Food & Beverage Market Place

Volume 2

2015

Fourteenth Edition

Food & Beverage Market Place

Volume 2

Equipment, Supplies & Services

Product Categories

Company Profiles

Grey House Publishing

AMENIA, NY 12501

PUBLISHER: Leslie Mackenzie
EDITOR: Richard Gottlieb
EDITORIAL DIRECTOR: Laura Mars

PRODUCTION MANAGER: Kristen Thatcher
COMPOSITION: David Garoogian
PRODUCTION ASSISTANTS: Kevin Bierfeldt; Diana Delgado; Brittany O'Brien

MARKETING DIRECTOR: Jessica Moody

Grey House Publishing, Inc.
4919 Route 22
Amenia, NY 12501
518.789.8700
FAX 845.373.6390
www.greyhouse.com
e-mail: books @greyhouse.com

First edition published 2001
Fourteenth edition published 2014
Printed in Canada

Food & beverage market place. - 14th ed. (2015) -
3 v. ; 27.5 cm. Annual
Includes index.
ISSN: 1554-6334

1. Food industry and trade-United States-Directories. 2. Food industry and trade-Canada-Directories. 3. Beverage industry-United States-Directories. 4. Beverage industry-Canada-Directories. I. Grey House Publishing, Inc. II. Title: Food & beverage market place.

HD9003.T48
338-dc21

3-Volume Set ISBN: 978-1-61925-274-5
Volume 1 ISBN: 978-1-61925-275-2
Volume 2 ISBN: 978-1-61925-276-9
Volume 3 ISBN: 978-1-61925-277-6

Table of Contents

VOLUME 1

VOLUME 2

VOLUME 3

Introduction

This 2015 edition of *Food & Beverage Market Place* represents the largest, most comprehensive resource of food and beverage manufacturers and service suppliers on the market today. These three volumes include over 45,000 company profiles that address all sectors of the industry—finished goods and ingredients manufacturers, equipment manufacturers, and third-party logistics providers, including transportation, warehousing, wholesalers, brokers, importers and exporters.

Praise for previous edition:

> "*. . . This publication is essential for researchers in the food industry, and large academic and public libraries.*"
>
> —American Reference Books Annual, 2013

The food and beverage industry continues its upward trend. While most food sectors have seen increased growth, *The Food Institute Report* confirms that the snack food category has experienced more growth than other sectors, and is the one to watch. Changing consumer behavior has not only changed the meaning of "snack," but also has increased how much we do it! Consumer behavior is also responsible for a drop in the purchase of breakfast cereals—so be on the look-out for ways that cereal manufacturers find to entice buyers. Also high on the list of what's important to consumers are fresh, local, and organic foods, and "farm-to-table" is an important claim for restaurants these days.

As consumer needs change, this industry—and *Food & Beverage Market Place*—continues to keep pace. Whatever slice of the market you cater to, you will find your buyers, sellers, and users in this comprehensive reference tool—three volumes of the complete coverage our subscribers have come to expect. Our extensive indexing makes quick work of locating exactly the company, product or service you are looking for.

Data Statistics

Each of the eight chapters in *Food & Beverage Market Place* reflects a massive update effort. This 2015 edition includes hundreds of new company profiles and thousands of updates throughout the three volumes. You will find 85,480 key executives, 32,099 fax numbers, 26,615 web sites, and 22,446 e-mails. The volumes breakdown as follows:

Volume 1 Food, Beverage & Ingredient Manufacturers – 12,888

Volume 2 Equipment, Supply & Service Providers – 13,421

Volume 3 Third Party Logistics
Brokers – 1,341
Importers & Exporters – 9,043
Transportation Firms – 681
Warehouse Companies – 1,301
Wholesalers & Distributors – 5,827

Arrangement

The product category sections for both food and beverage products in Volume 1 and equipment and supplies in Volume 2 begin with Product Category Lists. These include over 6,000 alphabetical terms for everything from Abalone to Zinc Citrate, from Adhesive Tapes to Zipper Application Systems. Use the detailed cross-references to find the full entry in the Product Category sections that immediately follow. Here you will find up to three levels of detail, for example—*Fish & Seafood: Fish: Abalone* or *Ingredients, Flavors & Additives: Vitamins & Supplements: Zinc Citrate*—with the name, location, phone number and packaging format of companies who manufacturer/ process the product you are looking for. Organic and Gluten-Free categories make it easy to locate those manufacturers who focus on these food types.

In addition to company profiles, this edition has 19 indexes, 17 chapter-specific, arranged by geographic region, product or company type, and two—All Brands and All Companies—that comprise all three volumes. See the Table of Contents for a complete list of specific indexes. Plus, chapters include User Guides that help you navigate chapter-specific data.

We are confident that this reference is the foremost research tool in the food and beverage industry. It will prove invaluable to manufacturers, buyers, specifiers, market researchers, consultants, and anyone working in food and beverage—one of the largest industries in the country.

Online Database & Mailing Lists

Food & Beverage Market Place is also available for subscription on http://gold.greyhouse.com for even faster, easier access to this wealth of information. Subscribers can search by product category, state, sales volume, employee size, personnel name, title and much more. Plus, users can print out prospect sheets or download data into their own spreadsheet or database. This database is a must for anyone marketing a product or service to this vast industry. Visit the site, or call 800-562-2139 for a free trial.

EQUIPMENT, SUPPLIES & SERVICES

Equipment User Guide

The **Equipment, Supplies and Services Chapter** of *Food & Beverage Market Place* includes companies that manufacturer equipment and supplies, or offer services, in the food and beverage industry. The chapter begins with a **Category Listing** of equipment, supplies and services that are offered by companies in this chapter. This category list is followed by a **Product Category Index**, organized first by state, then alphabetical by company. Each company listing includes packaging type, city and phone number.

Following the **Product Category Index** are the descriptive listings, which are organized alphabetically. Following the A – Z Equipment, Supplies and Services listings are two indexes: **Brand Name Index**, which lists the brand names of the equipment and supplies in this chapter, and **Geographic Index**, which lists all companies by state. These Indexes refers to listing numbers, not page numbers.

Below is a sample listing illustrating the kind of information that is or might be included in an Equipment, Supplies and Services listing. Each numbered item of information is described in the User Key on the following page.

---

1 → 245600

2 → **(HQ) A.A. A La Carte**

3 → 5600 Bloomingdale Avenue

New Berlin, WI 53151

4 → 062-789-1500

5 → 062-789-1501

6 → 888-789-1501

7 → info@AlaCarte.com

8 → www.AlaCarte.com

9 → Contract packager and exporter of hard candy in decorative tins, jars, and boxes.

10 → President: James Gold
CFO: James Filbert
COO: Gail King
Vice President: Elizabeth Timely
Marketing: Donna Paige

11 → *Estimated Sales*: $1-5 Million

12 → *Number Employees*: 35

13 → *Sq. Footage*: 25000

14 → *Parent Co.*: A.A. Special Lines

15 → *Company is also listed in the following section(s)*: Exporter

16 → Brands: Pierell, Apresa, Cocolot

Equipment Companies User Key

1 → **Record Number:** Entries are listed alphabetically within each category and numbered sequentially. The entry number, rather than the page number, is used in the indexes to refer to listings.

2 → **Company Name:** Formal name of company. HQ indicates headquarter location. If names are completely capitalized, the listing will appear at the beginning of the alphabetized section.

3 → **Address:** Location or permanent address of the company. If the mailing address differs from the street address, it will appear second.

4 → **Phone Number:** The listed phone number is usually for the main office, but may also be for the sales, marketing, or public relations office as provided.

5 → **Fax Number:** This is listed when provided by the company.

6 → **Toll-Free Number:** This is listed when provided by the company.

7 → **E-Mail:** This is listed when provided, and is generally the main office e-mail.

8 → **Web Site:** This is listed when provided by the company and is also referred to as an URL address. These web sites are accessed through the Internet by typing http:// before the URL address.

9 → **Description**: This paragraph contains a brief description of the products or services that are brokered, sometimes including markets served.

10 → **Key Personnel:** Names and titles of company executives.

11 → **Estimated Sales:** This is listed when provided by the company.

12 → **Number of Employees:** Total number of employees within the company.

13 → Indicates what other section in ***Food & Beverage Market Place*** this company is listed: Volume 1: Manufacturers. Volume 2: Equipment, Supplies & Services; Transportation; Warehouse; Wholesalers/Distributors. Volume 3: Brokers; Importers/Exporters.

14 → **Markets Served:** This further defines the company as serving one or more markers, such as Super Market Chains, Wholesale Distributors, Food Service Operators, etc. Companies are indexed by market.

15 → **Primary Brands Brokered include:** A list of brand names that the company brokers.

16 → **Brokered Products include**: This describes the type of product that the broker handles, such as alcoholic beverages, frozen foods, exports, ingredients, etc. Companies are indexed by product.

A

Adhesive *See Packaging Materials & Supplies: Tapes: Adhesive*

Advertising Novelties & Specialties *See Consultants & Services: Advertising Services: Advertising Novelties & Specialties*

Advertising Services *See Consultants & Services: Advertising Services*

Advertising Signs *See Foodservice Equipment & Supplies: Signs: Advertising*

Aerosol *See Equipment & Machinery: Food Processing: Aerosol*

Agglomeration *See Consultants & Services: Custom Services: Agglomeration*

Agitators *See Equipment & Machinery: Food Processing: Agitators*

Air Curtain Doors *See Building Equipment & Supplies: Doors: Air Curtain*

Air Curtains *See Building Equipment & Supplies: Air Curtains*

Air Filters *See Building Equipment & Supplies: Air Filters*

Air Knives *See Equipment & Machinery: Food Processing: Air Knives*

Airport Facilities *See Consultants & Services: Foodservice: Airport Facilities*

Alarm Systems *See Safety & Security Equipment & Supplies: Alarm Systems*

Aluminum Bottles *See Packaging Materials & Supplies: Bottles: Aluminum*

Aluminum Cans *See Packaging Materials & Supplies: Cans: Aluminum*

Aluminum Foil *See Packaging Materials & Supplies: Foil: Aluminum*

Aluminum Ware *See Food Preparation Equipment, Utensils & Cookware: Aluminum Ware*

Amino Acid, Nitrogen Analyzers *See Instrumentation & Laboratory Equipment: Analyzers: Amino Acid, Nitrogen*

Ammonia *See Sanitation Equipment & Supplies: Ammonia*

Amusement & Theme Parks *See Consultants & Services: Foodservice: Amusement & Theme Parks*

Anaerobic & Aerobic *See Sanitation Equipment & Supplies: Wastewater Treatment Systems: Anaerobic & Aerobic*

Analytical Services *See Consultants & Services: Analytical Services*

Analyzers *See Instrumentation & Laboratory Equipment: Analyzers*

Anti-Slip Flooring *See Building Equipment & Supplies: Flooring: Anti-Slip*

Aprons *See Clothing & Protective Apparel: Aprons*

Architects *See Consultants & Services: Architects*

Architectural & Engineering Designers *See Consultants & Services: Designers: Architectural & Engineering*

Aseptic Packaging *See Packaging Materials & Supplies: Packaging: Aseptic*

Augers *See Equipment & Machinery: Food Processing: Augers*

Auto Scrubbing & Burnishing Scrubbers *See Equipment & Machinery: Scrubbers: Auto Scrubbing & Burnishing*

Automated Guided Vehicles *See Transportation & Storage: Automated Guided Vehicles*

Automatic/Random Case Sealing Packaging *See Equipment & Machinery: Packaging: Automatic/Random Case Sealing*

Automation & Controls *See Instrumentation & Laboratory Equipment: Controls: Automation & Controls*

Automation *See Instrumentation & Laboratory Equipment: Automation*

Awnings *See Building Equipment & Supplies: Awnings*

B

Backers Magnetic Label *See Foodservice Equipment & Supplies: Magnetic Label: Backers*

Bag Closing *See Equipment & Machinery: Packaging: Bag Closing*

Bag Filling *See Equipment & Machinery: Packaging: Bag Filling*

Bag Holders *See Foodservice Equipment & Supplies: Holders: Bag*

Bag Opening *See Equipment & Machinery: Packaging: Bag Opening*

Bag Ties *See Packaging Materials & Supplies: Ties: Bag*

Bag, Cellophane & Pliofilm *See Equipment & Machinery: Packaging: Bag, Cellophane & Pliofilm*

Bag, Paper *See Equipment & Machinery: Packaging: Bag, Paper*

Bagel Slicer *See Food Preparation Equipment, Utensils & Cookware: Slicer: Bagel*

Bags *See Packaging Materials & Supplies: Bags*

Bakers' & Confectioners' Brushes *See Food Preparation Equipment, Utensils & Cookware: Brushes: Bakers' & Confectioners'*

Bakers' & Confectioners' Molds *See Food Preparation Equipment, Utensils & Cookware: Molds: Bakers' & Confectioners'*

Bakers' & Confectioners' Utensils *See Food Preparation Equipment, Utensils & Cookware: Utensils: Bakers' & Confectioners'*

Bakers' Boxes *See Packaging Materials & Supplies: Boxes: Bakers'*

Bakers' Gloves *See Clothing & Protective Apparel: Gloves: Bakers'*

Bakers' Mixers *See Equipment & Machinery: Food Processing: Mixers: Bakers'*

Bakers' Trays & Pans *See Food Preparation Equipment, Utensils & Cookware: Trays & Pans: Bakers'*

Bakery *See Consultants & Services: Contract Manufacturing: Bakery*

Bakery Racks *See Foodservice Equipment & Supplies: Racks: Bakery*

Baking & Roasting Pans *See Food Preparation Equipment, Utensils & Cookware: Pans: Baking & Roasting*

Baking Industry *See Equipment & Machinery: Baking Industry*

Balances *See Instrumentation & Laboratory Equipment: Balances*

Balers or Baling Presses *See Equipment & Machinery: Food Processing: Balers or Baling Presses*

Ball & Pebble Mills *See Equipment & Machinery: Food Processing: Mills: Ball & Pebble*

Bamboo Chopsticks *See Food Preparation Equipment, Utensils & Cookware: Utensils: Chopsticks: Bamboo*

Banquet Carts *See Foodservice Equipment & Supplies: Carts: Banquet*

Bar Code Devices *See Equipment & Machinery: Packaging: Bar Code Devices*

Barbecue Equipment & Supplies *See Equipment & Machinery: Barbecue Equipment & Supplies*

Barley Processing *See Equipment & Machinery: Food Processing: Barley Processing*

Barrel & Drum Draining Racks *See Transportation & Storage: Racks: Barrel & Drum Draining*

Barrel & Drum Filling *See Equipment & Machinery: Packaging: Barrel & Drum Filling*

Barrel Packers *See Equipment & Machinery: Packaging: Barrel Packers*

Bars & Bar Supplies *See Foodservice Equipment & Supplies: Bars & Bar Supplies*

Baskets *See Food Preparation Equipment, Utensils & Cookware: Baskets; Foodservice Equipment & Supplies: Baskets; Packaging Materials & Supplies: Baskets*

Batching, Blending, Weighing *See Instrumentation & Laboratory Equipment: Process Controls: Batching, Blending, Weighing*

Beam Scales *See Equipment & Machinery: Scales: Beam*

Bean & Grain Sorters *See Equipment & Machinery: Food Processing: Sorters: Bean & Grain*

Bean & Pea Hullers *See Equipment & Machinery: Food Processing: Hullers: Bean & Pea*

Bean, Pea Separators *See Equipment & Machinery: Food Processing: Separators: Bean, Pea*

Beaters *See Food Preparation Equipment, Utensils & Cookware: Beaters*

Beer & Ale Cans *See Packaging Materials & Supplies: Cans: Beer & Ale*

Beer Dispensers *See Foodservice Equipment & Supplies: Dispensers: Beer*

Beer Keg Movers *See Transportation & Storage: Beer Keg Movers*

Belt Conveyors *See Equipment & Machinery: Conveyors: Belt*

Belting *See Equipment & Machinery: Belting*

Belts *See Equipment & Machinery: Belts*

Beverage Bins *See Packaging Materials & Supplies: Bins: Beverage*

Beverage Carts *See Foodservice Equipment & Supplies: Carts: Beverage*

Beverage Coolers *See Refrigeration & Cooling Equipment: Coolers: Beverage*

Beverage Dispensers *See Foodservice Equipment & Supplies: Dispensers: Beverage*

Beverage Hoses *See Equipment & Machinery: Hoses: Beverage*

Beverage Industry *See Equipment & Machinery: Beverage Industry*

Beverages, Hot Fill Packaging *See Equipment & Machinery: Packaging: Beverages, Hot Fill*

Bins *See Packaging Materials & Supplies: Bins*

Biodegradable, Recyclable Plastic *See Packaging Materials & Supplies: Plastic: Biodegradable, Recyclable*

Biscuit & Cookie Cutters *See Food Preparation Equipment, Utensils & Cookware: Cutters: Biscuit & Cookie*

Biscuit Making *See Equipment & Machinery: Food Processing: Biscuit Making*

Blades *See Equipment & Machinery: Food Processing: Blades*

Blast Chillers *See Refrigeration & Cooling Equipment: Chillers: Blast*

Bleaches *See Sanitation Equipment & Supplies: Bleaches*

Blenders *See Equipment & Machinery: Food Processing: Blenders*

Blending & Mixing *See Consultants & Services: Contract Manufacturing: Blending & Mixing*

Blending *See Consultants & Services: Custom Services: Blending; Equipment & Machinery: Food Processing: Blending*

Blister Packaging *See Packaging Materials & Supplies: Packaging: Blister*

Blocks *See Food Preparation Equipment, Utensils & Cookware: Blocks*

Blowers *See Equipment & Machinery: Food Processing: Blowers*

Boards *See Food Preparation Equipment, Utensils & Cookware: Boards*

Boiler & Steam Controls *See Instrumentation & Laboratory Equipment: Controls: Boiler & Steam*

Boilers *See Equipment & Machinery: Food Processing: Boilers*

Borax *See Sanitation Equipment & Supplies: Borax*

Bottle & Jar Sealing *See Equipment & Machinery: Packaging: Bottle & Jar Sealing; Packaging Materials & Supplies: Seals: Bottle & Jar*

Bottle (Compounds) Cleaners *See Sanitation Equipment & Supplies: Cleaners: Bottle (Compounds)*

Bottle Brushes *See Sanitation Equipment & Supplies: Brushes: Bottle*

Bottle Cap, Plastic & Metal *See Equipment & Machinery: Packaging: Bottle Cap, Plastic & Metal*

Bottle Capping & Crowning *See Equipment & Machinery: Packaging: Bottle Capping & Crowning*

Bottle Cartoning *See Equipment & Machinery: Packaging: Bottle Cartoning*

Bottle Conveyors *See Equipment & Machinery: Conveyors: Bottle*

Bottle Corking *See Equipment & Machinery: Packaging: Bottle Corking*

Bottle Crates *See Packaging Materials & Supplies: Crates: Bottle*

Bottle Drying *See Equipment & Machinery: Packaging: Bottle Drying*

Bottle Filling *See Equipment & Machinery: Packaging: Bottle Filling*

Bottle Openers *See Equipment & Machinery: Openers: Bottle*

Bottle Racks *See Transportation & Storage: Racks: Bottle*

Bottle Sleeves *See Packaging Materials & Supplies: Sleeves: Bottle*

EXAMPLE: **Dairy Cooling Vats** *See Equipment & Machinery: Food Processing: Vats: Dairy Cooling*
(1 = Dairy Cooling Vats; 2 = See Equipment & Machinery:; 3 = Food Processing:; 4 = Vats:; 5 = Dairy Cooling)

1. Product or Service you are looking for
2. Main Category, in alphabetical order, located in the page headers starting on page 13
3. Category Description, located in black bars and in page headers
4. Product Category, located in gray bars
5. Product Type, located under gray bars, centered in bold

Bottle Sorters *See Equipment & Machinery: Packaging: Sorters: Bottle*
Bottle Washing, Soaking & Rinsing *See Equipment & Machinery: Packaging: Bottle Washing, Soaking & Rinsing*
Bottle, Can & Jar Caps *See Packaging Materials & Supplies: Caps: Bottle, Can & Jar*
Bottled for Cleaning Ammonia *See Sanitation Equipment & Supplies: Ammonia: Bottled for Cleaning*
Bottles *See Packaging Materials & Supplies: Bottles*
Bottling *See Equipment & Machinery: Packaging: Bottling*
Bowls *See Food Preparation Equipment, Utensils & Cookware: Bowls*
Box Closing *See Equipment & Machinery: Packaging: Box Closing*
Box Cutters *See Transportation & Storage: Box Cutters; Equipment & Machinery: Packaging: Box Cutting*
Box Strapping *See Equipment & Machinery: Packaging: Box Strapping; See also Packaging Materials & Supplies: Seals: Box Strapping*
Box, Carton, Case & Crate *See Packaging Materials & Supplies: Linings: Box, Carton, Case & Crate*
Box, Crate, Carton Openers *See Equipment & Machinery: Openers: Box, Crate, Carton*
Box, Paper *See Equipment & Machinery: Packaging: Box, Paper*
Boxes *See Packaging Materials & Supplies: Boxes*
Bread & Cake Slicers *See Equipment & Machinery: Food Processing: Slicers: Bread & Cake*
Bread & Pastry Bags *See Packaging Materials & Supplies: Bags: Bread & Pastry*
Bread Coolers *See Refrigeration & Cooling Equipment: Coolers: Bread*
Bread Knives *See Food Preparation Equipment, Utensils & Cookware: Knives: Bread*
Bread Slicer *See Food Preparation Equipment, Utensils & Cookware: Slicer: Bread*
Bread, Cake & Steak Wood Boards *See Food Preparation Equipment, Utensils & Cookware: Boards: Wood: Bread, Cake & Steak*
Brewery Cookers *See Equipment & Machinery: Food Processing: Cookers: Brewery; Equipment & Machinery: Food Processing: Brewery*
Brine Making Equipment *See Equipment & Machinery: Food Processing: Brine Making Equipment*
Broilers *See Equipment & Machinery: Food Processing: Broilers*
Broom Holders *See Sanitation Equipment & Supplies: Holders: Broom*
Brooms *See Sanitation Equipment & Supplies: Brooms*
Brushes *See Food Preparation Equipment, Utensils & Cookware: Brushes; See also Sanitation Equipment & Supplies: Brushes*
Bulk Bags *See Packaging Materials & Supplies: Bags: Bulk*
Bulk Grinding Grinders *See Equipment & Machinery: Food Processing: Grinders: Bulk Grinding*
Bundle, Package Ties *See Packaging Materials & Supplies: Ties: Bundle, Package*
Bussing Carts *See Foodservice Equipment & Supplies: Carts: Bussing*
Butchers' Blades *See Equipment & Machinery: Food Processing: Saws: Butchers' Blades*
Butchers' Block Scrapers *See Food Preparation Equipment, Utensils & Cookware: Scrapers: Butchers' Block*
Butchers' Blocks *See Food Preparation Equipment, Utensils & Cookware: Blocks: Butchers'*
Butchers' Cleavers *See Food Preparation Equipment, Utensils & Cookware: Cleavers: Butchers'*
Butchers' Coolers *See Refrigeration & Cooling Equipment: Coolers: Butchers'*
Butchers' Knives *See Food Preparation Equipment, Utensils & Cookware: Knives: Butchers'*
Butchers' Scales *See Equipment & Machinery: Scales: Butchers'*
Butchers' Trays *See Foodservice Equipment & Supplies: Trays: Butchers'*
Butter & Cheese Molds *See Food Preparation Equipment, Utensils & Cookware: Molds: Butter & Cheese*

C

Cabinets *See Refrigeration & Cooling Equipment: Cabinets*
Cafeteria Trays *See Foodservice Equipment & Supplies: Trays: Cafeteria*
Cafeteria, Restaurant Counters *See Foodservice Equipment & Supplies: Counters: Cafeteria, Restaurant*
Cafeteria, Restaurant, Foodservice Kitchen Tables *See Foodservice Equipment & Supplies: Tables: Cafeteria, Restaurant, Foodservice Kitchen*
Cake Cutters *See Food Preparation Equipment, Utensils & Cookware: Cutters: Cake*
Cake Knives *See Food Preparation Equipment, Utensils & Cookware: Knives: Cake*
Cake Pan Liners *See Food Preparation Equipment, Utensils & Cookware: Liners: Cake Pan*
Cake Tins *See Food Preparation Equipment, Utensils & Cookware: Tins: Cake*
Cake Turners *See Foodservice Equipment & Supplies: Cake Turners*
Can & Glass Crushers *See Equipment & Machinery: Food Processing: Crushers: Can & Glass*
Can Body Forming *See Equipment & Machinery: Packaging: Can Body Forming*
Can Capping *See Equipment & Machinery: Packaging: Can Capping*
Can Closing *See Equipment & Machinery: Packaging: Can Closing*
Can Drying *See Equipment & Machinery: Packaging: Can Drying*
Can Filling *See Equipment & Machinery: Packaging: Can Filling*
Can Openers *See Equipment & Machinery: Openers: Can*
Can Racks *See Transportation & Storage: Racks: Can*
Can Sealing *See Equipment & Machinery: Packaging: Can Sealing*
Can Seaming *See Equipment & Machinery: Packaging: Can Seaming*
Can Washing *See Equipment & Machinery: Packaging: Can Washing*
Can, Drum & Barrel Linings *See Packaging Materials & Supplies: Linings: Can, Drum & Barrel*
Candles *See Foodservice Equipment & Supplies: Candles*
Candy (Confectioners') Coolers *See Refrigeration & Cooling Equipment: Coolers: Candy (Confectioners')*
Candy Boxes *See Packaging Materials & Supplies: Boxes: Candy*
Candy Sticks *See Packaging Materials & Supplies: Sticks: Candy*
Candy Wrapping Paper *See Packaging Materials & Supplies: Paper: Candy Wrapping*
Cane Shredders *See Equipment & Machinery: Food Processing: Shredders: Cane*
Canners' & Packers' Aprons *See Clothing & Protective Apparel: Aprons: Canners' & Packers'*
Canners' Cookers *See Equipment & Machinery: Food Processing: Cookers: Canners'*
Canners' Coolers *See Refrigeration & Cooling Equipment: Coolers: Canners'*
Canners' Knives *See Food Preparation Equipment, Utensils & Cookware: Knives: Canners'*
Canners *See Consultants & Services: Canners*
Canning & Food Packing *See Equipment & Machinery: Packaging: Canning & Food Packing*
Canning & Preserving Jars *See Packaging Materials & Supplies: Jars: Canning & Preserving*
Canning & Preserving Kettles *See Food Preparation Equipment, Utensils & Cookware: Kettles: Canning & Preserving*
Canning Exhausters *See Equipment & Machinery: Packaging: Exhausters: Canning*
Canning Retorts *See Packaging Materials & Supplies: Retorts: Canning*
Cans *See Packaging Materials & Supplies: Cans*
Cap Torque Test *See Equipment & Machinery: Packaging: Cap Torque Test*
Cappers *See Equipment & Machinery: Packaging: Cappers*
Caps *See Clothing & Protective Apparel: Caps; Packaging Materials & Supplies: Caps*
Carriers *See Packaging Materials & Supplies: Carriers*
Carton *See Equipment & Machinery: Packaging: Carton*
Carton, Case, Box Sealing *See Equipment & Machinery: Packaging: Carton, Case, Box Sealing*
Cartons *See Packaging Materials & Supplies: Cartons*
Carts *See Foodservice Equipment & Supplies: Carts; Sanitation Equipment & Supplies: Carts; See also Transportation & Storage: Carts*
Carving Knives *See Food Preparation Equipment, Utensils & Cookware: Knives: Carving*
Cases *See Foodservice Equipment & Supplies: Cases*
Cash Registers *See Foodservice Equipment & Supplies: Cash Registers*
Cash, Money Drawers *See Foodservice Equipment & Supplies: Drawers: Cash, Money*
Casters *See Transportation & Storage: Casters*
Caustic Soda *See Sanitation Equipment & Supplies: Caustic Soda*
Ceiling Fans *See Building Equipment & Supplies: Fans: Ceiling*
Ceiling Surfaces & Panels *See Building Equipment & Supplies: Ceiling Surfaces & Panels*
Cellophane Bags *See Packaging Materials & Supplies: Bags: Cellophane*
Cellulose & Fiber Tags *See Packaging Materials & Supplies: Tags: Cellulose & Fiber*
Cellulose Acetate Film *See Packaging Materials & Supplies: Film: Cellulose Acetate*
Centrifuge Bags *See Packaging Materials & Supplies: Bags: Centrifuge*
Centrifuges *See Instrumentation & Laboratory Equipment: Centrifuges*
Cereal Contract Manufacturing *See Consultants & Services: Contract Manufacturing: Cereal*
Cereal Cookers *See Equipment & Machinery: Food Processing: Cookers: Cereal*
Cereal Making *See Equipment & Machinery: Food Processing: Cereal Making*
Certification *See Instrumentation & Laboratory Equipment: Certification*
Chafers *See Foodservice Equipment & Supplies: Chafers*
Chain Conveyors *See Equipment & Machinery: Conveyors: Chain*
Chairs *See Foodservice Equipment & Supplies: Chairs*
Chamois Cloths *See Sanitation Equipment & Supplies: Cloths: Chamois*
Changeable Letter Signs *See Foodservice Equipment & Supplies: Signs: Changeable Letter*
Changers *See Foodservice Equipment & Supplies: Changers*
Charcoal Briquette *See Equipment & Machinery: Food Processing: Cooking & Heating Equipment: Charcoal Briquettes*
Charcoal: Mesquite *See Equipment & Machinery: Food Processing: Cooking & Heating Equipment: Charcoal: Mesquite*
Check & Credit Card Verification Systems *See Foodservice Equipment & Supplies: Scanners: Check & Credit Card Verification Systems*
Check Weighing Systems *See Equipment & Machinery: Systems: Check Weighing*
Check, Bill & Voucher Sorters *See Foodservice Equipment & Supplies: Sorters: Check, Bill & Voucher*
Cheese Coating *See Packaging Materials & Supplies: Wax: Cheese Coating*
Cheese Cookers *See Equipment & Machinery: Food Processing: Cookers: Cheese*
Cheese Cutters *See Food Preparation Equipment, Utensils & Cookware: Cutters: Cheese*
Cheese Hoops *See Food Preparation Equipment, Utensils & Cookware: Hoops: Cheese*
Cheese Knives *See Food Preparation Equipment, Utensils & Cookware: Knives: Cheese*
Cheese Making *See Equipment & Machinery: Food Processing: Cheese Making*
Cheese Processing *See Equipment & Machinery: Food Processing: Cheese Processing*
Cheese Shredders *See Equipment & Machinery: Food Processing: Shredders: Cheese*
Cheese Vats *See Equipment & Machinery: Food Processing: Vats: Cheese; See also Transportation & Storage: Vats: Cheese*
Cheesecloth *See Equipment & Machinery: Food Processing: Cheesecloth*
Chemical Dispensing *See Equipment & Machinery: Systems: Chemical Dispensing & Feed*
Chemicals *See Instrumentation & Laboratory Equipment: Chemicals*
Chewing Gum *See Equipment & Machinery: Food Processing: Chewing Gum Processing*
Chicken, Prepared Containers *See Packaging Materials & Supplies: Containers: Chicken, Prepared*
Chillers *See Refrigeration & Cooling Equipment: Chillers*
China *See Foodservice Equipment & Supplies: China*
Chips Clear & Colored Plastic *See Foodservice Equipment & Supplies: Clear & Colored Plastic: Chips*

Chips Wood Grain Plastic *See Foodservice Equipment & Supplies: Wood Grain Plastic: Chips*

Chlorine *See Sanitation Equipment & Supplies: Chlorine*

Chocolate Grinding Mills *See Equipment & Machinery: Food Processing: Mills: Chocolate Grinding*

Chocolate Processing *See Equipment & Machinery: Food Processing: Chocolate Processing*

Chopsticks Utensils *See Food Preparation Equipment, Utensils & Cookware: Utensils: Chopsticks*

Clean Rooms *See Instrumentation & Laboratory Equipment: Laboratory Equipment: Clean Rooms*

Clean-In-Place Controls *See Instrumentation & Laboratory Equipment: Controls: Clean-In-Place*

Cleaners & Shellers *See Equipment & Machinery: Food Processing: Peanut Processing: Cleaners & Shellers*

Cleaners *See Sanitation Equipment & Supplies: Cleaners*

Cleaning & Scouring Powder *See Sanitation Equipment & Supplies: Powder: Cleaning & Scouring*

Cleaning Compound Dispensers *See Sanitation Equipment & Supplies: Dispensers: Cleaning Compound*

Cleaning Equipment & Supplies *See Sanitation Equipment & Supplies: Cleaning Equipment & Supplies*

Cleaning Oils *See Sanitation Equipment & Supplies: Oils: Cleaning*

Cleansing Tissue *See Sanitation Equipment & Supplies: Tissue: Cleansing*

Clear & Colored Plastic *See Foodservice Equipment & Supplies: Clear & Colored Plastic*

Clear Plastic *See Foodservice Equipment & Supplies: Clear Plastic*

Cleavers *See Food Preparation Equipment, Utensils & Cookware: Cleavers*

Closures & Closing Devices *See Packaging Materials & Supplies: Closures & Closing Devices*

Cloths *See Sanitation Equipment & Supplies: Cloths*

Clutches & Brakes *See Transportation & Storage: Clutches & Brakes*

Coasters *See Foodservice Equipment & Supplies: Coasters*

Cocktail Forks *See Food Preparation Equipment, Utensils & Cookware: Utensils: Forks: Cocktail*

Cocoa Processing *See Equipment & Machinery: Food Processing: Cocoa Processing*

Coding, Dating & Marking Equipment *See Equipment & Machinery: Packaging: Coding, Dating & Marking Equipment*

Coffee & Tea Urns *See Foodservice Equipment & Supplies: Urns: Coffee & Tea*

Coffee Dispensers *See Foodservice Equipment & Supplies: Dispensers: Coffee*

Coffee Filters *See Equipment & Machinery: Food Processing: Filters: Coffee*

Coffee Hoppers *See Equipment & Machinery: Food Processing: Hoppers: Coffee*

Coffee Industry *See Equipment & Machinery: Coffee Industry*

Coffee Makers *See Equipment & Machinery: Food Processing: Coffee Makers*

Coffee Pot Cleaners *See Sanitation Equipment & Supplies: Cleaners: Coffee Pot*

Coffee Pots *See Equipment & Machinery: Coffee Industry: Stainless Steel: Coffee Pots*

Coffee Processing *See Equipment & Machinery: Food Processing: Coffee Processing*

Coin Counters *See Foodservice Equipment & Supplies: Counters: Coin*

Coin Machinery *See Foodservice Equipment & Supplies: Coin Machinery*

Cold Cream *See Sanitation Equipment & Supplies: Skin Cream & Lotions: Cold Cream*

Cold Storage Doors *See Refrigeration & Cooling Equipment: Doors: Cold Storage*

Cold Storage Room Racks *See Transportation & Storage: Racks: Cold Storage Room*

Colleges & Universities *See Consultants & Services: Foodservice: Colleges & Universities*

Colloid Mills *See Equipment & Machinery: Food Processing: Mills: Colloid*

Color Measuring *See Instrumentation & Laboratory Equipment: Instrumentation: Color Measuring*

Colored Plastic *See Foodservice Equipment & Supplies: Colored Plastic*

Combination Oven/Steamers *See Equipment & Machinery: Food Processing: Combination Oven/Steamers*

Compounds *See Sanitation Equipment & Supplies: Compounds*

Compressors *See Equipment & Machinery: Food Processing: Compressors; Refrigeration & Cooling Equipment: Compressors*

Computer Software, Systems & Services *See Consultants & Services: Computer Software, Systems & Services*

Computing, Weighing *See Equipment & Machinery: Scales: Computing, Weighing*

Concession Supplies & Equipment *See Foodservice Equipment & Supplies: Concession Supplies & Equipment*

Condensed Milk *See Equipment & Machinery: Food Processing: Condensed Milk Processing*

Condensers *See Equipment & Machinery: Food Processing: Condensers*

Condiment Carts *See Foodservice Equipment & Supplies: Carts: Condiment*

Confectioners' Bags *See Packaging Materials & Supplies: Bags: Confectioners'*

Confectioners' Kettles *See Food Preparation Equipment, Utensils & Cookware: Kettles: Confectioners'*

Confectioners', Continuous Cookers *See Equipment & Machinery: Food Processing: Cookers: Confectioners', Continuous*

Confectionery *See Equipment & Machinery: Food Processing: Confectionery*

Confectionery Industry *See Equipment & Machinery: Confectionery Industry*

Construction *See Consultants & Services: Construction*

Consultants *See Consultants & Services: Consultants*

Container *See Equipment & Machinery: Packaging: Container; Packaging Materials & Supplies: Containers*

Containment Systems *See Safety & Security Equipment & Supplies: Containment Systems*

Contract Manufacturing *See Consultants & Services: Contract Manufacturing*

Contract Packaging *See Consultants & Services: Contract Packaging*

Control Panels *See Instrumentation & Laboratory Equipment: Process Controls: Control Panels*

Controls *See Instrumentation & Laboratory Equipment: Controls*

Convection Ovens *See Equipment & Machinery: Food Processing: Convection Ovens*

Convex Mirrors *See Equipment & Machinery: Mirrors: Convex*

Conveyors *See Equipment & Machinery: Conveyors*

Cookers *See Equipment & Machinery: Food Processing: Cookers*

Cookie Sheets *See Food Preparation Equipment, Utensils & Cookware: Sheets: Cookie*

Cooking & Baking Glassware *See Food Preparation Equipment, Utensils & Cookware: Glassware: Cooking & Baking*

Cooking & Heating Equipment *See Equipment & Machinery: Food Processing: Cooking & Heating Equipment*

Cookware *See Food Preparation Equipment, Utensils & Cookware: Cookware*

Coolers *See Equipment & Machinery: Water Treatment: Coolers*

Cooperage *See Equipment & Machinery: Cooperage*

Copper Kettles *See Food Preparation Equipment, Utensils & Cookware: Kettles: Copper*

Copra Grinding & Crushing Mills *See Equipment & Machinery: Food Processing: Mills: Copra Grinding & Crushing*

Cordage, Rope & Twine *See Transportation & Storage: Cordage, Rope & Twine*

Corers *See Equipment & Machinery: Food Processing: Corers*

Corks *See Packaging Materials & Supplies: Corks*

Corkscrews *See Foodservice Equipment & Supplies: Corkscrews*

Corn & Fodder Shredders *See Equipment & Machinery: Food Processing: Shredders: Corn & Fodder*

Corn Chip Processing *See Equipment & Machinery: Food Processing: Corn Chip Processing*

Corn Cob Holders *See Food Preparation Equipment, Utensils & Cookware: Holders: Corn Cob*

Corn Huskers *See Equipment & Machinery: Food Processing: Huskers: Corn*

Corn Meal & Corn Flour Mills *See Equipment & Machinery: Food Processing: Mills: Corn Meal & Corn Flour*

Corn Poppers *See Equipment & Machinery: Food Processing: Corn Poppers*

Corn Processing *See Equipment & Machinery: Food Processing: Co rn Processing*

Correctional Facilities *See Consultants & Services: Foodservice: Correctional Facilities*

Corrosion Resistant Doors *See Building Equipment & Supplies: Doors: Corrosion Resistant*

Corrugated Boxes *See Packaging Materials & Supplies: Boxes: Corrugated*

Corrugated Paper *See Packaging Materials & Supplies: Paper: Corrugated*

Cost Systems *See Equipment & Machinery: Systems: Cost*

Counter Scales *See Equipment & Machinery: Scales: Counter*

Counters *See Foodservice Equipment & Supplies: Counters*

Covers *See Food Preparation Equipment, Utensils & Cookware: Covers*

Crates *See Packaging Materials & Supplies: Crates*

Creamery Cans *See Packaging Materials & Supplies: Cans: Creamery*

Creamery, Dairy Tanks *See Equipment & Machinery: Food Processing: Tanks: Creamery, Dairy*

Crown Corks *See Packaging Materials & Supplies: Corks: Crown*

Cruise Lines *See Consultants & Services: Foodservice: Cruise Lines*

Crumb Belts *See Equipment & Machinery: Belts: Crumb*

Crushers *See Equipment & Machinery: Food Processing: Crushers*

Culinary Knives *See Food Preparation Equipment, Utensils & Cookware: Knives: Culinary*

Culinary Ladles *See Food Preparation Equipment, Utensils & Cookware: Ladles: Culinary*

Culinary, Frying *See Food Preparation Equipment, Utensils & Cookware: Baskets: Culinary, Frying, Etc.*

Cup & Napkin Dispensers *See Foodservice Equipment & Supplies: Dispensers: Cup & Napkin*

Cups *See Packaging Materials & Supplies: Cups*

Curd Knives *See Food Preparation Equipment, Utensils & Cookware: Knives: Curd*

Curd Mills *See Equipment & Machinery: Food Processing: Mills: Curd*

Currency Changers *See Foodservice Equipment & Supplies: Changers: Currency*

Custom Printed Promotional Products *See Consultants & Services: Advertising Services: Custom Printed Promotional Products*

Custom Services *See Consultants & Services: Custom Services*

Cutlery *See Food Preparation Equipment, Utensils & Cookware: Cutlery*

Cutters *See Food Preparation Equipment, Utensils & Cookware: Cutters*

Cutting & Trimming Tables *See Food Preparation Equipment, Utensils & Cookware: Tables: Cutting & Trimming*

Cutting Block *See Food Preparation Equipment, Utensils & Cookware: Boards: Cutting Block*

Cylinders *See Equipment & Machinery: Cylinders*

D

Dairy & Creamery *See Equipment & Machinery: Food Processing: Dairy & Creamery*

Dairy Aprons *See Clothing & Protective Apparel: Aprons: Dairy*

Dairy Cleaners *See Sanitation Equipment & Supplies: Cleaners: Dairy*

EXAMPLE: **Dairy Cooling Vats** (1) *See Equipment & Machinery:* (2) *Food Processing:* (3) *Vats:* (4) *Dairy Cooling* (5)

1. Product or Service you are looking for
2. Main Category, in alphabetical order, located in the page headers starting on page 13
3. Category Description, located in black bars and in page headers
4. Product Category, located in gray bars
5. Product Type, located under gray bars, centered in bold

Dairy Cooling *See Equipment & Machinery: Food Processing: Vats: Dairy Cooling; Refrigeration & Cooling Equipment: Vats: Dairy Cooling*
Dairy Industry *See Equipment & Machinery: Dairy Industry*
Data Loggers *See Instrumentation & Laboratory Equipment: Process Controls: Pressure: Data Loggers*
Dating & Numbering *See Packaging Materials & Supplies: Stamps: Dating & Numbering*
Deaerators *See Equipment & Machinery: Food Processing: Deaerators*
Dealers *See Consultants & Services: Dealers*
Decking *See Building Equipment & Supplies: Decking*
Decorative Items *See Foodservice Equipment & Supplies: Decorative Items*
Deep Fryer Hose *See Equipment & Machinery: Hoses: Deep Fryer*
Deep Fryers *See Equipment & Machinery: Food Processing: Deep Fryers*
Dehydration Equipment *See Equipment & Machinery: Food Processing: Dehydration Equipment*
Delivery Truck Ramps *See Transportation & Storage: Ramps: Delivery Truck*
Depositors *See Equipment & Machinery: Depositors*
Design Consultants *See Consultants & Services: Consultants: Design*
Designers *See Consultants & Services: Designers*
Dessert, Pastry Carts *See Foodservice Equipment & Supplies: Carts: Dessert, Pastry*
Detectors & Alarms *See Safety & Security Equipment & Supplies: Detectors & Alarms*
Detectors *See Equipment & Machinery: Packaging: Detectors; Safety & Security Equipment & Supplies: Detectors*
Detergents *See Sanitation Equipment & Supplies: Detergents*
Dicing Cutters *See Food Preparation Equipment, Utensils & Cookware: Cutters: Dicing*
Dish & Plate Warmers *See Foodservice Equipment & Supplies: Warmers: Dish & Plate*
Dish Cloths *See Sanitation Equipment & Supplies: Cloths: Dish*
Dish Washing Machinery *See Sanitation Equipment & Supplies: Dish Washing Machinery*
Dish, Food Display & Tray Covers *See Food Preparation Equipment, Utensils & Cookware: Covers: Dish, Food Display & Tray*
Dishes *See Foodservice Equipment & Supplies: Dishes*
Dishwasher *See Sanitation Equipment & Supplies: Dishwasher*
Dishwashing Compounds *See Sanitation Equipment & Supplies: Compounds: Dishwashing*
Disinfectants & Germicides *See Sanitation Equipment & Supplies: Disinfectants & Germicides*
Disintegrators *See Equipment & Machinery: Food Processing: Disintegrators*
Dispensers *See Foodservice Equipment & Supplies: Dispensers; Sanitation Equipment & Supplies: Dispensers*
Display Cases *See Foodservice Equipment & Supplies: Cases: Display*
Display Tables *See Foodservice Equipment & Supplies: Tables: Display*
Display, Store Hooks *See Foodservice Equipment & Supplies: Hooks: Display, Store*
Display, Store Racks *See Foodservice Equipment & Supplies: Racks: Display, Store*
Displays *See Foodservice Equipment & Supplies: Displays*
Disposable Gloves *See Clothing & Protective Apparel: Gloves: Disposable*
Disposable Towels *See Foodservice Equipment & Supplies: Towels: Disposable*
Disposable Wipers *See Sanitation Equipment & Supplies: Wipers: Disposable*
Doilies *See Foodservice Equipment & Supplies: Doilies*
Doors *See Building Equipment & Supplies: Doors; Foodservice Equipment & Supplies: Doors; Refrigeration & Cooling Equipment: Doors*
Double Acting Doors *See Building Equipment & Supplies: Doors: Double Acting*
Dough Make-up *See Equipment & Machinery: Food Processing: Dough Make-up*
Dough Sheeter *See Food Preparation Equipment, Utensils & Cookware: Sheeter: Dough*
Drawers *See Foodservice Equipment & Supplies: Drawers*
Drink Mixing *See Equipment & Machinery: Food Processing: Drink Mixing*
Drinking Glasses *See Food Preparation Equipment, Utensils & Cookware: Glasses: Drinking*
Drinking Straws *See Foodservice Equipment & Supplies: Straws: Drinking*
Drive-Thru & Pass-Thru Windows *See Building Equipment & Supplies: Windows: Drive-Thru & Pass-Thru*
Drum Mixers *See Equipment & Machinery: Food Processing: Mixers: Drum*
Drums *See Transportation & Storage: Drums*
Dry Measures *See Equipment & Machinery: Measures: Dry*
Dry Product Contract Packaging *See Consultants & Services: Contract Packaging: Dry Product*
Dry Products Filling *See Equipment & Machinery: Food Processing: Dry Products Filling*
Dryer Systems *See Sanitation Equipment & Supplies: Dryer Systems*
Dryers *See Equipment & Machinery: Food Processing: Dryers*
Drying *See Consultants & Services: Custom Services: Drying*
Drying, Evaporating Tanks *See Equipment & Machinery: Food Processing: Tanks: Drying, Evaporating*
Dumpers *See Equipment & Machinery: Food Processing: Dumpers*
Dust Collectors *See Sanitation Equipment & Supplies: Dust Collectors*
Dust Pans *See Sanitation Equipment & Supplies: Dust Pans*
Dusting Cloths *See Sanitation Equipment & Supplies: Cloths: Dusting*

E

Egg Baskets *See Packaging Materials & Supplies: Baskets: Egg*
Egg Crates *See Packaging Materials & Supplies: Crates: Egg*
Egg Processing *See Equipment & Machinery: Food Processing: Egg Processing & Cleaning*
Egg Slicers *See Equipment & Machinery: Food Processing: Slicers: Egg*
Egg, Cream, Culinary *See Food Preparation Equipment, Utensils & Cookware: Beaters: Egg, Cream, Culinary*
Electric Alarm Mats *See Safety & Security Equipment & Supplies: Mats: Electric Alarm*
Electric Heating *See Building Equipment & Supplies: Heating, Ventilation & Air Conditioning: Heating: Electric*
Electric Lighting *See Building Equipment & Supplies: Lighting Equipment: Lighting Fixtures: Electric*
Electric Signs *See Foodservice Equipment & Supplies: Signs: Electric*
Electric Steam Boilers *See Equipment & Machinery: Food Processing: Boilers: Electric Steam*
Electronic Survey *See Instrumentation & Laboratory Equipment: Process Analysis & Development: Electronic Survey*
Emergency Lighting *See Building Equipment & Supplies: Lighting Equipment: Lighting Fixtures: Emergency*
Employment Agencies *See Consultants & Services: Personnel Services: Employment Agencies*
Envelopes *See Foodservice Equipment & Supplies: Envelopes*
Equipment & Machinery *See Equipment & Machinery*
Equipment & Supplies *See Consultants & Services: Construction: Equipment & Supplies*
Equipment *See Equipment & Machinery: Food Processing: Equipment*
Equipment Packaging *See Equipment & Machinery: Packaging: Equipment*
Espresso & Cappuccino *See Equipment & Machinery: Food Processing: Espresso & Cappuccino Processing*
Ethyl Alcohol *See Instrumentation & Laboratory Equipment: Analyzers: Ethyl Alcohol*
Evaporative Condensers *See Equipment & Machinery: Food Processing: Condensers: Evaporative*
Evaporators *See Equipment & Machinery: Food Processing: Evaporators*
Exhausters *See Equipment & Machinery: Packaging: Exhausters*
Exterminators *See Sanitation Equipment & Supplies: Pest Control: Exterminators*
Extractors *See Equipment & Machinery: Food Processing: Extractors*
Extruders *See Equipment & Machinery: Food Processing: Extruders*
Extrusion *See Consultants & Services: Custom Services: Extrusion*

F

Facility Design *See Consultants & Services: Construction: Facility Design*
Factory, Warehouse, Shop & Industrial Trucks *See Transportation & Storage: Trucks: Factory, Warehouse, Shop & Industrial*
Fancy Boxes *See Packaging Materials & Supplies: Boxes: Fancy*
Fans *See Building Equipment & Supplies: Fans*
Fast Food *See Consultants & Services: Fast Food & Franchises*
Fast Food Restaurants *See Consultants & Services: Foodservice: Fast Food Restaurants*
Fats, Oils Analyzers *See Instrumentation & Laboratory Equipment: Analyzers: Fats, Oils*
Feed Mills *See Equipment & Machinery: Food Processing: Mills: Feed*
Feeders *See Equipment & Machinery: Feeders*
Fiber Boxes *See Packaging Materials & Supplies: Boxes: Fiber*
Fiber, Starch *See Instrumentation & Laboratory Equipment: Analyzers: Fiber, Starch*
Fillers *See Equipment & Machinery: Food Processing: Fillers*
Filling *See Equipment & Machinery: Packaging: Carton: Filling*
Film *See Packaging Materials & Supplies: Film*
Filters *See Equipment & Machinery: Food Processing: Filters*
Filtration and Separation *See Equipment & Machinery: Food Processing: Filtration and Separation*
Filtration Devices & Systems *See Equipment & Machinery: Filtration Devices & Systems*
Fire Alarm Systems *See Safety & Security Equipment & Supplies: Fire Alarm Systems*
Fire Extinguishers *See Safety & Security Equipment & Supplies: Fire Extinguishers*
Fire, Heat & Smoke Detectors & Alarms *See Safety & Security Equipment & Supplies: Detectors & Alarms: Fire, Heat & Smoke*
Fish Cleaning *See Equipment & Machinery: Food Processing: Fish Cleaning*
Fish Cookers *See Equipment & Machinery: Food Processing: Cookers: Fish*
Fish Scalers *See Equipment & Machinery: Food Processing: Scalers: Fish*
Fish Scaling & Slitting Knives *See Food Preparation Equipment, Utensils & Cookware: Knives: Fish Scaling & Slitting*
Fish, Meat & Produce Smokers *See Equipment & Machinery: Food Processing: Smokers: Fish, Meat & Produce*
Fittings *See Equipment & Machinery: Fittings*
Fixtures *See Foodservice Equipment & Supplies: Fixtures*
Flags, Pennants & Banners *See Consultants & Services: Advertising Services: Flags, Pennants & Banners*
Flakers or Flaking Drums *See Equipment & Machinery: Food Processing: Flakers or Flaking Drums*
Flashlights *See Safety & Security Equipment & Supplies: Flashlights*
Flexible Materials *See Packaging Materials & Supplies: Packaging: Flexible Materials*
Floor Cleaning Machinery *See Sanitation Equipment & Supplies: Floor Cleaning Machinery*
Floor Electric Alarm Mats *See Safety & Security Equipment & Supplies: Mats: Electric Alarm: Floor*
Floor Mats *See Building Equipment & Supplies: Flooring: Floor Mats*
Floor Polish *See Sanitation Equipment & Supplies: Polish: Floor*
Floor, Sweeping, Polishing & Waxing Brushes *See Sanitation Equipment & Supplies: Brushes: Floor, Sweeping, Polishing & Waxing*
Flooring *See Building Equipment & Supplies: Flooring*
Flour & Bakers' Sifters *See Food Preparation Equipment, Utensils & Cookware: Sifters: Flour & Bakers'*
Flour & Cereal Mills *See Equipment & Machinery: Food Processing: Mills: Flour & Cereal*

Flour Blending See *Equipment & Machinery: Food Processing: Blending: Flour*

Flour Hoppers See *Equipment & Machinery: Food Processing: Hoppers: Flour*

Flour Mill See *Equipment & Machinery: Food Processing: Flour Mill*

Flour, Meal & Feed Bags See *Packaging Materials & Supplies: Bags: Flour, Meal & Feed*

Flow Measurement See *Instrumentation & Laboratory Equipment: Instrumentation: Flow Measurement, Gas & Liquid*

Flow Meters See *Instrumentation & Laboratory Equipment: Meters: Flow*

Flow Regulators See *Equipment & Machinery: Flow Regulators*

Fluid, Liquid, Weighing Scales See *Equipment & Machinery: Scales: Fluid, Liquid, Weighing*

Fluorescent Lighting See *Building Equipment & Supplies: Lighting Equipment: Fluorescent*

Fluorescent Lighting Fixtures See *Building Equipment & Supplies: Lighting Equipment: Lighting Fixtures: Fluorescent*

Foil See *Packaging Materials & Supplies: Foil*

Folding Tables See *Foodservice Equipment & Supplies: Tables: Folding*

Food & Restaurant Trucks See *Transportation & Storage: Trucks: Food & Restaurant*

Food Bags See *Packaging Materials & Supplies: Bags: Food*

Food Carriers See *Packaging Materials & Supplies: Carriers: Food*

Food Certification See *Instrumentation & Laboratory Equipment: Certification: Food*

Food Closeouts See *Consultants & Services: Food Closeouts, Surplus, Salvage & Liquidators*

Food Deaerators See *Equipment & Machinery: Food Processing: Deaerators: Food*

Food Dispensers See *Foodservice Equipment & Supplies: Dispensers: Food*

Food Dryers See *Equipment & Machinery: Food Processing: Dryers: Food*

Food Filters See *Equipment & Machinery: Food Processing: Filters: Food*

Food Handlers' Protective Apparel See *Clothing & Protective Apparel: Protective Apparel: Food Handlers'*

Food Handling Hoses See *Equipment & Machinery: Hoses: Food Handling*

Food Industry Brushes See *Food Preparation Equipment, Utensils & Cookware: Brushes: Food Industry*

Food Inspection See *Instrumentation & Laboratory Equipment: Testers: Food Inspection*

Food Processing Agitators See *Equipment & Machinery: Food Processing: Agitators: Food Processing*

Food Processing See *Equipment & Machinery: Food Processing: Food Processing: Food*

Food Processing Machine Blades See *Equipment & Machinery: Food Processing: Blades: Food Processing Machine*

Food Processing Machine Knives See *Food Preparation Equipment, Utensils & Cookware: Knives: Food Processing Machine*

Food Processing Mixers See *Equipment & Machinery: Food Processing: Mixers: Food Processing*

Food Processing See *Equipment & Machinery: Food Processing*

Food Protective Packaging See *Packaging Materials & Supplies: Packaging: Food Protective*

Food Pumps See *Equipment & Machinery: Pumps: Food;* Instrumentation & Laboratory Equipment: Pumps: Food

Food Research See *Consultants & Services: Laboratories: Food Research & Development*

Food Storage Supplies See *Transportation & Storage: Food Storage Supplies*

Food Technology Consultants See *Consultants & Services: Consultants: Food Technology*

Food Tongs See *Food Preparation Equipment, Utensils & Cookware: Tongs: Food*

Food Trays See *Foodservice Equipment & Supplies: Trays: Food*

Food Warmers See *Foodservice Equipment & Supplies: Warmers: Food*

Food, Artificial Displays See *Foodservice Equipment & Supplies: Displays: Food, Artificial*

Food, Household, Hotel & Restaurant Mixers See *Equipment & Machinery: Food Processing: Mixers: Food, Household, Hotel & Restaurant*

Foodservice Architects See *Consultants & Services: Architects: Foodservice*

Foodservice Doors See *Foodservice Equipment & Supplies: Doors: Foodservice*

Foodservice Preparation Utensils See *Foodservice Equipment & Supplies: Utensils: Foodservice Preparation*

Foodservice See *Consultants & Services: Foodservice*

Forks See *Food Preparation Equipment, Utensils & Cookware: Utensils: Forks*

Form, Fill & Seal See *Equipment & Machinery: Packaging: Form, Fill & Seal*

Formulations See *Consultants & Services: Custom Services: Formulations*

Freeze Dryers See *Equipment & Machinery: Food Processing: Dryers: Freeze*

Freezer & Frozen Foods See *Refrigeration & Cooling Equipment: Cabinets: Freezer & Frozen Foods*

Freezer Doors See *Refrigeration & Cooling Equipment: Doors: Freezer*

Freezer Tapes See *Packaging Materials & Supplies: Tapes: Freezer*

Freezers See *Refrigeration & Cooling Equipment: Freezers*

Frozen Custard Processing See *Equipment & Machinery: Food Processing: Frozen Custard Processing*

Frozen Food Displays See *Foodservice Equipment & Supplies: Displays: Frozen Food*

Frozen Food Lockers See *Refrigeration & Cooling Equipment: Lockers: Frozen Food*

Frozen Food Wrappers See *Packaging Materials & Supplies: Wrappers: Frozen Food*

Frozen Foods Processing See *Equipment & Machinery: Food Processing: Frozen Foods Processing*

Fruit & Vegetable Bags See *Packaging Materials & Supplies: Bags: Fruit & Vegetable*

Fruit & Vegetable Baskets See *Packaging Materials & Supplies: Baskets: Fruit & Vegetable*

Fruit & Vegetable Boxes See *Packaging Materials & Supplies: Boxes: Fruit & Vegetable*

Fruit & Vegetable Corers See *Equipment & Machinery: Food Processing: Corers: Fruit & Vegetable*

Fruit & Vegetable Juice Extractors See *Equipment & Machinery: Food Processing: Extractors: Fruit & Vegetable Juice*

Fruit & Vegetable Juice Filters See *Equipment & Machinery: Food Processing: Filters: Fruit & Vegetable Juice*

Fruit & Vegetable Parers & Peelers See *Food Preparation Equipment, Utensils & Cookware: Parers & Peelers: Fruit & Vegetable*

Fruit & Vegetable Washers See *Equipment & Machinery: Food Processing: Washers: Fruit & Vegetable*

Fruit & Vegetable Waxers See *Equipment & Machinery: Food Processing: Waxers: Fruit & Vegetable*

Fruit Crushers See *Equipment & Machinery: Food Processing: Crushers: Fruit*

Fruit Dryers See *Equipment & Machinery: Food Processing: Dryers: Fruit*

Fruit Industry See *Equipment & Machinery: Fruit Industry*

Fruit Jar Openers See *Equipment & Machinery: Openers: Fruit Jar*

Fruit Juice Evaporators See *Equipment & Machinery: Food Processing: Evaporators: Fruit Juice*

Fruit Knives See *Food Preparation Equipment, Utensils & Cookware: Knives: Fruit*

Fruit Packers See *Consultants & Services: Packers: Fruit*

Fruit Processing See *Equipment & Machinery: Food Processing: Fruit Processing*

Fruit, Vegetable & Nut Graders See *Equipment & Machinery: Food Processing: Graders: Fruit, Vegetable & Nut*

Frying Pans See *Food Preparation Equipment, Utensils & Cookware: Pans: Frying*

Funnels See *Equipment & Machinery: Funnels*

Furniture Polish See *Sanitation Equipment & Supplies: Polish: Furniture*

G

Garbage & Waste See *Sanitation Equipment & Supplies: Incinerators: Garbage & Waste*

Garbage Bags See *Sanitation Equipment & Supplies: Garbage Bags*

Garbage Compactors See *Sanitation Equipment & Supplies: Garbage Compactors*

Garbage Control Units & Systems See *Sanitation Equipment & Supplies: Garbage Control Units & Systems*

Garbage Disposal Units See *Sanitation Equipment & Supplies: Garbage Disposal Units*

Gas Connectors See *Equipment & Machinery: Gas Connectors*

Gas Fired Boilers See *Equipment & Machinery: Food Processing: Boilers: Gas Fired*

Gas Leak Detectors See *Safety & Security Equipment & Supplies: Detectors: Gas Leak*

Gauges;Sanitary See *Instrumentation & Laboratory Equipment: Process Controls: Pressure: Gauges;Sanitary*

Gesticide Analyses See *Instrumentation & Laboratory Equipment: Gesticide Analyses*

Gift Baskets See *Packaging Materials & Supplies: Baskets: Gift*

Glass Bottles See *Packaging Materials & Supplies: Bottles: Glass*

Glass Dispensers See *Foodservice Equipment & Supplies: Dispensers: Glass*

Glass Jars See *Packaging Materials & Supplies: Jars: Glass*

Glass Trays See *Foodservice Equipment & Supplies: Trays: Glass*

Glasses See *Food Preparation Equipment, Utensils & Cookware: Glasses*

Glassine See *Packaging Materials & Supplies: Paper: Glassine*

Glassware See *Food Preparation Equipment, Utensils & Cookware: Glassware*

Gloves See *Clothing & Protective Apparel: Gloves*

Graders See *Equipment & Machinery: Food Processing: Graders*

Grain & Oat Crushers See *Equipment & Machinery: Food Processing: Crushers: Grain & Oat*

Grain & Seed Cleaners See *Sanitation Equipment & Supplies: Cleaners: Grain & Seed*

Grain Bags See *Packaging Materials & Supplies: Bags: Grain*

Grain Blending See *Equipment & Machinery: Food Processing: Blending: Grain*

Grain Dryers See *Equipment & Machinery: Food Processing: Dryers: Grain*

Grain Elevator See *Equipment & Machinery: Food Processing: Grain Elevator*

Grain, Flour Mill See *Equipment & Machinery: Food Processing: Separators: Grain, Flour Mill*

Grain, Rice & Seed Graders See *Equipment & Machinery: Food Processing: Graders: Grain, Rice & Seed*

Graters See *Equipment & Machinery: Food Processing: Graters*

Grating See *Building Equipment & Supplies: Grating*

Gravimetric, Volumetric, Loss-In-Weight, Etc. Feeders See *Equipment & Machinery: Feeders: Gravimetric, Volumetric, Loss-In-Weight, Etc.*

Grease & Oil Resistant Paper See *Packaging Materials & Supplies: Paper: Grease & Oil Resistant*

Grease Filters See *Equipment & Machinery: Food Processing: Filters: Grease*

Greaseproof Bags See *Packaging Materials & Supplies: Bags: Greaseproof*

Grilles See *Refrigeration & Cooling Equipment: Refrigerators: Grilles*

Grinders See *Equipment & Machinery: Food Processing: Grinders*

Grinding See *Consultants & Services: Custom Services: Grinding*

Grinding Mills See *Equipment & Machinery: Food Processing: Mills: Grinding*

EXAMPLE: **Dairy Cooling Vats** *See Equipment & Machinery: Food Processing: Vats: Dairy Cooling* (1: Dairy Cooling Vats; 2: Equipment & Machinery; 3: Food Processing; 4: Vats; 5: Dairy Cooling)

1. Product or Service you are looking for
2. Main Category, in alphabetical order, located in the page headers starting on page 13
3. Category Description, located in black bars and in page headers
4. Product Category, located in gray bars
5. Product Type, located under gray bars, centered in bold

Gummed Tapes *See Packaging Materials & Supplies: Tapes: Gummed*

H

Hair Nets *See Clothing & Protective Apparel: Hair Nets*
Hamburger & Meat Patty Processing *See Equipment & Machinery: Food Processing: Hamburger & Meat Patty Processing*
Hammer Mills *See Equipment & Machinery: Food Processing: Mills: Hammer*
Hand Carts *See Transportation & Storage: Carts: Hand*
Hand Cleaners *See Sanitation Equipment & Supplies: Cleaners: Hand*
Hand Trucks *See Transportation & Storage: Trucks: Hand*
Heat Exchangers *See Equipment & Machinery: Food Processing: Heat Exchangers*
Heat Resistant Glassware *See Food Preparation Equipment, Utensils & Cookware: Glassware: Heat Resistant*
Heat Sealed Bags *See Packaging Materials & Supplies: Bags: Heat Sealed*
Heat Sealers *See Equipment & Machinery: Packaging: Sealers: Heat*
Heat Sealing *See Equipment & Machinery: Packaging: Heat Sealing*
Heat Sealing Paper *See Packaging Materials & Supplies: Paper: Heat Sealing*
Heat Sealing Tapes *See Packaging Materials & Supplies: Tapes: Heat Sealing*
Heat Transfer Fluids *See Equipment & Machinery: Food Processing: Heat Transfer Fluids*
Heaters *See Equipment & Machinery: Heaters*
Heating, Ventilation & Air Conditioning *See Building Equipment & Supplies: Heating, Ventilation & Air Conditioning: Heating*
Hoists & Lifting Equipment *See Transportation & Storage: Hoists & Lifting Equipment*
Holders *See Clothing & Protective Apparel: Holders; Food Preparation Equipment, Utensils & Cookware: Holders; Foodservice Equipment & Supplies: Holders; Sanitation Equipment & Supplies: Holders*
Holding & Warming Equipment *See Foodservice Equipment & Supplies: Holding & Warming Equipment*
Holding, Storage Tanks *See Transportation & Storage: Tanks: Holding, Storage*
Hollowware *See Food Preparation Equipment, Utensils & Cookware: Hollowware*
Homogenizers *See Equipment & Machinery: Food Processing: Homogenizers*
Honey Processing *See Equipment & Machinery: Food Processing: Honey Processing*
Hoods *See Building Equipment & Supplies: Hoods*
Hooks *See Food Preparation Equipment, Utensils & Cookware: Hooks; Foodservice Equipment & Supplies: Hooks*
Hoops *See Food Preparation Equipment, Utensils & Cookware: Hoops*
Hoppers *See Equipment & Machinery: Food Processing: Hoppers*
Horizontal Form, Fill & Seal *See Equipment & Machinery: Packaging: Form, Fill & Seal: Horizontal*
Hose Reels *See Equipment & Machinery: Hose Reels*
Hoses *See Equipment & Machinery: Hoses*
Hospitals & Healthcare Foodservice *See Consultants & Services: Foodservice: Hospitals & Healthcare*
Hotel & Restaurant Glassware *See Food Preparation Equipment, Utensils & Cookware: Glassware: Hotel & Restaurant*
Hotel, Bar, Restaurant Interiors *See Foodservice Equipment & Supplies: Interiors: Hotel, Bar, Restaurant*
Household, Consumer Detergents *See Sanitation Equipment & Supplies: Detergents: Household, Consumer*
Household, Kitchen Utensils *See Food Preparation Equipment, Utensils & Cookware: Utensils: Household, Kitchen*
Housekeeping Carts *See Sanitation Equipment & Supplies: Carts: Housekeeping*
Hullers *See Equipment & Machinery: Food Processing: Hullers*
Humidity Loggers *See Instrumentation & Laboratory Equipment: Process Controls: Humidity Loggers*
Huskers *See Equipment & Machinery: Food Processing: Huskers*

I

Ice Breaking, Chipping, Crushing *See Equipment & Machinery: Food Processing: Ice Breaking, Chipping, Crushing*
Ice Carts *See Foodservice Equipment & Supplies: Carts: Ice*
Ice Coolers *See Refrigeration & Cooling Equipment: Coolers: Ice*
Ice Cream & Frozen Yogurt Dispensers *See Foodservice Equipment & Supplies: Dispensers: Ice Cream & Frozen Yogurt*
Ice Cream Cans *See Packaging Materials & Supplies: Cans: Ice Cream*
Ice Cream Cone, Bar, Biscuit Processing *See Equipment & Machinery: Food Processing: Ice Cream Cone, Bar, Biscuit Processing*
Ice Cream Coolers *See Refrigeration & Cooling Equipment: Coolers: Ice Cream*
Ice Cream Freezers *See Refrigeration & Cooling Equipment: Freezers: Ice Cream*
Ice Cream Processing *See Equipment & Machinery: Food Processing: Ice Cream Processing*
Ice Cream Sticks *See Packaging Materials & Supplies: Sticks: Ice Cream*
Ice Cubing *See Equipment & Machinery: Food Processing: Ice Cubing*
Ice Making Plants *See Consultants & Services: Ice Making Plants*
Ice Making, Refrigerating & Cooling *See Equipment & Machinery: Food Processing: Ice Making, Refrigerating & Cooling*
Ice Tongs *See Food Preparation Equipment, Utensils & Cookware: Tongs: Ice*
Incandescent Lighting *See Building Equipment & Supplies: Lighting Equipment: Incandescent*
Incinerators *See Sanitation Equipment & Supplies: Incinerators*
Incubators & Brooders *See Equipment & Machinery: Incubators & Brooders*
Indelible Inks *See Packaging Materials & Supplies: Inks: Indelible*
Indoor Sign Holders *See Foodservice Equipment & Supplies: Clear & Colored Plastic: Indoor Sign Holders*
Industrial Clutches & Brakes *See Transportation & Storage: Clutches & Brakes: Industrial*
Industrial Detergents *See Sanitation Equipment & Supplies: Detergents: Industrial*
Industrial Flooring *See Building Equipment & Supplies: Flooring: Industrial Flooring*
Industrial Lubricants *See Equipment & Machinery: Lubricants: Industrial*
Industrial Plant Serving *See Foodservice Equipment & Supplies: Serving Equipment: Industrial Plant*
Industrial Vacuum Cleaners *See Sanitation Equipment & Supplies: Vacuum Cleaners: Industrial*
Ingredient Water Coolers *See Refrigeration & Cooling Equipment: Coolers: Ingredient Water*
Inks *See Packaging Materials & Supplies: Inks*
Insecticides & Insect Control Systems *See Sanitation Equipment & Supplies: Insecticides & Insect Control Systems*
Inspection & Analysis *See Instrumentation & Laboratory Equipment: Inspection & Analysis Instrumentation & Systems*
Instrumentation *See Instrumentation & Laboratory Equipment: Instrumentation*
Insulated Bins *See Packaging Materials & Supplies: Bins: Insulated*
Insulated Panels *See Building Equipment & Supplies: Panels: Insulated*
Insulated Warehouses *See Transportation & Storage: Warehouses: Insulated*
Insulation *See Refrigeration & Cooling Equipment: Insulation*
Interchangeable Signs *See Foodservice Equipment & Supplies: Signs: Interchangeable*
Interior & Store Fixture Designers *See Consultants & Services: Designers: Interior & Store Fixture*
Interiors *See Foodservice Equipment & Supplies: Interiors*
Irradiation Preservation *See Equipment & Machinery: Food Processing: Preservation: Irradiation*
Irradiation Processing *See Equipment & Machinery: Food Processing: Irradiation Processing*
Isopropyl Alcohol *See Sanitation Equipment & Supplies: Isopropyl Alcohol*

J

Jackets *See Clothing & Protective Apparel: Jackets*
Jar Filling *See Equipment & Machinery: Packaging: Jar Filling*
Jars *See Packaging Materials & Supplies: Jars*

K

Kettles *See Food Preparation Equipment, Utensils & Cookware: Kettles*
Kiosks *See Foodservice Equipment & Supplies: Kiosks*
Kitchen (Commercial, Institutional, Restaurant) Designers *See Consultants & Services: Designers: Kitchen (Commercial, Institutional, Restaurant)*
Kitchen Racks *See Transportation & Storage: Racks: Kitchen*
Knife Sharpeners *See Food Preparation Equipment, Utensils & Cookware: Knife Sharpeners*
Knives *See Food Preparation Equipment, Utensils & Cookware: Knives*
Kosher Food Consultants *See Consultants & Services: Consultants: Kosher Food*
Kraft Paper *See Packaging Materials & Supplies: Paper: Kraft*
Kraut & Slaw Cutters *See Food Preparation Equipment, Utensils & Cookware: Cutters: Kraut & Slaw*

L

Label Holders *See Foodservice Equipment & Supplies: Plastic Back Tag: Label Holders*
Label Paper *See Packaging Materials & Supplies: Paper: Label*
Label Printing *See Equipment & Machinery: Packaging: Label Printing*
Labeling *See Equipment & Machinery: Packaging: Labeling*
Labels *See Packaging Materials & Supplies: Labels*
Laboratories *See Consultants & Services: Laboratories*
Laboratory Balances *See Instrumentation & Laboratory Equipment: Balances: Laboratory*
Laboratory Chemicals *See Instrumentation & Laboratory Equipment: Chemicals: Laboratory*
Laboratory Equipment *See Instrumentation & Laboratory Equipment: Laboratory Equipment*
Laboratory Testers *See Instrumentation & Laboratory Equipment: Testers: Laboratory*
Ladder Covers *See Safety & Security Equipment & Supplies: Ladder Covers*
Ladder Rungs *See Safety & Security Equipment & Supplies: Ladder Rungs*
Ladles *See Food Preparation Equipment, Utensils & Cookware: Ladles*
Laminated Bags *See Packaging Materials & Supplies: Bags: Laminated*
Laminated Paper *See Packaging Materials & Supplies: Paper: Laminated*
Lard Kettles *See Food Preparation Equipment, Utensils & Cookware: Kettles: Lard*
Level, Liquid & Dry Controls *See Instrumentation & Laboratory Equipment: Controls: Level, Liquid & Dry*
Lift Truck Pallets *See Transportation & Storage: Pallets: Lift Truck*
Lighting Equipment *See Building Equipment & Supplies: Lighting Equipment*
Lighting Fixtures *See Building Equipment & Supplies: Lighting Equipment: Lighting Fixtures*
Linen Goods *See Foodservice Equipment & Supplies: Linen Goods*
Liners *See Food Preparation Equipment, Utensils & Cookware: Liners*
Lining Paper *See Packaging Materials & Supplies: Paper: Lining*
Linings *See Packaging Materials & Supplies: Linings*
Liquid Chlorine *See Sanitation Equipment & Supplies: Chlorine: Liquid*
Liquid Product *See Consultants & Services: Contract Packaging: Liquid Product*
Liquid-Solid Separators *See Equipment & Machinery: Food Processing: Separators: Liquid-Solid*

Liquor, Wine Carts See *Foodservice Equipment & Supplies: Carts: Liquor, Wine*
Live Skid Pallets See *Transportation & Storage: Pallets: Live Skid*
Load Cells & Indicators See *Equipment & Machinery: Load Cells & Indicators*
Lockers See *Refrigeration & Cooling Equipment: Lockers*
Loin Knives See *Food Preparation Equipment, Utensils & Cookware: Knives: Loin*
Lotion See *Sanitation Equipment & Supplies: Skin Cream & Lotions: Lotion*
Lubricants See *Equipment & Machinery: Lubricants*
Luminous Tube Signs See *Foodservice Equipment & Supplies: Signs: Luminous Tube*

M

Machine Knives See *Food Preparation Equipment, Utensils & Cookware: Knives: Machine*
Magnetic Chips See *Foodservice Equipment & Supplies: Magnetic Chips*
Magnetic Label See *Foodservice Equipment & Supplies: Magnetic Label*
Magnetic Pocket See *Foodservice Equipment & Supplies: Magnetic Pocket*
Magnets See *Food Preparation Equipment, Utensils & Cookware: Magnets*
Malt Mills See *Equipment & Machinery: Food Processing: Mills: Malt*
Management See *Consultants & Services: Construction: Management*
Manufacturing Screening See *Equipment & Machinery: Screening: Manufacturing*
Markers, Pens & Pencils See *Packaging Materials & Supplies: Markers, Pens & Pencils; Foodservice Equipment & Supplies: Markers*
Marketing & Promotion Consultants See *Consultants & Services: Consultants: Marketing & Promotion*
Marking & Coding Inks See *Packaging Materials & Supplies: Inks: Marking & Coding*
Marking Tapes See *Packaging Materials & Supplies: Tapes: Marking*
Master Planning & Logistics See *Consultants & Services: Master Planning & Logistics*
Matches See *Food Preparation Equipment, Utensils & Cookware: Matches*
Material Handling & Distribution Equipment See *Transportation & Storage: Material Handling & Distribution Equipment*
Material Handling Consultants See *Consultants & Services: Consultants: Material Handling*
Materials See *Equipment & Machinery: Packaging: Equipment: Materials*
Mats & Matting Flooring See *Building Equipment & Supplies: Flooring: Mats & Matting*
Mats See *Safety & Security Equipment & Supplies: Mats*
Measurement Systems See *Instrumentation & Laboratory Equipment: Measurement Systems*
Measures See *Equipment & Machinery: Measures*
Meat Bags See *Packaging Materials & Supplies: Bags: Meat*
Meat Branding See *Packaging Materials & Supplies: Inks: Meat Branding*
Meat Curing See *Equipment & Machinery: Food Processing: Vats: Meat Curing*
Meat Cutters See *Food Preparation Equipment, Utensils & Cookware: Cutters: Meat*
Meat Dealers See *Consultants & Services: Dealers: Meat*
Meat Hooks See *Food Preparation Equipment, Utensils & Cookware: Hooks: Meat*
Meat Micer See *Food Preparation Equipment, Utensils & Cookware: Micer: Meat*
Meat Mincer See *Food Preparation Equipment, Utensils & Cookware: Mincer: Meat*
Meat Packers See *Consultants & Services: Packers: Meat*
Meat Packing Knives See *Food Preparation Equipment, Utensils & Cookware: Knives: Meat Packing*
Meat Preparation Equipment See *Equipment & Machinery: Food Processing: Meat Preparation Equipment*
Meat Slicers See *Equipment & Machinery: Food Processing: Slicers: Meat*
Meat Trucks See *Transportation & Storage: Trucks: Meat*
Menu Boards See *Foodservice Equipment & Supplies: Menu Boards*
Menus See *Foodservice Equipment & Supplies: Menus*
Mercury, High Intensity Lighting Equipment See *Building Equipment & Supplies: Lighting Equipment: Mercury, High Intensity*
Metal & Contamination Detection Systems See *Equipment & Machinery: Systems: Metal & Contamination Detection*
Metal Decking See *Building Equipment & Supplies: Decking: Metal*
Metal Detectors See *Safety & Security Equipment & Supplies: Detectors: Metal; See also Safety & Security Equipment & Supplies: Metal Detectors*
Metal Fabricators See *Consultants & Services: Construction: Metal Fabricators*
Metal Flooring See *Building Equipment & Supplies: Flooring: Metal*
Metal Grating See *Building Equipment & Supplies: Grating: Metal*
Metal Plating See *Building Equipment & Supplies: Plating: Metal*
Meters See *Instrumentation & Laboratory Equipment: Meters*
Micer See *Food Preparation Equipment, Utensils & Cookware: Micer*
Microbiology Instruments & Supplies See *Instrumentation & Laboratory Equipment: Microbiology Instruments & Supplies*
Microprocessor Controls See *Instrumentation & Laboratory Equipment: Controls: Microprocessor*
Microwave Ovens See *Equipment & Machinery: Food Processing: Microwave Ovens*
Milk & Cream Coolers See *Refrigeration & Cooling Equipment: Coolers: Milk & Cream*
Milk & Cream Regenerators See *Equipment & Machinery: Food Processing: Regenerators: Milk & Cream*
Milk & Cream Testers See *Instrumentation & Laboratory Equipment: Testers: Milk & Cream*
Milk Agitators See *Equipment & Machinery: Food Processing: Agitators: Milk*
Milk Bottle Carriers See *Packaging Materials & Supplies: Carriers: Milk Bottle*
Milk Cans See *Packaging Materials & Supplies: Cans: Milk*
Milk Evaporators See *Equipment & Machinery: Food Processing: Evaporators: Milk*
Milking See *Equipment & Machinery: Food Processing: Milking*
Mills See *Equipment & Machinery: Food Processing: Mills*
Mincer See *Food Preparation Equipment, Utensils & Cookware: Mincer*
Mirrors See *Equipment & Machinery: Mirrors*
Mist Collection See *Equipment & Machinery: Systems: Mist Collection*
Mixers See *Equipment & Machinery: Food Processing: Mixers*
Mixing Kettles See *Food Preparation Equipment, Utensils & Cookware: Kettles: Mixing*
Mobile Food Vending Carts See *Foodservice Equipment & Supplies: Carts: Mobile Food Vending*
Modular Tanks See *Transportation & Storage: Tanks: Modular*
Moldings See *Foodservice Equipment & Supplies: Plastic Store Shelf: Moldings*
Molds See *Food Preparation Equipment, Utensils & Cookware: Molds*
Mop Wringers See *Sanitation Equipment & Supplies: Mop Wringers*
Mops See *Sanitation Equipment & Supplies: Mops*
Multi-Wall Bags See *Packaging Materials & Supplies: Bags: Multi-Wall*
Mycotoxins See *Instrumentation & Laboratory Equipment: Analyzers: Mycotoxins*

N

Name Badges See *Clothing & Protective Apparel: Name Badges*
Napery See *Foodservice Equipment & Supplies: Napery*
Napkins See *Foodservice Equipment & Supplies: Napkins*
Netting, Open Mesh Bags See *Packaging Materials & Supplies: Bags: Netting, Open Mesh*
Nitrites, Nitrosamines See *Instrumentation & Laboratory Equipment: Analyzers: Nitrites, Nitrosamines*
Nozzles See *Equipment & Machinery: Nozzles*
Numerical Controls See *Instrumentation & Laboratory Equipment: Controls: Numerical*
Nut Cracking, Shelling & Salting See *Equipment & Machinery: Food Processing: Nut Cracking, Shelling & Salting*
Nut Grinding Mills See *Equipment & Machinery: Food Processing: Mills: Nut Grinding*
Nutritional Analyses & Labeling See *Consultants & Services: Nutritional Analyses & Labeling*

O

Oil Cake Grinding Mills See *Equipment & Machinery: Food Processing: Mills: Oil Cake Grinding*
Oil Extraction See *Equipment & Machinery: Food Processing: Oil Extraction*
Oil, Cottonseed & Linseed Presses See *Equipment & Machinery: Food Processing: Presses: Oil, Cottonseed & Linseed*
Oils See *Sanitation Equipment & Supplies: Oils*
Openers See *Equipment & Machinery: Openers*
Organic Acids See *Instrumentation & Laboratory Equipment: Analyzers: Organic Acids*
Outdoor Lighting See *Building Equipment & Supplies: Lighting Equipment: Outdoor*
Oven Mits See *Clothing & Protective Apparel: Oven Mits*
Ovens See *Equipment & Machinery: Food Processing: Ovens*
Oyster & Clam Knives See *Food Preparation Equipment, Utensils & Cookware: Knives: Oyster & Clam*

P

Package Tying See *Equipment & Machinery: Packaging: Package Tying*
Package, Carton & Display See *Consultants & Services: Designers: Package, Carton & Display*
Packaging & Containerizing See *Packaging Materials & Supplies: Packaging & Containerizing Products*
Packaging Consultants See *Consultants & Services: Consultants: Packaging*
Packaging Line Controls See *Instrumentation & Laboratory Equipment: Controls: Packaging Line*
Packaging Line Detectors See *Equipment & Machinery: Packaging: Detectors: Packaging Line*
Packaging Materials See *Instrumentation & Laboratory Equipment: Testers: Packaging Materials/Containers*
Packaging Services See *Consultants & Services: Packaging Services*
Packaging Systems See *Equipment & Machinery: Systems: Packaging*
Packaging See *Equipment & Machinery: Packaging; Packaging Materials & Supplies: Packaging*
Packers' & Butchers' Processing See *Equipment & Machinery: Food Processing: Packers' & Butchers'*
Packers' Glassware See *Food Preparation Equipment, Utensils & Cookware: Glassware: Packers'*
Packers See *Consultants & Services: Packers*
Packing House Racks See *Transportation & Storage: Racks: Packing House*
Packing House Supplies See *Packaging Materials & Supplies: Packing House Supplies*
Packing House Tables See *Equipment & Machinery: Packaging: Tables: Packing House*
Packing House Trucks See *Transportation & Storage: Trucks: Packing House*
Packing See *Equipment & Machinery: Packaging: Packing*
Paging Systems See *Building Equipment & Supplies: Paging Systems*
Pails See *Equipment & Machinery: Pails*
Pallet Handling Equipment See *Transportation & Storage: Pallet Handling Equipment*

EXAMPLE: **Dairy Cooling Vats** See *Equipment & Machinery: Food Processing: Vats: Dairy Cooling*
(1 = Dairy Cooling Vats; 2 = Equipment & Machinery; 3 = Food Processing; 4 = Vats; 5 = Dairy Cooling)

1. Product or Service you are looking for
2. Main Category, in alphabetical order, located in the page headers starting on page 13
3. Category Description, located in black bars and in page headers
4. Product Category, located in gray bars
5. Product Type, located under gray bars, centered in bold

Pallet Handling Trucks *See Transportation & Storage: Trucks: Pallet Handling*
Pallet Racks *See Transportation & Storage: Racks: Pallet*
Palletizers *See Transportation & Storage: Palletizers*
Pallets *See Transportation & Storage: Pallets; Building Equipment & Supplies: Panels*
Panomatic-Flour Collection System *See Equipment & Machinery: Food Processing: Panomatic-Flour Collection System*
Pans *See Food Preparation Equipment, Utensils & Cookware: Pans*
Paper Bags *See Packaging Materials & Supplies: Bags: Paper*
Paper Boxes *See Packaging Materials & Supplies: Boxes: Paper*
Paper Containers *See Packaging Materials & Supplies: Containers: Paper*
Paper Cups *See Packaging Materials & Supplies: Cups: Paper*
Paper Dishes *See Foodservice Equipment & Supplies: Dishes: Paper*
Paper Filters *See Equipment & Machinery: Food Processing: Filters: Paper*
Paper Lined Bags *See Packaging Materials & Supplies: Bags: Paper Lined*
Paper Napkins *See Foodservice Equipment & Supplies: Napkins: Paper*
Paper Plates *See Food Preparation Equipment, Utensils & Cookware: Plates: Paper*
Paper Towels *See Foodservice Equipment & Supplies: Towels: Paper*
Paper Wrappers *See Packaging Materials & Supplies: Wrappers: Paper*
Paper, Folding Boxes *See Packaging Materials & Supplies: Boxes: Paper, Folding*
Paper *See Foodservice Equipment & Supplies: Paper; Packaging Materials & Supplies: Paper*
Paraffin Wax *See Packaging Materials & Supplies: Wax: Paraffin*
Parers & Peelers *See Food Preparation Equipment, Utensils & Cookware: Parers & Peelers*
Parts Food Processing *See Equipment & Machinery: Food Processing: Food Processing: Parts*
Parts *See Equipment & Machinery: Parts*
Pasta Processing *See Equipment & Machinery: Food Processing: Pasta Processing*
Paste Products Mixers *See Equipment & Machinery: Food Processing: Mixers: Paste Products*
Pasteurizers *See Equipment & Machinery: Food Processing: Pasteurizers*
Peanut Butter Mills *See Equipment & Machinery: Food Processing: Mills: Peanut Butter*
Peanut Processing *See Equipment & Machinery: Food Processing: Peanut Processing*
Personnel Services *See Consultants & Services: Personnel Services*
Pest Control *See Sanitation Equipment & Supplies: Pest Control Systems & Devices; Sanitation Equipment & Supplies: Pest Control*
Pesticide Residue *See Instrumentation & Laboratory Equipment: Analyzers: Pesticide Residue, Antibiotics*
pH Loggers *See Instrumentation & Laboratory Equipment: Process Controls: pH Loggers*
pH Meters *See Instrumentation & Laboratory Equipment: Meters: pH*
Pharmaceutical Industry *See Equipment & Machinery: Pharmaceutical Industry*
Pickers *See Equipment & Machinery: Food Processing: Pickers*
Pickle Cutters *See Food Preparation Equipment, Utensils & Cookware: Cutters: Pickle*
Pie Pans *See Food Preparation Equipment, Utensils & Cookware: Pans: Pie*
Pie Plates *See Food Preparation Equipment, Utensils & Cookware: Plates: Pie*
Pizza & Pizza Products *See Equipment & Machinery: Food Processing: Pizza & Pizza Products Processing*
Place Mats *See Foodservice Equipment & Supplies: Place Mats*
Plastic Back Tag *See Foodservice Equipment & Supplies: Plastic Back Tag*
Plastic Bags *See Packaging Materials & Supplies: Bags: Plastic*
Plastic Bottles *See Packaging Materials & Supplies: Bottles: Plastic*
Plastic Boxes *See Packaging Materials & Supplies: Boxes: Plastic*
Plastic Coated Paper *See Packaging Materials & Supplies: Paper: Plastic Coated*
Plastic Containers *See Packaging Materials & Supplies: Containers: Plastic*
Plastic Cups *See Packaging Materials & Supplies: Cups: Plastic*
Plastic Doors *See Building Equipment & Supplies: Doors: Plastic*
Plastic Fabricators *See Equipment & Machinery: Plastic Fabricators*
Plastic Film *See Packaging Materials & Supplies: Film: Plastic*
Plastic Jars *See Packaging Materials & Supplies: Jars: Plastic*
Plastic Packaging *See Packaging Materials & Supplies: Packaging: Plastic*
Plastic Pallets *See Transportation & Storage: Pallets: Plastic*
Plastic Shelf Covers *See Foodservice Equipment & Supplies: Plastic Shelf Covers*
Plastic Signs *See Foodservice Equipment & Supplies: Signs: Plastic*
Plastic Store Shelf *See Foodservice Equipment & Supplies: Plastic Store Shelf*
Plastic Trays *See Foodservice Equipment & Supplies: Trays: Plastic*
Plastic Tubing *See Equipment & Machinery: Tubing: Plastic*
Plastic Utensils *See Foodservice Equipment & Supplies: Utensils: Plastic*
Plastic, Reusable Plates *See Food Preparation Equipment, Utensils & Cookware: Plates: Plastic, Reusable*
Plastic, Rubber Gloves *See Clothing & Protective Apparel: Gloves: Plastic, Rubber*
Plastic *See Packaging Materials & Supplies: Plastic*
Plastics Printing *See Equipment & Machinery: Packaging: Printing: Plastics*
Plate & Tray Dispensers *See Foodservice Equipment & Supplies: Dispensers: Plate & Tray*
Plate/Frame Exchanger *See Equipment & Machinery: Plate/Frame Exchanger*
Plates *See Food Preparation Equipment, Utensils & Cookware: Plates*
Platforms *See Building Equipment & Supplies: Platforms*
Plating *See Building Equipment & Supplies: Plating*
Platters *See Food Preparation Equipment, Utensils & Cookware: Platters*
Plumbing & Drainage *See Sanitation Equipment & Supplies: Plumbing & Drainage Equipment*
Point of Purchase Displays *See Foodservice Equipment & Supplies: Displays: Point of Purchase*
Point of Purchase Signs *See Foodservice Equipment & Supplies: Signs: Point of Purchase*
Point of Sale Systems *See Foodservice Equipment & Supplies: Point of Sale Systems*
Polarimeters *See Instrumentation & Laboratory Equipment: Measurement Systems: Polarimeters*
Polish *See Sanitation Equipment & Supplies: Polish*
Polishing, Refinishing, Sanding & Scrubbing *See Sanitation Equipment & Supplies: Floor Cleaning Machinery: Polishing, Refinishing, Sanding & Scrubbing*
Polyethylene Bags *See Packaging Materials & Supplies: Bags: Polyethylene*
Polypropylene Bags *See Packaging Materials & Supplies: Bags: Polypropylene*
Popcorn Bags *See Packaging Materials & Supplies: Bags: Popcorn*
Portion Control Equipment *See Equipment & Machinery: Packaging: Portion Control Equipment*
Pot Holders *See Clothing & Protective Apparel: Holders: Pot*
Potato & Onion Sorters *See Equipment & Machinery: Food Processing: Sorters: Potato & Onion*
Potato Chip Processing *See Equipment & Machinery: Food Processing: Potato Chip Processing*
Poultry Pickers *See Equipment & Machinery: Food Processing: Pickers: Poultry*
Poultry Processing *See Equipment & Machinery: Food Processing: Poultry Processing*
Poultry Shears *See Food Preparation Equipment, Utensils & Cookware: Shears: Poultry*
Powder Soap *See Sanitation Equipment & Supplies: Soap: Powder*
Powder *See Sanitation Equipment & Supplies: Powder*
Power Meat Cutters *See Food Preparation Equipment, Utensils & Cookware: Cutters: Meat: Power*
Powered Beer Keg Movers *See Transportation & Storage: Beer Keg Movers: Powered*
Preservation *See Equipment & Machinery: Food Processing: Preservation*
Presses *See Equipment & Machinery: Food Processing: Presses*
Pressure Cookers *See Equipment & Machinery: Food Processing: Cookers: Pressure*
Pressure Process Controls *See Instrumentation & Laboratory Equipment: Process Controls: Pressure*
Pressure Sensitive Film *See Packaging Materials & Supplies: Film: Pressure Sensitive*
Pressure Sensitive Foil *See Packaging Materials & Supplies: Foil: Pressure Sensitive*
Pressure Sensitive Labels *See Packaging Materials & Supplies: Labels: Pressure Sensitive*
Pressure Sensitive Paper *See Packaging Materials & Supplies: Paper: Pressure Sensitive*
Pressure Sensitive Seals *See Packaging Materials & Supplies: Seals: Pressure Sensitive*
Pressure Sensitive Tags *See Packaging Materials & Supplies: Tags: Pressure Sensitive*
Pressure Sensitive Tapes *See Packaging Materials & Supplies: Tapes: Pressure Sensitive*
Pressure Washers *See Sanitation Equipment & Supplies: Pressure Washers*
Pretzel Processing *See Equipment & Machinery: Food Processing: Pretzel Processing*
Price & Sign Markers *See Foodservice Equipment & Supplies: Markers: Price & Sign*
Price Card, Ticket, Etc. Holders *See Foodservice Equipment & Supplies: Holders: Price Card, Ticket, Etc.*
Price Tag Seals *See Packaging Materials & Supplies: Seals: Price Tag*
Price Tags *See Packaging Materials & Supplies: Tags: Price*
Pricer Signs *See Foodservice Equipment & Supplies: Pricer Signs*
Pricing Systems *See Equipment & Machinery: Systems: Pricing*
Primary & Secondary Schools Foodservice *See Consultants & Services: Foodservice: Primary & Secondary Schools*
Printed & Laminated Foil *See Packaging Materials & Supplies: Foil: Printed & Laminated*
Printing Carton *See Equipment & Machinery: Packaging: Carton: Printing*
Printing *See Equipment & Machinery: Packaging: Printing*
Private Label *See Packaging Materials & Supplies: Labels: Private Label*
Private Label Packaging *See Packaging Materials & Supplies: Packaging: Private Label*
Process & Production Systems *See Equipment & Machinery: Systems: Process & Production*
Process Analysis & Development *See Instrumentation & Laboratory Equipment: Process Analysis & Development*
Process Controls *See Instrumentation & Laboratory Equipment: Process Controls*
Process Vessels & Tanks *See Consultants & Services: Designers: Process Vessels & Tanks*
Programmable Process Controls *See Instrumentation & Laboratory Equipment: Process Controls: Programmable*
Project Management *See Consultants & Services: Project Management*
Protective Apparel *See Clothing & Protective Apparel: Protective Apparel*
Protective Gloves *See Clothing & Protective Apparel: Gloves: Protective*
Pulpers *See Equipment & Machinery: Food Processing: Pulpers*
Pulverizers *See Equipment & Machinery: Food Processing: Pulverizers*
Pump feeders *See Equipment & Machinery: Pump feeders*
Pumps *See Equipment & Machinery: Pumps; Foodservice Equipment & Supplies: Pumps; Instrumentation & Laboratory Equipment: Pumps*
Purifiers *See Equipment & Machinery: Water Treatment: Purifiers*

Q

Quality Control *See Consultants & Services: Quality Control*

Quick Freezing *See Refrigeration & Cooling Equipment: Freezers: Quick Freezing*

R

Racks Dishwasher *See Sanitation Equipment & Supplies: Dishwasher: Racks*

Racks Refrigerators *See Refrigeration & Cooling Equipment: Refrigerators: Racks*

Racks *See Foodservice Equipment & Supplies: Racks; Transportation & Storage: Racks*

Radios Paging Systems *See Building Equipment & Supplies: Paging Systems: Radios*

Ramps *See Transportation & Storage: Ramps*

Rat & Mouse Traps *See Sanitation Equipment & Supplies: Pest Control Systems & Devices: Traps: Rat & Mouse*

Rebuilt & Used *See Equipment & Machinery: Food Processing: Food Processing: Rebuilt & Used*

Rebuilt & Used Packaging *See Equipment & Machinery: Packaging: Rebuilt & Used*

Rechargable Flashlights *See Safety & Security Equipment & Supplies: Flashlights: Rechargable*

Recorders *See Instrumentation & Laboratory Equipment: Process Controls: Recorders*

Refinishing *See Consultants & Services: Refinishing & Refurbishing Services*

Refractometers *See Instrumentation & Laboratory Equipment: Measurement Systems: Refractometers*

Refrigerated Display Case Doors *See Refrigeration & Cooling Equipment: Doors: Refrigerated Display Case*

Refrigerated Trailers *See Transportation & Storage: Trailers: Refrigerated*

Refrigerating & Cooling Rooms *See Refrigeration & Cooling Equipment: Refrigerating & Cooling Rooms*

Refrigerating Equipment & Machinery *See Refrigeration & Cooling Equipment: Refrigerating Equipment & Machinery*

Refrigerating Units *See Refrigeration & Cooling Equipment: Refrigerating Units*

Refrigeration & Cold Storage Insulation *See Refrigeration & Cooling Equipment: Insulation: Refrigeration & Cold Storage*

Refrigeration Systems *See Instrumentation & Laboratory Equipment: Controls: Refrigeration Systems*

Refrigeration Valves *See Refrigeration & Cooling Equipment: Valves: Refrigeration*

Refrigerator & Stove Shelves *See Equipment & Machinery: Shelves: Refrigerator & Stove*

Refrigerator Baskets *See Packaging Materials & Supplies: Baskets: Refrigerator*

Refrigerator Doors *See Refrigeration & Cooling Equipment: Doors: Refrigerator*

Refrigerators *See Refrigeration & Cooling Equipment: Refrigerators*

Regenerators *See Equipment & Machinery: Food Processing: Regenerators*

Research & Development *See Consultants & Services: Research & Development*

Resistant Flooring *See Building Equipment & Supplies: Flooring: Thermal Shock: Resistant Flooring*

Restaurant Design *See Consultants & Services: Consultants: Restaurant Design*

Restaurant Supplies & Equipment *See Foodservice Equipment & Supplies: Restaurant Supplies & Equipment*

Retail Architects *See Consultants & Services: Architects: Retail*

Retail Foodservice *See Consultants & Services: Foodservice: Retail*

Retort Pouch *See Equipment & Machinery: Packaging: Retort Pouch Processing*

Retorts *See Packaging Materials & Supplies: Retorts*

Reverse Osmosis *See Equipment & Machinery: Systems: Reverse Osmosis*

Reverse Vending *See Foodservice Equipment & Supplies: Vending Machinery: Reverse*

Rice Grinding Mills *See Equipment & Machinery: Food Processing: Mills: Rice Grinding*

Rice Processing *See Equipment & Machinery: Food Processing: Rice Processing*

Road Plates *See Equipment & Machinery: Road Plates*

Roasters *See Equipment & Machinery: Food Processing: Roasters*

Roasting *See Equipment & Machinery: Food Processing: Roasting*

Rolling Pins *See Food Preparation Equipment, Utensils & Cookware: Rolling Pins*

Room Service *See Foodservice Equipment & Supplies: Tables: Room Service*

Rotisseries *See Equipment & Machinery: Food Processing: Rotisseries*

Routing & Scheduling for Food Industry *See Consultants & Services: Computer Software, Systems & Services: Software: Routing & Scheduling for Food Industry*

Rubber Stamps *See Packaging Materials & Supplies: Stamps: Rubber*

Rubber, Bottle Stoppers *See Instrumentation & Laboratory Equipment: Stoppers: Rubber, Bottle*

S

Safety & Security *See Safety & Security Equipment & Supplies*

Safety Flooring *See Building Equipment & Supplies: Flooring: Safety*

Salad Bars *See Foodservice Equipment & Supplies: Salad Bars*

Salad Carts *See Foodservice Equipment & Supplies: Carts: Salad*

Salt & Pepper Shakers *See Packaging Materials & Supplies: Shakers: Salt & Pepper*

Salt *See Instrumentation & Laboratory Equipment: Analyzers: Salt (Sodium Chloride)*

Salt Processing *See Equipment & Machinery: Food Processing: Salt Processing*

Sampling & Testing *See Instrumentation & Laboratory Equipment: Sampling & Testing Equipment & Instrumentation*

Sandwich Bags *See Packaging Materials & Supplies: Bags: Sandwich*

Sandwich Processing *See Equipment & Machinery: Food Processing: Sandwich Processing*

Sanitary Wall *See Sanitation Equipment & Supplies: Sanitary Wall*

Sanitation Equipment & Supplies *See Sanitation Equipment & Supplies*

Sanitation, Testing & Analysis *See Consultants & Services: Consultants: Sanitation, Testing & Analysis*

Sanitizers *See Sanitation Equipment & Supplies: Sanitizers*

Sauce Pans *See Food Preparation Equipment, Utensils & Cookware: Pans: Sauce*

Sausage Meat Cutters *See Food Preparation Equipment, Utensils & Cookware: Cutters: Meat: Sausage*

Sausage Stuffers *See Equipment & Machinery: Food Processing: Stuffers: Sausage*

Sawdust Smokers *See Equipment & Machinery: Food Processing: Smokers: Sawdust*

Saws *See Equipment & Machinery: Food Processing: Saws*

Scalers *See Equipment & Machinery: Food Processing: Scalers*

Scales *See Instrumentation & Laboratory Equipment: Scales & Weighing Systems; Equipment & Machinery: Scales*

Scanners *See Foodservice Equipment & Supplies: Scanners*

Scoops, Dishers & Spades *See Food Preparation Equipment, Utensils & Cookware: Scoops, Dishers & Spades*

Scouring Pads *See Sanitation Equipment & Supplies: Scouring Pads*

Scrapers *See Food Preparation Equipment, Utensils & Cookware: Scrapers*

Screening *See Equipment & Machinery: Screening*

Scrubbers *See Equipment & Machinery: Scrubbers; See also Sanitation Equipment & Supplies: Scrubbers*

Seafood Preparation *See Equipment & Machinery: Food Processing: Seafood Preparation Equipment*

Sealers *See Equipment & Machinery: Packaging: Sealers*

Sealing Wax *See Packaging Materials & Supplies: Wax: Sealing*

Seals *See Packaging Materials & Supplies: Seals*

Sensors *See Instrumentation & Laboratory Equipment: Sensors*

Separators *See Equipment & Machinery: Food Processing: Separators*

Service Carts *See Foodservice Equipment & Supplies: Carts: Service*

Serving Equipment *See Foodservice Equipment & Supplies: Serving Equipment*

Shakers *See Packaging Materials & Supplies: Shakers*

Shears *See Food Preparation Equipment, Utensils & Cookware: Shears*

Sheeter *See Food Preparation Equipment, Utensils & Cookware: Sheeter*

Sheets *See Food Preparation Equipment, Utensils & Cookware: Sheets*

Shelf Covers *See Foodservice Equipment & Supplies: Wood Grain Plastic: Shelf Covers*

Shelf Strips Clear Plastic *See Foodservice Equipment & Supplies: Clear Plastic: Shelf Strips*

Shelf Strips Colored Plastic *See Foodservice Equipment & Supplies: Colored Plastic: Shelf Strips*

Shelves *See Equipment & Machinery: Shelves*

Shelving *See Foodservice Equipment & Supplies: Shelving; See also Transportation & Storage: Shelving*

Shirts *See Clothing & Protective Apparel: Shirts*

Shish Kebab *See Equipment & Machinery: Food Processing: Shish Kebab Systems*

Shoplifting Detectors *See Safety & Security Equipment & Supplies: Detectors: Shoplifting*

Shopping Bags *See Packaging Materials & Supplies: Bags: Shopping*

Shopping Baskets *See Foodservice Equipment & Supplies: Baskets: Shopping*

Shopping Carts *See Foodservice Equipment & Supplies: Carts: Shopping*

Shredded Paper *See Packaging Materials & Supplies: Paper: Shredded*

Shredders *See Equipment & Machinery: Food Processing: Shredders*

Shrimp Processing *See Equipment & Machinery: Food Processing: Shrimp Processing Equipment*

Shrink Packaging *See Packaging Materials & Supplies: Packaging: Shrink*

Shrinkers: Plastic *See Equipment & Machinery: Packaging: Shrinkers: Plastic Packaging*

Sieves *See Food Preparation Equipment, Utensils & Cookware: Sieves*

Sifters *See Food Preparation Equipment, Utensils & Cookware: Sifters*

Sign & Card Holders *See Foodservice Equipment & Supplies: Magnetic Pocket: Sign & Card Holders*

Signs *See Foodservice Equipment & Supplies: Signs*

Silver Cleaners *See Sanitation Equipment & Supplies: Cleaners: Silver*

Silverware Boxes *See Packaging Materials & Supplies: Boxes: Silverware*

Silverware Cleaning *See Sanitation Equipment & Supplies: Silverware Cleaning Machinery*

Sinks *See Building Equipment & Supplies: Sinks*

Sizers *See Equipment & Machinery: Sizers*

Skewers *See Food Preparation Equipment, Utensils & Cookware: Skewers*

Skids Systems *See Equipment & Machinery: Systems: Skids*

Skids *See Transportation & Storage: Skids*

Skin Cream & Lotions *See Sanitation Equipment & Supplies: Skin Cream & Lotions; Sanitation Equipment & Supplies: Skin Cream & Lotions: Skin Cream*

Skinning *See Equipment & Machinery: Food Processing: Skinning*

Sleeves *See Packaging Materials & Supplies: Sleeves*

Slicer *See Food Preparation Equipment, Utensils & Cookware: Slicer*

Slicers *See Equipment & Machinery: Food Processing: Slicers*

Slicing Knives *See Food Preparation Equipment, Utensils & Cookware: Knives: Slicing*

Smokers *See Equipment & Machinery: Food Processing: Smokers*

EXAMPLE: [1] **Dairy Cooling Vats** [2] *See Equipment & Machinery:* [3] *Food Processing:* [4] *Vats:* [5] *Dairy Cooling*

1. Product or Service you are looking for
2. Main Category, in alphabetical order, located in the page headers starting on page 13
3. Category Description, located in black bars and in page headers
4. Product Category, located in gray bars
5. Product Type, located under gray bars, centered in bold

Snack Food *See Equipment & Machinery: Food Processing: Snack Food Processing*

Sneeze Guards *See Sanitation Equipment & Supplies: Sneeze Guards*

Soap Dispensers *See Sanitation Equipment & Supplies: Dispensers: Soap*

Soap *See Sanitation Equipment & Supplies: Soap*

Soda Fountain, Syrup & Fruit Juice Dispensers *See Foodservice Equipment & Supplies: Dispensers: Soda Fountain, Syrup & Fruit Juice*

Softeners *See Equipment & Machinery: Water Treatment: Softeners*

Software Computer *See Consultants & Services: Computer Software, Systems & Services: Software*

Software Process Controls *See Instrumentation & Laboratory Equipment: Process Controls: Software*

Sorters *See Equipment & Machinery: Food Processing: Sorters; Equipment & Machinery: Packaging: Sorters; Foodservice Equipment & Supplies: Sorters*

Soybean Processing *See Equipment & Machinery: Food Processing: Soybean Processing*

Speed Reducer *See Equipment & Machinery: Feeders: Gravimetric, Volumetric, Loss-In-Weight, Etc.: Speed Reducer*

Spice Grinding *See Equipment & Machinery: Food Processing: Mills: Spice Grinding*

Spice Racks *See Transportation & Storage: Racks: Spice*

Sponges *See Sanitation Equipment & Supplies: Sponges*

Spoons *See Food Preparation Equipment, Utensils & Cookware: Spoons*

Spray Dryers *See Equipment & Machinery: Food Processing: Dryers: Spray*

Spray Drying Services *See Consultants & Services: Spray Drying Services*

Spray Nozzles *See Equipment & Machinery: Nozzles: Spray*

Sprinkling Systems *See Sanitation Equipment & Supplies: Sprinkling Systems*

Squeegees *See Sanitation Equipment & Supplies: Squeegees*

Stacking *See Equipment & Machinery: Stacking*

Stainless Steel *See Food Preparation Equipment, Utensils & Cookware: Pans: Baking & Roasting: Stainless Steel; Equipment & Machinery: Coffee Industry: Stainless Steel*

Stainless Steel Hoods *See Building Equipment & Supplies: Hoods: Stainless Steel*

Stainless Steel Tables *See Food Preparation Equipment, Utensils & Cookware: Tables: Stainless Steel*

Stainless Steel Tanks *See Transportation & Storage: Tanks: Stainless Steel*

Stainless Steel Tubing *See Equipment & Machinery: Tubing: Stainless Steel*

Stamps *See Packaging Materials & Supplies: Stamps*

Stands *See Packaging Materials & Supplies: Stands*

Steak Knives *See Food Preparation Equipment, Utensils & Cookware: Knives: Steak*

Steam Cookers *See Equipment & Machinery: Food Processing: Cookers: Steam*

Steam Generators *See Equipment & Machinery: Steam Generators*

Steam Tables *See Equipment & Machinery: Steam Tables*

Steaming *See Food Preparation Equipment, Utensils & Cookware: Kettles: Steaming*

Steel Shelving *See Transportation & Storage: Shelving: Steel*

Stemmers *See Equipment & Machinery: Food Processing: Stemmers*

Sterilizers *See Sanitation Equipment & Supplies: Sterilizers*

Sticks *See Packaging Materials & Supplies: Sticks*

Stirrers & Picks *See Food Preparation Equipment, Utensils & Cookware: Stirrers & Picks: Cocktail, Hors D'oeuvres*

Stock Racks *See Transportation & Storage: Racks: Stock*

Stoppers *See Instrumentation & Laboratory Equipment: Stoppers*

Storage & Holding Equipment *See Transportation & Storage: Storage & Holding Equipment*

Storage Units *See Transportation & Storage: Storage Units*

Store Fixtures *See Foodservice Equipment & Supplies: Fixtures: Store*

Store Shelving *See Foodservice Equipment & Supplies: Shelving: Store*

Stoves *See Equipment & Machinery: Food Processing: Stoves*

Strainers *See Food Preparation Equipment, Utensils & Cookware: Strainers*

Straws *See Foodservice Equipment & Supplies: Straws*

Strech Sleeve *See Equipment & Machinery: Packaging: Strech Sleeve Application Equipment*

Strip Doors *See Building Equipment & Supplies: Doors: Strip*

Strips Wood Grain *See Foodservice Equipment & Supplies: Wood Grain Plastic: Strips*

Stuffers *See Equipment & Machinery: Food Processing: Stuffers*

Styrofoam Cups *See Packaging Materials & Supplies: Cups: Styrofoam*

Sub-Zero Freezers *See Refrigeration & Cooling Equipment: Freezers: Sub-Zero*

Sugar & Sugar Cane Mills *See Equipment & Machinery: Food Processing: Mills: Sugar & Sugar Cane*

Sugar & Syrup Kettles *See Food Preparation Equipment, Utensils & Cookware: Kettles: Sugar & Syrup*

Sugar & Syrup Processing *See Equipment & Machinery: Food Processing: Sugar & Syrup Processing*

Sugar Pulverizers *See Equipment & Machinery: Food Processing: Pulverizers: Sugar*

Sugars *See Instrumentation & Laboratory Equipment: Analyzers: Sugars (Dextrose, Fructose, Galactose, Lactose, Sucrose)*

Sweeping *See Sanitation Equipment & Supplies: Compounds: Sweeping*

Syrup & Soda Fountain Pumps *See Foodservice Equipment & Supplies: Pumps: Syrup & Soda Fountain*

Systems & Component *See Equipment & Machinery: Conveyors: Systems & Components*

Systems Process Controls *See Instrumentation & Laboratory Equipment: Process Controls: Systems*

Systems *See Equipment & Machinery: Systems*

T

Table Cloths *See Foodservice Equipment & Supplies: Table Cloths*

Tables *See Equipment & Machinery: Packaging: Tables; Food Preparation Equipment, Utensils & Cookware: Tables; Foodservice Equipment & Supplies: Tables*

Tabletop Supplies *See Equipment & Machinery: Tabletop Supplies*

Tags *See Packaging Materials & Supplies: Tags*

Tanks *See Equipment & Machinery: Food Processing:Tanks; Transportation & Storage: Tanks*

Tapes *See Packaging Materials & Supplies: Tapes*

Tea Bag *See Packaging Materials & Supplies: Tags: Tea Bag*

Tea Industry *See Equipment & Machinery: Tea Industry*

Tea Packaging *See Packaging Materials & Supplies: Tea Packaging Materials*

Temperature Controlled *See Transportation & Storage: Storage Units: Temperature Controlled*

Temperature Process Controls *See Instrumentation & Laboratory Equipment: Process Controls: Temperature*

Testers *See Instrumentation & Laboratory Equipment: Testers*

Testing & Sampling Services *See Consultants & Services: Testing & Sampling Services*

Thermal Shock Flooring *See Building Equipment & Supplies: Flooring: Thermal Shock*

Thermometers *See Instrumentation & Laboratory Equipment: Thermometers*

Ties *See Packaging Materials & Supplies: Ties*

Tilt Trucks *See Transportation & Storage: Trucks: Tilt*

Time Process *See Instrumentation & Laboratory Equipment: Process Controls: Time*

Timers *See Equipment & Machinery: Timers*

Tin Cans *See Packaging Materials & Supplies: Cans: Tin*

Tins *See Food Preparation Equipment, Utensils & Cookware: Tins*

Tinware *See Food Preparation Equipment, Utensils & Cookware: Tinware*

Tissue *See Sanitation Equipment & Supplies: Tissue*

Toasters *See Equipment & Machinery: Food Processing: Toasters*

Tongs *See Food Preparation Equipment, Utensils & Cookware: Tongs*

Toothpicks *See Food Preparation Equipment, Utensils & Cookware: Toothpicks*

Tortilla Making *See Equipment & Machinery: Food Processing: Tortilla Making*

Tote Bags *See Foodservice Equipment & Supplies: Tote Bags*

Towels *See Foodservice Equipment & Supplies: Towels*

Trailers *See Transportation & Storage: Trailers*

Transparent Wrappers *See Packaging Materials & Supplies: Wrappers: Transparent*

Transportation Loggers *See Instrumentation & Laboratory Equipment: Process Controls: Transportation Loggers*

Traps *See Sanitation Equipment & Supplies: Pest Control Systems & Devices: Traps*

Tray Sealers *See Equipment & Machinery: Packaging: Sealers: Tray*

Tray Stands *See Packaging Materials & Supplies: Stands: Tray*

Tray, Silverware Carts *See Foodservice Equipment & Supplies: Carts: Tray, Silverware*

Trays & Pans *See Food Preparation Equipment, Utensils & Cookware: Trays & Pans*

Trays Refrigerators *See Refrigeration & Cooling Equipment: Refrigerators: Trays*

Trays *See Foodservice Equipment & Supplies: Trays; Packaging Materials & Supplies: Trays*

Treatment Systems *See Equipment & Machinery: Water Treatment: Treatment Systems*

Truck, Trailer & Refrigerator Car *See Refrigeration & Cooling Equipment: Refrigerating Units: Truck, Trailer & Refrigerator Car*

Trucks *See Transportation & Storage: Trucks*

Tubing *See Equipment & Machinery: Tubing*

Tubularaseptic Processing *See Equipment & Machinery: Systems: Tubularaseptic Processing*

Turn Key *See Consultants & Services: Construction: Turn Key*

U

Ultrasonic Cutters *See Food Preparation Equipment, Utensils & Cookware: Cutters: Ultrasonic*

Uniforms *See Clothing & Protective Apparel: Uniforms & Special Clothing*

Unit, Packaging *See Instrumentation & Laboratory Equipment: Automation: Unit, Packaging, Bulk Handling*

Unscramblers *See Equipment & Machinery: Unscramblers*

Urns *See Foodservice Equipment & Supplies: Urns*

Utensils *See Food Preparation Equipment, Utensils & Cookware: Utensils; See also Foodservice Equipment & Supplies: Utensils*

Utility Carts *See Transportation & Storage: Carts: Utility*

Utility Vault Covers *See Transportation & Storage: Utility Vault Covers*

V

Vacuum Bags *See Sanitation Equipment & Supplies: Vaccuum Bags*

Vacuum Cleaners *See Sanitation Equipment & Supplies: Vacuum Cleaners*

Vacuum Packing *See Equipment & Machinery: Packaging: Vacuum Packing*

Vacuum Process *See Instrumentation & Laboratory Equipment: Process Controls: Vacuum*

Valve Control *See Equipment & Machinery: Systems: Valve Control*

Valves *See Equipment & Machinery: Valves; Refrigeration & Cooling Equipment: Valves*

Vats *See Equipment & Machinery: Food Processing: Vats; Refrigeration & Cooling Equipment: Vats; Transportation & Storage: Vats*

Vegetable & Fruit Shredders *See Equipment & Machinery: Food Processing: Shredders: Vegetable & Fruit*

Vegetable & Fruit Slicers *See Equipment & Machinery: Food Processing: Slicers: Vegetable & Fruit*

Vegetable Cookers *See Equipment & Machinery: Food Processing: Cookers: Vegetable*

Vegetable Knives *See Food Preparation Equipment, Utensils & Cookware: Knives: Vegetable*

Vegetable Oil *See Sanitation Equipment & Supplies: Soap: Vegetable Oil*

Vegetable Preparation *See Equipment & Machinery: Food Processing: Vegetable Preparation Equipment*

Vegetable Processing *See Equipment & Machinery: Food Processing: Vegetable Processing*

Vender & Visi-Cooler Installation Systems *See Refrigeration & Cooling Equipment: Vender & Visi-Cooler Installation Systems*

Vending Carts *See Foodservice Equipment & Supplies: Vending Carts*

Vending Machinery *See Foodservice Equipment & Supplies: Vending Machinery*
Vertical Form, Fill & Seal *See Equipment & Machinery: Packaging: Form, Fill & Seal: Vertical*
Vibrators *See Equipment & Machinery: Food Processing: Vibrators*
Viscous Products *See Equipment & Machinery: Pumps: Viscous Products*
Vision Verification *See Equipment & Machinery: Systems: Vision Verification*
Vitamin Analyzers *See Instrumentation & Laboratory Equipment: Analyzers: Vitamin*
VOC Control *See Equipment & Machinery: Food Processing: VOC Control*

W

Waffle Irons *See Equipment & Machinery: Food Processing: Waffle Irons*
Walk-In Coolers *See Refrigeration & Cooling Equipment: Coolers: Walk-In*
Walk-In Freezers *See Refrigeration & Cooling Equipment: Freezers: Walk-In*
Warehouses *See Transportation & Storage: Warehouses*
Warmers *See Foodservice Equipment & Supplies: Warmers*
Washers & Fillers *See Equipment & Machinery: Food Processing: Tanks: Washers & Fillers*
Washers *See Equipment & Machinery: Food Processing: Washers*
Washing Compounds *See Sanitation Equipment & Supplies: Compounds: Washing*
Washing Machinery *See Sanitation Equipment & Supplies: Washing Machinery*
Washing, Drying & Polishing *See Sanitation Equipment & Supplies: Silverware Cleaning Machinery: Washing, Drying & Polishing*
Waste Boxes *See Packaging Materials & Supplies: Boxes: Waste*
Waste Handling & Disposal *See Sanitation Equipment & Supplies: Waste Handling & Disposal Equipment*
Wastewater Treatment *See Sanitation Equipment & Supplies: Wastewater Treatment Systems*
Water Activity *See Instrumentation & Laboratory Equipment: Analyzers: Water Activity*
Water Boilers*See Equipment & Machinery: Food Processing: Boilers: Water*
Water Heaters *See Equipment & Machinery: Heaters: Water*
Water Treatment *See Equipment & Machinery: Water Treatment*
Wax *See Packaging Materials & Supplies: Wax*
Waxed Paper *See Packaging Materials & Supplies: Paper: Waxed*
Waxers *See Equipment & Machinery: Food Processing: Waxers*
Waxing*See Equipment & Machinery: Food Processing: Waxing*
Webtension & Torque Controls *See Instrumentation & Laboratory Equipment: Controls: Webtension & Torque*
Weighing *See Equipment & Machinery: Packaging: Weighing*
Wet Strength Paper *See Packaging Materials & Supplies: Paper: Wet Strength*
Windows *See Building Equipment & Supplies: Windows*
Wine Presses *See Equipment & Machinery: Food Processing: Presses: Wine*
Wine Racks *See Transportation & Storage: Racks: Wine*
Wine Storage *See Transportation & Storage: Wine Storage Units*
Wipers *See Sanitation Equipment & Supplies: Wipers*
Wire Cloths *See Sanitation Equipment & Supplies: Cloths: Wire*
Wire Racks *See Transportation & Storage: Racks: Wire*
Wire Shelving *See Transportation & Storage: Shelving: Wire*
Wire Stitching *See Equipment & Machinery: Packaging: Wire Stitching*
Wirebound Boxes *See Packaging Materials & Supplies: Boxes: Wirebound*
Wood Boards *See Food Preparation Equipment, Utensils & Cookware: Boards: Wood*
Wood Grain Plastic *See Foodservice Equipment & Supplies: Wood Grain Plastic*
Wooden Boxes *See Packaging Materials & Supplies: Boxes: Wooden*
Wooden Forks *See Food Preparation Equipment, Utensils & Cookware: Utensils: Forks: Wooden*
Wooden Pallets *See Transportation & Storage: Pallets: Wooden*
Wooden Shipping Crates *See Packaging Materials & Supplies: Crates: Wooden Shipping*
Work Tables *See Food Preparation Equipment, Utensils & Cookware: Tables: Work*
Wrappers *See Packaging Materials & Supplies: Wrappers*
Wrapping *See Equipment & Machinery: Packaging: Wrapping*
Wrapping Paper *See Packaging Materials & Supplies: Paper: Wrapping*
Writing, Forms, Sales & Order Books *See Foodservice Equipment & Supplies: Paper: Writing, Forms, Sales & Order Books*

X

X-ray Contaminant Detection *See Equipment & Machinery: Systems: X-ray Contaminant Detection*

Y

Yeast Processing *See Equipment & Machinery: Food Processing: Yeast Processing*

Z

Zipper Application *See Equipment & Machinery: Systems: Zipper Application*

1 2 3 4 5

EXAMPLE: **Dairy Cooling Vats** *See Equipment & Machinery: Food Processing: Vats: Dairy Cooling*

1. Product or Service you are looking for
2. Main Category, in alphabetical order, located in the page headers starting on page 13
3. Category Description, located in black bars and in page headers
4. Product Category, located in gray bars
5. Product Type, located under gray bars, centered in bold

Building Equipment & Supplies

Air Curtains

Apollo Sheet Metal
Kennewick, WA 509-586-1104
Atlas Equipment Company
Kansas City, MO.................. 800-842-9188
Berner International Corporation
New Castle, PA.................. 800-245-4455
Carnes Company
Verona, WI 608-845-6411
Chase-Doors
Cincinnati, OH 800-543-4455
Curtainaire
Los Angeles, CA.................. 323-753-4266
Curtron Products
Pittsburgh, PA.................. 800-833-5005
Donovan Enterprises
Lagrange, GA.................. 800-233-6180
Emco Industrial Plastics
Cedar Grove, NJ 800-292-9906
Insect-O-Cutor
Stone Mountain, GA.................. 800-988-5359
Kason Industries
Newnan, GA.................. 770-254-0553
Kason Industries, Inc.
Lewis Center, OH 740-549-2100
King Company
Dallas, TX.................. 507-451-3770
Lechler
St Charles, IL 800-777-2926
Mankato Tent & Awning Company
North Mankato, MN 866-747-3524
Mars Air Systems
Gardena, CA 800-421-1266
Plas-Ties, Co.
Tustin, CA.................. 800-854-0137
Quickserv Corporation
Houston, TX 800-388-8307
Ready Access
West Chicago, IL 800-621-5045
Universal Jet Industries
Hialeah, FL.................. 305-887-4378

Air Filters

Air Quality Engineering
Brooklyn Park, MN.................. 800-328-0787
Air-Maze Corporation
Cuyahoga Falls, OH 330-928-4100
Airguard Industries
Jeffersonville, IN 866-247-4827
Airsan Corporation
Milwaukee, WI.................. 800-558-5494
Allergen Air Filter Corporation
Houston, TX 800-333-8880
Amsoil
Superior, WI 715-392-7101
Beach Filter Products
Glen Rock, PA.................. 800-232-2485
Blue Tech
Hickory, NC 828-324-5900
Dwyer Instruments
Michigan City, IN.................. 800-872-3141
Eco-Air Products
San Diego, CA 800-284-8111
Elwood Safety Company
Buffalo, NY.................. 866-326-6060
Flanders Corporation
Washington, NC 800-637-2803
Freudenberg Nonwovens
Hopkinsville, KY 270-887-5115
G.W. Dahl Company
Greensboro, NC 800-852-4449
Gaylord Industries
Tualatin, OR 800-547-9696
Halton Company
Scottsville, KY 800-442-5866
Hunter Fan Company
Cordova, TN 901-743-1360
Ketch
Wichita, KS.................. 800-766-3777
King Bag & Manufacturing Company
Cincinnati, OH 800-444-5464
King Company
Dallas, TX.................. 507-451-3770
King Engineering - King-Gage
Newell, WV 800-242-8871
Lamports Filter Media
Cleveland, OH 216-881-2050
Mars Air Systems
Gardena, CA.................. 800-421-1266
Monroe Environmental Corporation
Monroe, MI.................. 800-992-7707
Parker Hannifin Corporation
Indianapolis, IN 800-272-7537
Refractron Technologies Corporation
Newark, NY 315-331-6222
Rolfs @ Boone
Boone, IA 800-265-2010
Stein DSI
Sandusky, OH.................. 800-447-2630
The Clyde Bergemann Power Group
Baltimore, MD 410-368-6800
Ultra Industries
Racine, WI 800-358-5872
United Air Specialists
Cincinnati, OH 800-992-4422
United States Systems
Kansas City, KS 888-281-2454
Vent Master
Mississauga, ON.................. 800-565-2981
VMC Signs Inc.
Victoria, TX 361-575-0548

Awnings

A&A International
Virginia Beach, VA.................. 800-252-1446
AAA Awning Co. Inc
Houston, TX 800-281-6193
Academy Awning
Los Angeles, CA.................. 310-277-8383
Acme Awning Company
Bronx, NY.................. 718-409-1881
Acme Awning Company
Salinas, CA 831-424-7134
Advanced Design Awning & Sign
Cloquet, MN.................. 800-566-8368
Allied Electric Sign & Aing
Salt Lake City, UT 801-972-5503
Alpha Canvas & Awning
Charlotte, NC 704-333-1581
Alpha Productions, Inc.
Los Angeles, CA.................. 800-223-0883
American Sun Control Awnings
Alpharetta, GA 800-245-6746
Anchor Industries
Evansville, IN 812-867-2421
Andgar Corporation
Ferndale, WA 360-366-9900
Arrow Sign & Awning Company
Ham Lake, MN.................. 800-621-9231
Avalon Canvas & Upholstery
Houston, TX 713-697-0156
Avondale Mills
Monroe, GA 770-267-2226
Awnco
Chicago, IL 800-339-6522
Awning Company
Sag Harbor, NY.................. 631-725-3651
Awning Enterprises
Frederick, MD.................. 301-631-0500
Awnings by Dee
Little Neck, NY.................. 516-487-6688
Awnings Plus
Addison, IL.................. 888-627-4770
B&W Awning ManufacturingCompany
Lexington, KY 859-252-1619
Belle Isle Awning Company
Roseville, MI 586-294-6050
BH Awning & Tent Company
Benton Harbor, MI 800-272-2187
Bowers Awning & Shade
Lebanon, PA 717-273-2351
Brock Awnings
Hampton Bays, NY.................. 631-728-3367
C.B. Dombach & Son
Lancaster, PA 717-392-0578
Cain Awning Company
Birmingham, AL.................. 205-323-8379
Camel Custom Canvas Shop
Knoxville, TN.................. 800-524-2704
Canvas Products Company
Grand Junction, CO 970-242-1453
Capitol Awning Company
Jamaica, NY 800-241-3539
Centredale Sign Company
Warwick, RI 401-231-1440
Certain Teed Shade Systems
Columbus, OH 800-894-3801
Charlotte Tent & Awning
Charlotte, NC 704-394-1616
Chattin Awning Company
Edison, NJ.................. 800-394-3500
Chesterfield Awning Company
South Holland, IL 800-339-6522
Childres Custom Canvas
Duncanville, TX 972-298-4943
Chilson's Shops
Easthampton, MA.................. 413-529-8062
City Canvas
San Jose, CA.................. 408-287-2688
Coastal Canvas Products Company
Savannah, GA.................. 800-476-5174
Creative Canopy Design
Hernando Beach, FL.................. 866-970-5200
Custom Tarpolin Products
Youngstown, OH.................. 330-758-1801
Dade Canvas Products Company
Silver Spring, MD.................. 301-680-2500
Danieli Awnings
Napa, CA.................. 707-257-6100
Dean Custom Awnings
Orangeburg, NY 845-425-1193
Delta Signs
Haltom City, TX 866-643-3582
Despro Manufacturing
Cedar Grove, NJ 800-292-9906
Dize Company
Winston Salem, NC.................. 336-722-5181
Dualite Sales & Service
Williamsburg, OH.................. 513-724-7100
Durasol Awnings
Middletown, NY.................. 800-444-6131
Ehmke Manufacturing Company
Philadelphia, PA 215-324-4200
Eide Industries
Cerritos, CA 800-422-6827
Elegant Awnings
Chino, CA.................. 800-541-9011
Engineered Textile Products, Inc.
Mobile, AL.................. 800-222-8277
Evanston Awning Company
Evanston, IL 847-864-4520
F&S Awning & Blind Company
Edison, NJ.................. 732-738-4110
French Awning & Screen Company
Jackson, MS 800-898-1132
Fresno Tent & Awning Company
Fresno, CA 559-264-4771
Ft. Wayne Awning Company
Fort Wayne, IN 260-478-1636
FTL/Happold Tensil Structure Design & Engineering
New York, NY 212-732-4691
G&J Awning & Canvas
Sauk Rapids, MN 800-467-1744
Geneva Awning & Tent Works Inc
Geneva, NY.................. 800-789-3151
Georgia Tent & Awning
Atlanta, GA.................. 800-252-2391
Glawe Manufacturing Company
Fairborn, OH.................. 800-434-8368
Glen Raven Custom Fabrics, LLC
Glen Raven, NC 336-227-6211
Globe Canvas Products Company
Philadelphia, PA 610-622-7211
Goodwin-Cole Company
Sacramento, CA 800-752-4477
Greeley Tent & Awning
Greeley, CO.................. 970-352-0253
Greenville Awning Company
Mauldin, SC 864-288-0063
H.B. Wall & Sons
Springfield, MO 417-869-0791
Hamilton Awning Company
Beaver, PA.................. 724-774-7644
Hendee Enterprises
Houston, TX 800-323-3641

Hogshire Industries
Norfolk, VA. 757-877-2297
J W Hulme Company
Saint Paul, MN 800-442-8212
J&J Sliding & Windows SaInc
Chesterfield, MO 636-532-3320
J.R. McCullough Company
Lancaster, PA 717-735-8772
Jamestown Awning
Jamestown, NY. 716-483-1435
Kohler Awning
Cheektowaga, NY. 716-685-3333
L.F. Pease Company
East Providence, RI 401-438-2850
LA Graphics
Greenville, SC. 864-297-1111
Lafayette Tent & Awning Company
Lafayette, IN. 800-458-2955
Laggren's
Monroe Township, NJ 908-756-1948
Laurel Awning Company
Apollo, PA. 888-567-5689
Lawrence Fabric Structures
Saint Louis, MO 800-527-3840
Leavitt & Parris
Portland, ME. 800-833-6679
Lincoln Tent & Awning
Lincoln, NE. 800-567-4559
Lloyd's of Millville
Millville, NJ 856-825-0345
Macon Tent & Awning Company
Macon, GA 478-743-2684
Maple Leaf Canvas Company
Sherwood, AR. 800-947-4233
Mason City Tent & AwningCompany
Mason City, IA 641-423-0044
Merrillville Awning
Merrillville, IN 800-781-6100
Metal Master
Tucson, AZ 800-488-8729
Miami Beach Awning Company
Miami, FL. 800-576-0222
Mid State Awning & PatioCompany
Bellefonte, PA. 814-355-8979
Milliken Industries
Englewood, FL 800-255-0094
Modesto Tent & Awning
Modesto, CA. 209-545-6150
Moran Canvas Products
La Mesa, CA. 800-515-1130
Mt. Lebanon Awning & Tent Company
Presto, PA 412-221-2233
Muskegon Awning & Fabrication
Muskegon, MI. 800-968-3686
Neilson Canvas Company
Sandusky, OH 419-625-0581
New Haven Awning Company
New Haven, CT 800-560-5650
Niantic Awning Company
Niantic, CT 860-739-0161
O'Brian Tarping Systems
Wilson, NC 800-334-8277
Oklahoma Neon
Tulsa, OK 888-707-6366
Omar Canvas & Awning Company
Johnson City, TN 800-274-6627
Ontario Neon Company
Ontario, CA. 909-986-4632
Ottumwa Tent & Awning Company
Ottumwa, IA 641-682-2257
Palo Alto Awning
San Jose, CA. 800-400-4270
Parasol Awnings
Memphis, TN 901-368-4477
Patio Center Inc
Lafayette, LA 337-233-9896
Peoria Tent & Awning
Peoria, IL. 309-674-1128
Pike Tent & Awning Company
Portland, OR 800-866-9172
Pride Neon
Sioux Falls, SD. 605-336-3563
Quality Aluminum & Canvas
Columbus, MS 662-329-2525
Queen City Awning
Cincinnati, OH 513-530-9660
Reliable Tent & Awning Co.
Billings, MT 800-544-1039
Rose City Awning Company
Portland, OR 800-446-4104
S.L. Doery & Son Corporation
Lawrence, NY. 516-239-8090

San Jose Awning Co., Inc.
San Jose, CA. 800-872-9646
Shaffer Sports & Events
Houston, TX 713-699-0088
Signtech Electrical Adv ertising Inc
San Diego, CA 619-527-6100
Sommer Awning Company
Indianapolis, IN 317-844-4744
South Akron Awning Company
Akron, OH. 330-848-7611
South Jersey Awning
Egg Harbor Township, NJ 609-646-2002
Southern Awning & Sign Company
Woodstock, GA. 770-516-8652
Sundance Architectural Products, LLC
Orlando, FL. 800-940-1337
Sunmaster of Naples
Naples, FL. 239-261-3581
Taylor Made Custom Products
Gloversville, NY. 518-725-0681
TCT&A Industries
Urbana, IL. 800-252-1355
The Canvas Exchange Inc
Cleveland, OH 216-749-2233
Thermal Bags by Ingrid
Gilberts, IL 800-622-5560
Total Identity Group
Cambridge, ON. 877-551-5529
Tucker Manufacturing Company
Cedar Rapids, IA. 800-553-8131
USA Canvas Shoppe
Dallas, TX. 877-626-8468
Van Nuys Awning Company
Van Nuys, CA 818-780-4868
Vermont Tent Company
South Burlington, VT 800-696-8368
Vernon Plastics
Haverhill, MA. 978-373-1551
Walker Sign Company
Sun Valley, CA 818-252-7788
Wilcox Canvas Awning
Perrysburg Wood, OH. 419-837-2821
William J. Mills & Company
Greenport, NY 800-477-1535
Williams Shade & Awning Company
Memphis, TN 901-368-5055
York Tent & Awning Company
York, PA 800-864-3510

Ceiling Surfaces & Panels

Arcoplast Wall & Ceiling Systems
St Peters, MO 888-736-2726

Decking

Metal

Slipnot Metal Safety Flooring
Detroit, MI 800-754-7668

Doors

Air Curtain

Aleco Food Service Div
Muscle Shoals, AL 800-633-3120
Apple-A-Day Nutritional Labeling Service
San Clemente, CA. 949-855-8954
Atlas Equipment Company
Kansas City, MO. 800-842-9188
Berner International Corporation
New Castle, PA. 800-245-4455
Curtron Products
Pittsburgh, PA. 800-833-5005
Kason Vinyl Products
Newnan, GA. 800-472-7450

Corrosion Resistant

Air-Lec Industries, Inc
Madison, WI. 608-244-4754
Chem-Pruf Door Company
Brownsville, TX 800-444-6924

Double Acting

Carlson Products
Maize, KS. 800-234-1069
Coldmatic Refrigeration
Concord, ON. 905-326-7600
Curtron Products
Pittsburgh, PA. 800-833-5005

Eliason Corporation
Kalamazoo, MI. 800-828-3655
Super Seal ManufacturingLimited
Woodbridge, ON. 800-337-3239

Plastic

Aleco
Muscle Shoals, AL 800-633-3120
Chase-Doors
Cincinnati, OH 800-543-4455
Coldmatic Refrigeration
Concord, ON. 905-326-7600
Curtron Products
Pittsburgh, PA 800-833-5005
FIB-R-DOR
Cincinnati, OH 800-342-7367
Firl Industries
Fond Du Lac, WI 800-558-4890
Hormann Flexan Llc
Leetsdale, PA 800-365-3667
Reese Enterprises
Rosemount, MN 800-328-0953
Seville Display Door
Temecula, CA 800-634-0412
Trimline Corporation
Elkhart Lake, WI. 920-876-3611
VT Industries
Holstein, IA. 800-827-1615
Western Laminates
Omaha, NE 402-556-4600

Strip

Aleco
Muscle Shoals, AL 800-633-3120
Aleco Food Service Div
Muscle Shoals, AL 800-633-3120
Berner International Corporation
New Castle, PA. 800-245-4455
Coastal Canvas Products Company
Savannah, GA. 800-476-5174
Coverall
Worcester, MA 800-356-2961
Curtron Products
Pittsburgh, PA. 800-833-5005
Davlynne International
Cudahy, WI. 800-558-5208
Environmental Products Company
North Aurora, IL. 800-677-8479
Firl Industries
Fond Du Lac, WI 800-558-4890
Flame Gard
Lakewood, NJ. 800-526-3694
Kason Industries
Newnan, GA. 770-254-0553
Kason Vinyl Products
Newnan, GA. 800-472-7450
Kelley Company
Carrollton, TX. 800-558-6960
Manufacturing Warehouse
Miami, FL. 305-635-8886
Reese Enterprises
Rosemount, MN 800-328-0953
Super Seal ManufacturingLimited
Woodbridge, ON. 800-337-3239
Superior Products Company
Saint Paul, MN 800-328-9800
Tuckahoe Manufacturing Company
Vineland, NJ 800-220-3368

Fans

Ceiling

Acme Engineering & Manufacturing Corporation
Muskogee, OK 918-682-7791
Airmaster Fan Company
Jackson, MI. 800-255-3084
Canarm, Ltd.
Brockville, ON 613-342-5424
Carnes Company
Verona, WI 608-845-6411
Ceilcote Air Pollution Control
Cleveland, OH 800-554-8673
Con-tech/Conservation Technology
Northbrook, IL 800-728-0312
Fountainhead
Bensalem, PA 800-326-8998
Halton Company
Scottsville, KY 800-442-5866
Hartzell Fan
Piqua, OH 800-336-3267

Hunter Fan Company
Cordova, TN 901-743-1360
Larkin Industries
Birmingham, AL 800-322-4036
Main Lamp Corporation
Brooklyn, NY 718-436-2207
Nalge Process Technologies Group
Rochester, NY 585-586-8800
Nu-Con Equipment
Chanhassen, MN 877-939-0510
Panasonic Commercial Food Service
Secaucus, NJ 800-553-0384
PennBarry
Plano, TX 972-212-4700
SEC
Plymouth, MI 734-455-4500
Stegall Metal Industries
Birmingham, AL 800-633-4373
West Metals
London, ON 800-300-6667

Flooring

Ahlstrom Filtration LLC
Madisonville, KY 270-821-0140
Kalman Floor Company
Evergreen, CO 866-266-7146
VibroFloors World
Fayetteville, GA 770-632-9701

Anti-Slip

Advanced Surfaces Corporation
Villa Rica, GA 800-963-4632
Slipnot Metal Safety Flooring
Detroit, MI 800-754-7668

Floor Mats

A&A Line & Wire Corporation
Flushing, NY 800-886-2657
Airomat Corporation
Fort Wayne, IN 800-348-4905
Atlantic Rubber Products
East Wareham, MA 800-695-0446
Boardman Molded Products/Space-Links
Youngstown, OH 800-233-4575
Cactus Mat ManufacturingCompany
El Monte, CA 626-579-6287
Collins & Aikman
Canton, OH 800-321-0244
Corson Rubber Products Inc
Clover, SC 803-222-7779
Durable Corporation
Norwalk, OH 800-537-1603
Golden Star
N Kansas City, MO 800-821-2792
JCH International
Rome, GA 800-328-9203
John Rohrer Contracting Company
Kansas City, KS 913-236-5005
Matrix Engineering
Vero Beach, FL 800-926-0528
Musson Rubber Company
Akron, OH 800-321-2381
Reese Enterprises
Rosemount, MN 800-328-0953
Superior Products Company
Saint Paul, MN 800-328-9800
Tepromark International
Skokie, IL 800-645-2622
United Textile Distribution
Garner, NC 800-262-7624
Wearwell/Tennessee Mat Company
Nashville, TN 615-254-8381

Industrial Flooring

Corro-Shield International, Inc.
Rosemont, IL 800-298-7637
Dur A Flex
East Hartford, CT 877-251-5418
Grating Pacific/Ross Technology Corporation
Los Alamitos, CA 800-321-4314
Kagetec
Montgomery, MN 612-435-7640
Kwasny/Sanicrete
Farmington Hills, MI 248-893-1000
Tufco International
Gentry, AR 800-364-0836
VibroFloors World
Fayetteville, GA 770-632-9701

Mats & Matting

Airomat Corporation
Fort Wayne, IN 800-348-4905
AMCO Corporation
City of Industry, CA 626-855-2550
Artex International
Highland, IL 618-654-2113
Atlantic Rubber Products
East Wareham, MA 800-695-0446
Atlas Equipment Company
Kansas City, MO 800-842-9188
Baker Concrete Construction
Monroe, OH 513-539-4000
Best Brands Home Products
New York, NY 212-684-7456
Boardman Molded Products/Space-Links
Youngstown, OH 800-233-4575
C.R. Manufacturing
Waverly, NE 877-789-5844
Cactus Mat ManufacturingCompany
El Monte, CA 626-579-6287
Coast Scientific
Rancho Santa Fe, CA 800-445-1544
Coburn Company
Whitewater, WI 800-776-7042
Collins & Aikman
Canton, OH 800-321-0244
Conimar Corporation
Ocala, FL 800-874-9735
Continental Identification
Sparta, MI 800-247-2499
Continental Industrial Supply
South Pasadena, FL 727-341-1100
Corson Rubber Products Inc
Clover, SC 803-222-7779
Custom Table Pads
St Paul, MN 651-714-5720
Dorado Carton Company
Dorado, PR 787-796-1670
Drehmann Paving & Flooring Company
Pennsauken, NJ 800-523-3800
Durable Corporation
Norwalk, OH 800-537-1603
Golden Star
N Kansas City, MO 800-821-2792
Gourmet Tableskirts
Houston, TX 800-527-0440
Have Our Plastic Inc
Mississauga, ON 800-263-5995
IKG Industries
Garrett, IN 800-467-2345
J. James
Brooklyn, NY 718-384-6144
J.M. Rogers & Sons
Moss Point, MS 228-475-7584
J.V. Reed & Company
Louisville, KY 877-258-7333
Jack the Ripper Table Skirting
Stafford, TX 800-331-7831
JCH International
Rome, GA 800-328-9203
John Rohrer Contracting Company
Kansas City, KS 913-236-5005
JR Mats
West Chester, PA 800-526-7763
K-C Products Company
Van Nuys, CA 818-267-1600
Lancaster Colony Commercial Products
Columbus, OH 800-528-2278
Larco
Brainerd, MN 800-523-6996
Matrix Engineering
Vero Beach, FL 800-926-0528
Millard Manufacturing Corporation
La Vista, NE 800-662-4263
Musson Rubber Company
Akron, OH 800-321-2381
Northland Process Piping
Isle, MN 320-679-2119
Paradise Products
El Cerrito, CA 800-227-1092
Proffitt Manufacturing Company
Dalton, GA 800-241-4682
Reese Enterprises
Rosemount, MN 800-328-0953
Royal Paper Products
Coatesville, PA 800-666-6655
Rubbermaid Commercial Products
Winchester, VA 800-336-9880
Saunders Manufacturing Co.
N Kansas City, MO 800-821-2792
SCA Tissue
Neenah, WI 866-722-6659
Scranton Lace Company
Forest City, PA 800-822-1036
Smith-Lee Company
Oshkosh, WI 800-327-9774
Sultan Linens
New York, NY 212-689-8900
Summitville Tiles
Summitville, OH 330-223-1511
Superior Products Company
Saint Paul, MN 800-328-9800
Tag-Trade Associated Group
Chicago, IL 800-621-8350
Tara Linens
Sanford, NC 800-476-8272
Tennant Company
Minneapolis, MN 800-553-8033
Tepromark International
Skokie, IL 800-645-2622
United Textile Distribution
Garner, NC 800-262-7624
US Lace Paper Works
Oshkosh, WI 800-873-6459
Wearwell/Tennessee Mat Company
Nashville, TN 615-254-8381

Metal

Slipnot Metal Safety Flooring
Detroit, MI 800-754-7668

Safety

Slipnot Metal Safety Flooring
Detroit, MI 800-754-7668

Thermal Shock

Resistant Flooring

Dur A Flex
East Hartford, CT 877-251-5418

Grating

Metal

Slipnot Metal Safety Flooring
Detroit, MI 800-754-7668

Heating, Ventilation & Air Conditioning

A.C. Horn & Co
Dallas, TX 800-657-6155
A.K. Robins
Baltimore, MD 800-486-9656
A.O. Smith Water Products Company
Irving, TX 800-527-1953
ABB SSAC
Baldwinsville, NY 888-385-1221
Acme Engineering & Manufacturing Corporation
Muskogee, OK 918-682-7791
ADDCHEK Coils
Fort Mill, SC 803-547-7566
Advanced Control Technologies
Indianapolis, IN 800-886-2281
AEI Corporation
Irvine, CA 949-474-3070
Aerco International
Northvale, NJ 201-768-2400
Aerolator Systems
Monroe, NC 800-843-8286
Aerovent
Minneapolis, MN 763-551-7500
AFGO Mechanical Services, Inc.
Long Island City, NY 800-438-2346
Air Quality Engineering
Brooklyn Park, MN 800-328-0787
Airmaster Fan Company
Jackson, MI 800-255-3084
Airsan Corporation
Milwaukee, WI 800-558-5494
AK Steel
West Chester, OH 800-331-5050
All State Fabricators Corporation
Florida, RI 800-322-9925
Allergen Air Filter Corporation
Houston, TX 800-333-8880
Allied Engineering
North Vancouver, BC 877-929-1214

Allstrong Restaurant Equipment
South El Monte, CA ... 800-933-8913
ALPI Food Preparation Equipment
Bolton, ON ... 800-928-2574
American Coolair Corporation
Jacksonville, FL ... 904-389-3646
American Radionic Company
Palm Coast, FL ... 800-445-6033
American Range & Hood Corporation
Pacoima, CA ... 888-753-9898
American Ventilation Company
Grafton, OH ... 800-854-3267
Andersen 2000
Peachtree City, GA ... 800-241-5424
Anderson Snow Corporation
Schiller Park, IL ... 800-346-2645
Andgar Corporation
Ferndale, WA ... 360-366-9900
Apollo Sheet Metal
Kennewick, WA ... 509-586-1104
ARI Industries
Addison, IL ... 800-237-6725
Armstrong International
Three Rivers, MI ... 269-273-1415
Ayr-King Corporation
Jeffersontown, KY ... 866-266-6290
Babcock & Wilcox Power Generation Group
Barberton, OH ... 800-222-2625
Baltimore Aircoil Company
Jessup, MD ... 410-799-6200
Barbeque Wood Flavors Enterprises
Ennis, TX ... 972-875-8391
BBC Industries
Pacific, MO ... 800-654-4205
Becker Brothers GraphiteCorporation
Maywood, IL ... 708-410-0700
Berner International Corporation
New Castle, PA ... 800-245-4455
Bessam-Aire
Cleveland, OH ... 800-321-5992
Betz Entec
Horsham, PA ... 800-877-1940
Bioclimatic Air Systems
Delran, NJ ... 800-962-5594
BKI Worldwide
Simpsonville, SC ... 800-927-6887
Bryan Boilers
Peru, IN ... 765-473-6651
Caddy Corporation of America
Bridgeport, NJ ... 856-467-4222
Canarm, Ltd.
Brockville, ON ... 613-342-5424
Carnes Company
Verona, WI ... 608-845-6411
Carroll Manufacturing International
Florham Park, NJ ... 800-444-9696
Ceilcote Air Pollution Control
Cleveland, OH ... 800-554-8673
CEM Corporation
Matthews, NC ... 800-726-3331
Chesmont Engineering Company
Exton, PA ... 610-594-9200
Cleaver-Brooks
Milwaukee, WI ... 414-359-0600
Climate Master
Oklahoma City, OK ... 877-436-0263
CMT
Hamilton, MA ... 978-768-2555
Commercial Kitchen Company
Los Angeles, CA ... 323-732-2291
Con-tech/Conservation Technology
Northbrook, IL ... 800-728-0312
Control Pak International
Fenton, MI ... 810-735-2800
Convectronics
Haverhill, MA ... 800-633-0166
Cook & Beals
Loup City, NE ... 308-745-0154
Cooling Products
Tulsa, OK ... 918-251-8588
Cooperheat/MQS
Alvin, TX ... 800-526-4233
Copeland Corporation
Sidney, OH ... 937-498-3011
Crispy Lite
St. Louis, MO ... 888-356-5362
Curtainaire
Los Angeles, CA ... 323-753-4266
Curtron Products
Pittsburgh, PA ... 800-833-5005
Custom Food Machinery
Stockton, CA ... 209-463-4343
Delfield Company
Mt Pleasant, MI ... 800-733-8821
Delta Cooling Towers
Rockaway, NJ ... 800-289-3358
Direct Fire Technical
Benbrook, TX ... 888-920-2468
Doucette Industries
York, PA ... 800-445-7511
Dreaco Products
Elyria, OH ... 800-368-3267
Duke Manufacturing Company
Saint Louis, MO ... 800-735-3853
Duo-Aire
Winter Haven, FL ... 863-294-2272
Dwyer Instruments
Michigan City, IN ... 800-872-3141
Dynamic Cooking Systems
Huntington Beach, CA ... 800-433-8466
Eclipse Innovative Ther mal Solutions
Toledo, OH ... 800-662-3966
Economy Paper & Restaurant Supply Company
Clifton, NJ ... 973-279-5500
Edwards Engineering Corporation
Pompton Plains, NJ ... 800-526-5201
Eldorado Miranda Manufacturing Company
Largo, FL ... 800-330-0708
Elmwood Sensors
Pawtucket, RI ... 800-356-9663
Energymaster
Walled Lake, MI ... 248-624-6900
Environmental Products Company
North Aurora, IL ... 800-677-8479
Epcon Industrial Systems
Conroe, TX ... 800-447-7872
ET International Technologies
Wheat Ridge, CO ... 855-412-5726
Exhausto
Atlanta, GA ... 800-255-2923
F.M. Corporation
Deerfield Beach, FL ... 954-570-9860
Flame Gard
Lakewood, NJ ... 800-526-3694
Flanders Corporation
Washington, NC ... 800-637-2803
Floaire
Blue Bell, PA ... 800-726-5623
Fountainhead
Bensalem, PA ... 800-326-8998
G.W. Berkheimer Company
Fort Wayne, IN ... 800-535-6696
Gardner Denver Inc.
Toronto, ON ... 416-763-4681
Garland Commercial Ranges
Mississauga, ON ... 905-624-0260
Gaylord Industries
Tualatin, OR ... 800-547-9696
Glo-Quartz Electric Heater Company
Mentor, OH ... 800-321-3574
Governair Corporation
Oklahoma City, OK ... 405-525-6546
Grease Master
Matthews, NC ... 704-844-6907
Greenheck Fan Corporation
Schofield, WI ... 715-359-6171
Greitzer
Elizabeth City, NC ... 252-338-4000
Grillco
Aurora, IL ... 800-644-0067
Grinnell Fire ProtectionSystems Company
Sauk Rapids, MN ... 888-870-6894
Hallock Fabricating Corporation
Riverhead, NY ... 631-727-2441
Halton Company
Scottsville, KY ... 800-442-5866
Hanson Lab Furniture
Newbury Park, CA ... 805-498-3121
Hartzell Fan
Piqua, OH ... 800-336-3267
Harvey W. Hottel
Gaithersburg, MD ... 301-921-9599
Heatrex
Meadville, PA ... 800-394-6589
HEMCO Corporation
Independence, MO ... 800-779-4362
Hercules Food Equipment
Weston, ON ... 416-742-9673
Holman Boiler Works
Dallas, TX ... 800-331-1956
Hunter Fan Company
Cordova, TN ... 901-743-1360
Hydro-Thermal
Waukesha, WI ... 800-952-0121
Ice-Cap
Piermont, NY ... 888-423-2270
ICM Controls
Cicero, NY ... 800-411-4270
Illinois Range Company
Schiller Park, IL ... 800-535-7041
Indiana Supply Company
Fort Wayne, IN ... 260-497-0533
J.L. Becker Company
Plymouth, MI ... 800-837-4328
Jacob Tubing LP
Memphis, TN ... 901-566-1110
Jarvis-Cutter Company
Boston, MA ... 617-567-7532
JennFan
Jacksonville, FL ... 904-731-4711
KEMCO
Wareham, MA ... 800-231-5955
King Company
Dallas, TX ... 507-451-3770
Lakewood Engineering & Manufacturing Company
Chicago, IL ... 800-621-4277
Larkin Industries
Birmingham, AL ... 800-322-4036
LDI Manufacturing Company
Logansport, IN ... 800-366-2001
Loren Cook Company
Springfield, MO ... 800-289-3267
Low Humidity Systems
Covington, GA ... 770-788-6744
Ludell Manufacturing Company
Milwaukee, WI ... 800-558-0800
Lumsden Flexx Flow
Lancaster, PA ... 800-367-3664
Machine Ice Company, Inc
Houston, TX ... 800-423-8822
Mars Air Systems
Gardena, CA ... 800-421-1266
Marshall Air Systems
Charlotte, NC ... 800-722-3474
Master Air
Lebanon, IN ... 800-248-8368
MCM Fixture Company
Hazel Park, MI ... 248-547-9280
Meadows Mills, Inc.
North Wilkesboro, NC ... 800-626-2282
Met-Pro Corporation
Owosso, MI ... 989-725-8184
Metal Master
Tucson, AZ ... 800-488-8729
Microtechnologies
Plainville, CT ... 888-248-7103
Milvan Food Equipment Manufacturing
Rexdale, ON ... 416-674-3456
Moli-Tron Company
Lakewood, CO ... 800-525-9494
Monroe Environmental Corporation
Monroe, MI ... 800-992-7707
Monroe Kitchen Equipment
Rochester, NY ... 585-235-3310
MovinCool/Denso Sales ofCalifornia
Long Beach, CA ... 310-834-6352
Muckler Industries, Inc
Saint Louis, MO ... 800-444-0283
Muellermist Irrigation Company
Broadview, IL ... 708-450-9595
Munters Corporation
Amesbury, MA ... 800-843-5360
Nalge Process Technologies Group
Rochester, NY ... 585-586-8800
National FABCO Manufacturing
St Louis, MO ... 314-842-4571
National Refrigeration
Bensalem, PA ... 800-523-7138
NewTech
Randolph, VT ... 800-210-2361
Noren Products
Menlo Park, CA ... 866-936-6736
Novar
Cleveland, OH ... 800-348-1235
Nu-Con Equipment
Chanhassen, MN ... 877-939-0510
NuTone
Cincinnati, OH ... 888-336-3948
Omnitemp Refrigeration
Downey, CA ... 800-423-9660
Pacific Steam Equipment, Inc.
Santa Fe Springs, CA ... 800-321-4114
Panasonic Commercial Food Service
Secaucus, NJ ... 800-553-0384
Parkland
Houston, TX ... 713-926-5055

Partnership Resources, Inc.
Minneapolis, MN 612-331-2075

Patterson-Kelley
East Stroudsburg, PA 570-421-7500

Peerless of America
Lincolnshire, IL 847-634-7500

Penn Barry
Plano, TX 972-212-4700

PennBarry
Plano, TX 972-212-4700

Precision Temp
Cincinnati, OH 800-934-9690

Premium Air Systems
Troy, MI 877-430-0333

Process Heating Company
Seattle, WA 866-682-1582

Process Heating Corporation
Shrewsbury, MA 508-842-5200

Proheatco Manufacturing
Pomona, CA 800-423-4195

R-K Electronics
Mason, OH 800-543-4936

Raypak
Oxnard, CA 805-278-5300

Roberts Gordon
Buffalo, NY 800-828-7450

Ron Vallort & Associates
Oak Brook, IL 630-734-3821

Royal Prestige Health Moguls
Westbury, NY 888-802-7433

Season's 4
Douglasville, GA 770-489-0716

Seattle Boiler Works
Seattle, WA 206-762-0737

Sellers Engineering Division
Danville, KY 859-236-3181

South Valley Manufacturing
Gilroy, CA 408-842-5457

Southern Metal Fabricators
Albertville, AL 800-989-1330

Spencer Turbine Company
Windsor, CT 800-232-4321

Spiral Manufacturing Company
Minneapolis, MN 800-426-3643

Stainless International
Rancho Cordova, CA 888-300-6196

Stainless Steel Fabricators
Tyler, TX 903-595-6625

Standex International Corporation
Salem, NH 603-893-9701

Stegall Metal Industries
Birmingham, AL 800-633-4373

Sterling
New Berlin, WI 262-641-8610

Storm Industrial
Shawnee Mission, KS 800-745-7483

Sturdi-Bilt Restaurant Equipment
Whitmore Lake, MI 800-521-2895

Super Radiator Coils
Richmond, VA 800-229-2645

Thermalogic Corporation
Hudson, MA 978-562-5974

Toronto Kitchen Equipment
North York, ON 416-745-4944

Trane Company
La Crosse, WI 608-787-2000

Tru-Form Plastics
Gardena, CA 800-510-7999

Ultrafryer Systems
San Antonio, TX 800-545-9189

United Fire & Safety Service
Yonkers, NY 914-968-4459

Universal Jet Industries
Hialeah, FL 305-887-4378

USECO
Murfreesboro, TN 615-893-4820

Vapor Corporation
Franklin Park, IL 888-874-9020

Vent Master
Mississauga, ON 800-565-2981

Vent-A-Hood Company
Richardson, TX 972-235-5201

Vilter Manufacturing Corporation
Cudahy, WI 414-744-0111

Vulcan Electric Company
Porter, ME 800-922-3027

Waterfurnace International
Fort Wayne, IN 260-478-5667

Welbilt Corporation
Stamford, CT 203-325-8300

West Metals
London, ON 800-300-6667

West Star Industries
Stockton, CA 800-326-2288

Westfield Sheet Metal Works
Kenilworth, NJ 908-276-5500

ZMD International
Long Beach, CA 800-222-9674

Heating

Electric

INDEECO
St Louis, MO 800-243-8162

Hoods

Stainless Steel

Aget Manufacturing Company
Adrian, MI 517-263-5781

Lighting Equipment

Fluorescent

Insect-O-Cutor
Stone Mountain, GA 800-988-5359

Lumax Industries
Altoona, PA 814-944-2537

Nemco Electric Company
Seattle, WA 206-622-1551

Oetiker Inc
Marlette, MI 800-959-0398

Trojan
Mount Sterling, KY 800-264-0526

UDEC Corporation
Woburn, MA 800-990-8332

Incandescent

Apex Fountain Sales
Philadelphia, PA 800-523-4586

Boyd Lighting Company
Sausalito, CA 415-778-4300

Candle Lamp Company
Riverside, CA 877-526-7748

Command Electronics
Schoolcraft, MI 269-679-4011

Dura Electric Lamp Company
Newark, NJ 973-624-0014

G Lighting
St Louis, MO 800-331-2425

GE Lighting
Cleveland, OH 800-435-4448

Holcor
Riverdale, IL 708-841-3800

Hubbell Lighting
Greenville, SC 540-382-6111

Hybrinetics
Santa Rosa, CA 800-247-6900

Indy Lighting
Fishers, IN 317-849-1233

Le-Jo Enterprises
Phoenixville, PA 484-921-9000

Luxo Corporation
Elmsford, NY 800-222-5896

Mason Candlelight Company
New Albany, MS 800-556-2766

Nova Industries
San Leandro, CA 510-357-0171

Osram Sylvania
Danvers, MA 800-544-4828

Philips Lighting Company
Somerset, NJ 732-563-3000

Prescolite
Vallejo, CA 707-562-3500

QSR Industrial Supply
Cherry Hill, NJ 800-257-8282

Renovator's Supply
Conway, NH 800-659-0203

Sterno
Lombard, IL 630-792-0080

Strand Lighting
Dallas, TX

Super Vision International
Orlando, FL 407-857-9900

Superior-Studio Specialties Ltd
Commerce, CA 800-354-3049

SuppliesForLess
Hampton, VA 800-235-2201

Trojan
Mount Sterling, KY 800-264-0526

Lighting Fixtures

Electric

Action Lighting
Bozeman, MT 800-248-0076

ALP Lighting & Ceiling Products
Pennsauken, NJ 800-633-7732

Apogee Translite
Deer Park, NY 631-254-6975

Apollo Acme Lighting Fixture
Mount Vernon, NY 800-833-9006

Architectural Products
Highland, NY 845-691-8500

Art Craft Lighting
Champlain, NY 718-387-8000

Azz/R-A-L
Houston, TX 713-943-0340

Boyd Lighting Company
Sausalito, CA 415-778-4300

Brinkmann Corporation
Dallas, TX 800-468-5252

C.W. Cole & Company
South El Monte, CA 626-443-2473

Capitol Hardware, Inc.,
Middlebury, IN 800-327-6083

Caselites
Hialeah, FL 305-819-7766

Casella Lighting Company
Sacramento, CA 888-252-7874

Chapman Manufacturing Company
Avon, MA 508-588-3200

Claude Neon Signs
Baltimore, MD 410-685-7575

Columbia Jet/JPL
Houston, TX 800-876-4511

Columbia Lighting
Greenville, SC 864-599-6000

Commercial Lighting Design
Memphis, TN 800-774-5799

Con-tech/Conservation Technology
Northbrook, IL 800-728-0312

Coronet Chandelier Originals
Brentwood, NY 631-273-1177

County Neon Sign Corporation
Plainview, NY 516-349-9550

Custom Lights & Iron
National City, CA 619-474-8593

Custom Metalcraft, Architectural Lighting
Boston, MA 617-242-0868

D'Lights
Glendale, CA 818-956-5656

DAC Lighting
New York, NY 914-698-5959

E-Lite Technologies
Trumbull, CT 877-520-3951

Eclipse Electric Manufacturing
St Louis Park, MN 952-929-2500

Econo Frost Night Covers
Shawnigan Lake, BC 800-519-1222

Edison Price Lighting
Long Island City, NY 718-685-0700

EGS Electrical Group
Skokie, IL 847-679-7800

Electrodex
Bradenton, FL 800-362-1972

Energy Saving Devices
Saint Paul, MN 651-222-0849

Eximco Manufacturing Company
Chicago, IL 773-463-1470

Fenton Art Glass Company
Williamstown, WV 800-933-6766

Forum Lighting
Pittsburgh, PA 412-781-5970

Fredrick Ramond Company
Cerritos, CA 800-743-7266

G Lighting
St Louis, MO 800-331-2425

GE Lighting
Cleveland, OH 800-435-4448

Gem Electric Manufacturing Company
Hauppauge, NY 800-275-4361

Genlyte Thomas Group
Burlington, MA 662-842-7212

GERM-O-RAY
Stone Mountain, GA 800-966-8480

Glass Industries
Wallingford, CT 203-269-6700

Greene Brothers
Brooklyn, NY 718-388-6800

Guth Lighting
Saint Louis, MO 314-533-3200

H&H Metal Fabrications
Belden, MS 662-489-4626
Hart Associates
Ruston, LA 800-592-3500
Hub Electric Company
Crystal Lake, IL 815-455-4400
Hubbell Lighting
Greenville, SC. 540-382-6111
Hydrel Corporation
Sylmar, CA 818-362-9465
Indy Lighting
Fishers, IN. 317-849-1233
Insect-O-Cutor
Stone Mountain, GA. 800-988-5359
JDO/LNR Lighting
Live Oak, TX 800-597-1570
Jet Lite Products
Highland, IL 618-654-2217
JJI Lighting Group, Inc.
Franklin Park, IL. 847-451-0700
Kensington Lighting
Greensburg, PA. 724-850-2433
Kim Lighting
City of Industry, CA 626-968-5666
Kreissle Forge Inc
Sarasota, FL 941-355-6795
LBL Lighting
Skokie, IL 800-323-3226
Le-Jo Enterprises
Phoenixville, PA 484-921-9000
Legion Lighting Company
Brooklyn, NY 800-453-4466
Light Waves Concept
Brooklyn, NY 800-670-8137
Lightolier
Wilmington, MA. 978-657-7600
Lights On
Yonkers, NY 914-961-0588
Linear Lighting Corporation
Long Island City, NY 718-361-7552
Litecontrol Corporation
Plympton, MA. 781-294-0100
Lithonia Lighting
Conyers, GA 770-922-9000
Little Giant Pump Company
Oklahoma City, OK. 405-947-2511
Louis Baldinger & Sons
New York, NY 718-204-5700
LSI Industries
Cincinnati, OH 800-436-7600
Luminiere Corporation
Bronx, NY. 718-295-5450
Luxo Corporation
Elmsford, NY 800-222-5896
Main Lamp Corporation
Brooklyn, NY 718-436-2207
Majestic
Bridgeport, CT 203-367-7900
Manning Lighting
Sheboygan, WI 920-458-2184
Meil Electric Fixture Manufacturing Company
Philadelphia, PA 215-228-8528
Mobern Electric Corporation
Laurel, MD 800-444-9288
Modulighter
New York, NY 212-371-0336
Mulholland-Harper Company
Denton, MD 800-882-3052
Natale Machine & Tool Company
Carlstadt, NJ 800-883-8382
Nemco Electric Company
Seattle, WA 206-622-1551
Neo-Ray Products
Brooklyn, NY 800-221-0946
Newstamp Lighting Corp.
North Easton, MA. 508-238-7071
Nova Industries
San Leandro, CA. 510-357-0171
Nulco Lighting
Providence, RI 401-728-5200
Osram Sylvania
Danvers, MA. 800-544-4828
Palmer Distributors
St Clair Shores, MI 800-444-1912
Peerless Lighting Corporation
Berkeley, CA. 510-845-2760
Philadelphia Glass Bending Company
Philadelphia, PA 215-726-8468
Prescolite
Vallejo, CA 707-562-3500
Primlite Manufacturing Corporation
Freeport, NY 800-327-7583

Remcraft Lighting Products
Miami, FL. 800-327-6585
Rewdco & Hanson Brass Products
Sun Valley, CA 888-841-3773
Ryther-Purdy Lumber Company
Old Saybrook, CT. 860-388-4405
Sea Gull Lighting Products, LLC
Corona, CA 800-347-5483
Simkar Corporation
Philadelphia, PA 800-523-3602
Staff Lighting
Highland, NY 845-691-6262
Standex International Corporation
Salem, NH. 603-893-9701
Sterner Lighting Systems
Eden Prairie, MN 800-328-7480
Strand Lighting
Dallas, TX
Super Vision International
Orlando, FL. 407-857-9900
Swivelier Company
Blauvelt, NY. 845-353-1455
Thomas Lighting Residential
Rosemont, IL. 800-825-5844
Toronto Fabricating & Manufacturing
Mississauga, ON. 905-891-2516
Troy Lighting
City of Industry, CA 800-533-8769
Tru-Form Plastics
Gardena, CA 800-510-7999
UDEC Corporation
Woburn, MA 800-990-8332
UL Lighting Fixtures Co rp.
Long Island City, NY 718-726-7500
V&R Metal Enterprises
Brooklyn, NY 718-768-8142
Versailles Lighting
Delray Beach, FL 888-564-0240
Vimco Inc.
King of Prussia, PA. 610-768-0500
Voigt Lighting Industries Inc.
Leonia, NJ. 201-461-2493
Western Lighting
Franklin Park, IL. 847-451-7200
Weston Emergency Light Company
Waltham, MA 800-649-3756
Yorkraft
York, PA 800-872-2044
Zelco Industries
Mount Vernon, NY 800-431-2486

Emergency

ALP Lighting & Ceiling Products
Pennsauken, NJ. 800-633-7732
Architectural Products
Highland, NY 845-691-8500
Big Beam Emergency Systems
Crystal Lake, IL 815-459-6100
Brinkmann Corporation
Dallas, TX. 800-468-5252
Carpenter Emergency Lighting
Hamilton, NJ. 888-884-2270
Claude Neon Signs
Baltimore, MD 410-685-7575
Cooper Crouse-Hinds, LLC
Syracuse, NY 315-477-7000
Cooper Lighting
Peachtree City, GA 770-486-4800
Gilbert Insect Light Traps
Jonesboro, AR. 800-643-0400
HD Electric Company
Waukegan, IL 847-473-4980
Hubbell Lighting
Greenville, SC. 540-382-6111
Natale Machine & Tool Company
Carlstadt, NJ 800-883-8382
Roflan Associates
Tulsa, OK 978-475-0100
UDEC Corporation
Woburn, MA. 800-990-8332
Weston Emergency Light Company
Waltham, MA 800-649-3756

Fluorescent

ALP Lighting & Ceiling Products
Pennsauken, NJ. 800-633-7732
American Houver Company
Skokie, IL 800-772-0355
Apollo Acme Lighting Fixture
Mount Vernon, NY 800-833-9006

C.W. Cole & Company
South El Monte, CA 626-443-2473
Claude Neon Signs
Baltimore, MD 410-685-7575
Columbia Lighting
Greenville, SC. 864-599-6000
Command Electronics
Schoolcraft, MI 269-679-4011
Crownlite Manufacturing Corporation
Bohemia, NY 631-589-9100
DAC Lighting
New York, NY 914-698-5959
Day-O-Lite ManufacturingCompany
Warwick, RI 401-808-6849
Diversified Lighting Diffusers Inc
Copiague, NY 800-234-5464
Dura Electric Lamp Company
Newark, NJ 973-624-0014
Edison Price Lighting
Long Island City, NY 718-685-0700
Energy Saving Devices
Saint Paul, MN 651-222-0849
Eximco Manufacturing Company
Chicago, IL 773-463-1470
Forum Lighting
Pittsburgh, PA. 412-781-5970
GE Lighting
Cleveland, OH 800-435-4448
Genesta Manufacturing
Rockwall, TX 972-771-1653
Genlyte Thomas Group
Burlington, MA. 662-842-7212
GERM-O-RAY
Stone Mountain, GA. 800-966-8480
Guth Lighting
Saint Louis, MO 314-533-3200
H&H Metal Fabrications
Belden, MS 662-489-4626
Hasco Electric Corporation
Greenwich, CT 203-531-9400
Hastings Lighting Company
Los Angeles, CA. 213-622-2009
Holcor
Riverdale, IL. 708-841-3800
Hybrinetics
Santa Rosa, CA. 800-247-6900
Illumination Products
San Juan, PR 787-754-7193
Indy Lighting
Fishers, IN. 317-849-1233
Insect-O-Cutor
Stone Mountain, GA. 800-988-5359
Kensington Lighting
Greensburg, PA. 724-850-2433
Legion Lighting Company
Brooklyn, NY 800-453-4466
Lightolier
Wilmington, MA. 978-657-7600
Lithonia Lighting
Conyers, GA 770-922-9000
Louisville Lamp Company
Louisville, KY 502-964-4094
Lumax Industries
Altoona, PA. 814-944-2537
Luxo Corporation
Elmsford, NY 800-222-5896
Meil Electric Fixture Manufacturing Company
Philadelphia, PA 215-228-8528
Nemco Electric Company
Seattle, WA 206-622-1551
Neo-Ray Products
Brooklyn, NY 800-221-0946
NT Industries
Franklin Park, IL. 847-451-6500
Osram Sylvania
Danvers, MA. 800-544-4828
Panasonic Commercial Food Service
Secaucus, NJ. 800-553-0384
Paramount Industries
Croswell, MI. 800-521-5405
Peerless Lighting Corporation
Berkeley, CA. 510-845-2760
Philips Lighting Company
Somerset, NJ. 732-563-3000
Prudential Lighting Corporation
Los Angeles, CA. 800-421-5483
Remcraft Lighting Products
Miami, FL. 800-327-6585
Roflan Associates
Tulsa, OK 978-475-0100
Ryther-Purdy Lumber Company
Old Saybrook, CT. 860-388-4405

Shat-R-Shield
Salisbury, NC 800-223-0853
Shelden, Dickson, & Steven Company
Omaha, NE 402-571-4848
Simkar Corporation
Philadelphia, PA 800-523-3602
Staff Lighting
Highland, NY 845-691-6262
Steel Craft Fluorescent Company
Newark, NJ 973-349-1614
Super Vision International
Orlando, FL. 407-857-9900
Toronto Fabricating & Manufacturing
Mississauga, ON. 905-891-2516
Trojan
Mount Sterling, KY 800-264-0526
UDEC Corporation
Woburn, MA 800-990-8332
Varco Products
Chardon, OH. 216-481-6895
Versailles Lighting
Delray Beach, FL 888-564-0240
Visual Marketing Associates
Santee, CA 619-258-0393

Mercury, High Intensity

GE Lighting
Cleveland, OH 800-435-4448
Grating Pacific/Ross Technology Corporation
Los Alamitos, CA. 800-321-4314
Guth Lighting
Saint Louis, MO 314-533-3200
Holcor
Riverdale, IL. 708-841-3800
Hubbell Lighting
Greenville, SC. 540-382-6111
JM Canty, Inc.
Buffalo, NY. 716-625-4227
Prescolite
Vallejo, CA 707-562-3500

Outdoor

Apollo Acme Lighting Fixture
Mount Vernon, NY. 800-833-9006
Brinkmann Corporation
Dallas, TX. 800-468-5252
Claude Neon Signs
Baltimore, MD 410-685-7575
Cooper Crouse-Hinds, LLC
Syracuse, NY 315-477-7000
Cooper Lighting
Peachtree City, GA 770-486-4800
Faribo Manufacturing Company
Faribault, MN 800-447-6043
GE Lighting
Cleveland, OH 800-435-4448
Genlyte Thomas Group
Burlington, MA. 662-842-7212
Glolite
Des Plaines, IL 847-803-4500
Hub Electric Company
Crystal Lake, IL 815-455-4400
Hubbell Lighting
Greenville, SC. 540-382-6111
Lightolier
Wilmington, MA. 978-657-7600
Linear Lighting Corporation
Long Island City, NY 718-361-7552
Little Giant Pump Company
Oklahoma City, OK. 405-947-2511
Natale Machine & Tool Company
Carlstadt, NJ 800-883-8382
Prescolite
Vallejo, CA 707-562-3500
Primlite Manufacturing Corporation
Freeport, NY. 800-327-7583
Progress Lighting
Greenville, SC. 864-678-1000
QSR Industrial Supply
Cherry Hill, NJ 800-257-8282
Remcraft Lighting Products
Miami, FL. 800-327-6585
Shakespeare Company
Newberry, SC 800-800-9008
Sterner Lighting Systems
Eden Prairie, MN 800-328-7480
Thomas Lighting Residential
Rosemont, IL. 800-825-5844
Troy Lighting
City of Industry, CA 800-533-8769

Zelco Industries
Mount Vernon, NY. 800-431-2486

Paging Systems

Command Communications
Centennial, CO 800-288-3491
Instacomm Canada
Oakville, ON. 877-426-2783
Long Range Systems
Addison, TX 800-577-8101
NTN Wireless
Norcross, GA 800-637-8639
UAA
Chicago, IL 800-813-1711

Radios

Long Range Systems
Addison, TX 800-577-8101

Panels

Insulated

Advance Energy Technologies
Clifton Park, NY. 800-724-0198
Extrutech Plastics Inc.
Manitowoc, WI. 888-818-0118
Kingspan Insulated Panels, Ltd.
Langley, BC, BC. 877-638-3266
Zeroloc
Kirkland, WA 425-823-4888

Platforms

C&R Refrigation Inc,
Center, TX. 800-438-6182
Delkor Systems, Inc
Minneapolis, MN 800-328-5558
Slipnot Metal Safety Flooring
Detroit, MI 800-754-7668

Plating

Metal

Slipnot Metal Safety Flooring
Detroit, MI 800-754-7668

Sinks

Advance Tabco
Edgewood, NY 800-645-3166
Aero Manufacturing Company
Clifton, NJ. 800-631-8378
All State Fabricators Corporation
Florida, RI. 800-322-9925
Amtekco Industries
Columbus, OH 800-336-4677
Baker Sheet Metal Corporation
Norfolk, VA. 800-909-4325
Bar Equipment Corporation of America
Downey, CA 888-870-2322
Baxter Manufacturing Company
Orting, WA 800-777-2828
Best Sanitizers
Penn Valley, CA 888-225-3267
Carts Food Equipment Corporation
Brooklyn, NY 718-788-5540
Component Hardware Group
Lakewood, NJ. 800-526-3694
Crown Steel Manufacturing
San Marcos, CA 760-471-1188
D.A. Berther
West Allis, WI. 877-357-9622
Denmar Corporation
North Dartmouth, MA 508-999-3295
Duke Manufacturing Company
Saint Louis, MO 800-735-3853
Duluth Sheet Metal
Duluth, MN. 218-722-2613
Dunhill Food Equipment Corporation
Armonk, NY. 800-847-4206
Eagle Foodservice Equipment
Clayton, DE. 800-441-8440
Eldorado Miranda Manufacturing Company
Largo, FL 800-330-0708
Erwin Food Service Equipment
Fort Worth, TX 817-535-0021
Eskay Metal Fabricating Company
Buffalo, NY. 800-836-8015

Fab-X/Metals
Washington, NC 800-677-3229
FabWright, Inc
Garden Grove, CA 800-854-6464
Fisher Manufacturing Company
Tulare, CA. 800-421-6162
GKL
Dickerson, MD 301-948-5538
Griffin Products
Wills Point, TX. 800-379-9709
Hercules Food Equipment
Weston, ON. 416-742-9673
IMC Teddy Food Service Equipment
Amityville, NY 800-221-5644
Insinger Machine Company
Philadelphia, PA 800-344-4802
John Boos & Company
Effingham, IL 217-347-7701
KEMCO
Wareham, MA. 800-231-5955
Kitchen Equipment Fabricating Company
Houston, TX 713-747-3611
Kitcor Corporation
Sun Valley, CA 818-767-4800
Krowne Metal Corporation
Wayne, NJ. 800-631-0442
La Crosse
Onalaska, WI. 800-345-0018
Lambertson Industries
Sparks, NV 800-548-3324
Load King Manufacturing Company
Jacksonville, FL 800-531-4975
M-One Specialties Inc
Salt Lake City, UT 800-525-9223
Marlo Manufacturing Company
Boonton, NJ 800-222-0450
MCM Fixture Company
Hazel Park, MI 248-547-9280
Metal Equipment Fabricators
Columbia, SC 803-776-9250
Metal Kitchen Fabricators
Houston, TX 713-683-8375
Metal Master
Tucson, AZ 800-488-8729
Metal Masters Food Service Equipment Company
Clayton, DE. 800-441-8440
Missouri Equipment Company
St Louis, MO. 800-727-6326
Moli-International
Denver, CO 800-525-8468
National Bar Systems
Huntington Beach, CA 714-848-1688
National FABCO Manufacturing
St Louis, MO. 314-842-4571
National Scoop & Equipment Company
Spring House, PA 215-646-2040
Polar Ware Company
Sheboygan, WI 800-237-3655
Premium Air Systems
Troy, MI 877-430-0333
Reliable Food Service Equipment
Concord, ON. 416-738-6840
Sefi Fabricators
Amityville, NY 631-842-2200
St. Louis Stainless Service
Fenton, MO. 888-507-1578
Stainless
La Vergne, TN. 800-877-5177
Stainless Equipment Manufacturing
Dallas, TX. 800-736-2038
Stainless Fabricating Company
Denver, CO 800-525-8966
Stainless International
Rancho Cordova, CA 888-300-6196
Stainless Steel Fabricators
Tyler, TX. 903-595-6625
Starlite Food Service Equipment
Detroit, MI 888-521-6603
Super Sturdy
Weldon, NC. 800-253-4833
Superior Products Company
Saint Paul, MN 800-328-9800
Supreme Metal
Alpharetta, GA 800-645-2526
T&S Brass & Bronze Works
Travelers Rest, SC 800-476-4103
Terriss Consolidated Industries
Asbury Park, NJ 800-342-1611
Tru-Form Plastics
Gardena, CA. 800-510-7999
United Fabricators
Fort Smith, AR 800-235-4101

Universal Stainless
Aurora, CO 800-223-8332
Universal Stainless
Titusville, PA 800-295-1909
Weiss Sheet Metal
Avon, MA 508-583-8300
West Metals
London, ON 800-300-6667
West Star Industries
Stockton, CA 800-326-2288

Windows

Drive-Thru & Pass-Thru

Ayr-King Corporation
Jeffersontown, KY 866-266-6290
Bullet Guard Corporation
West Sacramento, CA 800-233-5632
Creative Industries
Indianapolis, IN 800-776-2068
Quickserv Corporation
Houston, TX 800-388-8307
Ready Access
West Chicago, IL 800-621-5045

Clothing & Protective Apparel

Aprons

A.D. Cowdrey Company
Modesto, CA 209-538-4677
Adcapitol
Monroe, NC 800-868-7111
ADEX Medical Inc
Riverside, CA 800-873-4776
Akron Cotton Products
Akron, OH 800-899-7173
Alex Delvecchio Enterprises
Troy, MI 248-619-9600
Allred Marketing
Birmingham, AL 205-251-3700
American Advertising & Shop Cap Company
Old Tappan, NJ 800-442-8837
American Apron Inc.
Foxboro, MA 800-262-7766
American Bag & Linen Company
Cornelia, GA 706-778-5377
ATD-American Company
Wyncote, PA 800-523-2300
Atlantic Mills
Lakewood, NJ 800-242-7374
Bennett's Auto Inc.
Neenah, WI 800-215-5464
Best Brands Home Products
New York, NY 212-684-7456
Best Manufacturing
Jersey City, NJ 201-356-3800
Best Value Textiles
Elkhorn, WI 800-248-9826
Boss Manufacturing Company
Kewanee, IL 800-447-4581
Bragard Professional Uniforms
New York, NY 800-488-2433
Carson Manufacturing Company
Petaluma, CA 800-423-2380
Celebrity Promotions
Remsen, IA 800-332-6847
Champaign Plastics Company
Champaign, IL 800-575-0170
Charles Craft
Laurinburg, NC 910-844-3521
Christman Screenprint
Springfield, MI 800-962-9330
Coast Scientific
Rancho Santa Fe, CA 800-445-1544
David Dobbs Enterprise & Menu Design
St Augustine, FL 800-889-6368
Dove Screen Printing Company
Royston, GA 706-245-4975
Elwood Safety Company
Buffalo, NY 866-326-6060
Erell Manufacturing Company
Elk Grove Vlg, IL 800-622-6334
Erie Cotton Products Company
Erie, PA 800-289-4737
FabOhio
Uhrichsville, OH 740-922-4233
Fabriko
Altavista, VA 888-203-8098
Fashion Seal Uniforms
Seminole, FL 727-397-9611
Flavor Wear
Valley Center, CA 800-647-8372
Foley's Famous Aprons
Wayne, MI 800-634-3245
Gary Manufacturing Company
Chula Vista, CA 800-775-0804
Gourmet Tableskirts
Houston, TX 800-527-0440
Gril-Del
Mankato, MN 800-782-7320
Hall's Safety Apparel
Uhrichsville, OH 800-232-3671
Handgards
El Paso, TX 800-351-8161
Hank Rivera Associates
Dearborn, MI 313-581-8300
Hygrade Gloves
Brooklyn, NY 800-233-8100
Island Poly
Westbury, NY 800-338-4433
Jomac Products
Niles, IL 800-566-2289
Kennedy's Specialty Sewing
Erin, ON 519-833-9306
Keystone Adjustable Cap Company
Pennsauken, NJ 800-663-5439
Klever Kuvers
Pasadena, CA 626-355-8441
LaCrosse Safety and Industrial
Portland, OR 800-557-7246
Landau Uniforms
Olive Branch, MS 800-238-7513
Lexidyne of Pennsylvania
Pittsburgh, PA 800-543-2233
Libertyware
Clearfield, UT 888-500-5885
Locknane
Everett, WA 800-848-9854
Mell & Company
Niles, IL 800-262-6355
Midwest Promotional Group
Summit, IL 800-305-3388
Milliken & Company
Spartanburg, SC 864-503-2020
National Embroidery Service
Portsmouth, RI 800-227-1451
New Chef Fashion
Vernon, CA 323-581-0300
New Hatchwear Company
Calgary, AB 800-661-9249
Omni Apparel Inc.
Carrollton, GA 770-838-1008
Pacific Oasis Enterprises
Santa Fe Springs, CA 800-424-1475
PolyConversions
Rantoul, IL 888-893-3330
Pop Tops Company
South Easton, MA 508-238-8585
Rodes Professional Apparel
Louisville, KY 502-584-3112
Royal Paper Products
Coatesville, PA 800-666-6655
S&H Uniform Corporation
White Plains, NY 800-210-5295
Seven Mile Creek Corporation
Eaton, OH 800-497-6324
Shen Manufacturing Company
W Conshohocken, PA 610-825-2790
ST Restaurant Supplies
Delta, BC 888-448-4244
Sultan Linens
New York, NY 212-689-8900
Superior Linen & Work Wear
Kansas City, MO 800-798-7987
Tara Linens
Sanford, NC 800-476-8272
The Funny Apron Company
Lake Dallas, TX 800-835-5802
Triad Products Company
Springfield, OH 937-323-9422
Tronex Industries
Denville, NJ 800-833-1181
Tucker Industries
Colorado Springs, CO 800-786-7287
Universal Overall Company
Chicago, IL 800-621-3344
Vicmore Manufacturing Company
Brooklyn, NY 800-458-8663
Whiting & Davis
Attleboro Falls, MA 800-876-6374
World Pride
St Petersburg, FL 800-533-2433

Canners' & Packers'

A.D. Cowdrey Company
Modesto, CA 209-538-4677
Alabama Bag Company Inc
Talladega, AL 800-888-4921
American Apron Inc.
Foxboro, MA 800-262-7766
American Bag & Linen Company
Cornelia, GA 706-778-5377
Bennett's Auto Inc.
Neenah, WI 800-215-5464
Champaign Plastics Company
Champaign, IL 800-575-0170
Elwood Safety Company
Buffalo, NY 866-326-6060
Erell Manufacturing Company
Elk Grove Vlg, IL 800-622-6334
Gary Manufacturing Company
Chula Vista, CA 800-775-0804
Hall's Safety Apparel
Uhrichsville, OH 800-232-3671
Island Poly
Westbury, NY 800-338-4433
Kennedy's Specialty Sewing
Erin, ON 519-833-9306
Locknane
Everett, WA 800-848-9854
Seven Mile Creek Corporation
Eaton, OH 800-497-6324
Whiting & Davis
Attleboro Falls, MA 800-876-6374

Dairy

American Apron Inc.
Foxboro, MA 800-262-7766
Champaign Plastics Company
Champaign, IL 800-575-0170
Erell Manufacturing Company
Elk Grove Vlg, IL 800-622-6334
Seven Mile Creek Corporation
Eaton, OH 800-497-6324

Caps

Allred Marketing
Birmingham, AL 205-251-3700

Gloves

Bakers'

Best Value Textiles
Elkhorn, WI 800-248-9826
Golden Needles Knitting & Glove Company
Coshocton, OH 919-667-5102
Great Southern Corporation
Memphis, TN 800-421-7802
Hygrade Gloves
Brooklyn, NY 800-233-8100
Jomac Products
Niles, IL 800-566-2289
Panhandler, Inc.
Cordova, TN 800-654-7237

Disposable

ADEX Medical Inc
Riverside, CA 800-873-4776
AFASSCO
Minden, NV 800-441-6774
Alabama Bag Company Inc
Talladega, AL 800-888-4921
Ansell Healthcare
Iselin, NJ 800-800-0444
Atlantis Plastics Institutional Products
Mankato, MN 800-999-2374
Bennett's Auto Inc.
Neenah, WI 800-215-5464
Boss Manufacturing Company
Kewanee, IL 800-447-4581
Champaign Plastics Company
Champaign, IL 800-575-0170
Coast Scientific
Rancho Santa Fe, CA 800-445-1544
Erie Cotton Products Company
Erie, PA 800-289-4737
Gann Manufacturing
Baltimore, MD 800-922-9832
George Glove Company, Inc
Midland Park, NJ 800-631-4292
Goldmax Industries
City of Industry, CA 626-964-8820
Great Southern Corporation
Memphis, TN 800-421-7802
Handgards
El Paso, TX 800-351-8161
Hygrade Gloves
Brooklyn, NY 800-233-8100

John Plant Company
Ramseur, NC 800-334-2711
Libertyware
Clearfield, UT 888-500-5885
Omron Health Care
Bannockburn, IL 800-323-1482
Ontario Glove and Safety Products
Kitchener, ON 800-265-4554
Pacific Oasis Enterprises
Santa Fe Springs, CA 800-424-1475
Playtex Products, LLC
New Providence, NJ 888-310-4290
Rochester Midland
Rochester, NY 800-387-7174
Royal Paper Products
Coatesville, PA 800-666-6655
Superior Products Company
Saint Paul, MN 800-328-9800
Textile Buff & Wheel Company, Inc.
Charlestown, MA 617-241-8100
Triad Scientific
Manasquan, NJ 800-867-6690
Tronex Industries
Denville, NJ 800-833-1181
Wilkens-Anderson Company
Chicago, IL 800-847-2222
Y-Pers
Philadelphia, PA 800-421-0242

Plastic, Rubber

Allied Glove Corporation
Milwaukee, WI 800-558-9263
Ansell Healthcare
Iselin, NJ 800-800-0444
Boss Manufacturing Company
Kewanee, IL 800-447-4581
Carolina Glove
Conover, NC 800-335-1918
Champaign Plastics Company
Champaign, IL 800-575-0170
Choctaw-Kaul Distribution Company
Detroit, MI 313-894-9494
Coast Scientific
Rancho Santa Fe, CA 800-445-1544
Comasec Safety, Inc.
Enfield, CT 800-333-0219
Eagle Home Products
Huntington, NY
Erie Cotton Products Company
Erie, PA 800-289-4737
George Glove Company, Inc
Midland Park, NJ 800-631-4292
Glover Latex
Anaheim, CA 800-243-5110
Goldmax Industries
City of Industry, CA 626-964-8820
Great Southern Corporation
Memphis, TN 800-421-7802
Hall's Safety Apparel
Uhrichsville, OH 800-232-3671
Handgards
El Paso, TX 800-351-8161
Hygrade Gloves
Brooklyn, NY 800-233-8100
Island Poly
Westbury, NY 800-338-4433
Lambert Company
Chillicothe, MO 800-821-7667
Monte Glove Company
Wilkesboro, NC 662-263-5353
Omron Health Care
Bannockburn, IL 800-323-1482
Ontario Glove and Safety Products
Kitchener, ON 800-265-4554
Pacific Oasis Enterprises
Santa Fe Springs, CA 800-424-1475
Playtex Products, LLC
New Providence, NJ 888-310-4290
Quality Mop & Brush Manufacturers
Needham, MA 617-884-2999
Rochester Midland
Rochester, NY 800-387-7174
Sterling Rubber
Fergus, ON 519-843-4032
Tronex Industries
Denville, NJ 800-833-1181
Wells-Lamont Corporation
Niles, IL 800-323-2830
Y-Pers
Philadelphia, PA 800-421-0242

Protective

Alabama Bag Company Inc
Talladega, AL 800-888-4921
Allied Glove Corporation
Milwaukee, WI 800-558-9263
Bennett's Auto Inc.
Neenah, WI 800-215-5464
Best Manufacturing Company
Menlo, GA 800-241-0323
Carolina Glove
Conover, NC 800-335-1918
Century Glove
Summerville, GA 973-751-0300
Champaign Plastics Company
Champaign, IL 800-575-0170
Coast Scientific
Rancho Santa Fe, CA 800-445-1544
Comasec Safety, Inc.
Enfield, CT 800-333-0219
Fairfield Line Inc
Fairfield, IA 800-423-7437
Gann Manufacturing
Baltimore, MD 800-922-9832
George Glove Company, Inc
Midland Park, NJ 800-631-4292
Glover Latex
Anaheim, CA 800-243-5110
Golden Needles Knitting & Glove Company
Coshocton, OH 919-667-5102
Gril-Del
Mankato, MN 800-782-7320
Healthline Products
Los Angeles, CA 800-473-4003
Island Poly
Westbury, NY 800-338-4433
Micro Flex
Reno, NV 800-876-6866
Midwest Quality Gloves
Chillicothe, MO 800-821-3028
Omron Health Care
Bannockburn, IL 800-323-1482
Ontario Glove and Safety Products
Kitchener, ON 800-265-4554
Panhandler, Inc.
Cordova, TN 800-654-7237
Parvin Manufacturing Company
Los Angeles, CA 800-648-0770
Playtex Products, LLC
New Providence, NJ 888-310-4290
Royal Paper Products
Coatesville, PA 800-666-6655
Samco Freezewear Company
St Paul, MN 651-638-3888
ST Restaurant Supplies
Delta, BC 888-448-4244
Star Glove Company
Odon, IN 800-832-7101
Superior Distributing
Louisville, KY 800-365-6661
Textile Buff & Wheel Company, Inc.
Charlestown, MA 617-241-8100
Triad Scientific
Manasquan, NJ 800-867-6690
Tronex Industries
Denville, NJ 800-833-1181
Wells Lamont Industrial
Niles, IL 800-247-3295
Wells Lamont Industry Group
Niles, IL 800-323-2830
Whiting & Davis
Attleboro Falls, MA 800-876-6374
Work Well Company
Gahanna, OH 614-759-8003
Worksafe Industries
Huntington Station, NY 800-929-9000
Y-Pers
Philadelphia, PA 800-421-0242

Hair Nets

ADEX Medical Inc
Riverside, CA 800-873-4776
Cellucap
Philadelphia, PA 800-523-3814
Champaign Plastics Company
Champaign, IL 800-575-0170
Erie Cotton Products Company
Erie, PA 800-289-4737
Hairnet Corporation of America
New York, NY 212-675-5840
Hygrade Gloves
Brooklyn, NY 800-233-8100
Island Poly
Westbury, NY 800-338-4433
Joseph Titone & Sons
Burlington, NJ 800-220-4102
Keystone Adjustable Cap Company
Pennsauken, NJ 800-663-5439
Peekskill Hair Net
Peekskill, NY 914-737-1524
ST Restaurant Supplies
Delta, BC 888-448-4244
Sta-Rite Ginnie Lou
Shelbyville, IL 800-782-7483
Superior Distributing
Louisville, KY 800-365-6661

Holders

Pot

Arden Companies
Southfield, MI 248-415-8500
Best Brands Home Products
New York, NY 212-684-7456
Best Value Textiles
Elkhorn, WI 800-248-9826
Charles Craft
Laurinburg, NC 910-844-3521
Grayline Housewares
Carol Stream, IL 800-222-7388
Hank Rivera Associates
Dearborn, MI 313-581-8300
Healthline Products
Los Angeles, CA 800-473-4003
Jomac Products
Niles, IL 800-566-2289
Monte Glove Company
Wilkesboro, NC 662-263-5353
Panhandler, Inc.
Cordova, TN 800-654-7237
Shen Manufacturing Company
W Conshohocken, PA 610-825-2790
Standard Terry Mills
Souderton, PA 215-723-8121
Stevens Linen Association
Dudley, MA 508-943-0813

Jackets

Allred Marketing
Birmingham, AL 205-251-3700

Name Badges

Ace Stamp & Engraving
Lakewood, WA 253-582-3322
Alex Delvecchio Enterprises
Troy, MI 248-619-9600
Artcraft Badge & Sign Company
Olney, MD 800-739-0709
ATL-East Tag & Label Company
West Chester, PA 866-381-8744
Atlas Labels
Montreal, QC 514-852-7000
BAW Plastics
Jefferson Hills, PA 800-783-2229
Berlekamp Plastics
Fremont, OH 419-334-4481
Cawley
Manitowoc, WI 800-822-9539
Central Decal Company
Burr Ridge, IL 800-869-7654
Chemi-Graphic
Ludlow, MA 413-589-0151
City Stamp & Seal Company
Austin, TX 800-950-6074
Corpus Christi Stamp Works
Corpus Christi, TX 800-322-4515
Crown Marking
Minneapolis, MN 800-305-5249
Custom I.D.
Venice, FL 800-242-8430
Custom Rubber Stamp Company
Crosby, MN 888-606-4579
Custom Stamp Company
Anza, CA 323-292-0753
Darson Corporation
Detroit, MI 800-783-7781
Design Mark Corporation
Wareham, MA 800-451-3275
Dinosaur Plastics
Houston, TX 713-923-2278
E.C. Shaw Company
Cincinnati, OH 866-532-7429

Economy Novelty & Printing Company
New York, NY ... 212-481-3022
Ed Smith's Stencil Works
New Orleans, LA ... 504-525-2128
Ehrgott Rubber Stamp Company
Indianapolis, IN ... 317-353-2222
Elliot Lee
Cedarhurst, NY ... 516-569-9595
Emblem & Badge
Providence, RI ... 800-875-5444
Engraving Services Co.
Woodville South, SA
Engraving Specialists
Royal Oak, MI ... 248-542-2244
EPI World Graphics
Midlothian, IL ... 708-389-7500
Executive Line
Chatham, NY ... 800-333-5761
Fort Hill Sign Products, Inc.
Hopedale, MA ... 508-381-0357
Fox Stamp, Sign & Specialty
Menasha, WI ... 800-236-3699
Frost Manufacturing Corporation
Worcester, MA ... 800-462-0216
George Lauterer Corporation
Chicago, IL ... 312-913-1881
GM Nameplate
Seattle, WA ... 800-366-7668
Granite State Stamps, Inc.
Manchester, NH ... 800-937-3736
Graphics Unlimited
San Diego, CA ... 858-453-4031
Hartford Stamp Works
Hartford, CT ... 860-249-6205
IdentaBadge
Lafayette, LA ... 800-325-8247
Impact Awards & Promotions
Avon Park, FL ... 888-203-4225
ITC Systems
Toronto, ON ... 877-482-8326
King Badge & Button Company
Huntingtn Bch, CA ... 714-847-3060
Kraus & Sons
New York, NY ... 212-620-0408
Label Systems & Solutions
Bohemia, NY ... 800-811-2560
Labels Systems, Inc
Addison, TX ... 800-220-9552
Legible Signs
Loves Park, IL ... 800-435-4177
Martco Engravers
Fremont, NH ... 603-895-3561
Mastercraft Manufacturing Company
Long Island City, NY ... 718-729-5620
Midwest Badge & Novelty Company Inc
Minneapolis, MN ... 952-927-9901
Modern Stamp Company
Baltimore, MD ... 800-727-3029
MTL Etching Industries
Woodmere, NY ... 516-295-9733
My Serenity Pond
Cold Spring, MN ... 320-363-0411
N.G. Slater Corporation
New York, NY ... 800-848-4621
Nameplates
St Paul, MN ... 651-228-1522
Orber Manufacturing Company
Cranston, RI ... 800-761-4059
Paperweights Plus
Medford, NY ... 631-924-3222
Patrick & Company
Dallas, TX ... 214-761-0900
Photo-Graphics Company
Grandview, MO ... 816-761-3333
Plastic Tag & Trade Check Company
Essexville, MI ... 989-892-7913
Print Source
Wakefield, RI ... 401-789-9339
Pro-Ad-Company
Portland, OR ... 800-287-5885
Rebel Stamp & Sign Company, Inc.
Baton Rouge, LA ... 800-860-5120
Regal Plastics
North Kansas City, MO ... 816-471-6390
Richardson's Stamp Works
Houston, TX ... 713-973-0300
Royal Label Company
Boston, MA ... 617-825-6050
Sesame Label System
New York, NY ... 800-551-3020
Sign Shop
Rancho Cucamonga, CA ... 909-945-5888
Stoffel Seals Corporation
Tallapoosa, GA ... 800-422-8247
Strong Group
Gloucester, MA ... 800-332-6025
Sutherland Stamp Company
San Diego, CA ... 858-233-7784
V. Loria & Sons
Yonkers, NY ... 800-540-2927
Volk Corporation
Farmington Hills, MI ... 800-521-6799
Winmark Stamp & Sign
Salt Lake City, UT ... 800-438-0480
Yeuell Nameplate & Label
Woburn, MA ... 781-933-2984

Oven Mits

Abond Plastic Corporation
Lachine, QC ... 800-886-7947
Arden Companies
Southfield, MI ... 248-415-8500
Best Brands Home Products
New York, NY ... 212-684-7456
Best Value Textiles
Elkhorn, WI ... 800-248-9826
C.R. Manufacturing
Waverly, NE ... 877-789-5844
Gril-Del
Mankato, MN ... 800-782-7320
Jomac Products
Niles, IL ... 800-566-2289
Monte Glove Company
Wilkesboro, NC ... 662-263-5353
Parvin Manufacturing Company
Los Angeles, CA ... 800-648-0770
Shen Manufacturing Company
W Conshohocken, PA ... 610-825-2790
Standard Terry Mills
Souderton, PA ... 215-723-8121
Tucker Industries
Colorado Springs, CO ... 800-786-7287
Work Well Company
Gahanna, OH ... 614-759-8003

Protective Apparel

Food Handlers'

Abond Plastic Corporation
Lachine, QC ... 800-886-7947
ADEX Medical Inc
Riverside, CA ... 800-873-4776
Aero Company
Indianapolis, IN ... 800-225-9038
Akron Cotton Products
Akron, OH ... 800-899-7173
Allied Glove Corporation
Milwaukee, WI ... 800-558-9263
American Advertising & Shop Cap Company
Old Tappan, NJ ... 800-442-8837
American Apron Inc.
Foxboro, MA ... 800-262-7766
American Bag & Linen Company
Cornelia, GA ... 706-778-5377
Atlantis Plastics Institutional Products
Mankato, MN ... 800-999-2374
Best Brands Home Products
New York, NY ... 212-684-7456
Best Manufacturing Company
Menlo, GA ... 800-241-0323
Best Value Textiles
Elkhorn, WI ... 800-248-9826
Boss Manufacturing Company
Kewanee, IL ... 800-447-4581
Bragard Professional Uniforms
New York, NY ... 800-488-2433
Carolina Glove
Conover, NC ... 800-335-1918
Carry All Canvas Bag Company
Brooklyn, NY ... 888-425-5224
Century Glove
Summerville, GA ... 973-751-0300
Champaign Plastics Company
Champaign, IL ... 800-575-0170
Choctaw-Kaul Distribution Company
Detroit, MI ... 313-894-9494
Commercial Textiles Corporation-Best Buy Uniforms
Homestead, PA ... 800-345-1924
Dalloz Safety
Smithfield, RI ... 800-977-9177
Eagle Home Products
Huntington, NY
FabOhio
Uhrichsville, OH ... 740-922-4233
Fashion Seal Uniforms
Seminole, FL ... 727-397-9611
Golden Needles Knitting & Glove Company
Coshocton, OH ... 919-667-5102
Gourmet Gear
Los Angeles, CA ... 800-682-4635
Gril-Del
Mankato, MN ... 800-782-7320
Hall's Safety Apparel
Uhrichsville, OH ... 800-232-3671
Hygrade Gloves
Brooklyn, NY ... 800-233-8100
Island Poly
Westbury, NY ... 800-338-4433
John Plant Company
Ramseur, NC ... 800-334-2711
Jomac Products
Niles, IL ... 800-566-2289
Joseph Titone & Sons
Burlington, NJ ... 800-220-4102
Kennedy's Specialty Sewing
Erin, ON ... 519-833-9306
Keystone Adjustable Cap Company
Pennsauken, NJ ... 800-663-5439
Kimberly-Clark Corporation
Roswell, GA ... 888-525-8388
Knapp Shoes
Penn Yan, NY
Koch Equipment
Kansas City, MO ... 816-753-2150
Lambert Company
Chillicothe, MO ... 800-821-7667
Landau Uniforms
Olive Branch, MS ... 800-238-7513
Lexidyne of Pennsylvania
Pittsburgh, PA ... 800-543-2233
Micro Flex
Reno, NV ... 800-876-6866
New Chef Fashion
Vernon, CA ... 323-581-0300
New England Overshoe Company
Williston, VT ... 888-289-6367
Omron Health Care
Bannockburn, IL ... 800-323-1482
Onguard Industries
Havre De Grace, MD ... 800-304-2282
Parvin Manufacturing Company
Los Angeles, CA ... 800-648-0770
Playtex Products, LLC
New Providence, NJ ... 888-310-4290
PolyConversions
Rantoul, IL ... 888-893-3330
Quality Mop & Brush Manufacturers
Needham, MA ... 617-884-2999
Refrigiwear
Dahlonega, GA ... 800-645-3744
Rodes Professional Apparel
Louisville, KY ... 502-584-3112
Samco Freezewear Company
St Paul, MN ... 651-638-3888
Seven Mile Creek Corporation
Eaton, OH ... 800-497-6324
Sta-Rite Ginnie Lou
Shelbyville, IL ... 800-782-7483
Star Glove Company
Odon, IN ... 800-832-7101
Sultan Linens
New York, NY ... 212-689-8900
Superior Distributing
Louisville, KY ... 800-365-6661
Superior Linen & Work Wear
Kansas City, MO ... 800-798-7987
Triad Scientific
Manasquan, NJ ... 800-867-6690
Tronex Industries
Denville, NJ ... 800-833-1181
Tucker Industries
Colorado Springs, CO ... 800-786-7287
Universal Overall Company
Chicago, IL ... 800-621-3344
Valeo
Elmsford, Ny ... 800-634-2704
Work Well Company
Gahanna, OH ... 614-759-8003
Worksafe Industries
Huntington Station, NY ... 800-929-9000
Y-Pers
Philadelphia, PA ... 800-421-0242

Shirts

Allred Marketing
Birmingham, AL. . . . 205-251-3700

Uniforms & Special Clothing

Abond Plastic Corporation
Lachine, QC 800-886-7947
Acme Laundry Products
Chatsworth, CA 818-341-0700
Adcapitol
Monroe, NC. . . . 800-868-7111
ADEX Medical Inc
Riverside, CA 800-873-4776
Alex Delvecchio Enterprises
Troy, MI 248-619-9600
Allied Glove Corporation
Milwaukee, WI 800-558-9263
Allred Marketing
Birmingham, AL. . . . 205-251-3700
American Advertising & Shop Cap Company
Old Tappan, NJ 800-442-8837
American Design Studios
Carlsbad, CA. . . . 800-899-7104
American Identity
Orange City, IA. . . . 800-369-2277
Ansell Healthcare
Iselin, NJ 800-800-0444
Apparel Manufacturing Company
Lilburn, GA. . . . 800-366-1608
ARAMARK Uniform Services
Burbank, CA. . . . 800-272-6275
ATD-American Company
Wyncote, PA 800-523-2300
Bennett's Auto Inc.
Neenah, WI 800-215-5464
Best Brands Home Products
New York, NY 212-684-7456
Best Manufacturing
Jersey City, NJ 201-356-3800
Best Manufacturing Company
Menlo, GA 800-241-0323
Best Value Textiles
Elkhorn, WI. . . . 800-248-9826
Big Front Uniforms
Los Angeles, CA. . . . 800-234-8383
Blue Ridge Converting
Asheville, NC 800-438-3893
Boss Manufacturing Company
Kewanee, IL 800-447-4581
Bragard Professional Uniforms
New York, NY 800-488-2433
Bunzl Processor Division
Dallas, TX. . . . 800-456-5624
Campus Collection, Inc.
Tuscaloosa, AL 800-289-8744
Carlisle Food Service Products
Oklahoma City, OK 800-654-8210
Carnegie Textile Company
Solon, OH 800-633-4136
Carry All Canvas Bag Company
Brooklyn, NY 888-425-5224
Carson Manufacturing Company
Petaluma, CA 800-423-2380
CCP Industries, Inc.
Cleveland, OH 800-321-2840
Celebrity Promotions
Remsen, IA 800-332-6847
Cellucap
Philadelphia, PA 800-523-3814
Century Glove
Summerville, GA 973-751-0300
Champaign Plastics Company
Champaign, IL 800-575-0170
Charles Craft
Laurinburg, NC. . . . 910-844-3521
Chef Revival
Elkhorn, WI. . . . 800-248-9826
Chefwear
Addison, IL. . . . 800-568-2433
Christman Screenprint
Springfield, MI 800-962-9330
Cintas Corporation
Cincinnati, OH 800-246-8271
Coast Scientific
Rancho Santa Fe, CA 800-445-1544
Comasec Safety, Inc.
Enfield, CT 800-333-0219
Commercial Textiles Corporation-Best Buy Uniforms
Homestead, PA 800-345-1924
Dalloz Safety
Smithfield, RI 800-977-9177
David Dobbs Enterprise & Menu Design
St Augustine, FL. . . . 800-889-6368
Dow Cover Company
New Haven, CT 800-735-8877
Dunrite
Fremont, NE 800-782-3061
Elwood Safety Company
Buffalo, NY. . . . 866-326-6060
Erell Manufacturing Company
Elk Grove Vlg, IL. . . . 800-622-6334
Erie Cotton Products Company
Erie, PA 800-289-4737
F & F and A. Jacobs & Sons, Inc.
Baltimore, MD 410-727-6397
FabOhio
Uhrichsville, OH. . . . 740-922-4233
Fabriko
Altavista, VA. . . . 888-203-8098
Fairfield Line Inc
Fairfield, IA 800-423-7437
Fashion Seal Uniforms
Seminole, FL. . . . 727-397-9611
Flavor Wear
Valley Center, CA. . . . 800-647-8372
Foley's Famous Aprons
Wayne, MI. . . . 800-634-3245
Franklin Uniform Corporation
Baltimore, MD 410-235-8151
Gann Manufacturing
Baltimore, MD 800-922-9832
Gary Manufacturing Company
Chula Vista, CA 800-775-0804
George Glove Company, Inc
Midland Park, NJ 800-631-4292
Glover Latex
Anaheim, CA 800-243-5110
Golden Needles Knitting & Glove Company
Coshocton, OH 919-667-5102
Goldmax Industries
City of Industry, CA 626-964-8820
Gourmet Gear
Los Angeles, CA. . . . 800-682-4635
Gourmet Tableskirts
Houston, TX 800-527-0440
Graphic Apparel
Inniasfil, ON 800-757-4867
Great Southern Corporation
Memphis, TN 800-421-7802
Green Seams
Maple Grove, MN. . . . 612-929-3213
Gril-Del
Mankato, MN 800-782-7320
Haas Tailoring Company
Baltimore, MD 410-732-3804
Hairnet Corporation of America
New York, NY 212-675-5840
Hall's Safety Apparel
Uhrichsville, OH 800-232-3671
Handgards
El Paso, TX. . . . 800-351-8161
Hank Rivera Associates
Dearborn, MI 313-581-8300
Happy Chef
Butler, NJ 800-347-0288
Healthline Products
Los Angeles, CA. . . . 800-473-4003
Hygrade Gloves
Brooklyn, NY 800-233-8100
Image Experts Uniforms
Schenectady, NY. . . . 800-789-2433
Island Poly
Westbury, NY 800-338-4433
John Plant Company
Ramseur, NC. . . . 800-334-2711
Jomac Products
Niles, IL 800-566-2289
Kennedy's Specialty Sewing
Erin, ON 519-833-9306
Key Industries
Fort Scott, KS 800-835-0365
Keystone Adjustable Cap Company
Pennsauken, NJ. . . . 800-663-5439
Kingston McKnight
Redwood City, CA 800-900-0463
Klever Kuvers
Pasadena, CA 626-355-8441
Knapp Shoes
Penn Yan, NY
Koch Equipment
Kansas City, MO. . . . 816-753-2150
LaCrosse Safety and Industrial
Portland, OR 800-557-7246
Lambert Company
Chillicothe, MO 800-821-7667
Landau Uniforms
Olive Branch, MS. . . . 800-238-7513
Lehigh Safety Shoe Company
Nelsonville, OH 866-442-5429
Lexidyne of Pennsylvania
Pittsburgh, PA 800-543-2233
Libertyware
Clearfield, UT 888-500-5885
Lion Apparel
Dayton, OH. . . . 800-548-6614
Locknane
Everett, WA. . . . 800-848-9854
Marv Holland Industries
Edmonton, AB 800-661-7269
Metz Premiums
New York, NY 212-315-4660
Midwest Promotional Group
Summit, IL 800-305-3388
Midwest Quality Gloves
Chillicothe, MO 800-821-3028
Monte Glove Company
Wilkesboro, NC 662-263-5353
National Embroidery Service
Portsmouth, RI 800-227-1451
National Scoop & Equipment Company
Spring House, PA 215-646-2040
New Chef Fashion
Vernon, CA 323-581-0300
New Hatchwear Company
Calgary, AB. . . . 800-661-9249
OK Uniform Company
New York, NY 866-700-5765
Omron Health Care
Bannockburn, IL. . . . 800-323-1482
Pacific Oasis Enterprises
Santa Fe Springs, CA 800-424-1475
Panhandler, Inc.
Cordova, TN 800-654-7237
Parvin Manufacturing Company
Los Angeles, CA. . . . 800-648-0770
Paul G. Gallin Company
Yonkers, NY 914-964-5800
Peekskill Hair Net
Peekskill, NY 914-737-1524
PolyConversions
Rantoul, IL 888-893-3330
Pop Tops Company
South Easton, MA. . . . 508-238-8585
Print Ons/Express Mark
Monroe, NC 704-289-8261
Protexall
Greenville, IL 800-334-8939
Put-Ons USA
Brooklyn Park, MN. . . . 888-425-1215
Quality Mop & Brush Manufacturers
Needham, MA. . . . 617-884-2999
R&R Industries
San Clemente, CA. . . . 800-234-1434
Radio Cap Company
San Antonio, TX. . . . 210-472-1649
Red Kap Industries
Nashville, TN 615-565-5000
Refrigiwear
Dahlonega, GA. . . . 800-645-3744
Riverside Manufacturing Company
Moultrie, GA. . . . 800-841-8677
Rocky Shoes & Boots
Nelsonville, OH 740-753-1951
Rodes Professional Apparel
Louisville, KY. . . . 502-584-3112
Royal Paper Products
Coatesville, PA 800-666-6655
S&H Uniform Corporation
White Plains, NY 800-210-5295
Samco Freezewear Company
St Paul, MN. . . . 651-638-3888
Scafati Uniforms
New York, NY 212-695-4944
Scorpio Apparel
Northbrook, IL 800-559-3338
Seven Mile Creek Corporation
Eaton, OH 800-497-6324
Shen Manufacturing Company
W Conshohocken, PA. . . . 610-825-2790
Signco/Stylecraft
Cincinnati, OH 800-733-0045
ST Restaurant Supplies
Delta, BC. . . . 888-448-4244
Standard Terry Mills
Souderton, PA. . . . 215-723-8121

Star Glove Company
Odon, IN 800-832-7101
Sterling Rubber
Fergus, ON 519-843-4032
Sultan Linens
New York, NY 212-689-8900
Superior Distributing
Louisville, KY 800-365-6661
Superior Linen & Work Wear
Kansas City, MO. 800-798-7987
Task Footwear
Chippewa Falls, WI 800-962-0166
Terry Manufacturing Company
Birmingham, AL. 205-250-0062
Textile Buff & Wheel Company, Inc.
Charlestown, MA 617-241-8100
The Funny Apron Company
Lake Dallas, TX 800-835-5802
Todd Uniform
Saint Louis, MO 800-458-3402
Triad Products Company
Springfield, OH. 937-323-9422
Tronex Industries
Denville, NJ 800-833-1181
Tru-Form Plastics
Gardena, CA 800-510-7999
Tucker Industries
Colorado Springs, CO. 800-786-7287
UniFirst Corporation
Wilmington, MA. 800-455-7654
Uniforms to You & Company
Chicago, IL 800-864-3676
Universal Overall Company
Chicago, IL 800-621-3344
Univogue
Dallas, TX. 800-527-3374
Valeo
Elmsford, Ny. 800-634-2704
VCG Uniform
Chicago, IL 800-447-6502
Vicmore Manufacturing Company
Brooklyn, NY 800-458-8663
Weinbrenner Shoe Company
Merrill, WI 800-826-0002
Wells-Lamont Corporation
Niles, IL 800-323-2830
Whiting & Davis
Attleboro Falls, MA 800-876-6374
Work Well Company
Gahanna, OH. 614-759-8003
Worksafe Industries
Huntington Station, NY 800-929-9000
World Pride
St Petersburg, FL 800-533-2433
Y-Pers
Philadelphia, PA 800-421-0242

Consultants & Services

Advertising Services

Advertising Novelties & Specialties

AAA Electrical Signs
McAllen, TX . . . 800-825-5376
Access Solutions
Knoxville, TN . . . 865-531-0971
Ace Signs
Little Rock, AR . . . 501-562-0800
Adcapitol
Monroe, NC . . . 800-868-7111
Admatch Corporation
New York, NY . . . 800-777-9909
Alex Delvecchio Enterprises
Troy, MI . . . 248-619-9600
Alger Creations
Miami, FL . . . 954-454-3272
Allen Sign Company
Knoxville, TN . . . 800-844-3524
Alliance Rubber Corporation
Hot Springs National Par, AR . . . 800-626-5940
Allred Marketing
Birmingham, AL . . . 205-251-3700
Altrua Marketing Designs
Tallahassee, FL . . . 800-443-6939
AM Graphics
Minneapolis, MN . . . 612-341-2020
American Advertising & Shop Cap Company
Old Tappan, NJ . . . 800-442-8837
American Identification Industries
West Chicago, IL . . . 800-255-8890
American Identity
Orange City, IA . . . 800-369-2277
Ameritech Signs
Santa Monica, CA . . . 310-829-9359
Ampersand Label
Green Bay, WI . . . 800-325-0589
Andersen Sign Company
Woodsville, NH . . . 603-787-6806
Apparel Manufacturing Company
Lilburn, GA . . . 800-366-1608
Art Poly Bag Company
Brooklyn, NY . . . 800-278-7659
Atlas Match Corporation
Euless, TX . . . 800-628-2426
Audsam Printing
Marion, OH . . . 740-387-6252
B.E. Industries
Stamford, CT . . . 203-357-8055
Baldwin/Priesmeyer
Saint Louis, MO . . . 314-535-2800
Bayard Kurth Company
Detroit, MI . . . 313-891-0800
Betsy Ross ManufacturingCompany
Paterson, NJ . . . 877-238-7976
Bill Carr Signs
Flint, MI . . . 810-232-1569
BK Graphics
Morristown, TN . . . 800-581-9159
Black Horse Manufacturing Company
Chattanooga, TN . . . 423-624-0798
Blanks United
Oakbrook Terrace, IL . . . 847-257-1213
Blue Feather Product
Ashland, OR . . . 800-472-2487
Brewer-Cantelmo Company
New York, NY . . . 212-244-4600
Brown's Sign & Screen Printing
Covington, GA . . . 800-540-3107
Bynoe Printers
New York, NY . . . 212-662-5041
C.R. Manufacturing
Waverly, NE . . . 877-789-5844
California Toytime Balloons
San Pedro, CA . . . 310-548-1234
Capital Plastics
Middlefield, OH . . . 440-632-5800
Caraustar
Franklin, KY . . . 270-586-9565
Carlton Industries
La Grange, TX . . . 800-231-5988
Carry All Canvas Bag Company
Brooklyn, NY . . . 888-425-5224
Cawley
Manitowoc, WI . . . 800-822-9539
CCL Label
Cold Spring, KY . . . 800-422-6633
Central Decal Company
Burr Ridge, IL . . . 800-869-7654
Central Missouri Sheltered Enterprises
Columbia, MO . . . 573-442-6935
Chain Store Graphics
Decatur, IL . . . 800-443-7446
Charles E. Roberts Company
Wyckoff, NJ . . . 800-237-2684
Chicago Show
Buffalo Grove, IL . . . 847-955-0200
Christman Screenprint
Springfield, MI . . . 800-962-9330
Chroma Tone
Saint Clair, PA . . . 800-878-1552
City Grafx
Eugene, OR . . . 800-258-2489
Classy Basket
San Diego, CA . . . 888-449-4901
Coast Signs & Graphics
Hermosa Beach, CA . . . 310-379-9921
Comm-Pak
Opelika, AL . . . 334-749-6201
Commercial Printing Company
Birmingham, AL . . . 800-989-9203
Connecticut Laminating Company
New Haven, CT . . . 800-753-9119
Contemporary Products Company
Garner, NC . . . 919-779-4228
Continental Identification
Sparta, MI . . . 800-247-2499
Courtesy Sign Company
Amarillo, TX . . . 806-373-6609
Creative Enterprises
Kendall Park, NJ . . . 732-422-0300
Creegan Animation Company
Steubenville, OH . . . 740-283-3708
Crown Label Company
Santa Ana, CA . . . 800-422-3590
Curzon Promotional Graphics
Omaha, NE . . . 800-769-7446
Cyrk
Monroe, WA . . . 800-426-3125
Dave's Imports
Jacksonville, FL . . . 800-553-2837
David Dobbs Enterprise & Menu Design
St Augustine, FL . . . 800-889-6368
Dayton Bag & Burlap Company
Dayton, OH . . . 800-543-3400
Deadline Press
Kennesaw, GA . . . 770-419-2232
Deborah Sales, LLC
Newark, NJ . . . 973-344-8466
Decal Techniques
West Babylon, NY . . . 800-735-3322
Design Label Manufacturing
East Lyme, CT . . . 800-666-1575
Design Mark Corporation
Wareham, MA . . . 800-451-3275
Designers Plastics
Clearwater, FL . . . 727-573-1643
Diamond Packaging
Rochester, NY . . . 800-333-4079
Diamond Sign Company
Costa Mesa, CA . . . 714-545-1440
Dinosaur Plastics
Houston, TX . . . 713-923-2278
Distinctive Embedments
Pawtucket, RI . . . 401-729-0770
DLX Industries
Pomona, NY . . . 845-517-2200
Dominion Regala
Toronto, ON . . . 866-423-4086
Dove Screen Printing Company
Royston, GA . . . 706-245-4975
Dynamic Packaging
Minneapolis, MN . . . 800-878-9380
E.G. Staats & Company
Mount Pleasant, IA . . . 800-553-1853
Ebenezer Flag Company
Newport, RI . . . 401-846-1891
Eco-Bag Products
Ossining, NY . . . 800-720-2247
Economy Novelty & Printing Company
New York, NY . . . 212-481-3022
Einson Freeman
Paramus, NJ . . . 201-226-0300
EIT
Elmhurst, IL . . . 630-279-3400
Elliot Lee
Cedarhurst, NY . . . 516-569-9595
Emblem & Badge
Providence, RI . . . 800-875-5444
Emco Industrial Plastics
Cedar Grove, NJ . . . 800-292-9906
Empire Screen Printing, Inc.
Onalaska, WI . . . 608-783-3301
Endurart
New York, NY . . . 212-779-8522
Engraving Specialists
Royal Oak, MI . . . 248-542-2244
Erell Manufacturing Company
Elk Grove Vlg, IL . . . 800-622-6334
Executive Line
Chatham, NY . . . 800-333-5761
Fair Publishing House
Norwalk, OH . . . 800-824-3247
Flexo Transparent
Buffalo, NY . . . 877-993-5396
Forbes Products
Rush, NY . . . 800-316-5235
Forest Manufacturing Company
Twinsburg, OH . . . 330-425-3805
Forrest Engraving Company
New Rochelle, NY . . . 914-632-9892
Fox Stamp, Sign & Specialty
Menasha, WI . . . 800-236-3699
Foxfire Marketing Solutions
Newark, DE . . . 800-497-0512
Francis & Lusky Company
Nashville, TN . . . 800-251-3711
FRS Industries
Fargo, ND . . . 800-747-4795
Fun-Time International
Philadelphia, PA . . . 800-776-4386
Gallimore Industries
Lake Villa, IL . . . 800-927-8020
Gannett Outdoor of New J
Fairfield, NJ . . . 973-575-6900
Garland Writing Instruments
Coventry, RI . . . 401-821-1450
Gary Plastic Packaging Corporation
Bronx, NY . . . 800-227-4279
Geiger
Lewiston, ME . . . 215-672-8782
General Foam Plastics Corporation
Norfolk, VA . . . 757-857-0153
General Formulations
Sparta, MI . . . 800-253-3664
General Methods Corporation
Peoria, IL . . . 309-497-3344
George Lauterer Corporation
Chicago, IL . . . 312-913-1881
Globe Ticket & Label Company
Warminster, PA . . . 800-523-5968
Gold Bond
Hixson, TN . . . 423-842-5844
Gonterman & Associates
Saint Louis, MO . . . 314-771-0600
Graphic Calculator Company
Barrington, IL . . . 847-381-4480
Graphics Unlimited
San Diego, CA . . . 858-453-4031
Graydon Lettercraft
Great Neck, NY . . . 516-482-0531
Grays Harbor Stamp Works
Aberdeen, WA . . . 800-894-3830
Green Mountain Graphics
Long Island City, NY . . . 718-472-3377
Greenfield Packaging
White Plains, NY . . . 914-993-0233
H.C. Bainbridge, Inc
Syracuse, NY . . . 315-475-5313
Harco Enterprises
Peterborough, ON . . . 800-361-5361
HMG Worldwide
Morton Grove, IL . . . 847-965-7100
Hughes Manufacturing Company
Giddings, TX . . . 800-414-0765
IdentaBadge
Lafayette, LA . . . 800-325-8247

IDL
Monroeville, PA 724-733-2234
Image Plastics
Houston, TX 800-289-2811
Imperial Plastics
Lakeville, MN 952-469-4951
INOVAR Packaging Group
Arlington, TX 800-285-2235
Insignia Systems
Minneapolis, MN 800-874-4648
Jessup Paper Box
Brookston, IN 765-490-9043
Killion Industries
Vista, CA 800-421-5352
King Badge & Button Company
Huntingtn Bch, CA 714-847-3060
Koza's
Pearland, TX 800-594-5555
Kraus & Sons
New York, NY 212-620-0408
Krimstock Enterprises
Pennsauken, NJ 856-665-3676
Kuepper Favor Company, Celebrate Line
Peru, IN 800-321-5823
Label Systems & Solutions
Bohemia, NY 800-811-2560
LabelPrint Corporation
Newburyport, MA 978-463-4004
LabelQuest
Elmhurst, IL 800-999-5301
Labels Systems, Inc
Addison, TX 800-220-9552
Lake City Signs
Boulder City, NV 702-293-5805
Lane Award Manufacturing
Phoenix, AZ 800-843-2581
Legible Signs
Loves Park, IL 800-435-4177
Lewisburg Printing Company
Lewisburg, TN 800-559-1526
Lewtan Industries Corporation
Hartford, CT 860-278-9800
License Ad Plate Company
Cleveland, OH 216-265-4200
Lion Circle
Chicago, IL 773-582-5481
Logo Specialty Advertising Tems
Tampa, FL 800-704-0094
Lone Star Banners and Flags
Fort Worth, TX 800-288-9625
M&M Displays
Philadelphia, PA 800-874-7171
Maier Sign Systems
Saddle Brook, NJ 201-845-7555
Mansfield Rubber Stamp
Mansfield, OH 419-524-1442
Mar-Boro Printing & Advertising Specialties
Brooklyn, NY 718-336-4051
Martco Engravers
Fremont, NH 603-895-3561
Mastercraft Manufacturing Company
Long Island City, NY 718-729-5620
MDR International
North Miami, FL 305-944-5019
Memphis Delta Tent & Awning Company
Memphis, TN 901-522-1238
Meraz & Associates
Chico, CA 888-244-4463
Merchandising Inventives
Waukegan, IL 800-367-5653
Metz Premiums
New York, NY 212-315-4660
Midwest Badge & Novelty Company Inc
Minneapolis, MN 952-927-9901
Midwest Promotional Group
Summit, IL 800-305-3388
Minges Printing & Advertising Specialties
Gastonia, NC 704-867-6791
Minnesuing Acres
Lake Nebagamon, WI 715-374-2262
Modagrafics
Rolling Meadows, IL 847-392-3980
Modern Stamp Company
Baltimore, MD 800-727-3029
Moore Efficient Communication Aids
Denver, CO 303-433-8456
MTL Etching Industries
Woodmere, NY 516-295-9733
N.G. Slater Corporation
New York, NY 800-848-4621
Nameplates
St Paul, MN 651-228-1522

National Emblem
Carson, CA 800-877-5325
National Marking Products, Inc.
Richmond, VA 800-482-1553
Nationwide Pennant & Flag Manufacturing
San Antonio, TX 800-383-3524
Norgus Silk Screen Company
Clifton, NJ 973-365-0600
North American PackagingCorporation
New York, NY 800-499-3521
Novelty Advertising Company
Coshocton, OH 800-848-9163
Nutty Bavarian
Sanford, FL 800-382-4788
Orber Manufacturing Company
Cranston, RI 800-761-4059
PAK 2000
Mirror Lake, NH 603-569-3700
Palmer Displays
San Leandro, CA 510-632-8597
Paperweights Plus
Medford, NY 631-924-3222
Paradise Products
El Cerrito, CA 800-227-1092
Party Yards
Casselberry, FL 877-501-4400
Pelican Products Company
Bronx, NY 800-552-8820
Photo-Graphics Company
Grandview, MO 816-761-3333
Pierrepont Visual Graphics
Rochester, NY 585-235-5620
Pilgrim Plastic ProductsCompany
Brockton, MA 800-343-7810
Plastic Fantastics/Buck Signs
Ashland, OR 800-482-1776
Plastic Printing
Dayton, KY 877-581-7748
Pop Tops Company
South Easton, MA 508-238-8585
Print Ons/Express Mark
Monroe, NC 704-289-8261
Print Source
Wakefield, RI 401-789-9339
Pro-Ad-Company
Portland, OR 800-287-5885
Process Displays
New Berlin, WI 800-533-1764
Quick Point
Fenton, MO 800-638-1369
R&R Industries
San Clemente, CA 800-234-1434
Radio Cap Company
San Antonio, TX 210-472-1649
Ram Industries
Erwin, TN 800-523-3883
Ray-Craft
Cleveland, OH 216-651-3330
Rex Art Manufacturing Corp.
Lindenhurst, NY 631-884-4600
Riverside Manufacturing Company
Arlington Hts, IL 800-877-3349
Roxanne Signs
Gaithersburg, MD 301-428-4911
Rutler Screen Printing
Phillipsburg, NJ 908-859-3327
Samsill Corporation
Fort Worth, TX 800-255-1100
Sanders Manufacturing Company
Nashville, TN 866-254-6611
Sayco Yo-Yo Molding Company
Cumberland, RI 401-724-5296
Scott Sign Systems
Sarasota, FL 800-237-9447
Screen Print, Etc.
Anaheim, CA 714-630-1100
Semco Plastic Company
Saint Louis, MO 314-487-4557
Sesame Label System
New York, NY 800-551-3020
Shild Company
New York, NY 866-435-2949
Sign Factory
Cerritos, CA 562-809-1443
Sign Shop
Rancho Cucamonga, CA 909-945-5888
Signs & Shapes International
Omaha, NE 800-806-6069
Sillcocks Plastics International
Hudson, MA 800-526-4919
Smyth Companies, LLC
Saint Paul, MN 800-473-3464

Source for Packaging
New York, NY 800-223-2527
Southern Tailors
Atlanta, GA 877-655-2321
Spartan Flag Company
Northport, MI 231-386-5150
Special Events Supply Company
Hauppauge, NY
Steingart Associates
South Fallsburg, NY 845-434-4321
Sterling Novelty Products
Northbrook, IL 847-291-0070
Stoffel Seals Corporation
Tallapoosa, GA 800-422-8247
Stubblefield Screen Print Company
Albuquerque, NM 505-202-9802
Superior-Studio Specialties Ltd
Commerce, CA 800-354-3049
SuppliesForLess
Hampton, VA 800-235-2201
Sutherland Stamp Company
San Diego, CA 858-233-7784
The Tin Box Company
Farmingdale, NY 800-888-8467
Thermal Bags by Ingrid
Gilberts, IL 800-622-5560
Token Factory
La Crosse, WI 888-486-5367
Tomsed Corporation
Lillington, NC 800-334-5552
Trevor Owen Limited
Scarborough, ON 866-487-2224
Twenty/Twenty Graphics
Gaithersburg, MD 240-243-0511
Union Pen Company
Hagaman, NY 518-842-6000
Unique Manufacturing
Visalia, CA 888-737-1007
Universal Tag
Dudley, MA 800-332-8247
US Magnetix
Golden Valley, MN 800- 3-0
V. Loria & Sons
Yonkers, NY 800-540-2927
Variant
Eden Prairie, MN 612-927-8611
Volk Corporation
Farmington Hills, MI 800-521-6799
Vonco Products
Lake Villa, IL 800-323-9077
Vynatex
Port Washington, NY 516-944-6130
Wendell August Forge
Grove City, PA 800-923-1390
West Hawk Industries
Ann Arbor, MI 800-678-1286
WGN Flag & Decorating
Chicago, IL 773-768-8076
Whirley Industries
Warren, PA 800-825-5575
Willson Industries
Marmora, NJ 800-894-4169
Wishbone Utensil Tableware Line
Wheat Ridge, CO 866-266-5928
World Division
Dallas, TX 800-433-9843
WS Packaging Group Inc
Green Bay, WI 920-866-6300

Custom Printed Promotional Products

Allred Marketing
Birmingham, AL 205-251-3700
Eco-Bag Products
Ossining, NY 800-720-2247
Tangerine Promotions
Northbrook, IL 847-313-6000

Flags, Pennants & Banners

AAA Flag & Banner Manufacturing
Los Angeles, CA 800-266-4222
Ace Signs
Little Rock, AR 501-562-0800
AD/Mart
Calumet City, IL 708-891-0990
Adcapitol
Monroe, NC 800-868-7111
Allen Sign Company
Knoxville, TN 800-844-3524
Altrua Marketing Designs
Tallahassee, FL 800-443-6939

AM Graphics
Minneapolis, MN . . . 612-341-2020
American Flag & Banner
Clawson, MI . . . 800-892-5168
Ameritech Signs
Santa Monica, CA . . . 310-829-9359
Baldwin/Priesmeyer
Saint Louis, MO . . . 314-535-2800
Baltimore Sign Company
Arnold, MD . . . 410-276-1500
Banner Idea
Newport Beach, CA . . . 949-559-6600
Bannerland
Santa Fe Springs, CA . . . 800-654-0294
Betsy Ross ManufacturingCompany
Paterson, NJ . . . 877-238-7976
BH Awning & Tent Company
Benton Harbor, MI . . . 800-272-2187
Brown's Sign & Screen Printing
Covington, GA . . . 800-540-3107
Capitol Awning Company
Jamaica, NY . . . 800-241-3539
Coast Signs & Graphics
Hermosa Beach, CA . . . 310-379-9921
Coastal Canvas Products Company
Savannah, GA . . . 800-476-5174
Collegeville Flag & Manufacturing Company
Collegeville, PA . . . 800-523-5630
Courtesy Sign Company
Amarillo, TX . . . 806-373-6609
Creative Canopy Design
Hernando Beach, FL . . . 866-970-5200
Curzon Promotional Graphics
Omaha, NE . . . 800-769-7446
Deadline Press
Kennesaw, GA . . . 770-419-2232
Decal Techniques
West Babylon, NY . . . 800-735-3322
Diamond Sign Company
Costa Mesa, CA . . . 714-545-1440
Dimension Graphics
Grand Rapids, MI . . . 855-476-1281
Dinosaur Plastics
Houston, TX . . . 713-923-2278
Dixie Flag ManufacturingCompany
San Antonio, TX . . . 800-356-4085
Dominion Regala
Toronto, ON . . . 866-423-4086
Ebenezer Flag Company
Newport, RI . . . 401-846-1891
EIT
Elmhurst, IL . . . 630-279-3400
EMED Company
Buffalo, NY . . . 800-442-3633
Flexo Transparent
Buffalo, NY . . . 877-993-5396
Florart Flock Process
North Miami, FL . . . 800-292-3524
Forest Manufacturing Company
Twinsburg, OH . . . 330-425-3805
France Personalized Signs
Cleveland, OH . . . 216-241-2198
Frost Manufacturing Corporation
Worcester, MA . . . 800-462-0216
Fuller Flag Company
Holden, MA . . . 800-348-6723
George Lauterer Corporation
Chicago, IL . . . 312-913-1881
Goodwin-Cole Company
Sacramento, CA . . . 800-752-4477
Graphics Unlimited
San Diego, CA . . . 858-453-4031
Green Mountain Awning Company
West Rutland, VT . . . 800-479-2951
H. Arnold Wood Turning
Tarrytown, NY . . . 888-314-0088
H.C. Bainbridge, Inc
Syracuse, NY . . . 315-475-5313
Hammar & Sons Sign Company
Pelham, NH . . . 800-527-7446
Handicap Sign
Grand Rapids, MI . . . 800-690-4888
Harting Graphics
Wilmington, DE . . . 800-848-1373
Hollywood Banners
Copiague, NY . . . 800-691-5652
Hughes Manufacturing Company
Giddings, TX . . . 800-414-0765
Industrial Sign Company
South El Monte, CA . . . 800-596-3720
INOVAR Packaging Group
Arlington, TX . . . 800-285-2235
KD Kanopy
Westminster, CO . . . 800-432-4435
Kennedy's Specialty Sewing
Erin, ON . . . 519-833-9306
Keplinger & Son
Eagleville, PA . . . 610-666-6191
Kraus & Sons
New York, NY . . . 212-620-0408
Ladder Works
Lombard, IL . . . 800-419-5880
Lake City Signs
Boulder City, NV . . . 702-293-5805
Lone Star Banners and Flags
Fort Worth, TX . . . 800-288-9625
Metropolitan Flag Company
Philadelphia, PA . . . 215-426-2775
Nationwide Pennant & Flag Manufacturing
San Antonio, TX . . . 800-383-3524
Norgus Silk Screen Company
Clifton, NJ . . . 973-365-0600
Oates Flag Company
Louisville, KY . . . 502-267-8200
Paradise Products
El Cerrito, CA . . . 800-227-1092
Pierrepont Visual Graphics
Rochester, NY . . . 585-235-5620
Plasti-Clip Corporation
Milford, NH . . . 800-882-2547
Pratt Poster Company
Indianapolis, IN . . . 317-545-0842
Radio Cap Company
San Antonio, TX . . . 210-472-1649
Riverside Manufacturing Company
Arlington Hts, IL . . . 800-877-3349
Rose City Awning Company
Portland, OR . . . 800-446-4104
Roxanne Signs
Gaithersburg, MD . . . 301-428-4911
Screen Print, Etc.
Anaheim, CA . . . 714-630-1100
Sign Factory
Cerritos, CA . . . 562-809-1443
Sign Shop
Rancho Cucamonga, CA . . . 909-945-5888
Signet Graphic Products
St Louis, MO . . . 314-426-0200
Signmasters
Huntington Beach, CA . . . 949-364-9128
Southern Tailors
Atlanta, GA . . . 877-655-2321
Spartan Flag Company
Northport, MI . . . 231-386-5150
Special Events Supply Company
Hauppauge, NY
Sterling Novelty Products
Northbrook, IL . . . 847-291-0070
Stubblefield Screen Print Company
Albuquerque, NM . . . 505-202-9802
T&M Distributing Company
Henderson, NV . . . 702-458-1962
Timely Signs
Elmont, NY . . . 800-457-4467
Trevor Owen Limited
Scarborough, ON . . . 866-487-2224
US Flag & Signal Company
Portsmouth, VA . . . 757-497-8947
Volk Corporation
Farmington Hills, MI . . . 800-521-6799
Vomela/Harbor Graphics
St Paul, MN . . . 800-645-1012
Walker Companies
Oklahoma City, OK . . . 800-522-3015
Walker Sign Company
Sun Valley, CA . . . 818-252-7788
West Hawk Industries
Ann Arbor, MI . . . 800-678-1286
WGN Flag & Decorating
Chicago, IL . . . 773-768-8076
World Division
Dallas, TX . . . 800-433-9843

Analytical Services

A&L Western Ag Lab
Modesto, CA . . . 209-529-4080
Accra Laboratory
Cleveland, OH . . . 800-567-7200
Accu-Labs Research
Golden, CO . . . 303-277-9514
AgriTech
Columbus, OH . . . 614-488-2772
Airflow Sciences Corporation
Livonia, MI . . . 734-525-0300
Altek Company
Torrington, CT . . . 860-482-7626
AM Test Laboratories
Kirkland, WA . . . 425-885-1664
American Technical Services Group
Norcross, GA . . . 770-447-9444
Analytical Labs
Boise, ID . . . 800-574-5773
Anresco
San Francisco, CA . . . 800-359-0920
Barrow-Agee Laboratories
Memphis, TN . . . 901-332-1590
Barry-Wehmiller Design Group
Saint Louis, MO . . . 314-862-8000
BCN Research Laboratories
Rockford, TN . . . 800-236-0505
Bjorksten Research Laboratories
Northbrook, IL . . . 847-714-9662
BluMetric Environmental Inc.
Ottawa, ON . . . 613-839-3053
Brown & Caldwell
Walnut Creek, CA . . . 800-727-2224
Celsis Laboratory Group
Chicago, IL . . . 800-222-8260
Coffee Enterprises
Burlington, VT . . . 800-375-3398
Covance Laboratories Inc.
Madison, WI . . . 608-241-4471
CxR Company
Warsaw, IN . . . 800-817-5763
Deibel Laboratories
Madison, WI . . . 847-329-9900
DFL Laboratories
Chicago, IL . . . 312-938-5151
DQCI Services
Saint Paul, MN . . . 763-785-0484
ELISA Technologies
Gainesville, FL . . . 352-337-3929
ENSCO
Springfield, VA . . . 703-321-9000
Enviro-Test/Perry Laboratories
Woodridge, IL . . . 630-324-6685
Environmental Systems Service
Culpeper, VA . . . 800-541-2116
ESA
Chelmsford, MA . . . 978-250-7000
Eurofins Scientific
Des Moines, IA . . . 800-841-1110
Eurofins Scientific
Dayton, NJ . . . 800-880-1038
Fettig Laboratories
Grand Rapids, MI . . . 616-245-3000
Food & Agrosystems
Sunnyvale, CA . . . 408-245-8450
Food Consulting Company
Del Mar, CA . . . 800-793-2844
Food Quality Lab
Lake Oswego, OR . . . 800-977-3636
Food Safety Net Services
San Antonio, TX . . . 888-525-9788
Galbraith Laboratories
Knoxville, TN . . . 877-449-8797
Gaynes Labs
Bridgeview, IL . . . 708-233-6655
Great Lakes Scientific
Stevensville, MI . . . 269-429-1000
Hahn Laboratories
Columbia, SC . . . 803-799-1614
Harold Wainess & Associates
Arlington Heights, IL . . . 847-722-8744
Healthy Dining
San Diego, CA . . . 800-266-2049
Industrial Laboratories
Wheat Ridge, CO . . . 800-456-5288
Ingman Laboratories
Minneapolis, MN . . . 612-724-0121
International Approval Services
Cleveland, OH . . . 877-235-9791
Irvine Analytical Labs
Irvine, CA . . . 949-951-4425
ITS/ETL Testing Laboratories
Laguna Niguel, CA . . . 949-448-4100
J.L. Analytical Services
Modesto, CA . . . 209-538-8111
J.Leek Associates
Edenton, NC . . . 252-482-4456
Jel-Sert Company
West Chicago, IL . . . 800-323-2592
Krueger Food Laboratories
Chelmsford, MA . . . 978-256-1220
Lancaster Laboratories
Lancaster, PA . . . 717-656-2300

Laucks' Testing Laboratories
Seattle, WA 206-767-5060
Lebensmittel Consulting
Fostoria, OH 419-435-2774
Libra Laboratories Inc
Metuchen, NJ 732-321-5200
Libra Technical Center
Metuchen, NJ 732-321-5487
McCrone Associates
Westmont, IL. 630-887-7100
Medallion Laboratories
Minneapolis, MN 800-245-5615
Microbac Laboratories
Pittsburgh, PA 412-459-1060
Microbac Laboratories
Worcester, MA 866-515-4668
Midwest Laboratories
Omaha, NE 402-334-7770
Milligan & Higgins
Johnstown, NY 518-762-4638
Minnesota Valley TestingLaboratories
New Ulm, MN. 800-782-3557
National Food Laboratory
Livermore, CA 925-551-4209
Northeast Laboratory Services
Waterville, ME 866-591-7120
Northland Laboratories
Northbrook, IL 800-366-3522
Northview Laboratories
Spartanburg, SC 864-574-7728
Northwest Laboratories of Seattle
Seattle, WA 206-763-6252
Nutrinfo Corporation
Watertown, MA. 800-676-6686
Oklabs
Oklahoma City, OK 405-843-6832
Pearson Research
Santa Cruz, CA 831-429-9797
POS Pilot Plant Corporation
Saskatoon, SK. 800-230-2751
PSI
Oakbrook Terrace, IL 817-640-4162
QC
Southampton, PA 215-355-3900
Quest
San Clemente, CA. 949-643-1333
R-TECH Laboratories
Saint Paul, MN 800-328-9687
R.C. Keller & Associates
Barnegat, NJ 973-694-8810
Richardson Researches
South San Francisco, CA 650-589-5764
RTI Laboratories Inc
Livonia, MI 734-422-8000
S&J Laboratories
Portage, MI 269-324-7383
S-F Analytical Labs
New Berlin, WI. 800-300-6700
Sani-Pure Food Laboratories
Saddle Brook, NJ 201-843-2525
Sensory Spectrum
New Providence, NJ 908-376-7000
Shear Kershman Laboratories
Chesterfield, MO 636-519-8900
Shuster Laboratories
Canton, MA 800-444-8705
Silliker, Inc
Chicago, IL 312-938-5151
Southern Testing & Research Labs
Wilson, NC 252-237-4175
Soyatech
Bar Harbor, ME. 800-424-7692
Spencer Research
Columbus, OH 800-488-3242
Strasburger & Siegel
Hanover, MD 888-726-3753
Suburban Laboratories
Hillside, IL 800-783-5227
TEI Analytical
Niles, IL 847-647-1345
The Phytopia Garden
Dallas, TX. 888-750-9336
Total Quality Corporation
Branford, CT. 800-453-9729
Truesdail Laboratories
Tustin, CA. 714-730-6239
Underwriters Laboratories
Camas, WA 877-854-3577
VICAM, A Waters Business
Milford, MA 800-338-4381
Warren Analytical Laboratory
Greeley, CO. 800-945-6669
Winston Laboratories
Vernon Hills, IL 800-946-5229
Woodson-Tenent Laboratories
Des Moines, IA. 515-265-1461
Woodson-Tenent Laboratories
Gainesville, GA 770-536-5909
Woodson-Tenent Laboratories
Dayton, OH. 937-236-5756
X-Ray Industries
Troy, MI 800-973-4800
YottaMark
Redwood City, CA 866-768-7878

Architects

Foodservice

Excel Engineering
Fond Du Lac, WI 920-926-9800
Stahlman Group
New London, NH 866-526-2585

Retail

Mead & Hunt
Madison, WI. 888-364-7272

Canners

Chiquita Brands International, Inc.
Charlotte, NC 800-438-0015
Hormel Foods Corporation
Austin, MN 800-523-4635
LaMonica Fine Foods
Millville, NJ 856-825-8111
RDM International
North Hollywood, CA 818-985-7654
SOPAKCO Foods
Mullins, SC. 800-276-9678
Sportsmen's Cannery & Smokehouse
Winchester Bay, OR 800-457-8048
Truitt Brothers Inc
Salem, OR. 800-547-8712
Washington Frontier
Grandview, WA. 509-469-7662
Whitlock Packaging Corporation
Fort Gibson, OK 918-478-4300

Computer Software, Systems & Services

AC Label Company
Provo, UT 801-642-3500
Acromag Inc.
Wixom, MI 248-624-1541
Acumen Data Systems
West Springfield, MA 888-816-0933
Advanced Food Systems
Phoenix, AZ 602-522-8282
Advanced Micro Controls
Terryville, CT 860-585-1254
Advanced Software Designs
Chesterfield, MO 636-532-6021
Advanced Technology Corporation/Vetstar
Ramsey, NJ 201-934-7127
Agilysys, Inc.
Alpharetta, GA 800-241-8768
Airflow Sciences Corporation
Livonia, MI 734-525-0300
AL Systems
Rockaway, NJ 888-960-8324
Allpax Products
Covington, LA 888-893-9277
American Forms & Labels
Boise, ID 800-388-3554
American Technical Services Group
Norcross, GA 770-447-9444
Amplexus Corporation
Novato, CA 800-423-8268
Ann Arbor Computer
Farmington Hills, MI 800-526-9322
Apigent Solutions
Oklahoma City, OK 800-664-8228
ASAP Automation
Addison, IL 800-409-0383
ASI Datamyto
Minneapolis, MN 800-455-4359
ASI/Restaurant Manager
Silver Spring, MD. 800-356-6037
Assembly Technology & Test
Livonia, MI. 734-522-1900
At-Your-Service Software
Bronxville, NY 888-325-6937
Auto Quotes
Jacksonville, FL 904-384-2279
Automation Group
Houston, TX 713-860-5200
BatchMaster Software Corporation
Laguna Hills, CA 949-583-1646
Berg Company
Monona, WI 608-221-4281
BSI Instruments
Aliquippa, PA 800-274-9851
Buypass Corporation
Atlanta, GA. 770-953-2664
CA, Inc.
Islandia, NY 800-225-5224
Cache Box
Arlington, VA 800-603-4834
Cambar Software
North Charleston, SC 843-856-2822
Camstar Systems
San Jose, CA. 800-237-2841
Catalyst International
Milwaukee, WI 800-236-4600
CaterMate
Ithaca, NY. 800-486-2283
Cbord
Ithaca, NY. 800-982-4643
CBORD Group
Ithaca, NY. 607-257-2140
Coconut Code
Lighthouse Point, FL 954-786-0252
Comalex
Van Buren, AR 866-343-2594
Command Line Corporation
Edison, NJ. 732-738-6500
Compris Technologies
Duluth, GA 800-615-3301
Computer Aid, Inc.
Allentown, PA. 800-327-4243
Computer Aided Marketing
Chapel Hill, NC 919-401-0996
Computer Communications Specialists
Marietta, GA. 888-231-4227
Computrition
Chatsworth, CA 800-222-4488
Comstar Printing Solutions
Streetsboro, OH 330-528-2800
Comtrex Systems Corporation
Moorestown, NJ 800-220-2669
Comus Restaurant Systems
Frederick, MD. 301-698-6208
Control Module
Enfield, CT 800-722-6654
Crunch Time Information Systems
Boston, MA. 857-202-3000
Custom Business Solutions
Irvine, CA 800-551-7674
Cycle Computer Consultants
Hicksville, NY 516-733-1892
Cyplex
Los Angeles, CA
Danfoss
Baltimore, MD 410-931-8250
Data Management
San Angelo, TX 800-749-8463
Data Specialist
Elkhorn, WI. 800-211-1545
Decartes Systems Group
Waterloo, ON 519-746-8110
Digital Dining/Menusoft
Springfield, VA. 703-912-3000
Digital Dynamics
Scotts Valley, CA 800-765-1288
Digital Image & Sound Corporation
Rochester, NY. 585-381-0410
Domino Amjet
Gurnee, IL. 800-444-4512
DSA-Software
Foxboro, MA 508-543-0400
E2M
Duluth, GA 800-622-4326
Eatec Corporation
Emeryville, CA. 877-374-4783
Eaton Filtration, LLC
Tinton Falls, NJ. 800-859-9212
EBS
Houston, TX 713-939-1000
Ecklund-Harrison Technologies
Fort Myers, FL 239-936-6032
Economic Sciences Corporation
Berkeley, CA. 510-841-6869

Edgerton Corporation
Strongsville, OH 440-268-0000
Efficient Frontiers
Livermore, CA 888-433-4725
Electro Cam Corporation
Roscoe, IL. 800-228-5487
Electrol Specialties Company
South Beloit, IL 815-389-2291
Elo Touch Systems
Menlo Park, CA 800-557-1458
Elreha Controls Corporation
St Petersburg, FL 727-327-6236
Emtrol
York, PA 800-634-4927
EPD Technology Corporation
Elmsford, NY 800-892-8926
ERC Parts
Kennesaw, GA 800-241-6880
Esha Research
Salem, OR. 800-659-3742
ExecuChef Software
San Anselmo, CA 415-488-9600
Famous Software
Fresno, CA 800-444-8301
First DataBank
San Bruno, CA 800-633-3453
Fred D. Pfening Company
Columbus, OH 614-294-1633
GCA Bar Code Specialist
Huntington Beach, CA 714-379-4911
Genesis Total Solutions
Fultondale, AL 205-877-3228
Gerber Innovations
Tolland, CT 800-331-5797
Graphic Technology
New Century, KS 800-767-9920
Great Plains Software
Fargo, ND 800-456-0025
GTCO CalComp
Scottsdale, AZ. 800-856-0732
H.K. Systems
Milwaukee, WI 800-424-7365
Hampton-Tilley Associates
Chesterfield, MO 636-537-3353
Heart Smart International
Scottsdale, AZ. 800-762-7819
Helm Software
Phoenix, AZ 602-522-2999
Hope Industrial Systems Inc.
Roswell, GA 877-762-9790
Horizon Software International
Duluth, GA 800-741-7100
HSI
Scottsdale, AZ. 480-596-5456
Hudson Control Group
Springfield, NJ 973-376-7400
Iconics
Foxborough, MA 800-946-9679
ID Images
Brunswick, OH 866-516-7300
Illinois Wholesale Cash Register Corporation
Elgin, IL 800-544-5493
IMAS Corporation
St. Charles, IL. 847-274-9383
Industrious Software Solutions
Inglewood, CA 800-351-4225
InFood Corporation
Evanston, IL 773-338-8485
Infopro, Inc.
Aurora, IL 630-978-9231
Information Access
Cleveland, OH 216-328-0100
Insignia Systems
Minneapolis, MN 800-874-4648
Integrated Distribution
Omaha, NE 402-397-8757
Integrated Restaurant Software/RMS Touch
Timonium, MD. 201-461-9096
Intelligent Controls
Saco, ME. 800-872-3455
Interactive Sales Solutions
Coppell, TX 800-352-9575
Interlake Material Handling
Naperville, IL 800-468-3752
Intermec Systems & Solutions
Everett, WA. 800-755-5505
Intermec Technologies Corporation
Everett, WA. 800-755-5505
Invictus Systems Corporation
Falls Church, VA
ITC Systems
Toronto, ON 877-482-8326

Junction Solutions
Englewood, CO. 877-502-6355
Kaye Instruments
N Billerica, MA 800-343-4624
Kenray Associates
Greenville, IN 812-923-9884
Kistler-Morse Corporation
Spartanburg, SC 800-426-9010
Kochman Consultants Limited
Morton Grove, IL 847-470-1195
Konica Minolta Corporation
Ramsey, NJ 888-473-3637
LABLynx
Atlanta, GA. 800-585-5969
LDJ Electronics
Troy, MI 248-528-2202
Least Cost Formulations
Virginia Beach, VA. 757-467-0954
Ley Norback & Associates
Middleton, WI. 608-233-3814
Lighthouse for the Blindin New Orleans
New Orleans, LA 504-899-4501
LIS Warehouse Systems
Charlotte, NC 888-547-9670
Logility Transportation Group
Des Plaines, IL 847-699-6620
Long Range Systems
Addison, TX 800-577-8101
LPI Information Systems
Overland Park, KS 888-729-2020
Magnetic Technologies
Oxford, MA. 508-987-3303
Management Tech of America
Scottsdale, AZ. 480-998-0200
MAPS Software
Columbus, MS 662-328-6110
Marcam Solutions
Newton, MA 800-962-7226
MenuLink Computer Solutions
Huntington Beach, CA 714-934-6368
Micros Systems/Fidelio Software Company
Columbia, MD 800-638-0985
Microtouch Systems
Methuen, MA 978-851-9939
Microworks POS Solutions
Webster, NY 800-787-2068
Moisture Register Products
Rancho Cucamonga, CA 800-966-4788
Montalbano Development
Ronkonkoma, NY. 800-739-9152
Munck Automation Technology
Newport News, VA. 800-777-6862
Murata Automated Systems
Charlotte, NC 800-428-8469
National Computer Corporation
Greenville, SC. 866-944-5164
National Controls Corporation
West Chicago, IL 800-323-5293
Newmarket International
Portsmouth, NH 888-829-8871
Northwest Analytical
Portland, OR. 888-692-7638
Novax Group/Point of Sales
New York, NY 212-684-1244
Nutrition & Food Associates
Minneapolis, MN 763-550-9475
Omron Systems
Schaumburg, IL. 847-519-9465
Order-Matic Corporation
Oklahoma City, OK 800-767-6733
Parity Corporation
Bothell, WA. 425-408-9511
Party Perfect Catering
Houston, TX 800-522-5440
PC/Poll Systems
Dubuque, IA 800-670-1736
PEAK Technologies, Inc.
Columbia, MD 800-926-9212
PeopleSoft USA
Atlanta, GA. 800-380-7638
Preston Scientific
Anaheim, CA 714-632-3700
Prime ProData
North Canton, OH. 877-497-2578
Prism Visual Software, Inc
Port Washington, NY 516-944-5920
Progressive Software
Charlotte, NC 704-295-7000
Ramco Systems Corporation
Lawrence Township, NJ 800-472-6461
RDS of Florida
Largo, FL

Redi-Print
West Babylon, NY 631-491-6373
Reflex International
Norcross, GA 800-642-7640
ReMACS
Ocean, NJ 732-493-9596
Remote Equipment Systems
Alpharetta, GA 800-803-9488
Restaurant Technology
Marietta, GA. 770-590-4300
Retail Automations Products
New York, NY 800-237-9144
Retalix
Miamisburg, OH. 800-533-2277
Rice Lake Weighing Systems
Rice Lake, WI. 800-472-6703
Rockland Technology
Lewisville, TX 972-221-6190
ROI Software, LLC
Knoxville, TN. 865-522-2211
Ross Computer Systems
Knoxville, TN. 865-690-3008
Round Noon Software
Dallas, TX. 972-789-5191
Sable Technologies
Eagan, MN 800-722-5390
Sales Partner System
Ormond Beach, FL 800-777-2924
SalesData Software
San Jose, CA. 408-281-5811
Sanderson Computers
Worthington, OH 614-781-2525
SBA Software
Doral, FL. 800-222-8324
SBS of Financial Industries
Washington, NJ. 908-689-5520
Scan Corporation
Brandon, FL 800-881-7226
Schneider Automation
North Andover, MA 978-691-1400
Schoneman, Inc
Ashtabula, OH 800-255-4439
Schreck Software
Woodbury, MN 651-731-6822
Serti Information Solution
Montreal, QC 800-361-6615
Shared Data Systems
Charlotte, NC 800-622-2140
SICOM Systems
Doylestown, PA 800-547-4266
Siemens Measurement Systems
Pittsford, NY. 800-568-7721
Simply Products
Kunkletown, PA 610-681-6894
Squirrel Systems
Vancouver, BC 800-388-6824
Sterling Scale Company
Southfield, MI. 800-331-9931
Stoltz Enterprises
Slidell, LA. 800-738-1000
Stratix Corporation
Norcross, GA 800-883-8300
Success Systems
Stamford, GA 800-653-3345
SweetWARE
Oakland, CA 800-526-7900
System Concepts, Inc/FOOD-TRAK
Scottsdale, AZ. 800-553-2438
Tablecheck Technologies, Inc
Austin, TX. 800-522-1347
TallyGenicom
Irvine, CA 800-665-6210
Tangible Vision
Franklin, TN. 800-763-8634
Tekvisions California
Temecula, CA 800-466-8005
Televend
Baltimore, MD 410-532-7818
Texture Technologies Corporation
Scarsdale, NY. 914-472-0531
Tharo Systems, Inc
Brunswick, OH 800-878-6833
Tibersoft Corporation
Westborough, MA. 888-888-1969
Tinadre
Tampa, FL. 813-866-0033
TMT Software Company
Durham, NC 800-401-6682
Touch Menus
Bellevue, WA 800-688-6368
Tricor Systems
Elgin, IL 800-575-0161

TriCore
Racine, WI 262-886-3630
Trola Industries
York, PA 717-848-3700
Unisoft Systems Associates
Dublin, OH 800-448-1574
Universal Dynamics Technologies
Richmond, BC 888-912-7246
Vande Berg Scales
Sioux Center, IA 712-722-1181
Vertex Interactive
Clifton, NJ. 973-777-3500
W&H Systems
Carlstadt, NJ 201-933-9849
Wallace Computer Services
Elk Grove Vlg, IL 888-925-8324
Weber Packaging Solutions, Inc.
Arlington Hts, IL 800-843-4242
X-Rite, Inc.
Grand Rapids, MI 616-803-2100
Xcel Tower Controls
Gilbertsville, NY. 800-288-7362
Zebra Technologies Corporation
Lincolnshire, IL 866-230-9494

Software

Routing & Scheduling for Food Industry

Formulator Software,LLC
Clinton, NJ 908-735-2248
Prism Visual Software
Port Washington, NY 516-944-5920

Construction

Facility Design

BE&K Building Group
Birmingham, AL. 205-972-6000
Boldt Company
Appleton, WI 920-739-6321
Dennis Group
Springfield, MA 413-787-1785
Klinger Constructors LLC
Albuquerque, NM 505-822-9990
Shambaugh & Son
Fort Wayne, IN 260-487-7777
Tippmann Group
Fort Wayne, IN 260-490-3000

Management

BE&K Building Group
Birmingham, AL. 205-972-6000
Dennis Group
Springfield, MA 413-787-1785
Facility Group
Smyrna, GA 770-437-2700
Stellar Group
Jacksonville, FL 800-260-2900

Metal Fabricators

A&B Process Systems
Stratford, WI 888-258-2789
A-Z Factory Supply
Schiller Park, IL 800-323-4511
A.J. Antunes & Company
Carol Stream, IL 800-253-2991
Abalon Precision Manufacturing Corporation
Bronx, NY. 800-888-2225
ABC Letter Art
Los Angeles, CA. 888-261-5367
ABCO Industries Limited
Lunenburg, NS 866-634-8821
Ace Fabrication
Mobile, AL 251-478-0401
Ace Stamp & Engraving
Lakewood, WA 253-582-3322
Acme International
Maplewood, NJ. 973-416-0400
ACS Industries, Inc.
Lincoln, RI 866-783-4838
Adams Signs & Graphics
Massillon, OH. 888-886-9911
Adapto Storage Products
Hialeah, FL. 305-499-4800
Advance Fitting Corporation
Elkhorn, WI. 262-723-6699
Advance Tabco
Edgewood, NY 800-645-3166
Advanced Uniflo Technologies
Wichita, KS. 800-688-0400
Aero Manufacturing Company
Clifton, NJ. 800-631-8378
AFGO Mechanical Services, Inc.
Long Island City, NY 800-438-2346
AHP Machine & Tool Company
Lancaster, OH 740-681-6709
AK Steel
West Chester, OH 800-331-5050
Alegacy Food Service Products Group, Inc.
Santa Fe Springs, CA 800-848-4440
All American Containers
Medley, FL 305-887-0797
All Power
Sioux City, IA 712-258-0681
All Southern Fabricators
Clearwater, FL 727-573-4846
All Spun Metal Products
Des Plaines, IL 847-824-4117
All State Fabricators Corporation
Florida, RI. 800-322-9925
All-Clad Metalcrafters
Canonsburg, PA 800-255-2523
Allegheny Bradford Corporation
Bradford, PA. 800-542-0650
Alliance Products, LLC
Murfreesboro, TN. 800-522-3973
Allied Engineering
North Vancouver, BC 877-929-1214
Alloy Products Corporation
Waukesha, WI. 800-236-6603
Allstrong Restaurant Equipment
South El Monte, CA 800-933-8913
ALP Lighting & Ceiling Products
Pennsauken, NJ. 800-633-7732
ALPI Food Preparation Equipment
Bolton, ON 800-928-2574
Alumaworks
Sunny Isle Beach, FL 800-277-7267
AMCO Corporation
City of Industry, CA 626-855-2550
American Art Stamp
Gardena, CA 310-965-9004
American Lifts
Guthrie, OK. 877-360-6777
American Manufacturing &Engineering Company
Cleveland, OH 800-822-9402
American Metal Door Company
Richmond, IN 800-428-2737
American Production Company
Redwood City, CA 650-368-5334
Ametco Manufacturing Corporation
Willoughby, OH 800-321-7042
Amscor
Brooklyn, NY 800-825-9800
Amtekco Industries
Columbus, OH 800-336-4677
Anderson-Crane Company
Minneapolis, MN 800-314-2747
Andgar Corporation
Ferndale, WA 360-366-9900
Apache Stainless Equipment Corporation
Beaver Dam, WI. 800-444-0398
APW Wyott Food Service Equipment Company
Cheyenne, WY 800-527-2100
ARC Specialties
Valencia, CA. 661-775-8500
Archer Wire International
Bedford Park, IL 708-563-1700
Arizona Store Equipment
Phoenix, AZ 800-624-8395
Arkfeld Mfg & Distr Company
Norfolk, NE. 800-533-0676
Armbrust Paper Tubes
Chicago, IL 773-586-3232
ATD-American Company
Wyncote, PA 800-523-2300
Atlas Tag & Label
Neenah, WI 800-558-6418
Audrey Signs
New York, NY 212-769-4992
Auger-Fabrication
Exton, PA 800-334-1529
Automatic Specialities Inc.
Marlborough, MA. 800-445-2370
B Way Corporation
Atlanta, GA. 800-527-2267
B.C. Holland
Dousman, WI 262-965-2939
Baldewein Company
Lake Forrest, IL 800-424-5544
Ball Corporation
Broomfield, CO 920-261-5105
Ballymore Company
West Chester, PA. 610-696-3250
Baltimore Sign Company
Arnold, MD. 410-276-1500
Barker Wire Products
Keosauqua, IA 319-293-3176
Barn Furniture Mart
Van Nuys, CA 888-302-2276
Bayhead Products Corporation
Dover, NH. 800-229-4323
Beayl Weiner/Pak
Pacific Palisades, CA 310-454-1354
Behlen Mfg. Co.
Columbus, NE. 402-564-3111
Bennett Manufacturing Company
Alden, NY. 800-345-2142
Berloc Manufacturing & Sign Company
Sun Valley, CA 818-503-9823
Berlon Industries
Hustisford, WI 800-899-3580
Berndorf Belt Technology USA
Elgin, IL 877-232-7322
Bertels Can Company
Belcamp, MD 410-272-0090
BG Industries
Lemont, IL 800-800-5761
BMH
City of Industry, CA 909-349-2530
Boehringer Mfg. Co. Inc.
Felton, CA. 800-630-8665
Bohn & Dawson
Saint Louis, MO 800-225-5011
Borroughs Corporation
Kalamazoo, MI 800-748-0227
Bowers Process Equipment
Stratford, ON. 800-567-3223
Bradford A Ducon Company
Pewaukee, WI 800-789-1718
Bremer Manufacturing Company
Elkhart Lake, WI. 920-894-2944
Brenner Tank
Fond Du Lac, WI 800-558-9750
Brute Fabricators
Castroville, TX 800-777-2788
Bulman Products Inc
Grand Rapids, MI 616-363-4416
Burgess Manufacturing ofOklahoma
Guthrie, OK. 800-804-1913
Burrows Paper Corporation
Little Falls, NY 800-272-7122
C&H Store Equipment Company
Los Angeles, CA. 800-648-4979
C. Nelson Manufacturing Company
Oak Harbor, OH 800-922-7339
C.E. Rogers Company
Mora, MN 800-279-8081
Caddy Corporation of America
Bridgeport, NJ. 856-467-4222
California Caster & Handtruck
San Francisco, CA 800-950-8750
Canton Sign Company
Canton, OH 330-456-7151
Caraustar Industries, Inc.
Archdale, NC 800-223-1373
Carbis
Florence, SC 800-948-7750
Carmun International
San Antonio, TX. 800-531-7907
Carrier Vibrating Equipment
Louisville, KY 502-969-3171
Carter-Hoffman Corp LLC
Mundelein, IL 800-323-9793
Carton Closing Company
Butler, PA 724-287-7759
Carts Food Equipment Corporation
Brooklyn, NY 718-788-5540
Central Fabricators
Cincinnati, OH 800-909-8265
Charlton & Hill
Lethbridge, AB 403-328-3388
Chef Specialties Company
Smethport, PA. 800-440-2433
Chemdet
Sebastian, FL 800-645-1510
Cherry's Industrial Equipment Corporation
Elk Grove Vlg, IL. 800-350-0011
Chester-Jensen Company, Inc.
Chester, PA 800-685-3750
Chip-Makers Tooling Supply
Whittier, CA 800-659-5840

Claridge Products & Equipment
Harrison, AR
Classico Seating
Peru, IN. 800-968-6655
Clawson Container Company
Clarkston, MI 800-325-8700
Clayton & Lambert Manufacturing
Buckner, KY 800-626-5819
Cleveland Metal StampingCompany
Berea, OH 440-234-0010
Cleveland Wire Cloth & Manufacturing Company
Cleveland, OH 800-321-3234
Cobb & Zimmer
Detroit, MI 313-923-0350
Columbian TecTank
Parsons, KS. 800-421-2788
Commercial Kitchen Company
Los Angeles, CA. 323-732-2291
Complex Steel & Wire Corporation
Wayne, MI. 734-326-1600
Consolidated Can
Paramount, CA 888-793-2199
Consolidated Commercial Controls
Winsted, CT 800-332-2500
Container Supply Company
Garden Grove, CA 714-891-4896
Containment Technology
St Gabriel, LA. 800-388-2467
Continental-Fremont
Tiffin, OH 419-448-4045
Corby Hall
Randolph, NJ .973-366-8300
Cotter Corporation
Danvers, MA
Cotterman Company
Croswell, MI. .800-552-3337
COW Industries
Columbus, OH 800-542-9353
Cr. Manufacturing
Waverly, NE 877-789-5844
Cramer
Kansas City, MO. 800-366-6700
CRC
Council Bluffs, IA. 712-323-9477
Creative Mobile Systems
Manchester, CT. 800-646-8364
Crown Cork & Seal Company
Philadelphia, PA 215-698-5100
Crown Custom Metal Spinning
Concord, ON. .800-750-1924
Crown Holdings, Inc.
Philadelphia, PA 215-698-5100
Crown Manufacturing Corporation
Waterford, CT .860-442-4325
Crown Metal Manufacturing Company
Alta Loma, CA 909-948-9300
Crown Verity
Brantford, ON. 888-505-7240
Custom Diamond International
Laval, QC 800-326-5926
Custom Fabricating & Repair
Marshfield, WI 800-236-8773
D&D Sign Company
Wichita Falls, TX 940-692-4643
D&W Fine Pack
Lake Zurich, IL. 800-323-0422
D. Picking & Company
Bucyrus, OH 419-562-6891
D.A. Berther
West Allis, WI. 877-357-9622
Damascus/Bishop Tube Company
Greenville, PA. 724-646-1500
Dansk International Designs
White Plains, NY 914-697-6400
Davron Technologies
Chattanooga, TN. 423-870-1888
Dayco
Clearwater, FL 727-573-9330
DCI
St Cloud, MN .320-252-8200
Denmar Corporation
North Dartmouth, MA 508-999-3295
Designer's Choice Stainless
Peoria, AZ. 800-592-3274
Despro Manufacturing
Cedar Grove, NJ 800-292-9906
Dimension Graphics
Grand Rapids, MI 855-476-1281
Dinosaur Plastics
Houston, TX 713-923-2278
Doering Company
Clear Lake, MN 320-743-2276

Doran Scales
Batavia, IL. 800-365-0084
Dormont Manufacturing Company
Export, PA. 800-367-6668
Dover Parkersburg
Follansbee, WV
Dreaco Products
Elyria, OH. 800-368-3267
Dubuque Steel Products Company
Dubuque, IA 563-556-6288
Duke Manufacturing Company
Saint Louis, MO 800-735-3853
Duluth Sheet Metal
Duluth, MN. 218-722-2613
Durham Manufacturing Company
Durham, CT 413-781-7900
Durham Manufacturing Company
Duham, CT 800-243-3744
E.C. Shaw Company
Cincinnati, OH 866-532-7429
Eagle Foodservice Equipment
Clayton, DE. 800-441-8440
Eastern Silver Tabletop Manufacturing Company
Brooklyn, NY .888-422-4142
Easy Up Storage Systems
Seattle, WA 800-426-9234
EB Metal Industries
Whitehall, NY. 518-499-1222
Econofrost Night Covers
Shawnigan Lake, BC 800-519-1222
Economy Paper & Restaurant Supply Company
Clifton, NJ. 973-279-5500
Eldorado Miranda Manufacturing Company
Largo, FL 800-330-0708
Elite Trading Worldwide
Brooklyn, NY .888-354-8388
Ellett Industries
Port Coquitlam, BC. 604-941-8211
EMC Solutions, Inc
Celina, OH 419-586-2388
EMED Company
Buffalo, NY. 800-442-3633
Enerfab, Inc.
Cincinnati, OH 513-641-0500
Engineered Products Group
Madison, WI 800-626-3111
English Manufacturing Inc
Rancho Cordova, CA 800-651-2711
Enterprise Products
Bell Gardens, CA 562-928-1918
Erwin Food Service Equipment
Fort Worth, TX 817-535-0021
Etube and Wire
Shrewsbury, PA. 800-618-4720
Eugene Welding Company
Marysville, MI 810-364-7421
Eurodib
Champlain, NY. 888-956-6866
Ex-Cell Kaiser
Franklin Park, IL. 847-451-0451
F&A Fabricating
Battle Creek, MI 269-965-3268
F.P. Smith Wire Cloth Company
Northlake, IL. .800-323-6842
Fabricating & Welding Corporation
Chicago, IL 773-928-2050
FabWright, Inc
Garden Grove, CA 800-854-6464
Falco
La Prairie, CA. 450-444-0566
Falcon Fabricators
Nashville, TN .615-832-0027
Fata Automation
Sterling Heights, MI 586-323-9400
Faubion Central States Tank Company
Shawnee Mission, KS. 800-450-8265
Federal Sign
Carmel, IN. 800-527-9495
FEI
Mansfield, TX. 800-346-5908
Feldmeier Equipment
Syracuse, NY .315-454-8608
Ferrer Corporation
San Juan, PR 787-761-5151
Fine Woods Manufacturing
Phoenix, AZ 800-279-2871
Finn & Son's Metal Spinning Specialists
South Lebanon, OH 513-494-2898
Fisher Manufacturing Company
Tulare, CA. 800-421-6162
Fishmore
Melbourne,, FL 321-723-4751

Fiskars Brands Inc.
Baldwinsville, NY 315-635-9911
Fixtur-World
Cookeville, TN 800-634-9887
Flame Gard
Lakewood, NJ. 800-526-3694
Flat Plate
York, PA 888-854-2500
Folding Guard Company
Chicago, IL 312-829-3500
Forrest Engraving Company
New Rochelle, NY 914-632-9892
Forster & Son
Ada, OK 580-332-6020
Fountainhead
Bensalem, PA .800-326-8998
Frazier Industrial Company
Long Valley, NJ. 800-859-1342
Frazier Signs
Decatur, IL 217-429-2349
FRC Environmental
Gainesville, GA 770-534-3681
Friskem Infinetics
Wilmington, DE 302-658-2471
Fuller Box Company
North Attleboro, MA 508-695-2525
FWE/Food Warming Equipment Company, Inc
Crystal Lake, IL 800-222-4393
GA Systems
Huntington Beach, CA 714-848-7529
Gasser Chair Company
Youngstown, OH. 800-323-2234
Geerpres
Muskegon, MI. 231-773-3211
General Industries
Goldsboro, NC 888-735-2882
Gillis Associated Industries
Prospect Heights, IL 847-541-6500
Glaro
Hauppauge, NY 631-234-1717
Glo-Quartz Electric Heater Company
Mentor, OH. 800-321-3574
GM Nameplate
Seattle, WA 800-366-7668
Goergen-Mackwirth Company
Buffalo, NY. 716-874-4800
Gorbel
Fishers, NY 585-924-6262
Graff Tank Erection
Harrisville, PA. 814-385-6671
Great Lakes Brush
Centralia, MO .573-682-2128
Green Brothers
Barrington, RI .401-245-9043
Green Metal Fabricated Company
West Sacramento, CA. 916-371-0192
Gribble Stamp & Stencil Company
Houston, TX 713-228-5358
Grief Brothers Corporation
Delaware, OH .740-549-6000
Griffin Products
Wills Point, TX. 800-379-9709
Grindmaster-Cecilware Corporation
Louisville, KY 800-695-4500
H&H Metal Fabrications
Belden, MS 662-489-4626
Hallock Fabricating Corporation
Riverhead, NY 631-727-2441
Halton Company
Scottsville, KY 800-442-5866
Hamilton Kettles
Weirton, WV. .800-535-1882
Hank Rivera Associates
Dearborn, MI .313-581-8300
Hanset Stainless
Portland, OR 800-360-7030
Hantover
Kansas City, MO. 800-821-7849
Hardware-Components
New Matamoras, OH 740-865-2424
Hercules Food Equipment
Weston, ON. 416-742-9673
Hewitt Manufacturing Company
Waldron, IN. 765-525-9829
Hillside Metal Ware Company
Union, NJ 908-964-3080
Hines III
Jacksonville, FL 904-398-5110
HMG Worldwide In-Store Marketing
New York, NY 212-736-2300
Hodge Manufacturing Company
Springfield, MA 800-262-4634

Hodges
Vienna, IL 800-444-0011
Holmco Container Manufacturing, LTD
Baltic, OH 330-897-4503
Holsman Sign Services
Cleveland, OH 216-761-4433
Hot Food Boxes
Mooresville, IN 800-733-8073
Houston Wire Works, Inc.
South Houston, TX 800-468-9477
Howard Fabrication
City of Industry, CA 626-961-0114
Hurri-Kleen Corporation
Birmingham, AL 800-455-8265
Ideal of America/Valley Rio Enterprise
Atlanta, GA 770-352-0210
Ideal Wire Works
Alhambra, CA 626-282-1302
Illinois Range Company
Schiller Park, IL 800-535-7041
IMC Teddy Food Service Equipment
Amityville, NY 800-221-5644
IMO Foods
Yarmouth, NS 902-742-3519
Imperial Schrade Corporation
Ellenville, NY 212-210-8600
Independent Can Company
Belcamp, MD 909-923-6150
Indiana Cash Drawer Company
Shelbyville, IN 800-227-4379
Indiana Wire Company
Fremont, IN 877-786-6883
Industrial Air Conditioning Systems
Chicago, IL 773-486-4236
Industrial Sheet Metal
Cleveland, OH 216-431-9650
Institutional Equipment
Bolingbrook, IL 630-771-0990
Intrex
Bethel, CT 203-792-7400
Irby
Rocky Mount, NC 252-442-0154
J.L. Clark
Rockford, IL 815-962-8861
J.V. Reed & Company
Louisville, KY 877-258-7333
JanTec
Traverse City, MI 800-992-3303
Jarke Corporation
Prospect Hts, IL 800-722-5255
Jay Bee Manufacturing
Tyler, TX 800-445-0610
JEM Wire Products
Middletown, CT 860-347-0447
Jesco Industries, Inc.
Litchfield, MI 800-455-0019
JH Display & Fixture
Greenwood, IN 317-888-0631
John Boos & Company
Effingham, IL 217-347-7701
Johnson-Rose Corporation
Lockport, NY 800-456-2055
Joyce Engraving Company, Inc.
Dallas, TX 214-638-1262
Jupiter Mills Corporation
Roslyn, NY 800-853-5121
JW Leser Company
Los Angeles, CA 323-731-4173
K&I Creative Plastics
Jacksonville, FL 904-387-0438
Kaines West Michigan Company
Ludington, MI 231-845-1281
Kamflex Corporation
Chicago, IL 800-323-2440
Karyall-Telday
Cleveland, OH 216-281-4063
Kason Central
Columbus, OH 614-885-1992
KC Booth Company
Kansas City, MO 800-866-5226
KEMCO
Wareham, MA 800-231-5955
Key Material Handling
Simi Valley, CA 800-539-7225
Keystone Adjustable Cap
Pennsauken, NJ 800-663-5439
Kiefer Industries
Random Lake, WI 920-994-2332
King Sign Company
Akron, OH 330-762-7421
Kitchen Equipment Fabricating Company
Houston, TX 713-747-3611

Kitcor Corporation
Sun Valley, CA 818-767-4800
Klinger Constructors LLC
Albuquerque, NM 505-822-9990
Kloppenberg & Company
Englewood, CO 800-346-3246
Koehler Gibson Marking &Graphics
Buffalo, NY 800-875-1562
KOFAB
Algona, IA 515-295-7265
Kosempel Manufacturing Company
Philadelphia, PA 800-733-7122
L&H Wood Manufacturing Company
Farmington, MI 248-474-9000
L&L Engraving Company
Gilford, NH 888-524-3032
L&S Products
Coldwater, MI 517-279-9526
L.C. Thompson Company
Kenosha, WI 800-558-4018
La Crosse
Onalaska, WI 800-345-0018
Laidig Industrial Systems
Mishawaka, IN 574-256-0204
Lake Shore Industries
Erie, PA 800-458-0463
Lakeside Manufacturing
Milwaukee, WI 888-558-8574
Lakeside-Aris Manufacturing
Milwaukee, WI 800-558-8565
Lambert Material Handling
Syracuse, NY 800-253-5103
Lambertson Industries
Sparks, NV 800-548-3324
Lancaster Colony Commercial Products
Columbus, OH 800-528-2278
Lancaster Colony Corporation
Columbus, OH 800-292-7260
Langer Manufacturing Company
Cedar Rapids, IA 800-728-6445
Lask Seating Company
Chicago, IL 888-573-2846
Laughlin Corporation
Fort Worth, TX 817-625-7756
Lavi Industries
Valencia, CA 800-624-6225
Lawrence Metal Products
Bay Shore, NY 800-441-0019
Lazy-Man
Belvidere, NJ 800-475-1950
Le Smoker
Salisbury, MD 410-677-3233
Lee Industries Fluid Transfer
Philipsburg, PA 814-342-0802
Leeds Conveyor Manufacturer Company
Guilford, CT 800-724-1088
Leggett & Platt StorageP
Vernon Hills, IL 847-816-6246
Legible Signs
Loves Park, IL 800-435-4177
License Ad Plate Company
Cleveland, OH 216-265-4200
Lincoln Foodservice
Cleveland, OH 800-374-3004
Linvar
Hartford, CT 800-282-5288
Little Rock Crate & Basket Company
Little Rock, AR 800-223-7823
Lloyd Disher Company
Decatur, IL 217-429-0593
Load King Manufacturing Company
Jacksonville, FL 800-531-4975
Lodge Manufacturing Company
South Pittsburg, TN 423-837-5919
Loewenstein
Liberty, NC 800-327-2548
Lorenz Couplings
Cobourg, ON 800-263-7782
Lorenzen's Cookie Cutters
Wantagh, NY 516-781-7116
Low Temp Industries
Jonesboro, GA 770-478-8803
Loyal Manufacturing Corporation
Indianapolis, IN 317-359-3185
LPI Imports
Chicago, IL 877-389-6563
Lyco Wausau
Wausau, WI 715-845-7867
Lyon Metal Products
Aurora, IL 630-892-8941
M&E Manufacturing Company
Kingston, NY 845-331-2110

Madsen Wire Products
Orland, IN 260-829-6561
Magline
Pinconning, MI 800-624-5463
Magsys
Milwaukee, WI 414-543-2177
Malco Manufacturing Corporation
Los Angeles, CA 866-477-7267
Mar-Con Wire Belt
Richmond, BC 877-962-7266
Market Sign Systems
Portland, ME 800-421-1799
Marlin Steel Wire Products
Baltimore, MD 877-762-7546
Marlo Manufacturing Company
Boonton, NJ 800-222-0450
Marston Manufacturing
Cleveland, OH 216-587-3400
Martin/Baron
Irwindale, CA 626-960-5153
Material Storage Systems
Gadsden, AL 877-543-2467
MCM Fixture Company
Hazel Park, MI 248-547-9280
Memphis Delta Tent & Awning Company
Memphis, TN 901-522-1238
Metal Container Corporation
St Louis, MO 314-957-9500
Metal Equipment Company
Cleveland, OH 800-700-6326
Metal Equipment Fabricators
Columbia, SC 803-776-9250
Metal Kitchen Fabricators
Houston, TX 713-683-8375
Metal Master
Tucson, AZ 800-488-8729
Metal Masters Food Service Equipment Company
Clayton, DE 800-441-8440
Metal Masters Northwest
Lynnwood, WA 425-775-4481
Metcraft
Grandview, MO 800-444-9624
METKO
New Holstein, WI 920-898-4221
Mettler-Toledo
Columbus, OH 800-523-5123
Metz Premiums
New York, NY 212-315-4660
Micelli Chocolate Mold Company
West Babylon, NY 631-752-2888
Micro Wire Products Inc.
Brockton, MA 508-584-0200
MicroPure Filtration
Mound, MN 800-654-7873
Mid-State Metal Casting & Manufacturing
Fresno, CA 559-445-1974
Mid-States Manufacturing & Engineering
Milton, IA 800-346-1792
Mid-West Wire Products, Inc
Ferndale, MI 800-989-9881
Midwest Metalcraft & Equipment
Windsor, MO 800-647-3167
Midwest Stainless
Menomonie, WI 715-235-5472
Midwest Wire Products
Sturgeon Bay, WI 800-445-0225
MLS Signs
Chesterfield, MI 586-948-0200
MO Industries
Whippany, NJ 973-386-9228
Modern Brewing & Design
Santa Rosa, CA 707-542-6620
Modern Metalcraft
Midland, MI 800-948-3182
Modern Metals Industries
El Segundo, CA 800-437-6633
Montebello Packaging
Hawkesbury, ON 613-632-7096
Mouli Manufacturing Corporation
Belleville, NJ 800-789-8285
Mouron & Company
Indianapolis, IN 317-243-7955
Mulholland-Harper Company
Denton, MD 800-882-3052
Multi-Vac
Union Grove, WI 800-640-4213
Music City Metals
Nashville, TN 800-251-2674
Myers Container Corporation
Hayward, CA 510-652-6847
N. Wasserstrom & Sons
Columbus, OH 800-999-9277

National Bar Systems
Huntington Beach, CA 714-848-1688
National Metal Industries
West Springfield, MA 800-628-8850
New Age Industrial Corporation
Norton, KS 800-255-0104
New Court
Texarkana, TX 903-838-0521
Nexel Industries
Port Washington, NY 800-245-6682
Northern Stainless Fabricating
Traverse City, MI 231-947-4580
Northern Wire Products
St Cloud, MN 800-458-5549
Northwind
Alpena, AR 870-437-2585
Novelis Foil Products
Lagrange, GA 800-776-8701
Nowakowski
Franklin, WI 800-394-5866
Ohlson Packaging
Taunton, MA 508-977-0004
Old Dominion Wood Products
Lynchburg, VA 800-245-6382
Olde Country Reproductions
York, PA 800-358-3997
Olde Thompson/Leeds Engineering Corporation
Oxnard, CA 800-827-1565
Olive Can Company
Elgin, IL 847-468-7474
Omega Industrial Products
Saukville, WI 800-279-6634
Omicron Steel Products Company
Jamaica, NY 718-805-3400
Oneida Food Service
Oneida, NY 315-361-3000
Orber Manufacturing Company
Cranston, RI 800-761-4059
OSF
Toronto, ON 800-465-4000
OTD Corporation
Hinsdale, IL 630-321-9232
Pacific Northwest Wire Works
Dupont, WA 800-222-7699
Pacific Scale Company
Clackamas, OR 800-537-1886
Packaging Aids Corporation
San Rafael, CA 415-454-4868
Padinox
Winsloe, PE 800-263-9768
Pallet Management Systems
Lawrenceville, VA 800-446-1804
Parisi/Royal Store Fixture
Newtown, PA 215-968-6677
Patrick & Company
Dallas, TX 214-761-0900
Paul Mueller Company
Springfield, MO 800-683-5537
Paul O. Abbe
Bensenville, IL 630-350-2200
PBC
Mahwah, NJ 800-514-2739
Penasack Contract Manufacturer
Albion, NY 585-589-7044
Penco Products
Skippack, PA 800-562-1000
Pengo Corporation
Cokato, MN 800-599-0211
Pentwater Wire Products
Pentwater, MI 877-869-6911
Perfection Equipment
Gurnee, IL 800-356-6301
Peter Gray Corporation
Andover, MA 978-470-0990
Peterson Manufacturing Company
Plainfield, IL 800-547-8995
Petro Moore Manufacturing Corporation
Long Island City, NY 718-784-2516
Pinquist Tool & Die Company
Brooklyn, NY 800-752-0414
Pittsburgh Tank Corporation
Monongahela, PA 800-634-0243
Plasti-Line
Knoxville, TN 800-444-7446
Polar Process
Plattsville, ON 877-896-8077
Polar Ware Company
Sheboygan, WI 800-237-3655
Pollard Brothers Manufacturing
Chicago, IL 773-763-6868
Polyplastic Forms, Inc
Farmingdale, NY 800-428-7659

Precision Printing & Packaging
Clarksville, TN 800-500-4526
Prince Seating
Brooklyn, NY 800-577-4623
Pro-Ad-Company
Portland, OR 800-287-5885
Process Solutions
Riviera Beach, FL 561-840-0050
Production Equipment Company
Meriden, CT 800-758-5697
Proluxe
Paramount, CA 800-594-5528
Pronto Products Company
Arcadia, CA 800-377-6680
Pulva Corporation
Saxonburg, PA 800-878-5828
Purolator Products Company
Greensboro, NC 800-852-4449
Quality Fabrication & Design
Coppell, TX 972-393-0502
Quality Industries
La Vergne, TN 615-793-3000
Quantum Storage Systems
Miami, FL 800-685-4665
Quickserv Corporation
Houston, TX 800-388-8307
Quipco Products
Sauget, IL 314-993-1442
R&D Brass
Wappingers Falls, NY 800-447-6050
R.G. Stephens Engineering
Long Beach, CA 800-499-3001
R.H. Saw Corporation
Barrington, IL 847-381-8777
Randell Manufacturing Unified Brands
Weidman, MI 888-994-7636
Randware Industries
Prospect Heights, IL 847-299-8884
Rath Manufacturing Company
Janesville, WI 800-367-7284
Redi-Call, Incorporated
Reno, NV 800-648-1849
Reese Enterprises
Rosemount, MN 800-328-0953
Regal Manufacturing Company
Chicago, IL 773-921-3071
Regal Ware
Kewaskum, WI 262-626-2121
Reinke & Schomann
Milwaukee, WI 414-964-1100
Republic Storage Systems LLC
Canton, OH 800-477-1255
Rex Art Manufacturing Corp.
Lindenhurst, NY 631-884-4600
Rexam Beverage Can Company
Chicago, IL 773-399-3000
Rice Lake Weighing Systems
Rice Lake, WI 800-472-6703
Richards Industries Systems
West Caldwell, NJ 973-575-7480
Rigidized Metals Corporation
Buffalo, NY 800-836-2580
RJR Packaging, Inc.
Oakland, CA 510-638-5901
RMF Steel Products
Grandview, MO 816-765-4101
Robby Vapor Systems
Sunrise, FL 800-888-8711
Robert-James Sales
Buffalo, NY 800-777-1325
Robertson Furniture Company
Toccoa, GA 800-241-0713
RoMatic Manufacturing Company
Southbury, CT 203-264-8203
Rome Machine & Foundry Company, Inc
Rome, GA 800-538-7663
Ross Engineering
Savannah, GA 800-524-7677
Royal Display Corporation
Middletown, CT 800-569-1295
Royal Paper Products
Coatesville, PA 800-666-6655
Royal Welding & Fabricating
Fullerton, CA 714-680-6669
Royce-Rolls Ringer Company
Grand Rapids, MI 800-253-9638
RTI Shelving Systems
Elmhurst, NY 800-223-6210
Rubicon Industries Corporation
Brooklyn, NY 800-662-6999
Russell-Stanley Corporation
Woodbridge, NJ 800-229-6001

Rytec Corporation
Milwaukee, WI 888-467-9832
S&L Store Fixture Company
Miami, FL 800-205-4536
S. Howes
Silver Creek, NY 888-255-2611
S.S.I. Schaefer System International Limited
Brampton, ON 905-458-5399
Salem China Company
Salem, OH 330-337-8771
Samuel Strapping Systems
Woodridge, IL 800-323-4424
Sani-Fit
Pasadena, CA 626-395-7895
Sarasota Restaurant Equipment
Sarasota, FL 800-434-1410
Savage Brothers Company
Elk Grove Vlg, IL 800-342-0973
Scherping Systems
Winsted, MN 320-485-4401
Schwaab, Inc
Milwaukee, WI 800-935-9877
Seating Concepts
Rockdale, IL 800-421-2036
Seattle Boiler Works
Seattle, WA 206-762-0737
Sefi Fabricators
Amityville, NY 631-842-2200
Seneca Environmental Products
Tiffin, OH 419-447-1282
SFB Plastics
Wichita, KS 800-343-8133
Sharpsville Container
Sharpsville, PA 800-645-1248
Shaw & Slavsky
Detroit, MI 800-521-7527
Sigma Industries
Concord, MI 517-857-6520
Sign Shop
Rancho Cucamonga, CA 909-945-5888
Sign Systems, Inc.
Warren, MI 586-758-1600
Signet Marking Devices
Costa Mesa, CA 800-421-5150
Sims Machinery Company
Lanett, AL 334-576-2101
Sirco Systems
Birmingham, AL 205-731-7800
Solar Group
Taylorsville, MS 800-647-7063
Solve Needs International
White Lake, MI 800-783-2462
Sossner Steel Stamps
Elizabethton, TN 800-828-9515
South Valley Manufacturing
Gilroy, CA 408-842-5457
Southern Metal Fabricators
Albertville, AL 800-989-1330
Spanco
Morgantown, PA 800-869-2080
Spartanburg Stainless Products
Spartanburg, SC 800-974-7500
Specialty Blades
Staunton, VA 540-248-2200
Specific Mechanical Systems
Victoria, BC 250-652-2111
Speedrack Products GroupLtd.
Sparta, MI 616-887-0002
Speedways Conveyors
Lancaster, NY 800-800-1022
SPG International LLC
Covington, GA 877-503-4774
Spot Wire Works Company
Philadelphia, PA 215-627-6124
Spring USA Corporation
Naperville, IL 800-535-8974
Springfield Metal Products Company
Springfield, NJ 973-379-4600
Springport Steel Wire Products
Concord, MI 517-857-3010
SSW Holding Company, Inc.
Elizabethtown, KY 270-769-5526
Stainless
La Vergne, TN 800-877-5177
Stainless Equipment Manufacturing
Dallas, TX 800-736-2038
Stainless Fabricating Company
Denver, CO 800-525-8966
Stainless Fabrication
Springfield, MO 800-397-8265
Stainless International
Rancho Cordova, CA 888-300-6196

Stainless Products
Somers, WC 800-558-9446
Stainless Specialists
Wausau, WI 800-236-4155
Stainless Steel Fabricators
La Mirada, CA 714-739-9904
Stainless Steel Fabricators
Tyler, TX 903-595-6625
Star Filters
Timmonsville, SC 800-845-5381
Starlite Food Service Equipment
Detroit, MI 888-521-6603
Steel City Corporation
Youngstown, OH 800-321-0350
Steel Specialty Equipment Corporation
Ridgewood, NY 800-521-7732
Stegall Metal Industries
Birmingham, AL 800-633-4373
Stello Products
Spencer, IN 800-868-2246
Sterling Process Engineering
Columbus, OH 800-783-7875
Sterling Scale Company
Southfield, MI 800-331-9931
Stogsdill Tile Company
Huntley, IL 800-323-7504
Storm Industrial
Shawnee Mission, KS 800-745-7483
Straits Steel & Wire Company
Ludington, MI 231-843-3416
Streator Dependable Manufacturing
Streator, IL 800-798-0551
Stryco Wire Products
North York, ON 416-663-7000
Suburban Signs
College Park, MD 301-474-5051
Super Steel Products Corporation
Milwaukee, WI 414-355-4800
Super Sturdy
Weldon, NC 800-253-4833
Super Systems
Wausau, WI 800-558-5880
Superior Brush Company
Cleveland, OH 216-941-6987
Supreme Fabricators
Artesia, CA 323-583-8944
Supreme Metal
Alpharetta, GA 800-645-2526
Swanson Wire Works Industries, Inc.
Mesquite, TX 972-288-7465
T&A Metal Products Company
Deptford, NJ 856-227-1700
T&T Industries
Fort Mohave, AZ 800-437-6246
Table De France: North America
New York, NY 212-725-3461
Talbot Industries
Neosho, MO 417-451-5900
Tampa Sheet Metal Company
Tampa, FL 813-251-1845
Tar-Hong Melamine USA
City of Industry, CA 626-935-1612
The Tin Box Company
Farmingdale, NY 800-888-8467
Thermo Wisconsin
De Pere, WI 920-766-7200
Tilly Industries
St Laurent, QC 514-331-4922
Top Line Process Equipment Company
Bradford, PA 800-458-6095
Tops Manufacturing Company
Darien, CT 203-655-9367
Traulsen & Company
Fort Worth, TX 800-825-8220
Travelon
Elk Grove Vlg, IL 800-537-5544
Travis Manufacturing Company
Alliance, OH 330-875-1661
Tri-Boro Shelving & Partition
Farmville, VA 434-315-5600
Triner Scale & Manufacturing Co., Inc.
Olive Branch, MS 800-238-0152
Triple-A Manufacturing Company
Toronto, ON 800-786-2238
Tropic-Kool Engineering Corporation
Largo, FL 727-581-2824
TWM Manufacturing
Leamington, ON 888-495-4831
Ultratainer
St Jean-Sur-Richelie, QC 514-359-3651
Unifoil Corporation
Fairfield, NJ 973-244-9900

United Industries
Beloit, WI 608-365-8891
United Receptacle
Pottsville, PA 800-233-0314
United Steel Products Company
East Stroudsburg, PA 570-476-1010
UniTrak Corporation
Port Hope, ON 866-883-5749
Universal Stainless
Aurora, CO 800-223-8332
Universal Stainless
Titusville, PA 800-295-1909
Uniweb
Corona, CA 800-486-4932
Update International
Los Angeles, CA 800-747-7124
Upham & Walsh Lumber
Hoffman Estates, IL 847-519-1010
US Can Company
Rosedale, MD 800-436-8021
US Seating Products
Apopka, FL 407-884-4411
US Standard Sign Company
Franklin Park, IL 800-537-4790
USECO
Murfreesboro, TN 615-893-4820
V&R Metal Enterprises
Brooklyn, NY 718-768-8142
Vacumet Corp
Wayne, NJ 973-628-1067
Vacuum Depositing
Okolona, KY 502-969-4227
Valley Craft
Lake City, MN 800-328-1480
Valvinox
Iberville, QC 450-346-1981
Vasconia Housewares
San Antonio, TX 800-377-6723
Venus Corporation
Blytheville, AR 870-763-3830
Versailles Lighting
Delray Beach, FL 888-564-0240
Victone Manufacturing Company
Chicago, IL 312-738-3211
Viking Machine & Design
De Pere, WI 888-286-2116
Vollrath Company
Sheboygan, WI 920-457-4851
Vulcan Industries
Moody, AL 888-444-4417
Vulcanium Metals International, LLC
Northbrook, IL 888-922-0040
W.J. Egli Company
Alliance, OH 330-823-3666
Wahlstrom Manufacturing
Fontana, CA 909-822-4677
Walco Stainless
Utica, NY 800-879-2526
Walker Stainless Equipment
New Lisbon, WI 800-356-5734
Waukesha Foundry
Waukesha, WI 262-542-0741
Waukesha Specialty Company
Darien, WI 262-724-3700
Wayne Industries
Clanton, AL 800-225-3148
Weavewood, Inc.
Golden Valley, MN 800-367-6460
Weiss Sheet Metal
Avon, MA 508-583-8300
Wemas Metal Products
Calgary, AB 403-276-4451
Wendell August Forge
Grove City, PA 800-923-1390
West Star Industries
Stockton, CA 800-326-2288
Western Pacific Storage Systems
San Dimas, CA 800-888-5707
Western Plastics
Calhoun, GA 800-752-4106
Westfield Sheet Metal Works
Kenilworth, NJ 908-276-5500
Wheel Tough Company
Terre Haute, IN 888-765-8833
White Cap
Downers Grove, IL 800-515-1565
White Rabbit Dye Company
Saint Louis, MO 800-466-6588
Whiting & Davis
Attleboro Falls, MA 800-876-6374
Wilder Manufacturing Company
Port Jervis, NY 800-832-1319

Williamsburg Metal Spinning & Stamping Corporation
Brooklyn, NY 888-535-5402
Winmark Stamp & Sign
Salt Lake City, UT 800-438-0480
Winston Industries
Louisville, KY 800-234-5286
Wire Belt Company of America
Londonderry, NH 603-644-2500
Wire Products Corporation
Greensboro, NC 800-334-0807
Wirefab
Worcester, MA 877-877-4445
Wiremaid Products
Coral Springs, FL 800-770-4700
Witt Industries
Mason, OH 800-543-7417
Woerner Wire Works
Omaha, NE 402-451-5414
Woodard
Coppell, TX 800-877-2290
Yargus Manufacturing
Marshall, IL 217-826-6352
Yates Industries
Saint Clair Shores, MI 586-778-7680
YW Yacht Basin
Easton, MD 410-822-0414
Zelco Industries
Mount Vernon, NY 800-431-2486
Zol-Mark Industries
Winnipeg, NB 204-943-7393

Turn Key

Stahlman Group
New London, NH 866-526-2585

Consultants

Austin Company
Cleveland, OH 440-544-2600
BKI
Oakland, CA 510-444-8707
Boldt Company
Appleton, WI 920-739-6321
Burdock Group
Orlando, FL 407-802-1400
Consulting Nutritional Services
Calabasas, CA 818-880-6774
Cretel Food Equipment
Holland, MI 616-786-3980
Excel-A-Tec
Brookfield, WI 262-252-3600
Murray Runin
Mahwah, NJ 201-512-3885
Serti Information Solution
Montreal, QC 800-361-6615
Shambaugh & Son
Fort Wayne, IN 260-487-7777

Design

A&B Process Systems
Stratford, WI 888-258-2789
AAMD
Liverpool, NY 800-887-4167
Accommodation Program
New York, NY 800-929-1414
Aidi International Hotels of America
Washington, DC 202-331-9299
Aldo Locascio
Tucson, AZ 800-488-8729
ALPI Food Preparation Equipment
Bolton, ON 800-928-2574
ALY Group of New York
Pleasantville, NY 914-747-0052
American Agribusiness Assistance
Alexandria, VA 202-429-0500
American Handling
Cleveland, OH 800-482-5801
American Systems Associates
Hampton Bays, NY 800-584-3663
Anhydro Inc
Olympia Fields, IL 708-747-7000
APA
Omaha, NE 402-905-2696
Architectural Products
Highland, NY 845-691-8500
Art-Tech Restaurant Design
Lynbrook, NY 516-593-7787
Aseptic Resources
Overland Park, KS 913-897-4125
Aspect Engineering
Westerville, OH 614-638-7106

Asset Design LLC
Mooresville, NC 888-293-1740
AWB Engineers
Salisbury, MD 410-742-7299
B-T Engineering
Bala Cynwyd, PA 610-664-9500
Baker Group
Grand Rapids, MI 800-968-4011
Bargreen-Ellingson
Tacoma, WA 800-322-4441
Barry-Wehmiller Design Group
Saint Louis, MO 314-862-8000
Basic Leasing Corporation
Kearny, NJ 973-817-7373
BEC International
Louisville, KY 877-232-4687
Best Restaurant Equipment & Design
Columbus, OH 800-837-2378
Big-D Construction Corporation
Salt Lake City, UT 800-748-4481
Bintz Restaurant Supply Company
Salt Lake City, UT 800-443-4746
Birmingham Restaurant Supply
Birmingham, AL 205-252-0076
Brevard Restaurant Equipment
Cocoa, FL 321-636-7750
Brown/Millunzi & Associates
Houston, TX 800-460-3387
Cadence Technologies
Alpharetta, GA 800-667-6250
Carmona Designs
Chula Vista, CA 619-425-2800
Center for Packaging Education
Somers, NY 914-276-0425
CH2M Hill
Englewood, CO 303-771-0900
CHL Systems
Souderton, PA 215-723-7284
Chroust Associates International
Woodland Hills, CA 818-348-1438
CII Food Service Design
Lapeer, MI 810-667-3100
Citra-Tech
Lakeland, FL 863-646-3868
Clevenger Frable LaVallee
White Plains, NY 914-997-9660
Coastal Mechanical Services
Stamford, CT 203-359-3070
Cober Electronics, Inc.
Norwalk, CT 800-709-5948
Concepts & Design International, Ltd
West Nyack, NY 845-358-1558
Container-Quinn Testing Laboratories
Wheeling, IL 847-537-9470
Cooper Decoration Company
Weston, MA 315-475-1661
Crepas & Associates
Elmhurst, IL 630-833-4880
Curtis Restaurant Equipment
Springfield, OR 541-746-7480
D'Addario Design Associates
New York, NY 212-302-0059
DCS IPAL Consultants
Laval, QC 450-973-3338
DECI Corporation
Burgettstown, PA 724-947-3300
Dembling & Dembling Architects
Albany, NY 518-463-8066
Dennis Group
Springfield, MA 413-787-1785
Design Group Inc
Clearwater, FL 727-441-2825
Diamond & Lappin
Fair Lawn, NJ 877-527-7461
Digital Image & Sound Corporation
Rochester, NY 585-381-0410
Display Specialties
Wilder, KY 800-545-9362
Don Walters Company
Stanton, CA 714-892-0275
Donalds & Associates
Long Beach, CA 562-290-8440
Eagle-Concordia Paper Corporation
Farmingdale, NY 212-255-3860
Encompass Ind./Merch Services of Texas
Grand Prairie, TX 800-299-4824
Fabricon Products
River Rouge, MI 313-841-8200
Fenster Consulting
Port Washington, NY 516-944-7108
First Bank of Highland P
Northbrook, IL 847-272-1300

Fleet Wood Goldco Wyard
Cockeysville, MD 410-785-1934
FMB Company
Broken Bow, OK 580-513-5309
Food & Agrosystems
Sunnyvale, CA 408-245-8450
Food Industry ConsultingGroup
Dunnellon, FL 800-443-5820
Food Technologies
Golden Valley, MN 763-544-8586
Foodpro International
San Jose, CA 408-227-2332
Foodservice Design Associates
Orlando, FL 407-896-4115
Foster-Miller
Waltham, MA 781-890-3200
Foth & Van Dyke
Green Bay, WI 920-497-2500
Graphic Impressions of Illinois
River Grove, IL 708-453-1100
Group One
South Boston, MA 617-268-7000
H&H Metal Fabrications
Belden, MS 662-489-4626
Hampton-Tilley Associates
Chesterfield, MO 636-537-3353
Hanson Lab Furniture
Newbury Park, CA 805-498-3121
Hunter Graphics
Umatilla, FL 407-644-2060
Hy-Ten Plastics
Milford, NH 603-673-1611
Industrial Consortium
Sulphur Springs, TX 903-885-6610
Inman Foodservices Group
Nashville, TN 615-321-5591
Innovations by Design
Chadds Ford, PA 610-558-0160
Innovative Space Management
Woodside, NY 718-278-4300
Intelplex
Olivette, MO 314-983-9996
Interbrand Corporation
San Francisco, CA 877-692-7263
IPG International Packaging Group
Agoura Hills, CA 818-865-1428
Item Products
Houston, TX 800-333-4932
J/W Design Associates
San Francisco, CA 415-546-7707
Janows Design Associates
Lincolnwood, IL 847-763-0620
Jel-Sert Company
West Chicago, IL 800-323-2592
Jenike & Johanson
Tyngsboro, MA 978-649-3300
Joul, Engineering StaffiSolutions
Edison, NJ 877-494-8835
Kochman Consultants Limited
Morton Grove, IL 847-470-1195
Kohlenberger Associates Consulting Engineering
Fullerton, CA 714-738-7733
Landmark Kitchen Design
Phoenix, AZ 866-621-3192
Laschober & Sovich
Woodland Hills, CA 818-713-9011
Legge & Associates
Rockwood, ON 519-856-0444
Lobsters Alive Company
Johnsburg, IL 708-562-7837
Lockwood Greene Engineers
Knoxville, TN 251-476-2400
Lockwood Greene Engineers
Knoxville, TN 256-533-9907
Lockwood Greene Engineers
Brentwood, TN 615-221-5031
Lockwood Greene Engineers
Augusta, GA 706-724-8225
Lockwood Greene Engineers
Somerset, NJ 732-560-5700
Lockwood Greene Engineers
Atlanta, GA 770-829-6500
Lockwood Greene Engineers
Guaynabo, PR 787-781-9050
Lockwood Greene Engineers
Knoxville, TN 865-218-5377
Lockwood Greene Engineers
Pooler, GA 912-330-3000
Lockwood Greene Engineers
Dallas, TX 972-991-5505
Lockwood Greene Technologies
Augusta, GA 505-889-3831

Lorrich & Associates
San Diego, CA 858-586-0823
Management Insight
Malborough, MA 508-485-2100
Material Systems Engineering
Stilesville, IN 800-634-0904
McNichols Conveyor Company
Southfield, MI 800-331-1926
Mead & Hunt
Madison, WI 888-364-7272
Metcalf & Eddy
Wakefield, MA 781-246-5200
Michael Blackman & Associates
Santa Monica, CA 800-889-4925
Moseley Corporation
Franklin, MA 800-667-3539
Nicosia Creative Expresso
New York, NY 212-515-6600
Nimbus Water Systems
Murrieta, CA 800-451-9343
Nina Mauritz Design Service
Libertyville, IL 847-968-4438
Northeast Box Company
Ashtabula, OH 800-362-8100
Nutrinfo Corporation
Watertown, MA 800-676-6686
O.B.S. Trading
Jackson, MO 573-243-6999
Omega Company
Stamford, CT 800-848-4286
Ottenheimer Equipment Company
Lutherville Timonium, MD 410-597-9700
PacTech Engineering
Cincinnati, OH 513-792-1090
Patrick E. Panzarello Consulting Services
Sunland, CA 818-353-0431
Pharmaceutical & Food Special
San Jose, CA 408-275-0161
Phoenix & Eclectic Network
Elmhurst, IL 630-530-4373
Premier Restaurant Equipment
Minneapolis, MN 763-544-8800
Product Solutions
Wilkes Barre, PA 888-776-3765
R.C. Keller & Associates
Barnegat, NJ 973-694-8810
Raque Food Systems
Louisville, KY 502-267-9641
Raytheon Company
Waltham, MA 617-522-3000
RGN Developers
New Providence, NJ
RMF Steel Products
Grandview, MO 816-765-4101
Robert C. Vincek Design Associates LLC
Sussex, NJ 973-702-8553
Robinett & Associates
Richardson, TX 972-234-1945
ROI Software, LLC
Knoxville, TN 865-522-2211
Ron Vallort & Associates
Oak Brook, IL 630-734-3821
SBS of Financial Industries
Washington, NJ 908-689-5520
Schroeder Sewing Technologies
San Marcos, CA 760-591-9733
Seattle Menu Specialists
Kent, WA 800-622-2826
Seiberling Associates
Beloit, WI 608-313-1235
Setter, Leach & Lindstrom
Minneapolis, MN 612-338-8741
Shook Design Group
Charlotte, NC 704-377-0661
Southern Store Fixtures
Bessemer, AL 800-552-6283
Sprinkman Corporation
Franksville, WI 800-816-1610
SSOE Group
Toledo, OH 419-255-3830
St Onge Ruff & Associates
Kansas City, MO 800-800-5261
Stahlman Group
New London, NH 866-526-2585
Stokes Material HandlingSystems
Doylestown, PA 215-340-2200
Stratecon International Consultants
Winston Salem, NC 336-768-6808
Sverdrup Facilities
Saint Louis, MO 800-325-7910
T.E. Ibberson Company
Hopkins, MN 952-938-7007

TDF Automation
Cedar Falls, IA 800-553-1777
Tecton/Divercon
Omaha, NE 402-571-5115
Tetra Pak
Vernon Hills, IL 800-358-3872
Tuchenhagen
Columbia, MD 410-910-6000
Twenty First Century Design
Albany, NY 518-446-0939
UAA
Chicago, IL 800-813-1711
United Industries Group
Newport Beach, CA 949-759-3200
US Magnetix
Golden Valley, MN 800- 3-0
Washington Group International
Birmingham, AL 800-877-0980
Wayne Combustion Systems
Fort Wayne, IN 260-425-9200
Webber/Smith Associates
Lancaster, PA 800-231-0392
Wesley-Kind Associates
Mineola, NY 516-747-3434
Westfield Sheet Metal Works
Kenilworth, NJ 908-276-5500
Wyssmont Company
Fort Lee, NJ 201-947-4600

Food Technology

A&L Western Ag Lab
Modesto, CA 209-529-4080
ABIC International Consultant
Fairfield, NJ 973-227-7060
ADD Testing & Research
Valley Stream, NY 516-568-9197
AgriTech
Columbus, OH 614-488-2772
AM Test Laboratories
Kirkland, WA 425-885-1664
American Style Foods
Old Hickory, TN 615-847-0410
Ameritech Laboratories
Flushing, NY 718-461-0475
Anresco
San Francisco, CA 800-359-0920
Arthur D Little Inc.
Boston, MA 617-532-9550
ASI Food Safety Consultants
Saint Louis, MO 800-477-0778
Aspect Engineering
Westerville, OH 614-638-7106
Aspen Research Corporation
White Bear Lake, MN 651-773-7961
Bedrosian & Associates
Redwood City, CA 650-367-0259
Bernard Wolnak & Associates
Northbrook, IL 847-480-0427
BFB Consultants
Mississauga, ON 905-819-9856
Bioenergetics
Madison, WI 608-255-4028
Biovail Technologies
Chantilly, VA 703-995-2400
Brand Specialists
Duncanville, TX 888-323-3708
Broadmoor Baker
Seattle, WA 206-624-3660
Cardinal Kitchens
Louisville, KY 800-928-0832
Chaska Chocolate
Chaska, MN 952-448-5699
Codema
Maple Grove, MN 763-428-2266
Conatech Consulting Group, Inc
Saint Louis, MO 314-995-9767
Concepts & Design International, Ltd
West Nyack, NY 845-358-1558
Culinar
Montreal, QC 514-255-2811
Cynter Con Technology Adviser
Gaithersburg, MD 800-287-1811
Cyntergy Corporation
Rockville, MD 800-825-5787
Damon Industries
Alliance, OH 800-362-9850
Deibel Laboratories
Madison, WI 847-329-9900
Dow Chemical Company
Spring House, PA 800-447-4369
Eastern Regional Research Center
Wyndmoor, PA 215-233-6595
ELISA Technologies
Gainesville, FL 352-337-3929
EPL Technologies
Philadelphia, PA 800-637-3743
ESA
Chelmsford, MA 978-250-7000
Food & Agrosystems
Sunnyvale, CA 408-245-8450
Food & Beverage Consultants
Cranston, RI 401-463-5784
Food Consulting Company
Del Mar, CA 800-793-2844
Food Development Centre
Portage La Prairie, NB 800-870-1044
Food Industry ConsultingGroup
Dunnellon, FL 800-443-5820
Food Quality Lab
Lake Oswego, OR 800-977-3636
Food Science Associates
Crugers, NY 914-739-7541
Food Science Consulting
Walnut Creek, CA 925-947-6785
Food Technologies
Golden Valley, MN 763-544-8586
Food-Tek
Whippany, NJ 800-648-8114
Foods Research Laboratories
Boston, MA 617-442-3322
Future Foods
Chicago, IL 312-987-9342
George G. Giddings
Randolph, NJ 973-361-4687
George Lapgley Enterpri ses
Pipersville, PA 267-221-2426
Healthy Dining
San Diego, CA 800-266-2049
Industrial Laboratories
Wheat Ridge, CO 800-456-5288
Ingman Laboratories
Minneapolis, MN 612-724-0121
Innovative Food Solutions LLC
Columbus, OH 800-884-3314
Inter-Access
Etobicoke, ON 514-744-6262
International ProcessingCorporation
Winchester, KY 859-745-2200
J.L. Analytical Services
Modesto, CA 209-538-8111
J.Leek Associates
Edenton, NC 252-482-4456
James V. Hurson Associates
Arlington, VA 800-642-6564
Jonessco Enterprises
Plano, TX 972-985-7961
Kashrus Technical Consultants
Lakewood, NJ 732-364-8046
Kelley Advisory Services
Northbrook, IL 847-412-9234
KOF-K Kosher Supervision
Teaneck, NJ 201-837-0500
Landmark Kitchen Design
Phoenix, AZ 866-621-3192
Lawrence-Allen Group
San Mateo, CA 800-609-2909
Lebensmittel Consulting
Fostoria, OH 419-435-2774
Libra Technical Center
Metuchen, NJ 732-321-5487
Line of Snacks Consultants
Dallas, TX 972-484-1155
M-Tech & Associates
Downers Grove, IL 630-810-9714
Malcolm Stogo Associates
Scarsdale, NY 914-472-7255
Matrix Group Inc
Bloomfield, NJ 973-338-5638
MC Creation
San Francisco, CA 415-775-1135
Merlin Development, Inc
Plymouth, MN 763-475-0224
Micro-Chem Laboratory
Mississauga, ON 905-795-0490
Microwave Research Center
Eagan, MN 651-456-9190
Midwest Laboratories
Omaha, NE 402-334-7770
Miles Willard Technologies
Idaho Falls, ID 208-523-4741
Milligan & Higgins
Johnstown, NY 518-762-4638
Minnesota Valley TestingLaboratories
New Ulm, MN 800-782-3557
National Food Laboratory
Livermore, CA 925-551-4209
Natural Marketing Institute
Harleysville, PA 215-513-7300
NorCrest Consulting
Divide, CO 719-687-7635
Northeast Laboratory Services
Waterville, ME 866-591-7120
Northland Laboratories
Northbrook, IL 800-366-3522
Northwest Laboratories of Seattle
Seattle, WA 206-763-6252
Nutrinfo Corporation
Watertown, MA 800-676-6686
Nutrition Network
Irvine, CA 949-753-7998
Nutrition Research
Livingston, MT 406-686-4915
O.B.S. Trading
Jackson, MO 573-243-6999
Oklabs
Oklahoma City, OK 405-843-6832
Omega Company
Stamford, CT 800-848-4286
Petal
New York, NY 212-947-3662
Peter Kalustian Associates
Boonton, NJ 973-334-3008
POS Pilot Plant Corporation
Saskatoon, SK 800-230-2751
Positive Employment Practice
New City, NY 845-638-6442
Power Packaging, Inc.
Westerville, OH 877-272-1054
Protein Research Associates
Livermore, CA 800-948-1991
PSI
Oakbrook Terrace, IL 817-640-4162
Q Laboratories
Cincinnati, OH 513-471-1300
Quality Bakers of America
Allentown, PA 973-263-6970
R F Schiffmann Associates
New York, NY 212-362-7021
Riceselect
Alvin, TX 800-993-7423
Richardson Researches
South San Francisco, CA 650-589-5764
Robin Shepherd Group
Jacksonville, FL 888-447-2823
S-F Analytical Labs
New Berlin, WI 800-300-6700
Schiff & Company
West Caldwell, NJ 973-227-1830
Schroeder Sewing Technologies
San Marcos, CA 760-591-9733
Sensory Spectrum
New Providence, NJ 908-376-7000
Sentinel Lubricants Corporation
Miami, FL 800-842-6400
Shear Kershman Laboratories
Chesterfield, MO 636-519-8900
Simon S. Jackel Plymouth
Tarpon Springs, FL 727-942-3991
Solganik & Associates
Dayton, OH 800-253-8512
Southern Testing & Research Labs
Wilson, NC 252-237-4175
Soyatech
Bar Harbor, ME 800-424-7692
SoyNut Butter Company
Glenview, IL 800-288-1012
Spencer Research
Columbus, OH 800-488-3242
SSOE Group
Toledo, OH 419-255-3830
Stratecon International Consultants
Winston Salem, NC 336-768-6808
The Phytopia Garden
Dallas, TX 888-750-9336
Thomas J. Payne Market Development
San Mateo, CA 650-340-8311
Tiax LLC
Lexington, MA 800-677-3000
Trans-Chemco
Bristol, WI 800-880-2498
Volumetric Technologies
Cannon Falls, MN 507-263-0034
Warren Analytical Laboratory
Greeley, CO 800-945-6669

Wilhelmsen Consulting
Milpitas, CA . . . 408-946-4525

XL Corporate & Research Services
New York, NY . . . 800-221-2972

Yaloom Marketing Corporation
South Hackensack, NJ . . . 201-488-3535

Kosher Food

KOF-K Kosher Supervision
Teaneck, NJ. . . 201-837-0500

Orthodox Union
New York, NY . . . 212-563-4000

Star-K Kosher Certification
Baltimore, MD . . . 410-484-4110

Marketing & Promotion

ABIC International Consultant
Fairfield, NJ . . . 973-227-7060

AgriTech
Columbus, OH . . . 614-488-2772

Aidi International Hotels of America
Washington, DC . . . 202-331-9299

Alpert/Siegel & Associates
Los Angeles, CA. . . 310-571-0777

American Agribusiness Assistance
Alexandria, VA . . . 202-429-0500

Arthur D Little Inc.
Boston, MA. . . 617-532-9550

Axces Systems
Westbury, NY . . . 800-355-3534

BFB Consultants
Mississauga, ON. . . 905-819-9856

Broadmoor Baker
Seattle, WA . . . 206-624-3660

California Canning PeachAssociation
Sacramento, CA . . . 916-925-9131

Cannon Equipment Company
Rosemount, MN . . . 800-825-8501

Chain Restaurant Resolutions
Toronto, ON . . . 416-934-4334

Coffee Enterprises
Burlington, VT . . . 800-375-3398

Colonial Marketing Associates
Freehold, NJ . . . 732-431-3419

Conatech Consulting Group, Inc
Saint Louis, MO . . . 314-995-9767

Concept Hospitality Group
Foster City, CA. . . 650-357-1224

Connecticut Culinary Institute
Farmington, CT. . . 860-677-7869

Container-Quinn Testing Laboratories
Wheeling, IL. . . 847-537-9470

Cooper Decoration Company
Weston, MA . . . 315-475-1661

Cycle Computer Consultants
Hicksville, NY . . . 516-733-1892

Dakota Valley Products, Inc.
Willow Lake, SD. . . 605-625-2526

Decision Analyst
Arlington, TX. . . 800-262-5974

DMG Financial
Denver, CO. . . 888-331-3882

Dover Hospitality Consulting
Etobicoke, ON . . . 416-622-9294

Edge Resources
Hopedale, MA. . . 888-849-0998

Engineering & ManagementConsultants
Franklin Lakes, NJ . . . 201-847-0748

Feedback Plus
Dallas, TX. . . 800-882-7467

First Bank of Highland P
Northbrook, IL . . . 847-272-1300

Food & Beverage Consultants
Cranston, RI . . . 401-463-5784

Food Business Associates
Temple, ME. . . 207-778-2251

Food Industry ConsultingGroup
Dunnellon, FL. . . 800-443-5820

Food Insights
Washington, DC . . . 202-296-6540

Food Science Consulting
Walnut Creek, CA. . . 925-947-6785

Food Technologies
Golden Valley, MN . . . 763-544-8586

Francorp
Olympia Fields, IL . . . 800-327-6244

Future Foods
Chicago, IL . . . 312-987-9342

Graphic Promotions
Topeka, KS . . . 785-234-6684

Grocery Products Distribution Services
Cedar Knolls, NJ. . . 973-538-1035

Groth International
Stafford, TX . . . 800-354-7684

HealthFocus
Atlanta, GA. . . 770-645-1999

Healthy Dining
San Diego, CA . . . 800-266-2049

Heart Smart International
Scottsdale, AZ. . . 800-762-7819

HMG Worldwide In-Store Marketing
New York, NY . . . 212-736-2300

InnaVision Global Marketing Consultants
Racine, WI . . . 262-633-1000

Inter-Access
Etobicoke, ON . . . 514-744-6262

Interbrand Corporation
San Francisco, CA . . . 877-692-7263

Interliance
Santa Ana, CA . . . 800-540-7917

IPG International Packaging Group
Agoura Hills, CA . . . 818-865-1428

J.R. Ralph Marketing Company
Syracuse, NY . . . 315-445-0255

JDG Consulting
Chicago, IL . . . 800-243-7037

Jel-Sert Company
West Chicago, IL . . . 800-323-2592

Jonesco Enterprises
Plano, TX . . . 972-985-7961

Kelley Advisory Services
Northbrook, IL . . . 847-412-9234

Kilcher Company
South Pasadena, FL . . . 727-367-5839

Landmark Kitchen Design
Phoenix, AZ . . . 866-621-3192

Line of Snacks Consultants
Dallas, TX. . . 972-484-1155

Lorrich & Associates
San Diego, CA . . . 858-586-0823

Main Course Consultants
Skokie, IL . . . 847-869-7633

Malcolm Stogo Associates
Scarsdale, NY. . . 914-472-7255

Management Insight
Malborough, MA . . . 508-485-2100

Marketing Management
Fort Worth, TX. . . 800-433-2004

Mastio & Company
Saint Joseph, MO . . . 816-364-6200

Maui Wowi Fresh Hawaiin Blends
Greenwood Village, CO . . . 877-849-6992

MC Creation
San Francisco, CA . . . 415-775-1135

Mic-Ellen Associates
Collegeville, PA . . . 800-872-1252

Michigan Agricultural Cooperative Marketing Association
Lansing, MI. . . 800-824-3779

Minnesuing Acres
Lake Nebagamon, WI. . . 715-374-2262

Monterey Bay Food Group
Aptos, CA. . . 831-685-8600

Murray Runin
Mahwah, NJ . . . 201-512-3885

National Food Laboratory
Livermore, CA . . . 925-551-4209

National Food Product Research Corporation
West Newbury, MA. . . 800-363-2144

Natural Marketing Institute
Harleysville, PA . . . 215-513-7300

Nicholas Marketing Associates
Bogota, NJ . . . 201-343-9414

Nicosia Creative Expresso
New York, NY . . . 212-515-6600

Northland Consultants
Sault Ste. Marie, ON. . . 705-541-8490

Nutrinfo Corporation
Watertown, MA. . . 800-676-6686

Partners International
Hanover, NH. . . 603-643-8574

Pearson Research
Santa Cruz, CA. . . 831-429-9797

Peter Kalustian Associates
Boonton, NJ . . . 973-334-3008

Pioneer Marketing International
Los Gatos, CA. . . 408-356-4990

Positive Employment Practice
New City, NY . . . 845-638-6442

Premier Restaurant Equipment
Minneapolis, MN . . . 763-544-8800

Pro Media
Menomonee Falls, WI. . . 800-328-0439

Putnam Group
Trumbull, CT . . . 203-452-7270

Quality Bakers of America
Allentown, PA. . . 973-263-6970

R-TECH Laboratories
Saint Paul, MN . . . 800-328-9687

Radiant Systems
Pleasanton, CA . . . 800-767-4554

Restaurant Development Services
Bethesda, MD . . . 301-263-0400

Restaurant Partners
Orlando, FL. . . 407-839-5070

Robert C. Vincek Design Associates LLC
Sussex, NJ. . . 973-702-8553

Robin Shepherd Group
Jacksonville, FL . . . 888-447-2823

RQA
Orland Park, IL . . . 708-364-7060

Sales Building Systems
Mentor, OH. . . 800-435-7576

Sensors Quality Management
Toronto, ON . . . 800-866-2624

Simonson Group
Winchester, MA . . . 781-729-8906

Solganik & Associates
Dayton, OH. . . 800-253-8512

Sorensen Associates
Troutdale, OR . . . 800-542-4321

Source Distribution Logistics
Batavia, IL. . . 630-761-1231

SoyNut Butter Company
Glenview, IL . . . 800-288-1012

Specialty Cheese Group Limited
New York, NY . . . 212-243-7274

Stewart Marketing Services
Kirkland, WA . . . 425-889-2455

Stratecon
Winston Salem, NC. . . 336-768-6808

Stratecon International Consultants
Winston Salem, NC. . . 336-768-6808

Superior Product Pickup Services
Niles, IL . . . 847-647-4720

Supermarket Associates
Durham, NC . . . 919-493-0994

Swander Pace & Company
San Francisco, CA . . . 415-477-8500

Tara Communications
Dunedin, FL . . . 303-417-9602

Technomic
Chicago, IL . . . 312-876-0004

Thomas J. Payne Market Development
San Mateo, CA . . . 650-340-8311

Tiax LLC
Lexington, MA . . . 800-677-3000

TLC & Associates
Amarillo, TX. . . 806-353-1517

Tourtellot & Company
Providence, RI . . . 401-331-2385

Tragon Corporation
Redwood Shores, CA . . . 800-841-1177

US Magnetix
Golden Valley, MN . . . 800- 3-0

Vegetarian Resource Group
Baltimore, MD . . . 410-366-8343

Vine Solutions
Corte Madera, CA. . . 415-927-3308

W.A. Golomski & Associates
Algoma, WI. . . 920-487-9864

Yaloom Marketing Corporation
South Hackensack, NJ . . . 201-488-3535

Material Handling

California Vibratory Feeders
Anaheim, CA . . . 800-354-0972

Jel-Sert Company
West Chicago, IL . . . 800-323-2592

Kleenline Corporation
Newburyport, MA. . . 800-259-5973

Polyair
Toronto, ON . . . 888-765-9847

Packaging

BFB Consultants
Mississauga, ON. . . 905-819-9856

Conatech Consulting Group, Inc
Saint Louis, MO . . . 314-995-9767

DCS IPAL Consultants
Laval, QC . . . 450-973-3338

Food Development Centre
Portage La Prairie, NB 800-870-1044
Interbrand Corporation
San Francisco, CA 877-692-7263
Jel-Sert Company
West Chicago, IL 800-323-2592
Landmark Kitchen Design
Phoenix, AZ 866-621-3192
Pater & Associates
Cincinnati, OH 513- 24- 215
R F Schiffmann Associates
New York, NY 212-362-7021
R.C. Keller & Associates
Barnegat, NJ 973-694-8810
Raque Food Systems
Louisville, KY 502-267-9641
Schroeder Sewing Technologies
San Marcos, CA 760-591-9733
Stratecon International Consultants
Winston Salem, NC. 336-768-6808

Restaurant Design

Top Source Industries
Addison, IL 800-362-9625

Sanitation, Testing & Analysis

A&B Process Systems
Stratford, WI 888-258-2789
A&L Western Ag Lab
Modesto, CA. 209-529-4080
Accra Laboratory
Cleveland, OH 800-567-7200
Accu-Labs Research
Golden, CO 303-277-9514
Accu-Ray Inspection Services
Elmhurst, IL 800-378-1226
ADD Testing & Research
Valley Stream, NY 516-568-9197
Advanced Ergonomics
Frisco, TX. 800-682-0169
AgriTech
Columbus, OH 614-488-2772
Airflow Sciences Corporation
Livonia, MI. 734-525-0300
AM Test Laboratories
Kirkland, WA 425-885-1664
American Services Group
Memphis, TN 800-333-6678
Ameritech Laboratories
Flushing, NY. 718-461-0475
Analytical Labs
Boise, ID. 800-574-5773
Anresco
San Francisco, CA 800-359-0920
Applied Technologies Inc
Brookfield, WI 262-784-7690
Arthur D Little Inc.
Boston, MA. 617-532-9550
ASI Food Safety Consultants
Saint Louis, MO 800-477-0778
Aspect Engineering
Westerville, OH. 614-638-7106
Barrow-Agee Laboratories
Memphis, TN 901-332-1590
BCN Research Laboratories
Rockford, TN 800-236-0505
Betz Entec
Horsham, PA. 800-877-1940
Biological Services
Kansas City, MO. 913-236-6868
Bjorksten Research Laboratories
Northbrook, IL 847-714-9662
Brown & Caldwell
Walnut Creek, CA. 800-727-2224
Cal Western Pest Control
Arcadia, CA 800-326-2847
Cardinal Kitchens
Louisville, KY 800-928-0832
Celsis Laboratory Group
Chicago, IL 800-222-8260
Chilton Consulting Group
Rocky Face, GA 706-694-8325
Conam Inspection
Glendale Heights, IL. 630-681-0008
Container Testing Lab
Mamaroneck, NY 800-221-5170
Container-Quinn Testing Laboratories
Wheeling, IL. 847-537-9470
Covance Laboratories
Princeton, NJ. 609-452-4440
Covance Laboratories Inc.
Madison, WI 608-241-4471
Cynter Con Technology Adviser
Gaithersburg, MD. 800-287-1811
Cyntergy Corporation
Rockville, MD 800-825-5787
Dalare Associates
Philadelphia, PA 215-567-1953
Deibel Laboratories
Madison, WI 847-329-9900
DFL Laboratories
Chicago, IL 312-938-5151
Engineering & ManagementConsultants
Franklin Lakes, NJ 201-847-0748
Enviro-Test/Perry Laboratories
Woodridge, IL. 630-324-6685
Environmental Consultants
Clarksville, IN. 812-282-8481
Environmental Systems Service
Culpeper, VA. 800-541-2116
ESA
Chelmsford, MA 978-250-7000
Eurofins Scientific
Des Moines, IA 800-841-1110
Fettig Laboratories
Grand Rapids, MI 616-245-3000
Food & Beverage Consultants
Cranston, RI 401-463-5784
Food Consulting Company
Del Mar, CA 800-793-2844
Food Development Centre
Portage La Prairie, NB 800-870-1044
Food Industry ConsultingGroup
Dunnellon, FL. 800-443-5820
Food Quality Lab
Lake Oswego, OR. 800-977-3636
Food Sanitation Consultant Service
New York, NY 212-732-9540
Foodpro International
San Jose, CA. 408-227-2332
Foods Research Laboratories
Boston, MA. 617-442-3322
Foodworks
La Grange, KY 502-222-0135
Galbraith Laboratories
Knoxville, TN. 877-449-8797
Gaynes Labs
Bridgeview, IL 708-233-6655
Gems Sensors
Plainville, CT 860-747-3000
Genysis Nutritional Labs
Salt Lake City, UT 801-973-8824
George Lapgley Enterpri ses
Pipersville, PA. 267-221-2426
Gilbert Insect Light Traps
Jonesboro, AR. 800-643-0400
Great Lakes Scientific
Stevensville, MI 269-429-1000
Hahn Laboratories
Columbia, SC 803-799-1614
Harold Wainess & Associates
Arlington Heights, IL 847-722-8744
Industrial Laboratories
Wheat Ridge, CO 800-456-5288
Ingman Laboratories
Minneapolis, MN 612-724-0121
Innovative Food Solutions LLC
Columbus, OH 800-884-3314
Insect-O-Cutor
Stone Mountain, GA. 800-988-5359
International Approval Services
Cleveland, OH 877-235-9791
ITS/ETL Testing Laboratories
Laguna Niguel, CA. 949-448-4100
J.L. Analytical Services
Modesto, CA. 209-538-8111
J.Leek Associates
Edenton, NC 252-482-4456
Judith Quick & Associates
Hancock, MD 301-678-5737
Krueger Food Laboratories
Chelmsford, MA. 978-256-1220
Labelmax
Laredo, TX 956-722-6493
Lancaster Laboratories
Lancaster, PA 717-656-2300
Landmark Kitchen Design
Phoenix, AZ 866-621-3192
Laucks' Testing Laboratories
Seattle, WA. 206-767-5060
Lawrence-Allen Group
San Mateo, CA 800-609-2909
Lebensmittel Consulting
Fostoria, OH. 419-435-2774
Libra Technical Center
Metuchen, NJ 732-321-5487
M-Tech & Associates
Downers Grove, IL. 630-810-9714
Main Course Consultants
Skokie, IL 847-869-7633
McCrone Associates
Westmont, IL. 630-887-7100
Medallion Laboratories
Minneapolis, MN 800-245-5615
Metcalf & Eddy
Wakefield, MA 781-246-5200
Microbac Laboratories
Pittsburgh, PA. 412-459-1060
Microbac Laboratories
Worcester, MA 866-515-4668
Midwest Laboratories
Omaha, NE 402-334-7770
Midwest Labs
Omaha, NE 402-334-7770
Miles Willard Technologies
Idaho Falls, ID 208-523-4741
Milligan & Higgins
Johnstown, NY 518-762-4638
Minnesota Valley TestingLaboratories
New Ulm, MN. 800-782-3557
Monarch Analytical Laboratories
Maumee, OH. 419-897-9000
Nelson Company
Baltimore, MD 410-477-3000
Nimbus Water Systems
Murrieta, CA. 800-451-9343
Northeast Laboratory Services
Waterville, ME 866-591-7120
Northland Laboratories
Northbrook, IL 800-366-3522
Northview Laboratories
Spartanburg, SC 864-574-7728
Northview Pacific Laboratories
Hercules, CA. 510-741-3744
Nutrinfo Corporation
Watertown, MA. 800-676-6686
O.D. Kurtz Associates
Palm Bay, FL. 321-723-0135
Oerlikon Balzers
Elgin, IL 847-695-5200
Oklabs
Oklahoma City, OK 405-843-6832
Optipure
Plano, TX 972-422-1212
Orthodox Union
New York, NY 212-563-4000
Pearson Research
Santa Cruz, CA. 831-429-9797
POS Pilot Plant Corporation
Saskatoon, SK. 800-230-2751
PSI
Oakbrook Terrace, IL 817-640-4162
Q Laboratories
Cincinnati, OH 513-471-1300
QC
Southampton, PA 215-355-3900
Quest
San Clemente, CA. 949-643-1333
R.C. Keller & Associates
Barnegat, NJ 973-694-8810
Richardson Researches
South San Francisco, CA 650-589-5764
Ron Vallort & Associates
Oak Brook, IL. 630-734-3821
RQA
Orland Park, IL. 708-364-7060
RTI Laboratories Inc
Livonia, MI 734-422-8000
S-F Analytical Labs
New Berlin, WI. 800-300-6700
San Diego Health & Nutrition
Bonita, CA 619-470-3345
Sani-Pure Food Laboratories
Saddle Brook, NJ 201-843-2525
Schiff & Company
West Caldwell, NJ. 973-227-1830
Sensory Spectrum
New Providence, NJ 908-376-7000
SERCO Laboratories
St. Anthony, MN. 800-388-7173
Sheahan Sanitation Consulting
Oakley, CA. 800-554-4243
Shear Kershman Laboratories
Chesterfield, MO 636-519-8900

Shepard Brothers
La Habra, CA 562-697-1366
Shuster Laboratories
Canton, MA 800-444-8705
Silliker Laboratories
Allentown, PA 312-938-5151
Silliker Laboratories
Columbus, OH 614-486-0150
Silliker Laboratories
Stone Mountain, GA 770-469-2701
Silliker, Inc
Chicago, IL 312-938-5151
Simon S. Jackel Plymouth
Tarpon Springs, FL 727-942-3991
Smith-Emery Company
Los Angeles, CA 213-745-5333
Southern Testing & Research Labs
Wilson, NC 252-237-4175
SoyNut Butter Company
Glenview, IL 800-288-1012
Spencer Research
Columbus, OH 800-488-3242
Statex
Montreal, QC 514-527-6039
Stay Tuned Industries
Clinton, NJ 908-730-8455
Steritech Food Safety & Environmental Hygiene
Charlotte, NC 800-868-0089
Strasburger & Siegel
Hanover, MD 888-726-3753
Stratecon International Consultants
Winston Salem, NC 336-768-6808
Structure Probe
West Chester, PA 800-242-4774
Suburban Laboratories
Hillside, IL 800-783-5227
TEI Analytical
Niles, IL 847-647-1345
The Phytopia Garden
Dallas, TX 888-750-9336
TLC & Associates
Amarillo, TX 806-353-1517
Total Quality Corporation
Branford, CT 800-453-9729
Tragon Corporation
Redwood Shores, CA 800-841-1177
Trap Zap Environmental Systems
Wyckoff, NJ 800-282-8727
Triad Scientific
Manasquan, NJ 800-867-6690
Truesdail Laboratories
Tustin, CA 714-730-6239
Tuchenhagen
Columbia, MD 410-910-6000
Underwriters Laboratories
Camas, WA 877-854-3577
Universal Sanitizers & Supplies
Knoxville, TN 888-634-3196
Vivolac Cultures
Greenfield, IN 800-848-6522
Warren Analytical Laboratory
Greeley, CO 800-945-6669
West Agro
Kansas City, MO 816-891-1600
Wilhelmsen Consulting
Milpitas, CA 408-946-4525
Winston Laboratories
Vernon Hills, IL 800-946-5229
Woodson-Tenent Laboratories
Des Moines, IA 515-265-1461
Woodson-Tenent Laboratories
Gainesville, GA 770-536-5909
Woodson-Tenent Laboratories
Dayton, OH 937-236-5756
X-Ray Industries
Troy, MI 800-973-4800

Contract Manufacturing

Bakery

Interbake Foods
Richmond, VA 804-755-7107
PacMoore
Hammond, IN 866-610-2666

Blending & Mixing

Albion Laboratories
Clearfield, UT 800-453-2406
American Fruit Processors
Pacoima, CA 818-899-9574
Jel-Sert Company
West Chicago, IL 800-323-2592
PacMoore
Hammond, IN 866-610-2666
Sweeteners Plus
Lakeville, NY 858-346-2318

Contract Packaging

A La Carte
Chicago, IL 800-722-2370
Aaron Thomas Company
Garden Grove, CA 800-394-4776
All American Seasonings
Denver, CO 303-623-2320
AmeriQual Foods
Evansville, IN 812-867-1444
Athea Laboratories
Milwaukee, WI 800-743-6417
Atlantic Quality Spice &Seasonings
New Brunswick, NJ 800-584-0422
Austin Packaging Company
Austin, MN 507-433-6623
Baldwin Richardson Foods
Frankfort, IL 866-644-2732
Baron Spice
St Louis, MO 314-535-9020
Blendco
Hattiesburg, MS 800-328-3687
Bloomer Candy Company
Zanesville, OH 740-452-7501
Carton Service
Shelby, OH 800-533-7744
Century Foods International
Sparta, WI 800-269-1901
Chem-Pack
Cincinnati, OH 800-421-2700
Cloud Corporation
Des Plaines, IL 847-390-9410
Cobitco, Inc
Denver, CO 303-296-8575
Compact Industries
St Charles, IL 800-513-4262
Conpac
Warminster, PA 215-322-2755
Contact Industries
Bronx, NY 908-351-5900
Contract Comestibles
East Troy, WI 262-642-9400
Crest Foods Company
Ashton, IL 877-273-7893
Crown Chemical Products
Mississauga, ON 905-564-0904
Cup Pac Contract PackageRs
South Beloit, IL 877-347-9725
Diamond Packaging
Rochester, NY 800-333-4079
Do-It Corporation
South Haven, MI 800-426-4822
Douglas Products & Packaging
Liberty, MO 800-223-3684
Flexpak Corporation
Phoenix, AZ 602-269-7648
General Methods Corporation
Peoria, IL 309-497-3344
General Packaging Service
Clifton, NJ 973-472-4900
GKI Foods
Brighton, MI 248-486-0055
Hamilton Soap & Oil Products
Paterson, NJ 973-225-1031
Hearthside Food Solutions LLC
Downers Grove, IL 630-967-3600
IFP
Faribault, MN 800-997-4437
Innovative Food Solutions LLC
Columbus, OH 800-884-3314
Inter-Pack Corporation
Monroe, MI 734-242-7755
Jel-Sert Company
West Chicago, IL 800-323-2592
Ketch
Wichita, KS 800-766-3777
KIK Custom Products
Concord, ON 800-479-6603
LaMonica Fine Foods
Millville, NJ 856-825-8111
Longhorn Packaging
San Antonio, TX 800-433-7974
LRM Packaging
South Hackensack, NJ 201-342-2530
Mallet & Company
Carnegie, PA 800-245-2757
Marietta Corporation
Cortland, NY 800-950-7772
Max Packaging Company
Attalla, AL 800-543-5369
McClancy Seasoning Company
Fort Mill, SC 800-843-1968
Mid-Atlantic Packaging
Dover, DE 800-284-1332
Milani Gourmet
Melrose Park, IL 800-333-0003
Modern Packaging
Duluth, GA 770-622-1500
New Horizon Foods
Union City, CA 510-489-8600
Pacific Harvest Products
Bellevue, WA 425-401-7990
Packaging Associates
Randolph, NJ 973-252-8890
Packaging Service Company
Pearland, TX 800-826-2949
PacMoore
Hammond, IN 866-610-2666
Paket Corporation
Chicago, IL 773-221-7300
Per Pak/Orlandi
Farmingdale, NY 631-756-0110
Plaze
Saint Clair, MO 800-986-9509
Pluto Corporation
French Lick, IN 812-936-9988
Power Group
St Charles, IL 630-587-3770
Power Packaging, Inc.
Westerville, OH 877-272-1054
Precision Foods
Saint Louis, MO 800-442-5242
ProAct, Inc.
Eagan, MN 877-245-0405
Q&B Foods
Irwindale, CA 626-334-8090
Rempak Industries
Fort Lee, NJ 201-585-9007
Riverside Industries
St Helens, OR 503-397-1922
Robert's Packaging
Des Plaines, IL 800-707-5070
SOPAKCO Foods
Mullins, SC 800-276-9678
Specialty Food America
Hopkinsville, KY 888-881-1633
Specialty Lubricants Corporation
Macedonia, OH 800-238-5823
Techform
Mount Airy, NC 336-789-2115
Threshold Rehabilitation Services
Reading, PA 610-777-7691
Todd's
Des Moines, IA 800-247-5363
Triple X Packaging Company
North Chicago, IL 847-689-2200
Truitt Brothers Inc
Salem, OR 800-547-8712
Unette Corporation
Randolph, NJ 973-328-6800
Vita Key Packaging
Riverside, CA 909-355-1023
Vitatech International
Tustin, CA 714-832-9700
W H Wildman Company
New Hampshire, OH 419-568-7531
WePackItAll
Duarte, CA 626-301-9214
West Penn Oil Company
Warren, PA 814-723-9000
Westvaco Corporation
Richmond, VA 804-233-9205
Whitlock Packaging Corporation
Fort Gibson, OK 918-478-4300

Dry Product

All American Seasonings
Denver, CO 303-623-2320
Jel-Sert Company
West Chicago, IL 800-323-2592
Magic Seasoning Blends
New Orleans, LA 800-457-2857
Mallet & Company
Carnegie, PA 800-245-2757

Liquid Product

Jel-Sert Company
West Chicago, IL 800-323-2592
LaMonica Fine Foods
Millville, NJ 856-825-8111
Mallet & Company
Carnegie, PA 800-245-2757

Custom Services

Blending

AC Legg
Calera, AL. 800-422-5344
All American Seasonings
Denver, CO 303-623-2320
American Casein Company (AMCO)
Burlington, NJ. 609-387-3130
ARRO Corporation
Hodgkins, IL 877-929-2776
Calhoun Bend Mill
Libuse, LA 800-519-6455
California Blending Corp
El Monte, CA 626-448-1918
Continental Custom Ingredients
Oakville, ON. 905-815-8158
Elite Spice
Jessup, MD 800-232-3531
Invensys APV Products
Houston, TX 713-329-1600
Jel-Sert Company
West Chicago, IL 800-323-2592
Mallet & Company
Carnegie, PA 800-245-2757
Milani Gourmet
Melrose Park, IL 800-333-0003
Popcorn Connection
North Hollywood, CA 800-852-2676
Shashi Foods
Toronto, ON 866-748-7441
Technical Oil Products
Newton, NJ
Texas Spice Company
Round Rock, TX. 800-880-8007
W H Wildman Company
New Hampshire, OH. 419-568-7531
Washington State Juice
Pacoima, CA 818-899-1195
Wild Flavors
Erlanger, KY 888-945-3352

Drying

American Casein Company (AMCO)
Burlington, NJ. 609-387-3130

Extrusion

LPI, Legacy Plastics
Henderson, KY 270-827-1318

Formulations

American Casein Company (AMCO)
Burlington, NJ. 609-387-3130
American Fruit Processors
Pacoima, CA 818-899-9574
Apotheca Naturale
Woodbine, IA 800-736-3130
Atlantic Quality Spice &Seasonings
New Brunswick, NJ 800-584-0422
Century Foods International
Sparta, WI. 800-269-1901
Clofine Dairy & Food Products
Linwood, NJ 800-441-1001
Compact Industries
St Charles, IL 800-513-4262
GKI Foods
Brighton, MI 248-486-0055
Gold Coast Ingredients
Commerce, CA 800-352-8673
Innovative Food Solutions LLC
Columbus, OH 800-884-3314
Jel-Sert Company
West Chicago, IL 800-323-2592
Jimbo's Jumbos
Edenton, NC 800-334-4771
Kline Process Systems
Reading, PA 610-371-0200
Magic Seasoning Blends
New Orleans, LA 800-457-2857
Main Street Gourmet
Cuyahoga Falls, OH 800-533-6246
Mancini Packing Company
Zolfo Springs, FL 863-735-2000
Milani Gourmet
Melrose Park, IL 800-333-0003
Old Mansion Foods
Petersburg, VA 800-476-1877
Sokol & Company
Countryside, IL 800-328-7656
SOPAKCO Foods
Mullins, SC 800-276-9678
Thiel Cheese & Ingredients
Hilbert, WI 920-989-1440
Vita Key Packaging
Riverside, CA 909-355-1023
W H Wildman Company
New Hampshire, OH. 419-568-7531

Grinding

Shashi Foods
Toronto, ON 866-748-7441

Dealers

Meat

Becker Foods
Westminster, CA 714-315-9447
Boones Butcher Shop
Bardstown, KY 888-253-3384
Dick's Packing Plant
New Lexington, OH 740-342-4150
Fresh Mark
Massillon, OH. 330-832-7491
Graham Ice & Locker Plant
Graham, TX 940-549-1975
Hormel Foods Corporation
Austin, MN 800-523-4635
Lowell Packing Company
Fitzgerald, GA 800-342-0313
Marketing Management
Fort Worth, TX 800-433-2004
Moyer Packing Company
Elroy, PA 800-967-8325
O Chili Frozen Foods Inc
Northbrook, IL 847-562-1991
Sausage Shoppe
Cleveland, OH 216-351-5213
Weber-Stephen Products Company
Palatine, IL 800-446-1071
Welch Brothers
Bartlett, IL. 847-741-6134

Designers

Architectural & Engineering

Austin Company
Cleveland, OH 440-544-2600
Boldt Company
Appleton, WI 920-739-6321
Concepts & Design International, Ltd
West Nyack, NY 845-358-1558
Facility Group
Smyrna, GA 770-437-2700
Kleenline Corporation
Newburyport, MA. 800-259-5973
Select Technologies Inc.
Belmont, MI 616-866-6700
Stellar Group
Jacksonville, FL 800-260-2900
Tippmann Group
Fort Wayne, IN 260-490-3000

Interior & Store Fixture

Accommodation Program
New York, NY 800-929-1414
Acryline
North Attleboro, MA 508-695-7124
Air Pak Products & Services
Winter Park, FL. 800-824-7725
Aldo Locascio
Tucson, AZ 800-488-8729
Atlas Restaurant Supply
Indianapolis, IN 877-528-5275
Bargreen-Ellingson
Tacoma, WA 800-322-4441
Big-D Construction Corporation
Salt Lake City, UT 800-748-4481
Cannon Equipment Company
Rosemount, MN 800-825-8501
Carmona Designs
Chula Vista, CA 619-425-2800
Citra-Tech
Lakeland, FL. 863-646-3868
Custom Design Interiors Service & Manufacturing
Largo, FL 727-536-2207
Design Group Inc
Clearwater, FL 727-441-2825
Fenster Consulting
Port Washington, NY 516-944-7108
Group One
South Boston, MA 617-268-7000
Inman Foodservices Group
Nashville, TN 615-321-5591
Innovations by Design
Chadds Ford, PA. 610-558-0160
Intelplex
Olivette, MO 314-983-9996
Landmark Kitchen Design
Phoenix, AZ 866-621-3192
Legge & Associates
Rockwood, ON 519-856-0444
Leotta Designers
Miami, FL. 305-371-4949
Material Systems Engineering
Stilesville, IN 800-634-0904
Mead & Hunt
Madison, WI. 888-364-7272
Nina Mauritz Design Service
Libertyville, IL 847-968-4438
Refrigerated Warehousing
Jasper, GA. 800-873-2008
RGN Developers
New Providence, NJ
Ridg-U-Rak
North East, PA. 866-479-7225
RMF Steel Products
Grandview, MO. 816-765-4101
Shook Design Group
Charlotte, NC 704-377-0661
Southern Express
Saint Louis, MO 800-444-9157
Southern Store Fixtures
Bessemer, AL 800-552-6283
Spartan Showcase
Union, MO 800-325-0775
SSOE Group
Toledo, OH 419-255-3830
Tecton/Divercon
Omaha, NE 402-571-5115
TKF
Cincinnati, OH 513-241-5910
Triad Scientific
Manasquan, NJ 800-867-6690
TSG Merchandising
Perkasie, PA 215-453-9220
United Insulated Structures Corporation
Berkeley, IL. 800-821-5538

Kitchen (Commercial, Institutional, Restaurant)

Andgar Corporation
Ferndale, WA 360-366-9900
Atlas Restaurant Supply
Indianapolis, IN 877-528-5275
Best Restaurant Equipment & Design
Columbus, OH 800-837-2378
Carmona Designs
Chula Vista, CA 619-425-2800
G.V. Aikman Company
Indianapolis, IN 800-886-4029
Klinger Constructors LLC
Albuquerque, NM. 505-822-9990
Landmark Kitchen Design
Phoenix, AZ 866-621-3192
St Onge Ruff & Associates
Kansas City, MO. 800-800-5261

Package, Carton & Display

AD/Mart
Calumet City, IL 708-891-0990
AdPro
Solon, OH 440-542-1111
Ball Design Group
Fresno, CA 559-434-6100
Center for Packaging Education
Somers, NY. 914-276-0425

CF/NAPA
Napa, CA 707-265-1891
D'Addario Design Associates
New York, NY 212-302-0059
Dunn Woodworks
Shrewsbury, PA 877-835-8592
E2M
Duluth, GA 800-622-4326
Eagle-Concordia Paper Corporation
Farmingdale, NY 212-255-3860
Fasteners for Retail
Cincinnati, OH 800-422-2547
Filet Menu
Los Angeles, CA 310-202-8000
Gary Plastic Packaging Corporation
Bronx, NY 800-221-8151
Graphic Arts Center
Melbourne, FL 888-345-7436
Graphic Impressions of Illinois
River Grove, IL 708-453-1100
Greenfield Paper Box Company
Greenfield, MA 413-773-9414
HMG Worldwide In-Store Marketing
New York, NY 212-736-2300
Hunter Graphics
Umatilla, FL 407-644-2060
IPG International Packaging Group
Agoura Hills, CA 818-865-1428
Jel-Sert Company
West Chicago, IL 800-323-2592
Krimstock Enterprises
Pennsauken, NJ 856-665-3676
Landmark Kitchen Design
Phoenix, AZ 866-621-3192
LSI Industries Inc.
Cincinnati, OH 513-793-3200
Menu Graphics
Olmsted Falls, OH 216-696-1460
Nottingham-Spirk Design Associates
Cleveland, OH 216-231-7830
Omnicraft, Inc.
Minnetonka, MN 952-988-9944
PacTech Engineering
Cincinnati, OH 513-792-1090
Pharmaceutical & Food Special
San Jose, CA 408-275-0161
Presentations South
Orlando, FL 407-657-2108
R.C. Keller & Associates
Barnegat, NJ 973-694-8810
Robin Shepherd Group
Jacksonville, FL 888-447-2823
Roxanne Signs
Gaithersburg, MD 301-428-4911
Seattle Menu Specialists
Kent, WA 800-622-2826
THE Corporation
Terre Haute, IN 800-783-2151
Thomson-Leeds Company
New York, NY 800-535-9361
TSG Merchandising
Perkasie, PA 215-453-9220
US Magnetix
Golden Valley, MN 800- 3-0
Weatherchem Corporation
Twinsburg, OH 330-425-4206
Wishbone Utensil Tableware Line
Wheat Ridge, CO 866-266-5928
WNA Hopple Plastics
Florence, KY 800-446-4622

Process Vessels & Tanks

Four Corporation
Green Bay, WI 920-336-0621

Food Closeouts, Surplus, Salvage & Liquidators

CSV Sales
Plymouth, MI 800-886-6866
Mar-Khem Industries
Cinnaminson, NJ

Foodservice

McClancy Seasoning Company
Fort Mill, SC 800-843-1968

Amusement & Theme Parks

Better Health Lab
Hackensack, NJ 800-810-1888

Branded Concepts

Hixson Architects and Engineers
Cincinnati, OH 513-241-1230

Retail

Canon Potato Company
Center, CO 719-754-3445

Supermarkets

99 Ranch Market
Hacienda Hts, CA 626-839-2899
Certified Grocers Midwest
Hodgkins, IL 708-579-2100
Deko International Co, Ltd
Clifton, NJ 973-778-0212
Ingles Markets
Black Mountain, NC 828-669-2941
Schnuck Markets, Inc.
St Louis, MO 800-829-9901
Sprouts Farmers Market
Phoenix, AZ 888-577-7688
Weis Markets
Sunbury, PA 866-999-9347

Ice Making Plants

Blast-it-Clean
Kansas City, MO 877-379-4233
Boise Cold Storage Company
Boise, ID 208-344-9946
Buck Ice & Coal Company
Columbus, GA 706-322-5451
Carbonic Reserves
San Antonio, TX 800-880-1911
Four Corners Ice
Farmington, NM 505-325-3813
Girton Manufacturing Company, Inc.
Millville, PA 570-458-5521
Graham Ice & Locker Plant
Graham, TX 940-549-1975
Home City Ice
Cincinnati, OH 800-759-4411
Martin's Ice
Ephrata, PA 800-713-7968
Myers Ice Company
Garden City, KS 800-767-5751
Polar Ice
Bloomington, IN 800-733-0423
Reddy Ice Holdings, Inc.
Dallas, TX 800-683-4423
Scotsman Ice Systems
Vernon Hills, IL 800-726-8762
Turbo Refrigerating Company
Denton, TX 940-387-4301

Laboratories

Food Research & Development

A&L Western Ag Lab
Modesto, CA 209-529-4080
ABC Laboratories
Columbia, MO 800-538-5227
Accra Laboratory
Cleveland, OH 800-567-7200
ADD Testing & Research
Valley Stream, NY 516-568-9197
Advance Energy Technologies
Clifton Park, NY 800-724-0198
Analytical Labs
Boise, ID 800-574-5773
Anresco
San Francisco, CA 800-359-0920
Aspen Research Corporation
White Bear Lake, MN 651-773-7961
Baskin-Robbins National Laboratories
Burbank, CA 818-843-4651
BCN Research Laboratories
Rockford, TN 800-236-0505
Bjorksten Research Laboratories
Northbrook, IL 847-714-9662
Blendco
Hattiesburg, MS 800-328-3687
BluMetric Environmental Inc.
Ottawa, ON 613-839-3053
Celsis Laboratory Group
Chicago, IL 800-222-8260
Coffee Enterprises
Burlington, VT 800-375-3398
Culinar
Montreal, QC 514-255-2811
Deibel Laboratories
Madison, WI 847-329-9900
Eastern Regional Research Center
Wyndmoor, PA 215-233-6595
ENSCO
Springfield, VA 703-321-9000
Environmental Express Inc.
Charleston, SC 800-343-5319
Eurofins Scientific
Des Moines, IA 800-841-1110
Eurofins Scientific
Dayton, NJ 800-880-1038
Flow International Corporation
Kent, WA 800-610-1798
Food Quality Lab
Lake Oswego, OR 800-977-3636
Food Safety Net Services
San Antonio, TX 888-525-9788
Food-Tek
Whippany, NJ 800-648-8114
Foods Research Laboratories
Boston, MA 617-442-3322
Hahn Laboratories
Columbia, SC 803-799-1614
Hollander Horizon International
Princeton, NJ 609-924-7577
Hydro-Thermal
Waukesha, WI 800-952-0121
Industrial Laboratories
Wheat Ridge, CO 800-456-5288
Ingman Laboratories
Minneapolis, MN 612-724-0121
Innovative Food Solutions LLC
Columbus, OH 800-884-3314
Intertek Testing ServiceETL SEMKO
Boxborough, MA 800-967-5352
Irvine Analytical Labs
Irvine, CA 949-951-4425
ITS/ETL Testing Laboratories
Laguna Niguel, CA 949-448-4100
J.Leek Associates
Edenton, NC 252-482-4456
Jel-Sert Company
West Chicago, IL 800-323-2592
Jenike & Johanson
Tyngsboro, MA 978-649-3300
Krueger Food Laboratories
Chelmsford, MA 978-256-1220
Lebensmittel Consulting
Fostoria, OH 419-435-2774
Libra Laboratories Inc
Metuchen, NJ 732-321-5200
Libra Technical Center
Metuchen, NJ 732-321-5487
Medallion Laboratories
Minneapolis, MN 800-245-5615
Micro-Chem Laboratory
Mississauga, ON 905-795-0490
Microbac Laboratories
Pittsburgh, PA 412-459-1060
Microbac Laboratories
Worcester, MA 866-515-4668
Midwest Laboratories
Omaha, NE 402-334-7770
Miles Willard Technologies
Idaho Falls, ID 208-523-4741
National Food Laboratory
Livermore, CA 925-551-4209
Northeast Laboratory Services
Waterville, ME 866-591-7120
Northview Laboratories
Spartanburg, SC 864-574-7728
Northwest Laboratories of Seattle
Seattle, WA 206-763-6252
Norton Performance Plastics
Wayne, NJ 973-696-4700
Nutrition Research
Livingston, MT 406-686-4915
O.D. Kurtz Associates
Palm Bay, FL 321-723-0135
Oklabs
Oklahoma City, OK 405-843-6832
Phytotherapy Research Laboratory
Lobelville, TN 800-274-3727
POS Pilot Plant Corporation
Saskatoon, SK 800-230-2751
Protein Research Associates
Livermore, CA 800-948-1991
Q Laboratories
Cincinnati, OH 513-471-1300

Quality Bakers of America
Allentown, PA. 973-263-6970
R F Schiffmann Associates
New York, NY 212-362-7021
R-TECH Laboratories
Saint Paul, MN 800-328-9687
Roskamp Champion
Waterloo, IA 800-366-2563
RQA
Orland Park, IL 708-364-7060
S&J Laboratories
Portage, MI 269-324-7383
S-F Analytical Labs
New Berlin, WI. 800-300-6700
Sani-Pure Food Laboratories
Saddle Brook, NJ 201-843-2525
Silliker, Inc
Chicago, IL 312-938-5151
Southern Testing & Research Labs
Wilson, NC 252-237-4175
Soyatech
Bar Harbor, ME. 800-424-7692
Strasburger & Siegel
Hanover, MD 888-726-3753
Structure Probe
West Chester, PA. 800-242-4774
TEI Analytical
Niles, IL 847-647-1345
Terriss Consolidated Industries
Asbury Park, NJ 800-342-1611
Trans-Chemco
Bristol, WI. 800-880-2498
Truesdail Laboratories
Tustin, CA. 714-730-6239
USDA-NASS
Washington, DC 800-727-9540
Valley Lea Laboratories
Mishawaka, IN 800-822-1283
Vivolac Cultures
Greenfield, IN. 800-848-6522
Warren Analytical Laboratory
Greeley, CO. 800-945-6669
Winston Laboratories
Vernon Hills, IL 800-946-5229

Master Planning & Logistics

Dennis Group
Springfield, MA 413-787-1785
Jel-Sert Company
West Chicago, IL 800-323-2592

Nutritional Analyses & Labeling

AIBMR Life Sciences
Puyallup, WA 253-286-2888
Buchi Analytical
New Castle, DE. 877-692-8844
Q Laboratories
Cincinnati, OH 513-471-1300

Packaging Services

A La Carte
Chicago, IL. 800-722-2370
Aaron Thomas Company
Garden Grove, CA 800-394-4776
Agrinorthwest Division of Agreserves, Inc.
Kennewick, WA 509-734-1195
Austin Packaging Company
Austin, MN 507-433-6623
Baron Spice
St Louis, MO. 314-535-9020
Basic Leasing Corporation
Kearny, NJ. 973-817-7373
Bluegrass Packaging Industries
Louisville, KY 800-489-3159
Camco Chemical Company
Florence, KY. 800-554-1001
Century Foods International
Sparta, WI. 800-269-1901
Compact Industries
St Charles, IL 800-513-4262
David's Goodbatter
Bausman, PA. 717-872-0652
Decko Products
Sandusky, OH 800-537-6143
Diamond Packaging
Rochester, NY. 800-333-4079
Douglas Products & Packaging
Liberty, MO. 800-223-3684
Faribault Foods, Inc.
Minneapolis, MN 612-333-6461
Gary Plastic Packaging Corporation
Bronx, NY. 800-221-8151
Great Western Products
Ontario, CA. 888-598-5588
Hearthside Food Solutions LLC
Downers Grove, IL 630-967-3600
Hogtown Brewing Company
Mississauga, ON 905-855-9065
IFP
Faribault, MN 800-997-4437
Jess Jones Farms
Dixon, CA. 503-304-3806
Laundry Aids
Carlstadt, NJ 201-933-3500
Linker Machines
Rockaway, NJ 973-983-0001
LRM Packaging
South Hackensack, NJ 201-342-2530
Luke's Almond Acres
Reedley, CA 559-638-3483
Mallet & Company
Carnegie, PA 800-245-2757
Nature Most Laboratories
Middletown, CT 800-234-2112
Pacific Spice Company
Commerce, CA 800-281-0614
Packaging Associates
Randolph, NJ 973-252-8890
Packaging Service Company
Pearland, TX 800-826-2949
Pluto Corporation
French Lick, IN. 812-936-9988
Power Group
St Charles, IL 630-587-3770
Power Packaging, Inc.
Westerville, OH. 877-272-1054
Precision Foods
Saint Louis, MO 800-442-5242
ProAct, Inc.
Eagan, MN 877-245-0405
Q&B Foods
Irwindale, CA 626-334-8090
Rempak Industries
Fort Lee, NJ 201-585-9007
Robert's Packaging
Des Plaines, IL 800-707-5070
Robin Shepherd Group
Jacksonville, FL 888-447-2823
Schroeder Sewing Technologies
San Marcos, CA 760-591-9733
Sokol & Company
Countryside, IL. 800-328-7656
Sungjae Corporation
Irvine, CA. 949-757-1727
Techform
Mount Airy, NC 336-789-2115
Todd's
Des Moines, IA. 800-247-5363
Twelve Baskets Sales & Market
Atlanta, GA. 800-420-8840
Vita Key Packaging
Riverside, CA 909-355-1023
Welch Brothers
Bartlett, IL. 847-741-6134
WePackItAll
Duarte, CA 626-301-9214
Westvaco Corporation
Richmond, VA. 804-233-9205

Packers

Agrinorthwest Division of Agreserves, Inc.
Kennewick, WA 509-734-1195
Austin Packaging Company
Austin, MN 507-433-6623
Baron Spice
St Louis, MO. 314-535-9020
Bluegrass Packaging Industries
Louisville, KY 800-489-3159
Compact Industries
St Charles, IL 800-513-4262
Copper Hills Fruit Sales
Fresno, CA 559-432-5400
Family Tree Farms
Reedley, CA 866-352-8671
Food Pak Corporation
San Mateo, CA 650-341-6559
Ful-Flav-R Foods
Alamo, CA 925-838-0300
Hogtown Brewing Company
Mississauga, ON 905-855-9065
Jess Jones Farms
Dixon, CA. 503-304-3806
Luke's Almond Acres
Reedley, CA 559-638-3483
Moyer Packing Company
Elroy, PA 800-967-8325
Nebraska Popcorn
Clearwater, NE 800-253-6502
O Chili Frozen Foods Inc
Northbrook, IL 847-562-1991
Pacific Spice Company
Commerce, CA 800-281-0614
Power Packaging, Inc.
Westerville, OH. 877-272-1054
Precision Foods
Saint Louis, MO 800-442-5242
Q&B Foods
Irwindale, CA 626-334-8090
Rempak Industries
Fort Lee, NJ 201-585-9007
Robin Shepherd Group
Jacksonville, FL 888-447-2823
Twelve Baskets Sales & Market
Atlanta, GA. 800-420-8840
Welch Brothers
Bartlett, IL. 847-741-6134

Fruit

Copper Hills Fruit Sales
Fresno, CA 559-432-5400
Family Tree Farms
Reedley, CA 866-352-8671

Meat

Lynden Meat Company
Lynden, WA 360-354-2449
O Chili Frozen Foods Inc
Northbrook, IL 847-562-1991
Welch Brothers
Bartlett, IL. 847-741-6134

Personnel Services

Bristol Associates
Los Angeles, CA. 310-670-0525
Capitol Recruiting Group
Newport News, VA. 757-277-7934
Clanton & Company
Orange, CA. 714-282-7980
Cook Associates
Chicago, IL 312-329-0900
Dallas Roth Young
Richardson, TX. 972-233-5000
David E. Moley & Associates
Wrightsville Beach, NC 910-256-3826
Dixie Search Associates
Marietta, GA. 770-675-7300
Executive Referral Services
Chicago, IL 866-466-3339
Focus
Minneapolis, MN 612-706-4444
Food Executives Network
Milwaukee, WI 414-962-7684
Fox-Morris Associates
Charlotte, NC 800-777-6503
Futures
Barrington, NH 603-664-5811
Harper Associates
Farmington Hills, MI 248-932-1170
Inter-Access
Etobicoke, ON 514-744-6262
Johnson Associates
Wheaton, IL 630-690-9200
Judge
W Conshohocken, PA. 888-228-7162
Kent R Hedman & Associates
Arlington, TX. 817-277-0888
Landsman Foodservice Net
Owing Mills, MD 410-363-7038
Lawless Link
San Antonio, TX
Lawrence Glaser Associates
Moorestown, NJ 856-778-9500
Management Recruiters
Bradenton, FL. 941-756-3001
McGraw Hill/London House
Park Ridge, IL. 800-221-8378
Metroplex Corporation
Houston, TX 281-586-0559
Nelson & Associates Recruiting
Kirkland, WA 425-823-0956
North Company
Waupaca, WI. 715-258-6104

P&A Food Industry Recruiters
Deptford, NJ ... 856-384-4774
Resources in Food & FoodTeam
St Louis, MO. ... 800-875-1028
Riley Cole Professional Recruitment
Oakland, CA ... 510-336-2333
Ritt-Ritt & Associates
Rolling Meadows, IL ... 847-827-7771
Rjo Associates
Bradenton, FL ... 941-756-3001
RJR Executive Search
Houston, TX ... 281-368-8550
Roth Young Bellevue
Bellevue, WA ... 425-454-0677
Roth Young Chicago
Mount Prospect, IL ... 847-797-9211
Roth Young Farmington Hills
Farmington Hills, MI ... 248-539-9242
Roth Young Hicksville
Hicksville, NY ... 516-822-6000
Roth Young Minneapolis
Minneapolis, MN ... 800-356-6655
Roth Young Murrysville
Murrysville, PA. ... 724-733-5900
Roth Young New York
New York, NY ... 212-557-8181
Roth Young of Tampa Bay
Tampa, FL. ... 800-646-1513
Roth Young Washougal
Washougal, WA. ... 360-835-3136
S-H-S International of Wilkes
Wilkes Barre, PA. ... 570-825-3411
SBB & Associates
Norcross, GA ... 770-449-7610
Search West
Los Angeles, CA. ... 310-203-9797
Tom McCall & Associates
Millsboro, DE ... 410-539-0700
Wayne Group
San Francisco, CA ... 415-421-2010
William Willis Worldwide
Greenwich, CT

Employment Agencies

Bristol Associates
Los Angeles, CA. ... 310-670-0525
Capitol Recruiting Group
Newport News, VA. ... 757-277-7934
Clanton & Company
Orange, CA ... 714-282-7980
Cook Associates
Chicago, IL ... 312-329-0900
Dallas Roth Young
Richardson, TX. ... 972-233-5000
David E. Moley & Associates
Wrightsville Beach, NC ... 910-256-3826
Dixie Search Associates
Marietta, GA ... 770-675-7300
Executive Referral Services
Chicago, IL ... 866-466-3339
Focus
Minneapolis, MN ... 612-706-4444
Food Executives Network
Milwaukee, WI ... 414-962-7684
Food Management Search
Springfield, MA ... 413-732-2666
Fox-Morris Associates
Charlotte, NC ... 800-777-6503
Futures
Barrington, NH ... 603-664-5811
Harper Associates
Farmington Hills, MI ... 248-932-1170
Inter-Access
Etobicoke, ON ... 514-744-6262
Johnson Associates
Wheaton, IL ... 630-690-9200
Judge
W Conshohocken, PA. ... 888-228-7162
Kent R Hedman & Associates
Arlington, TX ... 817-277-0888
Landsman Foodservice Net
Owing Mills, MD ... 410-363-7038
Lawless Link
San Antonio, TX
Lawrence Glaser Associates
Moorestown, NJ ... 856-778-9500
Management Recruiters
Bradenton, FL. ... 941-756-3001
McGraw Hill/London House
Park Ridge, IL. ... 800-221-8378

Metroplex Corporation
Houston, TX ... 281-586-0559
Nelson & Associates Recruiting
Kirkland, WA ... 425-823-0956
North Company
Waupaca, WI. ... 715-258-6104
P&A Food Industry Recruiters
Deptford, NJ ... 856-384-4774
Resources in Food & FoodTeam
St Louis, MO. ... 800-875-1028
Riley Cole Professional Recruitment
Oakland, CA ... 510-336-2333
Ritt-Ritt & Associates
Rolling Meadows, IL ... 847-827-7771
Rjo Associates
Bradenton, FL. ... 941-756-3001
RJR Executive Search
Houston, TX ... 281-368-8550
Roth Young Bellevue
Bellevue, WA ... 425-454-0677
Roth Young Chicago
Mount Prospect, IL ... 847-797-9211
Roth Young Farmington Hills
Farmington Hills, MI ... 248-539-9242
Roth Young Hicksville
Hicksville, NY ... 516-822-6000
Roth Young Minneapolis
Minneapolis, MN ... 800-356-6655
Roth Young Murrysville
Murrysville, PA. ... 724-733-5900
Roth Young New York
New York, NY ... 212-557-8181
Roth Young of Tampa Bay
Tampa, FL. ... 800-646-1513
Roth Young Washougal
Washougal, WA. ... 360-962-3136
S-H-S International of Wilkes
Wilkes Barre, PA. ... 570-825-3411
SBB & Associates
Norcross, GA ... 770-449-7610
Search West
Los Angeles, CA. ... 310-203-9797
Tom McCall & Associates
Millsboro, DE ... 410-539-0700
Wayne Group
San Francisco, CA ... 415-421-2010
William Willis Worldwide
Greenwich, CT

Project Management

Dennis Group
Springfield, MA ... 413-787-1785

Quality Control

Delta Trak
Pleasanton, CA ... 800-962-6776
Formax/Provisur Technologies
Mokena, IL ... 708-479-3500
Hollander Horizon International
Princeton, NJ. ... 609-924-7577
Lixi, Inc.
Huntley, IL ... 847-961-6666
Orthodox Union
New York, NY ... 212-563-4000
Raque Food Systems
Louisville, KY ... 502-267-9641

Refinishing & Refurbishing Services

AmeriGlobe FIBC Solutions
Lafayette, LA ... 337-234-3212
B&B Neon Sign Company
Austin, TX. ... 800-791-6366
B.A.G. Corporation
Dallas, TX. ... 800-331-9200
Big State Spring Companyy
Corpus Christi, TX ... 800-880-0244
Custom Design Interiors Service & Manufacturing
Largo, FL ... 727-536-2207
Cutler Brothers Box & Lumber Company
Fairview, NJ ... 201-943-2535
Harrison of Texas
Houston, TX ... 800-245-5707
Illinois Wholesale Cash Register Corporation
Elgin, IL ... 800-544-5493
J.L. Honing Company
milwaukee, WI ... 800-747-9501
Refinishing Touch
Alpharetta, GA ... 800-523-9448
Sonoma Pacific Company
Montebello, CA ... 323-838-4374

Research & Development

Raque Food Systems
Louisville, KY ... 502-267-9641
Stratecon International Consultants
Winston Salem, NC. ... 336-768-6808
Terriss Consolidated Industries
Asbury Park, NJ ... 800-342-1611
Tiax LLC
Lexington, MA ... 800-677-3000

Spray Drying Services

APV Americas
Delavan, WI ... 800-252-5200
Brady Enterprises
East Weymouth, MA. ... 781-337-5000
IFP
Faribault, MN ... 800-997-4437
Vector Corporation
Marion, IA. ... 319-377-8263

Testing & Sampling Services

A&L Western Ag Lab
Modesto, CA. ... 209-529-4080
Accra Laboratory
Cleveland, OH ... 800-567-7200
Accu-Labs Research
Golden, CO ... 303-277-9514
Advanced Instruments
Norwood, MA. ... 800-225-4034
Airflow Sciences Corporation
Livonia, MI ... 734-525-0300
Altek Company
Torrington, CT ... 860-482-7626
AM Test Laboratories
Kirkland, WA ... 425-885-1664
Barrow-Agee Laboratories
Memphis, TN ... 901-332-1590
Biological Services
Kansas City, MO. ... 913-236-6868
Bjorksten Research Laboratories
Northbrook, IL ... 847-714-9662
BluMetric Environmental Inc.
Ottawa, ON. ... 613-839-3053
Celsis Laboratory Group
Chicago, IL ... 800-222-8260
Coffee Enterprises
Burlington, VT ... 800-375-3398
Covance Laboratories Inc.
Madison, WI ... 608-241-4471
Deibel Laboratories
Madison, WI ... 847-329-9900
Delta Trak
Pleasanton, CA ... 800-962-6776
DFL Laboratories
Chicago, IL ... 312-938-5151
DQCI Services
Saint Paul, MN ... 763-785-0484
ELISA Technologies
Gainesville, FL ... 352-337-3929
ENSCO
Springfield, VA. ... 703-321-9000
Enviro-Test/Perry Laboratories
Woodridge, IL. ... 630-324-6685
Environmental Systems Service
Culpeper, VA. ... 800-541-2116
ESA
Chelmsford, MA ... 978-250-7000
Eurofins Scientific
Dayton, NJ ... 800-880-1038
Gaynes Labs
Bridgeview, IL ... 708-233-6655
Healthy Dining
San Diego, CA ... 800-266-2049
Industrial Laboratories
Wheat Ridge, CO ... 800-456-5288
Innovative Food Solutions LLC
Columbus, OH ... 800-884-3314
International Approval Services
Cleveland, OH ... 877-235-9791
Intertek Testing ServiceETL SEMKO
Boxborough, MA ... 800-967-5352
ITS/ETL Testing Laboratories
Laguna Niguel, CA. ... 949-448-4100
J.L. Analytical Services
Modesto, CA. ... 209-538-8111
Krueger Food Laboratories
Chelmsford, MA. ... 978-256-1220
Libra Technical Center
Metuchen, NJ ... 732-321-5487

Medallion Laboratories
Minneapolis, MN 800-245-5615
Microbac Laboratories
Pittsburgh, PA 412-459-1060
Midwest Laboratories
Omaha, NE 402-334-7770
Milligan & Higgins
Johnstown, NY 518-762-4638
Minnesota Valley TestingLaboratories
New Ulm, MN. 800-782-3557
Miroil
Allentown, PA. 800-523-9844
Northland Laboratories
Northbrook, IL 800-366-3522
Northview Laboratories
Spartanburg, SC 864-574-7728
Pearson Research
Santa Cruz, CA. 831-429-9797
POS Pilot Plant Corporation
Saskatoon, SK. 800-230-2751
PSI
Oakbrook Terrace, IL 817-640-4162
Q Laboratories
Cincinnati, OH 513-471-1300
QC
Southampton, PA 215-355-3900
R-TECH Laboratories
Saint Paul, MN 800-328-9687
Richardson Researches
South San Francisco, CA 650-589-5764
S-F Analytical Labs
New Berlin, WI. 800-300-6700
Sani-Pure Food Laboratories
Saddle Brook, NJ 201-843-2525
Sensory Spectrum
New Providence, NJ 908-376-7000
Shear Kershman Laboratories
Chesterfield, MO 636-519-8900
Soyatech
Bar Harbor, ME. 800-424-7692
Suburban Laboratories
Hillside, IL 800-783-5227
TEI Analytical
Niles, IL 847-647-1345
The Phytopia Garden
Dallas, TX. 888-750-9336
Underwriters Laboratories
Camas, WA 877-854-3577
Valley Lea Laboratories
Mishawaka, IN 800-822-1283
Vivolac Cultures
Greenfield, IN 800-848-6522
Warren Analytical Laboratory
Greeley, CO. 800-945-6669
Woodson-Tenent Laboratories
Des Moines, IA. 515-265-1461
Woodson-Tenent Laboratories
Gainesville, GA 770-536-5909
Woodson-Tenent Laboratories
Dayton, OH. 937-236-5756

Equipment & Machinery

Baking Industry

Allied Bakery and Food Service Equipment
Santa Fe Springs, CA 562-945-6506
Andy J. Egan Co.
Grand Rapids, MI 800-594-9244
Charles H. Baldwin & Sons
West Stockbridge, MA 413-232-7785
Cr. Manufacturing
Waverly, NE 877-789-5844
ECS Warehouse
Buffalo, NY. 716-829-7356
ENJAY Converters Limited
Cobourg, ON. 800-427-5517
Henry Group
Greenville, TX 903-883-2002
Lucks Food Equipment Company
Kent, WA. 811-824-0696
LVO Manufacturing
Rock Rapids, IA 712-472-3734
Marel Food Systems, Inc.
Lenexa, KS 913-888-9110
Meraz & Associates
Chico, CA 888-244-4463
Nijal USA
Minneapolis, MN 651-353-6702
Oshikiri Corporation of America
Philadelphia, PA 215-637-6005
Pro Bake
Twinsburg, OH 800-837-4427
Reiser
Canton, MA 781-575-9941
Render
Buffalo, NY. 888-446-1010
Rheon, U.S.A.
Irvine, CA 949-768-1900
Spray Dynamics, Ltd
Saint Clair, MO. 800-260-7366
Sunset Paper Products
Simi Valley, CA. 800-228-7882
Superior Products Company
Saint Paul, MN 800-328-9800
WP Bakery Group
Shelton, CT. 203-929-6530

Barbecue Equipment & Supplies

AMCO Corporation
City of Industry, CA 626-855-2550
Archer Wire International
Bedford Park, IL. 708-563-1700
Bar-B-Q Woods
Newton, KS. 800-528-0819
BBQ Pits by Klose
Houston, TX 800-487-7487
Belson Outdoors
North Aurora, IL. 800-323-5664
Best Brands Home Products
New York, NY 212-684-7456
Big John Grills & Rotisseries
Pleasant Gap, PA. 800-326-9575
Boehringer Mfg. Co. Inc.
Felton, CA. 800-630-8665
BR Machine Company
Wedron, IL 800-310-7057
Century Foods International
Sparta, WI. 800-269-1901
Cleveland Metal StampingCompany
Berea, OH 440-234-0010
Cookshack
Ponca City, OK. 800-423-0698
Crown Verity
Brantford, ON. 888-505-7240
Dar-B-Ques Barbecue Equipment
Imperial, MO. 636-296-4408
Dynamic Cooking Systems
Huntington Beach, CA 800-433-8466
Esquire Mechanical Corp.
Armonk, NY 800-847-4206
F.P. Smith Wire Cloth Company
Northlake, IL. 800-323-6842
G.S. Blodgett Corporation
Burlington, VT 800-331-5842
GBS Foodservice Equipment, Inc.
Mississauga, ON. 888-402-1242
Gril-Del
Mankato, MN 800-782-7320
Grill Greats
Saxonburg, PA. 724-352-1511
Grillco
Aurora, IL. 800-644-0067
Grills to Go
Fresno, CA 877-869-2253
Hasty-Bake
Tulsa, OK 800-426-6836
Hercules Food Equipment
Weston, ON. 416-742-9673
Hickory Industries
North Bergen, NJ 800-732-9153
Holstein Manufacturing
Holstein, IA. 800-368-4342
J&R Manufacturing
Mesquite, TX 800-527-4831
Jackson Restaurant Supply
Jackson, TN 800-424-8943
Jensen Luhr & Sons
Hood River, OR 541-386-3811
Kay Home Products
Antioch, IL 800-600-7009
King Packaging Corporation
Schenectady, NY. 518-370-5464
Lazy-Man
Belvidere, NJ 800-475-1950
Lazzari Fuel Company
San Francisco, CA 800-242-7265
Lignetics of Missouri
Sandpoint, ID 800-544-3834
M.E. Heuck Company
Mason, OH 800-359-3200
Magikitch'n
Concord, NH. 800-441-1492
Magnum Custom Trailer & BBQ Pits
Austin, TX. 800-662-4686
Mali's All Natural Barbecue Supply Company
East Amherst, NY. 800-289-6254
Masterbuilt Manufacturing
Columbus, GA 800-489-1581
Meraz & Associates
Chico, CA 888-244-4463
Mosshaim Innovations
Jacksonville, FL 888-995-7775
Mr. Bar-B-Q
Old Bethpage, NY. 800-333-2124
Music City Metals
Nashville, TN 800-251-2674
Napoleon Appliance Corporation
Barrie, ON. 866-820-8686
Nashville Wire Products
Nashville, TN 615-743-2480
Nature's Own
Attleboro, MA. 130- 13- 612
Old Mansion Foods
Petersburg, VA 800-476-1877
Ole Hickory Pits
Cape Girardeau, MO. 800-223-9667
Patio King
Cutler Bay, FL. 786-258-8508
Porcelain Metals Corporation
Louisville, KY 502-635-7421
Prince Castle
Carol Stream, IL 800-722-7853
Profire Stainless Steel Barbecue
Miami, FL. 305-665-5313
Roseville Charcoal & Manufacturing
Zanesville, OH 740-452-5473
Roto-Flex Oven Company
San Antonio, TX. 877-859-1463
Smokaroma
Boley, OK. 800-331-5565
Southbend Company
Fuquay Varina, NC 800-348-2558
Southern Pride Distributing
Marion, IL. 800-851-8180
Standex International Corporation
Salem, NH. 603-893-9701
Stryco Wire Products
North York, ON. 416-663-7000
Super Cooker
Lake Park, GA 800-841-7452
Superior Products Company
Saint Paul, MN 800-328-9800
Swanson Wire Works Industries, Inc.
Mesquite, TX 972-288-7465
Thermal Engineering Corporation
Columbia, SC 800-331-0097
Toastmaster
Elgin, IL 847-741-3300
Town Food Service Equipment Company
Brooklyn, NY 800-221-5032
West Oregon Wood Products
Columbia City, OR 503-397-6707
Wilch Manufacturing
Topeka, KS 785-267-2762
Wood Stone Corporation
Bellingham, WA 800-988-8103

Belting

Ace Manufacturing
Cincinnati, OH 800-653-5692
Ammeraal Beltech
Grand Rapids, MI 616-791-0292
Ammeraal Beltech
Skokie, IL 800-323-4170
Andgar Corporation
Ferndale, WA 360-366-9900
ASGCO Manufacturing
Allentown, PA. 800-344-4000
Bamco Belting Products
Greenville, SC. 800-258-2358
Belt Technologies
Agawam, MA 413-786-9922
BMH
City of Industry, CA 909-349-2530
BNW Industries
Tippecanoe, IN 574-353-7855
Bowman Hollis Manufacturing
Charlotte, NC 888-269-2358
Boyd Corp.
Modesto, CA. 888-244-6931
Burrell Leder Beltech
Skokie, IL 800-323-4170
C.R. Daniels Inc.
Ellicott City, MD. 800-933-2638
California Vibratory Feeders
Anaheim, CA 800-354-0972
Cambridge
Cambridge, MD 877-649-7492
Change Parts
Ludington, MI. 231-845-5107
Clipper Belt Lacer Company
Grand Rapids, MI 616-459-3196
Dearborn Mid-West Company
Lenexa, KS 913-384-9950
Dresco Belting Company
East Weymouth, MA. 781-335-1350
Dyna-Veyor
Newark, NJ 800-930-4760
Elmo Rietschle - A Gardner Denver Product
Qunicy, IL. 217-222-5400
Emco Industrial Plastics
Cedar Grove, NJ 800-292-9906
Fabreeka International
Boise, ID 800-423-4469
Fenner Dunlop Engineered Conveyer Solutions
Pittsburgh, PA. 412-249-0700
Forbo Siegling LLC
Huntersville, NC. 800-255-5581
Furnace Belt Company
Buffalo, NY. 800-354-7213
Georgia Duck & Cordage Mill
Scottdale, GA 404-297-3170
Greenbelt Industries
Buffalo, NY. 800-668-1114
Habasit America
Suwanee, GA 800-458-6431
Habasit Canada Limited
Oakville, ON. 905-827-4131
Hoffmeyer Company
San Leandro, CA. 800-350-2358
Home Rubber Company
Trenton, NJ 800-257-9441
Hudson Belting & ServiceCompany
Worcester, MA 508-756-0090
Intralox
New Orleans, LA 800-535-8848
J.L. Becker Company
Plymouth, MI 800-837-4328

Keystone Rubber Corporation
Greenbackville, VA. 800-394-5661
KVP Falcon Plastic Belting
Reading, PA 800-445-7898
Lambeth Band Corporation
New Bedford, MA 508-984-4700
Lumsden Flexx Flow
Lancaster, PA 800-367-3664
M&R Sales & Service, Inc
Glen Ellyn, IL 800-736-6431
Mar-Con Wire Belt
Richmond, BC 877-962-7266
Maryland Wire Belts
Cambridge, MD 800-677-2358
Mell & Company
Niles, IL 800-262-6355
Meriwether Industries
Bloomfield, NJ 800-332-2358
Michigan Industrial Belting
Livonia, MI 800-778-1650
Midwest Rubber & Supply Company
Commerce City, CO 800-537-7457
Monarch-McLaren
Weston, ON. 416-741-9675
Northwind
Alpena, AR 870-437-2585
Omni Metalcraft Corporation
Alpena, MI 989-358-7000
Our Name is Mud
New York, NY 877-683-7867
Rademaker USA
Hudson, OH 330-650-2345
Rahmann Belting & Industrial Rubber Products
Gastonia, NC. 888-248-8148
Regina USA, Inc
Oak Creek, WI 414-571-0032
Shingle Belting
King of Prussia, PA. 800-345-6294
Slip-Not Belting Corporation
Kingsport, TN. 423-246-8141
Stiles Enterprises
Rockaway, NJ 800-325-4232
Tecweigh/Tecnetics Industries
White Bear Lake, MN. 800-536-4880
Universal Die & Stamping
Prairie Du Sac, WI 608-643-2477
Vaughn Belting Company
Spartanburg, SC 800-325-3303
Westfield Sheet Metal Works
Kenilworth, NJ 908-276-5500
Wire Belt Company of America
Londonderry, NH 603-644-2500

Belts

Crumb

American Conveyor Corporation
Astoria, NY. 718-386-0480
King Bag & Manufacturing Company
Cincinnati, OH 800-444-5464

Beverage Industry

Alard Equipment Corporation
Williamson, NY 315-589-4511
Bottom Line Processing Technologies, Inc.
Largo, GA. 888-834-4552
C.F.F. Stainless Steels
Hamilton, ON 800-263-4511
Dacam Machinery
Madison Heights, VA 434-369-1259
Distillata Company
Cleveland, OH 800-999-2906
Harrison Electropolishing
Houston, TX 832-467-3100
Ipec
New Castle, PA. 800-377-4732
Kamflex Corporation
Chicago, IL 800-323-2440
Maselli Measurements Incc.
Stockton, CA. 800-964-9600
Midwest Juice and Syrup Company
Grand Rapids, MI 877-265-8243
Rocheleau Blow Molding Systems
Fitchburg, MA 978-345-1723
Severn Trent Services
Fort Washington, PA. 215-646-9201
Sick Inc.
Minneapolis, MN 800-325-7425
Spinzer
Glen Ellyn, IL 630-469-7184

Coffee Industry

San Marco Coffee, Inc.
Charlotte, NC 800-715-9298
Stratecon International Consultants
Winston Salem, NC. 336-768-6808
U Roast Em
Hayward, WI. 715-634-6255
West Coast Specialty Coffee
Campbell, CA 650-259-9308

Stainless Steel

Coffee Pots

Castella Imports
Hauppauge, NY 866-227-8355

Confectionery Industry

A&B Process Systems
Stratford, WI 888-258-2789
Aerotech Enterprise Inc
Chesterland, OH 440-729-2616
Aladdin Transparent Packaging Corporation
Hauppauge, NY 631-273-4747
Andy J. Egan Co.
Grand Rapids, MI 800-594-9244
Bakers Choice Products
Beacon Falls, CT. 203-720-1000
Braun Brush Company
Albertson, NY 800-645-4111
Bryce Company
Memphis, TN 800-238-7277
C. Cretors & Company
Chicago, IL 800-228-1885
Catty Corporation
Harvard, IL 815-943-2288
Chocolate Concepts
Hartville, OH 330-877-3322
Esterle Mold & Machine Company
Stow, OH. 800-411-4086
Hebeler Corporation
Tonawanda, NY 800-486-4709
Insect-O-Cutor
Stone Mountain, GA. 800-988-5359
Kamflex Corporation
Chicago, IL 800-323-2440
Kaufman Paper Box Company
Providence, RI 401-272-7508
Liberty Engineering Company
Roscoe, IL. 877-623-9065
McCarter Corporation
Norristown, PA 610-272-3203
Micelli Chocolate Mold Company
West Babylon, NY 631-752-2888
Pacquet Oneida
Charlotte, NC 800-631-8388
Precision Brush Company
Cleveland, OH 800-252-4747
Reiser
Canton, MA 781-575-9941
Rheo-Tech
Gurnee, IL. 847-367-1557
Ritz Packaging Company
Brooklyn, NY 718-366-2300
Saunder Brothers
Bridgton, ME 207-647-3331
Six Hardy Brush Manufacturing
Suffield, CT. 860-623-8465
Stephan Machinery GmbH
Mandelein, IL 847-247-0182
Taconic
Petersburg, NY 800-833-1805
Taylor Precision Products
Las Cruces, NM 630-954-1250
Voorhees Rubber Manufacturing Co., Inc.
Newark, MD 410-632-1582
West Hawk Industries
Ann Arbor, MI 800-678-1286
Wilton Industries CanadaLtd.
Etobicoke, ON 800-387-3300

Conveyors

Belt

A.K. Robins
Baltimore, MD 800-486-9656
A.T. Ferrell Company
Bluffton, IN. 800-248-8318
ABI Limited
Concord, ON. 800-297-8666
Advanced Uniflo Technologies
Wichita, KS. 800-688-0400
AFECO
Algona, IA. 888-295-1116
All Power
Sioux City, IA 712-258-0681
Amark Packaging Systems
Kansas City, MO. 816-965-9000
Anderson-Crane Company
Minneapolis, MN 800-314-2747
Andgar Corporation
Ferndale, WA 360-366-9900
Andritz
Muncy, PA. 570-546-8211
ASGCO Manufacturing
Allentown, PA. 800-344-4000
Bamco Belting Products
Greenville, SC. 800-258-2358
Berkshire PPM
Litchfield, CT 860-567-3118
Berndorf Belt Technology USA
Elgin, IL 877-232-7322
Bilt-Rite Conveyors
New London, WI 920-982-6600
BMH
City of Industry, CA 909-349-2530
BMH Equipment
Sacramento, CA 800-350-8828
Bowman Hollis Manufacturing
Charlotte, NC 888-269-2358
C S Bell Company
Tiffin, OH 888-958-6381
C&R Refrigation Inc,
Center, TX. 800-438-6182
C.R. Daniels Inc.
Ellicott City, MD. 800-933-2638
California Vibratory Feeders
Anaheim, CA 800-354-0972
Cambelt International Corporation
Salt Lake City, UT 801-972-5511
Cambridge
Cambridge, MD 877-649-7492
Chantland-MHS Company
Dakota City, IA. 515-332-4045
Cleveland Vibrator Company
Cleveland, OH 800-221-3298
Commercial Manufacturing& Supply Company
Fresno, CA 559-237-1855
Conesco Conveyor Corporation
Clifton, NJ. 973-365-1440
Conveyor Supply
Deerfield, IL 847-945-5670
Custom Conveyor & SupplyCorporation
Racine, WI 262-634-4920
Davron Technologies
Chattanooga, TN. 423-870-1888
Dearborn Mid-West Company
Lenexa, KS 913-384-9950
Descon EDM
Brocton, NY 716-792-9300
Design Technology Corporation
Billerica, MA 978-663-7000
Dorner Manufacturing Corporation
Hartland, WI 800-397-8664
Duplex Mill & Manufacturing Company
Springfield, OH. 937-325-5555
Dyna-Veyor
Newark, NJ 800-930-4760
Dynamic Storage Systems Inc.
Brooksville, FL 800-974-8211
E-ZLIFT Conveyors
Denver, CO 800-821-9966
Eckels-Bilt, Inc
Fort Worth, TX 800-343-9020
Eisenmann Corporation
Crystal Lake, IL 815-455-4100
Ermanco
Norton Shores, MI 231-798-4547
F&A Fabricating
Battle Creek, MI 269-965-3268
Filling Equipment Company
Flushing, NY. 800-247-7127
Fleetwood
Romeoville, IL 630-759-6800
FleetwoodGoldcoWyard
Romeoville, IL 630-759-6800
Flodin
Moses Lake, WA. 509-766-2996
Flow-Turn, Inc.
Union, NJ 908-687-3225
FreesTech
Sinking Spring, PA 717-560-7560

Gem Equipment of Oregon	Woodburn, OR	503-982-9902
General Machinery Corporation	Sheboygan, WI	888-243-6622
Georgia Duck & Cordage Mill	Scottdale, GA	404-297-3170
Globe International	Tacoma, WA	800-523-6575
Goodnature Products	Orchard Park, NY	800-875-3381
Grain Machinery Manufacturing Corporation	Miami, FL	305-620-2525
Graybill Machines	Lititz, PA	717-626-5221
Greenline Corporation	Charlotte, NC	800-331-5312
Gulf Arizona Packaging	Humble, TX	800-364-3887
Gulf Systems	Oklahoma City, OK	405-528-2293
Gulf Systems	Brownsville, TX	800-217-4853
Gulf Systems	Oklahoma City, OK	800-364-3887
Gulf Systems	Arlington, TX	817-261-1915
Habasit Canada Limited	Oakville, ON	905-827-4131
Herche Warehouse	Denver, CO	303-371-8186
Hi Roller Enclosed Belt Conveyors	Sioux Falls, SD	800-328-1785
HMC Corporation	Hopkinton, NH	603-746-4691
Hurt Conveyor Equipment Company	Los Angeles, CA	323-541-0433
Hydro Power	Terre Haute, IN	812-232-0156
Industrial Design Fabrication & Installation, Inc.	Sioux City, IA	877-873-5858
Industrial Kinetics	Downers Grove, IL	800-655-0306
Inter-City Welding & Manufacturing	Independence, MO	816-252-1770
Intralox, L.L.C., USA	Harahan, LA	504-733-0463
JanTec	Traverse City, MI	800-992-3303
Kamflex Corporation	Chicago, IL	800-323-2440
Kaufman Engineered Systems	Waterville, OH	419-878-9727
Keenline Conveyor Systems	Omro, WI	920-685-0365
Key Material Handling	Simi Valley, CA	800-539-7225
Kinergy Corporation	Louisville, KY	502-366-5685
Kornylak Corporation	Hamilton, OH	800-837-5676
KWS Manufacturing Company	Burleson, TX	800-543-6558
LaRos Equipment Company	Portage, MI	269-323-1441
Laughlin Corporation	Fort Worth, TX	817-625-7756
Le Fiell Company, Inc.	Reno, NV	775-677-5300
Leeds Conveyor Manufacturer Company	Guilford, CT	800-724-1088
Lesco Design & Manufacturing Company	La Grange, KY	502-222-7101
LEWCO	Sandusky, OH	419-625-4014
Lewis M. Carter Manufacturing Company	Donalsonville, GA	229-524-2197
Magnetic Products	Highland, MI	800-544-5930
Mar-Con Wire Belt	Richmond, BC	877-962-7266
Marlen International	Astoria, OR	800-862-7536
Martin Engineering	Neponset, IL	800-766-2786
Maryland Wire Belts	Cambridge, MD	800-677-2358
Matthiesen Equipment Company	San Antonio, TX	800-624-8635
McCormick Enterprises	Delton, MI	800-223-3683
McNichols Conveyor Company	Southfield, MI	800-331-1926
Mell & Company	Niles, IL	800-262-6355
Meyer Machine & Garroutte Products	San Antonio, TX	210-736-1811
Michigan Industrial Belting	Livonia, MI	800-778-1650
Midwest Metalcraft & Equipment	Windsor, MO	800-647-3167
Millard Manufacturing Corporation	La Vista, NE	800-662-4263
Molding Automation Concepts	Woodstock, IL	800-435-6979
Monarch-McLaren	Weston, ON	416-741-9675
National Conveyor Corporation	Commerce, CA	323-725-0355
Northwind	Alpena, AR	870-437-2585
OCC Systems	Ferndale, MI	800-396-2554
Ohio Conveyor & Supply	Findlay, OH	419-422-3825
Omni Metalcraft Corporation	Alpena, MI	989-358-7000
Our Name is Mud	New York, NY	877-683-7867
P&F Metals	Turlock, CA	209-667-4716
Package Conveyor Company	Fort Worth, Fo.	800-792-1243
Packaging & Processing Equipment	Ayr, ON	519-622-6666
Packaging Systems International	Denver, CO	303-296-4445
Parkson Corporation	Berkeley Heights, NJ	908-464-0700
Peerless Conveyor and Manufacturing Corporation	Kansas City, KS	913-342-2240
Portec Flowmaster	Canon City, CO	800-777-7471
Power-Pack Conveyor Company	Willoughby, OH	440-975-9955
Priority One Packaging	Waterloo, ON	800-387-9102
Prodo-Pak Corporation	Garfield, NJ	973-777-7770
Quickdraft	Canton, OH	330-477-4574
R.G. Stephens Engineering	Long Beach, CA	800-499-3001
Rapat Corporation	Hawley, MN	800-325-6377
Rexnord Corporation	Milwaukee, WI	866-739-6673
San Fab Conveyor Systems	Sandusky, OH	419-626-4465
Schneider Packing Equipment Company	Brewerton, NY	315-676-3035
Screw Conveyor Corporation	Hammond, IN	219-931-1450
Simplex Filler Company	Napa, CA	800-796-7539
Smetco	Aurora, OR	800-253-5400
Southern Automatics	Lakeland, FL	800-441-4604
Span Tech	Glasgow, KY	270-651-9166
Speedways Conveyors	Lancaster, NY	800-800-1022
Sperling Industries	Omaha, NE	800-647-5062
Spurgeon Company	Ferndale, MI	800-396-2554
Stokes Material HandlingSystems	Doylestown, PA	215-340-2200
Svedala Industries	Colorado Springs, CO	719-471-3443
Sweet Manufacturing Company	Springfield, OH	800-334-7254
TGS Engineering & Conveying	Houston, TX	713-466-0426
The National Provisioner	Deerfield, IL	847-763-9534
Thomas L. Green & Company	Robenosia, PA	610-693-5816
Transnorm System	Grand Prairie, TX	800-259-2303
Traycon	Carlstadt, NJ	201-939-5555
Tri-Pak Machinery, Inc.	Harlingen, TX	956-423-5140
TWM Manufacturing	Leamington, ON	888-495-4831
UniTrak Corporation	Port Hope, ON	866-883-5749
Universal Die & Stamping	Prairie Du Sac, WI	608-643-2477
Universal Industries, In	Cedar Falls, IA	800-553-4446
US Rubber Supply Company	Brooklyn, NY	718-782-7888
Vande Berg Scales	Sioux Center, IA	712-722-1181
Vaughn Belting Company	Spartanburg, SC	800-325-3303
Versa Conveyor	London, OH	740-852-5609
Viking Machine & Design	De Pere, WI	888-286-2116
Volta Belting Technology, Inc.	Pine Brook, NJ	973-276-7905
Volumetric Technologies	Cannon Falls, MN	507-263-0034
W.A. Powers Company	Fort Worth, TX	800-792-1243
Wall Conveyor & Manufacturing	Huntington, WV	800-456-1335
Washington Frontier	Grandview, WA	509-469-7662
Yakima Wire Works	Reedley, CA	509-248-6790
Yargus Manufacturing	Marshall, IL	217-826-6352
Ziniz	Louisville, KY	502-955-6573

Bottle

Alliance Industrial Corporation	Lynchburg, VA	800-368-3556
Anderson Machine Sales	Fort Lee, NJ	
Berkshire PPM	Litchfield, CT	860-567-3118
Bilt-Rite Conveyors	New London, WI	920-982-6600
BMH Equipment	Sacramento, CA	800-350-8828
California Vibratory Feeders	Anaheim, CA	800-354-0972
Climax Packaging Machinery	Hamilton, OH	513-874-1233
Conveyor Supply	Deerfield, IL	847-945-5670
Ermanco	Norton Shores, MI	231-798-4547
Filling Equipment Company	Flushing, NY	800-247-7127
FleetwoodGoldcoWyard	Romeoville, IL	630-759-6800
Ipec	New Castle, PA	800-377-4732
Kinsley Inc	Doylestown, PA	800-414-6664
Laughlin Corporation	Fort Worth, TX	817-625-7756
LEWCO	Sandusky, OH	419-625-4014
Ohio Conveyor & Supply	Findlay, OH	419-422-3825
OnTrack Automation Inc	Waterloo, ON	519-886-9090
Priority One Packaging	Waterloo, ON	800-387-9102
Rexnord Corporation	Milwaukee, WI	866-739-6673
San Fab Conveyor Systems	Sandusky, OH	419-626-4465
Simplex Filler Company	Napa, CA	800-796-7539

Chain

A.K. Robins	Baltimore, MD	800-486-9656
ABI Limited	Concord, ON	800-297-8666
Advanced Uniflo Technologies	Wichita, KS	800-688-0400
Airfloat/HSI Systems	Decatur, IL	217-423-6001
All Power	Sioux City, IA	712-258-0681

Andritz
Muncy, PA....570-546-8211
Berkshire PPM
Litchfield, CT....860-567-3118
BEVCO
Canada, BC....800-663-0090
Bilt-Rite Conveyors
New London, WI....920-982-6600
BMH Equipment
Sacramento, CA....800-350-8828
California Vibratory Feeders
Anaheim, CA....800-354-0972
Cannon Equipment Company
Rosemount, MN....800-825-8501
Conesco Conveyor Corporation
Clifton, NJ....973-365-1440
Conveyor Supply
Deerfield, IL....847-945-5670
Custom Conveyor & SupplyCorporation
Racine, WI....262-634-4920
Davron Technologies
Chattanooga, TN....423-870-1888
Diamond Chain Company
Indianapolis, IN....800-872-4246
Donahower & Company
Olathe, KS....913-829-2650
Dorner Manufacturing Corporation
Hartland, WI....800-397-8664
Duplex Mill & Manufacturing Company
Springfield, OH....937-325-5555
Dyna-Veyor
Newark, NJ....800-930-4760
Eisenmann Corporation
Crystal Lake, IL....815-455-4100
EMC Solutions, Inc
Celina, OH....419-586-2388
Filling Equipment Company
Flushing, NY....800-247-7127
Fleetwood
Romeoville, IL....630-759-6800
Flodin
Moses Lake, WA....509-766-2996
FreesTech
Sinking Spring, PA....717-560-7560
Gem Equipment of Oregon
Woodburn, OR....503-982-9902
Graybill Machines
Lititz, PA....717-626-5221
Greenline Corporation
Charlotte, NC....800-331-5312
Hurt Conveyor Equipment Company
Los Angeles, CA....323-541-0433
Industrial Kinetics
Downers Grove, IL....800-655-0306
Laughlin Corporation
Fort Worth, TX....817-625-7756
Le Fiell Company, Inc.
Reno, NV....775-677-5300
LEWCO
Sandusky, OH....419-625-4014
Magnetic Products
Highland, MI....800-544-5930
Martin Cab
Cleveland, OH....216-651-3882
Material Systems Engineering
Stilesville, IN....800-634-0904
McNichols Conveyor Company
Southfield, MI....800-331-1926
Mell & Company
Niles, IL....800-262-6355
Michigan Industrial Belting
Livonia, MI....800-778-1650
New London Engineering
New London, WI....800-437-1994
Ohio Conveyor & Supply
Findlay, OH....419-422-3825
Omni Metalcraft Corporation
Alpena, MI....989-358-7000
Our Name is Mud
New York, NY....877-683-7867
Packaging & Processing Equipment
Ayr, ON....519-622-6666
Priority One Packaging
Waterloo, ON....800-387-9102
R.G. Stephens Engineering
Long Beach, CA....800-499-3001
Rexnord Corporation
Milwaukee, WI....866-739-6673
Richards Industries Systems
West Caldwell, NJ....973-575-7480
San Fab Conveyor Systems
Sandusky, OH....419-626-4465
Simplex Filler Company
Napa, CA....800-796-7539
Spurgeon Company
Ferndale, MI....800-396-2554
Sweet Manufacturing Company
Springfield, OH....800-334-7254
Tri-Pak Machinery, Inc.
Harlingen, TX....956-423-5140
TWM Manufacturing
Leamington, ON....888-495-4831
Versa Conveyor
London, OH....740-852-5609
Washington Frontier
Grandview, WA....509-469-7662
Wilkie Brothers Conveyors
Marysville, MI....810-364-4820
Yargus Manufacturing
Marshall, IL....217-826-6352
Ziniz
Louisville, KY....502-955-6573

Systems & Components

A P Dataweigh Systems
Cumming, GA....877-409-2562
A-Z Factory Supply
Schiller Park, IL....800-323-4511
A.C. Horn & Co
Dallas, TX....800-657-6155
A.K. Robins
Baltimore, MD....800-486-9656
A.T. Ferrell Company Inc
Bluffton, IN....800-248-8318
ABI Limited
Concord, ON....800-297-8666
Accutek Packaging Equipment Company
Vista, CA....800-989-1828
Adamation
Commerce, CA....800-225-3075
Advance Weight Systems
Grafton, OH....440-926-3691
Advanced Detection Systems
Milwaukee, WI....414-672-0553
Advanced Uniflo Technologies
Wichita, KS....800-688-0400
Aerocon
Langhorne, PA....215-860-6056
Aerowerks
Mississauga, ON....888-774-1616
AFECO
Algona, IA....888-295-1116
Airfloat/HSI Systems
Decatur, IL....217-423-6001
All Power
Sioux City, IA....712-258-0681
Allen Systems
Newberg, OR....800-246-2034
Alliance Bakery Systems
Blythewood, SC....803-691-9227
Alliance Industrial Corporation
Lynchburg, VA....800-368-3556
Alliance Products, LLC
Murfreesboro, TN....800-522-3973
Allied Bakery and Food Service Equipment
Santa Fe Springs, CA....562-945-6506
Allied Uniking Corporation
Memphis, TN....901-365-7240
Alpha MOS America
Hanover, MD....410-553-9736
Amark Packaging Systems
Kansas City, MO....816-965-9000
American Auger & Accesories
West Chester, PA....866-219-9619
American Extrusion International
South Beloit, IL....815-624-6616
American Food Equipment Company
Hayward, CA....510-783-0255
Ametek Technical & Industrial Products
Kent, OH....215-256-6601
Ammeraal Beltech
Grand Rapids, MI....616-791-0292
Anderson Machine Sales
Fort Lee, NJ
Anderson-Crane Company
Minneapolis, MN....800-314-2747
Andgar Corporation
Ferndale, WA....360-366-9900
Andritz
Muncy, PA....570-546-8211
Anver Corporation
Hudson, MA....800-654-3500
Apache Inc.
Cedar Rapids, IA....800-553-5455
Apache Stainless Equipment Corporation
Beaver Dam, WI....800-444-0398
Apollo Sheet Metal
Kennewick, WA....509-586-1104
APV Baker
Goldsboro, NC....919-736-4309
ASGCO Manufacturing
Allentown, PA....800-344-4000
Ashworth Bros
Winchester, VA....800-682-4594
Atlas Equipment Company
Kansas City, MO....800-842-9188
Automated Food Systems
Waxahachie, TX....972-298-5719
Automated Production Systems Corporation
New Freedom, PA....888-345-5377
Automatic Handling
Erie, MI....734-847-0633
Automotion
Oak Lawn, IL....708-229-3700
Baking Machines
Livermore, CA....925-449-3369
Belco Packaging Systems
Monrovia, CA....800-833-1833
Belshaw Adamatic Bakery Group
Auburn, WA....800-578-2547
Belt Technologies
Agawam, MA....413-786-9922
Berndorf Belt Technology USA
Elgin, IL....877-232-7322
Best
Brunswick, OH....800-827-9237
Best Diversified Products
Jonesboro, AR....800-327-9209
Bettendorf Stanford
Salem, IL....800-548-2253
BEVCO
Canada, BC....800-663-0090
Bilt-Rite Conveyors
New London, WI....920-982-6600
Biner Ellison
Vista, CA....800-733-8162
BMH
City of Industry, CA....909-349-2530
BMH Equipment
Sacramento, CA....800-350-8828
Bowman Hollis Manufacturing
Charlotte, NC....888-269-2358
Boyd Corp.
Modesto, CA....888-244-6931
Brothers Metal Products
Santa Ana, CA....714-972-3008
Brush Research Manufacturing Company
Los Angeles, CA....323-261-2193
Bryant Products
Ixonia, WI....800-825-3874
Buffalo Technologies Corporation
Buffalo, NY....800-332-2419
Buhler Group
Raleigh, NC....919-851-2000
Bulldog Factory Service
Madison Heights, MI....248-541-3500
Bunting Magnetics Company
Newton, KS....800-835-2526
C S Bell Company
Tiffin, OH....888-958-6381
C&R Refrigation Inc,
Center, TX....800-438-6182
C.H. Babb Company
Raynham, MA....508-977-0600
C.J. Machine
Fridley, MN....763-767-4630
C.R. Daniels Inc.
Ellicott City, MD....800-933-2638
Cable Conveyor Systems
Columbia, SC....800-624-6064
Caddy Corporation of America
Bridgeport, NJ....856-467-4222
California Vibratory Feeders
Anaheim, CA....800-354-0972
Caljan America
Denver, CO....303-321-3600
Cambelt International Corporation
Salt Lake City, UT....801-972-5511
Can Lines Engineering
Downey, CA....562-861-2996
Cannon Conveyor Specialty Systems
Rosemount, MN....800-533-2071
Cannon Equipment Company
Rosemount, MN....800-825-8501

Capway Systems
York, PA 877-222-7929
Carman Industries
Jeffersonville, IN 800-456-7560
Carrier Vibrating Equipment
Louisville, KY 502-969-3171
Carron Net Company
Two Rivers, WI........................ 800-558-7768
Casso-Solar Corporation
Pomona, NY 800-988-4455
Chantland-MHS Company
Dakota City, IA........................ 515-332-4045
Charlton & Hill
Lethbridge, AB 403-328-3388
Chase-Logeman Corporation
Greensboro, NC 336-665-0754
Checker Engineering
New Hope, MN........................ 888-800-5001
Chicago Conveyor Corporation
Addison, IL........................ 630-543-6300
CHL Systems
Souderton, PA........................ 215-723-7284
Chocolate Concepts
Hartville, OH 330-877-3322
Christianson Systems
Blomkest, MN........................ 800-328-8896
Christy Machine Company
Fremont, OH........................ 888-332-6451
CIM Bakery Equipment of USA
Arlington Heights, IL 847-818-8121
Cincinnati Boss Company
Omaha, NE 402-556-4070
Cincinnati Industrial Machinery
Mason, OH 800-677-0076
Cintex of America
Carol Stream, IL 800-424-6839
Cleveland Vibrator Company
Cleveland, OH 800-221-3298
Climax Packaging Machinery
Hamilton, OH 513-874-1233
Clipper Belt Lacer Company
Grand Rapids, MI 616-459-3196
Coastline Equipment
Bellingham, WA 360-739-2480
Colborne Foodbotics
Lake Forest, IL 847-371-0101
Columbus McKinnon Corporation
Amherst, NY........................ 800-888-0985
Command Belt Cleaning Systems
Jamaica, NY 800-433-7627
Commercial Dehydrator Systems Inc
Eugene, OR........................ 800-369-4283
Commercial Manufacturing& Supply Company
Fresno, CA 559-237-1855
Conesco Conveyor Corporation
Clifton, NJ........................ 973-365-1440
Conveyance Technologies LLC
Cleveland, OH 800-701-2278
Conveying Industries
Denver, CO........................ 877-600-4874
Conveyor Accessories
Burr Ridge, IL........................ 800-323-7093
Conveyor Components Company
Croswell, MI........................ 800-233-3233
Conveyor Supply
Deerfield, IL........................ 847-945-5670
Cook King
Laguna Beach, CA 949-497-1235
Corn States Metal Fabricators
West Des Moines, IA 515-225-7961
Coss Engineering Sales Company
Rochester Hills, MI........................ 800-446-1365
Crippen Manufacturing Company
St. Louis, MI........................ 800-872-2474
Crown Simplimatic Company
Lynchburg, VA 434-582-1200
Cugar Machine Company
Fort Worth, TX 817-927-0411
Currie Machinery Company
Santa Clara, CA 408-727-0424
Custom Conveyor & SupplyCorporation
Racine, WI 262-634-4920
Custom Food Machinery
Stockton, CA........................ 209-463-4343
Custom Metal Designs
Oakland, FL 800-334-1777
Custom Systems Integration Company
Carlsbad, CA........................ 760-635-1099
Cyclonaire Corporation
York, NE........................ 800-445-0730
Davron Technologies
Chattanooga, TN........................ 423-870-1888
Dearborn Mid-West Company
Lenexa, KS........................ 913-384-9950
Delavan Spray Technologies
Bamberg, SC........................ 800-982-6943
Delta/Ducon
Malvern, PA 800-238-2974
Dematic Corp
Grand Rapids, MI 877-725-7500
Descon EDM
Brocton, NY 716-792-9300
Design Systems
Farmington Hills, MI 800-660-4374
Design Technology Corporation
Billerica, MA 978-663-7000
Dillin Engineered Systems Corporation
Perrysburg, OH........................ 419-666-6789
Diversified Capping Equipment
Perrysburg, OH........................ 419-666-2566
Diversified Metal Engineering
Charlottetown, PE........................ 902-628-6900
Donahower & Company
Olathe, KS........................ 913-829-2650
Douglas Machine
Alexandria, MN 320-763-6587
Dresco Belting Company
East Weymouth, MA........................ 781-335-1350
Duke Manufacturing Company
Saint Louis, MO 800-735-3853
Duluth Sheet Metal
Duluth, MN........................ 218-722-2613
Dunkley International
Kalamazoo, MI 800-666-1264
Dunrite
Fremont, NE 800-782-3061
Duplex Mill & Manufacturing Company
Springfield, OH........................ 937-325-5555
Dupps Company
Germantown, OH 937-855-6555
Durand-Wayland, Inc.
Lagrange, GA 800-241-2308
Dyco
Bloomsburg, PA 800-545-3926
Dyna-Veyor
Newark, NJ 800-930-4760
Dynamet
Kalamazoo, MI........................ 269-385-0006
Dynamic Air
Saint Paul, MN 651-484-2900
Dynamic Automation
Simi Valley, CA........................ 805-584-8476
Dynamic Storage Systems Inc.
Brooksville, FL 800-974-8211
E-ZLIFT Conveyors
Denver, CO 800-821-9966
E.F. Bavis & Associates Drive-Thru
Maineville, OH 513-677-0500
Eckels-Bilt, Inc
Fort Worth, TX 800-343-9020
ECS Warehouse
Buffalo, NY........................ 716-829-7356
Edmeyer
Minneapolis, MN 651-450-1210
Eisenmann Corporation
Crystal Lake, IL 815-455-4100
Electrical Engineering &Equipment Company
Des Moines, IA .... 800-33 -722
ELF Machinery
La Porte, IN........................ 800-328-0466
EMC Solutions, Inc
Celina, OH 419-586-2388
En-Hanced Products, Inc.
Westerville, OH........................ 800-783-7400
Engineered Products Corporation
Greenville, SC........................ 800-868-0145
Equipment Outlet
Meridian, ID 208-887-1472
Eriez Magnetics
Erie, PA........................ 800-346-4946
Ermanco
Norton Shores, MI 231-798-4547
F&A Fabricating
Battle Creek, MI 269-965-3268
F.B. Pease Company
Rochester, NY........................ 585-475-1870
F.N. Smith Corporation
Oregon, IL........................ 815-732-2171
Fabreeka International
Boise, ID 800-423-4469
Fata Automation
Sterling Heights, MI 586-323-9400
FEI
Mansfield, TX........................ 800-346-5908
Fenner Dunlop Engineered Conveyer Solutions
Pittsburgh, PA........................ 412-249-0700
Filler Specialties
Zeeland, MI........................ 616-772-9235
Filling Equipment Company
Flushing, NY........................ 800-247-7127
Fillit
Kirkland, QC........................ 514-694-2390
Fishmore
Melbourne,, FL 321-723-4751
Fleet Wood Goldco Wyard
Cockeysville, MD 410-785-1934
Fleetwood
Romeoville, IL 630-759-6800
Fleetwood Systems
Orlando, FL........................ 407-855-0230
FleetwoodGoldcoWyard
Romeoville, IL 630-759-6800
Flexco
Downers Grove, IL 800-323-3444
Flexco
Downers Grove, IL 800-541-8028
Flexible Material Handling
Suwanee, GA 800-669-1501
Flexicell
Ashland, VA 804-550-7300
Flexicon Corporation
Bethlehem, PA 610-814-2400
Flodin
Moses Lake, WA........................ 509-766-2996
Flow-Turn, Inc.
Union, NJ 908-687-3225
Fogg Company
Holland, MI........................ 616-786-3644
Food Engineering Unlimited
Fullerton, CA 714-879-8762
Food Machinery Sales
Bogart, GA 706-549-2207
Food Processing Equipment Company
Santa Fe Springs, CA 479-751-9392
Forbo Siegling LLC
Huntersville, NC 800-255-5581
FPEC Corporation
Santa Fe Springs, CA 562-802-3727
Franz Haas Machinery of America
Richmond, VA........................ 804-222-6022
FreesTech
Sinking Spring, PA 717-560-7560
Frelco
Stephenville, NL........................ 709-643-5668
Frigoscandia Equipment
Northfield, MN........................ 800-426-1283
Frost Food Handling Products
Grand Rapids, MI 616-453-7781
G.S. Blodgett Corporation
Burlington, VT 800-331-5842
Gardner Denver Inc.
Toronto, ON 416-763-4681
Garvey Corporation
Hammonton, NJ 800-257-8581
Gates Manufacturing Company
Saint Louis, MO 800-237-9226
GBN Machine & Engineering Corporation
Woodford, VA........................ 800-446-9871
Gebo Conveyors, Consultants & Systems
Laval, QC 450-973-3337
Gebo Corporation
Bradenton, FL........................ 941-727-1400
Gem Equipment of Oregon
Woodburn, OR 503-982-9902
Gemini Bakery Equipment Company
Philadelphia, PA 800-468-9046
General Machinery Corporation
Sheboygan, WI 888-243-6622
General Tank
Berwick, PA 800-435-8265
Georgia Duck & Cordage Mill
Scottdale, GA 404-297-3170
Globe International
Tacoma, WA 800-523-6575
Goergen-Mackwirth Company
Buffalo, NY........................ 716-874-4800
Goldco Industries
Loveland, CO 970-278-4400
Gough Econ, Inc.
Charlotte, NC 800-204-6844
Grain Machinery Manufacturing Corporation
Miami, FL........................ 305-620-2525
Graybill Machines
Lititz, PA........................ 717-626-5221
Greenbelt Industries
Buffalo, NY........................ 800-668-1114

Greenline Corporation
Charlotte, NC 800-331-5312
Greitzer
Elizabeth City, NC 252-338-4000
Griffin Automation
Buffalo, NY. 716-674-2300
Griffin Cardwell, Ltd
Louisville, KY 502-636-1374
Gulf Arizona Packaging
Humble, TX 800-364-3887
Gulf Systems
Oklahoma City, OK 405-528-2293
Gulf Systems
Brownsville, TX 800-217-4853
Gulf Systems
Oklahoma City, OK 800-364-3887
Gulf Systems
Arlington, TX 817-261-1915
H.G. Weber & Company
Kiel, WI. 920-894-2221
H.K. Systems
Milwaukee, WI 800-424-7365
Habasit America
Suwanee, GA 800-458-6431
Habasit Canada Limited
Oakville, ON. 905-827-4131
Halton Packaging Systems
Oakville, ON. 905-847-9141
Hapman Conveyors
Kalamazoo, MI 800-968-7722
Hardy Systems Corporation
Northbrook, IL 800-927-3956
Hart Design & Manufacturing
Green Bay, WI. 920-468-5927
Hartness International
Greenville, SC. 800-845-8791
Heinzen Sales International
Gilroy, CA. 408-842-7233
Herche Warehouse
Denver, CO 303-371-8186
Hi Roller Enclosed Belt Conveyors
Sioux Falls, SD 800-328-1785
HMC Corporation
Hopkinton, NH 603-746-4691
Hoffmeyer Company
San Leandro, CA. 800-350-2358
Hoppmann Corporation
Elkwood, VA. 800-368-3582
Hudson Belting & ServiceCompany
Worcester, MA 508-756-0090
Hughes Equipment Company LLC
Columbus, WI. 866-535-9303
Hurt Conveyor Equipment Company
Los Angeles, CA. 323-541-0433
Hydro Power
Terre Haute, IN. 812-232-0156
IJ White Corporation
Farmingdale, NY. 631-293-2211
Industrial Automation Systems
Santa Clarita, CA 888-484-4427
Industrial Kinetics
Downers Grove, IL. 800-655-0306
Industrial Magnetics
Boyne City, MI 800-662-4638
Inline Filling Systems
Venice, FL. 941-486-8800
Inter-City Welding & Manufacturing
Independence, MO 816-252-1770
Interlake Material Handling
Naperville, IL 800-468-3752
Interroll Corporation
Wilmington, NC 800-830-9680
Intralox
New Orleans, LA 800-535-8848
Irby
Rocky Mount, NC. 252-442-0154
J.C. Ford Company
La Habra, CA 714-871-7361
J.H. Thornton Company
Olathe, KS. 913-764-6550
J.L. Becker Company
Plymouth, MI 800-837-4328
JanTec
Traverse City, MI 800-992-3303
Jervis B. Webb Company
Farmington Hills, MI 248-553-1000
Jetstream Systems
Denver, CO 303-371-9002
K-Tron
Salina, KS 785-825-1611
K.F. Logistics
Cincinnati, OH 800-347-9100

Kamflex Corporation
Chicago, IL 800-323-2440
Kaps-All Packaging Systems
Riverhead, NY 631-727-0300
Kasel Associated Industries
Denver, CO 800-218-4417
Kaufman Engineered Systems
Waterville, OH 419-878-9727
Keenline Conveyor Systems
Omro, WI 920-685-0365
Key Material Handling
Simi Valley, CA. 800-539-7225
Key Technology
Walla Walla, WA. 509-529-2161
Kinergy Corporation
Louisville, KY 502-366-5685
Kinetic Equipment Company
Appleton, WI 806-293-4471
Kinsley Inc
Doylestown, PA 800-414-6664
Kisco Manufacturing
Greendale, BC. 604-823-7456
KISS Packaging Systems
Vista, CA. 888-522-3538
Kleenline Corporation
Newburyport, MA. 800-259-5973
Kline Process Systems
Reading, PA 610-371-0200
Klippenstein Corporation
Fresno, CA 888-834-4258
KLS Lubriquip
Minneapolis, MN 612-623-6000
KOFAB
Algona, IA. 515-295-7265
Kohler Industries, Inc.
Lincoln, NE. 800-365-6708
Kornylak Corporation
Hamilton, OH 800-837-5676
KVP Falcon Plastic Belting
Reading, PA 800-445-7898
KWS Manufacturing Company
Burleson, TX. 800-543-6558
Laidig Industrial Systems
Mishawaka, IN 574-256-0204
Lambert Material Handling
Syracuse, NY 800-253-5103
LaRos Equipment Company
Portage, MI 269-323-1441
Laughlin Corporation
Fort Worth, TX 817-625-7756
Le Fiell Company, Inc.
Reno, NV 775-677-5300
Leeds Conveyor Manufacturer Company
Guilford, CT 800-724-1088
LEWCO
Sandusky, OH 419-625-4014
Lewis M. Carter Manufacturing Company
Donalsonville, GA 229-524-2197
Lock Inspection Systems
Fitchburg, MA 800-227-5539
Lorenz Couplings
Cobourg, ON. 800-263-7782
Louisville Dryer Company
Louisville, KY 800-735-3613
LPS Technology
Grafton, OH 800-586-1410
Lumsden Flexx Flow
Lancaster, PA 800-367-3664
Lyco Manufacturing
Wausau, WI. 715-845-7867
Lyco Wausau
Wausau, WI. 715-845-7867
MAC Equipment
Kansas City, MO. 800-821-2476
Machine Builders and Design
Shelby, NC 704-482-3456
Magnetic Products
Highland, MI. 800-544-5930
Magsys
Milwaukee, WI 414-543-2177
Mar-Con Wire Belt
Richmond, BC 877-962-7266
Marlen International
Astoria, OR 800-862-7536
Martin Engineering
Neponset, IL. 800-766-2786
Martin/Baron
Irwindale, CA 626-960-5153
Maryland Wire Belts
Cambridge, MD 800-677-2358
Material Systems Engineering
Stilesville, IN 800-634-0904

Materials TransportationCompany
Temple, TX 800-433-3110
Mathews Conveyor
Danville, KY. 800-628-4397
Matthiesen Equipment Company
San Antonio, TX. 800-624-8635
McCormick Enterprises
Delton, MI. 800-223-3683
McNichols Conveyor Company
Southfield, MI. 800-331-1926
MeGa Industries
Burlington, ON 800-665-6342
Mell & Company
Niles, IL 800-262-6355
Merco/Savory
Mt. Pleasant, MI 800-733-8821
Meriwether Industries
Bloomfield, NJ 800-332-2358
METKO
New Holstein, WI. 920-898-4221
Metzgar Conveyor Company
Comstock Park, MI. 888-266-8390
Meyer Machine & Garroutte Products
San Antonio, TX. 210-736-1811
Michigan Industrial Belting
Livonia, MI 800-778-1650
Midwest Metalcraft & Equipment
Windsor, MO. 800-647-3167
Midwest Rubber & Supply Company
Commerce City, CO 800-537-7457
Millard Manufacturing Corporation
La Vista, NE 800-662-4263
Miller Hofft Brands
Indianapolis, IN 317-638-6576
Miller Metal Fabricators
Staunton, VA. 540-886-5575
Molding Automation Concepts
Woodstock, IL. 800-435-6979
Moline Machinery
Duluth, MN. 800-767-5734
Monarch-McLaren
Weston, ON. 416-741-9675
Mp Equip. Co.
Buford, GA 770-614-5355
Mumper Machine Corporation
Butler, WI 262-781-8908
Murata Automated Systems
Charlotte, NC 800-428-8469
National Conveyor Corporation
Commerce, CA 323-725-0355
National Drying Machinery Company
Philadelphia, PA 215-464-6070
NECO
Omaha, NE 402-453-6912
Neos
Elk River, MN. 888-441-6367
Nercon Engineering & Manufacturing
Oshkosh, WI 920-233-3268
New London Engineering
New London, WI 800-437-1994
Newcastle Company, Inc.
New Castle, PA 724-658-4516
Niro Inc
Hudson, WI. 715-386-9371
North American Roller Products, Inc
Glen Ellyn, IL 630-858-9161
Northland Stainless
Tomahawk, WI 715-453-5326
Northwind
Alpena, AR 870-437-2585
Nothum Food Processing Systems
Springfield, MO 800-435-1297
Nu-Con Equipment
Chanhassen, MN. 877-939-0510
NuTec Manufacturing
New Lenox, IL 815-722-5348
Ohio Magnetics-Stearns Magnetics
Cleveland, OH 800-486-6446
Omega Industrial Products
Saukville, WI 800-279-6634
Omicron Steel Products Company
Jamaica, NY 718-805-3400
Omni Metalcraft Corporation
Alpena, MI 989-358-7000
Omni-Lift
Salt Lake City, UT 801-486-3776
OnTrack Automation Inc
Waterloo, ON 519-886-9090
Optek
Galena, OH 800-533-8400
Oshikiri Corporation of America
Philadelphia, PA 215-637-6005

Ouellette Machinery Systems
Fenton, MO. 800-545-7619
Our Name is Mud
New York, NY 877-683-7867
Oyster Bay Pump Works
Hicksville, NY 516-933-4500
Pacific Pneumatics
Rancho Cucamonga, CA 800-221-0961
Package Conveyor Company
Fort Worth, Fo. 800-792-1243
Packaging Equipment & Conveyors, Inc
Elkhart, IN. 574-266-6995
Packaging Machinery
Montgomery, AL. 334-265-9211
Packaging Progressions
Collegeville, PA 610-489-8601
Paget Equipment Company
Marshfield, WI 715-384-3158
Palace Packaging Machines
Downingtown, PA. 610-873-7252
Par Systems
Saint Paul, MN 800-464-1320
Parkson Corporation
Berkeley Heights, NJ 908-464-0700
Parkson Illinois
Vernon Hills, IL 847-816-3700
Paxton Products
Cincinnati, OH 800-441-7475
Peerless Conveyor and Manufacturing Corporation
Kansas City, KS 913-342-2240
Peerless Dough Mixing and Make-Up
Sidney, OH 800-999-3327
Peerless Food Inc
Sidney, OH 937-494-2870
Peerless-Winsmith
Springville, NY. 716-592-9310
Pengo Corporation
Cokato, MN. 800-599-0211
Peterson Fiberglass Laminates
Shell Lake, WI 715-468-2306
Piab Vacuum Products
Hingham, MA 800-321-7422
PlexPack Corp
Toronto, ON 855-635-9238
Pneumatic Conveying, Inc.
Ontario, CA. 800-655-4481
Polar Process
Plattsville, ON. 877-896-8077
Power-Pack Conveyor Company
Willoughby, OH 440-975-9955
Precision
Miami, FL. 800-762-7565
Priority One America
Waterloo, ON 519-746-6950
Priority One Packaging
Waterloo, ON 800-387-9102
Process Engineering & Fabrication
Afton, VA 800-852-7975
Prodo-Pak Corporation
Garfield, NJ. 973-777-7770
Production Systems
Marietta, GA. 800-235-9734
Professional EngineeringAssociation
Louisville, KY 502-429-0432
PTI Packaging
Portage, WI. 800-501-4077
Puritan Manufacturing
Omaha, NE 800-331-0487
Quadrant
Fort Wayne, IN 800-628-7264
R.G. Stephens Engineering
Long Beach, CA 800-499-3001
Rahmann Belting & Industrial Rubber Products
Gastonia, NC. 888-248-8148
Ralphs-Pugh Company
Benicia, CA. 800-486-0021
Rapat Corporation
Hawley, MN 800-325-6377
Rapid Industries
Louisville, KY 800-787-4381
Raque Food Systems
Louisville, KY 502-267-9641
Reading Plastic Fabricators
Temple, PA 610-926-3245
Reese Enterprises
Rosemount, MN 800-328-0953
Regina USA, Inc
Oak Creek, WI 414-571-0032
Reinke & Schomann
Milwaukee, WI. 414-964-1100
Renold Products
Westfield, NY 800-879-2529
Rexnord Corporation
Milwaukee, WI 866-739-6673
REYCO Systems
Caldwell, ID 208-795-5700
Rhodes Machinery International
Louisville, KY 502-778-7377
Richards Industries Systems
West Caldwell, NJ. 973-575-7480
Rigidized Metals Corporation
Buffalo, NY. 800-836-2580
RMF Freezers
Grandview, MO. 816-765-4101
Roechling Engineered Plastics
Gastonia, NC. 800-541-4419
Rome Machine & Foundry Company, Inc
Rome, GA 800-538-7663
Ruiz Flour Tortillas
Riverside, CA 909-947-7811
S. Howes
Silver Creek, NY. 888-255-2611
Sadler Conveyor Systems
Montreal, QC 888-887-5129
San Fab Conveyor Systems
Sandusky, OH 419-626-4465
Sardee Industries
Orlando, FL. 407-295-2114
Sasib North America
Plano, TX 972-422-5808
Schloss Engineered Equipment
Aurora, CO 303-695-4500
Schlueter Company
Janesville, WI. 800-359-1700
Schneider Electric Sensor Competency Center
Dayton, OH. 800-435-2121
Schneider Packaging Equipment
Brewerton, NY 315-676-3035
Schroeder Sewing Technologies
San Marcos, CA 760-591-9733
Scientific Process & Research
Kendall Park, NJ. 800-868-4777
Screw Conveyor Corporation
Hammond, IN 219-931-1450
Servco Co.
St Louis, MO. 314-781-3189
Shelcon
Ontario, CA. 909-947-4877
Shingle Belting
King of Prussia, PA. 800-345-6294
Shouldice Brothers SheetMetal
Battle Creek, MI 269-962-5579
Shuttleworth
Huntington, IN 800-444-7412
SI Systems
Easton, PA. 800-523-9464
Sidney Manufacturing Company
Sidney, OH 800-482-3535
Simplex Filler Company
Napa, CA. 800-796-7539
Sinco
Red Wing, MN 800-243-6753
Slip-Not Belting Corporation
Kingsport, TN. 423-246-8141
Smalley Manufacturing Company
Knoxville, TN 865-966-5866
Smetco
Aurora, OR 800-253-5400
Southern Ag Company
Blakely, GA. 229-723-4262
Southworth Products Corporation
Portland, ME. 800-743-1000
Span Tech
Glasgow, KY. 270-651-9166
Spanco
Morgantown, PA. 800-869-2080
Speedways Conveyors
Lancaster, NY 800-800-1022
Sperling Industries
Omaha, NE 800-647-5062
Spiral Manufacturing Company
Minneapolis, MN 800-426-3643
Springport Steel Wire Products
Concord, MI 517-857-3010
Spudnik Equipment
Blackfoot, ID 208-785-0480
Spurgeon Company
Ferndale, MI 800-396-2554
Stainless Specialists
Wausau, WI. 800-236-4155
Steel Storage Systems
Commerce City, CO 800-442-0291
Stein DSI
Sandusky, OH 800-447-2630
Steinmetz Machine Works
Stamford, CT. 203-327-0118
Sterling Net & Twine Company
Cedar Knolls, NJ. 800-342-0316
Stokes Material HandlingSystems
Doylestown, PA 215-340-2200
Superior Industries
Morris, MN. 800-321-1558
Svedala Industries
Colorado Springs, CO. 719-471-3443
TEMP-AIR
Burnsville, MN 800-836-7432
TGS Engineering & Conveying
Houston, TX 713-466-0426
The National Provisioner
Deerfield, IL 847-763-9534
Thomas L. Green & Company
Robenosia, PA. 610-693-5816
Titan Industries
New London, WI 800-558-3616
TKF
Cincinnati, OH 513-241-5910
Transnorm System
Grand Prairie, TX 800-259-2303
Traycon
Carlstadt, NJ 201-939-5555
Tridyne Process Systems Inc.
South Burlington, VT 802-863-6873
Triple/S Dynamics
Dallas, TX. 800-527-2116
True Manufacturing Company
O Fallon, MO 636-240-2400
TWM Manufacturing
Leamington, ON 888-495-4831
Uhrden
Sugarcreek, OH. 800-852-2411
Unex Manufacturing
Jackson, NJ 800-695-7726
United Pentek
Indianapolis, IN 800-357-9299
United States Systems
Kansas City, KS 888-281-2454
UniTrak Corporation
Port Hope, ON 866-883-5749
Universal Die & Stamping
Prairie Du Sac, WI 608-643-2477
Universal Industries, In
Cedar Falls, IA 800-553-4446
Universal Labeling Systems
St Petersburg, FL 877-236-0266
Universal Packaging
Houston, TX 800-324-2610
US Rubber Supply Company
Brooklyn, NY 718-782-7888
Vac-U-Max
Belleville, NJ 800-822-8629
Van Der Graaf Corporation
Lithia Springs, GA 770-819-6650
Vertical Systems
Ft. Michelle, KY. 859-485-9650
Vesco
New Hyde Park, NY. 516-746-5139
W.A. Powers Company
Fort Worth, TX 800-792-1243
W.G. Durant Corporation
Whittier, CA 562-946-5555
Walker Magnetics
Worcester, MA 800-962-4638
Wall Conveyor & Manufacturing
Huntington, WV 800-456-1335
Ward Ironworks
Welland, ON 888-441-9273
Wardcraft Conveyor
Spring Arbor, MI 800-782-2779
Washington Frontier
Grandview, WA. 509-469-7662
Webb-Stiles Company
Valley City, OH. 330-225-7761
Weigh Right Automatic Scale Company
Joliet, IL 800-571-0249
Weiler & Company
Whitewater, WI. 800-558-9507
Westfield Sheet Metal Works
Kenilworth, NJ 908-276-5500
Whirl Air Flow Corporation
Big Lake, MN. 800-373-3461
Wilkie Brothers Conveyors
Marysville, MI 810-364-4820
Wilson Steel Products Company
Memphis, TN 901-527-8742
Win-Holt Equipment Group
Westbury, NY 800-444-3595

Wire Belt Company of America
Londonderry, NH 603-644-2500
Witte Company
Washington, NJ 908-689-6500
Yakima Wire Works
Reedley, CA 509-248-6790
Yargus Manufacturing
Marshall, IL 217-826-6352
YW Yacht Basin
Easton, MD 410-822-0414
Ziniz
Louisville, KY 502-955-6573

Cooperage

Brooks Barrel Company
Baltimore, MD 800-398-2766
EGW Bradbury Enterprises
Bridgewater, ME 800-332-6021
Fetzer Vineyards
Hopland, CA 800-846-8637
Gibbs Brothers Cooperage Company
Hot Springs, AR 501-623-8881
Oak Barrel Winecraft
Berkeley, CA 510-849-0400
Ramoneda Brothers
Culpeper, VA 540-825-9166
Trilla Steel Drum Corporation
Chicago, IL 773-847-7588
Warwick Products Company
Cleveland, OH 800-535-4404

Cylinders

Catalina Cylinders
Garden Grove, CA 714-890-0999

Dairy Industry

Elmo Rietschle - A Gardner Denver Product
Qunicy, IL 217-222-5400
GEA Niro Soavi North America
Bedford, NH 603-606-4060
GEA Process Engineering,Inc.
Columbia, MD 410-997-8700
GEA Tuchenhagen North America, USA, LLC
Portland, ME 207-797-9500
Invensys APV Products
Houston, TX 713-329-1600
Marel Food Systems, Inc.
Lenexa, KS 913-888-9110
Reiser
Canton, MA 781-575-9941
Sanchelima Intl. Inc.
Miami, FL 305-591-4343
Schwartz ManufacturingcoCompany
Two Rivers, WI 920-793-1375
Stephan Machinery GmbH
Mandelein, IL 847-247-0182
Stratecon International Consultants
Winston Salem, NC 336-768-6808
Unitherm Food Systems Innc.
Bristow, OK 918-367-0197

Depositors

Alard Equipment Corporation
Williamson, NY 315-589-4511
Bogner Industries
Ronkonkoma, NY 631-981-5123
Edhard Corporation
Hackettstown, NJ 888-334-2731
Polar Process
Plattsville, ON 877-896-8077
Raque Food Systems
Louisville, KY 502-267-9641
Reiser
Canton, MA 781-575-9941

Feeders

Alard Equipment Corporation
Williamson, NY 315-589-4511
All Power
Sioux City, IA 712-258-0681
Anderson-Crane Company
Minneapolis, MN 800-314-2747
Applied Chemical Technology
Florence, AL 800-228-3217
Automated Flexible Conveyor
Clifton, NJ 800-694-7271
Buffalo Technologies Corporation
Buffalo, NY 800-332-2419
California Vibratory Feeders
Anaheim, CA 800-354-0972
Campbell Wrapper Corporation
De Pere, WI 920-983-7100
Carman Industries
Jeffersonville, IN 800-456-7560
Carrier Vibrating Equipment
Louisville, KY 502-969-3171
Chicago Conveyor Corporation
Addison, IL 630-543-6300
Cleveland Vibrator Company
Cleveland, OH 800-221-3298
Creative Automation
Passaic, NJ 973-778-0061
Custom Systems Integration Company
Carlsbad, CA 760-635-1099
Dema Engineering Company
Saint Louis, MO 800-325-3362
Eriez Magnetics
Erie, PA 800-346-4946
Flow of Solids
Westford, MA 978-392-0300
Fuller Weighing Systems
Columbus, OH 614-882-8121
Gebo Corporation
Bradenton, FL 941-727-1400
Gram Equipment of America
Tampa, FL 813-248-1978
Graybill Machines
Lititz, PA 717-626-5221
Hart Design & Manufacturing
Green Bay, WI 920-468-5927
Hoppmann Corporation
Elkwood, VA 800-368-3582
Hydro Power
Terre Haute, IN 812-232-0156
Ilapak
Newtown, PA 215-579-2900
Ipec
New Castle, PA 800-377-4732
Key Technology
Walla Walla, WA 509-529-2161
Kinergy Corporation
Louisville, KY 502-366-5685
KISS Packaging Systems
Vista, CA 888-522-3538
Magnuson Corporation
Pueblo, CO 719-948-9500
Martin Vibration Systems
Marine City, MI 800-474-4538
MeGa Industries
Burlington, ON 800-665-6342
Mell & Company
Niles, IL 800-262-6355
Merrick Industries
Lynn Haven, FL 800-271-7834
Meyer Machine & Garroutte Products
San Antonio, TX 210-736-1811
Modular King Packaging Systems
Randolph, NJ 973-970-9393
National Drying Machinery Company
Philadelphia, PA 215-464-6070
Norden
Branchburg, NJ 908-252-9483
Norwalt Design Inc.
Randolph, NJ 973-927-3200
Nu-Con Equipment
Chanhassen, MN 877-939-0510
Omega Design Corporation
Exton, PA 800-346-0191
Open Date Systems
Georges Mills, NH 877-673-6328
Our Name is Mud
New York, NY 877-683-7867
Pacific Process Technology
La Jolla, CA 858-551-3298
Palace Packaging Machines
Downingtown, PA 610-873-7252
Paramount Packaging Corp.
Melville, NY 516-333-8100
Pfankuch Machinery Corporation
Apple Valley, MN 952-891-3311
PFI Prasence From Innovation
St Louis, MO 314-423-9777
Polar Process
Plattsville, ON 877-896-8077
Professional EngineeringAssociation
Louisville, KY 502-429-0432
Ram Equipment
Waukesha, WI 262-513-1114
Schenck Process LLC
Whitewater, WI 888-742-1249
Schneider Packing Equipment Company
Brewerton, NY 315-676-3035
Shenck AccuRate
Whitewater, WI 888-742-1249
Shiffer Industries
Kihei, HI 800-642-1774
Smalley Manufacturing Company
Knoxville, TN 865-966-5866
Summit Machine Builders Corporation
Denver, CO 800-274-6741
Superior Food Machinery
Pico Rivera, CA 800-944-0396
Tecweigh/Tecnetics Industries
White Bear Lake, MN 800-536-4880
Thayer Scale
Pembroke, MA 781-826-8101
Thermo Ramsey
Coon Rapids, MN 763-783-2500
Universal Labeling Systems
St Petersburg, FL 877-236-0266
Vesco
New Hyde Park, NY 516-746-5139
Ward Ironworks
Welland, ON 888-441-9273
Waukesha Cherry-Burrell
Louisville, KY 502-491-4310
Weigh Right Automatic Scale Company
Joliet, IL 800-571-0249
Wyssmont Company
Fort Lee, NJ 201-947-4600

Gravimetric, Volumetric, Loss-In-Weight, Etc.

Applied Chemical Technology
Florence, AL 800-228-3217
Automated Flexible Conveyor
Clifton, NJ 800-694-7271
Chicago Conveyor Corporation
Addison, IL 630-543-6300
Cleveland Vibrator Company
Cleveland, OH 800-221-3298
Ilapak
Newtown, PA 215-579-2900
Merrick Industries
Lynn Haven, FL 800-271-7834
Polar Process
Plattsville, ON 877-896-8077
Shenck AccuRate
Whitewater, WI 888-742-1249
Tecweigh/Tecnetics Industries
White Bear Lake, MN 800-536-4880
Thayer Scale
Pembroke, MA 781-826-8101
Thermo Ramsey
Coon Rapids, MN 763-783-2500
Weigh Right Automatic Scale Company
Joliet, IL 800-571-0249

Speed Reducer

Boston Gear
Boston, MA 888-999-9860
FR Drake Company
Waynesboro, VA 540-451-2790

Filtration Devices & Systems

A&B Process Systems
Stratford, WI 888-258-2789
ACS Industries, Inc.
Lincoln, RI 866-783-4838
Advance Fitting Corporation
Elkhorn, WI 262-723-6699
Air Quality Engineering
Brooklyn Park, MN 800-328-0787
Air-Maze Corporation
Cuyahoga Falls, OH 330-928-4100
Airguard Industries
Jeffersonville, IN 866-247-4827
Airsan Corporation
Milwaukee, WI 800-558-5494
Alard Equipment Corporation
Williamson, NY 315-589-4511
Alexander Machinery
Spartanburg, SC 864-963-3624
Allegheny Bradford Corporation
Bradford, PA 800-542-0650
Allergen Air Filter Corporation
Houston, TX 800-333-8880
Ametek Technical & Industrial Products
Kent, OH 215-256-6601

Anguil Environmental Systems
Milwaukee, WI 800-488-0230
Applied Chemical Technology
Florence, AL 800-228-3217
APV Americas
Delavan, WI 800-252-5200
Aqua-Aerobic Systems
Loves Park, IL. 800-940-5008
Aquathin Corporation
Pompano Beach, FL 800-462-7634
Astro-Pure Water Purifiers
Deerfield Beach, FL 954-422-8966
Avery Filter Company
Westwood, NJ 201-666-9664
Avestin
Ottawa, ON 888-283-7846
Beach Filter Products
Glen Rock, PA. 800-232-2485
Berkshire PPM
Litchfield, CT 860-567-3118
Better Health Lab
Hackensack, NJ. 800-810-1888
Bird Machine Company
Houston, TX 800-229-7447
Bloomfield Industries
St. Louis, MO 888-356-5362
Blue Tech
Hickory, NC 828-324-5900
BluMetric Environmental Inc.
Ottawa, ON 613-839-3053
Bunn Corporation
Springfield, IL. 800-637-8606
CE International Trading Corporation
Miami, FL 800-827-1169
Cellulo Company
Fresno, CA 866-213-1131
Climate Master
Oklahoma City, OK 877-436-0263
Complete Automation
Lake Orion, MI 248-693-0500
Cook King
Laguna Beach, CA 949-497-1235
Corrigan Corporation of America
Gurnee, IL. 800-462-6478
Crane Environmental
Norristown, PA 800-633-7435
Crispy Lite
St. Louis, MO 888-356-5362
Croll-Reynolds Engineering Company
Trumbull, CT 203-371-1983
Culligan Company
Northbrook, IL 800-527-8637
Cuno
Meriden, CT 800-243-6894
Custom Fabricating & Repair
Marshfield, WI 800-236-8773
Dallas Group of America
Whitehouse, NJ. 800-367-4188
Dedert Corporation
Olympia Fields, IL 708-747-7000
Delta Pure Filtration
Ashland, VA 800-785-9450
Diamond Water Conditioning
Hortonville, WI. 800-236-8931
Diebolt & Company
Old Lyme, CT. 800-343-2658
Dow Chemical Company
Spring House, PA 800-447-4369
Durastill
Kansas City, MO. 800-449-5260
Dwyer Instruments
Michigan City, IN. 800-872-3141
Eaton Filtration, LLC
Tinton Falls, NJ. 800-859-9212
Eco-Air Products
San Diego, CA 800-284-8111
Elwood Safety Company
Buffalo, NY. 866-326-6060
Enting Water Condition g
Dayton, OH. 800-735-5100
Enviro-Clear Company, Inc
High Bridge, NJ 908-638-5507
Ertel Alsop
Kingston, NY 800-553-7835
Ertelalsop Inc.
Kingston, NY 800-553-7835
Etube and Wire
Shrewsbury, PA. 800-618-4720
Everfilt Corporation
Mira Loma, CA. 800-360-8380
Everpure, LLC
Hanover Park, IL. 630-307-3000
F.P. Smith Wire Cloth Company
Northlake, IL. 800-323-6842
Falcon Fabricators
Nashville, TN 615-832-0027
Filtercorp
Fresno, CA 800-473-4526
Filtration Systems
Sunrise, FL 954-572-2700
Filtration Systems Products
Saint Louis, MO 800-444-4720
Flame Gard
Lakewood, NJ 800-526-3694
Flanders Corporation
Washington, NC 800-637-2803
Freudenberg Nonwovens
Hopkinsville, KY 270-887-5115
Frymaster, LLC.
Shreveport, LA 800-221-4583
Fuller Ultraviolet CorpoRation
Frankfort, IL 815-469-3301
G.S. Blodgett Corporation
Burlington, VT 800-331-5842
G.W. Dahl Company
Greensboro, NC 800-852-4449
Gardner Denver Inc.
Toronto, ON 416-763-4681
Gaylord Industries
Tualatin, OR 800-547-9696
Globe International
Tacoma, WA 800-523-6575
Goodnature Products
Orchard Park, NY 800-875-3381
Greig Filters
Lafayette, LA 800-456-0177
Halton Company
Scottsville, KY 800-442-5866
Hankison International
Canonsburg, PA. 724-746-1100
Harborlite Corporation
Lompoc, CA 800-342-8667
Hayes & Stolz IndustrialManufacturing Company
Fort Worth, TX 800-725-7272
Hayward Industrial Products
Clemmons, NC 908-355-7995
HEMCO Corporation
Independence, MO 800-779-4362
Hess Machine International
Ephrata, PA 800-735-4377
Holland Applied Technologies
Burr Ridge, IL. 630-325-5130
HTI Filteration
Rancho Santa Margarita, CA 877-404-9372
Hungerford & Terry
Clayton, NJ 856-881-3200
Hunter Fan Company
Cordova, TN 901-743-1360
HydroMax
Emmitsburg, MD 800-326-0602
Hydropure Water Treatment Company
Coral Springs, FL 800-753-1547
I.W. Tremont Company
Hawthorne, NJ 973-427-3800
Imperial Commercial Cooking Equipment
Corona, CA 800-343-7790
Introdel Products
Itasca, IL. 800-323-4772
Kason Central
Columbus, OH 614-885-1992
Kason Industries
Newnan, GA 770-254-0553
Keating of Chicago
Mc Cook, IL 800-532-8464
Kentwood Spring Water Company
Patterson, LA 985-395-9313
Ketch
Wichita, KS. 800-766-3777
KHS
Waukesha, WI 262-798-1102
Kinetico
Newbury, OH 440-564-9111
King Bag & Manufacturing Company
Cincinnati, OH 800-444-5464
King Company
Dallas, TX. 507-451-3770
King Engineering - King-Gage
Newell, WV 800-242-8871
Kiss International/Di-tech Systems
Vista, CA. 800-527-5477
Kraissl Company
Hackensack, NJ. 800-572-4775
L&A Process Systems
Modesto, CA. 209-581-0205
L.C. Thompson Company
Kenosha, WI 800-558-4018
Lamports Filter Media
Cleveland, OH 216-881-2050
Lenser Filtration
Lakewood, NJ 732-370-1600
Lewis M. Carter Manufacturing Company
Donalsonville, GA 229-524-2197
Mars Air Systems
Gardena, CA 800-421-1266
Melvina Can Machinery Company
Hudson Falls, NY 518-743-0606
Membrane System Specialists
Wisconsin Rapids, WI 715-421-2333
Metlar LLC
Riverhead, NC 631-252-5574
MicroPure Filtration
Mound, MN 800-654-7873
Mies Products
West Bend, WI 800-480-6437
Miroil
Allentown, PA. 800-523-9844
Moli-Tron Company
Lakewood, CO 800-525-9494
Mountain Safety Research
Seattle, WA 800-877-9677
Muckler Industries, Inc
Saint Louis, MO 800-444-0283
NETZSCH
Exton, PA 610-363-8010
New Wave Enviro Water Products
Englewood, CO. 800-592-8371
Newark Wire Cloth Company
Clifton, NJ. 800-221-0392
Niro
Hudson, WI. 715-386-9371
Nordfab Systems
Thomasville, NC. 800-533-5286
Norton Performance Plastics
Wayne, NJ. 973-696-4700
Nothum Food Processing Systems
Springfield, MO 800-435-1297
O C Lugo Company
New City, NY 845-480-5121
Optipure
Plano, TX 972-422-1212
Ozotech
Yreka, CA. 530-842-4189
Pacific Process Technology
La Jolla, CA 858-551-3298
Pall Filtron
Northborough, MA 800-345-8766
Pall Food and Beverage
Port Washington, NY 866-905-7255
Par-Kan Company
Silver Lake, IN 800-291-5487
Parker Hannifin Corporation
Cleveland, OH 609-586-5151
Parker Hannifin Corporation
Indianapolis, IN 800-272-7537
Parkson Illinois
Vernon Hills, IL 847-816-3700
Piab Vacuum Products
Hingham, MA. 800-321-7422
Premier Manufactured Systems
Peoria, AZ. 800-752-5582
Prince Castle
Carol Stream, IL 800-722-7853
Pro-Flo Products
Cedar Grove, NJ 800-325-1057
PURA
Sun Valley, CA 800-292-7872
Purolator Products Company
Greensboro, NC 800-852-4449
R.F. Hunter Company
Dover, NH. 800-332-9565
R.R. Street & Co., Inc.
Naperville, IL 630-416-4244
Refractron Technologies Corporation
Newark, NY 315-331-6222
Reynolds Water Conditioning Company
Farmington Hills, MI 800-572-9575
Robinson/Kirshbaum Industries
Inglewood, CA 800-929-3812
Rolfs @ Boone
Boone, IA 800-265-2010
Sartorius Corporation
Edgewood, NY 800-635-2906
Schlueter Company
Janesville, WI 800-359-1700
Scienco Systems
Saint Louis, MO 314-621-2536

Scotsman Ice Systems
Vernon Hills, IL ... 800-726-8762

Selecto Scientific
Suwanee, GA ... 800-635-4017

SERFILCO Ltd
Northbrook, IL ... 800-323-5431

Sermia International
Blainville, QC ... 800-567-7483

Severn Trent Services
Fort Washington, PA ... 215-646-9201

Shick Tube-Veyor Corporation
Kansas City, MO ... 816-861-7224

Siemens Water Technologies Corp.
Warrendale, PA ... 866-926-8420

Sparkler Filters
Conroe, TX ... 936-756-4471

Spencer Strainer Systems
Jeffersonville, IN ... 800-801-4977

Star Filters
Timmonsville, SC ... 800-845-5381

Stearns Technical Textiles Company
Cincinnati, OH ... 800-543-7173

Stein DSI
Sandusky, OH ... 800-447-2630

Steri Technologies
Bohemia, NY ... 800-253-7140

Straight Line Filters
Wilmington, DE ... 302-654-8805

Tema Systems
Cincinnati, OH ... 513-489-7811

Therm Tec, Inc
Tualatin, OR ... 800-292-9163

Thomas Technical Services
Neillsville, WI. ... 715-743-4666

Trenton Mills
Trenton, TN. ... 731-855-1323

Triad Scientific
Manasquan, NJ ... 800-867-6690

Ultra Industries
Racine, WI ... 800-358-5872

Ultrafilter
Norcross, GA ... 800-543-3634

United Air Specialists
Cincinnati, OH ... 800-992-4422

United Filters
Amarillo, TX. ... 806-373-8386

United Industries Group
Newport Beach, CA ... 949-759-3200

United States Systems
Kansas City, KS ... 888-281-2454

US Filter Dewatering Systems
Holland, MI. ... 800-245-3006

Van Air Systems
Lake City, PA ... 800-840-9906

Vent Master
Mississauga, ON ... 800-565-2981

VMC Signs Inc.
Victoria, TX ... 361-575-0548

Washington Frontier
Grandview, WA. ... 509-469-7662

Water & Power Technologies
Salt Lake City, UT ... 888-271-3295

Water Sciences Services ,Inc.
Jackson, TN ... 973-584-4131

Water System Group
Santa Clarita, CA ... 800-350-9283

Waterlink/Sanborn Technologies
Canton, OH ... 800-343-3381

Whatman
Piscataway, NJ ... 973-245-8300

Whatman
Haverhill, MA. ... 978-374-7400

Williams & Mettle Company
Houston, TX ... 800-526-4954

Womack International
Vallejo, CA ... 707-647-2370

Yardney Water ManagementSystems
Riverside, CA ... 800-854-4788

Zander
Nashville, TN ... ÿ80- 35- 428

Fittings

Accutek Packaging Equipment Company
Vista, CA. ... 800-989-1828

Ace Manufacturing
Cincinnati, OH ... 800-653-5692

Advance Fitting Corporation
Elkhorn, WI. ... 262-723-6699

Anver Corporation
Hudson, MA ... 800-654-3500

ARCHON Industries
Suffern, NY. ... 800-554-1394

Baldewein Company
Lake Forrest, IL ... 800-424-5544

Bradford A Ducon Company
Pewaukee, WI. ... 800-789-1718

C.F.F. Stainless Steels
Hamilton, ON ... 800-263-4511

Carmun International
San Antonio, TX. ... 800-531-7907

Crown Industries
East Orange, NJ ... 877-747-2457

Dormont Manufacturing Company
Export, PA. ... 800-367-6668

Eischen Enterprises
Fresno, CA ... 559-834-0013

Ellett Industries
Port Coquitlam, BC. ... 604-941-8211

Gems Sensors
Plainville, CT ... 860-747-3000

General Tank
Berwick, PA ... 800-435-8265

Hoffmeyer Company
San Leandro, CA. ... 800-350-2358

Hydra-Flex
Livonia, MI ... 800-234-0832

Keystone Rubber Corporation
Greenbackville, VA. ... 800-394-5661

Kuriyama of America
Schaumburg, IL. ... 800-800-0320

Lake Process Systems
Lake Barrington, IL ... 800-331-9260

Magnatech
East Granby, CT ... 888-393-3602

Nalge Process Technologies Group
Rochester, NY. ... 585-586-8800

Norgren
Littleton, CO ... 303-794-2611

Parker Hannifin Corporation
Cleveland, OH ... 609-586-5151

Processing Machinery & Supply
Philadelphia, PA ... 215-425-4320

Pure Fit
Allentown, PA. ... 866-787-3348

Qosina Corporation
Edgewood, NY ... 631-242-3000

Qualtech
Quebec, QC. ... 888-339-3801

Robert-James Sales
Buffalo, NY. ... 800-777-1325

Rolfs @ Boone
Boone, IA ... 800-265-2010

Rolland Machining & Fabricating
Moneta, VA. ... 973-827-6911

Rubber Fab
Sparta, NJ ... 866-442-2959

Sanitary Couplers
Springboro, OH. ... 513-743-0144

Southern Metal Fabricators
Albertville, AL ... 800-989-1330

Special Products
Springfield, MO ... 417-881-6114

Spencer Turbine Company
Windsor, CT ... 800-232-4321

Spraying Systems Company
Wheaton, IL ... 630-655-5000

Standex International Corporation
Salem, NH. ... 603-893-9701

T&S Brass & Bronze Works
Travelers Rest, SC ... 800-476-4103

Tomlinson Industries
Cleveland, OH ... 800-945-4589

Top Line Process Equipment Company
Bradford, PA ... 800-458-6095

Tuchenhagen
Columbia, MD ... 410-910-6000

Unisource Manufacturing
Portland, OR ... 800-234-2566

Valvinox
Iberville, QC. ... 450-346-1981

Waukesha Cherry-Burrell
Louisville, KY ... 502-491-4310

Waukesha Specialty Company
Darien, WI. ... 262-724-3700

Windhorst Blowmold
Euless, TX. ... 817-540-6639

World Wide Fittings
Niles, IL ... 800-393-9894

Flow Regulators

Alard Equipment Corporation
Williamson, NY ... 315-589-4511

American LEWA
Holliston, MA ... 888-539-2123

Boston Gear
Boston, MA. ... 888-999-9860

Carmun International
San Antonio, TX. ... 800-531-7907

Cashco
Ellsworth, KS ... 785-472-4461

Linde Gas LLC
Cleveland, OH ... 800-983-5615

Lumenite Control Technology
Franklin Park, IL. ... 800-323-8510

Meltric Corporation
Franklin, WI ... 800-824-4031

Monitor Technologies
Elburn, IL ... 800-601-6319

Music City Metals
Nashville, TN ... 800-251-2674

Norgren
Littleton, CO ... 303-794-2611

Samson Controls
Baytown, TX. ... 281-383-3677

Spraying Systems Company
Wheaton, IL ... 630-655-5000

Standard Pump
Auburn, GA. ... 866-558-8611

Food Processing

Aerosol

Nalbach Engineering Company, Inc.
Countryside, IL. ... 708-579-9100

Packaging Equipment & Conveyors, Inc
Elkhart, IN. ... 574-266-6995

Agitators

Food Processing

A&B Process Systems
Stratford, WI. ... 888-258-2789

APV Americas
Delavan, WI ... 800-252-5200

Berkshire PPM
Litchfield, CT ... 860-567-3118

Bowers Process Equipment
Stratford, ON. ... 800-567-3223

Bush Tank Fabricators
Newark, NJ ... 973-596-1121

Chemineer
Dayton, OH. ... 937-454-3200

Chemineer-Kenics/Greerco
North Andover, MA ... 800-643-0641

Coastline Equipment
Bellingham, WA ... 360-739-2480

E.T. Oakes Corporation
Hauppauge, NY ... 631-232-0002

EKATO Corporation
St Ramsey, NJ ... 201-825-4684

Expert Industries
Brooklyn, NY ... 718-434-6060

Falco Technologies
La Prairie, QC. ... 450-444-0566

Fernholtz Engineering
Van Nuys, CA ... 818-785-5800

Hamilton Kettles
Weirton, WV ... 800-535-1882

Lee Industries Fluid Transfer
Philipsburg, PA ... 814-342-0802

Norvell Company
Fort Scott, KS ... 800-653-3147

Patterson Industries
Scarborough, ON ... 800-336-1110

Process Systems
Barrington, IL ... 847-842-8618

Sonic Corporation
Stratford, CT ... 866-493-1378

Washington Frontier
Grandview, WA. ... 509-469-7662

Milk

Alard Equipment Corporation
Williamson, NY ... 315-589-4511

Bowers Process Equipment
Stratford, ON. ... 800-567-3223

Chemineer-Kenics/Greerco
North Andover, MA ... 800-643-0641

Falco Technologies
La Prairie, QC. ... 450-444-0566

Liquid Scale
New Brighton, MN. ... 888-633-2969

Relco Unisystems Corporation
Willmar, MN. ... 320-231-2210

Washington Frontier
Grandview, WA 509-469-7662
Whey Systems
Willmar, MN 320-905-4122

Air Knives

Ametek Technical & Industrial Products
Kent, OH 215-256-6601
Paxton Products
Cincinnati, OH 800-441-7475
Spencer Turbine Company
Windsor, CT 800-232-4321

Augers

A.T. Ferrell Company Inc
Bluffton, IN 800-248-8318
Apollo Sheet Metal
Kennewick, WA 509-586-1104
Auger-Fabrication
Exton, PA 800-334-1529
Cal-Coast Manufacturing
Turlock, CA 209-668-9378
Polar Process
Plattsville, ON 877-896-8077
Relco Unisystems Corporation
Willmar, MN 320-231-2210
Spee-Dee Packaging Machinery
Sturtevant, WI 877-387-5212
TWM Manufacturing
Leamington, ON 888-495-4831
Universal Packaging
Houston, TX 800-324-2610
Viking Machine & Design
De Pere, WI 888-286-2116
Washington Frontier
Grandview, WA 509-469-7662
Whey Systems
Willmar, MN 320-905-4122

Bakers'

A&J Mixing International
Oakville, ON 800-668-3470
Aaburco Piemaster
Grass Valley, CA 800-533-7437
ABI Limited
Concord, ON 800-297-8666
Adamatic
Auburn, WA 800-578-2547
Allied Bakery and Food Service Equipment
Santa Fe Springs, CA 562-945-6506
American Eagle Food Machinery
Chicago, IL 800-836-5756
AMF Bakery Systems
Richmond, VA 800-225-3771
AMF CANADA
Sherbrooke, QC 800-255-3869
Andgar Corporation
Ferndale, WA 360-366-9900
Arcobaleno Pasta Machines
Lancaster, PA 800-875-7096
Attias Oven Corporation
Brooklyn, NY 800-928-8427
Bakery Associates
Setauket, NY 631-751-4156
Baking Machines
Livermore, CA 925-449-3369
Belshaw Adamatic Bakery Group
Auburn, WA 800-578-2547
Bettendorf Stanford
Salem, IL 800-548-2253
Bevles Company
Dallas, TX 800-441-1601
Bolling Oven & Machine Company
Avon, OH 440-937-6112
Breddo Likwifier
Kansas City, MO 800-669-4092
Buss America
Carol Stream, IL 630-933-9100
C&K Machine Company
Holyoke, MA 413-536-8122
C. Palmer Manufacturing
West Newton, PA 724-872-8200
C.H. Babb Company
Raynham, MA 508-977-0600
Cannon Equipment Company
Rosemount, MN 800-825-8501
Christy Machine Company
Fremont, OH 888-332-6451
Cinelli Esperia
Woodbridge, ON 905-856-1820
Clayton Manufacturing Company
Derby, NY 716-549-0392
CMC America Corporation
Joliet, IL 815-726-4337
Cobatco
Peoria, IL 800-426-2282
Comtec Industries
Woodridge, IL 630-759-9000
Custom Diamond International
Laval, QC 800-326-5926
D.R. McClain & Son
Commerce, CA 800-428-2263
Dawn Equipment Company
Jackson, MI 800-248-1844
DBE Inc
Concord, ON 800-461-5313
Delta Machine & Manufacturing
Saint Rose, LA 504-949-8304
Deluxe Equipment Company
Bradenton, FL 800-367-8931
Don Lee
Escondido, CA 760-745-0707
Doyon Equipment
Liniere, QC 800-463-4273
Dutchess Bakers' Machinery Company
Superior, WI 800-777-4498
E.T. Oakes Corporation
Hauppauge, NY 631-232-0002
Edhard Corporation
Hackettstown, NJ 888-334-2731
Empire Bakery Equipment
Hicksville, NY 800-878-4070
Epcon Industrial Systems
Conroe, TX 800-447-7872
Everedy Automation
Frederick, PA 610-754-1775
Exact Mixing Systems
Memphis, TN 901-362-8501
Fish Oven & Equipment Corporation
Wauconda, IL 877-526-8720
Food Engineering Unlimited
Fullerton, CA 714-879-8762
Food Machinery Sales
Bogart, GA 706-549-2207
FoodTools
Santa Barbara, CA 877-836-6386
Franz Haas Machinery of America
Richmond, VA 804-222-6022
Fred D. Pfening Company
Columbus, OH 614-294-1633
Friedrich Metal ProductsCompany
Browns Summit, NC 800-772-0326
Garland Commercial Ranges
Mississauga, ON 905-624-0260
Good Idea
Northampton, MA 800-462-9237
Goodway Industries
Bohemia, NY 800-943-4501
Graybill Machines
Lititz, PA 717-626-5221
Hayon Manufacturing & Engineering Corporation
Las Vegas, NV 702-562-3377
IJ White Corporation
Farmingdale, NY 631-293-2211
IKA Works
Wilmington, NC 800-733-3037
Imperial Commercial Cooking Equipment
Corona, CA 800-343-7790
Indiana Wire Company
Fremont, IN 877-786-6883
Industrial Air Conditioning Systems
Chicago, IL 773-486-4236
Industrial Products Corporation
Ho Ho Kus, NJ 800-472-5913
JAS Manufacturing Company
Carrollton, TX 972-380-1150
KB Systems Baking Machinery Design Company
Bangor, PA 610-588-7788
Knott Slicers
Canton, MA 781-821-0925
Lanly Company
Cleveland, OH 216-731-1115
Latendorf Corporation
Brielle, NJ 800-526-4057
Lawrence Equipment
South El Monte, CA 800-423-4500
LeMatic
Jackson, MI 517-787-3301
Lil' Orbits
Minneapolis, MN 800-228-8305
LVO Manufacturing
Rock Rapids, IA 712-472-3734
Maddox/Adams International
Miami, FL 305-592-3337
Magna Machine Co.
Cincinnati, OH 800-448-3475
Mallet & Company
Carnegie, PA 800-245-2757
McCall Refrigeration
Parsons, TN 888-732-2446
Merco/Savory
Mt. Pleasant, MI 800-733-8821
Mercury Equipment Company
Chino, CA 800-273-6688
Moffat
San Antonio, TX 800-551-8795
Moline Machinery
Duluth, MN 800-767-5734
Motom Corporation
Bensenville, IL 630-787-1995
National Manufacturing Company
Lincoln, NE 402-475-3400
Nemeth Engineering Associates
Crestwood, KY 502-241-1502
Nothum Food Processing Systems
Springfield, MO 800-435-1297
Oshikiri Corporation of America
Philadelphia, PA 215-637-6005
Pavailler Distribution Company
Northvale, NJ 201-767-0766
Peerless Food Inc
Sidney, OH 937-494-2870
Peerless Machinery Corporation
Sidney, OH 800-999-3327
PMI Food Equipment Group
Troy, OH 937-332-3000
Radio Frequency Company
Millis, MA 508-376-9555
Ram Equipment
Waukesha, WI 262-513-1114
Reading Bakery Systems
Robesonia, PA 610-693-5816
Reed Oven Company
Kansas City, MO 816-842-7446
Regal Ware
Kewaskum, WI 262-626-2121
Reiser
Canton, MA 781-575-9941
Revent
Piscataway, NJ 732-777-9433
Rheon USA
Huntersville, NC 704-875-9191
Rhodes Bakery Equipment
Portland, OR 800-426-3813
Rondo Inc.
Moonachie, NJ 800-882-0633
Roto-Flex Oven Company
San Antonio, TX 877-859-1463
Ruiz Flour Tortillas
Riverside, CA 909-947-7811
Sasib North America
Plano, TX 972-422-5808
SOCO System
Waukesha, WI 800-441-6293
Somerset Industries
Billerica, MA 800-772-4404
Southbend Company
Fuquay Varina, NC 800-348-2558
T.K. Products
Anaheim, CA 714-621-0267
Thomas L. Green & Company
Robenosia, PA 610-693-5816
Thompson Bagel Machine MFg. Corp.
Los Angeles, CA 310-836-0900
Toastmaster
Elgin, IL 847-741-3300
Unifiller Systems
Delta, BC 888-733-8444
United Bakery Equipment Company
Shawnee Mission, KS 913-541-8700
US Tsubaki
Wheeling, IL 800-323-7790
Varimixer
Charlotte, NC 800-221-1138
Warwick Manufacturing & Equipment
North Brunswick, NJ 732-241-9263
Wilder Manufacturing Company
Port Jervis, NY 800-832-1319
Woody Associates
York, PA 717-843-3975
X-Press Manufacturing
New Braunfels, TX 830-629-2651

Balers or Baling Presses

Advance Lifts
St Charles, IL 800-843-3625
Balemaster
Crown Point, IN 219-663-4525
Consolidated Baling Machine Company
Jacksonville, FL 800-231-9286
Enterprise Company
Santa Ana, CA 714-835-0541
Galbreath LLC
Winamac, IN 574-946-6631
Incinerator International
Houston, TX 713-227-1466
Load King Manufacturing Company
Jacksonville, FL 800-531-4975
Logemann Brothers Company
Milwaukee, WI 414-445-2700
Marathon Equipment Company
Vernon, AL 800-633-8974
Maren Engineering Corporation
South Holland, IL 800-875-1038
Orwak
Minneapolis, MN 800-747-0449
Ouachita Packaging Machinery
West Monroe, LA 318-396-1468
PTR Baler and Compactor Company
Philadelphia, PA 800-523-3654
Schleicher & Company of America
Sanford, NC 800-775-7570
SP Industries
Hopkins, MI 800-592-5959
Waste Away Systems
Newark, OH 800-223-4741
Wastequip
Charlotte, NC 877-468-9278

Barley Processing

Andritz
Muncy, PA 570-546-8211

Biscuit Making

Rademaker USA
Hudson, OH 330-650-2345
Reading Bakery Systems
Robesonia, PA 610-693-5816
Reiser
Canton, MA 781-575-9941
Rheon USA
Huntersville, NC 704-875-9191

Blades

Food Processing Machine

Atlanta SharpTech
Peachtree City, GA 800-462-7297
Bettendorf Stanford
Salem, IL 800-548-2253
Boehringer Mfg. Co. Inc.
Felton, CA 800-630-8665
CB Manufacturing & SalesCompany
Miamisburg, OH 800-543-6860
Cozzini
Chicago, IL 773-478-9700
E-Z Edge
West New York, NJ 800-232-4470
Garvey Products
Cincinnati, OH 513-771-8710
Good Idea
Northampton, MA 800-462-9237
Hansaloy Corporation
Davenport, IA 800-553-4992
Huther Brothers
Rochester, NY 800-334-1115
Industrial Products Corporation
Ho Ho Kus, NJ 800-472-5913
Industrial Razor Blade Company
Orange, NJ 973-673-4286
KSW Corporation
Des Moines, IA 515-265-5269
PIECO, Inc.
Manchester, IA 800-334-3929
R.H. Saw Corporation
Barrington, IL 847-381-8777
Ranger Blade Manufacturing Company
Traer, IA 800-377-7860
Save-O-Seal Corporation
Elmsford, NY 800-831-9720
Simmons Engineering Corporation
Wheeling, IL 800-252-3381
Simonds International
Fitchburg, MA 800-343-1616
Specialty Blades
Staunton, VA 540-248-2200
Specialty Saw
Simsbury, CT 800-225-0772
TGW International
Florence, KY 800-407-0173
Thomas Precision, Inc.
Rice Lake, WI 800-657-4808

Blenders

A&B Process Systems
Stratford, WI 888-258-2789
Aaron Equipment Company
Bensenville, IL 630-350-2200
Acrison
Moonachie, NJ 800-422-4266
Apache Stainless Equipment Corporation
Beaver Dam, WI 800-444-0398
APV Americas
Delavan, WI 800-252-5200
Attias Oven Corporation
Brooklyn, NY 800-928-8427
Automated Food Systems
Waxahachie, TX 972-298-5719
Axiflow Technologies, Inc.
Kennesaw, GA 770-795-1195
Bepex International,LLC
Minneapolis, MN 800-607-2470
Blentech Corporation
Santa Rosa, CA 707-523-5949
Blue Tech
Hickory, NC 828-324-5900
Bowers Process Equipment
Stratford, ON 800-567-3223
Breddo Likwifier
Kansas City, MO 800-669-4092
Bush Tank Fabricators
Newark, NJ 973-596-1121
Century Foods International
Sparta, WI 800-269-1901
Charles Ross & Son Company
Hauppauge, NY 800-243-7677
Cleveland-Eastern Mixers
Clinton, CT 800-243-1188
CRC
Council Bluffs, IA 712-323-9477
Dito Dean Food Prep
Rocklin, CA 800-331-7958
Dorton Incorporated
Arlington Hts, IL 800-299-8600
Drum-Mates Inc.
Lumberton, NJ 800-621-3786
E.T. Oakes Corporation
Hauppauge, NY 631-232-0002
Ederback Corporation
Ann Arbor, MI 800-422-2558
Eirich Machines
Gurnee, IL 847-336-2444
Eurodib
Champlain, NY 888-956-6866
Expert Industries
Brooklyn, NY 718-434-6060
Falco Technologies
La Prairie, QC 450-444-0566
Fernholtz Engineering
Van Nuys, CA 818-785-5800
Ferrell-Ross
Amarillo, TX 800-299-9051
Fleet Wood Goldco Wyard
Cockeysville, MD 410-785-1934
Flow of Solids
Westford, MA 978-392-0300
Food Processing Equipment Company
Santa Fe Springs, CA 479-751-9392
FPEC Corporation
Santa Fe Springs, CA 562-802-3727
Glen Mills, Inc.
Clifton, NJ 973-777-0777
Gold Medal Products Company
Cincinnati, OH 800-543-0862
Hamilton Beach/Proctor-Silex
Southern Pines, NC 800-711-6100
Hayes & Stolz IndustrialManufacturing Company
Fort Worth, TX 800-725-7272
Hosokawa/Bepex Corporation
Santa Rosa, CA 707-586-6000
International Reserve Equipment Corporation
Clarendon Hills, IL 708-531-0680
Jenike & Johanson
Tyngsboro, MA 978-649-3300
Karl Schnell
New London, WI 920-982-9974
Kemutec Group
Bristol, PA 215-788-8013
Kinetic Equipment Company
Appleton, WI 806-293-4471
Krones
Franklin, WI 414-409-4000
Lee Industries Fluid Transfer
Philipsburg, PA 814-342-0802
Lowe Industries
Marion, IA 319-447-9724
Machanix Fabrication
Chino, CA 800-700-9701
Matcon USA
Elmhurst, IL 856-256-1330
Materials TransportationCompany
Temple, TX 800-433-3110
Midwest Metalcraft & Equipment
Windsor, MO 800-647-3167
MO Industries
Whippany, NJ 973-386-9228
Munson Machinery Company
Utica, NY 800-944-6644
Paget Equipment Company
Marshfield, WI 715-384-3158
Patterson Industries
Scarborough, ON 800-336-1110
Patterson-Kelley Hars Company
East Stroudsburg, PA 570-421-7500
Paul O. Abbe
Bensenville, IL 630-350-2200
Peerless Machinery Corporation
Sidney, OH 800-999-3327
Polar Process
Plattsville, ON 877-896-8077
Pro Scientific
Oxford, CT 800-584-3776
Reiser
Canton, MA 781-575-9941
Robot Coupe USA, Inc.
Jackson, MS 800-824-1646
Rubicon Industries Corporation
Brooklyn, NY 800-662-6999
Stephan Machinery, Inc.
Mundelein, IL 800-783-7426
Stricklin Company
Dallas, TX 214-637-1030
Superior Products Company
Saint Paul, MN 800-328-9800
Swirl Freeze Corp
Salt Lake City, UT 800-262-4275
T.D. Sawvel Company
Maple Plain, MN 877-488-1816
TSA Griddle Systems
Kelowna, BC 250-491-9025
Vita-Mix Corporation
Cleveland, OH 800-437-4654
VitaMinder Company
Providence, RI 800-858-8840
Waring Products
Torrington, CT 800-492-7464
Wilch Manufacturing
Topeka, KS 785-267-2762
Yargus Manufacturing
Marshall, IL 217-826-6352

Blending

Flour

Automated Food Systems
Waxahachie, TX 972-298-5719
Breddo Likwifier
Kansas City, MO 800-669-4092
Glen Mills, Inc.
Clifton, NJ 973-777-0777
Hosokawa/Bepex Corporation
Santa Rosa, CA 707-586-6000
Patterson-Kelley Hars Company
East Stroudsburg, PA 570-421-7500
Peerless Machinery Corporation
Sidney, OH 800-999-3327
Tuchenhagen
Columbia, MD 410-910-6000

Grain

Andritz
Muncy, PA 570-546-8211

Breddo Likwifier
Kansas City, MO 800-669-4092
Davron Technologies
Chattanooga, TN 423-870-1888
Glen Mills, Inc.
Clifton, NJ 973-777-0777
Hosokawa/Bepex Corporation
Santa Rosa, CA 707-586-6000
MO Industries
Whippany, NJ 973-386-9228
Patterson-Kelley Hars Company
East Stroudsburg, PA 570-421-7500
Tuchenhagen
Columbia, MD 410-910-6000

Blowers

Aerovent
Minneapolis, MN 763-551-7500
Andgar Corporation
Ferndale, WA 360-366-9900
Ceilcote Air Pollution Control
Cleveland, OH 800-554-8673
Chicago Conveyor Corporation
Addison, IL 630-543-6300
Gardner Denver Inc.
Toronto, ON 416-763-4681
Hartzell Fan
Piqua, OH 800-336-3267
Loren Cook Company
Springfield, MO 800-289-3267
Nalge Process Technologies Group
Rochester, NY 585-586-8800
Nu-Con Equipment
Chanhassen, MN 877-939-0510
Palace Packaging Machines
Downingtown, PA 610-873-7252
Paxton Products
Cincinnati, OH 800-441-7475
Ross Cook
San Jose, CA 800-233-7339
Spencer Turbine Company
Windsor, CT 800-232-4321
Tuthill Vacuum & Blower Systems
Springfield, MO 800-825-6937
Yakima Wire Works
Reedley, CA 509-248-6790

Boilers

Electric Steam

Sussman Electric Boilers
Long Island City, NY 800-238-3535

Gas Fired

ECS Warehouse
Buffalo, NY 716-829-7356

Steam

Pick Heaters Inc.
West Bend, WI 800-233-9030

Water

A.O. Smith Water Products Company
Irving, TX 800-527-1953
Bryan Boilers
Peru, IN 765-473-6651
Cleaver-Brooks
Milwaukee, WI 414-359-0600
Holman Boiler Works
Dallas, TX 800-331-1956
Pacific Steam Equipment, Inc.
Santa Fe Springs, CA 800-321-4114
PVI Industries
Fort Worth, TX 800-784-8326
QuikWater, Inc.
Sand Springs, OK 918-241-8880
Sellers Engineering Division
Danville, KY 859-236-3181
Sussman Electric Boilers
Long Island City, NY 800-238-3535
Vanguard Technology
Eugene, OR 800-624-4809
Washington Frontier
Grandview, WA 509-469-7662

Brewery

Alfa Laval
Newburyport, MA 978-465-5777
Andritz
Muncy, PA 570-546-8211
Anver Corporation
Hudson, MA 800-654-3500
API Heat Transfer
Buffalo, NY 877-274-4328
Berkshire PPM
Litchfield, CT 860-567-3118
Brew Store
Oakville, ON 905-845-2120
BVL Controls
Bois-Des-Filion, QC 866-285-2668
Chester-Jensen Company, Inc.
Chester, PA 800-685-3750
Criveller East
Niagara Falls, ON 888-894-2266
Crown Cork & Seal Company
Philadelphia, PA 215-698-5100
Crown-Simplimatic
Baltimore, MD 410-563-6700
Diversified Metal Engineering
Charlottetown, PE 902-628-6900
Falco
La Prairie, CA 450-444-0566
FleetwoodGoldcoWyard
Romeoville, IL 630-759-6800
Globe International
Tacoma, WA 800-523-6575
Goodnature Products
Orchard Park, NY 800-875-3381
MacDonald Steel Ltd
Cambridge, ON 800-563-8247
McNab
Buena Vista, VA 540-261-1045
Metal Master
Tucson, AZ 800-488-8729
Micropub Systems International
Rochester, NY 585-385-3990
Modern Brewing & Design
Santa Rosa, CA 707-542-6620
Newlands Systems
Abbotsford, BC 604-855-4890
O.I. Analytical
College Station, TX 979-690-1711
Oak Barrel Winecraft
Berkeley, CA 510-849-0400
San-Rec-Pak
Tualatin, OR 503-692-5552
Simplex Filler Company
Napa, CA 800-796-7539
The Pub Brewing Company
Mahwah, NJ 201-512-0387
The Pub Brewing Company
Santa Rosa, CA 707- 58- 179
Vincent Corporation
Tampa, FL 813-248-2650
Vineco International Products
St Catharines, ON 905-685-9342

Brine Making Equipment

Berg Chilling Systems
Toronto, ON 416-755-2221
Membrane System Specialists
Wisconsin Rapids, WI 715-421-2333
Northland Process Piping
Isle, MN 320-679-2119
Peterson Fiberglass Laminates
Shell Lake, WI 715-468-2306
Reiser
Canton, MA 781-575-9941
South Valley Manufacturing
Gilroy, CA 408-842-5457

Broilers

American Range & Hood Corporation
Pacoima, CA 888-753-9898
Anetsberger
Concord, NH 603-225-6684
APW Wyott Food Service Equipment Company
Cheyenne, WY 800-527-2100
Bakers Pride Oven Company
New Rochelle, NY 800-431-2745
Broaster Company
Beloit, WI 800-365-8278
Comstock-Castle Stove Company
Quincy, IL 800-637-9188
Connerton Company
Santa Ana, CA 714-547-9218
Cook King
Laguna Beach, CA 949-497-1235
CPM Wolverine Proctor
Horsham, PA 215-443-5200
Dynamic Cooking Systems
Huntington Beach, CA 800-433-8466
Ember-Glo
Chicago, IL 866-705-0515
Garland Commercial Ranges
Mississauga, ON 905-624-0260
Garland Commercial Ranges Ltd.
Mississauga, ON 905-624-0260
Grande Chef Company
Orangeville, ON 519-942-4470
Holman Cooking Equipment
Saint Louis, MO 888-356-5362
Imperial Commercial Cooking Equipment
Corona, CA 800-343-7790
J&R Manufacturing
Mesquite, TX 800-527-4831
Lang Manufacturing Company
Everett, WA 800-882-6368
Leedal Inc
Northbrook, IL 847-498-0111
Magikitch'n
Concord, NH 800-441-1492
Marshall Air Systems
Charlotte, NC 800-722-3474
Merco/Savory
Mt. Pleasant, MI 800-733-8821
Middleby Marshall, CTX
Elgin, IL 800-323-5575
Montague Company
Hayward, CA 800-345-1830
Nieco Corporation
Windsor, CA 800-643-2656
Rankin-DeLux
Eastwale, CA 951-685-0081
Renato Specialty Product
Garland, TX 866-575-6316
Southbend Company
Fuquay Varina, NC 800-348-2558
Star Manufacturing International
Saint Louis, MO 800-264-7827
Stein DSI
Sandusky, OH 800-447-2630
Super-Chef Manufacturing Company
Houston, TX 800-231-3478
Thermal Engineering Corporation
Columbia, SC 800-331-0097
Toastmaster
Elgin, IL 847-741-3300
Trimen Foodservice Equipment
North York, ON 877-437-1422
Vulcan-Hart Company
Louisville, KY 800-814-2028
Welbilt Corporation
Stamford, CT 203-325-8300
Wells Manufacturing Company
Verdi, NV 800-777-0450
Wolf Range Company
Louisville, KY 800-366-9653
Wood Stone Corporation
Bellingham, WA 800-988-8103

Cereal Making

A&B Process Systems
Stratford, WI 888-258-2789
Andgar Corporation
Ferndale, WA 360-366-9900
Andritz
Muncy, PA 570-546-8211
Buffalo Technologies Corporation
Buffalo, NY 800-332-2419
Coperion Corporation
Ramsey, NJ 201-327-6300
Ferrell-Ross
Amarillo, TX 800-299-9051
Kamflex Corporation
Chicago, IL 800-323-2440
Lanly Company
Cleveland, OH 216-731-1115
Munson Machinery Company
Utica, NY 800-944-6644
Pavan USA, Inc.
Emigsville, PA 717-767-4889
Polar Process
Plattsville, ON 877-896-8077
Puritan Manufacturing
Omaha, NE 800-331-0487
UniTrak Corporation
Port Hope, ON 866-883-5749

Wolverine Proctor & Schwartz
Lexington, NC 336-248-5181

Cheese Making

A&B Process Systems
Stratford, WI 888-258-2789
Breddo Likwifier
Kansas City, MO 800-669-4092
Custom Fabricating & Repair
Marshfield, WI 800-236-8773
Damrow Company
Fond Du Lac, WI 800-236-1501
Dito Dean Food Prep
Rocklin, CA 800-331-7958
Eischen Enterprises
Fresno, CA 559-834-0013
Johnson Industries International, Inc.
Windsor, WI 608-846-4499
Kusel Equipment Company
Watertown, WI 920-261-4112
Len E. Ivarson
Milwaukee, WI 414-351-0700
Midwest Stainless
Menomonie, WI 715-235-5472
Pacific Process Technology
La Jolla, CA 858-551-3298
Peterson Fiberglass Laminates
Shell Lake, WI 715-468-2306
Polar Process
Plattsville, ON 877-896-8077
Rheo-Tech
Gurnee, IL 847-367-1557
Rosenwach Tank Company
Long Island City, NY 718-729-4900
Sanchelima Intl. Inc.
Miami, FL 305-591-4343
Scherping Systems
Winsted, MN 320-485-4401
Viking Machine & Design
De Pere, WI 888-286-2116
Washington Frontier
Grandview, WA 509-469-7662
Whey Systems
Willmar, MN 320-905-4122

Cheese Processing

Corenco
Santa Rosa, CA 888-267-3626
Loos Machine & Automation
Colby, WI 715-223-2844
Millerbernd Process Sytems
Winsted, MN 320-485-2685
Reiser
Canton, MA 781-575-9941

Cheesecloth

Ace-Tex Enterprises
Detroit, MI 800-444-3800
Akron Cotton Products
Akron, OH 800-899-7173
Armaly Brands
Walled Lake, MI 800-772-1222
Cadie Products Corporation
Paterson, NJ 973-278-8300
Canton Sterilized WipingCloth Company
Canton, OH 330-455-5179
Clayton L. Hagy & Son
Philadelphia, PA 215-844-6470
De Royal Textiles
Camden, SC 800-845-1062
Erie Cotton Products Company
Erie, PA 800-289-4737
James Thompson & Company
New York, NY 212-686-4242
King Bag & Manufacturing Company
Cincinnati, OH 800-444-5464
Lexidyne of Pennsylvania
Pittsburgh, PA 800-543-2233
Mednik Wiping Materials Company
Saint Louis, MO 800-325-7193
Mill Wiping Rags/The Rag Factory
Bronx, NY 718-994-7100
Nu-Tex Styles, Inc.
Somerset, NJ 732-485-5456
Paley-Lloyd-Donohue
Elizabeth, NJ 908-352-5835
Textile Buff & Wheel Company, Inc.
Charlestown, MA 617-241-8100
Textile Products Company
Anaheim, CA 714-761-0401

Wipe-Tex
Bronx, NY 800-643-9607
Y-Pers
Philadelphia, PA 800-421-0242

Chewing Gum Processing

A&B Process Systems
Stratford, WI 888-258-2789
LIST
Acton, MA 978-635-9521
UniTrak Corporation
Port Hope, ON 866-883-5749

Chocolate Processing

A&B Process Systems
Stratford, WI 888-258-2789
Buffalo Technologies Corporation
Buffalo, NY 800-332-2419
Chocolate Concepts
Hartville, OH 330-877-3322
Dadant & Sons
Hamilton, IL 888-922-1293
Glen Mills, Inc.
Clifton, NJ 973-777-0777
Hilliard's Chocolate System
West Bridgewater, MA 800-258-1530
LIST
Acton, MA 978-635-9521
Savage Brothers Company
Elk Grove Vlg, IL 800-342-0973
Tricor Systems
Elgin, IL 800-575-0161
Union Process
Akron, OH 330-929-3333
UniTrak Corporation
Port Hope, ON 866-883-5749
US Tsubaki
Wheeling, IL 800-323-7790
Woody Associates
York, PA 717-843-3975

Cocoa Processing

A&B Process Systems
Stratford, WI 888-258-2789
Andritz
Muncy, PA 570-546-8211
Glen Mills, Inc.
Clifton, NJ 973-777-0777
LIST
Acton, MA 978-635-9521
Union Process
Akron, OH 330-929-3333

Coffee Makers

Acorto
Bellevue, WA 800-995-9019
AK Steel
West Chester, OH 800-331-5050
Astoria General Espresso
Greensboro, NC 336-393-0224
Bloomfield Industries
St. Louis, MO 888-356-5362
Boyd Coffee Company
Portland, OR 800-545-4077
Brewmatic Company
Torrance, CA 800-421-6860
Bunn Corporation
Springfield, IL 800-637-8606
Carriage Works
Klamath Falls, OR 541-882-0700
Chemex Division/International Housewares Corporation
Pittsfield, MA 800-243-6399
CPI Importers
Dallas, TX 214-353-0328
Formula Espresso
Brooklyn, NY 718-834-8724
Gabriella Imports
Cleveland, OH 800-544-8117
Grand Silver Company
Bronx, NY 718-585-1930
Grindmaster Corporation
Louisville, KY 800-695-4500
LaVazza Premium Coffee
New York, NY 212-725-8800
Melitta USA
Clearwater, FL 888-635-4880
Newco Enterprises
Saint Charles, MO 800-325-7867

Nuova Distribution Centre
Ferndale, WA 360-366-2226
Pasquini Espresso
Los Angeles, CA 800-724-6225
Regal Ware
Kewaskum, WI 262-626-2121
Rexcraft Fine Chafers
Long Island City, NY 888-739-2723
Saeco
Cleveland, OH 440-528-2000
Schaerer Corporation
Signal Hill, CA 562-989-3004
Sheffield Platers
San Diego, CA 800-227-9242
Steel Products
Marion, IA 800-333-9451
Superior Products Company
Saint Paul, MN 800-328-9800
Supramatic
Toronto, ON 877-465-2883
T.J. Topper Company
Redwood City, CA 650-365-6962
Tops Manufacturing Company
Darien, CT 203-655-9367
Wells Manufacturing Company
Verdi, NV 800-777-0450
Wilbur Curtis Company
Montebello, CA 800-421-6150
World Kitchen
Elmira, NY 800-999-3436
Zelco Industries
Mount Vernon, NY 800-431-2486

Coffee Processing

Acorto
Bellevue, WA 800-995-9019
Alfa Laval
Newburyport, MA 978-465-5777
American Production Company
Redwood City, CA 650-368-5334
Ascaso
Bensenville, IL 630-350-0066
Astoria General Espresso
Greensboro, NC 336-393-0224
Astra Manufacturing
Canoga Park, CA 877-340-1800
Boyd Coffee Company
Portland, OR 800-545-4077
Brewmatic Company
Torrance, CA 800-421-6860
Bunn Corporation
Springfield, IL 800-637-8606
Bunn-O-Matic Corporation
Aurora, ON 905-841-2866
Carriage Works
Klamath Falls, OR 541-882-0700
Chemex Division/International Housewares Corporation
Pittsfield, MA 800-243-6399
Ditting USA
Glendale, CA 800-835-5992
Eastern Silver Tabletop Manufacturing Company
Brooklyn, NY 888-422-4142
Eurodib
Champlain, NY 888-956-6866
FETCO - Food Equipment Technologies Corporation
Lake Zurich, IL 800-338-2699
Formula Espresso
Brooklyn, NY 718-834-8724
Gabriella Imports
Cleveland, OH 800-544-8117
Gensaco Marketing
New York, NY 800-506-1935
Grindmaster Corporation
Louisville, KY 800-695-4500
Grindmaster-Cecilware Corporation
Louisville, KY 800-695-4500
Hamilton Beach/Proctor-Silex
Southern Pines, NC 800-711-6100
Kentwood Spring Water Company
Patterson, LA 985-395-9313
LaVazza Premium Coffee
New York, NY 212-725-8800
Melitta USA
Clearwater, FL 888-635-4880
Modern Process Equipment
Chicago, IL 773-254-3929
Newco Enterprises
Saint Charles, MO 800-325-7867
Pasquini Espresso
Los Angeles, CA 800-724-6225

PolyMaid Company
Largo, FL 800-206-9188
Regal Ware
Kewaskum, WI 262-626-2121
Rexcraft Fine Chafers
Long Island City, NY 888-739-2723
Saeco
Cleveland, OH 440-528-2000
Schaerer Corporation
Signal Hill, CA 562-989-3004
Sivetz Coffee
Corvallis, OR 541-753-9713
Steel Products
Marion, IA 800-333-9451
Supramatic
Toronto, ON 877-465-2883
Tops Manufacturing Company
Darien, CT 203-655-9367
UniTrak Corporation
Port Hope, ON 866-883-5749
Wega USA
Bensenville, IL 630-350-0066
Wells Manufacturing Company
Verdi, NV 800-777-0450
Wilbur Curtis Company
Montebello, CA 800-421-6150
Zelco Industries
Mount Vernon, NY 800-431-2486

Combination Oven/Steamers

Superior Products Company
Saint Paul, MN 800-328-9800

Compressors

Berkshire PPM
Litchfield, CT 860-567-3118
Blackmer
Grand Rapids, MI 616-241-1611
C&R Refrigeration
Center, TX 800-438-6182
Cooper Turbocompressor
Buffalo, NY 877-805-7911
Copeland Corporation
Sidney, OH 937-498-3011
Domnick Hunter
Charlotte, NC 800-345-8462
Howe Corporation
Chicago, IL 773-235-0200
Ingersoll Rand
Annandale, NJ 800-376-8665
International Machinery Exchange
Deerfield, WI 800-279-0191
Kopykake Enterprises
Torrance, CA 800-999-5253
Paxton Products
Cincinnati, OH 800-441-7475
Seattle Refrigeration & Manufacturing
Seattle, WA 800-228-8881
Tecumseh Products Company
Ann Arbor, MI 734-585-9500
Vilter Manufacturing Corporation
Cudahy, WI 414-744-0111
York Refrigeration Marine US
Seattle, WA 800-282-0904
Zander
Nashville, TN ÿ80- 35- 428

Condensed Milk Processing

A&B Process Systems
Stratford, WI 888-258-2789
C.E. Rogers Company
Mora, MN 800-279-8081

Condensers

Evaporative

Baltimore Aircoil Company
Jessup, MD 410-799-6200
Berkshire PPM
Litchfield, CT 860-567-3118
Central Fabricators
Cincinnati, OH 800-909-8265
Chil-Con Products
Brantford, ON 800-263-0086
Cooling Products
Tulsa, OK 918-251-8588
Croll-Reynolds Company
Parsippany, NJ 908-232-4200

Doucette Industries
York, PA 800-445-7511
EVAPCO
Taneytown, MD 410-756-2600
FES Systems
York, PA 800-888-4337
Governair Corporation
Oklahoma City, OK 405-525-6546
Howe Corporation
Chicago, IL 773-235-0200
Imeco
Polo, IL 815-946-2351
Industrial Piping
Pineville, NC 800-951-0988
Membrane System Specialists
Wisconsin Rapids, WI 715-421-2333
Niagara Blower Company
Buffalo, NY 800-426-5169
Paget Equipment Company
Marshfield, WI 715-384-3158
Ron Vallort & Associates
Oak Brook, IL 630-734-3821
Seattle Refrigeration & Manufacturing
Seattle, WA 800-228-8881
Vilter Manufacturing Corporation
Cudahy, WI 414-744-0111

Confectionery

A&B Process Systems
Stratford, WI 888-258-2789
A&M Industries
Sioux Falls, SD 800-888-2615
Aerotech Enterprise Inc
Chesterland, OH 440-729-2616
Automated Food Systems
Waxahachie, TX 972-298-5719
C. Cretors & Company
Chicago, IL 800-228-1885
Chocolate Concepts
Hartville, OH 330-877-3322
Coperion Corporation
Ramsey, NJ 201-327-6300
Davron Technologies
Chattanooga, TN 423-870-1888
Design Technology Corporation
Billerica, MA 978-663-7000
DT Converting Technologies - Stokes
Bristol, PA 800-635-0036
E.T. Oakes Corporation
Hauppauge, NY 631-232-0002
Goodway Industries
Bohemia, NY 800-943-4501
Graybill Machines
Lititz, PA 717-626-5221
Griffin Cardwell, Ltd
Louisville, KY 502-636-1374
Ideal Wrapping Machine Company
Middletown, NY 845-343-7700
Matiss
St Georges, QC 888-562-8477
Munson Machinery Company
Utica, NY 800-944-6644
Polar Process
Plattsville, ON 877-896-8077
TSA Griddle Systems
Kelowna, BC 250-491-9025
Unifiller Systems
Delta, BC 888-733-8444
Union Process
Akron, OH 330-929-3333
UniTrak Corporation
Port Hope, ON 866-883-5749
Woody Associates
York, PA 717-843-3975

Convection Ovens

ALPI Food Preparation Equipment
Bolton, ON 800-928-2574
Anetsberger
Concord, NH 603-225-6684
Apollo Sheet Metal
Kennewick, WA 509-586-1104
Coast Scientific
Rancho Santa Fe, CA 800-445-1544
Cres Cor
Mentor, OH 877-273-7267
Davron Technologies
Chattanooga, TN 423-870-1888
Dynamic Cooking Systems
Huntington Beach, CA 800-433-8466

Foster Refrigerator Corporation
Kinderhook, NY 888-828-3311
G.S. Blodgett Corporation
Burlington, VT 800-331-5842
Garland Commercial Ranges
Mississauga, ON 905-624-0260
Garland Commercial Ranges Ltd.
Mississauga, ON 905-624-0260
Gehnrich Oven Sales Company
Smithtown, NY 631-585-8787
Imperial Commercial Cooking Equipment
Corona, CA 800-343-7790
Lang Manufacturing Company
Everett, WA 800-882-6368
Merco/Savory
Mt. Pleasant, MI 800-733-8821
Middleby Corporation
Elgin, IL 847-741-3300
Moffat
San Antonio, TX 800-551-8795
Montague Company
Hayward, CA 800-345-1830
Nevo Corporation
Ronkonkoma, NY 631-585-8787
Piper Products
Wausau, WI 800-544-3057
Roto-Flex Oven Company
San Antonio, TX 877-859-1463
Southbend Company
Fuquay Varina, NC 800-348-2558
Super Systems
Wausau, WI 800-558-5880
Superior Products Company
Saint Paul, MN 800-328-9800
Welbilt Corporation
Stamford, CT 203-325-8300

Cookers

Brewery

Custom Food Machinery
Stockton, CA 209-463-4343
Falco Technologies
La Prairie, QC 450-444-0566

Canners'

A.K. Robins
Baltimore, MD 800-486-9656
Custom Food Machinery
Stockton, CA 209-463-4343
Hamilton Kettles
Weirton, WV 800-535-1882

Cereal

Andritz
Muncy, PA 570-546-8211
Central Fabricators
Cincinnati, OH 800-909-8265
Hamilton Kettles
Weirton, WV 800-535-1882
Lauhoff Corporation
Detroit, MI 313-259-0027

Cheese

A&B Process Systems
Stratford, WI 888-258-2789
Damrow Company
Fond Du Lac, WI 800-236-1501
Hamilton Kettles
Weirton, WV 800-535-1882
Viking Machine & Design
De Pere, WI 888-286-2116

Confectioners', Continuous

A&B Process Systems
Stratford, WI 888-258-2789
Dupps Company
Germantown, OH 937-855-6555
Hamilton Kettles
Weirton, WV 800-535-1882

Fish

Brinkmann Corporation
Dallas, TX 800-468-5252
Coastline Equipment
Bellingham, WA 360-739-2480
Diversified Metal Engineering
Charlottetown, PE 902-628-6900

Hamilton Kettles
Weirton, WV 800-535-1882

Pressure

A&B Process Systems
Stratford, WI 888-258-2789
Hamilton Kettles
Weirton, WV 800-535-1882
Henny Penny, Inc.
Detroit, MI 313-877-9550
Littleford Day
Florence, KY 800-365-8555
Vasconia Housewares
San Antonio, TX 800-377-6723
Winston Industries
Louisville, KY 800-234-5286

Steam

A.K. Robins
Baltimore, MD 800-486-9656
AccuTemp Products
Fort Wayne, IN 800-210-5907
Alumaworks
Sunny Isle Beach, FL 800-277-7267
Aroma Manufacturing Company
San Diego, CA 800-276-6286
Blodgett
Burlington, VT 800-331-5842
Brinkmann Corporation
Dallas, TX 800-468-5252
Cleveland Range Company
Cleveland, OH 800-338-2204
ColburnTreat
Winooski, VT 877-877-1224
Ember-Glo
Chicago, IL 866-705-0515
Garland Commercial Ranges
Mississauga, ON 905-624-0260
Garvis Manufacturing Company
Des Moines, IA 515-243-8054
Hamilton Kettles
Weirton, WV 800-535-1882
J.C. Ford Company
La Habra, CA 714-871-7361
Key Technology
Walla Walla, WA 509-529-2161
Komline-Sanderson
Peapack, NJ 800-225-5457
Legion Industries
Waynesboro, GA 800-887-1988
Market Forge Industries
Everett, MA 866-698-3188
Middleby Corporation
Elgin, IL 847-741-3300
Sandvik Process Systems
Totowa, NJ 973-790-1600
Southbend Company
Fuquay Varina, NC 800-348-2558
Stellar Steam
Winooski, VT 802-654-8603
Superior Products Company
Saint Paul, MN 800-328-9800
Viatec
Hastings, MI 800-942-4702
Vulcan-Hart Company
Louisville, KY 800-814-2028
Washington Frontier
Grandview, WA 509-469-7662
Welbilt Corporation
Stamford, CT 203-325-8300

Vegetable

A.K. Robins
Baltimore, MD 800-486-9656
Alkar
Lodi, WI 608-592-3211
AMCO Corporation
City of Industry, CA 626-855-2550
Brinkmann Corporation
Dallas, TX 800-468-5252
Hamilton Kettles
Weirton, WV 800-535-1882
J.C. Ford Company
La Habra, CA 714-871-7361
Market Forge Industries
Everett, MA 866-698-3188
Pick Heaters
West Bend, WI 800-233-9030
Washington Frontier
Grandview, WA 509-469-7662

Cooking & Heating Equipment

A.C. Horn & Co
Dallas, TX 800-657-6155
Abalon Precision Manufacturing Corporation
Bronx, NY 800-888-2225
Abco International
Melville, NY 866-240-2226
AccuTemp Products
Fort Wayne, IN 800-210-5907
Acra Electric Corporation
Tulsa, OK 800-223-4328
Adamatic
Auburn, WA 800-578-2547
Advance Tabco
Edgewood, NY 800-645-3166
AK Steel
West Chester, OH 800-331-5050
Alegacy Food Service Products Group, Inc.
Santa Fe Springs, CA 800-848-4440
ALKAR
Lodi, WI 608-592-3211
All Spun Metal Products
Des Plaines, IL 847-824-4117
All State Fabricators Corporation
Florida, RI 800-322-9925
Alliance Products, LLC
Murfreesboro, TN 800-522-3973
Allied Metal Spinning Corp
Bronx, NY 800-615-2266
Alloy Hardfacing & Engineering Company, Inc
Jordan, MN 800-328-8408
Allstrong Restaurant Equipment
South El Monte, CA 800-933-8913
ALPI Food Preparation Equipment
Bolton, ON 800-928-2574
Alto-Shaam
Menomonee Falls, WI 800-558-8744
Amana Commercial Products
Cedar Rapids, IA 319-368-8198
American Extrusion International
South Beloit, IL 815-624-6616
American Housewares Manufacturing Corporation
Bronx, NY 718-665-9500
American Metal Stamping & Spinning
Brooklyn, NY 718-384-1500
American Range & Hood Corporation
Pacoima, CA 888-753-9898
American Systems Associates
Hampton Bays, NY 800-584-3663
AMF CANADA
Sherbrooke, QC 800-255-3869
AMI
Richmond, CA 800-942-7466
Anchor Hocking Company
Lancaster, OH 800-562-7511
Anetsberger
Concord, NH 603-225-6684
Antrim Manufacturing
Brookfield, WI 262-781-6860
Apollo Sheet Metal
Kennewick, WA 509-586-1104
APW Wyott Food Service Equipment Company
Cheyenne, WY 800-527-2100
Archer Wire International
Bedford Park, IL 708-563-1700
Arcobaleno Pasta Machines
Lancaster, PA 800-875-7096
Aroma Manufacturing Company
San Diego, CA 800-276-6286
Astoria General Espresso
Greensboro, NC 336-393-0224
Attias Oven Corporation
Brooklyn, NY 800-928-8427
Autofry
Northborough, MA 800-348-2976
Automated Food Systems
Waxahachie, TX 972-298-5719
Automatic Specialities Inc.
Marlborough, MA 800-445-2370
Avalon Manufacturing
Corona, CA 800-676-3040
Awmco
Orland Park, IL 708-478-6032
Aztec Grill
Dallas, TX 800-346-8114
Bakers Pride Oven Company
New Rochelle, NY 800-431-2745
Bakery Associates
Setauket, NY 631-751-4156
Ballantyne Food Service Equipment
Omaha, NE 800-424-1215

Bar-B-Q Woods
Newton, KS 800-528-0819
Baxter Manufacturing Company
Orting, WA 800-777-2828
BBC Industries
Pacific, MO 800-654-4205
BBQ Pits by Klose
Houston, TX 800-487-7487
BE & SCO
San Antonio, TX 800-683-0928
Becker Brothers GraphiteCorporation
Maywood, IL 708-410-0700
Belshaw Adamatic Bakery Group
Auburn, WA 800-578-2547
Belson Outdoors
North Aurora, IL 800-323-5664
Benchmark Thermal Corporation
Grass Valley, CA 530-477-5011
Benko Products
Sheffield Village, OH 440-934-2180
Bethel Engineering & Equipment Inc
New Hampshire, OH 800-889-6129
Bevles Company
Dallas, TX 800-441-1601
Big John Grills & Rotisseries
Pleasant Gap, PA 800-326-9575
BKI Worldwide
Simpsonville, SC 800-927-6887
Blentech Corporation
Santa Rosa, CA 707-523-5949
Blodgett
Burlington, VT 800-331-5842
Bolling Oven & Machine Company
Avon, OH 440-937-6112
BR Machine Company
Wedron, IL 800-310-7057
Brinkmann Corporation
Dallas, TX 800-468-5252
Britt's Barbecue
Birmingham, AL 205-612-6538
Broaster Company
Beloit, WI 800-365-8278
Buhler Group
Raleigh, NC 919-851-2000
C.H. Babb Company
Raynham, MA 508-977-0600
Carlisle Food Service Products
Oklahoma City, OK 800-654-8210
Casa Herrera
Pomona, CA 800-624-3916
Casso-Solar Corporation
Pomona, NY 800-988-4455
Central Fabricators
Cincinnati, OH 800-909-8265
Checker Engineering
New Hope, MN 888-800-5001
Chef's Choice Mesquite Charcoal
Carpinteria, CA 805-684-8284
Chesmont Engineering Company
Exton, PA 610-594-9200
Chester-Jensen Company, Inc.
Chester, PA 800-685-3750
Chromalox
Pittsburgh, PA 800-443-2640
Cincinnati Industrial Machine
Mason, OH 800-677-0076
Cleveland Range Company
Cleveland, OH 800-338-2204
Coast Scientific
Rancho Santa Fe, CA 800-445-1544
Cobatco
Peoria, IL 800-426-2282
Cober Electronics, Inc.
Norwalk, CT 800-709-5948
ColburnTreat
Winooski, VT 877-877-1224
Commercial Dehydrator Systems Inc
Eugene, OR 800-369-4283
Comstock-Castle Stove Company
Quincy, IL 800-637-9188
Connerton Company
Santa Ana, CA 714-547-9218
Cook King
Laguna Beach, CA 949-497-1235
Cooking Systems International
Stratford, CT 203-377-4174
Cookshack
Ponca City, OK 800-423-0698
CookTek
Chicago, IL 888-266-5835
Cool Curtain/CCI Industries
Costa Mesa, CA 800-854-5719

Cove Four Slide & Stamping Corporation
Freeport, NY 516-379-4232
CPM Wolverine Proctor
Horsham, PA 215-443-5200
Craft Industries
Long Island City, NY 252-753-3152
Cres Cor
Mentor, OH 877-273-7267
Crispy Lite
St. Louis, MO 888-356-5362
Crown Verity
Brantford, ON 888-505-7240
Custom Diamond International
Laval, QC 800-326-5926
Custom Diamond International
Laval, QC 800-363-5926
Cutler Industries
Morton Grove, IL 800-458-5593
D. Picking & Company
Bucyrus, OH 419-562-6891
Damrow Company
Fond Du Lac, WI 800-236-1501
Dar-B-Ques Barbecue Equipment
Imperial, MO 636-296-4408
Davron Technologies
Chattanooga, TN 423-870-1888
Dawn Equipment Company
Jackson, MI 800-248-1844
DBE Inc
Concord, ON 800-461-5313
Dean Industries
Gardena, CA 800-995-1210
Defreeze Corporation
Southborough, MA 508-485-8512
Deluxe Equipment Company
Bradenton, FL 800-367-8931
Diversified Metal Engineering
Charlottetown, PE 902-628-6900
Doyon Equipment
Liniere, QC 800-463-4273
Duke Manufacturing Company
Saint Louis, MO 800-735-3853
Dupps Company
Germantown, OH 937-855-6555
Dura-Ware Company of America
Oklahoma City, OK 800-664-3872
Duralite
Riverton, CT 888-432-8797
Dynamic Cooking Systems
Huntington Beach, CA 800-433-8466
Dynynstyl
Delray Beach, FL 800-774-7895
Earthstone Wood-Fire Ovens
Glendale, CA 800-840-4915
Electro-Steam Generator Corporation
Rancocas, NJ 866-617-0764
Ember-Glo
Chicago, IL 866-705-0515
Empire Bakery Equipment
Hicksville, NY 800-878-4070
Epcon Industrial Systems
Conroe, TX 800-447-7872
Equipex Limited
Providence, RI 800-649-7885
Erwin Food Service Equipment
Fort Worth, TX 817-535-0021
Esquire Mechanical Corp.
Armonk, NY 800-847-4206
Eurodib
Champlain, NY 888-956-6866
Fab-X/Metals
Washington, NC 800-677-3229
Filtercorp
Fresno, CA 800-473-4526
Fish Oven & Equipment Corporation
Wauconda, IL 877-526-8720
FlashBake Ovens Food Service
Fremont, CA 800-843-6836
FleetwoodGoldcoWyard
Romeoville, IL 630-759-6800
Flodin
Moses Lake, WA 509-766-2996
Food Automation Service Techniques
Stratford, CT 800-327-8766
Food Engineering Unlimited
Fullerton, CA 714-879-8762
Foster Refrigerator Corporation
Kinderhook, NY 888-828-3311
Franrica Systems
Stockton, CA 209-948-2811
Franz Haas Machinery of America
Richmond, VA 804-222-6022

Friedrich Metal ProductsCompany
Browns Summit, NC 800-772-0326
Fry Tech Corporation
Dubuque, IA 319-583-1559
Frymaster, LLC.
Shreveport, LA 800-221-4583
G.S. Blodgett Corporation
Burlington, VT 800-331-5842
Garland Commercial Ranges
Mississauga, ON 905-624-0260
Garland Commercial Ranges Ltd.
Mississauga, ON 905-624-0260
Garvis Manufacturing Company
Des Moines, IA 515-243-8054
GBS Foodservice Equipment, Inc.
Mississauga, ON 888-402-1242
Gehnrich Oven Sales Company
Smithtown, NY 631-585-8787
Gem Equipment of Oregon
Woodburn, OR 503-982-9902
General Cage
Elwood, IN 800-428-6403
Giles Enterprises
Montgomery, AL 800-288-1555
Glenro
Paterson, NJ 800-922-0106
Glowmaster Corporation
Clifton, NJ 800-272-7008
Gold Medal Products Company
Cincinnati, OH 800-543-0862
GraLab Corporation
Centerville, OH 800-876-8353
Grand Silver Company
Bronx, NY 718-585-1930
Grande Chef Company
Orangeville, ON 519-942-4470
Grill Greats
Saxonburg, PA 724-352-1511
Grillco
Aurora, IL 800-644-0067
Grills to Go
Fresno, CA 877-869-2253
GSW Jackes-Evans Manufacturing Company
Saint Louis, MO 800-325-6173
H.F. Coors China Company
New Albany, MS 800-782-6677
Hamilton Kettles
Weirton, WV 800-535-1882
Hardt Equipment Manufacturing
Lachine, QC 888-848-4408
Hasty-Bake
Tulsa, OK 800-426-6836
HATCO Corporation
Milwaukee, WI 800-558-0607
Heat-It Manufacturing
San Antonio, TX 800-323-9336
Henny Penny, Inc.
Detroit, MI 313-877-9550
Hercules Food Equipment
Weston, ON 416-742-9673
HH Controls Company
Arilington, MA 781-646-2626
Hickory Industries
North Bergen, NJ 800-732-9153
Hobart Corporation
Troy, OH 888-446-2278
Holman Boiler Works
Dallas, TX 800-331-1956
Holman Cooking Equipment
Saint Louis, MO 888-356-5362
Holstein Manufacturing
Holstein, IA 800-368-4342
House of Webster
Rogers, AR 800-369-4641
Hughes Equipment Company LLC
Columbus, WI 866-535-9303
Hydro-Thermal
Waukesha, WI 800-952-0121
Idaho Steel Products Company
Idaho Falls, ID 208-522-1275
Illinois Range Company
Schiller Park, IL 800-535-7041
Imperial Commercial Cooking Equipment
Corona, CA 800-343-7790
Industrial Ceramic Products
Marysville, OH 800-427-2278
Industrial Sheet Metal
Cleveland, OH 216-431-9650
Intedge Manufacturing
Woodruff, SC 866-969-9605
IR Systems
Jupiter, FL 800-893-7540

Iwatani International Corporation of America
Houston, TX 800-775-5506
J&R Manufacturing
Mesquite, TX 800-527-4831
J.C. Ford Company
La Habra, CA 714-871-7361
Jackson MSC
Barbourville, KY 888-800-5672
Jackson Restaurant Supply
Jackson, TN 800-424-8943
Jade Range
Brea, CA 800-884-5233
Kady International
Scarborough, ME 800-367-5239
Karl Schnell
New London, WI 920-982-9974
Kay Home Products
Antioch, IL 800-600-7009
Keating of Chicago
Mc Cook, IL 800-532-8464
Kelmin Products
Plymouth, FL 407-886-6079
Key Technology
Walla Walla, WA 509-529-2161
King Packaging Corporation
Schenectady, NY 518-370-5464
Knox Stove Works
Knoxville, TN 865-524-4113
Komline-Sanderson
Peapack, NJ 800-225-5457
Krispy Kist Company
Chicago, IL 312-733-0900
Lancaster Colony Corporation
Columbus, OH 800-292-7260
Lang Manufacturing Company
Everett, WA 800-882-6368
Lanly Company
Cleveland, OH 216-731-1115
Lauhoff Corporation
Detroit, MI 313-259-0027
Lazy-Man
Belvidere, NJ 800-475-1950
Le Smoker
Salisbury, MD 410-677-3233
Leedal Inc
Northbrook, IL 847-498-0111
Legion Industries
Waynesboro, GA 800-887-1988
Libertyware
Clearfield, UT 888-500-5885
Lignetics of Missouri
Sandpoint, ID 800-544-3834
Lil' Orbits
Minneapolis, MN 800-228-8305
Lincoln Foodservice
Cleveland, OH 800-374-3004
Littleford Day
Florence, KY 800-365-8555
LPS Technology
Grafton, OH 800-586-1410
Magikitch'n
Concord, NH 800-441-1492
Market Forge Industries
Everett, MA 866-698-3188
Marshall Air Systems
Charlotte, NC 800-722-3474
Martin/Baron
Irwindale, CA 626-960-5153
Masterbuilt Manufacturing
Columbus, GA 800-489-1581
Mastex Industries
Petersburg, VA 804-732-8300
Maytag Corporation
Benton Harbor, MI 800-344-1274
Merco/Savory
Mt. Pleasant, MI 800-733-8821
Metal Masters Food Service Equipment Company
Clayton, DE 800-441-8440
Metal Masters Northwest
Lynnwood, WA 425-775-4481
Metro Corporation
Wilkes Barre, PA 800-433-2233
Microdry
Crestwood, KY 502-241-8933
Middleby Corporation
Elgin, IL 847-741-3300
Middleby Marshall, CTX
Elgin, IL 800-323-5575
Midwest Aircraft Products Company
Mansfield, OH 419-522-2231
Midwest Wire Products
Sturgeon Bay, WI 800-445-0225

Mies Products
West Bend, WI 800-480-6437
Miracle Exclusives
Danbury, CT 203-796-5493
Mirro Company
Lancaster, OH 800-848-7200
Moffat
San Antonio, TX 800-551-8795
Moli-International
Denver, CO 800-525-8468
Moline Machinery
Duluth, MN 800-767-5734
Montague Company
Hayward, CA 800-345-1830
Mosshaim Innovations
Jacksonville, FL 888-995-7775
Motion Technology
Northborough, MA 800-468-2976
Motom Corporation
Bensenville, IL 630-787-1995
Mouli Manufacturing Corporation
Belleville, NJ 800-789-8285
Mountain Safety Research
Seattle, WA 800-877-9677
Mr. Bar-B-Q
Old Bethpage, NY 800-333-2124
Music City Metals
Nashville, TN 800-251-2674
Napoleon Appliance Corporation
Barrie, ON 866-820-8686
National Drying Machinery Company
Philadelphia, PA 215-464-6070
National Hotpack
Stone Ridge, NY 800-431-8232
Nature's Own
Attleboro, MA 130- 13- 612
Nemeth Engineering Associates
Crestwood, KY 502-241-1502
Nevo Corporation
Ronkonkoma, NY 631-585-8787
Nieco Corporation
Windsor, CA 800-643-2656
Normandie Metal Fabricators
Port Washington, NY 800-221-2398
Northern Stainless Fabricating
Traverse City, MI 231-947-4580
Nothum Food Processing Systems
Springfield, MO 800-435-1297
NuTone
Cincinnati, OH 888-336-3948
Ogden Manufacturing Company
Pittsburgh, PA 412-967-3906
Olde Country Reproductions
York, PA 800-358-3997
Ole Hickory Pits
Cape Girardeau, MO 800-223-9667
Otto Braun Bakery Equipment
Buffalo, NY 716-824-1252
Padinox
Winsloe, PE 800-263-9768
Panasonic Commercial Food Service
Secaucus, NJ 800-553-0384
Paragon International
Nevada, IA 800-433-0333
Patio King
Cutler Bay, FL 786-258-8508
Peerless Ovens
Sandusky, OH 800-548-4514
Peerless-Premier Appliance Company
Belleville, IL 618-233-0475
Perfect Fry Company
Calgary, AB 800-265-7711
Peter Gray Corporation
Andover, MA 978-470-0990
Pick Heaters
West Bend, WI 800-233-9030
Pier 1 Imports
Woodcliff Lake, NJ 800-448-9993
Pino's Pasta Veloce
Staten Island, NY 718-273-6660
Piper Products
Wausau, WI 800-544-3057
Pitco Frialator
Concord, NH 800-258-3708
PMI Food Equipment Group
Troy, OH 937-332-3000
Polar Ware Company
Sheboygan, WI 800-237-3655
Porcelain Metals Corporation
Louisville, KY 502-635-7421
Power Flame
Parsons, KS 800-862-4256

Precision
Miami, FL 800-762-7565
Prince Castle
Carol Stream, IL 800-722-7853
Process Heating Corporation
Shrewsbury, MA 508-842-5200
Process Systems
Barrington, IL 847-842-8618
Profire Stainless Steel Barbecue
Miami, FL 305-665-5313
Proheatco Manufacturing
Pomona, CA 800-423-4195
Proluxe
Paramount, CA 800-594-5528
Q-Matic Technologies
Carol Stream, IL 800-880-6836
QNC
Dallas, TX 888-668-3687
Quadra-Tech
Columbus, OH 800-443-2766
Quality Fabrication & Design
Coppell, TX 972-393-0502
Quantem Corporation
Ewing, NJ 609-883-9879
Quasar Industries
Rochester Hills, MI 248-852-0300
Randell Manufacturing Unified Brands
Weidman, MI 888-994-7636
Rankin-DeLux
Eastwale, CA 951-685-0081
Rational Cooking Systems
Schaumburg, IL 888-320-7274
Reading Bakery Systems
Robesonia, PA 610-693-5816
Reed Oven Company
Kansas City, MO 816-842-7446
Regal Ware
Kewaskum, WI 262-626-2121
Reliable Food Service Equipment
Concord, ON 416-738-6840
Remco Industries International
Fort Lauderdale, FL 800-987-3626
Renato Specialty Product
Garland, TX 866-575-6316
Revent
Piscataway, NJ 732-777-9433
Ricoh Technologies
Grand Prairie, TX 800-585-9367
Rival Manufacturing Company
Kansas City, MO 816-943-4100
Rotisol France Inc
Inglewood, CA 800-651-5969
Roto-Flex Oven Company
San Antonio, TX 877-859-1463
Roundup Food Equipment
Carol Stream, IL 800-253-2991
Royal Oak Enterprises
Roswell, GA 770-393-1430
Royalton Foodservice Equipment
Cleveland, OH 800-662-8765
Sandvik Process Systems
Totowa, NJ 973-790-1600
Sasib North America
Plano, TX 972-422-5808
Saunder Brothers
Bridgton, ME 207-647-3331
Savage Brothers Company
Elk Grove Vlg, IL 800-342-0973
Seidman Brothers
Chelsea, MA 800-437-7770
Server Products
Richfield, WI 800-558-8722
Sharp Electronics Corporation
Mahwah, NJ 800-237-4277
Sharpsville Container
Sharpsville, PA 800-645-1248
Shat-R-Shield
Salisbury, NC 800-223-0853
Shelcon
Ontario, CA 909-947-4877
Shouldice Brothers SheetMetal
Battle Creek, MI 269-962-5579
Silesia Grill Machines
Saint Petersburg, FL 800-267-4766
Silesia Velox Grill Machines, Inc.
Saint Petersburg, FL 800-237-4766
Silver Weibull
Aurora, CO 303-373-2311
Smokaroma
Boley, OK 800-331-5565
South Valley Manufacturing
Gilroy, CA 408-842-5457

Southbend Company
Fuquay Varina, NC 800-348-2558
Southern Pride Distributing
Marion, IL 800-851-8180
Spring USA Corporation
Naperville, IL 800-535-8974
Standex International Corporation
Salem, NH 603-893-9701
Star Manufacturing International
Saint Louis, MO 800-264-7827
Starkey Chemical ProcessCompany
La Grange, IL 800-323-3040
State Products
Long Beach, CA 800-730-5150
Stein DSI
Sandusky, OH 800-447-2630
Stricklin Company
Dallas, TX 214-637-1030
Stryco Wire Products
North York, ON 416-663-7000
Super Cooker
Lake Park, GA 800-841-7452
Super Systems
Wausau, WI 800-558-5880
Super-Chef Manufacturing Company
Houston, TX 800-231-3478
Superior Food Machinery
Pico Rivera, CA 800-944-0396
Superior Products Company
Saint Paul, MN 800-328-9800
Svedala Industries
Colorado Springs, CO 719-471-3443
Swanson Wire Works Industries, Inc.
Mesquite, TX 972-288-7465
T&H Trading Corporation
Redmond, WA 425-883-2131
Tablecraft Products
Gurnee, IL 800-323-8321
Tekmatex
New York, NY 800-392-9890
TEMP-TECH Company
Springfield, MA 800-343-5579
Tempco Electric Heater Corporation
Wood Dale, IL 888-268-6396
Texas Corn Roasters
Granbury, TX 800-772-4345
Thermal Engineering Corporation
Columbia, SC 800-331-0097
Thermo King Corporation
Minneapolis, MN 952-887-2200
Thermodyne Food Service
Fort Wayne, IN 800-526-9182
Thermoquest
Riviera Beach, FL 800-532-4752
Thermos Company
Schaumburg, IL 800-243-0745
Thomas L. Green & Company
Robenosia, PA 610-693-5816
Toastmaster
Elgin, IL 847-741-3300
Tolan Machinery Company
Rockaway, NJ 973-983-7212
Tomlinson Industries
Cleveland, OH 800-945-4589
Toronto Kitchen Equipment
North York, ON 416-745-4944
Town Food Service Equipment Company
Brooklyn, NY 800-221-5032
Traeger Industries
Mount Angel, OR 800-872-3437
Trak-Air/Rair
Denver, CO 800-688-8725
Tramontina USA
Sugar Land, TX 800-221-7809
Trimen Foodservice Equipment
North York, ON 877-437-1422
TruHeat Corporation
Allegan, MI 800-879-6199
Tupperware Brand Corporation
Orlando, FL 800-366-3800
TURBOCHEF Technologies
Carrollton, TX 800-908-8726
Ultrafryer Systems
San Antonio, TX 800-545-9189
Utility Refrigerator Company
Los Angeles, CA 800-884-5233
Valad Electric Heating Corporation
Tarrytown, NY
Vasconia Housewares
San Antonio, TX 800-377-6723
Vimco Inc.
King of Prussia, PA 610-768-0500

Vortron Smokehouse/Ovens
Iron Ridge, WI 800-874-1949
Vulcan-Hart Company
Louisville, KY 800-814-2028
Wayne Combustion Systems
Fort Wayne, IN 260-425-9200
Welbilt Corporation
Stamford, CT. 203-325-8300
Wells Manufacturing Company
Verdi, NV 800-777-0450
West Oregon Wood Products
Columbia City, OR 503-397-6707
Western Combustion Engineering
Carson, CA 310-834-9389
Wheel Tough Company
Terre Haute, IN 888-765-8833
Whitford Corporation
Frazer, PA 610-296-3200
Wilch Manufacturing
Topeka, KS 785-267-2762
Wilder Manufacturing Company
Port Jervis, NY 800-832-1319
Wilton Industries
Woodridge, IL 630-963-1818
Win-Holt Equipment Group
Westbury, NY 800-444-3595
Winston Industries
Louisville, KY 800-234-5286
Wisco Industries
Oregon, WI 800-999-4726
Wittco Food Service Equipment
Milwaukee, WI 800-367-8413
Wittco Foodservice Equipment, Inc.
Milwaukee, WI 800-821-3912
Wolf Range Company
Louisville, KY 800-366-9653
Wolverine Proctor & Schwartz
Lexington, NC 336-248-5181
Wood Stone Corporation
Bellingham, WA 800-988-8103
World Kitchen
Elmira, NY 800-999-3436
X-Press Manufacturing
New Braunfels, TX. 830-629-2651

Charcoal Briquettes

Grill Greats
Saxonburg, PA. 724-352-1511
King Packaging Corporation
Schenectady, NY. 518-370-5464
Lazzari Fuel Company
San Francisco, CA 800-242-7265
Le Smoker
Salisbury, MD 410-677-3233
Mali's All Natural Barbecue Supply Company
East Amherst, NY. 800-289-6254
Mex-Char
Douglas, AZ 520-364-2138
Music City Metals
Nashville, TN 800-251-2674
Nature's Own
Attleboro, MA. 130- 13- 612
Roseville Charcoal & Manufacturing
Zanesville, OH 740-452-5473
Royal Oak Enterprises
Roswell, GA 770-393-1430

Charcoal: Mesquite

Chef's Choice Mesquite Charcoal
Carpinteria, CA. 805-684-8284
Lazzari Fuel Company
San Francisco, CA 800-242-7265
Le Smoker
Salisbury, MD 410-677-3233
Lignetics of Missouri
Sandpoint, ID 800-544-3834
Mali's All Natural Barbecue Supply Company
East Amherst, NY. 800-289-6254
Mex-Char
Douglas, AZ 520-364-2138
Music City Metals
Nashville, TN 800-251-2674

Corers

Fruit & Vegetable

A.D. Cowdrey Company
Modesto, CA. 209-538-4677
AMCO Corporation
City of Industry, CA 626-855-2550

F.B. Pease Company
Rochester, NY. 585-475-1870
Globe International
Tacoma, WA 800-523-6575
Goodnature Products
Orchard Park, NY. 800-875-3381

Corn Chip Processing

A.C. Horn & Co
Dallas, TX. 800-657-6155
Casa Herrera
Pomona, CA 800-624-3916
Graybill Machines
Lititz, PA. 717-626-5221
J.C. Ford Company
La Habra, CA 714-871-7361
Krispy Kist Company
Chicago, IL 312-733-0900
Maddox/Adams International
Miami, FL. 305-592-3337
Pavan USA, Inc.
Emigsville, PA 717-767-4889
Polar Process
Plattsville, ON. 877-896-8077

Corn Poppers

A.C. Horn & Co
Dallas, TX. 800-657-6155
C. Cretors & Company
Chicago, IL 800-228-1885
Dunbar Manufacturing Company
South Elgin, IL 847-741-6394
Fun City Popcorn
Las Vegas, NV 800-423-1710
Gold Medal Products Company
Cincinnati, OH 800-543-0862
Great Western Products Company
Assumption, IL 217-226-3241
Great Western Products Company
Hollywood, AL. 256-259-3578
Great Western Products Company
Hollywood, AL. 800-239-2143
Maddox/Adams International
Miami, FL. 305-592-3337
Paragon International
Nevada, IA 800-433-0333
Server Products
Richfield, WI 800-558-8722
Star Manufacturing International
Saint Louis, MO 800-264-7827
Treier Popcorn Farms
Bloomdale, OH 419-454-2811

Corn Processing

Andritz
Muncy, PA. 570-546-8211
Automated Food Systems
Waxahachie, TX 972-298-5719
Custom Millers Supply Company
Monmouth, IL. 309-734-6312
Hughes Equipment Company LLC
Columbus, WI. 866-535-9303
J.C. Ford Company
La Habra, CA 714-871-7361
Lee Financial Corporation
Dallas, TX. 972-960-1001
OXBO International Corporation
Clear Lake, WI 800-628-6196
Texas Corn Roasters
Granbury, TX 800-772-4345

Crushers

Can & Glass

A.T. Ferrell Company Inc
Bluffton, IN. 800-248-8318
Berkshire PPM
Litchfield, CT 860-567-3118
C S Bell Company
Tiffin, OH 888-958-6381
Compactors
Hilton Head Island, SC. 800-423-4003
Consolidated Baling Machine Company
Jacksonville, FL 800-231-9286
Ertel Alsop
Kingston, NY 800-553-7835
Glen Mills, Inc.
Clifton, NJ. 973-777-0777

Langsenkamp Manufacturing
Indianapolis, IN 877-585-1950
Maren Engineering Corporation
South Holland, IL 800-875-1038
Waring Products
Torrington, CT 800-492-7464

Fruit

A.K. Robins
Baltimore, MD 800-486-9656
Globe International
Tacoma, WA 800-523-6575
Goodnature Products
Orchard Park, NY. 800-875-3381
Healdsburg Machine Company
Santa Rosa, CA. 707-433-3348
Oak Barrel Winecraft
Berkeley, CA. 510-849-0400

Grain & Oat

C S Bell Company
Tiffin, OH 888-958-6381
Glen Mills, Inc.
Clifton, NJ. 973-777-0777
MO Industries
Whippany, NJ 973-386-9228
Roskamp Champion
Waterloo, IA 800-366-2563
Schutte-Buffalo HammermilLl
Buffalo, NY. 800-447-4634

Dairy & Creamery

A&B Process Systems
Stratford, WI 888-258-2789
Advance Energy Technologies
Clifton Park, NY. 800-724-0198
Apex Packing & Rubber Company
Farmingdale, NY. 800-645-9110
Armfield
Ringwood, EN 142- 47-781
AW Company
Franksville, WI 800-850-6110
B-T Engineering
Bala Cynwyd, PA 610-664-9500
Babson Brothers Company
Galesville, WI. 608-582-2221
Ben H. Anderson Manufacturers
Morrisonville, WI 608-846-5474
Berlon Industries
Hustisford, WI 800-899-3580
Bowers Process Equipment
Stratford, ON. 800-567-3223
C&R Refrigation Inc,
Center, TX. 800-438-6182
C.E. Rogers Company
Mora, MN 800-279-8081
Cal-Coast Manufacturing
Turlock, CA 209-668-9378
Cannon Equipment Company
Rosemount, MN 800-825-8501
Chester-Jensen Company, Inc.
Chester, PA 800-685-3750
Coburn Company
Whitewater, WI. 800-776-7042
Custom Fabricating & Repair
Marshfield, WI 800-236-8773
Custom Food Machinery
Stockton, CA. 209-463-4343
Damrow Company
Fond Du Lac, WI 800-236-1501
Dipwell Company
Northampton, MA. 413-587-4673
Diversified Metal Engineering
Charlottetown, PE. 902-628-6900
Doering Machines, Inc.
San Francisco, CA 415-526-2131
Dyna-Veyor
Newark, NJ 800-930-4760
Dynamic Automation
Simi Valley, CA. 805-584-8476
Eischen Enterprises
Fresno, CA 559-834-0013
Equipment Specialists
Haines City, FL. 863-421-4567
Falco
La Prairie, CA. 450-444-0566
Food Resources International
Redlands, CA 714-299-8829
GEA Tuchenhagen North America, USA, LLC
Portland, ME. 207-797-9500

General Machinery Corporation
Sheboygan, WI 888-243-6622
Girton Manufacturing Company, Inc.
Millville, PA 570-458-5521
Globe Food Equipment Company
Dayton, OH. 800-347-5423
Gruenewald ManufacturingCompany
Danvers, MA. 800-229-9447
IKA Works
Wilmington, NC 800-733-3037
Johnson Industries International, Inc.
Windsor, WI 608-846-4499
Kusel Equipment Company
Watertown, WI 920-261-4112
Leland
South Plainfield, NJ 800-984-9793
Len E. Ivarson
Milwaukee, WI. 414-351-0700
Lyco Manufacturing
Wausau, WI. 715-845-7867
Lyco Wausau
Wausau, WI. 715-845-7867
Master-Bilt
New Albany, MS. 800-647-1284
Membrane System Specialists
Wisconsin Rapids, WI 715-421-2333
Millerbernd Process Sytems
Winsted, MN. 320-485-2685
Nicholas Machine and Grinding
Houston, TX 800-747-1256
NIMCO Corporation
Crystal Lake, IL 815-459-4200
Omni International
Kennesaw, GA 800-776-4431
Opal Manufacturing Ltd
Toronto, ON 416-646-5232
Pacific Process Technology
La Jolla, CA 858-551-3298
Papertech
North Vancouver, BC 877-787-2737
Paradigm Technologies
Eugene, OR. 541-345-5543
Peterson Fiberglass Laminates
Shell Lake, WI 715-468-2306
Polar Process
Plattsville, ON. 877-896-8077
Pro Scientific
Oxford, CT 800-584-3776
Processing Machinery & Supply
Philadelphia, PA 215-425-4320
Reiser
Canton, MA 781-575-9941
Relco Unisystems Corporation
Willmar, MN. 320-231-2210
Rheo-Tech
Gurnee, IL. 847-367-1557
Sanchelima International
Doral, FL. 305-591-4343
Scherping Systems
Winsted, MN. 320-485-4401
Schlueter Company
Janesville, WI 800-359-1700
Sepragen Corporation
Hayward, CA 510-475-0650
Sonic Corporation
Stratford, CT 866-493-1378
Stanfos
Edmonton, AB 800-661-5648
Superflex
Brooklyn, NY 800-394-3665
Swirl Freeze Corp
Salt Lake City, UT 800-262-4275
T.D. Sawvel Company
Maple Plain, MN. 877-488-1816
Tetra Pak
Chicago, IL 312-553-9200
Tindall Packaging
Vicksburg, MI 269-649-1163
Westfalia-Surge, Inc.
Naperville, IL 630-548-8374
Whey Systems
Willmar, MN. 320-905-4122

Deaerators

Food

B.A.G. Corporation
Dallas, TX. 800-331-9200
Bryan Boilers
Peru, IN. 765-473-6651

Cornell Machine Company
Springfield, NJ 973-379-6860
Hebeler Corporation
Tonawanda, NY 800-486-4709
Sellers Engineering Division
Danville, KY. 859-236-3181
South Valley Manufacturing
Gilroy, CA. 408-842-5457

Deep Fryers

Abalon Precision Manufacturing Corporation
Bronx, NY. 800-888-2225
All State Fabricators Corporation
Florida, RI. 800-322-9925
Alumaworks
Sunny Isle Beach, FL 800-277-7267
American Extrusion International
South Beloit, IL 815-624-6616
Apollo Sheet Metal
Kennewick, WA 509-586-1104
Autofry
Northborough, MA 800-348-2976
Automated Food Systems
Waxahachie, TX 972-298-5719
Ballantyne Food Service Equipment
Omaha, NE 800-424-1215
Baxter Manufacturing Company
Orting, WA 800-777-2828
Belshaw Adamatic Bakery Group
Auburn, WA 800-578-2547
Broaster Company
Beloit, WI 800-365-8278
Comstock-Castle Stove Company
Quincy, IL 800-637-9188
Cook King
Laguna Beach, CA 949-497-1235
Crispy Lite
St. Louis, MO 888-356-5362
Davron Technologies
Chattanooga, TN. 423-870-1888
Dawn Equipment Company
Jackson, MI. 800-248-1844
Dean Industries
Gardena, CA 800-995-1210
Fry Tech Corporation
Dubuque, IA 319-583-1559
Frymaster, LLC.
Shreveport, LA 800-221-4583
G.S. Blodgett Corporation
Burlington, VT 800-331-5842
Garland Commercial Ranges
Mississauga, ON. 905-624-0260
Gem Equipment of Oregon
Woodburn, OR 503-982-9902
Giles Enterprises
Montgomery, AL. 800-288-1555
Gold Medal Products Company
Cincinnati, OH 800-543-0862
Imperial Commercial Cooking Equipment
Corona, CA 800-343-7790
Keating of Chicago
Mc Cook, IL 800-532-8464
Krispy Kist Company
Chicago, IL 312-733-0900
Lang Manufacturing Company
Everett, WA. 800-882-6368
Lucks Food Equipment Company
Kent, WA. 811-824-0696
Market Forge Industries
Everett, MA. 866-698-3188
Masterbuilt Manufacturing
Columbus, GA 800-489-1581
Meyer Machine & Garroutte Products
San Antonio, TX. 210-736-1811
Middleby Corporation
Elgin, IL 847-741-3300
Mies Products
West Bend, WI 800-480-6437
Moline Machinery
Duluth, MN. 800-767-5734
Motion Technology
Northborough, MA 800-468-2976
Nothum Food Processing Systems
Springfield, MO 800-435-1297
Otto Braun Bakery Equipment
Buffalo, NY. 716-824-1252
Perfect Fry Company
Calgary, AB. 800-265-7711
Pitco Frialator
Concord, NH. 800-258-3708

Ricoh Technologies
Grand Prairie, TX 800-585-9367
Southbend Company
Fuquay Varina, NC 800-348-2558
Stafford - Smith
Kalamazoo, MI 800-968-2442
Star Manufacturing International
Saint Louis, MO 800-264-7827
Stein DSI
Sandusky, OH 800-447-2630
Super-Chef Manufacturing Company
Houston, TX 800-231-3478
Superior Products Company
Saint Paul, MN 800-328-9800
Tekmatex
New York, NY 800-392-9890
Toastmaster
Elgin, IL 847-741-3300
Trak-Air/Rair
Denver, CO 800-688-8725
TWM Manufacturing
Leamington, ON 888-495-4831
Ultrafryer Systems
San Antonio, TX. 800-545-9189
Vulcan-Hart Company
Louisville, KY 800-814-2028
Welbilt Corporation
Stamford, CT. 203-325-8300
Wells Manufacturing Company
Verdi, NV 800-777-0450
Western Combustion Engineering
Carson, CA 310-834-9389
Wheel Tough Company
Terre Haute, IN 888-765-8833
Wolf Range Company
Louisville, KY 800-366-9653

Dehydration Equipment

A&J Mixing International
Oakville, ON. 800-668-3470
American Drying Systems
Miami, FL. 800-762-7565
Andritz
Muncy, PA. 570-546-8211
B.A.G. Corporation
Dallas, TX. 800-331-9200
BNW Industries
Tippecanoe, IN 574-353-7855
Brothers Metal Products
Santa Ana, CA 714-972-3008
Brown International Corporation
Winter Haven, FL 626-966-8361
Buhler Group
Raleigh, NC 919-851-2000
C.E. Rogers Company
Mora, MN 800-279-8081
Commercial Dehydrator Systems Inc
Eugene, OR. 800-369-4283
Davenport Machine
Rock Island, IL 309-786-1500
Davron Technologies
Chattanooga, TN. 423-870-1888
Dito Dean Food Prep
Rocklin, CA 800-331-7958
EnWave Corporation
Vancouver, BC 604-822-4425
Evaporator Dryer Technologies Inc
Hammond, WI. 715-796-2313
Flodin
Moses Lake, WA. 509-766-2996
Fluid Air
Aurora, IL 630-665-5001
Fluid Energy Processing and Equipment Company
Hatfield, PA. 215-368-2510
French Oil Mill Machinery Company
Piqua, OH 937-773-3420
Globe International
Tacoma, WA 800-523-6575
Goodnature Products
Orchard Park, NY 800-875-3381
H. Gartenberg & Company
Buffalo Grove, IL 847-821-7590
Joneca Corporation
Anaheim, CA 714-993-5997
Lanly Company
Cleveland, OH. 216-731-1115
Littleford Day
Florence, KY. 800-365-8555
Low Humidity Systems
Covington, GA 770-788-6744

M-E-C Company
Neodesha, KS 620-325-2673
National Drying Machinery Company
Philadelphia, PA 215-464-6070
P&F Metals
Turlock, CA 209-667-4716
Patterson Industries
Scarborough, ON 800-336-1110
Raytheon Company
Waltham, MA 617-522-3000
SP Industries
Warminster, PA 800-523-2327
Sphinx Adsorbents
Springfield, MA 800-388-0157
Thermex Thermatron
Louisville, KY 502-493-1299
Thoreson-McCosh
Troy, MI 800-959-0805
United McGill Corporation
Groveport, OH 614-829-1200
Van Air Systems
Lake City, PA 800-840-9906
Wittemann Company
Palm Coast, FL 386-445-4200
Wolverine Proctor & Schwartz
Lexington, NC 336-248-5181

Disintegrators

Schutte-Buffalo HammermilLl
Buffalo, NY 800-447-4634

Dough Make-up

Benier
Lithia Springs, GA 770-745-2200
La Poblana Food Machines
Mesa, AZ 480-258-2091
Rheon, U.S.A.
Irvine, CA 949-768-1900

Drink Mixing

A&B Process Systems
Stratford, WI 888-258-2789
Component Hardware Group
Lakewood, NJ 800-526-3694
Nuova Distribution Centre
Ferndale, WA 360-366-2226
Polar Beer Systems
Sun City, CA 951-928-8171
Vita-Mix Corporation
Cleveland, OH 800-437-4654

Dry Products Filling

GEA Tuchenhagen North America, USA, LLC
Portland, ME 207-797-9500
Inspired Automation
Agoura Hills, CA 818-991-4598

Dryers

Domnick Hunter
Charlotte, NC 800-345-8462
GEA Procomac
Hudson, WI 800-376-6476
Relco Unisystems Corporation
Willmar, MN 320-231-2210
Spiral Systems
Fair Oaks, CA 800-998-6111

Food

A&B Process Systems
Stratford, WI 888-258-2789
American Drying Systems
Miami, FL 800-762-7565
Ametek Technical & Industrial Products
Kent, OH 215-256-6601
Anhydro Inc
Olympia Fields, IL 708-747-7000
Apollo Sheet Metal
Kennewick, WA 509-586-1104
Applied Chemical Technology
Florence, AL 800-228-3217
APV Americas
Delavan, WI 800-252-5200
Berg Chilling Systems
Toronto, ON, ON 416-755-2221
BNW Industries
Tippecanoe, IN 574-353-7855
Brothers Metal Products
Santa Ana, CA 714-972-3008
Buffalo Technologies Corporation
Buffalo, NY 800-332-2419
Buhler Group
Raleigh, NC 919-851-2000
C.E. Rogers Company
Mora, MN 800-279-8081
Carrier Vibrating Equipment
Louisville, KY 502-969-3171
Casso-Solar Corporation
Pomona, NY 800-988-4455
Columbus Instruments
Columbus, OH 800-669-5011
Commercial Dehydrator Systems Inc
Eugene, OR 800-369-4283
Davron Technologies
Chattanooga, TN 423-870-1888
Delux Manufacturing Company
Kearney, NE 800-658-3240
Dito Dean Food Prep
Rocklin, CA 800-331-7958
Dupps Company
Germantown, OH 937-855-6555
Dynamic International
Pewaukee, WI 800-267-7794
Fernholtz Engineering
Van Nuys, CA 818-785-5800
FFI Corporation
Assumption, IL 217-226-5100
Fitzpatrick Company
Elmhurst, IL 630-530-3333
Fluid Air
Aurora, IL 630-665-5001
Fluid Energy Processing and Equipment Company
Hatfield, PA 215-368-2510
French Oil Mill Machinery Company
Piqua, OH 937-773-3420
Gaston County Dyeing Machine Company
Stanley, NC 704-822-5000
Glatt Air Techniques
Ramsey, NJ 201-825-8700
Great Western Products
Ontario, CA 888-598-5588
Hebeler Corporation
Tonawanda, NY 800-486-4709
Heinzen Sales International
Gilroy, CA 408-842-7233
Idaho Steel Products Company
Idaho Falls, ID 208-522-1275
International Reserve Equipment Corporation
Clarendon Hills, IL 708-531-0680
Komline-Sanderson
Peapack, NJ 800-225-5457
Lanly Company
Cleveland, OH 216-731-1115
LIST
Acton, MA 978-635-9521
Littleford Day
Florence, KY 800-365-8555
M-E-C Company
Neodesha, KS 620-325-2673
Mannhart
Fort Worth, TX 817-421-0100
Marriott Walker Corporation
Bingham Farms, MI 248-644-6868
MCD Technologies
Tacoma, WA 253-476-0968
National Drying Machinery Company
Philadelphia, PA 215-464-6070
Nemeth Engineering Associates
Crestwood, KY 502-241-1502
Paget Equipment Company
Marshfield, WI 715-384-3158
Patterson Industries
Scarborough, ON 800-336-1110
Patterson-Kelley Hars Company
East Stroudsburg, PA 570-421-7500
Paul O. Abbe
Bensenville, IL 630-350-2200
Paxton Products
Cincinnati, OH 800-441-7475
Plainview Milk Products Cooperative
Plainview, MN 800-356-5606
Procedyne Corporation
New Brunswick, NJ 732-249-8347
Radio Frequency Company
Millis, MA 508-376-9555
Raytheon Company
Waltham, MA 617-522-3000
Sandvik Process Systems
Totowa, NJ 973-790-1600
Shanzer Grain Dryer
Sioux Falls, SD 800-843-9887
Shivvers
Corydon, IA 641-872-1007
SP Industries
Warminster, PA 800-523-2327
Spray Drying Systems
Eldersberg, MD 410-549-8090
Steri Technologies
Bohemia, NY 800-253-7140
Thermex Thermatron
Louisville, KY 502-493-1299
Ultrafilter
Norcross, GA 800-543-3634
United McGill Corporation
Groveport, OH 614-829-1200
Van Air Systems
Lake City, PA 800-840-9906
Vector Corporation
Marion, IA 319-377-8263
Vortron Smokehouse/Ovens
Iron Ridge, WI 800-874-1949
Witte Company
Washington, NJ 908-689-6500
Wittemann Company
Palm Coast, FL 386-445-4200
Wolverine Proctor & Schwartz
Lexington, NC 336-248-5181
Wyssmont Company
Fort Lee, NJ 201-947-4600
Zeeco
Broken Arrow, OK 918-258-8551

Freeze

Apollo Sheet Metal
Kennewick, WA 509-586-1104
Berg Chilling Systems
Toronto, ON, ON 416-755-2221
Berndorf Belt Technology USA
Elgin, IL 877-232-7322
SP Industries
Warminster, PA 800-523-2327

Fruit

American Drying Systems
Miami, FL 800-762-7565
Ametek Technical & Industrial Products
Kent, OH 215-256-6601
Apollo Sheet Metal
Kennewick, WA 509-586-1104
BNW Industries
Tippecanoe, IN 574-353-7855
Davron Technologies
Chattanooga, TN 423-870-1888
Globe International
Tacoma, WA 800-523-6575
Goodnature Products
Orchard Park, NY 800-875-3381
Paxton Products
Cincinnati, OH 800-441-7475
Sandvik Process Systems
Totowa, NJ 973-790-1600
Wolverine Proctor & Schwartz
Lexington, NC 336-248-5181

Grain

American Drying Systems
Miami, FL 800-762-7565
Apollo Sheet Metal
Kennewick, WA 509-586-1104
Chief Industries
Kearney, NE 800-359-8833
Davenport Machine
Rock Island, IL 309-786-1500
Davron Technologies
Chattanooga, TN 423-870-1888
Delux Manufacturing Company
Kearney, NE 800-658-3240
DMC-David Manufacturing Company
Mason City, IA 641-424-7010
DriAll
Attica, IN 765-295-2255
FFI Corporation
Assumption, IL 217-226-5100
Forster & Son
Ada, OK 580-332-6020
Grain Machinery Manufacturing Corporation
Miami, FL 305-620-2525
NECO
Omaha, NE 402-453-6912
Patterson-Kelley Hars Company
East Stroudsburg, PA 570-421-7500

Sandvik Process Systems
Totowa, NJ 973-790-1600
Shanzer Grain Dryer
Sioux Falls, SD 800-843-9887
Shivvers
Corydon, IA 641-872-1007
Wolverine Proctor & Schwartz
Lexington, NC 336-248-5181

Spray

A&B Process Systems
Stratford, WI 888-258-2789
Armfield
Ringwood, EN 142- 47-781
Davron Technologies
Chattanooga, TN 423-870-1888
Evaporator Dryer Technologies Inc
Hammond, WI 715-796-2313
Food Resources International
Redlands, CA 714-299-8829
Gardner Denver Inc.
Toronto, ON 416-763-4681
Marriott Walker Corporation
Bingham Farms, MI 248-644-6868
Niro
Hudson, WI 715-386-9371
Paget Equipment Company
Marshfield, WI 715-384-3158
Spray Drying Systems
Eldersberg, MD 410-549-8090
Spraying Systems Company
Wheaton, IL 630-655-5000
Stainless Fabrication
Springfield, MO 800-397-8265

Dumpers

AFECO
Algona, IA 888-295-1116
American Food Equipment Company
Hayward, CA 510-783-0255
Andgar Corporation
Ferndale, WA 360-366-9900
Apache Stainless Equipment Corporation
Beaver Dam, WI 800-444-0398
Automated Flexible Conveyor
Clifton, NJ 800-694-7271
Bridge Machine Company
Palmyra, NJ 856-829-1800
Cecor
Verona, WI 800-356-9042
Cleasby Manufacturing Company
San Francisco, CA 415-822-6565
Coastline Equipment
Bellingham, WA 360-739-2480
Cugar Machine Company
Fort Worth, TX 817-927-0411
Custom Food Machinery
Stockton, CA 209-463-4343
Dynamet
Kalamazoo, MI 269-385-0006
Flodin
Moses Lake, WA 509-766-2996
Food Processing Equipment Company
Santa Fe Springs, CA 479-751-9392
Gem Equipment of Oregon
Woodburn, OR 503-982-9902
Heinzen Sales International
Gilroy, CA 408-842-7233
Jesco Industries, Inc.
Litchfield, MI 800-455-0019
Kinetic Equipment Company
Appleton, WI 806-293-4471
MAF Industries
Traver, CA 559-897-2905
Materials TransportationCompany
Temple, TX 800-433-3110
Midwest Metalcraft & Equipment
Windsor, MO 800-647-3167
Palace Packaging Machines
Downingtown, PA 610-873-7252
Phelps Industries
Little Rock, AR 501-568-5550
Pucel Enterprises
Cleveland, OH 800-336-4986
Reiser
Canton, MA 781-575-9941
RMF Freezers
Grandview, MO 816-765-4101
Screw Conveyor Corporation
Hammond, IN 219-931-1450

SP Industries
Hopkins, MI 800-592-5959
TWM Manufacturing
Leamington, ON 888-495-4831
Uhrden
Sugarcreek, OH 800-852-2411
Vanmark Corporation
Creston, IA 800-523-6261
Vertical Systems
Ft. Michelle, KY 859-485-9650

Egg Processing & Cleaning

A&B Process Systems
Stratford, WI 888-258-2789
ADSI, Inc.
Durant, OK 580-924-4461
Behrens Manufacturing Company
Winona, MN 507-454-4664
Brush Research Manufacturing Company
Los Angeles, CA 323-261-2193
Davidson's Safest Choice Eggs
Lansing, IL 800-410-7619
Diamond Automation
Farmington Hills, MI 248-426-9394
Eggboxes Inc
Deerfield Beach, FL 800-326-6667
H. Gartenberg & Company
Buffalo Grove, IL 847-821-7590
Hayon Manufacturing & Engineering Corporation
Las Vegas, NV 702-562-3377
KL Products, Ltd.
London, ON, ON 800-388-5744
Kuhl Corporation
Flemington, NJ 908-782-5696

Equipment

Advance Energy Technologies
Clifton Park, NY 800-724-0198
American Process Systems
Gurnee, IL 847-336-2444
Dresser Instruments
Stratford, CT 800-328-8258
Ever Extruder
Festus, MO 636-937-8830
Famco Automatic Sausage Linkers
Pittsburgh, PA 412-241-6410
Formax/Provisur Technologies
Mokena, IL 708-479-3500
GEA Process Engineering,Inc.
Columbia, MD 410-997-8700
Graybill Machines
Lititz, PA 717-626-5221
Gridpath, Inc.
Stony Creek, ON 905-643-0955
I. Fm Usa Inc.
Franklin Park, IL 866-643-6872
Lyco Manufacturing
Wausau, WI 715-845-7867
Lyco Manufacturing
Columbus, WI 920-623-4152
M-Vac Systems
Bluffdale, UT 801-523-3962
Marlen Research Corporation
Shawnee Mission, KS 913-888-3333
MPS North America, Inc.
Lenexa, KS 913-310-0055
Murzan
Norcross, GA 770-448-0583
Paramount Packaging Corp.
Melville, NY 516-333-8100
Reiser
Canton, MA 781-575-9941
Rheon, U.S.A.
Irvine, CA 949-768-1900
Risco USA Corporation
South Easton, MA 888-474-7267
Ross Industries
Midland, VA 800-336-6010
Ryowa Company America
Elk Grove Village, IL 800-700-9692
Stephan Machinery GmbH
Mandelein, IL 847-247-0182
Sympak, Inc.
Mundelein, IL 847-247-0182
Terlet USA
Swedesboro, NJ 856-241-9970

Espresso & Cappuccino Processing

Acorto
Bellevue, WA 800-995-9019
Ascaso
Bensenville, IL 630-350-0066
Astoria General Espresso
Greensboro, NC 336-393-0224
Boston's Best Coffee Roa
South Easton, MA 800-898-8393
Carriage Works
Klamath Falls, OR 541-882-0700
Espresso Roma Corporation
Emeryville, CA 800-437-1668
Formula Espresso
Brooklyn, NY 718-834-8724
Gabriella Imports
Cleveland, OH 800-544-8117
Gensaco Marketing
New York, NY 800-506-1935
Grindmaster Corporation
Louisville, KY 800-695-4500
LaVazza Premium Coffee
New York, NY 212-725-8800
Michaelo Espresso
Seattle, WA 800-545-2883
Nuova Distribution Centre
Ferndale, WA 360-366-2226
Pasquini Espresso
Los Angeles, CA 800-724-6225
Pier 1 Imports
Woodcliff Lake, NJ 800-448-9993
Saeco
Cleveland, OH 440-528-2000
Schaerer Corporation
Signal Hill, CA 562-989-3004
Specialty Equipment Company
Farmington, CT 630-585-5111
Steel Products
Marion, IA 800-333-9451
Supramatic
Toronto, ON 877-465-2883
Wega USA
Bensenville, IL 630-350-0066
Wells Manufacturing Company
Verdi, NV 800-777-0450

Evaporators

Fruit Juice

A&B Process Systems
Stratford, WI 888-258-2789
Berkshire PPM
Litchfield, CT 860-567-3118
Central Fabricators
Cincinnati, OH 800-909-8265
Custom Food Machinery
Stockton, CA 209-463-4343
Dedert Corporation
Olympia Fields, IL 708-747-7000
Globe International
Tacoma, WA 800-523-6575
Goodnature Products
Orchard Park, NY 800-875-3381
L&A Process Systems
Modesto, CA 209-581-0205
South Valley Manufacturing
Gilroy, CA 408-842-5457
Washington Frontier
Grandview, WA 509-469-7662

Milk

A&B Process Systems
Stratford, WI 888-258-2789
Central Fabricators
Cincinnati, OH 800-909-8265
LIST
Acton, MA 978-635-9521
Marriott Walker Corporation
Bingham Farms, MI 248-644-6868
Membrane System Specialists
Wisconsin Rapids, WI 715-421-2333
Niro
Hudson, WI 715-386-9371

Extractors

Fruit & Vegetable Juice

A.K. Robins
Baltimore, MD 800-486-9656
Berkshire PPM
Litchfield, CT 860-567-3118
Brown International Corporation
Winter Haven, FL 626-966-8361

Chop-Rite Two, Inc.
Harleysville, PA 800-683-5858
Custom Food Machinery
Stockton, CA 209-463-4343
Dorton Incorporated
Arlington Hts, IL 800-299-8600
Dynamic International
Pewaukee, WI 800-267-7794
Eurodib
Champlain, NY 888-956-6866
FMC FoodTech
Madera, CA 559-673-2766
FMC FoodTech
Lakeland, FL 863-683-5411
French Oil Mill Machinery Company
Piqua, OH 937-773-3420
Globe International
Tacoma, WA 800-523-6575
Goodnature Products
Orchard Park, NY 800-875-3381
Hollymatic Corporation
Countryside, IL 708-579-3700
Juice Tree
Omaha, NE 714-891-4425
Mandeville Company
Minneapolis, MN 800-328-8490
Mulligan Associates
Mequon, WI 800-627-2886
Nutrifaster
Seattle, WA 800-800-2641
Omega Products
Harrisburg, PA 800-633-3401
Ruby Manufacturing
South El Monte, CA 626-443-1171
Technium
Medford, NJ 609-702-5910
Waring Products
Torrington, CT 800-492-7464
Washington Frontier
Grandview, WA 509-469-7662

Extruders

Bogner Industries
Ronkonkoma, NY 631-981-5123
Polar Process
Plattsville, ON 877-896-8077
Reiser
Canton, MA 781-575-9941

Fillers

Bogner Industries
Ronkonkoma, NY 631-981-5123
Edhard Corporation
Hackettstown, NJ 888-334-2731
Fogg Company
Holland, MI 616-786-3644
G&F Manufacturing Comp any
Oak Lawn, IL 800-282-1574
HAMBA USA, Inc
Saint Peters, MO
Handtmann, Inc.
Lake Forest, IL 800-477-3585
Innovative Foods, Inc.
South San Francisco, CA 650-871-8912
Niro Inc
Hudson, WI 715-386-9371
Raque Food Systems
Louisville, KY 502-267-9641
Reiser
Canton, MA 781-575-9941
Risco USA Corporation
South Easton, MA 888-474-7267
SeamTech
Acampo, CA 209-464-4610
Statco Engineering & Fabricators
Huntington Beach, CA 800-421-0362
T.D. Sawvel Company
Maple Plain, MN 877-488-1816
Terlet USA
Swedesboro, NJ 856-241-9970

Filters

Coffee

ANDEX Corporation
Rochester, NY 585-328-3790
Boston's Best Coffee Roa
South Easton, MA 800-898-8393
Bunn Corporation
Springfield, IL 800-637-8606
Chemex Division/International Housewares Corporation
Pittsfield, MA 800-243-6399
Coffee Sock Company
Eugene, OR 541-344-7698
Green Mountain Coffee Roasters, Inc.
Waterbury, VT 888-879-4627
Kennedy's Specialty Sewing
Erin, ON 519-833-9306
Lamports Filter Media
Cleveland, OH 216-881-2050
Melitta Canada
Vaughan, ON 800-565-4882
Melitta USA
Clearwater, FL 888-635-4880
Rockline Industries
Sheboygan, WI 800-558-7790
Superior Products Company
Saint Paul, MN 800-328-9800
Tops Manufacturing Company
Darien, CT 203-655-9367

Food

Alexander Machinery
Spartanburg, SC 864-963-3624
Avalon Manufacturing
Corona, CA 800-676-3040
Bird Machine Company
Houston, TX 800-229-7447
Cambridge
Cambridge, MD 877-649-7492
Cellulo Company
Fresno, CA 866-213-1131
Crispy Lite
St. Louis, MO 888-356-5362
Eaton Filtration, LLC
Tinton Falls, NJ 800-859-9212
Ertel Alsop
Kingston, NY 800-553-7835
Falcon Fabricators
Nashville, TN 615-832-0027
Filtercorp
Fresno, CA 800-473-4526
Globe International
Tacoma, WA 800-523-6575
Goodnature Products
Orchard Park, NY 800-875-3381
Greig Filters
Lafayette, LA 800-456-0177
International Reserve Equipment Corporation
Clarendon Hills, IL 708-531-0680
Komline-Sanderson
Peapack, NJ 800-225-5457
L.C. Thompson Company
Kenosha, WI 800-558-4018
MicroPure Filtration
Mound, MN 800-654-7873
Mies Products
West Bend, WI 800-480-6437
Pall Filtron
Northborough, MA 800-345-8766
Piab Vacuum Products
Hingham, MA 800-321-7422
Prince Castle
Carol Stream, IL 800-722-7853
Purolator Products Company
Greensboro, NC 800-852-4449
Refractron Technologies Corporation
Newark, NY 315-331-6222
Sparkler Filters
Conroe, TX 936-756-4471
Stein DSI
Sandusky, OH 800-447-2630
Steri Technologies
Bohemia, NY 800-253-7140
Ultrafilter
Norcross, GA 800-543-3634
Ultrafryer Systems
San Antonio, TX 800-545-9189
Williams & Mettle Company
Houston, TX 800-526-4954
Womack International
Vallejo, CA 707-647-2370

Fruit & Vegetable Juice

Berkshire PPM
Litchfield, CT 860-567-3118
Delta Pure Filtration
Ashland, VA 800-785-9450
Domnick Hunter
Charlotte, NC 800-345-8462
F.P. Smith Wire Cloth Company
Northlake, IL 800-323-6842
FDP
Santa Rosa, CA 707-547-1776
Filtration Systems
Sunrise, FL 954-572-2700
Globe International
Tacoma, WA 800-523-6575
Goodnature Products
Orchard Park, NY 800-875-3381
Komline-Sanderson
Peapack, NJ 800-225-5457
Lenser Filtration
Lakewood, NJ 732-370-1600
Metlar LLC
Riverhead, NC 631-252-5574
NSW Corporation
Roanoke, VA 800-368-3610
Refractron Technologies Corporation
Newark, NY 315-331-6222
Washington Frontier
Grandview, WA 509-469-7662

Grease

Component Hardware Group
Lakewood, NJ 800-526-3694
Flame Gard
Lakewood, NJ 800-526-3694
Trine Corporation
Bronx, NY 800-223-8075

Paper

ANDEX Corporation
Rochester, NY 585-328-3790
Avery Filter Company
Westwood, NJ 201-666-9664

Filtration and Separation

Westech Engineering
Salt Lake City, UT 801-265-1000

Fish Cleaning

Coastline Equipment
Bellingham, WA 360-739-2480
Crane Research & Engineering Company
Hampton, VA 757-826-1707
Design Technology Corporation
Billerica, MA 978-663-7000
Diversified Metal Engineering
Charlottetown, PE 902-628-6900
Fishmore
Melbourne,, FL 321-723-4751
Skrmetta Machinery Corporation
New Orleans, LA 504-488-4413
Steamway Corporation
Scottsburg, IN 800-259-8171
TWM Manufacturing
Leamington, ON 888-495-4831

Flakers or Flaking Drums

Biro Manufacturing Company
Marblehead, OH 419-798-4451
Buffalo Technologies Corporation
Buffalo, NY 800-332-2419
Ferrell-Ross
Amarillo, TX 800-299-9051
General Machinery Corporation
Sheboygan, WI 888-243-6622
Hoshizaki America
Peachtree City, GA 800-438-6087
Lauhoff Corporation
Detroit, MI 313-259-0027
Roskamp Champion
Waterloo, IA 800-366-2563
Scotsman Ice Systems
Vernon Hills, IL 800-726-8762

Flour Mill

Buffalo Technologies Corporation
Buffalo, NY 800-332-2419
Commodity Traders International
Trilla, IL 217-235-4322
Forster & Son
Ada, OK 580-332-6020

Food Processing

A-One Manufacturing
Strafford, MO 417-736-2195
Advance Energy Technologies
Clifton Park, NY. 800-724-0198
Alard Equipment Corporation
Williamson, NY 315-589-4511
AMFEC
Hayward, CA 510-783-0255
Anderson Chemical Company
Litchfield, MN 320-693-2477
Anritsu Industrial Solutions
Elk Grove Village, IL 847-419-9729
Axiflow Technologies, Inc.
Kennesaw, GA 770-795-1195
Beehive/Provisur Technologies
Mokena, IL 708-479-3500
Bizerba USA
Piscataway, NJ 732-565-6000
Bogner Industries
Ronkonkoma, NY. 631-981-5123
CPM Wolverine Proctor
Horsham, PA. 215-443-5200
Cresco Food Technologies, LLC
Cresco, IA. 563-547-4241
Eischen Enterprises
Fresno, CA 559-834-0013
Ennio International
Aurora, IL. 630-851-5808
Evonik Corporation
Parsippany, NJ. 973-541-8000
Four Corporation
Green Bay, WI. 920-336-0621
FR Drake Company
Waynesboro, VA 540-451-2790
Frost, Inc.
Grand Rapids, MI 800-253-9382
GEA Process Engineering,Inc.
Columbia, MD 410-997-8700
Grasselli SSI
Throop, PA 800-789-4353
Gridpath, Inc.
Stony Creek, ON. 905-643-0955
Incomec-Cerex Industries
Fairfield, CT 203-335-1050
Insect-O-Cutor
Stone Mountain, GA. 800-988-5359
JCS Controls, Inc.
Rochester, NY. 585-227-5910
Kasel Engineering
Dayton, OH. 937-854-8875
KL Products, Ltd.
London, ON, ON 800-388-5744
Lechler
St Charles, IL 800-777-2926
Libra Technical Center
Metuchen, NJ 732-321-5487
Loeb Equipment & Appraisal Company
Chicago, IL. 773-548-4131
Loos Machine & Automation
Colby, WI 715-223-2844
Lyco Manufacturing
Wausau, WI. 715-845-7867
Marel Food Systems, Inc.
Lenexa, KS 913-888-9110
Marlen
Riverside, MO. 913-888-3333
Micro Thermics
Raleigh, NC 919-878-8076
MTC Food Equipment
Poulsbo, WA 360-697-6319
Qualtech
Quebec, QC. 888-339-3801
Raque Food Systems
Louisville, KY 502-267-9641
Reiser
Canton, MA 781-575-9941
Ripon Manufacturing Company
Ripon, CA. 800-800-1232
Risco USA Corporation
South Easton, MA. 888-474-7267
Robot Coupe USA, Inc.
Jackson, MS 800-824-1646
Roskamp Champion
Waterloo, IA 800-366-2563
Scott Process Equipment & Controls
Guelph, ON. 888-343-5421
Sick Inc.
Minneapolis, MN 800-325-7425
Simply Manufacturing
Prairie Du Sac, WI 608-643-6656
Sperling Boss
Sperling, MB. 877-626-3401
Statco Engineering & Fabricators
Huntington Beach, CA 800-421-0362
Stone Enterprises Inc.
Omaha, NE 877-653-0500
Superior Products Company
Saint Paul, MN 800-328-9800
Thunderbird Food Machinery
Blaine, WA 800-764-9377
Ultra Process Systems
Oak Ridge, TN 865-483-2772
Warren Rupp
Mansfield, OH 419-524-8388
Washington Frontier
Grandview, WA. 509-469-7662
Weiler Equipment
Whitewater, WI. 800-558-9507
Young & Associates
Kenosha, WI 262-657-6394

Food

A C Tool & Machine Company
Louisville, KY 502-447-5505
A&B Process Systems
Stratford, WI. 888-258-2789
A&J Mixing International
Oakville, ON. 800-668-3470
A&M Industries
Sioux Falls, SD. 800-888-2615
A&M Process Equipment
Ajax, ON. 905-619-8001
A.C. Horn & Co
Dallas, TX. 800-657-6155
A.K. Robins
Baltimore, MD 800-486-9656
A.T. Ferrell Company Inc
Bluffton, IN. 800-248-8318
Aaburco Piemaster
Grass Valley, CA. 800-533-7437
Aaron Equipment Company
Bensenville, IL 630-350-2200
ABCO Industries Limited
Lunenburg, NS 866-634-8821
Abel Pumps
Sewickley, PA 412-741-3222
ABI Limited
Concord, ON. 800-297-8666
ABO Industries
San Diego, CA 858-566-9750
Acra Electric Corporation
Tulsa, OK 800-223-4328
Acraloc Corporation
Oak Ridge, TN 865-483-1368
Acrison
Moonachie, NJ 800-422-4266
ADMIX
Manchester, NH 800-466-2369
ADSI, Inc.
Durant, OK 580-924-4461
Aerotech Enterprise Inc
Chesterland, OH 440-729-2616
AEW Thurne
Lake Zurich, IL. 800-239-7297
AFECO
Algona, IA. 888-295-1116
Agricultural Data Systems
Laguna Niguel, CA. 800-328-2246
Albion Machine & Tool Company
Albion, MI 517-629-9135
Alfa Laval
Newburyport, MA. 978-465-5777
ALKAR
Lodi, WI 608-592-3211
Allegheny Bradford Corporation
Bradford, PA. 800-542-0650
Allen Gauge & Tool Company
Pittsburgh, PA. 412-241-6410
Alloy Hardfacing & Engineering Company, Inc
Jordan, MN. 800-328-8408
Allpax Products
Covington, LA 888-893-9277
Alpha Omega Technology
Cedar Knolls, NJ. 800-442-1969
ALPI Food Preparation Equipment
Bolton, ON 800-928-2574
Altman Industries
Gray, GA. 478-986-3116
Am-Mac Incorporated
Fairfield, NJ 800-829-2018
American Extrusion International
South Beloit, IL 815-624-6616
American Food Equipment Company
Hayward, CA 510-783-0255
American Housewares Manufacturing Corporation
Bronx, NY. 718-665-9500
American Manufacturing &Engineering Company
Cleveland, OH 800-822-9402
American Metal Stamping & Spinning
Brooklyn, NY 718-384-1500
Ametek Technical & Industrial Products
Kent, OH. 215-256-6601
AMF Bakery Systems
Richmond, VA. 800-225-3771
AMF CANADA
Sherbrooke, QC 800-255-3869
Anderson International Corporation
Stow, OH. 800-336-4730
Andgar Corporation
Ferndale, WA 360-366-9900
Andritz
Muncy, PA. 570-546-8211
Anhydro Inc
Olympia Fields, IL 708-747-7000
Apache Stainless Equipment Corporation
Beaver Dam, WI 800-444-0398
APEC
Lake Odessa, MI. 616-374-1000
API Heat Transfer
Buffalo, NY. 877-274-4328
Apollo Sheet Metal
Kennewick, WA 509-586-1104
Applied Chemical Technology
Florence, AL. 800-228-3217
APV Americas
Delavan, WI 800-252-5200
Arcobaleno Pasta Machines
Lancaster, PA 800-875-7096
Arde Barinco
Carlstadt, NJ 800-909-6070
Armfield
Ringwood, EN 142- 47-781
Arrow Tank Company
Buffalo, NY. 716-893-7200
Artisan Controls Corporation
Randolph, NJ 800-457-4950
Artisan Industries
Waltham, MA 781-893-6800
Ashbrook Corporation
Houston, TX 800-362-9041
Ashlock Company
San Leandro, CA. 510-351-0560
Astoria General Espresso
Greensboro, NC 336-393-0224
Atlanta SharpTech
Peachtree City, GA 800-462-7297
Atlas Minerals & Chemicals
Mertztown, PA 800-523-8269
Atlas Pacific Engineering Company
Pueblo, CO 719-948-3040
Auger-Fabrication
Exton, PA 800-334-1529
Automated Food Systems
Waxahachie, TX 972-298-5719
Avestin
Ottawa, ON. 888-283-7846
Ay Machine Company
Ephrata, PA. 717-733-0335
Ayr-King Corporation
Jeffersontown, KY 866-266-6290
B&P Process Equipment & Systems
Saginaw, MI 989-757-1300
B-T Engineering
Bala Cynwyd, PA 610-664-9500
B.A.G. Corporation
Dallas, TX. 800-331-9200
B.C. Holland
Dousman, WI 262-965-2939
Babson Brothers Company
Galesville, WI. 608-582-2221
Backwoods Smoker
Shreveport, LA 318-220-0380
Bake Star
Somerset, WI. 763-427-7611
Bakery Machinery Dealers
Holbrook, NY 631-567-6666
Baking Machines
Livermore, CA 925-449-3369
Baldewein Company
Lake Forrest, IL 800-424-5544
BE & SCO
San Antonio, TX. 800-683-0928
Bean Machines
Sonoma, CA 707-996-0706

BEI
South Haven, MI....800-364-7425
Belshaw Adamatic Bakery Group
Auburn, WA....800-578-2547
Bematek Systems
Salem, MA....877-236-2835
Ben H. Anderson Manufacturers
Morrisonville, WI....608-846-5474
Bepex International,LLC
Minneapolis, MN....800-607-2470
Berg Chilling Systems
Toronto, ON....416-755-2221
Berkshire PPM
Litchfield, CT....860-567-3118
Bermar America
Malvern, PA....888-289-5838
Bernhard
Kennett Square, PA....800-541-7874
Best & Donovan
Cincinnati, OH....800-553-2378
Bete Fog Nozzle
Greenfield, MA....800-235-0049
Bettcher Industries
Birmingham, OH....800-321-8763
Bettendorf Stanford
Salem, IL....800-548-2253
BFM Equipment Sales
Fall River, WI....920-484-3341
Bijur Lubricating Corporation
Morrisville, NC....800-631-0168
Billington Manufacturing/BWM
Modesto, CA....800-932-9312
Bird Machine Company
Houston, TX....800-229-7447
Biro Manufacturing Company
Marblehead, OH....419-798-4451
Blackmer
Grand Rapids, MI....616-241-1611
Blakeslee, Inc.
Addison, IL....630-532-5021
Blentech Corporation
Santa Rosa, CA....707-523-5949
Bloomfield Industries
St. Louis, MO....888-356-5362
Blue Tech
Hickory, NC....828-324-5900
BluMetric Environmental Inc.
Ottawa, ON....613-839-3053
BMH Equipment
Sacramento, CA....800-350-8828
Boehringer Mfg. Co. Inc.
Felton, CA....800-630-8665
Bonnot Company
Uniontown, OH....330-896-6544
Bowers Process Equipment
Stratford, ON....800-567-3223
Branson Ultrasonics Corporation
Danbury, CT....203-796-0400
Breddo Likwifier
Kansas City, MO....800-669-4092
Brew Store
Oakville, ON....905-845-2120
Bridge Machine Company
Palmyra, NJ....856-829-1800
Brothers Metal Products
Santa Ana, CA....714-972-3008
Brower
Houghton, IA....800-553-1791
Brown International Corporation
Winter Haven, FL....626-966-8361
Buffalo Technologies Corporation
Buffalo, NY....800-332-2419
Buhler Group
Raleigh, NC....919-851-2000
Bulldog Factory Service
Madison Heights, MI....248-541-3500
Bunting Magnetics Company
Newton, KS....800-835-2526
Buss America
Carol Stream, IL....630-933-9100
BVL Controls
Bois-Des-Filion, QC....866-285-2668
C S Bell Company
Tiffin, OH....888-958-6381
C. Cretors & Company
Chicago, IL....800-228-1885
C.E. Rogers Company
Mora, MN....800-279-8081
C.H. Babb Company
Raynham, MA....508-977-0600
Cal-Coast Manufacturing
Turlock, CA....209-668-9378

Capway Systems
York, PA....877-222-7929
Carolina Knife
Asheville, NC....800-520-5030
Carrier Vibrating Equipment
Louisville, KY....502-969-3171
Carter Day International, Inc.
Minneapolis, MN....763-571-1000
Casa Herrera
Pomona, CA....800-624-3916
Casso-Solar Corporation
Pomona, NY....800-988-4455
Challenge-RMF
Grandview, MO....816-765-0515
Champion Trading Corporation
Marlboro, NJ....732-780-4200
Charles Ross & Son Company
Hauppauge, NY....800-243-7677
Chemicolloid Laboratories, Inc.
New Hyde Park, NY....516-747-2666
Chemineer-Kenics/Greerco
North Andover, MA....800-643-0641
Chester-Jensen Company, Inc.
Chester, PA....800-685-3750
Chicago Stainless Equipment
Palm City, FL....800-927-8575
Chil-Con Products
Brantford, ON....800-263-0086
Chocolate Concepts
Hartville, OH....330-877-3322
Chop-Rite Two, Inc.
Harleysville, PA....800-683-5858
Cincinnati Boss Company
Omaha, NE....402-556-4070
Cleveland-Eastern Mixers
Clinton, CT....800-243-1188
Clextral, Inc
Tampa, FL....813-854-4434
CMC America Corporation
Joliet, IL....815-726-4337
Coastline Equipment
Bellingham, WA....360-739-2480
Cobatco
Peoria, IL....800-426-2282
Coburn Company
Whitewater, WI....800-776-7042
Codema
Maple Grove, MN....763-428-2266
Columbus Instruments
Columbus, OH....800-669-5011
Commercial Dehydrator Systems Inc
Eugene, OR....800-369-4283
Commercial Manufacturing& Supply Company
Fresno, CA....559-237-1855
Commodity Traders International
Trilla, IL....217-235-4322
Computer Controlled Machines
Pueblo, CO....719-948-9500
Controls Unlimited
Perry, OH....440-259-2500
Convay Systems
Etobicoke, ON....800-811-5511
Cook & Beals
Loup City, NE....308-745-0154
Cooper Turbocompressor
Buffalo, NY....877-805-7911
Coperion Corporation
Ramsey, NJ....201-327-6300
Corenco
Santa Rosa, CA....888-267-3626
Cornell Machine Company
Springfield, NJ....973-379-6860
Cornell Pump Company
Portland, OR....503-653-0330
Cozzini
Chicago, IL....773-478-9700
Crane Research & Engineering Company
Hampton, VA....757-826-1707
CRC
Council Bluffs, IA....712-323-9477
Croll-Reynolds Company
Parsippany, NJ....908-232-4200
Crown Iron Works Company
Minneapolis, MN....888-703-7500
Crown Simplimatic Company
Lynchburg, VA....434-582-1200
Cugar Machine Company
Fort Worth, TX....817-927-0411
Custom Fabricating & Repair
Marshfield, WI....800-236-8773
Custom Food Machinery
Stockton, CA....209-463-4343

Custom Metalcraft
Springfield, MO....417-862-0707
Custom Pools & Spas
Newington, NH....800-323-9509
Cutrite Company
Fremont, OH....800-928-8748
D&S Manufacturing Company
Auburn, MA....508-799-7812
D.A. Berther
West Allis, WI....877-357-9622
D.R. McClain & Son
Commerce, CA....800-428-2263
Dadant & Sons
Hamilton, IL....888-922-1293
Daily Printing
Plymouth, MN....800-622-6596
Daleco
West Chester, PA....610-429-0181
Damrow Company
Fond Du Lac, WI....800-236-1501
Davenport Machine
Rock Island, IL....309-786-1500
Davron Technologies
Chattanooga, TN....423-870-1888
DBE Inc
Concord, ON....800-461-5313
DCI
St Cloud, MN....320-252-8200
Dedert Corporation
Olympia Fields, IL....708-747-7000
Defreeze Corporation
Southborough, MA....508-485-8512
Dehyco Company
Memphis, TN....901-774-3322
Delta Machine & Manufacturing
Saint Rose, LA....504-949-8304
Delux Manufacturing Company
Kearney, NE....800-658-3240
Demaco
Ridgewood, NY
Design Technology Corporation
Billerica, MA....978-663-7000
Designer's Choice Stainless
Peoria, AZ....800-592-3274
Designpro Engineering
Clearwater, MN....800-221-4144
Diamond Automation
Farmington Hills, MI....248-426-9394
Dipwell Company
Northampton, MA....413-587-4673
Direct South
Macon, GA....478-746-3518
Dito Dean Food Prep
Rocklin, CA....800-331-7958
Diversified Metal Engineering
Charlottetown, PE....902-628-6900
Dixie Canner Company
Athens, GA....706-549-1914
Doering Company
Clear Lake, MN....320-743-2276
Doering Machines, Inc.
San Francisco, CA....415-526-2131
Dole Refrigerating Company
Lewisburg, TN....800-251-8990
Dorton Incorporated
Arlington Hts, IL....800-299-8600
DriAll
Attica, IN....765-295-2255
Drum-Mates Inc.
Lumberton, NJ....800-621-3786
DSW Converting Knives
Birmingham, AL....205-322-2021
DT Converting Technologies - Stokes
Bristol, PA....800-635-0036
Dunbar Manufacturing Company
South Elgin, IL....847-741-6394
Dunkley International
Kalamazoo, MI....800-666-1264
Duplex Mill & Manufacturing Company
Springfield, OH....937-325-5555
Dupps Company
Germantown, OH....937-855-6555
Duralite
Riverton, CT....888-432-8797
Dutchess Bakers' Machinery Company
Superior, WI....800-777-4498
Dynamic Automation
Simi Valley, CA....805-584-8476
Dynamic International
Pewaukee, WI....800-267-7794
E.T. Oakes Corporation
Hauppauge, NY....631-232-0002

Eaton Sales & Service
Denver, CO 800-208-2657
Ecklund-Harrison Technologies
Fort Myers, FL 239-936-6032
Eclipse Systems
Milpitas, CA 408-263-2201
Edhard Corporation
Hackettstown, NJ 888-334-2731
Edlund Company Inc
Burlington, VT 800-772-2126
Eirich Machines
Gurnee, IL 847-336-2444
EKATO Corporation
St Ramsey, NJ 201-825-4684
Electro Cam Corporation
Roscoe, IL 800-228-5487
Elliott Manufacturing Company Inc.
Fresno, CA 559-233-6235
Emery Thompson Machine &Supply Company
Brooksville, FL 718-588-7300
Empire Bakery Equipment
Hicksville, NY 800-878-4070
Engineered Products Group
Madison, WI 800-626-3111
Equipment Specialists
Haines City, FL 863-421-4567
Ertel Alsop
Kingston, NY 800-553-7835
ESCO
Houston, TX 800-966-5514
Eurodib
Champlain, NY 888-956-6866
Evaporator Dryer Technologies Inc
Hammond, WI. 715-796-2313
Everedy Automation
Frederick, PA 610-754-1775
Exact Mixing Systems
Memphis, TN 901-362-8501
Expert Industries
Brooklyn, NY 718-434-6060
F.B. Pease Company
Rochester, NY 585-475-1870
F.N. Smith Corporation
Oregon, IL 815-732-2171
Falco
La Prairie, CA 450-444-0566
Falcon Fabricators
Nashville, TN 615-832-0027
Feldmeier Equipment
Syracuse, NY 315-454-8608
Fernholtz Engineering
Van Nuys, CA 818-785-5800
Fish Oven & Equipment Corporation
Wauconda, IL 877-526-8720
Fishmore
Melbourne,, FL 321-723-4751
Fitzpatrick Company
Elmhurst, IL 630-530-3333
Fleet Wood Goldco Wyard
Cockeysville, MD 410-785-1934
FleetwoodGoldcoWyard
Romeoville, IL 630-759-6800
Flex-Hose Company
East Syracuse, NY 315-437-1611
Flodin
Moses Lake, WA 509-766-2996
Flow Autoclave Systems
Columbus, OH 614-891-2732
Flow International Corporation
Kent, WA 800-610-1798
Flow of Solids
Westford, MA 978-392-0300
Flow Robotics
Jeffersonville, IN 812-283-7888
Fluid Air
Aurora, IL 630-665-5001
Fluid Energy Processing and Equipment Company
Hatfield, PA 215-368-2510
Fluid Metering
Syosset, NY 800-223-3388
Flux Pumps Corporation
Atlanta, GA 800-367-3589
FMC FoodTech
Madera, CA 559-673-2766
FMC FoodTech
Lakeland, FL 863-683-5411
Food Engineering Unlimited
Fullerton, CA 714-879-8762
Food Processing Equipment Company
Santa Fe Springs, CA 479-751-9392
Food Resources International
Redlands, CA 714-299-8829
Food Service Equipment Corporation
Cape Coral, FL 941-574-7767
FoodTools
Santa Barbara, CA 877-836-6386
Forster & Son
Ada, OK 580-332-6020
Foster-Miller
Waltham, MA 781-890-3200
FPEC Corporation
Santa Fe Springs, CA 562-802-3727
Franrica Systems
Stockton, CA 209-948-2811
Frelco
Stephenville, NL 709-643-5668
French Oil Mill Machinery Company
Piqua, OH 937-773-3420
Friedr Dick Corporation
Farmingdale, NY 800-554-3425
Frosty Factory of America
Ruston, LA 800-544-4071
Gabriella Imports
Cleveland, OH 800-544-8117
Garroutte
San Antonio, TX 888-457-4997
Gem Equipment of Oregon
Woodburn, OR 503-982-9902
General Machinery Corporation
Sheboygan, WI 888-243-6622
General, Inc
Weston, FL 954-202-7419
Giles Enterprises
Montgomery, AL 800-288-1555
Gilson Company Incorporated
Lewis Center, OH 800-444-1508
Glatt Air Techniques
Ramsey, NJ 201-825-8700
Global Manufacturing
Little Rock, AR 800-551-3569
Globe Food Equipment Company
Dayton, OH 800-347-5423
Goodnature Products
Orchard Park, NY 800-875-3381
Goodway Industries
Bohemia, NY 800-943-4501
Grain Machinery Manufacturing Corporation
Miami, FL 305-620-2525
Gram Equipment of America
Tampa, FL 813-248-1978
Granco Pumps
San Ramon, CA 925-359-3290
Grant-Letchworth
Tonawanda, NY 716-692-1000
Graybill Machines
Lititz, PA 717-626-5221
Great Western Manufacturing Company
Leavenworth, KS 800-682-3121
Greenbelt Industries
Buffalo, NY 800-668-1114
Gregor Jonsson, Inc
Lake Forest, IL 847-831-2030
Griffin Cardwell, Ltd
Louisville, KY 502-636-1374
Grote Company
Columbus, OH 888-534-7683
H. Gartenberg & Company
Buffalo Grove, IL 847-821-7590
Hamilton Beach/Proctor-Silex
Southern Pines, NC 800-711-6100
Hamilton Kettles
Weirton, WV 800-535-1882
Hartel International LLC
Fort Atkinson, WI 920-563-6597
Hayes & Stolz IndustrialManufacturing Company
Fort Worth, TX 800-725-7272
HBD Industries
Salisbury, NC 800-438-2312
Healdsburg Machine Company
Santa Rosa, CA 707-433-3348
Health Star
Randolph, MA 800-545-3639
Helken Equipment Company
Crystal Lake, IL 847-697-3690
Hinds-Bock Corporation
Bothell, WA 425-885-1183
Hobart Corporation
Troy, OH 888-446-2278
Hollymatic Corporation
Countryside, IL 708-579-3700
Hosokawa/Bepex Corporation
Santa Rosa, CA 707-586-6000
Howard Fabrication
City of Industry, CA 626-961-0114
Hughes Equipment Company LLC
Columbus, WI 866-535-9303
Hydro-Miser
San Marcos, CA 800-736-5083
Hydro-Thermal
Waukesha, WI 800-952-0121
IBA Food Safety
Memphis, TN 800-777-9012
Idaho Steel Products Company
Idaho Falls, ID 208-522-1275
IKA Works
Wilmington, NC 800-733-3037
Indiana Wire Company
Fremont, IN 877-786-6883
Industrial Automation Systems
Santa Clarita, CA 888-484-4427
Industrial Piping
Pineville, NC 800-951-0988
Industrial Sheet Metal
Cleveland, OH 216-431-9650
Insta Pro International
Des Moines, IA 800-383-4524
International Knife & Saw
Florence, SC 800-354-9872
International Machinery Exchange
Deerfield, WI 800-279-0191
International Reserve Equipment Corporation
Clarendon Hills, IL 708-531-0680
J.C. Ford Company
La Habra, CA 714-871-7361
Jarvis Products Corporation
Middletown, CT 860-347-7271
Jay Bee Manufacturing
Tyler, TX 800-445-0610
Jayhawk Manufacturing Company, Inc.
Hutchinson, KS 866-886-8269
Jenike & Johanson
Tyngsboro, MA 978-649-3300
Jensen Luhr & Sons
Hood River, OR 541-386-3811
Jescorp
Des Plaines, IL 847-299-7800
Johnson Food Equipment
Kansas City, KS 800-288-3434
Johnson Industries International, Inc.
Windsor, WI 608-846-4499
Johnson Pumps of America
Hanover Park, IL 847-671-7867
Juice Tree
Omaha, NE 714-891-4425
JW Leser Company
Los Angeles, CA 323-731-4173
Kady International
Scarborough, ME 800-367-5239
Karl Schnell
New London, WI 920-982-9974
Kasel Associated Industries
Denver, CO 800-218-4417
Kemutec Group
Bristol, PA 215-788-8013
Kerian Machines
Grafton, ND 701-352-0480
Key Technology
Walla Walla, WA 509-529-2161
Kinetic Equipment Company
Appleton, WI 806-293-4471
King Company
Dallas, TX 507-451-3770
KIRKCO
Monroe, NC 704-289-7090
Kitcor Corporation
Sun Valley, CA 818-767-4800
Knott Slicers
Canton, MA 781-821-0925
Koch Equipment
Kansas City, MO 816-753-2150
KOFAB
Algona, IA 515-295-7265
Kohler Industries
Lincoln, NE 800-365-6708
Krispy Kist Company
Chicago, IL 312-733-0900
Krogh Pump Company
Benicia, CA 800-225-7644
Krones
Franklin, WI 414-409-4000
Kuest Enterprise
Filer, ID 208-326-4084
Kusel Equipment Company
Watertown, WI 920-261-4112
L&A Process Systems
Modesto, CA 209-581-0205

Laciny Brothers
Saint Louis, MO . . . 314-862-8330
Langsenkamp Manufacturing
Indianapolis, IN . . . 877-585-1950
Latendorf Corporation
Brielle, NJ . . . 800-526-4057
Lauhoff Corporation
Detroit, MI . . . 313-259-0027
Le-Jo Enterprises
Phoenixville, PA . . . 484-921-9000
Lee Financial Corporation
Dallas, TX . . . 972-960-1001
Lee Industries Fluid Transfer
Philipsburg, PA . . . 814-342-0802
Leland
South Plainfield, NJ . . . 800-984-9793
Leland
South Plainfield, NJ . . . 908-668-1008
LeMatic
Jackson, MI . . . 517-787-3301
Len E. Ivarson
Milwaukee, WI . . . 414-351-0700
Lewis M. Carter Manufacturing Company
Donalsonville, GA . . . 229-524-2197
Liberty Engineering Company
Roscoe, IL . . . 877-623-9065
Lil' Orbits
Minneapolis, MN . . . 800-228-8305
Lima Sheet Metal
Lima, OH . . . 419-229-1161
LineSource
Springfield, MA . . . 413-747-9488
Linker Machines
Rockaway, NJ . . . 973-983-0001
Liquid Controls
Lake Bluff, IL . . . 800-458-5262
Liquid Scale
New Brighton, MN . . . 888-633-2969
LIST
Acton, MA . . . 978-635-9521
Littleford Day
Florence, KY . . . 800-365-8555
Louisville Dryer Company
Louisville, KY . . . 800-735-3613
Lowe Industries
Marion, IA . . . 319-447-9724
Lumenite Control Technology
Franklin Park, IL . . . 800-323-8510
Luthi Machinery Company, Inc.
Pueblo, CO . . . 719-948-1110
Lyco Wausau
Wausau, WI . . . 715-845-7867
M-One Specialties Inc
Salt Lake City, UT . . . 800-525-9223
Machanix Fabrication
Chino, CA . . . 800-700-9701
Maddox/Adams International
Miami, FL . . . 305-592-3337
Magna Machine Co.
Cincinnati, OH . . . 800-448-3475
Magnetool
Troy, MI . . . 248-588-5400
Magnuson Corporation
Pueblo, CO . . . 719-948-9500
Maja Equipment Company
Omaha, NE . . . 402-346-6252
Mandeville Company
Minneapolis, MN . . . 800-328-8490
Mar-Con Wire Belt
Richmond, BC . . . 877-962-7266
Marion Mixers
Marion, IA . . . 319-377-6371
Market Forge Industries
Everett, MA . . . 866-698-3188
Marlen International
Astoria, OR . . . 800-862-7536
Marlo Manufacturing Company
Boonton, NJ . . . 800-222-0450
Marriott Walker Corporation
Bingham Farms, MI . . . 248-644-6868
Martin Engineering
Neponset, IL . . . 800-766-2786
Martin/Baron
Irwindale, CA . . . 626-960-5153
Matcon USA
Elmhurst, IL . . . 856-256-1330
Materials TransportationCompany
Temple, TX . . . 800-433-3110
Matfer
Van Nuys, CA . . . 800-766-0333
Matiss
St Georges, QC . . . 888-562-8477

Maurer North America
Kansas City, MO . . . 816-914-3518
May-Wes Manufacturing
Hutchinson, MN . . . 800-788-6483
MBC Food Machinery Corporation
Hackensack, NJ . . . 201-489-7000
McCarter Corporation
Norristown, PA . . . 610-272-3203
McCormick Enterprises
Delton, MI . . . 800-223-3683
MCD Technologies
Tacoma, WA . . . 253-476-0968
MDS Nordion
Ottawa, ON . . . 800-465-3666
Meadows Mills, Inc.
North Wilkesboro, NC . . . 800-626-2282
Membrane System Specialists
Wisconsin Rapids, WI . . . 715-421-2333
Mepsco
Batavia, IL . . . 800-323-8535
Mercury Equipment Company
Chino, CA . . . 800-273-6688
Merlin Process Equipment
Houston, TX . . . 713-221-1651
Mesa Laboratories
Lakewood, CO . . . 800-525-1215
Met-Pro Environmental Air Solutions
Owosso, MI . . . 800-392-7621
Metal Master
Tucson, AZ . . . 800-488-8729
Metcraft
Grandview, MO . . . 800-444-9624
Meyer & Garroutte Systems
San Antonio, TX . . . 210-736-1811
Microdry
Crestwood, KY . . . 502-241-8933
Microfluidics International Corporation
Newton, MA . . . 800-370-5452
Micropub Systems International
Rochester, NY . . . 585-385-3990
Microthermics
Raleigh, NC . . . 919-878-8045
Mid-Western Research & Supply
Wichita, KS . . . 800-835-2832
Middleby Corporation
Elgin, IL . . . 847-741-3300
Middleby Worldwide
Elgin, IL . . . 847-468-6068
Midwest Metalcraft & Equipment
Windsor, MO . . . 800-647-3167
Midwest Stainless
Menomonie, WI . . . 715-235-5472
Millard Manufacturing Corporation
La Vista, NE . . . 800-662-4263
Miller's Technical Service
Canton, MI . . . 734-738-1970
Minnesota Valley Engineering
New Prague, MN . . . 800-428-3777
MO Industries
Whippany, NJ . . . 973-386-9228
Modern Electronics
Mansfield, LA . . . 318-872-4764
Modern Process Equipment
Chicago, IL . . . 773-254-3929
Moline Machinery
Duluth, MN . . . 800-767-5734
Monroe Environmental Corporation
Monroe, MI . . . 800-992-7707
Morris & Associates
Garner, NC . . . 919-582-9200
Motom Corporation
Bensenville, IL . . . 630-787-1995
Mouli Manufacturing Corporation
Belleville, NJ . . . 800-789-8285
Moyno
Springfield, OH . . . 937-327-3111
Mulligan Associates
Mequon, WI . . . 800-627-2886
Mumper Machine Corporation
Butler, WI . . . 262-781-8908
Munson Machinery Company
Utica, NY . . . 800-944-6644
Murotech Corporation
Torrance, CA . . . 800-565-6876
National Band Saw Company
Santa Clarita, CA . . . 800-851-5050
National Drying Machinery Company
Philadelphia, PA . . . 215-464-6070
National Equipment Corporation
Bronx, NY . . . 800-237-8873
NECO
Omaha, NE . . . 402-453-6912

Nemeth Engineering Associates
Crestwood, KY . . . 502-241-1502
NETZSCH
Exton, PA . . . 610-363-8010
Newlands Systems
Abbotsford, BC . . . 604-855-4890
NIMCO Corporation
Crystal Lake, IL . . . 815-459-4200
Niro
Hudson, WI . . . 715-386-9371
Nordfab Systems
Thomasville, NC . . . 800-533-5286
Northland Stainless
Tomahawk, WI . . . 715-453-5326
Northwind
Alpena, AR . . . 870-437-2585
Norton Performance Plastics
Wayne, NJ . . . 973-696-4700
Norvell Company
Fort Scott, KS . . . 800-653-3147
Nothum Food Processing Systems
Springfield, MO . . . 800-435-1297
Nowakowski
Franklin, WI . . . 800-394-5866
NST Metals
Louisville, KY . . . 502-584-5846
NuCO2
Stuart, FL . . . 772-221-1754
NuTec Manufacturing
New Lenox, IL . . . 815-722-5348
Nutrifaster
Seattle, WA . . . 800-800-2641
Nydree Flooring
Forest, VA . . . 800-682-5698
Oak Barrel Winecraft
Berkeley, CA . . . 510-849-0400
Oden Corporation
Tonawanda, NY . . . 800-658-3622
Odenberg Engineering
West Sacramento, CA . . . 800-688-8396
Omcan Inc.
Mississauga, ON . . . 800-465-0234
Omega Products
Harrisburg, PA . . . 800-633-3401
Omni International
Kennesaw, GA . . . 800-776-4431
Organon Teknika Corporation
Durham, NC . . . 800-682-2666
OXBO International Corporation
Clear Lake, WI . . . 800-628-6196
P&F Metals
Turlock, CA . . . 209-667-4716
Pacific Process Technology
La Jolla, CA . . . 858-551-3298
Pacific Tank
Adelanto, CA . . . 800-449-5838
Packaging & Processing Equipment
Ayr, ON . . . 519-622-6666
Packaging Progressions
Collegeville, PA . . . 610-489-8601
Paget Equipment Company
Marshfield, WI . . . 715-384-3158
Paradigm Technologies
Eugene, OR . . . 541-345-5543
Paragon Group USA
St Petersburg, FL . . . 800-835-6962
Parkson Corporation
Fort Lauderdale, FL . . . 954-974-6610
Patterson Industries
Scarborough, ON . . . 800-336-1110
Patterson-Kelley Hars Company
East Stroudsburg, PA . . . 570-421-7500
Paul O. Abbe
Bensenville, IL . . . 630-350-2200
Pavailler Distribution Company
Northvale, NJ . . . 201-767-0766
Pavan USA, Inc.
Emigsville, PA . . . 717-767-4889
Paxton Corporation
Bristol, RI
Peerless Food Inc
Sidney, OH . . . 937-494-2870
Peerless Machinery Corporation
Sidney, OH . . . 800-999-3327
Peerless-Winsmith
Springville, NY . . . 716-592-9310
Peterson Fiberglass Laminates
Shell Lake, WI . . . 715-468-2306
Phase II Pasta Machines
Farmingdale, NY . . . 800-457-5070
Piab Vacuum Products
Hingham, MA . . . 800-321-7422

Pickwick Company
Cedar Rapids, IA. 800-397-9797
Pier 1 Imports
Woodcliff Lake, NJ. 800-448-9993
Planet Products Corporation
Blue Ash, OH 513-984-5544
Polar Process
Plattsville, ON. 877-896-8077
PolyMaid Company
Largo, FL 800-206-9188
Prawnto Systems
Caddo Mills, TX 800-426-7254
Preferred Machining Corporation
Englewood, CO. 303-761-1535
Pressure Pack
Williamsburg, VA 757-220-3693
Prince Castle
Carol Stream, IL 800-722-7853
Prince Industries
Murrayville, GA 800-441-3303
Pro Scientific
Oxford, CT 800-584-3776
Procedyne Corporation
New Brunswick, NJ 732-249-8347
Process Engineering & Fabrication
Afton, VA 800-852-7975
Process Systems
Barrington, IL 847-842-8618
Processing Machinery & Supply
Philadelphia, PA 215-425-4320
Production Packaging & Processing Equipment Company
Phoenix, AZ 602-254-7878
Professional EngineeringAssociation
Louisville, KY 502-429-0432
Pulva Corporation
Saxonburg, PA 800-878-5828
Puritan Manufacturing
Omaha, NE 800-331-0487
Putsch
Asheville, NC 800-847-8427
Quality Fabrication & Design
Coppell, TX 972-393-0502
Quality Industries
Cleveland, OH 216-961-5566
Quantum Topping Systems Quantum Technical Services Inc
Frankfort, IL 888-464-1540
R. Murphy Company
Ayer, MA. 888-772-3481
R.G. Stephens Engineering
Long Beach, CA 800-499-3001
Ram Equipment
Waukesha, WI 262-513-1114
Ranger Blade Manufacturing Company
Traer, IA 800-377-7860
Raque Food Systems
Louisville, KY 502-267-9641
RAS Process Equipment
Robbinsville, NJ 609-371-1000
Raytheon Company
Waltham, MA 617-522-3000
RBS Fab
Hummelstown, PA 717-566-9513
Readco Kuimoto, LLC
York, PA 800-395-4959
Reading Bakery Systems
Robesonia, PA. 610-693-5816
Regal Ware
Kewaskum, WI 262-626-2121
Renard Machine Company
Green Bay, WI. 920-432-8412
Respirometry Plus, LLC
Fond Du Lac, WI 800-328-7518
Rheo-Tech
Gurnee, IL. 847-367-1557
Rheon USA
Huntersville, NC. 704-875-9191
Rhodes Bakery Equipment
Portland, OR 800-426-3813
RMF Steel Products
Grandview, MO. 816-765-4101
Robot Coupe USA
Jackson, MS 800-824-1646
Rome Machine & Foundry Company, Inc
Rome, GA 800-538-7663
Rondo Inc.
Moonachie, NJ 800-882-0633
Rosenwach Tank Company
Long Island City, NY 718-729-4900
Roskamp Champion
Waterloo, IA 800-366-2563

Ross Cook
San Jose, CA. 800-233-7339
Ross Engineering
Savannah, GA. 800-524-7677
Ruiz Flour Tortillas
Riverside, CA 909-947-7811
Samson Controls
Baytown, TX. 281-383-3677
Samuel Underberg
Brooklyn, NY 718-363-0787
San-Rec-Pak
Tualatin, OR 503-692-5552
Sanchelima International
Doral, FL. 305-591-4343
Sandvik Process Systems
Totowa, NJ 973-790-1600
Sanford Redmond Company
Stamford, CT. 203-351-9800
Sanifab
Stratford, WI 715-687-4332
SaniServ
Mooresville, IN. 800-733-8073
Sasib Beverage & Food North America
Plano, TX 800-558-3814
Satake USA
Stafford, TX 281-276-3600
Savage Brothers Company
Elk Grove Vlg, IL 800-342-0973
Scherping Systems
Winsted, MN. 320-485-4401
Schlagel
Cambridge, MN 800-328-8002
Schlueter Company
Janesville, WI 800-359-1700
Schutte-Buffalo HammermilLl
Buffalo, NY. 800-447-4634
Scientific Process & Research
Kendall Park, NJ. 800-868-4777
Scott Turbon Mixer
Adelanto, CA 800-285-8512
Seepex
Enon, OH 800-695-3659
Sellers Engineering Division
Danville, KY. 859-236-3181
Semi-Bulk Systems
Fenton, MO. 800-732-8769
Separators
Indianapolis, IN 800-233-9022
Sepragen Corporation
Hayward, CA 510-475-0650
Shanzer Grain Dryer
Sioux Falls, SD. 800-843-9887
Sharp Brothers
Bayonne, NJ 201-339-0404
Sharpsville Container
Sharpsville, PA 800-645-1248
Silver Weibull
Aurora, CO 303-373-2311
Silverson Machines
East Longmeadow, MA 800-204-6400
Simmons Engineering Corporation
Wheeling, IL. 800-252-3381
Sine Pump
Arvada, CO 888-504-8301
SJ Controls
Signal Hill, CA 562-494-1400
Smico Manufacturing Company
Valley Brook, OK 800-351-9088
Smith-Berger Marine
Seattle, WA. 206-764-4650
Solbern
Fairfield, NJ 973-227-3030
Somerset Industries
Billerica, MA 800-772-4404
Sonic Corporation
Stratford, CT 866-493-1378
Sonics & Materials, Inc
Newtown, CT 800-745-1105
Sortex
Fremont, CA 510-797-5000
South River Machine
Hackensack, NJ. 201-487-1736
Southern Ag Company
Blakely, GA. 229-723-4262
SP Industries
Warminster, PA 800-523-2327
Specialty Equipment Company
Farmington, CT. 630-585-5111
Sperling Industries
Omaha, NE 800-647-5062
Spray Dynamics, Ltd
Saint Clair, MO. 800-260-7366

SPX Flow Technology
Charlotte, NC 800-252-5200
Stainless Fabrication
Springfield, MO 800-397-8265
Stainless Specialists
Wausau, WI. 800-236-4155
Stainless Steel Fabricators
La Mirada, CA 714-739-9904
Standard Casing Company
Lyndhurst, NJ 800-847-4141
Stanfos
Edmonton, AB 800-661-5648
STARMIX srl
Marano, VI 044- 57- 659
Stein DSI
Sandusky, OH 800-447-2630
Stephan Machinery, Inc.
Mundelein, IL 800-783-7426
Stephen Paoli Manufacturing Corporation
Rockford, IL 815-965-0621
Steri Technologies
Bohemia, NY 800-253-7140
Stock America Inc
Grafton, WI. 262-375-4100
Stork Gamco
Gainesville, GA 770-532-7041
Stork Townsend Inc.
Des Moines, IA. 800-247-8609
Straight Line Filters
Wilmington, DE 302-654-8805
Strategic Equipment & Supply
Scottsdale, AZ. 480-905-5530
Straub Company
Minneapolis, MN 952-546-6686
Stricklin Company
Dallas, TX. 214-637-1030
Sturdi-Bilt Restaurant Equipment
Whitmore Lake, MI 800-521-2895
Stutz Products Corporation
Hartford City, IN. 765-348-2510
Superior Food Machinery
Pico Rivera, CA 800-944-0396
SWECO
Florence, KY. 800-807-9326
Swirl Freeze Corp
Salt Lake City, UT 800-262-4275
T&H Trading Corporation
Redmond, WA. 425-883-2131
T.D. Sawvel Company
Maple Plain, MN. 877-488-1816
T.K. Products
Anaheim, CA 714-621-0267
Taylor Manufacturing Company
Moultrie, GA. 229-985-5445
TDH Manufacturing
Sand Springs, OK 888-251-7961
Techno-Design
Garfield, NJ. 973-478-0930
Tema Systems
Cincinnati, OH 513-489-7811
Tetra Pak
Chicago, IL 312-553-9200
Tetra Pak Inc.
Vernon Hills, IL 847-955-6000
TGW International
Florence, KY. 800-407-0173
Thayer Scale
Pembroke, MA 781-826-8101
Thomas L. Green & Company
Robenosia, PA. 610-693-5816
Thoreson-McCosh
Troy, MI 800-959-0805
Tindall Packaging
Vicksburg, MI. 269-649-1163
Todd's
Des Moines, IA. 800-247-5363
Tolan Machinery Company
Rockaway, NJ. 973-983-7212
Torpac Capsules
Fairfield, NJ 973-244-1125
Tranter Pite
Wichita Falls, TX 940-723-7125
Tri-Pak Machinery, Inc.
Harlingen, TX. 956-423-5140
Triple/S Dynamics
Dallas, TX. 800-527-2116
Tru-Form Plastics
Gardena, CA 800-510-7999
TSA Griddle Systems
Kelowna, BC. 250-491-9025
Turner & Seymour Manufacturing
Torrington, CT 888-856-4864

Tuthill Vacuum & Blower Systems
Springfield, MO 800-825-6937
TWM Manufacturing
Leamington, ON 888-495-4831
Unifiller Systems
Delta, BC. 888-733-8444
Union Process
Akron, OH. 330-929-3333
United McGill Corporation
Groveport, OH 614-829-1200
UniTrak Corporation
Port Hope, ON 866-883-5749
Univex Corporation
Salem, NH. 800-258-6358
Vacuum Barrier Corporation
Woburn, MA 781-933-3570
Van Air Systems
Lake City, PA 800-840-9906
Vanmark Corporation
Creston, IA 800-523-6261
Varimixer
Charlotte, NC 800-221-1138
Vector Corporation
Marion, IA. 319-377-8263
Viatec
Hastings, MI 800-942-4702
Viking Machine & Design
De Pere, WI. 888-286-2116
Vincent Corporation
Tampa, FL. 813-248-2650
Vineco International Products
St Catharines, ON 905-685-9342
Virginia Industrial Services
Waynesboro, VA 800-825-3050
Vita-Mix Corporation
Cleveland, OH 800-437-4654
VitaMinder Company
Providence, RI 800-858-8840
Vortron Smokehouse/Ovens
Iron Ridge, WI 800-874-1949
Vulcan-Hart Company
Louisville, KY 800-814-2028
Vulcanium Metals International, LLC
Northbrook, IL 888-922-0040
Waring Products
Torrington, CT 800-492-7464
Warwick Manufacturing & Equipment
North Brunswick, NJ 732-241-9263
Washington Frontier
Grandview, WA. 509-469-7662
Waukesha Cherry-Burrell
Louisville, KY 502-491-4310
Waukesha Cherry-Burrell
Louisville, KY 800-252-5200
Webb's Machine Design Company
Clearwater, FL 727-799-1768
Weiler & Company
Whitewater, WI. 800-558-9507
Weinman/Midland Pump
Piqua, OH 937-773-2442
Welbilt Corporation
Stamford, CT. 203-325-8300
Welliver Metal Products Corporation
Salem, OR. 503-362-1568
Wemas Metal Products
Calgary, AB. 403-276-4451
Western Polymer Corporation
Moses Lake, WA. 800-362-6845
Westfalia Separator
Northvale, NJ 800-722-6622
Westfalia-Surge, Inc.
Naperville, IL 630-548-8374
White Mountain Freezer
Kansas City, MO. 816-943-4100
Wilch Manufacturing
Topeka, KS 785-267-2762
Wilevco
Billerica, MA 978-667-0400
Wolverine Proctor & Schwartz
Lexington, NC 336-248-5181
Wyssmont Company
Fort Lee, NJ 201-947-4600
X-Press Manufacturing
New Braunfels, TX. 830-629-2651
Yargus Manufacturing
Marshall, IL 217-826-6352
York Saw & Knife Company
York, PA 800-233-1969
Zenith Cutter Company
Loves Park, IL. 800-223-5202
Zitropack Ltd
Addison, IL 630-543-1016

Parts

A C Tool & Machine Company
Louisville, KY 502-447-5505
A-L-L Magnetics
Anaheim, CA 800-262-4638
ABB
Norwalk, CT 203-750-2200
Accuflex Industrial Hose
Romulus, MI 734-451-0080
Action Technology
Prussia, PA 217-935-8311
AFT Advanced Fiber Technologies
Sherbrooke, QC 800-668-7273
AGC Engineering
Bristow, VA. 800-825-8820
Alard Equipment Corporation
Williamson, NY 315-589-4511
All Weather Energy Systems
Plymouth, MI 888-636-8324
American Extrusion International
South Beloit, IL 815-624-6616
American Manufacturing &Engineering Company
Cleveland, OH 800-822-9402
Andgar Corporation
Ferndale, WA 360-366-9900
Apex Packing & Rubber Company
Farmingdale, NY. 800-645-9110
APV Americas
Delavan, WI 800-252-5200
Artisan Controls Corporation
Randolph, NJ 800-457-4950
Automatic Specialities Inc.
Marlborough, MA. 800-445-2370
Ay Machine Company
Ephrata, PA. 717-733-0335
Baader Johnson
Kansas City, KS 800-288-3434
Baldewein Company
Lake Forrest, IL 800-424-5544
Baldor Electric Company
Fort Smith, AR 479-646-4711
Bardo Abrasives
Ridgewood, NY 718-456-6400
Beacon Specialties
New York, NY 800-221-9405
Becker Brothers GraphiteCorporation
Maywood, IL. 708-410-0700
Bert Manufacturing
Gardnerville, NV 775-265-3900
Bird Machine Company
Houston, TX 800-229-7447
Bodine Electric Company
Northfield, IL
Boston Gear
Boston, MA. 888-999-9860
Bradford A Ducon Company
Pewaukee, WI. 800-789-1718
Cal Controls
Gurnee, IL. 800-866-6659
Candy Manufacturing
Niles, IL 847-588-2639
Chicago Stainless Equipment
Palm City, FL 800-927-8575
Chip-Makers Tooling Supply
Whittier, CA 800-659-5840
Continental Disc Corporation
Liberty, MO. 816-792-1500
Conxall Corporation
Villa Park, IL. 630-834-7504
Corenco
Santa Rosa, CA. 888-267-3626
Cornell Pump Company
Portland, OR 503-653-0330
Crouzet Corporation
Carrollton, TX. 800-677-5311
Debbie Wright Sales
Fort Worth, TX 800-935-7883
Duralite
Riverton, CT 888-432-8797
Dyna-Veyor
Newark, NJ 800-930-4760
Electro Cam Corporation
Roscoe, IL. 800-228-5487
ESCO
Houston, TX 800-966-5514
Fabreeka International
Boise, ID 800-423-4469
Falcon Fabricators
Nashville, TN 615-832-0027
Florida Knife Company
Sarasota, FL 800-966-5643

Gary W. Pritchard Engineer
Huntington Beach, CA 714-893-5441
GED, LLC
Laurel, DE. 302-856-1756
General Grinding
Oakland, CA 800-806-6037
Glo-Quartz Electric Heater Company
Mentor, OH 800-321-3574
Good Idea
Northampton, MA. 800-462-9237
Granco Pumps
San Ramon, CA 925-359-3290
Graphite Metallizing Corporation
Yonkers, NY 914-968-8400
Greenbelt Industries
Buffalo, NY. 800-668-1114
Gridpath, Inc.
Stony Creek, ON. 905-643-0955
H. Yamamoto
Port Washington, NY 718-821-7700
Habasit Canada Limited
Oakville, ON. 905-827-4131
Hansaloy Corporation
Davenport, IA 800-553-4992
Harrington Equipment Company
Fairfield, PA 800-468-8467
Hayes & Stolz IndustrialManufacturing Company
Fort Worth, TX 800-725-7272
Hi-Temp
Tuscumbia, AL 800-239-5066
Home Rubber Company
Trenton, NJ 800-257-9441
Hydra-Flex
Livonia, MI 800-234-0832
Industrial Products Corporation
Ho Ho Kus, NJ 800-472-5913
Infitec
Syracuse, NY 800-334-0837
International Tank & Pipe Co
Clackamas, OR 888-988-0011
Introdel Products
Itasca, IL 800-323-4772
Jokamsco Group
Mechanicville, NY 518-237-6416
Keystone Rubber Corporation
Greenbackville, VA. 800-394-5661
Kinetic Equipment Company
Appleton, WI 806-293-4471
King Company
Dallas, TX. 507-451-3770
Knobs Unlimited
Bowling Green, OH 419-353-8215
L.C. Thompson Company
Kenosha, WI. 800-558-4018
Lako Tool & Manufacturing
Perrysburg, OH 800-228-2982
Lambeth Band Corporation
New Bedford, MA 508-984-4700
LEESON Electric Corporation
Grafton, WI. 262-377-8810
Len E. Ivarson
Milwaukee, WI 414-351-0700
Leybold Vacuum
Export, PA. 724-327-5700
Lil' Orbits
Minneapolis, MN 800-228-8305
Lucas Industrial
Cedar Hill, TX 800-877-1720
M-One Specialties Inc
Salt Lake City, UT 800-525-9223
Master Magnetics
Castle Rock, CO 800-525-3536
McKey Perforating Company
New Berlin, WI. 800-345-7373
Meadows Mills, Inc.
North Wilkesboro, NC 800-626-2282
Metal Master
Tucson, AZ 800-488-8729
Miller's Technical Service
Canton, MI 734-738-1970
Modern Process Equipment
Chicago, IL 773-254-3929
Moyno
Springfield, OH. 937-327-3111
Nalge Process Technologies Group
Rochester, NY. 585-586-8800
National Band Saw Company
Santa Clarita, CA 800-851-5050
National Metal Industries
West Springfield, MA. 800-628-8850
Newman Sanitary Gasket Company
Lebanon, OH. 513-932-7379

Northland Process Piping
Isle, MN 320-679-2119
Pacer Pumps
Lancaster, PA 800-233-3861
Paramount Packing & Rubber
Baltimore, MD 866-727-7225
Paul Mueller Company
Springfield, MO 800-683-5537
Payne Engineering
Scott Depot, WV.................. 800-331-1345
Piab Vacuum Products
Hingham, MA.................... 800-321-7422
Polychem International
Mentor, OH...................... 440-357-1500
Pres-Air-Trol Corporation
Mamaroneck, NY 800-431-2625
Pure Fit
Allentown, PA.................... 866-787-3348
Qosina Corporation
Edgewood, NY 631-242-3000
Quadrant
Fort Wayne, IN 800-628-7264
Quality Industries
Cleveland, OH 216-961-5566
Rath Manufacturing Company
Janesville, WI 800-367-7284
Rigidized Metals Corporation
Buffalo, NY...................... 800-836-2580
Robert-James Sales
Buffalo, NY...................... 800-777-1325
Salem-Republic Rubber Company
Sebring, OH 800-686-4199
Sanchelima International
Doral, FL........................ 305-591-4343
Sani-Fit
Pasadena, CA 626-395-7895
Sanifab
Stratford, WI..................... 715-687-4332
Sanitary Couplers
Springboro, OH.................. 513-743-0144
Schwartz ManufacturingcoCompany
Two Rivers, WI.................. 920-793-1375
Sellers Engineering Division
Danville, KY..................... 859-236-3181
Senior Flexonics
Bartlett, IL...................... 800-473-0474
SEW Eurodrive
Lyman, SC....................... 864-439-8792
Sharon Manufacturing Company
Deer Park, NY.................... 800-424-6455
Simolex Rubber Corporation
Plymouth, MI 734-453-4500
Simply Manufacturing
Prairie Du Sac, WI 608-643-6656
Sine Pump
Arvada, CO 888-504-8301
Specialty Blades
Staunton, VA..................... 540-248-2200
STD Precision Gear & Instrument
West Bridgewater, MA 888-783-4327
Strahman Valves
Bethlehem, PA 877-787-2462
Stutz Products Corporation
Hartford City, IN.................. 765-348-2510
Thomas Precision, Inc.
Rice Lake, WI.................... 800-657-4808
Top Line Process Equipment Company
Bradford, PA 800-458-6095
TWM Manufacturing
Leamington, ON 888-495-4831
Union Cord Products Company
Schaumburg, IL................... 877-237-9098
US Tsubaki
Wheeling, IL..................... 800-323-7790
Valvinox
Iberville, QC 450-346-1981
Vaughn Belting Company
Spartanburg, SC 800-325-3303
Viking Machine & Design
De Pere, WI...................... 888-286-2116
Vulcanium Metals International, LLC
Northbrook, IL 888-922-0040
Warner Electric
South Beloit, IL 800-234-3369
Washington Frontier
Grandview, WA................... 509-469-7662
Waukesha Cherry-Burrell
Louisville, KY 800-252-5200
Wilden Pump & Engineering LLC
Grand Terrace, CA 909-422-1700
Wire Belt Company of America
Londonderry, NH 603-644-2500
Wolverine Proctor & Schwartz
Lexington, NC 336-248-5181
Womack International
Vallejo, CA 707-647-2370
World Wide Fittings
Niles, IL 800-393-9894
Yates Industries
Saint Clair Shores, MI 586-778-7680
Zenith Cutter Company
Loves Park, IL.................... 800-223-5202

Rebuilt & Used

A C Tool & Machine Company
Louisville, KY 502-447-5505
A&M Industries
Sioux Falls, SD................... 800-888-2615
Alard Equipment Corporation
Williamson, NY 315-589-4511
Albion Machine & Tool Company
Albion, MI 517-629-9135
Alpha Resources Inc.
Stevensville, MI 800-833-3083
Ay Machine Company
Ephrata, PA...................... 717-733-0335
Berkshire PPM
Litchfield, CT 860-567-3118
Big State Spring Companyy
Corpus Christi, TX 800-880-0244
Buffalo Wire Works
Buffalo, NY...................... 800-828-7028
Champion Trading Corporation
Marlboro, NJ..................... 732-780-4200
Commodity Traders International
Trilla, IL 217-235-4322
CPM Century Extrusion
Traverse City, MI 231-947-6400
Custom Food Machinery
Stockton, CA..................... 209-463-4343
Delphi International
Tempe, AZ 480-483-8361
Denman Equipment
Memphis, TN 901-755-7135
Equipment Specialists
Haines City, FL................... 863-421-4567
ESCO
Houston, TX 800-966-5514
Food Resources International
Redlands, CA 714-299-8829
GED, LLC
Laurel, DE....................... 302-856-1756
Hallmark Equipment
Morgan Hill, CA.................. 408-782-2600
Harrington Equipment Company
Fairfield, PA 800-468-8467
Health Star
Randolph, MA 800-545-3639
Helken Equipment Company
Crystal Lake, IL 847-697-3690
International Machinery Exchange
Deerfield, WI 800-279-0191
Jarboe Equipment
Georgetown, DE 800-699-7988
Lehman Sales Associates
Sun Prairie, WI 608-575-7712
Machinery Corporation ofAmerica
Capitola, CA 831-479-9901
Mandeville Company
Minneapolis, MN 800-328-8490
Mba Suppliers Inc.
Bellevue, NE..................... 800-467-1201
McNeil Food Machinery
Stockton, CA..................... 209-463-4343
Miller's Technical Service
Canton, MI 734-738-1970
National Equipment Corporation
Bronx, NY....................... 800-237-8873
Naughton Equipment Company
Fort Calhoun, NE 866-858-4682
Pacific Process Machinery
Santa Rosa, CA................... 707-523-4122
Packaging & Processing Equipment
Ayr, ON......................... 519-622-6666
Paxton Corporation
Bristol, RI
Peerless Machinery Corporation
Sidney, OH 800-999-3327
Polar Process
Plattsville, ON.................... 877-896-8077
Regal Equipment
Ravenna, OH..................... 330-325-9000
Separators
Indianapolis, IN 800-233-9022
Stone Enterprises Inc.
Omaha, NE 877-653-0500
Thomas Precision, Inc.
Rice Lake, WI.................... 800-657-4808
Warwick Manufacturing & Equipment
North Brunswick, NJ 732-241-9263
Wohl Associates
Bohemia, NY 631-244-7979
Wolverine Proctor & Schwartz
Lexington, NC 336-248-5181
Zitropack Ltd
Addison, IL...................... 630-543-1016

Frozen Custard Processing

Emery Thompson Machine &Supply Company
Brooksville, FL................... 718-588-7300

Frozen Foods Processing

Automated Food Systems
Waxahachie, TX 972-298-5719
Design Technology Corporation
Billerica, MA 978-663-7000
Dipwell Company
Northampton, MA................. 413-587-4673
Dole Refrigerating Company
Lewisburg, TN 800-251-8990
Emery Thompson Machine &Supply Company
Brooksville, FL................... 718-588-7300
Flodin
Moses Lake, WA.................. 509-766-2996
Food Engineering Unlimited
Fullerton, CA 714-879-8762
Frazier & Son
Conroe, TX 800-365-5438
Gabriella Imports
Cleveland, OH.................... 800-544-8117
Kamflex Corporation
Chicago, IL 800-323-2440
MBC Food Machinery Corporation
Hackensack, NJ................... 201-489-7000
Millard Manufacturing Corporation
La Vista, NE 800-662-4263
Minnesota Valley Engineering
New Prague, MN 800-428-3777
Multi-Fill Inc
West Jordan, UT 801-280-1570
Raque Food Systems
Louisville, KY 502-267-9641
RMF Freezers
Grandview, MO................... 816-765-4101
Specialty Equipment Company
Farmington, CT................... 630-585-5111
Techno-Design
Garfield, NJ...................... 973-478-0930
TWM Manufacturing
Leamington, ON 888-495-4831
UniTrak Corporation
Port Hope, ON 866-883-5749

Fruit Processing

A.K. Robins
Baltimore, MD 800-486-9656
ABCO Industries Limited
Lunenburg, NS 866-634-8821
Advance Energy Technologies
Clifton Park, NY.................. 800-724-0198
Altman Industries
Gray, GA........................ 478-986-3116
Ametek Technical & Industrial Products
Kent, OH........................ 215-256-6601
Andgar Corporation
Ferndale, WA 360-366-9900
Ashlock Company
San Leandro, CA.................. 510-351-0560
Atlas Pacific Engineering Company
Pueblo, CO 719-948-3040
Autoline
Reedley, CA 559-638-5432
Automated Food Systems
Waxahachie, TX 972-298-5719
Bake Star
Somerset, WI..................... 763-427-7611
BEI
South Haven, MI.................. 800-364-7425
BMH Equipment
Sacramento, CA 800-350-8828
BNW Industries
Tippecanoe, IN 574-353-7855
Branson Ultrasonics Corporation
Danbury, CT 203-796-0400

Brown International Corporation
Winter Haven, FL 626-966-8361
Chop-Rite Two, Inc.
Harleysville, PA 800-683-5858
Citra-Tech
Lakeland, FL 863-646-3868
Coastline Equipment
Bellingham, WA 360-739-2480
Commercial Dehydrator Systems Inc
Eugene, OR 800-369-4283
Corenco
Santa Rosa, CA 888-267-3626
Custom Food Machinery
Stockton, CA 209-463-4343
Dixie Canner Company
Athens, GA 706-549-1914
Dunkley International
Kalamazoo, MI 800-666-1264
Durand-Wayland, Inc.
Lagrange, GA 800-241-2308
Elliott Manufacturing Company Inc.
Fresno, CA 559-233-6235
Everedy Automation
Frederick, PA 610-754-1775
F.B. Pease Company
Rochester, NY 585-475-1870
FMC FoodTech
Madera, CA 559-673-2766
FMC FoodTech
Lakeland, FL 863-683-5411
Globe International
Tacoma, WA 800-523-6575
Goodnature Products
Orchard Park, NY 800-875-3381
Healdsburg Machine Company
Santa Rosa, CA 707-433-3348
Juice Tree
Omaha, NE 714-891-4425
Kerian Machines
Grafton, ND 701-352-0480
Key Technology
Walla Walla, WA 509-529-2161
Lyco Wausau
Wausau, WI 715-845-7867
Mulligan Associates
Mequon, WI 800-627-2886
Murotech Corporation
Torrance, CA 800-565-6876
Odenberg Engineering
West Sacramento, CA 800-688-8396
Paxton Corporation
Bristol, RI
Paxton Products
Cincinnati, OH 800-441-7475
Pick Heaters
West Bend, WI 800-233-9030
Tew Manufacturing Corporation
Penfield, NY 800-380-5839
Tri-Pak Machinery, Inc.
Harlingen, TX 956-423-5140
TWM Manufacturing
Leamington, ON 888-495-4831
UniTrak Corporation
Port Hope, ON 866-883-5749
Vanmark Corporation
Creston, IA 800-523-6261
Vincent Corporation
Tampa, FL 813-248-2650
Webb's Machine Design Company
Clearwater, FL 727-799-1768
White Mountain Freezer
Kansas City, MO 816-943-4100

Graders

Fruit, Vegetable & Nut

A.K. Robins
Baltimore, MD 800-486-9656
Berkshire PPM
Litchfield, CT 860-567-3118
Commercial Manufacturing& Supply Company
Fresno, CA 559-237-1855
Descon EDM
Brocton, NY 716-792-9300
Durand-Wayland, Inc.
Lagrange, GA 800-241-2308
Hughes Equipment Company LLC
Columbus, WI 866-535-9303
Kerian Machines
Grafton, ND 701-352-0480
Key Technology
Walla Walla, WA 509-529-2161
Sortex
Fremont, CA 510-797-5000
Tri-Pak Machinery, Inc.
Harlingen, TX 956-423-5140
Welliver Metal Products Corporation
Salem, OR 503-362-1568

Grain, Rice & Seed

Andritz
Muncy, PA 570-546-8211
Commercial Manufacturing& Supply Company
Fresno, CA 559-237-1855
Commodity Traders International
Trilla, IL 217-235-4322
Crippen Manufacturing Company
St. Louis, MI 800-872-2474
Grain Machinery Manufacturing Corporation
Miami, FL 305-620-2525
Sortex
Fremont, CA 510-797-5000
Welliver Metal Products Corporation
Salem, OR 503-362-1568

Grain Elevator

Andritz
Muncy, PA 570-546-8211
Chief Industries
Kearney, NE 800-359-8833
Dunrite
Fremont, NE 800-782-3061
NECO
Omaha, NE 402-453-6912
Schlagel
Cambridge, MN 800-328-8002
Screw Conveyor Corporation
Hammond, IN 219-931-1450
Universal Industries, In
Cedar Falls, IA 800-553-4446
Yargus Manufacturing
Marshall, IL 217-826-6352

Graters

Acme International
Maplewood, NJ 973-416-0400
AMCO Corporation
City of Industry, CA 626-855-2550
Browne & Company
Markham, ON 905-475-6104
Corenco
Santa Rosa, CA 888-267-3626
Giunta Brothers
Philadelphia, PA 215-389-9670
Leggett & Platt StorageP
Vernon Hills, IL 847-816-6246
Polar Process
Plattsville, ON 877-896-8077
Samuel Underberg
Brooklyn, NY 718-363-0787

Grinders

Bulk Grinding

Ditting USA
Glendale, CA 800-835-5992
La Poblana Food Machines
Mesa, AZ 480-258-2091
Marlen Research Corporation
Shawnee Mission, KS 913-888-3333
Provisur Technologies/Weiler
Whitewater, WI 800-558-9507
Reiser
Canton, MA 781-575-9941
Risco USA Corporation
South Easton, MA 888-474-7267
Weiler Equipment
Whitewater, WI 800-558-9507

Hamburger & Meat Patty Processing

Bridge Machine Company
Palmyra, NJ 856-829-1800
Daleco
West Chester, PA 610-429-0181
Design Technology Corporation
Billerica, MA 978-663-7000
Hollymatic Corporation
Countryside, IL 708-579-3700
Nieco Corporation
Windsor, CA 800-643-2656
NuTec Manufacturing
New Lenox, IL 815-722-5348
Provisur Technologies/Weiler
Whitewater, WI 800-558-9507
Reiser
Canton, MA 781-575-9941

Heat Exchangers

A&B Process Systems
Stratford, WI 888-258-2789
AFGO Mechanical Services, Inc.
Long Island City, NY 800-438-2346
AGC Engineering
Bristow, VA 800-825-8820
Allegheny Bradford Corporation
Bradford, PA 800-542-0650
Allied Engineering
North Vancouver, BC 877-929-1214
Alloy Hardfacing & Engineering Company, Inc
Jordan, MN 800-328-8408
Andgar Corporation
Ferndale, WA 360-366-9900
API Heat Transfer
Buffalo, NY 877-274-4328
Apollo Sheet Metal
Kennewick, WA 509-586-1104
APV Americas
Delavan, WI 800-252-5200
Armfield
Ringwood, EN 142- 47-781
Baltimore Aircoil Company
Jessup, MD 410-799-6200
Bimetalix
Sullivan, WI 262-593-8066
Buffalo Technologies Corporation
Buffalo, NY 800-332-2419
Carmel Engineering
Kirklin, IN 888-427-0497
Carnes Company
Verona, WI 608-845-6411
Central Fabricators
Cincinnati, OH 800-909-8265
Chemineer-Kenics/Greerco
North Andover, MA 800-643-0641
Chester-Jensen Company, Inc.
Chester, PA 800-685-3750
Chil-Con Products
Brantford, ON 800-263-0086
Cooling Products
Tulsa, OK 918-251-8588
Doucette Industries
York, PA 800-445-7511
E.L. Nickell Company
Constantine, MI 269-435-2475
Eclipse Innovative Ther mal Solutions
Toledo, OH 800-662-3966
Eischen Enterprises
Fresno, CA 559-834-0013
Ellett Industries
Port Coquitlam, BC 604-941-8211
Enerquip, LLC
Medford, WI 715-748-5888
EVAPCO
Taneytown, MD 410-756-2600
Feldmeier Equipment
Syracuse, NY 315-454-8608
Flat Plate
York, PA 888-854-2500
Franrica Systems
Stockton, CA 209-948-2811
Gaston County Dyeing Machine Company
Stanley, NC 704-822-5000
GEA Refrigeration North America, Inc.
York, PA 800-888-4337
Gram Equipment of America
Tampa, FL 813-248-1978
Harris Equipment
Melrose Park, IL 800-365-0315
Hebeler Corporation
Tonawanda, NY 800-486-4709
International Machinery Exchange
Deerfield, WI 800-279-0191
Lake Process Systems
Lake Barrington, IL 800-331-9260
Louisville Dryer Company
Louisville, KY 800-735-3613
Ludell Manufacturing Company
Milwaukee, WI 800-558-0800

M.G. Newell
Greensboro, NC 800-334-0231
MadgeTech, Inc.
Contoocook, NH 603-456-2011
Midwest Stainless
Menomonie, WI 715-235-5472
Noren Products
Menlo Park, CA 866-936-6736
Northland Stainless
Tomahawk, WI 715-453-5326
Patterson Industries
Scarborough, ON 800-336-1110
Pick Heaters
West Bend, WI 800-233-9030
RAS Process Equipment
Robbinsville, NJ 609-371-1000
Seattle Boiler Works
Seattle, WA 206-762-0737
Seattle Refrigeration & Manufacturing
Seattle, WA 800-228-8881
Standard Refrigeration Company
Wood Dale, IL 708-345-5400
Statco Engineering & Fabricators
Huntington Beach, CA 800-421-0362
Svedala Industries
Colorado Springs, CO 719-471-3443
Tolan Machinery Company
Rockaway, NJ 973-983-7212
Tranter Pite
Wichita Falls, TX 940-723-7125
Ultra Process Systems
Oak Ridge, TN 865-483-2772
Vilter Manufacturing Corporation
Cudahy, WI 414-744-0111
Washington Frontier
Grandview, WA 509-469-7662
Waukesha Cherry-Burrell
Louisville, KY 800-252-5200
Wilevco
Billerica, MA 978-667-0400

Heat Transfer Fluids

Dow Chemical Company
Spring House, PA 800-447-4369
Enercon Systems
Elyria, OH 440-323-7080
Paratherm Corporation
Conshohocken, PA 800-222-3611
QuikWater, Inc.
Sand Springs, OK 918-241-8880
Washington Frontier
Grandview, WA 509-469-7662

Homogenizers

APV Americas
Delavan, WI 800-252-5200
Armfield
Ringwood, EN 142- 47-781
Avestin
Ottawa, ON 888-283-7846
Bematek Systems
Salem, MA 877-236-2835
Berkshire PPM
Litchfield, CT 860-567-3118
Chemineer-Kenics/Greerco
North Andover, MA 800-643-0641
Cornell Machine Company
Springfield, NJ 973-379-6860
E.T. Oakes Corporation
Hauppauge, NY 631-232-0002
Ederback Corporation
Ann Arbor, MI 800-422-2558
Eischen Enterprises
Fresno, CA 559-834-0013
GEA Niro Soavi North America
Bedford, NH 603-606-4060
Glen Mills, Inc.
Clifton, NJ 973-777-0777
Goodway Industries
Bohemia, NY 800-943-4501
IKA Works
Wilmington, NC 800-733-3037
JW Leser Company
Los Angeles, CA 323-731-4173
Omni International
Kennesaw, GA 800-776-4431
Pro Scientific
Oxford, CT 800-584-3776
Processing Machinery & Supply
Philadelphia, PA 215-425-4320
Sanchelima International
Doral, FL 305-591-4343
Silverson Machines
East Longmeadow, MA 800-204-6400
Sonic Corporation
Stratford, CT 866-493-1378
Special Products
Springfield, MO 417-881-6114
Statco Engineering & Fabricators
Huntington Beach, CA 800-421-0362
Stephan Machinery, Inc.
Mundelein, IL 800-783-7426

Honey Processing

Cook & Beals
Loup City, NE 308-745-0154
Dadant & Sons
Hamilton, IL 888-922-1293

Hoppers

Anderson-Crane Company
Minneapolis, MN 800-314-2747
Andgar Corporation
Ferndale, WA 360-366-9900
Andritz
Muncy, PA 570-546-8211
Bonar Plastics
West Chicago, IL 800-295-3725
COW Industries
Columbus, OH 800-542-9353
Food Processing Equipment Company
Santa Fe Springs, CA 479-751-9392
Galbreath LLC
Winamac, IN 574-946-6631
Jesco Industries, Inc.
Litchfield, MI 800-455-0019
Midwest Metalcraft & Equipment
Windsor, MO 800-647-3167
Our Name is Mud
New York, NY 877-683-7867
Palace Packaging Machines
Downingtown, PA 610-873-7252
Pittsburgh Tank Corporation
Monongahela, PA 800-634-0243
Puritan Manufacturing
Omaha, NE 800-331-0487
Schlueter Company
Janesville, WI 800-359-1700
Sharpsville Container
Sharpsville, PA 800-645-1248
Shick Tube-Veyor Corporation
Kansas City, MO 816-861-7224
TWM Manufacturing
Leamington, ON 888-495-4831
UniTrak Corporation
Port Hope, ON 866-883-5749
Wilson Steel Products Company
Memphis, TN 901-527-8742

Coffee

Bonar Plastics
West Chicago, IL 800-295-3725
Pittsburgh Tank Corporation
Monongahela, PA 800-634-0243
Sharpsville Container
Sharpsville, PA 800-645-1248
Shick Tube-Veyor Corporation
Kansas City, MO 816-861-7224
TWM Manufacturing
Leamington, ON 888-495-4831
UniTrak Corporation
Port Hope, ON 866-883-5749

Flour

Anderson-Crane Company
Minneapolis, MN 800-314-2747
Andritz
Muncy, PA 570-546-8211
Bonar Plastics
West Chicago, IL 800-295-3725
COW Industries
Columbus, OH 800-542-9353
Food Processing Equipment Company
Santa Fe Springs, CA 479-751-9392
Galbreath LLC
Winamac, IN 574-946-6631
Midwest Metalcraft & Equipment
Windsor, MO 800-647-3167
Pittsburgh Tank Corporation
Monongahela, PA 800-634-0243
Puritan Manufacturing
Omaha, NE 800-331-0487
Schlueter Company
Janesville, WI 800-359-1700
Sharpsville Container
Sharpsville, PA 800-645-1248
Shick Tube-Veyor Corporation
Kansas City, MO 816-861-7224
TWM Manufacturing
Leamington, ON 888-495-4831
Wilson Steel Products Company
Memphis, TN 901-527-8742

Hullers

Bean & Pea

A.C. Horn & Co
Dallas, TX 800-657-6155
A.K. Robins
Baltimore, MD 800-486-9656
Grain Machinery Manufacturing Corporation
Miami, FL 305-620-2525
Lee Financial Corporation
Dallas, TX 972-960-1001

Huskers

Corn

Berkshire PPM
Litchfield, CT 860-567-3118
Hughes Equipment Company LLC
Columbus, WI 866-535-9303

Ice Breaking, Chipping, Crushing

Clawson Machine
Franklin, NJ 800-828-4088
Flodin
Moses Lake, WA 509-766-2996
Great Western Products Company
Hollywood, AL 800-239-2143
Hoshizaki America
Peachtree City, GA 800-438-6087
Howe Corporation
Chicago, IL 773-235-0200
International Cooling Systems
Richmond Hill, ON 888-213-5566
Machine Ice Company, Inc
Houston, TX 800-423-8822
Swing-A-Way Manufacturing Company
St Louis, MO 314-773-1488
Vita-Mix Corporation
Cleveland, OH 800-437-4654
Vogt-Tube Ice
Louisville, KY 800-853-8648
Waring Products
Torrington, CT 800-492-7464
Welbilt Corporation
Stamford, CT 203-325-8300

Ice Cream Cone, Bar, Biscuit Processing

Darifill, Inc.
Westerville, OH 614-890-3274
Eischen Enterprises
Fresno, CA 559-834-0013
NDS
Columbus, OH 614-294-4931
Norse Dairy Systems
Columbus, OH 800-338-7465
Schroeder Sewing Technologies
San Marcos, CA 760-591-9733

Ice Cream Processing

A&B Process Systems
Stratford, WI 888-258-2789
Advance Energy Technologies
Clifton Park, NY 800-724-0198
Carpigiani Corporation of America
Winston Salem, NC 800-648-4389
Dipwell Company
Northampton, MA 413-587-4673
Emery Thompson Machine &Supply Company
Brooksville, FL 718-588-7300
Frosty Factory of America
Ruston, LA 800-544-4071
Gram Equipment of America
Tampa, FL 813-248-1978
H.C. Duke & Son
East Moline, IL 309-755-4553

Master-Bilt
New Albany, MS. 800-647-1284
Norse Dairy Systems
Columbus, OH 800-338-7465
Swirl Freeze Corp
Salt Lake City, UT 800-262-4275
Tetra Pak Inc.
Vernon Hills, IL 847-955-6000
Tindall Packaging
Vicksburg, MI. 269-649-1163
Vita-Mix Corporation
Cleveland, OH 800-437-4654
White Mountain Freezer
Kansas City, MO. 816-943-4100

Ice Cubing

Hoshizaki America
Peachtree City, GA 800-438-6087
Ice-O-Matic
Denver, CO 800-423-3367
Machine Ice Company, Inc
Houston, TX 800-423-8822
Morris & Associates
Garner, NC 919-582-9200
Scotsman Ice Systems
Vernon Hills, IL 800-726-8762
SerVend International
Sellersburg, IN 800-367-4233
Vogt-Tube Ice
Louisville, KY 800-853-8648
Water Sciences Services ,Inc.
Jackson, TN 973-584-4131
Welbilt Corporation
Stamford, CT. 203-325-8300

Ice Making, Refrigerating & Cooling

A-1 Refrigeration Company
Ontario, CA. 800-669-4423
Advance Energy Technologies
Clifton Park, NY. 800-724-0198
American Food & Equipment
Miami, FL. 305-377-8991
Applied Chemical Technology
Florence, AL. 800-228-3217
Attias Oven Corporation
Brooklyn, NY 800-928-8427
Berg Chilling Systems
Toronto, ON, ON 416-755-2221
BVL Controls
Bois-Des-Filion, QC. 866-285-2668
C&R Refrigeration
Center, TX. 800-438-6182
Carbonic Machines
Minneapolis, MN 612-824-0745
Cooling Technology
Charlotte, NC 800-872-1448
Cornelius Wilshire Corporation
Schaumburg, IL. 847-397-4600
Delta Cooling Towers
Rockaway, NJ 800-289-3358
Dole Refrigerating Company
Lewisburg, TN 800-251-8990
Flakice Corporation
Metuchen, NJ 800-654-4630
Follett Corporation
Easton, PA. 800-523-9361
Happy Ice
Winnepeg, MB 888-573-9237
Hoshizaki America
Peachtree City, GA 800-438-6087
Howe Corporation
Chicago, IL 773-235-0200
Ice-O-Matic
Denver, CO 800-423-3367
IMI Cornelius
Garner, IA 641-424-6150
IMI Cornelius
Schaumburg, IL. 800-323-4789
IMI Cornelius
Osseo, MN 800-838-3600
International Cooling Systems
Richmond Hill, ON. 888-213-5566
Kloppenberg & Company
Englewood, CO. 800-346-3246
Leer Limited Partnership
New Lisbon, WI 800-766-5337
Leer, Inc.
New Lisbon, WI 800-237-8350
Louisville Dryer Company
Louisville, KY 800-735-3613
Machine Ice Company, Inc
Houston, TX 800-423-8822
Maja Equipment Company
Omaha, NE 402-346-6252
Manitowoc Foodservice Companies, Inc.
New Port Richey, FL. 877-375-9300
Mannhardt Inc
Sheboygan Falls, WI. 800-423-2327
Master-Bilt
New Albany, MS. 800-647-1284
Matthiesen Equipment Company
San Antonio, TX. 800-624-8635
Maximicer
Georgetown, TX. 800-289-9098
McCormack Manufacturing Company
Lake Oswego, OR. 800-395-1593
Middleby Worldwide
Elgin, IL 847-468-6068
Morris & Associates
Garner, NC 919-582-9200
North Star Ice EquipmentCorporation
Seattle, WA 800-321-1381
Polyfoam Packers Corporation
Arlington Hts, IL 800-323-7442
Scotsman Ice Systems
Vernon Hills, IL 800-726-8762
Seattle Refrigeration & Manufacturing
Seattle, WA 800-228-8881
Semco Manufacturing Company
Pharr, TX. 956-787-4203
SerVend International
Sellersburg, IN 800-367-4233
Superior Products Company
Saint Paul, MN 800-328-9800
Tom Lockerbie
Edmeston, NY. 315-737-5612
Turbo Refrigerating Company
Denton, TX 940-387-4301
U-Line Corporation
Milwaukee, WI 414-354-0300
Vilter Manufacturing Corporation
Cudahy, WI 414-744-0111
Welbilt Corporation
Stamford, CT. 203-325-8300
Wittemann Company
Palm Coast, FL 386-445-4200

Irradiation Processing

Alpha Omega Technology
Cedar Knolls, NJ. 800-442-1969
IBA Food Safety
Memphis, TN 800-777-9012
Insect-O-Cutor
Stone Mountain, GA. 800-988-5359
MDS Nordion
Ottawa, ON. 800-465-3666
New Horizon Technologies
Richland, WA 509-372-4868

Meat Preparation Equipment

A C Tool & Machine Company
Louisville, KY 502-447-5505
AEW Thurne
Lake Zurich, IL. 800-239-7297
AFECO
Algona, IA. 888-295-1116
Alfa Laval
Newburyport, MA. 978-465-5777
Allen Gauge & Tool Company
Pittsburgh, PA 412-241-6410
Am-Mac Incorporated
Fairfield, NJ 800-829-2018
Andgar Corporation
Ferndale, WA 360-366-9900
Ankom Technology
Macedon, NY 315-986-8090
Atlanta SharpTech
Peachtree City, GA 800-462-7297
Automated Food Systems
Waxahachie, TX 972-298-5719
Beacon, Inc.
Alsip, IL 800-445-4203
BH Bunn Company
Lakeland, FL. 800-222-2866
Biro Manufacturing Company
Marblehead, OH 419-798-4451
Blakeslee, Inc.
Addison, IL. 630-532-5021
Boehringer Mfg. Co. Inc.
Felton, CA. 800-630-8665
Bridge Machine Company
Palmyra, NJ. 856-829-1800
Challenge-RMF
Grandview, MO. 816-765-0515
Chop-Rite Two, Inc.
Harleysville, PA 800-683-5858
Cincinnati Boss Company
Omaha, NE 402-556-4070
Cozzini
Chicago, IL 773-478-9700
Cutrite Company
Fremont, OH 800-928-8748
Daleco
West Chester, PA. 610-429-0181
DC Tech
Kansas City, MO. 877-742-9090
Design Technology Corporation
Billerica, MA 978-663-7000
Dresser Instruments
Stratford, CT 800-328-8258
E-Z Edge
West New York, NJ. 800-232-4470
Eze Lap Diamond Products
Carson City, NV 800-843-4815
Formax/Provisur Technologies
Mokena, IL 708-479-3500
Friedr Dick Corporation
Farmingdale, NY 800-554-3425
Friedrich Metal ProductsCompany
Browns Summit, NC. 800-772-0326
G.F. Frank & Sons
Fairfield, OH. 513-870-9075
General Machinery Corporation
Sheboygan, WI 888-243-6622
General, Inc
Weston, FL 954-202-7419
Globe Food Equipment Company
Dayton, OH. 800-347-5423
Greenline Corporation
Charlotte, NC 800-331-5312
Haban Saw Company
St.Louis, MO. 314-968-3991
Handtmann, Inc.
Lake Forest, IL 800-477-3585
Hansaloy Corporation
Davenport, IA 800-553-4992
Hobart Corporation
Troy, OH 888-446-2278
Hoegger Food Technology Inc.
Minneapolis, MN 877-789-5400
Hollingsworth Custom Wood Products
Sault Ste. Marie, ON. 705-759-1756
Hollymatic Corporation
Countryside, IL. 708-579-3700
I. Fm Usa Inc.
Franklin Park, IL. 866-643-6872
Indeco Products
San Marcos, TX 512-396-5814
Jarvis Products Corporation
Middletown, CT 860-347-7271
Kasel Associated Industries
Denver, CO. 800-218-4417
Kentmaster ManufacturingCompany
Monrovia, CA 800-421-1477
Key Technology
Walla Walla, WA. 509-529-2161
Koch Equipment
Kansas City, MO. 816-753-2150
Le Fiell Company, Inc.
Reno, NV 775-677-5300
Linker Machines
Rockaway, NJ 973-983-0001
Loos Machine & Automation
Colby, WI 715-223-2844
Luthi Machinery Company, Inc.
Pueblo, CO 719-948-1110
M-One Specialties Inc
Salt Lake City, UT 800-525-9223
Maja Equipment Company
Omaha, NE 402-346-6252
Mandeville Company
Minneapolis, MN 800-328-8490
Marlen
Riverside, MO. 913-888-3333
Marlen International
Astoria, OR 800-862-7536
Mba Suppliers Inc.
Bellevue, NE. 800-467-1201
Mepsco
Batavia, IL. 800-323-8535
Michigan Maple Block Company
Petoskey, MI 800-447-7975

Mid-Western Research & Supply
Wichita, KS 800-835-2832
Mp Equip. Co.
Buford, GA 770-614-5355
MPS North America, Inc.
Lenexa, KS 913-310-0055
National Band Saw Company
Santa Clarita, CA 800-851-5050
Nieco Corporation
Windsor, CA 800-643-2656
NuTec Manufacturing
New Lenox, IL 815-722-5348
Packaging Progressions
Collegeville, PA 610-489-8601
Paragon Group USA
St Petersburg, FL 800-835-6962
Patty-O-Matic
Farmingdale, NJ 877-938-5244
Pemberton & Associates
Brooklyn, NY 800-736-2664
Planet Products Corporation
Blue Ash, OH 513-984-5544
Prince Castle
Carol Stream, IL 800-722-7853
Prince Industries
Murrayville, GA 800-441-3303
Quickdraft
Canton, OH 330-477-4574
R. Murphy Company
Ayer, MA 888-772-3481
Ranger Tool Company
Memphis, TN 800-737-9999
Reiser
Canton, MA 781-575-9941
Rheo-Tech
Gurnee, IL 847-367-1557
Rollstock, Inc.
Kansas City, MO 800-954-6020
SFK Danfotech, Inc.
Kansas City, MO 816-891-7357
Simmons Engineering Corporation
Wheeling, IL 800-252-3381
Simonds International
Fitchburg, MA 978-424-0100
Sperling Industries
Omaha, NE 800-647-5062
Standard Casing Company
Lyndhurst, NJ 800-847-4141
Stanfos
Edmonton, AB 800-661-5648
Stephan Machinery GmbH
Mandelein, IL 847-247-0182
Stephen Paoli Manufacturing Corporation
Rockford, IL 815-965-0621
Stone Enterprises Inc.
Omaha, NE 877-653-0500
Stork Townsend Inc.
Des Moines, IA 800-247-8609
Superior Distributing
Louisville, KY 800-365-6661
Tech-Roll, Inc.
Blaine, WA 888-946-3929
TGW International
Florence, KY 800-407-0173
TNI Packaging
West Chicago, IL 800-383-0990
Trenton Mills
Trenton, TN 731-855-1323
Unitherm Food Systems Innc.
Bristow, OK 918-367-0197
Univex Corporation
Salem, NH 800-258-6358
Weber North America
Kansas City, MO 816-891-0072

Microwave Ovens

AccuTemp Products
Fort Wayne, IN 800-210-5907
AK Steel
West Chester, OH 800-331-5050
Amana Commercial Products
Cedar Rapids, IA 319-368-8198
Cober Electronics, Inc.
Norwalk, CT 800-709-5948
Defreeze Corporation
Southborough, MA 508-485-8512
Hickory Industries
North Bergen, NJ 800-732-9153
Kreative Koncepts
Marquette, MI 800-638-2019
Microdry
Crestwood, KY 502-241-8933
Panasonic Commercial Food Service
Secaucus, NJ 800-553-0384
Quasar Industries
Rochester Hills, MI 248-852-0300
R F Schiffmann Associates
New York, NY 212-362-7021
Sharp Electronics Corporation
Mahwah, NJ 800-237-4277

Milking

Ben H. Anderson Manufacturers
Morrisonville, WI 608-846-5474
Coburn Company
Whitewater, WI 800-776-7042
Lyco Wausau
Wausau, WI 715-845-7867
Schlueter Company
Janesville, WI 800-359-1700

Mills

Ball & Pebble

Fernholtz Engineering
Van Nuys, CA 818-785-5800
Glen Mills, Inc.
Clifton, NJ 973-777-0777
NaraKom
Peapack, NJ 908-234-1776
Paul O. Abbe
Bensenville, IL 630-350-2200
Union Process
Akron, OH 330-929-3333

Chocolate Grinding

Glen Mills, Inc.
Clifton, NJ 973-777-0777
Union Process
Akron, OH 330-929-3333

Colloid

Bematek Systems
Salem, MA 877-236-2835
Berkshire PPM
Litchfield, CT 860-567-3118
Chemicolloid Laboratories, Inc.
New Hyde Park, NY 516-747-2666
Chemineer-Kenics/Greerco
North Andover, MA 800-643-0641
Glen Mills, Inc.
Clifton, NJ 973-777-0777
Silverson Machines
East Longmeadow, MA 800-204-6400
Sonic Corporation
Stratford, CT 866-493-1378
Waukesha Cherry-Burrell
Louisville, KY 502-491-4310

Copra Grinding & Crushing

Andritz
Muncy, PA 570-546-8211
Corenco
Santa Rosa, CA 888-267-3626

Corn Meal & Corn Flour

C S Bell Company
Tiffin, OH 888-958-6381
ConAgra Corn Processing Company
Atchison, KS 800-541-2556
Glen Mills, Inc.
Clifton, NJ 973-777-0777
International Reserve Equipment Corporation
Clarendon Hills, IL 708-531-0680
La Poblana Food Machines
Mesa, AZ 480-258-2091
MO Industries
Whippany, NJ 973-386-9228

Curd

Damrow Company
Fond Du Lac, WI 800-236-1501

Feed

A.T. Ferrell Company Inc
Bluffton, IN 800-248-8318
Amherst Milling Company
Amherst, VA 434-946-7601
Andritz
Muncy, PA 570-546-8211
C S Bell Company
Tiffin, OH 888-958-6381
Custom Millers Supply Company
Monmouth, IL 309-734-6312
Forster & Son
Ada, OK 580-332-6020
Germantown Milling Company
Germantown, KY 606-728-5857
Meadows Mills, Inc.
North Wilkesboro, NC 800-626-2282
Summit Machine Builders Corporation
Denver, CO 800-274-6741

Flour & Cereal

Bartlett Milling Company
Statesville, NC 800-222-8626
CHS Inc.
Inver Grove Heights, MN 800-232-3639
Fernholtz Engineering
Van Nuys, CA 818-785-5800
Ferrell-Ross
Amarillo, TX 800-299-9051
Germantown Milling Company
Germantown, KY 606-728-5857
International Reserve Equipment Corporation
Clarendon Hills, IL 708-531-0680
Lauhoff Corporation
Detroit, MI 313-259-0027
Lehi Roller Mills
Lehi, UT 800-660-4346
Meadows Mills, Inc.
North Wilkesboro, NC 800-626-2282
Mill Engineering & Machinery Company
Oakland, CA 510-562-1832
Norvell Company
Fort Scott, KS 800-653-3147
Satake USA
Stafford, TX 281-276-3600

Grinding

A.C. Horn & Co
Dallas, TX 800-657-6155
Andritz
Muncy, PA 570-546-8211
Autio Company
Astoria, OR 800-483-8884
C S Bell Company
Tiffin, OH 888-958-6381
Corenco
Santa Rosa, CA 888-267-3626
Daily Printing
Plymouth, MN 800-622-6596
Ferrell-Ross
Amarillo, TX 800-299-9051
Fitzpatrick Company
Elmhurst, IL 630-530-3333
Fluid Air
Aurora, IL 630-665-5001
Fluid Energy Processing and Equipment Company
Hatfield, PA 215-368-2510
Gilson Company Incorporated
Lewis Center, OH 800-444-1508
Glen Mills, Inc.
Clifton, NJ 973-777-0777
Globe International
Tacoma, WA 800-523-6575
Goodnature Products
Orchard Park, NY 800-875-3381
Jayhawk Manufacturing Company, Inc.
Hutchinson, KS 866-886-8269
Kemutec Group
Bristol, PA 215-788-8013
Lasermation
Philadelphia, PA 800-523-2759
MO Industries
Whippany, NJ 973-386-9228
Modern Process Equipment
Chicago, IL 773-254-3929
NaraKom
Peapack, NJ 908-234-1776
NETZSCH
Exton, PA 610-363-8010
Nordfab Systems
Thomasville, NC 800-533-5286
Straub Company
Minneapolis, MN 952-546-6686
Union Process
Akron, OH 330-929-3333

Hammer

A.C. Horn & Co
Dallas, TX....800-657-6155
A.T. Ferrell Company
Bluffton, IN....800-248-8318
Andritz
Muncy, PA....570-546-8211
Berkshire PPM
Litchfield, CT....860-567-3118
C S Bell Company
Tiffin, OH....888-958-6381
Corenco
Santa Rosa, CA....888-267-3626
Dehyco Company
Memphis, TN....901-774-3322
Duplex Mill & Manufacturing Company
Springfield, OH....937-325-5555
Fernholtz Engineering
Van Nuys, CA....818-785-5800
Fitzpatrick Company
Elmhurst, IL....630-530-3333
Forster & Son
Ada, OK....580-332-6020
Glen Mills, Inc.
Clifton, NJ....973-777-0777
Globe International
Tacoma, WA....800-523-6575
Goodnature Products
Orchard Park, NY....800-875-3381
Jay Bee Manufacturing
Tyler, TX....800-445-0610
Meadows Mills, Inc.
North Wilkesboro, NC....800-626-2282
NaraKom
Peapack, NJ....908-234-1776
Roskamp Champion
Waterloo, IA....800-366-2563
Schutte-Buffalo HammermilLl
Buffalo, NY....800-447-4634

Malt

Andritz
Muncy, PA....570-546-8211

Nut Grinding

A.C. Horn & Co
Dallas, TX....800-657-6155
Andritz
Muncy, PA....570-546-8211
Corenco
Santa Rosa, CA....888-267-3626
Straub Company
Minneapolis, MN....952-546-6686

Oil Cake Grinding

Andritz
Muncy, PA....570-546-8211
Corenco
Santa Rosa, CA....888-267-3626

Peanut Butter

A.C. Horn & Co
Dallas, TX....800-657-6155
Berkshire PPM
Litchfield, CT....860-567-3118
Glen Mills, Inc.
Clifton, NJ....973-777-0777

Rice Grinding

Andritz
Muncy, PA....570-546-8211
Satake USA
Stafford, TX....281-276-3600

Spice Grinding

Andritz
Muncy, PA....570-546-8211
Berkshire PPM
Litchfield, CT....860-567-3118
Browne & Company
Markham, ON....905-475-6104
C S Bell Company
Tiffin, OH....888-958-6381
Chef Specialties Company
Smethport, PA....800-440-2433
Corenco
Santa Rosa, CA....888-267-3626
Ferrell-Ross
Amarillo, TX....800-299-9051
Glen Mills, Inc.
Clifton, NJ....973-777-0777

Sugar & Sugar Cane

Silver Weibull
Aurora, CO....303-373-2311

Mixers

American Process Systems
Gurnee, IL....847-336-2444
G&F Manufacturing Comp any
Oak Lawn, IL....800-282-1574
Hamilton Beach/Proctor-Silex
Southern Pines, NC....800-711-6100
Quadro Engineering
Waterloo, ON....519-884-9660
Reiser
Canton, MA....781-575-9941
Thunderbird Food Machinery
Blaine, WA....800-764-9377

Bakers'

A&J Mixing International
Oakville, ON....800-668-3470
ABI Limited
Concord, ON....800-297-8666
Adamatic
Auburn, WA....800-578-2547
Alliance Bakery Systems
Blythewood, SC....803-691-9227
American Eagle Food Machinery
Chicago, IL....800-836-5756
AMF CANADA
Sherbrooke, QC....800-255-3869
Arcobaleno Pasta Machines
Lancaster, PA....800-875-7096
Arde Barinco
Carlstadt, NJ....800-909-6070
Benier USA
Lithia Springs, GA....770-745-2200
Blakeslee, Inc.
Addison, IL....630-532-5021
Breddo Likwifier
Kansas City, MO....800-669-4092
CMC America Corporation
Joliet, IL....815-726-4337
DBE Inc
Concord, ON....800-461-5313
Empire Bakery Equipment
Hicksville, NY....800-878-4070
Exact Mixing Systems
Memphis, TN....901-362-8501
Excellent Bakery Equipment Company
Fairfield, NJ....888-BAG-ELS1
Food Engineering Unlimited
Fullerton, CA....714-879-8762
Gemini Bakery Equipment Company
Philadelphia, PA....800-468-9046
Goodway Industries
Bohemia, NY....800-943-4501
Hayes & Stolz IndustrialManufacturing Company
Fort Worth, TX....800-725-7272
Hebeler Corporation
Tonawanda, NY....800-486-4709
International Reserve Equipment Corporation
Clarendon Hills, IL....708-531-0680
Kemper Bakery Systems
Rockaway, NJ....973-625-1566
Leland
South Plainfield, NJ....908-668-1008
Magna Machine Co.
Cincinnati, OH....800-448-3475
Marion Mixers
Marion, IA....319-377-6371
Moline Machinery
Duluth, MN....800-767-5734
National Manufacturing Company
Lincoln, NE....402-475-3400
Packaging & Processing Equipment
Ayr, ON....519-622-6666
Pavailler Distribution Company
Northvale, NJ....201-767-0766
Peerless Dough Mixing and Make-Up
Sidney, OH....800-999-3327
Peerless Food Inc
Sidney, OH....937-494-2870
Peerless Machinery Corporation
Sidney, OH....800-999-3327
Pro Bake
Twinsburg, OH....800-837-4427
Rondo Inc.
Moonachie, NJ....800-882-0633
Shaffer Manufacturing Corporation
Lemont, IL....800-652-2151
T.K. Products
Anaheim, CA....714-621-0267
Thomas L. Green & Company
Robenosia, PA....610-693-5816
Varimixer
Charlotte, NC....800-221-1138

Drum

Arde Barinco
Carlstadt, NJ....800-909-6070
Chemineer-Kenics/Greerco
North Andover, MA....800-643-0641
Custom Food Machinery
Stockton, CA....209-463-4343
Drum-Mates Inc.
Lumberton, NJ....800-621-3786
Eclipse Systems
Milpitas, CA....408-263-2201
Glen Mills, Inc.
Clifton, NJ....973-777-0777
Munson Machinery Company
Utica, NY....800-944-6644
Packaging & Processing Equipment
Ayr, ON....519-622-6666
Scott Turbon Mixer
Adelanto, CA....800-285-8512

Food Processing

A&B Process Systems
Stratford, WI....888-258-2789
A&J Mixing International
Oakville, ON....800-668-3470
A&M Process Equipment
Ajax, ON....905-619-8001
ADMIX
Manchester, NH....800-466-2369
Am-Mac Incorporated
Fairfield, NJ....800-829-2018
American Extrusion International
South Beloit, IL....815-624-6616
American Food Equipment Company
Hayward, CA....510-783-0255
American Manufacturing &Engineering Company
Cleveland, OH....800-822-9402
AMF CANADA
Sherbrooke, QC....800-255-3869
Apache Stainless Equipment Corporation
Beaver Dam, WI....800-444-0398
APEC
Lake Odessa, MI....616-374-1000
APV Americas
Delavan, WI....800-252-5200
Arcobaleno Pasta Machines
Lancaster, PA....800-875-7096
Arde Barinco
Carlstadt, NJ....800-909-6070
Automated Food Systems
Waxahachie, TX....972-298-5719
AZO Food
Memphis, TN....901-794-9480
B.C. Holland
Dousman, WI....262-965-2939
Baldewein Company
Lake Forrest, IL....800-424-5544
Bematek Systems
Salem, MA....877-236-2835
Bepex International,LLC
Minneapolis, MN....800-607-2470
Berkshire PPM
Litchfield, CT....860-567-3118
Biro Manufacturing Company
Marblehead, OH....419-798-4451
Blakeslee, Inc.
Addison, IL....630-532-5021
Blue Tech
Hickory, NC....828-324-5900
Bowers Process Equipment
Stratford, ON....800-567-3223
Breddo Likwifier
Kansas City, MO....800-669-4092
Bulldog Factory Service
Madison Heights, MI....248-541-3500
Bush Tank Fabricators
Newark, NJ....973-596-1121
California Vibratory Feeders
Anaheim, CA....800-354-0972

Carlisle Food Service Products
Oklahoma City, OK ... 800-654-8210
Charles Ross & Son Company
Hauppauge, NY ... 800-243-7677
Chemineer-Kenics/Greerco
North Andover, MA ... 800-643-0641
Cinelli Esperia
Woodbridge, ON ... 905-856-1820
Cleveland-Eastern Mixers
Clinton, CT ... 800-243-1188
CMC America Corporation
Joliet, IL ... 815-726-4337
Coastline Equipment
Bellingham, WA ... 360-739-2480
Columbus Instruments
Columbus, OH ... 800-669-5011
Cornell Machine Company
Springfield, NJ ... 973-379-6860
CRC
Council Bluffs, IA ... 712-323-9477
Custom Food Machinery
Stockton, CA ... 209-463-4343
Davron Technologies
Chattanooga, TN ... 423-870-1888
Dito Dean Food Prep
Rocklin, CA ... 800-331-7958
Dorton Incorporated
Arlington Hts, IL ... 800-299-8600
Drum-Mates Inc.
Lumberton, NJ ... 800-621-3786
Duplex Mill & Manufacturing Company
Springfield, OH ... 937-325-5555
Dynamic International
Pewaukee, WI ... 800-267-7794
E.T. Oakes Corporation
Hauppauge, NY ... 631-232-0002
Eclipse Systems
Milpitas, CA ... 408-263-2201
Eirich Machines
Gurnee, IL ... 847-336-2444
EKATO Corporation
St Ramsey, NJ ... 201-825-4684
Empire Bakery Equipment
Hicksville, NY ... 800-878-4070
Ertel Alsop
Kingston, NY ... 800-553-7835
Exact Mixing Systems
Memphis, TN ... 901-362-8501
Expert Industries
Brooklyn, NY ... 718-434-6060
Falco Technologies
La Prairie, QC ... 450-444-0566
Fernholtz Engineering
Van Nuys, CA ... 818-785-5800
Fish Oven & Equipment Corporation
Wauconda, IL ... 877-526-8720
Fitzpatrick Company
Elmhurst, IL ... 630-530-3333
Food Engineering Unlimited
Fullerton, CA ... 714-879-8762
Food Processing Equipment Company
Santa Fe Springs, CA ... 479-751-9392
Gem Equipment of Oregon
Woodburn, OR ... 503-982-9902
General, Inc
Weston, FL ... 954-202-7419
Glen Mills, Inc.
Clifton, NJ ... 973-777-0777
Goodway Industries
Bohemia, NY ... 800-943-4501
Grant-Letchworth
Tonawanda, NY ... 716-692-1000
Hamilton Beach/Proctor-Silex
Southern Pines, NC ... 800-711-6100
Hayes & Stolz IndustrialManufacturing Company
Fort Worth, TX ... 800-725-7272
Hebeler Corporation
Tonawanda, NY ... 800-486-4709
Hobart Corporation
Troy, OH ... 888-446-2278
Hollymatic Corporation
Countryside, IL ... 708-579-3700
Hosokawa/Bepex Corporation
Santa Rosa, CA ... 707-586-6000
Howard Fabrication
City of Industry, CA ... 626-961-0114
International Reserve Equipment Corporation
Clarendon Hills, IL ... 708-531-0680
JW Leser Company
Los Angeles, CA ... 323-731-4173
Kady International
Scarborough, ME ... 800-367-5239
Karl Schnell
New London, WI ... 920-982-9974
Kelmin Products
Plymouth, FL ... 407-886-6079
Kemutec Group
Bristol, PA ... 215-788-8013
Kinetic Equipment Company
Appleton, WI ... 806-293-4471
Koflo Corporation
Cary, IL ... 800-782-8427
Lee Industries Fluid Transfer
Philipsburg, PA ... 814-342-0802
Leland
South Plainfield, NJ ... 908-668-1008
LIST
Acton, MA ... 978-635-9521
Littleford Day
Florence, KY ... 800-365-8555
Machanix Fabrication
Chino, CA ... 800-700-9701
Mandeville Company
Minneapolis, MN ... 800-328-8490
Marel Food Systems, Inc.
Lenexa, KS ... 913-888-9110
Marion Mixers
Marion, IA ... 319-377-6371
Matcon USA
Elmhurst, IL ... 856-256-1330
Matfer
Van Nuys, CA ... 800-766-0333
McCarter Corporation
Norristown, PA ... 610-272-3203
Merlin Process Equipment
Houston, TX ... 713-221-1651
Microfluidics International Corporation
Newton, MA ... 800-370-5452
Midwest Metalcraft & Equipment
Windsor, MO ... 800-647-3167
Modern Process Equipment
Chicago, IL ... 773-254-3929
Munson Machinery Company
Utica, NY ... 800-944-6644
Nalge Process Technologies Group
Rochester, NY ... 585-586-8800
Pacific Process Technology
La Jolla, CA ... 858-551-3298
Packaging & Processing Equipment
Ayr, ON ... 519-622-6666
Patterson-Kelley Hars Company
East Stroudsburg, PA ... 570-421-7500
Paul Mueller Company
Springfield, MO ... 800-683-5537
Paul O. Abbe
Bensenville, IL ... 630-350-2200
Paxton Corporation
Bristol, RI
Peerless Machinery Corporation
Sidney, OH ... 800-999-3327
Polar Process
Plattsville, ON ... 877-896-8077
PolyMaid Company
Largo, FL ... 800-206-9188
Prince Castle
Carol Stream, IL ... 800-722-7853
Process Systems
Barrington, IL ... 847-842-8618
Production Packaging & Processing Equipment Company
Phoenix, AZ ... 602-254-7878
Provisur Technologies
Mokena, IL ... 708-479-3500
Provisur Technologies/Weiler
Whitewater, WI ... 800-558-9507
Puritan Manufacturing
Omaha, NE ... 800-331-0487
Readco Kuimoto, LLC
York, PA ... 800-395-4959
Reading Bakery Systems
Robesonia, PA ... 610-693-5816
Reiser
Canton, MA ... 781-575-9941
RMF Freezers
Grandview, MO ... 816-765-4101
Ross Engineering
Savannah, GA ... 800-524-7677
S. Howes
Silver Creek, NY ... 888-255-2611
Savage Brothers Company
Elk Grove Vlg, IL ... 800-342-0973
Scott Turbon Mixer
Adelanto, CA ... 800-285-8512
Semi-Bulk Systems
Fenton, MO ... 800-732-8769
Silverson Machines
East Longmeadow, MA ... 800-204-6400
Sonic Corporation
Stratford, CT ... 866-493-1378
South River Machine
Hackensack, NJ ... 201-487-1736
Specific Mechanical Systems
Victoria, BC ... 250-652-2111
Stainless Fabrication
Springfield, MO ... 800-397-8265
Stein DSI
Sandusky, OH ... 800-447-2630
Stephan Machinery, Inc.
Mundelein, IL ... 800-783-7426
Stricklin Company
Dallas, TX ... 214-637-1030
Superior Products Company
Saint Paul, MN ... 800-328-9800
T.K. Products
Anaheim, CA ... 714-621-0267
TDH Manufacturing
Sand Springs, OK ... 888-251-7961
Thomas L. Green & Company
Robenosia, PA ... 610-693-5816
TSA Griddle Systems
Kelowna, BC ... 250-491-9025
Varimixer
Charlotte, NC ... 800-221-1138
Viatec
Hastings, MI ... 800-942-4702
Vita-Mix Corporation
Cleveland, OH ... 800-437-4654
Waring Products
Torrington, CT ... 800-492-7464
Washington Frontier
Grandview, WA ... 509-469-7662
Weiler & Company
Whitewater, WI ... 800-558-9507
Welbilt Corporation
Stamford, CT ... 203-325-8300
Wilevco
Billerica, MA ... 978-667-0400

Food, Household, Hotel & Restaurant

Arcobaleno Pasta Machines
Lancaster, PA ... 800-875-7096
Attias Oven Corporation
Brooklyn, NY ... 800-928-8427
Blakeslee, Inc.
Addison, IL ... 630-532-5021
CRC
Council Bluffs, IA ... 712-323-9477
Custom Food Machinery
Stockton, CA ... 209-463-4343
Dorton Incorporated
Arlington Hts, IL ... 800-299-8600
General, Inc
Weston, FL ... 954-202-7419
Hobart Corporation
Troy, OH ... 888-446-2278
Jiffy Mixer Company
Corona, CA ... 951-272-0838
Leland
South Plainfield, NJ ... 908-668-1008
Mandeville Company
Minneapolis, MN ... 800-328-8490
Marion Mixers
Marion, IA ... 319-377-6371
Matfer
Van Nuys, CA ... 800-766-0333
Nalge Process Technologies Group
Rochester, NY ... 585-586-8800
Packaging & Processing Equipment
Ayr, ON ... 519-622-6666
Paul Mueller Company
Springfield, MO ... 800-683-5537
Paxton Corporation
Bristol, RI
Prince Castle
Carol Stream, IL ... 800-722-7853
Puritan Manufacturing
Omaha, NE ... 800-331-0487
Superior Products Company
Saint Paul, MN ... 800-328-9800
T.K. Products
Anaheim, CA ... 714-621-0267
Toronto Kitchen Equipment
North York, ON ... 416-745-4944
Univex Corporation
Salem, NH ... 800-258-6358

Varimixer
Charlotte, NC 800-221-1138
VitaMinder Company
Providence, RI 800-858-8840
Welbilt Corporation
Stamford, CT....................203-325-8300

Paste Products

A&B Process Systems
Stratford, WI....................888-258-2789
Breddo Likwifier
Kansas City, MO....................800-669-4092
Chemineer-Kenics/Greerco
North Andover, MA 800-643-0641
Kelmin Products
Plymouth, FL 407-886-6079
McCarter Corporation
Norristown, PA....................610-272-3203
Packaging & Processing Equipment
Ayr, ON....................519-622-6666
Paxton Corporation
Bristol, RI
Polar Process
Plattsville, ON....................877-896-8077
Reiser
Canton, MA 781-575-9941

Nut Cracking, Shelling & Salting

A.C. Horn & Co
Dallas, TX....................800-657-6155
Carolina Cracker
Garner, NC 919-779-6899
Design Technology Corporation
Billerica, MA 978-663-7000
Key Technology
Walla Walla, WA....................509-529-2161
Krispy Kist Company
Chicago, IL 312-733-0900
Lewis M. Carter Manufacturing Company
Donalsonville, GA 229-524-2197
Maddox/Adams International
Miami, FL....................305-592-3337
Modern Electronics
Mansfield, LA....................318-872-4764
Nutty Bavarian
Sanford, FL....................800-382-4788
Satake USA
Stafford, TX 281-276-3600

Oil Extraction

Abanaki Corporation
Chagrin Falls, OH....................800-358-7546
Alfa Laval
Newburyport, MA....................978-465-5777
Anderson International Corporation
Stow, OH....................800-336-4730
Caron Products & Services
Marietta, OH....................800-648-3042
Crown Iron Works Company
Minneapolis, MN 888-703-7500
French Oil Mill Machinery Company
Piqua, OH....................937-773-3420

Ovens

A.C. Horn & Co
Dallas, TX....................800-657-6155
ABI Limited
Concord, ON....................800-297-8666
AccuTemp Products
Fort Wayne, IN 800-210-5907
Adamatic
Auburn, WA 800-578-2547
AK Steel
West Chester, OH 800-331-5050
Allied Bakery and Food Service Equipment
Santa Fe Springs, CA 562-945-6506
ALPI Food Preparation Equipment
Bolton, ON 800-928-2574
Alto-Shaam
Menomonee Falls, WI....................800-558-8744
Amana Commercial Products
Cedar Rapids, IA....................319-368-8198
American Extrusion International
South Beloit, IL 815-624-6616
American Range & Hood Corporation
Pacoima, CA....................888-753-9898
AMF CANADA
Sherbrooke, QC 800-255-3869
Anetsberger
Concord, NH....................603-225-6684
Antrim Manufacturing
Brookfield, WI 262-781-6860
Apollo Sheet Metal
Kennewick, WA 509-586-1104
Attias Oven Corporation
Brooklyn, NY 800-928-8427
Bakers Pride Oven Company
New Rochelle, NY 800-431-2745
Bakery Associates
Setauket, NY....................631-751-4156
Ballantyne Food Service Equipment
Omaha, NE 800-424-1215
Baxter Manufacturing Company
Orting, WA 800-777-2828
BBC Industries
Pacific, MO....................800-654-4205
Benier USA
Lithia Springs, GA 770-745-2200
Benko Products
Sheffield Village, OH....................440-934-2180
Bethel Engineering & Equipment Inc
New Hampshire, OH....................800-889-6129
Bevles Company
Dallas, TX....................800-441-1601
BKI Worldwide
Simpsonville, SC 800-927-6887
Blodgett
Burlington, VT 800-331-5842
Bolling Oven & Machine Company
Avon, OH 440-937-6112
C.H. Babb Company
Raynham, MA....................508-977-0600
Casso-Solar Corporation
Pomona, NY 800-988-4455
Chase Industries
Carson, CA 310-763-9900
Checker Engineering
New Hope, MN....................888-800-5001
Chesmont Engineering Company
Exton, PA 610-594-9200
Cincinnati Industrial Machine
Mason, OH 800-677-0076
Cinelli Esperia
Woodbridge, ON....................905-856-1820
Cleveland Range Company
Cleveland, OH 800-338-2204
Coast Scientific
Rancho Santa Fe, CA 800-445-1544
Cober Electronics, Inc.
Norwalk, CT....................800-709-5948
Comstock-Castle Stove Company
Quincy, IL....................800-637-9188
Cook King
Laguna Beach, CA 949-497-1235
Cookshack
Ponca City, OK....................800-423-0698
Custom Diamond International
Laval, QC 800-363-5926
Cutler Industries
Morton Grove, IL 800-458-5593
Davron Technologies
Chattanooga, TN....................423-870-1888
DBE Inc
Concord, ON....................800-461-5313
Defreeze Corporation
Southborough, MA 508-485-8512
Deluxe Equipment Company
Bradenton, FL....................800-367-8931
Doyon Equipment
Liniere, QC 800-463-4273
Duke Manufacturing Company
Saint Louis, MO 800-735-3853
Dynamic Cooking Systems
Huntington Beach, CA 800-433-8466
Earthstone Wood-Fire Ovens
Glendale, CA 800-840-4915
Empire Bakery Equipment
Hicksville, NY 800-878-4070
Ensign Ribbon Burners
Pelham, NY....................914-738-0600
Epcon Industrial Systems
Conroe, TX 800-447-7872
Equipex Limited
Providence, RI 800-649-7885
Excellent Bakery Equipment Company
Fairfield, NJ....................888-BAG-ELS1
Fab-X/Metals
Washington, NC 800-677-3229
FBM/Baking Machines Inc
Cranbury, NJ 800-449-0433
FECO/MOCO
Cleveland, OH 216-531-1599
Fish Oven & Equipment Corporation
Wauconda, IL 877-526-8720
FlashBake Ovens Food Service
Fremont, CA....................800-843-6836
Food Engineering Unlimited
Fullerton, CA 714-879-8762
Foster Refrigerator Corporation
Kinderhook, NY 888-828-3311
Franz Haas Machinery of America
Richmond, VA....................804-222-6022
Friedrich Metal ProductsCompany
Browns Summit, NC....................800-772-0326
G.S. Blodgett Corporation
Burlington, VT 800-331-5842
Garland Commercial Ranges
Mississauga, ON....................905-624-0260
Garland Commercial Ranges Ltd.
Mississauga, ON....................905-624-0260
Gehnrich Oven Sales Company
Smithtown, NY....................631-585-8787
Gemini Bakery Equipment Company
Philadelphia, PA 800-468-9046
Glenro
Paterson, NJ 800-922-0106
Grande Chef Company
Orangeville, ON 519-942-4470
Hardt Equipment Manufacturing
Lachine, QC 888-848-4408
Hasty-Bake
Tulsa, OK 800-426-6836
HATCO Corporation
Milwaukee, WI 800-558-0607
Henry Group
Greenville, TX 903-883-2002
Hercules Food Equipment
Weston, ON....................416-742-9673
Hickory Industries
North Bergen, NJ 800-732-9153
Holman Cooking Equipment
Saint Louis, MO 888-356-5362
House of Webster
Rogers, AR 800-369-4641
Illinois Range Company
Schiller Park, IL 800-535-7041
Imperial Commercial Cooking Equipment
Corona, CA....................800-343-7790
Industronics Service Company
South Windsor, CT....................800-878-1551
IR Systems
Jupiter, FL....................800-893-7540
J.C. Ford Company
La Habra, CA 714-871-7361
Jackson MSC
Barbourville, KY 888-800-5672
KB Systems Baking Machinery Design Company
Bangor, PA 610-588-7788
Kemper Bakery Systems
Rockaway, NJ....................973-625-1566
La Poblana Food Machines
Mesa, AZ....................480-258-2091
Laboratory Devices
Holliston, MA....................508-429-1716
Lang Manufacturing Company
Everett, WA....................800-882-6368
Lanly Company
Cleveland, OH....................216-731-1115
Legion Industries
Waynesboro, GA....................800-887-1988
LPS Technology
Grafton, OH 800-586-1410
LTG Technologies
Spartanburg, SC 864-599-6340
Lucks Food Equipment Company
Kent, WA....................811-824-0696
Market Forge Industries
Everett, MA....................866-698-3188
Martin/Baron
Irwindale, CA 626-960-5153
Mayekawa USA, Inc.
Chicago, IL....................773-516-5070
Merco/Savory
Mt. Pleasant, MI 800-733-8821
Meyer Machine & Garroutte Products
San Antonio, TX....................210-736-1811
MF&B Restaurant Systems
Dunbar, PA 724-628-3050
Microdry
Crestwood, KY....................502-241-8933
Middleby Corporation
Elgin, IL 847-741-3300

Middleby Marshall, CTX
Elgin, IL 800-323-5575
Moffat
San Antonio, TX 800-551-8795
Montague Company
Hayward, CA 800-345-1830
Mosshaim Innovations
Jacksonville, FL 888-995-7775
Motom Corporation
Bensenville, IL 630-787-1995
Mugnaini Imports
Watsonville, CA 888-887-7206
National Drying Machinery Company
Philadelphia, PA 215-464-6070
National Hotpack
Stone Ridge, NY 800-431-8232
Nevo Corporation
Ronkonkoma, NY 631-585-8787
Normandie Metal Fabricators
Port Washington, NY 800-221-2398
Nothum Food Processing Systems
Springfield, MO 800-435-1297
Nu-Vu Food Service Systems
Menominee, MI 800-338-9886
Panasonic Commercial Food Service
Secaucus, NJ 800-553-0384
Pavailler Distribution Company
Northvale, NJ 201-767-0766
Peerless Ovens
Sandusky, OH 800-548-4514
Peerless-Premier Appliance Company
Belleville, IL 618-233-0475
Pier 1 Imports
Woodcliff Lake, NJ 800-448-9993
Piper Products
Wausau, WI 800-544-3057
PMI Food Equipment Group
Troy, OH 937-332-3000
Pro Scientific
Oxford, CT 800-584-3776
Process Heating Corporation
Shrewsbury, MA 508-842-5200
Proheatco Manufacturing
Pomona, CA 800-423-4195
Proluxe
Paramount, CA 800-594-5528
Q-Matic Technologies
Carol Stream, IL 800-880-6836
QNC
Dallas, TX 888-668-3687
Quasar Industries
Rochester Hills, MI 248-852-0300
Randell Manufacturing Unified Brands
Weidman, MI 888-994-7636
Rankin-DeLux
Eastwale, CA 951-685-0081
Rational Cooking Systems
Schaumburg, IL 888-320-7274
Reading Bakery Systems
Robesonia, PA 610-693-5816
Reed Oven Company
Kansas City, MO 816-842-7446
Reliable Food Service Equipment
Concord, ON 416-738-6840
Remco Industries International
Fort Lauderdale, FL 800-987-3626
Renato Specialty Product
Garland, TX 866-575-6316
Revent
Piscataway, NJ 732-777-9433
Rotisol France Inc
Inglewood, CA 800-651-5969
Roto-Flex Oven Company
San Antonio, TX 877-859-1463
Royalton Foodservice Equipment
Cleveland, OH 800-662-8765
Ruiz Flour Tortillas
Riverside, CA 909-947-7811
Sasib North America
Plano, TX 972-422-5808
Server Products
Richfield, WI 800-558-8722
Sharp Electronics Corporation
Mahwah, NJ 800-237-4277
Shouldice Brothers SheetMetal
Battle Creek, MI 269-962-5579
Solbern
Fairfield, NJ 973-227-3030
Southbend Company
Fuquay Varina, NC 800-348-2558
Southern Pride Distributing
Marion, IL 800-851-8180
Stafford - Smith
Kalamazoo, MI 800-968-2442
Standex International Corporation
Salem, NH 603-893-9701
Stein DSI
Sandusky, OH 800-447-2630
Super Systems
Wausau, WI 800-558-5880
Super-Chef Manufacturing Company
Houston, TX 800-231-3478
Superior Products Company
Saint Paul, MN 800-328-9800
Thermodyne Food Service
Fort Wayne, IN 800-526-9182
Thomas L. Green & Company
Robenosia, PA 610-693-5816
Toastmaster
Elgin, IL 847-741-3300
Toronto Kitchen Equipment
North York, ON 416-745-4944
Town Food Service Equipment Company
Brooklyn, NY 800-221-5032
Trak-Air/Rair
Denver, CO 800-688-8725
Triad Scientific
Manasquan, NJ 800-867-6690
Trimen Foodservice Equipment
North York, ON 877-437-1422
TURBOCHEF Technologies
Carrollton, TX 800-908-8726
Valad Electric Heating Corporation
Tarrytown, NY
Vortron Smokehouse/Ovens
Iron Ridge, WI 800-874-1949
Vulcan-Hart Company
Louisville, KY 800-814-2028
Welbilt Corporation
Stamford, CT 203-325-8300
Western Combustion Engineering
Carson, CA 310-834-9389
Win-Holt Equipment Group
Westbury, NY 800-444-3595
Winston Industries
Louisville, KY 800-234-5286
Wisco Industries
Oregon, WI 800-999-4726
Wittco Food Service Equipment
Milwaukee, WI 800-367-8413
Wolf Range Company
Louisville, KY 800-366-9653
Wolverine Proctor & Schwartz
Lexington, NC 336-248-5181
Wood Stone Corporation
Bellingham, WA 800-988-8103

Packers' & Butchers'

Aaron Equipment Company
Bensenville, IL 630-350-2200
Allen Gauge & Tool Company
Pittsburgh, PA 412-241-6410
Am-Mac Incorporated
Fairfield, NJ 800-829-2018
API
Tampa, FL 813-888-8488
Automated Food Systems
Waxahachie, TX 972-298-5719
Best & Donovan
Cincinnati, OH 800-553-2378
BH Bunn Company
Lakeland, FL 800-222-2866
Biro Manufacturing Company
Marblehead, OH 419-798-4451
Chop-Rite Two, Inc.
Harleysville, PA 800-683-5858
Cincinnati Boss Company
Omaha, NE 402-556-4070
CMC America Corporation
Joliet, IL 815-726-4337
Compacker Systems LLC
Davenport, IA 563-391-2751
Customized Equipment SE
Tucker, GA 770-934-9300
DC Tech
Kansas City, MO 877-742-9090
Doering Company
Clear Lake, MN 320-743-2276
Durable Packaging Corporation
Countryside, IL 800-700-5677
Ennio International
Aurora, IL 630-851-5808
Friedr Dick Corporation
Farmingdale, NY 800-554-3425
Globe Food Equipment Company
Dayton, OH 800-347-5423
Grant-Letchworth
Tonawanda, NY 716-692-1000
Hollymatic Corporation
Countryside, IL 708-579-3700
Indeco Products
San Marcos, TX 512-396-5814
Kasel Associated Industries
Denver, CO 800-218-4417
Kohler Industries
Lincoln, NE 800-365-6708
Linker Machines
Rockaway, NJ 973-983-0001
Marlen International
Astoria, OR 800-862-7536
Molins/Sandiacre Richmond
Richmond, VA 804-421-8795
Pemberton & Associates
Brooklyn, NY 800-736-2664
Pickwick Company
Cedar Rapids, IA 800-397-9797
Preferred Machining Corporation
Englewood, CO 303-761-1535
Pressure Pack
Williamsburg, VA 757-220-3693
Professional Marketing Group
Seattle, WA 800-227-3769
Ranger Tool Company
Memphis, TN 800-737-9999
Schroeder Sewing Technologies
San Marcos, CA 760-591-9733
Stork Townsend Inc.
Des Moines, IA 800-247-8609
Walsroder Packaging
Willowbrook, IL 800-882-9987

Panomatic-Flour Collection System

Aget Manufacturing Company
Adrian, MI 517-263-5781

Pasta Processing

A.K. Robins
Baltimore, MD 800-486-9656
ALPI Food Preparation Equipment
Bolton, ON 800-928-2574
APV Baker
Goldsboro, NC 919-736-4309
Arcobaleno Pasta Machines
Lancaster, PA 800-875-7096
Demaco
Ridgewood, NY
Design Technology Corporation
Billerica, MA 978-663-7000
Gemini Bakery Equipment Company
Philadelphia, PA 800-468-9046
IJ White Corporation
Farmingdale, NY 631-293-2211
Industrial Products Corporation
Ho Ho Kus, NJ 800-472-5913
Kemper Bakery Systems
Rockaway, NJ 973-625-1566
Lawrence Equipment
South El Monte, CA 800-423-4500
Lyco Manufacturing
Wausau, WI 715-845-7867
MBC Food Machinery Corporation
Hackensack, NJ 201-489-7000
Molded Fiber Glass Tray Company
Linesville, PA 800-458-6050
Mouli Manufacturing Corporation
Belleville, NJ 800-789-8285
Multi-Fill Inc
West Jordan, UT 801-280-1570
Oshikiri Corporation of America
Philadelphia, PA 215-637-6005
Pavan USA, Inc.
Emigsville, PA 717-767-4889
Peerless Dough Mixing and Make-Up
Sidney, OH 800-999-3327
Phase II Pasta Machines
Farmingdale, NY 800-457-5070
Pier 1 Imports
Woodcliff Lake, NJ 800-448-9993
Pro Bake
Twinsburg, OH 800-837-4427
Rademaker USA
Hudson, OH 330-650-2345

Reiser
Canton, MA 781-575-9941
Rheon USA
Huntersville, NC....................704-875-9191
Shick Tube-Veyor Corporation
Kansas City, MO....................816-861-7224
South River Machine
Hackensack, NJ....................201-487-1736
Spraying Systems Company
Wheaton, IL 630-655-5000
Stephan Machinery, Inc.
Mundelein, IL 800-783-7426
Techno-Design
Garfield, NJ....................973-478-0930
TWM Manufacturing
Leamington, ON 888-495-4831
UniTrak Corporation
Port Hope, ON 866-883-5749
US Tsubaki
Wheeling, IL....................800-323-7790
Wohl Associates
Bohemia, NY 631-244-7979

Pasteurizers

AGC Engineering
Bristow, VA....................800-825-8820
API Heat Transfer
Buffalo, NY....................877-274-4328
Arcobaleno Pasta Machines
Lancaster, PA 800-875-7096
B-T Engineering
Bala Cynwyd, PA 610-664-9500
Chad Company
Olathe, KS....................800-444-8360
Chester-Jensen Company, Inc.
Chester, PA 800-685-3750
Convay Systems
Etobicoke, ON....................800-811-5511
Eischen Enterprises
Fresno, CA 559-834-0013
Feldmeier Equipment
Syracuse, NY 315-454-8608
FleetwoodGoldcoWyard
Romeoville, IL 630-759-6800
Frigoscandia
Redmond, WA....................800-423-1743
Globe International
Tacoma, WA 800-523-6575
Goodnature Products
Orchard Park, NY....................800-875-3381
Krones
Franklin, WI 414-409-4000
Microthermics
Raleigh, NC 919-878-8045
Pacific Process Technology
La Jolla, CA 858-551-3298
Packaging & Processing Equipment
Ayr, ON....................519-622-6666
Pneumatic Scale Corporation
Cuyahoga Falls, OH 330-923-0491
Relco Unisystems Corporation
Willmar, MN....................320-231-2210
Sanchelima International
Doral, FL....................305-591-4343
Schlueter Company
Janesville, WI 800-359-1700
South Valley Manufacturing
Gilroy, CA....................408-842-5457
Stanfos
Edmonton, AB 800-661-5648
Stephan Machinery, Inc.
Mundelein, IL 800-783-7426
Unitherm Food Systems Innc.
Bristow, OK 918-367-0197
Whey Systems
Willmar, MN....................320-905-4122

Peanut Processing

A.C. Horn & Co
Dallas, TX....................800-657-6155
Andritz
Muncy, PA....................570-546-8211
Krispy Kist Company
Chicago, IL 312-733-0900
Lewis M. Carter Manufacturing Company
Donalsonville, GA 229-524-2197
Star Manufacturing International
Saint Louis, MO 800-264-7827
Straub Company
Minneapolis, MN 952-546-6686

Suffolk Iron Works
Suffolk, VA....................757-539-2353
UniTrak Corporation
Port Hope, ON 866-883-5749
Wolverine Proctor & Schwartz
Lexington, NC 336-248-5181

Cleaners & Shellers

Southern Ag Company
Blakely, GA....................229-723-4262

Pickers

Poultry

Brower
Houghton, IA 800-553-1791
M & M Poultry Equipment
Hollister, MO 800-872-9687
MSSH
Greensburg, IN 812-663-2180
Pickwick Company
Cedar Rapids, IA....................800-397-9797

Pizza & Pizza Products Processing

ABI Limited
Concord, ON....................800-297-8666
AC Dispensing Equipment
Lower Sackville, NS....................888-777-9990
ALPI Food Preparation Equipment
Bolton, ON 800-928-2574
APV Baker
Goldsboro, NC 919-736-4309
Bakers Pride Oven Company
New Rochelle, NY 800-431-2745
Benier USA
Lithia Springs, GA 770-745-2200
C.H. Babb Company
Raynham, MA....................508-977-0600
Christy Machine Company
Fremont, OH....................888-332-6451
CIM Bakery Equipment of USA
Arlington Heights, IL 847-818-8121
Comtec Industries
Woodridge, IL....................630-759-9000
DBE Inc
Concord, ON....................800-461-5313
Doughpro
Perris, CA 800-594-5528
DoughXpress
Pittsburg, KS....................800-835-0606
Doyon Equipment
Liniere, QC 800-463-4273
Dutchess Bakers' Machinery Company
Superior, WI 800-777-4498
Garland Commercial Ranges
Mississauga, ON....................905-624-0260
Garland Commercial Ranges Ltd.
Mississauga, ON....................905-624-0260
Gemini Bakery Equipment Company
Philadelphia, PA 800-468-9046
Grote Company
Columbus, OH 888-534-7683
IJ White Corporation
Farmingdale, NY....................631-293-2211
Industrial Ceramic Products
Marysville, OH 800-427-2278
Kemper Bakery Systems
Rockaway, NJ 973-625-1566
Lanly Company
Cleveland, OH....................216-731-1115
Lawrence Equipment
South El Monte, CA 800-423-4500
Martin/Baron
Irwindale, CA 626-960-5153
Matiss
St Georges, QC 888-562-8477
Merco/Savory
Mt. Pleasant, MI 800-733-8821
Molded Fiber Glass Tray Company
Linesville, PA 800-458-6050
Normandie Metal Fabricators
Port Washington, NY 800-221-2398
Oshikiri Corporation of America
Philadelphia, PA 215-637-6005
Paxton Corporation
Bristol, RI
Peerless Dough Mixing and Make-Up
Sidney, OH 800-999-3327
Peerless Food Inc
Sidney, OH 937-494-2870

Peerless Ovens
Sandusky, OH 800-548-4514
Piper Products
Wausau, WI....................800-544-3057
Pizzamatic Corporation
South Holland, IL....................888-749-9279
Pro Bake
Twinsburg, OH 800-837-4427
Proluxe
Paramount, CA 800-594-5528
Rademaker USA
Hudson, OH 330-650-2345
Raque Food Systems
Louisville, KY 502-267-9641
Reiser
Canton, MA 781-575-9941
Remco Industries International
Fort Lauderdale, FL 800-987-3626
Renato Specialty Product
Garland, TX 866-575-6316
Rheon USA
Huntersville, NC....................704-875-9191
Roto-Flex Oven Company
San Antonio, TX....................877-859-1463
Server Products
Richfield, WI 800-558-8722
Shick Tube-Veyor Corporation
Kansas City, MO....................816-861-7224
Southbend Company
Fuquay Varina, NC....................800-348-2558
Stephan Machinery, Inc.
Mundelein, IL....................800-783-7426
Trak-Air/Rair
Denver, CO 800-688-8725
US Tsubaki
Wheeling, IL....................800-323-7790
Vulcan-Hart Company
Louisville, KY 800-814-2028
Wolverine Proctor & Schwartz
Lexington, NC 336-248-5181
Wood Stone Corporation
Bellingham, WA 800-988-8103

Potato Chip Processing

Graybill Machines
Lititz, PA....................717-626-5221
Krispy Kist Company
Chicago, IL 312-733-0900
Pavan USA, Inc.
Emigsville, PA 717-767-4889
Paxton Corporation
Bristol, RI
Polar Process
Plattsville, ON....................877-896-8077

Poultry Processing

Advance Energy Technologies
Clifton Park, NY....................800-724-0198
Automated Food Systems
Waxahachie, TX 972-298-5719
Bluffton Motor Works
Bluffton, IN....................800-579-8527
Brower
Houghton, IA 800-553-1791
Designpro Engineering
Clearwater, MN....................800-221-4144
Doering Company
Clear Lake, MN 320-743-2276
Ennio International
Aurora, IL 630-851-5808
Falcon Fabricators
Nashville, TN 615-832-0027
Gainco, Inc.
Gainesville, GA 800-467-2828
Greenline Corporation
Charlotte, NC 800-331-5312
Johnson Food Equipment
Kansas City, KS 800-288-3434
Kamflex Corporation
Chicago, IL....................800-323-2440
Kent Company, Inc.
Miami, FL....................800-521-4886
Lyco Wausau
Wausau, WI....................715-845-7867
Maja Equipment Company
Omaha, NE 402-346-6252
Marlen International
Astoria, OR....................800-862-7536
Mepsco
Batavia, IL....................800-323-8535

Millard Manufacturing Corporation
La Vista, NE....................800-662-4263
Miller Metal Fabricators
Staunton, VA....................540-886-5575
Morris & Associates
Garner, NC....................919-582-9200
Mp Equip. Co.
Buford, GA....................770-614-5355
MSSH
Greensburg, IN....................812-663-2180
P&F Metals
Turlock, CA....................209-667-4716
Pemberton & Associates
Brooklyn, NY....................800-736-2664
Pickwick Company
Cedar Rapids, IA....................800-397-9797
Polar Process
Plattsville, ON....................877-896-8077
Preferred Machining Corporation
Englewood, CO....................303-761-1535
Prince Industries
Murrayville, GA....................800-441-3303
Reiser
Canton, MA....................781-575-9941
Stephen Paoli Manufacturing Corporation
Rockford, IL....................815-965-0621
Stork Gamco
Gainesville, GA....................770-532-7041
Stork Townsend Inc.
Des Moines, IA....................800-247-8609
Tech-Roll, Inc.
Blaine, WA....................888-946-3929

Preservation

Irradiation

Nydree Flooring
Forest, VA....................800-682-5698
Paragon Group USA
St Petersburg, FL....................800-835-6962

Presses

Oil, Cottonseed & Linseed

Anderson International Corporation
Stow, OH....................800-336-4730
Ashbrook Corporation
Houston, TX....................800-362-9041
Davenport Machine
Rock Island, IL....................309-786-1500
French Oil Mill Machinery Company
Piqua, OH....................937-773-3420
Packaging & Processing Equipment
Ayr, ON....................519-622-6666

Wine

Ashbrook Corporation
Houston, TX....................800-362-9041
Globe International
Tacoma, WA....................800-523-6575
Goodnature Products
Orchard Park, NY....................800-875-3381
Oak Barrel Winecraft
Berkeley, CA....................510-849-0400
P&F Metals
Turlock, CA....................209-667-4716

Pretzel Processing

Design Technology Corporation
Billerica, MA....................978-663-7000
Graybill Machines
Lititz, PA....................717-626-5221
IJ White Corporation
Farmingdale, NY....................631-293-2211
Industrial Products Corporation
Ho Ho Kus, NJ....................800-472-5913
Krispy Kist Company
Chicago, IL....................312-733-0900
Lanly Company
Cleveland, OH....................216-731-1115
Peerless Dough Mixing and Make-Up
Sidney, OH....................800-999-3327
Rademaker USA
Hudson, OH....................330-650-2345
Rheon USA
Huntersville, NC....................704-875-9191
Shick Tube-Veyor Corporation
Kansas City, MO....................816-861-7224

Stephan Machinery, Inc.
Mundelein, IL....................800-783-7426
UniTrak Corporation
Port Hope, ON....................866-883-5749
US Tsubaki
Wheeling, IL....................800-323-7790

Pulpers

Brown International Corporation
Winter Haven, FL....................626-966-8361
Corenco
Santa Rosa, CA....................888-267-3626
Custom Food Machinery
Stockton, CA....................209-463-4343
Dixie Canner Company
Athens, GA....................706-549-1914
Somat Company
Lancaster, PA....................800-237-6628

Pulverizers

Sugar

Glen Mills, Inc.
Clifton, NJ....................973-777-0777
Pro Scientific
Oxford, CT....................800-584-3776

Regenerators

Milk & Cream

Chester-Jensen Company, Inc.
Chester, PA....................800-685-3750

Rice Processing

Andritz
Muncy, PA....................570-546-8211
Grain Machinery Manufacturing Corporation
Miami, FL....................305-620-2525
Multi-Fill Inc
West Jordan, UT....................801-280-1570

Roasters

A.C. Horn & Co
Dallas, TX....................800-657-6155
Alumaworks
Sunny Isle Beach, FL....................800-277-7267
AMCO Corporation
City of Industry, CA....................626-855-2550
Browne & Company
Markham, ON....................905-475-6104
Commercial Dehydrator Systems Inc
Eugene, OR....................800-369-4283
Davron Technologies
Chattanooga, TN....................423-870-1888
Gourmet Coffee Roasters
Wixom, MI....................866-933-6300
Imperial Commercial Cooking Equipment
Corona, CA....................800-343-7790
Krispy Kist Company
Chicago, IL....................312-733-0900
National Drying Machinery Company
Philadelphia, PA....................215-464-6070
Star Manufacturing International
Saint Louis, MO....................800-264-7827
Superior Products Company
Saint Paul, MN....................800-328-9800
Sweet Manufacturing Company
Springfield, OH....................800-334-7254
Texas Corn Roasters
Granbury, TX....................800-772-4345
Unitherm Food Systems Innc.
Bristow, OK....................918-367-0197
Wolverine Proctor & Schwartz
Lexington, NC....................336-248-5181

Roasting

A.C. Horn & Co
Dallas, TX....................800-657-6155
Gourmet Coffee Roasters
Wixom, MI....................866-933-6300
Imperial Commercial Cooking Equipment
Corona, CA....................800-343-7790
Krispy Kist Company
Chicago, IL....................312-733-0900
Renato Specialty Product
Garland, TX....................866-575-6316

Sivetz Coffee
Corvallis, OR....................541-753-9713
Wolverine Proctor & Schwartz
Lexington, NC....................336-248-5181

Rotisseries

American Range & Hood Corporation
Pacoima, CA....................888-753-9898
Attias Oven Corporation
Brooklyn, NY....................800-928-8427
Aztec Grill
Dallas, TX....................800-346-8114
Ballantyne Food Service Equipment
Omaha, NE....................800-424-1215
Belson Outdoors
North Aurora, IL....................800-323-5664
BKI Worldwide
Simpsonville, SC....................800-927-6887
Broaster Company
Beloit, WI....................800-365-8278
Esquire Mechanical Corp.
Armonk, NY....................800-847-4206
Friedrich Metal ProductsCompany
Browns Summit, NC....................800-772-0326
Grillco
Aurora, IL....................800-644-0067
Hardt Equipment Manufacturing
Lachine, QC....................888-848-4408
Henny Penny, Inc.
Detroit, MI....................313-877-9550
Hickory Industries
North Bergen, NJ....................800-732-9153
J&R Manufacturing
Mesquite, TX....................800-527-4831
Merco/Savory
Mt. Pleasant, MI....................800-733-8821
Music City Metals
Nashville, TN....................800-251-2674
Remco Industries International
Fort Lauderdale, FL....................800-987-3626
Renato Specialty Product
Garland, TX....................866-575-6316
Roto-Flex Oven Company
San Antonio, TX....................877-859-1463
Shelcon
Ontario, CA....................909-947-4877
Southern Pride Distributing
Marion, IL....................800-851-8180
Super Systems
Wausau, WI....................800-558-5880
Superior Products Company
Saint Paul, MN....................800-328-9800
Toastmaster
Elgin, IL....................847-741-3300
Welbilt Corporation
Stamford, CT....................203-325-8300
Win-Holt Equipment Group
Westbury, NY....................800-444-3595
Wood Stone Corporation
Bellingham, WA....................800-988-8103

Salt Processing

A.C. Horn & Co
Dallas, TX....................800-657-6155
Viking Machine & Design
De Pere, WI....................888-286-2116

Sandwich Processing

APV Baker
Goldsboro, NC....................919-736-4309
Design Technology Corporation
Billerica, MA....................978-663-7000
Machine Builders and Design
Shelby, NC....................704-482-3456
Nuova Distribution Centre
Ferndale, WA....................360-366-2226
Peerless Food Equipment
Sidney, OH....................937-492-4158
Polar Process
Plattsville, ON....................877-896-8077

Saws

Butchers' Blades

Acraloc Corporation
Oak Ridge, TN....................865-483-1368
AEW Thurne
Lake Zurich, IL....................800-239-7297

Atlanta SharpTech
Peachtree City, GA ... 800-462-7297
Best & Donovan
Cincinnati, OH ... 800-553-2378
Biro Manufacturing Company
Marblehead, OH ... 419-798-4451
California Saw & Knife Works
San Francisco, CA ... 888-729-6533
Carter Products Company
Grand Rapids, MI ... 888-622-7837
Cass Saw & Tool Sharpening
Westmont, IL ... 630-968-1617
Eze Lap Diamond Products
Carson City, NV ... 800-843-4815
Haban Saw Company
St.Louis, MO ... 314-968-3991
Hollymatic Corporation
Countryside, IL ... 708-579-3700
Jarvis Products Corporation
Middletown, CT ... 860-347-7271
Kentmaster ManufacturingCompany
Monrovia, CA ... 800-421-1477
Mandeville Company
Minneapolis, MN ... 800-328-8490
PIECO, Inc.
Manchester, IA ... 800-334-3929
Simmons Engineering Corporation
Wheeling, IL ... 800-252-3381
Simonds International
Fitchburg, MA ... 800-343-1616
Specialty Saw
Simsbury, CT ... 800-225-0772

Scalers

Fish

Cretel Food Equipment
Holland, MI ... 616-786-3980
Fishmore
Melbourne,, FL ... 321-723-4751
Samuel Underberg
Brooklyn, NY ... 718-363-0787

Seafood Preparation Equipment

Alfa Laval
Newburyport, MA ... 978-465-5777
Buck Knives
Post Falls, ID ... 800-326-2825
Crane Research & Engineering Company
Hampton, VA ... 757-826-1707
Defreeze Corporation
Southborough, MA ... 508-485-8512
Design Technology Corporation
Billerica, MA ... 978-663-7000
E-Z Edge
West New York, NJ ... 800-232-4470
Fishmore
Melbourne,, FL ... 321-723-4751
Gregor Jonsson, Inc
Lake Forest, IL ... 847-831-2030
Kamflex Corporation
Chicago, IL ... 800-323-2440
Key Technology
Walla Walla, WA ... 509-529-2161
Mp Equip. Co.
Buford, GA ... 770-614-5355
Nieco Corporation
Windsor, CA ... 800-643-2656
Patty-O-Matic
Farmingdale, NJ ... 877-938-5244
Prawnto Systems
Caddo Mills, TX ... 800-426-7254
R. Murphy Company
Ayer, MA ... 888-772-3481
Simmons Engineering Corporation
Wheeling, IL ... 800-252-3381
Skrmetta Machinery Corporation
New Orleans, LA ... 504-488-4413
Smith-Berger Marine
Seattle, WA ... 206-764-4650
Steamway Corporation
Scottsburg, IN ... 800-259-8171
Stephen Paoli Manufacturing Corporation
Rockford, IL ... 815-965-0621
Stork Townsend Inc.
Des Moines, IA ... 800-247-8609
Superior Products Company
Saint Paul, MN ... 800-328-9800
Universal Stainless
Aurora, CO ... 800-223-8332
Universal Stainless
Titusville, PA ... 800-295-1909

Separators

Bean, Pea

A.C. Horn & Co
Dallas, TX ... 800-657-6155
A.K. Robins
Baltimore, MD ... 800-486-9656
Andritz
Muncy, PA ... 570-546-8211
Crippen Manufacturing Company
St. Louis, MI ... 800-872-2474
Hebeler Corporation
Tonawanda, NY ... 800-486-4709
Lewis M. Carter Manufacturing Company
Donalsonville, GA ... 229-524-2197
Lyco Manufacturing
Columbus, WI ... 920-623-4152
Magnetool
Troy, MI ... 248-588-5400
Pro Scientific
Oxford, CT ... 800-584-3776
Thomas Precision, Inc.
Rice Lake, WI ... 800-657-4808
TWM Manufacturing
Leamington, ON ... 888-495-4831

Grain, Flour Mill

A.T. Ferrell Company
Bluffton, IN ... 800-248-8318
Alfa Laval
Newburyport, MA ... 978-465-5777
Andritz
Muncy, PA ... 570-546-8211
Cleland Manufacturing Company
Columbia Heights, MN ... 763-571-4606
Crippen Manufacturing Company
St. Louis, MI ... 800-872-2474
Dehyco Company
Memphis, TN ... 901-774-3322
Eischen Enterprises
Fresno, CA ... 559-834-0013
Hebeler Corporation
Tonawanda, NY ... 800-486-4709
International Reserve Equipment Corporation
Clarendon Hills, IL ... 708-531-0680
Magnetic Products
Highland, MI ... 800-544-5930
Magnetool
Troy, MI ... 248-588-5400
Meadows Mills, Inc.
North Wilkesboro, NC ... 800-626-2282
Pro Scientific
Oxford, CT ... 800-584-3776
Southern Ag Company
Blakely, GA ... 229-723-4262
TWM Manufacturing
Leamington, ON ... 888-495-4831

Liquid-Solid

Abanaki Corporation
Chagrin Falls, OH ... 800-358-7546
AFL Industries
West Palm Beach, FL ... 800-807-2709
Alfa Laval
Newburyport, MA ... 978-465-5777
Alkota Cleaning Systems
Alcester, SD ... 800-255-6823
Alpha MOS
Hanover, MD ... 410-553-9736
Bird Machine Company
Houston, TX ... 800-229-7447
Bunting Magnetics Company
Newton, KS ... 800-835-2526
Chil-Con Products
Brantford, ON ... 800-263-0086
Compatible Components Corporation
Houston, TX ... 713-688-2008
Cook & Beals
Loup City, NE ... 308-745-0154
Dedert Corporation
Olympia Fields, IL ... 708-747-7000
Dings Company/Magnetic Group
Milwaukee, WI ... 414-672-7830
Enviro-Clear Company, Inc
High Bridge, NJ ... 908-638-5507
Everfilt Corporation
Mira Loma, CA ... 800-360-8380
Fernholtz Engineering
Van Nuys, CA ... 818-785-5800
Filtration Systems
Sunrise, FL ... 954-572-2700
French Oil Mill Machinery Company
Piqua, OH ... 937-773-3420
General Industries
Goldsboro, NC ... 888-735-2882
Globe International
Tacoma, WA ... 800-523-6575
Goodnature Products
Orchard Park, NY ... 800-875-3381
Hebeler Corporation
Tonawanda, NY ... 800-486-4709
Hosokawa/Bepex Corporation
Santa Rosa, CA ... 707-586-6000
Jay R. Smith Manufacturing Company
Montgomery, AL ... 334-277-8520
Lyco Manufacturing
Columbus, WI ... 920-623-4152
Membrane Process & Controls
Edgar, WI ... 715-352-3206
Membrane System Specialists
Wisconsin Rapids, WI ... 715-421-2333
Monroe Environmental Corporation
Monroe, MI ... 800-992-7707
Pacific Process Technology
La Jolla, CA ... 858-551-3298
Pall Filtron
Northborough, MA ... 800-345-8766
Pro Scientific
Oxford, CT ... 800-584-3776
Provisur Technologies
Mokena, IL ... 708-479-3500
Relco Unisystems Corporation
Willmar, MN ... 320-231-2210
Scienco Systems
Saint Louis, MO ... 314-621-2536
Sermia International
Blainville, QC ... 800-567-7483
Statco Engineering & Fabricators
Huntington Beach, CA ... 800-421-0362
SWECO
Florence, KY ... 800-807-9326
Tema Systems
Cincinnati, OH ... 513-489-7811
TWM Manufacturing
Leamington, ON ... 888-495-4831
Ultrafilter
Norcross, GA ... 800-543-3634
Van Air Systems
Lake City, PA ... 800-840-9906
Vincent Corporation
Tampa, FL ... 813-248-2650
Waterlink/Sanborn Technologies
Canton, OH ... 800-343-3381
Welliver Metal Products Corporation
Salem, OR ... 503-362-1568
Westfalia Separator
Northvale, NJ ... 800-722-6622

Shish Kebab Systems

Automated Food Systems
Waxahachie, TX ... 972-298-5719
Wishbone Utensil Tableware Line
Wheat Ridge, CO ... 866-266-5928

Shredders

Cane

Silver Weibull
Aurora, CO ... 303-373-2311

Cheese

Corenco
Santa Rosa, CA ... 888-267-3626
Deville Technologies
St Laurent, QC ... 866-404-4545
Reiser
Canton, MA ... 781-575-9941

Corn & Fodder

Dito Dean Food Prep
Rocklin, CA ... 800-331-7958
Grote Company
Columbus, OH ... 888-534-7683

Vegetable & Fruit

Corenco
Santa Rosa, CA 888-267-3626
Globe International
Tacoma, WA 800-523-6575
Goodnature Products
Orchard Park, NY 800-875-3381
Paxton Corporation
Bristol, RI
Reiser
Canton, MA 781-575-9941
Rival Manufacturing Company
Kansas City, MO 816-943-4100
Superior Products Company
Saint Paul, MN 800-328-9800
Univex Corporation
Salem, NH 800-258-6358

Shrimp Processing Equipment

Steamway Corporation
Scottsburg, IN 800-259-8171
Tri-Pak Machinery, Inc.
Harlingen, TX 956-423-5140

Skinning

Cretel Food Equipment
Holland, MI 616-786-3980
Grasselli SSI
Throop, PA 800-789-4353
MTC Food Equipment
Poulsbo, WA 360-697-6319

Slicers

Bread & Cake

ABI Limited
Concord, ON 800-297-8666
Am-Mac Incorporated
Fairfield, NJ 800-829-2018
American Eagle Food Machinery
Chicago, IL 800-836-5756
AMF CANADA
Sherbrooke, QC 800-255-3869
Bettendorf Stanford
Salem, IL 800-548-2253
C&K Machine Company
Holyoke, MA 413-536-8122
Chicago Scale & Slicer Company
Franklin Park, IL 847-455-3400
Clayton Manufacturing Company
Derby, NY 716-549-0392
Deluxe Equipment Company
Bradenton, FL 800-367-8931
DoughXpress
Pittsburg, KS 800-835-0606
Empire Bakery Equipment
Hicksville, NY 800-878-4070
FoodTools
Santa Barbara, CA 877-836-6386
Good Idea
Northampton, MA 800-462-9237
Grote Company
Columbus, OH 888-534-7683
Hansaloy Corporation
Davenport, IA 800-553-4992
Hobart Corporation
Troy, OH 888-446-2278
Knott Slicers
Canton, MA 781-821-0925
LeMatic
Jackson, MI 517-787-3301
SOCO System
Waukesha, WI 800-441-6293
Solbern
Fairfield, NJ 973-227-3030
Steinmetz Machine Works
Stamford, CT 203-327-0118
Toronto Kitchen Equipment
North York, ON 416-745-4944
United Bakery Equipment Company
Shawnee Mission, KS 913-541-8700
Waring Products
Torrington, CT 800-492-7464

Egg

Acme International
Maplewood, NJ 973-416-0400
AMCO Corporation
City of Industry, CA 626-855-2550
Grote Company
Columbus, OH 888-534-7683
Hobart Corporation
Troy, OH 888-446-2278
Polar Process
Plattsville, ON 877-896-8077
Superior Products Company
Saint Paul, MN 800-328-9800

Meat

AEW Thurne
Lake Zurich, IL 800-239-7297
Am-Mac Incorporated
Fairfield, NJ 800-829-2018
Automated Food Systems
Waxahachie, TX 972-298-5719
Bettcher Industries
Birmingham, OH 800-321-8763
Biro Manufacturing Company
Marblehead, OH 419-798-4451
Bizerba USA
Piscataway, NJ 732-565-6000
Blakeslee, Inc.
Addison, IL 630-532-5021
Bridge Machine Company
Palmyra, NJ 856-829-1800
Browne & Company
Markham, ON 905-475-6104
Chicago Scale & Slicer Company
Franklin Park, IL 847-455-3400
Edlund Company Inc
Burlington, VT 800-772-2126
Formax/Provisur Technologies
Mokena, IL 708-479-3500
General Machinery Corporation
Sheboygan, WI 888-243-6622
General, Inc
Weston, FL 954-202-7419
Globe Food Equipment Company
Dayton, OH 800-347-5423
Grasselli SSI
Throop, PA 800-789-4353
Grote Company
Columbus, OH 888-534-7683
Handtmann, Inc.
Lake Forest, IL 800-477-3585
Hobart Corporation
Troy, OH 888-446-2278
I. Fm Usa Inc.
Franklin Park, IL 866-643-6872
Kasel Associated Industries
Denver, CO 800-218-4417
Machanix Fabrication
Chino, CA 800-700-9701
Mandeville Company
Minneapolis, MN 800-328-8490
Marlen International
Astoria, OR 800-862-7536
MTC Food Equipment
Poulsbo, WA 360-697-6319
Planet Products Corporation
Blue Ash, OH 513-984-5544
Prince Castle
Carol Stream, IL 800-722-7853
Quantum Topping Systems Quantum Technical Services Inc
Frankfort, IL 888-464-1540
Reiser
Canton, MA 781-575-9941
Ross Industries
Midland, VA 800-336-6010
Spiral Slices Ham Market
Detroit, MI 313-259-6262
Spirocut Equipment
Fort Worth, TX 888-887-4267
Standex International Corporation
Salem, NH 603-893-9701
STARMIX srl
Marano, VI 044- 57- 659
Superior Products Company
Saint Paul, MN 800-328-9800
Toronto Kitchen Equipment
North York, ON 416-745-4944
TWM Manufacturing
Leamington, ON 888-495-4831
Univex Corporation
Salem, NH 800-258-6358
Waring Products
Torrington, CT 800-492-7464
Weber Inc.
Kansas City, MO 800-505-9591
Weber North America
Kansas City, MO 816-891-0072

Vegetable & Fruit

A.K. Robins
Baltimore, MD 800-486-9656
Am-Mac Incorporated
Fairfield, NJ 800-829-2018
Ashlock Company
San Leandro, CA 510-351-0560
Atlas Pacific Engineering Company
Pueblo, CO 719-948-3040
Automated Food Systems
Waxahachie, TX 972-298-5719
Blakeslee, Inc.
Addison, IL 630-532-5021
Bluffton Slaw Cutter Company
Bluffton, OH 419-358-9840
Brothers Metal Products
Santa Ana, CA 714-972-3008
C.M. Slicechief Company, Inc.
Toledo, OH 419-241-7647
Chicago Scale & Slicer Company
Franklin Park, IL 847-455-3400
Dito Dean Food Prep
Rocklin, CA 800-331-7958
Edlund Company Inc
Burlington, VT 800-772-2126
F.B. Pease Company
Rochester, NY 585-475-1870
General, Inc
Weston, FL 954-202-7419
Goodnature Products
Orchard Park, NY 800-875-3381
Grote Company
Columbus, OH 888-534-7683
Hobart Corporation
Troy, OH 888-446-2278
Insinger Machine Company
Philadelphia, PA 800-344-4802
International Knife & Saw
Florence, SC 800-354-9872
Keen Kutter
Torrance, CA 310-370-6941
Knott Slicers
Canton, MA 781-821-0925
Lincoln Foodservice
Cleveland, OH 800-374-3004
Machanix Fabrication
Chino, CA 800-700-9701
Mandeville Company
Minneapolis, MN 800-328-8490
Mannhart
Fort Worth, TX 817-421-0100
Matfer
Van Nuys, CA 800-766-0333
Nemco Food Equipment
Hicksville, OH 800-782-6761
Paxton Corporation
Bristol, RI
Prince Castle
Carol Stream, IL 800-722-7853
Reiser
Canton, MA 781-575-9941
Rival Manufacturing Company
Kansas City, MO 816-943-4100
South Valley Manufacturing
Gilroy, CA 408-842-5457
Stafford - Smith
Kalamazoo, MI 800-968-2442
Superior Products Company
Saint Paul, MN 800-328-9800
Toronto Kitchen Equipment
North York, ON 416-745-4944
TWM Manufacturing
Leamington, ON 888-495-4831
Univex Corporation
Salem, NH 800-258-6358
Urschel Laboratories
Valparaiso, IN 219-464-4811
Waring Products
Torrington, CT 800-492-7464

Smokers

Fish, Meat & Produce

Alto-Shaam
Menomonee Falls, WI 800-558-8744
Backwoods Smoker
Shreveport, LA 318-220-0380

Ballantyne Food Service Equipment
Omaha, NE 800-424-1215
BBQ Pits by Klose
Houston, TX 800-487-7487
Brinkmann Corporation
Dallas, TX 800-468-5252
Britt's Barbecue
Birmingham, AL 205-612-6538
Cookshack
Ponca City, OK 800-423-0698
Custom Diamond International
Laval, QC 800-326-5926
Friedrich Metal ProductsCompany
Browns Summit, NC 800-772-0326
Gregg
Waunakee, WI 608-846-5143
Jensen Luhr & Sons
Hood River, OR 541-386-3811
Le Smoker
Salisbury, MD 410-677-3233
Masterbuilt Manufacturing
Columbus, GA 800-489-1581
Reiser
Canton, MA 781-575-9941
Roto-Flex Oven Company
San Antonio, TX 877-859-1463
Seven B Plus
Sandy, OR 503-668-5079
Smokaroma
Boley, OK 800-331-5565
Southern Pride Distributing
Marion, IL 800-851-8180
Super Cooker
Lake Park, GA 800-841-7452
Superior Products Company
Saint Paul, MN 800-328-9800
Town Food Service Equipment Company
Brooklyn, NY 800-221-5032
Traeger Industries
Mount Angel, OR 800-872-3437
Unitherm Food Systems Innc.
Bristow, OK 918-367-0197
Vortron Smokehouse/Ovens
Iron Ridge, WI 800-874-1949
Win-Holt Equipment Group
Westbury, NY 800-444-3595

Sawdust

American Wood Fibers
Columbia, MD 800-624-9663
Northeastern Products Corporation
Warrensburg, NY 800-873-8233
West Oregon Wood Products
Columbia City, OR 503-397-6707

Snack Food Processing

A&B Process Systems
Stratford, WI 888-258-2789
A.C. Horn & Co
Dallas, TX 800-657-6155
Automated Food Systems
Waxahachie, TX 972-298-5719
Berkshire PPM
Litchfield, CT 860-567-3118
Coperion Corporation
Ramsey, NJ 201-327-6300
Design Technology Corporation
Billerica, MA 978-663-7000
E.T. Oakes Corporation
Hauppauge, NY 631-232-0002
Food Machinery Sales
Bogart, GA 706-549-2207
Formost Packaging Machines
Woodinville, WA 425-483-9090
Graybill Machines
Lititz, PA 717-626-5221
Industrial Products Corporation
Ho Ho Kus, NJ 800-472-5913
J.C. Ford Company
La Habra, CA 714-871-7361
Kamflex Corporation
Chicago, IL 800-323-2440
Krispy Kist Company
Chicago, IL 312-733-0900
Lanly Company
Cleveland, OH 216-731-1115
Oshikiri Corporation of America
Philadelphia, PA 215-637-6005
Pavan USA, Inc.
Emigsville, PA 717-767-4889
Peerless Dough Mixing and Make-Up
Sidney, OH 800-999-3327
Polar Process
Plattsville, ON 877-896-8077
Pro Bake
Twinsburg, OH 800-837-4427
Reading Bakery Systems
Robesonia, PA 610-693-5816
Reiser
Canton, MA 781-575-9941
Stephan Machinery, Inc.
Mundelein, IL 800-783-7426
Superior Food Machinery
Pico Rivera, CA 800-944-0396
UniTrak Corporation
Port Hope, ON 866-883-5749
US Tsubaki
Wheeling, IL 800-323-7790
Wolverine Proctor & Schwartz
Lexington, NC 336-248-5181
Woody Associates
York, PA 717-843-3975

Sorters

Bean & Grain

A.K. Robins
Baltimore, MD 800-486-9656
OXBO International Corporation
Clear Lake, WI 800-628-6196
Sortex
Fremont, CA 510-797-5000
Welliver Metal Products Corporation
Salem, OR 503-362-1568

Potato & Onion

A.K. Robins
Baltimore, MD 800-486-9656
Andgar Corporation
Ferndale, WA 360-366-9900
Atlas Pacific Engineering Company
Pueblo, CO 719-948-3040
Odenberg Engineering
West Sacramento, CA 800-688-8396
Southern Automatics
Lakeland, FL 800-441-4604
Welliver Metal Products Corporation
Salem, OR 503-362-1568

Soybean Processing

A.K. Robins
Baltimore, MD 800-486-9656
Andritz
Muncy, PA 570-546-8211
Bean Machines
Sonoma, CA 707-996-0706
Corenco
Santa Rosa, CA 888-267-3626
Insta Pro International
Des Moines, IA 800-383-4524
Wolverine Proctor & Schwartz
Lexington, NC 336-248-5181

Stemmers

Healdsburg Machine Company
Santa Rosa, CA 707-433-3348

Stoves

AK Steel
West Chester, OH 800-331-5050
American Range & Hood Corporation
Pacoima, CA 888-753-9898
Connerton Company
Santa Ana, CA 714-547-9218
Dynamic Cooking Systems
Huntington Beach, CA 800-433-8466
Gold Star Products
Oak Park, MI 800-800-0205
House of Webster
Rogers, AR 800-369-4641
Imperial Commercial Cooking Equipment
Corona, CA 800-343-7790
Iwatani International Corporation of America
Houston, TX 800-775-5506
Krispy Kist Company
Chicago, IL 312-733-0900
Maytag Corporation
Benton Harbor, MI 800-344-1274
Mosshaim Innovations
Jacksonville, FL 888-995-7775
Mountain Safety Research
Seattle, WA 800-877-9677
Mr. Bar-B-Q
Old Bethpage, NY 800-333-2124
Savage Brothers Company
Elk Grove Vlg, IL 800-342-0973
Seidman Brothers
Chelsea, MA 800-437-7770
Superior Products Company
Saint Paul, MN 800-328-9800
Toronto Kitchen Equipment
North York, ON 416-745-4944
Town Food Service Equipment Company
Brooklyn, NY 800-221-5032

Stuffers

Sausage

Biro Manufacturing Company
Marblehead, OH 419-798-4451
Famco Automatic Sausage Linkers
Pittsburgh, PA 412-241-6410
Friedr Dick Corporation
Farmingdale, NY 800-554-3425
Handtmann, Inc.
Lake Forest, IL 800-477-3585
Hitec Food Equip. Inc.
Wood Dale, IL 630-521-9460
Marlen
Riverside, MO 913-888-3333
Polar Process
Plattsville, ON 877-896-8077
Reiser
Canton, MA 781-575-9941
Stork Townsend Inc.
Des Moines, IA 800-247-8609

Sugar & Syrup Processing

Alfa Laval
Newburyport, MA 978-465-5777
Broussard Cane Equipment
Parks, LA 337-845-5080
Custom Food Machinery
Stockton, CA 209-463-4343
HONIRON Corporation
Jeanerette, LA 337-276-6314
Mulligan Associates
Mequon, WI 800-627-2886
Putsch
Asheville, NC 800-847-8427
Raytheon Company
Waltham, MA 617-522-3000
Silver Weibull
Aurora, CO 303-373-2311
Vendome Copper & Brass Works
Louisville, KY 888-384-5161

Tanks

Creamery, Dairy

A&B Process Systems
Stratford, WI 888-258-2789
Bowers Process Equipment
Stratford, ON 800-567-3223
C.E. Rogers Company
Mora, MN 800-279-8081
Chester-Jensen Company, Inc.
Chester, PA 800-685-3750
DCI
St Cloud, MN 320-252-8200
Diversified Metal Engineering
Charlottetown, PE 902-628-6900
Eischen Enterprises
Fresno, CA 559-834-0013
Electrol Specialties Company
South Beloit, IL 815-389-2291
Enerfab, Inc.
Cincinnati, OH 513-641-0500
Falco
La Prairie, CA 450-444-0566
Falco Technologies
La Prairie, QC 450-444-0566
Feldmeier Equipment
Syracuse, NY 315-454-8608
Howard Fabrication
City of Industry, CA 626-961-0114
Lee Industries Fluid Transfer
Philipsburg, PA 814-342-0802

Midwest Stainless
Menomonie, WI 715-235-5472
Northland Process Piping
Isle, MN 320-679-2119
Packaging & Processing Equipment
Ayr, ON 519-622-6666
Paul Mueller Company
Springfield, MO 800-683-5537
Puritan Manufacturing
Omaha, NE 800-331-0487
Rosenwach Tank Company
Long Island City, NY 718-729-4900
Sanchelima International
Doral, FL 305-591-4343
Sanifab
Stratford, WI 715-687-4332
Scherping Systems
Winsted, MN 320-485-4401
Schlueter Company
Janesville, WI 800-359-1700
Sharpsville Container
Sharpsville, PA 800-645-1248
Stainless Fabrication
Springfield, MO 800-397-8265
Viatec
Hastings, MI 800-942-4702
Walker Stainless Equipment
New Lisbon, WI 800-356-5734

Drying, Evaporating

A&B Process Systems
Stratford, WI 888-258-2789
Behlen Mfg. Co.
Columbus, NE 402-564-3111
DCI
St Cloud, MN 320-252-8200
Electrol Specialties Company
South Beloit, IL 815-389-2291
Ellett Industries
Port Coquitlam, BC 604-941-8211
Falco Technologies
La Prairie, QC 450-444-0566
Gaston County Dyeing Machine Company
Stanley, NC 704-822-5000
Northland Process Piping
Isle, MN 320-679-2119
Packaging & Processing Equipment
Ayr, ON 519-622-6666
Paget Equipment Company
Marshfield, WI 715-384-3158
Pittsburgh Tank Corporation
Monongahela, PA 800-634-0243
Sharpsville Container
Sharpsville, PA 800-645-1248
Stainless Fabrication
Springfield, MO 800-397-8265

Washers & Fillers

ABCO Automation
Browns Summit, NC 336-375-6400

Toasters

APW Wyott Food Service Equipment Company
Cheyenne, WY 800-527-2100
Attias Oven Corporation
Brooklyn, NY 800-928-8427
HATCO Corporation
Milwaukee, WI 800-558-0607
Holman Cooking Equipment
Saint Louis, MO 888-356-5362
Machanix Fabrication
Chino, CA 800-700-9701
Merco/Savory
Mt. Pleasant, MI 800-733-8821
Middleby Corporation
Elgin, IL 847-741-3300
Middleby Marshall, CTX
Elgin, IL 800-323-5575
Prince Castle
Carol Stream, IL 800-722-7853
Roundup Food Equipment
Carol Stream, IL 800-253-2991
Superior Products Company
Saint Paul, MN 800-328-9800
Toastmaster
Elgin, IL 847-741-3300
Welbilt Corporation
Stamford, CT 203-325-8300

Tortilla Making

Alliance Bakery Systems
Blythewood, SC 803-691-9227
Baking Machines
Livermore, CA 925-449-3369
BE & SCO
San Antonio, TX 800-683-0928
Bettendorf Stanford
Salem, IL 800-548-2253
Burford Corporation
Maysville, OK 877-287-3673
Casa Herrera
Pomona, CA 800-624-3916
Christy Machine Company
Fremont, OH 888-332-6451
Design Technology Corporation
Billerica, MA 978-663-7000
Dutchess Bakers' Machinery Company
Superior, WI 800-777-4498
FoodTools
Santa Barbara, CA 877-836-6386
Formost Packaging Machines
Woodinville, WA 425-483-9090
Gemini Bakery Equipment Company
Philadelphia, PA 800-468-9046
IJ White Corporation
Farmingdale, NY 631-293-2211
J.C. Ford Company
La Habra, CA 714-871-7361
KB Systems Baking Machinery Design Company
Bangor, PA 610-588-7788
Lanly Company
Cleveland, OH 216-731-1115
Lawrence Equipment
South El Monte, CA 800-423-4500
Maddox/Adams International
Miami, FL 305-592-3337
Peerless Dough Mixing and Make-Up
Sidney, OH 800-999-3327
Peerless Food Inc
Sidney, OH 937-494-2870
Pinckney Molded Plastics
Howell, MI 800-854-2920
Proluxe
Paramount, CA 800-594-5528
Rademaker USA
Hudson, OH 330-650-2345
Rheon USA
Huntersville, NC 704-875-9191
Shick Tube-Veyor Corporation
Kansas City, MO 816-861-7224
SOCO System
Waukesha, WI 800-441-6293
Stephan Machinery, Inc.
Mundelein, IL 800-783-7426
Superior Food Machinery
Pico Rivera, CA 800-944-0396
Wolverine Proctor & Schwartz
Lexington, NC 336-248-5181
X-Press Manufacturing
New Braunfels, TX 830-629-2651

VOC Control

Anguil Environmental Systems
Milwaukee, WI 800-488-0230
Dennis Group
Springfield, MA 413-787-1785
Lyco Manufacturing
Wausau, WI 715-845-7867

Vats

Cheese

Relco Unisystems Corporation
Willmar, MN 320-231-2210

Dairy Cooling

Relco Unisystems Corporation
Willmar, MN 320-231-2210

Meat Curing

DC Tech
Kansas City, MO 877-742-9090
Dubuque Steel Products Company
Dubuque, IA 563-556-6288

Vegetable Preparation Equipment

A.K. Robins
Baltimore, MD 800-486-9656
Altman Industries
Gray, GA 478-986-3116
Berkshire PPM
Litchfield, CT 860-567-3118
Bluffton Slaw Cutter Company
Bluffton, OH 419-358-9840
Brothers Metal Products
Santa Ana, CA 714-972-3008
Brown International Corporation
Winter Haven, FL 626-966-8361
Computer Controlled Machines
Pueblo, CO 719-948-9500
Design Technology Corporation
Billerica, MA 978-663-7000
Diversified Metal Engineering
Charlottetown, PE 902-628-6900
Eurodib
Champlain, NY 888-956-6866
F. Harold Haines Manufacturing
Presque Isle, ME 207-762-1411
French Oil Mill Machinery Company
Piqua, OH 937-773-3420
General, Inc
Weston, FL 954-202-7419
Globe International
Tacoma, WA 800-523-6575
Goodnature Products
Orchard Park, NY 800-875-3381
Hobart Corporation
Troy, OH 888-446-2278
Hughes Equipment Company LLC
Columbus, WI 866-535-9303
Keen Kutter
Torrance, CA 310-370-6941
Kerian Machines
Grafton, ND 701-352-0480
Key Technology
Walla Walla, WA 509-529-2161
Knott Slicers
Canton, MA 781-821-0925
Kusel Equipment Company
Watertown, WI 920-261-4112
Lee Financial Corporation
Dallas, TX 972-960-1001
Mannhart
Fort Worth, TX 817-421-0100
Matfer
Van Nuys, CA 800-766-0333
Mumper Machine Corporation
Butler, WI 262-781-8908
Murotech Corporation
Torrance, CA 800-565-6876
Nemco Food Equipment
Hicksville, OH 800-782-6761
Odenberg Engineering
West Sacramento, CA 800-688-8396
Oxo International
New York, NY 800-545-4411
Patty-O-Matic
Farmingdale, NJ 877-938-5244
Paxton Corporation
Bristol, RI
Pick Heaters
West Bend, WI 800-233-9030
Power Brushes, Inc
Toledo, OH 800-968-9600
Prince Castle
Carol Stream, IL 800-722-7853
Reiser
Canton, MA 781-575-9941
Simmons Engineering Corporation
Wheeling, IL 800-252-3381
South Valley Manufacturing
Gilroy, CA 408-842-5457
Superior Products Company
Saint Paul, MN 800-328-9800
Taylor Manufacturing Company
Moultrie, GA 229-985-5445
Univex Corporation
Salem, NH 800-258-6358
Urschel Laboratories
Valparaiso, IN 219-464-4811
Vanmark Corporation
Creston, IA 800-523-6261

Vegetable Processing

A.K. Robins
Baltimore, MD 800-486-9656

ABCO Industries Limited
Lunenburg, NS 866-634-8821
Altman Industries
Gray, GA 478-986-3116
Am-Mac Incorporated
Fairfield, NJ 800-829-2018
Ametek Technical & Industrial Products
Kent, OH 215-256-6601
Andgar Corporation
Ferndale, WA 360-366-9900
Berkshire PPM
Litchfield, CT 860-567-3118
Brown International Corporation
Winter Haven, FL 626-966-8361
C.M. Slicechief Company, Inc.
Toledo, OH 419-241-7647
Computer Controlled Machines
Pueblo, CO 719-948-9500
Corenco
Santa Rosa, CA 888-267-3626
Custom Food Machinery
Stockton, CA 209-463-4343
Dipwell Company
Northampton, MA 413-587-4673
Dito Dean Food Prep
Rocklin, CA 800-331-7958
Diversified Metal Engineering
Charlottetown, PE 902-628-6900
Dixie Canner Company
Athens, GA 706-549-1914
F. Harold Haines Manufacturing
Presque Isle, ME 207-762-1411
F.B. Pease Company
Rochester, NY 585-475-1870
Franrica Systems
Stockton, CA 209-948-2811
Globe International
Tacoma, WA 800-523-6575
Goodnature Products
Orchard Park, NY 800-875-3381
Hughes Equipment Company LLC
Columbus, WI 866-535-9303
Kerian Machines
Grafton, ND 701-352-0480
Key Technology
Walla Walla, WA 509-529-2161
Kusel Equipment Company
Watertown, WI 920-261-4112
Lyco Wausau
Wausau, WI 715-845-7867
Mannhart
Fort Worth, TX 817-421-0100
Mouli Manufacturing Corporation
Belleville, NJ 800-789-8285
Multi-Fill Inc
West Jordan, UT 801-280-1570
Mumper Machine Corporation
Butler, WI 262-781-8908
Murotech Corporation
Torrance, CA 800-565-6876
Nemco Food Equipment
Hicksville, OH 800-782-6761
Paxton Corporation
Bristol, RI
Paxton Products
Cincinnati, OH 800-441-7475
Reiser
Canton, MA 781-575-9941
Semco Manufacturing Company
Pharr, TX 956-787-4203
Taylor Manufacturing Company
Moultrie, GA 229-985-5445
Tew Manufacturing Corporation
Penfield, NY 800-380-5839
UniTrak Corporation
Port Hope, ON 866-883-5749
Urschel Laboratories
Valparaiso, IN 219-464-4811
Vanmark Corporation
Creston, IA 800-523-6261
Wolverine Proctor & Schwartz
Lexington, NC 336-248-5181

Vibrators

MeGa Industries
Burlington, ON 800-665-6342

Waffle Irons

Superior Products Company
Saint Paul, MN 800-328-9800

Washers

Fruit & Vegetable

A.K. Robins
Baltimore, MD 800-486-9656
Atlas Pacific Engineering Company
Pueblo, CO 719-948-3040
Berkshire PPM
Litchfield, CT 860-567-3118
Brogdex Company
Pomona, CA 909-622-1021
Davron Technologies
Chattanooga, TN 423-870-1888
F. Harold Haines Manufacturing
Presque Isle, ME 207-762-1411
Globe International
Tacoma, WA 800-523-6575
Goodnature Products
Orchard Park, NY 800-875-3381
Hughes Equipment Company LLC
Columbus, WI 866-535-9303
Key Technology
Walla Walla, WA 509-529-2161
Leon C. Osborn Company
Houston, TX 281-488-0755
N&A Manufacturing Spraymatic Sprayers
Mallard, IA 712-425-3512
Tew Manufacturing Corporation
Penfield, NY 800-380-5839
Tri-Pak Machinery, Inc.
Harlingen, TX 956-423-5140
Vanmark Corporation
Creston, IA 800-523-6261

Waxers

International Wax Refining Company
Warren, NJ 908-561-2500
Sandvik Process Systems
Totowa, NJ 973-790-1600

Waxing

Kent Company, Inc.
Miami, FL 800-521-4886
MAF Industries
Traver, CA 559-897-2905
Tri-Pak Machinery, Inc.
Harlingen, TX 956-423-5140

Yeast Processing

Alfa Laval
Newburyport, MA 978-465-5777
Sharp Brothers
Bayonne, NJ 201-339-0404
Tuchenhagen
Columbia, MD 410-910-6000
Vendome Copper & Brass Works
Louisville, KY 888-384-5161

Fruit Industry

Alard Equipment Corporation
Williamson, NY 315-589-4511
Ocs Checkweighers, Inc.
Snellville, GA 678-344-8030

Funnels

American Metalcraft
Melrose Park, IL 800-333-9133
Behrens Manufacturing Company
Winona, MN 507-454-4664
Jacob Tubing LP
Memphis, TN 901-566-1110
Kosempel Manufacturing Company
Philadelphia, PA 800-733-7122
Lorann Oils
Lansing, MI 800-862-8620
MO Industries
Whippany, NJ 973-386-9228
Southern Metal Fabricators
Albertville, AL 800-989-1330
Superior Products Company
Saint Paul, MN 800-328-9800
Tolco Corporation
Toledo, OH 800-537-4786
Wilks Precision Instrument Company
Union Bridge, MD 410-775-7917
World Kitchen
Elmira, NY 800-999-3436

Zeier Plastic & Manufacturing
Madison, WI 608-244-5782

Gas Connectors

Dormont Manufacturing Company
Export, PA 800-367-6668
Hose Master
Cleveland, OH 216-481-2020
Linde Gas LLC
Cleveland, OH 800-983-5615
Spraying Systems Company
Wheaton, IL 630-655-5000
Superior Products Company
Saint Paul, MN 800-328-9800

General

Alard Equipment Corporation
Williamson, NY 315-589-4511
ALLCAMS Machine Company
Folsom, PA 610-534-9004
Allied Purchasing Company
Mason City, IA 800-247-5956
Altra Industrial Motion
Braintree, MA 781-917-0600
American Conveyor Corporation
Astoria, NY 718-386-0480
AmeriVap Systems Inc
Dawsonville, GA 800-763-7687
Amsler Equipment Inc
Richmond Hill, ON, ON 877-738-2569
Annie's Frozen Yogurt
Eding, MN 800-969-9648
Automation Ideas Inc.
Rockford, MI 877-254-3327
Baldor Electric Company
Fort Smith, AR 479-646-4711
Boston Gear
Boston, MA 888-999-9860
Bunzl Processor Division
Dallas, TX 800-456-5624
Butler Winery
Bloomington, IN 812-332-6660
Carmel Engineering
Kirklin, IN 888-427-0497
Century Extrusion
Traverse City, MI 231-947-6400
Cipriani Harrison Valves
Rcho Sta Marg, CA 949-589-3978
Cold Jet LLC
Rancho Cucamonga, CA 800-777-9101
Ecolab, Inc
St Paul, MN 800-232-6522
Gates Mectrol
Salem, NH 800-394-4844
Ickler Machine Company
Saint Cloud, MN 800-243-8382
La Poblana Food Machines
Mesa, AZ 480-258-2091
Leeson Electric Corporation
Grafton, WI 262-377-8810
Lepel Corporation
Waukesha, WI 800-231-6008
Liburdi Group of Companies
Mooresville, NC 800-533-9353
Lumaco
Hackensack, NJ 800-735-8258
Material Handling Technology, Inc
Morrisville, NC 800-779-2475
Meltric Corporation
Franklin, WI 800-824-4031
Motoman
West Carrollton, OH 937-847-6200
Mountain States Processing & Rendering Equipment
Fort Lupton, CO 303-857-1060
Nigrelli Systems Inc
Kiel, WI 920-693-3161
Nijal USA
Minneapolis, MN 651-353-6702
PCM Delasco
Houston, TX 713-896-4888
Plymouth Tube Company
East Troy, WI 262-642-8201
Precision Plus Vacuum Parts
Sanborn, NY 800-526-2707
Quadro Engineering
Waterloo, ON 519-884-9660
Reiser
Canton, MA 781-575-9941
Rocheleau Blow Molding Systems
Fitchburg, MA 978-345-1723

Rockwell Automation
Milwaukee, WI 414-382-2000
Ryowa Company America
Elk Grove Village, IL 800-700-9692
Schneider Packing Equipment Company
Brewerton, NY 315-676-3035
Scrivner Equipment Company
Carthage, MS 601-267-7614
Septimatech Group
Waterloo, ON 888-777-6775
Serac
Carol Stream, IL 630-510-9343
Sick Inc.
Minneapolis, MN 800-325-7425
Specialty Food America
Hopkinsville, KY 888-881-1633
Spencer Strainer Systems
Jeffersonville, IN 800-801-4977
Stainless Motors Inc
Rio Rancho, NM 505-867-0224
Standard Pump
Auburn, GA 866-558-8611
Sterling Electric
Indianapolis, IN 800-654-6220
Strongarm
Horsham, PA 215-443-3400
Sundyne Corporation
Arvada, CO 303-425-0800
T-Drill Industries
Norcross, GA 800-554-2730
Technical Tool Solutions Inc.
Lake Forest, IL 847-235-5551
Tente Casters
Hebron, KY 800-783-2470
Uhrden
Sugarcreek, OH 800-852-2411
Ultra Process Systems
Oak Ridge, TN 865-483-2772
Unisource Manufacturing
Portland, OR 800-234-2566
Volumetric Technologies
Cannon Falls, MN 507-263-0034
World Water Works
Elmsford, NY 800-607-7873
Young & Associates
Kenosha, WI 262-657-6394

Heaters

Water

Alard Equipment Corporation
Williamson, NY 315-589-4511
Andgar Corporation
Ferndale, WA 360-366-9900
HATCO Corporation
Milwaukee, WI 800-558-0607
Hubbell Electric Heater Company
Stratford, CT 800-647-3165
PVI Industries
Fort Worth, TX 800-784-8326
QuikWater, Inc.
Sand Springs, OK 918-241-8880
Vanguard Technology
Eugene, OR 800-624-4809

Hose Reels

Hannay Reels
Westerlo, NY 877-467-3357
Kuriyama of America
Schaumburg, IL 800-800-0320
Reelcraft Industries
Columbia City, IN 800-444-3134
Unisource Manufacturing
Portland, OR 800-234-2566

Hoses

Beverage

Accuflex Industrial Hose
Romulus, MI 734-451-0080
Action Technology
Prussia, PA 217-935-8311
Alard Equipment Corporation
Williamson, NY 315-589-4511
Associated Industrial Rubber
Magna, UT 800-526-6288
Cardinal Rubber & Seal
Roanoke, VA 800-542-5737
Emco Industrial Plastics
Cedar Grove, NJ 800-292-9906
Nalge Process Technologies Group
Rochester, NY 585-586-8800
Parker Hannifin Corporation/Industrial Hose Products Division
Strongsville, OH 800-272-7537
Simolex Rubber Corporation
Plymouth, MI 734-453-4500
Superflex
Brooklyn, NY 800-394-3665
Superior Products Company
Saint Paul, MN 800-328-9800
Union Plastics Company
Marshville, NC 704-624-2112

Deep Fryer

Diebolt & Company
Old Lyme, CT 800-343-2658

Food Handling

Accuflex Industrial Hose
Romulus, MI 734-451-0080
Action Technology
Prussia, PA 217-935-8311
Baldewein Company
Lake Forrest, IL 800-424-5544
Cardinal Rubber & Seal
Roanoke, VA 800-542-5737
Emco Industrial Plastics
Cedar Grove, NJ 800-292-9906
FabWright, Inc
Garden Grove, CA 800-854-6464
Flex-Hose Company
East Syracuse, NY 315-437-1611
HBD Industries
Salisbury, NC 800-438-2312
Hoffmeyer Company
San Leandro, CA 800-350-2358
Home Rubber Company
Trenton, NJ 800-257-9441
Hydra-Flex
Livonia, MI 800-234-0832
Keystone Rubber Corporation
Greenbackville, VA 800-394-5661
L.C. Thompson Company
Kenosha, WI 800-558-4018
Nalge Process Technologies Group
Rochester, NY 585-586-8800
Parker Hannifin Corporation/Industrial Hose Products Division
Strongsville, OH 800-272-7537
Pure Fit
Allentown, PA 866-787-3348
Salem-Republic Rubber Company
Sebring, OH 800-686-4199
Sanitary Couplers
Springboro, OH 513-743-0144
Strahman Valves
Bethlehem, PA 877-787-2462
Superflex
Brooklyn, NY 800-394-3665
Union Plastics Company
Marshville, NC 704-624-2112
US Rubber Supply Company
Brooklyn, NY 718-782-7888
Vaughn Belting Company
Spartanburg, SC 800-325-3303
Watson-Marlow
Wilmington, MA 800-282-8823

Incubators & Brooders

Kuhl Corporation
Flemington, NJ 908-782-5696
National Hotpack
Stone Ridge, NY 800-431-8232
Pro Scientific
Oxford, CT 800-584-3776
Triad Scientific
Manasquan, NJ 800-867-6690

Load Cells & Indicators

Tedea-Huntliegh
Chatsworth, CA 800-423-5483

Lubricants

Industrial

Alex C. Fergusson
Chambersburg, PA 800-345-1329
Amsoil
Superior, WI 715-392-7101
Bel-Ray Company
Farmingdale, NJ 732-938-2421
Boyer Corporation
La Grange, IL 800-323-3040
Cantol
Markham, ON 800-387-9773
Cellier Corporation
Taunton, MA 508-655-5906
CRC Industries, Inc.
Warminster, PA 800-556-5074
Dow Corning Corporation
Midland, MI 989-496-4000
Haynes Manufacturing Company
Cleveland, OH 800-992-2166
Huskey Specialty Lubricants
Norco, CA 888-448-7539
KLS Lubriquip
Minneapolis, MN 612-623-6000
Kluber Lubrication NorthAmerica LP
Londonderry, NH 800-447-2238
Kurtz Oil Company
Winston Salem, NC 336-768-1515
Linker Machines
Rockaway, NJ 973-983-0001
Lubriplate Lubricants
Newark, NJ 800-733-4755
Lubriquip
Minneapolis, MN 800-USA-LUBE
Moly-XL Company
Westville, NJ 856-848-2880
Momar
Atlanta, GA 800-556-3967
National-Purity
Brooklyn Center, MN 612-672-0022
Rock Valley Oil & Chemical Company
Rockford, IL 815-654-2400
Sentinel Lubricants Corporation
Miami, FL 800-842-6400
Specialty Lubricants Corporation
Macedonia, OH 800-238-5823
Stoner
Quarryville, PA 800-227-5538
The Orelube Corporation
Bellport, NY 800-645-9124
Thermoil Corporation
Brooklyn, NY 718-855-0544
Tribology/Tech-Lube
Yaphank, NY 800-569-1757
US Industrial Lubricants
Cincinnati, OH 800-562-5454

Measures

Dry

Alard Equipment Corporation
Williamson, NY 315-589-4511
Frye's Measure Mill
Wilton, NH 603-654-6581
Optek-Danulat, Inc
Germantown, WI 888-551-4288

Mirrors

Convex

American Houver Company
Skokie, IL 800-772-0355
American Store Fixtures
Skokie, IL
Emco Industrial Plastics
Cedar Grove, NJ 800-292-9906
EMED Company
Buffalo, NY 800-442-3633
Mirror-Tech
Yonkers, NY 914-423-1600
Rosco, Inc
Jamaica, NY 800-227-2095
Se-Kure Controls
Franklin Park, IL 800-250-9260

Nozzles

Spray

Arthur Products Company
Medina, OH. 800-322-0510
Bete Fog Nozzle
Greenfield, MA. 800-235-0049
California Vibratory Feeders
Anaheim, CA 800-354-0972
Delavan Spray Technologies
Charlotte, NC 704-423-7000
Greenfield Packaging
White Plains, NY 914-993-0233
Lechler
St Charles, IL 800-777-2926
Paxton Products
Cincinnati, OH 800-441-7475
Sani-Matic
Madison, WI. 800-356-3300
Spraying Systems Company
Wheaton, IL 630-655-5000
Superior Products Company
Saint Paul, MN 800-328-9800
Viking Corporation
Hastings, MI. 800-968-9501

Openers

Bottle

AMCO Corporation
City of Industry, CA 626-855-2550
Brown Manufacturing Company
Decatur, GA 404-378-8311
Browne & Company
Markham, ON. 905-475-6104
C.R. Manufacturing
Waverly, NE 877-789-5844
Cleveland Metal StampingCompany
Berea, OH 440-234-0010
G.G. Greene Enterprises
Warren, PA 814-723-5700
Superior Products Company
Saint Paul, MN 800-328-9800

Box, Crate, Carton

Climax Packaging Machinery
Hamilton, OH 513-874-1233
Edson Packaging Machinery
Hamilton, ON 905-385-3201
Gulf Arizona Packaging
Humble, TX 800-364-3887
Innovative Marketing
Eden Prairie, MN 800-438-4627
Listo Pencil Corporation
Alameda, CA. 800-547-8648
Samuel Underberg
Brooklyn, NY 718-363-0787
Seal-O-Matic Company
Jacksonville, OR. 800-631-2072
Thiele Technologies
Reedley, CA 800-344-8951

Can

Berkshire PPM
Litchfield, CT 860-567-3118
C.R. Manufacturing
Waverly, NE 877-789-5844
CanPacific Engineering
Delta, BC. 604-946-1680
Dorton Incorporated
Arlington Hts, IL 800-299-8600
Edlund Company Inc
Burlington, VT 800-772-2126
G.G. Greene Enterprises
Warren, PA 814-723-5700
Langsenkamp Manufacturing
Indianapolis, IN 877-585-1950
Lincoln Foodservice
Cleveland, OH 800-374-3004
Morrison Timing Screw Company
Glenwood, IL 708-331-6600
Rival Manufacturing Company
Kansas City, MO. 816-943-4100
Swing-A-Way Manufacturing Company
St Louis, MO. 314-773-1488
Turner & Seymour Manufacturing
Torrington, CT 888-856-4864

Fruit Jar

Swing-A-Way Manufacturing Company
St Louis, MO. 314-773-1488

Packaging

A&M Industries
Sioux Falls, SD. 800-888-2615
A-B-C Packaging Machine Corporation
Tarpon Springs, FL 800-237-5975
A.B. Sealer, Inc.
Beaver Dam, WI. 877-885-9299
A.K. Robins
Baltimore, MD 800-486-9656
Aabbitt Adhesives
Chicago, IL 800-222-2488
AAMD
Liverpool, NY. 800-887-4167
Aaron Equipment Company
Bensenville, IL 630-350-2200
About Packaging Robotics
Thornton, CO 303-449-2559
Accu-Pak
Akron, OH 330-644- 301
Accumetric
Elizabethtown, KY 800-928-2677
Accurate Paper Box Company
Knoxville, TN 865-690-0311
Accutek Packaging Equipment Company
Vista, CA. 800-989-1828
Ace Technical Plastics
Hartford, CT 860-305-8138
Achilles USA
Everett, WA. 425-353-7000
ACMA/GD
Richmond, VA. 800-525-2735
Acraloc Corporation
Oak Ridge, TN 865-483-1368
Actionpac Scales & Automation
Oxnard, CA. 800-394-0154
Adco Manufacturing
Sanger, CA 559-875-5563
Adhesive Products, Inc.
Vernon, CA 800-669-5516
Adhesive Technologies
Hampton, NH 800-458-3486
ADM Corporation
Middlesex, NJ. 800-327-0718
AdPro
Solon, OH 440-542-1111
Advance Engineering Company
Township, MI 800-497-6388
Advance Weight Systems
Grafton, OH 440-926-3691
Advanced Poly-Packaging
Akron, OH. 800-754-4403
AEP Industries
South Hackensack, NJ 800-999-2374
Ag-Pak
Gasport, NY 716-772-2651
AGR International
Butler, PA 724-482-2163
Air Products and Chemicals
Allentown, PA. 800-654-4567
Air Technical Industries
Mentor, OH. 888-857-6265
Aladdin Transparent Packaging Corporation
Hauppauge, NY 631-273-4747
Alard Equipment Corporation
Williamson, NY 315-589-4511
Alcoa Foil Products
St Louis, MO. 314-481-7000
Alcoa Packaging Machinery
Randolph, NY. 716-358-6451
Alcon Packaging
Weston, ON. 416-742-8910
Alfa Production Systems
Westfield, NJ. 908-654-0255
Aline Heat Seal Corporation
Cerritos, CA 888-285-3917
All American Poly Corporation
Piscataway, NJ 800-526-3551
All Packaging Machinery Corporation
Ronkonkoma, NY. 800-637-8808
All Sorts Premium Packaging
Buffalo, NY. 888-565-9727
All-Fill
Exton, PA 866-255-4455
Alliance Rubber Corporation
Hot Springs National Par, AR 800-626-5940
Allied Graphics
St Michael, MN. 800-490-9931
Alloyd Brands
Dekalb, IL. 800-756-7639
Allpac
Dallas, TX. 214-630-8804
Amark Packaging Systems
Kansas City, MO. 816-965-9000
AMCO Products Company
Fort Smith, AR 479-646-8949
Amcor Flexibles - North America
Hagerstown, MD. 800-332-7928
American Bag & Burlap Company
Chelsea, MA 617-884-7600
American Excelsior Inc
Arlington, TX 800-777-7645
American Label Mark
Chicago, IL 800-621-5808
American Manufacturing &Engineering Company
Cleveland, OH 800-822-9402
American Printpak
Sussex, WI 800-441-8003
AmeriPak
Warrington, PA 215-343-1530
AmeriVacs
San Diego, CA
AMF Bakery Systems
Richmond, VA. 800-225-3771
AMF CANADA
Sherbrooke, QC 800-255-3869
Ampak
Cleveland, OH 800-342-6329
Amplas
Green Bay, WI. 800-950-4362
AMS Filling Systems
Glenmoore, PA 800-647-5390
Anderson Machine Sales
Fort Lee, NJ
Anderson Tool & Engineering Company
Anderson, IN. 765-643-6691
Andy Printed Products
Lagrangeville, NY 845-223-5101
Anver Corporation
Hudson, MA 800-654-3500
API
Tampa, FL. 813-888-8488
Applied Product Sales
Lilburn, GA. 650-218-3104
APS Packaging Systems
Fairfield, NJ 800-526-2276
Arthur G. Russell Company (The)
Bristol, CT 860-583-4109
Artistic Packaging Concepts
Massapequa Pk, NY 516-797-4020
ARY
Kansas City, MO. 800-821-7849
ASCENT Technics Corporation
Brick, NJ. 800-774-7077
Associated Packaging Equipment Corporation
Markham, ON. 905-475-6647
Astoria Laminations
Saint Clair Shores, MI 800-526-7325
Atlantic Foam & Packaging Company
Sanford, FL. 407-328-9444
Atlas Packaging & Displays Inc
Miami, FL. 800-662-0630
Atlas Tag & Label
Neenah, WI. 800-558-6418
Audion Automation
Carrollton, TX. 972-389-0777
Auger-Fabrication
Exton, PA 800-334-1529
Automated Packaging Systems
Streetsboro, OH 888-288-6224
Automated Production Systems Corporation
New Freedom, PA. 888-345-5377
Autoprod
Davenport, IA 563-391-1100
Avon Tape
Chestnut Hill, MA 508-584-8273
B&R Machine Inc.
Wedron, IL 815-434-0427
B-T Engineering
Bala Cynwyd, PA 610-664-9500
B.A.G. Corporation
Dallas, TX. 800-331-9200
BagcraftPapercon
Chicago, IL 800-621-8468
Baldwin Staub
San Bernardino, CA 909-799-9950
Balemaster
Crown Point, IN 219-663-4525
Barnes Machine Company
Saint Petersburg, FL 727-327-9452

Barrette - Outdoor Livin
Middleburg Hts., OH 800-336-2383
Batching Systems
Prince Frederick, MD 800-311-0851
Baur Tape & Label Company
San Antonio, TX. 877-738-3222
Bedford Industries
Worthington, MN 800-533-5314
BEI
St Charles, IL 630-879-0300
BEI
South Haven, MI. 800-364-7425
Bemis Company
Neenah, WI. 920-727-4100
Berlin Foundry & MachineCompany
Berlin, NH. 603-752-4550
Bernal, Inc
Rochester Hills, MI. 800-237-6251
Berry Plastics
Evansville, IN 800-234-1930
Bertek Systems
Georgia, VT 800-367-0210
Bettendorf Stanford
Salem, IL. 800-548-2253
Better Packages
Shelton, CT 800-237-9151
BH Bunn Company
Lakeland, FL. 800-222-2866
Biner Ellison
Vista, CA. 800-733-8162
Bivac Enterprise
Brick, NJ 732-920-0080
Black Brothers Company
Mendota, IL 800-252-2568
Blako Industries
Dunbridge, OH 419-833-4491
Blodgett Company
Houston, TX 281-933-6195
Blue Ridge Paper Products, Inc.
Canton, NC 828-454-0676
BluePrint Automation
Colonial Heights, VA 804-520-5400
BP Amoco
Naperville, IL 630-369-0128
Bradman Lake Inc
Rock Hill, SC 704-588-3301
Branson Ultrasonics Corporation
Danbury, CT 203-796-0400
Brechteen
Chesterfield, MI 586-949-2240
Brenton LLC
Alexandria, MN 800-535-2730
Brentwood Plastic Films
St Louis, MO. 314-968-1137
Brothers Metal Products
Santa Ana, CA 714-972-3008
Brown Machine
Beaverton, MI. 877-702-4142
Bulman Products Inc
Grand Rapids, MI 616-363-4416
Burghof Engineering & Manufacturing Company
Prairie View, IL. 847-634-0737
C&K Machine Company
Holyoke, MA 413-536-8122
C.J. Machine
Fridley, MN. 763-767-4630
California Vibratory Feeders
Anaheim, CA 800-354-0972
Campbell Wrapper Corporation
De Pere, WI. 800-727-4210
Campbell Wrapper Corporation
De Pere, WI. 920-983-7100
Can Creations
Pembroke Pines, FL 954-581-3312
Cannon Equipment Company
Rosemount, MN 800-825-8501
Cantech Industries
Johnson City, TN 800-654-3947
Capmatic, Ltd.
Monreal North, QC 514-332-0062
Carando Machine Works
Stockton, CA. 209-948-6500
Caraustar
Warrensville Heights, OH. 800-362-1125
Care Controls, Inc.
Mill Creek, WA. 800-593-6050
Carlisle Plastics
Minneapolis, MN 952-884-1309
Carpenter-Hayes Paper Box Company
East Hampton, CT. 203-267-4436
Carroll Packaging
Dearborn, MI 313-584-0400
Carroll Products
Garland, TX 800-527-5722
Carton Closing Company
Butler, PA 724-287-7759
Cartpac
Franklin Park, IL. 630-629-9900
Catty Corporation
Harvard, IL 815-943-2288
Cello Pack Corporation
Cheektowaga, NY 800-778-3111
Cellotape
Fremont, CA 800-231-0608
Central Bag & Burlap Company
Denver, CO 800-783-1224
Central Coated Products
Alliance, OH 330-821-9830
Central Fine Pack
Fort Wayne, IN 260-432-3027
Central Ohio Bag & Burlap
Columbus, OH 800-798-9405
Central Products Company
Menasha, WI. 800-558-5006
Chaffee Company
Rocklin, CA 916-630-3980
Chambers Container Company
Gastonia, NC. 704-377-6317
Champion Trading Corporation
Marlboro, NJ. 732-780-4200
Change Parts
Ludington, MI. 231-845-5107
Charles Beck Machine Corporation
King of Prussia, PA. 610-265-0500
Chase Industries
Carson, CA 310-763-9900
Chase-Logeman Corporation
Greensboro, NC 336-665-0754
Circle Packaging Machinery Inc
De Pere, WI. 920-983-3420
City Box Company
Aurora, IL 773-277-5500
CL&D Graphics
Oconomowoc, WI 800-777-1114
Clamco Corporation
Berea, OH 216-267-1911
Clark Stek-O Corporation
Bayonne, NJ 201-437-0770
Clayton Corporation
Fenton, MO. 800-729-8220
Clearwater Packaging
Clearwater, FL 800-299-2596
Cleveland Plastic Films
Elyria, OH. 800-832-6799
Cleveland Wire Cloth & Manufacturing Company
Cleveland, OH 800-321-3234
Climax Packaging Machinery
Hamilton, OH 513-874-1233
Cloud Corporation
Des Plaines, IL 847-390-9410
CMD Corporation
Appleton, WI 920-730-0930
CMS Gilbreth Packaging Systems
Croydon, PA 800-630-2413
Coastal Sleeve Label
Brunswick, GA 877-753-3837
Collector's Gallery
Saint Charles, IL. 800-346-3063
Colonial Transparent Products Company
Hicksville, NY 516-822-4430
Colter & Peterson
Paterson, NJ 973-684-0901
Columbia Labeling Machinery
Benton City, WA 888-791-9590
Columbus Container
Columbus, IN 812-376-9301
Combi Packaging Systems
Canton, OH 800-521-9072
Compacker Systems LLC
Davenport, IA 563-391-2751
Conflex, Inc.
Germantown, WI. 800-225-4296
Continental Packaging Corporation
Elgin, IL 847-289-6400
Contour Products
Kansas City, KS 800-638-3626
Control & Metering
Mississauga, ON. 800-736-5739
CoolBrands International
Ronkonkoma, NY 631-737-9700
Corfab
Chicago, IL 708-458-8750
Corrugated Inner-Pak Corporation
Conshohocken, PA 610-825-0200
Corrugated Packaging
Sarasota, FL 941-371-0000
Cortec Corporation
St. Paul, MN 800-426-7832
Coz Plastics
Dayville, CT 860-774-3770
Cozzoli Machine Company
Somerset, NJ 732-564-0400
CPT
Edgerton, WI. 608-884-2244
CR Plastics
Council Bluffs, IA. 866-869-6293
Crandall Filling Machinery
Buffalo, NY. 800-280-8551
Crayex Corporation
Piqua, OH 800-837-1747
Creative Automation
Passaic, NJ 973-778-0061
Creative Coatings Corporation
Nashua, NH. 800-229-1957
Creative Foam Corporation
Fenton, MI 810-629-4149
Crowell Corporation
Wilmington, DE 800-441-7525
Crown Simplimatic Company
Lynchburg, VA 434-582-1200
Crystal Creative Products
Middletown, OH 800-776-6762
Crystal-Flex Packaging Corporation
Rockville Centre, NY 888-246-7325
Crystal-Vision PackagingSystems
Torrance, CA. 800-331-3240
CSS International Corporation
Philadelphia, PA 800-278-8107
CTK Plastics
Moose Jaw, SK 800-667-8847
Cup Pac Contract PackageRs
South Beloit, IL 877-347-9725
Custom Card & Label Corporation
Lincoln Park, NJ. 973-492-0022
Custom Foam Molders
Foristell, MO. 636-441-2307
Custom Food Machinery
Stockton, CA. 209-463-4343
Custom Metal Designs
Oakland, FL 800-334-1777
Customized Equipment SE
Tucker, GA 770-934-9300
CVP Systems
Downers Grove, IL 800-422-4720
Cyro Industries/Degussa
Parsippany, NJ. 800-631-5384
D & L Manufacturing
Milwaukee, WI 414-256-8160
Dacam Corporation
Madison Heights, VA 434-929-4001
Dacam Machinery
Madison Heights, VA 434-369-1259
Dalemark Industries
Lakewood, NJ. 732-367-3100
Danafilms
Westborough, MA. 508-366-8884
Data Scale
Fremont, CA 800-651-7350
Davis Core & Pad Company
Cave Spring, GA. 800-235-7483
Decko Products
Sandusky, OH 800-537-6143
Dehyco Company
Memphis, TN 901-774-3322
Delta Cyklop Orga Pac
Charlotte, NC 800-446-4347
Delta Engineering Corporation
Walpole, MA. 781-729-8650
Desert Box & Supply Corporation
Thermal, CA 760-399-5161
Design Mark Corporation
Wareham, MA. 800-451-3275
Design Packaging Company
Glencoe, IL 800-321-7659
Design Plastics
Omaha, NE 800-491-0786
Design Technology Corporation
Billerica, MA 978-663-7000
Developak Corporation
Vista, CA. 760-598-7404
Diamond Automation
Farmington Hills, MI 248-426-9394
Dimension Industries
Alexandria, MN 763-425-3955
Diversified Capping Equipment
Perrysburg, OH 419-666-2566

Diversified Metal Engineering
Charlottetown, PE. 902-628-6900
Dixie Canner Company
Athens, GA 706-549-1914
Dolco Packaging
Decatur, IN 260-422-0796
Domnick Hunter
Charlotte, NC 800-345-8462
Donahower & Company
Olathe, KS. 913-829-2650
Dorell Equipment Inc
Somerset, NJ. 732-247-5400
Douglas Machine
Alexandria, MN 320-763-6587
DT Converting Technologies - Stokes
Bristol, PA. 800-635-0036
DT Industries
Dayton, OH. 937-586-5600
DuPont
Wilmington, DE 800-441-7515
Durable Engravers
Franklin Park, IL. 800-869-9565
Durable Packaging Corporation
Countryside, IL 800-700-5677
Durand-Wayland, Inc.
Lagrange, GA 800-241-2308
Durango-Georgia Paper
Tampa, FL. 813-286-2718
Dyco
Bloomsburg, PA 800-545-3926
Dynaclear Packaging
Wyckoff, NJ 201-337-1001
Dynamic Packaging
Minneapolis, MN 800-878-9380
Dynamic Pak
Syracuse, NY 315-474-8593
Dynaric
Virginia Beach, VA 800-526-0827
East Coast Group New York
Springfield Gardens, NY 718-527-8464
Eastern Machine
Middlebury, CT. 203-598-0066
Ebel Tape & Label
Cincinnati, OH 513-471-1067
Econocorp
Randolph, MA 781-986-7500
EDL Packaging Engineers
Green Bay, WI. 920-336-7744
Edmeyer
Minneapolis, MN 651-450-1210
Edson Packaging Machinery
Hamilton, ON 905-385-3201
Electro Cam Corporation
Roscoe, IL. 800-228-5487
ELF Machinery
La Porte, IN. 800-328-0466
Ellay
Commerce, CA 323-725-2974
Ellehammer Industries
Langley, BC 604-882-9326
Elliott Manufacturing Company Inc.
Fresno, CA 559-233-6235
Elmar Worldwide
Depew, NY 800-433-3562
Elmark Packaging
West Chester, PA. 800-670-9688
Elopak
New Hudson, MI. 248-486-4600
Emerald Packaging
Union City, CA 510-429-5700
Energy Sciences Inc.
Wilmington, MA. 978-694-9000
Engineered Automation
Comstock Park, MI. 616-784-4227
Enhance Packaging Technologies
Whitby, ON 905-668-5811
Ensinger Hyde Company
Grenloch, NJ 856-227-0500
EnviroPAK Corporation
Earth City, MO 314-739-1202
Equipment Outlet
Meridian, ID 208-887-1472
Esselte Meto
Morris Plains, NJ 800-645-3290
Evergreen Packaging Equipment
Cedar Rapids, IA
Exact Equipment Corporation
Morrisville, PA 215-295-2000
Excelsior Transparent Bag Manufacturing
Yonkers, NY 914-968-1300
F.N. Smith Corporation
Oregon, IL. 815-732-2171

Fabricon Products
River Rouge, MI 313-841-8200
Fairchild Industrial Products Company
Winston Salem, NC. 800-334-8422
Fallas Automation
Waco, TX 254-772-9524
Farnell Packaging
Dartmouth, NS 800-565-9378
Fawema Packaging Machinery
Palmetto, FL 941-351-9597
Federal Label Systems
Elmhurst, NY 800-238-0015
Fehlig Brothers Box & Lumber Company
St Louis, MO. 314-241-6900
Felco Bag & Burlap Company
Baltimore, MD 800-673-8488
Felins USA
Milwaukee, WI 800-336-3220
Fibre Converters
Constantine, MI 269-279-1700
Fibre Leather Manufacturing Company
New Bedford, MA 800-358-6012
Fiedler Technology
Maple, ON. 905-832-0493
Filler Specialties
Zeeland, MI. 616-772-9235
Filling Equipment Company
Flushing, NY. 800-247-7127
Film-Pak
Crowley, TX 800-526-1838
Filmco
Aurora, OH 800-545-8457
Fischbein Company
Statesville, NC 704-871-1159
Fitec International
Memphis, TN 800-332-6387
Fleetwood
Romeoville, IL 630-759-6800
Flexicell
Ashland, VA 804-550-7300
Flojet
Foothill Ranch, CA. 800-235-6538
Florida Knife Company
Sarasota, FL 800-966-5643
Foam Concepts
Uxbridge, MA. 508-278-7255
Foam Pack Industries
Springfield, NJ 973-376-3700
Fogg Company
Holland, MI. 616-786-3644
Folding Carton/Flexible Packaging
North Hollywood, CA 818-896-3449
Food Equipment Manufacturing Company
Bedford Heights, OH 216-663-1208
Food Pak Corporation
San Mateo, CA 650-341-6559
Formax/Provisur Technologies
Mokena, IL 708-479-3500
FormFlex
Bloomingdale, IN 800-255-7659
Formost Packaging Machines
Woodinville, WA. 425-483-9090
Four M Manufacturing Group
San Jose, CA 408-998-1141
Fowler Products Company
Athens, GA 877-549-3301
Framarx/Waxstar
S Chicago Hts, IL 800-336-3936
Frazier & Son
Conroe, TX. 800-365-5438
Free Flow Packaging Corporation
Redwood City, CA 800-888-3725
Fremont Die Cut Products
Fremont, OH 800-223-3177
Friendly City Box Company
Johnstown, PA. 814-266-6287
Frontier Bag Company
Grandview, MO. 816-765-4811
Fuller Weighing Systems
Columbus, OH 614-882-8121
Fulton-Denver Company
Denver, CO 800-776-6715
Future Commodities/Bestpack
Rancho Cucamonga, CA 888-588-2378
Gallo Manufacturing Company
Racine, WI 262-752-9950
Ganz Brothers
Paramus, NJ 201-845-6010
Garvey Products
Cincinnati, OH 513-771-8710
GBS Corporate
North Canton, OH. 800-552-2427

GCA Bar Code Specialist
Huntington Beach, CA 714-379-4911
GEI Autowrappers
Exton, PA. 610-321-1115
GEI Turbo
Exton, PA 800-345-1308
Gemini Plastic Films Corporation
Garfield, NJ. 800-789-4732
General Bag Corporation
Cleveland, OH 800-837-9396
General Corrugated Machinery Company
Palisades Park, NJ. 201-944-0644
General Electric Company
Louisville, KY. 502-452-4311
General Formulations
Sparta, MI 800-253-3664
General Methods Corporation
Peoria, IL. 309-497-3344
General Packaging Equipment Company
Houston, TX 713-686-4331
General Processing Systems
Holland, MI. 800-547-9370
Genpak
Peterborough, ON 800-461-1995
GHM Industries
Charlton, MA 800-793-7013
Giltron
Medfield, MA 508-359-4310
Gleason Industries
Roseville, CA 916-784-1302
Glenmarc Manufacturing
Chicago, IL 800-323-5350
Glopak
St Leonard, QC 800-361-6994
Goex Corporation
Janesville, WI 608-754-3303
Goldco Industries
Loveland, CO 970-278-4400
Goodwrappers/J.C. Parry & Sons Company
Halethorpe, MD 800-638-1127
Gram Equipment of America
Tampa, FL. 813-248-1978
Grand Valley Labels
Grand Rapids, MI
Graphic Impressions of Illinois
River Grove, IL. 708-453-1100
Graybill Machines
Lititz, PA. 717-626-5221
Great Southern Corporation
Memphis, TN 800-421-7802
Great Western Products
Ontario, CA. 888-598-5588
Green-Tek
Janesville, WI 800-747-6440
Greenbush Tape & Label, Inc.
Albany, NY 518-465-2389
Greenfield Packaging
White Plains, NY 914-993-0233
Grief Brothers Corporation
Delaware, OH 740-549-6000
GTI
Arvada, CO 303-420-6699
Gulf Arizona Packaging
Humble, TX 800-364-3887
Gulf Packaging Company
Safety Harbor, FL 800-749-3466
Gulf States Paper Corporation
Tuscaloosa, AL 205-562-5000
Gulf Systems
Oklahoma City, OK 405-528-2293
Gulf Systems
Brownsville, TX 800-217-4853
Gulf Systems
Oklahoma City, OK 800-364-3887
Gulf Systems
Arlington, TX 817-261-1915
H&H Lumber Company
Amarillo, TX. 806-335-1813
H&N Packaging
Colmar, PA 215-997-6222
H.B. Fuller Company
St Paul, MN. 651-236-5900
H.G. Weber & Company
Kiel, WI. 920-894-2221
Halpak Plastics
Deer Park, NY. 800-442-5725
Halton Packaging Systems
Oakville, ON. 905-847-9141
Hampden Papers
Holyoke, MA 413-536-1000
Hamrick Manufacturing & Service
Mogadore, OH 800-321-9590

Handy Wacks Corporation
Sparta, MI 800-445-4434
Hannan Products Corporation
Corona, CA 800-954-4266
Hantover
Kansas City, MO 800-821-7849
Harbro Packaging
Chicago, IL 877-428-5812
Hart Design & Manufacturing
Green Bay, WI 920-468-5927
Hartel International LLC
Fort Atkinson, WI 920-563-6597
Hartford Containers
Terryville, CT 860-584-1194
Hartness International
Greenville, SC 800-845-8791
Harwil Corporation
Oxnard, CA 800-562-2447
Haumiller Engineering
Elgin, IL 847-695-9111
Hayes Machine Company
Des Moines, IA 800-860-6224
Hayssen
Duncan, SC 864-486-4000
Health Star
Randolph, MA 800-545-3639
Heisler Industries, Inc
Fairfield, NJ 973-227-6300
Henkel Consumer Adhesive
Avon, OH 800-321-0253
Henley Paper Company
Greensboro, NC 336-668-0081
Henschel Coating & Laminating
New Berlin, WI 262-786-1750
Herche Warehouse
Denver, CO 303-371-8186
Highland Plastics
Mira Loma, CA 800-368-0491
Highland Supply Company
Highland, IL 800-472-3645
Highlight Industries
Wyoming, MI 800-531-2465
Hinchcliff Products Company
Strongsville, OH 440-238-5200
Holland Applied Technologies
Burr Ridge, IL 630-325-5130
Hollymatic Corporation
Countryside, IL 708-579-3700
Hoppmann Corporation
Elkwood, VA 800-368-3582
Hudson Control Group
Springfield, NJ 973-376-7400
Hudson Poly Bag
Hudson, MA 800-229-7566
Hudson-Sharp Machine Company
Green Bay, WI 920-494-4571
Huhtamaki Food Service Plastics
Lake Forest, IL 800-244-6382
Huntsman Packaging
South Deerfield, MA 413-665-2145
Hurst Corporation
Devon, PA 610-687-2404
IBC/Shell Containers
New Hyde Park, NY 516-352-4505
ID Images
Brunswick, OH 866-516-7300
Ideal of America
Charlotte, NC 704-523-1604
Ideal of America/Valley Rio Enterprise
Atlanta, GA 770-352-0210
Ideal Wrapping Machine Company
Middletown, NY 845-343-7700
Ilapak
Newtown, PA 215-579-2900
Iman Pack
Westland, MI 800-810-4626
Imar
Miami Beach, FL 305-531-5757
In-Line Corporation
Hopkins, MN 952-938-0046
Indeco Products
San Marcos, TX 512-396-5814
Indiana Carton Company
Bremen, IN 800-348-2390
Industrial Automation Systems
Santa Clarita, CA 888-484-4427
Industrial Devices Corporation
Petaluma, CA 707-789-1000
Industrial Machine Manufacturing
Richmond, VA 804-271-6979
Industrial Magnetics
Boyne City, MI 800-662-4638

Inland Paperboard & Packaging
Rock Hill, SC 803-366-4103
Inline Filling Systems
Venice, FL 941-486-8800
Innovative Packaging Solution
Martin, MI 616-656-2100
Inspired Automation
Agoura Hills, CA 818-991-4598
Instabox
Calgary, AB 800-482-6173
Inter-Pack Corporation
Monroe, MI 734-242-7755
International Omni-Pac Corporation
La Verne, CA 909-593-2833
International Packaging Machinery
Naples, FL 800-237-6496
International Paper Box Machine Company
Nashua, NH 603-889-6651
International Tape Company
Windham, NH 800-253-4450
Interstate Packaging
White Bluff, TN 800-251-1072
Intertape Polymer Group
Bradenton, FL 877-318-5752
ITW Stretch Packaging System
Glenview, IL 847-657-4444
Ives-Way Products
Round Lake Beach, IL 847-740-0658
Jagenberg
Enfield, CT 860-741-2501
January & Wood Company
Maysville, KY 606-564-3301
Jarisch Paper Box Company
North Adams, MA 413-663-5396
Jay Packaging Group
Warwick, RI 401-739-7200
Jeb Plastics
Wilmington, DE 800-556-2247
Jel-Sert Company
West Chicago, IL 800-323-2592
Jescorp
Des Plaines, IL 847-299-7800
Jetstream Systems
Denver, CO 303-371-9002
Jif-Pak Manufacturing
Vista, CA 800-777-6613
Jilson Group
Lodi, NJ 800-969-5400
JMC Packaging Equipment
Burlington, ON 800-263-5252
John Dusenbery Company
Paramus, NJ 973-366-7500
John E. Ruggles & Company
New Bedford, MA 508-992-9766
Johnson Corrugated Products Corporation
Thompson, CT 860-923-9563
Jones Packaging Machinery
Ooltewah, TN 423-238-4558
JW Leser Company
Los Angeles, CA 323-731-4173
Kama Corporation
Hazleton, PA 570-455-0958
Kammann Machine
Portsmouth, NH 978-463-0050
Kapak Corporation
Minneapolis, MN 952-541-0730
KAPCO
Kent, OH 800-843-5368
Kaps-All Packaging Systems
Riverhead, NY 631-727-0300
Karolina Polymers
Hickory, NC 828-328-2247
Kaufman Engineered Systems
Waterville, OH 419-878-9727
Kennedy Group
Willoughby, OH 440-951-7660
Key Automation
Eagan, MN 651-455-0547
Keystone Packaging Service
Phillipsburg, NJ 800-473-8567
KHL Engineered Packaging
Montebello, CA 323-721-5300
KHS
Waukesha, WI 262-798-1102
Kinsley Inc
Doylestown, PA 800-414-6664
KIRKCO
Monroe, NC 704-289-7090
Kisters Kayat
Sarasota, FL 386-424-0101
Kliklok-Woodman
Decatur, GA 770-981-5200

Klippenstein Corporation
Fresno, CA 888-834-4258
Klockner Bartelt
Sarasota, FL 877-227-8358
Klockner Pentaplast of America
Gordonsville, VA 540-832-3600
Kloppenberg & Company
Englewood, CO 800-346-3246
KM International
Kenton, TN 731-749-8700
Knapp Container
Beacon Falls, CT 203-888-0511
Koch Equipment
Kansas City, MO 816-753-2150
Kohler Industries
Lincoln, NE 800-365-6708
Korab Engineering Company
Los Angeles, CA 310-670-7710
Kord Products Inc.
Brantford, ON 800-452-9070
Krones
Franklin, WI 414-409-4000
Kwik Lok Corporation
Yakima, WA 800-688-5945
Kwik-Lok Corporation
Yakima, WA 800-688-5945
L&H Wood Manufacturing Company
Farmington, MI 248-474-9000
LAB Equipment
Skaneateles, NY 800-522-5781
Label Makers
Pleasant Prairie, WI 800-208-3331
Label Technology
Merced, CA 800-388-1990
Lako Tool & Manufacturing
Perrysburg, OH 800-228-2982
Lamcraft
Lees Summit, MO 800-821-1333
Langen Packaging
Mississauga, ON 905-670-7200
Laub/Hunt Packaging Systems
Norwalk, CA 888-671-9338
Lawrence Schiff Silk Mills
New York, NY 800-272-4433
Lawson Mardon Flexible
Bellwood, IL 708-544-1600
Lawson Mardon Flexible Labels
Weston, ON 416-742-8910
Leader Engineering-Fabrication
Napoleon, OH 419-592-0008
Leal True Form Corporation
Freeport, NY 516-379-2008
Leco Plastics
Hackensack, NJ 201-343-3330
LeMatic
Jackson, MI 517-787-3301
Len E. Ivarson
Milwaukee, WI 414-351-0700
Lenkay Sani Products Corporation
Brooklyn, NY 718-927-9260
Lester Box & Manufacturing
Long Beach, CA 562-437-5123
Levin Brothers Paper
Cicero, IL 800-666-8484
Liqui-Box
Allentown, PA 610-264-5420
Livingston-Wilbor Corporation
Edison, NJ 908-322-8403
Lockwood Packaging
Woburn, MA 800-641-3100
Loeb Equipment & Appraisal Company
Chicago, IL 773-548-4131
Longford Equipment US
Glastonbury, CT 860-659-0762
Longhorn Packaging
San Antonio, TX 800-433-7974
Longview Fibre Company
Longview, WA 800-929-8111
Lorann Oils
Lansing, MI 800-862-8620
Los Angeles Paper Box & Board Mills
Los Angeles, CA 323-685-8900
Loveshaw
South Canaan, PA 800-572-3434
Luetzow Industries
South Milwaukee, WI 800-558-6055
Lunn Industries
Glen Cove, NY 516-671-9000
Lyco Wausau
Wausau, WI 715-845-7867
Lydall
Doswell, VA 804-266-9611

Lynch Corporation
Greenwich, CT 203-622-1150
M S Willett Inc
Cockeysville, MD 410-771-0460
M&G Packaging Corporation
Floral Park, NY 800-240-5288
M&Q Packaging Corporation
North Wales, PA 267-498-4000
M&R Flexible Packaging
Springboro, OH 800-543-3380
Machine Electronics Company
Brooklyn, NY 718-384-3211
Mactac
Stow, OH 800-233-4291
Madison County Wood Products
Saint Louis, MO 314-772-1722
MAF Industries
Traver, CA 559-897-2905
Magnuson Corporation
Pueblo, CO 719-948-9500
Mail-Well Label
Sparks, NV 775-359-1703
Malnove Packaging Systems
Omaha, NE 800-228-9877
Malo/Loveless Manufacturing
Tulsa, OK 918-583-2743
Manchester Tool & Die
Manchester, IN 260-982-8524
Maren Engineering Corporation
South Holland, IL 800-875-1038
Mark Products Company
Denville, NJ 973-983-8818
Markwell Manufacturing Company
Norwood, MA 800-666-1123
Marlen International
Astoria, OR 800-862-7536
Maro Paper Products Company
Bellwood, IL 708-649-9982
Marq Packaging Systems
Yakima, WA 800-998-4301
Marshall Paper Products
East Norwich, NY
Marshall Plastic Film
Martin, MI 269-672-5511
Maryland Packaging Corporation
Baltimore, MD 410-347-0365
Massachusetts Container Corporation
Marlborough, MA 508-481-1100
Mastercraft International
Charlotte, NC 704-392-7436
Material Handling Technology, Inc
Morrisville, NC 800-779-2475
Matiss
St Georges, QC 888-562-8477
Matrix Packaging Machinery
Saukville, WI 262-268-8300
Matthiesen Equipment Company
San Antonio, TX 800-624-8635
Maull-Baker Box Company
Brookfield, WI 414-463-1290
Maxco Supply
Parlier, CA 559-646-6700
Maypak
Wayne, NJ 973-696-0780
Measurex/S&L Plastics
Nazareth, PA 800-752-0650
Merix Chemical Company
Chicago, IL 312-573-1400
Merryweather Foam
Sylacauga, AL 256-249-8546
Micro Solutions Enterprises
Van Nuys, CA 800-673-4968
Mid Cities Paper Box Company
Downey, CA 877-277-6272
Miller's Technical Service
Canton, MI 734-738-1970
Milliken Packaging
Spartanburg, SC 864-598-0100
Milprint
Oshkosh, WI 920-303-8600
Milwaukee Tool & MachineCompany
Okauchee, WI 262-821-0160
Minipack
Orange, CA 714-283-4200
Mitsubishi Polyester Film, Inc.
Greer, SC 864-879-5000
Modern Packaging
Deer Park, NY 631-595-2437
Modular King Packaging Systems
Randolph, NJ 973-970-9393
Moen Industries
Santa Fe Springs, CA 800-732-7766

Molins/Sandiacre Richmond
Richmond, VA 804-421-8795
Monument Industries
Bennington, VT 802-442-8187
Moore Production Tool Specialties
Farmington Hills, MI 248-476-1200
Morphy Container Company
Brantford, ON 519-752-5428
Mount Hope Machinery Company
Westborough, MA 508-616-9458
Mount Vernon Plastics
Mamaroneck, NY 914-698-1122
MS Plastics & Packaging Company
Butler, NJ 800-593-1802
Multisorb Technologies
West Seneca, NY 800-445-9890
Nalbach Engineering Company, Inc.
Countryside, IL 708-579-9100
Namco Controls Corporation
Cleveland, OH 800-626-8324
NAP Industries
Brooklyn, NY 877-635-4948
Nashua Corporation
Nashua, NH 603-661-2004
National Equipment Corporation
Bronx, NY 800-237-8873
National Instrument Company
Baltimore, MD 800-526-1301
National Package SealingCompany
Santa Ana, CA 714-630-1505
National Packaging
Rumford, RI 401-434-1070
National Poly Bag Manufacturing Corporation
Brooklyn, NY 718-629-9800
National Velour
Warwick, RI 401-737-8300
NDS
Columbus, OH 614-294-4931
Neos
Elk River, MN 888-441-6367
New England Machinery Inc
Bradenton, FL 941-755-5550
New Jersey Wire Stitching Machine Company
Cherry Hill, NJ 856-428-2572
Nichols Specialty Products
Southborough, MA 508-481-4367
Nigrelli Systems Inc
Kiel, WI 920-693-3161
NIMCO Corporation
Crystal Lake, IL 815-459-4200
Niro
Hudson, WI 715-386-9371
Nitech
Columbus, NE 800-397-1100
NJM/CLI
Pointe Claire, QC 514-630-6990
Norden
Branchburg, NJ 908-252-9483
Nordson Corporation
Duluth, GA 800-683-2314
Norpak Corporation
Newark, NJ 800-631-6970
North American ContainerCorporation
Maretta, GA 800-929-0610
Northeast Packaging Materials
Monsey, NY 845-426-2900
Norwalt Design Inc.
Randolph, NJ 973-927-3200
Norwood Paper
Chicago, IL 773-788-1508
Novelis Foil Products
Lagrange, GA 800-776-8701
Now Plastics
East Longmeadow, MA 413-525-1010
Nu-Con Equipment
Chanhassen, MN 877-939-0510
NU-Trend Plastic/Corrigan & Company
Jacksonville, FL 904-353-5936
NYP Corporation
Leola, PA 800-541-0961
Ocme America Corporation
York, PA 717-843-6263
OCS Checkweighers Inc
Snellville, GA 678-344-8300
Oden Corporation
Tonawanda, NY 800-658-3622
Oerlikon Leybold Vacuum USA Inc
Export, PA 800-764-5369
Old Dominion Box Company
Burlington, NC 336-226-4491
Olney Machinery
Westernville, NY 315-827-4208

Omega Design Corporation
Exton, PA 800-346-0191
Omnitech International
Midland, MI 989-631-3377
OMNOVA Solutions
Fairlawn, OH 330-869-4200
OnTrack Automation Inc
Waterloo, ON 519-886-9090
Orange Plastics
Compton, CA 310-609-2121
Orics Industries
Farmingdale, NY 718-461-8613
Orion Packaging Systems
Alexandria, MN 800-333-6556
Osgood Industries
Oldsmar, FL 813-855-7337
OSSID LLC
Rocky Mount, NC 800-334-8369
Ouachita Packaging Machinery
West Monroe, LA 318-396-1468
Outlook Packaging
Neenah, WI 920-722-1666
Oystar North America
Edison, NJ 732-343-7600
Pacemaker Packaging Corporation
Flushing, NY 718-458-1188
Pack Line Corporation
Racine, WI 800-248-6868
Pack West Machinery Company
Irwindale, CA 626-814-4766
Pack-Rite
Racine, WI 800-248-6868
Package Machinery Company
West Springfield, MA 413-732-4000
Package Service Company of Colorado
Northmoor, MO 800-748-7799
Package Systems Corporation
Danielson, CT 800-522-3548
Packaging & Processing Equipment
Ayr, ON 519-622-6666
Packaging Aids Corporation
San Rafael, CA 415-454-4868
Packaging Associates
Randolph, NJ 973-252-8890
Packaging By Design
Elgin, IL 847-741-5600
Packaging Dynamics
Chicago, IL 773-843-8000
Packaging Dynamics
Walnut Creek, CA 925-938-2711
Packaging Dynamics International
Caldwell, OH 740-732-5665
Packaging Enterprises
Jenkintown, PA 763-257-3687
Packaging Equipment & Conveyors, Inc
Elkhart, IN 574-266-6995
Packaging Machinery & Equipment
West Orange, NJ 973-325-2418
Packaging Machinery International
Elk Grove Village, IL 800-871-4764
Packaging Materials
Cambridge, OH 800-565-8550
Packaging Products Corporation
Mission, KS 913-262-3033
Packaging Progressions
Collegeville, PA 610-489-8601
Packing Material Company
Southfield, MI 248-489-7000
PackRite
Racine, WI 800-248-6868
Packrite Packaging
Archdale, NC 336-431-1111
Packworld USA
Nazareth, PA 610-746-2765
Paco Manufacturing Comp any
Clarksville, IN 888-283-7963
Pacur
Oshkosh, WI 920-236-2888
Page Slotting & Saw Company
Toledo, OH 419-476-5131
Pak-Rapid
Conshohocken, PA 610-828-3511
Pakmark
Chesterfield, MO 800-423-1379
Palmetto Canning Company
Palmetto, FL 941-722-1100
Paper Box & Specialty Company
Sheboygan, WI 888-240-3756
Paper Converting MachineCompany
Green Bay, WI 920-336-4300
Paper Machinery Corporation
Milwaukee, WI 414-354-8050

Paper Pak Industries
La Verne, CA 909-392-1750
Paper Service
Hinsdale, NH 603-239-6344
Par Systems
Saint Paul, MN 800-464-1320
Paragon Films
Broken Arrow, OK 800-274-9727
Partola Packaging
Naperville, IL 800-727-8652
Pasco
Saint Louis, MO 800-489-3300
Pater & Associates
Cincinnati, OH 513- 24- 215
PDC International
Austin, TX. 512-302-0194
PDMP
Leesburg, VA 703-777-8400
Pearson Packaging Systems
Spokane, WA. 800-732-7766
Peco Controls Corporation
Modesto, CA. 800-732-6285
Peerless Food Equipment
Sidney, OH 937-492-4158
Peerless-Winsmith
Springville, NY. 716-592-9310
Penny Plate
Haddonfield, NJ 856-429-7583
Pepperell Paper Company
Lawrence, MA 978-433-6951
Per-Fil Industries Inc
Riverside, NJ. 856-461-5700
Performance Packaging
Trail Creek, IN 219-874-6226
Perl Packaging Systems
Middlebury, CT. 800-864-2853
Pfankuch Machinery Corporation
Apple Valley, MN 952-891-3311
PFM Packaging Machinery Corporation
Newmarket, ON 905-836-6709
Phase Fire Systems
Vista, CA. 888-741-2341
Phoenix Closures
Naperville, IL 630-544-3475
Plas-Ties
Tustin, CA. 800-854-0137
Plastech Corporation
Atlanta, GA. 404-355-9682
Plasti-Mach Corporation
Valley Cottage, NY 800-394-1128
Plastic Packaging Inc
Hickory, NC 800-333-2466
Plastic Suppliers
Columbus, OH 800-722-5577
PlexPack Corp
Toronto, ON 855-635-9238
Pneumatic Scale Corporation
Cuyahoga Falls, OH 330-923-0491
Polar Tech Industries
Genoa, IL 800-423-2749
Poly Plastic Products
Delano, PA 570-467-3000
Poly Shapes Corporation
Elyria, OH. 800-605-9359
Poly-Seal Corporation
Baltimore, MD 410-633-1990
Polypack
Pinellas Park, FL. 727-578-5000
Polyplastics
Austin, TX. 800-753-7659
Portco Corporation
Vancouver, WA 800-426-1794
Portola Packaging
Naperville, IL 800-767-8652
Powertex
Rouses Point, NY 800-769-3783
Praxair
Danbury, CT 800-772-9247
Preferred Packaging Systems
San Dimas, CA 800-378-4777
Premier Plastics Company
Waukesha, WI. 800-878-8430
Premium Foil Products Company
Louisville, KY 502-459-2820
Pres-On Products
Addison, IL. 800-323-7467
Pressure Pack
Williamsburg, VA 757-220-3693
Prestige Label Company
Burgaw, NC. 800-969-4449
Print & Peel
New York, NY 800-451-0807
Print Pack
Atlanta, GA. 404-460-7000
Printpack
Atlanta, GA. 404-460-7000
Priority One America
Waterloo, ON 519-746-6950
Priority One Packaging
Waterloo, ON 800-387-9102
Processing Machinery & Supply
Philadelphia, PA 215-425-4320
Prodo-Pak Corporation
Garfield, NJ. 973-777-7770
Production Packaging & Processing Equipment
Company
Phoenix, AZ 602-254-7878
Production Systems
Marietta, GA. 800-235-9734
Professional Marketing Group
Seattle, WA 800-227-3769
Progressive Packaging
Plymouth, MN. 800-844-7889
Promotional Packaging Group
Addison, TX 972-733-3199
Prototype Equipment Corporation
Libertyville, IL 847-680-4433
PTI Packaging
Portage, WI. 800-501-4077
Pure & Secure, LLC
Lincoln, NE. 800-875-5915
QPF
Streamwood, IL. 800-323-6963
Quality Films
Three Rivers, MI. 269-679-5263
Quality Industries
Cleveland, OH 216-961-5566
Racine Paper Box Manufacturing
Chicago, IL 773-227-3900
RAM Center
Red Wing, MN 800-762-6842
Ramoneda Brothers
Culpeper, VA. 540-825-9166
Ranger Blade Manufacturing Company
Traer, IA 800-377-7860
Raque Food Systems
Louisville, KY 502-267-9641
Ray C. Sprosty Bag Company
Wooster, OH 330-264-8559
Refrigiwear
Dahlonega, GA 800-645-3744
Reilly Foam Corporation
Conshohocken, PA 610-834-1900
Reiser
Canton, MA 781-575-9941
Remcon Plastics
West Reading, PA 800-360-3636
Renard Machine Company
Green Bay, WI. 920-432-8412
Rennco
Homer, MI. 800-409-5225
Republic Foil
Danbury, CT 800-722-3645
RER Services
Northridge, CA 818-993-1826
Resina
Brooklyn, NY 800-207-4804
Rexam Beverage Can Company
Chicago, IL 773-399-3000
Rexford Paper Company
Racine, WI 262-886-9100
Rico Packaging Company
Chicago, IL 773-523-9190
Rigidized Metals Corporation
Buffalo, NY. 800-836-2580
Riverwood International
Atlanta, GA. 770-984-5477
RMF Freezers
Grandview, MO. 816-765-4101
RMF Steel Products
Grandview, MO. 816-765-4101
Robert Bosch Corporation
Carol Stream, IL 708-865-5200
Robert's Packaging
Des Plaines, IL 800-707-5070
Roberts PolyPro
Charlotte, NC 800-269-7409
Rock-Tenn Company
Scarborough, ME 207-883-8921
Rockford-Midland Corporation
Rockford, IL 800-327-7908
Rockwell Automation/Electro
Eden Prairie, MN 800-328-3983
Rohrer Corporation
Buford, GA 800-243-6640
Rollprint Packaging Products
Addison, IL. 800-276-7629
Romanow Container Inc
Westwood, MA. 781-320-9200
Rondo of America
Naugatuck, CT 203-723-7474
Ropak Manufacturing Company
Decatur, AL. 256-350-4241
Roplast Industries Inc.
Oroville, CA 800-767-5278
Rose City Awning Company
Portland, OR 800-446-4104
Rose Forgrove
Saint Charles, IL 630-443-1317
Ross Industries
Midland, VA 800-336-6010
Rowland Technologies
Wallingford, CT 203-269-9500
Royal Box Group
Cicero, IL 708-656-2020
Royal Label Company
Boston, MA. 617-825-6050
RR Donnelley
Chicago, IL 800-742-4455
RTS Packaging
Hillside, IL 708-338-2800
Rudd Container Corporation
Chicago, IL 773-847-7600
Ruffino Paper Box Manufacturing
Hackensack, NJ. 201-487-1260
Rutan Polyethylene Supply Bag & Manufacturing
Company
Mahwah, NJ 800-872-1474
Rutherford Engineering
Rockford, IL 815-623-2141
S.V. Dice Designers
Rowland Heights, CA. 888-478-3423
Sabel Engineering Corporation
Villard, MN. 320-554-3611
Salinas Valley Wax PaperCompany
Salinas, CA 831-424-2747
Salwasser Manufacturing Company
Reedley, CA 800-344-8951
Samuel P. Harris
Rumford, RI 401-438-4020
Samuel Strapping Systems
Woodridge, IL. 800-323-4424
San Fab Conveyor Systems
Sandusky, OH 419-626-4465
Sanchelima International
Doral, FL. 305-591-4343
Sanford Redmond Company
Stamford, CT. 203-351-9800
Sasib Beverage & Food North America
Plano, TX 800-558-3814
Scandia Packaging Machinery Company
Fairfield, NJ 973-473-6100
Schaefer Machine Company Inc.
Deep River, CT. 800-243-5143
Schneider Packing Equipment Company
Brewerton, NY 315-676-3035
Scholle Corporation
Northlake, IL. 888-224-6269
Schroeder Sewing Technologies
San Marcos, CA 760-591-9733
Seal-O-Matic Company
Jacksonville, OR. 800-631-2072
Sealant Equipment & Engiineering
Plymouth, MI 734-459-8600
Sealstrip Corporation
Boyertown, PA 610-367-6282
Seepex
Enon, OH 800-695-3659
Seiler Plastics Corporation
Saint Louis, MO 314-815-3030
Sekisui TA Industries
Brea, CA 800-258-8273
Serac
Carol Stream, IL 630-510-9343
Serpa Packaging Solutions
Visalia, CA 800-348-5453
Sertapak Packaging Corporation
Woodstock, ON. 800-265-1162
Servpak Corporation
Hollywood, FL 800-782-0840
Seville Flexpack Corporation
Oak Creek, WI 414-761-2751
Shamrock Paper Company
Saint Louis, MO 314-241-2370

Shanklin Corporation
Ayer, MA. 978-772-3200
Shawans Specialty Papers
Shawano, WI. 800-543-5554
Sherwood Tool
Owings Mills, MD 860-828-4161
Shields Bag & Printing Company
Yakima, WA 800-541-8630
Shields Products
West Pittston, PA. 570-655-4596
Shippers Supply
Saskatoon, SK. 800-661-5639
Shippers Supply, Labelgraphic
Calgary, AB. 800-661-5639
ShockWatch
Dallas, TX. 800-527-9497
Shrinkfast Marketing
Newport, NH. 800-867-4746
Sierra Dawn Products
Graton, CA 707-535-0172
SIG Combibloc USA, Inc.
Chester, PA 610-546-4200
SIG Doboy
New Richmond, WI 715-246-6511
SIG Pack Eagle Corporation
Oakland, CA 800-824-3245
Signature Packaging
West Orange, NJ 800-376-2299
Signode Packaging Systems
Glenview, IL 800-323-2464
Silver Spur Corporation
Cerritos, CA 562-921-6880
Simolex Rubber Corporation
Plymouth, MI 734-453-4500
Simplex Filler Company
Napa, CA. 800-796-7539
Sitma USA
Spilamberto, MO 800-728-1254
SKW Gelatin & Specialties
Waukesha, WI. 800-654-2396
SL Sanderson & Company
Berry Creek, CA 800-763-7845
Slautterback Corporation
Duluth, GA 800-827-3308
SleeveCo Inc
Dawsonville, GA. 706-216-3110
Snapware
Fullerton, CA 800-334-3062
Snow Craft Company
Garden City Park, NY. 516-739-1399
Sohn Manufacturing
Elkhart Lake, WI. 920-876-3361
Somerville Packaging
Scarborough, ON 416-291-1161
Somerville Packaging
Mississauga, ON. 905-678-8211
SONOCO
Hartsville, SC 800-576-6626
Sonoco Flexible Packaging
Hartsville, SC 800-377-2692
Southern Automatics
Lakeland, FL. 800-441-4604
Southern Container Corporation
Deer Park, NY. 631-586-6006
Southern Film Extruders
High Point, NC 800-334-6101
Southern Packaging & Bottling
Athens, GA 706-208-0814
Southern Pallet
Memphis, TN 901-942-4603
Southern Tool
West Monroe, LA 318-387-2263
Spartec Plastics
Conneaut, OH. 800-325-5176
Spartech Plastics
Wichita, KS. 316-722-8621
Spartech Plastics
Portage, WI. 800-998-7123
Spartech Poly Com
Clayton, MI. 888-721-4242
Specialty Films & Associates
Hebron, KY. 800-984-3346
Specialty Packaging
Fort Worth, TX 800-284-7722
Spee-Dee Packaging Machinery
Sturtevant, WI. 877-387-5212
Sphinx Adsorbents
Springfield, MA 800-388-0157
St. Clair Pakwell
Bellwood, IL. 800-323-1922
St. Pierre Box & Lumber Company
Canton, CT 860-693-2089

Stainless Specialists
Wausau, WI. 800-236-4155
Standard-Knapp
Portland, CT 800-628-9565
Star Poly Bag, Inc.
Brooklyn, NY 718-384-3130
Starview Packaging Machinery
Dorval, QC 888-278-5555
Steven's International
New Berlin, WI. 262-827-3800
Stewart Mechanical Seals & Supply
Bakersfield, CA 661-391-9332
Stiles Enterprises
Rockaway, NJ 800-325-4232
Stock America Inc
Grafton, WI. 262-375-4100
Stone Container
Chicago, IL 312-346-6600
Stormax International
Concord, NH. 800-874-7629
Straub Design Company
Minneapolis, MN 800-959-3708
Stretch-Vent Packaging System
Ontario, CA. 800-822-8368
Sungjae Corporation
Irvine, CA 949-757-1727
Superior Distributing
Louisville, KY 800-365-6661
Superior Packaging Equipment Corporation
Fairfield, NJ 973-575-8818
Surekap
Winder, GA. 770-867-5793
SWF McDowell
Orlando, FL. 800-877-7971
Sycamore Containers
Sycamore, IL. 815-895-2343
T&T Industries
Fort Mohave, AZ 800-437-6246
T.D. Sawvel Company
Maple Plain, MN. 877-488-1816
T.O. Plastics
Minneapolis, MN 952-854-2131
Taconic
Petersburg, NY 800-833-1805
Target Industries
Flanders, NJ 973-927-0011
Taylor Products Company A Division Of Magnum Systems
Parsons, KS. 888-882-9567
TDF Automation
Cedar Falls, IA 800-553-1777
Technistar Corporation
Denver, CO 303-651-0188
Tecweigh/Tecnetics Industries
White Bear Lake, MN. 800-536-4880
Telesonic Packaging Corporation
Wilmington, DE 302-658-6945
Temco
Oakland, CA 707-746-5966
Templock Corporation
Santa Barbara, CA 800-777-1715
TEQ
Huntley, IL 800-874-7113
Terkelsen Machine Company
Hyannis, MA. 508-775-6229
Terphane
Bloomfield, NY 585-657-5800
THARCO
San Lorenzo, CA. 800-772-2332
Tharo Systems, Inc
Brunswick, OH 800-878-6833
The Staplex Company
Brooklyn, NY 800-221-0822
Thiele Engineering Company
Fergus Falls, MN 218-739-3321
Thiele Technologies
Reedley, CA 800-344-8951
Thieley Technolgies
Minneapolis, MN 612-782-1200
Thomas Tape Company
Springfield, OH. 937-325-6414
Tieco-Unadilla Corporation
Unadilla, NY. 877-889-6540
Tilly Industries
St Laurent, QC 514-331-4922
Tisma Machinery Corporation
Elk Grove Village, IL 847-427-9525
TMT Vacuum Filters
Danville, IL. 217-446-0742
TNA Packaging Solutions
Coppell, TX 972-462-6500

Tolas Health Care Packaging
Feasterville Trevose, PA. 215-322-7900
Tomac Packaging
Woburn, MA 800-641-3100
Trans World Services
Melrose, MA. 800-882-2105
Trenton Mills
Trenton, TN. 731-855-1323
Tri-Sterling
Altamonte Spgs, FL 407-260-0330
Triangle Package Machinery Company
Chicago, IL 800-621-4170
Trico Converting
Fullerton, CA 714-563-0701
Tridyne Process Systems Inc.
South Burlington, VT 802-863-6873
True Pack Ltd
New Castle, DE. 800-825-7890
Tucson Container Corporation
Tucson, AZ 520-746-3171
Tuscarora
New Brighton, PA. 724-843-8200
Tyco Plastics
Lakeville, MN. 800-328-4080
UCB Films
Smyrna, GA 877-822-3456
ULMA Packaging Systems, Inc.
Ball Ground, GA. 770-345-5300
Ultra Pac
Rogers, MN. 800-324-8541
Unifoil Corporation
Fairfield, NJ 973-244-9900
Unique Boxes
Chicago, IL 800-281-1670
Unisource
Farmington, NY 800-864-7687
United Desiccants
Louisville, KY 505-864-6691
United Flexible
Westbury, NY 516-222-2150
United Silicone
Lancaster, NY 716-681-8222
United States Systems
Kansas City, KS 888-281-2454
UniTrak Corporation
Port Hope, ON 866-883-5749
Universal Labeling Systems
St Petersburg, FL 877-236-0266
Universal Packaging
Houston, TX 800-324-2610
Universal Paper Box
Seattle, WA 800-228-1045
Upaco Adhesives
Richmond, VA. 800-446-9984
US Label Corporation
Greensboro, NC 336-332-7000
US Line Company
Westfield, MA. 413-562-3629
Vacumet Corp
Wayne, NJ. 973-628-1067
Vacumet Corporation
Austell, GA. 800-776-0865
Vacuum Depositing
Okolona, KY. 502-969-4227
Valco
Cincinnati, OH 513-874-6550
VC999 Packaging Systems
Kansas City, MO. 800-728-2999
Vc999 Packaging Systems Inc.
Kansas City, MO. 800-728-2999
VIFAN
Lanoraie, QC. 800-557-0192
Viking Industries
New Smyma Beach, FL 888-605-5560
Viking Packaging & Display
San Jose, CA. 408-998-1000
Virginia Plastics
Roanoke, VA. 800-777-8541
Vista International Packaging
Kenosha, WI 800-558-4058
Volk Corporation
Farmington Hills, MI 800-521-6799
Volumetric Technologies
Cannon Falls, MN. 507-263-0034
VPI Mirrex Corporation
Bear, DE 800-488-7608
W.G. Durant Corporation
Whittier, CA 562-946-5555
Warwick Manufacturing & Equipment
North Brunswick, NJ 732-241-9263
Washington Frontier
Grandview, WA. 509-469-7662

Wasserman Bag Company
Center Moriches, NY 631-909-8656
Water Sciences Services ,Inc.
Jackson, TN 973-584-4131
Waukesha Cherry-Burrell
Louisville, KY 502-491-4310
Wayne Automation Corporation
Norristown, PA 610-630-8900
WE Killam Enterprises
Waterford, ON. 519-443-7421
Weatherchem Corporation
Twinsburg, OH 330-425-4206
Weber Display & Packaging
Philadelphia, PA 215-426-3500
Weigh Right Automatic Scale Company
Joliet, IL 800-571-0249
WeighPack Systems/PaxiomGroup
Montreal, QC 888-934-4472
Welliver Metal Products Corporation
Salem, OR. 503-362-1568
Wepackit
Orangeville, ON 519-942-1700
West-Pak
Dallas, TX. 214-337-8984
Western Plastics
Calhoun, GA 800-752-4106
Western Plastics California
Portland, TN 615-325-7331
Wexxar Corporation
Chicago, IL 630-983-6666
Wexxar Packaging Inc
Richmond, BC 888-565-3219
Whirley Industries
Warren, PA 800-825-5575
White Cap
Downers Grove, IL 800-515-1565
Wick's Packaging Service
Cutler, IN 574-967-3104
Wilks Precision Instrument Company
Union Bridge, MD 410-775-7917
Williamson & Company
Greer, SC. 800-849-3263
Winpak Portion Packaging
Langhorne, PA 800-841-2600
Winpak Technologies
Toronto, ON 416-421-1700
Winzen Film
Sulphur Springs, TX 800-779-7595
Wisconsin Film & Bag
Shawano, WI. 800-765-9224
Witt Plastics
Greenville, OH 800-227-9181
Woodstock Line Company
Putnam, CT. 860-928-6557
Woodward Manufacturing
Paramus, NJ 201-262-6700
Wrap-Pak
Yakima, WA 800-879-9727
Wrapade Packaging Systems, LLC
Fairfield, NJ 888-815-8564
Wraps
East Orange, NJ 973-673-7873
WS Packaging Group Inc
Green Bay, WI. 920-866-6300
Y-Z Sponge & Foam Products
Delta, BC. 604-525-1665
Yakima Wire Works
Reedley, CA 509-248-6790
Yohay Baking Company
Lindenhurst, NY 631-225-0300
Zed Industries
Vandalia, OH. 937-667-8407
Zepf Technologies
Clearwater, FL 727-535-4100
Zimmer Custom-Made Packaging
Indianapolis, IN 317-263-3436
Zitropack Ltd
Addison, IL. 630-543-1016

Automatic/Random Case Sealing

Alard Equipment Corporation
Williamson, NY 315-589-4511
Reiser
Canton, MA 781-575-9941
S&R Machinery
Olyphant, PA. 800-229-4896
Tetra Pak
Vernon Hills, IL 800-358-3872

Bag Closing

About Packaging Robotics
Thornton, CO 303-449-2559
Alard Equipment Corporation
Williamson, NY 315-589-4511
Aline Heat Seal Corporation
Cerritos, CA 888-285-3917
Amark Packaging Systems
Kansas City, MO. 816-965-9000
American Bag & Burlap Company
Chelsea, MA 617-884-7600
Andgar Corporation
Ferndale, WA 360-366-9900
Automated Packaging Systems
Streetsboro, OH 888-288-6224
Branson Ultrasonics Corporation
Danbury, CT 203-796-0400
Chaffee Company
Rocklin, CA 916-630-3980
Clamco Corporation
Berea, OH 216-267-1911
Crystal-Vision PackagingSystems
Torrance, CA. 800-331-3240
Custom Food Machinery
Stockton, CA. 209-463-4343
Customized Equipment SE
Tucker, GA 770-934-9300
Dynamic Automation
Simi Valley, CA. 805-584-8476
Fawema Packaging Machinery
Palmetto, FL 941-351-9597
Fischbein Company
Statesville, NC 704-871-1159
Gulf Arizona Packaging
Humble, TX 800-364-3887
Gulf Systems
Oklahoma City, OK 405-528-2293
Gulf Systems
Brownsville, TX 800-217-4853
Gulf Systems
Oklahoma City, OK 800-364-3887
Gulf Systems
Arlington, TX 817-261-1915
Harwil Corporation
Oxnard, CA. 800-562-2447
Herche Warehouse
Denver, CO 303-371-8186
Hermann Ultrasonics Inc
Bartlett, IL. 630-736-7400
ID Images
Brunswick, OH 866-516-7300
Iman Pack
Westland, MI. 800-810-4626
Industrial Automation Systems
Santa Clarita, CA 888-484-4427
JMC Packaging Equipment
Burlington, ON 800-263-5252
Kwik-Lok Corporation
Yakima, WA 800-688-5945
Lockwood Packaging
Woburn, MA 800-641-3100
Matthiesen Equipment Company
San Antonio, TX. 800-624-8635
New Jersey Wire Stitching Machine Company
Cherry Hill, NJ 856-428-2572
Pacemaker Packaging Corporation
Flushing, NY. 718-458-1188
Pack-Rite
Racine, WI 800-248-6868
Packaging Systems International
Denver, CO 303-296-4445
Pacmac
Fayetteville, AR 479-521-0525
Plas-Ties
Tustin, CA. 800-854-0137
PlexPack Corp
Toronto, ON 855-635-9238
Prodo-Pak Corporation
Garfield, NJ. 973-777-7770
Save-O-Seal Corporation
Elmsford, NY 800-831-9720
SIG Doboy
New Richmond, WI 715-246-6511
The Staplex Company
Brooklyn, NY 800-221-0822
Tomac Packaging
Woburn, MA 800-641-3100
Triangle Package Machinery Company
Chicago, IL 800-621-4170
Weigh Right Automatic Scale Company
Joliet, IL 800-571-0249

Bag Filling

About Packaging Robotics
Thornton, CO 303-449-2559
Actionpac Scales & Automation
Oxnard, CA. 800-394-0154
Ag-Pak
Gasport, NY 716-772-2651
Alard Equipment Corporation
Williamson, NY 315-589-4511
Amark Packaging Systems
Kansas City, MO. 816-965-9000
American Bag & Burlap Company
Chelsea, MA 617-884-7600
AmeriGlobe FIBC Solutions
Lafayette, LA 337-234-3212
Amplas
Green Bay, WI. 800-950-4362
Andgar Corporation
Ferndale, WA 360-366-9900
Audion Automation
Carrollton, TX. 972-389-0777
Automated Packaging Systems
Streetsboro, OH 888-288-6224
Batching Systems
Prince Frederick, MD 800-311-0851
Bettendorf Stanford
Salem, IL. 800-548-2253
California Vibratory Feeders
Anaheim, CA 800-354-0972
Chantland-MHS Company
Dakota City, IA. 515-332-4045
Circle Packaging Machinery Inc
De Pere, WI. 920-983-3420
Control & Metering
Mississauga, ON. 800-736-5739
Crystal-Vision PackagingSystems
Torrance, CA. 800-331-3240
Custom Food Machinery
Stockton, CA. 209-463-4343
Custom Metal Designs
Oakland, FL 800-334-1777
Customized Equipment SE
Tucker, GA 770-934-9300
Enhance Packaging Technologies
Whitby, ON. 905-668-5811
Fawema Packaging Machinery
Palmetto, FL 941-351-9597
Franrica Systems
Stockton, CA. 209-948-2811
Glopak
St Leonard, QC 800-361-6994
ID Images
Brunswick, OH 866-516-7300
Ideal of America
Charlotte, NC 704-523-1604
Iman Pack
Westland, MI. 800-810-4626
JMC Packaging Equipment
Burlington, ON 800-263-5252
Klockner Bartelt
Sarasota, FL 877-227-8358
Kloppenberg & Company
Englewood, CO. 800-346-3246
Liqui-Box
Allentown, PA. 610-264-5420
Liqui-Box Corporation
Worthington, OH 614-888-9280
Lockwood Packaging
Woburn, MA. 800-641-3100
Machine Electronics Company
Brooklyn, NY 718-384-3211
Multi-Fill Inc
West Jordan, UT 801-280-1570
Oden Corporation
Tonawanda, NY 800-658-3622
Pacemaker Packaging Corporation
Flushing, NY. 718-458-1188
Packaging Enterprises
Jenkintown, PA. 763-257-3687
Packaging Systems International
Denver, CO 303-296-4445
Pacmac
Fayetteville, AR 479-521-0525
Palace Packaging Machines
Downingtown, PA. 610-873-7252
PlexPack Corp
Toronto, ON 855-635-9238
Pneumatic Scale Corporation
Cuyahoga Falls, OH 330-923-0491
Processing Machinery & Supply
Philadelphia, PA 215-425-4320

Prodo-Pak Corporation
Garfield, NJ....973-777-7770
Prototype Equipment Corporation
Libertyville, IL....847-680-4433
Reiser
Canton, MA....781-575-9941
Save-O-Seal Corporation
Elmsford, NY....800-831-9720
Simplex Filler Company
Napa, CA....800-796-7539
Summit Machine Builders Corporation
Denver, CO....800-274-6741
Taylor Products Company A Division Of Magnum Systems
Parsons, KS....888-882-9567
Telesonic Packaging Corporation
Wilmington, DE....302-658-6945
Temco
Oakland, CA....707-746-5966
TMT Vacuum Filters
Danville, IL....217-446-0742
Triangle Package Machinery Company
Chicago, IL....800-621-4170
Tridyne Process Systems Inc.
South Burlington, VT....802-863-6873
United States Systems
Kansas City, KS....888-281-2454
UniTrak Corporation
Port Hope, ON....866-883-5749
Vc999 Packaging Systems Inc.
Kansas City, MO....800-728-2999
Water Sciences Services ,Inc.
Jackson, TN....973-584-4131
Weigh Right Automatic Scale Company
Joliet, IL....800-571-0249

Bag Opening

About Packaging Robotics
Thornton, CO....303-449-2559
Alard Equipment Corporation
Williamson, NY....315-589-4511
Audion Automation
Carrollton, TX....972-389-0777
Automated Packaging Systems
Streetsboro, OH....888-288-6224
General Processing Systems
Holland, MI....800-547-9370
Gulf Arizona Packaging
Humble, TX....800-364-3887
Gulf Systems
Oklahoma City, OK....405-528-2293
Gulf Systems
Brownsville, TX....800-217-4853
Gulf Systems
Oklahoma City, OK....800-364-3887
Gulf Systems
Arlington, TX....817-261-1915
Herche Warehouse
Denver, CO....303-371-8186
Lockwood Packaging
Woburn, MA....800-641-3100
Our Name is Mud
New York, NY....877-683-7867
Packaging Systems International
Denver, CO....303-296-4445
Pacmac
Fayetteville, AR....479-521-0525
Temco
Oakland, CA....707-746-5966

Bag, Cellophane & Pliofilm

Alard Equipment Corporation
Williamson, NY....315-589-4511
Amplas
Green Bay, WI....800-950-4362
Automated Packaging Systems
Streetsboro, OH....888-288-6224
Batching Systems
Prince Frederick, MD....800-311-0851
Com-Pac International
Carbondale, IL....800-824-0817
Dynaclear Packaging
Wyckoff, NJ....201-337-1001
Fawema Packaging Machinery
Palmetto, FL....941-351-9597
Hudson-Sharp Machine Company
Green Bay, WI....920-494-4571
Liqui-Box
Allentown, PA....610-264-5420
M&Q Packaging Corporation
North Wales, PA....267-498-4000

Bag, Paper

About Packaging Robotics
Thornton, CO....303-449-2559
Alard Equipment Corporation
Williamson, NY....315-589-4511
B&R Machine Inc.
Wedron, IL....815-434-0427
H.G. Weber & Company
Kiel, WI....920-894-2221
New Jersey Wire Stitching Machine Company
Cherry Hill, NJ....856-428-2572
PlexPack Corp
Toronto, ON....855-635-9238
Vc999 Packaging Systems Inc.
Kansas City, MO....800-728-2999

Bar Code Devices

Accu-Sort Systems
Telford, PA....800-227-2633
Alard Equipment Corporation
Williamson, NY....315-589-4511
Alfa Production Systems
Westfield, NJ....908-654-0255
American Forms & Labels
Boise, ID....800-388-3554
Baublys Control Laser
Orlando, FL....866-612-8619
Cognitive
Golden, CO....800-765-6600
Columbia Labeling Machinery
Benton City, WA....888-791-9590
Command Line Corporation
Edison, NJ....732-738-6500
Computype
Saint Paul, MN....800-328-0852
Comstar Printing Solutions
Streetsboro, OH....330-528-2800
Concept Packaging Technologies
Carson City, NV....800-796-2769
Control Module
Enfield, CT....800-722-6654
Creative Automation
Passaic, NJ....973-778-0061
CRS Marking Systems
Portland, OR....800-547-7158
Diagraph Corporation
St Charles, MO....800-722-1125
Durable Engravers
Franklin Park, IL....800-869-9565
Esselte Meto
Morris Plains, NJ....800-645-3290
Exact Equipment Corporation
Morrisville, PA....215-295-2000
Fairbanks Scales
Kansas City, MO....800-451-4107
Fernqvist Labeling Solutions
Mountain View, CA....800-426-8215
Formulator Software,LLC
Clinton, NJ....908-735-2248
Fotel
Lombard, IL....800-834-4920
GCA Bar Code Specialist
Huntington Beach, CA....714-379-4911
Graphic Technology
New Century, KS....800-767-9920
Herche Warehouse
Denver, CO....303-371-8186
ID Images
Brunswick, OH....866-516-7300
Imaging Technologies
Cookeville, TN....800-488-2804
Imaje
Kennesaw, GA....770-421-7700
Indiana Cash Drawer Company
Shelbyville, IN....800-227-4379
Intermec Technologies Corporation
Everett, WA....800-755-5505
Label Products
Bloomington, MN....877-370-0688
LGInternational, Inc.
Portland, OR....800-345-0534
Los Angeles Label Company
Commerce, CA....800-606-5223
Marsh Company
Belleville, IL....800-527-6275
Microscan Systems
Renton, WA....800-762-1149
Quik-Stik Labels
Everett, MA....800-225-3496
SATO America
Charlotte, NC....888-871-8741
Southern Atlantic Label Company
Chesapeake, VA....800-456-5999
Stratix Corporation
Norcross, GA....800-883-8300
TallyGenicom
Irvine, CA....800-665-6210
Tharo Systems, Inc
Brunswick, OH....800-878-6833
Trident
Brookfield, CT....203-740-9333
Vertex Interactive
Clifton, NJ....973-777-3500
Videx, Inc.
Corvallis, OR....541-758-0521
Wallace Computer Services
Elk Grove Vlg, IL....888-925-8324
Zebra Technologies Corporation
Warwick, RI....800-556-7266
Zebra Technologies Corporation
Lincolnshire, IL....866-230-9494

Barrel & Drum Filling

Alard Equipment Corporation
Williamson, NY....315-589-4511
Custom Food Machinery
Stockton, CA....209-463-4343
Data Scale
Fremont, CA....800-651-7350
J.G. Machine Works
Holmdel, NJ....732-203-2077
Washington Frontier
Grandview, WA....509-469-7662

Barrel Packers

Alard Equipment Corporation
Williamson, NY....315-589-4511
Buffalo Technologies Corporation
Buffalo, NY....800-332-2419
Centennial Molding LLC
Hastings, NE....888-883-2189

Beverages, Hot Fill

Alard Equipment Corporation
Williamson, NY....315-589-4511
Innovative Food Solutions LLC
Columbus, OH....800-884-3314
Power Packaging, Inc.
Westerville, OH....877-272-1054
Promens
St. John, NB....800-295-3725
Washington Frontier
Grandview, WA....509-469-7662

Bottle & Jar Sealing

AAMD
Liverpool, NY....800-887-4167
AHP Machine & Tool Company
Lancaster, OH....740-681-6709
Alard Equipment Corporation
Williamson, NY....315-589-4511
Anderson Machine Sales
Fort Lee, NJ
Custom Food Machinery
Stockton, CA....209-463-4343
Giltron
Medfield, MA....508-359-4310
Hermann Ultrasonics Inc
Bartlett, IL....630-736-7400
Lyco Wausau
Wausau, WI....715-845-7867
New England Machinery Inc
Bradenton, FL....941-755-5550
Pack Line Corporation
Racine, WI....800-248-6868
Packaging & Processing Equipment
Ayr, ON....519-622-6666
Promens
St. John, NB....800-295-3725
Resina
Brooklyn, NY....800-207-4804
Sanchelima International
Doral, FL....305-591-4343

Bottle Cap, Plastic & Metal

AAMD
Liverpool, NY....800-887-4167
AHP Machine & Tool Company
Lancaster, OH....740-681-6709

Alard Equipment Corporation
Williamson, NY 315-589-4511
Anderson Machine Sales
Fort Lee, NJ
Auto-Mate Technologies LLC
Riverhead, NY 631-727-8886
Berkshire PPM
Litchfield, CT 860-567-3118
California Vibratory Feeders
Anaheim, CA 800-354-0972
Custom Food Machinery
Stockton, CA.................. 209-463-4343
International Plastics &Equipment Corporation
New Castle, PA.................. 724-658-3004
Maverick Enterprises
Ukiah, CA.................. 707-463-5591
Partola Packaging
Naperville, IL 800-727-8652
Surekap
Winder, GA.................. 770-867-5793

Bottle Capping & Crowning

AAMD
Liverpool, NY.................. 800-887-4167
Accutek Packaging Equipment Company
Vista, CA.................. 800-989-1828
AHP Machine & Tool Company
Lancaster, OH 740-681-6709
Alard Equipment Corporation
Williamson, NY 315-589-4511
Alcoa Packaging Machinery
Randolph, NY.................. 716-358-6451
Anderson Machine Sales
Fort Lee, NJ
Automated Production Systems Corporation
New Freedom, PA.................. 888-345-5377
Berkshire PPM
Litchfield, CT 860-567-3118
Biner Ellison
Vista, CA.................. 800-733-8162
California Vibratory Feeders
Anaheim, CA 800-354-0972
Chase-Logeman Corporation
Greensboro, NC 336-665-0754
Closure Systems International
Indianapolis, IN 800-311-2740
Cozzoli Machine Company
Somerset, NJ.................. 732-564-0400
Custom Food Machinery
Stockton, CA.................. 209-463-4343
Diversified Capping Equipment
Perrysburg, OH.................. 419-666-2566
Donahower & Company
Olathe, KS.................. 913-829-2650
Dynamic Automation
Simi Valley, CA.................. 805-584-8476
Eastern Machine
Middlebury, CT.................. 203-598-0066
ELF Machinery
La Porte, IN.................. 800-328-0466
Elmar Worldwide
Depew, NY 800-433-3562
Filler Specialties
Zeeland, MI.................. 616-772-9235
Filling Equipment Company
Flushing, NY.................. 800-247-7127
Fillit
Kirkland, QC.................. 514-694-2390
Fogg Company
Holland, MI.................. 616-786-3644
Fowler Products Company
Athens, GA 877-549-3301
Giltron
Medfield, MA 508-359-4310
Haumiller Engineering
Elgin, IL 847-695-9111
Horix Manufacturing Company
Mc Kees Rocks, PA.................. 412-771-1111
Inline Filling Systems
Venice, FL.................. 941-486-8800
International Plastics &Equipment Corporation
New Castle, PA.................. 724-658-3004
Kaps-All Packaging Systems
Riverhead, NY 631-727-0300
Kinsley Inc
Doylestown, PA 800-414-6664
KISS Packaging Systems
Vista, CA.................. 888-522-3538
Lake Eyelet Manufacturing Company
Weatogue, CT 860-628-5543
National Instrument Company
Baltimore, MD 800-526-1301
New England Machinery Inc
Bradenton, FL.................. 941-755-5550
Nichols Specialty Products
Southborough, MA.................. 508-481-4367
NJM/CLI
Pointe Claire, QC 514-630-6990
Norwalt Design Inc.
Randolph, NJ 973-927-3200
Packaging & Processing Equipment
Ayr, ON 519-622-6666
Palace Packaging Machines
Downingtown, PA.................. 610-873-7252
Perl Packaging Systems
Middlebury, CT.................. 800-864-2853
Portola Packaging
Naperville, IL 800-767-8652
Production Packaging & Processing Equipment Company
Phoenix, AZ 602-254-7878
Resina
Brooklyn, NY 800-207-4804
Silgan Containers
Woodland Hills, CA 818-710-3700
Simplex Filler Company
Napa, CA.................. 800-796-7539
Surekap
Winder, GA.................. 770-867-5793
Universal Labeling Systems
St Petersburg, FL 877-236-0266
US Bottlers Machinery Company
Charlotte, NC 704-588-4750
White Cap
Downers Grove, IL.................. 800-515-1565

Bottle Cartoning

Alard Equipment Corporation
Williamson, NY 315-589-4511
Berkshire PPM
Litchfield, CT 860-567-3118
Cannon Equipment Company
Rosemount, MN 800-825-8501
Packaging & Processing Equipment
Ayr, ON.................. 519-622-6666
Sasib Beverage & Food North America
Plano, TX 800-558-3814

Bottle Corking

Alard Equipment Corporation
Williamson, NY 315-589-4511
Poly-Seal Corporation
Baltimore, MD 410-633-1990
Power Packaging, Inc.
Westerville, OH.................. 877-272-1054

Bottle Drying

Alard Equipment Corporation
Williamson, NY 315-589-4511
Ametek Technical & Industrial Products
Kent, OH.................. 215-256-6601
Custom Food Machinery
Stockton, CA.................. 209-463-4343
Gardner Denver Inc.
Toronto, ON 416-763-4681
Paxton Products
Cincinnati, OH 800-441-7475

Bottle Filling

A.K. Robins
Baltimore, MD 800-486-9656
Accutek Packaging Equipment Company
Vista, CA.................. 800-989-1828
Alard Equipment Corporation
Williamson, NY 315-589-4511
B-T Engineering
Bala Cynwyd, PA 610-664-9500
Berkshire PPM
Litchfield, CT 860-567-3118
Biner Ellison
Vista, CA.................. 800-733-8162
California Vibratory Feeders
Anaheim, CA 800-354-0972
Chase-Logeman Corporation
Greensboro, NC 336-665-0754
Cozzoli Machine Company
Somerset, NJ.................. 732-564-0400
Custom Food Machinery
Stockton, CA.................. 209-463-4343
E2M
Duluth, GA 800-622-4326
Eischen Enterprises
Fresno, CA 559-834-0013
Elmar Worldwide
Depew, NY 800-433-3562
Federal Mfg Co
Milwaukee, WI 414-384-3200
Filler Specialties
Zeeland, MI.................. 616-772-9235
Fogg Company
Holland, MI.................. 616-786-3644
Globe International
Tacoma, WA 800-523-6575
Goodnature Products
Orchard Park, NY.................. 800-875-3381
Horix Manufacturing Company
Mc Kees Rocks, PA.................. 412-771-1111
J.G. Machine Works
Holmdel, NJ 732-203-2077
Jetstream Systems
Denver, CO 303-371-9002
Kaps-All Packaging Systems
Riverhead, NY 631-727-0300
KHS
Waukesha, WI.................. 262-798-1102
Kinsley Inc
Doylestown, PA 800-414-6664
KISS Packaging Systems
Vista, CA.................. 888-522-3538
Liqui-Box Corporation
Worthington, OH 614-888-9280
Lyco Wausau
Wausau, WI.................. 715-845-7867
Morrison Timing Screw Company
Glenwood, IL 708-331-6600
Multi-Fill Inc
West Jordan, UT 801-280-1570
Nalbach Engineering Company, Inc.
Countryside, IL.................. 708-579-9100
National Instrument Company
Baltimore, MD 800-526-1301
Oden Corporation
Tonawanda, NY 800-658-3622
Packaging & Processing Equipment
Ayr, ON.................. 519-622-6666
Packaging Dynamics
Walnut Creek, CA.................. 925-938-2711
Packaging Enterprises
Jenkintown, PA.................. 763-257-3687
Per-Fil Industries Inc
Riverside, NJ.................. 856-461-5700
Perl Packaging Systems
Middlebury, CT.................. 800-864-2853
Pneumatic Scale Corporation
Cuyahoga Falls, OH 330-923-0491
Power Packaging, Inc.
Westerville, OH.................. 877-272-1054
Sanchelima International
Doral, FL.................. 305-591-4343
Sasib Beverage & Food North America
Plano, TX 800-558-3814
Simplex Filler Company
Napa, CA.................. 800-796-7539
Tindall Packaging
Vicksburg, MI.................. 269-649-1163
Universal Labeling Systems
St Petersburg, FL 877-236-0266
US Bottlers Machinery Company
Charlotte, NC 704-588-4750
Volckening
Brooklyn, NY 718-748-0294

Bottle Washing, Soaking & Rinsing

Alard Equipment Corporation
Williamson, NY 315-589-4511
Alliance Industrial Corporation
Lynchburg, VA 800-368-3556
Berkshire PPM
Litchfield, CT 860-567-3118
BEVCO
Canada, BC.................. 800-663-0090
Custom Food Machinery
Stockton, CA.................. 209-463-4343
Davron Technologies
Chattanooga, TN.................. 423-870-1888
Horix Manufacturing Company
Mc Kees Rocks, PA.................. 412-771-1111
Jetstream Systems
Denver, CO 303-371-9002

Krones
Franklin, WI 414-409-4000
McBrady Engineering
Joliet, IL 815-744-8900
Metal Equipment Company
Cleveland, OH 800-700-6326
Namco Machinery
Maspeth, NY
National Hotpack
Stone Ridge, NY 800-431-8232
Palace Packaging Machines
Downingtown, PA 610-873-7252
Priority One Packaging
Waterloo, ON 800-387-9102
Sasib Beverage & Food North America
Plano, TX 800-558-3814
US Bottlers Machinery Company
Charlotte, NC 704-588-4750

Bottling

AC Label Company
Provo, UT 801-642-3500
Alard Equipment Corporation
Williamson, NY 315-589-4511
AMCO Products Company
Fort Smith, AR 479-646-8949
Ametek Technical & Industrial Products
Kent, OH 215-256-6601
Anver Corporation
Hudson, MA 800-654-3500
Berkshire PPM
Litchfield, CT 860-567-3118
Capmatic, Ltd.
Monreal North, QC 514-332-0062
Crown Cork & Seal Company
Philadelphia, PA 215-698-5100
Custom Food Machinery
Stockton, CA 209-463-4343
Filling Equipment Company
Flushing, NY 800-247-7127
Fowler Products Company
Athens, GA 877-549-3301
Horix Manufacturing Company
Mc Kees Rocks, PA 412-771-1111
Improved Blow Molding
Hollis, NH 800-256-1766
Jel-Sert Company
West Chicago, IL 800-323-2592
Kaps-All Packaging Systems
Riverhead, NY 631-727-0300
Kinsley Inc
Doylestown, PA 800-414-6664
Krones
Franklin, WI 414-409-4000
New England Machinery Inc
Bradenton, FL 941-755-5550
Oak Barrel Winecraft
Berkeley, CA 510-849-0400
OnTrack Automation Inc
Waterloo, ON 519-886-9090
Pace Packaging Corporation
Fairfield, NJ 800-867-2726
Packaging & Processing Equipment
Ayr, ON 519-622-6666
Packaging Dynamics
Walnut Creek, CA 925-938-2711
Palace Packaging Machines
Downingtown, PA 610-873-7252
Paxton Products
Cincinnati, OH 800-441-7475
Pearson Packaging Systems
Spokane, WA 800-732-7766
Peerless-Winsmith
Springville, NY 716-592-9310
Pneumatic Scale Corporation
Cuyahoga Falls, OH 330-923-0491
Pure & Secure, LLC
Lincoln, NE 800-875-5915
Rocheleau Blow Molding Systems
Fitchburg, MA 978-345-1723
Silver Spur Corporation
Cerritos, CA 562-921-6880
Simplex Filler Company
Napa, CA 800-796-7539
Universal Aqua Technologies
Torrance, CA 800-777-6939

Box Closing

Berkshire PPM
Litchfield, CT 860-567-3118
Charles Beck Machine Corporation
King of Prussia, PA 610-265-0500
Custom Food Machinery
Stockton, CA 209-463-4343
Gulf Arizona Packaging
Humble, TX 800-364-3887
Gulf Systems
Oklahoma City, OK 405-528-2293
Gulf Systems
Brownsville, TX 800-217-4853
Gulf Systems
Oklahoma City, OK 800-364-3887
Gulf Systems
Arlington, TX 817-261-1915
Herche Warehouse
Denver, CO 303-371-8186
Iman Pack
Westland, MI 800-810-4626
Moen Industries
Santa Fe Springs, CA 800-732-7766
Sealant Equipment & Engiineering
Plymouth, MI 734-459-8600
Thiele Technologies
Reedley, CA 800-344-8951
WE Killam Enterprises
Waterford, ON 519-443-7421
Weigh Right Automatic Scale Company
Joliet, IL 800-571-0249

Box Cutting

Accurate Paper Box Company
Knoxville, TN 865-690-0311
Charles Beck Machine Corporation
King of Prussia, PA 610-265-0500
D & L Manufacturing
Milwaukee, WI 414-256-8160
Premier Packages
Saint Louis, MO 800-466-6588

Box Strapping

Delta Cyklop Orga Pac
Charlotte, NC 800-446-4347
Dynaric
Virginia Beach, VA 800-526-0827
Gulf Arizona Packaging
Humble, TX 800-364-3887
Gulf Systems
Oklahoma City, OK 405-528-2293
Gulf Systems
Brownsville, TX 800-217-4853
Gulf Systems
Oklahoma City, OK 800-364-3887
Gulf Systems
Arlington, TX 817-261-1915
Herche Warehouse
Denver, CO 303-371-8186

Box, Paper

Accurate Paper Box Company
Knoxville, TN 865-690-0311
AmeriPak
Warrington, PA 215-343-1530
Barnes Machine Company
Saint Petersburg, FL 727-327-9452
Colter & Peterson
Paterson, NJ 973-684-0901
D & L Manufacturing
Milwaukee, WI 414-256-8160
Fuller Box Company
North Attleboro, MA 508-695-2525
General Corrugated Machinery Company
Palisades Park, NJ 201-944-0644
Gram Equipment of America
Tampa, FL 813-248-1978
International Paper Box Machine Company
Nashua, NH 603-889-6651
Jel-Sert Company
West Chicago, IL 800-323-2592
MarquipWardUnited
Phillips, WI 715-339-2191
Moen Industries
Santa Fe Springs, CA 800-732-7766
New Jersey Wire Stitching Machine Company
Cherry Hill, NJ 856-428-2572
Standard Paper Box Machine Company
Bronx, NY 800-367-8755
Superior Packaging Equipment Corporation
Fairfield, NJ 973-575-8818
Thiele Technologies
Reedley, CA 800-344-8951

Can Body Forming

Custom Food Machinery
Stockton, CA 209-463-4343
Dietzco
Hudson, MA 508-481-4000
M S Willett Inc
Cockeysville, MD 410-771-0460
Melvina Can Machinery Company
Hudson Falls, NY 518-743-0606
Omnitech International
Midland, MI 989-631-3377
Precision Component Industries
Canton, OH 330-477-6287
Reynolds Metals Company
Richmond, VA 804-743-6723

Can Capping

Accutek Packaging Equipment Company
Vista, CA 800-989-1828
Alcoa Packaging Machinery
Randolph, NY 716-358-6451
Anderson Machine Sales
Fort Lee, NJ
Berkshire PPM
Litchfield, CT 860-567-3118
Custom Food Machinery
Stockton, CA 209-463-4343
Filling Equipment Company
Flushing, NY 800-247-7127
Fleetwood
Romeoville, IL 630-759-6800
Nichols Specialty Products
Southborough, MA 508-481-4367
Pack Line Corporation
Racine, WI 800-248-6868
Pneumatic Scale Corporation
Cuyahoga Falls, OH 330-923-0491
Production Packaging & Processing Equipment Company
Phoenix, AZ 602-254-7878
Resina
Brooklyn, NY 800-207-4804
Silgan Containers
Woodland Hills, CA 818-710-3700

Can Closing

Berkshire PPM
Litchfield, CT 860-567-3118
Custom Food Machinery
Stockton, CA 209-463-4343
Dixie Canner Company
Athens, GA 706-549-1914
Heisler Industries, Inc
Fairfield, NJ 973-227-6300
Hermann Ultrasonics Inc
Bartlett, IL 630-736-7400
Schroeder Sewing Technologies
San Marcos, CA 760-591-9733

Can Drying

Ametek Technical & Industrial Products
Kent, OH 215-256-6601
BFM Equipment Sales
Fall River, WI 920-484-3341
Custom Food Machinery
Stockton, CA 209-463-4343
Gardner Denver Inc.
Toronto, ON 416-763-4681
Mountaingate Engineering
Campbell, CA 408-866-5100
Paxton Products
Cincinnati, OH 800-441-7475

Can Filling

A.K. Robins
Baltimore, MD 800-486-9656
Berkshire PPM
Litchfield, CT 860-567-3118
Custom Food Machinery
Stockton, CA 209-463-4343
E2M
Duluth, GA 800-622-4326
Elmar Worldwide
Depew, NY 800-433-3562
Horix Manufacturing Company
Mc Kees Rocks, PA 412-771-1111
J.G. Machine Works
Holmdel, NJ 732-203-2077

Jetstream Systems
Denver, CO … 303-371-9002
KHS
Waukesha, WI … 262-798-1102
KISS Packaging Systems
Vista, CA … 888-522-3538
Luthi Machinery Company, Inc.
Pueblo, CO … 719-948-1110
Marlen International
Astoria, OR … 800-862-7536
Multi-Fill Inc
West Jordan, UT … 801-280-1570
Nalbach Engineering Company, Inc.
Countryside, IL … 708-579-9100
Nu-Con Equipment
Chanhassen, MN … 877-939-0510
Oden Corporation
Tonawanda, NY … 800-658-3622
Per-Fil Industries Inc
Riverside, NJ … 856-461-5700
Pneumatic Scale Corporation
Cuyahoga Falls, OH … 330-923-0491
Pressure Pack
Williamsburg, VA … 757-220-3693
Rutherford Engineering
Rockford, IL … 815-623-2141
Sasib Beverage & Food North America
Plano, TX … 800-558-3814
SeamTech
Acampo, CA … 209-464-4610
Sick Inc.
Minneapolis, MN … 800-325-7425
Simplex Filler Company
Napa, CA … 800-796-7539
Temco
Oakland, CA … 707-746-5966
Tindall Packaging
Vicksburg, MI … 269-649-1163
Weigh Right Automatic Scale Company
Joliet, IL … 800-571-0249

Can Sealing

AAMD
Liverpool, NY … 800-887-4167
Alcoa Packaging Machinery
Randolph, NY … 716-358-6451
Anderson Machine Sales
Fort Lee, NJ
Berkshire PPM
Litchfield, CT … 860-567-3118
Custom Food Machinery
Stockton, CA … 209-463-4343
Fleetwood
Romeoville, IL … 630-759-6800
Hermann Ultrasonics Inc
Bartlett, IL … 630-736-7400
Ives-Way Products
Round Lake Beach, IL … 847-740-0658
Nu-Con Equipment
Chanhassen, MN … 877-939-0510

Can Seaming

Berkshire PPM
Litchfield, CT … 860-567-3118
Custom Food Machinery
Stockton, CA … 209-463-4343
Fleetwood
Romeoville, IL … 630-759-6800
Jescorp
Des Plaines, IL … 847-299-7800
Melvina Can Machinery Company
Hudson Falls, NY … 518-743-0606
Pneumatic Scale Corporation
Cuyahoga Falls, OH … 330-923-0491
SeamTech
Acampo, CA … 209-464-4610

Can Washing

A.K. Robins
Baltimore, MD … 800-486-9656
BFM Equipment Sales
Fall River, WI … 920-484-3341
Cincinnati Industrial Machine
Mason, OH … 800-677-0076
Custom Food Machinery
Stockton, CA … 209-463-4343
Davron Technologies
Chattanooga, TN … 423-870-1888
IMC Teddy Food Service Equipment
Amityville, NY … 800-221-5644

Canning & Food Packing

A.K. Robins
Baltimore, MD … 800-486-9656
ABCO Industries Limited
Lunenburg, NS … 866-634-8821
Acraloc Corporation
Oak Ridge, TN … 865-483-1368
Ametek Technical & Industrial Products
Kent, OH … 215-256-6601
Apollo Sheet Metal
Kennewick, WA … 509-586-1104
Berkshire PPM
Litchfield, CT … 860-567-3118
BluePrint Automation
Colonial Heights, VA … 804-520-5400
Custom Food Machinery
Stockton, CA … 209-463-4343
Dixie Canner Company
Athens, GA … 706-549-1914
Douglas Machine
Alexandria, MN … 320-763-6587
E.T. Oakes Corporation
Hauppauge, NY … 631-232-0002
E2M
Duluth, GA … 800-622-4326
Fleetwood
Romeoville, IL … 630-759-6800
FMC FoodTech
Madera, CA … 559-673-2766
Horix Manufacturing Company
Mc Kees Rocks, PA … 412-771-1111
Hughes Equipment Company LLC
Columbus, WI … 866-535-9303
Krones
Franklin, WI … 414-409-4000
Langsenkamp Manufacturing
Indianapolis, IN … 877-585-1950
Leader Engineering-Fabrication
Napoleon, OH … 419-592-0008
Lima Sheet Metal
Lima, OH … 419-229-1161
M S Willett Inc
Cockeysville, MD … 410-771-0460
Magnuson Corporation
Pueblo, CO … 719-948-9500
Melco Steel
Azusa, CA … 626-334-7875
Millard Manufacturing Corporation
La Vista, NE … 800-662-4263
Muskogee Rubber Stamp & Seal Company
Fort Gibson, OK … 918-478-3046
Olney Machinery
Westernville, NY … 315-827-4208
Paxton Products
Cincinnati, OH … 800-441-7475
Reid Boiler Works
Bellingham, WA … 360-714-6157
Riverwood International
Atlanta, GA … 770-984-5477
RMF Steel Products
Grandview, MO … 816-765-4101
T.D. Sawvel Company
Maple Plain, MN … 877-488-1816
Techno-Design
Garfield, NJ … 973-478-0930
Welliver Metal Products Corporation
Salem, OR … 503-362-1568

Cap Torque Test

Vibrac Corporation
Amherst, NH … 603-882-6777

Cappers

Blackhawk Molding
Addison, IL … 630-458-2100
G&F Manufacturing Comp any
Oak Lawn, IL … 800-282-1574

Carton

Adco Manufacturing
Sanger, CA … 559-875-5563
Berkshire PPM
Litchfield, CT … 860-567-3118
Bradman Lake Inc
Rock Hill, SC … 704-588-3301
C&K Machine Company
Holyoke, MA … 413-536-8122
Campbell Wrapper Corporation
De Pere, WI … 800-727-4210
Combi Packaging Systems
Canton, OH … 800-521-9072
Custom Food Machinery
Stockton, CA … 209-463-4343
D & L Manufacturing
Milwaukee, WI … 414-256-8160
Delkor Systems, Inc
Minneapolis, MN … 800-328-5558
Dimension Industries
Alexandria, MN … 763-425-3955
Econocorp
Randolph, MA … 781-986-7500
F.N. Smith Corporation
Oregon, IL … 815-732-2171
Future Commodities/Bestpack
Rancho Cucamonga, CA … 888-588-2378
Gram Equipment of America
Tampa, FL … 813-248-1978
Hayes Machine Company
Des Moines, IA … 800-860-6224
Heisler Industries, Inc
Fairfield, NJ … 973-227-6300
International Paper Box Machine Company
Nashua, NH … 603-889-6651
Jel-Sert Company
West Chicago, IL … 800-323-2592
Micro Solutions Enterprises
Van Nuys, CA … 800-673-4968
Packaging Machinery & Equipment
West Orange, NJ … 973-325-2418
Prototype Equipment Corporation
Libertyville, IL … 847-680-4433
San Fab Conveyor Systems
Sandusky, OH … 419-626-4465
Scandia Packaging Machinery Company
Fairfield, NJ … 973-473-6100
Serpa Packaging Solutions
Visalia, CA … 800-348-5453
TDF Automation
Cedar Falls, IA … 800-553-1777
Thiele Technologies
Reedley, CA … 800-344-8951
Tisma Machinery Corporation
Elk Grove Village, IL … 847-427-9525

Filling

Adco Manufacturing
Sanger, CA … 559-875-5563
Bradman Lake Inc
Rock Hill, SC … 704-588-3301
C&K Machine Company
Holyoke, MA … 413-536-8122
Campbell Wrapper Corporation
De Pere, WI … 800-727-4210
Cannon Equipment Company
Rosemount, MN … 800-825-8501
Crystal-Vision PackagingSystems
Torrance, CA … 800-331-3240
Custom Food Machinery
Stockton, CA … 209-463-4343
Design Technology Corporation
Billerica, MA … 978-663-7000
Doering Machines, Inc.
San Francisco, CA … 415-526-2131
Eischen Enterprises
Fresno, CA … 559-834-0013
Elliott Manufacturing Company Inc.
Fresno, CA … 559-233-6235
Iman Pack
Westland, MI … 800-810-4626
Key Automation
Eagan, MN … 651-455-0547
Klockner Bartelt
Sarasota, FL … 877-227-8358
MAF Industries
Traver, CA … 559-897-2905
Multi-Fill Inc
West Jordan, UT … 801-280-1570
NIMCO Corporation
Crystal Lake, IL … 815-459-4200
Optek
Galena, OH … 800-533-8400
Packaging Dynamics
Walnut Creek, CA … 925-938-2711
Pomona Service & Supply Company
Yakima, WA … 509-452-7121
RA Jones & Company
Covington, KY … 859-341-0400
Schneider Packaging Equipment
Brewerton, NY … 315-676-3035
Simplex Filler Company
Napa, CA … 800-796-7539

Summit Machine Builders Corporation
Denver, CO 800-274-6741
TDF Automation
Cedar Falls, IA 800-553-1777
Temco
Oakland, CA 707-746-5966
Thiele Engineering Company
Fergus Falls, MN 218-739-3321
Tindall Packaging
Vicksburg, MI 269-649-1163
Tisma Machinery Corporation
Elk Grove Village, IL 847-427-9525
Tridyne Process Systems Inc.
South Burlington, VT 802-863-6873
Universal Labeling Systems
St Petersburg, FL 877-236-0266
Weigh Right Automatic Scale Company
Joliet, IL 800-571-0249

Printing

Algene Marking EquipmentCompany
Garfield, NJ 973-478-9041
Blue Ridge Paper Products, Inc.
Canton, NC 828-454-0676
Custom Food Machinery
Stockton, CA 209-463-4343
Matthews International Corporation
Pittsburgh, PA 412-665-3640
Trident
Brookfield, CT 203-740-9333
WE Killam Enterprises
Waterford, ON 519-443-7421

Carton, Case, Box Sealing

A.B. Sealer, Inc.
Beaver Dam, WI 877-885-9299
Accutek Packaging Equipment Company
Vista, CA 800-989-1828
Adco Manufacturing
Sanger, CA 559-875-5563
Barnes Machine Company
Saint Petersburg, FL 727-327-9452
Belco Packaging Systems
Monrovia, CA 800-833-1833
Berkshire PPM
Litchfield, CT 860-567-3118
Better Packages
Shelton, CT 800-237-9151
Bradman Lake Inc
Rock Hill, SC 704-588-3301
Brenton LLC
Alexandria, MN 800-535-2730
C.J. Machine
Fridley, MN 763-767-4630
Campbell Wrapper Corporation
De Pere, WI 800-727-4210
Central Products Company
Menasha, WI 800-558-5006
Charles Beck Machine Corporation
King of Prussia, PA 610-265-0500
Combi Packaging Systems
Canton, OH 800-521-9072
Compacker Systems LLC
Davenport, IA 563-391-2751
Custom Food Machinery
Stockton, CA 209-463-4343
Customized Equipment SE
Tucker, GA 770-934-9300
Dimension Industries
Alexandria, MN 763-425-3955
Douglas Machine
Alexandria, MN 320-763-6587
Durable Packaging Corporation
Countryside, IL 800-700-5677
Econocorp
Randolph, MA 781-986-7500
Elliott Manufacturing Company Inc.
Fresno, CA 559-233-6235
Future Commodities/Bestpack
Rancho Cucamonga, CA 888-588-2378
General Corrugated Machinery Company
Palisades Park, NJ 201-944-0644
Gulf Arizona Packaging
Humble, TX 800-364-3887
Gulf Systems
Oklahoma City, OK 405-528-2293
Gulf Systems
Brownsville, TX 800-217-4853
Gulf Systems
Arlington, TX 817-261-1915
Hayes Machine Company
Des Moines, IA 800-860-6224
Heisler Industries, Inc
Fairfield, NJ 973-227-6300
Herche Warehouse
Denver, CO 303-371-8186
Hermann Ultrasonics Inc
Bartlett, IL 630-736-7400
Iman Pack
Westland, MI 800-810-4626
KIRKCO
Monroe, NC 704-289-7090
Kisters Kayat
Sarasota, FL 386-424-0101
Klippenstein Corporation
Fresno, CA 888-834-4258
Liqui-Box Corporation
Worthington, OH 614-888-9280
Loveshaw
South Canaan, PA 800-572-3434
Markwell Manufacturing Company
Norwood, MA 800-666-1123
Marq Packaging Systems
Yakima, WA 800-998-4301
Mastercraft International
Charlotte, NC 704-392-7436
Moen Industries
Santa Fe Springs, CA 800-732-7766
On-Hand Adhesives
Lake Zurich, IL 800-323-5158
Packaging & Processing Equipment
Ayr, ON 519-622-6666
Peace Industries
Rolling Meadows, IL 800-873-2239
Pearson Packaging Systems
Spokane, WA 800-732-7766
Prototype Equipment Corporation
Libertyville, IL 847-680-4433
Rockford-Midland Corporation
Rockford, IL 800-327-7908
S.V. Dice Designers
Rowland Heights, CA 888-478-3423
Sabel Engineering Corporation
Villard, MN 320-554-3611
Samuel Strapping Systems
Woodridge, IL 800-323-4424
San Fab Conveyor Systems
Sandusky, OH 419-626-4465
Scandia Packaging Machinery Company
Fairfield, NJ 973-473-6100
Sekisui TA Industries
Brea, CA 800-258-8273
Superior Packaging Equipment Corporation
Fairfield, NJ 973-575-8818
SWF McDowell
Orlando, FL 800-877-7971
TDF Automation
Cedar Falls, IA 800-553-1777
Technistar Corporation
Denver, CO 303-651-0188
Temco
Oakland, CA 707-746-5966
The Staplex Company
Brooklyn, NY 800-221-0822
Thiele Engineering Company
Fergus Falls, MN 218-739-3321
Thiele Technologies
Reedley, CA 800-344-8951
Triangle Package Machinery Company
Chicago, IL 800-621-4170
WE Killam Enterprises
Waterford, ON 519-443-7421
Weigh Right Automatic Scale Company
Joliet, IL 800-571-0249
Wepackit
Orangeville, ON 519-942-1700
Wexxar Corporation
Chicago, IL 630-983-6666
Wexxar Packaging Inc
Richmond, BC 888-565-3219
Zed Industries
Vandalia, OH 937-667-8407

Coding, Dating & Marking Equipment

A.D. Johnson Engraving Company
Kalamazoo, MI 269-342-5500
A.D. Joslin Manufacturing Company
Manistee, MI 231-723-2908
ABC Stamp Company
Boise, ID 208-375-4470
ABM Marking Company
Belleville, IL 800-626-9012
Accent Mark
Palmdale, CA 661-274-8191
Accu-Sort Systems
Telford, PA 800-227-2633
Ace Stamp & Engraving
Lakewood, WA 253-582-3322
Allmark Impressions
Fort Worth, TX 817-834-0080
American Art Stamp
Gardena, CA 310-965-9004
American Forms & Labels
Boise, ID 800-388-3554
Ameristamp Sign-A-Rama
Evansville, IN 800-543-6693
Applied Products Company
El Segundo, CA 888-551-0447
Astoria Laminations
Saint Clair Shores, MI 800-526-7325
Atlas Rubber Stamp Company
York, PA 717-755-1105
Authentic Biocode Corp
Addison, TX 866-434-1402
Axiohm USA
Myrtle Beach, SC 843-443-3155
Baublys Control Laser
Orlando, FL 866-612-8619
Bell-Mark Corporation
Pine Brook, NJ 973-882-0202
Bishop Machine
Zanesville, OH 740-453-8818
Bren Instruments
Franklin, TN 615-794-6825
Chattanooga Rubber Stamp& Stencil Works
Sale Creek, TN 800-894-1164
City Stamp & Seal Company
Austin, TX 800-950-6074
Cognitive
Golden, CO 800-765-6600
Columbia Labeling Machinery
Benton City, WA 888-791-9590
Computype
Saint Paul, MN 800-328-0852
Comstar Printing Solutions
Streetsboro, OH 330-528-2800
Concept Packaging Technologies
Carson City, NV 800-796-2769
Control Module
Enfield, CT 800-722-6654
Corpus Christi Stamp Works
Corpus Christi, TX 800-322-4515
Crown Marking
Minneapolis, MN 800-305-5249
CRS Marking Systems
Portland, OR 800-547-7158
Cup Pac Contract PackageRs
South Beloit, IL 877-347-9725
Custom Food Machinery
Stockton, CA 209-463-4343
Custom Rubber Stamp Company
Crosby, MN 888-606-4579
Custom Stamp Company
Anza, CA 323-292-0753
Custom Stamping & Manufacturing
Portland, OR 503-238-3700
D & L Manufacturing
Milwaukee, WI 414-256-8160
Dalemark Industries
Lakewood, NJ 732-367-3100
Day Mark/Food Safety Systems
Bowling Green, OH 419-353-2458
Dayton Marking Devices Company
Dayton, OH 937-432-0285
Design Technology Corporation
Billerica, MA 978-663-7000
Detroit Marking Products
Detroit, MI 800-833-8222
Diagraph Corporation
St Charles, MO 800-722-1125
Dixie Rubber Stamp & Seal Company
Atlanta, GA 404-875-8883
Domino Amjet
Gurnee, IL 800-444-4512
Dorell Equipment Inc
Somerset, NJ 732-247-5400
DRS Designs
Bethel, CT 888-792-3740
Durable Engravers
Franklin Park, IL 800-869-9565
E.C. Shaw Company
Cincinnati, OH 866-532-7429

E2M
Duluth, GA 800-622-4326
East Memphis Rubber Stamp Company
Bartlett, TN 901-384-0887
Easterday Fluid Technologies
Saint Francis, WI 414-482-4488
Ed Smith's Stencil Works
New Orleans, LA 504-525-2128
Ehrgott Rubber Stamp Company
Indianapolis, IN 317-353-2222
ELF Machinery
La Porte, IN. 800-328-0466
Elmark Packaging
West Chester, PA. 800-670-9688
EMCO
Miamisburg, OH 800-722-3626
Everett Stamp Works
Everett, WA. 425-258-6747
Fairbanks Scales
Kansas City, MO. 800-451-4107
Fas-Co Coders
Lithia Springs, GA 800-478-0685
Federal Stamp & Seal Manufacturing Company
Atlanta, GA. 800-333-7726
Fleming Packaging Corporation
Peoria, IL. 309-676-7657
Flint Rubber Stamp Works
Flint, MI 810-235-2341
Fox Stamp, Sign & Specialty
Menasha, WI. 800-236-3699
Franklin Rubber Stamp Company
Wilmington, DE 302-654-8841
Fraser Stamp & Seal
Chicago, IL 800-540-8565
Frost Manufacturing Corporation
Worcester, MA 800-462-0216
Fuller Box Company
North Attleboro, MA 508-695-2525
G&R Graphics
South Orange, NJ 813-503-8592
Garvey Products
Cincinnati, OH 513-771-8710
Garvey Products
West Chester, OH 800-543-1908
GCA Bar Code Specialist
Huntington Beach, CA 714-379-4911
Glover Rubber Stamp Corporation
Wills Point, TX. 214-824-6900
Gotham Pen & Pencil Company
Bronx, NY. 800-334-7970
Granite State Stamps, Inc.
Manchester, NH 800-937-3736
Graphic Impressions of Illinois
River Grove, IL 708-453-1100
Graphic Technology
New Century, KS 800-767-9920
Grays Harbor Stamp Works
Aberdeen, WA. 800-894-3830
Gribble Stamp & Stencil Company
Houston, TX 713-228-5358
Grueny's Rubber Stamps
Little Rock, AR. 501-376-0393
Gulf Systems
Oklahoma City, OK 405-528-2293
Gulf Systems
Arlington, TX 817-261-1915
H.G. Weber & Company
Kiel, WI. 920-894-2221
Hartford Stamp Works
Hartford, CT 860-249-6205
Hathaway Stamp Company
Cincinnati, OH 513-621-1052
Herche Warehouse
Denver, CO 303-371-8186
House Stamp Works
Chicago, IL 312-939-7177
Houston Label
Pasadena, TX 800-477-6995
Houston Stamp & Stencil Company
Houston, TX 713-869-4337
Howard Imprinting Machine Company
Tampa, FL. 800-334-6943
Hub Pen Company
Quincy, MA. 617-471-9900
Huntington Park Rubber Stamp Company
Huntington Park, CA 800-882-0029
ID Images
Brunswick, OH 866-516-7300
Ideal Stencil Machine & Tape Company
Marion, IL. 800-388-0162
Imaging Technologies
Cookeville, TN 800-488-2804
Imaje
Kennesaw, GA 770-421-7700
Independent Ink
Gardena, CA 800-446-5538
Indiana Cash Drawer Company
Shelbyville, IN 800-227-4379
Innovative Ceramic Corp.
East Liverpool, OH. 330-385-6515
Irby
Rocky Mount, NC. 252-442-0154
Jim Lake Companies
Dallas, TX. 214-741-5018
Joyce Engraving Company, Inc.
Dallas, TX. 214-638-1262
Justrite Rubber Stamp & Seal Company
Kansas City, MO. 800-229-5010
KIRKCO
Monroe, NC 704-289-7090
Koehler Gibson Marking &Graphics
Buffalo, NY. 800-875-1562
Kwikprint Manufacturing Company, Inc.
Jacksonville, FL 800-940-5945
L&L Engraving Company
Gilford, NH. 888-524-3032
Label Aire
Fullerton, CA 714-441-0700
Label Art
Tucker, GA 800-652-1072
LabelPrint Corporation
Newburyport, MA. 978-463-4004
Lake Eyelet Manufacturing Company
Weatogue, CT 860-628-5543
Lakeland Rubber Stamp Company
Lakeland, FL 863-682-5111
Lakeview Rubber Stamp Company
Chicago, IL 773-539-1525
Larry B. Newman PrintingCompany
Knoxville, TN 888-835-4566
Lasertechnics Marking Corporation
Nepean, ON. 613-749-4895
Listo Pencil Corporation
Alameda, CA. 800-547-8648
Long Island Stamp Corporation
Flushing, NY. 800-547-8267
Lord Label Machine Systems
Charlotte, NC 704-644-1650
Loveshaw
South Canaan, PA 800-572-3434
Mankuta Brothers Rubber Stamp Company, Inc.
Bohemia, NY 800-223-4481
Mansfield Rubber Stamp
Mansfield, OH 419-524-1442
Mark-It Rubber Stamp & Label Company
Stamford, CT. 203-348-3204
Marking Devices
Cleveland, OH 216-861-4498
Marking Methods
Alhambra, CA. 626-282-8823
Marsh Company
Belleville, IL. 800-527-6275
Mastermark
Kent, WA. 206-762-9610
Matthews International Corporation
Pittsburgh, PA. 412-665-3640
Mecco Marking & Traceability
Cranberry Township, PA. 888-369-9190
Menke Marking Devices
Santa Fe Springs, CA 800-231-6023
Mettler-Toledo
Columbus, OH 800-523-5123
Modern Stamp Company
Baltimore, MD 800-727-3029
Moore Efficient Communication Aids
Denver, CO 303-433-8456
Muskogee Rubber Stamp & Seal Company
Fort Gibson, OK 918-478-3046
My Serenity Pond
Cold Spring, MN. 320-363-0411
National Metal Industries
West Springfield, MA 800-628-8850
National Pen Corporation
San Diego, CA 858-675-3000
NCR Corporation
Duluth, GA 800-225-5627
Newstamp Lighting Corp.
North Easton, MA. 508-238-7071
Northern Berkshire Manufacturing Company
North Adams, MA 413-663-9204
Norwood Marking Systems
Downers Grove, IL 800-626-3464
O.K. Marking Devices
Regina, SK 306-522-2856
Oak International
Sturgis, MI 269-651-9790
OK Stamp & Seal Company
Oklahoma City, OK 405-235-7853
Open Date Systems
Georges Mills, NH 877-673-6328
Oration Rubber Stamp Company
Columbus, NJ 908-496-4161
Organic Products Company
Dallas, TX. 972-438-7321
Oshikiri Corporation of America
Philadelphia, PA 215-637-6005
Packaging & Processing Equipment
Ayr, ON 519-622-6666
Packaging Machinery & Equipment
West Orange, NJ 973-325-2418
Plastimatic Arts Corporation
Mishawaka, IN 800-442-3593
Printcraft Marking Devices
Buffalo, NY. 716-873-8181
Pulse Systems
Los Alamos, NM. 505-662-7599
Quick Stamp & Sign Mfg
Lafayette, LA 337-232-2171
Quik-Stik Labels
Everett, MA. 800-225-3496
R.P. Childs Stamp Company
Ludlow, MA 413-733-1211
Rebel Stamp & Sign Company, Inc.
Baton Rouge, LA 800-860-5120
Richardson's Stamp Works
Houston, TX 713-973-0300
RR Donnelley
Chicago, IL 800-742-4455
Rubber Stamp Shop
Accokeek, MD 800-835-0839
Sancoa International
Lumberton, NJ 609-953-5050
Sanifab
Stratford, WI 715-687-4332
SATO America
Charlotte, NC 888-871-8741
Schwaab, Inc
Milwaukee, WI 800-935-9877
Signet Marking Devices
Costa Mesa, CA 800-421-5150
Sioux Falls Rubber StampWork
Sioux Falls, SD. 605-334-5990
Smyth Companies, LLC
Saint Paul, MN 800-473-3464
Sossner Steel Stamps
Elizabethton, TN. 800-828-9515
Southern Rubber Stamp Company
Tulsa, OK 888-826-4304
Spectrum Enterprises
Evansville, IN 812-425-1771
Spencer Business Form Company
Spencer, WV 304-372-8877
Sprinter Marking
Zanesville, OH 740-453-1000
Steven's International
New Berlin, WI. 262-827-3800
Stratix Corporation
Norcross, GA 800-883-8300
Sutherland Stamp Company
San Diego, CA 858-233-7784
TallyGenicom
Irvine, CA 800-665-6210
Tharo Systems, Inc
Brunswick, OH 800-878-6833
TNA Packaging Solutions
Coppell, TX 972-462-6500
Trident
Brookfield, CT 203-740-9333
United Ribtype Company
Fort Wayne, IN 800-473-4039
Universal Die & Stamping
Prairie Du Sac, WI 608-643-2477
Universal Packaging
Houston, TX 800-324-2610
Vande Berg Scales
Sioux Center, IA 712-722-1181
Varitronic Systems
Brooklyn Park, MN. 763-536-6400
Videojet Technologies, Inc
Wood Dale, IL. 800-843-3610
Videx, Inc.
Corvallis, OR 541-758-0521
Volk Corporation
Farmington Hills, MI 800-521-6799
Walker Companies
Oklahoma City, OK 800-522-3015

Wallace Computer Services
Elk Grove Vlg, IL 888-925-8324
WE Killam Enterprises
Waterford, ON. . . . 519-443-7421
Weber Packaging Solutions, Inc.
Arlington Hts, IL 800-843-4242
Wichita Stamp & Seal
Wichita, KS. . . . 316-263-4223
Wildes - Spirit Design & Printing
White Plains, MD 301-870-4141
Willett America
Wood Dale, IL. . . . 800-259-2600
Winmark Stamp & Sign
Salt Lake City, UT 800-438-0480
Zanasi USA
Brooklyn Park, MN. . . . 800-627-2633
Zebra Technologies Corporation
Warwick, RI 800-556-7266

Coding, Marking, Dating

A.D. Johnson Engraving Company
Kalamazoo, MI 269-342-5500
A.D. Joslin Manufacturing Company
Manistee, MI. . . . 231-723-2908
Algene Marking EquipmentCompany
Garfield, NJ. . . . 973-478-9041
American Art Stamp
Gardena, CA 310-965-9004
American Forms & Labels
Boise, ID 800-388-3554
Ameristamp Sign-A-Rama
Evansville, IN 800-543-6693
Astoria Laminations
Saint Clair Shores, MI 800-526-7325
Baublys Control Laser
Orlando, FL. . . . 866-612-8619
Bell-Mark Corporation
Pine Brook, NJ 973-882-0202
Berkshire PPM
Litchfield, CT 860-567-3118
Bishop Machine
Zanesville, OH 740-453-8818
Bren Instruments
Franklin, TN 615-794-6825
Century Rubber Stamp Company
New York, NY 212-962-6165
Cognitive
Golden, CO 800-765-6600
Columbia Labeling Machinery
Benton City, WA 888-791-9590
Computype
Saint Paul, MN 800-328-0852
Crown Marking
Minneapolis, MN 800-305-5249
Cup Pac Contract PackageRs
South Beloit, IL 877-347-9725
Custom Food Machinery
Stockton, CA. . . . 209-463-4343
D & L Manufacturing
Milwaukee, WI 414-256-8160
Dalemark Industries
Lakewood, NJ 732-367-3100
Day Mark/Food Safety Systems
Bowling Green, OH 419-353-2458
Dayton Marking Devices Company
Dayton, OH. . . . 937-432-0285
Diagraph Corporation
St Charles, MO 800-722-1125
Dorell Equipment Inc
Somerset, NJ. . . . 732-247-5400
E.C. Shaw Company
Cincinnati, OH 866-532-7429
E2M
Duluth, GA 800-622-4326
Easterday Fluid Technologies
Saint Francis, WI 414-482-4488
Ed Smith's Stencil Works
New Orleans, LA 504-525-2128
ELF Machinery
La Porte, IN. . . . 800-328-0466
Elmark Packaging
West Chester, PA. . . . 800-670-9688
Esselte Meto
Morris Plains, NJ 800-645-3290
Everett Stamp Works
Everett, WA. . . . 425-258-6747
Fairbanks Scales
Kansas City, MO. . . . 800-451-4107
Fas-Co Coders
Lithia Springs, GA 800-478-0685
Federal Stamp & Seal Manufacturing Company
Atlanta, GA 800-333-7726
Franklin Rubber Stamp Company
Wilmington, DE 302-654-8841
FSI Technologies, Inc.
Lombard, IL 800-468-6009
Fuller Box Company
North Attleboro, MA 508-695-2525
Garvey Products
Cincinnati, OH 513-771-8710
GCA Bar Code Specialist
Huntington Beach, CA 714-379-4911
Glover Rubber Stamp Corporation
Wills Point, TX. . . . 214-824-6900
Granite State Stamps, Inc.
Manchester, NH 800-937-3736
Graphic Technology
New Century, KS 800-767-9920
Gulf Arizona Packaging
Humble, TX 800-364-3887
Gulf Systems
Oklahoma City, OK 405-528-2293
Gulf Systems
Brownsville, TX 800-217-4853
Gulf Systems
Arlington, TX 817-261-1915
H.G. Weber & Company
Kiel, WI. . . . 920-894-2221
Herche Warehouse
Denver, CO 303-371-8186
Howard Imprinting Machine Company
Tampa, FL. . . . 800-334-6943
Huntington Park Rubber Stamp Company
Huntington Park, CA 800-882-0029
ID Images
Brunswick, OH 866-516-7300
Ideal Stencil Machine & Tape Company
Marion, IL. . . . 800-388-0162
Imaje
Kennesaw, GA 770-421-7700
Independent Ink
Gardena, CA 800-446-5538
Indiana Cash Drawer Company
Shelbyville, IN 800-227-4379
Irby
Rocky Mount, NC. . . . 252-442-0154
Joyce Engraving Company, Inc.
Dallas, TX. . . . 214-638-1262
KIRKCO
Monroe, NC 704-289-7090
Koehler Gibson Marking &Graphics
Buffalo, NY. . . . 800-875-1562
Kwikprint Manufacturing Company, Inc.
Jacksonville, FL 800-940-5945
LabelPrint Corporation
Newburyport, MA. . . . 978-463-4004
Lake Eyelet Manufacturing Company
Weatogue, CT 860-628-5543
Lasertechnics Marking Corporation
Nepean, ON. . . . 613-749-4895
Loveshaw
South Canaan, PA 800-572-3434
Marking Methods
Alhambra, CA. . . . 626-282-8823
Marsh Company
Belleville, IL. . . . 800-527-6275
Matthews International Corporation
Pittsburgh, PA. . . . 412-665-3640
Mecco Marking & Traceability
Cranberry Township, PA. . . . 888-369-9190
Menke Marking Devices
Santa Fe Springs, CA 800-231-6023
Moore Efficient Communication Aids
Denver, CO 303-433-8456
Muskogee Rubber Stamp & Seal Company
Fort Gibson, OK 918-478-3046
National Metal Industries
West Springfield, MA. . . . 800-628-8850
Newstamp Lighting Corp.
North Easton, MA. . . . 508-238-7071
Norwood Marking Systems
Downers Grove, IL 800-626-3464
Oration Rubber Stamp Company
Columbus, NJ 908-496-4161
Packaging & Processing Equipment
Ayr, ON 519-622-6666
Precision Component Industries
Canton, OH 330-477-6287
Pulse Systems
Los Alamos, NM. . . . 505-662-7599
R.P. Childs Stamp Company
Ludlow, MA 413-733-1211
Rebel Stamp & Sign Company, Inc.
Baton Rouge, LA 800-860-5120
Rubber Stamp Shop
Accokeek, MD 800-835-0839
Schwaab, Inc
Milwaukee, WI 800-935-9877
Shiffer Industries
Kihei, HI 800-642-1774
Signet Marking Devices
Costa Mesa, CA 800-421-5150
Sossner Steel Stamps
Elizabethton, TN. . . . 800-828-9515
Southern Rubber Stamp Company
Tulsa, OK 888-826-4304
Sprinter Marking
Zanesville, OH 740-453-1000
Steven's International
New Berlin, WI. . . . 262-827-3800
TallyGenicom
Irvine, CA 800-665-6210
Tharo Systems, Inc
Brunswick, OH 800-878-6833
Trident
Brookfield, CT 203-740-9333
Universal Die & Stamping
Prairie Du Sac, WI 608-643-2477
Vande Berg Scales
Sioux Center, IA 712-722-1181
Varitronic Systems
Brooklyn Park, MN. . . . 763-536-6400
Videojet Technologies, Inc
Wood Dale, IL. . . . 800-843-3610
Videx, Inc.
Corvallis, OR 541-758-0521
Volk Corporation
Farmington Hills, MI 800-521-6799
WE Killam Enterprises
Waterford, ON. . . . 519-443-7421
Weber Packaging Solutions, Inc.
Arlington Hts, IL 800-843-4242
Wichita Stamp & Seal
Wichita, KS. . . . 316-263-4223
Willett America
Wood Dale, IL. . . . 800-259-2600
Zanasi USA
Brooklyn Park, MN. . . . 800-627-2633
Zebra Technologies Corporation
Warwick, RI 800-556-7266

Container

About Packaging Robotics
Thornton, CO 303-449-2559
Barnes Machine Company
Saint Petersburg, FL. . . . 727-327-9452
Berry Plastics
Evansville, IN 800-234-1930
Burd & Fletcher
Independence, MO 800-821-2776
Carando Machine Works
Stockton, CA. . . . 209-948-6500
Carleton Helical Technologies
New Britain, PA 215-230-8900
Dietzco
Hudson, MA 508-481-4000
Heisler Industries, Inc
Fairfield, NJ 973-227-6300
Heuft
Downers Grove, IL 630-968-9011
Hoegger Food Technology Inc.
Minneapolis, MN 877-789-5400
MarquipWardUnited
Phillips, WI. . . . 715-339-2191
Neos
Elk River, MN. . . . 888-441-6367
Osgood Industries
Oldsmar, FL 813-855-7337
Paradise
Plant City, FL 800-330-8952
Peco Controls Corporation
Modesto, CA. . . . 800-732-6285
Plastic Ingenuity, Inc.
Cross Plains, WI 608-798-3071
Plastipak Industries
La Prairie, QC. . . . 800-387-7452
Promens
St. John, NB 800-295-3725
Rotonics Manufacturing
Gardena, CA 310-327-5401
Silver Spur Corporation
Cerritos, CA 562-921-6880

Solbern
Fairfield, NJ 973-227-3030
Southworth Products Corporation
Portland, ME 800-743-1000
Stormax International
Concord, NH 800-874-7629
Tindall Packaging
Vicksburg, MI 269-649-1163
Vc999 Packaging Systems Inc.
Kansas City, MO 800-728-2999

Detectors

Packaging Line

AW Company
Franksville, WI 800-850-6110
Binks Industries
Montgomery, IL 630-801-1100
Care Controls, Inc.
Mill Creek, WA 800-593-6050
Carter Products Company
Grand Rapids, MI 888-622-7837
Daystar
Glen Arm, MD 800-494-6537
Eaton Corporation
Cleveland, OH 800-386-1911
Eriez Magnetics
Erie, PA 800-346-4946
Industrial Dynamics Company
Torrance, CA 888-434-5832
LDJ Electronics
Troy, MI 248-528-2202
Lixi
Huntley, IL 847-961-6666
Lock Inspection Systems
Fitchburg, MA 800-227-5539
Mettler Toldeo Safeline
Tampa, FL 800-447-4439
MOCON
Minneapolis, MN 763-493-6370
Nikka Densok
Lakewood, CO 800-806-4587
Norman N. Axelrod Associates
New York, NY 212-741-6302
Ohio Magnetics-Stearns Magnetics
Cleveland, OH 800-486-6446
Peco Controls Corporation
Modesto, CA 800-732-6285
ShockWatch
Dallas, TX 800-527-9497
Vande Berg Scales
Sioux Center, IA 712-722-1181

Equipment

Materials

Loeb Equipment & Appraisal Company
Chicago, IL 773-548-4131
Lyco Manufacturing
Wausau, WI 715-845-7867
Priority One Packaging
Waterloo, ON 800-387-9102

Exhausters

Canning

A.K. Robins
Baltimore, MD 800-486-9656
Dixie Canner Company
Athens, GA 706-549-1914
Ross Cook
San Jose, CA 800-233-7339

Form, Fill & Seal

Horizontal

ACMA/GD
Richmond, VA 800-525-2735
Bradman Lake Inc
Rock Hill, SC 704-588-3301
Campbell Wrapper Corporation
De Pere, WI 920-983-7100
Circle Packaging Machinery Inc
De Pere, WI 920-983-3420
Elopak
New Hudson, MI 248-486-4600
Enhance Packaging Technologies
Whitby, ON 905-668-5811
Equipment Outlet
Meridian, ID 208-887-1472
Formost Packaging Machines
Woodinville, WA 425-483-9090
Hermann Ultrasonics Inc
Bartlett, IL 630-736-7400
Ilapak
Newtown, PA 215-579-2900
Iman Pack
Westland, MI 800-810-4626
Maryland Packaging Corporation
Baltimore, MD 410-347-0365
OSSID LLC
Rocky Mount, NC 800-334-8369
Packaging Dynamics
Walnut Creek, CA 925-938-2711
Prodo-Pak Corporation
Garfield, NJ 973-777-7770
Reiser
Canton, MA 781-575-9941
Sitma USA
Spilamberto, MO 800-728-1254
Southern Packaging & Bottling
Athens, GA 706-208-0814
Zed Industries
Vandalia, OH 937-667-8407

Vertical

Accu-Pak
Akron, OH 330-644- 301
ACMA/GD
Richmond, VA 800-525-2735
Amark Packaging Systems
Kansas City, MO 816-965-9000
Blodgett Company
Houston, TX 281-933-6195
Bradman Lake Inc
Rock Hill, SC 704-588-3301
Campbell Wrapper Corporation
De Pere, WI 800-727-4210
Circle Packaging Machinery Inc
De Pere, WI 920-983-3420
Elopak
New Hudson, MI 248-486-4600
Enhance Packaging Technologies
Whitby, ON 905-668-5811
Equipment Outlet
Meridian, ID 208-887-1472
Formost Packaging Machines
Woodinville, WA 425-483-9090
General Packaging Equipment Company
Houston, TX 713-686-4331
Hayssen
Duncan, SC 864-486-4000
Hermann Ultrasonics Inc
Bartlett, IL 630-736-7400
Ilapak
Newtown, PA 215-579-2900
Iman Pack
Westland, MI 800-810-4626
Key-Pak Machines
Lebanon, NJ 908-236-2111
Korab Engineering Company
Los Angeles, CA 310-670-7710
Longhorn Packaging
San Antonio, TX 800-433-7974
Matrix Packaging Machinery
Saukville, WI 262-268-8300
OSSID LLC
Rocky Mount, NC 800-334-8369
Packaging Dynamics
Walnut Creek, CA 925-938-2711
Pacmac
Fayetteville, AR 479-521-0525
PFM Packaging Machinery Corporation
Newmarket, ON 905-836-6709
Prodo-Pak Corporation
Garfield, NJ 973-777-7770
TNA Packaging Solutions
Coppell, TX 972-462-6500
Universal Packaging
Houston, TX 800-324-2610
Wick's Packaging Service
Cutler, IN 574-967-3104
Zed Industries
Vandalia, OH 937-667-8407

Heat Sealing

AAMD
Liverpool, NY 800-887-4167
Audion Automation
Carrollton, TX 972-389-0777
Branson Ultrasonics Corporation
Danbury, CT 203-796-0400
Chaffee Company
Rocklin, CA 916-630-3980
Chase Industries
Carson, CA 310-763-9900
Circle Packaging Machinery Inc
De Pere, WI 920-983-3420
Custom Food Machinery
Stockton, CA 209-463-4343
Design Technology Corporation
Billerica, MA 978-663-7000
Edson Packaging Machinery
Hamilton, ON 905-385-3201
Food Equipment Manufacturing Company
Bedford Heights, OH 216-663-1208
Giltron
Medfield, MA 508-359-4310
Green-Tek
Janesville, WI 800-747-6440
Harwil Corporation
Oxnard, CA 800-562-2447
Key-Pak Machines
Lebanon, NJ 908-236-2111
Kliklok-Woodman
Decatur, GA 770-981-5200
On-Hand Adhesives
Lake Zurich, IL 800-323-5158
PlexPack Corp
Toronto, ON 855-635-9238
Pressure Pack
Williamsburg, VA 757-220-3693
Reiser
Canton, MA 781-575-9941
Rockford-Midland Corporation
Rockford, IL 800-327-7908
Save-O-Seal Corporation
Elmsford, NY 800-831-9720
Servpak Corporation
Hollywood, FL 800-782-0840
SIG Doboy
New Richmond, WI 715-246-6511
Stock America Inc
Grafton, WI 262-375-4100
Wraps
East Orange, NJ 973-673-7873
Zed Industries
Vandalia, OH 937-667-8407

Jar Filling

A.K. Robins
Baltimore, MD 800-486-9656
Berkshire PPM
Litchfield, CT 860-567-3118
Custom Food Machinery
Stockton, CA 209-463-4343
Dana Labels
Beaverton, OR 800-255-1492
Delta Plastics
Hot Springs, AR 501-760-3000
Elmar Worldwide
Depew, NY 800-433-3562
J.G. Machine Works
Holmdel, NJ 732-203-2077
Morrison Timing Screw Company
Glenwood, IL 708-331-6600
Multi-Fill Inc
West Jordan, UT 801-280-1570
Oden Corporation
Tonawanda, NY 800-658-3622
Packaging Enterprises
Jenkintown, PA 763-257-3687
Sick Inc.
Minneapolis, MN 800-325-7425
Simplex Filler Company
Napa, CA 800-796-7539
Tindall Packaging
Vicksburg, MI 269-649-1163
Weigh Right Automatic Scale Company
Joliet, IL 800-571-0249

Label Printing

Advent Machine Company
Commerce, CA 800-846-7716
Apex Machine Company
Fort Lauderdale, FL 954-566-1572
Auto Labe
Fort Pierce, FL 800-634-5376

Cam Tron Systems
Addison, IL 630-543-2884
Comstar Printing Solutions
Streetsboro, OH 330-528-2800
Dana Labels
Beaverton, OR 800-255-1492
Dorell Equipment Inc
Somerset, NJ 732-247-5400
Fairbanks Scales
Kansas City, MO 800-451-4107
Fernqvist Labeling Solutions
Mountain View, CA 800-426-8215
Grand Valley Labels
Grand Rapids, MI
ID Images
Brunswick, OH 866-516-7300
LabelPrint Corporation
Newburyport, MA 978-463-4004
Lord Label Group
Charlotte, NC 800-341-5225
Mateer Burt
Exton, PA 800-345-1308
Matthews International Corporation
Pittsburgh, PA 412-665-3640
Paper Converting Machine Company Aquaflex
Duncansville, PA 814-695-5521
PEAK Technologies, Inc.
Columbia, MD 800-926-9212
Robbie Manufacturing
Shawnee Mission, KS 800-255-6328
Sohn Manufacturing
Elkhart Lake, WI 920-876-3361
Tharo Systems, Inc
Brunswick, OH 800-878-6833
W.T. Nickell Label Company
Batavia, OH 888-899-1991
Wishbone Utensil Tableware Line
Wheat Ridge, CO 866-266-5928
WS Packaging-Superior Label
Green Bay, WI 800-818-5481
Zebra Technologies Corporation
Warwick, RI 800-556-7266

Labeling

A.D. Joslin Manufacturing Company
Manistee, MI 231-723-2908
About Packaging Robotics
Thornton, CO 303-449-2559
AC Label Company
Provo, UT 801-642-3500
Accraply/Trine
Burlington Ontario, ON 800-387-6742
Accutek Packaging Equipment Company
Vista, CA 800-989-1828
ASCENT Technics Corporation
Brick, NJ 800-774-7077
Associated Packaging Equipment Corporation
Markham, ON 905-475-6647
Auto Labe
Fort Pierce, FL 800-634-5376
Automated Packaging Systems
Streetsboro, OH 888-288-6224
Bell & Howell Company
Lincolnwood, IL 800-647-2290
Berkshire PPM
Litchfield, CT 860-567-3118
Cam Tron Systems
Addison, IL 630-543-2884
CMS Gilbreth Packaging Systems
Croydon, PA 800-630-2413
Cognitive
Golden, CO 800-765-6600
Columbia Labeling Machinery
Benton City, WA 888-791-9590
Concept Packaging Technologies
Carson City, NV 800-796-2769
Convergent Label Technology
Tampa, FL 800-252-6111
CRS Marking Systems
Portland, OR 800-547-7158
Custom Food Machinery
Stockton, CA 209-463-4343
CVP Systems
Downers Grove, IL 800-422-4720
D & L Manufacturing
Milwaukee, WI 414-256-8160
Dalemark Industries
Lakewood, NJ 732-367-3100
Day Mark/Food Safety Systems
Bowling Green, OH 419-353-2458
Diagraph Corporation
St Charles, MO 800-722-1125
Dispensa-Matic Label Dispense
Rocky Mount, MO 800-325-7303
Dorell Equipment Inc
Somerset, NJ 732-247-5400
Dow Industries
Wilmington, MA 800-776-1201
ELF Machinery
La Porte, IN 800-328-0466
Elmark Packaging
West Chester, PA 800-670-9688
EMCO
Miamisburg, OH 800-722-3626
EPI Labelers
New Freedom, PA 800-755-8344
Esselte Meto
Morris Plains, NJ 800-645-3290
Exact Equipment Corporation
Morrisville, PA 215-295-2000
Fairbanks Scales
Kansas City, MO 800-451-4107
Fast Industries
Fort Lauderdale, FL 800-775-5345
Fernqvist Labeling Solutions
Mountain View, CA 800-426-8215
Garvey Products
West Chester, OH 800-543-1908
GCA Bar Code Specialist
Huntington Beach, CA 714-379-4911
GEI PPM
Exton, PA 800-345-1308
Glen Mills, Inc.
Clifton, NJ 973-777-0777
Gluemaster
Kenosha, WI 262-857-7212
Gulf Arizona Packaging
Humble, TX 800-364-3887
Gulf Systems
Oklahoma City, OK 405-528-2293
Gulf Systems
Brownsville, TX 800-217-4853
Gulf Systems
Oklahoma City, OK 800-364-3887
Gulf Systems
Arlington, TX 817-261-1915
Heisler Industries, Inc
Fairfield, NJ 973-227-6300
Herche Warehouse
Denver, CO 303-371-8186
Horix Manufacturing Company
Mc Kees Rocks, PA 412-771-1111
Houston Label
Pasadena, TX 800-477-6995
Hurst Corporation
Devon, PA 610-687-2404
Hurst Labeling Systems
Chatsworth, CA 800-969-1705
Industrial Automation Systems
Santa Clarita, CA 888-484-4427
Innovative Packaging Solution
Martin, MI 616-656-2100
KISS Packaging Systems
Vista, CA 888-522-3538
Krones
Franklin, WI 414-409-4000
Label Aire
Fullerton, CA 714-441-0700
Label Technology
Merced, CA 800-388-1990
Labelette Company
Forest Park, IL 708-366-2010
LabelPrint Corporation
Newburyport, MA 978-463-4004
Livingston-Wilbor Corporation
Edison, NJ 908-322-8403
Lord Label Group
Charlotte, NC 800-341-5225
Lord Label Machine Systems
Charlotte, NC 704-644-1650
Loveshaw
South Canaan, PA 800-572-3434
Marking Methods
Alhambra, CA 626-282-8823
Master Magnetics
Castle Rock, CO 800-525-3536
Mateer Burt
Exton, PA 800-345-1308
Matthews International Corporation
Pittsburgh, PA 412-665-3640
Miken Cosmpanies
Buffalo, NY 716-668-6311
Modular King Packaging Systems
Randolph, NJ 973-970-9393
MRI Flexible Packaging
Newtown, PA 800-448-8183
National Label Company
Lafayette Hill, PA 610-825-3250
National Package SealingCompany
Santa Ana, CA 714-630-1505
Nercon Engineering & Manufacturing
Oshkosh, WI 920-233-3268
New Way Packaging Machinery
Hanover, PA 800-522-3537
NJM/CLI
Pointe Claire, QC 514-630-6990
Nordson Corporation
Duluth, GA 800-683-2314
OnTrack Automation Inc
Waterloo, ON 519-886-9090
Package Systems Corporation
Danielson, CT 800-522-3548
Packaging & Processing Equipment
Ayr, ON 519-622-6666
Paragon Labeling Systems
White Bear Lake, MN 800-429-7722
PDC International
Austin, TX 512-302-0194
PEAK Technologies, Inc.
Columbia, MD 800-926-9212
Perl Packaging Systems
Middlebury, CT 800-864-2853
PMI Food Equipment Group
Troy, OH 937-332-3000
Priority One Packaging
Waterloo, ON 800-387-9102
Production Packaging & Processing Equipment Company
Phoenix, AZ 602-254-7878
Quadrel Labeling Systems
Mentor, OH 800-321-8509
Quik-Stik Labels
Everett, MA 800-225-3496
Renard Machine Company
Green Bay, WI 920-432-8412
Roberts PolyPro
Charlotte, NC 800-269-7409
Sasib Beverage & Food North America
Plano, TX 800-558-3814
Schaefer Machine Company Inc.
Deep River, CT 800-243-5143
Seal-O-Matic Company
Jacksonville, OR 800-631-2072
Smyth Companies, LLC
Saint Paul, MN 800-473-3464
Tamarack Products
Wauconda, IL 847-526-9333
Tharo Systems, Inc
Brunswick, OH 800-878-6833
Universal Labeling Systems
St Petersburg, FL 877-236-0266
Vande Berg Scales
Sioux Center, IA 712-722-1181
Varitronic Systems
Brooklyn Park, MN 763-536-6400
Wallace Computer Services
Elk Grove Vlg, IL 888-925-8324
WE Killam Enterprises
Waterford, ON 519-443-7421
Weber Packaging Solutions, Inc.
Arlington Hts, IL 800-843-4242
WS Packaging-Superior Label
Green Bay, WI 800-818-5481
Zebra Technologies Corporation
Warwick, RI 800-556-7266
Zebra Technologies Corporation
Lincolnshire, IL 866-230-9494

Package Tying

BH Bunn Company
Lakeland, FL 800-222-2866
Delta Cyklop Orga Pac
Charlotte, NC 800-446-4347
Felins USA
Milwaukee, WI 800-336-3220
Gulf Arizona Packaging
Humble, TX 800-364-3887
Gulf Systems
Oklahoma City, OK 405-528-2293
Gulf Systems
Brownsville, TX 800-217-4853
Gulf Systems
Arlington, TX 817-261-1915

Herche Warehouse
Denver, CO 303-371-8186
Kwik Lok Corporation
Yakima, WA 800-688-5945
Machine Electronics Company
Brooklyn, NY 718-384-3211
Plas-Ties
Tustin, CA 800-854-0137
Steinmetz Machine Works
Stamford, CT 203-327-0118

Packing

A.K. Robins
Baltimore, MD 800-486-9656
Aaron Equipment Company
Bensenville, IL 630-350-2200
About Packaging Robotics
Thornton, CO 303-449-2559
Adco Manufacturing
Sanger, CA 559-875-5563
Amark Packaging Systems
Kansas City, MO 816-965-9000
API
Tampa, FL 813-888-8488
Arthur G. Russell Company (The)
Bristol, CT 860-583-4109
Automated Production Systems Corporation
New Freedom, PA 888-345-5377
B-T Engineering
Bala Cynwyd, PA 610-664-9500
BEI
South Haven, MI 800-364-7425
Belco Packaging Systems
Monrovia, CA 800-833-1833
BH Bunn Company
Lakeland, FL 800-222-2866
BluePrint Automation
Colonial Heights, VA 804-520-5400
Bradman Lake Inc
Rock Hill, SC 704-588-3301
Branson Ultrasonics Corporation
Danbury, CT 203-796-0400
Brechteen
Chesterfield, MI 586-949-2240
C.J. Machine
Fridley, MN 763-767-4630
Campbell Wrapper Corporation
De Pere, WI 800-727-4210
Clamco Corporation
Berea, OH 216-267-1911
Cleveland Vibrator Company
Cleveland, OH 800-221-3298
Climax Packaging Machinery
Hamilton, OH 513-874-1233
Coastline Equipment
Bellingham, WA 360-739-2480
Combi Packaging Systems
Canton, OH 800-521-9072
Compacker Systems LLC
Davenport, IA 563-391-2751
Custom Food Machinery
Stockton, CA 209-463-4343
CVP Systems
Downers Grove, IL 800-422-4720
Data Scale
Fremont, CA 800-651-7350
Design Technology Corporation
Billerica, MA 978-663-7000
Diversified Metal Engineering
Charlottetown, PE 902-628-6900
Domnick Hunter
Charlotte, NC 800-345-8462
Dorell Equipment Inc
Somerset, NJ 732-247-5400
Douglas Machine
Alexandria, MN 320-763-6587
Durable Packaging Corporation
Countryside, IL 800-700-5677
Durand-Wayland, Inc.
Lagrange, GA 800-241-2308
Eastern Machine
Middlebury, CT 203-598-0066
EDL Packaging Engineers
Green Bay, WI 920-336-7744
Edmeyer
Minneapolis, MN 651-450-1210
Edson Packaging Machinery
Hamilton, ON 905-385-3201
Elliott Manufacturing Company Inc.
Fresno, CA 559-233-6235
Fillit
Kirkland, QC 514-694-2390
Fleetwood
Romeoville, IL 630-759-6800
Fogg Company
Holland, MI 616-786-3644
Gainco, Inc.
Gainesville, GA 800-467-2828
GEI Autowrappers
Exton, PA 610-321-1115
General Bag Corporation
Cleveland, OH 800-837-9396
General Processing Systems
Holland, MI 800-547-9370
Gram Equipment of America
Tampa, FL 813-248-1978
GTI
Arvada, CO 303-420-6699
Halton Packaging Systems
Oakville, ON 905-847-9141
Hamrick Manufacturing & Service
Mogadore, OH 800-321-9590
Hart Design & Manufacturing
Green Bay, WI 920-468-5927
Hartness International
Greenville, SC 800-845-8791
Hermann Ultrasonics Inc
Bartlett, IL 630-736-7400
Hoegger Food Technology Inc.
Minneapolis, MN 877-789-5400
Hudson Control Group
Springfield, NJ 973-376-7400
ID Images
Brunswick, OH 866-516-7300
Ideal of America
Charlotte, NC 704-523-1604
Ilapak
Newtown, PA 215-579-2900
Iman Pack
Westland, MI 800-810-4626
Industrial Magnetics
Boyne City, MI 800-662-4638
International Omni-Pac Corporation
La Verne, CA 909-593-2833
Jagenberg
Enfield, CT 860-741-2501
Jeb Plastics
Wilmington, DE 800-556-2247
Jetstream Systems
Denver, CO 303-371-9002
Kisters Kayat
Sarasota, FL 386-424-0101
Kohler Industries
Lincoln, NE 800-365-6708
Krones
Franklin, WI 414-409-4000
L&H Wood Manufacturing Company
Farmington, MI 248-474-9000
Lako Tool & Manufacturing
Perrysburg, OH 800-228-2982
Langen Packaging
Mississauga, ON 905-670-7200
Longford Equipment US
Glastonbury, CT 860-659-0762
Machine Builders and Design
Shelby, NC 704-482-3456
Malo/Loveless Manufacturing
Tulsa, OK 918-583-2743
Maren Engineering Corporation
South Holland, IL 800-875-1038
Marq Packaging Systems
Yakima, WA 800-998-4301
Mateer Burt
Exton, PA 800-345-1308
Matthiesen Equipment Company
San Antonio, TX 800-624-8635
Melco Steel
Azusa, CA 626-334-7875
Molins/Sandiacre Richmond
Richmond, VA 804-421-8795
NDS
Columbus, OH 614-294-4931
Newcastle Company, Inc.
New Castle, PA 724-658-4516
Nigrelli Systems Inc
Kiel, WI 920-693-3161
NIMCO Corporation
Crystal Lake, IL 815-459-4200
Nu-Con Equipment
Chanhassen, MN 877-939-0510
Olney Machinery
Westernville, NY 315-827-4208
Pacemaker Packaging Corporation
Flushing, NY 718-458-1188
Package Systems Corporation
Danielson, CT 800-522-3548
Peco Controls Corporation
Modesto, CA 800-732-6285
Per-Fil Industries Inc
Riverside, NJ 856-461-5700
Pneumatic Scale Corporation
Cuyahoga Falls, OH 330-923-0491
Pressure Pack
Williamsburg, VA 757-220-3693
Priority One America
Waterloo, ON 519-746-6950
Professional Marketing Group
Seattle, WA 800-227-3769
Promarks, Inc.
Ontario, CA 909-923-3888
Prototype Equipment Corporation
Libertyville, IL 847-680-4433
PTI Packaging
Portage, WI 800-501-4077
RAM Center
Red Wing, MN 800-762-6842
Reiser
Canton, MA 781-575-9941
Remcon Plastics
West Reading, PA 800-360-3636
Rennco
Homer, MI 800-409-5225
Riverwood International
Atlanta, GA 770-984-5477
Rockford-Midland Corporation
Rockford, IL 800-327-7908
Ropak Manufacturing Company
Decatur, AL 256-350-4241
Rose Forgrove
Saint Charles, IL 630-443-1317
Sabel Engineering Corporation
Villard, MN 320-554-3611
Schneider Packaging Equipment
Brewerton, NY 315-676-3035
Schroeder Sewing Technologies
San Marcos, CA 760-591-9733
Semco Manufacturing Company
Pharr, TX 956-787-4203
Serpa Packaging Solutions
Visalia, CA 800-348-5453
Southern Automatics
Lakeland, FL 800-441-4604
Standard-Knapp
Portland, CT 800-628-9565
T.D. Sawvel Company
Maple Plain, MN 877-488-1816
TDF Automation
Cedar Falls, IA 800-553-1777
Thiele Engineering Company
Fergus Falls, MN 218-739-3321
Thiele Technologies
Reedley, CA 800-344-8951
Trio Packaging Corporation
Ronkonkoma, NY 800-331-0492
Ulma Packaging Systems
Taunton, MA 508-884-2500
Universal Packaging
Houston, TX 800-324-2610
W.G. Durant Corporation
Whittier, CA 562-946-5555
Wayne Automation Corporation
Norristown, PA 610-630-8900
WE Killam Enterprises
Waterford, ON 519-443-7421
WeighPack Systems/PaxiomGroup
Montreal, QC 888-934-4472
Wick's Packaging Service
Cutler, IN 574-967-3104
Wrapade Packaging Systems, LLC
Fairfield, NJ 888-815-8564
Zepf Technologies
Clearwater, FL 727-535-4100

Portion Control Equipment

AC Dispensing Equipment
Lower Sackville, NS 888-777-9990
Acme Scale Company
San Leandro, CA 888-638-5040
AEW Thurne
Lake Zurich, IL 800-239-7297
Am-Mac Incorporated
Fairfield, NJ 800-829-2018

Avery Weigh-Tronix
Fairmont, MN 877-888-1646
Beer Magic Devices
Hamilton, ON 905-522-3081
BVL Controls
Bois-Des-Filion, QC 866-285-2668
CCi Scale Company
Ventura, CA 800-900-0224
Challenge-RMF
Grandview, MO 816-765-0515
Crestware
North Salt Lake City, UT 800-345-0513
Daleco
West Chester, PA 610-429-0181
Design Technology Corporation
Billerica, MA 978-663-7000
Detecto Scale Company
Webb City, MO 800-641-2008
Diversified Metal Engineering
Charlottetown, PE 902-628-6900
Doering Machines, Inc.
San Francisco, CA 415-526-2131
Edlund Company Inc
Burlington, VT 800-772-2126
Genpak
Peterborough, ON 800-461-1995
Hoegger Food Technology Inc.
Minneapolis, MN 877-789-5400
Hollymatic Corporation
Countryside, IL 708-579-3700
Industrial Laboratory Equipment
Charlotte, NC 704-357-3930
Label Makers
Pleasant Prairie, WI 800-208-3331
Libertyware
Clearfield, UT 888-500-5885
Little Squirt
Toronto, ON 416-665-6605
Magnuson Industries
Rockford, IL 800-435-2816
Opal Manufacturing Ltd
Toronto, ON 416-646-5232
Packaging Progressions
Collegeville, PA 610-489-8601
Patty-O-Matic
Farmingdale, NJ 877-938-5244
Pelouze Scale Company
Bridgeview, IL 800-323-8363
Pino's Pasta Veloce
Staten Island, NY 718-273-6660
Plastic Fantastics/Buck Signs
Ashland, OR 800-482-1776
Proluxe
Paramount, CA 800-594-5528
Quantum Topping Systems Quantum Technical Services Inc
Frankfort, IL 888-464-1540
Reiser
Canton, MA 781-575-9941
Superior Products Company
Saint Paul, MN 800-328-9800
Traex
Dane, WI 800-356-8006
TWM Manufacturing
Leamington, ON 888-495-4831
Unifiller Systems
Delta, BC 888-733-8444
Weiler & Company
Whitewater, WI 800-558-9507
Zeroll Company
Fort Pierce, FL 800-872-5000

Printing

ABM Marking Company
Belleville, IL 800-626-9012
Accurate Paper Box Company
Knoxville, TN 865-690-0311
Advanced Poly-Packaging
Akron, OH 800-754-4403
Algene Marking EquipmentCompany
Garfield, NJ 973-478-9041
Apex Machine Company
Fort Lauderdale, FL 954-566-1572
Axiohm USA
Myrtle Beach, SC 843-443-3155
Bell-Mark Corporation
Pine Brook, NJ 973-882-0202
Bren Instruments
Franklin, TN 615-794-6825
Carl Strutz & Company
Mars, PA 724-625-1501
Cognitive
Golden, CO 800-765-6600
Columbia Labeling Machinery
Benton City, WA 888-791-9590
Computype
Saint Paul, MN 800-328-0852
Comstar Printing Solutions
Streetsboro, OH 330-528-2800
D & L Manufacturing
Milwaukee, WI 414-256-8160
Dana Labels
Beaverton, OR 800-255-1492
Dependable Machine Company
Verona, NJ 800-356-3237
Desco Equipment Corporation
Twinsburg, OH 330-405-1581
Domino Amjet
Gurnee, IL 800-444-4512
Donnick Label Systems
Jacksonville, FL 800-334-7849
Dorell Equipment Inc
Somerset, NJ 732-247-5400
Durable Engravers
Franklin Park, IL 800-869-9565
EMCO
Miamisburg, OH 800-722-3626
Esselte Meto
Morris Plains, NJ 800-645-3290
Exact Equipment Corporation
Morrisville, PA 215-295-2000
Fernqvist Labeling Solutions
Mountain View, CA 800-426-8215
GCA Bar Code Specialist
Huntington Beach, CA 714-379-4911
GM Nameplate
Seattle, WA 800-366-7668
GTCO CalComp
Scottsdale, AZ 800-856-0732
H.G. Weber & Company
Kiel, WI 920-894-2221
Howard Imprinting Machine Company
Tampa, FL 800-334-6943
ID Images
Brunswick, OH 866-516-7300
Imaging Technologies
Cookeville, TN 800-488-2804
Indiana Cash Drawer Company
Shelbyville, IN 800-227-4379
Kammann Machine
Portsmouth, NH 978-463-0050
Kase Equipment Corporation
Cleveland, OH 216-642-9040
Kurz Transfer Products
Charlotte, NC 800-333-2306
Kwikprint Manufacturing Company, Inc.
Jacksonville, FL 800-940-5945
Label Systems & Solutions
Bohemia, NY 800-811-2560
Labelmart
Maple Grove, MN 888-577-0141
Loveshaw
South Canaan, PA 800-572-3434
Marsh Company
Belleville, IL 800-527-6275
Mettler-Toledo
Columbus, OH 800-523-5123
Norwood Marking Systems
Downers Grove, IL 800-626-3464
Packaging Machinery & Equipment
West Orange, NJ 973-325-2418
Paper Converting Machine Company Aquaflex
Duncansville, PA 814-695-5521
Paper Converting MachineCompany
Green Bay, WI 920-336-4300
Paragon Labeling Systems
White Bear Lake, MN 800-429-7722
Reflex International
Norcross, GA 800-642-7640
Rice Lake Weighing Systems
Rice Lake, WI 800-472-6703
Service Stamp Works
Chicago, IL 312-666-8839
Sohn Manufacturing
Elkhart Lake, WI 920-876-3361
Star Micronics
Edison, NJ 800-782-7636
Steven's International
New Berlin, WI 262-827-3800
Stratix Corporation
Norcross, GA 800-883-8300
TallyGenicom
Irvine, CA 800-665-6210
Tamarack Products
Wauconda, IL 847-526-9333
TEC America
Atlanta, GA 770-453-0868
Tharo Systems, Inc
Brunswick, OH 800-878-6833
Trident
Brookfield, CT 203-740-9333
Varitronic Systems
Brooklyn Park, MN 763-536-6400
Videojet Technologies, Inc
Wood Dale, IL 800-843-3610
W.T. Nickell Label Company
Batavia, OH 888-899-1991
Wallace Computer Services
Elk Grove Vlg, IL 888-925-8324
Wichita Stamp & Seal
Wichita, KS 316-263-4223
Yamato Corporation
Colorado Springs, CO 800-538-1762
Zebra Technologies Corporation
Warwick, RI 800-556-7266
Zebra Technologies Corporation
Lincolnshire, IL 866-230-9494

Plastics

Carl Strutz & Company
Mars, PA 724-625-1501
Desco Equipment Corporation
Twinsburg, OH 330-405-1581
Trident
Brookfield, CT 203-740-9333
Uniloy Milacron
Manchester, MI 800-666-8852
WE Killam Enterprises
Waterford, ON 519-443-7421

Rebuilt & Used

A&M Industries
Sioux Falls, SD 800-888-2615
American Equipment Company
Aberdeen, MD 410-272-2626
AmeriPak
Warrington, PA 215-343-1530
Automated Packaging Systems
Streetsboro, OH 888-288-6224
Berkshire PPM
Litchfield, CT 860-567-3118
Cartpac
Franklin Park, IL 630-629-9900
Champion Trading Corporation
Marlboro, NJ 732-780-4200
Change Parts
Ludington, MI 231-845-5107
Circle Packaging Machinery Inc
De Pere, WI 920-983-3420
Colter & Peterson
Paterson, NJ 973-684-0901
Custom Food Machinery
Stockton, CA 209-463-4343
Eischen Enterprises
Fresno, CA 559-834-0013
Equipment Specialists
Haines City, FL 863-421-4567
Gulf Systems
Oklahoma City, OK 405-528-2293
Gulf Systems
Oklahoma City, OK 800-364-3887
Gulf Systems
Arlington, TX 817-261-1915
Hallmark Equipment
Morgan Hill, CA 408-782-2600
Health Star
Randolph, MA 800-545-3639
Ilapak
Newtown, PA 215-579-2900
Lehman Sales Associates
Sun Prairie, WI 608-575-7712
Madison County Wood Products
Saint Louis, MO 314-772-1722
McNeil Food Machinery
Stockton, CA 209-463-4343
Miller's Technical Service
Canton, MI 734-738-1970
National Equipment Corporation
Bronx, NY 800-237-8873
Package Machinery Company
West Springfield, MA 413-732-4000
Packaging & Processing Equipment
Ayr, ON 519-622-6666

Packaging Machinery & Equipment
West Orange, NJ ... 973-325-2418
Palace Packaging Machines
Downingtown, PA ... 610-873-7252
Plasti-Mach Corporation
Valley Cottage, NY ... 800-394-1128
Production Packaging & Processing Equipment Company
Phoenix, AZ ... 602-254-7878
Professional Marketing Group
Seattle, WA ... 800-227-3769
QMS International, Inc.
Mississauga, Ontario, ON ... 905-820-7225
Schroeder Sewing Technologies
San Marcos, CA ... 760-591-9733
Warwick Manufacturing & Equipment
North Brunswick, NJ ... 732-241-9263
Wick's Packaging Service
Cutler, IN ... 574-967-3104

Retort Pouch Processing

AmeriQual Foods
Evansville, IN ... 812-867-1444
SOPAKCO Foods
Mullins, SC ... 800-276-9678
Stock America Inc
Grafton, WI ... 262-375-4100
Sungjae Corporation
Irvine, CA ... 949-757-1727

Sealers

Heat

AAMD
Liverpool, NY ... 800-887-4167
Audion Automation
Carrollton, TX ... 972-389-0777
Branson Ultrasonics Corporation
Danbury, CT ... 203-796-0400
Carson Manufacturing Company
Petaluma, CA ... 800-423-2380
Chaffee Company
Rocklin, CA ... 916-630-3980
Chase Industries
Carson, CA ... 310-763-9900
Durable Packaging Corporation
Countryside, IL ... 800-700-5677
Giltron
Medfield, MA ... 508-359-4310
Gulf Arizona Packaging
Humble, TX ... 800-364-3887
Herche Warehouse
Denver, CO ... 303-371-8186
Jeb Plastics
Wilmington, DE ... 800-556-2247
Korab Engineering Company
Los Angeles, CA ... 310-670-7710
Lako Tool & Manufacturing
Perrysburg, OH ... 800-228-2982
Matthiesen Equipment Company
San Antonio, TX ... 800-624-8635
Moen Industries
Santa Fe Springs, CA ... 800-732-7766
Nordson Corporation
Duluth, GA ... 800-683-2314
Osgood Industries
Oldsmar, FL ... 813-855-7337
Pack-Rite
Racine, WI ... 800-248-6868
Packaging & Processing Equipment
Ayr, ON ... 519-622-6666
Packaging Aids Corporation
San Rafael, CA ... 415-454-4868
Packworld USA
Nazareth, PA ... 610-746-2765
Plasti-Mach Corporation
Valley Cottage, NY ... 800-394-1128
PlexPack Corp
Toronto, ON ... 855-635-9238
Pressure Pack
Williamsburg, VA ... 757-220-3693
Reiser
Canton, MA ... 781-575-9941
Rockford-Midland Corporation
Rockford, IL ... 800-327-7908
Seal-O-Matic Company
Jacksonville, OR ... 800-631-2072
Servpak Corporation
Hollywood, FL ... 800-782-0840
United Silicone
Lancaster, NY ... 716-681-8222

Wraps

East Orange, NJ ... 973-673-7873
Zed Industries
Vandalia, OH ... 937-667-8407

Tray

Great Western Products
Ontario, CA ... 888-598-5588
Reiser
Canton, MA ... 781-575-9941

Shrinkers: Plastic Packaging

ADEX Medical Inc
Riverside, CA ... 800-873-4776
Alfa Production Systems
Westfield, NJ ... 908-654-0255
Aline Heat Seal Corporation
Cerritos, CA ... 888-285-3917
API
Tampa, FL ... 813-888-8488
Atlantis Plastics Institutional Products
Mankato, MN ... 800-999-2374
Audion Automation
Carrollton, TX ... 972-389-0777
Bollore
Dayville, CT ... 860-774-2930
Brenton LLC
Alexandria, MN ... 800-535-2730
Chase Industries
Carson, CA ... 310-763-9900
Cima-Pak Corporation
Dorval, QC ... 877-631-2462
Clamco Corporation
Berea, OH ... 216-267-1911
Conflex, Inc.
Germantown, WI ... 800-225-4296
Douglas Machine
Alexandria, MN ... 320-763-6587
Ideal of America
Charlotte, NC ... 704-523-1604
Ideal of America/Valley Rio Enterprise
Atlanta, GA ... 770-352-0210
Iman Pack
Westland, MI ... 800-810-4626
L&H Wood Manufacturing Company
Farmington, MI ... 248-474-9000
M&Q Packaging Corporation
North Wales, PA ... 267-498-4000
MS Plastics & Packaging Company
Butler, NJ ... 800-593-1802
Packaging Machinery International
Elk Grove Village, IL ... 800-871-4764
Phase Fire Systems
Vista, CA ... 888-741-2341
Polypack
Pinellas Park, FL ... 727-578-5000
Reiser
Canton, MA ... 781-575-9941
Rennco
Homer, MI ... 800-409-5225
Robbie Manufacturing
Shawnee Mission, KS ... 800-255-6328
SEAL-IT
Farmingdale, NY ... 800-325-3965
Triune Enterprises
Gardena, CA ... 310-719-1600
VC999 Packaging Systems
Kansas City, MO ... 800-728-2999
Vector Packaging
Oak Brook, IL ... 800-435-9100
Zepf Technologies
Clearwater, FL ... 727-535-4100

Sorters

Bottle

California Vibratory Feeders
Anaheim, CA ... 800-354-0972
Heuft
Downers Grove, IL ... 630-968-9011
Kinsley Inc
Doylestown, PA ... 800-414-6664
Packaging & Processing Equipment
Ayr, ON ... 519-622-6666
Palace Packaging Machines
Downingtown, PA ... 610-873-7252

Strech Sleeve Application Equipment

SleeveCo, Inc
Dawsonville, GA ... 706-216-3110

Tables

Packing House

A.K. Robins
Baltimore, MD ... 800-486-9656
AFECO
Algona, IA ... 888-295-1116
Atlas Equipment Company
Kansas City, MO ... 800-842-9188
Belco Packaging Systems
Monrovia, CA ... 800-833-1833
Brothers Metal Products
Santa Ana, CA ... 714-972-3008
Cleveland Vibrator Company
Cleveland, OH ... 800-221-3298
Columbus McKinnon Corporation
Amherst, NY ... 800-888-0985
DC Tech
Kansas City, MO ... 877-742-9090
Key Material Handling
Simi Valley, CA ... 800-539-7225
MeGa Industries
Burlington, ON ... 800-665-6342
MSSH
Greensburg, IN ... 812-663-2180
Packaging & Processing Equipment
Ayr, ON ... 519-622-6666
Sperling Industries
Omaha, NE ... 800-647-5062

Vacuum Packing

Cretel Food Equipment
Holland, MI ... 616-786-3980
Elmo Rietschle - A Gardner Denver Product
Qunicy, IL ... 217-222-5400
Market Sales Company
Newton, MA ... 617-232-0239
Promarks, Inc.
Ontario, CA ... 909-923-3888
Reiser
Canton, MA ... 781-575-9941
Rollstock, Inc.
Kansas City, MO ... 800-954-6020

Weighing

A P Dataweigh Systems
Cumming, GA ... 877-409-2562
A&D Weighing
San Jose, CA ... 800-726-3364
Abel Manufacturing Company
Appleton, WI ... 920-734-4443
Accu-Pak
Akron, OH ... 330-644- 301
Acme Scale Company
San Leandro, CA ... 888-638-5040
Action Packaging Automation
Roosevelt, NJ ... 800-241-2724
Actionpac Scales & Automation
Oxnard, CA ... 800-394-0154
Ag-Pak
Gasport, NY ... 716-772-2651
All-Fill
Exton, PA ... 866-255-4455
Amark Packaging Systems
Kansas City, MO ... 816-965-9000
American Bag & Burlap Company
Chelsea, MA ... 617-884-7600
AmeriGlobe FIBC Solutions
Lafayette, LA ... 337-234-3212
Andgar Corporation
Ferndale, WA ... 360-366-9900
APEC
Lake Odessa, MI ... 616-374-1000
Arkfeld Mfg & Distr Company
Norfolk, NE ... 800-533-0676
Avery Weigh-Tronix
Fairmont, MN ... 877-368-2039
Bell & Howell Company
Lincolnwood, IL ... 800-647-2290
BLH Electronics
Canton, MA ... 781-821-2000
Blodgett Company
Houston, TX ... 281-933-6195
Campbell Wrapper Corporation
De Pere, WI ... 800-727-4210

Cardinal Scale Manufacturing Company
Webb City, MO 800-441-4237
Care Controls, Inc.
Mill Creek, WA 800-593-6050
CCi Scale Company
Ventura, CA 800-900-0224
Chemi-Graphic
Ludlow, MA 413-589-0151
Chlorinators Inc
Stuart, FL 800-327-9761
Cintex of America
Carol Stream, IL 800-424-6839
Convergent Label Technology
Tampa, FL 800-252-6111
Crestware
North Salt Lake City, UT 800-345-0513
Crystal-Vision PackagingSystems
Torrance, CA 800-331-3240
Delta Engineering Corporation
Walpole, MA 781-729-8650
Detecto Scale Company
Webb City, MO 800-641-2008
Doran Scales
Batavia, IL 800-365-0084
Edlund Company Inc
Burlington, VT 800-772-2126
Emery Winslow Scale Company
Seymour, CT 203-881-9333
Equipment Outlet
Meridian, ID 208-887-1472
Exact Equipment Corporation
Morrisville, PA 215-295-2000
Fairbanks Scales
Kansas City, MO 800-451-4107
Fawema Packaging Machinery
Palmetto, FL 941-351-9597
Fuller Weighing Systems
Columbus, OH 614-882-8121
Gainco, Inc.
Gainesville, GA 800-467-2828
General Packaging Equipment Company
Houston, TX 713-686-4331
Grain Machinery Manufacturing Corporation
Miami, FL 305-620-2525
Hardy Systems Corporation
Northbrook, IL 800-927-3956
IEW
Niles, OH 330-652-0113
Ilapak
Newtown, PA 215-579-2900
Iman Pack
Westland, MI 800-810-4626
Industrial Laboratory Equipment
Charlotte, NC 704-357-3930
Inspired Automation
Agoura Hills, CA 818-991-4598
IWS Scales
San Diego, CA 800-881-9755
Key Material Handling
Simi Valley, CA 800-539-7225
Kistler-Morse Corporation
Spartanburg, SC 800-426-9010
Kliklok-Woodman
Decatur, GA 770-981-5200
Lock Inspection Systems
Fitchburg, MA 800-227-5539
Lockwood Packaging
Woburn, MA 800-641-3100
Loma International
Carol Stream, IL 800-872-5662
Mandeville Company
Minneapolis, MN 800-328-8490
Merrick Industries
Lynn Haven, FL 800-271-7834
Mettler-Toledo
Columbus, OH 800-523-5123
Micro-Strain
Spring City, PA 610-948-4550
Mortec Industries
Brush, CO 800-541-9983
National Scoop & Equipment Company
Spring House, PA 215-646-2040
O.A. Newton & Son Company
Bridgeville, DE 800-726-5745
Ocs Checkweighers, Inc.
Snellville, GA 678-344-8030
Ohaus Corporation
Parsippany, NJ 800-672-7722
Ohlson Packaging
Taunton, MA 508-977-0004
Pacific Scale Company
Clackamas, OR 800-537-1886
Peco Controls Corporation
Modesto, CA 800-732-6285
Pelouze Scale Company
Bridgeview, IL 800-323-8363
PMI Food Equipment Group
Troy, OH 937-332-3000
Pomona Service & Supply Company
Yakima, WA 509-452-7121
Quest Corporation
North Royalton, OH 440-230-9400
Renard Machine Company
Green Bay, WI 920-432-8412
Rice Lake Weighing Systems
Rice Lake, WI
Rice Lake Weighing Systems
Rice Lake, WI 800-472-6703
S. Howes
Silver Creek, NY 888-255-2611
Sartorius Corporation
Edgewood, NY 800-635-2906
Schaffer Poidometer Company
Pittsburgh, PA 412-281-9031
Scientech, Inc
Boulder, CO 800-525-0522
Si-Lodec
Tukwila, WA 800-255-8274
SIG Pack Eagle Corporation
Oakland, CA 800-824-3245
Sterling Controls
Sterling, IL 800-257-7214
Sterling Scale Company
Southfield, MI 800-331-9931
Sunbeam Health & Safety
Bridgeview, IL 708-598-9100
Taylor Precision Products
Las Cruces, NM 630-954-1250
Taylor Products Company A Division Of Magnum Systems
Parsons, KS 888-882-9567
TEC America
Atlanta, GA 770-453-0868
Tecweigh/Tecnetics Industries
White Bear Lake, MN 800-536-4880
Temco
Oakland, CA 707-746-5966
Thayer Scale
Pembroke, MA 781-826-8101
Thermo Ramsey
Coon Rapids, MN 763-783-2500
Tomac Packaging
Woburn, MA 800-641-3100
Toroid Corporation
Huntsville, AL 256-837-7510
Triangle Package Machinery Company
Chicago, IL 800-621-4170
Tridyne Process Systems Inc.
South Burlington, VT 802-863-6873
Triner Scale & Manufacturing Co., Inc.
Olive Branch, MS 800-238-0152
Vande Berg Scales
Sioux Center, IA 712-722-1181
VitaMinder Company
Providence, RI 800-858-8840
Water Sciences Services ,Inc.
Jackson, TN 973-584-4131
Weigh Right Automatic Scale Company
Joliet, IL 800-571-0249
WeighPack Systems/PaxiomGroup
Montreal, QC 888-934-4472
Yakima Wire Works
Reedley, CA 509-248-6790
Yargus Manufacturing
Marshall, IL 217-826-6352

Wire Stitching

New Jersey Wire Stitching Machine Company
Cherry Hill, NJ 856-428-2572

Wrapping

Air Technical Industries
Mentor, OH 888-857-6265
Aline Heat Seal Corporation
Cerritos, CA 888-285-3917
Allpac
Dallas, TX 214-630-8804
Ampak
Cleveland, OH 800-342-6329
API
Tampa, FL 813-888-8488
APS Packaging Systems
Fairfield, NJ 800-526-2276
Audion Automation
Carrollton, TX 972-389-0777
Automatic Electronic Machines Company
Brooklyn, NY 718-384-3211
B W Cooney & Associates
Bolton, Ontario, ON 905-857-7880
Berkshire PPM
Litchfield, CT 860-567-3118
Berlin Foundry & MachineCompany
Berlin, NH 603-752-4550
Brenton LLC
Alexandria, MN 800-535-2730
C&K Machine Company
Holyoke, MA 413-536-8122
Campbell Wrapper Corporation
De Pere, WI 800-727-4210
Campbell Wrapper Corporation
De Pere, WI 920-983-7100
Charles Beseler Corporation
Stroudsburg, PA 800-237-3537
Chase Industries
Carson, CA 310-763-9900
Circle Packaging Machinery Inc
De Pere, WI 920-983-3420
Conflex, Inc.
Germantown, WI 800-225-4296
Crystal-Vision PackagingSystems
Torrance, CA 800-331-3240
Delkor Systems, Inc
Minneapolis, MN 800-328-5558
Design Technology Corporation
Billerica, MA 978-663-7000
Doering Machines, Inc.
San Francisco, CA 415-526-2131
Dorell Equipment Inc
Somerset, NJ 732-247-5400
EDL Packaging Engineers
Green Bay, WI 920-336-7744
Exact Equipment Corporation
Morrisville, PA 215-295-2000
Felins USA
Milwaukee, WI 800-336-3220
Formost Packaging Machines
Woodinville, WA 425-483-9090
Ganz Brothers
Paramus, NJ 201-845-6010
GEI Autowrappers
Exton, PA 610-321-1115
Goodwrappers/J.C. Parry & Sons Company
Halethorpe, MD 800-638-1127
Halton Packaging Systems
Oakville, ON 905-847-9141
Hart Design & Manufacturing
Green Bay, WI 920-468-5927
Hayssen
Duncan, SC 864-486-4000
Highlight Industries
Wyoming, MI 800-531-2465
Ideal of America
Charlotte, NC 704-523-1604
Ideal of America/Valley Rio Enterprise
Atlanta, GA 770-352-0210
Ideal Wrapping Machine Company
Middletown, NY 845-343-7700
Ilapak
Newtown, PA 215-579-2900
International Packaging Machinery
Naples, FL 800-237-6496
ITW Stretch Packaging System
Glenview, IL 847-657-4444
Kisters Kayat
Sarasota, FL 386-424-0101
Machine Electronics Company
Brooklyn, NY 718-384-3211
Mark Products Company
Denville, NJ 973-983-8818
MarquipWard United
Phillips, WI 715-339-2191
Maryland Packaging Corporation
Baltimore, MD 410-347-0365
Nitech
Columbus, NE 800-397-1100
Orion Packaging Systems
Alexandria, MN 800-333-6556
OSSID LLC
Rocky Mount, NC 800-334-8369
Pack Line Corporation
Racine, WI 800-248-6868
Packaging & Processing Equipment
Ayr, ON 519-622-6666
Packaging Dynamics
Walnut Creek, CA 925-938-2711

Peerless Food Equipment
Sidney, OH 937-492-4158
Pfankuch Machinery Corporation
Apple Valley, MN 952-891-3311
PMI Food Equipment Group
Troy, OH 937-332-3000
Polypack
Pinellas Park, FL. 727-578-5000
Renard Machine Company
Green Bay, WI. 920-432-8412
Rose Forgrove
Saint Charles, IL 630-443-1317
Sanford Redmond Company
Stamford, CT. 203-351-9800
Scan Coin
Ashburn, VA 800-336-3311
Scandia Packaging Machinery Company
Fairfield, NJ 973-473-6100
Seal-O-Matic Company
Jacksonville, OR 800-631-2072
Shanklin Corporation
Ayer, MA. 978-772-3200
Shrinkfast Marketing
Newport, NH. 800-867-4746
Sitma USA
Spilamberto, MO 800-728-1254
Telesonic Packaging Corporation
Wilmington, DE 302-658-6945

Pails

Acra Electric Corporation
Tulsa, OK 800-223-4328
All American Containers
Medley, FL 305-887-0797
Container Supply Company
Garden Grove, CA 714-891-4896
Greenfield Packaging
White Plains, NY 914-993-0233
Hedwin Corporation
Baltimore, MD 800-638-1012
Indianapolis Container Company
Indianapolis, IN 800-760-3318
IPL Inc
Saint-Damien, QC. 800-463-4755
Landis Plastics
Alsip, IL 708-396-1470
Louisville Container Company
Indianapolis, IN 888-539-7225
National Scoop & Equipment Company
Spring House, PA 215-646-2040
Prolon
Port Gibson, MS 888-480-9828
Reliance Product
Winnipeg, MB. 800-665-0258
Spartech Industries
Etobicoke, ON 416-744-4220

Parts

A C Tool & Machine Company
Louisville, KY 502-447-5505
ABB
Norwalk, CT 203-750-2200
Accuflex Industrial Hose
Romulus, MI 734-451-0080
Acromag Inc.
Wixom, MI 248-624-1541
Action Technology
Prussia, PA 217-935-8311
Advance Fitting Corporation
Elkhorn, WI. 262-723-6699
Advanced Control Technologies
Indianapolis, IN 800-886-2281
AFT Advanced Fiber Technologies
Sherbrooke, QC 800-668-7273
AGC Engineering
Bristow, VA. 800-825-8820
Air Quality Engineering
Brooklyn Park, MN. 800-328-0787
Alkota Cleaning Systems
Alcester, SD 800-255-6823
All Packaging Machinery Corporation
Ronkonkoma, NY 800-637-8808
American Extrusion International
South Beloit, IL 815-624-6616
American Radionic Company
Palm Coast, FL 800-445-6033
Ampco Pumps Company
Glendale, WI. 800-737-8671
Andantex USA
Ocean, NJ 800-713-6170
ANVER Corporation
Hudson, MA 800-654-3500
Apex Packing & Rubber Company
Farmingdale, NY. 800-645-9110
API
Tampa, FL. 813-888-8488
APV Americas
Delavan, WI 800-252-5200
Arc Machines
Pacoima, CA 818-896-9556
Arctic Seal & Gasket of the Americas
Stuart, FL 800-881-4663
Armstrong-Lynnwood
Three Rivers, MI. 269-273-1415
Arthur Products Company
Medina, OH. 800-322-0510
Artisan Controls Corporation
Randolph, NJ 800-457-4950
Automatic Specialities Inc.
Marlborough, MA. 800-445-2370
Bal Seal Engineering Company
Foothill Ranch, CA. 800-366-1006
Baldewein Company
Lake Forrest, IL 800-424-5544
Banner Equipment Comp any
Morris, IL 800-621-4625
Bardo Abrasives
Ridgewood, NY 718-456-6400
Basiloid Products Corporation
Elnora, IN 866-692-5511
Bassick Casters
Shiner, TX. 888-527-3526
Bayside Motion Group
Port Washington, NY 800-305-4555
Beacon Specialties
New York, NY 800-221-9405
Beam Industries
Webster City, IA 800-369-2326
Becker Brothers GraphiteCorporation
Maywood, IL. 708-410-0700
Benchmark Thermal Corporation
Grass Valley, CA. 530-477-5011
Bert Manufacturing
Gardnerville, NV 775-265-3900
Bettendorf Stanford
Salem, IL. 800-548-2253
BFM Equipment Sales
Fall River, WI 920-484-3341
Bodine Electric Company
Northfield, IL
Bohn & Dawson
Saint Louis, MO 800-225-5011
Boilzoni Auramo, Inc.
Homewood, IL 800-358-5438
Boston Gear
Boston, MA. 888-999-9860
Bradford A Ducon Company
Pewaukee, WI. 800-789-1718
Brudi Bolzoni Auramo, Inc
Homewood, IL 800-358-5438
C&D Valve Manufacturing Company, Inc.
Oklahoma City, OK 800-654-9233
Cal Controls
Gurnee, IL. 800-866-6659
Caldwell Group
Rockford, IL 800-628-4263
Caloritech
Greensburg, IN 800-473-2403
Carmun International
San Antonio, TX. 800-531-7907
Carter Products Company
Grand Rapids, MI 888-622-7837
Cashco
Ellsworth, KS 785-472-4461
CAT PUMPS
Blaine, MN 763-780-5440
Change Parts
Ludington, MI. 231-845-5107
Chicago Stainless Equipment
Palm City, FL 800-927-8575
Chip-Makers Tooling Supply
Whittier, CA 800-659-5840
Chromalox
Pittsburgh, PA. 800-443-2640
Clark-Cooper Division Magnatrol Valve Corporation
Cinnaminson, NJ. 856-829-4580
Clean Water Systems International
Klamath Falls, OR 866-273-9993
Consolidated Commercial Controls
Winsted, CT 800-332-2500
Continental Disc Corporation
Liberty, MO. 816-792-1500
Conveyor Accessories
Burr Ridge, IL. 800-323-7093
Conxall Corporation
Villa Park, IL. 630-834-7504
Cornell Pump Company
Portland, OR 503-653-0330
Cramer Company
South Windsor, CT 877-684-6464
Crown Battery Manufacturing Company
Fremont, OH 800-487-2879
CSS International Corporation
Philadelphia, PA 800-278-8107
Delavan Spray Technologies
Charlotte, NC 704-423-7000
Doering Company
Clear Lake, MN 320-743-2276
Dormont Manufacturing Company
Export, PA. 800-367-6668
Dyna-Veyor
Newark, NJ 800-930-4760
Electro Cam Corporation
Roscoe, IL. 800-228-5487
Elite Forming Design Solutions, Inc.
Rome, GA. 706-232-3021
Ellett Industries
Port Coquitlam, BC. 604-941-8211
Ernst Timing Screw Company
Bensalem, PA 215-639-1438
ESCO
Houston, TX 800-966-5514
Fabreeka International
Boise, ID 800-423-4469
Falcon Fabricators
Nashville, TN 615-832-0027
Faribo Manufacturing Company
Faribault, MN 800-447-6043
Federal Machines
Des Moines, IA. 800-247-2446
FEI
Mansfield, TX. 800-346-5908
Fleetwood Systems
Orlando, FL. 407-855-0230
Flomatic International
Clackamas, OR 800-435-2550
Florida Knife Company
Sarasota, FL 800-966-5643
Fluid Metering
Syosset, NY. 800-223-3388
Fluid Transfer
Philipsburg, PA. 814-342-0902
Frost Food Handling Products
Grand Rapids, MI 616-453-7781
Furnace Belt Company
Buffalo, NY. 800-354-7213
G.W. Dahl Company
Greensboro, NC 800-852-4449
Garvey Products
West Chester, OH 800-543-1908
GE Interlogix Industrial
Tualatin, OR 800-247-9447
Gems Sensors
Plainville, CT 860-747-3000
Glo-Quartz Electric Heater Company
Mentor, OH. 800-321-3574
Globe Fire Sprinkler Corporation
Standish, MI 800-248-0278
Good Idea
Northampton, MA. 800-462-9237
Granco Pumps
San Ramon, CA 925-359-3290
Graphite Metallizing Corporation
Yonkers, NY 914-968-8400
Greenbelt Industries
Buffalo, NY. 800-668-1114
H&H Metal Fabrications
Belden, MS 662-489-4626
H.A. Phillips & Company
DeKalb, IL 630-377-0050
Habasit Canada Limited
Oakville, ON. 905-827-4131
Hansaloy Corporation
Davenport, IA 800-553-4992
Haumiller Engineering
Elgin, IL 847-695-9111
Hayes & Stolz IndustrialManufacturing Company
Fort Worth, TX 800-725-7272
Hi-Temp
Tuscumbia, AL 800-239-5066
Hoffmeyer Company
San Leandro, CA. 800-350-2358
Home Rubber Company
Trenton, NJ 800-257-9441

Hose Master
Cleveland, OH 216-481-2020
IKA Works
Wilmington, NC 800-733-3037
IMI Norgren
Brookville, OH 937-833-4033
Indemax
Vernon, NJ. 800-345-7185
Industrial Products Corporation
Ho Ho Kus, NJ 800-472-5913
Infitec
Syracuse, NY 800-334-0837
International Tank & Pipe Co
Clackamas, OR 888-988-0011
Introdel Products
Itasca, IL 800-323-4772
Irby
Rocky Mount, NC. 252-442-0154
J&J Industries
Bensenville, IL 630-595-8878
Jilson Group
Lodi, NJ. 800-969-5400
Jokamsco Group
Mechanicville, NY 518-237-6416
Kason Central
Columbus, OH 614-885-1992
Kinetic Equipment Company
Appleton, WI 806-293-4471
King Company
Dallas, TX. 507-451-3770
Kinsley Inc
Doylestown, PA 800-414-6664
Knobs Unlimited
Bowling Green, OH 419-353-8215
Kraissl Company
Hackensack, NJ. 800-572-4775
KWS Manufacturing Company
Burleson, TX. 800-543-6558
L.C. Thompson Company
Kenosha, WI 800-558-4018
Lake Process Systems
Lake Barrington, IL 800-331-9260
Lakeside Manufacturing
Milwaukee, WI 888-558-8574
Lako Tool & Manufacturing
Perrysburg, OH 800-228-2982
Lambeth Band Corporation
New Bedford, MA 508-984-4700
Len E. Ivarson
Milwaukee, WI 414-351-0700
Liburdi Group of Companies
Mooresville, NC 800-533-9353
Lil' Orbits
Minneapolis, MN 800-228-8305
Livingston-Wilbor Corporation
Edison, NJ. 908-322-8403
Lorenz Couplings
Cobourg, ON. 800-263-7782
Lucas Industrial
Cedar Hill, TX 800-877-1720
Lumsden Flexx Flow
Lancaster, PA 800-367-3664
M&R Sales & Service, Inc
Glen Ellyn, IL 800-736-6431
M.H. Rhodes Cramer
South Windsor, CT 877-684-6464
Master Magnetics
Castle Rock, CO 800-525-3536
Mastercraft Industries
Newburgh, NY 800-835-7812
McCormack Manufacturing Company
Lake Oswego, OR. 800-395-1593
McKey Perforating Company
New Berlin, WI. 800-345-7373
Meadows Mills, Inc.
North Wilkesboro, NC 800-626-2282
Membrane Process & Controls
Edgar, WI 715-352-3206
Metal Master
Tucson, AZ 800-488-8729
Micro Solutions Enterprises
Van Nuys, CA. 800-673-4968
Midwest Rubber & Supply Company
Commerce City, CO 800-537-7457
Midwest Stainless
Menomonie, WI 715-235-5472
Miller Metal Fabricators
Staunton, VA. 540-886-5575
Miller's Technical Service
Canton, MI 734-738-1970
MO Industries
Whippany, NJ 973-386-9228

Mollenberg-Betz
Buffalo, NY. 716-614-7473
Monarch-McLaren
Weston, ON. 416-741-9675
Morse Manufacturing Company
East Syracuse, NY 315-437-8475
Motion Industries
Birmingham, AL. 877-609-7975
Moyno
Springfield, OH. 937-327-3111
Murtech Manufacturing
Kenilworth, NJ 908-245-1556
Nalge Process Technologies Group
Rochester, NY. 585-586-8800
National Band Saw Company
Santa Clarita, CA 800-851-5050
National Metal Industries
West Springfield, MA. 800-628-8850
Nelles Automation
Houston, TX 713-939-9399
Newman Sanitary Gasket Company
Lebanon, OH. 513-932-7379
Norgren
Littleton, CO 303-794-2611
Northland Process Piping
Isle, MN 320-679-2119
Ogden Manufacturing Company
Pittsburgh, PA. 412-967-3906
Pacer Pumps
Lancaster, PA 800-233-3861
Package Machinery Company
West Springfield, MA. 413-732-4000
Parker Hannifin Corporation
Cleveland, OH 609-586-5151
Partex Corporation
Flint, MI 810-736-5656
Pengo Corporation
Cokato, MN. 800-599-0211
Piab Vacuum Products
Hingham, MA. 800-321-7422
Plasti-Clip Corporation
Milford, NH 800-882-2547
Polychem International
Mentor, OH. 440-357-1500
Pres-Air-Trol Corporation
Mamaroneck, NY 800-431-2625
Pure Fit
Allentown, PA. 866-787-3348
Pyromation
Fort Wayne, IN 260-484-2580
Qosina Corporation
Edgewood, NY 631-242-3000
Quadrant
Fort Wayne, IN 800-628-7264
Quality Industries
Cleveland, OH 216-961-5566
R-K Electronics
Mason, OH 800-543-4936
R.H. Chandler Company
Saint Louis, MO 314-962-9353
Ralphs-Pugh Company
Benicia, CA. 800-486-0021
Ranger Blade Manufacturing Company
Traer, IA 800-377-7860
Rath Manufacturing Company
Janesville, WI 800-367-7284
Reading Plastic Fabricators
Temple, PA 610-926-3245
Rees
Fremont, IN. 260-495-9811
Refrigeration Research
Brighton, MI 810-227-1151
Reid Boiler Works
Bellingham, WA 360-714-6157
Rigidized Metals Corporation
Buffalo, NY. 800-836-2580
RM Waite Inc
Clintonville, WI 715-823-4327
Robert-James Sales
Buffalo, NY. 800-777-1325
Rolland Machining & Fabricating
Moneta, VA. 973-827-6911
Salem-Republic Rubber Company
Sebring, OH 800-686-4199
Sanchelima International
Doral, FL. 305-591-4343
Sani-Fit
Pasadena, CA 626-395-7895
Sanifab
Stratford, WI. 715-687-4332
Sanitary Couplers
Springboro, OH. 513-743-0144

Schneider Electric Sensor Competency Center
Dayton, OH. 800-435-2121
Seattle Refrigeration & Manufacturing
Seattle, WA 800-228-8881
Sellers Engineering Division
Danville, KY. 859-236-3181
Senior Flexonics
Bartlett, IL. 800-473-0474
SEW Eurodrive
Lyman, SC. 864-439-8792
Sharon Manufacturing Company
Deer Park, NY. 800-424-6455
Shingle Belting
King of Prussia, PA. 800-345-6294
Shivvers
Corydon, IA 641-872-1007
Simolex Rubber Corporation
Plymouth, MI 734-453-4500
Sine Pump
Arvada, CO 888-504-8301
Smokehouse Limited
Franklinville, NC 800-554-8385
Southern Metal Fabricators
Albertville, AL 800-989-1330
Special Products
Springfield, MO 417-881-6114
Specialty Blades
Staunton, VA. 540-248-2200
Spot Wire Works Company
Philadelphia, PA. 215-627-6124
Stainless Products
Somers, WC 800-558-9446
Standex International Corporation
Salem, NH. 603-893-9701
STD Precision Gear & Instrument
West Bridgewater, MA 888-783-4327
Step Products
Round Rock, TX. 800-777-7837
Storm Industrial
Shawnee Mission, KS. 800-745-7483
Strahman Valves
Bethlehem, PA 877-787-2462
Stroter Inc
Freeport, IL. 815-616-2506
Stutz Products Corporation
Hartford City, IN. 765-348-2510
Super Radiator Coils
Richmond, VA. 800-229-2645
Super Steel Products Corporation
Milwaukee, WI 414-355-4800
Svedala Industries
Colorado Springs, CO. 719-471-3443
T&S Brass & Bronze Works
Travelers Rest, SC 800-476-4103
Tema Systems
Cincinnati, OH 513-489-7811
TENTE CASTERS
Hebron, KY. 800-783-2470
Top Line Process Equipment Company
Bradford, PA. 800-458-6095
Travis Manufacturing Company
Alliance, OH. 330-875-1661
Tropic-Kool Engineering Corporation
Largo, FL 727-581-2824
TruHeat Corporation
Allegan, MI. 800-879-6199
Tuchenhagen
Columbia, MD 410-910-6000
Unifiller Systems
Delta, BC. 888-733-8444
US Tsubaki
Wheeling, IL. 800-323-7790
Valvinox
Iberville, QC 450-346-1981
Vaughn Belting Company
Spartanburg, SC 800-325-3303
Vilter Manufacturing Corporation
Cudahy, WI 414-744-0111
Vulcanium Metals International, LLC
Northbrook, IL 888-922-0040
W.T. Nickell Label Company
Batavia, OH. 888-899-1991
Wade Manufacturing Company
Tigard, OR 800-222-7246
Warner Electric
South Beloit, IL 800-234-3369
Waukesha Cherry-Burrell
Louisville, KY 502-491-4310
Waukesha Cherry-Burrell
Louisville, KY 800-252-5200
Waukesha Foundry
Waukesha, WI. 262-542-0741

Waukesha Specialty Company
Darien, WI. 262-724-3700
Wico Corporation
Niles, IL 800-367-9426
Wiegmann & Rose
Oakland, CA 510-632-8828
Wilden Pump & Engineering LLC
Grand Terrace, CA 909-422-1700
Windhorst Blowmold
Euless, TX. 817-540-6639
Wire Belt Company of America
Londonderry, NH 603-644-2500
Wolverine Proctor & Schwartz
Lexington, NC 336-248-5181
Womack International
Vallejo, CA 707-647-2370
World Wide Fittings
Niles, IL 800-393-9894
Wright Metal Products
Greenville, SC. 864-297-6610
Yates Industries
Saint Clair Shores, MI 586-778-7680

Pharmaceutical Industry

ARRO Corporation
Hodgkins, IL. 877-929-2776
Covance Laboratories Inc.
Madison, WI 608-241-4471

Plastic Fabricators

A La Carte
Chicago, IL 800-722-2370
Abbott Industries
Paterson, NJ
ABC Letter Art
Los Angeles, CA. 888-261-5367
ABI Limited
Concord, ON. 800-297-8666
Abond Plastic Corporation
Lachine, QC 800-886-7947
Ace Stamp & Engraving
Lakewood, WA 253-582-3322
Ace Technical Plastics
Hartford, CT 860-305-8138
Achilles USA
Everett, WA. 425-353-7000
Acme Bag Company
Chula Vista, CA 800-275-2263
Aco Container Systems
Pickering, ON 800-542-9942
Adams Signs & Graphics
Massillon, OH. 888-886-9911
ADM Corporation
Middlesex, NJ. 800-327-0718
Advance Engineering Company
Township, MI 800-497-6388
Advantage Puck Group
Corry, PA. 814-664-4810
AEP Industries
South Hackensack, NJ 800-999-2374
Aero Housewares
Fayetteville, GA 770-914-4240
Aero Manufacturing Company
Clifton, NJ. 800-631-8378
Aeromat Plastics
Burnsville, MN 888-286-8729
Alger Creations
Miami, FL. 954-454-3272
All American Containers
Medley, FL 305-887-0797
All American Poly Corporation
Piscataway, NJ 800-526-3551
Allred Marketing
Birmingham, AL. 205-251-3700
ALP Lighting & Ceiling Products
Pennsauken, NJ. 800-633-7732
Alpack
Centerville, MA 508-771-9131
Altira
Miami, FL. 305-687-8074
Aluf Plastics
Orangeburg, NY 800-394-2247
Amcel
Watertown, MA. 800-225-7992
AMCO Corporation
City of Industry, CA 626-855-2550
Amcor Twinpak
Dorval, QC 514-684-7070
American Bag & Burlap Company
Chelsea, MA 617-884-7600
American Identification Industries
West Chicago, IL 800-255-8890
AmeriGlobe FIBC Solutions
Lafayette, LA 337-234-3212
Ametco Manufacturing Corporation
Willoughby, OH 800-321-7042
AR Arena Products
Rochester, NY. 800-836-2528
Art Plastics Handy Home Helpers
Leominster, MA 978-537-0367
Art Poly Bag Company
Brooklyn, NY 800-278-7659
Artcraft Badge & Sign Company
Olney, MD. 800-739-0709
Artistic Packaging Concepts
Massapequa Pk, NY 516-797-4020
Atlantis Industries
Milton, DE 302-684-8542
Atlantis Plastics Institutional Products
Mankato, MN 800-999-2374
Audrey Signs
New York, NY 212-769-4992
B&B Neon Sign Company
Austin, TX. 800-791-6366
Bag Company
Kennesaw, GA 800-533-1931
BagcraftPapercon
Chicago, IL 800-621-8468
Baltimore Sign Company
Arnold, MD. 410-276-1500
Bardes Plastics
Milwaukee, WI 800-558-5161
Barrette - Outdoor Livin
Middleburg Hts., OH 800-336-2383
BAW Plastics
Jefferson Hills, PA 800-783-2229
Bayhead Products Corporation
Dover, NH. 800-229-4323
Beayl Weiner/Pak
Pacific Palisades, CA 310-454-1354
Bel-Art Products
Wayne, NJ 800-423-5278
Belleview
Brookline, NH. 603-878-1583
Bergen Barrel & Drum Company
Kearny, NJ. 201-998-3500
Berloc Manufacturing & Sign Company
Sun Valley, CA 818-503-9823
Berry Plastics
Evansville, IN 800-234-1930
Berry Plastics
Evansville, IN 812-424-2904
Berry Plastics Corporati
Evansville, IN 812-424-2904
Berry Plastics Corporation
Evansville, IN 812-424-2904
BG Industries
Lemont, IL 800-800-5761
Blako Industries
Dunbridge, OH 419-833-4491
Bloomfield Industries
St. Louis, MO 888-356-5362
BOC Plastics Inc
Winston Salem, NC. 800-334-8687
Bonar Plastics
West Chicago, IL 800-295-3725
Boss Manufacturing Company
Kewanee, IL 800-447-4581
Brechteen
Chesterfield, MI 586-949-2240
Brentwood Plastic Films
St Louis, MO. 314-968-1137
Brown Paper Goods Company
Waukegan, IL 847-688-1451
Browns International & Company
St. Laurent, QC 514-737-1326
Buckhorn Canada
Brampton, ON. 800-461-7579
Buckhorn Inc
Milford, OH 800-543-4454
Budget Blinds
Orange, CA. 800-800-9250
Bulk Lift International
Carpentersville, IL 800-992-6372
Burgess Manufacturing ofOklahoma
Guthrie, OK. 800-804-1913
C.R. Daniels Inc.
Ellicott City, MD. 800-933-2638
C.R. Manufacturing
Waverly, NE 877-789-5844
Canton Sign Company
Canton, OH. 330-456-7151
Caraustar
Franklin, KY 270-586-9565
Caraustar Industries, Inc.
Archdale, NC 800-223-1373
Cardinal Packaging
Evansville, IN 812-424-2904
Cardinal Rubber & Seal
Roanoke, VA. 800-542-5737
Carlisle Food Service Products
Oklahoma City, OK 800-654-8210
Carlisle Plastics
Minneapolis, MN 952-884-1309
Carolina Glove
Conover, NC. 800-335-1918
Carroll Products
Garland, TX 800-527-5722
Carson Industries
Pomona, CA 800-735-5566
Cash Caddy
Palm Desert, CA. 888-522-2221
Castle Bag Company
Wilmington, DE 302-656-1001
Cayne Industrial Sales Corporation
Bronx, NY. 718-993-5800
CCW Products, Inc.
Arvada, CO 303-427-9663
CDF Corporation
Plymouth, MA. 800-443-1920
Cell-O-Core Company
Sharon Center, OH 800-239-4370
Cello Bag Company
Bowling Green, KY 800-347-0338
Cello Pack Corporation
Cheektowaga, NY. 800-778-3111
Central Bag & Burlap Company
Denver, CO 800-783-1224
Central Bag Company
Leavenworth, KS 913-250-0325
Central Container Corporation
Minneapolis, MN 763-425-7444
Central Fine Pack
Fort Wayne, IN 260-432-3027
Chalmur Bag Company, LLC
Philadelphia, PA 800-349-2247
Champion Plastics
Clifton, NJ. 800-526-1230
Chase-Doors
Cincinnati, OH 800-543-4455
Checker Bag Company
Saint Louis, MO 800-489-3130
Chem-Tainer Industries
West Babylon, NY 800-275-2436
Chem-Tainer Industries
West Babylon, NY 800-938-8896
Chester Plastics
Chester, NS 902-275-3522
Chili Plastics
Rochester, NY. 585-889-4680
Chinet Company
Laguna Niguel, CA. 949-348-1711
Chip-Makers Tooling Supply
Whittier, CA 800-659-5840
Chocolate Concepts
Hartville, OH 330-877-3322
Choctaw-Kaul Distribution Company
Detroit, MI 313-894-9494
Choklit Molds Ltd
Lincoln, RI 800-777-6653
City Signs
Jackson, TN 877-248-9744
CKS Packaging
Atlanta, GA. 800-800-4257
Clawson Container Company
Clarkston, MI 800-325-8700
Clear Pack Company
Franklin Park, IL. 847-957-6282
Clear View Bag Company
Thomasville, NC. 336-885-8131
Clear View Bag Company
Albany, NY. 800-458-7153
Clearplass Containers
Penn Yan, NY 315-536-5690
Cleveland Plastic Films
Elyria, OH. 800-832-6799
Cleveland Specialties Company
Loveland, OH 513-677-9787
CMD Corporation
Appleton, WI 920-730-6888
CMS Gilbreth Packaging Systems
Croydon, PA 800-630-2413
Coast Scientific
Rancho Santa Fe, CA 800-445-1544

Coastal Sleeve Label
Brunswick, GA ... 877-753-3837
Collins & Aikman
Canton, OH ... 800-321-0244
Colonial Transparent Products Company
Hicksville, NY ... 516-822-4430
Com-Pac International
Carbondale, IL ... 800-824-0817
Connecticut Container Corporation
North Haven, CT ... 203-248-2161
Connecticut Laminating Company
New Haven, CT ... 800-753-9119
Consolidated Container Company
Atlanta, GA ... 888-831-2184
Consolidated Plastics
Stow, OH ... 800-858-5001
Container Specialties
Melrose Park, IL ... 800-548-7513
Container Supply Company
Garden Grove, CA ... 714-891-4896
Contico Container
Norwalk, CA ... 562-921-9967
Continental Commercial Products
Bridgeton, MO ... 800-325-1051
Continental Packaging Corporation
Elgin, IL ... 847-289-6400
Continental Products
Mexico, MO ... 800-325-0216
Contour Packaging
Philadelphia, PA ... 215-457-1600
Convoy
Canton, OH ... 800-899-1583
Cope Plastics
Alton, IL ... 800-851-5510
Cork Specialties
Miami, FL ... 305-477-1506
Corning Costar
Acton, MA ... 800-492-1110
Coverall
Worcester, MA ... 800-356-2961
CPT
Edgerton, WI ... 608-884-2244
CR Plastics
Council Bluffs, IA ... 866-869-6293
Cr. Manufacturing
Waverly, NE ... 877-789-5844
Crayex Corporation
Piqua, OH ... 800-837-1747
Creative Essentials
Ronkonkoma, NY ... 800-355-5891
Creative Forming
Ripon, WI ... 920-748-7285
Crespac Incorporated
Tucker, GA ... 800-438-1900
Crown Holdings, Inc.
Philadelphia, PA ... 215-698-5100
Crystal-Flex Packaging Corporation
Rockville Centre, NY ... 888-246-7325
CTK Plastics
Moose Jaw, SK ... 800-667-8847
Curwood
Oshkosh, WI ... 800-544-4672
Custom Bottle of Connecticut
Naugatuck, CT ... 203-723-6661
Custom Foam Molders
Foristell, MO ... 636-441-2307
Custom I.D.
Venice, FL ... 800-242-8430
Custom Molders
Rocky Mount, NC ... 919-688-8061
Custom Plastics
Decatur, GA ... 404-373-1691
Cuutom Poly Packaging
Fort Wayne, IN ... 800-548-6603
Dadant & Sons
Hamilton, IL ... 888-922-1293
Danafilms
Westborough, MA ... 508-366-8884
Danbury Plastics
Cumming, GA ... 678-455-7391
Dansk International Designs
White Plains, NY ... 914-697-6400
Dart Container Corporation
Mason, MI ... 800-248-5960
Dashco
Gloucester, ON ... 613-834-6825
Davron Technologies
Chattanooga, TN ... 423-870-1888
Dayton Bag & Burlap Company
Dayton, OH ... 800-543-3400
De Ster Corporation
Atlanta, GA ... 800-237-8270

DEFCO
Landenberg, PA ... 215-274-8245
Del-Tec Packaging
Greenville, SC ... 800-747-8683
Delfin Design & Manufacturing
Rcho Sta Marg, CA ... 800-354-7919
Delta Cooling Towers
Rockaway, NJ ... 800-289-3358
Den Ray Sign Company
Jackson, TN ... 800-530-7291
Design Packaging Company
Glencoe, IL ... 800-321-7659
Design Plastics
Omaha, NE ... 800-491-0786
Design Specialties
Hamden, CT ... 800-999-1584
Designers Plastics
Clearwater, FL ... 727-573-1643
Detroit Forming
Southfield, MI ... 248-352-8108
Development Workshop
Idaho Falls, ID ... 800-657-5597
Diamond Brands
Cloquet, MN ... 218-879-6700
Dimension Graphics
Grand Rapids, MI ... 855-476-1281
Dinosaur Plastics
Houston, TX ... 713-923-2278
Display Specialties
Wilder, KY ... 800-545-9362
Display Tray
Mont-Royal, QC ... 800-782-8861
Dispoz-O Plastics
Fountain Inn, SC ... 864-862-4004
Diversified Lighting Diffusers Inc
Copiague, NY ... 800-234-5464
Dixie Poly Packaging
Greenville, SC ... 864-268-3751
Do-It Corporation
South Haven, MI ... 800-426-4822
Donoco Industries
Huntington Beach, CA ... 888-822-8763
Dordan Manufacturing Company
Woodstock, IL ... 800-663-5460
Douglas Stephen Plastics
Paterson, NJ ... 973-523-3030
Dowling Company
Fredericksburg, VA ... 800-572-2100
Dub Harris Corporation
Pomona, CA ... 909-596-6300
Dwinell's Central Neon
Yakima, WA ... 800-932-8832
Dyna-Veyor
Newark, NJ ... 800-930-4760
E.S. Robbins Corporation
Muscle Shoals, AL ... 800-800-2235
East Coast Group New York
Springfield Gardens, NY ... 718-527-8464
Eastern Poly Packaging Company
Brooklyn, NY ... 800-421-6006
Eaton Manufacturing Company
Houston, TX ... 800-328-6610
Eaton-Quade Company
Oklahoma City, OK ... 405-236-4475
Economy Label Sales Company
Daytona Beach, FL ... 386-253-4741
Ed Smith's Stencil Works
New Orleans, LA ... 504-525-2128
Edco Industries
Bridgeport, CT ... 203-333-8982
Edge Paper Box Company
Cudahy, CA ... 323-771-7733
Ellay
Commerce, CA ... 323-725-2974
Ellehammer Industries
Langley, BC ... 604-882-9326
Elliot Lee
Cedarhurst, NY ... 516-569-9595
Elopak
New Hudson, MI ... 248-486-4600
Elrene Home Fashions
New York, NY ... 212-213-0425
Emco Industrial Plastics
Cedar Grove, NJ ... 800-292-9906
EMED Company
Buffalo, NY ... 800-442-3633
Encore Plastics
Huntington Beach, CA ... 888-822-8763
Engineered Plastics
Gibsonville, NC ... 800-711-1740
Engraving Services Co.
Woodville South, SA

Erell Manufacturing Company
Elk Grove Vlg, IL ... 800-622-6334
Esterle Mold & Machine Company
Stow, OH ... 800-411-4086
Everett Stamp Works
Everett, WA ... 425-258-6747
Exhibitron Corporation
Grants Pass, OR ... 800-437-4571
FabOhio
Uhrichsville, OH ... 740-922-4233
Fabreeka International
Boise, ID ... 800-423-4469
Fabri-Form Company
Byesville, OH ... 740-685-0424
Fabri-Kal Corporation
Kalamazoo, MI ... 800-888-5054
Fan Bag Company
Chicago, IL ... 773-342-2752
Faribo Manufacturing Company
Faribault, MN ... 800-447-6043
Farnell Packaging
Dartmouth, NS ... 800-565-9378
Fast Bags
Fort Worth, TX ... 800-321-3687
Fato Fiberglass Company
Kankakee, IL ... 815-932-3015
Federal Sign
Carmel, IN ... 800-527-9495
Ferrer Corporation
San Juan, PR ... 787-761-5151
Field Manufacturing Corporation
Torrance, CA ... 310-781-9292
Film X
Dayville, CT ... 800-628-6128
Film-Pak
Crowley, TX ... 800-526-1838
Filmco
Aurora, OH ... 800-545-8457
Filmpack Plastic Corporation
Dayton, NJ ... 732-329-6523
Finn Industries
Ontario, CA ... 909-930-1500
Firl Industries
Fond Du Lac, WI ... 800-558-4890
Five-M Plastics Company
Marion, OH ... 740-383-6246
Flex Products
Carlstadt, NJ ... 800-526-6273
FLEXcon Company
Spencer, MA ... 508-885-8200
Flexible Foam Products
Elkhart, IN ... 800-678-3626
FMI Display
Elkins Park, PA ... 215-663-1998
Foamex
Cornelius, NC ... 704-892-8081
Fonda Group
Oshkosh, WI ... 800-367-2877
Fonda Group
Oshkosh, WI ... 800-558-9300
FormFlex
Bloomingdale, IN ... 800-255-7659
Forrest Engraving Company
New Rochelle, NY ... 914-632-9892
Fort Hill Sign Products, Inc.
Hopedale, MA ... 508-381-0357
Fort James Canada
Toronto, ON ... 416-784-1621
Fortune Plastics, Inc
Old Saybrook, CT ... 800-243-0306
France Personalized Signs
Cleveland, OH ... 216-241-2198
Franklin Rubber Stamp Company
Wilmington, DE ... 302-654-8841
Frankston Paper Box Company of Texas
Frankston, TX ... 903-876-2550
Fredman Bag Company
Milwaukee, WI ... 800-945-5686
Freeman Electric Company
Panama City, FL ... 850-785-7448
Fremont Die Cut Products
Fremont, OH ... 800-223-3177
Fresno Pallet, Inc.
Sultana, CA ... 559-591-4111
Frontier Bag Company
Grandview, MO ... 816-765-4811
Fuller Brush Company
Great Bend, KS ... 800-522-0499
Fulton-Denver Company
Denver, CO ... 800-776-6715
Gary Manufacturing Company
Chula Vista, CA ... 800-775-0804

Gary Plastic Packaging Corporation
Bronx, NY....................800-221-8151
Gary Plastic Packaging Corporation
Bronx, NY....................800-227-4279
Gastro-Gnomes
West Hartford, CT....................800-747-4666
Geerpres
Muskegon, MI....................231-773-3211
Gelberg Signs
Washington, DC....................800-443-5237
Gemini Plastic Films Corporation
Garfield, NJ....................800-789-4732
General Electric Company
Louisville, KY....................502-452-4311
General Films
Covington, OH....................888-436-3456
General Foam Plastics Corporation
Norfolk, VA....................757-857-0153
General Neon Sign Company
San Antonio, TX....................210-227-1203
Genesta Manufacturing
Rockwall, TX....................972-771-1653
Genpak
Peterborough, ON....................800-461-1995
Genpak
Glens Falls, NY....................800-626-6695
Genpak LLC
Lakeville, MN....................800-328-4556
Gessner Products Company
Ambler, PA....................800-874-7808
Gibraltar Packaging Group
Hastings, NE....................402-463-1366
Glover Latex
Anaheim, CA....................800-243-5110
GM Nameplate
Seattle, WA....................800-366-7668
Goebel Fixture Company
Hutchinson, MN....................888-339-0509
Goex Corporation
Janesville, WI....................608-754-3303
Golden West Packaging Concept
Lake Forest, CA....................949-855-9646
Goldmax Industries
City of Industry, CA....................626-964-8820
Graham Engineering Corporation
York, PA....................717-848-3755
GraLab Corporation
Centerville, OH....................800-876-8353
Grande Ronde Sign Company
La Grande, OR....................541-963-5841
Great Northern Corporation
Appleton, WI....................800-236-3671
Great Southern Corporation
Memphis, TN....................800-421-7802
Green-Tek
Janesville, WI....................800-747-6440
Grief Brothers Corporation
Delaware, OH....................740-549-6000
Gulf Arizona Packaging
Humble, TX....................800-364-3887
Gulf Coast Plastics
Tampa, FL....................800-277-7491
Gulf Packaging Company
Safety Harbor, FL....................800-749-3466
H&H Lumber Company
Amarillo, TX....................806-335-1813
Hal-One Plastics
Olathe, KS....................800-626-5784
Hall Manufacturing Corporation
Ringwood, NJ....................973-962-6022
Hall's Safety Apparel
Uhrichsville, OH....................800-232-3671
Hampel Corporation
Germantown, WI....................800-494-4762
Handgards
El Paso, TX....................800-351-8161
Handy Wacks Corporation
Sparta, MI....................800-445-4434
Hank Rivera Associates
Dearborn, MI....................313-581-8300
Harbor Pallet Company
Anaheim, CA....................714-533-4940
Harco Enterprises
Peterborough, ON....................800-361-5361
Hardin Signs
Peoria, IL....................309-688-4111
Have Our Plastic Inc
Mississauga, ON....................800-263-5995
Hayward Industrial Products
Clemmons, NC....................908-355-7995
Heath & Company
Alhambra, CA....................800-421-9069

Hedwin Corporation
Baltimore, MD....................800-638-1012
Herche Warehouse
Denver, CO....................303-371-8186
Heritage Bag Company
Carrollton, TX....................972-241-5525
Highland Plastics
Mira Loma, CA....................800-368-0491
Himolene
Carrollton, TX....................800-777-4411
HMG Worldwide In-Store Marketing
New York, NY....................212-736-2300
Hoarel Sign Company
Amarillo, TX....................806-373-2175
Hollywood Banners
Copiague, NY....................800-691-5652
Holsman Sign Services
Cleveland, OH....................216-761-4433
Home Plastics
Des Moines, IA....................515-265-2562
Hood Flexible Packaging
St Paul, MN....................800-448-0682
Hood Packaging
Burlington, ON....................877-637-5066
Horn Packaging Corporation
Lancaster, MA....................800-832-7020
HP Manufacturing
Cleveland, OH....................216-361-6500
HPI North America/ Plastics
Eagan, MN....................800-752-7462
HPI North America/Plastics
Saint Paul, MN....................800-752-7462
HUBCO Inc.
Hutchinson, KS....................800-563-1867
Hudson Poly Bag
Hudson, MA....................800-229-7566
Hughes Manufacturing Company
Giddings, TX....................800-414-0765
Huntsman Packaging
South Deerfield, MA....................413-665-2145
Huntsman Packaging Corporation
Birmingham, Bi....................205-328-4720
I.H. McBride Sign Company
Lynchburg, VA....................434-847-4151
Ideal Office Supply & Rubber Stamp Company
Kingsport, TN....................423-246-7371
Image Plastics
Houston, TX....................800-289-2811
In the Bag
St Petersburg, FL....................800-330-2247
Indeco Products
San Marcos, TX....................512-396-5814
Indian Valley Industries
Johnson City, NY....................800-659-5111
Indiana Bottle Company Inc.
Scottsburg, IN....................800-752-8702
Indiana Vac-Form
Warsaw, IN....................574-269-1725
Indianapolis Container Company
Indianapolis, IN....................800-760-3318
Industrial Nameplates
Ivyland, PA....................800-878-6263
Inland Showcase & Fixture Company
Fresno, CA....................559-237-4158
Inline Plastics Corporation
Shelton, CT....................800-826-5567
Innovative Molding
Sebastopol, CA....................707-829-2666
Innovative Plastics Corporation
Orangeburg, NY....................845-359-7500
Insulair
Vernalis, CA....................800-343-3402
Inteplast Bags & Films Corporation
Delta, BC....................604-946-5431
Intermold Corporation
Greenville, SC....................864-627-0300
International Polymers Corporation
Allentown, PA....................800-526-0953
Interplast
Troy, OH....................937-332-1110
Interstate Packaging
White Bluff, TN....................800-251-1072
Intralox
New Orleans, LA....................800-535-8848
Intrex
Bethel, CT....................203-792-7400
IPL Plastics
Edmundston, NB....................800-739-9595
Island Poly
Westbury, NY....................800-338-4433
ITW Minigrip/Zip-Pak
Manteno, IL....................800-488-6973

J.E. Roy
St Claire, QC....................418-883-2711
J.L. Clark
Rockford, IL....................815-962-8861
James River Canada
North York, ON....................416-789-5151
Jamison Plastic Corporation
Allentown, PA....................610-391-1400
Jarden Home Brands
Daleville, IN....................800-392-2575
Jarisch Paper Box Company
North Adams, MA....................413-663-5396
Jeb Plastics
Wilmington, DE....................800-556-2247
Jeffcoat Signs
Gainesville, FL....................877-377-4248
Jescorp
Des Plaines, IL....................847-299-7800
Jet Plastica Industries
Hatfield, PA
Jewell Bag Company
Dallas, TX....................214-749-1223
JH Display & Fixture
Greenwood, IN....................317-888-0631
Jilson Group
Lodi, NJ....................800-969-5400
Jim Scharf Holdings
Perdue, SK....................800-667-9727
Johnson Refrigerated Truck Bodies
Rice Lake, WI....................800-922-8360
Johnstown Manufacturing
Columbus, OH....................614-236-8853
Jomar Corporation
Pleasantville, NJ....................609-646-8000
Jomar Plastics Industry
Nanty Glo, PA....................800-681-4039
Jones-Zylon Company
West Lafayette, OH....................800-848-8160
Joseph Struhl Company
Garden City Park, NY....................800-552-0023
Juice Merchandising Corporation
Kansas City, MO....................800-950-1998
Juice Tree
Omaha, NE....................714-891-4425
Jupiter Mills Corporation
Roslyn, NY....................800-853-5121
Just Plastics
New York, NY....................212-569-8500
K&I Creative Plastics
Jacksonville, FL....................904-387-0438
K-C Products Company
Van Nuys, CA....................818-267-1600
Kadon Corporation
Milford, OH....................937-299-0088
Kal Pac Corporation
New Windsor, NY....................845-567-0095
Kama Corporation
Hazleton, PA....................570-455-0958
Keena Corporation
Newton, MA....................617-244-9800
Kendrick Johnson & Associates
Bloomington, MN....................800-826-1271
Kenro
Fredonia, WI....................262-692-2411
Key Packaging Company
Sarasota, FL....................941-355-2728
KHM Plastics
Gurnee, IL....................847-249-4910
Kimball Companies
East Longmeadow, MA....................413-525-1881
King Plastics
North Port, FL....................941-493-5502
Kitchener Plastics
Kitchener, ON....................800-429-5633
Klever Kuvers
Pasadena, CA....................626-355-8441
Klockner Pentaplast of America
Gordonsville, VA....................540-832-3600
KM International
Kenton, TN....................731-749-8700
Knobs Unlimited
Bowling Green, OH....................419-353-8215
Kord Products Inc.
Brantford, ON....................800-452-9070
Kornylak Corporation
Hamilton, OH....................800-837-5676
Kuriyama of America
Schaumburg, IL....................800-800-0320
KVP Falcon Plastic Belting
Reading, PA....................800-445-7898
L&C Plastic Bags
Covington, OH....................937-473-2968

L&H Wood Manufacturing Company
Farmington, MI. 248-474-9000
L&L Engraving Company
Gilford, NH. 888-524-3032
Lafayette Sign Company
Little Falls, NJ. 800-343-5366
Lakeside Manufacturing
Milwaukee, WI .888-558-8574
Lakeside-Aris Manufacturing
Milwaukee, WI .800-558-8565
Lamb Sign
Manassas, VA .703-791-7960
Lambert Company
Chillicothe, MO 800-821-7667
Lamcraft
Lees Summit, MO. 800-821-1333
Landis Plastics
Alsip, IL 708-396-1470
Laughlin Corporation
Fort Worth, TX .817-625-7756
Laydon Company
Brown City, MI. 810-346-2952
Leathertone
Findlay, OH. 419-429-0188
Leeds Conveyor Manufacturer Company
Guilford, CT 800-724-1088
Legible Signs
Loves Park, IL. .800-435-4177
Letica Corporation
Rochester, MI 800-538-4221
Linvar
Hartford, CT 800-282-5288
Liqui-Box
Allentown, PA. .610-264-5420
Liquitane
Berwick, PA 570-759-6200
LMK Containers
Centerville, UT .626-821-9984
Locknane
Everett, WA. 800-848-9854
Long Island Stamp Corporation
Flushing, NY. 800-547-8267
Longhorn Packaging
San Antonio, TX. 800-433-7974
LoTech Industries
Lakewood, CO .800-295-0199
LPI Imports
Chicago, IL. 877-389-6563
Luetzow Industries
South Milwaukee, WI. 800-558-6055
Lynn Sign
Andover, MA 800-225-5764
M&E Manufacturing Company
Kingston, NY 845-331-2110
M&G Packaging Corporation
Floral Park, NY. 800-240-5288
M&R Flexible Packaging
Springboro, OH. 800-543-3380
Maco Bag Corporation
Newark, NY 315-226-1000
Majestic
Bridgeport, CT .203-367-7900
Malpack Polybag
Ajax, ON. 905-428-3751
Marco Products
Adrian, MI. 517-265-3333
Marpac Industries
Philmont, NY 888-462-7722
Marshall Plastic Film
Martin, MI. 269-672-5511
Martin/Baron
Irwindale, CA 626-960-5153
Mason Transparent Package Company
Armonk, NY 718-792-6000
Max Packaging Company
Attalla, AL 800-543-5369
May-Wes Manufacturing
Hutchinson, MN 800-788-6483
Maypak
Wayne, NJ. 973-696-0780
MBX Packaging
Wausau, WI. 715-845-1171
McQueen Sign & Lighting
Canton, OH 330-452-5769
MDR International
North Miami, FL. 305-944-5019
Measurex/S&L Plastics
Nazareth, PA 800-752-0650
Melmat, Inc.
Huntington Beach, CA 800-635-6289
Menasha Corporation
Oconomowoc, WI. 262-560-0228

Merchandising Inventives
Waukegan, IL 800-367-5653
Merryweather Foam
Sylacauga, AL. .256-249-8546
Micelli Chocolate Mold Company
West Babylon, NY 631-752-2888
Micro Qwik
Cross Plains, WI 608-798-3071
Microplas Industries
Dunwoody, GA .800-952-4528
Midco Plastics
Enterprise, KS. .800-235-2729
Midland Manufacturing Company
Monroe, IA 800-394-2625
Millhiser
Richmond, VA. .800-446-2247
Mimi et Cie
Seattle, WA 206-545-1850
Mini-Bag Company
Farmingdale, NY 631-694-3325
MIT Poly-Cart Corporation
New York, NY .800-234-7659
Mohawk Northern Plastics
Auburn, WA 800-426-1100
Molded Container Corporation
Portland, OR 503-233-8601
Monument Industries
Bennington, VT .802-442-8187
Moser Bag & Paper Company
Cleveland, OH 800-433-6638
Mount Vernon Plastics
Mamaroneck, NY 914-698-1122
Mr. Ice Bucket
New Brunswick, NJ 732-545-0420
MRI Flexible Packaging
Newtown, PA 800-448-8183
MS Plastics & Packaging Company
Butler, NJ 800-593-1802
Mulholland-Harper Company
Denton, MD 800-882-3052
Mullinix Packages
Fort Wayne, IN .260-747-3149
Naltex
Austin, TX. 800-531-5112
NAP Industries
Brooklyn, NY 877-635-4948
National Marker Company
North Smithfield, RI. 800-453-2727
National Poly Bag Manufacturing Corporation
Brooklyn, NY 718-629-9800
National Sign Corporation
Seattle, WA 206-282-0700
Nelson Company
Baltimore, MD .410-477-3000
Neo-Kraft Signs
Lewiston, ME 800-339-2258
Net Pack Systems
Oakland, ME. 207-465-4531
Newman Sanitary Gasket Company
Lebanon, OH. 513-932-7379
Nolon Industries
Mantua, OH. 330-274-2283
Norgus Silk Screen Company
Clifton, NJ. 973-365-0600
North American PackagingCorporation
New York, NY .800-499-3521
North American Plastic Manufacturing Company
Bethel, CT. 800-934-7752
Northeast Packaging Materials
Monsey, NY 845-426-2900
Northwind
Alpena, AR 870-437-2585
Noteworthy Company
Amsterdam, NY 800-696-7849
Novelty Crystal Corporation
Groveland, FL. .352-429-9036
Novelty Crystal Corporation
Long Island City, NY 800-622-0250
Now Plastics
East Longmeadow, MA 413-525-1010
NU-Trend Plastic/Corrigan & Company
Jacksonville, FL 904-353-5936
Nucon Corporation
Deerfield, IL 877-545-0070
Nutty Bavarian
Sanford, FL. 800-382-4788
Nyman Manufacturing Company
Rumford, RI 401-438-3410
NYP Corporation
Leola, PA. 800-524-1052
NYP Corporation
Leola, PA. 800-541-0961

O-I
Perrysburg, OH
Occidental Chemical Corporation
Dallas, TX. 800-733-3665
Ockerlund Industries
Forest Park, IL .708-771-7707
Oklahoma Neon
Tulsa, OK 888-707-6366
Olcott Plastics
Saint Charles, IL. 888-313-5277
Olde Thompson/Leeds Engineering Corporation
Oxnard, CA. 800-827-1565
OMNOVA Solutions
Fairlawn, OH. 330-869-4200
Ontario Glove and Safety Products
Kitchener, ON. .800-265-4554
Orbis Corp.
Rexdale, ON 800-890-7292
ORBIS Corporation
Oconomowoc, WI. 800-890-7292
OWD
Tupper Lake, NY 800-836-1693
Pace Packaging Corporation
Fairfield, NJ 800-867-2726
Pacific Oasis Enterprises
Santa Fe Springs, CA 800-424-1475
Packaging Associates
Randolph, NJ 973-252-8890
Packaging Corporation of America
Lake Forest, IL .800-456-4725
Packing Material Company
Southfield, MI. .248-489-7000
Pactiv LLC
Lake Forest, IL .888-828-2850
PAK 2000
Mirror Lake, NH. 603-569-3700
Pak Sak Industries
Sparta, MI 800-748-0431
Pallet Management Systems
Lawrenceville, VA 800-446-1804
Palmer Snyder
Brookfield, WI .800-762-0415
Pan Pacific Plastics Manufacturing
Hayward, CA 888-475-6888
Papelera Puertorriquena
Utuado, PR 787-894-2098
Par-Pak
Houston, TX 713-686-6700
Par-Pak
Houston, TX 888-272-7725
Parade Packaging
Mundelein, IL. .847-566-6264
Paragon Packaging
Ferndale, CA. 888-615-0065
Parisian Novelty Company
Homewood, IL .773-847-1212
Park Custom Molding
Linden, NJ. 908-486-8882
Parkway Plastics
Piscataway, NJ .732-752-3636
Parsons Manufacturing Corp.
Menlo Park, CA 650-324-4726
PARTA
Kent, OH. 800-543-5781
Party Yards
Casselberry, FL. 877-501-4400
Peerless Packages
Cleveland, OH 216-464-3620
Pelco Packaging Corporation
Stirling, NJ 908-647-3500
Pelican Displays
Homer, IL 800-627-1517
Pelican Products Company
Bronx, NY. 800-552-8820
Penley Corporation
West Paris, ME .800-368-6449
Penn Bottle & Supply Company
Philadelphia, PA 215-365-5700
Penn Products
Portland, CT 800-490-7366
Perfex Corporation
Poland, NY. 800-848-8483
Peter Gray Corporation
Andover, MA 978-470-0990
Pexco Packaging Corporation
Toledo, OH 800-227-9950
Pfeil & Holing, Inc.
Flushing, NY. 800-247-7955
Phoenix Sign Company
Aberdeen, WA. .360-532-1111
Pilgrim Plastic ProductsCompany
Brockton, MA. .800-343-7810

Pioneer Packaging
Dixon, KY....800-951-1551
Plaint Corporation
Bloomington, IN....800-366-3525
Plascal Corporation
Farmingdale, NY....800-899-7527
Plastech Corporation
Atlanta, GA....404-355-9682
Plasti-Clip Corporation
Milford, NH....800-882-2547
Plasti-Line
Knoxville, TN....800-444-7446
Plasti-Print
Burlingame, CA....650-652-4950
Plastic Assembly Corporation
Ayer, MA....978- 77- 472
Plastic Fantastics/Buck Signs
Ashland, OR....800-482-1776
Plastic Industries
Athens, TN....800-894-4876
Plastic Packaging Corporation
Hickory, NC....828-328-2466
Plastic Packaging Inc
Hickory, NC....800-333-2466
Plastic Suppliers
Columbus, OH....800-722-5577
Plastic Tag & Trade Check Company
Essexville, MI....989-892-7913
Plastic Turning Company
Leominster, MA....978-534-8326
Plastic-Craft Products Corp
West Nyack, NY....800-627-3010
Plastican Corporation
Fairfield, NJ....973-227-7817
Plastipak Packaging
Plymouth, MI....734-354-3510
Plastipro
Denver, CO....800-654-0409
Plastiques Cascades Group
Montreal, QC....888-703-6515
Plaxall
Long Island City, NY....800-876-5706
PM Plastics
Pewaukee, WI....262-691-1700
Pocono PET
Hazle Twp, PA....570-459-1800
Podnar Plastics
Kent, OH....800-673-5277
Polar Plastics
St Laurent, QC....514-331-0207
Polar Plastics
Mooresville, NC....704-660-6600
Poliplastic
Granby, QC....450-378-8417
Poly Processing Company
French Camp, CA....877-325-3142
Poly Shapes Corporation
Elyria, OH....800-605-9359
Poly-Seal Corporation
Baltimore, MD....410-633-1990
Polybottle Group
Brampton, ON....905-450-3600
PolyConversions
Rantoul, IL....888-893-3330
Polyplastic Forms, Inc
Farmingdale, NY....800-428-7659
Port Erie Plastics
Harborcreek, PA....814-899-7602
Portco Corporation
Vancouver, WA....800-426-1794
Pretium Packaging
Seymour, IN....812-522-8177
Primepak Company
Teaneck, NJ....201-836-5060
Printpack
Atlanta, GA....404-460-7000
Pro-Gram Plastics
Geneva, OH....440-466-8080
Progressive Plastics
Cleveland, OH....800-252-0053
Prolon
Port Gibson, MS....888-480-9828
QPF
Streamwood, IL....800-323-6963
Quality Container Company
Ypsilanti, MI....734-481-1373
Quality Films
Three Rivers, MI....269-679-5263
Quality Plastic Bag Corporation
Flushing, NY....800-532-2247
Quantum Storage Systems
Miami, FL....800-685-4665
Quintex Corporation
Spokane Valley, WA....509-924-7900
Qyk Syn Industries
Miami, FL....800-354-5640
R.H. Saw Corporation
Barrington, IL....847-381-8777
Rainbow Neon Sign Company
Houston, TX....713-923-2759
Ram Industries
Erwin, TN....800-523-3883
RAPAC
Oakland, TN....800-280-6333
Ray C. Sprosty Bag Company
Wooster, OH....330-264-8559
Rayne Plastic Signs
Rayne, LA....337-334-4276
RC Molding Inc.
Greer, SC....864-879-7279
Reading Plastic Fabricators
Temple, PA....610-926-3245
Redi-Call, Incorporated
Reno, NV....800-648-1849
Reese Enterprises
Rosemount, MN....800-328-0953
Regal Plastic Company
Mission, KS....800-852-1556
Regal Plastics
North Kansas City, MO....816-471-6390
Regina USA, Inc
Oak Creek, WI....414-571-0032
Reidler Decal Corporation
Saint Clair, PA....800-628-7770
Reilly Foam Corporation
Conshohocken, PA....610-834-1900
Reliance Product
Winnipeg, MB....800-665-0258
Rexam Beverage Can Company
Chicago, IL....773-399-3000
Rez-Tech Corporation
Kent, OH....800-673-5277
Richard Read Construction Company
Arcadia, CA....888-450-7343
Richards Packaging
Memphis, TN....800-361-6453
Richards Packaging
Memphis, TN....800-583-0327
Riverside Manufacturing Company
Arlington Hts, IL....800-877-3349
RJR Packaging, Inc.
Oakland, CA....510-638-5901
RMI-C/Rotonics Manufacturing
Bensenville, IL....630-773-9510
Roberts PolyPro
Charlotte, NC....800-269-7409
Robinson Cone
Burlington, ON....905-333-1515
Robinson Industries
Coleman, MI....989-465-6111
Rochester Midland
Rochester, NY....800-387-7174
Rock-Tenn Company
St Paul, MN....651-641-4874
Rock-Tenn Company
Norcross, GA....770-448-2193
Roechling Engineered Plastics
Gastonia, NC....800-541-4419
Roll-O-Sheets Canada
Barrie, ON....888-767-3456
Rolland Machining & Fabricating
Moneta, VA....973-827-6911
Ropak
Oak Brook, IL....800-527-2267
Roplast Industries Inc.
Oroville, CA....800-767-5278
Ross & Wallace Paper Products
Hammond, LA....800-854-2300
Rosson Sign Company
Macon, GA....478-788-3905
Roth Sign Systems
Petaluma, CA....800-585-7446
Rowland Technologies
Wallingford, CT....203-269-9500
Royal Ecoproducts
Vaughan, ON....800-465-7670
RubaTex Polymer
Middlefield, OH....440-632-1691
Rubbermaid Commercial Products
Winchester, VA....800-336-9880
Rutan Polyethylene Supply Bag & Manufacturing Company
Mahwah, NJ....800-872-1474
RXI Silgan Specialty Plastics
Triadelphia, WV....304-547-9100
Rytec Corporation
Milwaukee, WI....888-467-9832
Sabert Corporation
Sayreville, NJ....800-722-3781
Sacramento Bag Manufacturing
Woodland, CA....800-287-2247
Saeplast Canada
St John, NB....800-567-3966
Samuel P. Harris
Rumford, RI....401-438-4020
Samuel Strapping Systems
Woodridge, IL....800-323-4424
San Miguel Label Manufacturing
Ciales, PR....787-871-3120
Sani-Top Products
De Leon Springs, FL....800-874-6094
Schlueter Company
Janesville, WI....800-359-1700
Schoeneck Containers
New Berlin, WI....262-786-9360
Scott Sign Systems
Sarasota, FL....800-237-9447
Sealed Air Corporation
Elmwood Park, NJ....800-648-9093
Seiler Plastics Corporation
Saint Louis, MO....314-815-3030
Selby Sign Company
Pocomoke City, MD....410-957-1541
Semco Plastic Company
Saint Louis, MO....314-487-4557
Senior Housing Options
Denver, CO....800-659-2656
Sertapak Packaging Corporation
Woodstock, ON....800-265-1162
Service Neon Signs
Springfield, VA....703-354-3000
Setco
Monroe Twp, NJ....609-655-4600
Setco
Anaheim, CA....714-777-5200
Seton Identification Products
Branford, CT....800-571-2596
Seville Display Door
Temecula, CA....800-634-0412
SFB Plastics
Wichita, KS....800-343-8133
Shamrock Plastics
Mount Vernon, OH....800-765-1611
Sharpsville Container
Sharpsville, PA....800-645-1248
Shaw-Clayton Corporation
San Rafael, CA....800-537-6712
Sheboygan Paper Box Company
Sheboygan, WI....800-458-8373
Sheffield Plastics
Sheffield, MA....800-628-5084
Shields Bag & Printing Company
Yakima, WA....800-541-8630
Shingle Belting
King of Prussia, PA....800-345-6294
Ship Rite Packaging
Bergenfield, NJ....800-721-7447
Shippers Supply
Saskatoon, SK....800-661-5639
Sho-Me Container
Grinnell, IA....800-798-3512
Sign Graphics
Evansville, IN....812-476-9151
Sign Systems, Inc.
Warren, MI....586-758-1600
SignArt Advertising
Van Buren, AR....479-474-8581
Signature Packaging
West Orange, NJ....800-376-2299
Silgan Plastics
Chesterfield, MO....800-274-5426
Silgan Plastics Canada
Chesterfield, MO....800-274-5426
SKD Distribution Corp
Jamaica, NY....800-458-8753
SleeveCo Inc
Dawsonville, GA....706-216-3110
Smurfit Flexible Packaging
Milwaukee, WI....414-355-2700
Smurfit Stone Container
San Jose, CA....408-925-9391
Snapware
Fullerton, CA....800-334-3062
Snyder Crown
Marked Tree, AR....870-358-3400

Snyder Industries Inc.
Lincoln, NE. 800-351-1363
Solo Cup Canada
Toronto, ON 800-465-9696
Sommers Plastic ProductsCompany
Clifton, NJ. 800-225-7677
Soodhalter Plastics
Los Angeles, CA. 213-747-0231
Southern Film Extruders
High Point, NC 800-334-6101
Spartanburg Stainless Products
Spartanburg, SC 800-974-7500
Spartec Plastics
Conneaut, OH 800-325-5176
Spartech Plastics
Portage, WI 800-998-7123
Spartech Poly Com
Clayton, MI. 888-721-4242
Specialty Films & Associates
Hebron, KY. 800-984-3346
Spectrum Plastics
Las Vegas, NV 702-876-8650
Spir-It/Zoo Piks
Andover, MA 800-343-0996
Spirit Foodservice, Inc.
Andover, MA 800-343-0996
Star Container Company
Phoenix, AZ 480-281-4200
Star Filters
Timmonsville, SC. 800-845-5381
Steel City Corporation
Youngstown, OH. 800-321-0350
Stelray Plastic Products, Inc.
Ansonia, CT 800-735-2331
Step Products
Round Rock, TX. 800-777-7837
Sterling Net & Twine Company
Cedar Knolls, NJ. 800-342-0316
Sterling Novelty Products
Northbrook, IL 847-291-0070
Stoffel Seals Corporation
Tallapoosa, GA 800-422-8247
Storm Industrial
Shawnee Mission, KS. 800-745-7483
Stratis Plastic Pallets
Indianapolis, IN 800-725-5387
Straubel Company
De Pere, WI. 888-336-1412
Stripper Bags
Henderson, NV 800-354-2247
Suburban Sign Company
Anoka, MN 763-753-8849
Suburban Signs
College Park, MD 301-474-5051
Sun Plastics
Clearwater, MN. 800-862-1673
Sunland Manufacturing Company
Minneapolis, MN 800-790-1905
Superfos Packaging
Cumberland, MD 800-537-9242
Superior Quality Products
Schenectady, NY. 800-724-1129
Sutherland Stamp Company
San Diego, CA 858-233-7784
T&S Blow Molding
Scarborough, ON 416-752-8330
T&T Industries
Fort Mohave, AZ 800-437-6246
T.O. Plastics
Minneapolis, MN 952-854-2131
Tablet & Ticket Company
West Chicago, IL 800-438-4959
Tar-Hong Melamine USA
City of Industry, CA 626-935-1612
Target Industries
Flanders, NJ 973-927-0011
Taymar Industries
Palm Desert, CA. 800-624-1972
Techform
Mount Airy, NC 336-789-2115
TEMP-TECH Company
Springfield, MA 800-343-5579
Templock Corporation
Santa Barbara, CA 800-777-1715
TEQ
Huntley, IL 800-874-7113
Terphane
Bloomfield, NY 585-657-5800
Thermo-Serv
Dallas, TX. 800-635-5559
Thermodynamics
Commerce City, CO 800-627-9037
Thermodyne International
Ontario, CA. 909-923-9945
Thombert
Newton, IA 800-433-3572
Thornton Plastics
Salt Lake City, UT 800-248-3434
Three P
Salt Lake City, UT 801-486-7407
Tolas Health Care Packaging
Feasterville Trevose, PA. 215-322-7900
Tolco Corporation
Toledo, OH 800-537-4786
Toledo Sign
Toledo, OH 419-244-4444
Toscarora
Sandusky, OH 419-625-7343
Total Identity Group
Cambridge, ON. 877-551-5529
Trans Container Corporation
Upland, CA. 909-985-2750
Trans Flex Packagers
Unionville, CT 860-673-2531
Tray Pak
Reading, PA 610-926-5800
Trevor Industries
Eden, NY. 716-992-4775
Tri-State Plastics
Henderson, KY. 270-826-8361
Tri-State Plastics
Glenwillard, PA. 724-457-6900
Triad Scientific
Manasquan, NJ 800-867-6690
Trident Plastics
Ivyland, PA 800-222-2318
TriEnda Corporation
Portage, WI. 800-356-8150
Triple Dot Corporation
Santa Ana, CA 714-241-0888
Triple-A Manufacturing Company
Toronto, ON 800-786-2238
Tru-Form Plastics
Gardena, CA 800-510-7999
Tuckahoe Manufacturing Company
Vineland, NJ 800-220-3368
Tulsa Plastics Company
Tulsa, OK 888-273-5303
Tupperware Brand Corporation
Orlando, FL. 800-366-3800
Tyco Plastics
Lakeville, MN. 800-328-4080
UCB Films
Smyrna, GA 877-822-3456
Ultra Pac
Rogers, MN. 800-324-8541
Uniloy Milacron
Manchester, MI. 800-666-8852
Union Carbide Corporation
Danbury, CT 800-568-4000
Union Industries
Providence, RI 800-556-6454
Uniplast Films
Palmer, MA. 800-343-1295
Unique Manufacturing
Visalia, CA 888-737-1007
Unique Plastics
Rio Rico, AZ. 800-658-5946
United Bags
Saint Louis, MO 800-550-2247
United Commercial Corporation
Shrewsbury, NJ. 800-498-7147
United Flexible
Westbury, NY 516-222-2150
United Seal & Tag Corporation
Port Charlotte, FL. 800-211-9552
Universal Container Corporation
Odessa, FL 800-582-7477
Universal Paper Box
Seattle, WA. 800-228-1045
Universal Sign Company and Manufacturing Company
Lafayette, LA 337-234-1466
Upham & Walsh Lumber
Hoffman Estates, IL 847-519-1010
Vacumet Corporation
Austell, GA. 800-776-0865
Valley City Sign Company
Comstock Park, MI. 616-784-5711
Valley Packaging Supply Company, Inc.
Green Bay, WI. 920-336-9012
Vermont Bag & Film
Bennington, VT 802-442-3166
Vicmore Manufacturing Company
Brooklyn, NY 800-458-8663
VIFAN
Lanoraie, QC. 800-557-0192
Virginia Plastics
Roanoke, VA. 800-777-8541
Visual Packaging Corporation
Haskell, NJ 973-835-7055
Volk Corporation
Farmington Hills, MI 800-521-6799
Vollrath Company
Sheboygan, WI 920-457-4851
Vonco Products
Lake Villa, IL 800-323-9077
VPI Manufacturing
Draper, UT 801-495-2310
VPI Mirrex Corporation
Bear, DE 800-488-7608
Vulcan Industries
Moody, AL 888-444-4417
Waddington North America
Chelmsford, MA. 888-962-2877
Waddington North AmericaCups Illustrated
Lancaster, TX 800-334-2877
Wasserman Bag Company
Center Moriches, NY 631-909-8656
Weatherchem Corporation
Twinsburg, OH 330-425-4206
Wedlock Paper ConvertersLtd.
Mississauga, ON. 800-388-0447
Wells-Lamont Corporation
Niles, IL 800-323-2830
Western Plastics
Calhoun, GA. 800-752-4106
Western Plastics California
Portland, TN 615-325-7331
White Cap
Downers Grove, IL. 800-515-1565
White Swan Fruit Products
Plant City, FL 800-330-8952
Wilks Precision Instrument Company
Union Bridge, MD 410-775-7917
Winmark Stamp & Sign
Salt Lake City, UT 800-438-0480
Winnebago Sign Company
Fond Du Lac, WI 920-922-5930
Winpak Portion Packaging
Langhorne, PA 800-841-2600
Winzen Film
Sulphur Springs, TX. 800-779-7595
Wisconsin Film & Bag
Shawano, WI. 800-765-9224
Witt Plastics
Greenville, OH 800-227-9181
WNA-Comet West
City of Industry, CA 800-225-0939
WNA-Cups Illustrated
Lancaster, TX 800-334-2877
Wolens Company
Dallas, TX. 214-634-0800
Woodstock Plastics Company
Marengo, IL 815-568-5281
Wright Plastics Company
Prattville, AL 800-874-7659
Zeier Plastic & Manufacturing
Madison, WI 608-244-5782
Zimmer Custom-Made Packaging
Indianapolis, IN 317-263-3436

Plate/Frame Exchanger

Harris Equipment
Melrose Park, IL. 800-365-0315

Pump feeders

John Crane Mechanical Sealing Devices
Morton Grove, IL 800-732-5464
Polar Process
Plattsville, ON. 877-896-8077
Warren Rupp
Mansfield, OH 419-524-8388

Pumps

Food

A.K. Robins
Baltimore, MD 800-486-9656
Abel Pumps
Sewickley, PA 412-741-3222
ABO Industries
San Diego, CA 858-566-9750
Alloy Hardfacing & Engineering Company, Inc
Jordan, MN 800-328-8408

American LEWA
Holliston, MA....................888-539-2123
APV Americas
Delavan, WI....................800-252-5200
Arcobaleno Pasta Machines
Lancaster, PA....................800-875-7096
Autio Company
Astoria, OR....................800-483-8884
Automated Food Systems
Waxahachie, TX....................972-298-5719
Axiflow Technologies, Inc.
Kennesaw, GA....................770-795-1195
Baldewein Company
Lake Forrest, IL....................800-424-5544
Blackmer
Grand Rapids, MI....................616-241-1611
Bran & Luebbe
Schaumburg, IL....................847-882-8116
Calmar
Richmond, VA....................804-444-1000
Chocolate Concepts
Hartville, OH....................330-877-3322
Commercial Manufacturing& Supply Company
Fresno, CA....................559-237-1855
Cook & Beals
Loup City, NE....................308-745-0154
Cornell Pump Company
Portland, OR....................503-653-0330
Custom Food Machinery
Stockton, CA....................209-463-4343
Doering Machines, Inc.
San Francisco, CA....................415-526-2131
Dupps Company
Germantown, OH....................937-855-6555
Eirich Machines
Gurnee, IL....................847-336-2444
Eischen Enterprises
Fresno, CA....................559-834-0013
ESCO
Houston, TX....................800-966-5514
Flojet
Foothill Ranch, CA....................800-235-6538
Flow of Solids
Westford, MA....................978-392-0300
Flux Pumps Corporation
Atlanta, GA....................800-367-3589
Franrica Systems
Stockton, CA....................209-948-2811
Fristam Pumps
Middleton, WI....................800-841-5001
Fristam Pumps, USA, Ltd.Partnership
Middleton, WI....................608-831-5001
GEA Niro Soavi North America
Bedford, NH....................603-606-4060
GEA Tuchenhagen North America, USA, LLC
Portland, ME....................207-797-9500
General Tank
Berwick, PA....................800-435-8265
Granco Pumps
San Ramon, CA....................925-359-3290
Greenfield Packaging
White Plains, NY....................914-993-0233
Handtmann, Inc.
Lake Forest, IL....................800-477-3585
Healdsburg Machine Company
Santa Rosa, CA....................707-433-3348
Hinds-Bock Corporation
Bothell, WA....................425-885-1183
John Crane Mechanical Sealing Devices
Morton Grove, IL....................800-732-5464
Johnson Pumps of America
Hanover Park, IL....................847-671-7867
Karl Schnell
New London, WI....................920-982-9974
Kelmin Products
Plymouth, FL....................407-886-6079
Key Technology
Walla Walla, WA....................509-529-2161
Kinetic Equipment Company
Appleton, WI....................806-293-4471
Krogh Pump Company
Benicia, CA....................800-225-7644
L.C. Thompson Company
Kenosha, WI....................800-558-4018
Langsenkamp Manufacturing
Indianapolis, IN....................877-585-1950
Lear Romec
Elyria, OH....................440-323-3211
Leybold Vacuum
Export, PA....................724-327-5700
Liberty Engineering Company
Roscoe, IL....................877-623-9065

Lyco Manufacturing
Wausau, WI....................715-845-7867
Lyco Wausau
Wausau, WI....................715-845-7867
Marlen
Riverside, MO....................913-888-3333
MBC Food Machinery Corporation
Hackensack, NJ....................201-489-7000
Met-Pro Environmental Air Solutions
Owosso, MI....................800-392-7621
Mid-Western Research & Supply
Wichita, KS....................800-835-2832
Midwest Stainless
Menomonie, WI....................715-235-5472
Moyno
Springfield, OH....................937-327-3111
Murzan
Norcross, GA....................770-448-0583
Pacer Pumps
Lancaster, PA....................800-233-3861
Pacific Pneumatics
Rancho Cucamonga, CA....................800-221-0961
Pacific Process Technology
La Jolla, CA....................858-551-3298
Piab Vacuum Products
Hingham, MA....................800-321-7422
Polar Process
Plattsville, ON....................877-896-8077
Preferred Machining Corporation
Englewood, CO....................303-761-1535
Prince Industries
Murrayville, GA....................800-441-3303
Processing Machinery & Supply
Philadelphia, PA....................215-425-4320
Raque Food Systems
Louisville, KY....................502-267-9641
Redi-Call, Incorporated
Reno, NV....................800-648-1849
Reiser
Canton, MA....................781-575-9941
Rheo-Tech
Gurnee, IL....................847-367-1557
Rieke Packaging Systems
Auburn, IN....................260-925-3700
Roto-Jet Pump
Salt Lake City, UT....................801-359-8731
Seepex
Enon, OH....................800-695-3659
Server Products
Richfield, WI....................800-558-8722
SHURflo
Cypress, CA....................800-854-3218
Sine Pump
Arvada, CO....................888-504-8301
Special Products
Springfield, MO....................417-881-6114
Stainless Products
Somers, WC....................800-558-9446
TDH Manufacturing
Sand Springs, OK....................888-251-7961
Top Line Process Equipment Company
Bradford, PA....................800-458-6095
Valvinox
Iberville, QC....................450-346-1981
Watson-Marlow
Wilmington, MA....................800-282-8823
Waukesha Cherry-Burrell
Louisville, KY....................502-491-4310
Waukesha Cherry-Burrell
Louisville, KY....................800-252-5200
Weinman/Midland Pump
Piqua, OH....................937-773-2442
Wilden Pump & Engineering LLC
Grand Terrace, CA....................909-422-1700

Viscous Products

Invensys APV Products
Houston, TX....................713-329-1600
John Crane Mechanical Sealing Devices
Morton Grove, IL....................800-732-5464
Murzan
Norcross, GA....................770-448-0583
PCM Delasco
Houston, TX....................713-896-4888
Polar Process
Plattsville, ON....................877-896-8077
Precision Plus Vacuum Parts
Sanborn, NY....................800-526-2707
Qualtech
Quebec, QC....................888-339-3801

Raque Food Systems
Louisville, KY....................502-267-9641
Reiser
Canton, MA....................781-575-9941
Standard Pump
Auburn, GA....................866-558-8611
Sundyne Corporation
Arvada, CO....................303-425-0800
Warren Rupp
Mansfield, OH....................419-524-8388

Road Plates

Slipnot Metal Safety Flooring
Detroit, MI....................800-754-7668

Scales

Beam

Fairbanks Scales
Kansas City, MO....................800-451-4107
QA Supplies, LLC
Norfolk, VA....................800-472-7205
Vande Berg Scales
Sioux Center, IA....................712-722-1181

Butchers'

Acme Scale Company
San Leandro, CA....................888-638-5040
Arkfeld Mfg & Distr Company
Norfolk, NE....................800-533-0676
Exact Equipment Corporation
Morrisville, PA....................215-295-2000
Fairbanks Scales
Kansas City, MO....................800-451-4107
Mandeville Company
Minneapolis, MN....................800-328-8490
Marel Food Systems, Inc.
Lenexa, KS....................913-888-9110
QA Supplies, LLC
Norfolk, VA....................800-472-7205
Vande Berg Scales
Sioux Center, IA....................712-722-1181

Computing, Weighing

Acme Scale Company
San Leandro, CA....................888-638-5040
Automated Packaging Systems
Streetsboro, OH....................888-288-6224
Avery Weigh-Tronix
Fairmont, MN....................877-368-2039
Avery Weigh-Tronix
Fairmont, MN....................877-888-1646
Bizerba USA
Piscataway, NJ....................732-565-6000
Brechbuhler Scales
Canton, OH....................330-453-2424
Browne & Company
Markham, ON....................905-475-6104
Bunzl Processor Division
Dallas, TX....................800-456-5624
Campbell Wrapper Corporation
De Pere, WI....................800-727-4210
Cardinal Scale Manufacturing Company
Webb City, MO....................800-441-4237
Detecto Scale Company
Webb City, MO....................800-641-2008
Emery Winslow Scale Company
Seymour, CT....................203-881-9333
Exact Equipment Corporation
Morrisville, PA....................215-295-2000
Fairbanks Scales
Kansas City, MO....................800-451-4107
Gainco, Inc.
Gainesville, GA....................800-467-2828
Ilapak
Newtown, PA....................215-579-2900
Iman Pack
Westland, MI....................800-810-4626
Industrial Laboratory Equipment
Charlotte, NC....................704-357-3930
Intercomp Company
Hamel, MN....................800-328-3336
IWS Scales
San Diego, CA....................800-881-9755
Key-Pak Machines
Lebanon, NJ....................908-236-2111
Kisco Manufacturing
Greendale, BC....................604-823-7456

Mandeville Company
Minneapolis, MN 800-328-8490
Mettler-Toledo
Columbus, OH 800-523-5123
QA Supplies, LLC
Norfolk, VA. 800-472-7205
Rice Lake Weighing Systems
Rice Lake, WI
Si-Lodec
Tukwila, WA. 800-255-8274
SIG Pack Eagle Corporation
Oakland, CA 800-824-3245
Sterling Scale Company
Southfield, MI. 800-331-9931
Taylor Precision Products
Las Cruces, NM 630-954-1250
Thermo BLH
Canton, MA 781-821-2000
Tridyne Process Systems Inc.
South Burlington, VT 802-863-6873
Vande Berg Scales
Sioux Center, IA 712-722-1181
Weigh Right Automatic Scale Company
Joliet, IL 800-571-0249
Yamato Corporation
Colorado Springs, CO. 800-538-1762

Counter

Acme Scale Company
San Leandro, CA. 888-638-5040
Action Packaging Automation
Roosevelt, NJ 800-241-2724
Automated Packaging Systems
Streetsboro, OH 888-288-6224
Detecto Scale Company
Webb City, MO 800-641-2008
Fairbanks Scales
Kansas City, MO. 800-451-4107
Iman Pack
Westland, MI. 800-810-4626
Industrial Laboratory Equipment
Charlotte, NC 704-357-3930
Mettler-Toledo
Columbus, OH 800-523-5123
NJM/CLI
Pointe Claire, QC 514-630-6990
QA Supplies, LLC
Norfolk, VA. 800-472-7205
Vande Berg Scales
Sioux Center, IA 712-722-1181
Yamato Corporation
Colorado Springs, CO. 800-538-1762

Fluid, Liquid, Weighing

APEC
Lake Odessa, MI. 616-374-1000
Fairbanks Scales
Kansas City, MO. 800-451-4107
Fuller Weighing Systems
Columbus, OH 614-882-8121
Industrial Laboratory Equipment
Charlotte, NC 704-357-3930
Magnetic Products
Highland, MI. 800-544-5930
Rice Lake Weighing Systems
Rice Lake, WI
Sartorius Corporation
Edgewood, NY 800-635-2906
Thermo BLH
Canton, MA 781-821-2000
Vande Berg Scales
Sioux Center, IA 712-722-1181
Yamato Corporation
Colorado Springs, CO. 800-538-1762

Screening

Manufacturing

ANKOM Technology
Macedon, NY 315-986-8090
Buffalo Wire Works
Buffalo, NY. 800-828-7028

Scrubbers

Auto Scrubbing & Burnishing

Surtec, Inc.
Tracy, CA 800-877-6330

Shelves

Refrigerator & Stove

BMH Equipment
Sacramento, CA 800-350-8828
E-Z Shelving Systems
Merriam, KS. 800-353-1331
Fasteners for Retail
Cincinnati, OH 800-422-2547
G.F. Frank & Sons
Fairfield, OH. 513-870-9075
Grillco
Aurora, IL 800-644-0067
Kaines West Michigan Company
Ludington, MI. 231-845-1281
Kason Industries
Newnan, GA. 770-254-0553
Marlin Steel Wire Products
Baltimore, MD 877-762-7546
Metro Corporation
Wilkes Barre, PA. 800-433-2233
Mid-West Wire Specialties
Chicago, IL 800-238-0228
Olson Wire Products Company
Halethorpe, MD 410-242-1945
Pacific Northwest Wire Works
Dupont, WA 800-222-7699
Princeton Shelving
Cedar Rapids, IA. 319-369-0355
SSW Holding Company, Inc.
Elizabethtown, KY 270-769-5526
Straits Steel & Wire Company
Ludington, MI. 231-843-3416
Superior Products Company
Saint Paul, MN 800-328-9800
Triple-A Manufacturing Company
Toronto, ON 800-786-2238
Wald Wire & Manufacturing Company
Oshkosh, WI 800-236-0053

Sizers

Andgar Corporation
Ferndale, WA 360-366-9900
Bepex International,LLC
Minneapolis, MN 800-607-2470
Brown International Corporation
Winter Haven, FL 626-966-8361
Carter Day International, Inc.
Minneapolis, MN 763-571-1000
Durand-Wayland, Inc.
Lagrange, GA 800-241-2308
F. Harold Haines Manufacturing
Presque Isle, ME 207-762-1411
Glen Mills, Inc.
Clifton, NJ. 973-777-0777
Hosokawa/Bepex Corporation
Santa Rosa, CA. 707-586-6000
Kerian Machines
Grafton, ND 701-352-0480
Lewis M. Carter Manufacturing Company
Donalsonville, GA 229-524-2197
MAF Industries
Traver, CA. 559-897-2905
Southern Ag Company
Blakely, GA. 229-723-4262
Southern Automatics
Lakeland, FL. 800-441-4604
Suffolk Iron Works
Suffolk, VA. 757-539-2353
Tri-Pak Machinery, Inc.
Harlingen, TX. 956-423-5140

Stacking

Anver Corporation
Hudson, MA 800-654-3500
API
Tampa, FL. 813-888-8488
BMH Equipment
Sacramento, CA 800-350-8828
C.J. Machine
Fridley, MN. 763-767-4630
Food Equipment Manufacturing Company
Bedford Heights, OH 216-663-1208
GBN Machine & Engineering Corporation
Woodford, VA. 800-446-9871
Graybill Machines
Lititz, PA. 717-626-5221
Kisters Kayat
Sarasota, FL 386-424-0101
Lift Rite
Mississauga, ON. 905-456-2603
MarquipWard United
Phillips, WI. 715-339-2191
Packaging Systems International
Denver, CO. 303-296-4445
Peerless Food Equipment
Sidney, OH 937-492-4158
Planet Products Corporation
Blue Ash, OH 513-984-5544
Roberts PolyPro
Charlotte, NC 800-269-7409
Vertical Systems
Ft. Michelle, KY. 859-485-9650

Steam Generators

Aerco International
Northvale, NJ 201-768-2400
Direct Fire Technical
Benbrook, TX. 888-920-2468
Electro-Steam Generator Corporation
Rancocas, NJ. 866-617-0764
PVI Industries
Fort Worth, TX 800-784-8326
Vapor Corporation
Franklin Park, IL. 888-874-9020

Steam Tables

Allstrong Restaurant Equipment
South El Monte, CA 800-933-8913
Caselites
Hialeah, FL 305-819-7766
Craig Manufacturing
Irvington, NJ. 800-631-7936
Custom Diamond International
Laval, QC 800-326-5926
Delfield Company
Mt Pleasant, MI. 800-733-8821
Denmar Corporation
North Dartmouth, MA 508-999-3295
Duke Manufacturing Company
Saint Louis, MO 800-735-3853
Dunhill Food Equipment Corporation
Armonk, NY. 800-847-4206
Habco
Concord, CA. 925-682-6203
Hot Food Boxes
Mooresville, IN. 800-733-8073
Institutional Equipment
Bolingbrook, IL 630-771-0990
Lambertson Industries
Sparks, NV 800-548-3324
LaRosa Refrigeration & Equipment Company
Detroit, MI 800-527-6723
Lazy-Man
Belvidere, NJ 800-475-1950
Leedal Inc
Northbrook, IL 847-498-0111
M&S Manufacturing
Arnold, MO. 636-464-2739
Mayekawa USA, Inc.
Chicago, IL 773-516-5070
N. Wasserstrom & Sons
Columbus, OH 800-999-9277
Professional Bakeware Company
Willis, TX 800-440-9547
Randell Manufacturing Unified Brands
Weidman, MI 888-994-7636
Reliable Food Service Equipment
Concord, ON. 416-738-6840
Rexcraft Fine Chafers
Long Island City, NY 888-739-2723
Rubbermaid Commercial Products
Winchester, VA 800-336-9880
Superior Products Company
Saint Paul, MN 800-328-9800
Supreme Metal
Alpharetta, GA 800-645-2526
Update International
Los Angeles, CA. 800-747-7124
West Metals
London, ON 800-300-6667

Systems

Check Weighing

Cintex of America
Carol Stream, IL 800-424-6839
Gainco, Inc.
Gainesville, GA 800-467-2828

New-Ma Co. Llc
Grand Rapids, MI 616-942-5500
Sick Inc.
Minneapolis, MN 800-325-7425
Thompson Scale Company
Houston, TX 713-932-9071

Chemical Dispensing & Feed

Solvox Manufacturing Company
Milwaukee, WI 414-774-5664

Cost

Berg Company
Monona, WI 608-221-4281
InFood Corporation
Evanston, IL 773-338-8485

Metal & Contamination Detection

Cintex of America
Carol Stream, IL 800-424-6839
Loma Systems
Carol Stream, IL 800-872-5662

Mist Collection

Aget Manufacturing Company
Adrian, MI. 517-263-5781

Packaging

Advance Weight Systems
Grafton, OH 440-926-3691
AGA Gas
Cleveland, OH 216-642-6600
Alfa Production Systems
Westfield, NJ. 908-654-0255
Bradman Lake Inc
Rock Hill, SC 704-588-3301
California Vibratory Feeders
Anaheim, CA 800-354-0972
Campbell Wrapper Corporation
De Pere, WI. 920-983-7100
Creative Foam Corporation
Fenton, MI 810-629-4149
Crown Simplimatic Company
Lynchburg, VA 434-582-1200
Indeco Products
San Marcos, TX 512-396-5814
New-Ma Co. Llc
Grand Rapids, MI 616-942-5500
Niro
Hudson, WI. 715-386-9371
Palace Packaging Machines
Downingtown, PA. 610-873-7252
Par Systems
Saint Paul, MN 800-464-1320
Parish Manufacturing
Indianapolis, IN 800-592-2268
Promarks, Inc.
Ontario, CA. 909-923-3888
Raque Food Systems
Louisville, KY 502-267-9641
Reiser
Canton, MA 781-575-9941
Schroeder Sewing Technologies
San Marcos, CA 760-591-9733
Sealpac USA LLC
Richmond, VA. 804-261-0580
Sertapak Packaging Corporation
Woodstock, ON. 800-265-1162
SIG Combibloc USA, Inc.
Chester, PA 610-546-4200
Somerville Packaging
Scarborough, ON 416-291-1161
Stock America Inc
Grafton, WI. 262-375-4100
TNA Packaging Solutions
Coppell, TX 972-462-6500

Pricing

Astoria Laminations
Saint Clair Shores, MI 800-526-7325
Eaton Filtration, LLC
Tinton Falls, NJ. 800-859-9212
Garvey Products
West Chester, OH 800-543-1908
L.A. Darling Company
Paragould, AR. 800-643-3499

Stratecon International Consultants
Winston Salem, NC. 336-768-6808

Process & Production

Ace Manufacturing
Cincinnati, OH 800-653-5692
All-Fill, Inc.
Exton, PA 800-334-1529
ANKOM Technology
Macedon, NY 315-986-8090
Cog-Veyor Systems, Inc.
Woodbridge, Ontario, ON. 888-337-2358
Dennis Group
Springfield, MA 413-787-1785
FR Drake Company
Waynesboro, VA 540-451-2790
Gainco, Inc.
Gainesville, GA 800-467-2828
NewTech
Randolph, VT 800-210-2361
Reiser
Canton, MA 781-575-9941
Spray Dynamics, Ltd
Saint Clair, MO. 800-260-7366
Strongarm
Horsham, PA. 215-443-3400

Reverse Osmosis

Aquathin Corporation
Pompano Beach, FL 800-462-7634
Armfield
Ringwood, EN 142- 47-781
Culligan Company
Northbrook, IL 800-527-8637
Ecodyne Water Treatment,LLC
Naperville, IL 800-228-9326
Enting Water Condition g
Dayton, OH. 800-735-5100
Hungerford & Terry
Clayton, NJ 856-881-3200
Hydropure Water Treatment Company
Coral Springs, FL 800-753-1547
Kiss International/Di-tech Systems
Vista, CA. 800-527-5477
Multiplex Company, Inc.
Sellersburg, IN 800-787-8880
Pacific Process Technology
La Jolla, CA 858-551-3298
Thomas Technical Services
Neillsville, WI. 715-743-4666
Water & Power Technologies
Salt Lake City, UT 888-271-3295
Waterlink/Sanborn Technologies
Canton, OH 800-343-3381

Skids

Relco Unisystems Corporation
Willmar, MN. 320-231-2210

Tubularaseptic Processing

Excel-A-Tec
Brookfield, WI 262-252-3600

Valve Control

Andersen 2000
Peachtree City, GA 800-241-5424

Vision Verification

Cintex of America
Carol Stream, IL 800-424-6839
Cotton Goods Manufacturing Company
Chicago, IL 773-265-0088
Sick Inc.
Minneapolis, MN 800-325-7425

X-ray Contaminant Detection

Cintex of America
Carol Stream, IL 800-424-6839

Zipper Application

Com-Pac International
Carbondale, IL 888-297-2824
Zip-Pak
Manteno, IL 815-468-6500

Tabletop Supplies

A-1 Tablecloth Company
S Hackensack, NJ 800-727-8987
Abco International
Melville, NY 866-240-2226
Adcapitol
Monroe, NC. 800-868-7111
AJM Packaging Corporation
Bloomfield Hills, MI 248-901-0040
Aladdin's Hookah & Loung Bar
Nashville, TN 615-329-3558
Amcel
Watertown, MA. 800-225-7992
Anchor Hocking Company
Lancaster, OH 800-562-7511
Artex International
Highland, IL 618-654-2113
Arthur Corporation
Huron, OH. 419-433-7202
Atlantis Industries
Milton, DE 302-684-8542
AWP Butcher Block Inc
Horse Cave, KY 800-764-7840
Babco International, Inc
Tucson, AZ 520-628-7596
Benner China & Glassware of Florida
Jacksonville, FL 904-733-4620
Bib Pak
Racine, WI 262-633-5803
Bright of America
Summersville, WV 304-872-3000
Brooklace
Oshkosh, WI 800-572-4552
Browne & Company
Markham, ON 905-475-6104
Buffalo China
Buffalo, NY. 716-824-8515
Carnegie Textile Company
Solon, OH 800-633-4136
Carthage Cup Company
Longview, TX 903-238-9833
Ceramica De Espana
Doral, FL. 305-597-9161
Chef Specialties Company
Smethport, PA 800-440-2433
China Lenox Incorporated
Bristol, PA. 267-525-7800
Chinet Company
Winter Springs, FL 800-539-3726
Chinet Company
Laguna Niguel, CA 949-348-1711
City Grafx
Eugene, OR. 800-258-2489
Colonial Paper Company
Silver Springs, FL. 352-622-4171
Commercial Textiles Corporation-Best Buy Uniforms
Homestead, PA 800-345-1924
Cr. Manufacturing
Waverly, NE 877-789-5844
Creative Converting
Clintonville, WI 800-826-0418
Custom Table Pads
St Paul, MN. 651-714-5720
Cyclamen Collection
Oakland, CA 510-434-7620
Dansk International Designs
White Plains, NY 914-697-6400
Dart Container Corporation
Mason, MI. 800-248-5960
De Ster Corporation
Atlanta, GA. 800-237-8270
Delco Tableware
Port Washington, NY 800-221-9557
Delfin Design & Manufacturing
Rcho Sta Marg, CA. 800-354-7919
Design Specialties
Hamden, CT 800-999-1584
Diamond Brands
Cloquet, MN 218-879-6700
Dorado Carton Company
Dorado, PR 787-796-1670
Drapes 4 Show
Sylmar, CA 800-525-7469
Durango-Georgia Paper
Tampa, FL. 813-286-2718
Dynynstyl
Delray Beach, FL 800-774-7895
Eastern Silver Tabletop Manufacturing Company
Brooklyn, NY 888-422-4142
Eide Industries
Cerritos, CA 800-422-6827

Elrene Home Fashions
New York, NY 212-213-0425
Erving Industries
Erving, MA 413-422-2700
Fabri-Kal Corporation
Kalamazoo, MI 800-888-5054
Fenton Art Glass Company
Williamstown, WV 800-933-6766
Filet Menu
Los Angeles, CA 310-202-8000
Filmpack Plastic Corporation
Dayton, NJ 732-329-6523
Flamingo Food Service Products
Hialeah, FL 800-432-8269
Fonda Group
Goshen, IN 574-534-2515
Fonda Group
Oshkosh, WI 800-367-2877
Fonda Group
Oshkosh, WI 800-558-9300
Fort James Canada
Toronto, ON 416-784-1621
Fort James Corporation
Norwalk, CT 800-257-9744
Four M Manufacturing Group
San Jose, CA 408-998-1141
Franke Commercial Systems
Hatfield, PA 800-626-5771
Gaetano America
El Monte, CA 626-442-2858
Genpak
Peterborough, ON 800-461-1995
Genpak
Glens Falls, NY 800-626-6695
Georgia Pacific
Green Bay, WI 920-435-8821
Gourmet Tableskirts
Houston, TX 800-527-0440
Grand Silver Company
Bronx, NY 718-585-1930
H.F. Coors China Company
New Albany, MS 800-782-6677
Hal-One Plastics
Olathe, KS 800-626-5784
Hall China Company
East Liverpool, OH 800-445-4255
Hartstone
Zanesville, OH 740-452-9999
Have Our Plastic Inc
Mississauga, ON 800-263-5995
Hilden Halifax
South Boston, VA 800-431-2514
Hofmann & Leavy/Tasseldepot
Deerfield Beach, FL 954-698-0001
Hollowick
Manlius, NY 800-367-3015
Homer Laughlin China Company
Newell, WV 800-452-4462
HPI North America/ Plastics
Eagan, MN 800-752-7462
HPI North America/Plastics
Saint Paul, MN 800-752-7462
Image Plastics
Houston, TX 800-289-2811
International Paper Co.
Memphis, TN 800-207-4003
J. James
Brooklyn, NY 718-384-6144
Jack the Ripper Table Skirting
Stafford, TX 800-331-7831
JBC Plastics
St Louis, MO 877-834-5526
Jet Plastica Industries
Hatfield, PA
Jones-Zylon Company
West Lafayette, OH 800-848-8160
K-C Products Company
Van Nuys, CA 818-267-1600
Kenro
Fredonia, WI 262-692-2411
Klever Kuvers
Pasadena, CA 626-355-8441
Kuepper Favor Company, Celebrate Line
Peru, IN 800-321-5823
Libbey
Toledo, OH
Libby Canada
Mississauga, ON 905-607-8280
Libertyware
Clearfield, UT 888-500-5885
Louis Jacobs & Son
Brooklyn, NY 718-782-3500

Mack-Chicago Corporation
Chicago, IL 800-992-6225
Majestic
Bridgeport, CT 203-367-7900
Marston Manufacturing
Cleveland, OH 216-587-3400
Mason Candlelight Company
New Albany, MS 800-556-2766
Master Piece Crystal
Jane Lew, WV 304-884-7841
Mastercraft
Appleton, WI 800-242-6602
Metal Master
Tucson, AZ 800-488-8729
Michael Leson Dinnerware
Youngstown, OH 800-821-3541
Milliken & Company
Spartanburg, SC 864-503-2020
Mr. Ice Bucket
New Brunswick, NJ 732-545-0420
Novelty Crystal Corporation
Long Island City, NY 800-622-0250
Olde Country Reproductions
York, PA 800-358-3997
Oneida Canada, Limited
Oneida, NY 888-263-7195
Oneida Food Service
Oneida, NY 315-361-3000
OWD
Tupper Lake, NY 800-836-1693
Palmland Paper Company
Fort Lauderdale, FL 800-266-9067
Paradise Products
El Cerrito, CA 800-227-1092
Party Linens
Chicago, IL 800-281-0003
Party Yards
Casselberry, FL 877-501-4400
Penley Corporation
West Paris, ME 800-368-6449
Philmont Manufacturing Co.
Englewood, NJ 888-379-6483
Placemat Printers
Fogelsville, PA 800-628-7746
Plastiques Cascades Group
Montreal, QC 888-703-6515
Polar Plastics
Mooresville, NC 704-660-6600
Potlatch Corporation
Spokane, WA 509-835-1500
Premier Industries
Cincinnati, OH 800-354-9817
Premier Skirting Products
Lawrence, NY 800-544-2516
Prestige Skirting & Tablecloths
Orangeburg, NY 800-635-3313
Racket Group
Kansas City, MO 816-842-2380
Reed & Barton Food Service
Taunton, MA 800-797-9675
Resource One/Resource Two
Reseda, CA 818-343-3451
Ronnie's Ceramic Company
San Francisco, CA 800-888-8218
Royal Paper Products
Coatesville, PA 800-666-6655
Royal Prestige Health Moguls
Westbury, NY 888-802-7433
Rubbermaid Canada
Mississauga, ON 905-279-1010
Sabert Corporation
Sayreville, NJ 800-722-3781
Salem China Company
Salem, OH 330-337-8771
Sani-Top Products
De Leon Springs, FL 800-874-6094
SCA Tissue
Neenah, WI 866-722-6659
Scan Group
Appleton, WI 920-730-9150
Sims Superior Seating
Locust Grove, GA 800-729-9178
Smith-Lee Company
Oshkosh, WI 800-327-9774
Snap-Drape
Carrollton, TX 800-527-5147
Solo Cup Canada
Toronto, ON 800-465-9696
Solo Cup Company
Lake Forest, IL 800-367-2877
Something Different Linen
Clifton, NJ 800-422-2180

Sonoco
Pottstown, PA 800-377-2692
Spir-It/Zoo Piks
Andover, MA 800-343-0996
Spirit Foodservice, Inc.
Andover, MA 800-343-0996
Stanley Roberts
Piscataway, NJ 973-778-5900
Sterling Paper Company
Philadelphia, PA 215-744-5350
Stevens Linen Association
Dudley, MA 508-943-0813
Straubel Company
De Pere, WI 888-336-1412
Superior Linen & Work Wear
Kansas City, MO 800-798-7987
Superior Products Company
Saint Paul, MN 800-328-9800
Table De France: North America
New York, NY 212-725-3461
Tag-Trade Associated Group
Chicago, IL 800-621-8350
Tango Shatterproof Drinkware
Walpole, MA 888-898-2646
Tar-Hong Melamine USA
City of Industry, CA 626-935-1612
TEMP-TECH Company
Springfield, MA 800-343-5579
Town Food Service Equipment Company
Brooklyn, NY 800-221-5032
Tradeco International
Addison, IL 800-628-3738
Traex
Dane, WI 800-356-8006
Uhtamaki Foods Services
Waterville, ME 207-873-3351
Ullman Company
New York, NY 212-571-0068
Ultimate Textile
Paterson, NJ 973-523-5866
Unisource Converting
Jacksonville, FL 904-783-0550
US Lace Paper Works
Oshkosh, WI 800-873-6459
Vertex China
Walnut, CA 800-483-7839
Vicmore Manufacturing Company
Brooklyn, NY 800-458-8663
Victoria Porcelain
Miami, FL 888-593-2353
Waddington North America
Chelmsford, MA 888-962-2877
Waddington North AmericaCups Illustrated
Lancaster, TX 800-334-2877
Wiltec
Leominster, MA 978-537-1497
Wilton Armetale Company
Mount Joy, PA 800-779-4586
Wishbone Utensil Tableware Line
Wheat Ridge, CO 866-266-5928
WNA-Comet West
City of Industry, CA 800-225-0939
Xtreme Beverages, LLC
Dana Point, CA 949-495-7929

Tea Industry

Washington Frontier
Grandview, WA 509-469-7662

Timers

ABB SSAC
Baldwinsville, NY 888-385-1221
Alarm Controls Corporation
Deer Park, NY 800-645-5538
AMCO Corporation
City of Industry, CA 626-855-2550
American Time & Signal
Dassel, MN 800-328-8996
Automatic Timing & Controls
Newell, WV 800-727-5646
Chaney Instrument
Lake Geneva, WI 800-777-0565
Coley Industries
Wayland, NY 716-728-2390
Control Products
Chanhassen, MN 800-947-9098
Cooper Instrument Corporation
Middlefield, CT 800-835-5011
Cramer Company
South Windsor, CT 877-684-6464

Dayton Marking Devices Company
Dayton, OH. .937-432-0285
Elreha Controls Corporation
St Petersburg, FL 727-327-6236
ERC Parts
Kennesaw, GA 800-241-6880
Food Automation Service Techniques
Stratford, CT 800-327-8766
GraLab Corporation
Centerville, OH. 800-876-8353
M.H. Rhodes Cramer
South Windsor, CT 877-684-6464
National Controls Corporation
West Chicago, IL 800-323-5293
National Time Recording Equipment Company
New York, NY 212-227-3310
Pelouze Scale Company
Bridgeview, IL 800-323-8363
Prince Castle
Carol Stream, IL 800-722-7853
R.P. Childs Stamp Company
Ludlow, MA .413-733-1211
Superior Products Company
Saint Paul, MN 800-328-9800
Wilkens-Anderson Company
Chicago, IL 800-847-2222

Tubing

Plastic

AR-BEE Transparent
Elk Grove Vlg, IL 800-642-2247
Emco Industrial Plastics
Cedar Grove, NJ 800-292-9906
Flexo Transparent
Buffalo, NY. .877-993-5396
Hall Manufacturing Corporation
Ringwood, NJ 973-962-6022
Home Plastics
Des Moines, IA 515-265-2562
LPI, Legacy Plastics
Henderson, KY 270-827-1318
MS Plastics & Packaging Company
Butler, NJ 800-593-1802
Roechling Engineered Plastics
Gastonia, NC. 800-541-4419
Rubber Fab
Sparta, NJ 866-442-2959
Target Industries
Flanders, NJ .973-927-0011
Trident Plastics
Ivyland, PA 800-222-2318
Wilkens-Anderson Company
Chicago, IL 800-847-2222

Stainless Steel

Accutek Packaging Equipment Company
Vista, CA. 800-989-1828
Arc Machines
Pacoima, CA .818-896-9556
Baldewein Company
Lake Forrest, IL 800-424-5544
Damascus/Bishop Tube Company
Greenville, PA. 724-646-1500
J.L. Honing Company
milwaukee, WI 800-747-9501
Jacob Tubing LP
Memphis, TN 901-566-1110
L&S Products
Coldwater, MI. 517-279-9526
L.C. Thompson Company
Kenosha, WI .800-558-4018
Liburdi Group of Companies
Mooresville, NC 800-533-9353
Melrose Displays
Passaic, NJ 973-471-7700
Northland Process Piping
Isle, MN 320-679-2119
Pinquist Tool & Die Company
Brooklyn, NY 800-752-0414
Plymouth Tube Company
East Troy, WI 262-642-8201
Rath Manufacturing Company
Janesville, WI 800-367-7284
Robert-James Sales
Buffalo, NY. .800-777-1325
Spencer Turbine Company
Windsor, CT .800-232-4321
Sterling Process Engineering
Columbus, OH 800-783-7875

Sudmo North America, Inc
Machesney Park, IL 800-218-3915
T-Drill Industries
Norcross, GA 800-554-2730
Top Line Process Equipment Company
Bradford, PA. 800-458-6095
United Industries
Beloit, WI 608-365-8891
Valvinox
Iberville, QC .450-346-1981

Unscramblers

A.K. Robins
Baltimore, MD 800-486-9656
BEVCO
Canada, BC. .800-663-0090
Chase-Logeman Corporation
Greensboro, NC 336-665-0754
ELF Machinery
La Porte, IN. .800-328-0466
Fogg Company
Holland, MI. .616-786-3644
Inline Filling Systems
Venice, FL. 941-486-8800
JW Leser Company
Los Angeles, CA. 323-731-4173
Kaps-All Packaging Systems
Riverhead, NY 631-727-0300
Kinsley Inc
Doylestown, PA 800-414-6664
Leader Engineering-Fabrication
Napoleon, OH. 419-592-0008
Leeds Conveyor Manufacturer Company
Guilford, CT .800-724-1088
McBrady Engineering
Joliet, IL 815-744-8900
Nalbach Engineering Company, Inc.
Countryside, IL. 708-579-9100
New England Machinery Inc
Bradenton, FL. 941-755-5550
Norwalt Design Inc.
Randolph, NJ 973-927-3200
Omega Design Corporation
Exton, PA 800-346-0191
Pace Packaging Corporation
Fairfield, NJ .800-867-2726
Palace Packaging Machines
Downingtown, PA. 610-873-7252
Pearson Packaging Systems
Spokane, WA. 800-732-7766
Perl Packaging Systems
Middlebury, CT. 800-864-2853
Simplex Filler Company
Napa, CA. 800-796-7539
Spurgeon Company
Ferndale, MI .800-396-2554
Stiles Enterprises
Rockaway, NJ 800-325-4232
Weigh Right Automatic Scale Company
Joliet, IL 800-571-0249

Valves

Advance Fitting Corporation
Elkhorn, WI. .262-723-6699
Anver Corporation
Hudson, MA .800-654-3500
APV Americas
Delavan, WI .800-252-5200
ARCHON Industries
Suffern, NY. .800-554-1394
Armstrong-Lynnwood
Three Rivers, MI. 269-273-1415
Baldewein Company
Lake Forrest, IL 800-424-5544
Boston Gear
Boston, MA. .888-999-9860
Bradford A Ducon Company
Pewaukee, WI. 800-789-1718
C&D Valve Manufacturing Company, Inc.
Oklahoma City, OK 800-654-9233
C&R Refrigration Inc,
Center, TX. 800-438-6182
C.F.F. Stainless Steels
Hamilton, ON 800-263-4511
Cashco
Ellsworth, KS 785-472-4461
Chlorinators Inc
Stuart, FL 800-327-9761
Cincinnati Industrial Machinery
Mason, OH 800-677-0076

Cipriani Harrison Valves
Rcho Sta Marg, CA. 949-589-3978
Clark-Cooper Division Magnatrol Valve Corporation
Cinnaminson, NJ. 856-829-4580
Conbraco Industries
Matthews, NC. 704-847-9191
Delavan Spray Technologies
Bamberg, SC. 800-982-6943
Doering Company
Clear Lake, MN 320-743-2276
Dormont Manufacturing Company
Export, PA. 800-367-6668
Duplex Mill & Manufacturing Company
Springfield, OH. 937-325-5555
EVAPCO
Taneytown, MD 410-756-2600
Firematic Sprinkler Devices
Shrewsbury, MA. 508-845-2121
Flomatic International
Clackamas, OR 800-435-2550
Fluid Transfer
Philipsburg, PA. 814-342-0902
Flynn Burner Corporation
New Rochelle, NY 800-643-8910
FMC Fluid Control
Stephenville, TX. 800-772-8582
GEA Tuchenhagen North America, USA, LLC
Portland, ME. 207-797-9500
General Tank
Berwick, PA .800-435-8265
Globe Fire Sprinkler Corporation
Standish, MI .800-248-0278
Harris Equipment
Melrose Park, IL. 800-365-0315
Hayes & Stolz IndustrialManufacturing Company
Fort Worth, TX 800-725-7272
Hayward Industrial Products
Clemmons, NC 908-355-7995
Heuft
Downers Grove, IL 630-968-9011
Hi-Temp
Tuscumbia, AL 800-239-5066
Hilliard Corporation
Elmira, NY 607-733-7121
Holland Applied Technologies
Burr Ridge, IL. 630-325-5130
Hydra-Flex
Livonia, MI 800-234-0832
IMI Norgren
Brookville, OH 937-833-4033
Invensys APV Products
Houston, TX .713-329-1600
Josam Company
Michigan City, IN 800-365-6726
K-Tron
Salina, KS 785-825-1611
Kemutec Group
Bristol, PA. 215-788-8013
Kraissl Company
Hackensack, NJ. 800-572-4775
L.C. Thompson Company
Kenosha, WI .800-558-4018
Lumaco
Hackensack, NJ. 800-735-8258
Lumaco Sanitary Valves
Hackensack, NJ. 800-735-8258
M-One Specialties Inc
Salt Lake City, UT 800-525-9223
Matcon USA
Elmhurst, IL .856-256-1330
Midwest Stainless
Menomonie, WI 715-235-5472
MO Industries
Whippany, NJ 973-386-9228
Moyno
Springfield, OH. 937-327-3111
Norgren
Littleton, CO .303-794-2611
Northland Process Piping
Isle, MN 320-679-2119
Numatics
Novi, MI 248-596-3200
Parker Hannifin Corporation
Cleveland, OH 609-586-5151
Paxton Corporation
Bristol, RI
PBM
Irwin, PA. 800-967-4PBM
Plast-O-Matic Valves
Cedar Grove, NJ 973-256-3000
Qosina Corporation
Edgewood, NY 631-242-3000

Qualtech
Quebec, QC....................888-339-3801
Robert-James Sales
Buffalo, NY....................800-777-1325
Rubber Fab
Sparta, NJ....................866-442-2959
Rutherford Engineering
Rockford, IL....................815-623-2141
Samson Controls
Baytown, TX....................281-383-3677
Sanchelima International
Doral, FL....................305-591-4343
SerVend International
Sellersburg, IN....................800-367-4233
Shick Tube-Veyor Corporation
Kansas City, MO....................816-861-7224
Special Products
Springfield, MO....................417-881-6114
Spraying Systems Company
Wheaton, IL....................630-655-5000
Stainless Products
Somers, WC....................800-558-9446
Storm Industrial
Shawnee Mission, KS....................800-745-7483
Strahman Valves
Bethlehem, PA....................877-787-2462
Sudmo North America, Inc
Machesney Park, IL....................800-218-3915
Top Line Process Equipment Company
Bradford, PA....................800-458-6095
Tuchenhagen
Columbia, MD....................410-910-6000
Valvinox
Iberville, QC....................450-346-1981
Van Air Systems
Lake City, PA....................800-840-9906
Viatec
Hastings, MI....................800-942-4702
Viking Corporation
Hastings, MI....................800-968-9501
Vilter Manufacturing Corporation
Cudahy, WI....................414-744-0111
Watts Regulator Company
North Andover, MA....................978-688-1811
Waukesha Cherry-Burrell
Louisville, KY....................800-252-5200
Waukesha Specialty Company
Darien, WI....................262-724-3700

Water Treatment

Alar Engineering Corporation
Mokena, IL....................708-479-6100
Amsoil
Superior, WI....................715-392-7101
Anderson Chemical Company
Litchfield, MN....................320-693-2477
Astro-Pure Water Purifiers
Deerfield Beach, FL....................954-422-8966
Better Health Lab
Hackensack, NJ....................800-810-1888
Bloomfield Industries
St. Louis, MO....................888-356-5362
Cellulo Company
Fresno, CA....................866-213-1131
Crane Environmental
Norristown, PA....................800-633-7435
Croll-Reynolds Engineering Company
Trumbull, CT....................203-371-1983
Culligan Company
Northbrook, IL....................800-527-8637
Cuno
Meriden, CT....................800-243-6894
Delta Pure Filtration
Ashland, VA....................800-785-9450
Diamond Water Conditioning
Hortonville, WI....................800-236-8931
Eaton Filtration, LLC
Tinton Falls, NJ....................800-859-9212
Enting Water Condition g
Dayton, OH....................800-735-5100
Everpure, LLC
Hanover Park, IL....................630-307-3000
Filtrine Manufacturing Company
Keene, NH....................603-352-5500
Freudenberg Nonwovens
Hopkinsville, KY....................270-887-5115
G.W. Dahl Company
Greensboro, NC....................800-852-4449
Hess Machine International
Ephrata, PA....................800-735-4377
Holland Applied Technologies
Burr Ridge, IL....................630-325-5130
Hungerford & Terry
Clayton, NJ....................856-881-3200
HydroMax
Emmitsburg, MD....................800-326-0602
Hydropure Water Treatment Company
Coral Springs, FL....................800-753-1547
Introdel Products
Itasca, IL....................800-323-4772
Kinetico
Newbury, OH....................440-564-9111
King Bag & Manufacturing Company
Cincinnati, OH....................800-444-5464
Lamports Filter Media
Cleveland, OH....................216-881-2050
Miura Boiler Inc
Atlanta, GA....................770-916-1695
Moli-Tron Company
Lakewood, CO....................800-525-9494
Optipure
Plano, TX....................972-422-1212
Our Name is Mud
New York, NY....................877-683-7867
Parkson Illinois
Vernon Hills, IL....................847-816-3700
Premier Manufactured Systems
Peoria, AZ....................800-752-5582
PURA
Sun Valley, CA....................800-292-7872
RainSoft Water TreatmentSystem
Elk Grove Vlg, IL....................847-437-9400
Refractron Technologies Corporation
Newark, NY....................315-331-6222
Reynolds Water Conditioning Company
Farmington Hills, MI....................800-572-9575
Selecto Scientific
Suwanee, GA....................800-635-4017
Sermia International
Blainville, QC....................800-567-7483
Star Filters
Timmonsville, SC....................800-845-5381
Trisep Corporation
Goleta, CA....................805-964-8003
VMC Signs Inc.
Victoria, TX....................361-575-0548
Water Management Resources
Overton, NV....................800-552-5797
Water Sciences Services ,Inc.
Jackson, TN....................973-584-4131

Coolers

Allied Bakery and Food Service Equipment
Santa Fe Springs, CA....................562-945-6506
Baxter Manufacturing Company
Orting, WA....................800-777-2828
DBE Inc
Concord, ON....................800-461-5313
Deep Rock Water Company
Atlanta, GA....................800-695-2020
Distillata Company
Cleveland, OH....................800-999-2906
Fred D. Pfening Company
Columbus, OH....................614-294-1633
Girard Spring Water
North Providence, RI....................800-477-9287
Hoshizaki
Worthington, OH....................800-642-1140
Lucks Food Equipment Company
Kent, WA....................811-824-0696
Moli-International
Denver, CO....................800-525-8468
Oshikiri Corporation of America
Philadelphia, PA....................215-637-6005
Pavailler Distribution Company
Northvale, NJ....................201-767-0766
Perfection Equipment
Gurnee, IL....................800-356-6301
Pro Bake
Twinsburg, OH....................800-837-4427
Pro-Flo Products
Cedar Grove, NJ....................800-325-1057
Sunroc Corporation
Columbus, OH....................800-478-6762

Purifiers

Aquathin Corporation
Pompano Beach, FL....................800-462-7634
Astro-Pure Water Purifiers
Deerfield Beach, FL....................954-422-8966
Bestech
Pompano Beach, FL....................800-977-2378
Deep Rock Water Company
Atlanta, GA....................800-695-2020
Diamond Water Conditioning
Hortonville, WI....................800-236-8931
Distillata Company
Cleveland, OH....................800-999-2906
Durastill
Kansas City, MO....................800-449-5260
Enting Water Condition g
Dayton, OH....................800-735-5100
Fuller Ultraviolet CorpoRation
Frankfort, IL....................815-469-3301
HydroMax
Emmitsburg, MD....................800-326-0602
Hydropure Water Treatment Company
Coral Springs, FL....................800-753-1547
Joneca Corporation
Anaheim, CA....................714-993-5997
Kinetico
Newbury, OH....................440-564-9111
Kiss International/Di-tech Systems
Vista, CA....................800-527-5477
Pariser Industries
Paterson, NJ....................800-370-7627
Premier Manufactured Systems
Peoria, AZ....................800-752-5582
RainSoft Water TreatmentSystem
Elk Grove Vlg, IL....................847-437-9400
Reynolds Water Conditioning Company
Farmington Hills, MI....................800-572-9575
Royal Prestige Health Moguls
Westbury, NY....................888-802-7433
Ulcra Dynamics
Colmar, PA....................800-727-6931
United Industries Group
Newport Beach, CA....................949-759-3200
Water & Power Technologies
Salt Lake City, UT....................888-271-3295

Softeners

Aquathin Corporation
Pompano Beach, FL....................800-462-7634
Culligan Company
Northbrook, IL....................800-527-8637
Diamond Water Conditioning
Hortonville, WI....................800-236-8931
Ecodyne Water Treatment,LLC
Naperville, IL....................800-228-9326
Enting Water Condition g
Dayton, OH....................800-735-5100
Hungerford & Terry
Clayton, NJ....................856-881-3200
North American Salt Company
Overland Park, KS....................913-344-9100
Reynolds Water Conditioning Company
Farmington Hills, MI....................800-572-9575

Treatment Systems

A-L-L Magnetics
Anaheim, CA....................800-262-4638
ABJ/Sanitaire Corporation
Milwaukee, WI....................414-365-2200
Action Engineering
Temple City, CA....................626-447-8111
ADI Systems Inc
Fredericton, NB....................800-561-2831
Aeration Industries International
Chaska, MN....................800-328-8287
Aeromix Systems
Minneapolis, MN....................800-879-3677
AERTEC
North Andover, MA....................978-475-6385
AFL Industries
West Palm Beach, FL....................800-807-2709
Alar Engineering Corporation
Mokena, IL....................708-479-6100
ALCO Designs
Gardena, CA....................800-228-2346
Alkota Cleaning Systems
Alcester, SD....................800-255-6823
Alloy Hardfacing & Engineering Company, Inc
Jordan, MN....................800-328-8408
Andco Environmental Processes
Amherst, NY....................716-691-2100
API Industries
Tulsa, OK....................918-664-4010
Applied Membranes
Vista, CA....................800-321-9321
Aqua-Aerobic Systems
Loves Park, IL....................800-940-5008

Aqua-Dyne
Baxter Springs, KS . . . 800-826-9274
Aquathin Corporation
Pompano Beach, FL . . . 800-462-7634
Armfield
Ringwood, EN . . . 142- 47-781
Ashland Specialty Chemical Company
Covington, KY . . . 859-815-3333
Astro-Pure Water Purifiers
Deerfield Beach, FL . . . 954-422-8966
Atlantic Ultraviolet Corporation
Hauppauge, NY . . . 866-958-9085
Ayer Sales
East Syracuse, NY . . . 315-432-0550
Bestech
Pompano Beach, FL . . . 800-977-2378
Better Health Lab
Hackensack, NJ. . . . 800-810-1888
Betz Entec
Horsham, PA . . . 800-877-1940
Bio-Cide International
Norman, OK . . . 800-323-1398
Bioionix
Mc Farland, WI. . . . 608-838-0300
Biothane Corporation
Camden, NJ. . . . 856-541-3500
BluMetric Environmental Inc.
Ottawa, ON . . . 613-839-3053
Capital Controls Company/MicroChem
Colmar, PA . . . 215-997-4000
Centrisys Corporation
Kenosha, WI . . . 877-339-5496
ChemTreat, Inc.
Glen Allen, VA . . . 800-648-4579
Chicago Conveyor Corporation
Addison, IL . . . 630-543-6300
Chlorinators Inc
Stuart, FL . . . 800-327-9761
Clean Water Systems International
Klamath Falls, OR . . . 866-273-9993
Clean Water Technologies
Los Angeles, CA. . . . 310-380-4648
Conquest International LLC
Plainville, KS . . . 785-434-2483
Continental Industrial Supply
South Pasadena, FL. . . . 727-341-1100
Crane Environmental
Norristown, PA . . . 800-633-7435
Culligan Company
Northbrook, IL . . . 800-527-8637
Diamond Water Conditioning
Hortonville, WI. . . . 800-236-8931
Discovery Chemical
Marietta, GA . . . 800-973-9881
Durastill
Kansas City, MO. . . . 800-449-5260
Eaton Filtration, LLC
Tinton Falls, NJ. . . . 800-859-9212
Ecodyne Water Treatment,LLC
Naperville, IL . . . 800-228-9326
ECOLAB
St Paul, MN. . . . 800-352-5326
Enting Water Condition g
Dayton, OH. . . . 800-735-5100
Equipment Enterprises
Charlotte, NC . . . 800-221-3681
Eutek Systems
Hillsboro, OR . . . 503-615-8130
Everfilt Corporation
Mira Loma, CA. . . . 800-360-8380
Filtrine Manufacturing Company
Keene, NH. . . . 603-352-5500
FRC Environmental
Gainesville, GA . . . 770-534-3681
GE Betz
Trevose, PA. . . . 215-355-3300

Global Water Group
Dallas, TX. . . . 214-678-9866
Hess Machine International
Ephrata, PA . . . 800-735-4377
Hibrett Puratex
Pennsauken, NJ. . . . 800-260-5124
Hoshizaki
Worthington, OH. . . . 800-642-1140
Hubbell Electric Heater Company
Stratford, CT . . . 800-647-3165
Hungerford & Terry
Clayton, NJ . . . 856-881-3200
Hydrite Chemical Company
Brookfield, WI . . . 262-792-1450
HydroCal
Laguna Hills, CA . . . 800-877-0765
HydroMax
Emmitsburg, MD . . . 800-326-0602
Hydropure Water Treatment Company
Coral Springs, FL . . . 800-753-1547
Innova-Tech
Paoli, PA . . . 800-523-7299
InterBio
The Woodlands, TX . . . 888-876-2844
International Reserve Equipment Corporation
Clarendon Hills, IL. . . . 708-531-0680
Introdel Products
Itasca, IL . . . 800-323-4772
Jemolo Enterprises
Porterville, CA . . . 559-784-5566
Kinetico
Newbury, OH . . . 440-564-9111
Kiss International/Di-tech Systems
Vista, CA. . . . 800-527-5477
Komline-Sanderson
Peapack, NJ. . . . 800-225-5457
Lechler
St Charles, IL . . . 800-777-2926
Little Giant Pump Company
Oklahoma City, OK. . . . 405-947-2511
Loprest Water Treatment Company
Rodeo, CA. . . . 888-228-5982
Ludell Manufacturing Company
Milwaukee, WI . . . 800-558-0800
Membrane System Specialists
Wisconsin Rapids, WI . . . 715-421-2333
Midbrook
Jackson, MI. . . . 800-966-9274
Moli-Tron Company
Lakewood, CO . . . 800-525-9494
Momar
Atlanta, GA. . . . 800-556-3967
Mountain Safety Research
Seattle, WA . . . 800-877-9677
Multiplex Company, Inc.
Sellersburg, IN . . . 800-787-8880
Navy Brand ManufacturingCompany
St Louis, MO. . . . 800-325-3312
Nepcco
Ocala, FL. . . . 800-277-3279
Newco Enterprises
Saint Charles, MO . . . 800-325-7867
NewTech
Randolph, VT . . . 800-210-2361
Nijhuis Water Technology North America
Chicago, IL . . . 312-300-4103
Nimbus Water Systems
Murrieta, CA. . . . 800-451-9343
Otterbine Barebo
Emmaus, PA . . . 800-237-8837
Ozotech
Yreka, CA . . . 530-842-4189
Pariser Industries
Paterson, NJ . . . 800-370-7627
Parkson Corporation
Fort Lauderdale, FL . . . 954-974-6610

Parkson Illinois
Vernon Hills, IL . . . 847-816-3700
Polychem International
Mentor, OH. . . . 440-357-1500
Praxair
Danbury, CT . . . 800-772-9247
Premier Manufactured Systems
Peoria, AZ . . . 800-752-5582
Pro-Flo Products
Cedar Grove, NJ . . . 800-325-1057
PURA
Sun Valley, CA . . . 800-292-7872
Pure & Secure, LLC
Lincoln, NE. . . . 800-875-5915
Puronics Water Systems Inc
Livermore, CA . . . 925-456-7000
Quality Control Equipment Company
Des Moines, IA. . . . 515-266-2268
RainSoft Water TreatmentSystem
Elk Grove Vlg, IL. . . . 847-437-9400
Reynolds Water Conditioning Company
Farmington Hills, MI . . . 800-572-9575
Rochester Midland Corporation
Rochester, NY. . . . 800-836-1627
Ryter Corporation
Saint James, MN. . . . 800-643-2184
Scaltrol
Norcross, GA . . . 800-868-0629
Scienco Systems
Saint Louis, MO . . . 314-621-2536
Sermia International
Blainville, QC . . . 800-567-7483
Severn Trent Services
Fort Washington, PA. . . . 215-646-9201
Shepard Brothers
La Habra, CA . . . 562-697-1366
Siemens Water Technologies Corp.
Warrendale, PA . . . 866-926-8420
Somat Company
Lancaster, PA . . . 800-237-6628
Southeastern Filtration & Equipment
Canton, GA . . . 800-935-8500
Star Filters
Timmonsville, SC . . . 800-845-5381
Systems IV
Chandler, AZ. . . . 800-852-4221
Telechem Corporation
Atlanta, GA. . . . 800-637-0495
TLB Corporation
Newington, CT . . . 203-233-5109
TRITEN Corporation
Houston, TX . . . 832-214-5000
Ulcra Dynamics
Colmar, PA . . . 800-727-6931
United Industries Group
Newport Beach, CA . . . 949-759-3200
US Filter
Palm Desert, CA. . . . 760-340-0098
US Filter Davco Products
Thomasville, GA. . . . 800-841-1550
US Filter/Continental Water
San Antonio, TX. . . . 800-426-3426
Vulcan Materials Company
Birmingham, AL. . . . 205-298-3000
Wade Manufacturing Company
Tigard, OR . . . 800-222-7246
Water & Power Technologies
Salt Lake City, UT . . . 888-271-3295
Water System Group
Santa Clarita, CA . . . 800-350-9283
Waterlink/Sanborn Technologies
Canton, OH. . . . 800-343-3381
World Water Works
Elmsford, NY . . . 800-607-7873
Yardney Water ManagementSystems
Riverside, CA . . . 800-854-4788

Food Preparation Equipment, Utensils & Cookware

Aluminum Ware

Advance Tabco
Edgewood, NY .800-645-3166
Alegacy Food Service Products Group, Inc.
Santa Fe Springs, CA 800-848-4440
Alumaworks
Sunny Isle Beach, FL 800-277-7267
Cr. Manufacturing
Waverly, NE 877-789-5844
Dur-Able Aluminum Corporation
Hoffman Estates, IL 847-843-1100
Econofrost Night Covers
Shawnigan Lake, BC 800-519-1222
H. Yamamoto
Port Washington, NY 718-821-7700
Hillside Metal Ware Company
Union, NJ 908-964-3080
Johnson-Rose Corporation
Lockport, NY .800-456-2055
Lloyd Disher Company
Decatur, IL 217-429-0593
Montebello Packaging
Hawkesbury, ON. 613-632-7096
Regal Ware
Kewaskum, WI 262-626-2121
Vasconia Housewares
San Antonio, TX. 800-377-6723
Weavewood, Inc.
Golden Valley, MN 800-367-6460
Wilkinson Manufacturing Company
Fort Calhoun, NE 402-468-5511
Williamsburg Metal Spinning & Stamping Corporation
Brooklyn, NY .888-535-5402

Baskets

Culinary, Frying, Etc.

Archer Wire International
Bedford Park, IL. 708-563-1700
Atlanta Burning Bush
Newnan, GA 800-665-5611
Automatic Specialities Inc.
Marlborough, MA. 800-445-2370
Barker Wire Products
Keosauqua, IA 319-293-3176
Bluebird Manufacturing
Montreal, QC .800-406-2505
Dean Industries
Gardena, CA 800-995-1210
Etube and Wire
Shrewsbury, PA. 800-618-4720
F.P. Smith Wire Cloth Company
Northlake, IL. .800-323-6842
J.C. Products Inc.
Haddam, CT 860-267-5516
Jesco Industries, Inc.
Litchfield, MI .800-455-0019
Keating of Chicago
Mc Cook, IL 800-532-8464
Madsen Wire Products
Orland, IN 260-829-6561
Mid-West Wire Products, Inc
Ferndale, MI 800-989-9881
Midwest Wire Products
Sturgeon Bay, WI 800-445-0225
Mouli Manufacturing Corporation
Belleville, NJ .800-789-8285
Music City Metals
Nashville, TN .800-251-2674
Pitco Frialator
Concord, NH. .800-258-3708
Prince Castle
Carol Stream, IL 800-722-7853
Pronto Products Company
Arcadia, CA 800-377-6680
Quadra-Tech
Columbus, OH 800-443-2766
SSW Holding Company, Inc.
Elizabethtown, KY 270-769-5526
Stryco Wire Products
North York, ON. 416-663-7000
Technibilt/Cari-All
Newton, NC 800-233-3972
Wirefab
Worcester, MA 877-877-4445

Blocks

Butchers'

Anderson Wood Products Company
Louisville, KY 502-778-5591
Bally Block Company
Bally, PA 610-845-7511
Canada Goose Wood Produc
Gloucester, ON 888-890-6506
Emco Industrial Plastics
Cedar Grove, NJ 800-292-9906
Greensburg ManufacturingCompany
Greensburg, KY 270-932-5511
Hollingsworth Custom Wood Products
Sault Ste. Marie, ON. 705-759-1756
John Boos & Company
Effingham, IL .217-347-7701
M&E Manufacturing Company
Kingston, NY .845-331-2110
Meraz & Associates
Chico, CA 888-244-4463
Michigan Maple Block Company
Petoskey, MI 800-447-7975
Perfect Plank Company
Oroville, CA 800-327-1961

Boards

Cutting Block

Arrow Plastics
Elk Grove, IL .847-595-9000
Bally Block Company
Bally, PA 610-845-7511
Browne & Company
Markham, ON. 905-475-6104
C.R. Manufacturing
Waverly, NE 877-789-5844
Canada Goose Wood Produc
Gloucester, ON 888-890-6506
Capital Plastics
Middlefield, OH 440-632-5800
Catskill Craftsmen
Stamford, NY .607-652-7321
Chef Specialties Company
Smethport, PA. 800-440-2433
Ellingers
Sheboygan, WI 888-287-8906
Emco Industrial Plastics
Cedar Grove, NJ 800-292-9906
Goebel Fixture Company
Hutchinson, MN 888-339-0509
Greensburg ManufacturingCompany
Greensburg, KY 270-932-5511
Hollingsworth Custom Wood Products
Sault Ste. Marie, ON. 705-759-1756
John Boos & Company
Effingham, IL .217-347-7701
KTG
Cincinnati, OH 888-533-6900
M&E Manufacturing Company
Kingston, NY .845-331-2110
Meraz & Associates
Chico, CA 888-244-4463
Michigan Maple Block Company
Petoskey, MI 800-447-7975
Read Products
Seattle, WA 800-445-3416
Rubbermaid Commercial Products
Winchester, VA 800-336-9880
Spartec Plastics
Conneaut, OH .800-325-5176
Superior Products Company
Saint Paul, MN 800-328-9800
Vermillion Flooring Company
Springfield, MO 417-862-3785
Wolf Works
Arroyo Grande, CA. 800-549-3806
Wooster Novelty Company
Brooklyn, NY .718-852-8934

Wood

Bread, Cake & Steak

Enjay Converters Ltd.
Cobourg, ON. .800-427-5517
H A Stiles
Westbrook, ME 800-447-8537
Lady Mary
Rockingham, NC 910-997-7321
Lillsun Manufacturing Company, Inc.
Huntington, IN 260-356-6514
Marston Manufacturing
Cleveland, OH 216-587-3400
Michigan Maple Block Company
Petoskey, MI 800-447-7975
Sunset Paper Products
Simi Valley, CA. 800-228-7882
Wooster Novelty Company
Brooklyn, NY .718-852-8934

Bowls

AJM Packaging Corporation
Bloomfield Hills, MI 248-901-0040
AMCO Corporation
City of Industry, CA 626-855-2550
Apex Fountain Sales
Philadelphia, PA 800-523-4586
Atlantis Industries
Milton, DE 302-684-8542
BG Industries
Lemont, IL 800-800-5761
C.R. Manufacturing
Waverly, NE 877-789-5844
Cal-Mil Plastic Products
Oceanside, CA 800-321-9069
Carlisle Food Service Products
Oklahoma City, OK 800-654-8210
Carthage Cup Company
Longview, TX. 903-238-9833
Chef Specialties Company
Smethport, PA. 800-440-2433
Cleveland Metal StampingCompany
Berea, OH 440-234-0010
Coley Industries
Wayland, NY. .716-728-2390
Cr. Manufacturing
Waverly, NE 877-789-5844
Cyclamen Collection
Oakland, CA 510-434-7620
Delfin Design & Manufacturing
Rcho Sta Marg, CA. 800-354-7919
Design Specialties
Hamden, CT 800-999-1584
Dover Parkersburg
Follansbee, WV
Eastern Silver Tabletop Manufacturing Company
Brooklyn, NY .888-422-4142
Ellingers
Sheboygan, WI 888-287-8906
Engineered Plastics
Gibsonville, NC 800-711-1740
Finn & Son's Metal Spinning Specialists
South Lebanon, OH 513-494-2898
Fonda Group
Oshkosh, WI 800-558-9300
Gaetano America
El Monte, CA .626-442-2858
Genpak
Glens Falls, NY. 800-626-6695
Grand Silver Company
Bronx, NY. 718-585-1930
Granville Manufacturing Company
Granville, VT .800-828-1005
HPI North America/Plastics
Saint Paul, MN 800-752-7462
Jones-Zylon Company
West Lafayette, OH. 800-848-8160
Kendrick Johnson & Associates
Bloomington, MN. 800-826-1271
Kosempel Manufacturing Company
Philadelphia, PA 800-733-7122
Leggett & Platt StorageP
Vernon Hills, IL 847-816-6246
Majestic
Bridgeport, CT 203-367-7900

Novelty Crystal Corporation
Groveland, FL. 352-429-9036
Novelty Crystal Corporation
Long Island City, NY 800-622-0250
Olde Country Reproductions
York, PA 800-358-3997
Palmer Distributors
St Clair Shores, MI 800-444-1912
Polar Plastics
Mooresville, NC 704-660-6600
Polar Ware Company
Sheboygan, WI 800-237-3655
Prolon
Port Gibson, MS 888-480-9828
Sani-Top Products
De Leon Springs, FL. 800-874-6094
Savage Brothers Company
Elk Grove Vlg, IL. 800-342-0973
Service Ideas
Woodbury, MN 800-328-4493
Solo Cup Company
Lake Forest, IL 800-367-2877
Solo Cup Company
Owings Mills, MD 800-800-0300
Superior Products Company
Saint Paul, MN 800-328-9800
Tablecraft Products
Gurnee, IL. 800-323-8321
Techform
Mount Airy, NC 336-789-2115
Ullman Company
New York, NY 212-571-0068
Vertex China
Walnut, CA 800-483-7839
Victoria Porcelain
Miami, FL. 888-593-2353
Waddington North AmericaCups Illustrated
Lancaster, TX 800-334-2877
Weavewood, Inc.
Golden Valley, MN. 800-367-6460
Western Stoneware
Monmouth, IL. 309-734-2161
Wiltec
Leominster, MA 978-537-1497
WNA-Comet West
City of Industry, CA 800-225-0939

Brushes

Bakers' & Confectioners'

AMCO Corporation
City of Industry, CA 626-855-2550
Braun Brush Company
Albertson, NY. 800-645-4111
Carlisle Food Service Products
Oklahoma City, OK 800-654-8210
Kiefer Brushes, Inc
Franklin, NJ 800-526-2905
Kopykake Enterprises
Torrance, CA. 800-999-5253
Linzer Products Corporation
W Babylon, NY. 800-423-3254
Music City Metals
Nashville, TN 800-251-2674
Opie Brush Company
Independence, MO 800-877-6743
Precision Brush Company
Cleveland, OH 800-252-4747
Six Hardy Brush Manufacturing
Suffield, CT. 860-623-8465
Tucel Industries, Inc.
Forestdale, VT 800-558-8235

Food Industry

ABCO Products
Miami, FL. 888-694-2226
Akron Cotton Products
Akron, OH. 800-899-7173
All Weather Energy Systems
Plymouth, MI 888-636-8324
AMCO Corporation
City of Industry, CA 626-855-2550
American Brush Company
Portland, OR 800-826-8492
Anderson Products
Cresco, PA. 800-729-4694
Baldewein Company
Lake Forrest, IL 800-424-5544
Bouras Mop ManufacturingCompany
Saint Louis, MO 800-634-9153
Braun Brush Company
Albertson, NY. 800-645-4111
Brush Research Manufacturing Company
Los Angeles, CA. 323-261-2193
Carlisle Food Service Products
Oklahoma City, OK 800-654-8210
Carlisle Sanitary Maintenance Products
Oklahoma City, OK 800-654-8210
Cosgrove Enterprises
Miami Lakes, FL. 800-888-3396
DQB Industries
Livonia, MI 800-722-3037
Furgale Industries Ltd.
Winnipeg, NB 800-665-0506
Great Lakes Brush
Centralia, MO 573-682-2128
Greenwood Mop & Broom
Greenwood, SC. 800-635-6849
Harper Brush Works
Fairfield, IA 800-223-7894
Hoge Brush Company
New Knoxville, OH 800-494-4643
Hub City Brush
Petal, MS. 800-278-7452
Ideal Stencil Machine & Tape Company
Marion, IL. 800-388-0162
Industries for the Blind
West Allis, WI. 414-778-3040
Justman Brush Company
Omaha, NE 800-800-6940
Keating of Chicago
Mc Cook, IL 800-532-8464
Kiefer Brushes, Inc
Franklin, NJ 800-526-2905
Labpride Chemicals
Bronx, NY. 800-467-1255
Libman Company
Arcola, IL 877-818-3380
Maugus Manufacturing Company
Lancaster, PA 717-299-5681
Messina Brothers Manufacturing Company
Brooklyn, NY 800-924-6454
Mill-Rose Company
Mentor, OH. 800-321-3598
Murk Brush Company
New Britain, CT 860-249-2550
Music City Metals
Nashville, TN 800-251-2674
Nation/Ruskin
Montgomeryville, PA 800-523-2489
Nationwide Wire & Brush Manufacturing
Lodi, CA. 209-334-9660
Newton Broom Company
Newton, IL 618-783-4424
O'Dell Corporation
Ware Shoals, SC 800-342-2843
O-Cedar
Aurora, IL 800-543-8105
Opie Brush Company
Independence, MO 800-877-6743
Pepper Mill Company
Mobile, AL 800-669-5175
Power Brushes, Inc
Toledo, OH 800-968-9600
Precision Brush Company
Cleveland, OH 800-252-4747
Quality Mop & Brush Manufacturers
Needham, MA. 617-884-2999
Quickie Manufacturing Corp.
Cinnaminson, NJ. 856-829-7900
Remco Products Corporation
Zionsville, IN 800-585-8619
RidgeView Products LLC
La Crosse, WI. 888-782-1221
Rubbermaid Commercial Products
Winchester, VA. 800-336-9880
Six Hardy Brush Manufacturing
Suffield, CT. 860-623-8465
Special Products
Springfield, MO 417-881-6114
Superior Products Company
Saint Paul, MN 800-328-9800
TRC
Middlefield, OH 440-834-0078
Tucel Industries, Inc.
Forestdale, VT 800-558-8235
Urnex Brands, Inc.
Elmsford, NY 800-222-2826
Volckening
Brooklyn, NY. 718-748-0294
Walker Brush
Webster, NY 585-467-7850
Warren E. Conley Corporation
Carmel, IN. 800-367-7875
Wilen Professional Cleaning Products
Atlanta, GA. 800-241-7371
Wright-Bernet
Hamilton, OH 513-874-1800
Young & Swartz
Buffalo, NY. 800-466-7682
Zephyr Manufacturing
Sedalia, MO 660-827-0352
Zoia Banquetier Company
Cleveland, OH 216-631-6414

Cleavers

Butchers'

Lamson & Goodnow Manufacturing Company
Shelburne Falls, MA. 800-872-6564

Cookware

Alegacy Food Service Products Group, Inc.
Santa Fe Springs, CA 800-848-4440
All-Clad Metalcrafters
Canonsburg, PA 800-255-2523
Alumaworks
Sunny Isle Beach, FL 800-277-7267
APW Wyott Food Service Equipment Company
Cheyenne, WY 800-527-2100
Asian Foods
St. Paul, MN 800-274-2655
Baking Machines
Livermore, CA 925-449-3369
Bluebird Manufacturing
Montreal, QC 800-406-2505
Browne & Company
Markham, ON 905-475-6104
CookTek
Chicago, IL 888-266-5835
Crown Custom Metal Spinning
Concord, ON. 800-750-1924
Cyclamen Collection
Oakland, CA 510-434-7620
Danger Men Cooking
Highland, NY 845-691-7029
Dover Parkersburg
Follansbee, WV
Dura-Ware Company of America
Oklahoma City, OK 800-664-3872
Eagleware Manufacturing
Compton, CA 310-604-0404
Ember-Glo
Chicago, IL. 866-705-0515
Esterle Mold & Machine Company
Stow, OH. 800-411-4086
Eurodib
Champlain, NY. 888-956-6866
Finn & Son's Metal Spinning Specialists
South Lebanon, OH 513-494-2898
Floaire
Blue Bell, PA. 800-726-5623
H.F. Coors China Company
New Albany, MS. 800-782-6677
Harold Leonard SouthwestCorporation
Houston, TX 800-245-8105
Hartstone
Zanesville, OH 740-452-9999
Hillside Metal Ware Company
Union, NJ 908-964-3080
Johnson-Rose Corporation
Lockport, NY 800-456-2055
Lancaster Colony Commercial Products
Columbus, OH 800-528-2278
Lancaster Colony Corporation
Columbus, OH 800-292-7260
Legion Industries
Waynesboro, GA. 800-887-1988
Libertyware
Clearfield, UT. 888-500-5885
Lincoln Foodservice
Cleveland, OH 800-374-3004
Lodge Manufacturing Company
South Pittsburg, TN 423-837-5919
Marston Manufacturing
Cleveland, OH 216-587-3400
Mirro Company
Lancaster, OH 800-848-7200
Padinox
Winsloe, PE. 800-263-9768
Professional Bakeware Company
Willis, TX 800-440-9547

Regal Ware
Kewaskum, WI....................262-626-2121
Ricoh Technologies
Grand Prairie, TX..................800-585-9367
Royal Prestige Health Moguls
Westbury, NY.....................888-802-7433
Spring USA Corporation
Naperville, IL.....................800-535-8974
Superior Products Company
Saint Paul, MN...................800-328-9800
Thermoquest
Riviera Beach, FL..................800-532-4752
Thermos Company
Schaumburg, IL...................800-243-0745
Tomlinson Industries
Cleveland, OH....................800-945-4589
Tramontina USA
Sugar Land, TX....................800-221-7809
Tufty Ceramics
Andover, NY......................607-478-5150
Tupperware Brand Corporation
Orlando, FL.......................800-366-3800
Vasconia Housewares
San Antonio, TX..................800-377-6723
Vulcanium Metals International, LLC
Northbrook, IL....................888-922-0040
World Kitchen
Elmira, NY.......................800-999-3436
Xtreme Beverages, LLC
Dana Point, CA...................949-495-7929

Covers

Dish, Food Display & Tray

A-1 Tablecloth Company
S Hackensack, NJ..................800-727-8987
Acryline
North Attleboro, MA...............508-695-7124
AMCO Corporation
City of Industry, CA...............626-855-2550
American Metalcraft
Melrose Park, IL..................800-333-9133
Apple-A-Day Nutritional Labeling Service
San Clemente, CA.................949-855-8954
Arden Companies
Southfield, MI....................248-415-8500
Bardes Plastics
Milwaukee, WI...................800-558-5161
Brooklace
Oshkosh, WI.....................800-572-4552
C-Through Covers
San Diego, CA....................619-286-0671
Carlisle Food Service Products
Oklahoma City, OK................800-654-8210
Coverall
Worcester, MA....................800-356-2961
Curtron Products
Pittsburgh, PA....................800-833-5005
Davlynne International
Cudahy, WI......................800-558-5208
Delfin Design & Manufacturing
Rcho Sta Marg, CA................800-354-7919
Delta Plastics
Hot Springs, AR...................501-760-3000
Dilley Manufacturing Company
Des Moines, IA...................800-247-5087
Donovan Enterprises
Lagrange, GA.....................800-233-6180
Dow Cover Company
New Haven, CT...................800-735-8877
Dynynstyl
Delray Beach, FL..................800-774-7895
Eaton-Quade Company
Oklahoma City, OK................405-236-4475
Econofrost Night Covers
Shawnigan Lake, BC...............800-519-1222
Eide Industries
Cerritos, CA.....................800-422-6827
Eliason Corporation
Kalamazoo, MI...................800-828-3655
Erving Industries
Erving, MA......................413-422-2700
Fabri-Form Company
Byesville, OH....................740-685-0424
Fato Fiberglass Company
Kankakee, IL.....................815-932-3015
Golden West Sales
Cerritos, CA.....................800-827-6175
Great Western Products
Ontario, CA......................888-598-5588
Highland Supply Company
Highland, IL......................800-472-3645
J. James
Brooklyn, NY.....................718-384-6144
J.V. Reed & Company
Louisville, KY.....................877-258-7333
Jordan Specialty Company
Brooklyn, NY.....................877-567-3265
K-C Products Company
Van Nuys, CA....................818-267-1600
Kendrick Johnson & Associates
Bloomington, MN..................800-826-1271
Lakeside Manufacturing
Milwaukee, WI...................888-558-8574
Michael Leson Dinnerware
Youngstown, OH..................800-821-3541
Midco Plastics
Enterprise, KS....................800-235-2729
Morris Transparent Box Company
East Providence, RI................401-438-6116
MultiFab Plastics
Boston, MA......................888-293-5754
Nyman Manufacturing Company
Rumford, RI......................401-438-3410
Palmer Distributors
St Clair Shores, MI................800-444-1912
Polar Plastics
St Laurent, QC...................514-331-0207
Polar Ware Company
Sheboygan, WI...................800-237-3655
Reading Plastic Fabricators
Temple, PA......................610-926-3245
Samsill Corporation
Fort Worth, TX...................800-255-1100
Sani-Top Products
De Leon Springs, FL...............800-874-6094
Sims Superior Seating
Locust Grove, GA.................800-729-9178
Springprint Medallion
Augusta, GA.....................800-543-5990
Standard Terry Mills
Souderton, PA....................215-723-8121
Steril-Sil Company
Boston, MA......................800-784-5537
Superior Linen & Work Wear
Kansas City, MO..................800-798-7987
Superior Products Company
Saint Paul, MN...................800-328-9800
Tara Linens
Sanford, NC......................800-476-8272
TEMP-TECH Company
Springfield, MA...................800-343-5579
Thermal Bags by Ingrid
Gilberts, IL......................800-622-5560
Tri-State Plastics
Glenwillard, PA...................724-457-6900
US Lace Paper Works
Oshkosh, WI.....................800-873-6459
Zoia Banquetier Company
Cleveland, OH....................216-631-6414

Cutlery

A.G. Russell Knives Inc.
Rogers, AR......................800-255-9034
AceCo Precision Manufacturing
Boise, ID........................800-359-7012
Acme International
Maplewood, NJ...................973-416-0400
Amcel
Watertown, MA...................800-225-7992
American Housewares Manufacturing Corporation
Bronx, NY.......................718-665-9500
Babco International, Inc
Tucson, AZ......................520-628-7596
Bettendorf Stanford
Salem, IL........................800-548-2253
BOC Plastics Inc
Winston Salem, NC................800-334-8687
Boehringer Mfg. Co. Inc.
Felton, CA.......................800-630-8665
Brooklyn Boys
Boca Raton, FL...................561-477-3663
Browne & Company
Markham, ON....................905-475-6104
Buck Knives
Post Falls, ID.....................800-326-2825
Burrell Cutlery Company
Ellicottville, NY...................716-699-2343
C.R. Manufacturing
Waverly, NE.....................877-789-5844
CB Manufacturing & SalesCompany
Miamisburg, OH..................800-543-6860
Chef Revival
Elkhorn, WI......................800-248-9826
Chicago Scale & Slicer Company
Franklin Park, IL..................847-455-3400
Chuppa Knife Manufacturing
Jackson, TN......................731-424-1212
Conimar Corporation
Ocala, FL........................800-874-9735
Cutco Vector
Olean, NY.......................716-373-6148
Cutrite Company
Fremont, OH.....................800-928-8748
Dart Container Corporation
Mason, MI.......................800-248-5960
De Ster Corporation
Atlanta, GA......................800-237-8270
Delco Tableware
Port Washington, NY...............800-221-9557
Dexter-Russell
Southbridge, MA..................508-765-0201
Diamond Brands
Cloquet, MN.....................218-879-6700
Dispoz-O Plastics
Fountain Inn, SC..................864-862-4004
E-Z Edge
West New York, NJ................800-232-4470
E.K. Lay Company
Philadelphia, PA..................800-523-3220
Edge Resources
Hopedale, MA....................888-849-0998
EdgeCraft Corporation
Avondale, PA....................800-342-3255
F.N. Smith Corporation
Oregon, IL.......................815-732-2171
Fioriware
Zanesville, OH....................740-454-7400
Florida Knife Company
Sarasota, FL.....................800-966-5643
Fonda Group
Oshkosh, WI.....................800-367-2877
Fort James Corporation
Norwalk, CT.....................800-257-9744
Franke Commercial Systems
Hatfield, PA......................800-626-5771
Friedr Dick Corporation
Farmingdale, NY..................800-554-3425
General Cutlery
Fremont, OH.....................419-332-2316
Gerber Legendary Blades
Portland, OR.....................503-639-6161
Gril-Del
Mankato, MN.....................800-782-7320
Hansaloy Corporation
Davenport, IA....................800-553-4992
Hantover
Kansas City, MO..................800-821-7849
Hollymatic Corporation
Countryside, IL...................708-579-3700
Imperial Schrade Corporation
Ellenville, NY.....................212-210-8600
Izabel Lam International
Brooklyn, NY.....................718-797-3983
James River Canada
North York, ON...................416-789-5151
Jet Plastica Industries
Hatfield, PA
Jim Scharf Holdings
Perdue, SK......................800-667-9727
John J. Adams Die Corporation
Worcester, MA...................508-757-3894
Kinetic Company
Greendale, WI....................414-425-8221
KSW Corporation
Des Moines, IA...................515-265-5269
Lamson & Goodnow Manufacturing Company
Shelburne Falls, MA...............800-872-6564
Les Industries Touch Inc
Sherbrooke, QC...................800-267-4140
Lifetime Hoan Corporation
Garden City, NY..................516-683-6000
Mandeville Company
Minneapolis, MN..................800-328-8490
Max Packaging Company
Attalla, AL......................800-543-5369
Mundial
Norwood, MA....................800-487-2224
Omcan Manufacturing & Distributing Company
Mississauga, ON..................800-465-0234
Oneida Food Service
Oneida, NY......................315-361-3000
Penley Corporation
West Paris, ME...................800-368-6449

Polar Plastics
St Laurent, QC 514-331-0207
Polar Plastics
Mooresville, NC 704-660-6600
R. Murphy Company
Ayer, MA. 888-772-3481
R.H. Saw Corporation
Barrington, IL 847-381-8777
Ranger Blade Manufacturing Company
Traer, IA 800-377-7860
Replacements Ltd.
Greensboro, NC 800-737-5223
Royal Prestige Health Moguls
Westbury, NY 888-802-7433
Royal Silver Company
Norfolk, VA. 757-855-6004
Safe T Cut
Monson, MA. 413-267-9984
Salem China Company
Salem, OH. 330-337-8771
Simmons Engineering Corporation
Wheeling, IL 800-252-3381
Solo Cup Company
Lake Forest, IL 800-367-2877
Solo Cup Company
Owings Mills, MD 800-800-0300
Spir-It/Zoo Piks
Andover, MA 800-343-0996
Superior Products Company
Saint Paul, MN 800-328-9800
Tramontina USA
Sugar Land, TX. 800-221-7809
Utica Cutlery Company
Utica, NY 800-879-2526
Waddington North America
Chelmsford, MA 888-962-2877
Walco Stainless
Utica, NY 800-879-2526
Warther Museum
Dover, OH. 330-343-7513
Wishbone Utensil Tableware Line
Wheat Ridge, CO 866-266-5928
WNA-Comet West
City of Industry, CA 800-225-0939
Zelco Industries
Mount Vernon, NY 800-431-2486

Cutters

Biscuit & Cookie

AMCO Corporation
City of Industry, CA 626-855-2550
Ann Clark, LTD
Rutland, VT 800-252-6798
Arcobaleno Pasta Machines
Lancaster, PA 800-875-7096
Boehringer Mfg. Co. Inc.
Felton, CA. 800-630-8665
Browne & Company
Markham, ON. 905-475-6104
Dito Dean Food Prep
Rocklin, CA 800-331-7958
Don Lee
Escondido, CA 760-745-0707
Educational Products Company
Hope, NJ. 800-272-3822
Irresistible Cookie Jar
Hayden Lake, ID. 208-664-1261
Lee Financial Corporation
Dallas, TX. 972-960-1001
Lorenzen's Cookie Cutters
Wantagh, NY. 516-781-7116
LoTech Industries
Lakewood, CO 800-295-0199
Moline Machinery
Duluth, MN. 800-767-5734
Polar Process
Plattsville, ON. 877-896-8077
Pro Bake
Twinsburg, OH 800-837-4427
Rademaker USA
Hudson, OH 330-650-2345
Reading Bakery Systems
Robesonia, PA. 610-693-5816
Rhodes Bakery Equipment
Portland, OR 800-426-3813
SOCO System
Waukesha, WI. 800-441-6293
Superior Products Company
Saint Paul, MN 800-328-9800

Cake

Belshaw Adamatic Bakery Group
Auburn, WA 800-578-2547
Colborne Foodbotics
Lake Forest, IL 847-371-0101
Hinds-Bock Corporation
Bothell, WA. 425-885-1183
Matiss
St Georges, QC 888-562-8477
Polar Process
Plattsville, ON. 877-896-8077

Cheese

AMCO Corporation
City of Industry, CA 626-855-2550
Berkshire PPM
Litchfield, CT 860-567-3118
Bluffton Slaw Cutter Company
Bluffton, OH 419-358-9840
C&R Refrigation Inc,
Center, TX. 800-438-6182
General Machinery Corporation
Sheboygan, WI 888-243-6622
Globe Food Equipment Company
Dayton, OH. 800-347-5423
Hart Design & Manufacturing
Green Bay, WI. 920-468-5927
Lincoln Foodservice
Cleveland, OH 800-374-3004
Mouli Manufacturing Corporation
Belleville, NJ 800-789-8285
Polar Process
Plattsville, ON. 877-896-8077
Samuel Underberg
Brooklyn, NY 718-363-0787
Superior Products Company
Saint Paul, MN 800-328-9800
TGW International
Florence, KY. 800-407-0173

Dicing

Berkshire PPM
Litchfield, CT 860-567-3118
C.M. Slicechief Company, Inc.
Toledo, OH 419-241-7647
Custom Food Machinery
Stockton, CA. 209-463-4343
D&S Manufacturing Company
Auburn, MA 508-799-7812
General Machinery Corporation
Sheboygan, WI 888-243-6622
Insinger Machine Company
Philadelphia, PA 800-344-4802
Luthi Machinery Company, Inc.
Pueblo, CO 719-948-1110
Paxton Corporation
Bristol, RI
Superior Products Company
Saint Paul, MN 800-328-9800
Urschel Laboratories
Valparaiso, IN 219-464-4811

Kraut & Slaw

A.K. Robins
Baltimore, MD 800-486-9656
Bluffton Slaw Cutter Company
Bluffton, OH. 419-358-9840
Clawson Machine
Franklin, NJ 800-828-4088
Great Western Products Company
Hollywood, AL. 800-239-2143
Paxton Corporation
Bristol, RI

Meat

Power

AEW Thurne
Lake Zurich, IL. 800-239-7297
Berkshire PPM
Litchfield, CT 860-567-3118
Biro Manufacturing Company
Marblehead, OH 419-798-4451
Globe Food Equipment Company
Dayton, OH. 800-347-5423
Jarvis Products Corporation
Middletown, CT 860-347-7271
Prince Castle
Carol Stream, IL 800-722-7853
Superior Products Company
Saint Paul, MN 800-328-9800
TGW International
Florence, KY. 800-407-0173
Urschel Laboratories
Valparaiso, IN 219-464-4811

Sausage

Automated Food Systems
Waxahachie, TX 972-298-5719
Cincinnati Boss Company
Omaha, NE 402-556-4070
Cozzini
Chicago, IL 773-478-9700
General Machinery Corporation
Sheboygan, WI 888-243-6622
Handtmann, Inc.
Lake Forest, IL 800-477-3585
Linker Machines
Rockaway, NJ 973-983-0001
Marlen International
Astoria, OR. 800-862-7536
TGW International
Florence, KY. 800-407-0173

Pickle

A.K. Robins
Baltimore, MD 800-486-9656
Berkshire PPM
Litchfield, CT 860-567-3118
Custom Food Machinery
Stockton, CA. 209-463-4343

Ultrasonic

Polar Process
Plattsville, ON. 877-896-8077

Glasses

Drinking

Anchor Hocking Company
Lancaster, OH 800-562-7511
ATAGO USA Inc
Bellevue, WA 877-282-4687
Atlantis Industries
Milton, DE 302-684-8542
Babco International, Inc
Tucson, AZ 520-628-7596
Benner China & Glassware of Florida
Jacksonville, FL 904-733-4620
Browne & Company
Markham, ON. 905-475-6104
Carlisle Food Service Products
Oklahoma City, OK 800-654-8210
Design Specialties
Hamden, CT 800-999-1584
Donoco Industries
Huntington Beach, CA 888-822-8763
Edco Industries
Bridgeport, CT 203-333-8982
Encore Plastics
Huntington Beach, CA 888-822-8763
Epic Products
Santa Ana, CA 800-548-9791
Franke Commercial Systems
Hatfield, PA. 800-626-5771
HPI North America/Plastics
Saint Paul, MN 800-752-7462
Ideas Etc
Louisville, KY 800-733-0337
Image Plastics
Houston, TX 800-289-2811
Indiana Glass Company
Columbus, OH 800-543-0357
Izabel Lam International
Brooklyn, NY 718-797-3983
Jet Plastica Industries
Hatfield, PA
Jones-Zylon Company
West Lafayette, OH. 800-848-8160
Judel Products
Elmsford, NY 800-583-3526
Libby Canada
Mississauga, ON. 905-607-8280
Majestic
Bridgeport, CT 203-367-7900

MDR International
North Miami, FL. 305-944-5019
Michael Leson Dinnerware
Youngstown, OH. 800-821-3541
Mikasa Hotelware
Secaucus, NJ. 866-645-2721
Novelty Crystal Corporation
Long Island City, NY 800-622-0250
Polar Plastics
Mooresville, NC 704-660-6600
Prolon
Port Gibson, MS 888-480-9828
Royal Prestige Health Moguls
Westbury, NY 888-802-7433
Spirit Foodservice, Inc.
Andover, MA 800-343-0996
Superior Products Company
Saint Paul, MN 800-328-9800
Tango Shatterproof Drinkware
Walpole, MA. 888-898-2646
Tar-Hong Melamine USA
City of Industry, CA 626-935-1612
Ullman Company
New York, NY 212-571-0068
V. Loria & Sons
Yonkers, NY 800-540-2927
Wiltec
Leominster, MA 978-537-1497
Xtreme Beverages, LLC
Dana Point, CA. 949-495-7929

Glassware

Cooking & Baking

Anchor Hocking Company
Lancaster, OH 800-562-7511
Judel Products
Elmsford, NY 800-583-3526
Oneida Canada, Limited
Oneida, NY. 888-263-7195
World Kitchen
Elmira, NY 800-999-3436

Heat Resistant

Automated Packaging Systems
Streetsboro, OH 888-288-6224
Corning Life Sciences
Acton, MA. 800-492-1110
Hartstone
Zanesville, OH 740-452-9999
Judel Products
Elmsford, NY 800-583-3526
Triad Scientific
Manasquan, NJ 800-867-6690
World Kitchen
Elmira, NY 800-999-3436

Hotel & Restaurant

Abco International
Melville, NY. 866-240-2226
Anchor Hocking Company
Lancaster, OH 800-562-7511
ATAGO USA Inc
Bellevue, WA 877-282-4687
Browne & Company
Markham, ON. 905-475-6104
Epic Products
Santa Ana, CA 800-548-9791
Fenton Art Glass Company
Williamstown, WV 800-933-6766
Judel Products
Elmsford, NY 800-583-3526
Lancaster Colony Commercial Products
Columbus, OH. 800-528-2278
Lancaster Colony Corporation
Columbus, OH 800-292-7260
Libbey
Toledo, OH
Libby Canada
Mississauga, ON. 905-607-8280
Master Piece Crystal
Jane Lew, WV. 304-884-7841
Mikasa Hotelware
Secaucus, NJ. 866-645-2721
Minners Designs Inc.
New York, NY 212-688-7441
Mr. Ice Bucket
New Brunswick, NJ 732-545-0420
Novelty Crystal Corporation
Long Island City, NY 800-622-0250

Oneida Food Service
Oneida, NY. 315-361-3000
Royal Prestige Health Moguls
Westbury, NY 888-802-7433
Superior Products Company
Saint Paul, MN 800-328-9800
Tango Shatterproof Drinkware
Walpole, MA. 888-898-2646
Variety Glass
Cambridge, OH. 740-432-3643
World Kitchen
Elmira, NY 800-999-3436
Xtreme Beverages, LLC
Dana Point, CA. 949-495-7929

Packers'

All American Containers
Medley, FL 305-887-0797
Indianapolis Container Company
Indianapolis, IN 800-760-3318
Kelman Bottles
Glenshaw, PA 412-486-9100
St. Tobain Containers
Seattle, WA 206-762-0660

Holders

Corn Cob

Jarden Home Brands
Daleville, IN 800-392-2575

Hollowware

Abco International
Melville, NY. 866-240-2226
Browne & Company
Markham, ON. 905-475-6104
Corby Hall
Randolph, NJ 973-366-8300
Delco Tableware
Port Washington, NY 800-221-9557
Dynynstyl
Delray Beach, FL 800-774-7895
Grand Silver Company
Bronx, NY. 718-585-1930
Lenox
Bristol, PA. 800-223-4311
Libby Canada
Mississauga, ON. 905-607-8280
Oneida Canada, Limited
Oneida, NY. 888-263-7195
Oneida Food Service
Oneida, NY. 315-361-3000
Reed & Barton Food Service
Taunton, MA. 800-797-9675
Rexcraft Fine Chafers
Long Island City, NY 888-739-2723
Superior Products Company
Saint Paul, MN 800-328-9800
Tradeco International
Addison, IL. 800-628-3738
Walco Stainless
Utica, NY 800-879-2526
Xtreme Beverages, LLC
Dana Point, CA. 949-495-7929

Hooks

Meat

Boehringer Mfg. Co. Inc.
Felton, CA. 800-630-8665
G.F. Frank & Sons
Fairfield, OH. 513-870-9075
Le Fiell Company, Inc.
Reno, NV 775-677-5300
Samuel Underberg
Brooklyn, NY 718-363-0787

Hoops

Cheese

Damrow Company
Fond Du Lac, WI 800-236-1501
Viking Machine & Design
De Pere, WI. 888-286-2116

Kettles

G&F Manufacturing Comp any
Oak Lawn, IL 800-282-1574

Canning & Preserving

A.K. Robins
Baltimore, MD 800-486-9656
Berkshire PPM
Litchfield, CT 860-567-3118
Central Fabricators
Cincinnati, OH 800-909-8265
Custom Food Machinery
Stockton, CA. 209-463-4343
El Cerrito Steel
El Cerrito, CA. 510-529-0370
Hamilton Kettles
Weirton, WV. 800-535-1882
Packaging & Processing Equipment
Ayr, ON. 519-622-6666
Production Packaging & Processing Equipment Company
Phoenix, AZ 602-254-7878

Confectioners'

A&B Process Systems
Stratford, WI. 888-258-2789
Berkshire PPM
Litchfield, CT 860-567-3118
Chocolate Concepts
Hartville, OH 330-877-3322
D. Picking & Company
Bucyrus, OH 419-562-6891
Hamilton Kettles
Weirton, WV. 800-535-1882
Packaging & Processing Equipment
Ayr, ON. 519-622-6666
Vendome Copper & Brass Works
Louisville, KY 888-384-5161

Copper

All Spun Metal Products
Des Plaines, IL 847-824-4117
D. Picking & Company
Bucyrus, OH 419-562-6891
Packaging & Processing Equipment
Ayr, ON. 519-622-6666
Savage Brothers Company
Elk Grove Vlg, IL. 800-342-0973
Vendome Copper & Brass Works
Louisville, KY 888-384-5161

Lard

A&B Process Systems
Stratford, WI. 888-258-2789
Hamilton Kettles
Weirton, WV. 800-535-1882
Packaging & Processing Equipment
Ayr, ON. 519-622-6666

Mixing

A&B Process Systems
Stratford, WI. 888-258-2789
Berkshire PPM
Litchfield, CT 860-567-3118
Bowers Process Equipment
Stratford, ON. 800-567-3223
Chocolate Concepts
Hartville, OH 330-877-3322
Custom Food Machinery
Stockton, CA. 209-463-4343
DCI
St Cloud, MN 320-252-8200
Eischen Enterprises
Fresno, CA 559-834-0013
Hamilton Kettles
Weirton, WV. 800-535-1882
Lee Industries Fluid Transfer
Philipsburg, PA. 814-342-0802
Packaging & Processing Equipment
Ayr, ON. 519-622-6666
Savage Brothers Company
Elk Grove Vlg, IL. 800-342-0973
Sharpsville Container
Sharpsville, PA 800-645-1248
South Valley Manufacturing
Gilroy, CA. 408-842-5457

Stainless Fabrication
Springfield, MO 800-397-8265

Steaming

Berkshire PPM
Litchfield, CT 860-567-3118
Chester-Jensen Company, Inc.
Chester, PA 800-685-3750
Cleasby Manufacturing Company
San Francisco, CA 415-822-6565
Cleveland Range Company
Cleveland, OH 800-338-2204
Eischen Enterprises
Fresno, CA 559-834-0013
Electro-Steam Generator Corporation
Rancocas, NJ. 866-617-0764
Hamilton Kettles
Weirton, WV 800-535-1882
Legion Industries
Waynesboro, GA. 800-887-1988
Packaging & Processing Equipment
Ayr, ON 519-622-6666
Process Systems
Barrington, IL 847-842-8618
Sharpsville Container
Sharpsville, PA 800-645-1248
South Valley Manufacturing
Gilroy, CA. 408-842-5457
Southbend Company
Fuquay Varina, NC 800-348-2558
Welbilt Corporation
Stamford, CT. 203-325-8300
Welliver Metal Products Corporation
Salem, OR. 503-362-1568

Sugar & Syrup

A&B Process Systems
Stratford, WI 888-258-2789
Hamilton Kettles
Weirton, WV 800-535-1882
Packaging & Processing Equipment
Ayr, ON 519-622-6666

Knife Sharpeners

Browne & Company
Markham, ON 905-475-6104
Cass Saw & Tool Sharpening
Westmont, IL. 630-968-1617
Diamond Machining Technologies
Marlborough, MA. 800-666-4368
EdgeCraft Corporation
Avondale, PA 800-342-3255
Eze Lap Diamond Products
Carson City, NV 800-843-4815
Fortune Products
Cedar Park, TX 800-742-7797
Friedr Dick Corporation
Farmingdale, NY 800-554-3425
General Grinding
Oakland, CA 800-806-6037
Imperial Schrade Corporation
Ellenville, NY 212-210-8600
Rx Honing Machine Corporation
Mishawaka, IN 800-346-6464
Serr-Edge Machine Company
Cleveland, Cl 800-443-8097
Superior Products Company
Saint Paul, MN 800-328-9800
Tru Hone Corporation
Ocala, FL. 800-237-4663

Knives

Bread

Borden
Columbus, OH 614-225-4953
Brooklyn Boys
Boca Raton, FL. 561-477-3663
Lamson & Goodnow Manufacturing Company
Shelburne Falls, MA. 800-872-6564
Mundial
Norwood, MA. 800-487-2224
Simmons Engineering Corporation
Wheeling, IL 800-252-3381
Superior Products Company
Saint Paul, MN 800-328-9800

Butchers'

Atlanta SharpTech
Peachtree City, GA 800-462-7297
Boehringer Mfg. Co. Inc.
Felton, CA. 800-630-8665
Chicago Scale & Slicer Company
Franklin Park, IL. 847-455-3400
General Cutlery
Fremont, OH 419-332-2316
Jarvis Products Corporation
Middletown, CT 860-347-7271
Lamson & Goodnow Manufacturing Company
Shelburne Falls, MA. 800-872-6564
Mandeville Company
Minneapolis, MN 800-328-8490
Mundial
Norwood, MA. 800-487-2224
R. Murphy Company
Ayer, MA. 888-772-3481
Simmons Engineering Corporation
Wheeling, IL 800-252-3381
Superior Products Company
Saint Paul, MN 800-328-9800

Cake

C.R. Manufacturing
Waverly, NE 877-789-5844
Mundial
Norwood, MA. 800-487-2224
Polar Process
Plattsville, ON. 877-896-8077
Simmons Engineering Corporation
Wheeling, IL 800-252-3381

Canners'

A.D. Cowdrey Company
Modesto, CA. 209-538-4677
A.K. Robins
Baltimore, MD 800-486-9656
General Cutlery
Fremont, OH 419-332-2316

Carving

Browne & Company
Markham, ON 905-475-6104
Burrell Cutlery Company
Ellicottville, NY 716-699-2343
Cutco Vector
Olean, NY 716-373-6148
Dexter-Russell
Southbridge, MA 508-765-0201
General Cutlery
Fremont, OH 419-332-2316
Gerber Legendary Blades
Portland, OR 503-639-6161
Imperial Schrade Corporation
Ellenville, NY. 212-210-8600
Mandeville Company
Minneapolis, MN 800-328-8490
Mundial
Norwood, MA. 800-487-2224
R. Murphy Company
Ayer, MA. 888-772-3481
Superior Products Company
Saint Paul, MN 800-328-9800

Cheese

Browne & Company
Markham, ON 905-475-6104
General Cutlery
Fremont, OH 419-332-2316
Lamson & Goodnow Manufacturing Company
Shelburne Falls, MA. 800-872-6564
Mundial
Norwood, MA. 800-487-2224
Polar Process
Plattsville, ON. 877-896-8077
TGW International
Florence, KY. 800-407-0173

Culinary

Browne & Company
Markham, ON 905-475-6104
Buck Knives
Post Falls, ID. 800-326-2825
Burrell Cutlery Company
Ellicottville, NY 716-699-2343
Dexter-Russell
Southbridge, MA 508-765-0201
Gerber Legendary Blades
Portland, OR 503-639-6161
Imperial Schrade Corporation
Ellenville, NY. 212-210-8600
John J. Adams Die Corporation
Worcester, MA 508-757-3894
Lamson & Goodnow Manufacturing Company
Shelburne Falls, MA. 800-872-6564
Lifetime Hoan Corporation
Garden City, NY 516-683-6000
Mundial
Norwood, MA. 800-487-2224
OWD
Tupper Lake, NY 800-836-1693
Superior Products Company
Saint Paul, MN 800-328-9800

Curd

Damrow Company
Fond Du Lac, WI 800-236-1501
Engineered Products Corporation
Greenville, SC. 800-868-0145

Fish Scaling & Slitting

Buck Knives
Post Falls, ID. 800-326-2825
Dexter-Russell
Southbridge, MA 508-765-0201
E-Z Edge
West New York, NJ. 800-232-4470
General Cutlery
Fremont, OH 419-332-2316
Imperial Schrade Corporation
Ellenville, NY. 212-210-8600
R. Murphy Company
Ayer, MA. 888-772-3481
Simmons Engineering Corporation
Wheeling, IL. 800-252-3381
Steamway Corporation
Scottsburg, IN. 800-259-8171
TGW International
Florence, KY. 800-407-0173

Food Processing Machine

AceCo Precision Manufacturing
Boise, ID 800-359-7012
Am-Mac Incorporated
Fairfield, NJ 800-829-2018
Branson Ultrasonics Corporation
Danbury, CT 203-796-0400
Brooklyn Boys
Boca Raton, FL. 561-477-3663
California Saw & Knife Works
San Francisco, CA 888-729-6533
Carolina Knife
Asheville, NC 800-520-5030
Chapman Corporation
Saint Louis, MO 800-843-1404
Dexter-Russell
Southbridge, MA 508-765-0201
DSW Converting Knives
Birmingham, AL. 205-322-2021
Florida Knife Company
Sarasota, FL 800-966-5643
Huther Brothers
Rochester, NY. 800-334-1115
International Knife & Saw
Florence, SC 800-354-9872
KSW Corporation
Des Moines, IA. 515-265-5269
Lako Tool & Manufacturing
Perrysburg, OH. 800-228-2982
Pappas Inc.
Detroit, MI 800-521-0888
R.H. Saw Corporation
Barrington, IL. 847-381-8777
Simmons Engineering Corporation
Wheeling, IL. 800-252-3381
Simonds International
Fitchburg, MA 800-343-1616
Simonds International
Fitchburg, MA 978-424-0100
Specialty Blades
Staunton, VA. 540-248-2200
Stutz Products Corporation
Hartford City, IN. 765-348-2510
TGW International
Florence, KY. 800-407-0173

York Saw & Knife Company
York, PA 800-233-1969
Zenith Cutter Company
Loves Park, IL 800-223-5202

Fruit

AMCO Corporation
City of Industry, CA 626-855-2550
Burrell Cutlery Company
Ellicottville, NY 716-699-2343
Globe International
Tacoma, WA 800-523-6575
Goodnature Products
Orchard Park, NY 800-875-3381
International Knife & Saw
Florence, SC 800-354-9872
Mundial
Norwood, MA 800-487-2224
QA Supplies, LLC
Norfolk, VA 800-472-7205
Simmons Engineering Corporation
Wheeling, IL 800-252-3381
TGW International
Florence, KY 800-407-0173

Loin

Mound Tool Company
Saint Louis, MO 314-968-3991

Machine

AceCo Precision Manufacturing
Boise, ID 800-359-7012
Bettendorf Stanford
Salem, IL 800-548-2253
California Saw & Knife Works
San Francisco, CA 888-729-6533
Carolina Knife
Asheville, NC 800-520-5030
D&S Manufacturing Company
Auburn, MA 508-799-7812
DSW Converting Knives
Birmingham, AL 205-322-2021
Florida Knife Company
Sarasota, FL 800-966-5643
Greenfield Disston
Greensboro, NC 336-855-4200
Huther Brothers
Rochester, NY 800-334-1115
International Knife & Saw
Florence, SC 800-354-9872
Kinetic Company
Greendale, WI 414-425-8221
KSW Corporation
Des Moines, IA 515-265-5269
Lako Tool & Manufacturing
Perrysburg, OH 800-228-2982
Moore Production Tool Specialties
Farmington Hills, MI 248-476-1200
Nitsch Tool Company
Syracuse, NY 315-472-4044
Page Slotting & Saw Company
Toledo, OH 419-476-5131
Polar Process
Plattsville, ON 877-896-8077
Rudolph Industries
Mississauga, ON 905-564-6160
Simonds International
Fitchburg, MA 800-343-1616
Simonds International
Fitchburg, MA 978-424-0100
Specialty Blades
Staunton, VA 540-248-2200
Stutz Products Corporation
Hartford City, IN 765-348-2510
TGW International
Florence, KY 800-407-0173
York Saw & Knife Company
York, PA 800-233-1969
Zenith Cutter Company
Loves Park, IL 800-223-5202

Meat Packing

Cutrite Company
Fremont, OH 800-928-8748
E-Z Edge
West New York, NJ 800-232-4470
General Cutlery
Fremont, OH 419-332-2316
Lamson & Goodnow Manufacturing Company
Shelburne Falls, MA 800-872-6564
Mandeville Company
Minneapolis, MN 800-328-8490
Omcan Manufacturing & Distributing Company
Mississauga, ON 800-465-0234
Specialty Blades
Staunton, VA 540-248-2200
TGW International
Florence, KY 800-407-0173

Oyster & Clam

Mundial
Norwood, MA 800-487-2224
Superior Products Company
Saint Paul, MN 800-328-9800
TGW International
Florence, KY 800-407-0173

Slicing

Bettendorf Stanford
Salem, IL 800-548-2253
Browne & Company
Markham, ON 905-475-6104
Burrell Cutlery Company
Ellicottville, NY 716-699-2343
Dexter-Russell
Southbridge, MA 508-765-0201
Friedr Dick Corporation
Farmingdale, NY 800-554-3425
Gerber Legendary Blades
Portland, OR 503-639-6161
Gril-Del
Mankato, MN 800-782-7320
Huther Brothers
Rochester, NY 800-334-1115
Industrial Razor Blade Company
Orange, NJ 973-673-4286
International Knife & Saw
Florence, SC 800-354-9872
Lamson & Goodnow Manufacturing Company
Shelburne Falls, MA 800-872-6564
Mundial
Norwood, MA 800-487-2224
Pappas Inc.
Detroit, MI 800-521-0888
R.H. Saw Corporation
Barrington, IL 847-381-8777
Rudolph Industries
Mississauga, ON 905-564-6160
Simmons Engineering Corporation
Wheeling, IL 800-252-3381
Stutz Products Corporation
Hartford City, IN 765-348-2510
TGW International
Florence, KY 800-407-0173

Steak

Browne & Company
Markham, ON 905-475-6104
Burrell Cutlery Company
Ellicottville, NY 716-699-2343
Delco Tableware
Port Washington, NY 800-221-9557
General Cutlery
Fremont, OH 419-332-2316
Gerber Legendary Blades
Portland, OR 503-639-6161
Lamson & Goodnow Manufacturing Company
Shelburne Falls, MA 800-872-6564
Mundial
Norwood, MA 800-487-2224
Superior Products Company
Saint Paul, MN 800-328-9800
Walco Stainless
Utica, NY 800-879-2526

Vegetable

Am-Mac Incorporated
Fairfield, NJ 800-829-2018
Brooklyn Boys
Boca Raton, FL 561-477-3663
Browne & Company
Markham, ON 905-475-6104
International Knife & Saw
Florence, SC 800-354-9872
Jim Scharf Holdings
Perdue, SK 800-667-9727
Mundial
Norwood, MA 800-487-2224
Simmons Engineering Corporation
Wheeling, IL 800-252-3381
Superior Products Company
Saint Paul, MN 800-328-9800
TGW International
Florence, KY 800-407-0173

Ladles

Culinary

AMCO Corporation
City of Industry, CA 626-855-2550
Browne & Company
Markham, ON 905-475-6104
Carlisle Food Service Products
Oklahoma City, OK 800-654-8210
Eastern Silver Tabletop Manufacturing Company
Brooklyn, NY 888-422-4142
Leggett & Platt StorageP
Vernon Hills, IL 847-816-6246
Libertyware
Clearfield, UT 888-500-5885
Olde Country Reproductions
York, PA 800-358-3997
Superior Products Company
Saint Paul, MN 800-328-9800
Vollrath Company
Sheboygan, WI 920-457-4851
Wiltec
Leominster, MA 978-537-1497

Liners

Cake Pan

Brown Paper Goods Company
Waukegan, IL 847-688-1451
MS Plastics & Packaging Company
Butler, NJ 800-593-1802
Norpak Corporation
Newark, NJ 800-631-6970
State Products
Long Beach, CA 800-730-5150
Taconic
Petersburg, NY 800-833-1805
Zenith Specialty Bag Company
City of Industry, CA 800-925-2247

Magnets

Industrial Magnetics
Boyne City, MI 800-662-4638

Matches

Admatch Corporation
New York, NY 800-777-9909
Atlas Match Company
Toronto, ON 888-285-2783
Atlas Match Corporation
Euless, TX 800-628-2426
Bradley Industries
Westchester, IL 815-469-2314
D.D. Bean & Sons Company
Jaffrey, NH 800-326-8311
Diamond Brands
Cloquet, MN 218-879-6700
Great Western Products
Ontario, CA 888-598-5588
Palmland Paper Company
Fort Lauderdale, FL 800-266-9067
Penley Corporation
West Paris, ME 800-368-6449

Micer

Meat

Thunderbird Food Machinery
Blaine, WA 800-764-9377

Mincer

Thunderbird Food Machinery
Blaine, WA 800-764-9377

Molds

Bakers' & Confectioners'

AMCO Corporation
City of Industry, CA 626-855-2550
Carnegie Manufacturing Company
Fairfield, NJ 973-575-3449
Chocolate Concepts
Hartville, OH 330-877-3322
Choklit Molds Ltd
Lincoln, RI 800-777-6653
D.R. McClain & Son
Commerce, CA 800-428-2263
Edhard Corporation
Hackettstown, NJ 888-334-2731
Hartstone
Zanesville, OH 740-452-9999
Hillside Metal Ware Company
Union, NJ 908-964-3080
Intermold Corporation
Greenville, SC. 864-627-0300
Liberty Engineering Company
Roscoe, IL. 877-623-9065
Lorann Oils
Lansing, MI. 800-862-8620
Matfer
Van Nuys, CA 800-766-0333
Micelli Chocolate Mold Company
West Babylon, NY 631-752-2888
Moline Machinery
Duluth, MN. 800-767-5734
Somerset Industries
Billerica, MA 800-772-4404
Voorhees Rubber Manufacturing Co., Inc.
Newark, MD 410-632-1582
White Swan Fruit Products
Plant City, FL 800-330-8952

Butter & Cheese

Carnegie Manufacturing Company
Fairfield, NJ 973-575-3449
Lancaster Colony Corporation
Columbus, OH 800-292-7260
Sanchelima International
Doral, FL. 305-591-4343
Viking Machine & Design
De Pere, WI. 888-286-2116

Pans

Baking & Roasting

ABI Limited
Concord, ON. 800-297-8666
Advance Tabco
Edgewood, NY 800-645-3166
Allied Metal Spinning Corp
Bronx, NY. 800-615-2266
Alumaworks
Sunny Isle Beach, FL 800-277-7267
American Metal Stamping & Spinning
Brooklyn, NY. 718-384-1500
APW Wyott Food Service Equipment Company
Cheyenne, WY 800-527-2100
Baking Machines
Livermore, CA 925-449-3369
Bluebird Manufacturing
Montreal, QC 800-406-2505
Browne & Company
Markham, ON. 905-475-6104
Cambro Manufacturing Company
Huntington Beach, CA 800-848-1555
Carlson Products
Maize, KS 800-234-1069
Crestware
North Salt Lake City, UT 800-345-0513
Crown Custom Metal Spinning
Concord, ON. 800-750-1924
D&W Fine Pack
Lake Zurich, IL. 800-323-0422
Dur-Able Aluminum Corporation
Hoffman Estates, IL 847-843-1100
Dura-Ware Company of America
Oklahoma City, OK 800-664-3872
G&S Metal Products Company
Cleveland, OH 216-441-0700
Hillside Metal Ware Company
Union, NJ 908-964-3080
Kosempel Manufacturing Company
Philadelphia, PA 800-733-7122
Legion Industries
Waynesboro, GA. 800-887-1988
Lincoln Foodservice
Cleveland, OH 800-374-3004
Magna Industries
Lakewood, NJ. 800-510-9856
Matfer
Van Nuys, CA 800-766-0333
Mouli Manufacturing Corporation
Belleville, NJ 800-789-8285
National Cart Company
Saint Charles, MO 636-947-3800
Pfeil & Holing, Inc.
Flushing, NY. 800-247-7955
Piper Products
Wausau, WI. 800-544-3057
Southbend Company
Fuquay Varina, NC 800-348-2558
State Products
Long Beach, CA 800-730-5150
Superior Products Company
Saint Paul, MN 800-328-9800
Vollrath Company
Sheboygan, WI 920-457-4851
Williamsburg Metal Spinning & Stamping Corporation
Brooklyn, NY 888-535-5402
World Kitchen
Elmira, NY 800-999-3436

Stainless Steel

Castella Imports
Hauppauge, NY 866-227-8355

Frying

Adcraft
Hicksville, NY 800-223-7750
Alumaworks
Sunny Isle Beach, FL 800-277-7267
Bluebird Manufacturing
Montreal, QC 800-406-2505
Browne & Company
Markham, ON. 905-475-6104
Crown Custom Metal Spinning
Concord, ON. 800-750-1924
Dura-Ware Company of America
Oklahoma City, OK 800-664-3872
Imperial Commercial Cooking Equipment
Corona, CA 800-343-7790
Libertyware
Clearfield, UT 888-500-5885
Market Forge Industries
Everett, MA. 866-698-3188
Matfer
Van Nuys, CA 800-766-0333
Olde Country Reproductions
York, PA 800-358-3997
Regal Ware
Kewaskum, WI 262-626-2121
Superior Products Company
Saint Paul, MN 800-328-9800
Vollrath Company
Sheboygan, WI 920-457-4851

Pie

ABI Limited
Concord, ON. 800-297-8666
Allied Metal Spinning Corp
Bronx, NY. 800-615-2266
Browne & Company
Markham, ON. 905-475-6104
Carlson Products
Maize, KS 800-234-1069
Crown Custom Metal Spinning
Concord, ON. 800-750-1924
D&W Fine Pack
Lake Zurich, IL. 800-323-0422
Lincoln Foodservice
Cleveland, OH 800-374-3004
Malco Manufacturing Corporation
Los Angeles, CA. 866-477-7267
Revere Packaging
Shelbyville, KY 800-626-2668
Superior Products Company
Saint Paul, MN 800-328-9800
V&R Metal Enterprises
Brooklyn, NY 718-768-8142

Sauce

Alumaworks
Sunny Isle Beach, FL 800-277-7267
Bluebird Manufacturing
Montreal, QC 800-406-2505
Dover Parkersburg
Follansbee, WV
Dura-Ware Company of America
Oklahoma City, OK 800-664-3872
Lincoln Foodservice
Cleveland, OH 800-374-3004
Regal Ware
Kewaskum, WI 262-626-2121
Superior Products Company
Saint Paul, MN 800-328-9800

Parers & Peelers

Fruit & Vegetable

A.K. Robins
Baltimore, MD 800-486-9656
AMCO Corporation
City of Industry, CA 626-855-2550
Atlas Pacific Engineering Company
Pueblo, CO 719-948-3040
Blakeslee, Inc.
Addison, IL. 630-532-5021
Browne & Company
Markham, ON. 905-475-6104
Conimar Corporation
Ocala, FL. 800-874-9735
F.B. Pease Company
Rochester, NY. 585-475-1870
Insinger Machine Company
Philadelphia, PA 800-344-4802
Juice Tree
Omaha, NE 714-891-4425
Magnuson Corporation
Pueblo, CO 719-948-9500
Mouli Manufacturing Corporation
Belleville, NJ 800-789-8285
Murotech Corporation
Torrance, CA. 800-565-6876
Odenberg Engineering
West Sacramento, CA. 800-688-8396
Superior Products Company
Saint Paul, MN 800-328-9800
Univex Corporation
Salem, NH. 800-258-6358
Vanmark Corporation
Creston, IA 800-523-6261
White Mountain Freezer
Kansas City, MO. 816-943-4100

Plates

Paper

AJM Packaging Corporation
Bloomfield Hills, MI 248-901-0040
Bergschrond
Seattle, WA 206-763-3502
Carthage Cup Company
Longview, TX. 903-238-9833
Chinet Company
Laguna Niguel, CA. 949-348-1711
Creative Converting
Clintonville, WI 800-826-0418
Durango-Georgia Paper
Tampa, FL. 813-286-2718
E.K. Lay Company
Philadelphia, PA 800-523-3220
Enviro-Ware
Pittsburgh, PA. 888-233-7857
Fonda Group
Goshen, IN 574-534-2515
Fonda Group
Oshkosh, WI. 800-558-9300
Fort James Corporation
Norwalk, CT 800-257-9744
Four M Manufacturing Group
San Jose, CA. 408-998-1141
Genpak
Glens Falls, NY. 800-626-6695
Gulf States Paper Corporation
Tuscaloosa, AL 205-562-5000
James River Canada
North York, ON. 416-789-5151
Jones-Zylon Company
West Lafayette, OH. 800-848-8160

Premier Industries
Cincinnati, OH 800-354-9817
Primary Liquidation Corporation
Bohemia, NY 631-244-1410
Scan Group
Appleton, WI 920-730-9150
Smith-Lee Company
Oshkosh, WI 800-327-9774
Solo Cup Canada
Toronto, ON 800-465-9696
Solo Cup Company
Lake Forest, IL 800-367-2877
Solo Cup Company
Owings Mills, MD 800-800-0300
Sterling Paper Company
Philadelphia, PA 215-744-5350

Pie

Carlisle Food Service Products
Oklahoma City, OK 800-654-8210
Norandal
Franklin, TX 615-771-5700

Plastic, Reusable

De Ster Corporation
Atlanta, GA 800-237-8270
Fonda Group
Oshkosh, WI 800-367-2877
Great Western Products
Ontario, CA 888-598-5588
HPI North America/Plastics
Saint Paul, MN 800-752-7462
Kendrick Johnson & Associates
Bloomington, MN 800-826-1271
OWD
Tupper Lake, NY 800-836-1693
Plastiques Cascades Group
Montreal, QC 888-703-6515
Solo Cup Canada
Toronto, ON 800-465-9696
Solo Cup Company
Lake Forest, IL 800-367-2877
Solo Cup Company
Owings Mills, MD 800-800-0300
Wiltec
Leominster, MA 978-537-1497

Platters

Art Plastics Handy Home Helpers
Leominster, MA 978-537-0367
Browne & Company
Markham, ON 905-475-6104
Cal-Mil Plastic Products
Oceanside, CA 800-321-9069
Carlisle Food Service Products
Oklahoma City, OK 800-654-8210
Cyclamen Collection
Oakland, CA 510-434-7620
Delfin Design & Manufacturing
Rcho Sta Marg, CA 800-354-7919
Gaetano America
El Monte, CA 626-442-2858
Gril-Del
Mankato, MN 800-782-7320
M&E Manufacturing Company
Kingston, NY 845-331-2110
Michael Leson Dinnerware
Youngstown, OH 800-821-3541
Olde Country Reproductions
York, PA 800-358-3997
Olde Thompson/Leeds Engineering Corporation
Oxnard, CA 800-827-1565
Prolon
Port Gibson, MS 888-480-9828
Ronnie's Ceramic Company
San Francisco, CA 800-888-8218
Sabert Corporation
Sayreville, NJ 800-722-3781
Sims Superior Seating
Locust Grove, GA 800-729-9178
Superior Products Company
Saint Paul, MN 800-328-9800
Tomlinson Industries
Cleveland, OH 800-945-4589
Ullman Company
New York, NY 212-571-0068
Vertex China
Walnut, CA 800-483-7839
Waddington North AmericaCups Illustrated
Lancaster, TX 800-334-2877

Weavewood, Inc.
Golden Valley, MN 800-367-6460

Rolling Pins

H. Arnold Wood Turning
Tarrytown, NY 888-314-0088
Read Products
Seattle, WA 800-445-3416
Superior Products Company
Saint Paul, MN 800-328-9800
Thorpe Rolling Pin Company
Hamden, CT 800-344-6966

Scoops, Dishers & Spades

AMCO Corporation
City of Industry, CA 626-855-2550
Bremer Manufacturing Company
Elkhart Lake, WI. 920-894-2944
C.R. Manufacturing
Waverly, NE 877-789-5844
Carlisle Food Service Products
Oklahoma City, OK 800-654-8210
Cr. Manufacturing
Waverly, NE 877-789-5844
Landis Plastics
Alsip, IL 708-396-1470
Lloyd Disher Company
Decatur, IL 217-429-0593
Measurex/S&L Plastics
Nazareth, PA 800-752-0650
National Scoop & Equipment Company
Spring House, PA 215-646-2040
Penn Scale ManufacturingCompany
Philadelphia, PA 215-739-9644
Prolon
Port Gibson, MS 888-480-9828
Superior Products Company
Saint Paul, MN 800-328-9800
Tolco Corporation
Toledo, OH 800-537-4786
Zeroll Company
Fort Pierce, FL 800-872-5000

Scrapers

Butchers' Block

Boehringer Mfg. Co. Inc.
Felton, CA. 800-630-8665
C.R. Manufacturing
Waverly, NE 877-789-5844
Goodell Tools
New Hope, MN 800-542-3906

Shears

Poultry

AMCO Corporation
City of Industry, CA 626-855-2550
Cutrite Company
Fremont, OH 800-928-8748
E-Z Edge
West New York, NJ 800-232-4470
Imperial Schrade Corporation
Ellenville, NY 212-210-8600
Mundial
Norwood, MA 800-487-2224
Superior Products Company
Saint Paul, MN 800-328-9800

Sheeter

Dough

Thunderbird Food Machinery
Blaine, WA 800-764-9377

Sheets

Cookie

Browne & Company
Markham, ON 905-475-6104
Dover Parkersburg
Follansbee, WV
Lincoln Foodservice
Cleveland, OH 800-374-3004
Matfer
Van Nuys, CA 800-766-0333

State Products
Long Beach, CA 800-730-5150
Superior Products Company
Saint Paul, MN 800-328-9800

Sieves

Andritz
Muncy, PA 570-546-8211
ATM Corporation
New Berlin, WI 800-511-2096
Browne & Company
Markham, ON 905-475-6104
Cleveland Vibrator Company
Cleveland, OH 800-221-3298
CSC Scientific Company
Fairfax, VA 800-621-4778
Gilson Company Incorporated
Lewis Center, OH 800-444-1508
Glen Mills, Inc.
Clifton, NJ 973-777-0777
Great Western Manufacturing Company
Leavenworth, KS 800-682-3121
Newark Wire Cloth Company
Clifton, NJ 800-221-0392
Norvell Company
Fort Scott, KS 800-653-3147
Vorti-Siv
Salem, OH 800-227-7487

Sifters

Flour & Bakers'

AMCO Corporation
City of Industry, CA 626-855-2550
Ayr-King Corporation
Jeffersontown, KY 866-266-6290
B&P Process Equipment & Systems
Saginaw, MI 989-757-1300
Browne & Company
Markham, ON 905-475-6104
Buffalo Technologies Corporation
Buffalo, NY 800-332-2419
F.P. Smith Wire Cloth Company
Northlake, IL 800-323-6842
Fred D. Pfening Company
Columbus, OH 614-294-1633
Great Western Manufacturing Company
Leavenworth, KS 800-682-3121
KB Systems Baking Machinery Design Company
Bangor, PA 610-588-7788
Kemutec Group
Bristol, PA 215-788-8013
Meadows Mills, Inc.
North Wilkesboro, NC 800-626-2282
Norvell Company
Fort Scott, KS 800-653-3147
S. Howes
Silver Creek, NY 888-255-2611
Sasib North America
Plano, TX 972-422-5808
Shick Tube-Veyor Corporation
Kansas City, MO 816-861-7224
Sifters Parts & Service
Wesley Chapel, FL 800-367-3591
Smico Manufacturing Company
Valley Brook, OK 800-351-9088

Skewers

AMCO Corporation
City of Industry, CA 626-855-2550
Asian Foods
St. Paul, MN 800-274-2655
Automated Food Systems
Waxahachie, TX 972-298-5719
C.R. Manufacturing
Waverly, NE 877-789-5844
Chicago Dowel Company
Chicago, IL 800-333-6935
Coastline Equipment
Bellingham, WA 360-739-2480
G.F. Frank & Sons
Fairfield, OH 513-870-9075
Great Western Products
Ontario, CA 888-598-5588
H. Arnold Wood Turning
Tarrytown, NY 888-314-0088
Hardwood Products Company
Guilford, ME 800-289-3340
Jarden Home Brands
Daleville, IN 800-392-2575

Les Industries Touch Inc
Sherbrooke, QC 800-267-4140
Lynch-Jamentz Company
Lakewood, CA 800-828-6217
Royal Paper Products
Coatesville, PA 800-666-6655
Saunder Brothers
Bridgton, ME 207-647-3331
Trepte's Wire & Metal Works
Bellflower, CA 800-828-6217

Slicer

Bagel

Larien Products
Northampton, MA. 800-462-9237

Bread

Paramount Packaging Corp.
Melville, NY. 516-333-8100
Thunderbird Food Machinery
Blaine, WA 800-764-9377

Spoons

Abco International
Melville, NY. 866-240-2226
AMCO Corporation
City of Industry, CA 626-855-2550
American Housewares Manufacturing Corporation
Bronx, NY. 718-665-9500
C.R. Manufacturing
Waverly, NE 877-789-5844
Carlisle Food Service Products
Oklahoma City, OK 800-654-8210
Cr. Manufacturing
Waverly, NE 877-789-5844
Cutco Vector
Olean, NY. 716-373-6148
Design Specialties
Hamden, CT 800-999-1584
Fab-X/Metals
Washington, NC 800-677-3229
Fioriware
Zanesville, OH 740-454-7400
Hal-One Plastics
Olathe, KS. 800-626-5784
Harco Enterprises
Peterborough, ON. 800-361-5361
Hardwood Products Company
Guilford, ME. 800-289-3340
Imperial Schrade Corporation
Ellenville, NY. 212-210-8600
Jarden Home Brands
Daleville, IN 800-392-2575
Jones-Zylon Company
West Lafayette, OH. 800-848-8160
Lifetime Hoan Corporation
Garden City, NY 516-683-6000
LoTech Industries
Lakewood, CO 800-295-0199
Lynch-Jamentz Company
Lakewood, CA 800-828-6217
OWD
Tupper Lake, NY 800-836-1693
Polar Plastics
St Laurent, QC 514-331-0207
Polar Ware Company
Sheboygan, WI 800-237-3655
Solo Cup Canada
Toronto, ON 800-465-9696
Solon Manufacturing Company
North Haven, CT. 800-341-6640
Superior Products Company
Saint Paul, MN 800-328-9800
Tops Manufacturing Company
Darien, CT. 203-655-9367
Trepte's Wire & Metal Works
Bellflower, CA 800-828-6217
Vollrath Company
Sheboygan, WI 920-457-4851
Weavewood, Inc.
Golden Valley, MN 800-367-6460
Wiltec
Leominster, MA 978-537-1497

Stirrers & Picks: Cocktail, Hors D'oeuvres

C.R. Manufacturing
Waverly, NE 877-789-5844
Cell-O-Core Company
Sharon Center, OH 800-239-4370
Epic Products
Santa Ana, CA 800-548-9791
Goldmax Industries
City of Industry, CA 626-964-8820
Harco Enterprises
Peterborough, ON. 800-361-5361
Hardwood Products Company
Guilford, ME. 800-289-3340
Jarden Home Brands
Daleville, IN 800-392-2575
Johnstown Manufacturing
Columbus, OH 614-236-8853
Pelican Products Company
Bronx, NY. 800-552-8820
Royal Paper Products
Coatesville, PA 800-666-6655
Soodhalter Plastics
Los Angeles, CA. 213-747-0231
Spinzer
Glen Ellyn, IL 630-469-7184
Spir-It/Zoo Piks
Andover, MA 800-343-0996
Spirit Foodservice, Inc.
Andover, MA 800-343-0996
Superior Products Company
Saint Paul, MN 800-328-9800
Superior Quality Products
Schenectady, NY. 800-724-1129
Token Factory
La Crosse, WI 888-486-5367
Tops Manufacturing Company
Darien, CT. 203-655-9367
Trevor Industries
Eden, NY. 716-992-4775
Ursini Plastics
Bracebridge, ON. 705-646-2701
Waddington North America
Chelmsford, MA 888-962-2877

Strainers

AMCO Corporation
City of Industry, CA 626-855-2550
American Metal Stamping & Spinning
Brooklyn, NY 718-384-1500
C.R. Manufacturing
Waverly, NE 877-789-5844
Eaton Filtration, LLC
Tinton Falls, NJ. 800-859-9212
Feldmeier Equipment
Syracuse, NY 315-454-8608
Giunta Brothers
Philadelphia, PA 215-389-9670
Globe International
Tacoma, WA 800-523-6575
Goodnature Products
Orchard Park, NY 800-875-3381
L.C. Thompson Company
Kenosha, WI 800-558-4018
Lincoln Foodservice
Cleveland, OH 800-374-3004
Mouli Manufacturing Corporation
Belleville, NJ 800-789-8285
Schlueter Company
Janesville, WI 800-359-1700
South Valley Manufacturing
Gilroy, CA. 408-842-5457
Superior Products Company
Saint Paul, MN 800-328-9800

Tables

Cutting & Trimming

Bally Block Company
Bally, PA 610-845-7511
BMH Equipment
Sacramento, CA 800-350-8828
Catskill Craftsmen
Stamford, NY 607-652-7321
Dunhill Food Equipment Corporation
Armonk, NY 800-847-4206
Fishmore
Melbourne,, FL 321-723-4751
Frelco
Stephenville, NL 709-643-5668
Michigan Maple Block Company
Petoskey, MI 800-447-7975
MSSH
Greensburg, IN 812-663-2180
Rheon USA
Huntersville, NC 704-875-9191
Triple-A Manufacturing Company
Toronto, ON 800-786-2238
Ultrafryer Systems
San Antonio, TX 800-545-9189

Stainless Steel

A-1 Booth Manufacturing
Burley, ID 800-820-3285
A.J. Antunes & Company
Carol Stream, IL 800-253-2991
Advance Tabco
Edgewood, NY 800-645-3166
All State Fabricators Corporation
Florida, RI. 800-322-9925
Allstrong Restaurant Equipment
South El Monte, CA 800-933-8913
Amtekco Industries
Columbus, OH 800-336-4677
Andgar Corporation
Ferndale, WA 360-366-9900
ARC Specialties
Valencia, CA 661-775-8500
Atlas Equipment Company
Kansas City, MO. 800-842-9188
Avalon Manufacturing
Corona, CA 800-676-3040
California Vibratory Feeders
Anaheim, CA 800-354-0972
Carts Food Equipment Corporation
Brooklyn, NY 718-788-5540
Cobb & Zimmer
Detroit, MI 313-923-0350
Commercial Kitchen Company
Los Angeles, CA. 323-732-2291
Custom Diamond International
Laval, QC 800-326-5926
D.A. Berther
West Allis, WI. 877-357-9622
Dayco
Clearwater, FL 727-573-9330
Denmar Corporation
North Dartmouth, MA 508-999-3295
Duluth Sheet Metal
Duluth, MN. 218-722-2613
Eldorado Miranda Manufacturing Company
Largo, FL 800-330-0708
Erwin Food Service Equipment
Fort Worth, TX 817-535-0021
FabWright, Inc
Garden Grove, CA 800-854-6464
Falcon Fabricators
Nashville, TN 615-832-0027
Fixtur-World
Cookeville, TN 800-634-9887
Gasser Chair Company
Youngstown, OH. 800-323-2234
Griffin Products
Wills Point, TX 800-379-9709
Hot Food Boxes
Mooresville, IN. 800-733-8073
IMC Teddy Food Service Equipment
Amityville, NY 800-221-5644
Institutional Equipment
Bolingbrook, IL 630-771-0990
John Boos & Company
Effingham, IL 217-347-7701
KEMCO
Wareham, MA. 800-231-5955
Kiefer Industries
Random Lake, WI. 920-994-2332
Kitchen Equipment Fabricating Company
Houston, TX 713-747-3611
Lakeside Manufacturing
Milwaukee, WI. 888-558-8574
Load King Manufacturing Company
Jacksonville, FL 800-531-4975
M&E Manufacturing Company
Kingston, NY 845-331-2110
Marlo Manufacturing Company
Boonton, NJ 800-222-0450
MCM Fixture Company
Hazel Park, MI 248-547-9280

Metal Equipment Fabricators
Columbia, SC 803-776-9250
Metal Master
Tucson, AZ 800-488-8729
Metal Masters Food Service Equipment Company
Clayton, DE. 800-441-8440
Miami Metal
Miami, FL 305-576-3600
Midwest Folding Products
Chicago, IL 800-344-2864
Mouron & Company
Indianapolis, IN 317-243-7955
N. Wasserstrom & Sons
Columbus, OH 800-999-9277
New Age Industrial Corporation
Norton, KS 800-255-0104
Northern Stainless Fabricating
Traverse City, MI 231-947-4580
Omicron Steel Products Company
Jamaica, NY 718-805-3400
Pollard Brothers Manufacturing
Chicago, IL 773-763-6868
Premium Air Systems
Troy, MI 877-430-0333
Quipco Products
Sauget, IL 314-993-1442
Randell Manufacturing Unified Brands
Weidman, MI 888-994-7636
Sarasota Restaurant Equipment
Sarasota, FL 800-434-1410
Savage Brothers Company
Elk Grove Vlg, IL. 800-342-0973
Schlueter Company
Janesville, WI 800-359-1700
Sefi Fabricators
Amityville, NY 631-842-2200
South Valley Manufacturing
Gilroy, CA. 408-842-5457
Southwestern Porcelain Steel
Sand Springs, OK 918-245-1375
Stainless
La Vergne, TN. 800-877-5177
Stainless Fabricating Company
Denver, CO 800-525-8966
Stainless International
Rancho Cordova, CA 888-300-6196
Stainless Steel Fabricators
Tyler, TX. 903-595-6625
Starlite Food Service Equipment
Detroit, MI 888-521-6603
Super Sturdy
Weldon, NC. 800-253-4833
Superior Products Company
Saint Paul, MN 800-328-9800
Supreme Metal
Alpharetta, GA 800-645-2526
Travis Manufacturing Company
Alliance, OH. 330-875-1661
Unarco Industries
Wagoner, OK. 800-654-4100
Universal Stainless
Aurora, CO 800-223-8332
Universal Stainless
Titusville, PA 800-295-1909
Vande Berg Scales
Sioux Center, IA 712-722-1181
Weiss Sheet Metal
Avon, MA 508-583-8300
West Star Industries
Stockton, CA. 800-326-2288
Wilder Manufacturing Company
Port Jervis, NY 800-832-1319
Zol-Mark Industries
Winnipeg, NB 204-943-7393

Work

Advance Tabco
Edgewood, NY 800-645-3166
Allstrong Restaurant Equipment
South El Monte, CA 800-933-8913
BMH Equipment
Sacramento, CA 800-350-8828
Carts Food Equipment Corporation
Brooklyn, NY 718-788-5540
Eldorado Miranda Manufacturing Company
Largo, FL 800-330-0708
Falcon Fabricators
Nashville, TN 615-832-0027
John Boos & Company
Effingham, IL 217-347-7701
Lakeside Manufacturing
Milwaukee, WI 888-558-8574
MCM Fixture Company
Hazel Park, MI 248-547-9280
Metro Corporation
Wilkes Barre, PA. 800-433-2233
National Bar Systems
Huntington Beach, CA 714-848-1688
Stainless Equipment Manufacturing
Dallas, TX. 800-736-2038
Superior Products Company
Saint Paul, MN 800-328-9800
Weiss Sheet Metal
Avon, MA 508-583-8300

Tins

Cake

Browne & Company
Markham, ON. 905-475-6104
Dover Parkersburg
Follansbee, WV
Independent Can Company
Belcamp, MD 909-923-6150
Olive Can Company
Elgin, IL 847-468-7474

Tinware

B Way Corporation
Atlanta, GA. 800-527-2267
Dover Parkersburg
Follansbee, WV
Greenfield Packaging
White Plains, NY 914-993-0233
Independent Can Company
Belcamp, MD 909-923-6150
Xtreme Beverages, LLC
Dana Point, CA. 949-495-7929

Tongs

Food

AMCO Corporation
City of Industry, CA 626-855-2550
Art Plastics Handy Home Helpers
Leominster, MA 978-537-0367
Atlanta Burning Bush
Newnan, GA 800-665-5611
Browne & Company
Markham, ON. 905-475-6104
C.R. Manufacturing
Waverly, NE 877-789-5844
Carlisle Food Service Products
Oklahoma City, OK 800-654-8210
Gril-Del
Mankato, MN 800-782-7320
Libertyware
Clearfield, UT. 888-500-5885
LoTech Industries
Lakewood, CO 800-295-0199
Music City Metals
Nashville, TN 800-251-2674
Superior Products Company
Saint Paul, MN 800-328-9800
Vollrath Company
Sheboygan, WI 920-457-4851
Weavewood, Inc.
Golden Valley, MN. 800-367-6460
Wiltec
Leominster, MA 978-537-1497
Wishbone Utensil Tableware Line
Wheat Ridge, CO 866-266-5928

Ice

Browne & Company
Markham, ON. 905-475-6104
C.R. Manufacturing
Waverly, NE 877-789-5844
Superior Products Company
Saint Paul, MN 800-328-9800
Weavewood, Inc.
Golden Valley, MN. 800-367-6460
Wiltec
Leominster, MA 978-537-1497

Toothpicks

Admatch Corporation
New York, NY 800-777-9909
Atlas Match Company
Toronto, ON 888-285-2783
C.R. Manufacturing
Waverly, NE 877-789-5844
Cell-O-Core Company
Sharon Center, OH 800-239-4370
Diamond Brands
Cloquet, MN 218-879-6700
Goldmax Industries
City of Industry, CA 626-964-8820
Great Western Products
Ontario, CA. 888-598-5588
H A Stiles
Westbrook, ME 800-447-8537
Jarden Home Brands
Daleville, IN 800-392-2575
Les Industries Touch Inc
Sherbrooke, QC 800-267-4140
Penley Corporation
West Paris, ME 800-368-6449
Royal Paper Products
Coatesville, PA 800-666-6655
Unique Manufacturing
Visalia, CA 888-737-1007
Z 2000 The Pick of the Millenium
Bartlesville, OK 800-654-7311

Trays & Pans

Bakers'

Aeromat Plastics
Burnsville, MN 888-286-8729
Allied Bakery and Food Service Equipment
Santa Fe Springs, CA 562-945-6506
Allied Metal Spinning Corp
Bronx, NY. 800-615-2266
American Metal Stamping & Spinning
Brooklyn, NY 718-384-1500
American Metalcraft
Melrose Park, IL. 800-333-9133
Browne & Company
Markham, ON. 905-475-6104
Buckhorn Inc
Milford, OH 800-543-4454
COW Industries
Columbus, OH 800-542-9353
D&W Fine Pack
Lake Zurich, IL. 800-323-0422
Dur-Able Aluminum Corporation
Hoffman Estates, IL 847-843-1100
Green-Tek
Janesville, WI 800-747-6440
Music City Metals
Nashville, TN 800-251-2674
National Cart Company
Saint Charles, MO 636-947-3800
Omega Industries
St Louis, MO. 314-961-1668
Paper Products Company
Cincinnati, OH 513-921-4717
Polar Ware Company
Sheboygan, WI 800-237-3655
Superior Products Company
Saint Paul, MN 800-328-9800
Toscarora
Sandusky, OH 419-625-7343
Unique Plastics
Rio Rico, AZ. 800-658-5946

Utensils

Bakers' & Confectioners'

Allied Metal Spinning Corp
Bronx, NY. 800-615-2266
AMCO Corporation
City of Industry, CA 626-855-2550
August Thomsen Corporation
Glen Cove, NY 800-645-7170
Automated Food Systems
Waxahachie, TX 972-298-5719
Belshaw Adamatic Bakery Group
Auburn, WA 800-578-2547
Browne & Company
Markham, ON. 905-475-6104
Dur-Able Aluminum Corporation
Hoffman Estates, IL 847-843-1100
Esterle Mold & Machine Company
Stow, OH 800-411-4086
Florida Knife Company
Sarasota, FL 800-966-5643

H. Arnold Wood Turning
Tarrytown, NY 888-314-0088
Hodges
Vienna, IL 800-444-0011
Johnson Corrugated Products Corporation
Thompson, CT 860-923-9563
Kosempel Manufacturing Company
Philadelphia, PA 800-733-7122
Lady Mary
Rockingham, NC 910-997-7321
Leggett & Platt StorageP
Vernon Hills, IL 847-816-6246
Leon Bush Manufacturer
Glenview, IL 847-657-8888
Lorann Oils
Lansing, MI 800-862-8620
Measurex/S&L Plastics
Nazareth, PA 800-752-0650
Pfeil & Holing, Inc.
Flushing, NY 800-247-7955
Saunder Brothers
Bridgton, ME 207-647-3331
State Products
Long Beach, CA 800-730-5150
Turner & Seymour Manufacturing
Torrington, CT 888-856-4864
Unifiller Systems
Delta, BC 888-733-8444
Wishbone Utensil Tableware Line
Wheat Ridge, CO 866-266-5928
Zeier Plastic & Manufacturing
Madison, WI 608-244-5782

Chopsticks

Bamboo

Asian Foods
St. Paul, MN 800-274-2655
Great Western Products
Ontario, CA 888-598-5588

Forks

Cocktail

AMCO Corporation
City of Industry, CA 626-855-2550
C.R. Manufacturing
Waverly, NE 877-789-5844
Jarden Home Brands
Daleville, IN 800-392-2575
Pelican Products Company
Bronx, NY 800-552-8820
Soodhalter Plastics
Los Angeles, CA 213-747-0231
Wishbone Utensil Tableware Line
Wheat Ridge, CO 866-266-5928

Wooden

Coley Industries
Wayland, NY 716-728-2390
Jarden Home Brands
Daleville, IN 800-392-2575
Weavewood, Inc.
Golden Valley, MN 800-367-6460

Household, Kitchen

A.G. Russell Knives Inc.
Rogers, AR 800-255-9034
Abco International
Melville, NY 866-240-2226
Abond Plastic Corporation
Lachine, QC 800-886-7947
Ace Fabrication
Mobile, AL 251-478-0401
Acme International
Maplewood, NJ 973-416-0400
All-Clad Metalcrafters
Canonsburg, PA 800-255-2523
AMCO Corporation
City of Industry, CA 626-855-2550
American Housewares Manufacturing Corporation
Bronx, NY 718-665-9500
American Time & Signal
Dassel, MN 800-328-8996
Bally Block Company
Bally, PA 610-845-7511
Best Manufacturers
Portland, OR 800-500-1528
Bluffton Slaw Cutter Company
Bluffton, OH 419-358-9840
Bremer Manufacturing Company
Elkhart Lake, WI 920-894-2944
Brown Manufacturing Company
Decatur, GA 404-378-8311
Browne & Company
Markham, ON 905-475-6104
Buck Knives
Post Falls, ID 800-326-2825
Burrell Cutlery Company
Ellicottville, NY 716-699-2343
C.M. Slicechief Company, Inc.
Toledo, OH 419-241-7647
C.R. Manufacturing
Waverly, NE 877-789-5844
Carlisle Food Service Products
Oklahoma City, OK 800-654-8210
Carolina Cracker
Garner, NC 919-779-6899
Chef Revival
Elkhorn, WI 800-248-9826
Chef Specialties Company
Smethport, PA 800-440-2433
Chicago Scale & Slicer Company
Franklin Park, IL 847-455-3400
Cleveland Metal StampingCompany
Berea, OH 440-234-0010
Coley Industries
Wayland, NY 716-728-2390
Conimar Corporation
Ocala, FL 800-874-9735
Corby Hall
Randolph, NJ 973-366-8300
Cr. Manufacturing
Waverly, NE 877-789-5844
Cutco Vector
Olean, NY 716-373-6148
Cyclamen Collection
Oakland, CA 510-434-7620
Dart Container Corporation
Mason, MI 800-248-5960
Dexter-Russell
Southbridge, MA 508-765-0201
Diamond Machining Technologies
Marlborough, MA 800-666-4368
Dorton Incorporated
Arlington Hts, IL 800-299-8600
Dynynstyl
Delray Beach, FL 800-774-7895
E.K. Lay Company
Philadelphia, PA 800-523-3220
Edco Industries
Bridgeport, CT 203-333-8982
Educational Products Company
Hope, NJ 800-272-3822
Fab-X/Metals
Washington, NC 800-677-3229
Fioriware
Zanesville, OH 740-454-7400
Fortune Products
Cedar Park, TX 800-742-7797
Fun-Time International
Philadelphia, PA 800-776-4386
G&S Metal Products Company
Cleveland, OH 216-441-0700
G.G. Greene Enterprises
Warren, PA 814-723-5700
Giunta Brothers
Philadelphia, PA 215-389-9670
Goebel Fixture Company
Hutchinson, MN 888-339-0509
Gold Star Products
Oak Park, MI 800-800-0205
Good Idea
Northampton, MA 800-462-9237
Goodell Tools
New Hope, MN 800-542-3906
Grand Silver Company
Bronx, NY 718-585-1930
Gril-Del
Mankato, MN 800-782-7320
H A Stiles
Westbrook, ME 800-447-8537
H. Arnold Wood Turning
Tarrytown, NY 888-314-0088
Hardwood Products Company
Guilford, ME 800-289-3340
Harold Leonard SouthwestCorporation
Houston, TX 800-245-8105
Hillside Metal Ware Company
Union, NJ 908-964-3080
Insinger Machine Company
Philadelphia, PA 800-344-4802
James River Canada
North York, ON 416-789-5151
Jim Scharf Holdings
Perdue, SK 800-667-9727
Kosempel Manufacturing Company
Philadelphia, PA 800-733-7122
Lady Mary
Rockingham, NC 910-997-7321
Lamson & Goodnow Manufacturing Company
Shelburne Falls, MA 800-872-6564
Lancaster Colony Corporation
Columbus, OH 800-292-7260
Leading Industry
Oxnard, CA 805-385-4100
Leggett & Platt StorageP
Vernon Hills, IL 847-816-6246
Lenox
Bristol, PA 800-223-4311
Libby Canada
Mississauga, ON 905-607-8280
Libertyware
Clearfield, UT 888-500-5885
Lifetime Hoan Corporation
Garden City, NY 516-683-6000
Lincoln Foodservice
Cleveland, OH 800-374-3004
Lloyd Disher Company
Decatur, IL 217-429-0593
Lodge Manufacturing Company
South Pittsburg, TN 423-837-5919
Lorenzen's Cookie Cutters
Wantagh, NY 516-781-7116
Luce Corporation
Hamden, CT 800-344-6966
Lynch-Jamentz Company
Lakewood, CA 800-828-6217
M&E Manufacturing Company
Kingston, NY 845-331-2110
M.E. Heuck Company
Mason, OH 800-359-3200
Majestic
Bridgeport, CT 203-367-7900
Mastex Industries
Petersburg, VA 804-732-8300
Maugus Manufacturing Company
Lancaster, PA 717-299-5681
Measurex/S&L Plastics
Nazareth, PA 800-752-0650
Michael Leson Dinnerware
Youngstown, OH 800-821-3541
Michigan Maple Block Company
Petoskey, MI 800-447-7975
Mid-West Wire Products, Inc
Ferndale, MI 800-989-9881
Mundial
Norwood, MA 800-487-2224
Music City Metals
Nashville, TN 800-251-2674
New Age Industrial Corporation
Norton, KS 800-255-0104
Novelty Crystal Corporation
Long Island City, NY 800-622-0250
Olde Country Reproductions
York, PA 800-358-3997
Olde Thompson/Leeds Engineering Corporation
Oxnard, CA 800-827-1565
Oneida Canada, Limited
Oneida, NY 888-263-7195
Oneida Food Service
Oneida, NY 315-361-3000
OWD
Tupper Lake, NY 800-836-1693
Oxo International
New York, NY 800-545-4411
Penley Corporation
West Paris, ME 800-368-6449
Polar Plastics
Mooresville, NC 704-660-6600
Polar Ware Company
Sheboygan, WI 800-237-3655
Ranger Blade Manufacturing Company
Traer, IA 800-377-7860
Regal Ware
Kewaskum, WI 262-626-2121
Reiner Products
Waterbury, CT 800-345-6775
Replacements Ltd.
Greensboro, NC 800-737-5223
Rival Manufacturing Company
Kansas City, MO 816-943-4100

RubaTex Polymer
Middlefield, OH 440-632-1691
Samuel Underberg
Brooklyn, NY 718-363-0787
Saunder Brothers
Bridgton, ME 207-647-3331
Serr-Edge Machine Company
Cleveland, Cl 800-443-8097
Spir-It/Zoo Piks
Andover, MA 800-343-0996
ST Restaurant Supplies
Delta, BC. 888-448-4244
Stanley Roberts
Piscataway, NJ 973-778-5900
Sturdi-Bilt Restaurant Equipment
Whitmore Lake, MI 800-521-2895
Swing-A-Way Manufacturing Company
St Louis, MO. 314-773-1488
T&A Metal Products Company
Deptford, NJ 856-227-1700
Table De France: North America
New York, NY 212-725-3461
Tar-Hong Melamine USA
City of Industry, CA 626-935-1612
Techform
Mount Airy, NC 336-789-2115
Thorpe Rolling Pin Company
Hamden, CT 800-344-6966
Tops Manufacturing Company
Darien, CT. 203-655-9367
Traeger Industries
Mount Angel, OR 800-872-3437
TRC
Middlefield, OH 440-834-0078
Trepte's Wire & Metal Works
Bellflower, CA 800-828-6217
Tru Hone Corporation
Ocala, FL. 800-237-4663
Turner & Seymour Manufacturing
Torrington, CT 888-856-4864
Ultrafryer Systems
San Antonio, TX. 800-545-9189
Unique Manufacturing
Visalia, CA 888-737-1007
United Showcase Company
Wood Ridge, NJ 800-526-6382
Utica Cutlery Company
Utica, NY 800-879-2526
Vermillion Flooring Company
Springfield, MO 417-862-3785
Vita Craft Corporation
Shawnee, KS. 800-359-3444
Vollrath Company
Sheboygan, WI 920-457-4851
Vulcanium Metals International, LLC
Northbrook, IL 888-922-0040
Waddington North America
Chelmsford, MA. 888-962-2877
Walco Stainless
Utica, NY 800-879-2526
Warren E. Conley Corporation
Carmel, IN. 800-367-7875
Warther Museum
Dover, OH. 330-343-7513
Waukesha Cherry-Burrell
Louisville, KY 502-491-4310
Weavewood, Inc.
Golden Valley, MN 800-367-6460
Western Stoneware
Monmouth, IL. 309-734-2161
Wiltec
Leominster, MA 978-537-1497
Wilton Industries
Woodridge, IL. 630-963-1818
Wishbone Utensil Tableware Line
Wheat Ridge, CO 866-266-5928
World Kitchen
Elmira, NY 800-999-3436
York Saw & Knife Company
York, PA 800-233-1969
Zelco Industries
Mount Vernon, NY 800-431-2486
Zeroll Company
Fort Pierce, FL 800-872-5000

Foodservice Equipment & Supplies

Bars & Bar Supplies

Admatch Corporation
New York, NY 800-777-9909
Advanced Design Manufacturing
Concord, CA. 800-690-0002
Alpine Store Equipment Corporation
Long Island City, NY 718-361-1213
Alvarado Manufacturing Company
Chino, CA. 800-445-7401
AMC Industries
Tampa, FL. 813-989-9663
AMCO Corporation
City of Industry, CA 626-855-2550
American Coaster Company
Sanborn, NY 888-423-8628
American Metalcraft
Melrose Park, IL 800-333-9133
AMI
Richmond, CA 800-942-7466
Amtekco Industries
Columbus, OH 800-336-4677
Anchor Hocking Company
Lancaster, OH 800-562-7511
Atlas Match Company
Toronto, ON 888-285-2783
Atlas Match Corporation
Euless, TX. 800-628-2426
Automatic Bar Controls
Vacaville, CA 800-722-6738
Ballantyne Food Service Equipment
Omaha, NE 800-424-1215
Bar Equipment Corporation of America
Downey, CA 888-870-2322
Bar-Maid Minibars
Garfield, NJ. 800-227-6243
Berg Company
Monona, WI 608-221-4281
Best Brands Home Products
New York, NY 212-684-7456
Booth
Dallas, TX. 800-497-2958
Bradley Industries
Westchester, IL 815-469-2314
Brass Smith
Denver, CO 800-662-9595
Brown Manufacturing Company
Decatur, GA 404-378-8311
Browne & Company
Markham, ON. 905-475-6104
C.R. Manufacturing
Waverly, NE 877-789-5844
Carlisle Food Service Products
Oklahoma City, OK 800-654-8210
Carnegie Textile Company
Solon, OH 800-633-4136
Carpigiani Corporation of America
Winston Salem, NC. 800-648-4389
Carroll Chair Company
Onalaska, WI. 800-331-4707
Carts Food Equipment Corporation
Brooklyn, NY 718-788-5540
CCS Stone, Inc.
Moonachie, NJ 800-227-7785
Cell-O-Core Company
Sharon Center, OH 800-239-4370
Chaircraft
Hickory, NC 828-326-8458
Classico Seating
Peru, IN. 800-968-6655
Co-Rect Products
Golden Valley, MN. 800-328-5702
Coastal Canvas Products Company
Savannah, GA. 800-476-5174
Cobb & Zimmer
Detroit, MI 313-923-0350
Commercial Seating Specialist
Santa Clara, CA 408-453-8983
Commercial Textiles Corporation-Best Buy Uniforms
Homestead, PA 800-345-1924
Conimar Corporation
Ocala, FL. 800-874-9735
Control Beverage
Adelanto, CA 330-549-5376
Cork Specialties
Miami, FL. 305-477-1506
Cove Woodworking
Gloucester, MA. 800-273-0037
Cr. Manufacturing
Waverly, NE 877-789-5844
Craig Manufacturing
Irvington, NJ. 800-631-7936
Cruvinet Winebar Company
Reno, NV 800-278-8463
Custom Design Interiors Service & Manufacturing
Largo, FL 727-536-2207
D.D. Bean & Sons Company
Jaffrey, NH 800-326-8311
De Felsko Corporation
Ogdensburg, NY 800-448-3835
Designer's Choice Stainless
Peoria, AZ. 800-592-3274
Diamond Brands
Cloquet, MN 218-879-6700
Dometic Mini Bar
Elkhart, IN. 800-301-8118
Dorado Carton Company
Dorado, PR 787-796-1670
Eagle Products Company
Houston, TX 713-690-1161
Eclectic Contract Furniture Industries
New York, NY. 888-311-6272
Edco Industries
Bridgeport, CT 203-333-8982
Ellingers
Sheboygan, WI 888-287-8906
English Manufacturing Inc
Rancho Cordova, CA 800-651-2711
Epic Products
Santa Ana, CA 800-548-9791
Erie Cotton Products Company
Erie, PA 800-289-4737
Ex-Cell Kaiser
Franklin Park, IL. 847-451-0451
Felix Storch
Bronx, NY. 800-932-4267
Flojet
Foothill Ranch, CA. 800-235-6538
Fun-Time International
Philadelphia, PA 800-776-4386
Gar Products
Lakewood, NJ. 800-424-2477
Gasser Chair Company
Youngstown, OH. 800-323-2234
Gensaco Marketing
New York, NY 800-506-1935
Glastender
Saginaw, MI 800-748-0423
Goldmax Industries
City of Industry, CA 626-964-8820
GSW Jackes-Evans Manufacturing Company
Saint Louis, MO 800-325-6173
H A Stiles
Westbrook, ME. 800-447-8537
Harbour House Bar Crafting
Stamford, CT. 800-755-1227
Harco Enterprises
Peterborough, ON. 800-361-5361
Hardwood Products Company
Guilford, ME. 800-289-3340
Hines III
Jacksonville, FL 904-398-5110
Hoshizaki America
Peachtree City, GA 800-438-6087
Ideas Etc
Louisville, KY 800-733-0337
ILC Dover
Frederica, DE 800-631-9567
IMI Cornelius
Schaumburg, IL. 800-323-4789
Infra Corporation
Waterford, MI 888-434-6372
J.H. Carr & Sons
Seattle, WA 800-523-8842
Jarden Home Brands
Daleville, IN 800-392-2575
Jarlan Manufacturing Company
Los Angeles, CA. 323-752-1211
Johnstown Manufacturing
Columbus, OH 614-236-8853
K&I Creative Plastics
Jacksonville, FL 904-387-0438
K-Way Products
Mount Carroll, IL 800-622-9163
Karma
Watertown, WI 800-558-9565
Kings River Casting
Sanger, CA 888-545-5157
Krowne Metal Corporation
Wayne, NJ. 800-631-0442
La Crosse
Onalaska, WI. 800-345-0018
Lakeside Manufacturing
Milwaukee, WI 888-558-8574
Lask Seating Company
Chicago, IL 888-573-2846
Lauritzen & Makin
Fort Worth, TX 817-921-0218
Lavi Industries
Valencia, CA 800-624-6225
Lawrence Metal Products
Bay Shore, NY 800-441-0019
Leggett & Platt StorageP
Vernon Hills, IL 847-816-6246
Les Industries Touch Inc
Sherbrooke, QC 800-267-4140
Loewenstein
Liberty, NC 800-327-2548
Long Range Systems
Addison, TX 800-577-8101
Magnuson Industries
Rockford, IL 800-435-2816
Majestic
Bridgeport, CT 203-367-7900
Manitowoc Foodservice
Sellersburg, IN 800-367-4233
Marcal Paper Mills
Elmwood Park, NJ 800-631-8451
Mars Systems
Dallas, TX. 214-634-7441
Meraz & Associates
Chico, CA 888-244-4463
Metal Master
Tucson, AZ 800-488-8729
Metal Masters Food Service Equipment Company
Clayton, DE. 800-441-8440
Milvan Food Equipment Manufacturing
Rexdale, ON 416-674-3456
MTS Seating
Temperance, MI 734-847-3875
N. Wasserstrom & Sons
Columbus, OH 800-999-9277
National Bar Systems
Huntington Beach, CA 714-848-1688
National Plastic Companyof California
Santa Fe Springs, CA 800-221-9149
Omicron Steel Products Company
Jamaica, NY 718-805-3400
OWD
Tupper Lake, NY 800-836-1693
Palmland Paper Company
Fort Lauderdale, FL 800-266-9067
Parisi/Royal Store Fixture
Newtown, PA 215-968-6677
Pelican Products Company
Bronx, NY. 800-552-8820
Penley Corporation
West Paris, ME 800-368-6449
Perfection Equipment
Gurnee, IL. 800-356-6301
Perlick Corporation
Milwaukee, WI 800-558-5592
Peter Gray Corporation
Andover, MA 978-470-0990
Placemat Printers
Fogelsville, PA 800-628-7746
Polar Hospitality Products
Philadelphia, PA 800-831-7823
Polar Ware Company
Sheboygan, WI 800-237-3655
Precision Pours
Plymouth, MN. 800-549-4491
Prince Seating
Brooklyn, NY 800-577-4623
ProBar Systems Inc.
Barrie, ON. 800-521-7294
Redi-Call, Incorporated
Reno, NV 800-648-1849

Regal Manufacturing Company
Chicago, IL 773-921-3071
Richardson Seating Corporation
Chicago, IL 800-522-1883
Rodo Industries
London, ON 519-668-3711
Royal Oak Enterprises
Roswell, GA 770-393-1430
Royal Paper Products
Coatesville, PA 800-666-6655
Rubbermaid Commercial Products
Winchester, VA 800-336-9880
S&R Products/Mr. Party
Bronson, MI 800-328-3887
Salem China Company
Salem, OH. 330-337-8771
San Jamar
Elkhorn, WI. 800-248-9826
SaniServ
Mooresville, IN 800-733-8073
Scheb International
North Barrington, IL 847-381-2573
Scotsman Ice Systems
Vernon Hills, IL 800-726-8762
Semco Plastic Company
Saint Louis, MO 314-487-4557
Sentry/Bevcon North America
Adelanto, CA 800-661-3003
Servco Co.
St Louis, MO. 314-781-3189
Server Products
Richfield, WI 800-558-8722
Sipco Products
Peoria Heights, IL 309-682-5400
Smith-Lee Company
Oshkosh, WI 800-327-9774
Smoke Right
Chicago, IL 888-375-8885
Sneezeguard Solutions
Columbia, MO 800-569-2056
Sonoco
Pottstown, PA 800-377-2692
Soodhalter Plastics
Los Angeles, CA 213-747-0231
Spir-It/Zoo Piks
Andover, MA 800-343-0996
Spirit Foodservice, Inc.
Andover, MA 800-343-0996
Springprint Medallion
Augusta, GA 800-543-5990
Stainless International
Rancho Cordova, CA 888-300-6196
Strong Group
Gloucester, MA 800-332-6025
Summit Appliance Division
Bronx, NY 800-932-4267
Summit Commercial
Bronx, NY 800-932-4267
Superior Quality Products
Schenectady, NY 800-724-1129
Supreme Metal
Alpharetta, GA 800-645-2526
Token Factory
La Crosse, WI 888-486-5367
Tops Manufacturing Company
Darien, CT. 203-655-9367
Toronto Fabricating & Manufacturing
Mississauga, ON 905-891-2516
Trevor Industries
Eden, NY. 716-992-4775
True Food Service Equipment, Inc.
O Fallon, MO 800-325-6152
U.B. Klem Furniture Company
Saint Anthony, IN 800-264-1995
United Showcase Company
Wood Ridge, NJ 800-526-6382
Ursini Plastics
Bracebridge, ON 705-646-2701
Valley Fixtures
Sparks, NV 775-331-1050
Vintage
Jasper, IN 800-992-3491
Vitro Seating Products
Saint Louis, MO 800-325-7093
Vynatex
Port Washington, NY 516-944-6130
Waddington North America
Chelmsford, MA 888-962-2877
Wag Industries
Skokie, IL 800-621-3305
Wallace & Hinz
Blue Lake, CA 800-831-8282
Walsh & Simmons Seating
Saint Louis, MO 800-727-0364
Weavewood, Inc.
Golden Valley, MN 800-367-6460
West Metals
London, ON 800-300-6667
Wizard Art Glass
Chatsworth, CA 800-438-9565
Wood & Laminates
Lodi, NJ. 973-773-7475
Wylie Systems
Mississauga, ON 800-525-6609
Yorkraft
York, PA 800-872-2044
Z 2000 The Pick of the Millenium
Bartlesville, OK 800-654-7311
Zol-Mark Industries
Winnipeg, NB 204-943-7393

Baskets

Shopping

American Houver Company
Skokie, IL 800-772-0355
American Store Fixtures
Skokie, IL
Clamp Swing Pricing Company
Oakland, CA 800-227-7615
Day Basket Factory
North East, MD. 410-287-8100
Pentwater Wire Products
Pentwater, MI 877-869-6911
Peterboro Basket Company
Peterborough, NH 603-924-3861
Southern Imperial
Rockford, IL 800-747-4665

Cake Turners

American Housewares Manufacturing Corporation
Bronx, NY. 718-665-9500
Dexter-Russell
Southbridge, MA 508-765-0201

Candles

AMCO Corporation
City of Industry, CA 626-855-2550
Culinart
Cincinnati, OH 800-333-5678
Diamond Brands
Cloquet, MN 218-879-6700
Empire Candle
Kansas City, KS 800-231-9398
General Wax & Candle Company
North Hollywood, CA 800-929-7867
Hollowick
Manlius, NY 800-367-3015
Mason Candlelight Company
New Albany, MS. 800-556-2766
Neo-Image Candle Light
Mississauga, ON 800-375-8023
Spin-Tech Corporation
Hoboken, NJ 800-977-4692
Sterno
Lombard, IL 630-792-0080
Will & Baumer
Syracuse, NY 315-451-1000
Xtreme Beverages, LLC
Dana Point, CA. 949-495-7929

Carts

Banquet

AMCO Corporation
City of Industry, CA 626-855-2550
BMH Equipment
Sacramento, CA 800-350-8828
Carter-Hoffman Corp LLC
Mundelein, IL. 800-323-9793
Duke Manufacturing Company
Saint Louis, MO 800-735-3853
EPCO
Murfreesboro, TN 800-251-3398
Forbes Industries
Ontario, CA. 909-923-4559
Hot Food Boxes
Mooresville, IN. 800-733-8073
Lakeside Manufacturing
Milwaukee, WI 888-558-8574
Leggett & Platt StorageP
Vernon Hills, IL 847-816-6246
Shammi Industries/Sammons Equipment
Corona, CA 800-417-9260
Superior Products Company
Saint Paul, MN 800-328-9800
Wilder Manufacturing Company
Port Jervis, NY 800-832-1319

Beverage

ARC Specialties
Valencia, CA. 661-775-8500
BMH Equipment
Sacramento, CA 800-350-8828
Cannon Equipment Company
Rosemount, MN 800-825-8501
Carlisle Food Service Products
Oklahoma City, OK 800-654-8210
Carriage Works
Klamath Falls, OR 541-882-0700
Custom Sales & Service Inc.
Hammonton, NJ 800-257-7855
Duke Manufacturing Company
Saint Louis, MO 800-735-3853
Espresso Carts and Supplies
Lindenwold, NJ 800-972-CART
Hot Food Boxes
Mooresville, IN. 800-733-8073
Lakeside Manufacturing
Milwaukee, WI 888-558-8574
Meraz & Associates
Chico, CA 888-244-4463
Midwest Aircraft Products Company
Mansfield, OH 419-522-2231
Prestige Metal Products
Antioch, IL 847-395-0775
Superior Products Company
Saint Paul, MN 800-328-9800

Bussing

AMCO Corporation
City of Industry, CA 626-855-2550
BMH Equipment
Sacramento, CA 800-350-8828
Forbes Industries
Ontario, CA. 909-923-4559
Lakeside Manufacturing
Milwaukee, WI 888-558-8574
Leggett & Platt StorageP
Vernon Hills, IL 847-816-6246
Paxton Corporation
Bristol, RI
Shammi Industries/Sammons Equipment
Corona, CA 800-417-9260
Sneezeguard Solutions
Columbia, MO 800-569-2056
Superior Products Company
Saint Paul, MN 800-328-9800

Condiment

BMH Equipment
Sacramento, CA 800-350-8828
Lakeside Manufacturing
Milwaukee, WI 888-558-8574
Meraz & Associates
Chico, CA 888-244-4463

Dessert, Pastry

ARC Specialties
Valencia, CA. 661-775-8500
BMH Equipment
Sacramento, CA 800-350-8828
Lakeside Manufacturing
Milwaukee, WI 888-558-8574
Meraz & Associates
Chico, CA 888-244-4463
Merchandising Frontiers
Winterset, IA. 800-421-2278
Superior Products Company
Saint Paul, MN 800-328-9800

Ice

BMH Equipment
Sacramento, CA 800-350-8828
Cannon Equipment Company
Rosemount, MN 800-825-8501
Kloppenberg & Company
Englewood, CO. 800-346-3246

Lakeside Manufacturing
Milwaukee, WI 888-558-8574
Tooterville Trolley Company
Newburgh, IN 812-858-8585

Liquor, Wine

AMCO Corporation
City of Industry, CA 626-855-2550
BMH Equipment
Sacramento, CA 800-350-8828
Cannon Equipment Company
Rosemount, MN 800-825-8501
La Crosse
Onalaska, WI. 800-345-0018
Lakeside Manufacturing
Milwaukee, WI 888-558-8574
Leggett & Platt StorageP
Vernon Hills, IL 847-816-6246

Mobile Food Vending

800Buy Cart
Jamaica, NY 800-289-2278
All A Cart Manufacturing
Columbus, OH 800-695-2278
All Star Carts & Vehicles
Bay Shore, NY 800-831-3166
All State Fabricators Corporation
Florida, RI. 800-322-9925
Alliance Products, LLC
Murfreesboro, TN. 800-522-3973
Alto-Shaam
Menomonee Falls, WI. 800-558-8744
AMCO Corporation
City of Industry, CA 626-855-2550
AMI
Richmond, CA 800-942-7466
ARC Specialties
Valencia, CA. 661-775-8500
Automated Food Systems
Waxahachie, TX 972-298-5719
Barrette - Outdoor Livin
Middleburg Hts., OH 800-336-2383
BBQ Pits by Klose
Houston, TX 800-487-7487
Boyd Coffee Company
Portland, OR 800-545-4077
BR Machine Company
Wedron, IL 800-310-7057
Burgess Enterprises, Inc
Renton, WA. 800-927-3286
C. Nelson Manufacturing Company
Oak Harbor, OH 800-922-7339
Caddy Corporation of America
Bridgeport, NJ. 856-467-4222
Carlin Manufacturing
Fresno, CA 888-212-0801
Carlisle Food Service Products
Oklahoma City, OK 800-654-8210
Carriage Works
Klamath Falls, OR 541-882-0700
Carts of Colorado
Greenwood Vlg, CO. 800-227-8634
Continental Cart by Kullman Industries
Lebanon, NJ 888-882-2278
Corsair Display Systems
Canandalgua, NY 800-347-5245
Creative Mobile Systems
Manchester, CT. 800-646-8364
Custom Diamond International
Laval, QC 800-326-5926
Custom Sales & Service Inc.
Hammonton, NJ 800-257-7855
Delfield Company
Mt Pleasant, MI. 800-733-8821
Dometic Mini Bar
Elkhart, IN. 800-301-8118
Duke Manufacturing Company
Saint Louis, MO 800-735-3853
Embee Sunshade Company
Brooklyn, NY 718-387-8566
EPCO
Murfreesboro, TN. 800-251-3398
Eskay Metal Fabricating Company
Buffalo, NY. 800-836-8015
Ex-Cell Kaiser
Franklin Park, IL. 847-451-0451
FETCO - Food Equipment Technologies Corporation
Lake Zurich, IL. 800-338-2699
G.S. Blodgett Corporation
Burlington, VT 800-331-5842
Gensaco Marketing
New York, NY 800-506-1935
Global Carts and Equipment
Jackson, NJ 800-653-0881
Gold Medal Products Company
Cincinnati, OH 800-543-0862
Hot Food Boxes
Mooresville, IN. 800-733-8073
Hot Shot Delivery Systems
Bloomingdale, IL 630-924-8817
International Thermal Dispensers
Boston, MA. 617-239-3600
King Arthur
Statesville, NC 800-257-7244
Lakeside Manufacturing
Milwaukee, WI 888-558-8574
Lakeside-Aris Manufacturing
Milwaukee, WI 800-558-8565
Leggett & Platt StorageP
Vernon Hills, IL 847-816-6246
Lil' Orbits
Minneapolis, MN 800-228-8305
Magnum Custom Trailer & BBQ Pits
Austin, TX. 800-662-4686
Merchandising Frontiers
Winterset, IA. 800-421-2278
Metal Master
Tucson, AZ 800-488-8729
Metro Corporation
Wilkes Barre, PA. 800-433-2233
METRO Material Handling & Storage Products
Wilkes Barre, PA. 800-433-2232
Michaelo Espresso
Seattle, WA 800-545-2883
Midwest Aircraft Products Company
Mansfield, OH 419-522-2231
National FABCO Manufacturing
St Louis, MO. 314-842-4571
New Age Industrial Corporation
Norton, KS 800-255-0104
Palmer Snyder
Brookfield, WI 800-762-0415
Paragon International
Nevada, IA 800-433-0333
Plastocon
Oconomowoc, WI. 800-966-0103
Polyfoam Packers Corporation
Arlington Hts, IL 800-323-7442
Precision
Miami, FL. 800-762-7565
Prestige Metal Products
Antioch, IL 847-395-0775
Proluxe
Paramount, CA 800-594-5528
Quantum Storage Systems
Miami, FL. 800-685-4665
SICO America
Minneapolis, MN 800-328-6138
Sopralco
Plantation, FL 954-584-2225
Sould Manufacturing
Winnepeg, NB. 204-339-3499
Southern Express
Saint Louis, MO 800-444-9157
SPG International LLC
Covington, GA 877-503-4774
Star Manufacturing International
Saint Louis, MO 800-264-7827
Steamway Corporation
Scottsburg, IN. 800-259-8171
Super Sturdy
Weldon, NC. 800-253-4833
Super-Chef Manufacturing Company
Houston, TX 800-231-3478
Supreme Products
Waco, TX 254-799-4941
Technibilt/Cari-All
Newton, NC 800-233-3972
Tooterville Trolley Company
Newburgh, IN 812-858-8585
USECO
Murfreesboro, TN. 615-893-4820
Vollrath Company
Sheboygan, WI 920-457-4851
Wag Industries
Skokie, IL 800-621-3305
Wittco Foodservice Equipment, Inc.
Milwaukee, WI. 800-821-3912
WR Key
Scarborough, ON 416-291-6246
Yorkraft
York, PA 800-872-2044

Salad

BMH Equipment
Sacramento, CA 800-350-8828
Lakeside Manufacturing
Milwaukee, WI. 888-558-8574
Steamway Corporation
Scottsburg, IN. 800-259-8171
Tooterville Trolley Company
Newburgh, IN 812-858-8585

Service

AMCO Corporation
City of Industry, CA 626-855-2550
ARC Specialties
Valencia, CA. 661-775-8500
BMH Equipment
Sacramento, CA 800-350-8828
Cannon Equipment Company
Rosemount, MN 800-825-8501
Duke Manufacturing Company
Saint Louis, MO 800-735-3853
G.S. Blodgett Corporation
Burlington, VT 800-331-5842
Gillis Associated Industries
Prospect Heights, IL. 847-541-6500
Glowmaster Corporation
Clifton, NJ. 800-272-7008
Hot Food Boxes
Mooresville, IN. 800-733-8073
Infanti International
Staten Island, NY 800-874-8590
King Arthur
Statesville, NC 800-257-7244
Lakeside Manufacturing
Milwaukee, WI 888-558-8574
Leggett & Platt StorageP
Vernon Hills, IL 847-816-6246
Marlen
Riverside, MO. 913-888-3333
Meraz & Associates
Chico, CA 888-244-4463
Moli-International
Denver, CO 800-525-8468
Paxton Corporation
Bristol, RI
Princeton Shelving
Cedar Rapids, IA. 319-369-0355
Rewdco & Hanson Brass Products
Sun Valley, CA 888-841-3773
Shammi Industries/Sammons Equipment
Corona, CA. 800-417-9260
SICO America
Minneapolis, MN 800-328-6138
Superior Products Company
Saint Paul, MN 800-328-9800
Tri-Boro Shelving & Partition
Farmville, VA 434-315-5600
USECO
Murfreesboro, TN. 615-893-4820

Shopping

Assembled Products
Rogers, AR 800-548-3373
Seymour Housewares
Seymour, IN 800-457-9881
Technibilt/Cari-All
Newton, NC 800-233-3972
Unarco Industries
Wagoner, OK. 800-654-4100

Tray, Silverware

Alliance Products, LLC
Murfreesboro, TN. 800-522-3973
Duke Manufacturing Company
Saint Louis, MO 800-735-3853
EPCO
Murfreesboro, TN. 800-251-3398
Hot Food Boxes
Mooresville, IN. 800-733-8073
Lakeside Manufacturing
Milwaukee, WI. 888-558-8574
National Cart Company
Saint Charles, MO 636-947-3800
Paramount Packaging Corp.
Melville, NY. 516-333-8100
Traycon
Carlstadt, NJ 201-939-5555
Wilder Manufacturing Company
Port Jervis, NY 800-832-1319

Cases

Display

Accent Store Fixtures
Kenosha, WI 800-545-1144
Acme Display Fixture Company
Los Angeles, CA 800-959-5657
ALCO Designs
Gardena, CA 800-228-2346
All State Fabricators Corporation
Florida, RI 800-322-9925
Allstate Manufacturing Company
Manchester, OH 800-262-2340
Alto-Shaam
Menomonee Falls, WI 800-558-8744
Arctica Showcase Company
Calgary, AB 800-839-5536
Arizona Store Equipment
Phoenix, AZ 800-624-8395
Arneg
Lexington, NC 800-276-3487
Bailly Showcase & Fixture Company
Las Vegas, NV 702-947-6885
Barker Company
Keosauqua, IA 319-293-3777
BKI Worldwide
Simpsonville, SC 800-927-6887
Brass Smith
Denver, CO 800-662-9595
C&H Store Equipment Company
Los Angeles, CA 800-648-4979
Carman And Company
Burlington, MA 781-221-3500
Caselites
Hialeah, FL 305-819-7766
Claridge Products & Equipment
Harrison, AR
Coldstream Products Corporation
Crossfield, AB 888-946-4097
Corsair Display Systems
Canandalgua, NY 800-347-5245
Craig Manufacturing
Irvington, NJ 800-631-7936
Crispy Lite
St. Louis, MO 888-356-5362
Crown Metal Manufacturing Company
Elmhurst, IL 630-279-9800
Cruvinet Winebar Company
Reno, NV 800-278-8463
CSC Worldwide
Columbus, OH 800-848-3573
Delfield Company
Mt Pleasant, MI 800-733-8821
Display Creations
Brooklyn, NY 718-257-2300
Dunhill Food Equipment Corporation
Armonk, NY 800-847-4206
Dunn Woodworks
Shrewsbury, PA 877-835-8592
Empire Bakery Equipment
Hicksville, NY 800-878-4070
Esquire Mechanical Corp.
Armonk, NY 800-847-4206
Federal Industries
Belleville, WI 800-356-4206
Fogel Jordon Commercial Refrigeration Company
Philadelphia, PA 800-523-0171
Forbes Industries
Ontario, CA 909-923-4559
Greene Industries
East Greenwich, RI 401-884-7530
Handy Store Fixtures
Newark, NJ 800-631-4280
Hardt Equipment Manufacturing
Lachine, QC 888-848-4408
Hercules Food Equipment
Weston, ON 416-742-9673
Hoshizaki America
Peachtree City, GA 800-438-6087
Interstate Showcase & Fixture Company
West Orange, NJ 973-483-5555
Jordan Specialty Company
Brooklyn, NY 877-567-3265
Kedco Wine Storage Systems
Farmingdale, NY 800-654-9988
Langer Manufacturing Company
Cedar Rapids, IA 800-728-6445
Leggett and Platt, Inc.
Carthage, MO 417-358-8131
Lynn Sign
Andover, MA 800-225-5764
Madix
Goodwater, AL 256-839-6354
Mayworth Showcase Works
Tampa, FL 813-251-1558
McCall Refrigeration
Parsons, TN 888-732-2446
Merco/Savory
Mt. Pleasant, MI 800-733-8821
Mercury Equipment Company
Chino, CA 800-273-6688
Merix Chemical Company
Chicago, IL 312-573-1400
Modar
Benton Harbor, MI 800-253-6186
Modern Store Fixtures Company
Dallas, TX 800-634-7777
Moli-International
Denver, CO 800-525-8468
MultiFab Plastics
Boston, MA 888-293-5754
N. Wasserstrom & Sons
Columbus, OH 800-999-9277
Nor-Lake
Salem, NH 603-893-9701
Northwestern
Van Nuys, CA 818-786-1581
Omega Industries
St Louis, MO 314-961-1668
Omnitemp Refrigeration
Downey, CA 800-423-9660
OSF
Toronto, ON 800-465-4000
Palmer Distributors
St Clair Shores, MI 800-444-1912
Parisi/Royal Store Fixture
Newtown, PA 215-968-6677
Plastic Supply Incorporated
Manchester, NH 800-752-7759
Poblocki
Milwaukee, WI 414-453-4010
Premier Brass
Atlanta, GA 800-251-5800
Process Displays
New Berlin, WI 800-533-1764
QBD Modular Systems
Santa Clara, CA 800-663-3005
Rathe Productions
New York, NY 212-242-9000
Refcon
Norwood, NJ 201-750-5060
Refrigeration Engineering
Grand Rapids, MI 800-968-3227
Regal Custom Fixture Company
Westampton, NJ 800-525-3092
Retail Decor
Ironton, OH 800-726-3402
Robelan Displays
Hempstead, NY 865-564-8600
RW Products
Edgewood, NY 800-345-1022
Sani-Top Products
De Leon Springs, FL 800-874-6094
Seattle Plastics
Seattle, WA 800-441-0679
Silver King
Minneapolis, MN 800-328-3329
Sitka Store Fixtures
Kansas City, MO 800-821-7558
Southern Store Fixtures
Bessemer, AL 800-552-6283
Spartan Showcase
Union, MO 800-325-0775
Standex International Corporation
Salem, NH 603-893-9701
Taymar Industries
Palm Desert, CA 800-624-1972
Top Source Industries
Addison, IL 800-362-9625
True Food Service Equipment, Inc.
O Fallon, MO 800-325-6152
Tyler Refrigeration Corporation
Niles, MI 800-992-3744
United Showcase Company
Wood Ridge, NJ 800-526-6382
Universal Folding Box
East Orange, NJ 973-482-4300
West Metals
London, ON 800-300-6667
William Hecht
Philadelphia, PA 215-925-6223

Cash Registers

Data Visible Corporation
Charlottesville, VA 800-368-3494
Geac Computers
Nashua, NH 603-889-5152
Indiana Cash Drawer Company
Shelbyville, IN 800-227-4379
Kelmin Products
Plymouth, FL 407-886-6079
Omron Systems
Schaumburg, IL 847-519-9465
ParTech
New Hartford, NY 800-448-6505
Superior Products Company
Saint Paul, MN 800-328-9800
TEC America
Atlanta, GA 770-453-0868

Chafers

Apex Fountain Sales
Philadelphia, PA 800-523-4586
ARC Specialties
Valencia, CA 661-775-8500
Bon Chef
Lafayette, NJ 800-331-0177
Browne & Company
Markham, ON 905-475-6104
Candle Lamp Company
Riverside, CA 877-526-7748
Crestware
North Salt Lake City, UT 800-345-0513
Dura-Ware Company of America
Oklahoma City, OK 800-664-3872
Dynynstyl
Delray Beach, FL 800-774-7895
Eastern Silver Tabletop Manufacturing Company
Brooklyn, NY 888-422-4142
Glowmaster Corporation
Clifton, NJ 800-272-7008
Kelmin Products
Plymouth, FL 407-886-6079
King Arthur
Statesville, NC 800-257-7244
Mack-Chicago Corporation
Chicago, IL 800-992-6225
Mosshaim Innovations
Jacksonville, FL 888-995-7775
Polar Ware Company
Sheboygan, WI 800-237-3655
Randware Industries
Prospect Heights, IL 847-299-8884
Rexcraft Fine Chafers
Long Island City, NY 888-739-2723
Superior Products Company
Saint Paul, MN 800-328-9800

Chairs

A-1 Booth Manufacturing
Burley, ID 800-820-3285
AMC Industries
Tampa, FL 813-989-9663
Barn Furniture Mart
Van Nuys, CA 888-302-2276
Beaufurn LLC
Advance, NC 888-766-7706
Beka Furniture
Concord, ON 905-669-4255
Bennington Furniture Corporation
Bennington, PA 724-962-2234
Brill Manufacturing Company
Ludington, MI 866-896-6420
Carroll Chair Company
Onalaska, WI 800-331-4707
CCS Stone, Inc.
Moonachie, NJ 800-227-7785
Chaircraft
Hickory, NC 828-326-8458
Classico Seating
Peru, IN 800-968-6655
Commercial Furniture Group
Newport, TN 800-873-3252
Commercial Seating Specialist
Santa Clara, CA 408-453-8983
Cosco
Columbus, IN 812-372-0141
Cramer
Kansas City, MO 800-366-6700
Eagle Products Company
Houston, TX 713-690-1161

Eclectic Contract Furniture Industries
New York, NY 888-311-6272
Elite Trading Worldwide
Brooklyn, NY 888-354-8388
Fab-X/Metals
Washington, NC 800-677-3229
FDL/Flair Designs
Kokomo, IN 765-452-6000
Fiskars Brands Inc.
Baldwinsville, NY 315-635-9911
Fixtur-World
Cookeville, TN 800-634-9887
Fixtures Furniture
Florence, AL 855-321-4999
Fred Beesley's Booth & Upholstery
Centerville, UT 801-364-8189
Furniture Lab
Carrboro, NC 800-449-8677
Gar Products
Lakewood, NJ 800-424-2477
Gasser Chair Company
Youngstown, OH 800-323-2234
Gaychrome Division of CSL
Crystal Lake, IL 800-873-4370
Hines III
Jacksonville, FL 904-398-5110
Imperial
Carlstadt, NJ 800-526-6261
Infanti International
Staten Island, NY 800-874-8590
International Patterns, Inc.
Bay Shore, NY 631-952-2000
J.A. Thurston Company
Rumford, ME 207-364-7921
J.H. Carr & Sons
Seattle, WA 800-523-8842
John Boos & Company
Effingham, IL 217-347-7701
KC Booth Company
Kansas City, MO 800-866-5226
Ken Coat
Bardstown, KY 888-536-2628
Kings River Casting
Sanger, CA 888-545-5157
Krueger International
Green Bay, WI 800-424-2432
Lask Seating Company
Chicago, IL 888-573-2846
Lauritzen & Makin
Fort Worth, TX 817-921-0218
LB Furniture Industries
Hudson, NY 800-221-8752
Line-Master Products
Cocolalla, ID 208-265-4743
Loewenstein
Liberty, NC 800-327-2548
Marston Manufacturing
Cleveland, OH 216-587-3400
Merric
Bridgeton, MO 314-770-9944
Miami Metal
Miami, FL 305-576-3600
Mity-Lite
Orem, UT 800-909-8034
MLP Seating
Elk Grove Vlg, IL 800-723-3030
MTS Seating
Temperance, MI 734-847-3875
Old Dominion Wood Products
Lynchburg, VA 800-245-6382
Omicron Steel Products Company
Jamaica, NY 718-805-3400
Palmer Snyder
Brookfield, WI 800-762-0415
Pinnacle Furnishing
Aberdeen, NC 866-229-5704
Plymold
Kenyon, MN 800-759-6653
Prince Castle
Carol Stream, IL 800-722-7853
Prince Seating
Brooklyn, NY 800-577-4623
Quality Highchairs
Pacoima, CA 800-969-9635
Quality Seating Company
Youngstown, OH 800-765-7096
Regal Manufacturing Company
Chicago, IL 773-921-3071
Richardson Seating Corporation
Chicago, IL 800-522-1883
Robertson Furniture Company
Toccoa, GA 800-241-0713
Rodo Industries
London, ON 519-668-3711
Rollhaus Seating Products
New York, NY 800-822-6684
Rosenwach Tank Company
Long Island City, NY 718-729-4900
Sandler Seating
Atlanta, GA 404-982-9000
Sauvagnat Inc
Huntersville, NC 800-258-5619
Seating Concepts
Rockdale, IL 800-421-2036
Shafer Commercial Seating
Denver, CO 303-322-7792
Shelby Williams Industries
Newport, TN 800-873-3252
Sims Superior Seating
Locust Grove, GA 800-729-9178
Superior Products Company
Saint Paul, MN 800-328-9800
Thorpe & Associates
Siler City, NC 919-742-5516
Toronto Fabricating & Manufacturing
Mississauga, ON 905-891-2516
Trojan Commercial Furni ture Inc.
Montereal, QC 877-271-3878
U.B. Klem Furniture Company
Saint Anthony, IN 800-264-1995
US Seating Products
Apopka, FL 407-884-4411
Vintage
Jasper, IN 800-992-3491
Vitro Seating Products
Saint Louis, MO 800-325-7093
Walsh & Simmons Seating
Saint Louis, MO 800-727-0364
Waymar Industries
Burnsville, MN 888-474-1112
Wheel Tough Company
Terre Haute, IN 888-765-8833
Woodard
Coppell, TX 800-877-2290
World Wide Hospitality Furniture
Paramount, CA 800-728-8262
Xiaoping Design
New York, NY 800-891-9896
Zol-Mark Industries
Winnipeg, NB 204-943-7393

Changers

Currency

Advantus Corp.
Jacksonville, FL 904-482-0091
Automated Business Products
Hackensack, NJ 800-334-1440
G&D America
Sterling, VA 800-856-7712
Hamilton Manufacturing Corporation
Holland, OH 419-867-4858
Rowe International
Grand Rapids, MI 616-246-0483

China

Abco International
Melville, NY 866-240-2226
Americana Art China Company
Sebring, OH 800-233-6133
Asian Foods
St. Paul, MN 800-274-2655
Babco International, Inc
Tucson, AZ 520-628-7596
Bel-Terr China
Warren, OH 800-900-2371
Benner China & Glassware of Florida
Jacksonville, FL 904-733-4620
Brooklyn Boys
Boca Raton, FL 561-477-3663
Buffalo China
Buffalo, NY 716-824-8515
China Lenox Incorporated
Bristol, PA 267-525-7800
Crestware
North Salt Lake City, UT 800-345-0513
Dansk International Designs
White Plains, NY 914-697-6400
Delco Tableware
Port Washington, NY 800-221-9557
Dynynstyl
Delray Beach, FL 800-774-7895
H.F. Coors China Company
New Albany, MS 800-782-6677
Hall China Company
East Liverpool, OH 800-445-4255
Hartstone
Zanesville, OH 740-452-9999
Homer Laughlin China Company
Newell, WV 800-452-4462
Izabel Lam International
Brooklyn, NY 718-797-3983
Lenox
Bristol, PA 800-223-4311
Libby Canada
Mississauga, ON 905-607-8280
Michael Leson Dinnerware
Youngstown, OH 800-821-3541
Mikasa Hotelware
Secaucus, NJ 866-645-2721
Minners Designs Inc.
New York, NY 212-688-7441
Oneida Canada, Limited
Oneida, NY 888-263-7195
Oneida Food Service
Oneida, NY 315-361-3000
Pickard
Antioch, IL 847-395-3800
Prolon
Port Gibson, MS 888-480-9828
Rego China Corporation
Melville, NY 800-221-1707
Rexcraft Fine Chafers
Long Island City, NY 888-739-2723
Royal Prestige Health Moguls
Westbury, NY 888-802-7433
Salem China Company
Salem, OH 330-337-8771
Sterling China Company
Wellsville, OH 800-682-7628
Superior Products Company
Saint Paul, MN 800-328-9800
Syracuse China Company
Syracuse, NY 800-448-5711
Town Food Service Equipment Company
Brooklyn, NY 800-221-5032
Tradeco International
Addison, IL 800-628-3738
Vertex China
Walnut, CA 800-483-7839
Victoria Porcelain
Miami, FL 888-593-2353
Wedgwood USA
Wall Township, NJ 800-999-9936
Xtreme Beverages, LLC
Dana Point, CA 949-495-7929

Clear & Colored Plastic

Chips

Hopp Companies
New Hyde Park, NY 800-889-8425

Indoor Sign Holders

Hopp Companies
New Hyde Park, NY 800-889-8425

Clear Plastic

Shelf Strips

Hopp Companies
New Hyde Park, NY 800-889-8425

Coasters

Admatch Corporation
New York, NY 800-777-9909
AMCO Corporation
City of Industry, CA 626-855-2550
American Coaster Company
Sanborn, NY 888-423-8628
Atlas Match Company
Toronto, ON 888-285-2783
Best Brands Home Products
New York, NY 212-684-7456
Conimar Corporation
Ocala, FL 800-874-9735
Edco Industries
Bridgeport, CT 203-333-8982
Gessner Products Company
Ambler, PA 800-874-7808

Harco Enterprises
Peterborough, ON.................800-361-5361
IB Concepts
Elizabeth, NJ.....................888-671-0800
Majestic
Bridgeport, CT 203-367-7900
Pelican Products Company
Bronx, NY.........................800-552-8820
Polar Hospitality Products
Philadelphia, PA..................800-831-7823
Royal Paper Products
Coatesville, PA...................800-666-6655
Sonoco
Pottstown, PA.....................800-377-2692
Springprint Medallion
Augusta, GA.......................800-543-5990
Tops Manufacturing Company
Darien, CT........................203-655-9367
Unique Manufacturing
Visalia, CA.......................888-737-1007
Weavewood, Inc.
Golden Valley, MN.................800-367-6460

Coin Machinery

G&D America
Sterling, VA......................800-856-7712
Scan Coin
Ashburn, VA.......................800-336-3311
Wico Corporation
Niles, IL.........................800-367-9426

Colored Plastic

Shelf Strips

Hopp Companies
New Hyde Park, NY.................800-889-8425

Concession Supplies & Equipment

All Star Carts & Vehicles
Bay Shore, NY.....................800-831-3166
Alliance Products, LLC
Murfreesboro, TN..................800-522-3973
Automated Food Systems
Waxahachie, TX....................972-298-5719
Carlin Manufacturing
Fresno, CA........................888-212-0801
Carriage Works
Klamath Falls, OR.................541-882-0700
Century Industries
Sellersburg, IN...................800-248-3371
Creative Mobile Systems
Manchester, CT....................800-646-8364
Delfield Company
Mt Pleasant, MI...................800-733-8821
Fun City Popcorn
Las Vegas, NV.....................800-423-1710
Gold Medal Products Company
Cincinnati, OH....................800-543-0862
Great Western Products Company
Assumption, IL....................217-226-3241
Great Western Products Company
Hollywood, AL.....................256-259-3578
Great Western Products Company
Hollywood, AL.....................800-239-2143
Holstein Manufacturing
Holstein, IA......................800-368-4342
International Thermal Dispensers
Boston, MA........................617-239-3600
Karma
Watertown, WI.....................800-558-9565
Lazy-Man
Belvidere, NJ.....................800-475-1950
Magnum Custom Trailer & BBQ Pits
Austin, TX........................800-662-4686
Marston Manufacturing
Cleveland, OH.....................216-587-3400
New Centennial
Columbus, GA......................800-241-7541
Rio Syrup Company
Saint Louis, MO...................800-325-7666
Server Products
Richfield, WI.....................800-558-8722
Steamway Corporation
Scottsburg, IN....................800-259-8171
Supreme Products
Waco, TX..........................254-799-4941
Texas Corn Roasters
Granbury, TX......................800-772-4345
Thermal Bags by Ingrid
Gilberts, IL......................800-622-5560
Yorkraft
York, PA..........................800-872-2044

Corkscrews

AMCO Corporation
City of Industry, CA..............626-855-2550
C.R. Manufacturing
Waverly, NE.......................877-789-5844
Cove Four Slide & Stamping Corporation
Freeport, NY......................516-379-4232
Pelican Products Company
Bronx, NY.........................800-552-8820
Superior Products Company
Saint Paul, MN....................800-328-9800
Swing-A-Way Manufacturing Company
St Louis, MO......................314-773-1488

Counters

Cafeteria, Restaurant

Accent Store Fixtures
Kenosha, WI.......................800-545-1144
Ace Fabrication
Mobile, AL........................251-478-0401
All State Fabricators Corporation
Florida, RI.......................800-322-9925
Alpine Store Equipment Corporation
Long Island City, NY..............718-361-1213
Atlas Metal Industries
Kenton, HR........................208-907-1374
Baker Sheet Metal Corporation
Norfolk, VA.......................800-909-4325
Barn Furniture Mart
Van Nuys, CA......................888-302-2276
Borroughs Corporation
Kalamazoo, MI.....................800-748-0227
Cara Products Company
Jonesboro, GA.....................770-478-9802
Carman And Company
Burlington, MA....................781-221-3500
Catskill Craftsmen
Stamford, NY......................607-652-7321
Cobb & Zimmer
Detroit, MI.......................313-923-0350
Custom Diamond International
Laval, QC.........................800-326-5926
Delfield Company
Mt Pleasant, MI...................800-733-8821
Designer's Choice Stainless
Peoria, AZ........................800-592-3274
Duke Manufacturing Company
Saint Louis, MO...................800-735-3853
Duluth Sheet Metal
Duluth, MN........................218-722-2613
Dunhill Food Equipment Corporation
Armonk, NY........................800-847-4206
Economy Paper & Restaurant Supply Company
Clifton, NJ.......................973-279-5500
Erwin Food Service Equipment
Fort Worth, TX....................817-535-0021
Eskay Metal Fabricating Company
Buffalo, NY.......................800-836-8015
Fixtur-World
Cookeville, TN....................800-634-9887
Fred Beesley's Booth & Upholstery
Centerville, UT...................801-364-8189
Gervasi Wood Products
Madison, WI.......................608-274-6752
Habco
Concord, CA.......................925-682-6203
Hallock Fabricating Corporation
Riverhead, NY.....................631-727-2441
Hercules Food Equipment
Weston, ON........................416-742-9673
IGS Store Fixtures
Peabody, MA.......................978-532-0010
Inland Showcase & Fixture Company
Fresno, CA........................559-237-4158
Institutional Equipment
Bolingbrook, IL...................630-771-0990
Kitchen Equipment Fabricating Company
Houston, TX.......................713-747-3611
Kitcor Corporation
Sun Valley, CA....................818-767-4800
Lauritzen & Makin
Fort Worth, TX....................817-921-0218
Load King Manufacturing Company
Jacksonville, FL..................800-531-4975
Low Temp Industries
Jonesboro, GA.....................770-478-8803
Marlo Manufacturing Company
Boonton, NJ.......................800-222-0450
MCM Fixture Company
Hazel Park, MI....................248-547-9280
McRoyal Industries
Youngstown, OH....................800-785-2556
Merric
Bridgeton, MO.....................314-770-9944
Metal Kitchen Fabricators
Houston, TX.......................713-683-8375
Metal Master
Tucson, AZ........................800-488-8729
Missouri Equipment Company
St Louis, MO......................800-727-6326
Monroe Kitchen Equipment
Rochester, NY.....................585-235-3310
Mouron & Company
Indianapolis, IN..................317-243-7955
National FABCO Manufacturing
St Louis, MO......................314-842-4571
Omicron Steel Products Company
Jamaica, NY.......................718-805-3400
Paramount Manufacturing Company
Wilmington, MA....................978-657-4300
Parisi/Royal Store Fixture
Newtown, PA.......................215-968-6677
Perfect Plank Company
Oroville, CA......................800-327-1961
Pierce Laminated Products
Rockford, IL......................815-968-9651
PMI Food Equipment Group
Troy, OH..........................937-332-3000
Quipco Products
Sauget, IL........................314-993-1442
Sarasota Restaurant Equipment
Sarasota, FL......................800-434-1410
Seating Concepts
Rockdale, IL......................800-421-2036
Sefi Fabricators
Amityville, NY....................631-842-2200
Shelley Cabinet Company
Shelley, ID.......................208-357-3700
Solid Surface Acrylics
North Tonawanda, NY...............888-595-4114
Southwestern Porcelain Steel
Sand Springs, OK..................918-245-1375
Spartan Showcase
Union, MO.........................800-325-0775
St. Louis Stainless Service
Fenton, MO........................888-507-1578
Stainless Equipment Manufacturing
Dallas, TX........................800-736-2038
Stainless Fabricating Company
Denver, CO........................800-525-8966
Stainless International
Rancho Cordova, CA................888-300-6196
Stainless Steel Fabricators
Tyler, TX.........................903-595-6625
Top Source Industries
Addison, IL.......................800-362-9625
Trojan Commercial Furni ture Inc.
Montereal, QC.....................877-271-3878
United Fabricators
Fort Smith, AR....................800-235-4101
Universal Stainless
Aurora, CO........................800-223-8332
Universal Stainless
Titusville, PA....................800-295-1909
Walsh & Simmons Seating
Saint Louis, MO...................800-727-0364
Weiss Sheet Metal
Avon, MA..........................508-583-8300
West Coast Industries
San Francisco, CA.................800-243-3150
Western Laminates
Omaha, NE.........................402-556-4600

Coin

Automated Business Products
Hackensack, NJ....................800-334-1440
G&D America
Sterling, VA......................800-856-7712
Scan Coin
Ashburn, VA.......................800-336-3311

Decorative Items

Hollowick
Manlius, NY.......................800-367-3015
Irresistible Cookie Jar
Hayden Lake, ID...................208-664-1261

Stanpac, Inc.
Smithville, ON 905-957-3326
Xtreme Beverages, LLC
Dana Point, CA 949-495-7929

Dishes

Paper

Design Specialties
Hamden, CT 800-999-1584
Fonda Group
Oshkosh, WI 800-558-9300
Primary Liquidation Corporation
Bohemia, NY 631-244-1410

Dispensers

Beer

Autobar Systems
Asbury Park, NJ 732-922-3355
Automatic Bar Controls
Vacaville, CA 800-722-6738
Banner Equipment Comp any
Morris, IL 800-621-4625
Beer Magic Devices
Hamilton, ON 905-522-3081
Berg Company
Monona, WI 608-221-4281
Bijur Lubricating Corporation
Morrisville, NC 800-631-0168
Carbonic Machines
Minneapolis, MN 612-824-0745
Carmun International
San Antonio, TX 800-531-7907
Custom Diamond International
Laval, QC 800-363-5926
Easybar Beverage Management Systems
Tualatin, OR 888-294-7405
Flojet
Foothill Ranch, CA 800-235-6538
IMI Cornelius
Schaumburg, IL 800-323-4789
K-Way Products
Mount Carroll, IL 800-622-9163
Multiplex Company, Inc.
Sellersburg, IN 800-787-8880
Perlick Corporation
Milwaukee, WI 800-558-5592
Sentry/Bevcon North America
Adelanto, CA 800-661-3003
Stainless One DispensingSystem
Vacaville, CA 888-723-3827
Summit Appliance Division
Bronx, NY 800-932-4267
Summit Commercial
Bronx, NY 800-932-4267
Superior Products Company
Saint Paul, MN 800-328-9800
True Food Service Equipment, Inc.
O Fallon, MO 800-325-6152

Beverage

Action Technology
Prussia, PA 217-935-8311
AK Steel
West Chester, OH 800-331-5050
American Manufacturing &Engineering Company
Cleveland, OH 800-822-9402
Apex Fountain Sales
Philadelphia, PA 800-523-4586
Autobar Systems
Asbury Park, NJ 732-922-3355
Automatic Bar Controls
Vacaville, CA 800-722-6738
Automatic Products
Williston, SC 800-523-8363
Azbar Plus
Qu,bec, QC 418-687-3672
Banner Equipment Comp any
Morris, IL 800-621-4625
Beer Magic Devices
Hamilton, ON 905-522-3081
Berg Company
Monona, WI 608-221-4281
Bevistar
Oswego, IL 877-238-7827
BG Industries
Lemont, IL 800-800-5761
Bijur Lubricating Corporation
Morrisville, NC 800-631-0168
Booth
Dallas, TX 800-497-2958
C.R. Manufacturing
Waverly, NE 877-789-5844
Carbonic Machines
Minneapolis, MN 612-824-0745
Carlisle Food Service Products
Oklahoma City, OK 800-654-8210
Carmun International
San Antonio, TX 800-531-7907
Carpigiani Corporation of America
Winston Salem, NC 800-648-4389
Chill Rite/Desco
Slidell, LA 800-256-2190
Cleland Sales Corporation
Los Alamitos, CA 562-598-6616
Commercial Refrigeration Service, Inc.
Phoenix, AZ 623-869-8881
Control Beverage
Adelanto, CA 330-549-5376
Cornelius Wilshire Corporation
Schaumburg, IL 847-397-4600
Cr. Manufacturing
Waverly, NE 877-789-5844
Cruvinet Winebar Company
Reno, NV 800-278-8463
Cuno
Meriden, CT 800-243-6894
Custom Diamond International
Laval, QC 800-363-5926
Delfield Company
Mt Pleasant, MI 800-733-8821
Easybar Beverage Management Systems
Tualatin, OR 888-294-7405
Elmeco SRL
Bartlett, TN 901-385-0490
Eurodib
Champlain, NY 888-956-6866
Federal Machines
Des Moines, IA 800-247-2446
FETCO - Food Equipment Technologies Corporation
Lake Zurich, IL 800-338-2699
Flojet
Foothill Ranch, CA 800-235-6538
FMC FoodTech
Lakeland, FL 863-683-5411
Fountainhead
Bensalem, PA 800-326-8998
Grindmaster Corporation
Louisville, KY 800-695-4500
Grindmaster-Cecilware Corporation
Louisville, KY 800-695-4500
Hedwin Corporation
Baltimore, MD 800-638-1012
Hoshizaki America
Peachtree City, GA 800-438-6087
Icee-USA Corporation
Ontario, CA 800-426-4233
Igloo Products
Katy, TX 800-364-5566
IMI Cornelius
Schaumburg, IL 800-323-4789
IMI Cornelius
Osseo, MN 800-838-3600
In-Sink-Erator
Racine, WI 800-558-5700
Juicy Whip
La Verne, CA 909-392-7500
K-Way Products
Mount Carroll, IL 800-622-9163
Karma
Watertown, WI 800-558-9565
Lancaster Colony Corporation
Columbus, OH 800-292-7260
Lancer Corporation
San Antonio, TX 800-729-1565
Leland
South Plainfield, NJ 800-984-9793
Little Squirt
Toronto, ON 416-665-6605
Magnuson Industries
Rockford, IL 800-435-2816
Manitowoc Foodservice
Sellersburg, IN 800-367-4233
Moli-International
Denver, CO 800-525-8468
Mulligan Associates
Mequon, WI 800-627-2886
Multiplex Company, Inc.
Sellersburg, IN 800-787-8880
Norris Dispenser Company
Minneapolis, MN 800-252-5561
Perfection Equipment
Gurnee, IL 800-356-6301
Perlick Corporation
Milwaukee, WI 800-558-5592
Polar Beer Systems
Sun City, CA 951-928-8171
Precision Pours
Plymouth, MN 800-549-4491
Pro-Flo Products
Cedar Grove, NJ 800-325-1057
ProBar Systems Inc.
Barrie, ON 800-521-7294
Procon Products
Murfreesboro, TN 615-890-5710
Prolon
Port Gibson, MS 888-480-9828
Regal Ware
Kewaskum, WI 262-626-2121
Remco Products Company
Zionsville, IN 800-585-8619
Rieke Packaging Systems
Auburn, IN 260-925-3700
Robinson/Kirshbaum Industries
Inglewood, CA 800-929-3812
Rocket Man
Louisville, KY 800-365-6661
S&R Products/Mr. Party
Bronson, MI 800-328-3887
SaniServ
Mooresville, IN 800-733-8073
Scotsman Ice Systems
Vernon Hills, IL 800-726-8762
Sea Breeze Fruit Flavors
Towaco, NJ 800-732-2733
Sentry/Bevcon North America
Adelanto, CA 800-661-3003
SerVend International
Sellersburg, IN 800-367-4233
Server Products
Richfield, WI 800-558-8722
Silver King
Minneapolis, MN 800-328-3329
Sopralco
Plantation, FL 954-584-2225
Spin-Tech Corporation
Hoboken, NJ 800-977-4692
Spinco Metal Products
Newark, NY 315-331-6285
Stainless One DispensingSystem
Vacaville, CA 888-723-3827
Star Manufacturing International
Saint Louis, MO 800-264-7827
Steel Products
Marion, IA 800-333-9451
Summit Appliance Division
Bronx, NY 800-932-4267
Summit Commercial
Bronx, NY 800-932-4267
Sunroc Corporation
Columbus, OH 800-478-6762
Superflex
Brooklyn, NY 800-394-3665
Superior Products Company
Saint Paul, MN 800-328-9800
Tablecraft Products
Gurnee, IL 800-323-8321
Technium
Medford, NJ 609-702-5910
Thermos Company
Schaumburg, IL 800-243-0745
Tops Manufacturing Company
Darien, CT 203-655-9367
True Food Service Equipment, Inc.
O Fallon, MO 800-325-6152
Wells Manufacturing Company
Verdi, NV 800-777-0450
Wilch Manufacturing
Topeka, KS 785-267-2762
Wine Chillers of California
Santa Ana, CA 800-331-4274
Winekeeper
Santa Barbara, CA 805-963-3451

Coffee

American Production Company
Redwood City, CA 650-368-5334
Bevistar
Oswego, IL 877-238-7827

Custom Diamond International
Laval, QC 800-363-5926
FETCO - Food Equipment Technologies Corporation
Lake Zurich, IL 800-338-2699
Grindmaster-Cecilware Corporation
Louisville, KY 800-695-4500
K-Way Products
Mount Carroll, IL 800-622-9163
Karma
Watertown, WI 800-558-9565
Midwest Juice and Syrup Company
Grand Rapids, MI 877-265-8243
Regal Ware
Kewaskum, WI 262-626-2121
Sopralco
Plantation, FL 954-584-2225
Steel Products
Marion, IA 800-333-9451
Superior Products Company
Saint Paul, MN 800-328-9800
Thermos Company
Schaumburg, IL 800-243-0745
Tops Manufacturing Company
Darien, CT 203-655-9367
Wells Manufacturing Company
Verdi, NV 800-777-0450

Cup & Napkin

Atlas Metal Industries
Kenton, HR 208-907-1374
Browne & Company
Markham, ON 905-475-6104
C.R. Manufacturing
Waverly, NE 877-789-5844
Component Hardware Group
Lakewood, NJ 800-526-3694
Custom Diamond International
Laval, QC 800-363-5926
Dispense Rite
Northbrook, IL 800-772-2877
Diversified Metal Products
Northbrook, IL 800-772-2877
Georgia Pacific
Green Bay, WI 920-435-8821
Great Western Products
Ontario, CA 888-598-5588
Igloo Products
Katy, TX 800-364-5566
Levelmatic
Miami, FL 800-762-7565
M-One Specialties Inc
Salt Lake City, UT 800-525-9223
Palmer Fixture Company
Green Bay, WI 800-558-8678
Plastic Fantastics/Buck Signs
Ashland, OR 800-482-1776
Pronto Products Company
Arcadia, CA 800-377-6680
Redi-Call, Incorporated
Reno, NV 800-648-1849
San Jamar
Elkhorn, WI 800-248-9826
Sanitor Manufacturing Company
Portage, MI 800-379-5314
SerVend International
Sellersburg, IN 800-367-4233
Superior Products Company
Saint Paul, MN 800-328-9800
Tomlinson Industries
Cleveland, OH 800-945-4589
Tops Manufacturing Company
Darien, CT 203-655-9367
Traex
Dane, WI 800-356-8006

Food

AC Dispensing Equipment
Lower Sackville, NS 888-777-9990
Action Technology
Prussia, PA 217-935-8311
American Production Company
Redwood City, CA 650-368-5334
Automatic Bar Controls
Vacaville, CA 800-722-6738
Belshaw Adamatic Bakery Group
Auburn, WA 800-578-2547
Bijur Lubricating Corporation
Morrisville, NC 800-631-0168
Calmar
Richmond, VA 804-444-1000
Carlisle Food Service Products
Oklahoma City, OK 800-654-8210
Carpigiani Corporation of America
Winston Salem, NC 800-648-4389
Cornelius Wilshire Corporation
Schaumburg, IL 847-397-4600
Creamery Plastics Products, Ltd
Chilliwack, BC 604-792-0232
Custom Diamond International
Laval, QC 800-363-5926
Design Technology Corporation
Billerica, MA 978-663-7000
Dispense Rite
Northbrook, IL 800-772-2877
Diversified Metal Products
Northbrook, IL 800-772-2877
Drum-Mates Inc.
Lumberton, NJ 800-621-3786
Dunkin Brands Inc.
Canton, MA 800-458-7731
Eurodispenser
Decatur, IL 217-864-4061
Federal Machines
Des Moines, IA 800-247-2446
Great Western Products
Ontario, CA 888-598-5588
Gruenewald ManufacturingCompany
Danvers, MA 800-229-9447
Hoshizaki America
Peachtree City, GA 800-438-6087
Karma
Watertown, WI 800-558-9565
Lakeside Manufacturing
Milwaukee, WI 888-558-8574
LBP Manufacturing
Cicero, IL 708-652-5600
Lincoln Foodservice
Cleveland, OH 800-374-3004
Mid-Southwest Marketing
Edmond, OK 405-341-3962
National Scoop & Equipment Company
Spring House, PA 215-646-2040
Neos
Elk River, MN 888-441-6367
Nuova Distribution Centre
Ferndale, WA 360-366-2226
Opal Manufacturing Ltd
Toronto, ON 416-646-5232
Perfection Equipment
Gurnee, IL 800-356-6301
Plastic Fantastics/Buck Signs
Ashland, OR 800-482-1776
Precision Pours
Plymouth, MN 800-549-4491
Prestige Metal Products
Antioch, IL 847-395-0775
Prince Castle
Carol Stream, IL 800-722-7853
Pro-Flo Products
Cedar Grove, NJ 800-325-1057
Ragtime
Ceres, CA 209-634-8475
Rieke Packaging Systems
Auburn, IN 260-925-3700
San Jamar
Elkhorn, WI 800-248-9826
SaniServ
Mooresville, IN 800-733-8073
Server Products
Richfield, WI 800-558-8722
Silver King
Minneapolis, MN 800-328-3329
Steril-Sil Company
Boston, MA 800-784-5537
Summit Machine Builders Corporation
Denver, CO 800-274-6741
Tablecraft Products
Gurnee, IL 800-323-8321
Texican Specialty Products
Houston, TX 800-869-5918
Thermos Company
Schaumburg, IL 800-243-0745
Tomlinson Industries
Cleveland, OH 800-945-4589
Traex
Dane, WI 800-356-8006
Viking Industries
New Smyma Beach, FL 888-605-5560
Wells Manufacturing Company
Verdi, NV 800-777-0450
Wilch Manufacturing
Topeka, KS 785-267-2762

Glass

Lakeside Manufacturing
Milwaukee, WI 888-558-8574

Ice Cream & Frozen Yogurt

Carpigiani Corporation of America
Winston Salem, NC 800-648-4389
Custom Diamond International
Laval, QC 800-363-5926
Delfield Company
Mt Pleasant, MI 800-733-8821
Dispense Rite
Northbrook, IL 800-772-2877
Diversified Metal Products
Northbrook, IL 800-772-2877
Dunkin Brands Inc.
Canton, MA 800-458-7731
Federal Machines
Des Moines, IA 800-247-2446
Flavor Burst Company
Danville, IN 800-264-3528
Frosty Factory of America
Ruston, LA 800-544-4071
Gruenewald ManufacturingCompany
Danvers, MA 800-229-9447
H.C. Duke & Son
East Moline, IL 309-755-4553
NDS
Columbus, OH 614-294-4931
SaniServ
Mooresville, IN 800-733-8073
Superior Products Company
Saint Paul, MN 800-328-9800
Wilch Manufacturing
Topeka, KS 785-267-2762

Plate & Tray

APW Wyott Food Service Equipment Company
Cheyenne, WY 800-527-2100
Atlas Metal Industries
Kenton, HR 208-907-1374
Custom Diamond International
Laval, QC 800-363-5926
Delfield Company
Mt Pleasant, MI 800-733-8821
Great Western Products
Ontario, CA 888-598-5588
Lakeside Manufacturing
Milwaukee, WI 888-558-8574

Soda Fountain, Syrup & Fruit Juice

Automatic Bar Controls
Vacaville, CA 800-722-6738
Bevistar
Oswego, IL 877-238-7827
Carbonic Machines
Minneapolis, MN 612-824-0745
Commercial Refrigeration Service, Inc.
Phoenix, AZ 623-869-8881
Control Beverage
Adelanto, CA 330-549-5376
Custom Diamond International
Laval, QC 800-363-5926
Easybar Beverage Management Systems
Tualatin, OR 888-294-7405
Eurodispenser
Decatur, IL 217-864-4061
Follett Corporation
Easton, PA 800-523-9361
IMI Cornelius
Schaumburg, IL 800-323-4789
K-Way Products
Mount Carroll, IL 800-622-9163
Karma
Watertown, WI 800-558-9565
Leland
South Plainfield, NJ 800-984-9793
Manitowoc Foodservice
Sellersburg, IN 800-367-4233
Sentry/Bevcon North America
Adelanto, CA 800-661-3003
Server Products
Richfield, WI 800-558-8722

Displays

Food, Artificial

Accent Store Fixtures
Kenosha, WI 800-545-1144
Buffet Enhancements International
Fairhope, AL 251-990-6119
Cal-Mil Plastic Products
Oceanside, CA 800-321-9069
Consolidated Display Company
Oswego, IL 888-851-7669
Despro Manufacturing
Cedar Grove, NJ 800-292-9906
Display Studios Inc.
Kansas City, KS 800-648-8479
Dufeck Manufacturing Company
Denmark, WI. 888-603-9663
Fax Foods
Vista, CA. 760-599-6030
GCJ Mattei Company
Louisville, KY 502-583-4774
Hiclay Studios
St Louis, MO. 314-533-8393
Madix
Goodwater, AL 256-839-6354
Marineland Commercial Aquariums
Blacksburg, VA. 800-322-1266
Merchandising Frontiers
Winterset, IA. 800-421-2278
Rathe Productions
New York, NY 212-242-9000
Schmidt Progressive, LLC
Lebanon, OH. 800-272-3706
Trade Fixtures
Little Rock, AR. 800-872-3490
Vomela/Harbor Graphics
St Paul, MN. 800-645-1012

Frozen Food

Arneg
Lexington, NC 800-276-3487
Coldstream Products Corporation
Crossfield, AB 888-946-4097
Display Studios Inc.
Kansas City, KS 800-648-8479
GA Systems
Huntington Beach, CA 714-848-7529
GCJ Mattei Company
Louisville, KY 502-583-4774
Hercules Food Equipment
Weston, ON. 416-742-9673
Hiclay Studios
St Louis, MO. 314-533-8393
Novelty Baskets
Hurst, TX 817-268-5426
Oscartielle Equipment Company
Burlingame, CA 800-672-2784
Refcon
Norwood, NJ. 201-750-5060
Retail Decor
Ironton, OH. 800-726-3402
Vomela/Harbor Graphics
St Paul, MN. 800-645-1012

Point of Purchase

3M Dynamic Message Systems
Spokane Valley, WA 800-727-9111
ABC Letter Art
Los Angeles, CA. 888-261-5367
Accent Store Fixtures
Kenosha, WI 800-545-1144
ALCO Designs
Gardena, CA 800-228-2346
Alger Creations
Miami, FL. 954-454-3272
Alphabet Signs
Gap, PA 800-582-6366
American LED-gible
Columbus, OH 614-851-1100
AMI
Richmond, CA 800-942-7466
Archer Wire International
Bedford Park, IL. 708-563-1700
Arlington Display Industries
Detroit, MI 313-837-1212
Art Wire Works
Bedford Park, IL. 708-458-3993
Art-Phyl Creations
Hialeah, FL 800-327-8318
Atlas Packaging & Displays Inc
Miami, FL. 800-662-0630
B&B Neon Sign Company
Austin, TX. 800-791-6366
Baltimore Sign Company
Arnold, MD. 410-276-1500
Barrette - Outdoor Livin
Middleburg Hts., OH 800-336-2383
Beemak Plastics
La Mirada, CA 800-421-4393
Better Bilt Products
Addison, OH. 800-544-4550
Bill Carr Signs
Flint, MI 810-232-1569
Blue Ridge Signs
Weatherford, TX 800-659-5645
Boston Retail Products
Medford, MA 800-225-1633
Boxes.com
Livingston, NJ. 201-646-9050
Cannon Equipment Company
Rosemount, MN 800-825-8501
Canton Sign Company
Canton, OH. 330-456-7151
Capitol Hardware, Inc.,
Middlebury, IN 800-327-6083
CCW Products, Inc.
Arvada, CO 303-427-9663
Cellox Corporation
Reedsburg, WI 608-524-2316
Chesapeake Packaging Company
Binghamton, NY. 607-775-1550
Chicago Show
Buffalo Grove, IL 847-955-0200
Chroma Tone
Saint Clair, PA. 800-878-1552
Chrysler Jeep Dodge Ram of Kirkland
Kirkland, WA 877-606-8196
Clearr Corporation
Minneapolis, MN 800-548-3269
Collegeville Flag & Manufacturing Company
Collegeville, PA 800-523-5630
Columbus Container
Columbus, IN 812-376-9301
Comm-Pak
Opelika, AL. 334-749-6201
Commercial Corrugated Corporation
Baltimore, MD 800-242-8861
Connecticut Container Corporation
North Haven, CT. 203-248-2161
Containair Packaging Corporation
Paterson, NJ 888-276-6500
Corfab
Chicago, IL 708-458-8750
Corman & Associates
Lexington, KY 859-233-0544
Corr-Pak Corporation
Mc Cook, IL 708-442-7806
Courtesy Sign Company
Amarillo, TX. 806-373-6609
Creative Enterprises
Kendall Park, NJ. 732-422-0300
Curry Enterprises
Atlanta, GA. 800-241-7308
Curzon Promotional Graphics
Omaha, NE 800-769-7446
Custom I.D.
Venice, FL. 800-242-8430
Custom Packaging
Richmond, VA. 804-232-3299
Daytech Limited
Toronto, ON 877-329-1907
Denver Sign Systems
Denver, CO 888-295-7446
Derse
Milwaukee, WI. 800-562-2300
Designers Plastics
Clearwater, FL 727-573-1643
Despro Manufacturing
Cedar Grove, NJ 800-292-9906
Diamond Packaging
Rochester, NY. 800-333-4079
Dinosaur Plastics
Houston, TX 713-923-2278
Display Concepts
Trenton, ME 800-446-0033
Display Studios Inc.
Kansas City, KS 800-648-8479
Drake Container Corporation
Houston, TX 800-299-5644
Dunn Woodworks
Shrewsbury, PA. 877-835-8592
Eastern Container Corporation
Mansfield, MA 508-337-0400
Eastern Plastics
Pawtucket, RI 800-442-8585
Eaton-Quade Company
Oklahoma City, OK 405-236-4475
EGW Bradbury Enterprises
Bridgewater, ME. 800-332-6021
Einson Freeman
Paramus, NJ 201-226-0300
Embro Manufacturing Company
East Canton, OH 330-489-3500
Emco Industrial Plastics
Cedar Grove, NJ 800-292-9906
Empire Container Corporation
Carson, CA 323-537-8190
Enterprise Products
Bell Gardens, CA 562-928-1918
ERC Parts
Kennesaw, GA 800-241-6880
ERS International
Norwalk, CT 800-377-4685
Esco Manufacturer
Watertown, SD 800-843-3726
Everbrite
Greenfield, WI 800-558-3888
Exhibitron Corporation
Grants Pass, OR 800-437-4571
ExpoDisplays
Birmingham, AL. 800-747-3976
Fasteners for Retail
Cincinnati, OH 800-422-2547
Filet Menu
Los Angeles, CA. 310-202-8000
First Bank of Highland P
Northbrook, IL 847-272-1300
Fitzpatrick Container Company
North Wales, PA 215-699-3515
Five-M Plastics Company
Marion, OH. 740-383-6246
Fleetwood International Paper
Vernon, CA 323-588-7121
Flexpak Corporation
Phoenix, AZ 602-269-7648
Florida Plastics International
Evergreen Park, IL 708-499-0400
FMI Display
Elkins Park, PA. 215-663-1998
Foxfire Marketing Solutions
Newark, DE. 800-497-0512
France Personalized Signs
Cleveland, OH 216-241-2198
Freely Display
Cleveland, OH 216-721-6056
Fresno Neon Sign Company
Fresno, CA 559-292-2944
Fuller Packaging
Central Falls, RI 401-725-4300
GCJ Mattei Company
Louisville, KY 502-583-4774
Gelberg Signs
Washington, DC 800-443-5237
Genesta Manufacturing
Rockwall, TX 972-771-1653
Glolite
Des Plaines, IL 847-803-4500
Gordon Sign Company
Denver, CO 303-629-6121
Green Bay Packaging
Coon Rapids, MN. 800-236-6456
Greif Inc.
Delaware, OH 800-476-1635
Hager Containers
Carrollton, TX. 972-417-7660
Handicap Sign
Grand Rapids, MI 800-690-4888
Hanley Sign Company
Latham, NY. 518-783-6183
Harmar Products
Sarasota, FL 800-833-0478
Harting Graphics
Wilmington, DE 800-848-1373
Hiclay Studios
St Louis, MO. 314-533-8393
HMG Worldwide
Morton Grove, IL. 847-965-7100
HMG Worldwide In-Store Marketing
New York, NY 212-736-2300
Hoarel Sign Company
Amarillo, TX. 806-373-2175
Hunter Packaging Corporation
South Elgin, IL 800-428-4747

IBC/Shell Containers
New Hyde Park, NY 516-352-4505
Icee-USA Corporation
Ontario, CA. 800-426-4233
Illuma Display
Brookfield, WI 800-501-0128
Industrial Nameplates
Ivyland, PA 800-878-6263
Industrial Sign Company
South El Monte, CA 800-596-3720
Innovative Space Management
Woodside, NY. 718-278-4300
International Patterns, Inc.
Bay Shore, NY 631-952-2000
J.C. Products Inc.
Haddam, CT 860-267-5516
Jay Packaging Group
Warwick, RI 401-739-7200
JBC Plastics
St Louis, MO. 877-834-5526
JEM Wire Products
Middletown, CT 860-347-0447
Jesse Jones Box Corporation
Philadelphia, PA 215-425-6600
Just Plastics
New York, NY 212-569-8500
K&I Creative Plastics
Jacksonville, FL 904-387-0438
Kehr-Buffalo Wire Frame Company
Grand Island, NY 800-875-4212
Kell Container Corporation
Chippewa Falls, WI 800-472-1800
King Products
Mississauga, ON. 866-454-6757
Koch Container Corporation
Victor, NY. 585-924-1600
Krimstock Enterprises
Pennsauken, NJ. 856-665-3676
L.A. Darling Company
Paragould, AR. 800-643-3499
LBP Manufacturing
Cicero, IL 708-652-5600
Lil' Orbits
Minneapolis, MN 800-228-8305
Lorac/Union Tool Company
Providence, RI 888-680-3236
Loy-Lange Box Company
Saint Louis, MO 800-886-4712
LSI Industries Inc.
Cincinnati, OH 513-793-3200
M&M Displays
Philadelphia, PA 800-874-7171
Mack-Chicago Corporation
Chicago, IL 800-992-6225
Madsen Wire Products
Orland, IN. 260-829-6561
Mainstreet Menu Systems
Brookfield, WI 800-782-6222
Mall City Containers
Kalamazoo, MI 800-643-6721
Mannkraft Corporation
Newark, NJ 973-589-7400
Mark Slade ManufacturingCompany
Seymour, WI 920-833-6557
Market Sign Systems
Portland, ME. 800-421-1799
McCall Refrigeration
Parsons, TN. 888-732-2446
McRoyal Industries
Youngstown, OH. 800-785-2556
MDI WorldWide
Farmington Hills, MI 800-228-8925
Meilahn Manufacturing Company
Chicago, IL 773-581-5204
Melrose Displays
Passaic, NJ 973-471-7700
Merchandising Inventives
Waukegan, IL 800-367-5653
Merric
Bridgeton, MO 314-770-9944
Metaline Products Company
South Amboy, NJ 732-721-1373
Michigan Box Company
Detroit, MI 888-642-4269
Micro Wire Products Inc.
Brockton, MA. 508-584-0200
Mid Cities Paper Box Company
Downey, CA 877-277-6272
Mid-West Wire Products, Inc
Ferndale, MI 800-989-9881
Mid-West Wire Specialties
Chicago, IL 800-238-0228

Miller Multiplex Displays Fixtures
Dupo, IL 800-325-3350
Mirro Products Company
High Point, NC 336-885-4166
Modar
Benton Harbor, MI 800-253-6186
Modern Metalcraft
Midland, MI 800-948-3182
Morrissey Displays & Models
Port Washington, NY 516-883-6944
Moseley Corporation
Franklin, MA 800-667-3539
Multi-Panel Display Corporation
Brooklyn, NY 800-439-0879
MultiFab Plastics
Boston, MA. 888-293-5754
Nashville Display Manufacturing Company
Nashville, TN 800-251-1150
National Manufacturing Company
Lincoln, NE. 402-475-3400
Neal Walters Poster Corporation
Bentonville, AR 501-273-2489
North American Plastic Manufacturing Company
Bethel, CT. 800-934-7752
Northeast Box Company
Ashtabula, OH 800-362-8100
Northern Wire Products
St Cloud, MN 800-458-5549
Northwestern
Van Nuys, CA 818-786-1581
NT Industries
Franklin Park, IL. 847-451-6500
Omega Industries
St Louis, MO. 314-961-1668
Omnicraft, Inc.
Minnetonka, MN. 952-988-9944
OSF
Toronto, ON 800-465-4000
Pacific Store Designs
Garden Grove, CA 800-772-5661
Pentwater Wire Products
Pentwater, MI 877-869-6911
Peter Pepper Products
Compton, CA 310-639-0390
PFI Displays
Rittman, OH 800-925-9075
Philipp Lithographing Company
Grafton, WI. 800-657-0871
Pilgrim Plastic ProductsCompany
Brockton, MA. 800-343-7810
Plastech
Monrovia, CA. 626-358-9306
Plasti-Clip Corporation
Milford, NH 800-882-2547
Plasti-Line
Knoxville, TN. 800-444-7446
Plastic Fantastics/Buck Signs
Ashland, OR 800-482-1776
PM Plastics
Pewaukee, WI. 262-691-1700
PMI Food Equipment Group
Troy, OH 937-332-3000
Prengler Products
Sherman, TX. 903-892-0242
Presentations South
Orlando, FL. 407-657-2108
Prestige Plastics Corporation
Delta, BC. 604-930-2931
Princeton Shelving
Cedar Rapids, IA. 319-369-0355
Pro-Ad-Company
Portland, OR 800-287-5885
Process Displays
New Berlin, WI. 800-533-1764
Propak
Burlington, ON 800-263-4872
R. Wireworks
Elmira, NY 800-550-4009
Racks
San Diego, CA 619-661-0987
Rand-Whitney Container Corporation
Worcester, MA 508-791-2301
Randware Industries
Prospect Heights, IL 847-299-8884
Rapid Displays
Chicago, IL. 800-356-5775
Rathe Productions
New York, NY 212-242-9000
Reading Plastic Fabricators
Temple, PA 610-926-3245
Reeve Store Equipment Company
Pico Rivera, CA 800-927-3383

Refcon
Norwood, NJ. 201-750-5060
Reflex International
Norcross, GA 800-642-7640
Render
Buffalo, NY. 888-446-1010
Retail Decor
Ironton, OH. 800-726-3402
Rex Art Manufacturing Corp.
Lindenhurst, NY 631-884-4600
Rice Packaging
Ellington, CT 800-367-6725
Robelan Displays
Hempstead, NY. 865-564-8600
Rock-Tenn Company
Norcross, GA 770-448-2193
Royal Display Corporation
Middletown, CT 800-569-1295
Royce Phoenix
Glendale, AZ. 602-256-0006
RPA Process Technologies
Marblehead, MA. 800-631-9707
RR Donnelley
Chicago, IL 800-742-4455
RTC Industries
Rolling Meadows, IL 847-640-2400
Rudd Container Corporation
Chicago, IL 773-847-7600
Russell-William
Odenton, MD 410-551-3602
Rutler Screen Printing
Phillipsburg, NJ 908-859-3327
Sam Pievac Company
Santa Fe Springs, CA 800-742-8585
San Juan Signs
Farmington, NM 505-326-5511
Schiffenhaus Industries
Newark, NJ 973-484-5000
SEMCO
Ocala, FL. 800-749-6894
Sign Shop
Rancho Cucamonga, CA 909-945-5888
Smurfit Stone Container
San Jose, CA. 408-925-9391
Smyth Companies, LLC
Saint Paul, MN 800-473-3464
Source Packaging
Mahwah, NJ 888-665-9768
Southern Container Corporation
Deer Park, NY. 631-586-6006
Southern Imperial
Rockford, IL 800-747-4665
Special Events Supply Company
Hauppauge, NY
St Joseph Packaging Inc
St Joseph, MO. 800-383-3000
St. Elizabeth Street Display Corporation
Hackensack, NJ. 201-883-0333
Standex International Corporation
Salem, NH. 603-893-9701
Steel City Corporation
Youngstown, OH. 800-321-0350
Stoffel Seals Corporation
Tallapoosa, GA 800-422-8247
Stone Container
Santa Fe Springs, CA 714-774-0100
Stout Sign Company
Saint Louis, MO 800-325-8530
Stricker & Company
La Plata, MD. 301-934-8346
Sutton Designs
Ithaca, NY. 800-326-8119
Talbot Industries
Neosho, MO 417-451-5900
THARCO
San Lorenzo, CA. 800-772-2332
Thomson-Leeds Company
New York, NY 800-535-9361
Top Source Industries
Addison, IL. 800-362-9625
Traitech Industries
Vaughan, ON. 877-872-4835
Traub Container Corporation
Cleveland, OH 216-475-5100
Travelon
Elk Grove Vlg, IL. 800-537-5544
Trinkle Signs & Displays
Youngstown, OH. 330-747-9712
Tru-Form Plastics
Gardena, CA 800-510-7999
Twenty/Twenty Graphics
Gaithersburg, MD 240-243-0511

Universal Folding Box
East Orange, NJ . . . 973-482-4300
Uniweb
Corona, CA . . . 800-486-4932
US Magnetix
Golden Valley, MN . . . 800- 3-0
Vacuform Industries
Columbus, OH . . . 800-366-7446
Vega Mfg Ltd.
Port Coquitlam, BC . . . 800-224-8342
Viking Packaging & Display
San Jose, CA . . . 408-998-1000
VIP Real Estate Ltd
Chicago, IL . . . 773-376-5000
Visual Marketing Associates
Santee, CA . . . 619-258-0393
Vomela/Harbor Graphics
St Paul, MN . . . 800-645-1012
Vulcan Industries
Moody, AL . . . 888-444-4417
Wahlstrom Manufacturing
Fontana, CA . . . 909-822-4677
Warwick Products Company
Cleveland, OH . . . 800-535-4404
Wayne Industries
Clanton, AL . . . 800-225-3148
Webster Packaging Corporation
Loveland, OH . . . 513-683-5666
Welbilt Corporation
Stamford, CT . . . 203-325-8300
White Way Sign & Maintenance
Mt Prospect, IL . . . 800-621-4122
Willamette Industries
Beaverton, OR . . . 503-641-1131
Willson Industries
Marmora, NJ . . . 800-894-4169
Wire Products Corporation
Greensboro, NC . . . 800-334-0807
Wiremaid Products
Coral Springs, FL . . . 800-770-4700
Woodstock Plastics Company
Marengo, IL . . . 815-568-5281
WS Packaging Group, Inc.
Neenah, WI . . . 888-532-3334

Doilies

American Pan Company
Urbana, OH . . . 800-652-2151
Brooklace
Oshkosh, WI . . . 800-572-4552
Cannon Equipment Company
Rosemount, MN . . . 800-825-8501
Dorado Carton Company
Dorado, PR . . . 787-796-1670
Frost, Inc.
Grand Rapids, MI . . . 800-253-9382
IB Concepts
Elizabeth, NJ . . . 888-671-0800
Pinckney Molded Plastics
Howell, MI . . . 800-854-2920
Pro Bake
Twinsburg, OH . . . 800-837-4427
Smith-Lee Company
Oshkosh, WI . . . 800-327-9774
Sunset Paper Products
Simi Valley, CA . . . 800-228-7882
US Lace Paper Works
Oshkosh, WI . . . 800-873-6459

Doors

Foodservice

Aleco
Muscle Shoals, AL . . . 800-633-3120
American Metal Door Company
Richmond, IN . . . 800-428-2737
Andgar Corporation
Ferndale, WA . . . 360-366-9900
Beta Tech Corporation
Carlstadt, NJ . . . 800-272-7336
Curtron Products
Pittsburgh, PA . . . 800-833-5005
Eliason Corporation
Kalamazoo, MI . . . 800-828-3655
FIB-R-DOR
Cincinnati, OH . . . 800-342-7367
Hoffman Company
Corpus Christi, TX . . . 262-391-8664
Hormann Flexan Llc
Leetsdale, PA . . . 800-365-3667
Kedco Wine Storage Systems
Farmingdale, NY . . . 800-654-9988
Marlite
Dover, OH . . . 800-377-1221
Plas-Ties, Co.
Tustin, CA . . . 800-854-0137
Rasco Industries
Hamel, MN . . . 800-537-3802
Rite-Hite Corporation
Milwaukee, WI . . . 888-841-4283
Stanley Access Technologies
Farmington, CT . . . 800-722-2377
Super Seal ManufacturingLimited
Woodbridge, ON . . . 800-337-3239
Trimline Corporation
Elkhart Lake, WI . . . 920-876-3611
Woodfold-Marco Manufacturing
Forest Grove, OR . . . 503-357-7181

Drawers

Cash, Money

APG Cash Drawer
Fridley, MN . . . 763-571-5000
E.F. Bavis & Associates Drive-Thru
Maineville, OH . . . 513-677-0500
Indiana Cash Drawer Company
Shelbyville, IN . . . 800-227-4379
Leggett and Platt, Inc.
Carthage, MO . . . 417-358-8131
Loyal Manufacturing Corporation
Indianapolis, IN . . . 317-359-3185
Superior Products Company
Saint Paul, MN . . . 800-328-9800

Envelopes

ADM Corporation
Middlesex, NJ . . . 800-327-0718
Appleson Press
Syosset, NY . . . 800-888-2775
Artistic Packaging Concepts
Massapequa Pk, NY . . . 516-797-4020
Barkley Filing Supplies
Hattiesburg, MS . . . 800-647-3070
BAW Plastics
Jefferson Hills, PA . . . 800-783-2229
Cenveo, Inc.
Chicago, IL . . . 800-388-8406
Check Savers
Dallas, TX . . . 972-272-7533
Coleman Resources
Greensboro, NC . . . 336-852-4006
Commercial Envelope Manufacturing Company
Hauppauge, NY
Continental Envelope Corporation
Geneva, IL . . . 800-621-8155
Dagher Printing
Jacksonville, FL . . . 904-998-0911
Double Envelope Corporation
Roanoke, VA . . . 540-362-3311
Eastern Envelope
Flanders, NJ . . . 973-584-3311
Eaton Manufacturing Company
Houston, TX . . . 800-328-6610
Enterprise Box Company
Montclair, NJ . . . 973-509-2200
Enterprise Envelope Inc
Grand Rapids, MI . . . 800-422-4255
Excelsior Transparent Bag Manufacturing
Yonkers, NY . . . 914-968-1300
Flexo Transparent
Buffalo, NY . . . 877-993-5396
Forbes Products
Rush, NY . . . 800-316-5235
Grand Valley Labels
Grand Rapids, MI
Heinrich Envelope Corporation
Minneapolis, MN . . . 800-346-7957
Innova Envelopes
La Salle, QC . . . 514-595-0555
International Envelope Company
Exton, PA . . . 610-363-0900
MAC Paper Converters
Jacksonville, FL . . . 800-334-7026
Miami Systems Corporation
Blue Ash, OH . . . 800-543-4540
Murray Envelope Corporation
Hattiesburg, MS . . . 601-583-8292
North American PackagingCorporation
New York, NY . . . 800-499-3521
Oles of Puerto Rico
Bayamon, PR . . . 787-786-1700
Poser Envelope
Oakland, CA . . . 800-208-6100
Steingart Associates
South Fallsburg, NY . . . 845-434-4321
Stone Container
Chicago, IL . . . 312-346-6600
Unisource Converting
Jacksonville, FL . . . 904-783-0550
Volk Corporation
Farmington Hills, MI . . . 800-521-6799
Westrick Paper Company
Jacksonville, FL . . . 904-737-2122
Worcester Envelope Company
Auburn, MA . . . 508-832-5394

Fixtures

Store

A.T. Foote Woodworking Company
Hartford, CT . . . 860-249-6821
AAA Mill
Austin, TX . . . 512-385-2215
Acme Display Fixture Company
Los Angeles, CA . . . 800-959-5657
Acme Fixture Company
Los Angeles, CA . . . 888-379-9566
Acraloc Corporation
Oak Ridge, TN . . . 865-483-1368
ALCO Designs
Gardena, CA . . . 800-228-2346
Amscor
Brooklyn, NY . . . 800-825-9800
Amtekco Industries
Columbus, OH . . . 800-336-4677
Andrew's Fixture Company
Tacoma, WA . . . 253-627-8388
Arizona Store Equipment
Phoenix, AZ . . . 800-624-8395
Art-Phyl Creations
Hialeah, FL . . . 800-327-8318
Bailly Showcase & Fixture Company
Las Vegas, NV . . . 702-947-6885
Baker Cabinet Company
Costa Mesa, CA . . . 714-540-5515
BJ Wood Products
Ladysmith, WI . . . 715-532-6626
Blue Ridge Signs
Weatherford, TX . . . 800-659-5645
Boston Retail Products
Medford, MA . . . 800-225-1633
C&H Store Equipment Company
Los Angeles, CA . . . 800-648-4979
Cannon Equipment Company
Rosemount, MN . . . 800-825-8501
Capitol Hardware, Inc.,
Middlebury, IN . . . 800-327-6083
Chicago Show
Buffalo Grove, IL . . . 847-955-0200
Chrysler Jeep Dodge Ram of Kirkland
Kirkland, WA . . . 877-606-8196
Clearr Corporation
Minneapolis, MN . . . 800-548-3269
Corman & Associates
Lexington, KY . . . 859-233-0544
Crown Metal Manufacturing Company
Elmhurst, IL . . . 630-279-9800
Crown Metal Manufacturing Company
Alta Loma, CA . . . 909-948-9300
CSC Worldwide
Columbus, OH . . . 800-848-3573
Custom Business Interiors
Henderson, NV . . . 702-564-6661
Custom Craft Laminates
Tampa, FL . . . 800-486-4367
Display Craft Manufacturing Company
Halethorpe, MD . . . 410-242-0400
Display Creations
Brooklyn, NY . . . 718-257-2300
Dunn Woodworks
Shrewsbury, PA . . . 877-835-8592
East Bay Fixture Company
Oakland, CA . . . 800-995-4521
EGW Bradbury Enterprises
Bridgewater, ME . . . 800-332-6021
Emco Industrial Plastics
Cedar Grove, NJ . . . 800-292-9906
Enterprise Products
Bell Gardens, CA . . . 562-928-1918

Exhibits and More
Liverpool, NY 888-326-9100
Fab-X/Metals
Washington, NC 800-677-3229
Fasteners for Retail
Cincinnati, OH 800-422-2547
Field Manufacturing Corporation
Torrance, CA 310-781-9292
Fine Woods Manufacturing
Phoenix, AZ 800-279-2871
Freely Display
Cleveland, OH 216-721-6056
Garvey Products
West Chester, OH 800-543-1908
GDM Concepts
Paramount, CA 562-633-0195
General Cage
Elwood, IN 800-428-6403
Handy Store Fixtures
Newark, NJ 800-631-4280
Heartwood Cabinets
Montclair, CA 909-626-8104
Henry Hanger & Fixture Corporation of America
New York City, NY 877-279-0852
Hoffman Company
Corpus Christi, TX 262-391-8664
Huck Store Fixture Company
Quincy, IL 800-680-4823
Hurlingham Company
San Pedro, CA 310-538-0236
IGS Store Fixtures
Peabody, MA 978-532-0010
Industrial Sheet Metal
Cleveland, OH 216-431-9650
Inland Showcase & Fixture Company
Fresno, CA 559-237-4158
Interior Systems
Milwaukee, WI 800-837-8373
Interstate Showcase & Fixture Company
West Orange, NJ 973-483-5555
Ironwood Displays
Niles, MI 231-683-8500
J.K. Harman, Inc.
Hamden, CT 800-248-1627
Kedco Wine Storage Systems
Farmingdale, NY 800-654-9988
Kehr-Buffalo Wire Frame Company
Grand Island, NY 800-875-4212
Kent Corporation
Birmingham, AL 800-252-5368
Killion Industries
Vista, CA 800-421-5352
L&S Products
Coldwater, MI 517-279-9526
L.A. Darling Company
Paragould, AR 800-643-3499
LA Cabinet & Finishing Company
Los Angeles, CA 323-233-7245
Lauritzen & Makin
Fort Worth, TX 817-921-0218
Leggett and Platt, Inc.
Carthage, MO 417-358-8131
Lozier Corporation
Omaha, NE 800-228-9882
Madix
Goodwater, AL 256-839-6354
Madix, Inc.
Terrell, TX 800-776-2349
Mark Slade ManufacturingCompany
Seymour, WI 920-833-6557
Melrose Displays
Passaic, NJ 973-471-7700
Merchandising Systems Manufacturing
Union City, CA 800-523-1468
Metal Master
Tucson, AZ 800-488-8729
Micro Wire Products Inc.
Brockton, MA 508-584-0200
Modar
Benton Harbor, MI 800-253-6186
Modern Store Fixtures Company
Dallas, TX 800-634-7777
New Court
Texarkana, TX 903-838-0521
Northern Wire Products
St Cloud, MN 800-458-5549
Northwestern
Van Nuys, CA 818-786-1581
Omaha Fixture International
Omaha, NE 800-637-2257
Omicron Steel Products Company
Jamaica, NY 718-805-3400

Omnicraft, Inc.
Minnetonka, MN 952-988-9944
OSF
Toronto, ON 800-465-4000
Pacific Store Designs
Garden Grove, CA 800-772-5661
Paramount Manufacturing Company
Wilmington, MA 978-657-4300
Peacock Crate Factory
Jacksonville, TX 800-657-2200
Pentwater Wire Products
Pentwater, MI 877-869-6911
Peter Pepper Products
Compton, CA 310-639-0390
PFI Displays
Rittman, OH 800-925-9075
Pierce Laminated Products
Rockford, IL 815-968-9651
Premier Brass
Atlanta, GA 800-251-5800
Primlite Manufacturing Corporation
Freeport, NY 800-327-7583
Quality Cabinets & Fixtures Company
San Diego, CA 619-266-1011
R. Wireworks
Elmira, NY 800-550-4009
R.C. Smith Company
Burnsville, MN 800-747-7648
Reeve Store Equipment Company
Pico Rivera, CA 800-927-3383
Reeves Enterprises
La Verne, CA 909-392-9999
Regal Plastics
North Kansas City, MO 816-471-6390
Russell-William
Odenton, MD 410-551-3602
RW Products
Edgewood, NY 800-345-1022
S&L Store Fixture Company
Miami, FL 800-205-4536
Sam Pievac Company
Santa Fe Springs, CA 800-742-8585
SEMCO
Ocala, FL 800-749-6894
Shelley Cabinet Company
Shelley, ID 208-357-3700
Sinicrope & Sons
Alhambra, CA 323-283-5131
Sitka Store Fixtures
Kansas City, MO 800-821-7558
Southern Store Fixtures
Bessemer, AL 800-552-6283
Spartan Showcase
Union, MO 800-325-0775
Specialty Wood Products
Clanton, AL 800-322-5343
Stanly Fixtures Company
Norwood, NC 704-474-3184
Streater LLC
Albert Lea, MN 800-527-4197
Tables Cubed
Chesterfield, MO 800-878-3001
Talbert Display
Fort Worth, TX 817-429-4504
Thomson-Leeds Company
New York, NY 800-535-9361
Thorco Industries LLC
Lamar, MO 800-445-3375
Tulsa Plastics Company
Tulsa, OK 888-273-5303
Unarco Industries
Wagoner, OK 800-654-4100
Uniweb
Corona, CA 800-486-4932
Valley Fixtures
Sparks, NV 775-331-1050
Vandereems ManufacturingCompany
Hawthorne, NJ 973-427-2355
View-Rite Manufacturing
Daly City, CA 415-468-3856
Vulcan Industries
Moody, AL 888-444-4417
Warwick Products Company
Cleveland, OH 800-535-4404
William Hecht
Philadelphia, PA 215-925-6223

Holders

Bag

Eastern Plastics
Pawtucket, RI 800-442-8585
Grayline Housewares
Carol Stream, IL 800-222-7388
Seattle Plastics
Seattle, WA 800-441-0679
Sipco Products
Peoria Heights, IL 309-682-5400
Thorco Industries LLC
Lamar, MO 800-445-3375
UniTrak Corporation
Port Hope, ON 866-883-5749

Price Card, Ticket, Etc.

AMCO Corporation
City of Industry, CA 626-855-2550
BAW Plastics
Jefferson Hills, PA 800-783-2229
Beemak Plastics
La Mirada, CA 800-421-4393
C.R. Manufacturing
Waverly, NE 877-789-5844
Cannon Equipment Company
Rosemount, MN 800-825-8501
Clamp Swing Pricing Company
Oakland, CA 800-227-7615
Cleveland Menu Printing
Cleveland, OH 800-356-6368
Creative Essentials
Ronkonkoma, NY 800-355-5891
Crown Metal Manufacturing Company
Alta Loma, CA 909-948-9300
Fast Industries
Fort Lauderdale, FL 800-775-5345
Fasteners for Retail
Cincinnati, OH 800-422-2547
Forbes Industries
Ontario, CA 909-923-4559
Gastro-Gnomes
West Hartford, CT 800-747-4666
Illuma Display
Brookfield, WI 800-501-0128
JBC Plastics
St Louis, MO 877-834-5526
Jordan Specialty Company
Brooklyn, NY 877-567-3265
Just Plastics
New York, NY 212-569-8500
Lorac/Union Tool Company
Providence, RI 888-680-3236
Lynn Sign
Andover, MA 800-225-5764
Market Sign Systems
Portland, ME 800-421-1799
Menu Men
Palm Harbor, FL 727-934-7191
MultiFab Plastics
Boston, MA 888-293-5754
National Plastic Companyof California
Santa Fe Springs, CA 800-221-9149
Plasti-Clip Corporation
Milford, NH 800-882-2547
Ram Industries
Erwin, TN 800-523-3883
Redi-Call, Incorporated
Reno, NV 800-648-1849
Reeve Store Equipment Company
Pico Rivera, CA 800-927-3383
RPA Process Technologies
Marblehead, MA 800-631-9707
Spirit Foodservice, Inc.
Andover, MA 800-343-0996
Sutton Designs
Ithaca, NY 800-326-8119
US Magnetix
Golden Valley, MN 800- 3-0

Holding & Warming Equipment

Acra Electric Corporation
Tulsa, OK 800-223-4328
Aladdin Temp-Rite, LLC
Hendersonville, TN 800-888-8018
Alliance Products, LLC
Murfreesboro, TN 800-522-3973
Alto-Shaam
Menomonee Falls, WI 800-558-8744

American Metalcraft
Melrose Park, IL 800-333-9133
American Production Company
Redwood City, CA 650-368-5334
Antrim Manufacturing
Brookfield, WI 262-781-6860
Apex Fountain Sales
Philadelphia, PA 800-523-4586
APW Wyott Food Service Equipment Company
Cheyenne, WY 800-527-2100
ARC Specialties
Valencia, CA 661-775-8500
Arctica Showcase Company
Calgary, AB. 800-839-5536
Aroma Manufacturing Company
San Diego, CA 800-276-6286
Ballantyne Food Service Equipment
Omaha, NE 800-424-1215
BEVCO
Canada, BC 800-663-0090
Bevles Company
Dallas, TX. 800-441-1601
BG Industries
Lemont, IL 800-800-5761
BKI Worldwide
Simpsonville, SC 800-927-6887
Bon Chef
Lafayette, NJ. 800-331-0177
Brass Smith
Denver, CO 800-662-9595
Brewmatic Company
Torrance, CA. 800-421-6860
Broaster Company
Beloit, WI 800-365-8278
Canadian Display Systems
Concord, ON. 800-895-5862
Candle Lamp Company
Riverside, CA 877-526-7748
Carlisle Food Service Products
Oklahoma City, OK 800-654-8210
Carter-Hoffman Corp LLC
Mundelein, IL 800-323-9793
Caselites
Hialeah, FL 305-819-7766
Convay Systems
Etobicoke, ON. 800-811-5511
Craig Manufacturing
Irvington, NJ. 800-631-7936
Creative Mobile Systems
Manchester, CT. 800-646-8364
Cres Cor
Mentor, OH. 877-273-7267
Crispy Lite
St. Louis, MO 888-356-5362
Curtron Products
Pittsburgh, PA. 800-833-5005
Custom Diamond International
Laval, QC 800-326-5926
D'Lights
Glendale, CA 818-956-5656
Delfield Company
Mt Pleasant, MI. 800-733-8821
Deluxe Equipment Company
Bradenton, FL. 800-367-8931
Duke Manufacturing Company
Saint Louis, MO 800-735-3853
Dynynstyl
Delray Beach, FL 800-774-7895
Eagle Foodservice Equipment
Clayton, DE. 800-441-8440
EPCO
Murfreesboro, TN. 800-251-3398
Esquire Mechanical Corp.
Armonk, NY 800-847-4206
Faubion Central States Tank Company
Shawnee Mission, KS. 800-450-8265
Fixtur-World
Cookeville, TN 800-634-9887
FleetwoodGoldcoWyard
Romeoville, IL 630-759-6800
Fred D. Pfening Company
Columbus, OH 614-294-1633
FWE/Food Warming Equipment Company, Inc
Crystal Lake, IL 800-222-4393
Galley
Jupiter, FL. 800-537-2772
Garland Commercial Ranges
Mississauga, ON 905-624-0260
Gold Medal Products Company
Cincinnati, OH 800-543-0862
Habco
Concord, CA 925-682-6203
HATCO Corporation
Milwaukee, WI 800-558-0607
Heat-It Manufacturing
San Antonio, TX. 800-323-9336
Henny Penny, Inc.
Detroit, MI 313-877-9550
Hickory Industries
North Bergen, NJ 800-732-9153
Hot Food Boxes
Mooresville, IN. 800-733-8073
InfraTech Corporation
Azusa, CA. 800-955-2476
Intedge Manufacturing
Woodruff, SC 866-969-9605
J.V. Reed & Company
Louisville, KY 877-258-7333
Karma
Watertown, WI 800-558-9565
Keating of Chicago
Mc Cook, IL 800-532-8464
Kelmin Products
Plymouth, FL 407-886-6079
King Arthur
Statesville, NC 800-257-7244
Lakeside Manufacturing
Milwaukee, WI 888-558-8574
Lambertson Industries
Sparks, NV 800-548-3324
LaRosa Refrigeration & Equipment Company
Detroit, MI 800-527-6723
Lazy-Man
Belvidere, NJ 800-475-1950
Leedal Inc
Northbrook, IL 847-498-0111
LEWCO
Sandusky, OH 419-625-4014
Lincoln Foodservice
Cleveland, OH 800-374-3004
Low Temp Industries
Jonesboro, GA 770-478-8803
M&S Manufacturing
Arnold, MO. 636-464-2739
Marshall Air Systems
Charlotte, NC 800-722-3474
Mastex Industries
Petersburg, VA 804-732-8300
Merco/Savory
Mt. Pleasant, MI 800-733-8821
Metal Masters Food Service Equipment Company
Clayton, DE. 800-441-8440
Metal Masters Northwest
Lynnwood, WA. 425-775-4481
Metro Corporation
Wilkes Barre, PA. 800-433-2233
Mies Products
West Bend, WI 800-480-6437
Moffat
San Antonio, TX. 800-551-8795
Monroe Kitchen Equipment
Rochester, NY. 585-235-3310
Mosshaim Innovations
Jacksonville, FL 888-995-7775
Mr. Bar-B-Q
Old Bethpage, NY. 800-333-2124
N. Wasserstrom & Sons
Columbus, OH 800-999-9277
Nutty Bavarian
Sanford, FL. 800-382-4788
Parvin Manufacturing Company
Los Angeles, CA. 800-648-0770
Piper Products
Wausau, WI. 800-544-3057
Plastocon
Oconomowoc, WI. 800-966-0103
Polyfoam Packers Corporation
Arlington Hts, IL 800-323-7442
Prince Castle
Carol Stream, IL 800-722-7853
Proluxe
Paramount, CA 800-594-5528
Randell Manufacturing Unified Brands
Weidman, MI 888-994-7636
Randware Industries
Prospect Heights, IL 847-299-8884
Reliable Food Service Equipment
Concord, ON. 416-738-6840
Remco Industries International
Fort Lauderdale, FL 800-987-3626
Rexcraft Fine Chafers
Long Island City, NY 888-739-2723
Royalton Foodservice Equipment
Cleveland, OH 800-662-8765
Server Products
Richfield, WI 800-558-8722
Sheffield Platers
San Diego, CA 800-227-9242
SICO America
Minneapolis, MN 800-328-6138
Sould Manufacturing
Winnepeg, NB. 204-339-3499
Southern Pride Distributing
Marion, IL. 800-851-8180
Super Systems
Wausau, WI. 800-558-5880
Super-Chef Manufacturing Company
Houston, TX 800-231-3478
Superior Products Company
Saint Paul, MN 800-328-9800
Tempco Electric Heater Corporation
Wood Dale, IL. 888-268-6396
Texican Specialty Products
Houston, TX 800-869-5918
Thermal Bags by Ingrid
Gilberts, IL 800-622-5560
Tomlinson Industries
Cleveland, OH 800-945-4589
Tranter Pite
Wichita Falls, TX 940-723-7125
Ultrafryer Systems
San Antonio, TX. 800-545-9189
Update International
Los Angeles, CA. 800-747-7124
Valad Electric Heating Corporation
Tarrytown, NY
Vimco Inc.
King of Prussia, PA. 610-768-0500
Vollrath Company
Sheboygan, WI 920-457-4851
Vulcan-Hart Company
Louisville, KY 800-814-2028
Welbilt Corporation
Stamford, CT. 203-325-8300
Wells Manufacturing Company
Verdi, NV 800-777-0450
West Metals
London, ON 800-300-6667
Wilder Manufacturing Company
Port Jervis, NY 800-832-1319
Will & Baumer
Syracuse, NY 315-451-1000
Williamsburg Metal Spinning & Stamping Corporation
Brooklyn, NY 888-535-5402
Win-Holt Equipment Group
Westbury, NY 800-444-3595
Wisco Industries
Oregon, WI 800-999-4726
Wittco Food Service Equipment
Milwaukee, WI 800-367-8413
Wittco Foodservice Equipment, Inc.
Milwaukee, WI 800-821-3912
Zoia Banquetier Company
Cleveland, OH 216-631-6414

Hooks

Display, Store

Cannon Equipment Company
Rosemount, MN 800-825-8501
Clamp Swing Pricing Company
Oakland, CA 800-227-7615
Etube and Wire
Shrewsbury, PA. 800-618-4720
Fasteners for Retail
Cincinnati, OH 800-422-2547
Mark Slade ManufacturingCompany
Seymour, WI. 920-833-6557
Merchandising Inventives
Waukegan, IL 800-367-5653
SEMCO
Ocala, FL. 800-749-6894
Southern Imperial
Rockford, IL 800-747-4665

Interiors

Hotel, Bar, Restaurant

Commercial Furniture Group
Newport, TN. 800-873-3252

Kiosks

All A Cart Manufacturing
Columbus, OH ... 800-695-2278

Burgess Enterprises, Inc
Renton, WA ... 800-927-3286

Carriage Works
Klamath Falls, OR ... 541-882-0700

Carts of Colorado
Greenwood Vlg, CO ... 800-227-8634

Corsair Display Systems
Canandalgua, NY ... 800-347-5245

Daytech Limited
Toronto, ON ... 877-329-1907

Lakeside Manufacturing
Milwaukee, WI ... 888-558-8574

Landmark Kitchen Design
Phoenix, AZ ... 866-621-3192

McRoyal Industries
Youngstown, OH ... 800-785-2556

Merchandising Frontiers
Winterset, IA ... 800-421-2278

Michaelo Espresso
Seattle, WA ... 800-545-2883

Moseley Corporation
Franklin, MA ... 800-667-3539

Reflex International
Norcross, GA ... 800-642-7640

Southern Express
Saint Louis, MO ... 800-444-9157

Steamway Corporation
Scottsburg, IN ... 800-259-8171

Linen Goods

A-1 Tablecloth Company
S Hackensack, NJ ... 800-727-8987

Artex International
Highland, IL ... 618-654-2113

ATD-American Company
Wyncote, PA ... 800-523-2300

Babco International, Inc
Tucson, AZ ... 520-628-7596

Best Brands Home Products
New York, NY ... 212-684-7456

Bragard Professional Uniforms
New York, NY ... 800-488-2433

Commercial Textiles Corporation-Best Buy Uniforms
Homestead, PA ... 800-345-1924

Cotton Goods Manufacturing Company
Chicago, IL ... 773-265-0088

Drapes 4 Show
Sylmar, CA ... 800-525-7469

Fashion Industries
Griffin, GA ... 770-412-9214

Gary Manufacturing Company
Chula Vista, CA ... 800-775-0804

Gourmet Tableskirts
Houston, TX ... 800-527-0440

Happy Chef
Butler, NJ ... 800-347-0288

Hilden Halifax
South Boston, VA ... 800-431-2514

Jack the Ripper Table Skirting
Stafford, TX ... 800-331-7831

Jones-Zylon Company
West Lafayette, OH ... 800-848-8160

K Katen & Company
Rahway, NJ ... 732-381-0220

Marko
Spartanburg, SC ... 866-466-2756

Party Linens
Chicago, IL ... 800-281-0003

Philmont Manufacturing Co.
Englewood, NJ ... 888-379-6483

Premier Skirting Products
Lawrence, NY ... 800-544-2516

Prestige Skirting & Tablecloths
Orangeburg, NY ... 800-635-3313

Radius Display Products
Dallas, TX ... 888-322-7429

Stevens Linen Association
Dudley, MA ... 508-943-0813

Sultan Linens
New York, NY ... 212-689-8900

Tara Linens
Sanford, NC ... 800-476-8272

Magnetic Chips

Hopp Companies
New Hyde Park, NY ... 800-889-8425

Magnetic Label

Backers

Hopp Companies
New Hyde Park, NY ... 800-889-8425

Magnetic Pocket

Sign & Card Holders

Hopp Companies
New Hyde Park, NY ... 800-889-8425

Markers

Price & Sign

Atlas Rubber Stamp Company
York, PA ... 717-755-1105

Century Rubber Stamp Company
New York, NY ... 212-962-6165

Courtesy Sign Company
Amarillo, TX ... 806-373-6609

Display Concepts
Trenton, ME ... 800-446-0033

Ed Smith's Stencil Works
New Orleans, LA ... 504-525-2128

Fasteners for Retail
Cincinnati, OH ... 800-422-2547

Garvey Products
Cincinnati, OH ... 513-771-8710

Grueny's Rubber Stamps
Little Rock, AR ... 501-376-0393

Lamb Sign
Manassas, VA ... 703-791-7960

Muskogee Rubber Stamp & Seal Company
Fort Gibson, OK ... 918-478-3046

Neal Walters Poster Corporation
Bentonville, AR ... 501-273-2489

Plastimatic Arts Corporation
Mishawaka, IN ... 800-442-3593

Quick Stamp & Sign Mfg
Lafayette, LA ... 337-232-2171

US Magnetix
Golden Valley, MN ... 800- 3-0

Wildes - Spirit Design & Printing
White Plains, MD ... 301-870-4141

Menu Boards

Qyk Syn Industries
Miami, FL ... 800-354-5640

Menus

Ad Art Litho.
Cleveland, OH ... 800-875-6368

Allred Marketing
Birmingham, AL ... 205-251-3700

Beaverite Corporation
Croghan, NY ... 800-424-6337

Brass Smith
Denver, CO ... 800-662-9595

Charles Mayer Studios
Akron, OH ... 330-535-6121

City Grafx
Eugene, OR ... 800-258-2489

Cleveland Menu Printing
Cleveland, OH ... 800-356-6368

Corsair Display Systems
Canandalgua, NY ... 800-347-5245

Creative Essentials
Ronkonkoma, NY ... 800-355-5891

Creative Impressions
Buena Park, CA ... 800-524-5278

Creative Menus
Burr Ridge, IL ... 630-734-3244

CustomColor Corporation
Lenexa, KS ... 888-605-4050

David Dobbs Enterprise & Menu Design
St Augustine, FL ... 800-889-6368

Dilley Manufacturing Company
Des Moines, IA ... 800-247-5087

Ennis Inc.
Midlothian, TX ... 800-972-1069

Everbrite
Greenfield, WI ... 800-558-3888

Filet Menu
Los Angeles, CA ... 310-202-8000

Florida Plastics International
Evergreen Park, IL ... 708-499-0400

Forbes Industries
Ontario, CA ... 909-923-4559

Frost Manufacturing Corporation
Worcester, MA ... 800-462-0216

Futura 2000 Corporation
Miami, FL ... 305-256-5877

GA Design Menu Company
Wixom, MI ... 313-561-2530

Gastro-Gnomes
West Hartford, CT ... 800-747-4666

Have Our Plastic Inc
Mississauga, ON ... 800-263-5995

Impulse Signs
Toronto, ON ... 866-636-8273

International Patterns, Inc.
Bay Shore, NY ... 631-952-2000

Jordan Specialty Company
Brooklyn, NY ... 877-567-3265

Kenyon Press
Signal Hill, CA ... 800-752-9395

Landmark Kitchen Design
Phoenix, AZ ... 866-621-3192

Legible Signs
Loves Park, IL ... 800-435-4177

Lynn Sign
Andover, MA ... 800-225-5764

Maier Sign Systems
Saddle Brook, NJ ... 201-845-7555

Mainstreet Menu Systems
Brookfield, WI ... 800-782-6222

Mastercraft
Appleton, WI ... 800-242-6602

MDI WorldWide
Farmington Hills, MI ... 800-228-8925

Menu Graphics
Olmsted Falls, OH ... 216-696-1460

Menu Men
Palm Harbor, FL ... 727-934-7191

Menu Promotions
Bronx, NY ... 718-324-3800

Milwaukee Sign Company
Grafton, WI ... 262-375-5740

National Menuboard
Auburn, WA ... 800-800-5237

National Plastic Companyof California
Santa Fe Springs, CA ... 800-221-9149

National Sign Systems
Hilliard, OH ... 800-544-6726

Ontario Neon Company
Ontario, CA ... 909-986-4632

Placemat Printers
Fogelsville, PA ... 800-628-7746

Polar Hospitality Products
Philadelphia, PA ... 800-831-7823

Posterloid Corporation
Long Island City, NY ... 800-651-5000

Ram Industries
Erwin, TN ... 800-523-3883

RAO Contract Sales
Paterson, NJ ... 888-324-0020

Redi-Print
West Babylon, NY ... 631-491-6373

Retail Decor
Ironton, OH ... 800-726-3402

Roxanne Signs
Gaithersburg, MD ... 301-428-4911

Samsill Corporation
Fort Worth, TX ... 800-255-1100

School Marketing Partners
San Juan Cpstrno, CA ... 800-565-7778

Seattle Menu Specialists
Kent, WA ... 800-622-2826

Signets/Menu-Quik
Mentor, OH ... 800-775-6368

Spokane House of Hose
Spokane Valley, WA ... 800-541-6351

Strong Group
Gloucester, MA ... 800-332-6025

Sutton Designs
Ithaca, NY ... 800-326-8119

Tablet & Ticket Company
West Chicago, IL ... 800-438-4959

Unique Manufacturing
Visalia, CA ... 888-737-1007

Vacuform Industries
Columbus, OH ... 800-366-7446

VC Menus
Eastland, TX ... 800-826-3687

Visual Marketing Associates
Santee, CA ... 619-258-0393

Visual Planning Corp
Champlain, NY ... 800-361-1192

VMC Signs Inc.
Victoria, TX 361-575-0548
Vynatex
Port Washington, NY 516-944-6130
Wayne Industries
Clanton, AL 800-225-3148
Western Manufacturing Company
San Francisco, CA 415-431-1458
Your Place Menu Systems
Carson City, NV 800-321-8105

Napery

A-1 Tablecloth Company
S Hackensack, NJ 800-727-8987
Adcapitol
Monroe, NC 800-868-7111
Americo
West Memphis, AR 800-626-2350
Artex International
Highland, IL 618-654-2113
Asian Foods
St. Paul, MN 800-274-2655
Best Brands Home Products
New York, NY 212-684-7456
Carnegie Textile Company
Solon, OH 800-633-4136
Commercial Textiles Corporation-Best Buy Uniforms
Homestead, PA 800-345-1924
Connecticut Laminating Company
New Haven, CT 800-753-9119
Cotton Goods Manufacturing Company
Chicago, IL 773-265-0088
Drapes 4 Show
Sylmar, CA 800-525-7469
Erving Industries
Erving, MA 413-422-2700
Fashion Industries
Griffin, GA 770-412-9214
Filet Menu
Los Angeles, CA 310-202-8000
Gary Manufacturing Company
Chula Vista, CA 800-775-0804
Gourmet Tableskirts
Houston, TX 800-527-0440
Happy Chef
Butler, NJ 800-347-0288
Hilden Halifax
South Boston, VA 800-431-2514
Jack the Ripper Table Skirting
Stafford, TX 800-331-7831
Jones-Zylon Company
West Lafayette, OH 800-848-8160
K Katen & Company
Rahway, NJ 732-381-0220
K-C Products Company
Van Nuys, CA 818-267-1600
Marcal Paper Mills
Elmwood Park, NJ 800-631-8451
Marko
Spartanburg, SC 866-466-2756
Palmland Paper Company
Fort Lauderdale, FL 800-266-9067
Paper Service
Hinsdale, NH 603-239-6344
Party Linens
Chicago, IL 800-281-0003
Premier Skirting Products
Lawrence, NY 800-544-2516
Prestige Skirting & Tablecloths
Orangeburg, NY 800-635-3313
Resource One/Resource Two
Reseda, CA 818-343-3451
Scan Group
Appleton, WI 920-730-9150
Scranton Lace Company
Forest City, PA 800-822-1036
Shen Manufacturing Company
W Conshohocken, PA 610-825-2790
Showeray Corporation
Brooklyn, NY 718-965-3633
Smith-Lee Company
Oshkosh, WI 800-327-9774
Something Different Linen
Clifton, NJ 800-422-2180
Springprint Medallion
Augusta, GA 800-543-5990
Sultan Linens
New York, NY 212-689-8900
Tag-Trade Associated Group
Chicago, IL 800-621-8350
Tara Linens
Sanford, NC 800-476-8272
Ultimate Textile
Paterson, NJ 973-523-5866

Napkins

Paper

Admatch Corporation
New York, NY 800-777-9909
Alex Delvecchio Enterprises
Troy, MI 248-619-9600
Atlas Match Company
Toronto, ON 888-285-2783
Chinet Company
Laguna Niguel, CA 949-348-1711
Creative Converting
Clintonville, WI 800-826-0418
Encore Paper Company
South Glens Falls, NY 800-362-6735
Erving Industries
Erving, MA 413-422-2700
Flamingo Food Service Products
Hialeah, FL 800-432-8269
Fonda Group
Oshkosh, WI 800-367-2877
Fonda Group
Oshkosh, WI 800-558-9300
Fort James Corporation
Norwalk, CT 800-257-9744
Georgia Pacific
Green Bay, WI 920-435-8821
Gold Star Products
Oak Park, MI 800-800-0205
Great Western Products
Ontario, CA 888-598-5588
Kentfield's
Greenbrae, CA 888-461-7454
Kimberly-Clark Corporation
Roswell, GA 888-525-8388
Lasermation
Philadelphia, PA 800-523-2759
Marcal Paper Mills
Elmwood Park, NJ 800-631-8451
Palmland Paper Company
Fort Lauderdale, FL 800-266-9067
Paper Service
Hinsdale, NH 603-239-6344
Paradise Products
El Cerrito, CA 800-227-1092
Potlatch Corporation
Spokane, WA 509-835-1500
Primary Liquidation Corporation
Bohemia, NY 631-244-1410
SCA Tissue
Neenah, WI 866-722-6659
Scan Group
Appleton, WI 920-730-9150
Schroeder Sewing Technologies
San Marcos, CA 760-591-9733
Sorg Paper Company
Middletown, OH 513-420-5300
Spirit Foodservice, Inc.
Andover, MA 800-343-0996
Springprint Medallion
Augusta, GA 800-543-5990
Superior Quality Products
Schenectady, NY 800-724-1129

Paper

Writing, Forms, Sales & Order Books

Access Solutions
Knoxville, TN 865-531-0971
Adams Business Forms
Topeka, KS 785-233-4101
Appleson Press
Syosset, NY 800-888-2775
Atlas Match Corporation
Euless, TX 800-628-2426
Conimar Corporation
Ocala, FL 800-874-9735
Dagher Printing
Jacksonville, FL 904-998-0911
Double Envelope Corporation
Roanoke, VA 540-362-3311
Durango-Georgia Paper
Tampa, FL 813-286-2718
Ennis Inc.
Midlothian, TX 800-972-1069
Fay Paper Products
Foxboro, MA 800-765-4620
Graydon Lettercraft
Great Neck, NY 516-482-0531
Hazen Paper Company
Holyoke, MA 413-538-8204
Holden Graphic Services
Minneapolis, MN 612-339-0241
Larry B. Newman PrintingCompany
Knoxville, TN 888-835-4566
Miami Systems Corporation
Blue Ash, OH 800-543-4540
Mohawk Paper Mills
Clifton Park, NY 518-371-6700
Monadnock Paper Mills
Bennington, NH 603-588-3311
NCR Corporation
Duluth, GA 800-225-5627
Neal Walters Poster Corporation
Bentonville, AR 501-273-2489
North American PackagingCorporation
New York, NY 800-499-3521
Old English Printing & Label Company
Delray Beach, FL 561-997-9990
Pan American Papers
Miami, FL 305-635-2534
Patrick & Company
Dallas, TX 214-761-0900
Randall Printing
Brockton, MA 508-588-3830
Salinas Valley Wax PaperCompany
Salinas, CA 831-424-2747
Steingart Associates
South Fallsburg, NY 845-434-4321
Unisource Converting
Jacksonville, FL 904-783-0550
Visual Planning Corp
Champlain, NY 800-361-1192
Westrick Paper Company
Jacksonville, FL 904-737-2122

Place Mats

Abond Plastic Corporation
Lachine, QC 800-886-7947
Admatch Corporation
New York, NY 800-777-9909
Artex International
Highland, IL 618-654-2113
Bright of America
Summersville, WV 304-872-3000
Brooklace
Oshkosh, WI 800-572-4552
Conimar Corporation
Ocala, FL 800-874-9735
Connecticut Laminating Company
New Haven, CT 800-753-9119
Creative Essentials
Ronkonkoma, NY 800-355-5891
Custom Table Pads
St Paul, MN 651-714-5720
Decolin
Montreal, QC 514-384-2910
Dorado Carton Company
Dorado, PR 787-796-1670
Elrene Home Fashions
New York, NY 212-213-0425
Ennis Inc.
Midlothian, TX 800-972-1069
Erving Industries
Erving, MA 413-422-2700
Filet Menu
Los Angeles, CA 310-202-8000
Fonda Group
Oshkosh, WI 800-367-2877
Gourmet Tableskirts
Houston, TX 800-527-0440
Have Our Plastic Inc
Mississauga, ON 800-263-5995
J. James
Brooklyn, NY 718-384-6144
Jack the Ripper Table Skirting
Stafford, TX 800-331-7831
K-C Products Company
Van Nuys, CA 818-267-1600
Louisville Bedding Company
Jeffersontown, KY 502-491-3370
Marko
Spartanburg, SC 866-466-2756
Mastercraft
Appleton, WI 800-242-6602
Milliken & Company
Spartanburg, SC 864-503-2020
Palmland Paper Company
Fort Lauderdale, FL 800-266-9067

Paradise Products
El Cerrito, CA 800-227-1092
Placemat Printers
Fogelsville, PA 800-628-7746
Premier Skirting Products
Lawrence, NY 800-544-2516
Process Displays
New Berlin, WI 800-533-1764
Royal Paper Products
Coatesville, PA 800-666-6655
SCA Tissue
Neenah, WI 866-722-6659
Scranton Lace Company
Forest City, PA 800-822-1036
Seattle Menu Specialists
Kent, WA 800-622-2826
Shen Manufacturing Company
W Conshohocken, PA 610-825-2790
Smith-Lee Company
Oshkosh, WI 800-327-9774
Sonoco
Pottstown, PA 800-377-2692
Springprint Medallion
Augusta, GA 800-543-5990
Stevens Linen Association
Dudley, MA 508-943-0813
Sultan Linens
New York, NY 212-689-8900
Tag-Trade Associated Group
Chicago, IL 800-621-8350
Tara Linens
Sanford, NC 800-476-8272
US Lace Paper Works
Oshkosh, WI 800-873-6459

Plastic Back Tag

Label Holders

Hopp Companies
New Hyde Park, NY 800-889-8425

Plastic Shelf Covers

Hopp Companies
New Hyde Park, NY 800-889-8425

Plastic Store Shelf

Moldings

Hopp Companies
New Hyde Park, NY 800-889-8425

Point of Sale Systems

APG Cash Drawer
Fridley, MN 763-571-5000
ASI/Restaurant Manager
Silver Spring, MD 800-356-6037
Astoria Laminations
Saint Clair Shores, MI 800-526-7325
Business Control Systems
Iselin, NJ 800-233-5876
Cache Box
Arlington, VA 800-603-4834
Compris Technologies
Duluth, GA 800-615-3301
Comtek Systems
San Antonio, TX 210-340-8253
Comtrex Systems Corporation
Moorestown, NJ 800-220-2669
Comus Restaurant Systems
Frederick, MD 301-698-6208
Custom Business Solutions
Irvine, CA 800-551-7674
Custom Design Interiors Service & Manufacturing
Largo, FL 727-536-2207
Cyplex
Los Angeles, CA
Data Management
San Angelo, TX 800-749-8463
Digital Dining/Menusoft
Springfield, VA 703-912-3000
Eaton Filtration, LLC
Tinton Falls, NJ 800-859-9212
Elo Touch Systems
Menlo Park, CA 800-557-1458
Fasteners for Retail
Cincinnati, OH 800-422-2547
Geac Computers
Nashua, NH 603-889-5152
Illinois Wholesale Cash Register Corporation
Elgin, IL 800-544-5493
Indiana Cash Drawer Company
Shelbyville, IN 800-227-4379
ITC Systems
Toronto, ON 877-482-8326
Lowen Color Graphics
Hutchinson, KS 800-545-5505
Loyal Manufacturing Corporation
Indianapolis, IN 317-359-3185
Madix, Inc.
Terrell, TX 800-776-2349
MAPS Software
Columbus, MS 662-328-6110
Metro Corporation
Wilkes Barre, PA 800-433-2233
Microcheck Solutions
Humble, TX 800-647-4524
Microtouch Systems
Methuen, MA 978-851-9939
National Computer Corporation
Greenville, SC 866-944-5164
Novax Group/Point of Sales
New York, NY 212-684-1244
Omron Systems
Schaumburg, IL 847-519-9465
Order-Matic Corporation
Oklahoma City, OK 800-767-6733
ParTech
New Hartford, NY 800-448-6505
PC/Poll Systems
Dubuque, IA 800-670-1736
RDS of Florida
Largo, FL
Reflex International
Norcross, GA 800-642-7640
Retail Automations Products
New York, NY 800-237-9144
Retail Decor
Ironton, OH 800-726-3402
Retalix
Miamisburg, OH 800-533-2277
Sable Technologies
Eagan, MN 800-722-5390
SalesData Software
San Jose, CA 408-281-5811
Scan Corporation
Brandon, FL 800-881-7226
SICOM Systems
Doylestown, PA 800-547-4266
Simply Products
Kunkletown, PA 610-681-6894
Southern Atlantic Label Company
Chesapeake, VA 800-456-5999
Squirrel Systems
Vancouver, BC 800-388-6824
Star Micronics
Edison, NJ 800-782-7636
Stoffel Seals Corporation
Tallapoosa, GA 800-422-8247
TEC America
Atlanta, GA 770-453-0868
Tinadre
Tampa, FL 813-866-0033
Touch Menus
Bellevue, WA 800-688-6368
US Magnetix
Golden Valley, MN 800- 3-0
VeriFone
Alpharetta, GA 770-410-0890
Zebra Technologies Corporation
Warwick, RI 800-556-7266

Pricer Signs

Dualite Sales & Service
Williamsburg, OH 513-724-7100

Pumps

Syrup & Soda Fountain

Fristam Pumps
Middleton, WI 800-841-5001
John Crane Mechanical Sealing Devices
Morton Grove, IL 800-732-5464
Manitowoc Foodservice
Sellersburg, IN 800-367-4233
Procon Products
Murfreesboro, TN 615-890-5710
Rio Syrup Company
Saint Louis, MO 800-325-7666
Server Products
Richfield, WI 800-558-8722
SHURflo
Cypress, CA 800-854-3218
Standex International Corporation
Salem, NH 603-893-9701
Superflex
Brooklyn, NY 800-394-3665

Racks

Bakery

AFCO Manufacturing
Cincinnati, OH 800-747-7332
Allied Bakery and Food Service Equipment
Santa Fe Springs, CA 562-945-6506
AMCO Corporation
City of Industry, CA 626-855-2550
ARC Specialties
Valencia, CA 661-775-8500
Better Bilt Products
Addison, OH 800-544-4550
BMH Equipment
Sacramento, CA 800-350-8828
California Caster & Handtruck
San Francisco, CA 800-950-8750
Cannon Equipment Company
Rosemount, MN 800-825-8501
Crown Custom Metal Spinning
Concord, ON 800-750-1924
Curtron Products
Pittsburgh, PA 800-833-5005
DBE Inc
Concord, ON 800-461-5313
Dubuque Steel Products Company
Dubuque, IA 563-556-6288
EPCO
Murfreesboro, TN 800-251-3398
Esterle Mold & Machine Company
Stow, OH 800-411-4086
Hodges
Vienna, IL 800-444-0011
Lakeside Manufacturing
Milwaukee, WI 888-558-8574
Langer Manufacturing Company
Cedar Rapids, IA 800-728-6445
Leggett & Platt StorageP
Vernon Hills, IL 847-816-6246
Lynch-Jamentz Company
Lakewood, CA 800-828-6217
M&E Manufacturing Company
Kingston, NY 845-331-2110
Magna Industries
Lakewood, NJ 800-510-9856
Malco Manufacturing Corporation
Los Angeles, CA 866-477-7267
Market Forge Industries
Everett, MA 866-698-3188
Marlin Steel Wire Products
Baltimore, MD 877-762-7546
Metro Corporation
Wilkes Barre, PA 800-433-2233
Micro Wire Products Inc.
Brockton, MA 508-584-0200
National Cart Company
Saint Charles, MO 636-947-3800
Olson Wire Products Company
Halethorpe, MD 410-242-1945
Omega Industries
St Louis, MO 314-961-1668
Otto Braun Bakery Equipment
Buffalo, NY 716-824-1252
Piper Products
Wausau, WI 800-544-3057
Proluxe
Paramount, CA 800-594-5528
Sitka Store Fixtures
Kansas City, MO 800-821-7558
SPG International LLC
Covington, GA 877-503-4774
Storage Unlimited
Nixa, MO 800-478-6642
Straits Steel & Wire Company
Ludington, MI 231-843-3416
Super Systems
Wausau, WI 800-558-5880
Superior Products Company
Saint Paul, MN 800-328-9800
Trepte's Wire & Metal Works
Bellflower, CA 800-828-6217

Wirefab
Worcester, MA 877-877-4445

Display, Store

Abalon Precision Manufacturing Corporation
Bronx, NY 800-888-2225
Acryline
North Attleboro, MA 508-695-7124
ARC Specialties
Valencia, CA 661-775-8500
Arlington Display Industries
Detroit, MI 313-837-1212
Art Wire Works
Bedford Park, IL 708-458-3993
Art-Phyl Creations
Hialeah, FL 800-327-8318
Beemak Plastics
La Mirada, CA 800-421-4393
Best Brands Home Products
New York, NY 212-684-7456
Better Bilt Products
Addison, OH 800-544-4550
BMH Equipment
Sacramento, CA 800-350-8828
Cannon Equipment Company
Rosemount, MN 800-825-8501
Chroma Tone
Saint Clair, PA 800-878-1552
Despro Manufacturing
Cedar Grove, NJ 800-292-9906
Display Creations
Brooklyn, NY 718-257-2300
Dubuque Steel Products Company
Dubuque, IA 563-556-6288
Dunn Woodworks
Shrewsbury, PA 877-835-8592
E-Z Shelving Systems
Merriam, KS 800-353-1331
Eastern Plastics
Pawtucket, RI 800-442-8585
Emco Industrial Plastics
Cedar Grove, NJ 800-292-9906
Enterprise Products
Bell Gardens, CA 562-928-1918
Fab-X/Metals
Washington, NC 800-677-3229
General Cage
Elwood, IN 800-428-6403
Harmar Products
Sarasota, FL 800-833-0478
Hewitt Manufacturing Company
Waldron, IN 765-525-9829
HMG Worldwide In-Store Marketing
New York, NY 212-736-2300
Hodges
Vienna, IL 800-444-0011
Houston Wire Works, Inc.
South Houston, TX 800-468-9477
Ideal Wire Works
Alhambra, CA 626-282-1302
Ironwood Displays
Niles, MI 231-683-8500
JEM Wire Products
Middletown, CT 860-347-0447
Kaines West Michigan Company
Ludington, MI 231-845-1281
Key Material Handling
Simi Valley, CA 800-539-7225
L&S Products
Coldwater, MI 517-279-9526
L.A. Darling Company
Paragould, AR 800-643-3499
Langer Manufacturing Company
Cedar Rapids, IA 800-728-6445
Load King Manufacturing Company
Jacksonville, FL 800-531-4975
Loyal Manufacturing Corporation
Indianapolis, IN 317-359-3185
Marlin Steel Wire Products
Baltimore, MD 877-762-7546
McMillin Manufacturing Corporation
Los Angeles, CA 323-268-1900
Melrose Displays
Passaic, NJ 973-471-7700
Merchandising Systems Manufacturing
Union City, CA 800-523-1468
Metaline Products Company
South Amboy, NJ 732-721-1373
Metro Corporation
Wilkes Barre, PA 800-433-2233
METRO Material Handling & Storage Products
Wilkes Barre, PA 800-433-2232
Midwest Wire Products
Sturgeon Bay, WI 800-445-0225
Mirro Products Company
High Point, NC 336-885-4166
Multi-Panel Display Corporation
Brooklyn, NY 800-439-0879
Olson Wire Products Company
Halethorpe, MD 410-242-1945
Omega Industries
St Louis, MO 314-961-1668
Peterson Manufacturing Company
Plainfield, IL 800-547-8995
Pinquist Tool & Die Company
Brooklyn, NY 800-752-0414
Piper Products
Wausau, WI 800-544-3057
Polaris Industrial Corporation
Dayton, OH 937-236-8000
Princeton Shelving
Cedar Rapids, IA 319-369-0355
Quality Industries
La Vergne, TN 615-793-3000
R&D Brass
Wappingers Falls, NY 800-447-6050
R.I. Enterprises
Hernando, MS 662-429-7863
Racks
San Diego, CA 619-661-0987
Rex Art Manufacturing Corp.
Lindenhurst, NY 631-884-4600
Ridg-U-Rak
North East, PA 866-479-7225
Riverside Wire & Metal Co.
Ionia, MI 616-527-3500
Royal Display Corporation
Middletown, CT 800-569-1295
Royce Phoenix
Glendale, AZ 602-256-0006
Selma Wire Products Company
Selma, IN 765-282-3532
SEMCO
Ocala, FL 800-749-6894
Southern Imperial
Rockford, IL 800-747-4665
Southwest Fixture Company
Dallas, TX 214-634-2800
Spot Wire Works Company
Philadelphia, PA 215-627-6124
Steel City Corporation
Youngstown, OH 800-321-0350
Straits Steel & Wire Company
Ludington, MI 231-843-3416
Superior Products Company
Saint Paul, MN 800-328-9800
Swanson Wire Works Industries, Inc.
Mesquite, TX 972-288-7465
Technibilt/Cari-All
Newton, NC 800-233-3972
Thorco Industries LLC
Lamar, MO 800-445-3375
Toledo Wire Products
Toledo, OH 888-430-7445
Vomela/Harbor Graphics
St Paul, MN 800-645-1012
Vulcan Industries
Moody, AL 888-444-4417
W.J. Egli Company
Alliance, OH 330-823-3666
Wahlstrom Manufacturing
Fontana, CA 909-822-4677
Wald Wire & Manufacturing Company
Oshkosh, WI 800-236-0053
Wire Products Manufacturing Company
Merrill, WI 715-536-7144
Wiremaid Products
Coral Springs, FL 800-770-4700
Woerner Wire Works
Omaha, NE 402-451-5414
Xtreme Beverages, LLC
Dana Point, CA 949-495-7929
Yeager Wire Works
Berwick, PA 570-752-2769

Restaurant Supplies & Equipment

Action Lighting
Bozeman, MT 800-248-0076
Advance Energy Technologies
Clifton Park, NY 800-724-0198
Alegacy Food Service Products Group, Inc.
Santa Fe Springs, CA 800-848-4440
AMC Industries
Tampa, FL 813-989-9663
American Restaurant Supply
Everett, WA 888-770-2424
Anderson Wood Products Company
Louisville, KY 502-778-5591
ASI/Restaurant Manager
Silver Spring, MD 800-356-6037
Asian Foods
St. Paul, MN 800-274-2655
Bargreen-Ellingson
Tacoma, WA 800-322-4441
Blue Line Foodservice Distributing
Farmington Hills, MI 800-892-8272
Borden
Columbus, OH 614-225-4953
Browne & Company
Markham, ON 905-475-6104
Carroll Chair Company
Onalaska, WI 800-331-4707
Charles Mayer Studios
Akron, OH 330-535-6121
Co-Rect Products
Golden Valley, MN 800-328-5702
Coastal Canvas Products Company
Savannah, GA 800-476-5174
Commercial Textiles Corporation-Best Buy Uniforms
Homestead, PA 800-345-1924
Cove Woodworking
Gloucester, MA 800-273-0037
Curtron Products
Pittsburgh, PA 800-833-5005
Daga Restaurant Ware
Honolulu, HI 808-847-3100
Dorado Carton Company
Dorado, PR 787-796-1670
Electro-Steam Generator Corporation
Rancocas, NJ 866-617-0764
Ex-Cell Kaiser
Franklin Park, IL 847-451-0451
Fashion Seal Uniforms
Seminole, FL 727-397-9611
Great Western Products
Ontario, CA 888-598-5588
Green Metal Fabricated Company
West Sacramento, CA 916-371-0192
H.A. Sparke Company
Shreveport, LA 318-222-0927
Industrial Sheet Metal
Cleveland, OH 216-431-9650
Inland Showcase & Fixture Company
Fresno, CA 559-237-4158
Instacomm Canada
Oakville, ON 877-426-2783
Kessenich's Restaurant Supplies
Madison, WI 800-248-0555
Lauritzen & Makin
Fort Worth, TX 817-921-0218
Libra Technical Center
Metuchen, NJ 732-321-5487
Lockwood Manufacturing
Livonia, MI 800-521-0238
Menu Graphics
Olmsted Falls, OH 216-696-1460
Metal Masters Northwest
Lynnwood, WA 425-775-4481
Metro Corporation
Wilkes Barre, PA 800-433-2233
Mosshaim Innovations
Jacksonville, FL 888-995-7775
NTN Wireless
Norcross, GA 800-637-8639
Order-Matic Corporation
Oklahoma City, OK 800-767-6733
Pinnacle Furnishing
Aberdeen, NC 866-229-5704
RDS of Florida
Largo, FL
Rx Honing Machine Corporation
Mishawaka, IN 800-346-6464
Sable Technologies
Eagan, MN 800-722-5390
Sandler Seating
Atlanta, GA 404-982-9000
Sarasota Restaurant Equipment
Sarasota, FL 800-434-1410
Shanker Industries
Deer Park, NY 877-742-6561
Sign Classics
San Jose, CA 408-298-1600
Sign Products
Sheridan, WY 800-532-4753

Sims Superior Seating
Locust Grove, GA. 800-729-9178
Standex International Corporation
Salem, NH. 603-893-9701
Sturdi-Bilt Restaurant Equipment
Whitmore Lake, MI 800-521-2895
Superior Products Company
Saint Paul, MN 800-328-9800
Tango Shatterproof Drinkware
Walpole, MA. 888-898-2646
TEC America
Atlanta, GA. 770-453-0868
Tec Art Industries Inc
Wixom, MI 800-886-6615
Trojan Commercial Furni ture Inc.
Montereal, QC 877-271-3878
Univogue
Dallas, TX. 800-527-3374
Valley Fixtures
Sparks, NV 775-331-1050
Waymar Industries
Burnsville, MN 888-474-1112
Wheel Tough Company
Terre Haute, IN 888-765-8833
Woodard
Coppell, TX 800-877-2290

Salad Bars

Advanced Design Manufacturing
Concord, CA. 800-690-0002
Atlas Metal Industries
Kenton, HR. 208-907-1374
Brass Smith
Denver, CO 800-662-9595
Craig Manufacturing
Irvington, NJ. 800-631-7936
Custom Plastics
Decatur, GA 404-373-1691
Delfield Company
Mt Pleasant, MI. 800-733-8821
Duke Manufacturing Company
Saint Louis, MO 800-735-3853
Forbes Industries
Ontario, CA. 909-923-4559
Galley
Jupiter, FL. 800-537-2772
Just Plastics
New York, NY 212-569-8500
LaRosa Refrigeration & Equipment Company
Detroit, MI 800-527-6723
Lavi Industries
Valencia, CA. 800-624-6225
Load King Manufacturing Company
Jacksonville, FL 800-531-4975
N. Wasserstrom & Sons
Columbus, OH 800-999-9277
Northern Stainless Fabricating
Traverse City, MI 231-947-4580
Plymold
Kenyon, MN. 800-759-6653
PMI Food Equipment Group
Troy, OH 937-332-3000
R&D Brass
Wappingers Falls, NY. 800-447-6050
Steamway Corporation
Scottsburg, IN. 800-259-8171
Stryco Wire Products
North York, ON. 416-663-7000
Superior Products Company
Saint Paul, MN 800-328-9800
Tables Cubed
Chesterfield, MO 800-878-3001
United Showcase Company
Wood Ridge, NJ 800-526-6382
Wizard Art Glass
Chatsworth, CA 800-438-9565
Wylie Systems
Mississauga, ON. 800-525-6609
Yorkraft
York, PA 800-872-2044

Scanners

Check & Credit Card Verification Systems

Axiohm USA
Myrtle Beach, SC 843-443-3155
Bruins Instruments
Salem, NH. 603-898-6527
CSPI
Billerica, MA 978-663-7598
Intercard
St Louis, MO. 314-275-8066
Reflex International
Norcross, GA 800-642-7640
Retalix
Miamisburg, OH 800-533-2277
Scan Corporation
Brandon, FL 800-881-7226
TEC America
Atlanta, GA. 770-453-0868

Serving Equipment

A.J. Antunes & Company
Carol Stream, IL 800-253-2991
Ace Fabrication
Mobile, AL 251-478-0401
Advance Engineering Company
Township, MI 800-497-6388
Advanced Plastic Coating
Parsons, KS. 620-421-1660
Aero Manufacturing Company
Clifton, NJ. 800-631-8378
Aladdin Temp-Rite, LLC
Hendersonville, TN. 800-888-8018
Aladdin's Hookah & Loung Bar
Nashville, TN 615-329-3558
All State Fabricators Corporation
Florida, RI. 800-322-9925
AMCO Corporation
City of Industry, CA 626-855-2550
AMI
Richmond, CA 800-942-7466
Apex Fountain Sales
Philadelphia, PA 800-523-4586
ARC Specialties
Valencia, CA. 661-775-8500
Art Wire Works
Bedford Park, IL 708-458-3993
Asian Foods
St. Paul, MN 800-274-2655
Aurora Design Associates, Inc.
Salt Lake City, UT. 801-588-0111
Automatic Specialities Inc.
Marlborough, MA. 800-445-2370
Bakers Choice Products
Beacon Falls, CT. 203-720-1000
Bardes Plastics
Milwaukee, WI 800-558-5161
Bloomfield Industries
St. Louis, MO 888-356-5362
Bon Chef
Lafayette, NJ. 800-331-0177
Boyd Coffee Company
Portland, OR 800-545-4077
Brooklace
Oshkosh, WI 800-572-4552
C.R. Manufacturing
Waverly, NE 877-789-5844
Cal-Mil Plastic Products
Oceanside, CA 800-321-9069
California Vibratory Feeders
Anaheim, CA 800-354-0972
Carlisle Food Service Products
Oklahoma City, OK 800-654-8210
Carter-Hoffman Corp LLC
Mundelein, IL 800-323-9793
Component Hardware Group
Lakewood, NJ. 800-526-3694
Cr. Manufacturing
Waverly, NE 877-789-5844
Creative Forming
Ripon, WI 920-748-7285
Crespac Incorporated
Tucker, GA 800-438-1900
Crestware
North Salt Lake City, UT 800-345-0513
Custom Diamond International
Laval, QC 800-363-5926
Custom Molders
Rocky Mount, NC. 919-688-8061
Cyclamen Collection
Oakland, CA 510-434-7620
Dart Container Corporation
Mason, MI. 800-248-5960
De Ster Corporation
Atlanta, GA. 800-237-8270
Delco Tableware
Port Washington, NY 800-221-9557
Delfin Design & Manufacturing
Rcho Sta Marg, CA. 800-354-7919
Detroit Forming
Southfield, MI. 248-352-8108
Douglas Stephen Plastics
Paterson, NJ 973-523-3030
Duke Manufacturing Company
Saint Louis, MO 800-735-3853
Dura-Ware Company of America
Oklahoma City, OK 800-664-3872
Dynynstyl
Delray Beach, FL 800-774-7895
Eastern Silver Tabletop Manufacturing Company
Brooklyn, NY 888-422-4142
Edco Industries
Bridgeport, CT 203-333-8982
Ellingers
Sheboygan, WI 888-287-8906
Engineered Plastics
Gibsonville, NC 800-711-1740
EPCO
Murfreesboro, TN. 800-251-3398
Epic Products
Santa Ana, CA 800-548-9791
Eskay Metal Fabricating Company
Buffalo, NY. 800-836-8015
FETCO - Food Equipment Technologies Corporation
Lake Zurich, IL. 800-338-2699
Fold-Pak South
Columbus, GA 706-689-2924
FWE/Food Warming Equipment Company, Inc
Crystal Lake, IL 800-222-4393
Gaetano America
El Monte, CA 626-442-2858
Galley
Jupiter, FL. 800-537-2772
Gaychrome Division of CSL
Crystal Lake, IL 800-873-4370
Gessner Products Company
Ambler, PA 800-874-7808
Glaro
Hauppauge, NY 631-234-1717
Gourmet Display
Kent, WA. 800-767-4711
Grand Silver Company
Bronx, NY. 718-585-1930
Great Western Products
Ontario, CA. 888-598-5588
Gril-Del
Mankato, MN 800-782-7320
Grindmaster-Cecilware Corporation
Louisville, KY 800-695-4500
Hal-One Plastics
Olathe, KS. 800-626-5784
Hot Food Boxes
Mooresville, IN. 800-733-8073
HPI North America/ Plastics
Eagan, MN 800-752-7462
HPI North America/Plastics
Saint Paul, MN 800-752-7462
Infanti International
Staten Island, NY 800-874-8590
Innovative Plastics Corporation
Orangeburg, NY 845-359-7500
Institutional & Supermarket Equipment
Plantation, FL 954-584-3100
International Patterns, Inc.
Bay Shore, NY 631-952-2000
Jackstack
Inwood, NY. 800-999-9840
Jones-Zylon Company
West Lafayette, OH. 800-848-8160
K&I Creative Plastics
Jacksonville, FL 904-387-0438
Keating of Chicago
Mc Cook, IL 800-532-8464
Kelmin Products
Plymouth, FL 407-886-6079
Key Packaging Company
Sarasota, FL 941-355-2728
King Arthur
Statesville, NC 800-257-7244
Lakeside Manufacturing
Milwaukee, WI 888-558-8574
Lambertson Industries
Sparks, NV 800-548-3324
Lancaster Colony Corporation
Columbus, OH 800-292-7260
Leggett & Platt StorageP
Vernon Hills, IL 847-816-6246
Leon Bush Manufacturer
Glenview, IL. 847-657-8888
Lincoln Foodservice
Cleveland, OH 800-374-3004

Lodge Manufacturing Company
South Pittsburg, TN 423-837-5919
LoTech Industries
Lakewood, CO 800-295-0199
Low Temp Industries
Jonesboro, GA 770-478-8803
M&E Manufacturing Company
Kingston, NY 845-331-2110
Mack-Chicago Corporation
Chicago, IL 800-992-6225
Madsen Wire Products
Orland, IN 260-829-6561
Majestic
Bridgeport, CT 203-367-7900
Metal Master
Tucson, AZ 800-488-8729
Metal Masters Northwest
Lynnwood, WA 425-775-4481
Mid-West Wire Products, Inc
Ferndale, MI 800-989-9881
Middleby Worldwide
Elgin, IL 847-468-6068
Moli-International
Denver, CO 800-525-8468
Mosshaim Innovations
Jacksonville, FL 888-995-7775
Mr. Ice Bucket
New Brunswick, NJ 732-545-0420
National Scoop & Equipment Company
Spring House, PA 215-646-2040
Normandie Metal Fabricators
Port Washington, NY 800-221-2398
Novelty Crystal Corporation
Groveland, FL 352-429-9036
Novelty Crystal Corporation
Long Island City, NY 800-622-0250
Olde Country Reproductions
York, PA 800-358-3997
Olde Thompson/Leeds Engineering Corporation
Oxnard, CA 800-827-1565
Olive Can Company
Elgin, IL 847-468-7474
Orbis Corp.
Rexdale, ON 800-890-7292
Packtive Corporation
Belvidere, IL 815-547-1200
Palmer Distributors
St Clair Shores, MI 800-444-1912
Par-Pak
Houston, TX 888-272-7725
Plastocon
Oconomowoc, WI 800-966-0103
Polar Beer Systems
Sun City, CA 951-928-8171
Polar Ware Company
Sheboygan, WI 800-237-3655
Precision
Miami, FL 800-762-7565
Process Displays
New Berlin, WI 800-533-1764
Prolon
Port Gibson, MS 888-480-9828
Quipco Products
Sauget, IL 314-993-1442
Rexcraft Fine Chafers
Long Island City, NY 888-739-2723
Robinson Industries
Coleman, MI 989-465-6111
Rolland Machining & Fabricating
Moneta, VA 973-827-6911
Ronnie's Ceramic Company
San Francisco, CA 800-888-8218
Sani-Top Products
De Leon Springs, FL 800-874-6094
Server Products
Richfield, WI 800-558-8722
Service Ideas
Woodbury, MN 800-328-4493
Shammi Industries/Sammons Equipment
Corona, CA 800-417-9260
Sheffield Platers
San Diego, CA 800-227-9242
SICO America
Minneapolis, MN 800-328-6138
Spin-Tech Corporation
Hoboken, NJ 800-977-4692
Superior Products Company
Saint Paul, MN 800-328-9800
Techform
Mount Airy, NC 336-789-2115
TEMP-TECH Company
Springfield, MA 800-343-5579
Thermo-Serv
Dallas, TX 800-635-5559
Thermodynamics
Commerce City, CO 800-627-9037
Thermos Company
Schaumburg, IL 800-243-0745
Tomlinson Industries
Cleveland, OH 800-945-4589
Tops Manufacturing Company
Darien, CT 203-655-9367
Toscarora
Sandusky, OH 419-625-7343
Toska Foodservice Systems
Lannon, WI 262-253-4782
Tramontina USA
Sugar Land, TX 800-221-7809
Tray Pak
Reading, PA 610-926-5800
Tri-State Plastics
Glenwillard, PA 724-457-6900
Ullman Company
New York, NY 212-571-0068
Unique Plastics
Rio Rico, AZ 800-658-5946
Update International
Los Angeles, CA 800-747-7124
Vermillion Flooring Company
Springfield, MO 417-862-3785
Vollrath Company
Sheboygan, WI 920-457-4851
Waddington North America
Chelmsford, MA 888-962-2877
Weavewood, Inc.
Golden Valley, MN 800-367-6460
Wells Manufacturing Company
Verdi, NV 800-777-0450
Wilton Armetale Company
Mount Joy, PA 800-779-4586
WR Key
Scarborough, ON 416-291-6246
Yorkraft
York, PA 800-872-2044
Zeier Plastic & Manufacturing
Madison, WI 608-244-5782
Zeroll Company
Fort Pierce, FL 800-872-5000
Zoia Banquetier Company
Cleveland, OH 216-631-6414

Industrial Plant

Andgar Corporation
Ferndale, WA 360-366-9900
BMH Equipment
Sacramento, CA 800-350-8828
Dresser Instruments
Stratford, CT 800-328-8258
Institutional & Supermarket Equipment
Plantation, FL 954-584-3100
National Scoop & Equipment Company
Spring House, PA 215-646-2040
Quipco Products
Sauget, IL 314-993-1442
Standex International Corporation
Salem, NH 603-893-9701

Shelving

Store

Accent Store Fixtures
Kenosha, WI 800-545-1144
Amscor
Brooklyn, NY 800-825-9800
Arizona Store Equipment
Phoenix, AZ 800-624-8395
BMH Equipment
Sacramento, CA 800-350-8828
Borroughs Corporation
Kalamazoo, MI 800-748-0227
Cannon Equipment Company
Rosemount, MN 800-825-8501
Continental Commercial Products
Bridgeton, MO 800-325-1051
Despro Manufacturing
Cedar Grove, NJ 800-292-9906
E-Z Shelving Systems
Merriam, KS 800-353-1331
Easy Up Storage Systems
Seattle, WA 800-426-9234
Handy Store Fixtures
Newark, NJ 800-631-4280
Hodge Manufacturing Company
Springfield, MA 800-262-4634
Hodges
Vienna, IL 800-444-0011
Kent Corporation
Birmingham, AL 800-252-5368
L.A. Darling Company
Paragould, AR 800-643-3499
Leggett and Platt, Inc.
Carthage, MO 417-358-8131
LPI Imports
Chicago, IL 877-389-6563
Lyon Metal Products
Aurora, IL 630-892-8941
Madix, Inc.
Terrell, TX 800-776-2349
Madsen Wire Products
Orland, IN 260-829-6561
Metro Corporation
Wilkes Barre, PA 800-433-2233
METRO Material Handling & Storage Products
Wilkes Barre, PA 800-433-2232
Modar
Benton Harbor, MI 800-253-6186
Newcourt, Inc.
Madison, IN 800-933-0006
Pacific Store Designs
Garden Grove, CA 800-772-5661
Princeton Shelving
Cedar Rapids, IA 319-369-0355
Quantum Storage Systems
Miami, FL 800-685-4665
RTI Shelving Systems
Elmhurst, NY 800-223-6210
S&L Store Fixture Company
Miami, FL 800-205-4536
Sefi Fabricators
Amityville, NY 631-842-2200
SPG International LLC
Covington, GA 877-503-4774
Strong Hold Products
Louisville, KY 800-880-2625
Teilhaber Manufacturing Corporation
Broomfield, CO 800-358-7225
Tennsco Corporation
Dickson, TN 800-251-8184
Triple-A Manufacturing Company
Toronto, ON 800-786-2238
Western Pacific Storage Systems
San Dimas, CA 800-888-5707

Signs

Advertising

AAA Electrical Signs
McAllen, TX 800-825-5376
AAA Flag & Banner Manufacturing
Los Angeles, CA 800-266-4222
ABC Letter Art
Los Angeles, CA 888-261-5367
Ace Signs
Little Rock, AR 501-562-0800
Ace Stamp & Engraving
Lakewood, WA 253-582-3322
Acme Sign Corporation
Peabody, MA 978-535-6600
AD/Mart
Calumet City, IL 708-891-0990
Adams Signs & Graphics
Massillon, OH 888-886-9911
Affiliated Resources
Chicago, IL 800-366-9336
Alex Delvecchio Enterprises
Troy, MI 248-619-9600
Allen Industries
Greensboro, NC 336-668-2791
Allen Sign Company
Knoxville, TN 800-844-3524
Allred Marketing
Birmingham, AL 205-251-3700
Altrua Marketing Designs
Tallahassee, FL 800-443-6939
AM Graphics
Minneapolis, MN 612-341-2020
American Art Stamp
Gardena, CA 310-965-9004
American Label Mark
Chicago, IL 800-621-5808
American LED-gible
Columbus, OH 614-851-1100

American Menu Displays
Long Island City, NY 718-392-1032
Ameritech Signs
Santa Monica, CA. 310-829-9359
Andersen Sign Company
Woodsville, NH. 603-787-6806
Andrew H. Lawson Company
Philadelphia, PA 800-411-6628
Arrow Sign & Awning Company
Ham Lake, MN. 800-621-9231
Art Kraft-Strauss Sign Corporation
New York, NY 212-265-5155
Artcraft Badge & Sign Company
Olney, MD. 800-739-0709
Audrey Signs
New York, NY 212-769-4992
B&B Neon Sign Company
Austin, TX. 800-791-6366
Baltimore Sign Company
Arnold, MD. 410-276-1500
Banner Idea
Newport Beach, CA 949-559-6600
Barlo Signs/Screengraphics
Hudson, NH 800-227-5674
Berloc Manufacturing & Sign Company
Sun Valley, CA 818-503-9823
Blue Ridge Signs
Weatherford, TX. 800-659-5645
Brown's Sign & Screen Printing
Covington, GA 800-540-3107
Cal-Mil Plastic Products
Oceanside, CA 800-321-9069
Canton Sign Company
Canton, OH 330-456-7151
Capital City Neon Sign Company
Monona, WI 608-222-1881
Cascade Signs & Neon
Salem, OR. 503-378-0012
Centredale Sign Company
Warwick, RI 401-231-1440
Century Sign Company
Fargo, ND 701-235-5323
Chain Store Graphics
Decatur, IL 800-443-7446
Chapman Sign
Warren, MI 586-758-1600
Charles Mayer Studios
Akron, OH. 330-535-6121
Chatelain Plastics
Findlay, OH. 419-422-4323
Chicago Show
Buffalo Grove, IL 847-955-0200
Christman Screenprint
Springfield, MI 800-962-9330
Chroma Tone
Saint Clair, PA. 800-878-1552
City Grafx
Eugene, OR 800-258-2489
City Neon Sign Company
Spokane, WA. 509-483-5171
City Sign Services
Dallas, TX. 214-826-4475
City Signs
Jackson, TN 877-248-9744
City Stamp & Seal Company
Austin, TX. 800-950-6074
Classic Signs
Amherst, NH. 800-734-7446
Clearr Corporation
Minneapolis, MN 800-548-3269
Coleman Stamps, Signs & Recognition Products
Daytona Beach, FL. 386-253-1206
Color Ad Tech Signs
Amarillo, TX. 806-374-8117
Comco Signs
Charlotte, NC 704-375-2338
Comet Neon Advertising Company
San Antonio, TX. 210-341-7245
Command Packaging
Vernon, CA 800-996-2247
Connecticut Laminating Company
New Haven, CT. 800-753-9119
Cook Neon Signs
Tullahoma, TN 931-455-0944
Corsair Display Systems
Canandalgua, NY 800-347-5245
Couch & Philippi
Stanton, CA. 800-854-3360
Courtesy Sign Company
Amarillo, TX. 806-373-6609
Creative Signage System,
College Park, MD 800-220-7446

Crown Marking
Minneapolis, MN 800-305-5249
Cuerden Sign Company
Conway, AR 501-329-6317
Cummings
Nashville, TN 615-673-8999
Curzon Promotional Graphics
Omaha, NE 800-769-7446
Custom I.D.
Venice, FL 800-242-8430
CustomColor Corporation
Lenexa, KS 888-605-4050
D&D Sign Company
Wichita Falls, TX 940-692-4643
Day Nite Neon Signs
Dartmouth, NS 902-469-7095
Daytech Limited
Toronto, ON 877-329-1907
Delta Signs
Haltom City, TX 866-643-3582
Denver Sign Systems
Denver, CO 888-295-7446
Derse
Milwaukee, WI 800-562-2300
Dewey & Wilson Displays
Lincoln, NE. 402-489-0868
Diamond Sign Company
Costa Mesa, CA 714-545-1440
Dimension Graphics
Grand Rapids, MI 855-476-1281
Dinosaur Plastics
Houston, TX 713-923-2278
Display Concepts
Trenton, ME 800-446-0033
Dixie Neon Company
Tampa, FL 813-248-2531
Dixie Signs
Lakeland, FL. 863-644-3521
Dove Screen Printing Company
Royston, GA 706-245-4975
Dowling Company
Fredericksburg, VA. 800-572-2100
Doyle Signs
Addison, IL 630-543-9490
DRS Designs
Bethel, CT. 888-792-3740
Dualite Sales & Service
Williamsburg, OH. 513-724-7100
Dwinell's Central Neon
Yakima, WA 800-932-8832
Dynamic Packaging
Minneapolis, MN 800-878-9380
Ehrgott Rubber Stamp Company
Indianapolis, IN 317-353-2222
Electric City Signs & Neon Inc.
Anderson, SC 800-270-5851
Elro Sign Company
Gardena, CA 800-927-4555
Empire Screen Printing, Inc.
Onalaska, WI. 608-783-3301
Engraving Specialists
Royal Oak, MI 248-542-2244
Esco Manufacturer
Watertown, SD 800-843-3726
ESCO Manufacturing, Inc
Watertown, SD 800-843-3726
Everett Stamp Works
Everett, WA. 425-258-6747
Exhibitron Corporation
Grants Pass, OR 800-437-4571
F.O. Carlson Company
Chicago, IL 773-847-6900
Fair Publishing House
Norwalk, OH. 800-824-3247
Federal Sign
Carmel, IN. 800-527-9495
Federal Sign of Rhode Island
Providence, RI 401-421-3400
Ferrer Corporation
San Juan, PR 787-761-5151
Fiber Does
San Jose, CA. 408-453-5533
First Choice Sign & Lighting
Escondido, CA 800-659-0629
Flexlume Sign Corporation
Buffalo, NY. 716-884-2020
FMI Display
Elkins Park, PA. 215-663-1998
Foley Sign Company
Seattle, WA. 206-324-3040
FormFlex
Bloomingdale, IN 800-255-7659

Fort Hill Sign Products, Inc.
Hopedale, MA. 508-381-0357
Fox Stamp, Sign & Specialty
Menasha, WI. 800-236-3699
France Personalized Signs
Cleveland, OH 216-241-2198
Franklin Rubber Stamp Company
Wilmington, DE 302-654-8841
Frazier Signs
Decatur, IL 217-429-2349
Frost Manufacturing Corporation
Worcester, MA 800-462-0216
Futura 2000 Corporation
Miami, FL. 305-256-5877
Gannett Outdoor of New J
Fairfield, NJ 973-575-6900
Gardenville Signs
Baltimore, MD 410-485-4800
Gary Sign Company
Merrillville, IN 219-942-3191
Gelberg Signs
Washington, DC 800-443-5237
General Neon Sign Company
San Antonio, TX. 210-227-1203
General Sign Company
Sheffield, AL. 256-383-3176
Gessner Products Company
Ambler, PA 800-874-7808
Glaro
Hauppauge, NY 631-234-1717
Glolite
Des Plaines, IL 847-803-4500
Glover Rubber Stamp Corporation
Wills Point, TX. 214-824-6900
Gordon Sign Company
Denver, CO 303-629-6121
Grays Harbor Stamp Works
Aberdeen, WA. 800-894-3830
Green Mountain Graphics
Long Island City, NY 718-472-3377
Gribble Stamp & Stencil Company
Houston, TX 713-228-5358
Gulf Coast Sign Company
Pensacola, FL 800-768-3549
Haden Signs of Texas
Lubbock, TX. 806-744-4404
Hammar & Sons Sign Company
Pelham, NH. 800-527-7446
Handicap Sign
Grand Rapids, MI 800-690-4888
Hanley Sign Company
Latham, NY. 518-783-6183
Hardin Signs
Peoria, IL. 309-688-4111
Harlan Laws Corporation
Durham, NC 800-596-7602
Harting Graphics
Wilmington, DE 800-848-1373
Heath & Company
Roswell, GA 770-650-2724
Heath & Company
Alhambra, CA. 800-421-9069
Hiclay Studios
St Louis, MO. 314-533-8393
HMG Worldwide In-Store Marketing
New York, NY 212-736-2300
Hoarel Sign Company
Amarillo, TX. 806-373-2175
Holsman Sign Services
Cleveland, OH 216-761-4433
Horn & Todak
Fairfax, VA 703-352-7330
Hub-Federal Signs
Providence, RI 401-421-9643
Hutz Sign & Awning
Youngstown, OH. 330-743-5168
I.H. McBride Sign Company
Lynchburg, VA 434-847-4151
IdentaBadge
Lafayette, LA 800-325-8247
Image National
Nampa, ID. 208-345-4020
Imperial Plastics
Lakeville, MN. 952-469-4951
Imperial Signs & Manufacturing
Rapid City, SD 605-348-2511
Industrial Sign Company
South El Monte, CA 800-596-3720
Industrial Signs
New Orleans, LA 504-736-0600
INOVAR Packaging Group
Arlington, TX 800-285-2235

Insignia Systems
Minneapolis, MN 800-874-4648
Interior Systems
Milwaukee, WI 800-837-8373
International Patterns, Inc.
Bay Shore, NY 631-952-2000
J.V. Reed & Company
Louisville, KY 877-258-7333
Jack Stone Lighting & Electrical
Landover, MD 301-322-3323
Janedy Sign Company
Everett, MA 617-776-5700
JBC Plastics
St Louis, MO 877-834-5526
Jeffcoat Signs
Gainesville, FL 877-377-4248
John I. Nissly Company
Lancaster, PA 717-393-3841
Johnson Brothers Sign Company
South Whitley, IN 800-477-7516
Joseph Struhl Company
Garden City Park, NY 800-552-0023
Jutras Signs
Manchester, NH 800-924-3524
K&I Creative Plastics
Jacksonville, FL 904-387-0438
K&M International
Twinsburg, OH 330-425-2550
Kessler Sign Company
Zanesville, OH 800-686-1870
King Electric Sign Co
Nampa, ID 208-466-2000
King Sign Company
Akron, OH 330-762-7421
Krimstock Enterprises
Pennsauken, NJ 856-665-3676
Krusoe Sign Company
Cleveland, OH 216-447-1177
L&L Engraving Company
Gilford, NH 888-524-3032
Lake Shore Industries
Erie, PA 800-458-0463
Lamar
Pearl, MS 800-893-2560
Lamar Advertising Co
Baton Rouge, LA 225-926-1000
Lasermation
Philadelphia, PA 800-523-2759
Lawrence Signs
St Paul, MN 800-998-8901
Leathertone
Findlay, OH 419-429-0188
License Ad Plate Company
Cleveland, OH 216-265-4200
Lion Labels
South Easton, MA 800-875-5300
Little Rock Sign
Conway, AR 501-327-4166
Lone Star Banners and Flags
Fort Worth, TX 800-288-9625
Long Island Stamp Corporation
Flushing, NY 800-547-8267
LSI Industries Inc.
Cincinnati, OH 513-793-3200
Lynn Sign
Andover, MA 800-225-5764
M&M Displays
Philadelphia, PA 800-874-7171
MacDonald's Magnetic Signs
Alamo, TX 956-787-0016
Maier Sign Systems
Saddle Brook, NJ 201-845-7555
Maltese Signs
Norcross, GA 770-368-0911
Mankuta Brothers Rubber Stamp Company, Inc.
Bohemia, NY 800-223-4481
Mansfield Rubber Stamp
Mansfield, OH 419-524-1442
Master Printers
Canon City, CO 719-275-8608
Master Signs
Dallas, TX 214-338-4727
Mastermark
Kent, WA 206-762-9610
McNeill Signs
Pompano Beach, FL 954-946-3474
MDI WorldWide
Farmington Hills, MI 800-228-8925
Metro Signs
N Las Vegas, NV 702-649-9333
Milwaukee Sign Company
Grafton, WI 262-375-5740
Mirro Products Company
High Point, NC 336-885-4166
MLS Signs
Chesterfield, MI 586-948-0200
Modagrafics
Rolling Meadows, IL 847-392-3980
Modern Stamp Company
Baltimore, MD 800-727-3029
Morrow Technologies Corporation
St Petersburg, FL 877-526-8711
Mulholland-Harper Company
Denton, MD 800-882-3052
Muskogee Rubber Stamp & Seal Company
Fort Gibson, OK 918-478-3046
Nameplates
St Paul, MN 651-228-1522
National Sign Corporation
Seattle, WA 206-282-0700
National Sign Systems
Hilliard, OH 800-544-6726
National Stock Sign Company
Santa Cruz, CA 800-462-7726
Neal Walters Poster Corporation
Bentonville, AR 501-273-2489
Nebraska Neon Sign Company
Lincoln, NE 402-476-6563
Nelson Custom Signs
Plymouth, MI 734-455-0500
Neon Design-a-Sign
Laguna Niguel, CA 888-636-6327
Norgus Silk Screen Company
Clifton, NJ 973-365-0600
North American Signs
South Bend, IN 800-348-5000
O.K. Marking Devices
Regina, SK 306-522-2856
Ontario Neon Company
Ontario, CA 909-986-4632
Parisian Novelty Company
Homewood, IL 773-847-1212
Patrick & Company
Dallas, TX 214-761-0900
Patrick Signs
Rockville, MD 301-770-6200
Pearson Signs Service
Hampstead, MD 410-239-3838
Perfect Plank Company
Oroville, CA 800-327-1961
Peterson Sign Company
Honolulu, HI 808-521-6785
Phoenix Sign Company
Aberdeen, WA 360-532-1111
Pierrepont Visual Graphics
Rochester, NY 585-235-5620
Pioneer Sign Company
Lewiston, ID 208-743-1275
Plasti-Line
Knoxville, TN 800-444-7446
Plastic Fantastics/Buck Signs
Ashland, OR 800-482-1776
Plastic Turning Company
Leominster, MA 978-534-8326
Plastic-Craft Products Corp
West Nyack, NY 800-627-3010
Poblocki
Milwaukee, WI 414-453-4010
Polyplastic Forms, Inc
Farmingdale, NY 800-428-7659
Posterloid Corporation
Long Island City, NY 800-651-5000
Pratt Poster Company
Indianapolis, IN 317-545-0842
Pride Neon
Sioux Falls, SD 605-336-3563
Print Source
Wakefield, RI 401-789-9339
Pro-Ad-Company
Portland, OR 800-287-5885
Process Displays
New Berlin, WI 800-533-1764
Qyk Syn Industries
Miami, FL 800-354-5640
R. Wireworks
Elmira, NY 800-550-4009
Radding Signs
Springfield, MA 413-736-5400
Rainbow Neon Sign Company
Houston, TX 713-923-2759
Ramsay Signs
Portland, OR 503-777-4555
Rapid Displays
Chicago, IL 800-356-5775
Rayne Plastic Signs
Rayne, LA 337-334-4276
Reading Plastic Fabricators
Temple, PA 610-926-3245
Regal Plastics
North Kansas City, MO 816-471-6390
Reinhold Sign Service
Green Bay, WI 920-494-7161
Retail Decor
Ironton, OH 800-726-3402
Rex Art Manufacturing Corp.
Lindenhurst, NY 631-884-4600
Rock-Tenn Company
St Paul, MN 651-641-4874
Rosson Sign Company
Macon, GA 478-788-3905
Roth Sign Systems
Petaluma, CA 800-585-7446
Roxanne Signs
Gaithersburg, MD 301-428-4911
RPA Process Technologies
Marblehead, MA 800-631-9707
RR Donnelley
Chicago, IL 800-742-4455
RTC Industries
Rolling Meadows, IL 847-640-2400
Rueff Sign Company
Louisville, KY 502-582-1714
Rutler Screen Printing
Phillipsburg, NJ 908-859-3327
S&S Metal & Plastics
Jacksonville, FL 904-731-4655
San Juan Signs
Farmington, NM 505-326-5511
Scott Sign Systems
Sarasota, FL 800-237-9447
Screen Print, Etc.
Anaheim, CA 714-630-1100
Seiz Signs Company
Hot Springs, AR 501-623-3181
Selby Sign Company
Pocomoke City, MD 410-957-1541
Service Neon Signs
Springfield, VA 703-354-3000
Seton Identification Products
Branford, CT 800-571-2596
Sexton Sign
Anderson, SC 864-226-6071
Shaw & Slavsky
Detroit, MI 800-521-7527
Sheridan Sign Company
Salisbury, MD 410-749-7441
Sign Classics
San Jose, CA 408-298-1600
Sign Experts
Pacific, MO 800-874-9942
Sign Factory
Cerritos, CA 562-809-1443
Sign Graphics
Evansville, IN 812-476-9151
Sign Products
Sheridan, WY 800-532-4753
Sign Shop
Rancho Cucamonga, CA 909-945-5888
Sign Systems, Inc.
Warren, MI 586-758-1600
Sign Warehouse, Inc.
Denison, TX 800-699-5512
SignArt Advertising
Van Buren, AR 479-474-8581
Signco
Kansas City, KS 913-722-1377
Signet Graphic Products
St Louis, MO 314-426-0200
Signmasters
Huntington Beach, CA 949-364-9128
Signs & Designs
Palmdale, CA 888-480-7446
Signs & Shapes International
Omaha, NE 800-806-6069
Signs O' Life
Avon, MA 800-750-1475
Southwest Neon Signs
San Antonio, TX 800-927-3221
Southwestern Porcelain Steel
Sand Springs, OK 918-245-1375
Steel Art Company
Norwood, MA 800-322-2828
Steingart Associates
South Fallsburg, NY 845-434-4321
Stello Products
Spencer, IN 800-868-2246

Stoffel Seals Corporation
Tallapoosa, GA 800-422-8247
Stout Sign Company
Saint Louis, MO 800-325-8530
Stricker & Company
La Plata, MD 301-934-8346
Suburban Sign Company
Anoka, MN 763-753-8849
Suburban Signs
College Park, MD 301-474-5051
Sun-Ray Sign & Glass
Holland, MI 616-392-2824
Super Vision International
Orlando, FL 407-857-9900
Superior Neon Sign, Inc.
Oklahoma City, OK 405-528-5515
SuppliesForLess
Hampton, VA 800-235-2201
Sutherland Stamp Company
San Diego, CA 858-233-7784
Symmetry Products Group
Lincoln, RI 401-365-6272
Tec Art Industries Inc
Wixom, MI 800-886-6615
The Shelby Company
Cleveland, OH 800-842-1650
Timely Signs
Elmont, NY 800-457-4467
Toledo Sign
Toledo, OH 419-244-4444
Total Identity Group
Cambridge, ON 877-551-5529
Triangle Sign Service Company
Halethorpe, MD 410-247-5300
Trident Plastics
Ivyland, PA 800-222-2318
Trinkle Signs & Displays
Youngstown, OH 330-747-9712
Trumbull Nameplates
New Smyrna Beach, FL 386-423-1105
Twenty/Twenty Graphics
Gaithersburg, MD 240-243-0511
Twin State Signs
Essex Junction, VT 802-872-8949
Universal Sign Company and Manufacturing Company
Lafayette, LA 337-234-1466
University-Brink
Foxboro, MA 617-926-4400
US Magnetix
Golden Valley, MN 800- 3-0
US Standard Sign Company
Franklin Park, IL 800-537-4790
Vacuform Industries
Columbus, OH 800-366-7446
Valley City Sign Company
Comstock Park, MI 616-784-5711
Varco Products
Chardon, OH 216-481-6895
Visual Marketing Associates
Santee, CA 619-258-0393
VMC Signs Inc.
Victoria, TX 361-575-0548
Volk Corporation
Farmington Hills, MI 800-521-6799
Vomela/Harbor Graphics
St Paul, MN 800-645-1012
Walker Companies
Oklahoma City, OK 800-522-3015
Walker Sign Company
Sun Valley, CA 818-252-7788
Wayne Industries
Clanton, AL 800-225-3148
Webster Packaging Corporation
Loveland, OH 513-683-5666
Wedlock Paper ConvertersLtd.
Mississauga, ON 800-388-0447
Welch Stencil Company
Scarborough, ME 800-635-3506
West Hawk Industries
Ann Arbor, MI 800-678-1286
Western Lighting
Franklin Park, IL 847-451-7200
WGN Flag & Decorating
Chicago, IL 773-768-8076
Winmark Stamp & Sign
Salt Lake City, UT 800-438-0480
Winnebago Sign Company
Fond Du Lac, WI 920-922-5930
Wisco Signs
Eau Claire, WI 715-835-6189
World Division
Dallas, TX 800-433-9843
Young Electric Sign Company
Salt Lake City, UT 800-444-3847

Changeable Letter

AAA Electrical Signs
McAllen, TX 800-825-5376
ABC Letter Art
Los Angeles, CA 888-261-5367
Acme Sign Corporation
Peabody, MA 978-535-6600
AD/Mart
Calumet City, IL 708-891-0990
Alex Delvecchio Enterprises
Troy, MI 248-619-9600
Arrow Sign & Awning Company
Ham Lake, MN 800-621-9231
Audrey Signs
New York, NY 212-769-4992
Charles Mayer Studios
Akron, OH 330-535-6121
Claridge Products & Equipment
Harrison, AR
Classic Signs
Amherst, NH 800-734-7446
Comco Signs
Charlotte, NC 704-375-2338
Exhibitron Corporation
Grants Pass, OR 800-437-4571
Fasteners for Retail
Cincinnati, OH 800-422-2547
Gelberg Signs
Washington, DC 800-443-5237
Glolite
Des Plaines, IL 847-803-4500
Hardin Signs
Peoria, IL 309-688-4111
Heath & Company
Roswell, GA 770-650-2724
Hiclay Studios
St Louis, MO 314-533-8393
Hoarel Sign Company
Amarillo, TX 806-373-2175
I.H. McBride Sign Company
Lynchburg, VA 434-847-4151
International Patterns, Inc.
Bay Shore, NY 631-952-2000
Lamb Sign
Manassas, VA 703-791-7960
Lynn Sign
Andover, MA 800-225-5764
MDI WorldWide
Farmington Hills, MI 800-228-8925
Neon Design-a-Sign
Laguna Niguel, CA 888-636-6327
Omaha Neon Sign Co, Inc.
Omaha, NE 800-786-6366
Poblocki
Milwaukee, WI 414-453-4010
Roth Sign Systems
Petaluma, CA 800-585-7446
Selby Sign Company
Pocomoke City, MD 410-957-1541
Seton Identification Products
Branford, CT 800-571-2596
Signets/Menu-Quik
Mentor, OH 800-775-6368
Signs O' Life
Avon, MA 800-750-1475
Super Vision International
Orlando, FL 407-857-9900
Tablet & Ticket Company
West Chicago, IL 800-438-4959
Toledo Sign
Toledo, OH 419-244-4444
Total Identity Group
Cambridge, ON 877-551-5529
Vomela/Harbor Graphics
St Paul, MN 800-645-1012

Electric

3M Dynamic Message Systems
Spokane Valley, WA 800-727-9111
AAA Electrical Signs
McAllen, TX 800-825-5376
Acme Sign Corporation
Peabody, MA 978-535-6600
AD/Mart
Calumet City, IL 708-891-0990
Adams Signs & Graphics
Massillon, OH 888-886-9911
Affiliated Resources
Chicago, IL 800-366-9336
Allen Industries
Greensboro, NC 336-668-2791
Allen Sign Company
Knoxville, TN 800-844-3524
Allred Marketing
Birmingham, AL 205-251-3700
Alphabet Signs
Gap, PA 800-582-6366
American LED-gible
Columbus, OH 614-851-1100
Attracta Sign
Rogers, MN 763-428-6377
Barlo Signs/Screengraphics
Hudson, NH 800-227-5674
Big Beam Emergency Systems
Crystal Lake, IL 815-459-6100
Canton Sign Company
Canton, OH 330-456-7151
Cascade Signs & Neon
Salem, OR 503-378-0012
Centredale Sign Company
Warwick, RI 401-231-1440
Chapman Sign
Warren, MI 586-758-1600
City Neon Sign Company
Spokane, WA 509-483-5171
City Sign Services
Dallas, TX 214-826-4475
City Signs
Jackson, TN 877-248-9744
Classic Signs
Amherst, NH 800-734-7446
Claude Neon Signs
Baltimore, MD 410-685-7575
Clearr Corporation
Minneapolis, MN 800-548-3269
Comco Signs
Charlotte, NC 704-375-2338
Comet Neon Advertising Company
San Antonio, TX 210-341-7245
Cook Neon Signs
Tullahoma, TN 931-455-0944
Corsair Display Systems
Canandalgua, NY 800-347-5245
County Neon Sign Corporation
Plainview, NY 516-349-9550
Cuerden Sign Company
Conway, AR 501-329-6317
Cummings
Nashville, TN 615-673-8999
Custom I.D.
Venice, FL 800-242-8430
Day Nite Neon Signs
Dartmouth, NS 902-469-7095
Delta Signs
Haltom City, TX 866-643-3582
Den Ray Sign Company
Jackson, TN 800-530-7291
Denver Sign Systems
Denver, CO 888-295-7446
Dixie Neon Company
Tampa, FL 813-248-2531
Dowling Company
Fredericksburg, VA 800-572-2100
Doyle Signs
Addison, IL 630-543-9490
Dualite Sales & Service
Williamsburg, OH 513-724-7100
Dwinell's Central Neon
Yakima, WA 800-932-8832
Electric City Signs & Neon Inc.
Anderson, SC 800-270-5851
Electro-Lite Signs
Rancho Cucamonga, CA 909-945-3555
Elro Sign Company
Gardena, CA 800-927-4555
Engraving Services Co.
Woodville South, SA
ESCO Manufacturing, Inc
Watertown, SD 800-843-3726
Everbrite
Greenfield, WI 800-558-3888
Everbrite LLC
Greenfield, WI 800-558-3888
Federal Sign of Rhode Island
Providence, RI 401-421-3400
Ferrer Corporation
San Juan, PR 787-761-5151
Fiber Does
San Jose, CA 408-453-5533

First Choice Sign & Lighting
Escondido, CA 800-659-0629
Frank Torrone & Sons
Staten Island, NY 718-273-7600
Frazier Signs
Decatur, IL 217-429-2349
Freeman Electric Company
Panama City, FL 850-785-7448
Fresno Neon Sign Company
Fresno, CA 559-292-2944
Frohling Sign Company
Nanuet, NY 845-623-2258
Gainesville Neon & Signs
Gainesville, FL 800-852-1407
Gelberg Signs
Washington, DC 800-443-5237
General Neon Sign Company
San Antonio, TX 210-227-1203
General Sign Company
Sheffield, AL 256-383-3176
Genlyte Thomas Group
Burlington, MA 662-842-7212
Gilbert Insect Light Traps
Jonesboro, AR 800-643-0400
Glolite
Des Plaines, IL 847-803-4500
Gordon Sign Company
Denver, CO 303-629-6121
Grande Ronde Sign Company
La Grande, OR 541-963-5841
Gulf Coast Sign Company
Pensacola, FL 800-768-3549
Haden Signs of Texas
Lubbock, TX 806-744-4404
Hammar & Sons Sign Company
Pelham, NH 800-527-7446
Harlan Laws Corporation
Durham, NC 800-596-7602
Heath & Company
Roswell, GA 770-650-2724
Heath & Company
Alhambra, CA 800-421-9069
Heath Signs
Reno, NV 775-359-9007
Hiclay Studios
St Louis, MO 314-533-8393
Hoarel Sign Company
Amarillo, TX 806-373-2175
Holsman Sign Services
Cleveland, OH 216-761-4433
Houser Neon Sign Company
Houston, TX 713-691-5765
Hub-Federal Signs
Providence, RI 401-421-9643
I.H. McBride Sign Company
Lynchburg, VA 434-847-4151
Image National
Nampa, ID 208-345-4020
Industrial Neon Sign Corporation
Houston, TX 713-748-6600
Industrial Sign Company
South El Monte, CA 800-596-3720
Industrial Signs
New Orleans, LA 504-736-0600
International Patterns, Inc.
Bay Shore, NY 631-952-2000
Jack Stone Lighting & Electrical
Landover, MD 301-322-3323
Johnson Brothers Sign Company
South Whitley, IN 800-477-7516
Jutras Signs
Manchester, NH 800-924-3524
K&M International
Twinsburg, OH 330-425-2550
King Electric Sign Co
Nampa, ID 208-466-2000
Lafayette Sign Company
Little Falls, NJ 800-343-5366
Lake City Signs
Boulder City, NV 702-293-5805
Leroy Signs, Inc.
Brooklyn Park, MN 763-535-0080
Little Rock Sign
Conway, AR 501-327-4166
Master Signs
Dallas, TX 214-338-4727
McNeill Signs
Pompano Beach, FL 954-946-3474
McQueen Sign & Lighting
Canton, OH 330-452-5769
MDI WorldWide
Farmington Hills, MI 800-228-8925

Milwaukee Sign Company
Grafton, WI 262-375-5740
Mirro Products Company
High Point, NC 336-885-4166
MLS Signs
Chesterfield, MI 586-948-0200
Mt. Vernon Neon Company
Mt Vernon, IL 618-242-0645
Mulholland-Harper Company
Denton, MD 800-882-3052
MultiMedia Electronic Displays
Rancho Cordova, CA 800-888-3007
National Menuboard
Auburn, WA 800-800-5237
National Sign Corporation
Seattle, WA 206-282-0700
National Sign Systems
Hilliard, OH 800-544-6726
Nelson Custom Signs
Plymouth, MI 734-455-0500
Neon Design-a-Sign
Laguna Niguel, CA 888-636-6327
North American Signs
South Bend, IN 800-348-5000
Oklahoma Neon
Tulsa, OK 888-707-6366
Omaha Neon Sign Co, Inc.
Omaha, NE 800-786-6366
Ontario Neon Company
Ontario, CA 909-986-4632
Pearson Signs Service
Hampstead, MD 410-239-3838
Phoenix Sign Company
Aberdeen, WA 360-532-1111
Plastic Arts Sign Company
Pensacola, FL 866-662-7060
Poblocki
Milwaukee, WI 414-453-4010
Pride Neon
Sioux Falls, SD 605-336-3563
Radding Signs
Springfield, MA 413-736-5400
Rainbow Neon Sign Company
Houston, TX 713-923-2759
Ramsay Signs
Portland, OR 503-777-4555
Rock-Tenn Company
St Paul, MN 651-641-4874
Rosson Sign Company
Macon, GA 478-788-3905
Roth Sign Systems
Petaluma, CA 800-585-7446
Roxanne Signs
Gaithersburg, MD 301-428-4911
Rueff Sign Company
Louisville, KY 502-582-1714
Sasser Signs
Danville, VA 800-752-6091
Selby Sign Company
Pocomoke City, MD 410-957-1541
Service Neon Signs
Springfield, VA 703-354-3000
Sexton Sign
Anderson, SC 864-226-6071
Sheridan Sign Company
Salisbury, MD 410-749-7441
Signart
Charlotte, NC 800-929-3521
SignArt Advertising
Van Buren, AR 479-474-8581
Signs & Designs
Palmdale, CA 888-480-7446
Signs O' Life
Avon, MA 800-750-1475
Southwest Neon Signs
San Antonio, TX 800-927-3221
Spann Sign Company
Kenosha, WI 262-658-1288
Steel Art Signs
Markham, ON 800-771-6971
Super Vision International
Orlando, FL 407-857-9900
Superior Neon Sign, Inc.
Oklahoma City, OK 405-528-5515
Superior Products Company
Saint Paul, MN 800-328-9800
Tec Art Industries Inc
Wixom, MI 800-886-6615
Texas Neon Advertising Company
San Antonio, TX 210-734-6694
Thomson-Leeds Company
New York, NY 800-535-9361

Toledo Sign
Toledo, OH 419-244-4444
Total Identity Group
Cambridge, ON 877-551-5529
Triple A Neon Company
Valley Village, CA 323-877-5381
Twin State Signs
Essex Junction, VT 802-872-8949
United Sign Company
Kansas City, MO 816-923-8208
Universal Sign Company and Manufacturing Company
Lafayette, LA 337-234-1466
University-Brink
Foxboro, MA 617-926-4400
Valley City Sign Company
Comstock Park, MI 616-784-5711
Varco Products
Chardon, OH 216-481-6895
Visual Marketing Associates
Santee, CA 619-258-0393
VMC Signs Inc.
Victoria, TX 361-575-0548
Western Lighting
Franklin Park, IL 847-451-7200
Weston Emergency Light Company
Waltham, MA 800-649-3756
White Way Sign & Maintenance
Mt Prospect, IL 800-621-4122
Wilhite Sign Company
Joplin, MO 417-623-1411
Winnebago Sign Company
Fond Du Lac, WI 920-922-5930
Wisco Signs
Eau Claire, WI 715-835-6189
Young Electric Sign Company
Salt Lake City, UT 800-444-3847

Interchangeable

Acme Sign Corporation
Peabody, MA 978-535-6600
AD/Mart
Calumet City, IL 708-891-0990
Allen Industries
Greensboro, NC 336-668-2791
American Menu Displays
Long Island City, NY 718-392-1032
Audrey Signs
New York, NY 212-769-4992
Claridge Products & Equipment
Harrison, AR
Comco Signs
Charlotte, NC 704-375-2338
Diskey Architectural Signage Inc.
Fort Wayne, IN 260-424-0233
Display Concepts
Trenton, ME 800-446-0033
Everbrite
Greenfield, WI 800-558-3888
Exhibitron Corporation
Grants Pass, OR 800-437-4571
Forbes Industries
Ontario, CA 909-923-4559
Frost Manufacturing Corporation
Worcester, MA 800-462-0216
Gelberg Signs
Washington, DC 800-443-5237
Gordon Sign Company
Denver, CO 303-629-6121
Heath & Company
Roswell, GA 770-650-2724
Hoarel Sign Company
Amarillo, TX 806-373-2175
I.H. McBride Sign Company
Lynchburg, VA 434-847-4151
Impulse Signs
Toronto, ON 866-636-8273
Lynn Sign
Andover, MA 800-225-5764
Maier Sign Systems
Saddle Brook, NJ 201-845-7555
Mainstreet Menu Systems
Brookfield, WI 800-782-6222
McQueen Sign & Lighting
Canton, OH 330-452-5769
MDI WorldWide
Farmington Hills, MI 800-228-8925
Menu Men
Palm Harbor, FL 727-934-7191
Norgus Silk Screen Company
Clifton, NJ 973-365-0600

Plasti-Line
Knoxville, TN 800-444-7446
Roth Sign Systems
Petaluma, CA 800-585-7446
Screen Print, Etc.
Anaheim, CA 714-630-1100
Tablet & Ticket Company
West Chicago, IL 800-438-4959
Toledo Sign
Toledo, OH 419-244-4444
Total Identity Group
Cambridge, ON 877-551-5529
US Magnetix
Golden Valley, MN 800- 3-0
Vomela/Harbor Graphics
St Paul, MN 800-645-1012
Wayne Industries
Clanton, AL 800-225-3148
Your Place Menu Systems
Carson City, NV 800-321-8105

Luminous Tube

AAA Electrical Signs
McAllen, TX 800-825-5376
Acme Sign Corporation
Peabody, MA 978-535-6600
Adams Signs & Graphics
Massillon, OH 888-886-9911
Allred Marketing
Birmingham, AL 205-251-3700
Alphabet Signs
Gap, PA 800-582-6366
Arrow Sign & Awning Company
Ham Lake, MN 800-621-9231
Audrey Signs
New York, NY 212-769-4992
B&B Neon Sign Company
Austin, TX 800-791-6366
Capital City Neon Sign Company
Monona, WI 608-222-1881
Cascade Signs & Neon
Salem, OR 503-378-0012
Centredale Sign Company
Warwick, RI 401-231-1440
Century Sign Company
Fargo, ND 701-235-5323
Cheshire Signs
Keene, NH 603-352-5985
City Neon Sign Company
Spokane, WA 509-483-5171
City Signs
Jackson, TN 877-248-9744
Claude Neon Signs
Baltimore, MD 410-685-7575
Clearr Corporation
Minneapolis, MN 800-548-3269
Cobb Sign Company
Burlington, NC 336-227-0181
Comco Signs
Charlotte, NC 704-375-2338
Cook Neon Signs
Tullahoma, TN 931-455-0944
County Neon Sign Corporation
Plainview, NY 516-349-9550
Custom I.D.
Venice, FL 800-242-8430
D&D Sign Company
Wichita Falls, TX 940-692-4643
Day Nite Neon Signs
Dartmouth, NS 902-469-7095
Den Ray Sign Company
Jackson, TN 800-530-7291
Denver Sign Systems
Denver, CO 888-295-7446
Display Concepts
Trenton, ME 800-446-0033
Dowling Company
Fredericksburg, VA 800-572-2100
Dualite Sales & Service
Williamsburg, OH 513-724-7100
Dwinell's Central Neon
Yakima, WA 800-932-8832
Electric City Signs & Neon Inc.
Anderson, SC 800-270-5851
Elro Sign Company
Gardena, CA 800-927-4555
ESCO Manufacturing, Inc
Watertown, SD 800-843-3726
Everbrite
Greenfield, WI 800-558-3888
Federal Sign of Rhode Island
Providence, RI 401-421-3400
Ferrer Corporation
San Juan, PR 787-761-5151
Frazier Signs
Decatur, IL 217-429-2349
Freeman Electric Company
Panama City, FL 850-785-7448
Fresno Neon Sign Company
Fresno, CA 559-292-2944
Frohling Sign Company
Nanuet, NY 845-623-2258
Gainesville Neon & Signs
Gainesville, FL 800-852-1407
General Neon Sign Company
San Antonio, TX 210-227-1203
General Sign Company
Sheffield, AL 256-383-3176
Grande Ronde Sign Company
La Grande, OR 541-963-5841
Gulf Coast Sign Company
Pensacola, FL 800-768-3549
Haden Signs of Texas
Lubbock, TX 806-744-4404
Hammar & Sons Sign Company
Pelham, NH 800-527-7446
Hardin Signs
Peoria, IL 309-688-4111
Harlan Laws Corporation
Durham, NC 800-596-7602
Heath & Company
Roswell, GA 770-650-2724
Heath & Company
Alhambra, CA 800-421-9069
Heath Signs
Reno, NV 775-359-9007
Hedges Neon Sales
Salina, KS 785-827-9341
Hoarel Sign Company
Amarillo, TX 806-373-2175
Holsman Sign Services
Cleveland, OH 216-761-4433
Houser Neon Sign Company
Houston, TX 713-691-5765
I.H. McBride Sign Company
Lynchburg, VA 434-847-4151
Imperial Signs & Manufacturing
Rapid City, SD 605-348-2511
Industrial Signs
New Orleans, LA 504-736-0600
Jeffcoat Signs
Gainesville, FL 877-377-4248
Jenkins Sign Company
Youngstown, OH 330-799-3205
Jet Lite Products
Highland, IL 618-654-2217
Jim Did It Sign Company
Allston, MA 617-782-2410
Johnson Brothers Sign Company
South Whitley, IN 800-477-7516
Jutras Signs
Manchester, NH 800-924-3524
K&M International
Twinsburg, OH 330-425-2550
King Electric Sign Co
Nampa, ID 208-466-2000
Lafayette Sign Company
Little Falls, NJ 800-343-5366
Leroy Signs, Inc.
Brooklyn Park, MN 763-535-0080
Maier Sign Systems
Saddle Brook, NJ 201-845-7555
Master Signs
Dallas, TX 214-338-4727
McNeill Signs
Pompano Beach, FL 954-946-3474
McQueen Sign & Lighting
Canton, OH 330-452-5769
MDI WorldWide
Farmington Hills, MI 800-228-8925
Mt. Vernon Neon Company
Mt Vernon, IL 618-242-0645
National Sign Corporation
Seattle, WA 206-282-0700
National Sign Systems
Hilliard, OH 800-544-6726
Nebraska Neon Sign Company
Lincoln, NE 402-476-6563
Neo-Kraft Signs
Lewiston, ME 800-339-2258
Neonetics
Hampstead, MD 410-374-8057
North American Signs
South Bend, IN 800-348-5000
Oklahoma Neon
Tulsa, OK 888-707-6366
Omaha Neon Sign Co, Inc.
Omaha, NE 800-786-6366
Ontario Neon Company
Ontario, CA 909-986-4632
Pacific Sign Construction
Poway, CA 858-486-8006
Pearson Signs Service
Hampstead, MD 410-239-3838
Peskin Neon Sign Company
Youngstown, OH 330-783-2470
Phoenix Sign Company
Aberdeen, WA 360-532-1111
Plastic Arts Sign Company
Pensacola, FL 866-662-7060
Poblocki
Milwaukee, WI 414-453-4010
Porter Bowers Signs
Des Moines, IA 515-253-9622
Pride Neon
Sioux Falls, SD 605-336-3563
Qyk Syn Industries
Miami, FL 800-354-5640
Rainbow Neon Sign Company
Houston, TX 713-923-2759
Rainbow Neon Sign Company
Salt Lake City, UT 801-466-7856
Ramsay Signs
Portland, OR 503-777-4555
Rosson Sign Company
Macon, GA 478-788-3905
Roth Sign Systems
Petaluma, CA 800-585-7446
Roxanne Signs
Gaithersburg, MD 301-428-4911
RR Donnelley
Chicago, IL 800-742-4455
Ruggles Sign Company
Versailles, KY 859-879-1199
Safety Light Corporation
Bloomsburg, PA 570-784-4344
Sasser Signs
Danville, VA 800-752-6091
Selby Sign Company
Pocomoke City, MD 410-957-1541
Service Neon Signs
Springfield, VA 703-354-3000
Sheridan Sign Company
Salisbury, MD 410-749-7441
Sign Products
Sheridan, WY 800-532-4753
SignArt Advertising
Van Buren, AR 479-474-8581
Signs & Designs
Palmdale, CA 888-480-7446
Signs O' Life
Avon, MA 800-750-1475
Spann Sign Company
Kenosha, WI 262-658-1288
Super Vision International
Orlando, FL 407-857-9900
SuppliesForLess
Hampton, VA 800-235-2201
Tablet & Ticket Company
West Chicago, IL 800-438-4959
Tec Art Industries Inc
Wixom, MI 800-886-6615
Texas Neon Advertising Company
San Antonio, TX 210-734-6694
Toledo Sign
Toledo, OH 419-244-4444
Total Identity Group
Cambridge, ON 877-551-5529
Triangle Sign Service Company
Halethorpe, MD 410-247-5300
Twin State Signs
Essex Junction, VT 802-872-8949
United Sign Company
Kansas City, MO 816-923-8208
Universal Sign Company and Manufacturing Company
Lafayette, LA 337-234-1466
University-Brink
Foxboro, MA 617-926-4400
VMC Signs Inc.
Victoria, TX 361-575-0548
Western Lighting
Franklin Park, IL 847-451-7200
Wilhite Sign Company
Joplin, MO 417-623-1411

Winnebago Sign Company
Fond Du Lac, WI 920-922-5930
Wisco Signs
Eau Claire, WI 715-835-6189
Your Place Menu Systems
Carson City, NV 800-321-8105

Plastic

ABC Letter Art
Los Angeles, CA 888-261-5367
Ace Stamp & Engraving
Lakewood, WA 253-582-3322
AD/Mart
Calumet City, IL 708-891-0990
Adams Signs & Graphics
Massillon, OH 888-886-9911
Allred Marketing
Birmingham, AL 205-251-3700
Audrey Signs
New York, NY 212-769-4992
B&B Neon Sign Company
Austin, TX 800-791-6366
Baltimore Sign Company
Arnold, MD 410-276-1500
Berlekamp Plastics
Fremont, OH 419-334-4481
Berryhill Signs
Memphis, TN 901-324-1730
Canton Sign Company
Canton, OH 330-456-7151
Capital City Neon Sign Company
Monona, WI 608-222-1881
Century Sign Company
Fargo, ND 701-235-5323
Chain Store Graphics
Decatur, IL 800-443-7446
Chatelain Plastics
Findlay, OH 419-422-4323
Cheshire Signs
Keene, NH 603-352-5985
Chroma Tone
Saint Clair, PA 800-878-1552
City Neon Sign Company
Spokane, WA 509-483-5171
City Signs
Jackson, TN 877-248-9744
City Stamp & Seal Company
Austin, TX 800-950-6074
Clearr Corporation
Minneapolis, MN 800-548-3269
Cobb Sign Company
Burlington, NC 336-227-0181
Comco Signs
Charlotte, NC 704-375-2338
Continental Commercial Products
Bridgeton, MO 800-325-1051
Creative Signage System,
College Park, MD 800-220-7446
Custom I.D.
Venice, FL 800-242-8430
Custom Plastics
Decatur, GA 404-373-1691
Custom Rubber Stamp Company
Crosby, MN 888-606-4579
Den Ray Sign Company
Jackson, TN 800-530-7291
Dimension Graphics
Grand Rapids, MI 855-476-1281
Dinosaur Plastics
Houston, TX 713-923-2278
Diskey Architectural Signage Inc.
Fort Wayne, IN 260-424-0233
Dixie Neon Company
Tampa, FL 813-248-2531
Dowling Company
Fredericksburg, VA 800-572-2100
Dwinell's Central Neon
Yakima, WA 800-932-8832
Eaton-Quade Company
Oklahoma City, OK 405-236-4475
Ed Smith's Stencil Works
New Orleans, LA 504-525-2128
Electric City Signs & Neon Inc.
Anderson, SC 800-270-5851
Elro Sign Company
Gardena, CA 800-927-4555
Emco Industrial Plastics
Cedar Grove, NJ 800-292-9906
EMED Company
Buffalo, NY 800-442-3633
Engraving Services Co.
Woodville South, SA
Engraving Specialists
Royal Oak, MI 248-542-2244
Everett Stamp Works
Everett, WA 425-258-6747
Exhibitron Corporation
Grants Pass, OR 800-437-4571
Federal Sign
Carmel, IN 800-527-9495
Ferrer Corporation
San Juan, PR 787-761-5151
Five-M Plastics Company
Marion, OH 740-383-6246
Forrest Engraving Company
New Rochelle, NY 914-632-9892
Fort Hill Sign Products, Inc.
Hopedale, MA 508-381-0357
France Personalized Signs
Cleveland, OH 216-241-2198
Franklin Rubber Stamp Company
Wilmington, DE 302-654-8841
Frazier Signs
Decatur, IL 217-429-2349
Freeman Electric Company
Panama City, FL 850-785-7448
Fresno Neon Sign Company
Fresno, CA 559-292-2944
Frohling Sign Company
Nanuet, NY 845-623-2258
Gelberg Signs
Washington, DC 800-443-5237
General Neon Sign Company
San Antonio, TX 210-227-1203
General Sign Company
Sheffield, AL 256-383-3176
Grande Ronde Sign Company
La Grande, OR 541-963-5841
Gulf Coast Sign Company
Pensacola, FL 800-768-3549
Hardin Signs
Peoria, IL 309-688-4111
Heath & Company
Roswell, GA 770-650-2724
Heath & Company
Alhambra, CA 800-421-9069
HMG Worldwide In-Store Marketing
New York, NY 212-736-2300
Hoarel Sign Company
Amarillo, TX 806-373-2175
Holsman Sign Services
Cleveland, OH 216-761-4433
Houser Neon Sign Company
Houston, TX 713-691-5765
Houston Stamp & Stencil Company
Houston, TX 713-869-4337
I.H. McBride Sign Company
Lynchburg, VA 434-847-4151
Ideal Office Supply & Rubber Stamp Company
Kingsport, TN 423-246-7371
Impact Awards & Promotions
Avon Park, FL 888-203-4225
Imperial Plastics
Lakeville, MN 952-469-4951
Imperial Signs & Manufacturing
Rapid City, SD 605-348-2511
Industrial Neon Sign Corporation
Houston, TX 713-748-6600
Jeffcoat Signs
Gainesville, FL 877-377-4248
Jenkins Sign Company
Youngstown, OH 330-799-3205
Jim Did It Sign Company
Allston, MA 617-782-2410
John I. Nissly Company
Lancaster, PA 717-393-3841
Johnson Brothers Sign Company
South Whitley, IN 800-477-7516
Joseph Struhl Company
Garden City Park, NY 800-552-0023
Just Plastics
New York, NY 212-569-8500
K&I Creative Plastics
Jacksonville, FL 904-387-0438
King Electric Sign Co
Nampa, ID 208-466-2000
King Products
Mississauga, ON 866-454-6757
King Sign Company
Akron, OH 330-762-7421
Kitchener Plastics
Kitchener, ON 800-429-5633
Krusoe Sign Company
Cleveland, OH 216-447-1177
L&L Engraving Company
Gilford, NH 888-524-3032
Lafayette Sign Company
Little Falls, NJ 800-343-5366
Lamb Sign
Manassas, VA 703-791-7960
Leathertone
Findlay, OH 419-429-0188
Legible Signs
Loves Park, IL 800-435-4177
Leroy Signs, Inc.
Brooklyn Park, MN 763-535-0080
License Ad Plate Company
Cleveland, OH 216-265-4200
Little Rock Sign
Conway, AR 501-327-4166
LPI, Legacy Plastics
Henderson, KY 270-827-1318
Lynn Sign
Andover, MA 800-225-5764
Maier Sign Systems
Saddle Brook, NJ 201-845-7555
Mansfield Rubber Stamp
Mansfield, OH 419-524-1442
Master Signs
Dallas, TX 214-338-4727
McNeill Signs
Pompano Beach, FL 954-946-3474
McQueen Sign & Lighting
Canton, OH 330-452-5769
MDI WorldWide
Farmington Hills, MI 800-228-8925
Mirro Products Company
High Point, NC 336-885-4166
Mulholland
Fort Worth, TX 817-624-1153
Mulholland-Harper Company
Denton, MD 800-882-3052
National Marker Company
North Smithfield, RI 800-453-2727
National Marking Products, Inc.
Richmond, VA 800-482-1553
National Sign Corporation
Seattle, WA 206-282-0700
National Stock Sign Company
Santa Cruz, CA 800-462-7726
Neo-Kraft Signs
Lewiston, ME 800-339-2258
Norgus Silk Screen Company
Clifton, NJ 973-365-0600
Oklahoma Neon
Tulsa, OK 888-707-6366
Omaha Neon Sign Co, Inc.
Omaha, NE 800-786-6366
Parisian Novelty Company
Homewood, IL 773-847-1212
Pearson Signs Service
Hampstead, MD 410-239-3838
Peskin Neon Sign Company
Youngstown, OH 330-783-2470
Phoenix Sign Company
Aberdeen, WA 360-532-1111
Plastech Corporation
Atlanta, GA 404-355-9682
Plasti-Line
Knoxville, TN 800-444-7446
Plastic Arts Sign Company
Pensacola, FL 866-662-7060
Plastic Turning Company
Leominster, MA 978-534-8326
Plastic-Craft Products Corp
West Nyack, NY 800-627-3010
Plastimatic Arts Corporation
Mishawaka, IN 800-442-3593
PM Plastics
Pewaukee, WI 262-691-1700
Print Source
Wakefield, RI 401-789-9339
Qyk Syn Industries
Miami, FL 800-354-5640
Rainbow Neon Sign Company
Houston, TX 713-923-2759
Rayne Plastic Signs
Rayne, LA 337-334-4276
Regal Plastics
North Kansas City, MO 816-471-6390
Reidler Decal Corporation
Saint Clair, PA 800-628-7770
Reinhold Sign Service
Green Bay, WI 920-494-7161

Richardson's Stamp Works
Houston, TX 713-973-0300
Rock-Tenn Company
St Paul, MN 651-641-4874
Rosson Sign Company
Macon, GA 478-788-3905
Roth Sign Systems
Petaluma, CA 800-585-7446
RR Donnelley
Chicago, IL 800-742-4455
Rueff Sign Company
Louisville, KY 502-582-1714
Ruggles Sign Company
Versailles, KY 859-879-1199
S&S Metal & Plastics
Jacksonville, FL 904-731-4655
Scott Sign Systems
Sarasota, FL 800-237-9447
Service Neon Signs
Springfield, VA 703-354-3000
Seton Identification Products
Branford, CT 800-571-2596
Sign Graphics
Evansville, IN 812-476-9151
Sign Systems, Inc.
Warren, MI 586-758-1600
SignArt Advertising
Van Buren, AR 479-474-8581
Signet Graphic Products
St Louis, MO 314-426-0200
Signs & Designs
Palmdale, CA 888-480-7446
Spann Sign Company
Kenosha, WI 262-658-1288
Stoffel Seals Corporation
Tallapoosa, GA 800-422-8247
Suburban Sign Company
Anoka, MN 763-753-8849
Suburban Signs
College Park, MD 301-474-5051
Superior Neon Sign, Inc.
Oklahoma City, OK 405-528-5515
Sutherland Stamp Company
San Diego, CA 858-233-7784
Tablet & Ticket Company
West Chicago, IL 800-438-4959
Three P
Salt Lake City, UT 801-486-7407
Toledo Sign
Toledo, OH 419-244-4444
Total Identity Group
Cambridge, ON 877-551-5529
Triangle Sign Service Company
Halethorpe, MD 410-247-5300
Trident Plastics
Ivyland, PA 800-222-2318
Tulsa Plastics Company
Tulsa, OK 888-273-5303
United Sign Company
Kansas City, MO 816-923-8208
Universal Sign Company and Manufacturing Company
Lafayette, LA 337-234-1466
University-Brink
Foxboro, MA 617-926-4400
Valley City Sign Company
Comstock Park, MI 616-784-5711
Volk Corporation
Farmington Hills, MI 800-521-6799
Vomela/Harbor Graphics
St Paul, MN 800-645-1012
Wilhite Sign Company
Joplin, MO 417-623-1411
Winnebago Sign Company
Fond Du Lac, WI 920-922-5930
Wisco Signs
Eau Claire, WI 715-835-6189
Wolens Company
Dallas, TX 214-634-0800

Point of Purchase

Acme Sign Corporation
Peabody, MA 978-535-6600
Allred Marketing
Birmingham, AL 205-251-3700
Arlington Display Industries
Detroit, MI 313-837-1212
B&B Neon Sign Company
Austin, TX 800-791-6366
Barlo Signs/Screengraphics
Hudson, NH 800-227-5674
Blanc Industries
Dover, NJ 888-332-5262
Carlton Industries
La Grange, TX 800-231-5988
Chicago Show
Buffalo Grove, IL 847-955-0200
City Signs
Jackson, TN 877-248-9744
Clearr Corporation
Minneapolis, MN 800-548-3269
Comco Signs
Charlotte, NC 704-375-2338
Curzon Promotional Graphics
Omaha, NE 800-769-7446
Daytech Limited
Toronto, ON 877-329-1907
Dimension Graphics
Grand Rapids, MI 855-476-1281
Dunn Woodworks
Shrewsbury, PA 877-835-8592
Emco Industrial Plastics
Cedar Grove, NJ 800-292-9906
Empire Screen Printing, Inc.
Onalaska, WI 608-783-3301
Fasteners for Retail
Cincinnati, OH 800-422-2547
Federal Stamp & Seal Manufacturing Company
Atlanta, GA 800-333-7726
Florida Plastics International
Evergreen Park, IL 708-499-0400
FMI Display
Elkins Park, PA 215-663-1998
Futura 2000 Corporation
Miami, FL 305-256-5877
Gelberg Signs
Washington, DC 800-443-5237
Greif Inc.
Delaware, OH 800-476-1635
Hammar & Sons Sign Company
Pelham, NH 800-527-7446
Harting Graphics
Wilmington, DE 800-848-1373
Heath & Company
Roswell, GA 770-650-2724
Hoarel Sign Company
Amarillo, TX 806-373-2175
I.H. McBride Sign Company
Lynchburg, VA 434-847-4151
Impulse Signs
Toronto, ON 866-636-8273
Insignia Systems
Minneapolis, MN 800-874-4648
JBC Plastics
St Louis, MO 877-834-5526
MDI WorldWide
Farmington Hills, MI 800-228-8925
National Sign Systems
Hilliard, OH 800-544-6726
Neal Walters Poster Corporation
Bentonville, AR 501-273-2489
Norgus Silk Screen Company
Clifton, NJ 973-365-0600
Pilgrim Plastic ProductsCompany
Brockton, MA 800-343-7810
Plasti-Line
Knoxville, TN 800-444-7446
Pratt Poster Company
Indianapolis, IN 317-545-0842
Prestige Plastics Corporation
Delta, BC 604-930-2931
Rex Art Manufacturing Corp.
Lindenhurst, NY 631-884-4600
Royal Display Corporation
Middletown, CT 800-569-1295
RPA Process Technologies
Marblehead, MA 800-631-9707
Stoffel Seals Corporation
Tallapoosa, GA 800-422-8247
The Shelby Company
Cleveland, OH 800-842-1650
Toledo Sign
Toledo, OH 419-244-4444
Total Identity Group
Cambridge, ON 877-551-5529
Trident Plastics
Ivyland, PA 800-222-2318
Twin State Signs
Essex Junction, VT 802-872-8949
US Magnetix
Golden Valley, MN 800- 3-0
Vomela/Harbor Graphics
St Paul, MN 800-645-1012
Wayne Industries
Clanton, AL 800-225-3148
Welch Stencil Company
Scarborough, ME 800-635-3506
Wichita Stamp & Seal
Wichita, KS 316-263-4223
Willson Industries
Marmora, NJ 800-894-4169

Sorters

Check, Bill & Voucher

Automated Business Products
Hackensack, NJ 800-334-1440
Bell & Howell Company
Lincolnwood, IL 800-647-2290
C.R. Manufacturing
Waverly, NE 877-789-5844
Savasort
West Palm Beach, FL 800-255-8744
Scan Coin
Ashburn, VA 800-336-3311
Sortie/Kohlhaas
Monee, IL 708-534-3940

Straws

Drinking

C.R. Manufacturing
Waverly, NE 877-789-5844
Cell-O-Core Company
Sharon Center, OH 800-239-4370
Fun-Time International
Philadelphia, PA 800-776-4386
Goldmax Industries
City of Industry, CA 626-964-8820
Great Western Products
Ontario, CA 888-598-5588
Jet Plastica Industries
Hatfield, PA
Johnstown Manufacturing
Columbus, OH 614-236-8853
OWD
Tupper Lake, NY 800-836-1693
Penley Corporation
West Paris, ME 800-368-6449
Robinson Cone
Burlington, ON 905-333-1515
RubaTex Polymer
Middlefield, OH 440-632-1691
Semco Plastic Company
Saint Louis, MO 314-487-4557
Solo Cup Company
Lake Forest, IL 800-367-2877
Spinzer
Glen Ellyn, IL 630-469-7184
Spir-It/Zoo Piks
Andover, MA 800-343-0996
Spirit Foodservice, Inc.
Andover, MA 800-343-0996
Superior Products Company
Saint Paul, MN 800-328-9800
Superior Quality Products
Schenectady, NY 800-724-1129
Trevor Industries
Eden, NY 716-992-4775
Unisource Converting
Jacksonville, FL 904-783-0550
Waddington North America
Chelmsford, MA 888-962-2877

Table Cloths

A-1 Tablecloth Company
S Hackensack, NJ 800-727-8987
Abond Plastic Corporation
Lachine, QC 800-886-7947
Adcapitol
Monroe, NC 800-868-7111
Americo
West Memphis, AR 800-626-2350
Artex International
Highland, IL 618-654-2113
Atlantis Plastics Institutional Products
Mankato, MN 800-999-2374
Best Brands Home Products
New York, NY 212-684-7456
Best Value Textiles
Elkhorn, WI 800-248-9826

Carnegie Textile Company
Solon, OH 800-633-4136
Commercial Textiles Corporation-Best Buy Uniforms
Homestead, PA 800-345-1924
Cotton Goods Manufacturing Company
Chicago, IL 773-265-0088
Creative Converting
Clintonville, WI 800-826-0418
Custom Table Pads
St Paul, MN. 651-714-5720
Decolin
Montreal, QC 514-384-2910
Drapes 4 Show
Sylmar, CA 800-525-7469
Elrene Home Fashions
New York, NY 212-213-0425
Erving Industries
Erving, MA 413-422-2700
Fashion Industries
Griffin, GA 770-412-9214
Fonda Group
Oshkosh, WI 800-558-9300
Gary Manufacturing Company
Chula Vista, CA 800-775-0804
Gourmet Tableskirts
Houston, TX 800-527-0440
Hilden Halifax
South Boston, VA 800-431-2514
Jack the Ripper Table Skirting
Stafford, TX 800-331-7831
K Katen & Company
Rahway, NJ 732-381-0220
K-C Products Company
Van Nuys, CA 818-267-1600
Klever Kuvers
Pasadena, CA 626-355-8441
Louis Jacobs & Son
Brooklyn, NY 718-782-3500
Louisville Bedding Company
Jeffersontown, KY 502-491-3370
Marko
Spartanburg, SC 866-466-2756
Milliken & Company
Spartanburg, SC 864-503-2020
Party Linens
Chicago, IL 800-281-0003
Philmont Manufacturing Co.
Englewood, NJ 888-379-6483
Premier Skirting Products
Lawrence, NY 800-544-2516
Radius Display Products
Dallas, TX 888-322-7429
Resource One/Resource Two
Reseda, CA 818-343-3451
SCA Tissue
Neenah, WI 866-722-6659
Showeray Corporation
Brooklyn, NY 718-965-3633
Something Different Linen
Clifton, NJ 800-422-2180
Straubel Company
De Pere, WI 888-336-1412
Sultan Linens
New York, NY 212-689-8900
Superior Products Company
Saint Paul, MN 800-328-9800
Tag-Trade Associated Group
Chicago, IL 800-621-8350
Tara Linens
Sanford, NC 800-476-8272
Ultimate Textile
Paterson, NJ 973-523-5866
Vicmore Manufacturing Company
Brooklyn, NY 800-458-8663

Tables

Cafeteria, Restaurant, Foodservice Kitchen

A-1 Booth Manufacturing
Burley, ID 800-820-3285
A.J. Antunes & Company
Carol Stream, IL 800-253-2991
Advance Tabco
Edgewood, NY 800-645-3166
Aero Manufacturing Company
Clifton, NJ 800-631-8378
All State Fabricators Corporation
Florida, RI 800-322-9925
Allstrong Restaurant Equipment
South El Monte, CA 800-933-8913
AMC Industries
Tampa, FL 813-989-9663
AMI
Richmond, CA 800-942-7466
AMTAB Manufacturing Company
Aurora, IL 800-878-2257
Anderson Wood Products Company
Louisville, KY 502-778-5591
ARC Specialties
Valencia, CA 661-775-8500
ATD-American Company
Wyncote, PA 800-523-2300
Atlas Metal Industries
Kenton, HR 208-907-1374
AWP Butcher Block Inc
Horse Cave, KY 800-764-7840
Barn Furniture Mart
Van Nuys, CA 888-302-2276
Barrette - Outdoor Livin
Middleburg Hts., OH 800-336-2383
Beaufurn LLC
Advance, NC 888-766-7706
Beka Furniture
Concord, ON 905-669-4255
Berco Furniture Solutions
St Louis, MO 888-772-4788
Bessco Tube Bending & Pipe Fabricating
Thornton, IL 800-337-3977
Brill Manufacturing Company
Ludington, MI 866-896-6420
Carts Food Equipment Corporation
Brooklyn, NY 718-788-5540
Catskill Craftsmen
Stamford, NY 607-652-7321
CCS Stone, Inc.
Moonachie, NJ 800-227-7785
Charter House
Holland, MI 616-399-6000
Chocolate Concepts
Hartville, OH 330-877-3322
Classico Seating
Peru, IN 800-968-6655
Cobb & Zimmer
Detroit, MI 313-923-0350
Colecraft Commercial Furnishings
Jamestown, NY 800-622-2777
Commercial Furniture Group
Newport, TN 800-873-3252
Commercial Seating Specialist
Santa Clara, CA 408-453-8983
Component Hardware Group
Lakewood, NJ 800-526-3694
Cove Woodworking
Gloucester, MA 800-273-0037
Crown Industries
East Orange, NJ 877-747-2457
Crown Steel Manufacturing
San Marcos, CA 760-471-1188
Custom Design Interiors Service & Manufacturing
Largo, FL 727-536-2207
Custom Diamond International
Laval, QC 800-326-5926
Custom Diamond International
Laval, QC 800-363-5926
Dayco
Clearwater, FL 727-573-9330
Delfield Company
Mt Pleasant, MI 800-733-8821
Denmar Corporation
North Dartmouth, MA 508-999-3295
Duke Manufacturing Company
Saint Louis, MO 800-735-3853
Duluth Sheet Metal
Duluth, MN 218-722-2613
Dunhill Food Equipment Corporation
Armonk, NY 800-847-4206
Eagle Foodservice Equipment
Clayton, DE 800-441-8440
Eagle Products Company
Houston, TX 713-690-1161
Eash Industries
Elkhart, IN 574-295-4450
Eclectic Contract Furniture Industries
New York, NY 888-311-6272
Economy Paper & Restaurant Supply Company
Clifton, NJ 973-279-5500
Edgemold Products
Oconomowoc, WI 800-334-3665
Eldorado Miranda Manufacturing Company
Largo, FL 800-330-0708
Empire Bakery Equipment
Hicksville, NY 800-878-4070
Erwin Food Service Equipment
Fort Worth, TX 817-535-0021
Eskay Metal Fabricating Company
Buffalo, NY 800-836-8015
Fab-X/Metals
Washington, NC 800-677-3229
FCD Tabletops
Brooklyn, NY 800-822-5399
Fiskars Brands Inc.
Baldwinsville, NY 315-635-9911
Fixtur-World
Cookeville, TN 800-634-9887
Fixtures Furniture
Florence, AL 855-321-4999
Forbes Industries
Ontario, CA 909-923-4559
Franke Commercial Systems
Hatfield, PA 800-626-5771
Fred Beesley's Booth & Upholstery
Centerville, UT 801-364-8189
Furniture Lab
Carrboro, NC 800-449-8677
Gar Products
Lakewood, NJ 800-424-2477
Gasser Chair Company
Youngstown, OH 800-323-2234
Gates Manufacturing Company
Saint Louis, MO 800-237-9226
Harbour House Bar Crafting
Stamford, CT 800-755-1227
Hines III
Jacksonville, FL 904-398-5110
Hot Food Boxes
Mooresville, IN 800-733-8073
Industrial Plastics Company
Fort Smith, AR 800-850-0916
J.H. Carr & Sons
Seattle, WA 800-523-8842
John Boos & Company
Effingham, IL 217-347-7701
KaiRak
Fullerton, CA 714-870-8661
Kamran & Company
Santa Barbara, CA 800-480-9418
Kay Home Products
Antioch, IL 800-600-7009
KC Booth Company
Kansas City, MO 800-866-5226
Ken Coat
Bardstown, KY 888-536-2628
Kiefer Industries
Random Lake, WI 920-994-2332
Kings River Casting
Sanger, CA 888-545-5157
Krueger International
Green Bay, WI 800-424-2432
Lakeside Manufacturing
Milwaukee, WI 888-558-8574
Lambertson Industries
Sparks, NV 800-548-3324
Lask Seating Company
Chicago, IL 888-573-2846
LB Furniture Industries
Hudson, NY 800-221-8752
Load King Manufacturing Company
Jacksonville, FL 800-531-4975
Loewenstein
Liberty, NC 800-327-2548
M&E Manufacturing Company
Kingston, NY 845-331-2110
M&S Manufacturing
Arnold, MO 636-464-2739
MCM Fixture Company
Hazel Park, MI 248-547-9280
McRoyal Industries
Youngstown, OH 800-785-2556
Meraz & Associates
Chico, CA 888-244-4463
Merric
Bridgeton, MO 314-770-9944
Metal Equipment Fabricators
Columbia, SC 803-776-9250
Metal Master
Tucson, AZ 800-488-8729
Metal Masters Food Service Equipment Company
Clayton, DE 800-441-8440
Metro Corporation
Wilkes Barre, PA 800-433-2233
Miami Metal
Miami, FL 305-576-3600
Michigan Maple Block Company
Petoskey, MI 800-447-7975

Midwest Folding Products
Chicago, IL 800-344-2864
Migali Industries
Camden, NJ 800-852-5292
Milvan Food Equipment Manufacturing
Rexdale, ON 416-674-3456
Missouri Equipment Company
St Louis, MO 800-727-6326
Mity-Lite
Orem, UT 800-909-8034
MLP Seating
Elk Grove Vlg, IL 800-723-3030
Monroe Kitchen Equipment
Rochester, NY 585-235-3310
Mosshaim Innovations
Jacksonville, FL 888-995-7775
Mouron & Company
Indianapolis, IN 317-243-7955
MTS Seating
Temperance, MI 734-847-3875
N. Wasserstrom & Sons
Columbus, OH 800-999-9277
National Bar Systems
Huntington Beach, CA 714-848-1688
National FABCO Manufacturing
St Louis, MO 314-842-4571
Nor-Lake
Salem, NH 603-893-9701
Normandie Metal Fabricators
Port Washington, NY 800-221-2398
Northern Stainless Fabricating
Traverse City, MI 231-947-4580
Old Dominion Wood Products
Lynchburg, VA 800-245-6382
Palmer Snyder
Brookfield, WI 800-762-0415
Paramount Manufacturing Company
Wilmington, MA 978-657-4300
Parisi/Royal Store Fixture
Newtown, PA 215-968-6677
Peter Pepper Products
Compton, CA 310-639-0390
Petro Moore Manufacturing Corporation
Long Island City, NY 718-784-2516
Pinnacle Furnishing
Aberdeen, NC 866-229-5704
Plymold
Kenyon, MN 800-759-6653
PMI Food Equipment Group
Troy, OH 937-332-3000
Pollard Brothers Manufacturing
Chicago, IL 773-763-6868
Prince Seating
Brooklyn, NY 800-577-4623
Quadra-Tech
Columbus, OH 800-443-2766
Quality Seating Company
Youngstown, OH 800-765-7096
Quipco Products
Sauget, IL 314-993-1442
R.R. Scheibe Company
Newton Center, MA 508-584-4900
Robertson Furniture Company
Toccoa, GA 800-241-0713
Rodo Industries
London, ON 519-668-3711
Rollhaus Seating Products
New York, NY 800-822-6684
Sandler Seating
Atlanta, GA 404-982-9000
Sarasota Restaurant Equipment
Sarasota, FL 800-434-1410
Sauvagnat Inc
Huntersville, NC 800-258-5619
Seating Concepts
Rockdale, IL 800-421-2036
Sefi Fabricators
Amityville, NY 631-842-2200
Shafer Commercial Seating
Denver, CO 303-322-7792
Shammi Industries/Sammons Equipment
Corona, CA 800-417-9260
SICO America
Minneapolis, MN 800-328-6138
Silver King
Minneapolis, MN 800-328-3329
Solid Surface Acrylics
North Tonawanda, NY 888-595-4114
St. Louis Stainless Service
Fenton, MO 888-507-1578
Stainless
La Vergne, TN 800-877-5177
Stainless Equipment Manufacturing
Dallas, TX 800-736-2038
Stainless Steel Fabricators
Tyler, TX 903-595-6625
Standard Signs
Macedonia, OH 800-258-1997
Starlite Food Service Equipment
Detroit, MI 888-521-6603
Straubel Company
De Pere, WI 888-336-1412
Super Sturdy
Weldon, NC 800-253-4833
Superior Products Company
Saint Paul, MN 800-328-9800
Supreme Metal
Alpharetta, GA 800-645-2526
Thorpe & Associates
Siler City, NC 919-742-5516
Toronto Fabricating & Manufacturing
Mississauga, ON 905-891-2516
Trimen Foodservice Equipment
North York, ON 877-437-1422
Trojan Commercial Furni ture Inc.
Montereal, QC 877-271-3878
True Food Service Equipment, Inc.
O Fallon, MO 800-325-6152
U.B. Klem Furniture Company
Saint Anthony, IN 800-264-1995
United Fabricators
Fort Smith, AR 800-235-4101
Universal Stainless
Aurora, CO 800-223-8332
Universal Stainless
Titusville, PA 800-295-1909
US Seating Products
Apopka, FL 407-884-4411
Versailles Lighting
Delray Beach, FL 888-564-0240
Vintage
Jasper, IN 800-992-3491
Vitro Seating Products
Saint Louis, MO 800-325-7093
Walsh & Simmons Seating
Saint Louis, MO 800-727-0364
Waymar Industries
Burnsville, MN 888-474-1112
Weiss Sheet Metal
Avon, MA 508-583-8300
West Coast Industries
San Francisco, CA 800-243-3150
West Metals
London, ON 800-300-6667
Wheel Tough Company
Terre Haute, IN 888-765-8833
Wilder Manufacturing Company
Port Jervis, NY 800-832-1319
Woodard
Coppell, TX 800-877-2290
Woodgoods Industries
Luck, WI 715-472-2226
World Wide Hospitality Furniture
Paramount, CA 800-728-8262
Xiaoping Design
New York, NY 800-891-9896
Zol-Mark Industries
Winnipeg, NB 204-943-7393

Display

Altrua Marketing Designs
Tallahassee, FL 800-443-6939
BMH Equipment
Sacramento, CA 800-350-8828
Cal-Mil Plastic Products
Oceanside, CA 800-321-9069
Dunn Woodworks
Shrewsbury, PA 877-835-8592
Eskay Metal Fabricating Company
Buffalo, NY 800-836-8015
Juice Tree
Omaha, NE 714-891-4425
Kehr-Buffalo Wire Frame Company
Grand Island, NY 800-875-4212
Schmidt Progressive, LLC
Lebanon, OH 800-272-3706
Southern Store Fixtures
Bessemer, AL 800-552-6283

Folding

AMTAB Manufacturing Company
Aurora, IL 800-878-2257

Mity-Lite
Orem, UT 800-909-8034
Palmer Snyder
Brookfield, WI 800-762-0415
Rheon USA
Huntersville, NC 704-875-9191
Rollhaus Seating Products
New York, NY 800-822-6684
Superior Products Company
Saint Paul, MN 800-328-9800

Room Service

Forbes Industries
Ontario, CA 909-923-4559
Lakeside Manufacturing
Milwaukee, WI 888-558-8574

Tote Bags

Eco-Bag Products
Ossining, NY 800-720-2247

Towels

Disposable

ADEX Medical Inc
Riverside, CA 800-873-4776
Akron Cotton Products
Akron, OH 800-899-7173
American Textile Mills
Kansas City, MO 816-842-2909
Atlantic Mills
Lakewood, NJ 800-242-7374
Best Brands Home Products
New York, NY 212-684-7456
Blue Ridge Converting
Asheville, NC 800-438-3893
Browne & Company
Markham, ON 905-475-6104
C.R. Manufacturing
Waverly, NE 877-789-5844
Diamond Wipes International
Chino, CA 800-454-1077
Erie Cotton Products Company
Erie, PA 800-289-4737
Fort James Corporation
Norwalk, CT 800-257-9744
Georgia Pacific
Green Bay, WI 920-435-8821
Healthline Products
Los Angeles, CA 800-473-4003
IFC Disposables
Brownsville, TN 800-432-9473
Kimberly-Clark Corporation
Roswell, GA 888-525-8388
Lexidyne of Pennsylvania
Pittsburgh, PA 800-543-2233
Mainline Industries
Springfield, MA 800-527-7917
Mednik Wiping Materials Company
Saint Louis, MO 800-325-7193
National Towelette Company
Bensalem, PA 215-245-7300
Nosaj Disposables
Paterson, NJ 800-631-3809
Nu-Towel Company
Kansas City, MO 800-800-7247
Rockline Industries
Sheboygan, WI 800-558-7790
SCA Tissue
Neenah, WI 866-722-6659
Superior Linen & Work Wear
Kansas City, MO 800-798-7987
Wipeco, Inc.
Hillside, IL 708-544-7247

Paper

Bro-Tex
Saint Paul, MN 800-328-2282
Diamond Wipes International
Chino, CA 800-454-1077
Encore Paper Company
South Glens Falls, NY 800-362-6735
Erie Cotton Products Company
Erie, PA 800-289-4737
Fort James Corporation
Norwalk, CT 800-257-9744
Georgia Pacific
Green Bay, WI 920-435-8821

Goodman Wiper & Paper
Auburn, ME 800-439-9473
Great Western Products
Ontario, CA. . . . 888-598-5588
Kentfield's
Greenbrae, CA 888-461-7454
Kimberly-Clark Corporation
Neenah, WI. . . . 888-525-8388
Marcal Paper Mills
Elmwood Park, NJ 800-631-8451
Mednik Wiping Materials Company
Saint Louis, MO 800-325-7193
Nice-Pak Products
Orangeburg, NY 800-999-6423
Nosaj Disposables
Paterson, NJ 800-631-3809
Potlatch Corporation
Spokane, WA. . . . 509-835-1500
SCA Hygiene Paper
San Ramon, CA 800-992-8675
SCA Tissue
Neenah, WI. . . . 866-722-6659
Sorg Paper Company
Middletown, OH. . . . 513-420-5300
United Textile Distribution
Garner, NC 800-262-7624
Wipeco, Inc.
Hillside, IL 708-544-7247

Trays

Butchers'

Buckhorn Inc
Milford, OH 800-543-4454
COW Industries
Columbus, OH 800-542-9353
Quality Industries
La Vergne, TN. . . . 615-793-3000
Tenneco Specialty Packaging
Smyrna, GA 800-241-4402

Cafeteria

Browne & Company
Markham, ON. . . . 905-475-6104
Carlisle Food Service Products
Oklahoma City, OK 800-654-8210
Central Fine Pack
Fort Wayne, IN 260-432-3027
Fonda Group
Oshkosh, WI. . . . 800-558-9300
Innovative Plastics Corporation
Orangeburg, NY. . . . 845-359-7500
Kendrick Johnson & Associates
Bloomington, MN. . . . 800-826-1271
Lincoln Foodservice
Cleveland, OH 800-374-3004
Polar Ware Company
Sheboygan, WI 800-237-3655
Prolon
Port Gibson, MS 888-480-9828
Superior Products Company
Saint Paul, MN 800-328-9800
Traex
Dane, WI. . . . 800-356-8006
Wiltec
Leominster, MA 978-537-1497
Xtreme Beverages, LLC
Dana Point, CA. . . . 949-495-7929

Food

Advance Engineering Company
Township, MI 800-497-6388
Advanced Plastic Coating
Parsons, KS. . . . 620-421-1660
ALCO Designs
Gardena, CA 800-228-2346
Allied Metal Spinning Corp
Bronx, NY. . . . 800-615-2266
Ample Industries
Franklin, OH 888-818-9700
Art Wire Works
Bedford Park, IL. . . . 708-458-3993
Automatic Specialities Inc.
Marlborough, MA. . . . 800-445-2370
Bakers Choice Products
Beacon Falls, CT. . . . 203-720-1000
Bardes Plastics
Milwaukee, WI 800-558-5161
Brooklace
Oshkosh, WI 800-572-4552
Browne & Company
Markham, ON. . . . 905-475-6104
Buckhorn Inc
Milford, OH 800-543-4454
Cal-Mil Plastic Products
Oceanside, CA 800-321-9069
Canada Goose Wood Produc
Gloucester, ON 888-890-6506
Carlisle Food Service Products
Oklahoma City, OK 800-654-8210
Delfin Design & Manufacturing
Rcho Sta Marg, CA. . . . 800-354-7919
Designers-Folding Box Corporation
Buffalo, NY. . . . 716-853-5141
Detroit Forming
Southfield, MI. . . . 248-352-8108
Display Tray
Mont-Royal, QC 800-782-8861
Dynynstyl
Delray Beach, FL 800-774-7895
Eastern Silver Tabletop Manufacturing Company
Brooklyn, NY 888-422-4142
Ellingers
Sheboygan, WI 888-287-8906
Engineered Plastics
Gibsonville, NC 800-711-1740
Esterle Mold & Machine Company
Stow, OH. . . . 800-411-4086
Ex-Cell Kaiser
Franklin Park, IL. . . . 847-451-0451
Foam Packaging
Footsville, WI 608-876-4217
Fold-Pak South
Columbus, GA 706-689-2924
Fonda Group
Oshkosh, WI. . . . 800-558-9300
Great Western Products
Ontario, CA. . . . 888-598-5588
Gulf States Paper Corporation
Tuscaloosa, AL. . . . 205-562-5000
Handy Wacks Corporation
Sparta, MI. . . . 800-445-4434
K&I Creative Plastics
Jacksonville, FL 904-387-0438
Kay Home Products
Antioch, IL 800-600-7009
Kendrick Johnson & Associates
Bloomington, MN. . . . 800-826-1271
Key Packaging Company
Sarasota, FL 941-355-2728
Lakeside Manufacturing
Milwaukee, WI 888-558-8574
Lancaster Colony Corporation
Columbus, OH 800-292-7260
Leading Industry
Oxnard, CA. . . . 805-385-4100
Lin Pac Plastics
Roswell, GA 770-751-6006
Meraz & Associates
Chico, CA 888-244-4463
Olive Can Company
Elgin, IL 847-468-7474
Packtive Corporation
Belvidere, IL. . . . 815-547-1200
Par-Pak
Houston, TX 888-272-7725
Plastiques Cascades Group
Montreal, QC 888-703-6515
Plastocon
Oconomowoc, WI. . . . 800-966-0103
Polar Ware Company
Sheboygan, WI 800-237-3655
Premier Industries
Cincinnati, OH 800-354-9817
Process Displays
New Berlin, WI. . . . 800-533-1764
Promens
St. John, NB 800-295-3725
R.R. Scheibe Company
Newton Center, MA 508-584-4900
Rubbermaid Commercial Products
Winchester, VA 800-336-9880
Sani-Top Products
De Leon Springs, FL. . . . 800-874-6094
Sealpac USA LLC
Richmond, VA. . . . 804-261-0580
Spin-Tech Corporation
Hoboken, NJ 800-977-4692
Sterling Paper Company
Philadelphia, PA 215-744-5350
Stock America Inc
Grafton, WI. . . . 262-375-4100
Superior Products Company
Saint Paul, MN 800-328-9800
Superior Quality Products
Schenectady, NY. . . . 800-724-1129
Tenneco Packaging/Pressware
Lake Forest, IL 800-403-3393
Tenneco Specialty Packaging
Smyrna, GA 800-241-4402
Toscarora
Sandusky, OH 419-625-7343
Traex
Dane, WI. . . . 800-356-8006
Traitech Industries
Vaughan, ON. . . . 877-872-4835
Tuscarora
New Brighton, PA. . . . 724-843-8200
Unique Plastics
Rio Rico, AZ. . . . 800-658-5946
Vermillion Flooring Company
Springfield, MO 417-862-3785
Wiltec
Leominster, MA 978-537-1497
WNA Hopple Plastics
Florence, KY. . . . 800-446-4622
Xtreme Beverages, LLC
Dana Point, CA. . . . 949-495-7929

Glass

Browne & Company
Markham, ON. . . . 905-475-6104
Superior Products Company
Saint Paul, MN 800-328-9800
World Kitchen
Elmira, NY 800-999-3436

Plastic

ACO
Moore, OK 405-794-7662
Advance Engineering Company
Township, MI 800-497-6388
Aeromat Plastics
Burnsville, MN 888-286-8729
Anchor Packaging
Ballwin, MO 800-467-3900
Arthur Corporation
Huron, OH. . . . 419-433-7202
Asian Foods
St. Paul, MN 800-274-2655
Bardes Plastics
Milwaukee, WI 800-558-5161
Barrette - Outdoor Livin
Middleburg Hts., OH 800-336-2383
Buckhorn Inc
Milford, OH 800-543-4454
C.R. Manufacturing
Waverly, NE 877-789-5844
Cambro Manufacturing Company
Huntington Beach, CA 800-848-1555
Carlisle Food Service Products
Oklahoma City, OK 800-654-8210
Cash Caddy
Palm Desert, CA. . . . 888-522-2221
Central Fine Pack
Fort Wayne, IN 260-432-3027
Creative Forming
Ripon, WI 920-748-7285
Crespac Incorporated
Tucker, GA 800-438-1900
Custom Molders
Rocky Mount, NC. . . . 919-688-8061
Dart Container Corporation
Mason, MI. . . . 800-248-5960
De Ster Corporation
Atlanta, GA. . . . 800-237-8270
Del-Tec Packaging
Greenville, SC. . . . 800-747-8683
Delfin Design & Manufacturing
Rcho Sta Marg, CA. . . . 800-354-7919
Design Specialties
Hamden, CT 800-999-1584
Detroit Forming
Southfield, MI. . . . 248-352-8108
Display Tray
Mont-Royal, QC 800-782-8861
Douglas Stephen Plastics
Paterson, NJ 973-523-3030
Edco Industries
Bridgeport, CT 203-333-8982
Engineered Plastics
Gibsonville, NC 800-711-1740

Esterle Mold & Machine Company
Stow, OH........................800-411-4086
Fabri-Form Company
Byesville, OH....................740-685-0424
Fato Fiberglass Company
Kankakee, IL.....................815-932-3015
Fonda Group
Oshkosh, WI.....................800-558-9300
Gateway Plastics
Mequon, WI.....................262-242-2020
Gessner Products Company
Ambler, PA.......................800-874-7808
Hal-One Plastics
Olathe, KS........................800-626-5784
HPI North America/ Plastics
Eagan, MN.......................800-752-7462
Imperial Plastics
Lakeville, MN....................952-469-4951
Inline Plastics Corporation
Shelton, CT.......................800-826-5567
Innovative Plastics Corporation
Orangeburg, NY..................845-359-7500
iVEX Packaging Corporation
Lachine, QC.....................514-636-7951
Kendrick Johnson & Associates
Bloomington, MN.................800-826-1271
Kenro
Fredonia, WI.....................262-692-2411
Key Packaging Company
Sarasota, FL.....................941-355-2728
Majestic
Bridgeport, CT...................203-367-7900
Meraz & Associates
Chico, CA........................888-244-4463
Mr. Ice Bucket
New Brunswick, NJ...............732-545-0420
Novelty Crystal Corporation
Long Island City, NY..............800-622-0250
NU-Trend Plastic/Corrigan & Company
Jacksonville, FL..................904-353-5936
Orbis Corp.
Rexdale, ON.....................800-890-7292
Plastech Corporation
Atlanta, GA.......................404-355-9682
Plaxall
Long Island City, NY..............800-876-5706
Prolon
Port Gibson, MS..................888-480-9828
Promens
St. John, NB.....................800-295-3725
Robinson Industries
Coleman, MI.....................989-465-6111
Rolland Machining & Fabricating
Moneta, VA.......................973-827-6911
Sani-Top Products
De Leon Springs, FL..............800-874-6094
Snapware
Fullerton, CA.....................800-334-3062
Spirit Foodservice, Inc.
Andover, MA......................800-343-0996
Stock America Inc
Grafton, WI.......................262-375-4100
Techform
Mount Airy, NC...................336-789-2115
TEMP-TECH Company
Springfield, MA...................800-343-5579
Thermodynamics
Commerce City, CO...............800-627-9037
Toscarora
Sandusky, OH.....................419-625-7343
Tray Pak
Reading, PA......................610-926-5800
Tri-State Plastics
Glenwillard, PA...................724-457-6900
Tulip Corporation
Milwaukee, WI....................414-963-3120
Unique Plastics
Rio Rico, AZ......................800-658-5946
Wilks Precision Instrument Company
Union Bridge, MD.................410-775-7917
Wiltec
Leominster, MA...................978-537-1497
WNA Hopple Plastics
Florence, KY......................800-446-4622
Zeier Plastic & Manufacturing
Madison, WI......................608-244-5782

Urns

Coffee & Tea

Aladdin's Hookah & Loung Bar
Nashville, TN.....................615-329-3558
BG Industries
Lemont, IL.......................800-800-5761
Bon Chef
Lafayette, NJ.....................800-331-0177
Bunn Corporation
Springfield, IL....................800-637-8606
Eastern Silver Tabletop Manufacturing Company
Brooklyn, NY.....................888-422-4142
Grindmaster Corporation
Louisville, KY....................800-695-4500
Grindmaster-Cecilware Corporation
Louisville, KY....................800-695-4500
Kelmin Products
Plymouth, FL.....................407-886-6079
Lancaster Colony Commercial Products
Columbus, OH.....................800-528-2278
Lancaster Colony Corporation
Columbus, OH.....................800-292-7260
Lazy-Man
Belvidere, NJ.....................800-475-1950
Regal Ware
Kewaskum, WI....................262-626-2121
Rexcraft Fine Chafers
Long Island City, NY..............888-739-2723
Sheffield Platers
San Diego, CA....................800-227-9242
T.J. Topper Company
Redwood City, CA................650-365-6962
Wells Manufacturing Company
Verdi, NV.........................800-777-0450
World Kitchen
Elmira, NY.......................800-999-3436
Xtreme Beverages, LLC
Dana Point, CA...................949-495-7929

Utensils

Foodservice Preparation

Abond Plastic Corporation
Lachine, QC.....................800-886-7947
Ace Fabrication
Mobile, AL.......................251-478-0401
All Southern Fabricators
Clearwater, FL...................727-573-4846
AMCO Corporation
City of Industry, CA..............626-855-2550
American Metal Stamping & Spinning
Brooklyn, NY.....................718-384-1500
Asian Foods
St. Paul, MN.....................800-274-2655
Browne & Company
Markham, ON....................905-475-6104
C.M. Slicechief Company, Inc.
Toledo, OH.......................419-241-7647
C.R. Manufacturing
Waverly, NE......................877-789-5844
Carlisle Food Service Products
Oklahoma City, OK...............800-654-8210
Chef Revival
Elkhorn, WI......................800-248-9826
Chef Specialties Company
Smethport, PA....................800-440-2433
Chuppa Knife Manufacturing
Jackson, TN......................731-424-1212
Cr. Manufacturing
Waverly, NE......................877-789-5844
Crestware
North Salt Lake City, UT..........800-345-0513
Cugar Machine Company
Fort Worth, TX...................817-927-0411
Cutrite Company
Fremont, OH.....................800-928-8748
Cyclamen Collection
Oakland, CA......................510-434-7620
Delco Tableware
Port Washington, NY.............800-221-9557
Designer's Choice Stainless
Peoria, AZ.......................800-592-3274
Dur-Able Aluminum Corporation
Hoffman Estates, IL...............847-843-1100
E-Z Edge
West New York, NJ...............800-232-4470
Eagleware Manufacturing
Compton, CA.....................310-604-0404
Edge Resources
Hopedale, MA....................888-849-0998
EdgeCraft Corporation
Avondale, PA.....................800-342-3255
Ellingers
Sheboygan, WI....................888-287-8906
Fab-X/Metals
Washington, NC..................800-677-3229
Fioriware
Zanesville, OH....................740-454-7400
Fortune Products
Cedar Park, TX...................800-742-7797
Franke Commercial Systems
Hatfield, PA......................800-626-5771
Gerber Legendary Blades
Portland, OR.....................503-639-6161
Goebel Fixture Company
Hutchinson, MN...................888-339-0509
Good Idea
Northampton, MA.................800-462-9237
Goodell Tools
New Hope, MN....................800-542-3906
Grand Silver Company
Bronx, NY........................718-585-1930
Greensburg ManufacturingCompany
Greensburg, KY...................270-932-5511
H. Arnold Wood Turning
Tarrytown, NY....................888-314-0088
Hank Rivera Associates
Dearborn, MI.....................313-581-8300
Hantover
Kansas City, MO..................800-821-7849
Hodges
Vienna, IL........................800-444-0011
Hollingsworth Custom Wood Products
Sault Ste. Marie, ON...............705-759-1756
Imperial Schrade Corporation
Ellenville, NY.....................212-210-8600
Industrial Razor Blade Company
Orange, NJ.......................973-673-4286
John Boos & Company
Effingham, IL.....................217-347-7701
John J. Adams Die Corporation
Worcester, MA....................508-757-3894
Keen Kutter
Torrance, CA.....................310-370-6941
Kosempel Manufacturing Company
Philadelphia, PA..................800-733-7122
KTG
Cincinnati, OH....................888-533-6900
Lady Mary
Rockingham, NC..................910-997-7321
Lamson & Goodnow Manufacturing Company
Shelburne Falls, MA...............800-872-6564
Leggett & Platt StorageP
Vernon Hills, IL...................847-816-6246
Leon Bush Manufacturer
Glenview, IL......................847-657-8888
Lillsun Manufacturing Company, Inc.
Huntington, IN....................260-356-6514
Lodge Manufacturing Company
South Pittsburg, TN...............423-837-5919
LoTech Industries
Lakewood, CO....................800-295-0199
M&E Manufacturing Company
Kingston, NY.....................845-331-2110
Matfer
Van Nuys, CA.....................800-766-0333
Maugus Manufacturing Company
Lancaster, PA.....................717-299-5681
Mill-Rose Company
Mentor, OH.......................800-321-3598
Mosshaim Innovations
Jacksonville, FL..................888-995-7775
Mouli Manufacturing Corporation
Belleville, NJ.....................800-789-8285
Mulligan Associates
Mequon, WI......................800-627-2886
Mundial
Norwood, MA.....................800-487-2224
Nemco Food Equipment
Hicksville, OH....................800-782-6761
Novelty Crystal Corporation
Long Island City, NY..............800-622-0250
Olde Thompson/Leeds Engineering Corporation
Oxnard, CA.......................800-827-1565
Pepper Mill Company
Mobile, AL.......................800-669-5175
Polar Ware Company
Sheboygan, WI....................800-237-3655
Proluxe
Paramount, CA...................800-594-5528

R. Murphy Company
Ayer, MA . . . 888-772-3481
R.H. Saw Corporation
Barrington, IL . . . 847-381-8777
Read Products
Seattle, WA . . . 800-445-3416
Robinson Cone
Burlington, ON . . . 905-333-1515
Royal Paper Products
Coatesville, PA . . . 800-666-6655
Rx Honing Machine Corporation
Mishawaka, IN . . . 800-346-6464
Samuel Underberg
Brooklyn, NY . . . 718-363-0787
Spartec Plastics
Conneaut, OH . . . 800-325-5176
Sturdi-Bilt Restaurant Equipment
Whitmore Lake, MI . . . 800-521-2895
Superior Products Company
Saint Paul, MN . . . 800-328-9800
T&A Metal Products Company
Deptford, NJ . . . 856-227-1700
Tablecraft Products
Gurnee, IL . . . 800-323-8321
Thorpe Rolling Pin Company
Hamden, CT . . . 800-344-6966
Toronto Kitchen Equipment
North York, ON . . . 416-745-4944
Town Food Service Equipment Company
Brooklyn, NY . . . 800-221-5032
Turner & Seymour Manufacturing
Torrington, CT . . . 888-856-4864
Update International
Los Angeles, CA . . . 800-747-7124
Varimixer
Charlotte, NC . . . 800-221-1138
Vermillion Flooring Company
Springfield, MO . . . 417-862-3785
Vita Craft Corporation
Shawnee, KS . . . 800-359-3444
Vollrath Company
Sheboygan, WI . . . 920-457-4851
Wilton Armetale Company
Mount Joy, PA . . . 800-779-4586
Wishbone Utensil Tableware Line
Wheat Ridge, CO . . . 866-266-5928
Zeroll Company
Fort Pierce, FL . . . 800-872-5000

Plastic

Action Technology
Prussia, PA . . . 217-935-8311
Art Plastics Handy Home Helpers
Leominster, MA . . . 978-537-0367
BOC Plastics Inc
Winston Salem, NC . . . 800-334-8687
C.R. Manufacturing
Waverly, NE . . . 877-789-5844
Carlisle Food Service Products
Oklahoma City, OK . . . 800-654-8210
Chinet Company
Laguna Niguel, CA . . . 949-348-1711
Cr. Manufacturing
Waverly, NE . . . 877-789-5844
Design Specialties
Hamden, CT . . . 800-999-1584
Dispoz-O Plastics
Fountain Inn, SC . . . 864-862-4004
Fonda Group
Oshkosh, WI . . . 800-367-2877
Hal-One Plastics
Olathe, KS . . . 800-626-5784
Harold Leonard SouthwestCorporation
Houston, TX . . . 800-245-8105
HPI North America/Plastics
Saint Paul, MN . . . 800-752-7462
James River Canada
North York, ON . . . 416-789-5151
Jarden Home Brands
Daleville, IN . . . 800-392-2575
Jet Plastica Industries
Hatfield, PA
Jones-Zylon Company
West Lafayette, OH . . . 800-848-8160
LoTech Industries
Lakewood, CO . . . 800-295-0199
Max Packaging Company
Attalla, AL . . . 800-543-5369
Measurex/S&L Plastics
Nazareth, PA . . . 800-752-0650
Novelty Crystal Corporation
Long Island City, NY . . . 800-622-0250
Nyman Manufacturing Company
Rumford, RI . . . 401-438-3410
Olde Thompson/Leeds Engineering Corporation
Oxnard, CA . . . 800-827-1565
OWD
Tupper Lake, NY . . . 800-836-1693
Penley Corporation
West Paris, ME . . . 800-368-6449
Polar Plastics
St Laurent, QC . . . 514-331-0207
Polar Plastics
Mooresville, NC . . . 704-660-6600
R.H. Saw Corporation
Barrington, IL . . . 847-381-8777
Solo Cup Canada
Toronto, ON . . . 800-465-9696
Spir-It/Zoo Piks
Andover, MA . . . 800-343-0996
Tenneco Specialty Packaging
Smyrna, GA . . . 800-241-4402
Waddington North America
Chelmsford, MA . . . 888-962-2877
Waddington North AmericaCups Illustrated
Lancaster, TX . . . 800-334-2877
Wiltec
Leominster, MA . . . 978-537-1497
Wishbone Utensil Tableware Line
Wheat Ridge, CO . . . 866-266-5928

Vending Carts

800Buy Cart
Jamaica, NY . . . 800-289-2278
All Star Carts & Vehicles
Bay Shore, NY . . . 800-831-3166
All State Fabricators Corporation
Florida, RI . . . 800-322-9925
Alliance Products, LLC
Murfreesboro, TN . . . 800-522-3973
Alto-Shaam
Menomonee Falls, WI . . . 800-558-8744
AMCO Corporation
City of Industry, CA . . . 626-855-2550
ARC Specialties
Valencia, CA . . . 661-775-8500
Automated Food Systems
Waxahachie, TX . . . 972-298-5719
BBQ Pits by Klose
Houston, TX . . . 800-487-7487
Carriage Works
Klamath Falls, OR . . . 541-882-0700
Corsair Display Systems
Canandalgua, NY . . . 800-347-5245
Custom Sales & Service Inc.
Hammonton, NJ . . . 800-257-7855
Eskay Metal Fabricating Company
Buffalo, NY . . . 800-836-8015
Hackney Brothers
Washington, NC . . . 800-763-0700
Hot Food Boxes
Mooresville, IN . . . 800-733-8073
Hot Shot Delivery Systems
Bloomingdale, IL . . . 630-924-8817
International Thermal Dispensers
Boston, MA . . . 617-239-3600
Lakeside Manufacturing
Milwaukee, WI . . . 888-558-8574
Leggett & Platt StorageP
Vernon Hills, IL . . . 847-816-6246
Magnum Custom Trailer & BBQ Pits
Austin, TX . . . 800-662-4686
Merchandising Frontiers
Winterset, IA . . . 800-421-2278
Metal Master
Tucson, AZ . . . 800-488-8729
Michaelo Espresso
Seattle, WA . . . 800-545-2883
Moseley Corporation
Franklin, MA . . . 800-667-3539
Paragon International
Nevada, IA . . . 800-433-0333
Polyfoam Packers Corporation
Arlington Hts, IL . . . 800-323-7442
Prestige Metal Products
Antioch, IL . . . 847-395-0775
Proluxe
Paramount, CA . . . 800-594-5528
Southern Express
Saint Louis, MO . . . 800-444-9157
Steamway Corporation
Scottsburg, IN . . . 800-259-8171
Super Sturdy
Weldon, NC . . . 800-253-4833
Super-Chef Manufacturing Company
Houston, TX . . . 800-231-3478
Supreme Products
Waco, TX . . . 254-799-4941
Tooterville Trolley Company
Newburgh, IN . . . 812-858-8585
Vollrath Company
Sheboygan, WI . . . 920-457-4851
Wag Industries
Skokie, IL . . . 800-621-3305

Vending Machinery

Reverse

Can & Bottle Systems, Inc.
Milwaukie, OR . . . 866-302-2636
Environmental Products Corporation
Naugatuck, CT . . . 800-275-3861

Warmers

Dish & Plate

Bloomfield Industries
St. Louis, MO . . . 888-356-5362
Convay Systems
Etobicoke, ON . . . 800-811-5511
Cyclamen Collection
Oakland, CA . . . 510-434-7620
Kelmin Products
Plymouth, FL . . . 407-886-6079
Mastex Industries
Petersburg, VA . . . 804-732-8300
Metro Corporation
Wilkes Barre, PA . . . 800-433-2233
Monroe Kitchen Equipment
Rochester, NY . . . 585-235-3310
Super-Chef Manufacturing Company
Houston, TX . . . 800-231-3478
Wells Manufacturing Company
Verdi, NV . . . 800-777-0450

Food

Aroma Manufacturing Company
San Diego, CA . . . 800-276-6286
BG Industries
Lemont, IL . . . 800-800-5761
BKI Worldwide
Simpsonville, SC . . . 800-927-6887
Bon Chef
Lafayette, NJ . . . 800-331-0177
Broaster Company
Beloit, WI . . . 800-365-8278
Canadian Display Systems
Concord, ON . . . 800-895-5862
Cres Cor
Mentor, OH . . . 877-273-7267
Crispy Lite
St. Louis, MO . . . 888-356-5362
D'Lights
Glendale, CA . . . 818-956-5656
Deluxe Equipment Company
Bradenton, FL . . . 800-367-8931
Duke Manufacturing Company
Saint Louis, MO . . . 800-735-3853
Dynynstyl
Delray Beach, FL . . . 800-774-7895
Eagle Foodservice Equipment
Clayton, DE . . . 800-441-8440
Esquire Mechanical Corp.
Armonk, NY . . . 800-847-4206
Garland Commercial Ranges
Mississauga, ON . . . 905-624-0260
Gold Medal Products Company
Cincinnati, OH . . . 800-543-0862
HATCO Corporation
Milwaukee, WI . . . 800-558-0607
Henny Penny, Inc.
Detroit, MI . . . 313-877-9550
Hot Food Boxes
Mooresville, IN . . . 800-733-8073
InfraTech Corporation
Azusa, CA . . . 800-955-2476
Keating of Chicago
Mc Cook, IL . . . 800-532-8464
Lincoln Foodservice
Cleveland, OH . . . 800-374-3004

Merco/Savory
Mt. Pleasant, MI 800-733-8821
Metal Masters Food Service Equipment Company
Clayton, DE. 800-441-8440
Metro Corporation
Wilkes Barre, PA. 800-433-2233
Middleby Marshall, CTX
Elgin, IL 800-323-5575
Mies Products
West Bend, WI 800-480-6437
Monroe Kitchen Equipment
Rochester, NY. 585-235-3310
Mosshaim Innovations
Jacksonville, FL 888-995-7775
Prince Castle
Carol Stream, IL 800-722-7853
Remco Industries International
Fort Lauderdale, FL 800-987-3626
Rexcraft Fine Chafers
Long Island City, NY 888-739-2723
Server Products
Richfield, WI 800-558-8722
SICO America
Minneapolis, MN 800-328-6138
Southern Pride Distributing
Marion, IL 800-851-8180
Star Manufacturing International
Saint Louis, MO 800-264-7827
Super Systems
Wausau, WI. 800-558-5880
Super-Chef Manufacturing Company
Houston, TX 800-231-3478
Tomlinson Industries
Cleveland, OH 800-945-4589
Ultrafryer Systems
San Antonio, TX. 800-545-9189
Vulcan-Hart Company
Louisville, KY 800-814-2028
Welbilt Corporation
Stamford, CT. 203-325-8300
Wells Manufacturing Company
Verdi, NV 800-777-0450
Wilder Manufacturing Company
Port Jervis, NY 800-832-1319
Win-Holt Equipment Group
Westbury, NY 800-444-3595
Wisco Industries
Oregon, WI 800-999-4726
Zoia Banquetier Company
Cleveland, OH 216-631-6414

Wood Grain Plastic

Chips

Hopp Companies
New Hyde Park, NY. 800-889-8425

Shelf Covers

Hopp Companies
New Hyde Park, NY. 800-889-8425

Strips

Hopp Companies
New Hyde Park, NY. 800-889-8425

Instrumentation & Laboratory Equipment

Analyzers

Amino Acid, Nitrogen

Antek Instruments
Houston, TX....................800-444-8378
Bran & Luebbe
Schaumburg, IL....................847-882-8116

Ethyl Alcohol

Greer's Ferry Glass Work
Dubuque, IA....................501-589-2947
NDC Infrared EngineeringInc
Irwindale, CA....................626-960-3300
YSI
Yellow Springs, OH....................800-765-4974

Fats, Oils

ABB Bomem
Quebec, QC....................800-858-3847
Bran & Luebbe
Schaumburg, IL....................847-882-8116
CEM Corporation
Matthews, NC....................800-726-3331
Columbus Instruments
Columbus, OH....................800-669-5011
Dresser Instruments
Stratford, CT....................800-328-8258
Industrial Laboratories
Wheat Ridge, CO....................800-456-5288
Libra Laboratories Inc
Metuchen, NJ....................732-321-5200
Libra Technical Center
Metuchen, NJ....................732-321-5487
NDC Infrared EngineeringInc
Irwindale, CA....................626-960-3300
Nirsystems
Silver Spring, MD....................301-680-0252
Univex Corporation
Salem, NH....................800-258-6358

Fiber, Starch

Supelco
Bellefonte, PA....................800-247-6628
Texture Technologies Corporation
Scarsdale, NY....................914-472-0531

Mycotoxins

Supelco
Bellefonte, PA....................800-247-6628
VICAM, A Waters Business
Milford, MA....................800-338-4381

Nitrites, Nitrosamines

Supelco
Bellefonte, PA....................800-247-6628

Organic Acids

YSI
Yellow Springs, OH....................800-765-4974

Pesticide Residue, Antibiotics

Charm Sciences
Lawrence, MA....................978-683-6100
Neogen Corporation
Lansing, MI....................800-234-5333
Supelco
Bellefonte, PA....................800-247-6628

Salt (Sodium Chloride)

Dresser Instruments
Stratford, CT....................800-328-8258
Greer's Ferry Glass Work
Dubuque, IA....................501-589-2947
Hanna Instruments
Woonsocket, RI....................800-426-6287
Presto Tek Corporation
Santa Ana, CA....................800-639-7678
QA Supplies, LLC
Norfolk, VA....................800-472-7205

Sugars (Dextrose, Fructose, Galactose, Lactose, Su

Greer's Ferry Glass Work
Dubuque, IA....................501-589-2947
MISCO Refractometer
Cleveland, OH....................866-831-1999
Nirsystems
Silver Spring, MD....................301-680-0252
YSI
Yellow Springs, OH....................800-765-4974

Vitamin

Industrial Laboratories
Wheat Ridge, CO....................800-456-5288

Water Activity

Arizona Instrument LLC
Chandler, AZ....................800-528-7411
Astro/Polymetron Zellweger
League City, TX....................281-332-2484
Biopath
West Palm Beach, FL....................800-645-2302
Burkert Fluid Control Systems
Irvine, CA....................800-325-1405
Capital Controls Company/MicroChem
Colmar, PA....................215-997-4000
CEM Corporation
Matthews, NC....................800-726-3331
CHEMetrics
Midland, VA....................800-356-3072
CSC Scientific Company
Fairfax, VA....................800-621-4778
Forte Technology
South Easton, MA....................508-297-2363
Hach Company
Loveland, CO....................800-227-4224
Machine Applications Corporation
Sandusky, OH....................419-621-2322
MOCON
Minneapolis, MN....................763-493-6370
NDC Infrared EngineeringInc
Irwindale, CA....................626-960-3300
Nirsystems
Silver Spring, MD....................301-680-0252
Onset Computer Corporation
Buzzards Bay, MA....................800-564-4377
Orion Research
Beverly, MA....................800-225-1480
Precision Systems
Natick, MA....................508-655-7010
Rosemount Analytical
Irvine, CA....................800-543-8257
Rotronic Instrument
Hauppauge, NY....................800-628-7101
Suburban Laboratories
Hillside, IL....................800-783-5227
Thermo Detection
Franklin, MA....................866-269-0070
Troxler Electronic Laboratories
Research Triangle Park, NC....................919-549-8661

Automation

Unit, Packaging, Bulk Handling

Andgar Corporation
Ferndale, WA....................360-366-9900
Barclay & Associates
Arlington, TX....................817-274-5734
California Vibratory Feeders
Anaheim, CA....................800-354-0972
CH2M Hill
Englewood, CO....................303-771-0900
Falco Technologies
La Prairie, QC....................450-444-0566
Hampton-Tilley Associates
Chesterfield, MO....................636-537-3353
Lockwood Greene Engineers
Knoxville, TN....................251-476-2400
Lockwood Greene Engineers
Knoxville, TN....................256-533-9907
Lockwood Greene Engineers
Brentwood, TN....................615-221-5031
Lockwood Greene Engineers
Augusta, GA....................706-724-8225
Lockwood Greene Engineers
Somerset, NJ....................732-560-5700
Lockwood Greene Engineers
Atlanta, GA....................770-829-6500
Lockwood Greene Engineers
Guaynabo, PR....................787-781-9050
Lockwood Greene Engineers
Knoxville, TN....................865-218-5377
Lockwood Greene Engineers
Pooler, GA....................912-330-3000
Lockwood Greene Engineers
Dallas, TX....................972-991-5505
Lockwood Greene Technologies
Augusta, GA....................505-889-3831
Priority One Packaging
Waterloo, ON....................800-387-9102
Schroeder Sewing Technologies
San Marcos, CA....................760-591-9733
Stock America Inc
Grafton, WI....................262-375-4100
Vande Berg Scales
Sioux Center, IA....................712-722-1181
Washington Frontier
Grandview, WA....................509-469-7662

Balances

Laboratory

A&D Weighing
San Jose, CA....................800-726-3364
Denver Instrument Company
Bohemia, NY....................800-321-1135
Fairbanks Scales
Kansas City, MO....................800-451-4107
Precision Solutions
Quakertown, PA....................215-536-4400
QA Supplies, LLC
Norfolk, VA....................800-472-7205
Sartorius Corporation
Edgewood, NY....................800-635-2906
Vande Berg Scales
Sioux Center, IA....................712-722-1181
Vertex Interactive
Clifton, NJ....................973-777-3500
Wilkens-Anderson Company
Chicago, IL....................800-847-2222

Centrifuges

Alfa Laval
Newburyport, MA....................978-465-5777
Alpha MOS
Hanover, MD....................410-553-9736
Ampco Pumps Company
Glendale, WI....................800-737-8671
Bird Machine Company
Houston, TX....................800-229-7447
C&R Refrigation Inc,
Center, TX....................800-438-6182
Centrisys Corporation
Kenosha, WI....................877-339-5496
Commercial Manufacturing& Supply Company
Fresno, CA....................559-237-1855
Cooper Turbocompressor
Buffalo, NY....................877-805-7911
Dedert Corporation
Olympia Fields, IL....................708-747-7000
International Machinery Exchange
Deerfield, WI....................800-279-0191
International Reserve Equipment Corporation
Clarendon Hills, IL....................708-531-0680
Pacer Pumps
Lancaster, PA....................800-233-3861
Pacific Process Technology
La Jolla, CA....................858-551-3298
Pro Scientific
Oxford, CT....................800-584-3776
Ross Cook
San Jose, CA....................800-233-7339
Separators
Indianapolis, IN....................800-233-9022
Silver Weibull
Aurora, CO....................303-373-2311

Tecumseh Products Company
Ann Arbor, MI 734-585-9500
Tema Systems
Cincinnati, OH 513-489-7811

Certification

Food

International Kosher Supervision
Keller, TX 817-337-4700
KOF-K Kosher Supervision
Teaneck, NJ 201-837-0500
Lloyd's Register QualityAssurance
Houston, TX 888-877-8001
OK Labs Kosher Certification
Brooklyn, NY 718-756-7500
Orthodox Union
New York, NY 212-563-4000
Star-K Kosher Certification
Baltimore, MD 410-484-4110

Chemicals

Laboratory

Advance Energy Technologies
Clifton Park, NY 800-724-0198
Dow Chemical Company
Spring House, PA 800-447-4369
Exaxol Chemical Corporation
Clearwater, FL 800-739-2965
Fisher Scientific Company
Pittsburgh, PA 412-490-8300
Ricca Chemical Co.
Batesville, IN 888-467-4222
S&J Laboratories
Portage, MI 269-324-7383
Solvox Manufacturing Company
Milwaukee, WI 414-774-5664
Wilkens-Anderson Company
Chicago, IL 800-847-2222

Controls

Automation & Controls

Dennis Group
Springfield, MA 413-787-1785
M.G. Newell
Greensboro, NC 800-334-0231
Red Lion Controls
York, PA 717-767-6511
Sick Inc.
Minneapolis, MN 800-325-7425
Sterling Electric
Indianapolis, IN 800-654-6220

Boiler & Steam

ACME Control Service
Chicago, IL 800-621-6427
Heatrex
Meadville, PA 800-394-6589
Ohmart/VEGA
Cincinnati, OH 800-367-5383
Paxton Corporation
Bristol, RI
Sellers Engineering Division
Danville, KY 859-236-3181
Washington Frontier
Grandview, WA 509-469-7662

Clean-In-Place

A&B Process Systems
Stratford, WI 888-258-2789
Debelak Technical Systems
Greenville, WI 800-888-4207
Dresser Instruments
Stratford, CT 800-328-8258
Electrol Specialties Company
South Beloit, IL 815-389-2291
Hartel International LLC
Fort Atkinson, WI 920-563-6597
Lake Process Systems
Lake Barrington, IL 800-331-9260
Northland Process Piping
Isle, MN 320-679-2119
Papertech
North Vancouver, BC 877-787-2737

Scherping Systems
Winsted, MN 320-485-4401
Stainless Products
Somers, WC 800-558-9446
Sterling Process Engineering
Columbus, OH 800-783-7875
West Agro
Kansas City, MO 816-891-1600

Level, Liquid & Dry

A&B Process Systems
Stratford, WI 888-258-2789
Anderson Instrument
Fultonville, NY 800-833-0081
Anderson Instrument Company
Fultonville, NY 800-833-0081
ASI Electronics
Cypress, TX 800-231-6066
Azbar Plus
Qu,bec, QC 418-687-3672
Banner Engineering Corporation
Plymouth, MN 888-373-6767
Bernhard
Kennett Square, PA 800-541-7874
Berthold Technologies
Oak Ridge, TN 865-483-1488
Clean Water Systems International
Klamath Falls, OR 866-273-9993
Conveyor Components Company
Croswell, MI 800-233-3233
DistaView Corporation
Bowling Green, OH 800-795-9970
Gems Sensors
Plainville, CT 860-747-3000
Hartel International LLC
Fort Atkinson, WI 920-563-6597
Heuft
Downers Grove, IL 630-968-9011
Honeywell's
Freeport, IL 800-537-6945
Infitec
Syracuse, NY 800-334-0837
Innovative Components
Southington, CT 800-789-2851
Intelligent Controls
Saco, ME 800-872-3455
King Engineering - King-Gage
Newell, WV 800-242-8871
Knight Equipment International
Lake Forest, CA 800-854-3764
Liquid Scale
New Brighton, MN 888-633-2969
Lumenite Control Technology
Franklin Park, IL 800-323-8510
Ohmart/VEGA
Cincinnati, OH 800-367-5383
Peco Controls Corporation
Modesto, CA 800-732-6285
Sick Inc.
Minneapolis, MN 800-325-7425
Tokheim Company
Marion, IA 800-747-3442
Washington Frontier
Grandview, WA 509-469-7662

Microprocessor

GEA Refrigeration North America, Inc.
York, PA 800-888-4337

Numerical

American Autogard Corporation
Rockford, IL 815-229-3190
Candy Manufacturing
Niles, IL 847-588-2639
ENM Company
Chicago, IL 773-775-8400

Packaging Line

Alfa Production Systems
Westfield, NJ 908-654-0255
Andantex USA
Ocean, NJ 800-713-6170
ASI Electronics
Cypress, TX 800-231-6066
AW Company
Franksville, WI 800-850-6110
Banner Engineering Corporation
Plymouth, MN 888-373-6767

Blodgett Company
Houston, TX 281-933-6195
Cal Controls
Gurnee, IL 800-866-6659
Candy Manufacturing
Niles, IL 847-588-2639
Centent Company
Santa Ana, CA 714-979-6491
Container Machinery Corporation
Albany, NY 518-694-3310
Contrex
Maple Grove, MN 763-424-7800
Control & Metering
Mississauga, ON 800-736-5739
Conveyor Components Company
Croswell, MI 800-233-3233
Electro Cam Corporation
Roscoe, IL 800-228-5487
Emerson Electronic Motion Controls
Chanhassen, MN 800-397-3786
Fairchild Industrial Products Company
Winston Salem, NC 800-334-8422
Gebo Conveyors, Consultants & Systems
Laval, QC 450-973-3337
Harland Simon Control Systems USA
Oakbrook, IL 630-572-7650
Hartel International LLC
Fort Atkinson, WI 920-563-6597
Honeywell's
Freeport, IL 800-537-6945
Hoppmann Corporation
Elkwood, VA 800-368-3582
Hudson Control Group
Springfield, NJ 973-376-7400
Industrial Devices Corporation
Petaluma, CA 707-789-1000
Industrial Magnetics
Boyne City, MI 800-662-4638
Kinematics & Controls Corporation
Deer Park, NY 800-833-8103
Moeller Electric
Houston, TX 800-394-5687
Namco Controls Corporation
Cleveland, OH 800-626-8324
Omron Electronics
Schaumburg, IL 800-556-6766
Optek
Galena, OH 800-533-8400
Payne Engineering
Scott Depot, WV 800-331-1345
Peco Controls Corporation
Modesto, CA 800-732-6285
Rexroth Corporation
Hoffman Estates, IL 847-645-3600
Schroeder Sewing Technologies
San Marcos, CA 760-591-9733
Sure Torque
Sarasota, FL 800-387-6572
Tri-Tronics Company
Tampa, FL 800-237-0946
W.G. Durant Corporation
Whittier, CA 562-946-5555
Washington Frontier
Grandview, WA 509-469-7662

Refrigeration Systems

ABB SSAC
Baldwinsville, NY 888-385-1221
Andgar Corporation
Ferndale, WA 360-366-9900
Apollo Sheet Metal
Kennewick, WA 509-586-1104
Cooling Technology
Charlotte, NC 800-872-1448
Danfoss
Baltimore, MD 410-931-8250
Edwards Engineering Corporation
Pompton Plains, NJ 800-526-5201
Frigoscandia
Redmond, WA 800-423-1743
H.A. Phillips & Company
DeKalb, IL 630-377-0050
Hansen Technologies Corporation
Bolingbrook, IL 800-426-7368
Hartel International LLC
Fort Atkinson, WI 920-563-6597
Johnson Controls
Milwaukee, WI 800-950-7539
Novar
Cleveland, OH 800-348-1235

Paragon Electric Company
Two Rivers, WI 920-793-1161
Quantem Corporation
Ewing, NJ 609-883-9879
Ron Vallort & Associates
Oak Brook, IL 630-734-3821
Selco Products Company
Anaheim, CA 800-257-3526
WA Brown & Son
Salisbury, NC 704-636-5131

Webtension & Torque

Magpowr
Fenton, MO 800-624-7697

Inspection & Analysis Instrumentation & Systems

ABB Instrumentation
Rochester, NY 716-292-6050
Abbeon Cal
Santa Barbara, CA 800-922-0977
Accu-Ray Inspection Services
Elmhurst, IL 800-378-1226
ACR Systems
Surrey, BC 800-663-7845
Acrison
Moonachie, NJ 800-422-4266
Advanced Detection Systems
Milwaukee, WI 414-672-0553
Advanced Instruments
Norwood, MA 800-225-4034
AGR International
Butler, PA 724-482-2163
Agricultural Data Systems
Laguna Niguel, CA 800-328-2246
Agtron
Reno, NV 775-850-4600
Air Logic Power Systems
Milwaukee, WI 800-325-8717
Altek Company
Torrington, CT 860-482-7626
American Gas & Chemical Company Limited
Northvale, NJ 800-288-3647
Analytical Development
Lawrenceville, GA 770-237-2330
Analytical Measurements
Chester, NJ 800-635-5580
Anderson Instrument Company
Fultonville, NY 800-833-0081
Ansul Incorporated
Marinette, WI 800-862-6785
Antek Instruments
Houston, TX 800-444-8378
Aqua Measure Instrument Company
Rancho Cucamonga, CA 800-966-4788
Arizona Instrument LLC
Chandler, AZ 800-528-7411
Aromascan PLC
Hollis, NH 603-598-2922
Arthur G. Russell Company (The)
Bristol, CT 860-583-4109
Astro/Polymetron Zellweger
League City, TX 281-332-2484
Atkins Technical
Gainesville, FL 800-284-2842
ATS RheoSystems
Bordentown, NJ 609-298-2522
Automation Service
Earth City, MO 800-325-4808
Bailey Controls/ABB ation
Wickliffe, OH 440-585-8948
Baltimore Aircoil Company
Jessup, MD 410-799-6200
Banner Engineering Corporation
Plymouth, MN 888-373-6767
Barco Machine Vision
Duluth, GA 704-392-9371
Becton Dickinson & Company: Diagnostic Systems
Franklin Lakes, NJ 201-847-6800
Bel-Art Products
Wayne, NJ 800-423-5278
Bentley Instruments
Chaska, MN 952-448-7600
Bernhard
Kennett Square, PA 800-541-7874
Berthold Technologies
Oak Ridge, TN 865-483-1488
Binks Industries
Montgomery, IL 630-801-1100
BioControl Systems
Bellevue, WA 800-245-0113
Biolog
Hayward, CA 800-284-4949
Biological Services
Kansas City, MO 913-236-6868
Bioscience International, Inc
Rockville, MD 301-231-7400
Biotest Diagnostics Corporation
Rockaway, NJ 800-522-0090
Bran & Luebbe
Schaumburg, IL 847-882-8116
Brookfield Engineering Laboratories
Middleboro, MA 800-628-8139
Brooks Instrument
Hatfield, PA 888-554-3569
C.W. Brabender Instruments
South Hackensack, NJ 201-343-8425
CanPacific Engineering
Delta, BC 604-946-1680
Care Controls, Inc.
Mill Creek, WA 800-593-6050
Carleton Technologies
Orchard Park, NY 716-662-0006
Caron Products & Services
Marietta, OH 800-648-3042
Carter Products Company
Grand Rapids, MI 888-622-7837
CEA Instruments
Westwood, NJ 888-893-9640
CEM Corporation
Matthews, NC 800-726-3331
Charm Sciences
Lawrence, MA 978-683-6100
Chicago Stainless Equipment
Palm City, FL 800-927-8575
Chord Engineering
Niwot, CO 303-449-5812
Cintex of America
Carol Stream, IL 800-424-6839
Clean Water Systems International
Klamath Falls, OR 866-273-9993
Columbus Instruments
Columbus, OH 800-669-5011
Comark Instruments
Everett, WA 800-555-6658
Container Machinery Corporation
Albany, NY 518-694-3310
Control Instruments Corporation
Fairfield, NJ 973-575-9114
Cooperheat/MQS
Alvin, TX 800-526-4233
Crystal Chem Inc.
Downers Grove, IL 630-889-9003
CSC Scientific Company
Fairfax, VA 800-621-4778
CSPI
Billerica, MA 978-663-7598
Custom Pools & Spas
Newington, NH 800-323-9509
CxR Company
Warsaw, IN 800-817-5763
Datapaq
Wilmington, MA 800-326-5270
Debelak Technical Systems
Greenville, WI 800-888-4207
Delavan-Delta
Naugatuck, CT 203-720-5610
Delta F Corporation
Woburn, MA 781-935-4600
Design Technology Corporation
Billerica, MA 978-663-7000
Devar
Bridgeport, CT 800-566-6822
Dipix Technologies
Ottawa, ON 613-596-4942
Dresser Instruments
Stratford, CT 800-328-8258
Dunkley International
Kalamazoo, MI 800-666-1264
Dupps Company
Germantown, OH 937-855-6555
Ecklund-Harrison Technologies
Fort Myers, FL 239-936-6032
ELISA Technologies
Gainesville, FL 352-337-3929
Endress & Hauser
Greenwood, IN 800-428-4344
ENSCO
Springfield, VA 703-321-9000
EPD Technology Corporation
Elmsford, NY 800-892-8926
ESA
Chelmsford, MA 978-250-7000
Eurotherm Controls
Ashburn, VA 703-443-0000
Food Instrument Corporation
Federalsburg, MD 800-542-5688
Food Technology Corporation
Sterling, VA 703-444-1870
Forte Technology
South Easton, MA 508-297-2363
FSI Technologies, Inc.
Lombard, IL 800-468-6009
Garver Manufacturing
Union City, IN 765-964-5828
Gems Sensors
Plainville, CT 860-747-3000
Geo. Olcott Company
Scottsboro, AL 800-634-2769
Gerstel
Linthicum Hts, MD 800-413-8160
Gracey Instrument Corporation
Encinitas, CA 800-304-5859
GraLab Corporation
Centerville, OH 800-876-8353
Greer's Ferry Glass Work
Dubuque, IA 501-589-2947
Haake
Paramus, NJ 800-631-1369
Hach Company
Loveland, CO 800-227-4224
Hanna Instruments
Woonsocket, RI 800-426-6287
Heuft
Downers Grove, IL 630-968-9011
High-Purity Standards
North Charleston, SC 866-767-4771
Hoffer Flow Controls
Elizabeth City, NC 800-628-4584
I.W. Tremont Company
Hawthorne, NJ 973-427-3800
Idexx Laboratories
Westbrook, ME 800-321-0207
IMC Instruments
Menomonee Falls, WI 262-252-4620
Industrial Dynamics Company
Torrance, CA 888-434-5832
Innovative Components
Southington, CT 800-789-2851
International Equipment Trading
Vernon Hills, IL 800-438-4522
International Tank & Pipe Co
Clackamas, OR 888-988-0011
Interstate Monroe Machinery
Seattle, WA 206-682-4870
IQ Scientific Instruments
Carlsbad, CA 760-930-6501
JM Canty, Inc.
Buffalo, NY 716-625-4227
Kodex Inc
Nutley, NJ 800-325-6339
Koehler Instrument Company
Bohemia, NY 800-878-9070
Konica Minolta Corporation
Ramsey, NJ 888-473-3637
Labconco Corporation
Kansas City, MO 800-821-5525
LabVantage Solutions
Bridgewater, NJ 888-346-5467
Leeman Labs
Hudson, NH 603-886-8400
Leica Microsystems
Depew, NY 800-346-4560
Libra Laboratories Inc
Metuchen, NJ 732-321-5200
Lixi
Huntley, IL 847-961-6666
Lock Inspection Systems
Fitchburg, MA 800-227-5539
Loma International
Carol Stream, IL 800-872-5662
LT Industries
Gaithersburg, MD 301-990-4050
Lumenite Control Technology
Franklin Park, IL 800-323-8510
Machine Applications Corporation
Sandusky, OH 419-621-2322
Malthus Diagnostics
North Ridgeville, OH 800-346-7202
Maptech Packaging Inc.
Hilton Head Island, SC 843-342-5900
Maselli Measurements
Stockton, CA 800-964-9600

MDS
Valrico, FL 813-653-1180
Mesa Laboratories
Lakewood, CO 800-525-1215
Mettler Toldeo Safeline
Tampa, FL. 800-447-4439
Mettler Toledo-Rainin
Woburn, MA 800-662-7027
Miroil
Allentown, PA. 800-523-9844
MISCO Refractometer
Cleveland, OH 866-831-1999
MOCON
Minneapolis, MN 763-493-6370
Moisture Register Products
Rancho Cucamonga, CA 800-966-4788
Namco Controls Corporation
Cleveland, OH 800-626-8324
National Hotpack
Stone Ridge, NY. 800-431-8232
NDC Infrared EngineeringInc
Irwindale, CA 626-960-3300
Neogen Corporation
Lansing, MI. 800-234-5333
Neogen Gene-Trak Systems
Lansing, MI. 800-234-5333
New Brunswick ScientificCompany
Enfield, CT 800-645-3050
Nirsystems
Silver Spring, MD. 301-680-0252
Noral
Natick, MA 800-348-2345
Norton Performance Plastics
Wayne, NJ 973-696-4700
Ohio Magnetics-Stearns Magnetics
Cleveland, OH 800-486-6446
Omni Controls
Tampa, FL. 800-783-6664
Omnion
Rockland, MA. 781-878-7200
Omron Electronics
Schaumburg, IL. 800-556-6766
OneVision Corporation
Westerville, OH. 614-794-1144
Optel Vision
Quebec, QC. 866-688-0334
Organon Teknika Corporation
Durham, NC 800-682-2666
Orion Research
Beverly, MA 800-225-1480
Pacific Scientific Instrument
Grants Pass, OR 800-866-7889
Paktronics Controls
Richland Hills, TX 817-284-5241
Peco Controls Corporation
Modesto, CA. 800-732-6285
Perkin-Elmer Inc.
Shelton, CT. 800-762-4000
Perten Instruments
Springfield, IL. 888-773-7836
PolyScience
Niles, IL 800-229-7569
Process Sensors Corporation
Milford, MA 508-473-9901
Promega Corporation
Fitchburg, WI 608-274-4330
Pyrometer Instrument Company
Windsor, NJ. 800-468-7976
QA Supplies, LLC
Norfolk, VA. 800-472-7205
QMI
St Paul, MN. 651-501-2337
Quality Control Equipment Company
Des Moines, IA. 515-266-2268
Quest Corporation
North Royalton, OH 440-230-9400
Reotemp Instrument Corporation
San Diego, CA 800-648-7737
Rexroth Corporation
Hoffman Estates, IL 847-645-3600
Rheometric Scientific
New Castle, DE. 732-560-8550
Rosemount Analytical
Irvine, CA 800-543-8257
Rotronic Instrument
Hauppauge, NY 800-628-7101
Ryan Instruments
Redmond, WA. 425-883-7926
SDIX
Newark, DE. 800-544-8881
Sensidyne
Clearwater, FL 800-451-9444
Sensitech
Beverly, MA 800-843-8367
Sensortech Systems
Chatsworth, CA 818-341-5366
Sentry Equipment Corporation
Oconomowoc, WI. 262-567-7256
ShockWatch
Dallas, TX. 800-527-9497
SIGHTech Vision Systems
Santa Clara, CA 408-282-3770
Spectro
Marble Falls, TX. 800-580-6608
Spiral Biotech
Norwood, MA. 800-554-1620
Sure Torque
Sarasota, FL 800-387-6572
Tangent Systems
Charlotte, NC 800-992-7577
Technistar Corporation
Denver, CO 303-651-0188
Tekmar-Dohrmann
Mason, OH 800-874-2004
Teledyne Taptone
North Falmouth, MA 508-563-1000
Testing Machines, Inc
New Castle, DE. 800-678-3221
Texture Technologies Corporation
Scarsdale, NY 914-472-0531
Thermedics Detection
Chelmsford, MA. 888-846-7226
Thermo Detection
Franklin, MA 866-269-0070
Thermo Fisher Scientific, Inc.
Waltham, MA 800-678-5599
Thermo Ramsey
Coon Rapids, MN. 763-783-2500
ThermoQuest
Austin, TX. 800-876-6711
Theta Sciences
San Diego, CA 760-745-3311
Thorn Smith Laboratories
Beulah, MI 231-882-4672
Tricor Systems
Elgin, IL 800-575-0161
Troxler Electronic Laboratories
Research Triangle Park, NC 919-549-8661
TVC Systems
Portsmouth, NH 888-431-5251
Univex Corporation
Salem, NH. 800-258-6358
Vee Gee Scientific
Kirkland, WA 800-423-8842
Venture Measurement Company
Spartanburg, SC 864-574-8960
VICAM, A Waters Business
Milford, MA 800-338-4381
Washington Frontier
Grandview, WA. 509-469-7662
Whatman
Haverhill, MA. 978-374-7400
Wilkens-Anderson Company
Chicago, IL 800-847-2222
X-Ray Industries
Troy, MI 800-973-4800
Xylem, Inc.
White Plains, NY 914-323-5700
YSI
Yellow Springs, OH 800-765-4974
Zeltex
Hagerstown, MD. 800-732-1950

Instrumentation

Color Measuring

Byk-Gardner
Columbia, MD 301-483-6500
Hunterlab
Reston, VA 703-471-1920
Konica Minolta Corporation
Ramsey, NJ 888-473-3637
Sick Inc.
Minneapolis, MN 800-325-7425
Wilkens-Anderson Company
Chicago, IL 800-847-2222

Flow Measurement, Gas & Liquid

ACR Systems
Surrey, BC. 800-663-7845
Anderson Instrument Company
Fultonville, NY. 800-833-0081
Auburn Systems
Danvers, MA. 800-255-5008
Berthold Technologies
Oak Ridge, TN 865-483-1488
Brooks Instrument
Hatfield, PA. 888-554-3569
CEA Instruments
Westwood, NJ 888-893-9640
CEM Corporation
Matthews, NC. 800-726-3331
Columbus Instruments
Columbus, OH 800-669-5011
Endress & Hauser
Greenwood, IN 800-428-4344
Hach Company
Loveland, CO 800-227-4224
Hardy Systems Corporation
Northbrook, IL 800-927-3956
Hoffer Flow Controls
Elizabeth City, NC 800-628-4584
IMC Instruments
Menomonee Falls, WI. 262-252-4620
Interstate Monroe Machinery
Seattle, WA 206-682-4870
Labconco Corporation
Kansas City, MO. 800-821-5525
Maptech Packaging Inc.
Hilton Head Island, SC. 843-342-5900
MOCON
Minneapolis, MN 763-493-6370
Omni Controls
Tampa, FL. 800-783-6664
Optek
Galena, OH 800-533-8400
Rotronic Instrument
Hauppauge, NY 800-628-7101
Tuchenhagen
Columbia, MD 410-910-6000
Washington Frontier
Grandview, WA. 509-469-7662

Laboratory Equipment

Acme Scale Company
San Leandro, CA. 888-638-5040
Advance Energy Technologies
Clifton Park, NY. 800-724-0198
Advanced Technology Corporation/Vetstar
Ramsey, NJ 201-934-7127
Agri-Equipment International
Longs, SC 877-550-4709
Analytical Measurements
Chester, NJ 800-635-5580
Arizona Instrument LLC
Chandler, AZ. 800-528-7411
Atkins Technical
Gainesville, FL 800-284-2842
Barnant Company
Lake Barrington, IL 800-637-3739
Becton Dickinson & Company: Diagnostic Systems
Franklin Lakes, NJ 201-847-6800
Bel-Art Products
Wayne, NJ. 800-423-5278
Bematek Systems
Salem, MA 877-236-2835
Bentley Instruments
Chaska, MN 952-448-7600
Bernhard
Kennett Square, PA. 800-541-7874
BioControl Systems
Bellevue, WA 800-245-0113
Bioscience International, Inc
Rockville, MD 301-231-7400
Bran & Luebbe
Schaumburg, IL. 847-882-8116
Brookfield Engineering Laboratories
Middleboro, MA. 800-628-8139
C.W. Brabender Instruments
South Hackensack, NJ 201-343-8425
Caron Products & Services
Marietta, OH. 800-648-3042
Charm Sciences
Lawrence, MA 978-683-6100
ChemIndustrial Systems
Cedarburg, WI. 262-375-8570
Chemineer-Kenics/Greerco
North Andover, MA 800-643-0641
Clark-Cooper Division Magnatrol Valve Corporation
Cinnaminson, NJ. 856-829-4580
Cleveland Vibrator Company
Cleveland, OH 800-221-3298
Corning Life Sciences
Acton, MA. 800-492-1110

Cuutom Poly Packaging
Fort Wayne, IN 800-548-6603
Domnick Hunter
Charlotte, NC 800-345-8462
Dresser Instruments
Stratford, CT 800-328-8258
E & E Process Instrumentation
Concord, Ontario, ON. 905-669-4857
Ederback Corporation
Ann Arbor, MI 800-422-2558
ENSCO
Springfield, VA 703-321-9000
Food Technology Corporation
Sterling, VA. 703-444-1870
Gerstel
Linthicum Hts, MD. 800-413-8160
Glen Mills, Inc.
Clifton, NJ. 973-777-0777
Gracey Instrument Corporation
Encinitas, CA 800-304-5859
GraLab Corporation
Centerville, OH. 800-876-8353
Greer's Ferry Glass Work
Dubuque, IA 501-589-2947
Haake
Paramus, NJ 800-631-1369
Hanna Instruments
Woonsocket, RI. 800-426-6287
Hanson Lab Furniture
Newbury Park, CA 805-498-3121
HEMCO Corporation
Independence, MO 800-779-4362
Hunterlab
Reston, VA 703-471-1920
Idexx Laboratories
Westbrook, ME. 800-321-0207
IKA Works
Wilmington, NC 800-733-3037
IMC Instruments
Menomonee Falls, WI. 262-252-4620
IQ Scientific Instruments
Carlsbad, CA. 760-930-6501
Labconco Corporation
Kansas City, MO. 800-821-5525
Laboratory Devices
Holliston, MA 508-429-1716
LabVantage Solutions
Bridgewater, NJ 888-346-5467
Lauhoff Corporation
Detroit, MI 313-259-0027
Leeman Labs
Hudson, NH 603-886-8400
Leica Microsystems
Depew, NY 800-346-4560
Libra Laboratories Inc
Metuchen, NJ 732-321-5200
Libra Technical Center
Metuchen, NJ 732-321-5487
Maselli Measurements
Stockton, CA. 800-964-9600
Microthermics
Raleigh, NC 919-878-8045
National Hotpack
Stone Ridge, NY. 800-431-8232
National Manufacturing Company
Lincoln, NE. 402-475-3400
NDC Infrared EngineeringInc
Irwindale, CA 626-960-3300
Neogen Corporation
Lansing, MI. 800-234-5333
NETZSCH
Exton, PA 610-363-8010
New Brunswick ScientificCompany
Enfield, CT 800-645-3050
Nirsystems
Silver Spring, MD. 301-680-0252
Noral
Natick, MA 800-348-2345
Omnion
Rockland, MA. 781-878-7200
Pacific Scientific Instrument
Grants Pass, OR 800-866-7889
Par Systems
Saint Paul, MN 800-464-1320
Patterson-Kelley Hars Company
East Stroudsburg, PA 570-421-7500
Perkin-Elmer Inc.
Shelton, CT 800-762-4000
Perten Instruments
Springfield, IL. 888-773-7836
PolyScience
Niles, IL 800-229-7569
Pro Scientific
Oxford, CT 800-584-3776
Pro-Line
Haverhill, MA. 978-556-1695
QA Supplies, LLC
Norfolk, VA. 800-472-7205
Radiation Processing Division
Parsippany, NJ. 800-442-1969
Rosemount Analytical
Irvine, CA 800-543-8257
Schlueter Company
Janesville, WI 800-359-1700
Scott Turbon Mixer
Adelanto, CA 800-285-8512
Sefi Fabricators
Amityville, NY 631-842-2200
Silverson Machines
East Longmeadow, MA 800-204-6400
Spiral Biotech
Norwood, MA. 800-554-1620
Stewart Laboratories
Golden Valley, MN. 800-820-2333
Straub Company
Minneapolis, MN 952-546-6686
Texture Technologies Corporation
Scarsdale, NY 914-472-0531
Thermex Thermatron
Louisville, KY 502-493-1299
ThermoQuest
Austin, TX. 800-876-6711
Triad Scientific
Manasquan, NJ 800-867-6690
Tricor Systems
Elgin, IL 800-575-0161
Tromner
Thorofare, NJ 856-686-1600
Variety Glass
Cambridge, OH. 740-432-3643
Vee Gee Scientific
Kirkland, WA 800-423-8842
VICAM, A Waters Business
Milford, MA 800-338-4381
Weber Scientific
Hamilton, NJ. 800-328-8378
Whatman
Piscataway, NJ 973-245-8300
Whatman
Haverhill, MA. 978-374-7400
Wilkens-Anderson Company
Chicago, IL 800-847-2222
X-Ray Industries
Troy, MI 800-973-4800
X-Rite, Inc.
Grand Rapids, MI 616-803-2100
YSI
Yellow Springs, OH 800-765-4974

Clean Rooms

Advance Energy Technologies
Clifton Park, NY. 800-724-0198

Laboratory Sample Testing

Chr. Hansen, Inc.
Milwaukee, WI 800-558-0802

Measurement Systems

A&D Weighing
San Jose, CA. 800-726-3364
A&M Thermometer Corporation
Asheville, NC 800-685-9211
ABB Instrumentation
Rochester, NY. 716-292-6050
Abbeon Cal
Santa Barbara, CA 800-922-0977
Abel Manufacturing Company
Appleton, WI 920-734-4443
Acme Scale Company
San Leandro, CA. 888-638-5040
Acrison
Moonachie, NJ 800-422-4266
Action Packaging Automation
Roosevelt, NJ 800-241-2724
Advanced Instruments
Norwood, MA. 800-225-4034
Agri-Equipment International
Longs, SC 877-550-4709
Agtron
Reno, NV 775-850-4600
Alnor Instrument Company
Skokie, IL 800-424-7427
Ametek
Sellersville, PA 215-257-6531
Analytical Measurements
Chester, NJ 800-635-5580
Anderson Instrument
Fultonville, NY. 800-833-0081
Anderson Instrument Company
Fultonville, NY 800-833-0081
Aqua Measure Instrument Company
Rancho Cucamonga, CA 800-966-4788
Arkfeld Mfg & Distr Company
Norfolk, NE. 800-533-0676
ASI Electronics
Cypress, TX 800-231-6066
Athena Controls
Plymouth Meeting, PA 800-782-6776
Atkins Technical
Gainesville, FL 800-284-2842
ATM Corporation
New Berlin, WI. 800-511-2096
ATS RheoSystems
Bordentown, NJ 609-298-2522
AW Company
Franksville, WI 800-850-6110
Babson Brothers Company
Galesville, WI. 608-582-2221
Badger Meter
Milwaukee, WI 800-876-3837
Banner Engineering Corporation
Plymouth, MN. 888-373-6767
Barnant Company
Lake Barrington, IL 800-637-3739
Berthold Technologies
Oak Ridge, TN 865-483-1488
Blancett Fluid Flow Meters
Racine, WI 800-235-1638
BLH Electronics
Canton, MA 781-821-2000
Blodgett Company
Houston, TX 281-933-6195
Bowtemp
Mont-Royal, QC 514-735-5551
Brookfield Engineering Laboratories
Middleboro, MA. 800-628-8139
Brooks Instrument
Hatfield, PA. 888-554-3569
Bry-Air
Sunbury, OH 877-379-2479
Byk-Gardner
Columbia, MD 301-483-6500
Cambridge Viscosity, Inc.
Medford, MA 800-554-4639
CEA Instruments
Westwood, NJ. 888-893-9640
Chaney Instrument
Lake Geneva, WI 800-777-0565
ChemIndustrial Systems
Cedarburg, WI. 262-375-8570
Chocolate Concepts
Hartville, OH 330-877-3322
Clark-Cooper Division Magnatrol Valve Corporation
Cinnaminson, NJ. 856-829-4580
Clayton Industries
City of Industry, CA 800-423-4585
CMT
Hamilton, MA. 978-768-2555
Columbus Instruments
Columbus, OH 800-669-5011
Comark Instruments
Everett, WA. 800-555-6658
Conax Buffalo Technologies
Buffalo, NY. 800-223-2389
Control Products
Chanhassen, MN. 800-947-9098
Cooper Instrument Corporation
Middlefield, CT. 800-835-5011
Crystal-Vision PackagingSystems
Torrance, CA. 800-331-3240
Cyvex Nutrition
Irvine, CA 888-992-9839
Datapaq
Wilmington, MA. 800-326-5270
Debelak Technical Systems
Greenville, WI 800-888-4207
Delavan-Delta
Naugatuck, CT 203-720-5610
Devar
Bridgeport, CT 800-566-6822
Dwyer Instruments
Michigan City, IN. 800-872-3141
E & E Process Instrumentation
Concord, Ontario, ON. 905-669-4857

Electronic Weighing Systems
Opa Locka, FL 305-685-8067
Endress & Hauser
Greenwood, IN 800-428-4344
Enercon Systems
Elyria, OH 440-323-7080
ENM Company
Chicago, IL 773-775-8400
EPD Technology Corporation
Elmsford, NY 800-892-8926
ESCO
Houston, TX 800-966-5514
Exact Mixing Systems
Memphis, TN 901-362-8501
Flowdata
Tempe, AZ 800-833-2448
FMC Fluid Control
Stephenville, TX 800-772-8582
Food Technology Corporation
Sterling, VA 703-444-1870
Forte Technology
South Easton, MA 508-297-2363
Frazier Precision Instrument Company
Hagerstown, MD 301-790-2585
Frye's Measure Mill
Wilton, NH 603-654-6581
Gracey Instrument Corporation
Encinitas, CA 800-304-5859
Greer's Ferry Glass Work
Dubuque, IA 501-589-2947
Haake
Paramus, NJ 800-631-1369
Hanna Instruments
Woonsocket, RI 800-426-6287
HD Electric Company
Waukegan, IL 847-473-4980
Hoffer Flow Controls
Elizabeth City, NC 800-628-4584
Hunterlab
Reston, VA 703-471-1920
IAS Corporation
Hampton, VA 800-916-4272
IMC Instruments
Menomonee Falls, WI 262-252-4620
Industrial Laboratory Equipment
Charlotte, NC 704-357-3930
Inspired Automation
Agoura Hills, CA 818-991-4598
Intelligent Controls
Saco, ME 800-872-3455
IQ Scientific Instruments
Carlsbad, CA 760-930-6501
Ivek Corporation
N Springfield, VT 800-356-4746
Kason Central
Columbus, OH 614-885-1992
Kason Industries
Newnan, GA 770-254-0553
King Engineering - King-Gage
Newell, WV 800-242-8871
Kistler-Morse Corporation
Spartanburg, SC 800-426-9010
Konica Minolta Corporation
Ramsey, NJ 888-473-3637
L.C. Thompson Company
Kenosha, WI 800-558-4018
Leica Microsystems
Depew, NY 800-346-4560
Liquid Controls
Lake Bluff, IL 800-458-5262
Liquid Scale
New Brighton, MN 888-633-2969
Liquid Solids Control
Upton, MA 508-529-3377
Lockwood Packaging
Woburn, MA 800-641-3100
Loma International
Carol Stream, IL 800-872-5662
Loma Systems
Carol Stream, IL 800-872-5662
Lorann Oils
Lansing, MI 800-862-8620
Love Controls Division
Michigan City, IN 800-828-4588
Lumenite Control Technology
Franklin Park, IL 800-323-8510
M.H. Rhodes Cramer
South Windsor, CT 877-684-6464
Machine Applications Corporation
Sandusky, OH 419-621-2322
Maselli Measurements
Stockton, CA 800-964-9600
Mesa Laboratories
Lakewood, CO 800-525-1215
Micro Motion
Boulder, CO 800-760-8119
Micro-Strain
Spring City, PA 610-948-4550
Miljoco Corporation
Mount Clemens, MI 888-888-1498
Moisture Register Products
Rancho Cucamonga, CA 800-966-4788
Monitor Company
Modesto, CA 800-537-3201
Monitor Technologies
Elburn, IL 800-601-6319
MTL Etching Industries
Woodmere, NY 516-295-9733
Munters Corporation
Amesbury, MA 800-843-5360
Music City Metals
Nashville, TN 800-251-2674
National Time Recording Equipment Company
New York, NY 212-227-3310
NDC Infrared EngineeringInc
Irwindale, CA 626-960-3300
Nicol Scales
Dallas, TX 800-225-8181
Noral
Natick, MA 800-348-2345
Ogden Manufacturing Company
Pittsburgh, PA 412-967-3906
Optek-Danulat, Inc
Germantown, WI 888-551-4288
Orion Research
Beverly, MA 800-225-1480
Oyster Bay Pump Works
Hicksville, NY 516-933-4500
Pacific Scale Company
Clackamas, OR 800-537-1886
Pacific Scientific Instrument
Grants Pass, OR 800-866-7889
Paktronics Controls
Richland Hills, TX 817-284-5241
Paratherm Corporation
Conshohocken, PA 800-222-3611
Peco Controls Corporation
Modesto, CA 800-732-6285
Pelouze Scale Company
Bridgeview, IL 800-323-8363
Perten Instruments
Springfield, IL 888-773-7836
Prince Castle
Carol Stream, IL 800-722-7853
Process Sensors Corporation
Milford, MA 508-473-9901
Reotemp Instrument Corporation
San Diego, CA 800-648-7737
Rheometric Scientific
New Castle, DE 732-560-8550
Rosemount Analytical
Irvine, CA 800-543-8257
Rotronic Instrument
Hauppauge, NY 800-628-7101
Samson Controls
Baytown, TX 281-383-3677
Scientech, Inc
Boulder, CO 800-525-0522
Sensitech
Beverly, MA 800-843-8367
Sensortech Systems
Chatsworth, CA 818-341-5366
Sentron
Gig Harbor, WA 800-472-4361
Siko Products
Dexter, MI 800-447-7456
SJ Controls
Signal Hill, CA 562-494-1400
Spinco Metal Products
Newark, NY 315-331-6285
Sure Torque
Sarasota, FL 800-387-6572
Tangent Systems
Charlotte, NC 800-992-7577
Taylor Precision Products
Las Cruces, NM 630-954-1250
Tel-Tru Manufacturing Company
Rochester, NY 800-232-5335
Testing Machines, Inc
New Castle, DE 800-678-3221
Texture Technologies Corporation
Scarsdale, NY 914-472-0531
Thayer Scale
Pembroke, MA 781-826-8101
Thermalogic Corporation
Hudson, MA 978-562-5974
Thermo Detection
Franklin, MA 866-269-0070
Thermo Instruments
Yaphank, NY 631-924-0880
Thermo King Corporation
Minneapolis, MN 952-887-2200
Triad Scientific
Manasquan, NJ 800-867-6690
Tuchenhagen
Columbia, MD 410-910-6000
Venture Measurement Company
Spartanburg, SC 864-574-8960
VitaMinder Company
Providence, RI 800-858-8840
Water Sciences Services ,Inc.
Jackson, TN 973-584-4131
Weiss Instruments
Holtsville, NY 631-207-1200
Wescor
Logan, UT 800-453-2725
Whatman
Haverhill, MA 978-374-7400
Wika Instrument Corporation
Lawrenceville, GA 800-645-0606
X-Rite, Inc.
Grand Rapids, MI 616-803-2100
YSI
Yellow Springs, OH 800-765-4974

Polarimeters

Cyvex Nutrition
Irvine, CA 888-992-9839

Refractometers

Cyvex Nutrition
Irvine, CA 888-992-9839

Meters

Flow

ABB Instrumentation
Rochester, NY 716-292-6050
Ametek
Sellersville, PA 215-257-6531
Anderson Instrument
Fultonville, NY 800-833-0081
Auburn Systems
Danvers, MA 800-255-5008
AW Company
Franksville, WI 800-850-6110
Badger Meter
Milwaukee, WI 800-876-3837
Barnant Company
Lake Barrington, IL 800-637-3739
Bernhard
Kennett Square, PA 800-541-7874
Blancett Fluid Flow Meters
Racine, WI 800-235-1638
ChemIndustrial Systems
Cedarburg, WI 262-375-8570
Conflow Technologies, Inc.
Brampton, ON 800-275-9887
DMC-David Manufacturing Company
Mason City, IA 641-424-7010
Flowdata
Tempe, AZ 800-833-2448
FMC Fluid Control
Stephenville, TX 800-772-8582
Hayward Industrial Products
Clemmons, NC 908-355-7995
Hoffer Flow Controls
Elizabeth City, NC 800-628-4584
Kisco Manufacturing
Greendale, BC 604-823-7456
Liquid Controls
Lake Bluff, IL 800-458-5262
Lumenite Control Technology
Franklin Park, IL 800-323-8510
Machine Applications Corporation
Sandusky, OH 419-621-2322
Mesa Laboratories
Lakewood, CO 800-525-1215
Monitor Technologies
Elburn, IL 800-601-6319
Music City Metals
Nashville, TN 800-251-2674
Quality Control Equipment Company
Des Moines, IA 515-266-2268

Samson Controls
Baytown, TX. 281-383-3677
Shenck AccuRate
Whitewater, WI. 888-742-1249
SJ Controls
Signal Hill, CA 562-494-1400
Special Products
Springfield, MO 417-881-6114
Spinco Metal Products
Newark, NY 315-331-6285
TWM Manufacturing
Leamington, ON 888-495-4831

pH

Analytical Measurements
Chester, NJ 800-635-5580
Byk-Gardner
Columbia, MD 301-483-6500
ChemIndustrial Systems
Cedarburg, WI. 262-375-8570
Cyvex Nutrition
Irvine, CA 888-992-9839
DeltaTrak
Pleasanton, CA 800-962-6776
Devar
Bridgeport, CT 800-566-6822
Dresser Instruments
Stratford, CT 800-328-8258
E & E Process Instrumentation
Concord, Ontario, ON. 905-669-4857
Hanna Instruments
Woonsocket, RI. 800-426-6287
IQ Scientific Instruments
Carlsbad, CA. 760-930-6501
QA Supplies, LLC
Norfolk, VA. 800-472-7205
Tricor Systems
Elgin, IL 800-575-0161
Wilkens-Anderson Company
Chicago, IL 800-847-2222
X-Rite, Inc.
Grand Rapids, MI 616-803-2100
YSI
Yellow Springs, OH 800-765-4974

Microbiology Instruments & Supplies

Baltimore Aircoil Company
Jessup, MD 410-799-6200
Becton Dickinson & Company: Diagnostic Systems
Franklin Lakes, NJ 201-847-6800
Biolog
Hayward, CA 800-284-4949
Malthus Diagnostics
North Ridgeville, OH 800-346-7202
MicroBioLogics
Saint Cloud, MN. 800-599-2847
New Brunswick ScientificCompany
Enfield, CT 800-645-3050
Organon Teknika Corporation
Durham, NC 800-682-2666
QA Supplies, LLC
Norfolk, VA. 800-472-7205
VICAM, A Waters Business
Milford, MA 800-338-4381
Whatman
Piscataway, NJ 973-245-8300
Wilkens-Anderson Company
Chicago, IL 800-847-2222

Process Analysis & Development

A&B Process Systems
Stratford, WI. 888-258-2789
Asset Design LLC
Mooresville, NC 888-293-1740
Datapaq
Wilmington, MA. 800-326-5270
Food & Agrosystems
Sunnyvale, CA 408-245-8450
JM Canty, Inc.
Buffalo, NY. 716-625-4227
Vee Gee Scientific
Kirkland, WA 800-423-8842

Electronic Survey

Innovative Food Solutions LLC
Columbus, OH 800-884-3314
Libra Technical Center
Metuchen, NJ 732-321-5487

Long Range Systems
Addison, TX 800-577-8101

Process Controls

Batching, Blending, Weighing

A&B Process Systems
Stratford, WI. 888-258-2789
Abel Manufacturing Company
Appleton, WI 920-734-4443
APEC
Lake Odessa, MI. 616-374-1000
ASI Electronics
Cypress, TX 800-231-6066
Autocon Mixing Systems
St Helena, CA 800-225-6192
AZO Food
Memphis, TN 901-794-9480
Batching Systems
Prince Frederick, MD 800-311-0851
BLH Electronics
Canton, MA 781-821-2000
Chicago Conveyor Corporation
Addison, IL. 630-543-6300
Coastline Equipment
Bellingham, WA 360-739-2480
Conflow Technologies, Inc.
Brampton, ON. 800-275-9887
Digital Dynamics
Scotts Valley, CA 800-765-1288
Hartel International LLC
Fort Atkinson, WI. 920-563-6597
Hoffer Flow Controls
Elizabeth City, NC 800-628-4584
JCS Controls, Inc.
Rochester, NY. 585-227-5910
Liquid Solids Control
Upton, MA 508-529-3377
Matiss
St Georges, QC 888-562-8477
Merrick Industries
Lynn Haven, FL 800-271-7834
Nu-Con Equipment
Chanhassen, MN. 877-939-0510
Pickwick Company
Cedar Rapids, IA. 800-397-9797
Pro Scientific
Oxford, CT 800-584-3776
Quest Corporation
North Royalton, OH 440-230-9400
Rice Lake Weighing Systems
Rice Lake, WI
Schaffer Poidometer Company
Pittsburgh, PA. 412-281-9031
Shenck AccuRate
Whitewater, WI. 888-742-1249
Silverson Machines
East Longmeadow, MA 800-204-6400
Sterling Controls
Sterling, IL 800-257-7214
T.D. Sawvel Company
Maple Plain, MN. 877-488-1816
Tecweigh/Tecnetics Industries
White Bear Lake, MN. 800-536-4880
Thermedics Detection
Chelmsford, MA 888-846-7226
Trola Industries
York, PA 717-848-3700

Control Panels

A&B Process Systems
Stratford, WI. 888-258-2789
ASAP Automation
Addison, IL. 800-409-0383
Controls Unlimited
Perry, OH 440-259-2500
Digital Dynamics
Scotts Valley, CA 800-765-1288
Hartel International LLC
Fort Atkinson, WI. 920-563-6597
Novar
Cleveland, OH 800-348-1235
Our Name is Mud
New York, NY 877-683-7867
Pro Controls
Yakima, WA 800-488-3386
Process Solutions
Riviera Beach, FL. 561-840-0050
Red Lion Controls
York, PA 717-767-6511

Trola Industries
York, PA 717-848-3700
Viatran Corporation
North Tonawanda, NY 800-688-0030
Washington Frontier
Grandview, WA. 509-469-7662

Humidity Loggers

Dresser Instruments
Stratford, CT 800-328-8258

Pressure

ACR Systems
Surrey, BC. 800-663-7845
Acromag Inc.
Wixom, MI 248-624-1541
Alnor Instrument Company
Skokie, IL 800-424-7427
Anderson Instrument Company
Fultonville, NY. 800-833-0081
Chicago Stainless Equipment
Palm City, FL 800-927-8575
Control Products
Chanhassen, MN. 800-947-9098
Dresser Instruments
Stratford, CT 800-328-8258
Endress & Hauser
Greenwood, IN 800-428-4344
IMC Instruments
Menomonee Falls, WI. 262-252-4620
Omni Controls
Tampa, FL. 800-783-6664
Peco Controls Corporation
Modesto, CA. 800-732-6285
Samson Controls
Baytown, TX. 281-383-3677
United Electric ControlsCompany
Watertown, MA. 617-926-1000
Washington Frontier
Grandview, WA. 509-469-7662
Weiss Instruments
Holtsville, NY. 631-207-1200

Data Loggers

Dresser Instruments
Stratford, CT 800-328-8258
Jumo Process Control Incc
East Syracuse, NY 800-554-5866

Gauges;Sanitary

Dresser Instruments
Stratford, CT 800-328-8258

Programmable

ACR Systems
Surrey, BC. 800-663-7845
Allpax Products
Covington, LA 888-893-9277
American Autogard Corporation
Rockford, IL 815-229-3190
Boston Gear
Boston, MA. 888-999-9860
Chicago Conveyor Corporation
Addison, IL. 630-543-6300
Dresser Instruments
Stratford, CT 800-328-8258
Intelligent Controls
Saco, ME. 800-872-3455
Pro Scientific
Oxford, CT 800-584-3776
Selco Products Company
Anaheim, CA 800-257-3526
Sterling Controls
Sterling, IL 800-257-7214
Thermex Thermatron
Louisville, KY 502-493-1299
Theta Sciences
San Diego, CA 760-745-3311

Recorders

ABB Instrumentation
Rochester, NY. 716-292-6050
Datapaq
Wilmington, MA. 800-326-5270
Delta Trak
Pleasanton, CA 800-962-6776
Devar
Bridgeport, CT 800-566-6822

Dresser Instruments
Stratford, CT 800-328-8258
Hanna Instruments
Woonsocket, RI........ 800-426-6287
IAS Corporation
Hampton, VA 800-916-4272
Mesa Laboratories
Lakewood, CO 800-525-1215
Pyrometer Instrument Company
Windsor, NJ........ 800-468-7976
Ryan Instruments
Redmond, WA........ 425-883-7926
Simplex Time Recorder Company
Santa Ana, CA 949-724-5000

Software

Iconics
Foxborough, MA 800-946-9679
Loma Systems
Carol Stream, IL 800-872-5662

Systems

A&B Process Systems
Stratford, WI........ 888-258-2789
ABB Instrumentation
Rochester, NY........ 716-292-6050
Abel Manufacturing Company
Appleton, WI 920-734-4443
Ace Specialty Manufacturing Company
Rosemead, CA 626-444-3867
Acrison
Moonachie, NJ 800-422-4266
Acromag Inc.
Wixom, MI 248-624-1541
Advanced Instruments
Norwood, MA........ 800-225-4034
AL Systems
Rockaway, NJ 888-960-8324
Allegheny Bradford Corporation
Bradford, PA 800-542-0650
Allpax Products
Covington, LA 888-893-9277
Alnor Instrument Company
Skokie, IL 800-424-7427
American Autogard Corporation
Rockford, IL 815-229-3190
American LEWA
Holliston, MA........ 888-539-2123
American Metal Door Company
Richmond, IN 800-428-2737
Analite
Plainview, NY........ 800-229-3357
Andantex USA
Ocean, NJ 800-713-6170
Anderson Instrument
Fultonville, NY........ 800-833-0081
Anderson Instrument Company
Fultonville, NY........ 800-833-0081
Applexion
Chicago, IL........ 773-243-0454
APV Americas
Delavan, WI 800-252-5200
Artisan Controls Corporation
Randolph, NJ 800-457-4950
ASAP Automation
Addison, IL........ 800-409-0383
ASI Electronics
Cypress, TX 800-231-6066
Athena Controls
Plymouth Meeting, PA 800-782-6776
Auburn Systems
Danvers, MA........ 800-255-5008
Autocon Mixing Systems
St Helena, CA 800-225-6192
Automation Service
Earth City, MO 800-325-4808
Autotron
Oak Creek, WI 800-527-7500
AZO Food
Memphis, TN 901-794-9480
B-T Engineering
Bala Cynwyd, PA 610-664-9500
Bailey Controls/ABB ation
Wickliffe, OH 440-585-8948
Batching Systems
Prince Frederick, MD 800-311-0851
Bentley Instruments
Chaska, MN 952-448-7600
BLH Electronics
Canton, MA 781-821-2000
Blue Tech
Hickory, NC 828-324-5900
Branford Vibrator Company
Peru, IL 800-262-2106
Bry-Air
Sunbury, OH 877-379-2479
BSI Instruments
Aliquippa, PA 800-274-9851
Burling Instruments
Chatham, NJ 800-635-2526
Burns Engineering
Hopkins, MN 800-328-3871
Cal Controls
Gurnee, IL........ 800-866-6659
Cashco
Ellsworth, KS 785-472-4461
Centent Company
Santa Ana, CA 714-979-6491
Chil-Con Products
Brantford, ON........ 800-263-0086
Cleveland Motion Controls
Cleveland, OH 800-321-8072
Coastline Equipment
Bellingham, WA 360-739-2480
Conflow Technologies, Inc.
Brampton, ON........ 800-275-9887
Contrex
Maple Grove, MN........ 763-424-7800
Control Concepts
Chanhassen, MN........ 800-765-2799
Control Pak International
Fenton, MI 810-735-2800
Control Products
Chanhassen, MN........ 800-947-9098
Control Systems Design
Forest Hill, MD........ 410-296-0466
Control Technology Corporation
Hopkinton, MA........ 800-282-5008
Controls Unlimited
Perry, OH 440-259-2500
Conveyor Components Company
Croswell, MI 800-233-3233
Cotter Corporation
Danvers, MA
Cramer Company
South Windsor, CT 877-684-6464
Crouzet Corporation
Carrollton, TX........ 800-677-5311
Damrow Company
Fond Du Lac, WI 800-236-1501
Debelak Technical Systems
Greenville, WI 800-888-4207
DEFCO
Landenberg, PA........ 215-274-8245
Delavan-Delta
Naugatuck, CT 203-720-5610
Design Technology Corporation
Lexington, MA 800-597-7063
Devar
Bridgeport, CT 800-566-6822
Diamond Automation
Farmington Hills, MI 248-426-9394
Dickson
Addison, IL........ 800-757-3747
Digital Dynamics
Scotts Valley, CA 800-765-1288
Dipix Technologies
Ottawa, ON........ 613-596-4942
DistaView Corporation
Bowling Green, OH 800-795-9970
Dwyer Instruments
Michigan City, IN........ 800-872-3141
Ecklund-Harrison Technologies
Fort Myers, FL 239-936-6032
Edwards Engineering Corporation
Pompton Plains, NJ........ 800-526-5201
Electro Cam Corporation
Roscoe, IL........ 800-228-5487
Electrol Specialties Company
South Beloit, IL 815-389-2291
Endress & Hauser
Greenwood, IN 800-428-4344
Enercon Systems
Elyria, OH........ 440-323-7080
ESE, Inc
Marshfield, WI 800-236-4778
Eurotherm Controls
Ashburn, VA 703-443-0000
Fata Automation
Sterling Heights, MI 586-323-9400
Flow Robotics
Jeffersonville, IN 812-283-7888
Food Automation Service Techniques
Stratford, CT 800-327-8766
Forte Technology
South Easton, MA........ 508-297-2363
Foxboro Company
Foxboro, MA 888-369-2676
Gems Sensors
Plainville, CT 860-747-3000
Glatt Air Techniques
Ramsey, NJ 201-825-8700
GraLab Corporation
Centerville, OH........ 800-876-8353
H.K. Systems
Milwaukee, WI 800-424-7365
Hanna Instruments
Woonsocket, RI........ 800-426-6287
Harland Simon Control Systems USA
Oakbrook, IL........ 630-572-7650
Hartel International LLC
Fort Atkinson, WI........ 920-563-6597
Hectronic
Oklahoma City, OK 405-946-3574
Hoffer Flow Controls
Elizabeth City, NC 800-628-4584
Hudson Control Group
Springfield, NJ 973-376-7400
Innovative Components
Southington, CT 800-789-2851
Intelligent Controls
Saco, ME........ 800-872-3455
Interstate Monroe Machinery
Seattle, WA 206-682-4870
ITW Foamseal
Oxford, MI 248-628-2587
Kinematics & Controls Corporation
Deer Park, NY........ 800-833-8103
L.C. Thompson Company
Kenosha, WI 800-558-4018
Lake Process Systems
Lake Barrington, IL 800-331-9260
LDJ Electronics
Troy, MI 248-528-2202
Liquid Controls
Lake Bluff, IL........ 800-458-5262
Liquid Solids Control
Upton, MA 508-529-3377
Love Controls Division
Michigan City, IN........ 800-828-4588
LT Industries
Gaithersburg, MD........ 301-990-4050
Lumenite Control Technology
Franklin Park, IL........ 800-323-8510
Maselli Measurements
Stockton, CA........ 800-964-9600
MeGa Industries
Burlington, ON........ 800-665-6342
Membrane Process & Controls
Edgar, WI 715-352-3206
Merrick Industries
Lynn Haven, FL 800-271-7834
Micromeritics
Norcross, GA 770-662-3620
Midwest Stainless
Menomonie, WI 715-235-5472
Monitor Technologies
Elburn, IL 800-601-6319
Murata Automated Systems
Charlotte, NC 800-428-8469
Murzan
Norcross, GA 770-448-0583
Namco Controls Corporation
Cleveland, OH 800-626-8324
NAPCO Security Systems
Amityville, NY 631-842-9400
Nelles Automation
Houston, TX 713-939-9399
Norman N. Axelrod Associates
New York, NY 212-741-6302
Novar
Cleveland, OH 800-348-1235
Nu-Con Equipment
Chanhassen, MN........ 877-939-0510
Omni Controls
Tampa, FL........ 800-783-6664
Omron Electronics
Schaumburg, IL........ 800-556-6766
Onset Computer Corporation
Buzzards Bay, MA 800-564-4377
Optek
Galena, OH 800-533-8400
Paktronics Controls
Richland Hills, TX 817-284-5241

Papertech
North Vancouver, BC 877-787-2737
Partnership Resources, Inc.
Minneapolis, MN 612-331-2075
Payne Engineering
Scott Depot, WV. 800-331-1345
Peco Controls Corporation
Modesto, CA. 800-732-6285
Pro Controls
Yakima, WA 800-488-3386
Process Automation
Hurst, TX 800-460-9546
Process Solutions
Riviera Beach, FL. 561-840-0050
Process Systems
Barrington, IL 847-842-8618
Production Systems
Marietta, GA. 800-235-9734
Professional EngineeringAssociation
Louisville, KY 502-429-0432
Pyrometer Instrument Company
Windsor, NJ. 800-468-7976
Quest Corporation
North Royalton, OH 440-230-9400
R.G. Stephens Engineering
Long Beach, CA 800-499-3001
Ram Equipment
Waukesha, WI 262-513-1114
Relco Unisystems Corporation
Willmar, MN. 320-231-2210
Rexroth Corporation
Hoffman Estates, IL 847-645-3600
Rheometric Scientific
New Castle, DE. 732-560-8550
Rice Lake Weighing Systems
Rice Lake, WI
Roberts Gordon
Buffalo, NY. 800-828-7450
Samson Controls
Baytown, TX. 281-383-3677
Schneider Automation
North Andover, MA 978-691-1400
Scientech, Inc
Boulder, CO 800-525-0522
Seneca Environmental Products
Tiffin, OH 419-447-1282
Sepragen Corporation
Hayward, CA 510-475-0650
Simpson
Elgin, IL 847-697-2260
SJ Controls
Signal Hill, CA 562-494-1400
Spinco Metal Products
Newark, NY 315-331-6285
Stainless Products
Somers, WC 800-558-9446
Sterling
New Berlin, WI. 262-641-8610
Sterling Controls
Sterling, IL 800-257-7214
T.D. Sawvel Company
Maple Plain, MN. 877-488-1816
Tecweigh/Tecnetics Industries
White Bear Lake, MN. 800-536-4880
Thermedics Detection
Chelmsford, MA 888-846-7226
Thermo Detection
Franklin, MA 866-269-0070
Thermo King Corporation
Minneapolis, MN 952-887-2200
Theta Sciences
San Diego, CA 760-745-3311
Transbotics Corporation
Charlotte, NC 704-362-1115
Trola Industries
York, PA 717-848-3700
Tuchenhagen
Columbia, MD 410-910-6000
Tudor Technology
Plymouth Meeting, PA 800-777-0778
TVC Systems
Portsmouth, NH 888-431-5251
TWM Manufacturing
Leamington, ON 888-495-4831
Vee Gee Scientific
Kirkland, WA 800-423-8842
Videx, Inc.
Corvallis, OR 541-758-0521
Vulcan Electric Company
Porter, ME. 800-922-3027
W.G. Durant Corporation
Whittier, CA 562-946-5555
Watlow
St Louis, MO. 800-492-8569
Watlow Anafaze
Los Gatos, CA. 831-724-3800
Waukesha Cherry-Burrell
Louisville, KY 800-252-5200
Webb-Triax Company
Farmington Hills, MI 248-553-1000
WeighPack Systems/PaxiomGroup
Montreal, QC 888-934-4472
Williamson & Company
Greer, SC. 800-849-3263
Xcel Tower Controls
Gilbertsville, NY. 800-288-7362

Temperature

ACR Systems
Surrey, BC. 800-663-7845
Acromag Inc.
Wixom, MI 248-624-1541
Advance Energy Technologies
Clifton Park, NY 800-724-0198
Alnor Instrument Company
Skokie, IL 800-424-7427
Analite
Plainview, NY 800-229-3357
Anderson Instrument Company
Fultonville, NY 800-833-0081
ARI Industries
Addison, IL 800-237-6725
Artisan Controls Corporation
Randolph, NJ 800-457-4950
Athena Controls
Plymouth Meeting, PA 800-782-6776
Automatic Timing & Controls
Newell, WV 800-727-5646
Bry-Air
Sunbury, OH 877-379-2479
Burling Instruments
Chatham, NJ 800-635-2526
Burns Engineering
Hopkins, MN 800-328-3871
Chicago Stainless Equipment
Palm City, FL 800-927-8575
CMT
Hamilton, MA. 978-768-2555
Control Concepts
Chanhassen, MN. 800-765-2799
Control Pak International
Fenton, MI 810-735-2800
Control Products
Chanhassen, MN. 800-947-9098
Cooling Technology
Charlotte, NC 800-872-1448
Crouzet Corporation
Carrollton, TX. 800-677-5311
Danfoss
Baltimore, MD 410-931-8250
Debelak Technical Systems
Greenville, WI 800-888-4207
Dwyer Instruments
Michigan City, IN 800-872-3141
Enercon Systems
Elyria, OH 440-323-7080
Eurotherm Controls
Ashburn, VA 703-443-0000
Glo-Quartz Electric Heater Company
Mentor, OH. 800-321-3574
Hanna Instruments
Woonsocket, RI. 800-426-6287
Heatrex
Meadville, PA 800-394-6589
IMC Instruments
Menomonee Falls, WI. 262-252-4620
Kaye Instruments
N Billerica, MA 800-343-4624
L.C. Thompson Company
Kenosha, WI 800-558-4018
Laboratory Devices
Holliston, MA. 508-429-1716
Love Controls Division
Michigan City, IN 800-828-4588
Lumenite Control Technology
Franklin Park, IL. 800-323-8510
Munters Corporation
Amesbury, MA 800-843-5360
Novar
Cleveland, OH 800-348-1235
Ogden Manufacturing Company
Pittsburgh, PA 412-967-3906
Omni Controls
Tampa, FL. 800-783-6664
Omron Electronics
Schaumburg, IL. 800-556-6766
Paktronics Controls
Richland Hills, TX 817-284-5241
Paratherm Corporation
Conshohocken, PA 800-222-3611
Payne Engineering
Scott Depot, WV. 800-331-1345
PolyScience
Niles, IL 800-229-7569
Pyrometer Instrument Company
Windsor, NJ. 800-468-7976
Quantem Corporation
Ewing, NJ 609-883-9879
Selco Products Company
Anaheim, CA 800-257-3526
Sterling
New Berlin, WI. 262-641-8610
Thermalogic Corporation
Hudson, MA 978-562-5974
Thermo King Corporation
Minneapolis, MN 952-887-2200
Tudor Technology
Plymouth Meeting, PA 800-777-0778
United Electric ControlsCompany
Watertown, MA. 617-926-1000
Vulcan Electric Company
Porter, ME. 800-922-3027
Weiss Instruments
Holtsville, NY. 631-207-1200

Data Loggers

Dresser Instruments
Stratford, CT 800-328-8258

Time

Artisan Controls Corporation
Randolph, NJ 800-457-4950
Automatic Timing & Controls
Newell, WV 800-727-5646
Control Products
Chanhassen, MN. 800-947-9098
Dayton Marking Devices Company
Dayton, OH. 937-432-0285
Dresser Instruments
Stratford, CT 800-328-8258
M.H. Rhodes Cramer
South Windsor, CT 877-684-6464
Pro Scientific
Oxford, CT 800-584-3776

Transportation Loggers

Dresser Instruments
Stratford, CT 800-328-8258

Vacuum

Buchi Corporation
New Castle, DE. 877-692-8244
Dresser Instruments
Stratford, CT 800-328-8258
Lyco Wausau
Wausau, WI. 715-845-7867

pH Loggers

Dresser Instruments
Stratford, CT 800-328-8258

Pumps

Food

Barnant Company
Lake Barrington, IL 800-637-3739
Clark-Cooper Division Magnatrol Valve Corporation
Cinnaminson, NJ. 856-829-4580
Fluid Metering
Syosset, NY. 800-223-3388
Glen Mills, Inc.
Clifton, NJ. 973-777-0777
Kelmin Products
Plymouth, FL 407-886-6079
Lyco Wausau
Wausau, WI. 715-845-7867
NETZSCH
Exton, PA 610-363-8010

Northland Process Piping
Isle, MN ... 320-679-2119
Roto-Jet Pump
Salt Lake City, UT ... 801-359-8731
Savage Brothers Company
Elk Grove Vlg, IL ... 800-342-0973
Watson-Marlow
Wilmington, MA ... 800-282-8823
Waukesha Cherry-Burrell
Louisville, KY ... 800-252-5200

Sampling & Testing Equipment & Instrumentation

ACR Systems
Surrey, BC ... 800-663-7845
Advance Fitting Corporation
Elkhorn, WI ... 262-723-6699
Advanced Instruments
Norwood, MA ... 800-225-4034
Air Logic Power Systems
Milwaukee, WI ... 800-325-8717
Atkins Technical
Gainesville, FL ... 800-284-2842
Barco Machine Vision
Duluth, GA ... 704-392-9371
Binks Industries
Montgomery, IL ... 630-801-1100
BioControl Systems
Bellevue, WA ... 800-245-0113
Bioscience International, Inc
Rockville, MD ... 301-231-7400
Biotest Diagnostics Corporation
Rockaway, NJ ... 800-522-0090
Bran & Luebbe
Schaumburg, IL ... 847-882-8116
Charm Sciences
Lawrence, MA ... 978-683-6100
Comark Instruments
Everett, WA ... 800-555-6658
DeltaTrak
Pleasanton, CA ... 800-962-6776
Elwood Safety Company
Buffalo, NY ... 866-326-6060
ENSCO
Springfield, VA ... 703-321-9000
Gerstel
Linthicum Hts, MD ... 800-413-8160
Glen Mills, Inc.
Clifton, NJ ... 973-777-0777
Gracey Instrument Corporation
Encinitas, CA ... 800-304-5859
Hach Company
Loveland, CO ... 800-227-4224
HD Electric Company
Waukegan, IL ... 847-473-4980
I.W. Tremont Company
Hawthorne, NJ ... 973-427-3800
Idexx Laboratories
Westbrook, ME ... 800-321-0207
Industrial Dynamics Company
Torrance, CA ... 888-434-5832
IQ Scientific Instruments
Carlsbad, CA ... 760-930-6501
Kodex Inc
Nutley, NJ ... 800-325-6339
Konica Minolta Corporation
Ramsey, NJ ... 888-473-3637
LabVantage Solutions
Bridgewater, NJ ... 888-346-5467
LT Industries
Gaithersburg, MD ... 301-990-4050
Machine Applications Corporation
Sandusky, OH ... 419-621-2322
Maselli Measurements
Stockton, CA ... 800-964-9600
Mosshaim Innovations
Jacksonville, FL ... 888-995-7775
National Hotpack
Stone Ridge, NY ... 800-431-8232
Neogen Gene-Trak Systems
Lansing, MI ... 800-234-5333
Noral
Natick, MA ... 800-348-2345
Ohio Magnetics-Stearns Magnetics
Cleveland, OH ... 800-486-6446
Orion Research
Beverly, MA ... 800-225-1480
Peco Controls Corporation
Modesto, CA ... 800-732-6285
Perkin-Elmer Inc.
Shelton, CT ... 800-762-4000
Perten Instruments
Springfield, IL ... 888-773-7836
PolyScience
Niles, IL ... 800-229-7569
QMI
St Paul, MN ... 651-501-2337
Quality Control Equipment Company
Des Moines, IA ... 515-266-2268
Remel
Shawnee Mission, KS ... 800-255-6730
SDIX
Newark, DE ... 800-544-8881
Sensidyne
Clearwater, FL ... 800-451-9444
Sentry Equipment Corporation
Oconomowoc, WI ... 262-567-7256
Spiral Biotech
Norwood, MA ... 800-554-1620
The Staplex Company
Brooklyn, NY ... 800-221-0822
Tricor Systems
Elgin, IL ... 800-575-0161
Troxler Electronic Laboratories
Research Triangle Park, NC ... 919-549-8661
Univex Corporation
Salem, NH ... 800-258-6358
Vee Gee Scientific
Kirkland, WA ... 800-423-8842
Weber Scientific
Hamilton, NJ ... 800-328-8378
Whatman
Haverhill, MA ... 978-374-7400

Scales & Weighing Systems

A P Dataweigh Systems
Cumming, GA ... 877-409-2562
A&D Weighing
San Jose, CA ... 800-726-3364
Abel Manufacturing Company
Appleton, WI ... 920-734-4443
Accu-Pak
Akron, OH ... 330-644- 301
Acme Scale Company
San Leandro, CA ... 888-638-5040
Action Packaging Automation
Roosevelt, NJ ... 800-241-2724
Actionpac Scales & Automation
Oxnard, CA ... 800-394-0154
Adamatic
Auburn, WA ... 800-578-2547
Advance Weight Systems
Grafton, OH ... 440-926-3691
Ag-Pak
Gasport, NY ... 716-772-2651
All-Fill
Exton, PA ... 866-255-4455
Amark Packaging Systems
Kansas City, MO ... 816-965-9000
American Bag & Burlap Company
Chelsea, MA ... 617-884-7600
Andgar Corporation
Ferndale, WA ... 360-366-9900
APEC
Lake Odessa, MI ... 616-374-1000
Arkfeld Mfg & Distr Company
Norfolk, NE ... 800-533-0676
ASI Electronics
Cypress, TX ... 800-231-6066
Atlas Equipment Company
Kansas City, MO ... 800-842-9188
Automated Packaging Systems
Streetsboro, OH ... 888-288-6224
Avery Weigh-Tronix
Fairmont, MN ... 877-368-2039
Avery Weigh-Tronix
Fairmont, MN ... 877-888-1646
AZO Food
Memphis, TN ... 901-794-9480
B&P Process Equipment & Systems
Saginaw, MI ... 989-757-1300
BLH Electronics
Canton, MA ... 781-821-2000
Blodgett Company
Houston, TX ... 281-933-6195
Brechbuhler Scales
Canton, OH ... 330-453-2424
Cardinal Scale Manufacturing Company
Webb City, MO ... 800-441-4237
CCi Scale Company
Ventura, CA ... 800-900-0224
Chemi-Graphic
Ludlow, MA ... 413-589-0151
Chlorinators Inc
Stuart, FL ... 800-327-9761
Cintex of America
Carol Stream, IL ... 800-424-6839
Circuits & Systems
East Rockaway, NY ... 800-645-4301
Crestware
North Salt Lake City, UT ... 800-345-0513
Crystal-Vision PackagingSystems
Torrance, CA ... 800-331-3240
DBE Inc
Concord, ON ... 800-461-5313
Delavan Spray Technologies
Bamberg, SC ... 800-982-6943
Detecto Scale Company
Webb City, MO ... 800-641-2008
Dipix Technologies
Ottawa, ON ... 613-596-4942
Doran Scales
Batavia, IL ... 800-365-0084
Edlund Company Inc
Burlington, VT ... 800-772-2126
Electronic Weighing Systems
Opa Locka, FL ... 305-685-8067
Emery Winslow Scale Company
Seymour, CT ... 203-881-9333
Equipment Outlet
Meridian, ID ... 208-887-1472
Exact Equipment Corporation
Morrisville, PA ... 215-295-2000
Fairbanks Scales
Kansas City, MO ... 800-451-4107
Fawema Packaging Machinery
Palmetto, FL ... 941-351-9597
Frazier Precision Instrument Company
Hagerstown, MD ... 301-790-2585
Fred D. Pfening Company
Columbus, OH ... 614-294-1633
Fuller Weighing Systems
Columbus, OH ... 614-882-8121
General Bag Corporation
Cleveland, OH ... 800-837-9396
General Packaging Equipment Company
Houston, TX ... 713-686-4331
Grain Machinery Manufacturing Corporation
Miami, FL ... 305-620-2525
Hardy Systems Corporation
Northbrook, IL ... 800-927-3956
IEW
Niles, OH ... 330-652-0113
Ilapak
Newtown, PA ... 215-579-2900
Iman Pack
Westland, MI ... 800-810-4626
Industrial Laboratory Equipment
Charlotte, NC ... 704-357-3930
Inspired Automation
Agoura Hills, CA ... 818-991-4598
Intercomp Company
Hamel, MN ... 800-328-3336
IWS Scales
San Diego, CA ... 800-881-9755
Key Material Handling
Simi Valley, CA ... 800-539-7225
Key-Pak Machines
Lebanon, NJ ... 908-236-2111
Kisco Manufacturing
Greendale, BC ... 604-823-7456
Kliklok-Woodman
Decatur, GA ... 770-981-5200
Lock Inspection Systems
Fitchburg, MA ... 800-227-5539
Lockwood Packaging
Woburn, MA ... 800-641-3100
MAC Equipment
Kansas City, MO ... 800-821-2476
Mandeville Company
Minneapolis, MN ... 800-328-8490
Measurement Systems International
Tukwila, WA ... 800-874-4320
Merrick Industries
Lynn Haven, FL ... 800-271-7834
Micro-Strain
Spring City, PA ... 610-948-4550
MTL Etching Industries
Woodmere, NY ... 516-295-9733
National Scoop & Equipment Company
Spring House, PA ... 215-646-2040
Nicol Scales
Dallas, TX ... 800-225-8181
Ohaus Corporation
Parsippany, NJ ... 800-672-7722

Ohmart/VEGA
Cincinnati, OH 800-367-5383
Pacific Scale Company
Clackamas, OR 800-537-1886
Peco Controls Corporation
Modesto, CA 800-732-6285
Pelouze Scale Company
Bridgeview, IL 800-323-8363
Penn Scale ManufacturingCompany
Philadelphia, PA 215-739-9644
Precision Solutions
Quakertown, PA 215-536-4400
QA Supplies, LLC
Norfolk, VA 800-472-7205
Quest Corporation
North Royalton, OH 440-230-9400
Renard Machine Company
Green Bay, WI 920-432-8412
Renold Products
Westfield, NY 800-879-2529
Rice Lake Weighing Systems
Rice Lake, WI
Rice Lake Weighing Systems
Rice Lake, WI 800-472-6703
S. Howes
Silver Creek, NY 888-255-2611
Sartorius Corporation
Edgewood, NY 800-635-2906
Schaffer Poidometer Company
Pittsburgh, PA 412-281-9031
Scientech, Inc
Boulder, CO 800-525-0522
Si-Lodec
Tukwila, WA 800-255-8274
SIG Pack Eagle Corporation
Oakland, CA 800-824-3245
Sterling Controls
Sterling, IL 800-257-7214
Sterling Scale Company
Southfield, MI 800-331-9931
Summit Machine Builders Corporation
Denver, CO 800-274-6741
Sunbeam Health & Safety
Bridgeview, IL 708-598-9100
Superior Products Company
Saint Paul, MN 800-328-9800
Taylor Products Company A Division Of Magnum Systems
Parsons, KS 888-882-9567
TEC America
Atlanta, GA 770-453-0868
Tecweigh/Tecnetics Industries
White Bear Lake, MN 800-536-4880
Temco
Oakland, CA 707-746-5966
Thayer Scale
Pembroke, MA 781-826-8101
Thermo BLH
Canton, MA 781-821-2000
Thurman Scale
Groveport, OH 800-688-9741
Tomac Packaging
Woburn, MA 800-641-3100
Toroid Corporation
Huntsville, AL 256-837-7510
Triangle Package Machinery Company
Chicago, IL 800-621-4170
Tridyne Process Systems Inc.
South Burlington, VT 802-863-6873
Triner Scale & Manufacturing Co., Inc.
Olive Branch, MS 800-238-0152
Vande Berg Scales
Sioux Center, IA 712-722-1181
Vertex Interactive
Clifton, NJ 973-777-3500
VitaMinder Company
Providence, RI 800-858-8840
Weigh Right Automatic Scale Company
Joliet, IL 800-571-0249
WeighPack Systems/PaxiomGroup
Montreal, QC 888-934-4472
Yakima Wire Works
Reedley, CA 509-248-6790
Yamato Corporation
Colorado Springs, CO 800-538-1762
Yargus Manufacturing
Marshall, IL 217-826-6352

Sensors

ABB SSAC
Baldwinsville, NY 888-385-1221
Applied Robotics
Glenville, NY 800-309-3475
ARI Industries
Addison, IL 800-237-6725
Automatic Timing & Controls
Newell, WV 800-727-5646
AW Company
Franksville, WI 800-850-6110
Bailey Controls/ABB ation
Wickliffe, OH 440-585-8948
Banner Engineering Corporation
Plymouth, MN 888-373-6767
Burns Engineering
Hopkins, MN 800-328-3871
Clean Water Systems International
Klamath Falls, OR 866-273-9993
Conax Buffalo Technologies
Buffalo, NY 800-223-2389
Dresser Instruments
Stratford, CT 800-328-8258
Eaton Corporation
Cleveland, OH 800-386-1911
Eurotherm Controls
Ashburn, VA 703-443-0000
FSI Technologies, Inc.
Lombard, IL 800-468-6009
GE Interlogix Industrial
Tualatin, OR 800-247-9447
Honeywell's
Freeport, IL 800-537-6945
Industrial Devices Corporation
Petaluma, CA 707-789-1000
Infitec
Syracuse, NY 800-334-0837
Kinematics & Controls Corporation
Deer Park, NY 800-833-8103
Love Controls Division
Michigan City, IN 800-828-4588
LT Industries
Gaithersburg, MD 301-990-4050
Magpowr
Fenton, MO 800-624-7697
Mesa Laboratories
Lakewood, CO 800-525-1215
Migatron Corporation
Woodstock, IL 815-338-5800
Monitor Technologies
Elburn, IL 800-601-6319
Namco Controls Corporation
Cleveland, OH 800-626-8324
Norman N. Axelrod Associates
New York, NY 212-741-6302
Ohmart/VEGA
Cincinnati, OH 800-367-5383
Omron Electronics
Schaumburg, IL 800-556-6766
Ozotech
Yreka, CA 530-842-4189
ProMinent Fluid Controls
Pittsburgh, PA 412-787-2484
Pyrometer Instrument Company
Windsor, NJ 800-468-7976
Quantem Corporation
Ewing, NJ 609-883-9879
Raytek Corporation
Santa Cruz, CA 800-866-5478
Reflectronics
Lexington, KY 888-415-0441
Schneider Electric Sensor Competency Center
Dayton, OH 800-435-2121
Sick Inc.
Minneapolis, MN 800-325-7425
Tri-Tronics Company
Tampa, FL 800-237-0946
Tudor Technology
Plymouth Meeting, PA 800-777-0778
United Electric ControlsCompany
Watertown, MA 617-926-1000
Venture Measurement Company
Spartanburg, SC 864-574-8960
Viatran Corporation
North Tonawanda, NY 800-688-0030
Vulcan Electric Company
Porter, ME 800-922-3027
Watlow
Richmond, IL 815-678-2211

Stoppers

Rubber, Bottle

Crown Cork & Seal Company
Philadelphia, PA 215-698-5100
Imperial Plastics
Lakeville, MN 952-469-4951
Oak Barrel Winecraft
Berkeley, CA 510-849-0400
Poly-Seal Corporation
Baltimore, MD 410-633-1990
Qualiform, Inc
Wadsworth, OH 330-336-6777
RubaTex Polymer
Middlefield, OH 440-632-1691
Simolex Rubber Corporation
Plymouth, MI 734-453-4500
Wilkens-Anderson Company
Chicago, IL 800-847-2222

Testers

Food Inspection

Advanced Instruments
Norwood, MA 800-225-4034
Ameritech Laboratories
Flushing, NY 718-461-0475
Bio-Tek Instruments
Winooski, VT 802-655-4040
Charm Sciences
Lawrence, MA 978-683-6100
DeltaTrak
Pleasanton, CA 800-962-6776
Dresser Instruments
Stratford, CT 800-328-8258
ELISA Technologies
Gainesville, FL 352-337-3929
ESA
Chelmsford, MA 978-250-7000
Eurofins Scientific
Dayton, NJ 800-880-1038
Fettig Laboratories
Grand Rapids, MI 616-245-3000
Industrial Laboratories
Wheat Ridge, CO 800-456-5288
Kodex Inc
Nutley, NJ 800-325-6339
Libra Laboratories Inc
Metuchen, NJ 732-321-5200
Libra Technical Center
Metuchen, NJ 732-321-5487
Loma Systems
Carol Stream, IL 800-872-5662
Marshfield Food Safety
Marshfield, WI 888-780-9897
MISCO Refractometer
Cleveland, OH 866-831-1999
Neogen Corporation
Lansing, MI 800-234-5333
Neogen Gene-Trak Systems
Lansing, MI 800-234-5333
Northwest Laboratories of Seattle
Seattle, WA 206-763-6252
Pacific Scientific Instrument
Grants Pass, OR 800-866-7889
QA Supplies, LLC
Norfolk, VA 800-472-7205
Radiation Processing Division
Parsippany, NJ 800-442-1969
Raytek Corporation
Santa Cruz, CA 800-866-5478
Reichert Analytical Instruments
Depew, NY 716-686-4500
SDIX
Newark, DE 800-544-8881
Supelco
Bellefonte, PA 800-247-6628
Total Quality Corporation
Branford, CT 800-453-9729
Woodson-Tenent Laboratories
Des Moines, IA 515-265-1461
Woodson-Tenent Laboratories
Gainesville, GA 770-536-5909
Woodson-Tenent Laboratories
Dayton, OH 937-236-5756

Laboratory

Aerotech Laboratories
Phoenix, AZ 800-651-4802

Analytical Measurements
Chester, NJ 800-635-5580
BioControl Systems
Bellevue, WA 800-245-0113
BluMetric Environmental Inc.
Ottawa, ON 613-839-3053
C.W. Brabender Instruments
South Hackensack, NJ 201-343-8425
Charm Sciences
Lawrence, MA 978-683-6100
Chestnut Labs
Springfield, MO 417-829-3788
CSC Scientific Company
Fairfax, VA 800-621-4778
Dresser Instruments
Stratford, CT 800-328-8258
Enviro-Test/Perry Laboratories
Woodridge, IL 630-324-6685
Eurofins Scientific
Des Moines, IA 800-841-1110
Eurofins Scientific
Dayton, NJ 800-880-1038
Industrial Laboratories
Wheat Ridge, CO 800-456-5288
Libra Technical Center
Metuchen, NJ 732-321-5487
Northwest Laboratories of Seattle
Seattle, WA 206-763-6252
Oxoid
Nepean, ON 800-567-8378
Perten Instruments
Springfield, IL 888-773-7836
Radiation Processing Division
Parsippany, NJ 800-442-1969
Remel
Shawnee Mission, KS 800-255-6730
Spiral Biotech
Norwood, MA 800-554-1620
Tekmar-Dohrmann
Mason, OH 800-874-2004
Texture Technologies Corporation
Scarsdale, NY 914-472-0531
Troxler Electronic Laboratories
Research Triangle Park, NC 919-549-8661
Vee Gee Scientific
Kirkland, WA 800-423-8842
VICAM, A Waters Business
Milford, MA 800-338-4381
Wilkens-Anderson Company
Chicago, IL 800-847-2222
Woodson-Tenent Laboratories
Des Moines, IA 515-265-1461
Woodson-Tenent Laboratories
Gainesville, GA 770-536-5909
Woodson-Tenent Laboratories
Dayton, OH 937-236-5756

Milk & Cream

Advanced Instruments
Norwood, MA 800-225-4034

Packaging Materials/Containers

Air Logic Power Systems
Milwaukee, WI 800-325-8717
Altek Company
Torrington, CT 860-482-7626
Carleton Technologies
Orchard Park, NY 716-662-0006
Daystar
Glen Arm, MD 800-494-6537
Food Instrument Corporation
Federalsburg, MD 800-542-5688
Kodex Inc
Nutley, NJ 800-325-6339
Libra Technical Center
Metuchen, NJ 732-321-5487
MOCON
Minneapolis, MN 763-493-6370
NDC Infrared EngineeringInc
Irwindale, CA 626-960-3300
United Desiccants
Louisville, KY 505-864-6691

Thermometers

A&M Thermometer Corporation
Asheville, NC 800-685-9211
Agri-Equipment International
Longs, SC 877-550-4709
Alnor Instrument Company
Skokie, IL 800-424-7427
Ametek
Sellersville, PA 215-257-6531
Atkins Technical
Gainesville, FL 800-284-2842
Barnant Company
Lake Barrington, IL 800-637-3739
Bowtemp
Mont-Royal, QC 514-735-5551
Browne & Company
Markham, ON 905-475-6104
Chaney Instrument
Lake Geneva, WI 800-777-0565
Chicago Stainless Equipment
Palm City, FL 800-927-8575
Comark Instruments
Everett, WA 800-555-6658
Cooper Instrument Corporation
Middlefield, CT 800-835-5011
Crestware
North Salt Lake City, UT 800-345-0513
Datapaq
Wilmington, MA 800-326-5270
Delta Trak
Pleasanton, CA 800-962-6776
DeltaTrak
Pleasanton, CA 800-962-6776
Dresser Instruments
Stratford, CT 800-328-8258
Dynasys Technologies
Clearwater, FL 800-867-5968
E & E Process Instrumentation
Concord, Ontario, ON 905-669-4857
Elreha Controls Corporation
St Petersburg, FL 727-327-6236
EPD Technology Corporation
Elmsford, NY 800-892-8926
ESCO
Houston, TX 800-966-5514
Eurotherm Controls
Ashburn, VA 703-443-0000
Gracey Instrument Corporation
Encinitas, CA 800-304-5859
Greer's Ferry Glass Work
Dubuque, IA 501-589-2947
Hanna Instruments
Woonsocket, RI 800-426-6287
Kason Central
Columbus, OH 614-885-1992
Kason Industries
Newnan, GA 770-254-0553
L.C. Thompson Company
Kenosha, WI 800-558-4018
Libertyware
Clearfield, UT 888-500-5885
Lorann Oils
Lansing, MI 800-862-8620
Love Controls Division
Michigan City, IN 800-828-4588
LumaSense Technologies
Santa Clara, CA 800-631-0176
Marshall Instruments
Anaheim, CA 800-222-8476
Matfer
Van Nuys, CA 800-766-0333
Mesa Laboratories
Lakewood, CO 800-525-1215
Miljoco Corporation
Mount Clemens, MI 888-888-1498
Music City Metals
Nashville, TN 800-251-2674
National Controls Corporation
West Chicago, IL 800-323-5293
National Time Recording Equipment Company
New York, NY 212-227-3310
Noral
Natick, MA 800-348-2345
Pelouze Scale Company
Bridgeview, IL 800-323-8363
QA Supplies, LLC
Norfolk, VA 800-472-7205
Raytek Corporation
Santa Cruz, CA 800-866-5478
Reotemp Instrument Corporation
San Diego, CA 800-648-7737
Ryan Instruments
Redmond, WA 425-883-7926
Sensitech
Beverly, MA 800-843-8367
Special Products
Springfield, MO 417-881-6114
Superior Products Company
Saint Paul, MN 800-328-9800
Taylor Precision Products
Las Cruces, NM 630-954-1250
Taylor Precision Products
Las Cruces, NM 866-843-3905
Tel-Tru Manufacturing Company
Rochester, NY 800-232-5335
TESTO
Sparta, NJ 800-227-0729
Thermo Instruments
Yaphank, NY 631-924-0880
Trans World Services
Melrose, MA 800-882-2105
United Electric ControlsCompany
Watertown, MA 617-926-1000
Weiss Instruments
Holtsville, NY 631-207-1200
Wescor
Logan, UT 800-453-2725
Wika Instrument Corporation
Lawrenceville, GA 800-645-0606
Wilkens-Anderson Company
Chicago, IL 800-847-2222

Packaging Materials & Supplies

Bags

Ampac Packaging, LLC
Cincinnati, OH 800-543-7030
Bella Vita
Phoenix, AZ 877-827-3638
Can Creations
Pembroke Pines, FL 800-272-0235
Clorox Company
Oakland, CA 888-271-7000
Grayling Industries
Alpharetta, GA 800-635-1551
Libra Technical Center
Metuchen, NJ 732-321-5487
Nashville Wraps
Hendersonville, TN. . . . 800-547-9727
Revere Group
Seattle, WA 206-545-8150
S Walter Packaging Corporation
Philadelphia, PA 888-429-5673
Tenka Flexible Packaging
Chino, CA. . . . 888-836-5255
Vista International Packaging, Inc.
Kenosha, WI 800-558-4058

Bread & Pastry

Aladdin Transparent Packaging Corporation
Hauppauge, NY 631-273-4747
All American Poly Corporation
Piscataway, NJ 800-526-3551
AR-BEE Transparent
Elk Grove Vlg, IL. . . . 800-642-2247
Checker Bag Company
Saint Louis, MO 800-489-3130
Flexo Transparent
Buffalo, NY. . . . 877-993-5396
Jomar Plastics Industry
Nanty Glo, PA. . . . 800-681-4039
Malpack Polybag
Ajax, ON. . . . 905-428-3751
Mini-Bag Company
Farmingdale, NY 631-694-3325
Moser Bag & Paper Company
Cleveland, OH 800-433-6638
Pactiv LLC
Lake Forest, IL 888-828-2850
Pak-Sher Company
Kilgore, TX. . . . 800-642-2295
Pater & Associates
Cincinnati, OH 513- 24- 215
Pexco Packaging Corporation
Toledo, OH 800-227-9950
Pfeil & Holing, Inc.
Flushing, NY. . . . 800-247-7955
Seal-Tite Bag Company
Philadelphia, PA 717-917-1949
Sonoco Flexible Packaging
Hartsville, SC 800-377-2692
Specialty Paper Bag Company
Bronx, NY. . . . 718-893-8888
Star Poly Bag, Inc.
Brooklyn, NY 718-384-3130
Stewart Sutherland
Vicksburg, MI. . . . 269-649-5489

Bulk

King Bag & Manufacturing Company
Cincinnati, OH 800-444-5464

Cellophane

AR-BEE Transparent
Elk Grove Vlg, IL. . . . 800-642-2247
Beayl Weiner/Pak
Pacific Palisades, CA 310-454-1354
Chalmur Bag Company, LLC
Philadelphia, PA 800-349-2247
Checker Bag Company
Saint Louis, MO 800-489-3130
Collector's Gallery
Saint Charles, IL. . . . 800-346-3063
Dupont Liquid Packaging Systems
Worthington, OH 614-888-9280
Formel Industries
Franklin Park, IL. . . . 800-373-3300
Milprint
Oshkosh, WI 920-303-8600
Pater & Associates
Cincinnati, OH 513- 24- 215

Centrifuge

King Bag & Manufacturing Company
Cincinnati, OH 800-444-5464

Confectioners'

Accurate Flannel Bag Company
Paterson, NJ 800-234-9200
AR-BEE Transparent
Elk Grove Vlg, IL. . . . 800-642-2247
August Thomsen Corporation
Glen Cove, NY 800-645-7170
Checker Bag Company
Saint Louis, MO 800-489-3130
Collector's Gallery
Saint Charles, IL. . . . 800-346-3063
Colonial Transparent Products Company
Hicksville, NY 516-822-4430
Flexo Transparent
Buffalo, NY. . . . 877-993-5396
Milprint
Oshkosh, WI 920-303-8600
Mimi et Cie
Seattle, WA 206-545-1850
Star Poly Bag, Inc.
Brooklyn, NY 718-384-3130
Stewart Sutherland
Vicksburg, MI. . . . 269-649-5489
Wisconsin Converting of Green Bay
Green Bay, WI. . . . 800-544-1935

Flour, Meal & Feed

Accurate Flannel Bag Company
Paterson, NJ 800-234-9200
Chatfield & Woods Sack Company
Harrison, OH. . . . 513-202-9700
Dayton Bag & Burlap Company
Dayton, OH. . . . 800-543-3400
Exopack, LLC
Spartanburg, SC 877-447-3539
Flexo Transparent
Buffalo, NY. . . . 877-993-5396
Frontier Bag Company
Omaha, NE 800-278-2247
Fulton-Denver Company
Denver, CO 800-776-6715
HUBCO Inc.
Hutchinson, KS. . . . 800-563-1867
Indian Valley Industries
Johnson City, NY 800-659-5111
Set Point Paper Company
Mansfield, MA 800-225-0501
Star Poly Bag, Inc.
Brooklyn, NY 718-384-3130
Werthan Packaging
White House, TN 615-672-3336

Food

Accurate Flannel Bag Company
Paterson, NJ 800-234-9200
Aladdin Transparent Packaging Corporation
Hauppauge, NY 631-273-4747
All American Poly Corporation
Piscataway, NJ 800-526-3551
AR-BEE Transparent
Elk Grove Vlg, IL. . . . 800-642-2247
Automated Packaging Systems
Streetsboro, OH 888-288-6224
BagcraftPapercon
Chicago, IL. . . . 800-621-8468
Brown Paper Goods Company
Waukegan, IL 847-688-1451
Bryce Company
Memphis, TN 800-238-7277
Cadie Products Corporation
Paterson, NJ 973-278-8300
Castle Bag Company
Wilmington, DE 302-656-1001
Checker Bag Company
Saint Louis, MO 800-489-3130
Cincinnati Convertors
Cincinnati, OH 513-731-6600
Cleveland Plastic Films
Elyria, OH. . . . 800-832-6799
Collector's Gallery
Saint Charles, IL. . . . 800-346-3063
David Dobbs Enterprise & Menu Design
St Augustine, FL. . . . 800-889-6368
Development Workshop
Idaho Falls, ID 800-657-5597
Dixie Poly Packaging
Greenville, SC. . . . 864-268-3751
Dupont Liquid Packaging Systems
Worthington, OH 614-888-9280
Eco-Bag Products
Ossining, NY 800-720-2247
Emoshun
Rancho Cucamonga, CA 909-484-9559
Exopack
Tomah, WI 608-372-2153
Fabriko
Altavista, VA. . . . 888-203-8098
Fischer Paper Products
Antioch, IL 800-323-9093
Flexo Transparent
Buffalo, NY. . . . 877-993-5396
Food Pak Corporation
San Mateo, CA 650-341-6559
Fortune Plastics
Glendale, AZ. . . . 800-243-0306
Fulton-Denver Company
Denver, CO 800-776-6715
Glopak
St Leonard, QC 800-361-6994
GP Plastics Corporation
Medley, FL 305-888-3555
Great Western Products
Ontario, CA. . . . 888-598-5588
Gulf Arizona Packaging
Humble, TX 800-364-3887
Gulf Systems
Oklahoma City, OK 405-528-2293
Gulf Systems
Brownsville, TX 800-217-4853
Gulf Systems
Oklahoma City, OK 800-364-3887
Gulf Systems
Arlington, TX 817-261-1915
Hank Rivera Associates
Dearborn, MI 313-581-8300
Herche Warehouse
Denver, CO 303-371-8186
Hood Flexible Packaging
St Paul, MN. . . . 800-448-0682
HUBCO Inc.
Hutchinson, KS. . . . 800-563-1867
In the Bag
St Petersburg, FL 800-330-2247
Jomar Plastics Industry
Nanty Glo, PA. . . . 800-681-4039
Keeper Thermal Bag Company
Crystal Lake, IL 800-765-9244
Liqui-Box Corporation
Worthington, OH 614-888-9280
Masternet, Ltd
Mississauga, ON. . . . 800-216-2536
McDowell Industries
Memphis, TN 800-622-3695
Millhiser
Richmond, VA. . . . 800-446-2247
Mimi et Cie
Seattle, WA 206-545-1850
Mini-Bag Company
Farmingdale, NY 631-694-3325
Morgan Brothers Bag Company
Richmond, VA. . . . 804-355-9107
Moser Bag & Paper Company
Cleveland, OH 800-433-6638
Naltex
Austin, TX. . . . 800-531-5112
Net Pack Systems
Oakland, ME. . . . 207-465-4531
Noteworthy Company
Amsterdam, NY 800-696-7849

NSW Corporation
Roanoke, VA 800-368-3610
Orange Plastics
Compton, CA 310-609-2121
Pactiv LLC
Lake Forest, IL 888-828-2850
Pak-Sher Company
Kilgore, TX........ 800-642-2295
Pan Pacific Plastics Manufacturing
Hayward, CA 888-475-6888
Parvin Manufacturing Company
Los Angeles, CA........ 800-648-0770
Pater & Associates
Cincinnati, OH 513- 24- 215
Pexco Packaging Corporation
Toledo, OH 800-227-9950
Poly Plastic Products
Delano, PA 570-467-3000
Portco Corporation
Vancouver, WA........ 800-426-1794
Rapak
Romeoville, IL 630-296-2000
Ray C. Sprosty Bag Company
Wooster, OH 330-264-8559
Roplast Industries Inc.
Oroville, CA 800-767-5278
Ross & Wallace Paper Products
Hammond, LA 800-854-2300
Rutan Polyethylene Supply Bag & Manufacturing Company
Mahwah, NJ 800-872-1474
Scholle Corporation
Irvine, CA 949-955-1750
Service Manufacturing
Aurora, IL........ 888-325-2788
Sheboygan Paper Box Company
Sheboygan, WI 800-458-8373
Signature Packaging
West Orange, NJ........ 800-376-2299
Sonoco Flexible Packaging
Hartsville, SC 800-377-2692
Specialty Paper Bag Company
Bronx, NY........ 718-893-8888
Star Poly Bag, Inc.
Brooklyn, NY 718-384-3130
Sterling Net & Twine Company
Cedar Knolls, NJ........ 800-342-0316
Sterling Novelty Products
Northbrook, IL 847-291-0070
Stewart Sutherland
Vicksburg, MI........ 269-649-5489
Storsack
Houston, TX........ 800-841-4982
Stretch-Vent Packaging System
Ontario, CA........ 800-822-8368
TEMP-TECH Company
Springfield, MA 800-343-5579
Tenka Flexible Packaging
Chino, CA........ 888-836-5255
Tetosky Plastics
Morristown, TN 423-586-8917
Thermal Bags by Ingrid
Gilberts, IL 800-622-5560
Trevor Owen Limited
Scarborough, ON 866-487-2224
Urnex Brands, Inc.
Elmsford, NY 800-222-2826
Valley Packaging Supply Company, Inc.
Green Bay, WI........ 920-336-9012
Vonco Products
Lake Villa, IL 800-323-9077
Walnut Packaging
Farmingdale, NY 631-293-3836
Wins Paper Products
Springtown, TX 800-733-2420
Wisconsin Converting of Green Bay
Green Bay, WI........ 800-544-1935

Fruit & Vegetable

Accurate Flannel Bag Company
Paterson, NJ 800-234-9200
AR-BEE Transparent
Elk Grove Vlg, IL........ 800-642-2247
Eco-Bag Products
Ossining, NY 800-720-2247
Flexo Transparent
Buffalo, NY........ 877-993-5396
Frontier Bag Company
Omaha, NE 800-278-2247
Fulton-Denver Company
Denver, CO 800-776-6715
Gulf Arizona Packaging
Humble, TX 800-364-3887
Gulf Systems
Oklahoma City, OK 405-528-2293
Gulf Systems
Brownsville, TX 800-217-4853
Gulf Systems
Oklahoma City, OK 800-364-3887
Gulf Systems
Arlington, TX 817-261-1915
Herche Warehouse
Denver, CO 303-371-8186
Indian Valley Industries
Johnson City, NY 800-659-5111
Inteplast Bags & Films Corporation
Delta, BC........ 604-946-5431
Langston Bag Company
Memphis, TN 901-774-4440
Masternet, Ltd
Mississauga, ON........ 800-216-2536
McDowell Industries
Memphis, TN 800-622-3695
Mini-Bag Company
Farmingdale, NY 631-694-3325
Morgan Brothers Bag Company
Richmond, VA........ 804-355-9107
Naltex
Austin, TX........ 800-531-5112
Net Pack Systems
Oakland, ME........ 207-465-4531
NSW Corporation
Roanoke, VA........ 800-368-3610
Orange Plastics
Compton, CA 310-609-2121
Pan Pacific Plastics Manufacturing
Hayward, CA 888-475-6888
Pater & Associates
Cincinnati, OH 513- 24- 215
Portco Corporation
Vancouver, WA........ 800-426-1794
Roplast Industries Inc.
Oroville, CA 800-767-5278
Signature Packaging
West Orange, NJ........ 800-376-2299
Sterling Net & Twine Company
Cedar Knolls, NJ........ 800-342-0316
Urnex Brands, Inc.
Elmsford, NY 800-222-2826
Werthan Packaging
White House, TN 615-672-3336

Grain

Dayton Bag & Burlap Company
Dayton, OH........ 800-543-3400
Development Workshop
Idaho Falls, ID 800-657-5597
Exopack, LLC
Spartanburg, SC 877-447-3539
Flexo Transparent
Buffalo, NY........ 877-993-5396
Indian Valley Industries
Johnson City, NY 800-659-5111
McDowell Industries
Memphis, TN 800-622-3695
Portco Corporation
Vancouver, WA........ 800-426-1794
Storsack
Houston, TX 800-841-4982

Greaseproof

AR-BEE Transparent
Elk Grove Vlg, IL........ 800-642-2247
Brown Paper Goods Company
Waukegan, IL 847-688-1451
Cincinnati Convertors
Cincinnati, OH 513-731-6600
Dayton Bag & Burlap Company
Dayton, OH........ 800-543-3400
Exopack
Tomah, WI 608-372-2153
Exopack, LLC
Spartanburg, SC 877-447-3539
Mini-Bag Company
Farmingdale, NY 631-694-3325
Sonoco Flexible Packaging
Hartsville, SC 800-377-2692

Heat Sealed

Aladdin Transparent Packaging Corporation
Hauppauge, NY 631-273-4747
AR-BEE Transparent
Elk Grove Vlg, IL........ 800-642-2247
Atlas Tag & Label
Neenah, WI........ 800-558-6418
Automated Packaging Systems
Streetsboro, OH 888-288-6224
Beayl Weiner/Pak
Pacific Palisades, CA 310-454-1354
Chalmur Bag Company, LLC
Philadelphia, PA 800-349-2247
Cincinnati Convertors
Cincinnati, OH 513-731-6600
Exopack
Tomah, WI 608-372-2153
Exopack, LLC
Spartanburg, SC 877-447-3539
Flexo Transparent
Buffalo, NY........ 877-993-5396
Gulf Arizona Packaging
Humble, TX 800-364-3887
Gulf Systems
Oklahoma City, OK 405-528-2293
Gulf Systems
Oklahoma City, OK 800-364-3887
Gulf Systems
Arlington, TX........ 817-261-1915
Herche Warehouse
Denver, CO........ 303-371-8186
Home Plastics
Des Moines, IA........ 515-265-2562
Keystone Packaging Service
Phillipsburg, NJ 800-473-8567
Liqui-Box Corporation
Worthington, OH 614-888-9280
Mini-Bag Company
Farmingdale, NY 631-694-3325
NAP Industries
Brooklyn, NY 877-635-4948
Net Pack Systems
Oakland, ME........ 207-465-4531
Pater & Associates
Cincinnati, OH 513- 24- 215
Ram Industries
Erwin, TN........ 800-523-3883
Seal-Tite Bag Company
Philadelphia, PA 717-917-1949
Servin Company
New Baltimore, MI........ 800-824-0962
Set Point Paper Company
Mansfield, MA 800-225-0501
Star Poly Bag, Inc.
Brooklyn, NY 718-384-3130
Thermal Bags by Ingrid
Gilberts, IL 800-622-5560
Urnex Brands, Inc.
Elmsford, NY........ 800-222-2826

Laminated

Amcor Flexibles - North America
Hagerstown, MD........ 800-332-7928
AR-BEE Transparent
Elk Grove Vlg, IL........ 800-642-2247
BAW Plastics
Jefferson Hills, PA 800-783-2229
Cincinnati Convertors
Cincinnati, OH 513-731-6600
Exopack, LLC
Spartanburg, SC 877-447-3539
Gulf Arizona Packaging
Humble, TX 800-364-3887
Gulf Systems
Oklahoma City, OK 405-528-2293
Gulf Systems
Oklahoma City, OK 800-364-3887
Gulf Systems
Arlington, TX........ 817-261-1915
Herche Warehouse
Denver, CO........ 303-371-8186
Pater & Associates
Cincinnati, OH 513- 24- 215
Sheboygan Paper Box Company
Sheboygan, WI........ 800-458-8373
Sungjae Corporation
Irvine, CA 949-757-1727
Vonco Products
Lake Villa, IL 800-323-9077
Workman Packaging Inc.
Saint-Laurent, QC........ 800-252-5208

Meat

Accurate Flannel Bag Company
Paterson, NJ 800-234-9200
All American Poly Corporation
Piscataway, NJ 800-526-3551
AR-BEE Transparent
Elk Grove Vlg, IL 800-642-2247
Flexo Transparent
Buffalo, NY 877-993-5396
Frontier Bag Company
Grandview, MO 816-765-4811
Jomar Plastics Industry
Nanty Glo, PA 800-681-4039
Morgan Brothers Bag Company
Richmond, VA 804-355-9107
NAP Industries
Brooklyn, NY 877-635-4948
Net Pack Systems
Oakland, ME 207-465-4531
Pan Pacific Plastics Manufacturing
Hayward, CA 888-475-6888
VPI Manufacturing
Draper, UT 801-495-2310

Multi-Wall

Central Bag Company
Leavenworth, KS 913-250-0325
Colonial Transparent Products Company
Hicksville, NY 516-822-4430
Durango-Georgia Paper
Tampa, FL 813-286-2718
Exopack, LLC
Spartanburg, SC 877-447-3539
First Midwest of Iowa Corporation
Des Moines, IA 800-247-8411
Flexo Transparent
Buffalo, NY 877-993-5396
Indian Valley Industries
Johnson City, NY 800-659-5111
Langston Bag Company
Memphis, TN 901-774-4440
Northeast Packaging Company
Presque Isle, ME 207-764-6271
NYP Corporation
Leola, PA 800-541-0961
Ray C. Sprosty Bag Company
Wooster, OH 330-264-8559
Santa Fe Bag Company
Vernon, CA 323-585-7225
Southern Bag Corporation
Madison, MS 662-746-3631
Stone Container
Chicago, IL 312-346-6600
United Bags
Saint Louis, MO 800-550-2247
Werthan Packaging
White House, TN 615-672-3336

Netting, Open Mesh

Alabama Bag Company Inc
Talladega, AL 800-888-4921
Fitec International
Memphis, TN 800-332-6387
Friedman Bag Company
Manhattan Beach, CA 213-628-2341
Fulton-Denver Company
Denver, CO 800-776-6715
General Bag Corporation
Cleveland, OH 800-837-9396
Indian Valley Industries
Johnson City, NY 800-659-5111
Jif-Pak Manufacturing
Vista, CA 800-777-6613
Langston Bag Company
Memphis, TN 901-774-4440
Masternet, Ltd
Mississauga, ON 800-216-2536
Naltex
Austin, TX 800-531-5112
Net Pack Systems
Oakland, ME 207-465-4531
NSW Corporation
Roanoke, VA 800-368-3610
NYP Corporation
Leola, PA 800-541-0961
Sterling Net & Twine Company
Cedar Knolls, NJ 800-342-0316
TNI Packaging
West Chicago, IL 800-383-0990
Tree Saver
Englewood, CO 800-676-7741
United Bags
Saint Louis, MO 800-550-2247
Wasserman Bag Company
Center Moriches, NY 631-909-8656

Paper

Acme Bag Company
Chula Vista, CA 800-275-2263
AJM Packaging Corporation
Bloomfield Hills, MI 248-901-0040
American Bag & Burlap Company
Chelsea, MA 617-884-7600
Bancroft Bag
West Monroe, LA 318-387-2550
Brown Paper Goods Company
Waukegan, IL 847-688-1451
Burrows Paper Corporation
Little Falls, NY 800-272-7122
Central Bag & Burlap Company
Denver, CO 800-783-1224
Clearwater Paper Corporation
Spokane, WA 877-847-7831
Cuutom Poly Packaging
Fort Wayne, IN 800-548-6603
Dayton Bag & Burlap Company
Dayton, OH 800-543-3400
El Dorado Paper Bag Manufacturing Company
El Dorado, AR 870-862-4977
Exopack, LLC
Spartanburg, SC 877-447-3539
F&G Packaging
Yulee, FL 904-225-5121
Fabricon Products
River Rouge, MI 313-841-8200
Fast Bags
Fort Worth, TX 800-321-3687
Felco Bag & Burlap Company
Baltimore, MD 800-673-8488
First Midwest of Iowa Corporation
Des Moines, IA 800-247-8411
Fischer Paper Products
Antioch, IL 800-323-9093
Fortifiber Corporation
Fernley, NV 775-575-5557
Fulton-Denver Company
Denver, CO 800-776-6715
Gateway Packaging Company
Kansas City, MO 816-483-9800
General Bag Corporation
Cleveland, OH 800-837-9396
Gilchrist Bag Company
Camden, AR 800-643-1513
Indian Valley Industries
Johnson City, NY 800-659-5111
KapStone Paper and Packaging Corporation
Northbrook, IL 847-239-8800
Keystone Packaging Service
Phillipsburg, NJ 800-473-8567
Langston Bag Company
Memphis, TN 901-774-4440
Milprint
Oshkosh, WI 920-303-8600
Mimi et Cie
Seattle, WA 206-545-1850
Moser Bag & Paper Company
Cleveland, OH 800-433-6638
North American PackagingCorporation
New York, NY 800-499-3521
Northeast Packaging Company
Presque Isle, ME 207-764-6271
NYP Corporation
Leola, PA 800-524-1052
NYP Corporation
Leola, PA 800-541-0961
Package Containers
Canby, OR 800-266-5806
PAK 2000
Mirror Lake, NH 603-569-3700
Pak-Sher Company
Kilgore, TX 800-642-2295
Papelera Puertorriquena
Utuado, PR 787-894-2098
Peerless Packages
Cleveland, OH 216-464-3620
Portco Corporation
Vancouver, WA 800-426-1794
Ray C. Sprosty Bag Company
Wooster, OH 330-264-8559
Ross & Wallace Paper Products
Hammond, LA 800-854-2300
Samuels Products
Cincinnati, OH 800-543-7155
Santa Fe Bag Company
Vernon, CA 323-585-7225
Seaboard Bag Corporation
Richmond, VA
Shippers Paper Products
Sheridan, AR 800-468-1230
Solo Cup Company
Lake Forest, IL 800-367-2877
Southern Bag Corporation
Madison, MS 662-746-3631
Specialty Packaging
Fort Worth, TX 800-284-7722
Specialty Paper Bag Company
Bronx, NY 718-893-8888
Stone Container
Chicago, IL 312-346-6600
Surfine Central Corporation
Pine Bluff, AR 870-247-2387
Tulsack
Tulsa, OK 918-664-0664
United Bags
Saint Louis, MO 800-550-2247
Walker Bag ManufacturingCompany
Louisville, KY 800-642-4949
Wasserman Bag Company
Center Moriches, NY 631-909-8656
Wedlock Paper ConvertersLtd.
Mississauga, ON 800-388-0447
Wins Paper Products
Springtown, TX 800-733-2420
Wisconsin Converting of Green Bay
Green Bay, WI 800-544-1935
Zenith Specialty Bag Company
City of Industry, CA 800-925-2247

Paper Lined

Dayton Bag & Burlap Company
Dayton, OH 800-543-3400
Exopack, LLC
Spartanburg, SC 877-447-3539

Plastic

A La Carte
Chicago, IL 800-722-2370
Abond Plastic Corporation
Lachine, QC 800-886-7947
Acme Bag Company
Chula Vista, CA 800-275-2263
ADM Corporation
Middlesex, NJ 800-327-0718
Alabama Bag Company Inc
Talladega, AL 800-888-4921
Alger Creations
Miami, FL 954-454-3272
All American Poly Corporation
Piscataway, NJ 800-526-3551
Aluf Plastics
Orangeburg, NY 800-394-2247
Amcel
Watertown, MA 800-225-7992
American Bag & Burlap Company
Chelsea, MA 617-884-7600
AmeriGlobe FIBC Solutions
Lafayette, LA 337-234-3212
AMPAC Holdings, LLC
Cincinnati, OH 800-543-7030
AR-BEE Transparent
Elk Grove Vlg, IL 800-642-2247
Art Poly Bag Company
Brooklyn, NY 800-278-7659
Artistic Packaging Concepts
Massapequa Pk, NY 516-797-4020
Automated Packaging Systems
Streetsboro, OH 888-288-6224
Avantage Group
Redondo Beach, CA 310-379-3933
Bag Company
Kennesaw, GA 800-533-1931
Beayl Weiner/Pak
Pacific Palisades, CA 310-454-1354
Bennett's Auto Inc.
Neenah, WI 800-215-5464
Blako Industries
Dunbridge, OH 419-833-4491
Brown Paper Goods Company
Waukegan, IL 847-688-1451

Bulk Lift International
Carpentersville, IL 800-992-6372
Carlisle Plastics
Minneapolis, MN 952-884-1309
Carroll Products
Garland, TX 800-527-5722
Castle Bag Company
Wilmington, DE 302-656-1001
Cello Bag Company
Bowling Green, KY 800-347-0338
Cello Pack Corporation
Cheektowaga, NY 800-778-3111
Central Bag & Burlap Company
Denver, CO 800-783-1224
Central Bag Company
Leavenworth, KS 913-250-0325
Central Container Corporation
Minneapolis, MN 763-425-7444
Chalmur Bag Company, LLC
Philadelphia, PA 800-349-2247
Champion Plastics
Clifton, NJ 800-526-1230
Checker Bag Company
Saint Louis, MO 800-489-3130
Clear View Bag Company
Thomasville, NC 336-885-8131
Clear View Bag Company
Albany, NY 800-458-7153
Cleveland Plastic Films
Elyria, OH 800-832-6799
Coast Scientific
Rancho Santa Fe, CA 800-445-1544
Colonial Transparent Products Company
Hicksville, NY 516-822-4430
Com-Pac International
Carbondale, IL 800-824-0817
Command Packaging
Vernon, CA 800-996-2247
Continental Extrusion Corporation
Cedar Grove, NJ 800-822-4748
Continental Packaging Corporation
Elgin, IL 847-289-6400
Continental Products
Mexico, MO 800-325-0216
Cortec Corporation
St. Paul, MN 800-426-7832
CR Plastics
Council Bluffs, IA 866-869-6293
Crayex Corporation
Piqua, OH 800-837-1747
Crystal-Flex Packaging Corporation
Rockville Centre, NY 888-246-7325
Cuutom Poly Packaging
Fort Wayne, IN 800-548-6603
Dairyland Plastics Company
Colfax, WI 715-962-3425
Dashco
Gloucester, ON 613-834-6825
Dayton Bag & Burlap Company
Dayton, OH 800-543-3400
Design Packaging Company
Glencoe, IL 800-321-7659
Development Workshop
Idaho Falls, ID 800-657-5597
Dixie Poly Packaging
Greenville, SC 864-268-3751
Dub Harris Corporation
Pomona, CA 909-596-6300
Dynamic Packaging
Minneapolis, MN 800-878-9380
East Coast Group New York
Springfield Gardens, NY 718-527-8464
Eastern Poly Packaging Company
Brooklyn, NY 800-421-6006
Eaton Manufacturing Company
Houston, TX 800-328-6610
Ellehammer Industries
Langley, BC 604-882-9326
Elliot Lee
Cedarhurst, NY 516-569-9595
Exopack
Tomah, WI 608-372-2153
Exopack, LLC
Spartanburg, SC 877-447-3539
FabOhio
Uhrichsville, OH 740-922-4233
Fan Bag Company
Chicago, IL 773-342-2752
Fast Bags
Fort Worth, TX 800-321-3687
First Brands Corporation
Oakland, CA 203-731-2427
Flexo Transparent
Buffalo, NY 877-993-5396
Fortune Plastics
Glendale, AZ 800-243-0306
Fortune Plastics, Inc
Old Saybrook, CT 800-243-0306
Fredman Bag Company
Milwaukee, WI 800-945-5686
Friedman Bag Company
Manhattan Beach, CA 213-628-2341
Frontier Bag Company
Grandview, MO 816-765-4811
Fulton-Denver Company
Denver, CO 800-776-6715
Garvey Products
West Chester, OH 800-543-1908
Gemini Plastic Films Corporation
Garfield, NJ 800-789-4732
General Bag Corporation
Cleveland, OH 800-837-9396
General Films
Covington, OH 888-436-3456
Genpak LLC
Lakeville, MN 800-328-4556
Gibraltar Packaging Group
Hastings, NE 402-463-1366
Goldmax Industries
City of Industry, CA 626-964-8820
GP Plastics Corporation
Medley, FL 305-888-3555
Great Western Products
Ontario, CA 888-598-5588
Gulf Arizona Packaging
Humble, TX 800-364-3887
Gulf Coast Plastics
Tampa, FL 800-277-7491
Gulf Systems
Oklahoma City, OK 405-528-2293
Gulf Systems
Brownsville, TX 800-217-4853
Gulf Systems
Oklahoma City, OK 800-364-3887
Gulf Systems
Arlington, TX 817-261-1915
Handgards
El Paso, TX 800-351-8161
Hedwin Corporation
Baltimore, MD 800-638-1012
Herche Warehouse
Denver, CO 303-371-8186
Heritage Bag Company
Carrollton, TX 972-241-5525
Himolene
Carrollton, TX 800-777-4411
Hood Flexible Packaging
St Paul, MN 800-448-0682
HUBCO Inc.
Hutchinson, KS 800-563-1867
Hudson Poly Bag
Hudson, MA 800-229-7566
In the Bag
St Petersburg, FL 800-330-2247
Ina Company
San Carlos, CA 650-631-7066
Indian Valley Industries
Johnson City, NY 800-659-5111
Interstate Packaging
White Bluff, TN 800-251-1072
ITW Minigrip/Zip-Pak
Manteno, IL 800-488-6973
Jeb Plastics
Wilmington, DE 800-556-2247
Jomar Plastics Industry
Nanty Glo, PA 800-681-4039
Jupiter Mills Corporation
Roslyn, NY 800-853-5121
K-C Products Company
Van Nuys, CA 818-267-1600
Kal Pac Corporation
New Windsor, NY 845-567-0095
Kane Bag Supply Company
Baltimore, MD 410-732-5800
KM International
Kenton, TN 731-749-8700
L&C Plastic Bags
Covington, OH 937-473-2968
Luetzow Industries
South Milwaukee, WI 800-558-6055
M&G Packaging Corporation
Floral Park, NY 800-240-5288
M&R Flexible Packaging
Springboro, OH 800-543-3380
Maco Bag Corporation
Newark, NY 315-226-1000
Malpack Polybag
Ajax, ON 905-428-3751
Marshall Plastic Film
Martin, MI 269-672-5511
Mason Transparent Package Company
Armonk, NY 718-792-6000
Mercury Plastic Bag Company
Passaic, NJ 973-778-7200
Microplas Industries
Dunwoody, GA 800-952-4528
Midco Plastics
Enterprise, KS 800-235-2729
Millhiser
Richmond, VA 800-446-2247
Mini-Bag Company
Farmingdale, NY 631-694-3325
Mohawk Northern Plastics
Auburn, WA 800-426-1100
Mohawk Western Plastic
La Verne, CA 909-593-7547
Mount Vernon Plastics
Mamaroneck, NY 914-698-1122
MRI Flexible Packaging
Newtown, PA 800-448-8183
MS Plastics & Packaging Company
Butler, NJ 800-593-1802
Naltex
Austin, TX 800-531-5112
NAP Industries
Brooklyn, NY 877-635-4948
National Poly Bag Manufacturing Corporation
Brooklyn, NY 718-629-9800
Net Pack Systems
Oakland, ME 207-465-4531
North American PackagingCorporation
New York, NY 800-499-3521
Noteworthy Company
Amsterdam, NY 800-696-7849
Now Plastics
East Longmeadow, MA 413-525-1010
NSW Corporation
Roanoke, VA 800-368-3610
NYP Corporation
Leola, PA 800-524-1052
NYP Corporation
Leola, PA 800-541-0961
Osterneck Company
Lumberton, NC 800-682-2416
Packaging Enterprises
Rockledge, PA 215-379-1234
Packaging Materials
Cambridge, OH 800-565-8550
Pactiv LLC
Lake Forest, IL 888-828-2850
PAK 2000
Mirror Lake, NH 603-569-3700
Pak Sak Industries
Sparta, MI 800-748-0431
Pak-Sher Company
Kilgore, TX 800-642-2295
Pan Pacific Plastics Manufacturing
Hayward, CA 888-475-6888
Papelera Puertorriquena
Utuado, PR 787-894-2098
Parade Packaging
Mundelein, IL 847-566-6264
Paradise Plastics
Brooklyn, NY
Pater & Associates
Cincinnati, OH 513- 24- 215
Peerless Packages
Cleveland, OH 216-464-3620
Pexco Packaging Corporation
Toledo, OH 800-227-9950
Plaint Corporation
Bloomington, IN 800-366-3525
Plastic Packaging Inc
Hickory, NC 800-333-2466
Poliplastic
Granby, QC 450-378-8417
Poly Plastic Products
Delano, PA 570-467-3000
Poly Shapes Corporation
Elyria, OH 800-605-9359
Portco Corporation
Vancouver, WA 800-426-1794
Primepak Company
Teaneck, NJ 201-836-5060
Quality Plastic Bag Corporation
Flushing, NY 800-532-2247

Quality Transparent Bag
Bay City, MI 989-893-3561
Ram Industries
Erwin, TN 800-523-3883
Ray C. Sprosty Bag Company
Wooster, OH 330-264-8559
Roplast Industries Inc.
Oroville, CA 800-767-5278
Ross & Wallace Paper Products
Hammond, LA 800-854-2300
Rutan Polyethylene Supply Bag & Manufacturing Company
Mahwah, NJ 800-872-1474
Sacramento Bag Manufacturing
Woodland, CA 800-287-2247
San Miguel Label Manufacturing
Ciales, PR 787-871-3120
Seal-Tite Bag Company
Philadelphia, PA 717-917-1949
Seattle-Tacoma Box Co.
Kent, WA 253-854-9700
Senior Housing Options
Denver, CO 800-659-2656
Servin Company
New Baltimore, MI 800-824-0962
Shamrock Plastics
Mount Vernon, OH 800-765-1611
Sheboygan Paper Box Company
Sheboygan, WI 800-458-8373
Shields Bag & Printing Company
Yakima, WA 800-541-8630
Ship Rite Packaging
Bergenfield, NJ 800-721-7447
Shippers Paper Products
Sheridan, AR 800-468-1230
Signature Packaging
West Orange, NJ 800-376-2299
Silver State Plastics
Greeley, CO 800-825-2247
Smurfit Flexible Packaging
Milwaukee, WI 414-355-2700
Sonoco Flexible Packaging
Hartsville, SC 800-377-2692
Specialty Films & Associates
Hebron, KY 800-984-3346
Specialty Paper Bag Company
Bronx, NY 718-893-8888
Spectrum Plastics
Las Vegas, NV 702-876-8650
Star Poly Bag, Inc.
Brooklyn, NY 718-384-3130
Steel City Corporation
Youngstown, OH 800-321-0350
Sterling Net & Twine Company
Cedar Knolls, NJ 800-342-0316
Sterling Novelty Products
Northbrook, IL 847-291-0070
Stone Container
Chicago, IL 312-346-6600
Stretch-Vent Packaging System
Ontario, CA 800-822-8368
Stripper Bags
Henderson, NV 800-354-2247
Sungjae Corporation
Irvine, CA 949-757-1727
Sunland Manufacturing Company
Minneapolis, MN 800-790-1905
Target Industries
Flanders, NJ 973-927-0011
Thermal Bags by Ingrid
Gilberts, IL 800-622-5560
Trans Flex Packagers
Unionville, CT 860-673-2531
Tyco Plastics
Lakeville, MN 800-328-4080
United Bags
Saint Louis, MO 800-550-2247
United Flexible
Westbury, NY 516-222-2150
Universal Plastics
Greenville, SC 864-277-3623
US Plastic Corporation
Swampscott, MA 781-595-1030
Valley Packaging Supply Company, Inc.
Green Bay, WI 920-336-9012
Vermont Bag & Film
Bennington, VT 802-442-3166
Vonco Products
Lake Villa, IL 800-323-9077
VPI Manufacturing
Draper, UT 801-495-2310
Walker Bag ManufacturingCompany
Louisville, KY 800-642-4949
Walnut Packaging
Farmingdale, NY 631-293-3836
Wasserman Bag Company
Center Moriches, NY 631-909-8656
Wisconsin Film & Bag
Shawano, WI 800-765-9224
Wright Plastics Company
Prattville, AL 800-874-7659

Polyethylene

AEP Industries
South Hackensack, NJ 800-999-2374
Alabama Bag Company Inc
Talladega, AL 800-888-4921
All American Poly Corporation
Piscataway, NJ 800-526-3551
Aluf Plastics
Orangeburg, NY 800-394-2247
AMPAC Holdings, LLC
Cincinnati, OH 800-543-7030
AR-BEE Transparent
Elk Grove Vlg, IL 800-642-2247
Art Poly Bag Company
Brooklyn, NY 800-278-7659
Automated Packaging Systems
Streetsboro, OH 888-288-6224
Bag Company
Kennesaw, GA 800-533-1931
Beayl Weiner/Pak
Pacific Palisades, CA 310-454-1354
Bennett's Auto Inc.
Neenah, WI 800-215-5464
Blako Industries
Dunbridge, OH 419-833-4491
Carlisle Plastics
Minneapolis, MN 952-884-1309
Castle Bag Company
Wilmington, DE 302-656-1001
Cello Pack Corporation
Cheektowaga, NY 800-778-3111
Central Container Corporation
Minneapolis, MN 763-425-7444
Chalmur Bag Company, LLC
Philadelphia, PA 800-349-2247
Champion Plastics
Clifton, NJ 800-526-1230
Checker Bag Company
Saint Louis, MO 800-489-3130
Cleveland Plastic Films
Elyria, OH 800-832-6799
Coast Scientific
Rancho Santa Fe, CA 800-445-1544
Collector's Gallery
Saint Charles, IL 800-346-3063
Command Packaging
Vernon, CA 800-996-2247
Continental Packaging Corporation
Elgin, IL 847-289-6400
Cortec Corporation
St. Paul, MN 800-426-7832
CR Plastics
Council Bluffs, IA 866-869-6293
Crayex Corporation
Piqua, OH 800-837-1747
Crystal-Flex Packaging Corporation
Rockville Centre, NY 888-246-7325
Cuutom Poly Packaging
Fort Wayne, IN 800-548-6603
Dixie Poly Packaging
Greenville, SC 864-268-3751
Dynamic Packaging
Minneapolis, MN 800-878-9380
Eastern Poly Packaging Company
Brooklyn, NY 800-421-6006
Eaton Manufacturing Company
Houston, TX 800-328-6610
Emerald Packaging
Union City, CA 510-429-5700
Exopack, LLC
Spartanburg, SC 877-447-3539
Film-Pak
Crowley, TX 800-526-1838
Flexo Transparent
Buffalo, NY 877-993-5396
Fortune Plastics
Glendale, AZ 800-243-0306
Fortune Plastics, Inc
Old Saybrook, CT 800-243-0306
Fredman Bag Company
Milwaukee, WI 800-945-5686
Friedman Bag Company
Manhattan Beach, CA 213-628-2341
Frontier Bag Company
Grandview, MO 816-765-4811
Fulton-Denver Company
Denver, CO 800-776-6715
Gemini Plastic Films Corporation
Garfield, NJ 800-789-4732
Genpak LLC
Lakeville, MN 800-328-4556
Gibraltar Packaging Group
Hastings, NE 402-463-1366
GP Plastics Corporation
Medley, FL 305-888-3555
Gulf Arizona Packaging
Humble, TX 800-364-3887
Gulf Systems
Oklahoma City, OK 405-528-2293
Gulf Systems
Brownsville, TX 800-217-4853
Gulf Systems
Oklahoma City, OK 800-364-3887
Gulf Systems
Arlington, TX 817-261-1915
Herche Warehouse
Denver, CO 303-371-8186
Home Plastics
Des Moines, IA 515-265-2562
Hudson Poly Bag
Hudson, MA 800-229-7566
In the Bag
St Petersburg, FL 800-330-2247
Indian Valley Industries
Johnson City, NY 800-659-5111
Inteplast Bags & Films Corporation
Delta, BC 604-946-5431
Interstate Packaging
White Bluff, TN 800-251-1072
ITW Minigrip/Zip-Pak
Manteno, IL 800-488-6973
Jewell Bag Company
Dallas, TX 214-749-1223
King Bag & Manufacturing Company
Cincinnati, OH 800-444-5464
KM International
Kenton, TN 731-749-8700
L&C Plastic Bags
Covington, OH 937-473-2968
Luetzow Industries
South Milwaukee, WI 800-558-6055
Malpack Polybag
Ajax, ON 905-428-3751
Mason Transparent Package Company
Armonk, NY 718-792-6000
Microplas Industries
Dunwoody, GA 800-952-4528
Millhiser
Richmond, VA 800-446-2247
Mini-Bag Company
Farmingdale, NY 631-694-3325
Mohawk Northern Plastics
Auburn, WA 800-426-1100
Mohawk Western Plastic
La Verne, CA 909-593-7547
Monument Industries
Bennington, VT 802-442-8187
MRI Flexible Packaging
Newtown, PA 800-448-8183
MS Plastics & Packaging Company
Butler, NJ 800-593-1802
NAP Industries
Brooklyn, NY 877-635-4948
Net Pack Systems
Oakland, ME 207-465-4531
Noteworthy Company
Amsterdam, NY 800-696-7849
NYP Corporation
Leola, PA 800-524-1052
NYP Corporation
Leola, PA 800-541-0961
Packaging Materials
Cambridge, OH 800-565-8550
Pactiv LLC
Lake Forest, IL 888-828-2850
Pak Sak Industries
Sparta, MI 800-748-0431
Pater & Associates
Cincinnati, OH 513- 24- 215
Pexco Packaging Corporation
Toledo, OH 800-227-9950

Plaint Corporation
Bloomington, IN....................800-366-3525
Portco Corporation
Vancouver, WA....................800-426-1794
Primepak Company
Teaneck, NJ....................201-836-5060
Quality Transparent Bag
Bay City, MI....................989-893-3561
Rutan Polyethylene Supply Bag & Manufacturing Company
Mahwah, NJ....................800-872-1474
Sacramento Bag Manufacturing
Woodland, CA....................800-287-2247
Shields Bag & Printing Company
Yakima, WA....................800-541-8630
Ship Rite Packaging
Bergenfield, NJ....................800-721-7447
Signature Packaging
West Orange, NJ....................800-376-2299
Silver State Plastics
Greeley, CO....................800-825-2247
Smurfit Flexible Packaging
Milwaukee, WI....................414-355-2700
Sonoco Flexible Packaging
Hartsville, SC....................800-377-2692
Sungjae Corporation
Irvine, CA....................949-757-1727
Sunland Manufacturing Company
Minneapolis, MN....................800-790-1905
Superior Distributing
Louisville, KY....................800-365-6661
Target Industries
Flanders, NJ....................973-927-0011
Trans Flex Packagers
Unionville, CT....................860-673-2531
United Flexible
Westbury, NY....................516-222-2150
US Plastic Corporation
Swampscott, MA....................781-595-1030
VPI Manufacturing
Draper, UT....................801-495-2310
Walnut Packaging
Farmingdale, NY....................631-293-3836
Wasserman Bag Company
Center Moriches, NY....................631-909-8656
Workman Packaging Inc.
Saint-Laurent, QC....................800-252-5208
Wright Plastics Company
Prattville, AL....................800-874-7659

Polypropylene

AR-BEE Transparent
Elk Grove Vlg, IL....................800-642-2247
Astro Plastics
Oakland, NJ....................201-337-8170
Automated Packaging Systems
Streetsboro, OH....................888-288-6224
Bag Company
Kennesaw, GA....................800-533-1931
Beayl Weiner/Pak
Pacific Palisades, CA....................310-454-1354
Bulk Lift International
Carpentersville, IL....................800-992-6372
Central Bag Company
Leavenworth, KS....................913-250-0325
Checker Bag Company
Saint Louis, MO....................800-489-3130
Cuutom Poly Packaging
Fort Wayne, IN....................800-548-6603
Dayton Bag & Burlap Company
Dayton, OH....................800-543-3400
Design Packaging Company
Glencoe, IL....................800-321-7659
Eastern Poly Packaging Company
Brooklyn, NY....................800-421-6006
Eaton Manufacturing Company
Houston, TX....................800-328-6610
Flexo Transparent
Buffalo, NY....................877-993-5396
Gibraltar Packaging Group
Hastings, NE....................402-463-1366
Gulf Arizona Packaging
Humble, TX....................800-364-3887
Gulf Systems
Oklahoma City, OK....................405-528-2293
Gulf Systems
Brownsville, TX....................800-217-4853
Gulf Systems
Oklahoma City, OK....................800-364-3887
Gulf Systems
Arlington, TX....................817-261-1915
Herche Warehouse
Denver, CO....................303-371-8186
HUBCO Inc.
Hutchinson, KS....................800-563-1867
In the Bag
St Petersburg, FL....................800-330-2247
Indian Valley Industries
Johnson City, NY....................800-659-5111
Mason Transparent Package Company
Armonk, NY....................718-792-6000
Masternet, Ltd
Mississauga, ON....................800-216-2536
Mercury Plastic Bag Company
Passaic, NJ....................973-778-7200
Millhiser
Richmond, VA....................800-446-2247
Mimi et Cie
Seattle, WA....................206-545-1850
NYP Corporation
Leola, PA....................800-524-1052
NYP Corporation
Leola, PA....................800-541-0961
Pater & Associates
Cincinnati, OH....................513- 24- 215
Pexco Packaging Corporation
Toledo, OH....................800-227-9950
Ray C. Sprosty Bag Company
Wooster, OH....................330-264-8559
Sacramento Bag Manufacturing
Woodland, CA....................800-287-2247
Shields Bag & Printing Company
Yakima, WA....................800-541-8630
Sterling Net & Twine Company
Cedar Knolls, NJ....................800-342-0316
Storsack
Houston, TX....................800-841-4982
Target Industries
Flanders, NJ....................973-927-0011
Trans Flex Packagers
Unionville, CT....................860-673-2531
United Bags
Saint Louis, MO....................800-550-2247
Walker Bag ManufacturingCompany
Louisville, KY....................800-642-4949
Wasserman Bag Company
Center Moriches, NY....................631-909-8656
Workman Packaging Inc.
Saint-Laurent, QC....................800-252-5208

Popcorn

AR-BEE Transparent
Elk Grove Vlg, IL....................800-642-2247
Exopack, LLC
Spartanburg, SC....................877-447-3539
Flexo Transparent
Buffalo, NY....................877-993-5396
HUBCO Inc.
Hutchinson, KS....................800-563-1867
Stewart Sutherland
Vicksburg, MI....................269-649-5489

Sandwich

Aladdin Transparent Packaging Corporation
Hauppauge, NY....................631-273-4747
AR-BEE Transparent
Elk Grove Vlg, IL....................800-642-2247
Brown Paper Goods Company
Waukegan, IL....................847-688-1451
Castle Bag Company
Wilmington, DE....................302-656-1001
Colonial Transparent Products Company
Hicksville, NY....................516-822-4430
Food Pak Corporation
San Mateo, CA....................650-341-6559
Pater & Associates
Cincinnati, OH....................513- 24- 215
Stewart Sutherland
Vicksburg, MI....................269-649-5489
Vermont Bag & Film
Bennington, VT....................802-442-3166

Shopping

All American Poly Corporation
Piscataway, NJ....................800-526-3551
American Advertising & Shop Cap Company
Old Tappan, NJ....................800-442-8837
AR-BEE Transparent
Elk Grove Vlg, IL....................800-642-2247
Celebrity Promotions
Remsen, IA....................800-332-6847
Colonial Transparent Products Company
Hicksville, NY....................516-822-4430
Continental Extrusion Corporation
Cedar Grove, NJ....................800-822-4748
Continental Products
Mexico, MO....................800-325-0216
Cuutom Poly Packaging
Fort Wayne, IN....................800-548-6603
David Dobbs Enterprise & Menu Design
St Augustine, FL....................800-889-6368
Eco-Bag Products
Ossining, NY....................800-720-2247
Excelsior Transparent Bag Manufacturing
Yonkers, NY....................914-968-1300
Fabriko
Altavista, VA....................888-203-8098
Fischer Paper Products
Antioch, IL....................800-323-9093
Fitec International
Memphis, TN....................800-332-6387
Genpak LLC
Lakeville, MN....................800-328-4556
Green Seams
Maple Grove, MN....................612-929-3213
Hall Manufacturing Company
Henderson, TX....................903-657-4501
Memphis Delta Tent & Awning Company
Memphis, TN....................901-522-1238
Millhiser
Richmond, VA....................800-446-2247
Moser Bag & Paper Company
Cleveland, OH....................800-433-6638
NAP Industries
Brooklyn, NY....................877-635-4948
North American PackagingCorporation
New York, NY....................800-499-3521
Pater & Associates
Cincinnati, OH....................513- 24- 215
Pexco Packaging Corporation
Toledo, OH....................800-227-9950
Poliplastic
Granby, QC....................450-378-8417
Primepak Company
Teaneck, NJ....................201-836-5060
Save-A-Tree
Berkeley, CA....................510-843-5233
Shamrock Plastics
Mount Vernon, OH....................800-765-1611
Sheboygan Paper Box Company
Sheboygan, WI....................800-458-8373
Source for Packaging
New York, NY....................800-223-2527
Star Poly Bag, Inc.
Brooklyn, NY....................718-384-3130
Tree Saver
Englewood, CO....................800-676-7741
Vermont Bag & Film
Bennington, VT....................802-442-3166
Walker Bag ManufacturingCompany
Louisville, KY....................800-642-4949
Wisconsin Converting of Green Bay
Green Bay, WI....................800-544-1935

Baskets

Egg

Langer Manufacturing Company
Cedar Rapids, IA....................800-728-6445
Xtreme Beverages, LLC
Dana Point, CA....................949-495-7929

Fruit & Vegetable

Berlin Fruit Box Company
Berlin Heights, OH....................800-877-7721
Classy Basket
San Diego, CA....................888-449-4901
Collector's Gallery
Saint Charles, IL....................800-346-3063
Day Basket Factory
North East, MD....................410-287-8100
Farmers Co-op Elevator Co.
Hudsonville, MI....................800-439-9859
Frobisher Industries
Waterborough, NB....................506-362-2198
Fruit Growers Package Company
Grandville, MI....................616-724-1400
Harvey's Groves
Rockledge, FL....................800-327-9312
Langer Manufacturing Company
Cedar Rapids, IA....................800-728-6445

Little Rock Crate & Basket Company
Little Rock, AR.................... 800-223-7823
Longaberger Basket Company
Newark, OH..................... 740-322-7800
Peacock Crate Factory
Jacksonville, TX.................. 800-657-2200
Peterboro Basket Company
Peterborough, NH................. 603-924-3861
Shipley Basket Inc
Dayton, TN....................... 800-251-0806
Smalley Package Company
Berryville, VA.................... 540-955-2550
Specialty Wood Products
Clanton, AL...................... 800-322-5343
Straits Steel & Wire Company
Ludington, MI.................... 231-843-3416
Thorco Industries LLC
Lamar, MO....................... 800-445-3375
Traitech Industries
Vaughan, ON..................... 877-872-4835
Xtreme Beverages, LLC
Dana Point, CA................... 949-495-7929

Gift

All Sorts Premium Packaging
Buffalo, NY...................... 888-565-9727
Andrea Baskets
Bohemia, NY..................... 888-272-8826
Baskets Extraordinaires
Westbury, NY.................... 800-666-1685
Classy Basket
San Diego, CA................... 888-449-4901
Coe & Dru Inc.
San Dimas, CA................... 800-722-7538
Collector's Gallery
Saint Charles, IL................. 800-346-3063
Dufeck Manufacturing Company
Denmark, WI..................... 888-603-9663
Gril-Del
Mankato, MN..................... 800-782-7320
Harvey's Groves
Rockledge, FL.................... 800-327-9312
Houdini
Fullerton, CA.................... 714-525-0325
Mar-Boro Printing & Advertising Specialties
Brooklyn, NY..................... 718-336-4051
Metrovock Snacks
Maywood, CA..................... 800-428-0522
Peacock Crate Factory
Jacksonville, TX.................. 800-657-2200
Roofian
Sun Valley, CA................... 800-431-3886
Seymour Woodenware Company
Seymour, WI...................... 920-833-6551
United Basket Company
Maspeth, NY...................... 894-545- 555
Xtreme Beverages, LLC
Dana Point, CA................... 949-495-7929

Refrigerator

Coastline Equipment
Bellingham, WA................... 360-739-2480
Langer Manufacturing Company
Cedar Rapids, IA.................. 800-728-6445
Straits Steel & Wire Company
Ludington, MI.................... 231-843-3416

Bins

A-Z Factory Supply
Schiller Park, IL.................. 800-323-4511
ABI Limited
Concord, ON...................... 800-297-8666
American Pallet
Oakdale, CA...................... 209-847-6122
Anderson-Crane Company
Minneapolis, MN.................. 800-314-2747
Andgar Corporation
Ferndale, WA..................... 360-366-9900
Atlas Equipment Company
Kansas City, MO.................. 800-842-9188
AZO Food
Memphis, TN..................... 901-794-9480
BestBins Corporation
Chaska, MN....................... 866-448-3114
Bonar Plastics
West Chicago, IL.................. 800-295-3725
Bonar Plastics
Ridgefield, WA.................... 800-972-5252
Bowers Process Equipment
Stratford, ON..................... 800-567-3223
Buhler Group
Raleigh, NC...................... 919-851-2000
Cecor
Verona, WI....................... 800-356-9042
Centennial Molding LLC
Hastings, NE..................... 888-883-2189
Chief Industries
Kearney, NE...................... 800-359-8833
Clayton & Lambert Manufacturing
Buckner, KY...................... 800-626-5819
Containair Packaging Corporation
Paterson, NJ..................... 888-276-6500
Continental-Fremont
Tiffin, OH....................... 419-448-4045
Davron Technologies
Chattanooga, TN.................. 423-870-1888
DBE Inc
Concord, ON...................... 800-461-5313
Del-Tec Packaging
Greenville, SC.................... 800-747-8683
Despro Manufacturing
Cedar Grove, NJ.................. 800-292-9906
Duke Manufacturing Company
Saint Louis, MO.................. 800-735-3853
Durham Manufacturing Company
Durham, CT...................... 413-781-7900
Earl Soesbe Company
Romeoville, IL.................... 219-866-4191
Eastern Plastics
Pawtucket, RI.................... 800-442-8585
Electrical Engineering &Equipment Company
Des Moines, IA................... 800-33 -722
Emco Industrial Plastics
Cedar Grove, NJ.................. 800-292-9906
Expert Industries
Brooklyn, NY..................... 718-434-6060
F.E. Wood & Sons
East Baldwin, ME................. 207-286-5003
F.N. Smith Corporation
Oregon, IL....................... 815-732-2171
Falco Technologies
La Prairie, QC.................... 450-444-0566
Faribo Manufacturing Company
Faribault, MN.................... 800-447-6043
Flow of Solids
Westford, MA.................... 978-392-0300
Follett Corporation
Easton, PA....................... 800-523-9361
Forbes Industries
Ontario, CA...................... 909-923-4559
Fred D. Pfening Company
Columbus, OH.................... 614-294-1633
Frem Corporation
Worcester, MA.................... 508-791-3152
Fresno Pallet, Inc.
Sultana, CA...................... 559-591-4111
Gates Manufacturing Company
Saint Louis, MO.................. 800-237-9226
Goergen-Mackwirth Company
Buffalo, NY...................... 716-874-4800
Golden West Sales
Cerritos, CA...................... 800-827-6175
Graff Tank Erection
Harrisville, PA.................... 814-385-6671
Griffin Cardwell, Ltd
Louisville, KY.................... 502-636-1374
Hardy Systems Corporation
Northbrook, IL.................... 800-927-3956
Hedstrom Corporation
Ashland, OH...................... 700-765-9665
Hodge Manufacturing Company
Springfield, MA................... 800-262-4634
Hoshizaki America
Peachtree City, GA................ 800-438-6087
Imperial Industries Inc
Wausau, WI...................... 800-558-2945
InterMetro Industries Corporation
Wilkes Barre, PA.................. 800-441-2714
International Wood Industries
Snohomish, WA................... 800-922-6141
Jacksonville Box & Woodwork Company
Jacksonville, FL................... 800-683-2699
Jarlan Manufacturing Company
Los Angeles, CA.................. 323-752-1211
Jenike & Johanson
Tyngsboro, MA................... 978-649-3300
K&I Creative Plastics
Jacksonville, FL................... 904-387-0438
K-Tron
Salina, KS....................... 785-825-1611
Kason Industries, Inc.
Lewis Center, OH................. 740-549-2100
KHM Plastics
Gurnee, IL....................... 847-249-4910
Kimball Companies
East Longmeadow, MA............. 413-525-1881
Lakeside Manufacturing
Milwaukee, WI................... 888-558-8574
Leer Limited Partnership
New Lisbon, WI................... 800-766-5337
Longview Fibre Company
Beaverton, OR.................... 503-350-1600
Machine Ice Company, Inc
Houston, TX...................... 800-423-8822
Manitowoc Foodservice Companies, Inc.
New Port Richey, FL............... 877-375-9300
Mannhardt Inc
Sheboygan Falls, WI............... 800-423-2327
Material Storage Systems
Gadsden, AL...................... 877-543-2467
Matthiesen Equipment Company
San Antonio, TX.................. 800-624-8635
MeGa Industries
Burlington, ON................... 800-665-6342
Mell & Company
Niles, IL......................... 800-262-6355
Melmat, Inc.
Huntington Beach, CA............. 800-635-6289
Meyers Corbox Co, Inc.
Cleveland, OH.................... 800-321-7286
Michiana Box & Crate
Niles, MI......................... 800-677-6372
Miller Hofft Brands
Indianapolis, IN.................. 317-638-6576
Moli-International
Denver, CO...................... 800-525-8468
Mountain Valley Farms & Lumber Products, Inc.
Biglerville, PA.................... 717-677-6166
MultiFab Plastics
Boston, MA...................... 888-293-5754
Nelson Company
Baltimore, MD.................... 410-477-3000
Nepa Pallet & Container Company
Snohomish, WA................... 360-568-3185
NST Metals
Louisville, KY.................... 502-584-5846
Omega Industries
St Louis, MO..................... 314-961-1668
Our Name is Mud
New York, NY.................... 877-683-7867
Pallet One
Bartow, FL....................... 800-771-1148
Pelican Displays
Homer, IL........................ 800-627-1517
Pittsburgh Tank Corporation
Monongahela, PA.................. 800-634-0243
Precision Plastics Inc.
Beltsville, MD.................... 800-922-1317
Prestige Plastics Corporation
Delta, BC........................ 604-930-2931
Prince Castle
Carol Stream, IL.................. 800-722-7853
Pro Bake
Twinsburg, OH.................... 800-837-4427
Process Solutions
Riviera Beach, FL................. 561-840-0050
Pruitt's Packaging Services
Grand Rapids, MI................. 800-878-0553
Quantum Storage Systems
Miami, FL........................ 800-685-4665
Ram Equipment
Waukesha, WI.................... 262-513-1114
Remcon Plastics
West Reading, PA................. 800-360-3636
Render
Buffalo, NY...................... 888-446-1010
RMI-C/Rotonics Manaufacturing
Bensenville, IL................... 630-773-9510
Rotonics Manufacturing
Gardena, CA..................... 310-327-5401
Rubbermaid Commercial Products
Winchester, VA................... 800-336-9880
Schenck Process LLC
Whitewater, WI................... 888-742-1249
Scotsman Ice Systems
Vernon Hills, IL.................. 800-726-8762
Seattle Plastics
Seattle, WA...................... 800-441-0679
SEMCO
Ocala, FL........................ 800-749-6894
SerVend International
Sellersburg, IN................... 800-367-4233
Shouldice Brothers SheetMetal
Battle Creek, MI.................. 269-962-5579

Snyder Crown
Marked Tree, AR 870-358-3400
Solve Needs International
White Lake, MI. . . . 800-783-2462
Southern Ag Company
Blakely, GA. . . . 229-723-4262
Spudnik Equipment
Blackfoot, ID 208-785-0480
Stainless Fabrication
Springfield, MO 800-397-8265
Stearnswood
Hutchinson, MN 800-657-0144
Supreme Metal
Alpharetta, GA 800-645-2526
Thermodynamics
Commerce City, CO 800-627-9037
Tolan Machinery Company
Rockaway, NJ 973-983-7212
Trade Fixtures
Little Rock, AR. . . . 800-872-3490
Tri-Boro Shelving & Partition
Farmville, VA 434-315-5600
Triple-A Manufacturing Company
Toronto, ON 800-786-2238
Tulip Corporation
Milwaukee, WI 414-963-3120
Upham & Walsh Lumber
Hoffman Estates, IL 847-519-1010
Vande Berg Scales
Sioux Center, IA 712-722-1181
Vanmark Corporation
Creston, IA 800-523-6261
Warwick Products Company
Cleveland, OH 800-535-4404
Westeel
Saskatoon, SK. . . . 306-931-2855
Westfield Sheet Metal Works
Kenilworth, NJ 908-276-5500
Wilder Manufacturing Company
Port Jervis, NY 800-832-1319
Wilson Steel Products Company
Memphis, TN 901-527-8742
Woodstock Plastics Company
Marengo, IL 815-568-5281

Beverage

Crown Plastics
Plymouth, MN. . . . 800-423-2769
Falco Technologies
La Prairie, QC. . . . 450-444-0566
Lakeside Manufacturing
Milwaukee, WI 888-558-8574

Insulated

ABI Limited
Concord, ON. . . . 800-297-8666
Falco Technologies
La Prairie, QC. . . . 450-444-0566
Lakeside Manufacturing
Milwaukee, WI 888-558-8574
Melmat, Inc.
Huntington Beach, CA 800-635-6289
Promens
St. John, NB 800-295-3725

Bottles

Aluminum

California Vibratory Feeders
Anaheim, CA 800-354-0972
Mountain Safety Research
Seattle, WA. . . . 800-877-9677

Glass

Arkansas Glass Container Corporation
Jonesboro, AR. . . . 800-527-4527
Bal/Foster Glass Container Company
Port Allegany, PA 814-642-2521
Ball Foster Glass
Fairfield, CA. . . . 707-863-4061
Ball Foster Glass Container Company
Sapulpa, OK 918-224-1440
Ball Glass Container Corporation
El Monte, CA 626-448-9831
California Vibratory Feeders
Anaheim, CA 800-354-0972
Foster-Forbes Glass Company
Vernon, CA 800-767-4527
Greenfield Packaging
White Plains, NY 914-993-0233
Indiana Glass Company
Columbus, OH 800-543-0357
Indianapolis Container Company
Indianapolis, IN 800-760-3318
Kelman Bottles
Glenshaw, PA 412-486-9100
LMK Containers
Centerville, UT 626-821-9984
Louisville Container Company
Indianapolis, IN 888-539-7225
Oak Barrel Winecraft
Berkeley, CA. . . . 510-849-0400
Palmer Distributors
St Clair Shores, MI 800-444-1912
Penn Bottle & Supply Company
Philadelphia, PA 215-365-5700
Richards Packaging
Memphis, TN 800-583-0327
St. Tobain Containers
Seattle, WA 206-762-0660
Stanpac, Inc.
Smithville, ON 905-957-3326
World Kitchen
Elmira, NY 800-999-3436
Xtreme Beverages, LLC
Dana Point, CA. . . . 949-495-7929

Plastic

Abbott Industries
Paterson, NJ
Alpack
Centerville, MA 508-771-9131
Altira
Miami, FL 305-687-8074
Berry Plastics Corporation
Evansville, IN 812-424-2904
Browns International & Company
St. Laurent, QC 514-737-1326
California Vibratory Feeders
Anaheim, CA 800-354-0972
CapSnap Equipment
Jackson, MI. . . . 517-787-3481
Carmi Flavor & Fragrance Company
City of Commerce, CA. . . . 800-421-9647
Chester Plastics
Chester, NS 902-275-3522
Clearplass Containers
Penn Yan, NY 315-536-5690
CMD Corporation
Appleton, WI 920-730-6888
Consolidated Container Company
Atlanta, GA. . . . 888-831-2184
Consolidated Plastics
Stow, OH. . . . 800-858-5001
Constar International
Trevose, PA. . . . 215-552-3700
Container Specialties
Melrose Park, IL. . . . 800-548-7513
Continental Plastic Container
Dallas, TX. . . . 972-303-1825
Contour Packaging
Philadelphia, PA 215-457-1600
Crown Holdings, Inc.
Philadelphia, PA 215-698-5100
CTK Plastics
Moose Jaw, SK 800-667-8847
Custom Bottle of Connecticut
Naugatuck, CT 203-723-6661
Flexo Transparent
Buffalo, NY. . . . 877-993-5396
Fuller Brush Company
Great Bend, KS. . . . 800-522-0499
Graham Engineering Corporation
York, PA 717-848-3755
Greenfield Packaging
White Plains, NY 914-993-0233
Hartford Plastics
Omaha, NE
Hedwin Corporation
Baltimore, MD 800-638-1012
Indiana Bottle Company Inc.
Scottsburg, IN. . . . 800-752-8702
Indianapolis Container Company
Indianapolis, IN 800-760-3318
Intertech Corporation
Greensboro, NC 800-364-2255
J.E. Roy
St Claire, QC. . . . 418-883-2711
Juice Merchandising Corporation
Kansas City, MO. . . . 800-950-1998
Jupiter Mills Corporation
Roslyn, NY 800-853-5121
Liqui-Box Corporation
Worthington, OH 614-888-9280
Liquitane
Berwick, PA 570-759-6200
LMK Containers
Centerville, UT 626-821-9984
Louisville Container Company
Indianapolis, IN 888-539-7225
Marpac Industries
Philmont, NY 888-462-7722
O-I
Perrysburg, OH
Packaging Associates
Randolph, NJ 973-252-8890
Parkway Plastics
Piscataway, NJ 732-752-3636
Penn Bottle & Supply Company
Philadelphia, PA 215-365-5700
Plastic Industries
Athens, TN 800-894-4876
Plastipak Packaging
Plymouth, MI 734-354-3510
Plaxicon
West Chicago, IL 630-231-0850
Pocono PET
Hazle Twp, PA 570-459-1800
Podnar Plastics
Kent, OH. . . . 800-673-5277
Polycon Industries
Chicago, IL. . . . 773-374-5500
Pretium Packaging
Hermann, MO. . . . 573-486-2811
Pretium Packaging
Seymour, IN 812-522-8177
Pretium Packaging, LLC.
Chesterfield, MO 314-727-8200
Pro-Gram Plastics
Geneva, OH. . . . 440-466-8080
Progressive Plastics
Cleveland, OH 800-252-0053
Q Pak Corporation
Newark, NJ 973-483-4404
Quintex Corporation
Spokane Valley, WA 509-924-7900
RAPAC
Oakland, TN 800-280-6333
Redi-Call, Incorporated
Reno, NV 800-648-1849
Reliance Product
Winnipeg, MB. . . . 800-665-0258
Rexam Beverage Can Company
Chicago, IL. . . . 773-399-3000
Richard Read Construction Company
Arcadia, CA 888-450-7343
Richards Packaging
Memphis, TN 800-583-0327
RXI Silgan Specialty Plastics
Triadelphia, WV. . . . 304-547-9100
Schoeneck Containers
New Berlin, WI. . . . 262-786-9360
Setco
Monroe Twp, NJ 609-655-4600
Setco
Anaheim, CA 714-777-5200
Sho-Me Container
Grinnell, IA. . . . 800-798-3512
Silgan Plastics
Chesterfield, MO 800-274-5426
Silgan Plastics Canada
Chesterfield, MO 800-274-5426
Snapware
Fullerton, CA 800-334-3062
T&S Blow Molding
Scarborough, ON 416-752-8330
Thornton Plastics
Salt Lake City, UT 800-248-3434
Tolco Corporation
Toledo, OH 800-537-4786
Wheaton Plastic Containers
Millville, NJ 856-825-1400

Boxes

Bakers'

International Paper Co.
Memphis, TN 800-207-4003

Morris Transparent Box Company
East Providence, RI. 401-438-6116
Pater & Associates
Cincinnati, OH 513- 24- 215
Piper Products
Wausau, WI. 800-544-3057
Premier Packages
Saint Louis, MO 800-466-6588
Reliable Container Corporation
Downey, CA 562-745-0200
Ritz Packaging Company
Brooklyn, NY 718-366-2300
Schiefer Packaging Corporation
Syracuse, NY 315-422-0615
Schroeder Sewing Technologies
San Marcos, CA 760-591-9733
Smyrna Container Company
Smyrna, GA 800-868-4305
Xtreme Beverages, LLC
Dana Point, CA 949-495-7929

Candy

A La Carte
Chicago, IL 800-722-2370
Cardinal Packaging Products Inc.
Crystal Lake, IL 866-216-4942
Central Paper Box
Kansas City, MO. 816-753-3126
Collector's Gallery
Saint Charles, IL 800-346-3063
Creative Cookie
Easton, MD. 800-451-4005
Elegant Packaging
Cicero, IL 800-367-5493
Friend Box Company
Danvers, MA. 978-774-0240
Gary Plastic Packaging Corporation
Bronx, NY. 800-227-4279
H.P. Neun
Fairport, NY 585-388-1360
Impress Industries
Emmaus, PA 610-967-6027
Kaufman Paper Box Company
Providence, RI 401-272-7508
Lengsfield Brothers
New Orleans, LA 504-529-2235
Nashville Wraps
Hendersonville, TN. 800-547-9727
Pater & Associates
Cincinnati, OH 513- 24- 215
Ritz Packaging Company
Brooklyn, NY 718-366-2300
Schiefer Packaging Corporation
Syracuse, NY 315-422-0615
Taylor Box Company
Warren, RI. 800-304-6361
Visual Packaging Corporation
Haskell, NJ 973-835-7055
Xtreme Beverages, LLC
Dana Point, CA 949-495-7929

Corrugated

AdPro
Solon, OH 440-542-1111
American Containers
Plymouth, IN. 574-936-4068
Atlas Packaging & Displays Inc
Miami, FL. 800-662-0630
Bell Container Corporation
Newark, NJ 973-344-4400
Bell Packaging Corporation
Marion, IN. 800-382-0153
Boxes.com
Livingston, NJ. 201-646-9050
Cantwell-Cleary Company
Landover, MD. 301-773-9800
Capital City Container Corporation
Buda, TX. 512-312-1222
Capitol Carton Company
Sacramento, CA 916-388-7848
Capitol City Container Corporation
Indianapolis, IN 800-233-5145
Cardinal Container Corporation
Indianapolis, IN 800-899-2715
Cardinal Packaging Products Inc.
Crystal Lake, IL 866-216-4942
Carolina Container Company
High Point, NC 800-627-0825
Carpet City Paper Box Company
Amsterdam, NY 518-842-5430
Cedar Box Company
Minneapolis, MN 612-332-4287
Central Container Corporation
Minneapolis, MN 763-425-7444
Chambers Container Company
Gastonia, NC. 704-377-6317
Champlin Company
Hartford, CT 800-458-5261
Chesapeake Packaging
Scranton, PA 570-342-9217
Chesapeake Packaging Company
Binghamton, NY. 607-775-1550
City Box Company
Aurora, IL 773-277-5500
Color Carton
Bronx, NY. 718-665-0840
Columbus Container
Columbus, IN 812-376-9301
Columbus Paperbox Company
Columbus, OH 800-968-0797
Commencement Bay Corrugated
Orting, WA 253-845-3100
Commercial Corrugated Corporation
Baltimore, MD 800-242-8861
Complete Packaging & Shipping Supplies
Freeport, NY 877-269-3236
Connecticut Container Corporation
North Haven, CT. 203-248-2161
Corfab
Chicago, IL 708-458-8750
Corr-Pak Corporation
Mc Cook, IL 708-442-7806
Corrugated Packaging
Sarasota, FL 941-371-0000
Corrugated Specialties
Plainwell, MI 269-685-9821
Craft Corrugated Box
New Bedford, MA 508-998-2115
Cush-Pak Container Corporation
Henderson, TX 903-657-0555
Custom Packaging
Richmond, VA. 804-232-3299
Dakota Corrugated Box
Sioux Falls, SD 605-332-3501
Deline Box Company
Denver, CO 303-373-1430
Desert Box & Supply Corporation
Thermal, CA 760-399-5161
Diamond Packaging
Rochester, NY. 800-333-4079
Die Cut Specialties
Savage, MN. 952-890-7590
Display One
Hartford, WI 262-673-5880
Dixie Printing & Packaging
Glen Burnie, MD 800-433-4943
Dorado Carton Company
Dorado, PR 787-796-1670
Drake Container Corporation
Houston, TX 800-299-5644
Drescher Paper Box
Buffalo, NY. 716-854-0288
Dusobox Company
Haverhill, MA. 978-372-7192
Duval Container Company
Jacksonville, FL 800-342-8194
E-Cooler
Chicago, IL 866-955-3266
Eagle Box Company
Farmingdale, NY 212-255-3860
EB Box Company
Richmond Hill, ON. 800-513-2269
Englander Container Company
Waco, TX 888-314-5259
Felco Bag & Burlap Company
Baltimore, MD 800-673-8488
Ferguson Containers
Phillipsburg, NJ 908-454-9755
Field Container Company
Elk Grove Vlg, IL. 847-437-1700
Fitzpatrick Container Company
North Wales, PA 215-699-3515
Fleetwood International Paper
Vernon, CA 323-588-7121
Flint Boxmakers
Burton, MI 810-743-0400
Four M Manufacturing Group
San Jose, CA. 408-998-1141
Frankston Paper Box Company of Texas
Frankston, TX. 903-876-2550
Fuller Box Company
North Attleboro, MA 508-695-2525
Gateway Packaging Corporation
Murrysville, PA. 888-289-2693
Gaylord Container Corporation
Tampa, FL. 813-621-3591
General Bag Corporation
Cleveland, OH 800-837-9396
Genesee Corrugated
Flint, MI 810-235-6120
Georgia-Pacific LLC
Atlanta, GA. 404-652-4000
Goldman Manufacturing Company
Detroit, MI 313-834-5535
Great Lakes Corrugated
Toledo, OH 419-726-3491
Great Lakes-Triad Package Corporation
Grand Rapids, MI 616-241-6441
Great Northern Corporation
Racine, WI 800-558-4711
Green Bay Packaging
Coon Rapids, MN 800-236-6456
Green Bay Packaging
Tulsa, OK 918-446-3341
Green Bay Packaging
Green Bay, WI. 920-433-5111
Greenfield Packaging
White Plains, NY 914-993-0233
Gulf Arizona Packaging
Humble, TX 800-364-3887
Gulf Systems
Oklahoma City, OK 405-528-2293
Gulf Systems
Brownsville, TX 800-217-4853
Gulf Systems
Oklahoma City, OK 800-364-3887
Gulf Systems
Arlington, TX 817-261-1915
H.P. Neun
Fairport, NY 585-388-1360
Hager Containers
Carrollton, TX. 972-417-7660
Hawkeye Corrugated Box Company
Cedar Falls, IA 319-268-0407
Herche Warehouse
Denver, CO 303-371-8186
Hinkle Manufacturing
Perrysburg, OH 419-666-5550
Hope Paper Box Company
Pawtucket, RI 401-724-5700
Horn Packaging Corporation
Lancaster, MA. 800-832-7020
Hunter Packaging Corporation
South Elgin, IL 800-428-4747
Illinois Valley Container Corporation
Peru, IL 815-223-7200
Imperial Containers
City of Industry, CA 626-333-6363
Imperial Packaging Corporation
Pawtucket, RI 401-753-7778
Impress Industries
Emmaus, PA 610-967-6027
Indiana Box Company
Greenfield, IN 317-462-7743
Industrial Container Corporation
High Point, NC 336-886-7031
Industrial Crating & Packing, Inc.
Seattle, WA 800-942-0499
Inland Consumer Packaging
Harrington, DE 302-398-4211
Inland Paper Board & Packaging
Elizabethton, TN. 423-542-2112
Inland Paperboard & Packaging
Austin, TX. 512-434-5800
Inland Paperboard & Packaging
Rock Hill, SC 803-366-4103
Instabox
Calgary, AB. 800-482-6173
J&J Corrugated Box Corporation
Franklin, MA 508-528-6200
J&J Mid-South Container Corporation
Augusta, GA 800-395-1025
Jamestown Container Corporation
Macedonia, OH. 800-247-1033
Jayhawk Boxes
Fremont, NE 800-642-8363
Jesse Jones Box Corporation
Philadelphia, PA 215-425-6600
Jessup Paper Box
Brookston, IN 765-490-9043
Jet Age Containers Company
Chicago, IL 708-594-5260
Jet Box Company
Troy, MI 248-362-1260

Johnson Corrugated Products Corporation
Thompson, CT 860-923-9563
Jupiter Mills Corporation
Roslyn, NY 800-853-5121
K&H Container
Wallingford, CT 203-265-1547
K&H Corrugated Case Company
Walden, NY 845-778-1631
KapStone Paper and Packaging Corporation
Northbrook, IL 847-239-8800
Kell Container Corporation
Chippewa Falls, WI 800-472-1800
Kelly Box & Packaging Corporation
Fort Wayne, IN 260-432-4570
Kendel
Countryside, IL 800-323-1100
Kerrigan Paper Products
Haverhill, MA 978-374-4797
Kimball Companies
East Longmeadow, MA 413-525-1881
Knapp Container
Beacon Falls, CT 203-888-0511
Koch Container Corporation
Victor, NY 585-924-1600
Kole Industries
Miami, FL 305-633-2556
Lakeside Container Corporation
Plattsburgh, NY 518-561-6150
Lansing Corrugated Products
Lansing, MI 517-323-2752
Laval Paper Box
Pointe Claire, QC 450-669-3551
Lawrence Paper Company
Lawrence, KS 785-843-8111
Leaman Container
Fort Worth, TX 817-429-2660
Len E. Ivarson
Milwaukee, WI 414-351-0700
Levin Brothers Paper
Cicero, IL 800-666-8484
Liberty Carton Company
Minneapolis, MN 800-818-2698
LinPac
San Angelo, TX 800-453-7393
Lone Star Container Corporation
Irving, TX 800-552-6937
Love Box Company
Wichita, KS 316-838-0851
Loy-Lange Box Company
Saint Louis, MO 800-886-4712
Mack-Chicago Corporation
Chicago, IL 800-992-6225
MacMillan Bloedel Packaging
Montgomery, AL 800-239-4464
Mall City Containers
Kalamazoo, MI 800-643-6721
Mannkraft Corporation
Newark, NJ 973-589-7400
Manufacturers CorrugatedBox Company
Flushing, NY 718-894-7200
Marfred Industries
Sun Valley, CA 800-529-5156
Mark Container Corporation
San Leandro, CA 510-483-4440
Maro Paper Products Company
Bellwood, IL 708-649-9982
Massachusetts Container Corporation
Marlborough, MA 508-481-1100
Menasha Corporation
Neenah, WI 800-558-5073
Meyers Corbox Co, Inc.
Cleveland, OH 800-321-7286
Michiana Corrugated Products
Sturgis, MI 269-651-5225
Michigan Box Company
Detroit, MI 888-642-4269
Midwest Box Company
Cleveland, OH 216-281-3980
Midwest Fibre Products
Viola, IL 309-596-2955
Midwest Paper Products Company
Louisville, KY 502-636-2741
Morphy Container Company
Brantford, ON 519-752-5428
Neff Packaging Solutions
Mason, OH 800-445-4383
Negus Container & Packaging
Madison, WI 888-241-7482
Nelson Container Corporation
Germantown, WI 262-250-5000
New England Wooden Ware Corporation
Gardner, MA 800-252-9214

New York Corrugated Box Company
Paterson, NJ 973-742-5000
North Carolina Box
Raleigh, NC 919-872-3007
Northeast Box Company
Ashtabula, OH 800-362-8100
Northeast Container Corporation
Dumont, NJ 201-385-6200
Northern Box Company
Elkhart, IN 574-264-2161
Northern Package Corporation
Minneapolis, MN 952-881-5861
Ockerlund Industries
Forest Park, IL 708-771-7707
Old Dominion Box Company
Madison Heights, VA 434-929-6701
Packaging Design Corporation
Burr Ridge, IL 630-323-1354
Palmetto Packaging Corporation
Florence, SC 843-662-5800
Parlor City Paper Box Company
Binghamton, NY 607-772-0600
PCA Denver
Denver, CO 303-331-0400
Pel-Pak Container
Pell City, AL 800-239-2699
Performance Packaging
Trail Creek, IN 219-874-6226
Premier Packages
Saint Louis, MO 800-466-6588
President Container
Wood Ridge, NJ 201-933-7500
Propak
Burlington, ON 800-263-4872
Providence Packaging
Mooresville, NC 866-779-4945
Quality Packaging, Inc.
Fond du Lac, WI 800-923-3633
R&R Corrugated Container
Terryville, CT 860-584-1194
Rand-Whitney Container Corporation
Worcester, MA 508-791-2301
Rand-Whitney Container Corporation
Portsmouth, NH 603-822-7300
RDA Container Corporation
Gates, NY 585-247-2323
Regal Box Company
Milwaukee, WI 414-562-5890
Reliable Container Corporation
Downey, CA 562-745-0200
Reliance-Paragon
Philadelphia, PA 215-743-1231
Rex Carton Company
Chicago, IL 773-581-4115
Richmond Corrugated Box Company
Richmond, VA 804-222-1320
Rock Tenn/Alliance Group
Tullahoma, TN 931-455-3535
Romanow Container
Westwood, MA 781-320-9200
Romanow Container Inc
Westwood, MA 781-320-9200
Royal Box Group
Cicero, IL 708-656-2020
Rudd Container Corporation
Chicago, IL 773-847-7600
Ruffino Paper Box Manufacturing
Hackensack, NJ 201-487-1260
Rusken Packaging
Cullman, AL 256-734-0092
Schermerhorn
Chicopee, MA 413-598-8348
Schiffenhaus Industries
Newark, NJ 973-484-5000
Scope Packaging
Orange, CA 714-998-4411
Seattle-Tacoma Box Co.
Kent, WA 253-854-9700
Seattle-Tacoma Box Company
Kent, WA 253-854-9700
Sebring Container Corporation
Salem, OH 330-332-1533
Security Packaging
North Bergen, NJ 201-854-1955
Sheboygan Paper Box Company
Sheboygan, WI 800-458-8373
Shillington Box Company
Saint Louis, MO 636-225-5353
Shippers Supply
Saskatoon, SK 800-661-5639
Shippers Supply, Labelgraphic
Calgary, AB 800-661-5639

Simkins Industries
East Haven, CT 203-787-7171
Smith Packaging
Mississauga, ON 905-564-6640
Smurfit Stone Container
San Jose, CA 408-925-9391
Smurfit Stone Container
North Tonawanda, NY 716-692-6510
Solve Needs International
White Lake, MI 800-783-2462
Somerville Packaging
Scarborough, ON 416-291-1161
Southern Missouri Containers
Springfield, MO 800-999-7666
Southern Packaging Corporation
Bennettsville, SC 843-479-7154
Sphinx Adsorbents
Springfield, MA 800-388-0157
Spring Cove Container
Roaring Spring, PA 814-224-2222
St Joseph Packaging Inc
St Joseph, MO 800-383-3000
Stand Fast Packaging Products
Addison, IL 630-600-0900
Star Container Corporation
Leominster, MA 978-537-1676
State Container Corporation
Moonachie, NJ 201-933-5200
Stearnswood
Hutchinson, MN 800-657-0144
Stone Container
Moss Point, MS 502-491-4870
Stone Container
Santa Fe Springs, CA 714-774-0100
Stronghaven Inc.
Matthews, NC 800-222-7919
Suburban Corrugated Box Company
Indianhead Park, IL 630-920-1230
Superior Quality Products
Schenectady, NY 800-724-1129
Supply One
Tulsa, OK 800-832-4725
Tampa Corrugated Carton Company
Tampa, FL 813-623-5115
Taylor Box Company
Warren, RI 800-304-6361
Tenneco Packaging
Westmont, IL 630-850-7034
Tennessee Packaging
Loudon, TN 800-968-6894
THARCO
San Lorenzo, CA 800-772-2332
The Royal Group
Cicero, IL 262-723-6900
Traub Container Corporation
Cleveland, OH 216-475-5100
Trent Corporation
Trenton, NJ 609-587-7515
Triple A Containers
Buena Park, CA 714-521-2820
Tucson Container Corporation
Tucson, AZ 520-746-3171
Union Camp Corporation
Denver, CO 303-371-0760
Unique Boxes
Chicago, IL 800-281-1670
Universal Folding Box
East Orange, NJ 973-482-4300
Valley Container
Bridgeport, CT 203-336-6100
Valley Container Corporation
Saint Louis, MO 314-652-8050
Vermont Container
Bennington, VT 802-442-5455
Victory Box Corporation
Roselle, NJ 908-245-5100
Victory Packaging, Inc.
Houston, TX 800-486-5606
Volk Packaging Corporation
Biddeford, ME 800-341-0208
Wagner Brothers Containers
Baltimore, MD 410-354-0044
Wasserman Bag Company
Center Moriches, NY 631-909-8656
Weber Display & Packaging
Philadelphia, PA 215-426-3500
Webster Packaging Corporation
Loveland, OH 513-683-5666
Welch Packaging
Elkhart, IN 574-295-2460
Westvaco Corporation
Newark, DE 302-453-7200

Weyerhaeuser Company
Federal Way, WA 800-525-5440
Wil-Mac Container Corporation
Conyers, GA 800-428-9269
Willamette Industries
Beaverton, OR...................503-641-1131
Willard Packaging
Gaithersburg, MD 301-948-7700
Woodson Pallet
Anmoore, WV.....................304-623-2858
Xtreme Beverages, LLC
Dana Point, CA..................949-495-7929
York Container Company
York, PA 717-757-7611

Fancy

Can Creations
Pembroke Pines, FL 954-581-3312
Central Paper Box
Kansas City, MO.................816-753-3126
Colbert Packaging Corporation
Lake Forest, IL 847-367-5990
Collector's Gallery
Saint Charles, IL...............800-346-3063
Elegant Packaging
Cicero, IL 800-367-5493
Gates
West Peterborough, NH 888-543-6316
Godshall Paper Box Company
Oshkosh, WI 920-235-4040
H.P. Neun
Fairport, NY 585-388-1360
McGraw Box Company
Mc Graw, NY 607-836-6465
Nordic Printing & Packaging
New Hope, MN....................763-535-6440
North American PackagingCorporation
New York, NY 800-499-3521
Paragon Packaging
Ferndale, CA....................888-615-0065
Pater & Associates
Cincinnati, OH 513- 24- 215
Paul T. Freund Corporation
Palmyra, NY 800-333-0091
Racine Paper Box Manufacturing
Chicago, IL 773-227-3900
Smurfit Stone Container
San Jose, CA....................408-925-9391
Xtreme Beverages, LLC
Dana Point, CA..................949-495-7929

Fiber

Goldman Manufacturing Company
Detroit, MI 313-834-5535
Greenfield Packaging
White Plains, NY 914-993-0233
Jupiter Mills Corporation
Roslyn, NY 800-853-5121
Lansing Corrugated Products
Lansing, MI.....................517-323-2752
North American ContainerCorporation
Maretta, GA 800-929-0610
Palmetto Packaging Corporation
Florence, SC 843-662-5800
PCA Denver
Denver, CO 303-331-0400
Romanow Container
Westwood, MA....................781-320-9200
Round Paper Packages
Erlanger, KY 859-331-7200
Smith Packaging
Mississauga, ON.................905-564-6640
Solve Needs International
White Lake, MI..................800-783-2462
State Container Corporation
Moonachie, NJ 201-933-5200
The Royal Group
Cicero, IL 262-723-6900
Tucson Container Corporation
Tucson, AZ 520-746-3171
Union Camp Corporation
Denver, CO 303-371-0760
Volk Packaging Corporation
Biddeford, ME 800-341-0208

Fruit & Vegetable

Franklin Crates
Micanopy, FL 352-466-3141
Frobisher Industries
Waterborough, NB 506-362-2198

Jacksonville Box & Woodwork Company
Jacksonville, FL 800-683-2699
Luke's Almond Acres
Reedley, CA 559-638-3483
Remmey Wood Products
Southampton, PA 215-355-3335
Schiefer Packaging Corporation
Syracuse, NY 315-422-0615
Supply One
Tulsa, OK 800-832-4725
Upham & Walsh Lumber
Hoffman Estates, IL 847-519-1010
WNC Pallet & Forest Products
Candler, NC 828-667-5426
Xtreme Beverages, LLC
Dana Point, CA..................949-495-7929

Paper

Accurate Paper Box Company
Knoxville, TN...................865-690-0311
AdPro
Solon, OH 440-542-1111
Alcan Packaging
Baie D'Urfe, QC.................514-457-4555
Ample Industries
Franklin, OH....................888-818-9700
Artistic Carton
Auburn, IN 260-925-6060
Artistic Carton Company
Elgin, IL 847-741-0247
Bancroft Bag
West Monroe, LA 318-387-2550
Bell Packaging Corporation
Marion, IN......................800-382-0153
Boxes.com
Livingston, NJ..................201-646-9050
Brewer-Cantelmo Company
New York, NY 212-244-4600
Burrows Paper Corporation
Little Falls, NY 800-732-1933
C.W. Zumbiel Company
Cincinnati, OH 513-531-3600
Capitol Carton Company
Sacramento, CA 916-388-7848
Cardinal Packaging Products Inc.
Crystal Lake, IL 866-216-4942
Carpenter-Hayes Paper Box Company
East Hampton, CT................203-267-4436
Carpet City Paper Box Company
Amsterdam, NY 518-842-5430
Cedar Box Company
Minneapolis, MN 612-332-4287
Central Paper Box
Kansas City, MO.................816-753-3126
Chambers Container Company
Gastonia, NC....................704-377-6317
Cleveland Specialties Company
Loveland, OH 513-677-9787
Climax Manufacturing Company
Lowville, NY 800-225-4629
Coast Paper Box Company
San Bernardino, CA 909-382-3475
Colbert Packaging Corporation
Lake Forest, IL 847-367-5990
Color Box
Richmond, IN 765-966-7588
Color Carton
Bronx, NY.......................718-665-0840
Columbus Container
Columbus, IN 812-376-9301
Columbus Paperbox Company
Columbus, OH 800-968-0797
Commencement Bay Corrugated
Orting, WA 253-845-3100
Commercial Corrugated Corporation
Baltimore, MD 800-242-8861
Complete Packaging & Shipping Supplies
Freeport, NY....................877-269-3236
Connecticut Container Corporation
North Haven, CT.................203-248-2161
Corfab
Chicago, IL 708-458-8750
Corpak
San Juan, PR....................787-787-9085
Corr-Pak Corporation
Mc Cook, IL 708-442-7806
Corrobilt Container Company
Livermore, CA 925-373-0880
Corrugated Packaging
Sarasota, FL 941-371-0000

Corson Manufacturing Company
Lockport, NY 716-434-8871
Crane Carton Corporation
Chicago, IL 773-722-0555
Curtis Packaging Corporation
Sandy Hook, CT 203-426-5861
Custom Packaging
Richmond, VA....................804-232-3299
Day Manufacturing Company
Sherman, TX.....................903-893-1138
Designers-Folding Box Corporation
Buffalo, NY.....................716-853-5141
Diamond Packaging
Rochester, NY...................800-333-4079
Dixie Printing & Packaging
Glen Burnie, MD 800-433-4943
Dorado Carton Company
Dorado, PR 787-796-1670
Drescher Paper Box
Buffalo, NY.....................716-854-0288
Dusobox Company
Haverhill, MA...................978-372-7192
Duval Container Company
Jacksonville, FL 800-342-8194
Eagle Box Company
Farmingdale, NY 212-255-3860
EB Box Company
Richmond Hill, ON...............800-513-2269
Economy Folding Box Corporation
Chicago, IL.....................800-771-1053
Edge Paper Box Company
Cudahy, CA......................323-771-7733
Elegant Packaging
Cicero, IL 800-367-5493
Enterprise Box Company
Montclair, NJ 973-509-2200
Eureka Paper Box Company
Williamsport, PA................570-326-9147
Felco Bag & Burlap Company
Baltimore, MD 800-673-8488
Field Container Company
Elk Grove Vlg, IL...............847-437-1700
Finn Industries
Ontario, CA.....................909-930-1500
Fitzpatrick Container Company
North Wales, PA 215-699-3515
Flashfold Carton
Fort Wayne, IN 260-423-9431
Flour City Press-Pack Company
Minneapolis, MN 952-831-1265
Folding Carton/Flexible Packaging
North Hollywood, CA 818-896-3449
Food Pak Corporation
San Mateo, CA 650-341-6559
Four M Manufacturing Group
San Jose, CA....................408-998-1141
Frankston Paper Box Company of Texas
Frankston, TX...................903-876-2550
Friend Box Company
Danvers, MA.....................978-774-0240
Friendly City Box Company
Johnstown, PA...................814-266-6287
Fuller Box Company
North Attleboro, MA 508-695-2525
Fuller Packaging
Central Falls, RI 401-725-4300
Gateway Packaging Corporation
Murrysville, PA.................888-289-2693
Godshall Paper Box Company
Oshkosh, WI.....................920-235-4040
Goldman Manufacturing Company
Detroit, MI 313-834-5535
Great Lakes Corrugated
Toledo, OH 419-726-3491
Great Western Products
Ontario, CA.....................888-598-5588
Green Bay Packaging
Coon Rapids, MN.................800-236-6456
Green Bay Packaging
Tulsa, OK 918-446-3341
Green Bay Packaging
Green Bay, WI...................920-433-5111
Green Brothers
Barrington, RI..................401-245-9043
Greenfield Paper Box Company
Greenfield, MA..................413-773-9414
Grigsby Brothers Paper Box Manufacturers
Portland, OR 866-233-4690
Gulf Packaging Company
Safety Harbor, FL...............800-749-3466
H.P. Neun
Fairport, NY 585-388-1360

Hager Containers
Carrollton, TX. 972-417-7660
Harvard Folding Box Company
Lynn, MA 781-598-1600
Hope Paper Box Company
Pawtucket, RI 401-724-5700
Horn Packaging Corporation
Lancaster, MA. 800-832-7020
Hub Folding Box Company
Mansfield, MA 508-339-0005
Hunter Packaging Corporation
South Elgin, IL 800-428-4747
Imperial Packaging Corporation
Pawtucket, RI 401-753-7778
Impress Industries
Emmaus, PA 610-967-6027
Industrial Nameplates
Ivyland, PA 800-878-6263
Inland Consumer Packaging
Harrington, DE 302-398-4211
Inland Paper Board & Packaging
Elizabethton, TN. 423-542-2112
Inland Paperboard & Packaging
Rock Hill, SC 803-366-4103
Ira L Henry Company, Inc
Watertown, WI 920-261-0648
Jamestown Container Corporation
Macedonia, OH. 800-247-1033
Jarisch Paper Box Company
North Adams, MA 413-663-5396
Jesse Jones Box Corporation
Philadelphia, PA 215-425-6600
Jessup Paper Box
Brookston, IN 765-490-9043
Jet Age Containers Company
Chicago, IL 708-594-5260
Johnson Corrugated Products Corporation
Thompson, CT 860-923-9563
Jordan Box Company
Syracuse, NY 315-422-3419
Jordan Paper Box Company
Chicago, IL 773-287-5362
Jupiter Mills Corporation
Roslyn, NY 800-853-5121
K&H Container
Wallingford, CT 203-265-1547
K&H Corrugated Case Company
Walden, NY. 845-778-1631
KapStone Paper and Packaging Corporation
Northbrook, IL 847-239-8800
Kaufman Paper Box Company
Providence, RI 401-272-7508
Kell Container Corporation
Chippewa Falls, WI 800-472-1800
Kendel
Countryside, IL. 800-323-1100
Knight Paper Box Company
Chicago, IL 773-585-2035
Koch Container Corporation
Victor, NY. 585-924-1600
Lakeside Container Corporation
Plattsburgh, NY 518-561-6150
Lawson Mardon Radisson
Baldwinsville, NY 800-847-5677
Len E. Ivarson
Milwaukee, WI 414-351-0700
Levin Brothers Paper
Cicero, IL 800-666-8484
Liberty Carton Company
Minneapolis, MN 800-818-2698
LinPac
San Angelo, TX 800-453-7393
Lone Star Container Corporation
Irving, TX 800-552-6937
Los Angeles Paper Box & Board Mills
Los Angeles, CA. 323-685-8900
Lowell Paper Box Company
Nashua, NH. 603-595-0700
Loy-Lange Box Company
Saint Louis, MO 800-886-4712
Mack-Chicago Corporation
Chicago, IL 800-992-6225
MacMillan Bloedel Packaging
Montgomery, AL. 800-239-4464
Mall City Containers
Kalamazoo, MI. 800-643-6721
Malnove Packaging Systems
Omaha, NE 800-228-9877
Marcus Carton Company
Melville, NY. 631-752-4200
Marfred Industries
Sun Valley, CA 800-529-5156
Marion Paper Box Company
Marion, IN. 765-664-6435
Maro Paper Products Company
Bellwood, IL. 708-649-9982
Master Paper Box Company
Chicago, IL 877-927-0252
Maypak
Wayne, NJ 973-696-0780
Menasha Corporation
Neenah, WI 800-558-5073
Merchants Publishing Company
Kalamazoo, MI 269-345-1175
Meyer Packaging
Palmyra, PA. 717-838-6300
Meyers Corbox Co, Inc.
Cleveland, OH 800-321-7286
Michiana Corrugated Products
Sturgis, MI 269-651-5225
Michigan Box Company
Detroit, MI 888-642-4269
Mid Cities Paper Box Company
Downey, CA 877-277-6272
Midwest Fibre Products
Viola, IL 309-596-2955
Modern Paper Box Company
Providence, RI 401-861-7357
Moore Paper Boxes
Dayton, OH. 937-278-7327
Morphy Container Company
Brantford, ON. 519-752-5428
Mount Vernon Packaging
Mount Vernon, OH 888-397-3221
Nagel Paper & Box Company
Saginaw, MI 800-292-3654
Neff Packaging Solutions
Mason, OH 800-445-4383
New England Wooden Ware Corporation
Gardner, MA. 800-252-9214
New York Corrugated Box Company
Paterson, NJ 973-742-5000
New York Folding Box Company
Newark, NJ. 973-589-0654
Norristown Box Company
Norristown, PA 610-275-5540
Northeast Box Company
Ashtabula, OH 800-362-8100
Northeast Container Corporation
Dumont, NJ. 201-385-6200
Northern Package Corporation
Minneapolis, MN 952-881-5861
Oakes Carton Company
Kalamazoo, MI. 269-381-6022
Ockerlund Industries
Forest Park, IL 708-771-7707
Old Dominion Box Company
Burlington, NC 336-226-4491
Old Dominion Box Company
Madison Heights, VA 434-929-6701
Oracle Packaging
Toledo, OH 800-952-9536
Original Packaging & Display Company
Saint Louis, MO 314-772-7797
Ott Packagings
Selinsgrove, PA. 570-374-2811
Packaging Corporation of America
Lake Forest, IL 800-456-4725
Packaging Design Corporation
Burr Ridge, IL. 630-323-1354
Packrite Packaging
Archdale, NC. 336-431-1111
Paper Box & Specialty Company
Sheboygan, WI 888-240-3756
Paragon Packaging
Ferndale, CA. 888-615-0065
Parlor City Paper Box Company
Binghamton, NY. 607-772-0600
PARTA
Kent, OH. 800-543-5781
Pater & Associates
Cincinnati, OH 513-24- 215
Paul T. Freund Corporation
Palmyra, NY 800-333-0091
Peerless Packages
Cleveland, OH 216-464-3620
Pell Paper Box Company
Elizabeth City, NC 252-335-4361
Performance Packaging
Trail Creek, IN 219-874-6226
Pioneer Packaging
Chicopee, MA. 413-378-6930
Pioneer Packaging & Printing
Anoka, MN. 800-708-1705
Pohlig Brothers
Richmond, VA. 804-275-9000
Portland Paper Box Company
Portland, OR 800-547-2571
Premier Packages
Saint Louis, MO 800-466-6588
Quality Packaging, Inc.
Fond du Lac, WI. 800-923-3633
Rand-Whitney Container Corporation
Worcester, MA 508-791-2301
Rand-Whitney Container Corporation
Portsmouth, NH 603-822-7300
RDA Container Corporation
Gates, NY 585-247-2323
Reliable Container Corporation
Downey, CA 562-745-0200
Reliance-Paragon
Philadelphia, PA 215-743-1231
Rhoades Paper Box Corporation
Springfield, OH. 800-441-6494
Rice Paper Box Company
Colorado Springs, CO. 303-733-1000
Ritz Packaging Company
Brooklyn, NY 718-366-2300
Rock Tenn/Alliance Group
Tullahoma, TN 931-455-3535
Rock-Tenn Company
Norcross, GA 608-223-6272
Rock-Tenn Company
Norcross, GA 770-448-2193
Romanow Container
Westwood, MA 781-320-9200
Round Paper Packages
Erlanger, KY 859-331-7200
Roy's Folding Box
Cleveland, OH. 216-464-1191
Royal Box Group
Cicero, IL 708-656-2020
Royal Paper Box Company of California
Montebello, CA 323-728-7041
Ruffino Paper Box Manufacturing
Hackensack, NJ. 201-487-1260
Rusken Packaging
Cullman, AL 256-734-0092
Schermerhorn
Chicopee, MA. 413-598-8348
Schwarz
Morton Grove, IL 847-966-4050
Scope Packaging
Orange, CA 714-998-4411
Seaboard Carton Company
Downers Grove, IL. 708-344-0575
Seaboard Folding Box Company
Fitchburg, MA 800-255-6313
Seattle-Tacoma Box Company
Kent, WA. 253-854-9700
Sebring Container Corporation
Salem, OH. 330-332-1533
Security Packaging
North Bergen, NJ 201-854-1955
Sheboygan Paper Box Company
Sheboygan, WI 800-458-8373
Shillington Box Company
Saint Louis, MO 636-225-5353
Shippers Supply
Saskatoon, SK. 800-661-5639
Shippers Supply, Labelgraphic
Calgary, AB. 800-661-5639
Shore Paper Box Company
Mardela Springs, MD 410-749-7125
Shorewood Packaging
Carlstadt, NJ 201-933-3203
Simkins Industries
East Haven, CT. 203-787-7171
Smith-Lustig Paper Box Manufacturing
Cleveland, OH 216-621-0454
Smurfit Stone Container
San Jose, CA. 408-925-9391
Smyrna Container Company
Smyrna, GA 800-868-4305
Solve Needs International
White Lake, MI. 800-783-2462
Somerville Packaging
Scarborough, ON 416-291-1161
Sonderen Packaging
Spokane, WA. 800-727-9139
Southern Champion Tray
Chattanooga, TN. 800-468-2222
Southern Missouri Containers
Springfield, MO 800-999-7666
Southern Packaging Corporation
Bennettsville, SC 843-479-7154

Specialized Packaging London
London, ON 519-659-7011
Sphinx Adsorbents
Springfield, MA 800-388-0157
Spring Cove Container
Roaring Spring, PA................814-224-2222
St Joseph Packaging Inc
St Joseph, MO......................800-383-3000
St. Louis Carton Company
Saint Louis, MO 314-241-0990
Stand Fast Packaging Products
Addison, IL.........................630-600-0900
Stearnswood
Hutchinson, MN 800-657-0144
Sterling Packaging Company
Jeannette, PA.......................724-523-5565
Sterling Paper Company
Philadelphia, PA 215-744-5350
Stone Container
Moss Point, MS 502-491-4870
Stone Container
Santa Fe Springs, CA 714-774-0100
Stronghaven Inc.
Matthews, NC......................800-222-7919
Suburban Corrugated Box Company
Indianhead Park, IL 630-920-1230
Superior Quality Products
Schenectady, NY...................800-724-1129
T.J. Smith Box Company
Fort Smith, AR 877-540-7933
Tampa Corrugated Carton Company
Tampa, FL...........................813-623-5115
Taylor Box Company
Warren, RI...........................800-304-6361
THARCO
San Lorenzo, CA...................800-772-2332
The Piqua Paper Box Company
Piqua, OH 800-536-2136
Traub Container Corporation
Cleveland, OH 216-475-5100
Trent Corporation
Trenton, NJ 609-587-7515
UniPak
West Chester, PA..................610-436-6600
Unique Boxes
Chicago, IL 800-281-1670
Universal Folding Box
East Orange, NJ 973-482-4300
Universal Folding Box Company
Hoboken, NJ 201-659-7373
Universal Paper Box
Seattle, WA 800-228-1045
Utah Paper Box Company
Salt Lake City, UT 801-363-0093
Victory Box Corporation
Roselle, NJ 908-245-5100
Victory Packaging, Inc.
Houston, TX 800-486-5606
VIP Real Estate Ltd
Chicago, IL 773-376-5000
Volk Packaging Corporation
Biddeford, ME 800-341-0208
Wasserman Bag Company
Center Moriches, NY 631-909-8656
Western Container Company
Kansas City, MO..................816-924-5700
Westvaco Corporation
Newark, DE.........................302-453-7200
Willamette Industries
Beaverton, OR......................503-641-1131
Winchester Carton
Eutaw, AL 205-372-3337
Woodson Pallet
Anmoore, WV......................304-623-2858
Wright Brothers Paper Box Company
Fond Du Lac, WI 920-921-8270
Xtreme Beverages, LLC
Dana Point, CA....................949-495-7929
York Container Company
York, PA 717-757-7611

Paper, Folding

AdPro
Solon, OH 440-542-1111
Alcan Packaging
Baie D'Urfe, QC...................514-457-4555
Ample Industries
Franklin, OH........................888-818-9700
Artistic Carton
Auburn, IN 260-925-6060
Artistic Carton Company
Elgin, IL..............................847-741-0247
Bell Packaging Corporation
Marion, IN...........................800-382-0153
Boxes.com
Livingston, NJ......................201-646-9050
Brewer-Cantelmo Company
New York, NY 212-244-4600
Burrows Paper Corporation
Little Falls, NY.....................800-732-1933
C.W. Zumbiel Company
Cincinnati, OH 513-531-3600
Capitol Carton Company
Sacramento, CA 916-388-7848
Cardinal Packaging Products Inc.
Crystal Lake, IL 866-216-4942
Carpet City Paper Box Company
Amsterdam, NY 518-842-5430
Carton Service
Shelby, OH 800-533-7744
Cedar Box Company
Minneapolis, MN 612-332-4287
Central Paper Box
Kansas City, MO..................816-753-3126
Chambers Container Company
Gastonia, NC........................704-377-6317
Cleveland Specialties Company
Loveland, OH 513-677-9787
Climax Manufacturing Company
Lowville, NY 800-225-4629
Coast Paper Box Company
San Bernardino, CA 909-382-3475
Collector's Gallery
Saint Charles, IL 800-346-3063
Color Carton
Bronx, NY...........................718-665-0840
Columbus Container
Columbus, IN 812-376-9301
Columbus Paperbox Company
Columbus, OH 800-968-0797
Commencement Bay Corrugated
Orting, WA 253-845-3100
Commercial Corrugated Corporation
Baltimore, MD 800-242-8861
Complete Packaging & Shipping Supplies
Freeport, NY 877-269-3236
Connecticut Container Corporation
North Haven, CT..................203-248-2161
Corfab
Chicago, IL 708-458-8750
Corr-Pak Corporation
Mc Cook, IL 708-442-7806
Corrobilt Container Company
Livermore, CA 925-373-0880
Corrugated Packaging
Sarasota, FL 941-371-0000
Corson Manufacturing Company
Lockport, NY 716-434-8871
Crane Carton Corporation
Chicago, IL 773-722-0555
Curtis Packaging Corporation
Sandy Hook, CT 203-426-5861
Day Manufacturing Company
Sherman, TX........................903-893-1138
Designers-Folding Box Corporation
Buffalo, NY.........................716-853-5141
Diamond Packaging
Rochester, NY......................800-333-4079
Dixie Printing & Packaging
Glen Burnie, MD 800-433-4943
Dorado Carton Company
Dorado, PR 787-796-1670
Drescher Paper Box
Buffalo, NY.........................716-854-0288
Dusobox Company
Haverhill, MA......................978-372-7192
Duval Container Company
Jacksonville, FL 800-342-8194
Eagle Box Company
Farmingdale, NY 212-255-3860
EB Box Company
Richmond Hill, ON..............800-513-2269
Eureka Paper Box Company
Williamsport, PA..................570-326-9147
Felco Bag & Burlap Company
Baltimore, MD 800-673-8488
Field Container Company
Elk Grove Vlg, IL................847-437-1700
Finn Industries
Ontario, CA.........................909-930-1500
Fitzpatrick Container Company
North Wales, PA 215-699-3515
Flashfold Carton
Fort Wayne, IN 260-423-9431
Flour City Press-Pack Company
Minneapolis, MN 952-831-1265
Folding Carton/Flexible Packaging
North Hollywood, CA 818-896-3449
Food Pak Corporation
San Mateo, CA 650-341-6559
Four M Manufacturing Group
San Jose, CA........................408-998-1141
Frankston Paper Box Company of Texas
Frankston, TX.......................903-876-2550
Friendly City Box Company
Johnstown, PA.....................814-266-6287
Goldman Manufacturing Company
Detroit, MI 313-834-5535
Great Lakes Corrugated
Toledo, OH 419-726-3491
Green Bay Packaging
Tulsa, OK 918-446-3341
Green Bay Packaging
Green Bay, WI.....................920-433-5111
Greenfield Packaging
White Plains, NY 914-993-0233
Greenfield Paper Box Company
Greenfield, MA....................413-773-9414
Grigsby Brothers Paper Box Manufacturers
Portland, OR 866-233-4690
Gulf Packaging Company
Safety Harbor, FL 800-749-3466
H.P. Neun
Fairport, NY 585-388-1360
Hager Containers
Carrollton, TX.....................972-417-7660
Harvard Folding Box Company
Lynn, MA 781-598-1600
Heritage Corrugated Box Corporation
Brooklyn, NY 718-495-1500
Hope Paper Box Company
Pawtucket, RI 401-724-5700
Hub Folding Box Company
Mansfield, MA 508-339-0005
Hunter Packaging Corporation
South Elgin, IL 800-428-4747
Imperial Packaging Corporation
Pawtucket, RI 401-753-7778
Impress Industries
Emmaus, PA 610-967-6027
Indiana Carton Company
Bremen, IN 800-348-2390
Industrial Nameplates
Ivyland, PA 800-878-6263
Inland Consumer Packaging
Harrington, DE 302-398-4211
Inland Paper Board & Packaging
Elizabethton, TN.................423-542-2112
Inland Paperboard & Packaging
Rock Hill, SC 803-366-4103
International Paper Co.
Memphis, TN 800-207-4003
Jamestown Container Corporation
Macedonia, OH...................800-247-1033
Jarisch Paper Box Company
North Adams, MA 413-663-5396
Jesse Jones Box Corporation
Philadelphia, PA 215-425-6600
Jessup Paper Box
Brookston, IN 765-490-9043
Jupiter Mills Corporation
Roslyn, NY 800-853-5121
KapStone Paper and Packaging Corporation
Northbrook, IL 847-239-8800
Kell Container Corporation
Chippewa Falls, WI 800-472-1800
Kendel
Countryside, IL 800-323-1100
Knight Paper Box Company
Chicago, IL 773-585-2035
Koch Container Corporation
Victor, NY..........................585-924-1600
Lakeside Container Corporation
Plattsburgh, NY 518-561-6150
Lawson Mardon Radisson
Baldwinsville, NY 800-847-5677
Len E. Ivarson
Milwaukee, WI...................414-351-0700
Levin Brothers Paper
Cicero, IL 800-666-8484
Lone Star Container Corporation
Irving, TX...........................800-552-6937
Los Angeles Paper Box & Board Mills
Los Angeles, CA..................323-685-8900

Lowell Paper Box Company
Nashua, NH. 603-595-0700
Loy-Lange Box Company
Saint Louis, MO 800-886-4712
MacMillan Bloedel Packaging
Montgomery, AL. 800-239-4464
Malnove Packaging Systems
Omaha, NE 800-228-9877
Marcus Carton Company
Melville, NY 631-752-4200
Marfred Industries
Sun Valley, CA 800-529-5156
Marion Paper Box Company
Marion, IN. 765-664-6435
Maro Paper Products Company
Bellwood, IL 708-649-9982
Master Paper Box Company
Chicago, IL 877-927-0252
Menasha Corporation
Neenah, WI 800-558-5073
Merchants Publishing Company
Kalamazoo, MI 269-345-1175
Meyer Packaging
Palmyra, PA. 717-838-6300
Meyers Corbox Co, Inc.
Cleveland, OH .800-321-7286
Michigan Box Company
Detroit, MI 888-642-4269
Mid Cities Paper Box Company
Downey, CA 877-277-6272
Midvale Paper Box Corporation
Wilkes Barre, PA. 570-824-3577
Midwest Fibre Products
Viola, IL 309-596-2955
Nagel Paper & Box Company
Saginaw, MI 800-292-3654
Neff Packaging Solutions
Mason, OH 800-445-4383
New England Wooden Ware Corporation
Gardner, MA 800-252-9214
New York Corrugated Box Company
Paterson, NJ 973-742-5000
New York Folding Box Company
Newark, NJ 973-589-0654
Norristown Box Company
Norristown, PA 610-275-5540
Northeast Box Company
Ashtabula, OH .800-362-8100
Northeast Container Corporation
Dumont, NJ. 201-385-6200
Oakes Carton Company
Kalamazoo, MI 269-381-6022
Ockerlund Industries
Forest Park, IL 708-771-7707
Old Dominion Box Company
Burlington, NC 336-226-4491
Old Dominion Box Company
Madison Heights, VA 434-929-6701
Oracle Packaging
Toledo, OH 800-952-9536
Original Packaging & Display Company
Saint Louis, MO 314-772-7797
Ott Packagings
Selinsgrove, PA. 570-374-2811
Packaging Design Corporation
Burr Ridge, IL. 630-323-1354
Packrite Packaging
Archdale, NC. .336-431-1111
Paragon Packaging
Ferndale, CA. .888-615-0065
Parlor City Paper Box Company
Binghamton, NY. 607-772-0600
PARTA
Kent, OH. 800-543-5781
Pater & Associates
Cincinnati, OH .513- 24- 215
Peerless Cartons
Bartlett, IL. 312-226-7952
Peerless Packages
Cleveland, OH .216-464-3620
Pell Paper Box Company
Elizabeth City, NC 252-335-4361
Performance Packaging
Trail Creek, IN 219-874-6226
Pioneer Packaging
Chicopee, MA. .413-378-6930
Pioneer Packaging & Printing
Anoka, MN 800-708-1705
Pohlig Brothers
Richmond, VA. 804-275-9000
Portland Paper Box Company
Portland, OR 800-547-2571
Premier Packages
Saint Louis, MO 800-466-6588
Prystup Packaging Products
Livingston, AL 205-652-9583
Quality Packaging, Inc.
Fond du Lac, WI. 800-923-3633
Racine Paper Box Manufacturing
Chicago, IL 773-227-3900
Rand-Whitney Container Corporation
Worcester, MA 508-791-2301
Rand-Whitney Container Corporation
Portsmouth, NH 603-822-7300
RDA Container Corporation
Gates, NY 585-247-2323
Reliable Container Corporation
Downey, CA 562-745-0200
Reliance-Paragon
Philadelphia, PA 215-743-1231
Rhoades Paper Box Corporation
Springfield, OH. 800-441-6494
Rice Paper Box Company
Colorado Springs, CO. 303-733-1000
Ritz Packaging Company
Brooklyn, NY .718-366-2300
Rock Tenn/Alliance Group
Tullahoma, TN 931-455-3535
Rock-Tenn Company
Norcross, GA .608-223-6272
Rock-Tenn Company
Norcross, GA .770-448-2193
Romanow Container
Westwood, MA 781-320-9200
Rondo of America
Naugatuck, CT 203-723-7474
Roy's Folding Box
Cleveland, OH. 216-464-1191
Royal Box Group
Cicero, IL 708-656-2020
Royal Paper Box Company of California
Montebello, CA 323-728-7041
Ruffino Paper Box Manufacturing
Hackensack, NJ. 201-487-1260
Rusken Packaging
Cullman, AL 256-734-0092
San Diego Paper Box Company
Spring Valley, CA 619-660-9566
Schermerhorn
Chicopee, MA. .413-598-8348
Schiefer Packaging Corporation
Syracuse, NY .315-422-0615
Schwarz
Morton Grove, IL 847-966-4050
Scope Packaging
Orange, CA 714-998-4411
Scott & Daniells
Portland, CT 860-342-1932
Seaboard Carton Company
Downers Grove, IL. 708-344-0575
Seaboard Folding Box Company
Fitchburg, MA 800-255-6313
Seattle-Tacoma Box Company
Kent, WA. 253-854-9700
Sebring Container Corporation
Salem, OH. 330-332-1533
Security Packaging
North Bergen, NJ 201-854-1955
SFBC, LLC dba Seaboard Folding Box
Fitchburg, MA 800-225-6313
Sheboygan Paper Box Company
Sheboygan, WI 800-458-8373
Shillington Box Company
Saint Louis, MO 636-225-5353
Shippers Supply
Saskatoon, SK. 800-661-5639
Shippers Supply, Labelgraphic
Calgary, AB. 800-661-5639
Shore Paper Box Company
Mardela Springs, MD 410-749-7125
Shorewood Packaging
Carlstadt, NJ 201-933-3203
Simkins Industries
East Haven, CT. 203-787-7171
Smyrna Container Company
Smyrna, GA 800-868-4305
Somerville Packaging
Scarborough, ON 416-291-1161
Sonderen Packaging
Spokane, WA. .800-727-9139
Southern Champion Tray
Chattanooga, TN. 800-468-2222
Southern Missouri Containers
Springfield, MO 800-999-7666
Southern Packaging Corporation
Bennettsville, SC 843-479-7154
Spring Cove Container
Roaring Spring, PA 814-224-2222
St Joseph Packaging Inc
St Joseph, MO. .800-383-3000
St. Louis Carton Company
Saint Louis, MO 314-241-0990
Stand Fast Packaging Products
Addison, IL 630-600-0900
Stearnswood
Hutchinson, MN 800-657-0144
Sterling Packaging Company
Jeannette, PA. .724-523-5565
Stone Container
Moss Point, MS 502-491-4870
Stone Container
Santa Fe Springs, CA 714-774-0100
Stoneway Carton Company
Mercer Island, WA 800-498-2185
Suburban Corrugated Box Company
Indianhead Park, IL 630-920-1230
Superior Quality Products
Schenectady, NY. 800-724-1129
T.J. Smith Box Company
Fort Smith, AR 877-540-7933
Tampa Corrugated Carton Company
Tampa, FL. 813-623-5115
Taylor Box Company
Warren, RI. 800-304-6361
THARCO
San Lorenzo, CA. 800-772-2332
The Piqua Paper Box Company
Piqua, OH 800-536-2136
The Shelby Company
Cleveland, OH .800-842-1650
Traub Container Corporation
Cleveland, OH .216-475-5100
Trent Corporation
Trenton, NJ 609-587-7515
Unique Boxes
Chicago, IL 800-281-1670
Universal Folding Box
East Orange, NJ 973-482-4300
Universal Folding Box Company
Hoboken, NJ 201-659-7373
Utah Paper Box Company
Salt Lake City, UT 801-363-0093
Victory Box Corporation
Roselle, NJ 908-245-5100
Victory Packaging, Inc.
Houston, TX 800-486-5606
VIP Real Estate Ltd
Chicago, IL 773-376-5000
Volk Packaging Corporation
Biddeford, ME 800-341-0208
Warren Packaging
San Bernardino, CA 909-888-7008
Western Container Company
Kansas City, MO. 816-924-5700
Westvaco Corporation
Newark, DE. 302-453-7200
Willamette Industries
Beaverton, OR. .503-641-1131
Woodson Pallet
Anmoore, WV. .304-623-2858
Wright Brothers Paper Box Company
Fond Du Lac, WI 920-921-8270
Xtreme Beverages, LLC
Dana Point, CA 949-495-7929
York Container Company
York, PA 717-757-7611

Plastic

ACO
Moore, OK 405-794-7662
Alpack
Centerville, MA 508-771-9131
Bardes Plastics
Milwaukee, WI 800-558-5161
Berry Plastics Corporation
Evansville, IN .812-424-2904
Billie-Ann Plastics Packaging Corp
Brooklyn, NY .888-245-5432
Buckhorn Canada
Brampton, ON. .800-461-7579
Buckhorn Inc
Milford, OH 800-543-4454
Cambro Manufacturing Company
Huntington Beach, CA 800-848-1555

Central Plastics Corporation
Shawnee, OK 800-654-3872
CKS Packaging
Atlanta, GA 800-800-4257
Convoy
Canton, OH 800-899-1583
Del-Tec Packaging
Greenville, SC 800-747-8683
Edge Paper Box Company
Cudahy, CA 323-771-7733
Emco Industrial Plastics
Cedar Grove, NJ 800-292-9906
Finn Industries
Ontario, CA 909-930-1500
Frankston Paper Box Company of Texas
Frankston, TX 903-876-2550
Fremont Die Cut Products
Fremont, OH 800-223-3177
Gary Plastic Packaging Corporation
Bronx, NY 800-221-8151
Great Northern Corporation
Appleton, WI 800-236-3671
Great Western Products
Ontario, CA 888-598-5588
Gulf Packaging Company
Safety Harbor, FL 800-749-3466
Imperial Plastics
Lakeville, MN 952-469-4951
Jarisch Paper Box Company
North Adams, MA 413-663-5396
Jupiter Mills Corporation
Roslyn, NY 800-853-5121
Kimball Companies
East Longmeadow, MA 413-525-1881
Midland Manufacturing Company
Monroe, IA 800-394-2625
Morris Transparent Box Company
East Providence, RI 401-438-6116
Nolon Industries
Mantua, OH 330-274-2283
Ockerlund Industries
Forest Park, IL 708-771-7707
Paragon Packaging
Ferndale, CA 888-615-0065
Parkway Plastics
Piscataway, NJ 732-752-3636
Parsons Manufacturing Corp.
Menlo Park, CA 650-324-4726
Peerless Packages
Cleveland, OH 216-464-3620
Pelco Packaging Corporation
Stirling, NJ 908-647-3500
Penn Products
Portland, CT 800-490-7366
Plastic Packaging Corporation
Hickory, NC 828-328-2466
Prestige Plastics Corporation
Delta, BC 604-930-2931
Prolon
Port Gibson, MS 888-480-9828
Quantum Storage Systems
Miami, FL 800-685-4665
RC Molding Inc.
Greer, SC 864-879-7279
Regal Plastic Company
Mission, KS 800-852-1556
Reliance-Paragon
Philadelphia, PA 215-743-1231
Ropak
Oak Brook, IL 800-527-2267
Saeplast Canada
St John, NB 800-567-3966
Semco Plastic Company
Saint Louis, MO 314-487-4557
Sharpsville Container
Sharpsville, PA 800-645-1248
Snyder Industries Inc.
Lincoln, NE 800-351-1363
Spartech Plastics
Portage, WI 800-998-7123
Tectonics
Westmoreland, NH 603-352-8894
The Piqua Paper Box Company
Piqua, OH 800-536-2136
Thermodynamics
Commerce City, CO 800-627-9037
Thermodyne International
Ontario, CA 909-923-9945
Tri-State Plastics
Henderson, KY 270-826-8361
Tulip Corporation
Milwaukee, WI 414-963-3120
Visual Packaging Corporation
Haskell, NJ 973-835-7055
WES Plastics
Richmond Hill, ON 905-508-1546
Wilks Precision Instrument Company
Union Bridge, MD 410-775-7917
Wiltec
Leominster, MA 978-537-1497
Zero Corporation
Monson, MA 413-267-5561

Silverware

Gates Manufacturing Company
Saint Louis, MO 800-237-9226
Lakeside Manufacturing
Milwaukee, WI 888-558-8574
Leer Limited Partnership
New Lisbon, WI 800-766-5337
McGraw Box Company
Mc Graw, NY 607-836-6465
Rubbermaid Commercial Products
Winchester, VA 800-336-9880
Supreme Metal
Alpharetta, GA 800-645-2526

Waste

Anova
St Louis, MO 800-231-1327
Bennett Manufacturing Company
Alden, NY 800-345-2142
Continental Commercial Products
Bridgeton, MO 800-325-1051
Erwyn Products Company
Morganville, NJ 800-331-9208
Ex-Cell Kaiser
Franklin Park, IL 847-451-0451
Frem Corporation
Worcester, MA 508-791-3152
Glaro
Hauppauge, NY 631-234-1717
Hodge Manufacturing Company
Springfield, MA 800-262-4634
Intrex
Bethel, CT 203-792-7400
J.V. Reed & Company
Louisville, KY 877-258-7333
Lakeside Manufacturing
Milwaukee, WI 888-558-8574
United Receptacle
Pottsville, PA 800-233-0314

Wirebound

Corbett Package Company
Wilmington, NC 800-334-0684
Elberta Crate & Box Company
Carpentersville, IL 888-672-9260
Franklin Crates
Micanopy, FL 352-466-3141
Gulf Arizona Packaging
Humble, TX 800-364-3887
Gulf Systems
Oklahoma City, OK 405-528-2293
Gulf Systems
Brownsville, TX 800-217-4853
Gulf Systems
Oklahoma City, OK 800-364-3887
Gulf Systems
Arlington, TX 817-261-1915
Herche Warehouse
Denver, CO 303-371-8186
L&H Wood Manufacturing Company
Farmington, MI 248-474-9000
Milan Box Corporation
Milan, TN 800-225-8057
Wisconsin Box Company
Wausau, WI 800-876-6658

Wooden

A.M. Loveman Lumber & Box Company
Nashville, TN 615-297-1397
American Box Corporation
Lisbon, OH 330-424-8055
Auto Pallets-Boxes
Lathrup Village, MI 800-875-2699
Buckeye Group
South Charleston, OH 937-462-8361
Burgess Manufacturing ofOklahoma
Guthrie, OK 800-804-1913
Caravan Packaging
Cleveland, OH 440-243-4100
Cassel Box & Lumber Company
Grafton, WI 262-377-4420
Cedar Box Company
Minneapolis, MN 612-332-4287
Century Box Company
Chicago, IL 773-847-7070
Champlin Company
Hartford, CT 800-458-5261
Coastal Pallet Corporation
Bridgeport, CT 203-333-6222
Corinth Products
Corinth, ME 207-285-3387
Corrugated Inner-Pak Corporation
Conshohocken, PA 610-825-0200
Cush-Pak Container Corporation
Henderson, TX 903-657-0555
D&M Pallet Company
Neshkoro, WI 920-293-4616
Davis Brothers Produce Boxes
Evergreen, NC 910-654-4913
Denver Reel & Pallet Company
Denver, CO 303-321-1920
Desert Box & Supply Corporation
Thermal, CA 760-399-5161
Die Cut Specialties
Savage, MN 952-890-7590
Donnelly Industries, Inc
Wayne, NJ 973-672-1800
Dufeck Manufacturing Company
Denmark, WI 888-603-9663
Eichler Wood Products
Laurys Station, PA 610-262-6749
Farmers Co-op Elevator Co.
Hudsonville, MI 800-439-9859
Fehlig Brothers Box & Lumber Company
St Louis, MO 314-241-6900
Fox Valley Wood Products
Kaukauna, WI 920-766-4069
Frobisher Industries
Waterborough, NB 506-362-2198
Frye's Measure Mill
Wilton, NH 603-654-6581
Gates
West Peterborough, NH 888-543-6316
Gatewood Products LLC
Parkersburg, WV 800-827-5461
H. Arnold Wood Turning
Tarrytown, NY 888-314-0088
Hampton Roads Box Company
Suffolk, VA 757-934-2355
Hanson Box & Lumber Company
Wakefield, MA 617-245-0358
Harbor Pallet Company
Anaheim, CA 714-533-4940
Heritage Packaging
Victor, NY 585-742-3310
Herkimer Pallet & Wood Products Company
Herkimer, NY 315-866-4591
Hinchcliff Products Company
Strongsville, OH 440-238-5200
Horn Packaging Corporation
Lancaster, MA 800-832-7020
Hunter Woodworks
Carson, CA 800-966-4751
Industrial Contracting &Rigging Company
Mahwah, NJ 888-427-7444
Industrial Hardwood
Perrysburg, OH 419-666-2503
Industrial Lumber & Packaging
Spring Lake, MI 616-842-1457
Industrial WoodFab & Packaging Company
Riverview, MI 734-284-4808
Jacksonville Box & Woodwork Company
Jacksonville, FL 800-683-2699
Jupiter Mills Corporation
Roslyn, NY 800-853-5121
Kelley Wood Products
Fitchburg, MA 978-345-7531
Kelly Box & Packaging Corporation
Fort Wayne, IN 260-432-4570
Ketch
Wichita, KS 800-766-3777
Killington Wood ProductsCompany
Rutland, VT 802-773-9111
Kimball Companies
East Longmeadow, MA 413-525-1881
Kontane
Charleston, SC 843-352-0011
L&H Wood Manufacturing Company
Farmington, MI 248-474-9000

Lester Box & Manufacturing
Long Beach, CA 562-437-5123
Longhorn Imports
Irving, TX 800-641-8348
Luke's Almond Acres
Reedley, CA 559-638-3483
Lumber & Things
Keyser, WV 800-296-5656
Manufacturers Wood Supply Company
Cleveland, OH 216-771-7848
Marshall Boxes
Rochester, NY 585-458-7432
Maull-Baker Box Company
Brookfield, WI 414-463-1290
Maypak
Wayne, NJ 973-696-0780
McGraw Box Company
Mc Graw, NY 607-836-6465
McIntosh Box & Pallet Company
East Syracuse, NY 800-219-9552
Meriden Box Company
Southington, CT 860-621-7141
Michiana Box & Crate
Niles, MI 800-677-6372
Milan Box Corporation
Milan, TN 800-225-8057
Moorecraft Box & Crate
Tarboro, NC 252-823-2510
Nefab Packaging, Inc.
Coppell, TX 800-322-4425
New Mexico Products
Albuquerque, NM 877-345-7864
Oak Creek Pallet Company
Milwaukee, WI 414-762-7170
Ockerlund Industries
Forest Park, IL 708-771-7707
Pack-Rite
Newington, CT 860-953-0120
Packing Material Company
Southfield, MI 248-489-7000
Pallox Incorporated
Onsted, MI 517-456-4101
Perfect Packaging Company
Perrysburg, OH 419-874-3167
Precision Wood of Hawaii
Vancouver, WA 808-682-2055
Pruitt's Packaging Services
Grand Rapids, MI 800-878-0553
Reading Box Company
Reading, PA 610-372-7411
Red River Lumber Company
Saint Helena, CA 707-963-1251
Remmey Wood Products
Southampton, PA 215-355-3335
Roddy Products PackagingCompany
Aldan, PA 610-623-7040
Romanow Container Inc
Westwood, MA 781-320-9200
Saint Charles Lumber Products
St Charles, MI 989-865-9915
Seattle-Tacoma Box Co.
Kent, WA 253-854-9700
Seattle-Tacoma Box Company
Kent, WA 253-854-9700
Seymour Woodenware Company
Seymour, WI 920-833-6551
Smalley Package Company
Berryville, VA 540-955-2550
Smith Packaging
Mississauga, ON 905-564-6640
Smith Pallet Company
Hatfield, AR 870-389-6184
Southern Pallet
Memphis, TN 901-942-4603
Spring Wood Products
Geneva, OH 440-466-1135
St. Pierre Box & Lumber Company
Canton, CT 860-693-2089
Stearnswood
Hutchinson, MN 800-657-0144
Tampa Pallet Company
Tampa, FL 813-626-5700
Technipack, Inc.
Le Sueur, MN 507-665-6658
The Original Lincoln Logs
Chestertown, NY 800-833-2461
Thunder Pallet
Theresa, WI 800-354-0643
Treen Box & Pallet Corporation
Bensalem, PA 215-639-5100
Vandereems ManufacturingCompany
Hawthorne, NJ 973-427-2355
Volk Packaging Corporation
Biddeford, ME 800-341-0208
W.W. Babcock Company
Bath, NY 607-776-3341
Wisconsin Box Company
Wausau, WI 800-876-6658
WNC Pallet & Forest Products
Candler, NC 828-667-5426
Xtreme Beverages, LLC
Dana Point, CA 949-495-7929

Cans

Aluminum

Ball Corporation
Broomfield, CO 920-261-5105
Can Corporation of America
Blandon, PA 610-926-3044
CCL Container
Toronto, ON 416-756-8500
Crown Holdings, Inc.
Philadelphia, PA 215-698-5100
IMO Foods
Yarmouth, NS 902-742-3519
Metal Container Corporation
St Louis, MO 314-957-9500
Montebello Packaging
Hawkesbury, ON 613-632-7096
Rexam Beverage Can Company
Chicago, IL 773-399-3000
Schroeder Sewing Technologies
San Marcos, CA 760-591-9733
US Can Company
Rosedale, MD 800-436-8021

Beer & Ale

Crown Cork & Seal Company
Philadelphia, PA 215-698-5100
Metal Container Corporation
St Louis, MO 314-957-9500
Rexam Beverage Can Company
Chicago, IL 773-399-3000

Creamery

Schroeder Sewing Technologies
San Marcos, CA 760-591-9733

Ice Cream

Armbrust Paper Tubes
Chicago, IL 773-586-3232
Independent Can Company
Belcamp, MD 909-923-6150
Negus Container & Packaging
Madison, WI 888-241-7482

Milk

Schroeder Sewing Technologies
San Marcos, CA 760-591-9733

Tin

Bertels Can Company
Belcamp, MD 410-272-0090
Consolidated Can
Paramount, CA 888-793-2199
Container Supply Company
Garden Grove, CA 714-891-4896
Crown Cork & Seal Company
Philadelphia, PA 215-698-5100
Crown Holdings, Inc.
Philadelphia, PA 215-698-5100
GED, LLC
Laurel, DE 302-856-1756
Independent Can Company
Belcamp, MD 909-923-6150
J.L. Clark
Rockford, IL 815-962-8861
Jupiter Mills Corporation
Roslyn, NY 800-853-5121
Quality Containers
Weston, ON 416-749-6247
Rexam Beverage Can Company
Chicago, IL 773-399-3000
Schroeder Sewing Technologies
San Marcos, CA 760-591-9733
US Can Company
Rosedale, MD 800-436-8021
Xtreme Beverages, LLC
Dana Point, CA 949-495-7929

Caps

Bottle, Can & Jar

AHP Machine & Tool Company
Lancaster, OH 740-681-6709
All American Containers
Medley, FL 305-887-0797
Alpha Packaging
Saint Louis, MO 800-421-4772
Berry Plastics Corporati
Evansville, IN 812-424-2904
California Vibratory Feeders
Anaheim, CA 800-354-0972
Clayton Corporation
Fenton, MO 800-729-8220
Consolidated Can
Paramount, CA 888-793-2199
Crown Cork & Seal Company
Philadelphia, PA 215-698-5100
Danbury Plastics
Cumming, GA 678-455-7391
E.S. Robbins Corporation
Muscle Shoals, AL 800-800-2235
Eastern Cap & Closure Company
Baltimore, MD 410-327-5640
Greenfield Packaging
White Plains, NY 914-993-0233
Ideal Wire Works
Alhambra, CA 626-282-1302
Innovative Molding
Sebastopol, CA 707-829-2666
Keystone Adjustable Cap
Pennsauken, NJ 800-663-5439
Label Makers
Pleasant Prairie, WI 800-208-3331
Landis Plastics
Alsip, IL 708-396-1470
LMK Containers
Centerville, UT 626-821-9984
Maugus Manufacturing Company
Lancaster, PA 717-299-5681
Metal Container Corporation
St Louis, MO 314-957-9500
Nagel Paper & Box Company
Saginaw, MI 800-292-3654
Nyman Manufacturing Company
Rumford, RI 401-438-3410
Olcott Plastics
Saint Charles, IL 888-313-5277
Orca
New Britain, CT 860-223-4180
Parkway Plastics
Piscataway, NJ 732-752-3636
Partola Packaging
Naperville, IL 800-727-8652
Phoenix Closures
Naperville, IL 630-544-3475
RoMatic Manufacturing Company
Southbury, CT 203-264-8203
RXI Silgan Specialty Plastics
Triadelphia, WV 304-547-9100
Silgan Containers
Woodland Hills, CA 818-710-3700
Silgan Plastics Canada
Chesterfield, MO 800-274-5426
Smith-Lee Company
Oshkosh, WI 800-327-9774
Snapware
Fullerton, CA 800-334-3062
SONOCO
Hartsville, SC 800-576-6626
Sonoco Paper Board Specialties
Norcross, GA 800-264-7494
Van Blarcom Closures
Brooklyn, NY 718-855-3810
Wheaton Plastic Containers
Millville, NJ 856-825-1400

Carriers

Food

B&H Labeling Systems
Ceres, CA 209-537-5785
Cambro Manufacturing Company
Huntington Beach, CA 800-848-1555
Carlisle Food Service Products
Oklahoma City, OK 800-654-8210

Fold-Pak Corporation
Newark, NY 315-331-3159
Great Western Products
Ontario, CA. 888-598-5588
Hank Rivera Associates
Dearborn, MI 313-581-8300
Igloo Products
Katy, TX 800-364-5566
ITW Hi-Cone
Itasca, IL. 630-438-5300
Keeper Thermal Bag Company
Crystal Lake, IL 800-765-9244
Lawson Mardon Radisson
Baldwinsville, NY 800-847-5677
Naltex
Austin, TX. 800-531-5112
O-I
Perrysburg, OH
Plastocon
Oconomowoc, WI. 800-966-0103
Polyfoam Packers Corporation
Arlington Hts, IL 800-323-7442
Rubbermaid Commercial Products
Winchester, VA 800-336-9880
Service Manufacturing
Aurora, IL 888-325-2788
Sterling Paper Company
Philadelphia, PA 215-744-5350
Thermal Bags by Ingrid
Gilberts, IL 800-622-5560
Vollrath Company
Sheboygan, WI 920-457-4851

Milk Bottle

B&H Labeling Systems
Ceres, CA 209-537-5785
Graphic Packaging Corporation
Golden, CO 800-677-2886
Lawson Mardon Radisson
Baldwinsville, NY 800-847-5677

Cartons

A La Carte
Chicago, IL 800-722-2370
Accurate Paper Box Company
Knoxville, TN 865-690-0311
AdPro
Solon, OH 440-542-1111
Alcan Packaging
Baie D'Urfe, QC 514-457-4555
Americraft Carton
Saint Paul, MN 651-227-6655
Americraft Carton
Prairie Village, KS 913-387-3700
Artistic Carton
Auburn, IN 260-925-6060
Artistic Carton Company
Elgin, IL 847-741-0247
Atlas Packaging & Displays Inc
Miami, FL. 800-662-0630
B.F. Nelson Folding Corporation
Savage, MN. 800-328-2380
Boelter Industries
Winona, MN 507-452-2315
C.W. Zumbiel Company
Cincinnati, OH 513-531-3600
Cardinal Container Corporation
Indianapolis, IN 800-899-2715
Cardinal Packaging Products Inc.
Crystal Lake, IL 866-216-4942
Carpenter-Hayes Paper Box Company
East Hampton, CT. 203-267-4436
Carton Service
Shelby, OH 800-533-7744
Central Paper Box
Kansas City, MO. 816-753-3126
Central Plastics Corporation
Shawnee, OK 800-654-3872
City Box Company
Aurora, IL. 773-277-5500
CKS Packaging
Atlanta, GA. 800-800-4257
Cleveland Specialties Company
Loveland, OH 513-677-9787
Climax Manufacturing Company
Lowville, NY 800-225-4629
Coast Paper Box Company
San Bernardino, CA 909-382-3475
Color Box
Richmond, IN 765-966-7588
Columbus Container
Columbus, IN 812-376-9301
Columbus Paperbox Company
Columbus, OH 800-968-0797
Commencement Bay Corrugated
Orting, WA 253-845-3100
Commercial Corrugated Corporation
Baltimore, MD 800-242-8861
Complete Packaging & Shipping Supplies
Freeport, NY. 877-269-3236
Connecticut Container Corporation
North Haven, CT. 203-248-2161
Containair Packaging Corporation
Paterson, NJ 888-276-6500
Corrobilt Container Company
Livermore, CA 925-373-0880
Corson Manufacturing Company
Lockport, NY 716-434-8871
Curtis Packaging Corporation
Sandy Hook, CT 203-426-5861
Cush-Pak Container Corporation
Henderson, TX 903-657-0555
Day Manufacturing Company
Sherman, TX. 903-893-1138
Diamond Packaging
Rochester, NY. 800-333-4079
Donnelly Industries, Inc
Wayne, NJ. 973-672-1800
Dorado Carton Company
Dorado, PR 787-796-1670
Eagle Box Company
Farmingdale, NY 212-255-3860
EB Box Company
Richmond Hill, ON. 800-513-2269
Elopak
New Hudson, MI. 248-486-4600
Eureka Paper Box Company
Williamsport, PA. 570-326-9147
Farmers Co-op Elevator Co.
Hudsonville, MI 800-439-9859
Field Container Company
Elk Grove Vlg, IL. 847-437-1700
Finn Industries
Ontario, CA. 909-930-1500
Flashfold Carton
Fort Wayne, IN 260-423-9431
Flour City Press-Pack Company
Minneapolis, MN 952-831-1265
Foam Packaging
Footsville, WI. 608-876-4217
Fold-Pak Corporation
Newark, NY 315-331-3159
Folding Carton/Flexible Packaging
North Hollywood, CA 818-896-3449
Food Pak Corporation
San Mateo, CA. 650-341-6559
Four M Manufacturing Group
San Jose, CA. 408-998-1141
Friendly City Box Company
Johnstown, PA. 814-266-6287
Fulton-Denver Company
Denver, CO 800-776-6715
Gaylord Container Corporation
Tampa, FL. 813-621-3591
Gibraltar Packaging Group
Hastings, NE 402-463-1366
Goldman Manufacturing Company
Detroit, MI 313-834-5535
Graphic Packaging Corporation
Golden, CO 800-677-2886
Green Bay Packaging
Green Bay, WI. 920-433-5111
Greenfield Packaging
White Plains, NY 914-993-0233
Greif Brothers Corporation
Cleveland, OH 800-424-0342
Grigsby Brothers Paper Box Manufacturers
Portland, OR 866-233-4690
Gulf Arizona Packaging
Humble, TX 800-364-3887
Gulf States Paper Corporation
Tuscaloosa, AL 205-562-5000
Gulf Systems
Oklahoma City, OK 405-528-2293
Gulf Systems
Brownsville, TX 800-217-4853
Gulf Systems
Oklahoma City, OK 800-364-3887
Gulf Systems
Arlington, TX 817-261-1915
H.J. Jones & Sons
London, ON 800-667-0476
Hager Containers
Carrollton, TX. 972-417-7660
Herche Warehouse
Denver, CO 303-371-8186
Hope Paper Box Company
Pawtucket, RI 401-724-5700
Hunter Packaging Corporation
South Elgin, IL 800-428-4747
Impress Industries
Emmaus, PA 610-967-6027
Indiana Carton Company
Bremen, IN 800-348-2390
Inland Consumer Packaging
Harrington, DE 302-398-4211
Innovative Folding Carton Company
South Plainfield, NJ 908-757-0205
Instabox
Calgary, AB. 800-482-6173
International Paper Co.
Memphis, TN 800-207-4003
Jamestown Container Corporation
Macedonia, OH. 800-247-1033
Jarisch Paper Box Company
North Adams, MA 413-663-5396
Jordan Paper Box Company
Chicago, IL 773-287-5362
Jupiter Mills Corporation
Roslyn, NY 800-853-5121
KapStone Paper and Packaging Corporation
Northbrook, IL 847-239-8800
Kelly Box & Packaging Corporation
Fort Wayne, IN 260-432-4570
Kendel
Countryside, IL 800-323-1100
Laminated Paper Products
San Jose, CA. 408-888-0880
Lawrence Paper Company
Lawrence, KS 785-843-8111
Lawson Mardon Radisson
Baldwinsville, NY 800-847-5677
Lexel
Fort Worth, TX 817-332-4061
Liberty Carton Company
Minneapolis, MN 800-818-2698
Lin Pac Plastics
Roswell, GA 770-751-6006
Lowell Paper Box Company
Nashua, NH. 603-595-0700
Loy-Lange Box Company
Saint Louis, MO 800-886-4712
LTI Printing
Sturgis, MI 269-651-7574
M&G Packaging Corporation
Floral Park, NY. 800-240-5288
Malnove Packaging Systems
Omaha, NE 800-228-9877
Mannkraft Corporation
Newark, NJ 973-589-7400
Marcus Carton Company
Melville, NY 631-752-4200
Marfred Industries
Sun Valley, CA 800-529-5156
Marion Paper Box Company
Marion, IN. 765-664-6435
Maro Paper Products Company
Bellwood, IL. 708-649-9982
Massachusetts Container Corporation
Marlborough, MA. 508-481-1100
Maull-Baker Box Company
Brookfield, WI 414-463-1290
Maypak
Wayne, NJ. 973-696-0780
Melville Plastics
Haw River, NC 336-578-5800
Merchants Publishing Company
Kalamazoo, MI 269-345-1175
Mid Cities Paper Box Company
Downey, CA 877-277-6272
Midlands Packaging Corporation
Lincoln, NE. 402-464-9124
Neff Packaging Solutions
Mason, OH 800-445-4383
New York Corrugated Box Company
Paterson, NJ 973-742-5000
Northeast Container Corporation
Dumont, NJ. 201-385-6200
Nosco
Waukegan, IL 847-360-4806
Oakes Carton Company
Kalamazoo, MI 269-381-6022
Old Dominion Box Company
Burlington, NC 336-226-4491

Old Dominion Box Company
Madison Heights, VA 434-929-6701
Oracle Packaging
Toledo, OH 800-952-9536
Packaging Solutions
Los Altos Hills, CA 650-917-1022
Packrite Packaging
Archdale, NC. 336-431-1111
Pactiv LLC
Lake Forest, IL 888-828-2850
Paper Products Company
Cincinnati, OH 513-921-4717
PARTA
Kent, OH 800-543-5781
Pater & Associates
Cincinnati, OH 513- 24- 215
Peerless Cartons
Bartlett, IL 312-226-7952
Premier Packages
Saint Louis, MO 800-466-6588
Prestige Plastics Corporation
Delta, BC. 604-930-2931
Quantum Storage Systems
Miami, FL 800-685-4665
Rand-Whitney Container Corporation
Worcester, MA 508-791-2301
Reliance-Paragon
Philadelphia, PA 215-743-1231
Rex Carton Company
Chicago, IL 773-581-4115
Rice Packaging
Ellington, CT 800-367-6725
RJR Packaging, Inc.
Oakland, CA 510-638-5901
Rock Tenn/Alliance Group
Tullahoma, TN 931-455-3535
Rock-Tenn Company
Norcross, GA 608-223-6272
Rock-Tenn Company
Norcross, GA 770-448-2193
Rose City Printing & Packaging
Vancouver, WA 800-704-8693
Royal Box Group
Cicero, IL 708-656-2020
Rudd Container Corporation
Chicago, IL 773-847-7600
Rusken Packaging
Cullman, AL 256-734-0092
San Diego Paper Box Company
Spring Valley, CA 619-660-9566
Schroeder Sewing Technologies
San Marcos, CA 760-591-9733
Scott & Daniells
Portland, CT 860-342-1932
Seaboard Carton Company
Downers Grove, IL 708-344-0575
Security Packaging
North Bergen, NJ 201-854-1955
Set Point Paper Company
Mansfield, MA 800-225-0501
Sheboygan Paper Box Company
Sheboygan, WI 800-458-8373
Shippers Supply
Winnipeg, NB 800-661-5639
Shore Paper Box Company
Mardela Springs, MD 410-749-7125
Smith Packaging
Mississauga, ON 905-564-6640
Smurfit Stone Container
St Louis, MO 314-679-2300
Smurfit Stone Container
San Jose, CA 408-925-9391
Somerville Packaging
Scarborough, ON 416-291-1161
Somerville Packaging
Mississauga, ON 905-678-8211
Sonoco Flexible Packaging
Hartsville, SC 800-377-2692
Southern Champion Tray
Chattanooga, TN 800-468-2222
Southern Missouri Containers
Springfield, MO 800-999-7666
Southern Packaging Corporation
Bennettsville, SC 843-479-7154
Specialized Packaging London
London, ON 519-659-7011
Sphinx Adsorbents
Springfield, MA 800-388-0157
Spring Cove Container
Roaring Spring, PA 814-224-2222
St Joseph Packaging Inc
St Joseph, MO 800-383-3000
St. Louis Carton Company
Saint Louis, MO 314-241-0990
St. Pierre Box & Lumber Company
Canton, CT 860-693-2089
Standard Folding Cartons
Flushing, NY 718-335-5500
Stearnswood
Hutchinson, MN 800-657-0144
Sterling Paper Company
Philadelphia, PA 215-744-5350
Stone Container
Santa Fe Springs, CA 714-774-0100
Stoneway Carton Company
Mercer Island, WA 800-498-2185
Suburban Corrugated Box Company
Indianhead Park, IL 630-920-1230
Superior Quality Products
Schenectady, NY 800-724-1129
Tampa Corrugated Carton Company
Tampa, FL 813-623-5115
The Piqua Paper Box Company
Piqua, OH 800-536-2136
The Shelby Company
Cleveland, OH 800-842-1650
Thermodyne International
Ontario, CA 909-923-9945
Traub Container Corporation
Cleveland, OH 216-475-5100
UniPak
West Chester, PA 610-436-6600
Unique Boxes
Chicago, IL 800-281-1670
Universal Folding Box
East Orange, NJ 973-482-4300
Universal Folding Box Company
Hoboken, NJ 201-659-7373
Utah Paper Box Company
Salt Lake City, UT 801-363-0093
Victory Packaging, Inc.
Houston, TX 800-486-5606
VIP Real Estate Ltd
Chicago, IL 773-376-5000
Volk Packaging Corporation
Biddeford, ME 800-341-0208
Warren Packaging
San Bernardino, CA 909-888-7008
Weber Display & Packaging
Philadelphia, PA 215-426-3500
Welch Packaging
Elkhart, IN 574-295-2460
Western Container Company
Kansas City, MO 816-924-5700
Westvaco Corporation
Newark, DE 302-453-7200
Willamette Industries
Beaverton, OR 503-641-1131
Willard Packaging
Gaithersburg, MD 301-948-7700
Winchester Carton
Eutaw, AL 205-372-3337
Woodson Pallet
Anmoore, WV 304-623-2858
Wright Brothers Paper Box Company
Fond Du Lac, WI 920-921-8270
WS Packaging Group Inc
Green Bay, WI 920-866-6300
York Container Company
York, PA 717-757-7611

Closures & Closing Devices

AAMD
Liverpool, NY 800-887-4167
AHP Machine & Tool Company
Lancaster, OH 740-681-6709
All American Containers
Medley, FL 305-887-0797
Allendale Cork Company
Rye, NY 800-816-2675
Alliance Rubber Corporation
Hot Springs National Par, AR 800-626-5940
Alpha Packaging
Saint Louis, MO 800-421-4772
Amcor Twinpak
Dorval, QC 514-684-7070
American National Rubber
Ceredo, WV 304-453-1311
American Printpak
Sussex, WI 800-441-8003
American Star Cork Company
Woodside, NY 800-338-3581
Autoprod
Davenport, IA 563-391-1100
Bal Seal Engineering Company
Foothill Ranch, CA 800-366-1006
Ball Corporation
Broomfield, CO 920-261-5105
Bedford Industries
Worthington, MN 800-533-5314
Bericap North America, Inc.
CDN-Burlington, ON 905-634-2248
Berry Plastics
Evansville, IN 800-234-1930
Berry Plastics
Evansville, IN 812-424-2904
Berry Plastics Corporati
Evansville, IN 812-424-2904
Bettag & Associates
O Fallon, MO 800-325-0959
Blackhawk Molding Co, Inc
Addison, IL 800-222-7391
Browns International & Company
St. Laurent, QC 514-737-1326
Cameo Metal Products Inc
Brooklyn, NY 718-788-1106
Caraustar
Franklin, KY 270-586-9565
Carton Closing Company
Butler, PA 724-287-7759
Chaffee Company
Rocklin, CA 916-630-3980
Chase-Logeman Corporation
Greensboro, NC 336-665-0754
Clayton Corporation
Fenton, MO 800-729-8220
Cleveland Specialties Company
Loveland, OH 513-677-9787
Conax Buffalo Technologies
Buffalo, NY 800-223-2389
Consolidated Can
Paramount, CA 888-793-2199
Cork Specialties
Miami, FL 305-477-1506
Crandall Filling Machinery
Buffalo, NY 800-280-8551
Creative Packaging Corporation
Buffalo Grove, IL 847-459-1001
Cresthill Industries
Yonkers, NY 914-965-9510
Crown Cork & Seal Company
Philadelphia, PA 215-698-5100
Crown Holdings, Inc.
Philadelphia, PA 215-698-5100
Cup Pac Contract PackageRs
South Beloit, IL 877-347-9725
Danbury Plastics
Cumming, GA 678-455-7391
Dickey Manufacturing Company
St Charles, IL 630-584-2918
Diversified Capping Equipment
Perrysburg, OH 419-666-2566
E.T. Oakes Corporation
Hauppauge, NY 631-232-0002
Eastern Cap & Closure Company
Baltimore, MD 410-327-5640
Filler Specialties
Zeeland, MI 616-772-9235
Flex Products
Carlstadt, NJ 800-526-6273
Gallo Manufacturing Company
Racine, WI 262-752-9950
Gateway Plastics
Mequon, WI 262-242-2020
Gemini Plastic Films Corporation
Garfield, NJ 800-789-4732
General Press Corporation
Natrona Heights, PA 724-224-3500
Genpak
Peterborough, ON 800-461-1995
Greenfield Packaging
White Plains, NY 914-993-0233
Gulf Arizona Packaging
Humble, TX 800-364-3887
Gulf Systems
Oklahoma City, OK 405-528-2293
Gulf Systems
Brownsville, TX 800-217-4853
Gulf Systems
Oklahoma City, OK 800-364-3887
Gulf Systems
Arlington, TX 817-261-1915
H&N Packaging
Colmar, PA 215-997-6222
Herche Warehouse
Denver, CO 303-371-8186

Highland Plastics
Mira Loma, CA 800-368-0491
Innovative Molding
Sebastopol, CA 707-829-2666
IPEC
New Castle, PA 800-377-4732
Ipec
New Castle, PA 800-377-4732
Ives-Way Products
Round Lake Beach, IL 847-740-0658
J.E. Roy
St Claire, QC 418-883-2711
J.L. Clark
Rockford, IL 815-962-8861
Kapak Corporation
Minneapolis, MN 952-541-0730
Keystone Adjustable Cap
Pennsauken, NJ 800-663-5439
Kwik-Lok Corporation
Yakima, WA 800-688-5945
L&H Wood Manufacturing Company
Farmington, MI 248-474-9000
Label Makers
Pleasant Prairie, WI 800-208-3331
Landis Plastics
Alsip, IL 708-396-1470
Leco Plastics
Hackensack, NJ 201-343-3330
LMK Containers
Centerville, UT 626-821-9984
Maugus Manufacturing Company
Lancaster, PA 717-299-5681
Metal Container Corporation
St Louis, MO 314-957-9500
Molded Container Corporation
Portland, OR 503-233-8601
Montebello Packaging
Hawkesbury, ON 613-632-7096
New Jersey Wire Stitching Machine Company
Cherry Hill, NJ 856-428-2572
Nyman Manufacturing Company
Rumford, RI 401-438-3410
O-I
Perrysburg, OH
Olcott Plastics
Saint Charles, IL 888-313-5277
On-Hand Adhesives
Lake Zurich, IL 800-323-5158
Orca
New Britain, CT 860-223-4180
Package Containers
Canby, OR 800-266-5806
Packaging Associates
Randolph, NJ 973-252-8890
Par-Kan Company
Silver Lake, IN 800-291-5487
Parkway Plastics
Piscataway, NJ 732-752-3636
PARTA
Kent, OH 800-543-5781
Partola Packaging
Naperville, IL 800-727-8652
Perl Packaging Systems
Middlebury, CT 800-864-2853
Phoenix Closures
Naperville, IL 630-544-3475
Poly-Seal Corporation
Baltimore, MD 410-633-1990
Portola Packaging
Naperville, IL 800-767-8652
Qosina Corporation
Edgewood, NY 631-242-3000
Reotemp Instrument Corporation
San Diego, CA 800-648-7737
Richards Packaging
Memphis, TN 800-361-6453
Richards Packaging
Memphis, TN 800-583-0327
Rieke Packaging Systems
Auburn, IN 260-925-3700
RoMatic Manufacturing Company
Southbury, CT 203-264-8203
Scheidegger
Yorktown Heights, NY 914-245-7850
Schiffmayer Plastics Corp.
Algonquin, IL 847-658-8140
Signature Packaging
West Orange, NJ 800-376-2299
Silgan Plastics Canada
Chesterfield, MO 800-274-5426
Smith-Lee Company
Oshkosh, WI 800-327-9774
SONOCO
Hartsville, SC 800-576-6626
Sonoco Paper Board Specialties
Norcross, GA 800-264-7494
Stoffel Seals Corporation
Tallapoosa, GA 800-422-8247
Stormax International
Concord, NH 800-874-7629
T&T Industries
Fort Mohave, AZ 800-437-6246
Techform
Mount Airy, NC 336-789-2115
The Staplex Company
Brooklyn, NY 800-221-0822
Tipper Tie
Apex, NC 919-362-8811
Trans Container Corporation
Upland, CA 909-985-2750
Trent Corporation
Trenton, NJ 609-587-7515
US Bottlers Machinery Company
Charlotte, NC 704-588-4750
Van Blarcom Closures
Brooklyn, NY 718-855-3810
Vivid Packaging Inc
Cleveland, OH 877-752-2250
Weatherchem Corporation
Twinsburg, OH 330-425-4206
Wheaton Plastic Containers
Millville, NJ 856-825-1400
White Cap
Downers Grove, IL 800-515-1565
Zero Corporation
Monson, MA 413-267-5561

Containers

A La Carte
Chicago, IL 800-722-2370
A-Z Factory Supply
Schiller Park, IL 800-323-4511
Abbott Industries
Paterson, NJ
Accurate Paper Box Company
Knoxville, TN 865-690-0311
Aces Manufacturing Company
Sullivan, MO 800-325-6138
Aco Container Systems
Pickering, ON 800-542-9942
Acryline
North Attleboro, MA 508-695-7124
AdPro
Solon, OH 440-542-1111
Adrian Fabricators/Cargotainer
Adrian, MI 800-221-3794
Aero Tec Laboratories/ATL
Ramsey, NJ 800-526-5330
Alcan Packaging
Baie D'Urfe, QC 514-457-4555
All American Containers
Medley, FL 305-887-0797
All American Poly Corporation
Piscataway, NJ 800-526-3551
Allflex Packaging Products
Ambler, PA 800-448-2467
Alpack
Centerville, MA 508-771-9131
Althor Products
Bethel, CT 800-688-2693
AMCO Corporation
City of Industry, CA 626-855-2550
Amcor Twinpak
Dorval, QC 514-684-7070
American Box Corporation
Lisbon, OH 330-424-8055
American Production Company
Redwood City, CA 650-368-5334
Americraft Carton
Saint Paul, MN 651-227-6655
Ample Industries
Franklin, OH 888-818-9700
Anchor Packaging
Ballwin, MO 800-467-3900
Anova
St Louis, MO 800-231-1327
AR Arena Products
Rochester, NY 800-836-2528
Arkansas Glass Container Corporation
Jonesboro, AR 800-527-4527
Armbrust Paper Tubes
Chicago, IL 773-586-3232
Arthur Corporation
Huron, OH 419-433-7202
Artistic Carton
Auburn, IN 260-925-6060
Artistic Carton Company
Elgin, IL 847-741-0247
ATD-American Company
Wyncote, PA 800-523-2300
Atlas Case
Denver, CO 888-325-7102
Atlas Equipment Company
Kansas City, MO 800-842-9188
Atlas Packaging & Displays Inc
Miami, FL 800-662-0630
Auto Pallets-Boxes
Lathrup Village, MI 800-875-2699
B Way Corporation
Atlanta, GA 800-527-2267
B.A.G. Corporation
Dallas, TX 800-331-9200
B.C. Holland
Dousman, WI 262-965-2939
B.F. Nelson Folding Corporation
Savage, MN 800-328-2380
Bakers Choice Products
Beacon Falls, CT 203-720-1000
Bal/Foster Glass Container Company
Port Allegany, PA 814-642-2521
Ball Corporation
Broomfield, CO 920-261-5105
Ball Foster Glass
Fairfield, CA 707-863-4061
Ball Foster Glass Container Company
Sapulpa, OK 918-224-1440
Ball Glass Container Corporation
El Monte, CA 626-448-9831
Bardes Plastics
Milwaukee, WI 800-558-5161
Bareny Packaging Corporation
Menomonee Falls, WI 262-251-8787
Bayhead Products Corporation
Dover, NH 800-229-4323
Bell Packaging Corporation
Marion, IN 800-382-0153
Belleview
Brookline, NH 603-878-1583
Bennett Manufacturing Company
Alden, NY 800-345-2142
Bergen Barrel & Drum Company
Kearny, NJ 201-998-3500
Berlin Fruit Box Company
Berlin Heights, OH 800-877-7721
Berlon Industries
Hustisford, WI 800-899-3580
Berry Plastics
Evansville, IN 800-234-1930
Berry Plastics
Evansville, IN 812-424-2904
Berry Plastics Corporation
Evansville, IN 800-822-2342
Berry Plastics Corporation
Evansville, IN 812-424-2904
Bertels Can Company
Belcamp, MD 410-272-0090
Best
Brunswick, OH 800-827-9237
Boelter Industries
Winona, MN 507-452-2315
Boise Cascade Corporation
Burley, ID 208-678-3531
Bonar Plastics
West Chicago, IL 800-295-3725
Boxes.com
Livingston, NJ 201-646-9050
Brenner Tank
Fond Du Lac, WI 800-558-9750
Brewer-Cantelmo Company
New York, NY 212-244-4600
Brooks Barrel Company
Baltimore, MD 800-398-2766
Browns International & Company
St. Laurent, QC 514-737-1326
Bruni Glass Packaging
Lachine Montreal, QC 877-771-7856
Buckhorn Canada
Brampton, ON 800-461-7579
Buckhorn Inc
Milford, OH 800-543-4454
Buffet Enhancements International
Fairhope, AL 251-990-6119
Bulk Lift International
Carpentersville, IL 800-992-6372
Bulk Pack
Monroe, LA 800-498-4215

Bulk Sak
Malvern, AR 501-332-8745
Burd & Fletcher
Independence, MO 800-821-2776
Burgess Manufacturing ofOklahoma
Guthrie, OK 800-804-1913
Burrows Paper Corporation
Little Falls, NY 800-732-1933
C&L Wood Products
Hartselle, AL 800-483-2035
C&M Fine Pak
San Bernardino, CA 800-232-5959
Calzone Case Company
Bridgeport, CT 800-243-5152
Cambro Manufacturing Company
Huntington Beach, CA 800-848-1555
Can Corporation of America
Blandon, PA 610-926-3044
Cantwell-Cleary Company
Landover, MD 301-773-9800
Capital City Container Corporation
Buda, TX 512-312-1222
Capitol Carton Company
Sacramento, CA 916-388-7848
Capitol City Container Corporation
Indianapolis, IN 800-233-5145
Cardinal Packaging
Evansville, IN 812-424-2904
Cardinal Packaging Products Inc.
Crystal Lake, IL 866-216-4942
Carlisle Food Service Products
Oklahoma City, OK 800-654-8210
Carolina Container Company
High Point, NC 800-627-0825
Carpet City Paper Box Company
Amsterdam, NY 518-842-5430
Carrier Transicold
Farmington, CT 800-227-7437
Carson Industries
Pomona, CA 800-735-5566
Carton Service
Shelby, OH 800-533-7744
CCW Products, Inc.
Arvada, CO 303-427-9663
Cecor
Verona, WI 800-356-9042
Cedar Box Company
Minneapolis, MN 612-332-4287
Central Bag & Burlap Company
Denver, CO 800-783-1224
Central Plastics Corporation
Shawnee, OK 800-654-3872
Century Box Company
Chicago, IL 773-847-7070
Chambers Container Company
Gastonia, NC 704-377-6317
Champlin Company
Hartford, CT 800-458-5261
Charles Engineering & Service
Belcamp, MD 410-272-1090
Chem-Tainer Industries
West Babylon, NY 800-275-2436
Chem-Tainer Industries
West Babylon, NY 800-938-8896
Cherry's Industrial Equipment Corporation
Elk Grove Vlg, IL 800-350-0011
Chesapeake Packaging
Scranton, PA 570-342-9217
Chesapeake Packaging Company
Binghamton, NY 607-775-1550
Chili Plastics
Rochester, NY 585-889-4680
Cin-Made Packaging Group
Cincinnati, OH 513-681-3600
Cincinnati Foam Products
Cincinnati, OH 513-741-7722
City Box Company
Aurora, IL 773-277-5500
CKS Packaging
Atlanta, GA 800-800-4257
Clawson Container Company
Clarkston, MI 800-325-8700
Clearplass Containers
Penn Yan, NY 315-536-5690
Clearwater Paper Corporation
Spokane, WA 877-847-7831
Cleveland Canvas Goods Manufacturing Company
Cleveland, OH 216-361-4567
Clorox Company
Oakland, CA 888-271-7000
Coast Paper Box Company
San Bernardino, CA 909-382-3475

Coastal Pallet Corporation
Bridgeport, CT 203-333-6222
Colbert Packaging Corporation
Lake Forest, IL 847-367-5990
Cold Chain Technologies
Holliston, MA 800-370-8566
Collector's Gallery
Saint Charles, IL 800-346-3063
Color Box
Richmond, IN 765-966-7588
Color Carton
Bronx, NY 718-665-0840
Columbus Container
Columbus, IN 812-376-9301
Columbus Paperbox Company
Columbus, OH 800-968-0797
Commencement Bay Corrugated
Orting, WA 253-845-3100
Commercial Corrugated Corporation
Baltimore, MD 800-242-8861
Complete Packaging & Shipping Supplies
Freeport, NY 877-269-3236
Conductive Containers, I
New Hope, MN 800-327-2329
Connecticut Container Corporation
North Haven, CT 203-248-2161
Constar International
Trevose, PA 215-552-3700
Containair Packaging Corporation
Paterson, NJ 888-276-6500
Container Specialties
Melrose Park, IL 800-548-7513
Container Supply Company
Garden Grove, CA 714-891-4896
Containment Technology
St Gabriel, LA 800-388-2467
Contico Container
Norwalk, CA 562-921-9967
Continental Plastic Container
Dallas, TX 972-303-1825
Contour Packaging
Philadelphia, PA 215-457-1600
Convoy
Canton, OH 800-899-1583
Corbett Package Company
Wilmington, NC 800-334-0684
Corning Costar
Acton, MA 800-492-1110
Cornish Containers
Maumee, OH 419-893-7911
Corpak
San Juan, PR 787-787-9085
Corr-Pak Corporation
Mc Cook, IL 708-442-7806
Corrobilt Container Company
Livermore, CA 925-373-0880
Corrugated Inner-Pak Corporation
Conshohocken, PA 610-825-0200
Corrugated Packaging
Sarasota, FL 941-371-0000
Corson Manufacturing Company
Lockport, NY 716-434-8871
CPT
Edgerton, WI 608-884-2244
Craft Corrugated Box
New Bedford, MA 508-998-2115
Crate Ideas by Wilderness House
Cave Junction, OR 800-592-2206
Cream of the Valley Plastics
Arvada, CO 303-425-5499
Crespac Incorporated
Tucker, GA 800-438-1900
Crown Holdings, Inc.
Philadelphia, PA 215-698-5100
Crown Manufacturing Corporation
Waterford, CT 860-442-4325
CTK Plastics
Moose Jaw, SK 800-667-8847
Cumberland Container Corporation
Monterey, TN 931-839-2227
Curtis Packaging Corporation
Sandy Hook, CT 203-426-5861
Cush-Pak Container Corporation
Henderson, TX 903-657-0555
Custom Bottle of Connecticut
Naugatuck, CT 203-723-6661
Custom Stamping & Manufacturing
Portland, OR 503-238-3700
D&W Fine Pack
Lake Zurich, IL 800-323-0422
Dakota Corrugated Box
Sioux Falls, SD 605-332-3501

Dallas Container Corporation
Dallas, TX 214-381-7148
Dart Container Corporation
Mason, MI 800-248-5960
Davis Brothers Produce Boxes
Evergreen, NC 910-654-4913
Davis Core & Pad Company
Cave Spring, GA 800-235-7483
Day Lumber Company
Westfield, MA 413-568-3511
Day Manufacturing Company
Sherman, TX 903-893-1138
De Ster Corporation
Atlanta, GA 800-237-8270
Del-Tec Packaging
Greenville, SC 800-747-8683
Deline Box Company
Denver, CO 303-373-1430
Delta Container Corporation
New Orleans, LA 800-752-7292
Design Plastics
Omaha, NE 800-491-0786
Designers-Folding Box Corporation
Buffalo, NY 716-853-5141
Despro Manufacturing
Cedar Grove, NJ 800-292-9906
Diamond Packaging
Rochester, NY 800-333-4079
Display One
Hartford, WI 262-673-5880
Dixie Printing & Packaging
Glen Burnie, MD 800-433-4943
Donnelly Industries, Inc
Wayne, NJ 973-672-1800
Donovan Enterprises
Lagrange, GA 800-233-6180
Dorado Carton Company
Dorado, PR 787-796-1670
Double R Enterprises
New Castle, PA 724-658-2477
Douglas Stephen Plastics
Paterson, NJ 973-523-3030
Drescher Paper Box
Buffalo, NY 716-854-0288
Dufeck Manufacturing Company
Denmark, WI 888-603-9663
DuPont
Wilmington, DE 800-441-7515
Durham Manufacturing Company
Durham, CT 413-781-7900
Dusobox Company
Haverhill, MA 978-372-7192
Duval Container Company
Jacksonville, FL 800-342-8194
Dynabilt Products
Readville, MA 800-443-1008
E.K. Lay Company
Philadelphia, PA 800-523-3220
E.S. Robbins Corporation
Muscle Shoals, AL 800-800-2235
Eagle Box Company
Farmingdale, NY 212-255-3860
Eastern Container Corporation
Mansfield, MA 508-337-0400
EB Box Company
Richmond Hill, ON 800-513-2269
Economy Folding Box Corporation
Chicago, IL 800-771-1053
Edco Industries
Bridgeport, CT 203-333-8982
Edge Paper Box Company
Cudahy, CA 323-771-7733
EGA Products
Brookfield, WI 262-781-7899
EGW Bradbury Enterprises
Bridgewater, ME 800-332-6021
Eichler Wood Products
Laurys Station, PA 610-262-6749
Elberta Crate & Box Company
Carpentersville, IL 888-672-9260
Elm Packaging Company
Memphis, TN 901-795-2711
Elopak
New Hudson, MI 248-486-4600
Emco Industrial Plastics
Cedar Grove, NJ 800-292-9906
Empire Container Corporation
Carson, CA 323-537-8190
Enterprise Box Company
Montclair, NJ 973-509-2200
Erie Container Corporation
Cleveland, OH 216-631-1650

ERO/Goodrich Forest Products
Tualatin, OR 800-458-5545
Erwyn Products Company
Morganville, NJ 800-331-9208
Eureka Paper Box Company
Williamsport, PA.................... 570-326-9147
Expert Industries
Brooklyn, NY 718-434-6060
F.E. Wood & Sons
East Baldwin, ME.................... 207-286-5003
F.N. Smith Corporation
Oregon, IL.......................... 815-732-2171
F/G Products
Rice Lake, WI....................... 800-247-3854
Fabri-Kal Corporation
Kalamazoo, MI....................... 800-888-5054
Fabricated Components
Stroudsburg, PA 800-233-8163
Fabricon Products
River Rouge, MI..................... 313-841-8200
Faribo Manufacturing Company
Faribault, MN 800-447-6043
Farmers Co-op Elevator Co.
Hudsonville, MI 800-439-9859
Faubion Central States Tank Company
Shawnee Mission, KS................. 800-450-8265
Felco Bag & Burlap Company
Baltimore, MD 800-673-8488
Ferguson Containers
Phillipsburg, NJ 908-454-9755
Fibre Containers Company
City of Industry, CA 626-968-5897
Field Container Company
Elk Grove Vlg, IL................... 847-437-1700
Finn Industries
Ontario, CA......................... 909-930-1500
Fitzpatrick Container Company
North Wales, PA 215-699-3515
Flashfold Carton
Fort Wayne, IN 260-423-9431
Fleetwood International Paper
Vernon, CA 323-588-7121
Flex Products
Carlstadt, NJ 800-526-6273
Flexible Foam Products
Elkhart, IN......................... 800-678-3626
Flow of Solids
Westford, MA 978-392-0300
Foam Concepts
Uxbridge, MA........................ 508-278-7255
Foam Pack Industries
Springfield, NJ 973-376-3700
Foam Packaging
Footsville, WI...................... 608-876-4217
Fold-Pak Corporation
Newark, NY 315-331-3159
Fold-Pak South
Columbus, GA 706-689-2924
Folding Carton/Flexible Packaging
North Hollywood, CA 818-896-3449
Fonda Group
Oshkosh, WI......................... 800-558-9300
Food Pak Corporation
San Mateo, CA 650-341-6559
Foster Forbes Glass
Marion, IN.......................... 765-668-1200
Four M Manufacturing Group
San Jose, CA........................ 408-998-1141
Franklin Crates
Micanopy, FL 352-466-3141
Frankston Paper Box Company of Texas
Frankston, TX....................... 903-876-2550
Frem Corporation
Worcester, MA 508-791-3152
Fremont Die Cut Products
Fremont, OH......................... 800-223-3177
Fresno Pallet, Inc.
Sultana, CA......................... 559-591-4111
Friend Box Company
Danvers, MA......................... 978-774-0240
Friendly City Box Company
Johnstown, PA....................... 814-266-6287
Fruit Growers Package Company
Grandville, MI 616-724-1400
Frye's Measure Mill
Wilton, NH 603-654-6581
Fuller Box Company
North Attleboro, MA 508-695-2525
Fuller Brush Company
Great Bend, KS...................... 800-522-0499
Fuller Packaging
Central Falls, RI 401-725-4300
Fulton-Denver Company
Denver, CO 800-776-6715
Fun-Time International
Philadelphia, PA 800-776-4386
G.S. Laboratory Equipment
Asheville, NC 800-252-7100
Gabriel Container Company
Santa Fe Springs, CA 562-699-1051
Galbreath LLC
Winamac, IN......................... 574-946-6631
Gatewood Products LLC
Parkersburg, WV..................... 800-827-5461
Gaylord Container Corporation
Tampa, FL 813-621-3591
Geerpres
Muskegon, MI........................ 231-773-3211
General Bag Corporation
Cleveland, OH 800-837-9396
General Foam Plastics Corporation
Norfolk, VA......................... 757-857-0153
General Industries
Goldsboro, NC 888-735-2882
Genesee Corrugated
Flint, MI 810-235-6120
Genpak
Peterborough, ON.................... 800-461-1995
Genpak
Glens Falls, NY..................... 800-626-6695
Georgia-Pacific LLC
Atlanta, GA......................... 404-652-4000
Gibbs Brothers Cooperage Company
Hot Springs, AR 501-623-8881
Gibraltar Packaging Group
Hastings, NE 402-463-1366
Gillis Associated Industries
Prospect Heights, IL 847-541-6500
Glaro
Hauppauge, NY 631-234-1717
Glasko Plastics
Santa Ana, CA 714-751-7830
Global Equipment Company
Port Washington, NY 888-628-3466
Golden West Sales
Cerritos, CA 800-827-6175
Goldman Manufacturing Company
Detroit, MI 313-834-5535
Graff Tank Erection
Harrisville, PA..................... 814-385-6671
Graham Engineering Corporation
York, PA 717-848-3755
GranPac
Wetaskiwin, AB 780-352-3324
Graphic Packaging Corporation
Golden, CO 800-677-2886
Graphic Packaging Holding Company
Marietta, GA........................ 770-644-3000
Great Lakes Corrugated
Toledo, OH 419-726-3491
Great Lakes-Triad Package Corporation
Grand Rapids, MI 616-241-6441
Great Northern Corporation
Appleton, WI 800-236-3671
Great Southern Industries
Jackson, MS 601-948-5700
Great Western Products
Ontario, CA......................... 888-598-5588
Green Bay Packaging
Coon Rapids, MN..................... 763-786-7446
Green Bay Packaging
Coon Rapids, MN..................... 800-236-6456
Green Bay Packaging
Tulsa, OK 918-446-3341
Green Bay Packaging
Green Bay, WI....................... 920-433-5111
Green Brothers
Barrington, RI...................... 401-245-9043
Greenfield Packaging
White Plains, NY 914-993-0233
Greenfield Paper Box Company
Greenfield, MA...................... 413-773-9414
Greif Brothers Corporation
Cleveland, OH 800-424-0342
Grief Brothers Corporation
Delaware, OH 740-549-6000
Grigsby Brothers Paper Box Manufacturers
Portland, OR........................ 866-233-4690
Gulf Arizona Packaging
Humble, TX 800-364-3887
Gulf Packaging Company
Safety Harbor, FL................... 800-749-3466
Gulf Systems
Oklahoma City, OK 405-528-2293
Gulf Systems
Brownsville, TX 800-217-4853
Gulf Systems
Oklahoma City, OK 800-364-3887
Gulf Systems
Arlington, TX 817-261-1915
H&R Industries
Beecher, IL 800-526-3244
H. Arnold Wood Turning
Tarrytown, NY 888-314-0088
Hager Containers
Carrollton, TX...................... 972-417-7660
Hampton Roads Box Company
Suffolk, VA 757-934-2355
Hanson Box & Lumber Company
Wakefield, MA 617-245-0358
Harbor Pallet Company
Anaheim, CA 714-533-4940
Hardi-Tainer
South Deerfield, MA 800-882-9878
Hardy Systems Corporation
Northbrook, IL 800-927-3956
Hartford Containers
Terryville, CT 860-584-1194
Hartford Plastics
Omaha, NE
Harvard Folding Box Company
Lynn, MA 781-598-1600
Hedstrom Corporation
Ashland, OH......................... 700-765-9665
Hedwin Corporation
Baltimore, MD 800-638-1012
Heller Truck Body Corporation
Hillside, NJ 800-229-4148
Herche Warehouse
Denver, CO 303-371-8186
Heritage Packaging
Victor, NY.......................... 585-742-3310
Herkimer Pallet & Wood Products Company
Herkimer, NY 315-866-4591
Highland Plastics
Mira Loma, CA....................... 800-368-0491
Hinchcliff Products Company
Strongsville, OH 440-238-5200
Hinkle Manufacturing
Perrysburg, OH...................... 419-666-5550
Hodge Manufacturing Company
Springfield, MA 800-262-4634
Hodges
Vienna, IL 800-444-0011
Holmco Container Manufacturing, LTD
Baltic, OH.......................... 330-897-4503
Hoover Materials Handling Group
Alpharetta, GA 800-391-3561
Hope Paper Box Company
Pawtucket, RI 401-724-5700
Hot Food Boxes
Mooresville, IN..................... 800-733-8073
HS
Oklahoma City, OK 800-238-1240
Hunter Packaging Corporation
South Elgin, IL 800-428-4747
Hunter Woodworks
Carson, CA 800-966-4751
Hurri-Kleen Corporation
Birmingham, AL...................... 800-455-8265
IBC/Shell Containers
New Hyde Park, NY................... 516-352-4505
Ideas Etc
Louisville, KY 800-733-0337
Illinois Valley Container Corporation
Peru, IL 815-223-7200
IMO Foods
Yarmouth, NS 902-742-3519
Imperial Containers
City of Industry, CA 626-333-6363
Imperial Industries Inc
Wausau, WI.......................... 800-558-2945
Imperial Packaging Corporation
Pawtucket, RI 401-753-7778
Impress Industries
Emmaus, PA 610-967-6027
Incinerator International
Houston, TX 713-227-1466
Independent Can Company
Belcamp, MD 909-923-6150
Indiana Bottle Company Inc.
Scottsburg, IN...................... 800-752-8702
Indiana Box Company
Greenfield, IN...................... 317-462-7743
Indiana Vac-Form
Warsaw, IN 574-269-1725

Indianapolis Container Company
Indianapolis, IN 800-760-3318
Industrial Container Corporation
High Point, NC 336-886-7031
Industrial Contracting &Rigging Company
Mahwah, NJ 888-427-7444
Industrial Hardwood
Perrysburg, OH 419-666-2503
Industrial Lumber & Packaging
Spring Lake, MI 616-842-1457
Industrial Nameplates
Ivyland, PA 800-878-6263
Industrial WoodFab & Packaging Company
Riverview, MI 734-284-4808
Inland Consumer Packaging
Harrington, DE 302-398-4211
Inland Paper Board & Packaging
Elizabethton, TN 423-542-2112
Inland Paperboard & Packaging
Austin, TX 512-434-5800
Inland Paperboard & Packaging
Rock Hill, SC 803-366-4103
Innovative Folding Carton Company
South Plainfield, NJ 908-757-0205
Instabox
Calgary, AB 800-482-6173
Inter-Pack Corporation
Monroe, MI 734-242-7755
International Paper
Fort Worth, TX 817-338-4000
International Wood Industries
Snohomish, WA 800-922-6141
IPL Plastics
Edmundston, NB 800-739-9595
IPS International
Snohomish, WA 360-668-5050
Ira L Henry Company, Inc
Watertown, WI 920-261-0648
J&J Corrugated Box Corporation
Franklin, MA 508-528-6200
J&J Mid-South Container Corporation
Augusta, GA 800-395-1025
Jackson Corrugated Container
Middletown, CT 860-346-9671
Jacksonville Box & Woodwork Company
Jacksonville, FL 800-683-2699
Jamestown Container Corporation
Macedonia, OH 800-247-1033
Jarisch Paper Box Company
North Adams, MA 413-663-5396
Jenike & Johanson
Tyngsboro, MA 978-649-3300
Jescorp
Des Plaines, IL 847-299-7800
Jesse Jones Box Corporation
Philadelphia, PA 215-425-6600
Jessup Paper Box
Brookston, IN 765-490-9043
Jet Age Containers Company
Chicago, IL 708-594-5260
John Henry Packaging
Penngrove, CA 800-327-5997
Jordan Box Company
Syracuse, NY 315-422-3419
Jordan Paper Box Company
Chicago, IL 773-287-5362
Juice Merchandising Corporation
Kansas City, MO 800-950-1998
Juice Tree
Omaha, NE 714-891-4425
Jupiter Mills Corporation
Roslyn, NY 800-853-5121
Just Plastics
New York, NY 212-569-8500
K&H Container
Wallingford, CT 203-265-1547
Kadon Corporation
Milford, OH 937-299-0088
KapStone Paper and Packaging Corporation
Northbrook, IL 847-239-8800
Karyall-Telday
Cleveland, OH 216-281-4063
Kaufman Paper Box Company
Providence, RI 401-272-7508
KB Systems Baking Machinery Design Company
Bangor, PA 610-588-7788
Kell Container Corporation
Chippewa Falls, WI 800-472-1800
Kelley Wood Products
Fitchburg, MA 978-345-7531
Kendel
Countryside, IL 800-323-1100

Key Container Company
South Gate, CA 323-564-4211
Key Material Handling
Simi Valley, CA 800-539-7225
Key Packaging Company
Sarasota, FL 941-355-2728
KHM Plastics
Gurnee, IL 847-249-4910
Killington Wood ProductsCompany
Rutland, VT 802-773-9111
Kimball Companies
East Longmeadow, MA 413-525-1881
King Bag & Manufacturing Company
Cincinnati, OH 800-444-5464
King Plastics
North Port, FL 941-493-5502
Knapp Container
Beacon Falls, CT 203-888-0511
Knight Paper Box Company
Chicago, IL 773-585-2035
Koch Container Corporation
Victor, NY 585-924-1600
Kontane
Charleston, SC 843-352-0011
Konz Wood Products
Appleton, WI 877-610-5145
Label Makers
Pleasant Prairie, WI 800-208-3331
Lakeside Container Corporation
Plattsburgh, NY 518-561-6150
Lakeside Manufacturing
Milwaukee, WI 888-558-8574
Laminated Paper Products
San Jose, CA 408-888-0880
Landis Plastics
Alsip, IL 708-396-1470
Larose & Fils Ltée
Laval, QC 877-382-7001
Laval Paper Box
Pointe Claire, QC 450-669-3551
Lawrence Paper Company
Lawrence, KS 785-843-8111
Lawson Mardon Radisson
Baldwinsville, NY 800-847-5677
Lawson Mardon Wheaton Company
Mays Landing, NJ 609-625-2291
LBP Manufacturing
Cicero, IL 708-652-5600
Le Claire Packaging Corporation
Ixonia, WI 920-206-9902
Leading Industry
Oxnard, CA 805-385-4100
Leggett & Platt StorageP
Vernon Hills, IL 847-816-6246
Len E. Ivarson
Milwaukee, WI 414-351-0700
Lester Box & Manufacturing
Long Beach, CA 562-437-5123
Letica Corporation
Rochester, MI 800-538-4221
Levin Brothers Paper
Cicero, IL 800-666-8484
Lewis Steel Works
Wrens, GA 800-521-5239
Lewisburg Container Company
Lewisburg, OH 937-962-2681
Lexel
Fort Worth, TX 817-332-4061
Lima Barrel & Drum Company
Lima, OH 419-224-8916
Lin Pac Plastics
Roswell, GA 770-751-6006
LinPac
San Angelo, TX 800-453-7393
Linpac Materials Handling
Dallas, TX 214-599-9023
Linvar
Hartford, CT 800-282-5288
Liquitane
Berwick, PA 570-759-6200
Little Rock Crate & Basket Company
Little Rock, AR 800-223-7823
LMK Containers
Centerville, UT 626-821-9984
Lone Star Container Corporation
Irving, TX 800-552-6937
Longview Fibre Company
Beaverton, OR 503-350-1600
Longview Fibre Company
Longview, WA 800-929-8111
Lowell Paper Box Company
Nashua, NH 603-595-0700

Loy-Lange Box Company
Saint Louis, MO 800-886-4712
LTI Printing
Sturgis, MI 269-651-7574
Luce Corporation
Hamden, CT 800-344-6966
Luke's Almond Acres
Reedley, CA 559-638-3483
Lunn Industries
Glen Cove, NY 516-671-9000
M&G Packaging Corporation
Floral Park, NY 800-240-5288
M&H Crates
Jacksonville, TX 903-683-5351
M&L Plastics
Easthampton, MA 413-527-1330
Mack-Chicago Corporation
Chicago, IL 800-992-6225
MacMillan Bloedel Packaging
Montgomery, AL 800-239-4464
Madsen Wire Products
Orland, IN 260-829-6561
Malco Manufacturing Corporation
Los Angeles, CA 866-477-7267
Mall City Containers
Kalamazoo, MI 800-643-6721
Manitowoc Foodservice Companies, Inc.
New Port Richey, FL 877-375-9300
Mannkraft Corporation
Newark, NJ 973-589-7400
Marco Products
Adrian, MI 517-265-3333
Marcus Carton Company
Melville, NY 631-752-4200
Marfred Industries
Sun Valley, CA 800-529-5156
Marion Paper Box Company
Marion, IN 765-664-6435
Maro Paper Products Company
Bellwood, IL 708-649-9982
Marpac Industries
Philmont, NY 888-462-7722
Marshall Boxes
Rochester, NY 585-458-7432
Massachusetts Container Corporation
Marlborough, MA 508-481-1100
Massillon Container Company
Navarre, OH 330-879-5653
Master Containers
Mulberry, FL 800-881-6847
Master Package Corporation
Owen, WI 800-396-8425
Maull-Baker Box Company
Brookfield, WI 414-463-1290
Maypak
Wayne, NJ 973-696-0780
Measurex/S&L Plastics
Nazareth, PA 800-752-0650
MeGa Industries
Burlington, ON 800-665-6342
Mello Smello
Minneapolis, MN 888-574-2964
Melmat, Inc.
Huntington Beach, CA 800-635-6289
Melville Plastics
Haw River, NC 336-578-5800
Menasha Corporation
Oconomowoc, WI 262-560-0228
Menasha Corporation
Neenah, WI 800-558-5073
Merchants Publishing Company
Kalamazoo, MI 269-345-1175
Meyer Packaging
Palmyra, PA 717-838-6300
Meyers Corbox Co, Inc.
Cleveland, OH 800-321-7286
Michael Leson Dinnerware
Youngstown, OH 800-821-3541
Michiana Corrugated Products
Sturgis, MI 269-651-5225
Michigan Box Company
Detroit, MI 888-642-4269
Micro Qwik
Cross Plains, WI 608-798-3071
Micro Wire Products Inc.
Brockton, MA 508-584-0200
Mid Cities Paper Box Company
Downey, CA 877-277-6272
Mid-States Manufacturing & Engineering
Milton, IA 800-346-1792
Midland Manufacturing Company
Monroe, IA 800-394-2625

Midwest Aircraft Products Company
Mansfield, OH 419-522-2231
Midwest Box Company
Cleveland, OH 216-281-3980
Midwest Paper Products Company
Louisville, KY 502-636-2741
Midwest Paper Tube & CanCorporation
New Berlin, WI. 262-782-7300
Midwest Rubber & Supply Company
Commerce City, CO 800-537-7457
Milan Box Corporation
Milan, TN 800-225-8057
Miller Hofft Brands
Indianapolis, IN 317-638-6576
Modern Paper Box Company
Providence, RI 401-861-7357
Molded Container Corporation
Portland, OR 503-233-8601
Moli-International
Denver, CO 800-525-8468
Montebello Container Corporation
La Mirada, CA 714-994-2351
Montebello Packaging
Hawkesbury, ON. 613-632-7096
Morphy Container Company
Brantford, ON 519-752-5428
Morris Transparent Box Company
East Providence, RI. 401-438-6116
Mount Vernon Packaging
Mount Vernon, OH 888-397-3221
Mountain Safety Research
Seattle, WA 800-877-9677
Mullinix Packages
Fort Wayne, IN 260-747-3149
Multibulk Systems International
Wendell, NC 919-366-2100
MultiFab Plastics
Boston, MA. 888-293-5754
Nagel Paper & Box Company
Saginaw, MI 800-292-3654
Nefab Packaging Inc.
Coppell, TX 800-322-4425
Nefab Packaging, Inc.
Coppell, TX 800-322-4425
Neff Packaging Solutions
Mason, OH 800-445-4383
Negus Container & Packaging
Madison, WI 888-241-7482
Nelson Company
Baltimore, MD 410-477-3000
Nelson Container Corporation
Germantown, WI. 262-250-5000
Nepa Pallet & Container Company
Snohomish, WA 360-568-3185
New England Wooden Ware Corporation
Gardner, MA 800-252-9214
New Lisbon Wood ProductsManufacturing Company
New Lisbon, WI 608-562-3122
New Mexico Products
Albuquerque, NM. 877-345-7864
New York Corrugated Box Company
Paterson, NJ 973-742-5000
North American ContainerCorporation
Maretta, GA 800-929-0610
North American PackagingCorporation
New York, NY 800-499-3521
Northeast Box Company
Ashtabula, OH 800-362-8100
Northeast Container Corporation
Dumont, NJ. 201-385-6200
Nosco
Waukegan, IL 847-360-4806
Novelis Foil Products
Lagrange, GA 800-776-8701
NPC Display Group
Newark, NJ. 973-589-2155
NU-Trend Plastic/Corrigan & Company
Jacksonville, FL 904-353-5936
O-I
Perrysburg, OH
Oak Barrel Winecraft
Berkeley, CA. 510-849-0400
Oakes Carton Company
Kalamazoo, MI 269-381-6022
Ockerlund Industries
Forest Park, IL 708-771-7707
Olcott Plastics
Saint Charles, IL 888-313-5277
Old Dominion Box Company
Burlington, NC 336-226-4491
Old Dominion Box Company
Madison Heights, VA 434-929-6701

Oracle Packaging
Toledo, OH 800-952-9536
ORBIS Corporation
Oconomowoc, WI. 800-890-7292
Original Packaging & Display Company
Saint Louis, MO 314-772-7797
OTD Corporation
Hinsdale, IL 630-321-9232
Ott Packagings
Selinsgrove, PA. 570-374-2811
Pack-Rite
Newington, CT 860-953-0120
Packaging Associates
Randolph, NJ 973-252-8890
Packaging Corporation of America
Lake Forest, IL 800-456-4725
Packaging Design Corporation
Burr Ridge, IL. 630-323-1354
Packaging Dynamics International
Caldwell, OH 740-732-5665
Packaging Solutions
Los Altos Hills, CA 650-917-1022
Packing Material Company
Southfield, MI. 248-489-7000
Packing Specialities
Warren, MI 586-758-5240
Packrite Packaging
Archdale, NC. 336-431-1111
Pactiv LLC
Lake Forest, IL 888-828-2850
Pak-Sher Company
Kilgore, TX. 800-642-2295
Pallet One
Bartow, FL. 800-771-1148
Palmer Distributors
St Clair Shores, MI 800-444-1912
Pan Pacific Plastics Manufacturing
Hayward, CA 888-475-6888
Paper Systems
Des Moines, IA 800-342-2855
Par-Kan Company
Silver Lake, IN 800-291-5487
Par-Pak
Houston, TX 713-686-6700
Par-Pak
Houston, TX 888-272-7725
Paragon Packaging
Ferndale, CA 888-615-0065
Parkway Plastics
Piscataway, NJ 732-752-3636
Parlor City Paper Box Company
Binghamton, NY. 607-772-0600
PARTA
Kent, OH. 800-543-5781
Paul T. Freund Corporation
Palmyra, NY 800-333-0091
Pelco Packaging Corporation
Stirling, NJ 908-647-3500
Pell Paper Box Company
Elizabeth City, NC 252-335-4361
Penn Bottle & Supply Company
Philadelphia, PA 215-365-5700
Penn Products
Portland, CT 800-490-7366
Penny Plate
Haddonfield, NJ 856-429-7583
Pentwater Wire Products
Pentwater, MI 877-869-6911
Perfect Packaging Company
Perrysburg, OH 419-874-3167
Performance Packaging
Trail Creek, IN 219-874-6226
Peter Pepper Products
Compton, CA 310-639-0390
Pine Point Wood Products
Dayton, MN 763-428-4301
Pioneer Packaging
Dixon, KY. 800-951-1551
Pioneer Packaging & Printing
Anoka, MN 800-708-1705
Pittsburgh Tank Corporation
Monongahela, PA 800-634-0243
Plastic Assembly Corporation
Ayer, MA. 978- 77- 472
Plastic Industries
Athens, TN 800-894-4876
Plastic Packaging Corporation
Hickory, NC 828-328-2466
Plastican Corporation
Fairfield, NJ 973-227-7817
Plastics
Greensboro, AL 334-624-8801

Plastipak Packaging
Plymouth, MI 734-354-3510
Plastiques Cascades Group
Montreal, QC 888-703-6515
Plaxall
Long Island City, NY 800-876-5706
Plaxicon
West Chicago, IL 630-231-0850
Pocono PET
Hazle Twp, PA 570-459-1800
Podnar Plastics
Kent, OH. 800-673-5277
Pohlig Brothers
Richmond, VA. 804-275-9000
Polar Plastics
Mooresville, NC 704-660-6600
Polar Tech Industries
Genoa, IL 800-423-2749
Polar Ware Company
Sheboygan, WI 800-237-3655
Poliplastic
Granby, QC 450-378-8417
Poly Processing Company
French Camp, CA 877-325-3142
Polybottle Group
Brampton, ON. 905-450-3600
Polycon Industries
Chicago, IL 773-374-5500
Polyfoam Packers Corporation
Arlington Hts, IL 800-323-7442
Portland Paper Box Company
Portland, OR 800-547-2571
Precision Wood of Hawaii
Vancouver, WA 808-682-2055
Precision Wood Products
Vancouver, WA 360-694-8322
Premier Packages
Saint Louis, MO 800-466-6588
Premium Foil Products Company
Louisville, KY 502-459-2820
President Container
Wood Ridge, NJ 201-933-7500
Prestige Plastics Corporation
Delta, BC. 604-930-2931
Pretium Packaging
Seymour, IN 812-522-8177
Pride Container Corporation
Chicago, IL 773-227-6000
Princeton Shelving
Cedar Rapids, IA. 319-369-0355
Progressive Plastics
Cleveland, OH 800-252-0053
Prolon
Port Gibson, MS 888-480-9828
Propak
Burlington, ON 800-263-4872
Pruitt's Packaging Services
Grand Rapids, MI 800-878-0553
Quality Container Company
Ypsilanti, MI 734-481-1373
Quality Containers
Weston, ON. 416-749-6247
Quality Packaging, Inc.
Fond du Lac, WI 800-923-3633
Quantum Storage Systems
Miami, FL. 800-685-4665
Quintex Corporation
Spokane Valley, WA 509-924-7900
Ram Equipment
Waukesha, WI. 262-513-1114
Rand-Whitney Container Corporation
Worcester, MA 508-791-2301
Rand-Whitney Container Corporation
Portsmouth, NH 603-822-7300
RAPAC
Oakland, TN 800-280-6333
RC Molding Inc.
Greer, SC. 864-879-7279
RDA Container Corporation
Gates, NY 585-247-2323
Regal Plastic Company
Mission, KS 800-852-1556
Regal Plastics
North Kansas City, MO 816-471-6390
Reliable Container Corporation
Downey, CA 562-745-0200
Reliance Product
Winnipeg, MB. 800-665-0258
Reliance-Paragon
Philadelphia, PA 215-743-1231
Remcon Plastics
West Reading, PA 800-360-3636

Revere Packaging
Shelbyville, KY 800-626-2668
Rexam Beverage Can Company
Chicago, IL 773-399-3000
Rez-Tech Corporation
Kent, OH 800-673-5277
Rhoades Paper Box Corporation
Springfield, OH 800-441-6494
Rice Packaging
Ellington, CT 800-367-6725
Richard Read Construction Company
Arcadia, CA 888-450-7343
Richards Packaging
Memphis, TN 800-361-6453
Ritz Packaging Company
Brooklyn, NY 718-366-2300
RJR Packaging, Inc.
Oakland, CA 510-638-5901
RMI-C/Rotonics Manaufacturing
Bensenville, IL 630-773-9510
Robinson Cone
Burlington, ON 905-333-1515
Rock Tenn/Alliance Group
Tullahoma, TN 931-455-3535
Rock-Tenn Company
Norcross, GA 770-448-2193
Romanow Container
Westwood, MA 781-320-9200
Ronnie's Ceramic Company
San Francisco, CA 800-888-8218
Ropak
Oak Brook, IL 800-527-2267
Round Paper Packages
Erlanger, KY 859-331-7200
Rownd & Son
Dillon, SC 803-774-8264
Roy's Folding Box
Cleveland, OH 216-464-1191
Royal Box Group
Cicero, IL 708-656-2020
Rubbermaid Specialty Products
Freeport, IL 815-235-4171
Rudd Container Corporation
Chicago, IL 773-847-7600
Ruffino Paper Box Manufacturing
Hackensack, NJ 201-487-1260
Rusken Packaging
Cullman, AL 256-734-0092
Russell-Stanley Corporation
Woodbridge, NJ 800-229-6001
S.S.I. Schaefer System International Limited
Brampton, ON 905-458-5399
Sabert Corporation
Sayreville, NJ 800-722-3781
Saeplast Canada
St John, NB 800-567-3966
Saint Charles Lumber Products
St Charles, MI 989-865-9915
Sanchelima International
Doral, FL 305-591-4343
Schermerhorn
Chicopee, MA 413-598-8348
Schiefer Packaging Corporation
Syracuse, NY 315-422-0615
Schwarz
Morton Grove, IL 847-966-4050
Scope Packaging
Orange, CA 714-998-4411
Scott & Daniells
Portland, CT 860-342-1932
Seaboard Carton Company
Downers Grove, IL 708-344-0575
Seattle-Tacoma Box Company
Kent, WA 253-854-9700
Sebring Container Corporation
Salem, OH 330-332-1533
Security Packaging
North Bergen, NJ 201-854-1955
Semco Plastic Company
Saint Louis, MO 314-487-4557
Sertapak Packaging Corporation
Woodstock, ON 800-265-1162
Set Point Paper Company
Mansfield, MA 800-225-0501
Setco
Monroe Twp, NJ 609-655-4600
Setco
Anaheim, CA 714-777-5200
Seville Flexpack Corporation
Oak Creek, WI 414-761-2751
Seymour Woodenware Company
Seymour, WI 920-833-6551

SFB Plastics
Wichita, KS 800-343-8133
SFBC, LLC dba Seaboard Folding Box
Fitchburg, MA 800-225-6313
Sharpsville Container
Sharpsville, PA 800-645-1248
Shaw-Clayton Corporation
San Rafael, CA 800-537-6712
Sheboygan Paper Box Company
Sheboygan, WI 800-458-8373
Shillington Box Company
Saint Louis, MO 636-225-5353
Shipmaster Containers Ltd.
Markham, ON 416-493-9193
Shippers Supply
Saskatoon, SK 800-661-5639
Shippers Supply, Labelgraphic
Calgary, AB 800-661-5639
Sho-Me Container
Grinnell, IA 800-798-3512
Shore Paper Box Company
Mardela Springs, MD 410-749-7125
Shorewood Packaging
Carlstadt, NJ 201-933-3203
Sigma Industries
Concord, MI 517-857-6520
Silgan Plastics Canada
Chesterfield, MO 800-274-5426
Simkins Industries
East Haven, CT 203-787-7171
Sirco Systems
Birmingham, AL 205-731-7800
Smith Packaging
Mississauga, ON 905-564-6640
Smurfit Stone Container
St Louis, MO 314-679-2300
Smurfit Stone Container
San Jose, CA 408-925-9391
Smurfit Stone Container
North Tonawanda, NY 716-692-6510
Smyrna Container Company
Smyrna, GA 800-868-4305
Snapware
Fullerton, CA 800-334-3062
Snow Craft Company
Garden City Park, NY 516-739-1399
Snyder Crown
Marked Tree, AR 870-358-3400
Snyder Industries Inc.
Lincoln, NE 800-351-1363
Sobel Corrugated Containers
Cleveland, OH 216-475-2100
Solo Cup Company
Owings Mills, MD 800-800-0300
Somerville Packaging
Scarborough, ON 416-291-1161
Somerville Packaging
Mississauga, ON 905-678-8211
Sonderen Packaging
Spokane, WA 800-727-9139
SONOCO
Hartsville, SC 800-576-6626
SOPAKCO Foods
Mullins, SC 800-276-9678
Southern Bag Corporation
Madison, MS 662-746-3631
Southern Champion Tray
Chattanooga, TN 800-468-2222
Southern Metal Fabricators
Albertville, AL 800-989-1330
Southern Missouri Containers
Springfield, MO 800-999-7666
Southern Packaging Corporation
Bennettsville, SC 843-479-7154
Spartanburg Stainless Products
Spartanburg, SC 800-974-7500
Spartech Industries
Etobicoke, ON 416-744-4220
Spartech Plastics
Portage, WI 800-998-7123
Sphinx Adsorbents
Springfield, MA 800-388-0157
Spring Cove Container
Roaring Spring, PA 814-224-2222
Spring Wood Products
Geneva, OH 440-466-1135
Springport Steel Wire Products
Concord, MI 517-857-3010
St Joseph Packaging Inc
St Joseph, MO 800-383-3000
St. Tobain Containers
Seattle, WA 206-762-0660

Stand Fast Packaging Products
Addison, IL 630-600-0900
Standard Folding Cartons
Flushing, NY 718-335-5500
Star Container Company
Phoenix, AZ 480-281-4200
Star Container Corporation
Leominster, MA 978-537-1676
State Container Corporation
Moonachie, NJ 201-933-5200
Stearnswood
Hutchinson, MN 800-657-0144
Step Products
Round Rock, TX 800-777-7837
Steril-Sil Company
Boston, MA 800-784-5537
Stone Container
Moss Point, MS 502-491-4870
Stone Container
Santa Fe Springs, CA 714-774-0100
Streator Dependable Manufacturing
Streator, IL 800-798-0551
Stronghaven Inc.
Matthews, NC 800-222-7919
Suburban Corrugated Box Company
Indianhead Park, IL 630-920-1230
Superfos Packaging
Cumberland, MD 800-537-9242
Superior Quality Products
Schenectady, NY 800-724-1129
T&S Blow Molding
Scarborough, ON 416-752-8330
T.J. Smith Box Company
Fort Smith, AR 877-540-7933
Taylor Box Company
Warren, RI 800-304-6361
Technibilt/Cari-All
Newton, NC 800-233-3972
Technipack, Inc.
Le Sueur, MN 507-665-6658
TEMP-TECH Company
Springfield, MA 800-343-5579
Temple-Inland
Memphis, TN 901-419-9000
Tenneco Packaging
Westmont, IL 630-850-7034
TEQ
Huntley, IL 800-874-7113
TGR Container Sales
San Leandro, CA 800-273-6887
THARCO
San Lorenzo, CA 800-772-2332
The Royal Group
Cicero, IL 262-723-6900
The Shelby Company
Cleveland, OH 800-842-1650
Thermo Wisconsin
De Pere, WI 920-766-7200
Thermodynamics
Commerce City, CO 800-627-9037
Thermodyne International
Ontario, CA 909-923-9945
Thornton Plastics
Salt Lake City, UT 800-248-3434
TinWerks Packaging
Addison, IL 630-628-8600
Titan Plastics
East Rutherford, NJ 201-935-7700
TMS
San Francisco, CA 800-447-7223
Tolco Corporation
Toledo, OH 800-537-4786
Trade Fixtures
Little Rock, AR 800-872-3490
Traex
Dane, WI 800-356-8006
Trans Container Corporation
Upland, CA 909-985-2750
Transparent Container Company
Addison, IL 708-449-8520
Traub Container Corporation
Cleveland, OH 216-475-5100
Treen Box & Pallet Corporation
Bensalem, PA 215-639-5100
Trent Corporation
Trenton, NJ 609-587-7515
Tri-State Plastics
Henderson, KY 270-826-8361
Trilla Steel Drum Corporation
Chicago, IL 773-847-7588
Triple A Containers
Buena Park, CA 714-521-2820

Triple Dot Corporation
Santa Ana, CA 714-241-0888
True Pack Ltd
New Castle, DE. 800-825-7890
Tucson Container Corporation
Tucson, AZ 520-746-3171
Tupperware Brand Corporation
Orlando, FL. 800-366-3800
Tuscarora
New Brighton, PA. 724-843-8200
ULMA Packaging Systems, Inc.
Ball Ground, GA. 770-345-5300
Ultratainer
St Jean-Sur-Richelie, QC 514-359-3651
Unarco Industries
Wagoner, OK. 800-654-4100
UniPak
West Chester, PA. 610-436-6600
Unique Boxes
Chicago, IL 800-281-1670
Universal Container Corporation
Odessa, FL 800-582-7477
Universal Folding Box
East Orange, NJ 973-482-4300
Universal Folding Box Company
Hoboken, NJ 201-659-7373
Universal Paper Box
Seattle, WA 800-228-1045
US Can Company
Rosedale, MD 800-436-8021
Utah Paper Box Company
Salt Lake City, UT 801-363-0093
Valley Container
Bridgeport, CT 203-336-6100
Vandereems ManufacturingCompany
Hawthorne, NJ 973-427-2355
Victory Box Corporation
Roselle, NJ 908-245-5100
Victory Packaging, Inc.
Houston, TX 800-486-5606
Viking Packaging & Display
San Jose, CA 408-998-1000
VIP Real Estate Ltd
Chicago, IL. 773-376-5000
Visual Packaging Corporation
Haskell, NJ 973-835-7055
VitaMinder Company
Providence, RI 800-858-8840
Vivid Packaging Inc
Cleveland, OH 877-752-2250
Volk Packaging Corporation
Biddeford, ME 800-341-0208
Wald Imports
Kirkland, WA 800-426-2822
Wastequip Teem
Eagleville, TN. 800-843-3358
Waymar Industries
Burnsville, MN 888-474-1112
Weber Display & Packaging
Philadelphia, PA 215-426-3500
Webster Packaging Corporation
Loveland, OH 513-683-5666
WES Plastics
Richmond Hill, ON. 905-508-1546
Westeel
Saskatoon, SK. 306-931-2855
Wheaton Plastic Containers
Millville, NJ 856-825-1400
Willamette Industries
Beaverton, OR. 503-641-1131
Willamette Industries
Louisville, KY 800-465-3065
Willard Packaging
Gaithersburg, MD. 301-948-7700
Winchester Carton
Eutaw, AL 205-372-3337
Winzen Film
Sulphur Springs, TX 800-779-7595
Wisconsin Box Company
Wausau, WI. 800-876-6658
Wisconsinbox
Wausau, WI. 715-842-2248
WNA Hopple Plastics
Florence, KY. 800-446-4622
Woodson Pallet
Anmoore, WV. 304-623-2858
Woodstock Plastics Company
Marengo, IL 815-568-5281
World Kitchen
Rosemont, IL. 847-678-8600
Wright Brothers Paper Box Company
Fond Du Lac, WI 920-921-8270
Xtreme Beverages, LLC
Dana Point, CA. 949-495-7929
York Container Company
York, PA 717-757-7611
Zero Corporation
Monson, MA. 413-267-5561

Chicken, Prepared

Flexo Transparent
Buffalo, NY. 877-993-5396
Foam Packaging
Footsville, WI 608-876-4217

Paper

Accurate Paper Box Company
Knoxville, TN 865-690-0311
AdPro
Solon, OH 440-542-1111
Alcan Packaging
Baie D'Urfe, QC. 514-457-4555
Ample Industries
Franklin, OH 888-818-9700
Apache Inc.
Cedar Rapids, IA. 800-553-5455
Armbrust Paper Tubes
Chicago, IL 773-586-3232
Artistic Carton
Auburn, IN 260-925-6060
Artistic Carton Company
Elgin, IL 847-741-0247
Bell Packaging Corporation
Marion, IN. 800-382-0153
Boelter Industries
Winona, MN 507-452-2315
Boxes.com
Livingston, NJ. 201-646-9050
Brewer-Cantelmo Company
New York, NY 212-244-4600
Burrows Paper Corporation
Little Falls, NY 800-732-1933
Capitol Carton Company
Sacramento, CA 916-388-7848
Cardinal Packaging Products Inc.
Crystal Lake, IL 866-216-4942
Carpet City Paper Box Company
Amsterdam, NY 518-842-5430
Cedar Box Company
Minneapolis, MN 612-332-4287
Chambers Container Company
Gastonia, NC. 704-377-6317
Cin-Made Packaging Group
Cincinnati, OH 513-681-3600
Coast Paper Box Company
San Bernardino, CA 909-382-3475
Colbert Packaging Corporation
Lake Forest, IL 847-367-5990
Collector's Gallery
Saint Charles, IL. 800-346-3063
Color Box
Richmond, IN 765-966-7588
Color Carton
Bronx, NY. 718-665-0840
Columbus Container
Columbus, IN 812-376-9301
Columbus Paperbox Company
Columbus, OH 800-968-0797
Commencement Bay Corrugated
Orting, WA 253-845-3100
Commercial Corrugated Corporation
Baltimore, MD 800-242-8861
Complete Packaging & Shipping Supplies
Freeport, NY. 877-269-3236
Connecticut Container Corporation
North Haven, CT. 203-248-2161
Corpak
San Juan, PR. 787-787-9085
Corr-Pak Corporation
Mc Cook, IL 708-442-7806
Corrobilt Container Company
Livermore, CA 925-373-0880
Corrugated Packaging
Sarasota, FL 941-371-0000
Cumberland Container Corporation
Monterey, TN 931-839-2227
Curtis Packaging Corporation
Sandy Hook, CT 203-426-5861
Dallas Container Corporation
Dallas, TX. 214-381-7148
Day Manufacturing Company
Sherman, TX. 903-893-1138
Designers-Folding Box Corporation
Buffalo, NY. 716-853-5141
Diamond Packaging
Rochester, NY. 800-333-4079
Dixie Printing & Packaging
Glen Burnie, MD 800-433-4943
Dorado Carton Company
Dorado, PR 787-796-1670
Drescher Paper Box
Buffalo, NY. 716-854-0288
Dusobox Company
Haverhill, MA. 978-372-7192
Duval Container Company
Jacksonville, FL 800-342-8194
Eagle Box Company
Farmingdale, NY 212-255-3860
Eastern Container Corporation
Mansfield, MA 508-337-0400
EB Box Company
Richmond Hill, ON. 800-513-2269
Economy Folding Box Corporation
Chicago, IL 800-771-1053
Edge Paper Box Company
Cudahy, CA. 323-771-7733
Empire Container Corporation
Carson, CA 323-537-8190
Enterprise Box Company
Montclair, NJ 973-509-2200
Erie Container Corporation
Cleveland, OH 216-631-1650
Eureka Paper Box Company
Williamsport, PA. 570-326-9147
Fabricon Products
River Rouge, MI 313-841-8200
Felco Bag & Burlap Company
Baltimore, MD 800-673-8488
Fibre Containers Company
City of Industry, CA 626-968-5897
Field Container Company
Elk Grove Vlg, IL. 847-437-1700
Finn Industries
Ontario, CA. 909-930-1500
Fitzpatrick Container Company
North Wales, PA 215-699-3515
Flashfold Carton
Fort Wayne, IN 260-423-9431
Folding Carton/Flexible Packaging
North Hollywood, CA 818-896-3449
Fonda Group
Oshkosh, WI 800-558-9300
Food Pak Corporation
San Mateo, CA 650-341-6559
Four M Manufacturing Group
San Jose, CA 408-998-1141
Frankston Paper Box Company of Texas
Frankston, TX. 903-876-2550
Friend Box Company
Danvers, MA. 978-774-0240
Friendly City Box Company
Johnstown, PA. 814-266-6287
Fuller Box Company
North Attleboro, MA 508-695-2525
Fuller Packaging
Central Falls, RI 401-725-4300
Gabriel Container Company
Santa Fe Springs, CA 562-699-1051
Goldman Manufacturing Company
Detroit, MI 313-834-5535
Graphic Packaging Holding Company
Marietta, GA 770-644-3000
Great Lakes Corrugated
Toledo, OH 419-726-3491
Green Bay Packaging
Coon Rapids, MN. 763-786-7446
Green Bay Packaging
Coon Rapids, MN. 800-236-6456
Green Bay Packaging
Tulsa, OK 918-446-3341
Green Bay Packaging
Green Bay, WI. 920-433-5111
Green Brothers
Barrington, RI. 401-245-9043
Greenfield Paper Box Company
Greenfield, MA. 413-773-9414
Greif Brothers Corporation
Cleveland, OH 800-424-0342
Grief Brothers Corporation
Delaware, OH 740-549-6000
Grigsby Brothers Paper Box Manufacturers
Portland, OR 866-233-4690
Gulf Packaging Company
Safety Harbor, FL 800-749-3466

Hager Containers
Carrollton, TX....................972-417-7660
Harvard Folding Box Company
Lynn, MA....................781-598-1600
Hope Paper Box Company
Pawtucket, RI....................401-724-5700
Hunter Packaging Corporation
South Elgin, IL....................800-428-4747
Illinois Valley Container Corporation
Peru, IL....................815-223-7200
Imperial Containers
City of Industry, CA....................626-333-6363
Imperial Packaging Corporation
Pawtucket, RI....................401-753-7778
Impress Industries
Emmaus, PA....................610-967-6027
Industrial Container Corporation
High Point, NC....................336-886-7031
Industrial Nameplates
Ivyland, PA....................800-878-6263
Inland Consumer Packaging
Harrington, DE....................302-398-4211
Inland Paper Board & Packaging
Elizabethton, TN....................423-542-2112
Inland Paperboard & Packaging
Austin, TX....................512-434-5800
Inland Paperboard & Packaging
Rock Hill, SC....................803-366-4103
Instabox
Calgary, AB....................800-482-6173
Ira L Henry Company, Inc
Watertown, WI....................920-261-0648
J&J Mid-South Container Corporation
Augusta, GA....................800-395-1025
Jamestown Container Corporation
Macedonia, OH....................800-247-1033
Jarisch Paper Box Company
North Adams, MA....................413-663-5396
Jesse Jones Box Corporation
Philadelphia, PA....................215-425-6600
Jessup Paper Box
Brookston, IN....................765-490-9043
Jet Age Containers Company
Chicago, IL....................708-594-5260
Jordan Box Company
Syracuse, NY....................315-422-3419
Jupiter Mills Corporation
Roslyn, NY....................800-853-5121
K&H Container
Wallingford, CT....................203-265-1547
KapStone Paper and Packaging Corporation
Northbrook, IL....................847-239-8800
Kaufman Paper Box Company
Providence, RI....................401-272-7508
Kell Container Corporation
Chippewa Falls, WI....................800-472-1800
Kendel
Countryside, IL....................800-323-1100
Knight Paper Box Company
Chicago, IL....................773-585-2035
Koch Container Corporation
Victor, NY....................585-924-1600
Lakeside Container Corporation
Plattsburgh, NY....................518-561-6150
Lawson Mardon Radisson
Baldwinsville, NY....................800-847-5677
Len E. Ivarson
Milwaukee, WI....................414-351-0700
Levin Brothers Paper
Cicero, IL....................800-666-8484
Lewisburg Container Company
Lewisburg, OH....................937-962-2681
Lone Star Container Corporation
Irving, TX....................800-552-6937
Longview Fibre Company
Longview, WA....................800-929-8111
Lowell Paper Box Company
Nashua, NH....................603-595-0700
Loy-Lange Box Company
Saint Louis, MO....................800-886-4712
Mack-Chicago Corporation
Chicago, IL....................800-992-6225
MacMillan Bloedel Packaging
Montgomery, AL....................800-239-4464
Mall City Containers
Kalamazoo, MI....................800-643-6721
Marcus Carton Company
Melville, NY....................631-752-4200
Marfred Industries
Sun Valley, CA....................800-529-5156
Marion Paper Box Company
Marion, IN....................765-664-6435
Maro Paper Products Company
Bellwood, IL....................708-649-9982
Maypak
Wayne, NJ....................973-696-0780
Merchants Publishing Company
Kalamazoo, MI....................269-345-1175
Meyer Packaging
Palmyra, PA....................717-838-6300
Meyers Corbox Co, Inc.
Cleveland, OH....................800-321-7286
Michiana Corrugated Products
Sturgis, MI....................269-651-5225
Michigan Box Company
Detroit, MI....................888-642-4269
Mid Cities Paper Box Company
Downey, CA....................877-277-6272
Midwest Paper Tube & CanCorporation
New Berlin, WI....................262-782-7300
Modern Paper Box Company
Providence, RI....................401-861-7357
Morphy Container Company
Brantford, ON....................519-752-5428
Mount Vernon Packaging
Mount Vernon, OH....................888-397-3221
Nagel Paper & Box Company
Saginaw, MI....................800-292-3654
Neff Packaging Solutions
Mason, OH....................800-445-4383
Negus Container & Packaging
Madison, WI....................888-241-7482
New England Wooden Ware Corporation
Gardner, MA....................800-252-9214
New York Corrugated Box Company
Paterson, NJ....................973-742-5000
North American PackagingCorporation
New York, NY....................800-499-3521
Northeast Box Company
Ashtabula, OH....................800-362-8100
Northeast Container Corporation
Dumont, NJ....................201-385-6200
NPC Display Group
Newark, NJ....................973-589-2155
Oakes Carton Company
Kalamazoo, MI....................269-381-6022
Ockerlund Industries
Forest Park, IL....................708-771-7707
Old Dominion Box Company
Madison Heights, VA....................434-929-6701
Oracle Packaging
Toledo, OH....................800-952-9536
Original Packaging & Display Company
Saint Louis, MO....................314-772-7797
Ott Packagings
Selinsgrove, PA....................570-374-2811
Packaging Corporation of America
Lake Forest, IL....................800-456-4725
Packaging Design Corporation
Burr Ridge, IL....................630-323-1354
Packing Material Company
Southfield, MI....................248-489-7000
Packrite Packaging
Archdale, NC....................336-431-1111
Paragon Packaging
Ferndale, CA....................888-615-0065
Parlor City Paper Box Company
Binghamton, NY....................607-772-0600
PARTA
Kent, OH....................800-543-5781
Paul T. Freund Corporation
Palmyra, NY....................800-333-0091
Pell Paper Box Company
Elizabeth City, NC....................252-335-4361
Performance Packaging
Trail Creek, IN....................219-874-6226
Pioneer Packaging & Printing
Anoka, MN....................800-708-1705
Pohlig Brothers
Richmond, VA....................804-275-9000
Portland Paper Box Company
Portland, OR....................800-547-2571
Premier Packages
Saint Louis, MO....................800-466-6588
Pride Container Corporation
Chicago, IL....................773-227-6000
Quality Packaging, Inc.
Fond du Lac, WI....................800-923-3633
Rand-Whitney Container Corporation
Worcester, MA....................508-791-2301
Rand-Whitney Container Corporation
Portsmouth, NH....................603-822-7300
RDA Container Corporation
Gates, NY....................585-247-2323
Reliable Container Corporation
Downey, CA....................562-745-0200
Reliance-Paragon
Philadelphia, PA....................215-743-1231
Rhoades Paper Box Corporation
Springfield, OH....................800-441-6494
Rice Packaging
Ellington, CT....................800-367-6725
Ritz Packaging Company
Brooklyn, NY....................718-366-2300
RJR Packaging, Inc.
Oakland, CA....................510-638-5901
Rock Tenn/Alliance Group
Tullahoma, TN....................931-455-3535
Rock-Tenn Company
Norcross, GA....................770-448-2193
Romanow Container
Westwood, MA....................781-320-9200
Round Paper Packages
Erlanger, KY....................859-331-7200
Roy's Folding Box
Cleveland, OH....................216-464-1191
Royal Box Group
Cicero, IL....................708-656-2020
Ruffino Paper Box Manufacturing
Hackensack, NJ....................201-487-1260
Rusken Packaging
Cullman, AL....................256-734-0092
Schermerhorn
Chicopee, MA....................413-598-8348
Schwarz
Morton Grove, IL....................847-966-4050
Scope Packaging
Orange, CA....................714-998-4411
Scott & Daniells
Portland, CT....................860-342-1932
Seaboard Carton Company
Downers Grove, IL....................708-344-0575
Sebring Container Corporation
Salem, OH....................330-332-1533
Security Packaging
North Bergen, NJ....................201-854-1955
Set Point Paper Company
Mansfield, MA....................800-225-0501
SFBC, LLC dba Seaboard Folding Box
Fitchburg, MA....................800-225-6313
Shillington Box Company
Saint Louis, MO....................636-225-5353
Shippers Supply
Saskatoon, SK....................800-661-5639
Shippers Supply, Labelgraphic
Calgary, AB....................800-661-5639
Shore Paper Box Company
Mardela Springs, MD....................410-749-7125
Shorewood Packaging
Carlstadt, NJ....................201-933-3203
Simkins Industries
East Haven, CT....................203-787-7171
Smurfit Stone Container
San Jose, CA....................408-925-9391
Smyrna Container Company
Smyrna, GA....................800-868-4305
Somerville Packaging
Scarborough, ON....................416-291-1161
Sonderen Packaging
Spokane, WA....................800-727-9139
SONOCO
Hartsville, SC....................800-576-6626
Southern Bag Corporation
Madison, MS....................662-746-3631
Southern Champion Tray
Chattanooga, TN....................800-468-2222
Southern Missouri Containers
Springfield, MO....................800-999-7666
Southern Packaging Corporation
Bennettsville, SC....................843-479-7154
Sphinx Adsorbents
Springfield, MA....................800-388-0157
Spring Cove Container
Roaring Spring, PA....................814-224-2222
St Joseph Packaging Inc
St Joseph, MO....................800-383-3000
Stand Fast Packaging Products
Addison, IL....................630-600-0900
Standard Folding Cartons
Flushing, NY....................718-335-5500
Stearnswood
Hutchinson, MN....................800-657-0144
Stone Container
Moss Point, MS....................502-491-4870
Stone Container
Santa Fe Springs, CA....................714-774-0100

Stronghaven Inc.
Matthews, NC . . . 800-222-7919
Suburban Corrugated Box Company
Indianhead Park, IL . . . 630-920-1230
Superior Quality Products
Schenectady, NY . . . 800-724-1129
T.J. Smith Box Company
Fort Smith, AR . . . 877-540-7933
Taylor Box Company
Warren, RI . . . 800-304-6361
Tenneco Packaging
Westmont, IL . . . 630-850-7034
THARCO
San Lorenzo, CA . . . 800-772-2332
The Shelby Company
Cleveland, OH . . . 800-842-1650
Traub Container Corporation
Cleveland, OH . . . 216-475-5100
Trent Corporation
Trenton, NJ . . . 609-587-7515
Tucson Container Corporation
Tucson, AZ . . . 520-746-3171
UniPak
West Chester, PA . . . 610-436-6600
Unique Boxes
Chicago, IL . . . 800-281-1670
Universal Folding Box
East Orange, NJ . . . 973-482-4300
Universal Folding Box Company
Hoboken, NJ . . . 201-659-7373
Universal Paper Box
Seattle, WA . . . 800-228-1045
Utah Paper Box Company
Salt Lake City, UT . . . 801-363-0093
Victory Box Corporation
Roselle, NJ . . . 908-245-5100
Victory Packaging, Inc.
Houston, TX . . . 800-486-5606
Viking Packaging & Display
San Jose, CA . . . 408-998-1000
VIP Real Estate Ltd
Chicago, IL . . . 773-376-5000
Volk Packaging Corporation
Biddeford, ME . . . 800-341-0208
Willamette Industries
Beaverton, OR . . . 503-641-1131
Winchester Carton
Eutaw, AL . . . 205-372-3337
Woodson Pallet
Anmoore, WV . . . 304-623-2858
Wright Brothers Paper Box Company
Fond Du Lac, WI . . . 920-921-8270
York Container Company
York, PA . . . 717-757-7611

Plastic

Abbott Industries
Paterson, NJ
Aco Container Systems
Pickering, ON . . . 800-542-9942
All American Containers
Medley, FL . . . 305-887-0797
All American Poly Corporation
Piscataway, NJ . . . 800-526-3551
Alpack
Centerville, MA . . . 508-771-9131
Amcor Twinpak
Dorval, QC . . . 514-684-7070
Anchor Packaging
Ballwin, MO . . . 800-467-3900
AR Arena Products
Rochester, NY . . . 800-836-2528
Arthur Corporation
Huron, OH . . . 419-433-7202
Atlas Equipment Company
Kansas City, MO . . . 800-842-9188
Bardes Plastics
Milwaukee, WI . . . 800-558-5161
Belleview
Brookline, NH . . . 603-878-1583
Bergen Barrel & Drum Company
Kearny, NJ . . . 201-998-3500
Berry Plastics
Evansville, IN . . . 800-234-1930
Berry Plastics
Evansville, IN . . . 812-424-2904
Berry Plastics Corporation
Evansville, IN . . . 800-822-2342
Berry Plastics Corporation
Evansville, IN . . . 812-424-2904
Bonar Plastics
West Chicago, IL . . . 800-295-3725
Browns International & Company
St. Laurent, QC . . . 514-737-1326
Buckhorn Canada
Brampton, ON . . . 800-461-7579
Buckhorn Inc
Milford, OH . . . 800-543-4454
Bulk Lift International
Carpentersville, IL . . . 800-992-6372
Cardinal Packaging
Evansville, IN . . . 812-424-2904
Carson Industries
Pomona, CA . . . 800-735-5566
CCW Products, Inc.
Arvada, CO . . . 303-427-9663
Central Plastics Corporation
Shawnee, OK . . . 800-654-3872
Chem-Tainer Industries
West Babylon, NY . . . 800-275-2436
Chem-Tainer Industries
West Babylon, NY . . . 800-938-8896
Chili Plastics
Rochester, NY . . . 585-889-4680
CKS Packaging
Atlanta, GA . . . 800-800-4257
Clawson Container Company
Clarkston, MI . . . 800-325-8700
Clearplass Containers
Penn Yan, NY . . . 315-536-5690
Conductive Containers, I
New Hope, MN . . . 800-327-2329
Constar International
Trevose, PA . . . 215-552-3700
Container Specialties
Melrose Park, IL . . . 800-548-7513
Container Supply Company
Garden Grove, CA . . . 714-891-4896
Continental Plastic Container
Dallas, TX . . . 972-303-1825
Contour Packaging
Philadelphia, PA . . . 215-457-1600
Convoy
Canton, OH . . . 800-899-1583
Corning Costar
Acton, MA . . . 800-492-1110
CPT
Edgerton, WI . . . 608-884-2244
Crespac Incorporated
Tucker, GA . . . 800-438-1900
CTK Plastics
Moose Jaw, SK . . . 800-667-8847
Cube Plastics
Concord, Ontario, ON . . . 877-260-2823
Custom Bottle of Connecticut
Naugatuck, CT . . . 203-723-6661
Dahl Tech, Inc.
Stillwater, MN . . . 800-626-5812
Dart Container Corporation
Mason, MI . . . 800-248-5960
De Ster Corporation
Atlanta, GA . . . 800-237-8270
Del-Tec Packaging
Greenville, SC . . . 800-747-8683
Design Plastics
Omaha, NE . . . 800-491-0786
Double R Enterprises
New Castle, PA . . . 724-658-2477
Douglas Stephen Plastics
Paterson, NJ . . . 973-523-3030
E.S. Robbins Corporation
Muscle Shoals, AL . . . 800-800-2235
Edco Industries
Bridgeport, CT . . . 203-333-8982
Edge Paper Box Company
Cudahy, CA . . . 323-771-7733
Emco Industrial Plastics
Cedar Grove, NJ . . . 800-292-9906
Engineered Products
Hazelwood, MO . . . 314-731-5744
Fabri-Kal Corporation
Kalamazoo, MI . . . 800-888-5054
Finn Industries
Ontario, CA . . . 909-930-1500
Flex Products
Carlstadt, NJ . . . 800-526-6273
Frankston Paper Box Company of Texas
Frankston, TX . . . 903-876-2550
Fuller Brush Company
Great Bend, KS . . . 800-522-0499
Gary Plastic Packaging Corporation
Bronx, NY . . . 800-221-8151
Genpak
Peterborough, ON . . . 800-461-1995
Genpak
Glens Falls, NY . . . 800-626-6695
Glasko Plastics
Santa Ana, CA . . . 714-751-7830
Graham Engineering Corporation
York, PA . . . 717-848-3755
GranPac
Wetaskiwin, AB . . . 780-352-3324
Great Western Products
Ontario, CA . . . 888-598-5588
Greenfield Packaging
White Plains, NY . . . 914-993-0233
Gulf Packaging Company
Safety Harbor, FL . . . 800-749-3466
Hartford Plastics
Omaha, NE
Hedstrom Corporation
Ashland, OH . . . 700-765-9665
Hedwin Corporation
Baltimore, MD . . . 800-638-1012
Highland Plastics
Mira Loma, CA . . . 800-368-0491
Indiana Bottle Company Inc.
Scottsburg, IN . . . 800-752-8702
Indiana Vac-Form
Warsaw, IN . . . 574-269-1725
Indianapolis Container Company
Indianapolis, IN . . . 800-760-3318
Intertech Corporation
Greensboro, NC . . . 800-364-2255
IPL Plastics
Edmundston, NB . . . 800-739-9595
Jarisch Paper Box Company
North Adams, MA . . . 413-663-5396
Jescorp
Des Plaines, IL . . . 847-299-7800
Juice Merchandising Corporation
Kansas City, MO . . . 800-950-1998
Juice Tree
Omaha, NE . . . 714-891-4425
Jupiter Mills Corporation
Roslyn, NY . . . 800-853-5121
Just Plastics
New York, NY . . . 212-569-8500
Kadon Corporation
Milford, OH . . . 937-299-0088
Key Packaging Company
Sarasota, FL . . . 941-355-2728
KHM Plastics
Gurnee, IL . . . 847-249-4910
Kimball Companies
East Longmeadow, MA . . . 413-525-1881
King Plastics
North Port, FL . . . 941-493-5502
Landis Plastics
Alsip, IL . . . 708-396-1470
Letica Corporation
Rochester, MI . . . 800-538-4221
Lin Pac Plastics
Roswell, GA . . . 770-751-6006
Linvar
Hartford, CT . . . 800-282-5288
Liquitane
Berwick, PA . . . 570-759-6200
LMK Containers
Centerville, UT . . . 626-821-9984
Lunn Industries
Glen Cove, NY . . . 516-671-9000
M&L Plastics
Easthampton, MA . . . 413-527-1330
Marco Products
Adrian, MI . . . 517-265-3333
Marpac Industries
Philmont, NY . . . 888-462-7722
Melmat, Inc.
Huntington Beach, CA . . . 800-635-6289
Melville Plastics
Haw River, NC . . . 336-578-5800
Menasha Corporation
Oconomowoc, WI . . . 262-560-0228
Micro Qwik
Cross Plains, WI . . . 608-798-3071
Midland Manufacturing Company
Monroe, IA . . . 800-394-2625
Molded Container Corporation
Portland, OR . . . 503-233-8601
Morris Transparent Box Company
East Providence, RI . . . 401-438-6116
Mullinix Packages
Fort Wayne, IN . . . 260-747-3149

North American PackagingCorporation
New York, NY 800-499-3521
NU-Trend Plastic/Corrigan & Company
Jacksonville, FL 904-353-5936
O-I
Perrysburg, OH
Ockerlund Industries
Forest Park, IL 708-771-7707
Olcott Plastics
Saint Charles, IL 888-313-5277
ORBIS Corporation
Oconomowoc, WI 800-890-7292
Packaging Associates
Randolph, NJ 973-252-8890
Packaging Corporation of America
Lake Forest, IL 800-456-4725
Pactiv LLC
Lake Forest, IL 888-828-2850
Pan Pacific Plastics Manufacturing
Hayward, CA 888-475-6888
Par-Pak
Houston, TX 713-686-6700
Par-Pak
Houston, TX 888-272-7725
Paragon Packaging
Ferndale, CA 888-615-0065
Pelco Packaging Corporation
Stirling, NJ 908-647-3500
Penn Bottle & Supply Company
Philadelphia, PA 215-365-5700
Penn Products
Portland, CT 800-490-7366
Pinckney Molded Plastics
Howell, MI 800-854-2920
Pioneer Packaging
Dixon, KY 800-951-1551
Plastic Assembly Corporation
Ayer, MA 978- 77- 472
Plastic Industries
Athens, TN 800-894-4876
Plastic Packaging Corporation
Hickory, NC 828-328-2466
Plastics
Greensboro, AL 334-624-8801
Plastipak Packaging
Plymouth, MI 734-354-3510
Plastiques Cascades Group
Montreal, QC 888-703-6515
Plaxicon
West Chicago, IL 630-231-0850
Pocono PET
Hazle Twp, PA 570-459-1800
Podnar Plastics
Kent, OH 800-673-5277
Polar Plastics
Mooresville, NC 704-660-6600
Poliplastic
Granby, QC 450-378-8417
Poly Plastic Products
Delano, PA 570-467-3000
Poly Processing Company
French Camp, CA 877-325-3142
Polybottle Group
Brampton, ON 905-450-3600
Polycon Industries
Chicago, IL 773-374-5500
Prestige Plastics Corporation
Delta, BC 604-930-2931
Pretium Packaging
Seymour, IN 812-522-8177
Pretium Packaging, LLC.
Chesterfield, MO 314-727-8200
Print Source
Wakefield, RI 401-789-9339
Progressive Plastics
Cleveland, OH 800-252-0053
Prolon
Port Gibson, MS 888-480-9828
Promens
St. John, NB 800-295-3725
Quality Container Company
Ypsilanti, MI 734-481-1373
Quantum Storage Systems
Miami, FL 800-685-4665
Quintex Corporation
Spokane Valley, WA 509-924-7900
RAPAC
Oakland, TN 800-280-6333
RC Molding Inc.
Greer, SC 864-879-7279
Regal Plastic Company
Mission, KS 800-852-1556
Reliance Product
Winnipeg, MB 800-665-0258
Reliance-Paragon
Philadelphia, PA 215-743-1231
Rexam Beverage Can Company
Chicago, IL 773-399-3000
Rez-Tech Corporation
Kent, OH 800-673-5277
Richard Read Construction Company
Arcadia, CA 888-450-7343
Richards Packaging
Memphis, TN 800-361-6453
RMI-C/Rotonics Manaufacturing
Bensenville, IL 630-773-9510
Ropak
Oak Brook, IL 800-527-2267
S.S.I. Schaefer System International Limited
Brampton, ON 905-458-5399
Sabert Corporation
Sayreville, NJ 800-722-3781
Saeplast Canada
St John, NB 800-567-3966
Semco Plastic Company
Saint Louis, MO 314-487-4557
Set Point Paper Company
Mansfield, MA 800-225-0501
Setco
Monroe Twp, NJ 609-655-4600
Setco
Anaheim, CA 714-777-5200
SFB Plastics
Wichita, KS 800-343-8133
Sharpsville Container
Sharpsville, PA 800-645-1248
Shaw-Clayton Corporation
San Rafael, CA 800-537-6712
Sheboygan Paper Box Company
Sheboygan, WI 800-458-8373
Sho-Me Container
Grinnell, IA 800-798-3512
Silgan Plastics Canada
Chesterfield, MO 800-274-5426
Smurfit Stone Container
San Jose, CA 408-925-9391
Snapware
Fullerton, CA 800-334-3062
Snyder Industries Inc.
Lincoln, NE 800-351-1363
Spartanburg Stainless Products
Spartanburg, SC 800-974-7500
Spartech Plastics
Portage, WI 800-998-7123
Star Container Company
Phoenix, AZ 480-281-4200
Step Products
Round Rock, TX 800-777-7837
Stock America Inc
Grafton, WI 262-375-4100
Superfos Packaging
Cumberland, MD 800-537-9242
T&S Blow Molding
Scarborough, ON 416-752-8330
TEQ
Huntley, IL 800-874-7113
Thermodynamics
Commerce City, CO 800-627-9037
Thermodyne International
Ontario, CA 909-923-9945
Thornton Plastics
Salt Lake City, UT 800-248-3434
Titan Plastics
East Rutherford, NJ 201-935-7700
Trans Container Corporation
Upland, CA 909-985-2750
Tri-State Plastics
Henderson, KY 270-826-8361
Triple Dot Corporation
Santa Ana, CA 714-241-0888
Tupperware Brand Corporation
Orlando, FL 800-366-3800
Universal Container Corporation
Odessa, FL 800-582-7477
Visual Packaging Corporation
Haskell, NJ 973-835-7055
WES Plastics
Richmond Hill, ON 905-508-1546
Willamette Industries
Louisville, KY 800-465-3065
Wiltec
Leominster, MA 978-537-1497
Winzen Film
Sulphur Springs, TX 800-779-7595
WNA Hopple Plastics
Florence, KY 800-446-4622
WNA-Cups Illustrated
Lancaster, TX 800-334-2877
Woodstock Plastics Company
Marengo, IL 815-568-5281
World Kitchen
Rosemont, IL 847-678-8600
Zero Corporation
Monson, MA 413-267-5561

Corks

Crown

Cork Specialties
Miami, FL 305-477-1506
Fetzer Vineyards
Hopland, CA 800-846-8637
Palace Packaging Machines
Downingtown, PA 610-873-7252

Crates

Bottle

Langer Manufacturing Company
Cedar Rapids, IA 800-728-6445
Tulip Corporation
Milwaukee, WI 414-963-3120

Egg

Eggboxes Inc
Deerfield Beach, FL 800-326-6667
Jacksonville Box & Woodwork Company
Jacksonville, FL 800-683-2699

Wooden Shipping

American Box Corporation
Lisbon, OH 330-424-8055
American Pallet
Oakdale, CA 209-847-6122
Brooks Barrel Company
Baltimore, MD 800-398-2766
Burgess Manufacturing ofOklahoma
Guthrie, OK 800-804-1913
C&L Wood Products
Hartselle, AL 800-483-2035
Cassel Box & Lumber Company
Grafton, WI 262-377-4420
Corbett Package Company
Wilmington, NC 800-334-0684
Corrugated Inner-Pak Corporation
Conshohocken, PA 610-825-0200
Denver Reel & Pallet Company
Denver, CO 303-321-1920
Eichler Wood Products
Laurys Station, PA 610-262-6749
Elberta Crate & Box Company
Carpentersville, IL 888-672-9260
Farmers Co-op Elevator Co.
Hudsonville, MI 800-439-9859
Fehlig Brothers Box & Lumber Company
St Louis, MO 314-241-6900
Fox Valley Wood Products
Kaukauna, WI 920-766-4069
Franklin Crates
Micanopy, FL 352-466-3141
Fruit Growers Package Company
Grandville, MI 616-724-1400
Gatewood Products LLC
Parkersburg, WV 800-827-5461
Goeman's Wood Products
Hartford, WI 262-673-6090
Greene Industries
East Greenwich, RI 401-884-7530
H. Arnold Wood Turning
Tarrytown, NY 888-314-0088
Hampton Roads Box Company
Suffolk, VA 757-934-2355
Heritage Packaging
Victor, NY 585-742-3310
Herkimer Pallet & Wood Products Company
Herkimer, NY 315-866-4591
Hinchcliff Products Company
Strongsville, OH 440-238-5200
Horn Packaging Corporation
Lancaster, MA 800-832-7020
Hunter Woodworks
Carson, CA 800-966-4751

Indiana Box Company
Greenfield, IN....................317-462-7743
Industrial Contracting &Rigging Company
Mahwah, NJ....................888-427-7444
Industrial Crating & Packing, Inc.
Seattle, WA....................800-942-0499
Industrial Lumber & Packaging
Spring Lake, MI....................616-842-1457
Industrial WoodFab & Packaging Company
Riverview, MI....................734-284-4808
Jacksonville Box & Woodwork Company
Jacksonville, FL....................800-683-2699
Killington Wood ProductsCompany
Rutland, VT....................802-773-9111
Kontane
Charleston, SC....................843-352-0011
Konz Wood Products
Appleton, WI....................877-610-5145
Lawson Industries
Holden, MO....................816-732-4347
Lester Box & Manufacturing
Long Beach, CA....................562-437-5123
Lexel
Fort Worth, TX....................817-332-4061
Little Rock Crate & Basket Company
Little Rock, AR....................800-223-7823
Luke's Almond Acres
Reedley, CA....................559-638-3483
Lumber & Things
Keyser, WV....................800-296-5656
M&H Crates
Jacksonville, TX....................903-683-5351
Maull-Baker Box Company
Brookfield, WI....................414-463-1290
Michiana Box & Crate
Niles, MI....................800-677-6372
Michigan Box Company
Detroit, MI....................888-642-4269
Milan Box Corporation
Milan, TN....................800-225-8057
Moorecraft Box & Crate
Tarboro, NC....................252-823-2510
Nefab Packaging Inc.
Coppell, TX....................800-322-4425
Nefab Packaging, Inc.
Coppell, TX....................800-322-4425
Nelson Company
Baltimore, MD....................410-477-3000
New Lisbon Wood ProductsManufacturing Company
New Lisbon, WI....................608-562-3122
New Mexico Products
Albuquerque, NM....................877-345-7864
Oak Creek Pallet Company
Milwaukee, WI....................414-762-7170
Packing Material Company
Southfield, MI....................248-489-7000
Pallets
Fort Edward, NY....................800-PLT-SKID
Perfect Packaging Company
Perrysburg, OH....................419-874-3167
Pine Point Wood Products
Dayton, MN....................763-428-4301
Precision Wood of Hawaii
Vancouver, WA....................808-682-2055
Precision Wood Products
Vancouver, WA....................360-694-8322
Remmey Wood Products
Southampton, PA....................215-355-3335
Roddy Products PackagingCompany
Aldan, PA....................610-623-7040
Seattle-Tacoma Box Co.
Kent, WA....................253-854-9700
Seattle-Tacoma Box Company
Kent, WA....................253-854-9700
Smith Pallet Company
Hatfield, AR....................870-389-6184
Southern Pallet
Memphis, TN....................901-942-4603
Spring Wood Products
Geneva, OH....................440-466-1135
Stearnswood
Hutchinson, MN....................800-657-0144
Tampa Pallet Company
Tampa, FL....................813-626-5700
The Original Lincoln Logs
Chestertown, NY....................800-833-2461
Thunder Pallet
Theresa, WI....................800-354-0643
W.W. Babcock Company
Bath, NY....................607-776-3341
Wisconsin Box Company
Wausau, WI....................800-876-6658
Wisconsinbox
Wausau, WI....................715-842-2248
WNC Pallet & Forest Products
Candler, NC....................828-667-5426
Xtreme Beverages, LLC
Dana Point, CA....................949-495-7929

Cups

Paper

Acme International
Maplewood, NJ....................973-416-0400
AJM Packaging Corporation
Bloomfield Hills, MI....................248-901-0040
Aladdin's Hookah & Loung Bar
Nashville, TN....................615-329-3558
Bynoe Printers
New York, NY....................212-662-5041
Central Bag & Burlap Company
Denver, CO....................800-783-1224
Chinet Company
Laguna Niguel, CA....................949-348-1711
Creative Converting
Clintonville, WI....................800-826-0418
Dart Container Corporation
Mason, MI....................800-248-5960
Durango-Georgia Paper
Tampa, FL....................813-286-2718
Fonda Group
Oshkosh, WI....................800-558-9300
Fort James Canada
Toronto, ON....................416-784-1621
Fort James Corporation
Norwalk, CT....................800-257-9744
Four M Manufacturing Group
San Jose, CA....................408-998-1141
Insulair
Vernalis, CA....................800-343-3402
International Paper Co.
Memphis, TN....................800-207-4003
James River Canada
North York, ON....................416-789-5151
Jones-Zylon Company
West Lafayette, OH....................800-848-8160
Letica Corporation
Rochester, MI....................800-538-4221
Nyman Manufacturing Company
Rumford, RI....................401-438-3410
Primary Liquidation Corporation
Bohemia, NY....................631-244-1410
Rockline Industries
Sheboygan, WI....................800-558-7790
Scan Group
Appleton, WI....................920-730-9150
Solo Cup Canada
Toronto, ON....................800-465-9696
Solo Cup Company
Lake Forest, IL....................800-367-2877
Solo Cup Company
Owings Mills, MD....................800-800-0300
Tenneco Specialty Packaging
Smyrna, GA....................800-241-4402

Plastic

Arthur Corporation
Huron, OH....................419-433-7202
Carlisle Food Service Products
Oklahoma City, OK....................800-654-8210
Carthage Cup Company
Longview, TX....................903-238-9833
Central Bag & Burlap Company
Denver, CO....................800-783-1224
Chinet Company
Laguna Niguel, CA....................949-348-1711
Cr. Manufacturing
Waverly, NE....................877-789-5844
Creative Converting
Clintonville, WI....................800-826-0418
Dart Container Corporation
Mason, MI....................800-248-5960
De Ster Corporation
Atlanta, GA....................800-237-8270
Design Specialties
Hamden, CT....................800-999-1584
Donoco Industries
Huntington Beach, CA....................888-822-8763
Elliot Lee
Cedarhurst, NY....................516-569-9595
Fabri-Kal Corporation
Kalamazoo, MI....................800-888-5054
Filmpack Plastic Corporation
Dayton, NJ....................732-329-6523
Fonda Group
Oshkosh, WI....................800-558-9300
Fort James Canada
Toronto, ON....................416-784-1621
Genpak
Peterborough, ON....................800-461-1995
Highland Plastics
Mira Loma, CA....................800-368-0491
HPI North America/ Plastics
Eagan, MN....................800-752-7462
Huhtamaki Food Service Plastics
Lake Forest, IL....................800-244-6382
Image Plastics
Houston, TX....................800-289-2811
James River Canada
North York, ON....................416-789-5151
Jones-Zylon Company
West Lafayette, OH....................800-848-8160
Kendrick Johnson & Associates
Bloomington, MN....................800-826-1271
King Plastics
North Port, FL....................941-493-5502
Letica Corporation
Rochester, MI....................800-538-4221
Master Containers
Mulberry, FL....................800-881-6847
MDR International
North Miami, FL....................305-944-5019
Novelty Crystal Corporation
Groveland, FL....................352-429-9036
Nyman Manufacturing Company
Rumford, RI....................401-438-3410
OWD
Tupper Lake, NY....................800-836-1693
Party Yards
Casselberry, FL....................877-501-4400
Peter Gray Corporation
Andover, MA....................978-470-0990
Plaxall
Long Island City, NY....................800-876-5706
Polar Plastics
St Laurent, QC....................514-331-0207
Polar Plastics
Mooresville, NC....................704-660-6600
Set Point Paper Company
Mansfield, MA....................800-225-0501
Solo Cup Canada
Toronto, ON....................800-465-9696
Solo Cup Company
Lake Forest, IL....................800-367-2877
Solo Cup Company
Owings Mills, MD....................800-800-0300
Spirit Foodservice, Inc.
Andover, MA....................800-343-0996
Techform
Mount Airy, NC....................336-789-2115
Tenneco Specialty Packaging
Smyrna, GA....................800-241-4402
Thermo-Serv
Dallas, TX....................800-635-5559
Ullman Company
New York, NY....................212-571-0068
Whirley Industries
Warren, PA....................800-825-5575
Wiltec
Leominster, MA....................978-537-1497
WNA-Comet West
City of Industry, CA....................800-225-0939
WNA-Cups Illustrated
Lancaster, TX....................800-334-2877

Styrofoam

Solo Cup Company
Lake Forest, IL....................800-367-2877
Solo Cup Company
Owings Mills, MD....................800-800-0300

Film

Cellulose Acetate

Emco Industrial Plastics
Cedar Grove, NJ....................800-292-9906
Modern Plastics
Bridgeport, CT....................800-243-9696
Pater & Associates
Cincinnati, OH....................513- 24- 215
Star Poly Bag, Inc.
Brooklyn, NY....................718-384-3130

Teepak LLC
Lisle, IL........................800-621-0264
UCB Films
Smyrna, GA.......................877-822-3456

Plastic

Achilles USA
Everett, WA......................425-353-7000
AEP Industries
South Hackensack, NJ.............800-999-2374
Aep Industries Inc.
South Hackensack, NJ.............800-999-2374
Amcor Twinpak
Dorval, QC.......................514-684-7070
Anchor Packaging
Ballwin, MO......................800-467-3900
Atlantis Plastics Institutional Products
Mankato, MN......................800-999-2374
Atlantis Plastics LinearFilm
Tulsa, OK........................800-324-9727
BagcraftPapercon
Chicago, IL......................800-621-8468
Beayl Weiner/Pak
Pacific Palisades, CA............310-454-1354
Bemis Company
Neenah, WI.......................612-376-3000
Blako Industries
Dunbridge, OH....................419-833-4491
Bollore
Dayville, CT.....................860-774-2930
Brentwood Plastic Films
St Louis, MO.....................314-968-1137
Carlisle Plastics
Minneapolis, MN..................952-884-1309
Cello Bag Company
Bowling Green, KY................800-347-0338
Cello Pack Corporation
Cheektowaga, NY..................800-778-3111
Central Bag & Burlap Company
Denver, CO.......................800-783-1224
Champion Plastics
Clifton, NJ......................800-526-1230
Cincinnati Convertors
Cincinnati, OH...................513-731-6600
Cleveland Plastic Films
Elyria, OH.......................800-832-6799
Cleveland Specialties Company
Loveland, OH.....................513-677-9787
Colonial Transparent Products Company
Hicksville, NY...................516-822-4430
Command Packaging
Vernon, CA.......................800-996-2247
Cortec Corporation
St. Paul, MN.....................800-426-7832
Crayex Corporation
Piqua, OH........................800-837-1747
Crystal-Flex Packaging Corporation
Rockville Centre, NY.............888-246-7325
Curwood
Oshkosh, WI......................800-544-4672
Danafilms
Westborough, MA..................508-366-8884
DuPont
Wilmington, DE...................800-441-7515
Dynamic Packaging
Minneapolis, MN..................800-878-9380
Ellay
Commerce, CA.....................323-725-2974
Ellehammer Industries
Langley, BC......................604-882-9326
Exopack
Tomah, WI........................608-372-2153
Exopack, LLC
Spartanburg, SC..................877-447-3539
Farnell Packaging
Dartmouth, NS....................800-565-9378
Film X
Dayville, CT.....................800-628-6128
Film-Pak
Crowley, TX......................800-526-1838
Filmco
Aurora, OH.......................800-545-8457
FLEXcon Company
Spencer, MA......................508-885-8200
Flexo Transparent
Buffalo, NY......................877-993-5396
FormFlex
Bloomingdale, IN.................800-255-7659
Fredman Bag Company
Milwaukee, WI....................800-945-5686
GBS Corporate
North Canton, OH.................800-552-2427
Gemini Plastic Films Corporation
Garfield, NJ.....................800-789-4732
General Films
Covington, OH....................888-436-3456
Goodwrappers/J.C. Parry & Sons Company
Halethorpe, MD...................800-638-1127
Greenfield Packaging
White Plains, NY.................914-993-0233
Gulf Arizona Packaging
Humble, TX.......................800-364-3887
Gulf Systems
Oklahoma City, OK................405-528-2293
Gulf Systems
Brownsville, TX..................800-217-4853
Gulf Systems
Oklahoma City, OK................800-364-3887
Hedwin Corporation
Baltimore, MD....................800-638-1012
Herche Warehouse
Denver, CO.......................303-371-8186
Home Plastics
Des Moines, IA...................515-265-2562
Hudson Poly Bag
Hudson, MA.......................800-229-7566
Huntsman Packaging
South Deerfield, MA..............413-665-2145
Huntsman Packaging Corporation
Birmingham, Bi...................205-328-4720
Inteplast Bags & Films Corporation
Delta, BC........................604-946-5431
Jescorp
Des Plaines, IL..................847-299-7800
Kama Corporation
Hazleton, PA.....................570-455-0958
Karolina Polymers
Hickory, NC......................828-328-2247
Klockner Pentaplast of America
Gordonsville, VA.................540-832-3600
KM International
Kenton, TN.......................731-749-8700
Kurz Transfer Products
Charlotte, NC....................800-333-2306
L&H Wood Manufacturing Company
Farmington, MI...................248-474-9000
Longhorn Packaging
San Antonio, TX..................800-433-7974
Luetzow Industries
South Milwaukee, WI..............800-558-6055
Mark Products Company
Denville, NJ.....................973-983-8818
Marshall Plastic Film
Martin, MI.......................269-672-5511
Mason Transparent Package Company
Armonk, NY.......................718-792-6000
Merix Chemical Company
Chicago, IL......................312-573-1400
Microplas Industries
Dunwoody, GA.....................800-952-4528
Mitsubishi Polyester Film, Inc.
Greer, SC........................864-879-5000
Modern Plastics
Bridgeport, CT...................800-243-9696
Mohawk Northern Plastics
Auburn, WA.......................800-426-1100
MS Plastics & Packaging Company
Butler, NJ.......................800-593-1802
National Poly Bag Manufacturing Corporation
Brooklyn, NY.....................718-629-9800
Northeast Packaging Materials
Monsey, NY.......................845-426-2900
Now Plastics
East Longmeadow, MA..............413-525-1010
Occidental Chemical Corporation
Dallas, TX.......................800-733-3665
OMNOVA Solutions
Fairlawn, OH.....................330-869-4200
Packaging Materials
Cambridge, OH....................800-565-8550
Packing Material Company
Southfield, MI...................248-489-7000
Pactiv LLC
Lake Forest, IL..................888-828-2850
Pak Sak Industries
Sparta, MI.......................800-748-0431
Parade Packaging
Mundelein, IL....................847-566-6264
Pater & Associates
Cincinnati, OH...................513- 24- 215
Plascal Corporation
Farmingdale, NY..................800-899-7527
Plastic Suppliers
Columbus, OH.....................800-722-5577
Plastic-Craft Products Corp
West Nyack, NY...................800-627-3010
Poly Plastic Products
Delano, PA.......................570-467-3000
Portco Corporation
Vancouver, WA....................800-426-1794
Printpack
Atlanta, GA......................404-460-7000
QPF
Streamwood, IL...................800-323-6963
Quality Films
Three Rivers, MI.................269-679-5263
RJR Packaging, Inc.
Oakland, CA......................510-638-5901
Robbie Manufacturing
Shawnee Mission, KS..............800-255-6328
Roll-O-Sheets Canada
Barrie, ON.......................888-767-3456
Roplast Industries Inc.
Oroville, CA.....................800-767-5278
Rowland Technologies
Wallingford, CT..................203-269-9500
Rutan Polyethylene Supply Bag & Manufacturing Company
Mahwah, NJ.......................800-872-1474
Seal-Tite Bag Company
Philadelphia, PA.................717-917-1949
Sealed Air Corporation
Elmwood Park, NJ.................800-648-9093
Senior Housing Options
Denver, CO.......................800-659-2656
Shields Bag & Printing Company
Yakima, WA.......................800-541-8630
Ship Rite Packaging
Bergenfield, NJ..................800-721-7447
Shippers Supply
Saskatoon, SK....................800-661-5639
SleeveCo Inc
Dawsonville, GA..................706-216-3110
Sommers Plastic ProductsCompany
Clifton, NJ......................800-225-7677
Southern Film Extruders
High Point, NC...................800-334-6101
Spartech Plastics
Wichita, KS......................316-722-8621
Spartech Plastics
Portage, WI......................800-998-7123
Spartech Poly Com
Clayton, MI......................888-721-4242
Specialty Films & Associates
Hebron, KY.......................800-984-3346
Star Poly Bag, Inc.
Brooklyn, NY.....................718-384-3130
Stone Container
Chicago, IL......................312-346-6600
Sungjae Corporation
Irvine, CA.......................949-757-1727
Teknor Apex Co
City of Industry, CA.............800-556-3864
Terphane
Bloomfield, NY...................585-657-5800
Trident Plastics
Ivyland, PA......................800-222-2318
Trio Packaging Corporation
Ronkonkoma, NY...................800-331-0492
Triune Enterprises
Gardena, CA......................310-719-1600
Tyco Plastics
Lakeville, MN....................800-328-4080
UCB Films
Smyrna, GA.......................877-822-3456
ULMA Packaging Systems, Inc.
Ball Ground, GA..................770-345-5300
Uniplast Films
Palmer, MA.......................800-343-1295
Vacumet Corporation
Austell, GA......................800-776-0865
Vc999 Packaging Systems Inc.
Kansas City, MO..................800-728-2999
VIFAN
Lanoraie, QC.....................800-557-0192
Virginia Plastics
Roanoke, VA......................800-777-8541
Viskase Companies
Darien, IL.......................800-323-8562
VPI Mirrex Corporation
Bear, DE.........................800-488-7608
Western Plastics
Calhoun, GA......................800-752-4106

Western Plastics California
Portland, TN 615-325-7331
Wisconsin Film & Bag
Shawano, WI. 800-765-9224
Wright Plastics Company
Prattville, AL 800-874-7659
Zimmer Custom-Made Packaging
Indianapolis, IN 317-263-3436

Pressure Sensitive

Bemis Company
Neenah, WI. 920-727-4100
CL&D Graphics
Oconomowoc, WI. 800-777-1114
Creative Coatings Corporation
Nashua, NH. 800-229-1957
FLEXcon Company
Spencer, MA 508-885-8200
General Formulations
Sparta, MI 800-253-3664
Mactac
Stow, OH. 800-233-4291
Northstar Print Group
Green Bay, WI. 800-236-8208
Shippers Supply
Winnipeg, NB 800-661-5639
Tyco Plastics
Lakeville, MN. 800-328-4080

Foil

Aluminum

Alcoa Foil Products
St Louis, MO. 314-481-7000
All Foils
Strongsville, OH 800-521-0054
Alufoil Products
Hauppauge, NY 631-231-4141
Burrows Paper Corporation
Little Falls, NY. 800-272-7122
Norandal
Franklin, TX 615-771-5700
Novelis Foil Products
Lagrange, GA 800-776-8701
Packaging Dynamics International
Caldwell, OH 740-732-5665
Republic Foil
Danbury, CT 800-722-3645
RJR Packaging, Inc.
Oakland, CA 510-638-5901
Somerville Packaging
Mississauga, ON 905-678-8211
Source for Packaging
New York, NY 800-223-2527
Tilly Industries
St Laurent, QC 514-331-4922
Trinidad Benham Corporation
Denver, CO 303-220-1400
Unifoil Corporation
Fairfield, NJ 973-244-9900
Western Plastics
Calhoun, GA. 800-752-4106
Western Plastics California
Portland, TN 615-325-7331

Pressure Sensitive

Mactac
Stow, OH. 800-233-4291
Tag & Label Corporation
Anderson, SC 864-224-2122

Printed & Laminated

All Foils
Strongsville, OH 800-521-0054
Alufoil Products
Hauppauge, NY 631-231-4141
BagcraftPapercon
Chicago, IL 800-621-8468
Catty Corporation
Harvard, IL 815-943-2288
Cincinnati Convertors
Cincinnati, OH 513-731-6600
Clearwater Paper Corporation
Spokane, WA. 877-847-7831
FormFlex
Bloomingdale, IN 800-255-7659
Hampden Papers
Holyoke, MA 413-536-1000
Kurz Transfer Products
Charlotte, NC 800-333-2306
Label Makers
Pleasant Prairie, WI 800-208-3331
Milprint
Oshkosh, WI 920-303-8600
Norandal
Franklin, TX 615-771-5700
Pakmark
Chesterfield, MO 800-423-1379
Paper Products Company
Cincinnati, OH 513-921-4717
Pater & Associates
Cincinnati, OH 513- 24- 215
Tag & Label Corporation
Anderson, SC 864-224-2122
Tolas Health Care Packaging
Feasterville Trevose, PA. 215-322-7900
Unifoil Corporation
Fairfield, NJ 973-244-9900

Inks

Indelible

Chicago Ink & Research Company
Antioch, IL 847-395-1078
Ideal Stencil Machine & Tape Company
Marion, IL. 800-388-0162
Organic Products Company
Dallas, TX. 972-438-7321
Trident
Brookfield, CT 203-740-9333
Volk Corporation
Farmington Hills, MI 800-521-6799
Wichita Stamp & Seal
Wichita, KS. 316-263-4223

Marking & Coding

ABM Marking Company
Belleville, IL. 800-626-9012
Carteret Coding
Clark, NJ. 732-574-0900
Chicago Ink & Research Company
Antioch, IL 847-395-1078
Colorcon
Harleysville, PA 215-256-7700
Custom Rubber Stamp Company
Crosby, MN. 888-606-4579
Dixie Rubber Stamp & Seal Company
Atlanta, GA. 404-875-8883
Domino Amjet
Gurnee, IL. 800-444-4512
Easterday Fluid Technologies
Saint Francis, WI 414-482-4488
Federal Stamp & Seal Manufacturing Company
Atlanta, GA. 800-333-7726
Ferro Corporation
Pittsburgh, PA. 412-781-7519
Fox Stamp, Sign & Specialty
Menasha, WI. 800-236-3699
Fraser Stamp & Seal
Chicago, IL 800-540-8565
Frost Manufacturing Corporation
Worcester, MA 800-462-0216
Garvey Products
Cincinnati, OH 513-771-8710
Graphic Impressions of Illinois
River Grove, IL. 708-453-1100
Hartford Stamp Works
Hartford, CT 860-249-6205
Hiss Stamp Company
Columbus, OH 614-224-5119
Ideal Stencil Machine & Tape Company
Marion, IL. 800-388-0162
Imaje
Kennesaw, GA 770-421-7700
Independent Ink
Gardena, CA 800-446-5538
Innovative Ceramic Corp.
East Liverpool, OH. 330-385-6515
Koehler Gibson Marking &Graphics
Buffalo, NY. 800-875-1562
Marsh Company
Belleville, IL. 800-527-6275
Mastermark
Kent, WA. 206-762-9610
Modern Stamp Company
Baltimore, MD 800-727-3029
Muskogee Rubber Stamp & Seal Company
Fort Gibson, OK 918-478-3046
Organic Products Company
Dallas, TX. 972-438-7321
Quick Stamp & Sign Mfg
Lafayette, LA 337-232-2171
Richardson's Stamp Works
Houston, TX 713-973-0300
Sohn Manufacturing
Elkhart Lake, WI. 920-876-3361
Southern Rubber Stamp Company
Tulsa, OK 888-826-4304
Starkey Chemical ProcessCompany
La Grange, IL 800-323-3040
Tharo Systems, Inc
Brunswick, OH 800-878-6833
Trident
Brookfield, CT 203-740-9333
Videojet Technologies, Inc
Wood Dale, IL. 800-843-3610
Volk Corporation
Farmington Hills, MI 800-521-6799

Meat Branding

Ideal Stencil Machine & Tape Company
Marion, IL. 800-388-0162
Service Stamp Works
Chicago, IL 312-666-8839

Jars

Canning & Preserving

Alcoa Packaging Machinery
Randolph, NY 716-358-6451
Delta Plastics
Hot Springs, AR 501-760-3000

Glass

All American Containers
Medley, FL 305-887-0797
Arkansas Glass Container Corporation
Jonesboro, AR. 800-527-4527
Bal/Foster Glass Container Company
Port Allegany, PA 814-642-2521
Ball Glass Container Corporation
El Monte, CA 626-448-9831
Gessner Products Company
Ambler, PA 800-874-7808
Greenfield Packaging
White Plains, NY 914-993-0233
Indiana Glass Company
Columbus, OH 800-543-0357
Indianapolis Container Company
Indianapolis, IN 800-760-3318
LMK Containers
Centerville, UT 626-821-9984
Louisville Container Company
Indianapolis, IN 888-539-7225
Olcott Plastics
Saint Charles, IL. 888-313-5277
Promens
St. John, NB 800-295-3725
Richards Packaging
Memphis, TN 800-583-0327
St. Tobain Containers
Seattle, WA 206-762-0660
Vivid Packaging Inc
Cleveland, OH 877-752-2250
World Kitchen
Elmira, NY 800-999-3436

Plastic

Delta Plastics
Hot Springs, AR 501-760-3000
Vivid Packaging Inc
Cleveland, OH 877-752-2250

Labels

A-1 Business Supplies
Dover, NJ 800-631-3421
Aabbitt Adhesives
Chicago, IL 800-222-2488
About Packaging Robotics
Thornton, CO 303-449-2559
AC Label Company
Provo, UT 801-642-3500
Accuform Manufacturing, Inc.
Vacaville, CA 800-233-3352
AD/Mart
Calumet City, IL 708-891-0990

Adhesive Label
New Hope, MN ... 763-746-2900
Adhesive Products, Inc.
Vernon, CA ... 800-669-5516
Adstick Custom Labels
Denver, CO ... 800-255-7314
Advanced Labelworx, Inc
Oak Ridge, TN ... 865-966-8711
Ahlstrom Filtration LLC
Madisonville, KY ... 270-821-0140
Aigner Index
New Windsor, NY ... 800-242-3919
Alcan Packaging
Chicago, IL ... 773-444-0415
Allied Graphics
St Michael, MN ... 800-490-9931
Altrua Marketing Designs
Tallahassee, FL ... 800-443-6939
AM Graphics
Minneapolis, MN ... 612-341-2020
American Forms & Labels
Boise, ID ... 800-388-3554
American Label Mark
Chicago, IL ... 800-621-5808
Ampersand Label
Green Bay, WI ... 800-325-0589
Andrew H. Lawson Company
Philadelphia, PA ... 800-411-6628
Andy Printed Products
Lagrangeville, NY ... 845-223-5101
Appleson Press
Syosset, NY ... 800-888-2775
Artistic Packaging Concepts
Massapequa Pk, NY ... 516-797-4020
ASCENT Technics Corporation
Brick, NJ ... 800-774-7077
ATK
Chicago, IL ... 800-522-3582
ATL-East Tag & Label Company
West Chester, PA ... 866-381-8744
Atlas Labels
Montreal, QC ... 514-852-7000
Atlas Packaging & Displays Inc
Miami, FL ... 800-662-0630
Atlas Tag & Label
Neenah, WI ... 800-558-6418
Auburn Label & Tag Company
New York, NY ... 212-971-0338
Avery Dennison Corporation
Glendale, CA ... 626-304-2000
Axon Corporation/Styrotech
Raleigh, NC ... 800-598-8601
Baltimore Tape Products
Sykesville, MD ... 410-795-0063
Barkley Filing Supplies
Hattiesburg, MS ... 800-647-3070
Baur Tape & Label Company
San Antonio, TX ... 877-738-3222
Bedford Industries
Worthington, MN ... 800-533-5314
Bertek Systems
Georgia, VT ... 800-367-0210
Born Printing Company
Baltimore, MD ... 410-646-7768
Burford Corporation
Maysville, OK ... 877-287-3673
Bynoe Printers
New York, NY ... 212-662-5041
Carlton Industries
La Grange, TX ... 800-231-5988
CCL Label
Cold Spring, KY ... 800-422-6633
Cellotape
Fremont, CA ... 800-231-0608
Central Container Corporation
Minneapolis, MN ... 763-425-7444
Central Decal Company
Burr Ridge, IL ... 800-869-7654
Christman Screenprint
Springfield, MI ... 800-962-9330
Church Offset Printing Inc. & North American Label
Albert Lea, MN ... 800-345-2116
CL&D Graphics
Oconomowoc, WI ... 800-777-1114
CMS Gilbreth Packaging Systems
Croydon, PA ... 800-630-2413
Coast Label Company
Fountain Valley, CA ... 800-995-0483
Coastal Sleeve Label
Brunswick, GA ... 877-753-3837
Colonial Transparent Products Company
Hicksville, NY ... 516-822-4430

Comm-Pak
Opelika, AL ... 334-749-6201
Computerized Machinery System
Maple Grove, MN ... 763-493-0099
Computype
Saint Paul, MN ... 800-328-0852
Conimar Corporation
Ocala, FL ... 800-874-9735
Consolidated Label Company
Longwood, FL ... 800-475-2235
Continental Identification
Sparta, MI ... 800-247-2499
Covergent Label Technology
Tampa, FL ... 800-252-6111
Creative Label Designers
Lees Summit, MO ... 816-537-8757
Crown Label Company
Santa Ana, CA ... 800-422-3590
Cummins Label Company
Kalamazoo, MI ... 800-280-7589
Curtis 1000
Duluth, GA ... 877-287-8715
Curzon Promotional Graphics
Omaha, NE ... 800-769-7446
Custom Card & Label Corporation
Lincoln Park, NJ ... 973-492-0022
Custom Stamp Company
Anza, CA ... 323-292-0753
Daclabels
Dallas, TX ... 800-483-1700
Dana Labels
Beaverton, OR ... 800-255-1492
Darson Corporation
Detroit, MI ... 800-783-7781
Data Visible Corporation
Charlottesville, VA ... 800-368-3494
Day Mark/Food Safety Systems
Bowling Green, OH ... 419-353-2458
Daydots
Fort Worth, TX ... 800-321-3687
Deadline Press
Kennesaw, GA ... 770-419-2232
Decal Techniques
West Babylon, NY ... 800-735-3322
Deco Labels & Tags
Toronto, ON ... 888-496-9029
Decorated Products Company
Westfield, MA ... 413-568-0944
DeLeone Corporation
Redmond, OR ... 541-504-8311
Design Label Manufacturing
East Lyme, CT ... 800-666-1575
Design Mark Corporation
Wareham, MA ... 800-451-3275
Donnick Label Systems
Jacksonville, FL ... 800-334-7849
Dot-It Food Safety Products
Arlington, TX ... 800-642-3687
Double Envelope Corporation
Roanoke, VA ... 540-362-3311
Dow Industries
Wilmington, MA ... 800-776-1201
DRS Designs
Bethel, CT ... 888-792-3740
Eaton Manufacturing Company
Houston, TX ... 800-328-6610
Ebel Tape & Label
Cincinnati, OH ... 513-471-1067
Economy Label Sales Company
Daytona Beach, FL ... 386-253-4741
EMED Company
Buffalo, NY ... 800-442-3633
Engraving Services Co.
Woodville South, SA
EPI World Graphics
Midlothian, IL ... 708-389-7500
Epsen Hilmer Graphics Company
Omaha, NE ... 800-228-9940
ERS International
Norwalk, CT ... 800-377-4685
Esselte Meto
Morris Plains, NJ ... 800-645-3290
Farnell Packaging
Dartmouth, NS ... 800-565-9378
Fast Bags
Fort Worth, TX ... 800-321-3687
Fasteners for Retail
Cincinnati, OH ... 800-422-2547
Federal Label Systems
Elmhurst, NY ... 800-238-0015
Fernqvist Labeling Solutions
Mountain View, CA ... 800-426-8215

Ferro Corporation
Pittsburgh, PA ... 412-781-7519
Fleming Packaging Corporation
Peoria, IL ... 309-676-7657
FLEXcon Company
Spencer, MA ... 508-885-8200
Flexible Tape & Label Company
Memphis, TN ... 901-522-1410
Flexo Graphics
Amarillo, TX ... 866-533-5396
Forest Manufacturing Company
Twinsburg, OH ... 330-425-3805
Fort Dearborn Company
Niles, IL ... 773-774-4321
Fotel
Lombard, IL ... 800-834-4920
Foxon Company
Providence, RI ... 800-556-6943
France Personalized Signs
Cleveland, OH ... 216-241-2198
Frost Manufacturing Corporation
Worcester, MA ... 800-462-0216
Garvey Products
Cincinnati, OH ... 513-771-8710
Garvey Products
West Chester, OH ... 800-543-1908
GBS Corporate
North Canton, OH ... 800-552-2427
GCA Bar Code Specialist
Huntington Beach, CA ... 714-379-4911
General Press Corporation
Natrona Heights, PA ... 724-224-3500
General Tape & Supply
Wixom, MI ... 800-490-3633
General Trade Mark Labelcraft
Staten Island, NY ... 718-448-9800
Gintzler Graphics
Williamsville, NY ... 716-631-9700
Globe Ticket & Label Company
Warminster, PA ... 800-523-5968
GM Nameplate
Seattle, WA ... 800-366-7668
Grand Rapids Label Company
Grand Rapids, MI ... 616-459-8134
Grand Valley Labels
Grand Rapids, MI
Graphic Impressions of Illinois
River Grove, IL ... 708-453-1100
Graphic Packaging Corporation
Golden, CO ... 800-677-2886
Graphic Technology
New Century, KS ... 800-767-9920
Graphics Unlimited
San Diego, CA ... 858-453-4031
Green Bay Packaging
Green Bay, WI ... 920-433-5111
Greenbush Tape & Label, Inc.
Albany, NY ... 518-465-2389
Gulf Arizona Packaging
Humble, TX ... 800-364-3887
H.B. Fuller Company
St Paul, MN ... 651-236-5900
Hal Mather & Sons
Woodstock, IL ... 800-338-4007
Halpak Plastics
Deer Park, NY ... 800-442-5725
Hano Business Forms
Wilbraham, MA ... 413-781-7800
Harris & Company
Salem, OH ... 330-332-4127
Herche Warehouse
Denver, CO ... 303-371-8186
Home Plastics
Des Moines, IA ... 515-265-2562
Hub Labels
Hagerstown, MD ... 800-433-4532
Hurst Labeling Systems
Chatsworth, CA ... 800-969-1705
Imprinting Systems
Charlotte, NC ... 800-497-1403
Industrial Nameplates
Ivyland, PA ... 800-878-6263
Inland Label and Marketing Services, LLC
La Crosse, WI ... 800-657-4413
Innovative Folding Carton Company
South Plainfield, NJ ... 908-757-0205
Innovative Packaging Solution
Martin, MI ... 616-656-2100
INOVAR Packaging Group
Arlington, TX ... 800-285-2235
Intermec Technologies Corporation
Everett, WA ... 425-348-2600

Intermec Technologies Corporation
Everett, WA. 800-755-5505
Interstate Packaging
White Bluff, TN 800-251-1072
Itac Label
Brooklyn, NY 718-625-2148
J.M. Packaging/Detroit Tape & Label
Warren, MI 586-771-7800
J.V. Reed & Company
Louisville, KY 877-258-7333
John Henry Packaging
Penngrove, CA 800-327-5997
KAPCO
Kent, OH. 800-843-5368
Kemex Meat Brands
Washington, DC 301-277-2444
Kennedy Group
Willoughby, OH 440-951-7660
KHS Company
West Simsbury, CT 860-658-9454
Kwik Lok Corporation
Yakima, WA 800-688-5945
L&N Label Company
Clearwater, FL 800-944-5401
Label Art
Tucker, GA 800-652-1072
Label Graphix
Heath, OH. 740-929-2210
Label House
Fullerton, CA 800-499-5858
Label Products
Bloomington, MN. 877-370-0688
Label Specialties
Placentia, CA 800-635-2386
Label Systems
Bridgeport, CT 203-333-5503
Label Systems
Newmarket, ON 905-836-7844
Label Systems & Solutions
Bohemia, NY 800-811-2560
Label Technology
Merced, CA. 800-388-1990
Labelmart
Maple Grove, MN. 888-577-0141
Labelmax
Laredo, TX 956-722-6493
LabelPrint Corporation
Newburyport, MA. 978-463-4004
LabelQuest
Elmhurst, IL 800-999-5301
Labels By Pulizzi
Williamsport, PA. 570-326-1244
Labels Systems, Inc
Addison, TX 800-220-9552
Lacroix Packaging
St-Placide, Quebec, QC 450-258-2262
Lancaster Colony Corporation
Columbus, OH 614-224-7141
Lawrence Schiff Silk Mills
New York, NY 800-272-4433
Lawson Mardon Flexible Labels
Weston, ON. 416-742-8910
Lawson Mardon Packaging
New Hyde Park, NY. 516-775-8000
Lawson Mardon Packaging
Burnaby, BC 800-721-8211
Leathertone
Findlay, OH. 419-429-0188
Lewis Label Products Corporation
Fort Worth, TX 800-772-7728
Lewisburg Printing Company
Lewisburg, TN 800-559-1526
LGInternational, Inc.
Portland, OR 800-345-0534
Liberty Labels, LLC
Liberty, MO. 800-783-5285
License Ad Plate Company
Cleveland, OH 216-265-4200
LifeLines Technology
Morris Plains, NJ 973-984-0525
Lion Labels
South Easton, MA. 800-875-5300
Lone Peak Labeling Systems
Salt Lake City, UT 800-658-8599
Long Island Stamp Corporation
Flushing, NY. 800-547-8267
Lord Label Group
Charlotte, NC 800-341-5225
Los Angeles Label Company
Commerce, CA. 800-606-5223
Louis Roesch Company
Foster City, CA 415-621-4700

LPI Imports
Chicago, IL 877-389-6563
LTI Printing
Sturgis, MI 269-651-7574
Lustre-Cal Nameplate Corporation
Lodi, CA. 800-234-6264
Mail-Well Label
Sparks, NV 775-359-1703
Mail-Well Label
Baltimore, MD 800-637-4879
Mar-Boro Printing & Advertising Specialties
Brooklyn, NY 718-336-4051
Mark-It Rubber Stamp & Label Company
Stamford, CT. 203-348-3204
Marklite Line
Bellwood, IL. 708-668-4900
Master Tape Printers, Inc.
Chicago, IL 800-621-5801
Mateer Burt
Exton, PA 800-345-1308
McCourt Label Company
Lewis Run, PA 800-458-2390
Merchants Publishing Company
Kalamazoo, MI 269-345-1175
Meyer Label Company
Fort Myers, FL 239-489-0342
Meyers Printing Company
Minneapolis, MN 763-533-9730
Miami Systems Corporation
Blue Ash, OH 800-543-4540
Mid South Graphics
Nashville, TN 615-331-4210
Middleton Printing
Grand Rapids, MI 800-952-0076
Mister Label, Inc
Bluffton, SC 800-732-0439
Modern Stamp Company
Baltimore, MD 800-727-3029
Morris Industries
Forestville, MD. 301-568-5005
Moss Printing
Elk Grove Village, IL 800-341-1557
MRI Flexible Packaging
Newtown, PA 800-448-8183
Nameplates
St Paul, MN. 651-228-1522
Nashua Corporation
Nashua, NH. 603-661-2004
Nashua Corporation
Omaha, NE 800-662-7482
National Emblem
Carson, CA 800-877-5325
National Label Company
Lafayette Hill, PA 610-825-3250
National Marking Products, Inc.
Richmond, VA. 800-482-1553
National Printing Converters
Encino, CA 818-906-7936
National Tape Corporation
New Orleans, LA 800-535-8846
Nationwide Pennant & Flag Manufacturing
San Antonio, TX. 800-383-3524
Neal Walters Poster Corporation
Bentonville, AR 501-273-2489
New England Label
Barre, VT 800-368-3932
New Era Label Corporation
Belleville, NJ 973-759-2444
North American PackagingCorporation
New York, NY 800-499-3521
Northern Berkshire Manufacturing Company
North Adams, MA 413-663-9204
Northstar Print Group
Green Bay, WI. 800-236-8208
Nosco
Waukegan, IL 847-360-4806
Old English Printing & Label Company
Delray Beach, FL 561-997-9990
Ozark Tape & Label Company
Springfield, MO 417-831-1444
Pace Labels
Williamston, SC 800-789-1592
Package Containers
Canby, OR. 800-266-5806
Package Service Company of Colorado
Northmoor, MO 800-748-7799
Package Systems Corporation
Danielson, CT 800-522-3548
Packaging Materials Corporation/PM Label Corporation
El Paso, TX. 800-325-4195
Packaging Solutions
Los Altos Hills, CA 650-917-1022

Paco Label Systems
Tyler, TX. 800-346-4185
Pakmark
Chesterfield, MO 800-423-1379
Pamco Printed Tape & Label Company
Des Plaines, IL 847-803-2200
Panther Industries
Highlands Ranch, CO 800-530-6018
Paper Product Specialties
Waukesha, WI. 262-549-1730
Parisian Novelty Company
Homewood, IL 773-847-1212
Paxar
Paterson, NJ 973-684-6564
Phenix Label Company
Olathe, KS. 800-274-3649
Philipp Lithographing Company
Grafton, WI. 800-657-0871
Photo-Graphics Company
Grandview, MO. 816-761-3333
Piedmont Label/Smyth Company
Bedford, VA 800-950-7011
Pierrepont Visual Graphics
Rochester, NY. 585-235-5620
Pioneer Labels
Denver, CO 877-744-1606
Pittsfield Weaving Company
Pittsfield, NH 603-435-8301
Plasti-Print
Burlingame, CA 650-652-4950
Plastic Packaging Inc
Hickory, NC 800-333-2466
Precision Printing & Packaging
Clarksville, TN 800-500-4526
Premier Southern Ticket Company
Cincinnati, OH 800-331-2283
Prestige Label Company
Burgaw, NC. 800-969-4449
Prestolabels.Com
Tipp City, OH 800-201-7120
Primera Technology
Plymouth, MN. 800-797-2772
Print & Peel
New York, NY 800-451-0807
Print Source
Wakefield, RI 401-789-9339
Print-O-Tape
Mundelein, IL. 800-346-6311
Pro-Ad-Company
Portland, OR 800-287-5885
Promo Edge
Wall Township, NJ 732-938-4242
Quali-Tech Tape & Label
Denver, CO
Quik-Stik Labels
Everett, MA. 800-225-3496
Racine Company
Racine, WI 800-242-4202
Randall Printing
Brockton, MA. 508-588-3830
RayPress Corporation
Birmingham, AL. 800-423-3731
Recco Tape & Label
West Columbia, SC. 800-334-3008
Regency Label Corporation
Wood Ridge, NJ 201-342-2288
Reid Graphics
Andover, MA 978-474-1930
Reidler Decal Corporation
Saint Clair, PA. 800-628-7770
Rhode Island Label Works
West Warwick, RI. 401-828-6400
Rice Packaging
Ellington, CT 800-367-6725
Richmond Printed Tape & Label
Hatfield, PA. 800-522-3525
Robinson Tape & Label
Branford, CT. 800-433-7102
Rose City Label Company
Portland, OR 800-547-9920
Rothchild Printing Company
Flushing, NY. 800-238-0015
Royal Label Company
Boston, MA. 617-825-6050
RR Donnelley
Chicago, IL. 800-742-4455
RSI ID Technologies
St. Paul, MN 888-364-3577
S Walter Packaging Corporation
Philadelphia, PA 888-429-5673
Samuels Products
Cincinnati, OH 800-543-7155

San Miguel Label Manufacturing
Ciales, PR 787-871-3120
Sancoa International
Lumberton, NJ 609-953-5050
Seal-Tite Bag Company
Philadelphia, PA 717-917-1949
Seneca Tape & Label
Cleveland, OH 800-251-0514
Sesame Label System
New York, NY 800-551-3020
Seton Identification Products
Branford, CT 800-571-2596
SFBC, LLC dba Seaboard Folding Box
Fitchburg, MA 800-225-6313
Shippers Supply
Saskatoon, SK 800-661-5639
Shippers Supply, Labelgraphic
Calgary, AB 800-661-5639
Sign Shop
Rancho Cucamonga, CA 909-945-5888
Signature Packaging
West Orange, NJ 800-376-2299
SleeveCo Inc
Dawsonville, GA 706-216-3110
Smurfit Stone Container
St Louis, MO 314-679-2300
Smyth Companies, LLC
Saint Paul, MN 800-473-3464
Sohn Manufacturing
Elkhart Lake, WI 920-876-3361
Sonoco Engraph Labels
Trenton, NJ 609-586-1332
Sonoco Flexible Packaging
Hartsville, SC 800-377-2692
Source for Packaging
New York, NY 800-223-2527
Southern Atlantic Label Company
Chesapeake, VA 800-456-5999
Southern Imperial
Rockford, IL 800-747-4665
Steven Label Corporation
Santa Fe Springs, CA 800-752-4968
Stoffel Seals Corporation
Tallapoosa, GA 800-422-8247
Storad Tape Company
Marion, OH 740-382-6440
Stratix Corporation
Norcross, GA 800-883-8300
Stricker & Company
La Plata, MD 301-934-8346
Stripper Bags
Henderson, NV 800-354-2247
Superior Products Company
Saint Paul, MN 800-328-9800
Swan Label & Tag
Coraopolis, PA 412-264-9000
Syracuse Label Company
Liverpool, NY 315-422-1037
Systems Graphics
Saint Louis, MO 800-221-7858
T&T Industries
Fort Mohave, AZ 800-437-6246
TAC-PAD
Irvine, CA 800-947-1609
Tag & Label Corporation
Anderson, SC 864-224-2122
Tape & Label Converters
Santa Fe Springs, CA 888-285-2462
Tape & Label Engineering
St Petersburg, FL 800-237-8955
Tarason Packaging, LLC.
Conover, NC 828-464-4743
TeleTech Label Company
Fort Collins, CO 888-403-8253
Tharo Systems, Inc
Brunswick, OH 800-878-6833
Three P
Salt Lake City, UT 801-486-7407
Thunderbird Label Corportion
Fairfield, NJ 973-575-6677
Timely Signs
Elmont, NY 800-457-4467
Timemed Labeling Systems
Valencia, CA 818-897-1111
Toledo Ticket Company
Toledo, OH 419-476-5424
Trident
Brookfield, CT 203-740-9333
Trumbull Nameplates
New Smyrna Beach, FL 386-423-1105
Twin City Pricing & Label
Minneapolis, MN 800-328-5076
United Ad Label
Downers Grove, IL 800-423-4643
United Label Corporation
Newark, NJ 800-252-0917
United Seal & Tag Corporation
Port Charlotte, FL 800-211-9552
Universal Tag
Dudley, MA 800-332-8247
University Products
Holyoke, MA 800-628-9281
US Label Corporation
Greensboro, NC 336-332-7000
Vacumet Corp
Wayne, NJ 973-628-1067
Varitronic Systems
Brooklyn Park, MN 763-536-6400
Vetter Vineyards Winery
Westfield, NY 716-326-3100
Viking Identification Product
Hopkins, MN 952-935-5245
Viking Label & Packaging
Nisswa, MN 218-963-2575
Vomela/Harbor Graphics
St Paul, MN 800-645-1012
Voxcom Web Printing
Peachtree City, GA 770-487-7575
W.T. Nickell Label Company
Batavia, OH 888-899-1991
Wallace Computer Services
Elk Grove Vlg, IL 888-925-8324
Walle Corporation
New Orleans, LA 800-942-6761
Wishbone Utensil Tableware Line
Wheat Ridge, CO 866-266-5928
Wood & Jones Printers
Pasadena, CA 626-797-5700
Worthen Industries
Nashua, NH 603-888-5443
WS Packaging Group Inc
Green Bay, WI 920-866-6300
WS Packaging Group, Inc.
Neenah, WI 888-532-3334
WS Packaging-Superior Label
Green Bay, WI 800-818-5481
Yerecic Label Company
New Kensington, PA 724-335-2200
Yeuell Nameplate & Label
Woburn, MA 781-933-2984

Pressure Sensitive

AC Label Company
Provo, UT 801-642-3500
Accuform Manufacturing, Inc.
Vacaville, CA 800-233-3352
AD/Mart
Calumet City, IL 708-891-0990
Adhesive Products, Inc.
Vernon, CA 800-669-5516
Adstick Custom Labels
Denver, CO 800-255-7314
Advanced Labelworx, Inc
Oak Ridge, TN 865-966-8711
Allied Graphics
St Michael, MN 800-490-9931
AM Graphics
Minneapolis, MN 612-341-2020
American Forms & Labels
Boise, ID 800-388-3554
American Label Mark
Chicago, IL 800-621-5808
Ampersand Label
Green Bay, WI 800-325-0589
Andy Printed Products
Lagrangeville, NY 845-223-5101
Appleson Press
Syosset, NY 800-888-2775
ATL-East Tag & Label Company
West Chester, PA 866-381-8744
Atlas Tag & Label
Neenah, WI 800-558-6418
Auburn Label & Tag Company
New York, NY 212-971-0338
Avery Dennison Corporation
Glendale, CA 626-304-2000
Baltimore Tape Products
Sykesville, MD 410-795-0063
Barkley Filing Supplies
Hattiesburg, MS 800-647-3070
Bertek Systems
Georgia, VT 800-367-0210
CCL Label
Cold Spring, KY 800-422-6633
Cellotape
Fremont, CA 800-231-0608
Central Decal Company
Burr Ridge, IL 800-869-7654
CL&D Graphics
Oconomowoc, WI 800-777-1114
Comm-Pak
Opelika, AL 334-749-6201
Computerized Machinery System
Maple Grove, MN 763-493-0099
Consolidated Label Company
Longwood, FL 800-475-2235
Creative Label Designers
Lees Summit, MO 816-537-8757
Cummins Label Company
Kalamazoo, MI 800-280-7589
Custom Card & Label Corporation
Lincoln Park, NJ 973-492-0022
Custom Stamp Company
Anza, CA 323-292-0753
Daclabels
Dallas, TX 800-483-1700
Dana Labels
Beaverton, OR 800-255-1492
Deadline Press
Kennesaw, GA 770-419-2232
Deco Labels & Tags
Toronto, ON 888-496-9029
DeLeone Corporation
Redmond, OR 541-504-8311
Design Label Manufacturing
East Lyme, CT 800-666-1575
Double Envelope Corporation
Roanoke, VA 540-362-3311
Dow Industries
Wilmington, MA 800-776-1201
DRS Designs
Bethel, CT 888-792-3740
Eagles Printing & Label Co., Inc.
Eau Claire, WI 715-835-6631
Ebel Tape & Label
Cincinnati, OH 513-471-1067
Economy Label Sales Company
Daytona Beach, FL 386-253-4741
Elmark Packaging
West Chester, PA 800-670-9688
EMED Company
Buffalo, NY 800-442-3633
Epsen Hilmer Graphics Company
Omaha, NE 800-228-9940
Farnell Packaging
Dartmouth, NS 800-565-9378
Federal Label Systems
Elmhurst, NY 800-238-0015
FLEXcon Company
Spencer, MA 508-885-8200
Flexible Tape & Label Company
Memphis, TN 901-522-1410
Flexo Graphics
Amarillo, TX 866-533-5396
Forest Manufacturing Company
Twinsburg, OH 330-425-3805
Fort Dearborn Company
Niles, IL 773-774-4321
Foxon Company
Providence, RI 800-556-6943
Garvey Products
Cincinnati, OH 513-771-8710
Garvey Products
West Chester, OH 800-543-1908
GBS Corporate
North Canton, OH 800-552-2427
General Tape & Supply
Wixom, MI 800-490-3633
General Trade Mark Labelcraft
Staten Island, NY 718-448-9800
Gintzler Graphics
Williamsville, NY 716-631-9700
Globe Ticket & Label Company
Warminster, PA 800-523-5968
Grand Rapids Label Company
Grand Rapids, MI 616-459-8134
Grand Valley Labels
Grand Rapids, MI
Graphic Impressions of Illinois
River Grove, IL 708-453-1100
Graphic Technology
New Century, KS 800-767-9920
Greenbush Tape & Label, Inc.
Albany, NY 518-465-2389

Greenfield Packaging
White Plains, NY 914-993-0233
Gulf Arizona Packaging
Humble, TX 800-364-3887
Herche Warehouse
Denver, CO.......................303-371-8186
Houston Label
Pasadena, TX 800-477-6995
Hub Labels
Hagerstown, MD...................800-433-4532
Hurst Labeling Systems
Chatsworth, CA 800-969-1705
Imprinting Systems
Charlotte, NC 800-497-1403
Innovative Folding Carton Company
South Plainfield, NJ 908-757-0205
Innovative Packaging Solution
Martin, MI.......................616-656-2100
Interstate Packaging
White Bluff, TN 800-251-1072
Itac Label
Brooklyn, NY 718-625-2148
KAPCO
Kent, OH.........................800-843-5368
KHS Company
West Simsbury, CT 860-658-9454
L&N Label Company
Clearwater, FL 800-944-5401
Label Aire
Fullerton, CA 714-441-0700
Label Graphix
Heath, OH........................740-929-2210
Label House
Fullerton, CA 800-499-5858
Label Products
Bloomington, MN..................877-370-0688
Label Specialties
Placentia, CA 800-635-2386
Label Systems
Bridgeport, CT 203-333-5503
Label Systems
Newmarket, ON 905-836-7844
Label Systems & Solutions
Bohemia, NY 800-811-2560
Label Technology
Merced, CA.......................800-388-1990
Labelmart
Maple Grove, MN..................888-577-0141
Labelmax
Laredo, TX 956-722-6493
LabelPrint Corporation
Newburyport, MA..................978-463-4004
Labels By Pulizzi
Williamsport, PA.................570-326-1244
Labels Systems, Inc
Addison, TX 800-220-9552
Lewis Label Products Corporation
Fort Worth, TX...................800-772-7728
LGInternational, Inc.
Portland, OR 800-345-0534
Liberty Labels, LLC
Liberty, MO......................800-783-5285
License Ad Plate Company
Cleveland, OH 216-265-4200
Lion Labels
South Easton, MA.................800-875-5300
Long Island Stamp Corporation
Flushing, NY.....................800-547-8267
M&M Displays
Philadelphia, PA 800-874-7171
Marklite Line
Bellwood, IL.....................708-668-4900
Master Tape Printers, Inc.
Chicago, IL 800-621-5801
McCourt Label Company
Lewis Run, PA 800-458-2390
Met-Speed Label
Levittown, PA....................888-886-0638
Meyer Label Company
Fort Myers, FL 239-489-0342
Meyers Printing Company
Minneapolis, MN 763-533-9730
Mid South Graphics
Nashville, TN 615-331-4210
Middleton Printing
Grand Rapids, MI.................800-952-0076
Mister Label, Inc
Bluffton, SC 800-732-0439
Morris Industries
Forestville, MD..................301-568-5005
Moss Printing
Elk Grove Village, IL 800-341-1557

MPI Label Systems
Sebring, OH 800-837-2134
Nashua Corporation
Nashua, NH.......................603-661-2004
Nashua Corporation
Omaha, NE 800-662-7482
National Printing Converters
Encino, CA 818-906-7936
National Tape Corporation
New Orleans, LA 800-535-8846
Neal Walters Poster Corporation
Bentonville, AR 501-273-2489
New England Label
Barre, VT 800-368-3932
New Era Label Corporation
Belleville, NJ 973-759-2444
NJM Packaging
Lebanon, NH......................800-432-2990
Northstar Print Group
Green Bay, WI....................800-236-8208
Ozark Tape & Label Company
Springfield, MO 417-831-1444
Pace Labels
Williamston, SC 800-789-1592
Package Service Company of Colorado
Northmoor, MO 800-748-7799
Package Systems Corporation
Danielson, CT....................800-522-3548
Packaging Materials Corporation/PM Label Corporation
El Paso, TX......................800-325-4195
Pakmark
Chesterfield, MO 800-423-1379
Pamco Printed Tape & Label Company
Des Plaines, IL 847-803-2200
Paper Product Specialties
Waukesha, WI.....................262-549-1730
Piedmont Label/Smyth Company
Bedford, VA 800-950-7011
Pierrepont Visual Graphics
Rochester, NY....................585-235-5620
Plasti-Print
Burlingame, CA 650-652-4950
Premier Southern Ticket Company
Cincinnati, OH 800-331-2283
Print & Peel
New York, NY 800-451-0807
Print Source
Wakefield, RI 401-789-9339
Print-O-Tape
Mundelein, IL....................800-346-6311
Promo Edge
Wall Township, NJ 732-938-4242
Quali-Tech Tape & Label
Denver, CO
Racine Company
Racine, WI 800-242-4202
RayPress Corporation
Birmingham, AL...................800-423-3731
Regency Label Corporation
Wood Ridge, NJ 201-342-2288
Rhode Island Label Works
West Warwick, RI.................401-828-6400
Rice Packaging
Ellington, CT 800-367-6725
Richmond Printed Tape & Label
Hatfield, PA.....................800-522-3525
Robinson Tape & Label
Branford, CT.....................800-433-7102
Rose City Label Company
Portland, OR.....................800-547-9920
Royal Label Company
Boston, MA.......................617-825-6050
RR Donnelley
Chicago, IL......................800-742-4455
Samuels Products
Cincinnati, OH 800-543-7155
Sancoa International
Lumberton, NJ 609-953-5050
Seneca Tape & Label
Cleveland, OH 800-251-0514
Seton Identification Products
Branford, CT.....................800-571-2596
Sign Shop
Rancho Cucamonga, CA 909-945-5888
Smyth Companies, LLC
Saint Paul, MN...................800-473-3464
Sonoco Engraph Labels
Trenton, NJ......................609-586-1332
Source for Packaging
New York, NY 800-223-2527
Southern Atlantic Label Company
Chesapeake, VA 800-456-5999

Steven Label Corporation
Santa Fe Springs, CA.............800-752-4968
Stoffel Seals Corporation
Tallapoosa, GA 800-422-8247
Storad Tape Company
Marion, OH.......................740-382-6440
Stratix Corporation
Norcross, GA 800-883-8300
Stripper Bags
Henderson, NV 800-354-2247
Swan Label & Tag
Coraopolis, PA 412-264-9000
Syracuse Label Company
Liverpool, NY....................315-422-1037
Systems Graphics
Saint Louis, MO 800-221-7858
TAC-PAD
Irvine, CA.......................800-947-1609
Tag & Label Corporation
Anderson, SC 864-224-2122
Tape & Label Converters
Santa Fe Springs, CA.............888-285-2462
Tape & Label Engineering
St Petersburg, FL 800-237-8955
Tarason Packaging, LLC.
Conover, NC......................828-464-4743
TeleTech Label Company
Fort Collins, CO 888-403-8253
Tharo Systems, Inc
Brunswick, OH 800-878-6833
Three P
Salt Lake City, UT 801-486-7407
Thunderbird Label Corportion
Fairfield, NJ 973-575-6677
Timemed Labeling Systems
Valencia, CA 818-897-1111
Trident
Brookfield, CT 203-740-9333
Trumbull Nameplates
New Smyrna Beach, FL 386-423-1105
United Ad Label
Downers Grove, IL................800-423-4643
United Seal & Tag Corporation
Port Charlotte, FL...............800-211-9552
Universal Tag
Dudley, MA.......................800-332-8247
University Products
Holyoke, MA 800-628-9281
Viking Identification Product
Hopkins, MN 952-935-5245
Vomela/Harbor Graphics
St Paul, MN......................800-645-1012
Voxcom Web Printing
Peachtree City, GA 770-487-7575
W.T. Nickell Label Company
Batavia, OH......................888-899-1991
Wallace Computer Services
Elk Grove Vlg, IL................888-925-8324
Wishbone Utensil Tableware Line
Wheat Ridge, CO 866-266-5928
WS Packaging-Superior Label
Green Bay, WI....................800-818-5481
Yerecic Label Company
New Kensington, PA...............724-335-2200

Private Label

Adrienne's Gourmet Foods
Santa Barbara, CA 800-937-7010
Alewel's Country Meats
Warrensburg, MO 800-353-8553
Baldwin Richardson Foods
Frankfort, IL....................866-644-2732
Bunzl Distribution USA
St Louis, MO.....................888-997-5959
Century Foods International
Sparta, WI.......................800-269-1901
Main Street Gourmet
Cuyahoga Falls, OH 800-533-6246
Old Mansion Foods
Petersburg, VA 800-476-1877
Treofan America, LLC
Winston-Salem, NC 800-424-6273

Linings

Box, Carton, Case & Crate

Atlantic Foam & Packaging Company
Sanford, FL......................407-328-9444
Chalmur Bag Company, LLC
Philadelphia, PA 800-349-2247

Grayling Industries
Alpharetta, GA 800-635-1551
Greenfield Packaging
White Plains, NY 914-993-0233
Gulf Arizona Packaging
Humble, TX 800-364-3887
Herche Warehouse
Denver, CO 303-371-8186
IB Concepts
Elizabeth, NJ 888-671-0800
Midco Plastics
Enterprise, KS 800-235-2729
Naltex
Austin, TX 800-531-5112
NSW Corporation
Roanoke, VA 800-368-3610
Paper Pak Industries
La Verne, CA 909-392-1750
Powertex
Rouses Point, NY 800-769-3783
Primepak Company
Teaneck, NJ 201-836-5060
Target Industries
Flanders, NJ 973-927-0011
Weyerhaeuser Company
Federal Way, WA 800-525-5440

Can, Drum & Barrel

Carson Manufacturing Company
Petaluma, CA 800-423-2380
CDF Corporation
Plymouth, MA 800-443-1920
Chalmur Bag Company, LLC
Philadelphia, PA 800-349-2247
Enerfab, Inc.
Cincinnati, OH 513-641-0500
FabOhio
Uhrichsville, OH 740-922-4233
Fortifiber Corporation
Fernley, NV 775-575-5557
Greenfield Packaging
White Plains, NY 914-993-0233
Gulf Arizona Packaging
Humble, TX 800-364-3887
Hedwin Corporation
Baltimore, MD 800-638-1012
Herche Warehouse
Denver, CO 303-371-8186
Home Plastics
Des Moines, IA 515-265-2562
Indiana Vac-Form
Warsaw, IN 574-269-1725
Inteplast Bags & Films Corporation
Delta, BC 604-946-5431
Mello Smello
Minneapolis, MN 888-574-2964
Midco Plastics
Enterprise, KS 800-235-2729
Nosaj Disposables
Paterson, NJ 800-631-3809
Packaging Dynamics International
Caldwell, OH 740-732-5665
Powertex
Rouses Point, NY 800-769-3783
Pres-On Products
Addison, IL 800-323-7467
Primepak Company
Teaneck, NJ 201-836-5060
Scholle Corporation
Irvine, CA 949-955-1750
Target Industries
Flanders, NJ 973-927-0011
Tri-Seal
Blauvelt, NY 845-353-3300

Markers, Pens & Pencils

Dri Mark Products
Port Washington, NY 800-645-9118
Elliot Lee
Cedarhurst, NY 516-569-9595
Garland Writing Instruments
Coventry, RI 401-821-1450
Gold Bond
Hixson, TN 423-842-5844
Gotham Pen & Pencil Company
Bronx, NY 800-334-7970
Hub Pen Company
Quincy, MA 617-471-9900
Industries of the Blind
Greensboro, NC 336-274-1591
Listo Pencil Corporation
Alameda, CA 800-547-8648
Markwell Manufacturing Company
Norwood, MA 800-666-1123
Micropoint
Mountain View, CA 650-969-3097
National Pen Corporation
San Diego, CA 858-675-3000
Pelican Products Company
Bronx, NY 800-552-8820
Union Pen Company
Hagaman, NY 518-842-6000
Visual Planning Corp
Champlain, NY 800-361-1192
Volk Corporation
Farmington Hills, MI 800-521-6799

Packaging

Aseptic

Century Foods International
Sparta, WI 800-269-1901
Elopak
New Hudson, MI 248-486-4600
Green Spot Packaging
Claremont, CA 800-456-3210
Innovative Food Solutions LLC
Columbus, OH 800-884-3314
JCS Controls, Inc.
Rochester, NY 585-227-5910
Power Packaging, Inc.
Westerville, OH 877-272-1054
Pressure Pack
Williamsburg, VA 757-220-3693
Professional Marketing Group
Seattle, WA 800-227-3769
Scholle Corporation
Irvine, CA 949-955-1750
SONOCO
Hartsville, SC 800-576-6626

Blister

Accurate Paper Box Company
Knoxville, TN 865-690-0311
Ace Technical Plastics
Hartford, CT 860-305-8138
Artistic Packaging Concepts
Massapequa Pk, NY 516-797-4020
California Vibratory Feeders
Anaheim, CA 800-354-0972
Dynamic Pak
Syracuse, NY 315-474-8593
Gulf Arizona Packaging
Humble, TX 800-364-3887
Gulf Packaging Company
Safety Harbor, FL 800-749-3466
Gulf Systems
Oklahoma City, OK 405-528-2293
Gulf Systems
Brownsville, TX 800-217-4853
Gulf Systems
Arlington, TX 817-261-1915
H.J. Jones & Sons
London, ON 800-667-0476
Hannan Products Corporation
Corona, CA 800-954-4266
Herche Warehouse
Denver, CO 303-371-8186
In-Touch Products
North Salt Lake, UT 801-298-4466
Jay Packaging Group
Warwick, RI 401-739-7200
Key Packaging Company
Sarasota, FL 941-355-2728
Kord Products Inc.
Brantford, ON 800-452-9070
Leading Industry
Oxnard, CA 805-385-4100
Leal True Form Corporation
Freeport, NY 516-379-2008
Maro Paper Products Company
Bellwood, IL 708-649-9982
Packaging & Processing Equipment
Ayr, ON 519-622-6666
Plastech Corporation
Atlanta, GA 404-355-9682
Power Packaging, Inc.
Westerville, OH 877-272-1054
Professional Marketing Group
Seattle, WA 800-227-3769
Rohrer Corporation
Buford, GA 800-243-6640
Rose City Printing & Packaging
Vancouver, WA 800-704-8693
Scott Packaging Corporation
Philadelphia, PA 215-925-5595
Sheboygan Paper Box Company
Sheboygan, WI 800-458-8373
TEQ
Huntley, IL 800-874-7113
Thermex Thermatron
Louisville, KY 502-493-1299
ULMA Packaging Systems, Inc.
Ball Ground, GA 770-345-5300
Woodstock Plastics Company
Marengo, IL 815-568-5281

Flexible Materials

Ace Technical Plastics
Hartford, CT 860-305-8138
Achilles USA
Everett, WA 425-353-7000
ADM Corporation
Middlesex, NJ 800-327-0718
Aladdin Transparent Packaging Corporation
Hauppauge, NY 631-273-4747
Alcan Packaging
Chicago, IL 773-444-0415
Alcoa Foil Products
St Louis, MO 314-481-7000
Alcon Packaging
Weston, ON 416-742-8910
All Foils
Strongsville, OH 800-521-0054
All Sorts Premium Packaging
Buffalo, NY 888-565-9727
Alufoil Products
Hauppauge, NY 631-231-4141
Amcor Twinpak
Dorval, QC 514-684-7070
American Printpak
Sussex, WI 800-441-8003
Anchor Packaging
Ballwin, MO 800-467-3900
AR-BEE Transparent
Elk Grove Vlg, IL 800-642-2247
Atlantis Plastics LinearFilm
Tulsa, OK 800-324-9727
B.A.G. Corporation
Dallas, TX 800-331-9200
BagcraftPapercon
Chicago, IL 800-621-8468
Banner Packaging
Oshkosh, WI 920-303-2300
Beayl Weiner/Pak
Pacific Palisades, CA 310-454-1354
Bemis Company
Neenah, WI 612-376-3000
Bemis Company
Neenah, WI 920-727-4100
Blako Industries
Dunbridge, OH 419-833-4491
Brentwood Plastic Films
St Louis, MO 314-968-1137
Bryce Company
Memphis, TN 800-238-7277
Burrows Paper Corporation
Little Falls, NY 800-272-7122
Can Creations
Pembroke Pines, FL 954-581-3312
Carlisle Plastics
Minneapolis, MN 952-884-1309
Catty Corporation
Harvard, IL 815-943-2288
Cello Bag Company
Bowling Green, KY 800-347-0338
Cello Pack Corporation
Cheektowaga, NY 800-778-3111
Central Bag & Burlap Company
Denver, CO 800-783-1224
Central Bag Company
Leavenworth, KS 913-250-0325
Champion Plastics
Clifton, NJ 800-526-1230
Cincinnati Convertors
Cincinnati, OH 513-731-6600
Circle Packaging Machinery Inc
De Pere, WI 920-983-3420
CL&D Graphics
Oconomowoc, WI 800-777-1114

Cleveland Plastic Films
Elyria, OH 800-832-6799
Cleveland Specialties Company
Loveland, OH 513-677-9787
Cloud Corporation
Des Plaines, IL 847-390-9410
Connecticut Container Corporation
North Haven, CT 203-248-2161
Continental Packaging Corporation
Elgin, IL 847-289-6400
Continental Products
Mexico, MO 800-325-0216
CoolBrands International
Ronkonkoma, NY 631-737-9700
Crystal-Flex Packaging Corporation
Rockville Centre, NY 888-246-7325
Curwood
Oshkosh, WI 800-544-4672
Danafilms
Westborough, MA 508-366-8884
Design Packaging Company
Glencoe, IL 800-321-7659
Dow Chemical Company
Spring House, PA 800-447-4369
Dynamic Packaging
Minneapolis, MN 800-878-9380
Ellay
Commerce, CA 323-725-2974
Ensinger Hyde Company
Grenloch, NJ 856-227-0500
Excelsior Transparent Bag Manufacturing
Yonkers, NY 914-968-1300
Exopack, LLC
Spartanburg, SC 877-447-3539
Fabricon Products
River Rouge, MI 313-841-8200
Farnell Packaging
Dartmouth, NS 800-565-9378
Film X
Dayville, CT 800-628-6128
Filmco
Aurora, OH 800-545-8457
Flexicon
Cary, IL 847-639-3530
Flexo Transparent
Buffalo, NY 877-993-5396
Foam Pack Industries
Springfield, NJ 973-376-3700
Food Pak Corporation
San Mateo, CA 650-341-6559
FormFlex
Bloomingdale, IN 800-255-7659
Gemini Plastic Films Corporation
Garfield, NJ 800-789-4732
General Films
Covington, OH 888-436-3456
Gibraltar Packaging Group
Hastings, NE 402-463-1366
Glopak
St Leonard, QC 800-361-6994
Gulf Arizona Packaging
Humble, TX 800-364-3887
Gulf Systems
Oklahoma City, OK 405-528-2293
Gulf Systems
Brownsville, TX 800-217-4853
Gulf Systems
Oklahoma City, OK 800-364-3887
Gulf Systems
Arlington, TX 817-261-1915
H&H Lumber Company
Amarillo, TX 806-335-1813
Hedwin Corporation
Baltimore, MD 800-638-1012
Herche Warehouse
Denver, CO 303-371-8186
Home Plastics
Des Moines, IA 515-265-2562
Hood Flexible Packaging
St Paul, MN 800-448-0682
Hudson Poly Bag
Hudson, MA 800-229-7566
Huntsman Packaging Corporation
Birmingham, Bi. 205-328-4720
In-Line Corporation
Hopkins, MN 952-938-0046
Interstate Packaging
White Bluff, TN 800-251-1072
Jif-Pak Manufacturing
Vista, CA 800-777-6613
Kama Corporation
Hazleton, PA 570-455-0958

Kapak Corporation
Minneapolis, MN 952-541-0730
KAPCO
Kent, OH 800-843-5368
Karolina Polymers
Hickory, NC 828-328-2247
KHL Engineered Packaging
Montebello, CA 323-721-5300
Klockner Pentaplast of America
Gordonsville, VA 540-832-3600
KM International
Kenton, TN 731-749-8700
Label Technology
Merced, CA 800-388-1990
Lawson Mardon Flexible
Bellwood, IL 708-544-1600
Longhorn Packaging
San Antonio, TX 800-433-7974
LPS Industries
Moonachie, NJ 800-275-4577
Luetzow Industries
South Milwaukee, WI 800-558-6055
M&R Flexible Packaging
Springboro, OH 800-543-3380
Maco Bag Corporation
Newark, NY 315-226-1000
Mactac
Stow, OH 800-233-4291
Mark Products Company
Denville, NJ 973-983-8818
Marshall Plastic Film
Martin, MI 269-672-5511
Masternet, Ltd
Mississauga, ON 800-216-2536
Microplas Industries
Dunwoody, GA 800-952-4528
Milprint
Oshkosh, WI 920-303-8600
Mimi et Cie
Seattle, WA 206-545-1850
Mohawk Northern Plastics
Auburn, WA 800-426-1100
Mohawk Western Plastic
La Verne, CA 909-593-7547
Morris Industries
Forestville, MD 301-568-5005
Multibulk Systems International
Wendell, NC 919-366-2100
National Poly Bag Manufacturing Corporation
Brooklyn, NY 718-629-9800
Net Pack Systems
Oakland, ME 207-465-4531
Northeast Packaging Materials
Monsey, NY 845-426-2900
Now Plastics
East Longmeadow, MA 413-525-1010
OMNOVA Solutions
Fairlawn, OH 330-869-4200
Outlook Packaging
Neenah, WI 920-722-1666
Packaging Enterprises
Rockledge, PA 215-379-1234
Packaging Products Corporation
Mission, KS 913-262-3033
Paco Manufacturing Comp any
Clarksville, IN 888-283-7963
Pak Sak Industries
Sparta, MI 800-748-0431
Pater & Associates
Cincinnati, OH 513- 24- 215
PDMP
Leesburg, VA 703-777-8400
Phoenix Closures
Naperville, IL 630-544-3475
Plascal Corporation
Farmingdale, NY 800-899-7527
Plastic Packaging Corporation
Kansas City, KS 800-468-0029
Plastic Packaging Inc
Hickory, NC 800-333-2466
Plastic Suppliers
Columbus, OH 800-722-5577
Plastic-Craft Products Corp
West Nyack, NY 800-627-3010
Poly Shapes Corporation
Elyria, OH 800-605-9359
Polyplastics
Austin, TX 800-753-7659
Portco Corporation
Vancouver, WA 800-426-1794
Power Packaging, Inc.
Westerville, OH 877-272-1054

Primepak Company
Teaneck, NJ 201-836-5060
Print & Peel
New York, NY 800-451-0807
Print Pack
Atlanta, GA 404-460-7000
Printpack
Atlanta, GA 404-460-7000
Professional Marketing Group
Seattle, WA 800-227-3769
QPF
Streamwood, IL 800-323-6963
Quality Films
Three Rivers, MI 269-679-5263
Ray C. Sprosty Bag Company
Wooster, OH 330-264-8559
Rexam Beverage Can Company
Chicago, IL 773-399-3000
Rico Packaging Company
Chicago, IL 773-523-9190
RJR Packaging, Inc.
Oakland, CA 510-638-5901
Rohrer Corporation
Buford, GA 800-243-6640
Roll-O-Sheets Canada
Barrie, ON 888-767-3456
Rollprint Packaging Products
Addison, IL 800-276-7629
Roplast Industries Inc.
Oroville, CA 800-767-5278
Rowland Technologies
Wallingford, CT 203-269-9500
Rutan Polyethylene Supply Bag & Manufacturing Company
Mahwah, NJ 800-872-1474
Scholle Corporation
Northlake, IL 888-224-6269
Schwab Paper Products Company
Romeoville, IL 800-837-7225
Seal-Tite Bag Company
Philadelphia, PA 717-917-1949
Sealed Air Corporation
Elmwood Park, NJ 800-648-9093
Seiler Plastics Corporation
Saint Louis, MO 314-815-3030
Seville Flexpack Corporation
Oak Creek, WI 414-761-2751
Shields Bag & Printing Company
Yakima, WA 800-541-8630
Shields Products
West Pittston, PA 570-655-4596
Ship Rite Packaging
Bergenfield, NJ 800-721-7447
Shippers Supply
Saskatoon, SK 800-661-5639
Shippers Supply, Labelgraphic
Calgary, AB 800-661-5639
SleeveCo Inc
Dawsonville, GA 706-216-3110
Smurfit Flexible Packaging
Milwaukee, WI 414-355-2700
Sonoco Flexible Packaging
Hartsville, SC 800-377-2692
Southern Film Extruders
High Point, NC 800-334-6101
Spartech Poly Com
Clayton, MI 888-721-4242
Specialty Films & Associates
Hebron, KY 800-984-3346
Star Poly Bag, Inc.
Brooklyn, NY 718-384-3130
Sterling Novelty Products
Northbrook, IL 847-291-0070
Stock America Inc
Grafton, WI 262-375-4100
Sungjae Corporation
Irvine, CA 949-757-1727
Sunland Manufacturing Company
Minneapolis, MN 800-790-1905
Terphane
Bloomfield, NY 585-657-5800
Trans Flex Packagers
Unionville, CT 860-673-2531
Trico Converting
Fullerton, CA 714-563-0701
Trident Plastics
Ivyland, PA 800-222-2318
Trio Packaging Corporation
Ronkonkoma, NY 800-331-0492
Tyco Plastics
Lakeville, MN 800-328-4080

UCB Films
Smyrna, GA 877-822-3456
Ultra Pac
Rogers, MN..................... 800-324-8541
Unifoil Corporation
Fairfield, NJ 973-244-9900
Union Industries
Providence, RI 800-556-6454
Uniplast Films
Palmer, MA..................... 800-343-1295
United Flexible
Westbury, NY 516-222-2150
Vacumet Corp
Wayne, NJ..................... 973-628-1067
Vacumet Corporation
Austell, GA..................... 800-776-0865
Vacuum Depositing
Okolona, KY..................... 502-969-4227
VIFAN
Lanoraie, QC..................... 800-557-0192
Viskase Companies
Darien, IL..................... 800-323-8562
VPI Mirrex Corporation
Bear, DE 800-488-7608
Western Plastics
Calhoun, GA..................... 800-752-4106
Western Plastics California
Portland, TN 615-325-7331
Winpak Technologies
Toronto, ON 416-421-1700
Witt Plastics
Greenville, OH 800-227-9181
Wraps
East Orange, NJ 973-673-7873
Zimmer Custom-Made Packaging
Indianapolis, IN 317-263-3436

Food Protective

Accurate Flannel Bag Company
Paterson, NJ 800-234-9200
Alkar-Rapidpak-MP Equipment, Inc
Lodi, WI 609-592-3211
Allflex Packaging Products
Ambler, PA 800-448-2467
American Excelsior Inc
Arlington, TX 800-777-7645
Ample Industries
Franklin, OH..................... 888-818-9700
Anchor Packaging
Ballwin, MO 800-467-3900
AR-BEE Transparent
Elk Grove Vlg, IL..................... 800-642-2247
BEI
St Charles, IL 630-879-0300
Berry Plastics Corporation
Evansville, IN..................... 800-822-2342
Bryce Company
Memphis, TN 800-238-7277
Burrows Paper Corporation
Little Falls, NY..................... 800-732-1933
Catty Corporation
Harvard, IL..................... 815-943-2288
CCW Products, Inc.
Arvada, CO..................... 303-427-9663
Central Bag & Burlap Company
Denver, CO..................... 800-783-1224
Central Coated Products
Alliance, OH..................... 330-821-9830
Central Fine Pack
Fort Wayne, IN..................... 260-432-3027
Cincinnati Convertors
Cincinnati, OH 513-731-6600
Colbert Packaging Corporation
Lake Forest, IL 847-367-5990
Collector's Gallery
Saint Charles, IL..................... 800-346-3063
Crystal-Flex Packaging Corporation
Rockville Centre, NY..................... 888-246-7325
Curwood, Inc.
Oshkosh, WI..................... 800-544-4672
Custom Foam Molders
Foristell, MO..................... 636-441-2307
Design Plastics
Omaha, NE 800-491-0786
Elmo Rietschle - A Gardner Denver Product
Quincy, IL..................... 217-222-5400
Ensinger Hyde Company
Grenloch, NJ..................... 856-227-0500
Fabri-Kal Corporation
Kalamazoo, MI..................... 800-888-5054
First Brands Corporation
Oakland, CA..................... 203-731-2427
Flexo Transparent
Buffalo, NY..................... 877-993-5396
Foam Concepts
Uxbridge, MA..................... 508-278-7255
Free Flow Packaging Corporation
Redwood City, CA 800-888-3725
Glopak
St Leonard, QC 800-361-6994
Great Western Products
Ontario, CA..................... 888-598-5588
Greenfield Paper Box Company
Greenfield, MA..................... 413-773-9414
Gulf Arizona Packaging
Humble, TX 800-364-3887
Gulf Systems
Oklahoma City, OK 405-528-2293
Gulf Systems
Brownsville, TX 800-217-4853
Gulf Systems
Oklahoma City, OK 800-364-3887
Gulf Systems
Arlington, TX 817-261-1915
Handy Wacks Corporation
Sparta, MI..................... 800-445-4434
Herche Warehouse
Denver, CO 303-371-8186
Hood Flexible Packaging
St Paul, MN..................... 800-448-0682
HUBCO Inc.
Hutchinson, KS..................... 800-563-1867
In the Bag
St Petersburg, FL 800-330-2247
Indian Valley Industries
Johnson City, NY 800-659-5111
Jewel Case Corporation
Providence, RI 800-441-4447
Kalco Enterprises
New York, NY 800-396-6600
King Plastics
North Port, FL..................... 941-493-5502
Lenkay Sani Products Corporation
Brooklyn, NY 718-927-9260
Letica Corporation
Rochester, MI 800-538-4221
Maco Bag Corporation
Newark, NY 315-226-1000
Milliken Packaging
Spartanburg, SC 864-598-0100
Mullinix Packages
Fort Wayne, IN 260-747-3149
Multisorb Technologies
West Seneca, NY 800-445-9890
Norpak Corporation
Newark, NJ 800-631-6970
ORBIS
Oconomowoc, WI..................... 800-890-7292
Osgood Industries Inc.
Oldsmar, FL 813-855-7337
Packaging Progressions
Collegeville, PA 610-489-8601
Packing Material Company
Southfield, MI..................... 248-489-7000
Pacquet Oneida
Charlotte, NC 800-631-8388
Pater & Associates
Cincinnati, OH 513- 24- 215
Patty Paper, Inc.
Plymouth, IN..................... 800-782-1703
Plastilite Corporation
Omaha, NE 800-228-9506
Polyfoam Packers Corporation
Arlington Hts, IL 800-323-7442
Polytainers
Toronto, ON 800-268-2424
Professional Marketing Group
Seattle, WA 800-227-3769
Promarks, Inc.
Ontario, CA..................... 909-923-3888
Roll-O-Sheets Canada
Barrie, ON..................... 888-767-3456
Roplast Industries Inc.
Oroville, CA 800-767-5278
Rownd & Son
Dillon, SC..................... 803-774-8264
Rutan Polyethylene Supply Bag & Manufacturing Company
Mahwah, NJ 800-872-1474
Saeplast Canada
St John, NB..................... 800-567-3966
Salinas Valley Wax PaperCompany
Salinas, CA 831-424-2747
Schroeder Sewing Technologies
San Marcos, CA 760-591-9733
Schwab Paper Products Company
Romeoville, IL 800-837-7225
Schwarz
Morton Grove, IL 847-966-4050
Shields Products
West Pittston, PA..................... 570-655-4596
Shippers Paper Products
Sheridan, AR..................... 800-933-7731
SIG Combibloc USA, Inc.
Chester, PA 610-546-4200
SONOCO
Hartsville, SC 800-576-6626
Southern Film Extruders
High Point, NC 800-334-6101
Sun Plastics
Clearwater, MN..................... 800-862-1673
T.D. Sawvel Company
Maple Plain, MN..................... 877-488-1816
TEMP-TECH Company
Springfield, MA 800-343-5579
Tenneco Packaging
Westmont, IL..................... 630-850-7034
Trans World Services
Melrose, MA..................... 800-882-2105
Trevor Owen Limited
Scarborough, ON 866-487-2224
Tri-State Plastics
Henderson, KY 270-826-8361
Triune Enterprises
Gardena, CA..................... 310-719-1600
ULMA Packaging Systems, Inc.
Ball Ground, GA..................... 770-345-5300
Union Industries
Providence, RI 800-556-6454
Unipac International
Rochester, NY..................... 800-586-2711
United Desiccants
Louisville, KY 505-864-6691
Urnex Brands, Inc.
Elmsford, NY 800-222-2826
Valley Packaging Supply Company, Inc.
Green Bay, WI..................... 920-336-9012
Viscofan USA
Montgomery, AL..................... 800-521-3577
Vista International Packaging
Kenosha, WI 800-558-4058
Vista International Packaging, Inc.
Kenosha, WI..................... 800-558-4058
VPI Mirrex Corporation
Bear, DE 800-488-7608
West-Pak
Dallas, TX..................... 214-337-8984
Wisconsin Converting of Green Bay
Green Bay, WI..................... 800-544-1935

Plastic

Ace Technical Plastics
Hartford, CT 860-305-8138
Acme Bag Company
Chula Vista, CA 800-275-2263
AEP Industries
South Hackensack, NJ 800-999-2374
Alcan Packaging
Chicago, IL 773-444-0415
Alcoa Packaging Machinery
Randolph, NY..................... 716-358-6451
Alkar-Rapidpak-MP Equipment, Inc
Lodi, WI 609-592-3211
Amcor Twinpak
Dorval, QC 514-684-7070
Anchor Packaging
Ballwin, MO 800-467-3900
AR-BEE Transparent
Elk Grove Vlg, IL..................... 800-642-2247
Atlantis Plastics Institutional Products
Mankato, MN 800-999-2374
Atlantis Plastics LinearFilm
Tulsa, OK 800-324-9727
Automated Packaging Systems
Streetsboro, OH 888-288-6224
Beayl Weiner/Pak
Pacific Palisades, CA 310-454-1354
Berry Plastics
Evansville, IN..................... 812-424-2904
Blako Industries
Dunbridge, OH 419-833-4491

Brechteen
Chesterfield, MI 586-949-2240
Brentwood Plastic Films
St Louis, MO. 314-968-1137
Buckhorn Inc
Milford, OH 800-543-4454
Bunzl Distribution USA
St Louis, MO. 888-997-5959
CCW Products, Inc.
Arvada, CO 303-427-9663
CDF Corporation
Plymouth, MA. 800-443-1920
Central Bag & Burlap Company
Denver, CO 800-783-1224
Central Fine Pack
Fort Wayne, IN 260-432-3027
Century Foods International
Sparta, WI. 800-269-1901
Champion Plastics
Clifton, NJ. 800-526-1230
Chem-Tainer Industries
West Babylon, NY 800-275-2436
Chester Plastics
Chester, NS 902-275-3522
Cincinnati Convertors
Cincinnati, OH 513-731-6600
Clawson Container Company
Clarkston, MI 800-325-8700
Clorox Company
Oakland, CA 888-271-7000
Connecticut Container Corporation
North Haven, CT. 203-248-2161
Consolidated Container Company
Atlanta, GA. 888-831-2184
Contour Packaging
Philadelphia, PA 215-457-1600
CR Plastics
Council Bluffs, IA. 866-869-6293
Crayex Corporation
Piqua, OH 800-837-1747
Crown Holdings, Inc.
Philadelphia, PA 215-698-5100
CTK Plastics
Moose Jaw, SK 800-667-8847
Curwood
Oshkosh, WI 800-544-4672
Custom Foam Molders
Foristell, MO. 636-441-2307
Danafilms
Westborough, MA. 508-366-8884
Davis Core & Pad Company
Cave Spring, GA. 800-235-7483
Denice & Filice Packing Company
Hollister, CA. 831-636-0544
Design Packaging Company
Glencoe, IL 800-321-7659
Design Plastics
Omaha, NE 800-491-0786
Dub Harris Corporation
Pomona, CA 909-596-6300
Eaton Manufacturing Company
Houston, TX 800-328-6610
Fabri-Kal Corporation
Kalamazoo, MI 800-888-5054
Farnell Packaging
Dartmouth, NS 800-565-9378
Film X
Dayville, CT 800-628-6128
Flexo Transparent
Buffalo, NY. 877-993-5396
Fredman Bag Company
Milwaukee, WI 800-945-5686
Fremont Die Cut Products
Fremont, OH 800-223-3177
Fulton-Denver Company
Denver, CO 800-776-6715
Gary Plastic Packaging Corporation
Bronx, NY. 800-221-8151
Gary Plastic Packaging Corporation
Bronx, NY. 800-227-4279
Gateway Plastics
Mequon, WI 262-242-2020
Genpak LLC
Lakeville, MN. 800-328-4556
Gibraltar Packaging Group
Hastings, NE. 402-463-1366
Goex Corporation
Janesville, WI 608-754-3303
Golden West Packaging Concept
Lake Forest, CA 949-855-9646
Goodwrappers/J.C. Parry & Sons Company
Halethorpe, MD 800-638-1127

Great Western Products
Ontario, CA. 888-598-5588
Grief Brothers Corporation
Delaware, OH 740-549-6000
Gulf Arizona Packaging
Humble, TX 800-364-3887
Gulf Coast Plastics
Tampa, FL. 800-277-7491
Gulf Systems
Oklahoma City, OK 405-528-2293
Gulf Systems
Brownsville, TX 800-217-4853
Gulf Systems
Oklahoma City, OK 800-364-3887
Gulf Systems
Arlington, TX 817-261-1915
H&H Lumber Company
Amarillo, TX. 806-335-1813
Handy Wacks Corporation
Sparta, MI 800-445-4434
Herche Warehouse
Denver, CO 303-371-8186
Hinkle Manufacturing
Perrysburg, OH 419-666-5550
Hood Flexible Packaging
St Paul, MN. 800-448-0682
Hood Packaging
Burlington, ON 877-637-5066
HUBCO Inc.
Hutchinson, KS. 800-563-1867
Hudson Poly Bag
Hudson, MA 800-229-7566
Huntsman Packaging
South Deerfield, MA 413-665-2145
Indianapolis Container Company
Indianapolis, IN 800-760-3318
Inline Plastics Corporation
Shelton, CT. 800-826-5567
Interstate Packaging
White Bluff, TN 800-251-1072
IPL Plastics
Edmundston, NB. 800-739-9595
iVEX Packaging Corporation
Lachine, QC 514-636-7951
Jomar Plastics Industry
Nanty Glo, PA. 800-681-4039
Kimball Companies
East Longmeadow, MA 413-525-1881
Klockner Pentaplast of America
Gordonsville, VA 540-832-3600
KM International
Kenton, TN. 731-749-8700
Kord Products Inc.
Brantford, ON. 800-452-9070
L&H Wood Manufacturing Company
Farmington, MI. 248-474-9000
Letica Corporation
Rochester, MI 800-538-4221
Luetzow Industries
South Milwaukee, WI. 800-558-6055
Maco Bag Corporation
Newark, NY 315-226-1000
Marpac Industries
Philmont, NY 888-462-7722
Marshall Plastic Film
Martin, MI. 269-672-5511
Mason Transparent Package Company
Armonk, NY 718-792-6000
Masternet, Ltd
Mississauga, ON. 800-216-2536
Maypak
Wayne, NJ. 973-696-0780
Melville Plastics
Haw River, NC 336-578-5800
Microplas Industries
Dunwoody, GA. 800-952-4528
Midco Plastics
Enterprise, KS. 800-235-2729
Mohawk Western Plastic
La Verne, CA 909-593-7547
MRI Flexible Packaging
Newtown, PA 800-448-8183
MS Plastics & Packaging Company
Butler, NJ 800-593-1802
Mullinix Packages
Fort Wayne, IN 260-747-3149
National Poly Bag Manufacturing Corporation
Brooklyn, NY 718-629-9800
Net Pack Systems
Oakland, ME. 207-465-4531
Nolon Industries
Mantua, OH. 330-274-2283

North American PackagingCorporation
New York, NY 800-499-3521
Noteworthy Company
Amsterdam, NY 800-696-7849
ORBIS RPM
Madison, WI 608-852-8840
Packaging Materials
Cambridge, OH. 800-565-8550
Packing Material Company
Southfield, MI. 248-489-7000
Papelera Puertorriquena
Utuado, PR 787-894-2098
Par-Pak
Houston, TX 713-686-6700
Pater & Associates
Cincinnati, OH 513- 24- 215
Pelco Packaging Corporation
Stirling, NJ 908-647-3500
Pioneer Packaging
Dixon, KY. 800-951-1551
Plaint Corporation
Bloomington, IN. 800-366-3525
Plascal Corporation
Farmingdale, NY 800-899-7527
Plastic Packaging Inc
Hickory, NC 800-333-2466
Plastic Suppliers
Columbus, OH 800-722-5577
Plastipak Packaging
Plymouth, MI 734-354-3510
Pocono PET
Hazle Twp, PA 570-459-1800
Polar Plastics
Mooresville, NC 704-660-6600
Poly Plastic Products
Delano, PA 570-467-3000
Portco Corporation
Vancouver, WA 800-426-1794
Power Packaging, Inc.
Westerville, OH. 877-272-1054
Primepak Company
Teaneck, NJ. 201-836-5060
Printpack
Atlanta, GA. 404-460-7000
Professional Marketing Group
Seattle, WA 800-227-3769
QPF
Streamwood, IL. 800-323-6963
Quality Transparent Bag
Bay City, MI 989-893-3561
Quintex Corporation
Spokane Valley, WA. 509-924-7900
Reliance Product
Winnipeg, MB. 800-665-0258
Ropak
Oak Brook, IL. 800-527-2267
Roplast Industries Inc.
Oroville, CA 800-767-5278
Ross & Wallace Paper Products
Hammond, LA 800-854-2300
Rowland Technologies
Wallingford, CT 203-269-9500
Rutan Polyethylene Supply Bag & Manufacturing Company
Mahwah, NJ 800-872-1474
Saeplast Canada
St John, NB 800-567-3966
Samuel Strapping Systems
Woodridge, IL. 800-323-4424
San Miguel Label Manufacturing
Ciales, PR 787-871-3120
Sealed Air Corporation
Elmwood Park, NJ 800-648-9093
Shamrock Plastics
Mount Vernon, OH 800-765-1611
Sheffield Plastics
Sheffield, MA 800-628-5084
Shields Bag & Printing Company
Yakima, WA 800-541-8630
Shields Products
West Pittston, PA. 570-655-4596
Ship Rite Packaging
Bergenfield, NJ. 800-721-7447
Shippers Supply
Saskatoon, SK. 800-661-5639
SleeveCo Inc
Dawsonville, GA. 706-216-3110
Smurfit Flexible Packaging
Milwaukee, WI 414-355-2700
Snapware
Fullerton, CA 800-334-3062

Spartec Plastics
Conneaut, OH ... 800-325-5176
Star Container Company
Phoenix, AZ ... 480-281-4200
Steel City Corporation
Youngstown, OH ... 800-321-0350
Stock America Inc
Grafton, WI ... 262-375-4100
Stripper Bags
Henderson, NV ... 800-354-2247
Sun Plastics
Clearwater, MN ... 800-862-1673
Sungjae Corporation
Irvine, CA ... 949-757-1727
T&S Blow Molding
Scarborough, ON ... 416-752-8330
Target Industries
Flanders, NJ ... 973-927-0011
Templock Corporation
Santa Barbara, CA ... 800-777-1715
Terphane
Bloomfield, NY ... 585-657-5800
Tolas Health Care Packaging
Feasterville Trevose, PA ... 215-322-7900
Trans Flex Packagers
Unionville, CT ... 860-673-2531
Trident Plastics
Ivyland, PA ... 800-222-2318
Trio Products
Elyria, OH ... 440-323-5457
Ultra Pac
Rogers, MN ... 800-324-8541
Union Industries
Providence, RI ... 800-556-6454
Uniplast Films
Palmer, MA ... 800-343-1295
United Flexible
Westbury, NY ... 516-222-2150
United Seal & Tag Corporation
Port Charlotte, FL ... 800-211-9552
Vacumet Corporation
Austell, GA ... 800-776-0865
VIFAN
Lanoraie, QC ... 800-557-0192
Virginia Plastics
Roanoke, VA ... 800-777-8541
VPI Mirrex Corporation
Bear, DE ... 800-488-7608
Western Plastics
Calhoun, GA ... 800-752-4106
Witt Plastics
Greenville, OH ... 800-227-9181
Woodstock Plastics Company
Marengo, IL ... 815-568-5281
Zimmer Custom-Made Packaging
Indianapolis, IN ... 317-263-3436

Private Label

Cache Creek Foods
Woodland, CA ... 530-662-1764
Calhoun Bend Mill
Libuse, LA ... 800-519-6455
Century Foods International
Sparta, WI ... 800-269-1901
Couprie Fenton
Augusta, GA ... 706-650-7017
MacKinlay Teas
Ann Arbor, MI ... 734-846-0966
MRI Flexible Packaging
Newtown, PA ... 800-448-8183
Professional Image Inc
Tulsa, OK ... 800-722-8550
Real Foods Group
Springfield, OH ... 937-322-2040
River Road Vineyards
Sebastopol, CA ... 707-887-2243
Tri-Connect
Oak Park, IL ... 708-660-8190
Truitt Brothers Inc
Salem, OR ... 800-547-8712
Vetter Vineyards Winery
Westfield, NY ... 716-326-3100
Wholesome Classics
Moraga, CA

Shrink

AdPro
Solon, OH ... 440-542-1111
Atlantis Plastics Institutional Products
Mankato, MN ... 800-999-2374
Audion Automation
Carrollton, TX ... 972-389-0777
Campbell Wrapper Corporation
De Pere, WI ... 920-983-7100
Can Creations
Pembroke Pines, FL ... 800-272-0235
Can Creations
Pembroke Pines, FL ... 954-581-3312
Central Bag Company
Leavenworth, KS ... 913-250-0325
Chem-Pack
Cincinnati, OH ... 800-421-2700
Cima-Pak Corporation
Dorval, QC ... 877-631-2462
Collector's Gallery
Saint Charles, IL ... 800-346-3063
Crayex Corporation
Piqua, OH ... 800-837-1747
Exopack, LLC
Spartanburg, SC ... 877-447-3539
Flexo Transparent
Buffalo, NY ... 877-993-5396
Gulf Arizona Packaging
Humble, TX ... 800-364-3887
Gulf Systems
Oklahoma City, OK ... 405-528-2293
Gulf Systems
Oklahoma City, OK ... 800-364-3887
Gulf Systems
Arlington, TX ... 817-261-1915
Halpak Plastics
Deer Park, NY ... 800-442-5725
Herche Warehouse
Denver, CO ... 303-371-8186
Ilapak
Newtown, PA ... 215-579-2900
Mark Products Company
Denville, NJ ... 973-983-8818
Marshall Plastic Film
Martin, MI ... 269-672-5511
Mimi et Cie
Seattle, WA ... 206-545-1850
MS Plastics & Packaging Company
Butler, NJ ... 800-593-1802
Oaklee International
Ronkonkoma, NY ... 800-333-7250
Pack Line Corporation
Racine, WI ... 800-248-6868
Packaging Materials
Cambridge, OH ... 800-565-8550
Power Packaging, Inc.
Westerville, OH ... 877-272-1054
Preferred Packaging Systems
San Dimas, CA ... 800-378-4777
QPF
Streamwood, IL ... 800-323-6963
Seal-O-Matic Company
Jacksonville, OR ... 800-631-2072
Shippers Supply
Saskatoon, SK ... 800-661-5639
Shrinkfast Marketing
Newport, NH ... 800-867-4746
SleeveCo Inc
Dawsonville, GA ... 706-216-3110
Sungjae Corporation
Irvine, CA ... 949-757-1727
Templock Corporation
Santa Barbara, CA ... 800-777-1715
Tri-Sterling
Altamonte Spgs, FL ... 407-260-0330
United Flexible
Westbury, NY ... 516-222-2150
Willow Specialties
Batavia, NY ... 800-724-7300

Packaging & Containerizing Products

A La Carte
Chicago, IL ... 800-722-2370
A-Z Factory Supply
Schiller Park, IL ... 800-323-4511
Aabbitt Adhesives
Chicago, IL ... 800-222-2488
Abbott Industries
Paterson, NJ
Abond Plastic Corporation
Lachine, QC ... 800-886-7947
AC Label Company
Provo, UT ... 801-642-3500
Accurate Flannel Bag Company
Paterson, NJ ... 800-234-9200
Accurate Paper Box Company
Knoxville, TN ... 865-690-0311
Ace Technical Plastics
Hartford, CT ... 860-305-8138
Aces Manufacturing Company
Sullivan, MO ... 800-325-6138
Acme Bag Company
Chula Vista, CA ... 800-275-2263
Aco Container Systems
Pickering, ON ... 800-542-9942
Adcapitol
Monroe, NC ... 800-868-7111
ADM Corporation
Middlesex, NJ ... 800-327-0718
AdPro
Solon, OH ... 440-542-1111
Adrian Fabricators/Cargotainer
Adrian, MI ... 800-221-3794
Adstick Custom Labels
Denver, CO ... 800-255-7314
Advanced Poly-Packaging
Akron, OH ... 800-754-4403
Advantage Puck Group
Corry, PA ... 814-664-4810
Aero Tec Laboratories/ATL
Ramsey, NJ ... 800-526-5330
AJM Packaging Corporation
Bloomfield Hills, MI ... 248-901-0040
Aladdin Transparent Packaging Corporation
Hauppauge, NY ... 631-273-4747
Alcan Packaging
Baie D'Urfe, QC ... 514-457-4555
Alcoa Packaging Machinery
Randolph, NY ... 716-358-6451
Alger Creations
Miami, FL ... 954-454-3272
All American Containers
Medley, FL ... 305-887-0797
All American Poly Corporation
Piscataway, NJ ... 800-526-3551
All Foils
Strongsville, OH ... 800-521-0054
All Sorts Premium Packaging
Buffalo, NY ... 888-565-9727
Allflex Packaging Products
Ambler, PA ... 800-448-2467
Alpack
Centerville, MA ... 508-771-9131
Alpha Packaging
Saint Louis, MO ... 800-421-4772
Althor Products
Bethel, CT ... 800-688-2693
Altira
Miami, FL ... 305-687-8074
Amcel
Watertown, MA ... 800-225-7992
AMCO Corporation
City of Industry, CA ... 626-855-2550
Amcor Twinpak
Dorval, QC ... 514-684-7070
American Advertising & Shop Cap Company
Old Tappan, NJ ... 800-442-8837
American Bag & Burlap Company
Chelsea, MA ... 617-884-7600
American Box Corporation
Lisbon, OH ... 330-424-8055
American Containers
Plymouth, IN ... 574-936-4068
American Label Mark
Chicago, IL ... 800-621-5808
American Pallet
Oakdale, CA ... 209-847-6122
American Production Company
Redwood City, CA ... 650-368-5334
Americraft Carton
Saint Paul, MN ... 651-227-6655
Americraft Carton
Prairie Village, KS ... 913-387-3700
AmeriGlobe FIBC Solutions
Lafayette, LA ... 337-234-3212
AMPAC Holdings, LLC
Cincinnati, OH ... 800-543-7030
Ample Industries
Franklin, OH ... 888-818-9700
Anchor Packaging
Ballwin, MO ... 800-467-3900
Appleson Press
Syosset, NY ... 800-888-2775
AR Arena Products
Rochester, NY ... 800-836-2528
Arkansas Glass Container Corporation
Jonesboro, AR ... 800-527-4527
Armbrust Paper Tubes
Chicago, IL ... 773-586-3232

Art Poly Bag Company
Brooklyn, NY 800-278-7659
Artistic Carton
Auburn, IN 260-925-6060
Artistic Carton Company
Elgin, IL 847-741-0247
Artistic Packaging Concepts
Massapequa Pk, NY 516-797-4020
Atlantis Plastics Institutional Products
Mankato, MN 800-999-2374
Atlantis Plastics LinearFilm
Tulsa, OK 800-324-9727
Atlas Case
Denver, CO 888-325-7102
Atlas Packaging & Displays Inc
Miami, FL 800-662-0630
Atlas Tag & Label
Neenah, WI 800-558-6418
Aurora Design Associates, Inc.
Salt Lake City, UT 801-588-0111
Auto Pallets-Boxes
Lathrup Village, MI 800-875-2699
Automatic Electronic Machines Company
Brooklyn, NY 718-384-3211
Automatic Specialities Inc.
Marlborough, MA 800-445-2370
Avantage Group
Redondo Beach, CA 310-379-3933
Avon Tape
Chestnut Hill, MA 508-584-8273
B Way Corporation
Atlanta, GA 800-527-2267
B.A.G. Corporation
Dallas, TX 800-331-9200
B.F. Nelson Folding Corporation
Savage, MN 800-328-2380
Bag Company
Kennesaw, GA 800-533-1931
BagcraftPapercon
Chicago, IL 800-621-8468
Bakers Choice Products
Beacon Falls, CT 203-720-1000
Bal/Foster Glass Container Company
Port Allegany, PA 814-642-2521
Ball Corporation
Broomfield, CO 920-261-5105
Ball Foster Glass
Fairfield, CA 707-863-4061
Ball Foster Glass Container Company
Sapulpa, OK 918-224-1440
Bancroft Bag
West Monroe, LA 318-387-2550
Barbour Threads
Anniston, AL 256-237-9461
Bardes Plastics
Milwaukee, WI 800-558-5161
Bareny Packaging Corporation
Menomonee Falls, WI 262-251-8787
Baskets Extraordinaires
Westbury, NY 800-666-1685
Bayard Kurth Company
Detroit, MI 313-891-0800
Beayl Weiner/Pak
Pacific Palisades, CA 310-454-1354
BEI
St Charles, IL 630-879-0300
Bell Container Corporation
Newark, NJ 973-344-4400
Bell Packaging Corporation
Marion, IN 800-382-0153
Belleview
Brookline, NH 603-878-1583
Bennett's Auto Inc.
Neenah, WI 800-215-5464
Bergen Barrel & Drum Company
Kearny, NJ 201-998-3500
Berlin Fruit Box Company
Berlin Heights, OH 800-877-7721
Berlon Industries
Hustisford, WI 800-899-3580
Berry Plastics
Evansville, IN 800-234-1930
Berry Plastics
Evansville, IN 812-424-2904
Berry Plastics Corporation
Evansville, IN 800-822-2342
Berry Plastics Corporation
Evansville, IN 812-424-2904
Bertels Can Company
Belcamp, MD 410-272-0090
Blackhawk Molding Co, Inc
Addison, IL 800-222-7391
Blako Industries
Dunbridge, OH 419-833-4491
Boelter Industries
Winona, MN 507-452-2315
Boise Cascade Corporation
Burley, ID 208-678-3531
Bonar Plastics
West Chicago, IL 800-295-3725
Bonar Plastics
Ridgefield, WA 800-972-5252
Boxes.com
Livingston, NJ 201-646-9050
Brechteen
Chesterfield, MI 586-949-2240
Brewer-Cantelmo Company
New York, NY 212-244-4600
Brooks Barrel Company
Baltimore, MD 800-398-2766
Brown Paper Goods Company
Waukegan, IL 847-688-1451
Browns International & Company
St. Laurent, QC 514-737-1326
Bryce Company
Memphis, TN 800-238-7277
Buckeye Group
South Charleston, OH 937-462-8361
Buckhorn Canada
Brampton, ON 800-461-7579
Buckhorn Inc
Milford, OH 800-543-4454
Bulk Lift International
Carpentersville, IL 800-992-6372
Bulk Pack
Monroe, LA 800-498-4215
Bulk Sak
Malvern, AR 501-332-8745
Burgess Manufacturing ofOklahoma
Guthrie, OK 800-804-1913
Burrows Paper Corporation
Little Falls, NY 800-272-7122
Burrows Paper Corporation
Little Falls, NY 800-732-1933
C&L Wood Products
Hartselle, AL 800-483-2035
C&M Fine Pak
San Bernardino, CA 800-232-5959
C.R. Daniels Inc.
Ellicott City, MD 800-933-2638
C.W. Zumbiel Company
Cincinnati, OH 513-531-3600
Calzone Case Company
Bridgeport, CT 800-243-5152
Cambro Manufacturing Company
Huntington Beach, CA 800-848-1555
Can Corporation of America
Blandon, PA 610-926-3044
Can Creations
Pembroke Pines, FL 954-581-3312
Cannon Equipment Company
Rosemount, MN 800-825-8501
Cantwell-Cleary Company
Landover, MD 301-773-9800
Capital City Container Corporation
Buda, TX 512-312-1222
Capitol Carton Company
Sacramento, CA 916-388-7848
Capitol City Container Corporation
Indianapolis, IN 800-233-5145
Caraustar Industries, Inc.
Archdale, NC 800-223-1373
Caravan Packaging
Cleveland, OH 440-243-4100
Cardinal Container Corporation
Indianapolis, IN 800-899-2715
Cardinal Packaging
Evansville, IN 812-424-2904
Cardinal Packaging Products Inc.
Crystal Lake, IL 866-216-4942
Caristrap International
Laval, QC 800-361-9466
Carlisle Food Service Products
Oklahoma City, OK 800-654-8210
Carlisle Plastics
Minneapolis, MN 952-884-1309
Carpenter-Hayes Paper Box Company
East Hampton, CT 203-267-4436
Carpet City Paper Box Company
Amsterdam, NY 518-842-5430
Carrier Transicold
Farmington, CT 800-227-7437
Carroll Products
Garland, TX 800-527-5722
Carson Industries
Pomona, CA 800-735-5566
Carton Service
Shelby, OH 800-533-7744
Castle Bag Company
Wilmington, DE 302-656-1001
CCL Container
Toronto, ON 416-756-8500
CCW Products, Inc.
Arvada, CO 303-427-9663
CDF Corporation
Plymouth, MA 800-443-1920
Cedar Box Company
Minneapolis, MN 612-332-4287
Cello Bag Company
Bowling Green, KY 800-347-0338
Cello Pack Corporation
Cheektowaga, NY 800-778-3111
Centennial Molding LLC
Hastings, NE 888-883-2189
Central Bag & Burlap Company
Denver, CO 800-783-1224
Central Bag Company
Leavenworth, KS 913-250-0325
Central Container Corporation
Minneapolis, MN 763-425-7444
Central Missouri Sheltered Enterprises
Columbia, MO 573-442-6935
Central Ohio Bag & Burlap
Columbus, OH 800-798-9405
Central Paper Box
Kansas City, MO 816-753-3126
Central Plastics Corporation
Shawnee, OK 800-654-3872
Century Foods International
Sparta, WI 800-269-1901
Chalmur Bag Company, LLC
Philadelphia, PA 800-349-2247
Chambers Container Company
Gastonia, NC 704-377-6317
Champion Plastics
Clifton, NJ 800-526-1230
Checker Bag Company
Saint Louis, MO 800-489-3130
Chem-Tainer Industries
West Babylon, NY 800-275-2436
Chem-Tainer Industries
West Babylon, NY 800-938-8896
Cherry's Industrial Equipment Corporation
Elk Grove Vlg, IL 800-350-0011
Chesapeake Packaging
Scranton, PA 570-342-9217
Chester Plastics
Chester, NS 902-275-3522
Chili Plastics
Rochester, NY 585-889-4680
Cin-Made Packaging Group
Cincinnati, OH 513-681-3600
Cincinnati Foam Products
Cincinnati, OH 513-741-7722
City Box Company
Aurora, IL 773-277-5500
CKS Packaging
Atlanta, GA 800-800-4257
Clawson Container Company
Clarkston, MI 800-325-8700
Clayton L. Hagy & Son
Philadelphia, PA 215-844-6470
Clear Pack Company
Franklin Park, IL 847-957-6282
Clear View Bag Company
Thomasville, NC 336-885-8131
Clear View Bag Company
Albany, NY 800-458-7153
Clearplass Containers
Penn Yan, NY 315-536-5690
Clearwater Paper Corporation
Spokane, WA 877-847-7831
Cleveland Canvas Goods Manufacturing Company
Cleveland, OH 216-361-4567
Cleveland Plastic Films
Elyria, OH 800-832-6799
Cleveland Specialties Company
Loveland, OH 513-677-9787
Climax Manufacturing Company
Lowville, NY 800-225-4629
CMD Corporation
Appleton, WI 920-730-6888
Coast Label Company
Fountain Valley, CA 800-995-0483
Coast Paper Box Company
San Bernardino, CA 909-382-3475

Coast Scientific
Rancho Santa Fe, CA 800-445-1544
Coastal Pallet Corporation
Bridgeport, CT 203-333-6222
Coffee Sock Company
Eugene, OR 541-344-7698
Colbert Packaging Corporation
Lake Forest, IL 847-367-5990
Cold Chain Technologies
Holliston, MA 800-370-8566
Collector's Gallery
Saint Charles, IL 800-346-3063
Colonial Transparent Products Company
Hicksville, NY 516-822-4430
Color Box
Richmond, IN 765-966-7588
Color Carton
Bronx, NY 718-665-0840
Columbus Container
Columbus, IN 812-376-9301
Columbus Paperbox Company
Columbus, OH 800-968-0797
Commencement Bay Corrugated
Orting, WA 253-845-3100
Commercial Corrugated Corporation
Baltimore, MD 800-242-8861
Complete Packaging & Shipping Supplies
Freeport, NY 877-269-3236
Conductive Containers, I
New Hope, MN 800-327-2329
Connecticut Container Corporation
North Haven, CT 203-248-2161
Consolidated Can
Paramount, CA 888-793-2199
Consolidated Container Company
Atlanta, GA 888-831-2184
Consolidated Plastics
Stow, OH 800-858-5001
Consolidated Thread Mills, Inc.
Fall River, MA 508-672-0032
Constar International
Trevose, PA 215-552-3700
Containair Packaging Corporation
Paterson, NJ 888-276-6500
Container Specialties
Melrose Park, IL 800-548-7513
Container Supply Company
Garden Grove, CA 714-891-4896
Containment Technology
St Gabriel, LA 800-388-2467
Contico Container
Norwalk, CA 562-921-9967
Continental Extrusion Corporation
Cedar Grove, NJ 800-822-4748
Continental Packaging Corporation
Elgin, IL 847-289-6400
Continental Plastic Container
Dallas, TX 972-303-1825
Continental Products
Mexico, MO 800-325-0216
Continental-Fremont
Tiffin, OH 419-448-4045
Contour Packaging
Philadelphia, PA 215-457-1600
Convoy
Canton, OH 800-899-1583
Corbett Package Company
Wilmington, NC 800-334-0684
Corfab
Chicago, IL 708-458-8750
Corinth Products
Corinth, ME 207-285-3387
Corning Costar
Acton, MA 800-492-1110
Cornish Containers
Maumee, OH 419-893-7911
Corpak
San Juan, PR 787-787-9085
Corr-Pak Corporation
Mc Cook, IL 708-442-7806
Corrobilt Container Company
Livermore, CA 925-373-0880
Corrugated Inner-Pak Corporation
Conshohocken, PA 610-825-0200
Corrugated Packaging
Sarasota, FL 941-371-0000
Corrugated Specialties
Plainwell, MI 269-685-9821
Corrugated Supplies
Chicago, IL 888-826-2738
Corson Manufacturing Company
Lockport, NY 716-434-8871

Cortec Corporation
St. Paul, MN 800-426-7832
CPT
Edgerton, WI 608-884-2244
CR Plastics
Council Bluffs, IA 866-869-6293
Craft Corrugated Box
New Bedford, MA 508-998-2115
Crane Carton Corporation
Chicago, IL 773-722-0555
Crate Ideas by Wilderness House
Cave Junction, OR 800-592-2206
Crayex Corporation
Piqua, OH 800-837-1747
Cream of the Valley Plastics
Arvada, CO 303-425-5499
Creative Packaging Corporation
Buffalo Grove, IL 847-459-1001
Creative Techniques
Auburn Hills, MI 800-473-0284
Crespac Incorporated
Tucker, GA 800-438-1900
Cresthill Industries
Yonkers, NY 914-965-9510
Crown Cork & Seal Company
Philadelphia, PA 215-698-5100
Crown Holdings, Inc.
Philadelphia, PA 215-698-5100
Crystal-Flex Packaging Corporation
Rockville Centre, NY 888-246-7325
CTK Plastics
Moose Jaw, SK 800-667-8847
Cumberland Container Corporation
Monterey, TN 931-839-2227
Curtis Packaging Corporation
Sandy Hook, CT 203-426-5861
Curwood
Oshkosh, WI 800-544-4672
Cush-Pak Container Corporation
Henderson, TX 903-657-0555
Custom Bottle of Connecticut
Naugatuck, CT 203-723-6661
Custom Card & Label Corporation
Lincoln Park, NJ 973-492-0022
Custom Foam Molders
Foristell, MO 636-441-2307
Custom Pack
Exton, PA 800-722-7005
Custom Packaging
Richmond, VA 804-232-3299
Custom Stamping & Manufacturing
Portland, OR 503-238-3700
Cuutom Poly Packaging
Fort Wayne, IN 800-548-6603
D&M Pallet Company
Neshkoro, WI 920-293-4616
D&W Fine Pack
Lake Zurich, IL 800-323-0422
Dahl Tech, Inc.
Stillwater, MN 800-626-5812
Dairyland Plastics Company
Colfax, WI 715-962-3425
Dakota Corrugated Box
Sioux Falls, SD 605-332-3501
Dallas Container Corporation
Dallas, TX 214-381-7148
Dart Container Corporation
Mason, MI 800-248-5960
Dashco
Gloucester, ON 613-834-6825
Davis Brothers Produce Boxes
Evergreen, NC 910-654-4913
Davis Core & Pad Company
Cave Spring, GA 800-235-7483
Davron Technologies
Chattanooga, TN 423-870-1888
Day Lumber Company
Westfield, MA 413-568-3511
Day Manufacturing Company
Sherman, TX 903-893-1138
Dayton Bag & Burlap Company
Dayton, OH 800-543-3400
DBE Inc
Concord, ON 800-461-5313
De Ster Corporation
Atlanta, GA 800-237-8270
Deccofelt Corporation
Glendora, CA 800-543-3226
Deco Labels & Tags
Toronto, ON 888-496-9029
Decorated Products Company
Westfield, MA 413-568-0944

Del-Tec Packaging
Greenville, SC 800-747-8683
Deline Box Company
Denver, CO 303-373-1430
Delta Container Corporation
New Orleans, LA 800-752-7292
Delta Plastics
Hot Springs, AR 501-760-3000
Denver Reel & Pallet Company
Denver, CO 303-321-1920
Desert Box & Supply Corporation
Thermal, CA 760-399-5161
Design Plastics
Omaha, NE 800-491-0786
Designers-Folding Box Corporation
Buffalo, NY 716-853-5141
Despro Manufacturing
Cedar Grove, NJ 800-292-9906
Detroit Forming
Southfield, MI 248-352-8108
Development Workshop
Idaho Falls, ID 800-657-5597
Diamond Packaging
Rochester, NY 800-333-4079
Die Cut Specialties
Savage, MN 952-890-7590
Display One
Hartford, WI 262-673-5880
Dixie Poly Packaging
Greenville, SC 864-268-3751
Dixie Printing & Packaging
Glen Burnie, MD 800-433-4943
Donnelly Industries, Inc
Wayne, NJ 973-672-1800
Donovan Enterprises
Lagrange, GA 800-233-6180
Dorado Carton Company
Dorado, PR 787-796-1670
Dordan Manufacturing Company
Woodstock, IL 800-663-5460
Double R Enterprises
New Castle, PA 724-658-2477
Douglas Stephen Plastics
Paterson, NJ 973-523-3030
Drake Container Corporation
Houston, TX 800-299-5644
Drescher Paper Box
Buffalo, NY 716-854-0288
Dub Harris Corporation
Pomona, CA 909-596-6300
Dubuque Steel Products Company
Dubuque, IA 563-556-6288
Dufeck Manufacturing Company
Denmark, WI 888-603-9663
DuPont
Wilmington, DE 800-441-7515
Dupont Liquid Packaging Systems
Worthington, OH 614-888-9280
Durango-Georgia Paper
Tampa, FL 813-286-2718
Durham Manufacturing Company
Durham, CT 413-781-7900
Dusobox Company
Haverhill, MA 978-372-7192
Duval Container Company
Jacksonville, FL 800-342-8194
Dynamic Packaging
Minneapolis, MN 800-878-9380
Dynamic Pak
Syracuse, NY 315-474-8593
E.K. Lay Company
Philadelphia, PA 800-523-3220
E.S. Robbins Corporation
Muscle Shoals, AL 800-800-2235
E2M
Duluth, GA 800-622-4326
Eagle Box Company
Farmingdale, NY 212-255-3860
Eastern Container Corporation
Mansfield, MA 508-337-0400
Eastern Plastics
Pawtucket, RI 800-442-8585
Eastern Poly Packaging Company
Brooklyn, NY 800-421-6006
Eaton Manufacturing Company
Houston, TX 800-328-6610
EB Box Company
Richmond Hill, ON 800-513-2269
EB Eddy Paper
Port Huron, MI 810-982-0191
Eco-Bag Products
Ossining, NY 800-720-2247

Economy Folding Box Corporation
Chicago, IL 800-771-1053
Edge Paper Box Company
Cudahy, CA. 323-771-7733
EGA Products
Brookfield, WI 262-781-7899
EGW Bradbury Enterprises
Bridgewater, ME. 800-332-6021
Eichler Wood Products
Laurys Station, PA 610-262-6749
El Dorado Paper Bag Manufacturing Company
El Dorado, AR 870-862-4977
Elberta Crate & Box Company
Carpentersville, IL 888-672-9260
Electrol Specialties Company
South Beloit, IL 815-389-2291
Elegant Packaging
Cicero, IL 800-367-5493
Ellehammer Industries
Langley, BC 604-882-9326
Elm Packaging Company
Memphis, TN 901-795-2711
Elopak
New Hudson, MI. 248-486-4600
Emoshun
Rancho Cucamonga, CA 909-484-9559
Empire Container Corporation
Carson, CA 323-537-8190
Engineered Products
Hazelwood, MO 314-731-5744
Englander Container Company
Waco, TX 888-314-5259
Ensinger Hyde Company
Grenloch, NJ. 856-227-0500
Enterprise Box Company
Montclair, NJ 973-509-2200
Epsen Hilmer Graphics Company
Omaha, NE 800-228-9940
Erie Container Corporation
Cleveland, OH 216-631-1650
ERO/Goodrich Forest Products
Tualatin, OR 800-458-5545
Erwyn Products Company
Morganville, NJ 800-331-9208
Eureka Paper Box Company
Williamsport, PA. 570-326-9147
Excelsior Transparent Bag Manufacturing
Yonkers, NY 914-968-1300
Exopack
Tomah, WI 608-372-2153
Expert Industries
Brooklyn, NY 718-434-6060
F&G Packaging
Yulee, FL. 904-225-5121
F.E. Wood & Sons
East Baldwin, ME. 207-286-5003
F.N. Smith Corporation
Oregon, IL. 815-732-2171
F/G Products
Rice Lake, WI. 800-247-3854
FabOhio
Uhrichsville, OH. 740-922-4233
Fabri-Kal Corporation
Kalamazoo, MI 800-888-5054
Fabricated Components
Stroudsburg, PA 800-233-8163
Fabriko
Altavista, VA. 888-203-8098
Fan Bag Company
Chicago, IL 773-342-2752
Faribo Manufacturing Company
Faribault, MN 800-447-6043
Farmers Co-op Elevator Co.
Hudsonville, MI 800-439-9859
Fashion Seal Uniforms
Seminole, FL. 727-397-9611
Fast Bags
Fort Worth, TX 800-321-3687
Fehlig Brothers Box & Lumber Company
St Louis, MO. 314-241-6900
Felco Bag & Burlap Company
Baltimore, MD 800-673-8488
Ferguson Containers
Phillipsburg, NJ 908-454-9755
Fibre Containers Company
City of Industry, CA 626-968-5897
Field Container Company
Elk Grove Vlg, IL. 847-437-1700
Film X
Dayville, CT 800-628-6128
Film-Pak
Crowley, TX 800-526-1838

Finn Industries
Ontario, CA. 909-930-1500
First Brands Corporation
Oakland, CA 203-731-2427
First Midwest of Iowa Corporation
Des Moines, IA 800-247-8411
Fischer Paper Products
Antioch, IL 800-323-9093
Fitec International
Memphis, TN 800-332-6387
Fitzpatrick Container Company
North Wales, PA 215-699-3515
Flashfold Carton
Fort Wayne, IN 260-423-9431
Flex Products
Carlstadt, NJ 800-526-6273
FLEXcon Company
Spencer, MA 508-885-8200
Flexible Foam Products
Elkhart, IN. 800-678-3626
Flexicon
Cary, IL 847-639-3530
Flexo Transparent
Buffalo, NY. 877-993-5396
Flint Boxmakers
Burton, MI 810-743-0400
Flour City Press-Pack Company
Minneapolis, MN 952-831-1265
Foam Concepts
Uxbridge, MA. 508-278-7255
Foam Pack Industries
Springfield, NJ 973-376-3700
Foam Packaging
Footsville, WI 608-876-4217
Foamex
Cornelius, NC 704-892-8081
Foamold Corporation
Oneida, NY. 315-363-5350
Fold-Pak Corporation
Newark, NY 315-331-3159
Fold-Pak South
Columbus, GA 706-689-2924
Folding Carton/Flexible Packaging
North Hollywood, CA 818-896-3449
Food Pak Corporation
San Mateo, CA 650-341-6559
Formel Industries
Franklin Park, IL. 800-373-3300
Fortune Plastics
Glendale, AZ. 800-243-0306
Fortune Plastics, Inc
Old Saybrook, CT. 800-243-0306
Four M Manufacturing Group
San Jose, CA. 408-998-1141
Franklin Crates
Micanopy, FL 352-466-3141
Frankston Paper Box Company of Texas
Frankston, TX. 903-876-2550
Fredman Bag Company
Milwaukee, WI. 800-945-5686
Freedom Press Packaging
Watsonville, CA 831-722-3565
Frem Corporation
Worcester, MA 508-791-3152
Fremont Die Cut Products
Fremont, OH 800-223-3177
Fresno Pallet, Inc.
Sultana, CA. 559-591-4111
Friedman Bag Company
Manhattan Beach, CA. 213-628-2341
Friend Box Company
Danvers, MA. 978-774-0240
Friendly City Box Company
Johnstown, PA. 814-266-6287
Frobisher Industries
Waterborough, NB 506-362-2198
Frontier Bag Company
Omaha, NE 800-278-2247
Frontier Bag Company
Grandview, MO. 816-765-4811
Fruit Growers Package Company
Grandville, MI 616-724-1400
Frye's Measure Mill
Wilton, NH 603-654-6581
Fuller Box Company
North Attleboro, MA 508-695-2525
Fuller Brush Company
Great Bend, KS. 800-522-0499
Fuller Packaging
Central Falls, RI 401-725-4300
Fulton-Denver Company
Denver, CO 800-776-6715

G.S. Laboratory Equipment
Asheville, NC 800-252-7100
Gabriel Container Company
Santa Fe Springs, CA 562-699-1051
Garvey Products
Cincinnati, OH 513-771-8710
Gary Plastic Packaging Corporation
Bronx, NY. 800-221-8151
Gates
West Peterborough, NH 888-543-6316
Gateway Packaging Company
Kansas City, MO. 816-483-9800
Gateway Packaging Corporation
Murrysville, PA. 888-289-2693
Gatewood Products LLC
Parkersburg, WV. 800-827-5461
Gaylord Container Corporation
Tampa, FL. 813-621-3591
Gemini Plastic Films Corporation
Garfield, NJ. 800-789-4732
General Bag Corporation
Cleveland, OH 800-837-9396
General Films
Covington, OH 888-436-3456
General Press Corporation
Natrona Heights, PA. 724-224-3500
Genesee Corrugated
Flint, MI 810-235-6120
Genpak
Peterborough, ON. 800-461-1995
Genpak
Glens Falls, NY. 800-626-6695
Genpak LLC
Lakeville, MN. 800-328-4556
Georgia-Pacific LLC
Atlanta, GA 404-652-4000
Gessner Products Company
Ambler, PA 800-874-7808
Gibbs Brothers Cooperage Company
Hot Springs, AR 501-623-8881
Gibraltar Packaging Group
Hastings, NE. 402-463-1366
Gilchrist Bag Company
Camden, AR 800-643-1513
Glasko Plastics
Santa Ana, CA 714-751-7830
Glopak
St Leonard, QC. 800-361-6994
Goeman's Wood Products
Hartford, WI 262-673-6090
Goergen-Mackwirth Company
Buffalo, NY. 716-874-4800
Golden West Packaging Concept
Lake Forest, CA 949-855-9646
Golden West Sales
Cerritos, CA 800-827-6175
Goldman Manufacturing Company
Detroit, MI 313-834-5535
Goldmax Industries
City of Industry, CA 626-964-8820
GP Plastics Corporation
Medley, FL. 305-888-3555
Graff Tank Erection
Harrisville, PA. 814-385-6671
Graham Engineering Corporation
York, PA 717-848-3755
Grand Valley Labels
Grand Rapids, MI
GranPac
Wetaskiwin, AB 780-352-3324
Graphic Impressions of Illinois
River Grove, IL. 708-453-1100
Graphic Packaging Corporation
Golden, CO. 800-677-2886
Graphic Packaging Holding Company
Marietta, GA. 770-644-3000
Great Lakes Corrugated
Toledo, OH 419-726-3491
Great Lakes-Triad Package Corporation
Grand Rapids, MI. 616-241-6441
Great Northern Corporation
Appleton, WI 800-236-3671
Great Northern Corporation
Racine, WI. 800-558-4711
Great Southern Industries
Jackson, MS 601-948-5700
Green Bay Packaging
Coon Rapids, MN. 763-786-7446
Green Bay Packaging
Coon Rapids, MN. 800-236-6456
Green Bay Packaging
Tulsa, OK 918-446-3341

Green Bay Packaging
Green Bay, WI....................920-433-5111
Green Brothers
Barrington, RI....................401-245-9043
Green Seams
Maple Grove, MN....................612-929-3213
Greenfield Packaging
White Plains, NY....................914-993-0233
Greenfield Paper Box Company
Greenfield, MA....................413-773-9414
Greif Brothers Corporation
Cleveland, OH....................800-424-0342
Greif Inc.
Delaware, OH....................800-476-1635
Gribble Stamp & Stencil Company
Houston, TX....................713-228-5358
Grief Brothers Corporation
Delaware, OH....................740-549-6000
Grigsby Brothers Paper Box Manufacturers
Portland, OR....................866-233-4690
Gulf Coast Plastics
Tampa, FL....................800-277-7491
Gulf Packaging Company
Safety Harbor, FL....................800-749-3466
H&R Industries
Beecher, IL....................800-526-3244
H. Arnold Wood Turning
Tarrytown, NY....................888-314-0088
H.J. Jones & Sons
London, ON....................800-667-0476
H.P. Neun
Fairport, NY....................585-388-1360
Hager Containers
Carrollton, TX....................972-417-7660
Hampton Roads Box Company
Suffolk, VA....................757-934-2355
Handgards
El Paso, TX....................800-351-8161
Hank Rivera Associates
Dearborn, MI....................313-581-8300
Hanson Box & Lumber Company
Wakefield, MA....................617-245-0358
Harbor Pallet Company
Anaheim, CA....................714-533-4940
Hardi-Tainer
South Deerfield, MA....................800-882-9878
Hardy Systems Corporation
Northbrook, IL....................800-927-3956
Hartford Containers
Terryville, CT....................860-584-1194
Hartford Plastics
Omaha, NE
Harvard Folding Box Company
Lynn, MA....................781-598-1600
Hawkeye Corrugated Box Company
Cedar Falls, IA....................319-268-0407
Hedstrom Corporation
Ashland, OH....................700-765-9665
Hedwin Corporation
Baltimore, MD....................800-638-1012
Heritage Bag Company
Carrollton, TX....................972-241-5525
Heritage Packaging
Victor, NY....................585-742-3310
Herkimer Pallet & Wood Products Company
Herkimer, NY....................315-866-4591
Hibco Plastics
Yadkinville, NC....................800-849-8683
Highland Plastics
Mira Loma, CA....................800-368-0491
Hinchcliff Products Company
Strongsville, OH....................440-238-5200
Hinkle Manufacturing
Perrysburg, OH....................419-666-5550
Hodge Manufacturing Company
Springfield, MA....................800-262-4634
Hodges
Vienna, IL....................800-444-0011
Holmco Container Manufacturing, LTD
Baltic, OH....................330-897-4503
Home Plastics
Des Moines, IA....................515-265-2562
Hood Flexible Packaging
St Paul, MN....................800-448-0682
Hood Packaging
Burlington, ON....................877-637-5066
Hoover Materials Handling Group
Alpharetta, GA....................800-391-3561
Hope Paper Box Company
Pawtucket, RI....................401-724-5700
Horn Packaging Corporation
Lancaster, MA....................800-832-7020
HS
Oklahoma City, OK....................800-238-1240
Hub Folding Box Company
Mansfield, MA....................508-339-0005
HUBCO Inc.
Hutchinson, KS....................800-563-1867
Hudson Poly Bag
Hudson, MA....................800-229-7566
Hunter Packaging Corporation
South Elgin, IL....................800-428-4747
Huntsman Packaging Corporation
Birmingham, Bi....................205-328-4720
Hurri-Kleen Corporation
Birmingham, AL....................800-455-8265
IB Concepts
Elizabeth, NJ....................888-671-0800
IBC/Shell Containers
New Hyde Park, NY....................516-352-4505
Ideal Wire Works
Alhambra, CA....................626-282-1302
Illinois Valley Container Corporation
Peru, IL....................815-223-7200
Imperial Containers
City of Industry, CA....................626-333-6363
Imperial Industries Inc
Wausau, WI....................800-558-2945
Imperial Packaging Corporation
Pawtucket, RI....................401-753-7778
Impress Industries
Emmaus, PA....................610-967-6027
In the Bag
St Petersburg, FL....................800-330-2247
In-Touch Products
North Salt Lake, UT....................801-298-4466
Incinerator International
Houston, TX....................713-227-1466
Independent Can Company
Belcamp, MD....................909-923-6150
Indian Valley Industries
Johnson City, NY....................800-659-5111
Indiana Bottle Company Inc.
Scottsburg, IN....................800-752-8702
Indiana Box Company
Greenfield, IN....................317-462-7743
Indiana Carton Company
Bremen, IN....................800-348-2390
Indiana Vac-Form
Warsaw, IN....................574-269-1725
Indianapolis Container Company
Indianapolis, IN....................800-760-3318
Industrial Container Corporation
High Point, NC....................336-886-7031
Industrial Contracting &Rigging Company
Mahwah, NJ....................888-427-7444
Industrial Crating & Packing, Inc.
Seattle, WA....................800-942-0499
Industrial Hardwood
Perrysburg, OH....................419-666-2503
Industrial Lumber & Packaging
Spring Lake, MI....................616-842-1457
Industrial Nameplates
Ivyland, PA....................800-878-6263
Industrial WoodFab & Packaging Company
Riverview, MI....................734-284-4808
Inland Consumer Packaging
Harrington, DE....................302-398-4211
Inland Paper Board & Packaging
Elizabethton, TN....................423-542-2112
Inland Paperboard & Packaging
Austin, TX....................512-434-5800
Inland Paperboard & Packaging
Rock Hill, SC....................803-366-4103
Inline Plastics Corporation
Shelton, CT....................800-826-5567
Innova Envelopes
La Salle, QC....................514-595-0555
Innovative Folding Carton Company
South Plainfield, NJ....................908-757-0205
Instabox
Calgary, AB....................800-482-6173
Inteplast Bags & Films Corporation
Delta, BC....................604-946-5431
International Paper
Fort Worth, TX....................817-338-4000
International Wood Industries
Snohomish, WA....................800-922-6141
Interstate Packaging
White Bluff, TN....................800-251-1072
Intertech Corporation
Greensboro, NC....................800-364-2255
IPL Inc
Saint-Damien, QC....................800-463-4755
IPL Plastics
Edmundston, NB....................800-739-9595
IPS International
Snohomish, WA....................360-668-5050
Ira L Henry Company, Inc
Watertown, WI....................920-261-0648
ITW Angleboard
Villa Rica, GA....................770-459-5747
ITW Hi-Cone
Itasca, IL....................630-438-5300
ITW Minigrip/Zip-Pak
Manteno, IL....................800-488-6973
iVEX Packaging Corporation
Lachine, QC....................514-636-7951
J&J Corrugated Box Corporation
Franklin, MA....................508-528-6200
J&J Mid-South Container Corporation
Augusta, GA....................800-395-1025
J.C. Products Inc.
Haddam, CT....................860-267-5516
J.L. Clark
Rockford, IL....................815-962-8861
J.M. Packaging/Detroit Tape & Label
Warren, MI....................586-771-7800
J.V. Reed & Company
Louisville, KY....................877-258-7333
Jackson Corrugated Container
Middletown, CT....................860-346-9671
Jacksonville Box & Woodwork Company
Jacksonville, FL....................800-683-2699
James Thompson & Company
New York, NY....................212-686-4242
Jamestown Container Corporation
Macedonia, OH....................800-247-1033
Jamison Plastic Corporation
Allentown, PA....................610-391-1400
Jarisch Paper Box Company
North Adams, MA....................413-663-5396
Java Jackets
Portland, OR....................800-208-4128
Jayhawk Boxes
Fremont, NE....................800-642-8363
Jeb Plastics
Wilmington, DE....................800-556-2247
Jeco Plastic Products
Plainfield, IN....................800-593-5326
JEM Wire Products
Middletown, CT....................860-347-0447
Jesco Industries, Inc.
Litchfield, MI....................800-455-0019
Jescorp
Des Plaines, IL....................847-299-7800
Jesse Jones Box Corporation
Philadelphia, PA....................215-425-6600
Jessup Paper Box
Brookston, IN....................765-490-9043
Jet Age Containers Company
Chicago, IL....................708-594-5260
Jewel Case Corporation
Providence, RI....................800-441-4447
Jewell Bag Company
Dallas, TX....................214-749-1223
Johnson Corrugated Products Corporation
Thompson, CT....................860-923-9563
Jomar Plastics Industry
Nanty Glo, PA....................800-681-4039
Jordan Box Company
Syracuse, NY....................315-422-3419
Jordan Paper Box Company
Chicago, IL....................773-287-5362
JP Plastics, Inc.
Foxboro, MA....................508-203-2420
Juice Tree
Omaha, NE....................714-891-4425
Jupiter Mills Corporation
Roslyn, NY....................800-853-5121
K&H Container
Wallingford, CT....................203-265-1547
K&H Corrugated Case Company
Walden, NY....................845-778-1631
K-C Products Company
Van Nuys, CA....................818-267-1600
Kadon Corporation
Milford, OH....................937-299-0088
Kal Pac Corporation
New Windsor, NY....................845-567-0095
Kane Bag Supply Company
Baltimore, MD....................410-732-5800
KAPCO
Kent, OH....................800-843-5368
KapStone Paper and Packaging Corporation
Northbrook, IL....................847-239-8800

Karyall-Telday
Cleveland, OH 216-281-4063
Kaufman Paper Box Company
Providence, RI 401-272-7508
Keeper Thermal Bag Company
Crystal Lake, IL 800-765-9244
Kell Container Corporation
Chippewa Falls, WI 800-472-1800
Kelley Wood Products
Fitchburg, MA 978-345-7531
Kelly Box & Packaging Corporation
Fort Wayne, IN 260-432-4570
Kelman Bottles
Glenshaw, PA 412-486-9100
Kendel
Countryside, IL....................800-323-1100
Kerrigan Paper Products
Haverhill, MA....................978-374-4797
Ketch
Wichita, KS....................800-766-3777
Key Container Company
South Gate, CA....................323-564-4211
Key Packaging Company
Sarasota, FL 941-355-2728
Keystone Packaging Service
Phillipsburg, NJ 800-473-8567
KHM Plastics
Gurnee, IL....................847-249-4910
Killington Wood ProductsCompany
Rutland, VT....................802-773-9111
Kimball Companies
East Longmeadow, MA 413-525-1881
King Plastics
North Port, FL....................941-493-5502
KM International
Kenton, TN 731-749-8700
Knapp Container
Beacon Falls, CT....................203-888-0511
Knight Paper Box Company
Chicago, IL 773-585-2035
Koch Container Corporation
Victor, NY....................585-924-1600
Koch Equipment
Kansas City, MO....................816-753-2150
Kole Industries
Miami, FL....................305-633-2556
Kontane
Charleston, SC 843-352-0011
Konz Wood Products
Appleton, WI 877-610-5145
L&C Plastic Bags
Covington, OH 937-473-2968
L&H Wood Manufacturing Company
Farmington, MI....................248-474-9000
Label Makers
Pleasant Prairie, WI 800-208-3331
Labels Systems, Inc
Addison, TX....................800-220-9552
Lakeside Container Corporation
Plattsburgh, NY 518-561-6150
Lakeside Manufacturing
Milwaukee, WI....................888-558-8574
Laminated Paper Products
San Jose, CA....................408-888-0880
Landis Plastics
Alsip, IL....................708-396-1470
Langer Manufacturing Company
Cedar Rapids, IA....................800-728-6445
Langston Bag Company
Memphis, TN 901-774-4440
Lansing Corrugated Products
Lansing, MI....................517-323-2752
Laval Paper Box
Pointe Claire, QC 450-669-3551
Lawrence Paper Company
Lawrence, KS 785-843-8111
Lawrence Schiff Silk Mills
New York, NY 800-272-4433
Lawson Mardon Radisson
Baldwinsville, NY 800-847-5677
Lawson Mardon Wheaton Company
Mays Landing, NJ....................609-625-2291
LBP Manufacturing
Cicero, IL 708-652-5600
Le Claire Packaging Corporation
Ixonia, WI....................920-206-9902
Leading Industry
Oxnard, CA....................805-385-4100
Leaman Container
Fort Worth, TX 817-429-2660
Leggett & Platt StorageP
Vernon Hills, IL 847-816-6246

Len E. Ivarson
Milwaukee, WI....................414-351-0700
Lengsfield Brothers
New Orleans, LA 504-529-2235
Lenkay Sani Products Corporation
Brooklyn, NY 718-927-9260
Lester Box & Manufacturing
Long Beach, CA 562-437-5123
Letica Corporation
Rochester, MI 800-538-4221
Levin Brothers Paper
Cicero, IL 800-666-8484
Lewis Steel Works
Wrens, GA....................800-521-5239
Lewisburg Container Company
Lewisburg, OH 937-962-2681
Lexel
Fort Worth, TX 817-332-4061
Liberty Carton Company
Minneapolis, MN 800-818-2698
Lima Barrel & Drum Company
Lima, OH 419-224-8916
Lin Pac Plastics
Roswell, GA 770-751-6006
LinPac
San Angelo, TX 800-453-7393
Linvar
Hartford, CT 800-282-5288
Liqui-Box Corporation
Worthington, OH 614-888-9280
Liquitane
Berwick, PA 570-759-6200
Little Rock Crate & Basket Company
Little Rock, AR....................800-223-7823
LMK Containers
Centerville, UT....................626-821-9984
Lone Star Container Corporation
Irving, TX....................800-552-6937
Longview Fibre Company
Beaverton, OR 503-350-1600
Longview Fibre Company
Longview, WA....................800-929-8111
Los Angeles Paper Box & Board Mills
Los Angeles, CA....................323-685-8900
Love Box Company
Wichita, KS....................316-838-0851
Lowell Paper Box Company
Nashua, NH....................603-595-0700
Loy-Lange Box Company
Saint Louis, MO 800-886-4712
LPS Industries
Moonachie, NJ 800-275-4577
LTI Printing
Sturgis, MI 269-651-7574
Luce Corporation
Hamden, CT 800-344-6966
Luetzow Industries
South Milwaukee, WI....................800-558-6055
Luke's Almond Acres
Reedley, CA 559-638-3483
Lunn Industries
Glen Cove, NY 516-671-9000
Lustre-Cal Nameplate Corporation
Lodi, CA....................800-234-6264
M&G Packaging Corporation
Floral Park, NY....................800-240-5288
M&H Crates
Jacksonville, TX....................903-683-5351
M&L Plastics
Easthampton, MA....................413-527-1330
M&R Flexible Packaging
Springboro, OH....................800-543-3380
Mack-Chicago Corporation
Chicago, IL 800-992-6225
MacMillan Bloedel Packaging
Montgomery, AL....................800-239-4464
Maco Bag Corporation
Newark, NY 315-226-1000
Madsen Wire Products
Orland, IN....................260-829-6561
Malco Manufacturing Corporation
Los Angeles, CA....................866-477-7267
Mall City Containers
Kalamazoo, MI 800-643-6721
Malnove Packaging Systems
Omaha, NE 800-228-9877
Malpack Polybag
Ajax, ON....................905-428-3751
Mannkraft Corporation
Newark, NJ 973-589-7400
Manufacturers CorrugatedBox Company
Flushing, NY....................718-894-7200

Manufacturers Wood Supply Company
Cleveland, OH 216-771-7848
Mar-Boro Printing & Advertising Specialties
Brooklyn, NY 718-336-4051
Marco Products
Adrian, MI....................517-265-3333
Marcus Carton Company
Melville, NY....................631-752-4200
Marden Edwards
Antioch, CA 800-332-1838
Marfred Industries
Sun Valley, CA 800-529-5156
Marion Paper Box Company
Marion, IN....................765-664-6435
Mark Container Corporation
San Leandro, CA....................510-483-4440
Maro Paper Products Company
Bellwood, IL....................708-649-9982
Marpac Industries
Philmont, NY 888-462-7722
Marshall Boxes
Rochester, NY....................585-458-7432
Marshall Plastic Film
Martin, MI....................269-672-5511
Mason Transparent Package Company
Armonk, NY....................718-792-6000
Massachusetts Container Corporation
Marlborough, MA....................508-481-1100
Massillon Container Company
Navarre, OH 330-879-5653
Master Containers
Mulberry, FL....................800-881-6847
Master Package Corporation
Owen, WI 800-396-8425
Master Paper Box Company
Chicago, IL 877-927-0252
Maull-Baker Box Company
Brookfield, WI 414-463-1290
Maypak
Wayne, NJ....................973-696-0780
McDowell Industries
Memphis, TN 800-622-3695
McGraw Box Company
Mc Graw, NY 607-836-6465
MeadWestvaco Corporation
Richmond, VA....................804-444-1000
MeGa Industries
Burlington, ON 800-665-6342
Mello Smello
Minneapolis, MN 888-574-2964
Melmat, Inc.
Huntington Beach, CA 800-635-6289
Melville Plastics
Haw River, NC 336-578-5800
Memphis Delta Tent & Awning Company
Memphis, TN 901-522-1238
Menasha Corporation
Oconomowoc, WI....................262-560-0228
Menasha Corporation
Neenah, WI....................800-558-5073
Merchants Publishing Company
Kalamazoo, MI 269-345-1175
Meriden Box Company
Southington, CT 860-621-7141
Metal Container Corporation
St Louis, MO....................314-957-9500
Meyer Packaging
Palmyra, PA....................717-838-6300
Meyers Corbox Co, Inc.
Cleveland, OH 800-321-7286
Michiana Box & Crate
Niles, MI....................800-677-6372
Michiana Corrugated Products
Sturgis, MI 269-651-5225
Michigan Box Company
Detroit, MI 888-642-4269
Micro Qwik
Cross Plains, WI 608-798-3071
Micro Wire Products Inc.
Brockton, MA....................508-584-0200
Microplas Industries
Dunwoody, GA....................800-952-4528
Mid Cities Paper Box Company
Downey, CA 877-277-6272
Mid-States Manufacturing & Engineering
Milton, IA 800-346-1792
Mid-West Wire Specialties
Chicago, IL....................800-238-0228
Midco Plastics
Enterprise, KS....................800-235-2729
Midland Manufacturing Company
Monroe, IA 800-394-2625

Midlands Packaging Corporation
Lincoln, NE 402-464-9124
Midvale Paper Box Corporation
Wilkes Barre, PA. 570-824-3577
Midwest Aircraft Products Company
Mansfield, OH 419-522-2231
Midwest Box Company
Cleveland, OH 216-281-3980
Midwest Fibre Products
Viola, IL 309-596-2955
Midwest Paper Products Company
Louisville, KY 502-636-2741
Midwest Paper Tube & CanCorporation
New Berlin, WI. 262-782-7300
Midwest Rubber & Supply Company
Commerce City, CO 800-537-7457
Milan Box Corporation
Milan, TN 800-225-8057
Millhiser
Richmond, VA. 800-446-2247
Milliken Packaging
Spartanburg, SC 864-598-0100
Milprint
Oshkosh, WI 920-303-8600
Mimi et Cie
Seattle, WA 206-545-1850
Mini-Bag Company
Farmingdale, NY 631-694-3325
MO Industries
Whippany, NJ 973-386-9228
Modern Packaging
Deer Park, NY. 631-595-2437
Modern Paper Box Company
Providence, RI 401-861-7357
Mohawk Northern Plastics
Auburn, WA 800-426-1100
Mohawk Western Plastic
La Verne, CA 909-593-7547
Molded Container Corporation
Portland, OR 503-233-8601
Molded Materials
Plymouth, MI 800-825-2566
Monte Package Company
Riverside, MI 800-653-2807
Montebello Container Corporation
La Mirada, CA 714-994-2351
Montebello Packaging
Hawkesbury, ON. 613-632-7096
Moore Paper Boxes
Dayton, OH. 937-278-7327
Moorecraft Box & Crate
Tarboro, NC 252-823-2510
Morgan Brothers Bag Company
Richmond, VA. 804-355-9107
Morphy Container Company
Brantford, ON. 519-752-5428
Morris Industries
Forestville, MD. 301-568-5005
Morris Transparent Box Company
East Providence, RI. 401-438-6116
Moser Bag & Paper Company
Cleveland, OH 800-433-6638
Mount Vernon Packaging
Mount Vernon, OH 888-397-3221
Mountain Safety Research
Seattle, WA 800-877-9677
MRI Flexible Packaging
Newtown, PA 800-448-8183
Mullinix Packages
Fort Wayne, IN 260-747-3149
Multibulk Systems International
Wendell, NC 919-366-2100
MultiFab Plastics
Boston, MA. 888-293-5754
Murray Envelope Corporation
Hattiesburg, MS 601-583-8292
Nagel Paper & Box Company
Saginaw, MI 800-292-3654
Naltex
Austin, TX. 800-531-5112
Nameplates
St Paul, MN. 651-228-1522
NAP Industries
Brooklyn, NY 877-635-4948
Nashua Corporation
Nashua, NH. 603-661-2004
National Marking Products, Inc.
Richmond, VA. 800-482-1553
National Poly Bag Manufacturing Corporation
Brooklyn, NY 718-629-9800
Neal Walters Poster Corporation
Bentonville, AR 501-273-2489

Nefab
EGV, IL. 630-451-5300
Nefab Packaging Inc.
Coppell, TX 800-322-4425
Nefab Packaging, Inc.
Coppell, TX 800-322-4425
Neff Packaging Solutions
Mason, OH 800-445-4383
Negus Container & Packaging
Madison, WI 888-241-7482
Nelson Company
Baltimore, MD 410-477-3000
Nelson Container Corporation
Germantown, WI. 262-250-5000
Neos
Elk River, MN. 888-441-6367
Net Pack Systems
Oakland, ME. 207-465-4531
New England Wooden Ware Corporation
Gardner, MA 800-252-9214
New Era Label Corporation
Belleville, NJ 973-759-2444
New Lisbon Wood ProductsManufacturing Company
New Lisbon, WI 608-562-3122
New Mexico Products
Albuquerque, NM. 877-345-7864
New York Corrugated Box Company
Paterson, NJ 973-742-5000
New York Folding Box Company
Newark, NJ 973-589-0654
Nolon Industries
Mantua, OH. 330-274-2283
Nordic Printing & Packaging
New Hope, MN. 763-535-6440
North American ContainerCorporation
Maretta, GA 800-929-0610
North American PackagingCorporation
New York, NY 800-499-3521
North Carolina Box
Raleigh, NC 919-872-3007
Northeast Box Company
Ashtabula, OH 800-362-8100
Northeast Container Corporation
Dumont, NJ. 201-385-6200
Northeast Packaging Company
Presque Isle, ME. 207-764-6271
Northeast Packaging Materials
Monsey, NY 845-426-2900
Northern Box Company
Elkhart, IN. 574-264-2161
Northern Package Corporation
Minneapolis, MN 952-881-5861
Nosco
Waukegan, IL 847-360-4806
Noteworthy Company
Amsterdam, NY 800-696-7849
Nottingham-Spirk Design Associates
Cleveland, OH 216-231-7830
Novelis Foil Products
Lagrange, GA 800-776-8701
Now Plastics
East Longmeadow, MA 413-525-1010
NPC Display Group
Newark, NJ. 973-589-2155
NSW Corporation
Roanoke, VA. 800-368-3610
NU-Trend Plastic/Corrigan & Company
Jacksonville, FL 904-353-5936
NYP Corporation
Leola, PA. 800-524-1052
O-I
Perrysburg, OH
O.C. Adhesives Corporation
Ridgefield, NJ. 800-662-1595
Oak Barrel Winecraft
Berkeley, CA. 510-849-0400
Oak Creek Pallet Company
Milwaukee, WI 414-762-7170
Oakes Carton Company
Kalamazoo, MI 269-381-6022
Occidental Chemical Corporation
Dallas, TX. 800-733-3665
Ockerlund Industries
Forest Park, IL 708-771-7707
Okura USA
Shawnee Mission, KS 800-772-1187
Olcott Plastics
Saint Charles, IL 888-313-5277
Old Dominion Box Company
Burlington, NC 336-226-4491
Old Dominion Box Company
Madison Heights, VA 434-929-6701

Old English Printing & Label Company
Delray Beach, FL 561-997-9990
Olive Can Company
Elgin, IL 847-468-7474
Oracle Packaging
Toledo, OH 800-952-9536
Orange Plastics
Compton, CA 310-609-2121
Oration Rubber Stamp Company
Columbus, NJ 908-496-4161
ORBIS Corporation
Oconomowoc, WI. 800-890-7292
Original Packaging & Display Company
Saint Louis, MO 314-772-7797
Osterneck Company
Lumberton, NC 800-682-2416
OTD Corporation
Hinsdale, IL 630-321-9232
P&E
Altamonte Spgs, FL 800-438-0674
Pack-Rite
Newington, CT 860-953-0120
Package Containers
Canby, OR. 800-266-5806
Packaging Associates
Randolph, NJ 973-252-8890
Packaging Corporation of America
Lake Forest, IL 800-456-4725
Packaging Design Corporation
Burr Ridge, IL. 630-323-1354
Packaging Dynamics International
Caldwell, OH 740-732-5665
Packaging Enterprises
Rockledge, PA. 215-379-1234
Packaging Solutions
Los Altos Hills, CA 650-917-1022
Packing Material Company
Southfield, MI. 248-489-7000
Packing Specialities
Warren, MI 586-758-5240
Packrite Packaging
Archdale, NC. 336-431-1111
Pacquet Oneida
Charlotte, NC 800-631-8388
Pactiv LLC
Lake Forest, IL 888-828-2850
Pak Sak Industries
Sparta, MI 800-748-0431
Pak-Sher Company
Kilgore, TX. 800-642-2295
Pakmark
Chesterfield, MO 800-423-1379
Pallet One
Bartow, FL. 800-771-1148
Pallets
Fort Edward, NY. 800-PLT-SKID
Pallox Incorporated
Onsted, MI 517-456-4101
Palmer Distributors
St Clair Shores, MI 800-444-1912
Palmetto Packaging Corporation
Florence, SC 843-662-5800
Pan Pacific Plastics Manufacturing
Hayward, CA 888-475-6888
Papelera Puertorriquena
Utuado, PR 787-894-2098
Paper Box & Specialty Company
Sheboygan, WI 888-240-3756
Paper Products Company
Cincinnati, OH 513-921-4717
Paper Systems
Des Moines, IA. 800-342-2855
Par-Kan Company
Silver Lake, IN 800-291-5487
Par-Pak
Houston, TX 713-686-6700
Par-Pak
Houston, TX 888-272-7725
Parade Packaging
Mundelein, IL. 847-566-6264
Paragon Packaging
Ferndale, CA. 888-615-0065
Parisian Novelty Company
Homewood, IL 773-847-1212
Park Custom Molding
Linden, NJ. 908-486-8882
Parkway Plastics
Piscataway, NJ 732-752-3636
Parlor City Paper Box Company
Binghamton, NY. 607-772-0600
Parsons Manufacturing Corp.
Menlo Park, CA 650-324-4726

PARTA
Kent, OH 800-543-5781
Partola Packaging
Naperville, IL 800-727-8652
Parvin Manufacturing Company
Los Angeles, CA 800-648-0770
Paul T. Freund Corporation
Palmyra, NY 800-333-0091
PBC
Mahwah, NJ 800-514-2739
PCA Denver
Denver, CO 303-331-0400
Peace Industries
Rolling Meadows, IL 800-873-2239
Peacock Crate Factory
Jacksonville, TX 800-657-2200
Peerless Cartons
Bartlett, IL 312-226-7952
Peerless Packages
Cleveland, OH 216-464-3620
Pel-Pak Container
Pell City, AL 800-239-2699
Pelco Packaging Corporation
Stirling, NJ 908-647-3500
Pelican Displays
Homer, IL 800-627-1517
Pell Paper Box Company
Elizabeth City, NC 252-335-4361
Peninsula Plastics Compny
Auburn Hills, MI 800-394-8698
Penn Bottle & Supply Company
Philadelphia, PA 215-365-5700
Penn Products
Portland, CT 800-490-7366
Penny Plate
Haddonfield, NJ 856-429-7583
Pentwater Wire Products
Pentwater, MI 877-869-6911
Perfect Packaging Company
Perrysburg, OH 419-874-3167
Performance Packaging
Trail Creek, IN 219-874-6226
Peter Pepper Products
Compton, CA 310-639-0390
Peterboro Basket Company
Peterborough, NH 603-924-3861
Pexco Packaging Corporation
Toledo, OH 800-227-9950
Pfeil & Holing, Inc.
Flushing, NY 800-247-7955
Phoenix Closures
Naperville, IL 630-544-3475
Piedmont Label/Smyth Company
Bedford, VA 800-950-7011
Pine Point Wood Products
Dayton, MN 763-428-4301
Pioneer Packaging
Chicopee, MA 413-378-6930
Pioneer Packaging
Dixon, KY 800-951-1551
Pioneer Packaging & Printing
Anoka, MN 800-708-1705
Pittsburgh Tank Corporation
Monongahela, PA 800-634-0243
Plaint Corporation
Bloomington, IN 800-366-3525
Plas-Ties
Tustin, CA 800-854-0137
Plastic Assembly Corporation
Ayer, MA 978- 77- 472
Plastic Industries
Athens, TN 800-894-4876
Plastic Packaging Corporation
Hickory, NC 828-328-2466
Plastic Packaging Inc
Hickory, NC 800-333-2466
Plastican Corporation
Fairfield, NJ 973-227-7817
Plastics
Greensboro, AL 334-624-8801
Plastilite Corporation
Omaha, NE 800-228-9506
Plastipak Packaging
Plymouth, MI 734-354-3510
Plastiques Cascades Group
Montreal, QC 888-703-6515
Plaxall
Long Island City, NY 800-876-5706
Plaxicon
West Chicago, IL 630-231-0850
PM Plastics
Pewaukee, WI 262-691-1700

Pocono PET
Hazle Twp, PA 570-459-1800
Pohlig Brothers
Richmond, VA 804-275-9000
Polar Plastics
Mooresville, NC 704-660-6600
Polar Tech Industries
Genoa, IL 800-423-2749
Poly Plastic Products
Delano, PA 570-467-3000
Poly Processing Company
French Camp, CA 877-325-3142
Poly Shapes Corporation
Elyria, OH 800-605-9359
Polybottle Group
Brampton, ON 905-450-3600
Polycon Industries
Chicago, IL 773-374-5500
Polyfoam Packers Corporation
Arlington Hts, IL 800-323-7442
Polyplastics
Austin, TX 800-753-7659
Polytainers
Toronto, ON 800-268-2424
Pop Tops Company
South Easton, MA 508-238-8585
Portco Corporation
Vancouver, WA 800-426-1794
Portland Paper Box Company
Portland, OR 800-547-2571
Power Packaging, Inc.
Westerville, OH 877-272-1054
Pratt Industries
New Orleans, LA 504-733-7292
Precision Printing & Packaging
Clarksville, TN 800-500-4526
Precision Wood of Hawaii
Vancouver, WA 808-682-2055
Precision Wood Products
Vancouver, WA 360-694-8322
Premier Packages
Saint Louis, MO 800-466-6588
Premium Foil Products Company
Louisville, KY 502-459-2820
President Container
Wood Ridge, NJ 201-933-7500
Prestige Plastics Corporation
Delta, BC 604-930-2931
Pretium Packaging
Hermann, MO 573-486-2811
Pretium Packaging
Seymour, IN 812-522-8177
Pride Container Corporation
Chicago, IL 773-227-6000
Primepak Company
Teaneck, NJ 201-836-5060
Pro-Gram Plastics
Geneva, OH 440-466-8080
Process Solutions
Riviera Beach, FL 561-840-0050
Processing Machinery & Supply
Philadelphia, PA 215-425-4320
Professional Marketing Group
Seattle, WA 800-227-3769
Progressive Plastics
Cleveland, OH 800-252-0053
Promo Edge
Wall Township, NJ 732-938-4242
Promotional Packaging Group
Addison, TX 972-733-3199
Propak
Burlington, ON 800-263-4872
Pruitt's Packaging Services
Grand Rapids, MI 800-878-0553
Prystup Packaging Products
Livingston, AL 205-652-9583
PTI-Packaging Technologies & Inspection
Tuckahoe, NY 914-337-2005
Q Pak Corporation
Newark, NJ 973-483-4404
Quality Container Company
Ypsilanti, MI 734-481-1373
Quality Containers
Weston, ON 416-749-6247
Quality Containers of New England
Yarmouth, ME 800-639-1550
Quality Packaging, Inc.
Fond du Lac, WI 800-923-3633
Quality Plastic Bag Corporation
Flushing, NY 800-532-2247
Quality Transparent Bag
Bay City, MI 989-893-3561

Quantum Storage Systems
Miami, FL 800-685-4665
Quintex Corporation
Spokane Valley, WA 509-924-7900
R&R Corrugated Container
Terryville, CT 860-584-1194
Racine Paper Box Manufacturing
Chicago, IL 773-227-3900
Ram Equipment
Waukesha, WI 262-513-1114
Rand-Whitney Container Corporation
Worcester, MA 508-791-2301
Rand-Whitney Container Corporation
Portsmouth, NH 603-822-7300
RAPAC
Oakland, TN 800-280-6333
Ray C. Sprosty Bag Company
Wooster, OH 330-264-8559
RC Molding Inc.
Greer, SC 864-879-7279
RDA Container Corporation
Gates, NY 585-247-2323
Reading Box Company
Reading, PA 610-372-7411
Red River Lumber Company
Saint Helena, CA 707-963-1251
Regal Box Company
Milwaukee, WI 414-562-5890
Regal Plastic Company
Mission, KS 800-852-1556
Regal Plastics
North Kansas City, MO 816-471-6390
Regency Label Corporation
Wood Ridge, NJ 201-342-2288
Reliable Container Corporation
Downey, CA 562-745-0200
Reliance Product
Winnipeg, MB 800-665-0258
Reliance-Paragon
Philadelphia, PA 215-743-1231
Remcon Plastics
West Reading, PA 800-360-3636
Remmey Wood Products
Southampton, PA 215-355-3335
Rex Carton Company
Chicago, IL 773-581-4115
Rexam Beverage Can Company
Chicago, IL 773-399-3000
Rez-Tech Corporation
Kent, OH 800-673-5277
Rhoades Paper Box Corporation
Springfield, OH 800-441-6494
Rice Packaging
Ellington, CT 800-367-6725
Rice Paper Box Company
Colorado Springs, CO 303-733-1000
Richard Read Construction Company
Arcadia, CA 888-450-7343
Richards Packaging
Memphis, TN 800-361-6453
Richards Packaging
Memphis, TN 800-583-0327
Richmond Corrugated Box Company
Richmond, VA 804-222-1300
Ritz Packaging Company
Brooklyn, NY 718-366-2300
RJR Packaging, Inc.
Oakland, CA 510-638-5901
RMI-C/Rotonics Manufacturing
Bensenville, IL 630-773-9510
Robinette Company
Bristol, TN 423-968-7800
Robinson Cone
Burlington, ON 905-333-1515
Robinson Industries
Coleman, MI 989-465-6111
Rock Tenn/Alliance Group
Tullahoma, TN 931-455-3535
Rock-Tenn Company
Norcross, GA 608-223-6272
Rock-Tenn Company
Norcross, GA 770-448-2193
Roddy Products PackagingCompany
Aldan, PA 610-623-7040
Roll-O-Sheets Canada
Barrie, ON 888-767-3456
Romanow Container
Westwood, MA 781-320-9200
Romanow Container Inc
Westwood, MA 781-320-9200
Rondo of America
Naugatuck, CT 203-723-7474

Ropak
Oak Brook, IL 800-527-2267
Roplast Industries Inc.
Oroville, CA 800-767-5278
Rose City Printing & Packaging
Vancouver, WA 800-704-8693
Ross & Wallace Paper Products
Hammond, LA 800-854-2300
Round Paper Packages
Erlanger, KY 859-331-7200
Rownd & Son
Dillon, SC 803-774-8264
Roy's Folding Box
Cleveland, OH 216-464-1191
Royal Box Group
Cicero, IL 708-656-2020
Royal Paper Box Company of California
Montebello, CA 323-728-7041
RubaTex Polymer
Middlefield, OH 440-632-1691
Rudd Container Corporation
Chicago, IL 773-847-7600
Ruffino Paper Box Manufacturing
Hackensack, NJ 201-487-1260
Rusken Packaging
Cullman, AL 256-734-0092
Russell-Stanley Corporation
Woodbridge, NJ 800-229-6001
RXI Silgan Specialty Plastics
Triadelphia, WV 304-547-9100
S.S.I. Schaefer System International Limited
Brampton, ON 905-458-5399
Sabert Corporation
Sayreville, NJ 800-722-3781
Sacramento Bag Manufacturing
Woodland, CA 800-287-2247
Saeplast Canada
St John, NB 800-567-3966
Saint Charles Lumber Products
St Charles, MI 989-865-9915
San Diego Paper Box Company
Spring Valley, CA 619-660-9566
San Miguel Label Manufacturing
Ciales, PR 787-871-3120
Sanchelima International
Doral, FL 305-591-4343
Santa Fe Bag Company
Vernon, CA 323-585-7225
Saunders Corporation
Azusa, CA 888-932-8836
Save-A-Tree
Berkeley, CA 510-843-5233
Scheb International
North Barrington, IL 847-381-2573
Schermerhorn
Chicopee, MA 413-598-8348
Schiefer Packaging Corporation
Syracuse, NY 315-422-0615
Schiffenhaus Industries
Newark, NJ 973-484-5000
Schiffmayer Plastics Corp.
Algonquin, IL 847-658-8140
Schoeneck Containers
New Berlin, WI 262-786-9360
Scholle Corporation
Northlake, IL 888-224-6269
Scholle Corporation
Irvine, CA 949-955-1750
Schroeder Sewing Technologies
San Marcos, CA 760-591-9733
Schwab Paper Products Company
Romeoville, IL 800-837-7225
Schwarz
Morton Grove, IL 847-966-4050
Scope Packaging
Orange, CA 714-998-4411
Scott & Daniells
Portland, CT 860-342-1932
Scott Packaging Corporation
Philadelphia, PA 215-925-5595
Seaboard Bag Corporation
Richmond, VA
Seaboard Carton Company
Downers Grove, IL 708-344-0575
Seaboard Folding Box Company
Fitchburg, MA 800-255-6313
Seal-Tite Bag Company
Philadelphia, PA 717-917-1949
Sealed Air Corporation
Elmwood Park, NJ 201-791-7600
Sealed Air Corporation
Elmwood Park, NJ 800-648-9093
Sealstrip Corporation
Boyertown, PA 610-367-6282
Seattle Plastics
Seattle, WA 800-441-0679
Seattle-Tacoma Box Company
Kent, WA 253-854-9700
Sebring Container Corporation
Salem, OH 330-332-1533
SECO Industries
Commerce, CA 323-726-9721
Security Packaging
North Bergen, NJ 201-854-1955
Sekisui TA Industries
Brea, CA 800-258-8273
Semco Plastic Company
Saint Louis, MO 314-487-4557
Sertapak Packaging Corporation
Woodstock, ON 800-265-1162
SerVend International
Sellersburg, IN 800-367-4233
Service Manufacturing
Aurora, IL 888-325-2788
Servin Company
New Baltimore, MI 800-824-0962
Set Point Paper Company
Mansfield, MA 800-225-0501
Setco
Monroe Twp, NJ 609-655-4600
Setco
Anaheim, CA 714-777-5200
Seton Identification Products
Branford, CT 800-571-2596
Setterstix Corporation
Cattaraugus, NY 716-257-3451
Seville Flexpack Corporation
Oak Creek, WI 414-761-2751
Seymour Woodenware Company
Seymour, WI 920-833-6551
SFB Plastics
Wichita, KS 800-343-8133
SFBC, LLC dba Seaboard Folding Box
Fitchburg, MA 800-225-6313
Shamrock Plastics
Mount Vernon, OH 800-765-1611
Sharpsville Container
Sharpsville, PA 800-645-1248
Shaw-Clayton Corporation
San Rafael, CA 800-537-6712
Sheboygan Paper Box Company
Sheboygan, WI 800-458-8373
Sheffield Plastics
Sheffield, MA 800-628-5084
Shields Bag & Printing Company
Yakima, WA 800-541-8630
Shillington Box Company
Saint Louis, MO 636-225-5353
Ship Rite Packaging
Bergenfield, NJ 800-721-7447
Shipley Basket Inc
Dayton, TN 800-251-0806
Shipmaster Containers Ltd.
Markham, ON 416-493-9193
Shippers Paper Products
Sheridan, AR 800-468-1230
Shippers Paper Products
Sheridan, AR 800-933-7731
Shippers Supply
Saskatoon, SK 800-661-5639
Shippers Supply, Labelgraphic
Calgary, AB 800-661-5639
Sho-Me Container
Grinnell, IA 800-798-3512
Shore Paper Box Company
Mardela Springs, MD 410-749-7125
Shorewood Packaging
Carlstadt, NJ 201-933-3203
Shouldice Brothers SheetMetal
Battle Creek, MI 269-962-5579
Sicht-Pack Hagner
Dornstetten/ Hallwangen, QC 800-454-5269
SIG Combibloc USA, Inc.
Chester, PA 610-546-4200
Sigma Industries
Concord, MI 517-857-6520
Signature Packaging
West Orange, NJ 800-376-2299
Silgan Plastics
Chesterfield, MO 800-274-5426
Silgan Plastics Canada
Chesterfield, MO 800-274-5426
Silver State Plastics
Greeley, CO 800-825-2247
Simkins Industries
East Haven, CT 203-787-7171
Sirco Systems
Birmingham, AL 205-731-7800
SKD Distribution Corp
Jamaica, NY 800-458-8753
SleeveCo Inc
Dawsonville, GA 706-216-3110
Smalley Package Company
Berryville, VA 540-955-2550
Smith Pallet Company
Hatfield, AR 870-389-6184
Smith-Lee Company
Oshkosh, WI 800-327-9774
Smith-Lustig Paper Box Manufacturing
Cleveland, OH 216-621-0454
Smurfit Flexible Packaging
Milwaukee, WI 414-355-2700
Smurfit Stone Container
St Louis, MO 314-679-2300
Smurfit Stone Container
San Jose, CA 408-925-9391
Smurfit Stone Container
North Tonawanda, NY 716-692-6510
Smyrna Container Company
Smyrna, GA 800-868-4305
Snapware
Fullerton, CA 800-334-3062
Snyder Crown
Marked Tree, AR 870-358-3400
Snyder Industries Inc.
Lincoln, NE 800-351-1363
Sobel Corrugated Containers
Cleveland, OH 216-475-2100
Solve Needs International
White Lake, MI 800-783-2462
Somerville Packaging
Scarborough, ON 416-291-1161
Somerville Packaging
Mississauga, ON 905-678-8211
Sommers Plastic ProductsCompany
Clifton, NJ 800-225-7677
Sonderen Packaging
Spokane, WA 800-727-9139
SONOCO
Hartsville, SC 800-576-6626
Sonoco Flexible Packaging
Hartsville, SC 800-377-2692
SOPAKCO Foods
Mullins, SC 800-276-9678
Source for Packaging
New York, NY 800-223-2527
Source Packaging
Mahwah, NJ 888-665-9768
Southern Bag Corporation
Madison, MS 662-746-3631
Southern Champion Tray
Chattanooga, TN 800-468-2222
Southern Film Extruders
High Point, NC 800-334-6101
Southern Metal Fabricators
Albertville, AL 800-989-1330
Southern Missouri Containers
Springfield, MO 800-999-7666
Southern Packaging Corporation
Bennettsville, SC 843-479-7154
Southern Pallet
Memphis, TN 901-942-4603
Spartanburg Stainless Products
Spartanburg, SC 800-974-7500
Spartech Industries
Etobicoke, ON 416-744-4220
Spartech Plastics
Portage, WI 800-998-7123
Specialized Packaging London
London, ON 519-659-7011
Specialty Films & Associates
Hebron, KY 800-984-3346
Specialty Packaging
Fort Worth, TX 800-284-7722
Specialty Paper Bag Company
Bronx, NY 718-893-8888
SpecTape, Inc.
Erlanger, KY 859-283-2044
Spectrum Plastics
Las Vegas, NV 702-876-8650
Sphinx Adsorbents
Springfield, MA 800-388-0157
Spring Cove Container
Roaring Spring, PA 814-224-2222
Spring Wood Products
Geneva, OH 440-466-1135

Squire Corrugated Container Company
South Plainfield, NJ 908-561-8550
SSW Holding Company, Inc.
Elizabethtown, KY 270-769-5526
St Joseph Packaging Inc
St Joseph, MO. 800-383-3000
St. Louis Carton Company
Saint Louis, MO 314-241-0990
St. Pierre Box & Lumber Company
Canton, CT 860-693-2089
Stand Fast Packaging Products
Addison, IL 630-600-0900
Standard Folding Cartons
Flushing, NY. 718-335-5500
Star Container Company
Phoenix, AZ 480-281-4200
Star Container Corporation
Leominster, MA 978-537-1676
Star Poly Bag, Inc.
Brooklyn, NY 718-384-3130
State Container Corporation
Moonachie, NJ 201-933-5200
Steel City Corporation
Youngstown, OH. 800-321-0350
Step Products
Round Rock, TX. 800-777-7837
Steril-Sil Company
Boston, MA. 800-784-5537
Sterling Net & Twine Company
Cedar Knolls, NJ. 800-342-0316
Sterling Novelty Products
Northbrook, IL 847-291-0070
Sterling Packaging Company
Jeannette, PA. 724-523-5565
Sterling Paper Company
Philadelphia, PA 215-744-5350
Stewart Sutherland
Vicksburg, MI 269-649-5489
Stik-2 Products
Easthampton, MA 800-356-3572
Stock America Inc
Grafton, WI 262-375-4100
Stoffel Seals Corporation
Tallapoosa, GA 800-422-8247
Stone Container
Chicago, IL 312-346-6600
Stone Container
Moss Point, MS 502-491-4870
Stone Container
Santa Fe Springs, CA 714-774-0100
Stoneway Carton Company
Mercer Island, WA 800-498-2185
Streator Dependable Manufacturing
Streator, IL 800-798-0551
Stretch-Vent Packaging System
Ontario, CA. 800-822-8368
Stripper Bags
Henderson, NV 800-354-2247
Stronghaven Inc.
Matthews, NC. 800-222-7919
Stryco Wire Products
North York, ON. 416-663-7000
Suburban Corrugated Box Company
Indianhead Park, IL 630-920-1230
Sun Plastics
Clearwater, MN. 800-862-1673
Sunland Manufacturing Company
Minneapolis, MN 800-790-1905
Superfos Packaging
Cumberland, MD 800-537-9242
Superior Quality Products
Schenectady, NY. 800-724-1129
Supply One
Tulsa, OK 800-832-4725
Surfine Central Corporation
Pine Bluff, AR 870-247-2387
T&S Blow Molding
Scarborough, ON 416-752-8330
T&T Industries
Fort Mohave, AZ 800-437-6246
T.J. Smith Box Company
Fort Smith, AR 877-540-7933
Tampa Corrugated Carton Company
Tampa, FL. 813-623-5115
Tampa Pallet Company
Tampa, FL. 813-626-5700
Tampa Sheet Metal Company
Tampa, FL. 813-251-1845
Target Industries
Flanders, NJ 973-927-0011
Taylor Box Company
Warren, RI. 800-304-6361

Technipack, Inc.
Le Sueur, MN 507-665-6658
TEMP-TECH Company
Springfield, MA 800-343-5579
Temple-Inland
Memphis, TN 901-419-9000
Tenneco Packaging
Westmont, IL. 630-850-7034
Tenneco Packaging/Pressware
Lake Forest, IL 800-403-3393
Tenneco Specialty Packaging
Smyrna, GA 800-241-4402
TEQ
Huntley, IL 800-874-7113
Tesa Tape
Charlotte, NC 800-429-8273
Tetosky Plastics
Morristown, TN 423-586-8917
TGR Container Sales
San Leandro, CA. 800-273-6887
THARCO
San Lorenzo, CA. 800-772-2332
The Original Lincoln Logs
Chestertown, NY 800-833-2461
The Royal Group
Cicero, IL 262-723-6900
The Shelby Company
Cleveland, OH 800-842-1650
The Tin Box Company
Farmingdale, NY 800-888-8467
Thermal Bags by Ingrid
Gilberts, IL 800-622-5560
Thermodynamics
Commerce City, CO 800-627-9037
Thermodyne International
Ontario, CA. 909-923-9945
Thermos Company
Schaumburg, IL. 800-243-0745
Thomas Tape Company
Springfield, OH. 937-325-6414
Thornton Plastics
Salt Lake City, UT 800-248-3434
Thunder Pallet
Theresa, WI. 800-354-0643
Tipper Tie
Apex, NC 919-362-8811
TMS
San Francisco, CA 800-447-7223
TNI Packaging
West Chicago, IL 800-383-0990
Tolan Machinery Company
Rockaway, NJ. 973-983-7212
Tolco Corporation
Toledo, OH 800-537-4786
Trade Fixtures
Little Rock, AR. 800-872-3490
Trans Container Corporation
Upland, CA. 909-985-2750
Trans Flex Packagers
Unionville, CT 860-673-2531
Trans World Services
Melrose, MA. 800-882-2105
Transparent Container Company
Addison, IL. 708-449-8520
Traub Container Corporation
Cleveland, OH 216-475-5100
Tree Saver
Englewood, CO. 800-676-7741
Treen Box & Pallet Corporation
Bensalem, PA 215-639-5100
Trent Corporation
Trenton, NJ. 609-587-7515
Trevor Owen Limited
Scarborough, ON 866-487-2224
Tri-Seal
Blauvelt, NY. 845-353-3300
Tri-State Plastics
Henderson, KY 270-826-8361
Tri-Sterling
Altamonte Spgs, FL 407-260-0330
Trident Plastics
Ivyland, PA 800-222-2318
Trinidad Benham Corporation
Denver, CO 303-220-1400
Trio Packaging Corporation
Ronkonkoma, NY. 800-331-0492
Trio Products
Elyria, OH. 440-323-5457
Triple A Containers
Buena Park, CA 714-521-2820
Triple Dot Corporation
Santa Ana, CA 714-241-0888

True Pack Ltd
New Castle, DE. 800-825-7890
Tucson Container Corporation
Tucson, AZ 520-746-3171
Tudor Pulp & Paper Corporation
Prospect, CT 203-758-4494
Tulsack
Tulsa, OK 918-664-0664
Tupperware Brand Corporation
Orlando, FL. 800-366-3800
Tuscarora
New Brighton, PA. 724-843-8200
Tuscarora
New Brighton, PA. 724-847-2601
Tyco Plastics
Lakeville, MN. 800-328-4080
ULMA Packaging Systems, Inc.
Ball Ground, GA. 770-345-5300
Ultratainer
St Jean-Sur-Richelie, QC 514-359-3651
Union Camp Corporation
Denver, CO 303-371-0760
Union Industries
Providence, RI 800-556-6454
Unipac International
Rochester, NY. 800-586-2711
UniPak
West Chester, PA. 610-436-6600
Uniplast Films
Palmer, MA. 800-343-1295
Unique Boxes
Chicago, IL 800-281-1670
United Bags
Saint Louis, MO 800-550-2247
United Flexible
Westbury, NY 516-222-2150
United Seal & Tag Corporation
Port Charlotte, FL. 800-211-9552
Universal Container Corporation
Odessa, FL 800-582-7477
Universal Folding Box
East Orange, NJ 973-482-4300
Universal Folding Box Company
Hoboken, NJ 201-659-7373
Universal Paper Box
Seattle, WA 800-228-1045
Universal Plastics
Greenville, SC. 864-277-3623
Upham & Walsh Lumber
Hoffman Estates, IL 847-519-1010
Urnex Brands, Inc.
Elmsford, NY 800-222-2826
US Can Company
Rosedale, MD 800-436-8021
US Plastic Corporation
Swampscott, MA 781-595-1030
US Tsubaki
Wheeling, IL. 800-323-7790
Utah Paper Box Company
Salt Lake City, UT 801-363-0093
Vacumet Corporation
Austell, GA 800-776-0865
Valley Container
Bridgeport, CT 203-336-6100
Valley Container Corporation
Saint Louis, MO 314-652-8050
Valley Packaging Supply Company, Inc.
Green Bay, WI. 920-336-9012
Vandereems ManufacturingCompany
Hawthorne, NJ 973-427-2355
Vermont Bag & Film
Bennington, VT 802-442-3166
Vermont Container
Bennington, VT 802-442-5455
Victory Box Corporation
Roselle, NJ 908-245-5100
Victory Packaging, Inc.
Houston, TX 800-486-5606
VIFAN
Lanoraie, QC. 800-557-0192
Viking Packaging & Display
San Jose, CA. 408-998-1000
VIP Real Estate Ltd
Chicago, IL 773-376-5000
Virginia Plastics
Roanoke, VA. 800-777-8541
Visual Packaging Corporation
Haskell, NJ 973-835-7055
VitaMinder Company
Providence, RI 800-858-8840
Volk Packaging Corporation
Biddeford, ME 800-341-0208

Vonco Products
Lake Villa, IL 800-323-9077
VPI Manufacturing
Draper, UT 801-495-2310
W.W. Babcock Company
Bath, NY 607-776-3341
Wagner Brothers Containers
Baltimore, MD 410-354-0044
Walker Bag ManufacturingCompany
Louisville, KY 800-642-4949
Warner Electric
South Beloit, IL 800-234-3369
Warren Packaging
San Bernardino, CA 909-888-7008
Wasserman Bag Company
Center Moriches, NY 631-909-8656
Wastequip Teem
Eagleville, TN 800-843-3358
Waymar Industries
Burnsville, MN 888-474-1112
Weber Display & Packaging
Philadelphia, PA 215-426-3500
Webster Packaging Corporation
Loveland, OH 513-683-5666
Wedlock Paper ConvertersLtd.
Mississauga, ON 800-388-0447
Welch Packaging
Elkhart, IN 574-295-2460
Werthan Packaging
White House, TN 615-672-3336
Westeel
Saskatoon, SK 306-931-2855
Western Container Company
Kansas City, MO 816-924-5700
Westvaco Corporation
Newark, DE 302-453-7200
Weyerhaeuser Company
Federal Way, WA 800-525-5440
Wil-Mac Container Corporation
Conyers, GA 800-428-9269
Wilks Precision Instrument Company
Union Bridge, MD 410-775-7917
Willamette Industries
Beaverton, OR 503-641-1131
Willamette Industries
Louisville, KY 800-465-3065
Willard Packaging
Gaithersburg, MD 301-948-7700
Winchester Carton
Eutaw, AL 205-372-3337
Wins Paper Products
Springtown, TX 800-733-2420
Winzen Film
Sulphur Springs, TX 800-779-7595
Wisconsin Box Company
Wausau, WI 800-876-6658
Wisconsin Converting of Green Bay
Green Bay, WI 800-544-1935
Wisconsin Film & Bag
Shawano, WI 800-765-9224
WNA Hopple Plastics
Florence, KY 800-446-4622
WNA-Cups Illustrated
Lancaster, TX 800-334-2877
WNC Pallet & Forest Products
Candler, NC 828-667-5426
Woodson Pallet
Anmoore, WV 304-623-2858
Woodstock Plastics Company
Marengo, IL 815-568-5281
Workman Packaging Inc.
Saint-Laurent, QC 800-252-5208
World Kitchen
Rosemont, IL 847-678-8600
Wrap-Pak
Yakima, WA 800-879-9727
Wright Brothers Paper Box Company
Fond Du Lac, WI 920-921-8270
WS Packaging Group Inc
Green Bay, WI 920-866-6300
Yerecic Label Company
New Kensington, PA 724-335-2200
Yeuell Nameplate & Label
Woburn, MA 781-933-2984
York Container Company
York, PA 717-757-7611
Zenith Specialty Bag Company
City of Industry, CA 800-925-2247
Zero Corporation
Monson, MA 413-267-5561

Packing House Supplies

Acme Scale Company
San Leandro, CA 888-638-5040
Actionpac Scales & Automation
Oxnard, CA 800-394-0154
AFECO
Algona, IA 888-295-1116
All Power
Sioux City, IA 712-258-0681
Allflex Packaging Products
Ambler, PA 800-448-2467
Auto Pallets-Boxes
Lathrup Village, MI 800-875-2699
Barrette - Outdoor Livin
Middleburg Hts., OH 800-336-2383
Base Manufacturing
Monroe, GA 800-367-0572
Belco Packaging Systems
Monrovia, CA 800-833-1833
Bennett Box & Pallet Company
Winston, NC 800-334-8741
C.J. Machine
Fridley, MN 763-767-4630
Campbell Wrapper Corporation
De Pere, WI 800-727-4210
Carton Closing Company
Butler, PA 724-287-7759
Cincinnati Foam Products
Cincinnati, OH 513-741-7722
Columbia Machine
Vancouver, WA 800-628-4065
Columbus McKinnon Corporation
Amherst, NY 800-888-0985
Crowell Corporation
Wilmington, DE 800-441-7525
Crown Equipment Corporation
New Bremen, OH 419-629-2311
Cutler Brothers Box & Lumber Company
Fairview, NJ 201-943-2535
Dearborn Mid-West Company
Lenexa, KS 913-384-9950
Dimension Industries
Alexandria, MN 763-425-3955
Donovan Enterprises
Lagrange, GA 800-233-6180
Dorell Equipment Inc
Somerset, NJ 732-247-5400
Douglas Machine
Alexandria, MN 320-763-6587
Dynabilt Products
Readville, MA 800-443-1008
Edson Packaging Machinery
Hamilton, ON 905-385-3201
Elliott Manufacturing Company Inc.
Fresno, CA 559-233-6235
Exact Equipment Corporation
Morrisville, PA 215-295-2000
F.E. Wood & Sons
East Baldwin, ME 207-286-5003
Fabricating & Welding Corporation
Chicago, IL 773-928-2050
Fabrication Specialties Corporation
Centerville, TN 931-729-2283
Florida Knife Company
Sarasota, FL 800-966-5643
Food Equipment Manufacturing Company
Bedford Heights, OH 216-663-1208
Frazier Industrial Company
Long Valley, NJ 800-859-1342
FreesTech
Sinking Spring, PA 717-560-7560
Fresno Pallet, Inc.
Sultana, CA 559-591-4111
Gemini Plastic Films Corporation
Garfield, NJ 800-789-4732
Genesee Corrugated
Flint, MI 810-235-6120
Girard Wood Products
Puyallup, WA 253-845-0505
Goldco Industries
Loveland, CO 970-278-4400
Goldman Manufacturing Company
Detroit, MI 313-834-5535
Gram Equipment of America
Tampa, FL 813-248-1978
H.J. Jones & Sons
London, ON 800-667-0476
Halpak Plastics
Deer Park, NY 800-442-5725
Halton Packaging Systems
Oakville, ON 905-847-9141
Hanson Box & Lumber Company
Wakefield, MA 617-245-0358
Hudson Control Group
Springfield, NJ 973-376-7400
Iman Pack
Westland, MI 800-810-4626
Industrial Hardwood
Perrysburg, OH 419-666-2503
Industrial Lumber & Packaging
Spring Lake, MI 616-842-1457
International Paper Box Machine Company
Nashua, NH 603-889-6651
J.M. Rogers & Sons
Moss Point, MS 228-475-7584
Jetstream Systems
Denver, CO 303-371-9002
Kimball Companies
East Longmeadow, MA 413-525-1881
Kisters Kayat
Sarasota, FL 386-424-0101
Konz Wood Products
Appleton, WI 877-610-5145
Krones
Franklin, WI 414-409-4000
L&H Wood Manufacturing Company
Farmington, MI 248-474-9000
Landis Plastics
Alsip, IL 708-396-1470
Le Fiell Company, Inc.
Reno, NV 775-677-5300
Load King Manufacturing Company
Jacksonville, FL 800-531-4975
Longford Equipment US
Glastonbury, CT 860-659-0762
M&R Flexible Packaging
Springboro, OH 800-543-3380
Market Forge Industries
Everett, MA 866-698-3188
Matthiesen Equipment Company
San Antonio, TX 800-624-8635
Michiana Box & Crate
Niles, MI 800-677-6372
New Age Industrial Corporation
Norton, KS 800-255-0104
New Jersey Wire Stitching Machine Company
Cherry Hill, NJ 856-428-2572
Old English Printing & Label Company
Delray Beach, FL 561-997-9990
Packaging & Processing Equipment
Ayr, ON 519-622-6666
Packaging Dynamics
Walnut Creek, CA 925-938-2711
Pallet Pro
Moss, TN 800-489-3661
PDC International
Austin, TX 512-302-0194
Pneumatic Scale Corporation
Cuyahoga Falls, OH 330-923-0491
Precision Printing & Packaging
Clarksville, TN 800-500-4526
Premier Packages
Saint Louis, MO 800-466-6588
Premium Pallet
Philadelphia, PA 800-648-7347
Priority One America
Waterloo, ON 519-746-6950
Production Systems
Marietta, GA 800-235-9734
PTI Packaging
Portage, WI 800-501-4077
RAM Center
Red Wing, MN 800-762-6842
Ratcliff Hoist Company
San Carlos, CA 650-595-3840
Refrigiwear
Dahlonega, GA 800-645-3744
Remcon Plastics
West Reading, PA 800-360-3636
Rennco
Homer, MI 800-409-5225
Rockford-Midland Corporation
Rockford, IL 800-327-7908
Saeplast Canada
St John, NB 800-567-3966
Sapac International
Fond Du Lac, WI 800-257-2722
Seal-O-Matic Company
Jacksonville, OR 800-631-2072
Seattle-Tacoma Box Co.
Kent, WA 253-854-9700
Sekisui TA Industries
Brea, CA 800-258-8273

Shields Products
West Pittston, PA. 570-655-4596
Shippers Supply
Saskatoon, SK. 800-661-5639
Sinco
Red Wing, MN 800-243-6753
Solve Needs International
White Lake, MI. 800-783-2462
Sonoma Pacific Company
Montebello, CA 323-838-4374
Sperling Industries
Omaha, NE 800-647-5062
Standard-Knapp
Portland, CT 800-628-9565
Steel King Industries
Stevens Point, WI 800-553-3096
Studd & Whipple Company
Conewango Valley, NY. 716-287-3791
Swift Creek Forest Products
Amelia Court Hse, VA 804-561-4498
Technibilt/Cari-All
Newton, NC 800-233-3972
Thiele Technologies
Reedley, CA 800-344-8951
Tier-Rack Corporation
Ballwin, MO 800-325-7869
Trenton Mills
Trenton, TN. 731-855-1323
Trident Plastics
Ivyland, PA 800-222-2318
Triple-A Manufacturing Company
Toronto, ON 800-786-2238
Unirak Storage Systems
Taylor, MI 800-348-7225
Upaco Adhesives
Richmond, VA. 800-446-9984
Upham & Walsh Lumber
Hoffman Estates, IL 847-519-1010
UPN Pallet Company
Penns Grove, NJ 856-299-1192
Vertical Systems
Ft. Michelle, KY 859-485-9650
Viking Pallet Corporation
Osseo, MN 763-425-6707
W.G. Durant Corporation
Whittier, CA 562-946-5555
WE Killam Enterprises
Waterford, ON. 519-443-7421
Western Plastics California
Portland, TN 615-325-7331
Whallon Machinery
Royal Center, IN 574-643-9561
Williamsburg Millwork Corporation
Bowling Green, VA. 804-994-2151
Williamson, Lannes, Pallets
Southside, WV 304-675-2716
Woodson Pallet
Anmoore, WV. 304-623-2858
Wrap-Pak
Yakima, WA 800-879-9727
Zed Industries
Vandalia, OH. 937-667-8407

Paper

Candy Wrapping

Alufoil Products
Hauppauge, NY 631-231-4141
IB Concepts
Elizabeth, NJ. 888-671-0800

Corrugated

Clearwater Paper Corporation
Spokane, WA. 877-847-7831
Corfab
Chicago, IL 708-458-8750
Corrugated Specialties
Plainwell, MI 269-685-9821
Corrugated Supplies
Chicago, IL 888-826-2738
Field Container Company
Elk Grove Vlg, IL. 847-437-1700
Inland Paperboard & Packaging
Austin, TX. 512-434-5800
Inter-Pack Corporation
Monroe, MI. 734-242-7755
iVEX Packaging Corporation
Lachine, QC 514-636-7951
Lumber & Things
Keyser, WV. 800-296-5656
Marshall Paper Products
East Norwich, NY
National Packaging
Rumford, RI 401-434-1070
RTS Packaging
Hillside, IL 708-338-2800
Shipmaster Containers Ltd.
Markham, ON. 416-493-9193

Glassine

Brooklace
Oshkosh, WI. 800-572-4552
Simkins Industries
East Haven, CT. 203-787-7171

Grease & Oil Resistant

Brooklace
Oshkosh, WI. 800-572-4552
Central Coated Products
Alliance, OH. 330-821-9830
Pepperell Paper Company
Lawrence, MA 978-433-6951
Printpack
Atlanta, GA. 404-460-7000
Simkins Industries
East Haven, CT. 203-787-7171
Sorg Paper Company
Middletown, OH. 513-420-5300
Tudor Pulp & Paper Corporation
Prospect, CT 203-758-4494

Heat Sealing

Hazen Paper Company
Holyoke, MA 413-538-8204
Paper Product Specialties
Waukesha, WI. 262-549-1730
Printpack
Atlanta, GA. 404-460-7000

Kraft

Caraustar
Warrensville Heights, OH. 800-362-1125
Durango-Georgia Paper
Tampa, FL. 813-286-2718
Lumber & Things
Keyser, WV. 800-296-5656
MeadWestvaco Corporation
Richmond, VA. 804-444-1000
Pepperell Paper Company
Lawrence, MA 978-433-6951
Salinas Valley Wax PaperCompany
Salinas, CA 831-424-2747
Shamrock Paper Company
Saint Louis, MO 314-241-2370

Label

Graphic Impressions of Illinois
River Grove, IL. 708-453-1100
Harris & Company
Salem, OH. 330-332-4127
Lancaster Colony Corporation
Columbus, OH 614-224-7141
Print & Peel
New York, NY 800-451-0807
Southern Imperial
Rockford, IL 800-747-4665
Vande Berg Scales
Sioux Center, IA 712-722-1181

Laminated

Alufoil Products
Hauppauge, NY 631-231-4141
Burrows Paper Corporation
Little Falls, NY. 800-272-7122
Cello Pack Corporation
Cheektowaga, NY. 800-778-3111
Fibre Converters
Constantine, MI 269-279-1700
Fortifiber Corporation
Fernley, NV. 775-575-5557
Hampden Papers
Holyoke, MA 413-536-1000
Hazen Paper Company
Holyoke, MA 413-538-8204
Henschel Coating & Laminating
New Berlin, WI. 262-786-1750
Lamcraft
Lees Summit, MO. 800-821-1333
Laminated Papers
Holyoke, MA 413-533-3906
Lancaster Colony Corporation
Columbus, OH 614-224-7141
Mail-Well Label
Baltimore, MD 800-637-4879
Norpak Corporation
Newark, NJ. 800-631-6970
Packaging Dynamics International
Caldwell, OH 740-732-5665
Rock-Tenn Company
Norcross, GA 770-448-2193
Salinas Valley Wax PaperCompany
Salinas, CA 831-424-2747
Sorg Paper Company
Middletown, OH. 513-420-5300
Zimmer Custom-Made Packaging
Indianapolis, IN 317-263-3436

Lining

Cellier Corporation
Taunton, MA. 508-655-5906
Gardiner Paperboard
Gardiner, ME 207-582-3230
International Tray Pads & Packaging, Inc.
Aberdeen, NC. 910-944-1800
Salinas Valley Wax PaperCompany
Salinas, CA 831-424-2747

Plastic Coated

Central Coated Products
Alliance, OH. 330-821-9830
Fibre Leather Manufacturing Company
New Bedford, MA 800-358-6012
Henschel Coating & Laminating
New Berlin, WI. 262-786-1750
International Tray Pads & Packaging, Inc.
Aberdeen, NC 910-944-1800
Jen-Coat, Inc.
Westfield, MA. 877-536-2628
Salinas Valley Wax PaperCompany
Salinas, CA 831-424-2747
Zimmer Custom-Made Packaging
Indianapolis, IN 317-263-3436

Pressure Sensitive

KAPCO
Kent, OH. 800-843-5368
Mactac
Stow, OH. 800-233-4291
Print & Peel
New York, NY 800-451-0807

Waxed

Burrows Paper Corporation
Little Falls, NY 800-272-7122
Clearwater Paper Corporation
Spokane, WA. 877-847-7831
Fabricon Products
River Rouge, MI. 313-841-8200
Framarx/Waxstar
S Chicago Hts, IL 800-336-3936
Handy Wacks Corporation
Sparta, MI 800-445-4434
Norpak Corporation
Newark, NJ. 800-631-6970
Patty Paper, Inc.
Plymouth, IN. 800-782-1703
Rochester Midland
Rochester, NY. 800-387-7174
Salinas Valley Wax PaperCompany
Salinas, CA. 831-424-2747
Schwab Paper Products Company
Romeoville, IL 800-837-7225
Shields Products
West Pittston, PA. 570-655-4596

Wet Strength

SCA Hygiene Paper
San Ramon, CA 800-992-8675
Shawans Specialty Papers
Shawano, WI. 800-543-5554
Sorg Paper Company
Middletown, OH. 513-420-5300

Wrapping

Alufoil Products
Hauppauge, NY 631-231-4141
Caraustar
Warrensville Heights, OH 800-362-1125
Dorado Carton Company
Dorado, PR 787-796-1670
Hampden Papers
Holyoke, MA 413-536-1000
Jupiter Mills Corporation
Roslyn, NY 800-853-5121
Mimi et Cie
Seattle, WA 206-545-1850
Norpak Corporation
Newark, NJ 800-631-6970
North American PackagingCorporation
New York, NY 800-499-3521
Paper Service
Hinsdale, NH 603-239-6344
Patty Paper, Inc.
Plymouth, IN 800-782-1703
Pepperell Paper Company
Lawrence, MA 978-433-6951
Robinette Company
Bristol, TN 423-968-7800
Salinas Valley Wax PaperCompany
Salinas, CA 831-424-2747
Shamrock Paper Company
Saint Louis, MO 314-241-2370
Sorg Paper Company
Middletown, OH 513-420-5300
St. Clair Pakwell
Bellwood, IL 800-323-1922

Plastic

Biodegradable, Recyclable

AR-BEE Transparent
Elk Grove Vlg, IL 800-642-2247
Berry Plastics
Evansville, IN 812-424-2904
Gateway Plastics
Mequon, WI 262-242-2020
Hinkle Manufacturing
Perrysburg, OH 419-666-5550
International Polymers Corporation
Allentown, PA 800-526-0953
Stock America Inc
Grafton, WI 262-375-4100
Tectonics
Westmoreland, NH 603-352-8894
Tolas Health Care Packaging
Feasterville Trevose, PA 215-322-7900
Ultra Pac
Rogers, MN 800-324-8541

Retorts

Canning

A.K. Robins
Baltimore, MD 800-486-9656
Allpax Products
Covington, LA 888-893-9277
Dixie Canner Company
Athens, GA 706-549-1914
Innovative Food Solutions LLC
Columbus, OH 800-884-3314
Melco Steel
Azusa, CA 626-334-7875
Reid Boiler Works
Bellingham, WA 360-714-6157
Stock America Inc
Grafton, WI 262-375-4100

Seals

Bottle & Jar

AHP Machine & Tool Company
Lancaster, OH 740-681-6709
American National Rubber
Ceredo, WV 304-453-1311
Crown Cork & Seal Company
Philadelphia, PA 215-698-5100
Dickey Manufacturing Company
St Charles, IL 630-584-2918
Greenfield Packaging
White Plains, NY 914-993-0233
Pack Line Corporation
Racine, WI 800-248-6868
Phoenix Closures
Naperville, IL 630-544-3475
RoMatic Manufacturing Company
Southbury, CT 203-264-8203
Simolex Rubber Corporation
Plymouth, MI 734-453-4500
SONOCO
Hartsville, SC 800-576-6626
Tri-Seal
Blauvelt, NY 845-353-3300

Box Strapping

Gulf Arizona Packaging
Humble, TX 800-364-3887
Herche Warehouse
Denver, CO 303-371-8186
L&H Wood Manufacturing Company
Farmington, MI 248-474-9000

Pressure Sensitive

Cantech Industries
Johnson City, TN 800-654-3947
City Stamp & Seal Company
Austin, TX 800-950-6074
Coleman Stamps, Signs & Recognition Products
Daytona Beach, FL 386-253-1206
Cummins Label Company
Kalamazoo, MI 800-280-7589
Deco Labels & Tags
Toronto, ON 888-496-9029
Grand Rapids Label Company
Grand Rapids, MI 616-459-8134
Innovative Packaging Solution
Martin, MI 616-656-2100
Long Island Stamp Corporation
Flushing, NY 800-547-8267
M&M Displays
Philadelphia, PA 800-874-7171
New Era Label Corporation
Belleville, NJ 973-759-2444
Reotemp Instrument Corporation
San Diego, CA 800-648-7737
Rhode Island Label Works
West Warwick, RI 401-828-6400
Schwaab, Inc
Milwaukee, WI 800-935-9877
Stoffel Seals Corporation
Tallapoosa, GA 800-422-8247
Timemed Labeling Systems
Valencia, CA 818-897-1111

Price Tag

General Trade Mark Labelcraft
Staten Island, NY 718-448-9800
House Stamp Works
Chicago, IL 312-939-7177
Muskogee Rubber Stamp & Seal Company
Fort Gibson, OK 918-478-3046
Stoffel Seals Corporation
Tallapoosa, GA 800-422-8247

Shakers

Salt & Pepper

AMCO Corporation
City of Industry, CA 626-855-2550
Browne & Company
Markham, ON 905-475-6104
C.R. Manufacturing
Waverly, NE 877-789-5844
Carlisle Food Service Products
Oklahoma City, OK 800-654-8210
Coley Industries
Wayland, NY 716-728-2390
Gril-Del
Mankato, MN 800-782-7320
Libertyware
Clearfield, UT 888-500-5885
Michael Leson Dinnerware
Youngstown, OH 800-821-3541
Reiner Products
Waterbury, CT 800-345-6775
Superior Products Company
Saint Paul, MN 800-328-9800
Tablecraft Products
Gurnee, IL 800-323-8321
Traex
Dane, WI 800-356-8006

Sleeves

Bottle

Flexo Transparent
Buffalo, NY 877-993-5396
SleeveCo Inc
Dawsonville, GA 706-216-3110
Wilkens-Anderson Company
Chicago, IL 800-847-2222

Stamps

Dating & Numbering

A.D. Johnson Engraving Company
Kalamazoo, MI 269-342-5500
A.D. Joslin Manufacturing Company
Manistee, MI 231-723-2908
ABC Stamp Company
Boise, ID 208-375-4470
Accent Mark
Palmdale, CA 661-274-8191
American Art Stamp
Gardena, CA 310-965-9004
Century Rubber Stamp Company
New York, NY 212-962-6165
City Stamp & Seal Company
Austin, TX 800-950-6074
Des Moines Stamp Manufacturing Company
Des Moines, IA 888-236-7739
DRS Designs
Bethel, CT 888-792-3740
Durable Engravers
Franklin Park, IL 800-869-9565
E.C. Shaw Company
Cincinnati, OH 866-532-7429
Fleming Packaging Corporation
Peoria, IL 309-676-7657
Fraser Stamp & Seal
Chicago, IL 800-540-8565
G&R Graphics
South Orange, NJ 813-503-8592
Hartford Stamp Works
Hartford, CT 860-249-6205
Hiss Stamp Company
Columbus, OH 614-224-5119
Innovative Ceramic Corp.
East Liverpool, OH 330-385-6515
Joyce Engraving Company, Inc.
Dallas, TX 214-638-1262
L&L Engraving Company
Gilford, NH 888-524-3032
Mecco Marking & Traceability
Cranberry Township, PA 888-369-9190
Modern Stamp Company
Baltimore, MD 800-727-3029
Nameplates
St Paul, MN 651-228-1522
National Metal Industries
West Springfield, MA 800-628-8850
Pinquist Tool & Die Company
Brooklyn, NY 800-752-0414
Plastimatic Arts Corporation
Mishawaka, IN 800-442-3593
R.P. Childs Stamp Company
Ludlow, MA 413-733-1211
Sanifab
Stratford, WI 715-687-4332
Schwaab, Inc
Milwaukee, WI 800-935-9877
Southern Atlantic Label Company
Chesapeake, VA 800-456-5999
The Southwell Company
San Antonio, TX 210-223-1831
United Ribtype Company
Fort Wayne, IN 800-473-4039
Volk Corporation
Farmington Hills, MI 800-521-6799

Rubber

ABC Stamp Company
Boise, ID 208-375-4470
Accent Mark
Palmdale, CA 661-274-8191
Ace Stamp & Engraving
Lakewood, WA 253-582-3322

Allmark Impressions
Fort Worth, TX....................817-834-0080
American Art Stamp
Gardena, CA....................310-965-9004
Ameristamp Sign-A-Rama
Evansville, IN....................800-543-6693
Atlas Rubber Stamp Company
York, PA....................717-755-1105
Century Rubber Stamp Company
New York, NY....................212-962-6165
Chattanooga Rubber Stamp& Stencil Works
Sale Creek, TN....................800-894-1164
City Stamp & Seal Company
Austin, TX....................800-950-6074
Coleman Stamps, Signs & Recognition Products
Daytona Beach, FL....................386-253-1206
Corpus Christi Stamp Works
Corpus Christi, TX....................800-322-4515
Crown Marking
Minneapolis, MN....................800-305-5249
Custom Rubber Stamp Company
Crosby, MN....................888-606-4579
Custom Stamp Company
Anza, CA....................323-292-0753
Dayton Marking Devices Company
Dayton, OH....................937-432-0285
Des Moines Stamp Manufacturing Company
Des Moines, IA....................888-236-7739
Detroit Marking Products
Detroit, MI....................800-833-8222
Dixie Rubber Stamp & Seal Company
Atlanta, GA....................404-875-8883
DRS Designs
Bethel, CT....................888-792-3740
East Memphis Rubber Stamp Company
Bartlett, TN....................901-384-0887
Ed Smith's Stencil Works
New Orleans, LA....................504-525-2128
Ehrgott Rubber Stamp Company
Indianapolis, IN....................317-353-2222
Everett Stamp Works
Everett, WA....................425-258-6747
Federal Stamp & Seal Manufacturing Company
Atlanta, GA....................800-333-7726
Fleming Packaging Corporation
Peoria, IL....................309-676-7657
Flint Rubber Stamp Works
Flint, MI....................810-235-2341
Fox Stamp, Sign & Specialty
Menasha, WI....................800-236-3699
Franklin Rubber Stamp Company
Wilmington, DE....................302-654-8841
Fraser Stamp & Seal
Chicago, IL....................800-540-8565
Frost Manufacturing Corporation
Worcester, MA....................800-462-0216
G&R Graphics
South Orange, NJ....................813-503-8592
Glover Rubber Stamp Corporation
Wills Point, TX....................214-824-6900
Granite State Stamps, Inc.
Manchester, NH....................800-937-3736
Grays Harbor Stamp Works
Aberdeen, WA....................800-894-3830
Gribble Stamp & Stencil Company
Houston, TX....................713-228-5358
Grueny's Rubber Stamps
Little Rock, AR....................501-376-0393
Hartford Stamp Works
Hartford, CT....................860-249-6205
Hathaway Stamp Company
Cincinnati, OH....................513-621-1052
Hiss Stamp Company
Columbus, OH....................614-224-5119
House Stamp Works
Chicago, IL....................312-939-7177
Houston Stamp & Stencil Company
Houston, TX....................713-869-4337
Huntington Park Rubber Stamp Company
Huntington Park, CA....................800-882-0029
Ideal Office Supply & Rubber Stamp Company
Kingsport, TN....................423-246-7371
Innovative Ceramic Corp.
East Liverpool, OH....................330-385-6515
Jim Lake Companies
Dallas, TX....................214-741-5018
Justrite Rubber Stamp & Seal Company
Kansas City, MO....................800-229-5010
JVC Rubber Stamp Company
Elkhart, IN....................574-293-0113
L&L Engraving Company
Gilford, NH....................888-524-3032
Lakeland Rubber Stamp Company
Lakeland, FL....................863-682-5111
Lakeview Rubber Stamp Company
Chicago, IL....................773-539-1525
Larry B. Newman PrintingCompany
Knoxville, TN....................888-835-4566
Lobues Rubber Stamp Company
Houston, TX....................713-652-0031
Long Island Stamp Corporation
Flushing, NY....................800-547-8267
Mankuta Brothers Rubber Stamp Company, Inc.
Bohemia, NY....................800-223-4481
Mansfield Rubber Stamp
Mansfield, OH....................419-524-1442
Mark-It Rubber Stamp & Label Company
Stamford, CT....................203-348-3204
Marking Devices
Cleveland, OH....................216-861-4498
Martco Engravers
Fremont, NH....................603-895-3561
Mastermark
Kent, WA....................206-762-9610
Modern Stamp Company
Baltimore, MD....................800-727-3029
Moore Efficient Communication Aids
Denver, CO....................303-433-8456
Muskogee Rubber Stamp & Seal Company
Fort Gibson, OK....................918-478-3046
My Serenity Pond
Cold Spring, MN....................320-363-0411
Nameplates
St Paul, MN....................651-228-1522
National Marking Products, Inc.
Richmond, VA....................800-482-1553
Northern Berkshire Manufacturing Company
North Adams, MA....................413-663-9204
O.K. Marking Devices
Regina, SK....................306-522-2856
OK Stamp & Seal Company
Oklahoma City, OK....................405-235-7853
Oration Rubber Stamp Company
Columbus, NJ....................908-496-4161
Plastimatic Arts Corporation
Mishawaka, IN....................800-442-3593
Printcraft Marking Devices
Buffalo, NY....................716-873-8181
Quick Stamp & Sign Mfg
Lafayette, LA....................337-232-2171
R.P. Childs Stamp Company
Ludlow, MA....................413-733-1211
Rebel Stamp & Sign Company, Inc.
Baton Rouge, LA....................800-860-5120
Richardson's Stamp Works
Houston, TX....................713-973-0300
Royal Acme Corporation
Cleveland, OH....................216-241-1477
Rubber Stamp Shop
Accokeek, MD....................800-835-0839
Schwaab, Inc
Milwaukee, WI....................800-935-9877
Service Stamp Works
Chicago, IL....................312-666-8839
Sioux Falls Rubber StampWork
Sioux Falls, SD....................605-334-5990
Southern Rubber Stamp Company
Tulsa, OK....................888-826-4304
Spectrum Enterprises
Evansville, IN....................812-425-1771
Spencer Business Form Company
Spencer, WV....................304-372-8877
Sutherland Stamp Company
San Diego, CA....................858-233-7784
The Southwell Company
San Antonio, TX....................210-223-1831
United Ribtype Company
Fort Wayne, IN....................800-473-4039
Volk Corporation
Farmington Hills, MI....................800-521-6799
Walker Companies
Oklahoma City, OK....................800-522-3015
Welch Stencil Company
Scarborough, ME....................800-635-3506
Wichita Stamp & Seal
Wichita, KS....................316-263-4223
Wildes - Spirit Design & Printing
White Plains, MD....................301-870-4141
Winmark Stamp & Sign
Salt Lake City, UT....................800-438-0480

Stands

Tray

C.R. Manufacturing
Waverly, NE....................877-789-5844
Carlisle Food Service Products
Oklahoma City, OK....................800-654-8210
Creative Essentials
Ronkonkoma, NY....................800-355-5891
Duke Manufacturing Company
Saint Louis, MO....................800-735-3853
Ex-Cell Kaiser
Franklin Park, IL....................847-451-0451
Fixtur-World
Cookeville, TN....................800-634-9887
Gaychrome Division of CSL
Crystal Lake, IL....................800-873-4370
Glaro
Hauppauge, NY....................631-234-1717
International Patterns, Inc.
Bay Shore, NY....................631-952-2000
Marston Manufacturing
Cleveland, OH....................216-587-3400
MLS Signs
Chesterfield, MI....................586-948-0200
Quality Highchairs
Pacoima, CA....................800-969-9635
R.R. Scheibe Company
Newton Center, MA....................508-584-4900
Superior Products Company
Saint Paul, MN....................800-328-9800
US Seating Products
Apopka, FL....................407-884-4411
WES Plastics
Richmond Hill, ON....................905-508-1546

Sticks

Candy

Automated Food Systems
Waxahachie, TX....................972-298-5719
Jarden Home Brands
Daleville, IN....................800-392-2575
Lorann Oils
Lansing, MI....................800-862-8620
Saunder Brothers
Bridgton, ME....................207-647-3331
Setterstix Corporation
Cattaraugus, NY....................716-257-3451

Ice Cream

Diamond Brands
Cloquet, MN....................218-879-6700
Global Sticks, Inc.
Surrey, BC....................866-433-5770
Hardwood Products Company
Guilford, ME....................800-289-3340
Norse Dairy Systems
Columbus, OH....................800-338-7465
Solon Manufacturing Company
North Haven, CT....................800-341-6640

Tags

Cellulose & Fiber

Atlas Tag & Label
Neenah, WI....................800-558-6418
Connecticut Laminating Company
New Haven, CT....................800-753-9119
InterMetro Industries Corporation
Wilkes Barre, PA....................800-441-2714
LabelPrint Corporation
Newburyport, MA....................978-463-4004

Pressure Sensitive

ATL-East Tag & Label Company
West Chester, PA....................866-381-8744
Carlton Industries
La Grange, TX....................800-231-5988
Daclabels
Dallas, TX....................800-483-1700
Deco Labels & Tags
Toronto, ON....................888-496-9029
EMED Company
Buffalo, NY....................800-442-3633
GBS Corporate
North Canton, OH....................800-552-2427

Grand Valley Labels
Grand Rapids, MI
Itac Label
Brooklyn, NY 718-625-2148
Label House
Fullerton, CA 800-499-5858
Label Technology
Merced, CA........................ 800-388-1990
Labelmart
Maple Grove, MN................. 888-577-0141
LabelPrint Corporation
Newburyport, MA................ 978-463-4004
Met-Speed Label
Levittown, PA..................... 888-886-0638
Mid South Graphics
Nashville, TN 615-331-4210
Nameplates
St Paul, MN........................ 651-228-1522
Northstar Print Group
Green Bay, WI..................... 800-236-8208
Ozark Tape & Label Company
Springfield, MO 417-831-1444
Paper Product Specialties
Waukesha, WI..................... 262-549-1730
Royal Label Company
Boston, MA........................ 617-825-6050
Seton Identification Products
Branford, CT...................... 800-571-2596
Southern Atlantic Label Company
Chesapeake, VA 800-456-5999
Stoffel Seals Corporation
Tallapoosa, GA 800-422-8247
Swan Label & Tag
Coraopolis, PA 412-264-9000
TAC-PAD
Irvine, CA.......................... 800-947-1609
Tag & Label Corporation
Anderson, SC 864-224-2122
Three P
Salt Lake City, UT 801-486-7407
Universal Tag
Dudley, MA........................ 800-332-8247

Price

Andrew H. Lawson Company
Philadelphia, PA 800-411-6628
Bedford Industries
Worthington, MN 800-533-5314
Clamp Swing Pricing Company
Oakland, CA....................... 800-227-7615
Esselte Meto
Morris Plains, NJ 800-645-3290
Federal Label Systems
Elmhurst, NY 800-238-0015
General Trade Mark Labelcraft
Staten Island, NY 718-448-9800
Intermec Technologies Corporation
Everett, WA........................ 425-348-2600
KHS Company
West Simsbury, CT 860-658-9454
LabelPrint Corporation
Newburyport, MA................. 978-463-4004
Los Angeles Label Company
Commerce, CA..................... 800-606-5223
National Marking Products, Inc.
Richmond, VA..................... 800-482-1553
Plasti-Clip Corporation
Milford, NH 800-882-2547
Plastic Tag & Trade Check Company
Essexville, MI...................... 989-892-7913
Reeve Store Equipment Company
Pico Rivera, CA 800-927-3383
Rothchild Printing Company
Flushing, NY....................... 800-238-0015
Royal Label Company
Boston, MA........................ 617-825-6050
SFBC, LLC dba Seaboard Folding Box
Fitchburg, MA 800-225-6313
Stoffel Seals Corporation
Tallapoosa, GA 800-422-8247
United Seal & Tag Corporation
Port Charlotte, FL................. 800-211-9552

Tea Bag

Cincinnati Convertors
Cincinnati, OH 513-731-6600
Stoffel Seals Corporation
Tallapoosa, GA 800-422-8247

Tapes

Adhesive

AFASSCO
Minden, NV 800-441-6774
Cantech Industries
Johnson City, TN 800-654-3947
Deccofelt Corporation
Glendora, CA 800-543-3226
Dunrite
Fremont, NE 800-782-3061
Fasteners for Retail
Cincinnati, OH 800-422-2547
Felco Bag & Burlap Company
Baltimore, MD 800-673-8488
Gulf Arizona Packaging
Humble, TX 800-364-3887
Herche Warehouse
Denver, CO 303-371-8186
International Tape Company
Windham, NH...................... 800-253-4450
Intertape Polymer Group
Bradenton, FL..................... 877-318-5752
Jupiter Mills Corporation
Roslyn, NY 800-853-5121
Label Systems & Solutions
Bohemia, NY 800-811-2560
Levin Brothers Paper
Cicero, IL.......................... 800-666-8484
Master Tape Printers, Inc.
Chicago, IL........................ 800-621-5801
Miller Products, Inc
New Philadelphia, OH 800-332-0050
Nashua Corporation
Nashua, NH........................ 603-661-2004
National Tape Corporation
New Orleans, LA 800-535-8846
O.C. Adhesives Corporation
Ridgefield, NJ...................... 800-662-1595
On-Hand Adhesives
Lake Zurich, IL.................... 800-323-5158
Quali-Tech Tape & Label
Denver, CO
Recco Tape & Label
West Columbia, SC............... 800-334-3008
Saunders Corporation
Azusa, CA.......................... 888-932-8836
Sekisui TA Industries
Brea, CA........................... 800-258-8273
SpecTape, Inc.
Erlanger, KY....................... 859-283-2044
Stik-2 Products
Easthampton, MA................. 800-356-3572
Tesa Tape
Charlotte, NC 800-429-8273
Thomas Tape Company
Springfield, OH.................... 937-325-6414
US Label Corporation
Greensboro, NC 336-332-7000
Wasserman Bag Company
Center Moriches, NY 631-909-8656
Worthen Industries
Nashua, NH........................ 603-888-5443
WS Packaging Group Inc
Green Bay, WI..................... 920-866-6300

Freezer

Gulf Arizona Packaging
Humble, TX 800-364-3887
Herche Warehouse
Denver, CO 303-371-8186
Verilon Products Company
Wheeling, IL....................... 800-323-1056

Gummed

Adhesive Products, Inc.
Vernon, CA 800-669-5516
Cantech Industries
Johnson City, TN 800-654-3947
Central Products Company
Menasha, WI...................... 800-558-5006
Crowell Corporation
Wilmington, DE 800-441-7525
Ebel Tape & Label
Cincinnati, OH 513-471-1067
Gulf Arizona Packaging
Humble, TX 800-364-3887
Herche Warehouse
Denver, CO 303-371-8186

Intertape Polymer Group
Bradenton, FL..................... 877-318-5752
Keena Corporation
Newton, MA 617-244-9800
Master Tape Printers, Inc.
Chicago, IL 800-621-5801
Rexford Paper Company
Racine, WI 262-886-9100
Rudd Container Corporation
Chicago, IL 773-847-7600
Thomas Tape Company
Springfield, OH.................... 937-325-6414
Timemed Labeling Systems
Valencia, CA 818-897-1111
Volk Corporation
Farmington Hills, MI 800-521-6799

Heat Sealing

International Tape Company
Windham, NH...................... 800-253-4450
Intertape Polymer Group
Bradenton, FL..................... 877-318-5752
National Tape Corporation
New Orleans, LA 800-535-8846
Rexford Paper Company
Racine, WI 262-886-9100

Marking

Carlton Industries
La Grange, TX 800-231-5988
Felco Bag & Burlap Company
Baltimore, MD 800-673-8488
Master Tape Printers, Inc.
Chicago, IL 800-621-5801
National Tape Corporation
New Orleans, LA 800-535-8846

Pressure Sensitive

Adhesive Products, Inc.
Vernon, CA 800-669-5516
Adstick Custom Labels
Denver, CO 800-255-7314
Advanced Labelworx, Inc
Oak Ridge, TN 865-966-8711
Avon Tape
Chestnut Hill, MA 508-584-8273
Baltimore Tape Products
Sykesville, MD 410-795-0063
Cantech Industries
Johnson City, TN 800-654-3947
Central Products Company
Menasha, WI...................... 800-558-5006
Daclabels
Dallas, TX.......................... 800-483-1700
Deccofelt Corporation
Glendora, CA 800-543-3226
Ebel Tape & Label
Cincinnati, OH 513-471-1067
Emco Industrial Plastics
Cedar Grove, NJ 800-292-9906
Fibre Leather Manufacturing Company
New Bedford, MA 800-358-6012
Gulf Arizona Packaging
Humble, TX 800-364-3887
Henkel Consumer Adhesive
Avon, OH 800-321-0253
Herche Warehouse
Denver, CO 303-371-8186
International Tape Company
Windham, NH...................... 800-253-4450
Intertape Polymer Group
Bradenton, FL..................... 877-318-5752
J.M. Packaging/Detroit Tape & Label
Warren, MI 586-771-7800
Jupiter Mills Corporation
Roslyn, NY 800-853-5121
KAPCO
Kent, OH........................... 800-843-5368
Label Systems & Solutions
Bohemia, NY 800-811-2560
Marklite Line
Bellwood, IL....................... 708-668-4900
Master Tape Printers, Inc.
Chicago, IL 800-621-5801
Merryweather Foam
Sylacauga, AL..................... 256-249-8546
Miller Products, Inc
New Philadelphia, OH 800-332-0050
NAP Industries
Brooklyn, NY 877-635-4948

National Tape Corporation
New Orleans, LA 800-535-8846
Ozark Tape & Label Company
Springfield, MO 417-831-1444
Pakmark
Chesterfield, MO 800-423-1379
Pamco Printed Tape & Label Company
Des Plaines, IL 847-803-2200
Print-O-Tape
Mundelein, IL 800-346-6311
RayPress Corporation
Birmingham, AL.................800-423-3731
Rexford Paper Company
Racine, WI 262-886-9100
Richmond Printed Tape & Label
Hatfield, PA.................800-522-3525
Robinson Tape & Label
Branford, CT.................800-433-7102
Saunders Corporation
Azusa, CA.................888-932-8836
Sekisui TA Industries
Brea, CA.................800-258-8273
Shippers Supply
Saskatoon, SK.................800-661-5639
Shippers Supply, Labelgraphic
Calgary, AB.................800-661-5639
Source for Packaging
New York, NY 800-223-2527
SpecTape, Inc.
Erlanger, KY.................859-283-2044
St. Gobain Performance Plastics
New Haven, CT 203-777-2822
Tag & Label Corporation
Anderson, SC 864-224-2122
Tape & Label Engineering
St Petersburg, FL 800-237-8955
Tesa Tape
Charlotte, NC 800-429-8273
Thomas Tape Company
Springfield, OH.................937-325-6414
Volk Corporation
Farmington Hills, MI 800-521-6799

Tea Packaging Materials

Cin-Made Packaging Group
Cincinnati, OH 513-681-3600
Packaging Dynamics
Walnut Creek, CA.................925-938-2711
Xtreme Beverages, LLC
Dana Point, CA.................949-495-7929

Ties

Bag

AR-BEE Transparent
Elk Grove Vlg, IL.................800-642-2247
Bedford Industries
Worthington, MN 800-533-5314
Cavert Wire Company
Rural Hall, NC 800-245-4042
Gulf Arizona Packaging
Humble, TX.................800-364-3887
Herche Warehouse
Denver, CO.................303-371-8186
Leco Plastics
Hackensack, NJ.................201-343-3330
Package Containers
Canby, OR.................800-266-5806
Plas-Ties
Tustin, CA.................800-854-0137
Superior Products Company
Saint Paul, MN 800-328-9800
T&T Industries
Fort Mohave, AZ 800-437-6246

Bundle, Package

Bedford Industries
Worthington, MN 800-533-5314
Cavert Wire Company
Rural Hall, NC 800-245-4042

Emco Industrial Plastics
Cedar Grove, NJ 800-292-9906
Gulf Arizona Packaging
Humble, TX 800-364-3887
Herche Warehouse
Denver, CO.................303-371-8186
Indeco Products
San Marcos, TX 512-396-5814
Jilson Group
Lodi, NJ.................800-969-5400
Leco Plastics
Hackensack, NJ.................201-343-3330
Lorann Oils
Lansing, MI.................800-862-8620
Package Containers
Canby, OR.................800-266-5806
QMS International, Inc.
Mississauga, Ontario, ON.................905-820-7225
T&T Industries
Fort Mohave, AZ 800-437-6246

Trays

Ace Technical Plastics
Hartford, CT 860-305-8138
Bayhead Products Corporation
Dover, NH.................800-229-4323
Collector's Gallery
Saint Charles, IL.................800-346-3063
Del-Tec Packaging
Greenville, SC.................800-747-8683
Douglas Stephen Plastics
Paterson, NJ 973-523-3030
Flexpak Corporation
Phoenix, AZ 602-269-7648
Great Western Products
Ontario, CA.................888-598-5588
In-Touch Products
North Salt Lake, UT 801-298-4466
iVEX Packaging Corporation
Lachine, QC 514-636-7951
Jay Packaging Group
Warwick, RI 401-739-7200
Key Packaging Company
Sarasota, FL 941-355-2728
Leading Industry
Oxnard, CA.................805-385-4100
Leal True Form Corporation
Freeport, NY.................516-379-2008
Madsen Wire Products
Orland, IN.................260-829-6561
Molded Materials
Plymouth, MI 800-825-2566
NU-Trend Plastic/Corrigan & Company
Jacksonville, FL 904-353-5936
Olive Can Company
Elgin, IL 847-468-7474
Packaging Solutions
Los Altos Hills, CA 650-917-1022
Pactiv LLC
Lake Forest, IL 888-828-2850
Palace Packaging Machines
Downingtown, PA.................610-873-7252
Parlor City Paper Box Company
Binghamton, NY.................607-772-0600
Revere Group
Seattle, WA 206-545-8150
Schroeder Sewing Technologies
San Marcos, CA 760-591-9733
Scott Packaging Corporation
Philadelphia, PA 215-925-5595
Sealpac USA LLC
Richmond, VA.................804-261-0580
Tenneco Packaging/Pressware
Lake Forest, IL 800-403-3393
Tenneco Specialty Packaging
Smyrna, GA 800-241-4402
Vc999 Packaging Systems Inc.
Kansas City, MO.................800-728-2999
WNA Hopple Plastics
Florence, KY.................800-446-4622
Xtreme Beverages, LLC
Dana Point, CA.................949-495-7929

Wax

Cheese Coating

Frank B. Ross Company
Rahway, NJ.................732-669-0810
International Group
Oshkosh, WI 920-233-5500

Paraffin

Hollowick
Manlius, NY 800-367-3015

Sealing

Frank B. Ross Company
Rahway, NJ.................732-669-0810
Stevenson-Cooper, Inc.
Philadelphia, PA 215-223-2600

Wrappers

Frozen Food

Campbell Wrapper Corporation
De Pere, WI.................920-983-7100
Schwab Paper Products Company
Romeoville, IL 800-837-7225

Paper

Alufoil Products
Hauppauge, NY 631-231-4141
Burrows Paper Corporation
Little Falls, NY.................800-272-7122
Campbell Wrapper Corporation
De Pere, WI.................920-983-7100
Gardiner Paperboard
Gardiner, ME 207-582-3230
Handy Wacks Corporation
Sparta, MI 800-445-4434
Patty Paper, Inc.
Plymouth, IN.................800-782-1703
Printpack
Atlanta, GA.................404-460-7000
Ross & Wallace Paper Products
Hammond, LA 800-854-2300
Salinas Valley Wax PaperCompany
Salinas, CA 831-424-2747
Schwab Paper Products Company
Romeoville, IL 800-837-7225
Signature Packaging
West Orange, NJ.................800-376-2299
Stewart Sutherland
Vicksburg, MI.................269-649-5489
Wrap-Pak
Yakima, WA 800-879-9727

Transparent

AR-BEE Transparent
Elk Grove Vlg, IL.................800-642-2247
Campbell Wrapper Corporation
De Pere, WI.................920-983-7100
Curwood
Oshkosh, WI 800-544-4672
DuPont
Wilmington, DE 800-441-7515
Flexo Transparent
Buffalo, NY.................877-993-5396
Goodwrappers/J.C. Parry & Sons Company
Halethorpe, MD 800-638-1127
MS Plastics & Packaging Company
Butler, NJ 800-593-1802
MSK Covertech
Marietta, GA.................770-928-1099
Trans World Services
Melrose, MA.................800-882-2105

Refrigeration & Cooling Equipment

Cabinets

Freezer & Frozen Foods

AAA Mill
Austin, TX. . . . 512-385-2215
Andgar Corporation
Ferndale, WA . . . 360-366-9900
Arkfeld Mfg & Distr Company
Norfolk, NE. . . . 800-533-0676
Bacchus Wine Cellars
Houston, TX . . . 800-487-8812
Bettag & Associates
O Fallon, MO . . . 800-325-0959
Bevles Company
Dallas, TX. . . . 800-441-1601
C. Nelson Manufacturing Company
Oak Harbor, OH . . . 800-922-7339
Crown Manufacturing Corporation
Waterford, CT . . . 860-442-4325
Cryochem
St Simons Island, GA . . . 800-237-4001
Delfield Company
Mt Pleasant, MI. . . . 800-733-8821
Duke Manufacturing Company
Saint Louis, MO . . . 800-735-3853
EPCO
Murfreesboro, TN. . . . 800-251-3398
Eskay Metal Fabricating Company
Buffalo, NY. . . . 800-836-8015
Fogel Jordon Commercial Refrigeration Company
Philadelphia, PA . . . 800-523-0171
Foster Refrigerator Corporation
Kinderhook, NY . . . 888-828-3311
FWE/Food Warming Equipment Company, Inc
Crystal Lake, IL . . . 800-222-4393
GA Systems
Huntington Beach, CA . . . 714-848-7529
Habco
Concord, CA. . . . 925-682-6203
Hoshizaki America
Peachtree City, GA . . . 800-438-6087
IMC Teddy Food Service Equipment
Amityville, NY . . . 800-221-5644
J.H. Carr & Sons
Seattle, WA . . . 800-523-8842
Kedco Wine Storage Systems
Farmingdale, NY . . . 800-654-9988
LaRosa Refrigeration & Equipment Company
Detroit, MI . . . 800-527-6723
Lauritzen & Makin
Fort Worth, TX . . . 817-921-0218
Lyon Metal Products
Aurora, IL . . . 630-892-8941
Master-Bilt
New Albany, MS. . . . 800-647-1284
McCall Refrigeration
Parsons, TN. . . . 888-732-2446
Merric
Bridgeton, MO . . . 314-770-9944
Metal Master
Tucson, AZ . . . 800-488-8729
Normandie Metal Fabricators
Port Washington, NY . . . 800-221-2398
Omicron Steel Products Company
Jamaica, NY . . . 718-805-3400
Piper Products
Wausau, WI. . . . 800-544-3057
Sefi Fabricators
Amityville, NY . . . 631-842-2200
Shammi Industries/Sammons Equipment
Corona, CA. . . . 800-417-9260
Silver King
Minneapolis, MN . . . 800-328-3329
St. Louis Stainless Service
Fenton, MO. . . . 888-507-1578
Super Sturdy
Weldon, NC. . . . 800-253-4833
Talbert Display
Fort Worth, TX . . . 817-429-4504
Texican Specialty Products
Houston, TX . . . 800-869-5918
Valad Electric Heating Corporation
Tarrytown, NY
Welbilt Corporation
Stamford, CT. . . . 203-325-8300
Western Laminates
Omaha, NE . . . 402-556-4600
Wine Chillers of California
Santa Ana, CA . . . 800-331-4274
Zero Corporation
Monson, MA. . . . 413-267-5561

Chillers

Blast

Advance Energy Technologies
Clifton Park, NY. . . . 800-724-0198
ALKAR
Lodi, WI . . . 608-592-3211
Edwards Engineering Corporation
Pompton Plains, NJ. . . . 800-526-5201
Elliott-Williams Company
Indianapolis, IN . . . 800-428-9303
Gea Intec, Llc
Durham, NC . . . 919-433-0131
Glastender
Saginaw, MI . . . 800-748-0423
Henny Penny, Inc.
Detroit, MI . . . 313-877-9550
Pacific Pneumatics
Rancho Cucamonga, CA . . . 800-221-0961
RMF Freezers
Grandview, MO. . . . 816-765-4101
Superior Products Company
Saint Paul, MN . . . 800-328-9800
USECO
Murfreesboro, TN. . . . 615-893-4820
Williams Refrigeration
Hillsdale, NJ . . . 800-445-9979

Compressors

GEA FES, Inc.
York, PA . . . 025-119-1051
GEA Refrigeration North America, Inc.
York, PA . . . 800-888-4337
Paxton Products
Cincinnati, OH . . . 800-441-7475
Tecumseh Products Company
Ann Arbor, MI . . . 734-585-9500

Coolers

Beverage

Advance Energy Technologies
Clifton Park, NY. . . . 800-724-0198
Alkar
Lodi, WI . . . 608-592-3211
Aurora Design Associates, Inc.
Salt Lake City, UT. . . . 801-588-0111
Bar Equipment Corporation of America
Downey, CA . . . 888-870-2322
Berkshire PPM
Litchfield, CT . . . 860-567-3118
Beverage-Air
Winston Salem, NC. . . . 800-845-9800
Chester-Jensen Company, Inc.
Chester, PA . . . 800-685-3750
Cleland Sales Corporation
Los Alamitos, CA . . . 562-598-6616
Convay Systems
Etobicoke, ON. . . . 800-811-5511
Cool-Pitch Company
Jacksonville, FL . . . 800-938-0128
Cramer Products
New York, NY . . . 212-645-2368
Duke Manufacturing Company
Saint Louis, MO . . . 800-735-3853
Elwood Safety Company
Buffalo, NY. . . . 866-326-6060
Felix Storch
Bronx, NY. . . . 800-932-4267
FleetwoodGoldcoWyard
Romeoville, IL . . . 630-759-6800
Fogel Jordon Commercial Refrigeration Company
Philadelphia, PA . . . 800-523-0171
Foster Refrigerator Corporation
Kinderhook, NY . . . 888-828-3311
General Foam Plastics Corporation
Norfolk, VA. . . . 757-857-0153
Girard Spring Water
North Providence, RI . . . 800-477-9287
Glastender
Saginaw, MI . . . 800-748-0423
Hebeler Corporation
Tonawanda, NY . . . 800-486-4709
Hoshizaki America
Peachtree City, GA . . . 800-438-6087
ILC Dover
Frederica, DE . . . 800-631-9567
International Patterns, Inc.
Bay Shore, NY . . . 631-952-2000
Perlick Corporation
Milwaukee, WI. . . . 800-558-5592
Pro-Flo Products
Cedar Grove, NJ . . . 800-325-1057
QBD Modular Systems
Santa Clara, CA . . . 800-663-3005
RubaTex Polymer
Middlefield, OH . . . 440-632-1691
Rubbermaid Specialty Products
Freeport, IL. . . . 815-235-4171
Summit Appliance Division
Bronx, NY. . . . 800-932-4267
Summit Commercial
Bronx, NY. . . . 800-932-4267
Superior Products Company
Saint Paul, MN . . . 800-328-9800
True Food Service Equipment, Inc.
O Fallon, MO . . . 800-325-6152
Tuscarora
New Brighton, PA. . . . 724-847-2601
Wine Chillers of California
Santa Ana, CA . . . 800-331-4274
Wine Well Chiller Company
Milford, CT. . . . 203-878-2465

Bread

Advance Energy Technologies
Clifton Park, NY. . . . 800-724-0198
Fred D. Pfening Company
Columbus, OH . . . 614-294-1633
IJ White Corporation
Farmingdale, NY. . . . 631-293-2211
Industrial Air Conditioning Systems
Chicago, IL . . . 773-486-4236
Peerless Food Inc
Sidney, OH . . . 937-494-2870

Butchers'

Advance Energy Technologies
Clifton Park, NY. . . . 800-724-0198

Candy (Confectioners')

Advance Energy Technologies
Clifton Park, NY. . . . 800-724-0198
Applied Thermal Technologies
San Marcos, CA . . . 800-736-5083
Hebeler Corporation
Tonawanda, NY . . . 800-486-4709
Komline-Sanderson
Peapack, NJ. . . . 800-225-5457

Canners'

Advance Energy Technologies
Clifton Park, NY. . . . 800-724-0198
Berkshire PPM
Litchfield, CT . . . 860-567-3118
Custom Food Machinery
Stockton, CA. . . . 209-463-4343
Hebeler Corporation
Tonawanda, NY . . . 800-486-4709
Horix Manufacturing Company
Mc Kees Rocks, PA. . . . 412-771-1111
Nercon Engineering & Manufacturing
Oshkosh, WI . . . 920-233-3268
South Valley Manufacturing
Gilroy, CA. . . . 408-842-5457

Ice

Eskay Metal Fabricating Company
Buffalo, NY. 800-836-8015
General Foam Plastics Corporation
Norfolk, VA. 757-857-0153
Hoshizaki America
Peachtree City, GA 800-438-6087
Igloo Products
Katy, TX 800-364-5566
Majestic
Bridgeport, CT 203-367-7900
Mid-Lands Chemical Company
Omaha, NE 402-455-9975
Midwest Aircraft Products Company
Mansfield, OH 419-522-2231
Northfield Freezing Systems
Northfield, MN 800-426-1283
Olde Country Reproductions
York, PA 800-358-3997
PFI Prasence From Innovation
St Louis, MO. 314-423-9777
Plastilite Corporation
Omaha, NE 800-228-9506
Polyfoam Packers Corporation
Arlington Hts, IL 800-323-7442
Rubbermaid Specialty Products
Freeport, IL 815-235-4171
Semco Manufacturing Company
Pharr, TX. 956-787-4203
Superior Products Company
Saint Paul, MN 800-328-9800

Ice Cream

Advance Energy Technologies
Clifton Park, NY. 800-724-0198
Jack Langston Manufacturing Company
Dallas, TX. 214-821-9844
Manufacturing Warehouse
Miami, FL. 305-635-8886
Superior Products Company
Saint Paul, MN 800-328-9800
WA Brown & Son
Salisbury, NC 704-636-5131

Ingredient Water

Advance Energy Technologies
Clifton Park, NY. 800-724-0198
Applied Thermal Technologies
San Marcos, CA 800-736-5083
Bevistar
Oswego, IL 877-238-7827
Filtrine Manufacturing Company
Keene, NH. 603-352-5500
Girard Spring Water
North Providence, RI 800-477-9287
Komline-Sanderson
Peapack, NJ. 800-225-5457
Koolant Koolers
Kalamazoo, MI 800-968-5665
Perfection Equipment
Gurnee, IL. 800-356-6301
Wine Well Chiller Company
Milford, CT. 203-878-2465

Milk & Cream

Advance Energy Technologies
Clifton Park, NY. 800-724-0198
Applied Thermal Technologies
San Marcos, CA 800-736-5083
Babson Brothers Company
Galesville, WI. 608-582-2221
Beverage-Air
Winston Salem, NC. 800-845-9800
C.E. Rogers Company
Mora, MN 800-279-8081
Carrier Vibrating Equipment
Louisville, KY 502-969-3171
Chester-Jensen Company, Inc.
Chester, PA 800-685-3750
Foster Refrigerator Corporation
Kinderhook, NY 888-828-3311
Hebeler Corporation
Tonawanda, NY 800-486-4709
Precision
Miami, FL. 800-762-7565
Viatec
Hastings, MI 800-942-4702

Walk-In

Advance Energy Technologies
Clifton Park, NY. 800-724-0198
American Panel Corporation
Ocala, FL. 800-327-3015
Arctic Industries
Medley, FL 800-325-0123
B.N.W. Industries
Tippecanoe, IN 574-353-7855
Bally Refrigerated Boxes
Morehead City, NC. 800-242-2559
C.M. Lingle Company
Henderson, TX 800-256-6963
Crown/Tonka Walk-Ins
Plymouth, MN. 800-523-7337
Dade Engineering
Tampa, FL. 800-321-2112
David A. Lingle & Son Manufacturing Company
Russellville, AR 479-968-2500
Elliott-Williams Company
Indianapolis, IN 800-428-9303
Emjac Industries
Hialeah, FL 305-883-2194
Erickson Industries
River Falls, WI 800-729-9941
FleetwoodGoldcoWyard
Romeoville, IL 630-759-6800
Flo-Cold
Wixom, MI 248-348-6666
Harford Duracool LLC
Aberdeen, MD 410-272-9999
International Cold Storage
Andover, KS 800-835-0001
Jack Langston Manufacturing Company
Dallas, TX. 214-821-9844
KEMCO
Wareham, MA. 800-231-5955
Kolpak
Parsons, TN. 800-826-7036
Kolpak Walk-ins
Parsons, TN. 800-826-7036
Kysor Panel Systems
Fort Worth, TX 800-633-3426
Kysor/Kalt
Portland, OR 503-235-0776
Kysor/Warren
Columbus, GA 800-866-5596
Leer Limited Partnership
New Lisbon, WI 800-766-5337
M&S Manufacturing
Arnold, MO. 636-464-2739
Manufacturing Warehouse
Miami, FL. 305-635-8886
Marquis Products
Concord, ON. 800-268-1282
Mollenberg-Betz
Buffalo, NY. 716-614-7473
Nor-Lake
Salem, NH. 603-893-9701
Pacific Refrigerator Company
San Bernardino, CA 909-381-5669
Penn Refrigeration Service Corporation
Wilkes Barre, PA. 800-233-8354
Perley-Halladay Associates, Inc.
West Chester, PA. 800-248-5800
Polar King International
Fort Wayne, IN 800-752-7178
Portable Cold Storage
Edison, NJ. 800-535-2445
QBD Modular Systems
Santa Clara, CA 800-663-3005
Refrigeration Engineering
Grand Rapids, MI 800-968-3227
Superior Products Company
Saint Paul, MN 800-328-9800
Tafco-TMP Company
Hyde, PA. 800-233-1954
US Cooler Company
Quincy, IL. 800-521-2665
WA Brown & Son
Salisbury, NC 704-636-5131
Zero-Temp
Santa Ana, CA 714-538-3177

Doors

Cold Storage

Advance Energy Technologies
Clifton Park, NY. 800-724-0198
Advanced Insulation Concepts
Florence, KY. 800-826-3100
Air-Lec Industries, Inc
Madison, WI 608-244-4754
Aleco
Muscle Shoals, AL 800-633-3120
Aluma Shield
Deland, FL 877-638-3266
Andgar Corporation
Ferndale, WA 360-366-9900
Apple-A-Day Nutritional Labeling Service
San Clemente, CA. 949-855-8954
Berner International Corporation
New Castle, PA 800-245-4455
C.M. Lingle Company
Henderson, TX 800-256-6963
Carlson Products
Maize, KS 800-234-1069
Chase Doors
Cincinnati, OH 800-543-4455
Coldmatic Refrigeration
Concord, ON. 905-326-7600
Curtron Products
Pittsburgh, PA 800-833-5005
Dade Engineering
Tampa, FL. 800-321-2112
David A. Lingle & Son Manufacturing Company
Russellville, AR 479-968-2500
Dole Refrigerating Company
Lewisburg, TN 800-251-8990
Jamison Door Company
Hagerstown, MD. 800-532-3667
Kingspan Insulated Panels, Ltd.
Langley, BC, BC. 877-638-3266
Manufacturing Warehouse
Miami, FL. 305-635-8886
Rite-Hite Co.
Milwaukee, WI 888-841-4283
Rytec Corporation
Milwaukee, WI 888-467-9832
Therm-L-Tec Building Systems LLC
Basehor, KS 913-728-2662

Freezer

Advance Energy Technologies
Clifton Park, NY. 800-724-0198
Advanced Insulation Concepts
Florence, KY. 800-826-3100
Air-Lec Industries, Inc
Madison, WI 608-244-4754
Aleco
Muscle Shoals, AL 800-633-3120
Berner International Corporation
New Castle, PA. 800-245-4455
Chase Doors
Cincinnati, OH 800-543-4455
Curtron Products
Pittsburgh, PA. 800-833-5005
Dole Refrigerating Company
Lewisburg, TN 800-251-8990
Jamison Door Company
Hagerstown, MD. 800-532-3667
Kingspan Insulated Panels, Ltd.
Langley, BC, BC. 877-638-3266
Rite-Hite Co.
Milwaukee, WI. 888-841-4283
Rytec Corporation
Milwaukee, WI. 888-467-9832
Superior Products Company
Saint Paul, MN 800-328-9800

Refrigerated Display Case

Advance Energy Technologies
Clifton Park, NY. 800-724-0198
Kedco Wine Storage Systems
Farmingdale, NY 800-654-9988
Seville Display Door
Temecula, CA 800-634-0412
Superior Products Company
Saint Paul, MN 800-328-9800

Refrigerator

Advance Energy Technologies
Clifton Park, NY. 800-724-0198
Advanced Insulation Concepts
Florence, KY. 800-826-3100
Aleco
Muscle Shoals, AL 800-633-3120
Berner International Corporation
New Castle, PA. 800-245-4455

Carlson Products
Maize, KS 800-234-1069

Chase Doors
Cincinnati, OH 800-543-4455

Coldmatic Refrigeration
Concord, ON 905-326-7600

Curtron Products
Pittsburgh, PA 800-833-5005

Dole Refrigerating Company
Lewisburg, TN 800-251-8990

Jumo Process Control Incc
East Syracuse, NY 800-554-5866

Kason Industries
Newnan, GA 770-254-0553

Seville Display Door
Temecula, CA 800-634-0412

Therm-L-Tec Building Systems LLC
Basehor, KS 913-728-2662

Freezers

Advance Energy Technologies
Clifton Park, NY 800-724-0198

Advanced Equipment
Richmond, BC 604-276-8989

Alpha MOS America
Hanover, MD 410-553-9736

American Food & Equipment
Miami, FL 305-377-8991

APV Americas
Delavan, WI 800-252-5200

Arctic Air
Eden Prairie, MN 952-941-2270

Arctic Industries
Medley, FL 800-325-0123

Attias Oven Corporation
Brooklyn, NY 800-928-8427

Bally Refrigerated Boxes
Morehead City, NC 800-242-2559

Berndorf Belt Technology USA
Elgin, IL 877-232-7322

BOC Gases
New Providence, NJ 908-464-8100

C. Nelson Manufacturing Company
Oak Harbor, OH 800-922-7339

C.M. Lingle Company
Henderson, TX 800-256-6963

Carbonic Reserves
San Antonio, TX 800-880-1911

Carpigiani Corporation of America
Winston Salem, NC 800-648-4389

Checker Engineering
New Hope, MN 888-800-5001

Chrysler & Koppin Company
Detroit, MI 800-441-0038

Cloudy & Britton
Mountlake Ter, WA 425-775-7424

Coldstream Products Corporation
Crossfield, AB 888-946-4097

Cool Curtain/CCI Industries
Costa Mesa, CA 800-854-5719

Crown/Tonka Walk-Ins
Plymouth, MN 800-523-7337

Cryochem
St Simons Island, GA 800-237-4001

Dade Engineering
Tampa, FL 800-321-2112

David A. Lingle & Son Manufacturing Company
Russellville, AR 479-968-2500

Delfield Company
Mt Pleasant, MI 800-733-8821

Dole Refrigerating Company
Lewisburg, TN 800-251-8990

Duke Manufacturing Company
Saint Louis, MO 800-735-3853

Elliott-Williams Company
Indianapolis, IN 800-428-9303

Emjac Industries
Hialeah, FL 305-883-2194

Empire Bakery Equipment
Hicksville, NY 800-878-4070

Erickson Industries
River Falls, WI 800-729-9941

ESCO
Houston, TX 800-966-5514

Felix Storch
Bronx, NY 800-932-4267

Flo-Cold
Wixom, MI 248-348-6666

FMC FoodTech
Madera, CA 559-673-2766

Fogel Jordon Commercial Refrigeration Company
Philadelphia, PA 800-523-0171

Food Engineering Unlimited
Fullerton, CA 714-879-8762

Foster Refrigerator Corporation
Kinderhook, NY 888-828-3311

FreesTech
Sinking Spring, PA 717-560-7560

Frigidaire
St Cloud, MN 320-253-1212

Frigoscandia
Redmond, WA 800-423-1743

Frigoscandia Equipment
Northfield, MN 800-426-1283

G.S. Laboratory Equipment
Asheville, NC 800-252-7100

Galley
Jupiter, FL 800-537-2772

Gem Refrigerator Company
Philadelphia, PA 215-426-8700

General Electric Company
Fairfield, CT 203-373-2211

Glastender
Saginaw, MI 800-748-0423

Gold Star Products
Oak Park, MI 800-800-0205

Gram Equipment of America
Tampa, FL 813-248-1978

Griffin Cardwell, Ltd
Louisville, KY 502-636-1374

HABCO Beverage Systems
Toronto, ON 800-448-0244

Hobart Corporation
Troy, OH 888-446-2278

Howard McCray
Philadelphia, PA 800-344-8222

IJ White Corporation
Farmingdale, NY 631-293-2211

Imeco
Polo, IL 815-946-2351

International Cold Storage
Andover, KS 800-835-0001

Jack Langston Manufacturing Company
Dallas, TX 214-821-9844

Jordon Commercial Refrigerator
Philadelphia, PA 800-523-0171

KEMCO
Wareham, MA 800-231-5955

Kold Pack
Jackson, MI 800-824-2661

Kolpak
Parsons, TN 800-826-7036

Kolpak Walk-ins
Parsons, TN 800-826-7036

Kysor/Kalt
Portland, OR 503-235-0776

Kysor/Warren
Columbus, GA 800-866-5596

LaRosa Refrigeration & Equipment Company
Detroit, MI 800-527-6723

Leer Limited Partnership
New Lisbon, WI 800-766-5337

Manitowoc Foodservice Companies, Inc.
New Port Richey, FL 877-375-9300

Manufacturing Warehouse
Miami, FL 305-635-8886

Mar-Con Wire Belt
Richmond, BC 877-962-7266

Marc Refrigeration
Miami, FL 305-691-0500

Marquis Products
Concord, ON 800-268-1282

Martin Cab
Cleveland, OH 216-651-3882

Martin/Baron
Irwindale, CA 626-960-5153

Master-Bilt
New Albany, MS 800-647-1284

McCall Refrigeration
Parsons, TN 888-732-2446

McCormack Manufacturing Company
Lake Oswego, OR 800-395-1593

Migali Industries
Camden, NJ 800-852-5292

Mollenberg-Betz
Buffalo, NY 716-614-7473

National Hotpack
Stone Ridge, NY 800-431-8232

Nor-Lake
Salem, NH 603-893-9701

Northfield Freezing Systems
Northfield, MN 800-426-1283

Northland Refrigeration Company
Greenville, MI 800-223-3900

Nothum Food Processing Systems
Springfield, MO 800-435-1297

Odenberg Engineering
West Sacramento, CA 800-688-8396

Pacific Refrigerator Company
San Bernardino, CA 909-381-5669

Penn Refrigeration Service Corporation
Wilkes Barre, PA 800-233-8354

Perley-Halladay Associates, Inc.
West Chester, PA 800-248-5800

Polar King International
Fort Wayne, IN 800-752-7178

Praxair
Danbury, CT 800-772-9247

Processing Machinery & Supply
Philadelphia, PA 215-425-4320

Ransco Industries
Ventura, CA 805-487-7777

Refrigerated Warehousing
Jasper, GA 800-873-2008

Reliable Food Service Equipment
Concord, ON 416-738-6840

Rival Manufacturing Company
Kansas City, MO 816-943-4100

Ron Vallort & Associates
Oak Brook, IL 630-734-3821

Ross Industries
Midland, VA 800-336-6010

Sandvik Process Systems
Totowa, NJ 973-790-1600

SaniServ
Mooresville, IN 800-733-8073

Seattle Refrigeration & Manufacturing
Seattle, WA 800-228-8881

Semco Manufacturing Company
Pharr, TX 956-787-4203

Silver King
Minneapolis, MN 800-328-3329

SP Industries
Warminster, PA 800-523-2327

Stafford - Smith
Kalamazoo, MI 800-968-2442

Starlite Food Service Equipment
Detroit, MI 888-521-6603

Summit Appliance Division
Bronx, NY 800-932-4267

Summit Commercial
Bronx, NY 800-932-4267

Superior Products Company
Saint Paul, MN 800-328-9800

Supreme Corporation
Goshen, IN 800-642-4889

Systemate Numafa
Canton, GA 800-240-3770

Tafco-TMP Company
Hyde, PA 800-233-1954

Thermo King Corporation
Minneapolis, MN 952-887-2200

Traulsen & Company
Fort Worth, TX 800-825-8220

True Food Service Equipment, Inc.
O Fallon, MO 800-325-6152

U-Line Corporation
Milwaukee, WI 414-354-0300

US Cooler Company
Quincy, IL 800-521-2665

Utility Refrigerator Company
Los Angeles, CA 800-884-5233

Victory Refrigeration
Cherry Hill, NJ 856-428-4200

WA Brown & Son
Salisbury, NC 704-636-5131

Waukesha Cherry-Burrell
Louisville, KY 502-491-4310

White Mountain Freezer
Kansas City, MO 816-943-4100

Wilch Manufacturing
Topeka, KS 785-267-2762

Zero-Temp
Santa Ana, CA 714-538-3177

Ice Cream

Advance Energy Technologies
Clifton Park, NY 800-724-0198

C. Nelson Manufacturing Company
Oak Harbor, OH 800-922-7339

Carpigiani Corporation of America
Winston Salem, NC 800-648-4389

Delfield Company
Mt Pleasant, MI 800-733-8821

Eischen Enterprises
Fresno, CA 559-834-0013
FreesTech
Sinking Spring, PA 717-560-7560
Glastender
Saginaw, MI 800-748-0423
Howard McCray
Philadelphia, PA 800-344-8222
LaRosa Refrigeration & Equipment Company
Detroit, MI 800-527-6723
Manufacturing Warehouse
Miami, FL 305-635-8886
Marc Refrigeration
Miami, FL 305-691-0500
Rival Manufacturing Company
Kansas City, MO 816-943-4100
SaniServ
Mooresville, IN 800-733-8073
Schroeder Sewing Technologies
San Marcos, CA 760-591-9733
Stainless Fabrication
Springfield, MO 800-397-8265
Summit Appliance Division
Bronx, NY 800-932-4267
Summit Commercial
Bronx, NY 800-932-4267
White Mountain Freezer
Kansas City, MO 816-943-4100
Wilch Manufacturing
Topeka, KS 785-267-2762

Quick Freezing

Advance Energy Technologies
Clifton Park, NY 800-724-0198
Advanced Equipment
Richmond, BC 604-276-8989
Carbonic Reserves
San Antonio, TX 800-880-1911
Dole Refrigerating Company
Lewisburg, TN 800-251-8990
Foster Refrigerator Corporation
Kinderhook, NY 888-828-3311
FreesTech
Sinking Spring, PA 717-560-7560
Frigoscandia
Redmond, WA 800-423-1743
Griffin Cardwell, Ltd
Louisville, KY 502-636-1374
Linde
Murray Hill, NJ 800-755-9277
Manufacturing Warehouse
Miami, FL 305-635-8886
Mar-Con Wire Belt
Richmond, BC 877-962-7266
Mayekawa USA, Inc.
Chicago, IL 773-516-5070
McCormack Manufacturing Company
Lake Oswego, OR 800-395-1593
Praxair Food Technologies
Burr Ridge, IL 630-320-4000
Stainless Fabrication
Springfield, MO 800-397-8265
Witte Brothers Exchange
Troy, MO 800-325-8151

Sub-Zero

Advance Energy Technologies
Clifton Park, NY 800-724-0198
C.M. Lingle Company
Henderson, TX 800-256-6963
Cryochem
St Simons Island, GA 800-237-4001
Fogel Jordon Commercial Refrigeration Company
Philadelphia, PA 800-523-0171
Foster Refrigerator Corporation
Kinderhook, NY 888-828-3311
Frigidaire
St Cloud, MN 320-253-1212
Hoshizaki America
Peachtree City, GA 800-438-6087
Howard McCray
Philadelphia, PA 800-344-8222
Imeco
Polo, IL 815-946-2351
Martin/Baron
Irwindale, CA 626-960-5153
McCormack Manufacturing Company
Lake Oswego, OR 800-395-1593
Portable Cold Storage
Edison, NJ 800-535-2445
Ransco Industries
Ventura, CA 805-487-7777
RMF Freezers
Grandview, MO 816-765-4101
Ron Vallort & Associates
Oak Brook, IL 630-734-3821
Semco Manufacturing Company
Pharr, TX 956-787-4203
SP Industries
Warminster, PA 800-523-2327

Walk-In

Advance Energy Technologies
Clifton Park, NY 800-724-0198
Arctic Industries
Medley, FL 800-325-0123
Bally Refrigerated Boxes
Morehead City, NC 800-242-2559
C.M. Lingle Company
Henderson, TX 800-256-6963
Chrysler & Koppin Company
Detroit, MI 800-441-0038
Coldstream Products Corporation
Crossfield, AB 888-946-4097
Crown/Tonka Walk-Ins
Plymouth, MN 800-523-7337
Dade Engineering
Tampa, FL 800-321-2112
David A. Lingle & Son Manufacturing Company
Russellville, AR 479-968-2500
Elliott-Williams Company
Indianapolis, IN 800-428-9303
Emjac Industries
Hialeah, FL 305-883-2194
Foster Refrigerator Corporation
Kinderhook, NY 888-828-3311
Gem Refrigerator Company
Philadelphia, PA 215-426-8700
HABCO Beverage Systems
Toronto, ON 800-448-0244
Howard McCray
Philadelphia, PA 800-344-8222
International Cold Storage
Andover, KS 800-835-0001
Jack Langston Manufacturing Company
Dallas, TX 214-821-9844
Jordon Commercial Refrigerator
Philadelphia, PA 800-523-0171
KEMCO
Wareham, MA 800-231-5955
Kolpak
Parsons, TN 800-826-7036
Kolpak Walk-ins
Parsons, TN 800-826-7036
Kysor/Kalt
Portland, OR 503-235-0776
Leer Limited Partnership
New Lisbon, WI 800-766-5337
Manufacturing Warehouse
Miami, FL 305-635-8886
Martin Cab
Cleveland, OH 216-651-3882
Nor-Lake
Salem, NH 603-893-9701
Pacific Refrigerator Company
San Bernardino, CA 909-381-5669
Penn Refrigeration Service Corporation
Wilkes Barre, PA 800-233-8354
Polar King International
Fort Wayne, IN 800-752-7178
Portable Cold Storage
Edison, NJ 800-535-2445
RMF Freezers
Grandview, MO 816-765-4101
Semco Manufacturing Company
Pharr, TX 956-787-4203
Superior Products Company
Saint Paul, MN 800-328-9800
Tafco-TMP Company
Hyde, PA 800-233-1954
US Cooler Company
Quincy, IL 800-521-2665
WA Brown & Son
Salisbury, NC 704-636-5131
Zero-Temp
Santa Ana, CA 714-538-3177

Insulation

Refrigeration & Cold Storage

Advanced Insulation Concepts
Florence, KY 800-826-3100
Andgar Corporation
Ferndale, WA 360-366-9900
Cellofoam North America
Conyers, GA 800-241-3634
David A. Lingle & Son Manufacturing Company
Russellville, AR 479-968-2500
Foam Pack Industries
Springfield, NJ 973-376-3700
Modular Panel Company
New Bedford, MA 508-993-9955
Reilly Foam Corporation
Conshohocken, PA 610-834-1900
Republic Refrigeration IInc.
Monroe, NC 704-282-0399
Ron Vallort & Associates
Oak Brook, IL 630-734-3821
Therm-L-Tec Building Systems LLC
Basehor, KS 913-728-2662
WA Brown & Son
Salisbury, NC 704-636-5131

Lockers

Frozen Food

Cayne Industrial Sales Corporation
Bronx, NY 718-993-5800
Remcon Plastics
West Reading, PA 800-360-3636
Welch Brothers
Bartlett, IL 847-741-6134

Refrigerating & Cooling Rooms

Advance Energy Technologies
Clifton Park, NY 800-724-0198
AeroFreeze, Inc.
Richmond, BC, BC 604-278-4118
American Panel Corporation
Ocala, FL 800-327-3015
Arctic Industries
Medley, FL 800-325-0123
Bakery Refrigeration & Services
Lake Park, FL 561-882-1655
C.M. Lingle Company
Henderson, TX 800-256-6963
Cool Care
Boynton Beach, FL 561-364-5711
David A. Lingle & Son Manufacturing Company
Russellville, AR 479-968-2500
Elliott-Williams Company
Indianapolis, IN 800-428-9303
Erickson Industries
River Falls, WI 800-729-9941
Fogel Jordon Commercial Refrigeration Company
Philadelphia, PA 800-523-0171
Kysor Panel Systems
Fort Worth, TX 800-633-3426
Kysor/Kalt
Portland, OR 503-235-0776
Kysor/Warren
Columbus, GA 800-866-5596
M&S Manufacturing
Arnold, MO 636-464-2739
Master-Bilt
New Albany, MS 800-647-1284
Mollenberg-Betz
Buffalo, NY 716-614-7473
National Hotpack
Stone Ridge, NY 800-431-8232
Pacific Refrigerator Company
San Bernardino, CA 909-381-5669
Perley-Halladay Associates, Inc.
West Chester, PA 800-248-5800
Praxair Food Technologies
Burr Ridge, IL 630-320-4000
QBD Modular Systems
Santa Clara, CA 800-663-3005
Ransco Industries
Ventura, CA 805-487-7777
Refrigerated Warehousing
Jasper, GA 800-873-2008
Refrigerator Manufacturers LLC
Cerritos, CA 562-926-2006
Ron Vallort & Associates
Oak Brook, IL 630-734-3821

Tafco-TMP Company
Hyde, PA 800-233-1954
Thermal Technologies
Broomall, PA. 610-353-8887
US Cooler Company
Quincy, IL. 800-521-2665
Zero-Temp
Santa Ana, CA 714-538-3177

Refrigerating Equipment & Machinery

ABCO Industries Limited
Lunenburg, NS 866-634-8821
Advance Energy Technologies
Clifton Park, NY. 800-724-0198
Advanced Equipment
Richmond, BC 604-276-8989
Advanced Insulation Concepts
Florence, KY. 800-826-3100
AeroFreeze, Inc.
Richmond, BC, BC 604-278-4118
AGA Gas
Cleveland, OH 216-642-6600
AK Steel
West Chester, OH 800-331-5050
Aleco
Muscle Shoals, AL 800-633-3120
ALKAR
Lodi, WI 608-592-3211
Alto-Shaam
Menomonee Falls, WI. 800-558-8744
Aluma Shield
Deland, FL 877-638-3266
American Food & Equipment
Miami, FL. 305-377-8991
American Panel Corporation
Ocala, FL. 800-327-3015
American Systems Associates
Hampton Bays, NY. 800-584-3663
Applied Thermal Technologies
San Marcos, CA 800-736-5083
Arctic Air
Eden Prairie, MN 952-941-2270
Arctic Industries
Medley, FL 800-325-0123
Arctica Showcase Company
Calgary, AB. 800-839-5536
Attias Oven Corporation
Brooklyn, NY 800-928-8427
Baltimore Aircoil Company
Jessup, MD 410-799-6200
Bar Equipment Corporation of America
Downey, CA 888-870-2322
Bar-Maid Minibars
Garfield, NJ. 800-227-6243
Barker Company
Keosauqua, IA 319-293-3777
Beacon Specialties
New York, NY 800-221-9405
Benko Products
Sheffield Village, OH 440-934-2180
Berg Chilling Systems
Toronto, ON, ON 416-755-2221
Berner International Corporation
New Castle, PA 800-245-4455
Beverage-Air
Winston Salem, NC. 800-845-9800
BNW Industries
Tippecanoe, IN 574-353-7855
Buffalo Technologies Corporation
Buffalo, NY. 800-332-2419
Buhler Group
Raleigh, NC 919-851-2000
Bush Refrigeration
Camden, NJ. 800-220-2874
C&R Refrigeration
Center, TX. 800-438-6182
C.M. Lingle Company
Henderson, TX 800-256-6963
Caddy Corporation of America
Bridgeport, NJ. 856-467-4222
Carbonic Reserves
San Antonio, TX. 800-880-1911
Carpigiani Corporation of America
Winston Salem, NC. 800-648-4389
Carrier Transicold
Farmington, CT. 800-227-7437
Carter-Hoffman Corp LLC
Mundelein, IL. 800-323-9793
Carts Food Equipment Corporation
Brooklyn, NY 718-788-5540

Century Refrigeration
Pryor, OK 918-825-6363
Checker Engineering
New Hope, MN. 888-800-5001
Chrysler & Koppin Company
Detroit, MI 800-441-0038
Cloudy & Britton
Mountlake Ter, WA. 425-775-7424
Coldmatic Refrigeration
Concord, ON. 905-326-7600
Coldstream Products Corporation
Crossfield, AB 888-946-4097
ColdZone
Anaheim, CA
Control Beverage
Adelanto, CA 330-549-5376
Controls Unlimited
Perry, OH 440-259-2500
Cool Care
Boynton Beach, FL. 561-364-5711
Cool Curtain/CCI Industries
Costa Mesa, CA 800-854-5719
Copeland Corporation
Sidney, OH 937-498-3011
Cornell Pump Company
Portland, OR. 503-653-0330
Craig Manufacturing
Irvington, NJ 800-631-7936
Cramer Products
New York, NY 212-645-2368
Cres Cor
Mentor, OH. 877-273-7267
Crown/Tonka Walk-Ins
Plymouth, MN. 800-523-7337
Cryochem
St Simons Island, GA 800-237-4001
Curtron Products
Pittsburgh, PA. 800-833-5005
Custom Diamond International
Laval, QC 800-363-5926
Davenport Machine
Rock Island, IL 309-786-1500
David A. Lingle & Son Manufacturing Company
Russellville, AR 479-968-2500
Dole Refrigerating Company
Lewisburg, TN 800-251-8990
Doucette Industries
York, PA 800-445-7511
Duke Manufacturing Company
Saint Louis, MO 800-735-3853
Econofrost Night Covers
Shawnigan Lake, BC 800-519-1222
Eliason Corporation
Kalamazoo, MI 800-828-3655
Elliott-Williams Company
Indianapolis, IN 800-428-9303
Elwood Safety Company
Buffalo, NY. 866-326-6060
Emjac Industries
Hialeah, FL. 305-883-2194
Empire Bakery Equipment
Hicksville, NY 800-878-4070
EPCO
Murfreesboro, TN. 800-251-3398
Erickson Industries
River Falls, WI 800-729-9941
EVAPCO
Taneytown, MD 410-756-2600
F/G Products
Rice Lake, WI. 800-247-3854
Federal Industries
Belleville, WI 800-356-4206
Felix Storch
Bronx, NY. 800-932-4267
FES Systems
York, PA 800-888-4337
Flakice Corporation
Metuchen, NJ 800-654-4630
Flat Plate
York, PA 888-854-2500
FleetwoodGoldcoWyard
Romeoville, IL 630-759-6800
Flo-Cold
Wixom, MI 248-348-6666
Food Engineering Unlimited
Fullerton, CA 714-879-8762
FreesTech
Sinking Spring, PA 717-560-7560
Frick by Johnson Controls
Milwaukee, WI. 414-524-1200
Frigidaire
St Cloud, MN 320-253-1212

Frigoscandia
Redmond, WA. 800-423-1743
FWE/Food Warming Equipment Company, Inc
Crystal Lake, IL 800-222-4393
Galley
Jupiter, FL. 800-537-2772
Gates Manufacturing Company
Saint Louis, MO 800-237-9226
Gem Refrigerator Company
Philadelphia, PA 215-426-8700
Gold Star Products
Oak Park, MI. 800-800-0205
Governair Corporation
Oklahoma City, OK 405-525-6546
Griffin Cardwell, Ltd
Louisville, KY 502-636-1374
H.A. Phillips & Company
DeKalb, IL 630-377-0050
Hackney Brothers
Washington, NC 800-763-0700
Hall Manufacturing Corporation
Ringwood, NJ 973-962-6022
Hansen Technologies Corporation
Bolingbrook, IL 800-426-7368
Harford Duracool LLC
Aberdeen, MD 410-272-9999
Harford Systems
Aberdeen, MD 800-638-7620
Hartel International LLC
Fort Atkinson, WI. 920-563-6597
Harvey W. Hottel
Gaithersburg, MD. 301-921-9599
Heatcraft
Stone Mountain, GA. 770-465-5600
Hobart Corporation
Troy, OH 888-446-2278
Hoshizaki America
Peachtree City, GA 800-438-6087
Howard McCray
Philadelphia, PA 800-344-8222
Howe Corporation
Chicago, IL 773-235-0200
Hussmann International
Bridgeton, MO 314-291-2000
Hydro-Miser
San Marcos, CA 800-736-5083
Imeco
Polo, IL 815-946-2351
IMI Cornelius
Osseo, MN 800-838-3600
International Cold Storage
Andover, KS 800-835-0001
International Cooling Systems
Richmond Hill, ON. 888-213-5566
Interstate Showcase & Fixture Company
West Orange, NJ 973-483-5555
Jack Langston Manufacturing Company
Dallas, TX. 214-821-9844
Jade Range
Brea, CA 800-884-5233
Jamison Door Company
Hagerstown, MD. 800-532-3667
Johnson Refrigerated Truck Bodies
Rice Lake, WI. 800-922-8360
Jordon Commercial Refrigerator
Philadelphia, PA 800-523-0171
KaiRak
Fullerton, CA 714-870-8661
Kason Central
Columbus, OH 614-885-1992
Kason Industries
Newnan, GA 770-254-0553
Kedco Wine Storage Systems
Farmingdale, NY 800-654-9988
KEMCO
Wareham, MA. 800-231-5955
Kidron
Kidron, OH 800-321-5421
Kold Pack
Jackson, MI. 800-824-2661
Kold-Hold
Edgefield, SC 803-637-3166
Kolpak
Parsons, TN. 800-826-7036
Kolpak Walk-ins
Parsons, TN. 800-826-7036
Koolant Koolers
Kalamazoo, MI 800-968-5665
Krewson Enterprises
Cleveland, OH 800-521-2282
Kysor Panel Systems
Fort Worth, TX 800-633-3426

Kysor/Kalt
Portland, OR 503-235-0776
Kysor/Warren
Columbus, GA 800-866-5596
LaRosa Refrigeration & Equipment Company
Detroit, MI 800-527-6723
Leer Limited Partnership
New Lisbon, WI 800-766-5337
Liberty Machine Company
York, PA 800-745-8152
Little Squirt
Toronto, ON 416-665-6605
M&S Manufacturing
Arnold, MO 636-464-2739
Manitowoc Foodservice Companies, Inc.
New Port Richey, FL 877-375-9300
Mannhardt Inc
Sheboygan Falls, WI 800-423-2327
Manufacturing Warehouse
Miami, FL 305-635-8886
Marc Refrigeration
Miami, FL 305-691-0500
Marquis Products
Concord, ON 800-268-1282
Martin Cab
Cleveland, OH 216-651-3882
Martin/Baron
Irwindale, CA 626-960-5153
Master-Bilt
New Albany, MS 800-647-1284
McCall Refrigeration
Parsons, TN 888-732-2446
McCormack Manufacturing Company
Lake Oswego, OR 800-395-1593
MCM Fixture Company
Hazel Park, MI 248-547-9280
Middleby Worldwide
Elgin, IL 847-468-6068
Migali Industries
Camden, NJ 800-852-5292
MMR Technologies
Mountain View, CA 855-962-9620
Mollenberg-Betz
Buffalo, NY 716-614-7473
Mycom Group
Richmond, BC 604-270-1544
N. Wasserstrom & Sons
Columbus, OH 800-999-9277
National Drying Machinery Company
Philadelphia, PA 215-464-6070
National Refrigeration
Bensalem, PA 800-523-7138
Niagara Blower Company
Buffalo, NY 800-426-5169
Nor-Lake
Salem, NH 603-893-9701
Noren Products
Menlo Park, CA 866-936-6736
Norris Dispenser Company
Minneapolis, MN 800-252-5561
Northfield Freezing Systems
Northfield, MN 800-426-1283
Northland Refrigeration Company
Greenville, MI 800-223-3900
Odenberg Engineering
West Sacramento, CA 800-688-8396
Omnitemp Refrigeration
Downey, CA 800-423-9660
Pacific Refrigerator Company
San Bernardino, CA 909-381-5669
Paragon Electric Company
Two Rivers, WI 920-793-1161
Parkland
Houston, TX 713-926-5055
Peerless of America
Lincolnshire, IL 847-634-7500
Penn Refrigeration Service Corporation
Wilkes Barre, PA 800-233-8354
Perley-Halladay Associates, Inc.
West Chester, PA 800-248-5800
Perlick Corporation
Milwaukee, WI 800-558-5592
PFI Prasence From Innovation
St Louis, MO 314-423-9777
Pioneer Manufacturing Company
Cleveland, OH 800-877-1500
Pittsburgh Corning Corporation
Pittsburgh, PA 724-327-6100
PMI Food Equipment Group
Troy, OH 937-332-3000
Polar King International
Fort Wayne, IN 800-752-7178
Praxair
Danbury, CT 800-772-9247
Precision
Miami, FL 800-762-7565
Premium Air Systems
Troy, MI 877-430-0333
Pro-Flo Products
Cedar Grove, NJ 800-325-1057
Process Engineering & Fabrication
Afton, VA 800-852-7975
Randall Manufacturing
Elmhurst, IL 800-323-7424
Randell Manufacturing Unified Brands
Weidman, MI 888-994-7636
Ransco Industries
Ventura, CA 805-487-7777
Refrigerated Design Texas
Waxahachie, TX 800-736-9518
Refrigerated Warehousing
Jasper, GA 800-873-2008
Refrigeration Engineering
Grand Rapids, MI 800-968-3227
Refrigeration Research
Brighton, MI 810-227-1151
Reliable Food Service Equipment
Concord, ON 416-738-6840
Ron Vallort & Associates
Oak Brook, IL 630-734-3821
RTC Industries
Rolling Meadows, IL 847-640-2400
Rubbermaid Specialty Products
Freeport, IL 815-235-4171
Sandvik Process Systems
Totowa, NJ 973-790-1600
Schmidt Progressive, LLC
Lebanon, OH 800-272-3706
Scotsman Ice Systems
Vernon Hills, IL 800-726-8762
Seattle Refrigeration & Manufacturing
Seattle, WA 800-228-8881
Seidman Brothers
Chelsea, MA 800-437-7770
Semco Manufacturing Company
Pharr, TX 956-787-4203
Servco Co.
St Louis, MO 314-781-3189
Silver King
Minneapolis, MN 800-328-3329
SP Industries
Warminster, PA 800-523-2327
Spartan Showcase
Union, MO 800-325-0775
Specialty Equipment Company
Farmington, CT 630-585-5111
Spinco Metal Products
Newark, NY 315-331-6285
Standard Refrigeration Company
Wood Dale, IL 708-345-5400
Starlite Food Service Equipment
Detroit, MI 888-521-6603
Summit Appliance Division
Bronx, NY 800-932-4267
Summit Commercial
Bronx, NY 800-932-4267
Superflex
Brooklyn, NY 800-394-3665
Supreme Corporation
Goshen, IN 800-642-4889
Sure-Kol Refrigerator Company
Brooklyn, NY 718-625-0601
Tecumseh Products Company
Ann Arbor, MI 734-585-9500
Tetra Pak Inc.
Vernon Hills, IL 847-955-6000
Therm-L-Tec Building Systems LLC
Basehor, KS 913-728-2662
Thermo King Corporation
Minneapolis, MN 952-887-2200
THERMO-KOOL/Mid-South Industries
Laurel, MS 601-649-4600
Toromont Process Systems
North Salt Lake, UT 801-292-1747
Tranter Pite
Wichita Falls, TX 940-723-7125
Traulsen & Company
Fort Worth, TX 800-825-8220
Trimen Foodservice Equipment
North York, ON 877-437-1422
True Food Service Equipment, Inc.
O Fallon, MO 800-325-6152
Tyler Refrigeration Corporation
Niles, MI 800-992-3744
US Cooler Company
Quincy, IL 800-521-2665
USECO
Murfreesboro, TN 615-893-4820
Utility Refrigerator Company
Los Angeles, CA 800-884-5233
Victory Refrigeration
Cherry Hill, NJ 856-428-4200
Vilter Manufacturing Corporation
Cudahy, WI 414-744-0111
WA Brown & Son
Salisbury, NC 704-636-5131
West Star Industries
Stockton, CA 800-326-2288
Wilevco
Billerica, MA 978-667-0400
Williams Refrigeration
Hillsdale, NJ 800-445-9979
Wine Chillers of California
Santa Ana, CA 800-331-4274
Wine Well Chiller Company
Milford, CT 203-878-2465
Wittemann Company
Palm Coast, FL 386-445-4200
York Refrigeration Marine US
Seattle, WA 800-282-0904

Refrigerating Units

Truck, Trailer & Refrigerator Car

Advanced Distribution & Packaging
Louisville, KY 502-449-1720
American Food & Equipment
Miami, FL 305-377-8991
Carrier Transicold
Farmington, CT 800-227-7437
Collins Manufacturing Company Ltd
Langley, BC 800-663-6761
Dole Refrigerating Company
Lewisburg, TN 800-251-8990
Hackney Brothers
Washington, NC 800-763-0700
Johnson Refrigerated Truck Bodies
Rice Lake, WI 800-922-8360
Kidron
Kidron, OH 800-321-5421
Kold-Hold
Edgefield, SC 803-637-3166
Martin Cab
Cleveland, OH 216-651-3882
National FABCO Manufacturing
St Louis, MO 314-842-4571
New Centennial
Columbus, GA 800-241-7541
Portable Cold Storage
Edison, NJ 800-535-2445
Supreme Corporation
Goshen, IN 800-642-4889
Thermo King Corporation
Minneapolis, MN 952-887-2200

Refrigerators

Adamatic
Auburn, WA 800-578-2547
Advance Energy Technologies
Clifton Park, NY 800-724-0198
AK Steel
West Chester, OH 800-331-5050
Arctic Air
Eden Prairie, MN 952-941-2270
Arctic Industries
Medley, FL 800-325-0123
Attias Oven Corporation
Brooklyn, NY 800-928-8427
Bally Refrigerated Boxes
Morehead City, NC 800-242-2559
Bar Equipment Corporation of America
Downey, CA 888-870-2322
Bar-Maid Minibars
Garfield, NJ 800-227-6243
Benko Products
Sheffield Village, OH 440-934-2180
C.M. Lingle Company
Henderson, TX 800-256-6963
Carts Food Equipment Corporation
Brooklyn, NY 718-788-5540
Caselites
Hialeah, FL 305-819-7766
Chrysler & Koppin Company
Detroit, MI 800-441-0038

Cloudy & Britton
Mountlake Ter, WA 425-775-7424
Coldstream Products Corporation
Crossfield, AB 888-946-4097
Continental Refrigerator
Bensalem, PA 800-523-7138
Craig Manufacturing
Irvington, NJ 800-631-7936
Custom Diamond International
Laval, QC 800-363-5926
Delfield Company
Mt Pleasant, MI 800-733-8821
Duke Manufacturing Company
Saint Louis, MO 800-735-3853
Elliott-Williams Company
Indianapolis, IN 800-428-9303
Empire Bakery Equipment
Hicksville, NY 800-878-4070
EPCO
Murfreesboro, TN 800-251-3398
Erickson Industries
River Falls, WI 800-729-9941
Eskay Metal Fabricating Company
Buffalo, NY 800-836-8015
Fogel Jordon Commercial Refrigeration Company
Philadelphia, PA 800-523-0171
Follett Corporation
Easton, PA 800-523-9361
Foster Refrigerator Corporation
Kinderhook, NY 888-828-3311
Gates Manufacturing Company
Saint Louis, MO 800-237-9226
GEA FES, Inc.
York, PA 800-888-4337
Gem Refrigerator Company
Philadelphia, PA 215-426-8700
HABCO Beverage Systems
Toronto, ON 800-448-0244
Helmer
Noblesville, IN 317-773-9082
Hobart Corporation
Troy, OH 888-446-2278
Hoshizaki America
Peachtree City, GA 800-438-6087
Howard McCray
Philadelphia, PA 800-344-8222
Hussmann International
Bridgeton, MO 314-291-2000
International Cold Storage
Andover, KS 800-835-0001
Jack Langston Manufacturing Company
Dallas, TX 214-821-9844
Jade Range
Brea, CA 800-884-5233
Jordon Commercial Refrigerator
Philadelphia, PA 800-523-0171
Kolpak Walk-ins
Parsons, TN 800-826-7036
Lockwood Manufacturing
Livonia, MI 800-521-0238
Manitowoc Foodservice Companies, Inc.
New Port Richey, FL 877-375-9300
Marc Refrigeration
Miami, FL 305-691-0500
Master-Bilt
New Albany, MS 800-647-1284
Mayekawa USA, Inc.
Chicago, IL 773-516-5070
McCall Refrigeration
Parsons, TN 888-732-2446
MCM Fixture Company
Hazel Park, MI 248-547-9280
N. Wasserstrom & Sons
Columbus, OH 800-999-9277
National Hotpack
Stone Ridge, NY 800-431-8232
Nor-Lake
Salem, NH 603-893-9701
Northland Refrigeration Company
Greenville, MI 800-223-3900
Parkland
Houston, TX 713-926-5055
Polar King International
Fort Wayne, IN 800-752-7178
Portable Cold Storage
Edison, NJ 800-535-2445
QBD Modular Systems
Santa Clara, CA 800-663-3005
Randell Manufacturing Unified Brands
Weidman, MI 888-994-7636
Ransco Industries
Ventura, CA 805-487-7777
Seidman Brothers
Chelsea, MA 800-437-7770
Servco Co.
St Louis, MO 314-781-3189
Silver King
Minneapolis, MN 800-328-3329
Spartan Showcase
Union, MO 800-325-0775
Springer-Penguin
Mount Vernon, NY 800-835-8500
Stafford - Smith
Kalamazoo, MI 800-968-2442
Summit Appliance Division
Bronx, NY 800-932-4267
Summit Commercial
Bronx, NY 800-932-4267
Superior Products Company
Saint Paul, MN 800-328-9800
Sure-Kol Refrigerator Company
Brooklyn, NY 718-625-0601
Tafco-TMP Company
Hyde, PA 800-233-1954
THERMO-KOOL/Mid-South Industries
Laurel, MS 601-649-4600
Toromont Process Systems
North Salt Lake, UT 801-292-1747
Traulsen & Company
Fort Worth, TX 800-825-8220
Triad Scientific
Manasquan, NJ 800-867-6690
Tru-Form Plastics
Gardena, CA 800-510-7999
True Food Service Equipment, Inc.
O Fallon, MO 800-325-6152
Tyler Refrigeration Corporation
Niles, MI 800-992-3744
U-Line Corporation
Milwaukee, WI 414-354-0300
USECO
Murfreesboro, TN 615-893-4820
Utility Refrigerator Company
Los Angeles, CA 800-884-5233
Victory Refrigeration
Cherry Hill, NJ 856-428-4200
Williams Refrigeration
Hillsdale, NJ 800-445-9979

Grilles

Gea Intec, Llc
Durham, NC 919-433-0131
Liberty Machine Company
York, PA 800-745-8152

Racks

ABI Limited
Concord, ON 800-297-8666
Caddy Corporation of America
Bridgeport, NJ 856-467-4222
ColdZone
Anaheim, CA
Dubuque Steel Products Company
Dubuque, IA 563-556-6288
Eagle Wire Works
Cleveland, OH 216-341-8550
Hewitt Manufacturing Company
Waldron, IN 765-525-9829
Houston Wire Works, Inc.
South Houston, TX 800-468-9477
Kedco Wine Storage Systems
Farmingdale, NY 800-654-9988
Metro Corporation
Wilkes Barre, PA 800-433-2233
Olson Wire Products Company
Halethorpe, MD 410-242-1945
Straits Steel & Wire Company
Ludington, MI 231-843-3416
Unirak Storage Systems
Taylor, MI 800-348-7225
Universal Coatings
Twinsburg, OH 330-963-6776
Wald Wire & Manufacturing Company
Oshkosh, WI 800-236-0053

Trays

Flexpak Corporation
Phoenix, AZ 602-269-7648
Kaines West Michigan Company
Ludington, MI 231-845-1281
Olson Wire Products Company
Halethorpe, MD 410-242-1945
Spot Wire Works Company
Philadelphia, PA 215-627-6124
World Kitchen
Elmira, NY 800-999-3436

Valves

Refrigeration

C&D Valve Manufacturing Company, Inc.
Oklahoma City, OK 800-654-9233
Doering Company
Clear Lake, MN 320-743-2276
EVAPCO
Taneytown, MD 410-756-2600
H.A. Phillips & Company
DeKalb, IL 630-377-0050
Hansen Technologies Corporation
Bolingbrook, IL 800-426-7368
Parker Hannifin Corporation
Cleveland, OH 609-586-5151
Vilter Manufacturing Corporation
Cudahy, WI 414-744-0111

Vats

Dairy Cooling

Dubuque Steel Products Company
Dubuque, IA 563-556-6288
Falco Technologies
La Prairie, QC 450-444-0566

Vender & Visi-Cooler Installation Systems

Ultra Lift Corporation
San Jose, CA 800-346-3057

Safety & Security Equipment & Supplies

Alarm Systems

Acromag Inc.
Wixom, MI 248-624-1541
ADT Security Systems
Fort Wayne, IN 260-483-6370
ADT Security Systems
Indianapolis, IN 317-848-1181
Alarm Controls Corporation
Deer Park, NY. 800-645-5538
AMSECO
Carson, CA 800-421-1096
Christy Industries
Brooklyn, NY 800-472-2078
CMT
Hamilton, MA. 978-768-2555
Control Products
Chanhassen, MN. 800-947-9098
Electro Alarms
Tiffin, OH 800-261-9174
Ellenco
Brentwood, MD 301-927-4370
Faraday
Tecumseh, MI 517-423-2111
Flair Electronics
Pomona, CA 800-532-3492
Gamewell Corporation
Northborough, MA 888-347-3269
George Risk Industries
Kimball, NE 800-523-1227
Globe Fire Sprinkler Corporation
Standish, MI 800-248-0278
GraLab Corporation
Centerville, OH. 800-876-8353
Harford Systems
Aberdeen, MD 800-638-7620
Honeywell
Morristown, NJ. 877-841-2840
Iconics
Foxborough, MA 800-946-9679
King Research Laboratory
Maywood, IL. 708-344-7877
Krewson Enterprises
Cleveland, OH 800-521-2282
Liquid Scale
New Brighton, MN. 888-633-2969
Long Range Systems
Addison, TX 800-577-8101
NAPCO Security Systems
Amityville, NY 631-842-9400
Optex
Chino, CA. 800-966-7839
Permaloc Security Devices
Silver Spring, MD. 301-681-6300
Quantis Secure Systems
Hanover, MD 800-325-6124
RACO Manufacturing
Emeryville, CA. 800-722-6999
Sargent & Greenleaf
Nicholasville, KY 800-826-7652
Security Link
Danville, IL. 217-446-4871
Sensidyne
Clearwater, FL 800-451-9444
Silent Watchman Security Services LLC
Danbury, CT 800-932-3822
Simplex Time Recorder Company
Santa Ana, CA 800-746-7539
Star Micronics
Edison, NJ. 800-782-7636
Sterling Alarm Company
Glendora, CA 800-932-9561
The WL Jenkins Company
Canton, OH. 330-477-3407
Ultrak
Westminster, CO. 303-428-9480
Viking Corporation
Hastings, MI 800-968-9501

Containment Systems

Arcoplast Wall & Ceiling Systems
St Peters, MO 888-736-2726
Blome International
O'Fallon, MO 636-379-9119
Modutank
Long Island City, NY 800-245-6964

Detectors

Gas Leak

American Gas & Chemical Company Limited
Northvale, NJ 800-288-3647
Chlorinators Inc
Stuart, FL 800-327-9761
Control Instruments Corporation
Fairfield, NJ 973-575-9114
Gems Sensors
Plainville, CT 860-747-3000
QA Supplies, LLC
Norfolk, VA. 800-472-7205
Rosemount Analytical
Irvine, CA 800-543-8257
Sensidyne
Clearwater, FL 800-451-9444
Teledyne Taptone
North Falmouth, MA 508-563-1000

Metal

Accu-Pak
Akron, OH 330-644- 301
Accu-Ray Inspection Services
Elmhurst, IL 800-378-1226
Advanced Detection Systems
Milwaukee, WI 414-672-0553
Andgar Corporation
Ferndale, WA 360-366-9900
Berkshire PPM
Litchfield, CT 860-567-3118
Bunting Magnetics Company
Newton, KS. 800-835-2526
Cintex of America
Carol Stream, IL 800-424-6839
Eriez Magnetics
Erie, PA. 800-346-4946
Friskem Infinetics
Wilmington, DE 302-658-2471
Geo. Olcott Company
Scottsboro, AL 800-634-2769
Leeman Labs
Hudson, NH 603-886-8400
Lock Inspection Systems
Fitchburg, MA 800-227-5539
Loma International
Carol Stream, IL 800-872-5662
Magnetic Products
Highland, MI. 800-544-5930
Mettler Toldeo Safeline
Tampa, FL. 800-447-4439
Ohio Magnetics-Stearns Magnetics
Cleveland, OH 800-486-6446
Thermo Ramsey
Coon Rapids, MN. 763-783-2500
TNA Packaging Solutions
Coppell, TX 972-462-6500
Vande Berg Scales
Sioux Center, IA 712-722-1181

Shoplifting

Engineered Security Systems
Towaco, NJ 800-742-1263
Friskem Infinetics
Wilmington, DE 302-658-2471
King Research Laboratory
Maywood, IL. 708-344-7877
Protex International Corp.
Bohemia, NY 800-835-3580
Se-Kure Controls
Franklin Park, IL. 800-250-9260
Silent Watchman Security Services LLC
Danbury, CT 800-932-3822

Detectors & Alarms

Fire, Heat & Smoke

Alarm Controls Corporation
Deer Park, NY. 800-645-5538
CMT
Hamilton, MA. 978-768-2555
Krewson Enterprises
Cleveland, OH 800-521-2282
Migatron Corporation
Woodstock, IL. 815-338-5800
NAPCO Security Systems
Amityville, NY 631-842-9400
Protectowire Company
Pembrook, MA 781-826-3878
Silent Watchman Security Services LLC
Danbury, CT 800-932-3822
Simplex Time Recorder Company
Santa Ana, CA 800-746-7539
Sterling Alarm Company
Glendora, CA 800-932-9561

Fire Alarm Systems

ADT Security Systems
Indianapolis, IN 317-848-1181
Ansul Incorporated
Marinette, WI 800-862-6785
Carroll Manufacturing International
Florham Park, NJ 800-444-9696
Charles Gratz Fire Protection
Philadelphia, PA 215-235-5800
Christy Industries
Brooklyn, NY 800-472-2078
Duke Manufacturing Company
Saint Louis, MO 800-735-3853
Ellenco
Brentwood, MD 301-927-4370
Faraday
Tecumseh, MI 517-423-2111
Gamewell Corporation
Northborough, MA 888-347-3269
Globe Fire Sprinkler Corporation
Standish, MI 800-248-0278
Grinnell Fire ProtectionSystems Company
Sauk Rapids, MN 320-253-8665
Honeywell
Morristown, NJ. 877-841-2840
Monroe Kitchen Equipment
Rochester, NY. 585-235-3310
NAPCO Security Systems
Amityville, NY 631-842-9400
Protectowire Company
Pembrook, MA 781-826-3878
Quantis Secure Systems
Hanover, MD 800-325-6124
Scientific Fire Prevention
Brooklyn, NY 516-222-1715
Signal Equipment
Seattle, WA 800-542-0884
Silent Watchman Security Services LLC
Danbury, CT 800-932-3822
Simplex Time Recorder Company
Santa Ana, CA 800-746-7539
Simplex Time Recorder Company
Santa Ana, CA 949-724-5000
Sterling Alarm Company
Glendora, CA 800-932-9561
The WL Jenkins Company
Canton, OH. 330-477-3407
Viking Corporation
Hastings, MI 800-968-9501

Fire Extinguishers

Ansul Incorporated
Marinette, WI 800-862-6785
Charles Gratz Fire Protection
Philadelphia, PA 215-235-5800
Greenheck Fan Corporation
Schofield, WI 715-359-6171
Grinnell Fire ProtectionSystems Company
Sauk Rapids, MN 888-870-6894
Kidde Safety Products
Mebane, NC 919-563-5911
National Foam
Exton, PA 610-363-1400
Pacific Scientific
Radford, VA 815-226-3100
Pyro-Chem
Marinette, WI 800-526-1079
Scientific Fire Prevention
Brooklyn, NY 516-222-1715
United Fire & Safety Service
Yonkers, NY 914-968-4459

Flashlights

Rechargable

Natale Machine & Tool Company
Carlstadt, NJ 800-883-8382

General

A&B Safe Corporation
Glassboro, NJ 800-253-1267
Accuform Manufacturing, Inc.
Vacaville, CA 800-233-3352
ADT Security Systems
Fort Wayne, IN 260-483-6370
ADT Security Systems
Indianapolis, IN 317-848-1181
Aero Company
Indianapolis, IN 800-225-9038
AFASSCO
Minden, NV 800-441-6774
Alarm Controls Corporation
Deer Park, NY. 800-645-5538
Alvarado Manufacturing Company
Chino, CA 800-445-7401
American Houver Company
Skokie, IL 800-772-0355
American Store Fixtures
Skokie, IL
AMSECO
Carson, CA 800-421-1096
Ansul Incorporated
Marinette, WI 800-862-6785
Applied Robotics
Glenville, NY 800-309-3475
Atlantic Rubber Products
East Wareham, MA. 800-695-0446
Atlas Equipment Company
Kansas City, MO. 800-842-9188
Ballymore Company
West Chester, PA. 610-696-3250
Banner Engineering Corporation
Plymouth, MN. 888-373-6767
Best Value Textiles
Elkhorn, WI. 800-248-9826
BMH Equipment
Sacramento, CA 800-350-8828
Boston Retail Products
Medford, MA 800-225-1633
Bullet Guard Corporation
West Sacramento, CA. 800-233-5632
CCP Industries, Inc.
Cleveland, OH 800-321-2840
Cesco Magnetics
Santa Rosa, CA. 877-624-8727
Charles Gratz Fire Protection
Philadelphia, PA 215-235-5800
Christy Industries
Brooklyn, NY 800-472-2078
Cintex of America
Carol Stream, IL 800-424-6839
Claude Neon Signs
Baltimore, MD 410-685-7575
Continental Commercial Products
Bridgeton, MO 800-325-1051
Control Instruments Corporation
Fairfield, NJ 973-575-9114
Conveyor Components Company
Croswell, MI. 800-233-3233
Corporate Safe Specialists
Posen, IL. 800-342-3033
Cotterman Company
Croswell, MI. 800-552-3337
Creative Industries
Indianapolis, IN 800-776-2068
Dalloz Safety
Smithfield, RI 800-977-9177
Detex Corporation
New Braunfels, TX. 800-729-3839
Diamond Electronics
Lancaster, OH 800-443-6680
Dickey Manufacturing Company
St Charles, IL 630-584-2918
Diversified Lighting Diffusers Inc
Copiague, NY 800-234-5464
Dometic Mini Bar
Elkhart, IN. 800-301-8118
Dresser Instruments
Stratford, CT 800-328-8258
Dri Mark Products
Port Washington, NY 800-645-9118
Duke Manufacturing Company
Saint Louis, MO 800-735-3853
Durable Corporation
Norwalk, OH. 800-537-1603
Durham Manufacturing Company
Durham, CT 413-781-7900
Dynamic Storage Systems Inc.
Brooksville, FL. 800-974-8211
EJ Brooks Company
Livingston, NJ. 800-458-7325
Ellenco
Brentwood, MD 301-927-4370
Elwood Safety Company
Buffalo, NY. 866-326-6060
EMED Company
Buffalo, NY. 800-442-3633
Empire Safe Company
New York, NY 212-226-2255
Engineered Security Systems
Towaco, NJ 800-742-1263
Etube and Wire
Shrewsbury, PA. 800-618-4720
Firematic Sprinkler Devices
Shrewsbury, MA. 508-845-2121
Flair Electronics
Pomona, CA 800-532-3492
Flame Gard
Lakewood, NJ. 800-526-3694
Folding Guard Company
Chicago, IL. 312-829-3500
Friskem Infinetics
Wilmington, DE 302-658-2471
Gamewell Corporation
Northborough, MA 888-347-3269
Gaylord Industries
Tualatin, OR 800-547-9696
George Risk Industries
Kimball, NE 800-523-1227
Gilbert Insect Light Traps
Jonesboro, AR. 800-643-0400
Glaro
Hauppauge, NY 631-234-1717
Globe Fire Sprinkler Corporation
Standish, MI 800-248-0278
Grecon, Inc.
Tigard, OR 503-641-7731
Grinnell Fire ProtectionSystems Company
Sauk Rapids, MN 320-253-8665
Grinnell Fire ProtectionSystems Company
Sauk Rapids, MN 888-870-6894
Halton Company
Scottsville, KY 800-442-5866
Harford Systems
Aberdeen, MD 800-638-7620
HD Electric Company
Waukegan, IL 847-473-4980
Hodge Manufacturing Company
Springfield, MA 800-262-4634
Honeywell
Morristown, NJ. 877-841-2840
Iconics
Foxborough, MA 800-946-9679
IDESCO Corporation
New York, NY 800-336-1383
J.L. Industries
Minneapolis, MN 800-554-6077
Jesco Industries, Inc.
Litchfield, MI 800-455-0019
Kason Industries, Inc.
Lewis Center, OH 740-549-2100
Kidde Safety Products
Mebane, NC 919-563-5911
King Research Laboratory
Maywood, IL. 708-344-7877
Koke
Queensbury, NY 800-535-5303
Krewson Enterprises
Cleveland, OH 800-521-2282
KTG
Cincinnati, OH 888-533-6900
Larco
Brainerd, MN 800-523-6996
Lavi Industries
Valencia, CA. 800-624-6225
LDJ Electronics
Troy, MI 248-528-2202
Lima Sheet Metal
Lima, OH. 419-229-1161
Linde Gas LLC
Cleveland, OH 800-983-5615
Lixi, Inc.
Huntley, IL 847-961-6666
Locknetics
Carmel, IN
Lomont IMT
Mt. Pleasant, IA 800-776-0380
Long Range Systems
Addison, TX 800-577-8101
Loyal Manufacturing Corporation
Indianapolis, IN 317-359-3185
McGunn Safe Company
Chicago, IL 800-621-2816
Metro Corporation
Wilkes Barre, PA. 800-433-2233
Mettler Toldeo Safeline
Tampa, FL. 800-447-4439
Micro Affiliates
Fairfax, VA 800-430-1099
Mirror-Tech
Yonkers, NY 914-423-1600
Monroe Kitchen Equipment
Rochester, NY. 585-235-3310
Nalge Process Technologies Group
Rochester, NY. 585-586-8800
NAPCO Security Systems
Amityville, NY 631-842-9400
National Foam
Exton, PA 610-363-1400
National Marker Company
North Smithfield, RI. 800-453-2727
National Stock Sign Company
Santa Cruz, CA. 800-462-7726
Nelson-Jameson
Marshfield, WI 800-826-8302
New Pig Corporation
Tipton, PA 800-468-4647
Newstamp Lighting Corp.
North Easton, MA. 508-238-7071
Niroflex, USA
Deerfield, IL 847-400-2638
NRD LLC
Grand Island, NY 800-525-8076
O'Brien Brothers
West Springfield, MA. 800-343-0949
Omicron Steel Products Company
Jamaica, NY 718-805-3400
Optex
Chino, CA. 800-966-7839
Our Name is Mud
New York, NY 877-683-7867
Pacific Scientific
Radford, VA 815-226-3100
PAK 2000
Mirror Lake, NH. 603-569-3700
Patlite Corporation
Torrance, CA. 888-214-2580
Penco Products
Skippack, PA. 800-562-1000
Permaloc Security Devices
Silver Spring, MD. 301-681-6300
PLI (Plasticard-Locktech International
Asheville, NC 800-752-1017
Pro-Com Security Systems
Mount Vernon, NY. 914-667-8400
Protectowire Company
Pembrook, MA. 781-826-3878
Protex International Corp.
Bohemia, NY 800-835-3580
Quickserv Corporation
Houston, TX 800-388-8307
R&D Brass
Wappingers Falls, NY. 800-447-6050
RACO Manufacturing
Emeryville, CA. 800-722-6999
Reidler Decal Corporation
Saint Clair, PA. 800-628-7770
Remcon Plastics
West Reading, PA 800-360-3636
Rocky Shoes & Boots
Nelsonville, OH 740-753-1951
RonI, Inc.
Charlotte, NC 866-543-8635
Rosco, Inc
Jamaica, NY 800-227-2095
Safety Light Corporation
Bloomsburg, PA 570-784-4344
Sargent & Greenleaf
Nicholasville, KY. 800-826-7652
Scientific Fire Prevention
Brooklyn, NY 516-222-1715
Se-Kure Controls
Franklin Park, IL. 800-250-9260
Security Link
Danville, IL. 217-446-4871

Sensidyne
Clearwater, FL 800-451-9444
Sensormatic Electronics Corporation
Boca Raton, FL....... 561-912-6000
Server Products
Richfield, WI 800-558-8722
Seton Identification Products
Branford, CT....... 800-571-2596
Shelden, Dickson, & Steven Company
Omaha, NE 402-571-4848
Sick Inc.
Minneapolis, MN 800-325-7425
Signal Equipment
Seattle, WA....... 800-542-0884
Silent Watchman Security Services LLC
Danbury, CT 800-932-3822
Simplex Time Recorder Company
Santa Ana, CA 800-746-7539
Simplex Time Recorder Company
Santa Ana, CA 949-724-5000
Sinco
Red Wing, MN 800-243-6753
Sipco Products
Peoria Heights, IL....... 309-682-5400
Slipnot Metal Safety Flooring
Detroit, MI 800-754-7668
Stanley Access Technologies
Farmington, CT....... 800-722-2377
Star Micronics
Edison, NJ....... 800-782-7636
Steel King Industries
Stevens Point, WI 800-553-3096
Sterling Alarm Company
Glendora, CA 800-932-9561

Stoffel Seals Corporation
Tallapoosa, GA....... 800-422-8247
Technibilt/Cari-All
Newton, NC 800-233-3972
Tepromark International
Skokie, IL 800-645-2622
The WL Jenkins Company
Canton, OH....... 330-477-3407
Theta Sciences
San Diego, CA 760-745-3311
Tomsed Corporation
Lillington, NC....... 800-334-5552
Torbeck Industries
Harrison, OH....... 800-333-0080
Tucker Industries
Colorado Springs, CO....... 800-786-7287
Tyco Fire Protection Products
Lansdale, PA 800-558-5236
UAA
Chicago, IL 800-813-1711
Ultrak
Westminster, CO 303-428-9480
United Fire & Safety Service
Yonkers, NY 914-968-4459
Valeo
Elmsford, Ny....... 800-634-2704
Vent Master
Mississauga, ON....... 800-565-2981
Viking Corporation
Hastings, MI 800-968-9501
Wearwell/Tennessee Mat Company
Nashville, TN 615-254-8381
Weinbrenner Shoe Company
Merrill, WI 800-826-0002

Wiginton Fire Sprinklers
Sanford, FL....... 407-831-3414
World Wide Safe Brokers
Woodbury, NJ 800-593-2893
Wylie Systems
Mississauga, ON....... 800-525-6609
YottaMark
Redwood City, CA 866-768-7878

Ladder Covers

Slipnot Metal Safety Flooring
Detroit, MI 800-754-7668

Ladder Rungs

Slipnot Metal Safety Flooring
Detroit, MI 800-754-7668

Mats

Electric Alarm

Floor

Larco
Brainerd, MN 800-523-6996

Metal Detectors

Industrial Magnetics
Boyne City, MI 800-662-4638

Sanitation Equipment & Supplies

Ammonia

Bottled for Cleaning

James Austin Company
Mars, PA 724-625-1535
Laundry Aids
Carlstadt, NJ 201-933-3500
Patterson Laboratories
Detroit, MI 313-843-4500
Rooto Corporation
Howell, MI 517-546-8330
Sewell Products
Salem, VA 540-389-5401

Bleaches

Bio Pac
Incline Village, NV 800-225-2855
Blue Cross Laboratories
Santa Clarita, CA
Country Save Corporation
Arlington, WA 360-435-9868
Delta Chemical Corporation
Baltimore, MD 800-282-5322
Diamond Chemical Compan y
East Rutherford, NJ 800-654-7627
Dover Chemical Corporation
Dover, OH 800-321-8805
DuPont
Wilmington, DE 800-441-7515
Hilex Company
Eagan, MN 651-454-1160
Hydrite Chemical Company
Brookfield, WI 262-792-1450
James Austin Company
Mars, PA 724-625-1535
Kuehne Chemical Company
Kearny, NJ 973-589-0700
Patterson Laboratories
Detroit, MI 313-843-4500
Rooto Corporation
Howell, MI 517-546-8330
Sewell Products
Salem, VA 540-389-5401
Venturetech Corporation
Knoxville, TN 800-826-4095

Borax

Ceramic Color & ChemicalManufacturing Company
New Brighton, PA 724-846-4000

Brooms

ABCO Products
Miami, FL 888-694-2226
Amarillo Mop & Broom Company
Amarillo, TX 800-955-8596
American Broom Company
Mattoon, IL 217-235-1992
American Brush Company
Portland, OR 800-826-8492
American Water Broom
Atlanta, GA 800-241-6565
Anderson Products
Cresco, PA 800-729-4694
Birmingham Mop Manufacturing Company
Birmingham, AL 205-942-6101
Bouras Mop ManufacturingCompany
Saint Louis, MO 800-634-9153
Bruske Products
Tinley Park, IL 708-532-3800
Carlisle Food Service Products
Oklahoma City, OK 800-654-8210
Carolina Mop Company
Anderson, SC 800-845-9725
Chickasaw Broom Manufacturing
Little Rock, AR 501-532-0311
Cleveland Mop Manufacturing Company
Cleveland, OH 800-767-9934
Cornelia Broom Company
Cornelia, GA 800-228-2551
Cosgrove Enterprises
Miami Lakes, FL 800-888-3396
Costa Broom Works
Tampa, FL 813-385-1722
Crystal Lake Manufacturing
Autaugaville, AL 800-633-8720
Culicover & Shapiro
Bay Shore, NY 631-918-4560
DQB Industries
Livonia, MI 800-722-3037
Fuller Brush Company
Great Bend, KS 800-522-0499
Furgale Industries Ltd.
Winnipeg, NB 800-665-0506
Greenwood Mop & Broom
Greenwood, SC 800-635-6849
H. Arnold Wood Turning
Tarrytown, NY 888-314-0088
Harper Brush Works
Fairfield, IA 800-223-7894
Hoge Brush Company
New Knoxville, OH 800-494-4643
Howard Overman & Sons
Baltimore, MD 410-276-8445
Hub City Brush
Petal, MS 800-278-7452
Imperial Broom Company
Richmond, VA 888-353-7840
Industries for the Blind
West Allis, WI 414-778-3040
Industries of the Blind
Greensboro, NC 336-274-1591
J.I. Holcomb Manufacturing
Independence, OH 800-458-3222
John L. Denning & Company
Wichita, KS 316-264-2357
Labpride Chemicals
Bronx, NY 800-467-1255
Libman Company
Arcola, IL 877-818-3380
Lighthouse for the Blindin New Orleans
New Orleans, LA 504-899-4501
Little Rock Broom Works
Little Rock, AR 501-562-0311
LMCO
Rosenberg, TX 281-342-8888
Luco Mop Company
St Louis, MO 800-522-5826
Messina Brothers Manufacturing Company
Brooklyn, NY 800-924-6454
Michigan Brush Manufacturing Company, Inc.
Detroit, MI 800-642-7874
Milwaukee Dustless BrushCompany
Delavan, WI 800-632-3220
Minuteman Power Boss
Aberdeen, NC 800-323-9420
Nationwide Wire & Brush Manufacturing
Lodi, CA 209-334-9660
Newton Broom Company
Newton, IL 618-783-4424
O'Dell Corporation
Ware Shoals, SC 800-342-2843
O-Cedar
Aurora, IL 800-543-8105
Perfex Corporation
Poland, NY 800-848-8483
Quality Mop & Brush Manufacturers
Needham, MA 617-884-2999
Quickie Manufacturing Corp.
Cinnaminson, NJ 856-829-7900
Reit-Price ManufacturingCompany
Union City, IN 800-521-5343
RidgeView Products LLC
La Crosse, WI 888-782-1221
Royal Broom & Mop Factory
Harahan, LA 800-537-6925
S&M Manufacturing Company
Cisco, TX 800-772-8532
Tucel Industries, Inc.
Forestdale, VT 800-558-8235
Waco Broom & Mop Factory
Waco, TX 800-548-7716
Warren E. Conley Corporation
Carmel, IN 800-367-7875
Whitley Manufacturing Company
Midland, NC 704-888-2625
Wright-Bernet
Hamilton, OH 513-874-1800
Young & Swartz
Buffalo, NY 800-466-7682

Brushes

Bottle

Braun Brush Company
Albertson, NY 800-645-4111
Carlisle Food Service Products
Oklahoma City, OK 800-654-8210
Justman Brush Company
Omaha, NE 800-800-6940
Volckening
Brooklyn, NY 718-748-0294

Floor, Sweeping, Polishing & Waxing

ABCO Products
Miami, FL 888-694-2226
Anderson Products
Cresco, PA 800-729-4694
Braun Brush Company
Albertson, NY 800-645-4111
Bruske Products
Tinley Park, IL 708-532-3800
Carlisle Food Service Products
Oklahoma City, OK 800-654-8210
Carlisle Sanitary Maintenance Products
Oklahoma City, OK 800-654-8210
Cornelia Broom Company
Cornelia, GA 800-228-2551
Costa Broom Works
Tampa, FL 813-385-1722
Culicover & Shapiro
Bay Shore, NY 631-918-4560
DQB Industries
Livonia, MI 800-722-3037
Fox Brush Company
Oxford, ME 207-539-2208
Fuller Brush Company
Great Bend, KS 800-522-0499
Harper Brush Works
Fairfield, IA 800-223-7894
Hoge Brush Company
New Knoxville, OH 800-494-4643
Kiefer Brushes, Inc
Franklin, NJ 800-526-2905
Labpride Chemicals
Bronx, NY 800-467-1255
Lighthouse for the Blindin New Orleans
New Orleans, LA 504-899-4501
Michigan Brush Manufacturing Company, Inc.
Detroit, MI 800-642-7874
Microtron Abrasives
Pineville, NC 800-476-7237
Milwaukee Dustless BrushCompany
Delavan, WI 800-632-3220
O'Dell Corporation
Ware Shoals, SC 800-342-2843
O-Cedar
Aurora, IL 800-543-8105
Perfex Corporation
Poland, NY 800-848-8483
Reit-Price ManufacturingCompany
Union City, IN 800-521-5343
Superior Brush Company
Cleveland, OH 216-941-6987
Tucel Industries, Inc.
Forestdale, VT 800-558-8235
Walker Brush
Webster, NY 585-467-7850
Wilen Professional Cleaning Products
Atlanta, GA 800-241-7371
Wright-Bernet
Hamilton, OH 513-874-1800
Young & Swartz
Buffalo, NY 800-466-7682
Zephyr Manufacturing
Sedalia, MO 660-827-0352

Carts

Housekeeping

AMCO Corporation
City of Industry, CA 626-855-2550
BMH Equipment
Sacramento, CA 800-350-8828

Geerpres
Muskegon, MI....................231-773-3211
James Varley & Sons
Saint Louis, MO..................800-325-3303
Lakeside Manufacturing
Milwaukee, WI....................888-558-8574
Princeton Shelving
Cedar Rapids, IA.................319-369-0355

Caustic Soda

ATOFINA Chemicals
Philadelphia, PA.................800-225-7788

Chlorine

Liquid

ATOFINA Chemicals
Philadelphia, PA.................800-225-7788
Delta Chemical Corporation
Baltimore, MD....................800-282-5322
Selig Chemical Industries
Atlanta, GA......................404-876-5511

Cleaners

Bottle (Compounds)

American Formula
Atlanta, GA......................800-282-1215
American Municipal Chemical Company
West Allis, WI...................800-598-3106
Champion Chemical Co.
Whittier, CA.....................800-621-7868
Church & Dwight Company
Princeton, NJ....................800-833-9532
Delta Foremost Chemical Corporation
Memphis, TN......................800-238-5150
Diamond Chemical Compan y
East Rutherford, NJ..............800-654-7627
ELF Machinery
La Porte, IN.....................800-328-0466
Essential Industries
Merton, WI.......................800-551-9679
Hy-Trous/Flash Sales
Woburn, MA.......................781-933-5772
James Varley & Sons
Saint Louis, MO..................800-325-3303
Lubar Chemical
Kansas City, MO..................816-471-2560
Magnuson Products
Clifton, NJ......................973-472-9292
Mertz L. Carlton Company
Bedford Park, IL.................708-594-1050
National Interchem Corporation
Blue Island, IL...................800-638-6688
Oakite Products
New Providence, NJ...............800-526-4473
Occidental Chemical Corporation
Niagara Falls, NY................716-278-7027
Pneumatic Scale Corporation
Cuyahoga Falls, OH...............330-923-0491
Seatex Ltd
Rosenberg, TX....................800-829-3020
Shepard Brothers
La Habra, CA.....................562-697-1366
Warren E. Conley Corporation
Carmel, IN.......................800-367-7875
Warsaw Chemical Company
Warsaw, IN.......................800-548-3396

Coffee Pot

Urnex Brands, Inc.
Elmsford, NY.....................800-222-2826

Dairy

Hoge Brush Company
New Knoxville, OH................800-494-4643
Hy-Ko Enviro-MaintenanceProducts
Salt Lake City, UT...............801-973-6099
Lechler
St Charles, IL...................800-777-2926
Magnuson Products
Clifton, NJ......................973-472-9292
Westfalia-Surge, Inc.
Naperville, IL...................630-548-8374
Winn-Sol Products
Oshkosh, WI......................920-231-2031

Grain & Seed

A.C. Horn & Co
Dallas, TX.......................800-657-6155
A.K. Robins
Baltimore, MD....................800-486-9656
A.T. Ferrell Company
Bluffton, IN.....................800-248-8318
Carter Day International, Inc.
Minneapolis, MN..................763-571-1000
Cleland Manufacturing Company
Columbia Heights, MN.............763-571-4606
Crippen Manufacturing Company
St. Louis, MI....................800-872-2474
DMC-David Manufacturing Company
Mason City, IA...................641-424-7010
En-Hanced Products, Inc.
Westerville, OH..................800-783-7400
Forster & Son
Ada, OK..........................580-332-6020
Grain Machinery Manufacturing Corporation
Miami, FL........................305-620-2525
Lewis M. Carter Manufacturing Company
Donalsonville, GA................229-524-2197
NECO
Omaha, NE........................402-453-6912

Hand

AFASSCO
Minden, NV.......................800-441-6774
Amodex Products
Bridgeport, CT...................877-866-1255
Athea Laboratories
Milwaukee, WI....................800-743-6417
Buckeye International
Maryland Heights, MO.............314-291-1900
CCP Industries, Inc.
Cleveland, OH....................800-321-2840
Chef Revival
Elkhorn, WI......................800-248-9826
Coleman Manufacturing Company
Everett, MA......................617-389-0380
Concord Chemical Company
Camden, NJ.......................800-282-2436
CRC Industries, Inc.
Warminster, PA...................800-556-5074
Cresset Chemical Company
Weston, OH.......................800-367-2020
Critzas Industries
St Louis, MO.....................800-537-1418
Crown Chemical Products
Mississauga, ON..................905-564-0904
Deb Canada
Waterford, ON....................888-332-7627
Development Workshop
Idaho Falls, ID..................800-657-5597
Diamond Wipes International
Chino, CA........................800-454-1077
Dickler Chemical Labs
Philadelphia, PA.................800-426-1127
Dober Chemical Corporation
Midlothian, IL...................800-323-4983
Dreumex USA
York, PA.........................800-233-9382
Du-Good Chemical Laboratory & Manufacturing Company
Saint Louis, MO..................314-773-5007
ECOLAB
St Paul, MN......................800-352-5326
Emulso Corporation
Tonawanda, NY....................800-724-7667
Essential Industries
Merton, WI.......................800-551-9679
Fishers Investment
Cincinnati, OH...................800-833-5916
Galaxy Chemical Corporation
Sarasota, FL.....................941-755-8545
Go-Jo Industries
Akron, OH........................800-321-9647
Hallberg Manufacturing Corporation
Tampa, FL........................800-633-7627
Hewitt Soap Company
Dayton, OH.......................800-543-2245
Hill Manufacturing Company
Atlanta, GA......................404-522-8364
Hy-Ko Enviro-MaintenanceProducts
Salt Lake City, UT...............801-973-6099
Hy-Trous/Flash Sales
Woburn, MA.......................781-933-5772
Industrial EnvironmentalPollution Control
Bronx, NY........................718-585-2410
Inksolv 30, LLC.
Emerson, NE......................515-537-5344
ITW Dymon
Olathe, KS.......................800-443-9536
J.C. Whitlam Manufacturing Co.
Wadsworth, OH....................800-321-8358
J.I. Holcomb Manufacturing
Independence, OH.................800-458-3222
James Austin Company
Mars, PA.........................724-625-1535
James Varley & Sons
Saint Louis, MO..................800-325-3303
Kildon Manufacturing
Ingersoll, ON....................800-485-4930
Kleen Products
Oklahoma City, OK................800-392-1792
L&M Chemicals
Tampa, FL........................800-362-3331
Lee Products Company
Bloomington, MN..................952-854-3544
Man-O Products
Cincinnati, OH...................888-210-6266
Martin Laboratories
Owensboro, KY....................800-345-9352
Micro-Brush Pro Soap
Rockwall, TX.....................800-776-7627
Milburn Company
Detroit, MI......................313-259-3410
Mione Manufacturing Company
Mickleton, NJ....................800-257-0497
Mission Laboratories
Los Angeles, CA..................888-201-8866
Nice-Pak Products
Orangeburg, NY...................800-999-6423
Nosaj Disposables
Paterson, NJ.....................800-631-3809
Nuance Solutions
Chicago, IL......................800-621-8553
R&C Pro Brands
Wayne, NJ........................973-633-7374
Rochester Midland Corporation
Rochester, NY....................800-535-5053
Rochester Midland Corporation
Rochester, NY....................800-836-1627
S&S Soap Company
Bronx, NY........................718-585-2900
Sanitek Products, Inc
Los Angeles, CA..................818-242-1071
Savogran Company
Norwood, MA......................800-225-9872
SCA Hygiene Paper
San Ramon, CA....................800-992-8675
Starkey Chemical ProcessCompany
La Grange, IL....................800-323-3040
Steiner Company
Holland, IL......................800-222-4638
Stone Soap Company
Sylvan Lake, MI..................800-952-7627
Sunbeam Product
Toledo, OH.......................419-691-1551
Syndett Products
Bolton, CT.......................860-646-0172
Telechem Corporation
Atlanta, GA......................800-637-0495
Tropical Soap Company
Carrollton, TX...................800-527-2368
Verax Chemical Company
Bothell, WA......................800-637-7771
W.M. Barr & Company
Memphis, TN......................800-238-2672
Whisk Products
Wentzville, MO...................800-204-7627

Silver

Burnishine Products
Gurnee, IL.......................800-818-8275
Casabar
Morristown, NJ...................877-745-8700
Copper Clad Products
Reading, PA......................610-375-4596
Dynynstyl
Delray Beach, FL.................800-774-7895
George Basch Company
Freeport, NY.....................516-378-8100
Sanolite Corporation
Elizabeth, NJ....................800-221-0806

Cleaning Equipment & Supplies

9-12 Corporation
Caguas, PR.......................787-747-0405

A&L Laboratories
Minneapolis, MN 800-225-3832
A.J. Funk & Company
Elgin, IL 877-225-3865
A.K. Robins
Baltimore, MD 800-486-9656
A.L. Wilson Chemical Company
Kearny, NJ. 800-526-1188
ABCO Products
Miami, FL 888-694-2226
Abicor Binzel
Frederick, MD. 800-542-4867
Absorbco
Walterboro, SC 888-335-6439
Ace-Tex Enterprises
Detroit, MI 800-444-3800
Acme Sponge & Chamois Company
Tarpon Springs, FL 727-937-3222
Acro Dishwashing Service
Kansas City, KS 913-342-4282
ACS Industries, Inc.
Lincoln, RI 866-783-4838
Activon Products
Beaver Dam, WI 800-841-0410
Adamation
Commerce, CA 800-225-3075
ADCO
Albany, GA 800-821-7556
Advance Cleaning Products
Milwaukee, WI 800-925-5326
Air-Scent International
Pittsburgh, PA 800-247-0770
Airosol Company
Neodesha, KS 800-633-9576
Akron Cotton Products
Akron, OH. 800-899-7173
Alconox
White Plains, NY 914-948-4040
Alex C. Fergusson
Chambersburg, PA 800-345-1329
Alkota Cleaning Systems
Alcester, SD 800-255-6823
All American Containers
Medley, FL 305-887-0797
Alumin-Nu Corporation
Lyndhurst, OH 800-899-7097
Amarillo Mop & Broom Company
Amarillo, TX. 800-955-8596
AMCO Corporation
City of Industry, CA 626-855-2550
Ameri-Khem
Port Orange, FL 800-224-9950
American Broom Company
Mattoon, IL. 217-235-1992
American Brush Company
Portland, OR 800-826-8492
American Formula
Atlanta, GA. 800-282-1215
American Municipal Chemical Company
West Allis, WI. 800-598-3106
American Textile Mills
Kansas City, MO. 816-842-2909
American Water Broom
Atlanta, GA. 800-241-6565
American Wax Company
Long Island City, NY 888-929-7587
Ametek Technical & Industrial Products
Kent, OH. 215-256-6601
Amodex Products
Bridgeport, CT 877-866-1255
Andersen 2000
Peachtree City, GA 800-241-5424
Anderson Products
Cresco, PA. 800-729-4694
APEX
Neodesha, KS 800-633-9576
Aqua-Dyne
Baxter Springs, KS 800-826-9274
Aquafine Corporation
Valencia, CA 800-423-3015
Aquionics
Erlanger, KY. 800-925-0440
ARC Specialties
Valencia, CA 661-775-8500
Arden Companies
Southfield, MI. 248-415-8500
Argo & Company
Spartanburg, SC 864-583-9766
Armaly Brands
Walled Lake, MI 800-772-1222
Armstrong Manufacturing
Mississauga, ON 866-627-6588
Armstrong-Lynnwood
Three Rivers, MI. 269-273-1415
Arrow Magnolia International, Inc.
Dallas, TX. 800-527-2101
Assembled Products
Rogers, AR 800-548-3373
Associated Products
Glenshaw, PA 800-243-5689
Athea Laboratories
Milwaukee, WI 800-743-6417
Atlantic Mills
Lakewood, NJ 800-242-7374
ATOFINA Chemicals
Philadelphia, PA 800-225-7788
Auto Chlor Systems
Memphis, TN 800-477-3693
Banner Chemical Corporation
Orange, NJ 973-676-2900
Bar Maid Corporation
Pompano Beach, FL 954-960-1468
Beam Industries
Webster City, IA 800-369-2326
Bel-Art Products
Wayne, NJ 800-423-5278
Bete Fog Nozzle
Greenfield, MA. 800-235-0049
Bethel Engineering & Equipment Inc
New Hampshire, OH. 800-889-6129
Bex Inc.
Ann Arbor, MI 734-464-8282
Bi-O-Kleen Industries
Portland, OR 503-224-6246
Bio Industries
Luxemburg, WI. 920-845-2355
Bio Pac
Incline Village, NV. 800-225-2855
Bio Zapp Laboratorie Inc
San Antonio, TX. 210-805-9199
Bio-Cide International
Norman, OK 800-323-1398
Birko Corporation
Henderson, CO 800-525-0476
Birmingham Mop Manufacturing Company
Birmingham, AL. 205-942-6101
Black's Products of HighPoint
High Point, NC 336-886-5011
Blue Cross Laboratories
Santa Clarita, CA
Blue Feather Product
Ashland, OR 800-472-2487
Blue Ridge Converting
Asheville, NC 800-438-3893
Boston Chemical Industries
Randolph, MA 800-255-8651
Bouras Mop ManufacturingCompany
Saint Louis, MO 800-634-9153
Boyer Corporation
La Grange, IL 800-323-3040
Branson Ultrasonics Corporation
Danbury, CT 203-796-0400
Braun Brush Company
Albertson, NY 800-645-4111
Bro-Tex
Saint Paul, MN 800-328-2282
Brulin & Company
Indianapolis, IN 800-776-7149
Bruske Products
Tinley Park, IL 708-532-3800
Buckeye International
Maryland Heights, MO. 314-291-1900
Bunzl Distribution USA
St Louis, MO. 888-997-5959
Burnishine Products
Gurnee, IL. 800-818-8275
Butterworth Systems
Houston, TX 281-821-7300
C&H Chemical
St Paul, MN. 651-227-4343
C&R Refrigation Inc,
Center, TX. 800-438-6182
C.P. Industries
Salt Lake City, UT 800-453-4931
Cadie Products Corporation
Paterson, NJ 973-278-8300
Cal Ben Soap Company
Oakland, CA 800-340-7091
Cam Spray
Iowa Falls, IA 800-648-5011
Candy & Company/Peck's Products Company
Chicago, IL 800-837-9189
Cantol
Markham, ON 800-387-9773
Canton Sterilized WipingCloth Company
Canton, OH 330-455-5179
Carbon Clean Products
Kingston, PA 570-288-1155
Carhoff Company
Cleveland, OH 216-541-4835
Carlisle Food Service Products
Oklahoma City, OK 800-654-8210
Carlisle Sanitary Maintenance Products
Oklahoma City, OK 800-654-8210
Carnegie Textile Company
Solon, OH 800-633-4136
Carolina Mop Company
Anderson, SC 800-845-9725
Carroll Company
Garland, TX 800-527-5722
Casabar
Morristown, NJ. 877-745-8700
CC Custom Technology Corporation
Cleveland, OH 216-662-5500
CCP Industries, Inc.
Cleveland, OH 800-321-2840
Central Solutions
Kansas City, KS 800-255-0662
Century Chemical Corporation
Elkhart, IN. 800-348-3505
Ceramic Color & ChemicalManufacturing Company
New Brighton, PA. 724-846-4000
Chad Company
Olathe, KS. 800-444-8360
Champion Chemical Co.
Whittier, CA 800-621-7868
Champion Industries
Winston Salem, NC. 800-532-8591
Chef Revival
Elkhorn, WI. 800-248-9826
Chemclean Corporation
Jamaica, NY 800-538-2436
Chemdet
Sebastian, FL 800-645-1510
Chemifax
Santa Fe Springs, CA 800-527-5722
Chickasaw Broom Manufacturing
Little Rock, AR. 501-532-0311
Cincinnati Industrial Machine
Mason, OH 800-677-0076
Claire Manufacturing Company
Addison, IL 800-252-4731
Clarke
Plymouth, MN. 800-253-0367
Clarkson Chemical Company
Williamsport, PA. 800-326-9457
Clayton L. Hagy & Son
Philadelphia, PA 215-844-6470
Clean All
Syracuse, NY 315-472-9189
Clean Freak
Appleton, WI 888-722-5508
Clearly Natural Products
Kennesaw, GA 800-451-7096
Cleveland Mop Manufacturing Company
Cleveland, OH 800-767-9934
Clorox Company
Oakland, CA 888-271-7000
Cloud Company
San Luis Obispo, CA 800-234-5650
CMA/Dishmachines
Garden Grove, CA 800-854-6417
Coast Scientific
Rancho Santa Fe, CA 800-445-1544
Cobitco, Inc
Denver, CO 303-296-8575
Coburn Company
Whitewater, WI. 800-776-7042
Cold Jet
Loveland, OH 800-337-9423
Coleman Manufacturing Company
Everett, MA. 617-389-0380
Colgate-Palmolive
Morristown, NJ. 800-432-8226
Colonial Paper Company
Silver Springs, FL. 352-622-4171
Command Belt Cleaning Systems
Jamaica, NY 800-433-7627
Common Sense Natural Soap & Bodycare Products
Rutland, VT 802-773-0582
Compliance Control
Hyattsville, MD 800-810-4000
Composition Materials Company
Milford, CT. 800-262-7763
Concord Chemical Company
Camden, NJ. 800-282-2436

Continental Commercial Products
Bridgeton, MO 800-325-1051
Continental Equipment Corporation
Milwaukee, WI 414-463-0500
Continental Girbau
Oshkosh, WI 800-256-1073
Conveyor Components Company
Croswell, MI 800-233-3233
Copper Brite
Santa Barbara, CA 805-565-1566
Copper Clad Products
Reading, PA 610-375-4596
Core Products Company
Canton, TX 800-825-2673
Cornelia Broom Company
Cornelia, GA 800-228-2551
Cosgrove Enterprises
Miami Lakes, FL 800-888-3396
Costa Broom Works
Tampa, FL 813-385-1722
Country Save Corporation
Arlington, WA 360-435-9868
CRC Industries, Inc.
Warminster, PA 800-556-5074
Cresset Chemical Company
Weston, OH 800-367-2020
Critzas Industries
St Louis, MO 800-537-1418
Crown Chemical Products
Mississauga, ON 905-564-0904
Cryogenesis
Cleveland, OH 216-696-8797
Crystal Lake Manufacturing
Autaugaville, AL 800-633-8720
Culicover & Shapiro
Bay Shore, NY 631-918-4560
D&M Products
Santa Monica, CA 800-245-0485
D.W. Davies & Company
Racine, WI 800-888-6133
Damas Corporation
Trenton, NJ 609-695-9121
Damon Industries
Alliance, OH 800-362-9850
Damp Rid
Memphis, TN 888-326-7743
De Royal Textiles
Camden, SC 800-845-1062
Deb Canada
Waterford, ON 888-332-7627
DeLaval Cleaning Solutions
Kansas City, MO 816-891-1530
Delta Carbona
Fairfield, NJ 888-746-5599
Delta Chemical Corporation
Baltimore, MD 800-282-5322
Delta Foremost Chemical Corporation
Memphis, TN 800-238-5150
Dema Engineering Company
Saint Louis, MO 800-325-3362
Development Workshop
Idaho Falls, ID 800-657-5597
Diablo Products
Fort Dodge, IA 800-548-1385
Dial Corporation
Scottsdale, AZ 480-754-3425
Diamond Chemical Compan y
East Rutherford, NJ 800-654-7627
Diamond Wipes International
Chino, CA 800-454-1077
Dickler Chemical Labs
Philadelphia, PA 800-426-1127
Dirt Killer Pressure Washers, Inc
Baltimore, MD 800-544-1188
Distribution Results
Akron, OH 800-737-9671
DL Enterprises
Etters, PA 717-938-1292
Dober Chemical Corporation
Midlothian, IL 800-323-4983
Donaldson Company
Minneapolis, MN 800-767-0702
Dorden & Company
Detroit, MI 313-834-7910
Douglas Machines Corporation
Clearwater, FL 800-331-6870
Dover Chemical Corporation
Dover, OH 800-321-8805
Dover Parkersburg
Follansbee, WV
Downeast Chemical
Westbrook, ME 800-287-2225

DPC
Norristown, PA 800-220-9473
DQB Industries
Livonia, MI 800-722-3037
DR Technology
Freehold, NJ 732-780-4664
Drackett Professional
Cincinnati, OH 513-583-3900
Dreumex USA
York, PA 800-233-9382
Du-Good Chemical Laboratory & Manufacturing Company
Saint Louis, MO 314-773-5007
Dynablast Manufacturing
Mississauga, ON 888-242-8597
Dynynstyl
Delray Beach, FL 800-774-7895
Eagle Home Products
Huntington, NY
ECOLAB
St Paul, MN 800-352-5326
Ecolab
St. Paul, MN 651-293-2233
Ecolo Odor Control Systems Worldwide
North York, ON 800-667-6355
Economy Paper & Restaurant Supply Company
Clifton, NJ 973-279-5500
Ecover
Los Angeles, CA 323-720-5730
Electro-Steam Generator Corporation
Rancocas, NJ 866-617-0764
ELF Machinery
La Porte, IN 800-328-0466
Elgene
Hamden, CT 800-922-4623
Emulso Corporation
Tonawanda, NY 800-724-7667
Encore Paper Company
South Glens Falls, NY 800-362-6735
Erie Cotton Products Company
Erie, PA 800-289-4737
Essential Industries
Merton, WI 800-551-9679
Ettore Products Company
Alameda, CA 510-748-4130
Eureka Company
Bloomington, IL 800-282-2886
Ex-Cell Kaiser
Franklin Park, IL 847-451-0451
Excel Chemical Company
Jacksonville, FL 904-356-0446
Faciltec Corporation
Elgin, IL 800-284-8273
Falls Chemical Products
Oconto Falls, WI 920-846-3561
Fast Industries
Fort Lauderdale, FL 800-775-5345
Feather Duster Corporation
Amsterdam, NY 800-967-8659
Fiebing Company
Milwaukee, WI 800-558-1033
Fishers Investment
Cincinnati, OH 800-833-5916
Fitzpatrick Brothers
Pleasant Prairie, WI 800-233-8064
FleetwoodGoldcoWyard
Romeoville, IL 630-759-6800
Flo-Matic Corporation
Belvidere, IL 800-959-1179
Floormaster
Chattanooga, TN 423-867-4525
Flow International Corporation
Kent, WA 800-610-1798
Fort James Corporation
Norwalk, CT 800-257-9744
Fuller Brush Company
Great Bend, KS 800-522-0499
Furgale Industries Ltd.
Winnipeg, NB 800-665-0506
FX-Lab Company
Union, NJ 908-810-1212
Galaxy Chemical Corporation
Sarasota, FL 941-755-8545
Gamajet Cleaning Systems
Exton, PA 800-289-5387
Game Cock Chemical Company
Sumter, SC 803-773-7391
Gardner Denver Inc.
Toronto, ON 416-763-4681
Garman Company
Valley Park, MO 800-466-5150

Geerpres
Muskegon, MI 231-773-3211
GEMTEK Products, LLC
Phoenix, AZ 800-331-7022
General Floor Craft
Little Silver, NJ 973-742-7400
General Steel Fabricators
Joplin, MO 800-820-8644
General, Inc
Weston, FL 954-202-7419
Geo. Olcott Company
Scottsboro, AL 800-634-2769
George Basch Company
Freeport, NY 516-378-8100
Georgia Pacific
Green Bay, WI 920-435-8821
Ghibli North American
Wilmington, DE 302-654-5908
Girton Manufacturing Company, Inc.
Millville, PA 570-458-5521
Glass Pro
Addison, IL 888-641-8919
Glastender
Saginaw, MI 800-748-0423
Glit Microtron
Bridgetown, MO 800-325-1051
Glover Latex
Anaheim, CA 800-243-5110
Go-Jo Industries
Akron, OH 800-321-9647
Golden Star
N Kansas City, MO 800-821-2792
Goodman Wiper & Paper
Auburn, ME 800-439-9473
Goodway Technologies Corporation
Stamford, CT 800-333-7467
Goodwin Company
Garden Grove, CA 714-894-0531
Grace-Lee Products
Minneapolis, MN 612-379-2711
Graco
Minneapolis, MN 877-844-7226
Great Western Chemical Company
Portland, OR 800-547-1400
Greenwood Mop & Broom
Greenwood, SC 800-635-6849
Griffin Brothers
Salem, OR 800-456-4743
Guardsman/Valspar Corp
Grand Rapids, MI 616-940-2900
Guest Supply
Monmouth Jct, NJ 800-448-3787
H. Arnold Wood Turning
Tarrytown, NY 888-314-0088
H.F. Staples & Company
Merrimack, NH 800-682-0034
H.L. Diehl Company
South Windham, CT 860-423-7741
Hallberg Manufacturing Corporation
Tampa, FL 800-633-7627
Hamilton Soap & Oil Products
Paterson, NJ 973-225-1031
Hanco Manufacturing Company
Memphis, TN 800-530-7364
Hardt Equipment Manufacturing
Lachine, QC 888-848-4408
Hardwood Products Company
Guilford, ME 800-289-3340
Harper Brush Works
Fairfield, IA 800-223-7894
Haviland Products Company
Grand Rapids, MI 800-456-1134
Hedgetree Chemical Manufacturing
Savannah, GA 912-691-0408
Hewitt Soap Company
Dayton, OH 800-543-2245
Hibrett Puratex
Pennsauken, NJ 800-260-5124
Hilex Company
Eagan, MN 651-454-1160
Hill Manufacturing Company
Atlanta, GA 404-522-8364
Hillyard
Saint Joseph, MO 800-365-1555
Hodges
Vienna, IL 800-444-0011
Hoge Brush Company
New Knoxville, OH 800-494-4643
Hohn Manufacturing Company
Fenton, MO 800-878-1440
Holland Applied Technologies
Burr Ridge, IL 630-325-5130

Holland Chemicals Company
Windsor, ON 519-948-4373
Hollowell Products Corporation
Wyandotte, MI 734-282-8200
Hoover Company
North Canton, OH. 330-499-9200
Hope Chemical Corporation
Pawtucket, RI 401-724-8000
Hosch Company
Oakdale, PA 800-695-3310
Howard Overman & Sons
Baltimore, MD 410-276-8445
Howell Brothers ChemicalLaboratories
Philadelphia, PA 215-477-0260
Hub City Brush
Petal, MS. 800-278-7452
Hy-Ko Enviro-MaintenanceProducts
Salt Lake City, UT 801-973-6099
Hy-Trous/Flash Sales
Woburn, MA 781-933-5772
Hydrite Chemical Company
Brookfield, WI 262-792-1450
Idexx Laboratories
Westbrook, ME 800-321-0207
IFC Disposables
Brownsville, TN 800-432-9473
Imperial Broom Company
Richmond, VA. 888-353-7840
Indian Valley Industries
Johnson City, NY 800-659-5111
Indiana Wiping Cloth
Mishawaka, IN 800-446-9645
Industries for the Blind
West Allis, WI. 414-778-3040
Industries of the Blind
Greensboro, NC 336-274-1591
Insect-O-Cutor
Stone Mountain, GA. 800-988-5359
Insinger Machine Company
Philadelphia, PA 800-344-4802
InterBio
The Woodlands, TX 888-876-2844
International Environmental Solutions
South Pasadena, FL 800-972-8348
Iron Out
Fort Wayne, IN 888-476-6688
ITW Dymon
Olathe, KS. 800-443-9536
J.C. Whitlam Manufacturing Co.
Wadsworth, OH. 800-321-8358
J.I. Holcomb Manufacturing
Independence, OH 800-458-3222
J.V. Reed & Company
Louisville, KY 877-258-7333
Jacks Manufacturing Company
Mendota, MN 800-821-2089
James Austin Company
Mars, PA 724-625-1535
James Varley & Sons
Saint Louis, MO 800-325-3303
JAS Manufacturing Company
Carrollton, TX. 972-380-1150
John L. Denning & Company
Wichita, KS. 316-264-2357
Johnson Diversey
Sturtevant, WI. 262-631-4001
Johnson International Materials
Brownsville, TX 956-541-6364
Justman Brush Company
Omaha, NE 800-800-6940
Kafko International Ltd.
Skokie, IL. 800-528-0334
Kent Company, Inc.
Miami, FL. 800-521-4886
Kiefer Brushes, Inc
Franklin, NJ 800-526-2905
Kilgore Chemical Corporation
Layton, UT 801-546-9909
Kimberly-Clark Corporation
Neenah, WI. 888-525-8388
King of All Manufacturing
Clio, MI. 810-564-0139
Kleen Products
Oklahoma City, OK 800-392-1792
Knapp Manufacturing
Fresno, CA 559-251-8254
Knight Equipment International
Lake Forest, CA 800-854-3764
Kuehne Chemical Company
Kearny, NJ. 973-589-0700
L&M Chemicals
Tampa, FL. 800-362-3331

Lab-Tech Industries
Detroit, MI 800-525-8667
Labpride Chemicals
Bronx, NY. 800-467-1255
Lake Process Systems
Lake Barrington, IL 800-331-9260
Lakeside Manufacturing
Milwaukee, WI 888-558-8574
Lamco Chemical Company
Chelsea, MA 617-884-8470
Larose & Fils Ltêe
Laval, QC 877-382-7001
Laundry Aids
Carlstadt, NJ 201-933-3500
Laundrylux
Inwood, NY. 800-645-2205
Lavo Company
Milwaukee, WI 414-353-2140
Layflat Products
Shreveport, LA 800-551-8515
Lechler
St Charles, IL 800-777-2926
Lee Products Company
Bloomington, MN. 952-854-3544
Lee Soap Company
Commerce City, CO 800-888-1896
Leedal Inc
Northbrook, IL 847-498-0111
Leggett & Platt StorageP
Vernon Hills, IL 847-816-6246
Letraw Manufacturing Company
Rockford, IL 815-987-9670
Lexidyne of Pennsylvania
Pittsburgh, PA. 800-543-2233
Libman Company
Arcola, IL 877-818-3380
Lighthouse for the Blindin New Orleans
New Orleans, LA 504-899-4501
Lite-Weight Tool Manufacturing Company
Sun Valley, CA 800-859-3529
Little Rock Broom Works
Little Rock, AR. 501-562-0311
LMCO
Rosenberg, TX 281-342-8888
LPI Imports
Chicago, IL 877-389-6563
Lubar Chemical
Kansas City, MO. 816-471-2560
Luco Mop Company
St Louis, MO. 800-522-5826
Luseaux Laboratories Inc
Gardena, CA 800-266-1555
Machem Industries
Delta, BC. 604-526-5655
Magic American Corporation
Cleveland, OH 800-321-6330
Magnuson Products
Clifton, NJ. 973-472-9292
Mahoney Environmental
Joliet, IL 800-892-9392
Mainline Industries
Springfield, MA 800-527-7917
Majestic Industries, Inc
Macomb, MI. 586-786-9100
Mar-Len Supply
Hayward, CA 510-782-3555
Marcal Paper Mills
Elmwood Park, NJ 800-631-8451
Marko
Spartanburg, SC 866-466-2726
Martin Laboratories
Owensboro, KY 800-345-9352
Mastercraft Industries
Newburgh, NY 800-835-7812
Maxi-Vac Inc.
Dundee, IL 855-629-4538
Mba Suppliers Inc.
Bellevue, NE. 800-467-1201
McBrady Engineering
Joliet, IL 815-744-8900
Mednik Wiping Materials Company
Saint Louis, MO 800-325-7193
Meguiar's
Irvine, CA. 949-752-8000
Mercury Floor Machines
Englewood, NJ 888-568-4606
Meritech
Golden, CO. 800-932-7707
Mertz L. Carlton Company
Bedford Park, IL. 708-594-1050
Messina Brothers Manufacturing Company
Brooklyn, NY. 800-924-6454

Metalloid Corporation
Huntington, IN 260-356-3200
Metcraft
Grandview, MO. 800-444-9624
MGF.com
Atlanta, GA. 770-444-9686
Mia Rose Products
Newport Beach, CA 800-292-6339
Michigan Brush Manufacturing Company, Inc.
Detroit, MI 800-642-7874
Micro-Brush Pro Soap
Rockwall, TX 800-776-7627
Microbest Products
Waterbury, CT. 800-426-4246
Microtron Abrasives
Pineville, NC. 800-476-7237
MIFAB Manufacturing
Chicago, IL 800-465-2736
Mil-Du-Gas Company/Star Brite
Fort Lauderdale, FL 800-327-8583
Mill Wiping Rags/The Rag Factory
Bronx, NY. 718-994-7100
Milsek Furniture Polish Inc.
North Lima, OH 330-542-2700
Milwaukee Dustless BrushCompany
Delavan, WI 800-632-3220
Minuteman Power Boss
Aberdeen, NC 800-323-9420
Mione Manufacturing Company
Mickleton, NJ 800-257-0497
Mission Laboratories
Los Angeles, CA. 888-201-8866
Moly-XL Company
Westville, NJ. 856-848-2880
Momar
Atlanta, GA. 800-556-3967
Motom Corporation
Bensenville, IL 630-787-1995
Moyer-Diebel
Winston Salem, NC. 336-661-1992
Murk Brush Company
New Britain, CT 860-249-2550
Murnell Wax Company
Springfield, MA 781-395-1323
N&A Manufacturing Spraymatic Sprayers
Mallard, IA 712-425-3512
Nation/Ruskin
Montgomeryville, PA 800-523-2489
National Conveyor Corporation
Commerce, CA 323-725-0355
National Interchem Corporation
Blue Island, IL 800-638-6688
National Scoop & Equipment Company
Spring House, PA 215-646-2040
National Towelette Company
Bensalem, PA 215-245-7300
National-Purity
Brooklyn Center, MN 612-672-0022
Nationwide Wire & Brush Manufacturing
Lodi, CA 209-334-9660
Navy Brand ManufacturingCompany
St Louis, MO. 800-325-3312
New Klix Corporation
South San Francisco, CA 800-522-5544
New Pig Corporation
Tipton, PA 800-468-4647
Newton Broom Company
Newton, IL 618-783-4424
Nice-Pak Products
Orangeburg, NY 800-999-6423
Northwind
Alpena, AR 870-437-2585
Nosaj Disposables
Paterson, NJ 800-631-3809
Nova Hand Dryers
Herndon, VA. 703-615-3636
Novus
Savage, MN. 800-328-1117
Nu-Tex Styles, Inc.
Somerset, NJ. 732-485-5456
Nu-Towel Company
Kansas City, MO. 800-800-7247
Nuance Solutions
Chicago, IL 800-621-8553
NuTone
Cincinnati, OH 888-336-3948
Nyco Products Company
Countryside, IL. 800-752-4754
Nylonge Company
Elyria, OH. 440-323-6161
O'Dell Corporation
Ware Shoals, SC 800-342-2843

O-Cedar
Aurora, IL . . . 800-543-8105
O.A. Newton & Son Company
Bridgeville, DE . . . 800-726-5745
Occidental Chemical Corporation
Niagara Falls, NY . . . 716-278-7027
Oerlikon Balzers
Elgin, IL . . . 847-695-5200
Ohio Soap Products Company
Wickliffe, OH . . . 440-585-1100
Omni-Lift
Salt Lake City, UT . . . 801-486-3776
Opie Brush Company
Independence, MO . . . 800-877-6743
Oreck Corporation
Cookeville, TN . . . 800-989-3535
Original Bradford Soap Works
West Warwick, RI . . . 401-821-2141
Ostrem Chemical Co. Ltd
Edmonton, AB . . . 780-440-1911
Pacific Oasis Enterprises
Santa Fe Springs, CA . . . 800-424-1475
Packaging & Processing Equipment
Ayr, ON . . . 519-622-6666
Packaging Distribution Services, Inc
Des Moines, IA . . . 800-747-2699
Pagoda Products
Sinking Spring, PA . . . 610-678-8096
Paley-Lloyd-Donohue
Elizabeth, NJ . . . 908-352-5835
Panasonic Commercial Food Service
Secaucus, NJ . . . 800-553-0384
Paper-Pak Products
La Verne, CA . . . 909-392-1200
Parachem Corporation
Des Moines, IA . . . 515-280-9445
Paragon Group USA
St Petersburg, FL . . . 800-835-6962
Pariser Industries
Paterson, NJ . . . 800-370-7627
Patterson Laboratories
Detroit, MI . . . 313-843-4500
Paxton Products
Cincinnati, OH . . . 800-441-7475
PCI Inc.
Saint Louis, MO . . . 800-752-7657
Pepper Mill Company
Mobile, AL . . . 800-669-5175
Perfex Corporation
Poland, NY . . . 800-848-8483
Pioneer Chemical Company
Gardena, CA . . . 310-366-7393
Pioneer Manufacturing Company
Cleveland, OH . . . 800-877-1500
PM Chemical Company
San Diego, CA . . . 619-296-0191
Portion-Pac Chemical Corp.
Chicago, IL . . . 312-226-0400
Potlatch Corporation
Spokane, WA. . . . 509-835-1500
Pro-Tex-All Company
Evansville, IN . . . 800-755-5458
Proctor & Gamble Company
Cincinnati, OH . . . 513-983-1100
Productos Familia
Santurce, PR . . . 787-268-5929
Proffitt Manufacturing Company
Dalton, GA . . . 800-241-4682
ProRestore Products
Pittsburgh, PA . . . 800-332-6037
ProTeam
Boise, ID . . . 800-541-1456
Purdy Products Company
Wauconda, IL . . . 800-726-4849
Puritan/Churchill Chemical Company
Marietta, GA . . . 800-275-8914
Purity Products
Plainview, NY . . . 800-256-6102
Quaker Chemical Company
Columbia, SC . . . 800-849-9520
Quality Mop & Brush Manufacturers
Needham, MA . . . 617-884-2999
Quickie Manufacturing Corp.
Cinnaminson, NJ . . . 856-829-7900
R&C Pro Brands
Wayne, NJ . . . 973-633-7374
R.R. Street & Co., Inc.
Naperville, IL . . . 630-416-4244
Ready White
Holyoke, MA . . . 413-534-4864
Reeno Detergent & Soap Company
Saint Louis, MO . . . 314-429-6078
Reit-Price ManufacturingCompany
Union City, IN . . . 800-521-5343
Rem Ohio
Cincinnati, OH . . . 513-878-8188
Remco Products Corporation
Zionsville, IN . . . 800-585-8619
Rex Chemical Corporation
Miami, FL . . . 305-634-2471
RJS Carter Company
New Brighton, MN . . . 651-636-8818
Robby Vapor Systems
Sunrise, FL . . . 800-888-8711
Rochester Midland Corporation
Rochester, NY . . . 800-535-5053
Rochester Midland Corporation
Rochester, NY . . . 800-836-1627
Rockford Chemical Company
Belvidere, IL . . . 815-544-3476
Rockline Industries
Sheboygan, WI . . . 800-558-7790
Ronell Industries
Roselle, NJ . . . 908-245-5255
Rooto Corporation
Howell, MI . . . 517-546-8330
Roxide International
Larchmont, NY . . . 800-431-5500
Royal Broom & Mop Factory
Harahan, LA . . . 800-537-6925
Royal Chemical of Carolina
Albemarle, NC . . . 800-650-6346
Royal Paper Products
Coatesville, PA . . . 800-666-6655
Royal Welding & Fabricating
Fullerton, CA . . . 714-680-6669
Royce-Rolls Ringer Company
Grand Rapids, MI . . . 800-253-9638
Rubbermaid Commercial Products
Cleveland, TN . . . 423-476-4544
Rubbermaid Commercial Products
Winchester, VA . . . 800-336-9880
S&M Manufacturing Company
Cisco, TX . . . 800-772-8532
S&S Soap Company
Bronx, NY . . . 718-585-2900
San Joaquin Supply Company
Stockton, CA . . . 209-952-0680
SAN-AIRE Industries
Fort Worth, TX . . . 800-757-1912
Sangamon Mills
Cohoes, NY . . . 518-237-5321
Sani-Matic
Madison, WI . . . 800-356-3300
Sanitech Corporation
Lorton, VA . . . 800-486-4321
Sanitek Products, Inc
Los Angeles, CA . . . 818-242-1071
Sanolite Corporation
Elizabeth, NJ . . . 800-221-0806
Sasib Beverage & Food North America
Plano, TX . . . 800-558-3814
Saunders Manufacturing Co.
N Kansas City, MO . . . 800-821-2792
Savogran Company
Norwood, MA . . . 800-225-9872
SCA Hygiene Paper
San Ramon, CA . . . 800-992-8675
SCA Tissue
Neenah, WI . . . 866-722-6659
Schlueter Company
Janesville, WI . . . 800-359-1700
Scot Young Research
Saint Joseph, MO . . . 816-232-4100
Scott's Liquid Gold
Denver, CO . . . 800-447-1919
Seatex Ltd
Rosenberg, TX . . . 800-829-3020
Sedalia Janitorial & Paper Supplies
Sedalia, MO . . . 660-826-9899
Selig Chemical Industries
Atlanta, GA . . . 404-876-5511
Seneca Environmental Products
Tiffin, OH . . . 419-447-1282
SerVaas Laboratories
Indianapolis, IN . . . 800-433-5818
Sewell Products
Salem, VA . . . 540-389-5401
Shen Manufacturing Company
W Conshohocken, PA . . . 610-825-2790
Shepard Brothers
La Habra, CA . . . 562-697-1366
Sierra Dawn Products
Graton, CA . . . 707-535-0172
Sioux Corporation
Beresford, SD . . . 888-763-8833
Snee Chemical Company
Harahan, LA . . . 800-489-7633
Solvit
Monona, WI . . . 888-314-1072
Solvox Manufacturing Company
Milwaukee, WI . . . 414-774-5664
Sonicor Instrument Corporation
Deer Park, NY . . . 800-864-5022
Southend Janitorial Supply
Los Angeles, CA . . . 323-754-2842
Spartan Tool
Mendota, IL . . . 800-435-3866
Specialty Equipment Company
Mendota Heights, MN . . . 651-452-7909
Spencer Turbine Company
Windsor, CT . . . 800-232-4321
Spontex
Columbia, TN . . . 800-251-4222
Sprayway
Addison, IL . . . 800-332-9000
Spurrier Chemical Companies
Wichita, KS . . . 800-835-1059
Squar-Buff
Oakland, CA . . . 800-525-6955
ST Restaurant Supplies
Delta, BC . . . 888-448-4244
Stampendous
Anaheim, CA . . . 800-869-0474
Stanford Chemicals
Dallas, TX . . . 972-682-5600
Star Pacific
Union City, CA . . . 800-227-0760
Starkey Chemical ProcessCompany
La Grange, IL . . . 800-323-3040
State Industrial Products
Mayfield Heights, OH . . . 877-747-6986
Stearns Packaging Corporation
Madison, WI . . . 608-246-5150
Stearns Technical Textiles Company
Cincinnati, OH . . . 800-543-7173
Steiner Company
Holland, IL . . . 800-222-4638
Sterling Novelty Products
Northbrook, IL . . . 847-291-0070
Stero Company
Petaluma, CA . . . 800-762-7600
Stewart Laboratories
Golden Valley, MN . . . 800-820-2333
Stone Soap Company
Sylvan Lake, MI . . . 800-952-7627
Stoner
Quarryville, PA . . . 800-227-5538
Strahman Valves
Bethlehem, PA . . . 877-787-2462
Sun Paints & Coatings
Tampa, FL . . . 813-367-4444
Sunbeam Product
Toledo, OH . . . 419-691-1551
Sunpoint Products
Lawrence, MA . . . 978-794-3100
Superior Brush Company
Cleveland, OH . . . 216-941-6987
Superior Distributing
Louisville, KY . . . 800-365-6661
Superior Linen & Work Wear
Kansas City, MO . . . 800-798-7987
Superior Quality Products
Schenectady, NY . . . 800-724-1129
Surco Products
Pittsburgh, PA . . . 800-556-0111
Sure Clean Corporation
Two Rivers, WI . . . 920-793-3838
Surtec, Inc.
Tracy, CA . . . 800-877-6330
Swissh Commercial Equipment
Montreal, QC . . . 888-794-7749
Synthron
Morganton, NC . . . 828-437-8611
T&S Brass & Bronze Works
Travelers Rest, SC . . . 800-476-4103
Tate Western
Goleta, CA . . . 800-903-0200
Techni-Chem Corporation
Boise, ID . . . 800-635-8930
Telechem Corporation
Atlanta, GA . . . 800-637-0495
Tennant Company
Minneapolis, MN . . . 800-553-8033
Texas Refinery Corporation
Fort Worth, TX . . . 817-332-1161

Textile Buff & Wheel Company, Inc.
Charlestown, MA 617-241-8100
Textile Products Company
Anaheim, CA 714-761-0401
Thamesville Metal Products Ltd
Thamesville, ON. 519-692-3963
The Clyde Bergemann Power Group
Baltimore, MD 410-368-6800
Theochem Laboratories
Tampa, FL. 800-237-2591
Therma-Kleen
Plainfield, IL. 800-999-3120
Thermaco
Asheboro, NC 800-633-4204
Time Products
Atlanta, GA. 800-241-6681
Tolco Corporation
Toledo, OH 800-537-4786
Trap Zap Environmental Systems
Wyckoff, NJ 800-282-8727
TRC
Middlefield, OH 440-834-0078
TRITEN Corporation
Houston, TX 832-214-5000
Tropical Soap Company
Carrollton, TX. 800-527-2368
Tucel Industries, Inc.
Forestdale, VT 800-558-8235
Tuchenhagen
Columbia, MD 410-910-6000
Tucker Manufacturing Company
Cedar Rapids, IA. 800-553-8131
Turtle Wax
Westmont, IL. 905-470-6665
TuWay American Group
Rockford, OH 800-537-3750
Twi-Laq Industries
Bronx, NY. 800-950-7627
U.B. Klem Furniture Company
Saint Anthony, IN 800-264-1995
Ulmer Pharmacal Company
Park Rapids, MN. 218-732-2656
United Floor Machine Company
Chicago, IL 800-288-0848
United Textile Distribution
Garner, NC 800-262-7624
Universal Stainless
Aurora, CO 800-223-8332
Universal Stainless
Titusville, PA 800-295-1909
Upright
St Louis, MO. 800-248-7007
Urnex Brands, Inc.
Elmsford, NY 800-222-2826
US Chemical
Watertown, WI 800-558-9566
US Industrial Lubricants
Cincinnati, OH 800-562-5454
Valspar Corporation
Chicago, IL 800-637-7793
Vector Technologies
Milwaukee, WI. 800-832-4010
Venturetech Corporation
Knoxville, TN 800-826-4095
Verax Chemical Company
Bothell, WA. 800-637-7771
Vulcan Materials Company
Birmingham, AL. 205-298-3000
W.M. Barr & Company
Memphis, TN 800-238-2672
Waco Broom & Mop Factory
Waco, TX 800-548-7716
Wal-Vac
Wyoming, MI 616-241-6717
Warren E. Conley Corporation
Carmel, IN. 800-367-7875
Warsaw Chemical Company
Warsaw, IN 800-548-3396
Wave Chemical Company
New York, NY 973-243-5852
Waxine
Bow, NH 603-228-8241
WCS Corporation
Hayward, CA 510-782-8727
Wen-Don Corporation
Roanoke, VA. 800-223-1284
West Agro
Kansas City, MO. 816-891-1600
Whisk Products
Wentzville, MO. 800-204-7627
White Mop Wringer Company
Tampa, FL. 800-237-7582
Whitley Manufacturing Company
Midland, NC 704-888-2625
Wilen Professional Cleaning Products
Atlanta, GA. 800-241-7371
Windsor Industries
Englewood, CO. 800-444-7654
Windsor Wax Company
Carolina, RI. 800-243-8929
Winn-Sol Products
Oshkosh, WI 920-231-2031
Wipe-Tex
Bronx, NY. 800-643-9607
Wipeco, Inc.
Hillside, IL 708-544-7247
World Dryer Corporation
Berkeley, IL. 800-323-0701
Wright-Bernet
Hamilton, OH 513-874-1800
Y-Pers
Philadelphia, PA 800-421-0242
Young & Swartz
Buffalo, NY. 800-466-7682
Zealco Industries
Calvert City, KY 800-759-5531
Zephyr Manufacturing
Sedalia, MO 660-827-0352
Zipskin
Dexter, MI. 734-426-5559

Cloths

Chamois

Acme Sponge & Chamois Company
Tarpon Springs, FL 727-937-3222
Blue Feather Product
Ashland, OR 800-472-2487
Clayton L. Hagy & Son
Philadelphia, PA 215-844-6470
Kalle USA
Gurnee, IL. 847-775-0781

Dish

Arden Companies
Southfield, MI. 248-415-8500
Bro-Tex
Saint Paul, MN 800-328-2282
Charles Craft
Laurinburg, NC. 910-844-3521
Letraw Manufacturing Company
Rockford, IL 815-987-9670
Mednik Wiping Materials Company
Saint Louis, MO 800-325-7193
Nu-Tex Styles, Inc.
Somerset, NJ. 732-485-5456
Sangamon Mills
Cohoes, NY. 518-237-5321
Shen Manufacturing Company
W Conshohocken, PA. 610-825-2790
Standard Terry Mills
Souderton, PA. 215-723-8121
Wipe-Tex
Bronx, NY. 800-643-9607

Dusting

Cadie Products Corporation
Paterson, NJ 973-278-8300
CCP Industries, Inc.
Cleveland, OH 800-321-2840
Clayton L. Hagy & Son
Philadelphia, PA 215-844-6470
Lexidyne of Pennsylvania
Pittsburgh, PA. 800-543-2233
Majestic Industries, Inc
Macomb, MI 586-786-9100
Mednik Wiping Materials Company
Saint Louis, MO 800-325-7193
Mill Wiping Rags/The Rag Factory
Bronx, NY. 718-994-7100
Nu-Tex Styles, Inc.
Somerset, NJ. 732-485-5456
Ready White
Holyoke, MA 413-534-4864
Shen Manufacturing Company
W Conshohocken, PA. 610-825-2790
Superior Distributing
Louisville, KY 800-365-6661
TuWay American Group
Rockford, OH 800-537-3750
Wipe-Tex
Bronx, NY. 800-643-9607

Wire

Cleveland Wire Cloth & Manufacturing Company
Cleveland, OH 800-321-3234
F.P. Smith Wire Cloth Company
Northlake, IL. 800-323-6842
Newark Wire Cloth Company
Clifton, NJ. 800-221-0392

Compounds

Dishwashing

American Municipal Chemical Company
West Allis, WI. 800-598-3106
Cal Ben Soap Company
Oakland, CA 800-340-7091
Clarkson Chemical Company
Williamsport, PA. 800-326-9457
D.W. Davies & Company
Racine, WI 800-888-6133
Emulso Corporation
Tonawanda, NY 800-724-7667
Essential Industries
Merton, WI 800-551-9679
Falls Chemical Products
Oconto Falls, WI. 920-846-3561
Fishers Investment
Cincinnati, OH 800-833-5916
J.I. Holcomb Manufacturing
Independence, OH 800-458-3222
Labpride Chemicals
Bronx, NY. 800-467-1255
Magnuson Products
Clifton, NJ. 973-472-9292
Rochester Midland Corporation
Rochester, NY. 800-535-5053
Sanolite Corporation
Elizabeth, NJ. 800-221-0806
Syndett Products
Bolton, CT 860-646-0172
Texas Refinery Corporation
Fort Worth, TX 817-332-1161

Sweeping

American Municipal Chemical Company
West Allis, WI. 800-598-3106
Delta Foremost Chemical Corporation
Memphis, TN 800-238-5150
Floormaster
Chattanooga, TN. 423-867-4525
Game Cock Chemical Company
Sumter, SC 803-773-7391
Grayling Industries
Alpharetta, GA 800-635-1551
Mission Laboratories
Los Angeles, CA. 888-201-8866
Waxine
Bow, NH 603-228-8241
Windsor Wax Company
Carolina, RI. 800-243-8929

Washing

American Municipal Chemical Company
West Allis, WI. 800-598-3106
C&H Chemical
St Paul, MN. 651-227-4343
Candy & Company/Peck's Products Company
Chicago, IL 800-837-9189
Elgene
Hamden, CT 800-922-4623
Essential Industries
Merton, WI 800-551-9679
Fishers Investment
Cincinnati, OH 800-833-5916
Garman Company
Valley Park, MO 800-466-5150
Hibrett Puratex
Pennsauken, NJ. 800-260-5124
Hill Manufacturing Company
Atlanta, GA. 404-522-8364
Hohn Manufacturing Company
Fenton, MO. 800-878-1440
Hy-Ko Enviro-MaintenanceProducts
Salt Lake City, UT 801-973-6099
J.I. Holcomb Manufacturing
Independence, OH 800-458-3222
Labpride Chemicals
Bronx, NY. 800-467-1255
Magnuson Products
Clifton, NJ. 973-472-9292

Ostrem Chemical Co. Ltd
Edmonton, AB 780-440-1911
Pariser Industries
Paterson, NJ 800-370-7627
R&C Pro Brands
Wayne, NJ 973-633-7374
Sanolite Corporation
Elizabeth, NJ 800-221-0806
Sewell Products
Salem, VA 540-389-5401
Solvit
Monona, WI 888-314-1072
Stanford Chemicals
Dallas, TX 972-682-5600
Techni-Chem Corporation
Boise, ID 800-635-8930
Windsor Wax Company
Carolina, RI 800-243-8929

Detergents

Household, Consumer

9-12 Corporation
Caguas, PR 787-747-0405
A&L Laboratories
Minneapolis, MN 800-225-3832
A.L. Wilson Chemical Company
Kearny, NJ 800-526-1188
Abicor Binzel
Frederick, MD 800-542-4867
American Wax Company
Long Island City, NY 888-929-7587
Auto Chlor Systems
Memphis, TN 800-477-3693
Bar Maid Corporation
Pompano Beach, FL 954-960-1468
Bio Industries
Luxemburg, WI 920-845-2355
C.P. Industries
Salt Lake City, UT 800-453-4931
Cal Ben Soap Company
Oakland, CA 800-340-7091
Cantol
Markham, ON 800-387-9773
Chef Revival
Elkhorn, WI 800-248-9826
Chemifax
Santa Fe Springs, CA 800-527-5722
Clarkson Chemical Company
Williamsport, PA 800-326-9457
Clorox Company
Oakland, CA 888-271-7000
Cobitco, Inc
Denver, CO 303-296-8575
Concord Chemical Company
Camden, NJ 800-282-2436
Country Save Corporation
Arlington, WA 360-435-9868
Delta Foremost Chemical Corporation
Memphis, TN 800-238-5150
DeVere Chemical Company
Janesville, WI 800-833-8373
Diablo Products
Fort Dodge, IA 800-548-1385
Diamond Chemical Compan y
East Rutherford, NJ 800-654-7627
Dickler Chemical Labs
Philadelphia, PA 800-426-1127
Downeast Chemical
Westbrook, ME 800-287-2225
Du-Good Chemical Laboratory & Manufacturing Company
Saint Louis, MO 314-773-5007
Essential Industries
Merton, WI 800-551-9679
Falls Chemical Products
Oconto Falls, WI 920-846-3561
Fitzpatrick Brothers
Pleasant Prairie, WI 800-233-8064
Fuller Brush Company
Great Bend, KS 800-522-0499
Goodwin Company
Garden Grove, CA 714-894-0531
Grace-Lee Products
Minneapolis, MN 612-379-2711
Griffin Brothers
Salem, OR 800-456-4743
Hamilton Soap & Oil Products
Paterson, NJ 973-225-1031
Hanco Manufacturing Company
Memphis, TN 800-530-7364
Hohn Manufacturing Company
Fenton, MO 800-878-1440
Holland Chemicals Company
Windsor, ON 519-948-4373
James Austin Company
Mars, PA 724-625-1535
Knapp Manufacturing
Fresno, CA 559-251-8254
L&M Chemicals
Tampa, FL 800-362-3331
Labpride Chemicals
Bronx, NY 800-467-1255
Laundry Aids
Carlstadt, NJ 201-933-3500
Lee Soap Company
Commerce City, CO 800-888-1896
Lubar Chemical
Kansas City, MO 816-471-2560
MGF.com
Atlanta, GA 770-444-9686
Mione Manufacturing Company
Mickleton, NJ 800-257-0497
National-Purity
Brooklyn Center, MN 612-672-0022
New Klix Corporation
South San Francisco, CA 800-522-5544
Nyco Products Company
Countryside, IL 800-752-4754
Ostrem Chemical Co. Ltd
Edmonton, AB 780-440-1911
Portion-Pac Chemical Corp.
Chicago, IL 312-226-0400
Proctor & Gamble Company
Cincinnati, OH 513-983-1100
Reeno Detergent & Soap Company
Saint Louis, MO 314-429-6078
Rem Ohio
Cincinnati, OH 513-878-8188
Rochester Midland Corporation
Rochester, NY 800-535-5053
S&S Soap Company
Bronx, NY 718-585-2900
Sanolite Corporation
Elizabeth, NJ 800-221-0806
Snee Chemical Company
Harahan, LA 800-489-7633
Star Pacific
Union City, CA 800-227-0760
Stearns Packaging Corporation
Madison, WI 608-246-5150
Stone Soap Company
Sylvan Lake, MI 800-952-7627
Sunbeam Product
Toledo, OH 419-691-1551
Sure Clean Corporation
Two Rivers, WI 920-793-3838
Synthron
Morganton, NC 828-437-8611
Telechem Corporation
Atlanta, GA 800-637-0495
Texas Refinery Corporation
Fort Worth, TX 817-332-1161
Theochem Laboratories
Tampa, FL 800-237-2591
Twi-Laq Industries
Bronx, NY 800-950-7627
Ulmer Pharmacal Company
Park Rapids, MN 218-732-2656
US Industrial Lubricants
Cincinnati, OH 800-562-5454
Venturetech Corporation
Knoxville, TN 800-826-4095
Wave Chemical Company
New York, NY 973-243-5852
West Chemical Products
Princeton, NJ 609-921-0501

Industrial

9-12 Corporation
Caguas, PR 787-747-0405
A&L Laboratories
Minneapolis, MN 800-225-3832
Abicor Binzel
Frederick, MD 800-542-4867
Alconox
White Plains, NY 914-948-4040
American Wax Company
Long Island City, NY 888-929-7587
Auto Chlor Systems
Memphis, TN 800-477-3693
Bio Industries
Luxemburg, WI 920-845-2355
Church & Dwight Company
Princeton, NJ 800-833-9532
Clarkson Chemical Company
Williamsport, PA 800-326-9457
Colgate-Palmolive
Morristown, NJ 800-432-8226
Country Save Corporation
Arlington, WA 360-435-9868
Diablo Products
Fort Dodge, IA 800-548-1385
Dial Corporation
Scottsdale, AZ 480-754-3425
Ecolab
St. Paul, MN 651-293-2233
Falls Chemical Products
Oconto Falls, WI 920-846-3561
Fitzpatrick Brothers
Pleasant Prairie, WI 800-233-8064
Hope Chemical Corporation
Pawtucket, RI 401-724-8000
Hydrite Chemical Company
Brookfield, WI 262-792-1450
King of All Manufacturing
Clio, MI 810-564-0139
Knapp Manufacturing
Fresno, CA 559-251-8254
Labpride Chemicals
Bronx, NY 800-467-1255
Lubar Chemical
Kansas City, MO 816-471-2560
Luseaux Laboratories Inc
Gardena, CA 800-266-1555
Mione Manufacturing Company
Mickleton, NJ 800-257-0497
Original Bradford Soap Works
West Warwick, RI 401-821-2141
Pagoda Products
Sinking Spring, PA 610-678-8096
Pariser Industries
Paterson, NJ 800-370-7627
Patterson Laboratories
Detroit, MI 313-843-4500
PM Chemical Company
San Diego, CA 619-296-0191
Reeno Detergent & Soap Company
Saint Louis, MO 314-429-6078
Sanolite Corporation
Elizabeth, NJ 800-221-0806
Seatex Ltd
Rosenberg, TX 800-829-3020
Snee Chemical Company
Harahan, LA 800-489-7633
Spurrier Chemical Companies
Wichita, KS 800-835-1059
Stewart Laboratories
Golden Valley, MN 800-820-2333
US Industrial Lubricants
Cincinnati, OH 800-562-5454
Whisk Products
Wentzville, MO 800-204-7627

Dish Washing Machinery

Acro Dishwashing Service
Kansas City, KS 913-342-4282
Adamation
Commerce, CA 800-225-3075
Ali Group
Winston Salem, NC 800-532-8591
American Dish Service
Edwardsville, KS 800-922-2178
Attias Oven Corporation
Brooklyn, NY 800-928-8427
Blakeslee, Inc.
Addison, IL 630-532-5021
Burns Chemical Systems
Cleveland, OH 724-327-7600
Champion Industries
Winston Salem, NC 800-532-8591
CMA/Dishmachines
Garden Grove, CA 800-854-6417
Colonial Paper Company
Silver Springs, FL 352-622-4171
Convay Systems
Etobicoke, ON 800-811-5511
Custom Diamond International
Laval, QC 800-363-5926
Douglas Machines Corporation
Clearwater, FL 800-331-6870
Hartstone
Zanesville, OH 740-452-9999

Hobart Corporation
Troy, OH 888-446-2278
Insinger Machine Company
Philadelphia, PA 800-344-4802
Jackson MSC
Barbourville, KY 888-800-5672
Knight Equipment Canada
Mississauga, ON 800-854-3764
Knight Equipment International
Lake Forest, CA 800-854-3764
Moyer-Diebel
Winston Salem, NC. 336-661-1992
National Hotpack
Stone Ridge, NY. 800-431-8232
Proctor & Gamble Company
Cincinnati, OH 513-983-1100
Stero Company
Petaluma, CA 800-762-7600
Swissh Commercial Equipment
Montreal, QC 888-794-7749
TNN-Jeros, Inc.
Byron, IL. 815-978-2210
Vanguard Technology
Eugene, OR. 800-624-4809

Dishwasher

Racks

AMCO Corporation
City of Industry, CA 626-855-2550
Blakeslee, Inc.
Addison, IL 630-532-5021
Carlisle Food Service Products
Oklahoma City, OK 800-654-8210
Duke Manufacturing Company
Saint Louis, MO 800-735-3853
Marlin Steel Wire Products
Baltimore, MD 877-762-7546
Metro Corporation
Wilkes Barre, PA. 800-433-2233
Micro Wire Products Inc.
Brockton, MA. 508-584-0200
Straits Steel & Wire Company
Ludington, MI. 231-843-3416
Superior Products Company
Saint Paul, MN 800-328-9800
Traex
Dane, WI. 800-356-8006

Disinfectants & Germicides

Accommodation Mollen
Philadelphia, PA 800-872-6268
ADCO
Albany, GA. 800-821-7556
AFASSCO
Minden, NV 800-441-6774
American Wax Company
Long Island City, NY 888-929-7587
Bio-Cide International
Norman, OK 800-323-1398
Burnishine Products
Gurnee, IL. 800-818-8275
Candy & Company/Peck's Products Company
Chicago, IL 800-837-9189
Carroll Company
Garland, TX 800-527-5722
Central Solutions
Kansas City, KS 800-255-0662
Chemifax
Santa Fe Springs, CA 800-527-5722
Church & Dwight Company
Princeton, NJ. 800-833-9532
Claire Manufacturing Company
Addison, IL. 800-252-4731
Cobitco, Inc
Denver, CO 303-296-8575
Colgate-Palmolive
Morristown, NJ 800-432-8226
Concord Chemical Company
Camden, NJ. 800-282-2436
Crown Chemical Products
Mississauga, ON. 905-564-0904
Damon Industries
Alliance, OH. 800-362-9850
DeVere Chemical Company
Janesville, WI 800-833-8373
Diamond Chemical Compan y
East Rutherford, NJ 800-654-7627
Dickler Chemical Labs
Philadelphia, PA 800-426-1127
ECOLAB
St Paul, MN. 800-352-5326
Emulso Corporation
Tonawanda, NY 800-724-7667
GERM-O-RAY
Stone Mountain, GA. 800-966-8480
Griffin Brothers
Salem, OR. 800-456-4743
Hanco Manufacturing Company
Memphis, TN 800-530-7364
Hilex Company
Eagan, MN 651-454-1160
Hill Manufacturing Company
Atlanta, GA. 404-522-8364
Hy-Ko Enviro-MaintenanceProducts
Salt Lake City, UT 801-973-6099
Hydrite Chemical Company
Brookfield, WI 262-792-1450
Insect-O-Cutor
Stone Mountain, GA. 800-988-5359
ITW Dymon
Olathe, KS. 800-443-9536
J.I. Holcomb Manufacturing
Independence, OH 800-458-3222
James Austin Company
Mars, PA 724-625-1535
Johnson Diversey
Sturtevant, WI. 262-631-4001
Knapp Manufacturing
Fresno, CA 559-251-8254
L&M Chemicals
Tampa, FL. 800-362-3331
Labpride Chemicals
Bronx, NY. 800-467-1255
Larose & Fils Ltêe
Laval, QC 877-382-7001
Lubar Chemical
Kansas City, MO. 816-471-2560
Marko
Spartanburg, SC 866-466-2726
MGF.com
Atlanta, GA. 770-444-9686
Mission Laboratories
Los Angeles, CA. 888-201-8866
Nuance Solutions
Chicago, IL 800-621-8553
Paley-Lloyd-Donohue
Elizabeth, NJ. 908-352-5835
Pioneer Chemical Company
Gardena, CA 310-366-7393
Proctor & Gamble Company
Cincinnati, OH 513-983-1100
ProRestore Products
Pittsburgh, PA. 800-332-6037
Puritan/Churchill Chemical Company
Marietta, GA. 800-275-8914
R&C Pro Brands
Wayne, NJ. 973-633-7374
Rochester Midland Corporation
Rochester, NY. 800-535-5053
Rochester Midland Corporation
Rochester, NY. 800-836-1627
San Joaquin Supply Company
Stockton, CA. 209-952-0680
Sanco Products Company
Greenville, OH 937-548-2225
Sanolite Corporation
Elizabeth, NJ. 800-221-0806
Seatex Ltd
Rosenberg, TX 800-829-3020
Selig Chemical Industries
Atlanta, GA. 404-876-5511
State Industrial Products
Mayfield Heights, OH 877-747-6986
Sunpoint Products
Lawrence, MA 978-794-3100
Syndett Products
Bolton, CT 860-646-0172
Ulmer Pharmacal Company
Park Rapids, MN. 218-732-2656
Verax Chemical Company
Bothell, WA. 800-637-7771
Vulcan Materials Company
Birmingham, AL. 205-298-3000
West Chemical Products
Princeton, NJ. 609-921-0501
Whisk Products
Wentzville, MO. 800-204-7627

Dispensers

Cleaning Compound

Auto Chlor Systems
Memphis, TN 800-477-3693
Carbon Clean Products
Kingston, PA. 570-288-1155
CRC Industries, Inc.
Warminster, PA 800-556-5074
Eurodispenser
Decatur, IL 217-864-4061
Go-Jo Industries
Akron, OH. 800-321-9647
Graco
Minneapolis, MN 877-844-7226
Hygiene-Technik
Beamsville, ON. 905-563-4987
Knight Equipment Canada
Mississauga, ON. 800-854-3764
Knight Equipment International
Lake Forest, CA 800-854-3764
Labpride Chemicals
Bronx, NY. 800-467-1255
Steiner Company
Chicago, IL 800-222-4638
Tate Western
Goleta, CA 800-903-0200

Soap

Best Sanitizers
Penn Valley, CA 888-225-3267
Deb Canada
Waterford, ON. 888-332-7627
Dema Engineering Company
Saint Louis, MO 800-325-3362
Dreumex USA
York, PA 800-233-9382
Eurodispenser
Decatur, IL 217-864-4061
Go-Jo Industries
Akron, OH. 800-321-9647
Hygiene-Technik
Beamsville, ON. 905-563-4987
Micro-Brush Pro Soap
Rockwall, TX 800-776-7627
Milburn Company
Detroit, MI 313-259-3410
Parachem Corporation
Des Moines, IA. 515-280-9445
Steiner Company
Holland, IL 800-222-4638
Superior Products Company
Saint Paul, MN 800-328-9800
Tate Western
Goleta, CA 800-903-0200
Tolco Corporation
Toledo, OH 800-537-4786
Whisk Products
Wentzville, MO. 800-204-7627
World Dryer Corporation
Berkeley, IL. 800-323-0701

Dryer Systems

A&B Process Systems
Stratford, WI 888-258-2789
A&J Mixing International
Oakville, ON. 800-668-3470
AmeriVap Systems Inc
Dawsonville, GA 800-763-7687
Ametek Technical & Industrial Products
Kent, OH. 215-256-6601
Applied Chemical Technology
Florence, AL. 800-228-3217
Bepex International,LLC
Minneapolis, MN 800-607-2470
BFM Equipment Sales
Fall River, WI 920-484-3341
Brothers Metal Products
Santa Ana, CA 714-972-3008
Buffalo Technologies Corporation
Buffalo, NY. 800-332-2419
Carman Industries
Jeffersonville, IN 800-456-7560
Casso-Solar Corporation
Pomona, NY 800-988-4455
Chief Industries
Kearney, NE 800-359-8833
Convay Systems
Etobicoke, ON. 800-811-5511

Crown Iron Works Company
Minneapolis, MN 888-703-7500
Damas Corporation
Trenton, NJ 609-695-9121
Davenport Machine
Rock Island, IL 309-786-1500
Davron Technologies
Chattanooga, TN 423-870-1888
Dito Dean Food Prep
Rocklin, CA 800-331-7958
Evaporator Dryer Technologies Inc
Hammond, WI. 715-796-2313
Fitzpatrick Company
Elmhurst, IL 630-530-3333
Flodin
Moses Lake, WA. 509-766-2996
Fluid Energy Processing and Equipment Company
Hatfield, PA. 215-368-2510
Gardner Denver Inc.
Toronto, ON 416-763-4681
Gaston County Dyeing Machine Company
Stanley, NC 704-822-5000
Glatt Air Techniques
Ramsey, NJ. 201-825-8700
Grain Machinery Manufacturing Corporation
Miami, FL. 305-620-2525
Hankison International
Canonsburg, PA. 724-746-1100
Hoyt Corporation
Westport, MA 508-636-8811
Insinger Machine Company
Philadelphia, PA. 800-344-4802
International Reserve Equipment Corporation
Clarendon Hills, IL 708-531-0680
Kinergy Corporation
Louisville, KY 502-366-5685
Laundrylux
Inwood, NY. 800-645-2205
LIST
Acton, MA 978-635-9521
Littleford Day
Florence, KY. 800-365-8555
Louisville Dryer Company
Louisville, KY 800-735-3613
M-E-C Company
Neodesha, KS 620-325-2673
Midbrook
Jackson, MI. 800-966-9274
National Drying Machinery Company
Philadelphia, PA 215-464-6070
National Hotpack
Stone Ridge, NY. 800-431-8232
NECO
Omaha, NE 402-453-6912
Nemeth Engineering Associates
Crestwood, KY. 502-241-1502
Niro
Hudson, WI. 715-386-9371
Paget Equipment Company
Marshfield, WI 715-384-3158
Patterson Industries
Scarborough, ON 800-336-1110
Patterson-Kelley Hars Company
East Stroudsburg, PA 570-421-7500
Paul O. Abbe
Bensenville, IL 630-350-2200
Paxton Products
Cincinnati, OH 800-441-7475
Procedyne Corporation
New Brunswick, NJ 732-249-8347
Professional EngineeringAssociation
Louisville, KY 502-429-0432
Radio Frequency Company
Millis, MA 508-376-9555
SAN-AIRE Industries
Fort Worth, TX 800-757-1912
Shanzer Grain Dryer
Sioux Falls, SD. 800-843-9887
Spencer Turbine Company
Windsor, CT 800-232-4321
Spray Drying Systems
Eldersberg, MD. 410-549-8090
Steri Technologies
Bohemia, NY 800-253-7140
Tuthill Vacuum & Blower Systems
Springfield, MO 800-825-6937
United McGill Corporation
Groveport, OH 614-829-1200
Vector Corporation
Marion, IA. 319-377-8263
Vortron Smokehouse/Ovens
Iron Ridge, WI 800-874-1949
Wittemann Company
Palm Coast, FL 386-445-4200
Wolverine Proctor & Schwartz
Lexington, NC 336-248-5181
World Dryer Corporation
Berkeley, IL. 800-323-0701
Zeeco
Broken Arrow, OK 918-258-8551

Dust Collectors

Chicago Conveyor Corporation
Addison, IL. 630-543-6300
Paget Equipment Company
Marshfield, WI 715-384-3158
Rupp Industries
Burnsville, MN. 800-836-7432
Spencer Turbine Company
Windsor, CT 800-232-4321

Dust Pans

Carlisle Food Service Products
Oklahoma City, OK 800-654-8210
Ex-Cell Kaiser
Franklin Park, IL. 847-451-0451
J.V. Reed & Company
Louisville, KY 877-258-7333
Superior Products Company
Saint Paul, MN 800-328-9800

Floor Cleaning Machinery

Polishing, Refinishing, Sanding & Scrubbing

Clarke
Plymouth, MN. 800-253-0367
Clean Freak
Appleton, WI 888-722-5508
Dynamic Coatings Inc
Fresno, CA 559-225-4605
Larose & Fils Ltêe
Laval, QC. 877-382-7001
Mercury Floor Machines
Englewood, NJ 888-568-4606
Microtron Abrasives
Pineville, NC. 800-476-7237
Squar-Buff
Oakland, CA 800-525-6955
Surtec, Inc.
Tracy, CA 800-877-6330
United Floor Machine Company
Chicago, IL. 800-288-0848
Windsor Industries
Englewood, CO. 800-444-7654

Garbage Bags

All American Poly Corporation
Piscataway, NJ 800-526-3551
AR-BEE Transparent
Elk Grove Vlg, IL. 800-642-2247
Brown Paper Goods Company
Waukegan, IL 847-688-1451
Carlisle Plastics
Minneapolis, MN 952-884-1309
Cuutom Poly Packaging
Fort Wayne, IN 800-548-6603
Dashco
Gloucester, ON 613-834-6825
Development Workshop
Idaho Falls, ID 800-657-5597
East Coast Group New York
Springfield Gardens, NY 718-527-8464
Exopack
Tomah, WI 608-372-2153
Fortune Plastics
Glendale, AZ. 800-243-0306
GP Plastics Corporation
Medley, FL 305-888-3555
Himolene
Carrollton, TX. 800-777-4411
KM International
Kenton, TN. 731-749-8700
Lakeside Manufacturing
Milwaukee, WI. 888-558-8574
Luetzow Industries
South Milwaukee, WI. 800-558-6055
Marshall Plastic Film
Martin, MI. 269-672-5511
Nosaj Disposables
Paterson, NJ 800-631-3809
Package Containers
Canby, OR. 800-266-5806
Pactiv LLC
Lake Forest, IL 888-828-2850
Pan Pacific Plastics Manufacturing
Hayward, CA 888-475-6888
Paradise Plastics
Brooklyn, NY
Primepak Company
Teaneck, NJ. 201-836-5060
S&O Corporation
Gallaway, TN 800-624-7858
Schroeder Sewing Technologies
San Marcos, CA 760-591-9733
Servin Company
New Baltimore, MI. 800-824-0962
Star Poly Bag, Inc.
Brooklyn, NY 718-384-3130
Tree Saver
Englewood, CO. 800-676-7741
Valley Packaging Supply Company, Inc.
Green Bay, WI. 920-336-9012
Wisconsin Converting of Green Bay
Green Bay, WI. 800-544-1935

Garbage Compactors

Chicago Trashpacker Corporation
Marengo, IL 800-635-5745
Compactors
Hilton Head Island, SC. 800-423-4003
Consolidated Baling Machine Company
Jacksonville, FL 800-231-9286
Dempster Systems
Toccoa, GA 706-886-2327
Enterprise Company
Santa Ana, CA 714-835-0541
Galbreath LLC
Winamac, IN. 574-946-6631
Incinerator International
Houston, TX 713-227-1466
Logemann Brothers Company
Milwaukee, WI 414-445-2700
Marathon Equipment Company
Vernon, AL 800-633-8974
Maren Engineering Corporation
South Holland, IL 800-875-1038
Multi-Pak Corporation
Hackensack, NJ. 201-342-7474
Orwak
Minneapolis, MN 800-747-0449
PAC Equipment Company
Garfield, NJ. 973-478-1008
PTR Baler and Compactor Company
Philadelphia, PA 800-523-3654
Robar International
Milwaukee, WI 800-279-7750
Schleicher & Company of America
Sanford, NC 800-775-7570
Schloss Engineered Equipment
Aurora, CO 303-695-4500
SP Industries
Hopkins, MI 800-592-5959
Universal Handling Equipment
Hamilton, ON 877-843-1122
Waste Away Systems
Newark, OH 800-223-4741
Wastequip
Charlotte, NC 877-468-9278
Wayne Engineering Corporation
Cedar Falls, IA 319-266-1721

Garbage Control Units & Systems

Chicago Trashpacker Corporation
Marengo, IL 800-635-5745
Compactors
Hilton Head Island, SC. 800-423-4003
Consolidated Baling Machine Company
Jacksonville, FL 800-231-9286
Convay Systems
Etobicoke, ON. 800-811-5511
FabWright, Inc
Garden Grove, CA 800-854-6464
Harmony Enterprises
Harmony, MN. 800-658-2320
JWC Environmental
Costa Mesa, CA 800-331-2277
Lodal
Kingsford, MI 800-435-3500

Maren Engineering Corporation
South Holland, IL 800-875-1038
Mell & Company
Niles, IL 800-262-6355
Multi-Pak Corporation
Hackensack, NJ. 201-342-7474
Our Name is Mud
New York, NY 877-683-7867
PAC Equipment Company
Garfield, NJ. 973-478-1008
PTR Baler and Compactor Company
Philadelphia, PA 800-523-3654
Robar International
Milwaukee, WI 800-279-7750
Tema Systems
Cincinnati, OH 513-489-7811
U.B. Klem Furniture Company
Saint Anthony, IN 800-264-1995
Universal Handling Equipment
Hamilton, ON 877-843-1122
Wastequip
Charlotte, NC 877-468-9278
Wayne Engineering Corporation
Cedar Falls, IA 319-266-1721

Garbage Disposal Units

Anaheim Manufacturing Company
Anaheim, CA 800-767-6293
Anova
St Louis, MO. 800-231-1327
Blower Application Company
Germantown, WI. 800-959-0880
Consolidated Baling Machine Company
Jacksonville, FL 800-231-9286
Convay Systems
Etobicoke, ON. 800-811-5511
Dempster Systems
Toccoa, GA 706-886-2327
Dover Parkersburg
Follansbee, WV
Dynabilt Products
Readville, MA. 800-443-1008
FabWright, Inc
Garden Grove, CA 800-854-6464
General Electric Company
Fairfield, CT 203-373-2211
Harmony Enterprises
Harmony, MN 800-658-2320
In-Sink-Erator
Racine, WI 800-558-5700
Insinger Machine Company
Philadelphia, PA 800-344-4802
Ken Coat
Bardstown, KY 888-536-2628
Larose & Fils Ltêe
Laval, QC 877-382-7001
Lewis Steel Works
Wrens, GA. 800-521-5239
Maren Engineering Corporation
South Holland, IL 800-875-1038
Old Dominion Wood Products
Lynchburg, VA 800-245-6382
PAC Equipment Company
Garfield, NJ. 973-478-1008
Pack-A-Drum
Satellite Beach, FL 800-694-6163
Robar International
Milwaukee, WI 800-279-7750
Salvajor Company
Kansas City, MO. 800-821-3136
Tema Systems
Cincinnati, OH 513-489-7811
U.B. Klem Furniture Company
Saint Anthony, IN 800-264-1995
Universal Handling Equipment
Hamilton, ON 877-843-1122
Wastequip
Charlotte, NC 877-468-9278
White Mop Wringer Company
Tampa, FL. 800-237-7582

General

9-12 Corporation
Caguas, PR 787-747-0405
A&B Process Systems
Stratford, WI 888-258-2789
A.K. Robins
Baltimore, MD 800-486-9656
Activon Products
Beaver Dam, WI 800-841-0410
Air-Scent International
Pittsburgh, PA 800-247-0770
Alconox
White Plains, NY 914-948-4040
All American Containers
Medley, FL 305-887-0797
Alumin-Nu Corporation
Lyndhurst, OH 800-899-7097
Ameri-Khem
Port Orange, FL 800-224-9950
AmeriVap Systems Inc
Dawsonville, GA 800-763-7687
Ampco Pumps Company
Glendale, WI. 800-737-8671
Andco Environmental Processes
Amherst, NY. 716-691-2100
APEX
Neodesha, KS 800-633-9576
Aquafine Corporation
Valencia, CA. 800-423-3015
Aquionics
Erlanger, KY. 800-925-0440
ARCHON Industries
Suffern, NY. 800-554-1394
Atlantic Ultraviolet Corporation
Hauppauge, NY 866-958-9085
ATOFINA Chemicals
Philadelphia, PA 800-225-7788
Bake Star
Somerset, WI. 763-427-7611
Bar Maid Corporation
Pompano Beach, FL 954-960-1468
Bennett Manufacturing Company
Alden, NY. 800-345-2142
Bio Zapp Laboratorie Inc
San Antonio, TX. 210-805-9199
Bio-Cide International
Norman, OK 800-323-1398
Birko Corporation
Henderson, CO 800-525-0476
Boston Chemical Industries
Randolph, MA 800-255-8651
C&R Refrigation Inc,
Center, TX. 800-438-6182
Cadie Products Corporation
Paterson, NJ 973-278-8300
Candy & Company/Peck's Products Company
Chicago, IL 800-837-9189
Carroll Company
Garland, TX 800-527-5722
Cashco
Ellsworth, KS 785-472-4461
Century Chemical Corporation
Elkhart, IN. 800-348-3505
Cesco Magnetics
Santa Rosa, CA. 877-624-8727
Champion Chemical Co.
Whittier, CA 800-621-7868
Chore-Boy Corporation
Centerville, IN 765-855-5434
Clean Water Systems International
Klamath Falls, OR 866-273-9993
Coburn Company
Whitewater, WI. 800-776-7042
Cold Jet
Loveland, OH 800-337-9423
Colgate-Palmolive
Morristown, NJ. 800-432-8226
Compliance Control
Hyattsville, MD 800-810-4000
Control Beverage
Adelanto, CA 330-549-5376
Cosgrove Enterprises
Miami Lakes, FL. 800-888-3396
Crown Chemical Products
Mississauga, ON. 905-564-0904
Damon Industries
Alliance, OH. 800-362-9850
Damrow Company
Fond Du Lac, WI 800-236-1501
DH/Sureflow
Portland, OR 800-654-2548
Diamond Wipes International
Chino, CA 800-454-1077
Dipwell Company
Northampton, MA. 413-587-4673
Discovery Chemical
Marietta, GA. 800-973-9881
DL Enterprises
Etters, PA 717-938-1292
Donaldson Company
Minneapolis, MN 800-767-0702
Dorden & Company
Detroit, MI 313-834-7910
DR Technology
Freehold, NJ 732-780-4664
Dresser Instruments
Stratford, CT 800-328-8258
DriAll
Attica, IN. 765-295-2255
Ecolab
St. Paul, MN 651-293-2233
Ecolo Odor Control Systems Worldwide
North York, ON. 800-667-6355
Electro-Steam Generator Corporation
Rancocas, NJ. 866-617-0764
Electrol Specialties Company
South Beloit, IL 815-389-2291
Elgene
Hamden, CT 800-922-4623
Encore Paper Company
South Glens Falls, NY 800-362-6735
Essential Industries
Merton, WI 800-551-9679
Faciltec Corporation
Elgin, IL 800-284-8273
Falls Chemical Products
Oconto Falls, WI. 920-846-3561
Fluid Transfer
Philipsburg, PA 814-342-0902
FX-Lab Company
Union, NJ 908-810-1212
Gamajet Cleaning Systems
Exton, PA 800-289-5387
Geerpres
Muskegon, MI. 231-773-3211
Graco
Minneapolis, MN 877-844-7226
GraLab Corporation
Centerville, OH. 800-876-8353
Great Western Chemical Company
Portland, OR 800-547-1400
Haviland Products Company
Grand Rapids, MI 800-456-1134
Hill Brush, Inc.
Baltimore, MD 800-998-1515
Hoge Brush Company
New Knoxville, OH 800-494-4643
Hubbell Electric Heater Company
Stratford, CT 800-647-3165
Hydrite Chemical Company
Brookfield, WI 262-792-1450
Insect-O-Cutor
Stone Mountain, GA. 800-988-5359
InterBio
The Woodlands, TX 888-876-2844
ITW Dymon
Olathe, KS. 800-443-9536
James Varley & Sons
Saint Louis, MO 800-325-3303
Joneca Corporation
Anaheim, CA 714-993-5997
Justman Brush Company
Omaha, NE 800-800-6940
KES Science & Technology, Inc.
Kennesaw, GA 800-627-4913
Kimberly-Clark Corporation
Neenah, WI 888-525-8388
Knapp Manufacturing
Fresno, CA 559-251-8254
Labpride Chemicals
Bronx, NY. 800-467-1255
Lake Process Systems
Lake Barrington, IL 800-331-9260
Laundry Aids
Carlstadt, NJ 201-933-3500
Lechler
St Charles, IL 800-777-2926
Little Giant Pump Company
Oklahoma City, OK. 405-947-2511
Luseaux Laboratories Inc
Gardena, CA 800-266-1555
Metcraft
Grandview, MO. 800-444-9624
Midbrook
Jackson, MI. 800-966-9274
Middleby Worldwide
Elgin, IL 847-468-6068
Mil-Du-Gas Company/Star Brite
Fort Lauderdale, FL 800-327-8583
Milsek Furniture Polish Inc.
North Lima, OH 330-542-2700
Mission Laboratories
Los Angeles, CA. 888-201-8866

Moly-XL Company
Westville, NJ....856-848-2880
Navy Brand ManufacturingCompany
St Louis, MO....800-325-3312
NETZSCH
Exton, PA....610-363-8010
Northwind
Alpena, AR....870-437-2585
Nuance Solutions
Chicago, IL....800-621-8553
Oakite Products
New Providence, NJ....800-526-4473
Omni Controls
Tampa, FL....800-783-6664
Orwak
Minneapolis, MN....800-747-0449
PAC Equipment Company
Garfield, NJ....973-478-1008
Parachem Corporation
Des Moines, IA....515-280-9445
Paragon Group USA
St Petersburg, FL....800-835-6962
Paramount Packaging Corp.
Melville, NY....516-333-8100
Pariser Industries
Paterson, NJ....800-370-7627
Paxton Corporation
Bristol, RI
Pioneer Chemical Company
Gardena, CA....310-366-7393
Pioneer Manufacturing Company
Cleveland, OH....800-877-1500
Portion-Pac Chemical Corp.
Chicago, IL....312-226-0400
Potlatch Corporation
Spokane, WA....509-835-1500
ProRestore Products
Pittsburgh, PA....800-332-6037
Purdy Products Company
Wauconda, IL....800-726-4849
Purolator Products Company
Greensboro, NC....800-852-4449
PVI Industries
Fort Worth, TX....800-784-8326
QuikWater, Inc.
Sand Springs, OK....918-241-8880
Radiation Processing Division
Parsippany, NJ....800-442-1969
Rea UltraVapor
Ancaster, ON....800-323-3865
Rochester Midland Corporation
Rochester, NY....800-535-5053
Rochester Midland Corporation
Rochester, NY....800-836-1627
Ronell Industries
Roselle, NJ....908-245-5255
Royal Paper Products
Coatesville, PA....800-666-6655
Royce-Rolls Ringer Company
Grand Rapids, MI....800-253-9638
Ryter Corporation
Saint James, MN....800-643-2184
Sanitech Corporation
Lorton, VA....800-486-4321
Sanitor Manufacturing Company
Portage, MI....800-379-5314
Sanolite Corporation
Elizabeth, NJ....800-221-0806
SCA Tissue
Neenah, WI....866-722-6659
Sedalia Janitorial & Paper Supplies
Sedalia, MO....660-826-9899
Selig Chemical Industries
Atlanta, GA....404-876-5511
Seneca Environmental Products
Tiffin, OH....419-447-1282
Siemens Water Technologies Corp.
Warrendale, PA....866-926-8420
Sigma Engineering Corporation
White Plains, NY....914-682-1820
Snee Chemical Company
Harahan, LA....800-489-7633
Southend Janitorial Supply
Los Angeles, CA....323-754-2842
Spartan Tool
Mendota, IL....800-435-3866
Spurrier Chemical Companies
Wichita, KS....800-835-1059
Sterling Novelty Products
Northbrook, IL....847-291-0070
T&S Brass & Bronze Works
Travelers Rest, SC....800-476-4103
Telechem Corporation
Atlanta, GA....800-637-0495
Tennant Company
Minneapolis, MN....800-553-8033
Thermaco
Asheboro, NC....800-633-4204
TRITEN Corporation
Houston, TX....832-214-5000
Tuchenhagen
Columbia, MD....410-910-6000
Tucker Manufacturing Company
Cedar Rapids, IA....800-553-8131
UniFirst Corporation
Wilmington, MA....800-455-7654
United Electric ControlsCompany
Watertown, MA....617-926-1000
United Floor Machine Company
Chicago, IL....800-288-0848
Upright
St Louis, MO....800-248-7007
US Industrial Lubricants
Cincinnati, OH....800-562-5454
Waco Broom & Mop Factory
Waco, TX....800-548-7716
Warren E. Conley Corporation
Carmel, IN....800-367-7875
Warsaw Chemical Company
Warsaw, IN....800-548-3396
Waste Away Systems
Newark, OH....800-223-4741
Water Sciences Services ,Inc.
Jackson, TN....973-584-4131
Water System Group
Santa Clarita, CA....800-350-9283
Wen-Don Corporation
Roanoke, VA....800-223-1284
West Chemical Products
Princeton, NJ....609-921-0501
Zipskin
Dexter, MI....734-426-5559

Holders

Broom

Geerpres
Muskegon, MI....231-773-3211

Incinerators

Garbage & Waste

Andersen 2000
Peachtree City, GA....800-241-5424
Chesmont Engineering Company
Exton, PA....610-594-9200
DriAll
Attica, IN....765-295-2255
Enercon Systems
Elyria, OH....440-323-7080
Incinerator International
Houston, TX....713-227-1466
Incinerator Specialty Company
Houston, TX....713-681-4207
Industronics Service Company
South Windsor, CT....800-878-1551
Jarvis-Cutter Company
Boston, MA....617-567-7532
Outotec
Jessup, ID....301-543-1200
Process Heating Corporation
Shrewsbury, MA....508-842-5200
Therm Tec, Inc
Tualatin, OR....800-292-9163
Zeeco
Broken Arrow, OK....918-258-8551

Insecticides & Insect Control Systems

Accommodation Mollen
Philadelphia, PA....800-872-6268
Actron
Tarzana, CA....800-866-8887
Air-Scent International
Pittsburgh, PA....800-247-0770
Airosol Company
Neodesha, KS....800-633-9576
All Weather Energy Systems
Plymouth, MI....888-636-8324
Arrow Magnolia International, Inc.
Dallas, TX....800-527-2101
Atlas Equipment Company
Kansas City, MO....800-842-9188
Bacon Products Corporation
Chattanooga, TN....800-251-6238
Bell Laboratories
Madison, WI....608-241-0202
Berner International Corporation
New Castle, PA....800-245-4455
Cantol
Markham, ON....800-387-9773
Cardinal Professional Products
Woodland, CA....800-548-2223
Claire Manufacturing Company
Addison, IL....800-252-4731
Commercial Dehydrator Systems Inc
Eugene, OR....800-369-4283
Contech
Grand Rapids, MI....800-767-8658
Cool Curtain/CCI Industries
Costa Mesa, CA....800-854-5719
Copper Brite
Santa Barbara, CA....805-565-1566
Delta Foremost Chemical Corporation
Memphis, TN....800-238-5150
Discovery Chemical
Marietta, GA....800-973-9881
ECOLAB
St Paul, MN....800-733-8705
Entech Systems Corporation
Kenner, LA....800-783-6561
Envirolights Manufacturing
Concord, ON....905-738-0357
Gardner Manufacturing Company
Horicon, WI....800-242-5513
Gilbert Industries, Inc
Jonesboro, AR....800-643-0400
Gilbert Insect Light Traps
Jonesboro, AR....800-643-0400
Grant Laboratories
San Leandro, CA....510-483-6070
Hanco Manufacturing Company
Memphis, TN....800-530-7364
Insect-O-Cutor
Stone Mountain, GA....800-988-5359
Insects
Westfield, IN....800-992-1991
J.I. Holcomb Manufacturing
Independence, OH....800-458-3222
Kincaid Enterprises
Nitro, WV....800-951-3377
L ChemCo Distribution
Louisville, KY....800-292-1977
Mars Air Systems
Gardena, CA....800-421-1266
Matson, LLC
North Bend, WA....800-308-3723
McLaughlin Gormley King Company
Golden Valley, MN....800-645-6466
Nozzle Nolen
Palm Springs, FL....561-964-6200
P.F. Harris Manufacturing Company
Alpharetta, GA....800-637-0317
Paraclipse
Columbus, NE....800-854-6379
Pioneer Manufacturing Company
Cleveland, OH....800-877-1500
Prentiss
Alpharetta, GA....770-552-8072
Research Products Company
Salina, KS....785-825-2181
Rochester Midland Corporation
Rochester, NY....800-535-5053
Rochester Midland Corporation
Rochester, NY....800-836-1627
Roxide International
Larchmont, NY....800-431-5500
Rupp Industries
Burnsville, MN....800-836-7432
Safety Fumigant Company
Hingham, MA....800-244-1199
Sanco Products Company
Greenville, OH....937-548-2225
Selig Chemical Industries
Atlanta, GA....404-876-5511
Solvit
Monona, WI....888-314-1072
Sprayway
Addison, IL....800-332-9000
Surco Products
Pittsburgh, PA....800-556-0111
Terminix Commercial Services
Flushing, NY....866-319-6528

Venturetech Corporation
Knoxville, TN 800-826-4095
Walco-Linck Company
Bellingham, WA 800-338-2329
Warren E. Conley Corporation
Carmel, IN. 800-367-7875
West Chemical Products
Princeton, NJ. 609-921-0501
Western Exterminator Company
Irvine, CA 800-698-2440
Whitmire Micro-Gen Research
St Louis, MO. 800-777-8570

Isopropyl Alcohol

AFASSCO
Minden, NV 800-441-6774
Hydrite Chemical Company
Brookfield, WI 262-792-1450
Union Carbide Corporation
Danbury, CT 800-568-4000

Maintenance

Bunzl Processor Division
Dallas, TX. 800-456-5624

Mop Wringers

Geerpres
Muskegon, MI. 231-773-3211
Royce-Rolls Ringer Company
Grand Rapids, MI 800-253-9638
Superior Products Company
Saint Paul, MN 800-328-9800

Mops

ABCO Products
Miami, FL. 888-694-2226
Amarillo Mop & Broom Company
Amarillo, TX. 800-955-8596
Argo & Company
Spartanburg, SC 864-583-9766
Birmingham Mop Manufacturing Company
Birmingham, AL. 205-942-6101
Bouras Mop ManufacturingCompany
Saint Louis, MO 800-634-9153
Bro-Tex
Saint Paul, MN 800-328-2282
Carlisle Food Service Products
Oklahoma City, OK 800-654-8210
Carnegie Textile Company
Solon, OH 800-633-4136
Carolina Mop Company
Anderson, SC 800-845-9725
Chickasaw Broom Manufacturing
Little Rock, AR. 501-532-0311
Cleveland Mop Manufacturing Company
Cleveland, OH 800-767-9934
Continental Commercial Products
Bridgeton, MO 800-325-1051
Cornelia Broom Company
Cornelia, GA. 800-228-2551
Cosgrove Enterprises
Miami Lakes, FL. 800-888-3396
Costa Broom Works
Tampa, FL. 813-385-1722
Crystal Lake Manufacturing
Autaugaville, AL 800-633-8720
Dover Parkersburg
Follansbee, WV
DQB Industries
Livonia, MI. 800-722-3037
Drackett Professional
Cincinnati, OH 513-583-3900
Fuller Brush Company
Great Bend, KS. 800-522-0499
Furgale Industries Ltd.
Winnipeg, NB 800-665-0506
Golden Star
N Kansas City, MO. 800-821-2792
Greenwood Mop & Broom
Greenwood, SC. 800-635-6849
H. Arnold Wood Turning
Tarrytown, NY 888-314-0088
Harper Brush Works
Fairfield, IA 800-223-7894
Hub City Brush
Petal, MS. 800-278-7452
Industries of the Blind
Greensboro, NC 336-274-1591
J.I. Holcomb Manufacturing
Independence, OH 800-458-3222
Kiefer Brushes, Inc
Franklin, NJ 800-526-2905
Labpride Chemicals
Bronx, NY. 800-467-1255
Layflat Products
Shreveport, LA 800-551-8515
Libman Company
Arcola, IL 877-818-3380
Lighthouse for the Blindin New Orleans
New Orleans, LA 504-899-4501
Little Rock Broom Works
Little Rock, AR. 501-562-0311
LMCO
Rosenberg, TX 281-342-8888
Luco Mop Company
St Louis, MO. 800-522-5826
Majestic Industries, Inc
Macomb, MI. 586-786-9100
Messina Brothers Manufacturing Company
Brooklyn, NY 800-924-6454
Milwaukee Dustless BrushCompany
Delavan, WI 800-632-3220
Newton Broom Company
Newton, IL 618-783-4424
O'Dell Corporation
Ware Shoals, SC 800-342-2843
Perfex Corporation
Poland, NY 800-848-8483
Pioneer Manufacturing Company
Cleveland, OH 800-877-1500
Quaker Chemical Company
Columbia, SC 800-849-9520
Quality Mop & Brush Manufacturers
Needham, MA. 617-884-2999
Quickie Manufacturing Corp.
Cinnaminson, NJ. 856-829-7900
Reit-Price ManufacturingCompany
Union City, IN. 800-521-5343
Royal Broom & Mop Factory
Harahan, LA 800-537-6925
Rubbermaid Commercial Products
Cleveland, TN. 423-476-4544
S&M Manufacturing Company
Cisco, TX 800-772-8532
Saunders Manufacturing Co.
N Kansas City, MO. 800-821-2792
Shen Manufacturing Company
W Conshohocken, PA 610-825-2790
Superior Products Company
Saint Paul, MN 800-328-9800
TuWay American Group
Rockford, OH 800-537-3750
UniFirst Corporation
Wilmington, MA. 800-455-7654
Verax Chemical Company
Bothell, WA. 800-637-7771
Waco Broom & Mop Factory
Waco, TX 800-548-7716
Whitley Manufacturing Company
Midland, NC 704-888-2625

Oils

Cleaning

GEMTEK Products, LLC
Phoenix, AZ 800-331-7022
Labpride Chemicals
Bronx, NY. 800-467-1255
Moly-XL Company
Westville, NJ. 856-848-2880
Oak International
Sturgis, MI 269-651-9790
Stoner
Quarryville, PA 800-227-5538
US Industrial Lubricants
Cincinnati, OH 800-562-5454

Pest Control

Exterminators

Nozzle Nolen
Palm Springs, FL 561-964-6200
Orkin Commercial Services
Anaheim, CA 866-949-6098
Western Exterminator Company
Irvine, CA 800-698-2440

Pest Control Systems & Devices

Actron
Tarzana, CA 800-866-8887
Air-Scent International
Pittsburgh, PA. 800-247-0770
All Weather Energy Systems
Plymouth, MI 888-636-8324
Bacon Products Corporation
Chattanooga, TN. 800-251-6238
Bell Laboratories
Madison, WI 608-241-0202
Cardinal Professional Products
Woodland, CA. 800-548-2223
Claire Manufacturing Company
Addison, IL. 800-252-4731
Contech
Grand Rapids, MI 800-767-8658
Copesan
Menomonee Falls, WI. 800-267-3726
ECOLAB
St Paul, MN. 800-352-5326
ECOLAB
St Paul, MN. 800-733-8705
Envirolights Manufacturing
Concord, ON. 905-738-0357
Gardner Manufacturing Company
Horicon, WI 800-242-5513
Gilbert Insect Light Traps
Jonesboro, AR. 800-643-0400
Grant Laboratories
San Leandro, CA. 510-483-6070
Insect-O-Cutor
Stone Mountain, GA. 800-988-5359
Insects
Westfield, IN. 800-992-1991
Kincaid Enterprises
Nitro, WV. 800-951-3377
L ChemCo Distribution
Louisville, KY 800-292-1977
Matson, LLC
North Bend, WA 800-308-3723
McLaughlin Gormley King Company
Golden Valley, MN 800-645-6466
Motomco
Madison, WI 800-418-9242
Nozzle Nolen
Palm Springs, FL 561-964-6200
P.F. Harris Manufacturing Company
Alpharetta, GA 800-637-0317
Paraclipse
Columbus, NE. 800-854-6379
Pioneer Manufacturing Company
Cleveland, OH 800-877-1500
Prentiss
Alpharetta, GA 770-552-8072
QA Supplies, LLC
Norfolk, VA. 800-472-7205
Rochester Midland Corporation
Rochester, NY. 800-535-5053
Roxide International
Larchmont, NY 800-431-5500
Rupp Industries
Burnsville, MN. 800-836-7432
Selig Chemical Industries
Atlanta, GA. 404-876-5511
Sprayway
Addison, IL. 800-332-9000
Superior Products Company
Saint Paul, MN 800-328-9800
Surco Products
Pittsburgh, PA 800-556-0111
Terminix Commercial Services
Flushing, NY. 866-319-6528
Truly Nolen
Brandon, FL 813-684-6665
Walco-Linck Company
Bellingham, WA 800-338-2329
Warren E. Conley Corporation
Carmel, IN. 800-367-7875
Western Exterminator Company
Irvine, CA 800-698-2440
Whitmire Micro-Gen Research
St Louis, MO. 800-777-8570

Traps

Rat & Mouse

Bell Laboratories
Madison, WI 608-241-0202

Motomco
Madison, WI 800-418-9242
Nozzle Nolen
Palm Springs, FL 561-964-6200
Roxide International
Larchmont, NY 800-431-5500

Plumbing & Drainage Equipment

ABT
Troutman, NC 800-438-6057
Advanced Detection Systems
Milwaukee, WI 414-672-0553
Alkota Cleaning Systems
Alcester, SD 800-255-6823
All Power
Sioux City, IA 712-258-0681
Alumin-Nu Corporation
Lyndhurst, OH 800-899-7097
Ampco Pumps Company
Glendale, WI 800-737-8671
Andco Environmental Processes
Amherst, NY 716-691-2100
Athea Laboratories
Milwaukee, WI 800-743-6417
Atlas Minerals & Chemicals
Mertztown, PA 800-523-8269
Beacon Specialties
New York, NY 800-221-9405
Boyer Corporation
La Grange, IL 800-323-3040
Browne & Company
Markham, ON 905-475-6104
Carts Food Equipment Corporation
Brooklyn, NY 718-788-5540
Continental Industrial Supply
South Pasadena, FL 727-341-1100
Croll-Reynolds Engineering Company
Trumbull, CT 203-371-1983
DH/Sureflow
Portland, OR 800-654-2548
Drehmann Paving & Flooring Company
Pennsauken, NJ 800-523-3800
Enpoco
Richmond, VA 800-338-2581
FX-Lab Company
Union, NJ 908-810-1212
GKL
Dickerson, MD 301-948-5538
Hankison International
Canonsburg, PA 724-746-1100
Hi-Temp
Tuscumbia, AL 800-239-5066
Hydrite Chemical Company
Brookfield, WI 262-792-1450
IMC Teddy Food Service Equipment
Amityville, NY 800-221-5644
InterBio
The Woodlands, TX 888-876-2844
Josam Company
Michigan City, IN 800-365-6726
Kason Central
Columbus, OH 614-885-1992
King of All Manufacturing
Clio, MI 810-564-0139
Kraissl Company
Hackensack, NJ 800-572-4775
Krogh Pump Company
Benicia, CA 800-225-7644
M-One Specialties Inc
Salt Lake City, UT 800-525-9223
Metcraft
Grandview, MO 800-444-9624
MIFAB Manufacturing
Chicago, IL 800-465-2736
NETZSCH
Exton, PA 610-363-8010
Newstamp Lighting Corp.
North Easton, MA 508-238-7071
Northland Process Piping
Isle, MN 320-679-2119
PCI Inc.
Saint Louis, MO 800-752-7657
Plastipro
Denver, CO 800-654-0409
Rochester Midland Corporation
Rochester, NY 800-836-1627
Rockford Sanitary Systems
Rockford, IL 800-747-5077
Sefi Fabricators
Amityville, NY 631-842-2200
Somat Company
Lancaster, PA 800-237-6628
StainlessDrains.com
Greenville, TX 888-785-2345
Stogsdill Tile Company
Huntley, IL 800-323-7504
Trap Zap Environmental Systems
Wyckoff, NJ 800-282-8727
Van Air Systems
Lake City, PA 800-840-9906
Vaughan Company
Montesano, WA 888-249-2467
Viking Corporation
Hastings, MI 800-968-9501
Warren E. Conley Corporation
Carmel, IN 800-367-7875
Watts Regulator Company
North Andover, MA 978-688-1811
World Dryer Corporation
Berkeley, IL 800-323-0701
Zurn Industries
Erie, PA 855-663-9876

Polish

Floor

ADCO
Albany, GA 800-821-7556
Advance Cleaning Products
Milwaukee, WI 800-925-5326
American Wax Company
Long Island City, NY 888-929-7587
Boston Chemical Industries
Randolph, MA 800-255-8651
Boyer Corporation
La Grange, IL 800-323-3040
Brulin & Company
Indianapolis, IN 800-776-7149
Buckeye International
Maryland Heights, MO 314-291-1900
Cantol
Markham, ON 800-387-9773
Chemifax
Santa Fe Springs, CA 800-527-5722
Claire Manufacturing Company
Addison, IL 800-252-4731
Cobitco, Inc
Denver, CO 303-296-8575
Concord Chemical Company
Camden, NJ 800-282-2436
D.W. Davies & Company
Racine, WI 800-888-6133
Dial Corporation
Scottsdale, AZ 480-754-3425
Emulso Corporation
Tonawanda, NY 800-724-7667
Essential Industries
Merton, WI 800-551-9679
Fuller Brush Company
Great Bend, KS 800-522-0499
Golden Star
N Kansas City, MO 800-821-2792
Griffin Brothers
Salem, OR 800-456-4743
H.F. Staples & Company
Merrimack, NH 800-682-0034
Hill Manufacturing Company
Atlanta, GA 404-522-8364
Hillyard
Saint Joseph, MO 800-365-1555
Holland Chemicals Company
Windsor, ON 519-948-4373
Hy-Ko Enviro-MaintenanceProducts
Salt Lake City, UT 801-973-6099
J.I. Holcomb Manufacturing
Independence, OH 800-458-3222
James Varley & Sons
Saint Louis, MO 800-325-3303
Johnson Diversey
Sturtevant, WI 262-631-4001
Knapp Manufacturing
Fresno, CA 559-251-8254
Lamco Chemical Company
Chelsea, MA 617-884-8470
Larose & Fils Ltêe
Laval, QC 877-382-7001
Lavo Company
Milwaukee, WI 414-353-2140
Lubar Chemical
Kansas City, MO 816-471-2560
Magic American Corporation
Cleveland, OH 800-321-6330
Marko
Spartanburg, SC 866-466-2726
Meguiar's
Irvine, CA 949-752-8000
Microbest Products
Waterbury, CT 800-426-4246
Mission Laboratories
Los Angeles, CA 888-201-8866
Murnell Wax Company
Springfield, MA 781-395-1323
Pioneer Manufacturing Company
Cleveland, OH 800-877-1500
Portion-Pac Chemical Corp.
Chicago, IL 312-226-0400
Quaker Chemical Company
Columbia, SC 800-849-9520
R&C Pro Brands
Wayne, NJ 973-633-7374
Rochester Midland Corporation
Rochester, NY 800-535-5053
Rochester Midland Corporation
Rochester, NY 800-836-1627
Sanitek Products, Inc
Los Angeles, CA 818-242-1071
Selig Chemical Industries
Atlanta, GA 404-876-5511
SerVaas Laboratories
Indianapolis, IN 800-433-5818
Twi-Laq Industries
Bronx, NY 800-950-7627
Valspar Corporation
Chicago, IL 800-637-7793
Verax Chemical Company
Bothell, WA 800-637-7771
Warren E. Conley Corporation
Carmel, IN 800-367-7875
West Chemical Products
Princeton, NJ 609-921-0501
Windsor Wax Company
Carolina, RI 800-243-8929

Furniture

ADCO
Albany, GA 800-821-7556
Black's Products of HighPoint
High Point, NC 336-886-5011
Boston Chemical Industries
Randolph, MA 800-255-8651
Burnishine Products
Gurnee, IL 800-818-8275
Claire Manufacturing Company
Addison, IL 800-252-4731
Golden Star
N Kansas City, MO 800-821-2792
H.F. Staples & Company
Merrimack, NH 800-682-0034
Hohn Manufacturing Company
Fenton, MO 800-878-1440
Meguiar's
Irvine, CA 949-752-8000
Milsek Furniture Polish Inc.
North Lima, OH 330-542-2700
Novus
Savage, MN 800-328-1117
Scott's Liquid Gold
Denver, CO 800-447-1919
SerVaas Laboratories
Indianapolis, IN 800-433-5818

Powder

Cleaning & Scouring

Church & Dwight Company
Princeton, NJ 800-833-9532
Fitzpatrick Brothers
Pleasant Prairie, WI 800-233-8064
Hill Manufacturing Company
Atlanta, GA 404-522-8364
J.I. Holcomb Manufacturing
Independence, OH 800-458-3222
Rochester Midland Corporation
Rochester, NY 800-836-1627
Savogran Company
Norwood, MA 800-225-9872
SerVaas Laboratories
Indianapolis, IN 800-433-5818

Pressure Washers

Aaladin Industries
Elk Point, SD 800-356-3325

Alkota Cleaning Systems
Alcester, SD 800-255-6823
Cam Spray
Iowa Falls, IA 800-648-5011
Clarke
Plymouth, MN. 800-253-0367
Cold Jet
Loveland, OH 800-337-9423
D&M Products
Santa Monica, CA. 800-245-0485
Davron Technologies
Chattanooga, TN. 423-870-1888
Dirt Killer Pressure Washers, Inc
Baltimore, MD 800-544-1188
General Tank
Berwick, PA 800-435-8265
Goodway Technologies Corporation
Stamford, CT. 800-333-7467
Hector Delorme & Sons
Farnham, QC. 450-293-5310
Industrial Washing Machine Corporation
Jackson, NJ 732-304-9203
Kew Cleaning Systems
Clearwater, FL 800-942-1690
Kewanee Washer Corporaton
Findlay, OH. 419-435-8269
Larose & Fils Ltêe
Laval, QC 877-382-7001
Lechler
St Charles, IL 800-777-2926
Maxi-Vac Inc.
Dundee, IL 855-629-4538
N&A Manufacturing Spraymatic Sprayers
Mallard, IA 712-425-3512
Pro Scientific
Oxford, CT 800-584-3776
Sani-Matic
Madison, WI 800-356-3300
Sioux Corporation
Beresford, SD 888-763-8833
SprayMaster Technologies
Rogers, AR 800-548-3373
Therma-Kleen
Plainfield, IL. 800-999-3120
Windsor Industries
Englewood, CO. 800-444-7654

Sanitary Wall

AlphaBio Inc
Rancho Santa Maragarita, CA 800-966-0716
Arcoplast Wall & Ceiling Systems
St Peters, MO 888-736-2726
Zeroloc
Kirkland, WA 425-823-4888

Sanitizers

A&L Laboratories
Minneapolis, MN 800-225-3832
Activon Products
Beaver Dam, WI. 800-841-0410
Air-Scent International
Pittsburgh, PA. 800-247-0770
Atlantic Mills
Lakewood, NJ. 800-242-7374
Bar Maid Corporation
Pompano Beach, FL 954-960-1468
Best Sanitizers
Penn Valley, CA 888-225-3267
Birko Corporation
Henderson, CO 800-525-0476
Boston Chemical Industries
Randolph, MA 800-255-8651
Burnishine Products
Gurnee, IL. 800-818-8275
Candy & Company/Peck's Products Company
Chicago, IL 800-837-9189
Century Chemical Corporation
Elkhart, IN. 800-348-3505
Cold Jet
Loveland, OH 800-337-9423
Colgate-Palmolive
Morristown, NJ. 800-432-8226
Discovery Chemical
Marietta, GA. 800-973-9881
ECOLAB
St Paul, MN. 800-352-5326
Electro-Steam Generator Corporation
Rancocas, NJ. 866-617-0764
Falls Chemical Products
Oconto Falls, WI. 920-846-3561

Glass Pro
Addison, IL. 888-641-8919
Hilex Company
Eagan, MN 651-454-1160
Hydrite Chemical Company
Brookfield, WI 262-792-1450
James Varley & Sons
Saint Louis, MO 800-325-3303
Labpride Chemicals
Bronx, NY. 800-467-1255
LEE Industries
Philipsburg, PA 814-342-0461
Luseaux Laboratories Inc
Gardena, CA 800-266-1555
Machem Industries
Delta, BC. 604-526-5655
Meritech
Golden, CO 800-932-7707
Nelson-Jameson
Marshfield, WI 800-826-8302
Nice-Pak Products
Orangeburg, NY 800-999-6423
Nuance Solutions
Chicago, IL 800-621-8553
Oakite Products
New Providence, NJ 800-526-4473
Paxton Corporation
Bristol, RI
Portion-Pac Chemical Corp.
Chicago, IL 312-226-0400
ProRestore Products
Pittsburgh, PA. 800-332-6037
Purdy Products Company
Wauconda, IL 800-726-4849
Rem Ohio
Cincinnati, OH 513-878-8188
Rochester Midland Corporation
Rochester, NY. 800-836-1627
Shepard Brothers
La Habra, CA 562-697-1366
Vulcan Materials Company
Birmingham, AL. 205-298-3000
Water Sciences Services ,Inc.
Jackson, TN 973-584-4131

Scouring Pads

ACS Industries, Inc.
Lincoln, RI 866-783-4838
Arden Companies
Southfield, MI. 248-415-8500
Argo & Company
Spartanburg, SC 864-583-9766
Armaly Brands
Walled Lake, MI. 800-772-1222
Banner Chemical Corporation
Orange, NJ 973-676-2900
Carlisle Food Service Products
Oklahoma City, OK 800-654-8210
Glit Microtron
Bridgetown, MO. 800-325-1051
Mainline Industries
Springfield, MA 800-527-7917
Microtron Abrasives
Pineville, NC. 800-476-7237
Nylonge Company
Elyria, OH. 440-323-6161
Pacific Oasis Enterprises
Santa Fe Springs, CA 800-424-1475
Quickie Manufacturing Corp.
Cinnaminson, NJ. 856-829-7900
Royal Paper Products
Coatesville, PA 800-666-6655
Stearns Technical Textiles Company
Cincinnati,.OH 800-543-7173
Thamesville Metal Products Ltd
Thamesville, ON. 519-692-3963
Tucel Industries, Inc.
Forestdale, VT 800-558-8235
TuWay American Group
Rockford, OH 800-537-3750
Wilen Professional Cleaning Products
Atlanta, GA. 800-241-7371

Scrubbers

Andersen 2000
Peachtree City, GA 800-241-5424

Silverware Cleaning Machinery

Washing, Drying & Polishing

Adamation
Commerce, CA. 800-225-3075
Middleby Worldwide
Elgin, IL 847-468-6068
Vanguard Technology
Eugene, OR. 800-624-4809

Skin Cream & Lotions

Cold Cream

Milburn Company
Detroit, MI 313-259-3410

Lotion

Milburn Company
Detroit, MI 313-259-3410

Skin Cream

Milburn Company
Detroit, MI 313-259-3410
Proctor & Gamble Company
Cincinnati, OH 513-983-1100

Sneeze Guards

Advanced Design Manufacturing
Concord, CA. 800-690-0002
Brass Smith
Denver, CO. 800-662-9595
Carlisle Food Service Products
Oklahoma City, OK 800-654-8210
Custom Plastics
Decatur, GA 404-373-1691
Duke Manufacturing Company
Saint Louis, MO 800-735-3853
Emco Industrial Plastics
Cedar Grove, NJ. 800-292-9906
English Manufacturing Inc
Rancho Cordova, CA 800-651-2711
K&I Creative Plastics
Jacksonville, FL 904-387-0438
Lavi Industries
Valencia, CA. 800-624-6225
Precision Plastics Inc.
Beltsville, MD. 800-922-1317
R&D Brass
Wappingers Falls, NY. 800-447-6050
Rewdco & Hanson Brass Products
Sun Valley, CA 888-841-3773
Sneezeguard Solutions
Columbia, MO 800-569-2056
Superior Products Company
Saint Paul, MN. 800-328-9800

Soap

Advance Cleaning Products
Milwaukee, WI 800-925-5326
Akron Cotton Products
Akron, OH. 800-899-7173
American Wax Company
Long Island City, NY 888-929-7587
Bi-O-Kleen Industries
Portland, OR 503-224-6246
Bio Pac
Incline Village, NV. 800-225-2855
Blue Cross Laboratories
Santa Clarita, CA
Boston Chemical Industries
Randolph, MA 800-255-8651
Buckeye International
Maryland Heights, MO. 314-291-1900
Cal Ben Soap Company
Oakland, CA 800-340-7091
Cantol
Markham, ON. 800-387-9773
Carroll Company
Garland, TX 800-527-5722
Chef Revival
Elkhorn, WI. 800-248-9826
Clearly Natural Products
Kennesaw, GA 800-451-7096
Colgate-Palmolive
Morristown, NJ. 800-432-8226
Common Sense Natural Soap & Bodycare Products
Rutland, VT 802-773-0582

Concord Chemical Company
Camden, NJ. 800-282-2436
CRC Industries, Inc.
Warminster, PA 800-556-5074
Critzas Industries
St Louis, MO. 800-537-1418
Crown Chemical Products
Mississauga, ON 905-564-0904
Deb Canada
Waterford, ON. 888-332-7627
Delta Foremost Chemical Corporation
Memphis, TN 800-238-5150
Diablo Products
Fort Dodge, IA 800-548-1385
Dial Corporation
Scottsdale, AZ. 480-754-3425
Dickler Chemical Labs
Philadelphia, PA 800-426-1127
Dirt Killer Pressure Washers, Inc
Baltimore, MD 800-544-1188
Dober Chemical Corporation
Midlothian, IL. 800-323-4983
Dreumex USA
York, PA 800-233-9382
ECOLAB
St Paul, MN. 800-352-5326
Economy Paper & Restaurant Supply Company
Clifton, NJ. 973-279-5500
Emulso Corporation
Tonawanda, NY 800-724-7667
Essential Industries
Merton, WI 800-551-9679
Falls Chemical Products
Oconto Falls, WI. 920-846-3561
Fiebing Company
Milwaukee, WI 800-558-1033
Fishers Investment
Cincinnati, OH 800-833-5916
Fort James Corporation
Norwalk, CT 800-257-9744
Go-Jo Industries
Akron, OH. 800-321-9647
Hallberg Manufacturing Corporation
Tampa, FL. 800-633-7627
Hamilton Soap & Oil Products
Paterson, NJ 973-225-1031
Hanco Manufacturing Company
Memphis, TN 800-530-7364
Hewitt Soap Company
Dayton, OH. 800-543-2245
Hohn Manufacturing Company
Fenton, MO. 800-878-1440
Hy-Trous/Flash Sales
Woburn, MA 781-933-5772
Inksolv 30, LLC.
Emerson, NE. 515-537-5344
J.I. Holcomb Manufacturing
Independence, OH 800-458-3222
James Austin Company
Mars, PA 724-625-1535
James Varley & Sons
Saint Louis, MO 800-325-3303
Kildon Manufacturing
Ingersoll, ON 800-485-4930
Larose & Fils Ltêe
Laval, QC 877-382-7001
Lavo Company
Milwaukee, WI 414-353-2140
Lee Soap Company
Commerce City, CO 800-888-1896
Man-O Products
Cincinnati, OH 888-210-6266
Martin Laboratories
Owensboro, KY 800-345-9352
Meritech
Golden, CO. 800-932-7707
Micro-Brush Pro Soap
Rockwall, TX 800-776-7627
Milburn Company
Detroit, MI 313-259-3410
Mione Manufacturing Company
Mickleton, NJ 800-257-0497
Mission Laboratories
Los Angeles, CA. 888-201-8866
National-Purity
Brooklyn Center, MN 612-672-0022
Nuance Solutions
Chicago, IL 800-621-8553
Ohio Soap Products Company
Wickliffe, OH 440-585-1100
Original Bradford Soap Works
West Warwick, RI. 401-821-2141
Parachem Corporation
Des Moines, IA. 515-280-9445
Pioneer Chemical Company
Gardena, CA 310-366-7393
PM Chemical Company
San Diego, CA 619-296-0191
Proctor & Gamble Company
Cincinnati, OH 513-983-1100
R.R. Street & Co., Inc.
Naperville, IL 630-416-4244
Rochester Midland Corporation
Rochester, NY. 800-535-5053
Rochester Midland Corporation
Rochester, NY. 800-836-1627
Rooto Corporation
Howell, MI 517-546-8330
S&S Soap Company
Bronx, NY. 718-585-2900
San Joaquin Supply Company
Stockton, CA. 209-952-0680
Sanitek Products, Inc
Los Angeles, CA. 818-242-1071
SCA Hygiene Paper
San Ramon, CA 800-992-8675
Selig Chemical Industries
Atlanta, GA. 404-876-5511
Sierra Dawn Products
Graton, CA 707-535-0172
Snee Chemical Company
Harahan, LA 800-489-7633
State Industrial Products
Mayfield Heights, OH 877-747-6986
Steiner Company
Holland, IL 800-222-4638
Stone Soap Company
Sylvan Lake, MI 800-952-7627
Sunbeam Product
Toledo, OH 419-691-1551
Sunpoint Products
Lawrence, MA 978-794-3100
Sure Clean Corporation
Two Rivers, WI. 920-793-3838
Syndett Products
Bolton, CT 860-646-0172
Tropical Soap Company
Carrollton, TX. 800-527-2368
Twi-Laq Industries
Bronx, NY. 800-950-7627
Ulmer Pharmacal Company
Park Rapids, MN. 218-732-2656
UniFirst Corporation
Wilmington, MA. 800-455-7654
US Industrial Lubricants
Cincinnati, OH 800-562-5454
Venturetech Corporation
Knoxville, TN. 800-826-4095
Verax Chemical Company
Bothell, WA. 800-637-7771
Whisk Products
Wentzville, MO. 800-204-7627

Powder

Hallberg Manufacturing Corporation
Tampa, FL. 800-633-7627

Vegetable Oil

National-Purity
Brooklyn Center, MN. 612-672-0022
US Industrial Lubricants
Cincinnati, OH 800-562-5454

Sponges

Acme Sponge & Chamois Company
Tarpon Springs, FL. 727-937-3222
ACS Industries, Inc.
Lincoln, RI 866-783-4838
Armaly Brands
Walled Lake, MI. 800-772-1222
Carlisle Food Service Products
Oklahoma City, OK 800-654-8210
Distribution Results
Akron, OH. 800-737-9671
Glit Microtron
Bridgetown, MO. 800-325-1051
Labpride Chemicals
Bronx, NY. 800-467-1255
Nation/Ruskin
Montgomeryville, PA 800-523-2489
Nylonge Company
Elyria, OH. 440-323-6161
Quickie Manufacturing Corp.
Cinnaminson, NJ. 856-829-7900
Royal Paper Products
Coatesville, PA 800-666-6655
Spontex
Columbia, TN. 800-251-4222
Tee-Jay Corporation
Shelton, CT. 203-924-4767
Tucel Industries, Inc.
Forestdale, VT 800-558-8235

Sprinkling Systems

American Fire Sprinkler Services, Inc
Hialeah, FL 305-628-0100
APEC
Lake Odessa, MI. 616-374-1000
Corrigan Corporation of America
Gurnee, IL. 800-462-6478
Doering Company
Clear Lake, MN 320-743-2276
Fire Protection Industries
Bensalem, PA 215-245-1830
Firematic Sprinkler Devices
Shrewsbury, MA. 508-845-2121
Globe Fire Sprinkler Corporation
Standish, MI 800-248-0278
Grinnell Fire ProtectionSystems Company
Sauk Rapids, MN 320-253-8665
Muellermist Irrigation Company
Broadview, IL 708-450-9595
Storm Industrial
Shawnee Mission, KS. 800-745-7483
Tyco Fire Protection Products
Lansdale, PA 800-558-5236
Viking Corporation
Hastings, MI 800-968-9501
Wiginton Fire Sprinklers
Sanford, FL. 407-831-3414

Squeegees

Carlisle Food Service Products
Oklahoma City, OK 800-654-8210
Continental Commercial Products
Bridgeton, MO 800-325-1051
Dorden & Company
Detroit, MI 313-834-7910
Ettore Products Company
Alameda, CA. 510-748-4130
Harper Brush Works
Fairfield, IA 800-223-7894
Kiefer Brushes, Inc
Franklin, NJ 800-526-2905
Labpride Chemicals
Bronx, NY. 800-467-1255
Lite-Weight Tool Manufacturing Company
Sun Valley, CA 800-859-3529
Milwaukee Dustless BrushCompany
Delavan, WI 800-632-3220
Perfex Corporation
Poland, NY 800-848-8483
Reit-Price ManufacturingCompany
Union City, IN. 800-521-5343
Superior Products Company
Saint Paul, MN 800-328-9800
Warren E. Conley Corporation
Carmel, IN. 800-367-7875

Sterilizers

A.K. Robins
Baltimore, MD 800-486-9656
Allpax Products
Covington, LA 888-893-9277
API Heat Transfer
Buffalo, NY. 877-274-4328
Atlantic Ultraviolet Corporation
Hauppauge, NY 866-958-9085
Burnishine Products
Gurnee, IL. 800-818-8275
Capital Controls Company/MicroChem
Colmar, PA 215-997-4000
Cleaver-Brooks
Milwaukee, WI. 414-359-0600
Electro-Steam Generator Corporation
Rancocas, NJ. 866-617-0764
GERM-O-RAY
Stone Mountain, GA. 800-966-8480
Hess Machine International
Ephrata, PA. 800-735-4377
Littleford Day
Florence, KY. 800-365-8555

Market Forge Industries
Everett, MA. 866-698-3188
Melco Steel
Azusa, CA. 626-334-7875
National Hotpack
Stone Ridge, NY. 800-431-8232
Pick Heaters Inc.
West Bend, WI 800-233-9030
San Joaquin Supply Company
Stockton, CA. 209-952-0680
Schlueter Company
Janesville, WI 800-359-1700
South Valley Manufacturing
Gilroy, CA. 408-842-5457
SP Industries
Warminster, PA 800-523-2327
TMI-USA
Reston, VA 703-668-0114
Triad Scientific
Manasquan, NJ 800-867-6690

Tissue

Cleansing

Carhoff Company
Cleveland, OH 216-541-4835
Georgia Pacific
Green Bay, WI. 920-435-8821
Kimberly-Clark Corporation
Roswell, GA 888-525-8388
Marcal Paper Mills
Elmwood Park, NJ 800-631-8451
Potlatch Corporation
Spokane, WA. 509-835-1500
Proctor & Gamble Company
Cincinnati, OH 513-983-1100
Productos Familia
Santurce, PR 787-268-5929
SCA Hygiene Paper
San Ramon, CA 800-992-8675
SCA Tissue
Neenah, WI. 866-722-6659
Sorg Paper Company
Middletown, OH. 513-420-5300
Superior Quality Products
Schenectady, NY. 800-724-1129
Vermont Tissue Paper Company
North Bennington, VT 802-447-7558

Vaccuum Bags

Cretel Food Equipment
Holland, MI. 616-786-3980

Vacuum Cleaners

Industrial

Beam Industries
Webster City, IA 800-369-2326
Clarke
Plymouth, MN. 800-253-0367
DL Enterprises
Etters, PA 717-938-1292
Eureka Company
Bloomington, IL 800-282-2886
Gardner Denver Inc.
Toronto, ON 416-763-4681
General Floor Craft
Little Silver, NJ. 973-742-7400
Goodway Technologies Corporation
Stamford, CT. 800-333-7467
H.L. Diehl Company
South Windham, CT 860-423-7741
Hollowell Products Corporation
Wyandotte, MI 734-282-8200
Hoover Company
North Canton, OH. 330-499-9200
Mastercraft Industries
Newburgh, NY 800-835-7812
Mercury Floor Machines
Englewood, NJ 888-568-4606
Multi-Vac
Union Grove, WI 800-640-4213
Oreck Corporation
Cookeville, TN 800-989-3535
ProTeam
Boise, ID. 800-541-1456
Spencer Turbine Company
Windsor, CT 800-232-4321
Superior Products Company
Saint Paul, MN 800-328-9800
United Floor Machine Company
Chicago, IL. 800-288-0848
Vector Technologies
Milwaukee, WI 800-832-4010
Windsor Industries
Englewood, CO. 800-444-7654

Washing Machinery

A.K. Robins
Baltimore, MD 800-486-9656
Aaladin Industries
Elk Point, SD 800-356-3325
Adamation
Commerce, CA 800-225-3075
Ali Group
Winston Salem, NC. 800-532-8591
Alkota Cleaning Systems
Alcester, SD 800-255-6823
Ametek Technical & Industrial Products
Kent, OH. 215-256-6601
Andgar Corporation
Ferndale, WA 360-366-9900
Assembled Products
Rogers, AR 800-548-3373
Atlas Pacific Engineering Company
Pueblo, CO 719-948-3040
Attias Oven Corporation
Brooklyn, NY 800-928-8427
Bar Maid Corporation
Pompano Beach, FL 954-960-1468
Bete Fog Nozzle
Greenfield, MA. 800-235-0049
Bethel Engineering & Equipment Inc
New Hampshire, OH. 800-889-6129
BFM Equipment Sales
Fall River, WI 920-484-3341
Burns Chemical Systems
Cleveland, OH 724-327-7600
Cam Spray
Iowa Falls, IA 800-648-5011
Cannon Equipment Company
Rosemount, MN 800-825-8501
Chad Company
Olathe, KS. 800-444-8360
Champion Industries
Winston Salem, NC. 800-532-8591
Chemdet
Sebastian, FL 800-645-1510
Cincinnati Industrial Machinery
Mason, OH 800-677-0076
Cloud Company
San Luis Obispo, CA 800-234-5650
CMA/Dishmachines
Garden Grove, CA 800-854-6417
Cold Jet
Loveland, OH 800-337-9423
Colonial Paper Company
Silver Springs, FL. 352-622-4171
Commercial Dehydrator Systems Inc
Eugene, OR. 800-369-4283
Commercial Manufacturing& Supply Company
Fresno, CA 559-237-1855
Component Hardware Group
Lakewood, NJ. 800-526-3694
Continental Equipment Corporation
Milwaukee, WI 414-463-0500
Continental Girbau
Oshkosh, WI 800-256-1073
Convay Systems
Etobicoke, ON. 800-811-5511
Cugar Machine Company
Fort Worth, TX 817-927-0411
Custom Diamond International
Laval, QC 800-363-5926
Custom Food Machinery
Stockton, CA. 209-463-4343
D&M Products
Santa Monica, CA. 800-245-0485
Damas Corporation
Trenton, NJ 609-695-9121
Davron Technologies
Chattanooga, TN. 423-870-1888
Dirt Killer Pressure Washers, Inc
Baltimore, MD 800-544-1188
Diversified Metal Engineering
Charlottetown, PE. 902-628-6900
Douglas Machines Corporation
Clearwater, FL 800-331-6870
Dynablast Manufacturing
Mississauga, ON. 888-242-8597
F. Harold Haines Manufacturing
Presque Isle, ME. 207-762-1411
FleetwoodGoldcoWyard
Romeoville, IL 630-759-6800
Flo-Matic Corporation
Belvidere, IL. 800-959-1179
Gamajet Cleaning Systems
Exton, PA 800-289-5387
Geo. Olcott Company
Scottsboro, AL 800-634-2769
Ghibli North American
Wilmington, DE 302-654-5908
Girton Manufacturing Company, Inc.
Millville, PA 570-458-5521
Glass Pro
Addison, IL. 888-641-8919
Glastender
Saginaw, MI 800-748-0423
Hector Delorme & Sons
Farnham, QC. 450-293-5310
Hobart Corporation
Troy, OH 888-446-2278
Horix Manufacturing Company
Mc Kees Rocks, PA. 412-771-1111
Hoyt Corporation
Westport, MA 508-636-8811
Hughes Equipment Company LLC
Columbus, WI. 866-535-9303
IMC Teddy Food Service Equipment
Amityville, NY 800-221-5644
Industrial Washing Machine Corporation
Jackson, NJ 732-304-9203
Insinger Machine Company
Philadelphia, PA 800-344-4802
Kew Cleaning Systems
Clearwater, FL 800-942-1690
Kewanee Washer Corporaton
Findlay, OH. 419-435-8269
Key Technology
Walla Walla, WA. 509-529-2161
Knight Equipment International
Lake Forest, CA 800-854-3764
Krones
Franklin, WI 414-409-4000
Krowne Metal Corporation
Wayne, NJ. 800-631-0442
Kuhl Corporation
Flemington, NJ 908-782-5696
Larose & Fils Ltêe
Laval, QC 877-382-7001
Laundrylux
Inwood, NY. 800-645-2205
Lechler
St Charles, IL 800-777-2926
Leedal Inc
Northbrook, IL 847-498-0111
Leon C. Osborn Company
Houston, TX 281-488-0755
LPS Technology
Grafton, OH 800-586-1410
LTG Technologies
Spartanburg, SC 864-599-6340
Magnuson Corporation
Pueblo, CO 719-948-9500
Matcon USA
Elmhurst, IL 856-256-1330
Maxi-Vac Inc.
Dundee, IL 855-629-4538
McBrady Engineering
Joliet, IL 815-744-8900
Meritech
Golden, CO. 800-932-7707
Metal Equipment Company
Cleveland, OH 800-700-6326
Metcraft
Grandview, MO. 800-444-9624
Midbrook
Jackson, MI. 800-966-9274
Moyer-Diebel
Winston Salem, NC. 336-661-1992
N&A Manufacturing Spraymatic Sprayers
Mallard, IA 712-425-3512
Namco Machinery
Maspeth, NY
National Conveyor Corporation
Commerce, CA 323-725-0355
Paxton Products
Cincinnati, OH 800-441-7475
Pellerin Milnor Corporation
Kenner, LA 800-469-8780
PMI Food Equipment Group
Troy, OH 937-332-3000

Pneumatic Scale Corporation
Cuyahoga Falls, OH 330-923-0491
Puritan/Churchill Chemical Company
Marietta, GA 800-275-8914
Roto-Jet Pump
Salt Lake City, UT 801-359-8731
Sani-Matic
Madison, WI 800-356-3300
Sanitech Corporation
Lorton, VA 800-486-4321
Sasib Beverage & Food North America
Plano, TX 800-558-3814
Schlueter Company
Janesville, WI 800-359-1700
Sioux Corporation
Beresford, SD 888-763-8833
Sonicor Instrument Corporation
Deer Park, NY 800-864-5022
Specialty Equipment Company
Mendota Heights, MN 651-452-7909
Spraying Systems Company
Wheaton, IL 630-655-5000
SprayMaster Technologies
Rogers, AR 800-548-3373
Stero Company
Petaluma, CA 800-762-7600
Superior Food Machinery
Pico Rivera, CA 800-944-0396
Swissh Commercial Equipment
Montreal, QC 888-794-7749
Therma-Kleen
Plainfield, IL 800-999-3120
Tri-Pak Machinery, Inc.
Harlingen, TX 956-423-5140
US Bottlers Machinery Company
Charlotte, NC 704-588-4750
Waring Products
Torrington, CT 800-492-7464
Washing Systems
Loveland, OH 800-272-1974
Windsor Industries
Englewood, CO 800-444-7654
Zealco Industries
Calvert City, KY 800-759-5531

Waste Handling & Disposal Equipment

Abel Pumps
Sewickley, PA 412-741-3222
Adamation
Commerce, CA 800-225-3075
Aeration Industries International
Chaska, MN 800-328-8287
Aeromix Systems
Minneapolis, MN 800-879-3677
Ali Group
Winston Salem, NC 800-532-8591
Alkota Cleaning Systems
Alcester, SD 800-255-6823
Alloy Hardfacing & Engineering Company, Inc
Jordan, MN 800-328-8408
Ameri-Khem
Port Orange, FL 800-224-9950
Ampco Pumps Company
Glendale, WI 800-737-8671
Anaheim Manufacturing Company
Anaheim, CA 800-767-6293
Andco Environmental Processes
Amherst, NY 716-691-2100
Anova
St Louis, MO 800-231-1327
Apache Stainless Equipment Corporation
Beaver Dam, WI 800-444-0398
API Industries
Tulsa, OK 918-664-4010
Armstrong International
Three Rivers, MI 269-273-1415
Athea Laboratories
Milwaukee, WI 800-743-6417
Bennett Manufacturing Company
Alden, NY 800-345-2142
Betz Entec
Horsham, PA 800-877-1940
Biothane Corporation
Camden, NJ 856-541-3500
Blower Application Company
Germantown, WI 800-959-0880
C S Bell Company
Tiffin, OH 888-958-6381
C.E. Rogers Company
Mora, MN 800-279-8081
Can & Bottle Systems, Inc.
Milwaukie, OR 866-302-2636
Cavert Wire Company
Rural Hall, NC 800-245-4042
Chesmont Engineering Company
Exton, PA 610-594-9200
Chicago Trashpacker Corporation
Marengo, IL 800-635-5745
Clean Water Systems International
Klamath Falls, OR 866-273-9993
Compactors
Hilton Head Island, SC 800-423-4003
Consolidated Baling Machine Company
Jacksonville, FL 800-231-9286
Continental Commercial Products
Bridgeton, MO 800-325-1051
Convay Systems
Etobicoke, ON 800-811-5511
Corenco
Santa Rosa, CA 888-267-3626
Cornell Pump Company
Portland, OR 503-653-0330
Dempster Systems
Toccoa, GA 706-886-2327
DriAll
Attica, IN 765-295-2255
Enercon Systems
Elyria, OH 440-323-7080
Ertel Alsop
Kingston, NY 800-553-7835
Erwyn Products Company
Morganville, NJ 800-331-9208
FabWright, Inc
Garden Grove, CA 800-854-6464
Foremost Machine Builders
Fairfield, NJ 973-227-0700
Frem Corporation
Worcester, MA 508-791-3152
Galbreath LLC
Winamac, IN 574-946-6631
Garb-El Products Company
Lockport, NY 800-242-7235
General Electric Company
Fairfield, CT 203-373-2211
General, Inc
Weston, FL 954-202-7419
Glaro
Hauppauge, NY 631-234-1717
Harmony Enterprises
Harmony, MN 800-658-2320
Himolene
Carrollton, TX 800-777-4411
Hines III
Jacksonville, FL 904-398-5110
Hodge Manufacturing Company
Springfield, MA 800-262-4634
Hygiene-Technik
Beamsville, ON 905-563-4987
In-Sink-Erator
Racine, WI 800-558-5700
Incinerator International
Houston, TX 713-227-1466
Incinerator Specialty Company
Houston, TX 713-681-4207
Industronics Service Company
South Windsor, CT 800-878-1551
Insect-O-Cutor
Stone Mountain, GA 800-988-5359
Insinger Machine Company
Philadelphia, PA 800-344-4802
International Reserve Equipment Corporation
Clarendon Hills, IL 708-531-0680
Intrex
Bethel, CT 203-792-7400
J.V. Reed & Company
Louisville, KY 877-258-7333
JC Industries
West Babylon, NY 800-322-1189
Joneca Corporation
Anaheim, CA 714-993-5997
Jones Environmental
Austin, TX 512-834-6040
JWC Environmental
Costa Mesa, CA 800-331-2277
Kew Cleaning Systems
Clearwater, FL 800-942-1690
Komline-Sanderson
Peapack, NJ 800-225-5457
Krogh Pump Company
Benicia, CA 800-225-7644
Lenser Filtration
Lakewood, NJ 732-370-1600
Lewis Steel Works
Wrens, GA 800-521-5239
Load King Manufacturing Company
Jacksonville, FL 800-531-4975
Lodal
Kingsford, MI 800-435-3500
Logemann Brothers Company
Milwaukee, WI 414-445-2700
Ludell Manufacturing Company
Milwaukee, WI 800-558-0800
Mahoney Environmental
Joliet, IL 800-892-9392
Marathon Equipment Company
Vernon, AL 800-633-8974
Maren Engineering Corporation
South Holland, IL 800-875-1038
Mell & Company
Niles, IL 800-262-6355
Metal Equipment Company
Cleveland, OH 800-700-6326
Midbrook
Jackson, MI 800-966-9274
Miller Manufacturing
Turlock, CA 209-632-3846
Multi-Pak Corporation
Hackensack, NJ 201-342-7474
National Conveyor Corporation
Commerce, CA 323-725-0355
NETZSCH
Exton, PA 610-363-8010
Oil Skimmers
Cleveland, OH 800-200-4603
Old Dominion Wood Products
Lynchburg, VA 800-245-6382
Olson Manufacturing/V-RAM Solids
Albert Lea, MN 888-373-3996
Orwak
Minneapolis, MN 800-747-0449
Our Name is Mud
New York, NY 877-683-7867
Outotec
Jessup, ID 301-543-1200
PAC Equipment Company
Garfield, NJ 973-478-1008
Pack-A-Drum
Satellite Beach, FL 800-694-6163
Paradise Plastics
Brooklyn, NY
Parkson Illinois
Vernon Hills, IL 847-816-3700
Peter Pepper Products
Compton, CA 310-639-0390
Plymold
Kenyon, MN 800-759-6653
PMI Food Equipment Group
Troy, OH 937-332-3000
PTR Baler and Compactor Company
Philadelphia, PA 800-523-3654
R.G. Stephens Engineering
Long Beach, CA 800-499-3001
Respirometry Plus, LLC
Fond Du Lac, WI 800-328-7518
REYCO Systems
Caldwell, ID 208-795-5700
Robar International
Milwaukee, WI 800-279-7750
Salvajor Company
Kansas City, MO 800-821-3136
Schleicher & Company of America
Sanford, NC 800-775-7570
Schloss Engineered Equipment
Aurora, CO 303-695-4500
Scienco Systems
Saint Louis, MO 314-621-2536
Seating Concepts
Rockdale, IL 800-421-2036
SERFILCO Ltd
Northbrook, IL 800-323-5431
Shepard Brothers
La Habra, CA 562-697-1366
Somat Company
Lancaster, PA 800-237-6628
SP Industries
Hopkins, MI 800-592-5959
Star Filters
Timmonsville, SC 800-845-5381
Tema Systems
Cincinnati, OH 513-489-7811
Terminix Commercial Services
Flushing, NY 866-319-6528
Therm Tec, Inc
Tualatin, OR 800-292-9163

TLB Corporation
Newington, CT 203-233-5109
U.B. Klem Furniture Company
Saint Anthony, IN 800-264-1995
United Receptacle
Pottsville, PA. 800-233-0314
Universal Handling Equipment
Hamilton, ON 877-843-1122
US Filter
Palm Desert, CA 760-340-0098
US Filter Davco Products
Thomasville, GA. 800-841-1550
US Filter Dewatering Systems
Holland, MI. 800-245-3006
Vaughan Company
Montesano, WA 888-249-2467
Vesco
New Hyde Park, NY 516-746-5139
VRAM Solids
Albert Lea, MN. 888-373-3996
Waste Away Systems
Newark, OH 800-223-4741
Wastequip
Charlotte, NC 877-468-9278
Waterlink/Sanborn Technologies
Canton, OH 800-343-3381
Waymar Industries
Burnsville, MN 888-474-1112
Wayne Engineering Corporation
Cedar Falls, IA 319-266-1721
White Mop Wringer Company
Tampa, FL 800-237-7582
Witt Industries
Mason, OH 800-543-7417
Worcester Industrial Products
Worcester, MA 800-533-5711
Zeeco
Broken Arrow, OK 918-258-8551

Wastewater Treatment Systems

Anaerobic & Aerobic

ADI Systems Inc
Fredericton, NB 800-561-2831
AERTEC
North Andover, MA 978-475-6385
Biothane Corporation
Camden, NJ. 856-541-3500
FRC Systems International
Roswell, GA 770-534-3681
GW&E Global Water & Energy
Austin, TX. 512-697-1930
Hach Co.
Loveland, CO 800-227-4224
Lightnin Mixers
Rochester, NY. 888-649-2377
M-Vac Systems
Bluffdale, UT 801-523-3962
Oakite Products
New Providence, NJ 800-526-4473
Radiant Industrial Solutions, Inc.
Houston, TX 713-972-0196
World Water Works Inc.
Oklahoma City, OK 800-607-7973

Wipers

Disposable

Absorbco
Walterboro, SC 888-335-6439
Akron Cotton Products
Akron, OH. 800-899-7173
Atlantic Mills
Lakewood, NJ. 800-242-7374
Blue Ridge Converting
Asheville, NC 800-438-3893
Bro-Tex
Saint Paul, MN 800-328-2282
Casabar
Morristown, NJ. 877-745-8700
CCP Industries, Inc.
Cleveland, OH 800-321-2840
Coast Scientific
Rancho Santa Fe, CA 800-445-1544
De Royal Textiles
Camden, SC 800-845-1062
DPC
Norristown, PA 800-220-9473
Georgia Pacific
Green Bay, WI. 920-435-8821
Goodman Wiper & Paper
Auburn, ME 800-439-9473
ITW Dymon
Olathe, KS. 800-443-9536
Johnson International Materials
Brownsville, TX 956-541-6364
Lexidyne of Pennsylvania
Pittsburgh, PA 800-543-2233
Mainline Industries
Springfield, MA 800-527-7917
Mednik Wiping Materials Company
Saint Louis, MO 800-325-7193
Mill Wiping Rags/The Rag Factory
Bronx, NY. 718-994-7100
Nosaj Disposables
Paterson, NJ 800-631-3809
Nu-Towel Company
Kansas City, MO. 800-800-7247
Packaging Distribution Services, Inc
Des Moines, IA. 800-747-2699
Rockline Industries
Sheboygan, WI 800-558-7790
SCA Hygiene Paper
San Ramon, CA 800-992-8675
Textile Products Company
Anaheim, CA 714-761-0401
United Textile Distribution
Garner, NC 800-262-7624
Wipeco, Inc.
Hillside, IL 708-544-7247

Transportation & Storage

Automated Guided Vehicles

FMC Technologies
Chalfont, PA 888-362-3622

Beer Keg Movers

Powered

Ultra Lift Corporation
San Jose, CA 800-346-3057

Box Cutters

Charles Beck Machine Corporation
King of Prussia, PA 610-265-0500
Garvey Products
West Chester, OH 800-543-1908
Handy Roll Company
San Marcos, CA 760-471-6214
Listo Pencil Corporation
Alameda, CA 800-547-8648
Safe T Cut
Monson, MA 413-267-9984

Carts

Hand

Alliance Products, LLC
Murfreesboro, TN 800-522-3973
AMCO Corporation
City of Industry, CA 626-855-2550
ARC Specialties
Valencia, CA 661-775-8500
Art Wire Works
Bedford Park, IL 708-458-3993
Atlas Equipment Company
Kansas City, MO 800-842-9188
Baking Machines
Livermore, CA 925-449-3369
Barrette - Outdoor Livin
Middleburg Hts., OH 800-336-2383
Bennett Manufacturing Company
Alden, NY 800-345-2142
Bessco Tube Bending & Pipe Fabricating
Thornton, IL 800-337-3977
BMH Equipment
Sacramento, CA 800-350-8828
Burgess Enterprises, Inc
Renton, WA 800-927-3286
C. Nelson Manufacturing Company
Oak Harbor, OH 800-922-7339
C.R. Daniels Inc.
Ellicott City, MD 800-933-2638
Caddy Corporation of America
Bridgeport, NJ 856-467-4222
California Caster & Handtruck
San Francisco, CA 800-950-8750
Cambro Manufacturing Company
Huntington Beach, CA 800-848-1555
Cannon Conveyor Specialty Systems
Rosemount, MN 800-533-2071
Cannon Equipment Company
Rosemount, MN 800-825-8501
Carlisle Food Service Products
Oklahoma City, OK 800-654-8210
Clark Caster Company
Forest Park, IL 800-538-0765
Clipper Products
Cincinnati, OH 800-543-0324
Conveyance Technologies LLC
Cleveland, OH 800-701-2278
Corsair Display Systems
Canandalgua, NY 800-347-5245
Custom Diamond International
Laval, QC 800-326-5926
Decoren Equipment
Willowbrook, IL 708-789-3367
Dubuque Steel Products Company
Dubuque, IA 563-556-6288
Dutro Company
Logan, UT 866-388-7660
EPCO
Murfreesboro, TN 800-251-3398
Equipment Design & Fabrication
Charlotte, NC 800-949-0165
Excel
Lincolnton, NC 704-735-6535
Fabricated Components
Stroudsburg, PA 800-233-8163
FETCO - Food Equipment Technologies Corporation
Lake Zurich, IL 800-338-2699
Forbes Industries
Ontario, CA 909-923-4559
Galbreath LLC
Winamac, IN 574-946-6631
Galley
Jupiter, FL 800-537-2772
Gillis Associated Industries
Prospect Heights, IL 847-541-6500
Glowmaster Corporation
Clifton, NJ 800-272-7008
Hodges
Vienna, IL 800-444-0011
Houston Wire Works, Inc.
South Houston, TX 800-468-9477
Item Products
Houston, TX 800-333-4932
Jesco Industries, Inc.
Litchfield, MI 800-455-0019
KEMCO
Wareham, MA 800-231-5955
Key Material Handling
Simi Valley, CA 800-539-7225
Lakeside Manufacturing
Milwaukee, WI 888-558-8574
Lambertson Industries
Sparks, NV 800-548-3324
Leggett & Platt StorageP
Vernon Hills, IL 847-816-6246
Line-Master Products
Cocolalla, ID 208-265-4743
Linett Company
Blawnox, PA 800-565-2165
Load King Manufacturing Company
Jacksonville, FL 800-531-4975
M&E Manufacturing Company
Kingston, NY 845-331-2110
Metal Equipment Company
Cleveland, OH 800-700-6326
Metal Master
Tucson, AZ 800-488-8729
Metro Corporation
Wilkes Barre, PA 800-433-2233
Mid-States Manufacturing & Engineering
Milton, IA 800-346-1792
Midwest Aircraft Products Company
Mansfield, OH 419-522-2231
Miller Metal Fabricators
Staunton, VA 540-886-5575
MIT Poly-Cart Corporation
New York, NY 800-234-7659
Moseley Corporation
Franklin, MA 800-667-3539
Mosshaim Innovations
Jacksonville, FL 888-995-7775
New Age Industrial Corporation
Norton, KS 800-255-0104
Nexel Industries
Port Washington, NY 800-245-6682
Normandie Metal Fabricators
Port Washington, NY 800-221-2398
Nu-Star
Shakopee, MN 952-445-8295
Omicron Steel Products Company
Jamaica, NY 718-805-3400
Ortmayer Materials Handling Inc
Brooklyn, NY 718-875-7995
Palmer Snyder
Brookfield, WI 800-762-0415
Piper Products
Wausau, WI 800-544-3057
Polar Beer Systems
Sun City, CA 951-928-8171
Princeton Shelving
Cedar Rapids, IA 319-369-0355
Pucel Enterprises
Cleveland, OH 800-336-4986
Reelcraft Industries
Columbia City, IN 800-444-3134
Royce-Rolls Ringer Company
Grand Rapids, MI 800-253-9638
Rubbermaid Commercial Products
Winchester, VA 800-336-9880
Schlueter Company
Janesville, WI 800-359-1700
Shammi Industries/Sammons Equipment
Corona, CA 800-417-9260
Sharpsville Container
Sharpsville, PA 800-645-1248
Shouldice Brothers SheetMetal
Battle Creek, MI 269-962-5579
Solve Needs International
White Lake, MI 800-783-2462
Steel Specialty Equipment Corporation
Ridgewood, NY 800-521-7732
Super Sturdy
Weldon, NC 800-253-4833
Superior Products Company
Saint Paul, MN 800-328-9800
Technibilt/Cari-All
Newton, NC 800-233-3972
Travelon
Elk Grove Vlg, IL 800-537-5544
Traycon
Carlstadt, NJ 201-939-5555
Tri-Boro Shelving & Partition
Farmville, VA 434-315-5600
Westfield Sheet Metal Works
Kenilworth, NJ 908-276-5500
White Mop Wringer Company
Tampa, FL 800-237-7582
Wilder Manufacturing Company
Port Jervis, NY 800-832-1319

Utility

AMCO Corporation
City of Industry, CA 626-855-2550
Antrim Manufacturing
Brookfield, WI 262-781-6860
ARC Specialties
Valencia, CA 661-775-8500
BMH Equipment
Sacramento, CA 800-350-8828
Caddy Corporation of America
Bridgeport, NJ 856-467-4222
Cannon Equipment Company
Rosemount, MN 800-825-8501
Continental Commercial Products
Bridgeton, MO 800-325-1051
Duke Manufacturing Company
Saint Louis, MO 800-735-3853
FWE/Food Warming Equipment Company, Inc
Crystal Lake, IL 800-222-4393
Galley
Jupiter, FL 800-537-2772
Hodge Manufacturing Company
Springfield, MA 800-262-4634
Hot Food Boxes
Mooresville, IN 800-733-8073
Lakeside Manufacturing
Milwaukee, WI 888-558-8574
Leggett & Platt StorageP
Vernon Hills, IL 847-816-6246
Linett Company
Blawnox, PA 800-565-2165
METRO Material Handling & Storage Products
Wilkes Barre, PA 800-433-2232
Princeton Shelving
Cedar Rapids, IA 319-369-0355
Steel Specialty Equipment Corporation
Ridgewood, NY 800-521-7732
Technibilt/Cari-All
Newton, NC 800-233-3972

Casters

Albion Industries
Albion, MI 800-835-8911
Atlas Equipment Company
Kansas City, MO 800-842-9188
Bassick Casters
Shiner, TX 888-527-3526
Beacon Specialties
New York, NY 800-221-9405
Berlon Industries
Hustisford, WI 800-899-3580

BMH Equipment
Sacramento, CA 800-350-8828
California Caster & Handtruck
San Francisco, CA 800-950-8750
Clark Caster Company
Forest Park, IL 800-538-0765
Colson Caster Corporation
Jonesboro, AR. 800-643-5515
Component Hardware Group
Lakewood, NJ 800-526-3694
Darcor Casters
Toronto, ON 800-387-7206
Fasteners for Retail
Cincinnati, OH 800-422-2547
Faultless Caster
Evansville, IN 800-322-7359
Hamilton
Hamilton, OH 888-699-7164
Jarvis Caster Company
Jackson, TN 800-995-9876
Jilson Group
Lodi, NJ. 800-969-5400
Lakeside Manufacturing
Milwaukee, WI 888-558-8574
LPI Imports
Chicago, IL 877-389-6563
Metro Corporation
Wilkes Barre, PA. 800-433-2233
Mid-State Metal Casting & Manufacturing
Fresno, CA 559-445-1974
Monarch-McLaren
Weston, ON. 416-741-9675
Par-Kan Company
Silver Lake, IN 800-291-5487
Roll Rite Corporation
Hayward, CA 800-345-9305
Solve Needs International
White Lake, MI. 800-783-2462
Standex International Corporation
Salem, NH. 603-893-9701
TENTE CASTERS
Hebron, KY. 800-783-2470

Clutches & Brakes

Industrial

Warner Electric
South Beloit, IL 800-234-3369

Cordage, Rope & Twine

A&A Line & Wire Corporation
Flushing, NY. 800-886-2657
Barbour Threads
Anniston, AL 256-237-9461
Caristrap International
Laval, QC 800-361-9466
Consolidated Thread Mills, Inc.
Fall River, MA 508-672-0032
Crown Industries
East Orange, NJ 877-747-2457
Fitec International
Memphis, TN 800-332-6387
Fulton-Denver Company
Denver, CO 800-776-6715
James Thompson & Company
New York, NY 212-686-4242
January & Wood Company
Maysville, KY. 606-564-3301
John E. Ruggles & Company
New Bedford, MA 508-992-9766
Pensacola Rope Company
Slidell, LA. 850-968-9760
Rose City Awning Company
Portland, OR 800-446-4104
Terkelsen Machine Company
Hyannis, MA. 508-775-6229
US Line Company
Westfield, MA. 413-562-3629
Woodstock Line Company
Putnam, CT 860-928-6557

Drums

Acra Electric Corporation
Tulsa, OK 800-223-4328
Bergen Barrel & Drum Company
Kearny, NJ. 201-998-3500
Centennial Molding LLC
Hastings, NE. 888-883-2189
Containair Packaging Corporation
Paterson, NJ 888-276-6500
Dubuque Steel Products Company
Dubuque, IA 563-556-6288
DuPont
Wilmington, DE 800-441-7515
Greenfield Packaging
White Plains, NY 914-993-0233
Grief Brothers Corporation
Delaware, OH 740-549-6000
Jupiter Mills Corporation
Roslyn, NY 800-853-5121
Lima Barrel & Drum Company
Lima, OH 419-224-8916
MO Industries
Whippany, NJ 973-386-9228
Munson Machinery Company
Utica, NY 800-944-6644
Myers Container Corporation
Hayward, CA 510-652-6847
Process Solutions
Riviera Beach, FL. 561-840-0050
Pucel Enterprises
Cleveland, OH 800-336-4986
Remcon Plastics
West Reading, PA 800-360-3636
RMI-C/Rotonics Manaufacturing
Bensenville, IL 630-773-9510
Russell-Stanley Corporation
Woodbridge, NJ 800-229-6001
Sharpsville Container
Sharpsville, PA 800-645-1248
Sirco Systems
Birmingham, AL. 205-731-7800
Smurfit Stone Container
San Jose, CA 408-925-9391
Trilla Steel Drum Corporation
Chicago, IL 773-847-7588

Food Storage Supplies

Abel Manufacturing Company
Appleton, WI 920-734-4443
Accent Store Fixtures
Kenosha, WI 800-545-1144
Acrison
Moonachie, NJ 800-422-4266
Advance Energy Technologies
Clifton Park, NY. 800-724-0198
Aero Tec Laboratories/ATL
Ramsey, NJ 800-526-5330
AFECO
Algona, IA. 888-295-1116
AFGO Mechanical Services, Inc.
Long Island City, NY 800-438-2346
Alliance Products, LLC
Murfreesboro, TN. 800-522-3973
Allied Engineering
North Vancouver, BC 877-929-1214
Althor Products
Bethel, CT. 800-688-2693
AMCO Corporation
City of Industry, CA 626-855-2550
Anderson-Crane Company
Minneapolis, MN 800-314-2747
Apache Stainless Equipment Corporation
Beaver Dam, WI 800-444-0398
ARC Specialties
Valencia, CA 661-775-8500
Art Plastics Handy Home Helpers
Leominster, MA 978-537-0367
Avalon Manufacturing
Corona, CA 800-676-3040
B Way Corporation
Atlanta, GA 800-527-2267
Barker Company
Keosauqua, IA 319-293-3777
Barker Wire Products
Keosauqua, IA 319-293-3176
Bennett Manufacturing Company
Alden, NY. 800-345-2142
Bergen Barrel & Drum Company
Kearny, NJ. 201-998-3500
Bertels Can Company
Belcamp, MD 410-272-0090
Bowers Process Equipment
Stratford, ON. 800-567-3223
Brenner Tank
Fond Du Lac, WI 800-558-9750
Brisker Dry Food Crisper
Oldsmar, FL 800-356-9080
Buckhorn Canada
Brampton, ON. 800-461-7579
Buckhorn Inc
Milford, OH 800-543-4454
Bulk Pack
Monroe, LA. 800-498-4215
C. Nelson Manufacturing Company
Oak Harbor, OH 800-922-7339
Cal-Mil Plastic Products
Oceanside, CA 800-321-9069
Cambro Manufacturing Company
Huntington Beach, CA 800-848-1555
Cardinal Packaging
Evansville, IN 812-424-2904
Carlisle Food Service Products
Oklahoma City, OK 800-654-8210
Carter-Hoffman Corp LLC
Mundelein, IL 800-323-9793
CCW Products, Inc.
Arvada, CO 303-427-9663
Central Fabricators
Cincinnati, OH 800-909-8265
Chem-Tainer Industries
West Babylon, NY 800-275-2436
Chem-Tainer Industries
West Babylon, NY 800-938-8896
Clayton & Lambert Manufacturing
Buckner, KY 800-626-5819
Columbian TecTank
Parsons, KS. 800-421-2788
Commercial Kitchen Company
Los Angeles, CA. 323-732-2291
Containair Packaging Corporation
Paterson, NJ 888-276-6500
Containment Technology
St Gabriel, LA. 800-388-2467
Continental Commercial Products
Bridgeton, MO 800-325-1051
Continental-Fremont
Tiffin, OH 419-448-4045
Cramer Products
New York, NY 212-645-2368
Cres Cor
Mentor, OH. 877-273-7267
Crown Custom Metal Spinning
Concord, ON. 800-750-1924
Cruvinet Winebar Company
Reno, NV 800-278-8463
Curtron Products
Pittsburgh, PA 800-833-5005
Custom Diamond International
Laval, QC 800-326-5926
Custom Metalcraft
Springfield, MO 417-862-0707
Custom Systems Integration Company
Carlsbad, CA. 760-635-1099
Denmar Corporation
North Dartmouth, MA 508-999-3295
Denstor Mobile Storage Systems
Walker, MI 800-234-7477
Design Plastics
Omaha, NE 800-491-0786
Despro Manufacturing
Cedar Grove, NJ 800-292-9906
Dubuque Steel Products Company
Dubuque, IA 563-556-6288
Duke Manufacturing Company
Saint Louis, MO 800-735-3853
E-Z Shelving Systems
Merriam, KS 800-353-1331
E.S. Robbins Corporation
Muscle Shoals, AL 800-800-2235
Easy Up Storage Systems
Seattle, WA 800-426-9234
Eaton Sales & Service
Denver, CO 800-208-2657
Edwards Fiberglass
Sedalia, MO 660-826-3915
Eldorado Miranda Manufacturing Company
Largo, FL 800-330-0708
Electrol Specialties Company
South Beloit, IL 815-389-2291
Eliason Corporation
Kalamazoo, MI 800-828-3655
Ellett Industries
Port Coquitlam, BC. 604-941-8211
Enerfab, Inc.
Cincinnati, OH 513-641-0500
Engineered Products Corporation
Greenville, SC. 800-868-0145
EPCO
Murfreesboro, TN. 800-251-3398
Epic Products
Santa Ana, CA 800-548-9791
Fab-X/Metals
Washington, NC 800-677-3229

Fabricated Components
Stroudsburg, PA 800-233-8163
Faribo Manufacturing Company
Faribault, MN 800-447-6043
Fato Fiberglass Company
Kankakee, IL. 815-932-3015
Faubion Central States Tank Company
Shawnee Mission, KS. 800-450-8265
Federal Industries
Belleville, WI 800-356-4206
Flexible Material Handling
Suwanee, GA 800-669-1501
Flexpak Corporation
Phoenix, AZ 602-269-7648
Flow of Solids
Westford, MA 978-392-0300
Forbes Industries
Ontario, CA. 909-923-4559
FreesTech
Sinking Spring, PA 717-560-7560
G.F. Frank & Sons
Fairfield, OH. 513-870-9075
G.S. Laboratory Equipment
Asheville, NC 800-252-7100
Gates Manufacturing Company
Saint Louis, MO 800-237-9226
General Industries
Goldsboro, NC 888-735-2882
Gillis Associated Industries
Prospect Heights, IL 847-541-6500
Grayline Housewares
Carol Stream, IL 800-222-7388
Hall-Woolford Tank Company
Philadelphia, PA 215-329-9022
Harmar Products
Sarasota, FL 800-833-0478
Hedstrom Corporation
Ashland, OH 700-765-9665
Hewitt Manufacturing Company
Waldron, IN. 765-525-9829
Hodges
Vienna, IL 800-444-0011
Hoover Materials Handling Group
Alpharetta, GA 800-391-3561
Houston Wire Works, Inc.
South Houston, TX 800-468-9477
Howard Fabrication
City of Industry, CA 626-961-0114
HS
Oklahoma City, OK 800-238-1240
Hughes Equipment Company LLC
Columbus, WI. 866-535-9303
IMC Teddy Food Service Equipment
Amityville, NY 800-221-5644
Industrial Air Conditioning Systems
Chicago, IL 773-486-4236
International Machinery Exchange
Deerfield, WI 800-279-0191
IPL Plastics
Edmundston, NB. 800-739-9595
Irby
Rocky Mount, NC. 252-442-0154
Item Products
Houston, TX 800-333-4932
J.H. Carr & Sons
Seattle, WA 800-523-8842
Jackstack
Inwood, NY. 800-999-9840
Jenike & Johanson
Tyngsboro, MA. 978-649-3300
Jesco Industries, Inc.
Litchfield, MI 800-455-0019
JH Display & Fixture
Greenwood, IN 317-888-0631
K&I Creative Plastics
Jacksonville, FL 904-387-0438
Kason Industries, Inc.
Lewis Center, OH 740-549-2100
Kedco Wine Storage Systems
Farmingdale, NY 800-654-9988
KHM Plastics
Gurnee, IL. 847-249-4910
Kisco Manufacturing
Greendale, BC. 604-823-7456
Kold-Hold
Edgefield, SC 803-637-3166
Lakeside Manufacturing
Milwaukee, WI 888-558-8574
Langer Manufacturing Company
Cedar Rapids, IA. 800-728-6445
Langsenkamp Manufacturing
Indianapolis, IN 877-585-1950
LaRosa Refrigeration & Equipment Company
Detroit, MI 800-527-6723
Leer Limited Partnership
New Lisbon, WI 800-766-5337
Leggett & Platt StorageP
Vernon Hills, IL 847-816-6246
Liberty Machine Company
York, PA 800-745-8152
Lodi Metal Tech
Lodi, CA 800-359-5999
Loyal Manufacturing Corporation
Indianapolis, IN 317-359-3185
LPI Imports
Chicago, IL 877-389-6563
Luce Corporation
Hamden, CT 800-344-6966
Lyon Metal Products
Aurora, IL 630-892-8941
M&E Manufacturing Company
Kingston, NY 845-331-2110
Machine Ice Company, Inc
Houston, TX 800-423-8822
Madix, Inc.
Terrell, TX. 800-776-2349
Madsen Wire Products
Orland, IN 260-829-6561
Manitowoc Foodservice Companies, Inc.
New Port Richey, FL. 877-375-9300
Marineland Commercial Aquariums
Blacksburg, VA 800-322-1266
Material Storage Systems
Gadsden, AL 877-543-2467
McCall Refrigeration
Parsons, TN. 888-732-2446
McMillin Manufacturing Corporation
Los Angeles, CA. 323-268-1900
Melville Plastics
Haw River, NC 336-578-5800
Metal Equipment Company
Cleveland, OH 800-700-6326
Metal Master
Tucson, AZ 800-488-8729
Metaline Products Company
South Amboy, NJ 732-721-1373
Metro Corporation
Wilkes Barre, PA. 800-433-2233
Meyer Machine & Garroutte Products
San Antonio, TX. 210-736-1811
Michiana Box & Crate
Niles, MI 800-677-6372
Midwest Aircraft Products Company
Mansfield, OH 419-522-2231
Miller Metal Fabricators
Staunton, VA 540-886-5575
MultiFab Plastics
Boston, MA. 888-293-5754
Myers Container Corporation
Hayward, CA 510-652-6847
Nalge Process Technologies Group
Rochester, NY. 585-586-8800
New Age Industrial Corporation
Norton, KS 800-255-0104
Nexel Industries
Port Washington, NY 800-245-6682
Normandie Metal Fabricators
Port Washington, NY 800-221-2398
NST Metals
Louisville, KY 502-584-5846
NSW Corporation
Roanoke, VA. 800-368-3610
Oak Barrel Winecraft
Berkeley, CA. 510-849-0400
OCC Systems
Ferndale, MI 800-396-2554
Omega Industries
St Louis, MO. 314-961-1668
Omicron Steel Products Company
Jamaica, NY 718-805-3400
Pallet One
Bartow, FL. 800-771-1148
Paltier
Michigan City, IN 800-348-3201
Paul Mueller Company
Springfield, MO 800-683-5537
PBC
Mahwah, NJ 800-514-2739
Peterboro Basket Company
Peterborough, NH 603-924-3861
Peterson Manufacturing Company
Plainfield, IL 800-547-8995
Piper Products
Wausau, WI. 800-544-3057
Plastic Supply Incorporated
Manchester, NH 800-752-7759
Plastilite Corporation
Omaha, NE 800-228-9506
Plastocon
Oconomowoc, WI. 800-966-0103
Polar Ware Company
Sheboygan, WI 800-237-3655
Polyfoam Packers Corporation
Arlington Hts, IL 800-323-7442
Precision
Miami, FL 800-762-7565
Process Solutions
Riviera Beach, FL. 561-840-0050
Prolon
Port Gibson, MS 888-480-9828
Pruitt's Packaging Services
Grand Rapids, MI 800-878-0553
QBD Modular Systems
Santa Clara, CA 800-663-3005
RAS Process Equipment
Robbinsville, NJ 609-371-1000
Ridg-U-Rak
North East, PA. 866-479-7225
Rose City Awning Company
Portland, OR 800-446-4104
Royal Display Corporation
Middletown, CT 800-569-1295
Royce Phoenix
Glendale, AZ. 602-256-0006
Rubbermaid Commercial Products
Winchester, VA 800-336-9880
S.S.I. Schaefer System International Limited
Brampton, ON. 905-458-5399
Saeplast Canada
St John, NB 800-567-3966
Scheb International
North Barrington, IL. 847-381-2573
Scherping Systems
Winsted, MN. 320-485-4401
Schiefer Packaging Corporation
Syracuse, NY 315-422-0615
Schlueter Company
Janesville, WI 800-359-1700
Seattle Plastics
Seattle, WA 800-441-0679
Sefi Fabricators
Amityville, NY 631-842-2200
Shammi Industries/Sammons Equipment
Corona, CA 800-417-9260
Shelley Cabinet Company
Shelley, ID. 208-357-3700
Silver King
Minneapolis, MN 800-328-3329
Sims Machinery Company
Lanett, AL. 334-576-2101
Solar Group
Taylorsville, MS 800-647-7063
Southern Ag Company
Blakely, GA. 229-723-4262
Spartan Showcase
Union, MO 800-325-0775
Specific Mechanical Systems
Victoria, BC. 250-652-2111
SPG International LLC
Covington, GA 877-503-4774
SSW Holding Company, Inc.
Elizabethtown, KY 270-769-5526
St. Louis Stainless Service
Fenton, MO. 888-507-1578
Stainless Steel Fabricators
Tyler, TX. 903-595-6625
Stearnswood
Hutchinson, MN 800-657-0144
Steel City Corporation
Youngstown, OH. 800-321-0350
Steelmaster Material Handling
Marietta, GA. 800-875-9900
Stock America Inc
Grafton, WI. 262-375-4100
Storage Unlimited
Nixa, MO 800-478-6642
Stryco Wire Products
North York, ON. 416-663-7000
Super Sturdy
Weldon, NC. 800-253-4833
Super Systems
Wausau, WI. 800-558-5880
Superior Products Company
Saint Paul, MN 800-328-9800
Supreme Metal
Alpharetta, GA 800-645-2526

Tag-Trade Associated Group
Chicago, IL 800-621-8350
Teilhaber Manufacturing Corporation
Broomfield, CO 800-358-7225
Tennsco Corporation
Dickson, TN 800-251-8184
Thermal Bags by Ingrid
Gilberts, IL 800-622-5560
Tosca Ltd
Green Bay, WI. 920-617-4000
Traex
Dane, WI. 800-356-8006
Triple-A Manufacturing Company
Toronto, ON 800-786-2238
Tupperware Brand Corporation
Orlando, FL. 800-366-3800
United States Systems
Kansas City, KS 888-281-2454
Universal Stainless
Aurora, CO 800-223-8332
Universal Stainless
Titusville, PA 800-295-1909
Upham & Walsh Lumber
Hoffman Estates, IL 847-519-1010
Valad Electric Heating Corporation
Tarrytown, NY
Vermillion Flooring Company
Springfield, MO 417-862-3785
Viatec
Hastings, MI 800-942-4702
Vollrath Company
Sheboygan, WI 920-457-4851
Wag Industries
Skokie, IL 800-621-3305
Walker Stainless Equipment
New Lisbon, WI 800-356-5734
Weiss Sheet Metal
Avon, MA 508-583-8300
Welbilt Corporation
Stamford, CT. 203-325-8300
Westfield Sheet Metal Works
Kenilworth, NJ 908-276-5500
Wilder Manufacturing Company
Port Jervis, NY 800-832-1319
Wine Chillers of California
Santa Ana, CA 800-331-4274
Wire Products Manufacturing Company
Merrill, WI 715-536-7144
Woerner Wire Works
Omaha, NE 402-451-5414
WR Key
Scarborough, ON 416-291-6246
Yorkraft
York, PA 800-872-2044
Zero Corporation
Monson, MA. 413-267-5561

Hoists & Lifting Equipment

A-Z Factory Supply
Schiller Park, IL 800-323-4511
A.C. Horn & Co
Dallas, TX. 800-657-6155
Abell-Howe Crane
Woodridge, IL. 800-366-0068
Ace Engineering Company
Fort Worth, TX 800-431-4223
Advance Lifts
St Charles, IL 800-843-3625
Air Technical Industries
Mentor, OH. 888-857-6265
Airfloat Systems
Decatur, IL 217-423-6001
Airfloat/HSI Systems
Decatur, IL 217-423-6001
ALM Corporation
Streator, IL 800-544-5438
American Crane & Equipment Company
Douglassville, PA 610-385-6061
American Lifts
Guthrie, OK. 877-360-6777
American Solving
Brook Park, OH 800-822-2285
AMF CANADA
Sherbrooke, QC 800-255-3869
Anchor Crane & Hoist Service Company
Houston, TX 800-835-2223
Anderson-Crane Company
Minneapolis, MN 800-314-2747
ANVER Corporation
Hudson, MA 800-654-3500
Anver Corporation
Hudson, MA 800-654-3500

Apache Stainless Equipment Corporation
Beaver Dam, WI 800-444-0398
Atlas Equipment Company
Kansas City, MO. 800-842-9188
Autoquip Corporation
Guthrie, OK. 877-360-6777
Baking Machines
Livermore, CA 925-449-3369
Ballymore Company
West Chester, PA. 610-696-3250
Basiloid Products Corporation
Elnora, IN 866-692-5511
Benko Products
Sheffield Village, OH 440-934-2180
BEVCO
Canada, BC 800-663-0090
Bishamon Industries Corporation
Ontario, CA. 800-358-8833
BMH Equipment
Sacramento, CA 800-350-8828
Boilzoni Auramo, Inc.
Homewood, IL 800-358-5438
Bradley Lifting Corporation
York, PA 717-848-3121
Brudi Bolzoni Auramo, Inc
Homewood, IL 800-358-5438
Buffalo Technologies Corporation
Buffalo, NY. 800-332-2419
Burns Industries
Line Lexington, PA. 800-223-6430
Bushman Equipment
Butler, WI 800-338-7810
C.J. Machine
Fridley, MN. 763-767-4630
Caldwell Group
Rockford, IL 800-628-4263
Century Crane & Hoist
Dravosburg, PA. 888-601-8801
Chester Hoist
Lisbon, OH 800-424-7248
Cleasby Manufacturing Company
San Francisco, CA 415-822-6565
Columbus McKinnon Corporation
Amherst, NY. 800-888-0985
Columbus McKinnon Corportion
Amherst, NY. 800-888-0985
Commercial Manufacturing& Supply Company
Fresno, CA 559-237-1855
Conveyance Technologies LLC
Cleveland, OH 800-701-2278
Corn States Metal Fabricators
West Des Moines, IA 515-225-7961
Cotterman Company
Croswell, MI. 800-552-3337
Crown Equipment Corporation
New Bremen, OH 419-629-2311
Currie Machinery Company
Santa Clara, CA 408-727-0424
Custom Conveyor & SupplyCorporation
Racine, WI 262-634-4920
Custom Metal Designs
Oakland, FL 800-334-1777
Delta Machine & Manufacturing
Saint Rose, LA 504-949-8304
Deshazo Crane Company
Alabaster, AL 205-664-2006
Downs Crane & Hoist Company
Los Angeles, CA. 800-748-5994
Duplex Mill & Manufacturing Company
Springfield, OH. 937-325-5555
Ederer
Seattle, WA 206-622-4421
Electrolift
Clifton, NJ. 973-471-0204
En-Hanced Products, Inc.
Westerville, OH. 800-783-7400
Equipment Outlet
Meridian, ID 208-887-1472
Frazier & Son
Conroe, TX 800-365-5438
Gem Equipment of Oregon
Woodburn, OR 503-982-9902
Gorbel
Fishers, NY. 585-924-6262
Gough Econ, Inc.
Charlotte, NC 800-204-6844
Grain Machinery Manufacturing Corporation
Miami, FL. 305-620-2525
Harrington Hoists
Manheim, PA 800-233-3010
Hayes & Stolz IndustrialManufacturing Company
Fort Worth, TX 800-725-7272

Heller Truck Body Corporation
Hillside, NJ 800-229-4148
Hydro Power
Terre Haute, IN 812-232-0156
Industrial Hoist Service
Angleton, TX 800-766-7077
Innovative Moving Systems, Inc.
Oostburg, WI. 800-619-0625
Joyce/Dayton Corporation
Kettering, OH 937-294-6261
Keenline Conveyor Systems
Omro, WI 920-685-0365
Key Material Handling
Simi Valley, CA. 800-539-7225
Knight Industries
Auburn Hills, MI 248-377-4950
Komatsu Forklift
Rolling Meadows, IL 847-437-5800
KWS Manufacturing Company
Burleson, TX. 800-543-6558
Landoo Corporation
Horsham, PA. 785-562-5381
Lift Rite
Mississauga, ON. 905-456-2603
Liftomatic Material Handling
Buffalo Grove, IL 800-837-6540
Linde Material Handling North America Corporation
Summerville, SC. 843-871-0312
Mannesmann Dematic Corporation
Solon, OH 440-248-2400
Matot - Commercial GradeLift Solutions
Bellwood, IL. 800-369-1070
Meyer Machine & Garroutte Products
San Antonio, TX 210-736-1811
NACCO Materials HandlingGroup
Fairview, OR. 503-721-6205
O'Brien Installations
Ontario, CA. 905-336-8245
Parkson Corporation
Berkeley Heights, NJ 908-464-0700
Pucel Enterprises
Cleveland, OH 800-336-4986
Quality Corporation
Denver, CO 303-777-6608
R.G. Stephens Engineering
Long Beach, CA 800-499-3001
Ratcliff Hoist Company
San Carlos, CA 650-595-3840
Raymond Corporation
Greene, NY 800-235-7200
Remstar International
Westbrook, ME. 800-639-5805
Richards Industries Systems
West Caldwell, NJ. 973-575-7480
S. Howes
Silver Creek, NY. 888-255-2611
Sackett Systems
Bensenville, IL 800-323-8332
Saturn Engineering Corporation
Newark, NJ 973-465-0224
Scaglia America
Charlotte, NC 704-357-8811
Screw Conveyor Corporation
Hammond, IN 219-931-1450
Shepard Niles
Montour Falls, NY 800-481-2260
Sidney Manufacturing Company
Sidney, OH 800-482-3535
Smetco
Aurora, OR 800-253-5400
Solve Needs International
White Lake, MI. 800-783-2462
Southern Ag Company
Blakely, GA. 229-723-4262
Southworth Products Corporation
Portland, ME. 800-743-1000
Spanco
Morgantown, PA. 800-869-2080
Sperling Industries
Omaha, NE 800-647-5062
TC/American Monorail
Saint Michael, MN 763-497-7000
Theimeg
Sharpsville, PA 724-962-3571
Toter
Statesville, NC 800-772-0071
Unidex
Warsaw, NY 800-724-1302
Unimove, LLC
Palmerton, PA. 610-826-7855
UniTrak Corporation
Port Hope, ON 866-883-5749

Valley Craft
Lake City, MN 800-328-1480
Vertical Systems
Ft. Michelle, KY..................859-485-9650
Ward Ironworks
Welland, ON......................888-441-9273
Wastequip
Charlotte, NC 877-468-9278
Weigh Right Automatic Scale Company
Joliet, IL..........................800-571-0249
Whit-Log Trailers Inc
Wilbur, OR 800-452-1234
Yargus Manufacturing
Marshall, IL 217-826-6352
Zenar Corporation
Oak Creek, WI 414-764-1800
Zimmerman Handling Systems
Madison Heights, MI 800-347-7047

Material Handling & Distribution Equipment

A P Dataweigh Systems
Cumming, GA......................877-409-2562
A-Z Factory Supply
Schiller Park, IL 800-323-4511
A.C. Horn & Co
Dallas, TX.......................800-657-6155
A.K. Robins
Baltimore, MD 800-486-9656
A.M. Loveman Lumber & Box Company
Nashville, TN 615-297-1397
A.T. Ferrell Company Inc
Bluffton, IN......................800-248-8318
AAMD
Liverpool, NY....................800-887-4167
Abel Manufacturing Company
Appleton, WI 920-734-4443
Abel Pumps
Sewickley, PA 412-741-3222
Abell-Howe Crane
Woodridge, IL....................800-366-0068
ACCO Systems
Warren, MI 800-342-2226
Accutek Packaging Equipment Company
Vista, CA.........................800-989-1828
Ace Engineering Company
Fort Worth, TX 800-431-4223
Ace Specialty Manufacturing Company
Rosemead, CA 626-444-3867
ACLA
Cranberry Twp, PA 724-776-0099
ACO
Moore, OK 405-794-7662
Acrison
Moonachie, NJ 800-422-4266
Action Engineering
Temple City, CA 626-447-8111
Adamation
Commerce, CA....................800-225-3075
Adrian Fabricators/Cargotainer
Adrian, MI........................800-221-3794
Advance Engineering Company
Township, MI 800-497-6388
Advance Lifts
St Charles, IL 800-843-3625
Advance Weight Systems
Grafton, OH 440-926-3691
Advanced Detection Systems
Milwaukee, WI....................414-672-0553
Advanced Uniflo Technologies
Wichita, KS.......................800-688-0400
Aerocon
Langhorne, PA 215-860-6056
Aerowerks
Mississauga, ON..................888-774-1616
AFCO Manufacturing
Cincinnati, OH 800-747-7332
AFECO
Algona, IA.......................888-295-1116
Air Technical Industries
Mentor, OH.......................888-857-6265
Airfloat Systems
Decatur, IL 217-423-6001
Airfloat/HSI Systems
Decatur, IL 217-423-6001
Albion Industries
Albion, MI........................800-835-8911
All Power
Sioux City, IA....................712-258-0681
All Star Carts & Vehicles
Bay Shore, NY 800-831-3166
Allen Systems
Newberg, OR 800-246-2034
Allflex Packaging Products
Ambler, PA 800-448-2467
Alliance Industrial Corporation
Lynchburg, VA 800-368-3556
Alliance Products, LLC
Murfreesboro, TN.................800-522-3973
Allied Uniking Corporation
Memphis, TN 901-365-7240
Alloy Products Corporation
Waukesha, WI....................800-236-6603
Amark Packaging Systems
Kansas City, MO..................816-965-9000
AMCO Corporation
City of Industry, CA 626-855-2550
American Box Corporation
Lisbon, OH.......................330-424-8055
American Crane & Equipment Company
Douglassville, PA 610-385-6061
American Extrusion International
South Beloit, IL 815-624-6616
American Food Equipment Company
Hayward, CA 510-783-0255
American Lifts
Guthrie, OK......................877-360-6777
American Pallet
Oakdale, CA 209-847-6122
American Solving
Brook Park, OH 800-822-2285
Ametek Technical & Industrial Products
Kent, OH.........................215-256-6601
AMF CANADA
Sherbrooke, QC 800-255-3869
Ampco Pumps Company
Glendale, WI.....................800-737-8671
Anchor Crane & Hoist Service Company
Houston, TX 800-835-2223
Anderson Machine Sales
Fort Lee, NJ
Anderson Tool & Engineering Company
Anderson, IN.....................765-643-6691
Anderson-Crane Company
Minneapolis, MN 800-314-2747
Andritz
Muncy, PA........................570-546-8211
Ann Arbor Computer
Farmington Hills, MI 800-526-9322
Antrim Manufacturing
Brookfield, WI 262-781-6860
ANVER Corporation
Hudson, MA 800-654-3500
Anver Corporation
Hudson, MA 800-654-3500
Apache Stainless Equipment Corporation
Beaver Dam, WI...................800-444-0398
Apollo Sheet Metal
Kennewick, WA 509-586-1104
Applied Chemical Technology
Florence, AL......................800-228-3217
ARC Specialties
Valencia, CA.....................661-775-8500
ARPAC LP
Schiller Park, IL 847-678-9034
Art Wire Works
Bedford Park, IL..................708-458-3993
ASGCO Manufacturing
Allentown, PA....................800-344-4000
Ashworth Bros
Winchester, VA...................800-682-4594
Assembly Technology & Test
Livonia, MI 734-522-1900
Atlas Equipment Company
Kansas City, MO..................800-842-9188
Auto Pallets-Boxes
Lathrup Village, MI 800-875-2699
Automated Flexible Conveyor
Clifton, NJ.......................800-694-7271
Automated Production Systems Corporation
New Freedom, PA.................888-345-5377
Automatic Handling
Erie, MI..........................734-847-0633
Automotion
Oak Lawn, IL 708-229-3700
Autoquip Corporation
Guthrie, OK.......................877-360-6777
AZO Food
Memphis, TN 901-794-9480
Baking Machines
Livermore, CA 925-449-3369
Balemaster
Crown Point, IN 219-663-4525
Ballymore Company
West Chester, PA.................610-696-3250
Bamco Belting Products
Greenville, SC....................800-258-2358
Barrette - Outdoor Livin
Middleburg Hts., OH 800-336-2383
Base Manufacturing
Monroe, GA 800-367-0572
Basiloid Products Corporation
Elnora, IN 866-692-5511
Bay Area Pallet Company/IFCO Systems
Houston, TX 877-430-4326
Bayhead Products Corporation
Dover, NH........................800-229-4323
BC Wood Products
Ashland, VA 804-798-9154
Bedford Enterprises
Santa Maria, CA 800-242-8884
Beech Engineering
Ashland, OH 419-281-0894
Belco Packaging Systems
Monrovia, CA.....................800-833-1833
Bell Packaging Corporation
Marion, IN........................800-382-0153
Belt Technologies
Agawam, MA 413-786-9922
Benko Products
Sheffield Village, OH 440-934-2180
Bennett Box & Pallet Company
Winston, NC 800-334-8741
Bergen Barrel & Drum Company
Kearny, NJ........................201-998-3500
Berndorf Belt Technology USA
Elgin, IL 877-232-7322
Bessco Tube Bending & Pipe Fabricating
Thornton, IL 800-337-3977
Best
Brunswick, OH 800-827-9237
Best Diversified Products
Jonesboro, AR.....................800-327-9209
Bettendorf Stanford
Salem, IL..........................800-548-2253
Beumer Corporation
Branchburg, NJ 732-560-8222
BEVCO
Canada, BC........................800-663-0090
Bevles Company
Dallas, TX.........................800-441-1601
Bilt-Rite Conveyors
New London, WI 920-982-6600
Biner Ellison
Vista, CA..........................800-733-8162
Bishamon Industries Corporation
Ontario, CA.......................800-358-8833
Black River Pallet Company
Zeeland, MI.......................800-427-6515
Blue Giant Equipment Corporation
Brampton, ON.....................800-668-7078
Bluff Manufacturing
Fort Worth, TX 800-433-2212
BMH
City of Industry, CA 909-349-2530
BMH Equipment
Sacramento, CA 800-350-8828
Boilzoni Auramo, Inc.
Homewood, IL 800-358-5438
Bowman Hollis Manufacturing
Charlotte, NC 888-269-2358
Bradley Lifting Corporation
York, PA..........................717-848-3121
Branford Vibrator Company
Peru, IL...........................800-262-2106
Brothers Metal Products
Santa Ana, CA 714-972-3008
Broussard Cane Equipment
Parks, LA 337-845-5080
Brudi Bolzoni Auramo, Inc
Homewood, IL 800-358-5438
Brute Fabricators
Castroville, TX 800-777-2788
Bryant Products
Ixonia, WI.........................800-825-3874
Buckhorn Canada
Brampton, ON.....................800-461-7579
Buffalo Technologies Corporation
Buffalo, NY.......................800-332-2419
Buhler Group
Raleigh, NC 919-851-2000
Bulldog Factory Service
Madison Heights, MI 248-541-3500
Bunting Magnetics Company
Newton, KS.......................800-835-2526

Burgess Enterprises, Inc
Renton, WA........................800-927-3286
Burgess Manufacturing ofOklahoma
Guthrie, OK........................800-804-1913
Burns Industries
Line Lexington, PA................800-223-6430
Bushman Equipment
Butler, WI........................800-338-7810
Busse/SJI
Randolph, WI......................800-882-4995
C S Bell Company
Tiffin, OH........................888-958-6381
C&L Wood Products
Hartselle, AL.....................800-483-2035
C&R Refrigation Inc,
Center, TX........................800-438-6182
C. Nelson Manufacturing Company
Oak Harbor, OH....................800-922-7339
C.H. Babb Company
Raynham, MA.......................508-977-0600
C.J. Machine
Fridley, MN.......................763-767-4630
C.R. Daniels Inc.
Ellicott City, MD.................800-933-2638
Cable Conveyor Systems
Columbia, SC......................800-624-6064
Caddy Corporation of America
Bridgeport, NJ....................856-467-4222
Caldwell Group
Rockford, IL......................800-628-4263
California Caster & Handtruck
San Francisco, CA.................800-950-8750
Caljan America
Denver, CO........................303-321-3600
Cambelt International Corporation
Salt Lake City, UT................801-972-5511
Can Lines Engineering
Downey, CA........................562-861-2996
Cannon Conveyor Specialty Systems
Rosemount, MN.....................800-533-2071
Cannon Equipment Company
Rosemount, MN.....................800-825-8501
Cantley-Ellis Manufacturing Company
Kingsport, TN.....................423-246-4671
Carbis
Florence, SC......................800-948-7750
Carleton Helical Technologies
New Britain, PA...................215-230-8900
Carman Industries
Jeffersonville, IN................800-456-7560
Carrier Vibrating Equipment
Louisville, KY....................502-969-3171
Carron Net Company
Two Rivers, WI....................800-558-7768
Carson Industries
Pomona, CA........................800-735-5566
Cassel Box & Lumber Company
Grafton, WI.......................262-377-4420
Casso-Solar Corporation
Pomona, NY........................800-988-4455
Cattron Group International
Sharpsville, PA...................724-962-1629
Cayne Industrial Sales Corporation
Bronx, NY.........................718-993-5800
Cedar Box Company
Minneapolis, MN...................612-332-4287
Century Crane & Hoist
Dravosburg, PA....................888-601-8801
Century Industries
Sellersburg, IN...................800-248-3371
Challenger Pallet & Supply
Idaho Falls, ID...................800-733-0205
Chantland-MHS Company
Dakota City, IA...................515-332-4045
Charles Tirschman Company
Baltimore, MD.....................410-282-6199
Charlton & Hill
Lethbridge, AB....................403-328-3388
Chase-Logeman Corporation
Greensboro, NC....................336-665-0754
Checker Engineering
New Hope, MN......................888-800-5001
Chem-Tainer Industries
West Babylon, NY..................800-938-8896
Cherry's Industrial Equipment Corporation
Elk Grove Vlg, IL.................800-350-0011
Chester Hoist
Lisbon, OH........................800-424-7248
Chicago Conveyor Corporation
Addison, IL.......................630-543-6300
Chief Industries
Kearney, NE.......................800-359-8833
CHL Systems
Souderton, PA.....................215-723-7284
Chocolate Concepts
Hartville, OH.....................330-877-3322
Christianson Systems
Blomkest, MN......................800-328-8896
Christy Machine Company
Fremont, OH.......................888-332-6451
Cimino Box Company
Cleveland, OH.....................216-961-7377
Cincinnati Boss Company
Omaha, NE.........................402-556-4070
Cintex of America
Carol Stream, IL..................800-424-6839
Citra-Tech
Lakeland, FL......................863-646-3868
Clamp Swing Pricing Company
Oakland, CA.......................800-227-7615
Clark Caster Company
Forest Park, IL...................800-538-0765
Cleasby Manufacturing Company
San Francisco, CA.................415-822-6565
CLECO Systems
Marietta, GA......................770-392-0330
Cleveland Vibrator Company
Cleveland, OH.....................800-221-3298
Climax Packaging Machinery
Hamilton, OH......................513-874-1233
Clipper Belt Lacer Company
Grand Rapids, MI..................616-459-3196
Clipper Products
Cincinnati, OH....................800-543-0324
Clymer Enterprises
Pandora, OH.......................800-448-0784
Coastal Pallet Corporation
Bridgeport, CT....................203-333-6222
Coblentz Brothers
Apple Creek, OH...................330-857-7211
Coddington Lumber Company
Frostburg, MD.....................301-689-8816
Collins Manufacturing Company Ltd
Langley, BC.......................800-663-6761
Colson Caster Corporation
Jonesboro, AR.....................800-643-5515
Columbia Machine
Vancouver, WA.....................800-628-4065
Columbus McKinnon Corporation
Amherst, NY.......................800-888-0985
Columbus McKinnon Corportion
Amherst, NY.......................800-888-0985
Commercial Manufacturing& Supply Company
Fresno, CA........................559-237-1855
Conesco Conveyor Corporation
Clifton, NJ.......................973-365-1440
Continental Commercial Products
Bridgeton, MO.....................800-325-1051
Control & Metering
Mississauga, ON...................800-736-5739
Control Chief Corporation
Bradford, PA......................814-362-6811
Controls Unlimited
Perry, OH.........................440-259-2500
Conveyance Technologies LLC
Cleveland, OH.....................800-701-2278
Conveying Industries
Denver, CO........................877-600-4874
Conveyor Accessories
Burr Ridge, IL....................800-323-7093
Conveyor Components Company
Croswell, MI......................800-233-3233
Conveyor Dynamics Corporation
Saint Peters, MO..................636-279-1111
Conveyor Supply
Deerfield, IL.....................847-945-5670
Cook King
Laguna Beach, CA..................949-497-1235
Corinth Products
Corinth, ME.......................207-285-3387
Corn States Metal Fabricators
West Des Moines, IA...............515-225-7961
Coss Engineering Sales Company
Rochester Hills, MI...............800-446-1365
Cotter Corporation
Danvers, MA
Cotterman Company
Croswell, MI......................800-552-3337
Craft Industries
Long Island City, NY..............252-753-3152
Creative Foam Corporation
Fenton, MI........................810-629-4149
Creative Techniques
Auburn Hills, MI..................800-473-0284
Crippen Manufacturing Company
St. Louis, MI.....................800-872-2474
Crown Equipment Corporation
New Bremen, OH....................419-629-2311
Crown Simplimatic Company
Lynchburg, VA.....................434-582-1200
Cryovac
Duncan, SC........................800-845-3456
CSS International Corporation
Philadelphia, PA..................800-278-8107
Cugar Machine Company
Fort Worth, TX....................817-927-0411
Cumberland Box & Mill Company
Cumberland, MD....................301-724-1010
Currie Machinery Company
Santa Clara, CA...................408-727-0424
Custom Conveyor & SupplyCorporation
Racine, WI........................262-634-4920
Custom Diamond International
Laval, QC.........................800-326-5926
Custom Food Machinery
Stockton, CA......................209-463-4343
Custom Metal Designs
Oakland, FL.......................800-334-1777
Custom Metalcraft
Springfield, MO...................417-862-0707
Custom Millers Supply Company
Monmouth, IL......................309-734-6312
Custom Systems Integration Company
Carlsbad, CA......................760-635-1099
Cutler Brothers Box & Lumber Company
Fairview, NJ......................201-943-2535
Cutter Lumber Products
Livermore, CA.....................925-443-5959
Cyclonaire Corporation
York, NE..........................800-445-0730
D&M Pallet Company
Neshkoro, WI......................920-293-4616
Daewoo Heavy Industries America Corporation
Cleveland, OH.....................800-323-9662
Dairy Conveyor Corporation
Brewster, NY......................845-278-7878
Damrow Company
Fond Du Lac, WI...................800-236-1501
Daniel Boone Lumber Industries
Morehead, KY......................606-784-7586
Darcor Casters
Toronto, ON.......................800-387-7206
Darnell-Rose Corporation
City of Industry, CA..............800-327-6355
Davis Core & Pad Company
Cave Spring, GA...................800-235-7483
Davron Technologies
Chattanooga, TN...................423-870-1888
Day Lumber Company
Westfield, MA.....................413-568-3511
Dearborn Mid-West Company
Lenexa, KS........................913-384-9950
Dearborn Mid-West Conveyor Company
Taylor, MI........................734-288-4400
Decoren Equipment
Willowbrook, IL...................708-789-3367
Del-Tec Packaging
Greenville, SC....................800-747-8683
Delta Machine & Manufacturing
Saint Rose, LA....................504-949-8304
Delta/Ducon
Malvern, PA.......................800-238-2974
Dematic Corp
Grand Rapids, MI..................877-725-7500
Dempster Systems
Toccoa, GA........................706-886-2327
Denver Reel & Pallet Company
Denver, CO........................303-321-1920
Descon EDM
Brocton, NY.......................716-792-9300
Deshazo Crane Company
Alabaster, AL.....................205-664-2006
Design Systems
Farmington Hills, MI..............800-660-4374
Design Technology Corporation
Lexington, MA.....................800-597-7063
Development Workshop
Idaho Falls, ID...................800-657-5597
Dexco
Leola, PA.........................800-345-8170
Dillin Engineered Systems Corporation
Perrysburg, OH....................419-666-6789
Dimension Industries
Alexandria, MN....................763-425-3955
Diversified Capping Equipment
Perrysburg, OH....................419-666-2566

Diversified Metal Engineering
Charlottetown, PE 902-628-6900
DMC-David Manufacturing Company
Mason City, IA 641-424-7010
Dominion Pallet Company
Mineral, VA 800-227-5321
Donahower & Company
Olathe, KS 913-829-2650
Donovan Enterprises
Lagrange, GA 800-233-6180
Douglas Machine
Alexandria, MN 320-763-6587
Douglas Machines Corporation
Clearwater, FL 800-331-6870
Downs Crane & Hoist Company
Los Angeles, CA 800-748-5994
Dubuque Steel Products Company
Dubuque, IA 563-556-6288
Dufeck Manufacturing Company
Denmark, WI 888-603-9663
Duke Manufacturing Company
Saint Louis, MO 800-735-3853
Dunkley International
Kalamazoo, MI 800-666-1264
Dunrite
Fremont, NE 800-782-3061
Duplex Mill & Manufacturing Company
Springfield, OH 937-325-5555
Dupps Company
Germantown, OH 937-855-6555
Durable Corporation
Norwalk, OH 800-537-1603
Durand-Wayland, Inc.
Lagrange, GA 800-241-2308
Durant Box Factory
Durant, OK 580-924-4035
Dutro Company
Logan, UT 866-388-7660
Dyco
Bloomsburg, PA 800-545-3926
Dyna-Veyor
Newark, NJ 800-930-4760
Dynabilt Products
Readville, MA 800-443-1008
Dynamet
Kalamazoo, MI 269-385-0006
Dynamic Air
Saint Paul, MN 651-484-2900
Dynamic Automation
Simi Valley, CA 805-584-8476
Dynamic Storage Systems Inc.
Brooksville, FL 800-974-8211
E-ZLIFT Conveyors
Denver, CO 800-821-9966
E.F. Bavis & Associates Drive-Thru
Maineville, OH 513-677-0500
E2M
Duluth, GA 800-622-4326
Earl Soesbe Company
Romeoville, IL 219-866-4191
Eckels-Bilt, Inc
Fort Worth, TX 800-343-9020
Ederer
Seattle, WA 206-622-4421
Edmeyer
Minneapolis, MN 651-450-1210
Edson Packaging Machinery
Hamilton, ON 905-385-3201
Edwards Products
Cincinnati, OH 800-543-1835
EGA Products
Brookfield, WI 262-781-7899
Eichler Wood Products
Laurys Station, PA 610-262-6749
Eisenmann Corporation
Crystal Lake, IL 815-455-4100
Elba Pallets Company
Elba, AL 334-897-6034
Elberta Crate & Box Company
Carpentersville, IL 888-672-9260
Electrical Engineering &Equipment Company
Des Moines, IA . . . . . 800-33 -722
Electrolift
Clifton, NJ 973-471-0204
ELF Machinery
La Porte, IN 800-328-0466
Elwell Parker
Coraopolis, PA 800-272-9953
EMC Solutions, Inc
Celina, OH 419-586-2388
Emtrol
York, PA 800-634-4927

En-Hanced Products, Inc.
Westerville, OH 800-783-7400
Engineered Products Corporation
Greenville, SC 800-868-0145
Enrick Company
Zumbrota, MN 507-732-5215
Equipment Design & Fabrication
Charlotte, NC 800-949-0165
Equipment Outlet
Meridian, ID 208-887-1472
Eriez Magnetics
Erie, PA 800-346-4946
Ermanco
Norton Shores, MI 231-798-4547
ERO/Goodrich Forest Products
Tualatin, OR 800-458-5545
Esko Pallets
Cloquet, MN 218-879-8553
Eugene Welding Company
Marysville, MI 810-364-7421
Excalibur Miretti Group
Fairfield, NJ 973-808-8399
Excel
Lincolnton, NC 704-735-6535
F&A Fabricating
Battle Creek, MI 269-965-3268
F. Harold Haines Manufacturing
Presque Isle, ME 207-762-1411
F.E. Wood & Sons
East Baldwin, ME 207-286-5003
F.N. Smith Corporation
Oregon, IL 815-732-2171
Fabreeka International
Boise, ID 800-423-4469
Fabri-Form Company
Byesville, OH 740-685-0424
Fabricated Components
Stroudsburg, PA 800-233-8163
Fabricating & Welding Corporation
Chicago, IL 773-928-2050
Fabrication Specialties Corporation
Centerville, TN 931-729-2283
Fairborn
Upper Sandusky, OH 800-262-1188
Fata Automation
Sterling Heights, MI 586-323-9400
Faultless Caster
Evansville, IN 800-322-7359
Fehlig Brothers Box & Lumber Company
St Louis, MO 314-241-6900
FEI
Mansfield, TX 800-346-5908
Felco Bag & Burlap Company
Baltimore, MD 800-673-8488
Fenner Dunlop Engineered Conveyer Solutions
Pittsburgh, PA 412-249-0700
FETCO - Food Equipment Technologies Corporation
Lake Zurich, IL 800-338-2699
Fibre Converters
Constantine, MI 269-279-1700
Filler Specialties
Zeeland, MI 616-772-9235
Filling Equipment Company
Flushing, NY 800-247-7127
Fillit
Kirkland, QC 514-694-2390
Fishmore
Melbourne,, FL 321-723-4751
Fleet Wood Goldco Wyard
Cockeysville, MD 410-785-1934
Fleetwood
Romeoville, IL 630-759-6800
Fleetwood Systems
Orlando, FL 407-855-0230
FleetwoodGoldcoWyard
Romeoville, IL 630-759-6800
Flexco
Downers Grove, IL 800-323-3444
Flexible Material Handling
Suwanee, GA 800-669-1501
Flexicon Corporation
Bethlehem, PA 610-814-2400
Flodin
Moses Lake, WA 509-766-2996
Flow of Solids
Westford, MA 978-392-0300
Flow-Turn, Inc.
Union, NJ 908-687-3225
Fogg Company
Holland, MI 616-786-3644
Food Engineering Unlimited
Fullerton, CA 714-879-8762

Food Machinery Sales
Bogart, GA 706-549-2207
Food Processing Equipment Company
Santa Fe Springs, CA 479-751-9392
Forbo Siegling LLC
Huntersville, NC 800-255-5581
Foremost Machine Builders
Fairfield, NJ 973-227-0700
Fox Valley Wood Products
Kaukauna, WI 920-766-4069
FPEC Corporation
Santa Fe Springs, CA 562-802-3727
Frazier & Son
Conroe, TX 800-365-5438
Frazier Industrial Company
Long Valley, NJ 800-859-1342
Fred D. Pfening Company
Columbus, OH 614-294-1633
FreesTech
Sinking Spring, PA 717-560-7560
Frelco
Stephenville, NL 709-643-5668
Fresno Pallet, Inc.
Sultana, CA 559-591-4111
Frost Food Handling Products
Grand Rapids, MI 616-453-7781
G.F. Frank & Sons
Fairfield, OH 513-870-9075
Galbreath LLC
Winamac, IN 574-946-6631
Gardner Denver Inc.
Toronto, ON 416-763-4681
Garvey Corporation
Hammonton, NJ 800-257-8581
Gates Manufacturing Company
Saint Louis, MO 800-237-9226
Gatewood Products LLC
Parkersburg, WV 800-827-5461
GBN Machine & Engineering Corporation
Woodford, VA 800-446-9871
Gebo Conveyors, Consultants & Systems
Laval, QC 450-973-3337
Gebo Corporation
Bradenton, FL 941-727-1400
Gem Equipment of Oregon
Woodburn, OR 503-982-9902
General Corrugated Machinery Company
Palisades Park, NJ 201-944-0644
General Electric Company
Louisville, KY 502-452-4311
General Machinery Corporation
Sheboygan, WI 888-243-6622
General Steel Fabricators
Joplin, MO 800-820-8644
General Tank
Berwick, PA 800-435-8265
Georgia Duck & Cordage Mill
Scottdale, GA 404-297-3170
Gerrity Industries
Monmouth, ME 877-933-2804
Gillis Associated Industries
Prospect Heights, IL 847-541-6500
Girard Wood Products
Puyallup, WA 253-845-0505
GL Packaging Products
West Chicago, IL 866-935-8755
Glatt Air Techniques
Ramsey, NJ 201-825-8700
Goeman's Wood Products
Hartford, WI 262-673-6090
Goergen-Mackwirth Company
Buffalo, NY 716-874-4800
Goldco Industries
Loveland, CO 970-278-4400
Gorbel
Fishers, NY 585-924-6262
Gough Econ, Inc.
Charlotte, NC 800-204-6844
Graham Pallet Company
Tompkinsville, KY 888-525-0694
Grain Machinery Manufacturing Corporation
Miami, FL 305-620-2525
Gram Equipment of America
Tampa, FL 813-248-1978
Gray Woodproducts
Orrington, ME 207-825-3578
Graybill Machines
Lititz, PA 717-626-5221
Green-Tek
Janesville, WI 800-747-6440
Greenbelt Industries
Buffalo, NY 800-668-1114

Greenline Corporation
Charlotte, NC 800-331-5312
Greitzer
Elizabeth City, NC 252-338-4000
Griffin Cardwell, Ltd
Louisville, KY 502-636-1374
H&H Lumber Company
Amarillo, TX. 806-335-1813
H&H Wood Products
Hamburg, NY 716-648-5600
H.G. Weber & Company
Kiel, WI. 920-894-2221
H.K. Systems
Milwaukee, WI 800-424-7365
Habasit America
Suwanee, GA 800-458-6431
Hackney Brothers
Washington, NC 800-763-0700
Halton Packaging Systems
Oakville, ON. 905-847-9141
Hamilton
Hamilton, OH 888-699-7164
Hampel Corporation
Germantown, WI. 800-494-4762
Hampton Roads Box Company
Suffolk, VA 757-934-2355
Handling Specialty
Niagara Falls, NY 800-559-8366
Hanel Storage Systems
Pittsburgh, PA 412-787-3444
Hannay Reels
Westerlo, NY. 877-467-3357
Hanson Box & Lumber Company
Wakefield, MA 617-245-0358
Hapman Conveyors
Kalamazoo, MI 800-968-7722
Harbor Pallet Company
Anaheim, CA 714-533-4940
Hardy Systems Corporation
Northbrook, IL 800-927-3956
Harper Trucks
Wichita, KS. 800-835-4099
Harrington Hoists
Manheim, PA 800-233-3010
Hart Design & Manufacturing
Green Bay, WI. 920-468-5927
Hartness International
Greenville, SC. 800-845-8791
Hawkeye Pallet Company
Johnston, IA 515-276-0409
Hayes & Stolz IndustrialManufacturing Company
Fort Worth, TX 800-725-7272
HDT Manufacturing
Salem, OH. 800-968-7438
Hectronic
Oklahoma City, OK 405-946-3574
Heller Truck Body Corporation
Hillside, NJ 800-229-4148
Herkimer Pallet & Wood Products Company
Herkimer, NY 315-866-4591
Hevi-Haul International
Menomonee Falls, WI. 800-558-0577
HHP
Henniker, NH 603-428-3298
Hi Roller Enclosed Belt Conveyors
Sioux Falls, SD 800-328-1785
Hilderth Wood Products
Wadesboro, NC. 704-826-8326
Hinchcliff Products Company
Strongsville, OH 440-238-5200
Hodge Manufacturing Company
Springfield, MA 800-262-4634
Hodges
Vienna, IL 800-444-0011
Hoffmeyer Company
San Leandro, CA. 800-350-2358
Hoppmann Corporation
Elkwood, VA. 800-368-3582
Hormann Flexan Llc
Leetsdale, PA 800-365-3667
Horn Packaging Corporation
Lancaster, MA. 800-832-7020
Hot Food Boxes
Mooresville, IN. 800-733-8073
Hot Shot Delivery Systems
Bloomingdale, IL 630-924-8817
Houston Wire Works, Inc.
South Houston, TX 800-468-9477
Hovair Systems Inc
Kent, WA. 800-237-4518
Hunter Woodworks
Carson, CA 800-966-4751

Hurt Conveyor Equipment Company
Los Angeles, CA. 323-541-0433
Hydro Power
Terre Haute, IN 812-232-0156
Hyster Company
San Diego, CA 855-804-2118
IEW
Niles, OH 330-652-0113
Iman Pack
Westland, MI. 800-810-4626
Incinerator International
Houston, TX 713-227-1466
Industrial Automation Systems
Santa Clarita, CA 888-484-4427
Industrial Hardwood
Perrysburg, OH 419-666-2503
Industrial Kinetics
Downers Grove, IL 800-655-0306
Industrial Lumber & Packaging
Spring Lake, MI 616-842-1457
Industrial WoodFab & Packaging Company
Riverview, MI. 734-284-4808
Innovative Moving Systems, Inc.
Oostburg, WI. 800-619-0625
Inter-City Welding & Manufacturing
Independence, MO 816-252-1770
Interlake Material Handling
Naperville, IL 800-468-3752
International Wood Industries
Snohomish, WA 800-922-6141
Interroll Corporation
Wilmington, NC 800-830-9680
Intralox
New Orleans, LA 800-535-8848
Irby
Rocky Mount, NC. 252-442-0154
Item Products
Houston, TX 800-333-4932
J.C. Ford Company
La Habra, CA 714-871-7361
J.H. Thornton Company
Olathe, KS 913-764-6550
J.L. Becker Company
Plymouth, MI 800-837-4328
J.M. Rogers & Sons
Moss Point, MS 228-475-7584
JanTec
Traverse City, MI 800-992-3303
Jarke Corporation
Prospect Hts, IL 800-722-5255
Jarvis Caster Company
Jackson, TN 800-995-9876
Jervis B. Webb Company
Farmington Hills, MI 248-553-1000
Jesco Industries, Inc.
Litchfield, MI 800-455-0019
Jetstream Systems
Denver, CO 303-371-9002
Jilson Group
Lodi, NJ. 800-969-5400
John Rock Inc
Coatesville, PA 610-857-8080
Johnston Equipment
Delta, BC. 800-237-5159
Joyce/Dayton Corporation
Kettering, OH 937-294-6261
K-Tron
Salina, KS 785-825-1611
K.F. Logistics
Cincinnati, OH 800-347-9100
Kadon Corporation
Milford, OH 937-299-0088
Kamflex Corporation
Chicago, IL 800-323-2440
Kaps-All Packaging Systems
Riverhead, NY 631-727-0300
Kasel Associated Industries
Denver, CO 800-218-4417
Kaufman Engineered Systems
Waterville, OH 419-878-9727
Kauling Wood Products Company
Beckemeyer, IL. 618-594-2901
Keenline Conveyor Systems
Omro, WI 920-685-0365
Kelley Wood Products
Fitchburg, MA 978-345-7531
Kelly Dock Systems
Milwaukee, WI 414-352-1000
Kent District Library
Comstock Park, NE. 616-784-2007
Ketch
Wichita, KS. 800-766-3777

Key Material Handling
Simi Valley, CA. 800-539-7225
Key Technology
Walla Walla, WA. 509-529-2161
Killington Wood ProductsCompany
Rutland, VT. 802-773-9111
Kimball Companies
East Longmeadow, MA 413-525-1881
Kinergy Corporation
Louisville, KY 502-366-5685
Kinetic Equipment Company
Appleton, WI 806-293-4471
Kinsley Inc
Doylestown, PA 800-414-6664
Kisco Manufacturing
Greendale, BC. 604-823-7456
KISS Packaging Systems
Vista, CA. 888-522-3538
Klippenstein Corporation
Fresno, CA 888-834-4258
KLS Lubriquip
Minneapolis, MN 612-623-6000
Knight Industries
Auburn Hills, MI 248-377-4950
Koke
Queensbury, NY 800-535-5303
Komatsu Forklift
Rolling Meadows, IL 847-437-5800
Konz Wood Products
Appleton, WI 877-610-5145
Kornylak Corporation
Hamilton, OH 800-837-5676
Krones
Franklin, WI 414-409-4000
Kusel Equipment Company
Watertown, WI 920-261-4112
KVP Falcon Plastic Belting
Reading, PA 800-445-7898
KWS Manufacturing Company
Burleson, TX. 800-543-6558
L&H Wood Manufacturing Company
Farmington, MI. 248-474-9000
L&S Pallet Company
Houston, TX 281-443-6537
La Crosse
Onalaska, WI. 800-345-0018
La Marche Manufacturing Company
Des Plaines, IL 847-299-1188
La Menuiserie East Angus
East Angus, QC. 819-832-2746
Laidig Industrial Systems
Mishawaka, IN 574-256-0204
Lake Michigan Hardwood Company
Leland, MI. 231-256-9811
Lakeside Manufacturing
Milwaukee, WI 888-558-8574
Lakeside-Aris Manufacturing
Milwaukee, WI 800-558-8565
Lambert Material Handling
Syracuse, NY 800-253-5103
Landoo Corporation
Horsham, PA 785-562-5381
LaRos Equipment Company
Portage, MI 269-323-1441
Larson Pallet Company
Ogema, WI 715-767-5131
Laughlin Corporation
Fort Worth, TX 817-625-7756
Lawson Industries
Holden, MO 816-732-4347
Le Fiell Company, Inc.
Reno, NV 775-677-5300
Lear Romec
Elyria, OH 440-323-3211
Lee Engineering Company
Pawtucket, RI 401-725-6100
Leeds Conveyor Manufacturer Company
Guilford, CT 800-724-1088
Leggett & Platt StorageP
Vernon Hills, IL 847-816-6246
Lesco Design & Manufacturing Company
La Grange, KY 502-222-7101
Lester Box & Manufacturing
Long Beach, CA 562-437-5123
LEWCO
Sandusky, OH 419-625-4014
Lewis M. Carter Manufacturing Company
Donalsonville, GA 229-524-2197
Leyman Manufacturing Corporation
Cincinnati, OH 866-539-6261
Liberty Machine Company
York, PA 800-745-8152

Lift Rite
Mississauga, ON....905-456-2603
Liftomatic Material Handling
Buffalo Grove, IL....800-837-6540
Linde Material Handling North America Corporation
Summerville, SC....843-871-0312
Line-Master Products
Cocolalla, ID....208-265-4743
Linett Company
Blawnox, PA....800-565-2165
Lista International Corporation
Holliston, MA....800-722-3020
Load King Manufacturing Company
Jacksonville, FL....800-531-4975
LoadBank International
Orlando, FL....800-458-9010
Lock Inspection Systems
Fitchburg, MA....800-227-5539
Logemann Brothers Company
Milwaukee, WI....414-445-2700
Long Reach ManufacturingCompany
Westport, CT....800-285-7000
Longford Equipment US
Glastonbury, CT....860-659-0762
Longview Fibre Company
Longview, WA....800-929-8111
Lorenz Couplings
Cobourg, ON....800-263-7782
Louisville Dryer Company
Louisville, KY....800-735-3613
Love Box Company
Wichita, KS....316-838-0851
LPI Imports
Chicago, IL....877-389-6563
LPS Technology
Grafton, OH....800-586-1410
Lumsden Flexx Flow
Lancaster, PA....800-367-3664
M&E Manufacturing Company
Kingston, NY....845-331-2110
M&H Crates
Jacksonville, TX....903-683-5351
M.G. Newell
Greensboro, NC....800-334-0231
Madison County Wood Products
Saint Louis, MO....314-772-1722
Madsen Wire Products
Orland, IN....260-829-6561
Magline
Pinconning, MI....800-624-5463
Magna Power Controls
Milwaukee, WI....800-288-8178
Magnuson Corporation
Pueblo, CO....719-948-9500
Magsys
Milwaukee, WI....414-543-2177
Mannesmann Dematic Corporation
Solon, OH....440-248-2400
Manufacturers Wood Supply Company
Cleveland, OH....216-771-7848
Mar-Con Wire Belt
Richmond, BC....877-962-7266
Marion Body Works
Marion, WI....715-754-5261
Marion Pallet Company
Marion, OH....800-432-4117
Mark Slade ManufacturingCompany
Seymour, WI....920-833-6557
Marlen International
Astoria, OR....800-862-7536
Marshall Boxes
Rochester, NY....585-458-7432
Martin Cab
Cleveland, OH....216-651-3882
Martin Engineering
Neponset, IL....800-766-2786
Martin/Baron
Irwindale, CA....626-960-5153
Matcon USA
Elmhurst, IL....856-256-1330
Material Storage Systems
Humble, TX....800-881-6750
Material Systems Engineering
Stilesville, IN....800-634-0904
Materials TransportationCompany
Temple, TX....800-433-3110
Mathews Conveyor
Danville, KY....800-628-4397
Matot - Commercial GradeLift Solutions
Bellwood, IL....800-369-1070
Matthiesen Equipment Company
San Antonio, TX....800-624-8635

Maull-Baker Box Company
Brookfield, WI....414-463-1290
May-Wes Manufacturing
Hutchinson, MN....800-788-6483
MBX Packaging
Wausau, WI....715-845-1171
McCormick Enterprises
Delton, MI....800-223-3683
McCullough Industries
Kenton, OH....800-245-9490
McIntosh Box & Pallet Company
East Syracuse, NY....800-219-9552
McNeilly Wood Products, Inc.
Campbell Hall, NY....845-457-9651
McNichols Conveyor Company
Southfield, MI....800-331-1926
MeGa Industries
Burlington, ON....800-665-6342
Melcher Manufacturing Company
Spokane Valley, WA....800-541-4227
Menasha Corporation
Oconomowoc, WI....262-560-0228
Merco/Savory
Mt. Pleasant, MI....800-733-8821
Meriden Box Company
Southington, CT....860-621-7141
Meriwether Industries
Bloomfield, NJ....800-332-2358
Merrick Industries
Lynn Haven, FL....800-271-7834
Metal Equipment Company
Cleveland, OH....800-700-6326
METKO
New Holstein, WI....920-898-4221
Metro Corporation
Wilkes Barre, PA....800-433-2233
METRO Material Handling & Storage Products
Wilkes Barre, PA....800-433-2232
Metzgar Conveyor Company
Comstock Park, MI....888-266-8390
Meyer Machine & Garroutte Products
San Antonio, TX....210-736-1811
Michaelo Espresso
Seattle, WA....800-545-2883
Michiana Box & Crate
Niles, MI....800-677-6372
Michigan Box Company
Detroit, MI....888-642-4269
Michigan Industrial Belting
Livonia, MI....800-778-1650
Micro Solutions Enterprises
Van Nuys, CA....800-673-4968
Mid-States Manufacturing & Engineering
Milton, IA....800-346-1792
Mid-West Wire Products, Inc
Ferndale, MI....800-989-9881
Mid-West Wire Specialties
Chicago, IL....800-238-0228
Middleby Worldwide
Elgin, IL....847-468-6068
Midwest Metalcraft & Equipment
Windsor, MO....800-647-3167
Milan Box Corporation
Milan, TN....800-225-8057
Millard Manufacturing Corporation
La Vista, NE....800-662-4263
Miller Hofft Brands
Indianapolis, IN....317-638-6576
Miller Metal Fabricators
Staunton, VA....540-886-5575
MIT Poly-Cart Corporation
New York, NY....800-234-7659
MO Industries
Whippany, NJ....973-386-9228
Modern Metals Industries
El Segundo, CA....800-437-6633
Molding Automation Concepts
Woodstock, IL....800-435-6979
Moline Machinery
Duluth, MN....800-767-5734
Momence Pallet Corporation
Momence, IL....815-472-6451
Monarch-McLaren
Weston, ON....416-741-9675
Moorecraft Box & Crate
Tarboro, NC....252-823-2510
Morse Manufacturing Company
East Syracuse, NY....315-437-8475
Moseley Corporation
Franklin, MA....800-667-3539
Motom Corporation
Bensenville, IL....630-787-1995

Mountain Valley Farms & Lumber Products, Inc.
Biglerville, PA....717-677-6166
Multi-Vac
Union Grove, WI....800-640-4213
Mumper Machine Corporation
Butler, WI....262-781-8908
Munck Automation Technology
Newport News, VA....800-777-6862
Murata Automated Systems
Charlotte, NC....800-428-8469
NACCO Materials HandlingGroup
Fairview, OR....503-721-6205
Namco Controls Corporation
Cleveland, OH....800-626-8324
National Air Vibrator Company
Houston, TX....800-231-0164
National Conveyor Corporation
Commerce, CA....323-725-0355
National Distributor Services
Aurora, CO....303-755-4411
National Drying Machinery Company
Philadelphia, PA....215-464-6070
National Scoop & Equipment Company
Spring House, PA....215-646-2040
Native Lumber Company
Wallingford, CT....203-269-2625
Necedah Pallet Company
Necedah, WI....800-672-5538
NECO
Omaha, NE....402-453-6912
Nefab Packaging Inc.
Coppell, TX....800-322-4425
Nefab Packaging, Inc.
Coppell, TX....800-322-4425
Nelson Company
Baltimore, MD....410-477-3000
Neos
Elk River, MN....888-441-6367
Nepa Pallet & Container Company
Snohomish, WA....360-568-3185
Nercon Engineering & Manufacturing
Oshkosh, WI....920-233-3268
Net Material Handling
Milwaukee, WI....800-558-7260
Nevlen Co. 2, Inc.
Wakefield, MA....800-562-7225
New Age Industrial Corporation
Norton, KS....800-255-0104
New England Machinery Inc
Bradenton, FL....941-755-5550
New England Pallets & Skids
Ludlow, MA....413-583-6628
New Lisbon Wood ProductsManufacturing Company
New Lisbon, WI....608-562-3122
New London Engineering
New London, WI....800-437-1994
New Mexico Products
Albuquerque, NM....877-345-7864
New Pig Corporation
Tipton, PA....800-468-4647
New South Lumber Company
Myrtle Beach, SC....843-236-9399
Newcastle Company, Inc.
New Castle, PA....724-658-4516
Nexel Industries
Port Washington, NY....800-245-6682
Nissan Forklift Corporation of North America
Marengo, IL....800-871-5438
North Star Ice EquipmentCorporation
Seattle, WA....800-321-1381
Northland Stainless
Tomahawk, WI....715-453-5326
Northwest Products
Archbold, OH....419-445-1950
Northwind
Alpena, AR....870-437-2585
Norwalt Design Inc.
Randolph, NJ....973-927-3200
Nothum Food Processing Systems
Springfield, MO....800-435-1297
NST Metals
Louisville, KY....502-584-5846
Nu-Con Equipment
Chanhassen, MN....877-939-0510
Nu-Star
Shakopee, MN....952-445-8295
Nucon Corporation
Deerfield, IL....877-545-0070
NuTec Manufacturing
New Lenox, IL....815-722-5348
O'Brien Installations
Ontario, CA....905-336-8245

O.A. Newton & Son Company
Bridgeville, DE 800-726-5745

Oak Creek Pallet Company
Milwaukee, WI 414-762-7170

OCC Systems
Ferndale, MI 800-396-2554

Occidental Chemical Corporation
Dallas, TX 800-733-3665

Ohio Magnetics-Stearns Magnetics
Cleveland, OH 800-486-6446

Ohio Rack
Alliance, OH 800-344-4164

Olson Manufacturing/V-RAM Solids
Albert Lea, MN 888-373-3996

Omega Design Corporation
Exton, PA 800-346-0191

Omicron Steel Products Company
Jamaica, NY 718-805-3400

Omni Metalcraft Corporation
Alpena, MI 989-358-7000

Omni-Lift
Salt Lake City, UT 801-486-3776

OnTrack Automation Inc
Waterloo, ON 519-886-9090

ORBIS Corporation
Oconomowoc, WI 800-890-7292

Orion Packaging Systems
Alexandria, MN 800-333-6556

Ortmayer Materials Handling Inc
Brooklyn, NY 718-875-7995

OTD Corporation
Hinsdale, IL 630-321-9232

Otto Braun Bakery Equipment
Buffalo, NY 716-824-1252

Ouellette Machinery Systems
Fenton, MO 800-545-7619

Our Name is Mud
New York, NY 877-683-7867

Pacific Pneumatics
Rancho Cucamonga, CA 800-221-0961

Pacific Process Technology
La Jolla, CA 858-551-3298

Pacific Tank
Adelanto, CA 800-449-5838

Package Conveyor Company
Fort Worth, Fo. 800-792-1243

Packaging & Processing Equipment
Ayr, ON 519-622-6666

Packaging Equipment & Conveyors, Inc
Elkhart, IN 574-266-6995

Packaging Machinery
Montgomery, AL 334-265-9211

Packaging Systems International
Denver, CO 303-296-4445

Packing Material Company
Southfield, MI 248-489-7000

Paco Manufacturing Comp any
Clarksville, IN 888-283-7963

Paget Equipment Company
Marshfield, WI 715-384-3158

Palace Packaging Machines
Downingtown, PA 610-873-7252

Pallet Management Systems
Lawrenceville, VA 800-446-1804

Pallet Masters
Los Angeles, CA 800-675-2579

Pallet One
Bartow, FL 800-771-1148

Pallet Pro
Moss, TN 800-489-3661

Pallet Service Corporation
Maple Grove, MN 888-391-8020

PalletOne, Inc.
Bartow, FL 800-771-1148

Pallets
Fort Edward, NY 800-PLT-SKID

Pallister Pallet
Wapello, IA 319-523-8161

Pallox Incorporated
Onsted, MI 517-456-4101

Paltier
Michigan City, IN 800-348-3201

Paper Systems
Des Moines, IA 800-342-2855

Paradigm Technologies
Eugene, OR 541-345-5543

Parkson Corporation
Berkeley Heights, NJ 908-464-0700

Parkson Illinois
Vernon Hills, IL 847-816-3700

Paul Hawkins Lumber Company
Mannington, WV 304-986-2230

Paxton Products
Cincinnati, OH 800-441-7475

Payne Engineering
Scott Depot, WV 800-331-1345

Peerless Conveyor and Manufacturing Corporation
Kansas City, KS 913-342-2240

Peerless Food Inc
Sidney, OH 937-494-2870

Peerless-Winsmith
Springville, NY 716-592-9310

Pelco Packaging Corporation
Stirling, NJ 908-647-3500

Pengo Corporation
Cokato, MN 800-599-0211

Peregrine
Lincoln, NE 800-777-3433

Peterson Fiberglass Laminates
Shell Lake, WI 715-468-2306

PFI Prasence From Innovation
St Louis, MO 314-423-9777

Phelps Industries
Little Rock, AR 501-568-5550

Piab Vacuum Products
Hingham, MA 800-321-7422

Pine Bluff Crating & Pallet
Pine Bluff, AR 866-415-1075

Pine Point Wood Products
Dayton, MN 763-428-4301

Piper Products
Wausau, WI 800-544-3057

PlexPack Corp
Toronto, ON 855-635-9238

Pneumatic Conveying, Inc.
Ontario, CA 800-655-4481

Polar Beer Systems
Sun City, CA 951-928-8171

Pomona Service & Supply Company
Yakima, WA 509-452-7121

Port Erie Plastics
Harborcreek, PA 814-899-7602

Portec Flowmaster
Canon City, CO 800-777-7471

Porter & Porter Lumber
Fort Gay, WV 304-648-5133

Positech
Laurens, IA 800-831-6026

Power Electronics International
East Dundee, IL 800-362-7959

Power Ramp
Germantown, WI 800-643-5424

Power-Pack Conveyor Company
Willoughby, OH 440-975-9955

Prater Industries
Bolingbrook, IL 800-451-6958

Precision Wood of Hawaii
Vancouver, WA 808-682-2055

Precision Wood Products
Vancouver, WA 360-694-8322

Premium Pallet
Philadelphia, PA 800-648-7347

Priority One America
Waterloo, ON 519-746-6950

Priority One Packaging
Waterloo, ON 800-387-9102

Pro-Line
Haverhill, MA 978-556-1695

Process Engineering & Fabrication
Afton, VA 800-852-7975

Process Solutions
Riviera Beach, FL 561-840-0050

Prodo-Pak Corporation
Garfield, NJ 973-777-7770

Production Equipment Company
Meriden, CT 800-758-5697

Production Systems
Marietta, GA 800-235-9734

Professional EngineeringAssociation
Louisville, KY 502-429-0432

Pruitt's Packaging Services
Grand Rapids, MI 800-878-0553

PTI Packaging
Portage, WI 800-501-4077

PTR Baler and Compactor Company
Philadelphia, PA 800-523-3654

Pucel Enterprises
Cleveland, OH 800-336-4986

Puritan Manufacturing
Omaha, NE 800-331-0487

Quality Corporation
Denver, CO 303-777-6608

Quality Fabrication & Design
Coppell, TX 972-393-0502

R.G. Stephens Engineering
Long Beach, CA 800-499-3001

Rahmann Belting & Industrial Rubber Products
Gastonia, NC 888-248-8148

Ralph L. Mason,
Newark, MD 410-632-1766

Ralphs-Pugh Company
Benicia, CA 800-486-0021

RAM Center
Red Wing, MN 800-762-6842

Rapat Corporation
Hawley, MN 800-325-6377

Rapid Industries
Louisville, KY 800-787-4381

Rapid Pallet
Jermyn, PA 570-876-4000

Rapid Rack Industries
City of Industry, CA 800-736-7225

Ratcliff Hoist Company
San Carlos, CA 650-595-3840

Raymond Corporation
Greene, NY 800-235-7200

Reading Plastic Fabricators
Temple, PA 610-926-3245

Redding Pallet
Redding, CA 530-241-6321

Reelcraft Industries
Columbia City, IN 800-444-3134

Reese Enterprises
Rosemount, MN 800-328-0953

Regina USA, Inc
Oak Creek, WI 414-571-0032

Reinke & Schomann
Milwaukee, WI 414-964-1100

Reis Robotics
Elgin, IL 800-358-4245

Remco Products Corporation
Zionsville, IN 800-585-8619

Remcon Plastics
West Reading, PA 800-360-3636

Remmey Wood Products
Southampton, PA 215-355-3335

Remstar International
Westbrook, ME 800-639-5805

Renold Products
Westfield, NY 800-879-2529

RETROTECH, Inc
Victor, NY 585-924-6333

Rexnord Corporation
Milwaukee, WI 866-739-6673

REYCO Systems
Caldwell, ID 208-795-5700

Rhodes Machinery International
Louisville, KY 502-778-7377

Richards Industries Systems
West Caldwell, NJ 973-575-7480

Rigidized Metals Corporation
Buffalo, NY 800-836-2580

RMI-C/Rotonics Manaufacturing
Bensenville, IL 630-773-9510

Roberts Pallet Company
Ellington, MO 573-663-7877

Robinson Industries
Coleman, MI 989-465-6111

Roechling Engineered Plastics
Gastonia, NC 800-541-4419

Roll Rite Corporation
Hayward, CA 800-345-9305

Rome Machine & Foundry Company, Inc
Rome, GA 800-538-7663

Ron Vallort & Associates
Oak Brook, IL 630-734-3821

Roto-Jet Pump
Salt Lake City, UT 801-359-8731

Royal Ecoproducts
Vaughan, ON 800-465-7670

Royce Phoenix
Glendale, AZ 602-256-0006

Royce-Rolls Ringer Company
Grand Rapids, MI 800-253-9638

Rubbermaid Commercial Products
Winchester, VA 800-336-9880

Ruiz Flour Tortillas
Riverside, CA 909-947-7811

S&W Pallet Company
Camden, TN 800-640-0522

S. Howes
Silver Creek, NY 888-255-2611

Sackett Systems
Bensenville, IL 800-323-8332

Sadler Conveyor Systems
Montreal, QC 888-887-5129

Saeplast Canada
St John, NB 800-567-3966
Saint Charles Lumber Products
St Charles, MI 989-865-9915
Salwasser Manufacturing Company
Reedley, CA 800-344-8951
San Fab Conveyor Systems
Sandusky, OH 419-626-4465
Sapac International
Fond Du Lac, WI 800-257-2722
Sardee Industries
Orlando, FL 407-295-2114
Sardee Industries
Lisle, IL 630-824-4200
Sasib Beverage & Food North America
Plano, TX 800-558-3814
Sasib North America
Plano, TX 972-422-5808
Saturn Engineering Corporation
Newark, NJ 973-465-0224
Savanna Pallets
McGregor, MN 218-768-2077
Scaglia America
Charlotte, NC 704-357-8811
Schaeff
Bridgeview, IL 708-598-9099
Scheb International
North Barrington, IL 847-381-2573
Schenck Process LLC
Whitewater, WI 888-742-1249
Schloss Engineered Equipment
Aurora, CO 303-695-4500
Schlueter Company
Janesville, WI 800-359-1700
Schneider Packaging Equipment
Brewerton, NY 315-676-3035
Schroeder Sewing Technologies
San Marcos, CA 760-591-9733
Scientific Process & Research
Kendall Park, NJ 800-868-4777
Scott Pallets
Amelia Court House, VA 800-394-2514
Screw Conveyor Corporation
Hammond, IN 219-931-1450
Semco Manufacturing Company
Pharr, TX 956-787-4203
SencorpWhite
Hyannis, MA 508-771-9400
Sertapak Packaging Corporation
Woodstock, ON 800-265-1162
Servco Co.
St Louis, MO 314-781-3189
SFB Plastics
Wichita, KS 800-343-8133
Shammi Industries/Sammons Equipment
Corona, CA 800-417-9260
Sheffield Lumber & Pallet Company
Mocksville, NC 336-492-5565
Shelby Pallet & Box Company
Shelby, MI 231-861-4214
Shelcon
Ontario, CA 909-947-4877
Sheldon Wood Products
Toano, VA 757-566-8880
Shepard Niles
Montour Falls, NY 800-481-2260
Shick Tube-Veyor Corporation
Kansas City, MO 816-861-7224
Shiffer Industries
Kihei, HI 800-642-1774
Shingle Belting
King of Prussia, PA 800-345-6294
Shippers Supply
Saskatoon, SK 800-661-5639
Shippers Supply, Labelgraphic
Calgary, AB 800-661-5639
Shouldice Brothers SheetMetal
Battle Creek, MI 269-962-5579
Shuttleworth
Huntington, IN 800-444-7412
SI Systems
Easton, PA 800-523-9464
Sidney Manufacturing Company
Sidney, OH 800-482-3535
Sigma Industries
Concord, MI 517-857-6520
Simplex Filler Company
Napa, CA 800-796-7539
Sinco
Red Wing, MN 800-243-6753
Slip-Not Belting Corporation
Kingsport, TN 423-246-8141
Smalley Manufacturing Company
Knoxville, TN 865-966-5866
Smalley Package Company
Berryville, VA 540-955-2550
Smetco
Aurora, OR 800-253-5400
Smith Pallet Company
Hatfield, AR 870-389-6184
Solve Needs International
White Lake, MI 800-783-2462
Sonoma Pacific Company
Montebello, CA 323-838-4374
Sould Manufacturing
Winnepeg, NB 204-339-3499
Southern Ag Company
Blakely, GA 229-723-4262
Southern Pallet
Memphis, TN 901-942-4603
Southworth Products Corporation
Portland, ME 800-743-1000
SP Industries
Hopkins, MI 800-592-5959
Span Tech
Glasgow, KY 270-651-9166
Spanco
Morgantown, PA 800-869-2080
Sparks Belting Company
Grand Rapids, MI 800-451-4537
Speedways Conveyors
Lancaster, NY 800-800-1022
Spencer Turbine Company
Windsor, CT 800-232-4321
SPG International LLC
Covington, GA 877-503-4774
Spring Wood Products
Geneva, OH 440-466-1135
Springport Steel Wire Products
Concord, MI 517-857-3010
Spudnik Equipment
Blackfoot, ID 208-785-0480
Spurgeon Company
Ferndale, MI 800-396-2554
St. Pierre Box & Lumber Company
Canton, CT 860-693-2089
Stainless Specialists
Wausau, WI 800-236-4155
Stearnswood
Hutchinson, MN 800-657-0144
Steel King Industries
Stevens Point, WI 800-553-3096
Steel Specialty Equipment Corporation
Ridgewood, NY 800-521-7732
Steel Storage Systems
Commerce City, CO 800-442-0291
Stein DSI
Sandusky, OH 800-447-2630
Steinmetz Machine Works
Stamford, CT 203-327-0118
Sterling Net & Twine Company
Cedar Knolls, NJ 800-342-0316
Stiles Enterprises
Rockaway, NJ 800-325-4232
Stokes Material HandlingSystems
Doylestown, PA 215-340-2200
Storax
Bromsgrove, UK 845-130-3090
Stratis Plastic Pallets
Indianapolis, IN 800-725-5387
Streator Dependable Manufacturing
Streator, IL 800-798-0551
Studd & Whipple Company
Conewango Valley, NY 716-287-3791
Suffolk Iron Works
Suffolk, VA 757-539-2353
Summit Machine Builders Corporation
Denver, CO 800-274-6741
Super Sturdy
Weldon, NC 800-253-4833
Superior Industries
Morris, MN 800-321-1558
Svedala Industries
Colorado Springs, CO 719-471-3443
Sweet Manufacturing Company
Springfield, OH 800-334-7254
Swift Creek Forest Products
Amelia Court Hse, VA 804-561-4498
Tampa Pallet Company
Tampa, FL 813-626-5700
Tasler
Webster City, IA 515-832-5200
TC/American Monorail
Saint Michael, MN 763-497-7000
TDF Automation
Cedar Falls, IA 800-553-1777
Technibilt/Cari-All
Newton, NC 800-233-3972
Technipack, Inc.
Le Sueur, MN 507-665-6658
Technistar Corporation
Denver, CO 303-651-0188
Tecweigh/Tecnetics Industries
White Bear Lake, MN 800-536-4880
Tennessee Mills
Red Boiling Springs, TN 615-699-2253
TGS Engineering & Conveying
Houston, TX 713-466-0426
The National Provisioner
Deerfield, IL 847-763-9534
The Original Lincoln Logs
Chestertown, NY 800-833-2461
Theimeg
Sharpsville, PA 724-962-3571
Thermodynamics
Commerce City, CO 800-627-9037
Thieley Technolgies
Minneapolis, MN 612-782-1200
Thomas L. Green & Company
Robenosia, PA 610-693-5816
Thombert
Newton, IA 800-433-3572
Thorco Industries LLC
Lamar, MO 800-445-3375
Thoreson-McCosh
Troy, MI 800-959-0805
Thunder Pallet
Theresa, WI 800-354-0643
Timbertech Company
Milton, NH 800-572-5538
Titan Industries
New London, WI 800-558-3616
TKF
Cincinnati, OH 513-241-5910
Torbeck Industries
Harrison, OH 800-333-0080
Toter
Statesville, NC 800-772-0071
Tower Pallet Company
De Pere, WI 920-336-3495
Transbotics Corporation
Charlotte, NC 704-362-1115
Transnorm System
Grand Prairie, TX 800-259-2303
Travelon
Elk Grove Vlg, IL 800-537-5544
Traycon
Carlstadt, NJ 201-939-5555
Treen Box & Pallet Corporation
Bensalem, PA 215-639-5100
Tri-Pak Machinery, Inc.
Harlingen, TX 956-423-5140
Tri-State Plastics
Glenwillard, PA 724-457-6900
Tri-Tronics Company
Tampa, FL 800-237-0946
Triad Pallet Company
Greensboro, NC 336-292-8175
Tridyne Process Systems Inc.
South Burlington, VT 802-863-6873
TriEnda Corporation
Portage, WI 800-356-8150
Triple-A Manufacturing Company
Toronto, ON 800-786-2238
Triple/S Dynamics
Dallas, TX 800-527-2116
Tuscarora
New Brighton, PA 724-843-8200
TWM Manufacturing
Leamington, ON 888-495-4831
Uhrden
Sugarcreek, OH 800-852-2411
Unex Manufacturing
Jackson, NJ 800-695-7726
Unidex
Warsaw, NY 800-724-1302
United Pentek
Indianapolis, IN 800-357-9299
United States Systems
Kansas City, KS 888-281-2454
UniTrak Corporation
Port Hope, ON 866-883-5749
Universal Die & Stamping
Prairie Du Sac, WI 608-643-2477
Universal Industries, In
Cedar Falls, IA 800-553-4446

Universal Labeling Systems
St Petersburg, FL ... 877-236-0266
Universal Packaging
Houston, TX ... 800-324-2610
Upham & Walsh Lumber
Hoffman Estates, IL ... 847-519-1010
UPN Pallet Company
Penns Grove, NJ ... 856-299-1192
US Rubber Supply Company
Brooklyn, NY ... 718-782-7888
USECO
Murfreesboro, TN ... 615-893-4820
Vac-U-Max
Belleville, NJ ... 800-822-8629
Vancouver Manufacturing
Washougal, WA ... 360-835-8519
Vande Berg Scales
Sioux Center, IA ... 712-722-1181
Vandereems ManufacturingCompany
Hawthorne, NJ ... 973-427-2355
Vaughn Belting Company
Spartanburg, SC ... 800-325-3303
Versa Conveyor
London, OH ... 740-852-5609
Vertical Systems
Ft. Michelle, KY ... 859-485-9650
Vesco
New Hyde Park, NY ... 516-746-5139
Videojet Technologies, Inc
Wood Dale, IL ... 800-843-3610
W.A. Powers Company
Fort Worth, TX ... 800-792-1243
W.G. Durant Corporation
Whittier, CA ... 562-946-5555
Waldon Equipment, LLC
Fairview, OK ... 800-486-0023
Walker Magnetics
Worcester, MA ... 800-962-4638
Wall Conveyor & Manufacturing
Huntington, WV ... 800-456-1335
Walters Brothers Lumber Manufacturing
Radisson, WI ... 715-945-2217
Ward Ironworks
Welland, ON ... 888-441-9273
Wardcraft Conveyor
Spring Arbor, MI ... 800-782-2779
Warren Pallet Company
Bloomsbury, NJ ... 908-995-7172
Wastequip
Charlotte, NC ... 877-468-9278
Wayne Engineering Corporation
Cedar Falls, IA ... 319-266-1721
Webb-Stiles Company
Valley City, OH ... 330-225-7761
Weigh Right Automatic Scale Company
Joliet, IL ... 800-571-0249
Welch Packaging
Elkhart, IN ... 574-295-2460
Wesley International Corporation
Scottdale, GA ... 800-241-8649
Westfield Sheet Metal Works
Kenilworth, NJ ... 908-276-5500
Wetterau Wood Products
Antigo, WI ... 715-623-7907
Whallon Machinery
Royal Center, IN ... 574-643-9561
Whirl Air Flow Corporation
Big Lake, MN ... 800-373-3461
Whit-Log Trailers Inc
Wilbur, OR ... 800-452-1234
White Mop Wringer Company
Tampa, FL ... 800-237-7582
White Mountain Lumber Company
Berlin, NH ... 603-752-1000
Wilder Manufacturing Company
Port Jervis, NY ... 800-832-1319
Wilkie Brothers Conveyors
Marysville, MI ... 810-364-4820
Williams Pallet
West Chester, OH ... 513-874-4014
Williamsburg Millwork Corporation
Bowling Green, VA ... 804-994-2151
Williamson & Company
Greer, SC ... 800-849-3263
Williamson, Lannes, Pallets
Southside, WV ... 304-675-2716
Wilson Steel Products Company
Memphis, TN ... 901-527-8742
Win-Holt Equipment Group
Westbury, NY ... 800-444-3595
Wire Belt Company of America
Londonderry, NH ... 603-644-2500
Wire Way Husky
Denver, NC ... 704-483-1900
Wittco Foodservice Equipment, Inc.
Milwaukee, WI ... 800-821-3912
Witte Company
Washington, NJ ... 908-689-6500
WNC Pallet & Forest Products
Candler, NC ... 828-667-5426
Woodson Pallet
Anmoore, WV ... 304-623-2858
Yakima Wire Works
Reedley, CA ... 509-248-6790
Yargus Manufacturing
Marshall, IL ... 217-826-6352
Yerger Wood Products
East Greenville, PA ... 215-679-4413
York River Pallet Corporation
Shacklefords, VA ... 804-785-5811
YW Yacht Basin
Easton, MD ... 410-822-0414
Z-Loda Systems Engineering
Stamford, CT ... 203-325-8001
Zenar Corporation
Oak Creek, WI ... 414-764-1800
Zimmerman Handling Systems
Madison Heights, MI ... 800-347-7047
Ziniz
Louisville, KY ... 502-955-6573
Zoia Banquetier Company
Cleveland, OH ... 216-631-6414

Pallet Handling Equipment

Advanced Uniflo Technologies
Wichita, KS ... 800-688-0400
Air Technical Industries
Mentor, OH ... 888-857-6265
Anver Corporation
Hudson, MA ... 800-654-3500
Automated Production Systems Corporation
New Freedom, PA ... 888-345-5377
Bayhead Products Corporation
Dover, NH ... 800-229-4323
BMH Equipment
Sacramento, CA ... 800-350-8828
Burgess Manufacturing ofOklahoma
Guthrie, OK ... 800-804-1913
Bushman Equipment
Butler, WI ... 800-338-7810
Cannon Equipment Company
Rosemount, MN ... 800-825-8501
Cherry's Industrial Equipment Corporation
Elk Grove Vlg, IL ... 800-350-0011
CLECO Systems
Marietta, GA ... 770-392-0330
Clymer Enterprises
Pandora, OH ... 800-448-0784
Conveyance Technologies LLC
Cleveland, OH ... 800-701-2278
Currie Machinery Company
Santa Clara, CA ... 408-727-0424
Dimension Industries
Alexandria, MN ... 763-425-3955
Dynabilt Products
Readville, MA ... 800-443-1008
Edson Packaging Machinery
Hamilton, ON ... 905-385-3201
Equipment Design & Fabrication
Charlotte, NC ... 800-949-0165
Eugene Welding Company
Marysville, MI ... 810-364-7421
Fibre Converters
Constantine, MI ... 269-279-1700
FreesTech
Sinking Spring, PA ... 717-560-7560
Goldco Industries
Loveland, CO ... 970-278-4400
H.K. Systems
Milwaukee, WI ... 800-424-7365
Halton Packaging Systems
Oakville, ON ... 905-847-9141
Johnston Equipment
Delta, BC ... 800-237-5159
Krones
Franklin, WI ... 414-409-4000
Load King Manufacturing Company
Jacksonville, FL ... 800-531-4975
Long Reach ManufacturingCompany
Westport, CT ... 800-285-7000
Metal Equipment Company
Cleveland, OH ... 800-700-6326
Metzgar Conveyor Company
Comstock Park, MI ... 888-266-8390
Mitsubishi Caterpillar Fork
Houston, TX ... 800-228-5438
Ohio Rack
Alliance, OH ... 800-344-4164
Priority One Packaging
Waterloo, ON ... 800-387-9102
PTI Packaging
Portage, WI ... 800-501-4077
RAM Center
Red Wing, MN ... 800-762-6842
Reis Robotics
Elgin, IL ... 800-358-4245
Sadler Conveyor Systems
Montreal, QC ... 888-887-5129
San Fab Conveyor Systems
Sandusky, OH ... 419-626-4465
Schneider Packaging Equipment
Brewerton, NY ... 315-676-3035
SFB Plastics
Wichita, KS ... 800-343-8133
Shrinkfast Marketing
Newport, NH ... 800-867-4746
Sigma Industries
Concord, MI ... 517-857-6520
Smetco
Aurora, OR ... 800-253-5400
Solve Needs International
White Lake, MI ... 800-783-2462
Springport Steel Wire Products
Concord, MI ... 517-857-3010
Steel King Industries
Stevens Point, WI ... 800-553-3096
TriEnda Corporation
Portage, WI ... 800-356-8150
Webb-Stiles Company
Valley City, OH ... 330-225-7761
Wesley International Corporation
Scottdale, GA ... 800-241-8649
Wire Way Husky
Denver, NC ... 704-483-1900

Palletizers

Automated Production Systems Corporation
New Freedom, PA ... 888-345-5377
Bell Packaging Corporation
Marion, IN ... 800-382-0153
Berkshire PPM
Litchfield, CT ... 860-567-3118
Beumer Corporation
Branchburg, NJ ... 732-560-8222
Busse/SJI
Randolph, WI ... 800-882-4995
Cannon Conveyor Specialty Systems
Rosemount, MN ... 800-533-2071
Cannon Equipment Company
Rosemount, MN ... 800-825-8501
Chantland-MHS Company
Dakota City, IA ... 515-332-4045
Columbia Machine
Vancouver, WA ... 800-628-4065
Conveying Industries
Denver, CO ... 877-600-4874
Crown Simplimatic Company
Lynchburg, VA ... 434-582-1200
Currie Machinery Company
Santa Clara, CA ... 408-727-0424
Custom Metal Designs
Oakland, FL ... 800-334-1777
Dearborn Mid-West Company
Lenexa, KS ... 913-384-9950
Dimension Industries
Alexandria, MN ... 763-425-3955
Douglas Machine
Alexandria, MN ... 320-763-6587
Edmeyer
Minneapolis, MN ... 651-450-1210
FleetwoodGoldcoWyard
Romeoville, IL ... 630-759-6800
FreesTech
Sinking Spring, PA ... 717-560-7560
General Corrugated Machinery Company
Palisades Park, NJ ... 201-944-0644
Goldco Industries
Loveland, CO ... 970-278-4400
H.K. Systems
Milwaukee, WI ... 800-424-7365
Halton Packaging Systems
Oakville, ON ... 905-847-9141
Iman Pack
Westland, MI ... 800-810-4626
ITW Angleboard
Villa Rica, GA ... 770-459-5747

Jetstream Systems
Denver, CO . . . 303-371-9002
Krones
Franklin, WI . . . 414-409-4000
Kusel Equipment Company
Watertown, WI . . . 920-261-4112
Lambert Material Handling
Syracuse, NY . . . 800-253-5103
Magnuson Corporation
Pueblo, CO . . . 719-948-9500
Mathews Conveyor
Danville, KY . . . 800-628-4397
Newcastle Company, Inc.
New Castle, PA . . . 724-658-4516
Nitech
Columbus, NE . . . 800-397-1100
Ocme America Corporation
York, PA . . . 717-843-6263
Ouellette Machinery Systems
Fenton, MO . . . 800-545-7619
Packaging & Processing Equipment
Ayr, ON . . . 519-622-6666
Packaging Systems International
Denver, CO . . . 303-296-4445
Pasco
Saint Louis, MO . . . 800-489-3300
Priority One America
Waterloo, ON . . . 519-746-6950
Priority One Packaging
Waterloo, ON . . . 800-387-9102
Production Systems
Marietta, GA . . . 800-235-9734
PTI Packaging
Portage, WI . . . 800-501-4077
R.G. Stephens Engineering
Long Beach, CA . . . 800-499-3001
RAM Center
Red Wing, MN . . . 800-762-6842
Reis Robotics
Elgin, IL . . . 800-358-4245
Sapac International
Fond Du Lac, WI . . . 800-257-2722
Sardee Industries
Orlando, FL . . . 407-295-2114
Sardee Industries
Lisle, IL . . . 630-824-4200
Sasib Beverage & Food North America
Plano, TX . . . 800-558-3814
Schneider Packaging Equipment
Brewerton, NY . . . 315-676-3035
Southworth Products Corporation
Portland, ME . . . 800-743-1000
Technistar Corporation
Denver, CO . . . 303-651-0188
Thieley Technolgies
Minneapolis, MN . . . 612-782-1200
TriEnda Corporation
Portage, WI . . . 800-356-8150
W.G. Durant Corporation
Whittier, CA . . . 562-946-5555
Whallon Machinery
Royal Center, IN . . . 574-643-9561

Pallets

A.M. Loveman Lumber & Box Company
Nashville, TN . . . 615-297-1397
Advance Engineering Company
Township, MI . . . 800-497-6388
Allflex Packaging Products
Ambler, PA . . . 800-448-2467
American Box Corporation
Lisbon, OH . . . 330-424-8055
American Pallet
Oakdale, CA . . . 209-847-6122
Auto Pallets-Boxes
Lathrup Village, MI . . . 800-875-2699
Barrette - Outdoor Livin
Middleburg Hts., OH . . . 800-336-2383
Bay Area Pallet Company/IFCO Systems
Houston, TX . . . 877-430-4326
BC Wood Products
Ashland, VA . . . 804-798-9154
Bell Packaging Corporation
Marion, IN . . . 800-382-0153
Bennett Box & Pallet Company
Winston, NC . . . 800-334-8741
Bergen Barrel & Drum Company
Kearny, NJ . . . 201-998-3500
Black River Pallet Company
Zeeland, MI . . . 800-427-6515
Buckhorn Canada
Brampton, ON . . . 800-461-7579
Buckhorn Inc
Milford, OH . . . 800-543-4454
Burgess Manufacturing ofOklahoma
Guthrie, OK . . . 800-804-1913
C&L Wood Products
Hartselle, AL . . . 800-483-2035
Cantley-Ellis Manufacturing Company
Kingsport, TN . . . 423-246-4671
Carson Industries
Pomona, CA . . . 800-735-5566
Cascade Wood Components
Cascade Locks, OR . . . 541-374-8413
Cassel Box & Lumber Company
Grafton, WI . . . 262-377-4420
Cedar Box Company
Minneapolis, MN . . . 612-332-4287
Challenger Pallet & Supply
Idaho Falls, ID . . . 800-733-0205
Charles Tirschman Company
Baltimore, MD . . . 410-282-6199
Cimino Box Company
Cleveland, OH . . . 216-961-7377
Coblentz Brothers
Apple Creek, OH . . . 330-857-7211
Coddington Lumber Company
Frostburg, MD . . . 301-689-8816
Corinth Products
Corinth, ME . . . 207-285-3387
Cutler Brothers Box & Lumber Company
Fairview, NJ . . . 201-943-2535
Cutter Lumber Products
Livermore, CA . . . 925-443-5959
D&M Pallet Company
Neshkoro, WI . . . 920-293-4616
Daniel Boone Lumber Industries
Morehead, KY . . . 606-784-7586
Davis Core & Pad Company
Cave Spring, GA . . . 800-235-7483
Day Lumber Company
Westfield, MA . . . 413-568-3511
Denver Reel & Pallet Company
Denver, CO . . . 303-321-1920
Development Workshop
Idaho Falls, ID . . . 800-657-5597
Dufeck Manufacturing Company
Denmark, WI . . . 888-603-9663
Durant Box Factory
Durant, OK . . . 580-924-4035
Eichler Wood Products
Laurys Station, PA . . . 610-262-6749
Elba Pallets Company
Elba, AL . . . 334-897-6034
Elberta Crate & Box Company
Carpentersville, IL . . . 888-672-9260
ERO/Goodrich Forest Products
Tualatin, OR . . . 800-458-5545
Esko Pallets
Cloquet, MN . . . 218-879-8553
F.E. Wood & Sons
East Baldwin, ME . . . 207-286-5003
Fabri-Form Company
Byesville, OH . . . 740-685-0424
Fabricated Components
Stroudsburg, PA . . . 800-233-8163
Fabrication Specialties Corporation
Centerville, TN . . . 931-729-2283
Fehlig Brothers Box & Lumber Company
St Louis, MO . . . 314-241-6900
Felco Bag & Burlap Company
Baltimore, MD . . . 800-673-8488
Fresno Pallet, Inc.
Sultana, CA . . . 559-591-4111
Gatewood Products LLC
Parkersburg, WV . . . 800-827-5461
GBN Machine & Engineering Corporation
Woodford, VA . . . 800-446-9871
Gemini Plastic Films Corporation
Garfield, NJ . . . 800-789-4732
Gerrity Industries
Monmouth, ME . . . 877-933-2804
Girard Wood Products
Puyallup, WA . . . 253-845-0505
GL Packaging Products
West Chicago, IL . . . 866-935-8755
Goeman's Wood Products
Hartford, WI . . . 262-673-6090
Graham Pallet Company
Tompkinsville, KY . . . 888-525-0694
Gray Woodproducts
Orrington, ME . . . 207-825-3578
Green-Tek
Janesville, WI . . . 800-747-6440
H&H Lumber Company
Amarillo, TX . . . 806-335-1813
H&H Wood Products
Hamburg, NY . . . 716-648-5600
Hampel Corporation
Germantown, WI . . . 800-494-4762
Hampton Roads Box Company
Suffolk, VA . . . 757-934-2355
Hanson Box & Lumber Company
Wakefield, MA . . . 617-245-0358
Harbor Pallet Company
Anaheim, CA . . . 714-533-4940
Hawkeye Pallet Company
Johnston, IA . . . 515-276-0409
Herkimer Pallet & Wood Products Company
Herkimer, NY . . . 315-866-4591
HHP
Henniker, NH . . . 603-428-3298
Hilderth Wood Products
Wadesboro, NC . . . 704-826-8326
Hinchcliff Products Company
Strongsville, OH . . . 440-238-5200
Hunter Woodworks
Carson, CA . . . 800-966-4751
Industrial Hardwood
Perrysburg, OH . . . 419-666-2503
Industrial Lumber & Packaging
Spring Lake, MI . . . 616-842-1457
Industrial WoodFab & Packaging Company
Riverview, MI . . . 734-284-4808
International Wood Industries
Snohomish, WA . . . 800-922-6141
ITW Plastic Packaging
Denver, CO . . . 303-316-6816
J.M. Rogers & Sons
Moss Point, MS . . . 228-475-7584
Jarke Corporation
Prospect Hts, IL . . . 800-722-5255
Jeco Plastic Products
Plainfield, IN . . . 800-593-5326
John Rock Inc
Coatesville, PA . . . 610-857-8080
Kadon Corporation
Milford, OH . . . 937-299-0088
Kauling Wood Products Company
Beckemeyer, IL . . . 618-594-2901
Kelley Wood Products
Fitchburg, MA . . . 978-345-7531
Ketch
Wichita, KS . . . 800-766-3777
Killington Wood ProductsCompany
Rutland, VT . . . 802-773-9111
Kimball Companies
East Longmeadow, MA . . . 413-525-1881
Konz Wood Products
Appleton, WI . . . 877-610-5145
L&H Wood Manufacturing Company
Farmington, MI . . . 248-474-9000
L&S Pallet Company
Houston, TX . . . 281-443-6537
La Menuiserie East Angus
East Angus, QC . . . 819-832-2746
Lake Michigan Hardwood Company
Leland, MI . . . 231-256-9811
Larson Pallet Company
Ogema, WI . . . 715-767-5131
Lawson Industries
Holden, MO . . . 816-732-4347
Lester Box & Manufacturing
Long Beach, CA . . . 562-437-5123
Load King Manufacturing Company
Jacksonville, FL . . . 800-531-4975
Longview Fibre Company
Longview, WA . . . 800-929-8111
Love Box Company
Wichita, KS . . . 316-838-0851
Lumber & Things
Keyser, WV . . . 800-296-5656
Lydall
Doswell, VA . . . 804-266-9611
M&H Crates
Jacksonville, TX . . . 903-683-5351
Madison County Wood Products
Saint Louis, MO . . . 314-772-1722
Marion Pallet Company
Marion, OH . . . 800-432-4117
Mark Slade ManufacturingCompany
Seymour, WI . . . 920-833-6557
Marshall Boxes
Rochester, NY . . . 585-458-7432
Mason Ways Indestructible Plastics
West Palm Beach, FL . . . 800-837-2881

Maull-Baker Box Company
Brookfield, WI 414-463-1290
Mayco
Dallas, TX. 214-638-4848
MBX Packaging
Wausau, WI. 715-845-1171
McIntosh Box & Pallet Company
East Syracuse, NY 800-219-9552
McNeilly Wood Products, Inc.
Campbell Hall, NY 845-457-9651
Menasha Corporation
Oconomowoc, WI. 262-560-0228
Meriden Box Company
Southington, CT 860-621-7141
Michiana Box & Crate
Niles, MI. 800-677-6372
Michigan Box Company
Detroit, MI 888-642-4269
MO Industries
Whippany, NJ 973-386-9228
Momence Pallet Corporation
Momence, IL. 815-472-6451
Moorecraft Box & Crate
Tarboro, NC 252-823-2510
Mountain Valley Farms & Lumber Products, Inc.
Biglerville, PA. 717-677-6166
Native Lumber Company
Wallingford, CT 203-269-2625
Necedah Pallet Company
Necedah, WI 800-672-5538
Nefab Packaging Inc.
Coppell, TX 800-322-4425
Nefab Packaging, Inc.
Coppell, TX 800-322-4425
Nelson Company
Baltimore, MD 410-477-3000
Nepa Pallet & Container Company
Snohomish, WA 360-568-3185
New England Pallets & Skids
Ludlow, MA 413-583-6628
New Lisbon Wood ProductsManufacturing Company
New Lisbon, WI 608-562-3122
New Mexico Products
Albuquerque, NM 877-345-7864
New South Lumber Company
Myrtle Beach, SC 843-236-9399
Newcourt, Inc.
Madison, IN 800-933-0006
Northwest Products
Archbold, OH 419-445-1950
Nucon Corporation
Deerfield, IL 877-545-0070
Oak Creek Pallet Company
Milwaukee, WI 414-762-7170
Occidental Chemical Corporation
Dallas, TX. 800-733-3665
ORBIS Corporation
Oconomowoc, WI. 800-890-7292
OTD Corporation
Hinsdale, IL 630-321-9232
Packing Material Company
Southfield, MI. 248-489-7000
Pallet Management Systems
Lawrenceville, VA 800-446-1804
Pallet Masters
Los Angeles, CA. 800-675-2579
Pallet One
Bartow, FL. 800-771-1148
Pallet Pro
Moss, TN. 800-489-3661
Pallet Service Corporation
Maple Grove, MN. 888-391-8020
PalletOne, Inc.
Bartow, FL. 800-771-1148
Pallets
Fort Edward, NY. 800-PLT-SKID
Pallister Pallet
Wapello, IA. 319-523-8161
Pallox Incorporated
Onsted, MI 517-456-4101
Paper Systems
Des Moines, IA. 800-342-2855
Paul Hawkins Lumber Company
Mannington, WV 304-986-2230
Pinckney Molded Plastics
Howell, MI 800-854-2920
Pine Bluff Crating & Pallet
Pine Bluff, AR 866-415-1075
Pine Point Wood Products
Dayton, MN 763-428-4301
Port Erie Plastics
Harborcreek, PA 814-899-7602
Porter & Porter Lumber
Fort Gay, WV 304-648-5133
Precision Wood of Hawaii
Vancouver, WA 808-682-2055
Precision Wood Products
Vancouver, WA 360-694-8322
Premium Pallet
Philadelphia, PA 800-648-7347
Pruitt's Packaging Services
Grand Rapids, MI 800-878-0553
Ralph L. Mason,
Newark, MD 410-632-1766
Rapid Pallet
Jermyn, PA 570-876-4000
Redding Pallet
Redding, CA 530-241-6321
Remcon Plastics
West Reading, PA 800-360-3636
Remmey Wood Products
Southampton, PA 215-355-3335
Roberts Pallet Company
Ellington, MO. 573-663-7877
Robinson Industries
Coleman, MI 989-465-6111
Rotonics Manufacturing
Gardena, CA 310-327-5401
Royal Ecoproducts
Vaughan, ON. 800-465-7670
S&W Pallet Company
Camden, TN 800-640-0522
Saeplast Canada
St John, NB 800-567-3966
Saint Charles Lumber Products
St Charles, MI. 989-865-9915
Savanna Pallets
McGregor, MN 218-768-2077
Scott Pallets
Amelia Court House, VA 800-394-2514
Sertapak Packaging Corporation
Woodstock, ON. 800-265-1162
SFB Plastics
Wichita, KS. 800-343-8133
Shelby Pallet & Box Company
Shelby, MI. 231-861-4214
Sheldon Wood Products
Toano, VA 757-566-8880
Sigma Industries
Concord, MI 517-857-6520
Smalley Package Company
Berryville, VA. 540-955-2550
Smith Pallet Company
Hatfield, AR 870-389-6184
Sonoma Pacific Company
Montebello, CA 323-838-4374
Southern Pallet
Memphis, TN 901-942-4603
Spring Wood Products
Geneva, OH. 440-466-1135
Springport Steel Wire Products
Concord, MI 517-857-3010
St. Pierre Box & Lumber Company
Canton, CT 860-693-2089
Stearnswood
Hutchinson, MN 800-657-0144
Sterling Net & Twine Company
Cedar Knolls, NJ. 800-342-0316
Stratis Plastic Pallets
Indianapolis, IN 800-725-5387
Streator Dependable Manufacturing
Streator, IL 800-798-0551
Studd & Whipple Company
Conewango Valley, NY. 716-287-3791
Swift Creek Forest Products
Amelia Court Hse, VA 804-561-4498
Tampa Pallet Company
Tampa, FL. 813-626-5700
Tasler
Webster City, IA 515-832-5200
Technipack, Inc.
Le Sueur, MN 507-665-6658
The Original Lincoln Logs
Chestertown, NY 800-833-2461
Thermodynamics
Commerce City, CO 800-627-9037
Thunder Pallet
Theresa, WI. 800-354-0643
Timbertech Company
Milton, NH 800-572-5538
Tower Pallet Company
De Pere, WI. 920-336-3495
Treen Box & Pallet Corporation
Bensalem, PA 215-639-5100
Triad Pallet Company
Greensboro, NC 336-292-8175
TriEnda Corporation
Portage, WI. 800-356-8150
Tuscarora
New Brighton, PA. 724-843-8200
Upham & Walsh Lumber
Hoffman Estates, IL 847-519-1010
UPN Pallet Company
Penns Grove, NJ 856-299-1192
Vancouver Manufacturing
Washougal, WA. 360-835-8519
Viking Pallet Corporation
Osseo, MN 763-425-6707
Walters Brothers Lumber Manufacturing
Radisson, WI. 715-945-2217
Warren Pallet Company
Bloomsbury, NJ. 908-995-7172
Welch Packaging
Elkhart, IN. 574-295-2460
Wetterau Wood Products
Antigo, WI 715-623-7907
White Mountain Lumber Company
Berlin, NH. 603-752-1000
Williams Pallet
West Chester, OH 513-874-4014
Williamsburg Millwork Corporation
Bowling Green, VA. 804-994-2151
Williamson, Lannes, Pallets
Southside, WV 304-675-2716
WNC Pallet & Forest Products
Candler, NC 828-667-5426
Woodson Pallet
Anmoore, WV. 304-623-2858
Yerger Wood Products
East Greenville, PA. 215-679-4413
York River Pallet Corporation
Shacklefords, VA 804-785-5811

Lift Truck

BMH Equipment
Sacramento, CA 800-350-8828
Cantley-Ellis Manufacturing Company
Kingsport, TN. 423-246-4671
Central Pallet Mills
Central City, KY 270-754-2900
Dominion Pallet Company
Mineral, VA. 800-227-5321
Hampel Corporation
Germantown, WI. 800-494-4762
Hanson Box & Lumber Company
Wakefield, MA 617-245-0358
Paul Hawkins Lumber Company
Mannington, WV 304-986-2230

Live Skid

Hampel Corporation
Germantown, WI. 800-494-4762
Load King Manufacturing Company
Jacksonville, FL 800-531-4975

Plastic

Barrette - Outdoor Livin
Middleburg Hts., OH 800-336-2383
Buckhorn Inc
Milford, OH 800-543-4454
Burgess Manufacturing ofOklahoma
Guthrie, OK. 800-804-1913
Emco Industrial Plastics
Cedar Grove, NJ 800-292-9906
Fabri-Form Company
Byesville, OH 740-685-0424
Fresno Pallet, Inc.
Sultana, CA 559-591-4111
Green-Tek
Janesville, WI 800-747-6440
Gulf Arizona Packaging
Humble, TX 800-364-3887
Gulf Systems
Oklahoma City, OK 800-364-3887
Hampel Corporation
Germantown, WI. 800-494-4762
Harbor Pallet Company
Anaheim, CA 714-533-4940
Herche Warehouse
Denver, CO 303-371-8186
Kadon Corporation
Milford, OH 937-299-0088
Kimball Companies
East Longmeadow, MA 413-525-1881

Lumber & Things
Keyser, WV 800-296-5656
MBX Packaging
Wausau, WI 715-845-1171
Menasha Corporation
Oconomowoc, WI 262-560-0228
Nelson Company
Baltimore, MD 410-477-3000
Nucon Corporation
Deerfield, IL 877-545-0070
Occidental Chemical Corporation
Dallas, TX 800-733-3665
ORBIS Corporation
Oconomowoc, WI 800-890-7292
Pallet Management Systems
Lawrenceville, VA 800-446-1804
PDQ Plastics
Bayonne, NJ 800-447-7141
Port Erie Plastics
Harborcreek, PA 814-899-7602
Robinson Industries
Coleman, MI 989-465-6111
Royal Ecoproducts
Vaughan, ON 800-465-7670
Saeplast Canada
St John, NB 800-567-3966
SFB Plastics
Wichita, KS 800-343-8133
Stearnswood
Hutchinson, MN 800-657-0144
Stratis Plastic Pallets
Indianapolis, IN 800-725-5387
Thermodynamics
Commerce City, CO 800-627-9037
TMF Corporation
Havertown, PA 610-853-3080
TriEnda Corporation
Portage, WI 800-356-8150
Upham & Walsh Lumber
Hoffman Estates, IL 847-519-1010

Wooden

A.M. Loveman Lumber & Box Company
Nashville, TN 615-297-1397
American Box Corporation
Lisbon, OH 330-424-8055
Auto Pallets-Boxes
Lathrup Village, MI 800-875-2699
Bay Area Pallet Company/IFCO Systems
Houston, TX 877-430-4326
BC Wood Products
Ashland, VA 804-798-9154
Burgess Manufacturing ofOklahoma
Guthrie, OK 800-804-1913
C&L Wood Products
Hartselle, AL 800-483-2035
Cantley-Ellis Manufacturing Company
Kingsport, TN 423-246-4671
Cascade Wood Components
Cascade Locks, OR 541-374-8413
Cedar Box Company
Minneapolis, MN 612-332-4287
Coastal Pallet Corporation
Bridgeport, CT 203-333-6222
Coblentz Brothers
Apple Creek, OH 330-857-7211
Corinth Products
Corinth, ME 207-285-3387
Cutler Brothers Box & Lumber Company
Fairview, NJ 201-943-2535
D&M Pallet Company
Neshkoro, WI 920-293-4616
Daniel Boone Lumber Industries
Morehead, KY 606-784-7586
Day Lumber Company
Westfield, MA 413-568-3511
Development Workshop
Idaho Falls, ID 800-657-5597
Dufeck Manufacturing Company
Denmark, WI 888-603-9663
Durant Box Factory
Durant, OK 580-924-4035
Eichler Wood Products
Laurys Station, PA 610-262-6749
Elba Pallets Company
Elba, AL 334-897-6034
ERO/Goodrich Forest Products
Tualatin, OR 800-458-5545
F.E. Wood & Sons
East Baldwin, ME 207-286-5003

Fabrication Specialties Corporation
Centerville, TN 931-729-2283
Fehlig Brothers Box & Lumber Company
St Louis, MO 314-241-6900
Fox Valley Wood Products
Kaukauna, WI 920-766-4069
Fresno Pallet, Inc.
Sultana, CA 559-591-4111
Girard Wood Products
Puyallup, WA 253-845-0505
GL Packaging Products
West Chicago, IL 866-935-8755
Goeman's Wood Products
Hartford, WI 262-673-6090
Graham Pallet Company
Tompkinsville, KY 888-525-0694
H&H Lumber Company
Amarillo, TX 806-335-1813
H&H Wood Products
Hamburg, NY 716-648-5600
Hanson Box & Lumber Company
Wakefield, MA 617-245-0358
Harbor Pallet Company
Anaheim, CA 714-533-4940
Hawkeye Pallet Company
Johnston, IA 515-276-0409
Herkimer Pallet & Wood Products Company
Herkimer, NY 315-866-4591
HHP
Henniker, NH 603-428-3298
Hilderth Wood Products
Wadesboro, NC 704-826-8326
Hinchcliff Products Company
Strongsville, OH 440-238-5200
Hunter Woodworks
Carson, CA 800-966-4751
Industrial Hardwood
Perrysburg, OH 419-666-2503
Industrial WoodFab & Packaging Company
Riverview, MI 734-284-4808
International Wood Industries
Snohomish, WA 800-922-6141
John Rock Inc
Coatesville, PA 610-857-8080
Kauling Wood Products Company
Beckemeyer, IL 618-594-2901
Kelley Wood Products
Fitchburg, MA 978-345-7531
Ketch
Wichita, KS 800-766-3777
Killington Wood ProductsCompany
Rutland, VT 802-773-9111
L&S Pallet Company
Houston, TX 281-443-6537
La Menuiserie East Angus
East Angus, QC 819-832-2746
Lake Michigan Hardwood Company
Leland, MI 231-256-9811
Love Box Company
Wichita, KS 316-838-0851
Lumber & Things
Keyser, WV 800-296-5656
Lydall
Doswell, VA 804-266-9611
M&H Crates
Jacksonville, TX 903-683-5351
Madison County Wood Products
Saint Louis, MO 314-772-1722
Marion Pallet Company
Marion, OH 800-432-4117
Mark Slade ManufacturingCompany
Seymour, WI 920-833-6557
Marshall Boxes
Rochester, NY 585-458-7432
Maull-Baker Box Company
Brookfield, WI 414-463-1290
Mayco
Dallas, TX 214-638-4848
McIntosh Box & Pallet Company
East Syracuse, NY 800-219-9552
McNeilly Wood Products, Inc.
Campbell Hall, NY 845-457-9651
Meriden Box Company
Southington, CT 860-621-7141
Momence Pallet Corporation
Momence, IL 815-472-6451
Moorecraft Box & Crate
Tarboro, NC 252-823-2510
Mountain Valley Farms & Lumber Products, Inc.
Biglerville, PA 717-677-6166
Native Lumber Company
Wallingford, CT 203-269-2625

Nefab Packaging, Inc.
Coppell, TX 800-322-4425
Nelson Company
Baltimore, MD 410-477-3000
New England Pallets & Skids
Ludlow, MA 413-583-6628
New Lisbon Wood ProductsManufacturing Company
New Lisbon, WI 608-562-3122
New Mexico Products
Albuquerque, NM 877-345-7864
New South Lumber Company
Myrtle Beach, SC 843-236-9399
Northwest Products
Archbold, OH 419-445-1950
Oak Creek Pallet Company
Milwaukee, WI 414-762-7170
Packing Material Company
Southfield, MI 248-489-7000
Pallet Management Systems
Lawrenceville, VA 800-446-1804
Pallet One
Bartow, FL 800-771-1148
Pallets
Fort Edward, NY 800-PLT-SKID
Pallister Pallet
Wapello, IA 319-523-8161
Pallox Incorporated
Onsted, MI 517-456-4101
Paul Hawkins Lumber Company
Mannington, WV 304-986-2230
Pine Bluff Crating & Pallet
Pine Bluff, AR 866-415-1075
Pine Point Wood Products
Dayton, MN 763-428-4301
Porter & Porter Lumber
Fort Gay, WV 304-648-5133
Precision Wood of Hawaii
Vancouver, WA 808-682-2055
Precision Wood Products
Vancouver, WA 360-694-8322
Pruitt's Packaging Services
Grand Rapids, MI 800-878-0553
Ralph L. Mason,
Newark, MD 410-632-1766
Redding Pallet
Redding, CA 530-241-6321
Remmey Wood Products
Southampton, PA 215-355-3335
Roberts Pallet Company
Ellington, MO 573-663-7877
S&W Pallet Company
Camden, TN 800-640-0522
Saint Charles Lumber Products
St Charles, MI 989-865-9915
Scott Pallets
Amelia Court House, VA 800-394-2514
Sheffield Lumber & Pallet Company
Mocksville, NC 336-492-5565
Sheldon Wood Products
Toano, VA 757-566-8880
Smith Pallet Company
Hatfield, AR 870-389-6184
Sonoma Pacific Company
Montebello, CA 323-838-4374
Southern Pallet
Memphis, TN 901-942-4603
Spring Wood Products
Geneva, OH 440-466-1135
St. Pierre Box & Lumber Company
Canton, CT 860-693-2089
Stearnswood
Hutchinson, MN 800-657-0144
Studd & Whipple Company
Conewango Valley, NY 716-287-3791
Tampa Pallet Company
Tampa, FL 813-626-5700
Tasler
Webster City, IA 515-832-5200
Technipack, Inc.
Le Sueur, MN 507-665-6658
Tennessee Mills
Red Boiling Springs, TN 615-699-2253
The Original Lincoln Logs
Chestertown, NY 800-833-2461
Thunder Pallet
Theresa, WI 800-354-0643
Treen Box & Pallet Corporation
Bensalem, PA 215-639-5100
Triad Pallet Company
Greensboro, NC 336-292-8175
Upham & Walsh Lumber
Hoffman Estates, IL 847-519-1010

UPN Pallet Company, Penns Grove, NJ 856-299-1192
Vancouver Manufacturing, Washougal, WA 360-835-8519
Viking Pallet Corporation, Osseo, MN 763-425-6707
Warren Pallet Company, Bloomsbury, NJ 908-995-7172
White Mountain Lumber Company, Berlin, NH 603-752-1000
Williams Pallet, West Chester, OH 513-874-4014
Williamsburg Millwork Corporation, Bowling Green, VA 804-994-2151
Williamson, Lannes, Pallets, Southside, WV 304-675-2716
WNC Pallet & Forest Products, Candler, NC 828-667-5426
Yerger Wood Products, East Greenville, PA 215-679-4413
York River Pallet Corporation, Shacklefords, VA 804-785-5811

Racks

Barrel & Drum Draining

BMH Equipment, Sacramento, CA 800-350-8828
Key Material Handling, Simi Valley, CA 800-539-7225
Triple-A Manufacturing Company, Toronto, ON 800-786-2238

Bottle

Cannon Equipment Company, Rosemount, MN 800-825-8501
Dunn Woodworks, Shrewsbury, PA 877-835-8592
Houston Wire Works, Inc., South Houston, TX 800-468-9477
Metro Corporation, Wilkes Barre, PA 800-433-2233
Olson Wire Products Company, Halethorpe, MD 410-242-1945
Polymer Solutions International, Newtown Square, PA 877-444-7225
Supreme Metal, Alpharetta, GA 800-645-2526
Triple-A Manufacturing Company, Toronto, ON 800-786-2238
Vermillion Flooring Company, Springfield, MO 417-862-3785
Western Square Industries, Stockton, CA 800-367-8383
Xtreme Beverages, LLC, Dana Point, CA 949-495-7929

Can

AMCO Corporation, City of Industry, CA 626-855-2550
ARC Specialties, Valencia, CA 661-775-8500
EPCO, Murfreesboro, TN 800-251-3398
Grayline Housewares, Carol Stream, IL 800-222-7388
Lakeside Manufacturing, Milwaukee, WI 888-558-8574
Leggett & Platt StorageP, Vernon Hills, IL 847-816-6246
Metro Corporation, Wilkes Barre, PA 800-433-2233
New Age Industrial Corporation, Norton, KS 800-255-0104
Storage Unlimited, Nixa, MO 800-478-6642
Superior Products Company, Saint Paul, MN 800-328-9800
Triple-A Manufacturing Company, Toronto, ON 800-786-2238
Xtreme Beverages, LLC, Dana Point, CA 949-495-7929

Cold Storage Room

ABI Limited, Concord, ON 800-297-8666
Aces Manufacturing Company, Sullivan, MO 800-325-6138
BMH Equipment, Sacramento, CA 800-350-8828
Carlisle Food Service Products, Oklahoma City, OK 800-654-8210
ColdZone, Anaheim, CA
Jarke Corporation, Prospect Hts, IL 800-722-5255
Kaines West Michigan Company, Ludington, MI 231-845-1281
Marlin Steel Wire Products, Baltimore, MD 877-762-7546
Metal Equipment Company, Cleveland, OH 800-700-6326
Metro Corporation, Wilkes Barre, PA 800-433-2233
Ridg-U-Rak, North East, PA 866-479-7225
Ron Vallort & Associates, Oak Brook, IL 630-734-3821
RTI Shelving Systems, Elmhurst, NY 800-223-6210
Superior Products Company, Saint Paul, MN 800-328-9800
Triple-A Manufacturing Company, Toronto, ON 800-786-2238

Kitchen

Advance Tabco, Edgewood, NY 800-645-3166
AMCO Corporation, City of Industry, CA 626-855-2550
American Housewares Manufacturing Corporation, Bronx, NY 718-665-9500
ARC Specialties, Valencia, CA 661-775-8500
Archer Wire International, Bedford Park, IL 708-563-1700
Bevles Company, Dallas, TX 800-441-1601
BMH Equipment, Sacramento, CA 800-350-8828
California Caster & Handtruck, San Francisco, CA 800-950-8750
Dubuque Steel Products Company, Dubuque, IA 563-556-6288
Grayline Housewares, Carol Stream, IL 800-222-7388
H.A. Sparke Company, Shreveport, LA 318-222-0927
Hodges, Vienna, IL 800-444-0011
Jackstack, Inwood, NY 800-999-9840
Lavi Industries, Valencia, CA 800-624-6225
LPI Imports, Chicago, IL 877-389-6563
M&E Manufacturing Company, Kingston, NY 845-331-2110
Metro Corporation, Wilkes Barre, PA 800-433-2233
New Age Industrial Corporation, Norton, KS 800-255-0104
Princeton Shelving, Cedar Rapids, IA 319-369-0355
Quipco Products, Sauget, IL 314-993-1442
Storage Unlimited, Nixa, MO 800-478-6642
Thermal Bags by Ingrid, Gilberts, IL 800-622-5560
United Showcase Company, Wood Ridge, NJ 800-526-6382
Universal Stainless, Aurora, CO 800-223-8332
Universal Stainless, Titusville, PA 800-295-1909
Vermillion Flooring Company, Springfield, MO 417-862-3785
Westfield Sheet Metal Works, Kenilworth, NJ 908-276-5500
Wilder Manufacturing Company, Port Jervis, NY 800-832-1319

Packing House

AFECO, Algona, IA 888-295-1116
BMH Equipment, Sacramento, CA 800-350-8828
Cannon Equipment Company, Rosemount, MN 800-825-8501
Market Forge Industries, Everett, MA 866-698-3188
New Age Industrial Corporation, Norton, KS 800-255-0104
Tier-Rack Corporation, Ballwin, MO 800-325-7869
Unirak Storage Systems, Taylor, MI 800-348-7225
United Steel Products Company, East Stroudsburg, PA 570-476-1010
Westfield Sheet Metal Works, Kenilworth, NJ 908-276-5500
Xtreme Beverages, LLC, Dana Point, CA 949-495-7929

Pallet

Aces Manufacturing Company, Sullivan, MO 800-325-6138
Adrian Fabricators/Cargotainer, Adrian, MI 800-221-3794
Atlas Equipment Company, Kansas City, MO 800-842-9188
Base Manufacturing, Monroe, GA 800-367-0572
BMH Equipment, Sacramento, CA 800-350-8828
Brute Fabricators, Castroville, TX 800-777-2788
Dexco, Leola, PA 800-345-8170
Durham Manufacturing Company, Duham, CT 800-243-3744
Dynamic Storage Systems Inc., Brooksville, FL 800-974-8211
Engineered Products Corporation, Greenville, SC 800-868-0145
Equipment Design & Fabrication, Charlotte, NC 800-949-0165
Eugene Welding Company, Marysville, MI 810-364-7421
Frazier Industrial Company, Long Valley, NJ 800-859-1342
Global Equipment Company, Port Washington, NY 888-628-3466
Key Material Handling, Simi Valley, CA 800-539-7225
Lumber & Things, Keyser, WV 800-296-5656
Mason Ways Indestructible Plastics, West Palm Beach, FL 800-837-2881
Material Storage Systems, Humble, TX 800-881-6750
Omicron Steel Products Company, Jamaica, NY 718-805-3400
Penco Products, Skippack, PA 800-562-1000
Princeton Shelving, Cedar Rapids, IA 319-369-0355
Sackett Systems, Bensenville, IL 800-323-8332
Sigma Industries, Concord, MI 517-857-6520
Solve Needs International, White Lake, MI 800-783-2462
Steel King Industries, Stevens Point, WI 800-553-3096
Steelmaster Material Handling, Marietta, GA 800-875-9900
Teilhaber Manufacturing Corporation, Broomfield, CO 800-358-7225
Triple-A Manufacturing Company, Toronto, ON 800-786-2238
Unirak Storage Systems, Taylor, MI 800-348-7225
Wire Way Husky, Denver, NC 704-483-1900

Spice

Metro Corporation, Wilkes Barre, PA 800-433-2233
Storage Unlimited, Nixa, MO 800-478-6642
Xtreme Beverages, LLC, Dana Point, CA 949-495-7929

Stock

Acme Display Fixture Company, Los Angeles, CA 800-959-5657

Advance Storage Products
Garden Grove, CA 888-478-7422
ARC Specialties
Valencia, CA 661-775-8500
Bayhead Products Corporation
Dover, NH 800-229-4323
Bennett Manufacturing Company
Alden, NY 800-345-2142
BMH Equipment
Sacramento, CA 800-350-8828
Cres Cor
Mentor, OH 877-273-7267
Edwards Products
Cincinnati, OH 800-543-1835
Faribo Manufacturing Company
Faribault, MN 800-447-6043
Flexible Material Handling
Suwanee, GA 800-669-1501
Hodge Manufacturing Company
Springfield, MA 800-262-4634
Hodges
Vienna, IL 800-444-0011
Interlake Material Handling
Naperville, IL 800-468-3752
Irby
Rocky Mount, NC 252-442-0154
Item Products
Houston, TX 800-333-4932
Koser Iron Works
Barron, WI 715-537-5654
Lodi Metal Tech
Lodi, CA 800-359-5999
Metro Corporation
Wilkes Barre, PA 800-433-2233
Omicron Steel Products Company
Jamaica, NY 718-805-3400
Paltier
Michigan City, IN 800-348-3201
Princeton Shelving
Cedar Rapids, IA 319-369-0355
Pucel Enterprises
Cleveland, OH 800-336-4986
Rapid Rack Industries
City of Industry, CA 800-736-7225
RW Products
Edgewood, NY 800-345-1022
Southern Metal Fabricators
Albertville, AL 800-989-1330
Speedrack Products GroupLtd.
Sparta, MI 616-887-0002
SPG International LLC
Covington, GA 877-503-4774
Tier-Rack Corporation
Ballwin, MO 800-325-7869
Unirak Storage Systems
Taylor, MI 800-348-7225
United Steel Products Company
East Stroudsburg, PA 570-476-1010
W.A. Schmidt Company
Oaks, PA 800-523-6719
Wirefab
Worcester, MA 877-877-4445

Wine

AMCO Corporation
City of Industry, CA 626-855-2550
Cannon Equipment Company
Rosemount, MN 800-825-8501
Cramer Products
New York, NY 212-645-2368
Dunn Woodworks
Shrewsbury, PA 877-835-8592
Epic Products
Santa Ana, CA 800-548-9791
Harmar Products
Sarasota, FL 800-833-0478
Houston Wire Works, Inc.
South Houston, TX 800-468-9477
Kedco Wine Storage Systems
Farmingdale, NY 800-654-9988
Leggett & Platt StorageP
Vernon Hills, IL 847-816-6246
Metro Corporation
Wilkes Barre, PA 800-433-2233
Tag-Trade Associated Group
Chicago, IL 800-621-8350
Triple-A Manufacturing Company
Toronto, ON 800-786-2238
Vermillion Flooring Company
Springfield, MO 417-862-3785
Wine Chillers of California
Santa Ana, CA 800-331-4274
Wineracks by Marcus
Costa Mesa, CA 714-546-4922
Xtreme Beverages, LLC
Dana Point, CA 949-495-7929

Wire

Aces Manufacturing Company
Sullivan, MO 800-325-6138
Advanced Plastic Coating
Parsons, KS 620-421-1660
Aero Manufacturing Company
Clifton, NJ 800-631-8378
AMCO Corporation
City of Industry, CA 626-855-2550
American Housewares Manufacturing Corporation
Bronx, NY 718-665-9500
Automatic Specialities Inc.
Marlborough, MA 800-445-2370
Avalon Manufacturing
Corona, CA 800-676-3040
Barker Wire Products
Keosauqua, IA 319-293-3176
Better Bilt Products
Addison, OH 800-544-4550
Complex Steel & Wire Corporation
Wayne, MI 734-326-1600
Cramer Products
New York, NY 212-645-2368
Dubuque Steel Products Company
Dubuque, IA 563-556-6288
Eagle Wire Works
Cleveland, OH 216-341-8550
Embro Manufacturing Company
East Canton, OH 330-489-3500
Emco Industrial Plastics
Cedar Grove, NJ 800-292-9906
FMI Display
Elkins Park, PA 215-663-1998
Gillis Associated Industries
Prospect Heights, IL 847-541-6500
Grayline Housewares
Carol Stream, IL 800-222-7388
Harmar Products
Sarasota, FL 800-833-0478
Hewitt Manufacturing Company
Waldron, IN 765-525-9829
HMG Worldwide In-Store Marketing
New York, NY 212-736-2300
Hodges
Vienna, IL 800-444-0011
Houston Wire Works, Inc.
South Houston, TX 800-468-9477
Indiana Wire Company
Fremont, IN 877-786-6883
J.C. Products Inc.
Haddam, CT 860-267-5516
Jarke Corporation
Prospect Hts, IL 800-722-5255
JEM Wire Products
Middletown, CT 860-347-0447
Kaines West Michigan Company
Ludington, MI 231-845-1281
Key Material Handling
Simi Valley, CA 800-539-7225
Leggett & Platt StorageP
Vernon Hills, IL 847-816-6246
Liberty Machine Company
York, PA 800-745-8152
Load King Manufacturing Company
Jacksonville, FL 800-531-4975
LPI Imports
Chicago, IL 877-389-6563
Lynch-Jamentz Company
Lakewood, CA 800-828-6217
Marlin Steel Wire Products
Baltimore, MD 877-762-7546
McMillin Manufacturing Corporation
Los Angeles, CA 323-268-1900
Metaline Products Company
South Amboy, NJ 732-721-1373
Metro Corporation
Wilkes Barre, PA 800-433-2233
Micro Wire Products Inc.
Brockton, MA 508-584-0200
Mid-West Wire Specialties
Chicago, IL 800-238-0228
Midwest Wire Products
Sturgeon Bay, WI 800-445-0225
Nashville Wire Products
Nashville, TN 615-743-2480
New Age Industrial Corporation
Norton, KS 800-255-0104
Northern Wire Products
St Cloud, MN 800-458-5549
Olson Wire Products Company
Halethorpe, MD 410-242-1945
Pentwater Wire Products
Pentwater, MI 877-869-6911
Pinquist Tool & Die Company
Brooklyn, NY 800-752-0414
Princeton Shelving
Cedar Rapids, IA 319-369-0355
R.I. Enterprises
Hernando, MS 662-429-7863
Racks
San Diego, CA 619-661-0987
Randware Industries
Prospect Heights, IL 847-299-8884
Riverside Wire & Metal Co.
Ionia, MI 616-527-3500
Royal Display Corporation
Middletown, CT 800-569-1295
Schlueter Company
Janesville, WI 800-359-1700
Selma Wire Products Company
Selma, IN 765-282-3532
SEMCO
Ocala, FL 800-749-6894
Sipco Products
Peoria Heights, IL 309-682-5400
Spot Wire Works Company
Philadelphia, PA 215-627-6124
SSW Holding Company, Inc.
Elizabethtown, KY 270-769-5526
Steel City Corporation
Youngstown, OH 800-321-0350
Straits Steel & Wire Company
Ludington, MI 231-843-3416
Superior Products Company
Saint Paul, MN 800-328-9800
Tennsco Corporation
Dickson, TN 800-251-8184
Toledo Wire Products
Toledo, OH 888-430-7445
Trepte's Wire & Metal Works
Bellflower, CA 800-828-6217
Triple-A Manufacturing Company
Toronto, ON 800-786-2238
Victone Manufacturing Company
Chicago, IL 312-738-3211
W.J. Egli Company
Alliance, OH 330-823-3666
Wahlstrom Manufacturing
Fontana, CA 909-822-4677
Wald Wire & Manufacturing Company
Oshkosh, WI 800-236-0053
Wire Products Manufacturing Company
Merrill, WI 715-536-7144
Wirefab
Worcester, MA 877-877-4445
Wiremaid Products
Coral Springs, FL 800-770-4700
Woerner Wire Works
Omaha, NE 402-451-5414
Yeager Wire Works
Berwick, PA 570-752-2769

Ramps

Delivery Truck

Hormann Flexan Llc
Leetsdale, PA 800-365-3667
Melcher Manufacturing Company
Spokane Valley, WA 800-541-4227

Shelving

Steel

Aces Manufacturing Company
Sullivan, MO 800-325-6138
Advance Tabco
Edgewood, NY 800-645-3166
Allied Engineering
North Vancouver, BC 877-929-1214
AMCO Corporation
City of Industry, CA 626-855-2550
Amscor
Brooklyn, NY 800-825-9800

ARC Specialties
Valencia, CA 661-775-8500
ATD-American Company
Wyncote, PA 800-523-2300
Atlas Equipment Company
Kansas City, MO 800-842-9188
BMH Equipment
Sacramento, CA 800-350-8828
Borroughs Corporation
Kalamazoo, MI 800-748-0227
Cleveland Metal StampingCompany
Berea, OH 440-234-0010
Commercial Kitchen Company
Los Angeles, CA 323-732-2291
Custom Diamond International
Laval, QC 800-326-5926
Denmar Corporation
North Dartmouth, MA 508-999-3295
Despro Manufacturing
Cedar Grove, NJ 800-292-9906
Duluth Sheet Metal
Duluth, MN 218-722-2613
Durham Manufacturing Company
Duham, CT 800-243-3744
E-Z Shelving Systems
Merriam, KS 800-353-1331
Easy Up Storage Systems
Seattle, WA 800-426-9234
Eldorado Miranda Manufacturing Company
Largo, FL 800-330-0708
Emco Industrial Plastics
Cedar Grove, NJ 800-292-9906
Global Equipment Company
Port Washington, NY 888-628-3466
Hodges
Vienna, IL 800-444-0011
IMC Teddy Food Service Equipment
Amityville, NY 800-221-5644
Infra Corporation
Waterford, MI 888-434-6372
Institutional Equipment
Bolingbrook, IL 630-771-0990
Jarke Corporation
Prospect Hts, IL 800-722-5255
Kent Corporation
Birmingham, AL 800-252-5368
Key Material Handling
Simi Valley, CA 800-539-7225
Lambertson Industries
Sparks, NV 800-548-3324
Leggett & Platt StorageP
Vernon Hills, IL 847-816-6246
Linvar
Hartford, CT 800-282-5288
Lista International Corporation
Holliston, MA 800-722-3020
Loyal Manufacturing Corporation
Indianapolis, IN 317-359-3185
LPI Imports
Chicago, IL 877-389-6563
Lyon Metal Products
Aurora, IL 630-892-8941
M&E Manufacturing Company
Kingston, NY 845-331-2110
Madix, Inc.
Terrell, TX 800-776-2349
Market Forge Industries
Everett, MA 866-698-3188
Marlin Steel Wire Products
Baltimore, MD 877-762-7546
Metal Kitchen Fabricators
Houston, TX 713-683-8375
Metal Masters Food Service Equipment Company
Clayton, DE 800-441-8440
Metro Corporation
Wilkes Barre, PA 800-433-2233
METRO Material Handling & Storage Products
Wilkes Barre, PA 800-433-2232
New Age Industrial Corporation
Norton, KS 800-255-0104
Nexel Industries
Port Washington, NY 800-245-6682
Omicron Steel Products Company
Jamaica, NY 718-805-3400
OSF
Toronto, ON 800-465-4000
Princeton Shelving
Cedar Rapids, IA 319-369-0355
Pucel Enterprises
Cleveland, OH 800-336-4986
Quantum Storage Systems
Miami, FL 800-685-4665
Republic Storage Systems LLC
Canton, OH 800-477-1255
Royce Phoenix
Glendale, AZ 602-256-0006
RTI Shelving Systems
Elmhurst, NY 800-223-6210
Sefi Fabricators
Amityville, NY 631-842-2200
Solar Group
Taylorsville, MS 800-647-7063
Solve Needs International
White Lake, MI 800-783-2462
Spot Wire Works Company
Philadelphia, PA 215-627-6124
Stainless Fabricating Company
Denver, CO 800-525-8966
Stainless Steel Fabricators
Tyler, TX 903-595-6625
Starlite Food Service Equipment
Detroit, MI 888-521-6603
Steelmaster Material Handling
Marietta, GA 800-875-9900
Streater LLC
Albert Lea, MN 800-527-4197
Stryco Wire Products
North York, ON 416-663-7000
Travis Manufacturing Company
Alliance, OH 330-875-1661
Tri-Boro Shelving & Partition
Farmville, VA 434-315-5600
Triple-A Manufacturing Company
Toronto, ON 800-786-2238
Universal Stainless
Aurora, CO 800-223-8332
Universal Stainless
Titusville, PA 800-295-1909
Weiss Sheet Metal
Avon, MA 508-583-8300
Western Pacific Storage Systems
San Dimas, CA 800-888-5707

Wire

Aces Manufacturing Company
Sullivan, MO 800-325-6138
Advance Tabco
Edgewood, NY 800-645-3166
AMCO Corporation
City of Industry, CA 626-855-2550
Atlas Equipment Company
Kansas City, MO 800-842-9188
Barker Wire Products
Keosauqua, IA 319-293-3176
Bettag & Associates
O Fallon, MO 800-325-0959
BMH Equipment
Sacramento, CA 800-350-8828
Coast Scientific
Rancho Santa Fe, CA 800-445-1544
Despro Manufacturing
Cedar Grove, NJ 800-292-9906
Enterprise Products
Bell Gardens, CA 562-928-1918
Etube and Wire
Shrewsbury, PA 800-618-4720
Gillis Associated Industries
Prospect Heights, IL 847-541-6500
Global Equipment Company
Port Washington, NY 888-628-3466
Hodge Manufacturing Company
Springfield, MA 800-262-4634
Hodges
Vienna, IL 800-444-0011
Indiana Wire Company
Fremont, IN 877-786-6883
JEM Wire Products
Middletown, CT 860-347-0447
Kaines West Michigan Company
Ludington, MI 231-845-1281
Kotoff & Company
San Dimas, CA 626-443-7115
Langer Manufacturing Company
Cedar Rapids, IA 800-728-6445
Leggett & Platt StorageP
Vernon Hills, IL 847-816-6246
LPI Imports
Chicago, IL 877-389-6563
Luckner Steel Shelving
Maspeth, NY 800-888-4212
Madix, Inc.
Terrell, TX 800-776-2349
Madsen Wire Products
Orland, IN 260-829-6561
Marlin Steel Wire Products
Baltimore, MD 877-762-7546
McMillin Manufacturing Corporation
Los Angeles, CA 323-268-1900
Metaline Products Company
South Amboy, NJ 732-721-1373
Metro Corporation
Wilkes Barre, PA 800-433-2233
Midwest Wire Products
Sturgeon Bay, WI 800-445-0225
Nexel Industries
Port Washington, NY 800-245-6682
Ortmayer Materials Handling Inc
Brooklyn, NY 718-875-7995
Pacific Northwest Wire Works
Dupont, WA 800-222-7699
Pentwater Wire Products
Pentwater, MI 877-869-6911
Princeton Shelving
Cedar Rapids, IA 319-369-0355
Riverside Wire & Metal Co.
Ionia, MI 616-527-3500
Royal Display Corporation
Middletown, CT 800-569-1295
Royce Phoenix
Glendale, AZ 602-256-0006
RTI Shelving Systems
Elmhurst, NY 800-223-6210
Sefi Fabricators
Amityville, NY 631-842-2200
Solar Group
Taylorsville, MS 800-647-7063
Space Guard Products
Seymour, IN 800-841-0680
Spot Wire Works Company
Philadelphia, PA 215-627-6124
Springport Steel Wire Products
Concord, MI 517-857-3010
Straits Steel & Wire Company
Ludington, MI 231-843-3416
Stryco Wire Products
North York, ON 416-663-7000
Superior Products Company
Saint Paul, MN 800-328-9800
Swanson Wire Works Industries, Inc.
Mesquite, TX 972-288-7465
Technibilt/Cari-All
Newton, NC 800-233-3972
Tennsco Corporation
Dickson, TN 800-251-8184
Triad Scientific
Manasquan, NJ 800-867-6690
Triple-A Manufacturing Company
Toronto, ON 800-786-2238
Wirefab
Worcester, MA 877-877-4445
Wiremaid Products
Coral Springs, FL 800-770-4700

Skids

American Box Corporation
Lisbon, OH 330-424-8055
American Pallet
Oakdale, CA 209-847-6122
Bay Area Pallet Company/IFCO Systems
Houston, TX 877-430-4326
Bennett Box & Pallet Company
Winston, NC 800-334-8741
Black River Pallet Company
Zeeland, MI 800-427-6515
Burgess Manufacturing ofOklahoma
Guthrie, OK 800-804-1913
Cassel Box & Lumber Company
Grafton, WI 262-377-4420
Cedar Box Company
Minneapolis, MN 612-332-4287
Charles Tirschman Company
Baltimore, MD 410-282-6199
Cotter Corporation
Danvers, MA
Cumberland Box & Mill Company
Cumberland, MD 301-724-1010
Cutter Lumber Products
Livermore, CA 925-443-5959
D&M Pallet Company
Neshkoro, WI 920-293-4616
Daniel Boone Lumber Industries
Morehead, KY 606-784-7586
Day Lumber Company
Westfield, MA 413-568-3511

Denver Reel & Pallet Company
Denver, CO . . . 303-321-1920
Durant Box Factory
Durant, OK . . . 580-924-4035
Eichler Wood Products
Laurys Station, PA . . . 610-262-6749
F.E. Wood & Sons
East Baldwin, ME . . . 207-286-5003
Fabricating & Welding Corporation
Chicago, IL . . . 773-928-2050
Fabrication Specialties Corporation
Centerville, TN . . . 931-729-2283
Fresno Pallet, Inc.
Sultana, CA . . . 559-591-4111
Gatewood Products LLC
Parkersburg, WV . . . 800-827-5461
Gerrity Industries
Monmouth, ME . . . 877-933-2804
Girard Wood Products
Puyallup, WA . . . 253-845-0505
Global Equipment Company
Port Washington, NY . . . 888-628-3466
Goeman's Wood Products
Hartford, WI . . . 262-673-6090
Graham Pallet Company
Tompkinsville, KY . . . 888-525-0694
Gray Woodproducts
Orrington, ME . . . 207-825-3578
Hanson Box & Lumber Company
Wakefield, MA . . . 617-245-0358
Harbor Pallet Company
Anaheim, CA . . . 714-533-4940
Hilderth Wood Products
Wadesboro, NC . . . 704-826-8326
Hinchcliff Products Company
Strongsville, OH . . . 440-238-5200
Horn Packaging Corporation
Lancaster, MA . . . 800-832-7020
Industrial Hardwood
Perrysburg, OH . . . 419-666-2503
Industrial Lumber & Packaging
Spring Lake, MI . . . 616-842-1457
International Wood Industries
Snohomish, WA . . . 800-922-6141
J.M. Rogers & Sons
Moss Point, MS . . . 228-475-7584
Jarke Corporation
Prospect Hts, IL . . . 800-722-5255
Kauling Wood Products Company
Beckemeyer, IL . . . 618-594-2901
Kelley Wood Products
Fitchburg, MA . . . 978-345-7531
Kent District Library
Comstock Park, NE . . . 616-784-2007
Kimball Companies
East Longmeadow, MA . . . 413-525-1881
Konz Wood Products
Appleton, WI . . . 877-610-5145
L&H Wood Manufacturing Company
Farmington, MI . . . 248-474-9000
Lester Box & Manufacturing
Long Beach, CA . . . 562-437-5123
Load King Manufacturing Company
Jacksonville, FL . . . 800-531-4975
Lumber & Things
Keyser, WV . . . 800-296-5656
Maull-Baker Box Company
Brookfield, WI . . . 414-463-1290
May-Wes Manufacturing
Hutchinson, MN . . . 800-788-6483
McIntosh Box & Pallet Company
East Syracuse, NY . . . 800-219-9552
McNeilly Wood Products, Inc.
Campbell Hall, NY . . . 845-457-9651
Michiana Box & Crate
Niles, MI . . . 800-677-6372
Mountain Valley Farms & Lumber Products, Inc.
Biglerville, PA . . . 717-677-6166
Necedah Pallet Company
Necedah, WI . . . 800-672-5538
Nefab Packaging, Inc.
Coppell, TX . . . 800-322-4425
Nelson Company
Baltimore, MD . . . 410-477-3000
New England Pallets & Skids
Ludlow, MA . . . 413-583-6628
New Lisbon Wood ProductsManufacturing Company
New Lisbon, WI . . . 608-562-3122
Ortmayer Materials Handling Inc
Brooklyn, NY . . . 718-875-7995
Packing Material Company
Southfield, MI . . . 248-489-7000
Pallets
Fort Edward, NY . . . 800-PLT-SKID
Pallox Incorporated
Onsted, MI . . . 517-456-4101
Pine Bluff Crating & Pallet
Pine Bluff, AR . . . 866-415-1075
Pine Point Wood Products
Dayton, MN . . . 763-428-4301
Porter & Porter Lumber
Fort Gay, WV . . . 304-648-5133
Premium Pallet
Philadelphia, PA . . . 800-648-7347
Pruitt's Packaging Services
Grand Rapids, MI . . . 800-878-0553
Remmey Wood Products
Southampton, PA . . . 215-355-3335
S&W Pallet Company
Camden, TN . . . 800-640-0522
Saint Charles Lumber Products
St Charles, MI . . . 989-865-9915
Savanna Pallets
McGregor, MN . . . 218-768-2077
Sheffield Lumber & Pallet Company
Mocksville, NC . . . 336-492-5565
Shelby Pallet & Box Company
Shelby, MI . . . 231-861-4214
Sheldon Wood Products
Toano, VA . . . 757-566-8880
Smith Pallet Company
Hatfield, AR . . . 870-389-6184
Sonoma Pacific Company
Montebello, CA . . . 323-838-4374
St. Pierre Box & Lumber Company
Canton, CT . . . 860-693-2089
Streator Dependable Manufacturing
Streator, IL . . . 800-798-0551
Swift Creek Forest Products
Amelia Court Hse, VA . . . 804-561-4498
Technipack, Inc.
Le Sueur, MN . . . 507-665-6658
The Original Lincoln Logs
Chestertown, NY . . . 800-833-2461
Thunder Pallet
Theresa, WI . . . 800-354-0643
Tower Pallet Company
De Pere, WI . . . 920-336-3495
Treen Box & Pallet Corporation
Bensalem, PA . . . 215-639-5100
Triad Pallet Company
Greensboro, NC . . . 336-292-8175
Upham & Walsh Lumber
Hoffman Estates, IL . . . 847-519-1010
Vandereems ManufacturingCompany
Hawthorne, NJ . . . 973-427-2355
Westfield Sheet Metal Works
Kenilworth, NJ . . . 908-276-5500
Wetterau Wood Products
Antigo, WI . . . 715-623-7907
Williams Pallet
West Chester, OH . . . 513-874-4014
WNC Pallet & Forest Products
Candler, NC . . . 828-667-5426

Storage & Holding Equipment

A&B Safe Corporation
Glassboro, NJ . . . 800-253-1267
A-Z Factory Supply
Schiller Park, IL . . . 800-323-4511
Accent Store Fixtures
Kenosha, WI . . . 800-545-1144
Acme Display Fixture Company
Los Angeles, CA . . . 800-959-5657
Aco Container Systems
Pickering, ON . . . 800-542-9942
Acrison
Moonachie, NJ . . . 800-422-4266
Adapto Storage Products
Hialeah, FL . . . 305-499-4800
Advance Fitting Corporation
Elkhorn, WI . . . 262-723-6699
Advance Storage Products
Garden Grove, CA . . . 888-478-7422
Advance Tabco
Edgewood, NY . . . 800-645-3166
Aero Manufacturing Company
Clifton, NJ . . . 800-631-8378
AFECO
Algona, IA . . . 888-295-1116
AFGO Mechanical Services, Inc.
Long Island City, NY . . . 800-438-2346
Allegheny Bradford Corporation
Bradford, PA . . . 800-542-0650
Allen Systems
Newberg, OR . . . 800-246-2034
Alliance Products, LLC
Murfreesboro, TN . . . 800-522-3973
Allied Engineering
North Vancouver, BC . . . 877-929-1214
Alloy Products Corporation
Waukesha, WI . . . 800-236-6603
Althor Products
Bethel, CT . . . 800-688-2693
AMCO Corporation
City of Industry, CA . . . 626-855-2550
Amscor
Brooklyn, NY . . . 800-825-9800
Anderson-Crane Company
Minneapolis, MN . . . 800-314-2747
Andritz
Muncy, PA . . . 570-546-8211
Apache Stainless Equipment Corporation
Beaver Dam, WI . . . 800-444-0398
Apollo Sheet Metal
Kennewick, WA . . . 509-586-1104
APV Americas
Delavan, WI . . . 800-252-5200
ARC Specialties
Valencia, CA . . . 661-775-8500
Arizona Store Equipment
Phoenix, AZ . . . 800-624-8395
Arkfeld Mfg & Distr Company
Norfolk, NE . . . 800-533-0676
Art Wire Works
Bedford Park, IL . . . 708-458-3993
Art-Phyl Creations
Hialeah, FL . . . 800-327-8318
ATD-American Company
Wyncote, PA . . . 800-523-2300
Atlas Equipment Company
Kansas City, MO . . . 800-842-9188
Atlas Minerals & Chemicals
Mertztown, PA . . . 800-523-8269
Automatic Specialities Inc.
Marlborough, MA . . . 800-445-2370
B.C. Holland
Dousman, WI . . . 262-965-2939
Bacchus Wine Cellars
Houston, TX . . . 800-487-8812
Bailly Showcase & Fixture Company
Las Vegas, NV . . . 702-947-6885
Baldewein Company
Lake Forrest, IL . . . 800-424-5544
Barker Company
Keosauqua, IA . . . 319-293-3777
Barker Wire Products
Keosauqua, IA . . . 319-293-3176
Baxter Manufacturing Company
Orting, WA . . . 800-777-2828
Bayhead Products Corporation
Dover, NH . . . 800-229-4323
Bennett Manufacturing Company
Alden, NY . . . 800-345-2142
Bergen Barrel & Drum Company
Kearny, NJ . . . 201-998-3500
Best
Brunswick, OH . . . 800-827-9237
Bevles Company
Dallas, TX . . . 800-441-1601
BMH
City of Industry, CA . . . 909-349-2530
Bonar Plastics
West Chicago, IL . . . 800-295-3725
Bonar Plastics
Ridgefield, WA . . . 800-972-5252
Borroughs Corporation
Kalamazoo, MI . . . 800-748-0227
Bowers Process Equipment
Stratford, ON . . . 800-567-3223
Brenner Tank
Fond Du Lac, WI . . . 800-558-9750
Brisker Dry Food Crisper
Oldsmar, FL . . . 800-356-9080
Brothers Manufacturing
Hermansville, MI . . . 888-277-6117
Buckhorn Inc
Milford, OH . . . 800-543-4454
Buhler Group
Raleigh, NC . . . 919-851-2000
Bulk Pack
Monroe, LA . . . 800-498-4215
Bulk Sak
Malvern, AR . . . 501-332-8745
Bush Tank Fabricators
Newark, NJ . . . 973-596-1121

C&H Store Equipment Company
Los Angeles, CA ... 800-648-4979

C&R Refrigation Inc,
Center, TX ... 800-438-6182

C. Nelson Manufacturing Company
Oak Harbor, OH ... 800-922-7339

C.E. Rogers Company
Mora, MN ... 800-279-8081

Cal-Coast Manufacturing
Turlock, CA ... 209-668-9378

Calzone Case Company
Bridgeport, CT ... 800-243-5152

Carter-Hoffman Corp LLC
Mundelein, IL ... 800-323-9793

Cayne Industrial Sales Corporation
Bronx, NY ... 718-993-5800

Central Fabricators
Cincinnati, OH ... 800-909-8265

Chart Industries - MVE Beverage Systems
Cleveland, OH ... 800-247-4446

Chem-Tainer Industries
West Babylon, NY ... 800-938-8896

Chester-Jensen Company, Inc.
Chester, PA ... 800-685-3750

Chicago Conveyor Corporation
Addison, IL ... 630-543-6300

Clayton & Lambert Manufacturing
Buckner, KY ... 800-626-5819

Coast Scientific
Rancho Santa Fe, CA ... 800-445-1544

Columbian TecTank
Parsons, KS ... 800-421-2788

Commercial Kitchen Company
Los Angeles, CA ... 323-732-2291

Complex Steel & Wire Corporation
Wayne, MI ... 734-326-1600

Containair Packaging Corporation
Paterson, NJ ... 888-276-6500

Containment Technology
St Gabriel, LA ... 800-388-2467

Continental Commercial Products
Bridgeton, MO ... 800-325-1051

Continental-Fremont
Tiffin, OH ... 419-448-4045

Coss Engineering Sales Company
Rochester Hills, MI ... 800-446-1365

COW Industries
Columbus, OH ... 800-542-9353

Cres Cor
Mentor, OH ... 877-273-7267

Crown Custom Metal Spinning
Concord, ON ... 800-750-1924

Cruvinet Winebar Company
Reno, NV ... 800-278-8463

Curtron Products
Pittsburgh, PA ... 800-833-5005

Custom Diamond International
Laval, QC ... 800-326-5926

Custom Metalcraft
Springfield, MO ... 417-862-0707

DBE Inc
Concord, ON ... 800-461-5313

DCI
St Cloud, MN ... 320-252-8200

Dematic Corp
Grand Rapids, MI ... 877-725-7500

Denstor Mobile Storage Systems
Walker, MI ... 800-234-7477

Despro Manufacturing
Cedar Grove, NJ ... 800-292-9906

Dexco
Leola, PA ... 800-345-8170

Dubuque Steel Products Company
Dubuque, IA ... 563-556-6288

Duke Manufacturing Company
Saint Louis, MO ... 800-735-3853

Dunn Woodworks
Shrewsbury, PA ... 877-835-8592

Durham Manufacturing Company
Duham, CT ... 800-243-3744

Dynamic Storage Systems Inc.
Brooksville, FL ... 800-974-8211

E2M
Duluth, GA ... 800-622-4326

Earl Soesbe Company
Romeoville, IL ... 219-866-4191

Eastern Plastics
Pawtucket, RI ... 800-442-8585

Easy Up Storage Systems
Seattle, WA ... 800-426-9234

Eaton Sales & Service
Denver, CO ... 800-208-2657

Edwards Fiberglass
Sedalia, MO ... 660-826-3915

Edwards Products
Cincinnati, OH ... 800-543-1835

EGA Products
Brookfield, WI ... 262-781-7899

Eldorado Miranda Manufacturing Company
Largo, FL ... 800-330-0708

Electrol Specialties Company
South Beloit, IL ... 815-389-2291

Ellett Industries
Port Coquitlam, BC ... 604-941-8211

Enerfab, Inc.
Cincinnati, OH ... 513-641-0500

Engineered Products Group
Madison, WI ... 800-626-3111

Eskay Metal Fabricating Company
Buffalo, NY ... 800-836-8015

Etube and Wire
Shrewsbury, PA ... 800-618-4720

Eugene Welding Company
Marysville, MI ... 810-364-7421

Expert Industries
Brooklyn, NY ... 718-434-6060

F.E. Wood & Sons
East Baldwin, ME ... 207-286-5003

Fab-X/Metals
Washington, NC ... 800-677-3229

Fabricated Components
Stroudsburg, PA ... 800-233-8163

Falco
La Prairie, CA ... 450-444-0566

Faribo Manufacturing Company
Faribault, MN ... 800-447-6043

Feldmeier Equipment
Syracuse, NY ... 315-454-8608

Flexible Material Handling
Suwanee, GA ... 800-669-1501

Flexpak Corporation
Phoenix, AZ ... 602-269-7648

Flow of Solids
Westford, MA ... 978-392-0300

Follett Corporation
Easton, PA ... 800-523-9361

Foster Forbes Glass
Marion, IN ... 765-668-1200

Four Corporation
Green Bay, WI ... 920-336-0621

Frazier Industrial Company
Long Valley, NJ ... 800-859-1342

Frelco
Stephenville, NL ... 709-643-5668

G.F. Frank & Sons
Fairfield, OH ... 513-870-9075

GA Systems
Huntington Beach, CA ... 714-848-7529

Geerpres
Muskegon, MI ... 231-773-3211

General Industries
Goldsboro, NC ... 888-735-2882

General Steel Fabricators
Joplin, MO ... 800-820-8644

Gibbs Brothers Cooperage Company
Hot Springs, AR ... 501-623-8881

Golden West Sales
Cerritos, CA ... 800-827-6175

Graff Tank Erection
Harrisville, PA ... 814-385-6671

Greene Industries
East Greenwich, RI ... 401-884-7530

Grief Brothers Corporation
Delaware, OH ... 740-549-6000

Griffin Cardwell, Ltd
Louisville, KY ... 502-636-1374

Hall-Woolford Tank Company
Philadelphia, PA ... 215-329-9022

Handy Store Fixtures
Newark, NJ ... 800-631-4280

Hanel Storage Systems
Pittsburgh, PA ... 412-787-3444

Hardware-Components
New Matamoras, OH ... 740-865-2424

Hardy Systems Corporation
Northbrook, IL ... 800-927-3956

Hedstrom Corporation
Ashland, OH ... 700-765-9665

Hewitt Manufacturing Company
Waldron, IN ... 765-525-9829

Hodge Manufacturing Company
Springfield, MA ... 800-262-4634

Hodges
Vienna, IL ... 800-444-0011

Hoover Materials Handling Group
Alpharetta, GA ... 800-391-3561

Houston Wire Works, Inc.
South Houston, TX ... 800-468-9477

Howard Fabrication
City of Industry, CA ... 626-961-0114

Hughes Equipment Company LLC
Columbus, WI ... 866-535-9303

Hydro-Miser
San Marcos, CA ... 800-736-5083

Hyster Company
San Diego, CA ... 855-804-2118

Ideal Wire Works
Alhambra, CA ... 626-282-1302

IMC Teddy Food Service Equipment
Amityville, NY ... 800-221-5644

Imperial Industries Inc
Wausau, WI ... 800-558-2945

Indeco Products
San Marcos, TX ... 512-396-5814

Indiana Wire Company
Fremont, IN ... 877-786-6883

Interlake Material Handling
Naperville, IL ... 800-468-3752

International Machinery Exchange
Deerfield, WI ... 800-279-0191

International Tank & Pipe Co
Clackamas, OR ... 888-988-0011

Interroll Corporation
Wilmington, NC ... 800-830-9680

Item Products
Houston, TX ... 800-333-4932

J.H. Carr & Sons
Seattle, WA ... 800-523-8842

JBC Plastics
St Louis, MO ... 877-834-5526

JEM Wire Products
Middletown, CT ... 860-347-0447

Jenike & Johanson
Tyngsboro, MA ... 978-649-3300

Jesco Industries, Inc.
Litchfield, MI ... 800-455-0019

JH Display & Fixture
Greenwood, IN ... 317-888-0631

Jupiter Mills Corporation
Roslyn, NY ... 800-853-5121

JW Leser Company
Los Angeles, CA ... 323-731-4173

K&I Creative Plastics
Jacksonville, FL ... 904-387-0438

Kadon Corporation
Milford, OH ... 937-299-0088

Kedco Wine Storage Systems
Farmingdale, NY ... 800-654-9988

Key Material Handling
Simi Valley, CA ... 800-539-7225

KHM Plastics
Gurnee, IL ... 847-249-4910

Kisco Manufacturing
Greendale, BC ... 604-823-7456

Koser Iron Works
Barron, WI ... 715-537-5654

La Crosse
Onalaska, WI ... 800-345-0018

Laidig Industrial Systems
Mishawaka, IN ... 574-256-0204

Lakeside Manufacturing
Milwaukee, WI ... 888-558-8574

Lambertson Industries
Sparks, NV ... 800-548-3324

Langsenkamp Manufacturing
Indianapolis, IN ... 877-585-1950

Leer Limited Partnership
New Lisbon, WI ... 800-766-5337

Leggett & Platt StorageP
Vernon Hills, IL ... 847-816-6246

Liberty Machine Company
York, PA ... 800-745-8152

Linvar
Hartford, CT ... 800-282-5288

LoadBank International
Orlando, FL ... 800-458-9010

Lodi Metal Tech
Lodi, CA ... 800-359-5999

Longview Fibre Company
Beaverton, OR ... 503-350-1600

Loyal Manufacturing Corporation
Indianapolis, IN ... 317-359-3185

LPI Imports
Chicago, IL ... 877-389-6563

Luckner Steel Shelving
Maspeth, NY ... 800-888-4212

Ludell Manufacturing Company
Milwaukee, WI 800-558-0800
Lyon Metal Products
Aurora, IL 630-892-8941
M&E Manufacturing Company
Kingston, NY 845-331-2110
Madsen Wire Products
Orland, IN 260-829-6561
Manitowoc Foodservice Companies, Inc.
New Port Richey, FL 877-375-9300
Mannhardt Inc
Sheboygan Falls, WI 800-423-2327
Marineland Commercial Aquariums
Blacksburg, VA 800-322-1266
Marlin Steel Wire Products
Baltimore, MD 877-762-7546
Material Storage Systems
Humble, TX 800-881-6750
Material Storage Systems
Gadsden, AL 877-543-2467
McCall Refrigeration
Parsons, TN 888-732-2446
McCullough Industries
Kenton, OH 800-245-9490
MeGa Industries
Burlington, ON 800-665-6342
Melmat, Inc.
Huntington Beach, CA 800-635-6289
Merric
Bridgeton, MO 314-770-9944
Metal Equipment Company
Cleveland, OH 800-700-6326
Metal Master
Tucson, AZ 800-488-8729
Metal Masters Food Service Equipment Company
Clayton, DE 800-441-8440
Metro Corporation
Wilkes Barre, PA 800-433-2233
METRO Material Handling & Storage Products
Wilkes Barre, PA 800-433-2232
Meyer Machine & Garroutte Products
San Antonio, TX 210-736-1811
Meyers Corbox Co, Inc.
Cleveland, OH 800-321-7286
Michiana Box & Crate
Niles, MI 800-677-6372
Micro Wire Products Inc.
Brockton, MA 508-584-0200
Middleby Worldwide
Elgin, IL 847-468-6068
Midwest Aircraft Products Company
Mansfield, OH 419-522-2231
Midwest Stainless
Menomonie, WI 715-235-5472
Miller Hofft Brands
Indianapolis, IN 317-638-6576
Miller Metal Fabricators
Staunton, VA 540-886-5575
MO Industries
Whippany, NJ 973-386-9228
Modar
Benton Harbor, MI 800-253-6186
Modern Brewing & Design
Santa Rosa, CA 707-542-6620
Modern Metals Industries
El Segundo, CA 800-437-6633
MultiFab Plastics
Boston, MA 888-293-5754
Murata Automated Systems
Charlotte, NC 800-428-8469
Myers Container Corporation
Hayward, CA 510-652-6847
Nalge Process Technologies Group
Rochester, NY 585-586-8800
National Bar Systems
Huntington Beach, CA 714-848-1688
Nefab
EGV, IL 630-451-5300
Nelson Company
Baltimore, MD 410-477-3000
Nepa Pallet & Container Company
Snohomish, WA 360-568-3185
New Pig Corporation
Tipton, PA 800-468-4647
Nexel Industries
Port Washington, NY 800-245-6682
Oak Barrel Winecraft
Berkeley, CA 510-849-0400
Omicron Steel Products Company
Jamaica, NY 718-805-3400
Pacific Store Designs
Garden Grove, CA 800-772-5661

Pacific Tank
Adelanto, CA 800-449-5838
Pallet One
Bartow, FL 800-771-1148
Paltier
Michigan City, IN 800-348-3201
Paramount Manufacturing Company
Wilmington, MA 978-657-4300
PBC
Mahwah, NJ 800-514-2739
Pelican Displays
Homer, IL 800-627-1517
Penco Products
Skippack, PA 800-562-1000
Pentwater Wire Products
Pentwater, MI 877-869-6911
Peter Gray Corporation
Andover, MA 978-470-0990
Peterson Manufacturing Company
Plainfield, IL 800-547-8995
Piper Products
Wausau, WI 800-544-3057
Pittsburgh Tank Corporation
Monongahela, PA 800-634-0243
Plastic Supply Incorporated
Manchester, NH 800-752-7759
Plastilite Corporation
Omaha, NE 800-228-9506
Plastocon
Oconomowoc, WI 800-966-0103
Prestige Skirting & Tablecloths
Orangeburg, NY 800-635-3313
Prince Castle
Carol Stream, IL 800-722-7853
Princeton Shelving
Cedar Rapids, IA 319-369-0355
Process Solutions
Riviera Beach, FL 561-840-0050
Processing Machinery & Supply
Philadelphia, PA 215-425-4320
Production Packaging & Processing Equipment Company
Phoenix, AZ 602-254-7878
Proluxe
Paramount, CA 800-594-5528
Pucel Enterprises
Cleveland, OH 800-336-4986
QBD Modular Systems
Santa Clara, CA 800-663-3005
Quantum Storage Systems
Miami, FL 800-685-4665
R&D Brass
Wappingers Falls, NY 800-447-6050
Ram Equipment
Waukesha, WI 262-513-1114
Ransco Industries
Ventura, CA 805-487-7777
Rapid Rack Industries
City of Industry, CA 800-736-7225
Reflex International
Norcross, GA 800-642-7640
Remcon Plastics
West Reading, PA 800-360-3636
Remstar International
Westbrook, ME 800-639-5805
Republic Storage Systems LLC
Canton, OH 800-477-1255
RETROTECH, Inc
Victor, NY 585-924-6333
Ridg-U-Rak
North East, PA 866-479-7225
Rolland Machining & Fabricating
Moneta, VA 973-827-6911
Rosenwach Tank Company
Long Island City, NY 718-729-4900
Royal Welding & Fabricating
Fullerton, CA 714-680-6669
RTI Shelving Systems
Elmhurst, NY 800-223-6210
Rubbermaid Commercial Products
Winchester, VA 800-336-9880
Rubicon Industries Corporation
Brooklyn, NY 800-662-6999
Saeplast Canada
St John, NB 800-567-3966
Sanchelima International
Doral, FL 305-591-4343
Scheb International
North Barrington, IL 847-381-2573
Seattle Plastics
Seattle, WA 800-441-0679

Sefi Fabricators
Amityville, NY 631-842-2200
SEMCO
Ocala, FL 800-749-6894
SerVend International
Sellersburg, IN 800-367-4233
Sharpsville Container
Sharpsville, PA 800-645-1248
Shelley Cabinet Company
Shelley, ID 208-357-3700
Silver King
Minneapolis, MN 800-328-3329
Sirco Systems
Birmingham, AL 205-731-7800
Smalley Manufacturing Company
Knoxville, TN 865-966-5866
Snyder Crown
Marked Tree, AR 870-358-3400
Solar Group
Taylorsville, MS 800-647-7063
Solve Needs International
White Lake, MI 800-783-2462
Southern Imperial
Rockford, IL 800-747-4665
Spacesaver Corporation
Fort Atkinson, WI 800-492-3434
Spartanburg Stainless Products
Spartanburg, SC 800-974-7500
Specific Mechanical Systems
Victoria, BC 250-652-2111
Speedrack Products GroupLtd.
Sparta, MI 616-887-0002
SPG International LLC
Covington, GA 877-503-4774
Spirit Foodservice, Inc.
Andover, MA 800-343-0996
Springport Steel Wire Products
Concord, MI 517-857-3010
SSW Holding Company, Inc.
Elizabethtown, KY 270-769-5526
St. Louis Stainless Service
Fenton, MO 888-507-1578
Stackbin Corporation
Lincoln, RI 800-333-1603
Stainless Fabrication
Springfield, MO 800-397-8265
Stainless Specialists
Wausau, WI 800-236-4155
Stainless Steel Fabricators
Tyler, TX 903-595-6625
Starlite Food Service Equipment
Detroit, MI 888-521-6603
Stearnswood
Hutchinson, MN 800-657-0144
Steel King Industries
Stevens Point, WI 800-553-3096
Stor-Loc
Kankakee, IL 815-936-0700
Storage Unlimited
Nixa, MO 800-478-6642
Strong Hold Products
Louisville, KY 800-880-2625
Summit Commercial
Bronx, NY 800-932-4267
Super Sturdy
Weldon, NC 800-253-4833
Supreme Fabricators
Artesia, CA 323-583-8944
Supreme Metal
Alpharetta, GA 800-645-2526
Tag-Trade Associated Group
Chicago, IL 800-621-8350
Tampa Sheet Metal Company
Tampa, FL 813-251-1845
Technibilt/Cari-All
Newton, NC 800-233-3972
Tennsco Corporation
Dickson, TN 800-251-8184
TGR Container Sales
San Leandro, CA 800-273-6887
Thermal Bags by Ingrid
Gilberts, IL 800-622-5560
Thermo Wisconsin
De Pere, WI 920-766-7200
Thermodynamics
Commerce City, CO 800-627-9037
Tier-Rack Corporation
Ballwin, MO 800-325-7869
TMS
San Francisco, CA 800-447-7223
Traex
Dane, WI 800-356-8006

Travis Manufacturing Company
Alliance, OH....................330-875-1661
Tri-Boro Shelving & Partition
Farmville, VA....................434-315-5600
Triad Scientific
Manasquan, NJ....................800-867-6690
Tupperware Brand Corporation
Orlando, FL....................800-366-3800
Turbo Refrigerating Company
Denton, TX....................940-387-4301
Unex Manufacturing
Jackson, NJ....................800-695-7726
Unirak Storage Systems
Taylor, MI....................800-348-7225
United Industries Group
Newport Beach, CA....................949-759-3200
United Showcase Company
Wood Ridge, NJ....................800-526-6382
United States Systems
Kansas City, KS....................888-281-2454
United Steel Products Company
East Stroudsburg, PA....................570-476-1010
Universal Stainless
Aurora, CO....................800-223-8332
Universal Stainless
Titusville, PA....................800-295-1909
Upham & Walsh Lumber
Hoffman Estates, IL....................847-519-1010
Vac-U-Max
Belleville, NJ....................800-822-8629
Valad Electric Heating Corporation
Tarrytown, NY
Valley Fixtures
Sparks, NV....................775-331-1050
Victone Manufacturing Company
Chicago, IL....................312-738-3211
Vorti-Siv
Salem, OH....................800-227-7487
W.A. Schmidt Company
Oaks, PA....................800-523-6719
Walker Stainless Equipment
New Lisbon, WI....................800-356-5734
Waukesha Cherry-Burrell
Louisville, KY....................502-491-4310
Welbilt Corporation
Stamford, CT....................203-325-8300
Welliver Metal Products Corporation
Salem, OR....................503-362-1568
Westeel
Saskatoon, SK....................306-931-2855
Western Pacific Storage Systems
San Dimas, CA....................800-888-5707
Westfield Sheet Metal Works
Kenilworth, NJ....................908-276-5500
Wilder Manufacturing Company
Port Jervis, NY....................800-832-1319
Wiltec
Leominster, MA....................978-537-1497
Wine Chillers of California
Santa Ana, CA....................800-331-4274
Winekeeper
Santa Barbara, CA....................805-963-3451
Winston Industries
Louisville, KY....................800-234-5286
Wirefab
Worcester, MA....................877-877-4445
Woerner Wire Works
Omaha, NE....................402-451-5414
Workman Packaging Inc.
Saint-Laurent, QC....................800-252-5208

Storage Units

Temperature Controlled

Advance Energy Technologies
Clifton Park, NY....................800-724-0198
American Panel Corporation
Ocala, FL....................800-327-3015
B.C. Holland
Dousman, WI....................262-965-2939
Bacchus Wine Cellars
Houston, TX....................800-487-8812
Baltimore Aircoil Company
Jessup, MD....................410-799-6200
BMH Equipment
Sacramento, CA....................800-350-8828
Cool Care
Boynton Beach, FL....................561-364-5711
Cramer Products
New York, NY....................212-645-2368
Creative Mobile Systems
Manchester, CT....................800-646-8364
Cruvinet Winebar Company
Reno, NV....................800-278-8463
Dade Engineering
Tampa, FL....................800-321-2112
Davis Core & Pad Company
Cave Spring, GA....................800-235-7483
Edwards Fiberglass
Sedalia, MO....................660-826-3915
Elliott-Williams Company
Indianapolis, IN....................800-428-9303
Eskay Metal Fabricating Company
Buffalo, NY....................800-836-8015
Faubion Central States Tank Company
Shawnee Mission, KS....................800-450-8265
Graff Tank Erection
Harrisville, PA....................814-385-6671
HABCO Beverage Systems
Toronto, ON....................800-448-0244
Hoshizaki America
Peachtree City, GA....................800-438-6087
Interstate Showcase & Fixture Company
West Orange, NJ....................973-483-5555
Johanson TransportationsServices
Fresno, CA....................800-742-2053
Kold-Hold
Edgefield, SC....................803-637-3166
La Crosse
Onalaska, WI....................800-345-0018
National Bar Systems
Huntington Beach, CA....................714-848-1688
Polyfoam Packers Corporation
Arlington Hts, IL....................800-323-7442
Portable Cold Storage
Edison, NJ....................800-535-2445
Refrigerator Manufacturers LLC
Cerritos, CA....................562-926-2006
Starlite Food Service Equipment
Detroit, MI....................888-521-6603
Superior Products Company
Saint Paul, MN....................800-328-9800
TMS
San Francisco, CA....................800-447-7223
Tolan Machinery Company
Rockaway, NJ....................973-983-7212
Tranter Pite
Wichita Falls, TX....................940-723-7125
Winekeeper
Santa Barbara, CA....................805-963-3451
Zero-Temp
Santa Ana, CA....................714-538-3177

Tanks

Holding, Storage

A&B Process Systems
Stratford, WI....................888-258-2789
Abalon Precision Manufacturing Corporation
Bronx, NY....................800-888-2225
Aco Container Systems
Pickering, ON....................800-542-9942
Advance Fitting Corporation
Elkhorn, WI....................262-723-6699
AFECO
Algona, IA....................888-295-1116
AFGO Mechanical Services, Inc.
Long Island City, NY....................800-438-2346
Allegheny Bradford Corporation
Bradford, PA....................800-542-0650
Alloy Products Corporation
Waukesha, WI....................800-236-6603
Anderson-Crane Company
Minneapolis, MN....................800-314-2747
Andgar Corporation
Ferndale, WA....................360-366-9900
Apache Stainless Equipment Corporation
Beaver Dam, WI....................800-444-0398
Apollo Sheet Metal
Kennewick, WA....................509-586-1104
APV Americas
Delavan, WI....................800-252-5200
Arrow Tank Company
Buffalo, NY....................716-893-7200
Atlas Minerals & Chemicals
Mertztown, PA....................800-523-8269
Baldewein Company
Lake Forrest, IL....................800-424-5544
Bayhead Products Corporation
Dover, NH....................800-229-4323
Berkshire PPM
Litchfield, CT....................860-567-3118
Bonar Plastics
Ridgefield, WA....................800-972-5252
Bowers Process Equipment
Stratford, ON....................800-567-3223
Brenner Tank
Fond Du Lac, WI....................800-558-9750
Brothers Manufacturing
Hermansville, MI....................888-277-6117
Bush Tank Fabricators
Newark, NJ....................973-596-1121
C&R Refrigation Inc,
Center, TX....................800-438-6182
Cal-Coast Manufacturing
Turlock, CA....................209-668-9378
Centennial Molding LLC
Hastings, NE....................888-883-2189
Central Fabricators
Cincinnati, OH....................800-909-8265
Chart Industries - MVE Beverage Systems
Cleveland, OH....................800-247-4446
Chem-Tainer Industries
West Babylon, NY....................800-275-2436
Chem-Tainer Industries
West Babylon, NY....................800-938-8896
Chester-Jensen Company, Inc.
Chester, PA....................800-685-3750
Clayton & Lambert Manufacturing
Buckner, KY....................800-626-5819
Coastline Equipment
Bellingham, WA....................360-739-2480
Columbian TecTank
Parsons, KS....................800-421-2788
Davron Technologies
Chattanooga, TN....................423-870-1888
DCI
St Cloud, MN....................320-252-8200
Eaton Sales & Service
Denver, CO....................800-208-2657
Electrol Specialties Company
South Beloit, IL....................815-389-2291
Emco Industrial Plastics
Cedar Grove, NJ....................800-292-9906
Enerfab, Inc.
Cincinnati, OH....................513-641-0500
Engineered Products Group
Madison, WI....................800-626-3111
Expert Industries
Brooklyn, NY....................718-434-6060
Falco
La Prairie, CA....................450-444-0566
Falco Technologies
La Prairie, QC....................450-444-0566
General Industries
Goldsboro, NC....................888-735-2882
General Tank
Berwick, PA....................800-435-8265
Graff Tank Erection
Harrisville, PA....................814-385-6671
Howard Fabrication
City of Industry, CA....................626-961-0114
Hughes Equipment Company LLC
Columbus, WI....................866-535-9303
Imperial Industries Inc
Wausau, WI....................800-558-2945
International Tank & Pipe Co
Clackamas, OR....................888-988-0011
JW Leser Company
Los Angeles, CA....................323-731-4173
Langsenkamp Manufacturing
Indianapolis, IN....................877-585-1950
Melmat, Inc.
Huntington Beach, CA....................800-635-6289
Miller Metal Fabricators
Staunton, VA....................540-886-5575
Modern Brewing & Design
Santa Rosa, CA....................707-542-6620
Nalge Process Technologies Group
Rochester, NY....................585-586-8800
Northland Process Piping
Isle, MN....................320-679-2119
Northwind
Alpena, AR....................870-437-2585
Pacific Tank
Adelanto, CA....................800-449-5838
PBC
Mahwah, NJ....................800-514-2739
Pittsburgh Tank Corporation
Monongahela, PA....................800-634-0243
Polar Process
Plattsville, ON....................877-896-8077

Poly Processing Company
French Camp, CA 877-325-3142
Process Solutions
Riviera Beach, FL 561-840-0050
Processing Machinery & Supply
Philadelphia, PA 215-425-4320
Production Packaging & Processing Equipment Company
Phoenix, AZ 602-254-7878
PVI Industries
Fort Worth, TX 800-784-8326
RAS Process Equipment
Robbinsville, NJ 609-371-1000
Remcon Plastics
West Reading, PA 800-360-3636
Rolland Machining & Fabricating
Moneta, VA 973-827-6911
Rosenwach Tank Company
Long Island City, NY 718-729-4900
Royal Welding & Fabricating
Fullerton, CA 714-680-6669
Rubicon Industries Corporation
Brooklyn, NY 800-662-6999
Sanchelima International
Doral, FL 305-591-4343
Scherping Systems
Winsted, MN 320-485-4401
Sharpsville Container
Sharpsville, PA 800-645-1248
Sims Machinery Company
Lanett, AL 334-576-2101
Snyder Crown
Marked Tree, AR 870-358-3400
Southern Metal Fabricators
Albertville, AL 800-989-1330
Specific Mechanical Systems
Victoria, BC 250-652-2111
Stainless Specialists
Wausau, WI 800-236-4155
Sterling Process Engineering
Columbus, OH 800-783-7875
Supreme Fabricators
Artesia, CA 323-583-8944
Tampa Sheet Metal Company
Tampa, FL 813-251-1845
Thermo Wisconsin
De Pere, WI 920-766-7200
Tolan Machinery Company
Rockaway, NJ 973-983-7212
United Industries Group
Newport Beach, CA 949-759-3200
Vorti-Siv
Salem, OH 800-227-7487
Waukesha Cherry-Burrell
Louisville, KY 502-491-4310
Welliver Metal Products Corporation
Salem, OR 503-362-1568

Modular

Modutank
Long Island City, NY 800-245-6964

Stainless Steel

G&F Manufacturing Comp any
Oak Lawn, IL 800-282-1574

Trailers

Refrigerated

All A Cart Manufacturing
Columbus, OH 800-695-2278
Fruehauf Trailer Services
St Louis, MO 314-822-1113
Great Dane Trailers, Inc.
Savannah, GA 912-232-4471
Manufacturers Railway Company
Saint Louis, MO 314-577-1775
New Centennial
Columbus, GA 800-241-7541
Portable Cold Storage
Edison, NJ 800-535-2445
Texas Corn Roasters
Granbury, TX 800-772-4345

Trucks

Factory, Warehouse, Shop & Industrial

A-Z Factory Supply
Schiller Park, IL 800-323-4511
Ace Engineering Company
Fort Worth, TX 800-431-4223
AFCO Manufacturing
Cincinnati, OH 800-747-7332
All Power
Sioux City, IA 712-258-0681
Bell & Howell Company
Lincolnwood, IL 800-647-2290
Bessco Tube Bending & Pipe Fabricating
Thornton, IL 800-337-3977
Bishamon Industries Corporation
Ontario, CA 800-358-8833
C.R. Daniels Inc.
Ellicott City, MD 800-933-2638
Caddy Corporation of America
Bridgeport, NJ 856-467-4222
California Caster & Handtruck
San Francisco, CA 800-950-8750
Cannon Equipment Company
Rosemount, MN 800-825-8501
Cayne Industrial Sales Corporation
Bronx, NY 718-993-5800
Collins Manufacturing Company Ltd
Langley, BC 800-663-6761
Continental Commercial Products
Bridgeton, MO 800-325-1051
Conveyance Technologies LLC
Cleveland, OH 800-701-2278
Crown Equipment Corporation
New Bremen, OH 419-629-2311
Daewoo Heavy Industries America Corporation
Cleveland, OH 800-323-9662
Dubuque Steel Products Company
Dubuque, IA 563-556-6288
Dutro Company
Logan, UT 866-388-7660
Dynabilt Products
Readville, MA 800-443-1008
Edwards Products
Cincinnati, OH 800-543-1835
Elwell Parker
Coraopolis, PA 800-272-9953
Excalibur Miretti Group
Fairfield, NJ 973-808-8399
Excel
Lincolnton, NC 704-735-6535
FMC Technologies
Chalfont, PA 888-362-3622
General Body Manufacturing Company of Texas
Houston, TX 800-395-8585
Hackney Brothers
Washington, NC 800-763-0700
Hamilton
Hamilton, OH 888-699-7164
Harper Trucks
Wichita, KS 800-835-4099
HDT Manufacturing
Salem, OH 800-968-7438
Heller Truck Body Corporation
Hillside, NJ 800-229-4148
Hot Shot Delivery Systems
Bloomingdale, IL 630-924-8817
Hyster Company
San Diego, CA 855-804-2118
Incinerator International
Houston, TX 713-227-1466
Industrial Equipment Company
Derry, NH 603-432-2037
Jarke Corporation
Prospect Hts, IL 800-722-5255
Jesco Industries, Inc.
Litchfield, MI 800-455-0019
Johnston Equipment
Delta, BC 800-237-5159
Kent District Library
Comstock Park, NE 616-784-2007
Komatsu Forklift
Rolling Meadows, IL 847-437-5800
Lakeside Manufacturing
Milwaukee, WI 888-558-8574
Landoo Corporation
Horsham, PA 785-562-5381
Leyman Manufacturing Corporation
Cincinnati, OH 866-539-6261
Linde Material Handling North America Corporation
Summerville, SC 843-871-0312
Load King Manufacturing Company
Jacksonville, FL 800-531-4975
Long Reach ManufacturingCompany
Westport, CT 800-285-7000
Marion Body Works
Marion, WI 715-754-5261
Metal Equipment Company
Cleveland, OH 800-700-6326
Mid-States Manufacturing & Engineering
Milton, IA 800-346-1792
Mitsubishi Caterpillar Fork
Houston, TX 800-228-5438
NACCO Materials HandlingGroup
Fairview, OR 503-721-6205
National Scoop & Equipment Company
Spring House, PA 215-646-2040
Net Material Handling
Milwaukee, WI 800-558-7260
Nevlen Co. 2, Inc.
Wakefield, MA 800-562-7225
New Age Industrial Corporation
Norton, KS 800-255-0104
Nexel Industries
Port Washington, NY 800-245-6682
Nissan Forklift Corporation of North America
Marengo, IL 800-871-5438
Ortmayer Materials Handling Inc
Brooklyn, NY 718-875-7995
Peregrine
Lincoln, NE 800-777-3433
Pucel Enterprises
Cleveland, OH 800-336-4986
Raymond Corporation
Greene, NY 800-235-7200
Royce Phoenix
Glendale, AZ 602-256-0006
Schaeff
Bridgeview, IL 708-598-9099
Solve Needs International
White Lake, MI 800-783-2462
Steel Specialty Equipment Corporation
Ridgewood, NY 800-521-7732
Technibilt/Cari-All
Newton, NC 800-233-3972
Thermo King Corporation
Minneapolis, MN 952-887-2200
Thombert
Newton, IA 800-433-3572
Valley Craft
Lake City, MN 800-328-1480
Waldon Equipment, LLC
Fairview, OK 800-486-0023
Wesley International Corporation
Scottdale, GA 800-241-8649

Food & Restaurant

800Buy Cart
Jamaica, NY 800-289-2278
All A Cart Manufacturing
Columbus, OH 800-695-2278
All Star Carts & Vehicles
Bay Shore, NY 800-831-3166
Alliance Products, LLC
Murfreesboro, TN 800-522-3973
AMCO Corporation
City of Industry, CA 626-855-2550
ARC Specialties
Valencia, CA 661-775-8500
BMH Equipment
Sacramento, CA 800-350-8828
Century Industries
Sellersburg, IN 800-248-3371
Creative Mobile Systems
Manchester, CT 800-646-8364
Custom Sales & Service Inc.
Hammonton, NJ 800-257-7855
Hackney Brothers
Washington, NC 800-763-0700
Holstein Manufacturing
Holstein, IA 800-368-4342
Lakeside Manufacturing
Milwaukee, WI 888-558-8574
Lakeside-Aris Manufacturing
Milwaukee, WI 800-558-8565
Leggett & Platt StorageP
Vernon Hills, IL 847-816-6246
M&E Manufacturing Company
Kingston, NY 845-331-2110
Metro Corporation
Wilkes Barre, PA 800-433-2233

Technibilt/Cari-All
Newton, NC 800-233-3972
Wag Industries
Skokie, IL 800-621-3305

Hand

ARC Specialties
Valencia, CA 661-775-8500
BMH Equipment
Sacramento, CA 800-350-8828
California Caster & Handtruck
San Francisco, CA 800-950-8750
Clamp Swing Pricing Company
Oakland, CA 800-227-7615
Clark Caster Company
Forest Park, IL 800-538-0765
Enrick Company
Zumbrota, MN 507-732-5215
Hamilton
Hamilton, OH 888-699-7164
Hodge Manufacturing Company
Springfield, MA 800-262-4634
Innovative Moving Systems, Inc.
Oostburg, WI. 800-619-0625
Magline
Pinconning, MI 800-624-5463
Net Material Handling
Milwaukee, WI 800-558-7260
Otto Braun Bakery Equipment
Buffalo, NY. 716-824-1252
Roll Rite Corporation
Hayward, CA 800-345-9305
Steel Specialty Equipment Corporation
Ridgewood, NY 800-521-7732
Ultra Lift Corporation
San Jose, CA. 800-346-3057
Valley Craft
Lake City, MN 800-328-1480

Meat

Dubuque Steel Products Company
Dubuque, IA 563-556-6288
Techform
Mount Airy, NC 336-789-2115

Packing House

Bessco Tube Bending & Pipe Fabricating
Thornton, IL 800-337-3977
BMH Equipment
Sacramento, CA 800-350-8828
Cannon Equipment Company
Rosemount, MN 800-825-8501
DC Tech
Kansas City, MO. 877-742-9090
Elwell Parker
Coraopolis, PA 800-272-9953
Key Material Handling
Simi Valley, CA. 800-539-7225
Le Fiell Company, Inc.
Reno, NV 775-677-5300
Wesley International Corporation
Scottdale, GA 800-241-8649

Pallet Handling

Bishamon Industries Corporation
Ontario, CA. 800-358-8833
BMH Equipment
Sacramento, CA 800-350-8828
Cannon Equipment Company
Rosemount, MN 800-825-8501
Elwell Parker
Coraopolis, PA 800-272-9953
Key Material Handling
Simi Valley, CA. 800-539-7225
Landoll Corporation
Marysville, KS 785-562-5381
Lift Rite
Mississauga, ON. 905-456-2603
Long Reach ManufacturingCompany
Westport, CT. 800-285-7000
Lumber & Things
Keyser, WV. 800-296-5656
NACCO Materials HandlingGroup
Fairview, OR. 503-721-6205
Net Material Handling
Milwaukee, WI 800-558-7260
Sackett Systems
Bensenville, IL 800-323-8332
Wesley International Corporation
Scottdale, GA 800-241-8649

Tilt

Bayhead Products Corporation
Dover, NH. 800-229-4323
BMH Equipment
Sacramento, CA 800-350-8828
Pucel Enterprises
Cleveland, OH 800-336-4986
RMI-C/Rotonics Manufacturing
Bensenville, IL 630-773-9510

Utility Vault Covers

Slipnot Metal Safety Flooring
Detroit, MI 800-754-7668

Vats

Cheese

A&B Process Systems
Stratford, WI. 888-258-2789
Damrow Company
Fond Du Lac, WI 800-236-1501
DCI
St Cloud, MN 320-252-8200
Dubuque Steel Products Company
Dubuque, IA 563-556-6288
Peterson Fiberglass Laminates
Shell Lake, WI 715-468-2306
Rosenwach Tank Company
Long Island City, NY 718-729-4900

Warehouses

Insulated

Advance Energy Technologies
Clifton Park, NY. 800-724-0198

Wine Storage Units

Advance Energy Technologies
Clifton Park, NY. 800-724-0198
Bacchus Wine Cellars
Houston, TX 800-487-8812
Cramer Products
New York, NY 212-645-2368
Cruvinet Winebar Company
Reno, NV 800-278-8463
Dufeck Manufacturing Company
Denmark, WI. 888-603-9663
Falco Technologies
La Prairie, QC. 450-444-0566
Felix Storch
Bronx, NY. 800-932-4267
International Patterns, Inc.
Bay Shore, NY 631-952-2000
Kedco Wine Storage Systems
Farmingdale, NY 800-654-9988
Lockwood Manufacturing
Livonia, MI. 800-521-0238
Metro Corporation
Wilkes Barre, PA. 800-433-2233
PBC
Mahwah, NJ 800-514-2739
Summit Commercial
Bronx, NY. 800-932-4267
Winekeeper
Santa Barbara, CA 805-963-3451
Wineracks by Marcus
Costa Mesa, CA 714-546-4922

Equipment, Supply & Service Companies

A to Z Profiles

18000 3D Instruments
2900 E White Star Ave
Anaheim, CA 92806 714-399-9200
Fax: 714-399-9221 jmeng@3dhb.com
www.3dinstruments.com
Quality Control: Charlene L Lah
VP: Garey Cooper
Estimated Sales: $50 - 100 Million
Number Employees: 100-249

18001 3DT, LLC
N114 W18850 Clinton Dr
Germantown, WI 53022 262-253-6700
Fax: 262-253-6977 888-326-7662
sales@3dtllc.com www.3dtllc.com
Corona treaters
President: Morten Jorgensen
Sales/Marketing Manager: S. Erik Kiel
Estimated Sales: $2.5 - 5 Million
Number Employees: 20-49

18002 3Greenmoms LLC
Po Box 59033
Potomac, MD 20859-9033 301-802-9390
Fax: 888-236-9043 kirsten@3greenmoms.com
www.lunchskins.com
Maker of reuseable decorative sandwich bags.

18003 3M Company
Medical Dept # 220
St Paul, MN 55144-0001 651-733-0694
800-698-4595
www.3m.com/foodservice
President: Harry Borrelli
Estimated Sales: $100 - 500 Million
Number Employees: 1-4

18004 3M Company Filtration Products
3m Center
St Paul, MN 55144-1000 651-733-1110
Fax: 651-733-9973 caperman@mmm.com
www.mmm.com
CEO: George W Buckley
Estimated Sales: $500,000 - $1,000,000
Number Employees: 10,000

18005 3M Company Food ServiceTrades
3m Center
St Paul, MN 55144-1000 651-733-1110
Fax: 651-733-9973 www.mmm.com
CEO: George W Buckley
Estimated Sales: K
Number Employees: 10,000

18006 3M Corporation Packaging Systems
Medical Dept # 220
St Paul, MN 55144-0001 651-733-0694
Fax: 651-736-5516 800-722-5463
mcfaust1@mmm.com www.3m.com/packaging
Multi-packing opportunites including carry handles for customer convenience, as well as a variety of packaging tapes, equipment and attachment systems
President: Harry Borrelli
CEO: James McNerney
Estimated Sales: $100+ Million
Number Employees: 1-4

18007 3M Dynamic Message Systems
3808 N Sullivan Rd
Bldg 3G
Spokane Valley, WA 99216 509-891-1511
Fax: 509-891-0546 800-727-9111
rjmoore1@mmm.com www.ge.com
Manufacturer and exporter of electronic message signs and L.E.D. displays
Sales Director: Bob Moore
Brands:
Diamond Brite

18008 3M Microbiology
3M Center
St Paul, MN 55144-0001 651-575-1326
Fax: 651-733-2181 888-364-3577
microbiology@mmm.com www.mmm.com
Microbiological testing; 3m(TM) petrifilm(TM) Plates(TM) Tecra(TM) Clean-Trace(TM) and other microbiological testing and sampling products for the food industry.
President: George Buckley
CEO: James Mc Nerney Jr
Number Employees: 20-49

18009 3M Security Systems Division/Industrial Food Service Solutions
3 M Ctr
St Paul, MN 55144-0001 651-575-1326
Fax: 651-733-2181 888-364-3577
dmsayers@mmm.com www.mmm.com
Safety, maintenance and productivity services and products for the food and beverage industry.
Chairman/President/CEO: George Buckley
CEO: James Mc Nerney Jr
SVP/Chief Financial Officer: Patrick Campbell
EVP/Industrial and Transportation: Cheol Shin
EVP/Research and Development: Frederick Palensky
Marketing Development Supervisor: David Sayers
SVP/Marketing and Sales: Robert MacDonald
SVP/Legal Affairs and General Counsel: Richard Ziegler
EVP/International Operations: Inge Thulin
EVP/Consumer and Office Business: Moe Nozari
SVP/Corporate Supply Chain Operations: John Woodworth

18010 518 Corporation
518 Martin Luther King Jr.
Savannah, GA 31401-4881 912-232-1141
Fax: 912-236-7969
President: Louis C Mathews III
Estimated Sales: $5 - 10 Million
Number Employees: 10-19

18011 7 Seas Fisheries
11216 S Michigan Ave
Chicago, IL 60628-4910 773-785-0550
Fax: 312-942-0236
Owner: Natibad Cortez
Estimated Sales: $300,000-500,000
Number Employees: 1-4

18012 800Buy Cart
94-15 100th St
Jamaica, NY 11416-1707 718-322-2003
Fax: 718-529-4803 800-289-2278
vending@worksman.com www.800buycart.com
Manufacturer and exporter of vending carts, trucks, trailers and kiosks.
President: Wayne Sosin
Mobile Food Equity, VP: Jack Beller
Estimated Sales: $5-10 Million
Square Footage: 360000
Type of Packaging: Food Service
Brands:
Admar
Worksman Cycles

18013 9-12 Corporation
HC-1 Box 29030
Department 388
Caguas, PR 00725 787-747-0405
Fax: 787-747-0318 jlazoff@elevatewaters.net
www.elevatewaters.net
Manufacturers of elevate enhanced fiber water beverages.
President/CEO: Joe Lazoff
Estimated Sales: $1-5 Million
Number Employees: 10
Square Footage: 40000
Type of Packaging: Consumer, Food Service, Private Label
Brands:
Apres
Pirel

18014 99 Ranch Market
1625 S Azusa Avenue
Hacienda Hts, CA 91745-3832 626-839-2899
Fax: 626-839-2127 www.99ranch.com
Largest Asian American Supermarket chain on the West Coast. Has 37 stores primarily in California, with other stores in Nevada, Washington, and Texas. Founded in 1984. Has one manufacturing facility listed below.
Founder/CEO: Roger Chen
Estimated Sales: $500,000
Number Employees: 2,000
Other Locations:
Manufacturing Facility - Sugarland
Sugarland TX

18015 A C Tool & Machine Company
3711 Nobel Ct
Louisville, KY 40216-4113 502-447-5505
Fax: 502-363-4073 www.actoolandmachine.com
Sausage processing and packaging equipment; re-building of food processing equipment and replacement parts.
President: Matthew Thoben
Estimated Sales: $1-2.5 Million
Number Employees: 10-19
Square Footage: 48000
Type of Packaging: Food Service
Brands:
Ac Slit & Trim

18016 A Duda & Sons
P.O.Box 620257
Oviedo, FL 32762 407-365-2111
Fax: 407-365-2010 info@duda.com
www.duda.com
President: Ferdinand S Duda
Estimated Sales: $100 - 500 Million
Number Employees: 1,000-4,999

18017 A Epstein & Sons International
600 W Fulton St Fl 9
Chicago, IL 60661 312-454-9100
Fax: 312-559-1217 information@epstein-isi.com
www.epstein-isi.com
Design and construction of food manufacturing and distribution facilities
President: John Patelski
CFO: Jim Jirsa
Executive VP: Allen L Pomerance
Quality Control: Darrin McCormies
R&D: Andrea Velasquez
Estimated Sales: $20 - 50 Million
Number Employees: 250-499

18018 A La Carte
5610 W Bloomingdale Ave
Chicago, IL 60639-4110 773-237-3000
Fax: 773-237-3075 800-722-2370
service@alacarteline.com www.alacarteline.com
Custom promotional products including hard candy and popcorn in decorative tins, jars, boxes, etc.
President: Michael Shulkin
CEO: Adam Robins
Sales Director: James Janowski
Purchasing: Marly Robins
Estimated Sales: $10 - 20 Million
Number Employees: 50-99
Parent Co: David Scott Industries
Type of Packaging: Food Service, Private Label, Bulk

18019 A Line Corporation
5410 Powerhouse Court
Concord, NC 28027 704-793-1602
Fax: 704-793-1603 sales@aline1.com
www.aline1.com
Top-Load Carton Forming and Closing machinery
President: Maria Naas
Marketing: Jan Stull
Estimated Sales: $5 - 10 Million
Number Employees: 5-9

18020 (HQ)A P Dataweigh Systems
2730 Northgate Drive
Cumming, GA 30041 678-679-8000
Fax: 678-679-8001 877-409-2562
sales@APcheckweighers.com
www.apdataweigh.com
Manufacturer and exporter of check weighers, in-motion conveyor scales and checkweighers.
President: Patrick Hetzel
Operations Manager: Scott Gibson
Estimated Sales: $1 Million
Number Employees: 10-19
Number of Brands: 2
Number of Products: 14
Brands:
Ap Checkweigers

18021 A Tec Technologic
5335 Progress Boulevard
Bethel Park, PA 15102-2545 412-835-6270
Fax: 412-835-6205 info@tecnologicusa.com
www.technologicusa.com
President: Philip Bochicchio

18022 **A&A International**
544 Central Dr Ste 110
Virginia Beach, VA 23454 757-463-1446
Fax: 757-463-4917 800-252-1446
info@aaawnings.com www.aaawnings.com
Commercial awnings
Manager: Rhonda Yarborough
Estimated Sales: $1-2,500,000
Number Employees: 20-49

18023 **A&A Line & Wire Corporation**
5118 Grand Ave Ste 10
Flushing, NY 11378 718-456-2657
Fax: 718-366-8284 800-886-2657
jlach@aalinewire.com
Manufacturer, importer and exporter of rope, twine and doormats, also sausage and pastella twine
President: Wally Greenburg
Treasurer: F Lach
Estimated Sales: Below $5 Million
Number Employees: 10-19
Square Footage: 16000
Parent Co: Long Island Import Center
Brands:
Coco
Crown
Queen O Mat

18024 **A&A Manufacturing Company**
2300 S Calhoun Rd
New Berlin, WI 53151-2708 414-906-4200
Fax: 262-786-3280 sales@gortite.com
www.gortite.com
Protective walk-on covers
President: Jim O'Rourke
CEO: Jerry O'Rourke
CFO: Larry Kean
VP: Tom Schanover
Quality Control: Darol Varter
Marketing Manager: Ken Sczyzkwski
Estimated Sales: $20-50 Million
Number Employees: 100-249
Parent Co: Standalone

18025 **(HQ)A&B Process Systems**
P.O.Box 86
Stratford, WI 54484 715-687-4332
Fax: 715-687-3225 888-258-2789
awiess@abprocess.com www.abprocess.com
Manufacturer and exporter of ASME U stamps, process systems, tanks, vessels and custom components.
Chairman/Co-Founder: Ajay Hilgemann
Chief Financial Officer: Paul Kinate
Marketing Team Leader: Andrea Wiese
Automation Team Lead: Les Mammen
Safety Manager: Bill Thompson
Estimated Sales: $120 Million
Number Employees: 100-249
Square Footage: 200000
Type of Packaging: Food Service, Bulk
Brands:
Oc Guide Bearing
Vacushear

18026 **A&B Safe Corporation**
114 Delsea Dr S
Glassboro, NJ 08028 856-863-1186
Fax: 856-863-1208 800-253-1267
info@a-bsafecorp.com www.a-bsafecorp.com
Manufacturer, importer and exporter of depository, burglary and insulated safes and chests; also, insulated filing cabinets, safes and locks
President: Edward Dornisch
Sales Director: Edward C Dornisch
Operations Manager: Mildred Dornisch
Estimated Sales: $.5 - 1 million
Number Employees: 1-4
Number of Brands: 20
Square Footage: 10000
Brands:
A&B

18027 **A&D Sales and Marketing**
145 E Colt Dr
Fayetteville, AR 72703-2847 479-521-8665
Fax: 479-521-0841
President: Jim Stockland
Treasurer: Pam Stockland
Estimated Sales: $5 - 10 Million
Number Employees: 5-9

18028 **A&D Weighing**
1756 Automation Pkwy
San Jose, CA 95131-1873 408-263-5333
Fax: 408-263-0119 scales@andweighing.com
www.andonline.com
President: Paul Huver
President, Chief Executive Officer: Teruhisa Moriya
Quality Control: Maggie Tan
CEO: Peru Moriya
Estimated Sales: $20 - 50 Million
Number Employees: 20-49

18029 **A&D Weighing**
1756 Automation Pkwy
San Jose, CA 95131-1873 408-263-5333
Fax: 408-263-0119 800-726-3364
scales@andweighing.com www.andonline.com
Manufacturer and exporter of balances, scales and indicators
President: Paul Huber
President, Chief Executive Officer: Teruhisa Moriya
CEO: Peru Moriya
Marketing Communications Coordinator: Regina Starzyk
Director Sales: Dan Ashton
Estimated Sales: $20-50 Million
Number Employees: 20-49
Square Footage: 3000

18030 **A&E Conveyor Systems**
121 P Rickman Industrial Dr
Canton, GA 30115 770-345-7300
Fax: 770-345-7391 info@ae-conveyor.com
www.ae-conveyor.com
Waterless container cleaning systems, container handling, conveying systems
President: Raymond Young
Estimated Sales: Below $5 000,000
Number Employees: 1-4

18031 **A&F**
5355 115th Avenue N
Clearwater, FL 33760-4840 727-572-7753
Fax: 727-573-0367 sales@autoprodinc.com
www.autoprodinc.com
Filling and sealing machinery
President: Paul Desocio
Estimated Sales: $10-20 Million
Number Employees: 50-100
Parent Co: Jagenberg

18032 **A&F Automation**
1210 Campus Dr
Morganville, NJ 07751-1262 732-536-8770
Fax: 732-536-8850 sales@hassiausa.com
www.oystarusa.com
President: Charles Ravalli
Estimated Sales: $3 - 5 Million
Number Employees: 10-19
Parent Co: IWKA Company

18033 **A&G Machine Company**
50 Dunnell Lane
Pawtucket, RI 02860-5828 401-726-4180
Fax: 401-723-2333
Aerators, candy making equipment including stringers and cookers, batch and continuous cooking equipment, cream machines, heat exchangers, kettle lifters and marshmallow equipment
President: Paul Desocio
Estimated Sales: $300,000-500,000
Number Employees: 1-4

18034 **A&J Mixing International**
8-2345 Wyecroft Road
Oakville, ON L6L 6L8
Canada 905-827-7288
Fax: 905-827-5045 800-668-3470
lyndon@ajmixing.com www.ajmixing.com
Manufacturer and exporter of food dry ingredient mixers, mixing sytems, vacuum coaters, dryers and continuous mixers.
President: A Flower
Sales: Lyndon Flower
Estimated Sales: $2.5 Million
Square Footage: 2500
Other Locations:
Sycamore IL
Brands:
Phlauer High Performance Mixers

18035 **A&K Automation**
1010 N Ashland Avenue
Aurora, ON L4G4R6 905-713-3429
Fax: 920-432-4356 info@akautomation.ca
www.akautomation.ca
Bakery products and pizza crust equipment
President: Randy Charles
CFO: Jim Charles
R & D: Dennis Dolski
Estimated Sales: Below $5 Million
Number Employees: 10
Square Footage: 1600

18036 **A&K Development Company**
410 Chambers St
Eugene, OR 97402 541-686-0012
Fax: 541-485-2892 akdco@akdco.net
www.akdco.com
Sweet corn processing equipment: power huskers, power orienter, vibratory receiving conveyors, steam wilters, elevators, distribution systems, automatic feeding and lubrication systems, roll washers, short piece graders, scalpers, andsilage choppers
President and R&D: Ronald L Anderson
CFO: Bob King
Marketing Director: Zack Zachemtmayer
Office Manager: Darla Vicksie
Estimated Sales: $1 - 2.5 000,000
Number Employees: 20-49

18037 **A&L Analytical Laboratories**
2790 Whitten Rd
Memphis, TN 38133 901-213-2400
Fax: 901-213-2440 support@allabs.com
www.allabs.com
Fat testing, water treatment systems
President: Scott McKee
Estimated Sales: $1 - 3 000,000
Number Employees: 50-99

18038 **A&L Laboratories**
1001 Glenwood Ave
Minneapolis, MN 55405 612-374-9141
Fax: 612-374-5426 800-225-3832
info@aandl-labs.com www.aandl-labs
Detergents and sanitizers
President: Guy Pochard
VP: Gabreiele Wittenburg
Estimated Sales: $20-50 Million
Number Employees: 20-49

18039 **A&L Western Ag Lab**
1311 Woodland Avenue
Suite 1
Modesto, CA 95351-1221 209-529-4080
Fax: 209-529-4736 director@al-labs-west.com
www.al-labs-west.com
Testing laboratory providing sanitation and nutritional analysis for product labeling
President and Laboratory Director: Robert Butterfield
Estimated Sales: $1-2.5 Million
Number Employees: 10-19
Square Footage: 26000

18040 **A&M Industries**
3610 North Cliff Avenue
Sioux Falls, SD 57104 605-332-4877
Fax: 605-338-6015 800-888-2615
amindustries@amindustries.com
www.amindustries.com
Manufacturer and exporter of rebuilt packaging, food processing and confectionery machinery, carton over-wrappers and specialty tooling
Owner: Richard Miller
Estimated Sales: Below $5 Million
Number Employees: 1-4
Square Footage: 20000
Type of Packaging: Consumer, Food Service, Private Label

18041 **A&M Process Equipment**
487 Westney Rd.
S., Unit #1
Ajax, ON L1S 6W7
Canada 905-619-8001
Fax: 905-619-8816 info@amprocess.com
www.amprocess.com
Food processing equipment including powder mixing and size reduction; exporter of ribbon, conical and twin shell blenders
President: John Lang
Number Employees: 4
Square Footage: 8000

18042 A&M Thermometer Corporation
17 Piney Park Road
Asheville, NC 28806-1727 828-251-9092
Fax: 828-254-5611 800-685-9211
www.laboratorynetwork.com/sotrefronts/aandm.html
Manufacturer and exporter of glass thermometers
President: M Pflaumbaum
R&D: Armin Pflaumbaum
Marketing: Kathy Toomey
Production: Armin Pflaumbaum
Purchasing Director: M Pflaumbaun
Estimated Sales: $2.5-5 Million
Number Employees: 10-19
Type of Packaging: Private Label, Bulk
Brands:
Accutest
Asico

18043 A&R Ceka North America
1400 Northbrook Pkwy # 350
Suwanee, GA 30024-7232 770-623-8235
Fax: 770-623-8236 www.ar-carton.com
President, Chief Executive Officer: Harald Schulz
Vice President: Gerard Vries
Senior Vice President of Sales and Marke: Jean-Francois Roche

18044 A-1 Booth Manufacturing
375 S 250 E
Burley, ID 83318-3718 208-678-2877
Fax: 208-678-4243 800-820-3285
sales@a1booth.com www.a1booth.com
Manufacturer and exporter of tables, chairs and seats
President: Robert Silcock
Estimated Sales: $1-2.5 Million
Number Employees: 5-9
Type of Packaging: Food Service
Brands:
Patriot Plus
Patriot Series

18045 A-1 Business Supplies
158 W Clinton St Ste N
Dover, NJ 07801 973-366-3690
800-631-3421
salesa-1@garden.net
Tags, price tags, day dots and labels including inventory control
Manager: Janet Larkin
VP: Janet Larkin
Sales Manager: Dick Burbaum
Estimated Sales: $1-2,500,000
Number Employees: 1-4

18046 A-1 Refrigeration Company
1720 E Monticello Ct
Ontario, CA 91761 909-930-9910
Fax: 909-930-9026 800-669-4423
www.a1flakeice.com
Ice machines.
Plant Manager: Tony Gallinucci
Number Employees: 10-19
Number of Products: 10
Brands:
A-1

18047 A-1 Tablecloth Company
450 Huyler St Ste 102
S Hackensack, NJ 07606 201-727-4364
Fax: 201-727-8988 800-727-8987
a1@a1tablecloth.com www.a1tablecloth.com
Manufacturer and exporter of tablecloths, napkins, table skirting, chair covers and drapes
Owner: Robert Fox
Estimated Sales: $10 - 50,000,000
Number Employees: 50-99

18048 A-B-C Packaging Machine Corporation
811 Live Oak St
Tarpon Springs, FL 34689-4137 727-937-5144
Fax: 727-938-1239 800-237-5975
sales@abcpackaging.com
www.abcpackaging.com
Manufacturer and exporter of packaging machinery
President: Donald G Reichert
Director Sales/Marketing: Bryan Sinicrope
Estimated Sales: $10-20 Million
Number Employees: 100-249
Square Footage: 100000

18049 A-L-L Magnetics
2831 E Via Martens
Anaheim, CA 92806-1751 714-632-1754
Fax: 714-632-1757 800-262-4638
sales@allmagnetics.com
www.magnets-ceramic.com
Manufacturer, exporter and importer of magnets used for holding, separating and water treatment
President: John Nellessen
CFO: John Nellessen
Sales: Rosemary Kute
Estimated Sales: Below $5 Million
Number Employees: 10-19
Square Footage: 80000
Brands:
Magnet Source, The

18050 A-One Manufacturing
549 Evergreen Rd
Strafford, MO 65757 417-736-2195
Fax: 417-736-2833 www.a-onemfg.com
Poultry, seafood and meat processing equipment.
President: David Cobb
Sales & Purchasing: Debra Denney

18051 A-One Manufacturing
549 Evergreen Rd
Strafford, MO 65757 417-736-2195
Fax: 417-736-2833
d.denney@a-onemanufacturing.com
www.a-onemfg.com
Conveyors and accessories, pressure washers, blenders, massagers and tumblers
Estimated Sales: $5-10 000,000
Number Employees: 35

18052 A-Z Factory Supply
10512 United Pkwy
Schiller Park, IL 60176 820-323-4511
Fax: 800-233-4512 800-323-4511
sales@azsupply.com www.azsupply.com
Manufacturer and exporter of material handling and storage equipment, shelving, carts, shelf trucks, boxes, bins, hoppers, corrugated steel containers, conveyors, lifts, hoists, etc
Manager: Henry Bolden
VP: R Hannesson
Sales Manager: B Spurling
Estimated Sales: Below $5,000,000
Number Employees: 1-4

18053 A. Epstein & Sons International
600 W Fulton St Fl 9
Chicago, IL 60661 312-454-9100
Fax: 312-559-1217 information@epstein-isi.com
www.epstein-isi.com
Executive VP: Allen L Pomerance
Estimated Sales: $20-50 Million
Number Employees: 250-499

18054 A. Klein & Company
P.O.Box 670
Claremont, NC 28610 828-459-9261
Fax: 828-459-9608
Custom made boxes for the confectionery industry
President: Jesse Salwen
Estimated Sales: $50-100 Million
Number Employees: 100-249

18055 A. Mindle & Associates
115 Post Street
Santa Cruz, CA 95060 831-425-6625
Fax: 831-425-6627 ÿinfo@amindle.com
www.amindle.com
Number Employees: 1-4

18056 A.A. Pesce Glass Company
216 Birch St
Kennett Square, PA 19348-3606 610-444-5065
Fax: 610-444-3358 mcarroll@pesceglass.com
www.pesceglass.com
Scientific and laboratory glassware
Manager: Mike Carroll
Estimated Sales: $1-2.5 Million
Number Employees: 5-9

18057 A.B. Sealer, Inc.
N 7212 Farwell Road
PO Box 635
Beaver Dam, WI 53916-0635 920-885-9299
Fax: 920-885-0288 877-885-9299
sales@absealer.com www.absealer.com
Manufacturer and exporter of packaging machinery including portable case erectors and sealers and custom equipment systems
Owner: Lou Stikowsky
CEO: Russell Quandt
Estimated Sales: $1-2.5 Million
Number Employees: 50-99
Brands:
Aantek
Series 9000

18058 A.C. Horn & Co
1269 Majesty Dr
Dallas, TX 75247 214-630-3311
Fax: 214-630-0130 800-657-6155
mritter@achornco.com www.achornco.com
Food processing, packaging, and material handling equipment.
President: Doug Horn
Vice President: Mark Ritter
Research/Development: Paul Lima
Quality Control: Paul Lima
Director Marketing/Sales: Mark Ritter
Public Relations: Michael Horn, Jr
Plant/Production Manager: Tommy Galloway
Purchasing: Elizabeth Durban
Estimated Sales: $10-20 Million
Number Employees: 67
Square Footage: 80000
Parent Co: A.C. Horn & Company
Brands:
Radiant Ray
Ray-O-Matic

18059 A.D. Cowdrey Company
1442 Angie Avenue
Modesto, CA 95351-4952 209-538-4677
Fax: 209-538-6087 cvpsdp@aol.com
www.adcowdrey.com
Canners' and packers' knives, aprons and corers
President: David Racher
VP: John Hassapakis
Estimated Sales: Below $5 Million
Number Employees: 20
Parent Co: Central Valley Professional Service

18060 A.D. Johnson Engraving Company
229 Woodward Ave
Kalamazoo, MI 49007-3221 269-342-5500
Fax: 269-342-5511 www.adjohnson.com
Engraving and embossing dies and stamps; also, engraving for premium goods and advertising novelties
President: Donovan J Kindle
Estimated Sales: $500,000-$1 Million
Number Employees: 1-4

18061 A.D. Joslin Manufacturing Company
33 Artic St
Manistee, MI 49660 231-723-2908
Fax: 231-723-2908 adjoslin@cosco2000.com
www.manistee.com/joslin
Manufacturer and exporter of handheld and electric seal embossing machinery, dating machinery, steel code marking stamps, ticket validators and handheld case numbering machines
General Manager: Norman Ware
Office Manager: Carol Westberg
Estimated Sales: $3 - 5 Million
Number Employees: 10-19
Parent Co: Cosco Industries

18062 A.G. Russell Knives Inc.
2900 S 26th St
Rogers, AR 72758 800-255-9034
Fax: 479-631-8493 800-255-9034
ag@agrussell.com www.agrussell.com
Manufacturer and exporter of household knives
Owner: A G Russell
CFO: Michael Donnovan
Director Sales/Marketing: Will Sennell
Estimated Sales: $20-50 Million
Number Employees: 100-249
Brands:
Camillus Classic Cartridge
Cartridge
Dura-Tool
Promaster
Silver Sword
Sword
Western

Woodcraft
Yello-Jacket

18063 (HQ)A.J. Antunes & Company
180 Kehoe Blvd
Carol Stream, IL 60188 630-784-1000
Fax: 630-784-1650 800-253-2991
scott.march@antunes.com www.ajantunes.com
Manufacturer and exporter of stainless steel food service equipment for restaurants and concession operations including tables and serving equipment in addition to filtration products that remove particulates, bacteria, and virusesfrom water.
President: Glenn Bullock
CFO: Bill Nelson
Executive VP: William Hickey
Director New Business Development: Scott March
VP Sales/Marketing: Tom Krisch
Estimated Sales: $50 - 100 Million
Number Employees: 250-499
Type of Packaging: Food Service
Brands:
Antunes Control
Roundup

18064 A.J. Funk & Company
1471 Timber Dr
Elgin, IL 6012 847-741-6760
Fax: 847-741-6767 877-225-3865
info@glasscleaner.com www.glasscleaner.com
Glass cleaner. Also supply product and service to distributors and end-users
President: Patrick Funk
Estimated Sales: $4 Million
Number Employees: 50-99
Square Footage: 24000
Type of Packaging: Consumer, Food Service
Brands:
Sparkle

18065 A.K. Robins
4100 Pistorio Road
Baltimore, MD 21229-5509 410-247-4000
Fax: 410-247-9165 800-486-9656
Manufacturer and exporter of cleaners, conveyors, cookers, cutters, exhausters, extractors, etc.; also, CAD engineering and design and USDA services available
Sales Manager: Steve Ward
Operations Manager: Ken Vogel
Number Employees: 50

18066 (HQ)A.L. Wilson Chemical Company
PO Box 207
Kearny, NJ 07032 201-997-3300
Fax: 201-997-5122 800-526-1188
help@alwilson.com www.alwilson.com
Manufacturer and exporter of laundry and dry cleaning stain removers
President: F G Schwarzmann
Estimated Sales: $10 - 20 Million
Number Employees: 10-19

18067 A.M. Loveman Lumber & Box Company
PO Box 40123
Nashville, TN 37204-0123 615-297-1397
Wooden boxes and pallets
President: Andrew M Loveman
Estimated Sales: $500,000-$1 Million
Number Employees: 8
Square Footage: 12000

18068 A.M. Manufacturing
14151 Irving Ave
Dolton, IL 60419 708-841-0959
Fax: 708-841-0975 800-342-6744
info@ammfg.com www.ammfg.com
Baking equipment
Owner: Claudia Kunis
Co-owner: Holly Rentner
Estimated Sales: $5 - 10 Million
Number Employees: 20-49
Square Footage: 28000

18069 A.O. Smith Water Products Company
600 E John Carpenter Fwy # 200
Irving, TX 75062-3985 972-792-4371
Fax: 972-719-5967 800-527-1953
techctr@hotwater.com www.hotwater.com
Manufacturer and exporter of tank-type water heaters and boilers and booster heaters
Chairman, Chief Executive Officer: Paul Jones
Vice President, Controller: Daniel Kempken
President, Chief Operating Officer: Ajita Rajendra
Project Manager: Will Harris
Number Employees: 50-99
Square Footage: 4000000
Parent Co: A.O. Smith Corporation
Brands:
Burkay
Cyclone Xhe
Dura-Max
Legend
Master Fit

18070 A.P.M.
1500 Hillcrest Rd
Norcross, GA 30093-2617 770-921-6300
Fax: 770-925-7801 800-226-5557
sales@apminc.org www.apminc.org
President: James R Sabourin
Estimated Sales: $3 - 5 Million
Number Employees: 10-19

18071 A.R. Arena Products
2101 Mount Read Boulevard
Rochester, NY 14615-3708 585-254-2180
Fax: 716-254-1046 800-836-2528
sales@arenaproducts.com
www.arenaproducts.com
President: Anthony R Arena
Estimated Sales: $1 - 5 Million
Number Employees: 20

18072 A.T. Ferrell Company
1440 S Adams St
Bluffton, IN 46714 260-824-3400
Fax: 260-824-5463 800-248-8318
info@atferrell.com www.atferrell.com
Manufacturer and exporter of grain and seed cleaners and separators, hammer and roller mills, grain and feed coolers and vibrator and air conveyors
President: Steve Stuller
CFO: Roger Stackhouse
Vice President: Phillip Petrakos
Research & Development: Dan Johnson
Sales Director: John Hay
Plant Manager: Howard Vaughn
Purchasing Manager: Brian Dynes
Estimated Sales: $5 - 10 Million
Number Employees: 20-49
Square Footage: 50000
Other Locations:
Clipper Separation Technologies
Bluffton IN
Ferrell-Ross Division
Amarillo TX
Brands:
Clipper
Ferrell-Ross
Mix-Mill

18073 A.T. Ferrell Company Inc
1440 S Adams St
Bluffton, IN 46714 260-622-7831
Fax: 260-824-5463 800-248-8318
www.atferrell.com
Manufacturer and exporter of automatic electric feed mills, augers, pneumatic feed conveyors and aluminum beverage can crushers
President: Steve Stuller
Estimated Sales: $1-2.5 Million
Number Employees: 5-9
Number of Brands: 2
Brands:
Modern Mill
Monarch Can Crushers

18074 A.T. Foote Woodworking Company
726 Windsor Street
Hartford, CT 06120 860-249-6821
Fax: 860-249-6192
Store fixtures
President: Arthur Foote, Sr.
VP: Arthur Foote, Jr.
Estimated Sales: $20-50 Million
Number Employees: 4

18075 AAA Awning Co. Inc
8810 Madie Drive
Houston, TX 77022-2617 713-694-3930
Fax: 713-694-0863 800-281-6193
main@awning.net www.aaaawning.net
Commercial awnings
Owner: Paul Yee
VP: Randy Deaton
Estimated Sales: $2.5-5 Million
Number Employees: 1-4

18076 AAA Electrical Signs
P.O.Box 3245
McAllen, TX 78502 956-546-2735
Fax: 956-464-2408 800-825-5376
signs@3asigns.com www.3asigns.com
Custom electrical signs, brass plaques, illuminated letters and time and temperature units; also, electronic message centers and color elcetronic signs, we sell and lease.
President: Paul Sullivan
General Manager: Steve Smith
Plant Manager: Ken Bailey
Estimated Sales: $4 Million
Number Employees: 20-49
Square Footage: 10000
Parent Co: Tesoro Corporation

18077 AAA Flag & Banner Manufacturing
8955 National Blvd
Los Angeles, CA 90034-3307 310-836-3341
Fax: 310-836-7253 800-266-4222
www.aaaflag.com
Flags, pennants, banners and signs
Controller: Carol Hettiger
CEO: Howard Furst
Estimated Sales: $20 - 50 Million
Number Employees: 500-999

18078 AAA Mill
812 Airport Blvd
Austin, TX 78702-4106 512-385-2215
Fax: 512-385-0860
Wood and plastic laminated freezer cabinets and store fixtures
President: David Bockhorn
General Manager: David Bockhorn
Estimated Sales: Below $5 Million
Number Employees: 5 to 9
Square Footage: 10000

18079 AAF International
P.O.Box 267
Four Oaks, NC 27524-0267 919-207-1376
Fax: 704-365-1975 800-600-5546
info@aafintl.com www.aafintl.com
Heating, cooling, ventilating, noise pollution control and air cleaning products and systems
Manager: Sam C Price
Sales/Marketing Director: Bob Sturges
APC Sales Manager: Chris O'Connor
Estimated Sales: Below 1 Million
Number Employees: 5-9

18080 AAMD
7342 Tomwood Dr
Liverpool, NY 13090-3747 315-451-0951
Fax: 315-451-8740 800-887-4167
eeoaamd@a-znet.com
Manufacturer, importer and exporter of packaging machinery including tamper evident sealing equipment, closure lining equipment, assembly machines, metal closure threaders, tamper evident cap slitting machines, etc.; also, consultingservices available
VP Sales/Marketing: Eugene Orr
Estimated Sales: $1 - 3 Million
Number Employees: 1-4
Square Footage: 26000

18081 AANTEC
3116 N Pointer Rd
Appleton, WI 54911 920-830-9723
Fax: 920-830-9840 info@aantec.com
www.tissueexcellencecenter.com

Packaging equipment; case packers, palletizers, tray packers/formers, case erectors/sealers, napkin folders, towel and tissue interfolders, tissue rewinders, napkin wrappers and bundlers, roll wrappers, conveyors, grip per elevatorsand lowerators, high-speed case-packers
President: Robert Schuh
VP: Corben Hoffman
Sales: Jeffrey Aissen
Public Relations: Julia Kirsch
Operations: Paul Tassoul
Estimated Sales: $5 - 10 Million
Number Employees: 10-19
Type of Packaging: Consumer, Food Service, Private Label, Bulk
Brands:
Involvo
Tmc

18082 AB McLauchlan Company
P.O.Box 12006
Salem, OR 97309-0006 503-363-8611
Fax: 503-364-5546 www.abmclauchlan.com
Blenders, food processing, conveying, size grading, cleaning, slicing, sorting, filling, and mixing equipment, mixers
President: John Layton
Estimated Sales: $1-2.5 Million
Number Employees: 5-9

18083 AB6
17190 Grant Road
Cypress, TX 77429 713-824-7275
Fax: 775-366-0516 john@ab6.net
www.ab6.net
President: John de Penne rouge

18084 ABB
P.O.Box 5308
Norwalk, CT 06856-5308 203-750-2200
Fax: 203-750-2263 www.abb.com
Manufacturer and exporter of presses and drives for high-pressure food processing equipment for pasteurization and sterilization, generators, control systems, drives, motors, instrumentation and metering
CEO: Enrique Santacana
Estimated Sales: K
Number Employees: 10,000

18085 ABB Autoclave Systems
3721 Corporate Dr
Columbus, OH 43231-4964 614-891-2732
Fax: 614-891-4568 www.flowae.com
Isostatic presses and thermocouples
Manager: Melanie Harter
Estimated Sales: $1 - 5 Million
Number Employees: 20-49

18086 ABB Bomem
300-585 Charest Boulevard E
Quebec, QC G1K 9H4
Canada 418-877-2944
Fax: 418-877-2834 800-858-3847
ftir@ca.abb.com www.abb.com
Analyzers for fats, proteins, solids, etc.; FTIR spectrometers
President: Doug Brown
Vice President: Don Murray
Marketing Director: Jim Kelly
Sales Director: Jean-Noel Berube
Public Relations: Barbara Bayer
Production Manager: Daniel Lafoutaine
Estimated Sales: $48 Million
Number Employees: 250
Square Footage: 63000
Brands:
Mb Series
Networkir

18087 ABB Flexible Automation
PO Box 372
Milwaukee, WI 53201-0372 262-785-3200
Fax: 262-784-9779 www.abb.com
Executive VP: Joe Carney
Estimated Sales: $45.4 Million
Number Employees: 250

18088 ABB Industrial Systems
P.O.Box 372
Milwaukee, WI 53201-0372 262-785-3200
Fax: 262-784-9779 www.abb.com
Estimated Sales: $50 - 100 Million
Number Employees: 250-499

18089 ABB Instrumentation
PO Box 20550
Rochester, NY 14602-0550 716-292-6050
stephen.a.frate@ustay.mail.abb.com
www.abbinstrumentation.com
Manufacturer, importer and exporter of process control equipment including circular charts, flow meters and controls, DP transmitters and stripchart recorders
President: Stephen Frate
Estimated Sales: $25-50 Million
Number Employees: 250-499
Square Footage: 231000
Brands:
Commander
Fulscope
Mag Master
Mass Meter
Mod 30 Ml

18090 ABB Labels
1010 E 18th St
Los Angeles, CA 90021-3008 213-748-7480
Fax: 213-748-5838 888-22 -5 22
sales@abblabels.com www.abblabels.com
Labels and tags specialized in quick turnaround at competitive prices
President: Pedram Fararooy
Owner: Albert Khoshbin
Sales: Pedram Fararooy
Estimated Sales: $10 - 20 Million
Number Employees: 20-49

18091 ABB SSAC
222 Disk Drive Rapid City
Baldwinsville, NY 13027 315-638-1300
Fax: 315-451-2126 888-385-1221
ssac.info@us.abb.com www.ssac.com
Manufacturer and exporter of standard and custom HVAC, defrost controls, timers, current sensors, and time delay relays
Research & Development: Rob Southworth
Quality Control: Doug Storey
Marketing Director: Gary Weeks
Sales Director: Eric Biss
Plant Manager: Geri Downey
Purchasing Manager: Rich Foretino
Number Employees: 100-249
Number of Brands: 1
Square Footage: 60000

18092 ABB Waterjet Systems
1250 Brown Rd
Auburn Hills, MI 48326-1507 248-391-9000
Fax: 248-393-4602 www.abb.com
Senior VP: Kirk Goins
Estimated Sales: $100+ Million
Number Employees: 1,000-4,999

18093 (HQ)ABC Laboratories
7200 E Abc Ln
Columbia, MO 65202 573-443-9000
Fax: 573-443-9033 800-538-5227
lorenze@abclabs.com www.abclabs.com
Laboratory offering analysis, testing and field research to the food service industry
President/CEO: John D Bucksath
R&D: Eric Lawerence
VP: Kristein King
Quality Control: Kevins Roberfon
Estimated Sales: $10 - 20 Million
Number Employees: 100-249
Square Footage: 100000

18094 ABC Letter Art
1623 S Vermont Ave
Los Angeles, CA 90006 323-733-0191
Fax: 323-733-6505 888-261-5367
mshear1@abcletterart.com www.abcletterart.com
Displays and signs including interior and exterior graphics, wood, metal, plastic and 3-D letters; also, installation services available
Owner: Mark Shear
CEO: Mark Shear
Sales Director: Jerry Eckert
Estimated Sales: $1-2.5 Million
Number Employees: 10-19
Brands:
A Sign of Good Taste

18095 ABC Research Corporation
3437 SW 24th Ave
Gainesville, FL 32607 352-372-0436
Fax: 352-378-6483 info@abcr.com
www.abcr.com
Certified, third-party, independent contract food laboratory specializing in microbiological and chemical analyses of commercial food products.
President: William Brown
CEO: George Baker
VP: James Kennedy
Marketing Director: Larry Clement
COO/Executive Director: Gillian Folkes
Estimated Sales: $5 Million
Number Employees: 70
Square Footage: 33000

18096 ABC Scales
240 Boone Ave
Marion, OH 43302-3356 740-382-0551
Fax: 740-387-4869
Estimated Sales: $1 - 3 Million
Number Employees: 1-4
Parent Co: Fairfield Engineering Company

18097 ABC Stamp Company
407 North Orchard
Boise, ID 83706 208-375-4470
Fax: 208-377-3509 abcstamp@abcstamp.com
www.abcstamp.com
Rubber stamps
President: Richard Paulson
Estimated Sales: Below $5 Million
Number Employees: 10-19
Square Footage: 12800

18098 ABCO Automation
6202 Technology Dr
Browns Summit, NC 27214 336-375-6400
Fax: 336-375-0090 contact@goabco.com
www.goabco.com
Serving industry since 1977. Our extensive experience, broad capibilities and strong technical aptitude make ABCO a most capable supplier of automated solutions
President: W Graham Ricks
Marketing: Terry Love
Sales: Paul Game
Purchasing: Tammy Murphy
Estimated Sales: $5-10 000,000
Number Employees: 50-99
Type of Packaging: Consumer

18099 ABCO Industries
2675 E Us Highway 80
Abilene, TX 79601 915-677-2011
Fax: 915-677-1420 800-530-4060
sales@abcoboilers.com
Estimated Sales: Below $500,000
Number Employees: 20-49

18100 ABCO Industries Limited
PO Box 1120
Lunenburg, NS B0J 2C0
Canada 902-634-8821
Fax: 902-634-8583 866-634-8821
graham@abco.ca www.abco.ca
Manufacturer and exporter of aluminum and stainless steel food processing equipment including steam blanchers evaporative coolers
President: John Meisner
CEO: J Eisenhauer
Marketing Director: Graham Gerhardt
Sales Director: Dan Croft
Number Employees: 50-99
Square Footage: 120000
Brands:
Abco

18101 ABCO Laboratories
2450 S Watney Way
Fairfield, CA 94533 707-432-2200
Fax: 707-432-2240 800-678-2226
sales@abcolabs.com www.abcolabs.com

Nutraceutical products-liquids, tablets, capsules, powder blends. Foods-spices, dry blends, seasonings, functional food blends.
President: David Baron
Founder: Allen Baron
R&D: Dr Muhammed Al-Nasassrah
Quality Control: Rich Hale
Marketing: Greg Northam
Sales: Victoria Gonzales
Operations: Richard Snowden
Plant Manager: Dick Snowden
Purchasing Director: Carl Falcone
Number Employees: 150
Number of Brands: 10
Number of Products: 5000
Square Footage: 800000
Type of Packaging: Consumer, Food Service, Private Label, Bulk
Brands:
Nutra Naturally Essentials

18102 ABCO Products
6800 NW 36th Ave
Miami, FL 33147 305-694-2226
Fax: 305-694-0451 888-694-2226
sales@abcoproducts.com
www.abcoproducts.com
Manufacturer and exporter of mops, brooms, brushes and dust control treatment systems
President: Carlos Albir Sr
VP of Sales: Jonathan Clark
VP Sales/Marketing: Ricky Stamburry
VP Sales/Marketing: Marcel Brisebois
Estimated Sales: Below $500,000
Number Employees: 20-49
Type of Packaging: Food Service
Brands:
Abco

18103 ABI Limited
8900 Keele Street, Unit 1
Concord, ON L4K 2N2
Canada 905-738-6070
Fax: 905-738-6085 800-297-8666
info@abiltd.com www.abiltd.com
ABI Ltd. manufacturers automated food processing equipment with the emphasis on performance, durability, reliability and simplicity in maintenance.
President: Alex Kuperman
Marketing: Regine Kuperman
Production VP: Mike Kuperman
Number Employees: 20
Square Footage: 60000
Brands:
Belt Saver 2000
Bpl 10000
Bpl 12000
Bpl 24000
Bpl 6000
Bpl 8600
Df 5000
Superformer

18104 ABIC International Consultant
24 Spielman Rd
Fairfield, NJ 07004 973-227-7060
Fax: 973-227-0172 abakal@abic-consulting.com
www.abic-consulting.com
Consultant providing product development, evaluation and improvement of current products and processing and implementation of cost efficiencies; also, expertise in food science, process engineering and sensory evaluation
President: Abraham Bakal
CEO: Penny Cash
Estimated Sales: $2.5 - 5 Million
Number Employees: 10-19
Square Footage: 16000

18105 ABJ/Sanitaire Corporation
9333 N 49th St
Milwaukee, WI 53223-1472 414-365-2200
Fax: 414-365-2210 abjinfo@sanitairie.itt.com
www.sanitaire.com
Manufacturer and exporter of anaerobic wastewater systems including sequencing batch reactors
President: Tom Pokovsky
CFO: Tom Thompson
Finance Executive: Scott Tysen
R&D: Joe Krall
Marketing: Laurie Besch
Manager Sales/Marketing: Roger Byrne
Public Relations: Laurie Besch
Customer Service Manager: Ken George
Production: Loras Lux
Purchasing: Loras Lux
Estimated Sales: $50 Million
Number Employees: 100-249
Square Footage: 7000
Brands:
Iceas

18106 ABM Marking Company
2799 S Belt W
Belleville, IL 62226 618-277-3773
Fax: 618-277-3782 800-626-9012
abmmarking@aol.com www.abmmarking.com
Manufacturer and exporter of ink jet printers and coding inks for porous and nonporous surfaces including coated, plastic and polyethylene; importer of tape dispensers and machines
President: Barbara Merchiori
Sales Manager: Alberto Merchiori
Operations: Roger Schaefer
Estimated Sales: $3 - 5 Million
Number Employees: 5-9
Square Footage: 12000
Brands:
Abm
Abm's Safemark

18107 ABO Industries
13620 Lindamere Ln
San Diego, CA 92128 858-566-9750
Fax: 858-566-9590 mingli@abopumps.com
www.abopumps.com
Manufacturer, exporter and importer of industrial progressive cavity, peristaltic, gear, metering and air operated diaphragm pumps
President: Joseph Schulman
VP: Ming Li
Estimated Sales: $1 - 5 Million
Number Employees: 5-9
Square Footage: 2500
Brands:
Carmine
Carminic Acid

18108 ABT
P.O.Box 837
259 Murdock Road
Troutman, NC 28166 704-528-9806
Fax: 704-528-5478 800-438-6057
sales@abtdrains.com www.abtdrains.com
Pre-engineered drainage systems
President: Ralph Brafford
National Sales Manager: Jim DelRe
Estimated Sales: $2.5-5 Million
Number Employees: 20-49
Other Locations:
ABT
Lexington KY
Brands:
Polydrain
Polyduct
Trench Former System

18109 AC Dispensing Equipment
100 Dispensing Way
Lower Sackville, NS B4C 4H2
Canada 902-865-9602
Fax: 902-865-9604 888-777-9990
sales@sureshotdispensing.com
www.sureshotdispensing.com
Electronic portion controlled dispensers for cream, sugar, milk and oil
President: Michel Duck
R&D: Ian Maclen
CFO: Ian Tramble
Director Sales/Marketing: W William Morris
Number Employees: 80
Brands:
Sureshot

18110 AC Label Company
2101 East VallyVistaWay
Provo, UT 84606 801-642-3500
Fax: 801-642-3510
americanfork_info@aclabel.com
www.aclabel.com
Bottling equipment and supplies, computer software, labeling and packaging machinery and packaging materials; also, printer, bar code, pressure sensitive and security labels
Manager: Matt Schwanbeck
VP: Jim DiBona
Estimated Sales: $10 - 20,000,000
Number Employees: 50-99
Parent Co: Impaxx

18111 AC Legg
6330 Highway 31
PO Box 709
Calera, AL 35040 205-324-3451
Fax: 205-668-7835 800-422-5344
sales@ACLegg.com www.aclegg.com
Founded in 1923. Processor of custom-blended seasonings for meat, poultry, seafood and snack foods.
President: James Purvis
CEO: James Purvis
VP: Sandra Purvis
Estimated Sales: $20-50 Million
Number Employees: 100-249
Square Footage: 130000
Type of Packaging: Food Service, Private Label, Bulk
Brands:
Legg's Old Plantation

18112 AC Technology Corporation
630 Douglas St
Uxbridge, MA 01569 508-278-9100
Fax: 508-278-7873 www.actechdrives.com
President: Allen Ottoson
Estimated Sales: $100+ Million
Number Employees: 100-249

18113 ACCO Systems
12755 E 9 Mile Rd
Warren, MI 48089 845-456-2236
Fax: 586-758-1901 800-342-2226
sales@accosystems.com www.accosystems.co.uk
Manufacturer and exporter of material handling systems and equipment
President: Anthony Gore
Director Sales/Marketing: Mark Murray
Number Employees: 250-499
Parent Co: Durr GmbH

18114 ACH Rice Specialties
7171 Goodlett Farms Pkwy
Cordova, TN 38016-4909 901-381-3000
Fax: 901-381-2968 800-691-1106
information@achfood.com
www.achfood.com/index2.htm
President: Dan Antonelli
CFO: Jeff Atkins
R&D and Quality Control: Pete Sriedman
Estimated Sales: $20 - 30 Million
Number Employees: 1,000-4,999

18115 ACI
3731b San Gabriel River Pkwy
Pico Rivera, CA 90660-1404 562-699-4999
Fax: 562-699-0919 acil@worldnet.att.net
Industrial ink jet printers

18116 ACLA
509 Thomson Park Dr
Cranberry Twp, PA 16066-6425 724-776-0099
Fax: 724-776-0477 aclausa@nauticom.net
www.acla.org
Manufacturer and exporter of material handling equipment including rollers, tires, wheels, bumpers and seals
President: Andy Mc Intyre
Estimated Sales: $1-2.5 Million
Number Employees: 5-9
Parent Co: ACLA

18117 ACMA/GD
501 Southlake Blvd
Richmond, VA 23236-3078 804-794-6688
Fax: 804-379-2199 800-525-2735
paul.smith@gidi.it www.acmavolpak.com

Manufacturer, importer and exporter of liquid filling machinery and vertical and horizontal form/fill/seal equipment
CEO: Guiseppe Venturi
Marketing: Glen Coater
Estimated Sales: Below $500,000
Number Employees: 250-499
Square Footage: 800000

18118 ACME Control Service
6140 W Higgins Ave
Chicago, IL 60630 773-774-9191
Fax: 773-774-3737 800-621-6427
info@acmecontrols.com www.acmecontrols.com
Reconditioner of boiler and burner controls
President: Robert Huening
Estimated Sales: $5-10,000,000
Number Employees: 20-49

18119 ACME-McClain & Son
4759 Durfee Avenue
Pico Rivera, CA 90660-2037 562-692-0026
Fax: 800-428-2263

18120 ACO
501 SW 19th St
Moore, OK 73160-5427 405-794-7662
Fax: 405-236-4014 www.mcdonalds.com
Manufacturer and exporter of material handling boxes, trays and racks
Founder: Ray Kroc
Estimated Sales: $1-2.5 Million
Number Employees: 10-19

18121 ACO Polymer Products
12080 Ravenna Road
Chardon, OH 44024-7008 440-285-7000
Fax: 440-285-7005
President: Derek Humphries
Number Employees: 50-99

18122 ACR Systems
#210-15110 54A Avenue
Surrey, BC V3S 5X7
Canada 604-591-1128
Fax: 604-591-2252 800-663-7845
sales@acrsystems.com www.acrsystems.com
Data loggers-measure and record temperature and humidity, current, power quality, pressure, process signals and more
President: Albert C Rock
CFO: David McDougall
Director of Operations: Wayne Thompson
Number Employees: 30
Type of Packaging: Private Label
Brands:
Acr Jr.
Acr Powerwatch
Owl
Smartvision
Smartreader
Smartreader Plus
Trendreader

18123 ACS Industries, Inc.
One New England Way
Lincoln, RI 02865 866-783-4838
Fax: 401-333-2294 acsind@acsind.com
www.acsindustries.com
Stainless steel sponges, nylon scouring pads, screens, filter cones and grill cleaning systems; also, nonsulphate antioxidants
President: Steven N Buckler
Estimated Sales: $5 - 10 Million
Number Employees: 1,000-4,999
Square Footage: 1200000
Brands:
Acs Industries, Inc. Scrubble

18124 ACUair/York Refrigeration
5757 N. Green Bay Ave
P.O. Box 591
Milwaukee, WI 53201 414-524-1200
Fax: 305-887-7853 414-524-1200
juan.a.perez@york.com
www.johnsoncontrols.com
Chairman, President and Chief Executive: Alex A. Molinaroli
EVP and Chief Financial Officer: R. Bruce McDonald
Human Resources: William Hyland
VP and Chief Marketing Officer: Kim Metcalf-Kupres
Estimated Sales: Below $500,000
Parent Co: Johnson Controls, Inc.

18125 AD Products
2919 Industrial Park Dr
Finksburg, MD 21048 800-743-8815
Fax: 410-833-8817 800-743-8815
sales@adprods.com www.adprods.com
Material handling equipment - dollies, racks, carts, baskets, trays (stock and custom)
Manager: Nick Hailston
CFO: Ami Markle
R & D: William Fauntleroy
Sales: Nick Hailstone
Estimated Sales: Below $5 000,000
Number Employees: 10-19

18126 (HQ)AD/Mart
135 Pulaski Rd
Calumet City, IL 60409-4227 708-891-0990
Fax: 708-891-2250
Flags, pennants, banners, labels and signs; also, design services available
Owner: Lee Kline
Office Manager: Dana Sheets
Estimated Sales: $500,000-$1 Million
Number Employees: 1-4
Square Footage: 5000

18127 ADCO
P.O.Box 999
Sedalia, MO 65302-0999 660-826-3300
Fax: 660-826-1361 sales@adco-inc.com
www.adco-inc.com
President: Charles M Van Dyne
Quality Control: Archie Shrieman
Estimated Sales: $10 - 20 Million
Number Employees: 50-99
Parent Co: AlliedSignal Company

18128 ADCO
1909 West Oakridge
Albany, GA 31707 660-826-3300
Fax: 660-826-1361 800-821-7556
sales@adco-inc.com www.adco-inc.com
Disinfectants, polishes and dry cleaning compounds
Chief Executive Officer: Mark Grimaldi
EVP/Business Operations: Yalda Harris
Quality/Compliance Manager: Scott Stanfill
Chief Products/Technology Officer: Jim Schreiner
National Sales Manager: Greg Reinhardt
Estimated Sales: $5-10 Million
Number Employees: 50-99

18129 ADCO Manufacturing
2170 Academy Ave
Sanger, CA 93657 559-875-5563
Fax: 559-875-7665 sales@adcomfg.com
www.adcomfg.com
Packaging machinery
President: Frank Hoffman
CFO: Kate King
CEO: Kate King
Estimated Sales: $20 - 50 Million
Number Employees: 100-249

18130 ADD Testing & Research
19 Addison Pl
Valley Stream, NY 11580 516-568-9197
Fax: 516-568-3147 info@addtestinglab.com
www.addtestinglab.com
Laboratory providing research, development, food testing, spice analysis, sanitation testing, etc
President: Michael Schenoude
Owner: Aida Shenouga
Estimated Sales: Below 1 Million
Number Employees: 1-4
Square Footage: 3000

18131 ADDCHEK Coils
1285 Jim Wilson Rd
Fort Mill, SC 29715-7605 803-547-7566
Fax: 803-547-5250
Heat transfer equipment using aluminum, copper, cupro nickel and stainless steel
President: Anna D Wood
Corporate Secretary: Helen Wood
Estimated Sales: $5-10 Million
Number Employees: 10-19

18132 ADE
1430 E 130th St
Chicago, IL 60633 773-646-3400
Fax: 773-646-3919 800-222-0221
info@ade-usa.com www.ade-usa.com
Protective packaging alternatives, package designs using elastomeric film
Manager: Lewis Lofgren
Estimated Sales: $5-10 000,000
Number Employees: 20-49

18133 ADEX Medical Inc
6101 Quail Valley Court
Riverside, CA 92507 951-653-9122
Fax: 951-653-9133 800-873-4776
info@adexmed.com www.adexmed.com
Manufacturer, wholesaler/distributor, importer and exporter of disposable apparel including gloves, goggles, aprons, hair nets, caps, masks, shoe covers, etc.; also, towels, industrial safety products, emergency preparednessproducts
President/CEO: Michael Ghafouri
Estimated Sales: $5 Million
Number Employees: 35
Number of Brands: 3
Number of Products: 200
Square Footage: 44000
Type of Packaging: Consumer, Food Service, Private Label
Brands:
Adex
Dispomed

18134 ADI Systems Inc
370 Wilsey Road
Fredericton, NB E3B 6E9
Canada 506-452-7307
Fax: 506-452-7308 800-561-2831
systems@adi.ca www.adisystemsinc.com
ADI offers proprietary anaerobic and aerobic industrial wastewater treatment and waste-to-energy technologies, biogas cleaning and utilization, plus complete design-build services. ADI also conducts treatability studies, pilot testingbench-scale studies, operator training, and aftercare services to customers who need to anaerobically or aerobically treat industrial wastewater.
President: Graham Brown
CEO: Hazen Hawker
VP Technology: Shannon Grant
Marketing Assistant: Connie Smith
Manager Business Development: Scott Christian
Marketing & Communications Manager: Sarah Brown
Estimated Sales: $10-20 Million
Number Employees: 25
Square Footage: 4000
Parent Co: ADI Group
Other Locations:
Wolfeboro NH
Brands:
Adi-Anmbr
Adi-Bvf Digester
Adi-Hybrid
Adi-Mbr
Adi-Sbr

18135 ADM Corporation
100 Lincoln Blvd
Middlesex, NJ 08846-1090 732-469-0900
Fax: 732-469-0785 800-327-0718
www.packing-list.com
Manufacturer and exporter of pressure sensitive envelopes, stretch wrap and bags including poly and zip-lock
VP Finance: Mike Turner
Vice President of Sales and Marketing: Ed Yarber
Estimated Sales: $20-50 Million
Number Employees: 100-249
Parent Co: Archer Daniels Midland Company

18136 ADM Packaged Oils
4666 Faries Parkway
Decatur, IL 62526-5666 217-424-5200
Fax: 217-451-2689 800-637-5843
info@admworld.com www.admworld.com
Packaged oils
President: Todd Saathoff
R&D: Tom Tiffany
Quality Control: Kelly Singelton
Estimated Sales: Below $5 Million
Number Employees: 25
Parent Co: Archer Daniels Midland Company
Type of Packaging: Consumer, Food Service, Bulk
Brands:
Gold' N Flavor
Golden Chef
Superb
Superb Select
Tastee Pop

18137 ADM Refined Oils
4666 Faries Parkway
Decatur, IL 62525-1820 217-424-5200
Fax: 217-424-5467 800-637-5843
info@admworld.com www.admworld.com
Food grade oils for the food industry. Grains used and oil types include corn, soy, peanut, canola, sunflower, cottonseed, palm and coconut
CEO: Paul Mulhollem
Vice President, Treasurer: Douglas Ostermann
Technical Service Manager: Frank Friend
Parent Co: Archer Daniels Midland Company
Type of Packaging: Bulk

18138 ADM Western Star Mill
P.O.Box 1400
Salina, KS 67402-1400 785-825-1541
Fax: 785-825-9209 www.admworld.com
Wheat flour milling
Vice President, Treasurer: Douglas Ostermann
Marketing: Richard Nelson
Estimated Sales: $50-100 Million
Number Employees: 50-99
Parent Co: Archer Daniels Midland Company

18139 ADMIX
234 Abby Rd
Manchester, NH 03103-3332 603-627-2340
Fax: 603-627-2019 800-466-2369
mixing@admix.com www.admix.com
Sanitary mixing and dispersion, and particle size reduction equipment
General Manager: L Beaudette
President: Louis Beaudette
Sales Manager: P Leitner
Operations Manager: P Foskitt
Estimated Sales: Below $5 Million
Number Employees: 20-49
Square Footage: 60000
Brands:
Admixer
Boston Shearpump
Dynashear
Oprishear
Optifeed
Rotomixx
Rotosolver
Rotostat
Vacushear

18140 ADSI, Inc.
P.O.Box 667
Durant, OK 74702-0667 580-924-4461
Fax: 580-924-7375 adsi@adsiinc.com
www.adsiinc.com
Manufacturer & exporter of commercial egg breaking machinery, egg washing & sanitizing machines.
President, Sales, & Operations: Mike Maynard
VP, Sales, Production & Plant Mgr.: Steve Maynard
Estimated Sales: Below $5 Million
Type of Packaging: Food Service
Brands:
Centri-Matic Iii
Egg Valet
Sew 400
Sew 800

18141 ADT Security Systems
8750 Hague Rd
Indianapolis, IN 46256 317-848-1181
Fax: 317-816-2435 www.adt.com
Manufacturer and exporter of electronic security and fire alarm systems
President: Mike Snyder
Operations Manager: Doug Gabbard
Estimated Sales: $50-100 Million
Number Employees: 150

18142 ADT Security Systems
1710 Dividend Rd
Fort Wayne, IN 46808-1131 260-483-6370
Fax: 260-483-1896 www.adt.com
Security alarms and systems; also, installation services available
Manager: John Piroli
Area Manager: Rick Lyon
Estimated Sales: $10-20 Million
Number Employees: 20-49
Parent Co: ADT Security Systems

18143 (HQ)ADT Security Systems
P.O.Box 5035
Boca Raton, FL 33431-0835 561-988-3600
Fax: 561-988-3601 www.tyco.com
Wholesaler/distributor of general merchandise including burglar and fire alarm systems, access control systems, security equipment and closed circuit TV
President: John B Koch
CFO: Mike Lopez
VP Communication Sales/Marketing: Jamie Rosand
General Manager: Furney Griffin
Estimated Sales: $157 Million
Number Employees: 10,000
Parent Co: Tyco/Fire & Security

18144 AE Staley Manufacturing Company
2200 E Eldorado St
Decatur, IL 62521-1578 217-423-4411
Fax: 217-421-2881 800-526-5728
mamyers@tlna.com www.tateandlyle.com
President: Matt Wineinger
CFO: Don Schnake
Corporate Secretary: J P Mohan
Estimated Sales: Over $1 Billion
Number Employees: 1,000-4,999

18145 AEI Corporation
2641 DuBridge Avenue
Irvine, CA 92620-1900 949-474-3070
Fax: 949-474-0559
sales@patiocomfortheaters.com
www.patiocomfortheaters.com
Outdoor and infrared patio heaters and outdoor heating equipment
Owner: Yukali Aoi
CFO: Fred Speicher
Estimated Sales: $5-10 Million
Number Employees: 1-4
Brands:
Ducane
Infratech
Pgs
Profire
Sunglo
Sunpak

18146 AEP Industries
125 Phillips Ave
South Hackensack, NJ 07606 201-641-6600
Fax: 201-807-2567 800-999-2374
info@aepinc.com www.aepinc.com
Plastic sheeting, stretch films and liners and polyethylene products including bags, packaging and film
Manager: Don Drafford
Logistics Manager: Stacy LeMaster
Executive VP Sales/Marketing: Robert Cron
Estimated Sales: $75 Million - 1 Billion
Number Employees: 2900

18147 AERTEC
P.O.Box 488
North Andover, MA 01845-0488 978-475-6385
Fax: 978-475-6387 info@aertec.com
www.aertec.com
Waste and water aeration
President: R Gary Gilbert
Estimated Sales: $1 - 5 Million
Number Employees: 5-9

18148 AES Corporation
3412 Center Point Road NE
Suite A
Cedar Rapids, IA 52402 319-395-7751
Fax: 319-395-7693 info@aescorp.com
www.aescorp.com
Design and installation of aseptic processing and packaging systems specialize in fruit and vegetables; dairy; pharmaceuticals
Manager: David Garrelts
Estimated Sales: $1 - 5 Million
Number Employees: 10-19

18149 AET Films
15 Reads Way
New Castle, DE 19720-1648 302-326-5500
Fax: 302-326-5501 800-688-2044
info@aetinc.com www.aetfilms.com
ODP film for flexible packaging and labeling
President: David Terhuna
CFO: Bryan Crescenzo
CEO: Thomas Mohr
Estimated Sales: $20 - 50 Million
Number Employees: 500-999

18150 AEW Thurne
1148 Ensell Road
Lake Zurich, IL 60047-1539 847-726-8000
Fax: 847-726-1600 800-239-7297
chicago@aewdelford.com www.aewdelford.com
Manufacturer and exporter of high-speed bandsaws and automated portion control slicing systems
President: Chris Mason
Chief Operating Officer, Chief Executive: Sigsteinn Gretarsson
Regional Sales Manager: David Bertelsen
Estimated Sales: $300,000-500,000
Number Employees: 9
Square Footage: 32000
Brands:
Aew

18151 AFA Systems
8 Tilbury Court.
Brampton
Ontario, CA L6T 3T4 905-456-8700
Fax: 905-456-2343 info@afasystemsinc.com
www.afasystemsinc.com
Liquid fillers, software
Estimated Sales: $.5 - 1 million
Number Employees: 1-4

18152 AFASSCO
2244 Park Pl
Suite C
Minden, NV 89423 800-441-6774
Fax: 800-232-7726 afassco@intercomm.com
www.afassco.com
CEO: Don Schumaker

18153 AFCO
5121 Coffey Ave
Chambersburg, PA 17201-8384 610-647-3300
Fax: 610-644-8240 800-345-1329
sourcethree@afco.net www.afcocare.com
Cleaning and sanitizing soaps and chemicals
President: Michael Hinkle
Estimated Sales: Below $5 Million
Number Employees: 45

18154 AFCO Manufacturing
7007 Valley Lane
Cincinnati, OH 45244-3031 859-261-3585
Fax: 859-261-3590 800-747-7332
afco@one.net www.afcomanufacturing.com
Baking equipment including bakery pan racks, pan trucks, dough troughs, custom dollies and flow racks
President: Frank Eberle
CEO: Peter Sullivan
Sales Manager: Brion Walter
Estimated Sales: Below $5 Million
Number Employees: 25
Square Footage: 100000

18155 AFECO
2400 Highway 18 E
Algona, IA 50511-7204 888-295-1116
Fax: 515-295-9568 888-295-1116
sales@afeco.com www.afeco.com
Vat and barrel dumpers, belt and screw conveyors, curing and blending systems, pallet lifts, platforms, tables, tanks, and smokehouse racks
President: Jeffrey Christensen
Director Sales/Marketing: Mike Rooney
Manager Production/Engineering: Jeffery Philips
Number Employees: 50-99
Square Footage: 200000

18156 AFGO Mechanical Services, Inc.
36-14 32nd Street
Long Island City, NY 11106 718-478-5555
Fax: 718-476-2222 800-438-2346
info@afgo.com www.afgo.com
Heaters, heat exchangers and stainless steel tanks; also, repair services available
President/COO: Blaine Udell
CEO: Glenn S. Udell
Vice President: Gregory Oro
Director of Operations: Michael McGuire
Estimated Sales: $5 - 10 Million
Number Employees: 20-49
Square Footage: 280000
Parent Co: Heat Transfer

18157 **AFL Industries**
1751 W 10th St
West Palm Beach, FL 33404-6431 561-844-5200
Fax: 561-844-5246 800-807-2709
Sales@aflindustries.com www.aflindustries.com
Manufacturer and exporter of oil and water separators for wastewater treatment systems
CEO: Tom Bieneman
CEO: Thomas Bieneman
Sales Manager: Ray Lopez
Administrative VP: Beverly Willcox
Estimated Sales: $1 - 2.5 Million
Number Employees: 10-19
Square Footage: 40000

18158 **AFT Advanced Fiber Technologies**
72 Queen Street
Sherbrooke, QC J1M 2C3
Canada 819-562-4754
Fax: 819-562-6064 800-668-7273
info@aikawagroup.com www.aft-global.com
Manufacturer, importer and exporter of custom made screen and extraction plates
President: Roch Leblanc
CFO: Norman Pogdin
R&D: Robert Gooding
Quality Control: Serge Turcotte
Sales Manager: Jean Marc Brousseau
Number Employees: 175
Square Footage: 436560
Parent Co: CAE
Brands:
Cae Profile
Cae Select
Durachrome

18159 **AG Beverage**
7031 Cahill Rd
Minneapolis, MN 55439 952-943-8148
Markets beverages for the food and beverage industy
Estimated Sales: $2.5-5 000,000
Number Employees: 9

18160 **AGA Gas**
P.O.Box 94737
Cleveland, OH 44101-4737 216-642-6600
Fax: 216-642-6625 mike.klaasse@us.aga.com
www.airgas.com
Cryogenic gas packaging and freezing equipment; also, industrial gases including oxygen, nitrogen, argon and carbon dioxide for the food industry
President: Bob Bradshaw
Applications Engineer: Keith Davis
Vice President of HR: Ann Rice
Sales Manager: Jay Loo
Vice President of Operations: Don Goldschmidt
Estimated Sales: $1 - 5 Million
Number Employees: 100-249
Parent Co: AGA Gas AB

18161 **AGC Engineering**
10129 Piper Lane
Bristow, VA 20136-1418 703-257-1660
Fax: 703-330-7940 800-825-8820
info@agcengineering.com
www.agcheattransfer.com
Manufacturer and exporter sanitary plate heat exchangers and replacement parts
President: Wade Chamblerlan P.E.
Director, Resaerch & Development: George Tholl
Director, Sales & Marketing: John C. Bohn
Office Manager - Western Factory: Jill Davis
Estimated Sales: $3-$5 Million
Number Employees: 20-49
Square Footage: 160000
Type of Packaging: Bulk

18162 **AGC Engineering Portland**
9109 SE 64th Avenue
Portland, OR 97206-9505 503-774-7342
Fax: 503-774-2550 800-715-8820
wadec@agcengineering.com
www.agcengineering.com
Manufacturers of heat exchangers
President: Robert Bohn
Plant Manager: Patrick Palmer
Estimated Sales: $2.5-5 Million
Number Employees: 20-49

18163 **AGM Container Controls**
3526 E. Ft. Lowell Rd
Tucson, AZ 85716 520-881-2130
Fax: 520-881-4983 800-995-5590
sales@agmcontainer.com
www.agmcontainer.com
Container breather valves, tie-down straps and shelving and portable wheelchair lifts
President: Howard Stewart
Estimated Sales: $5-10 Million
Number Employees: 50-99

18164 **AGR International**
615 Whitestown Road
Butler, PA 16001 724-482-2163
Fax: 724-482-2767 agrsales@agrintl.com
www.agrintl.com
Quality Assurance & Process Control Systems for the Packaging Industry
CEO: Henry Dimmick Jr
Marketing: David Dineff
Operations: Robert Cowden
Estimated Sales: $20 - 50 Million
Number Employees: 180
Square Footage: 100000

18165 **AGRA Simons**
800 Marquette Ave # 1200
Minneapolis, MN 55402-5716 612-332-8326
Fax: 612-332-2423 info@vertmarkets.com
www.amec.com
Communications Manager: Harold Ashurst
Chief Operating Officer: Neil Bruce
Estimated Sales: $1 - 5 Million

18166 **AGRANA, Fruit US, Inc**
6850 Southpointe Pkwy
Brecksville, OH 44141 440-546-1199
Fax: 440-546-0038 800-477-3788
lori-rajewski@agrana.com www.agrana.com
Quality leader in refining agricultural raw materials into sugar, starch and processed fruits. Their passion is for quality and efficiency makes AGRANA the natural choice of food companies and for technical applications worldwide.
President/CEO: Johann Marihart
Board Member: Fritz Gattermeyer
Estimated Sales: $10-20 Million
Number Employees: 50
Parent Co: SIAS MPA
Type of Packaging: Food Service, Private Label, Bulk

18167 **AGV Products**
8012 Tower Point Dr
Charlotte, NC 28227 704-845-1110
Fax: 704-845-1111 saleslit@agvp.com
www.agvp.com
President: Mats Herrstromer
CEO: Terry Dunn
CFO: Bob Consoli
Quality Control: Janet Hill
Estimated Sales: $10 - 20 Million
Number Employees: 50-99

18168 **AHP Machine & Tool Company**
1765 W Fair Ave
Lancaster, OH 43130-2325 740-681-6709
Fax: 740-681-6527 sheila.heath@crowncork.com
www.ahpmachineandtool.com
Capping/sealing equipment since 1913. Formerly known as Anchor Hocking Packaging. Member of Crown Cork and Seal family of corporations. Precision CNC machining capabilities. Machine building and rebuilding
Operations Manager: Sheila Heath
Plant Manager: Ed Schott
Purchasing Manager: Greg Henwood
Estimated Sales: Below $5 Million
Number Employees: 20-49
Square Footage: 192000
Parent Co: Crown Cork & Seal

18169 **AIB International, Inc.**
1213 Bakers Way
P.O. Box 3999
Manhattan, KS 66505-3999 785-537-4750
Fax: 785-537-1493 800-633-5137
info@aibonline.org www.aibonline.org
Food safety education guides and classes for the packaging, distribution and food service operations industries
President: Virgil Smail
Estimated Sales: $10 - 20 Million
Number Employees: 100-249

18170 **AIBMR Life Sciences**
4117 S. Meridian
Puyallup, WA 98373 253-286-2888
Fax: 253-286-2451 aibmrinfo@aibmr.com
www.aibmr.com
Consulting firm specializing in nutraceutical research and product development.
Director of Operations: Laura Schauss

18171 **AIDCO International**
P.O.Box 15339
Cincinnati, OH 45215-339
Fax: 517-265-2131 contactus@aidcoint.com
www.aidcoint.com
Palletizers, depalletizers
Estimated Sales: $5-10 000,000
Number Employees: 10-19

18172 **AIM**
One Landmark North
20399 Route 19, Suite 203
Cranberry Township, PA 16066 724-742-4473
Fax: 724-742-4476 info@aim-na.org
www.aimusa.org
President: Dan Mullen
COO: Mary Bosco
Number Employees: 6

18173 **AIS Container Handling**
7000 Dutton Ind Pk Dr SE
Dutton, MI 49316 616-554-1000
Fax: 616-554-1008 800-253-4621
sales@aisontainerhandling.com
www.aiscontainerhandling.com
Manufacturer and exporter of bagging and debagging equipment, conveyor, insepction and analysis systems for plastic containers
President: Jerry Pollard
Sales Manager: Jim McDonald
Production Manager: Gary Shaw
Purchasing Manager: Mark Luebs
Estimated Sales: $5-10 000,000
Number Employees: 20-49
Square Footage: 25000

18174 **AJM Packaging Corporation**
E-4111 Andover Road
Bloomfield Hills, MI 48302 248-901-0040
Fax: 248-901-0061 sales@ajmpack.com
www.ajmpack.com
Paper plates, cups, bowls and bags
President: Robert Epstein
Manager: Robert Kelm
Chief Financial Officer/Controller: Terry Jackson
Marketing Manager: Bill Baumann
National Sales Manager: Ken Sherry
Plant Manager: Michael Leach
Estimated Sales: $111 Million
Number Employees: 1,000
Square Footage: 12000
Brands:
Designer's Choice
Green Label
Original Heavyweight
Penthouse

18175 **AK Robbins**
4030 Benson Avenue
Baltimore, MD 21227-1408 410-247-4000
Fax: 410-247-9165 800-486-9656
www.akrobins.com
Meat slicers, cooling tank elevators, tramp metal eliminators, length and diameter grading equipment, cutting equipment, vibratory and belt conveyors, pack-off tables, hydrators, jar washers, chemical peelers, laminar-flo liquidfiller, washers, cleaners
Estimated Sales: $2.5-5 Million
Number Employees: 19

18176 **AK Steel**
9227 Centre Pointe Drive
West Chester, OH 45069 513-425-4200
800-331-5050
www.aksteel.com
President: James L. Wainscott
Estimated Sales: $6,000,000,000
Number Employees: 6,100

18177 **(HQ)AK Steel**
9227 Center Pointe Drive
West Chester, OH 45069 513-425-5000
Fax: 513-425-5866 800-331-5050
lee.price@aksteel.com www.aksteel.com
Stainless steel ranges, hoods, ovens, stoves, microwaves, refrigerators, beverage dispensers and coffee makers
Manager: Vijay Madi
CEO and President: Jim Wainscott
Head of R&D: Doug Tyger
Director Quality Assurance: Glynn Mikaloff
Manager: Lee Price
Number Employees: 100-249
Other Locations:
AK Steel
Rockport IN

18178 **AL Systems**
385 Franklin Ave
Suite C
Rockaway, NJ 07866 973-586-8500
Fax: 973-586-8865 888-960-8324
info@alsysinc.com www.alsysinc.com
Manufacturer and exporter of automated control systems and software
President: Paul Lightfoot
Director Operations: Gary Oriani
Director of Product Management: Gary Clemens
Estimated Sales: $1 - 5 Million
Number Employees: 20-49

18179 **(HQ)ALCO Designs**
407 E Redondo Beach Blvd
Gardena, CA 90248-2312 310-353-2300
Fax: 310-353-2301 800-228-2346
vege@earthlink.net www.alcodesigns.com
Manufacturer and exporter of water treatment systems including outdoor fogging and standard and reverse osmosis misting, fogging and humidification
President: Samuel Cohen
Owner: Sam Cohen
CFO: Sam Cohen
VP: Issac Cohen
Marketing: Dick Wardlaw
Administrator: Liz Luna
Estimated Sales: $3 - 5 Million
Number Employees: 20-49
Square Footage: 2500
Other Locations:
Vege Mist
Tucker GA

18180 **ALCO Designs**
407 E Redondo Beach Blvd
Gardena, CA 90248 310-353-2300
Fax: 310-353-2301 800-228-2346
vege@earthlink.net www.alcodesigns.com
Vacuum-molded risers, step-ups, trays and extenders for produce, meat and deli/dairy cases and dry tables; also, wooden display items available
President: Sam Cohen
Quality Control: Carlos Sanchez
Director Marketing: Bob Matsie
Estimated Sales: Below $5 Million
Number Employees: 20-49
Parent Co: Vege Mist

18181 **ALKAR**
P.O.Box 260
Lodi, WI 53555-0260 608-592-3211
Fax: 608-592-4039 marketing@alkar.com
www.alkar.com
Manufacturer and exporter of chillers including air blast, brine and glycol; also, smokehouses and continuous cook/chill systems.
President: David Smith
Estimated Sales: $50-100 Million
Number Employees: 100-249
Square Footage: 80000

18182 **ALL-CON World Systems**
P.O.Box 647
Seaford, DE 19973 302-628-3380
Fax: 302-628-3390 sales@all-con.com
www.all-con.com
Feeding, weighing and conveying of dry powder ingredients for food and baking industries
President: G Barry Slater
Sales Director: Mark Allen
Estimated Sales: Below $5 Million
Number Employees: 10

18183 **ALLCAMS Machine Company**
116 Sycamore Ave
Folsom, PA 19033 610-534-9004
Fax: 610-534-7517 sales@allcams.net
www.allcams.net
Manufactures and designs CAMs for automated industrial machinery
Number Employees: 10

18184 **ALM Corporation**
200 Benchmark Industrial Dr
Streator, IL 61364-9400 815-673-5546
Fax: 815-673-2292 800-544-5438
sales@almcorp.com www.alm-autolift.com
US manufacturer of bulkbag discharge and fill lifts, welding and assembly positioner. ALM specializes in custom heavy duty lifting equipment.
President: Douglas F Grunnet
Sales Director: Patricia Galick
Estimated Sales: $10 - 20 Million
Number Employees: 20-49
Square Footage: 55000
Brands:
Ibc

18185 **ALP Lighting & Ceiling Products**
6965 Airport Highway Ln
Pennsauken, NJ 08109 856-663-0095
Fax: 856-661-0870 800-633-7732
www.alplighting.com
Manufacturer, importer and exporter of lighting fixtures including louvers, lens, fluorescent fixture diffusers and components
VP: Steven Dix
Estimated Sales: $1 - 5,000,000
Number Employees: 100-249
Square Footage: 120000

18186 **(HQ)ALPI Food Preparation Equipment**
511 Piercey Road
Bolton, ON L7E 5B8
Canada 905-951-1067
Fax: 905-951-1608 800-928-2574
www.alpiinc.com
Manufacturer, exporter and importer of stainless steel convection/steam ovens, pasta cookers, pizza equipment, exhaust hoods, etc; consultant specializing in restaurant equipment design services
President: Pier Luigi Odorico
VP: Gian Paolo O'Dorico
National Sales Manager: Nazareno Cavallaro
Number Employees: 2
Square Footage: 28000
Type of Packaging: Food Service
Other Locations:
ALPI Food Preparation Equipme
Fort Lauderdale FL

18187 **ALY Group of New York**
70 Memorial Plaza
Pleasantville, NY 10570-2931 914-747-0052
Fax: 914-747-4193 alygroup@bestweb.net
Consultant and designer of restaurant interiors; also, space planning available.
President: Dolores Jones
CEO: A Eric Arctandfer
Estimated Sales: Less than $500,000
Number Employees: 5

18188 **AM Graphics**
1099 Snelling Avenue N St. Paul
Minneapolis, MN 55108 612-341-2020
Fax: 612-333-3295
amgraphics@amgraphicsinc.com
www.amgraphicsinc.com
Pressure sensitive labels and promotional items including banners, decals and shirts
President: Craig Nygaard
Estimated Sales: Less than $500,000
Number Employees: 1-4

18189 **AM Test Laboratories**
13600 NE 126th PL
Suite C
Kirkland, WA 98034-8720 425-885-1664
Fax: 425-820-0245
customerservice@amtestlab.com
www.amtestlab.com
Laboratory providing environmental testing, microbial and chemical food analysis and industrial hygiene services
President and Project Manager: Kathleen Fugiel
QA/QC Manager: Heidi Limmer
Vice President/Lab Manager: Aaron Young
Food Lab Director: Jim Pratt
General Manager: Mark Fugiel
Estimated Sales: Below $5 Million
Number Employees: 10-19
Square Footage: 80000

18190 **AMAC Plastic Products Corporation**
P.O.Box 750249
Petaluma, CA 94975-0249 707-763-3700
Fax: 707-763-9500 800-852-7158
info@amacplastics.com
www.amacpackaging.com
Rigid plastic containers for fine packaging; production and shopping of AMAC boxes to retail and manufacturing outlets worldwide
President: Jone Catechi
Estimated Sales: $2.5-5 Million
Number Employees: 10-19

18191 **AMC Chemicals**
93 Main St
Woodbridge, NJ 07095-2863 732-636-8720
Fax: 732-636-8727 robert@amcchem.com
www.amcchemical.com
Essential oils, aroma chemicals
Owner: Jerry Bozio
Estimated Sales: $1 - 5 Million
Number Employees: 1-4

18192 **AMC Industries**
1120 N 28th St
P.O.Box 5006
Tampa, FL 33675-5006 813-989-9663
Fax: 813-989-8609 sales@amcind.com
www.restaurantbooths.com
Restaurant furniture including bars, tables and booths; custom manufacturing available
President: Don Walstad
CEO: Gene Cornish
Accounting Controller: Richard Lee
Sales Director: John Ogden
Estimated Sales: $10 - 20 Million
Number Employees: 50-99

18193 **AMCO Corporation**
461 S 7th Ave
City of Industry, CA 91746-3119 626-855-2550
Fax: 626-855-2551 info@amcocorporation.com
www.amcocorporation.com
Manufacturer and exporter of racks, utensils, carts, dollies, trucks, mobile storage equipment, shelving, etc
Owner: Fank Ko
Sales Director: Dennis Dominic
Estimated Sales: $20-50 Million
Number Employees: 100-249
Square Footage: 240000
Parent Co: Leggett & Platt Storage Products Group
Brands:
Amco
Amcoat
Amcoll
Amtrax
Challenger
Magic Wall
Mod-A-Flex
Plasteel
Plastic Plus
Polygard
Shelving By the Inch
Take 10
Ultra Density

18194 **AMCO Products Company**
PO Box 145
Fort Smith, AR 72902 479-646-8949
Fax: 479-648-1032 www.amcoprod.com
Bottling machinery
President: Wendell Martin
Estimated Sales: $20-50 Million
Number Employees: 20-49
Square Footage: 65000

18195 **AME Engineering**
209 Gateway Rd
Bensenville, IL 60106 630-694-1828
Fax: 630-694-1827 www.ame-engineering.com

Packaging systems for meat
General Manager: Mosha Epstein
Estimated Sales: $.5 - 1 000,000
Number Employees: 1-4

18196 AMETEK Drexelbrook
205 Keith Valley Rd
Horsham, PA 19044 215-674-1234
Fax: 215-674-2731 800-553-9092
drexelbrook.info@ametek.com
www.drexelbrook.com
Test and calibration instruments
General Manager: Jim Visnic
VP: Dave Hernance
Estimated Sales: E
Number Employees: 100-249

18197 AMETEK U.S. Gauge
205 Keith Valley Rd
Horsham, PA 19044 215-293-4100
Fax: 215-323-9450 usg.sales@ametek.com
www.usgauge.com
Test and calibration instruments
Manager: Joe Karpov
Number Employees: 100-249

18198 AMF Bakery Systems
2115 W Laburnum Ave
Richmond, VA 23227 804-355-7961
Fax: 804-342-9755 800-225-3771
service-us@amfbakery.com
www.amfbakery.com
Manufacturer and exporter of bakery and packaging equipment
President: Ken Newsome
CFO: Margaret Shaia
Director Product Marketing: Larry Gore
Sales Director: Richard MacArthur
Number Employees: 100-249
Square Footage: 200000
Parent Co: Bakery Holding
Type of Packaging: Consumer, Food Service, Private Label, Bulk
Other Locations:
AMF Bakery Systems
Sherbrooke, Quebec

18199 AMF CANADA
1025 Cabana Street
Sherbrooke, QC J1K 2M4
Canada 819-563-3111
Fax: 819-821-2832 800-255-3869
mbissonnette@amfcanada.com
www.amfbakery.com
Manufacturer and exporter of mixers, ovens, troughs, trough elevators, fermentation rooms, dividers, rounders, moulders, panners, final proofers, slicers and baggers for the baking industry
CFO: Manon Bissonnette
Vice President Sales & Marketing: Jason Ward
Research & Development: Alain Lemieux
Director of Sales & Marketing: Larry Gore
Public Relations: Marie-Eve Raqieot
Operations Manager: Claude La Jeunesse
Production Manager: Danny Morin
Purchasing Manager: Jean-Pierre Rosa
Number Employees: 180
Square Footage: 500000
Brands:
Etm
Etmw
Supermix
Supertilt
Versatilt

18200 AMFEC
21040 Forbes Street
Hayward, CA 94545 510-783-0255
Fax: 510-783-0409 www.amfec.com
Food processing equipment.
Equipment Sales: Adam Quick

18201 AMI
PO Box 70520
Richmond, CA 94807-0520 510-234-5050
Fax: 510-234-5055 800-942-7466
sales@amiincorporated.com
www.amiincorporated.com
Manufacturer and exporter of food service serving carts, portable bars, mirror display products, cooking carts, maitre d' desks, etc
President: Kent Brown
CEO: Josh Yarrington
Sales: Lois Kitiuk
Plant Manager: Dang Nuygen
Number Employees: 10-19
Square Footage: 32000
Brands:
Ami

18202 AMI Bearings
570 N Wheeling Rd
Mt Prospect, IL 60056-1280 847-759-0620
Fax: 847-759-0630 www.amibearings.com
President: Steve Zimmerman
Estimated Sales: $5-10 Million
Number Employees: 20-49

18203 AMI/RECPRO
4250 Northeast Expy
Atlanta, GA 30340-3304 770-458-9189
Fax: 770-454-7350 800-241-1833
jefgri@ami-recpro.com www.ami-recpro.com

18204 AMISTCO Separation Products
23147 Highway 6 Alvin
Friendswood, TX 77512 281-331-5956
Fax: 281-585-1780 800-839-6374
amistco@amistco.com www.amistco.com
Owner: Mia Romar
Estimated Sales: $1 - 5 Million
Number Employees: 50-99
Square Footage: 210

18205 AMPAC Holdings, LLC
12025 Tricon Rd
Cincinnati, OH 45246-1719 513-671-1777
Fax: 513-671-2920 800-543-7030
inquiry@ampaconline.com
www.ampaconline.com
Manufacturer and exporter of polythylene and paper bags, and specialty films. Custom plastic and paper shopping bags, polymailers and specialty films. (Blown film with six monolayer lines, two 3-layer lines and on 7-layer line)
President: John Baumann
CFO: Jon Oill
Estimated Sales: $121.7 Million
Number Employees: 1100
Square Footage: 815000
Type of Packaging: Consumer, Food Service, Private Label

18206 AMRI
2045 Silber Road
Houston, TX 77055 713-682-0000
Fax: 713-682-0080 info@amrivalves.com
www.amrivalves.com
President: William Leech
Estimated Sales: $5 - 10 Million
Number Employees: 20-49

18207 AMS Filling Systems
2500 Chestnut Tree Rd
Glenmoore, PA 19343 610-942-4200
Fax: 610-942-7123 800-647-5390
sales@amsfilling.com www.amsfilling.com
Auger filling equipment for powder, granules, liquids and pastes
President/CEO: Andy Baker
Sales: Mark Pezone
Estimated Sales: $3,000,000
Number Employees: 20-49
Square Footage: 140000
Brands:
Ams

18208 AMS Industries
1051 Clinton St
Buffalo, NY 14206-2823 716-855-3155
Fax: 905-479-9752 sales@amsindustries.com
www.amsindustries.com
Owner: Martin Malthouse
CFO: Ken Pice
Estimated Sales: Below $5 Million
Number Employees: 5-9

18209 AMSECO
228 E. Star of India Lane
236
Carson, CA 90746-1418 310-538-4670
Fax: 310-538-9932 800-421-1096
info@amseco-kai.com www.amseco-kai.com
Manufacturer and exporter of burglar and fire alarms, closed circuit televisions, annunciator systems and security equipment
President: Yukata Odawara
VP Sales: Tom Galvez
Advertising Manager: Sergio Galvez
Estimated Sales: $10-20 Million
Number Employees: 10-19
Parent Co: AMSECO
Brands:
Audeocam
Crimeshield
E2 D2
Pal
Select-A-Horn/Strobe
Select-A-Strobe
Shadow
Supershield

18210 AMTAB Manufacturing Company
652 N Highland Ave
Aurora, IL 60506 630-301-7600
Fax: 630-896-7945 800-878-2257
info@amtab.com www.amtab.com
Manufacturer and exporter of folding banquet tables
Owner: Greg Hanusiak
CEO: Chris Cornier
VP: Greg Hanusiak
Estimated Sales: $5-10 Million
Number Employees: 20-49
Square Footage: 35000
Type of Packaging: Food Service, Private Label

18211 ANDEX Corporation
69 Deep Rock Rd
Rochester, NY 14624-3575 585-328-3790
Fax: 585-328-3792
Manufacturer and exporter of paper coffee filters
President: Andrew Cherre
Estimated Sales: $1-2 Million
Number Employees: 20-49
Square Footage: 20000
Type of Packaging: Food Service, Private Label, Bulk
Brands:
Coffee's Choice
Gourmay
Tru Brew

18212 ANKOM Technology
2052 O'Neil Rd
Macedon, NY 14502 315-986-8090
Fax: 315-986-8091 info@ankom.com
www.ankom.com
Analytical instruments for analyzing foods, determinine solubility of dietary fiber contents, and increasing employee outputs.
President: Andrew Komarek
Production Coordinator, RF Systems: Dave Lauber
VP Research & Development: Ronald Komarek
Quality Control Testing: Kurt Ouwenga
VP Marketing & Sales: Christopher Kelley
Technical Sales Manager: Nick Tedesche
Director, Strategic Marketing: Greg Coutant
VP Manufacturing Operations: Shawn Ritchie
Sr Design Engineer: Rick Giannetti
Estimated Sales: $3.3 Million
Number Employees: 24
Square Footage: 100000

18213 (HQ)ANVER Corporation
36 Parmenter Rd
Hudson, MA 01749 978-568-0221
Fax: 978-568-1570 800-654-3500
sales@anver.com www.anver.com
Manufacturer and exporter of FDA approved vacuum lifting equipment and parts including components, pumps and cups
President: Frank Vernooy
Estimated Sales: $10 - 20 Million
Number Employees: 50-99
Square Footage: 60000
Brands:
Anver
Vacu-Lift
Veribor

18214 AOAC International
481 N Frederick Ave
Suite 500
Gaithersburg, MD 20877-2417 301-924-7077
Fax: 301-924-7089 800-379-2622
aoac@aoac.org www.aoac.org
CFO: Joyce Schumacher
Executive Director: James Bradford
Estimated Sales: $1 - 5 Million
Number Employees: 20-49

18215 AOKI Laboratory America
1240 Landmeier Rd
Elk Grove Vlg, IL 60007 847-981-6000
Fax: 847-981-6105 888-638-2323
info@aokiusa.com www.aokitech.co.jp
Injection stretch-blow molding machines with direct heat conditioning systems and designs and produces tooling for machines that produce plastic containers. Provides service, parts, training and sales support for customers in the USAand in Canada
President: Sumio Fujisawa
VP: Sumio Fujisawa
Sales: Hiroshi Chino
Estimated Sales: $200-500 Million
Number Employees: 5-9
Parent Co: Aoki Technical Laboratory

18216 APA
14536 Monroe Circle
Omaha, NE 68137-3962 402-905-2696
Fax: 402-390-2005
kathryn.a.hanson@ue.corp.com
Consultant specializing in conceptual and final design, scheduling and cost estimating, specification development, contract awards and construction oversight for food industry
CEO: Eddie Barvan
CFO: Ken Everett
VP: Bud Dose
VP: Ivan Vrtiska
Marketing Director: Kathryn Hanson
Estimated Sales: $10 Million
Number Employees: 50-99
Square Footage: 15000
Other Locations:
APA
Dublin CA

18217 APA
7011 S 19th St
Tacoma, WA 98466-5333 253-565-6600
Fax: 253-565-7265 help@apawood.com
www.apawood.org
President: David L Rogoway
Director: Dennis Hardman
Estimated Sales: F
Number Employees: 100-249

18218 APEC
1201 4th Ave
Lake Odessa, MI 48849 616-374-1000
Fax: 616-374-1010 sales@apecusa.com
www.apecusa.com
Process equipment including liquid scales, weighing and discharging systems, powder applicators, batch mixers, etc
President: Kendall Wilcox
Sales Director: Terry Stemler
Operations Manager: Garrett Billmire
Estimated Sales: $4,500,000
Number Employees: 20-49

18219 APEX
P.O.Box 120
Neodesha, KS 66757-0120 620-325-2666
Fax: 620-325-2602 800-633-9576
solutions@airosol.com www.airosol.com
Aerosol propelled drain opener
President: Carl G Stratemeier
Sales Coordinator: Linda Cushman
Estimated Sales: $20 - 50 Million
Number Employees: 20-49
Parent Co: Airosol Company
Brands:
Power Plumber

18220 APG Cash Drawer
5250 Industrial Blvd NE
Fridley, MN 55421 763-571-5000
Fax: 763-571-5771 apginfo@apgcd.com
www.apgcd.com
Heavy duty and standard duty cash draw for point of sales systems.
President: Mark Olson
Research & Development: Bob Daugs
Quality Control: Jan Leathers
Marketing Director: Bob Daugs
Sales Director: John Meilahn
Operations/Production: Dale Dahlberg
Plant Manager: Wally Szulga
Purchasing Manager: Sheila Weber
Estimated Sales: $22 Million
Number Employees: 100-249
Number of Brands: 12
Number of Products: 12
Square Footage: 60000
Parent Co: Upper Midwest Industries
Type of Packaging: Private Label
Brands:
Caddy
Series100
Series4000
Series6000c
Vasario

18221 API
6206 Benjamin Road
Suite 309
Tampa, FL 33634-5169 813-888-8488
Fax: 813-888-8113 api.tampa@worldnet.att.net
Manufacturer and exporter of aseptic packaging equipment and components, over and shrink wrappers and case packers, stackers and unstackers
President: Jean-Louis Limousin
VP Sales: Keith Wennik
Number Employees: 100
Brands:
Api
Durajet
Duratech
Mastertech
Multitech
Versajet
Versatech

18222 API Foils
3841 Greenway Cir
Lawrence, KS 66046 785-842-7674
Fax: 785-842-9748 800-255-4605
marketing@api-foils.com www.api-foils.com
Coding and marking foils
Estimated Sales: $50 Million
Number Employees: 50-99

18223 API Heat Transfer
2777 Walden Ave
Buffalo, NY 14225-4788 716-684-6700
Fax: 716-684-2155 877-274-4328
sales@apiheattransfer.com
www.apiheattransfer.com
Manufacturer and exporter of thermal processing equipment and systems including plate heat exchangers, pasteurizers, evaporators, sterilizers and de-alcoholization systems
President: Joseph Cordosi
CFO: Jeff Lennox
Quality Control: Barry Kent
R&D: David Sijas
Marketing Director: Gary Trumpfheller
General Manager: David Parrott
Estimated Sales: $50 - 100 Million
Number Employees: 250-499
Brands:
Advance Aroma System
Sigma Plates
Sigmastar
Sigmatec
Sigmatherm

18224 API Industries
6590 E 40th St
Tulsa, OK 74145 918-664-4010
Fax: 918-664-8741 info@apiindustriesinc.org
www.apiindustriesinc.org
Waste water pre-treatment systems
President: David Plumb
VP: John Roberds
Estimated Sales: $1-2.5 Million
Number Employees: 10-19
Square Footage: 5000
Brands:
Ech20
Point

18225 API Industries
560 Sylvan Avenue
Englewood Cliffs, NJ 07632-3119 201-569-1700
Fax: 201-569-8907 800-229-7659
Estimated Sales: $300,000-500,000
Number Employees: 1-4

18226 APM
7661 NW 68th Street
Miami, FL 33166-2850 305-888-0161
Estimated Sales: $1 - 3 Million
Number Employees: 10

18227 APM
441 Industrial Way
Benicia, CA 94510-1119 707-399-8706
Fax: 707-745-0371 800-487-7555
info@apmglobal.com www.apmglobal.com
Packaging supplies, plastic lids, closures, metal and plastic capsules, wine corks, and imported and domestic specialty glass
Estimated Sales: $20-50 Million
Number Employees: 50-100

18228 APM/NNZ Industrial Packaging
805 Marathon Pkwy # 170
Lawrenceville, GA 30045-2890 770-921-9210
Fax: 770-682-7340 lance@apminc.org
www.nnzusa.com
President: Marco Boot

18229 APN
921 Industry Rd
Caledonia, MN 55921-1838 507-725-3392
Fax: 507-725-2073
Batch control systems, filtration equipment, piping, fittings and tubing
President: Karl Paasch
Vice President: Neil Goetzinger
Estimated Sales: $2.5-5 000,000
Number Employees: 20-49

18230 APS Packaging Systems
1275 Bloomfield Ave Ste 7
Fairfield, NJ 07004 973-575-1040
Fax: 973-575-6540 800-526-2276
sales@apspackaging.net www.apspackaging.net
Manual and automatic shrink wrap machinery
VP Sales: Eric Verbeke
Estimated Sales: $2.5-5 Million
Number Employees: 10-19
Square Footage: 20000

18231 APS Plastic Systems
3 Bowerwalls Place
Crossmill Business Park, Gl G78 1BF141-880-6688
Fax: 517-423-5647 info@apssafetysystems.com
www.apssafetysystems.com
President: Joe Carr
VP: Rick Roberts
Estimated Sales: $1-2.5 Million
Number Employees: 19

18232 APTEC-NRC Inc
800 Research Pkwy
Meriden, CT 06450-7127 215-343-5900
Fax: 215-343-3087 800-656-1114
tomalley@aptec-nrcinc.com www.aptec-nrc.com
Temperature recorders and monitors

18233 APV
395 Fillmore Ave
Tonawanda, NY 14150-2495 716-695-1697
Fax: 716-692-1715 800-828-7391
answers@invensys.com www.apvamericas.com
Evaporators, dryers, membrane systems, distillation
Estimated Sales: $20-50 Million
Number Employees: 50-99

18234 APV Americas
611 Sugar Creek Road
Delavan, WI 53115 847-678-4300
Fax: 800-252-5012 800-252-5200
apvproducts.us@apv.com www.apv.com
Manufacturer and exporter of automation, process systems, heat exchangers, dryers, evaporizers, membrane filtration systems, tanks, mixers, blenders, evaporators, etc.; spray drying available
Marketing Director: Richard Johnston
Project Sales Manager: Enrique Hinojosa
Estimated Sales: $1 - 5 Million
Number Employees: 50-100
Square Footage: 1800000
Parent Co: Invensys

18235 APV Baker
3223 Kraft Ave SE
Grand Rapids, MI 49512-2027 616-784-3111
Fax: 616-784-0973 800-458-2560
eriknadig@invensys.com www.apvbaker.com

Manufacturer, importer and exporter of food processing equipment including bakers and confectioners, mixing, forming, baking and product handling equipment
VP: John Lucas
R&D: Mark Glover
Marketing: Erik Nagig
VP Sales: Paul Abbott
Manager Process Optimization: Dan Smith
Number Employees: 50-99
Square Footage: 240000
Parent Co: APV plc

18236 **APV Baker**
1200 W Ash St
Goldsboro, NC 27530 919-736-4309
Fax: 919-735-5275 infous@apvbaker.com
www.apvbaker.com
Manufacturer and exporter of baking equipment: conveyors, ovens and mixers
VP Sales Bakery Machinery: Ricahrd Kirkland
Estimated Sales: $50-100 Million
Number Employees: 2800
Brands:
Powerpro

18237 **APV Engineered Systems**
105 CrossPoint Pkwy
Getzville, NY 14068 800-462-6893
Fax: 716-692-6416 800-369-2782
apvservicena@apv.com www.apv.com
Agglomerators, custom fabrication, dryers, fluid bed, spray filtration equipment, processing and packaging
Project Sales Manager: Enrique Hinojosa
Estimated Sales: $1 - 5 Million

18238 **APV Fluid Handling**
100 S Cp Ave
Lake Mills, WI 53551-1726 920-648-8311
Fax: 920-648-1441 800-369-2782
www.apv.com
Sanitary and industrial rotary and centrifugal pumps, pumping assemblies, sanitary valves, stainless steel or rubber rotor pumps, W+ Series high efficiency centrifugal pumps, mixproof double seat or single seat, butterfly, diaphragmand control valves
Executive Director: Jim Keene
General Manager: Frank Wheelwright
Project Sales Manager: Enrique Hinojosa
Estimated Sales: $50-100 Million
Number Employees: 100-249

18239 **APV Heat Transfer**
P.O.Box 1718
Goldsboro, NC 27533-1718 919-735-4570
Fax: 919-735-5275 800-369-2787
infous@apvbaker.com www.apvbakery.com
Aseptic heat processing equipment
CEO: John Lucas
Estimated Sales: $10-25 Million
Number Employees: 250-499

18240 **APV Mixing & Blending**
100 S Cp Ave
Lake Mills, WI 53551-1726 920-648-8311
Fax: 920-648-1441 800-369-2782
ekiessli@apv.com www.apv.invensys.com
Mixing and blending equipment
Executive Director: Jim Keene
Marketing Communications Manager: Antonella Crimi
Estimated Sales: $20 - 50 Million
Number Employees: 100-249

18241 **APV Systems**
9525w Bryn Mawr Avenue
Rosemont, IL 60018-5205 847-678-4300
Fax: 847-678-4313 888-278-9087
answers@apv.com www.apv.com
Process to boardroom automation and systems for food, dairy, beverage, brewery
Project Sales Manager: Enrique Hinojosa
Estimated Sales: $1 - 5 Million
Number Employees: 500

18242 **APV Tanks & Fabricated Products**
100 S Cp Ave
Lake Mills, WI 53551-1726 920-648-8311
Fax: 920-648-1441 888-278-4321
ekiessling@apvlakemills.com
www.apv.invensys.com
Auger feed units, food blenders, dual ribbon blenders, pumping assemblies for viscous products and the multiverter that chops, mixes, heats and cools, in one tank
Executive Director: Jim Keene
Marketing Communications Manager: Antonella Crimi
Estimated Sales: $20 - 50 Million
Number Employees: 100-249

18243 **(HQ)APW Wyott Food Service Equipment Company**
1938 Wyott Dr
Cheyenne, WY 82007-2102 307-634-5801
Fax: 307-637-8071 800-527-2100
www.apwwyott.com
Manufacturer and exporter of hardware, stainless steel kitchen pans, bun toasters, hot plates, food wells, broiling grills, dish dispensers and commercial food warming equipment
President: Lawrence Rosenbloom
Director National Accounts: Bruce Deckard
VP: Jim Humphrey
VP Marketing: Jeff King
Estimated Sales: $20-50 Million
Number Employees: 100-249
Type of Packaging: Food Service
Other Locations:
APW/WYOTT Food Service Equipment
New Rochelle NY
Brands:
Lowerraters

18244 **AR Arena Products**
2101 Mount Read Boulevard
Rochester, NY 14615
800-836-2528
sales@arenaproducts.com
www.arenaproducts.com
Reusable, collapsible plastic containers for shipping liquid and cheese
President: Anthony Arena
Sales Director: Mike Brunhuber
Plant Manager: Jeff Reeves
Estimated Sales: $5-10 Million
Number Employees: 20
Brands:
Arena 330 Shipper
Arena Shipper
Atlas 640 Shipper

18245 **AR-BEE Transparent**
1450 Pratt Blvd
Elk Grove Vlg, IL 60007-5713 847-593-0400
Fax: 847-593-0291 800-642-2247
www.arbee.com
A supplier of Plastic Bags
President: Robert Harris
Estimated Sales: $20-50 Million
Number Employees: 100-249
Square Footage: 25000

18246 **ARAMARK Uniform Services**
P.O.Box 7891
Burbank, CA 91510-7891 818-973-3700
Fax: 818-973-3545 800-272-6275
www.aramark-uniform.com
Manufacturer and wholesaler/distributor of uniforms; serving the food service market
President: Brad Drummond
CFO: David Solomon
VP Marketing: Judith Weiss
Estimated Sales: $50-100 Million
Number Employees: 10,000
Parent Co: Aramark Services

18247 **ARBO Engineering**
3 White Horse Road
Unit 5
Toronto, ON M3J 3G8
Canada 416-636-7057
Fax: 416-630-9135 800-689-2726
sgicza@arbo-feeders.com
www.arbo-feeders.com
Manufacturer of feeding and closing equipment
President: Shlomo Gicza
Product Manager: David Gicza
Sales Manager: David Gicza
Estimated Sales: Below $5 Million
Number Employees: 10

18248 **ARC Specialties**
29120 Commerce Center Dr
Valencia, CA 91355-5404 661-775-8500
Fax: 661-775-1499 info@lpstorage.com
www.arc-specialties.com
Tables, racks, mobile storage equipment, cabinets, dollies, hand trucks, carts, chafers, chafing dishes and shelving
President: Jay Lateko
President, Chief Executive Officer: Steven DarnelL
Vice President of Business Development: Dave Mack
VP Sales: Bill Gage
Vice President of Operations: Bob Buehler
Estimated Sales: $10 - 20 Million
Number Employees: 20-49
Square Footage: 40000
Parent Co: Leggett & Platt

18249 **ARCHON Industries**
357 Spook Rock Road
Suffern, NY 10901 845-368-3600
Fax: 845-368-3040 800-554-1394
sales@archonind.com www.archonind.com
Manufacturer, importer and exporter of washdown stations, sanitary fittings and ball, butterfly, gage and sanitary valves
CEO: Mario Faustini
Sales Manager: Linda Kyriakos
Engineering Manager: Konrad Mayer
Estimated Sales: $5 - 10 Million
Number Employees: 25

18250 **ARDE Barinco**
875 Washington Ave
Carlstadt, NJ 07072 201-970-7297
Fax: 201-784-0483 800-909-6070
ABmix@Ardeinc.com www.arde-barinco.com
Mixing equipment for beverage, sauces, preserves
Manager: Roy Scott
Estimated Sales: $2.5 - 5 000,000
Number Employees: 20-49
Square Footage: 20000

18251 **ARI Industries**
381 S Ari Ct
Addison, IL 60101 630-953-9100
Fax: 630-953-0590 800-237-6725
sales@ariindustries.com www.ariindustries.com
Manufacturer and exporter of temperature sensors and electric heaters
President: Dan Malcolm
VP Sales/Marketing: Dan Malcolm
Public Relations: Darlene Sosnowski
Operations: John Mulvey
Estimated Sales: $5-10 Million
Number Employees: 20-49
Square Footage: 56000

18252 **ARMAC Industries**
400 Kidds Hill Rd
Hyannis, MA 02601-1850 508-771-9400
Fax: 508-790-0002 sales@sencorp-inc.com
www.sencorp-inc.com
Thermoforming
CEO: Brian Urban
Estimated Sales: $20 - 50 Million
Number Employees: 100-249

18253 **ARPAC**
9511 River St
Schiller Park, IL 60176 630-406-8359
Fax: 847-671-7006 info@arpac.com
www.arpac.com
Shrink wrappers, case packers and tray loaders
President: Michael Levy
Estimated Sales: $25-50 Million
Number Employees: 250

18254 **ARPAC Group**
9511 River St
Schiller Park, IL 60176 847-678-9034
Fax: 847-678-2109 info@arpac.com
www.arpac.com
Shrink wrap and pallett stretch wrappers
President: Michael Levy
Sales Manager: Greg Levy
Number Employees: 230
Square Footage: 180
Type of Packaging: Consumer, Food Service, Private Label, Bulk

18255 **(HQ)ARPAC LP**
9511 W. River Street
Schiller Park, IL 60176-1019 847-678-9034
Fax: 847-671-7006 info@arpac.com
www.arpac.com
One stop shop packaging solutions. Manufacture shrink bundles, multipackers, horizontal shrin wrappers, corrugated tray and case erectors, box formers, corrugated board try and case packers, pallet stretch wrappers and pallet stretchhooders.
President: Michael Levy
Marketing Manager: Greg Levy
VP Sales: Gary Ehmka
Estimated Sales: $10 - 50 Million
Number Employees: 100-250
Square Footage: 260000
Brands:
Brandpac
Tray Star

18256 **ARRO Corporation**
7440 Santa Fe Dr
Hodgkins, IL 60525 708-352-8200
Fax: 708-352-5293 877-929-2776
Sales@arro.com www.arro.com
Corn, peanut, salad, soybean and vegetable oils; warehouse providing dry storage for food and food related products. Rail siding available
Owner: Pat Gaughn
Estimated Sales: $500,000-1 Million
Number Employees: 1-4
Type of Packaging: Food Service, Private Label, Bulk
Other Locations:
Chicago IL
Hodgkins IL

18257 **ARY**
10301 Hickman Mills Dr Ste 200
Kansas City, MO 64137 816-761-2900
Fax: 816-761-0055 800-821-7849
davephilgreen@aryvacmaster.com
www.aryvacmaster.com
Commercial manufacturer of Professional Cutlery and Vacuum Packaging Equipment for the Food Processing and Food Service Industries
Administrator: David Philgreen
Marketing: Tracey Edwards
Sales: Gary Ralstin
General Manager: David Philgreen
Estimated Sales: $3 - 5 000,000
Number Employees: 5-9

18258 **ASAP Automation**
503 Westgate Drive
Suite C
Addison, IL 60101 630-628-5830
Fax: 630-628-5831 800-409-0383
info@asapauto.com www.asap-automation.com
Software and control systems
President: Damir Kantardzic
Board of Director: Bill Bastian II
Marketing Manager: Lynsey Thomann
Sales Manager: Eric Cameron
Operations Manager: Hal Frary
Estimated Sales: $5 - 10 Million
Number Employees: 250-499
Number of Products: 14
Type of Packaging: Private Label, Bulk

18259 **ASC Industries**
2100 International Parkway
North Canton, OH 44720-1373 330-899-0340
Fax: 330-899-0350 800-253-6009
info@asc-ind.com www.asc-ind.com
President: Ted Swaldo

18260 **ASCENT Technics Corporation**
PO Box 981
Brick, NJ 08723-0981 732-279-0144
Fax: 732-255-3152 800-774-7077
cgreenh1@optonline.net
www.ascentofnewjersey.com
Manufacturer and exporter of pressure sensitive label applicators including automatic, semi-automatic and handheld, also; labels and packaging systems
President: Ched Greenhill
Estimated Sales: Below $5 Million
Number Employees: 15
Number of Products: 6
Square Footage: 20000
Brands:
Air-Ply
Atc
Sharpshooter
Smart 300

18261 **ASEPCO**
355 Pioneer Way
Mountain View, CA 94041 650-691-9500
Fax: 650-691-9600 800-882-3886
www.asepco.com
President/CEO: Steve Joy
Executive Vice-President: Mark Embury
Quality Control Manager: Glenn Slusher
Purchasing: Ben Herbert
Estimated Sales: $3 - 5 Million
Number Employees: 10-19

18262 **(HQ)ASGCO Manufacturing**
PO Box 1999
Allentown, PA 18105-1999 610-821-0210
Fax: 610-778-8991 800-344-4000
panthony@asgco.com www.asgco.com
Conveyor and bulk material handling systems and components including impact beds, belt cleaner, conveyor components; also, lightweight belt for food applications
President: Todd Gibbs
CFO: George Anthony
Vice President: Aaron Gibbs
Research & Development: George Mott
Marketing: Peggy Anthony
Inside Sales Manager: Steve Strella
Plant Manager: Steve Schubert
Estimated Sales: $10-20 Million
Square Footage: 100000
Other Locations:
ASGCO Manufacturing
Newburgh NY

18263 **ASI Datamyto**
2800 Campus Dr Ste 60
Minneapolis, MN 55441 763-553-1040
Fax: 763-553-1041 800-455-4359
info@asidatamyte.com www.asidatamyte.com
Manufacturer and exporter of packaging and quality control software
CEO: Frank Voight
CFO: Larry Kachina
CEO: Frank Voigt
R&D: Cecil Nelson
Quality Control: Douglas Stohr
Marketing: Terry Gilbert
Sales: Mark Roos
Customer Manager: Mike McCalley
VP Operations: Ted Bergstrom
Number Employees: 5-9
Brands:
Applied Stats
M-Ware

18264 **ASI Electronics**
PO Box 578
Cypress, TX 77410-0578 281-373-3835
Fax: 281-256-1406 800-231-6066
www.asielectronics.com
Manufacturer, exporter and importer of process controllers including level, weight and gate
President: Bill Jackson
Vice President: Alice Jackson
Sales: Bill Jackson
Estimated Sales: $150,000
Number Employees: 2
Square Footage: 500
Type of Packaging: Food Service, Bulk
Brands:
Kasi-Weigh

18265 **ASI Food Safety Consultants**
7625 Page Ave
Saint Louis, MO 63133 314-725-2555
Fax: 314-727-2563 800-477-0778
asi@asifood.com www.asifood.com
Consultant specializing in food safety audits and training including manual and high pressure cleaning and sanitizing and foodborne illness prevention and pest control; also, HACCP literature, videos and training materials available
President: Tom Huge
CEO: Gary Huge
Quality Control: Michael Bushaw
Sales: Jeanette Huge
Number Employees: 65
Square Footage: 30000
Parent Co: Huge Company
Other Locations:
ASI Food Safety Consultants
Lakeland FL

18266 **(HQ)ASI International**
10 Shawnee Drive
Suite B5
Watchung, NJ 07069-5803 908-753-4448
Fax: 908-753-1917 sales@info-asi.net
www.info-asi.net
Importer and distributor of bulk raw material ingredients to the nutritional, food, beverage and cosmetic industries.
President/Owner: Roland Lornig
VP: Joseph Campis
Operations: John Wyckoff
Type of Packaging: Bulk
Other Locations:
Padre Warehouse - California
Anaheim CA
Arco Warehouse - New Jersey
Passaic NJ

18267 **ASI MeltPro Systems**
PO Box 1085
Auburn, GA 30011-1085 800-366-0568
Fax: 770-339-1308 www.asistickit.net
Hot melt tanks, heads, hoses and nozzles compatible with Nordson, Itw, slautterback at 50 % savings. M-Series applicator head modular that allows end user to adapt 1-2-3-4 modules and types, for carton, case sealing, non wovenapplication, replace all heads with one. Module types extrusion, spray, reduced cavity, zero cavity, and air on air off
Research & Development: Merk Morriseette
Sales Director: Steve Wages
Plant Manager: Jesse Owens
Estimated Sales: $1-2.5 Million
Number Employees: 19

18268 **ASI Technologies**
5848 N 95th Ct
Milwaukee, WI 53225 414-464-6200
Fax: 414-464-9863 800-558-7068
info@asidoors.com www.asidoors.com
Maunfacturer and exporter of cold storsge and industrial refrigerator doors including manual, powered, fiberglass and stainless steel
President: George C Balbach
CFO: Steve Contrucci
Estimated Sales: $5 - 10 000,000
Number Employees: 100-249
Square Footage: 60000

18269 **ASI/Restaurant Manager**
1734 Elton Rd Ste 219
Silver Spring, MD 20903 800-356-6037
Fax: 301-445-6104 800-356-6037
sales@actionsystems.com www.rmpoas.com
The most compreensive and user-friendly POS system available. Improve service, reduce labor costs and makes faster, more informed decisions to boost your bottom line with powerful backoffice tracking. Choose the traditional touchscreen POS or give your servers the Write-On Handheld for the ultimate in imporved tableside service.
Owner: Smiley Shu
VP: Lisa Wilson
Sales/Marketing Director: Craig Bednarovsky
Estimated Sales: $1-3 Million
Number Employees: 10-19
Square Footage: 6000
Type of Packaging: Food Service
Brands:
Restaurant Manager

18270 **AT Information Products**
575 Corporate Dr Ste 401
Mahwah, NJ 07430 201-529-0202
Fax: 201-529-5603 info@atip-usa.com
www.atip-usa.com
Ink jet printing systems
President: Joseph Traut
Estimated Sales: Below $5 000,000
Number Employees: 10-19

18271 **ATAGO USA Inc**
11811 NE First Street
Suite 101
Bellevue, WA 98005 425-637-2107
Fax: 425-637-2110 877-282-4687
customerservice@atago-usa.com www.atago.net
The Official Port Wine Glass
President: Yusuke Amamiya
Technical Sales Supervisor: Emerson Carillo
Marketing Director: Frank Young
Sales Director: Wesley LeMay, Jr.
Estimated Sales: A
Number Employees: 1-4

Type of Packaging: Consumer, Bulk

18272 ATC
4037 Guion Ln
Indianapolis, IN 46268-2564 317-328-8492
Fax: 317-328-2686 hsagi@atcinc.net
www.atcinc.net
President: Hemi Sagi
Estimated Sales: $1 - 3 Million
Number Employees: 5-9

18273 ATD-American Company
135 Greenwood Ave
Wyncote, PA 19095-1396 215-576-1000
Fax: 215-576-1827 800-523-2300
american@atd.com www.atd.com
Furniture, steel shelving, cabinets, bins, table linens and chef aprons; exporter of furniture, linens and food service equipment
President: Jerome M Zaslow
VP: S Zaslow
VP: A Zaslow
R&D: Eric Wischnia
Estimated Sales: $65Million
Number Employees: 100-249

18274 ATK
847 N Troy St
Chicago, IL 60622
Fax: 773-826-0696 800-522-3582
Labels
Estimated Sales: $500,000-$1 Million
Number Employees: 1-4

18275 ATL-East Tag & Label Company
1244 W Chester Pike
Suite 407, PO Box 3551
West Chester, PA 19382-3151 610-692-2999
Fax: 610-692-3044 866-381-8744
ndawson@atlas-tag.com www.atl-east.com
Roll, pressure sensitive and continuous self-adhesive labels; also, shipping and multiport tags, nameplates and seals
President: James W Gordon
Estimated Sales: $500,000-$1 Million
Number Employees: 1-4
Parent Co: Bissell Corporation

18276 ATM Corporation
2450 S Commerce Dr
New Berlin, WI 53151 414-453-1100
Fax: 262-786-5074 800-511-2096
atm@execpc.com www.atmcorporation.com
Manufacturer and exporter of testing sieves and particle size measurement equipment
President: James Lang
VP: Stephen Kohl
VP of Marketing: Tony Romano
Estimated Sales: $5-10,000,000
Number Employees: 20-49

18277 ATOFINA Chemicals
2000 Market St
Philadelphia, PA 19103-3231 215-419-7000
Fax: 215-419-7591 800-225-7788
bill.pernice@atofina.com
www.atofinachemicals.com
Manufacturer, importer and exporter of cleaning equipment and supplies including liquid chlorine and caustic soda
President: Doug Sharp
CFO: Larry Hartnett
R&D: Louis Hegedus
Number Employees: 500-999

18278 ATS
5025-C N. Royal Atlanta Dr.
Tucker, GA 30084 770-270-1688
Fax: 770-270-5919 800-358-0212
Info@ATSfurniture.com www.atsfurniture.com
Tables and seating manufacturer
President: Sandra Xing
Estimated Sales: $10,000,000 - $20,000,000
Number Employees: 50 - 90

18279 ATS RheoSystems
231 Crosswicks Rd Ste 7
Bordentown, NJ 08505 609-298-2522
Fax: 609-298-2795 info@atsrheosystems.com
www.atsrheosystems.com
A comprehensive analytical instrumentation, rheological consulting and materials testing, technical support and services company. Rheometer and viscometer design, viscometers and viscosity measurements, research level rheometers andrheology measurements, capillary rheometers, dynamic shear rheometers for asphalt testing, and dynamic mechanical thermal analysis. Other materials characterization techniques are also available, including thermal analysis, surface tension, andcontact angle.
President/CEO: Steven Colo
Brands:
Dynalyser
Stresstech
Viscoanalyser

18280 ATW Manufacturing Company
4065 W. 11th Ave
Eugene, OR 97402-0029 800-759-3388
Fax: 541-484-1493 800-759-3388
sales@atwmfg.com www.atwmfg.com
Shrink-wrapping, shrink banding, labeling and heat sealing, shrink tunnels, vacuum packaging.
President and CEO: Thomas Drew
Sales: Jeff Spencer
Operations: James Warren
Estimated Sales: $1-2.5 Million
Number Employees: 7

18281 AVC Industries Inc
20311 Valley Blvd
Suite H
Walnut, CA 91789 909-839-1188
Fax: 909-839-1060 info@avcfilms.com
www.avcfilms.com
POF Shrink Film and Cross Linked POF Film applications and uses of which include that of the food and beverage industry.
Owner: Bill Pan
Vice President Sales: Bill Pan

18282 AVG Press Automation
4140 Utica Ridge Road
Bettendorf, IA 52722 800-711-5109
Fax: 630-668-4676 800-TEC-ENGR
webmaster@avg.net www.avg.net
Microprocessor based PLS, programmable limit switches, and revolver decoders for packaging machines
Plant Manager: Hyder Khan
Number Employees: 100-249

18283 AVTEC Industries
9 Kane Industrial Drive
Hudson, MA 1749 978-562-2300
Fax: 978-562-8900 raysch@avtecind.com
www.avtecindustries.com
Estimated Sales: $1 - 5 Million
Parent Co: Dover Industries

18284 AW Company
8809 Industrial Dr
Franksville, WI 53126-9337 262-884-9800
Fax: 262-884-9810 800-850-6110
sales@aw-lake.com www.awcompany.com
Manufacturer and distributor of flow control products including positive displacement flow meters, turbine flow meters, electronic sensors, flow computers, on-line optical sensors and signal conditioners.
President: Roger Tambling
Estimated Sales: $5 - 10 Million
Number Employees: 20-49
Square Footage: 60000
Brands:
Fluidpro
Proscan
Ta-3

18285 AWB Engineers
1942 Northwood Drive
Salisbury, MD 21801 410-742-7299
Fax: 410-742-0273 awbengs@aol.com
www.awbengineers.com
Consultant specializing in architecture, civil, constructural and mechanical engineering services for food processing facilities
President: Matthew R Smith
Director: John Shahan
Estimated Sales: $3 - 5 Million
Number Employees: 10-19
Square Footage: 23200

18286 AWP Butcher Block Inc
320 Cherry St
Horse Cave, KY 42749 270-786-2319
Fax: 270-786-2321 800-764-7840
sales@awpbutcherblock.com
www.awpbutcherblock.com
Laminated butcher block tops including kitchen counter and island tops, table tops for restaurant, institutional and home use
Owner: Marcia Baugh
Estimated Sales: $1-2.5 Million
Number Employees: 20-49
Type of Packaging: Consumer

18287 AZCO Corporation
26 Just Road
Fairfield, NJ 07004 973-439-1428
Fax: 973-439-9411 cs@azcocorp.com
www.azcocorp.com
Dispensers, inserters, fan folders, cut-to-length assemblies
President: Andrew Zucaro
Marketing: Tetie Milligan
Sales: John Perona
Estimated Sales: $1-2.5 Million
Number Employees: 10-19

18288 AZO Food
P.O.Box 181070
4445 Malone Road
Memphis, TN 38181 901-794-9480
Fax: 901-794-9934 info@azo.com
www.azo-inc.com
Pneumatic and automated handling equipment and systems for ingredients; also, mixers, hoppers, bins, batching and mixing controls and process control and weighing systems
President: Robert Moore
CFO: Jack Kerwin
Executive VP: Jim Cavender
Sales Manager: Kevin Pecha
Estimated Sales: $10 - 20 Million
Number Employees: 50-99
Brands:
Componenter
Dositainer
Flexitainer
Ruberg

18289 Aabbitt Adhesives
2403 N Oakley Ave
Chicago, IL 60647-2093 773-227-2700
Fax: 773-227-2103 800-222-2488
info@aabbitt.com www.aabbitt.com
Manufacturer and exporter of hot melt and water based labeling adhesives, casein-based ice proof label glue and resin emulsion systems
President: Ben Sarmas
VP: Daniel Sarmas
Sales Manager: Greg Sarmas
General Manager/VP Sales: David Sarmas
Purchasing Director: Donna Hendrickson
Estimated Sales: $20-50 Million
Square Footage: 150000

18290 (HQ)Aaburco Piemaster
17745 Atwater Lane
Grass Valley, CA 95949 530-268-2734
Fax: 530-268-3038 800-533-7437
support@piemaster.com www.piemaster.com
Manufacturer, exporter and wholesaler/distributor of food processing equipment including manually operated, semi-automatic and electro-pneumatic machines and dough rollers for calzones, empanadas and pierogies
President: J Burgard
CFO: F Burgard
Estimated Sales: Less than $500,000
Number Employees: 4
Square Footage: 40000
Type of Packaging: Consumer, Food Service
Brands:
Mt20
Piemaster
Sa21

18291 Aaladin Industries
32584 477th Ave
Elk Point, SD 57025-6700 605-356-3325
Fax: 605-356-2330 800-356-3325
info@aaladin.com www.aaladin.com

Manufacturer and exporter of portable, stationary pressure and aqueous parts washers
President of Systems: Pat Wingen
Purchasing Manager: Don Klunder
Estimated Sales: $10-20 Million
Number Employees: 1-4
Square Footage: 450000
Brands:
Aaladin

18292 Aalint Fluid Measure Solutions
150 Venture Boulevard
Spartanburg, SC 29306-3805 864-574-8960
Fax: 864-578-7308 sales@venturemeas.com
www.venturemeas.com
President: Mark Earl
Number Employees: 50-99

18293 Aaron Equipment Company
735 E. Green Street
P.O. Box 80
Bensenville, IL 60106-0080 630-350-2200
Fax: 630-350-9047 sales@aaronequipment.com
www.aaronequipment.com
Provider of new, used and reconditioned process equipment and asset management services to the chemical, plastics, pharmaceutical, food, mining and related industries.
President: Jerrold V Cohen
Vice President of Business Development: Bruce Baird
Estimated Sales: $20-50 Million
Number Employees: 50
Square Footage: 250000

18294 Aaron Fink Group
501 Mulberry Street
Newark, NJ 07114-2740 973-824-1414
President: Aaron Fink
Estimated Sales: Below $500,000
Number Employees: 2

18295 Aaron Thomas Company
7421 Chapman Ave
Garden Grove, CA 92841 714-894-4468
Fax: 714-373-8633 800-394-4776
service@packaging.com www.packaging.com
Contract packager of promotional on-pack samples and coupons; shrink wrapping, over wrappings and display assemblies on pallets or racks available
President: Thomas Bacon
VP: Bob Cassens
CFO: James Chang
Quality Control: Danny Bacarrelaq
Sales Executive: Aaron Bacon
Purchasing Executive: Linda Bacon
Estimated Sales: $10-20 Million
Number Employees: 185
Square Footage: 350000

18296 Abacus Label Applications
20120 115a Avenue
Maple Ridge, BC V2X 0Z4
Canada 604-465-8633
Fax: 604-465-0818 888-595-8633
beverley@abacuslabel.com
www.abacuslabel.com
President: Roy Ashworth
Number Employees: 9

18297 Abalon Precision Manufacturing Corporation
1040 Home Street
Bronx, NY 10459 718-589-5682
Fax: 718-589-0300 800-888-2225
info@abalonmfg.com www.abalonmfg.com
Manufacturer and exporter of fryer tanks, display store racks and metal fabricated rack parts
President: Norman Orent
Estimated Sales: $2.5 Million
Number Employees: 25
Square Footage: 160000
Parent Co: Abalon Precision Manufacturing Corporation

18298 Abanaki Corporation
17387 Munn Rd
Chagrin Falls, OH 44023 440-543-7400
Fax: 440-543-7404 800-358-7546
skimmers@abanaki.com www.abanaki.com
Manufacturer and exporter of oil and grease skimming equipment including portable models and multi-belt systems
President/Owner: Tom Hobson
Estimated Sales: $1 - 2.5 Million
Number Employees: 10-19
Square Footage: 10000
Brands:
Abanaki Concentrators
Abanaki Mighty Minn
Abanaki Oil Grabber
Abanaki Petro Extractor
Abanaki Tote-Its
Grease Grabber
Mighty Mini
Oil Concentrator
Oil Grabber
Oil Grabber Multi-Belt
Petroxtractor
Tote-It

18299 Abanda
PO Box 2028
Decatur, AL 35602-2028 205-340-1400
Fax: 205-340-5777

18300 Abatron
5501 95th Ave
Kenosha, WI 53144 262-653-2000
Fax: 262-653-2019 800-445-1754
info@abatron.com www.abatron.com
Epoxy and plastic compounds, molds, adhesives, protective coatings, sealants, wood and concrete restoration products
President: John J P Caporaso
Estimated Sales: $10-25 000,000
Number Employees: 10-19
Type of Packaging: Consumer, Bulk

18301 Abbeon Cal
123 Gray Ave
Santa Barbara, CA 93101 805-966-0810
Fax: 805-966-7659 800-922-0977
abbeoncal@abbeon.com www.abbeon.com
Manufacturer, exporter and importer of temperature, humidity and moisture measurement instruments and plastic cutting, bending & welding tools.
President: Alice Wertheim
CEO: Mark Tubbs
CFO: Karen Barros
VP: Mara Hassenbein
Quality Control: Robyn Ramirez
Mktg/Sales/Pub Relations/Operations: Bob Brunsman
Estimated Sales: $2.5 - 5 Million
Number Employees: 8
Square Footage: 40000

18302 Abbotsford Farms
301ÿCarlsonÿParkwayÿ
Suiteÿ400ÿ
Abbotsford, WI 54405 877-203-7620
888-300-3447
nfo@abbotsfordfarms.com
Supplier of organic and cage free liquid eggs to the food service industry.

18303 Abbott Industries
1-11 Morris St
Paterson, NJ 07501 97- 34- 111
Fax: 973-345-9154 abbott.harold@verizon.net
www.abbottind.com
Plastic bottles including extrusion, blow molded and decoration
President: Leonard Grossman
Owner: Harold Sheck
VP: John Klandt
Operations Manager: Richard Lowe
Estimated Sales: $5-10 Million
Number Employees: 20-49
Square Footage: 19000
Brands:
Similac Toddler's Best

18304 Abbott Plastics
3302 Lonergan Dr
Rockford, IL 61109-2670 815-874-8500
Fax: 815-874-6297 800-850-8551
Sales@abbottplastics.com
www.abbottplastics.com
Abbott Plastics is a plastics distributor the product line of which includes sheets, rods, tubes or machined plastic parts that are applicable to a variety of industries including dairy and food processing.
Owner: Robert Nelson
Sales Representative: Steve Forberg

18305 Abco International
200 Broadhollow Rd
Suite 400
Melville, NY 11747 631-427-9000
Fax: 631-427-9001 866-240-2226
info@abcointl.com www.oneida.com
Tableware for the airline, cruise, and railroad industry
Manager: Bill Grannis
Estimated Sales: Below $500,000
Number Employees: 10-19
Parent Co: Oneida

18306 Abco International
200 Broadhollow Rd Ste 400
Melville, NY 11747 631-427-9000
Fax: 631-427-9001 866-240-2226
info@abcointl.com www.oneida.com
Manufacturer and exporter of dinnerware, flatware, glassware, hollowware and ovenware
Manager: Bill Grannis
Managing Director: Peter Kranes
Estimated Sales: Below $500,000
Number Employees: 10-19
Parent Co: Delco Tableware International
Type of Packaging: Food Service
Brands:
Abco International

18307 Abel Manufacturing Company
1100 North Mayflower Drive
Appleton, WI 54913 920-734-4443
Fax: 920-734-1084 sales@abel-usa.com
www.abel-usa.com
Manufacturer and exporter of material handling equipment and batch weighing and bulk storage systems
President: Donald Abel
Estimated Sales: $5 - 10 Million
Number Employees: 20-49
Type of Packaging: Bulk

18308 Abel Pumps
79 N Industrial Park # 207
Sewickley, PA 15143 412-741-3222
Fax: 412-741-2599 mail@abelpumps.com
www.abelpumps.com
Food processing pumps including solids handling, sanitary stainless steel centrifugal and positive displacement diaphragm
Manager: Carl Dawson
Manager Sales Support: Mark Neiderhauser
National Sales Manager: Cersten Jantzoh
Estimated Sales: $1-2.5 Million
Number Employees: 5-9
Square Footage: 96000
Parent Co: ABEL-Twiete 1
Brands:
Abel

18309 Abell-Howe Crane
10321 Werch Dr # 100
Woodridge, IL 60517-4812 630-783-2188
Fax: 630-972-0897 800-366-0068
gree.rodriguez@ces-cranes.com
www.cmworks.com
Overhead and stainless steel jib cranes
Sales: Eric Vach
Sales/Marketing Manager: Eric Vack
Number Employees: 50-99

18310 Abicor Binzel
650 Medimmune Court
Suite 110
Frederick, MD 21703 301-846-4196
Fax: 301-846-4497 800-542-4867
customerservice@abicorusa.com
www.binzel.com
Dishwashing and laundry detergents
President: John M. Kaylor
VP, Finance & Administration: John R. Kuhn
Marketing Specialist: Megan Ensminger
Director of Sales/ Marketing: Paul Pfingston
VP Operations: Jutilda Binzel
Estimated Sales: Below $5 Million
Number Employees: 5-9

18311 Able Brands Inc
10540 72nd St
Largo, FL 33777-1500 727-547-5222
Fax: 727-541-3182 800-854-5019
nutritionsale@hotmail.com
www.sportnutrition.com
Owner: David Mc Cabe

Estimated Sales: $5 - 10 Million
Number Employees: 5-9

18312 Abloy Security Locks
6005 Commerce Drive # 330
Irving, TX 75063-2664 972-753-1127
Fax: 972-753-0792 800-367-4598
info@abloyusa.com www.abloyusa.com
High security locks, T-handle cylinders, padlocks, key-ring padlocks, cam locks
President: Steve Timmons
CFO and QC and R&D: Jeff Carpenter
Sales Manager: Martha Bartley
Estimated Sales: $1 - 2.5 Million
Number Employees: 10-19
Parent Co: Assa Abloy

18313 Abond Plastic Corporation
10050 Chemin Cote De Liesse
Lachine, QC H8T 1A3
Canada 514-273-1523
Fax: 514-273-3155 800-886-7947
info@abondcorp.com www.abondcorp.com
Manufacturer and importer of tablecloths, oven mitts, place mats and vinyl bags
Sales Manager: R Katz
Estimated Sales: Below $500,000
Number Employees: 20

18314 About Packaging Robotics
2131 E 99th Pl
Thornton, CO 80229 303-449-2559
Fax: 303-449-2559 aboutpr@apris.com
www.apris.com
Open/fill/seal systems for pouches and bags; also, labeling machinery and applicators
President: Sal Beltrami
CFO: Lynda Muhlbauer
Estimated Sales: $5 - 10 Million
Number Employees: 10-19
Square Footage: 2500
Brands:
Labelmaster Applicator
Pal Labelmaster
Pouchmaster Abs System
Pouchmaster Pac's System
Pouchmaster Xii
Thermal Printmaster
Twin Abs Poucher

18315 Abresist Corporation
5541 N State Road 13
Urbana, IN 46990 260-774-3327
Fax: 260-774-8188 800-348-0717
info@abresist.com www.abresist.com
Wear resistant linings to extend equipment life
President: Joe Acceta
CEO: Joe Accetta
Estimated Sales: $5-10 000,000
Number Employees: 20-49

18316 Absolute Custom Extrusions
3868 N Fratney St
Milwaukee, WI 53212 414-332-8133
Fax: 414-332-1827 info@ace-extrusions.com
www.ace-extrusions.com
Cocktail stirrers and straws including custom size and color
President: Barbara Cupertino
Sales: Barb Cupertino
Engineering/Technical: Mark Winiger
Estimated Sales: $500,000 - $1 Million
Number Employees: 20-49
Type of Packaging: Food Service, Private Label, Bulk
Brands:
Ace
Rainbow of New Colors

18317 Absolute Process Instruments
1220 American Way
Libertyville, IL 60048 847-918-3510
Fax: 800-942-7502 800-942-0315
tgrimes@api-usa.com www.api-usa.com
Signal conditioners
President: William Sawyer
Estimated Sales: $5-10 000,000
Number Employees: 20-49

18318 Absorbco
68 Anderson Road
Walterboro, SC 29488
Fax: 843-538-8678 888-335-6439
www.absorbco.com
Manufacturer and exporter of disposable wipers
VP: Scott Brown
Director Marketing: Randy Schubert
Number Employees: 107
Type of Packaging: Consumer, Food Service, Private Label, Bulk
Brands:
Mighty Wipe

18319 Abundant Earth Corporation
495 Fernwood Dr
Ashland, OR 97520-1611
President: Brian Hoffman
Estimated Sales: $300,000-500,000
Number Employees: 1-4
Brands:
Abundant

18320 Academy Awning
2080 Century Park E # 803
Los Angeles, CA 90067-2011 310-277-8383
Fax: 323-277-8370
Commercial awnings
President: James D Richman
Estimated Sales: $2,500,000-5,000,000
Number Employees: 19-Oct

18321 Accent Mark
345 Morningside Terrace
Palmdale, CA 93551-4445 661-274-8191
Rubber date and number stamps including plastic and inspection
Owner: Mark Evans
Estimated Sales: Less than $500,000
Number Employees: 4
Brands:
Baselock
Cosco
Ideal
Just-Rite
Pullman
Ribtype
X-Stamper

18322 Accent Store Fixtures
9629 58th Place
Kenosha, WI 53144 262-857-9450
Fax: 262-857-6620 800-545-1144
sales@accentind.com www.accentind.com
Checkout counters, displays, shelving and self-service displays; equipment service and installation available
Owner/President: Dave Shaw
Sales Executive: Chris Osborn
Estimated Sales: $5-10 Million
Number Employees: 55
Square Footage: 30000
Brands:
Accent

18323 Access Solutions
8705 Unicorn Dr Ste C302
Knoxville, TN 37923 865-531-0971
Fax: 865-531-3547
order@accesssolutionsinc.com
www.accesssolutionsinc.com
Manufacturer and exporter of advertising specialties and forms; also, embroidery available
Owner: Randy Philipps
Estimated Sales: Below $5,000,000
Number Employees: 10-19

18324 Acco Systems
12755 E 9 Mile Rd
Warren, MI 48089 586-755-7501
Fax: 586-758-1901 sales@acco.durr-usa.com
www.accosystems.com
Industrial conveyors, automated storage and retrieval systems and electrified monorail systems
President: Anthony Gore
Estimated Sales: $10-25 000,000
Number Employees: 200
Parent Co: FKI Company

18325 Accommodation Mollen
2150 Kubach Rd
Philadelphia, PA 19116-4203 215-739-2115
Fax: 215-739-4571 800-872-6268
sales@accommodation-mollen.com
www.7392115.com
Disinfectants and insecticides
President: Dave Potack
CFO: Sara Botoss
Quality Control: Ray Brand
General Manager: Dave Potack
Estimated Sales: Below $5 Million
Number Employees: 20-49
Brands:
3m
Buckeye
Chemspec
Taski

18326 Accommodation Program
120 Park Avenue
New York, NY 10017-5577 917-663-4048
Fax: 917-663-5544 800-929-1414
Consultant specializing in providing plans for designated and nondesignated smoking seats in food service establishments
President: Tara Carraro
Number Employees: 20
Parent Co: Phillip Morris

18327 Accra Laboratory
2686 Lisbon Road
Cleveland, OH 44104-3145 216-721-4747
Fax: 216-721-8715 800-567-7200
Laboratory performing bacterial and nutritional analysis on food and water, shelf-life studies, FDA labeling, sanitation consulting and plant inspections
President: G Lancaster
Senior Microbiologist: Monique Panzeter
Estimated Sales: Below $500,000
Number Employees: 4
Square Footage: 5000
Parent Co: CWC Industries

18328 Accraply/Trine
3070 Mainway
Units 16-19
Burlington Ontario, ON L7M 3X1
Canada 905-336-8880
Fax: 905-335-5988 800-387-6742
sales@accraply.com www.accraply.com
Supplier of product identification and decorating systems, offering pressure sensitive labeling systems, stand-alone label applicators, pritn and apply labeling systems, trine roll-fed labeling systems, shrink sleeve applicators andRFID solutions.
Manager: Peter Nicholson
Vice President: Rob Leonard
Sales Director: Stuart Moss
Operations Manager: Peter Nicholson
Number Employees: 100-249
Number of Brands: 5
Square Footage: 88000
Parent Co: Barry-Wehmiller Companies Inc
Brands:
Avery Dennison
Ccl Label
Collamat
Graham Sleeving
Mateer Burt
Novexx
Sato
Trine Labeling
Zebra

18329 Accro-Seal
316 Briggs St
Vicksburg, MI 49097 269-649-1014
Fax: 269-649-1067 sales@accroseal.com
www.accroseal.com
Gaskets, seals, O-rings and machinery parts
President: Joe Messer
Sales/Marketing: Neil Patten
Estimated Sales: Below $5 000,000
Number Employees: 10-19

18330 Accu-Labs Research
4663 Table Mountain Drive
Golden, CO 80403-1650 303-277-9514
Fax: 303-277-9512 www.acculabs.com
Laboratory specializing in chemical and environmental analysis
President: William Gilgren
Lab Manager: Christopher Shugarts
Marketing Director: Thomas Balka
Estimated Sales: $2.5-5 Million
Number Employees: 20-49
Square Footage: 108000

18331 Accu-Pak
2422 Prikel Rd
Akron, OH 44312 330-644- 301
Fax: 330-644- 316 www.accu-pak.com
Vertical form/fill/seal packaging and metal detection systems
President: Bill Frievalt
Vice President: Roy Allen
Operations Manager: Richard Camps
Production Manager: Curt Frievalt
Purchasing Manager: Ron Rendessy
Estimated Sales: $10-20,000,000
Number Employees: 50-99
Type of Packaging: Food Service

18332 Accu-Ray Inspection Services
211 Spangler Avenue
Elmhurst, IL 60126-1129 630-833-4027
800-378-1226
Inquires@accu-ray.com www.accu-ray.com
X-ray inspection services, X-ray rentals, metal detector rentals, manufaturers of metal detection equipment;, X-ray inspection services available
Manager: Doug Bierma
Estimated Sales: Less than $500,000
Number Employees: 1-4
Brands:
Fortress Technology

18333 Accu-Seal Corporation
225 Bingham Dr Ste B
San Marcos, CA 92069 760-591-9800
Fax: 760-591-9117 800-452-6040
info@accu-seal.com www.accu-seal.com
Vacuum, modified-atmosphere, medical, validatable, long-line, tube and hand-held sealers
Manager: Lesley Jensen
R&D: Chris Moore
General Manager: Roger Ricky
Estimated Sales: $1 - 2.5 000,000
Number Employees: 10-19

18334 Accu-Sort Systems
511 School House Rd
Telford, PA 18969 800-227-2633
Fax: 215-996-8249 800-227-2633
info@accusort.com www.accusort.com
Manufacturer and exporter of bar code scanners, CCD cameras, RFID solutions, integrated solutions, and data collection systems for material handling applications
President: Bob Joyce
CFO: Greg Banning
Marketing: Mark Verheyden
Sales: Don De Lash
Production: John Broderick
Estimated Sales: $50-100 Million
Type of Packaging: Bulk

18335 AccuLife
PO Box 218
Blanchester, OH 45107-0218 937-783-5565
Fax: 937-783-5574 acculift@compuserve.com
www.acculift.com

18336 AccuTemp Products
8415 Clinton Park Dr
Fort Wayne, IN 46825 260-490-5870
Fax: 260-493-0318 800-210-5907
sswogger@accutemp.net www.accutemp.net
Manufacturer and exporter of vacuum steam cookers and flat top grills and griddles.
President/CEO: Scott Swogger
CFO: Dave Ogram
Research & Development: Dean Stanley
Estimated Sales: $20 Million
Number Employees: 50-99
Square Footage: 45000
Brands:
Flipper the Robocook
Steam 'n' Hold
World's Best Griddle

18337 Accubar
PO Box 6013
Suite 5
Newport News, VA 23606 757-873-9394
Fax: 757-873-8311
Distributor of Easy Bar
President: David Epps

18338 Accuflex Industrial Hose
36663 Van Born Rd Ste 300
Romulus, MI 48174 734-451-0080
Fax: 734-796-8090 sales@accuflex.com
www.accuflex.com
Manufacturer, exporter and importer of food and beverage pressure and vacuum hoses and tubing; NSF, FDA and USDA approved
President: Les Kraska
Estimated Sales: $5 - 10 Million
Number Employees: 10-19
Brands:
Accu-Clear
Accu-Flo
Accu-Poly
Bev-Flex
Bev-Seal
Bevlex
Kuni-Tec

18339 Accuform Manufacturing,Inc.
PO Box 6299
Vacaville, CA 95696-6299 707-452-1430
Fax: 707-452-1636 800-233-3352
www.accuform.com
Safety signs and pressure sensitive labels
Director of Product Development: Matt Johnson
Number Employees: 10

18340 Accumetric
350 Ring Rd
Elizabethtown, KY 42701-6777 270-769-3386
Fax: 270-765-2412 800-928-2677
www.accumetricinc.com
USDA approved silicone sealant used for packaging
CEO: James V Hartlage Jr
CFO: Charles Casper
VP: Alan Hartlage
VP Domestic Sales/Marketing: Ed Linz
Operations: Joe Fowler
Purchasing: Tim Patterson
Estimated Sales: $50-100 Million
Number Employees: 100-249
Square Footage: 75000
Brands:
Boss

18341 Accura Tool & Mold
101 W Terra Cotta Ave
Crystal Lake, IL 60014-3507 815-459-5520
Fax: 815-459-4434 www.accuratool.com
Die cast molds
Estimated Sales: $5-10 000,000
Number Employees: 50-99

18342 Accurate Flannel Bag Company
468 Totowa Ave. Ste 3
Paterson, NJ 07522-1573 973-720-1800
Fax: 973-689-6774 800-234-9200
Custom designed bags for ham, sea salt, spices, flour, beverage mixes, candy, coffee beans, fruits and vegetables
Executive VP: Fred Baron
Marketing Manager: Wanda Morales
Estimated Sales: $1 - 3 Million
Number Employees: 100
Square Footage: 25000
Brands:
Silverpak

18343 Accurate Paper Box Company
2635 Byington Solway Rd
Knoxville, TN 37931 865-690-0311
Fax: 865-690-0312
Paper boxes, cartons, containers, blister packaging and machinery including box making, cutting, folding, gluing, printing and sheeting
President: Carl Hutchison
Chairman: Virgil Lawson
Sales Manager: Michael Cox
Estimated Sales: $1-2,500,000
Number Employees: 20-49

18344 Accutek Packaging Equipment Company
1399 Specialty Dr
Vista, CA 92081 760-734-4177
Fax: 760-734-4188 800-989-1828
sales@accutekpackaging.com
www.accutekpackaging.com
President: Edward Chocholek
VP: Darren Chocholek
Estimated Sales: $3-5 Million
Number Employees: 20-49
Square Footage: 40000
Brands:
Accucap
Accucapper
Accuvac
Auto Pinch-25
Auto Pinch-50
Auto-Mini
Handle Capper
Mini-6
Mini-Pinch
Mini-Punch
Pinch-25

18345 Ace Engineering Company
10200 Jacksboro Hwy
Fort Worth, TX 76135 817-237-7700
Fax: 817-237-2777 800-431-4223
tchapman@aceworldcompanies.com
www.aceworldcompanies.com
Manufacturer and exporter of hoists, load blocks and end trucks
President: John Watson
CFO: Mike Harris
Vice President: Rick Reeves
Estimated Sales: $20 - 50 Million
Number Employees: 50-99

18346 Ace Fabrication
2715 Dauphin St
Mobile, AL 36606-4899 251-478-0401
Fax: 251-479-8080 acefab@bellsouth.com
www.acefab.com
Custom built stainless steel food serving equipment
President: Bill Stewart
Estimated Sales: Below $5 Million
Number Employees: 20-49
Square Footage: 30000
Parent Co: Ace Fabrication
Type of Packaging: Food Service
Brands:
Design Series Counters

18347 Ace Manufacturing
5031 Winton Rd
Cincinnati, OH 45232-1506 513-541-2490
Fax: 513-541-2492 800-653-5692
sales@acemanco.com www.acemanco.com
Precision machining services
President: Linda Fullbeck
Number Employees: 10-19

18348 Ace Signs
5512 Patterson Road
Little Rock, AR 72209-2450 501-562-0800
Fax: 501-423-2407 jason@ace-sign.com
www.ace-sign.com
Decals, posters and banners
President: Sam Peters
Estimated Sales: $2.5 - 5 Million
Number Employees: 10

18349 Ace Specialty Manufacturing Company
9616 Valley Blvd
Rosemead, CA 91770-1510 626-444-3867
Fax: 626-444-6395
Manufacturer and exporter of can ejectors.
President: Karl Anderson
Secretary/Treasurer: Keith Anderson
Estimated Sales: $500,000-$1 Million
Number Employees: 1-4
Square Footage: 6000
Brands:
Ace

18350 Ace Stamp & Engraving
10510 Bridgeport Way SW Ste 6
Lakewood, WA 98499 253-582-3322
Fax: 253-582-1955
Corporate and recognition awards, medals, plaques, seals, rubber stamps, signs, ID and name tags, seals.
Owner: Thomas Joseph
Number Employees: 1-4
Square Footage: 1200

18351 Ace Technical Plastics
PO Box 4519
Hartford, CT 06147-4519 860-305-8138
bob@acetechplastics.com
www.acetechplastics.com

Manufacturer, importer and exporter of packaging materials including skin, blister, shrink, trays, etc
President: Robert Pomerantz
Estimated Sales: Below $5 Million
Number Employees: 5-9
Square Footage: 12000

18352 (HQ)Ace-Tex Enterprises
7601 Central Avenue
Detroit, MI 48210 313-834-4000
Fax: 313-834-0260 800-444-3800
www.ace-tex.com
Wiping, lint free disposable and polyester cheese-cloths
Vice President: Martin Laker
Director, Marketing: Elliott Parr
General Manager, Operations: Dennis Hadel
Estimated Sales: $23 Million
Number Employees: 70
Square Footage: 122000

18353 AceCo Precision Manufacturing
4419 S Federal Way
Boise, ID 83716-5528 208-343-7712
Fax: 208-345-0740 800-359-7012
info@aceco.com www.aceco.com
Manufacturer and exporter of industrial knives and water knife assemblies; also, custom cutting assemblies available
President: Raleigh J Jensen
CFO: Sid Sullivan
VP: William Moynihan
Sales/Marketing: Joe Jensen
Technical Support: Larry Rupe
Estimated Sales: $10 - 20,000,000
Number Employees: 50-99
Brands:
Strapslicer System

18354 Acebright Inc.
13-15 Deangelo Dr
Bedford, MA 01730 484-919-8980
deana.wang@acebright.com
Supplier and marketer of nutraceutical products such as vitamin B2, B6, H; L-Lactic acid, Oxytetracycline and Griseofulvin, etc.
President: Ying Kan
Estimated Sales: $700 Thousand
Number Employees: 7
Parent Co: Hegno Corporation
Type of Packaging: Bulk

18355 Aceco Precision Industrial Knives
4419 S Federal Way
Boise, ID 83716-5528 208-343-7712
Fax: 208-345-0740 800-359-7012
cut@aceco.com www.aceco.com
President: Raleigh Jensen
CFO: Syd Sullivan
Estimated Sales: $10 - 20 Million
Number Employees: 50-99

18356 Aces Manufacturing Company
300 Ramsey Street
Sullivan, MO 63080 573-468-4181
Fax: 573-468-5584 800-325-6138
acesrmv@pacbell.net
Manufacturer and exporter of wire containers and decks, shelving and racks:cantilever, pallet, drive-in and push-back; also, repair services available
President: Richard Vartanian
Estimated Sales: $2.5-5 Million
Number Employees: 10-19
Square Footage: 46000

18357 Achem Industry AmericaInc.
938 Hatcher Ave
City of Industry, CA 91748 626-839-0800
Fax: 562-802-5069 800-442-8273
jonyeh@achem.com www.achem-usa.com
Polyvinyl Chloride (PVC) and double-sided Pressure Sensitive Tapes
Estimated Sales: $50 - 100 Million
Number Employees: 50-100
Other Locations:
ANCHEM Industry America
Chicago IL
ANCHEM Industry America
Charlotte NC
ANCHEM
China
ANCHEM
Taiwan
ANCHEM
South Asia
ANCHEM
Europe

18358 Achilles USA
1407 80th Street SW
Everett, WA 98203 425-353-7000
Fax: 425-347-5785 www.achillesusa.com
Manufacturer and exporter of flexible and semi-rigid polyvinyl chloride film and sheeting
President: Takuo Suzuki
Vice President, Finance: Jestin Fought
Research & Development Manager: Bach Nguyen
Human Resources Manager/Safety Manager: Mike Burrows
Quality Systems Manager: James Knosp
VP, Manufacturing Sales/Operations: Chad Turner
Estimated Sales: $34 Million
Number Employees: 185
Square Footage: 14910
Parent Co: Achilles Corporation
Type of Packaging: Bulk

18359 Acme
8563 Whittier Blvd
Pico Rivera, CA 90660 323-821-3930
Fax: 562-696-0026
Manufaturers of bakery and restaurant equipment
President: Mario Labat

18360 Acme Awning Company
210 N Main St
Salinas, CA 93901-2816 831-424-7134
Fax: 831-424-0328 info@acmeawn.com
www.acmeawnings.com
Commercial awnings, canopies and fabric products
Owner: Gale Rawitzer
Purchasing Manager: Jay Loiacono
Estimated Sales: $500,000-$1,000,000
Number Employees: 5-9
Square Footage: 16000

18361 Acme Awning Company
435 Van Nest Ave
Bronx, NY 10460 718-409-1881
Fax: 718-824-3571 info@acmeawn.com
www.acmeawn.com
Commercial awnings
President: Lawrence Lo Iacono
Estimated Sales: $1-2,500,000
Number Employees: 10-19
Square Footage: 25000

18362 Acme Bag Company
2528 Main St
Suite T
Chula Vista, CA 91911 619-429-9800
Fax: 619-429-0969 800-275-2263
acmebag@aol.com www.acmebag.com
Paper and plastic bags, also burlap and polypropylene bags
President: Stephen Short
Estimated Sales: $5-10 Million
Number Employees: 5-9

18363 Acme Display Fixture Company
1057 S Olive St
Los Angeles, CA 90015 800-379-9566
Fax: 213-749-9822 800-959-5657
sales@acmedisplay.com www.acmedisplay.com
Store fixtures including racks, display cases and store buildouts
President: Lewis J Berenzweig
Director Marketing: Mitch Blumenfeld
Estimated Sales: $10-20,000,000
Number Employees: 50-99

18364 (HQ)Acme Engineering & Manufacturing Corporation
P.O. Box 978
Muskogee, OK 74402 918-682-7791
Fax: 918-682-0134 marketing@acmefan.com
www.acmefan.com
Manufacturer and exporter of kitchen ventilation systems and fans
President: Lee Buddrus
Vice President: B Frederick
Chief Financial Officer: Brian Combs
Executive Vice President: Doug Yamashita
Chief Technology Officer: Brian Simon
Director, Marketing: Doughlas Kimashka
Executive Vice President, Operations: Forrest Hooks
Plant Manager: Larry Templeton
Senior Buyer: Robert Webb
Estimated Sales: $50 Million
Number Employees: 500
Square Footage: 358020
Other Locations:
Acme Engineering & Manufacture
Fort Smith AR
Brands:
Centrimaster
Dynamaster
Propmaster
Sky Master
Tube Mastervent
Windmaster

18365 Acme Equipment Corporation
2202 Vondron Road
Madison, WI 53718-6732 608-222-6302
Fax: 608-222-2940 tmartin@mailbag.com
Agitation systems, milk and tank, continuous cookers, fine savers, forks, cheese equipment, agitators, custom fabrication, heat exchangers, plates, scraped surface, tubular, piping, fittings and tubing
President: Todd Martin
Estimated Sales: $1-5 000,000
Number Employees: 30

18366 Acme Fixture Company
1057 S Olive Street
Los Angeles, CA 90015 888-388-2263
Fax: 888-411-1849 888-379-9566
www.acmedisplay.com
Store fixtures
Estimated Sales: Below $500,000
Number Employees: 20-50

18367 Acme International
1006 Chancellor Avenue
Maplewood, NJ 07040-3015 973-416-0400
Fax: 973-416-0499 info@acme-usa.com
www.acme-usa.com
Household kitchen gadgets and utensils including baking cups, cutlery, cheese graters, egg slicers, garlic presses, etc
President: Emil Gillotti
CEO: K Fischer
Estimated Sales: $20-50 Million
Number Employees: 50-100
Square Footage: 150000

18368 Acme International Limited
115 West Avenue
Jenkintown, PA 19046-2031 215-885-7750
Fax: 215-885-5182 acmeintusa@aol.com
Estimated Sales: Below $500,000

18369 Acme Laundry Products
21600 Lassen St
Chatsworth, CA 91311 818-341-0700
Fax: 818-341-1546 info@hi-tecgarments.com
www.hi-tecgarments.com
Uniforms
President: Doby Byers
Estimated Sales: $5 - 10 Million
Number Employees: 100-249

18370 Acme Scale Company
1801 Adams Avenue
PO Box 1922
San Leandro, CA 94577 510-638-5040
Fax: 510-638-5619 888-638-5040
www.acmescales.com
Manufacturer, importer and exporter of scales including butchers', counting, portable, portion control, warehouse, educational and laboratory
Owner: Lou Buran
CFO: Lou Buran
VP: Lou Buran
Quality Control: Ron Widgren
Sales Manager: Barbara Byrd
Estimated Sales: Below $5 Million
Number Employees: 20-49
Square Footage: 26000
Parent Co: Buran & Reed

Other Locations:
Acme Scale Co.
Santa Fe Springs CA
Brands:
Chatillon
Detecto
Homs
Ohaus
Toledo

18371 Acme Sign Corporation
3 Lakeland Park Dr
Peabody, MA 01960 978-535-6600
Fax: 978-536-5051 info@acmesigncorp.com
www.acmesigncorp.com
Custom sign manufacturer and supplier
President: Brian Brinkers
Estimated Sales: $1 Million
Number Employees: 1-4
Square Footage: 8000

18372 Acme Sponge & Chamois Company
855 East Pine Street
Tarpon Springs, FL 34689 727-937-3222
Fax: 727-942-3064 sales@acmesponge.com
www.acmesponge.com
Manufacturer, distributor and exporter of chamois and natural sponges
President: James Cantonis
VP of Sales/Marketing: Steve Heller
Sales Manager: Nancy Troio
Estimated Sales: $5-10 Million
Number Employees: 50-99
Square Footage: 100000
Type of Packaging: Consumer, Food Service, Private Label, Bulk
Brands:
Aqua
Careware
Duro
Tanners Select
Thenatura;

18373 Acme Wire Products Company
1 Broadway Ave
Mystic, CT 06355 860-572-0511
Fax: 860-572-9456 800-723-7015
www.acmewire.com
President: Mary Fitzgerald
Vice-President: Michael Planeta
VP Sales: Edward Planeta
Estimated Sales: $10 - 20 Million
Number Employees: 50-99

18374 Aco Container Systems
794 McKay Road
Pickering, ON L1W 2Y4
Canada 905-683-8222
Fax: 905-683-2969 800-542-9942
custserv@acotainers.com www.acotainers.com
Manufacturer and exporter of polyethylene tanks including full draining, transportable and semi-bulk; also, custom fabricator of liquid dispensing systems
President and CFO: Stefan Assmann
Order Desk: Kevin Wentzell
Quality Control: Dave Marsden
General Manager: Stephan Assman
Plant Manager: Mike Banas
Number Employees: 30
Square Footage: 25000

18375 Acorto
1287 120th Ave NE
Bellevue, WA 98005 425-453-2800
Fax: 425-453-2167 800-995-9019
contactus@concordiacoffee.com
Manufacturer and exporter of fully automatic espresso, cappuccino and latte machines
President: David Isett
Sales Director: Sue Rae
Estimated Sales: $10-20 Million
Number Employees: 20-49
Square Footage: 16000
Brands:
Acorto

18376 Acoustical Systems
P.O.Box 146
Vandalia, OH 45377-1046 937-898-3198
Fax: 937-898-5043 info@acousticalsystems.com
www.acousticalsystems.com
President: Rick Seitz
Estimated Sales: Below 1 Million
Number Employees: 1-4

18377 Acra Electric Corporation
P. O. Box 9889
Tulsa, OK 74157 918-224-6755
Fax: 918-224-6866 800-223-4328
info@deltamfg.com www.acraelectric.com
Manufacturer and exporter of electric heating elements for soup pots, food warmers, dispensers, popcorn machines and coffee brewing equipment; also, drum and pail heaters
President: Robert Browne
Sales Director: Gary Marschke
Estimated Sales: $10 - 20 Million
Number Employees: 85
Brands:
Acrawatt
Wrap-It-Heat

18378 (HQ)Acraloc Corporation
113 Flint Rd
Oak Ridge, TN 37830 865-483-1368
Fax: 865-483-3500 acraloc@comcast.net
www.acraloc.com
Manufacturer and exporter of food processing equipment, vacuum packaging equipment, robotic saws, fixtures, etc
President: George Andre
CFO: Kent Park
R&D: Scott Andre
Quality Control: David Dyer
Director Corporate Development: Scott Andre
VP Engineering: Harry Ailey
Estimated Sales: $5 - 10 Million
Number Employees: 20-49
Square Footage: 50000

18379 (HQ)Acrison
20 Empire Blvd
Moonachie, NJ 07074 201-440-8300
Fax: 201-440-4939 800-422-4266
informail@acrison.com
www.acrisonsystems.com
Manufacturer and exporter of metering equipment, hoppers, blenders and microprocessor controls and control systems.
Marketing/Sales: John Shaw
Estimated Sales: $50 - 100 Million
Number Employees: 100-249
Square Footage: 130000
Other Locations:
Acrison
Manchester, England
Brands:
Acrason
Acri Lok
Acrison
Batch Lok
Md-Ii
Md-Ii-200

18380 Acro Dishwashing Service
940 Miami Ave
Kansas City, KS 66105 913-342-4282
Fax: 913-342-8006
www.acrodishwashingservice.com
Commercial low-temperature dishwashers
Manager: Scott Nelson
Manager: Lisa Zane
Estimated Sales: $1-2.5 Million
Number Employees: 10-19
Parent Co: Acro Manufacturing & Chemical Company

18381 Acro Plastics
8630 Airport Hwy
Holland, OH 43528-8639 419-865-0256
Fax: 419-865-0256 wjllmi@megsinet.net
Plastic molds and products
President: William J Lowry
VP: Larry Lowry
Estimated Sales: $10 - 20 000,000
Number Employees: 5-9

18382 Acromag Inc.
30765 S Wixom Rd
P.O. Box 437
Wixom, MI 48393 248-624-1541
Fax: 248-624-9234 sales@acromag.com
www.acromag.com
Manufactures measurement and control instrumentation, signal conditioning products, network I/O modules, VMEbus, PCI, and CompactPCI Bus Boards as well as industry pack and PMC mezzanine modules
President: David Wolfe
Quality Control: Chuck Smith
Marketing: Robert Greenfield
Sales Director: Donald Lupo
Plant Manager: Bret Stephenson
Purchasing Agent: Reg Crawford
Estimated Sales: $10-20 Million
Number Employees: 50-99
Brands:
Intelli Pack

18383 Acrotech
4770 Chino Ave Ste E
Chino, CA 91710 909-465-0610
Fax: 909-465-0403
Industrial electronics for force, weight, pressure management and control
President: Dan Blessum
Estimated Sales: $1-2.5 000,000
Number Employees: 8

18384 Acryline
500 John L Dietsch Blvd
PO Box 872
North Attleboro, MA 02761 508-695-7124
Fax: 508-699-5636 rbaker@acryline.com
www.acryline.com
Merchandising displays
President: Russell Baker
Estimated Sales: $5 - 10 Million
Number Employees: 20-49

18385 Acta Health Products
380 N Pastoria Avenue
Sunnyvale, CA 94085-4108 408-732-6830
Fax: 408-732-0208 davidc@actaproducts.com
www.actaproducts.com
Processor and exporter of vitamins, minerals, herbal extracts and other dietary supplements; importer of raw materials
President: David Chang
VP: K Y Chang
Director Quality Control: Michael Chang
Director Marketing/Sales: Cal Bewicke
Director Purchasing: Leo Liu
Estimated Sales: $3 Million
Number Employees: 30
Square Footage: 124000
Type of Packaging: Private Label, Bulk

18386 Acta Products Corporation
1131 N Fairoaks Avenue
Sunnyvale, CA 94089-2102 408-732-6830
Fax: 408-732-0208 www.actaproducts.com

18387 Action Engineering
5645 Persimmon Ave
P.O. Box 505
Temple City, CA 91780 626-447-8111
Fax: 626-447-8112 actioneng@earthlink.net
Manufacturer and exporter of oil skimmers, separators, wastewater equipment, corn bins, mixers, heavy-duty, low-profile dollies and flexible tank liners
President: Amos Broughton
CFO: Patricia Broughton
Estimated Sales: $.5 - 1 million
Number Employees: 5-9
Number of Brands: 3
Brands:
Hi-Rise Lls Liquid Separator
Hunter Oil Skimmer
Tred-Ties Adjustable Railroad Ties

18388 Action Instruments Company
741 Miller Drive SE
Suite F1
Leesburg, VA 20175-8994 703-443-0000
Fax: 858-279-6290 sales@actionio.com
www.actionio.com
Modules for measurement and control, electronic instrumentation
President: William Perry
Estimated Sales: $10-20 000,000
Number Employees: 100-250

18389 **Action Lighting**
310 Ice Pond Road
P. O. Box 6428
Bozeman, MT 59715 406-586-5105
Fax: 406-585-3078 800-248-0076
action@actionlighting.com
www.actionlighting.com
Manufacturer and exporter of lighting for restaurants, bars, casinos, etc
President: Hubert Reid
CFO: Hubert Reid
Manager: Dan Corthes
Estimated Sales: $5 - 10,000,000
Number Employees: 10-19
Type of Packaging: Food Service

18390 **Action Packaging Automation**
P.O.Box 190
Roosevelt, NJ 08555 609-448-9210
Fax: 609-448-8116 800-241-2724
sales@apaiusa.com www.apaiusa.com
Manufacturer, exporter and importer of automatic packaging machinery for recloseable pouches including counters, scales and support equipment, high speed counting systems, blister packaging machines
Owner: John Wojnicki
Marketing Administrative Assistant: Robin Carroll
Sales Manager: John Wojnicki
Estimated Sales: $2.5-5 Million
Number Employees: 20-49

18391 **Action Technology**
1150 First Avenue
Suite 500
Prussia, PA 19406 217-935-8311
Fax: 217-935-9132 Info@tekni-plex.com
www.tekni-plex.com
Manufacturer and exporter of extruded tubing for beverage dispensing and food handling, extruded coffee stirrers, cheese spreader applicators, sticks and tubing for frozen foods, etc
Sales Manager: Frank Lofrano
Plant Manager: Jason Gribbins
Number Employees: 100-249
Square Footage: 240000
Parent Co: Tekni-Plex
Other Locations:
Action Technology
City of Industry CA
Brands:
Ablex

18392 **Actionpac Scales & Automation**
1300 Yarnell Pl
Oxnard, CA 93033 805-487-0403
Fax: 805-487-0719 800-394-0154
info@actionpacscales.com
www.actionpacscales.com
Manufacturer and exporter of packaging machinery including automated bag filling; also, weighing machinery
President: John Dishion
Sales & Services Manager: Johnathan Cantalupo
Sales Assistant: Jennifer Taylor
Purchasing Manager: Justin Pence
Estimated Sales: $500,000-$1 Million
Number Employees: 3
Square Footage: 4000

18393 **Activon Products**
123 Commercial Drive
Beaver Dam, WI 53916-1160 970-484-5560
Fax: 970-482-6184 800-841-0410
rjoseph@activon.com www.activon.com
Biodegradable sanitizers in tablet form
President: Todd Howe
Marketing Director: Jim Heeren
Parent Co: PR Pharmacuticals

18394 **Actron**
PO Box 572244
Tarzana, CA 91357-2244 818-654-9744
Fax: 818-654-9788 800-866-8887
flymaster@actroninc.com www.actroninc.com
Manufacturer and exporter of flying-insect control systems and washable and decorative insect light and glue traps
Director Marketing: Abe Thomas
Estimated Sales: Below $500,000
Brands:
Actron
Efk
G-T 200/100 Ilt
Gardner
Haccp
Industrial
Wall Sconce
Ws-50/Ws-50 Bl

18395 **Acuair**
1700 Cannon Road
Northfield, MN 55057-1680 952-707-1286
Fax: 952-707-0914 www.frickcompressors.com
Parent Co: York International

18396 **Acumen Data Systems**
2223 Westfield St
West Springfield, MA 01089 413-737-4800
Fax: 413-737-5544 888-816-0933
info@acumendatasystems.com
www.acumendatasystems.com
Manufacturer and exporter of computer software for bakery management including order, production, formulation, delivery, billing, etc
President: El Squires
VP: Dan Coffey
Estimated Sales: $2.5 - 5,000,000
Number Employees: 10-19
Brands:
Clockview
Inview
Laborview
Opmview
Proview

18397 **Ad Art Litho.**
3133 Chester Ave
Cleveland, OH 44114 216-696-1460
Fax: 216-696-1463 800-875-6368
menugrfx@ix.netcom.com
www.menugraphics.com
Menus and menu covers; also, printing and silk screening available
President: Felicia West
CFO: Felicia West
Director Operations: Felicia West
Estimated Sales: $1 - 2,500,000
Number Employees: 10

18398 **Ad-Pak Systems**
3545 North Pkwy
Cumming, GA 30040 770-889-0033
Fax: 770-889-0189 sales@adpacksystems.com
www.adpaksystems.com
Labeling equipment
President: Ray Hawkins
Estimated Sales: $1 - 3 Million
Number Employees: 5-9

18399 **AdPro**
30500 Solon Industrial Parkway
Solon, OH 44139 440-542-1111
www.adpro.net
Manufacturer and importer of boxes including folding, set-up and corrugated; shrink packaging available; also, designer of sales promotion and marketing materials
VP: Stephen Lebby
Estimated Sales: $2.5-5 Million
Number Employees: 20-49
Square Footage: 65000
Parent Co: ADPRO

18400 **Adamatic**
814 44th St NW Ste 103
Auburn, WA 98001 206-322-5474
Fax: 206-322-5425 800-578-2547
info@adamatic.com www.adamatic.com
Manufacturer and exporter of bakers' equipment including ovens and machinery; also, refrigerators
General manager and Controller: Michael Hartnett
R&D: Walter Kopp
Quality Control: Michael Liberatore
General Manager: John Muldowney
Estimated Sales: $10 - 20 Million
Number Employees: 55
Parent Co: PMI Food Equipment Group
Type of Packaging: Consumer, Food Service

18401 **Adamation**
7039 E Slauson Ave
Commerce, CA 90040-3620 323-722-7900
Fax: 323-726-4700 800-225-3075
info@adamationinc.com www.adamationinc.com
Manufacturer and exporter of dish washing and silver burnishing machinery, tray conveyors and food waste shredder disposal systems
Owner: Jeff Branstein
CEO: Hubert Perry, Jr.
CFO: Joe Braver
Operations Manager: John Onu
Plant Manager: Cliff Bergland
Purchasing Manager: Mike Schulng
Estimated Sales: $5 Million
Number Employees: 50-99
Square Footage: 42000
Parent Co: Winbro Group
Brands:
Adamation
Lusterator

18402 **Adams**
2131 16th St
Fargo, ND 58107-2048 701-277-9422
Fax: 701-277-9411 800-342-4748
info@adamsfargo.com www.adamsfargo.com
A leading maufacturers representative for hundreds of material handling and storage products.
Owner: Al Hager
Manager: Al Hager
Estimated Sales: $2.5-5 Million
Number Employees: 5-9
Square Footage: 6000
Type of Packaging: Consumer, Food Service, Private Label

18403 **Adams Business Forms**
200 Jackson St
Topeka, KS 66603 785-233-4101
Fax: 785-233-4291
customerservice@cardinalbrands.com
www.cardinalbrands.com
Business forms
President: Rodney Olson

18404 **Adams Signs & Graphics**
1100 Industrial Ave SW
Massillon, OH 44647 330-832-9844
Fax: 330-832-6999 888-886-9911
clevalandeast@adamsigns.com
www.adamsigns.com
Electric, neon, plastic and aluminum signs; also, interior graphics available, also message centers and reimaging
President: Joseph Pugliese
Estimated Sales: $10-15 Million
Number Employees: 50-99
Square Footage: 70000

18405 **Adapto Storage Products**
PO Box 111600
Hialeah, FL 33011-1600 305-499-4800
Fax: 305-885-8677 info@adapto.com
www.adapto.com
Steel storage equipment
President: Joe Carignan
Quality Control: Elisa Hannna
Plant Manager: Ernie Ignaza
Purchasing: Jim Shutes
Number Employees: 70
Square Footage: 320000

18406 **Adcapitol**
1400 Goldmire Road
Monroe, NC 28111-5017 704-283-2147
Fax: 704-289-6857 800-868-7111
sales@adcapitol.com www.adcapitol.com
Cut and sew uniforms and promotional printed aprons, tote bags, tablecloths, napkins, lunch bags, banners and caps
President: Lance Dunn
Estimated Sales: $50-100 Million
Number Employees: 300
Square Footage: 100000
Parent Co: Dunn Manufacturing
Type of Packaging: Bulk

18407 **Adco Manufacturing**
2170 Academy Ave
Sanger, CA 93657 559-875-5563
Fax: 559-875-7665 sales@adcomfg.com
www.adcomfg.com

Manufacturer and exporter of packaging machinery for cartons
President: Frank Hoffman
CEO: Kate King
VP Marketing: Scott Reed
VP Sales: Paul Kessock
Human Resources Manager: Maureen Say
Operations/Plant Manager: Dale Kingen
Purchasing Director: Juanita Johnson
Estimated Sales: $24 Million
Number Employees: 130
Square Footage: 76000
Type of Packaging: Consumer, Food Service, Private Label

18408 Adcraft
940 S Oyster Bay Rd
Hicksville, NY 11801 516-433-4534
Fax: 800-447-7751 800-223-7750
Sales@Hdsheldon.com www.admiralcraft.com
Equipment, utensils and supplies
President: Matthew Lobman
Owner: Brett Ashley
EVP: Richard Powers
Estimated Sales: $
Number Employees: 44
Square Footage: 100000
Type of Packaging: Food Service
Brands:
Atlas
Hercules

18409 Adept Solutions, Inc.
990 Klamath Lane
Suite 6
Yuba City, CA 95993 530-751-5100
Fax: 530-313-5447 help@adept-solutions.net
www.adept-solutions.net
Specialty ingredients and technical services
President: Bud Sanchez
Owner: Jason Neukirchner
Operations Manager: Geoffrey Granger
Estimated Sales: $370,000
Number Employees: 4
Square Footage: 2852
Type of Packaging: Consumer, Food Service

18410 Adept Technology
5960 Inglewood Dr Ste 300
Pleasanton, CA 94588 925-245-3400
Fax: 925-960-0452 www.adept.com
CEO: John Dulchinos
Estimated Sales: H
Number Employees: 100-249

18411 Adheron Coatings Corporation
16420 Kilbourne Ave
Oak Forest, IL 60452 708-687-0010
cgrinter@andheroncoatings.com
www.andheroncoatings.com

18412 Adhesive Label
2916 Nevada Ave N
New Hope, MN 55427 763-746-2900
www.adhesivelabelinc.com
Labels
President: Steve Ericcson
VP: Diane Hurley
Estimated Sales: $4 Million
Number Employees: 7
Square Footage: 14000

18413 Adhesive Products, Inc.
4727 E 48th St
Vernon, CA 90058-2799 323-589-5516
Fax: 323-589-6460 800-669-5516
wpshattuck@api-la.com
www.adhesiveproductsinc.com
Resin emulsion, starch based and hot melt adhesives, water activated paper and reinforced gummed tapes and custom printed self adhesive labels and tapes
Manager: Ted Tritlett
VP: W Shattuck
Operations Manager: William Almas
Estimated Sales: $2.5-5 Million
Number Employees: 10-19
Square Footage: 56000
Type of Packaging: Consumer, Bulk

18414 Adhesive Technologies
3 Merrill Industrial Dr
Hampton, NH 03842-1995
Fax: 603-926-1780 800-458-3486
marketing@adhesivetech.com
www.adhesivetech.com
Manufacturer, importer and exporter of application-based systems: hot melts, sprays, solids, 2-part reactives and a wide range of applicators (glue guns) from craft to industrial.
Chief Executive Officer, Founder: Peter Melendy
Chief Executive Officer, Founder: Peter Melendy
Marketing Director: Laura Scaccia
VP Sales: John Starer
Public Relations: Laura Scaccia
Estimated Sales: $20-50 Million
Number Employees: 50-99
Brands:
Crafty
Floralpro
Magic Melt

18415 Adhesives Research, Inc.
400 Seaks Run Rd.
Glen Rock, PA 17327 717-235-7979
Fax: 717-235-8320 880-445-6240
www.adhesivesresearch.com
Developer and manufacturer of custom, high-performance specialty films, pressure-sensitive adhesives, tapes, coatings including dissolvable films and laminates.
President & Director: George Stolakis
Estimated Sales: $118 Million
Number Employees: 415
Square Footage: 240000
Type of Packaging: Consumer

18416 Admatch Corporation
36 W 25th St
Fl 8
New York, NY 10010 212-696-2600
Fax: 212-696-0620 800-777-9909
ask@admatch.com www.admatch.com
Manufacturer, exporter and importer of wood and paper matches with custom printed boxes and books, wood toothpicks, paper napkins, place mats, coasters and tissues
President: Mark Nackman
Sales Manager: Agatha Laura
Estimated Sales: $10-20 Million
Number Employees: 10-19
Type of Packaging: Consumer, Food Service, Private Label, Bulk
Brands:
Admatch
Promotissues

18417 Admix Inc.
234 Abby Rd
Manchester, NH 03103 603-627-2340
Fax: 603-627-2019 800-466-2369
mixing@admix.com www.admix.com
President: Louis Beaudette
Estimated Sales: $5-10 Million
Number Employees: 20-49

18418 Adolph Gottscho
835 Lehigh Ave
Union, NJ 07083-7631 908-688-2400
Fax: 908-687-9250 sales@gottscho.com
www.gottscho.com
President: Eva Gottscho
Estimated Sales: $5 - 10 Million
Number Employees: 20-49

18419 Adrian Fabricators/Cargotainer
545 Industrial Dr
PO Box 518
Adrian, MI 49221-9755 517-266-5700
Fax: 517-266-5751 800-221-3794
sales@cargotainer.com www.cargotainer.com
Manufacturer and exporter of welded wire mesh products including pallet racks and containers
President: Geoffrey Scully
CFO: Geoffrey Scully
National Sales Manager: Larry Cunningham
Estimated Sales: $10 - 20 Million
Number Employees: 10-19

18420 Adrienne's Gourmet Foods
849 Ward Dr
Santa Barbara, CA 93111 805-964-6848
Fax: 805-964-8698 800-937-7010
www.adriennesgourmetfoods.com
Manufacturer, importer and exporter of the finest organic and kosher cookies, crackers and high protein pastas
President: John O'Donnell
Vice President: Adrienne O'Donnell
Estimated Sales: $5-10 Million
Number Employees: 20-49
Type of Packaging: Consumer, Food Service, Private Label, Bulk
Brands:
Appeteasers
California Crisps
Courtney's
Courtney's Organic Water Crackers
Darcia's Organic Crostini
Lavosh Hawaii
Lavosh-Hawaii
Papadina Pasta
Papadini Hi-Protein

18421 Adstick Custom Labels
11000 East 53rd Avenue
Denver, CO 80239 303-388-5821
Fax: 303-321-4536 800-255-7314
info@adstick.com www.adstick.com
Pressure sensitive tapes and labels
CEO: R Stillahn
CEO: Brad Stillahn
General Manager: Robert Morland
Estimated Sales: $3 - 5 Million
Number Employees: 5-9
Square Footage: 14000

18422 Advance Adhesives
2403 N Oakley Ave
Chicago, IL 60647 773-278-3988
Fax: 773-227-2103 www.aabbitt.com
President: Benjamin B Sarmas
Estimated Sales: $50 - 100 Million
Number Employees: 50-99

18423 Advance Automated Systems
3775 14 Mile Rd NW
PO Box 476
Sparta, MI 49345 616-887-0316
Fax: 616-887-8407
www.advanceautomatedsystems.com
President: Dale Montgomery
Estimated Sales: $1 - 2.5 000,000
Number Employees: 1-4

18424 Advance Cleaning Products
PO Box 170950
Milwaukee, WI 53217-8086 414-937-8181
Fax: 414-344-3458 800-925-5326
mark@advancecleaning.com
www.advancecleaningsupplies.com
Self-polishing floor polish and cleaners including all purpose, toilet bowl and liquid soap
President: Mark Halaska
Estimated Sales: Less than $1 Million
Number Employees: 10-19
Square Footage: 120000
Brands:
Easy Strip
Floor Suds
Perma Shine
Scrub 'n Shine
Shine-Off
Snappy
Ultrashine

18425 Advance Coating & Converting
1229 S Dickerson Road
Goodlettsville, TN 37072-2802 615-851-2000
Fax: 615-851-5683 advancedcoating1@aol.com
www.hotmeltcoating.com
Hot melt applicators and replacement parts, packaging
President: Gary D Faulkner
Estimated Sales: $1 - 3 Million
Number Employees: 5-9

18426 Advance Energy Technologies
1 Solar Dr
Clifton Park, NY 12065 518-371-2140
Fax: 518-371-0737 800-724-0198
sales@advanceet.com www.advanceet.com
Manufacturer and exporter of walk-in coolers and freezers, refrigerated warehouses, foam injected insulated panels, clean rooms and environmental chambers.
President: Tim Carlo
General Manager: Dan Carlo

Estimated Sales: $10-20 Million
Number Employees: 20-49
Square Footage: 30000
Type of Packaging: Bulk

18427 Advance Engineering Company
12025 Dixie Redfort charter
Township, MI 48239 313-537-3500
Fax: 989-435-2860 800-497-6388
sales@adveng.net www.adveng.net
Plastic trays, pallets and packaging
Manager: Keith Vining
Customer Service: Angela Frasher
General Manager: Gene Cook
Estimated Sales: $10-20,000,000
Number Employees: 20-49
Parent Co: L&W Engineering

18428 Advance Fitting Corporation
218 Centralia St
Elkhorn, WI 53121 262-723-6699
Fax: 262-723-6643 advance@genevaonline.com
www.advancefittings.com
Manufacturer, importer and exporter of filtration equipment, fittings, clamps, tanks, sampling devices, tube and pipe supports, tubes and valves; also, custom fabrications available
President: Edward W Mentzer
VP: Roger Klemp
Marketing/Sales: Jeffery Klemp
VP of Sales: Peter Mentzer
Estimated Sales: $5-10 Million
Number Employees: 20-49

18429 Advance Grower Solutions
3343 Locke Ave
Suite 107
Fort Worth, TX 76107 503-646-5581
Fax: 503-646-0622 800-367-7082
sales@advgrower.com www.advgrower.com
Wine industry computer software
Owner: Dan Harris
Estimated Sales: $3 - 5 Million
Number Employees: 10-19

18430 Advance Lifts
701 Kirk Rd
St Charles, IL 60174 630-584-9881
Fax: 630-584-9405 800-843-3625
sales@advancelifts.com www.advancelifts.com
Hydraulic scissor lifts and recycling equipment
President: Henry Renken
VP Sales: David Ferguson
Estimated Sales: $20-50 Million
Number Employees: 50-99
Square Footage: 120000

18431 Advance Storage Products
7341 Lincoln Way
Garden Grove, CA 92841 714-902-9000
Fax: 714-902-9001 888-478-7422
asp@advstore.com www.advancestorage.com
Technology-driven company dedicated to developing the most efficient and economical solution to our customers' material storage needs. State-of-the-art engineering-providing turnkey systems. In business over 40 years
President: Chuck Kish
CFO: Rick Callow
R&D: T J Imholte
Marketing/Public Relations: Judy Pugh
Sales Director: Adel Santner
Operations Manager: T Imholte
Purchasing Manager: Lisa Ramirez
Estimated Sales: $20 - 50 Million
Number Employees: 20-49
Brands:
Pushback

18432 (HQ)Advance Tabco
200 Heartland Blvd
Edgewood, NY 11717 631-242-8270
Fax: 631-242-6900 800-645-3166
greed@advancetobaco.com
www.advancetabco.com
Stainless steel sinks, worktables, shelving and dish tables; also, aluminum and racks and wire shelving
President: Penny Hutner
VP: Danny Schwartz
Estimated Sales: $50-100 Million
Number Employees: 50-99
Brands:
Advance Tabco

18433 Advance Weight Systems
409 Main St
PO Box 6
Grafton, OH 44044 440-926-3691
sales@advancew8.com
www.advancew8.com
Scales, weighers and conveyors for food packaging systems
President: Clar Lahl Jr
VP Sales: John Koliha
Estimated Sales: Below $5 Million
Number Employees: 10-19

18434 Advanced Coating & Converting Systems
1229 S Dickerson Road
Goodlettsville, TN 37072-2802 615-851-2000
Fax: 615-851-5683 advancedcoating1@aol.com
hotmeltcoating.com

18435 Advanced Control Technologies
6805 Hillsdale Court
P.O.Box 502948
Indianapolis, IN 46250-7948 317-806-2750
Fax: 317-806-2770 800-886-2281
info@act-solutions.com www.act-solutions.com
Manufacturer and exporter of HVAC controls
President: Gary Colip
Estimated Sales: $5-10,000,000
Number Employees: 50-99

18436 Advanced Design Awning& Sign
1600 29th St
Cloquet, MN 55720-2886 218-879-9712
Fax: 218-879-2936 800-566-8368
craig@advancedawning.com
www.advancedawningdesign.com
Commercial awnings
President and CFO: Craig Simensen
Estimated Sales: Below $5 Million
Number Employees: 10-19

18437 Advanced Design Manufacturing
1281-A Franquette Ave
Concord, CA 94520-5213 925-680-8764
Fax: 925-680-7252 800-690-0002
sales@sneezeguard.com www.sneezeguards.com
Stock and custom sneeze guards
Owner: David Murry
CFO: Richard Harris
R & D: Peter Otool
Sales Director: Jeff Bigby
Production Director: Andy McGrath
Estimated Sales: $5-10 Million
Number Employees: 10-19
Square Footage: 88000

18438 Advanced Detection Systems
4740 W Electric Ave
Milwaukee, WI 53219 414-672-0553
Fax: 414-672-5354 dsmith@adsdetection.com
www.adsdetection.com
Manufacturer and exporter of electronic metal detectors with reject devices, conveyors and pipeline systems; also, washdown severe-duty models
Human Resources: Sue Medbed
Sales Manager: Dave Smith
Production Manager: Chuck Morgan
Estimated Sales: $10-20,000,000
Number Employees: 50-99
Parent Co: Venturedyne

18439 Advanced Distribution &Packaging
2349 Millers Lane
Louisville, KY 40216 502-449-1720
Fax: 502-778-1718
contactADS@advancedistribution.com
www.advancedistribution.com
A packaging, warehouse and distributor company for the food industry
President: Aldo Dagnino
R&D: J Perrier
Quality Control: L Defaint
Sales: Judy Jaedine
Operations: Aldo Dagnino
Plant Manager: Jorge Monge
Estimated Sales: $300,000-500,000
Number Employees: 1-4
Square Footage: 2400000
Type of Packaging: Consumer, Food Service

18440 Advanced Equipment
2411 Vauxhall Place
Richmond, BC V6V 1Z5
Canada 604-276-8989
Fax: 604-276-8962 info@advancedfreezer.com
www.advancedfreezer.com
Manufacturer and exporter of freezers
President: Peter Pao
Purchasing Agent: Thomas Leung
Estimated Sales: Below $5 Million
Number Employees: 40
Square Footage: 80000
Brands:
Advanced Equipment

18441 Advanced Ergonomics
7460 Warren Pkwy
Suite 265
Frisco, TX 75034 972-294-7600
Fax: 972-294-7620 800-682-0169
aei@advancedergonomics.com
www.advancedergonomics.com
Consultant providing pre-employment testing services and job site analysis
President: Harry Broxson
CEO: Terry Broxson
Estimated Sales: Below $5,000,000
Number Employees: 15

18442 Advanced Food ProcessingEquipment
PO Box 470
Mount Vernon, OH 43050 740-392-4685
Fax: 740-392-4785 sales@afpe.com
www.afpe.com
Package spiral freezers and steam cookers, site-built spiral freezers, fluidized belt and tray freezers, car/dolley freezers, contact belt freezers, pouch water and prine chillers, case/box freezers and chillers
President: Michael Webber
R&D: John Webber
Estimated Sales: $1 - 5 000,000
Number Employees: 1-4

18443 Advanced Food Systems
133 Lake Bluff Drive
Columbus, OH 43235 888-871-9885
Fax: 888-807-9632 sendmeinfo@afsusa.net
www.advancedfoodsys.com
President: Denny Vincent
Estimated Sales: $300,000-500,000
Number Employees: 1-4

18444 Advanced Food Systems
2141 E Highland Ave # 10
Phoenix, AZ 85016-4736 602-522-8282
Fax: 602-522-1856 sales@afsi.com
www.afsi.com
Food-specific distribution and financial computer software
CEO: Kurien Jacob
CFO: Pam Cooper
Vice President of Services: Abe Nezvadovitz
Marketing Manager: Jody Schafer
Senior Vice President of Sales and Marke: Carl McCauley
Chief Technical Officer: Suhas Gudihal
Estimated Sales: $20-50 Million
Number Employees: 50-99
Brands:
Foodbis
Fooddistribute
Foodedi
Foodscan

18445 Advanced Industrial Systems
21068 Bake Pkwy
Suite 200
Lake Forest, CA 92630-2185 208-237-2222
Fax: 949-597-9898 800-658-3850
sales@advancedindustrial.com
www.advancedindustrial.com
Real-time process control systems, human-machine interfaces, supervisory and cell control - SCADA systems, statistical process control
President: Gene Kaplan
Estimated Sales: Below $500,000

18446 Advanced Ingredients, Inc.
8421 Wayzata Blvd.
Suite 225
Golden Valley, MN 55426
Fax: 763-201-5820 888-238-4647
info@advancedingredients.com
www.advancedingredients.com
Processor and exporter of specialty ingredients
President: Fred Greenland
Estimated Sales: $1 - 3 Million
Number Employees: 5-9
Brands:
Bakesmart®
Energysmart®
Energysource®
Fruitrim®
Fruitsavr®
Fruitsource®
Moisturlok®
Plus and Moisturlok®

18447 (HQ)Advanced Instruments
2 Technology Way
Norwood, MA 02062 781-320-9000
Fax: 781-320-8181 800-225-4034
info@aicompanies.comÿ www.aicompanies.com
Manufacturer and exporter of clinical, industrial laboratory and food and dairy quality control equipment.
President: John Coughlin
CEO: John Coughlin
Marketing Manager: Kristen Vuotto
Sales: John Ryder
Plant Manager: Mike Graham
Estimated Sales: $10-20 Million
Number Employees: 50-99
Number of Brands: 4
Number of Products: 6
Square Footage: 40000
Other Locations:
Advanced Instruments
Bethesda MD
Brands:
Advanced
Fiske
Fiske Associates
Fluorophos Test System

18448 Advanced Instruments Incc.
2 Technology Way
Norwood, MA 02062 781-320-9000
Fax: 781-320-8181 800-225-4034
info@aicompanies.com www.aicompanies.com
Equipment for the dairy and food industry.
Director: Blanton Wiggin
Vice President: Pierre Emond
Vice President Sales: John Ryder
Number Employees: 94

18449 Advanced Insulation Concepts
8055 Production Dr
Florence, KY 41042-3094 859-342-8550
Fax: 859-342-5445 800-826-3100
info@aicinsulate.com
www.advancedinsulationconcepts.com
Manufacturer and exporter of insulated panels and doors for refrigerated and other atmosphere-controlled rooms including horizontal sliding, bi-parting, vertical lift and swing. Also insulated fire wall panels
President: W Burton Lloyd
VP: Michael Lloyd
Sales: Michael Lloyd
Estimated Sales: $6-10 Million
Number Employees: 30
Square Footage: 62000
Brands:
Insulrock
Isowall
Regent

18450 (HQ)Advanced Labelworx, Inc
1006 Larson Drive
Oak Ridge, TN 37830 865-966-8711
Fax: 865-813-9918
marketing@advancedlabelworx.com
www.advancedlabelworx.com
Manufacturer and exporter of pressure sensitive paper labels and tapes
President: Lana Sellers
CFO: Clyde Duncan
Quality Control: Gabrina Kelly
Number Employees: 10
Square Footage: 120000
Type of Packaging: Bulk

18451 Advanced Micro Controls
20 Gear Dr
Terryville, CT 06786 860-585-1254
Fax: 860-584-1973 sales@amci.com
www.amci.com
Hardware and software for packaging machinery
President: William Herbs
VP: Peter Serv
Estimated Sales: $20 - 50 Million
Number Employees: 20-49
Brands:
Ez Pack

18452 Advanced Organics
701 W Johnson St
Upper Sandusky, OH 43351 419-209-0216
Fax: 419-209-5010 aoimkolarik@udata.com
Organic waste disposal service, sanitation
President: Doug Craig
Estimated Sales: $2.5-5 000,000
Number Employees: 20-49
Type of Packaging: Bulk

18453 Advanced Packaging Techniques Corporation
393 Bentley Place
Buffalo Grove, IL 60089-2500 847-808-9227
Fax: 630-887-0771 jayb@airprocesssystems.com
Packaging machinery soces consultants
President: Barbara Bloom
Number Employees: 2

18454 Advanced Plastic Coating
1407 Corporate Dr
Parsons, KS 67357 620-421-1660
Fax: 620-421-1662 adpowdergreg@par1.net
www.advcoatings.com
Custom manufacturer of plastic coated wire products including trays, ice cream cup holders and condiment holders for drive-in car service
President: Don Alexander
CFO: Don Alexander
R&D: Don Alexander
Quality Control: Don Alexander
Number Employees: 10
Square Footage: 20000
Brands:
Serv-A-Car
Wire Rite

18455 Advanced Poly-Packaging
P.O.Box 7040
Akron, OH 44306 330-785-4000
Fax: 330-785-4010 800-754-4403
sales@advancedpoly.com
www.advancedpoly.com
Bags including pre-opened and printed polyfilm and printers, ribbon and packaging equipment including automatic bagging
President: Tony Baker
VP of Sales: Stuart Baker
National Sales Manager: Dan Moute
Estimated Sales: $20-50 Million
Number Employees: 100-249
Brands:
Advanced Polybagger

18456 Advanced Process Solutions
221 Mount Zion Road
Henryville, IN 47126-8658 888-294-8118

18457 Advanced Separation Technologies
5315 Great Oak Drive
Lakeland, FL 33815-3113 863-687-4460
Fax: 863-687-9362 ast@calgoncarbon.com
www.asapsys.com
Ion exchange, biotechnology, chromatography, fermentation, separators
President: Robert O'Brian
Estimated Sales: $5-10 Million
Number Employees: 60

18458 Advanced Separations andProcess Systems
6111 Pepsi Way
Windsor, WI 53598-9642 608-846-1130
Fax: 608-846-1144 800-879-8461
bob.cadwalader@asapsys.com www.asapsys.com
Software, systems integrator, membrane systems, resource recovery, separation equipment
Number Employees: 120

18459 Advanced Software Designs
1350 Elbridge Payne Rd Ste 150
Chesterfield, MO 63017 636-532-6021
Fax: 636-532-2935 info@asdsoftware.com
www.asdsoftware.com
Formula management software for nutritional labeling, production assistance and quality control measures
President: Ray Cook
Marketing Director: Stephanie Hanebrink
Account Executive: Ted Pliakos
Estimated Sales: $5-10 Million
Number Employees: 10-19
Brands:
Product Vision

18460 Advanced Surfaces Corporation
3355 Liberty Road
Villa Rica, GA 30180 770-920-0066
Fax: 770-947-9737 800-963-4632
www.advancedsurfacescorp.com
Specializing in flooring for the food and beverage industries.
President: Paul Patuka
Vice President: Kerry Patuka
General Sales Manager: Tom Young
Florida/Southern GA&AL Sales: Brent Parrish
Tennesee Sales: Brian Krost
Mid-South Sales: Brad Krost
Alabama Sales: Don Holman
Operations Manager: Justo Castro
Estimated Sales: 5.67 Million
Number Employees: 49

18461 Advanced Technology Corporation/Vetstar
79 N Franklin Turnpike
Suite 103
Ramsey, NJ 07446 201-934-7127
Fax: 201-236-1891 sales@vetstar.com
www.vetstar.com
Manufacturer and exporter of laboratory information management system software
President: John Cummins
Sales Manager: Susan Cummins
Number Employees: 5-9
Brands:
V-Lims
Vetstar

18462 Advanced Uniflo Technologies
1850 N Ohio Ave
Wichita, KS 67214-1530 316-688-0000
Fax: 316-267-3387 800-688-0400
uniflo@gplains.com www.unifloconveyor.com
Conveyor systems including small package, pallet handling, belt, chain, live roller and accumulation; also, steel fabrication services available
CEO: Steve Nulty
Sales Manager: Chuck Driskell
Marketing Technical Specialist: Brenda Salvati
Estimated Sales: $10-20 Million
Number Employees: 50-99
Square Footage: 80000
Brands:
Uniflo

18463 Advantage Puck Group
1 Plastics Road
Corry, PA 16407 814-664-4810
Fax: 814-663-6081 sales@advantagepuck.com
www.adv-puck.com
Manufacturer and exporter of plastic product carriers for assembly line filling
President: Kurt Sieber
Estimated Sales: $1-2.5 Million
Number Employees: 19
Brands:
Puck

18464 Advantage Puck Technologies
1 Plastics Road
Corry, PA 16407 814-664-4810
Fax: 814-663-6081 800-396-7825
Sales@AdvantagePuck.com www.adv-puck.com
Pucks and puck handling machinery
Number Employees: 10

18465 **Advantec Process Systems**
95 Wyngate Dr
Newnan, GA 30265 770-253-1021
Fax: 770-251-3437 dgnann@charter.com
www.advantecprocesssystems.com

18466 **Advantek**
7900 West 78th Street
Suite 180
Eden Prairie, MN 55439 952-746-9850
Fax: 952-938-1800 info@advantek.com
www.advantek.com

President: Bruce Bratten
CEO: Bruce Batten
CFO: Mike Eggers
Owner: Jared Koll
Quality Control: Mike Miller
Number Employees: 250-499

18467 **Advantus Corp.**
12276 San Jose Blvd
Building 618
Jacksonville, FL 32223 904-482-0091
Fax: 904-482-0099 www.mcgillinc.com
Manufacturer and exporter of coin changers
President: Wayne Schwartzman
R&D: Becky McDaniel
VP Sales: Jim Booth
Estimated Sales: $5 - 10 Million
Number Employees: 10-19
Square Footage: 260000

18468 **Advent Machine Company**
6815 E Washington Blvd
Commerce, CA 90040-1905 323-728-5367
Fax: 323-728-2443 800-846-7716
info@adventmachine.net
www.adventmachine.net
Pressure-sensitive or plain paper labels
Owner: Richard G Ealy
Estimated Sales: $1 - 3 Million
Number Employees: 5-9

18469 **Adwest Technologies**
151 Trapping Brook Rd
Wellsville, NY 14895 585-593-1405
Fax: 585-593-6614 adwestny@adelphia.net
www.adwestusa.com
Air pollution control systems
President: Jack Preston
Sales: Brian Cannon
Number Employees: 50-100
Parent Co: Adwest Technologies

18470 **Aearo Company**
5457 W 79th St
Indianapolis, IN 46268 317-692-6666
Fax: 317-692-6772 800-225-9038
customer_service@aearo.com www.aearo.com
President: Michael McLain
Estimated Sales: I
Number Employees: 1,000-4,999

18471 **Aep Industries Inc.**
125 Phillips Ave
South Hackensack, NJ 07606 201-641-6600
Fax: 201-807-6801 800-999-2374
www.aepinc.com
Plastic packaging film.
President/CEO/Chairman of the Board: J. Brendan Barba
Managing Principal: Kenneth Avia
Executive VP/Finance/CFO: Paul M. Feeney
Vice President-Finance: Richard E. Davis
Vice President and Treasurer: James B. Rafferty
Executive Vice President, Sales/Marketin: John J. Powers
Executive Vice President, Operations: Paul C. Vegliante
Senior Vice President-Manufacturing: David J. Cron

18472 **Aeration Industries International**
4100 Peavey Rd
Chaska, MN 55318 952-448-6789
Fax: 952-448-7293 800-328-8287
aiii.info@aireo2.com www.aireo2.com
Manufactures waste water treatment systems & equipment, including the dual-process Triton aerator and mixer to provide solutions for challenging wastewater needs.
President: Daniel Durda
VP: Brian Cohen
Estimated Sales: $10-20 Million
Number Employees: 20-49
Square Footage: 250000
Brands:
Aire-02
Aire-02 Triton
Microfloat
Turbo
Unisystem

18473 **Aeration Technologies**
P.O.Box 488
North Andover, MA 01845-0488 978-475-6385
Fax: 978-475-6387 info@aertec.com
www.aertec.com
Wastewater aeration systems
Owner: R Gary Gilbert
Office Manager: Linda Corners
Estimated Sales: $500,000-$1 Million
Number Employees: 5-9

18474 **Aerco International**
159 Paris Ave
Northvale, NJ 07647-2095 201-768-2400
Fax: 201-768-7789 www.aerco.com
Water heaters, condensing boilers and steam generators
President: Fred Depuy
VP: Fred F Campagna
Marketing Director: Mark Croche
Estimated Sales: $10-20 Million
Number Employees: 100-249

18475 **Aercology**
8 Custom Drive
Old Saybrook, CT 06475-4009 860-399-7941
Fax: 860-399-7049 800-826-6123
aercolory@snet.net www.aercology.com
Air filtration
Chairman, President, Chief Executive Off: Bill Cook
Estimated Sales: $5-10 Million
Number Employees: 50-100

18476 **Aero Company**
5457 W 79th St
Indianapolis, IN 46268-1675 317-692-6666
Fax: 317-692-6772 800-225-9038
info@aearo.com www.aearo.com
Manufacturer and exporter of protective eye, face and headwear for the food processing industry
President: Micheal A McLain
CEO: Mike McClain
CFO: Jeffrey S Kulka
VP of Marketing: Jim Hall
Director Marketing: Jim Gray
Estimated Sales: I
Number Employees: 1,000-4,999
Brands:
Aosafety
E-A-R
Peltor
Srx

18477 **Aero Company**
90 Mechanic St
Southbridge, MA 01550-2555 508-764-5500
Fax: 508-764-3350 800-678-4163
aearo@mmcweb.com www.aearo.com
Manufactures and distributes safety equipment
President: Mike Mc Clain
Plant Manager: Earl Vancelette
Estimated Sales: $5 - 10 Million
Number Employees: 20-49
Parent Co: Aearo Company

18478 **Aero Housewares**
Ste C
600 Glynn St N
Fayetteville, GA 30214-6716 770-914-4240
Fax: 770-914-4236 www.aeroplastics.com
Injection molded plastic products including storage containers, bowls, tableware, plates, tumblers, microwave containers, snack trays, etc
President: Jeffry Goldberg
CFO: Andrew Rice
Director Marketing/Sales: Heather Plaster
National Sales Manager: Steven Waugh
Regional Sales Manager: Keith Gouin
Estimated Sales: $20-50 Million
Number Employees: 20

18479 **Aero Manufacturing Company**
310 Allwood Road
PO Box 1250
Clifton, NJ 07012 973-473-5300
Fax: 973-473-3794 800-631-8378
sales@aeromfg.com www.aeromfg.com
Stainless steel sinks, tables, dishtables, cabinets, shelving, and custom fabrication.
President/CEO: Wayne Phillips
Number Employees: 50-99
Square Footage: 600000
Brands:
Aerospec

18480 **(HQ)Aero Tec Laboratories/ATL**
45 Spear Rd Industrial Park
Ramsey, NJ 07446-1251 201-825-1400
Fax: 201-825-1962 800-526-5330
atl@atlinc.com www.atlinc.com
Collapsible pillow-style storage tanks
President: Peter J Regna
VP, Contracts: I. Janeiro
VP, R&D: R. Clark
VP of Sales: David Dack
VP, Operations: L. Damico
Estimated Sales: $3 - 5 Million
Number Employees: 50-99
Square Footage: 280000
Other Locations:
Aero Tec Laboratories/ATL
Bletchley, Milton Keynes

18481 **Aero-Motive Company**
333 Knightsbridge Pkwy
Suite 200
Lincolnshire, IL 60069 847-353-2500
Fax: 847-353-2500 800-999-8559
wctechsup@molex.com
www.woodhead.com/woodhead/index.jsp?langPref = english
President: Micheal Gies
Number Employees: 100-249
Parent Co: Woodhead Industries

18482 **Aero-Power Unitized Fueler**
103 Smithtown Blvd
Smithtown, NY 11787 631-366-4362
Fax: 631-366-0905 info@areotank.com
www.areotank.com
Owner: Rudy Benit
Estimated Sales: $1 - 3 Million
Number Employees: 1-4

18483 **AeroFreeze, Inc.**
2551 Viking Way
Richmond, BC, BC V6V 1N4
Canada 604-278-4118
Fax: 604-278-4847 sales@aerofreeze.com
www.aerofreeze.com
Manufacturers of freezers, chillers and air cooling products.

18484 **Aerocon**
1707 Langhorne Newtown Rd # 1
Langhorne, PA 19047 215-860-6056
Fax: 215-860-8606 www.inbusiness.com
Owner: Rosemary Caligiuri
Parent Co: Vac-U-Max

18485 **Aerofreeze**
P.O.Box 2439
Redmond, WA 98073 425-869-8889
Fax: 425-869-8839 sales@aerofreeze.com
www.aerofreeze.com
Freezing units, plate and belt freezers
Manager: Lars Johansson
Estimated Sales: $.5 - 1 000,000
Number Employees: 5-9

18486 **Aerolator Systems**
2716 Chamber Dr
Monroe, NC 28110 704-289-9585
Fax: 704-289-9580 800-843-8286
info@aerolator.com www.aerolator.com
Hood systems; wholesaler/distributor of exhaust fans; serving the food service market
President: Janet Griffen
Sales Manager: Steve Surratt
Estimated Sales: $10-20 Million
Number Employees: 50-99
Square Footage: 40000
Brands:
Aerolator

18487 Aeromat Plastics
801 Cliff Rd E # 104
Burnsville, MN 55337-1534 952-890-4697
Fax: 952-890-1814 888-286-8729
www.aeromatplastics.com
Manufacturer and exporter of plastic proofer trays and machined plastic parts
President: Bruce Dahlke
Estimated Sales: $2.5 Million
Number Employees: 10
Square Footage: 17000

18488 Aeromix Systems
7135 Madison Ave W
Minneapolis, MN 55427 763-746-8400
Fax: 763-746-8408 800-879-3677
aeromix@aeromix.com www.aeromix.com
Water and wastewater treatment equipment for the municipal, industrial and freshwater markets. Also offers a line of eco-friendly equipment that is completely powered by solar energy
President: Peter Gross
Estimated Sales: $5-10 Million
Number Employees: 25
Brands:
Cyclone
Hurricane
Tornado
Zephyr

18489 Aerotech Enterprise Inc
8511 Mulberry Rd
Chesterland, OH 44026 440-729-2616
Fax: 440-729-1620 amatic@aerotechcnc.com
www.aerotechcnc.com
Confectionery machinery
Owner: Andrea Maticci
Office Manager: Elizabeth Krukowski
Estimated Sales: $500,000-$1 Million
Number Employees: 5-9

18490 Aerotech Laboratories
1501 W Knudsen Dr
Phoenix, AZ 85027 623-780-4800
Fax: 623-780-7695 800-651-4802
info@aerotechlabs.com www.aerotechpk.com
Manager: Ben Sublasky

18491 (HQ)Aerovent
5959 Trenton Ln N
Minneapolis, MN 55442 763-551-7500
Fax: 763-551-7501
aerovent_sales@aerovent.com
www.aerovent.com
Industrial air handling equipment, fans and blowers
President: Zika Srejovic
CEO: Chuck Barry
Marketing Manager: Timothy Clifford
Estimated Sales: $50-100 Million
Number Employees: 100-249
Brands:
Axiad II
Axico
Axipal

18492 Aerovent
5959 Trenton Ln N
Minneapolis, MN 55442 763-551-7500
Fax: 763-551-7501
aerovent_sales@aerovent.com
www.aerovent.com
Manufacturer and exporter of fans
President: Charles Barry
CFO: Julie Dale
VP Sales: Dave Laclerc
Estimated Sales: $50 - 75 Million
Number Employees: 100-249
Parent Co: Twin City Fan Company

18493 Aerowerks
6625 millcreek drive
Mississauga, ON L5M 5M4
Canada 905-363-6999
Fax: 905-363-6998 888-774-1616
aman@aero-werks.com www.aero-werks.com
Manufacturer and exporter of conveyors
President: Balbir Singh
Sales Manager: Aman Singh
Number Employees: 35
Parent Co: Aerotool
Brands:
K-Flex Systems

18494 Aerzen USA Corporation
108 Independence Way
Coatesville, PA 19320 610-380-0244
Fax: 610-380-0278 800-444-1692
inquiries@aerzenusa.com www.aerzenusa.com
150 year old manufacturer of oil-free rotary lobe blower packages and screw compressor packages
President: Pierre Noack
CFO: Keith Rolfe
Marketing Manager: Ralph Wilton
Sales Manager: Darrel Hill
Production Manager: Steve Wark
Number Employees: 50-99
Square Footage: 60000
Parent Co: Aerzener/Maschinenfabrik

18495 Afeco
4300 West Bryn Mawr Ave
Chicago, IL 60646 773-478-9700
Fax: 773-478-8689 sales@cozzini.com
www.afeco.com

18496 Affiliated Resources
3839 N Western Ave
Chicago, IL 60618-3733 773-509-9300
Fax: 773-509-9929 800-366-9336
info@4ledsigns.com www.4ledsigns.com
Manufacturer, wholesaler/distributor of indoor and outdoor electronic signs
President: Stephen Stillman
National Sales Manager: Rick Markle
Regional Sales Manager: Pam Zayas
Estimated Sales: $1 - 3 Million
Number Employees: 1-4
Square Footage: 4000

18497 Aftermarket Specialties
980 Cobb Place Blvd NW Ste 100
Kennesaw, GA 30144-6801 678-819-2274
Fax: 678-819-2275 800-438-5931
sales@aftermkt.com www.aftermkt.com
Vending compressors, refrigeration compressors
President: Dallas Rohrer
CFO: Dallas Rohrer
Vice President: Dion Rohrer
Estimated Sales: $1 - 2.5 Million
Number Employees: 5-9

18498 Ag-Pak
8416 State Street
PO Box 304
Gasport, NY 14067 716-772-2651
Fax: 716-772-2555 info@agpak.com
www.agpak.com
Manufacturer and exporter of produce weighers and bag fillers
President and CFO: James Currie
Estimated Sales: Below $5 Million
Number Employees: 10-19

18499 AgTracker
2335 81st Ter
Vero Beach, FL 32966-1329 772-770-3293
Fax: 303-440-6162
Computer systems and software and weight control systems
Estimated Sales: $1 - 5 000,000
Number Employees: 3

18500 Aget Manufacturing Company
1408 E. Church St
PO Box 248
Adrian, MI 49221-0248 517-263-5781
Fax: 517-263-7154 sales@agetmfg.com
www.agetmfg.com
Cleaners and dust and mist collectors
President: Ray V Wakefield
CFO: Chuck Morrow
VP/Owner: Rich Olsaver
Sales: Rich Olsaver
Estimated Sales: $5-10 Million
Number Employees: 20
Square Footage: 200000
Brands:
Dustkop
Mistkup

18501 Aggreko
15600 J F Kenedy Blvd Ste 200
Houston, TX 77032 281-985-8200
Fax: 713-852-4590 877-244-7356
aggreko@aggreko.com www.aggreko.com
As the world leader in temporary utility services we are ready to satisfy your power, temperature and oil-free compressed air needs. Our unique fleet of equipment is custom designed and built for the rigors of the diverse anddemanding temporary utility industry
Manager: Gary Meador
Estimated Sales: $.5 - 1 000,000
Number Employees: 1-4

18502 Agilysys, Inc.
1000 Windward Concourse
Suite 250
Alpharetta, GA 30005 770-810-7800
800-241-8768
sales@agilysys.com www.agilysys.com
A leading developer and marketer of proprietary enterprise software, services and solutions to the hospitality and retail industries. Specializes in market-leading point-of-sale, property management, inventory & procurement and mobile& wireless solutions that are designed to streamline operations, improve efficiency and enhance the consumer's experience.
President & CEO: James Dennedy
Sr. VP, General Counsel & Secretary: Kyle C. Badger
Senior Vice President, Chief Financial O: Janine Seebeck
Senior Vice President, General Counsel a: Kyle C. Badger
Senior Vice President and Chief Technolo: Larry Steinberg
Sr. Vice President & General Manager: Paul Civils
Senior Vice President of Sales and Marke: Michael Buckham-White
VP of Sales: Tony Ross
Estimated Sales: $5 - 10 Million
Number Employees: 50-99
Square Footage: 80000
Parent Co: Agilysys/Alpharetta GA
Brands:
Infogenesis Gsa
Infogenesis Hospitality
Infogenesis Iqs
Infogenesis Its
Infogenesis Ticketing

18503 Agri-Business Services
PO Box 1237
Lakeville, MN 55044-1237 952-469-6767

18504 Agri-Equipment International
493 Colonial Trace Dr
Longs, SC 29568 864-220-6477
Fax: 864-343-0076 877-550-4709
ggaffney@mindspring.com
www.agri-equipmentonline.com
Manufacturer and wholesaler/distributor of release (interleaver) sheets, thermometers, temperature data loggers and probes
President: Tom Gaffney
VP Sales: Gary Gaffney
Estimated Sales: $1-2.5,000,000
Number Employees: 1-4

18505 Agri-Sales
209 Louise Ave
Nashville, TN 37203-1811 615-329-1141
Fax: 615-329-2770 800-251-1141
info@agri-sales.com www.agri-sales.com
Manufacturer's Representative Group
President/Founder: Jerry Bellar
VP: Phillip Ferrell
Estimated Sales: Less than $500,000
Number Employees: 20-49

18506 AgriTech
1989 W 5th Avenue
Columbus, OH 43212-1912 614-488-2772
Fax: 715-335-4390 agritech@iwaynet.net
Consultation firm offering market research and assessment, operations analysis, technology transfer and planning; specializing in food processing, agricultural development, grains, dairy products and foreign markets
President: William Riddle
Estimated Sales: less than $500,000
Number Employees: 1

18507 **Agribuys Incorporated**
3625 Del Amo Blvd
Suite 210
Torrance, CA 90503 310-944-9655
Fax: 310-944-9665 877-499-3052
info@agribuys.com www.agribuys.com
Online supply chain integrator for the food industry
Quality Control: Le Vu
Manager: B J Asneck
Number Employees: 20-49

18508 **Agricultural Data Systems**
24331 Los Arboles Dr
Laguna Niguel, CA 92677 949-363-5353
Fax: 949-495-7066 800-328-2246
sales@touchmemory.com
www.touchmemory.com
Automatic harvesting and data collection equipment
President: Carl Gennaro
VP: Carl Gennaro
National Sales Manager/Marketing: Paul Geisterfer
Estimated Sales: $3 - 5,000,000
Number Employees: 10-19

18509 **(HQ)Agrinorthwest Divisionof Agreserves, Inc.**
7404 W Hood Pl
Suite B
Kennewick, WA 99336-6718 509-734-1195
Grower & supplier of corn, wheat and potatoes
President: Don Sleight
General Manager: Tom Mackay
Director of Purchasing: Mike Monger
Estimated Sales: $31.6 Million
Number Employees: 150
Square Footage: 3340
Type of Packaging: Food Service, Bulk

18510 **Agripac**
PO Box 5110
Denver, CO 80217-5110 503-363-9255
Fax: 503-371-5666
Packaging of canned and frozen vegetables and fruit products
Number Employees: 150

18511 **Agtron**
9395 Double R Blvd
Reno, NV 89521-5919 775-850-4600
Fax: 775-850-4611 agtron@aol.com
www.agtron.net
Manufacturer and exporter of spectrophotometers used in the food industry to measure the degree of roasted, baked or fried goods or color grading of most food products
President: Carl Staub
CEO: Mike Rowley
CFO: Mike Rowley
Sales/Marketing: Kim Franke
Estimated Sales: $1 - 2.5 Million
Number Employees: 5-9
Square Footage: 80000
Brands:
Agtron

18512 **Ahlstrom Filtration LLC**
215 Nebo Road
PO Box 1708
Madisonville, KY 42431 270-821-0140
Fax: 270-326-3290 www.ahlstrom.com
Filters, wallcovers, wipes, flooring, labels and food packaging.
CEO/President: Jan L†ng
Research & Development: Ina Parker
Marketing/Sales Director: Gary Blevins
Estimated Sales: 1,000,000,000
Number Employees: 3,800
Square Footage: 5000
Type of Packaging: Food Service

18513 **Ahlstrom Technical Specialties**
P.O.Box A
Marysville, PA 17053-0016 717-957-3843
Fax: 717-486-6413 888-486-3438
jackramsay@ahlstrom.com www.ahlstrom.com
Filter media for filtration and laboratory including laboratory filters, glass, composites, cellulose, nonwoven
President: Christophe Coates
President, Chief Executive Officer: Jan Lang
CFO: Marie Bernard
Quality Control: Tonia Showers
R&D: Frank Cousart
Estimated Sales: $20 - 50 Million
Number Employees: 100-249

18514 **Aidco International**
P.O.Box 15339
Cincinnati, OH 45215-339
Fax: 517-265-2131 contactus@aidcoint.com
www.aidcoint.com
President: Salh Khan
Estimated Sales: $5 - 10000,000
Number Employees: 45

18515 **Aidi International Hotels of America**
1050-17th Street NW
Suite 600
Washington, DC 20036- 202-331-9299
Fax: 202-478-0367
sales@royalregencyhotels.com
www.royalregencyhotels.com
Engineering and marketing consultant specializing in construction, management, decoration and operations in overseas hotels; wholesaler/distributor and exporter of equipment, furniture and food
President: Ghassane Aidi
Chairman: Adnan Aidi
VP: Samia Aidi
Number Employees: 200
Square Footage: 28000
Parent Co: Aidi Group

18516 **Aigner Index**
P.O.Box 4084
New Windsor, NY 12553-0084 845-562-4510
Fax: 845-562-2638 800-242-3919
holdex@frontiernet.net www.holdex.com
High quality plastic insertable label holders
President: Mark Aigner
Estimated Sales: $5 - 10 Million
Number Employees: 10-19

18517 **Aim Blending Technologies Inc**
4196 Suffolk Way
Pleasanton, CA 94588 925-484-5000
Fax: 925-484-5007 800-328-6060
pahelman@comcast.net www.aimblending.com
Premium quality dry powder blending equipment, ribbon, paddle, fluidicers, continuous, V, cone and numerous other dry powder blender.
President: Phil Helman
Marketing Director: Kassandra Cunningham
Sales Director: Phil Helman
Estimated Sales: $5 - 10 000,000
Number Employees: 20-49
Square Footage: 20000

18518 **Aimcal Association Pavillion**
201 Springs St
Fort Mill, SC 29715-1723 803-802-7820
Fax: 803-802-7821 aimcal@aimcal.org
www.askaimcal.com
Executive Director: Craig Sheppard
Number Employees: 1-4

18519 **Air Barge Company**
26807 Springcreek Rd
Rancho Palos Verdes, CA 90275 310-378-2928
jvaughen@airbarge.com
www.airbarge.com
President: Carol Vaughen
R & D: Jack Vaughen
Estimated Sales: $5-10 Million
Number Employees: 1-4

18520 **Air Blast**
2050 W Pepper Street
Alhambra, CA 91801 626-576-0144
Fax: 626-289-2548 866-424-7252
sales@airblastinc.com www.airblastinc.com
President: Carl Von Wolffradt
Estimated Sales: Below 1 Million
Number Employees: 10-19

18521 **Air Economy Corporation**
PO Box 29
Flemington, NJ 08822-0029 908-782-8888

18522 **Air Liquide**
2700 Post Oak Blvd
Houston, TX 77056 877-855-9533
Fax: 713-624-8350 800-820-2522
www.airliquide.com
Complete line of industrial gases, develops custom freezing, chilling, or gas packaging systems
Chairman: Benoit Pottier
Vice President of Europe: Augustin Roubin
Vice President of Operations: Fabienne Lecorvaisier
Estimated Sales: $485.7 Million
Number Employees: 4400
Square Footage: 40000
Other Locations:
San Francisco CA
Los Angeles CA
Dallas TX
Chicago IL
Baton Rouge LA
Philadelphia PA

18523 **Air Liquide US Industrial**
3 Great Valley Pkwy
Malvern, PA 19355-1416 610-695-7400
Fax: 610-695-7481 800-869-6644
www.us.airliquide.com
Industrial gases for food processing and beverages; nitrogen, CO2, nitrogen injection, food freezing, and food processing
Chairman: Benoit Pottier
Vice President of Europe: Augustin Roubin
Vice President of Operations: Fabienne Lecorvaisier
Estimated Sales: $360 Million
Number Employees: 10
Parent Co: Messer Group

18524 **Air Logic Power Systems**
1745 S. 38th Street
Suite 100
Milwaukee, WI 53215 414-671-3332
Fax: 414-671-6645 800-325-8717
info@alpsleak.com www.alpsleak.com
On-line leak detection equipment for the plastic container manufacturing industry.
President: Roger Tambling
Sales Manager: Scott Heins
Estimated Sales: $5-10 Million
Number Employees: 20-49
Square Footage: 80000
Brands:
Alps Model 7385
Alps Smart Test Module
Alps Sx-Flex
Alps Vision Plus

18525 **Air Pak Products & Services**
2976 Forsyth Road
Winter Park, FL 32792-6628 407-678-1847
Fax: 407-679-5655 800-824-7725
info@air-pakpsi.com www.air-pakpsi.com
Designer/builder providing restaurant remodeling, renovation, cabinetry, millwork and HVAC services
President: David W McLeod
VP: Robert Nippes
Purchasing Manager: Sulyn McLeod
Estimated Sales: $20-50 Million
Number Employees: 100-249

18526 **(HQ)Air Products and Chemicals**
7201 Hamilton Blvd
Allentown, PA 18195 610-481-4911
Fax: 610-481-5900 800-654-4567
www.airproducts.com/food
President/COO: John McGlade
Estimated Sales: $10 Billion
Number Employees: 10,000
Other Locations:
Air Products and Chemicals Inc
Tempe AZ
Air Products and Chemicals Inc
Geismar LA
Air Products and Chemicals Inc
Carlsbad CA
Air Products and Chemicals Inc
Austin TX
Air Products and Chemicals Inc
Fountain Valley CA
Air Products and Chemicals Inc
Houston TX
Air Products and Chemicals Inc
Santa Clara CA
Air Products and Chemicals Inc
Irving TX
Brands:
Crustplus
Cryo Batch
Cyro Rotary
Cryo Dip
Cryo Quick

Freshpak
Vt Tune

18527 **Air Quality Engineering**
7140 Northland Dr N
Brooklyn Park, MN 55428-1520 888-883-3273
Fax: 763-531-9900 800-328-0787
info@air-quality-eng.com
www.air-quality-eng.com
Manufacturer and exporter of electronic and media air cleaners, parts and accessories
President/CEO: Heidi Oas
VP Sales: Ira Golden
Estimated Sales: $5 - 10 Million
Number Employees: 50-75
Square Footage: 142800
Brands:
Smokemaster

18528 **Air System Components, Inc.**
605 Shiloh Road
Plano, TX 75074 972-212-4888
www.airsysco.com
Market-leading supplier of heating, air conditioning and ventilation system components for commercial, industrial, and residential applications.
President: Terry O'Halloran
CFO: Ron Dewey
VP Operations: Tom Cromwell
Purchasing Manager: Steve Janiga
Estimated Sales: $212 Million
Number Employees: 100
Square Footage: 28800
Parent Co: Tomkins Industries, Inc.
Brands:
Titus
Krueger
Tuttle & Bailey
Pennbarry
Superior Rex
Trion Indoor Air Quality
Koch Filter

18529 **Air Technical Industries**
7501 Clover Ave.
Mentor, OH 44060 440-951-5191
Fax: 440-953-9237 888-857-6265
ati@airtechnical.com www.airtechnical.com
Manufacturer and exporter of material handling equipment including floor cranes, fork lifts and pallet inverters and handlers; also, automatic wrappers and hydraulic lift tables
President: Pero Novak
VP: Jane Goff
Estimated Sales: $10-20 Million
Number Employees: 50-99
Square Footage: 120000
Brands:
Articularm
Econo-Verter
Husky Master
Low Profile E-Z Wrap
Universal-Lift
V-Master

18530 **Air-Knife Systems/PaxtonProducts Corporation**
10125 Carver Rd
Cincinnati, OH 45242 513-891-7485
Fax: 513-891-4092 800-441-7475
sales@paxtonproducts.com
www.paxtonproducts.com
General Manager: Barbara Stefl
Engineering Manager: Steve Pucciani
Sales Engineer: Jeem Newland
Operations Manager: Stan Coley
Number Employees: 30

18531 **Air-Lec Industries, Inc**
3300 Commercial Ave
Madison, WI 53714 608-244-4754
Fax: 608-246-7676 info@air-lec.com
www.air-lec.com
Quality door operating devices, track systems and door hardware, providing industry with reliable, productivity enhancing products since 1921.
President: John Lunenschloss
Estimated Sales: $10 - 20,000,000
Number Employees: 10-19
Square Footage: 30000
Brands:
Air-Lec
Zephyr

18532 **Air-Maze Corporation**
115 E Steels Corners Rd
Cuyahoga Falls, OH 44224 330-928-4100
Fax: 330-928-0122 info@fallsfti.com
www.fallsfti.com
Air and oil filters
President: Tom Page
CFO: Bradley Lane
Quality Manager: Jeff Patrick
Director of Commercial Marketing: Andy Blair
Director of Sales: Andy Blair
Customer Service Rep.: Simone Edwards
Senior Buyer: Jean Balcer
Estimated Sales: $10 - 20 Million
Number Employees: 50-99

18533 **(HQ)Air-Scent International**
290 Alpha Drive RIDC Industrial Park
Pittsburgh, PA 15238 412-252-2000
Fax: 412-252-1010 800-247-0770
info@airscent.com www.airscent.com
Manufacturer and exporter of air fresheners, sanitizers and odor control systems including aerosol dispensers and refills; also, aerosol insecticides
President: Arnold Zlotnik
Estimated Sales: Below $5 Million
Number Employees: 50-99
Square Footage: 80000
Brands:
Air-Scent
Ch
Nature Scent
Scent Flo
Surcotta

18534 **Air/Tak**
107 W Main St
Worthington, PA 16262 724-297-3416
Fax: 724-297-5189 airtak@airtak.com
www.airtak.com
President: Donald Burk
Estimated Sales: $3-5 Million
Number Employees: 10-19

18535 **Aire-Mate**
17335 Us 31 N
Westfield, IN 46074-9119 317-896-2561
Fax: 317-896-3788 service@airemate.com
www.airemate.com
President: Conrad Mc Ginnis
Estimated Sales: $3 - 5 Million
Number Employees: 5-9

18536 **Airflex**
9919 Clinton Rd
Cleveland, OH 44144-1077 216-281-2211
Fax: 216-281-3890 edlunder@eaton.com
www.airflex.com
President: Alexander M Cutler
Executive: Ed Luehring
Estimated Sales: $20 - 50 Million
Number Employees: 100-249
Parent Co: Eaton Corporation

18537 **Airfloat Systems**
2230 N Brush College Rd
Decatur, IL 62526 217-423-6001
Fax: 217-422-1049 sales@airfloat.com
www.airfloat.com
Manufacturer and exporter of lift, tilt and turn tables
President: Jason Stoecker
Marketing Manager: Kara Demarjian
Estimated Sales: $10-20 Million
Number Employees: 100-250

18538 **Airfloat/HSI Systems**
2230 N Brush College Rd
Decatur, IL 62526-5522 217-423-6001
Fax: 217-422-1049 sales@airfloat.com
www.airfloat.com
Manufacturer and designer of bulk handling machinery, conveyors and bucket elevators for the food industry
President: Jason Stoecker
Marketing Manager: Gary Mollohan
Director of Sales: Ken Adkins
Estimated Sales: $10-20 Million
Number Employees: 20-49

18539 **Airflow Sciences Corporation**
12190 Hubbard Street
Livonia, MI 48150 734-525-0300
Fax: 734-525-0303 asc@airflowsciences.com
www.airflowsciences.com
Consultant specializing in product development testing, process trouble shooting, dryer, mixer, cooking, chilling and freezing reactions and computer simulations of heat transfer, fluid flow and chemical reactions
Manager: James C Paul PE
CEO: Robert Nelson
VP Western Office: James Paul PE
Estimated Sales: $2.5-5 Million
Number Employees: 20-49
Square Footage: 16000
Parent Co: Airflow Science Corporation

18540 **Airgas Carbonic**
6340 Sugarloaf Pkwy Ste 300
Duluth, GA 30097 770-717-2200
Fax: 770-717-2222 800-241-5882
www.airgas.com
Water treatment, temperature controls, gas packaging, refrigeration systems
President: Phil Filer
Estimated Sales: $50 Million
Number Employees: 50-99

18541 **Airgas Carbonic**
2530 Sever Road
Suite 300
Lawrenceville, GA 30043 770-717-2200
Fax: 770-717-2222 www.robartcompanies.com
Water pollution treatment and monitoring systems, cryogenics, carbon dioxide and nitrogen refrigeration systems, dry ice, blocks or pellets, freeze tunnels, refrigeration systems, trucks and trailers
President: Sharon Burton
Estimated Sales: $.5 - 1 million
Number Employees: 5-9

18542 **Airguard Industries**
100 River Ridge Circle
Jeffersonville, IN 47130 502-969-2305
Fax: 502-961-6804 866-247-4827
mailbag@airguard.com www.airguard.com
Air filtration products including extended surface pleated, pocket and cartridges filter media, bag filters, fiberglass filter media, panel filters, streamline polyester filter medias, and synthetic automatic roll filter media, HEPAfilters
President: Jeff Tumm
CFO: Jim Snoedy
R&D: Monroe Britt
Marketing Director: Gary Heilmann
Sales Director: Joe Hevekamp
Operations Manager: Tom Justire
Number Employees: 50-99
Brands:
Clean-Pak
Dp
Mieloguard
Powerguard
Vari-Pak

18543 **Airlite Plastics Company**
6110 Abbott Drive
Omaha, NE 68110-2834 402-341-7300
Fax: 402-346-2509 800-228-9545
mosler@airliteplastics.com
www.airliteplastics.com
Plastic injection molding and printing manufacturer product line of which includes drink cups, polystyrene coolers, ICF (Insulating Concrete Form) building blocks, and customized plastic products. Additional options include in-moldlabeling (IML), shrink sleeving and offset printing.
CEO: Brad Crosby
President: Pat Gredys
CFO: Pat Kenealy
VP Sales & Marketing: Michael Corrigan
Regional Sales Manager: Mark Osler
Estimated Sales: $100-125 Million
Number Employees: 700
Square Footage: 325000

18544 **Airlocke Dock Seal**
549 W Indianola Ave
Youngstown, OH 44511 330-788-6504
Fax: 330-788-6705 800-538-2388
www.onealawnings.com
President: Larry O Neal
Marketing: Marijo Rischar
Estimated Sales: $1 - 5 Million
Number Employees: 20-49
Parent Co: O'Neal Tarpaulin & Awning Company

18545 (HQ)Airmaster Fan Company
1300 Falahee Rd Ste 5
Jackson, MI 49203 517-764-2300
Fax: 517-764-2300 800-255-3084
sales@airmasterfan.com www.airmasterfan.com
Industrial and commercial fans, stainless steel fan guards, aluminum air circulator blades and explosion proof fans
President: Richard Stone
CEO: Robert Lazebrick
CFO: Ronald Johnson
Marketing: Maryann Talbot
Director Of Sales: Mike Pignataro
Product Manager: Mike Hemer
Estimated Sales: $10-20 Million
Number Employees: 50-99
Square Footage: 750000
Brands:
Airmaster
Chelsea
Nova
Powerline

18546 Airomat Corporation
2916 Engle Rd
Fort Wayne, IN 46809 260-747-7408
Fax: 260-747-7409 800-348-4905
airomat@airomat.com www.mymatting.com
Manufacturer and exporter of safety and fatigue relief matting
President: Joanne K Feasel
VP: Jody Feasel
Marketing/Sales: Claudia Logan
Operations Manager: Pam Peters
Plant Manager: John Solga
Estimated Sales: $1 - 3,000,000
Number Employees: 5-9
Square Footage: 6000
Brands:
Airomat

18547 (HQ)Airosol Company
1101 Illinois St
Neodesha, KS 66757 620-325-2666
Fax: 620-325-2602 800-633-9576
solutions@airosol.com www.airosol.com
Manufacturer and exporter of insecticides and counter cleaners
President: Carl G Stratemeier
Marketing Specialist: Jim Leiker
VP Sales/Marketing: Don Gillen
Estimated Sales: $20-50 Million
Number Employees: 50-99
Square Footage: 80000
Brands:
Aero-Counter
Blacknight

18548 Airsan Corporation
4554 W Woolworth Ave
Milwaukee, WI 53218 414-353-5800
Fax: 414-353-8402 800-558-5494
info@airsan.com www.airsan.com
Manufacturer and exporter of filters including air and restaurant grease extractor
President: Arlin R Ratajczak
Quality Control: Kurt Gleisner
VP Sales: Kurt Glaisner
Estimated Sales: $5-10 Million
Number Employees: 10-19
Type of Packaging: Food Service
Brands:
Airsan

18549 Ajinomoto Heartland, Inc
8430 W Bryn Mawr Ave
Suite 650
Chicago, IL 60631-3421 773-380-7000
Fax: 773-380-7006 ahisales@ajiusa.com
www.lysine.com
Flavorings including aspartame, enzymes, monosodium glutamate, nucleotides, glutamic salts, soy oligosaccharides and amino acids. Also liquid and dry sauces, including soy sauce, sesame oil
President: Tommy Teshima
Director Sales: David Barbour
Estimated Sales: $600,000
Number Employees: 5
Parent Co: Ajinomoto Company
Type of Packaging: Bulk
Brands:
Activa Tg
Koji-Aji
Transglutaminase

18550 Akers Group
1450 East North Blvd.
Suite 8
Leesburg, FL 34748 352-787-4112
Fax: 201-475-7667 877-253-7744
kendra@akersmediagroup.com
www.akersmediagroup.com
Computerized software for flavor and fragrance formula
Manager: Robert Sobel

18551 Akicorp
20145 NE 21st CT
N Miami Beach, FL 33179 786-426-5750
ysaac@akinin.com
www.akicorp.com
Oilseeds manufacturer and supplier
Manager: Ysaac Akinin

18552 Akro-Mils
P.O.Box 989
Akron, OH 44309 330-848-3773
Fax: 330-761-6133 market@po.akro-mills.com
www.myersindustries.com
Molded plastic bins, cabinets and trays
President: John Orr
CFO: Gregory Stodnick
Quality Control: Guy Lyon
Marketing Director: Joseph Gluzyn
Estimated Sales: $75-100 Million
Number Employees: 1,000-4,999

18553 (HQ)Akron Cotton Products
437 W Cedar St
Akron, OH 44307 330-434-7171
Fax: 330-434-7150 800-899-7173
akroncotton@akroncotton.com
www.akroncotton.com
Manufacturer filter bags: beer and winemaking
Owner: Mike Zwick
Estimated Sales: $1 - 3 Million
Number Employees: 5-9
Square Footage: 26000

18554 Alabama Bag Company Inc
PO Box 576
Talladega, AL 35161 256-362-4921
Fax: 256-362-1801 800-888-4921
www.alabamabag.com
Manufacturer and exporter of food bags, twine, uniforms, aprons, butcher frocks, disposable wipers, stockinettes, elastic netting, knit gloves, ham tubings, shrouds, money bags, courier bags, transit bags, locking bags and coin andcurrency bags, Poly money bags, coin wrappers, bill straps, tags, security seals.
Brands:
U.S. Bag

18555 Aladdin Temp-Rite, LLC
250 East Main Street
Hendersonville, TN 37075-2521 615-537-3600
Fax: 615-537-3634 800-888-8018
info@aladdin-atr.com www.aladdintemprite.com
Manufacturer and exporter of serving and heating equipment
President: Martin A. Rothshchild
VP Marketing: Marty Rothchild
VP Sales: Steve Avery
Estimated Sales: $300,000-500,000
Number Employees: 1-4
Parent Co: ENOCIS
Type of Packaging: Food Service
Brands:
Heat on Demand
Insul-Plus
Temp-Rite Excel Ii

18556 Aladdin Transparent Packaging Corporation
115 Engineers Road
Hauppauge, NY 11788 631-273-4747
Fax: 631-273-2523 info@aladiinpackaging.com
www.aladdinpackaging.com
Cellophane, polyethylene and polypropylene bags, rolls and sheets; also, baking and candy cups/padding
Owner: Abe Mandel
Product Manager: Donny Uccellini
Plant Manager: Larry O'Connell
Estimated Sales: $10-20 Million
Number Employees: 20-49
Square Footage: 40000
Parent Co: Bleyer Industries
Other Locations:
Aladdin Transparent Packaging
Peoria IL
Brands:
Pantry Bakers

18557 (HQ)Aladdin's Hookah & Loung Bar
2206 Elliston Place
Nashville, TN 37203 615-329-3558
www.aladdinshookahloungeandbar.com
Beverage pots and paper cups
President: Fred Mayer
CEO: Fred Meyer
CFO: Gary Warfield
Number Employees: 100-249
Brands:
Porteco
Rite Temp
Stanley

18558 Alar Engineering Corporation
9651 196th St
Mokena, IL 60448 708-479-6100
Fax: 708-479-9059 info@alareng.com
www.alarcorp.com
Manufacturer and exporter of water pollution control equipment including filters for dewatering sludges, clarifiers, separators, carbon columns, drum compactors and holding tanks
President: Paula Jackfert
CEO: Vickey Hassen
Estimated Sales: $5-10 Million
Number Employees: 20-49
Square Footage: 39000
Brands:
Alar
Auto-Vac
Clar-O-Floc
Flero Star
Microklear
Spiral Flow

18559 Alard Equipment Corporation
6483 Lake Avenue
PO Box 57
Williamson, NY 14589-0057 315-589-4511
Fax: 315-589-3871 sales@alard.com
www.alard-equipment.com
Buy, sell and refurbish food processing machinery and food packaging equipment for industrial fruit and vegetable canning, freezing, juice, bottling, and fresh cut applications, as well as all related packaging and labeling equipmentfor cans, jars, bottles, bags, etc.
President: Alvin E Shults
CEO: Susan Laird
VP: Edward Shults
Marketing Director: Michael Shults
Sales: Daryl Hoffman & Christopher Weigel
Purchasing: Diane Jenkins
Estimated Sales: $3 Million
Number Employees: 20-49
Square Footage: 40000

18560 Alarm Controls Corporation
19 Brandywine Drive
Deer Park, NY 11729 631-586-4220
Fax: 631-586-6500 800-645-5538
info@alarmcontrols.com
www.alarmcontrols.com
Manufacturer and exporter of electronic burglar and smoke alarm systems and timers
President: Howard Berger
Sales Manager: John Benedetto
Estimated Sales: $5-10 Million
Number Employees: 10-19

18561 Albany International
975 Old Norcross Rd # A
Lawrenceville, GA 30045-4321 770-338-5000
Fax: 770-338-5024 800-252-2691
sales.ads.us@albint.com
www.albanydoorsystems.com
Plant Manager: Dan Garrau
Estimated Sales: $20 - 50 Million
Number Employees: 100-249

18562 Albion Industries
800 N Clark St
Albion, MI 49224 517-629-9441
Fax: 517-629-9501 800-835-8911
email@albioninc.com www.albioninc.com

Casters and wheels.
President: Bill Winslow
R&D: Rob Jorden
Sales: Mike Thorne
Estimated Sales: $35-45 Million
Number Employees: 50-99
Number of Brands: 10
Square Footage: 165000
Brands:
Contender
Prevenz
Shockmaster
Trionix

18563 Albion Laboratories
101 N Main St
Clearfield, UT 84015 801-773-4631
Fax: 801-773-4633 800-453-2406
albionlabs@aol.com www.albionminerals.com
Manufacturer and exporter of nutritional mineral supplements including amino acid chelates, vitamin complexes, etc.
President: Dr H DeWayne
CFO: Charles Whiting
Sales/Marketing: Ronald Wheelwright
Purchasing Manager: Brett Ashmead
Number Employees: 20-49
Type of Packaging: Consumer, Bulk
Brands:
Albion
Chela-Zone
Chelavite
Chelazome
Metalosate

18564 Albion Machine & Tool Company
1001 Industrial Blvd
PO Box 239
Albion, MI 49224 517-629-9135
Fax: 517-629-6888 amtco@aol.com
www.albionmachine.com
Manufacturer and exporter of specialty and reworked food processing equipment; repair services available
President: Robert Herwarth
CEO/Chairman: William Stoffer
VP: James Herwarth
Estimated Sales: $3 - 5 Million
Number Employees: 10-19

18565 Alburt Labeling Systems
3130 Pintail Ln
Signal Mountain, TN 37377 423-886-1664
Fax: 423-886-1676 alburtl@bellsouth.net
Rollfed labeling, machines; foam labels
Owner: Alan Jones
*Estimated Sales:*less than $500,000
Number Employees: 1-4

18566 Alcan Foil Products
191 Evans Avenue
Etobicoke, ON M8Z 1J5
Canada 416-503-6709
Fax: 416-503-6720 www.foil.alcan.com
President: Kevin Kindllan
Quality Control: Pierre Achim
Number Employees: 150

18567 Alcan Packaging
6700 Midland Industrial Dr
Shelbyville, KY 40065 502-633-6800
Fax: 502-647-2211
lisa.apolinski@alcanpackaging.com
www.alcan.com
Manager: Herman Grilliot
Estimated Sales: $20 - 50 Million
Number Employees: 100-249

18568 Alcan Packaging
19701 Clark Graham Boulevard
Baie D'Urfe, QC H9X 3T1
Canada 514-457-4555
www.alcanpackaging.com
Folding cartons and paper boxes
President: Michael Rubensteil
CFO: Marcel Hetu
Research & Development: Martin Fogel
Plant Manager: Gilles Neron
Number Employees: 10
Square Footage: 300000
Parent Co: Algroup Wheaton Margo

18569 Alcan Packaging
8770 W Bryn Mawr Ave Fl 9
Chicago, IL 60631 773-444-0415
Fax: 773-399-8648 joyce.musgrave@alcan.com
www.alcanpackaging.com/
Flexible food packaging, product range includes a large portfolio of packaging based on plastic aluminum, paper, carton and other materials: plain and converted barrier foils and films, high barrier materials, container strips andcontainers, capsules and closures, labels, pouches, steel cans and decorated tins. Foils and films are available for technical and industrial applications.
President: Mike Schmitt
Product Manager Flexible Packaging: John Reiff
Marketing Manager: Joyce Musgrave
Estimated Sales: $118 Million
Number Employees: 10,000
Type of Packaging: Food Service, Bulk

18570 Alcoa
201 Isabella Street
Pittsburgh, PA 15212-5858 412-553-4545
Fax: 412-553-4498 www.alcoa.com
President: Jeff Kellar
Estimated Sales: $1 - 5 Million
Number Employees: 1,000-4,999

18571 Alcoa Closure Systems International
201 Isabella Street
Pittsburgh, PA 15212-5858 412-553-4545
Fax: 412-553-4498 800-311-2740
thomas.donat@alcoa.com www.alcoa.com
Canning and bottling packaging, capping equipment, plastic closures: 28mm, 38mm, 43mm, push-pull
President: Victor L Mitchell
Estimated Sales: $10-25 000,000
Number Employees: 1,000-4,999

18572 Alcoa Foil Products
6100 S Broadway
St Louis, MO 63111-2523 314-481-7000
Fax: 314-481-6174 www.jwaluminum.com
Aluminum foil
Chief Executive Officer: Lee McCarter
Marketing Manager: Mike Ilten
President, Chief Operating Officer: Ron Marchbanks
Estimated Sales: $1 - 5 Million
Number Employees: 10-19
Type of Packaging: Food Service

18573 Alcoa Packaging Equipment International
26 Center St
Randolph, NY 14772-1024 716-358-6451
Fax: 716-358-6459 janet.keeley@alcoa.com
www.alcoacsi.com
Testers, presses, sheet feeders, curlers and can beaders machinery
Manager: Steve La Furia
Chairman/CEO: Alan J Belda
Exective VP/CFO: Rochard Kelson
Marketing Services Manager: Janet Keeley
Estimated Sales: $10-20 Million
Number Employees: 50-99
Parent Co: Alcoa Closure Systems International

18574 Alcoa Packaging Machinery
26 Center St
Randolph, NY 14772 716-358-6451
Fax: 716-358-6459 www.alcoa.com
Manufacturer and exporter of freestanding rotary cappers, polyethylene and stretch film, and other packaging equipment
Manager: Steve La Furia
Plant Manager: John Flood
Estimated Sales: $1 Billion
Number Employees: 50-99
Parent Co: Alcoa Packaging Equipment
Type of Packaging: Bulk

18575 Alcoa Wheel Products International
1600 Harvard Ave
Cleveland, OH 44105-3040 216-641-3600
Fax: 216-641-5099 800-242-9898
www.alcoa.com
Aluminum wheels and accessories for heavy, medium and light duty trucks
CEO: Ray Mitchell
Estimated Sales: Over $1 Billion
Number Employees: 1,000-4,999

18576 Alcon Packaging
130 Arrow Road
Weston, ON M9M 2M1
Canada 416-742-8910
Fax: 416-742-7118 www.alcon.com
Rotogravure printed flexible packaging laminations for food, beverage and personal care products
Technical Director: Don Iwacha
Number Employees: 10
Parent Co: Lawson Mardon Group
Brands:
Mixpap

18577 Alconox
30 Glenn St Ste 309
White Plains, NY 10603 914-948-4040
Fax: 914-948-4088 cleaning@alconox.com
www.alconox.com
Manufacturer and exporter of USDA approved detergents for critical cleaning applications including food preparation surfaces
President: Rhoda Shemin
CFO: Elliot Lebowitz
CEO: Elliot M Lebowitz
General Manager: Malcolm McLaughlin
Estimated Sales: $3 - 5 Million
Number Employees: 5-9
Type of Packaging: Food Service
Brands:
Alco Tabs
Alcojet
Alconox
Citranox
Det-O-Jet
Detergent 8
Liqui-Nox
Terg-A-Zyme

18578 Alconox
30 Glenn St Ste 309
White Plains, NY 10603 914-948-4040
Fax: 914-948-4088 cleaning@alconox.com
www.alconox.com
Cleaning detergents
President: Rhoda Shemin
CEO: Elliot M Lebowitz
Estimated Sales: $1-2.5 000,000
Number Employees: 5-9

18579 Alcor PMC
3730 S Kalamath Street
Englewood, CO 80110-3460 303-761-1535
Fax: 303-789-9300
james.abbott@stollemachinery.com
www.pmc1.net
End liner technology for the food, beer and beverage packaging industry as well as its line of food equipment, which include stuffers, formers and portioners
President and Owner: David Groetsch
Sales: Tom Hoffmann
General Manager: Bob Geoffroy
Number Employees: 75
Number of Products: 20
Square Footage: 64000

18580 Aldo Locascio
1440 S Alvernon Way
Tucson, AZ 85711-5604 520-270-3059
Fax: 520-325-6776 800-488-8729
ilpaguino@home.com
Consultant specializing in industrial design of commercial kitchens, concept dining rooms and food service operations, BBQ's, tabletop accessories
President: John Richards
Number Employees: 36
Number of Brands: 2
Number of Products: 40
Square Footage: 12000
Parent Co: Richards Manufacturing Company

18581 Aldon Company
3410 Sunset Ave
Waukegan, IL 60087-3295 847-623-8800
Fax: 847-623-6139 e-rail@aldonco.com
aldonco.com
CFO: Ralph V Switzer
Estimated Sales: $1 - 5 Million
Number Employees: 14

18582 Aleco
2802 Avalon Avenue
Muscle Shoals, AL 35661-2708 256-248-2400
Fax: 800-750-9616 800-633-3120
info@aleco.com www.aleco.com
PVC vinyl strip and impact-type doors for walk-in coolers, freezers; also, traffic doors
Owner: Edward Robbins
CEO: Edward Robbins III
VP Sales/Marketing: Stan Denton
Estimated Sales: $1 - 3 Million
Number Employees: 100 to 249
Type of Packaging: Food Service
Brands:
Clear-Flex Ii
Impacdor

18583 Aleco Food Service Div
2802 Avalon Ave
Muscle Shoals, AL 35661-2708 256-381-4970
800-633-3120
info@aleco.com www.aleco.com
PVC door strips or walk-in coolers and freezers, impact doors for restaurants, insect control doors, air curtain doors.
President/CEO: Edward Robbins
CFO: Doug Sledge
Vice President: John Saylor
R&D/Quality Control: Steve Bacon
Marketing Director: Kelli Bush
Regional Account Manager: John Keddie
Public Relations: Bill May
Operations Manager: Ronald White
Production Manager: Jessie Hall
Plant Manager: Keith Rhodes
Purchasing Manager: Nancy Hamilton
Estimated Sales: $30,000,000
Number Employees: 100-249
Number of Brands: 10
Number of Products: 10
Square Footage: 100000
Parent Co: ER Robbins Corp
Type of Packaging: Food Service, Bulk
Brands:
Air Pro
Airflex
Clear-Flex Ii
Impacdoors
Maxbullet
Maxslide
Scratch-Guard

18584 Alegacy Food Service Products Group, Inc.
12683 Corral Pl
Santa Fe Springs, CA 90670 562-320-3100
Fax: 888-604-1066 800-848-4440
info@alegacy.com www.alegacy.com
Manufacturer and exporter of top-of-range aluminum cookware. Also, restaurant supplies and equipment
President: Brett Gross
Sales Director: Eric Gross
Estimated Sales: $1 - 5 Million
Square Footage: 320000
Other Locations:
Leonard, Harold, & Co.
Chicago IL
Brands:
Alegacy
Eagleware

18585 Alewel's Country Meats
911 North Simpson Drive
Junction 13 & 50
Warrensburg, MO 64093 660-747-8261
Fax: 660-747-1857 800-353-8553
ralewel@alewels.com www.country-meats.com
Dry, shelf stable, game and summer sausage, and game jerky including deer and buffalo. Cured meat mail order operation, custom processing and catering-whole hog specialties available
President: Roger Alewel
Estimated Sales: $2.5-5 Million
Number Employees: 5-9
Square Footage: 20000
Type of Packaging: Consumer, Food Service, Private Label, Bulk
Brands:
Alewel's Country Meats
Grandpa A'S

18586 Alex C. Fergusson
5000 Letterkenny Rd # 220
Chambersburg, PA 17201-8384 717-264-9147
Fax: 717-264-9182 800-345-1329
host342.ipowerweb.com www.afcocare.com
Sanitizing and cleaning products including pressure cleaners, cleaning compounds and lubricants
President: Michael Hinkle
VP Sales: Joseph Woodring
Estimated Sales: $20-50 Million
Number Employees: 20-49
Square Footage: 80000
Brands:
Afco

18587 Alex Delvecchio Enterprises
PO Box 516
Troy, MI 48099-516 248-619-9600
Fax: 248-619-9688 sales@theimprintshop.com
www.theimprintshop.com
Promotional products including changeable letter bulletin boards, plaques, name plates, signs, matches and napkins; also, special clothing and uniforms
President: Alex Delvecchio Sr
CFO: Alex Delvecchio Jr
Estimated Sales: $5-10 Million
Number Employees: 10-19

18588 Alexander Machinery
P.O.Box 6446
Spartanburg, SC 29304 864-963-3624
Fax: 864-963-7018 alexcoair@aol.com
www.alexco.com
Manufacturer and exporter of pneumatic coalescer filters and system drainage equipment
President: Martin Cornelson III
VP: W Spearman
Pneumatic Systems Design: Cliff Troutman
Estimated Sales: $20-50 Million
Number Employees: 20-49
Square Footage: 400000
Brands:
Alexco

18589 Alfa Chem
2 Harbor Way
Kings Point, NY 11024 516-504-0059
Fax: 516-504-0039 800-375-6869
alfachem@gmail.com www.alfachem1.com
President: Alfred Khalily
Estimated Sales: $2.5 000,000
Number Employees: 1-4
Number of Products: 300
Square Footage: 7500
Type of Packaging: Private Label, Bulk

18590 Alfa Laval
111 Parker St
Newburyport, MA 01950 978-465-5777
Fax: 978-465-6006 www.alfalaval.us
Manufacturer and exporter of centrifuges including liquid/liquid and liquid/solid separators for edible oil, fish, meat, starch, protein, grain, yeast, wine, beer, coffee and sugar processing
President: Craig Martin
Sales Director: Steve Schwalje
Public Relations: Craig Martin
Operations Manager: Craig Martin
Estimated Sales: $1 Billion+
Number Employees: 50-99
Brands:
Sharples

18591 Alfa Production Systems
522 Boulevard
Westfield, NJ 07090 908-654-0255
Fax: 908-654-0256 www.ALFASYSTEMS.biz
mysite.verizon.net
Manufacturer and exporter of custom automation equipment and packaging systems including tamper evident packaging, print registration systems, sealer mounted shrink tunnels, fragile product automatic infeeders, random product bar codescanning, etc
President: Charles Holhea
Vice President: Chuck Holata
Estimated Sales: $1.25 Million
Number Employees: 16
Square Footage: 3000

18592 Alfacel
20w201 101st Street
Lemont, IL 60439-9674 630-783-9702
Fax: 630-783-9780 info@alfacel.com
Casings, films, laminates, flexible packages, and shrink packaging materials
Estimated Sales: $1-2.5 000,000
Number Employees: 20-49

18593 Algene Marking EquipmentCompany
15 Wells Ct
P.O. Box 410
Garfield, NJ 07026 973-478-9041
Fax: 973-478-7644 algene@ix.netcom.com
www.algenemarking.com
Manufacturer, importer and exporter of marking and printing equipment, coders, hand marking tools, air feed systems and indenters.
President: Milton Mann
VP/Production: Garry Mann
Plant Manager: Garry Mann
Estimated Sales: $1-1.5 Million
Number Employees: 5-9
Number of Brands: 19
Number of Products: 15
Square Footage: 5000
Brands:
Algene

18594 Alger Creations
P.O.Box 800604
Miami, FL 32380 954-454-3272
Fax: 954-239-5773 luisa@algercreations.com
www.algercreations.com
Manufacturer and exporter of plastic bags, advertising specialties, displays and exhibits; importer of inflatable displays.
President: Alvin Brenner
Sales/Marketing: Ogden Farray
Estimated Sales: $2.5-5 Million
Number Employees: 20-49
Number of Brands: 1
Number of Products: 100
Square Footage: 40000
Type of Packaging: Private Label

18595 Algroup
17-17 State Route 208
Fair Lawn, NJ 07410-2820 201-794-2409
Fax: 201-794-2685 800-777-1875
braleigh@lonzausa.com www.algroupint.com
Chemicals, chemical manufacturing
CEO: Sergio Marchionne
CFO: Markus Hofer
VP: Michael Newman
Number Employees: 15
Parent Co: Algroup
Type of Packaging: Bulk

18596 Algus Packaging
1212 E Taylor Street
Dekalb, IL 60115 815-756-1881
Fax: 815-758-2281 800-266-8581
algus@algus.com www.algus.com
Packaging service providing equipment and materials
Founder, President: Art Gustafson
Estimated Sales: $5-10 Million
Number Employees: 50-99

18597 (HQ)Ali Group
P.O.Box 4149
Winston Salem, NC 27115-4149 336-661-1556
Fax: 336-661-1979 800-532-8591
champion@championindustries.com
www.championindustries.com
Manufacturer and exporter of dishwashers, dish tables, manual and powered glass washers, pot and pan washers and waste disposal systems
President: Dexter Laughlin
CFO: Christian Miller
CEO: Hank Holt
Estimated Sales: $20 - 50 Million
Number Employees: 100-249
Brands:
Champion
Coldelite
Moyer Diebel

18598 Aline Heat Seal Corporation
13844 Struikman Rd
Cerritos, CA 90703 562-229-9727
Fax: 562-229-1607 888-285-3917
aline@alinesys.com www.alinesys.com

Manufacturer and exporter of packaging machinery including shrink wrap, bundling, tube, bag and blister sealing and custom heat sealers for plastic films
President: Charles Schapira
Controller: Susanna Cano
VP: John Rydgren
Marketing and Sales: Charles Schapiraÿ
Customer Service: Pat Almanza
Plant Supervisor: Domingo Ayala
Estimated Sales: $5 - 10 Million
Number Employees: 10-19
Square Footage: 10000
Brands:
Aline

18599 **Aline Systems Corporation**
13700 South Broadwayÿ
Los Angeles, CA 90061 310-715-6600
Fax: 310-715-6606 888-825-3917
alineinfo@sorbentsystems.com
www.alinesys.com
Semi and automatic binders, shrink wrappers, heat sealing, blister sealing and custom machinery
President: Charles Schapira
Controller: Susanna Cano
Vice President of Manufacturing: Julio Gonzalez
Estimated Sales: Below $5 Million
Number Employees: 10-19

18600 **Alipack Americas**
525 S Shore Dr
Osprey, FL 34229-9620 847-607-0591
Fax: 847-607-0592 info@alipack.it
www.alipack.it

18601 **Alkar**
P.O. Box 260
Lodi, WI 53555 608-592-3211
Fax: 608-592-4039 sales@alcar.com
www.alkar.com
Manufacturers of cooking and chilling systems for the food service industry.
Vice President/Sales: Timothy Moskal

18602 **Alkar-Rapidpak-MP Equipment, Inc**
932 Development Drive
PO Box 260
Lodi, WI 53555 609-592-3211
Fax: 608-592-4039
Daryl.Shackelford@rapidpak.com
www.rapidpak.com
Food packaging machines for cook-in turkeys, hot dogs and string cheese.
President: Magdy Albert
Chief Financial Officer: Mary Jane Hansen
Research/Development: Seth Pulsfus
Marketing: Keith Shackleford
Plant Manager: Nick Cable
Parent Co: Middleby Corporation

18603 **Alkota Cleaning Systems**
105 Broad Street
PO Box 288
Alcester, SD 57001 605-934-2222
Fax: 605-934-1808 800-255-6823
info@alkota.com www.alkota.com
Manufacturer and exporter of high-pressure washers and parts, steam cleaners, water reclaim units and waste water/oil separators
President: Gary Scott
CEO: Joseph Bjorkman
Head of Engineering: Roger Walz
Marketing Manager: Jim Scott
VP Sales: Jeff Burros
Estimated Sales: $10-20 Million
Number Employees: 50-99
Square Footage: 50000
Brands:
Alkota

18604 **All A Cart Manufacturing**
2001 Courtright Road
Columbus, OH 43232 614-443-5544
Fax: 614-443-4248 800-695-2278
jjmorris@allacart.com www.allacart.com
Manufacturer and exporter of vending carts, kiosks, trucks, mobile kitchens, catering vehicles and trailers
President: Jeffrey Morris
Estimated Sales: $5 - 10 Million
Number Employees: 20-49
Square Footage: 120000
Brands:
All a Cart

18605 **All American Containers**
9330 NW 110th Ave
Medley, FL 33178-2519 305-887-0797
Fax: 305-888-4133
sales@americancontainers.com
www.americancontainers.com
Supplier of glass, plastic bottles and jars, can, pumps, sprayers and atomizers
President: Remedios Diaz-Oliver
CEO: Fausto Diaz-Oliver
CFO: A Alvarez
VP: Rosie Diaz
R&D: T Thompson
Quality Control: Dunny Perez
Marketing: Ken Massiello
Sales: F G Oliver
Public Relations: Mercy Yanes
Operations: Richard Flores
Production: Steve Maniscalco
Plant Manager: Rickie Rangel
Purchasing Director: I Bermuidez
Estimated Sales: $120 Million
Number Employees: 100-249
Number of Products: 5000
Square Footage: 260000
Other Locations:
All American Containers
Tampa FL

18606 **All American Poly Corporation**
40 Turner Pl
Piscataway, NJ 08854 732-752-3200
Fax: 732-752-5570 800-526-3551
steveb@allampoly.com www.allampoly.com
Extruders, converters and polyethylene bags including food, meat, shopping, plastic, shrink, liners and compactor
President: Jack Klein
Sales Manager: Joe Friedman
Estimated Sales: $20-50 Million
Number Employees: 50-99

18607 **All American Seasonings**
10600 E 54th Ave
Denver, CO 80239 303-623-2320
Fax: 303-623-1920
info@allamericanseasonings.com
www.allamericanseasonings.com
Custom blended seasonings and spices
Manager: Eric Willy
Marketing Director: Joseph Gallagher
Estimated Sales: $12 Million
Number Employees: 20-49
Square Footage: 40000
Type of Packaging: Consumer, Food Service, Private Label, Bulk
Brands:
All American

18608 **All Bake Technologies**
1930 Heck Avenue, Build 1
Suite 4
Neptune, NJ 07753 732-988-0060
Fax: 732-776-6418 info@allbaketech.com
www.allbaketech.com
Mixing, proofing, baking, makeup equipment, retarding
President: Robert Hassell
Number Employees: 20-49

18609 **All Foils**
16100 Imperial Pkwy
Strongsville, OH 44149 800-521-0054
Fax: 440-378-0161 800-521-0054
cjharris@allfoils.com www.allfoils.com
Manufacturer and exporter of aluminum, foil and sheet gauges; importer of aluminum and copper; also, printing and laminating services available
President: Robert B Papp
Estimated Sales: $20-50 Million
Number Employees: 50-99
Square Footage: 140000
Brands:
Metalix

18610 **All Packaging MachineryCorporation**
90 13th Ave
Unit 11
Ronkonkoma, NY 11779-6818 631-588-7310
Fax: 631-467-4690 800-637-8808
sales@apmpackaging.com
www.allpackagingmachinery.com
Manufacturer and exporter of packaging machinery and parts
President: Daniel Wood
Marketing/Sales: Lynn Miranda
Plant Manager: Dan Wood
Number Employees: 20-49
Square Footage: 80000
Parent Co: All Packaging Machinery & Supplies Corporation
Brands:
Speedy Bag Packager

18611 **All Power**
2228 Murray St
Sioux City, IA 51111 712-258-0681
Fax: 712-258-6561 www.allpowerinc.com
Manufacturer and wholesaler/distributor of packing house equipment, trolleys, shackles and stainless steel conveyors; also, sludge pumps, pressure vessels, indexers, auto feeders and drives including electric motor, gear boxeshydraulics and line shafting
President: Eugene Anderson
General Manager: Gene Anderson, Jr.
Purchasing Manager: Jim Tucker
Estimated Sales: $10-20 Million
Number Employees: 20-49
Square Footage: 35000

18612 **All Sorts Premium Packaging**
2495 Main Street
Suite 548
Buffalo, NY 14214-2154 716-831-1622
Fax: 716-831-1630 888-565-9727
sales@allsortswrap.com www.allsortswrap.com
Gift basket wrap and bags
VP: Penny Duke
Estimated Sales: less than $500,000
Number Employees: 1-4
Brands:
All Sorts

18613 **All Southern Fabricators**
5010 126th Ave N
Clearwater, FL 33760 727-573-4846
Fax: 727-573-2360 asf@allsouthern.com
www.allsouthern.com
Custom stainless steel food service equipment
President: Manuel Santana
CFO: Pav Willis
VP: Pavilyn Willis
Quality Control: Tom Richardson
Operations Manager: Tom Richardson
Estimated Sales: $10 - 20 Million
Number Employees: 50-99

18614 **All Spun Metal Products**
1877 Busse Hwy
Des Plaines, IL 60016 847-824-4117
Fax: 847-824-0419 allspun@allspunmetal.com
www.allspunmetal.com
Copper and stainless steel kettles; stainless steel sheet metal fabrication services available
President: Gianfranco Isaia
General Manager: Douglas Reed
Estimated Sales: $1-2.5 Million
Number Employees: 5-9
Parent Co: Spectracrafts

18615 **All Star Carts & Vehicles**
1565 5th Industrial Ct
Unit B
Bay Shore, NY 11706 631-666-5581
Fax: 631-666-1319 800-831-3166
info@allstarcarts.com www.allstarcarts.com
Quality carts, kiosks, trailers and trucks for the food service and general merchandise industries
President: Stephen Kronrad
Sales Director: Mark Weiner
VP: Robert Kronrad
Sales Executive: Michael Clark
Estimated Sales: $5 - 10 Million
Number Employees: 20-49
Square Footage: 25000

18616 All Star Dairy Foods, In
620 New Ludlow Road
South Hadley, MA 01075 413-538-5240
Fax: 413-532-4093 800-462-1129
allstardairyfoods.com
Dairy products
President: Russell D. Sawyer
Inside Sales Manager: Lynne Sawyer
Office Manager: Lynn Rivest
Estimated Sales: $7.5 Million
Number Employees: 40
Square Footage: 10400
Type of Packaging: Consumer
Other Locations:
Schenkel's Dairy
Fort Wayne IN

18617 All State Belting Company
520 S 18th St
West Des Moines, IA 50265-6449 515-223-5843
Fax: 515-223-8305 info@all-stateind.com
www.all-stateind.com
Food handling belting for conveyors and pulleys
President: Robert Pulver
Estimated Sales: $20 - 50 Million
Number Employees: 50-99
Square Footage: 120000

18618 All State Fabricators Corporation
1316 Tech Blvd Tampa
Florida, RI 33619 800-322-9925
Fax: 800-867-3609 info@allstatefab.com
www.emiindustries.com
Stainless steel food service equipment including counters, hoods, tables, sinks, dishtables, display cases, mobile food carts and ventless fryers
Manager: Steven Rooney
General Manager: Steven Rooney
Estimated Sales: $10 - 20 Million
Number Employees: 50-99
Square Footage: 70000
Brands:
Auto Fry

18619 All States Caster/F.I.R
Neils Thompson Drive
Suite 113
Austin, TX 78758-7653 512-832-9821
Fax: 512-832-9834 800-234-3882
daves@allstatescasters.com
www.allstatesequip.com
President: Dave Spencer
Estimated Sales: $5 - 10 Million
Number Employees: 10-19

18620 All Valley Packaging
PO Box 63201
Colorado Springs, CO 80962-3201
Fax: 425-650-5090 csr@allvalleypackaging.com
www.allvalleypackaging.com
Printed boxes, labels, bags, pouches, food service containers, pallets, janitorial maintenance supply
President: Cheryl Mikel
VP/Sales: Steve Hobden
Purchasing Manager: Cheryl Mikel
Number Employees: 5
Number of Brands: 100+
Number of Products: 1000
Type of Packaging: Food Service, Private Label
Brands:
3m
Clorox
Dixie
Dow
Dupont
Reynolds
Rubbermaid
Solo

18621 All Weather Energy Systems
PO Box 701064
Plymouth, MI 48170-0958 888-636-8324
Fax: 888-636-8304 escheatzle@aol.com
Door and dock leveler sealing systems, brushes, gaskets, containment seals, dust and infiltration control systems and pest control devices; design and installation services available
Owner/President: Elizabeth Scheatzle
Sales/Marketing Executive: Molly McCarville
Purchasing Agent: Mario Derrick
Number Employees: 5
Square Footage: 5000

18622 All-Clad Metalcrafters
424 Morganza Rd
Canonsburg, PA 15317 724-745-8300
Fax: 724-746-5035 800-255-2523
info@all-clad.com www.all-clad.com
Manufacturer and exporter of stainless steel, aluminum and copper cookware and utensils.
CEO: Peter Cameron
Estimated Sales: $20-50 Million
Number Employees: 100-249
Parent Co: Clad Metals
Brands:
Cop*R*Chef
Master Chef Ltd.
Stainless

18623 All-Fill
418 Creamery Way
Exton, PA 19341 800-334-1529
Fax: 610-524-7346 866-255-4455
info@all-fill.com www.all-fill.com
Manufacturer and exporter of auger and Liouis filling and check weighing machinery
President: Glenn Edginton
Executive VP/General Manager: Raymond Arra Jr
VP Sales: Jack Jones
Purchasing Manager: Nick Dienno
Estimated Sales: $10-20 Million
Number Employees: 50-99
Square Footage: 55000

18624 All-Fill, Inc.
418 Creamery Way
Exton, PA 19341 610-524-7350
Fax: 610-524-7346 800-334-1529
sales@all-fill.com www.all-fill.com
Powder and liquid filling machines and packaging equipment.
President: Glenn Edginton
Number Employees: 80
Square Footage: 55000

18625 All-Right Enterprises
2307 Conciliation Lane
Green Cove Springs, FL 32043-8240
Canada 904-400-1245
Fax: 604-528-6103 lallright@aol.com
Principal: Vern Smith

18626 All-State Belting Company
520 S 18th St
West Des Moines, IA 50265 515-223-5843
Fax: 515-223-8305 800-247-4178
dsmsales@all-statebelting.com
www.all-stateind.com
Wholesaler/distributor of food handling belting for conveyors
President: Robert Pulver
Vice President: Casey Price
Research & Development: Doug Tibkin
Quality Control: Sherry Wilkinson
Estimated Sales: $20 - 50 Million
Number Employees: 50-99
Parent Co: All-State Industries

18627 Allegheny Bradford Corporation
P.O.Box 200
Bradford, PA 16701-0200 814-362-2590
Fax: 814-362-2574 800-542-0650
sales@alleghenybradford.com
www.abccorporate.com
Manufacturer and exporter of sanitary stainless steel heat exchangers, filter housings, tanks, pressure vessels, manifolds and modular process systems; custom fabrication available
President: Dan McCune
VP Sales: Tom Harvey
VP Sales: Michael Zurat
Estimated Sales: $50 - 100 Million
Number Employees: 50-99
Square Footage: 40000

18628 Allegheny TechnologiesIncorporated
1000 6 Ppg Place
Pittsburgh, PA 15222-5479 412-394-2800
Fax: 412-394-3034 www.atimetals.com
President & Chairman & CEO: Richard Harshman
Executive VP & Chief Financial Officer: Dale Reid
Estimated Sales: $5.03 Billion
Number Employees: 11200

18629 Allen Coding & Marking Systems
501 90th Avenue NW
Minneapolis, MN 55433-8005 763-783-2734
Fax: 763-783-2580 877-611-1711
barb.jurek@ramsevtsr.com
www.allencoding.com
Coding and marking equipment, hot stamp and thermal processes
Estimated Sales: $500,000-$1 Million
Number Employees: 10

18630 Allen Gauge & Tool Company
P.O.Box 8647
Pittsburgh, PA 15221 412-241-6410
Fax: 412-242-8877 info@allengauges.com
www.allengauges.com
Manufacturer and exporter of sausage linking machinery and other meat processing equipment
Manager: C Moekle
Number Employees: 20-49
Parent Co: Allen Gauge & Tool Company

18631 (HQ)Allen Industries
6434 Burnt Poplar Rd
Greensboro, NC 27409 336-668-2791
Fax: 336-668-7875 info@allenindustries.com
www.allenindustries.com
Menu boards, advertising and electric signs
President: Thomas Allen
VP: John Allen
Estimated Sales: $10-20 Million
Number Employees: 100-249
Other Locations:
Allen Industries
Clearwater FL

18632 Allen Sign Company
2408 Chapman Hwy
Knoxville, TN 379201 865-579-1683
800-844-3524
sales@allensgin.com www.vexusstore.com
Manufacturer and exporter of advertising specialties, flags, pennants, banners, electric signs, lighting and flag poles, etc.; also, sign painting services available
President: Lisa Allen
CFO: Tom Allen
Public Relations: Scott Marshall
Operations Manager: Benjamin Booker
Plant Manager: Andrew Asbury
Estimated Sales: Below $5,000,000
Number Employees: 1-4
Square Footage: 7500

18633 Allen Systems
500 E Illinois St
Newberg, OR 97132-2307 503-538-3141
Fax: 503-538-8575 steve.austin@fmcti.com
www.fmctechnologies.com
Manager: Mark Eaton
Regional Sales Manager: Ellen Hao
Estimated Sales: $1 - 5 Million
Number Employees: 100-249

18634 Allen Systems
500 E Illinois St
Newberg, OR 97132-2307 503-538-3141
Fax: 503-538-8575 800-246-2034
allen.sales@fmcti.com
www.fmctechnologies.com
Vibratory and belt conveyors, bucket elevators, optical sorters, controls and ingredient application and storage systems
Manager: Mark Eaton
VP: Mark Eaton
Marketing: Neil Anderson
Regional Sales Manager: Ellen Hao
Estimated Sales: $1 - 5 Million
Number Employees: 100-249
Square Footage: 600000
Parent Co: FMC Technologies
Brands:
Allen
Fmc

18635 Allenair Corporation
255 E 2nd St
Mineola, NY 11501 516-747-5450
Fax: 516-747-5481 info@allenair.com
www.allenair.com

All stainless steel air cylinders
Owner: John Allen
Research Manager: Wayne Butner
Quality Control Director: Daniel Palladino
Sales Manager: Waler Scheid
Marketing Manager: Steve Santoriello
Human Resources Manager: Virginia Amato
Plant Manager: Stephen Werlinitsch
Purchasing Manager: Tin Byrnes
Estimated Sales: $12 Million
Number Employees: 100
Square Footage: 150000

18636 Allendale Cork Company
4 Walnut St
Rye, NY 10579 914-921-2787
Fax: 914-967-9605 800-816-2675
Manufacturer and exporter of wine and tapered cork stoppers and champagne corks; importer of cork
President: Dale Balun
Vice President: Ken Queen
Estimated Sales: $1-2,500,000
Number Employees: 10-19

18637 Allergen Air Filter Corporation
5205 Ashbrook Dr
Houston, TX 77081 713-668-2371
Fax: 713-668-6815 800-333-8880
Air filters
President: Michael Horan
Estimated Sales: Below $5 Million
Number Employees: 1-4

18638 Allflex Packaging Products
105 Race St
Ambler, PA 19002-4423 215-542-9200
Fax: 215-643-3339 800-448-2467
sales@allflex.com www.allflex.com
Promotional sales kits, material handling totes, trays and bins, cases, insulated and hazardous material containers and protective packaging
President: Joel Cohen
Marketing Director: Kristine Koelzer
Purchasing Manager: Joy Rudegeair
Estimated Sales: $3 - 5 Million
Number Employees: 10-19

18639 Alliance Bakery Systems
130 Northpoint Court
Blythewood, SC 29016-8875 803-691-9227
Fax: 803-691-9239 hncp7@msn.com
www.alliancebakerysystems.com
Equipment: baking systems, dough handling, transport and sheeting lines
President: Cory Bolkestein
Estimated Sales: $10-20 Million
Number Employees: 19

18640 Alliance Industrial Corporation
208 Tomahawk Industrial Park
Lynchburg, VA 24502 434-239-2641
Fax: 434-239-5692 800-368-3556
www.allianceindustrial.com
Designer and manufacturer of conveying systems, material handling machinery, and controls. Spiral Conveyers for bulk and case, Depalletisers, Elevators, and Lowerators for can, bottle and case, rinsers, case switches, bulk case, andair conveyer systems and much more.
President: Gary Garner
Marketing/Sales: David Loyd
Sales Manager: Wayne Walker
Purhasing: Todd Farrar
Estimated Sales: $20-50 Million
Number Employees: 100-249
Square Footage: 80000

18641 Alliance Knife
124 May Dr
Harrison, OH 45030 513-367-9000
Fax: 513-367-2233 800-852-7447
contactus@allianceknife.com
www.allianceknife.com
Produces and markets paper trimming knives, press knives, sheeters, slitter, granulator blades, woodworking knives, and packaging knives, as well as knives for the metal converting industry.
Owner: Lonnie Keith
Estimated Sales: $5 - 10 000,000
Number Employees: 20-49

18642 Alliance Products, LLC
820 Esther Lane
Murfreesboro, TN 37129 615-895-5333
Fax: 615-895-5334 800-522-3973
jparker@allianceproducts.net
www.allianceproducts.net
Custom and stock metal carts, nonpowered conveyors, heated cabinets, racks, heaters and proofers
President: Tony Story
Marketing Manager: Donna Sikes
Engineering Manager: Scott Marshall
Estimated Sales: $5 - 10 Million
Number Employees: 20-49
Square Footage: 80000
Parent Co: Win-Holt Equipment
Brands:
Alliance

18643 Alliance Rubber Corporation
P.O.Box 20950
Hot Springs National Par, AR 71903 501-262-2700
Fax: 501-262-3948 800-626-5940
sales@alliance-rubber.com
www.rubberband.com
Manufacturer and exporter of imprinted rubber bands for brand identification, logos, produce, etc.; also, UPC imprinted tape for produce
President: Bonnie Spencer Swayze
Marketing Manager: Jason Risa
Sales Manager: Rachel Atkinson
Operations Manager: Brandon Hughes
Estimated Sales: $50 - 100 Million
Number Employees: 100
Number of Brands: 10
Number of Products: 4500
Square Footage: 160000
Type of Packaging: Consumer, Food Service, Private Label, Bulk
Brands:
Advantage
Alliance
Eco
Pale Crepe Gold
Protape
Sterling

18644 Alliance Shippers
516 Sylvan Avenue
Englewood Cliffs, NJ 07632 201-227-0400
Fax: 708-802-5253 800-222-0451
info@allianceshippers.com www.alliance.com
President: Ronald Lefcourt
Estimated Sales: $10 - 20 Million
Number Employees: 50-99

18645 Alliance/PMS
267 Livingston St
Northvale, NJ 07647-1901 201-784-1101
Fax: 201-784-1116 usa@romaco.com
www.wcbicecream.com
Encapsulation equipment, qualification, validation and rebuilding services
Owner: Neal White
Estimated Sales: $10 - 20 Million
Number Employees: 50-99
Square Footage: 34000
Parent Co: SBX

18646 Allied Adhesive Corporation
P.O.Box 1866
Baldwin, NY 11510-8566 718-846-3200
President: Steve Pollack
Estimated Sales: $1 - 3 Million
Number Employees: 5-9

18647 Allied Bakery and Food Service Equipment
12015 E. Slauson Ave
Suite K
Santa Fe Springs, CA 90670-8542 562-945-6506
Fax: 562-945-4282 info@alliedbake.com
www.alliedbake.com
Supplier of bakery equipment and systems
President: Roger Harsted
CFO: Phillis Markle
Estimated Sales: $5 - 10 Million
Number Employees: 10-19

18648 Allied Electric Sign & Aing
1920 South 900 West
Salt Lake City, UT 84127-0911 801-972-5503
Fax: 801-972-5670 sales@alliedawning.com
www.allied-sign.com
Commercial awnings
President: Duane Millard
Estimated Sales: Below $5 Million
Number Employees: 30

18649 (HQ)Allied Engineering
94 Riverside Drive
North Vancouver, BC V7H 2M6
Canada 604-929-1214
Fax: 604-929-5184 877-929-1214
sales@alliedboilers.com www.alliedboilers.com
Manufacturers of gas and electric boilers, tankless coils and electric boosters.
President: George Gilbert
Quality Control: Brad Gilbert
Marketing Director: Garry Epstein
Sales Director: T Weaver
Operations Manager: Urbano Pandin
Plant Manager: Howard Larlee
Purchasing Manager: Harry Bowker
Number Employees: 60
Square Footage: 340000
Brands:
Aae Series
E-Z-Rect
Mini-Gas Series
Saturn Series
Super Hot
Trim-Line
Type 1

18650 Allied Gear & Machine Company
1101 Research Blvd.
St Louis, MO 63132 314-991-5900
Fax: 314-991-5911 800-896-1989
%20Sales@alliedgear.com www.alliedgear.com
General Manager: Skip Liu
Technical Manager: Amy Zhang
Regional Sales Manager: Dan Jahn
Estimated Sales: $1 - 5 Million

18651 Allied Glove Corporation
433 E Stewart St
Milwaukee, WI 53207 414-481-0900
Fax: 414-481-0700 800-558-9263
info@alliedglove.com www.alliedglove.com
Manufacturer, importer and exporter of safety products and disposable wear for food handlers including industrial gloves and X-ray protective materials
Manager: Sarah Cunningham
VP: Ray Sroka
Plant Manager: Dan Sroka
Estimated Sales: $1 - 3 Million
Number Employees: 10-19
Square Footage: 150000
Brands:
Security
Superguard
White Hawk

18652 Allied Graphics
16290 54th St NE
St Michael, MN 55376 763-428-8365
Fax: 763-428-8366 800-490-9931
sales@allied-graphics.com
www.allied-graphics.com
Pressure sensitive decals
President: Patrick Kohler
Estimated Sales: $1-2.5 Million
Number Employees: 10-19
Square Footage: 40000

18653 Allied Metal Spinning Corp
1290 Viele Ave
Bronx, NY 10474 718-893-3300
Fax: 800-374-2323 800-615-2266
www.alliedmetalusa.com
Woks, cake rings, pizza screens, trays, cutters and bakery, pizza and chinese cooking utensils; also, pans including cake, pie, pizza, black nonstick, anodized, sheet extenders, etc. Importer of 2000 items to complement manufacturedline
Owner: Arlene Saunders
Plant Manager: Carlos Heredia
Purchasing Manager: Arlene Saunders
Number Employees: 20-49
Type of Packaging: Food Service, Private Label, Bulk

18654 **Allied Purchasing Company**
PO Box 1249
Mason City, IA 50401-1249
Fax: 800-635-3775 800-247-5956
brian@alliedpurchasing.com
www.alliedpurchasing.com
Equipment, supplies, ingredients and services for the dairy, soft drink, bottled water, water treatment and brewery industries.
President/CFO: Brian Janssen
EVP: Steve Husome
Customer Service: Angela Stadtlander
Senior Account Manager - Bottled Water: Kari Mondt
Number Employees: 22
Square Footage: 10500
Type of Packaging: Food Service

18655 **Allied Trades of the Baking Industry**
PO Box 1853
Sonoma, CA 95476-1853 847-920-9885
Fax: 847-920-9886 www.atbi.org

18656 **Allied Uniking Corporation**
P.O.Box 18484
Memphis, TN 38181 901-365-7240
Fax: 901-365-7306 www.allieduniking.com
Conveyors including overhead monorail, overhead power and free and inverted power and free
President: Kenneth Anderson
CFO: Mike Baker
VP: Dolph Stritzel
Quality Control: Sharron Dean
Estimated Sales: $20 - 50 Million
Number Employees: 50-99
Square Footage: 100000

18657 **Allione Agrifood USA**
10390 Wilshire Boulevard
Apt 608
Los Angeles, CA 90024-6409 310-271-3663
Fax: 310-271-3664 usa@allione.com
www.allione.com/plant-en.html
Fruit processing, preparations, aromatic herbs, customized products, technology, quality control

18658 **Allison Systems**
245 Regency Ct.
Suite 210
Brookfield, WI 53045 262-522-9800
Fax: 262-522-9600 800-536-9077
info@allisonsystems.com
www.allisonsystems.com
Owner: Alan Doyle
Estimated Sales: $1 - 5 Million
Number Employees: 10-19

18659 **Allmark Impressions**
P.O.Box 7575
Fort Worth, TX 76111 817-834-0080
Fax: 817-838-2315 www.allmark7.com
Rubber stamps
Owner: Richard Spaberry
Estimated Sales: $1-2.5 Million
Number Employees: 10-19

18660 **Alloy Cast Products**
700 Swenson Dr
Kenilworth, NJ 07033 908-245-2255
Fax: 908-245-3267 rexalloy@aol.com
www.alloycastproducts.com
President: Frank Panico
Estimated Sales: $3 - 5 Million
Number Employees: 10-19

18661 **Alloy Fab**
200 Ryan St.
South Plainfield, NJ 07080-4208 908-753-9393
President: Larry Schillings
Estimated Sales: $10 - 20 Million
Number Employees: 50-99

18662 **Alloy Hardfacing & Engineering Company, Inc**
20425 Johnson Memorial Drive
Jordan, MN 55352 952-492-5569
Fax: 952-492-3100 800-328-8408
juliek@alloyhardfacing.net
www.alloyhardfacing.com
Manufacturer and exporter of primary waste water equipment, CIP-option pumps, heat exchangers and custom cooking vessels
President: Mark Aulik
Sales Director: Paul Rothenberger
Estimated Sales: $5-10 Million
Number Employees: 10-19

18663 **Alloy Products Corporation**
P.O.Box 529
Waukesha, WI 53187-0529 262-446-3654
Fax: 262-542-5421 800-236-6603
info@alloyproductscorp.com
www.alloyproductscorp.com
Stainless steel pharmaceutical, bio-tech, specialty chemicals and hygenic tanks; also, UN transport and ASME portable pressure vessels
President: Craig E Bear
Executive VP: Joe Vick
Quality Assurance Manager: Jeff Boerschinger
Assistant Manager of Sales: Stacy Vick
Customer Service Supervisor: Randy King
Estimated Sales: $10-20 Million
Number Employees: 50-99
Square Footage: 100000

18664 **Alloy Wire Belt Company**
2318 Tenaya Dr
Modesto, CA 95354 410-901-2660
Fax: 410-901-2680 877-649-7492
sales@cambridge-es.com
www.alloywirebelt.com
Market Sales Manager: Cory Bloodsworth
Market Sales Manager: Melissa Lewis
Plant Manager: Gene Ford
Estimated Sales: $1 - 5 Million
Number Employees: 10-19

18665 **Alloyd Brands**
1401 Pleasant St
Dekalb, IL 60115-2663 815-756-8452
Fax: 815-756-5187 800-756-7639
info@alloyd.com www.tegrant.com
Formerly SCA Consumer Packaging, manufacturers of light-gauge custom thermoformed retail packaging.
President: Ron Leach
Vice President of Business Development: Prakash Mahesh
Marketing: Rob VanGilse
Estimated Sales: $20 - 50 Million
Number Employees: 1-4
Type of Packaging: Bulk

18666 **Allpac**
P.O.Box 565685
Dallas, TX 75356-5685 214-630-8804
Fax: 214-630-3912 sales@allpacinc.com
www.allpacinc.com
Horizontal fin seal wrapping machines
President: Lawrence D Lakey
VP of Sales/Marketing: Cheryl DiMarzio
Estimated Sales: $2.5-5 Million
Number Employees: 20-49

18667 **Allpax Products**
13510 Seymour Meyers Blvd
Covington, LA 70433 985-893-9277
Fax: 985-893-9477 888-893-9277
info@allpax.com www.allpax.com
Manufacturer and exporter of loading, unloading and shuttle systems, retorts, autoclaves and control software
President: Steve Hudson
VP: Mike Blattner
Estimated Sales: $2.5-5 Million
Number Employees: 50-99
Brands:
2404
Monitor
Paxware
Rotopax
Stillpax

18668 **Allpoly/National Container**
13131 Almeda Rd
Houston, TX 77045-6603 713-433-5093
Estimated Sales: $10 - 20 Million
Number Employees: 50-99

18669 **Allred Marketing**
401 Graymont Ave W
Birmingham, AL 35204-4007 205-251-3700
Fax: 205-251-3706 allredpromos@gmail.com
www.logoprint.com
Advertising specialties, signs, uniforms, shirts, caps, jackets, menus, flag poles and promotional items; also, custom printing and embroidery available.
President: Larry Allred
Estimated Sales: $500,000-$1 Million
Number Employees: 5-9
Parent Co: Promotional Products

18670 **Allsorts Premium Packaging**
2495 Main St Ste 548
Buffalo, NY 14214 716-831-1622
Fax: 800-301-5301 888-565-9727
sales@allsortswrap.com www.allsortswrap.com
Gift basket packaging specialists, basket bags, candy bags, tissue paper
Business Manager: Rosemarie Duke
Estimated Sales: Less than $500,000
Number Employees: 1-4

18671 **Allstate Can Corporation**
1 Woodhollow Rd
Parsippany, NJ 07054-2821 973-560-9030
Fax: 973-560-9217 tincans@allstatecan.com
www.allstatecan.com
Decorative stock tins, to include round, square and rectangular shapes
President: Joseph Papera
CEO: Dave West
Estimated Sales: $5 - 10 Million
Number Employees: 50-99

18672 **Allstate Manufacturing Company**
20 East Seventh Street
PO Box 326
Manchester, OH 45144 937-549-3133
Fax: 937-549-2709 800-262-2340
sales@allstatemfgco.com
www.allstatemfgco.com
Portable display cases
President: Joel Birnbaum
Estimated Sales: $500,000-$1 Million
Number Employees: 5-9

18673 **(HQ)Allstrong Restaurant Equipment**
1839 N Durfee Ave
South El Monte, CA 91733 626-448-7878
Fax: 626-448-7838 800-933-8913
www.allstrong.com
Manufacturer and exporter of Chinese woks, exhaust systems and stainless steel work and steam tables
President: Yuancansing Situ
General Manager: Ken Situ
Estimated Sales: Less than $500,000
Number Employees: 30
Other Locations:
Allstrong Restaurant Equipmen
Alhambra CA
Brands:
Allstrong

18674 **Alltech**
3031 Catnip Hill Rd
Nicholasville, KY 40356 859-885-9613
Fax: 859-887-3223 globalfoods@alltech.com
www.alltech.com
Bulk supplier and manufacture natural, safe, and environmental products that enhance crop production
President: T Pearse Lyons
Product Manager: Elizabeth Graves
Estimated Sales: $20-50 Million
Number Employees: 250-499
Type of Packaging: Bulk

18675 **Allylix Inc**
7220 Trade St
Suite 209
San Diego, CA 92121 858-909-0595
Fax: 858-909-0695 info@allylix.com
www.allylix.com
Terpene products and their derivatives for the flavor, food ingredient, pharmaceutical and agricultural markets.
President & CEO: Carolyn Fritz
VP Business Development: Seth Goldblum
VP Research & Development: Richard Burlingame PhD
VP Sales & Marketing: Leandro Nonino

Estimated Sales: $280,000
Number Employees: 3

18676 Alnor Instrument Company
7555 Linder Avenue
Skokie, IL 60077-3223 800-424-7427
Fax: 847-677-3539 customerservice@alnor.com
www.alnor-usa.com
Measuring equipment including air volume, air velocity, humidity, pressure and temperature
Marketing Communications Manager: Danielle Kenney
National Sales Manager: John Rose
General Manager: Alan Traylor
Number Employees: 50-99
Parent Co: TSI

18677 Aloe Hi-Tech
7921 NW South River Drive
Medley, FL 33166-2515 305-884-0399
Fax: 305-884-0365
Aloe vera raw materials
Estimated Sales: $1 - 5 000,000

18678 Alpack
33 Pond Street
Centerville, MA 02632 508-771-9131
Fax: 508-771-3696 info@alpackplastics.com
www.alpackplastics.com
Plastic boxes, bottles, jars and packaging components
President: Joseph Kopelman
Type of Packaging: Consumer

18679 Alpert/Siegel & Associates
3272 Motor Ave
Suite J
Los Angeles, CA 90034 310-571-0777
Fax: 310-826-8311 Frontdesk@asaproperty.com
www.asaproperty.com
Consultant providing site selection for restaurants
President: Howard J Alpert
Estimated Sales: $500,000 - $1,000,000
Number Employees: 1-4

18680 Alpha Associates
2 Amboy Avenue
Woodbridge, NJ 07095-2699 732-634-5700
Fax: 732-634-1430 800-631-5399
ranton@alphainc.com www.alphainc.com
Industrial, coated, laminated and fiberglass insulation materials
President: Christopher Avallone
Estimated Sales: $20-50 Million
Number Employees: 50-99

18681 Alpha Associates Inc
145 Lehigh Ave.
Woodbridge, NJ 08701 732-730-1800
Fax: 732-634-1430 800-631-5399
www.alphainc.com
President: Christopher Avallone
Estimated Sales: $1 - 5 Million
Number Employees: 100-249

18682 Alpha Canvas & Awning
411 E 13th St
Charlotte, NC 28206 704-333-1581
Fax: 704-333-1599 coverpro@alphacanvas.com
www.alphacanvas.com
Commercial awnings
Owner: Angela Riggins
Quality Control: Eric Regans
VP: Brian Regans
Secretary: Jane Riggins
Estimated Sales: $1 - 2,500,000
Number Employees: 10-19
Square Footage: 4400

18683 Alpha Checkweigher
418 Creamery Way
Exton, PA 19341-2536 610-524-7350
Fax: 610-524-7346
info@alphacheckweighers.com
www.all-fill.com
President: Glenn Edginton
Estimated Sales: $20 - 50 Million
Number Employees: 50-99

18684 Alpha Gear Drives
1249 Humbracht Cir
Bartlett, IL 60103 847-439-0700
Fax: 847-439-0755 888-534-1222
info@wittenstein-us.com www.alphagear.com
Motion control products and planetary gear reducers
President: Karl Heinz Schwarz
General Manager/VP: Tim Herbst
Marketing: Ronald Larsen
National Sales Manager: Ray Hamilton
Estimated Sales: $15 000,000
Number Employees: 35

18685 Alpha MOS
7502 Connelley Dr # 110
Hanover, MD 21076-1705 410-553-9736
Fax: 410-553-9871 amusa@alpha-mos.com
www.alpha-mos.com
High quality provider of high speed centrifugal separator systems for the food, beverage, dairy and biotech industries. Provides reliable products with advanced technology and performance capabilities
Owner: J C Mifsud
VP: John Poling

18686 Alpha MOS America
7502 Connelley Drive
Suite 110
Hanover, MD 21076-1705 410-553-9736
Fax: 410-553-9871 market@alpha-mos.com
www.alpha-mos.com
Owner and CEO: Jean-Christophe Mifsud
Estimated Sales: Below $5 Million
Number Employees: 10-19

18687 (HQ)Alpha Omega Technology
14 Ridgedale Avenue #110
Cedar Knolls, NJ 07927-1106 973-537-0073
Fax: 973-292-4999 800-442-1969
info@karibafarms.com www.karibafarms.com
Designer, builder and wholesaler/distributor of turn-key facilities; also, irradiation processing facility for the sanitation and sterilization of food ingredients
CEO: Martin Welt
Office Manager: Ruth Welt
Estimated Sales: $500,000-$1 Million
Number Employees: 5-9
Square Footage: 120000

18688 Alpha Packaging
1555 Page Industrial Blvd
Saint Louis, MO 63132 314-427-4300
Fax: 314-427-5445 800-421-4772
sales@alphaplastic.com www.alphap.com
Manufacturer and exporter of jars, bottles and caps
President: David Spence
CEO: David Spence
CFO: Jim Flower
VP: Dan Creston
R&D: Robert Wilson
Quality Control: Shane Vorden
Sales: Paul Bonastia
Operations Manager: Roy Allen
Plant Manager: Darren Viernes
Estimated Sales: $20-50 Million
Number Employees: 100-249
Square Footage: 210000

18689 Alpha Productions, Inc.
5800 W Jefferson Blvd
Los Angeles, CA 90016-3109 310-559-1364
Fax: 310-559-2151 800-223-0883
john@alphaproductions.com?subject=Contact%20Form%20from%20Alpha%20Productions%20Website&body=How%20m
www.alphaproductions.com
Retractable awnings
President: Missak Azirian
Sales Manager: Howard Goldstein
Estimated Sales: $2.5-5 Million
Number Employees: 20-49

18690 Alpha Resources Inc.
3090 Johnson Rd
Stevensville, MI 49127 269-465-5559
Fax: 269-465-3629 800-833-3083
sales@alpharesources.com
www.alpharesources.com
Aftermarket parts Perkin Elmer, Leco & Specto machinery.

18691 AlphaBio Inc
29816 Avenida De Las Banderas
Rancho Santa Maragarita, CA 92688 949-858-4999
Fax: 949-858-4994 800-966-0716
info@alphabio.com www.alphabio.com
Sanitary pumps
Account Manager: Sean Pursaid
Estimated Sales: $25 Million
Number Employees: 100

18692 Alphabet Signs
91 Newport Pike Ste 102
Gap, PA 17527 610-979-0174
Fax: 610-979-0066 800-582-6366
info@alphabetsigns.com
www.alphabetsigns.com
Retailer of restaurant signs
President: Daniel Keane
Estimated Sales: $500,000-$1 Million
Number Employees: 1-4
Square Footage: 2500

18693 Alphasonics
15 Cottondale Rd
The Hills, TX 78738-1513 512-837-8088
Estimated Sales: $3 - 5 Million
Number Employees: 5-9

18694 Alpine Store Equipment Corporation
3710 10th St
Long Island City, NY 11101-6005 718-361-1213
Fax: 718-786-1220
Self-service food bars, restaurant counters and equipment
Estimated Sales: $2.5-5 Million
Number Employees: 20-49

18695 Alro Plastics
P.O.Box 927
Jackson, MI 49204 517-787-5500
Fax: 517-787-6390 800-877-2576
aglick@alro.com www.alro.com
Engineering plastics parts and shapes, delrin, teflon, UHMW, nylon, polycarbonate, Ertalyte Pet - P & TX, fiberglass grating and structurals
President: Dean Davis
Quality Control: Mike Mraz
CEO: Al Glick
Estimated Sales: $20 Million
Number Employees: 20-49
Parent Co: Alro Steel Corporation
Type of Packaging: Bulk

18696 Alstor America
PO Box 98
Stockbridge, WI 53088-0098 920-439-1777
Fax: 920-439-1002 pekaty1@fox.tds.net
www.tnk.net
Stainless steel, galvanized and epoxy coated bolted tanks, silos and bins for processing and storage of liquids, solids and semi-solids
Type of Packaging: Bulk

18697 Alta Refrigeration
403 Dividend Dr
Peachtree City, GA 30269-1905 678-554-1100
Fax: 678-554-1111 alexg@cold4u.com
www.cold4u.com
Owner: Rex Brown
Estimated Sales: $10 - 20 Million
Number Employees: 50-99

18698 Alteca
731 McCall Rd
Manhattan, KS 66502 785-537-9773
Fax: 785-537-1800 alteca@alteca.com
www.alteca.com
Food and beverage research and inspection
President: Lynn Bates
Marketing/Advertising: Lisa Bardmment
Estimated Sales: $500,000
Number Employees: 5-9

18699 Altech
888 Gilbert Highway
Fairfield, CT 06824-1645 203-259-1525
Fax: 203-259-1527 information@altech.co.jp
www.altech.co.jp
Anti-microbial materials, long term anto-mite solution and anti-static agent for thermoplastic materials
President: Hirokazu Yuri

18700 Altech Packaging Company
330 Himrod St
Brooklyn, NY 11237 718-386-8800
Fax: 718-366-2398 800-362-2247
mitchell@altechpackaging.com
www.altechpackaging.com

Company is a wholesaler of packaging/recycling management.
President: Mitchell Lomazow
Estimated Sales: $4 000,000
Number Employees: 10-19
Number of Brands: 50
Number of Products: 300
Square Footage: 45000

18701 **Altek Company**
P.O.Box 1128
Torrington, CT 06790 860-482-7626
Fax: 860-496-7113 info@altekcompany.com
www.altekcompany.com
Manufacturer and exporter of can testing equipment; also, food and beverage can and bottle testing services available
President: Stephen Altschuler
Marketing: Brian Mazurkivich
Office Manager: David Altschuler
Estimated Sales: $10-20,000,000
Number Employees: 100-249
Square Footage: 46000
Brands:
Tech

18702 **Altek Industries Corporation**
35 Vantage Point Drive
Rochester, NY 14624-1142 716-349-3500

18703 **Alternative Air & StoreFixtures Company**
30 Echo Lane
Willingboro, NJ 08046 609-267-5870
Fax: 609-261-5531 aainfo@aafixtures.com
www.aafixtures.com
Display Fixtures
Marketing: Mike Banks

18704 **Althor Products**
2 Turnage Lane
Bethel, CT 06801-2853 203-830-6060
Fax: 203-830-6064 800-688-2693
althor640@aol.com www.althor.com
FDA approved containers
President: Harold Shupack
Sales Manager: Judy Vivone
Estimated Sales: $1-2.5 Million
Number Employees: 5-9
Square Footage: 48000
Parent Co: American Hinge Corporation

18705 **Altira**
3225 NW 112th St
Miami, FL 33167 305-687-8074
Fax: 305-688-8029 sales@altira.com
www.altira.com
Manufacturer and exporter of blow molded plastic bottles; also, silk screening, pressure sensitive labeling and hot stamping available
President: Ramon Poo
General Manager: Art Hammel
Estimated Sales: $10-20 Million
Number Employees: 100-249

18706 **Altman Industries**
699 Altman Road
Gray, GA 31032-3431 478-986-3116
Fax: 478-986-1699 altcutter@aol.com
Manufacturer and exporter of processing machinery for peppers, citrus fruits, cabbage, cauliflower, carrots, celery, etc
President: James E Altman
OFC Administrator: Jeri Hastings
Secretary: Gwen Jones
Estimated Sales: Below $5 Million
Number Employees: 10
Square Footage: 20000

18707 **Alto-Shaam**
W164 N9221 Water Street
P.O. Box 450
Menomonee Falls, WI 53052 262-251-3800
Fax: 262-251-7067 800-558-8744
fdsvs@alto-shaam.com www.alto-shaam.com
Manufacturer and exporter of warming ovens, low temperature cook and holding equipment, hot deli display cases, smokers, combination oven/steamers, quick chillers, fryers and convection ovens.
President/Chief Operating Officer: Steven Maahs
Chief Executive Officer: Karen Hansen
Vice President, Finance: Kevin Noonan
Vice President: William Hansen
Director, Engineering: Tom Rand
Vice President, Marketing: John Muldowney
Senior VP, Sales & Marketing: Jack Scott
Plant Manager: Fred Barron
Purchasing: Dan Reichert
Estimated Sales: $29 Million
Number Employees: 300
Number of Brands: 3
Number of Products: 200
Square Footage: 350000
Type of Packaging: Food Service
Brands:
Combitherm
Frytech
Halo Heat
Quickchiller

18708 **(HQ)Altra Industrial Motion**
300 Granite Street
Suite 201
Braintree, MA 02184 781-917-0600
Fax: 781-843-0709 www.altramotion.com
Designer, producer and marketer of a wide range of mechanical power transmission products.
Chairman: Michael Hurt
Chief Executive Officer/Director: Carl Christenson
Vice President/Chief Financial Officer: Christian Storch
CEO: Carl Christenson
VP, Marketing & Business Development: Craig Schuele
Vice President, Global Sales: Gerald Ferris
Estimated Sales: $732 Million
Number Employees: 3,617
Brands:
Ameridrives Couplings
Bibby Transmission
Boston Gear
Warren Electric

18709 **Altrafilters**
200 Wanaque Ave # 401
Pompton Lakes, NJ 07442-2130 973-831-1010
Fax: 973-831-8181
Executive Director: Elaine Gordon

18710 **Altrua Marketing Designs**
3225 Hartsfield Rd
Tallahassee, FL 32303-3153 850-562-4564
Fax: 850-562-8511 800-443-6939
mfloyd@altrua.com www.altrua.com
Manufacturer and wholesaler/distributor of signs, banners, flags, pennants, table displays, decals and other printed promotional materials
President: Michael Floyd
Estimated Sales: $6 Million
Number Employees: 20-49
Square Footage: 160000

18711 **Alturdyne**
660 Steele St
El Cajon, CA 92020 619-440-5531
Fax: 619-442-0481 info@alturdyne.com
www.alturdyne.com
President: Frank Dverbeke
CEO: James Eggert
Estimated Sales: E
Number Employees: 100-249

18712 **Aluf Plastics**
4 Glenshaw St
Orangeburg, NY 10962 845-365-2200
Fax: 845-365-2294 800-394-2247
ron.s@alufplastics.com www.alufplastics.com
Plastic and polyethylene bags
President: Reuven Rosenberg
Estimated Sales: $20 - 50 Million
Number Employees: 100-249
Parent Co: API Industries
Brands:
Commander

18713 **Alufoil Products**
135 Oser Ave
Hauppauge, NY 11788 631-231-4141
Fax: 631-231-1435 sales@alufoil.com
www.alufoil.com
A supplier of aluminum foil, paper foil and foil board for food packaging and laminating. Uses include ham & turkey wrap, confectioners foil and general food service
President: Howard Lent
VP: Elliot Lent
Estimated Sales: $3-5 000,000
Number Employees: 10-19
Square Footage: 40000
Type of Packaging: Food Service

18714 **Aluma Shield**
725 Summerhill Drive
Deland, FL 32724-2024 386-626-6789
877-638-3266
mail@alumashield.com www.alumashield.com
Manufacturer and exporter of cold storage panels and doors
President: John Peters
Sales Director: Allen Rockafellow
Estimated Sales: $20-50 Million
Number Employees: 10

18715 **Alumar**
4809 N Armenia Avenue
Suite 05
Tampa, FL 33603-1447 813-870-0998
Fax: 813-870-0590 info@alumar.com
www.alumar.com
Food processing and can closing machinery
Estimated Sales: Below 1 Million
Number Employees: 1
Square Footage: 8000
Type of Packaging: Bulk
Brands:
Canco

18716 **Alumaworks**
16850-112 Collins Avenue #185
Sunny Isle Beach, FL 33160 305-635-6100
Fax: 866-790-2153 800-277-7267
rod@alumaworks.com www.alumaworks.com
Manufacturer and exporter of aluminum bakeware and cookware including frying, sauce, saute, cake and pizza pans, stock pots, deep fryers, pasta cookers, roasters, steamers, etc
President: Rod Haber
Sales Manager: Rod Haber
Number Employees: 14
Square Footage: 40000
Brands:
Alumaworks

18717 **Alumaworks**
16850-112 Collins Avenue #185
Sunny Isles Bch, FL 33160-4238 305-635-6100
Fax: 866-790-2153 800-277-7267
sales@alumaworks.com www.alumaworks.com
Bakeware, cookware, pizza pans and accessories
President: Rod Haber
Estimated Sales: $2.5-5 Million
Number Employees: 5-9

18718 **Alumin-Nu Corporation**
PO Box 24539
Lyndhurst, OH 44124 216-421-2116
Fax: 216-791-8018 800-899-7097
aluminnu@aol.com www.aluminnu.com
Cleaners for drains, septics, ponds, lakes, fish, bird bath cleaner, aluminum and vinyl doors, window, gutters, siding and boats.
President/Purchasing Director: Howard Kaufman
Plant Manager: Charles Moon
Number Employees: 3
Number of Products: 11
Square Footage: 15000
Type of Packaging: Consumer, Private Label, Bulk
Brands:
Alumin-Nu
Nice N Easy
Power

18719 **Alusett Precision Manufacturing**
3 Cecilia Ln
Pleasantville, NY 10570 914-769-4900
alusett@alusett-usa.com
www.alusett-usa.com
Estimated Sales: $1 - 3 Million
Number Employees: 1-4

18720 Alvarado Manufacturing Company
12660 Colony St
Chino, CA 91710 909-591-8431
Fax: 909-628-1403 800-445-7401
information@alvaradomfg.com
www.alvaradomfg.com
railings including ornamental, metal, brass, chrome and color; also, bar railings and glass partitions and stair and ramp rails
President: Jack Horener
Chairman: James P Armatas
CEO: Bret Armatas
VP Sales/Marketing: Bret Armatas
Estimated Sales: $10-20 Million
Number Employees: 50-99
Brands:
Escort

18721 Am-Mac Incorporated
311 Us Highway 46 Ste C
Fairfield, NJ 07004 973-575-7567
Fax: 973-575-1956 800-829-2018
ammac1@aol.com www.am-mac.com
Manufacturer and exporter of meat and bread slicers, mixers, vegetable cutters and meat grinders; wholesaler/distributor of food handling and storage equipment, wire shelving and ovens
President: Judith Spritzer
Vice President: Jon Spritzer
Estimated Sales: $10-20,000,000
Number Employees: 10-19
Brands:
Arimex
Lan Elec

18722 Amagic Holographics
1652 Deere Avenue
Irvine, CA 92606-4813 877-693-6457
Fax: 949-474-3979 800-262-4421
sales@amagicholo.com www.amagicholo.com
Vertically integrated holographic images including holographic security labels, pressure sensitive stickers, PET/PVC/OPP film and hot stamping foil
President: Howard Chen
Marketing Manager: Susan Chiang

18723 Amana Commercial Products
225 49th Avenue Drive SW
Cedar Rapids, IA 52204 319-368-8120
Fax: 319-622-8589 319-368-8198
commercialservice@acpsolutions.com
www.acpsolutions.com
Manufacturer and exporter of commercial microwave and combination ovens.
Marketing Communications Manager: Wendy Roltgen
Estimated Sales: $1 - 5 Million
Number Employees: 1000-4999
Square Footage: 7200000
Parent Co: Maytag Corporation
Type of Packaging: Food Service
Brands:
Amana
Menumaster
Radarange
Radarline

18724 Amano Artisan Chocolate
496 South, 1325 West
Orem, UT 84058 801-655-1996
amano@amanochocolate.com
www.amanochocolate.com
Fine chocolates
Founder/President/Head Chocolate Maker: Amano Artisan
Pastry Chef: Rebecca Millican
Number Employees: 12
Type of Packaging: Private Label
Brands:
Amano Ocumare
Amano Jenbrana

18725 Amarillo Mop & Broom Company
801 S Fillmore
Suite 205
Amarillo, TX 79101 806-372-8596
Fax: 806-379-8724 800-955-8596
mops4u@suddenlink.net
Mop manufacturer
President: E Bryan
VP: Sue Ann Bryan
Estimated Sales: $2.5-5 Million
Number Employees: 10-19
Square Footage: 48000
Type of Packaging: Private Label, Bulk
Brands:
Amco
Trouble Shooter

18726 Amark Packaging Systems
4717 E. 119th Streetÿÿÿ
PO Box 9824
Kansas City, MO 64134 816-965-9000
Fax: 816-965-9003 amarkpkg@sprintmail.com
www.amarkpackaging.com
Manufacturer,exporter of conveyors,bag closers, sewing machines, heat sealers,scales, and pinch closers; custom fabrications available.
Owner: Bob Mc Cullough
Plant Manager: Jack Groblebe
Estimated Sales: $2.5-5 Million
Number Employees: 10
Number of Products: 15
Square Footage: 80000
Brands:
Amark/Simionato
Dura-Pak

18727 Amax Nutrasource
1770 Prairie Rd
Eugene, OR 97402 541-688-4944
Fax: 541-688-4866 800-893-5306
info@amaxnutrasource.com
www.amaxnutrasource.com
Manufacturer and distributor of herbal extracts and nutritional ingredients.
President: Larry Martinez
CFO: Daniel Rothwell
Business Development Manager: Steve Light
Production Manager: Charles Lofton

18728 Ambaflex
2202 113th Street
Suite 112
Grand Prairie, TX 75050-1200 877-800-1634
Fax: 877-800-1635 877-800-1634
info@ambaflex.com www.ambaflex.com

18729 Ambient Engineering
5 Crescent Ave
Rocky Hill, NJ 08553 609-279-6888
Fax: 609-279-9444 john@ambienteng.com
www.ambienteng.com
President: Bruce Bruns
Estimated Sales: $.5 - 1 million
Number Employees: 1-4

18730 Ambitech Engineering Corporation
1411 Opus Pl Ste 200
Downers Grove, IL 60515 630-963-5800
Fax: 630-963-8099 www.ambitech.com
President: Allan Koenig
CFO: Christopher Hunt
Estimated Sales: $10 - 20 Million
Number Employees: 100-249

18731 Ambrose Company
2919 Fulton St
Everett, WA 98201-3733 425-317-9818
Fax: 425-317-8597 info@ambrosecompany.com
www.ambrosecompany.com
Manufacturer and exporterof liquid packaging equipment including turnkey systems, pail denesters, fillers, check weighters, conveyors, palletizers, controls and engineering services
President: John Bowman
CFO: Cindy Annyas
Vice President: Jeff Bowman
Sales Director: John Bowman
Operations Manager: Jeff Bowman
Estimated Sales: $1.5 Million
Number Employees: 5-9
Number of Products: 12
Square Footage: 24000
Brands:
Ambrose

18732 Amcel
1 Galen Street
Watertown, MA 02472-4501 617-924-0800
Fax: 617-924-2931 800-225-7992
mmilich@amcel.com www.amcel.com
Producers of linear low density and high density polyethylene liners, and stock-size polyethylene bags for food packaging applications; also a leading supplier of disposable plastic cutlery
President: Brad Gordon
Sales Manager: Mike Milich
Customer Service Manager: Laura Ott
Estimated Sales: $50-100 Million
Number Employees: 20-49
Square Footage: 18000
Brands:
Amcel

18733 Amco Warehouse & Transportation
1210 Kona Drive
Suite B
Compton, CA 90220-5405 310-635-1885
Fax: 310-604-9762
Samplers and weighing machinery

18734 Amcor Flexibles - NorthAmerica
747 Bowman Ave
Hagerstown, MD 21740-6871 301-745-5000
Fax: 301-745-5005 800-332-7928
www.amcor.com
Film rollstock, bags and laminations
President: Peter Brues
President: Ralf K. Wunderlich
Chairman - AMVIG: Billy Chan
Executive Vice President Financ: Ron Delia
Executive Vice President Human Resources: Steve Keogh
VP Sales/Marketing: John Fry
VP Manufacturing/Product Manager: Robert Sloan
Estimated Sales: $1 - 5 Million
Number Employees: 50-99
Square Footage: 20000
Parent Co: Amcor

18735 Amcor Group Limited
539 46th Avenue
Long Island City, NY 11101-5230 718-361-2700
Fax: 718-706-6058

18736 Amcor Twinpak
Suite 210
Dorval, QC H9P 2V4
Canada 514-684-7070
Fax: 514-684-2290 ngirard@twinpak.com
www.twinpak.com
Manufacturer and exporter of plastic packaging products and materials including polypropylene containers, pet containers and plastic closures; also, printed plastic films, laminations and converted products
President and COO: Gary Davis
General Manager: John Dale
Estimated Sales: $350 Million
Number Employees: 2400
Parent Co: Amcor

18737 Ameri-Khem
530 New Town Road
PO Box 291907
Port Orange, FL 32129-1907 386-756-9950
800-224-9950
akab@bellsouth.net www.truckcompaniesin.com
Anti-bacterial drain cleaner and waste reduction equipment
President: George Huth
Number Employees: 1-4
Brands:
Nature's Best Liquid Live

18738 AmeriGlobe FIBC Solutions
153 S Long St
Lafayette, LA 70506-3019 337-234-3212
Fax: 866-264-5623
marlener@ameriglobe-fibc.com
www.ameriglobe-fibc.com
Bulk bags and weigh/fill stations; also, bulk bag refurbishing services available
President: Dan Schnaars
CFO: Randy Girourard
Marketing Director: Blaine Beck
Sales Director: Marlene Rodrigue
Estimated Sales: $50-100 Million
Number Employees: 250-499

18739 AmeriPak
2001 County Line Rd
Warrington, PA 18976-2416 215-343-1530
Fax: 215-343-5293 info@ameripak-pes.com
www.ameripak-ops.com
Packaging equipment including horizontal wrappers, filled tray sealers, rigid box and thermoforming; rebuilt equipment available; importer of thermoforming equipment; exporter of rigid box machinery and horizontal wrappers
President: William T Schuman
VP Marketing/Sales: Phil Kelly
Estimated Sales: $5-10 Million
Number Employees: 20-49
Number of Products: 5
Square Footage: 240000
Parent Co: SKS Equipment Company

18740 AmeriQual Foods
18200 Highway 41 N
Evansville, IN 47725 812-867-1444
Fax: 812-867-0278 www.ameriqual.com
Processor and contract packager of shelf stable entrees using retort processing
CEO: Dan Hermman
VP Sales/Marketing: Michael Billing
VP Tech: John Dorris
Senior VP Operations: Tim Brauer
Estimated Sales: $50-100 Million
Number Employees: 100-249
Square Footage: 100000

18741 AmeriVacs
1518 Lancaster Point Way
San Diego, CA 92154-7700
Fax: 619-498-8222 info@amerivacs.com
www.amerivacs.com
Clean room compatible chamber and retractable nozzle vacuum sealers with gas purge for all heat sealable bags, including all ESD bags by using quiet, nonparticle generating, maintenance-free compressed air-driven vacuum pumps. Standardimpulse sealers also available. One week trial period. Custom designs upon request. One year limited warranty. Made in the USA
President: Peter Tadlock
Estimated Sales: $1 - 2.5 Million
Number Employees: 5-9
Number of Brands: 1
Number of Products: 8
Square Footage: 8000
Brands:
Amerivacs

18742 AmeriVap Systems Inc
31 Successful Way
Dawsonville, GA 30534 404-350-0239
Fax: 404-350-9214 800-763-7687
Sales@AmeriVap.com www.amerivap.com
Dry steam cleaning and sanitizing systems.
President: Werner Diercks
CFO: Paula Marshal
VP Marketing: Dolly Diercks
VP Sales: Gabriel Perez
Estimated Sales: $3 Million
Number Employees: 10-19
Square Footage: 10000

18743 America's Electric Cooperatives
4301 Wilson Boulevard
Arlington, VA 22203-1867 703-907-5707
Fax: 703-907-5531 nreca@nreca.coop
www.nreca.org
President: James Baker
Senior Vice President of Programs: Vivek Talvadkar

18744 American & Efird
24 American St
Mount Holly, NC 28120 704-827-4311
Fax: 704-861-8579
Industrial yarns
Plant Manager: Chris McGuret
Estimated Sales: $20 - 50 Million
Number Employees: 100-249

18745 American Adhesives
1730 Evergreen St
Duarte, CA 91010 626-256-4417
Fax: 626-256-4427 800-557-4747
info@americanadhesives.com
www.americanadhesives.com
President: John S. Sepulveda
Owner: Tim Thornton
Estimated Sales: $1 - 5 Million
Number Employees: 1-4

18746 American Advertising & Shop Cap Company
48 Bi State Plaza
Suite 231
Old Tappan, NJ 07675-7003 845-639-1596
Fax: 845-639-1597 800-442-8837
ameradvert@aol.com
Men's work headwear, imprinted painters' caps, aprons, cloth bags, baseball caps, t-shirts, tote bags sunvisors, golf shirts, sweatshirts and engineer caps.
President: Ronnie Ehrlich
Number Employees: 50

18747 American Agribusiness Assistance
2916 Dartmouth Road
Alexandria, VA 22314-4822 202-429-0500
Fax: 202-429-0525 agequip@aol.com
Export broker of processing and packaging equipment for baked goods, sausage, vegetables, fruits, cheese, dairy products, etc.; consultant offering plant design and equipment installation
President: James Roberts
VP: Dick Verga
Number Employees: 1-4

18748 American Apron Inc.
P.O.Box 318
Foxboro, MA 02035-0318 508-384-9600
Fax: 508-384-9601 800-262-7766
www.apron.com
Aprons, safety vests and screen printing
President: James Holicker
VP: Connie Holicker
Estimated Sales: Less than $500,000
Number Employees: 1-4

18749 American Art Stamp
17803 South Harvard Street
Suite B
Gardena, CA 90248 310-965-9004
amartstamp@aol.com
www.americanartstamp.com
Rubber, number, pre-inked and self-inking stamps; also, marking devices, signage and metal marking devices
Co-Owner: Robert Tepper
Estimated Sales: $300,000-500,000
Number Employees: 1-4
Square Footage: 6800

18750 American Auger & Accesories
325 Westtown Rd
Suite 8
West Chester, PA 19382 610-692-7811
Fax: 610-692-7886 866-219-9619
sales@americanauger.com
www.americanauger.com
Replacement augers and funnels for all make model of auger filling machines. We also make augers for conveyors and horizontal feeders
President: Jack Treptow
Estimated Sales: $.5 - 1 million
Number Employees: 1-4

18751 American Autoclave
P.O.Box 430
Sumner, WA 98390 253-863-1770
Fax: 253-863-1770 info@americanautoclave.com
www.americanautoclave.com
President: Robert Stack
Estimated Sales: Below $5 Million
Number Employees: 5-9

18752 American Autogard Corporation
5173 26th Avenue
Rockford, IL 61109 815-229-3190
Fax: 815-633-8488 www.autogard.com
Mechanical and pneumatic torque limiting/overload release clutches and monitors
Manager: Thomas Johnson
Customer Service Manager: Bob Wallace
Operations Ex: Les Wodecki

18753 American Bag & Burlap Company
36 Arlington St
P.O. Box 505649
Chelsea, MA 02150 617-884-7600
Fax: 617-437-7917 info@cormanbag.com
www.cormanbag.com
Manufacturer and importer of bags including burlap, paper and plastic; also, weighing, filling and closing machinery
President: Elliot Corman
VP: Barry Corman
VP: Julie Corman
Estimated Sales: $12 Million
Number Employees: 10-19
Square Footage: 25000
Type of Packaging: Private Label

18754 American Bag & Linen Company
339 West Airport Road
PO Box 8
Cornelia, GA 30531 706-778-5377
Fax: 706-778-9118 abl@abl-sewing.com
www.abl-sewing.com
Aprons
President: James Harris
Office Manager: Judy Porter
Plant Manager: Ramona Holt
Estimated Sales: $5-10 Million
Number Employees: 50-99

18755 American Bakery Equipment Company
435 Johnston St # B
PO Box 3135
Half Moon Bay, CA 94019 650-560-9970
Fax: 650-560-9971 800-341-5581
abeco@coastside.net
www.americanbakeryequipment.biz
Wholesaler/distributor of new and used bakery equipment for pastries, muffins, cookies, cakes, breads, pizzas, bagels, etc.; installation services available
Manager: John Candelori Jr
CEO: Ken Skelton
CFO: Norman Gwinn
VP: John Candelori, Jr.
Research & Development: Polly Vandersyde
CFO: Sabatino Compi
Estimated Sales: Below $5,000,000
Number Employees: 5-9
Number of Brands: 200
Number of Products: 1000
Square Footage: 4750

18756 American Bank Note Holographics
2 Applegate Dr
Robbinsville, NJ 08691 609-632-0800
Fax: 609-632-0850 abnhr@abnh.com
www.abnh.com
Holograms
President: Kenneth Traub
Number Employees: 50-99
Parent Co: JDS Uniphase Corporation

18757 American Box Corporation
PO Box 112
Lisbon, OH 44432-0112 330-424-8055
Fax: 330-424-7441 amboxcorp@aol.com
Custom, new and reconditioned wooden pallets, skids, boxes and crates
Estimated Sales: less than $500,000
Number Employees: 10

18758 American Broom Company
1200 Moultrie Ave
Mattoon, IL 61938 217-235-1992
Fax: 217-234-9180
Brooms
Manager: Clarence Gillispie
Manager: Clarence Gillespie
Estimated Sales: $1 - 2.5 Million
Number Employees: 5-9
Parent Co: Luco Mop Company

18759 American Brush Company
3150 NW 31st Avenue
Suite 3
Portland, OR 97210 503-234-5064
Fax: 503-234-1270 800-826-8492
info@americanbrush.com
www.americanbrush.com
Manufacturer and exporter of industrial and commercial brooms and brushes
President: Laddie Wirth
CEO: John Martin
President: Laddie Wirth, Sr.
Vice President: Janine Wirth
Customer Service: Leroy Raz

Estimated Sales: $2.5-5 Million
Number Employees: 10-19
Square Footage: 20000

18760 American Cart Company
12 Eccleston Avenue
North Kingstown, RI 02852-7406 401-885-5055
Fax: 401-885-5057

Coffee and espresso carts

18761 American Casein Company(AMCO)
109 Elbow Lane
Burlington, NJ 08016 609-387-3130
Fax: 609-387-7204 info@109elbow.com
www.americancasein.com
Developer and manufacturer of functional protein ingredients and protein polymers for the edible applications for customers around the world.
CEO: Dennis Bobker
CFO: Jack Pipala
Account Manager: Jane Macey
Sales Manager: Cliff Lang
Human Resources Manager/IT Manager: Ellen Iuliucci
Facilities Manager: Chris Lockard
Estimated Sales: $5.8 Million
Number Employees: 50
Square Footage: 120000
Type of Packaging: Bulk

18762 American Chocolate MouldCompany
1401 Church St Ste 5
Bohemia, NY 11716 631-589-5080
Fax: 516-908-3660 amerchoc@mindspring.com
www.americanchocolatemould.com
Chocolate equipment chocolate moulds, plain and printed aluminum foils, foil wrapping machines
President: Raymond J Cote Jr
Sales Director: David Cote
Public Relations: Katie Cote
Estimated Sales: $500,000-$1 000,000
Number Employees: 10-19
Square Footage: 1700
Type of Packaging: Private Label, Bulk

18763 American Coaster Company
3685 Lockport Rd
Sanborn, NY 14132-9404 716-731-9193
Fax: 716-731-4138 888-423-8628
info@american-coaster.com
www.americancoaster.com
Custom designed beverage coasters
President: Tom Muraca
Sales Manager: Tammy Gorzka
Customer Service: Stacy Sikora
Estimated Sales: $10-20 Million
Number Employees: 50-99
Parent Co: Gardei

18764 American Containers
2526 Western Ave
Plymouth, IN 46563 574-936-4068
Fax: 574-936-4036 info@acontainers.com
www.acontainers.com
Manufacturer and exporter of corrugated boxes
President: Michael Isban
CFO: Steve Tubes
Estimated Sales: $5 - 10 Million
Number Employees: 20-49

18765 American Conveyor Corporation
26-40 1st St.
Astoria, NY 11385-1002 718-386-0480
Fax: 718-456-1233 info@americanconveyor.net
www.americanconveyor.net
Supplier of belt and rollover conveyor, bagging & debagging, case packaging & unscrambling, case stackers, casers, checkweighers, corrugated case forming & top sealing, corrugated palletizing & banding, deunitizers, fillers, labeling &coding, metal detectors, palletizers, pushers, unitizers, unstackers, shrink wrap & stretch wrap, truck & dock leveling
Owner: Valdie Freidman
Estimated Sales: Below $5 Million
Number Employees: 20-49
Other Locations:
American Conveyor Corporation
Carlisle NY
American Conveyor Corporation
Overland Park KS
American Conveyor Corporation
Sarasota FL
American Conveyor Corporation
Uxbridge MA
American Conveyor Corporation
Murray KY
American Conveyor Corporation
St. Petersburg FL

18766 American Coolair Corporation
P.O.Box 2300
Jacksonville, FL 32203 904-389-3646
Fax: 904-387-3449 info@coolair.com
www.coolair.com
Manufacturer and exporter of ventilation fans and systems
President: Harry M Graves Jr
VP: Neal Taylor
Marketing/Sales Manager: Mark Fales
Estimated Sales: $20 - 50 Million
Number Employees: 100-249
Square Footage: 110000

18767 American Crane & Equipment Company
531 Old Swede Rd
Douglassville, PA 19518 610-385-6061
Fax: 610-385-3191 info@americancrane.com
www.americancrane.com
Cranes and hoist trolleys
President: Oddvar Norheim
CFO: Dave Hope
Quality Control: Frank Yurich
VP of Sales: David Schaeffer
Purchasing Manager: Sandy Hoffman
Estimated Sales: $20 - 50 Million
Number Employees: 50-99
Square Footage: 60000

18768 American Custom Drying Company
109 Elbow Ln
Burlington, NJ 08016-4123 609-387-3933
Fax: 609-387-7204 acd@109elbow.com
www.americancustomdrying.com
Spray drying and blending services
President: Richard Shipley
CFO: Michael Garger
Vice President: Svend Hansen
Quality Control: Fran Thornton
Public Relations: Jane Macey
Operations Manager: Larry Cutler
Estimated Sales: $10 - 20 Million
Number Employees: 50-99
Type of Packaging: Private Label, Bulk

18769 American Cutting Edge
480 Congress Park Drive
Centerville, OH 45459 937-488-2398
Fax: 937-866-6844 888-252-3372
info@americancuttingedge.com
www.americancuttingedge.com
Industry standard blades and knives, high tolerant blades and safety knives
President: Rich Pooter
CFO: Don Cain
Estimated Sales: $5 - 10 Million
Number Employees: 20
Square Footage: 400000
Parent Co: CB Manufacturing & Sales Company

18770 American Cylinder Company
481 S Governors Hwy
Peotone, IL 60468 708-258-3935
Fax: 708-258-3980
amcyl@americancylinder.com
www.americancylinder.com
President: Joseph White
Estimated Sales: $20 - 50 Million

18771 American Design & Machinery
430 Cummings Avenue NW
Grand Rapids, MI 49534-7984 616-791-4856
Fax: 616-791-4898 www@admach.com
Food processing machinery
Marketing Director: Robert Cisleil
Estimated Sales: $1-2.5 000,000
Number Employees: 19
Square Footage: 23000

18772 American Design Studios
6353 Corte Del Abeto Ste A106
Carlsbad, CA 92011 760-438-8880
Fax: 760-438-8488 800-899-7104
www.americandesignstudios.com
Manufacturer and importer of shirts with names and logos
President: Robert Peritz
Marketing Director: Judy Morrill
Estimated Sales: $10-20 Million
Number Employees: 10-19
Brands:
American Terrain

18773 American Dish Service
900 Blake St
Edwardsville, KS 66111-3820 913-422-3700
Fax: 913-422-6630 800-922-2178
www.americandish.com
Commercial dishwashers
President: Jamie Andrews
Estimated Sales: $20-50 Million
Number Employees: 100-249

18774 American Dixie Group
250 Osborne Rd
Albany, NY 12205-1300 518-453-9000
www.americandixie.com
Packaging machinery
Owner: Beth Wade
Estimated Sales: $5-10 Million
Number Employees: 5-9

18775 American Drying Systems
1135 NW 159th Drive
Miami, FL 33169 305-625-2451
Fax: 305-623-0475 800-762-7565
www.atlasfoodserv.com
Manufacturer and exporter of dehydrating and drying machinery
Estimated Sales: $50-100 Million
Number Employees: 100-249
Parent Co: Atlas Metal Industries
Brands:
Adsco

18776 American Eagle Food Machinery
3557 S Halsted St
Chicago, IL 60609 773-376-0800
Fax: 773-376-2010 800-836-5756
Info@AmericanEagleMachine.com
www.americaneaglemachine.com
Manufacturer, importer and exporter of bakery machinery including mixers, bread slicers and grinders-meat tenderizer, dough sheets, dough roller, dividers of rounders and dough molders.
Owner: Spencer Yang
Estimated Sales: $1-2,500,000
Number Employees: 10-19
Brands:
American Eagle

18777 American Electric Power
1 Riverside Plaza
Columbus, OH 43215-2372 614-716-1000
Fax: 918-599-3480 888-216-3523
ochathaway@aep.com www.aep.com
Electric utility systems, research
Estimated Sales: $1 - 5 000,000
Number Employees: 500

18778 American Electronic Components
1101 Lafayette St.
Elkhart, IN 46515-0280 574-295-6330
Fax: 574-293-8013 888-847-6552
www.aecsensors.com
Number Employees: 250-499

18779 American Engineering Corporation
PO Box 336
Collegedale, TN 37315-0336 423-396-3666
Fax: 423-396-3668 support@americanengr.com
www.americanengr.com
Food safety data collection
Estimated Sales: $5-10 Million
Number Employees: 3

18780 American Environmental International
1325 Remington Road
Schaumburg, IL 60173-4834 847-342-8600
Fax: 847-342-8500 800-343-8601
jstandon@aol.com www.aei-inc.com
Environmental control and resource recovery equipment, emission control, solvent recovery systems, air pollution control
Estimated Sales: $500,000-$1 Million
Number Employees: 5-9

18781 American Equipment Company
1080 Hardees Drive
Aberdeen, MD 21001 410-272-2626
Fax: 410-272-2011 aec@sprynet.com
www.seamers.com
Refurbisher of can seamers; also, parts available
President: Charles Adams
General Manager: Mike Mangone
Estimated Sales: Below $5 Million
Number Employees: 5-9

18782 American Equipment Systems
5456 Louie Ln.
Reno, NV 89510-7061 775-852-1114
President: Robert G Sapeta
Estimated Sales: $3 - 5 Million
Number Employees: 5-9
Parent Co: American European Systems

18783 American European Systems
5456 Louie Lane
Reno, NV 89510-7061 775-852-1114
Fax: 775-852-1163 info@aes-sorma.com
www.aes-sorma.com
Importer and wholesaler/distributor of cutting, peeling, bagging and weighing equipment
President: Robert Sapeta
Sales/Marketing Executive: Don Bergin
Estimated Sales: $3 - 5 Million
Number Employees: 5-9
Square Footage: 32000

18784 American Excelsior Company
850 Avenue H E
Arlington, TX 76011-7720 817-385-3500
Fax: 817-649-7816 800-777-7645
rstaley@americanexcelsior.com
www.amerexcel.com
Plastic packaging products, erosion control products, evaporative cooling products and foam padding
General Manager: Rice Lake
Chairman: Robert Gregerson
CEO: Terry A Sadowski
Vice President of Sales and Marketing: Ken Starrett
Vice President of Operations: Kevin Stew
Estimated Sales: $20-50 Million
Number Employees: 20-49

18785 American Excelsior Inc
850 Avenue H East
Arlington, TX 76011
Fax: 817-649-7816 800-777-7645
www.americanexcelsior.com
Manufacturer, custom molder and exporter of foam packaging products including inserts, contours, protectors, pads, liners and fillers
President, Chief Executive Officer: Terry A. Sadowski
VP, CFO: Todd A. Eblen
Vice President of Sales and Marketing: Ken Starrett
Vice President of Sales and Marketing: Ken Starrett
Vice President of Operations: Kevin Stew
Estimated Sales: $5-10 Million
Number Employees: 20-49

18786 (HQ)American Extrusion International
498 Prairie Hill Rd
South Beloit, IL 61080 815-624-6616
Fax: 815-624-6628
rickw@americanextrusion.com
www.americanextrusion.com
Supplier and exporter of direct expansion extruders and auxiliary equipment including forced air ovens, fryers, seasoning systems, wear parts, reel cutters, mixers, tumblers and conveyors
President: Richard J Warner
R&D: Dr. Samirў El-Shatter
Director of Sales: Rick Warner
Sales Director: Rick Warner
General Manager: Daniel Thompson
Estimated Sales: $.5-$1 million
Number Employees: 20-49
Square Footage: 27000
Other Locations:
American Extrusion Internatio
South Beloit IL
Brands:
American Extrusion International

18787 American Fabric Filter
29807 State Road 54
Wesley Chapel, FL 33543 813-991-9400
Fax: 813-991-9700 800-367-3591
info@americanfabricfilter.com
www.americanfabricfilter.com
Manufacturers of custom made filter bags, dust bags and transfer sleeves for the food, wood, processing and baking industries. Our products are made specifically to fit each application.
President: Derek Williams
CFO: Tim Robinson
Estimated Sales: Below $5 Million
Number Employees: 5-9

18788 American Felt & Filter Company
361 Walsh Ave
New Windsor, NY 12553 845-561-3560
Fax: 845-563-4422 questions@affco.com
www.affco.com
President/CEO: Wilson H. Pryne
Vice President: Scott H. Pryne
Sales Manager: Mark A. Pryne
Estimated Sales: $10 - 20 Million
Number Employees: 50-99

18789 American Fire SprinklerServices, Inc
16221 NW 57th Ave
Hialeah, FL 33014-6709 305-628-0100
Fax: 305-628-3556 Sprinklerheads@bellsouth.net
www.americanfiresprinklers.com
Manufacturer and exporter of sprinkler systems
Owner: Anisa Oweiss
Operations Director: Ken Oweis
Estimated Sales: $2.5-5 Million
Number Employees: 10-19
Type of Packaging: Consumer, Food Service

18790 American Flag & Banner
28 S Main St
Clawson, MI 48017 248-288-3010
Fax: 248-288-5630 800-892-5168
flagsetc@aol.com
www.americanflagandbanner.com
Manufacturer and exporter of flags, pennants and banners
President: William S Miles
Sales Manager: Michelle Angle
Estimated Sales: $500,000 - $1 Million
Number Employees: 5-9

18791 American Foam Corporation
61 John St
Johnston, RI 02919 401-944-4990
Fax: 401-944-0142 800-235-0010
info@americanfoam.com
www.americanfoam.com
Flocked foam packaging materials
President: Aram Manouelian
VP: Chad Martin
Estimated Sales: $20-50 Million
Number Employees: 50-99

18792 American Food & Equipment
1301 North Miami Ave
Miami, FL 33136 305-377-8991
Fax: 305-358-4328
michael@americanfoodequipment.com
www.americanfoodequipment.com
Manufacturer and supplier of restaurant equipment such as coolers, freezers, and ice machines
Founder: Robert Green
President/Owner: Michael Clements
Estimated Sales: $460,000
Number Employees: 5
Square Footage: 28000
Parent Co: American Grinding And Equipment Company.
Type of Packaging: Consumer, Private Label, Bulk

18793 American Food EquipmentCompany
21040 Forbes Ave
Hayward, CA 94545-1116 510-783-0255
Fax: 510-783-0409 amfec@amfec.com
www.amfec.com
Manufacturer and exporter of mixers, dumpers, belt and screw conveyors, vacuum stuffers, tumblers and massagers
President: Michael Botto
Quality Control: Melvin Hauss
Controller: Simone Manos
Plant Manager: Ron Balthasar
Estimated Sales: $5 - 10 Million
Number Employees: 20-49
Square Footage: 80000
Brands:
Amfec

18794 (HQ)American Forms & Labels
7448 W Mossy Cup St
Boise, ID 83709-2839 208-562-0750
Fax: 208-562-0151 800-388-3554
margie@crown-american.com
www.crown-american.com
Pressure sensitive labels; also, bar code systems and hardware
Owner: Kevin Curtin
Estimated Sales: $5-10 Million
Number Employees: 10-19
Square Footage: 60000

18795 American Formula
4720 Frederick Dr SW
Atlanta, GA 30336 404-691-7940
Fax: 404-691-7943 800-282-1215
pvcnet@aol.com www.americanformula.com
Industrial cleaning compounds
President: Don Hamilton
President: Phillip Consolino
General Manager: Michael Holtzman
Number Employees: 20-49
Parent Co: Holtco

18796 (HQ)American Fruit Processors
10725 Sutter Ave
Pacoima, CA 91331-2553 818-899-9574
Fax: 818-899-6042 sales@americanfruit.com
www.americanfruits-flavors.com
Manufacturer and exporter of fruit juice and custom blended concentrates and natural fruit sweeteners
President: Fred Farago
VP Marketing: Richard Linn
Purchasing Manager: Jack Haddad
Estimated Sales: $50-100 Million
Number Employees: 50-99
Square Footage: 40000
Parent Co: American Fruit & Flavors
Type of Packaging: Bulk
Other Locations:
American Fruit Processors
Los Angeles CA
Brands:
Juicy Moo
Moose Juice
Phytoceuticals
Pound-4-Pound Powdered

18797 American Fruits & Flavors
10725 Sutter Ave
Pacoima, CA 91331 818-899-9574
Fax: 818-899-6042 sales@americanfruit.com
www.americanfruit.com
Custom flavor, fruit juice blends, natural sweeteners and juice concentrates and liquid powder blends. Specializing in fruit, vegetable, sweet and savor flavors, clouds, flavor bases, fruit concentrates, WONFs®, WOJCs®, dietblends, coconut products, smoothies, tropical blends and phyto-ceuticals®.
President: Fred Farago
Controller: Michael Model
Account Executive: Shane Herman
Programmer/Analyst: Irene Shure
VP Sales & Marketing: Richard Linn
Manager Human Resources: Regina Rodriguez
Estimated Sales: $16.6 Million
Number Employees: 100
Square Footage: 20000

18798 American Fuji Seal
1051 Bloomfield Rd
Bardstown, KY 40004 502-348-9211
Fax: 502-348-9558 800-533-3854
mlane@afseal.com www.afseal.com
Shrink sleeves and application equipment
President: Takeo Sonoda
Estimated Sales: $20 - 50 Million
Number Employees: 50-99

18799 American Gas & ChemicalCompany Limited
220 Pegasus Ave
Northvale, NJ 07647 201-767-7300
Fax: 201-767-1741 800-288-3647
contact@amgas.com www.amgas.com

Leak detection products and gas monitoring systems
President: Gerald Anderson
Quality Control and CFO: Jim Zanosky
Controller: Jim Zanosky
R&D: Scott Bruce
Marketing Director: Gerald Anderson
Sales Manager: John Hamilton
Estimated Sales: $10 - 20 Million
Number Employees: 20-49
Square Footage: 25000
Brands:
Flaw Finder
Leak-Tec
Pin Point

18800 American Gas Association
400 North Capitol Street
Washington, DC 20001 202-824-7000
Fax: 703-841-8406 www.aga.org
Gas dispensing systems
President: Christopher Johns
President, Chief Executive Officer: Dave McCurdy
Senior Vice President: Chris Hermann
Sales Director: Axel Nordwall
Director of Public Relations: Jake Rubin
President, Chief Operating Officer: Lawrence Borgard
Estimated Sales: $1-5 Million
Number Employees: 5
Parent Co: Linde Technische

18801 American Gasket & RubberCompany
119 Commerce Dr
Schaumburg, IL 60173 847-882-9333
Fax: 847-882-9333 www.tekni-plex.com
Number Employees: 100-249

18802 American Handling
18029 Cleveland Pkwy Dr
Cleveland, OH 44135 501-375-6611
Fax: 501-375-8931 800-482-5801
ÿsales@amermaterial.comÿ
www.amermaterial.com
Wholesaler/distributor and exporter of material handling systems; also, design consultant
President: Thomas DiSieno
VP of Marketing: Albert Redding
VP of Sales: Jack Racer
Estimated Sales: $5-10 Million
Number Employees: 9
Square Footage: 40000
Parent Co: Cetrum Industries

18803 American Hawaiian Soy Company
274 Kalihi Street
Honolulu, HI 96819 808-841-8435
800-841-8435
Soybean manufacturer
President: John Morita

18804 American Holt Corporation
203 Carnegie Row
Norwood, MA 02062 781-440-9993
Fax: 781-440-9994 sales@americanholt.com
www.americanholt.com
Replacement parts for industry
President: John Levy
Estimated Sales: $3 - 5 Million
Number Employees: 5-9

18805 American Housewares Manufacturing Corporation
755 E 134th St
Bronx, NY 10454 718-665-9500
Fax: 718-292-0830
sales@americanhousewaresmfg.com
www.americanhousewaresmfg.com
Manufacturer and exporter of kitchen utensils and equipment including strainers, colanders, basting spoons, forks, pancake turners, mashers, fry baskets, splatter screens, roast racks, kitchen tools and gadgets
President: Paul Mayer
COO: Irving Spiegel
Estimated Sales: $5-10 Million
Number Employees: 50-99

18806 American Houver Company
7700 Austin Ave
Skokie, IL 60077 847-470-3300
Fax: 847-966-8074 800-772-0355
www.americanlouver.com
Manufacturer and exporter of fluorescent lighting louvers, acrylic mirror sheets, handheld shopping baskets and convex security mirrors
President: Geoff Glass Jr
Chairman the Board: Walter Glass
VP: Barry Peterson
CFO: Lucy Polk
Marketing Manager: Butch Cavello
Estimated Sales: $20 - 50 Million
Number Employees: 50-99
Brands:
Alumicube
Paracube

18807 American IdentificationIndustries
1319 Howard Drive
West Chicago, IL 60185-1625 630-231-4500
Fax: 630-231-4530 800-255-8890
Plastic cards
Sales Manager: Juan Sanjujo
Sales: Ginny Lacy
Sales Support: Sandy Brush
Estimated Sales: $5-10 Million
Number Employees: 5

18808 American Identity
1520 Albany Pl SE
Orange City, IA 51041 712-737-4925
Fax: 712-737-2408 800-369-2277
www.americanidentity.com
Manufacturer, importer and exporter of promotional items including caps, jackets, uniforms, etc
Manager: Larry Sanson
Marketing Manager: Greg Ebel
Estimated Sales: $50-100 Million
Number Employees: 250-499
Parent Co: American Marketing Industry
Brands:
Glengate
Identity
K-Products
Swingster

18809 American Industrial Supply Company
519 Potrero Ave
San Francisco, CA 94110-1431 415-826-1144
Fax: 415-552-3300
President: George Herbst
Estimated Sales: $50,000 - 1 Million
Number Employees: 1-4

18810 American Ingredients Company
3947 Broadway Street
Kansas City, MO 64111-2516 816-561-9050
Fax: 816-561-9909 800-669-4092
mhart@americaningredients.com
www.aic-breddo.com
Manufacturer and exporter of emulsifiers, blends, blending equipment, defoamers and softeners
President: Ron Ashton
CFO: Joe Christopher
VP: R Masa
Estimated Sales: $20-50 Million
Number Employees: 50-99
Parent Co: CSM
Brands:
Alphamim
Bfm
Breddo Likwifier
Emplex
Patcote
Verv

18811 American Insulated PanelCompany
75 John Hancock Rd
Taunton, MA 02780 508-823-7003
Fax: 508-880-6438 800-924-2774
sales@aipanel.com
www.americaninsulatedpanel.com
Manufacturer and installer of walk in coolers and freezers, cold storage doors, and glass display doors.
President: John Lynch
CFO: John Lynch
R&D: John Lynch
Quality Control: John Lynch
Estimated Sales: $5 - 10 Million
Number Employees: 20-49
Square Footage: 35000
Type of Packaging: Bulk

18812 American International Electric
2835 Pellissier Pl
City of Industry, CA 90601-1512 562-908-5058
Fax: 562-908-5059 800-732-5377
sealers@worldnet.att.net www.aieco.com
CEO: Charles Chen
Estimated Sales: $3 - 5 Million
Number Employees: 10-19

18813 American International Tooling
2516 Business Parkway
Suite A
Minden, NV 89423 775-267-6939
Fax: 775-267-697 866-248-8665
sales@seamertooling.com
www.seamertooling.org
Manufacturer seamer tooling for canning and bottling industry
President: Lee Bertucci
Vice President Sales: John Konvicka
Production Manager: Anna Westmorland
Estimated Sales: $1 - 3 Million
Number Employees: 5-9

18814 American LED-gible
1776 Lone Eagle St
Columbus, OH 43228 614-851-1100
Fax: 614-851-1121 sale@ledgible.com
www.ledgible.com
Light emitting electronic display signs
President: George Smith
Estimated Sales: $1-2.5 Million
Number Employees: 10-19
Square Footage: 20000
Brands:
American Led-Gible, Inc.

18815 American LEWA
132 Hopping Brook Road
Holliston, MA 01746 508-429-7403
Fax: 508-429-8615 888-539-2123
sales@lewa-inc.com www.lewa.com
Manufacturer and exporter of precision metering and mixing pumps and systems for blending and proportioning all liquids; also, seal-less controlled volume pumps for process services and moderate high pressures
President/Owner: Mike Meraji
Purchasing Director: Charlie Riordan
Number of Brands: 1
Number of Products: 4
Parent Co: OTT Holding Internationa GmbH
Brands:
Lewa Ecodos
Lewa Lab
Lewa Modular
Lewa Triplex

18816 (HQ)American Label Mark
5724 N Pulaski Rd
Chicago, IL 60646 773-478-0900
Fax: 800-723-4327 800-621-5808
sales@labelmaster.com www.labelmaster.com
Manufacturer and exporter of signs including indoor, outdoor, painted and silk screened for restaurants, food manufacturers, etc
President: Dwight Curtis
CFO: Ed Kaplan
VP/Marketing: Marilyn Paprocki
Estimated Sales: $30-50 Million
Number Employees: 5-9
Type of Packaging: Food Service

18817 American Lifts
P.O. Box 1058
Guthrie, OK 73044 405-282-5200
Fax: 405-282-8105 877-360-6777
sales@autoquip.com www.americanlifts.com
Manufacturer, importer and exporter of lifts including hydraulic scissor and stainless steel; also, hydraulic tilters, and pallet trucks
Manager: Clay Brinson
Estimated Sales: $10 - 20 Million
Number Employees: 50-99
Square Footage: 70000
Parent Co: Columbs McKinnon Corporation
Brands:
Torklift

18818 **American Liquid Packaging Systems**
440 N Wolfe Rd
Sunnyvale, CA 94085-3869 650-363-2900
Fax: 650-363-2901 alps@alps-aquaservice.com
www.alps-watersupply.com
Bottled water plants, accessories and plastic resin
Owner: Saeed Amidi
Estimated Sales: $20 - 50 Million
Number Employees: 5-9

18819 **American Machinery Corporation**
PO Box 3228
Orlando, FL 32802-3228 407-295-2581
Estimated Sales: $1 - 5 Million

18820 **American Manufacturing &Engineering Company**
910 Cahoon Rd
Cleveland, OH 44145-1228 440-899-9400
Fax: 440-899-9401 800-822-9402
info@ameco-usa.com www.ameco-usa.com
Steel and stainless steel fabricated beverage and liquid distribution/fillers, steam pressure vessels and mixer components; exporter of stainless and regular steel manufactured products
President and CEO: Michael Perkins
Sales/Marketing Manager: Fred Swanson
Sales Engineer: Tom Miller
Estimated Sales: $500,000-$1 Million
Number Employees: 5-9
Square Footage: 100000

18821 **American Marazzi Tile**
359 Clay Rd
Mesquite, TX 75182 972-226-0110
Fax: 972-226-5629 www.marazzitile.com
CEO: Gianni Mattioli
Estimated Sales: $100+ Million
Number Employees: 250-499

18822 **American Menu Displays**
4862 36th Street
Long Island City, NY 11101-1918 718-392-1032
Fax: 718-786-9310
www.americandiscounttableware.com
Display signs and menu boards
President: Robet Subaj
Estimated Sales: $10 - 20 Million
Number Employees: 100-249
Brands:
Panel Lite

18823 **American Metal Door Company**
PO Box 2008
Richmond, IN 47375-2008 800-428-2737
Fax: 800-626-1490 800-428-2737
amdco@americanmetaldoor.com
www.americanmetaldoor.com
Stainless steel and galvanized sliding doors; also, high speed electric and pneumatic operators
Marketing Coordinator: Jennifer George
Sales Manager: Doug HolmesMidwest
Estimated Sales: $3 Million
Number Employees: 35
Square Footage: 108000
Brands:
Doors
Electric & Pneumatic Op.
Hardware

18824 **American Metal Stamping& Spinning**
1 Nassau Ave
Brooklyn, NY 11222 718-384-1500
Fax: 718-384-1523
Heavy duty bakers' pans and trays, food strainers, institutional kitchen baking and roasting pans and equipment smallwares
President: Stephanie Eisenberg
Estimated Sales: $5 - 10 Million
Number Employees: 20-49

18825 **American Metalcraft**
2074 George St
Melrose Park, IL 60160-1515 800-333-9133
Fax: 800-333-6046 info@amnow.com
www.amnow.com
Manufacturer, importer, exporter and wholesaler/distributor of stainless steel restaurant/bar tabletop supplies, funnels, pizza trays and food covers; serving the food service market
President: David Kahn
Sales Manager: Richard Packer
Estimated Sales: $10-20 Million
Number Employees: 100
Square Footage: 120000
Type of Packaging: Food Service
Brands:
American Metalcraft

18826 **American Municipal Chemical Company**
1907 S 89th St
West Allis, WI 53227 414-329-2920
Fax: 414-329-9043 800-598-3106
info@chemicalbargains.net
www.chemicalbargains.net
Cleaning compounds
President: Wayne Benz
VP: Eric Benz
Estimated Sales: $5-10 Million
Number Employees: 5-9
Square Footage: 30000

18827 **American National Can Company**
8770 W Bryn Mawr Ave # 11t
Chicago, IL 60631-3515 773-399-3000
Fax: 773-399-3354 www.rexam.com
Metal packaging manufacturer, aluminum can packaging
President: William Francois
CEO: Harry Barto
Estimated Sales: $2.5-5 Million
Number Employees: 5,000-9,999

18828 **American National Rubber**
P.O. Box 878
Ceredo, WV 25507-6396 304-453-1311
Fax: 304-453-2347 www.anro.com
Manufacturer and exporter of sponge rubber including gaskets and seals
Sales Manager: Ed Littlehales
Estimated Sales: $20-50 Million
Number Employees: 250-500

18829 **American Olean Tile Company**
1000 N Cannon Ave
Lansdale, PA 19446 215-855-1111
Estimated Sales: $1 - 5 Million
Parent Co: Armstrong World Industries

18830 **American Packaging Corporation**
P.O.Box 16223
Philadelphia, PA 19114-0223 215-676-8888
Fax: 215-698-7119 bkemp@ampkcorp.com
www.swalter.com
Flexible packages
President: Peter Schottland
CEO: Peter Schottland
CFO: Tom May
CEO: Andrew N Wilson
Quality Control: Jim Carlson
Estimated Sales: $81.3 Million
Number Employees: 100-249

18831 **American Packaging Machinery**
2550 S Eastwood Dr
Woodstock, IL 60098 815-337-8580
Fax: 815-337-8583 sales@apm-machinery.com
www.apm-machinery.com
Owner: Tadiya Peric
Estimated Sales: Below $5 Million
Number Employees: 20-49

18832 **American Packaging Machinery**
2550 S Eastwood Dr
Woodstock, IL 60098 815-337-8580
Fax: 815-337-8583 888-755-2705
sales@apm-machinery.com
www.apm-machinery.com
High speed servo controlled shrink wrapping systems and high speed shrink bundling equipment
President: Tadia Peric
Estimated Sales: $10 - 20 000,000
Number Employees: 20-49
Type of Packaging: Bulk

18833 **American Pallet**
1001 Knox Rd
Oakdale, CA 95361 209-847-6122
Fax: 209-847-6154 www.americanpallet.com
Pallets, skids, bins and crates
President: Bill Montey
VP: John Fauria
VP: John Fauria
Estimated Sales: $20 - 50 Million
Number Employees: 20-49

18834 **American Pallets**
2069 New Castle Rd.
Box 201
Portersville, PA 16051 724-658-5747

18835 **American Pan Company**
417 E Water St
PO Box 678
Urbana, OH 43078 937-652-3232
Fax: 937-652-1384 800-652-2151
sales@americanpan.com www.americanpan.com
Commercial bakery pans
President: Gil T Bundy
Estimated Sales: $10-20 000,000
Number Employees: 50-99

18836 **American Panel Corporation**
5800 SE 78th St
Ocala, FL 34472 352-245-7055
Fax: 352-245-0726 800-327-3015
sales@americanpanel.com
www.americanpanel.com
Manufacturer and exporter of walk-in coolers and freezers, blast chillers, refrigerated warehouses and refrigeration systems
President: Danny Duncan
CEO: Marvin Duncan
VP: Harmon Lewis
Sales Manager: Kevin Graham
Sales Associate: Jenn Duncan
Estimated Sales: $20 - 50 Million
Number Employees: 100-249
Square Footage: 100000
Type of Packaging: Food Service
Brands:
American Panel

18837 **American Plant & Equipment**
4200 S Church Street Ext
Roebuck, SC 29376 864-574-0404
Fax: 864-576-7204
apesales@americanplantandequipment.com
www.americanplantandequipment.com
Owner: Victor Le Bron
Quality Control: Cindy Forster
Estimated Sales: Below $5 Million
Number Employees: 5-9

18838 **American Plywood**
7011 S 19th St
Tacoma, WA 98466-5333 253-565-6600
Fax: 253-565-7265 www.apawood.org
President: David L Rogoway
Director: Dennis Hardman
Estimated Sales: F
Number Employees: 100-249

18839 **American Printpak**
P.O.Box 304
Sussex, WI 53089-0304 262-246-7300
Fax: 262-246-7388 800-441-8003
cbh1@americanprintpak.com
www.americanprintpak.com
Flexible packaging material including cohesive tape, foil, rolls and sheets; also, heat seal coated lidding and roll stock
President: Joseph Dollak
Director Sales/Marketing: Charles Holbrook
Customer Service: Anjanette Goetz
Estimated Sales: $5-10 Million
Number Employees: 20-49
Square Footage: 116000
Brands:
Touchseal

18840 **American Process Systems**
4033 Ryan Rd
Gurnee, IL 60031-1255 847-336-2444
Fax: 847-336-0914 eirich@eirichusa.com
www.eirichusa.com
High quality mixers, dryers, reactors and ancillary equipment
Sales: Richard Zak
VP Sales: Richard Zak
Estimated Sales: $20-50 Million
Number Employees: 50-99
Parent Co: Elrich Machines

18841 American Production Company
2734 Spring Street
Redwood City, CA 94063 650-368-5334
Fax: 650-368-4547
info@americanproduction.com
www.americanproduction.com
Manufacturer and exporter of commercial and industrial stainless steel insulated food and beverage containers and thermal dispensers
Owner: Owen Conley
Estimated Sales: $2.5-5 Million
Number Employees: 5-9
Parent Co: Tilley Manufacturing Company
Brands:
Super Chef

18842 American Profol
4333 C St SW
Cedar Rapids, IA 52404 319-365-0599
Fax: 319-365-1696 sales@profol.com
www.americanprofol.com
Plastic industrial film
CEO: Mark Thoeny
Estimated Sales: $20 - 50 Million
Number Employees: 50-99

18843 American Radionic Company
P.O.Box 352919
Palm Coast, FL 32135-2919 386-445-6000
Fax: 386-445-6871 800-445-6033
www.americanradionic.com
HVAC capacitors
President: Robert Stockman
Estimated Sales: $10-20 Million
Number Employees: 50-99

18844 American Range & Hood Corporation
13592 Desmond St
Pacoima, CA 91331 818-896-2769
Fax: 818-897-1670 888-753-9898
info@americanrange.com
www.americanrange.com
Manufacturer and exporter of commercial cooking equipment including exhaust hoods, ranges, ovens, hot plates, open burners, stock pot stoves, broilers, griddles, woks, cheese melters, chicken rotisseries, etc
President: Shane Demirjian
Quality Control: Cristie Merriot
Estimated Sales: $10 - 20 Million
Number Employees: 100-249
Square Footage: 35000
Brands:
American Range

18845 American Resin Corporation
6250 Southwest Pkwy
Wichita Falls, TX 76310 940-692-8011
Fax: 940-692-8014
President: John Vitek
Estimated Sales: $.5 - 1 million
Number Employees: 1-4

18846 American Restaurant Supply
133 128th Street SW
Everett, WA 98204 425-740-2424
Fax: 425-740-2432 888-770-2424
www.bargreen.com OR
www.americanrestaurantsupply.com
Restaurant equipment, restaurant supplies, kitchen supplies, bar supplies, janitorial supplies, disposables, and restaurant design services.
President: Howard Bargreen
Sales Manager: Josh Pugh
Estimated Sales: $10-20 Million
Number Employees: 10-19
Parent Co: American Restaurant Supply
Brands:
Bargreens
Cafe Amore
Golden Drip

18847 American Roland Food Corp
71 West 23rd Street
New York, NY 10010 800-221-4030
Fax: 516-694-9177 www.americanroland.com
Development, manufacture and sale of antioxidants including ethoxyquin, propyl gallate and tocopherols for feed, food and industrial uses

18848 American Safety Technologies
565 Eagle Rock Ave
Roseland, NJ 07068-1501 973-403-2600
Fax: 973-403-1108 800-645-7546
info@insulcast.com www.insulcast.com
Operations: Don Motta
Number Employees: 50-99

18849 American Services Group
850 Ridge Lake Blvd
Memphis, TN 38120 800-333-6678
Fax: 630-271-2710
alison.boyle@servicemaster.com
www.servicemaster.com
Consultant providing energy and waste management, sanitation, maintenance and pest control services
CEO: Robert J Gillette
Senior Vice President, General Counsel: Greer McMullen
Senior Vice President of Corporate Commu: Peter Tosches

18850 American Sigma
P.O. Box 389
Loveland, CO 80539-0389 970-669-3050
Fax: 970-669-2932 800-227-4224
hachflowsales@hach.com
www.americansigma.com
President: William Hungerford

18851 (HQ)American Solving
6511 Eastland Plaza
Brook Park, OH 44142 440-234-7373
Fax: 440-234-9112 800-822-2285
sales@solvinginc.com
www.americansolving.com
Manufacturer, importer and exporter of pneumatic powered ergonomic load transporters, lifts, tilts, turntables and load upenders
President: Orley Aten
General Manager: Stanley Aten
Production Manager: Doug Eckert
Estimated Sales: $3 - 5 Million
Number Employees: 5-9
Square Footage: 6000
Brands:
American Solving
Numeri-Tech
Solving

18852 American Specialty Coffee & Culinary
204 14th Street NW
Atlanta, GA 30318-5304 404-607-1150
Fax: 404-876-1544
Espresso carts, espresso machines and accessories, espresso pod machines

18853 American Specialty Machinery
456 Lake Hamilton Drive
Hot Springs National Par, AR 71913-7423 713-828- 286
Fax: 713-926-2123 www.am-spec-mach.com
Estimated Sales: $1 - 5 Million

18854 American Star Cork Company
33-53 62nd Street
P.O. Box 770449
Woodside, NY 11377 718-335-3000
Fax: 718-335-3037 800-338-3581
info@amstarcork.com www.amstarcork.com
Manufacturer, exporter and importer of cork and cork products
President: Thomas Petrosino
Estimated Sales: $.5 - 1 million
Number Employees: 1-4

18855 American Store Fixtures
7700 Austin Avenue
Skokie, IL 60077-2603
Fax: 847-966-8074
www.americanstorefixtures.com
Manufacturer and exporter of shopping baskets, security mirrors
President/Owner: Geoff Glass Jr
CEO: Geoff Glass Jr
CFO: Lucy Polk
Quality Control: Carol Salas
Marketing: Donna Kelner
Sales Manager: Debi Greenberg
Public Relations: Donna Kelner
Operations: Carol Salas
Plant Manager: Carol Salas
Estimated Sales: $1 - 5 Million
Number Employees: 100-250
Square Footage: 480000
Parent Co: American Louver

18856 American Style Foods
809 Riverside Drive
Old Hickory, TN 37138 615-847-0410
bobgarrison@mindspring.com
Consultant for food extrusion and product formulation processes
President: Robert Garrison
Number Employees: 4

18857 American Sun Control Awnings
925 McFarland 400 Blvd
Alpharetta, GA 30004-3373 770-772-9900
Fax: 770-740-8668 800-245-6746
advantages@fabri-frame.com
www.fabri-frame.com
Commercial awnings
President: Glorio Patsy Jr.
Estimated Sales: $1-2,500,000
Number Employees: 10-19
Brands:
Fabri-Frame

18858 American Systems Associates
Leander Road
Hampton Bays, NY 11946 718-482-0408
800-584-3663
Gas powered cooking and refrigeration equipment; also, food service design available
President: Johndavid Hensley
VP: Joyce Jones
Regional Director: Diane David
Number Employees: 1-4
Square Footage: 2000
Parent Co: FOOD

18859 American Technical Services Group
680 Oakbrook Parkway
Suite 165
Norcross, GA 30093 770-447-9444
Fax: 770-447-0319
Service company providing instrumentation and control system services including I/C installation, ISO 9000 software, NIST calibration, integration, maintenance and contract staffing
President: Robert Russo
Marketing Manager: Vicci Cogswell
VP Operations: Ray Green
Number Employees: 200
Parent Co: Strategic Distribution

18860 (HQ)American Textile Mills
208 Bennington Ave
Kansas City, MO 64123-1914 816-842-2909
Fax: 816-842-8679
Disposable and reusable wiping towels
President: Dennis Wacknov
Estimated Sales: $5-10 Million
Number Employees: 10 to 19
Square Footage: 90000
Brands:
Nu-Wipes
Quik-Wipes

18861 American Time & Signal
140 3rd St
PO Box 707
Dassel, MN 55325 320-275-2101
Fax: 800-789-1882 800-328-8996
theclockexperts@atsclock.com
www.atsclock.com
Manufacturer and exporter of food preparation timers and clocks
President: Karen Sipola
Estimated Sales: $10-20 Million
Number Employees: 50-99
Square Footage: 40000

Brands:
American Time & Signal
James Remind-O-Timer

18862 American Variseal
510 Burbank St
Broomfield, CO 80020-1604 303-465-1727
Fax: 303-469-4874 variseal@ix.netcom.com
Manager: Tom Potosky
Estimated Sales: $20 - 50 Million
Number Employees: 100-249

18863 American Ventilation Company
P.O.Box 227
Grafton, OH 44044-0227 440-365-4533
Fax: 440-365-5858 800-854-3267
Exhaust and make-up air fans for the food service industry
Manager: Tammy Parron
General Manager: Michael Maynard
Estimated Sales: $1-2.5 Million
Number Employees: 5-9
Square Footage: 25000

18864 American Water Broom
3565 McCall Pl
Atlanta, GA 30340 770-451-2000
Fax: 770-455-4478 800-241-6565
info@waterbrooms.com
www.americanwaterbroom.com
Manufacturer and exporter of commercial and residential high pressure water brooms
VP: Beverly Roberts
Number Employees: 5-9
Brands:
Jetaway
Squirt

18865 American Wax Company
39-30 Review Avenue
PO Box 1943
Long Island City, NY 11101 718-784-0800
Fax: 718-482-9366 888-929-7587
solutions@cleaning-solutions.com
www.cleaning-solutions.com
Manufacturer and exporter of detergents, deodorants, disinfectants, germicides, floor polish and soap
President: Ronald Ingber
Vice President: Ronald Ingber
Sales Manager: Allen Winik
Purchasing Manager: Ron Ingber
Estimated Sales: $2.5 - 5 Million
Number Employees: 20-49
Square Footage: 62000

18866 American Whey Company
12 N State Route 17
Paramus, NJ 07652-2644 201-587-1444
Fax: 201-587-0310

18867 American Wholesale Refrigeration
4001 Hamilton Ave
Cleveland, OH 44114 216-426-8882
Fax: 216-426-8883 877-220-8882
info@awrco.com www.awrco.com
Refrigerating equipment and machinery
President: John Paris
Estimated Sales: Below $5 Million
Number Employees: 10-19

18868 American Wire Products
616 Industrial Park
Frankfort, KY 40601 502-695-0073
Manager: Carol Chamblain
Estimated Sales: $20 - 50 Million
Number Employees: 100-249

18869 American Wood Fibers
9841 Broken Land Pkwy Ste 302
Columbia, MD 21046 410-290-8700
Fax: 410-290-6660 800-624-9663
www.awf.com
Sawdust, firelogs and wood floors
CEO: Ed Leland
General Manager: Mark Fahner
Estimated Sales: $1 - 5 Million
Number Employees: 20-49

18870 American-Newlong
5310 S Harding St
Indianapolis, IN 46217 317-787-9421
Fax: 317-786-5225
newlong@american-newlong.com
www.american-newlong.com
Automated packaging equipment and bagging systems.
President/General Manager: Gary Wells
CFO: Connie Perrin
North American Sales Manager: Garnet McMillian
Warehouse Manager: Mark Banholzer
Estimated Sales: $10-20 Million
Number Employees: 10-19

18871 (HQ)Americana Art China Company
PO Box 310
Sebring, OH 44672 330-938-6133
Fax: 330-938-9546 800-233-6133
amerimug@sbcglobal.net
Custom decorator of ceramic and glassware.
President/CEO: James Puckett
Research & Development: Lisa Cox
Manager of Quality Control: Wendy Davidson
Marketing Director: Jim Puckett
Operations: Jim Puckett
Estimated Sales: $1-3 Million
Number Employees: 32
Number of Products: 126
Square Footage: 80000
Type of Packaging: Private Label, Bulk
Other Locations:
Americana Art China Co.
Sebring OH

18872 Americo
601 E Barton Ave
West Memphis, AR 72301 870-735-4848
Fax: 870-735-4129 800-626-2350
www.americo-inc.com
Laminated and vinyl table covers; also, upholstery fabrics
President: Ed Straub
Chairman of the Board: Wallace Dunbar
Sales Director: Jerry Van Houten
Estimated Sales: $1-2.5 Million
Number Employees: 20-49

18873 Americquest-Transportation And Logistics Resources
457 Haddonfield Rd # 220
Cherry Hill, NJ 08002-2201 856-773-0600
Fax: 856-773-0609 888-999-6957
feedback@fleetxchange.com
www.ameriquestcorp.com
President: Doug Clarck
CFO: Rich Spotts
CEO: Douglas W Clark
Estimated Sales: $50 - 75 Million
Number Employees: 20-49

18874 Americraft Carton
403 Fillmore Ave E
Saint Paul, MN 55107 651-227-6655
Fax: 651-227-4713 www.americraft.com
Folding cartons
Manager: Jim Maher
General Manager: Jim Maher
Plnt Mngr: Brian Lewindowski
Estimated Sales: $10 - 20 Million
Number Employees: 100-249
Parent Co: Americraft Carton

18875 Americraft Carton
7400 State Line Rd.
Suite 206
Prairie Village, KS 66208 913-387-3700
www.americraft.com
Folding cartons
Manager: Eric Hanson
Office Manager: L Large
Plant Manager: F Fess
Estimated Sales: $59 Million
Number Employees: 600
Square Footage: 135000
Parent Co: Americraft Carton Group

18876 Ameridia
20 Worlds Fair Drive
Somerset, NJ 08873 732-805-4003
Fax: 732-805-4008 dbar@ameridia.com
www.ameridia.com
Electrodialysis stacks X equipment chromatography X ion exchange systems, micro ultra and nonafiltration systems.
Quality Control: Daniel Bar
Estimated Sales: $5-10 Million
Number Employees: 9
Parent Co: Eurodia Industrie

18877 Amerikooler
575 East 10th Ave
Hialeah, FL 33010 305-884-8384
Fax: 305-884-8330 800-627-5665
marylo@amerikooler.net www.amerikooler.com
Walk-in coolers, freezers and refrigerated warehouses
President: Renate M Alonso
Vice President: Renato J. Alonso
Vice President of Sales: Gian Carlo Alonso
Purchasing: Macbeth Araque
Estimated Sales: $5 - 10 Million
Number Employees: 100-249

18878 Ameripak
2001 County Line Rd
Warrington, PA 18976-2416 ÿ80- 94- 919
Fax: 215-343-5293 info@ameripak-pes.com
www.ameripak.net
Horizontal form fill seals, flowpak wrapper, fill tray sealers for plastic or paperboard trays
General Manager: Rob Bowlin
Estimated Sales: $5-10 Million
Number Employees: 20-49

18879 Ameristamp Sign-A-Rama
1300 N Royal Ave
Evansville, IN 47715 812-477-7763
Fax: 812-477-7898 800-543-6693
websales@SignsOverAmerica.com
www.signsoveramerica.com
Manufacturer and exporter of marking devices, including rubber stamps
Owner: Walter Valiant
Estimated Sales: $1-2.5 Million
Number Employees: 10-19
Square Footage: 3000
Type of Packaging: Consumer, Food Service, Bulk

18880 Ameritech Laboratories
12817 20th Ave
Flushing, NY 11356-2401 718-461-0475
Fax: 718-461-0187 info@ameritechlabs.com
www.ameritechlabs.com
Consultant providing a complete range of chemical, microbiological and nutritional tests and product development services
President: John Bonnes
Estimated Sales: Below $5 Million
Number Employees: 5-9
Square Footage: 20000

18881 Ameritech Signs
3015 Pico Blvd
Santa Monica, CA 90405 310-829-9359
Fax: 310-998-1109 ameritechsigns@verizon.net
www.ameritechsigns.com
Pennants, signs and banners
Owner: Bill Gabriel
Estimated Sales: less than $500,000
Number Employees: 1-4

18882 Ameron International
P.O.Box 1629
Brea, CA 92822-1629 714-256-7755
Fax: 714-256-7750 www.ameron.com
General Manager: Edwin Steenis
Chairman of the Board, Chief Executive O: James Marlen
Vice President: Christine Stanley
Vice Division President of Operations: David Jones
Plant Manager: Ron Johnson
Estimated Sales: $1 - 5 Million
Number Employees: 1-4

18883 Ames Engineering Corporation
805 E 13th St
Wilmington, DE 19802 302-658-6945
Fax: 302-658-6946 800-628-7128
telesonics@aol.com www.telesoniconline.com
Horizontal form-fill, three and four side seal sachet, stand-up pouch and stick pack portion packaging machinery
Owner: Bernard Katz
Estimated Sales: $5 000,000
Number Employees: 1-4

18884 **Ametco Manufacturing Corporation**
P.O.Box 1210
Willoughby, OH 44096 440-951-4300
Fax: 440-951-2542 800-321-7042
ametco@ametco.com www.ametco.com
Iron and steel security fencing; also, perforated plastics and expanded, perforated, heavy weld and bar metal gratings
President: Steve Mitrovich
Sales Manager: Ludwig Weber
Estimated Sales: $5-10,000,000
Number Employees: 20-49

18885 **Ametek**
900 E Clymer Ave
Sellersville, PA 18960-2628 215-257-6531
Fax: 215-257-4711 chatillon.fl-lar@ametek.com
www.usgauge.com
Test and calibration instruments
Manager: Joe Karpov
Estimated Sales: $30-50 Million
Number Employees: 10-19

18886 **Ametek**
1100 Cassatt Rd.
Berwyn, PA 19312 610-647-2121
Fax: 215-323-9337 chatillon.fl-lar@ametek.com
www.ametek.com
Test and calibration instruments
President/GM: Timothy Jones
VP: Tom Marecic
R&D: Mark Coppler
Quality Control: Dennis Petro
Number Employees: 100-249

18887 **Ametek**
900 E Clymer Ave
Sellersville, PA 18960-2628 215-257-6531
Fax: 215-257-4711 chatillon.fl-lar@ametek.com
www.usgauge.com
Manufacturer and exporter of pressure and temperature gauges
Manager: Joe Karpov
Sales Manager: Amil Demicco
Estimated Sales: $1 - 5 Million
Number Employees: 500-999
Parent Co: Ametek
Brands:
U.S. Gauge

18888 **Ametek**
1100 Cassatt Road
PO Box 1764
Berwyn, PA 19301 610-647-2121
Fax: 215-323-9337 800-473-1286
webmaster@ametek.com www.ametek.com
Controls, meters, transducers, temperature and chart recorders, calibrating devices, temperature and pressure transmitters
President: Frank Hermance
Estimated Sales: $10-25 000,000
Number Employees: 10,000

18889 **Ametek**
8600 Somerset Dr
Largo, FL 33773-2700 727-536-7831
Fax: 727-538-2400 www.ametek.com
Force gauges, mechanical and motorized test stands, material test systems, packaging testers, puncture testers, peel strength testers, grips, fixtures and accessories
Manager: Mike Kern
Estimated Sales: $20 - 50 Million
Number Employees: 50-99

18890 **Ametek Technical & Industrial Products**
627 Lake St
Kent, OH 44240 215-256-6601
Fax: 330-677-3306 www.ametektip.com
Air blowers and air knives for drying, dewatering and sterilization degassing applications; food grade products available, combustion blowers
Manager: Shannon Booth
Sales Director: Jay Jarboe
Number Employees: 50-99
Parent Co: Ametek

18891 **Amherst Milling Company**
140 Union Hill Rd
Amherst, VA 24521-4049 434-946-7601
Grist mills
Manager: William H Wydner
General Manager/VP: Bill Wydner
Estimated Sales: $1 - 3 Million
Number Employees: 1 to 4
Square Footage: 3

18892 **Amiad Filtration Systems**
120-J Talbert Road
Mooresville, NC 28117 704-662-3133
Fax: 704-662-3155 info@amiadusa.com
www.amiadusa.com
President: Tom Akehurst
Chief Executive Officer: Rami Molcho
Finance Executive: Inko Evrard
Sales Executive: Jim Lauria
Operations Executive: Jerry Weynand
Estimated Sales: $5 - 10 Million
Number Employees: 20-49

18893 **Ammeraal Beltech**
7501 Saint Louis Ave
Skokie, IL 60076 847-673-6720
Fax: 847-673-6373 800-323-4170
info@ammeraalbeltechusa.com
www.ammeraal-beltechusa.com
Manufacturer, importer and exporter of belts for packaging machinery and the processing of cookies, crackers, confectionary items, bread, rolls, meat and poultry
President: Brian Mc Sharry
CFO: Jan Marion
Marketing Director: Mark Wierzbinski
Estimated Sales: $20 - 50 Million
Number Employees: 50-99
Square Footage: 55000
Brands:
Beltech
Burtex
Polytek
Rapplon
Rapptex
Volta

18894 **Ammeraal Beltech**
3720 3 Mile Rd NW
Grand Rapids, MI 49534-1270 616-791-0292
Fax: 616-791-1067 sales@ammeraalusa.com
www.ammeraalbeltech.com
Process and conveyor belting equipment
President: Paul Hamilton
Manager: Jim Honeycutt
Sales Manager: Mike Wilde
Technical Services Manager: Jim Honeycutt
Estimated Sales: $20-50 Million
Number Employees: 20-49
Parent Co: Ammeraal International

18895 **Amoco Polymers**
4500 McGinnis Ferry Rd
Alpharetta, GA 30005 770-772-5177
Fax: 800-621-4557
Research for industrial carbon fibers and engineering polymers
Number Employees: 600

18896 **Amodex Products**
989 Hancock Ave
PO Box 3332
Bridgeport, CT 06605 203-335-1255
Fax: 203-330-9988 877-866-1255
info@amodexink.com www.amodexink.com
Stain removers and all-purpose industrial and household cleaners for face and hands
Owner: Peter Satse
Estimated Sales: $.5 - 1 million
Number Employees: 1-4

18897 **Amot Controls**
401 1st Street
Richmond, CA 94801-2906 510-307-8300
info@amotusa.com
www.amot.com
President: James Mannebach
Estimated Sales: $5 - 10 Million
Number Employees: 20-49

18898 **Ampac Packaging, LLC**
12025 Tricon Road
Cincinnati, OH 45246 513-671-1777
Fax: 513-671-2920 800-543-7030
www.ampaconline.com
Flexible packaging and bags
Brands:
Ab Sealers
All Packaging Machinery
Chantland
Fischbein Bag Closing
Fujy
Highlight Stretch Rappers
Lift Products
New London Eng
Vaculet Usa

18899 **Ampak**
4580 E 71st St
Cleveland, OH 44125 216-341-2022
Fax: 216-341-2163 800-342-6329
custserv@ampakco.com www.ampakco.com
Manufacturer and exporter of packaging machinery including bag/cup wrapping, skin and die cutting
Southeast Equipment Sales Manager: Dan Barnes
Customer Service: Troy Roberts
General Manager: Les Szakallas
Estimated Sales: $5-10 Million
Number Employees: 20-49
Square Footage: 40000
Parent Co: Heat Sealing Equipment Manufacturing Company
Brands:
Master
Maxima
Rotocut

18900 **Ampco Pumps Company**
2045 West Mill Road
Glendale, WI 53209 414-643-1852
Fax: 414-643-4452 800-737-8671
ampcocs@ampcopumps.com
www.ampcopumps.com
Manufacturer and exporter of pumps including centrifugal, sanitary, wastewater and water
President: Michael Nicholson
CFO: Loori Neisner
R&D: Loori Neisner
Quality Control: Oori Neisner
Midwestern Regional Manager: Matt Schultz
Estimated Sales: $1 - 2.5 Million
Number Employees: 10-19

18901 **Ampersand Label**
2571 S. Hemlock Road
Green Bay, WI 54229 714-893-4343
Fax: 714-891-1213 800-325-0589
service@ampersandlabel.com
www.wspackaging.com
1-8 color print applications including pressure sensitive labels and coupons
President: Lowell Matthews
CFO: Lowell Matthews
VP of Sales: Paulette Carnes
Estimated Sales: $2.5 - 5 Million
Number Employees: 50-99
Square Footage: 84000

18902 **Amplas**
975 Lombardi Ave
Green Bay, WI 54304 920-497-2002
Fax: 920-496-1322 800-950-4362
info@amplas.com www.amplas.com
Manufacturer and exporter of packaging machinery including bag makers and pouch makers and fillers
President: Don Pansier
VP: Gilas Blaser
Sales Director: Dennis Jimmel
Plant Manager: Jack Hendrickson
Estimated Sales: $20-50 Million
Number Employees: 100-249
Square Footage: 60000
Brands:
Amplas Converting Equipment
Totani Pouch M/C

18903 **Ample Industries**
4000 Commerce Center Dr
Franklin, OH 45005 937-746-9700
Fax: 937-746-2234 888-818-9700
ample@ampleindustries.com
www.ampleindustries.com
Carry-out containers, food trays, french fry and pizza boxes and hot dog clam shells; exporter of pizza boxes
Vice President Of Sales: David Ernst
General Manager: Robert Fairchild, Jr.
Plant Manager: Bill Bausmith

Estimated Sales: $50 Million
Number Employees: 100-249
Square Footage: 110000

18904 Amplexus Corporation
7665 Redwood Blvd Ste 250
Novato, CA 94945 415-897-3700
Fax: 415-897-4897 800-423-8268
www.softwarefordistributors.com
Software for restaurant supply and food equipment distributors
President: Kenneth Levin
Marketing Manager: Rebecca Baker
Estimated Sales: $5 - 10 Million
Number Employees: 4
Brands:
Amplexus Advantage
Amplexus E3/Commerce

18905 Amscor
188 Dupont St
PO Box 262
Brooklyn, NY 11222 718-383-4900
Fax: 718-383-7787 800-825-9800
sales@amscorinc.com www.amscorinc.com
Steel shelving
President: Scott Silberglied
Estimated Sales: $1-2.5 Million
Number Employees: 10-19
Square Footage: 10000
Parent Co: American Steel Corporation

18906 Amsler Equipment Inc
1245 Reid Street
Unit 1
Richmond Hill, ON, ON L4B 1G4
Canada 905-707-6704
Fax: 905-707-6707 877-738-2569
sales@amslerequipment.net
www.amslerequipment.net
Reheat stretch blow molding machines and related equipment.
President/CEO: Werner Amsler
Quality Control: Jason Amsler
Sales: Heidi Amsler
Estimated Sales: $3 Million
Number Employees: 15

18907 Amsoil
925 Tower Ave
Superior, WI 54880 715-392-7101
Fax: 715-392-5225 www.amsoil.com
Manufacturer and exporter of lubricating oils and greases, vitamins and filters including air and water
President: Albert Amatuzio
COO: Alan Amatuzio
Estimated Sales: G
Number Employees: 100-249

18908 Amstat Industries
3012 N Lake Terrace
Glenview, IL 60026-1335 847-998-6210
Fax: 847-998-6218 800-783-9999
info@amstat.com www.amstat.com
Manufacturer and distributor of static electricity control products.
President: Larry Jacobson
Sales Director: Larry Jacobson
Estimated Sales: $3 - 5Million
Number Employees: 10-19

18909 Amster-Kirtz Company
2830 Cleveland Ave NW
Canton, OH 44709 330-493-1800
Fax: 330-437-2015 800-257-9338
www.amsterkirtz.com
Wholesaler/distributor of merchandise for convenience stores including; candy and grocery items
President: Jim U
General Manager: Larry H
Sales Manager: Everett M
Type of Packaging: Consumer, Bulk

18910 Amtekco Industries
1205 Refugee Rd
Columbus, OH 43207 614-228-6590
Fax: 614-737-8017 800-336-4677
www.amtekco.com
Manufacturer and exporter of stainless steel tables, commercial sinks, wood cabinets, fixtures, table tops, bars and back bars.
President/Owner: Bruce Wasserstrom
CFO: Robert Hudgins
Research & Development: Roger Henry
Sales Manager: Nancy Green
Public Relations: Adena Bogdan
Plant Manager: Ron Fishking
Purchasing Manager: Hans Woschkolup
Estimated Sales: $18-20 Million
Number Employees: 100-249
Square Footage: 200000
Type of Packaging: Bulk

18911 Amwell
600 N Commons Dr Ste 116
Aurora, IL 60504-4151 630-898-6900
Fax: 630-898-1647 amwell@amwell-inc.com
www.amwell-inc.com
Owner: Jim McNish
Quality Control: Jim Martin
Estimated Sales: $3 - 5 Million
Number Employees: 10-19
Parent Co: McNish Corporation

18912 Anaheim Manufacturing Company
P.O.Box 4146
Anaheim, CA 92803-4146 714-524-7770
Fax: 714-996-7073 800-767-6293
aoregel@ix.netcom.com www.anaheimmfg.com
Manufacturer and exporter of garbage disposal units
President: Tom Dugan
Sales Supervisor: Alicia Oregel
Commercial Sales Manager: Grevor Wainwright
Estimated Sales: $20-50 Million
Number Employees: 100-249
Square Footage: 60000
Parent Co: Western Industries
Brands:
Sinkmaster
Waste King
Whirlaway

18913 Analite
24 Newtown Plz
Plainview, NY 11803-4506 516-752-1818
Fax: 516-752-0554 800-229-3357
www.analite.com
Manufacturer and exporter of relative humidity and temperature probes, controllers and transmitters
President: Morris Wasser
Vice President: Julius Levin
Estimated Sales: $2.5-5 Million
Number Employees: 10-19
Square Footage: 15200
Brands:
A2000
Humitran
Humitran-C
Humitran-Dp
Humitran-T

18914 Analog Devices
1 Technology Way
Norwood, MA 02062 781-320-1901
Fax: 781-329-1241 www.analog.com
President: Jerald G Fishman
Estimated Sales: K
Number Employees: 5,000-9,999

18915 Analog Technology Corporation
5220 4th St # 18
Baldwin Park, CA 91706-6600 626-856-5690
Fax: 626-472-6069 atcsupport@atcprinters.com
www.atcprinters.com
Manufacturers of industrial-graphic, bar code forms and label printers
President: James Lawrence
Estimated Sales: Below $5 Million
Number Employees: 1-4

18916 Analogic Corporation
8 Centennial Dr
Peabody, MA 01960 978-977-3000
Fax: 978-977-6809 www.analogic.com
CEO: James W Green
Estimated Sales: I
Number Employees: 1,000-4,999

18917 Analytical Development
381 Pike Blvd Ste E2
Lawrenceville, GA 30046 770-237-2330
Fax: 770-237-2332 www.adi-instruments.com
Manufacturer and exporter of hand-held portable luminometers
President: Ed Nemec
Estimated Sales: $500,000-$1 Million
Number Employees: 5-9
Brands:
Inspector

18918 Analytical Labs
1804 North 33rd Street Boise
Boise, ID 83703-5814 208-342-5515
Fax: 208-342-5591 800-574-5773
ali@analyticallaboratories.com
www.analyticallaboratories.com
Laboratory specializing in microbiological and chemical analysis of food, water, waste water and fuel; also, nutritional labeling analysis and plant GMP inspections available
President: Mike Moore
Estimated Sales: Below $5 Million
Number Employees: 20-49
Square Footage: 24000

18919 Analytical Measurements
22 Mountain View Drive
Chester, NJ 07930
800-635-5580
phmeter@verizon.net
www.analyticalmeasurements.com
Manufacturer/supplier of pH and ORP instrumentation, probes, and other related materials
President: W Richard Adey
*Estimated Sales:*500,000
Number Employees: 3
Square Footage: 2000
Brands:
Universal Ph Doser

18920 Analytical Technologies
11 Holt St
Westfield, NY 14787 716-326-6444
Fax: 716-326-6468 800-345-1357
sales@testmilk.com www.testmilk.com
Dairy, electronic milk testing equipment
President: David Gross
Estimated Sales: $500,000-$1 000,000
Number Employees: 5-9

18921 Anbroco
7711 Old Plank Road
Stanley, NC 28164-7774 704-827-1255
Fax: 704-822-6266 800-228-4784
anbroco@bellsouth.net
Agitators, aseptic processing equipment, blenders, batching and blending systems
Sales Manager: Ken Fincham
Number Employees: 22

18922 Anchor Continental
2000 S Beltline Blvd
Columbia, SC 29201 803-799-8800
Fax: 803-376-5585 800-628-8856
info@anchortape.com
www.intertapepolymergroup.com
Pressure sensitive tapes, including paper and film carton sealing tapes, filament reinforced strapping tapes, cloth duct tapes, crepe masking tape and double coated and specialty tapes
Manager: Don Hoffmann
Estimated Sales: $100-500 Million
Number Employees: 250-499

18923 Anchor Conveyor Products
6830 Kingsley Ave.
Dearborn, MI 48126 313-846-6000
Fax: 313-846-6004 800-959-1347
sales@anchorconveyor.com
www.anchorconveyor.com
President: Bill Farmer
Estimated Sales: $1 - 3 Million
Number Employees: 10-19

18924 Anchor Crane & Hoist Service Company
455 Aldine Bender Road
Houston, TX 77060 281-405-9048
Fax: 281-448-7500 800-835-2223
anchor@anchorcrane.com
www.proservanchor.com

Manufacturer and exporter of overhead crane systems
Manager: Greg Salinas
Purchasing Manager: Bob Steward
Number Employees: 100-249
Parent Co: RPC

18925 Anchor Glass Container Corporation
401 East Jackson Street
Suite 2800
Tampa, FL 33602 813-884-0000
www.anchorglass.com
Chairman of the Board: Eugene Davis
Internal Audit: Victor Lukban
Vice President: Robert Stewart
VP, Quality & Technical Services: Mike Fair
Vice President, Sales & Marketing: Tom Wieclaw
Operations Manager: Gary Jarrett
Vice President, Product Development: Sam Wilson
Vice President, Supply Chain: Frank McDemott
Estimated Sales: $297 Million
Number Employees: 2,840
Parent Co: Ardagh Group

18926 Anchor Hocking Company
519 N Pierce Ave
Lancaster, OH 43130 740-681-6478
Fax: 740-681-6040 800-562-7511
consumerar@anchorhocking.com
www.anchorhocking.com
Manufacturer and exporter of glass tabletop products including beverageware, stemware, dinnerware, ovenware and floral and table accessories
President: J David Reed
CEO: Mark Eichorn
Vice President Sales & Marketing: Jackie Sokol
VP Sales: Bert Filice
Vice President Of Operations: Margaret Homers
Estimated Sales: $53 Million
Number Employees: 600
Parent Co: Newell Rubbermaid
Other Locations:
Anchor Hocking Glass Co.
Richmond Hill ON
Brands:
Clarisse
Excellency
Florentine
Optic Florentine
Stackables

18927 Anchor Industries
P.O.Box 3477
Evansville, IN 47733-3477 812-867-2421
Fax: 812-867-1429 custdiv@anchorinc.com
www.anchorinc.com
Commercial awnings
Founder: Louis Daus
CFO: Mike Elliott
Estimated Sales: $30 - 50 Million
Number Employees: 500-999

18928 (HQ)Anchor Packaging
13515 Barrett Pky Dr Ste 100
Ballwin, MO 63021 314-822-7800
Fax: 314-822-2035 800-467-3900
info@anchorpackaging.com
www.anchorpac.com
Manufacturer and exporter of plastic microwaveable packaging and container supplies including films, containers, trays, food protective and cling wrap.
President: Jeffrey Wolff
CFO: Steve Riek
CEO: Brad Jensen
Marketing: Michael Thaler
Sales: Frank Baumann
Public Relations: Michael Thaler
Operations: Staya Garg
Estimated Sales: $20 - 50 Million
Number Employees: 50
Type of Packaging: Food Service, Private Label
Brands:
Aurity Wrap
Bonfaire
Culinary Classics
Fresh View
Micro Raves
Purity Wrap
Ultra Wrap

18929 Anco-Eaglin
1420 Lorraine Ave
High Point, NC 27263 336-855-7800
Fax: 336-855-7831 info@ancoeaglin.com
www.ancoeaglin.com
Batch rendering systems, continuous rendering systems, hydrolizing equipment, inedible rendering equipment and systems, prebreakers and presses
President: Rick Eaglin
US/European Sales: Brian Eaglin
Estimated Sales: Below $5 000,000
Number Employees: 10-19

18930 Andantex USA
1705 Valley Rd
Ocean, NJ 07712-3949 732-493-2812
Fax: 732-493-2949 800-713-6170
info@andantex.com www.andantex.com
Power transmissions including robotic controls, speed reducers and right angle gear boxes
President: Michael Munn
Vice President of Engineering: Dave Regiec
Systems Engineer: John Tashjian
VP of Marketing: Bruce Bradley
Sales Manager of Sales: Al Schwartz
Estimated Sales: $2.5-5 Million
Number Employees: 20-49

18931 Andco Environmental Processes
415 Commerce Dr
Amherst, NY 14228 716-691-2100
Fax: 716-691-2880 andco@localnet.com
www.localnet.com/~buffalo/customer/andco/andco.htm
Manufacturer and exporter of waste and ground water pollution elimination systems
Sales Manager: Jack Reich
Chief Process Engineer: Michael Laschinger
Estimated Sales: less than $500,000
Number Employees: 5-9
Square Footage: 22000

18932 Andean Naturals, Inc.
393 Catamaran St
Foster City, CA 94404 888-547-9777
Fax: 707-202-2838 info@andeannaturals.com
www.andeannaturals.com
Processer of quinoa, including milled, flaked or puffed, quinoa germ and protein conccentrate, quinoa patent flour, quinoa in seed form, golden, red or black quinoa, quinoa color blends, baby quinoa also available. Certified Fair TradeUSA, Gluten-Free, Kosher, and Organic
Owner: Sergio Nunez De Arco
Finance & Operations Manager: Marcos Guevara
Estimated Sales: $100 Thousand
Number Employees: 2
Type of Packaging: Bulk

18933 Anderol Specialty Lubricants & Anderol Conoco
P.O.Box 518
East Hanover, NJ 07936-0518 973-887-7410
Fax: 973-887-6930 800-263-3765
info@anderol.com www.anderol.com
President: Joe Fuhrman
R & D: Ed Edelson
Human Resources: Kathy Ackerman
Estimated Sales: $100+ Million
Number Employees: 50-99

18934 Andersen 2000
2011 Commerce Dr N
Peachtree City, GA 30269 770-486-2000
Fax: 770-487-5066 800-241-5424
a2k@crownandersen.com
Manufacturer and exporter of air pollution control systems for odor control, spray dryer dust and visible aerosol.
President/CEO: Jack Brady
CFO: Randall Morgan
CEO: Randall Morgan
Marketing/Sales: Tom Van Remmen
Purchasing Manager: Doug Topley
Number Employees: 50-99
Square Footage: 30000
Parent Co: Crown Andersen
Other Locations:
Andersen 2000
Sevenum

18935 Andersen Sign Company
1580 French Pond Road
Woodsville, NH 03785 603-787-6806
Advertising specialties including signs
Owner: Don Bowman
Estimated Sales: Less than $500,000
Number Employees: 1-4
Square Footage: 2500

18936 Anderson & Dahlen
6850 Sunwood Dr NW
Ramsey, MN 55303 763-852-4700
Fax: 763-852-4795 877-205-0239
sales@andersondahlen.com
www.andersondahlen.com
President: Thomas Knoll
Estimated Sales: $20 - 50 Million
Number Employees: 100-249

18937 Anderson American Precision
2511 Friday Rd.
Cocoa, FL 32926 321-637-0728
www.feedscrewdesigns.com
Estimated Sales: $300,000-500,000
Number Employees: 1-4

18938 Anderson Chemical Company
325 South Davis
Litchfield, MN 55355 320-693-2477
Fax: 320-693-8238 www.accomn.com
Cleaning/sanitation and water treatment chemical compounds
President: J Terry Anderson
Number Employees: 50-99
Type of Packaging: Food Service

18939 Anderson Greenwood & Company
3950 Greenbriar Dr.
Stafford, TX 77477 281-274-4400
Fax: 281-274-4480 andersongreenwood.com
Plant Manager: Andy Masullo

18940 Anderson Instrument
156 Auriesville Rd
Fultonville, NY 12072 518-922-5315
Fax: 518-922-8997 800-833-0081
info@andinst.com www.andinst.com
Manufacturer and exporter of sanitary liquid flow meters
President: Jennifer Honeycutt
VP Marketing/Sales: Bill Wilson
VP Operations: Daniel Lawrence
Vice President, Marketing: Bill Wilson
Director Sales: Scott LeBrun
Estimated Sales: $5-10 Million
Number Employees: 20-49

18941 Anderson Instrument Company
156 Auriesville Rd
Fultonville, NY 12072 518-922-5315
Fax: 518-922-8997 800-833-0081
marc.cognetti@danaher.com www.andinst.com
Sanitary temperature, pressure, liquid level monitoring and control instrumentation
President: Jennifer Honeycutt
Marketing Manager: Bill Wilson
Sales Manager: George Simok
Estimated Sales: $50 - 100 Million
Number Employees: 50-99
Parent Co: Danaher Corporation

18942 Anderson International Corporation
4545 Boyce Pkwy
Stow, OH 44224 216-641-1112
Fax: 330-668-0117 800-336-4730
webcontact@andersonintl.net
www.andersonintl.net
Manufacturer and exporter of screw press machinery for the continuous extraction of vegetable oils and animal fats
President: Len Trocano
CFO: Kathleen O'Hearn
VP: Vincent Vavpot
Marketing: Vincent Vavpot
Sales: Bruce Brown
Plant Manager: Dave Botson
Estimated Sales: $10 - 20 Million
Brands:
Dox Expander
Expeller
Hivex Expander
Solvex Expander

18943 **Anderson Machine Sales**
1066 Harvard Pl
P.O. Box 220
Fort Lee, NJ 07024-1630
Fax: 201-641-7952 amscapper@aol.com
www.andersonmachinesales.com
Manufacturer and exporter of single spindle and rotary capping machines, pump placers and crimpers, conveyors and accumulating tables
Manager: Howard Cunningham
Estimated Sales: $2.5-5,000,000
Number Employees: 1-4
Parent Co: Anderson Machine Systems

18944 **Anderson Products**
3202 Caroline Dr
Haw River, NC 27258-9564 336-376-3000
Fax: 336-376-8153 www.anpro.com
President: H W Andersen
Quality Control: Lori Pfohl
R&D: John Lindley
Estimated Sales: $20 - 50 Million
Number Employees: 100-249

18945 **Anderson Products**
1 Weiler Dr
Cresco, PA 18326-9804 508-755-6100
Fax: 508-755-4694 800-729-4694
info@andersonproducts.com
www.andersonproducts.com
Power, paint and maintenance brushes including wide face and strip, adapters, maintenance and hand, rollers and accessories, etc
President: Richard Gommel
VP Sales/Marketing: Robert Levine
Estimated Sales: $20 - 50 Million
Number Employees: 100-249
Parent Co: Wilton Corporation

18946 **Anderson Snow Corporation**
9225 Ivanhoe St
Schiller Park, IL 60176 847-678-3823
Fax: 847-678-0413 800-346-2645
sales@anscorocoils.com www.anscorcoils.com
Heating and cooling coils
President: Ted Campbell
Estimated Sales: $20-50 Million
Number Employees: 20-49

18947 **Anderson Tool & Engineering Company**
P.O.Box 1158
Anderson, IN 46015-1158 765-643-6691
Fax: 765-643-5022 ate@ateinc.com
www.ateinc.com
Manufacturer and exporter of packaging, automation and material handling equipment; also, electrical design and assembly services available
President: Ted Fiock
Sales/Marketing Manager: David Keller
Operations Manager: Tom Tuterow
Purchasing Manager: Ron King
Estimated Sales: $10 - 20 Million
Number Employees: 100-249
Square Footage: 85000

18948 **Anderson Wood Products Company**
PO Box 11517
Louisville, KY 40251 502-778-5591
Fax: 502-778-5599 kenl@andersonwood.com
www.andersonwood.com
Wooden butchers' blocks and restaurant tabletops
VP: David Anderson III
Chairman Of The Board: Sidney W Anderson Jr
Estimated Sales: $20 - 50 Million
Number Employees: 100-249
Square Footage: 140000

18949 **Anderson-Crane Company**
1213 Harmon Pl
Minneapolis, MN 55403 612-332-0331
Fax: 612-332-0384 800-314-2747
jona@anderson-crane.com
www.anderson-crane.com
Manufacturers of stainless steel screw conveyors @ screw feeders to food grade specs.
President: J. Crane
Director Of Sales: Rob Crane
Co-Director Of Sales: Jack Crane
Estimated Sales: $10-20 Million
Number Employees: 20-49
Square Footage: 30000

18950 **Andex Industries**
1911 4th Ave N
Escanaba, MI 49829 906-786-6070
Fax: 906-786-3133 800-338-9882
andex@andex.net www.andex.net
Printed blister cards and skin boards
President: John Anthony
Estimated Sales: $10-20 000,000
Number Employees: 10-19

18951 **Andfel Corporation**
2350 W Fulton Street
Chicago, IL 60612-2256 312-666-6375

18952 **Andgar Corporation**
P.O.Box 2708
Ferndale, WA 98248-2708 360-366-9900
Fax: 360-366-5800 corporate@andgar.com
www.andgar.com
Conveyors, belts, vibrating feeders, custom stainless steel design and fabrication, packaging equipment, metal detectors, separators, scanning and sorting equipment, complete processing lines, refrigeration and freezing equipmenttemperature controls, stairways, railings, catwalks, fabricated metal products
President: Gary Van Lou
CFO: Gary Van Lou
CEO: Gary Van Loo
Quality Control: Gary Van Lou
R&D: Gary Van Lou
Estimated Sales: $10 - 20 Million
Number Employees: 100-249
Number of Brands: 4
Square Footage: 45000
Brands:
Andgar
Lakewood
Langser Camp
Sateline

18953 **Andover Control Corporation**
300 Brickstone Sq
Andover, MA 01810-1430 978-470-0555
Fax: 978-470-0946 www.andovercontrol.com
President and CEO: William J Lapointe
CFO: Jeffrey Templer
Estimated Sales: $100+ Million
Number Employees: 10

18954 **Andre Robin And Associates**
8630 Farley Way
Fair Oaks, CA 95628-5353 916-852-0177
Fax: 916-852-0192 800-998-6111
info@robin.com www.robin.com
President: Andre Robin
Estimated Sales: $5 - 10 Million
Number Employees: 10-19

18955 **Andrea Baskets**
1401 Lakeland Avenue
Bohemia, NY 11716 631-231-4888
Fax: 631-231-5635 888-272-8826
info@andreabaskets.com
www.andreabaskets.com
Various styles of decorative baskets
President: Andrea Lieberman
Estimated Sales: $3.4 Million
Number Employees: 20

18956 **Andrew H. Lawson Company**
2927 W Thompson St
Philadelphia, PA 19121 215-235-1119
Fax: 215-235-1727 800-411-6628
info@screengemsinc.com
www.screengemsinc.com
Tags, signs and labels
Owner: Edward Mitchell Sr
VP of Marketing: Regina Mitchell
Manager Operations: John Mitchell
Estimated Sales: $1 - 5 Million
Number Employees: 10-19
Square Footage: 20000

18957 **Andrew's Fixture Company**
1720 Puyallup Ave
Tacoma, WA 98421 253-627-8388
Fax: 253-627-8395 www.andrewsfixture.com
Store fixtures, custom cabinets and office furniture
President: Kenson Lee
Secretary/Treasurer: Andrea Lee
Estimated Sales: $1 - 2.5 Million
Number Employees: 5-9
Square Footage: 10000

18958 **Andritz**
35 Sherman St
Muncy, PA 17756 570-546-8211
www.andritz.com
Manufacturer and exporter of size reduction, screening, mixing, pelleting, material handling, conveyor, cereal cooking, dehydration, grading, barley, blending, milling, crushing, grinding, separating and storage equipment
Estimated Sales: $90 Million
Number Employees: 500-999
Square Footage: 400000
Parent Co: Andritz Maschinenfabrik AG
Brands:
Dynestene
Hydrasieve
Roto Shaker
Sonisift

18959 **Andritz-Ruthner**
1010 Commercial Blvd S
Arlington, TX 76001 817-465-5611
Fax: 817-468-3961 andritz@andritz-arl.com
www.andritz.com
President: John Madden
Estimated Sales: $10-20 000,000
Number Employees: 500-999

18960 **Andy J. Egan Co.**
2001 Waldorf NW
Grand Rapids, MI 49544 616-791-9952
Fax: 616-791-1037 800-594-9244
info@andyegan.com www.andyegan.com
Manufacturer processing equipment for the baking, confectionery and snack food industries.
Owner: Tom Jasper
Vice President/Treasurer: Casey Schellenboom
Engineer: Eric Schippers
Estimated Sales: 25 Million
Number Employees: 230
Square Footage: 70000

18961 **Andy Printed Products**
1258 Route 82
Lagrangeville, NY 12540-6015 845-223-5101
Fax: 845-223-7426
Pressure sensitive and gummed labels
Owner: Thakur Nandlal
Estimated Sales: Less than $500,000
Number Employees: 1-4
Square Footage: 2000

18962 **Anetsberger**
P.O. Box 501
Concord, NH 06062 603-225-6684
Fax: 603-225-8472 sales@anetsberger.com
www.anetsberger.com
ANETS - Gas & Electric Fryers, Filter Systems, Chrome Grills, Pasta Cookers
President: Paul Angrick
VP: Steve Spittle
VP Sales/Marketing: Bonnie Bolster
Estimated Sales: $10-20 Million
Number Employees: 50-99
Parent Co: Middleby Corp
Brands:
Anets'

18963 **(HQ)Anguil Environmental Systems**
8855 N 55th St
Milwaukee, WI 53223 414-365-6400
Fax: 414-365-6410 800-488-0230
sales@anguil.com www.anguil.com
Manufacturer and exporter of air pollution abatement and oxidation systems
President: Gene Anguil
CEO: Gene Anugil
Vice President: Chris Anguil
Marketing Director: Kevin Summ
Estimated Sales: $20-25 Million
Number Employees: 50-99
Square Footage: 25000

18964 **Angus Chemical Company**
1500 E Lake Cook Rd
Buffalo Grove, IL 60089 989-832- 156
Fax: 989-832-1465 www.angus.com
CEO: Mark Henning
Number Employees: 50-99

18965 **(HQ)Anheuser-Busch InBev**
250 Park Avenue
New York, NY 10177 212-573-8800
www.ab-inbev.com
Processor, importer, and exporter of beer, malt liquor, ales, lagers, and non-alcoholic brews.
Chief Executive Officer: Carlos Brito
Chief Financial & Technology Officer: Felipe Dutra
Chief Procurement Officer: Tony Milikin
Chief Strategy Officer: Jo Van Biesbroeck
Chief People Officer: Claudio Garcia
Chief Marketing Officer: Miguel Patricio
Chief Sales Officer: Bernardo Pinto Paiva
Chief Legal & Corporate Affairs Officer: Sabine Chalmers
Chief Procurement Officer: Tony Milikin
Chief Supply Officer: Claudio Braz Ferro
Estimated Sales: $36 Billion
Number Employees: 116,500
Type of Packaging: Consumer, Food Service, Bulk
Other Locations:
Brewery
Baldwinsville NY
Brewery
Cartersville GA
Brewery
Columbus OH
Brewery
Fairfield CA
Brewery
Fort Collins CO
Brewery
Houston TX
Brewery
Jacksonville FL
Brewery
Los Angeles CA
Brewery
Merrimack NH
Brewery
St. Louis MO
Brewery
Williamsburg VA
Brewery
Newark NJ
Brands:
180
Anheuser World Select
Be
Bacardi Silver
Bacardi Silver Limon
Bacardi Silver Low Carb Blackcherry
Bacardi Silver O3
Bacardi Silver Raz
Bare Knuckle Stout
Bud Dry
Bud Ice
Bud Ice Light
Bud Light
Budweiser
Busch
Busch Ice
Busch Light
Busch Na
Hurricane Ice
Hurricane Malt Liquor
King Cobra
Michelob
Michelob Amber Bock
Michelob Golden Draft
Michelob Golden Draft Light
Michelob Hefeweizen
Michelob Honey Lager
Michelob Light
Michelob Ultra
Natural Ice
Natural Light
O'Douls
O'Douls Amber
Redhook Ale
Tequiza
Tilt
Widmer Brothers
Ziegenlight

18966 **Anhydro Inc**
20000 Governors Dr Ste 301
Olympia Fields, IL 60461 708-747-7000
Fax: 708-755-8815 anhydroinc@anhydro.com
www.anhydro.com
Manufacturer and exporter of food drying equipment including spray, tower, flash, fluid bed and ring; also, consulting, design and engineering services available
President: Guy Lonergan
Number Employees: 20-49
Square Footage: 40000
Parent Co: Drytec

18967 **Anixter**
2301 Patriot Blvd
Glenview, IL 60026 224-521-8000
Fax: 224-521-8100 www.anixter.com
President: Bob Grubbs
CEO: Robert J Eck
CFO: Dennis Letham
Number Employees: 20-49

18968 **Anko Food Machine USA Company Limited**
390 Swift Ave # 2
S San Francisco, CA 94080-6221 650-624-8038
Fax: 650-624-8039 ankousa@lanset.com
www.ankofood.com
Owner: James Chung
Estimated Sales: $300,000-500,000
Number Employees: 1-4

18969 **Anko Products**
6012 33rd St E
Bradenton, FL 34203-5402
Fax: 941-748-2307 800-446-2656
sales@ankoproducts.com
www.ankoproducts.com
Manufacture of contamination-proof peristaltic pumps, and fractional horsepower gearmotors
President: Lawrence Kottke
Estimated Sales: $20 - 50 Million
Number Employees: 50-99
Brands:
Mitydrive
Mityflex

18970 **Ankom Technology**
2052 O'Neil Road
Macedon, NY 14502 315-986-8090
Fax: 315-986-8091 info@ankom.com
www.ankom.com
Instrumentation for the meat processing and food manufacturing industry.
President: Andrew Komarek
Vice President, Manufacturing Operations: Shawn Ritchie
Vice President, Research and Development: Ronald Komarek
Director, Strategic Marketing: Greg Coutant
Technical Sales Manager: Nick Tedesche
Office Manager/Accounting: Scott Giali
Production Coordinator-Extraction System: Tom Bopp
Domestic Administrator: Mary Lou Williams

18971 **Ann Arbor Computer**
34375 W 12 Mile Road
Farmington Hills, MI 48331-3375 248-553-1000
Fax: 248-553-1228 800-526-9322
info@jerviswebb.com
www.annarborcomputer.com
Manufacturer and exporter of computer software inventory control systems for warehouses and distribution centers; also, complete integrated control systems for material handling and factory automation
President & CEO: Brian Stewart
Sr. Vice President & CFO: John Doychich
Vice President Sales And Marketing: Bruce Buscher
Sales Manager: Art Fleischer
Vice President Of Operations: Lon McAllister
Number Employees: 80
Square Footage: 148000
Parent Co: Jervis B. Webb Company
Brands:
Basis
Pc/Aim

18972 **Ann Clark, LTD**
112B Quality Lane
Rutland, VT 05701 802-773-7886
Fax: 802-775-6864 800-252-6798
info@annclark.com www.annclark.com
Shaped and holiday themed cookie cutters
President: Ann Clark
VP: John Clark Jr
Sales Manager: Elizabeth Clark

18973 **Annette's Donuts Ltd.**
1965 Lawrence Ave W
Toronto, ON M9N 1H5
Canada 416-656-3444
Fax: 416-656-5400 888-839-7857
Bread, pastries and other bakery products
President: Nicolas Yannopoulos
Board Member: Ariadni Yannopoulos
Estimated Sales: $5.9 Million
Number Employees: 85
Square Footage: 124000
Type of Packaging: Consumer, Food Service, Bulk

18974 **Annie's Frozen Yogurt**
5200 West 74th St
Suite A
Eding, MN 55439 952-835-2110
800-969-9648
www.anniesfrozenyogurt.com
Soft serve equipment for frozen yogurt.
President: Lawrence Serf
Number Employees: 5-9
Brands:
Annie's

18975 **Anova**
211 N. Lindbergh Blvd.
St Louis, MO 63141-7809
Fax: 314-768-0835 800-231-1327
www.cleancitysquares.com
Waste and recycling receptacles
President: William Gilbert
CFO: John Mueller
Estimated Sales: $5-10 Million
Number Employees: 20-49

18976 **Anresco**
1375 Van Dyke Ave.
San Francisco, CA 94124-3313 415-822-1100
Fax: 415-822-6615 800-359-0920
info@anresco.com www.anresco.com
Laboratory providing consulting and analytical services including microbiology and food technology
Founder & President: David Eisenberg
Treasurer: Ngaly Frank
Lab Co-Direcotr: Mr. VuLam
Lab Co-Director: Ms. Cynthia Kushi
Quality Control Manager: Paleen Castenada
Marketing Director: Charleen Bizily
Purchasing Manager: Cynthia Kcohi
Estimated Sales: $3.85 Million
Number Employees: 30
Square Footage: 37600

18977 **Anritsu Industrial Solutions**
1001 Cambridge Dr
Elk Grove Village, IL 60007-2453 847-419-9729
Fax: 847-419-8266 www.anritsu-industry.com
Food inspection equipment.
President: Abe Takashi
Number Employees: 10

18978 **Ansell Healthcare**
111 Wood Avenue South Suite 210
Iselin, NJ 08830 732-345-5400
Fax: 732-219-5114 800-800-0444
info@ansell.com www.ansellpro.com
World's largest manufacturer of protective golves and clothing for the food service and processing industries.
Senior VP: Michael Zedalis
Manager: Willaim Gero
Number Employees: 250-499
Type of Packaging: Food Service

18979 **Ansul Incorporated**
1 Stanton St
Marinette, WI 54143 715-735-7411
Fax: 715-732-3471 800-862-6785
www.ansul.com
Manufacturer and exporter of fire protection products includes fire extinguishers and hand line units; pre-engineered restaurant, vehicle, and industrial systems; sophisticated fire detection/suppression systems and a complete line ofdry chemical, foam, and gaseoue extinguishing agents.
President: Colleen Repplier
CFO: Dennis Moraros
Operations: Sally Falkenberg
Director, R&D: Jay Thomas
Director, Global Marketing: David Pelton
VP Sales: William Smith
Number Employees: 500-999
Parent Co: Tyco International

Brands:
Ansul Automan
Ansulex
Foray
K-Guard
Piranha
Plus-50
R-102
Sentry

18980 Antek Industrial Instruments
PO Box 1130
Marble Falls, TX 78654-1130 830-693-5671
Fax: 830-798-8208 888-478-5387
salesantek@281.com www.antekhou.com
State-of-the-art testing and measurement of carbon dioxide and sulfur levels commonly found in the processing of soft drinks

18981 (HQ)Antek Instruments
8824 Fallbrook Drive
Houston, TX 77064-4855 281-940-1803
Fax: 281-580-0719 800-444-8378
sales@paclp.com www.paclp.com
Manufacturer and exporter of analyzers including total nitrogen, sulfur and fluoride; also, sulfur-selective and nitrogen-specific GC and HPLC detectors
President: Tom McMullen
CEO: Randy Wreyford
Marketing Director: Cindy Goodman
Sales Manager: Emmanuel Filaudeau
Number Employees: 70
Square Footage: 120000
Other Locations:
Antek Instruments
Dusseldorf

18982 Anton Paar
10215 Timber Ridge Dr
Ashland, VA 23005-8135 804-550-1051
Fax: 804-550-1057 800-722-7556
info.us@anton-paar.com www.anton-paar.com
Laboratory density and brix meters, process brix and diet monitors, carbon dioxide monitors, laboratory and process beer analyzers
Manager: Reinhard Eberl
CEO: Niels Haggound
Product Manager: Thomas Luxbacher
Sales Manager: Erich Windischbacher
Estimated Sales: $2.5-5 Million
Number Employees: 20-49

18983 Antrim Manufacturing
3530 N 127th St
Brookfield, WI 53005 262-781-6860
Metal stampings and restaurant equipment including ovens and utility carts
Owner: Dan Antrim
Office Manager: Patricia Antrim
Estimated Sales: $1 - 5 Million
Number Employees: 1-4

18984 Anver Corporation
36 Parmenter Rd
Hudson, MA 01749 978-568-0221
Fax: 978-568-1570 800-654-3500
rfq13@anver.com www.anver.com
Full range of vacuum system components, from suction cups and vacuum cups, air and electric vacuum pumps and vacuum generations, and ergonomic vacuum lifters, to complete lifting systems
President: Anton Vernooy
CFO: Lynne Butterworth
Marketing Director: Cully Murphy
Estimated Sales: $10 Million
Number Employees: 50-99
Square Footage: 60000

18985 Anzu Technology
3180 Imjin Rd Ste 155
Marina, CA 93933 831-883-4400
Fax: 831-855-0220 twhite@anzutech.com
www.anzutech.com
Products and services include equipment for food processing, inspection and packaging.
President: Tom White

18986 Apache Inc.
P.O.Box 1719
Cedar Rapids, IA 52406 319-365-0471
Fax: 319-365-2522 800-553-5455
info@apache-inc.com www.apache-inc.com
Wholesaler/distributor of hose and conveyor belting. Products for the food industry.
President/CEO: Tom Pientok
Chief Financial Officer: Randy Walter
Controller: Eric Hentges
Quality Engineer: Rick Coyle
Marketing & Communications Manager: Jill Miller
VP, Operations: Kyle Gingrich
VP, Business Development: John Shafer
VP, Product Management: Tom Weisenstine
Purchasing Manager: Randy James
Estimated Sales: $75-85 Million
Number Employees: 250
Square Footage: 125000

18987 (HQ)Apache Stainless Equipment Corporation
200 Industrial Drive
PO Box 538
Beaver Dam, WI 53916-0538 920-887-3721
Fax: 920-887-0206 800-444-0398
info@apachestainless.com
www.apachestainless.com
Manufacturer and exporter of stainless steel food processing machinery including sanitary and ASME pressure vessels, tanks, blenders, mixers, conveyors, sanitary lifts, stuffers, dumpers and paced boning systems
President and R&D: D Foulkes
CFO: D Seifert
VP: W Lynn
Quality Control: Jerome Scharrer
Plant Manager: Duane Crouse
Estimated Sales: $5 - 10 Million
Number Employees: 100-249
Square Footage: 100000
Other Locations:
Apache Stainless Equipment Co
Beloit WI
Brands:
Vortron

18988 Apco/Valve & Primer Corporation
1420 Wright Blvd
Schaumburg, IL 60193 847-524-9000
Fax: 847-524-9007 factory@apcovalves.com
www.apcovalves.com
President: Robert Mauriello
CEO: George Christofidis
CFO: Jack Mann
Engineering/Technical: Russell Voseurg
Estimated Sales: $10 - 20 Million
Number Employees: 50-99

18989 Apex Bakery Equipment
803 Main St
Belmar, NJ 07719-2783 888-571-3599
Fax: 954-364-6268 888-571-3599
sales@apex-equip.com www.apex-equip.com
President: Herbert Freedman
CFO: Barry McWatters
Quality Control: Mark Freedman
Estimated Sales: $10 - 20 Million
Number Employees: 20-49

18990 Apex Fountain Sales
1140 N American St
Philadelphia, PA 19123 215-627-4526
Fax: 215-627-7877 800-523-4586
apexfountains@att.net www.apexfountains.com
Manufacturer and exporter of champagne fountains, chafing dishes, punch bowls, candelabra and food stands
President: Abe Weinberg
Manager: Jody Clemente
Estimated Sales: $1-2.5 Million
Number Employees: 5-9

18991 Apex Machine Company
3000 NE 12th Terrace
Fort Lauderdale, FL 33334 954-566-1572
Fax: 954-563-2844 email@apexmachine.com
www.apexmachine.com
Manufacturer and exporter, designs and engineers austonized part handling and pricing solutions for 3D products.
President: Todd D Coningsby
CEO & Chairman: A. Robert Coningsby III
Corp. Controller: Chris Bardelang
National Sales Manager: Russell Coningsby
VP Sales: Bob Coningsby
Engineering Manager: Greg Coningsby
Purchasing Manager: Bill Irwin
Estimated Sales: $5-10 Million
Number Employees: 50-99

18992 Apex Packing & Rubber Company
1855 New Hwy
Farmingdale, NY 11735 631-420-8150
Fax: 631-756-9639 800-645-9110
info@apexgaskets.com www.apexgaskets.com
Manufacturer and exporter of sanitary replacement parts for the dairy, food, beverage and pharmaceutical industries
President: Ralph Oppenheim
General Manager: Larry Hodes
Purchasing Agent: Leon Davidson
Estimated Sales: $2.5-5,000,000
Number Employees: 10-19
Brands:
Apex

18993 Apex Tool Works
3200 Tollview Dr
Rolling Meadows, IL 60008 847-394-5810
Fax: 847-394-2739 apextool@apextool.com
www.apextool.com
President: William Collins
Engineering/Technical: Roger Thompson
Manufacturing Executive: Jim Whittenhall
Estimated Sales: $5 - 10 Million
Number Employees: 20-49

18994 Apex Welding
P.O.Box 46199
Cleveland, OH 44146 440-232-6770
Fax: 440-232-6747 info@apex-bulkhandlers.com
www.apex-bulkhandlers.com
Bins
President: D J Warner
Estimated Sales: $5-10 000,000
Number Employees: 10-19

18995 Apigent Solutions
5 N McCormick Street
Oklahoma City, OK 73127-6620 405-946-8228
Fax: 405-946-8242 800-664-8228
info@apigent.com www.apigent.com
Specializes in software products taht enhance business performance and profitability by delivering reaL-time information from legacy business systems to site, field, and corporate personnel
CEO: Jim Melvin
Sales VP of the Americas: John Luidens
Public Relations: Ann Dickerson

18996 Aplen Sierra Coffee Company
2222 Park Place
Minden, NV 89423 530-541-1053
Fax: 530-541-4412 800-531-1405
coffeentea@alpensierra.com
www.alpensierra.com
Estimated Sales: $1-2.5 Million
Number Employees: 5-9

18997 Apogee Translite
593 Acorn St Ste B
Deer Park, NY 11729 631-254-6975
Fax: 631-254-3860 www.apogeetranslite.com
Manufacturer and exporter of lighting fixtures for food processing range hoods, hose down and wet locations
President: Richard Nicolai
President: Mike Shada
Estimated Sales: $10 - 20,000,000
Number Employees: 20-49
Square Footage: 38000
Other Locations:
Apogee Lighting Group
Riverdale IL

18998 Apollo Acme Lighting Fixture
212 S 12th Ave
Mount Vernon, NY 10550 914-664-3600
Fax: 914-664-6091 800-833-9006

Fluorescent lighting fixtures
VP: Paul Verkleij
Estimated Sales: $1-2,500,000
Number Employees: 5-9
Square Footage: 33000

18999 Apollo Sheet Metal
1207 W Columbia Dr
Kennewick, WA 99336 509-586-1104
Fax: 509-586-3771 info@apollosm.com
www.apollosm.com
Food processing, handling and storage systems including conveyors, tanks, blanchers, ovens and fryers; also, installation services available.
President: Bruce Ratchford
CFO: Angie Haisch
VP: Keith Larson
Quality Control: Bill Meloy
Marketing Director: Connie Gillispie
Sales: Dan Briscoe
Production: Cal Method
Estimated Sales: $20-50 Million
Number Employees: 250-499
Square Footage: 200000

19000 Apotheca Naturale
201 Apple Boulevard
Woodbine, IA 51579 712-647-3133
Fax: 888-898-0401 800-736-3130
info@apothecacompany.com
www.apothecacompany.com
Homeopathics, botanical extracts, capsules, tablets and sports nutritionals
President: Kathryn Simon
Estimated Sales: $10-20 Million
Number Employees: 100
Square Footage: 70000

19001 Apparel Manufacturing Company
5405 Webb Pkwy NW
Lilburn, GA 30047 770-638-1100
Fax: 770-638-8030 800-366-1608
info@apparelmanufacturing.com
www.apparelmanufacturing.com
Advertising specialties and uniforms; importer of caps
President: Martin Tulis
Administrative Assistant to President: Chelley Young
Estimated Sales: $5 - 10,000,000
Number Employees: 50-99

19002 Apple-A-Day NutritionalLabeling Service
103 1/2 Avenida Del Mar
San Clemente, CA 92672-4017 949-855-8954
Fax: 949-855-8954 aplledata@home.com
www.qualspec.net/appleaday.htm
Provides computerized nutrutional analysis based on submited recipes. Nutritional facts labeling for food manufacturers following FDA quidelines and regulations

19003 Applegate Chemical Company
1325 N Old Rand Road
Wauconda, IL 60084-9764 847-487-2651
Fax: 847-487-2654
President: Donald F Colby
Estimated Sales: $5 - 10 Million
Number Employees: 10

19004 Appleson Press
25 Tacoma Lane
Building 11
Syosset, NY 11791-6232 516-496-0004
Fax: 516-496-0006 800-888-2775
info@applesonpress.com
www.applesonpress.com
Manufacturer of continuous business forms, envelopes and labels including printed cloth, linen, silk, pressure sensitive, promotional items; product labels
President: Kenneth Sands
CEO: Elyse Newman
Plant Manager: John Samuels
Estimated Sales: $3-5 Million
Number Employees: 20-49
Square Footage: 40000
Type of Packaging: Food Service, Private Label, Bulk

19005 Applexion
9400 W Foster Avenue
Chicago, IL 60656-2860 773-243-0454
Fax: 773-243-0460 applexion@aol.com
Process engineering systems including ion exchange, chromatographic and membrane separation, fermentation, etc
President: Francois Rousset
Sales: Brian Burris
Production: Martha Turner
Estimated Sales: $1-2.5 Million
Number Employees: 1-4
Parent Co: Applexion S.A.
Brands:
Fast

19006 Application Software
211 Main St
New Paltz, NY 12561-1312 845-255-3226
Fax: 845-255-3295 800-888-9470
info@ascqc.com www.ascqc.com
Bar code scanners, batching and blender systems
President: Greg Brandow
Estimated Sales: $1 - 3 Million
Number Employees: 1-4

19007 Applied Analytics
40 Kensington Cir
Chestnut Hill, MA 02467-2624 617-277-0906

19008 Applied Chemical Technology
4350 Helton Dr
Florence, AL 35630 256-760-9600
Fax: 256-760-9638 800-228-3217
act@appliedchemical.com
www.appliedchemical.com
Manufacturer and exporter of fluid beds, feeders and granulators. Development and engineering of processing plants available
President: A Ray Shirley
CFO: Ginger Lewey
VP: Curtis Lewey
Quality Control: Curtis Lewey
Marketing: Alan Nix
Purchasing Manager: Roger Kilburn
Estimated Sales: Below $5 Million
Number Employees: 50
Square Footage: 35000

19009 Applied Fabric Technologies
P.O.Box 575
Orchard Park, NY 14127-0575 716-662-0632
Fax: 716-662-0636 info@appliedfabric.com
www.afti.com
Conveyor belting including endless felts, endless belts, rotary moulder belts and bakery belts
President: Peter Lane
Sales Director: Matt Severied
Estimated Sales: $20-50 Million
Number Employees: 10-19

19010 Applied Handling NW
8531 South 222nd St
Kent, WA 98031 253-395-8500
Fax: 253-395-8585 888-395-3943
ahnwi@aol.com www.appliednw.com
Wholesaler/distributor of material handling equipment including package conveyors and pallet racks; rack jobber services available
President: Michael Tucker
Estimated Sales: $5-10 Million
Number Employees: 10-19
Brands:
H.K. Systems
Prest Rack
Rapid Rack
Unarco
Western Pacific Storage Systems

19011 Applied Industrial Technologies
1 Applied Plaza
Cleveland, OH 44115 216-426-4000
Fax: 216-426-4845 877-279-2799
appliedindustrial@applied.com
www.applied.com
CEO: David L Pugh
Estimated Sales: $1 - 5 Million
Number Employees: 1,000-4,999

19012 Applied Membranes
2325 Cousteau Ct
Vista, CA 92081 760-727-3711
Fax: 760-727-4427 800-321-9321
sales@appliedmembranes.com
www.appliedmembranes.com
Reverse osmosis, ultrafiltration and nano filtration systems, RO membranes, filters, pressure vessels, residential and commercial components and resins
President: Gil Dhawan
Marketing: Jande Wysocki
Estimated Sales: $5 - 10 000,000
Number Employees: 50-99

19013 Applied Product Sales
802 Angevine Court SW
Lilburn, GA 30047-4209 650-218-3104
Fax: 770-921-5814
info@appliedproductmarketing.com
www.appliedproductmarketing.com
Insulated shipping boxes and containers. Packaging and process machinery parts. Electro-mechanical power transmission components.
President: Tracey McHugh
CFO: Jim McHugh
Estimated Sales: $1.5 Million
Number Employees: 2
Number of Brands: 5
Type of Packaging: Food Service, Private Label, Bulk
Other Locations:
Applied Product Sales
Lilburn GA

19014 Applied Products Company
118 Sierra St
El Segundo, CA 90245 310-322-5972
Fax: 310-640-2975 888-551-0447
appliedprods@att.net www.appliedprodco.com
Marking and numbering equipment
Owner: Richard Panacek
Estimated Sales: $500,000-$1 Million
Number Employees: 1-4

19015 Applied Robotics
648 Saratoga Rd
Glenville, NY 12302 518-384-1000
Fax: 518-384-1200 800-309-3475
info@arobotics.com www.arobotics.com
ARI is a leading provider of automation end-of-arm connectivity solutions designed to bring greater speed and flexibility to automation-based processes.
CEO: Tom Petronis
CFO: Paul Cullen
CEO: Thomas J Petronis
Research & Development: Clay Cooper
Quality Control: Mike Gallo
Marketing Director: Joanne Brown
Public Relations: Joanne Brown
Production Manager: Bob Butterfield
Plant Manager: John Sezfilippi
Estimated Sales: $10-20,000,000
Number Employees: 50-99
Square Footage: 18000
Brands:
Quickstop
Smartscan
Xchange

19016 Applied Technologies Inc
16815 W Wisconsin Ave
Brookfield, WI 53005 262-784-7690
Fax: 262-784-6847 info@ati-ae.com
www.ati-ae.com
Consultant specializing in water and wastewater management
President: Dennis Totzke
Vice President: Dennis Totzke
Quality Control: Frank Tiefert
Marketing Director: Dennis Totzke
Number Employees: 20-49

19017 Applied Thermal Technologies
906 Boardwalk Ste B
San Marcos, CA 92069-4071 760-744-5083
Fax: 442-744-5031 800-736-5083
info@hydromiser.com www.hydromiser.com
Manufacturer and exporter of water chilling systems for batch cooling, food, confectionery and dairy products.
President: Kimberly Howard
Plant Manager: Dale Anderson
Estimated Sales: $500,000-$1 Million
Number Employees: 1-4
Square Footage: 5000
Brands:
Hydro-Miser

19018 **Apt-Li Specialty Brushes**
231 Red Rose Rd
Kerrville, TX 78028-8957 830-995-5198
Fax: 830-995-4036 aptprod@hctc.net
Brushes (for food and also for equipment) used in the food industry
Owner: Jerry O'Brien
Estimated Sales: $.5 - 1 million
Number Employees: 1-4

19019 **Aqua Blast Corporation**
1025 West Commerce Drive
Decatur, IN 46733 260-728-4433
Fax: 260-728-4517 800-338-7373
davidt@aquablast.com www.aquablast.com
High pressure cleaning systems. I order to meet certain food quality sterilization requirements, offers wash down motors, food grade oil and stainless steel.
Owner: David Tumbleson
Estimated Sales: $3 - 5 Million
Number Employees: 9

19020 **Aqua Brew**
3421 W Fordham Ave
Santa Ana, CA 92704 714-546-7117
Fax: 714-432-8802 800-888-BREW
sarah@cafejo.com www.aquabrew.com
Iced tea and coffee brewers, brewing devices and cleaners
Owner: Patrick Rolfes
Estimated Sales: $2.5 - 5 000,000
Number Employees: 20-49

19021 **(HQ)Aqua Measure InstrumentCompany**
9567 Arrow Route
Suite E
Rancho Cucamonga, CA 91730 909-941-7776
Fax: 909-941-1830 800-966-4788
sales@aquameasure.com
www.moistureregisterproducts.com
Manufacturer and exporter of moisture meters and systems for measuring moisture content in solids for the food processing industry
Owner: John Lundrstrom
Sales: Gabriel Cote Jr
Estimated Sales: $2.5-5 Million
Number Employees: 20-49
Other Locations:
Aqua Measure InstrumentCo.
La Verne CA

19022 **Aqua-Aerobic Systems**
6306 N Alpine Rd
Loves Park, IL 61111 815-654-2501
Fax: 815-654-2508 800-940-5008
solutions@aqua-aerobic.com
www.aqua-aerobic.com
Manufacturer and exporter of water and wastewater treatment systems for both municipal and industrial market, including direct drive aerators, down draft mixers and sequencing batch reactors; also, shallow bed, gravity sand and clothmedia filtration equipment
President: Robert J Wimmer
R&D: Lloyd Johnson
VP Marketing: Deb Lavelle
VP Sales: Steven Schupbach
VP International Sales: Sharon DeDoncker
Operations: Rick Reiland
Estimated Sales: $20-50 Million
Number Employees: 100-249
Square Footage: 100000
Brands:
Aqua Br
Aqua Cb12/24
Aqua Dm
Aqua Endura Disc
Aqua Endura Tube
Aqua Gf
Aqua-Jet Aerator
Aquadisk
Thermo F10

19023 **Aqua-Dyne**
635 West 12th St.
Baxter Springs, KS 66713 620-856-6222
Fax: 713-864-0313 800-826-9274
sales@aqua-dyne.com www.aqua-dyne.com
Manufacturer and exporter of water blasting and tank cleaning equipment; also pumps
Manager: Deiter Tischler
VP: Jennifer Rankin
Regional Sales Manager: Jorge Elarba
Marketing: Dennis Williams
Sales/Marketing: Paul Bako
Public Relations: Dennis Williams
Purchasing: Jennifer Rankin
Estimated Sales: $5-10,000,000
Number Employees: 20-49
Square Footage: 170000
Brands:
Aqua-Dyne

19024 **AquaTec**
1235 Shappert Dr
Rockford, IL 61115 815-654-1500
Fax: 815-654-0038 rj.ryan@aquatecinc.com
www.aquatecinc.com
President: Richard Ryan
Estimated Sales: $3 - 5 Million
Number Employees: 20-49

19025 **Aquafine Corporation**
29010 Avenue Paine
Valencia, CA 91355 661-257-4770
Fax: 661-257-2489 800-423-3015
techsupport@aquafineuv.com
www.aquafineuv.com
Ultra-violet water treatment equipment for pure and ultrapure applications. Aquafine meets the most stringent specifications in a variety of industries ranging from semiconductor to bio-pharmaceutical, food and beverage to powergeneration. The systems adhere to rigid industry standards of performance and are available with UL, CE and TUV specifications to meet all standards
Manager: Rick Clark
CEO: Michael Murphy
CFO: Steven Smith
VP Operations: John Maskaluk
Research & Development: Tony Ng
Quality Control: Robert Rivard
Sales/Marketing: Greg Hoffman
Public Relations: Alexis Bruhn
Human Resource Director: Julie Weith
Engineering: Mike Quinn
Purchasing Manager: Paul Contreras
Estimated Sales: $10-20 Million
Number Employees: 50-99
Square Footage: 110000

19026 **Aquair**
PO Box 777
Glen Ellen, CA 95442-0777 800-834-4474
Fax: 707-996-9234 www.aquair.com

19027 **Aquathin Corporation**
950 South Andrews Avenue
Pompano Beach, FL 33069 954-781-7777
Fax: 954-781-7336 800-462-7634
info@aquathin.com www.aquathin.com
Manufacturer and exporter of water purification systems including reverse osmosis, softening and filtration
President: Alfred Lipshultz
Estimated Sales: $5 -14 Million
Number Employees: 20-49
Square Footage: 65000
Brands:
Aqualite
Aquathin
Country Hutch
Lead Out
Megachar
Platinum 90
Sodia Lite
Soft N Clean
Yes

19028 **Aquionics**
1455 Jamike Avenue
Erlanger, KY 41018 859-341-0710
Fax: 859-341-0350 800-925-0440
sales@aquionics.com www.aquionics.net
Manufacturer and exporter of ultraviolet disinfection equipment
President: William Dekker
Manager: Rica Williams
Food/Beverage Sales Manager: Ralph Lopez
Number Employees: 10-19
Square Footage: 30000
Parent Co: Halma

19029 **(HQ)Arc Machines**
10500 Orbital Way
Pacoima, CA 91331 818-896-9556
Fax: 818-890-3724 sales@arcmachines.com
www.arcmachines.com
Automatic orbital welding equipment
President: Mindegas E Gedgaudas
Estimated Sales: $30 - 50 Million
Number Employees: 100-249

19030 **Arcar Graphics LLC**
450 Wegner Dr 500
West Chicago, IL 60185 630-231-7313
Fax: 630-231-3716
President: Mark Denboer

19031 **(HQ)Archer Daniels Midland Company**
4666 Faries Parkway
Decatur, IL 62526 217-424-5200
Fax: 217-424-6196 800-637-5843
info@admworld.com www.adm.com
Processors of soybeans, corn, wheat and cocoa
Chairman/President/CEO: Paticia woertz
Vice Chairman: John Rice
SVP/CFO: Ray Young
EVP/Performance & Growth: Steven Mills
VP/Chief Communications Officer: Victoria Podesta
Estimated Sales: $69 Billion
Number Employees: 28,200
Type of Packaging: Bulk
Other Locations:
ADM
Canada
ADM do Brasil Ltda
Sao Paulo, Brasil
ADM Paraguay S.A.E.C.A
Mingua Guaz£, Paraguay
ADM SAO S.A. Bolivia
Santa Cruz de la Sierra
ADM
Europe
ADM
Middle East
ADM
Africa
ADM Australia
Sydney, Australia
ADM Hong Kong
Wanchai, Hong Long
ADM Trading Company Ltd
Shanghai, China
ADM Tianjin
Tianjin, China
ADM Dalian
Dalian, China
ADM Far East
Bunkyo-Ku Tokyo, Japan
Brands:
Ambrosia®
Arcon®
Beakin
Capsulec
Clintoser
Cornsweet®
De Zaan®
Fibersol-2™
Merckens®
Novalipid™
Novasoy®
Novaxan™
Nusun®
Nutrisoy®
Nutrisoy® Next™
Optixan™
Pfl™
Pro-Fam®
Superb®
Thermolec
Ultralec®
Yelkin®

19032 **Archer Wire International**
7300 S Narragansett Ave
Bedford Park, IL 60638 708-563-1700
Fax: 708-563-1740
info@archeramericanwire.com
www.archerwire.com
Stainless steel fry and wire baskets, barbecue grills, point of purchase displays, oven racks and stove grates; also, metal stamping services available
Owner: Lawrence Svabek
VP Sales: Rick Svabek
National Sales Manager: Dale Brines
VP Finance: Larry Svabek

Estimated Sales: $10-20 Million
Number Employees: 100-249
Square Footage: 188000

19033 Architectural Products
1 Lockhart Ln
Highland, NY 12528 845-691-8500
Fax: 845-691-2501
Lighting fixtures and emergency lighting; also, energy consultants
President: Stephen Lockhart
Estimated Sales: $500,000-$1,000,000
Number Employees: 1-4
Brands:
Api

19034 Architectural SpecialtyProducts
6312 W 74th St
Bedford Park, IL 60638 708-563-8510
Fax: 708-563-1860 800-388-0111
www.a-s-p-inc.com
President: Rena Jahn
Owner: Lauren Jahn
Finance Executive: Tim Gibbons
Sales Executive: Warren Yoksas
Operations Executive: Pat Walsh
Estimated Sales: $1 - 5 Million
Number Employees: 20-49

19035 Archon Industries
200 William Street
Rye Brook, NY 10573-4620 914-937-8030
Estimated Sales: $1 - 5 Million
Number Employees: 20-50

19036 Arcobaleno Pasta Machines
160 Greenfield Road
Lancaster, PA 17601 717-394-1402
800-875-7096
ravioli@pastamachines.com
www.pastamachines.com
Pasta machinery and bakery processing lines, continuous and general purpose mixers, pasta preparation machinery, dough cutters and sheeters, pasteurizers, etc; exporter of calzone and pizza lines, ravioli machines and dough sheeters
President: Antonio Adiletta
VP, Marketing & Sales: Maja Adijetta
Number Employees: 11
Square Footage: 80000
Brands:
Arcobaleno

19037 Arcoplast Wall & Ceiling Systems
1873 Williamstown Drive
St Peters, MO 63376-8101 636-978-7781
Fax: 636-978-7782 888-736-2726
ghislain@arcoplast.com www.arcoplast.com
Integrated components necessary to design a contamination controlled environment. Product line includes ceilings, lights, air handling and microbial control systems, load-bearing and airtight walls and partitions, doors, windowspass-thru air locks, baseboards, structures, fasteners and other accessories.
President: Ghislain Beauregard
Estimated Sales: $1-$5 Million
Type of Packaging: Food Service, Bulk

19038 Arctic Air
6440 City West Pkwy Ste 2
Eden Prairie, MN 55344 952-941-2270
Fax: 952-941-3066 info@arcticairco.com
www.arcticairco.com
Manufacturer and exporter of refrigerators including reach-in and NSF approved chest freezers.
Owner: Walter Broich Sr
Estimated Sales: $10-20 Million
Number Employees: 4
Square Footage: 5000
Parent Co: Broich Enterprises
Brands:
Arctic Air

19039 Arctic Industries
9731 NW 114th Way
Medley, FL 33178 305-883-5581
Fax: 305-883-4651 800-325-0123
rio@arcticwalk-ins.com
www.arcticwalk-ins.com
Manufacturer and exporter of walk-in coolers, freezers and cold storage facilities, as well as step-in freezers and coolers.
President: Donald Goodstein
Vice President: Barbara Bowman
Sales Director: Rio Giardinieri
Office Manager: Barbara Bowman
Estimated Sales: $5 - 100 Million
Number Employees: 100-249
Square Footage: 50000
Brands:
Arctic
Penguin

19040 Arctic Seal & Gasket ofthe Americas
P.O.Box 3393
Stuart, FL 34995-3393 772-283-0080
Fax: 772-220-7437 800-881-4663
gaskets@bellsouth.net
Gaskets and seals for refrigeration units
Owner: Fred Frobert
VP: Fred Froberg
Sales: I Micheal Roth
Estimated Sales: $1-2.5,000,000
Number Employees: 1-4

19041 Arctic Stars of Texas
3540 W Pioneer Pkwy
Pantego, TX 76013-4625 817-860-1839
Fax: 817-277-4828 800-229-6567
www.arcticstar.com
Refrigerated store displays
Owner: Jim Dunnagan
Estimated Sales: $10-20 000,000
Number Employees: 20-49

19042 Arctica Showcase Company
33 2419 52nd Avenue SE
Calgary, AB T2C 4X7
Canada 403-246-2332
Fax: 403-246-2375 800-839-5536
caseinfo@arctica.ca www.arctica.ca
Hot Food, Deli, Meat, Seafood, Bakery, Candy Cafeteria showcases, Gelato Ice Cream Freezers and more
President: Mitchell Taylor
R&D Manager: Bruce May
President: Ron Rye
VP Operations: Joe Rankin
Number Employees: 30
Square Footage: 188000
Brands:
Diamond 49 Series
Diamond 52 Series
M850 Series
Maxima Series
Omega 48 Series
Omega 52 Series
Omega Buffet Series

19043 (HQ)Ardco
12400 S Laramie Ave
Alsip, IL 60803-3209 708-388-4300
Fax: 708-388-0952 800-323-3387
www.temperbent.com
Glass doors, curved display case glass, refrigerated display cases, compressorized refrigerated equipment, commercial refrigerators, and a variety of refrigeration accessories
President, Chief Executive Officer: Jeffrey Clark
Vice President of Supply Chain: Nathan Lowstuter
Vice President of Sales and Marketing: Michael Murth
Chief Operating Officer: William Pack
Estimated Sales: $100+ Million
Number Employees: 20-49

19044 Arde Barinco
875 Washington Ave
Carlstadt, NJ 07072 201-784-9880
Fax: 201-784-0483 800-909-6070
abmix@ardeinc.com www.arde-barinco.com
Manufacturer and exporter of mixing equipment systems used to disperse gums and stabilizers to prepare emulsions
Manager: Sue Belaus
Sales/Engineering Manager: Roy Scott
Public Relations: Cindy Roehling
Purchasing: Tom Stephens
Estimated Sales: $5 Million
Number Employees: 20-49
Square Footage: 280000
Parent Co: Arde, Inc.

19045 Arden Companies
30400 Telegraph Road
Southfield, MI 48025 248-415-8500
Fax: 248-415-8520
salesdept@ardencompanies.com
www.ardencompanies.com
Manufacturer and exporter of aprons, chef coats, baker's mits, handle holders, cleaners, outdoor pads and cushions, grill covers, pot holders and oven mitts
President: Robert Sachs
CFO: John Connell
Sales/Marketing: William Sachs
Estimated Sales: $20-50 Million
Number Employees: 50-99
Square Footage: 675000
Type of Packaging: Consumer, Food Service

19046 Arena Products
2101 Mount Read Blvd
Rochester, NY 14615 585-254-2180
Fax: 585-254-1046 800-836-2528
sales@arenaproducts.com
www.arenaproducts.com
Designer and manufacturer of plastic products for storage and tranportation of food or chemical products.
President: Anthony Arena
Quality Control: Don Wilcox
CFO: Jim Vlaakman
Estimated Sales: $20 - 50 Million
Number Employees: 20

19047 Argo & Company
182 Ezell Street
P.O. Box 2747
Spartanburg, SC 29304 864-583-9766
Fax: 864-585-5056 argosheen@bellsouth.net
www.argoco.com
Manufacturer and exporter of cleaning supplies including cotton pads, rug mops and carpet/upholstery chemicals and machines
President: Anne Sanders
Estimated Sales: $10-20 Million
Number Employees: 20-49
Square Footage: 100000
Brands:
Argomops
Argonaut
Argosheen

19048 Arizona Instrument LLC
3375 North Delaware Street
Chandler, AZ 85225 602-470-1414
Fax: 602-804-0656 800-528-7411
sales@azic.com www.azic.com
An ISO 9001:200 registered company that designs, manufactures, and markets Computrac precision moisture, solids, and ash analyzers and Jerome toxic gas analyzers.
President: George Hays
Research & Development: Tom Hatfield
Quality Control: Blaine Nelson
Marketing: Shari Houtler
Operations Manager: Ben Brown
Estimated Sales: $10 Million
Number Employees: 50-99
Number of Brands: 4
Number of Products: 13
Brands:
Computrac Max
Computrac Vapor Pro
Jerome

19049 Arizona Store Equipment
2523 N 16th St
Phoenix, AZ 85006 602-252-4823
Fax: 602-258-3064 800-624-8395
Acrylic displays, showcases, slatwall, wall systems, shelving and store fixtures
Administrator: Bill James
Estimated Sales: $2.5-5,000,000
Number Employees: 1-4
Brands:
Cal Tuf
Diack
Discovery Plastics
Jahabow
Lozier
Marlite

19050 **Arjo Wiggins**
10901 Westlake Drive
Charlotte, NC 28273 704-587-3000
Fax: 704-587-1174 800-765-9278
chris.pelle@arjoexamerica.com
www.polyart.com
Product and services are tag and label applications suitable for a variety of uses including that of: food labels; slaughterhouse meat tags; bar-coded labels, and self-adhesive labels.
Sales Representative: Chris Pelle

19051 **Arjobex/Polyart**
10901 Westlake Dr
Charlotte, NC 28273-3740 704-587-3000
Fax: 704-588-9506 800-POL-YART
polyartus@aol.com www.polyart.com
Synthetic paper products
VP: Vijay Yadav
Estimated Sales: $10-25 Million
Number Employees: 50-99

19052 **Arkansas Glass Container Corporation**
P.O.Box 1717
Jonesboro, AR 72403-1717 870-932-4564
Fax: 870-268-6217 800-527-4527
agcsalesdept@agcc.com www.agcc.com
Manufacturer and exporter of glass jars and bottles
CEO: Anthony M Ramplex
VP Sales: Melton Harrison
VP Operations: Joel Sharp
Estimated Sales: $30 - 50 Million
Number Employees: 250-499
Square Footage: 450000

19053 **Arkansas Tomato Shippers**
106 N John C Moss III St
Warren, AR 71671-2510 870-463-8258
brooks@dakotacom.net
Distributor and processor of fresh produce
President: Charlie Sarcey
Estimated Sales: $1 - 5 Million
Number Employees: 6

19054 **Arkfeld Mfg & Distr Company**
P.O. Box 54
Norfolk, NE 68702 402-371-9430
Fax: 402-371-5137 800-533-0676
arkfeldm@ncfcomm.com www.arkfelds.com
Manufacturer, distributor and exporter of custom metal fabricated poultry scales, livestock dial scales and feed/grain hopper dial scales, custom automatic watering systems and security and frozen product storage cabinets.
President: Robert Arkfeld
CEO: Janet Arkfeld
CFO: Anthony Arkfeld
Sales Director: Janet Arkfeld
Sales: Robert Arkfeld
Number Employees: 10-19
Square Footage: 2500
Brands:
Arkfeld Instant Way Dial Scales
Arkfeld Security Cabinets
Bunker Boxes

19055 **Arlin Manufacturing Company**
P.O.Box 222
Lowell, MA 01853-0222 978-454-9165
Fax: 978-454-5265 sales@arlinmfg.com
www.arlinmfg.com
Tear tapes, plastic film, plastic sheet
Chairman of the Board: John R Mitchell
Estimated Sales: $5-10 Million
Number Employees: 20-49

19056 **Arlington Display Industries**
19303 W Davison St
Detroit, MI 48223 313-837-1212
Fax: 313-837-3425 sales@arlingtondisplay.com
www.arlingtondisplay.com
Point-of-purchase displays
President: Carl Dumas
Number Employees: 50-99
Brands:
Safe-Lode
Traveler
Versa-Panel

19057 **Arlyn Johnson & Associates**
1339 E Hanover St
Springfield, MO 65804-4232 417-886-3367
Fax: 417-886-4859
Poultry, poultry products, primarily fresh & frozen turkey [roducts or further processing
President: Rex Johnson
Estimated Sales: Below $5,000,000
Number Employees: 1-4

19058 **Armac Industries Limited**
400 Kidds Hill Rd
Hyannis, MA 02601 508-771-9400
Fax: 508-790-0002 www.sencorp-inc.com
CEO: Brian Urban
Estimated Sales: $1 - 5 Million
Number Employees: 100-249

19059 **(HQ)Armaly Brands**
PO Box 611
Walled Lake, MI 48390-0611 248-669-2100
Fax: 248-669-3505 800-772-1222
orderdesk207@armalybrands.com
www.armalybrands.com
Manufacturer and exporter of sponges, scrubbers, cotton cheesecloth and scouring pads
Owner: John Armaly
VP: Gilbert Armaly
Estimated Sales: $1 - 5 Million
Number Employees: 20-49
Square Footage: 400
Type of Packaging: Consumer, Food Service, Private Label, Bulk
Brands:
Auto Show
Estracell
Scourlite

19060 **Armand Manufacturing**
2399 Silver Wolf Dr
Henderson, NV 89011-4431 702-565-7500
Fax: 702-565-3838 sales@armandmfg.net
www.armandmfg.com
President: Richard De Heras
Estimated Sales: $10 - 20 Million
Number Employees: 20-49

19061 **Armato & Associates**
7825 Carlisle Dr
Hanover Park, IL 60133-2405 630-837-1886
Fax: 630-837-0813 www.armatoenterprises.com
Owner: Sam Armato
Estimated Sales: $1 - 5 Million
Number Employees: 1-4

19062 **Armbrust Paper Tubes**
6255 S Harlem Ave
Chicago, IL 60638 773-586-3232
Fax: 773-586-8997 tubesrus@corecomm.net
www.tubesrus.com
Manufacturer and exporter of packaging products including paper tubes, cores, cans and push-ups for frozen sherbet, gyros, etc.; also, containers for dry goods
President: Bernerd Armbrust
VP: Chris Armbrust
Marketing: Bill Constable
Sales: Marc Armbrust
Secretary: Dorothee Johnstone
Plant Manager: Mike Johnstone
Estimated Sales: $5-10 Million
Number Employees: 20-49
Square Footage: 85000
Type of Packaging: Food Service, Private Label
Brands:
Artpak
Pinched Tube
Push-Pops

19063 **Armco**
385 Todhunter Road
Monroe, OH 45050-1113 800-231-3748

19064 **Armfield**
Bridge House, West Street
Ringwood, EN BH24 1DY 142- 47-781
Fax: 142- 47-916 sales@armfield.co.uk
www.armfield.co.uk
Edible oil processing equipment, reverse osmosis/ultrafiltration units, heat exchangers, carbonators, homogenizers and miniature heat treatment HTST/UHT, distillation and spray drying systems
Manager: Mike Dileo
Sales Manager: Mark Fillingham
Operations Manager: Mike Dileo
Estimated Sales: $1 - 3 Million
Number Employees: 1-4

19065 **Armstrong Engineering Associates**
PO Box 566
West Chester, PA 19381-0566 610-436-6080
Fax: 610-436-0374
sales@armstrong-chemtec.com
www.rmarmstrong.com
President: Richard M Armstrong Jr
Sales: Gail Justi
Estimated Sales: $1 - 5 Million
Number Employees: 50-99

19066 **Armstrong International**
900 Maple St
Three Rivers, MI 49093 269-273-1415
Fax: 269-278-6555 marketing@armintl.com
www.armstrong-intl.com
Steam traps, strainers, purgers, air vents, humidifiers and liquid drainers, pressure reducing valves, instantaneous water heaters, radiator products, mixing valves, hosestations, and heating and cooling coils
Chairman of the Board: Merrill Armstrong
Marketing Director: Tom Grubka
Estimated Sales: $50-100 Million
Number Employees: 250-499

19067 **Armstrong Manufacturing**
2485 Haines Road
Mississauga, ON L4Y 1Y7
Canada 905-566-1395
Fax: 905-566-8195 866-627-6588
info@armcoinc.ca
www.armstrongmaufacturing.com
Industrial cleaning products
CEO: David Armstrong
Estimated Sales: $1 - 5 Million
Number Employees: 100-250

19068 **Armstrong-Hunt**
816 Maple Street
Three Rivers, MI 49093 269-273-1415
Fax: 269-278-6555 armhunt@ah-milton.com
www.armstrong-hunt.com
President, Chief Executive Officer: Patrick Armstrong

19069 **Armstrong-Lynnwood**
221 Armstrong Blvd
Three Rivers, MI 49093 269-273-1415
Fax: 269-278-6555 www.armstrong-intl.com
Manufacturer and exporter of hose stations and thermostatic mixing valves
President: David Armstrong
General Manager/Sales/Marketing Exec.: Paul Knight
Purchasing Agent: Steven Shutes
Number Employees: 7
Parent Co: Armstrong International
Brands:
Rada
Steamix

19070 **Arneg**
750 Old Hargrave Rd
Lexington, NC 27295 336-956-5300
Fax: 610-746-9580 800-276-3487
www.arnegusa.com
Display cases for meat, seafood, fish, cheese, deli and frozen foods, etc
General Manager: Gianfrano Genovese
President: Rejean Lumiere
Sales Manager: Jim Christman
Secretary: Sharon Sherman
Estimated Sales: $10-20 Million
Number Employees: 4
Square Footage: 70000
Parent Co: Arneg
Brands:
Arneg

19071 **Arnold Equipment Company**
P.O.Box 1148
Twinsburg, OH 44087 216-831-8485
Fax: 216-831-8414 800-642-1824
arnold@arnoldeqp.com www.arnoldeqp.com
Wholesaler/distributor and exporter of blenders, ovens, agitators, filters, dryers, packaging plastic granulators, centrifuges, pumps, evaporators, condensers, kettles, homogenizers and material handling and laboratory testingequipment, etc
President: Jon Arnold
CEO: Jon Arnold
CFO: Seth Arnold

Estimated Sales: Below $5 Million
Number Employees: 1-4
Square Footage: 120000

19072 Arol Closure Systems Spa
237 Graves Mill Road
Lynchburg, VA 24502-4203 800-423-5822
Fax: 434-832-8352 info@belvac.com
www.belvac.com

19073 Aroma Manufacturing Company
6469 Flanders Dr
San Diego, CA 92121 858-558-6688
Fax: 858-558-7300 800-276-6286
www.aroma-housewares.com
Rice and steam cookers; also, soup and rice warmers
Manager: David Kellerman
Marketing Director: Howard Ong
Estimated Sales: $3 - 5 Million
Number Employees: 5-9

19074 Aromascan PLC
14 Clinton Drive
Hollis, NH 03049-6595 603-598-2922
Fax: 603-595-9916
Instrumentation for the analysis of odors
General Manager: Peter Debroczy
Estimated Sales: $1-2.5 Million
Number Employees: 24
Parent Co: Aromascan PLC
Brands:
The Aromo Scanner

19075 Aromatech USA
5770 Hoffner Avenue
Suite 103
Orlando, FL 32822 407-277-5727
Fax: 407-277-5725 americas@aromatech.fr
www.aromatech.fr/en/f.usa.htm
Manufacturer of flavorings for beverages, candies, baking, snacks and pastries

19076 Arpeco Engineering Ltd
7095 Ordan Drive
Mississauga, ON L5T 1K6
Canada 905-564-5150
Fax: 905-564-2943 sales@arpeco.com
Owner: Allan Prittie

19077 Arro Corporation
7440 Santa Fe Dr
Hodgkins, IL 60525 708-352-8200
Fax: 708-352-5293 877-929-2776
sales@arro.com www.arro.com
Dry & liquid blending, dry & liquid processing, bulk handling & storage.
Square Footage: 600

19078 Arrow Magnolia International, Inc.
2646 Rodney Lane
Dallas, TX 75229 972-247-7111
Fax: 972-484-2896 800-527-2101
info@arrowmagnolia.com
www.arrowmagnolia.com
Industrial insecticides, grill cleaners, drain cleaners and deodorizers
President: Curtis Shaw
CEO: David Tippeconnic
Vice President of Sales: Jim Purcell
Operations Manager: Michael Campanaro
Number Employees: 20-49
Square Footage: 160000

19079 Arrow Plastics
701 E Devon Ave
Elk Grove, IL 60007-6700 847-595-9000
Fax: 847-595-9122 info@arrowplastic.com
www.arrowplastic.com
Manufacturer and exporter of plastic cutting boards
President: Robert Kleckauskas
Estimated Sales: $20-50 Million
Number Employees: 100-249
Type of Packaging: Food Service

19080 Arrow Sign & Awning Company
13735 Aberdeen St NE
Ham Lake, MN 55304-6784 763-755-8873
Fax: 763-755-1473 800-621-9231
bruce@arrowsigninc.com
www.arrowsigninc.com
Design manufacturer of lit and unlit fabric and metal commercial awnings, neon signs and lighted channel letters, also pylon signs, LED lighting, parking lot lights, LED message centers.
President: Bruce Cardnial
CFO/VP: Connie Cardinal Ramberg
Research & Development: Kelli Keilty
Quality Control: Tony Ramberg
Marketing: Bruce Cardinal
Plant Manager: Tony Ramberg
Purchasing Manager: Ryan Thiede
Estimated Sales: $10 Million
Number Employees: 20-49
Square Footage: 36000

19081 Arrow Tank Company
16 Barnett Pl
Buffalo, NY 14215 716-893-7200
Fax: 716-893-0693 sales@arrowtankco.com
www.arrowtankco.com
Manufacturer, exporter of wood tanks and tank hoops
President: W M Wehr
Operations: W H Wehr
Plant Manager: R Willis
Estimated Sales: $1-3,000,000
Number Employees: 10-19
Square Footage: 25000

19082 Art Craft Lighting
East Service Road
P.O. Box 1526
Champlain, NY 11919 718-387-8000
Fax: 516-593-9239 www.artcraftlighting.com
Electric lighting fixtures
President: Barry Spade
Estimated Sales: $1-2.5 Million
Number Employees: 5-9
Parent Co: Artcraft Lighting Company

19083 Art Kraft-Strauss SignCorporation
1776 Broadway #1810
New York, NY 10019-2006 212-265-5155
Fax: 212-265-5159 info@artkraft.com
www.artkraft.com
Manufacturer and exporter of advertising signs
President: Tama Starr
CFO: Neil Vonknoblauch
Vice President Design & Engineering: Robert Jackowitz
VP Sales: Bob Neuberger
Estimated Sales: $10 - 20 Million
Number Employees: 250-499
Type of Packaging: Consumer, Food Service, Bulk

19084 Art Plastics Handy HomeHelpers
22 Jytek Road
Leominster, MA 01453-5966 978-537-0367
Fax: 978-840-6908 ed@firstplastics.com
www.firstplastics.com
Plastic restaurant supplies including cake keepers, round platters and salad tongs
President: Edward Mazzaferro
CEO: Mary Anne Taylor
Office Manager: Lisa Butler
Estimated Sales: Below $5 Million
Number Employees: 20-49
Square Footage: 120000
Parent Co: Art Plastics Manufacturing Corporation
Type of Packaging: Consumer
Brands:
Handy-Home Helpers

19085 Art Poly Bag Company
70 Franklin Ave
Brooklyn, NY 11205-1504 718-243-9417
Fax: 718-422-8689 800-278-7659
www.artpromos.com
Promotional poly tote bags
President: Erwin Katz
Estimated Sales: $500,000-$1 Million
Number Employees: 10-19

19086 Art Wire Works
6711 S Leclaire Ave
Bedford Park, IL 60638 708-458-3993
dcollignon@artwireworks.com
www.artwireworks.com
Manufacturer and exporter of display racks, point of purchase displays, back room trays and hand carts
President: David Collignon
CFO: Ksenia Nalysnyk
R&D/Quality Control: Danny Tomasevich
Sales: Gayle Blakeslee
Plant Manager: Wally Kaim
Purchasing: Gayle Blakeslee
Estimated Sales: $5 Million
Number Employees: 50-99
Square Footage: 40000

19087 Art's Welding
3902 230th St
PO Box 909
Winsted, MN 55395 320-485-2471
Fax: 320-485-4466 888-272-2600
customerservice@awimfg.com
www.awimfg.com
President: Gary Scherping
Sales Manager: Brent Johnson
Estimated Sales: $1 - 3 Million
Number Employees: 20-49
Square Footage: 90

19088 Art-Phyl Creations
16250 NW 8th Avenue
Hialeah, FL 33014-6415 305-624-2333
Fax: 305-621-4093 800-327-8318
info@art-phyl.com www.hookstore.com
Manufacturer and exporter of store display fixtures, peghooks, merchandising aids, point of purchase displays, etc.
President: Arthur Hochman
CEO: S Gwinn
CFO: C Pomerantz
Sales: William Rodriguez
Estimated Sales: $5 - 10 Million
Number Employees: 20-49
Number of Products: 400
Square Footage: 200000
Brands:
Kwik-Hook
Kwik-Hub
Poly-Pole
Scan-A-Plate
Short-Stop
Super Hook

19089 Art-Tech Restaurant Design
1 Station Plz
Lynbrook, NY 11563 516-593-7787
Fax: 516-593-9239 restrauntplans@aol.com
www.arttechdesigns.com
Consultant and designer of restaurant/food service interiors
President: Philip Starr
Consultant: Philip Starr
Estimated Sales: $1 - 2.5 Million
Number Employees: 5-9

19090 Artco Equipment Company
40 Tillman St
Westwood, NJ 07675-2627 201-664-4455
Fax: 201-666-9243 800-664-5686
bagelman@webc1.com www.bagelbagel.com
Ovens, bagel machines, mixers, bagel kettles and smallwares
President: Howard Goldberg
Estimated Sales: $1-2.5 Million
Number Employees: 1-4

19091 Artcraft Badge & Sign Company
3512 John Carroll Drive
Olney, MD 20832 301-519-2939
800-739-0709
artcraft@his.com
Plastic custom imprinted identification badges and interior signage. Produces personalized name badges, identification tags, signs, and deskplates
Owner: Janet Dinerman
Bookkeeper: Shirley Bowker
General Manager: Arthur Dinerman
Shipping Manager: Reina Roeder
Estimated Sales: $2.5-5 Million
Number Employees: 9
Square Footage: 1800
Type of Packaging: Bulk

19092 Artel Packaging SystemsLimited
PO Box 335
Gromley, ON L0H 1G0
Canada 905-888-9800
Fax: 905-888-9804 inquiry@artelsystems.com
www.artelsystems.com
President: Fred McCatrney
Estimated Sales: Below $5 Million
Number Employees: 10

19093 Artex International
1405 Walnut St
Highland, IL 62249 618-654-2113
Fax: 618-654-0200 www.bestmanufacturing.com
Manufacturer and exporter of table linens including covers, skirts, napkins and place mats, restaurant design, linen processing, trade show listing, linen presentations
Manager: Mike Kirchoff
Estimated Sales: $50-100 Million
Number Employees: 50-99

19094 Arthur Corporation
1305 Huron Avery Rd
Huron, OH 44839 419-433-7202
Fax: 419-433-7088
Plastic cups, trays and containers
President: Charles Hensel
Estimated Sales: $10-20 Million
Number Employees: 100-249
Square Footage: 75000

19095 (HQ)Arthur D Little Inc.
68 Fargo Street
Suite 2810
Boston, MA 02110 617-532-9550
Fax: 617-261-6630 www.adlittle.com
Consultant specializing in technology, product and marketing services; also, management, environmental, health, safety, product formulation, sensory evaluation, research and development.
CEO/Pres.: C LaMantia
Sr. VP: P Ranganath Nayak
VP/Managing Director: C Gail Greenwald
Estimated Sales: $.5 - 1 million
Number Employees: 1,000-4,999
Square Footage: 800000

19096 Arthur G. Russell Company (The)
750 Clark Avenue
P.O. Box 237
Bristol, CT 06011-0237 860-583-4109
Fax: 860-583-0686 agr@arthurgrussell.com
www.arthurgrussell.com
Manufacturer and exporter of automated packaging, counting, inspecting and assembling equipment for food and disposable manufacturers; custom design services available
President: Robert J Ensminger
Applications Engr.: John Picoli
Vice President Sales & Marketing: William Mis
Estimated Sales: $10-20 Million
Number Employees: 100-249
Square Footage: 83000
Brands:
Uniplace
Vibro-Block

19097 Arthur J. Kaufman SalesCompany
261 Narragansett Park Dr
Rumford, RI 02916 401-438-5600
Fax: 401-431-0606 800-556-6254
info@ajksales.com www.ajksales.com
Manufacturers' representative for disposable paper and plastic food service products and packaging; serving all markets
President: Arthur Kaufman
Controller: H John Madden
VP: Allan Kaufman
Marketing Sales Manager: Kenneth McAuliffe
Estimated Sales: $20-50 Million
Number Employees: 20-49
Type of Packaging: Food Service
Brands:
Aep Institutional Products
Austins
Cascades
Cascades Ifc Disposables
Destiny Plastics
Disposable Products Company
Dopaco
Fabri-Kal Corporation
Fold Pak Company
Genpak
Handi-Foil of America
Johnsondiversey
McNarin Packaging
Morgro
Plastirun Corporation
Poliback Plastics America
Quality Paper Products
Stewart Sutherland
Tradex International

19098 Arthur Products Company
1140 Industrial Pkwy
Medina, OH 44256 330-725-4905
Fax: 330-722-2698 800-322-0510
apc@apclsq.com www.arthurproducts.com
Vent tubes and nozzles
Owner: Richard Rauckhorst
Sales Manager: Bob Peck
Estimated Sales: Below $5 Million
Number Employees: 5-9
Square Footage: 10000

19099 Artisan Controls Corporation
111 Canfield Ave Ste B-18
Randolph, NJ 07869 973-598-9400
Fax: 973-598-9410 800-457-4950
sales@artisancontrols.com
www.artisancontrols.com
Controllers including time/temperature, dispensing, scheduling for pasta machines, fryers, ovens, etc.
President: Jack Murray
VP Sales: Leigh Stevens
Estimated Sales: $3 Million
Number Employees: 20-49
Square Footage: 12000
Type of Packaging: Private Label, Bulk
Brands:
Tyme Chef

19100 Artisan Industries
73 Pond St
Waltham, MA 02451-4594 781-893-6800
Fax: 781-647-0143 info@artisanind.com
www.artisanind.com
Equipment to purify, concentrate, deodorize or recover/remove solvents or fatty acids
President: Andrew Donevan
SVP/General Manager: Perry Alasti
Director Marketing/Sales: Richard Giberti
Pilot Plant Services: Robert DiLoreto
Estimated Sales: $5-10 Million
Number Employees: 100
Brands:
Rototherm

19101 Artist Coffee
51 Harvey Road
Unit D
Londonderry, NH 03053-7414 603-434-9385
Fax: 603-216-8029 866-440-4511
dan@artistcoffee.com www.artistcoffee.com
Producer of gourmet coffee, tea and candy for promotional trade. Specializing in Custom Labeling with very special products.
President: Tom Rushton
Marketing Director: Dan Sewell
Estimated Sales: $3 - 5 Million
Number Employees: 1-4
Type of Packaging: Consumer, Private Label
Other Locations:
Lambent Technologies
Gurnee IL
Brands:
Cirashine
Erucical
Hodag
Lamchem
Lumisolve
Lumisorb
Lumulse
Oleocal
Polycal

19102 Artiste Flavor
35 Franklin Tpke
Waldwick, NJ 07463 201-447-1311
Ingredients, flavors, colors and additives
President: Joseph Raimondo
Customer Service Manager: Tracy Raimondo
Estimated Sales: $500,000- 1 Million
Number Employees: 5-9
Type of Packaging: Consumer

19103 Artistic Carton
1201 S Grandstaff Dr
Auburn, IN 46706 260-925-6060
Fax: 260-925-1762
customerserviceauburn@artisticcarton.com
www.artisticcarton.com
Folding cartons
President: Peter A Traeger
CFO: Mark Hopkinson
Estimated Sales: $10-20 Million
Number Employees: 50-99

19104 (HQ)Artistic Carton Company
1975 Big Timber Rd
Elgin, IL 60123 847-741-0247
Fax: 847-741-8529 www.artisticcarton.com
Folding paper boxes and cartons
President: Peter A Traeger
CFO: Mark Hopkinfon
Sales Manager: Patrick Driscoll
Estimated Sales: $20 - 50 Million
Number Employees: 250

19105 Artistic Packaging Concepts
PO Box 196
Massapequa Pk, NY 11762-0196 516-797-4020
Fax: 516-797-4020
Plain and printed plastic bags; also, blisters, blister cards, labels and paper printing foam envelopes
VP: S Falciana
Estimated Sales: $1 - 5 Million
Number Employees: 5

19106 Artx Limited
1770 W Lexington
Cincinnati, OH 45212 513-631-0660
Fax: 513-631-3111
Owner: Mike Rawlings
Estimated Sales: $5 - 10 Million
Number Employees: 10-19

19107 Ascaso
524 North York Road
Bensenville, IL 60106 630-350-0066
Fax: 630-350-0005 info@expressoshoppe.com
www.expressoshoppe.com
Espresso equipment and espresso beans
Owner: David Dimbert
Estimated Sales: $300,000-500,000
Number Employees: 1-4
Parent Co: Ascaso Spa
Type of Packaging: Food Service
Brands:
Ascaso

19108 Asepak Corporation
645 S High St
Covington, OH 45318 937-473-2053
Fax: 937-473-2403 www.generalfilms.com
Owner: Roy Weikert
Estimated Sales: $1 - 5 Million
Number Employees: 50-99

19109 Aseptic Resources
10008 W 120th St
Overland Park, KS 66213-1647 913-897-4125
Fax: 913-327-5529
Consultant for aseptic systems
Estimated Sales: $1 - 5 Million

19110 Ash Enterprises
801 N 7th St
Salina, KS 67401 785-825-5280
Fax: 785-825-5072 888-825-5280
dave@ashenterprisesonline.com
www.ashenterprisesonline.com
President: Adrienne Ash
CEO: Adrienne Ash
Estimated Sales: $5-9.9,000,000
Number Employees: 1-4
Brands:
Chile Chews
Hot Pops
Jalea De Jalapeno
Salsa Primo

19111 Ashbrook Corporation
11600 E Hardy Rd
Houston, TX 77093-1098 281-449-0322
Fax: 281-449-1324 800-362-9041
ashbrook@ashbrookcorp.com
www.ashbrookcorp.com

Manufacturer and exporter of liquid solid separation equipment (presses) and thickeners
President: Robert T Williams
Marketing Director: Carl Boyd
Estimated Sales: $20-50 Million
Number Employees: 100-249
Brands:
Aquabelt
Klampress
Winklepress

19112 Ashland Distributing Company
5200 Blazer Pkwy
Dublin, OH 43017-5309 614-790-3333
Fax: 614-790-4427 877-343-3278
csr@ashchem.com www.ashchem.com
President: F L Hank Waters
Chairman, Chief Executive Officer: Jim OBrien
Vice President: Blair Boggs
Senior Vice President of Research and De: Fran Lockwood
Director of Marketing: John Stotz
Director of Corporate Communications: Gary Rhodes
Number Employees: 1,000-4,999

19113 Ashland Incorporated
50 East RiverCenter Boulevard
P.O. Box 391
Covington, KY 41012-0391 859-815-3333
Fax: 859-815-5053 www.ashland.com
Supplier of specialty resins, polymers, and adhesives. Ashland's Water Technologies unit provides papermaking chemicals and specialty chemicals to markets such as pulp and paper, food and beverage, municipal, and mining.
Chairman/Chief Executive Officer: James O'Brien Jr
Senior VP/Chief Financial Officer: Lamar Chambers
VP/CIO/CAO: Anne Schumann
Chief Engineer: Walter Shevchuk
Chief Marketing Officer: Dean Doza
Executive VP, Human Resources: Gregory Chesser
Plant Manager: Klaus Busam
Director, Purchasing: Isabelle Nicolas
Estimated Sales: $8.2 Billion
Number Employees: 15,000
Brands:
Advantage
Escalol
Ganex
Polyclar

19114 Ashland Nutritional Products
17751 Mitchell N
Irvine, CA 92614-6028 949-833-9500
Fax: 949-622-0954
Estimated Sales: $5 - 10 000,000
Number Employees: 5-9

19115 Ashland Specialty Chemical Company
50 E RiverCenter Blvd
PO Box 391
Covington, KY 41012-0391 859-815-3333
Fax: 859-815-5053 www.ashland.com
Water treatment chemicals for corrosion, scale inhibitors, gras polymer, oxidation and chlorine dioxide systems
Chairman/CEO: James O'Brien
SVP/CFO: Lamar Chambers
VP Ahsland Distribution: Robert Claycraft II
VP Functional Ingredients: John Panichella
VP Water Technologies: Paul Raymond III
VP Chief Growth Officer: Walter Solomon
VP Communications: Susan Esler
VP Global Supply Chain: Theodore Harris
VP Consumer Markets: Samuel Mitchell Jr
Estimated Sales: $8 Billion
Number Employees: 15000
Parent Co: Ashland Chemical
Brands:
Generox

19116 Ashlock Company
855 Montague St
P.O. Box 1676
San Leandro, CA 94577 510-351-0560
Fax: 510-357-0329 info@ashlockco.com
www.ashlockco.com
Manufacturer and exporter of pitters for dates, prunes, cherries and olives. Also olive slicers
President: Tom G Rettagliata
CFO: Sheryl Sullivan
R & D: Jeff Davis
Marketing Director: Alan Stender
Office Manager: S Sullivan
Manager, Operations: Jeff Davis
Estimated Sales: $5-10 Million
Number Employees: 10-19
Square Footage: 12400
Parent Co: Vistan Corporation
Brands:
Ashlock

19117 Ashworth Bros
450 Armour Dl
Winchester, VA 22601 540-662-3494
Fax: 540-662-3150 800-682-4594
ashworth@ashworth.com www.ashworth.com
Manufacturer and exporter of conveyor belts
President: Vincent Moretti
VP: Joe Lackner
Quality Control: Jonathan Lasecki
Commercial Support Manager: Kenneth King
Sales: Marty Tabaka
Estimated Sales: $20 - 50 Million
Number Employees: 100-249
Brands:
All Plastic Belting
Balanceo Weave
Cbs Baking Band
Flat Wire
Fusion Grid
Hybri Flex
Hybri Grio
Omni Grid
Omniflex
Washer Holddown Mats
Woven Wire

19118 Asia and Middle East Food Traders
340 Pine Street
Suite 401
San Francisco, CA 94104 415-677-9700
Fax: 415-677-9711 info@arabellaadvisors.com
www.blueprintrd.com
President: Lucy Bernholz
Number Employees: 10-19

19119 Asian Foods
1300 L Orient St
St. Paul, MN 55117 651-558-2400
Fax: 651-558-2404 800-274-2655
afiinfo@asianfoods.com www.asianfoods.com
Supplier of Asian products including; buttermilk biscuits, food containers, cooking oil, cream cheese, fortune cookies, fresh broccoli, yellow onions, napa, cabbage, canned fruit & vegetables, rice, broccoli crowns, cleaning suppliesfresh chicken (bone-in & boneless), sesame oil, soft-serve ice cream mix, vinegar
Owner: Avlina Litchnegger
Owner: Yeong Osato
Owner: Quyen Nguyen
MIS Director: Chris Nguyen
Marketing Director: Michon Sommers
VP Sales: Paul Hamel
Vice President Operations: Les Wong
Estimated Sales: $100+ Million
Number Employees: 300+
Square Footage: 68000
Parent Co: SYSCO
Type of Packaging: Food Service, Private Label
Other Locations:
Kansas City MO
Hampshire IL
Brands:
Ji Hao
Shang Pin

19120 Aspect Engineering
7911 Linksview Cir.
Westerville, OH 614-638-7106
Fax: 614-416-6919
Consultant for product development and facility design; management advisory for food service companies and suppliers
Commun. Mgr.: Mark Wegner
Estimated Sales: $1 - 5 Million
Number Employees: 4
Square Footage: 2000

19121 Aspen Research Corporation
8401 Jefferson Highway
Maple Grove, MN 55369 651-842-6100
Fax: 651-842-6199 answers@aspenresearch.com
www.aspenresearch.com
President/CEO: Richard Burnton
Vice President - Research & Development: Roger Pearson, Ph.D.
Analytical Sales: Jan Fouks
VP of Manufacturing: Brian Woodman
Estimated Sales: $5 - 10 Million
Number Employees: 50-99

19122 Aspen Research Corporation
1800 Buerkle Rd
White Bear Lake, MN 55110 651-773-7961
Fax: 651-264-6270 answers@aspenresearch.com
www.aspenresearch.com
Contract applied research and development firm specializing in research on flavors, off-flavors, off odors and the interaction between food and food packaging
President: Andy Marine
VP Operations: Roger Worm
Estimated Sales: $20 - 50 Million
Number Employees: 50-99
Square Footage: 250000

19123 Aspen Systems
6930 E. Chauncey Lane
Suite 100
Phoenix, AZ 85054 800-767-1970
Fax: 480-538-1971 800-767-1970
sales@aspen-systems.com
www.aspen-systems.com
Software developer for food industry
President: George Puype
CFO: Jerry King
Quality Control: Stewart Ward
Estimated Sales: $10 - 20 000,000
Number Employees: 20-49

19124 Aspeon
16832 Red Hill Avenue
Irvine, CA 92606-4803 949-440-8000
Fax: 949-440-8087 800-574-1622
info@aspeon.com www.aspeon.com
Leading manufacturer and provider of point-of-sales systems, services and enterprise technology solutions for the retail and food markets

19125 Assembled Products
115 East Linden Street
Rogers, AR 72756 479-636-5776
Fax: 479-636-5776 800-548-3373
techservice@assembledproducts.com
www.assembledproducts.com
Manufacturer and exporter of electric shopping carts for supermarkets and high pressure spray cleaning systems
President: George Panter
Sr. VP Sales/Marketing: Steve Scroggine
Estimated Sales: $5-10 Million
Number Employees: 100-249
Square Footage: 256000
Parent Co: Assembled Products Corporation
Brands:
Mart Cart
Spray Master Technologies

19126 Assembly Technology & Test
12841 Stark Rd
Livonia, MI 48150-1525 734-522-1900
Fax: 734-522-9344 www.assembly-testww.com
Designer and manufacturer of software for material handling implementation and electrified monorail systems for ingredient transport
Founder: Klaus Woerner
VP: James Diedrich
VP Sales/Marketing: Jim Anderson
Estimated Sales: $50-100 Million
Number Employees: 100-249
Square Footage: 200000
Parent Co: DT Industries

19127 Asset Design LLC
PO Box 3234
Mooresville, NC 28117 704-663-6170
Fax: 704-663-6177 888-293-1740
info@assetdesign.com www.assetdesign.com

Consultant providing engineering solutions for process design and automation, plant design and operating procedures, feasibility studies, machine modifications and custom design. Also, project management, start-up assistance andefficiency training
Manager and R&D: Jeff Demback
Estimated Sales: $500,000 - $1,000,000
Number Employees: 1-4

19128 **Assmann Corporation of America**
300 N Taylor Rd
Garrett, IN 46738 260-357-3181
Fax: 260-357-3738 888-357-3181
info@assmann-usa.com www.assmann-usa.com
President: David Crager
Quality Control: James Reynolds
Estimated Sales: $5 - 10 Million
Number Employees: 20-49

19129 **Associated Bag Company**
400 W Boden St
Milwaukee, WI 53207 414-769-1000
Fax: 414-769-1820 800-926-6100
customerservice@associatedbag.com
www.associatedbag.com
Wholesaler/distributor of food grade stretch wrap and bags, gloves and shipping and packaging products
President: Herb Rubenstein
CFO: Sue Zelga
Quality Control: Mary Samanski
Marketing/Sales Director: Scott Pietila
Customer Service Manager: Philip Roedel
Purchasing Manager: Sue Zylka
Estimated Sales: $20-50 Million
Number Employees: 100-249
Square Footage: 300000

19130 **Associated Industrial Rubber**
7550 West 2100 South
Magna, UT 84044 801-239-1670
Fax: 801-239-1675 800-526-6288
www.associated-rubber.com
Food handling hoses for beer, milk and juice
General Manager: Steve Williams
Controller: David George
Inside Sales: Steven Munz
Sales Agent: Wilson Dube
Branch Manager: Roger Morrison
Estimated Sales: $2.5-5 Million
Number Employees: 5-9
Square Footage: 120000
Parent Co: Associated Industrial Rubber

19131 **Associated Packaging Enterprises**
900 S Us Highway 1
Suite 207
Jupiter, FL 33477-6469 561-746-2414
Fax: 561-746-7192 info@aptechnologies.com
www.ape-i.com

19132 **Associated Packaging Equipment Corporation**
70 Gibson Drive
Units 5 & 6
Markham, ON L3R 2Z3
Canada 905-475-6647
Fax: 905-479-9752 apec@associpak.com
www.associpak.com
Manufacturer and exporter of roll fed labeling machinery
President: M Malthouse
Controller: Kenneth Bick
Sales Director: Klaus See
Plant Manager: John Malthouse
Purchasing Manager: R Manoharan
Estimated Sales: $1 Million
Number Employees: 15
Square Footage: 24000
Type of Packaging: Food Service, Private Label
Brands:
Polyclad

19133 **Associated Products**
1901 William Flynn Hwy
P.O. Box 8
Glenshaw, PA 15116 412-486-2255
Fax: 412-486-7710 800-243-5689
info@sani-air.com www.sani-air.com
Manufacturer and exporter of air fresheners, deodorants and deodorizers; importer of essential oils and aromatic chemicals
President: Ralph Simons
CFO: Harlan Simons
Estimated Sales: $2.5-5 Million
Number Employees: 20-49
Number of Products: 100
Square Footage: 180000
Type of Packaging: Consumer, Private Label, Bulk
Brands:
Ban Air
Mini Scents
Sani Air

19134 **Astoria General Espresso**
7912 Industrial Village Rd
Greensboro, NC 27409 336-393-0224
Fax: 336-393-0295 info@geec.com
usa.astoria.com
Manufacturer, importer and exporter of espresso and cappuccino machines, coffee grinders, espresso equipment accessories and sandwich grills
Owner: Roberto Daltio
CEO: Umberto Terreni
Accounting/Office Manager: Linda Sizemore
Sales & Marketing: Courtney Baber
Managing/Sales Director: Scott Gordon
Technical Support Specialist: Jimmy Wardell
Number Employees: 5-9
Number of Brands: 2
Number of Products: 36
Square Footage: 25000
Parent Co: CMA
Type of Packaging: Private Label
Brands:
Astoria
Grillmaster
Llsa

19135 **Astoria Laminations**
19803 E 9 Mile Rd
Saint Clair Shores, MI 48080 586-775-7990
Fax: 586-775-0010 800-526-7325
info@lamseal.com www.lamseal.com
Point of sales systems and equipment including bar coders and pricers; also, laminators including thermal, pouch and roll
President: Dennis Oster
R & D: Anthony Sagese
VP: Anthony Sagese
Estimated Sales: $5-10 Million
Number Employees: 1-4
Square Footage: 1300

19136 **(HQ)Astra Manufacturing**
21520 Blythe St # A
Canoga Park, CA 91304-6609 818-340-1800
Fax: 818-340-5830 877-340-1800
sales@astramfr.com www.astramfr.com
Manufacturer and exporter of espresso and cappuccino equipment including coffee grinders
President: Richard Hourizadeh
Estimated Sales: $3 Million
Number Employees: 5-9
Square Footage: 40000
Type of Packaging: Food Service
Brands:
Astra

19137 **Astro Arc Polysoude**
W133n5138 Campbell Dr
Menomonee Falls, WI 53051 262-783-2720
Fax: 262-783-2730 www.igmusa.com
President: Hans-Peter Mariner
Principal: Lynn Marek
Estimated Sales: $1 - 5 Million
Number Employees: 5-9

19138 **Astro Plastics**
PO Box 665
Oakland, NJ 07436-0665 201-337-8170
Manufacturer and extruder of plastic film bags
President: Steven Ringley
Estimated Sales: $5 - 10 Million
Number Employees: 25

19139 **Astro-Pure Water Purifiers**
1441 SW 1st Way
Deerfield Beach, FL 33441 954-422-8966
Fax: 954-422-8966
Manufacturer and exporter of water purifiers and filters
President and CFO: Roger Stefl
VP Sales: Mary Munn
Office Manager: Miki Kaye
Estimated Sales: Below $5 Million
Number Employees: 10
Number of Brands: 1
Number of Products: 39
Square Footage: 3000
Type of Packaging: Consumer, Food Service, Private Label, Bulk
Brands:
Astro-Pure

19140 **Astro/Polymetron Zellweger**
100 Park Avenue
League City, TX 77573-2446 281-332-2484
Fax: 970-669-2932 kcraig@hach.com
Water quality analyzers for silica, sodium, phosphate, chlorine, ozone, dissolved oxygen, hydrazine, pH/conductivity and on-line titrates
President: Tom Joyce
Marketing Manager: Karon Craig
Sales Mgr: Robert Blight
Number Employees: 500

19141 **Astrophysics Inc**
21481 Ferrero Parkway
City of Industry, CA 91789 909-598-5488
Fax: 310-513-6593 800-251-9750
sales@astrophysicsinc.com
www.astrophysicsinc.com
Estimated Sales: $1 - 3 Million
Number Employees: 5-9

19142 **At-Your-Service Software**
450 Bronxville Rd
Bronxville, NY 10708
Fax: 914-337-9031 888-325-6937
info@costguard.com www.costguard.com
Develops Cost Guard restaurant and foodservice software
President: Matthew Starobin
CEO: Pamela Terr
Estimated Sales: $2.5-5 Million
Number Employees: 10-19
Brands:
Cost Guard
Smart Scaling
Vendor Transport

19143 **Athea Laboratories**
7855 N Faulkner Rd
Milwaukee, WI 53224 414-354-6417
Fax: 414-354-9219 800-743-6417
info@athea.com www.athea.com
Manufacturer and exporter of chemical specialties including ground and sewer maintenance chemicals, insecticides, aerosol, liquid and waterless hand cleaners and lotion; packager of aerosol and other products
President: Steve Hipp
VP Technical: Pete Martin
National Sales Manager: Ron Lloyd
Estimated Sales: $20-50 Million
Number Employees: 10
Parent Co: Share Company

19144 **Athena Controls**
5145 Campus Dr
Plymouth Meeting, PA 19462 610-828-2490
Fax: 610-828-7084 800-782-6776
sales@athenacontrols.com
www.athenacontrols.com
Manufacturer and exporter of temperature, power and process controls
Manager: Bob Schlegel
Sales/Marketing: Jennifer Klinedinst
Estimated Sales: $10-20 Million
Number Employees: 50-99
Parent Co: Inductotherm Industries
Other Locations:
Athena Controls
Plymouth Meeting PA

19145 **Atkins Jemptec**
6911 NW 22nd St
Gainesville, FL 32653-1249 352-378-5555
Fax: 352-335-6736 sdiuguid@cooper-atkins.com
www.atkinstech.com
Estimated Sales: $20 - 50 Million
Number Employees: 50-99

19146 **Atkins Technical**
6911 NW 22nd St
Gainesville, FL 32653-1249 352-378-5555
Fax: 352-335-6736 800-284-2842
www.atkinstech.com
Temperature recorders, digital thermocouple and thermistor thermometers
President: Carol Wallace
Sales/Marketing Executive: Stelli Dounson

Estimated Sales: $10-20 Million
Number Employees: 50-99
Parent Co: Cooper Instrumental Corporation

19147 Atkinson Dynamics
2645 Federal Signal Dr
University Park, IL 60484-3167 708-534-3400
Fax: 708-534-4852 888-751-1500
tbarron@federalsignal.com
www.atkinsondynamics.com
President: Peter Guile
Quality Control: Dennis Stanberry
Number Employees: 500-999
Parent Co: Federal Signal Company

19148 Atlanta Burning Bush
3781 Happy Valley Cir
Newnan, GA 30263 770-253-4443
Fax: 770-253-9941 800-665-5611
information@atlantaburning.com
www.atlantaburning.com
Hot sauces, BBQ sauce. Supplier of food related products
Owner: Marilyn Witt
Estimated Sales: $500,000-$1,000,000
Number Employees: 1-4
Type of Packaging: Consumer, Bulk
Brands:
Atlanta Burning

19149 Atlanta SharpTech
403 Westpark Ct Ste 130
P.O. Box 11000
Peachtree City, GA 30269-3577
Fax: 404-752-9034 800-462-7297
info@sharptech.com www.sharptech.com
Manufacturer and exporter of meat and bone cutting equipment including bandsaw blades, grinder plates, grinder knives, handsaw frames and handsaw blades
CEO: Tom Orelup
Estimated Sales: $20-50 Million
Number Employees: 100-249
Brands:
Atlanta Sharptech
Double Cut System
Kam-Lok
One Way Bands
Powermate System
Swift Tooth Bands

19150 Atlantic Coast Crushers
128 Market Street
Kenilworth, NJ 07033 908-259-9292
Fax: 908-259-9280 info@gocrushers.com
www.gocrushers.com
Owner: Jack Paddock
Estimated Sales: $3 - 5 Million
Number Employees: 5-9

19151 Atlantic Foam & Packaging Company
2664 Jewett Ln
Sanford, FL 32771-1678 407-328-9444
Fax: 407-324-2299 www.atlanticfoam.com
Manufacturers and fabricators of polystyrene foam box liners for perishables and non perishables.
President: Peter Chorney
Estimated Sales: $2.5 - 5 Million
Number Employees: 10-19
Square Footage: 132000

19152 Atlantic Group
16830 Barker Springs Rd
Houston, TX 77084 281-578-0366
info@agivalves.com
www.atlanticgroupinc.com
Estimated Sales: $1 - 5 Million
Number Employees: 8

19153 Atlantic Mills
1295 Towbin Ave
Lakewood, NJ 08701 732-363-9281
Fax: 732-363-4302 800-242-7374
sales@atlanticmills.com www.atlanticmills.com
Antimicrobial, sanitizing, disposable kitchen and industrial towels; also, aprons
President: Peter P Donnelly
Finance Executive: Warren Agate
Sales Director: Peter Donnelly
Estimated Sales: $10 - 20,000,000
Number Employees: 20-49
Brands:
Katelin
Kerri Klean
Simple Solutions

19154 Atlantic Quality Spice &Seasonings
9 Elkins Rd
New Brunswick, NJ 08816 732-574-3200
Fax: 732-574-3344 800-584-0422
info@aqspice.com www.aqspice.com
Imports, processes and packs conventional and organic spices and blends thousands of seasoning formulations.
President: Stanley Gorski
COO: Robert Ferguson
Quality Control: Bob Machemer
Sales: Tom Schmidt
Plant Manager: Hector Herrera
Purchasing: Hector Herrera
Estimated Sales: $25 Million
Number Employees: 100
Square Footage: 150000
Type of Packaging: Consumer, Food Service, Private Label, Bulk
Brands:
Kingred
Rosered
Sunred
Saigon Select

19155 Atlantic Rubber Products
3065 Cranberry Hwy 13
East Wareham, MA 02538-1325 508-291-1211
Fax: 508-291-1123 800-695-0446
mats@atlrubber.com www.atlrubber.com
Manufacturer, importer and exporter of rubber safety flooring for kitchens, bars and entrance ways
Owner: John Donahue
Sales Director: Susan Boyens
General Manager: Jerry Donahue
Estimated Sales: $5-10 Million
Number Employees: 10-19
Number of Products: 85
Square Footage: 56000
Type of Packaging: Consumer, Food Service, Bulk
Brands:
Comfort Zone
Enter Clean
Modular Tile
Ultimate Comfort
Work Right
Work Right Interlock
Work Station Airlock

19156 Atlantic Ultraviolet Corporation
375 Marcus Blvd
Hauppauge, NY 11788 631-273-0500
Fax: 631-273-0771 866-958-9085
info@ultraviolet.com www.ultraviolet.com
Manufacturer and exporter of ultraviolet sterilization products for air, water and surfaces
President: Hilary Boehme
CEO: Hilary Boehme
CFO: Arlene Metzroth
VP: Thomas Dituro Sr.
Director of Marketing: Ann Wysocki
Estimated Sales: $10 - 20 Million
Number Employees: 20-49
Square Footage: 25000
Brands:
Hygeaire
Magnum
Megatron
Mighty-Pure
Minipure
Nutripure
Sanitaire
Sanitron
Tank Master

19157 Atlantis Industries
1 Park St
Milton, DE 19968 302-684-8542
Fax: 302-684-3367 contact@atlantisusa.com
www.atlantisusa.com
Manufacturer and exporter of injection molded plastic tumblers, dessert dishes, bowls, salad bowls and mugs
President: Kenneth Orr
VP: Ken Orr
Sales: Judie Brasure
Estimated Sales: $2.5-5 Million
Number Employees: 250-499
Square Footage: 28000
Brands:
Sparkle-Lite

19158 Atlantis Pak USA
75 Valencia Ave, Ste 701
Coral Gables, FL 33134 305-403-2603
Fax: 786-249-0454
customerservice@atlantis-pak.com
www.atlantis-pak.com
Meat Packing, manufacturer of acid free packing paper, and recycled paper for meat.
Principle: Vladimir Zhamgotsev
Number Employees: 5-9
Parent Co: Atlantis Pak

19159 Atlantis Plastics Institutional Products
1970 Excel Drive
Mankato, MN 56001 507-386-4420
Fax: 507-388-4420 800-999-2374
www.stadri.com
Manufacturer and exporter of disposable gloves, aprons, bibs, table covers, specialty bags and films including cling, polyethylene, stretch and shrink
President: Anthony F Bova
Research & Development: Thea Ellingson
Marketing Director: Mike Sauer
Sales Director: Ken Christensen
Operations/Purchasing: Mike Ellis
Estimated Sales: $20 - 50 Million
Number Employees: 100-249
Parent Co: Atlantis Plastics
Type of Packaging: Consumer, Food Service, Bulk
Other Locations:
Mankato-Institutional Operations
Mankato MN
Brands:
Linear
Sta-Dri

19160 Atlantis Plastics LinearFilm
PO Box 9769
Tulsa, OK 74157-0769 918-446-1651
Fax: 918-227-2454 800-324-9727
paul.saari@atlantisplastics.com
www.atlantisplastics.com
Manufacturer and exporter of polyethylene stretch film
Manager: Randy Goodman
CFO: Paul G Saari
VP Sales: John Buchan
Estimated Sales: $10-20 Million
Number Employees: 100-249
Parent Co: Atlantis Films

19161 Atlas Bakery Machinery Company
4800 S.W. 51st Street
Suite 104
Davie, FL 33314-5511 954-316-6160
Fax: 954-316-1360 atlasbaker@aol.com
www.atlasshardwarecorp.com
Bread and roll make-up including dividers, rounders, proofers and mixers
President: Robert Atlass
Estimated Sales: $2.5-5 Million
Number Employees: 5-9

19162 Atlas Body
PO Box 479
Amory, MS 38821-0479 601-256-5692
Fax: 601-256-2162 800-354-2192
Estimated Sales: $1 - 5 Million

19163 Atlas Case
1380 S Cherokee St
Denver, CO 80223 303-778-7058
Fax: 303-778-7102 888-325-7102
sales@atlascases.com www.atlascases.com
Trunks, cases and shipping containers
President: Randy Sabey
Estimated Sales: Below $5 Million
Number Employees: 5-9

19164 Atlas Copco Tools & Assembly
37735 Enterprise Court
Suite 300
Farmington Hills, MI 48331-3471 248-489-1260
Fax: 248-489-0130 800-359-3746
conan.crawley@os.atlascopco.com
www.atlascopco.com
President: Frederik Moeller
Vice President of Corporate Communicatio: Annika Berglund

19165 **Atlas Equipment Company**
3111 Wyandotte St # 102
Kansas City, MO 64111-1369 816-842-9188
Fax: 816-842-9192 800-842-9188
2info@atlasequipment.com
www.atlasequipment.com
Wholesaler/distributor of storage and material handling systems, belt conveyors, steel shelving and pallet racks
President: Julie Duvall
VP: Julie Duvall
Estimated Sales: $5-10 Million
Number Employees: 1-4
Square Footage: 600000

19166 **Atlas Inspection**
9001 Baltimore St NE
Minneapolis, MN 55449 763-783-7072
Fax: 763-783-7138 atlas@atlasinspection.com
www.atlasinspection.com
Xray inspection of food products
Founder: Ken Long
President: Jeffery Boisverg
Estimated Sales: $2 Million
Number Employees: 5

19167 **(HQ)Atlas Labels**
11200 boul Pie 1X,
CP 280
Montreal, QC H1H 5L4
Canada 514-852-7000
Fax: 514-852-2000 info@cubart.com
Self-stick labels, silk screen, gold stampings, badges and folding boxes.
President: Rock Navy
Estimated Sales: $3 Million
Number Employees: 13
Number of Brands: 2
Number of Products: 114
Square Footage: 18000
Type of Packaging: Consumer, Food Service, Private Label, Bulk

19168 **Atlas Match Company**
45 Leadale Avenue
Toronto, ON M4G 3E9
Canada 416-929-8147
Fax: 416-961-3275 888-285-2783
nmackay11@rogers.com www.atlasmatch.com
Manufacturer, importer and exporter of custom designed wooden and book matches; also, reusable board coasters and cocktail and dinner napkins.
President: N Mackay
CFO: Sohan Kansal
Sales: W Teltz
Operations: Esther Tarahdmi
Number Employees: 5-9
Number of Brands: 2
Number of Products: 5
Square Footage: 8000
Type of Packaging: Food Service, Private Label, Bulk
Brands:
Atlas
Coasters Plus

19169 **Atlas Match Corporation**
1801 S Airport Cir
Euless, TX 76040 817-354-7474
Fax: 817-354-7478 800-628-2426
www.atlasmatch.com
Manufacturer, exporter and importer of matchbooks, box matches, scratchbooks and scratchpads
President: David Bradley
COO: Doug Lamb
Estimated Sales: $10-20 Million
Number Employees: 50-99
Square Footage: 65000

19170 **Atlas Materials & Chemicals**
P.O.Box 38
Mertztown, PA 19539-0038 610-682-7171
Fax: 610-682-9200 800-532-8269
sales@atlasmin.com www.atlasmin.com
Flooring products include coating, sealers, polymer toppings and tile and brick floors
President: Francis X Hanson
Estimated Sales: $10-20 Million
Number Employees: 50-99

19171 **Atlas Metal Industries**
20 Kenton Park Road
Kenton, HR HA3 8TY 208-907-1374
dina@atlasmetalind.com
www.atlasfoodserv.com
Cafeteria and restaurant counters, salad bars, food service tables and dispensers including cup, plate, self leveling, tray, bowl and napkin
President: David Meade
VP Marketing: Howard Bolner
Estimated Sales: $10-20 Million
Number Employees: 100-249
Parent Co: Mercury Aircraft
Brands:
Levelmatic
Precision
Set-N-Serve

19172 **(HQ)Atlas Minerals & Chemicals**
1227 Valley Road
P.O. Box 38
Mertztown, PA 19539 610-682-7171
Fax: 610-682-9200 800-523-8269
sales@atlasmin.com www.atlasmin.com
Manufacturer and exporter of construction materials including floor plates, drains and coatings and corrosion prevention; also, tanks for processing and storage
President: Francis X Hanson
Marketing: Scott Gallagher
Sales: Steve Abernathy
Number Employees: 50-99
Type of Packaging: Food Service, Private Label

19173 **(HQ)Atlas Pacific Engineering Company**
1 Atlas Avenue
P.O. Box 500
Pueblo, CO 81002-0500 719-948-3040
Fax: 719-948-3058 sales@atlaspacific.com
www.atlaspacific.com
Manufacturer and exporter of decidious fruit and vegetable processing equipment including pitters, slicers, peelers, washers, cutters, sorters and scrubbers
President: Erik Teranchi
CFO: Don Freeman
VP Marketing: Robb Morris
Estimated Sales: $20-50 Million
Number Employees: 100-249
Square Footage: 175000
Parent Co: Gulftech
Brands:
Magnupeeler
Magnuwasher
N.F. Peeler
Shufflo
Super Carrot Cutter
Super Cutter

19174 **Atlas Packaging & Displays Inc**
13165 North West 38th Avenue
Miami, FL 33054 305-688-5096
Fax: 305-685-0843 800-662-0630
randy@atlaspackaginginc.com
www.atlaspackaginginc.com
Designer and manufacturer of all types of packaging, litho laminated boxes and displays. Also provides promotional items such as standers and casecards.
President: Walter Shields
Sales Manager: Randy Macias
Estimated Sales: $5-10 Million
Number Employees: 20-49
Square Footage: 112000

19175 **Atlas Restaurant Supply**
3329 N Shadeland Ave
Indianapolis, IN 46226 317-541-1111
Fax: 574-272-3329 877-528-5275
jculbertson@atlasrestaurantsupplies.com
www.atlasrestaurantsupplies.com
Manufacturers' representative for bar equipment, carts, concession supplies, dishwashers, display cases, ice machines, refrigerators, can openers, steam tables, etc.; serving supermarket chains and food service operators; kitchen andinterior design services
President: Thomas S Vavul
Estimated Sales: Below $5,000,000
Number Employees: 20-49

19176 **Atlas Rubber Stamp Company**
3755 East Market Street
York, PA 17402 717-755-1105
Fax: 717-751-0459 www.atlasrubberstamp.com
Stamps and markers
Owner: Donald Fontaine
Co-Owner: Hally Fontaine
Estimated Sales: Below $5 Million
Number Employees: 1-4

19177 **Atlas Tag & Label**
PO Box 638
Neenah, WI 54957-0638 920-722-1557
Fax: 920-720-7900 800-558-6418
info@atlas-tag.com www.atlas-tag.com
Heat sealed bags, labels and tags
President: Mark Bissell
CFO: Dennis Novell
VP: Jerry Bultt
Head of Marketing: Kent Salomon
Account Manager: Mark White
Estimated Sales: $10-20 Million
Number Employees: 100-249
Parent Co: Atlas Tag & Label

19178 **Atlas-Stord**
7011-F Albert Pick Road
Greensboro, NC 27409 816-799-0808
Fax: 816-799-0812 info-usa@haarslev.com
www.haarslev.com/
Manager: Denise Gardner
CFO: Brad Rodgers
Estimated Sales: Below $5 Million
Number Employees: 20-49
Parent Co: Haarslev Industries A/S

19179 **Atomizing Systems**
1 Hollywood Ave
Suite 1
Ho Ho Kus, NJ 07423 201-447-1222
Fax: 201-447-6932 www.coldfog.com
President: Michael Elkas
Estimated Sales: $3 - 5 Million
Number Employees: 10-19

19180 **(HQ)Attias Oven Corporation**
926 Third Ave
Brooklyn, NY 11232 718-499-0145
Fax: 718-499-0144 800-928-8427
info@attiasco.com www.attiasco.com
Manufacturer and exporter of pizza ovens, rotisseries, mixers, slicers, ice makers, refrigerators, freezers, dishwashers, toasters, blenders, sheeters, dividers and rounders
President: Simon Attias
Estimated Sales: $3 - 5 Million
Number Employees: 10-19

19181 **Attracta Sign**
14680 James Road
Rogers, MN 55374-9363 763-428-6377
Fax: 763-428-9097 attracta@earthlink.net
Painted and electric signs
President: Greg Rendall
CFO: Greg Rendall
R&D/Quality Control: Greg Rendall
Estimated Sales: $1 - 2.5 Million
Number Employees: 10

19182 **Attune Foods**
535 Pacific Ave, 3rd Fl
San Francisco, CA 94133 415-486-2101
www.attunefoods.com
President: Rob Hurlbut
Director of Finance: Mike Centron
Director of Marketing: Daniel Wiser
Director of Sales: Steve Bernier
Production Manager: Marvin Malvar
Estimated Sales: $15 Million
Parent Co: Post Foods
Brands:
UNCLE SAM
SKINNER'S
EREWHON
ATTUNE

19183 **Atwood Adhesives**
945 S Doris St
Seattle, WA 98108 206-762-7455
Fax: 206-762-9852 sales@atwoodadhesives.com
www.atwoodadhesives.com
Manager: Laurel Mangan

Estimated Sales: $5 - 10 Million
Number Employees: 10-19
Parent Co: Adhesive Products

19184 AuNutra Industries Inc
5625 Daniels Street
Chino, CA 91710 909-628-2600
Fax: 909-628-8110 info@aunutra.com
www.aunutra.com
Manufacturer and supplier of botanicals and nutritional ingredients
VP Sales/Marketing: Ken Guest
Regional Sales Manager: Tara Trainor

19185 Auburn International
8 Electronics Avenue
Danvers, MA 01923 978-777-2460
Fax: 978-777-8820 800-255-5008
sales@auburnsys.com www.auburnsys.com
President: Ronald L Dechene

19186 Auburn Label & Tag Company
225 W 34th St
New York, NY 10122-9001 212-971-0338
Fax: 212-244-4397 quntmler@aol.com
www.ragnewyork.com
Labels including pressure sensitive and nonpressure sensitive
Owner: Max Greenstein
Vice President: Susan Alfender
Estimated Sales: $5-10 Million
Number Employees: 5-9

19187 Auburn Systems
8 Electronics Ave
Danvers, MA 01923-1045 978-777-2460
Fax: 978-777-8820 800-255-5008
sales@auburnsys.com www.auburnsys.com
Auburn Systems, LLC designs, engineers, and manufactures dust monitoring equipment and systems. Auburn's product line ranges from simple broken bag detectors, flow switches and dust monitors to comprehensive bag leak detection systemsfor a wide variety of applications.
President: Ronald L Dechene
Director/Business Development: Justin Dechene
VP/Sales: Earl Parker

19188 (HQ)Audion Automation
1533 Crescent Dr Ste 100
Carrollton, TX 75006 972-389-0777
Fax: 216-267-8713 info@clamcopackaging.com
www.audionautomation.com
Manufacturer and exporter of flexible packaging machinery including bag opening, filling and heat sealing; also, shrink packaging
President: Mark Goldman
CFO: David Johnson
Vice President Marketing & Sales: Dennis McGrath
Sales Manager: Bob Sorrentino
Operations Manager: David Bibb
Estimated Sales: $20 - 50 Million
Number Employees: 110
Square Footage: 56000
Brands:
Sergeant
Titan
Vacumaster

19189 Audrey Signs
167 W 81st St
New York, NY 10024-7221 212-769-4992
Fax: 212-496-9649 audreysigns2@aol.com
www.audreysigns.com
Interior and exterior advertising signs including brass, aluminum, bronze, plastic, neon, cold cathode and cut-out letters; also, installation available
President and CEO: Harriet Black
Estimated Sales: Below $5 Million
Number Employees: 10-19

19190 Audsam Printing
175 Park Blvd
Marion, OH 43302-3534 740-387-6252
Fax: 740-387-6251 www.audsamprinting.com
Coupon books
President: J Saxby
VP: M Saxby
Secretary: S Saxby
Estimated Sales: $5-10 Million
Number Employees: 20-49

19191 Audubon Sales & Service
850 Pennsylvania Blvd
Feasterville Trevose, PA 19053 215-364-5451
Fax: 215-364-1783 800-523-0169
info@meshbelt.com www.meshbelt.com
President: Stephen I Weiss
Estimated Sales: $5 - 10 Million
Number Employees: 20-49

19192 Auger Manufacturing Specialists
22 A Bacton Hill Rd
Frazer, PA 19355 610-647-4677
Fax: 610-640-9085 800-544-1199
info@augermfgspec.com
www.augermfgspec.com
Bag formers/fillers/sealers, cocoa packaging equipment, packaging machines, weighing machines and augers
Owner: William E Day
Estimated Sales: $5-10 000,000
Number Employees: 10-19

19193 Auger-Fabrication
418 Creamery Way
Exton, PA 19341-2500
Fax: 610-363-2821 800-334-1529
info@auger-fab.com www.auger-fab.com
Manufacturer and exporter of stainless steel and plastic liquid and powder filling equipment including replacement augers and funnels
President: Glenn Edginton
Regional Sales Manager: Allen Stewart
Regional Sales Manager: Rich Vanden Mooren
Estimated Sales: $10-20 Million
Number Employees: 50-99
Square Footage: 50000

19194 Auger-Fabrication
418 Creamery Way
Exton, PA 19341-2500 610-524-3350
Fax: 610-363-2821 800-334-1529
info@all-fill.com www.augerfab.com
Augers
President: Glenn Edginton
Estimated Sales: $10-20 000,000
Number Employees: 50-99

19195 August Thomsen Corporation
36 Sea Cliff Ave
Glen Cove, NY 11542 516-676-7100
Fax: 516-676-7108 800-645-7170
cs@atecousa.com www.atecousa.com
Manufacturer, importer and exporter of pastry tubes, pastry bags and other baking utensils
President: Jeffrey Schneider
VP: Douglas Schneider
Estimated Sales: $10 - 20 Million
Number Employees: 20-49
Brands:
Ateco

19196 Aurora Air Products
231c N Eola Rd
Aurora, IL 60502-9603 630-851-4515
Fax: 630-851-5165 ron@auroraair.com
www.auroraair.com
Manager: Dan Cibulskis
Quality Control: Don Cibulskis
Estimated Sales: $10 - 20 Million
Number Employees: 20-49

19197 Aurora Design Associates, Inc.
1308 South 1700 East
Suite 203
Salt Lake City, UT 84108 801-588-0111
Fax: 801-588-0333
www.auroradesignproducts.com
Manufacturer and exporter of servers and ice buckets for wine, water and champagne
President: Rob Norton
Advertising Manager: Rick Daynes
Estimated Sales: Less than $500,000
Number Employees: 1-4
Number of Products: 6
Square Footage: 14000
Brands:
Chateau
Connoisseur
Evian Connoisseur

19198 Austin Brown Company
300 Reading Rd
Mason, OH 45050 513-492-7933
Fax: 513-492-7932 800-421-9355
info@austinbrownco.com
www.austinbrownco.com
Manufacturers reps for insulated panels, cold storage doors and high speed doors.
Founder/Outside Sales: Austin Brown
Marketing: Douglas Brown
Inside Sales: Kevin Browning
Estimated Sales: $.5 - 1 million
Number Employees: 1-4
Number of Brands: 4

19199 Austin Company
6095 Parkland Blvd Ste 100
Cleveland, OH 44124 440-544-2600
Fax: 440-544-2684 austin.info@theaustin.com
www.theaustin.com
Designing, engineering and construction architectural firm that specializes in food and beverage processing facilities including: production and bottling plants; formulation and packaging plants for bulk ingredients; researchlaboratories; operations centers; bulk storage warehouses; and automated distribution centers.
President: Patrick Flanagan
VP Food & Beverage: Robert Graham
Senior VP Marketing/Sales: Michael Pierce
Vice President/Facilities Director: Don Schjeldahl
Estimated Sales: $100+ Million
Number Employees: 1,000-4,999
Parent Co: Kajima USA

19200 Austin Packaging Company
1118 N Main St
Austin, MN 55912 507-433-6623
Fax: 507-433-9717 mail@austinpackaging.com
www.austinpackaging.com
Contract packager of meal kits, meat pouches, shelf stable entrees, pizza and portion control products; exporter of frozen liquid sauces
Contact: Steve Whiteis
Contact: Paul Natzger
Plant Manager: Jon Vietor
Estimated Sales: $20 Million
Number Employees: 300
Square Footage: 125000
Type of Packaging: Consumer, Food Service, Private Label

19201 Authentic Biocode Corp
4355 Excel Parkway
Suite 100
Addison, TX 75001 469-737-4400
Fax: 469-737-4409 866-434-1402
jslocum2@compuserve.com www.authentix.com
Invisible inks and food markers
Chief Financial/Operations Officer and P: Jeff Kupp
Chairman and CEO: Bernard C Bailey
CAO, General Counsel and Secretary: Mark L Weintrub
Senior Vice President: Kevin McKenna
Chief Technology Officer: Jeff Conroy, Ph.D.
Chief Sales and Marketing Officer: Ryon Packer
Director Business Development: Jeffrey Slocum
CPO, GM and President: Dr. Mohamed Lazzouni
Estimated Sales: $3 - 5 Million
Number Employees: 8

19202 Autio Company
93750 Autio Loop
Astoria, OR 97103 503-458-6191
Fax: 503-458-6409 800-483-8884
office@autioco.com www.autioco.com
Manufacturer and exporter of grinders and pumps
President: Marvin Autio
Office Manager: Marilyn Anderson
Estimated Sales: $1 - 3 Million
Number Employees: 10-19

19203 Auto Chlor Systems
1000 Ridgeway Loop Rd Ste 100
Memphis, TN 38120 901-684-0600
Fax: 901-684-0620 800-477-3693
Glass cleaner, dishwasher detergents and dispensers
H.R. Dir.: Marie Brain
VP: Kirk Northcutt
Estimated Sales: $1 - 5 Million
Number Employees: 20-49
Parent Co: Unilever USA

Brands:
Glass Klean
Laundry Detergent Ii
Machine Detergent Ii

19204 Auto Labe
3101 Industrial Avenue 2
Fort Pierce, FL 34946 772-465-4441
Fax: 772-465-5177 800-634-5376
info@autolabe.com www.autolabe.com
Manufacturer and exporter of labeling equipment for fruits and vegetables, bottles, cans, boxes, cartons, bar coding, etc
President: Robert Smith
Marketing/Sales: Bob Peterson
Public Relations: Roy Shepherd
Production/Plant Manager: Dean Stauffer
Estimated Sales: $10-20 Million
Number Employees: 50-99
Square Footage: 25000
Parent Co: Booth Manufacturing Company

19205 Auto Pallets-Boxes
28000 Southfield Rd Fl 2
Lathrup Village, MI 48076-2864 248-559-7744
Fax: 248-559-6584 800-875-2699
www.apallets.com
Manufacturer and recycler of wooden pallets and boxes
Owner: Mitchell B Foster
VP: Mitchell Foster
Estimated Sales: $1-2.5 Million
Number Employees: 10 to 19

19206 Auto Quotes
4425 Merrimac Ave
Jacksonville, FL 32210 904-384-2279
Fax: 904-384-1736 kmotes@aqnet.com
www.aqnet.com
Software for the food service market
President: Michael Greenwald
Chief Executive Officer: Kent Motes
CFO: Rene Butcher
Executive Vice President: Rob Morgan
VP, Program Development: Bill Kessler
Marketing Director: Kate Schmidt
EVP, Sales: Rosemary Connor
CFO, Database Manager: Martin Smith
Estimated Sales: $3 - 5 Million
Number Employees: 1-4
Square Footage: 9600

19207 Auto-Mate Technologies LLC
34 Hinda Blvd
Riverhead, NY 11901 631-727-8886
Fax: 631-369-3903 info@automatetech.com
www.auto-matetech.com
Bottle labeling systems, induction cap systems, and complete bottle inspection systems.
Owner: Kenneth Herzog
Estimated Sales: $9-12 Million
Number Employees: 20-49

19208 AutoPak Engineering Corporation
PO Box 9024155
San Juan, PR 00902-4155 787-723-8036
Fax: 787-745-0030 mailbox@autopak.com
www.autopak.com
President: Ignacio Munoz
CFO: Astrid Robriguze
Quality Control: Amarilys Rivera
Estimated Sales: $30-40 Million
Number Employees: 10

19209 Autobar Systems
1800 Bloomsbury Ave
Asbury Park, NJ 07712-3975 732-922-3355
Fax: 732-922-2221 autobarcorp@aol.com
Manufacturer and exporter of alcoholic beverage dispensers and control equipment for bars, convention centers and restaurants
President: Donald E Ullery Jr
CEO: Donald Ullery
Estimated Sales: Below $5 Million
Number Employees: 5-9
Square Footage: 4000
Brands:
Autobar
Autopor
Beermatic
Underbar
Winematic

19210 Autobox NA/Jit Box Machines
218 N Broadway Rd
Azle, TX 76020-3708 817-270-1019
Fax: 817-270-8430 debra@autoboxna.com
www.autoboxna.com
President: Jerry Jenkins
Estimated Sales: $10 - 20 Million
Number Employees: 10-19

19211 Autocon Mixing Systems
2360 Vallejo St
St Helena, CA 94574-2432 707-963-3998
Fax: 707-963-3978 800-225-6192
info@autoconsystems.com www.theosten.com
Manufacturer and exporter of continuous solid/liquid feeders and dry blending processing systems
President: Thomas Haas
Estimated Sales: $5 - 10 Million
Number Employees: 5-9
Square Footage: 5000

19212 Autocrat Coffee
10 Blackstone Valley Pl
Lincoln, RI 02865-1145 401-333-3300
Fax: 401-334-5972 800-288-6272
info@autocrat.com www.autocrat.com
President: Richard M Field Jr
VP: Cynthia Wall
Estimated Sales: $50 - 100 Million
Number Employees: 100-249

19213 Autofry
10 Forbes Rd
Northborough, MA 01532 508-460-9800
Fax: 508-393-5750 800-348-2976
gsantos@autofry.com www.autofry.com
Deep fryers
Mktg. Manager: Heather Guerriero
Regional Sales Manager: Laird Hansberger
Sales Manager: Gary Santos
Number Employees: 15
Brands:
Autofry

19214 Autoline
23243 Clayton Ave
Reedley, CA 93654-9547 559-638-5432
Fax: 559-638-6189 sales@autolinesorters.com
www.autolinesorters.com
Fruit sorting equipent
President: Clarence Rasmussen
R&D: Jack Wis
Sales: Kelvin Farris
Quality Control: Brudy Hieberp
Estimated Sales: $5 - 10 Million
Number Employees: 20-49

19215 Automated Business Products
50 Clinton Pl Ste 1
Hackensack, NJ 07601 201-489-1440
Fax: 201-489-9443 800-334-1440
www.abpdirect.com
Manufacturer, importer and exporter of money processing and handling systems, packagers, sorters, counters and automatic wrappers; also, food stamp counters, endorsers and microencoders
President: Robert J Mahalik
Estimated Sales: $1-2,500,000
Number Employees: 10-19

19216 Automated Container Sales Corporation
2758 Centennial Road
Toledo, OH 43617 419-536-8393
Fax: 419-536-9686
ezosales@automatedcontainer.com
www.automatedcontainer.com
President: John Morrison

19217 Automated Control Concepts
3535 State Route 66
Neptune, NJ 07753 732-922-6611
Fax: 732-922-9611
sysmail@automated-control.com
www.automated-control.com
Owner: Robert Tomasetta
Estimated Sales: $10 - 20 Million
Number Employees: 50-99

19218 Automated Feeding & Alignment
1921 W Wilson Street
Suite A171
Batavia, IL 60510-1680 630-761-3104
Fax: 630-761-3105
Controlled pick and place system and packaging automation special purpose machinery
Estimated Sales: $.5 - 1 000,000
Number Employees: 1-4

19219 Automated Flexible Conveyor
55 Walman Ave
Clifton, NJ 07011-3416 973-340-1695
Fax: 973-340-8216 800-694-7271
gfaria@afcsolutions.com www.afcsolutions.com
Spiral and volumetric feeders, cartridge type bag dump stations and bulk bag unloading equipment; exporter of spiral feeders
President: Kevin Devaney
Vice President: Grace Faria
Estimated Sales: Below $5 Million
Number Employees: 5-9
Square Footage: 88000
Brands:
Dump Clean
Spiralfeeder
True Flow

19220 Automated Food Systems
1000 Lofland Dr
Waxahachie, TX 75165 972-298-5719
Fax: 469-517-0476 sales@afstexas.com
www.afstexas.com
Manufacturer, exporter and importer of production systems for corn dogs, kebabs, skewering, sausage sticking and funnel cakes. Fryers, mixers, pumps; special design
President: Robert Walser
CFO: Tina Walser
Marketing Director/Sales: Chris Consalus
Marketing Coordinator: Robin Seeton
Production Manager: Jerry Reidel
Plant Manager: Charles Stone
Purchasing Manager: Robert Walser
Estimated Sales: $2.5-5 Million
Number Employees: 13
Square Footage: 48000
Brands:
Cd-3 Vendor Cart
Fc-950
Kw-2001
Ptl-Condos Systems

19221 Automated Machine Technologies
10404 Chapel Hill Road
Suite 100
Morrisville, NC 27560-1186 919-361-0121
Fax: 919- 48- 212
Office@AMTLiquidFilling.com
www.amtliquidfilling.com
Packaging liquid filling equipment
Estimated Sales: $500,000-$1 Million
Number Employees: 2

19222 Automated Packaging Systems
10175 Philipp Pkwy
Streetsboro, OH 44241 330-342-2000
Fax: 330-342-2400 888-288-6224
info@autobag.com www.autobag.com
Manual, semi and fully automatic bagging equipment; also, customer training and graphic design services available
CEO: Hershey Lerner
CEO: Hershey Lerner
VP Sales/Marketing: Brad Worman
Estimated Sales: $100-500 Million
Number Employees: 100-249
Brands:
Autobag

19223 Automated Production Systems Corporation
15556 Elm Dr
New Freedom, PA 17349 717-235-5220
Fax: 717-235-5274 888-345-5377
hfisher@apsautomation.com
www.apsautomation.com
Conveyor systems, robotic palletizing and packing machinery, cappers and in-line fillers
President: William Donohue
Estimated Sales: E
Number Employees: 95

19224 Automated Retail Systems
726 Boulevard Ste 18
Kenilworth, NJ 07033 908-245-2829
Fax: 908-276-2214 800-355-0173
arsnj@aol.com www.arsnj.com

Distributor touch screen point of sale systems for restaurants, software and peripherals
President: Robert Meyn
Vice President: Grace Ann Meyn
Estimated Sales: 500000
Number Employees: 5
Square Footage: 1200

19225 **Automatic Bar Controls**
790 Eubanks Dr
Vacaville, CA 95688 707-448-5151
Fax: 707-448-1521 800-722-6738
sales@wunderbar.com www.wunderbar.com
Portable bars and dispensers including soft drink, liquor, juice, wine, beer and condiment; importer of beer dipensers; exporter of liquor, soft drink and condiment dipensers
President: Rick Martindale
Sales/Marketing: Brent Baker
Purchasing Agent: Tim Schroeder
Estimated Sales: $50 - 100 Million
Number Employees: 100-249
Square Footage: 70000
Brands:
Wunder-Bar

19226 **Automatic Electronic Machines Company**
110 N 6th St
Brooklyn, NY 11211-3033 718-384-3211
Straw wrappers and automatic shears
Owner: Hannah Curtin
General Manager: George Casella
Estimated Sales: $1 - 5 Million
Number Employees: 1-4
Square Footage: 7000

19227 **Automatic Feeder Company**
921 Albion Ave
Schaumburg, IL 60193 847-534-2300
Fax: 847-534-2354 888-534-2340
sales@automaticfeeder.com
www.automaticfeeder.com
Manufacturer, designer, and builder of specialty conveyor, feed (centrifugal linear and elevator) and assembly systems
Owner: Ken Eversole
President: Ken Eversole
VP: Kirk Verhasselt
VP: Jerry Kuntz
Marketing: Suzanne Eversole
Public Relations: Rochelle Verhasselt
Estimated Sales: $1-5 000,000
Number Employees: 20-49
Number of Brands: 4
Square Footage: 30000
Brands:
Auto-Slide
Flexlink
Hoppmann

19228 **Automatic Filters**
2672 S La Cienega Blvd
Los Angeles, CA 90034 310-839-2828
Fax: 310-839-6878 800-336-1942
info@tekleen.com www.tekleen.com
Fully automatic, self cleaning water filters
President: Gideon Brunn
Estimated Sales: Less than $10,000,000
Number Employees: 5-9

19229 **Automatic Handling**
360 La Voy Rd
Erie, MI 48133 734-847-0633
Fax: 734-847-1823 www.automatichandling.com
Manufacturer and exporter of automatic material handling systems
President: David Pienta
Estimated Sales: $10-20 Million
Number Employees: 50-99

19230 **Automatic Handling**
360 Lavoy Rd
Erie, MI 48133 734-847-0633
Fax: 734-847-1823
sales@automatichandling.com
www.automatichandling.com
Manufacturer and exporter of conveyors and conveyor systems, platforms, walkways and stairs; also, custom fabrication and custom stainless steel machinery available
President: David Pienta
Operations Manager: Dennis Barutha
Estimated Sales: $1.5,000,000
Number Employees: 50-99
Square Footage: 33000
Parent Co: Automatic Handling

19231 **Automatic Liquid Packaging**
2200 Lake Shore Dr
Woodstock, IL 60098-6919 815-338-9500
Fax: 815-206-1335 solutions@alp-bfs.com
www.catalent.com
Pharmaceutical and nutritional research and development
President: David Heyens
President, Chief Executive Officer: John Chiminski
Vice President of Audit: Charles Silvey
Senior Vice President of Quality: Sharon Johnson
Senior Vice President of Sales and Marke: Will Downie
Senior Vice President of Operations: Steve Leonard
Estimated Sales: $100+ Million
Number Employees: 500-999

19232 **Automatic Products**
PO Drawer 719
Williston, SC 29853 803-266-8891
Fax: 803-266-5150 800-523-8363
mktg@automaticproducts.com
www.automaticproducts.com
Manufacturer and exporter of hot beverage vending machinery
President: Alan J Suitor
Sales Manager: Len McElhaney

19233 **Automatic Products International**
165 Bridgeport Drive South
Saint Paul, MN 55075 651-288-2975
www.automaticproducts.com
Manufacturer and exporter of vending machinery including candy, pastry, snacks, coffee, hot drinks, ice cream and refrigerated/frozen foods
President: Robert J Sutter
CFO: Scott Edgergon
VP Marketing: James Radant
Quality Control: Randy Denver
Estimated Sales: $50-100 Million
Number Employees: 250-499

19234 **Automatic SpecialitiesInc.**
422 Northboro Road Central
Marlborough, MA 01752 508-481-2370
Fax: 508-485-6276 800-445-2370
sales@auspin.com www.auspin.com
Manufacturer and exporter of wire racks and baskets, stainless steel fry baskets, trays and food machinery parts
President: Wilfred Moineau
Vice President: Bill Moineau
Marketing/Sales: Jay Graham
Public Relations: Jay Graham
Estimated Sales: $3 - 5 Million
Number Employees: 20-49
Square Footage: 30000

19235 **Automatic Timing & Controls**
P.O.Box 305
Newell, WV 26050
Fax: 304-387-1212 800-727-5646
info@automatictiming.com
www.marshbellowfram.com
Manufacturer and exporter of controls including temperature, counters, timers and photoelectric sensors
President: Arnold Siemer
CFO: Roger Bailey
R&D: Tom Villano
Production Manager: J Tornetta
Production: E Allgyer
Estimated Sales: $10 - 20 Million
Number Employees: 225
Square Footage: 60000
Parent Co: Desco Corporation

19236 **Automation Devices Limited**
7050 West Ridge Road
Fairview, PA 16415-2099
Canada 814-474-5561
Fax: 814-474-2131 sales@adlcan.com
www.autodev.com
General Manager: Wayne Charlton
CFO: Garry Projanowski
Estimated Sales: Below $5 Million
Number Employees: 10

19237 **Automation Equipment**
E. Notherwest Highway
Dallas, TX 75228 469-212-9212
Fax: 419-663-1187
info.automationequipment.com
www.automationequipment.com
Custom designed machinery, material handling systems, metal fabricating, printing presses and special automatic machinery
Estimated Sales: $5-10 Million
Number Employees: 20-49

19238 **Automation Group**
6100 Hillcroft Street
Suite 300
Houston, TX 77081-1010 713-860-5200
Fax: 713-860-5298 darrylh@tagsite.com
www.tagsite.com
Process control and automation and networking software
President: Steven E Paulson
Business Development Manager: Darryl Hazlett
Estimated Sales: $5 - 10 Million
Number Employees: 120

19239 **Automation Ideas Inc.**
9945 Greenland Ave NE
Rockford, MI 49341 616-874-4041
Fax: 616-874-3454 877-254-3327
jerry@automationideas.com
www.automationideas.com
Equipment for the water bottling, dairy and food processing industries.
President: Jerry Bott
Vice President: Mick Donahue
Sales, Midwest Region: Dave Westra
Operations Manager: Justin Bott
Parts orders / Purchasing / Logistics: Brandon Totten

19240 **Automation Intelligence**
P.O.Box 704
Loganville, GA 30052-0704 404-241-1000
Fax: 770-497-8666 888-531-8213
info@motiononline.com www.motiononline.com
Motion control
Owner: Jim Bowers
Estimated Sales: Below $5 Million
Number Employees: 5-9

19241 **Automation ONSPEC Software**
PO Box 743
Rancho Cordova, CA 95741-0743 916-362-5867
Fax: 916-362-5967 888-362-5867
sales@automationonspec.com
www.automationonspec.com
Provides SCADA/HMI software for process control and trending and reporting.
President: Mike McMann
CFO: Steve Schasser
Research & Development: Dedh Chisum
Quality Control: Mo Dhmed
Marketing Director: Ken Thompson
Sales Director: Ed Ireton
Estimated Sales: Below $5 Million
Number Employees: 12
Number of Brands: 1
Number of Products: 167

19242 **Automation Packaging**
6206 Benjamin Road
Suite 309
Tampa, FL 33634-5169 813-888-8488
Fax: 813-888-8113 api.tampa@worldnet.att.net
Form, fill and seal wrappers, side-seal, lap-seal, shrink bundlers, automatic L-sealers and corrugated equipment
President: Jean Limousin
Estimated Sales: $5-10 000,000
Number Employees: 50-99

19243 **Automation Products**
8620 Richmond Ave # D
Houston, TX 77063-5649 713-785-3600
Fax: 713-869-7332 800-231-2062
www.packaging-online.com
Analyzers, tests, plant operations, total solids, batch control systems, chillers, filler monitoring systems, margarine processing equipment, meters, flow, milk, solids, process control
Owner: Vincent Gabory
National Sales Manager of Board: Brian Olesinski
Estimated Sales: $300,000-500,000
Number Employees: 1-4

19244 **Automation Safety**
24850 Drake Road
Farmington Hills, MI 48335-2506 248-473-1133
Fax: 248-473-3997 info@pilzusa.com
www.machinetoolsonline.com/doc/
Safety controls, industrial computers

19245 **Automation Service**
13871 Parks Steed Drive
Earth City, MO 63045 314-785-6600
Fax: 314-785-6610 800-325-4808
info@automationservice.com
www.automationservice.com
Process control instrumentation
President: Rod Barnett
Quality Control: Bob Bokel
R&D: Alex Muller
Marketing Director: Deanna Coppeans
Sales Director: Curt Sykes
Operations Manager: Mike Brunts
Production Manager: Michael Pruett
Purchasing Manager: Rich Kruse
Estimated Sales: $10 - 20 Million
Number Employees: 100

19246 **Automotion**
11000 Lavergne Ave
Oak Lawn, IL 60453 708-229-3700
Fax: 708-229-3798
info@automotionconveyors.com
www.automotionconveyors.com
Conveyors and sortation equipment
President: Merle Davis
CFO: Dave Beesley
Vice President: John Hejmanowski
Marketing Director: Joe O'Connor
Estimated Sales: $20 - 50 Million
Number Employees: 100-249
Square Footage: 140000

19247 **Autoprod**
807 W Kimberly Rd
Davenport, IA 52806 563-391-1100
Fax: 563-391-0017 sales@oystar.packt.com
www.packt.com
Manufacturer and exporter of packaging machinery for filling and closing pre-formed metallic, paper and plastic containers
President: Paul Desocio
CEO: Barry Shoulders
R & D: Hans Koule
Vice President Marketing & Sales: Tom Riggins
Sales: Barb Peeters
Trade Show Coordinator/Marketing: Mary Baltzell
Plant Manager: Larry Loftus
Purchasing Manager: Harvey Cassell
Number Employees: 50-99
Parent Co: IWKA Company
Type of Packaging: Consumer, Food Service, Private Label

19248 **Autoquip Corporation**
1058 W Industrial Rd
Guthrie, OK 73044 405-282-5200
Fax: 405-282-8105 877-360-6777
dcrabtree@autoquip.com www.autoquip.com
Manufacturer and exporter of material handling equipment including scissor lifts, turntables and tilters
President: Joe Robillard
Plant Manager: Chris Curning
Manager, Marketing & Sales: Louis Coleman
Sales: Donnie Crabtree
Operations Director: Chris Kuehni
Engineering Director: Mike Adel
Supervisor, Parts & Services: Mike Calvert
Estimated Sales: $10 - 20 Million
Number Employees: 100-249
Parent Co: Autoquip Corporation

19249 **Autosplice**
10121 Barnes Canyon Rd
San Diego, CA 92121-5797 858-535-0077
Fax: 858-535-0130 www.autosplice.com
President: Michael T Reagan
Estimated Sales: $50 Million
Number Employees: 250-499

19250 **Autotron**
195 W Ryan Rd
Oak Creek, WI 53154-4400 414-764-7500
Fax: 414-764-4298 800-527-7500
info@elwood.com www.elwood.com
Manufacturer and exporter of industrial photoelectric controls
President: Robert Larsen
Vice President/CFO: Terry Levin
Vice President: David Johnson
Quality Manager: John Hoeppner
Estimated Sales: $5 - 10 Million
Number Employees: 20-49
Square Footage: 60000

19251 **Avalon Canvas & Upholstery**
4617 N Shepherd Dr
Houston, TX 77018-3315 713-697-0156
Fax: 713-697-9257
Commercial awnings
Manager: Michael Falahee
Estimated Sales: $1-2,500,000
Number Employees: 20-49

19252 **Avalon Foodservice, Inc.**
P.O.Box 536
Canal Fulton, OH 44614-0536 330-854-4551
Fax: 330-854-7108 800-362-0622
marketing@avalonfoods.com
www.avalonfoods.com
Founded in 1957. Fresh and frozen foods, dry and canned goods, produce, juices, ice cream, fresh dairy products, coffee and beverage programs, fresh and custom cut meats.
President: Andy Schroer
Estimated Sales: $58 Billion
Parent Co: United Food Service
Brands:
Nestle
Tyson
Stouffers

19253 **Avalon Manufacturing**
509 Bateman Circle
Corona, CA 92880 909-340-0280
Fax: 909-340-0283 800-676-3040
info@avalonmfg.com www.avalonmfg.com
Manufacturer and exporter of fryers, glazers and stainless steel (aluminum) proof boxes
President: Bill Enger
VP: Troy Enger
Estimated Sales: $2.5-5 Million
Number Employees: 10-19
Square Footage: 80000

19254 **Avantage Group**
250 N Harbor Dr
Suite 311
Redondo Beach, CA 90277 310-379-3933
Fax: 310-376-0591
Plastic bags
President: Mark E Daniels
Owner: Mark Daniels
Estimated Sales: Below $5 Million
Number Employees: 5-9

19255 **Avena Foods Ltd.**
316 1st Ave. E
Regina, SK S4N 5H2
Canada 306-757-3663
Fax: 306-757-1218 drichardson@avenafoods.com
www.avenafoods.com
Processor and supplier of gluten-free/wheat free oat products for private label/ingredients market. Allergen free plant with GFCO and OU Kosher Certification. Products include rolled oats, quick flakes, flour, steel cuts oats andbran.
Director: Kevin Meadows
Director: Maryellen Carlson
Quality Control: Nicole Gudmundsson
Sales: Dale Richardson
Operations: Rod Lechner
Plant Manager: Nathalie Paquin
Purchasing: Carryl Litzenberger
Estimated Sales: $746.93 Thousand
Number Employees: 26
Type of Packaging: Private Label, Bulk

19256 **(HQ)Avery Dennison Corporation**
207 Goode Avenue
Glendale, CA 91203-1222 626-304-2000
www.averydennison.com
Manufacturer and exporter of pressure sensitive labels.
President/CEO/Chairman: Dean Scarborough
SVP/General Counsel/Secretary: Susan Miller
SVP/CFO: Mitchell Butier
President, Materials Group: Donald Nolan
President, Retail Branding/Info Services: R. Shawn Neville
SVP/Chief Information Officer: Richard Hoffman
SVP/Chief Human Resources Officer: Anne Hill
Estimated Sales: $6 Billion
Number Employees: 29,800
Other Locations:
Avery Research Center (AEM)
Irwindale CA
Business Media
Buffalo NY
Corporate
Framingham MA
Corporate Int'l Manufacturing
Covina CA
Corporate Office at Brea
Brea CA
Corporate Office at Framingham
Framingham MA
Corporate Shared EHS at Milford
Milford MA
Engineered Films Division
Greenfield IN
Engineered Films Division
Painesville OH

19257 **Avery Dennison Printer Systems**
2100 Summit Ave
Philadelphia, PA 19114 215-725-4700
Fax: 215-725-6850 800-395-2282
PrinterSystems_philadelphia@averydennison.com
www.machines.averydennison.com
Manager: Tom Upshur
Estimated Sales: $10 - 20 Million
Number Employees: 20-49

19258 **Avery Filter Company**
99 Kinderkamack Rd Ste 105
Westwood, NJ 07675 201-666-9664
Fax: 201-666-3802 info@averyfilter.com
www.averyfilter.com
Filter presses of used filters
VP: Paul Homs Larry Avery
Vice President & Technical Director: Larry Avery
Square Footage: 1000

19259 **Avery Weigh-Tronix**
1000 Armstrong Dr
Fairmont, MN 56031 129-409-4400
Fax: 507-238-8258 877-888-1646
usinfo@awtxglobal.com
www.averyweigh-tronix.com
Manufacturer, importer and exporter of point-of-sale interface scales that link to cash registers and computers; also, portion control scales
VP: Peggy Trimble
Worldwide Marketing Director: P Trimble
Sales Director: D Cone
Number Employees: 250-499
Square Footage: 65000
Parent Co: Weigh-Tronix
Other Locations:
Weigh-Tronix
Tonbridge, Kent
Brands:
Nci

19260 **Avery Weigh-Tronix**
1000 Armstrong Drive
Fairmont, MN 56031-1439 507-238-4461
Fax: 507-238-4195 877-368-2039
usinfo@awtxglobal.com www.wtxweb.com
Manufacturer and exporter of industrial scales
President: Peggi Trimble
Director, Research & Development: Leon Lammers
Quality Assurance: Ray Bales
Sales & Marketing Manager: Stephen Cox
Director, Sales: Cathy Erickson
Product Manager: Tim Peterson
Estimated Sales: $533 Million
Number Employees: 5,500
Square Footage: 330000
Parent Co: Illinois Tool Works Inc.

19261 **Avestin**
2450 Don Reid Drive
Ottawa, ON K1H 1E1
Canada 613-736-0019
Fax: 613-736-8086 888-283-7846
avestin@avestin.com www.avestin.com
Manufacturer and exporter of high pressure homogenizers, filters, extruders and liposome extruders
President: Mark Ruzbie
Vice President: Hilde Linder
Marketing Manager: Sophie Sommerer
Number Employees: 10
Brands:
Emulsiflex
Liposofast

19262 **Avne Packaging Services**
PO Box 863
Bronx, NY 10457-0863 718-716-7600

19263 **Avon Tape**
79 Florence St Apt 310s
Chestnut Hill, MA 02467 508-584-8273
Manufacturer and exporter of pressure-sensitive tapes
President: Howard Shuman
Estimated Sales: $5-10 Million
Number Employees: 50-99

19264 **Avondale Mills**
506 S Broad St
Monroe, GA 30655 770-267-2226
Fax: 803-663-5839 www.avondalemills.com
Manufacturers of fabrics for awnings
Manager: Doug Johnson
VP: Kevin Crean
Estimated Sales: $20-50 Million
Number Employees: 100-249
Parent Co: Avondale Mills

19265 **Award's of America's**
The Cuisine Group 25 Kearny S
Suite 500
San Francisco, CA 94108 415-982-0701
Fax: 415-982-4580 info@usaota.com
www.usaota.com
Since 1985, has dedicated itself to the purveyance of taste and quality throughout the culinary industry and the search for the best of the best in food, beverage, and equipment. Expanded to include three division: American TestingInstitute, American Culinary Institute, and American Quality Institute

19266 **Awmco**
11560 184th Pl
Orland Park, IL 60467 708-478-6032
Fax: 708-478-6041 awmco@aol.com
bakingstone.com
Manufacturer and exporter of baking decks and cooking stones for pizza, pretzel and bagel ovens
President: Mark O'Toole
Estimated Sales: $2 Million
Number Employees: 10
Number of Brands: 4
Number of Products: 12
Square Footage: 72000
Type of Packaging: Food Service
Brands:
Fibrament Baking Stone
Oven Stone

19267 **Awnco**
9301 S Western Ave
Chicago, IL 60643 773-239-1511
Fax: 773-596-9469 800-339-6522
www.chesterfieldawning.com
Commercial awnings
Owner: David Ausema
Estimated Sales: $1 - 3,000,000
Number Employees: 10-19

19268 **Awning Company**
1668 Bridgehampton
P.O.Box 1647
Sag Harbor, NY 11963 631-725-3651
Fax: 631-725-7452
info@theawningcompany.com
www.awningcompany.com
Commercial awnings
President: Michael Moody
Co-Ownr.: Susan Oi
Estimated Sales: $500,000-$1,000,000
Number Employees: 5-9

19269 **Awning Enterprises**
P.O.Box 1063
Frederick, MD 21702 301-631-0500
Fax: 301-695-7651
awningenterprises@comcast.net
www.awningenterprises.com
Commercial awnings
Owner: Danny Baer
VP: Patrick O'Connell
Associate VP: Rita O'Connell
Estimated Sales: $.5 - 1,000,000
Number Employees: 1-4

19270 **Awnings Plus**
367 S Rohlwing Rd Ste I
Addison, IL 60101 630-627-4700
Fax: 630-627-4747 888-627-4770
www.awnings-plus.net
Commercial awnings
President: Kent Weber
CFO: Nancy Gomez
Marketing Director: Ken Miller
Sales Director: Erich Doering
Purchasing Manager: Michael Moreth
Estimated Sales: Below $5,000,000
Number Employees: 5-9
Square Footage: 6000

19271 **Awnings by Dee**
24913 Northern Boulevard
Little Neck, NY 11362-1260 516-487-6688
Fax: 718-224-5614
Commercial awnings
Secretary: Laura Dee
Estimated Sales: $1-2,500,000
Number Employees: 10-19

19272 **Axces Systems**
265 Post Ave
Westbury, NY 11590-2233 516-333-8585
Fax: 516-333-4992 800-355-3534
www.access-systems.com
Consultant and marketing information specialist for companies with 3-tier distribution networks
Owner: Charlie Richgat
Estimated Sales: $1-2.5 Million
Number Employees: 5-9
Square Footage: 4000

19273 **Axia Distribution Corporation**
247-2628 Granville Street
Vancouver, BC V6H 4B4
Canada 778-371-9885
Fax: 778-371-9000 info@axiadistribution.com
www.axiadistribution.com
Distributor & Manufacutuer of High Quality Rubber Mats. The Mats are molded with virgin rubber that offers durability, less odor, stability and anti-fatigue properties
Type of Packaging: Food Service

19274 **Axiflow Technologies, Inc.**
1955 Vaughn Road
Suite 103
Kennesaw, GA 30144 770-795-1195
Fax: 770-795-1342
info@proces-technologies.com
www.axiflowtechnologies.com
Pumps, blenders and food processing machines for the food & beverage industries.

19275 **Axiohm USA**
2411 N Oak Street
Suite 203 C
Myrtle Beach, SC 29577 843-443-3155
Fax: 888-505-9555 namsales@Axiohm.com
www.axiohm.com
Manufacturer and exporter of magnetic strip card readers and thermal laser receipt printers
President and CEO: Lindsey Allen
Director Marketing/Communications: Mark Basla
Number Employees: 60
Brands:
Axiohm

19276 **Axon Corporation/Styrotech**
3080 Business Park Dr Ste 103
Raleigh, NC 27610 919-772-8383
Fax: 919-772-5575 800-598-8601
info@axoncorp.com www.axoncorp.com
Tamper evident sleeve labels
President: H Lane
Quality Control: Andy Perry
General Manager: Victor Menayan
Estimated Sales: $10 - 20,000,000
Number Employees: 20-49
Brands:
E-Z Seal

19277 **Axon-Styrotech**
3080 Business Park Dr.
Suite 103
Raleigh, NC 27610 919-779-8383
Fax: 919-772-5575 800-598-8601
info@axoncorp.com www.axoncorp.com
Shrink and stretch sleeve labeling machines and systems
Sales Director: Ed Farley
Estimated Sales: $1-2.5 Million
Number Employees: 20-49

19278 **Axons Labeling**
Gristmill Road
Wanaque, NJ 07465 973-616-7448
Fax: 973-616-7449
Labeling machines, labeling applicators/jar unscramblers

19279 **Ay Machine Company**
East King Street
PO Box 608
Ephrata, PA 17522-0608 717-733-0335
Fax: 717-733-2933 info@aymachine.com
www.aymachine.com
Custom built food processing machinery; also, spare parts and rebuilt equipment
President: Richard Ay
CEO: Rick Ay, Jr.
Estimated Sales: $2.5-5 Million
Number Employees: 10-19
Square Footage: 128000

19280 **Ayer Sales**
3 Adler Dr
East Syracuse, NY 13057 315-432-0550
Fax: 781-935-3675
Waste water treatment systems
Marketing Coordinator: Peter Quinn
Estimated Sales: $3 - 5 Million
Number Employees: 15
Parent Co: Ayer Sales

19281 **Ayr-King Corporation**
2013 Cobalt Dr
Jeffersontown, KY 40299 502-266-6270
Fax: 502-266-6274 866-266-6290
aurking@aol.com www.ayrking.com
Breading sifters, hoods and drive-thru windows
President: Diane King
VP Engineering: Cha Harned
VP of Sales: James Bell
Estimated Sales: $500,000-$1 Million
Number Employees: 5-9

19282 **Azbar Plus**
2755, av Dalton
Qu,bec, QC G1P 3T1
Canada 418-687-3672
Fax: 418-687-2987 azbar@total.net
azbarplus.com
Liquor and beverage control equipment and dispensers including electric and beverage
Estimated Sales: $1 - 5 Million

19283 **Azonix Corporation**
101 Billerica Ave
Building 4
Billerica, MA 01862 978-670-6300
Fax: 978-670-8855 800-967-5558
market@azonix.com www.azonix.com
President: Greg Balesta
Training/Sales Support: Craig Yelenick
Estimated Sales: $13 Million
Number Employees: 50-99

19284 **Aztec Grill**
PO Box 820037
Dallas, TX 75382 214-343-1897
800-346-8114
www.aztecgrill.com
Manufacturer and exporter of wood burning grills and rotisseries
Estimated Sales: $1 - 5 Million
Number Employees: 2
Square Footage: 8000
Type of Packaging: Food Service

19285 **Azz/R-A-L**
8500 Hansen Rd
Houston, TX 77075 713-943-0340
Fax: 713-943-8354 garybarber@azz.com
www.azz.com
Lighting fixtures for the food service industry.

19286 **B W Cooney & Associates**
28 Simpson Road
Bolton, Ontario, ON L7E 1G9
Canada 905-857-7880
Fax: 905-857-7883 info@bwcooney.com
www.bwcooney.ca
Shrink wrapping and tray stretch machines, flow wrappers, verticle form fill & seal systems, packaging film and retail food trays.
President: Brian Cooney
Number Employees: 2

19287 **B Way Corporation**
8607 Roberts Dr # 250
Atlanta, GA 30350-2237 770-645-4800
Fax: 770-645-4810 800-527-2267
sales@bwaycorp.com www.bwaycorp.com
Cans for coffee, nuts, snacks and similar products
CEO: Kenneth M Roessler
VP Marketing: R Coleman
Executive Vice President of Sales and Ma: Michael Noel
Vice President of Operations: Darrell Davis
Vice President of Purchasing: Leslie Bradshaw
Estimated Sales: 460000
Number Employees: 50-99

19288 **B&B Neon Sign Company**
2305 Donley Dr # 116
Austin, TX 78758-4535 512-765-4470
Fax: 512-719-4490 800-791-6366
customerservice@everythingneon.com
www.everythingneon.com
Point of purchase displays including neon and plexiglass signs; also, sign maintenance, refurbishing and repair services available
Owner: Tim O'Day
Estimated Sales: $300,000 -$500,000
Number Employees: 5-9

19289 **B&G Machine Company**
9124 S 53rd Ave
Oak Lawn, IL 60453-1665 708-499-1626
Fax: 631-589-9466 800-645-1191
www.bgmachine.com
Bins, hoppers, totes, ASME code vessels, storage tanks and mixing tanks
President: Barbara Ruehl
Vice President: Greg Ruehl
Estimated Sales: $5-10 Million
Number Employees: 5-9

19290 **B&G Products Co Inc**
3631 44th St SE # E
Grand Rapids, MI 49512-3971 616-698-9050
Fax: 616-698-9271 sales@bgproducts.com
www.bgproducts.com
President: Kathleen Geddes
Vice President: Jacci Harding
Quality Control Manager: Mark Mastbergen
Sales: Paul Geddes
Estimated Sales: $5 - 10 Million
Number Employees: 95
Square Footage: 40000
Type of Packaging: Food Service

19291 **B&H Labeling Systems**
P.O.Box 247
Ceres, CA 95307 209-537-5785
Fax: 209-537-6854 marketing@bhlabeling.com
www.bhlabeling.com
Hot-melt roll-fed labeling machines capable of handling most container sizes, label substrates, and speeds for a diverse range of products and materials. Features and options include Computerized Registration System, Web TrackingOperator Alarms, Touch Screen Operation, Rapid Change Over Change Parts, ENDURA Shrink Labeling process, Precision Components
Owner: Carol Bright
CEO: Roman M Eckols
Plant Manager: Bruce Andrade
Number Employees: 100-249
Type of Packaging: Consumer, Food Service, Private Label

19292 **B&J Machinery**
11560 Rockfield Ct
Cincinnati, OH 45241-1919 513-771-7374
Fax: 513-771-3820 info@pe-us.com
www.pe-us.com
Packaging machinery and replacement parts
President: Bruno Negri
CFO: Bruno Negri
VP: Tom Kauffmann
Regional Sales Manager: Ryan Cooper
Estimated Sales: $10 - 20 Million
Number Employees: 20-49
Square Footage: 32000

19293 **(HQ)B&P Process Equipment &Systems**
1000 Hess Ave
Saginaw, MI 48601-3729 989-757-1300
Fax: 989-757-1301 sales@bpprocess.com
www.bpprocess.com
Manufacturer and exporter of food processing machinery and equipment including automatic scales, sifters, etc
President: Ray E Miller
R&D: Doug Hillman
Executive: Joe Flynn
CFO: Allen Martin
Estimated Sales: $20 - 50 Million
Number Employees: 50-99

19294 **B&R Machine Inc.**
PO Box 9
Wedron, IL 60557 815-434-0427
info@brmachine.us
www.wedrongrills.com
Grocery bag machinery
Owner: Robert Rogowski
VP: Denise Ritchey
Estimated Sales: $2.5-5 Million
Number Employees: 5-9
Square Footage: 60000
Brands:
Sakmaker
Sakpacker
Sakstacker

19295 **B&W Awning ManufacturingCompany**
219 Walton Ave
Lexington, KY 40502-1492 859-252-1619
Fax: 859-233-4354 igille3607@aol.com
www.bwawning.com
Commercial awnings
President: Larry Gillespie
Estimated Sales: $1 - 2,500,000
Number Employees: 5-9

19296 **B-T Engineering**
29 Bala Ave Ste 209
Bala Cynwyd, PA 19004 610-664-9500
Fax: 610-664-0317 bte123123@aol.com
Automated sanitary liquid food processing equipment and control systems including clean-in-place pipeline systems, pasteurizers and volumetric filling machines; exporter of skidded food systems; design services available
President/CEO: William Willard
CFO: Thomas Berger Sr
Secretary/Treasurer: Thomas Berger
Estimated Sales: $1-2.5 Million
Number Employees: 1-4
Square Footage: 2500
Type of Packaging: Food Service

19297 **B.A.G. Corporation**
11510 Data Dr
Dallas, TX 75218 800-331-9200
Fax: 214-340-4598 800-331-9200
bagcorp@bagcorp.com www.bagcorp.com
Manufacturer and exporter of the Super Sack container, a woven polypropylene FIBC for shipping, handling, and storing dry-flowable and fluid products
President: Karl Reimers
Estimated Sales: $5-10 Million
Number Employees: 20-49
Type of Packaging: Food Service, Bulk
Brands:
Super Sack

19298 **B.C. Holland**
45 Wilson Ave
Dousman, WI 53118 262-965-2939
Fax: 262-965-3546
Custom tanks and mixers
President: Brian Holland
CFO: Rom Able
VP: David Steward
Sales Manager: Jim Huth
VP Operations: Dave Stewart
Estimated Sales: $1-2.5 Million
Number Employees: 10-19
Square Footage: 10000

19299 **B.C.E. Technologies**
616 S Ware Blvd
Tampa, FL 33619-4443 813-621-8128
Fax: 813-620-1206
pnelson@convergentlabeltech.com
www.convergentlabeltech.com
President: Graham Lloyd
Number Employees: 20-49

19300 **B.E. Industries**
652 Glenbrook Rd # 4102
Stamford, CT 06906-1410 203-357-8055
Fax: 203-967-9537
Advertising specialties including key rings and magnets
President: Bruce Kahn
Estimated Sales: $2.5-5,000,000
Number Employees: 10-19

19301 **B.E.S.T.**
1071 Industrial Pkwy N
Brunswick, OH 44212 330-273-1277
Fax: 330-225-8740 sales@bestvibes.com
www.bestvibes.com
President: Ed Verbos
Estimated Sales: $5 - 10 Million
Number Employees: 20-49

19302 **B.F. Nelson Folding Corporation**
12900 Eagle Creek Pkwy
Savage, MN 55378-1271 952-746-6300
Fax: 952-746-6399 800-328-2380
sales@bfnelson.com www.bfnelson.com
Folding cartons
President: Larry Ross
Executive VP: Gary Sotebeer
VP Sales: Ron Anderson
Estimated Sales: $1 - 5 Million
Number Employees: 100-249

19303 **B.K. Coffee**
P.O.Box 1238
Oneonta, NY 13820-5238 607-432-1499
Fax: 607-432-1592 800-432-1499
www.bkcoffee.com
Founded in 1991. Manufacturer of coffee
Owner: Paul Karabins
Owner: Gene Bettiol
Estimated Sales: $10-24.9 Million
Number Employees: 20-49
Type of Packaging: Private Label
Brands:
B.K. Coffee

19304 **B.N.W. Industries**
7930 N 700 E
Tippecanoe, IN 46570 574-353-7855
Fax: 574-353-8152 sales@norristhermal.com
www.beltomatic.com
Founded in 1965. Manufacturer of dryers, roasters, and coolers for the food industry.
President: Dan Norris
Founder/Consultant: Lee Norris
Regional Sale Engineer: Dick Garner
Export Department: Les Haspl
Vice President Sales: Aaron Norris
Project Manager: Chuck Norris
Estimated Sales: $1 - 3 Million
Number Employees: 5-9

19305 **BAW Plastics**
2148 Century Dr
Jefferson Hills, PA 15025 412-384-3100
Fax: 412-384-2033 800-783-2229
bawplas@uas.or.com www.bawplastics.com
Coupon bags, transparent vinyl envelopes, vinyl checker aids, acrylic holders, lamination pouches, time and attendance badges and name tags, etc
President: James Slovonic
Sales Manager: Martin Slovonic
Sales Director: Francis Dusch III
Estimated Sales: $10-20 Million
Number Employees: 100-249
Square Footage: 65000

19306 **BBC Industries**
5 Capper Drive
Pacific, MO 63069 636-343-5600
Fax: 636-343-3952 800-654-4205
info@bbcind.com www.bbcind.com
Industrial conveyor ovens and heaters
President and CFO: Ronald Vinyard
Head of R&D and Quality Control: Everett Graham
Estimated Sales: $5 - 10 Million
Number Employees: 10-19
Square Footage: 90400
Brands:
Baker's Best

19307 **BBQ Pits by Klose**
1355 Judiway Street #B
Houston, TX 77018-6005 713-686-8720
Fax: 713-686-8793 800-487-7487
david@bbqpits.com www.bbqpits.com
Manufacturer, importer and exporter of barbecue equipment including grills and smokers; also, catering trailers; wood, charcoal and gas fired.
President: David Klose
Sales: Dana Harlow
Estimated Sales: $1-3 Million
Number Employees: 10-19
Number of Products: 500
Square Footage: 24000
Type of Packaging: Consumer, Food Service, Bulk
Brands:
Klose

19308 **BC Wood Products**
11364 Air Park Rd
Ashland, VA 23005 804-798-9154
Fax: 804-798-2672 bcwoodprod@aol.com
www.bcwoodonline.com
Wooden pallets
Owner: Gordon Murdock
Sales/Marketing: Reynolds Cowardin
Secretary/Treasurer: Carolyn Barrett
Purchasing Manager: Richard Barrett
Estimated Sales: $3-5 Million
Number Employees: 20-49
Square Footage: 50000

19309 **BCN Research Laboratories**
2491 Stock Creek Blvd
Rockford, TN 37853 865-573-7511
Fax: 865-573-7513 800-236-0505
emilia.rico@bcnlabs.com www.bcnlabs.com
Consultant providing laboratory and research services including sanitation, testing and analysis; also, plant audits and training available
President: Emilia Rico
VP: Shawn Johnson
Estimated Sales: $.5 - 1 million
Number Employees: 5-9
Square Footage: 6000

19310 **BE & SCO**
1623 N San Marcos
San Antonio, TX 78201-6436 210-734-6485
Fax: 210-737-3925 800-683-0928
sales@bescomfg.com www.bescomfg.com
Manufacturer and exporter of flour tortilla and tamale equipment and grills
President: Robert Escamilla
VP: Rosie Ecamilla
Estimated Sales: $2.5-5 Million
Number Employees: 10-19
Square Footage: 120000
Brands:
Beta Max
Beta-900
Mini-Wedge Press
Wedge Press

19311 **(HQ)BE&K Building Group**
P.O.Box 2332
Birmingham, AL 35201-2332 205-972-6000
Fax: 205-972-6651 www.bek.com
Meeting the complex needs of clients requiring construction services
President: Tom Vaughn
CEO/Chairman: Luther Cochrane
CFO: Trilby Carriker
Estimated Sales: K
Number Employees: 5,000-9,999
Other Locations:
Atlanta GA
Charlotte NC
Greenville SC
Brentwood TN
Maitland FL
Raleigh NC
Vienna VA

19312 **BEC International**
2330 S Preston St
Louisville, KY 40217-2163 502-637-3852
Fax: 502-637-3803 877-232-4687
beci2001@hotmail.com
Consultant specializing in engineering and project management services
President: Richard Sorensen
Executive VP: James Winn
Number Employees: 1
Square Footage: 3600

19313 **BEI**
1375 Kalamazoo St
South Haven, MI 49090 269-637-8541
Fax: 269-637-4233 800-364-7425
sakes@beiintl.com www.beiintl.com
Manufacturer and exporter of berry harvesters and packing equipment
President: William De Witt Jr
Vice President: Butch Greiffendorf
Manager: J Greiffendorf
Estimated Sales: $5-10 Million
Number Employees: 20-49
Square Footage: 24000

19314 **BEI**
1870 Dean St # B
St Charles, IL 60174 630-879-0300
Fax: 630-406-0310
Insulated packaging
VP: Bob Belick
Marketing Manager: Bob Belick
Estimated Sales: Less than $500,000
Number Employees: 1-4
Brands:
Thermal Cor

19315 **BEMA**
7101 College Boulevard
Suite 1505
Overland Park, KS 66210-2087 847-920-1230
Fax: 847-920-1253 info@bema.org
www.bema.org
President, Chief Executive Officer: Kerwin Brown
Operations Manager: Gay Poteet
Number Employees: 10

19316 **BEVCO**
9354-194th Street Surrey
Canada, BC V4N 4E9
Canada 604-888-1455
Fax: 604-888-2887 800-663-0090
info@bevco.net www.bevco.net
Manufacturer and exporter of material handling and distribution equipment including accumulators, conveyors, conveyor systems, depalletizers and elevators; also, warmers and bottle rinsers
President: Brian Fortier
CEO: D Hargrove
CFO: Dianne Hargrove
Sales/Marketing Executive: Murray Kendrick
Estimated Sales: $5 - 10 Million
Number Employees: 45
Square Footage: 80000

19317 **BFB Consultants**
5995 River Grove Avenue
Mississauga, ON L5M 4Z8
Canada 905-819-9856
Fax: 905-819-9857 bulcan1@ibm.net
Consultant specializing in food packaging, labeling and advertising in Canada and the U.S. in accordance with government regulations
Regional Affairs: Laurel Bellissimo
Sr. Technical Director: Gary Gnirss
Estimated Sales: $1 - 5 Million

19318 **BFD Corporation**
15544 E Hinsdale Cir
Centennial, CO 80112 303-363-6288
Fax: 303-363-6844 www.bfdcorp.com
Depackaging soft products/soft tissue separation; cutting-deboning-desinewing.
President: John Shook
CFO: Mark Thomas
Sales Director: Harold Hodges
Number Employees: 10-19

19319 **BFM Equipment Sales**
209 Steel Road
P.O. Box 117
Fall River, WI 53932-0117 920-484-3341
Fax: 920-484-3077 info@bfmequip.com
www.bfmequip.com
Manufacturer, importer, exporter and wholesaler/distributor of food processing machinery, can end cleaners and dryers, replacement parts and supplies
Owner: Richard Bindley
Executive Manager: Russell Quandt
Estimated Sales: Below $5 Million
Number Employees: 1-4
Square Footage: 40000
Brands:
Bfm

19320 **BFT**
3513 Transmitter Rd
Panama City, FL 32404 850-784-1231
Fax: 850-784-1343 800-871-1481
Gripper style air cleaner, bi-directional accumulation table, table top conveyors and a carry handle application machine for six-pack bottles and other containers and products
Estimated Sales: $2.5-5 000,000
Number Employees: 10

19321 **BG Industries**
305 Canal Street
Lemont, IL 60439-3603 630-257-1077
Fax: 630-257-0005 800-800-5761
www.bgindustry.com
Disposable plastic and metal catering products including chafing dishes, soup terrines and beverage urns
President: Paul Orednick
Estimated Sales: $1-2.5 Million
Number Employees: 9
Brands:
Hot Buffet To Go
Party Chafer

19322 **BH Awning & Tent Company**
2275 M 139
Benton Harbor, MI 49022-6190 269-925-2187
Fax: 888-272-2197 800-272-2187
sales@bhawning.com www.bhawning.com
Commercial awnings, banners, canopies and flags
President: Charles Dill
Number Employees: 10-19

19323 **BH Bunn Company**
2730 Drane Field Rd
Lakeland, FL 33811-1325 863-647-1555
Fax: 863-686-2866 800-222-2866
info@bunntyco.com www.bunntyco.com
Bunn tying machines for poultry, pork and beef
President: John Bunn
Estimated Sales: $3 - 5 Million
Number Employees: 10-19
Square Footage: 68000
Brands:
Bunn

19324 **BIRKO Corporation**
9152 Yosemite St
Henderson, CO 80640 303-289-1090
Fax: 303-289-1190 800-525-0476
info@birkocorp.com www.birkocorp.com
Inorganic industrial chemicals
President: Florence Powers
CFO: Kelly Heffer
CEO: Mark Swanson
R&D and QC: Kerry McAninch
Estimated Sales: $20 - 50 Million
Number Employees: 50-99

19325 **BJ Wood Products**
400 West 9th Street South
Ladysmith, WI 54848 715-532-6626
Fax: 715-532-7774 pauls@bjwood.com
www.bjwood.com
Custom wood and acrylic casework, cabinets, displays, counters and store fixtures
President: Paul Sieg
VP: John Sieg
Estimated Sales: $5-10 Million
Number Employees: 20-49
Square Footage: 47500

19326 **BJM Pumps**
123 Spencer Plain Rd
Old Saybrook, CT 06475 860-399-5937
Fax: 860-399-7784 www.bjmpumps.com
Pumps and pump accesories for food industry
Principle: Steve Bjorkman
Business Manager: Mike Bjorkman
Estimated Sales: $630,000
Number Employees: 5

19327 **BK Graphics**
5270 Cub Cir Ste A
Morristown, TN 37814 423-581-4288
Fax: 423-581-9159 800-581-9159
bkgraphi@usit.net www.bkgraphics.com
Advertising specialties; also, screen printing available
CEO: Brian Frankford
Quality Control: Kathy Frankford
Estimated Sales: $.5 - 1,000,000
Number Employees: 5-9

19328 **BKI**
1000 Broadway
Suite 410
Oakland, CA 94607 510-444-8707
Fax: 510-463-2690 contactus@bki.com
www.bki.com
Technical management consultants
President: Robert Knight
Vice President: Brian Gitt
Number Employees: 10

19329 **BKI Worldwide**
2812 Grandview Drive
Simpsonville, SC 29680 864-963-3471
Fax: 864-963-5316 800-927-6887
customerservice@bkideas.com
www.bkideas.com
Manufacturer and exporter of rotisseries, ovens, fryers, deli cases, ventless hood systems and food warmers
President: Randy A Karns
Controller: Reggy Skelton
COO: Dave Korcsmaros
Quality Control Manager: Wade Pitts
Operations Manager: Reed Walpole
Production Manager: Reed Walpole
Purchasing Manager: Wade Pitts
Number Employees: 100-249
Parent Co: Standex International Corporation
Brands:
Bar-B-Que King
Whisperflow

19330 **BLH Electronics**
75 Shawmut Rd
Canton, MA 02021 781-821-2000
Fax: 781-828-1451 sales@blh.com
www.blh.com
Manufacturer and exporter of process weighing and web tension systems, strain gauges and load systems/instruments
President: Robert E Murphy
Vice President: William Sheehan
Research & Development: David Scanlon
Sales Director: Art Koehler
Facilities Manager: Alan Sandman
Estimated Sales: $50-100 Million
Number Employees: 1-4
Square Footage: 55000
Parent Co: Spectra-Physics AB
Other Locations:
BLH Electronics
Toronto ON
Brands:
Gate-Weigh

19331 **BMA**
100 Springdale Road
Suite 110
Cherry Hill, NJ 08003-3300 609-239-1080
Fax: 610-455-1491 information@maskell.com
www.maskell.com
Consulting firm, serving the needs of manufacturers and distributors
CFO: Nicholas S Katko
Estimated Sales: $1 - 5 Million

19332 **BMH**
19135 San Jose Avenue
City of Industry, CA 91748-1407 909-349-2530
Fax: 626-912-2477
Belt conveyors, automatic storage and handling systems and metal belting
Estimated Sales: $2.5-5,000,000
Number Employees: 20

19333 **BMH Chronos Richardson**
2 Stewart Place
Fairfield, NJ 07004-2202 973-227-3522
Fax: 973-227-8478 800-284-3644
info@premiertechchronos.com
www.bmhchronosrichardson.com
Estimated Sales: $1 - 5 Million

19334 **BMH Equipment**
1217 Blumenfeld Drive
P.O. Box 162109
Sacramento, CA 95815 916-922-8828
Fax: 916-922-8820 800-350-8828
jack@bmhequipment.com
www.bmhequipment.com
Distributor/exporter of custom material handling equipment, hand trucks, casters, conveyor systems, dollies, pallet jacks and racks, aluminum ramps, dock boards, shelving and work tables; design and engineering for nonstandard materialhandling problems
President: Jack Alexander
VP: Jerry Berg
Conveyor Specialist: Richard Wales
Estimated Sales: $2.5-5 Million
Number Employees: 5-9
Square Footage: 20800

19335 **BNW Industries**
7930 N 700 E
Tippecanoe, IN 46570 574-353-7855
Fax: 574-353-8152 sales@norristhermal.com
www.beltomatic.com
Manufacturer and exporter of coolers and dehydrators; manufacturer of balance/single weave wire belts
Founder/President: Lee Norris
President: Dan Norris
Vice President Sales: Aaron Norris
Purchasing Manager: Troy Eaton
Estimated Sales: $1-3 Million
Number Employees: 5-9
Square Footage: 26000
Parent Co: Lee Norris Construction & Grain Company
Brands:
Belt-O-Matic
Indiana Woven Wire

19336 **BOC Gases**
575 Mountain Ave
New Providence, NJ 00974 908-464-8100
Fax: 908-771-1701 jobs@us.gases.boc.com
www.boc.com
Freezing Systems
President: Anthony E Isaac
Marketing: Jon Lederman
Number Employees: 1,000-4,999

19337 **BOC Gases**
575 Mountain Ave
New Providence, NJ 07974 908-464-8100
Fax: 908-771-1701 800-742-4726
jobs@us.gases.boc.com www.boc.com
Full line of freezing and chilling equipment for beverage processing and carbonating needs
Marketing: Jon Lederman
Estimated Sales: $5 000,000
Number Employees: 1,000-4,999

19338 **BOC Plastics Inc**
90 Piedmont Industrial Drive
Suite 100
Winston Salem, NC 27107 336-767-0277
Fax: 336-767-2338 800-334-8687
info@bocplastics.com www.bocplastics.com
Plastic cutlery kits
President: Robert Bach
CFO: Aren Petersen
Estimated Sales: $5 - 10 Million
Number Employees: 20-49

19339 **BONAR Engineering & Construction Company**
565 South Edgewood Avenue
Jacksonville, FL 32205 228-627-1986
Fax: 904-389-6003 henry3rd@bonareng.com
www.bonareng.com
Owner: Henry Bonar
Estimated Sales: $3 - 5 Million
Number Employees: 10-19

19340 **(HQ)BP Amoco**
150 W Warrenville Rd
Naperville, IL 60563 630-369-0128
Fax: 630-836-5045 stallwdl@bp.com
www.bp.com/barex
Packaging materials including FDA approved resins and film
President: Graham Hunt
President: Ross Pillari
CFO: Byron Jroce
Estimated Sales: $1 Billion
Number Employees: 5-9
Brands:
Barex

19341 **BPH Pump and Equipment**
4126 Orleans St.
McHenry, IL 60050 815-578-0100
Fax: 815-578-0400 866-295-9161
bphpumps@aol.com www.bphpumps.com
Fluid handling equipment, system design, system fabrications, system engineering
President: Brian Hoskins
Estimated Sales: $2.5 000,000
Number Employees: 1-4

19342 **BR Machine Company**
P.O.Box 9
Wedron, IL 60557-0009 815-434-0427
Fax: 815-434-0428 800-310-7057
info@brmachine.us www.wedrongrills.com
Portable propane and custom portable grills, gas grill carts, personalized custom canopy and grill accessories
President and CFO: Bob Rogowski
VP: Nancy Rogowski
VP of Sales: Tony Rogowski
Production Manager: Sam Brown
Estimated Sales: Below $5 Million
Number Employees: 5-9
Square Footage: 40000
Brands:
Wedron Grills

19343 **BRECOflex Company, LLC**
222 Industrial Way W
Eatontown, NJ 07724 732-460-9500
Fax: 732-542-6725 888-463-1400
info@brecoflex.com www.brecoflex.com
Manufacturer, and exporter of polyurethane, USDA and FDA approved timing belts, pulleys, and accessories
President: Willi Fulleman
VP: Rudolf Schoendienst
Research & Development: Johnathan Weir
Quality Control: Dararith Son
Marketing Director: Joy Guigo
Estimated Sales: $2.5 - 5,000,000
Brands:
Breco
Brecoflex
Esband

19344 **BS&B Safety Systems**
7455 East 46th Street
Tulsa, OK 74147-0590 918-622-5950
Fax: 918-665-3904 sales@bsbsystems.com
www.bsbsystems.com
VP: Dave Garrison
Number Employees: 5-9

19345 **BSI Instruments**
101 Corporation Drive
Aliquippa, PA 15001-4859 724-378-1900
Fax: 724-378-1926 800-274-9851
bsischwa@sgi.net www.biospherical.com
On-line process control instrumentation including noninvasive level density systems
President: Bud Smith
VP of Marketing: Whit Little
Sales Manager: Aaron Tufts
Estimated Sales: $2.5-5 Million
Number Employees: 9
Square Footage: 60000

19346 **BVL Controls**
661, The Pit
Bois-Des-Filion, QC J6Z 4T2
Canada 450-965-0502
Fax: 450-965-8751 866-285-2668
info@bvlcontrols.com www.bvlcontrols.com

Manufacturer, importer and exporter of portion control and cooling equipment and supplies for beer, wine, soft drinks and liquors
President: Alvin Guerette
Controller: Josee Merchand
Vice President: Gilles Guerette
Estimated Sales: $1-3 Million
Number Employees: 10-19
Square Footage: 48000
Brands:
Bvl
Oberdorfer
True Measure

19347 BW Controls
1080 North Crooks
Clawson, MI 48017 248-435-0700
Fax: 248-435-8120 800-635-0289
apt.orders@ametek.com www.ametekapt.com
Continuous and point level instruments, offering a line of 3-A approved magnetostictive level sensors
Manager: Bob Soeder
Bus Unit Manager: Robert Soeder
Business Development Director: Michael Geis
Estimated Sales: $5 Million
Number Employees: 100-249
Number of Brands: 4
Number of Products: 26
Square Footage: 520000

19348 BWI-PLC
1750 Corporate Drive
Suite 700
Norcross, GA 30093-2932 770-925-2004
800-605-6217
tom.riggins@bwi-kp.com www.bwi-plc.com
Packaging machinery, equipment and materials
Estimated Sales: $5-10 Million
Number Employees: 50

19349 Baader Johnson
2955 Fairfax Trafficway
Kansas City, KS 66115-1317 913-621-3366
Fax: 913-621-1729 800-288-3434
sales@baader-johnson.com
www.baader-johnson.com
Designer, manufacturer and distributors of poultry and fish processing equipment.
President: Andrew Miller
Controller: Shaun Nicolas
Corporate Accounts/Sales Manager - US: Gehrig Chandler
Estimated Sales: $15.10 Million
Number Employees: 80
Square Footage: 13209
Parent Co: Baader Food Processing Machinery

19350 Babco International, Inc
911 S Tyndall
Tucson, AZ 85719 520-628-7596
Fax: 520-628-9622 contactus@babcotucson.com
www.babcotucson.com
Glassware, china, skirting, linen and silverware
Owner: Patrick Brodecky
Marketing/Customer Service Director: Betsy Marco
Estimated Sales: $2.5-5 Million
Number Employees: 5-9
Brands:
Snap Drape
Syracuse

19351 Babcock & Wilcox Power Generation Group
20 S Van Buren Ave
Barberton, OH 44203-0351 330-753-4511
Fax: 330-860-1886 800-222-2625
slmccaulley@babcock.com www.babcock.com
Manufacturer and exporter of steam generation boilers and auxiliary equipment
President, COO: J. Randall Data
Senior Vice President, General Counsel,: James D. Canafax
SVP, CFO: Anthony S. Colatrella
SVP, Chief Administrative Officer: Kairus K. Tarapore
R&D Director: Stan Vecci
Manager Advertising: Phil Stillitano
Director of Operation: Alan Nethery
Number Employees: 1,000-4,999
Parent Co: McDermott International

19352 Babson Brothers Company
20903 W Gale Ave
Galesville, WI 54630 608-582-2221
Fax: 608-582-2581
Manufacturer, importer and exporter of dairy farm equipment and machinery including milk meters, processors and coolers
Manager: Ralph Rottier
VP: Ralph Rottier
Estimated Sales: $20-50 Million
Number Employees: 100-249
Square Footage: 140000
Parent Co: Babson Brothers Company
Brands:
Surge
Tru-Test

19353 Bacchus Wine Cellars
14027 Memorial Drive #228
Houston, TX 77079-9826 281-496-4495
Fax: 284-496-5855 800-487-8812
bacchuswinecellars.com
Manufacturer, importer and exporter of temperature and humidity controlled wine cellars, cabinets and storage equipment
President: Pierre Guinaudeau
Estimated Sales: Less than $500,000
Number Employees: 75
Square Footage: 40000
Brands:
Le Cellier

19354 Bacharach EIT Gas Detection Systems
621 Hunt Valley Circle
New Kensington, PA 15068-7074 724-334-5000
Fax: 724-334-5001 800-736-4666
Help@MyBacharach.com
www.bacharach-inc.com
Estimated Sales: $1 - 5 Million
Number Employees: 50-99

19355 Back Tech
388 2nd Avenue.
459
New York, NJ 10010 973-279-0838
Fax: 212-673-0386 backtech@liftsolutions.com
www.liftsolutions.com
Lightweight electrical lifting cart for up to 500 pounds, mobil, handling rolls and totes
Plant Manager: E Rydstedt
Estimated Sales: $1 000,000
Number Employees: 1-4

19356 Backus USA
602 W Dubois Ave
Suite 9
Du Bois, PA 15801 814-375-6999
Estimated Sales: $1 - 5 Million

19357 Backwoods Smoker
8245 Dixie Shreveport Rd
Shreveport, LA 71107-8439 318-220-0380
backwoodssmoker@hughes.net
www.backwoods-smoker.com
Meat smokers
Founder: Mike McGowan
VP: Charlene McGowan
Secy.: Larie McGowan
Estimated Sales: $1-2.5 Million
Number Employees: 5-9
Square Footage: 6000
Type of Packaging: Private Label
Brands:
Backwoods Smoker

19358 Bacon Products Corporation
P.O.Box 22187
Chattanooga, TN 37422 423-892-0414
Fax: 423-892-2065 800-251-6238
eagles7@baconmail.com
www.baconproducts.com
Rodenticides and insecticides including pellets, glue traps, organic fly control products, ant, roach and spider spray, etc
Owner: Reed Bacon
R&D: Reed Bacon
Sales/Marketing: Karen Romito
VP of Production: James Edwards
Estimated Sales: $20 - 50 Million
Number Employees: 20-49
Brands:
Ant, Roach & Spider
Eagles-7
Final Bite!
Fly Eaters
Fly Ribbons
Last Step
Roach Destroyer
Septic Clean
Spray-Kill With Nylar
Wasp & Hornet Destroyer

19359 Baden Baden Food Equipment
3947 W Columbus Ave
Chicago, IL 60652 773-284-9009
Fax: 773-284-9109 877-368-8375
sales@badenfoodequip.com
www.badenfoodequip.com
Sales of food and bakery equipment and wares
President: Vernon Condon
Estimated Sales: $1,500,000
Number Employees: 5-9
Square Footage: 6000

19360 Badger Meter
4545 W. Brown Deer Road
P.O. Box 245036
Milwaukee, WI 53224-9536 414-355-0400
Fax: 414-371-5956 800-876-3837
tulsaoperator@badgermeter.com
www.badgermeter.com
Manufacturer and exporter of water meters and flowmeters
President: Richard A Meeusen
Marketing Communications Manager: Laurie Richelt
Estimated Sales: I
Number Employees: 1,000-4,999

19361 Badger Meter
P.O.Box 581390
Tulsa, OK 74158 918-836-8411
Fax: 918-832-9962 rcv@badgermeter.com
www.badgermeter.com
Ultrasonic flow meters, research control valves and flow tubes
General Manager: Byron Bradley
Quality Control: Denny Thompson
Product Manager: Brian Crockett
Estimated Sales: $20 - 50 Million
Number Employees: 50-99

19362 Badger Paper Mills
P.O.Box 149
Peshtigo, WI 54157 715-582-4551
Fax: 715-582-4853 800-826-0494
cpo@badgerpaper.com www.bagerpaper.com
Bond, mimeograph, duplicator, computer, copier rolls, MG and MF manifold, laminating stock, printed and plain waxed papers
President: Ronald Swanson
Plant Manager: Mark Bruemmer
Estimated Sales: $60 Million
Number Employees: 100-249

19363 Badger Plug Company
P.O.Box 199
Greenville, WI 54942-0199 920-757-7300
Fax: 920-757-7339 sales@badgerplug.net
www.badgerplug.com
Plastic end plugs for cardboard tubes
President: Dan Voissem
Estimated Sales: $10 - 20 Million
Number Employees: 20-49

19364 Badger Wood Arts
PO Box 44698
Racine, WI 53404-7015 414-636-9902
Fax: 888-703-0383 800-331-9663
contact@badgerwoodarts.com
www.badgerwoodarts.com
We design and produce food displays for retail point of sale
Estimated Sales: $1 - 5 Million

19365 Bag Company
1650 Airport Rd NW
Suite 104
Kennesaw, GA 30144-7039 770-422-4187
Fax: 800-417-7273 800-533-1931
sales@bagco.com www.bagco.com
Manufacturer and exporter of polyethylene and polypropylene bags; importer of plastic bags.
Director of Marketing: Katherine Remick
Estimated Sales: $13 Million
Number Employees: 10-19
Type of Packaging: Consumer

19366 **BagcraftPapercon**
3900 W 43rd Street
Chicago, IL 60632 773-254-8000
Fax: 773-254-8204 800-621-8468
www.bagcraft.com
Manufacturer and exporter of foil, film, paper, window and coffee bags and tin-tie
Vice President, General Manager: Dan Vice
Director of Marketing: Barak Bright
Vice President of Sales: Chuck Hathaway
Customer Service Manager: Fredia Hess
Vice President - Operations: Grady Wetherington
Number Employees: 867
Square Footage: 1860000
Parent Co: Packaging Dynamics
Brands:
Cameo
Dubl-Fresh
Dubl-View
Dubl-Wax

19367 **Bags Go Green**
13 Ruths Place
Sequim, WA 98382 360-681-3876
Fax: 360-681-4877 info@bagsgogreen.com
www.bagsgogreen.com
Eco-friendly reusable bags
Marketing: Hena Marrero

19368 **Bailey Controls/ABBation**
29801 Euclid Ave
Wickliffe, OH 44092-1893 440-585-8948
Fax: 440-585-8688 automationinfo@us.abb.com
www.abb.com
Manufacturer and exporter of process control systems including ph sensors and other field instrumentation
Manager: Barbara Sopko
R&D: Brat Smith
CFO: Dave Lucas
Quality Control: Steve Hamnond
Media Relations Manager: Edward Gabosek
Estimated Sales: Below $5 Million
Number Employees: 1-4
Parent Co: Elsag Bailey Process Automation

19369 **Bailey Moore Glazer**
16 Lunar Dr
Woodbridge, CT 06525 203-397-7700
Fax: 203-397-7717 800-443-2362
info@baileymoore.com www.baileymoore.com
Tea and coffee industry espresso machines and accessories, grinders
Partner: John Mooney
Estimated Sales: Less than $500,000
Number Employees: 20-49

19370 **Bailly Showcase & Fixture Company**
2213 Paseo Ct
Las Vegas, NV 89117 702-947-6885
Fax: 323-232-6157 baillyshowcase@tacbell.net
www.bailyshowcase.com
Store fixtures, cabinets and showcases
President: Gus Bailly
Estimated Sales: $1 - 2,500,000
Number Employees: 20

19371 **(HQ)Baird & Bartlett Company**
157 Green Street
Foxboro, MA 02035-2868 508-923-6400
Fax: 508-923-6060 800-752-4958
sales@baird-bartlett.com
www.baird-bartlett.com
Cake collars and cardboard
President: Andrew Poce
CFO: George Whalen
Marketing Director: Andrew Londergan
Sales Director: Darck Ellwood
Plant Manager: Leo Sousa
Purchasing Manager: Lisa Omalley
Estimated Sales: $15 Million
Number Employees: 20
Square Footage: 30000
Type of Packaging: Consumer, Food Service, Private Label, Bulk
Other Locations:
Baird & Bartlett Co.
Edison NJ

19372 **Bake Star**
1881 County Road C
Somerset, WI 54025-7508 763-427-7611
Fax: 763-323-9821 engineering@bakestar.com
www.bakestar.com
Manufacturer and wholesaler/distributor of chocolate spiral shavers, pre-depanners, semi-automatic strawberry cappers, surplus topping removers and UV surface sterilizers
CEO: Sherri Stumpl
President: Gary Hanson
R & D: Roger Hanson
General Manager: Laura Tuckner
Estimated Sales: Below $5 Million
Number Employees: 10
Square Footage: 36000

19373 **Baker Cabinet Company**
2931 Grace Ln Ste A
Costa Mesa, CA 92626 714-540-5515
Fax: 714-540-5515
Wood cabinets and store fixtures
Manager: Jim Thomas
CEO: Tom Ouellette
Estimated Sales: Below $5 Million
Number Employees: 1-4

19374 **Baker Concrete Construction**
900 N Garver Rd
Monroe, OH 45050 513-539-4000
Fax: 513-539-4380 www.bakerconcrete.com
Industrial concrete floor slab systems
President: Daniel Baker
Chief Financial Officer: Tom Bell
Estimated Sales: $324.30 Million
Number Employees: 4000
Square Footage: 27000

19375 **Baker Group**
2220 East Paris Ave SE
Grand Rapids, MI 49546 616-942-4011
Fax: 616-940-1415 800-968-4011
Marketing@BakerGroup.com
www.bakergroup.com
Award-winning foodservice consulting firm that has provided expert support in evaluation, planning and design for over two decades.
President/Principal: James Sukenik
Estimated Sales: $1-2.5 Million
Number Employees: 5-9

19376 **Baker Material HandlingCorporation**
2450 W 5th North St
Summerville, SC 29483-9695 843-875-8000
www.lmh-na.com
President: Ryan Butler
Estimated Sales: $50 - 100 Million
Number Employees: 100-249

19377 **Baker Process**
2929 Allen Parkway
Suite 2100
Houston, TX 77019-2118 508-668-0400
Fax: 508-668-6855 800-229-7447
www.bakerhughes.com/bakerprocess
Estimated Sales: $1 - 5 Million
Number Employees: 20-49
Parent Co: Baker Huges

19378 **Baker Process**
Neponset Avenue
South Walpole, MA 02071 508-668-0400
Fax: 508-668-6855
Walpole_bakerprocess@bakerhughes.com
www.bakerhughes.com/bakerprocess
Photo/graphics centrifuges and dryers, and filters with video overview of company
Estimated Sales: $420 Million
Number Employees: 1000

19379 **Baker Sheet Metal Corporation**
3541 Argonne Ave
Norfolk, VA 23509 757-853-4325
Fax: 757-855-6252 800-909-4325
john@bakersheetmetal.com
www.bakersheetmetal.com
A fabricator of custom and standard stainless steel products including worktables, sinks, tables, worktables and workstations, shelves and shelving, countertops, furniture, range hoods, cabinets, galley furniture, food service linespartitions
President: John Faircloth
Treasurer: Randy Bristow
CFO: R E Baker
Quality Control: C Winkler
Sales Director: John Kronske
Plant Manager: Paul Johnson
Estimated Sales: $10 - 20 Million
Number Employees: 50-99
Square Footage: 50000

19380 **Bakers Choice Products**
P.O.Box 236
Railroad Avenue Ext.
Beacon Falls, CT 06403 203-720-1000
Fax: 203-720-1004
Manufacturer, importer and exporter of sanitary food containers and cups for candy, cookie and baking; also, hot dog trays
Estimated Sales: $1 - 5 Million
Number Employees: 1 to 4
Square Footage: 60000
Parent Co: Reynolds Metals Company
Brands:
Baker's Choice
Chef's Choice

19381 **Bakers Pride Oven Company**
145 Huguenot St Ste Mz1
New Rochelle, NY 10801 914-576-0745
Fax: 914-576-0605 800-431-2745
sales@bakerspride.com www.bakerspride.com
Manufacturer and exporter of char-broilers and pizza and counter top ovens
President: Hylton Jonas
VP: Tom Marston
Technical Writer: Daniel J Rivera
Quality Manager: Jim Ponnwitz
Estimated Sales: $20-50 Million
Number Employees: 100-249
Parent Co: APW/WYOTT Food Service Equipment
Brands:
Bakers Pride

19382 **Bakery Associates**
PO Box 535
Setauket, NY 11733 631-751-4156
Fax: 631-751-4156 yinfo@bakeryassociates.net
www.bakeryassociates.net
Computerized bakery systems and commerical bakery equipment including ovens, oven loaders and unloaders
President: John Granger
Estimated Sales: $1-2.5 Million
Number Employees: 1-4

19383 **Bakery Crafts**
P.O.Box 37
West Chester, OH 45071 513-942-0862
Fax: 513-942-3835 800-543-1673
info@bakerycrafts.com www.bakerycrafts.com
Cake decorations: kits, edible decorations, candles, and bakery supplies
President: San Guttman
Head of Marketing: Anne Rueho
Head of Sales: Keith Murcum
Head of Public Relations: Tony Dirheimer
Estimated Sales: $5 - 10 Million
Number Employees: 100-249

19384 **Bakery Equipment Service**
118 Nevin Ave
Richmond, CA 94801 510-233-8265
Fax: 510-236-7600 800-842-4005
bes-webmaster@exclusive-ent.com
www.bakery-equip.com
President: Kenneth Lind
Estimated Sales: $5 - 10 Million
Number Employees: 10-19

19385 **Bakery Innovative**
139 North Ocean Ave
Patchogue, NY 11772-2018 631-758-3081
Fax: 631-758-3779 sales@bit-corp.com
www.bit-corp.com
Software and automation: applying and installing computer and programmable controller automation for bakeries and food plants
President: Robert White

Estimated Sales: $2.5-5 Million
Number Employees: 10-19

19386 Bakery Machinery & Fabrication
307 Bakery Ave
Peru, IL 61354 815-224-1306
Fax: 815-224-1396 cjbarnes@insightbb.com
www.bakerymachine.com

New and remanufactured bakery machinery for the cookie, cracker, snack food and pet food industry
President: Cloyd Barnes
Estimated Sales: $1 - 2.5 000,000
Number Employees: 20-49

19387 Bakery Machinery Dealers
908 Colin Drive
Holbrook, NY 11741 631-567-6666
Fax: 631-567-6703

Bagel making and baking equipment
National Sales Manager: Rick Morrison
Number Employees: 12
Square Footage: 8000

19388 Bakery Refrigeration & Services
1125 Old Dixie Highway
Lake Park, FL 33403-2348 561-882-1655
Fax: 561-842-8106 waltman@flips.net
President: William Altman
Estimated Sales: Less than $500,000
Number Employees: 20-49

19389 Bakery Systems
7246 Beach Dr SW 1
Ocean Isle Beach, NC 28469 910-575-2253
Fax: 910-575-5057 800-526-2253
bakerysystems@juno.com
Importer, exporter and wholesaler/distributor of bakery equipment nd supplies
President: Hayden O'Neil
Sales Manager: Lee Wagner
Estimated Sales: $2.5 Million
Number Employees: 5-9
Square Footage: 1000

19390 Bakeware Coatings
2915 Wilmarco Avenue
Baltimore, MD 21223-3223 410-664-2211
Fax: 410-664-1766

Coatings for baking pans and equipment

19391 Baking Machines
4577b Las Positas Road
Livermore, CA 94551-9615 925-449-3369
Fax: 925-449-2144 info@bakingmachines.com
www.bakingmachines.com
Bagel, roll and variety systems, sheeter makeup lines, tortilla equipment, troughs, elevators, baking pans and carts, reciprocators, dustets, reservoirs, etc.; also, custom design engineering services available
President: James Long
VP of Sales: J William Long
Estimated Sales: $10-20 Million
Number Employees: 50-99
Square Footage: 15000

19392 Baking Technology Systems
5243 Royal Woods Pkwy # 120
Tucker, GA 30084-3081 770-270-5911
Fax: 770-270-5913 rmiller@baketech.com
www.baketech.com
VP: Bob Miller
Sales Project Manager: Ben Marcum
Vice President, Director of Operations: Robert Miller
Purchasing Manager: Glenda Arrington
Estimated Sales: $1 Million
Number Employees: 10-19

19393 Bakipan
9251 Van Horne Way
Richmond, BC V6X 1W2
Canada 604-278-1762
Fax: 604-278-3697 sales@bakipan.com
www.bakipan.com

Estimated Sales: $1 - 5 Million

19394 Bakon Food Equipment
10117 Sepulveda Boulevard
Suite 205
Mission Hills, CA 91345-2600 818-895-7303
Fax: 818-892-1095 800-TRY-BAKO
bakonusa@aol.com www.zeelandernetnl/bakon
Bakery equipment, glaze sprayers, chocolate machines, tartlet machine, whipping cream machine
Estimated Sales: 700000
Number Employees: 2

19395 Bal Seal Engineering Company
19650 Pauling
Foothill Ranch, CA 92610 949-460-2100
Fax: 949-460-2300 800-366-1006
sales@balseal.com www.balseal.com
Manufacturer and exporter of spring loaded PTFE seals
President: Rob Sjostedt
Sales Director: Michael Anderson
Estimated Sales: $20 - 50 Million
Number Employees: 100-249

19396 Bal/Foster Glass Container Company
1 Glass Pl
Port Allegany, PA 16743-1154 814-642-2521
Fax: 814-642-3204 www.sgcontainers.com
Manufacturer and exporter of glass bottles and jars
Plant Manager: Ed Stewart
Estimated Sales: $1 - 5 Million
Number Employees: 250-499

19397 Balchem Corporation
52 Sunrise Park Rd
New Hampton, NY 10958 845-326-5600
Fax: 845-326-5742 877-222-8811
bcp@balchem.com www.balchem.com
Extensive line of encapsulated ingredients
CEO: Dino A Rossi
Applications Specialist: Terry Bell
Customer Relations Product Specialist: Cheryl Pasiut
New Ventures Development Leader: Carl Pacifico
Estimated Sales: I
Number Employees: 250-499

19398 Baldewein Company
9109 Belden Avenue
Lake Forrest, IL 60045 847-455-1686
Fax: 847-455-1706 800-424-5544
info@baldeweinco.com www.baldeweinco.com
Manufacturer and exporter of food processing equipment including sanitary fittings, pumps, valves, hose assemblies, brushes, steelware and steam and water mixers
President: Valentin R Baldewein Jr
Sales: Tina Sanders
Treasurer: Val Baldwewin
Estimated Sales: Below $5 Million
Number Employees: 10
Square Footage: 40000
Brands:
Alpha Laval Flo
Lightnin
S.S.
S.S. Ware
Sani-Tech
Sparta
Strahman
Thermo-Tech
Tri-Clover
Vollrath

19399 Baldor Electric Company
5711 R.S. Boreham, Jr. St.
P.O. Box 2400
Fort Smith, AR 72901 479-646-4711
Fax: 479-648-5792 www.baldor.com
Marketers, designers and manufacturers of industrial electric motors, mechanical power transmission products, drive and generators, specializing in products for the food and pharmaceutical industries. A member of the ABB group since2011.
President: Ronald Tucker
CEO: Ronald Tucker
VP, Finance and Corporate Secretary: Larry Johnston
EVP: Edward Ralston
VP, Channel Management: Chris Keyser
VP Marketing: Tracy Long
Vice President, Sales: Randy Colip
COO, Baldor Operations: Wayne Thurman
Estimated Sales: $2.0 Million
Number Employees: 5,000-9,999
Square Footage: 4000000

19400 Baldor Electric Company
5711 R.S. Boreham, Jr. St
P.O. Box 2400
Fort Smith, AR 72901 479-646-4711
Fax: 479-648-5792 800-241-2886
rjfleig@ra.rockwell.com www.reliance.com
Controls, energy management
Chief Engineer: Alex McCutcheon
Estimated Sales: $.5 - 1 million
Number Employees: 5-9

19401 Baldwin Belting and Light Weight Belting
2306 Washington Ave N
Minneapolis, MN 55411 612-338-5070
Fax: 612-338-4877 800-897-1964
ghansen@baldwinsupply.com
www.baldwinsupply.com

President: Dave La Rue
Estimated Sales: $3 - 5 Million
Number Employees: 10-19

19402 Baldwin Richardson Foods
20201 S La Grange Rd, Ste 200
Frankfort, IL 60423 815-464-9994
Fax: 815-464-9995 866-644-2732
www.brfoods.com

Founded in 1916. Liquid ingredient manufacturer specializing in signature sauces, dessert toppings, beverage/pancake syrups, specialty fruit fillings and condiments
President/CEO: Eric Johnson
CFO: Evelyn White
Director: Michele Salva
Purchasing: Paula Bell
Estimated Sales: $5 - 10,000,000
Number Employees: 200
Square Footage: 900000
Type of Packaging: Consumer, Food Service, Private Label, Bulk
Brands:
Baldwin Ice Cream
Mrs Richardson Toppings
Nance's Mustards
Nance's Wing Sauce & Condiments

19403 Baldwin Staub
1351 Riverview Dr
San Bernardino, CA 92408 909-799-9950
Fax: 909-796-8297
info@systems-technology-inc.com
www.systems-technology-inc.com
Manufacturer and exporter of packaging machinery
President: John St John
CFO: Steve Fox
Estimated Sales: $10 - 20 Million
Number Employees: 50-99
Square Footage: 40000
Parent Co: Baldwin Technology Corporation

19404 Baldwin/Priesmeyer
1235 Hanley Industrial Ct
Saint Louis, MO 63144 314-535-2800
Fax: 314-535-2887 www.baldwinflags.com
Banners, flags, flagpoles and advertising specialties
Manager: Jim Schaper
CFO: Jannet Alexender
VP: Jim Schaper
Estimated Sales: $30-50 Million
Number Employees: 5-9
Parent Co: Baldwin Regalia

19405 Balemaster
980 Crown Ct
Crown Point, IN 46307 219-663-4525
Fax: 219-663-4591 sales@balemaster.com
www.balemaster.com

Automatic horizontal balers
President: Cornel Raab Jr
VP Sales/Marketing: Samuel Finlay
Estimated Sales: $300,000-500,000
Number Employees: 1-4

19406 Ball Corporation
9300 W 108th Cir
Broomfield, CO 80021 920-261-5105
Fax: 720-273-7401 corpinfo@ball.com
www.ball.com

Aluminum and steel beverage and food containers; also, lids, metal plastic food and beverage packaging, steel household packaging, plastic pails, ball aerospace
CEO: David Hoover
CFO: Ray Seabrook
Human Resources: Susan Normington
Marketing: Jim Peterson
Public Relations: Scott McCarty
Estimated Sales: $7.39 Billion
Number Employees: 10,000
Type of Packaging: Consumer, Food Service, Private Label

19407 **Ball Design Group**
1170 E Champlain Dr
Suite 120
Fresno, CA 93720-5026 559-434-6100
Fax: 559-447-8596 john@balldesign.com
www.balldesign.com
Log and brand mark design, advertising website design, package and label design, and trade show displays for the produce and fruit industry
President: John Ball
Estimated Sales: $1 - 3 Million
Number Employees: 5-9

19408 **Ball Foster Glass**
5195 Fermi Drive
Fairfield, CA 94534-1607 707-863-4061
Fax: 707-863-4042 www.sgcontainer.com
Glass bottles and containers for food, wine, liquor and beer
Estimated Sales: $50-100 Million
Number Employees: 100
Parent Co: Saint-Gobain

19409 **Ball Foster Glass Container Company**
1000 N Mission St
Sapulpa, OK 74066-3149 918-224-1440
Fax: 918-224-5280 us.verallia.com
Soft drink and tea glass bottles
Quality Control: Robert Beets
Plant Manager: Pat Hogan
Estimated Sales: $1 - 5 Million
Number Employees: 250-499
Square Footage: 4800000
Parent Co: American National Can Company

19410 **Ball Glass Container Corporation**
4000 Arden Drive
El Monte, CA 91731-1806 626-448-9831
Fax: 626-279-3225
Glass jars, bottles and containers
Plant Manager: Rich O'Neil
Estimated Sales: $50-100 Million
Number Employees: 250-499
Parent Co: St. Gobain

19411 **(HQ)Ballantyne Food ServiceEquipment**
4350 McKinley St
Omaha, NE 68112 402-453-4444
Fax: 402-453-7238 800-424-1215
www.ballantyne-omaha.com
Manufacturer and exporter of commercial restaurant equipment including electric pressure and gas pressure fryers, gourmet grills, cook and hold barbecue ovens, smokers and rotisseries
President/CEO: John Wilmers
Senior VP: Ray Boegner
VP: Michael Nulty
Estimated Sales: $1 - 5 Million
Number Employees: 100-249
Square Footage: 200000
Parent Co: Ballantyne of Omaha
Type of Packaging: Food Service, Private Label
Brands:
Ballatyne
Ballatyne Smokers
Bpe 2000

19412 **Ballard & Wolfe Company**
519 Interstate 30 #102
Rockwall, TX 75087-5408 214-704-8451
Fax: 817-652-1245 dbruner@ballardwolfe.com
www.ballardwolfe.com
Ice cream equipment
Estimated Sales: Below 1 Million
Number Employees: 2

19413 **Balluff**
8125 Holton Dr
Florence, KY 41042 859-727-2200
Fax: 859-727-4823 800-543-8390
balluff@balluff.com www.balluff.com
Sensor, transducers and ID systems for automation
CEO: Kent Howard
Number Employees: 100-249

19414 **(HQ)Bally Block Company**
PO Box 188
30 South Seventh Street
Bally, PA 19503 610-845-7511
Fax: 610-845-7726 bbc@ballyblock.com
www.ballyblock.com
Manufacturer and exporter of cutting benches, blocks, tables and boards
President: James Reichart
Vice President of Sales and Marketing: Joe Barbercheck
Vice President Sales & Marketing: Pat Stanley
Vice President, Production: Emmet Wood
Estimated Sales: $5-10 Million
Number Employees: 50-99
Square Footage: 500000

19415 **Bally Refrigerated Boxes**
135 Little Nine Rd
Morehead City, NC 28557 252-240-2829
Fax: 252-240-0384 800-242-2559
ballysales@ballyrefboxes.com
www.ballyrefboxes.com
Walk-in cooler and freezers, refrigerated buildings, modular structures, blast chillers and refrigeration for the foodservice and scientific industries.
President: Michael Coyle
Sales Manager: William Strompf
Plant Manager: Alan Summers
Purchasing Manager: William Stomps
Estimated Sales: $20-50 Million
Number Employees: 100-249
Parent Co: United Refrigeration
Type of Packaging: Food Service
Other Locations:
Bally Refrigerated Boxes
King of Prussia PA
Brands:
Thermo-Plug

19416 **Ballymore Company**
220 Garfield Ave
West Chester, PA 19380-4512 610-696-3250
Fax: 610-593-8615 ballymore@icdc.com
www.ballymore.com
Safety ladders, hydraulic lifts and special work platforms
Manager: Tom Richardson
Estimated Sales: $5 - 10 Million
Number Employees: 20-49

19417 **Balston Filter Products**
260 Neck Road
Haverhill, MA 01835-8030 978-374-7400
Fax: 978-374-7070 800-343-4048
www.whatman.com
Industrial filter products
President: Wood Rinz
Estimated Sales: $10-20 Million
Number Employees: 100-249

19418 **Balston/Whatman**
PO Box 1262
Tewksbury, MA 01876-0962 978-858-0505
Fax: 978-858-0625 support@balston.com
www.balston.com
Estimated Sales: $20-50 Million
Number Employees: 100-249

19419 **Baltimore Aircoil Company**
7600 Dorsey Run Road
Jessup, MD 20794 410-799-6200
Fax: 410-799-6416 info@baltimoreaircoil.com
www.baltaircoil.com
President: Steve Duerwachter
Quality Control: John Hawkins
CFO: Robert Landstra
Number Employees: 1,000-4,999

19420 **Baltimore Aircoil Company**
7600 Dorsey Run Rd
Jessup, MD 20794 410-799-6200
Fax: 410-799-6416 info@baltimoreaircoil.com
www.baltimoreaircoil.com
Manufacturer and marketer of heat transfer and ice thermal storage products that conserve resources and respect the environment.
President: Steve Duerwachter
Estimated Sales: $17 Million
Number Employees: 1,000-4,999
Parent Co: Amsted Industries
Brands:
Bacount
Bacross
Baltibond
Baltidrive
Easy Connect
Ejector
Energy Miser
High K
Ice Chiller
Ice Logic
Iobio
M Logic

19421 **Baltimore Sign Company**
472 Cedar Haven Road
Arnold, MD 21012-1167 410-276-1500
Fax: 410-675-2420 baltsign@erols.com
www.baltimoresign.com
Signs, banners, displays, etc.; also, screen process and offset printing and collation
President: John Ferretti
Plant Manager: Hank Barret
Account Director: Kathie Schisler
Estimated Sales: $5 - 10 Million
Number Employees: 50-99

19422 **Baltimore Spice**
9740 Reisterstown Rd
Owings Mills, MD 21117 410-363-3209
Fax: 410-363-6619 800-376-0316
kbittorie@baltimorespice.com
www.baltimorespice.com
Spices
President: Jack M Irvin Jr
R&D: Elizabeth Morris
Quality Control: Joe Walters
Estimated Sales: $5 - 10 Million
Number Employees: 100-249

19423 **Baltimore Tape Products**
27 W Obrecht Rd
Sykesville, MD 21784-7702 410-795-0063
Printed and converted pressure sensitive labels and tape
President: Jeff H Remmel
Estimated Sales: Less than $500,000
Number Employees: 1 to 4
Square Footage: 1000

19424 **Bambeck Systems**
1921 Carnegie Ave
Santa Ana, CA 92705 949-250-3100
Fax: 949-757-1610 800-334-3101
webmaster@bambecksystems.com
www.bambecksystems.com
President: Robert Bambeck
CFO: Anthony Fazzio
Quality Control: Anthony Fazzio
Estimated Sales: $5 - 10 Million
Number Employees: 20-49

19425 **Bamco Belting Products**
6 Andrews Street
PO Box 8678
Greenville, SC 29604 864-269-9750
Fax: 864-269-9754 800-258-2358
sales@bamcobelting.com
www.bamcobelting.com
Distributor of flat transmission belting and textile, conveyor belting, and hose belt conveyors
President: Leonard Chace IV
Estimated Sales: $5 - 10 Million
Number Employees: 10-19
Type of Packaging: Bulk

19426 **Bancroft Bag**
425 Bancroft Blvd
West Monroe, LA 71292 318-387-2550
Fax: 318-324-2318 bbisales@bancroftbag.com
www.bancroftbag.com
Paper bags
President: Louis Rothschild
Executive Assistant: Teresa Lucas
Estimated Sales: $50 - 100 Million
Number Employees: 250-499

19427 **Banner Chemical Corporation**
111 Hill Street
Orange, NJ 07050-3901 973-676-2900
Fax: 973-676-4564 info@bannerchemical.com
www.bannerchemical.com
Cleaning products and sanitary maintenance chemicals including glass cleaners, floor cleaners, wates and strippers, kitchen and bathroom cleaners, disinfectants and many other chemicals for food service and industry.
President: Stanley Reichel
VP: David Herman
Estimated Sales: $2.5 - 5 Million
Number Employees: 5-9

19428 **Banner Day Company**
1840 N Michigan Ave
Saginaw, MI 48602 877-837-0584
Fax: 989-775-1309 info@banner-day.com
www.banner-day.com
Project Engineer: Brian Lewis
Estimated Sales: $5 - 10 Million
Number Employees: 20-49

19429 **Banner Engineering Corporation**
9714 10th Ave N
Plymouth, MN 55441 763-544-3164
Fax: 763-544-3123 888-373-6767
sensors@bannerengineering.com
www.bannerengineering.com
Photoelectric sensor, safety light curtains, ultrasonics, measurement and inspection sensors, safety modules, safety switches, fiber optics and vision sensors
President: Robert Fayfield
CFO: Larry Evans
R&D: Neal Schumacher
Marketing: Christian E Benson
Sales: Charley Rapp
Estimated Sales: $50-100 Million
Number Employees: 250-499
Square Footage: 100000
Brands:
A Gage
Beam-Array
Beam-Tracker
Duo-Touch
Ez-Beam
Ez-Beam
Ez-Screen
Econo-Beam
L Gage
Machine-Guard
Maxi-Amo
Maxi-Beam
Micro-Amp
Micro-Screen
Mini-Array
Mini-Beam
Mini-Screen
Multi-Beam
Multi-Screen
Omni-Beam
Opto Touch
Pico Guard
Picodot
Presence Plus
Thin-Pak
Ultra-Beam
Ultra-Beam
Vall-Beam
Valu-Beam
World-Beam

19430 **Banner Equipment Company**
1370 Bungalow Rd
Morris, IL 60450 815-941-9600
Fax: 815-941-9700 800-621-4625
internetsales@bannerbeer.com
www.bannerbeer.com
Manufacturer and exporter of draft beer tapping and dispensing equipment
President: James Groh
VP: Michael Tannhauser
Estimated Sales: $10 - 20 Million
Number Employees: 50-99
Square Footage: 40000
Brands:
Insta-Balance
Perfecta Line
Perfecta Pour

19431 **Banner Idea**
1400 Quail St
Newport Beach, CA 92660-2730 949-559-6600
Fax: 949-559-0861
Flags, pennants, banners and signs
Estimated Sales: less than $500,000
Number Employees: 5-9

19432 **Banner Packaging**
3550 Moser St
Oshkosh, WI 54901 920-303-2300
Fax: 920-233-8159
Flexible packaging material including three-layer co-extrusion and recloseable bags
Estimated Sales: $1 - 5,000,000
Number Employees: 1000
Parent Co: Beemis Company

19433 **Bannerland**
13360 Firestone Blvd Ste Ee
Santa Fe Springs, CA 90670-7040
Fax: 714-554-0579 800-654-0294
bannerland@aol.com www.bannerland.com
Banners, flags and poly pennants; also, silk screening available
Manager: Travis Townsend
Marketing/Sales: Terry Melanson
Plant Manager: Mike Slater
Estimated Sales: $26 Million
Number Employees: 10-19
Square Footage: 10000
Parent Co: AAA Flag & Banner

19434 **Bar Equipment Corporation of America**
7300 Flores Street
Downey, CA 90242 323-838-1770
Fax: 323-838-1778 888-870-2322
sales@lynxgrills.com www.lynxgrills.com
Bar equipment including undercounter refrigerators, bottle coolers, mug frosters and hand sinks
President: Michael Edwards
Director Sales: Dale Seiden
Estimated Sales: $3 - 5 Million
Number Employees: 5-9

19435 **Bar Maid Corporation**
2950 NW 22nd Terrace
Pompano Beach, FL 33069 954-960-1468
Fax: 800-457-5612 info@barmaidwashers.com
www.barmaidwashers.com
Manufacturer and exporter of portable, submersible and upright electric glass and muffin pan washers; also, low-sud detergents and sanitizers
President: George E Shepherd
CEO: Diane Michaud
Marketing Director: Tammie Rice
Estimated Sales: Below $5 Million
Number Employees: 10-19
Number of Brands: 2
Square Footage: 8000
Brands:
Bar Maid
Losuds

19436 **Bar NA, Inc.**
PO Box 6599
Champaign, IL 61826-6599 217-687-4810
Fax: 217-687-4830 rboodram@baraninc.com
www.baraninc.com
Manufacturer, distribution and installation of small to medium capacity equipment for soy foods and vegetable oilseeds production and processing
President: Ramlakhan Boodram
Estimated Sales: $1-2.5 Million
Number Employees: 10-19

19437 **Bar-B-Q Woods**
800 E 14th Street
Newton, KS 67114-5700 316-284-0300
Fax: 316-283-8371 800-528-0819
bbqwoods@southwind.net www.flavorwood.com
Compressed wood in a can which is heated in a home Bar-B-Q grill to produce natural smoke blowing
President: Gary Hawkey
CEO: James Beery
Estimated Sales: $1-2.5,000,000
Number Employees: 4
Square Footage: 5000
Type of Packaging: Consumer, Food Service, Private Label, Bulk

19438 **Bar-Maid Minibars**
362 Midland Ave
Garfield, NJ 07026-1736 973-478-7070
Fax: 973-478-2106 800-227-6243
sales@bar-maid.com www.bar-maid.com
Refrigerators, minibars and freezers.
President: George Steele
CEO: James Steele
Vice President: John Steele
Marketing Director: Ken Lasini
Sales Director: K Zanda
Public Relations: Mike Castle
Estimated Sales: $50-100 Million
Number Employees: 50-99
Square Footage: 80000
Brands:
Bar-Maids

19439 **Bar-Ron Industries**
58 Bryant Drive
Livingston, NJ 07039-1725 973-535-1406
Fax: 973-597-1996 rasi@grillit.com
www.grillit.com
Owner: Barry N Rein
Sales: Cindy Blanga
Sales: Rafi Blanga
Estimated Sales: $3 - 5 Million
Number Employees: 20-49
Brands:
Grillit 1200
Grillit 12x12

19440 **Barbeque Wood Flavors Enterprises**
141 Lyons Road
Ennis, TX 75119 972-875-8391
Fax: 972-875-8872 www.bbqwoodflavors.com
Manufacturer and exporter of wood firelogs
President and CEO: George C Wartsbaugh
Sales Manager: Charles Wartsbaugh
Estimated Sales: $5 - 10 Million
Number Employees: 10
Square Footage: 92000
Parent Co: Stephen Weber Production Company

19441 **Barbour Threads**
128 W 7th St
Anniston, AL 36201-5645 256-237-9461
Fax: 256-237-0646
Industrial nets and sports nets
President: Tony Foran
Plant Manager: Jim Landers
Estimated Sales: $5 - 10 Million
Number Employees: 50-99
Square Footage: 424000

19442 **Barclay & Associates**
PO Box 210931
Arlington, TX 76006 817-274-5734
Fax: 817-795-2174 tmbarclay@aol.com
Consultant providing automation solutions
President: T Michael Barclay
Number Employees: 3
Brands:
Margin Minder Software
Watch Dog

19443 **Barco Machine Vision**
3078 Prospect Park Drive
Rancho Cordova, CA 95670 916-376-0316
Fax: 916-376-0318 888-414-7226
machine.vision.na@barco.com www.barco.com
President & Chief Executive Officer: Eric Van Zele
Chief Financial Officer: Carl Peeters
GM International Sales: Ney Corsino
Chief Human Resources Officer: Jan Van Acoleyen
Chief Operating Officer: Filip Pintelon
Estimated Sales: $59,000,000
Parent Co: Barco

19444 **Barco Machine Vision**
3059 Premiere Parkway
Duluth, GA 30097 704-392-9371
Fax: 704-399-5588 sales.ba@barco.com
www.barco.com
Optical and X-ray sorting inspection equipment
Chairman: Herman Daems
Operations: Danny Claeys
VP Sales/Marketing: Richard McConeghy
Estimated Sales: $5-10 Million
Number Employees: 10-19
Parent Co: Barco

Brands:
Elbicon
Pulsarr

19445 Barcoding Inc
2220 Boston St
Fl 2
Baltimore, MD 21231 410-385-8532
Fax: 410-385-8559 888-412-7226
info@barcoding.com www.barcoding.com
Barcoding Inc works with companies within the Food and Beverage Industry to streamline their operations through the implementation of barcode and RFID systems.
CEO: Jay Steinmetz
Media/Public Relations: Jon Stroz
Type of Packaging: Consumer

19446 Bardes Plastics
5225 W Clinton Ave
Milwaukee, WI 53223 414-354-5300
Fax: 414-354-6331 800-558-5161
sales@bardesplastics.com
www.bardesplastics.com
Plastic and display boxes, lids, covers, food trays, sleeves, beaded rounds and cylindrical trays
President: Michael Heyer
CEO: Randolph Hamner
Sales: Steve Kopiske
Estimated Sales: $5-10 Million
Number Employees: 20-49
Square Footage: 80000
Type of Packaging: Consumer, Food Service, Private Label, Bulk

19447 Bardo Abrasives
1666 Summerfield St
Ridgewood, NY 11385 718-456-6400
Fax: 718-366-2104 www.bardoabrasives.com
Manufacturer and exporter of blending, finishing and buffing wheels for food processing equipment
President: Edwin F Doyle
VP: Ted Wood
Estimated Sales: $20 - 50 Million
Number Employees: 100-249
Square Footage: 90000
Parent Co: Barker Brothers
Brands:
Bardo Flex
Bardo Flex Deburring Wheels
Barker Buffs

19448 Bareny Packaging Corporation
PO Box 831
Menomonee Falls, WI 53052-0831 262-251-8787
Fax: 262-251-4710 tom@berenzpacking.com
www.berenzpackaging.com
Corrugated containers
President: Tom Berenz
Estimated Sales: $10 - 20 Million
Number Employees: 20-49

19449 Bargreen-Ellingson
6626 Tacoma Mall Blvd # B
Tacoma, WA 98409-9002 253-475-9201
Fax: 253-473-1875 800-322-4441
becatalog@bargreen.com www.bargreen.com
Restaurant equipment and supplies; interior and engineering design services available
President: Paul Ellingson
President: Paul G Ellingson
Estimated Sales: $20 - 50 Million
Number Employees: 50-99

19450 Barker Company
703 Franklin St
P.O. Box 478
Keosauqua, IA 52565 319-293-3777
Fax: 319-293-3776 sales@bakercompany.com
www.barkercompany.com
Manufacturer and importer of refrigerated, hot and dry display cases
President: Pat Mahon
Estimated Sales: $10 - 20,000,000
Number Employees: 250-499
Square Footage: 42000

19451 Barker Wire Products
PO Box 457
Keosauqua, IA 52565-0457 319-293-3176
Fax: 319-293-3182 www.angolawire.com
Custom wire shelves, baskets and racks
Sales Manager: Roy Abriani
Plant Manager: Larry Begley
Estimated Sales: $10-20 Million
Number Employees: 50-99
Square Footage: 290000
Parent Co: Angola Wire Products
Other Locations:
Barker Wire Products
Angola IN

19452 Barkley Filing Supplies
PO Box 15789
Hattiesburg, MS 39404-5789 601-545-2200
Fax: 800-423-7589 800-647-3070
rmenter@intlfiling.com www.barkleyfiling.com
Stationery including envelopes and pressure sensitive labels
President: Joseph Compitello
Number Employees: 475

19453 Barksdale
3211 Fruitland Ave
Vernon, CA 90058 323-589-6181
Fax: 323-589-3463 mmueller@barksdale.com
www.barksdale.com
President: Ian Dodd
Estimated Sales: G
Number Employees: 100-249
Parent Co: Crane Company

19454 Barliant & Company
319 E Van Emmon St
Yorkville, IL 60560 630-553-6992
Fax: 630-553-6908 barliant@aol.com
www.barliant.com
Domestic and export broker of new and used food processing equipment including meat and poultry, as well as appraisals, liquidations, auctions and asset management programs.
Owner: Scott Swanson
Sales Manager: Kevin Chapman
Estimated Sales: $1.5 Million
Number Employees: 5
Square Footage: 152000

19455 Barlo Signs/Screengraphics
158 Greeley Street
Hudson, NH 03051-3422 603-882-2638
Fax: 603-882-7680 800-227-5674
randy@barlosigns.com www.barlosigns.com
Electric and interior point of purchase signs; also, screen printing available
VP: Randy Bartlett
Estimated Sales: $10-20 Million
Number Employees: 100-250
Parent Co: Barlo Group

19456 Barn Furniture Mart
6206 Sepulveda Blvd.
Van Nuys, CA 91411-1110 818-785-4253
888-302-2276
www.barnfurnituremart.com
Manufacturer and exporter of chairs, barstools, bars, tables and booths; custom designing services available
President: Mildred Tuberman
VP: Leon Tuberman
Number Employees: 45
Square Footage: 840000

19457 Barnant Company
28092 W Commercial Ave
Lake Barrington, IL 60010 847-381-7050
Fax: 847-381-7053 800-637-3739
barnant@barnant.com www.barnant.com
Thermometers, tubing and vacuum pumps, controllers, data loggers, flow meters and mixers, and OEM pumps
President: Duncan Ross
Marketing: Greg Johnson
Marketing Director: Gregg Johnson
Estimated Sales: $20-50 Million
Number Employees: 100-249

19458 Barnebey & Sutcliffe Corporation
835 North Cassady Ave
Columbus, OH 43219-2203 614-258-9501
Fax: 614-258-0222 www.bscairfiltration.com
Incharge: David Evans
CEO: William W Vogelhuber
Number Employees: 100-249
Parent Co: Calgon Carbon Corporation

19459 Barnes Machine Company
2462 Emerson Avenue S
Saint Petersburg, FL 33712-1644 727-327-9452
Fax: 727-323-8791 sales@barnesmachineco.com
www.barnesmachineco.com
Packaging machinery including carton erecting, closing, paper box, carton case, box sealing, etc
President: John Barnes
President: John Barnes
CFO: Carla Barnes
Quality Control: John Barnes
Estimated Sales: Below $5 Million
Number Employees: 10 to 19
Square Footage: 15000
Brands:
Barnes Machine Company Bamco

19460 Barnstead/Thermolyne Corporation
P.O.Box 797
Dubuque, IA 52004-0797 563-556-2241
Fax: 563-589-0516 800-553-0039
mkt@barnsteadthermolyne.com
www.barnstead.com
Laboratory equipment
President: Duncan Ross
CEO: Guy Broadband
Quality Control: Mike Reagan
Marketing Communication Officer: Kathy Regan
Estimated Sales: $50 - 100 Million
Number Employees: 250-499

19461 Baron Spice
1440 Kentucky Ave
St Louis, MO 63110 314-535-9020
Fax: 314-535-7227 sales@baronspices.com
www.baronspices.com
Wholesaler/distributor and contract packager of spices, seasonings, herbs, flavors and extracts
President: Jerry Wiegers
Estimated Sales: $5-10 Million
Number Employees: 10-19
Number of Products: 300
Square Footage: 220000
Type of Packaging: Food Service, Private Label, Bulk
Brands:
Baron

19462 Barr Engineering Company
4700 W 77th St Ste 200
Minneapolis, MN 55435 952-832-2600
Fax: 952-832-2601 800-632-2277
askbarr@barr.com www.barr.com
Consulting engineering services
President: Doug Connell
R&D: Karin Clemon
CEO: Doug Conell
CFO: Terry Krohnverg
Estimated Sales: $20 - 30 Million
Number Employees: 250-499

19463 Barr Refrigeration
1423 Planeview Dr
Oshkosh, WI 54904 920-231-1711
Fax: 920-231-1701 888-661-0871
info@barrinc.com www.barrinc.com
Refrigeration equipment
Vice President: Jamie Barr
VP Marketing: Steve Morehead
Number Employees: 55

19464 Barr Refrigeration
1423 Planeview Drive
Oshkosh, WI 54904 920-231-1711
Fax: 920-231-1701 888-661-0871
info@barrinc.com www.barrinc.com
Blast freezing units, compressors, condensors, refrigerated structures, refrigeration systems, walk-in coolers and freezers
Sales: Erick Allatore
Estimated Sales: D
Number Employees: 30

19465 Barr-Rosin
92 Boulevard Prevost
Boisbriand, QC J7G 2S2
Canada 450-437-5252
Fax: 450-437-6740 800-561-8305
sales.barr-rosin.ca@gea.com
www.barr-rosin.com
President: Dell Lonvrgan
Quality Control: Haldgoudrvaulg Goudrvaulg
R & D: Paull Goudrvaulg

Number Employees: 10

19466 Barrett Industrial Trucks

240 N Prospect St
Marengo, IL 60152 815-568-5500
Fax: 815-568-0179 nfcsales@nfcna.com
www.nissanforklift.com

President: Takanobu Tokugawa
Estimated Sales: I
Number Employees: 1,000-4,999
Parent Co: Nissan Forklift Corporation, North America

19467 Barrette - Outdoor Livin

7830 Freeway Circle
Middleburg Hts., OH 44130
Fax: 440-891-5267 800-336-2383
paynej@plasticsresearch.com
www.barretteoutdoorliving.com

Manufacturer and exporter of structural foam products, regular and tote trays, pallets, carts, plant displays, produce tables, lattice panels, plastic trellises, plastic arbors and plastic fencing
Manager: Mario Gaudreault
CFO: Nick Kokotovich
Vice President: William Goslin
Marketing Director: Ron Smith
Sales Director: John Payne
Product Manager: Mark Sprague
Purchasing Manager: Steve Armstrong
Number Employees: 100-249
Square Footage: 1400000

19468 Barrow-Agee Laboratories

1555 Three Pl
Memphis, TN 38116-3507 901-332-1590
Fax: 901-398-1518 mhawkins@balabs.com
www.balabs.com

Analytical testing firm offering chemical and microbiological services
President: Lynn Hawkins
VP: Mike Hawkins
VP: John Peden
Estimated Sales: $2.5-5 Million
Number Employees: 20-49

19469 Barrow-Agee Laboratories

1555 Three Place
Memphis, TN 38116-3507 901-332-1590
Fax: 901-398-1518 customerservice@balabs.com
www.balabs.com

Private analytical laboratory
President and CEO: Lynn Hawkins
Estimated Sales: $5 - 10 Million
Number Employees: 20-49

19470 Barry-Wehmiller Companies

820 Forsyth Boulevard
St Louis, MO 63105 314-862-8000
Fax: 314-862-2457 sales@barry-wehmiller.com
www.barrywehmiller.com

Leader in the packaging automation industry, world-wide provider of advanced technologies in filling, closing, converting, labeling, conveying, cartoning, case packing, and shrink-wrapping.
Chairman/CEO: Robert Chapman
President: Phil Ostapowicz
Managing Partner: Robyn Pikey
Director Operations: Bruce Kuebler
Estimated Sales: $440 Million
Number Employees: 1,000-4,999

19471 Barry-Wehmiller Design Group

8020 Forsyth Blvd
Saint Louis, MO 63105 314-862-8000
Fax: 314-862-2457 sales@barry-wehmiller.com
www.barrywehmiller.com

Engineer consultant specializing in turnkey and line monitoring systems and project site management; also, feasibility studies, training programs, electrical control panels, validation, servo-motion control systems, equipmentprocurement and installation services available
President: Phil Ostapowicz
Partner: Robyn Pikey
CEO: Robert H Chapman
Estimated Sales: F
Number Employees: 40
Square Footage: 8000
Parent Co: Barry-Wehmiller Company
Other Locations:
Barry-Wehmiller Design Group
Cuyahoga Falls OH

19472 Bartlett Milling Company

PO Box 831
701 South Center Street
Statesville, NC 28687
Fax: 704-873-8956 800-222-8626
jeffbanks@banksfarm.com
www.bartlettmillingfeed.com

Grain merchandising, flour and feed milling
President: George Bure
Manager: Ashley Glover
Principal: Herman Pekarek
Quality Control Manager: Dan Winslow
Sales Manager: Earl Law
General Manager: Danny Sprouse
Manufacturing Head of Operations: Wayne Speaks
Estimated Sales: $50-100 Million
Number Employees: 100-249
Square Footage: 49705
Parent Co: Bartlett & Company
Type of Packaging: Consumer, Food Service, Private Label, Bulk
Brands:
Diamond Cake
Fine Spun
Palace Pastry
White Rock
Wigwam

19473 Baruch Box Company

85 South Bragg Street
Suite 503
Alexandria, VA 22312 703-642-0472
Fax: 703-941-7645 800-242-6948
ahe@baruchco.com www.baruchco.com

Boxes, crates, and baskets made out of wood. Wire, wicker and combination baskets, terra cotta, porcelain, silverplate
President: Andrew Eyck
Estimated Sales: $2.5 - 5 000,000
Number Employees: 5-9

19474 Base Manufacturing

1118 W Spring St
Monroe, GA 30655 770-207-0002
Fax: 770-207-0101 800-367-0572
www.basemfg.com

Pallet rack systems; also, design and installation available
President: Steve South
Chairman of the Board: Dan South
VP Sales: Lee Bissell
Estimated Sales: $10-20 Million
Number Employees: 100-249
Square Footage: 180000

19475 Basic Adhesives

25 Knickerbocker Ave
Brooklyn, NY 11237 718-497-5200
Fax: 718-366-1425 info@basicadhesives.com
www.basicadhesives.com

President: Yale E Block Block
Estimated Sales: $5 - 10 Million
Number Employees: 60

19476 Basic Concepts

6907 Mount Pleasant Dr
West Bend, WI 53090 262-247-2536
Fax: 262-673-2069 bio@execpc.com
www.execpc.com

SIS-Automatic saltine systems for cheese
President: James C Fischer
Estimated Sales: $1.6 000,000
Number Employees: 5-9

19477 (HQ)Basic Leasing Corporation

12a Port Kearny
Kearny, NJ 07032-4612 973-817-7373

Consultant specializing in the design of industrial kitchens; exporter of ice makers, dishwashers, etc.; importer of ice machines; wholesaler/distributor of equipment and fixtures and frozen drink machines and coffee machines
President: Harold Weber
VP: Johnathan Weber
Estimated Sales: $20-50 Million
Number Employees: 50-99
Square Footage: 28500

19478 Basic Polymers Industrial Flooring Systems

3628 W Holland Ave
Fresno, CA 93722-7808 559-230-1500
Fax: 559-266-6007 877-225-2549
info@basicpolmers.com
www.basicpolymers.com/

Industrial flooring systems product line of which includes urethane, epoxy, MMA, flooring.
Owner: Jose Gonzalez
Sales Representative: Scott Hamilton

19479 Basiloid Products Corporation

312 N East St
Elnora, IN 47529 812-692-5511
Fax: 812-692-5512 866-692-5511
basiloid@dmrtc.net www.basiloid.com

Mechanical lift truck attachments
Owner: Eric Lane
Estimated Sales: $10-20 Million
Number Employees: 10-19

19480 Baskets Extraordinaires

1150 Shames Dr
Westbury, NY 11590 212-929-7259
Fax: 212-929-6124 800-666-1685
presentz@aol.com

Gift baskets
Owner: Michele Triester
*Estimated Sales:*less than $500,000
Number Employees: 5-9

19481 Baskin-Robbins NationalLaboratories

1201 S Victory Blvd
Burbank, CA 91502-2552 818-843-4651
Fax: 818-688-3918 www.31scoops.com

Laboratory providing flavor, color and texture research
Manager: Julie Djigardjian
Director R&D: Patty DeGrazzio
Estimated Sales: $500,000-$1 Million
Number Employees: 10-19

19482 Bassick Casters

959 Highway 95 North
P.O. Box 667
Shiner, TX 77984
888-527-3526
gchumchal@kasparwireworks.com
www.kaselco.com

Sheetmetal, wire and tubing products plus casters, glides, leveling jacks, floor locks, clamps/latches and water treatment facilities
President: Douglas Herber PE
Board Member: Douglas Kaspar
Vice President, Engineering: Bruce Lesikar Ph.D
Consulting Chemist: Paul Morkovsky
Estimated Sales: $500 Million to $1 Billion
Number Employees: 500-999
Square Footage: 500000
Brands:
Diamond Arrow
Honcho
Syncro Lock

19483 BatchMaster

P.O.Box 1303
Fayetteville, AR 72702-1303 479-521-9208
Fax: 479-442-5860 sales@bmaster.com
www.bmaster.com

Owner: Paul Reagan
Estimated Sales: $1 - 3 Million
Number Employees: 5-9

19484 BatchMaster Software Corporation

23191 La Cadena Drive
Suite 101
Laguna Hills, CA 92653 949-583-1646
Fax: 310-799-8833 info@batchmaster.com
www.batchmaster.com

PC-based software products designed specifically for controlling inventory, production, formulation, costing, etc
Owner: David Stanyo
President, Chief Executive Officer: Sahib Dudani
Vice President, General Manager: Ingrid Leon
VP of Sales: Christy Hudson
Technical Specialist: Jeremy Wheaton
Brands:
Batchmaster

19485 Batching Systems
50 Jibsail Dr
Prince Frederick, MD 20678 410-414-8111
Fax: 410-414-8121 800-311-0851
info@BatchingSystems.com
www.batchingsystems.com
Manufacturer and exporter of optical part counting, scanning, filling and batching machines.
President: Donald Wooldridge
Marketing: Raven Easton
Sales: David Wooldridge
Estimated Sales: $10-20 Million
Number Employees: 20-49
Brands:
Bagmaster
Batchmaster

19486 Batory Foods
1700 Higgins Road
Suite 300
Des Plaines, IL 60018 847-299-1999
Fax: 847-299-1669 info@batoryfoods.com
www.batoryfoods.com
Distributor of cocoa products, dairy products, cereals, candies and corn syrup solids, commodity syrups, condiments, sauces, egg powders, dough conditioners, emulsifiers and fibers.

19487 Battenfeld Gloucester Engineering
P.O.Box 900
Gloucester, MA 01931 978-281-1800
President: Brian Marvelley
Estimated Sales: $100+ Million
Number Employees: 250-499

19488 Battenfield Gloucester Engineering Company
P.O.Box 900
Gloucester, MA 01931-0900 978-281-1800
Fax: 978-282-9111
www.gloucesterbattenfield.com
President: Carl Johnson
Estimated Sales: $100+ Million
Number Employees: 250-499

19489 Baublys Control Laser
2419 Lake Orange Dr
Orlando, FL 32837 407-926-3500
Fax: 407-926-3590 866-612-8619
clcsales@controllaser.com
www.controllaser.com
Fully integrated lasers and mechanical coding, marking, engraving, deep engraving, and 3D engraving systems and solution for the aerospace, automotive, coining and jewerly, consumer/commercial, electronic, medical, mold and diepackaging, tooling and trophy and awards industries. Our Laser Markink Systems are available: 10 Watt, 25 Watt, 50 Watt and CO2 with wigh power Nd:YAD and Nd:YLF lamp and diode pumped infrared, Green, UV and Deep UV systems.
President: Steve Graham
CEO: Antoine Dominic
CEO: Antoine Dominic
Marketing Director: Monica Correal
Number Employees: 50-99
Number of Products: 20
Square Footage: 52000
Parent Co: Excel Technology
Brands:
Instamark Script
Instamark Signature
Instamark Stylus

19490 Bauermeister
601 Corporate Woods Pkwy
Vernon Hills, IL 60061 901-363-0921
Fax: 847-793-8611 info@bauermeisterusa.com
www.bauermeisterusa.com
Food processing and chocolate machinery
President: Jeff Soldan
Estimated Sales: Below $5 Million
Number Employees: 10

19491 Baumer Electric Limited
122 Spring St
Suite C6
Southington, CT 06489 860-628-6280
Fax: 860-628-6280 www.baumer.com
President: Mark Barber
Owner: Ken Talentino
Estimated Sales: $1 - 5 Million
Number Employees: 10-19

19492 Baumuller LNI
117 W Dudley Town Rd
Bloomfield, CT 06002 860-243-0232
Fax: 860-286-3080 info@baumuller.com
www.baumuller.com
Estimated Sales: $3 - 5 Million
Number Employees: 10-19

19493 Baur Tape & Label Company
130 Lombrano St
San Antonio, TX 78207 210-738-3000
Fax: 210-738-0070 877-738-3222
baurlabel@swbell.net www.baurlabel.com
Manufacturer and exporter of shipping and metal labels
President: Leonard Humble
Sales Manager: Peter Humble
Estimated Sales: $1-2.5 Million
Number Employees: 5-9
Square Footage: 4000
Type of Packaging: Consumer, Food Service, Private Label, Bulk

19494 Baxter Manufacturing Company
19220 State Route 162 E
Orting, WA 98360 360-893-5554
Fax: 360-893-6836 800-777-2828
www.hobart.com
Manufacturer and exporter of bakery and deli equipment including rack and revolving ovens, proof boxes, fryers, inventory supply items, ingredient bins, molders and dividers
Design/Marketing Manager: Laura Barrentine
Estimated Sales: $1 - 5 Million
Number Employees: 100-249
Square Footage: 114000
Parent Co: Hobart Corporation

19495 Bay Area Pallet Company/IFCO Systems
13100 Northwest Fwy # 625
Houston, TX 77040-6340 713-332-6145
Fax: 713-332-6146 877-430-4326
info@ifcosystems.com www.ifco-us.com
Re-manufacturer of wooden pallets and skids
President IFCO Systems North America: David Russell
Chairman: Bernd Malmstrom
Senior Vice President, Chief Financial O: Rich Hamlin
Senior VP: Mike Hachtman
Vice President of Sales: Dan Martin
Chief Operating Officer: Wolfgang Orgeldinger
Estimated Sales: $20-50 Million
Number Employees: 1,000-4,999
Parent Co: IFCO Systems

19496 Bayard Kurth Company
19321 Mount Elliott St
Detroit, MI 48234-2724 313-891-0800
Fax: 313-891-8966
Manufacturer and exporter of advertising displays, decalcomanias and packaging materials
President: Bayard Kurth Jr
VP: Bayard Kurth III
Estimated Sales: $5-10 Million
Number Employees: 5-9
Type of Packaging: Consumer, Food Service, Bulk

19497 Bayer Environmental
95 Chestnut Ridge Road
Montvale, NJ 07645 201-307-9700
Fax: 201-307-3438
firtname.lastname@bayercropsience.com
President: Helmut Schramm
Estimated Sales: Below $5 Million
Number Employees: 50-99

19498 Bayer/Wolff Walsrode
7330 S Madison St
Willowbrook, IL 60527-5588 630-789-8442
Fax: 630-789-8489 800-882-9987
Flexible packages, gas packaging materials, modified atmospheric packaging, vacuum packaging materials
CEO: Timothy McDivit
Estimated Sales: $5-10 000,000
Number Employees: 20-49

19499 Bayhead Products Corporation
173 Crosby Rd
Dover, NH 03820 603-742-3000
Fax: 603-743-4701 800-229-4323
sales@bayheadproducts.com
www.bayheadproducts.com
Plastic and steel industrial items, tilt and box trucks, self-dumping hoppers, pallet containers, barrels, boxes, containment trays, totes, cases, tanks, steel racks and carts; exporter of tilt trucks and boxes
President: Elissa Moore
Estimated Sales: $1.9,000,000
Number Employees: 20-49
Square Footage: 50000
Type of Packaging: Bulk
Brands:
Haul-All

19500 Bayou Container
14021 Hemley Rd
Coden, AL 36523-3146 251-824-2658
Fax: 251-824-2670
Owner/President: Mike Frederick
Estimated Sales: $3 - 5 Million
Number Employees: 1-4

19501 Bayou Packing
9155 Little River Rd
Bayou La Batre, AL 36509 251-824-7710
Fax: 251-824-4061
Packages seafood
Owner: Richard Roush

19502 Bayside Motion Group
27 Seaview Boulevard
Port Washington, NY 11050-4610 516-484-5482
Fax: 516-484-5496 800-305-4555
lduphily@baysidemotion.com
www.baysideinfo.com
Manufacturer and exporter of environmentally sealed gear heads
Marketing Coordinator: Paul Gallagher
Estimated Sales: $5 - 10 Million
Number Employees: 150

19503 Beach Filter Products
7682 Glenville Rd
Glen Rock, PA 17327 717-235-1136
Fax: 717-235-4858 800-232-2485
beachsta-dri@comcast.net www.beachfilters.com
Manufacturer and exporter of compressed air filters, desiccant dehumidification bags, and breather filters.
President: Wesley Jones III
Sales Manager: Lori Prickitt
Production Manager: Leslie Doll
Plant Manager/Purchasing: Leslie Doll
Estimated Sales: $500,000-$1 Million
Number Employees: 5-9
Square Footage: 16000
Brands:
Polyclear Ii

19504 Beacon Engineering Company
162 Don Westbrook Ave S
Jasper, GA 30143 706-692-6411
Fax: 706-692-3227 beacon6411@aol.com
www.beaconcan.com
Batch spinners, conveyors, cooling equipment, candy cutting machines, and automatic feeders
Owner: Susie Shields
Estimated Sales: $1-2.5 000,000
Number Employees: 10-19

19505 Beacon Specialties
345 Bloome Street
New York, NY 10013
800-221-9405
Food service equipment parts and supplies including drains, casters, burners, grates, faucets, mixer parts, gaskets, refrigeration hardware, etc
VP: Steven Levine
Sales Manager: L Levine
Estimated Sales: $1 - 5 Million
Number Employees: 10
Square Footage: 5000

19506 Beacon, Inc.
12223 S Laramie Ave
Alsip, IL 60803 708-544-9900
800-445-4203
www.beaconmetals.com

Stainless steel equipment for meat and poultry processing.

19507 Beam Industries
1700 W 2nd St
Webster City, IA 50595 515-832-4620
Fax: 515-832-6659 800-369-2326
lars.hybel@beamvac.com www.beamvac.com
Manufacturer and exporter of central vacuum cleaner systems and parts
President: Russell S Minick
CFO: Dave Thompson
Commercial Sales Manager: Bill Smith
Estimated Sales: $20-50 Million
Number Employees: 100-249
Square Footage: 100000
Brands:
Beam

19508 Bean Machines
18619 Middlefield Rd
Sonoma, CA 95476-1998 707-996-0706
Fax: 707-996-0704
Manufacturer and exporter of soybean processing equipment used to produce soy milk, tofu, yogurt, etc.; importer of multiple filter centrifuges
President: W Rogers
CEO: S Fiering
Estimated Sales: $350,000
Number Employees: 6
Square Footage: 2800
Type of Packaging: Food Service

19509 Beaufurn LLC
5269 U.S. Highway 158
Advance, NC 27006 336-768-2544
Fax: 336-766-2790 888-766-7706
info@beaufurn.com www.beaufurn.com
Manufacturer, importer and exporter of chairs and tables
President/CEO: Bill Bongaerts
CFO: Monique De Proost
Sales: Lou Ann Bogulski
Public Relations: Janet Stanford
Estimated Sales: $3-4 Million
Number Employees: 5-9

19510 Beaverite Corporation
9794 Bridge St
Croghan, NY 13327-2327 315-346-6011
Fax: 315-346-6221 800-424-6337
sales@beaverite.com www.beaverite.com
Menu covers
Manager: Lucy Kniseley
Quality Control: Tom Becker
VP Manufacturing: Bob Burns
Estimated Sales: $20-50 Million
Number Employees: 20-49
Brands:
Beaverite

19511 Beayl Weiner/Pak
610 Palisades Drive
Pacific Palisades, CA 90272-2849 310-454-1354
Fax: 310-459-6545 weinerb@aol.com
Manufacturer and importer of flexible packaging materials including printed and laminated roll stock, bags and pouches
Owner: Jeanne Weiner
Number Employees: 95
Square Footage: 100000
Type of Packaging: Food Service, Private Label, Bulk

19512 Beckart Environmental
6900 46th St
Kenosha, WI 53144 262-656-7680
Fax: 262-656-7699 information@beckart.com
www.beckart.com
Wastewater treatment equipment
President: Arthur Fedrigon
CFO: Shawn Jensen
Estimated Sales: $5 - 10 000,000
Number Employees: 20-49

19513 Becker Brothers GraphiteCorporation
39 E.Legion St
Maywood, IL 60153 708-410-0700
Fax: 708-410-0701 sales@beckergraphite.com
www.beckergraphite.com
Self-lubricating and heat resistant graphite bushings, bearings, seals, rings and plates
President: Cheryl Ivanovich
Sales: Linda Egelhart
Customer Service: Linda Egelhart
Director Operations: Pedro Espinoza
Plant Manager: Pedro Espinoza
Estimated Sales: $2.5-5,000,000
Number Employees: 10
Square Footage: 10000

19514 Becker Foods
15136 Goldenwest Cir
Westminster, CA 92683 714-315-9447
stan@beckerfoods.com
www.beckerfoods.com
Custom processor and packager of; fresh and frozen poultry, beef, pork, lamb, veal, cheese products, and more
President: Stan Becker
Vice President: Dian Vendel
Type of Packaging: Food Service, Private Label

19515 Beckhoff Automation
12150 Nicollet Ave S
Burnsville, MN 55337 952-890-0000
Fax: 952-890-2888 bechkoff.usa@bechkoff.com
www.beckhoffautomation.com
President: Gram Harris
R&D: Gram Harris
Quality Control: Gram Harris
Managing Director: Arnold Beckhoff
Estimated Sales: $5 - 10 Million
Number Employees: 20-49

19516 Becton Dickinson & Company: Diagnostic Systems
1 Becton Dr
Franklin Lakes, NJ 07417-1880 201-847-6800
www.bd.com
Manufacturer and exporter of diagnostic tests and instruments for microbiology
President: Edward Ludwig
CFO: Glen McKin
VP Strategic Planning: Caroline Popper
R & D: Bob Rosenstin
Senior Vice President of Quality: Pierre Boisier
Director of Public Relations: Alyssa Zeff
Estimated Sales: $100-500 Million
Number Employees: 500-999
Parent Co: Becton Dickinson & Company

19517 Bedford Enterprises
1940 W. Betteravia Road
Santa Maria, CA 93455 805-922-4977
Fax: 805-928-7241 800-242-8884
ÿbedfordscrap@gmail.com www.beibedford.com
Manufacturer and exporter of stainless platforms, hand railing, stair treads, ladders and decking; wholesaler/distributor of fiberglass gratings; installation services available
Owner: Reneshia Bedford
VP: David Thomas
Estimated Sales: $1-2.5 Million
Number Employees: 1-4
Brands:
Bestdeck
Bestread

19518 Bedford Industries
1659 Rowe Ave
P.O. Box 39
Worthington, MN 56187 507-376-4136
Fax: 507-376-6742 800-533-5314
bedford@bedfordind.com www.bedfordind.com
Manufacturer and exporter of identification ties and tags, twist ties, recloseable twist ties, and ElasitTag® Products.
President: Kim Milbrandt
CEO: Bob Ludlow
Marketing Director: Deb Houseman
Sales Director: Martin Rickers
Estimated Sales: $20 - 50 Million
Number Employees: 100-249
Square Footage: 84000

19519 Bedrosian & Associates
525 Veterans Boulevard
Suite 102
Redwood City, CA 94063 650-367-0259
www.bedrosian-associates.com
Consultant for new product development
Owner: Ron Bedrosian
Estimated Sales: less than $500,000
Number Employees: 1 to 4

19520 Beech Engineering
1134 Turnpike Road 73
Ashland, OH 44805 419-281-0894
Fax: 419-281-0894 hello@bright.net
Transfer carts, lift tables, mobile work stations, stocking systems, etc
General Manager: Tracy McBride
Number Employees: 7

19521 Beehive- Provisur
9950 191st St
Mokena, IL 60448 801-561-4211
Fax: 801-562-5857 800-621-8438
jim.varney@provisur.com
www.beehive-provisur.com
Food processing equipment, meat industry
President/CEO: Nick Lesar
Director: James Varney
Number Employees: 20-49

19522 Beehive/Provisur Technologies
9100 191st Street
Mokena, IL 60448 708-479-3500
Fax: 708-479-3598 www.provisur.com
Food processing equipment.

19523 Beemak Plastics
16711 Knott Ave
La Mirada, CA 90638 310-886-5880
Fax: 310-764-0330 800-421-4393
info@beemak.com www.beemak.com
Manufacturer and exporter of displays and holders for recipe cards, brochures and pamphlets
President: Robert Gram
CEO: Thomas Quinn
Finance Executive: Christy Harp
Manager Sales: Julia Alty
Estimated Sales: $10 - 20 Million
Number Employees: 20-49
Square Footage: 36000
Parent Co: Jordon Industries

19524 Beer Magic Devices
20 Railway Street
Hamilton, ON L8R 2R3
Canada 905-522-3081
Fax: 905-527-1957
Manufacturer, wholesaler/distributor and importer of portion control dispensing machines for beer, wine and liquor
President: Fred Palermo
Number Employees: 4

19525 Beford Technology
PO Box 609
Worthington, MN 56187-0609 507-372-5558
Fax: 507-372-5726 mail@bedfordtech.com
www.bedfordtech.com
Estimated Sales: $1 - 5 Million
Number Employees: 25-49

19526 Behlen Mfg. Co.
P.O. Box 569
4025 E. 23rd Street
Columbus, NE 68602-0569 402-564-3111
Fax: 402-563-7405 behlen@behlenmfg.com
www.behlenmfg.com
And grain storage bins, steel buildings, and grain dryers
Chairman & Coach: TR Raimondo
Purchassing: Bob Elsasser
Estimated Sales: $98.6 Million
Number Employees: 945
Number of Products: 3
Square Footage: 850000
Brands:
Behlen Big Bin
Berico Dryers

19527 Behn & Bates/Haver Filling Systems
460 Gees Mill Business Ct NE
Conyers, GA 30013-1569 770-760-1130
Fax: 770-760-1181 sales@haverusa.com
www.haverusa.com
High speed and in-line packaging systems
VP: Thomas Reckersdrees
Estimated Sales: $10 - 20 Million
Number Employees: 10-19

19528 Behnke Lubricants/JAX
W134 N 5373 Campbell Dr
Menomonee Falls, WI 53051 262-781-8850
Fax: 262-781-3906 800-782-8850
info@jax.com www.jax.com
Manufacturer and exporter of food grade and high temperature synthetic lubricants
President: Eric Peter
Manager Central Region: Carter Anderson
Manager Western Region: Mitch Clark
Estimated Sales: $10-20 Million
Number Employees: 20-49
Parent Co: JAX
Brands:
Jax

19529 Behrens Manufacturing Company
1250 East Sanborn Street
Winona, MN 55987 507-454-4664
Fax: 507-452-2106 info@behrensmfg.com
www.behrensmfg.com
Manufacturer and exporter of oil galvanized funnels and egg washers
President: Keith Dau Schmidt
Marketing Manager: Steve Moen
Estimated Sales: $10-20 Million
Number Employees: 50-99
Type of Packaging: Bulk

19530 Beistle Company
1 Beistle Plz
Shippensburg, PA 17257 717-532-2131
Fax: 717-532-7789 sales@beistle.com
www.beistle.com
New Year's Eve party goods
President: Tricia Lacy
VP Marketing: David Goode
Marketing Director: Michael Fague
Estimated Sales: $50 - 75 Million
Number Employees: 250-499
Number of Products: 4000
Type of Packaging: Private Label

19531 Beka Furniture
259 Bradwick Drive
Concord, ON L4K 1L5
Canada 905-669-4255
Fax: 905-669-3627 info@bekacasting.com
www.bekacasting.com
Tables, chairs and groupings
President: Maggie Dederian
National Sales Manager: Raffi Dayian
Parent Co: Beka Casting
Brands:
Beka

19532 Bekum America Corporation
1140 W Grand River Ave
Williamston, MI 48895 517-655-4331
Fax: 517-655-4121 sales@bekumamerica.com
www.bekumamerica.com
Blow molding machinery
Chairman of the Board: Gottfried Mehnert
President: Martin Stark
CEO: Martin Stark
CFO: Owen Johnston
Estimated Sales: $30 - 50 Million
Number Employees: 100-249

19533 (HQ)Bel-Art Products
661 Route 23
Wayne, NJ 07470 973-694-0500
Fax: 973-694-7199 800-423-5278
www.belart.com
Manufacturer and exporter of plastic laboratory supplies including sterile and nonsterile sampling devices and magnetic stirring bars; also, laboratory cleaning products
President: David Landsberger
Estimated Sales: $10 - 20 Million
Number Employees: 250-499
Square Footage: 80000
Type of Packaging: Consumer, Private Label, Bulk
Other Locations:
Bel-Art Products
Pequannock NJ
Brands:
Clavies
Cleanware
Spinbar
Sterileware

19534 Bel-Ray Company
P.O.Box 526
Farmingdale, NJ 07727 732-938-2421
Fax: 732-938-4232 belray@belray.com
www.belray.com
Formulated petroleum and synthetic oils and greases
President: Linda Kiefer
CFO: Lauren Volk
CEO: Daryl Brosnan
R&D: Bill Shen
Quality Control: Victor Odueanjo
Manager (Industrial Division): Roy Provost
Estimated Sales: $75 - 100 Million
Number Employees: 100-249
Square Footage: 150000
Brands:
Molyube
No-Tox

19535 Bel-Terr China
1001 Country Way SW
Warren, OH 44481-9699
Fax: 330-457-7524 800-900-2371
Pottery
President: Edward Massey
VP: Paul Ramponi
Estimated Sales: $10 - 20 Million
Number Employees: 20-49

19536 Belcan Corporation
10200 Anderson Way
Cincinnati, OH 45242 513-985-7125
Fax: 513-277-3102 888-263-3165
dlajoie@belcan.com www.belcan.com
President: Todd Cross
CEO: Mike McCaw
Chief Financial Officer: Michael J. Wirth
Sr. Vice President: Leigh Ann Pagnard
COO: Cleve Campbell
Number Employees: 250-499

19537 Belco Packaging Systems
910 S Mountain Ave
Monrovia, CA 91016 626-357-9566
Fax: 626-359-3440 800-833-1833
info@belcopackaging.com
www.belcopackaging.com
Manufacturer and wholesaler/distributor of shrink packaging equipment, carton sealers, shrink tunnels, conveyors and accumulating tables
President: Michael A. Misik
CEO: Helen Misik
R&D: Tom Bolby
Quality Control: Dave Macneil
National Sales Manager: Thomas Misik
Distributor Sales Manager: Bruce Miles
Estimated Sales: $10 - 20 Million
Number Employees: 20-49
Square Footage: 35000
Brands:
Belco

19538 Belgian Electronic Sorting Technology USA
65 Inverness Dr E
Suite 300
Englewood, CO 80112-5141
Fax: 720-870-2241 info@bestnv.com
www.bestnv.com
President: Eddy De Reyes
CEO: Bert Van Der Auwera
VP: Johan Peters
R & D: Mark Ruynen
Manager: Johan Peeters
Estimated Sales: $3 - 5 Million
Number Employees: 5-9

19539 (HQ)Bell & Howell Company
6802 N McCormick Boulevard
Lincolnwood, IL 60712-2709 847-675-7600
800-647-2290
Antoinette.Ramos@emsonusa.com
www.bellhowell.com
Weighing systems, inserting systems, automated guided mail delivery vehicles, remittance processing equipment, labeling machinery and sorters
Principal: Mike Swift
Quality Control: Josecer David
CFO: Tom Werner
President: John Lomdard
Number Employees: 160

19540 Bell Container Corporation
PO Box 5728
Newark, NJ 07105 973-344-4400
Fax: 973-344-0817 www.bellcontainer.com
Corrugated boxes
President: Arnold Kaplan
Estimated Sales: $20-50 Million
Number Employees: 100-249

19541 (HQ)Bell Flavors & Fragrances
500 Academy Dr
Northbrook, IL 60062 847-291-8300
Fax: 847-291-1217 800-323-4387
infousa@bellff.com www.bellff.com
Manufacturer and exporter of natural and artificial flavoring extracts for food and beverages; also, spice compounds
President: James Heinz
Manager of Business Development: Susan Tainton
VP Sales: Bernd-Dieter Neufang
VP Operations: Peter Speck
Estimated Sales: $39 Million
Number Employees: 200
Square Footage: 100000
Type of Packaging: Consumer, Food Service
Brands:
Yuccafoam

19542 Bell Laboratories
P.O.Box 8421
Madison, WI 53708 608-241-0202
Fax: 608-241-9631 mallen@belllabs.com
www.belllabs.com
Rodent control products including rodenticides, glue traps and tamper resistant bait stations
Chairman of the Board: Malcolm Stack
CEO: Steve Levy
Sales/Marketing Manager: John Schwerin
Estimated Sales: $100-500 Million
Number Employees: 100-249
Brands:
Contrac
Ditrac
Final
Protecta
Trapper
Zp

19543 Bell Packaging Corporation
3112 S Boots St
Marion, IN 46953 765-664-1261
Fax: 765-668-8127 800-382-0153
ryoung@prattindustries.com
www.prattindustries.com
Manufacturer corrugated shipping containers
President: Robert Young
Plant Manager: Terry Royal
Estimated Sales: $20 - 50 Million
Number Employees: 10
Square Footage: 250000
Parent Co: Pratt Industries

19544 (HQ)Bell-Mark Corporation
331 Changebridge Road
Pine Brook, NJ 07058 973-882-0202
Fax: 973-808-4616 info@bell-mark.com
www.bell-mark.com
Manufacturer and exporter of innovative coding and printing systems to the packaging and converting markets
President: John Marozzi
CFO: James Pontrella
VP: Tom Pugh
Marketing: Glenn Breslauer
Sales: Bob Batesko
Plant Manager: Dale Miller
Purchasing: Lou Ciccone
Estimated Sales: $16-20 Million
Number Employees: 50-99
Number of Brands: 5
Number of Products: 30
Square Footage: 45000
Brands:
Easyprint
Flexprint
Intelijet

19545 Bella Vita
PO Box 93204
Phoenix, AZ 85070 877-827-3638
Fax: 480-827-7630 sales@bellavitabags.com
www.bellavitabags.com

Wine bags and gourmet bags

19546 Belle Isle Awning Company
20220 Cornillie Dr
Roseville, MI 48066 586-294-6050
Fax: 586-294-2487 biawning@netscape.net
www.belleisleawning.com
Commercial awnings
Owner: Bill Belloumo
Estimated Sales: $2.5-5,000,000
Number Employees: 20-49

19547 Belleco, Inc
PO Box 880
Saco, ME 04072 207-854-8006
Fax: 207-283-8080 sales@bellecocooking.com
www.bellecocooking.com
Customized toasters, conveyor Pizza Ovens and Heat Lamps
President: Russell Bellrose
CFO: Kevin Roche
Quality Control Manager: Gil Cole
Sales: Mike Clavet
Materials Manager: Ron Hevey
Type of Packaging: Food Service

19548 Belleview
PO Box 122
Brookline, NH 03033 603-878-1583
Water and plastic milk cases
CEO: Alfred Stauble
Estimated Sales: $1 - 5 Million
Number Employees: 1-4

19549 Bellingham & Stanley
1000 Hurricane Shoals Rd NE
Lawrenceville, GA 30043 770-822-6898
Fax: 770-822-9165 800-678-8573
sales@bs-rfm-inc.com
www.bellinghamandstanley.com
Manufactures refractometers and polarimeters
Administrator: Susan Davis

19550 Belliss & Morcom
1800 Gardner expressway
Quincy, Il 62301 217-222-5400
Fax: 217-221-8728
belliss.red@gardnerdenver.com
www.belliss.com
High pressure oil-free air compressors for PET stretch blow molding
Marketing/Sales: Wendy Johnson
Estimated Sales: $1-2.5 Million
Number Employees: 5-9

19551 Bellsola-Pan Plus
7326 NW 46th Street
Miami, FL 33166-6425 305-406-9662
Fax: 305-406-9664 maquipanit@msn.com
Director of Product Development: Kirk Crowder

19552 Belltown Boxing Company
1717 Market St
Tacoma, WA 98402-3246 253-274-9000
Fax: 253-274-9009 lewing@belltownboxing.com
www.belltownboxing.com
Creative custom, packaging for the retail and food industries
President: Linda Ewing
VP: Andrew Levkass
Estimated Sales: $1-2.5 Million
Number Employees: 10-19
Type of Packaging: Private Label, Bulk

19553 Belly Treats, Inc.
210-200 Wellington St W
Toronto, ON M5V 3C7
Canada 416-418-3285
Fax: 905-479-4135 mail@bellytreats.com
www.bellytreats.com
Manufacturer, importer and exporter of candies and nuts in bulk. Also catered corporate events and candy festivals.
Owner/Sales & Marketing: George Tsioros
Estimated Sales: $1 Million
Number of Products: 500+
Type of Packaging: Bulk

19554 Belshaw Adamatic BakeryGroup
814 44th Street NW
Suite 103
Auburn, WA 98001 206-322-5474
Fax: 206-322-5425 800-578-2547
info@belshaw.com www.belshaw.com
Machinery and production solutions for donut producers in every retail and wholesale category. Doughnut systems fryers, glazers, and icers; also pancake and batter depositers; and piston filler depostiters. One-hundred percentdedicated to the donut and to donut-makers worldwide.
President: Michael Bontatibus
CFO: William Yee
Marketing Coordinator: Mike Baxter
Sales: John DeMarre
Estimated Sales: $20 - 50 Million
Number Employees: 100-249
Square Footage: 120000
Parent Co: Welbilt Corporation
Type of Packaging: Food Service

19555 Belson Outdoors
111 N River Rd
North Aurora, IL 60542 800-323-5664
Fax: 630-897-0573 800-323-5664
sales@belson.com www.belson.com
Manufacturer and distributor of the finest outdoor cooking equipment available. Don't be misled, insist on certified (ul, csa, nsf) safe equipment. product line includes gas and charcoal grills, pig roasters, steam tables, trailerpits, smokers and more.
Brands:
Porta-Grills

19556 Belt Corporation of America
253 Castleberry Industrial Dr
Cumming, GA 30040 770-887-9725
Fax: 770-887-4138 800-235-0947
info@beltcorp.com www.beltcorp.com
Industrial belting, packing belts
Owner: Bill Levensalor
Estimated Sales: $5-10 000,000
Number Employees: 50-99
Type of Packaging: Consumer, Food Service, Private Label, Bulk

19557 (HQ)Belt Technologies
11 Bowles Rd
Agawam, MA 01001 413-786-9922
Fax: 413-789-2786
engineer@belttechnologies.com
www.belttechnologies.com
Manufacturer and exporter of pulleys and metal belts used for conveyors, power transmissions, etc.; importer of backed belts
President: Alan Wosky
Quality Control: John Robertson
Sales Manager: Timothy Potrikus
Human Resources: Cindy Gadbois
Estimated Sales: Below $5 Million
Number Employees: 20-49
Square Footage: 23000
Other Locations:
Belt Technologies
Durham City
Brands:
Metrak
Transback

19558 Beltek Systems Design
30 Englehart Street
Suite C
Dieppe, NB E1A 6P8
Canada 506-857-4196
Fax: 506-857-0194 danleb@beltek.com
Chief Executive Officer: Michel Belzile
Chief Financial Officer: David Pugsley
Chief Technology Officer: Jason Janes
Estimated Sales: $15,000,000
Number Employees: 99
Parent Co: HighJump Software, LLC.

19559 Beltram Food Service Supply
6800 N Florida Ave
Tampa, FL 33604-5558
Fax: 813-471-2394 800-940-1136
bfgtampa@beltram.com www.beltram.com
Wholesaler/distributor of food service supplies and equipment; serving the food service market
President: Dan Beltram
CFO: Hal Herdman
VP: Allen Cope
VP: Kathy McCain
Purchasing Manager: John Zloch
Estimated Sales: $20 - 50 Million
Number Employees: 100-249
Parent Co: Beltram Foodservice Group

19560 Belvac Production Machinery
237 Graves Mill Rd
Lynchburg, VA 24502 434-239-0358
Fax: 434-239-1964 800-423-5822
info@belvac.com www.belvac.com
President: Richard S Steigerwald
Number Employees: 100-249

19561 Bematek Systems
96 Swampscott Rd Ste 7
Salem, MA 01970 978-744-5816
Fax: 978-744-2531 877-236-2835
bematek@bematek.com www.bematek.com
Manufacturer and exporter of food processing equipment including in-line mixers, colloid mills, homogenizers, grinders and dispersers; also, laboratory testing machinery for wet mixing and size reduction, continuous or batch
President: David Ekstrom
Technical Director: Stephen Masucci
Administration: Denise Raimo
Sales Manager: Lindsey Humphrey
Estimated Sales: $1 - 3 Million
Number Employees: 5-9
Square Footage: 4300
Brands:
Bematek
Colby
Speco

19562 Bemis Company
One Neenah Center, 4th Floorÿ
P.O.Box 669
Neenah, WI 54957-0669 612-376-3000
Fax: 612-376-3180 contactbemis@bemis.com
www.bemis.com
Packaging materials including low density film
Manager: Audrey Kirchner
President/CEO: Jeffrey Curler
Executive VP/COO: Henry J Thiesen
Number Employees: 500-999

19563 Bemis Company
P.O.Box 669
Neenah, WI 54957-0669 920-727-4100
Fax: 920-527-7600 contactbemis@bemis.com
www.bemis.com
The largest flexible packaging company in the Americas and a major manufacturer of pressure sensitive materials used for labels, decoration and signage.
CEO: Henry J Theisen
Estimated Sales: K
Number Employees: 10,000
Brands:
Bemistape
Tension-Master Ii

19564 Bemis Packaging Machinery Company
315 27th Ave NE
Minneapolis, MN 55418-2715 612-782-1200
Fax: 612-782-1203 800-542-3647
larry.smith@phieletech.com www.thieletech.com
Conveying, insulation converting and bagging equipment, conveyors
President: Larry Smith
CFO: Keith Skerrett
R&D: Bob Odom
Marketing/Sales Manager: Todd Sandell
Estimated Sales: $20 - 30 Million
Number Employees: 500-999

19565 Ben H. Anderson Manufacturers
7848 Morrison St
Morrisonville, WI 53571 608-846-5474
Fax: 608-846-8878 bklucey@merr.com
www.benhanderson.com
Dairy processing equipment
President: Dale Victor
Number Employees: 10

19566 Benchmark Thermal Corporation
13185 Nevada City Avenue
PO Box 1799
Grass Valley, CA 95945 530-477-5011
Fax: 530-477-6507
thermal@benchmarkthermal.com
www.benchmarkthermal.com
Heating elements
President: Gil Mathew
CEO: Myles McKelo

Estimated Sales: $5-10 Million
Number Employees: 50-99
Square Footage: 12000

19567 Bendow
1120 Federal Road
Brookfield, CT 06804-1122 203-775-6341
Fax: 203-746-3728
Tea and coffee filters
Estimated Sales: $1 - 5 000,000
Number Employees: 3

19568 Benhil-Gasti
5355 115th Avenue N
Clearwater, FL 33760-4840 727-572-7753
Fax: 727-573-0367 sales@autoprodinc.com
www.autoprodinc.com
President: Paul Desocio

19569 Benier
351 Thornton Rd # 123
Lithia Springs, GA 30122-1589 770-745-2200
Fax: 770-745-0050 wvdb@kaakgroup.com
www.benierusa.com
Provider of bakery equipment
President: Mike Hartnett
Estimated Sales: $5 - 10 Million
Number Employees: 20-49
Brands:
Benier
Daub
Diosna
Kaak
Oddy
Spiromatic

19570 Benier USA
351 Thornton Rd # 123
Lithia Springs, GA 30122-1589 770-745-2200
Fax: 770-745-0050 sales@kaakgroup.com
www.benierusa.com
Supplier of equipment for the automated production of bread, rolls, pizza crust and tortillas
President: Mike Hartnett
CFO: Ron Tabor
Estimated Sales: $5 - 10 Million
Number Employees: 20-49
Square Footage: 148000
Brands:
Benier
Daub
Diosna
Koak Oddy

19571 Benko Products
5350 Evergreen Pkwy
Sheffield Village, OH 44054 440-934-2180
Fax: 440-934-4052 info@benkoproducts.com
www.benkoproducts.com
Manufacturer or revolutionary ergonomic beverage cart that eliminates the need to bend when loading and unloading.
President: John Benko
VP: Robert Benko
Sales/Marketing Manager: Laurie Benko
Estimated Sales: $10 Million
Number Employees: 20-49
Square Footage: 35000
Brands:
G-Raff
Sahara Hot Box

19572 Benner China & Glassware of Florida
5329 Powers Ave
Jacksonville, FL 32207-8013 904-733-4620
Fax: 904-733-4622 custserv@odysseyfl.com
www.odysseyfl.com
Manufacturer, importer and exporter of glassware and china
Owner: James Wang
VP: Marie Wang
General Manager: Edward Mills
Estimated Sales: $5-10 Million
Number Employees: 20-49
Square Footage: 100000
Parent Co: Jacksonville Ginter Box Company
Brands:
Odyssey

19573 Bennett Box & Pallet Company
200 River Street
Winston, NC 27968-9681 252-332-5026
Fax: 252-332-5799 800-334-8741
benbox@coastalnet.com
Skids and new and remanufactured pallets; also, pallet repair and removal services available
President: Barbara Perry
VP of Marketing: Shirley Walker
Estimated Sales: $10-20 Million
Number Employees: 50-99
Square Footage: 85000

19574 Bennett Manufacturing Company
13315 Railroad St
Alden, NY 14004 716-937-9161
Fax: 716-937-3137 800-345-2142
info@bennettmfg.com www.bennettmfg.com
Custom built metal cabinets, waste receptacles, janitor carts, racks, frames, etc
President: Steven Yellen
Manager: David Maue
CFO: Tim Brien
Quality Control: Mike Wacht
Sales Engineer: Robert Cowing
Estimated Sales: $5-10 Million
Number Employees: 50-99
Square Footage: 150000

19575 Bennett's Auto Inc.
W8136 Winnegamie Dr
Neenah, WI 54956-9401 920-836-3534
Fax: 920-836-3873 800-215-5464
bauto@bennettsauto.com www.bennettsauto.com
Disposable polyethylene products including bags, aprons and gloves; also, latex gloves
Owner: Lowell Bennett
Product Manager (Film Sales): Larry Stelow
National Sales Manager (Healthcare): William Rusch
Product Manager (Food Service): Ronald Green
Estimated Sales: $3 - 5 Million
Number Employees: 1-4
Square Footage: 992000

19576 Bennington Furniture Corporation
1371 Historic Route 7A
Bennington, PA 05201 724-962-2234
Fax: 724-962-1588
sales@benningtonfurniture.com
www.benningtonfurniturecorp.com
Cushioned chairs and bar stools
President: Carol Bennington
VP: Joseph Bennington
VP: Robert Bennington
Estimated Sales: $2.5-5 Million
Number Employees: 50-99
Brands:
Bennington

19577 Bentley Instruments
4004 Peavey Rd
Chaska, MN 55318 952-448-7600
Fax: 952-368-3355 info@bentleyinstruments.com
www.bentleyinstruments.com
Manufacturer and exporter of milk analyzers and control systems
President: Bent Lyder
Estimated Sales: $2.5-$5 Million
Number Employees: 10-19
Square Footage: 19000
Type of Packaging: Food Service, Bulk
Brands:
Bentley
Somacount

19578 Bepex International,LLC
333 Taft St NE
Minneapolis, MN 55413 612-331-4370
Fax: 612-627-1444 800-607-2470
info@bepex.com www.bepex.com
Provider of thermal processing, polymer processing, drying, agglomeration, size reduction, compaction, briquetting, mixing and blending for the food, chemical and polymer markets
President: Ralph Imholte
Estimated Sales: $20 Million
Number Employees: 20-49
Number of Brands: 4
Number of Products: 30+
Brands:
Alpine
Disintegrator
Extructor
Hosokawa
Kg
Mikropul
Rietz
Schugi
Strong Scott

19579 Berco Furniture Solutions
1120 Montrose Avenue
St Louis, MO 63104 314-772-4700
Fax: 314-772-2744 888-772-4788
info@bercoinc.com www.bercoinc.com
Tables and components for the food service industry
President: Rick Berkowitz
Human Resources: Angie Balencie
Estimated Sales: $5-10 Million
Number Employees: 50-99
Square Footage: 340000

19580 Berg Chilling Systems
51 Nantucket Blvd.
Toronto, ON, ON M1P 2N5
Canada 416-755-2221
Fax: 416-755-3874 bergsales@berg-group.com
www.berg-group.com
Manufacturer and exporter of industrial cooling equipment, fluid recirculation, cold storage and pumping systems, ice machines, chillers and cooling towers
Chairman/CEO: Lorne Berggren
VP Sales: Stephanie Goudie
Estimated Sales: $20-50 Million
Number Employees: 100-249
Square Footage: 75000
Brands:
Berg

19581 Berg Chilling Systems
51 Nantucket Blvd.
Toronto, ON M1P 2N5 416-755-2221
Fax: 416-755-3874 bergsales@berg-group.com
www.berg-group.com
Manufacturer and exporter of process cooling equipment, large ice-making machines, freeze dryers, turnkey food processing/refrigeration systems and brine chillers for meat
VP: S Goudie
Estimated Sales: $1-2.5 Million
Number Employees: 1-4
Parent Co: Berg Chilling Systems

19582 Berg Company
2160 Industrial Drive
Monona, WI 53713 608-221-4281
Fax: 608-221-1416 sales@berg-controls.com
www.bergliquorcontrols.com
Liquor dispensers, beer equipment and beverage dispensing systems
Estimated Sales: $2.5-5 Million
Number Employees: 1-4
Parent Co: DEC International
Brands:
All-Bottle
Berg
Infinity
Laser
Tap 1

19583 Bergen Barrel & Drum Company
43 Obrien Rd
Kearny, NJ 07032-4212 201-998-3500
Fax: 201-998-0414
Tanks, pallets and plastic drums
Sales Coordinator: Lisa Goldstein
Estimated Sales: $1-2.5 Million
Number Employees: 5-9

19584 Berger Lahr Motion Technology
8001 Knightdale Blvd
Knightdale, NC 27545-9023 734-459-8300
Fax: 734-459-8622 info@bergerlahrmotion.com
www.bergerlahrmotion.com
Electric motors and drive controls
President: Steve Seabaugh
Sales Manager: Frank Eble
Estimated Sales: $1-5 Million
Number Employees: 10

19585 **Berghausen Corporation**
4524 Este Avenue
Cincinnati, OH 45232 530-677-8863
Fax: 530-683-4011 800-648-5887
mpuehse@berghausen.com
www.berghausen.com
Processor and finisher of quillaja and yucca extracts (powder and liquid forms) and food colors. Founded in 1863.
President: Fritz Berghausen
Quality Control Manager: Tom Davlin
Estimated Sales: $1-5 Million
Number Employees: 10-20

19586 **Bergschrond**
4458 51st Avenue SW
Seattle, WA 98116-4029 206-763-3502
Fax: 206-763-3767 sales@bergschrund.com
www.bergschrund.com
Sereware
President: Karl Stephenson
VP of Marketing: Babette Easley
Estimated Sales: $1-2.5 Million
Number Employees: 20

19587 **Bericap North America, Inc.**
835 Syscon Court
CDN-Burlington, ON L7L 6C5
Canada 905-634-2248
Fax: 905-634-7780 info.na@bericap.com
www.bericap.com
Manufacturer, importer and exporter of tamper-evident pourer closures, capsules for bottled liquids and flat top dispensing closures
President: Scott Ambrose
Number Employees: 10
Square Footage: 58000
Parent Co: Rical SA

19588 **Berkshire PPM**
PO Box 59
Litchfield, CT 06759 860-567-3118
Fax: 860-567-3014 jrindos@bershireppm.com
www.berkshireppm.com
Reconditioner and exporter of used food and beverage packaging, processing machinery and tanks
President: James Rindos
Estimated Sales: $3 - 5 Million
Number Employees: 3
Square Footage: 15000

19589 **Berlekamp Plastics**
2587 County Road 99
Fremont, OH 43420-9316 419-334-4481
Fax: 419-334-9094 sales@berlekamp.com
www.berlekamp.com
Manufacturer and exporter of plastic signs and badges
President: Kenneth Berlekamp Jr
Estimated Sales: $1-2.5 Million
Number Employees: 20 to 49

19590 **Berlin Foundry & MachineCompany**
489 Goebel St
P.O. Box 127
Berlin, NH 03570 603-752-4550
Fax: 603-752-2798 hardiff@berlinfoundry.com
www.berlinfoundry.com
Manufacturer and exporter of wrapping and packaging machines for paper towels and toilet tissue.
Owner: Gary Hamel
Sales/Plant Manager: Gary Hamel
Operations: Gary Hamel
Estimated Sales: $1.5 Million
Number Employees: 10-19
Square Footage: 30000

19591 **Berlin Fruit Box Company**
PO Box 47
Berlin Heights, OH 44814-0047 419-588-2081
Fax: 419-588-2800 800-877-7721
contact@samuelpattersonbaskets.com
www.samuelpattersonbaskets.com
Wood veneer baskets for fruit and vegetables
President: Matthew Adelman
Estimated Sales: $1 - 2.5 Million
Number Employees: 10-19
Square Footage: 160000
Brands:
Family Heritage

19592 **Berloc Manufacturing & Sign Company**
8010 Wheatland Ave
Ste G
Sun Valley, CA 91352-5317 818-503-9823
Fax: 818-503-0934
Signs including aluminum, engraved and vinyl; also, letters, directories and bulletin boards
Owner: Joan Adams
VP: Harry Adams
Sales Manager: Diana Gleason
Estimated Sales: $1 - 3 Million
Number Employees: 10
Square Footage: 5000

19593 **Berlon Industries**
434 Rubicon St
Hustisford, WI 53034 920-349-3580
Fax: 920-349-3081 800-899-3580
www.berlon.com
Custom stainless steel products including boxes, casters and dairy equipment
President: Lon Berndt
Shop Foreman: Scott Klumb
Estimated Sales: $1-2.5 Million
Number Employees: 20-49
Square Footage: 8600

19594 **Bermar America**
42 Lloyd Ave
Malvern, PA 19355 610-889-4900
Fax: 610-889-0289 888-289-5838
info@bermaramerica.com
www.bermaramerica.com
Manufacturer and importer of vacuum and pressure seal wine preservation systems
President: Richard Hewitt
Estimated Sales: Below $5 Million
Number Employees: 1-4

19595 **Bermingham Controls**
11144 Business Cir
Cerritos, CA 90703 562-860-1600
Fax: 562-402-0485 800-527-8326
sales@bermingham.com www.bermingham.com
President: Gregory Gass
Sales: Wes Selby

19596 **Bernal, Inc**
2960 Technology Dr
Rochester Hills, MI 48309 248-299-3600
Fax: 248-299-3601 800-237-6251
sales@bernalinc.com www.bernalinc.com
Manufacturer and exporter of die cutting and packaging machines for cereal, coffee, snack foods, etc
President: Luigi Pessarelli
CFO: Kelly Lang
Director: Rey Hsu, Ph. D.
Vice President Sales & Marketing: Mark Voorhees
Sales Manager: Steven Leigh
Plant Manager: Frank Penksa
Estimated Sales: $20 Million
Number Employees: 50-99
Square Footage: 45000

19597 **Bernard Wolnak & Associates**
1721 Mission Hills Rd Apt 205
Northbrook, IL 60062-5715 847-480-0427
Fax: 847-480-0427 www.wolnak.com
Consultant for the food processing industry providing consultation on food ingredients, processes, technology, planning, data acquisition and interpretation
President: Bernard Wolnak
Estimated Sales: $2.5-5 Million
Number Employees: 1 to 4
Square Footage: 3000

19598 **Berndorf Belt Technology USA**
2525 Bath Rd
Elgin, IL 60124 847-931-5264
Fax: 847-931-5299 877-232-7322
danielw@berndorf-usa.com
www.berndorf-usa.com
Manufacturer and service provider of solid steel belts, processing systems and complete turnkey plants for cooling, heat transfer, solidificationand casting applications.
VP: Larry Edwards
Marketing Director: Daniela Weiszhar
Estimated Sales: Below $5 Million
Number Employees: 10-19
Square Footage: 11500
Parent Co: Berndorf Band Gesmb

19599 **Berner International Corporation**
111 Progress Ave
New Castle, PA 16101 724-658-3551
Fax: 724-652-0682 800-245-4455
technicalsupport@berner.com www.berner.com
Berner International Corp. has established itself as the leading manufacturer of air doors for insect and climate control and cooler/freezer applications. Berner also has its own line of patio heaters, arctic seal doors, strip doorsand bakery rack covers.
Owner: Georgia Berner
Sales Manager: Michael Coscarelli
Estimated Sales: $10-20 Million
Number Employees: 50-99
Square Footage: 50000
Type of Packaging: Food Service
Brands:
Aristocrat
Berner
Flystop
Miniveil
Posi-Flow
Zephyr

19600 **Bernhard**
2075 Marlboro Rd
Kennett Square, PA 19348 610-444-6400
Fax: 215-444-1985 800-541-7874
www.crowncontrols.com
Manufacturer and exporter of level controls and open channel flow meters; also, food processing equipment
President: Charles Stevens
Number Employees: 20-49
Brands:
Capaciagage
Sonargage
Sonarswitch

19601 **(HQ)Berry Plastics**
PO Box 959
Evansville, IN 47706-0959 812-424-2904
Fax: 812-424-0128 800-234-1930
pscapinfo@berryplastics.com
www.berryplastics.com
Manufacturer and exporter of injection molded plastic containers and lids; also, container fillers
President: Ira Boots
CFO: Jim Kratochvil
Executive Vice President: Mark Miles
Production Line Supervisor: Jaclyn Burch
Estimated Sales: $408 Million
Number Employees: 10,000
Square Footage: 400000
Other Locations:
Berry Plastics
Henderson NV

19602 **Berry Plastics**
PO Box 959
Evansville, IN 47706-0959 812-306-2000
Fax: 757-538-2007 812-424-2904
www.berryplastics.com
Recycled loosefill, injection molded and printed containers and lids
Manager: Suzanne Mills
President/CEO: Ira G Boots
Executive VP/CFO: James M Kratochvil
Estimated Sales: $5 - 10 Million
Number Employees: 20-49
Square Footage: 420000

19603 **Berry Plastics Corporation**
P.O. Box 959
Evansville, IN 47706-0959 812-424-2904
www.berryplastics.com
Manufacturer of injection molded packaging
Estimated Sales: $91 Million
Number Employees: 1235

19604 **Berry Plastics Corporation**
PO Box 959
Evansville, IN 47706-0959 812-424-2904
Fax: 812-424-0128 800-822-2342
www.berryplastics.com
Plastic containers for food and dairy products
CFO: James Kratochvil
CEO: Ira G Boots
Regional Sales Manager: Dave Cote
Estimated Sales: less than $500,000
Number Employees: 10,000

Square Footage: 880000
Parent Co: Berry Plastics Corporation

19605 Berry Plastics Corporati
P.O. Box 959
Evansville, IN 47706-0959 812-424-2904
www.berryplastics.com
Manufacturer and exporter of plastic closures and molded plastics
President: Gary Caraker
Number Employees: 100-249

19606 Berryhill Signs
597 Vandalia St
Memphis, TN 38112 901-324-1730
Fax: 901-324-1732 patberryhill@msn.com
www.berryhillsigns.com
Commercial plastic signs and designs
President: Kenneth M Berryhill
Manager: Debbie Faber
Estimated Sales: Below $5 Million
Number Employees: 5-9

19607 Bert Manufacturing
811 Short Ct Ste F
Gardnerville, NV 89460 775-265-3900
Fax: 775-265-3939 bertmfg2@aol.com
www.bertmanufacturing.com
Manufacturer and exporter of chucks and rolls for food processing machinery
Owner: Dennis Bergucci
Sales: Brian Bertucci
Technical Director: Paul Coleman
Engineering & Programming: Luis Martinez
Estimated Sales: $1-2.5 Million
Number Employees: 1-4
Type of Packaging: Bulk

19608 (HQ)Bertek Systems
133 Bryce Blvd
Georgia, VT 05454 802-752-3170
800-367-0210
reinvent@berteksystems.com
www.berteksystems.com
Manufacturer and exporter of data processing and pressure sensitive labels
President: Samuel Peters
Sales and Marketing Director: Peter Kvam
00: Ken Whitcomb
MIS Systems Manager: Mike Saunders
Sales/Marketing Manager: Peter Kvam
Sales Representative: Danielle Ryea
HR/Ex Assistant: Amy Kimball
General Manager: Barney Kijeh
Account Executive: Debbie Chadwick
Estimated Sales: $10 - 20 Million
Number Employees: 100

19609 Bertels Can Company
1300 Brass Mill Road
Belcamp, MD 21017 410-272-0090
sales@independentcan.com
www.independentcan.com
Manufacturer of specialty metal cans and lithography
President: Rick Huether
Director Of Sales: Neil DeFrancisco
Plant Manager: Frank Sorokach
Estimated Sales: $20 - 50 Million
Number Employees: 20-49
Square Footage: 60000
Parent Co: Independent Can Company

19610 Berthold Technologies
99 Widway Lane
Oak Ridge, TN 37830 865-483-1488
Fax: 865-425-4309 Berthold-US@berthold.com
www.berthold-us.com
Measurement gauges and analyzers

19611 Beryl's Cake Decorating& Pastry Supplies
P.O.Box 1584
Springfield, VA 22151-0584 703-256-6951
Fax: 703-750-3779 800-488-2749
beryls@beryls.com www.beryls.com
Specializes in mail order cake decorating and party supplies.
Owner: Beryl Loveland
Sales: Linda Howe
Public Relations: Mara Lee
Estimated Sales: $.5 - 1 million
Number Employees: 1-4
Number of Products: 6000

19612 Besco Grain Ltd
PO Box 166
30 Railway Avenue
Brunkild, MB R0G 0E0
Canada 204-736-3570
Fax: 204-736-3575 mustard@bescograin.ca
www.bescograin.ca
Grains
President: Renee Caners
Quality Control: Carol Schulz
International Sales: Anthony Krijger
Sales Manager: Fred Nicholson
Office Manager: Sheri Hiebert
Plant Manager: Jamie Stelmachowich

19613 Bessam-Aire
26881 Cannon Rd
Cleveland, OH 44146 440-439-1200
Fax: 440-439-1625 800-321-5992
bill@bessamaire.com www.bessamaire.com
Manufacturer and exporter of indirect heating equipment for gas/oil, make-up air heating and summer evaporative cooling units.
Owner: Bill Sullivan
Marketing Director: Joseph Marg
Product Manager: Mark McGinty
National Sales Manager: Ron Dometla
Estimated Sales: $10 - 20 Million
Number Employees: 20-49
Number of Brands: 1
Number of Products: 9
Square Footage: 50000
Type of Packaging: Food Service
Brands:
Bessam-Aire

19614 Bessco Tube Bending & Pipe Fabricating
18 Blackhawk Dr
Thornton, IL 60476-1127 708-339-3977
Fax: 708-339-9472 800-337-3977
Folding tables and trucks including hand, chair and table
President: Ed Eggebrecht
CEO: Ruth Hartman
Marketing Director: Theresa Eggebrecht
Purchasing Manager: Henry De Vries
Estimated Sales: $1 - 3 Million
Number Employees: 5-9
Square Footage: 20000
Brands:
Handy-Cart
Hercules Tables

19615 Best
1071 Industrial Pkwy N
Brunswick, OH 44212 330-273-1277
Fax: 330-225-8740 800-827-9237
sales@bestvibes.com www.bestvibes.com
Manufacturer and exporter of pneumatic and electric vibrators, bulk bag unloaders, bulk bag loaders, conveyors, tables, screeners and dry process systems.
President: Ed Verbos
VP of Engineering: Tim Conway
Marketing: S Fitzpatrick
Sales Manager: R Breudigam
Estimated Sales: $1-2,500,000
Number Employees: 10-19
Number of Products: 100+
Square Footage: 30000
Type of Packaging: Bulk

19616 Best & Donovan
5570 Creek Rd
Cincinnati, OH 45242 513-791-5194
Fax: 513-791-0925 800-553-2378
info@bestanddonovan.com
www.bestanddonovan.com
Manufacturer and exporter of portable power meat saws, skinners, hock cutters, dehiders and dehorners
Owner: Scott Andre
Finance Executive: Ken Park
VP: Scott Andre
Estimated Sales: $5 - 10 Million
Number Employees: 25
Square Footage: 55000
Brands:
B&D
Best & Donovan

19617 Best Brands Home Products
20 W 33rd St Fl 5
New York, NY 10001 212-684-7456
att@bestbrands.com
www.bestbrands.com
Manufacturer and importer of towels, tablecloths, place mats, pot holders, linen goods, display racks, vinyl & fabric table cloths and place mats, oven and barbecue mitts, barbecue aprons and vinyl coasters, all bath towell products
President: Jack Albert
CEO: Jack Kassin
Vice President: Rodnie Gindi
Marketing Director: Cari Bennett
Sales Director: Rodnie Gindi
Secretary: David Meyer
Estimated Sales: $25 Million+
Number Employees: 15-20
Type of Packaging: Consumer, Private Label
Brands:
American Greetings
Cannon
Norman Rockwell

19618 Best Cooking Pulses, Inc.
124 10th St NE
Portage la Prairie, MB R1N 1B5
Canada 204-857-4451
margaret@bestcookingpulses.com
www.bestcookingpulses.com
Peas, chickpea, lentil and bean flours and pea fiber. Certified Kosher, Halal, Conventional or Certified-Organic, free of all major allergens, and gluten free.
President: Trudy Heal
Sales & Marketing: Margaret Hughes
General Manager: Mike Gallais
Estimated Sales: $11.25 Million
Number Employees: 23
Type of Packaging: Bulk

19619 Best Diversified Products
107 Flint Street
Jonesboro, AR 72401-6717 870-935-0970
Fax: 870-935-3661 800-327-9209
salesinfo@bestconveyors.com
www.bestconveyors.com
Manufacturer and exporter of conveyors including flexible, expandable, skatewheel and roller
President: James E Markley
Sales/Marketing Director: Charlie Appleby
Estimated Sales: $20-50 Million
Number Employees: 100-249

19620 Best Manufacturers
6105 NE 92nd Drive
Portland, OR 97220 503-253-1528
Fax: 503-253-0878 800-500-1528
sales@bestmfrs.com www.bestmfrs.com
Wire whips and mashers for beans and potatoes
President: John Merrifield
VP Sales: Jeff Merrifield
Estimated Sales: $2.5-5 Million
Number Employees: 10-19
Square Footage: 60000
Brands:
Best

19621 Best Manufacturing
10 Exchange Pl Unit 5
Jersey City, NJ 07302 201-356-3800
Fax: 201-356-3816 hospitality@bestmfg.com
www.bestmfg.com
Manufacturers of aprons, bathrobes, bedspreads and blankets, napkins, fabric, pillows, sheets and pillow cases tablecloths and napkins, towels, cotton or linen, uniforms, clothing
Manager: Eddie Chain
VP: Henry Garner
VP of Sales: Larry Miles
Number Employees: 100
Number of Products: 9

19622 Best Manufacturing Company
579 Edison St
P.O. Box 8
Menlo, GA 30731 800-241-0323
Fax: 888-393-2666 800-241-0323
usa@showabestglove.com
www.showabestglove.com

Manufacturer and exporter of protective gloves
CEO: Bill Alico
CFO: Andrew Akins
R&D: Bill Williams
Customer Service Rep: Deborah Ellenburg
Estimated Sales: $50 - 100 Million
Number Employees: 500-999
Brands:
Black Knight
D Flex
Ndex
Ndex Free
Nitri Pro
Nitty Gritty

19623 Best Restaurant Equipment & Design
4020 Business Park Dr
Columbus, OH 43204 614-488-2378
Fax: 614-488-4732 800-837-2378
www.bestrestaurant.com
Wholesaler/distributor of furniture, cookware and refrigeration, cooking and serving equipment; serving the food service market; installation and restaurant design services available
President: Jim Hanson
CFO: Suzane Yosick
Estimated Sales: $10 - 20,000,000
Number Employees: 50-99

19624 Best Sanitizers
P.O.Box 1360
Penn Valley, CA 95946 530-432-7460
Fax: 530-432-0752 888-225-3267
customerservice@bestsanitizers.com
www.bestsanitizers.com
Hand sanitizing lotion, infrared no touch hand sanitizer dispensers and sinks
President: Hillard Witt
VP Sales/Marketing: Ryan Witt
Marketing Manager: Suzette Pool
Number Employees: 10-19
Square Footage: 40000

19625 Best Value Textiles
555 Koopman Ln
Elkhorn, WI 53121 262-723-6133
Fax: 262-723-4204 800-248-9826
info@chefrevival.com www.chefrevival.com
Manufacturer, importer and exporter of chef/crew apparel and tools. Flame retardant items including gloves, table linens, aprons, uniforms and oven mitts
Manager: Alex Onda
CFO: Tone Long
R&D: Elizabeth Weiler
Marketing: Rob Johnson
Sales: Claude Brewer III
Production: Arturo Gomez
Purchasing Director: Elizabeth Weiler
Estimated Sales: $15 Million
Number Employees: 20-49
Square Footage: 42500
Parent Co: The Coleman Group
Type of Packaging: Food Service
Brands:
Gold Lion
Kut-Guard
Tri-Flex

19626 BestBins Corporation
1107 Hazeltine Blvd
Suite 470
Chaska, MN 55318 952-448-3114
Fax: 952-216-0155 866-448-3114
robert@bestbins.com www.bestbins.net
Provider of 'next generation' polycarbonate gravity bins for bulk foods such as coffee, candy and natural foods.
Owner: Robert Groenevelt
CEO: Robert Groenevelt
Vice President: Kyle McDonough
Estimated Sales: $1 - 3 Million
Number Employees: 1-4
Type of Packaging: Bulk

19627 Bestech
442 S Dixie Hwy E
Pompano Beach, FL 33060 954-785-4550
Fax: 954-785-4678 800-977-2378
info@bestek.net www.bestek.net
Manufacturer and exporter of water purification systems and vending machines
President: Gary Barr
Director Sales: Gary Barr
Estimated Sales: $1-2.5 Million
Number Employees: 5-9
Square Footage: 10000

19628 Bestpack Packaging Systems
10676 Fulton Ct
Rancho Cucamonga, CA 91730 909-987-4258
Fax: 909-987-5189 sales@bestpack.com
www.bestpack.com
High speed carton erector without vacuum suction cups and fully automatic L-sealer with shrink tunnel
President: David Lim
Estimated Sales: $1-2.5 000,000
Number Employees: 1-4

19629 Beta Tech Corporation
707 Commercial Ave
Carlstadt, NJ 07072-2685 201-939-2400
Fax: 201-939-7656 800-272-7336
info@betascreen.com www.betascreen.com
Manufacturer and exporter of vinyl doors for automatic kitchen dining room access
President: Arnold Serchuk
Public Relations Director: Stu Serchuk
Estimated Sales: $3 - 5 Million
Number Employees: 5-9
Parent Co: Beta Industries
Type of Packaging: Food Service
Brands:
Betadoor

19630 Bete Fog Nozzle
50 Greenfield St
Greenfield, MA 01301 413-772-0846
Fax: 413-772-6729 800-235-0049
sales@bete.com www.bete.com
Manufacturer and exporter of nozzles for food and dairy processing and spray drying nozzles for food processing
President: Mathew Bete
CEO: Lincoln Soule
Owner: David Bete
Research & Development: Dan Delesdernier
Quality Control: Tom Bassett
Sales Director: Susan Cole
Public Relations: Heidi Arnold
Estimated Sales: $15 Million
Number Employees: 100-249
Square Footage: 54000
Brands:
Bete Spiral
Mp Series
Sa Series
Xa Series

19631 Bethel Engineering & Equipment Inc
13830 McBeth Road
P.O.Box 67
New Hampshire, OH 45870 419-568-1100
Fax: 419-568-1807 800-889-6129
info@bethelengr.com www.bethelengr.com
Manufacturer and exporter of ovens, washers and spray booths
Owner: David Whitaker
Director Sales/Marketing: Tom Shield
Estimated Sales: $5 - 10 Million
Number Employees: 20-49
Parent Co: Finishing Systems Holdings

19632 Bethel Grain Company
4220 Commercial Way
Glenview, IL 60025-3597 847-635-9960
Fax: 847-635-6801
President: Steve Grubb
Estimated Sales: $1 - 3 Million
Number Employees: 5-9

19633 Betsy Ross ManufacturingCompany
251 Broadway
Paterson, NJ 07501-2033 973-278-7700
Fax: 973-278-5903 877-238-7976
brossmfg@aol.com
Flags and banners
Sales: Stacey Jung
Manager: Zahia Chehadeh
Estimated Sales: $1 - 5 Million
Number Employees: 5-9
Square Footage: 20000

19634 Bettag & Associates
116 N Central Dr
O Fallon, MO 63366-2337 636-272-4400
Fax: 636-272-1405 800-325-0959
customerservice@rdmproducts.net
www.rdmproducts.net
Cabinet enclosures for refrigeration units, theft deterrent cages, UL listed panel shop
President/CEO: Mike Bettag
Marketing: Carrie Ellis
Estimated Sales: Below $5 Million
Number Employees: 10-19
Square Footage: 15000
Brands:
Con-Pak
Ez-Lok
Pcu-2000

19635 Bettcher Industries
P.O.Box 336
Vermilion, OH 44089 440-965-4422
Fax: 440-965-4900 800-321-8763
vendas@bettcher.com.br www.bettcher.com
President: Laurence A Bettcher
Number Employees: 100-249

19636 Bettcher Industries
6801 State Route 60
Birmingham, OH 44889 440-965-4422
Fax: 440-328-4535 800-321-8763
sales@bettcher.com www.bettcher.com
Optimex® breading machine and power knife
President: Don Esch
Chairman and Chief Executive Officer: Laurence A. Bettcher
Chief Financial Officer: Tim McNeil
Research/Development: Ed Steele
Quality Control: Mike Casteel
VP/Marketing: Paul Pirozzola
Public Relations: Wayne Daggett
Plant Manager: David Mears
Purchasing Director: Ed Gross
Number Employees: 110
Type of Packaging: Food Service

19637 Bettendorf Stanford
1370 West Main
Salem, IL 62881 618-548-3555
Fax: 618-548-3557 800-548-2253
sales@bettendorfstanford.com
www.bettendorfstanford.com
Bread slicing and bagging equipment; also, cooling conveyors and slicing blades for bread, meat and fish
Manager: Matt Stanford
Sales: Chad Roberts
Shop Support: Merle Gwymon
Number Employees: 20-49

19638 Better Bilt Products
900 South Kay Avenue
P.O. Box 559
Addison, OH 60101-0559 630-543-6767
Fax: 630-543-0524 800-544-4550
www.bbponline.com
Wire, metal and tubular products and point of purchase displays
President: Scott Camp
General Manager: Patty Tournai
Sales & Design Manager: Harry Camp
Estimated Sales: $50-100 Million
Number Employees: 20-49

19639 Better Health Lab
200 South Newman St
Hackensack, NJ 07601 201-880-7966
Fax: 732-247-2001 800-810-1888
contactus@alkazone.com www.alkazone.com
Manufacturer and exporter of water ionizers and filters; processor and exporter of alkaline dietary supplements and teas
President: Robert Kim
Estimated Sales: $5-10 Million
Number Employees: 5-9
Square Footage: 80000
Type of Packaging: Consumer
Brands:
Alkaline
Alkazone
Alkazone Alkaline Booster Drops
Alkazone Antioxidant Water Ionizer
Alkazone Vitamins & Herbs
Antioxidant

Bhl
Better Health Lab

19640 Better Packages
255 Canal St
P.O. Box 711
Shelton, CT 06484 203-926-3722
800-237-9151
info@betterpackages.com
www.betterpackages.com
Manufacturer and exporter of carton sealing equipment, label moisteners and label and gum tape dispensers including electronic and manual.
President & CEO: Philip White
Vice President Sales & Marketing: Jeffrey Deacon
Director Research & Development: Allen Crowe
Marketing Director: Lynn Padell
Director of Sales: Marc Schaible
Operations Director: Paul Kromberg
Number Employees: 100-249
Brands:
Better Pack
Big Inch
Code Taper
Counterboy
Express
Packer
Penetron
Simplex
Tape Culator
Tape Shooter
Tape Squirt

19641 Betz Entec
200 Witmer Road
Horsham, PA 19044-2213 215-674-9200
800-877-1940
dan@hazard.com www.hazard.com
Water treatment products, boilers, process cooling systems, cookers and waste water treatment systems; also, engineering service available
President: Joseph Perugini
VP of Sales: A Moisey
VP Technical: D Henderson
Number Employees: 300
Square Footage: 240000
Parent Co: Betz Labs

19642 Beumer Corporation
191 Chambers Brook Rd
Branchburg, NJ 08876-3587 732-560-8222
Fax: 732-563-0905 usa@beumer.com
www.beumer.com
Manufacturer, importer and exporter of material handling equipment including automatic palletizing systems and automatic shrink and stretch hood unitizing systems
President: Matthias Erdsmannadoerf
VP: Hanno Behm
Number Employees: 20-49
Square Footage: 5200
Parent Co: Beumer Maschinenfabrik GmbH & Company KG

19643 Beverage Flavors International, LLC
3150 N Campbell Ave
Chicago, IL 60618 773-248-3860
Fax: 773-248-3862
info@beverageflavorsintl.com
www.beverageflavorsinternational.com
Beverage flavor emulsions and concentrates to bottlers. Flavor selection includes citrus punch, tropical fruit punch, pineapple-banana, mango peach, apple, strawberry-kiwi, aloha punch and pineapple-guava.
Manager: Daniel Manoogian
Office Manager: Barbara Martinez
Estimated Sales: $1.6 Million
Number Employees: 10
Type of Packaging: Bulk

19644 (HQ)Beverage-Air
3779 Champion Boulevard
Winston Salem, NC 27105 336-245-6400
Fax: 336-245-6453 800-845-9800
sales@bevair.com www.beverage-air.com
Manufacturer and exporter of commercial beverage coolers and food service refrigeration equipment
President: Philippo Berti
National Sales Manager: Bill Stowik
VP Sales/Marketing: Jack McDonald
National Service Manager: Loran Tucker
Estimated Sales: $1 - 5 Million
Number Employees: 500-999
Square Footage: 2000000
Parent Co: Specialty Equipment Companies
Type of Packaging: Food Service
Other Locations:
Beverage-Air
Honea Path SC
Brands:
Bever Marketeer
Bree
Maxi Marketeer

19645 Bevistar
615 Vista Drive
Oswego, IL 60543-8129 847-758-1581
Fax: 847-758-1617 877-238-7827
info@bevstarusa.com www.bevstarusa.com
Markets and distributes the newest technology in small-scale beverage dispensers and related consumable concentrate syrups. Specializes in systems comprised of patented technology ideal for the small volumeaccount/establishment/workplace
Marketing Director: Lynda Filicette
Sales Director: Saul Strankus
Plant Manager: Joe Rosado
Estimated Sales: $1 - 5 Million
Number of Brands: 1
Number of Products: 15
Square Footage: 18400
Parent Co: Isoworth Limited

19646 Bevles Company
729 3rd Ave
Dallas, TX 75230-2098 214-421-7366
Fax: 214-565-0976 800-441-1601
info@apwwyott.com www.apwwyott.com
Manufacturer and exporter of kitchen equipment including heated holding, transport and storage cabinets, low temperature roast and hold ovens, proofing cabinets and racks
President: Hylcon Jonas
CFO: Don Wall
Quality Control: Jim Austin
Marketing Assistant: Martha Patino
VP of Sales/Marketing: John Kossler
Estimated Sales: $20 - 50 Million
Number Employees: 100-249
Square Footage: 45000
Brands:
Climate 2000
Tendertouch
Transitray

19647 Bevstar
615 Vista Drive
Oswego, IL 60543-8129 847-758-1581
Fax: 847-758-1617 877-238-7827
info@bevstarusa.com www.bevstar.com
A beverage dispenser that dispenses hot, cold and sparkling bottled or filtered water, as well as soft drinks, juices, coffees and teas
General Manager/VP: Allan Wasserman
Estimated Sales: $1 - 5 Million

19648 Bex Inc.
836 Phoenix Dr
Ann Arbor, MI 48108 734-464-8282
Fax: 734-389-0470 sales@bex.com
www.bex.com
Manufacture of spray nozzels and accessories for parts cleaning, rinsing and food processing.

19649 Bi-O-Kleen Industries
820 SW 2nd Ave # 200
Portland, OR 97204-3087 503-224-6246
Fax: 503-557-7818 sales@bi-o-kleen.com
www.bi-o-kleen.com
Nonhazardous cleaning products including spray and glass cleaners, dish and laundry powders, enzyme stain and odor eliminator, carpet cleaning, dish soaps and laundry liquid
Owner: Robert C Kline Jr
CFO: Brian Barnett
VP Sales/Marketing: Cindy Rimer
Estimated Sales: $1.5 Million
Number Employees: 1-4
Number of Brands: 15
Number of Products: 15
Square Footage: 26000
Brands:
Bac Out
Bi-O-Kleen

19650 Bi-Star Enterprise
P.O.Box 14016
Torrance, CA 90503 310-532-5829
Fax: 310-532-4216 info@bi-star.com
www.bistar.com
Decorative tin boxes
President: Daniel Hsieh
Estimated Sales: $1-2.5 000,000
Number Employees: 1-4

19651 Biacore
200 Centennial Ave
Piscataway, NJ 08854-3950 732-885-5618
Fax: 732-885-5669 800-242-2599
pdaravingas@biacore.com www.biacore.com
Biosensor-based instrument: quantifying folic acid and biotin levels
President: Jerry Williamson
CFO: George Hogan
National Account Manager: Thomas Grace
Estimated Sales: $3 - 5 Million
Number Employees: 20-49

19652 Bib Pak
3205 Sheridan Road
Racine, WI 53403-3662 262-633-5803
Fax: 262-633-2606 www.bibpak.com
Disposable food service and catering equipment
President: John Geshay
Quality Control and R&D: Jim Geshay
VP Sales: Jim Geshay
Estimated Sales: Below $5 Million
Number Employees: 6
Square Footage: 56000
Parent Co: Standalone
Brands:
The Party Servers

19653 Bicknell & Fuller Paperbox Company
5600 Highway 169 N
Minneapolis, MN 55428-3027 617-361-8484
Fax: 617-361-3716
Quality Control: Manuel Santos
General Manager: George Preston
Estimated Sales: $5 - 10 Million
Number Employees: 130

19654 Big Apple Equipment Corporation
PO Box 408
Yonkers, NY 10705-0408 914-376-9300
Fax: 914-376-9375 800-225-2626
Commercial refrigeration
President: Sheldon J Bess
Estimated Sales: $5 - 10 000,000
Number Employees: 15

19655 Big Beam Emergency Systems
PO Box 518
Crystal Lake, IL 60039-0518 815-459-6100
Fax: 815-459-6126 info@bigbeam.com
www.bigbeam.com
Emergency lights and exit signs
President: Nick Shah
Controller: Steve Loria
Quotations Manager: Pat Huber
Product Specialist: Frank Drew
Estimated Sales: $5-10 Million
Number Employees: 50-99
Brands:
Big Beam

19656 Big Front Uniforms
4535 Huntington Dr S
Los Angeles, CA 90032 323-227-4222
Fax: 323-227-4111 800-234-8383
info@bigfront.com www.bigfrontuniforms.com
Uniforms
President: Karen Katz
Marketing: Rou Pope
Estimated Sales: Less than $500,000
Number Employees: 20-49

19657 (HQ)Big John Grills & Rotisseries
770 W College Ave
Pleasant Gap, PA 16823-5250 814-359-2755
Fax: 814-359-2621 800-326-9575
bjgrills@aol.com www.bigjohngrills.com
Barbecue grills including gas and charcoal
Owner: Jeff Derr
Sales & Marketing: Scott Gray
Sales Manager: Steve McLaughlin
Office Manager: Randy Czekaj

Estimated Sales: $2.5-5 Million
Number Employees: 10-19
Square Footage: 20000
Other Locations:
Big John Grills & Rotisseries
Frisco CO

19658 Big State Spring Companyy
2738 S Port Avenue
PO Box 5255
Corpus Christi, TX 78405-2035 361-884-6232
Fax: 361-884-1112 800-880-0244
billwilltx@aol.com
Refurbisher of food mixer whips
President: Bill Willette
Executive Officer: Armando Cantu
Craftsman: Manuel Ramos III
Number Employees: 1-4
Square Footage: 6000

19659 Big-D Construction Corporation
404 W 400 S
Salt Lake City, UT 84101-1108 801-415-6000
Fax: 801-415-6900 800-748-4481
lworell@big-d.com www.big-d.com
Designer and engineer providing construction management to food processors and distributors; turn key projects included
CFO: Larry Worrell
CEO: Bill Smith, Jr.
CFO: Steve Spurlock
CEO: Jack Livingood
Marketing Director: Greg Carlisle
Estimated Sales: $255 Million
Number Employees: 250-499

19660 Bijur Lubricating Corporation
2100 Gateway Centre Blvd
Suite 109
Morrisville, NC 27560 919-465-4448
Fax: 919-465-0516 800-631-0168
info@bijurlube.com www.bijur.com
Manufacturer, exporter and importer of automatic lubricating equipment and fluid dispensers
CEO: Thomas Arndt
Marketing Communications Manager: Peter Sweeney
Sales: Kevin Ryan
Estimated Sales: $10 - 20 Million
Number Employees: 20-49
Square Footage: 80000
Parent Co: Vesper Corporation
Brands:
Airmatic Lube
Fluidflex
Versa Iii Lub

19661 Bill Carr Signs
719 W 12th St
Flint, MI 48503 810-232-1569
Fax: 810-232-6879 billcarr@billcarrsign.com
www.billcarrsigns.com
Vacuum formed, silk screened and advertising displays
President: Jergmy Elfstrom
CFO: Jergmy Elfstrom
Sales Manager: Mike Ellithorpe
Estimated Sales: $1 - 2.5 Million
Number Employees: 5-9

19662 Bill Davis Engineering
222 Hickman Drive
Suite 103
Sanford, FL 32771 407-328-1117
Fax: 407-330-5231 billdaviseng@bellsouth.net
www.davis-engineering.net
Packaging machinery
President: Rick Paulsen
Estimated Sales: $5 - 10 Million
Number Employees: 20-49
Parent Co: Davis Engineering

19663 Billie-Ann Plastics Packaging Corp
360 Troutman St
Brooklyn, NY 11237 718-497-5555
Fax: 718-497-6095 888-245-5432
info@billieannplastics.com
www.billieannplastics.com
Cylinders and plastic boxes
President: William Rubinstein
Marketing: Bill Rubenstein
Estimated Sales: $3 Million
Number Employees: 30

19664 Billington Manufacturing/BWM
PO Box 4460
Modesto, CA 95352 209-526-9312
Fax: 209-521-4759 800-932-9312
info@billington-mfg.com
www.billington-mfg.com
Food processing equipment
President: Frances Billington
Marketing Manager: Charles Billington
Estimated Sales: $5-10 Million
Number Employees: 20-49

19665 Bilt-Rite Conveyors
735 Industrial Loop Road
New London, WI 54961-3530 920-982-6600
Fax: 920-982-7750 info@bilt-rite.com
www.bilt-rite.com
Manufacturer and exporter of stainless steel conveyors including belt, tabletop, chain and wire mesh
Owner: Jeffrey Bellig
R&D: Orlando Rojas
Estimated Sales: $5 - 10 Million
Number Employees: 20-49
Parent Co: Titan Industies, Inc.
Brands:
Bilt-Rite
Brico
Speed-Flow

19666 Bimba Manufacturing Company
P.O.Box 68
Monee, IL 60449-68
Fax: 708-534-9394 800-442-4622
support@bimba.com www.bimba.com
Rodless cylinders, double bore rectangular cross-section cylinders, rack and pinion rotary actuators, linear thrusters, hydraulic cylinders, inport flow control valves and position sensing switches
President: Patrick Orfstey
VP: Randy Dunlap
Head of Marketing Department: Dennis Kennedy
Head Of Operations.: Randy Dunlap
Number Employees: 250-499

19667 Bimetalix
P.O.Box 8
Sullivan, WI 53178-0008 262-593-8066
Fax: 262-593-8067 sales@bimetalix.com
www.bimetalix.com
A complete line of scraped surface heat exchanger cylinders for a variety of food processing
President: Forbes Hotchkiss

19668 Bindmax Proteins
16595 W Stratton Dr
New Berlin, WI 53151 262-796-2468
877-543-2463
tcolleton@bindmax.com www.bindmax.com
Protein products supplier utilized by meat, poultry and seafood companies to improve cook yield and flavor
Vice President: Tom Colleton
Estimated Sales: $1 Million
Number Employees: 5-9

19669 Biner Ellison
2685 South Melrose Drive
Vista, CA 92081 760-598-6500
Fax: 760-598-7600 800-733-8162
sales@binerellison.com www.binerellison.com
Manufacturer and exporter of bottle labeling, conveying, liquid filling and capping machinery and integrated packaging systems
President: Tom Ellison Jr
Operations: Jeff Schwarz
Estimated Sales: $2.5-5 Million
Number Employees: 10-19

19670 Binks Industries
1997a Aucutt Rd
Montgomery, IL 60538 630-801-1100
Fax: 630-801-0819 www.binksindustries.com
Manufacturer and exporter of pin hole detection equipment
President: Carolyn Calkins
Estimated Sales: $.5 - 1 million
Number Employees: 1-4
Square Footage: 6000
Brands:
Binks Industries, Inc.

19671 Bintz Restaurant SupplyCompany
P.O.Box 1350
Salt Lake City, UT 84110-1350 801-463-1515
Fax: 801-463-1693 800-443-4746
sales@bintzsupply.com www.bintzsupply.com
Wholesaler/distributor and design consultant of hotel and restaurant equipment and supplies
President: Roger Brown
CFO: Troy Hanson
Vice President: Brad Garner
Sales Manager: Michael Bailey
Purchasing Manager: Christie Smith
Estimated Sales: $10-20 Million
Number Employees: 20-49
Square Footage: 40000

19672 Bio Huma Netica
1331 W. Houston Ave.
Gilbert, AZ 85233 480-961-1220
Fax: 480-425-3061 800-961-1220
info@biohumanetics.com www.probiotic.com
Odor control, sludge management, environmental compliance
President: Lyndon Smith
Estimated Sales: $5-10 Million
Number Employees: 10-19

19673 Bio Industries
112 4th St
Luxemburg, WI 54217-8396 920-845-2355
Fax: 920-845-2439
Industrial and household cleaners including detergents, degreasers, etc
President: Irvin Vincent
Office Manager: Nancy Vincent
Estimated Sales: $1 - 5 Million
Number Employees: 3
Number of Brands: 2
Square Footage: 4000
Parent Co: NEW Plastics Corporation
Brands:
Gp 101
Hazel's

19674 Bio Pac
584 Pinto Ct
Incline Village, NV 89451 775-831-9493
Fax: 209-844-2134 800-225-2855
ceh@bio-pac.com www.bio-pac.com
Laundry and dish cleaners including citrus cleaner concentrates, liquid soap concentrate, laundry and bleach powder
President: Collin Harris
Estimated Sales: $1 Million
Number Employees: 1
Square Footage: 1000
Brands:
Biopac
Oasis

19675 Bio Zapp Laboratorie Inc
2110 Broken Oak St
San Antonio, TX 78232 210-805-9199
Fax: 210-805-9196 biozapp@biozapp.com
www.biozapp.com
Manufacturer and exporter of odor elimination systems, degreasers, glass ans surface cleaners
President: Miky Gershenson
Estimated Sales: $5,000,000
Number Employees: 5-9
Number of Products: 20
Type of Packaging: Consumer, Food Service, Private Label, Bulk
Brands:
Grease Off

19676 Bio-Cide International
P.O. Box 722170
Norman, OK 73070 405-329-5556
Fax: 405-329-2681 800-323-1398
info@bio-cide.com www.bio-cide.com
Manufacturer and exporter of chlorine dioxide based products for sanitization, disinfection, deodorization and water treatment
CEO: B C Danner
Sales Director: Damon Dickinson
Chairman: B Danner
Estimated Sales: $1-2.5 Million
Number Employees: 20-49
Square Footage: 80000
Brands:
Envirocon
Odorid
Oxine

Purogene
Sanogene

19677 Bio-Rad Laboratories

2000 Alfred Nobel Dr
Hercules, CA 94547 510-724-7000
Fax: 510-741-5630 800-424-6723
Laboratory equiptment and supplies for food industry
President/CEO: Norman Schwartz
VP/CFO: Christine Tsingos
Estimated Sales: $1.9 Billion
Number Employees: 900

19678 Bio-Tek Instruments

100 Tigan St
Winooski, VT 05404 802-655-4040
Fax: 802-655-7941 sales@biotek.com
www.biotek.com
Test kits for vitamins, mycotoxins, antibiotics, steroids/hormones, PSP, etc
President: Briar Alpert
CFO: Klus Deutfcher
Quality Control: Mike Sevigny
R&D: Mike Kontorovich
Estimated Sales: $20 - 50 Million
Number Employees: 100-249

19679 BioAmber

3850 Annapolis Ln N
Suite 180
Plymouth, MN 55447 763-253-4480
kristine.weigal@bio-amber.com
www.bio-amber.com
Succinic acid, BDO, plasticizers, polymers and C6 chemicals
President & CEO: Jean-Francois HUC
CTO: Jim Millis
CFO: Andrew Ashworth
Executive VP: Mike Hartmann
Chief Commercial Officer: Babette Pettersen
Chief Operations Officer: Fabrice Orecchioni
Estimated Sales: $560 Thousand
Number Employees: 74

19680 (HQ)BioControl Systems

12822 SE 32nd St Ste 100
Bellevue, WA 98005 425-603-1123
Fax: 425-603-0070 800-245-0113
bcs_us@biocontrolsys.com
www.biocontrolsys.com
Manufacturer and exporter of diagnostic microbiology test kits and equipment
President: Phillip Feldsine
R&D: David Kerr
Sr. Vice President: Carolyn Feldsine
Quality Control: Julia Terry
Director Marketing: Maritta Ko
Marketing Assistant: Jennifer Hawton
Estimated Sales: $3 - 5 Million
Number Employees: 5-9
Other Locations:
Biocontrol Systems
Westbrook ME

19681 BioExx Specialty Proteins

33 Fraser Ave
Suite G11
Toronto, ON M6K 3J9
Canada 416-588-4442
Fax: 416-588-1999 info@bioexx.com
www.bioexx.com
Oil and high-value proteins from Canola.
CEO & Director: Chris Schnarr
CFO: Greg Furyk CA
EVP: Samah Garringer
VP Operations: Clinton Smith

19682 BioSys

3810 Packard Street
Ann Arbor, MI 48108-2054 613-271-1144
Fax: 613-271-1148 800-458-5101
biosysinc@mail.com www.biosysinc.com
E coliform
President: Brian Leek
Estimated Sales: $1-2.5 Million
Number Employees: 5-9

19683 BioTech Films, LLC

Ste 115
5370 College Blvd
Leawood, KS 66211-1884 813-628-0424
Fax: 813-628-0162 800-633-2611
info@bioprogress.com www.bioprogress.com
Customized films made with food ingredients for packaging uses; edible, water-soluble films; edible plastic films; edible flakes for decoration
President: James Rossman
CEO: Graham Hind
Executive VP: Larry Shattles
Research & Development: Caroline Decker
Sales Director: Richard Fielder
VP Operations: George Tidy
Estimated Sales: $10 Million
Number Employees: 50-99
Number of Brands: 2
Number of Products: 20
Square Footage: 25000
Type of Packaging: Private Label, Bulk
Brands:
Aquafilm
Aquaflakes

19684 BioVittoria USA

357 N Milwaukee Rd
Libertyville, IL 60048 847-226-3467
paul_paslaski@biovittoria.com
www.biovittoria.com
Processor and supplier of monk fruit, a natural calorie-free sweetener that is a new alternative to sugar and artificial sweeteners.
President: Lan Fusheng
CEO: David Thorrold
CFO: Danny Wai Yen
VP: Garth Smith
VP Sales & Marketing: Paul Paslaski
Estimated Sales: $500 Thousand
Type of Packaging: Food Service, Private Label, Bulk

19685 Bioclimatic Air Systems

600 Delran Pkwy
Delran, NJ 08075-1269 856-764-4300
Fax: 856-764-4301 800-962-5594
mail@bioclimatic.com www.bioclimatic.com
Manufacturer and exporter of air purification systems
President: Michele Bottino
Estimated Sales: Below $5 Million
Number Employees: 10-19
Brands:
Aeromat
Aerotec

19686 Bioenergetics

P.O.Box 259096
Madison, WI 53725-9096 608-255-4028
Fax: 608-251-0658
Research on flavor and nutrition, consutation and formulation
President: Roy Schenk
CEO: Roy Schenk
CFO: Roy Schenk
Estimated Sales: Below $5 Million
Number Employees: 1 to 4

19687 Bioionix

4603 Triangle St
Mc Farland, WI 53558 608-838-0300
info@bioionix.com
www.bioionix.com
Disinfectants and oxidation systems for water treatment.
President/CEO: James Tretheway

19688 Biolog

21124 Cabot Blvd
Hayward, CA 94545 510-785-2585
Fax: 510-782-4639 800-284-4949
csorders@biolog.com www.biolog.com
Manufacturer and exporter of microbiological identification products
President/CEO & CSO: Barry R Bochner
Vice President Of Finance/CFO: Edwin R Fineman
Vice President Of Operations: Doug E Rife
Estimated Sales: E
Number Employees: 20-49
Brands:
Microlog
Microplate
Rainbow Agar

19689 Biological Services

10835 NW Ambassador Drive
Kansas City, MO 64153-1241 913-236-6868
Fax: 913-236-6868
Consultant offering testing services for all bacteria; also, sanitation inspections and sampling
Estimated Sales: less than $500,000
Number Employees: 1-4

19690 Biomist Inc

573 North Wolf Road
Wheeling, IL 60090 847-850-5530
Fax: 847-803-0875 prmartin@biomistinc.com
www.biomistinc.com
Biomist Power Disinfecting System Spray.
Director of Sales & Operations: Robert Cook
Director of Sales & Operations: Robert Cook II
Vice President Customer Service: Eileen Bowery
Director of Sales and Operations: Peter Martin

19691 Biopath

2611 Mercer Avenue
West Palm Beach, FL 33401-7415 800-645-2302
Fax: 888-645-2302 800-645-2302
rchiger@rxir.com www.biopathholdings.com
President: Peter Nielsen

19692 Bioscience International, Inc

11333 Woodglen Drive
Rockville, MD 20852-4365 301-231-7400
Fax: 301-231-7277 bioinfo@biosci-intl.com
www.biosci-intl.com
Manufacturer and wholesaler/distributor of microbial air samplers for the food and beverage industry.
President: Don Queen
VP: Marsha Pratt
Customer Service: Don Queen
Number Employees: 20
Square Footage: 140000
Brands:
Sas Super 90

19693 Biotest Diagnostics Corporation

400 Commons Way
Rockaway, NJ 07866-2030 973-625-1300
Fax: 973-625-9454 800-522-0090
customerservice@boitestusa.com
www.biotestusa.com
Manufacturer and exporter of environmental monitoring products
President: William Wiess
Quality Control: Lara Soltis
Marketing Director: Carol Julich
Production Manager: Dan Behler
Estimated Sales: $10 - 20 Million
Number Employees: 20-49
Parent Co: Biotest AG
Type of Packaging: Bulk
Brands:
Apc Particle Counters
Hycom Contact Slides
Rcs Air Samplers

19694 Biothane Corporation

2500 Broadway
Camden, NJ 08104 856-541-3500
Fax: 856-541-3366 sales@biothane.com
www.biothane.com
Manufacturer and exporter of anaerobic biological waste water treatment systems
President: Robert Sax
VP: Jay Murphy
VP Marketing/Sales: Denise Johnston
Estimated Sales: $3 - 5 Million
Number Employees: 30
Square Footage: 80000
Parent Co: Joseph Oat Corporation
Brands:
Biopuric
Biothane
Biobed

19695 Biovail Technologies

3701 Concorde Pkwy Ste 800
Chantilly, VA 20151 703-995-2400
Fax: 703-995-2490 biovail@btl.com
www.biovail.com
Consultant offering technology including controlled release and taste making applications, rapid dissolving tablets and long taste flavor systems
VP: Paul De Jardins
Estimated Sales: $20 - 50 Million
Number Employees: 100-249
Square Footage: 32000

19696 Bird Machine Company
2929 Allen Parkway
Suite 2100
Houston, TX 77019-2118 713-439-8600
Fax: 713-439-8699 800-229-7447
info@bakerhughes.com www.bakerhughes.com
Manufacturer and exporter of centrifuges and filters for liquid/solid separations
President/CEO: Chad Deaton
Sr. Vice President/COO: Martin Craighead
Communications Manager: Micki Baker
Estimated Sales: K
Number Employees: 10,000
Square Footage: 300000
Parent Co: Baker Hughes

19697 (HQ)Birko Corporation
9152 Yosemite St
Henderson, CO 80640 303-289-1090
Fax: 303-289-1190 800-525-0476
djohnson@birkocorp.com www.birkocorp.com
Manufactures 250 cleaning, sanitation and production chemicals, and specialized chemical delivery equipment for HACCP meat, poultry and food plants.
President: Mike Gangel
CEO: Mike Swanson
CEO: Mark Swanson
Research/Development VP: Terry MacAninch
VP sales: Philip Snellen
Customer Service: Rosey Hohendorf
Estimated Sales: $9 Million
Number Employees: 20-49
Other Locations:
Birko Distribution Center
Atlanta GA
Birko Distribution Center
Boise ID
Birko Distribution Center
Louisville KY
Birko Distribution Center
Modesto CA
Birko Distribution Center
Philadelphia PA
Birko Distribution Center
Phoenix AZ

19698 Birmingham Mop Manufacturing Company
115 Oxmoor Ln W
Birmingham, AL 35209-5901 205-942-6101
Fax: 205-942-6101
Mops, brooms, mopheads, etc
President: Glenn L Beacham Jr
CEO: Mary Williams
Secretary: Frank Beacham
Estimated Sales: Below $5 Million
Number Employees: 11
Square Footage: 6500

19699 Birmingham Restaurant Supply
2428 6th Ave S
Birmingham, AL 35233-3322 205-252-0076
Fax: 205-323-8630 sales@brescoinc.com
www.brescoinc.com
Wholesaler/distributor of restaurant equipment and supplies; design services available
President: George Tobia
Estimated Sales: $10-20 Million
Number Employees: 50-99

19700 Biro Manufacturing Company
1114 West Main Street
Marblehead, OH 43440 419-798-4451
Fax: 419-798-9106 sales@birosaw.com
www.birosaw.com
Manufacturer and exporter of meat cutting and processing equipment including grinders and mixer grinders, vacuum tumblers, tenderizers, horizontal slicing machines, cutters, meat mixers and industrial power saws; also, frozen foodflakers
President: Richard C Biro
VP of Sales & Marketing: D.L (Skip) Muir
Sales Manager: David Dursbacky
Estimated Sales: $5 - 10 Million
Number Employees: 50-99
Type of Packaging: Bulk
Brands:
Biro

19701 Bishamon Industries Corporation
5651 E Francis St
Ontario, CA 91761 909-390-0055
Fax: 909-390-0060 800-358-8833
info@bishamon.com www.bishamon.com
Scissor and skid lifts, pallet trucks and manual levelers/positioners and mobile loading docks; exporter of pallet levelers/positioners; importer of pallet jacks
President: Wataru Sugiura
Quality Control: Margie Giordano
VP Sales/Marketing: Robert Clark
Sales Manager: Steve O'Connell
Estimated Sales: $10-20 Million
Number Employees: 50-99
Square Footage: 130000
Brands:
Bishamon
Ecoa
Ez Loader
Tad

19702 Bishop Machine
2304 Hoge Ave
Zanesville, OH 43701-2166 740-453-8818
Fax: 740-453-6750 www.plantfloor.com
Automatic contact ink marking machinery
Manager: Ron Barnhouse
Sales Manager: Bob Bishop
Estimated Sales: $500,000-$1 Million
Number Employees: 5-9
Brands:
Ink-Koder

19703 Bison Gear & Engineering
3850 Ohio Ave
St Charles, IL 60174 630-377-4327
Fax: 630-377-6777 800-282-4766
info@bisongear.com www.bisongear.com
President: Ronald Bullock
CFO: James Winters
CEO: Martin Swarbrick
Quality Assurance Manager: Rick Wilson
Estimated Sales: $100+ Million
Number Employees: 100-249

19704 Bit Corporation
139 N Ocean Ave
Patchogue, NY 11772 631-758-3081
Fax: 631-758-3779 info@bit-corp.com
www.bit-corp.com
Owner: Robert White
Estimated Sales: $1 - 5 Million
Number Employees: 10-19

19705 Bivac Enterprise
357 Lake Shore Drive
Brick, NJ 08723-6013 732-920-0080
Fax: 609-693-8637
Thermoplastic sealing, vacuum and gas packing equipment

19706 Bivans Corporation
2431 Dallas St
Los Angeles, CA 90031 323-225-4248
Fax: 323-225-7316 sales@bivans.com
www.bivans.com
Packaging equipment for the food industry

19707 Bizerba USA
5200 Anthony Road
Suite F
Sandston, VA 23150 804-649- 206
Fax: 804-649-2064 us.info@bizerba.com
www.bizerbausa.com
Packaging equipment
President/CEO: Rob Sylkhuis
CFO: Cheryll Ziemblicki
VP, Engineered Solutions: Rainer DallaRosa
Marketing Manager: Chuck Saje
Director Retail Systems: Robert Weisz
Operations Manager: Joanne Scuccimarri

19708 Bizerba USA
31 Gordon Rd
Piscataway, NJ 08854 732-565-6000
Fax: 732-819-0429 us.info@bizerba.com
www.bizerbausa.com
Retial scales, slicers, weigh price labeling equipment as well as checkweighers, industrial scales and software
President/CEO: Andreas Kraut
VP/Controller: Frank Thiry
Marketing Specialist: Gaudy Cruz
Operations Manager: Keith Aumiller
Estimated Sales: $10-$20 000,000
Number Employees: 20-49
Type of Packaging: Food Service, Bulk

19709 Bjorksten Research Laboratories
3330 Dundee Road
Suite C7
Northbrook, IL 60062 847-714-9662
Fax: 608-224-0455 info@globalpdg.com
www.globalpdg.com
Laboratory providing research and development, consulting and contract research services
President: Michael Maloney
Estimated Sales: $1 - 3 Million
Number Employees: 5-9
Square Footage: 5000

19710 Black Bear Farm Winery
248 County Road 1
Chenango Forks, NY 13746 607-656-9863
mamabear@blackbearwinery.com
www.blackbearwinery.com
Wines
Owner: Mark Stacey
Co-Owner: Sandy Stacey
Chief of Cider Production: Joe Stacey

19711 (HQ)Black Brothers Company
501 9th Ave
PO Box 401
Mendota, IL 61342 815-539-7451
Fax: 815-538-2451 800-252-2568
info@blackbros.com www.blackbros.com
Manufacturer and exporter of gluing, coating and laminating machines for packaging of food products
President: Matthew Carroll
CFO: Jeff Simonton
Director Sales/Service: Walter Weiland
Sales: Todd Phalen
Estimated Sales: $10-20 Million
Number Employees: 50-99
Other Locations:
Black Brothers Co.
Warsaw IN
Brands:
Black

19712 Black Horse Manufacturing Company
601 Cumberland St
Chattanooga, TN 37404 423-624-0798
Fax: 423-624-7557 bhorse1178@aol.com
Advertising specialties
President: Larry Shope
Estimated Sales: Below $5,000,000
Number Employees: 5-9

19713 Black River Caviar
0075 Sunset Dr
Breckenridge, CO 80424-7218 970-547-1542
Fax: 970-547-9707 888-315-0575
graham@blackrivercaviar.com
www.blackrivercaviar.com
Caviar
President: Graham Gaspard
Estimated Sales: $500 Thousand
Number Employees: 5
Type of Packaging: Consumer, Food Service

19714 Black River Pallet Company
410 East Roosevelt Avenue
Zeeland, MI 49464 616-772-6271
Fax: 616-772-6206 800-427-6515
larry@blackriverpallet.com
www.blackriverpallet.com
Pallets and skids
President: Larry Slagh
Estimated Sales: $1 - 2.5 Million
Number Employees: 20-49
Square Footage: 14000

19715 Black's Products of HighPoint
2800 Westchester Drive
High Point, NC 27262-8039 336-886-5011
Fax: 336-886-4734 blacks@highpoint.net
www.blacksfurniture.com
Manufacturer and exporter of leather and restaurant furniture polishes
Estimated Sales: $1 - 5 Million
Number Employees: 20-49
Square Footage: 40000
Brands:
Antique Blend
Apple Polisher
Blodis
Garde
Leather Care
Wood Care

19716 Blackhawk Molding
120 W Interstate Rd
Addison, IL 60101 630-458-2100
Fax: 630-543-3904 info@blackhawkmolding.com
www.blackhawkmolding.com
Caps for dairy, juice and water bottling companies.

19717 Blackhawk Molding Co, Inc
120 W Interstate Rd
P.O. Box 419
Addison, IL 60101 630-628-6218
Fax: 630-543-3904 800-222-7391
info@blackhawkmolding.com
www.blackhawkmolding.com
Manufacturer and exporter of Tamper-Evident closures for the dairy, juice, and bottled water industires
Finance Executive: Richard Hogan
Estimated Sales: $100+ Million
Number Employees: 10-19
Number of Brands: 1
Number of Products: 6
Square Footage: 80000
Type of Packaging: Consumer, Food Service, Private Label, Bulk

19718 Blackmer
1809 Century Ave SW
Grand Rapids, MI 49503 616-241-1611
Fax: 616-241-3752 info@blackmer.com
www.blackmer.com
Pumps and compressors
President: Carmine Bosco
CFO: Tom Madden
VP: John Pepper
Quality Control: Dick Sowa
Sales Manager: Peter Sturgeon
Number Employees: 250-499

19719 Blackwing, Inc
17618 W Edwards Rd
Antioch, IL 60002 847-838-4888
Fax: 847-838-4899 800-326-7874
roger@blackwing.com www.blackwing.com
Organic piedmontese beef, chicken, buffalo and ostrich. Plus various game meats elk and venison. Fresh and frozen, food service and retail packed. Forty-One retail ready items, and two hundred food service ready items.
President: Beth Kaplan
VP: Roger Gerber
VP Marketing: Beth Allison
Office Manager: Sandy Maurer
Estimated Sales: $3.4 Million
Number Employees: 9
Number of Brands: 5
Number of Products: 140
Square Footage: 32000
Type of Packaging: Consumer, Food Service, Private Label, Bulk
Brands:
Blackwing Organics
Blackwing
Solomon Glatt Kosher
Sport Stick

19720 Blade Runners
P.O.Box 49
New London, WI 54961-0049 920-982-9974
Fax: 920-982-0580
Computer systems and software, used and rebuilt equipment, sausage linkers, smokehouses, accessories, stuffers and accessories, and vacuum pumps
Manager: John Mauthe
Estimated Sales: $1-2.5 000,000
Number Employees: 10-19

19721 Blake Corporation
W1902 Holy Hill Rd
Cecil, WI 54111 715-745-2700
Fax: 715-758-2080
Cheese equipment, cutters
Estimated Sales: $1 - 5 000,000
Number Employees: 1

19722 Blakeslee, Inc.
1228 Capital Drive
Addison, IL 60101 630-532-5021
Fax: 630-532-5020 blakeslee@blakesleeinc.com
www.blakesleeinc.com
Manufacturer and exporter of dishwashers, dishwasher racks, mixers, grinders, peelers and slicers
President: Pirjo Stafseth
CFO: Gary Stafseth
Executive VP: Chirs Berg
Marketing/Sales: Pirjo Stafsethh
Plant Manager: Gary Berg
Purchasing Manager: Ron Pentis
Square Footage: 400000
Parent Co: Blako
Brands:
Blakeslee

19723 Blako Industries
P.O.Box 179
Dunbridge, OH 43414 419-833-4491
Fax: 419-833-5733 sales@blako.com
FDA and USDA approved low density polyethylene films and bags. Polyethylene plastic film and bags
President: Ed Long
Quality Control: Brad Kickle
VP: Chuck Hansen
Director Sales: Ronald Rummel
Estimated Sales: $5 - 10 Million
Number Employees: 20-49
Square Footage: 25000

19724 Blanc Industries
88 King St Ste 1
Dover, NJ 07801-3655 973-537-0090
Fax: 973-537-0906 888-332-5262
email@blancind.com www.blancind.com
Manufacture, design and print point of sale promotional signage, displays and fixtures for the food and retail industry. Founded in 1997.
President: Didier Blanc
Operations: Dorothy Vitiello

19725 Blancett Fluid Flow Meters
8635 Washinton Avenue
Racine, WI 53406 262-639-6770
Fax: 262-417-1155 800-235-1638
info@blancett.com www.blancett.com
Manufacturer and exporter of 3-A sanitary liquid turbine flow meters
President: John Erskine
Sales: Jim Braden
Purchasing Manager: Chuck Tucker
Estimated Sales: $3 - 5 Million
Number Employees: 5-9
Square Footage: 40000
Parent Co: Racine Federated
Type of Packaging: Bulk
Brands:
Floclean

19726 Blanche P. Field, LLC
1 Design Center Pl
Boston, MA 02210 617-423-0715
Fax: 617-330-6876 800-895-0714
www.blanchefield.com
Manufacturer and exporter of custom lamp shades
President: Stephen G W Walk
CEO: Mitchell Massey
Estimated Sales: $2.5-5 Million
Number Employees: 20-49
Brands:
Glanz French

19727 Blanks United
18W140 Butterfield Road
15th Floor
Oakbrook Terrace, IL 60181 847-257-1213
Fax: 847-376-3313 847-257-1213
www.plastag.com
Supplier of blank plastic cards.
Estimated Sales: $50-100 Million
Number Employees: 100-249
Square Footage: 62000

19728 Blast-it-Clean
7800 E 12th St
Suite 7
Kansas City, MO 64126-2370 913-236-7776
Fax: 913-440-4725 877-379-4233
info@blast-it-clean.com blast-it-cleanonline.com
Warehouse providing cooler, freezer and dry storage of grocery products; rail siding, distribution, delivery and refrigerated space available; two facilities are available with a total of 160,000 Sq Ft of space
President: Bill Rieke
VP: Dan Haller
Estimated Sales: $83,000
Number Employees: 2
Square Footage: 80000

19729 Blaze Products Corporation
PO Box 1409
Shelbyville, KY 40066-1409 502-633-0650
Fax: 502-633-0657
blazesales@blazeproducts.com
www.blazeproducts.com
Manufacture chafing dish fuel
COO: Cindy Foster

19730 Blendco
8 J M Tatum Industrial Dr
Hattiesburg, MS 39401 601-544-9800
Fax: 601-544-5634 800-328-3687
csr@blendcoinc.com www.blendcoinc.com
Dry food manufacturer, do customize blending and packaging as well as private labeling and contract packaging. Founded in 1983.
President: Charles N Mc Caffrey Jr
Sales Executive: Carolyn Jones
Public Relations/Finance Executive: Ken Hrdlica
Purchasing Director: Charles Prescott
Estimated Sales: $10-20 Million
Number Employees: 30
Type of Packaging: Consumer, Food Service, Private Label, Bulk
Brands:
Ezy Time
Home Sensations

19731 Blendex Company
11208 Electron Dr
Louisville, KY 40299 502-267-1003
Fax: 502-267-1024 800-626-6325
sales@blendex.com www.blendex.com
Breadings, seasonings, flavors and marinades. Founded in 1979.
President: Jacquelyn Bailey
CEO: Ronald Pottinger
Vice President: Ron Carr
VP Research/Development: Jordan Stivers
Chief Marketing Officer: Olin Cook
VP Operations: Wayne McDowell
Estimated Sales: $10-20 Million
Number Employees: 100

19732 (HQ)Blentech Corporation
2899 Dowd Drive
Santa Rosa, CA 95407 707-523-5949
Fax: 707-523-5939 sales@blentech.com
www.blentech.com
Specialists in cooking and blending systems for batch and continuous operations. Over 26 years of experience in design and manufacturing of specialty process systems.
Chief Operating Officer: Dan Volt
Vice President: Nick Tellow
Asst. Marketing/Customer Service: Leanne Dunphy
Purchasing: Tom Corriveau
Estimated Sales: $6.8 Million
Number Employees: 50
Square Footage: 108000
Brands:
Blentech

19733 Blentech Corporation
2899 Dowd Dr.
Santa Rosa, CA 95407 707-523-5949
Fax: 707-523-5939 info@blentech.com
www.blentech.com
Batch cookers, continuous batch cookers, mixer-blenders, vacuum tumble mixers, tilt and hi-lift dumpers, screw conveyors, pump feeders
Founder: Darrell Horn
Estimated Sales: $5-10 Million
Number Employees: 50-99

19734 Blickman Supply Company
280 N Midland Avenue
Bldg M1
Saddle Brook, NJ 07663-5720 201-791-6680
Fax: 201-791-2288
Fry saver oil filtration machines for food service
Estimated Sales: $1-2.5 000,000
Number Employees: 19

19735 Blissfield Canning Company
PO Box 127
Blissfield, MI 49228-0127 517-486-3815
Fax: 517-486-4032

Canning
President: George Waigle
VP: Jerry Roessler
Estimated Sales: $2.5-5,000,000
Number Employees: 20-49

19736 Blodgett
44 Lakeside Ave
Burlington, VT 05401 802-860-3700
Fax: 802-864-0183 800-331-5842
literature@blodgett.com www.blodgett.com
Manufacturer and exporter of steamer ovens
President: Gary Mick
VP of Marketing: Des Hague
VP of Sales: Jeff Cook
Number Employees: 250-499
Parent Co: Maytag Corporation

19737 Blodgett Company
10840 Seaboard Loop
Houston, TX 77099 281-933-6195
Fax: 281-933-6196
sales@theblodgettcompany.com
www.theblodgettcompany.com
Manufacturer and exporter of packaging equipment including scales, controls and vertical form/fill/seal, packaging machines
President: S Bradley Blodgett
CFO and R&D: Bradley Blodgett
Purchasing Agent: Pete Duncan
Estimated Sales: $1 - 2.5 Million
Number Employees: 5-9
Square Footage: 5500

19738 Bloemhof
1215 South Swaner Road
Salt Lake City, UT 84104
Canada ÿ80- 42- 277
Fax: 801-973-6858 bert@bloemhof.com
www.bloemhof.com

19739 Blome International
1450 Hoff Industrial Drive
O'Fallon, MO 63366 636-379-9119
Fax: 636-379-0388 support@blome.com
www.blome.com
Corrosion resistance coating materials.
President: James Blome
CEO: Steve Bloom
Parent Co: Hempel

19740 (HQ)Blommer Chocolate Company
600 W Kinzie St
Chicago, IL 60654 312-226-7700
Fax: 312-226-4141 800-621-1606
www.blommer.com
Processor and exporter of chocolate ingredients for the bakery, dairy and confectionery industries including milk and dark chocolate, confectioner and pastel coatings, cookie drops, chocolate liquor, cocoa butter, cocoa powder, icecream ingredients, etc. Founded in 1939.
President: Peter Blommer
Founder, Chairman & CEO: Henry Blommer Jr
CFO: John Blommer
Vice President: Rich Blommer
Manager of Quality Assurance: Radka Kacena
Marketing & Purchasing Manager: Leanna Hicks
Sales Support: Chief Marketing Officer Kidd
VP of Operations: Rich Blommer
Plant Mnaager: Joe Chwala
Purchasing Manager: Faye Garcia
Estimated Sales: $38.4 Million
Number Employees: 130
Square Footage: 340000
Type of Packaging: Bulk
Other Locations:
Union City CA
East Greenville PA
Campbellford ON

19741 Bloomer Candy Company
2200 Linden Ave.
Zanesville, OH 43701 740-452-7501
Fax: 740-452-7865 website@bloomercandy.com
www.bloomercandy.com
Founded in 1879. Manufacturer and wholesaler/distributor of chocolate candy
CEO: Jerry Nolder
Purchasing Manager: Debbie Fogle
Estimated Sales: $3.50 Million
Number Employees: 40

Type of Packaging: Food Service, Private Label, Bulk
Brands:
Star
Starline Sweets

19742 Bloomfield Industries
10 Sunnen drive
St. Louis, MO 63143-3800 775-345-8200
Fax: 314-781-3445 888-356-5362
clientcare@wellsbloomfield.com
www.wellsbloomfield.com
Coffee and tea equipment including automatic and satellite brewers, airpots and thermal servers, decanters and accessories, coffee warmers and grinders and water filtration systems and filters
Vice President, Sales/Marketing, Wells-B: Paul Angrick
Senior VP: Dave Ek
Estimated Sales: $500,000-$1 Million
Number Employees: 1-4
Parent Co: Carrier Commercial Refrigeration
Brands:
Cafe Elite
Integrity
Koffe King

19743 Blower Application Company
N114w19125 Clinton Dr
PO Box 279
Germantown, WI 53022 262-255-5580
Fax: 262-255-3446 800-959-0880
sales@bloapco.com www.bloapco.com
Manufacturer and exporter of waste disposal systems and equipment shredders
President: John Stanislowski
Sales Director: Ric Johnson
Estimated Sales: $5 - 10 Million
Number Employees: 20-49
Square Footage: 40000
Brands:
Blo Apco

19744 BluMetric EnvironmentalInc.
3108 Carp Road
P.O. Box 430
Ottawa, ON K0A 1L0
Canada 613-839-3053
Fax: 613-839-5376 info@blumetric.ca
www.blumetric.ca
Manufacturer and exporter of food processing equipment including membrane and whey processing and brine systems; also, filtration equipment and water and waste water treatment systems.
President, Water: Dan L. Scroggins
CEO: Roger M. Woeller
Chief Financial Officer: Ian Malone, B.A. Hons.
Reaserch/Development: Sam Ali
Sales/Marketing: Gary Black
Director Process Development: Greg Choryhanna
Number Employees: 15
Square Footage: 34000
Type of Packaging: Bulk
Brands:
Sepro Flow
Sepro Kleen
Sepro Pure

19745 Blue Cross Laboratories
20950 Centre Pointe Pkwy
Santa Clarita, CA 91350
bmahler@bc-labs.com
www.bc-labs.com
Manufacturer and exporter of cleaning products including air fresheners, nonchlorine bleach, anti-bacterial liquid soap, health and beauty care products
President: Darrell Mahler
Secretary/Treasurer: Glenn Mahler
Director, Research & Development: J C Koshti
Vice President, Sales: Burke Mahler
Production Manager: Salvatore Tapia
Plant Engineer: Timothy Irvin
Estimated Sales: $28 Million
Number Employees: 160
Square Footage: 175000
Type of Packaging: Consumer, Private Label
Other Locations:
Blue Cross Laboratories
Phoenix AR
Brands:
Admire
Blue Too
Capn Clean
Carpet Scent
Class
Glass & More
Glass Brite
Mighty Pine
Mr. John
Now
Pan Pal
Royal Flush
Scent Sation
Sensation
True Pine
Ultra
Wash & Clean

19746 Blue Diamond Growers
1802 C St
Sacramento, CA 95811 916-442-8500
Fax: 916-446-8461 800-987-2329
www.bluediamond.com
Processor, grower and exporter of almonds, macadamians, pistachios and hazelnuts. Two thousand almond products in many cuts, styles, sizes and shapes for use in confectionery, bakery, dairy and processed foods. In house R/D for customproducts
President/Chief Executive Officer: Mark Jansen
Chairman of The Board: Clinton Shick
CFO: Dean LaVallee
Vice Chairman: Dale Van Groningen
Quality Assurance Lab Manager: Steven Phillips
Director, Marketing: Al Greenlee
Manager, Communications: Cassandra Keyse
Manager, Operations: Bruce Lisch
Manager, Product Development: Mike Stoddard
Senior Vice President, Procurement: David Hills
Estimated Sales: $709 Million
Number Employees: 1100
Type of Packaging: Consumer, Food Service, Private Label, Bulk
Brands:
Almond Breeze
Almond Toppers
Blue Diamond
Blue Diamond Almonds
Blue Diamond Hazelnut
Blue Diamond Macadamias
Breeze
Nut Thins
Smokehouse
California Nuts

19747 Blue Feather Product
165 Reiten Dr
Ashland, OR 97520 541-482-5268
Fax: 541-482-2338 800-472-2487
info@blue-feather.com
www.grabbitsewingtools.com
Manufacturer, importer and exporter of synthetic chamois, magnetic picture frames and refrigerator magnets
President: Feather W King
VP: John King
Marketing Manager: Ashley Black
Office Manager: Lisa Gentle
Estimated Sales: $5 - 10 Million
Number Employees: 5-9
Square Footage: 4000
Type of Packaging: Consumer
Brands:
Clipwell
Cougar Cloth
Magnamight
Vpeez

19748 Blue Giant Equipment Corporation
85 Heart Lake Road South
Brampton, ON L6W 3K2
Canada 905-457-3900
Fax: 905-457-2313 800-668-7078
sales@bluegiant.com www.bluegiant.com
Manufacturer and exporter of loading dock equipment, vehicle restraints, dock lifts, lift tables and industrial trucks and the Blue Genius Tech Control Panels
Chairman: Bill Kostenko
Director of Sales and Marketing: Steve Greco
VP of Sales/Marketing: Jeff Miller
Estimated Sales: $35 Million
Number Employees: 100-250
Square Footage: 85000

19749 Blue Lake Products
P.O.Box 16355
Irvine, CA 92623-6355 949-786-0108
Fax: 949-786-3108 800-257-3477
sales@bluelakeproducts.com
www.bluelakeproducts.com
Power transmission belting and specialty belting: O-ring drive belts, flat woven endless belts, custom fabricated belts and foam covered belts
President: Dean Smeaton
Estimated Sales: $3 - 5 Million
Number Employees: 5-9

19750 Blue Line Foodservice Distributing
24120 Haggerty Road
Farmington Hills, MI 48335 248-442-4502
Fax: 248-476-2084 800-892-8272
Patricia.McGuire@bldcorp.com
www.bluelinefd.com
Restaurant equipment and supplies
President: Matt Ilitch

19751 Blue Ridge Converting
100 Fairview Road
Asheville, NC 28803 828-274-2100
Fax: 828-274-0000 800-438-3893
info@brconverting www.brconverting.com
Manufacturer, importer and exporter of disposable and waterproof clothing and nonwoven wipers
CEO: Thomas Snell
Vice President: Daniel Neal
VP Sales: Daniel Neal
Purchasing: Jo Curtis
Estimated Sales: $2 Million
Number Employees: 24
Square Footage: 480000

19752 Blue Ridge Paper Products, Inc.
41 Main St.
Canton, NC 28716-4331 828-454-0676
Fax: 828-646-6101 www.blueridgepaper.com
Packaging materials
President: Richard Lozyniak
Estimated Sales: $315.90 Million
Number Employees: 2000
Type of Packaging: Bulk

19753 Blue Ridge Signs
1800 Barnett Dr
Weatherford, TX 76087-9440 817-596-7711
Fax: 817-598-0025 800-659-5645
blueridgesigns@aol.com
www.blueridgesigns.com
Indoor and outdoor painted signs including ply-wood, redwood and magnetic; also, display fixtures
Manager: Sherry Hamilton
Estimated Sales: Less than $500,000
Number Employees: 1-4

19754 Blue Tech
PO Box 2674
Hickory, NC 28603 828-324-5900
Fax: 828-324-9712 www.bluetechusa.com
Manufacturer and exporter of process control and air swept grinding systems, mixers, ribbon blenders, air filtration systems, etc
President: Dennis Harrow
VP: Charles Gero
Estimated Sales: $.5 - 1 million
Number Employees: 5-9
Square Footage: 8000

19755 BluePrint Automation
16037 Innovation Dr
Colonial Heights, VA 23834-5951 804-520-5400
Fax: 804-526-8164
sales@blueprintautomation.com
www.blueprintautomation.com
Fully integrated Turnkey Systems for applications that involve the loading of flexible and hard-to-handle packages into secondary containers such as cases, trays, cartons, crates and master bags
President: Mike Ganacoplos
CEO: Martin Prakken
CFO: Tom O'Connell
Director Sales/Marketing: John French
Sales Manager: John Kertesz
Operations Manager: David Schoon
Purchasing: Louis Spartano
Estimated Sales: $10 - 25 Million
Number Employees: 50-99
Square Footage: 160000

19756 Bluebird Manufacturing
6670 St. Patrick
Montreal, QC H8N 1V2
Canada 514-762-2505
800-406-2505
admin@bluebird.ca www.bluebird.ca
Manufacturer, exporter and importer of metal cook-ware including pots, pans, fry baskets, etc; also, custom services available
President: Harvey Engelberg
Brands:
Bluebird Products

19757 Bluegrass Packaging Industries
3651 Collins Lane
Louisville, KY 40245 502-425-6442
Fax: 502-425-7201 800-489-3159
ellen@bluegrasspackaging.com
www.bluegrasspackaging.com
Co-packer of dried foods and snacks, beans, grain, gum balls, candy, coffee, etc
President: Ellen Waddle
CEO: Auggie Chick
Estimated Sales: $3 - 5 Million
Number Employees: 20-49
Square Footage: 100000

19758 Blueprint Automation
16037 Innovation Dr
Colonial Heights, VA 23834-5951 804-520-5400
Fax: 804-526-8164
sales@blueprintautomation.com
www.blueprintautomation.com
Vision-guided robotics, case packing of flexible bags and rigid packages and complete turn-key packaging systems, taking control of the product in its naked state through packaging, utilizing and palletizing.
President: Mike Ganacoplos
President: Mike Ganacoplos
Quality Control: Tom O'Connell
Marketing Director: Robbie Quinlin
Sales Manager: John Kertesz
Operations Manager: Jason Estes
Estimated Sales: $10 - 20 Million
Number Employees: 50-99
Square Footage: 40000

19759 Bluewater Environmental
704 Mara Street
Suite No. 201
Point Edward, ON N7V 1X4
Canada 519-337-0228
Fax: 519-337-9178 888-808-9782
eng@blueh2o.ca www.blueh2o.ca

19760 Bluff Manufacturing
1400 Everman Pkwy Ste 120
Fort Worth, TX 76140 817-293-3018
Fax: 817-293-7570 800-433-2212
bluffmfg@bluffmanufacturing.com
www.bluffmanufacturing.com
Manufacturers exporter of dockboards, dock plates and edge-of-dock levelers
President: Clark Smith
Estimated Sales: $10-20 Million
Number Employees: 9

19761 Bluffton Motor Works
410 E Spring St
Bluffton, IN 46714 260-827-2200
Fax: 260-827-2303 800-579-8527
mburgan@blmworks.com www.blmworks.com
Electric motors for the dairy, beverage, meat and poultry industries.
Number Employees: 200

19762 Bluffton Slaw Cutter Company
331 N Main St Ste 1
Bluffton, OH 45817 419-358-9840
Fax: 419-358-9840
sales@blufftonslawcutter.com
www.blufftonslawcutter.com
Manufacturer and exporter of lid removers, cheese shredders, apple slicers and slaw cutters
President and CFO: Paul King
VP: T King
Quality Control: Louis Stier
Marketing Director: L King
Estimated Sales: Below $5 Million
Number Employees: 1-4
Square Footage: 1200
Brands:
Top Loose

19763 Blumer
800A Prospect Hill Road
Windsor, CT 06095-1570 860-688-1589
Fax: 860-688-1539 marketing@blumerusa.com
www.blumerusa.com
Banding and labeling production machines
President: Kevin Coyle
VP: David Olbria
Estimated Sales: $2.5 - 5 Million
Number Employees: 5-9

19764 Boardman Molded Products/Space-Links
P.O.Box 1858
Youngstown, OH 44501 330-788-2401
Fax: 330-788-9665 800-233-4575
tbobonick@spacelinks1.com
www.spacelinks1.com
Safety mats and flooring
President: Ronald N Kessler
Controller: Jim Bowser
QA Manager: Jeff Westlake
VP Marketing: Dan Kessler
VP of Sales: Tom Bobonick
Plant Manager: George Lolakis
Estimated Sales: $20 - 50 Million
Brands:
Aisle Pro
Econo Pro
Entry Pro
Grip Top
Super Links
Water Pro

19765 Bodine Electric Company
201 Northfield Rd
Northfield, IL 60093-3311
Fax: 773-478-3232 info@bodine-electric.com
www.bodine-electric.com
Components for food processing machinery including fractional hp and gear motors and controls
President: John Bodine
CFO: Jeff Stahl
Marketing Manager: Edmund Glueck
Estimated Sales: $20-50 Million
Number Employees: 250-499
Square Footage: 250000
Type of Packaging: Private Label, Bulk

19766 Bodolay Packaging Machinery
2401 Airport Rd
Plant City, FL 33563-1101 813-754-9960
Fax: 813-754-9321 www.bodolaypackaging.com
Horizontal form, fill and seal packaging machines
President: Mostafa Farid
Estimated Sales: Below $5 Million
Number Employees: 5-9
Number of Products: 2
Type of Packaging: Consumer

19767 Bodycote Materials Testing
7530 Frontage Rd
Skokie, IL 60077-3213 847-676-2100
Fax: 847-676-3065 800-323-3657
info@bodycoteusa.com www.bodycote.com
Materials testing, food and drug testing, packaging testing
Chief Executive Officer: Stephen Harris
CEO: Gordon Lawerance
Estimated Sales: $2.5-5 Million
Number Employees: 50-99

19768 Boedeker Plastics
904 West 6th Street
Shiner, TX 77984 361-594-2941
Fax: 361-594-2349 800-444-3485
info@boedeker.com ÿ www.boedeker.com
High performance engineering plastics such as vespel, torlon, ultem, peek, nylon, teflon, and delrin, in-house machine shop manufactures parts from prints or samples
President: Marvin Boedeker
Marketing Director: Mike Randall
Sales: Jake Jalufka
Estimated Sales: $5-10 Million
Number Employees: 50

19769 Boehringer Mfg. Co. Inc.
6500 Highway 9
Unit F
Felton, CA 95018 831-704-7732
Fax: 831-704-7731 800-630-8665
info@toolwizard.com www.bbq-tools.com

Manufacturer and exporter of burlap sack needles, block scrapers, dough cutters, boning, meat hooks, and specialty blades; custom plastic injection moldings; also bbq tools and accessories
Secretary: Mark Fowles
Estimated Sales: $300-500,000
Number Employees: 5-9
Number of Products: 50
Square Footage: 2500
Parent Co: Boehringer Manufacturing Company
Type of Packaging: Consumer, Private Label

19770 **Boekels**
P.O.Box 7004
Oakland, NJ 07436-7004 201-651-0500
Fax: 201-651-0505 info@boekels.com
www.iaiusa.com
President: Mark Schultz

19771 **Boelter Industries**
202 Galewski Dr
Winona, MN 55987 507-452-2315
Fax: 507-452-2649
dboelter@boelterindustries.com
www.boelterindustries.com
Folding cartons and special paper products
President: Dennis Boelter
CEO: Lester Boelter
VP: Dixie Breitenfeldt
R&D: Dean Boelter
Estimated Sales: $20 - 50 Million
Number Employees: 130
Square Footage: 325000
Type of Packaging: Consumer, Food Service, Private Label, Bulk

19772 **Bogner Industries**
199 Trade Zone Drive
Ronkonkoma, NY 11779-7362 631-981-5123
Fax: 631-981-3792 sales@bognerindustries.com
www.bognerindustries.com
Manufacturer, engineer and designer of hi-tech and high quality production of stainless steel processing and packaging equipment for the food and beverage industries.
Owner: Erwin Bogner
Owner: Ruediger Albrecht
Sales Director: Tina Hadizadeh
Type of Packaging: Food Service

19773 **Bohler Bleche**
11525 Brittmoore Park Drive
Houston, TX 77041-6916 800-852-8556
Fax: 281-856-5458 bohlr_jl@nol.net
www.iadd.org/LISTAD.HTM - 101k
Specialty steel sheet and plate products used in producing knives for food processing
Head of Marketing Dept.: John Leonard
Operations Manager: John Leonard

19774 **Bohn & Dawson**
3500 Tree Court Ind Blvd
Saint Louis, MO 63122 636-225-5011
Fax: 636-825-6111 800-225-5011
info@bohnanddawson.com
www.bohnanddawson.com
Manufacturer and exporter of metal fabricators, tubular parts and assemblies; also, tool and die services available
President: Steven L Hurster
Engineer: J Koopman
VP: R Wiele
CFO: Steve Leibach
Quality Control: Mike Schneider
Estimated Sales: $20 - 50 Million
Number Employees: 130

19775 **Bohnert Construction Company**
PO Box 34320
Kansas City, MO 64120-4320 816-231-2281
Fax: 816-241-5236 800-701-2281
bohnert@chiefind.com
www.bohnert.chiefind.com
Manager: Eric Limoges
Quality Control: Emmie Cobins
Estimated Sales: $5 - 10 Million
Number Employees: 10

19776 **Boilzoni Auramo, Inc.**
17635 Hoffman Way
Homewood, IL 60430 708-957-8809
Fax: 708-957-8832 800-358-5438
sales.us@bolzoni-auramo.com
www.bolzoni-auramo.ca
Manufacturer and exporter of lift truck attachments
President: Roberto Scotti
General Manager: Dick Fennessey
Estimated Sales: $5-10 Million
Number Employees: 10
Parent Co: Auramo O.Y.

19777 **Boise Cascade**
1111 West Jefferson Street
Suite 300
Boise, ID 83702-5389 509-924-5211
Fax: 509-924-6866 BCBrand@bc.com
www.bc.com
Corrugated containers
President: Stanley Bell
Chief Executive Officer: Thomas Carlile
Chief Financial Officer: Wayne Rancourt
Senior Vice President: Thomas Corrick
Manager: Bill Bialkowsky
Vice President of Sales & Marketing: Dennis Huston
Vice President of Operations: Dan Hutchinson
Estimated Sales: $1 - 5 Million
Number Employees: 1-4

19778 **Boise Cascade Corporation**
1544 W 27th St
Burley, ID 83318 208-678-3531
Fax: 208-677-7719 burley-box@bc.com
www.bc.com
Containers and boxes
Nnational Accounts Manager: Lee Gill
Estimated Sales: $50 - 100 Million
Number Employees: 100-249
Parent Co: Boise Cascade Corporation

19779 **Boise Cold Storage Company**
495 S 15th St
Boise, ID 83702 208-344-9946
Fax: 208-344-8598 tviehweg@micron.net
Ice; warehouse providing cold, dry and freezer storage; also, distribution available
Owner: Tim Johnson
Office Manager: B Grover
General Manager: M Tallent
Estimated Sales: $1-2,500,000
Number Employees: 20 to 49
Square Footage: 50000

19780 **Boldt Company**
P.O.Box 419
Appleton, WI 54912-0419 920-739-6321
Fax: 920-739-4409 info@boldt.com
www.theboldtcompany.com
Offering consulting, construction and maintenance solutions throughout the United States
President/COO: Robert DeKoch
CEO: Thomas Boldt
CFO: Dale Von Behren
CEO: Thomas J Boldt
Chairman: Oscar Boldt
Marketing Director: Paula Wydeven
President, Chief Operating Officer: Bob DeKoch
Estimated Sales: $1-$3 Million
Number Employees: 1,000-4,999

19781 **Boldt Technologies Corporation**
812 10th Street
West Des Moines, IA 50265-3507 515-277-4848
Fax: 515-277-2775
Pouch machines, bag formers/fillers/sealers, cocoa packaging equipment, teabag machinery
President: Donald Vanoort
Estimated Sales: Less than $500,000
Number Employees: 25

19782 **Bolling Oven & Machine Company**
1101 Jaycox Road
Avon, OH 44011-1394 440-937-6112
Fax: 440-937-6875
Compact revolving tray baking ovens
VP: Lynn Bolling
Sales: Dennis Szalai
Estimated Sales: less than $500,000
Number Employees: 6
Square Footage: 11000

19783 **Bollore**
60 Louisa Viens Dr
Dayville, CT 06241 860-774-2930
Fax: 860-774-8895 sales@bolloreinc.com
www.bolloreinc.com
Specialty plastic films; high performance multipurpose, specialty and cross-linked shrink packaging films. ISO 9001:2000 certified.
CEO: Stephen Brunetti
Estimated Sales: $20 - 50 Million
Number Employees: 100-249

19784 **Bolmet**
60 Louisa Viens Drive
Dayville, CT 06241-1106 860-774-7431
Fax: 860-774-8895 sales@bolloreinc.com
www.bolloreinc.com
Tea, coffee filters (paper) and shrinkfilms
Estimated Sales: $20-50 Million
Number Employees: 100-249

19785 **Bon Chef**
205 State Route 94
Lafayette, NJ 07848 973-383-8848
Fax: 973-383-1827 800-331-0177
info@bonchef.com www.bonchef.com
Chafing dishes, coffee urns and buffet/servingware
President: Salvatore Torre
VP: Anthony Lo Grippo
Estimated Sales: $2.5-5 Million
Number Employees: 20-49

19786 **Bonar Plastics**
1005 Atlantic Dr
West Chicago, IL 60185 630-293-0303
Fax: 630-293-0930 800-295-3725
bonar@foxvalley.net www.bonarplastics.com
Custom plastic rotational molded bulk bins, tanks, hoppers, drums, combo bins, etc
President: John Bielby
CFO: Don Layng
Quality Control: Gustavo Cuevas
Sales Director: Cliff Thomas
Plant Manager: Gustavo Cuevas
Estimated Sales: Below $5 Million
Number Employees: 50-99
Square Footage: 100000

19787 **Bonar Plastics**
6111 S 6th Way
Ridgefield, WA 98642 360-887-2230
Fax: 360-887-3553 800-972-5252
lhughes@bonarplastics.com
www.bonarplastics.com
Bulk food handling bins
President: John Bielby
CFO: Lee Robinson
Sales/Marketing: Larry Hughes
Plant Manager: Jeff Harms
Estimated Sales: $20-50 Million
Number Employees: 100-249
Square Footage: 100000
Parent Co: Low & Bonar
Brands:
Bonar
Payloader
Polar
Two-Can

19788 **(HQ)Bonneau Company**
3334 South Tech Boulevard
Miamisburg, OH 45342 937-886-9100
Fax: 937-886-9300 800-394-0678
www.bonneaucompany.com
Manufacturer, importer and exporter of commercial and industrial dyes including paraffin, microcrystalline waxes and blends
President: Timothy Muldoon
VP/Technical Director: Paul Guinn
Estimated Sales: $5 - 10 Million
Number Employees: 1-4
Square Footage: 60000
Brands:
Bonn Dye
Bonn Trace

19789 **Bonnot Company**
1520 Corp Woods Pkwy Ste 100
Uniontown, OH 44685 330-896-6544
Fax: 330-896-0822 info@thebonnotco.com
www.thebonnotco.com
Manufacturer and exporter of extruders for food, chemicals, ceramics, catalysts, etc
President: George Bain
CFO: Becky Goulden
VP: John Negrelli
Engineering Manager: Kurt Houk
Controller: Becky Bouldon

Estimated Sales: $2.5-5 Million
Number Employees: 5-9

19829 Bradford Derustit Corporation
PO Box 1194
Yorba Linda, CA 92885 714-695-0899
Fax: 714-965-0840 877-899-5315
derustit@albany.net www.derustit.com
Chemical metal cleaners
President: Lois R Squire
VP: Anne Denney

19830 Bradley Industries
1 Westbrook Corp Ctr Ste 300
Westchester, IL 60154 815-469-2314
Fax: 815-469-7089
customerservice@atlantismatch.com
www.bradleyindustries.com
Matchbooks
President: Jon Bradley
Vice President: John Bradley
Estimated Sales: $5-10 Million
Number Employees: 50-99
Square Footage: 60000

19831 Bradley Lifting Corporation
1030 Elm St
York, PA 17403 717-848-3121
Fax: 717-843-7102 info@bradleylift.com
www.bradleylifting.com
Manufacturer and exporter of material handling equipment including slab and ingot tongs, plate and sheet lifters and coil and paper roll grabs
President: Tom Thole
CFO: Winfred Bradley
Estimated Sales: $5 - 10 Million
Number Employees: 17
Parent Co: Xtek, Inc.

19832 Bradley Ward Systems
635 Montauk Way
Alpharetta, GA 30022-4704 770-754-5899
Fax: 770-754-5876 bward@bwsys.com
www.bwsys.com
Manufacturing execution systems for packaging
President: Garry Diver

19833 Bradman Lake Inc
3050 Southcross Blvd.
Rock Hill, SC 29730 704-588-3301
Fax: 704-588-3302 usa@bradmanlake.com
www.bradman-lake.com
Specializes in the design and manufacture of packaging machinery
Manager: Steve Irwin
Marketing Director: Mervat El RaFei
Sales Director: Nick Bishop
Plant Manager: Sam Hunnicutt
Estimated Sales: $50 Million
Number Employees: 20-49
Parent Co: Bradman Lake Ltd
Type of Packaging: Bulk
Other Locations:
Bradman Lake Group
Charlotte NC

19834 Brady Enterprises
167 Moore Road
East Weymouth, MA 02189-0002 781-337-5000
Fax: 781-337-5351 info@bradyenterprises.com
www.bradyenterprises.com
Manufacturer and exporter of cocktail, powdered drink, stuffing and meatloaf mixes and seasonings; importer of seasoning; also, spray drying and dish detergent
President: Kevin Maguire
Chairman/CEO: John Brady
CFO: Mary Gudalawicz
Director QC/R&D: Mike Waytowich
Director Sales/Marketing: Desi Gould
Human Resources: Jack Brady Jr.
Estimated Sales: $11.60 Million
Number Employees: 90
Number of Brands: 3
Number of Products: 16
Type of Packaging: Consumer, Food Service
Brands:
Bar-Tenders
Bells
Dishwasher Glisten

19835 Brady Worldwide
P.O.Box 2131
Milwaukee, WI 53201 414-358-6600
Fax: 414-228-5979 www.whbrady.com
Safety signage and regulatory training products: pipe markers, floor marking materials, numbering and coding markers, aluminum, fiberglass and vinyl siding
President: Katherine Hudson
CEO: Frank Jaehnert
Estimated Sales: $50 - 100 Million
Number Employees: 100-249

19836 Bragard Professional Uniforms
201 E 42nd St # 1805
New York, NY 10017-5710 212-759-0202
Fax: 212-353-0318 800-488-2433
customersupport@bragardusa.com
www.bragardusa.com
Manufacturer, importer and exporter of uniforms and special clothing including aprons, linens, chef's hats and coats, footwear, cloth towels, etc.; complete embroidery services available
CEO: Lu Aranzamendez
Vice President: Peter Isom
Chief Operating Officer: Benjamin Bragard
Estimated Sales: $1-2.5 Million
Number Employees: 1-4
Parent Co: Bragard SA
Brands:
Bragard
Cooking Star By Bargard

19837 Bran & Luebbe
1234 Remington Rd
Schaumburg, IL 60173-4812 847-882-8116
Fax: 847-882-2319 info@branluebbe.com
www.pumpsandprocess.com
Manufacturer and exporter of metering pumps, food blending systems and analyzers for determination of protein, fat, moisture and other parameters in food products
President: Robert Arcaro
Marketing Coordinator: Kelly Breitlando
Director Sales: Jim Hunson
Estimated Sales: $20-50 Million
Number Employees: 50-99
Square Footage: 36000
Parent Co: Bran & Luebbe GmbH

19838 Brand Castle
5111 Richmond Road
Bedford Heights, OH 44146 216-292-7700
Fax: 216-292-7701 jimmyz@brandcastle.com
www.brandcastle.com
Cookie making kits and decorations
President/Founder: Jimmy Zeilinger
Marketing: Jimmy Zellinger
VP Sales/Marketing: Jim Shlonsky
Operations Manager: Jeff Berger
Number Employees: 5

19839 Brand Specialists
PO Box 381146
Duncanville, TX 75138-1146 972-283-8491
Fax: 972-572-9292 888-323-3708
jond@brandspecialists.com
www.brandspecialists.com
Consultant specializing in product development including frozen, fresh and dry items for the retail and food service markets
President: Dalton Lott
Member of the Board: Daniel F Pickering
VP of Operations: Jon Davies
Estimated Sales: $5-10 Million
Number Employees: 10

19840 Brandstedt Controls Corporation
3600 NW 115th Ave
Doral, FL 33178 305-477-0034
Fax: 305-477-0035 800-426-5488
info@brandstedt.com www.brandstedt.com

19841 Branford Vibrator Company
3600 Cougar Drive
Peru, IL 61354-9336 815-224-1200
Fax: 815-224-1241 800-262-2106
www.cougarindustries.com
Manufacturer and exporter of electronic control systems including vibrators
President: D Pedritti
Estimated Sales: $20-50 Million
Number Employees: 50-99
Parent Co: Cougar Industries

19842 Branford Vibrator Company
3600 Cougar Drive
Peru, IL 61354-9336 815-224-1200
Fax: 815-224-1241 800-262-2106
www.cougarindustries.com
Manufacturer and exporter of pneumatic and electric vibrators
President: D Pedritti
Manager: T Zagorski
Estimated Sales: $20-50 Million
Number Employees: 50
Parent Co: Cougar Industries
Brands:
Branford

19843 Branson Ultrasonics Corporation
41 Eagle Road
P.O. Box 1961
Danbury, CT 06813-1961 203-796-0400
Fax: 203-796-0450 info@bransonultrasonics.com
www.bransonultrasonics.com
The industry leader in the design, development, manufacture, and marketing of plastics joining, precision cleaning, ultrasonic processing, and ultrasonic metal welding equipment.
President: Ed Boone
VP Finance: Robert Tibbets
VP/General Manager-North America: Richard Gehrin
VP Sales: Rodger Martin
VP Operations: Anthony Prioreschi
Number Employees: 1,000-4,999

19844 Brass Smith
5125 Race Court
Denver, CO 80216 303-331-8777
Fax: 303-331-8444 800-662-9595
SALES@BSIDESIGNS.COM www.zguard.com
Manufacturer and exporter of sneeze guards, hot merchandising display cases, railing systems, crowd control posts, menu stands, etc
Human Resources: Dave Carr
Marketing: Wayne Sirmons
Regional Sales Manager: Benny Martinez
Estimated Sales: $5-10 Million
Number Employees: 50-99
Square Footage: 400000
Parent Co: BSI
Brands:
Beltway
Brass Master
Lustre Rail
Z Guard

19845 Braun Brush Company
43 Albertson Ave
Albertson, NY 11507 516-741-6000
Fax: 516-741-6299 800-645-4111
sales@brush.com www.braunbrush.com
Manufacturer, importer and exporter of sanitary cleaning brushes used for baking, confectionery processing, etc
President: Lance Cheney
Business Development Director: Peter Lassen
Customer Service: Jerilyn Leis
Accounting: Joan Egidio
Estimated Sales: $2 Million
Number Employees: 20-49
Square Footage: 14000
Parent Co: Braun Industries
Type of Packaging: Consumer, Food Service, Private Label, Bulk
Brands:
Saniset

19846 Braun Brush Company
43 Albertson Ave
Albertson, NY 11507 516-741-6000
Fax: 516-741-6299 800-645-4111
sales@brush.com www.braunbrush.com
Manufacturer, importer and exporter of USDA standard and custom designed brushes
President: Lance Cheney
President: Max Cheney
Director of Business Development: Peter Lassen
Customer Service: Jerilyn Leis
Accounting: Joan Egidio
Estimated Sales: $2.5-5 Million
Number Employees: 20-49
Square Footage: 14000

19847 Brechbuhler Scales
1424 Scales St SW
Canton, OH 44706 330-453-2424
Fax: 330-453-5322 www.brechbuhler.com
Manufacturer and exporter of scales including dormant, flour, warehouse, portable, etc
Manager: Roger Doerr
Branch Manager: Rick Spradling
Estimated Sales: $1-2.5 Million
Number Employees: 160
Parent Co: Brechbuhler Scales
Type of Packaging: Bulk

19848 Brechteen
30060 23 Mile Rd
Chesterfield, MI 48047-5718 586-949-2240
Manufacturer and importer of packaging materials including plastic, cellulose, collagen and fibrous; manufacturer of stuffing equipment
VP of Sales: Roger Allen
Number Employees: 100-249

19849 Breddo Likwifier
1230 Taney N.
Kansas City, MO 64116 816-561-9050
Fax: 816-561-7778 800-669-4092
don.wolfe@corbion.com www.breddo.com
Manufacturer and exporter of high shear blender with scraped surface heat transfer
President: Ron Ashton
Sales: Don Wolfe
Estimated Sales: $5 Million
Number Employees: 10-19
Parent Co: American Ingredients Company

19850 Bremer Manufacturing Company
W2002 County Road Q
Elkhart Lake, WI 53020 920-894-2944
Fax: 920-894-2881 sales@bremermfg.com
www.bremermfg.com
Aluminum hand scoops
President: Tom Dolack
Sales: Tim St Clair
Purchasing: Glen Leahn
Shipping Manager: J Thome
Estimated Sales: $10 - 20 Million
Number Employees: 100-249
Square Footage: 60000

19851 Bren Instruments
308 Century Court
Franklin, TN 37064-3918 615-794-6825
Fax: 615-794-7478 info@breninc.com
www.breninc.com
Automated decal and stencil systems
President: Murray O Wilhoite
CFO: Brenda Wilhoite
Quality Control Manager: Phill Thomas
Director Marketing/VP: Murray Wilhoite
Estimated Sales: $500,000 - $1 Million
Number Employees: 8

19852 (HQ)Brenner Tank
450 Arlington Ave
Fond Du Lac, WI 54935 920-922-5020
Fax: 920-922-3303 800-558-9750
sales@brennertank.com www.brennertank.com
Manufacturer, importer and exporter of stainless steel tank transports and intermodal tank containers
Vice President of Sales: Jim Miller
Sales Manager: Thomas Ballon
Estimated Sales: $20-50 Million
Number Employees: 100-249
Square Footage: 300000
Parent Co: Wabash National Corp.

19853 Brenntag Pacific
10747 Patterson Place
Santa Fe Springs, CA 90670 562-903-9626
Fax: 559-268-0619 obates@brenntag.com
www.brenntagpacific.com
Wine industry chemicals
Manager: Joe Grossi
Quality Control: Ozzie Bates
Estimated Sales: $5 - 10 Million
Number Employees: 5-9

19854 Brenton LLC
4750 County Road 13 NE
Alexandria, MN 56308-8022
Fax: 320-852-7621 800-535-2730
bec@becmail.com www.brentonengineering.com
Manufacturer and exporter of case packers, handling, robotics, and shrink wrappers
President: Jeff Bigger
Sales: Scott Leuschke
Marketing Director: Karen Kielmeyer
Vice President Sales: Troy Snader
Estimated Sales: $20-50 Million
Number Employees: 100-249
Parent Co: ProMach
Brands:
Brenton

19855 Brentwood Plastic Films
8734 Suburban Trak
PO Box 440160
St Louis, MO 63144-2734 314-968-1137
Fax: 314-968-4276 www.brentwoodplastics.com
Polyethylene films
President: Sam Longstreth
Estimated Sales: $5-10 Million
Number Employees: 20-49
Square Footage: 40000

19856 Brevard Restaurant Equipment
1623 N Cocoa Boulevard
Cocoa, FL 32922-6935 321-636-7750
Fax: 321-636-0171
Wholesaler/distributor of new and used equipment; serving the food service market; also, design and layout plans
President: John Schneider
VP: Diana Schneider
General Manager: Glenn Pierson
Estimated Sales: $1-2.5 Million
Number Employees: 1-4
Square Footage: 15000

19857 Brew Store
114 Lakeshore Road E
Oakville, ON L6J 6N2
Canada 905-845-2120
Fax: 905-845-1104
Manufacturer and exporter of micro brewing equipment
President: Gary Deathe
Number Employees: 17

19858 Brewer-Cantelmo Company
55 W 39th St # 205
New York, NY 10018 212-244-4600
Fax: 212-244-1640 bc@brewer-cantelmo.com
www.brewer-cantelmo.com
Custom handed crafted menus, room directories, reservation books, check presenters, wine lists, presentation tools.
President: Steve Kirschenbaum
Vice President: David Kirschenbaum
Estimated Sales: $2 Million
Number Employees: 20-49
Square Footage: 37500

19859 Brewmatic Company
P.O.Box 2959
Torrance, CA 90509 310-787-5444
Fax: 310-787-5412 800-421-6860
brew@brewmaticusa.com www.brewmatic.com
Manufacturer and exporter of thermal coffee servers, commercial and domestic drip brewing equipment and accessories; importer of espresso machines
Manager: Ed Esteban
Research & Development: Traian Zaionciuc
Quality Control: Ron Mann
Marketing Director: Eddison Esteban
Sales Director: Cindi Watson Kramer
Plant Manager: John Galvin
Purchasing Manager: Frank Cherry
Number Employees: 50-99
Square Footage: 150000
Parent Co: Farmer Brothers Company
Type of Packaging: Food Service, Private Label
Other Locations:
Brewmatic Company
St. Louis MO
Brands:
Brewmatic

19860 Bridge Machine Company
614 Kennedy Street
P.O. Box 45
Palmyra, NJ 08065-0045 856-829-1800
Fax: 856-786-8147 sales@bridgeonline.com
www.bridgeonline.com
Designs and manufactures a complete line of food processing equipment such as patty formers, tenderizers, dumpers/meat tubs, hand tenderizers, cutlet flatteners, meatball formers, macerators, spreading conveyors, dicers and stripcutters
President: Terry Bridge
Estimated Sales: $10 - 20 Million
Number Employees: 50-99
Square Footage: 14000

19861 Briel America
3888 Bluffview Pt
Marietta, GA 30062 770-509-3006
Fax: 770-518-6624 www.ascasousa.net
Espresso machines, accessories, grinders
President: Wesley Smith
Estimated Sales: $.5 - 1 000,000
Number Employees: 1-4

19862 Bright Technologies
127 N. Water Street
PO Box 296
Hopkins, MI 49328 269-793-7183
Fax: 269-793-8793 800-253-0532
www.brightbeltpress.com
De-packaging compactors, hydraulic cart dumpers, factory direct installation, service, patented Xtractors, patented HighDensity Extruders, patented Belt Filter Presses, mobile, trailer mounted and stationary equipment.
President: Brent Sebright
R&D/Sales: Dennis Sprick
Marketing Director: Jeannie Jansma
Operations: T Stuart Sebright
VP Purchasing: Lee Murray
Estimated Sales: $5-10 Million
Number Employees: 50-99
Number of Brands: 2
Number of Products: 80

19863 Bright of America
300 Greenbrier Rd
Summersville, WV 26651 304-872-3000
Fax: 304-872-3033 www.greenbrier-scentex.com
Place and counter mats
President: Steve Pridemore
Estimated Sales: $10 - 20 Million
Number Employees: 20-49
Square Footage: 200000
Parent Co: Russ Berrie & Company

19864 Bril-Tech
1506 Baltimore Street
Defiance, OH 43512-1908 419-782-2430
Fax: 419-784-9717 briltech@defnet.com
Air pollution control, drying rooms, ovens, smokehouses, refrigeration systems and tempering systems

19865 Brill Manufacturing Company
715 S James St
Ludington, MI 49431 231-843-2430
Fax: 231-845-9966 866-896-6420
www.brillcompany.com
Pine and oak tables, chairs and booths
Owner: David Field
VP: D Lange
Estimated Sales: $2.5-5 Million
Number Employees: 50-99
Square Footage: 96000

19866 (HQ)Brinkmann Corporation
4215 McEwen Rd
Dallas, TX 75244 972-387-4939
800-468-5252
kdulic@cpsc.gov www.brinkmann.net
Manufacturer and exporter of smokers and cookers; also, lighting including portable emergency, flashlights, lanterns, electronic flashers and electronic assemblies
President: Jon Brinkmann
VP: Erma Eddins
Estimated Sales: $20-50 Million
Number Employees: 100-249

19867 Brinkmann Instruments, Inc.
6555 Pelican Creek Circle
Riverview, FL 33578-8653 813-316-4700
Fax: 516-334-7506 800-645-3050
info@brinkmann.com www.brinkmann.com
Seward blenders, grinding mills and sievers, binders and ovens, fat determination systems, universal solvent extraction systems and lab equipment
President & Chief Executive Officer: Michael Melingo

Estimated Sales: $20.40 Million
Number Employees: 143

19868 Brisker Dry Food Crisper
PO Box 7000
Oldsmar, FL 34677 813-854-5231
Fax: 800-854-3069 800-356-9080
info@briskercrisper.com
www.briskercrisper.com
Manufacturer and exporter of electric kitchen countertop storage appliances designed to keep crackers, chips, cereals, etc. free of humidity
CEO: Anita Rybicki
Estimated Sales: $1 - 5 Million
Number Employees: 7
Number of Brands: 1
Number of Products: 1
Square Footage: 48000
Type of Packaging: Consumer, Food Service
Brands:
Brisker

19869 Bristol Associates
5777 W Century Blvd Ste 865
Los Angeles, CA 90045 310-670-0525
Fax: 310-670-4075 lstern@bristolassoc.com
www.bristolassoc.com
Executive recruitment firm serving the food industry
President: Jim Bright
Ex VP: Lucy Faber
Director Marketing: Laurie Stern
Number Employees: 10-19

19870 Britt Food Equipment
684733 HWY 2
RR 3
Woodstock, ON N4S 7V7 519-533-0365
Fax: 519-533-6315
info@brittfoodequipment.com
www.brittfoodequipment.com
Equipment and machinery to the red meat, poultry, fish and pet food industries
President: Brad Britton
Vice President: Greg Britton
Estimated Sales: $750,000
Number Employees: 3

19871 Britt's Barbecue
1678 Montgomery Highway
Suite 104
Birmingham, AL 35216 205-612-6538
info@brittsbarbecue.com
www.brittsbarbecue.com
Stationery and trailer commercial smokers
Owner: James Britt

19872 Bro-Tex
800 Hampden Avenue
Saint Paul, MN 55114 651-645-5721
Fax: 651-646-1876 800-328-2282
www.brotex.com
Polishing cloths, industrial paper and cloth wipers and Turkish bar mops
President/Chief Executive Officer: Roger Greenberg
Secretary/Treasurer: Myra Greenberg
Senior Vice President: Ed Freeman
Director, Marketing: Erwin Rendall
Product Development Manager: Lee Gilbertson
Plant Manager: Greg Conroy
Purchasing Manager: Chris Keisling
Estimated Sales: $21 Million
Number Employees: 100
Square Footage: 200000
Brands:
Bx-100
Dual-Tex

19873 Broadmoor Baker
1301 5th Ave
Seattle, WA 98101-2603 206-624-3660
Fax: 206-464-1389
Consultant specializing in the development and marketing of specialty bread recipes
Owner: Paul Suzman
Estimated Sales: less than $500,000
Number Employees: 1-4

19874 Broadway Companies
6161 Ventnor Ave
Dayton, OH 45414 937-890-1888
Fax: 937-890-5678 billbirch@aol.com
Innovations for custom molds, preforms and bottle designs, prototyping and production, injection preform models, blow molds, family molds that combine multiple sizes and finishes
Owner: Bill Gaiser
Estimated Sales: $10-20 000,000
Number Employees: 100-249

19875 Broaster Company
2855 Cranston Rd
Beloit, WI 53511-3991 800-365-8278
Fax: 608-363-7957 800-365-8278
broaster@broaster.com www.broaster.com
Manufacturer and exporter of gas and electric pressure fryers, ventless fryers, warmers, broilers and rotisseries
President: Richard Schrank
Vice President: Tracy Choppi
Marketing Director: Mark Markwardt
Sales Director: Randy McKinney
Plant Manager: Gene Halley
Purchasing Manager: Lee Blehinger
Brands:
Aristo-Ray
Bro-Tisserie
Broaster
Broaster Chicken
Broaster Foods
Broaster Recipe
Perfect Hold Deli Case
Snack-Mate

19876 Brock Awnings
211 E Montauk Hwy Ste 1
Hampton Bays, NY 11946 631-728-3367
Fax: 631-728-0134 sales@brockawnings.com
www.brockawnings.com
Commercial awnings
President: Earl Brock
Estimated Sales: $500,000-$1,000,000
Number Employees: 5-9

19877 Brogdex Company
1441 W 2nd St
Pomona, CA 91766 909-622-1021
Fax: 909-629-4564
Manufacturer and exporter of cleaners and chemicals for use in film/wax coatings for fresh fruits and vegetables; exporter of fruit and vegetable processing and handling equipment
President: Kirk Bannerman
Vice President: Greg Appel
Number Employees: 50-99
Brands:
Britex

19878 Brookfield Engineering Laboratories
11 Commerce Blvd
Middleboro, MA 02346 508-946-6200
Fax: 508-946-6262 800-628-8139
sales@brookfieldengineering.com
www.brookfieldengineering.com
Rotational viscometers and rheometers and also Texture Analyzers and powder flow testers.
President: Donald Brookfield Jr
Chief Executive Officer: David Brookfield
Chief Operating Officer: Peter Bigelow
General Manager/Global Sales: Robert McGregor Jr.
Quality Control: Richard Rattey
Human Resources Manager: Sandra Bearce
Manufacturing Manager: Richard Ross
Purchasing Manager: Lisa Dwyer
Estimated Sales: $50-100 Million
Number Employees: 185
Number of Brands: 3
Square Footage: 100000
Parent Co: Brookfield Engineering Labs, Inc.
Type of Packaging: Private Label

19879 Brooklace
P.O.Box 2038
Oshkosh, WI 54903-2038
Fax: 203-937-4583 800-572-4552
info@brooklace.com www.brooklace.com
Manufacturer and exporter of paper, foil, glassine and grease-proof doilies, place mats, tray covers, baking cups, cake decorating triangles and hot dog trays
President: Charles Foster
VP of Sales: Brian Schofield
VP of Manufacturing: James Stryker
Estimated Sales: $30 - 50 Million
Number Employees: 50-99
Square Footage: 50000
Parent Co: Hoffmaster
Brands:
Brooklace

19880 Brooklyn Boys
9967 Glades Rd
Boca Raton, FL 33434 561-477-3663
Manufacturer and wholesaler of knives, cutlery, china, dinnerware and related table-setting products
Owner: Carlos Sierra
Estimated Sales: $1 - 5 Million
Number Employees: 10-19

19881 Brooks Barrel Company
8 W Hamilton St
Baltimore, MD 21201-5008 410-228-0790
Fax: 410-221-1693 800-398-2766
brooksbarrel@shorenet.net
www.brooksbarrel.com
Wooden barrels, kegs, planters and buckets; wholesaler/distributor of bushel baskets and crates for shipping and display
President: Kenneth Knox
Office Manager: Tammy Doege
Estimated Sales: $500,000 - $1 Million
Number Employees: 15
Square Footage: 40000

19882 Brooks Instrument
407 W Vine St
Hatfield, PA 19440 215-362-3500
Fax: 215-362-3745 888-554-3569
brooksam@brooksinstrument.com
www.brooksinstrument.com
Manufacturer and exporter of measurement instrumentation for gas and liquid flow
President: Jim Dale
CFO: Joe Doeters
Quality Control: Kevin Gallagher
R & D: Steve Glaudel
Marketing: T Hannigan
Sales: R Fravel
Number Employees: 10,000
Parent Co: Emerson Electric Company
Brands:
Brooks

19883 Brookshire Grocery
1600 West South W Loop 323
PO Box 1411
Tyler, TX 75710 903-534-3000
Fax: 903-534-2206 www.brookshires.com
A supermarket chain that has more than 150 stores throughout Texas, Louisiana, Arkansas, and Mississippi. Manufacturing facilities are internal and include bakery, ice cream, dairy, fresh-cut, ice and water plants.
President/CEO: Rick Rayford
Founder: Wood Brookshire
CFO: Tim King
SVP Category Management: David Krause
EVP Retail Operations: Mike Terry
Estimated Sales: $2.2 Billion
Number Employees: 12,000
Brands:
Food Club
Full Circle Organic
Sunnybrook Farms
Tasty Bakery Cakes
Brookshire's Best
Full Circle
Goldenbrrok Farms
Valutime
Topcare
Paws For Pets

19884 Brose Chemical Company
702 Bridge St
Twin Falls, ID 83301 208-733-1045
Fax: 208-733-1320 dbrose@brosechemical.com
Manufactures chemicals for food processing and mining industries
President: David Brose
Vice President: Susan Brose
Research & Development: Jim Brose
Sales Director: Ken Stewart
Production Manager: Dick Clarkson
Estimated Sales: 1-5 000,000
Number Employees: 10-19
Number of Brands: 1
Type of Packaging: Private Label, Bulk

19885 **Brothers Manufacturing**
PO Box 220
Hermansville, MI 49847-0220 906-498-7771
Fax: 906-498-2150 888-277-6117
brothers@portup.com
Storage tanks and liquid handling systems
Operations Manager: Bob Triest
Estimated Sales: $10-20,000,000
Number Employees: 50-99
Square Footage: 33000

19886 **Brothers Metal Products**
1780 E McFadden Ave #117
Santa Ana, CA 92705-4648 714-972-3008
Fax: 714-632-5032
Manufacturer and exporter of vegetable slicers and dryers; also, wash tank conveyors and packaging and receiving tables
President: Gregory Siegmann
Estimated Sales: $600,000
Number Employees: 4
Square Footage: 11000
Type of Packaging: Food Service
Brands:
Legrow

19887 **Broughton Foods Company**
1701 Greene St
Marietta, OH 45750 740-373-4121
Fax: 740-373-2861 800-283-2479
www.broughtonfoods.com
milks, premium and homestyle ice cream, novelty ice cream, juices and fruit drinks, cottage cheese, sour cream, and chip dip.
Principle: Michael McCullum
Executive Vice President: George Broughton
Manager of Sales: Neil Schilling
Plant Manager: Mike Depue
Purchasing Agent: Becci Becker
Estimated Sales: $46.6 Million
Number Employees: 260
Square Footage: 8000
Parent Co: Dean Foods
Type of Packaging: Consumer, Food Service, Bulk

19888 **(HQ)Broussard Cane Equipment**
4947 Bridge Street Hwy
Parks, LA 70582 337-845-5080
Fax: 337-845-5090 sales@broussardcane.com
www.broussardcane.com
Sugar cane loaders and harvesters
President: V Kenneth Broussard
Purchasing Manager: Trisha Brasseaux
Estimated Sales: $1 - 3 Million
Number Employees: 5-9
Square Footage: 28000
Brands:
Broussard

19889 **Brower**
Highway 16 West
P.O. Box 2000
Houghton, IA 52631 319-469-4141
Fax: 319-469-4402 800-553-1791
sales@hawkeyesteel.com
www.hawkeyesteel.com
Manufacturer and exporter of poultry processing equipment including scalders, pickers, evicerating equipment and related accessories. Specialize in small and medium plants.
President: Tom Wenstrand
VP Sales: Cindy Wellman
Estimated Sales: $10 - 20 Million
Number Employees: 50-99
Square Footage: 200000
Parent Co: Hawkeye Steel Products
Type of Packaging: Consumer
Brands:
Batch Pik
Brower
Super Pik
Super Scald

19890 **Brower Equipment Corporation**
3750 Getwell Cv
Memphis, TN 38118-5909 901-365-7991
Fax: 901-367-2925 info@browerequipment.net
www.browerequipment.net
Process tank, controls, installation pumps, fittings and valve designs
President: Ralph E Brower
Estimated Sales: $5-10 000,000
Number Employees: 10-19

19891 **Brown & Caldwell**
201 North Civic Drive
Suite 115
Walnut Creek, CA 94596 925-937-9010
Fax: 925-932-9026 800-727-2224
info@brwncald.com
www.brownandcaldwell.com
Environmental engineer and consultant offering sanitation, waste water, testing and analytical services
President: Craig Goehring
Finance Administration Manager: Angela Ferrif
Director Marekting: Diana Levin
Director Operations: Jim Meehan
Estimated Sales: $3 - 5 Million
Number Employees: 1,000-4,999

19892 **Brown Chemical Company**
302 W Oakland Ave
Oakland, NJ 07436 201-337-0900
Fax: 201-337-9026 800-888-9822
sales@brownchem.com www.brownchem.com
Liquid packaging, contract warehousing, vendor managed inventory programs, custom blending, regulatory compliance assistance, USP, food grade and kosher packaging
President: Doug Brown
VP: Patrick Brown
VP Finance and Operations: Dave Lyle
Executive Secretary: Eileen Lyness
Office Manager: Doug Blum
Manager Information Systems: Rob Eckert
Operations Manager: Mark Donatiello
Estimated Sales: $20-50 Million
Number Employees: 20-49

19893 **Brown International Corporation**
333 Avenue M NW
Winter Haven, FL 33881 626-966-8361
Fax: 863-294-2688 info@brown-intl.com
www.brown-intl.com
Manufacturer and exporter of fruit and vegetable processing equipment including extractors, pulpers, finishers, dewaterers, sizers and processing lines
President: Scott Alexander
VP: Ann Williams
Sales: Jim Sheppard
Operations: Bryce Adolph
Purchasing: Bruce Strong
Estimated Sales: $20-50 Million
Number Employees: 100-249
Number of Brands: 1
Number of Products: 85
Square Footage: 70000
Brands:
Brown

19894 **Brown Machine**
330 North Ross Street
Beaverton, MI 48612 989-435-7741
Fax: 989-435-2821 877-702-4142
sales@brown-machine.com
www.brown-machine.com
Manufacturer and exporter of thermoforming machinery
President: Bryan Redman
Chief Financial Officer: Kay McCandless
Marketing Administration: Lynn Govitz
Vice President, Sales & Marketing: Jim Robbins
Vice President, Operations: Brian Keeley
Vice President, Process Engineering: Jim Martin
Estimated Sales: $42 Million
Number Employees: 250
Number of Brands: 1
Square Footage: 140000
Parent Co: John Brown

19895 **Brown Manufacturing Company**
125 New St Ste A
Decatur, GA 30030 404-378-8311
Fax: 404-378-8311 david@bottleopener.com
www.bottleopener.com
Manufacturer and exporter of stationary bottle openers; custom imprinting available.
President: David Brim
Number Employees: 1-4
Square Footage: 2500
Brands:
Starr

19896 **Brown Paper Goods Company**
3530 Birchwood Dr
Waukegan, IL 60085 847-688-1451
Fax: 847-688-1458
jlabuda@brownpapergoods.com
www.brownpapergoods.com
Cake pan liners and bags including food, garbage, greaseproof, paper, plastic and sandwich
President: Alan Mones
Estimated Sales: $20-50 Million
Number Employees: 100-249

19897 **Brown Plastics & Equipment**
683 Main Street # 1
Falmouth, MA 02540-3221 508-540-3990
Fax: 508-540-3963 www.falmouthlawyer.com
Partner: Paula M Barbosa
Estimated Sales: $300,000-500,000
Number Employees: 1-4

19898 **Brown's Sign & Screen Printing**
8299 Hazelbrand Road NE
Covington, GA 30014-3406 770-786-2257
Fax: 770-784-1324 800-540-3107
Manufacturer and exporter of flags, pennants, banners, signs and advertising specialties; screen printing and lettering services available
President: Mike Brown
Estimated Sales: Less than $500,000
Number Employees: 4

19899 **Brown/Millunzi & Associates**
3305 Tampa St
Houston, TX 77021-1143 713-747-2870
Fax: 713-237-0761 800-460-3387
Consultant specializing in the design of food and beverage facilities; also, project management services available
Prin.: Daniel Brown
Prin.: Robert Millunzi
Prin.: Robert Pursell
Estimated Sales: $300,000-500,000
Number Employees: 1-4

19900 **Browne & Company**
100 Esna Park Drive
Markham, ON L3R 1E3
Canada 905-475-6104
Fax: 866-849-4719 sales@browneco.com
www.browneco.com
A leading supplier of glassware, dinnerware and smallwares to the food service industry in Canada
President: Michael Browne
CFO: Alen Budish
Vice President: Brian Wood
Marketing Director: Katherine Dilk
Sales Director: Brian Wood
Number Employees: 10
Type of Packaging: Food Service

19901 **Browns International & Company**
422 Isabey
St. Laurent, QC H4T 1V3
Canada 514-737-1326
Fax: 514-737-7599
Plastic bottles, closures and sprayers
President: Howard Bassel

19902 **Bruce Industrial Company**
4049 New Castle Ave
New Castle, DE 19720 302-655-9616
Fax: 302-656-4327 service@bruceindustrial.com
www.bruceindustrial.com
Wholesaler/distributor of material handling equipment including overhead and modular lifts, enclosures, rigging, etc
President: Clement Bason
CEO: Doug Johnston
Estimated Sales: $10 Million
Number Employees: 50-99
Square Footage: 20000
Brands:
Alm
Akro-Mils
Aleco
Ballymore
Bishamon
Bluegiant
Cm
Cotterman
Eagle
Faultless
Fred Silver
Gorbel

Hamilton
Hytrol
Keymaster
Langley
Lift-Rite
Magline
Omni Spaceguard
Palamatic
Presto
Republic

19903 **Brudi Bolzoni Auramo, Inc**
17635 Hoffman Way
Homewood, IL 60430 708-957-8809
Fax: 708-957-8832 800-358-5438
sales.us@bolzoni-auramo.com
www.bolzoni-auramo.com
Manufacturer, importer and exporter of lift truck attachments
VP: Ad Artuso
VP Sales: Ronnie Keene
VP Operations: Ed Artuso
Plant Manager: Jose Cardonas
Purchasing Manager: Brian Cummings
Estimated Sales: $20 Million
Number Employees: 20-49
Square Footage: 14700
Parent Co: Bolzoni SPA

19904 **Bruins Instruments**
P.O. Box 1023
Salem, NH 03079 603-898-6527
Fax: 978-485-0055 info@bruinsinstruments.com
www.bruinsinstruments.com
NIR analyzers for the agricultural and food industries.
President: Hans Joachim Bruins

19905 **Brulin & Company**
2920 Dr Andrew J Brown Ave
Indianapolis, IN 46205 317-923-3211
Fax: 317-925-4596 800-776-7149
brulin@brulin.com www.brulin.com
Manufacturer and exporter of sanitation products including disinfectants, hand care, food sanitation and floor care chemicals. ISO 9002 certified
President: Charles Pollnow
VP Sales/Marketing: Michael Falkowski
Marketing Coordinator: Janet Cleary Salisbury
Marketing Manager (Commerical Products): Garry Thornley
Estimated Sales: $10-20 Million
Number Employees: 100-249
Brands:
815 Mx
Quat Clean Sanitizer
Spotlight

19906 **Bruni Glass Packaging**
1449 46TH Ave
Lachine Montreal, QC H8T 3C5
Canada 514-633-9247
Fax: 514-633-9878 877-771-7856
info@bruniglass.com www.bruniglass.com
Glass containers for food, pharmaceutical and related products; bottles for distillates, wine, oil and vinegar
President: Roberto Delbon
CEO: Gino Delbon
Marketing: Mark Bassel
Number Employees: 26

19907 **Bruni Glass Packaging**
2750 Maxwell Way
Fairfield, CA 94534 707-752-6200
Fax: 707-752-6201 877-278-6445
info@bruniglass.com www.firenzevetro.com
Glass packaging, specialty and custom glass jars and bottles

19908 **Brush Research Manufacturing Company**
4642 Floral Dr
Los Angeles, CA 90022-1288 323-261-2193
Fax: 323-268-6587 info@brushresearch.com
www.brushresearch.com
Manufacturer and exporter of conveyor brushes.
President: Tara Rands
VP: Robert Fowlie
General Manager: Don Didier
Estimated Sales: $5-10 Million
Number Employees: 50-99
Square Footage: 300000
Brands:
2-Flap
Flex-Hone
Nam Power

19909 **Bruske Products**
7447 Duvan Dr
Tinley Park, IL 60477 708-532-3800
Fax: 708-532-3977
bruskeproducts@ameritech.net
www.bruskeproducts.com
Brushes and brooms
President: Edward Bruske
Sales/Marketing Executive: David Cohea
Estimated Sales: $10-20 Million
Number Employees: 50-99
Square Footage: 30000

19910 **Brute Fabricators**
PO Box 1621
Castroville, TX 78009-1621 210-648-2370
Fax: 210-648-5811 800-777-2788
brute@stic.net www.bruterack.com
Manufacturer and exporter of heavy structural steel pallet racks including drive-in, drive-thru and cantilever drive-in
President: Fred Siebrecht
CEO: Brandie Siebrecht
CFO: Ben Cogdell
Number Employees: 20
Square Footage: 81000
Parent Co: Brute Fabricators
Brands:
Brute Rack

19911 **Bry-Air**
10793 State Route 37 West
Sunbury, OH 43074 740-965-2974
Fax: 740-965-5470 877-379-2479
info@bry-air.com www.bry-air.com
Manufacturers of industrial dehumidifiers.
President/CEO: Mel Meyers
Executive VP: Doug Howery
Quality Control: Rick Frenier
Plant Manager: Ron Busch
Purchasing Director: Debra Kemmer
Estimated Sales: $5-10 Million
Number Employees: 34

19912 **Bryan Boilers**
783 Chili Ave
Peru, IN 46970 765-473-6651
Fax: 765-473-3074 inquires@bryansteam.com
www.bryanboilers.com
Manufacturer and exporter of boilers, blow down separators, boiler feed systems and de-aerators
President: Tom May
CEO: Dale Bowman
Sales/Marketing Manager: Dick Holmquist
Estimated Sales: G
Number Employees: 250-499
Parent Co: Bryan Steam LLC

19913 **Bryant Glass Co.**
619 Main Street
Wilmington, MA 01887-3215 978-988-9300
Fax: 978-988-9111 800-369-2782
bryantglass@verizon.net
www.bryantglassco.com
High pressure pumps and homogenizers
Owner: Bob Bryant
Number Employees: 50-99

19914 **Bryant Products**
W1388 Elmwood Ave
Ixonia, WI 53036 920-206-6920
Fax: 920-206-6929 800-825-3874
www.bryantpro.com
Manufacturer and exporter of tensioning devices for conveyors, straight and tapered rollers, machine grade conveyor pulleys
President: Fred Thimmel
Purchasing: Jody Mack
Estimated Sales: $20-50 Million
Number Employees: 20-49
Square Footage: 50000
Brands:
Airform
Telescoper
Tleltrack

19915 **Bryce Company**
4505 Old Lamary
P.O.Box 18338
Memphis, TN 38118 901-369-4400
Fax: 901-367-5670 800-238-7277
prickman@brycecorp.com www.brycecorp.com
Convertable flexible packaging including candy wrappers and potato chip bags
President: John Bryce
CEO: Tom Bryce
VP Sales: Paul Rickman
R & D: Mark Montsinger
Number Employees: 1,000-4,999

19916 **Bubbla**
7931 Deering Ave
Canoga Park, CA 91304 818-884-2000
Fax: 818-884-2164 support@bubbla.com
www.bubbla.com
President: Andrew Cooper
Marketing: Cindy Daley
Estimated Sales: $3 - 5 Million
Number Employees: 1-4

19917 **Buchi Analytical**
19 Lukens Drive
Suite 400
New Castle, DE 19720 302-652-3000
Fax: 302-652-8777 877-692-8844
us-sales@buchi.com www.buchi-analytical.com
Nutrition analysis systems
General Manager: Christopher Sopko
Finance Manager: Tony Casadei
Sales Director: John Pollard
Regional Sales Manager: Brad Miller
Regional Sales Manager: Charles Douglas
Estimated Sales: $5-10 Million
Number Employees: 5-9

19918 **Buchi Corporation**
19 Lukens Dr
Suite 400
New Castle, DE 19720 302-652-3000
Fax: 302-652-8777 877-692-8244
us-sales@buchi.com www.mybuchi.com
Lab instruments such as spray dryers, NIR spectroscopy instruments for quality control, solvent extraction equipment for food analysis, etc.
Finance Manager: Tony Casadei
Marketing Manager: Rudi Hartmann
Sales Director: John Pollard
General Manager: Vahe Iplikci
Estimated Sales: $6.3 Million
Number Employees: 37

19919 **Buck Ice & Coal Company**
P.O.Box 1457
Columbus, GA 31902-1457 706-322-5451
Fax: 706-322-5453 info@buckice.com
www.buckice.com
Manufacturer and packager of ice. Private label packaging available
President: William C Buck
CEO: W Buck, Jr.
Estimated Sales: $1 - 3 Million
Number Employees: 5-9
Number of Products: 1
Square Footage: 120000
Type of Packaging: Consumer, Food Service, Private Label
Brands:
Buck Ice

19920 **Buck Knives**
660 S Lochsa St
Post Falls, ID 83854 208-262-0500
Fax: 208-262-0738 800-326-2825
www.buckknives.com
Manufacturer and exporter of fish fillet knives and cutlery.
Chairman: Charles Buck
VP Sales/Marketing: Rob Morgan
Estimated Sales: $20-50 Million
Number Employees: 250-499
Square Footage: 200000
Brands:
Buck

19921 **(HQ)Buckeye Group**
4700 Wilmington Pike
South Charleston, OH 45368 937-462-8361
Fax: 937-462-7071
Wooden packaging including boxes
President: Sam McAdow

Estimated Sales: $10-20 Million
Number Employees: 50-99
Other Locations:
Buckeye Group
South Charleston OH

19922 Buckeye International
2700 Wagner Pl
Maryland Heights, MO 63043 314-291-1900
Fax: 314-298-2850
www.buckeyeinternational.com
Manufacturer and exporter of cleaning chemicals including hand soap and floor polish for restaurants
President: Kristopher Kosup
Estimated Sales: $20-50 Million
Number Employees: 50-99
Type of Packaging: Food Service, Bulk

19923 Buckhorn Canada
8028 Torbram Road
Brampton, ON L6T 3T2
Canada 905-791-6500
Fax: 905-791-9942 800-461-7579
sales@buckhorncanada.com
www.buckhorninc.com/
Manufacturer, importer and exporter of reusable plastic pallets and boxes for storage, processing, dipping and freezing
Sales Manager: Tim Walsh
Number Employees: 20
Square Footage: 180000
Parent Co: Myers Industries
Brands:
Akro-Bins
Ameri-Kart
Maxi-Bins
Nestier

19924 Buckhorn Canada
8032 Torbram Road
Brampton, ON L6T 3T2
Canada 905-791-6500
Fax: 905-791-9942 800-461-7579
sales@buckhorncanada.com
www.buckhorncanada.com
Manufacturer and exporter of polyethylene containers for processing and transporting; importer of plastic containers and pallets
President: Jim Morrison
Sales/Marketing: Tim Walsh
Account Executive: Jim Cavanaugh
Estimated Sales: $10-20 Million
Number Employees: 10
Square Footage: 42000
Parent Co: Buckhorn
Brands:
Buckhorn
Nestier

19925 (HQ)Buckhorn Inc
55 W Techne Center Dr
Milford, OH 45150-9779 513-831-4402
Fax: 513-831-5474 800-543-4454
sales@buckhorninc.com www.buckhorninc.com
Manufacturer and exporter of plastic totes, bulk boxes, containers, trays and pallets for shipping and in-process use; USDA and FDA approved
Executive Director: Joel Grant
District Sales Manager: Ray McKinney
Number Employees: 20-49
Brands:
Akro-Mils
Buckhoen

19926 Budenheim USA, Inc.
2219 Westbrooke Drive
Columbus, OH 43228 614-345-2400
info@gallard.com
www.gallard.com
Curing preparations and phosphates
President: Harold Schaub
CEO: Christian Kohlpaitner
VP: Michael Lesser
Estimated Sales: $55 Million
Number Employees: 25
Square Footage: 5016

19927 Budget Blinds
1927 N Glassell St
Orange, CA 92865-4313 714-637-2100
800-800-9250
corporateoffice@budgetblinds.com
www.budgetblinds.com
Manufacturer and exporter of decorative items including centerpieces, candleabras, vases, candlesticks, etc
Executive VP: Mark Frankel
Office Manager: Cindy Mason
Number Employees: 10-19
Square Footage: 60000
Brands:
Band-It
Finesse
Franklinware
Garden Romance

19928 Buffalo China
658 Bailey Avenue
Buffalo, NY 14206-3003 716-824-8515
Fax: 716-825-5783 lester.rickard@oneida.com
www.oneida.com
Tabletop products and supplies including china
Sales Manager: Frank Fan
Manager: Charles Goehrig
VP Engineering: Paul Graeber
Estimated Sales: $1 - 5 Million
Number Employees: 500-999
Parent Co: Oneida Foodservice

19929 (HQ)Buffalo Technologies Corporation
750 E Ferry Street
Buffalo, NY 14211-1106 716-895-2100
Fax: 716-895-8263 800-332-2419
sales@buflovak.com www.btcorp.com
Manufacturer and exporter of food dryers, flaking drums, material handling and lifting equipment, coolers, evaporators, heat exchangers, conveyors, mills, etc
CEO/Chairman: Theodore Dann
Product Manager: Todd Murray
Production Manager: Patrick Scanlon
Estimated Sales: $10-20 Million
Number Employees: 2
Square Footage: 250000
Brands:
Bke
Bar Nun
Buflovak
Gump

19930 Buffalo Wire Works
1165 Clinton St
Buffalo, NY 14206 716-826-4666
Fax: 716-826-8271 800-828-7028
info@buffalowire.com www.buffalowire.com
Buffalo Wire Works offers screening media for industrial and food processing, including circular screens, taped edge, hooked panel and rolled goods for all major OEM's
CEO: Joseph Abramo
CFO: George Ulrich
VP of Technalogy: Erich Steadman
R&D: Zach Hall
Quality Control: Rick Zimmer
Marketing: Melissa Kenneweg
Executive VP of Sales: Dominic Nasso
Customer Service: Beth Dajka
Operations: Kevin Shoemaker
Production: Terrie Battaglia
Plant Manager: Kevin Shoemaker
Purchasing Director: Tom Duriak
Estimated Sales: $10 - 20 Million
Number Employees: 100-249
Type of Packaging: Food Service

19931 Buffet Enhancements International
P.O.Box 476
Fairhope, AL 36533-0476 251-990-6119
Fax: 251-990-9373 www.buffetenhancements.com
Display products for banquets and catering including decorative fountains, illuminated ice displays, food display trays, beverage housings and centerpiece trays; also, seafood display containers
Owner: Mike Anderson
Quality Control: Paul Lepiane
Marketing Director: Mike Anderson
Estimated Sales: $10 - 20 Million
Number Employees: 50-99
Square Footage: 5000
Brands:
Banquet Boats
Chef Stone
Marquis Fountains

19932 (HQ)Buffet Partners
2701 E Plano Pkwy # 200
Plano, TX 75074 214-291-2900
Fax: 214-291-2467 888-626-6636
www.furrs.net
Food gift certificates
Manager: Jill Laird
CFO: Monty Standifer
Number Employees: 20-49

19933 Buffetts
1020 Discovery Rd Ste 100
Saint Paul, MN 55121-2096
Fax: 651-365-2356 www.buffet.com
Large restaurant chain and restaurant franchiser
CEO: R Michael Andrews Jr
Estimated Sales: K
Number Employees: 10,000

19934 Buhler
P.O.Box 9497
Minneapolis, MN 55440 763-847-9900
Fax: 763-847-9911
buhler.minneapolis@buhlergroup.com
www.buhlergroup.com
Industrial grinders, blending and mixing equipment for coffee, green coffee cleaners, air filters, automatic controls, bin silo systems and storage, conveying equipment including elevators, machiners and buckets
President: Achim Klotz
CFO: Steve Romer
CEO: Rene Steiner
Sales Manager: Albert Lucia
Purchasing Agent: Dan Hogan
Estimated Sales: $20 - 50 Million
Number Employees: 500-999
Square Footage: 150000
Parent Co: Buhler AG

19935 Buhler Group
P.O.Box 29505
Raleigh, NC 27626-0505 919-851-2000
Fax: 919-851-6029 sales@aeroglide.com
www.buhlergroup.com
Design and manufacture of custom industrial dryers, roasters, toasters and coolers for food processing.
President: Fred Kelly Jr
CEO: J Fredrick Kelly Jr
Sales Director: Tom Barber
Number Employees: 100-249
Brands:
C.G. Sargent's Sons
Fec
National Drying Wachinery

19936 Bulk Lift International
1013 Tamarac Dr
Carpentersville, IL 60110 847-428-6059
Fax: 847-428-7180 800-992-6372
sales@bulklift.com www.bulklift.com
Manufacturer and importer of woven polypropylene flexible bulk bags
VP: Gary Nattrass
VP Marketing: Michael Offenburger
Regional Sales Representative: Dave Flaks
Number Employees: 325
Square Footage: 100000
Brands:
Bulklift
Ohmega
Sea Bag

19937 Bulk Pack
1025 N 9th St
Monroe, LA 71201 318-387-3260
Fax: 318-387-6362 800-498-4215
sales@bulk-pack.com www.bulk-pack.com
Manufacturer and exporter of bulk containers including flexible and intermediate
President: Peter Anderson
Quality Control: Jane Burden
VP Marketing/Sales: Peter Anderson
Sales: Ron Shemwell
Estimated Sales: $1 - 3 Million
Number Employees: 5-9
Square Footage: 45000
Type of Packaging: Bulk

19938 (HQ)Bulk Sak
103 Industrial Dr
Malvern, AR 72104 501-332-8745
Fax: 501-332-8438 bags@bulksak.com
www.bulksak.com

Bulk shipping containers; importer and exporter of bulk bags
President: Jack Patterson
VP: Grant Patterson
Vice President/Sales: David Whitt
Plant Manager: Mike Nissen
Estimated Sales: $8,000,000
Number Employees: 50-99
Square Footage: 48500
Type of Packaging: Bulk
Other Locations:
Bulk Sak
Memphis TN

19939 Bulldog Factory Service
25880 Commerce Dr
Madison Heights, MI 48071 248-541-3500
Fax: 248-842-5063 bmullins@santannatool.com
www.bulldogfactory.com
Conveyors and mixing machinery
President: Joseph Newton
Mgr.: Jim Morrell
Estimated Sales: $5-10 Million
Number Employees: 5-9

19940 Bullet Guard Corporation
3963 Commerce Dr
West Sacramento, CA 95691 916-373-0402
Fax: 916-373-0208 800-233-5632
gale@bulletguardmail.com
www.bulletguard.com
Manufacturer and exporter of drive-through and walk-up windows including bullet resistant; also, interior counter enclosures; installation and custom fabrication available
President: Karlin Lynch
CFO: Marcia Lynch
Vice President: Ken Lynch
Production Manager: Kevin Lynch
Marketing Director: Jeannine Ricci
Sales Manager: Sheila Lynch
Estimated Sales: $3 - 5 Million
Number Employees: 25
Square Footage: 15000
Brands:
Bullet Guard
Food Chute

19941 Bulman Products Inc
1650 McReynolds Ave NW
Grand Rapids, MI 49504 616-363-4416
Fax: 616-363-0380
bulman@bulmanproducts.com
www.bulmanproducts.com
Manufacturer and exporter of metal dispensers for rolled butcher paper, films, aluminum foil, bag sealing tape, etc.; importer of bag sealers
President: Jack Kirkwood
R&D: Marc Wierenga
Operations: Ann Kirkwood
Plant Manager/Purchasing: Nils Reichert
Estimated Sales: $3-4 Million
Number Employees: 28
Square Footage: 26000

19942 (HQ)Bunn Corporation
1400 Stevenson Drive
Springfield, IL 62703 217-529-6601
800-637-8606
bunn@bunn.com www.bunnomatic.com
Manufacturer and exporter of coffee brewers, decanters, grinders and warmers as well as coffee and iced tea filters, hot water systems, iced tea brewers, water filtration systems, and hot powdered and frozen drink systems
President/CEO: Arthur Bunn
CFO: Gene Wilken
R&D: Robert Kobylarz
Quality Control: Kurt Powell
Sales: John Kielb
Public Relations: Melinda McDonald
Production: John Vanderveldt
Plant Manager: Doug Schwartz
Purchasing Director: John Essig
Estimated Sales: $10 - 20 Million
Number Employees: 100-249
Other Locations:
Bunn-O-Matic Corporation
Cerritos CA
Brands:
Bunn
Bunn-O-Matic
Easy Pour
Pour-O-Matic

19943 Bunn-O-Matic Corporation
280 Industrial Parkway S
Aurora, ON L4G 3T9
Canada 905-841-2866
Fax: 905-841-2775
Coffee brewing equipment
VP of Sales: Ken Cox
General Manager: Ross Anderson
Estimated Sales: $1 - 5,000,000
Number Employees: 100
Parent Co: Bunn-O-Matic Corporation

19944 Bunting Magnetics Company
500 S Spencer Rd
Newton, KS 67114 316-284-2020
Fax: 316-283-4975 800-835-2526
bmc@buntingmagnetics.com
www.buntingmagnetics.com
Magnetic and nonmagnetic conveyors in steel and aluminum extruded frames, magnetic separators and all metal detection equipment for both dry and wet lines
President: Robert Bunting
Vice President: Richard Meister
Marketing Director: Michael Wilks
Sales Director: Rod Henricks
Estimated Sales: $21.7 Million
Number Employees: 160
Square Footage: 61000
Other Locations:
Bunting Magnetics Company
Elk Grove Village IL
Brands:
Mag Slide
Powertrac

19945 Bunzl Distribution USA
P.O.Box 419111
St Louis, MO 63141-9111 314-997-5959
Fax: 314-997-0247 888-997-5959
www.bunzldistribution.com
Supplies a range of products including outsourced food packaging, disposable supplies, and cleaning and safety products to food processors, supermarkets, retailers, convenience stores and other users.
Distribution President, Chief Executive: Patrick Larmon
Executive VP: Jeff Earnhart
Estimated Sales: K
Number Employees: 1,000-4,999
Square Footage: 200000
Parent Co: Bunzl PLC
Type of Packaging: Food Service, Private Label, Bulk
Other Locations:
Bunzl Distribution
West Valley City UT

19946 Bunzl Processor Division
Ste 120
2005 Valley View Ln
Dallas, TX 75234-8936 214-631-4350
800-456-5624
dennis.moubray@bunzlusa.com
www.bunzlprocessor.com
Leading supplier to the meat and food processing industry, providing everything from packaging materials to work and safety apparel. Also available is a private label product line called Prime Source, featuring various products for thefoodservice, janitorial, industrial and healthcare industries
Sales: Dennis Moubray
Number Employees: 500-999
Type of Packaging: Food Service, Private Label
Brands:
Prime Source

19947 Burd & Fletcher
5151 E Geospace Dr
Independence, MO 64056 816-257-0291
Fax: 816-257-9928 800-821-2776
info@burdfletcher.com www.burdfletcher.com
Carton containers for food products
Number Employees: 250-499
Type of Packaging: Food Service, Bulk

19948 Burdock Group
859 Outer Road
Orlando, FL 32814-6652 407-802-1400
Fax: 407-802-1405 info@burdockgroup.com
www.burdockgroup.com
Consulting team that provides clients with solutions to scientific and regulatory issues affecting FDA and USDA regulated products
President: George Burdock Phd
Director of Toxicology: Ray A. Matulka, Ph.D
Manager Marketing/Sales: Ginger Mundy
Estimated Sales: $300,000-500,000
Number Employees: 10

19949 Burdock Group
859 Outer Road
Orlando, FL 32814-6652 40- 8-2 14
Fax: 40- 8-2 14 888-287-3625
info@burdockgroup.com
www.burdockgroup.com
Consulting team that provides clients with solutions to scientific safety and regulatory issues affecting fda and usda regulated products.
President: George Burdock
Estimated Sales: $300,000-500,000
Number Employees: 10

19950 Burford Corporation
PO Box 748
Maysville, OK 73057 405-867-4467
Fax: 405-867-4219 877-287-3673
cburford@burford.com www.burford.com
Bag and pouch sealers, bag labeling equipment, closing equipment, coders, daters, imprinters, computer systems, cooling equipment, cooling tunnels and computer programs
President: Fred Springer
Executive VP: Fred Springer
CFO: Fred Speringr
Vice President: Don Ivey
R & D: Scott Clemons
Sales Manager: Teresa Ruder
Estimated Sales: $10-20 000,000
Number Employees: 50-99
Type of Packaging: Private Label, Bulk

19951 Burger Maker Inc
666 16th Street
Carlstadt, NJ 07072 201-939-4747
Fax: 201-939-0444 ccrenshaw@burgermaker.com
www.burgermaker.com
Hamburger patties
President: David Schweid
EVP Operations: Brad Schweld
EVP Sales: Jamie Schweld
Regional Manager: Chip Crenshaw
Regional Manager: Bill Breslin
Regional Manager: John Jernagan

19952 Burgess Enterprises, Inc
1000 SW 34th St
Bldg W2 Suite A
Renton, WA 98057 206-763-0255
Fax: 206-763-8039 800-927-3286
marketing@burgessenterprises.net
www.burgessenterprises.net
Carts and kiosks; importer and exporter of espresso machines
President/CEO: Robert S Burgess
CFO: Don Paschal
Sales: Robert Connor
Estimated Sales: Below $2.5 Million
Number Employees: 5-9
Number of Brands: 4
Number of Products: 12
Brands:
Burgess
Faema

19953 Burgess Manufacturing ofOklahoma
1250 Roundhouse Rd
P.O. Box 237
Guthrie, OK 73044 405-282-1913
Fax: 405-282-7132 800-804-1913
bmfg@sbcglobal.net www.burgesspallets.com
Manufacturer and exporter of pallets, boxes, crating and lumber; wholesaler/distributor of lumber, plywood, stretch film, plastic pallets, chipboard and plastic components
Plant Manager: Lee Williams
Estimated Sales: $3 Million
Number Employees: 20-49
Square Footage: 21000

19954 **Burghof Engineering & Manufacturing Company**
16051 Deerfield Pkwy Ste 1
Prairie View, IL 60069 847-634-0737
Fax: 847-634-0870
Automatic fillers and packers
President: Kaspar Kammerer
Estimated Sales: $2.5-5 Million
Number Employees: 10-19

19955 **Burke Industrial Coatings**
6200 NE Campus Drive
Suite B
Vancouver, WA 98661-6800 360-944-8465
Fax: 360-759-4989 800-348-3245
mickie@burkeindustrialcoatings.com
www.burke-ind-coatings.com
USDA accepted water base industrial coatings
President: James P Harris
Quality Control: Barreal Badertscher
Vice President: Darrell Badertscher
Estimated Sales: Below $5 Million
Number Employees: 10

19956 **Burkert Fluid Control Systems**
2572 White Road
Irvine, CA 92614 949-223-3100
Fax: 949-223-3198 800-325-1405
marketing-usa@burkert.com
www.burkert-usa.com
Water treatment systems.
Inside Sales: Ebert Bautista

19957 **Burling Instruments**
16 River Road
P.O. Box 298
Chatham, NJ 07928-0298 973-635-9481
Fax: 973-635-9530 800-635-2526
mwetterer@burlinginstruments.com
www.burlinginstruments.com
Manufacturer and exporter of temperature controls, limits and sensors; importer of thermostats
President: Harry Bentas
Sr. VP: Roger Nation
VP of Sales: Michael Wetterer
Estimated Sales: $2.5-5 Million
Number Employees: 10-19
Square Footage: 44000

19958 **Burnett Brothers Engineering, Inc.**
P. O. Box 1224
Fullerton, CA 92836 714-526-2448
Fax: 714-526-4961 info@burnettbros.com
www.burnettbros.com
Manufacturers and importers of machinery including bunch and shrink wrappers, carton overwrappers, colloid, roll-fed labelers for water, soft drink and milk bottles. Also produce wrapper for cauliflower, cabbage, iceberg lettuceetc
President: Malcolm Burnett
Sales VP: Malcolm Burnett
Estimated Sales: Less than $500,000
Number Employees: 1-4

19959 **Burnishine Products**
755 Tri State Pkwy
Gurnee, IL 60031 847-356-0222
Fax: 253-856-1003 800-818-8275
gunser@burnishine.com www.burnishine.com
Sanitizers, disinfectants, sterilants, cleaners and polishers
President: Carl Demasi
Human Resources: Laura Welch
Purchasing Manager: Michelle Hogan
Number Employees: 20-49
Number of Brands: 4
Number of Products: 250
Square Footage: 100000
Parent Co: Herbert Stanley Company
Type of Packaging: Consumer, Private Label, Bulk

19960 **(HQ)Burns & McDonnell**
P.O.Box 419173
Kansas City, MO 64141-6173 816-333-9400
Fax: 816-333-3690 rdick@burnsmcd.com
www.burnsmcd.com
Consulting engineers and construction for various industries including the food
General Manager: Ronald Colas
CEO: Greg Graves
Estimated Sales: $5 Million
Number Employees: 1,000-4,999

19961 **Burns Chemical Systems**
3100 Hamilton Ave
Cleveland, OH 44114-3701 724-327-7600
Fax: 724-327-8049
Dish washers
President: John Burns
Product Manager: Marvin Katz
Controller: Robert Rummel
Estimated Sales: $10-20,000,000
Number Employees: 100-249

19962 **Burns Engineering**
10201 Bren Rd E
Hopkins, MN 55343-9066 952-935-4400
Fax: 952-935-8782 800-328-3871
info@burnsengineering.com
www.burnsengineering.com
Resistant thermometer devices (RTD) and thermocouple sanitary temperature sensors, transmitters and thermowells; calibration services available
President: Jim Burns
Sales Director: Stefan Tudor
Purchasing Manager: Wendi Fetter
Estimated Sales: $10 - 20 Million
Number Employees: 50-99

19963 **Burns Industries**
1150 Bethlehem Pike
Line Lexington, PA 18932 215-822-8778
Fax: 215-822-1006 800-223-6430
Vacuum lifting systems
Manager: Tim Burns
Number Employees: 50
Square Footage: 30000
Brands:
Vacuhoist

19964 **Burrell Cutlery Company**
100 Rockwell Ave.
Ellicottville, NY 14731 716-699-2343
Fax: 716-699-2683
Carving, culinary, fruit, slicing, steak, household, specialty and kitchen knives
President: John Burrell
Estimated Sales: $2.5-5 Million
Number Employees: 10

19965 **Burrell Leder Beltech**
7501 N. Saint Louis Ave
Skokie, IL 60076-4000 847-673-6720
Fax: 847-673-6373 800-323-4170
info@ammeraalbeltechusa.com
www.ammeraal-beltechusa.com
Manufacturer, importer and exporter of belts for packaging machinery and the processing of cookies, crackers, confectionery items, bread, rolls, meat and poultry
President: Brian Mc Sharry
Vice President: Jim Ekedahl
Estimated Sales: $20-50 Million
Number Employees: 50-99
Square Footage: 55000
Parent Co: Verseidag
Brands:
Beltech
Burtek
Polytek
Rapplon
Rapptex
Volta

19966 **Burrows Paper Corporation**
501 W Main St
Little Falls, NY 13365 800-272-7122
Fax: 315-823-3892 800-272-7122
papersales@burline.com
www.burrowspaper.com
Integrated paper manufacturer with operations in the US and Europe.
President/CEO: R W Burrows
Corporate Secretary: Margaret Goldman
Corporate VP: Michael Lengvarsky
VP/General Manager: Hai Ninh
Vice President, Sales: Duane Judd
Estimated Sales: $20-50 Million
Number Employees: 1,000-4,999
Square Footage: 120000
Type of Packaging: Food Service
Brands:
Plastawrap

19967 **Burrows Paper Corporation**
501 W Main St
Little Falls, NY 13365 315-823-2300
Fax: 315-823-3892 800-732-1933
papersales@burrowspaper.com
www.burrowspaper.com
Pizza boxes, carry-out food containers, sandwich wrap, and micro-flute packaging
President/CEO: R W Burrows
CFO: Philip Paras
Vice President: Hai Ninh
Research & Development: Terry McMillen
Quality Control: Melinda Bird
VP OF Sales: Duane Judd
Sales Director: Ed Amodei
Operations Manager: Jeffrey Hall
Production Manager: Jeffrey Hall
Plant Manager: Chris Kitchel
Purchasing Manager: Ralph Renzulli
Number Employees: 1,000-4,999
Type of Packaging: Consumer, Food Service, Private Label

19968 **Burry Foods**
1750 E Main Street
Suite 160
Saint Charles, IL 60174 630-584-9976
www.burryfoodservice.com
Frozen food service supplier of Thomas', Boboli and Entenmann's
CEO/Founder: Tony Hyler
CFO/VP Information Technology: Dave Phillips
Operations Manager/VP Supply Chain: Gerard Mitchell
Estimated Sales: $28.15 Million
Number Employees: 17
Square Footage: 7853
Type of Packaging: Food Service

19969 **Busch**
516 Viking Dr
Virginia Beach, VA 23452 757-463-7800
Fax: 757-463-7407 800-872-7867
marketing@buschinc.com www.buschpump.com
Vacuum packaging equipment, vacuum systems, rendering pumps, vacuum pumps
President: Charles Kane
CFO: Doug Clark
Quality Control: Kelly Wood
Marketing Director: Terry McMahan
VP of Engineering: Wayne Benson
Estimated Sales: $10 - 25 000,000
Number Employees: 100-249

19970 **Bush Refrigeration**
1700 Admiral Wilson Blvd
Camden, NJ 08109-3990 856-963-1800
Fax: 856-963-0770 800-220-2874
info@bushrefrigerators.com
www.bushrefrigeration.com
Manufacturer and exporter of walk in, display and storage coolers and freezers. Refrigerated deli and bakery display cases. Prep tables and under the counter prep tables.
President: Jeffery Bush
Estimated Sales: $2.5-5 Million
Number Employees: 20-49

19971 **Bush Tank Fabricators**
222 Thomas St
Newark, NJ 07114 973-596-1121
Fax: 973-596-1662
Ribbon blenders, custom fabricated tanks, mixers, agitators and hoppers
President: Thomas Horenburg
Vice President: Martin Koppel
Estimated Sales: $10-20,000,000
Number Employees: 5-9

19972 **Bushman Equipment**
P.O.Box 309
Butler, WI 53007 262-790-4200
Fax: 262-790-4202 800-338-7810
sales@BushmanAvonTec.com
www.bushman.com
Manufacturer and exporter of material handling equipment including cranes, hooks, coil, sheet and pallet lifters, beams, spreaders, blocks and tongs
President: Ralph Deger
Sales Manager: Chuck Nettesheim
Estimated Sales: $20-50 Million
Number Employees: 20-49

19973 Business Control Systems
1173 Green St
Iselin, NJ 08830 732-283-1300
Fax: 732-283-1192 800-233-5876
www.businesscontrol.com
Point of sale systems and software

19974 Buss America
455 Kehoe Blvd
Carol Stream, IL 60188-5203 630-933-9100
Fax: 630-933-0400 info.us@busscorp.com
www.busscompounding.com
Kneading extruders
Product Manager: Edmund Meier
Estimated Sales: $20-50 Million
Number Employees: 5-9
Square Footage: 66000
Parent Co: George Fisher

19975 Busse
124 N Columbus St
Randolph, WI 53956-1204 920-326-3131
Fax: 920-326-3134 www.arrowheadsystems.com
Conveyors
President: Thomas J Young
Estimated Sales: $10-25 Million
Number Employees: 50-99

19976 Busse/SJI
124 N Columbus St
Randolph, WI 53956 920-326-6348
Fax: 920-326-6551 800-882-4995
inquiry@arrowheadsystems.com
www.arrowheadsystems.com
Manufacturer and exporter of palletizers and depalletizers for glass, can and plastic beverage containers; also, retort crate loading and unloading
President: Thomas Young
Marketing Director: Nick Osterholt
Sales Manager: Dan Erdman
General Manager: George Vroom
Number Employees: 50-99
Parent Co: Arrowhead Systems
Other Locations:
Busse
Shelton CT
Brands:
Advantage
Eclipse
Turbo
Viper

19977 Butler Winery
6200 E Robinsion Rtd
Bloomington, IN 47408 812-332-6660
vineyard@butlerwinery.com
www.butlerwinery.com
Wine and wine making supplies
President/CEO: James Butler
Secretary/Treasurer: Susan Butler
Manager: Amy Butler
Estimated Sales: $540,000
Number Employees: 5
Brands:
Butler

19978 Butterbuds Food Ingredients
2330 Chicory Rd
Racine, WI 53403-4113 262-598-9900
Fax: 262-598-9999 800-426-1119
bbfi@bbuds.com www.bbuds.com
Processor and exporter of cholesterol-free butter flavored oils and sprays; also, natural dairy concentrates including butter, cheese and cream
President: Allen Buhler
Finance Executive: Tom Buhler
VP: John Buhler
Applications Scientist: Adam Small
International Marketing Manager: Thomas Buhler
Human Resources Executive: Jan Schmaus
General Manager: Bill Buhler
Production Manager: Dan Vice
Plant Manager: John Kueffer
Estimated Sales: $5-10 Million
Number Employees: 50
Square Footage: 5000
Parent Co: Cumberland Packing Corporation
Type of Packaging: Consumer, Food Service, Private Label, Bulk
Brands:
Alfredobuds
Butter Flo
Butterbuds
Buttermist
Cheesebuds

19979 Butterworth Systems
16737 W Hardy Rd
Houston, TX 77060-6241 281-821-7300
Fax: 281-821-5550 info@butterworth.com
www.butterworth.com
Tank cleaning machines
President: George Sherman
CFO: Craig Cooper
R & D: Dan Elko
Director Sales: James Slaughter
Estimated Sales: $1-2.5 Million
Number Employees: 10-19

19980 Buyers Laboratory CustomTesting Division
108 John St
Hackensack, NJ 07601-4130 201-489-6439
Fax: 201-488-0461 info@buyerslab.com
www.buyerslab.com
Owner: Burt Meerow
Chief Executive Officer: Michael Danziger
Vice President of Sales: Patti Clyne
Chief Operating Officer: Mark Lerch
Estimated Sales: $.5 - 1 million
Number Employees: 5-9

19981 Buypass Corporation
360 Interstate North Pkwy SE
Atlanta, GA 30339-2204 770-953-2664
Fax: 770-916-3391 www.firstdata.com
Electronic payment systems for debit, credit, EBT and check authorization purposes
Co- Founder: George Roberts
Chief Executive Officer, Chairman: Michael Capellas
Vice President of Community Relations: Ellen Sandberg
Client Executive: Rich Toland
Number Employees: 250-499
Parent Co: Electronic Payment Services

19982 Byk-Gardner
9104 Guilford Rd Ste 2
Columbia, MD 21046 301-483-6500
Fax: 301-483-6555 www.bykgardner.com
Colors and color meters
VP: Mike Gogoel
General Manager: Mike Goegel
Estimated Sales: $300,000-500,000
Number Employees: 1-4

19983 Bynoe Printers
167 W 126th Street
New York, NY 10027-4412 212-662-5041
bynoeprinters@juno.com
Manufacturer and wholesaler/distributor of advertising specialties including labels, raffle tickets and paper cups
President: Mark Bynoe
Estimated Sales: $1-2,500,000
Number Employees: 1-4

19984 Byrton Dairy Products
28354 N Ballard Dr
Lake Forest, IL 60045 847-367-8300
Fax: 847-367-8332
President: Richard Tondi
Estimated Sales: $2.5-5 000,000
Number Employees: 5-9

19985 C S Bell Company
PO Box 291
Tiffin, OH 44883 419-448-0791
Fax: 419-448-1203 888-958-6381
info@csbellco.com www.csbellco.com
Manufacturer and exporter of grist and hammer mills, conveyors and recycling and size reduction equipment; also, custom fabrication available.
President: Daniel White
Estimated Sales: $500,000-$1 Million
Number Employees: 5-9
Square Footage: 10000
Brands:
Bell

19986 C&D Robotics
4780 S 23rd St
Beaumont, TX 77705 409-840-5252
Fax: 409-840-4660 800-967-6268
jhayes@cdrobot.com www.cdrobot.com
Material handling for finished goods, industrial contry robots, specialty machinery, conveyers and material handling systems
President: Charles Davis
Estimated Sales: $10-20 000,000
Number Employees: 100-249

19987 C&D Valve ManufacturingCompany, Inc.
201 North West 67th Street
Oklahoma City, OK 73116
Fax: 800-840-0443 800-654-9233
www.cdvalve.com
Manufacturer and exporter of valves for refrigeration equipment
President: Bradford Denning
Estimated Sales: $5 - 10 Million
Number Employees: 20-49

19988 C&H Chemical
222 Starkey St
St Paul, MN 55107-1813 651-227-4343
Fax: 651-227-2485 info@chchemical.com
www.secole.com
Cleaning compounds
President: Greg Elliott
Food Industry Specialist: John Jesmok
Estimated Sales: $5-10 Million
Number Employees: 20-49

19989 C&H Packaging Company
1401 W Taylor St
Merrill, WI 54452 715-536-5400
Fax: 715-536-4678 www.chpack.com
Flexographic printing, lamination, pouching
VP: Gene Wagner
Marketing: Bob Madderom
Sales: Bob Madderom
Operations: Larry Offerman
Plant Manager: Dave Welch
Estimated Sales: $3.5 000,000
Number Employees: 100-249
Type of Packaging: Consumer, Food Service, Private Label

19990 C&H Store Equipment Company
2530 S Broadway
Los Angeles, CA 90007 213-748-7165
Fax: 213-749-6135 800-648-4979
www.chstore.com
Manufacturer, wholesaler/distributor and exporter of store fixtures, office furniture, showcases, and metal shelving
Owner: Cheonil Kim
CEO: Cheon Kim
Estimated Sales: $2.5-5,000,000
Number Employees: 10-19
Brands:
Lozier Reeve

19991 C&K Machine Company
56 Jackson St Ste 1
Holyoke, MA 01040 413-536-8122
Fax: 413-532-9819 email@ckmachine.com
www.ckmachine.com
Manufacturer and exporter of nonshrink, conforming wrapping machines for cookies, candies and sandwiches; also, bakery slicing machines and gum and candy cartoners
President: James Tallon
Sales/Marketing: James Tallon
Estimated Sales: $1-3 Million
Number Employees: 1-4
Square Footage: 12000
Brands:
Redington
Wrap King

19992 C&L Wood Products
62 Walnut Rd
Hartselle, AL 35640-8813 256-773-3233
Fax: 256-773-3238 800-483-2035
hbowman@clwoodproducts.com
www.clwoodproducts.com
Pallets and crates including hardwood and pine
Manager: Henry Bowman
Plant Manager: Rodger Glaz
Estimated Sales: $2.5-5 Million
Number Employees: 50-99
Square Footage: 15000

19993 C&M Fine Pak
4162 Georgia Blvd
San Bernardino, CA 92407-1852 909-880-1781
Fax: 909-474-4384 800-232-5959
www.cmfinepack.com

Disposable food containers
President: Andrew Falcon
Estimated Sales: G
Number Employees: 100-249
Brands:
Fine Pak

19994 C&R
5600 Clyde Moore Dr
Groveport, OH 43125 614-497-1130
Fax: 614-497-1585 888-497-1130
Fabrication and installation of stainless process equipment and process piping; distributors of G and H products and AMPCO centrifugal pumps, heat exchangers, tubular, ice equipment, ice builders, flow diversion stations, pipingfittings and tubing
President: R Murphy
Estimated Sales: $5-10 000,000
Number Employees: 20-49

19995 (HQ)C&R Refrigation Inc
405 Center St
Center, TX 75935 936-598-2761
Fax: 936-598-7858 800-438-6182
www.crrefrig.com
Custom Metal Fabrication-3A tanks, process piping installation, platforms, flow panels, valve clusters, hoppers, skid systems, dryers, orbital welding. Distributor for Alfalaval, Ampco Pumps, Definix Valves.
President: Ronald Murphy
VP: Phillip McKitrick
Sales Manager: Jim McAnaul
Estimated Sales: $5-10 Million
Number Employees: 11
Square Footage: 80000
Other Locations:
C&R
Largo FL

19996 C&R Refrigeration
405 Center St
Center, TX 75935 936-598-2761
Fax: 409-598-7858 800-438-6182
crrefrig@netdot.com www.crrefrig.com
Rebuilt ammonia compressors, ice machines and other industrial refrigeration equipment
President: Robert Reeves
Estimated Sales: $10-20 Million
Number Employees: 50-99

19997 C-Through Covers
4955 Curry Drive
San Diego, CA 92115-2631 619-286-0671
Fax: 619-286-7991
Reinforced vinyl and canvas covers for bakery rack, freezers, etc
Sales Manager: Marta Stulberger
Estimated Sales: $1 - 5 Million

19998 C. Cretors & Company
3243 N California Ave
Chicago, IL 60618 773-588-1690
Fax: 773-588-2171 800-228-1885
info@cretors.com www.cretors.com
Manufacturer and exporter of popcorn machines and cotton candy equipment and supplies
President: Andrew Cretors
CFO: Dan Williams
Quality Control: Walter Karzak
Marketing Manager: Beth Cretors
Product Manager: John Concannon
Estimated Sales: $10 - 20 Million
Number Employees: 100-249
Square Footage: 53000
Brands:
Caramelizer
Cretors
Flo-Thru
Ringmaster I
Ringmaster Ii

19999 C. Cretors & Company
3243 N California Ave
Chicago, IL 60618 773-588-1690
Fax: 773-588-2171 800-228-1885
flothru@cretors.com www.cretors.com
Savory, cheese and carmel popcorn equipment; systems for the hot-air expansion and coating of snack pellets
President: Andrew Cretors
CEO: Frank Jancewicz
CFO: Van Neathery
Quality Control: Walter Krzak
Estimated Sales: $10 - 20 000,000
Number Employees: 100-249
Square Footage: 19000

20000 C. Nelson ManufacturingCompany
265 N Lake Winds Pkwy
Oak Harbor, OH 43449 419-898-3305
Fax: 419-898-4098 800-922-7339
info@cnelson.com www.cnelson.com
Manufacturer and exporter of refrigerated pushcarts and ice cream storage cabinets
President: Kelly Smith
Sr. Engineer: Paul Cox
Sales Manager: Tammy Almendinger
Account Manager: Tammy Almendinger
Purchasing Manager: Michele Huffman
Estimated Sales: $10-20 Million
Number Employees: 20-49
Square Footage: 20000

20001 C. Nelson ManufacturingCompany
265 N Lake Winds Pkwy
Oak Harbor, OH 43449 419-898-3305
Fax: 419-898-4098 info@cnelson.com
www.cnelson.com
Owner: Kelley Smith
Estimated Sales: $10-20 000,000
Number Employees: 20-49

20002 C. Palmer Manufacturing
5 Palmers Rd
West Newton, PA 15089 724-872-8200
Fax: 724-872-8302 cpalmeri@yuklnwaltc.com
www.cpalmermfg.com
Pizelle irons
President: John Palmieri
CEO: John Palmeri
President: John Palmieri
VP: Kathryn Palmeri
CFO: Philpe Palmieri
Sales Manager: Parcy Smose
Estimated Sales: $1 - 2.5 Million
Number Employees: 5-9

20003 C.B. Dombach & Son
252 N Prince St
Lancaster, PA 17603 717-392-0578
Fax: 717-392-1210 info@cbdombach.com
www.cbdombach.com
Commercial awnings
President: Scott Underwood
Estimated Sales: $1 - 2.5 Million
Number Employees: 10-19

20004 C.E. Rogers Company
1895 Frontage Rd
PO Box 118
Mora, MN 55051 320-679-2172
Fax: 320-679-2180 800-279-8081
cerogers@cerogers.com www.cerogers.com
Manufacturer, exporter and importer of free-standing multi-effect and waste water evaporators, horizontal and vertical spray dryers and related heating and cooling equipment; installation service available
President/Sales: Howard Rogers
Chief Engineer: Steven Degeest
Parts: Carol Dutton
Estimated Sales: $5-10 Million
Number Employees: 20-49
Square Footage: 4000
Parent Co: CFR Group

20005 C.E. Rogers Company
1895 Frontage Rd
P.O. Box 118
Mora, MN 55051 320-679-2172
Fax: 320-679-2180 800-279-8081
cerogers@cerogers.com www.cerogers.com
President: Howard Rogers
Estimated Sales: $5-10 000,000
Number Employees: 20-49

20006 C.F.F. Stainless Steels
1840 Burlington Street East
Hamilton, ON L8H 3L4 905-549-2603
Fax: 905-549-2994 800-263-4511
sales@cffstainless.com www.cffstainless.com
Supplier of stainless steel products to the pharmaceutical, chemical, beverage, mining, water purification, food and dairy industries
President: Brian McComb
Vice President Sales: John Burns

20007 C.H. Babb Company
445 Paramount Dr
Raynham, MA 02767 508-977-0600
Fax: 508-977-1985 sales@chbabb.com
www.chbabb.com
Manufacturer and exporter of automated final proofers, tunnel ovens, cooling conveyors and complete systems for pizza, bagels, breads and rolls, pastries, pies, etc
President: Charles Foran
Sales Representative: William Foran
Number Employees: 20-49
Square Footage: 75000
Brands:
Babbco

20008 (HQ)C.H. Robinson Worldwide
14800 Charlson Rd Ste 400
Eden Prairie, MN 55347 952-933-4545
Fax: 952-937-6714 www.chrobinson.com
CH Robinson provides: freight transportation - TL, intermodal, ocean and air freight, cross docking, LTL, customs brokerage, freight forwarding and trucking services; fresh produce sourcing; and information services.
CEO and Chairman of the Board: John Wiehoff
Owner: Warren Frank
SVP & CFO: Chad Lindbloom
Estimated Sales: $3.27 Billion
Number Employees: 5,000-9,999
Type of Packaging: Consumer, Food Service, Bulk

20009 C.J. Machine
1183-73 1/2 Avenue NW
Fridley, MN 55432 763-767-4630
Fax: 763-767-4633
Conveyors, casers, stackers, dolly cart loaders and elevators
President: Chuck Voller
VP: Jeff Anderson
Number Employees: 10
Brands:
Built Rite

20010 C.J. Machine
11551 Eagle Street NW
Suite 1
Coon Rapids, MN 55448-3051 763-506-0968
Fax: 763-767-4633
Estimated Sales: $300,000-500,000
Number Employees: 1-4

20011 C.M. Lingle Company
100 Millard Drive
Henderson, TX 75652-5034 903-657-5557
Fax: 903-657-9749 800-256-6963
Walk-in coolers and freezers and cold storage doors
President: Fred Lingle
VP: James Lingle
Estimated Sales: $10-20 Million
Number Employees: 50-99
Square Footage: 70000

20012 C.M. Slicechief Company, Inc.
3333 Maple St
P.O. Box 80206
Toledo, OH 43608-0206 419-241-7647
Fax: 419-241-3513 slicechief@slicechief.com
www.slicechief.com
Manufacturer and exporter of nonelectric vegetable/fruit slicers and cheese shredders
President: Susan Brown
Estimated Sales: $2.5-5 Million
Number Employees: 5-9
Type of Packaging: Food Service
Brands:
Chief 900 Series

20013 C.P. Industries
560 N 500 W
Salt Lake City, UT 84116 801-521-0313
Fax: 801-539-0510 800-453-4931
info@cpindustries.net www.cpindustries.net

Manufacturer and exporter of industrial and household cleaners, ice melters and detergents
Owner: Ann Lieber
National Detergent Manager: Ted Olsen
Estimated Sales: $10 - 20 Million
Number Employees: 20-49
Square Footage: 250000
Type of Packaging: Consumer, Food Service, Private Label, Bulk
Brands:
Generic Liquid Dish
Generic Liquid Laundry
Mountain White
Power Clean
Sparkle

20014 C.R. Daniels Inc.
3451 Ellicott Center Dr
Ellicott City, MD 21043-4191
Fax: 410-461-2987 800-933-2638
info@crdaniels.com www.crdaniels.com
Manufacturer and exporter of conveyor belting, trucks and plastic totes, carts, hampers and tubs; importer of cotton duck
President: Gary Abel
Vice President: Vic Keeler
Quality Control: J Singh
Estimated Sales: $20 - 50 Million
Number Employees: 250-499
Square Footage: 250000
Brands:
Dandux

20015 C.R. Manufacturing
10240 Deer Park Rd
Waverly, NE 68462 402-786-2000
Fax: 402-786-2096 877-789-5844
lisag@pmc-group.com www.crmfg.com
Manufacturer and exporter of plastic pour spouts, scoops, spreaders, spatulas, funnels, knives, spoons, bowls, pitchers, corkscrews, tongs, etc
General Manager: Daryl Chapelle
Quality Control: Ace Dettinger
Estimated Sales: $5 - 10 Million
Number Employees: 100-249
Brands:
Betterway
Dispos-A-Way
Exacto-Pour
Ezy-Way
Jigg-All
Lidd Off
Magic-Flo
Magic-Mesh
Margarita Made Easy
Pop-N-Pull
Posi-Pour
Posi-Pour 2000
Pour Mor
Pour-Eaz
Save-A-Nail
Shooters Made Easy
Table Lev'lr
Whiskygate

20016 C.W. Brabender Instruments
50 E Wesley St
PO Box 2127
South Hackensack, NJ 07606 201-343-8425
Fax: 201-343-0608 foodsales@cwbrabender.com
www.cwbrabender.com
Instrumentation for testing physical properties and quality of various materials utilized in the food industry. Product line includes the world renowned Farinograph®, Extensograph®, several viscometers, mills, extruders andmuch more.
President: Richard Thoma
VP Sales/Marketing-Food Division: Sal Iaquez
Marketing Manager: Mike DiNatale
Account Manager: Terence Richards
Estimated Sales: $5 - 10 Million
Number Employees: 20-49
Brands:
Extensograph
Farinograph
Plasti-Corder

20017 C.W. Cole & Company
2560 Rosemead Blvd
South El Monte, CA 91733-1593 626-443-2473
Fax: 626-443-9253 info@colelighting.com
www.colelighting.com
Custom lighting fixtures for cooking hoods, walk-in coolers and salad bar/pie cases; also, refrigerator door light switches
Co-Owner: Stephen Cole
Co-Owner: Donald Cole
Sales Manager: Sam Serrano
Sales Engineer: Kevin Brummett
Engineering & Design: Dan Wilkins
Plant Manager: Gustavo Castillo
Purchasing Manager: Jim Cotney
Estimated Sales: $5 Million
Number Employees: 20-49
Square Footage: 25000

20018 C.W. Shasky & Associates Ltd.
2880 Portland Drive
Oakville, ON L4K 5P2
Canada 905-829-9414
Fax: 905-760-7715 jennifer@shasky.com
www.shasky.com
Manufacturers' representative for foodservice, club and HMR segments
President: Michael Shasky
VP: James Shasky
Estimated Sales: $7.3 Million
Number Employees: 25
Brands:
Angostura Bitters
Au Pain Dore
Catania-Spagna
Dole Food Products
Eli's Cheesecake Company
Farmland Foods
Haagen-Dazs®
Japan Food Canada/Kikkoman
McIlhenny Company Tabasco®
Mimi Foods
Mission Foods
National Importers/Twinnings
Nestle Ice Cream
Norpac
Otis Spunkmeyer
Patak's
Rosina Food Products
Sea Watch International
Stanislaus Food Products
Tate & Lyle

20019 (HQ)C.W. Zumbiel Company
2339 Harris Ave
Cincinnati, OH 45212-2715 513-531-3600
Fax: 513-531-0072 wbowman@zumbiel.com
www.zumbiel.com
Paper boxes, folding cartons and beverage carriers
President: R Zumbiel
VP: Thomas Zumbiel
Sales Manager Beverages: Charles Mace
Estimated Sales: $20 - 50 Million
Number Employees: 250-499
Square Footage: 700000

20020 CA Griffith International
PO Box 1785
Huntington, NY 11743-0460 631-385-7521
Fax: 631-424-3639
Meat packaging
Estimated Sales: $5-10 000,000

20021 CA, Inc.
1 CA Plaza
Islandia, NY 11749
Fax: 631-342-6800 800-225-5224
www.ca.com
Software for systems, financial and warehouse management, etc
Founder/Vice Chairman: Russell Artzt
Chief Executive Officer: Michael Gregoire
EVP/Chief Financial Officer: Richard Beckert
EVP Strategy & Corporate Development: Jacob Lamm
Chief Marketing Officer: Andrew Wittman
EVP/Group Executive Sales & Services: George Fischer
Chief Communications Officer: William Hughes
Estimated Sales: $4.6 Billion
Number Employees: 13600
Parent Co: Computer Associates International

20022 CAB Technology
87 Progress Ave Unit 1
Tyngsboro, MA 01879 978-649-0293
Fax: 978-649-0294 info.us@cab.de
www.cab.de/us/
President: Joachim Komus
Operations Executive: Mark Cavanaugh
Estimated Sales: Below $5 Million
Number Employees: 1-4

20023 CABOT NORIT Americas Inc
P.O. Box 790
Marshall, TX 75671 903-923-1000
Fax: 903-938-9701 800-641-9245
mark@norit-americas.com www.norit.com
Manufaturer activated carbon, a filter media
Parent Co: Cabot Corp

20024 CAE Alpheus
9370 7th Street
Unit E
Rancho Cucamonga, CA 91730-5509
Fax: 513-831-3672 800-777-9101
info@coldjet.com www.dryiceblasting.com
Dry Ice blasting machines
Estimated Sales: $1-2.5 Million
Number Employees: 1-4

20025 CAL Controls
1675 Delany Road
Gurnee, IL 60031 800-866-6659
Fax: 847-782-5223 800-447-6690
NA@West-CS.com www.cal-controls.com
Temperature and process controllers for OEM and Plant MRO
President: Alan Bates
Estimated Sales: $1-2.5 Million
Number Employees: 5-9

20026 CAM Campak/Technician
119 Naylon Ave
Livingston, NJ 07039-1005 973-597-1414
Fax: 973-992-4713 info@campak.com
www.campak.com
Thermoformers, intermittent motion horizontal cartoners, automatic wrappers, automatic bundlers and shrink tunnels
President: Thomas Miller
Estimated Sales: $5-10 Million
Number Employees: 10-19

20027 CAT PUMPS
1681 94th Ln NE
Blaine, MN 55449 763-780-5440
Fax: 763-780-2958 techsupport@catpumps.com
www.catpumps.com
Manufacturer and exporter of pumps including high-pressure, positive displacement, piston and plunger, stainless steel, hightemp, custom designed power units, submersible and end-suction centrifugal
CEO: William Bruggeman
Marketing Director: Darla Jean Thompson
Sales: Scott Stelzner
Estimated Sales: $50-100 Million
Number Employees: 50-99
Square Footage: 130000
Brands:
Cat Pumps

20028 (HQ)CB Manufacturing & SalesCompany
4475 Infirmary Rd
Miamisburg, OH 45342 937-866-5986
Fax: 937-866-6844 800-543-6860
sales@cbmfg.com www.cbmfg.com
Manufacturer and distributor of industrial knives and blades
Chief Executive Officer: Chuck Biehn
CFO: Don Cain
VP Manufacturing: Roger Adams
Purchasing Manager: Angie Matheney
Estimated Sales: $10-20 Million
Number Employees: 10
Square Footage: 100000
Type of Packaging: Private Label, Bulk
Other Locations:
CB Manufacturing & Sales Company
Centerville OH

20029 CBI Freezing Equipment
6202 214th St SW
Mountlake Terrace, WA 98043 425-775-7424
Fax: 425-775-1715 info@cbife.com
www.cbife.com
President: Ed Cloudy
Estimated Sales: $3 - 5 Million
Number Employees: 5-9

20030 (HQ)CBORD Group
61 Brown Rd
Ithaca, NY 14850 607-257-2140
Fax: 607-257-1902 sales@cbord.com
www.cbord.com
Looking for major food cost savings? Net-based foodservice programs? Cashless cafeteria system to increase revenue? The CBORD provides everything from enterprise-wide food production management to single-facility inventory tracking.Catering and event modules are also available. NetNutrition provides nutrition information with just the click of a mouse. The Nutrition Service Suite delivers support tools to clinical services. Award winning 24/7 telephone support. CBORD offerssuccess w/out risk
President: John Alexander
CEO: Tim Tighe
Estimated Sales: $10 - 20 Million
Number Employees: 250-499
Other Locations:
CBORD Group
Indianapolis IN
Brands:
Catermate
Foodservice Suite
Gerimenu
Nutrition Service Suite

20031 CBS International
P.O.Box 70
Currituck, NC 27929-0070 252-232-3378
Fax: 252-232-3470
Manager: Spence Castello
Estimated Sales: $1-2.5 000,000
Number Employees: 1-4

20032 CBi Freezing Equipment
6202 214th St SW
Mountlake Terrace, WA 98043-2097 425-775-7424
Fax: 425-775-1715 ecloudy@cbife.com
www.cbife.com
President: Ed Cloudy
Estimated Sales: $3 - 5 Million
Number Employees: 20

20033 CC Custom Technology Corporation
18201 S Miles Road
Cleveland, OH 44128-4231 216-662-5500
Fax: 216-662-2623 www.cctranstech.com
Waxes and cleaners
President: April Esner
Quality Control: Don Pierce
VP Manufacturing: Charles Silk
Estimated Sales: $2.5-5 Million
Number Employees: 10

20034 CCL Container
105 Gordon Baker Rd
Suite 500
Toronto, ON M2H 3P8 416-756-8500
ccl@cclind.com
www.cclind.com
Manufacturer and exporter of aluminum aerosol cans and tubes
President & CEO: Geoffrey Martin
Executive Chairman: Donald Lang
Vice President, General Manager: Andy Iseli
Sales Manager: Joe Meldrew
Senior Vice President of Corporate Commu: Janis Wade
Estimated Sales: $1 - 5 Million

20035 CCL Container
1 Llodio Dr
Hermitage, PA 16148 724-981-4420
Fax: 724-342-1116 www.cclcontainer.com
Collapsible metal tubes and plastic closures
Estimated Sales: $10-20 000,000
Number Employees: 50-99

20036 CCL Label
1187 Industrial Rd
Cold Spring, KY 41076 859-781-6161
Fax: 859-781-6339 800-422-6633
jarseneault@cclind.com www.ccllabel.com
Pressure sensitive and promotional labels
President: Eric Schaffer
Quality Control: Liary Guys
Director Operations: Tom McDonald
Estimated Sales: $10-20 Million
Number Employees: 10-19
Brands:
On-Pak

20037 CCL Labeling Equipment
1616 S California Avenue
Monrovia, CA 91016-4622 626-305-8056
Fax: 626-301-0405 800-423-6569
cusserv@cdf-liners.com www.ccllabel.com
Stepper motor labeling heads with integrated electronics, in-line and rotary labeling systems, synchronous and transfer label applicators; prime and promotional label designs including rotating labels and multipanel labels

20038 CCP Industries, Inc.
26301 Curtiss-Wright Parkway
Cleveland, OH 44143 440-449-6550
Fax: 800-445-8366 800-321-2840
ccporders@ccpind.com www.ccpind.com
Industrial wiping materials, hand, glass and all purpose cleaners, disposable clothing, uniforms and safety products
President: Allen Menard
Quality Control: James Fulls
V.P.: Norman Sull
Marketing Manager: Dave Williams
Number Employees: 1,000-4,999
Square Footage: 500000
Parent Co: Tranzonic Companies

20039 CCS Stone, Inc.
9-11 Caeser Place
Moonachie, NJ 07074-1702 201-933-1515
Fax: 201-933-5744 800-227-7785
info@ccsstone.com www.ccsstone.com
Manufacturer and importer of restaurant and bar furniture including chairs, barstools, marble and granite tabletops and bases
President: Donald Mitnick
Controller: Corey Mitnick
VP: John Mitnick
Purchasing Manager: Michael Rivkin
Estimated Sales: $5-10 Million
Number Employees: 20-49
Square Footage: 200000

20040 CCW Products, Inc.
5861 Tennyson St
Arvada, CO 80003-6902 303-427-9663
Fax: 303-427-1608 vickie.h@ccwproducts.com
www.ccwproducts.com
Manufacturer and exporter of clear wide-mouth plastic containers used for food packaging and point-of-purchase displays
President: David Teneyck
CEO: Mort Saffer
Sales Manager: Donald Johnston
Operations Manager: Roger Lamb
Estimated Sales: $10 - 20 Million
Number Employees: 50-99
Number of Products: 300+
Square Footage: 80000
Type of Packaging: Consumer, Food Service, Private Label, Bulk

20041 CCi Scale Company
4350 Transport St
Suite 108
Ventura, CA 93003 805-658-0422
Fax: 805-658-0436 800-900-0224
cciscale@hotmail.com www.cciscale.com
Manufacturer and importer of mechanical, electronic digital, portable, portion control, receiving, counting and battery operated scales
Owner: Tom Bouton
CEO: Tom Bouton
Sales Manager: Terri McGinn
Estimated Sales: Below $5 Million
Number Employees: 1-4
Brands:
Cci

20042 CDF Corporation
77 Industrial Park Rd
Plymouth, MA 02360 800-443-1920
Fax: 508-747-6333 800-443-1920
www.cdf1.com
Liners and other value added products used in industrial shipping and storage containers.CDF offers the following products: cheer pack; cheertainer bag in box; IBC aseptic; form-fit; pillow & high-barrier foil liners & accessories;DrumSaver liners for steel,plastic and fiber drums; PailSaver liners for steel & plastic pails & dust caps, cover sheets, lids and strainers for drums and pails.
President: Joe Sullivan
Marketing: Amanda Verash-Morris
Operations: Buddy Morgan
Number Employees: 100-249
Type of Packaging: Food Service, Bulk

20043 CE International Trading Corporation
13450 SW 134th Ave
Suite B-5
Miami, FL 33186-4530 305-254-3448
Fax: 305-254-3182 800-827-1169
edwin@ceinternationaltrading.com
http://ceinternational.marcorojas.com/index.htm
Vibratory and separation systems. Food and beverage usage includes batch operations to screen and scalp powders, granules, or liquids in different locations.
Sales Representative: Edwin Rojas

20044 CE Rogers Company
P.O.Box 118
Mora, MN 55051-0118 320-679-2172
Fax: 320-679-2180 800-279-8081
cerogers@cerogers.com www.cerogers.com
Dairy and food process equipment including evaporators and spray dryers
President: Howard Rogers
CFO: Renee Parent
Estimated Sales: $5-10 Million
Number Employees: 20-49

20045 CEA Instruments
160 Tillman St Ste 1
Westwood, NJ 07675 201-967-5660
Fax: 201-967-8450 888-893-9640
ceainstr@aol.com www.ceainstr.com
Manufacturer, importer and exporter of monitors for toxic and combustible gas and oxygen levels
Manager: Steven Adelman
Vice President: Steve Adelman
General Manager: Martin Adelman
Estimated Sales: $2-3 Million
Number Employees: 5-9
Number of Brands: 4
Number of Products: 18
Square Footage: 4000
Brands:
Cea 266
Gas Baron
Gas Baron 2
Md-16
Series U

20046 CECO/Compressor Engineering Corporation
5440 Alder Dr
Houston, TX 77081 713-664-7333
Fax: 713-664-6444 800-879-2326
sales@ceconet.com www.ceconet.com
President: Richard Hotze
CFO: Mark Hotze
Estimated Sales: $20 - 50 Million
Number Employees: 100-249

20047 CEM Corporation
P.O.Box 200
Matthews, NC 28106 704-821-7015
Fax: 704-821-7894 800-726-3331
info@cem.com www.cem.com
Manufacturer and exporter of microwave instruments for moisture/solids, protein and fat analysis; also, digestion and solvent extraction systems and muffle furnaces
President: Michael Collins
CFO: Richard Decker
R&D: Ed King
Director Sales/Marketing: Ken Corliss
Estimated Sales: $20 - 30 Million
Number Employees: 100-249
Square Footage: 60000
Brands:
Fas-9001
Mars 5
Mars-X
Mas-7000

Profat 2
Smart System 5
Star Systems

20048 **CF Chef**
4030 Black Gold Dr
Dallas, TX 75247-6304 214-905-1518
Fax: 214-905-9817 800-332-8812
cfmails@cfchefs.com www.cfchefs.com
Sell roux as an ingredient to chef and other food companies throughout the world
Owner: W R Seeds
R & D: Eugene Wisakowsky
Vice President, Controller: Campbell Tagg
Director Operations: Donald Capone Ph.D
Vice President of Production: James Michel
Estimated Sales: $10 - 20 Million
Number Employees: 20-49
Brands:
Cf Chefs
Country Flavor Kitchens
Flavor Roux
Skillet Style

20049 **CF/NAPA**
2787 Napa Valley Corporate Dr
Napa, CA 94558-6216 707-265-1891
Fax: 707-265-1899 dschuemann@cfnapa.com
www.cfnapa.com
Designer of labels, containers, boxes, etc
Owner: David Schuemann
Principal: John Farrell
Marketing Director: Susan Rouzie
Estimated Sales: Below $5 Million
Number Employees: 5-9
Square Footage: 18000

20050 **CFC Applied HolographicsCorporation**
500 State St
Chicago Heights, IL 60411 708-891-3456
Fax: 708-758-5989 cfcinfo@cfcintl.com
www.cfcintl.com
Film, foils and office product supplies
Chairman: Roger Huby
President: Richard Grathwaite
Sales: Mark Mitravich
Estimated Sales: $10-25 000,000
Number Employees: 250-499

20051 **CFC Holographics**
500 State St
Chicago Heights, IL 60411-1293 708-891-3456
Fax: 708-758-5989 salesinfo@cfcintl.com
www.cfcintl.com
President: Greg Jehlik
Sales: Mark Mitravich
Estimated Sales: $10 - 20 Million
Number Employees: 250-499

20052 **CFS North America**
5048 Tennyson Pkwy # 200
Plano, TX 75024-3080 972-618-1100
Fax: 214-618-1200 www.cfs.com
Specializes in performance focused solutions for the food industry, from a single machine or packaging material to a complete production line for the preparation, marination, processing, slicing and packaging of primarily meatpoultry, fish, seafood and cheese based products.
Owner: Robert Algiere
Estimated Sales: $100+ Million
Number Employees: 100-249

20053 **CGI Processing Equipment**
275 Innovation Drive
Romeoville, IL 60446 888-746-0275
Fax: 815-221-5301 info@cgimfg.com
www.cgimfg.com
Brine systems, bacon processing equipment and accesories, continuous sausage processing systems, cookers, smokehouses, accessories, trucks and cages
Sales Manager: Mike Willis
Estimated Sales: $5-10 Million
Number Employees: 60

20054 **CH Imports**
3410 Deep Green Dr
Greensboro, NC 27410 336-282-9734
Fax: 336-288-3375 jbollini@traid.rr.com
www.chimports.com
Essential oils and aromatherapy supplies
Owner: Jack Bollini
Estimated Sales: Below $5 000,000
Number Employees: 1-4

20055 **(HQ)CH2M Hill**
9191 South Jamaica St.
Englewood, CO 80112-5946 303-771-0900
Fax: 720-286-9250 foodandbev@ch2m.com
www.ch2m.com
Global, full-service engineering, procurement, construction management and operations firm that has supported the growth of the food and beverage industry for more than a quarter a century. from baked goods, processed foods and dairyproducts to carbonated and non-carbonated beverages, we offer a broad range of services to the food and beverage industry around the world.
Chairman & Chief Executive Officer: Lee McIntire
Chief Financial Officer: Michael Lucki CPA
SVP & Chief Human Resources Officer: John Madia
Estimated Sales: $5.5 Billion
Number Employees: 30,000
Other Locations:
Lockwood Greene
Atlanta GA
Lockwood Greene-Enterprise Mill
Augusta GA
Lockwood Greene
Cincinnati OH
Lockwood Greene
Dallas TX
Lockwood Greene
Hampton VA
Lockwood Greene
Knoxville TN
Lockwood Greene
Long Beach CA
Lockwood Greene
Nashville TN
Lockwood Greene
New York NY
Lockwood Greene
Moon Township PA
Lockwood Greene
Saint Louis MO
Lockwood Greene
Pooler GA
Lockwood Greene
Somerset NJ

20056 **CHEMetrics**
4295 Catlett Road
Midland, VA 22728 540-788-9026
Fax: 540-788-4856 800-356-3072
marketing@chemetrics.com
www.chemetrics.com
Water analysis test kits
President: Bruce Rampy
International Business Manager: Shirley Ward
Estimated Sales: $20 - 50 Million
Number Employees: 8

20057 **CHEP**
8517 S Park Cir
Orlando, FL 32819-9030 407-370-2437
Fax: 407-355-6211 800-243-7872
chep@brambles.com www.chep.com
President: Michael Lamb
Estimated Sales: $75 - 100 Million
Number Employees: 500-999

20058 **CHL Systems**
476 Meetinghouse Rd
Souderton, PA 18964 215-723-7284
Fax: 215-723-9115 sales@chlsystems.com
www.chlsystems.com
Food handling and conveyor systems, and material handling equipment; custom designed systems available
President: J Daniel Landis
CFO: Kevin Albvefer
Sales Manager: Leon Kartz
Estimated Sales: $20 - 50 Million
Number Employees: 100-249
Square Footage: 80000
Parent Co: Clayton H. Landis Company

20059 **(HQ)CHS Inc.**
5500 Cenex Drive
Inver Grove Heights, MN 55077 651-355-6000
800-232-3639
www.chsinc.com
Supplier of refined vegetable oils, soy and wheat flours, textured soy protein, and confectionary sunflower seeds, along with other small grains and processed nuts ingredients. Packaged foods for retail, foodservice and institutionalmarkets are manufactured and distributed through Ventura Foods.
President & CEO: Carl Casale
EVP/COO, Energy and Foods: Jay Debertin
EVP & CFO: David Kastelic
EVP/COO, Ag Business: Mark Palmquist
EVP & General Counsel: Lisa Zell
EVP, Business Solutions: Lynden Johnson
EVP, Enterprise Secretary: Shirley Cunningham
EVP, Country Operations: John McEnroe
Plant Manager: Dean Hjelden
Estimated Sales: $36.92 Billion
Number Employees: 9562
Square Footage: 320000
Type of Packaging: Consumer, Food Service, Private Label, Bulk
Brands:
Savorysoy®
Honeysoy®
Ultra-Soy®
Lems™
Curley's™
Agway®
Marie's®
Dean's Dips®

20060 **CIDA**
15895 SW 72nd Ave
Suite 200
Portland, OR 97224 503-226-1285
Fax: 503-226-1670 888-226-1285
www.cidainc.com
President: David G Welsh
Architect: Jennifer Beattie
Estimated Sales: $3 - 5 Million
Number Employees: 20-49

20061 **CII Food Service Design**
545a N Saginaw St
Lapeer, MI 48446 810-667-3100
cii@tir.com
www.ciifsd.com
Consultant specializing in food service design
President: Jim Peterson
Estimated Sales: $500,000 - $1 Million
Number Employees: 1-4

20062 **CIM Bakery Equipment ofUSA**
836 E Rand Road
Pmb 198
Arlington Heights, IL 60004-4008 847-818-8121
Fax: 847-818-8894 sales@cimbakery.com
www.cimbakery.com
Estimated Sales: $1 - 5 Million

20063 **CJ America**
105 Challenger Rd
Ridgefield Park, NJ 07660-2101 201-229-6050
Fax: 201-229-6058 kiyoung@dreammart.com
www.ccaworld.com
President: Ben Heo
Estimated Sales: $1 - 5 Million
Number Employees: 10-19

20064 **CK Products**
310 Racquet Dr
Fort Wayne, IN 46825-4229 260-484-2517
Fax: 800-837-2686 800-424-6839
mail@ckproducts.com www.ckproducts.com
Cake decorating and candy making products
President: Orlie Brand
Estimated Sales: $2.5-5 Million
Number Employees: 50-99

20065 **CKS Packaging**
445 Great Southwest Parkway
Atlanta, GA 30336 404-691-8900
Fax: 404-691-0086 800-800-4257
www.ckspackaging.com
Clear plastic containers
Manager: Bryan Reynolds
Manager: Bill Beard
Estimated Sales: $10-20,000,000
Number Employees: 100-249
Parent Co: CKS Packaging

20066 CL&D Graphics
1101 Wests 2nd Street
Oconomowoc, WI 53066-0644
Fax: 262-569-4075 800-777-1114
marketing@cldgraphics.com
www.cldgraphics.com
Manufacturer and exporter of pressure sensitive labels and unsupported opp film
President: Mike Dowling
CFO: Scott Demski
Quality Control: Patrick Dillon
R&D: Greg McLain
Sales Manager: Ned Price
Estimated Sales: $20 - 50 Million
Number Employees: 100-249
Type of Packaging: Bulk

20067 CLECO Systems
1395 S Marietta Pkwy SE
Bldg 750
Marietta, GA 30067-4440 770-392-0330
Fax: 770-795-8093 clecosales@fkilogistex.com
www.clecosys.com
Pallet and case handling systems and equipment
President: Kenneth Matson
Quality Control: Ban Santonato
Sales Manager: Paul Sartore
Estimated Sales: Below $5 Million
Number Employees: 10
Brands:
Condor
Maestro
Raven
Titan
Viking

20068 CM Ambrose Company
PO Box 3037
Arlington, WA 98223-3037 360-435-1411
Fax: 360-435-8200 ambroseinc@aol.com
Liquid packaging equipment
Estimated Sales: $2.5-5 000,000
Number Employees: 19

20069 CM Becker International
1604 Falcon Dr.
PO Box 1022
Desoto, TX 75123-1022 972-228-1690
Fax: 972-224-2191 Info@CMBecker.com
www.cmbecker.com
Precision parts for the beverage industry
Owner: Michael Korkisch
Estimated Sales: Below $5 000,000
Number Employees: 1-4

20070 CM Packaging
800 Ela Rd
Lake Zurich, IL 60047 847-438-2171
Fax: 847-438-0369 800-323-0422
info@cmpackaging.com www.cmpackaging.com
President: Mark Faber

20071 CM Processing Solutions
235 Benjamin Drive
Suite 102
Corona, CA 92879 951-808-4376
Fax: 951-808-8657 sales@cmpsolutions.net
www.cmpsolutions.net
Supplier of stainless steel hygiene equipment and food processing equipment for the beef, pork, poultry, seafood and produce industry

20072 CMA/Dishmachines
12700 Knott St
Garden Grove, CA 92841 714-898-8781
Fax: 714-891-9836 800-854-6417
kim.feldstein@cmadishmachines.com
www.cmadishmachines.com
Manufacturer, importer and exporter of commercial dishmachines, glasswashers and dishtables
President: David Crane
Marketing Director: Matt Swift
Sales Assistant: Kimberly Feldstein
Plant Manager: Mike Belleville
Number Employees: 50-99
Square Footage: 35000
Parent Co: S.C. Johnson & Son
Brands:
Energy Mizer

20073 CMC America Corporation
208 South Center Street
Joliet, IL 60436 815-726-4337
Fax: 815-726-7138 info@cmc-america.com
www.cmc-america.com
Bakery machinery including mixers, water handling equipment and cookie depositing systems
President: Edward Fay
Executive Consultant: James Fay
Plant Manager: Michael Baron
Estimated Sales: $3 Million
Number Employees: 10-19
Number of Brands: 1
Number of Products: 4
Square Footage: 40000
Brands:
Champion

20074 CMD Corporation
2901-3005 East Pershing Street
PO Box 1279
Appleton, WI 54912-1279 920-730-6888
Fax: 920-730-6880 info@cmd-corp.com
www.cmd-corp.com
Plastic bottles
President: John Smith
R & D: Larry Mikeosjy
Corporate Market Manager, Research and C: Lisa Karin
VP Marketing and Sales: Timothy B. Lewis
Regional Sales Manager: David Andrews
Director of Operations: Ron Buchinger
Product Line Manager: Scott Fuller
Number Employees: 10

20075 CMD Corporation
P.O.Box 1279
Appleton, WI 54912 920-730-0930
Fax: 920-730-6880 info@cmd-corp.com
www.cmd-corp.com
High speed plastic film converting equipment for the production of trash can liners and bag rolls. Also vertical form fill and seal packaging equipment and modular pouch making systems.
President: Steve Sakai
Research & Development: Ron Buchinger
Quality Control: Curt Frievalt
Marketing/Public Relations: Lisa Kain
Sales: Margaret Valinski
Sales: Rich Camp
Operations Manager: Don Wiedenheft
Production Manager: Curt Frievalt
Plant Manager: Don Wiedenheft
Purchasing Manager: Colleen Frederick
Estimated Sales: $20-50 Million
Number Employees: 100-249
Number of Brands: 2
Number of Products: 40
Square Footage: 50000
Parent Co: CMD Corporation
Type of Packaging: Consumer, Food Service, Private Label, Bulk
Brands:
Cmd Converting Solutions
Cmd Packaging Systems
Modular Pouch Machine
Vffs Packaging System

20076 CMD Corporation
2901 E Pershing Street
Appelton, WI 54911 920-730-6888
Fax: 920-434-5750 info@cmd-corp.com
www.cmd-corp.com
Vertical form, fill and seal packaging equipment, washdown equipment
Manager: Lynell Sazama
CFO: Tim Lamerf
Quality Control: Mark Heindel
Regional Sales Manager: David Andrews
Director of Operations: Ron Buchinger
Number Employees: 20-49

20077 CMF Corporation
1524 W 15th St
Long Beach, CA 90813 562-437-2166
Fax: 562-495-1857 800-350-8979
info@jack-frost.com www.jack-frost.com
President: Larry Sackrison
Estimated Sales: $3 - 5 Million
Number Employees: 10-19

20078 CMS Gilbreth Packaging Systems
3001 State Rd
Croydon, PA 19021 215-785-3350
Fax: 215-785-4077 800-630-2413
info@gilbrethusa.com www.gilbrethusa.com
Manufacturer and exporter of film label application equipment and heat shrinkable PVC/PETG and oriented polypropylene labels and bands
VP: Wanda Coulton
Director Sales: Tom Koslowsky
Estimated Sales: $20-50 Million
Number Employees: 100-249
Brands:
Base 1000
Cms Forced Air Heat Tunnels
Cms Tamp-R-Alert

20079 CMT
P.O.Box 297
Hamilton, MA 01936 978-768-2555
Fax: 978-768-2525 cmtinc@tiac.net
www.habitatmonitor.com
Manufacturer and exporter of temperature and humidity monitors, alarms and controls sustems for climate sensitive goods such as wine and cigars.
President: David C De Sieye
Estimated Sales: $500,000-$1 Million
Number Employees: 1-4
Number of Products: 50
Square Footage: 8000

20080 CNC Containers
3045 32nd Ave SW
Tumwater, WA 98512-6161 360-943-2527
Fax: 360-943-2587 cnc-info@cnc-containers.com
www.cnc-containers.com
PET bottles for the carbonated and noncarbonated beverages, bottles for the dairy, hot fill juice, edible oil, liquor and other special food markets
Manager: Ken Carlson
Estimated Sales: $50-100 Million
Number Employees: 100-249

20081 CNL Beverage Property Group
450 South Orange Avenue
Orlando, FL 32801-3383 407-650-1000
Fax: 407-316-0457 800-522-3863
www.cnl.com
President: Robert Bourne
CFO: Lynn Rose
CEO: James Seneff
R & D: Courtney Powell
Number Employees: 10-19

20082 COTT Technologies
14923 Proctor Ave
La Puente, CA 91746-3206 626-961-0370
Fax: 626-333-9307 800-373-1968
www.cotttechnologies.com
Sanitary Piston Pumps, Liquid Fillers, Custom Process Piping and machinery
Owner: Gilbert De Cardenas
Marketing: Dennis Gonzalez
Production: Westly Brown
Plant Manager: Westly Brown
Estimated Sales: $10 - 20 Million
Number Employees: 20-49
Number of Brands: 1
Brands:
Cott

20083 COW Industries
1875 Progress Ave
Columbus, OH 43207 614-443-6537
Fax: 614-443-9600 800-542-9353
www.cowind.com
Bakers' equipment, flour hoppers, pans, racks, tanks, trays, etc
President: John Burns
CFO: John Burns
Executive VP Sales: David Burns
VP Production: Rock Kauser
Estimated Sales: $20 - 50 Million
Number Employees: 50-99
Square Footage: 100000

20084 COZZINI, LLC.
4300 West Bryn Mawr Ave
Chicago, IL 60646 773-478-9700
Fax: 773-478-8689 888-295-1116
cozzini@cozzini.com www.afeco.com

Meat processing and packaging equipment: chutes, boning systems, canning systems, custom machinery
Estimated Sales: $5-10 Million
Number Employees: 48

20085 **CP Converters**
15 Grumbacher Rd
York, PA 17406-8417 717-764-1193
Fax: 717-764-2039 rsullivan@cpconverters.com
www.cpconverters.com
Snack food bags, cellophane lamination, polypropylene and polyethylene, slitting, resource recovery, quality assurance
President: Tony Vaudo
Information Technologist: Brad Gates
Estimated Sales: $20-50 Million
Number Employees: 100-249
Number of Products: 6
Square Footage: 120000

20086 **CPI Importers**
2324 Shorecrest Drive
Dallas, TX 75235-1804 214-353-0328
Fax: 214-353-0074 jerry@globexamerica.net
www.cavallinicoffee.com
Brewing devices
President: Bonnie Itzig
CFO: Jerry Itziq
R & D: Donnie Itziq
Estimated Sales: $1 - 3 Million
Number Employees: 5-9

20087 **CPI Packaging**
50 Jiffy Rd
Somerset, NJ 08873 732-431-3500
Fax: 732-568-0440 info@cpipgk.com
www.cpipkg.com
Foam and plastic packaging products
COO: Joseph Lomando
COO: Joseph Mormondo
Estimated Sales: $20 - 50 Million
Number Employees: 10,000

20088 **CPM Century Extrusion**
2412 W. Aero Park Court
Traverse City, MI 49686 231-947-6400
Fax: 231-947-8400 sales@centuryextrusion.com
www.centuryextrusion.com
Manufacturer & supplier of extruders and extrusion parts.
Global Sales Manager: Charlie Spearing

20089 **CPM Wolverine Proctor**
251 Gibraltar Rd
Horsham, PA 19044 215-443-5200
Fax: 215-443-5206
sales@cpmwolverineproctor.com
www.cpmwolverineproctor.com
Manufacturer and designer of processing equipment including energy efficient continuous dryers, roasters, toasters, coolers, impingement ovens, and the jetzone fluid bed dryer for the processing of fruits, vegetables, nuts/seedsbakery, snack foods, meat, poultry, pet foods, etc. Also batch drying equipment including tray, truck and laboratory dryers, also ultra sanitary design conveyor dryer and new pizza infrared fuser/melter.
Lab Manager: Lisa Geck
VP Sales: Paul Smith
VP Operations: Rick Diefes
General Manager: Paul Finnerty
Estimated Sales: $13.1 Million
Number Employees: 100
Square Footage: 180000
Type of Packaging: Food Service

20090 **CPS Damrow**
423 Arlington Ave
Fond Du Lac, WI 54935-5518 920-922-1500
Fax: 920-922-1502 800-236-1501
info@damrow.com www.damrow.com
Agitation systems, curd, clean rooms and equipment, custom fabrication, fillers, air, ladders, vat
Manager: Gary Ring
Estimated Sales: $5-10 Million
Number Employees: 5-9

20091 **CPT**
415 E Fulton St
Edgerton, WI 53534-1923 608-884-2244
Fax: 608-884-2288 info@cptplastics.com
www.cptplastics.com
Plastic containers, heat sealing films and packaging
President: Linda Bracha
VP: Eli Bracha
Estimated Sales: $10 - 20 Million
Number Employees: 20-49
Type of Packaging: Bulk

20092 **CPT**
415 E Fulton St
Edgerton, WI 53534-1923 608-884-2244
Fax: 608-884-2288 info@cptplastics.com
www.cptplastics.com
Manufacturers of foamed polypropylene rollstock and trays for case-ready and other applications requiring extended shelf life; pre-formed trays and barrier shrink lidstock, foamed barrier PP is microwaveable, lightweight andeasy-to-form, specializes in
President: Linda Bracha
Estimated Sales: $10 - 20 Million
Number Employees: 20-49

20093 **CR Plastics**
1104 2nd Ave
Council Bluffs, IA 51501-4012 712-323-9995
Fax: 712-328-8617 866-869-6293
donreiners@deckerplastics.com
www.deckerplastics.com
Polyethylene bags, tubes and sheeting
President: Robert A Decker
CFO: Sherry Deckar
Estimated Sales: $1-2.5 Million
Number Employees: 10-19
Square Footage: 50000

20094 **CRC**
3218 Nebraska Ave
Council Bluffs, IA 51501-7035 712-323-9477
Fax: 712-323-3573
Stainless steel variable speed blenders and mixers
President: Donald Crossley
Secretary: Joan Collins
VP: Jim Crossley
Estimated Sales: $2.5-5,000,000
Number Employees: 5-9

20095 **CRC Industries, Inc.**
885 Louis Dr
Warminster, PA 18974-2869 215-674-4300
Fax: 215-674-2196 800-556-5074
kcantwell@crcindustries.com
www.crcindustries.com
Manufacturer and exporter of cleaners, degreasers, lubricants, corrosion inhibitors, hand cleaners, adhesives and sealants; also, cleaning compound dispensers
President & Chief Executive Officer: Dennis Conlon
Estimated Sales: $91 Million
Number Employees: 165
Brands:
3-36
Hydroforce
Mechanix Orange
Power Lube
Screwloose
Super

20096 **CRF Technologies**
PO Box 32414
Charlotte, NC 28232-2414 704-554-2253
Fax: 704-554-3900 800-875-0275
Cut resistant gloves, apparel and uniforms
Estimated Sales: $1 - 5 000,000

20097 **CRS Marking Systems**
3315 NW 26th Ave #1
Portland, OR 97210-1856 503-228-7624
Fax: 503-228-2464 800-547-7158
info@crsdatasolutions.com
Manufacturer and wholesaler/distributor of marking, coding, printing, labeling and bar code equipment
CEO: Julia Farrenkopf
Customer Service: Dwaine Brandson
COO: David Snmodgrass
Estimated Sales: $1 - 3 Million
Number Employees: 10 to 19

20098 **CSAT America**
7007 Johnson Cir
Longmont, CO 80503-7667 303-652-0370
Fax: 303-652-8736 888-904-2728
www.csat.de

20099 **CSC Scientific Company**
2799-C, Merrilee Drive
Fairfax, VA 22031 703-876-4030
Fax: 703-280-5142 800-621-4778
csc@cscscientific.com www.cscscientific.com
Manufacturer and exporter of sieves and laboratory analyzers to measure water, moisture, filtration equipment, solids, surface tension, particle size and consistency; also, calibration services available
President: Arthur Gatenby
Vice President: Tim Comwell
Marketing Director: Wendy Liu
Operations Manager: Theresa Andreoni
Estimated Sales: $2.5 - 5 Million
Number Employees: 20
Brands:
Aquapal
Cfc Dunouy Tensiometer
Cfc Us Standard
Digital Moisture Balance

20100 **(HQ)CSC Worldwide**
4401 Equity Dr
Columbus, OH 43228-3856 614-850-1460
Fax: 614-850-0741 800-848-3573
www.cscww.com
Manufacturer, designer and exporter of refrigerated and heated display cases; also store fixtures
CEO: Carl J Aschinger Jr
Marketing: Jennier Bobbitt
Estimated Sales: $20-50 Million
Number Employees: 100-249

20101 **CSI Tools**
2700 N Partnership Blvd
Springfield, MO 65803-8208 417-831-1411
Fax: 417-831-5314 800-258-0133
sales@csitools.com www.csitools.com
Leading provider of tube and pipe facing and cutting equipment for the sanitary process piping industry; also supply users of this equipment with top quality consumables for these tools such as blades, bits
President: Mark Cook
CFO: Joe Reynolds
Vice President of Systems: Beth Ipock
Manager: Mark Wilson
Marketing Director: Ryan Tiller
Sales Manager: Liz Braden
Vice President of Operations: Bryan Billmyer
Estimated Sales: $10-20 Million
Number Employees: 50-99
Type of Packaging: Food Service

20102 **CSM Bakery ProductsBakery Supplies North America (BSNA)**
1912 Montreal Road
Tucker, GA 30084 800-892-3039
Fax: 770-939-2934 800-241-8526
contactcsmbp@csmglobal.com
www.csmbakeryproducts.com
Develops, produces and sells a wide selection of bakery ingredients and products to professional bakeries, top consumer food companies, grocers and retailers. Products include brownies, cakes, cookies croissants, fillings, glazesicing & toppings, mixes, muffins, puff pastry, sweet rolls, filled pastries, and turnovers.
President & CEO: Troy Hendricks
Research & Development Manager: Steve Wade
Food Scientist: Amber Dumaine
Quality Assurance Director: Michelle You
Product Marketing Manager: Jay Bryan
VP Sales: Jim Quinn
Director Human Resources: Rae Lynn Welk
Director of Operations: Kirk Heissel
Maintenance Facilities Management: Andrew Castongia
Estimated Sales: $2.1 Billion
Number Employees: 5000
Square Footage: 170000
Parent Co: CSM
Other Locations:
CSM Bakery Products
Atlanta GA
Caravan Ingredients
Kansas City MO
BakeMark USA
Pico Rivera CA
Brands:
Brill®
Henry & Henry®
Multifoods®
Transmart™
Sensibly Indulgent™ Cupcakes

Thaw-N-Sell
Scoop-N-Bake

20103 **CSM Worldwide**
1100 Globe Ave
Mountainside, NJ 07092 908-233-2882
Fax: 908-233-1064 www.csmworldwide.com
Tea and coffee industry pollution control equipment
President: Mike Torstup
Estimated Sales: $2.5-5 000,000
Number Employees: 20-49

20104 **CSPI**
43 Manning Rd
Billerica, MA 01821-3925 978-663-7598
Fax: 978-663-0150 info@cspi.com
www.cspi.com
Scanning equipment
CEO: Alexander R Lupinetti
Marketing Coordinator: Bernard Pelon
Estimated Sales: $30 - 35 Million
Number Employees: 100-249

20105 **CSS Inc**
122 Rogers St
Hartsville, TN 37074 615-374-0601
Fax: 615-374-0610
choicecutsurplus@comcast.net
www.choicecut.net
Meat packing and food handling equipment
President: Randy Beach
Chief Executive Officer: Robert Paxton

20106 **CSS International Corporation**
2061 E Glenwood Ave
PO Box 19560
Philadelphia, PA 19124 215-533-6110
Fax: 215-288-8030 800-278-8107
sales@cssintl.com www.cssintl.com
Manufacturer and exporter of container handling equipment and packaging machinery
President: Herbert Coulston
Vice President: Albert Andrew
VP Productions: Gene Fijalkowski
Parent Co: CSS International Corporation
Type of Packaging: Consumer, Food Service, Private Label

20107 **CSV Sales**
44450 Pinetree Dr
Plymouth, MI 48170-3869 734-453-4544
Fax: 248-669-3000 800-886-6866
info@nationalfoodgroup.com
www.csvsales.com
Supplier of closeouts, surplus, salvage and liquidator items including baked goods, poultry, meats and off-grade, frozen and value added foods
President: Bud Zecman
Owner: Sean Zecman
Finance Executive: Scott Kaman
Sales Executive: Justin Sarrach
Operations Manager: Justin Sarrach
Purchasing/Sales Support: Roger Cary
Estimated Sales: $5-10 Million
Number Employees: 5-9
Brands:
Awrey's
Bakery Chef
House of Raeford
Pierre
Pilgrim's Pride
Tyson

20108 **CTC**
11 York Ave
West Caldwell, NJ 07006 973-228-2300
Fax: 973-228-7076 info@ctcint.com
www.ctcint.com
Tea and fruit juices
President: Erwin L Herbert
Estimated Sales: $10-20 000,000
Number Employees: 20-49

20109 **CTC Parker Automation**
50 W Techne Center Dr Ste H
Milford, OH 45150 513-831-2340
Fax: 513-831-5042 800-233-3329
moreinfo@ctcusa.com www.ctcusa.com
PC-based control, HMI software, industrial PCs, OI workstations
CFO: Michael Hiemstra
Sales: Mark Cunningham
Estimated Sales: $20-50 Million
Number Employees: 20-49

20110 **CTI Celtek Electronics**
3609 Robertson St
Metairie, LA 70001-5844 504-832-0049
Fax: 504-832-8117 www.cticeltek.com
Level controls, inventory management
Owner: Jack Graves
Estimated Sales: $1 - 5 Million
Number Employees: 1-4

20111 **CTK Plastics**
1815 Stadacona Street W.
Moose Jaw, SK S6H 7K8
Canada 306-693-7075
Fax: 306-693-9944 800-667-8847
sales.ctk@sasktel.net www.ctkplastics.com
Plastic bottles and sheeting; importer of resin and bottling equipment; exporter of plastic bottles and rigid sheeting
President: Dennis Wastle
Sales/Marketing: Dennis Wastle
General Manager: Brian McGuigan
Supervisor: Bernice Larose
Number Employees: 10
Square Footage: 120000
Parent Co: CTK Developments

20112 **CTS Bulk Sales**
P.O.Box 8318
Northfield, IL 60093 847-267-0837
Fax: 847-267-0838
President: Charles L Brooks
R&D: Ginger Brooks
Estimated Sales: Below $5 000,000
Number Employees: 5-9

20113 **CVC Technologies**
10861 Business Dr
Fontana, CA 92337 909-355-0311
Fax: 909-355-0411 sales@cvcusa.com
www.cvcusa.com
Labelers with automatic job set up, memory for 50 jobs and self-diagnostics. Also counters, cappers, indexing cappers, cartoners and blister packers
Manager: Yulie Luo
Vice President: Andy Span
Quality Control: Oscar Esparza
Marketing Director: Brit Sten
Sales Director: Andy Span
Plant Manager: Oscar Esparza
Estimated Sales: $7-12 000,000
Number Employees: 5-9
Number of Brands: 1
Number of Products: 9
Brands:
302 Hawk Labelers
Cvc 300

20114 **CVP Systems**
2518 Wisconsin Ave
Downers Grove, IL 60515 630-852-1190
Fax: 630-874-0229 800-422-4720
sales@cvpsystems.com www.cvpsystems.com
Manufacturer and exporter of cost effective, bags and packaging machinery including microbial reduction units, wrap around label systems and vacuum and modified atmosphere systems
President: Wesley Bork
VP: L Mykleby
Estimated Sales: $10 - 20 Million
Number Employees: 20-49
Type of Packaging: Consumer, Food Service, Private Label, Bulk
Brands:
Cvp Fresh Vac
Dynarap

20115 **CYBER BEARINGS, INC**
4821 S. Eastern Ave
Bell, CA 90201 562-272-8032
Fax: 562-272-8588 888-288-9889
info@cyberbearings.com
www.cyberbearings.com
Solid stainless steel bearing inserts with theremoplastic housing, bearing units (pillow block, flange), bearing inserts with nickel plated cast iron housing, mast guide bearings, agricultural bearings and ISO-9002 certified
President: Kevin Lee

20116 **Cable Conveyor Systems**
205 Corporate Park Blvd
Columbia, SC 29223 803-786-9576
Fax: 803-786-9577 800-624-6064
info@cableconveyor.com
www.cableconveyor.com
Manufacturer and exporter of material handling equipment including case conveyors, car conveyors, diverter gates, fittings, and can rinsers
President: David M Rauscher
VP Sales/Marketing: David Rauscher, Jr.
Office Manager: Lea Ann O'Quinn
Estimated Sales: $2.5-5 Million
Number Employees: 10-19
Square Footage: 5000

20117 **Cabot Corporation**
2 Seaport Ln Ste 1300
Boston, MA 02210 617-345-0100
www.cabot-corp.com
Manufacturer and exporter of treated and untreated fumed silica
President/CEO: Patrick Prevost
Executive Vice President/CFO: Eduardo Cordeiro
Vice President: James Belmont
Vice President, Research & Development: Yakov Kutsovsky
National Sales Manager: James Litrun
Vice President, Operations: James Turner
Estimated Sales: $20-50 Million
Number Employees: 100-249
Parent Co: Cabot Corporation
Brands:
Cab-O-Sil

20118 **Cacao Prieto**
218 Conover Street
Brooklyn, NY 11231 347-225-0130
info@cacaoholdings.combusiness
www.cacaoprieto.com
Fine chocolates
President/CEO: Dan Preston
VP & Art Director: Michele Clark
Sales Director: Mike Dirksen
Chief Operating Officer: Dennis Walsh
Number Employees: 20

20119 **Cache Box**
2009 14th Street N
Suite 415
Arlington, VA 22201-2514 703-276-2500
Fax: 703-276-2504 800-603-4834
weinerj@tdg.net www.cachebox.com
Manufacturer and exporter of touchscreen turn-key point of sale systems
CEO: Lorenzo Salhi
VP Engineering: Murali Nagaraj
CTO: Dilip Ranade
VP, Technical Marketing: Shaloo Shalini
COO: John Groff
Estimated Sales: $5-10 Million
Number Employees: 20-49
Brands:
Chromium

20120 **Cache Creek Foods**
411 N Pioneer Ave
Woodland, CA 95776 530-662-1764
Fax: 530-662-2529
Custom flavoring and wholesale manufacturing of almond, cashew, pistachio, nut products and nut butters
President: Matthew Moorehart
CEO: Matthew Morehart
Sales and Marketing Executive: Mike Leonard
Office Manager: Connie Stephens
Production: Ana Contreras
Estimated Sales: $10 Million
Number Employees: 19
Number of Products: 75
Square Footage: 30000
Type of Packaging: Consumer, Food Service, Private Label, Bulk
Brands:
Private Label

20121 **Cactus Mat ManufacturingCompany**
4131 Arden Dr
El Monte, CA 91731-1999 626-579-6287
Fax: 626-401-2003 cactuskid@cactusmat.com
www.cactusmat.com

Floor mats including rigid wood, interlocking rubber, entrance and rubber for food preparation areas
President: C W Hartranft Jr
CEO: Debra De Ring
CFO: Les De Ring
Estimated Sales: $5 - 10 Million
Number Employees: 20-49
Square Footage: 120000
Brands:
Cactus Kid
Contempo
Cushion Walk
Kaktus
Monterey
Softread
Vip
Vip Lite

20122 Caddy Corporation of America
509 Sharptown Road
Bridgeport, NJ 08014-0345 856-467-4222
Fax: 856-467-5511 mbodine@caddycorp.com
www.caddycorp.com
Manufacturer and exporter of food service equipment including conveyors, transport/delivery carts, kitchen ventilation hoods and utility distribution systems
President: Harry Schmidt
CEO: Craig Cohen
CFO: John McNamee
VP of Corporate Services: Al Scuderi
Vice President, Sales: Phil Bailis
National Sales Manager: Donald Morrison
Engineering Manager: Brad Wallace
Purchasing: Robin Corma
Estimated Sales: $5-10 Million
Number Employees: 50-99
Square Footage: 288000
Brands:
21c
Caddy
Caddy Cold
Caddy Connections
Caddy-Flex
Caddy-Veyor
Caddymagic
Circle-Air
Ds Special
Dura-San Belt
Fogg-It
Mega-Temp
Pacemaker
Servi-Shelf
Simplex
Speed-Lift
Temp-Lock
Temp-Lock Ii
Thermo-Lock
Xl-1

20123 Cadence Technologies
1006 Windward Ridge Pkwy
Alpharetta, GA 30005 770-667-6250
Fax: 770-667-6251 800-667-6250
info@cadencetech.com www.cadencetech.com
Consultant and design engineer specializing in systems integration and project management; installation services available
Owner: G H Brink
VP: David Bryant
Estimated Sales: $5-10 Million
Number Employees: 20-49
Square Footage: 13000

20124 Cadie Products Corporation
151 E 11th St
Paterson, NJ 07524 973-278-8300
Fax: 973-278-0303 www.cadieproducts.com
Manufacturer and exporter of cloths including dusting, polishing, cheese, pastry and sponge; also, cooking parchment, microwave cooking bags, seat covers, salad bags, ice cube bags, hamburger (patty) bags, and non-stick oven liner
President: Edwin Meyers
CFO: Bob Appelbaum
Vice President: Kenny Meyers
Estimated Sales: $20 - 50 Million
Number Employees: 20-49
Square Footage: 35000
Type of Packaging: Consumer, Private Label, Bulk
Brands:
Cadie
Chef's Favorite
Krazy Kloth
Super Power

20125 Cadillac Pallets
7000 15 Mile Rd
Sterling Heights, MI 48312-4520 586-264-2525
Fax: 248-879-7420

20126 Cadillac Plastics
2855 Coolidge Highway
Suite 300
Troy, MI 48084-3217 248-205-3100
Fax: 248-205-3173 800-488-1200
www.cadillacplastic.com
Engraved plastics: rods, sheets, tubes and film; adhesive and graphic arts products
Estimated Sales: D
Number Employees: 19

20127 Cadillac Products
5800 Crooks Rd Ste 200
Troy, MI 48098 248-879-0683
Fax: 248-879-6402 cppc@cadprod.com
www.cadillacpackaging.com
Tea and coffee industry flexible packaging, bags and packaging film supplies materials
Chairman of the Board: Robert Williams Sr
CEO: Robert J Williams Jr
Estimated Sales: $50-100 Million
Number Employees: 100-249

20128 Cady Bag
41 Project Cir
Pearson, GA 31642 912-422-3298
Fax: 912-422-3155
Polypropylene, woven bags
President: William Cady
Vice President: John Moore
Estimated Sales: $20 - 50 Million
Number Employees: 100-249

20129 Cafe Del Mundo
229 E 51st Ave
Anchorage, AK 99503 907-562-2326
Fax: 907-562-3278 800-770-2326
www.cafedelmundo.com
Coffee, espresso equipment
Owner: Perry Merkel
Manager: Monique Johnston
Purchasing: Perry Merkel
Estimated Sales: $800,000
Number Employees: 12
Type of Packaging: Private Label, Bulk
Brands:
Cafe Del Mundo

20130 Cain Awning Company
1301 3RD Avenue South
P.O.Box 12044
Birmingham, AL 35233 205-323-8379
Fax: 205-323-6739 www.cainawning.com
Commercial awnings
Owner: Hank Lawson
Estimated Sales: $1-2,500,000
Number Employees: 10-19

20131 Cal Ben Soap Company
9828 Pearmain Street
Oakland, CA 94603 510-638-7091
Fax: 510-638-7827 800-340-7091
calbenco@yahoo.com www.calbenpuresoap.com
Soaps including laundry, dish, etc
President: Martin Schachter
Estimated Sales: Below $5 Million
Number Employees: 10

20132 Cal Controls
1675 Delany Road
Gurnee, IL 60031
Fax: 847-782-5223 800-866-6659
custserv.west@dancon.com
www.cal-controls.com
Manufacturer and exporter of temperature and machine controllers for packaging and processing equipment
Sales Manager: Dave Chylstek
Estimated Sales: $15 Million
Number Employees: 21
Brands:
Cal
Calcomms
Calgrafix
Calogix

20133 Cal Western Pest Control
5417 Peck Road
Arcadia, CA 91006-5847 661-808-7378
Fax: 323-721-0377 800-326-2847
calwestern@calwestern.com
Consultant for pest and sanitation control programs for food processors and distributors
Owner: John Lemm
Manager: Dave Conner
General Manager: Marc Canipe
Estimated Sales: $2.5-5 Million
Number Employees: 50-99

20134 Cal-Coast Manufacturing
P.O.Box 1864
Turlock, CA 95381-1864 209-668-9378
Fax: 209-668-9382
Dairy equipment, storage tanks and auger systems. Also dairy construction and public scale
President: L Baptista
Controller: D Baptista
Estimated Sales: $1 - 3,000,000
Number Employees: 5-9

20135 Cal-Mil Plastic Products
4079 Calle Platino
Oceanside, CA 92056 760-630-5100
Fax: 760-630-5010 800-321-9069
info@calmil.com www.calmil.com
Manufacturer, exporter and importer of acrylic counter top cabinets, mirrored displays, crocks, platters, risers, bowls, pedestals, tables, domes, etc. for the catering and banquet industries.
President: John F Callahan
Marketing Director: Mike Juneman
Sales Director: Mike Juneman
Estimated Sales: $10-20 Million
Number Employees: 20-49
Number of Products: 1460
Type of Packaging: Bulk

20136 Calcium Chloride Sales
713 W Main St
Grove City, PA 16127 724-458-7591
Fax: 724-458-4250 800-228-3879
cacl2@zoominternet.net
www.calciumchloridesales.com
Food grade calcium chloride including liquid and flake
President: Jim Mc Lean
Secretary: Larry Bowie
Estimated Sales: $2.5 Million
Number Employees: 10-19
Number of Products: 1
Square Footage: 8000
Type of Packaging: Private Label, Bulk

20137 Caldwell Group
5055 26th Avenue
Rockford, IL 61109 815-229-5667
Fax: 815-229-5686 800-628-4263
contact@caldwellinc.com www.caldwellinc.com
Manufacturer and exporter of crane lifting attachments
Owner: Howard Will
VP: William McLeod
Estimated Sales: $5-10 Million
Number Employees: 50-99

20138 Calgene
1920 5th St
Davis, CA 95616 530-753-6313
Fax: 530-753-1510 800-992-4363
rhonda.ryan@monsanto.com www.calgene.com
Research in genetics, and biotechnology of food
Estimated Sales: $10 - 15 000,000
Number Employees: 100-249

20139 Calgon Carbon Corporatio
P.O.Box 717
Pittsburgh, PA 15230-0717 412-787-6700
Fax: 412-787-4541 www.calgoncarbon.com
President: John S Stanik
Estimated Sales: $100 -500 Million
Number Employees: 500-999
Parent Co: Calgon Carbon Corporation

20140 Calhoun Bend Mill
PO BOX 520
Libuse, LA 71348 318-640-0060
Fax: 318-339-9099 800-519-6455
sales@calhounbendmill.com
www.calhounbendmill.com

Products include mixes for Peach Cobbler mix, Apple Cinnamon Crisp mix, Cherry Oatmeal Crunch mix, Awesome Onion Coating mix, Fish Fry & Seafood coating, Stoneground Cornmeal, Cornbread & Muffin mix, Mexican Cornbread mix, Honey ButterCornbread mix, Pecan Pie mix and Sopapilla mix. Food services sizes in Fruit Cobblers, Cornmeal and Fish Fry & Seafood coating.
President/CEO: Patrick Calhoun
Treasurer: Monica Calhoun
Vice President: Nathan Martin
Sales Manager: Emma Cash
Corporate Secretary: Martie Hoover
Estimated Sales: $400,000
Number Employees: 5
Number of Brands: 2
Number of Products: 25
Square Footage: 17000
Type of Packaging: Consumer, Food Service, Private Label, Bulk
Brands:
Calhoun Bend Mill
Orchard Mills

20141 **Calia Technical**
420 Jefferson Boulevard
Staten Island, NY 10312-2334 718-967-9757
Fax: 718-967-0275 anthony@caliatech.com
www.caliatech.com
Inspection, control systems, bar code verification systems, bottle and cap inspection and machine vision solutions; web bar code verification systems to verify multiple bar codes on thermoformer lidstock
President: Anthony Calia
VP: Robert Santagata
Engineer: Elias Hawileh
Estimated Sales: $.5 - 1 million
Number Employees: 1-4
Number of Products: 2

20142 **Calico Cottage**
210 New Highway
Amityville, NY 11701 631-841-2100
Fax: 631-841-2401 800-645-5345
info@calicocottage.com www.calicocottage.com
Equipment, ingredients and merchandising concepts for a profitable, small-space, fudge making program
President: Mark Wurzel
CFO: Michael Lobaccaro
VP: Larry Wurzel
Estimated Sales: $5 Million
Number Employees: 50
Square Footage: 45000
Brands:
Calico Cottage Fudge Mix
Mister Fudge

20143 **California Blending Corp**
2603 Seaman Ave
El Monte, CA 91733 626-448-1918
Pizza spices, dough mixes, dressing mixes, steak salts, and garlic blends. Also provided; custom blending
Owner/President: William Morehart
Vice President: Roger Morehart
Estimated Sales: $230,000
Number Employees: 3
Square Footage: 7300
Type of Packaging: Private Label, Bulk

20144 **California Canning PeachAssociation**
2300 River Plaza Dr # 110
Sacramento, CA 95833-4241 916-925-9131
Fax: 916-925-9030 ccpa@calpeach.com
www.calpeach.com
Cooperative for cling peach processors providing marketing, price negotiation, etc
President: Richard Hudgins
VP/COO: Rich Hudgins
Number Employees: 5-9

20145 **California Caster & Handtruck**
1400 17th St
San Francisco, CA 94107 415-552-6750
Fax: 415-552-0463 800-950-8750
www.californiacaster.com
Stainless steel hand trucks and carts, dollies, casters, leveling pads and oven and bun pan racks; wholesaler/distributor of casters
Owner: Alan Mc Clure
VP: Terry Cavannaugh
Estimated Sales: $5-10 Million
Number Employees: 10-19
Square Footage: 16500
Brands:
Dareon
Darnell
Dutro
Faultless
Magline
Meese
Morton Kaciff
Rack & Roll
Vlier
Werner

20146 **California Hi-Lites**
12500 Slauson Ave Ste C3
Santa Fe Springs, CA 90670-2631 562-696-1777
Fax: 562-696-8917 Hans@hilites.com
www.hilites.com
Co-packing, labeling, over wrapping, display construction, handwork, light assembly, bundling, gluing, collating, QC projects, order fulfillment, FDA approved cleanroom, alcoholic beverage license, organic food license and more
Owner: Hans Blom
Owner: Robert Landinl
Owner: Jim Yoder
Estimated Sales: $3-5 Million
Number Employees: 23
Square Footage: 80000
Type of Packaging: Consumer, Food Service, Private Label, Bulk
Brands:
Feast of Eden
Hi-Lites
Nature's Candy
Val Linda

20147 **California League of Food Processors**
1755 Creekside Oaks Drive
Suite 250
Sacramento, CA 95833 916-640-8150
Fax: 916-640-8156 jessica@clfp.com
www.clfp.com
President/CEO: Rob Neenan
COO/Treasurer: Janet Planck
Marketing Manager: Amy Alcorn
Meetings & Events Manager: Alissa Dillon
Estimated Sales: $1 - 5 Million
Number Employees: 7

20148 **California Saw & Knife Works**
721 Brannan St
San Francisco, CA 94103 415-861-0644
Fax: 415-861-0406 888-729-6533
calsaw@calsaw.com www.calsaw.com
Manufacturer and exporter of machine knives and circular saws for food processing equipment
President: Warren Bird
CFO: Mike Weber
Vice President: Benson Joseph
VP Production: S Bird
Estimated Sales: $5-10 Million
Number Employees: 20-49
Square Footage: 18000
Brands:
Calsaw

20149 **California ToytimeBalloons**
554 West Seventh Street
PO Box 1876
San Pedro, CA 90733 310-548-1234
Fax: 310-548-1237
Printed advertising specialties including buttons, balloons, golf tees, bumper stickers and emery boards
Chairman: Bob Bershad
Sales: Richard Petrosino
Estimated Sales: $5-10 Million
Number Employees: 10-19
Parent Co: Bershad Advertising Products Company

20150 **California Vibratory Feeders**
1725 N Orangethorpe Park
Anaheim, CA 92801 714-526-3359
Fax: 714-526-3515 800-354-0972
schester@calvibes.com www.calvibes.com
Custom design and build automation equipment
President: Donald Robinson
Marketing: Sandy Chester
Sales: Peter Speers
Operations: Kelly Reece
Estimated Sales: $5 - 10 Million
Number Employees: 20-49

20151 **Caljan America**
3600 E 45th Ave
Denver, CO 80216-6510 303-321-3600
Fax: 303-321-6767 www.caljan.com
Telescopic conveyors for trailer loading and unloading
President: Lonnie Watkins
Estimated Sales: $5-10 Million
Number Employees: 20-49

20152 **Callanan Company Alloy Company**
1844 Brummel Avenue
Elk Grove Village, IL 60007-2121 847-364-4242
Fax: 847-364-4373 800-732-5123
alloyd@alloyd.com www.alloyd.com
Radio frequency heat sealing and packaging equipment
Estimated Sales: $5-10 Million
Number Employees: 40

20153 **Calmar**
501 South 5th Street
Richmond, VA 23219-0501 804-444-1000
www.calmar.com
Manufacturer and exporter of plastic pump dispensers
President: James Buzzard
Chairman/Chief Executive Officer: John Luke Jr.
Chief Financial Officer: Mark Rajkowski
Senior Vice President: Linda Schreiner
General Counsel/Secretary: Wendell Willkie II
Vice President, Strategy & Marketing: Todd Fister
Communications: Donna Owens Cox
Supply Chain: Nik Hiremath
Estimated Sales: $50 - 100 Million
Number Employees: 200
Type of Packaging: Bulk

20154 **Caloritech**
1420 West Main Street
P.O. Box 146
Greensburg, IN 47240 812-663-4141
Fax: 812-663-4202 800-473-2403
info@ccithermal.com www.caloritech.com
Manufacturer and exporter of components for electrical cooking equipment, air heating immersion and clamp-on radiant equipment
President: Harold Roozen
VP Sales/Marketing: Bob Pender
Number Employees: 200
Square Footage: 440000
Parent Co: CCI Thermal Technologies
Brands:
X-Max

20155 **(HQ)Calzone Case Company**
225 Black Rock Ave
Bridgeport, CT 06605 203-367-5766
Fax: 203-336-4406 800-243-5152
www.calzonecase.com
Custom transporting cases including shipping and storage containers
President: Joe Calzone
CFO: Stephen Bajda
Executive VP: Vin Calzone
Marketing: Kim Bullard
Estimated Sales: $5 - 10,000,000
Number Employees: 20-49
Other Locations:
Calzone Case Co.
City of Industry CA

20156 **Cam Spray**
520 Brooks Rd
Iowa Falls, IA 50126 641-648-5011
Fax: 641-648-5013 800-648-5011
sales@camspray.com www.camspray.com
Manufacturer and exporter of high pressure washers; importer of pumps
Manager: Jim Gillestie
CFO: Jim Gillispie
Estimated Sales: $5-10 Million
Number Employees: 20-49
Square Footage: 75000
Parent Co: Campbell Supplies
Brands:
Cam Spray

20157 **Cam Tron Systems**
444 W Interstate Rd
Addison, IL 60101-4518 630-543-2884
Fax: 630-543-8153 www.camtronsystems.com
Pressure sensitive labeling equipment
President: Micheal Ahern
General Manager: Frank Ross
Estimated Sales: Below $5 Million
Number Employees: 20-49
Parent Co: Cameron Group
Brands:
Cam Tron

20158 **Cambar Software**
2430 Mall Dr Ste 320
North Charleston, SC 29406-6552 843-856-2822
Fax: 843-881-4893
marketingdept@cambarsoft.com
www.cambarsolutions.com
Computer software for order processing, inventory control, purchasing and warehouse management
President: Wade R Register
CEO: Robert A. Moore
CEO: Cecil Duffie
Number Employees: 100-249
Brands:
Csw
Control Ii

20159 **Cambelt International Corporation**
2820 W 1100 S
Salt Lake City, UT 84104-4594 801-972-5511
Fax: 801-972-5522 inquiries@cambelt.com
www.cambelt.com
Conveyor belt and automatic reclaiming systems
President: Colin Campbell
VP Marketing: Rex Wood
Estimated Sales: $20 - 50 Million
Number Employees: 50-99

20160 **(HQ)Cambridge**
105 Goodwill Road
PO Box 399
Cambridge, MD 21613 410-901-2660
Fax: 410-901-2680 877-649-7492
info@cambridge-es.com
www.cambridge-inc.com
Manufacturer and Exporter of conveyor belting, filters, vibration screens and filter leaves
Manager: Jody Padelko
International Sales Manager: Bart Shellabarger
Belt Sales Manager: Larry Windsor
Director of Sales: Larry Windsor
Customer Service Manager: Breanne Hemphill
Estimated Sales: $300,000-500,000
Number Employees: 1-4
Brands:
Cam-Grid
Cambri-Link
Continu-Weld

20161 **(HQ)Cambridge Viscosity, Inc.**
101 Station Lndg
Medford, MA 02155-5134 781-393-6500
Fax: 781-393-6515 800-554-4639
info@cambridgeviscosity.com
www.cambridgeapplied.com
Manufacturer and exporter of viscometers
President: Robert Kasameyer
Marketing Manager: Art MacNeill
Director Engineering: Dan Airey
Estimated Sales: $1 - 2.5 Million
Number Employees: 20-49
Brands:
Cambridge
Visco Lab 400
Visco Pro 1000
Visco Pro 2000

20162 **Cambro Manufacturing Company**
5801 Skylab Rd
Huntington Beach, CA 92647-2056 714-848-1555
800-848-1555
webmaster@cambro.com www.cambro.com
Manufacturer and exporter of food service equipment and supplies including bus boxes, insulated food carriers, carts and beverage containers, plastic insert pans, fiberglass trays and polyethylene boxes
President: Argyle Campbell
CFO: David Capestro
Estimated Sales: $74 Million
Number Employees: 850
Type of Packaging: Food Service
Brands:
Cambro

20163 **Camco Chemical Company**
8150 Holton Dr
Florence, KY 41042-3010 859-727-3200
Fax: 859-727-1508 800-554-1001
deerwesterr@camco-chem.com
www.camco-chem.com
Contract packager of janitorial supplies, laundry detergents, lubricants, soaps and cleaners
President: Thomas Cropper
CFO: Richard Rolfes
CEO: Richard Rolfes
Estimated Sales: $20 - 50 Million
Number Employees: 50-99

20164 **Camcorp**
8224 Nieman Rd
Lenexa, KS 66214-1507 913-894-6141
Fax: 913-831-9271 info@camcorpinc.com
www.camcorpinc.com
Owner: Frank Hanwork
VP Sales/Marketing: Ted Remmers
Estimated Sales: $5 - 10 Million
Number Employees: 20-49

20165 **Camel Custom Canvas Shop**
8910 Valgro Rd
Knoxville, TN 37920 865-573-2804
Fax: 865-573-9677 800-524-2704
camelcanvas@camelcanvas.com
www.camelcanvas.com
Commercial awnings, and custom canvas products
President: D Christian Cain
Sales: Brad Young
Plant Manager: Brenda Young
Purchasing: Rayma Stasen
Estimated Sales: $5 - 10 Million
Number Employees: 10-19
Square Footage: 6400

20166 **Cameo Metal Products Inc**
127 12th St
Brooklyn, NY 11215 718-788-1106
Fax: 718-788-3761 sales@cameometal.com
www.cameometal.com
Cameo Metal Products Manufactures metal closures for the food and beverage industry.
President: Vito Di Maio
Finance Manager: Adolsopoll Cruz
Director of Sales/Plant Manager: Robert Geddis
Director of Operations: Anthony Di Maio
Estimated Sales: $5.8 Million
Number Employees: 40
Square Footage: 100000

20167 **Camie Campbell**
9225 Watson Industrial Park
Saint Louis, MO 63126 314-968-3222
Fax: 314-968-0741 800-325-9572
camie@camie.com www.camie.com
Lubricants, pressure sensitive adhesives, rust corrosion silicones, spray adhesive and silicone sealants
President: Vince Doder
CEO: Tom Shelby
CFO: Vincent Doder
Natl. Sales Rep.: Steve Hartley
Credit Manager: Claudia Grissin
Estimated Sales: $10-20 000,000
Number Employees: 20-49
Type of Packaging: Bulk

20168 **Campak Technicam**
119 Naylon Ave
Livingston, NJ 07039-1005 973-597-1414
Fax: 973-992-4713 info@campak.com
www.campak.com
Thermoformer, intermittent motion horiziontal cartons, automatic wrapper, automatic bundler and shrink tunnel
CEO: Thomas Miller
Estimated Sales: $5-10 Million
Number Employees: 10-19

20169 **Campbell Wrapper Corporation**
1415 Fortune Ave
De Pere, WI 54115-8104 920-983-7100
Fax: 920-983-7300
calawaym@campbellwrapper.com
www.campbellwrapper.com
Manufactures Horizontal Fin Seal Wrappers for food and nonfood applications. Shrink and Polyethylene Wrappers for magazines, cards, and coupons. Dual Lane Wrappers for a variety of products. Side Seal Wrappers for the printing andmailing industries. On-Edge Wrappers for cookies and crackers. In-line Feed Systems for confectionery and bakery. Bar Distribution Systems for health bars, confectionery, bakery, etc.
President: John Dykema
VP Finance & Administration: Todd Goodwin
R&D Manager/Electrical Engineering Mgr: Jeff Ginzl
Mechanical Engineering Manager: Gary LeTourneau
Vice President Sales & Marketing: Don Stelzer
Product Manager: Steve Joosten
Service Manager: Marv Calaway
Materials Manager/Wrapper Assembly Mgr: Jeff Jende
Estimated Sales: $10 - 20 Million
Number Employees: 50-99
Type of Packaging: Consumer

20170 **Campbell Wrapper Corporation**
1415 Fortune Ave
De Pere, WI 54115 920-983-7100
Fax: 920-983-7300 800-727-4210
cwsales@campbellwrapper.com
www.campbellwrapper.com
Horizontal flow wrappers and feeders for various product types, sizes and speeds.
President: John Dykema
VP Finance/Administration: Todd Goodwin
R&D Manager/Electric Engineering Mgr: Jeff Ginzel
VP Sales/Marketing: Don Stelzer
International/Regional Sales Manager: Gus Skapek
Product Manager: Steve Joosten
Number Employees: 100+
Square Footage: 60000
Type of Packaging: Bulk
Brands:
Clyboura
Pak-Master
Parsons
Ricciarelli
Sasib

20171 **Campbell-Hardage**
305 Old Commerce Rd
Athens, GA 30607 706-548-4615
Fax: 706-543-2139 chsales@negia.net
www.campbell-hardage.com
Machinery for distribution systems and automatic product loading
President: Tim Wayne Hardage
CFO: Ark Campbell
Estimated Sales: $2.5 - 5 000,000
Number Employees: 30

20172 **Campus Collection, Inc.**
PO Box 2904
Tuscaloosa, AL 35403 205-758-0678
Fax: 205-758-4848 800-289-8744
sales@campuscollection.net
www.campuscollection.net
Manufacturer and exporter of printed and embroidered T-shirts, hats
President: Chet Goldstein

20173 **Camstar Systems**
100 Century Center Ct # 500
San Jose, CA 95112-4536 408-559-5700
Fax: 408-558-9350 800-237-2841
partners@camstar.com www.camstar.com
Production line software systems
President: James David Cone
President, Chief Executive Officer: Scott Toney
Vice President of Marketing: Karim Lokas
Chief Technical Officer: Scott Jones
Vice President of Sales: Jay Antonellis
Estimated Sales: $20 - 50 Million
Number Employees: 100-249

20174 **Camtech-AMF**
2115 West Laburnum Avenue
Richmond, VA 23227-4315 804-355-7961
Fax: 804-355-1074 sales@amfbakery.com
www.amfbakery.com
Industrial baking equipment
President: Ken Newsome
Number Employees: 100-249

20175 Camtron Systems
444 W Interstate Rd
Addison, IL 60101-4518 630-543-2884
Fax: 630-543-8153
Labels and label applicators
Owner: Mike Ahern
Estimated Sales: $1 - 2.5 000,000
Number Employees: 20-49

20176 Can & Bottle Systems, Inc.
2525 SE Stubb St
Milwaukie, OR 97222-7323 503-236-9010
Fax: 503-232-8453 866-302-2636
info@canandbottle.com www.canandbottle.com
Manufacturer, sales and service and exporter of reverse vending machines and systems for beverage container redemption and recycling. Can, plastic and glass beverage container crushers/recyclers
President: Bill Janner
Number Employees: 20-49
Number of Products: 15
Square Footage: 40000
Brands:
Cando

20177 (HQ)Can Corporation of America
326 June Ave
Blandon, PA 19510 610-926-3044
Fax: 610-926-5041
Steel food cans
President: Earl Jaunzemis
CEO: Ronald A Moreau
Estimated Sales: $100-500 Million
Number Employees: 100-249
Square Footage: 150000
Other Locations:
Can Corp. of America
Reading PA

20178 Can Creations
PO Box 848576
Pembroke Pines, FL 33084 954-581-3312
Fax: 954-581-2523 800-272-0235
orders@cancreations.com
www.cancreations.com
Bags, baskets and containers, boxes, cellophane, gift wrap, pull bows, shrink wrap.

20179 Can Creations
PO Box 8576
Pembroke Pines, FL 33084 954-581-3312
Fax: 954-581-2523 orders@cancreations.com
www.cancreations.com
Decorative boxes, shrink wrap, ribbons, bows and bags
Estimated Sales: $1 - 5 Million
Number Employees: 12
Brands:
Crystal Wrap

20180 Can Lines Engineering
9839 Downey-Norwalk Road
P.O. Box 7039
Downey, CA 90241-7039 562-861-2996
Fax: 562-869-5293
keenan.koplien@canlines.com
www.canlines.com
Manufacturer and exporter of can and bottle handling conveyors
President: Keenan Koplien
Vice President: Erik Koplien
Director, Mechanical Engineering: Steve Lusa
Director, Electrical Engineering: Brian Wedin
Director of Construction Sales & Ops: Darwin Smock
Estimated Sales: $20 Million
Number Employees: 100
Square Footage: 40000

20181 Can-Am Instruments
2851 Brighton Road
Oakville, ON L6H 6C9 905-829-0030
Fax: 905-829-4701 800-215-4469
psmyth@can-am.net www.can-am.net
Food machinery and equipment
President: Mark Reeves
Director: Richard Reeves
Director: Greg Reeves
Estimated Sales: $3 Million
Number Employees: 12

20182 CanPacific Engineering
7331 Vantage Way
Delta, BC V4G 1C9
Canada 604-946-1680
Fax: 604-946-1620 cpe@direct.ca
Industrial can openers and can seam inspection equipment
President: Wun Chong
Number Employees: 5-9
Brands:
Canguard

20183 Canada Coaster
44 Head St.
Dundas, ON L9H 3H3
Canada 905-627-6910
Fax: 905-627-7608 866-233-7628
sales@canadacoaster.com
www.canadacoaster.com
Manufacturers of beer and drink coasters
Type of Packaging: Food Service, Private Label, Bulk

20184 Canada Goose Wood Produc
2489 Del Zotto Avenue
Gloucester, ON K1T 3V6
Canada 613-822-2575
Fax: 613-822-2232 888-890-6506
sales@canadagoosewood.com
www.canada-goose.com
Wooden cutting boards, butcherblocks, trays and fajita griddle underliners

20185 Canada Pure Water Company Ltd
7 Kodiak Crescent
Toronto, ON M3J 3E5
Canada 416-631-5800
Fax: 416-635-1711 800-361-2369
info@canadapure.com www.canadapure.com
Wholesaler/distributor of flavored spring water and teas
President: David Tavares
Marketing Assistant: Sophia Ahmed
Director Purchasing: Tracy Tavares
Number Employees: 10-19

20186 Canadian Display Systems
60 Corstate Ave
Concord, ON L4K 4X2
Canada 905-265-7888
Fax: 905-265-7692 800-895-5862
cds1@on.aibn.com
www.canadiandisplaysystems.com
Display coolers
President: Gary Sohi
Number Employees: 15

20187 Canarm, Ltd.
2157 Parkedale Avenue
PO Box 367
Brockville, ON K6V 5V6
Canada 613-342-5424
Fax: 800-263-4598 info@canarm.ca
www.canarm.com
Manufacturer and importer of ceiling fans
President: James A. Cooper
Vice President - HVAC & Agri Products: Doug Matthews
Marketing Manager: John McBride
Sales Manager: Tim Sutton
Director Operations: Steven Read
Number Employees: 30
Type of Packaging: Consumer, Food Service, Private Label
Brands:
Four Seasons
Pleasantaire

20188 Candle Lamp Company
1799 Rustin Ave
Riverside, CA 92507 951-682-9600
Fax: 951-784-5801 877-526-7748
sales@candlelamp.com www.candlelamp.com
Chafing dish and lamp fuel; also, table lamps for the restaurant/hotel industry
President: Daniel Stoner
VP: L Murlin
Marketing Services: J Van Osdel
Estimated Sales: $10 - 20 Million
Number Employees: 100-249
Brands:
Safe Heat
Soft Light

20189 Candy & Company/Peck's Products Company
4100 West 76th Street
Chicago, IL 60652
800-837-9189
info@daleyinternational.com
Manufacturer and exporter of industrial disinfectant cleaners, janitorial supplies, sanitizers, laundry supplies and specialty cleaning chemicals
President: Joh Daley
Sales Manager: Joann Stoskoph
Estimated Sales: $1 - 5 Million
Number Employees: 1-4
Square Footage: 80000
Parent Co: J.F. Daley International
Brands:
Camagsolv
Pepcocide

20190 Candy Manufacturing
5633 W Howard St
Niles, IL 60714 847-588-2639
Fax: 847-588-0055 info@candycontrols.com
www.candycontrols.com
Manufacturer and exporter of industrial timing controls including differentials, positioners, cam switches, timing hubs, and web handling systems
President: Robert Hendershot
Quality Control: Al Rosenow
Sales Director: Jacob Ninan
Estimated Sales: Below $5 Million
Number Employees: 5-9
Square Footage: 60000

20191 Candymachines.com
P.O.Box 9
San Marcos, CA 92079 760-744-1550
Fax: 866-863-5867 800-853-3941
info@candymachines.com
www.candymachines.com
Distributor of gumball and candy vending machines, sticker, capsule machines, and bulk products, and refill supplies
Manager: Tonya Bryhie
CFO: Irving Korn
Vice President: Harris Harris
Marketing Director: Jerry Korn
Estimated Sales: $2 Million
Number Employees: 11
Number of Brands: 500+
Number of Products: 5000
Parent Co: RM Electronics
Type of Packaging: Consumer, Bulk

20192 Canning & Filling
PO Box 7501
Burlingame, CA 94011 650-401-6654
Fax: 650-401-6535 laurags@ix.netcom.com

20193 Cannon Conveyor Specialty Systems
15100 Business Pkwy
Rosemount, MN 55068-1794 651-322-6300
Fax: 651-322-1583 800-533-2071
careers@cannonequipment.com
www.cannonequipment.com
Material handling equipment and systems including casers, stackers, palletizers, robotic pattern formers, conveyors and mobile carts
President: Charles Gruber
CFO: Dale Quam
Vice President: Brian Benson
Marketing Director: Mark Hanson
Vice President of Sales: Bryce Malone
Manager of Operations: Adria Nelson
Estimated Sales: $30 - 50 Million
Number Employees: 100-249
Parent Co: Cannon Conveyor Systems

20194 Cannon Equipment Company
15100 Business Pkwy
Rosemount, MN 55068 651-322-6300
Fax: 651-322-1583 800-825-8501
info@cannonequipment.com
www.cannonequipment.com
Products are used in the exchange of goods and services between trading partners in the supply-chain. Core products consist of point-of-purchase displays, front-end merchandisers, distribution and display carts, and material handlingequipment and system
President: Chuck Gruber
Marketing: Jackie Black
Sales: Joe Rother
Operations: Colin Leyden

Estimated Sales: $100 - 250 Million
Number Employees: 250-499
Number of Brands: 15
Number of Products: 100
Square Footage: 10000000
Parent Co: IMI,PLC
Type of Packaging: Consumer, Food Service, Private Label, Bulk
Other Locations:
Cannon Equipment Company
Passaic NJ
Cannon Equipment Company
College Point NY
Cannon Equipment Company
Chattanooga TN
Cannon Equipment Company
Garden Grove CA
Cannon Equipment Company
Cannon Falls MN
Brands:
Connect-A-Bench
Ez-Lock
Ez-Reach
Magna-Bar
Ship 'n Shop
Slip

20195 **Canon Potato Company**
P.O.Box 880
Center, CO 81125 719-754-3445
Fax: 719-754-2227 sales@canonpotato.com
www.canonpotato.com
Potatoes including Centennials, McClures, Norkotahs, Nuggets, Reds, Russets, Sangres and Yukon Gold.
Manager: Jim Tonso
Sales Representative: Matt Glowczewski
Sales Manager: David Tonso
General Manager: Jim Tonso
Office Manager: Sandy Tonso
Estimated Sales: $10-20 Million
Number Employees: 50-99
Square Footage: 288340
Type of Packaging: Consumer, Food Service, Bulk

20196 **Canongate Technology**
2045 S Arl Hts Rd Ste 109
Arlington Hts, IL 60005 847-593-1832
Fax: 847-593-1629 800-221-4051
sales@canongatetechnology.co.uk
www.canongatetechnology.com
Inline instruments and analyzers sensing dissolved CO2, O2, % alcohol, O.G. and Brix
Group Managing Director: Robin Cuthbertson
VP: Ron Mc Rae
Estimated Sales: $500,000-$1 000,000
Number Employees: 1-4

20197 **Cantech Industries**
2222 Eddie Williams Rd
Johnson City, TN 37601 423-928-8331
Fax: 423-928-0311 800-654-3947
cii@cttgroup.com www.cantechtape.com
Manufacturer and exporter of pressure sensitive tapes including duct, masking, box sealing, filament, double-coated, and electrical for industrial, automotive and retail markets
President: L Cohen
CFO: H Cohen
Research & Development: H Matsuura
VP Marketing/Sales: Ronald Jacobs
VP Sales: P Cohen
Plant Manager: Mark Patton
Estimated Sales: $50 Million
Number Employees: 500
Number of Brands: 2
Number of Products: 70
Square Footage: 100000
Parent Co: Canadian Technical Tape
Type of Packaging: Consumer, Food Service, Private Label, Bulk
Brands:
Cantech
Clipper

20198 **Cantley-Ellis Manufacturing Company**
1200 South Eastman Road
Kingsport, TN 37660-5408 423-246-4671
Wooden pallets
General Manager: Jim Cantley
Estimated Sales: $2.5-5 Million
Number Employees: 20-49

20199 **Cantol**
199 Steelcase Road West
Markham, ON L3R 2M4 905-475-6141
800-387-9773
info@cantol.com www.cantol.com
Liquid detergents, soaps, herbicides, insecticides, lubricants, solvents and degreasers and floor care products, drain treatment chemicals, turf products, odor control, food processing and dietary chemicals
President: Elmer Snethen
VP: Richard Petscha
Plant Manager: Ellwood Barth
Estimated Sales: $10-20 Million
Number Employees: 20-49
Number of Products: 13
Parent Co: Cantol
Type of Packaging: Private Label, Bulk

20200 **(HQ)Canton Sign Company**
222 5th St NE
Canton, OH 44702 330-456-7151
Fax: 330-456-7152 cantonsign@aol.com
Metal, electric, plastic and wood signs and displays
President: Timothy Franta
VP: Mark Franta
VP: Timothy Franta
Estimated Sales: $500,000-$1 Million
Number Employees: 1-4

20201 **(HQ)Canton Sterilized WipingCloth Company**
1401 Waynesburg Dr SE
Canton, OH 44707-2115 330-455-5179
Fax: 330-455-2003
Cheesecloth wiping rags
President: Robert Shapiro
Estimated Sales: $5 - 10 Million
Number Employees: 10 to 19

20202 **Cantwell-Cleary Company**
2100 Beaver Rd
Landover, MD 20785 301-773-9800
Fax: 301-773-9257 info@cantwellcleary.com
www.cantwellcleary.com
Distributors of corrugated boxes and containers
Chairman/CEO: Vincent Cleary
Estimated Sales: $14 Million
Number Employees: 53
Square Footage: 45000

20203 **Canvas Products Company**
580 25 Rd
Grand Junction, CO 81505 970-242-1453
Fax: 970-241-4801 www.canvas-products.com
Commercial awnings
Owner: Greg Coren
Estimated Sales: $1-2,500,000
Number Employees: 5-9

20204 **CapSnap Equipment**
2080 Brooklyn Road
Jackson, MI 49203 517-787-3481
Fax: 517-787-2349
sales@capsnapequipment.com
www.capsnapequipment.com
HOD water bottling equipment and service.

20205 **Capco Plastics**
9231 Billy the Kid St
El Paso, TX 79907-4738 915-772-1395
Fax: 915-772-1396 sales@capcoplastics.com
www.capcoplastics.com
Thermoform company specializing in blister, clamshell and trifold packages.
President: Robert Arno
Vice President, General Manager: Bob Arno
Estimated Sales: $3 - 5 Million
Number Employees: 10-19

20206 **Cape Systems**
100 Allentown Parkway
Suite 218
Allen, TX 75002 800-229-3434
Fax: 908-756-2332 sales@capesystems.com
www.capesystems.com
Pallets, load planning, optimization, transportation-software; warehouse management software order fulfillment and inventory system
Executive Chairman: Hugo Biermann
Director/CEO/CFO: Nicholas Toms
CEO: Nicholas R Toms
International Marketing: Peter Ayling
Vice President Group Sales: Brad Leonard
Customer Service Manager: Kim Karl
Chief Operating Officer/CTO: David Sasson
Vice President Software Sales: Heidi Larsen
Estimated Sales: Below $5 Million
Number Employees: 20-49
Number of Brands: 8

20207 **Capital City Container Corporation**
150 Precision Drive
Buda, TX 78610 512-312-1222
Fax: 512-312-1349
Corrugated shipping containers
Manager: Mike McDonald
VP of Marketing: Doug King
Estimated Sales: $10 - 20 Million
Number Employees: 148

20208 **Capital City Neon Sign Company**
2714 Industrial Dr
Monona, WI 53713-2250 608-222-1881
Fax: 608-222-1889
Luminous tube and plastic signs
President: Rosemary Zimmerman
VP/Secretary: Rosemary Zimmerman
Estimated Sales: Below $5 Million
Number Employees: 5 to 9
Square Footage: 8000

20209 **Capital Controls Company/MicroChem**
3000 Advance Ln
Colmar, PA 18915-9432 215-997-4000
Fax: 215-997-4062
marketing@capitalcontrols.com
www.severntrentservices.com
Manufacturer and exporter of water treatment systems including chlorinators, ultraviolet sterilization systems, pH/orp monitors and chlorine, ammonia and fluoride residue analyzers
President, Chief Executive Officer: Martin Kane
Marketing Manager: Anne Penkal
Plant Manager: Jeff Dohnam
Estimated Sales: $20-50 Million
Number Employees: 100-249

20210 **Capital Industries**
PO Box 1693
Mattituck, NY 11952-0929 631-298-6300
Fax: 631-298-2077 info@kwikbond.com
www.kwikbond.com
Kwik-Bond, floor repair
Estimated Sales: $5 - 10 Million
Number Employees: 20-49

20211 **Capital Packaging**
PO Box 873
Panacea, FL 32346 229-228-0006
Fax: 912-228-6405
Packaging
C.E.O: Polybus B. Joseph
Secretary: Polybus T. Frances
Sales Manager: Randy Eason

20212 **(HQ)Capital Plastics**
15060 Madison Road
Middlefield, OH 44062-9407 440-632-5800
Fax: 440-632-0012 collector@capitalplastics.com
www.capitalplastics.com
Manufacturer and exporter of custom plastic displays for acrylic cutting boards, clip boards, plaques and trophies
President: Lyle Schwartz
Estimated Sales: $2.5 - 5 Million
Number Employees: 20

20213 **Capitol Awning Company**
10515 180th St
Jamaica, NY 11433 718-454-6444
Fax: 718-657-8374 800-241-3539
www.capitolawning.com
Commercial awnings, banners, sign faces and graphics
President: Fred Catalano
Estimated Sales: $2.5-5,000,000
Number Employees: 20-49

20214 **Capitol Carton Company**
8333 24th Avenue
Sacramento, CA 95826 916-388-7848
Fax: 916-388-7840
Corrugated boxes
President: Neal Gurevitz
VP: Thomas Milligan
Plant Supervisor: James Wodarczyk
Estimated Sales: $1 - 5 Million
Number Employees: 5-9
Square Footage: 50000

20215 **Capitol City Container Corporation**
8240 Zionsville Rd
Indianapolis, IN 46268 317-875-0290
Fax: 317-876-6694 800-233-5145
info@capcitycontainer.com
www.capcitycont.com
Custom corrugated boxes and stock packaging supplies
President: Richard Purcell
VP: Mike Purcell
Plant Manager: Jim Plank
Estimated Sales: $10 - 20 Million
Number Employees: 20-49
Square Footage: 65000

20216 **Capitol Hardware, Inc.**
402 N Main Street
P.O. Box 70
Middlebury, IN 46540-2573 800-327-6083
Fax: 800-544-4054 www.leggettsfg.com
Manufacturer and exporter of retail store fixtures, peripheral display hardware and electric lighting fixtures
President: Joe Shelby
Senior Vice President: David DeSonier
Executive Vice President of Sales: Joel Katterhagen
Executive Vice President of Operations: Ron McComas
Estimated Sales: $2.5-5 Million
Number Employees: 20-49
Square Footage: 1000000
Parent Co: Leggett & Platt Store Fixtures Group
Brands:
Capitol Hardware

20217 **Capitol Recruiting Group**
712 Gum Rock Court
Newport News, VA 757-277-7934
info@capitolrecruitinggroup.com
www.capitolrecruitinggroup.com
Executive search firm specializing in selection and placement of consumer packaged goods industry personnel including sales, marketing, category, broker and senior level management positions
General Manager: Buford Sims
Other Locations:
Washington DC
Boston MA
New York NY

20218 **Capitol Vial**
151 Riverside Drive
Fultonville, NY 12072-1824 518-853-3377
Fax: 518-853-3409 sales@capitolvial.com
www.capitolvial.com
Estimated Sales: $5-10 Million
Number Employees: 20-49

20219 **Capmatic, Ltd.**
12180 Boul. Albert-Hudon
Monreal North, QC H1G 3K7
Canada 514-332-0062
Fax: 514-322-0063 info@capmatic.com
www.capmatic.com
Manufacturer and exporter of packaging machinery and bottling equipment
President: Charles Lacasse
CFO: Nicole Murray
President: Alioscia Bassani
Sales Director: Christian Normandin
Number Employees: 20

20220 **Capricorn Coffees**
353 10th St
San Francisco, CA 94103 415-621-8500
Fax: 415-621-9875 800-541-0758
www.capricorncoffees.com
Coffee, Tea, Accessories
Manager: Annie Ngo
Estimated Sales: $1-2.5 Million
Number Employees: 10-19
Type of Packaging: Private Label

20221 **Capricorn Coffees**
353 10th St
San Francisco, CA 94103 415-621-8500
Fax: 415-621-9875 www.capricorncoffees.com
Espresso machines and accessories
Manager: Megan Patterson
CFO: Craig Edwards
Quality Control: Craig Edwards
Estimated Sales: $1 - 2.5 000,000
Number Employees: 10-19

20222 **Capriole Farmstead GoatCheeses**
10329 New Cut Road
Greenville, IN 47124 812-923-9408
cheese@capriolegoatcheese.com
www.capriolegoatcheese.com
Fresh goat cheese
President/Head Cheesemaker: Judy Schad
Number Employees: 4

20223 **Capway Systems**
725 Vogelsong Rd
York, PA 17404 717-843-0003
Fax: 717-843-1654 877-222-7929
sales@capwayusa.com www.capwayusa.com
Manufacturer and exporter of bakery and food processing equipment including depanners, proofers, coolers, pan storage systems, conveyors, etc
President: Frank Achterberg
General Manager: Frank Achterberg
Estimated Sales: $5-10 Million
Number Employees: 20-49
Square Footage: 36000
Parent Co: Capway Systems
Brands:
Capway

20224 **Capway Systems**
725 Vogelsong Rd
York, PA 17404 717-843-0003
Fax: 717-843-1654 877-222-7929
capwayusa@aol.com www.capwayusa.com
Bakery and egg handling conveyors and automated equipment systems
President: Frank Achterberg
Estimated Sales: $5 - 10 000,000
Number Employees: 20-49

20225 **Cara Products Company**
9192 Tara Boulevard
Jonesboro, GA 30236-4913 770-478-9802
Fax: 770-471-3715
Manufacturer and exporter of stainless steel, fiberglass and wood free standing and hot food counters. Custom stainless steel kitchen equipment, serving lines, buffets and salad bard, portable hot and cold carts and custom millwork
President: W Casey
VP: David Pearson
Marketing: Bill Steadman
Sales Manager: Bill Steadman
Purchasing: Dan Casey
Estimated Sales: $20-25 Million
Number Employees: 200

20226 **Carando Machine Works**
345 N Harrison St
Stockton, CA 95203 209-948-6500
Fax: 209-948-6757 sales@carando.net
www.carando.net
Manufacturer and exporter of container production machinery
President: Sid Schuetz
Sales Coordinator: Laura Keir
Estimated Sales: $5-10 Million
Number Employees: 10-19

20227 **Caraustar**
115 Quail Road
Franklin, KY 42134 270-586-9565
info@caraustar.com
www.carustar.com
Advertising novelties and specialties including plastic lids, tips and spouts
Division Manager: Mark Bamberger
Estimated Sales: $5-10 Million
Number Employees: 20-49

20228 **Caraustar**
25221 Miles Road
Warrensville Heights, OH 44128-5402 216-831-8823
Fax: 216-831-5240 800-362-1125
Kraft paper sleeves, tubes and cheese wrappers
National Sales Manager: Robert Isaacs
Estimated Sales: $1-2.5 Million
Number Employees: 9
Parent Co: Tranzonic Companies
Brands:
Whelan

20229 **Caraustar Industries, Inc.**
3900 Comanche Drive
Archdale, NC 27263-3158 770-948-3101
800-223-1373
info@caraustar.com www.caraustar.com
Manufacturer and exporter of composite cans, tubes, metal ends and injection molded plastic products used for packaging wet and dry, hot fill and frozen products
Marketing Director: Andrew McGowan
Type of Packaging: Consumer, Food Service

20230 **Caravan Company**
P.O.Box 1004
Totowa, NJ 07511-1004 973-256-8886
Fax: 973-256-8395 800-526-5261
info@caravanproducts.com
www.caravanproducts.com
Bulk supplier
President: John Stone
CFO: Neil Bonyor
VP: Joseph Solimini
Quality Control: Rick Jackson
Chairman of the Board: Jaap Wink
Estimated Sales: $20 - 50 Million
Number Employees: 100-249

20231 **Caravan Packaging**
6427 Eastland Rd
Cleveland, OH 44142 440-243-4100
Fax: 440-243-4383 info@caravanpackaging.com
www.caravanpackaging.com
Manufacturer and exporter of wooden boxes and custom packaging
President: Fred Hitti
Estimated Sales: $500,000-$1 Million
Number Employees: 5-9
Type of Packaging: Food Service, Bulk

20232 **Carbis**
1430 W Darlington St
Florence, SC 29501-2124 843-669-6668
Fax: 843-662-1536 800-948-7750
sales@carbissolutions.com www.carbis.net
Stainless steel products, including loading racks, arms, stairs, platforms and handrails
President: Sam Cramer
Marketing Director: Rob Cooksey
General Manager: Ron Bennett
Number Employees: 250-499
Square Footage: 1200000

20233 **Carboline Company**
2150 Schuetz Rd
St Louis, MO 63146-3517 314-644-1000
Fax: 314-644-3353 800-848-4645
www.carboline.com
High-performance, anti-corrosive coatings
President: Richard Wilson
Estimated Sales: $87 Million
Number Employees: 500

20234 **Carbon Clean Products**
216 Courtdale Ave
Kingston, PA 18704 570-288-1155
Fax: 570-288-1227 carbonclean@aol.com
Chemical cleaners for the removal of burnt and carbonized food products; also, dispensers
President: Ernest J Clamar
CFO: Ernest J Clamar Sr
Estimated Sales: $5 - 10,000,000
Number Employees: 10-19

20235 **Carbonic Machines**
2900 5th Ave S
Minneapolis, MN 55408-2497 612-824-0745
Fax: 612-824-1974 info@shamrockgroup.net
www.shamrockgroup.net
Ice machines and beer, wine and soda dispensing systems for restaurants
President and QC: David Kelly
VP Marketing: Steven Kelly

Estimated Sales: $20 - 50 Million
Number Employees: 20-49

20236 Carbonic Reserves
4754 Shavano Oak # 102
San Antonio, TX 78249-4027 210-479-0100
Fax: 210-479-0070 800-880-1911
www.airgas.com
Freezers and cooling tunnels and spirals; processor of dry ice
President: Bob Bradshaw
Vice President of HR: Ann Rice
Sales Manager: Jay Loo
Vice President of Operations: Don Goldschmidt
Estimated Sales: $1 - 5 Million
Number Employees: 100-249
Brands:
Penguin Brand

20237 Card Pak
29601 Solon Rd
Cleveland, OH 44139 440-542-3100
Fax: 440-542-3399 800-824-3342
sgraham@cardpak.com www.cardpak.com
President: Rick Peters
Estimated Sales: $20 - 50 Million
Number Employees: 50-99

20238 Cardan Design
227 Rutgers St
Maplewood, NJ 07040-3229 973-762-2186
Fax: 973-762-2753
Owner: Bert Ghavami
Estimated Sales: $1 - 5 000,000
Number Employees: 50-99

20239 Cardinal Container Corporation
750 S Post Rd
Indianapolis, IN 46239 317-898-2715
Fax: 317-899-6747 800-899-2715
www.cardinalcontainercorp.com
Corrugated cartons
President: Dale Farmer
Controller: Mark Prosser
Estimated Sales: $10-20 Million
Number Employees: 20-49

20240 Cardinal Kitchens
230 Hiawatha Avenue
Louisville, KY 40209
Canada 502-363-3871
Fax: 502-363-3873 800-928-0832
info@cardnalkitchens.com
www.cardinalkitchens.com
Laboratory providing food testing services
Parent Co: Cardinal Biologicals
Brands:
Snack Rite

20241 Cardinal PackagingProducts Inc.
300 Exchange Drive
Suite A
Crystal Lake, IL 60014 815-444-6000
Fax: 815-444-6379 866-216-4942
info@cardinalpack.com
www.cardinalpkgproducts.com
Manufacturer and exporter of set-up paper boxes, specialty folding cartons, incorporating domicut platforms, etc. Also hot leaf (foil) stamping
President: Julie Wancket
Sales: Steve Overlee
Estimated Sales: $1 - 3 Million
Number Employees: 10-19

20242 Cardinal Packaging
Po Box 959
Evansville, IN 47706-0959 812-424-2904
Fax: 330-562-4875 cardpkg@ibm.net
www.berryplastics.com
Plastic round and rectangular containers
President: Ira Booth
CFO: Mike Cutnam
VP: Bill Regan
Quality Control: Warren Blazy
VP Sales: Bill Regan
Regional Manager: Norma Seevers
Plant Manager: Kurt Hamlin
Number Employees: 100-249
Square Footage: 380000
Parent Co: Cardinal Packaging

20243 Cardinal Professional Products
57 Matmor Road
Woodland, CA 95776 831-637-1992
Fax: 530-666-3170 800-548-2223
info@cardinalproproducts.com??????
www.cardinalproproducts.com
Insecticides
President: John Sansone
Estimated Sales: $.5 - 1 million
Number Employees: 5-9
Parent Co: Cal-Ag Industrial Supply

20244 Cardinal Rubber & Seal
1545 Brownlee Ave SE
Roanoke, VA 24014 540-982-0091
Fax: 540-982-6750 800-542-5737
sales@cardinalrubber.com
www.cardinalrubber.com
Manufacturer and exporter of rubber seals, gaskets, O-rings, hoses, etc.
President: Loren Bruffey, Jr
CEO: Loren Bruffey, Sr.
Vice President: Pat Lawhorn
Sales: Bob Edwards
Purchasing: Connie Dowdy
Estimated Sales: $10-20 Million
Number Employees: 20-49

20245 Cardinal Scale Manufacturing Company
203 E Daugherty St
P.O. Box 151
Webb City, MO 64870 417-673-4631
Fax: 417-673-5001 800-441-4237
cardinal@cardet.com www.cardet.com
Manufacturer and exporter of scales
President: David H Perry
CEO: W Perry
CFO: Charles Nasters
Vice President: Herbert Harwood
Estimated Sales: $50 - 100 Million
Number Employees: 500-999
Square Footage: 400000

20246 (HQ)Care Controls, Inc.
PO Box 12014
Mill Creek, WA 98082 425-745-1252
Fax: 425-745-8934 800-593-6050
info@carecontrols.com www.carecontrols.com
Manufacturer and exporter of on-line inspection systems including check weighers, vacuum and pressure detectors, etc
President: Ray Pynsky
Marketing: Rob Laroche
Brands:
Canalyzer
Ivis
Quantum

20247 Carelton Helical Technologies
30 S Sand Rd
New Britain, PA 18901-5123 215-230-8900
Fax: 215-230-8033 sales@feedscrew.com
www.feedscrew.com
Packaging and container handling
President: Nick Carleton
Engineering Dept./ Manager: Connie McDermott
Estimated Sales: Below $5 Million
Number Employees: 10-19

20248 Cargill Foods
PO Box 9300
Minneapolis, MN 55440-9300
800-227-4455
www.cargill.com
Grains and oilseeds, sugar, chocolate, sweeteners and starches, meats, eggs and poultry, salt, cotton, dressings, sauces and oils.
President: David MacLennan
Executive Chairman: Gregory Page
CFO: Sergio Rial
SVP: William Buckner
Corp VP, Research & Development: Christopher Mallett
Corp VP Strategy & Business Development: Sarena Lin
Exec VP & Chief Risk Officer: Emery Koenig
Corp VP, Corporate Affairs: Michael Fernandez
Corp VP, Operations: Thomas Hayes
Corp VP & Controller: Kimberly Lattu
Number Employees: 139000
Type of Packaging: Food Service, Bulk
Brands:
Peter's™ Chocolate
Gerkens® Cacao
Maizewise™
Corowise™
Regenasure™
Clear Valley®
Grainwise™
Progressive Baker™
Sunny Fresh™
Diamond Crystal®
Liza™
Delicia®
Truvia™
Naturefresh™
Peter's® Chocolate
Wilbur® Chocolate
Honeysuckle White®
Shady Brook Farms®
Sterling Silver®
Rumba®
Tender Choice®
Good Nature™

20249 Cargill Kitchen Solutions
206 West Fourth Street
Monticello, MN 55362
800-872-3447
usaeggs@cargill.com www.sunnyfresh.com
Eggs and breakfast products for; foodservice operatos, convenience stores, chain restaurants, healthcare foodservice facilities, and schools.
Parent Co: Cargill Incorporated
Type of Packaging: Bulk
Brands:
Sunny Fresh™

20250 Cargill Sweeteners
P.O.Box 5621
Minneapolis, MN 55440-5621 952-984-8280
Fax: 952-984-3256 800-227-4455
cargillfoods@cargill.com www.cargillsalt.com
Dry sweeteners, food starches, high fructose corn syrup
President: Mike Venker
President/COO: Gregory Page
Senior VP/Director Corporate Affairs: Robin Johnson
C.V.P. Public Affairs: Bonnie Raquet
Estimated Sales: less than $500,000
Number Employees: 10,000
Number of Products: 19

20251 Cargill Texturizing Solutions
308 6th Avenue SE
Cedar Rapids, IA 52401 319-399-3627
Fax: 319-399-6170 877-650-7080
www.cargilltexturizing.com
Supplier of texturizing and emulsifiers to the global food and beverage industry, as well as the pharmaceutical and cosmetics markets.
President: Ralph Apple
R&D: Joe Holtwick
Marketing: Jim Kubczak
Sales: Andy Dederich
Operations: Bernard Cerles
Plant Manager: Mike Rizor
Parent Co: Cargill, Incorporated
Type of Packaging: Consumer, Food Service, Bulk
Brands:
Angus Pride®
Circle T Beef®
Excel®
Fressure™
Meadowland Farms™
Ranchers Registry®
Rumba™
Sterling Silver®
Valley Tradition
Goodnature™
Tender Choice®<RStoneside®
Harvest Provisions™
Honeysuckle White®
Shady Brook Farms®
Willow Brook®
Plantation™
Marval™
Riverside™

20252 Cargill Vegetable Oils
5858 Park Ave
Minneapolis, MN 55417 612-378-0551
Fax: 612-318-2597 info@crcmeetings.com
www.crcmeetings.com

Vegetable and soybean oils; also, soybean meal
Owner: Lisa Cargill
National Accounts Sales: Bill Bohmer
Estimated Sales: $300,000-500,000
Number Employees: 1-4
Parent Co: Cargill Foods
Type of Packaging: Bulk

20253 Carhartt
P.O.Box 600
Dearborn, MI 48121-0600 313-271-8460
Fax: 313-271-3455 800-358-3825
www.carhartt.com
CFO: Linda Hubbard
CEO: Mark Valade
Number Employees: 1,000-4,999

20254 Carhoff Company
13404 Saint Clair Ave
Cleveland, OH 44110 216-541-4835
Fax: 216-541-4022
Manufacturer and exporter of silicone and chemically treated cleansing tissues
V.P.: Jim Lauer
Estimated Sales: $5-10 Million
Number Employees: 10-19

20255 Carico Systems
4211 Clubview Dr
Fort Wayne, IN 46804 260-432-6738
Fax: 260-432-2461 800-466-6738
carico@caricosystems.com
www.caricosystems.com
Material handling, wire carts, containers
President: Jon Marler
Estimated Sales: $500,000 - $1 000,000
Number Employees: 1-4

20256 Caristrap International
1760 Fortin Boulevard
Laval, QC H7S 1N8
Canada 450-667-4700
Fax: 450-663-1520 800-361-9466
info@caristrap.com www.caristrap.com
Manufacturer and exporter of polyester cord strapping
President: Audrey Karass
Operations: Gerry Elis
Plant Manager: Norm Stevenson
Number Employees: 150
Brands:
Strapping

20257 Carl Strutz & Company
440 Mars-Valencia Road
PO Box 509
Mars, PA 16046 724-625-1501
Fax: 724-625-3570 info@strutz.com
www.strutz.com
Direct screen printing equipment for glass and plastic containers
Director: Frank Strutz Jr
Director: James Strutz
President: Carl Strutz Jr
General Manager: Edward Zwigert
Estimated Sales: $5 - 10 Million
Number Employees: 10-19
Square Footage: 26000

20258 Carleton Helical Technologies
30 South Sand Road
New Britain, PA 18901-5123 215-230-8900
Fax: 215-230-8033 sales@feedscrew.com
www.feedscrew.com
Container handling products and systems including timing screws, invertors, inline air rinsers, carton twisters, etc
President: Nick Carleton
Operations Manager: Connie McDermott
Production Manager: Mike Anrein
Production: Mark McDermott
Purchasing Manager: Edward Amrein
Estimated Sales: $2 - 3 Million
Number Employees: 10-19
Number of Brands: 5
Number of Products: 1
Square Footage: 52000

20259 Carleton Technologies
10 Cobham Dr
Orchard Park, NY 14127 716-662-0006
Fax: 716-662-0747 info@carltech.com
www.carltech.com
Manufacturer and exporter of testing equipment for flexible package seal integrity and strength
President/CEO: Paddy Cawdery
Estimated Sales: $20-50 Million
Number Employees: 100-249
Square Footage: 93000
Parent Co: FR Group PLC
Brands:
Test-A-Pack

20260 Carlin Manufacturing
466 West Fallbrook Avenue
Suite 106
Fresno, CA 93711 559-276-0123
Fax: 559-222-1538 888-212-0801
info@carlinmfg.com www.carlinmfg.com
Manufacturer and exporter of custom mobile kitchens, military field kitchens and specialty vehicles.
Owner: Kevin Carlin
Sales/FMP/CEO: Bob Farrar
Estimated Sales: $5-10 Million
Number Employees: 10-19
Number of Brands: 1
Square Footage: 37000

20261 Carlisle Food Service Products
4711 E Hefner Road
PO Box 53006
Oklahoma City, OK 73131 405-475-5600
Fax: 405-475-5607 800-654-8210
customerservice@carlislefsp.com
www.carlislefsp.com
Over 16,000 products including dishware, tabletop accessories, coffee and tea supplies, buffet service, food bars and accessories, food service trays, bar supplies, catering equipment, kitchen accessories, storage and handling andcleaning tools
President: Dave Shannon
CFO: Carolyn Ford
R&D: Rich McDonach
VP Marketing: Todd Manor
Sales Director: Jim Calamito
Operations Manager: Rich McDonagh
Estimated Sales: $238.8 Million
Number Employees: 500
Number of Brands: 100
Number of Products: 1600
Square Footage: 150000
Type of Packaging: Food Service
Other Locations:
Central Distribution Center
Oklahoma City OK
Western Distribution Center
Reno NV
Eastern Distribution Center
Charlotte NC
Brands:
Aria
Bistro
Bravo
Catarcooler
Celebration
Che Series
Classic
Clutter Busters
Coldmaster
Crescendo
Crystalite
Delivers
Designer Displpayer
Elan
Elegant
Elegant Impressions
Excelibur
Expressions
Fall'n Go
Festival Traus
Flex - All
Galaxy
Glasted
Griptite
Hi - Lo
Ice Sculptures
Lexington
Meteor
Miracryl
Mosar Design Displayware
Munchie
Napkin Deli
Omni
Orchid
Perma - Sam
Perma - Sil
Petal Mist
Poly - Tuf
Poura - Clam
Queen Anne
Sani - Pail
Save - All
Signature Select
Six Star
Sleep'n Bag
Sparta
Spectrum
Ssal 2000
Stackable
Star Plus
Steclite
Sted Stock Ii
Steeluminum
Store'n Pour
Suds - Pail
Supreme
Symphony
Textile Design Collection
The Gotham Collection
The Lions Head Collection
The Mediterranean Collection
The New World Collection
The Oceana Collection
The Resort Collection
Thermoinsulator
Top Notch
Trimlina
Thermoinsulator
Top Notch
Trimlina
Tulip Deli
Universal
Weavewear

20262 Carlisle Plastics
1401 W 94th St
Minneapolis, MN 55431 952-884-1309
Fax: 952-884-6438 www.tycoplastics.com
Polyethylene bags, film and sheeting; also, garbage bags
Number Employees: 250-499
Parent Co: Tyco International
Brands:
Color Scents
Film-Gard
Ruffies
Sure Sak

20263 Carlisle Sanitary Maintenance Products
PO Box 53006
Oklahoma City, OK 73152 405-475-5600
Fax: 405-475-5607 800-654-8210
custserv@carlislesmp.com www.carlislesmp.com
President: Trent Freiberg
Manager: Tim Larson
Estimated Sales: $10 - 20 Million
Number Employees: 50-99

20264 Carlisle Sanitary Maintenance Products
4711 E Hefner Road
PO Box 53006
Oklahoma City, OK 73152-3006 405-475-5600
Fax: 405-475-5607 800-654-8210
www.carlislesmp.com
Manufacturer and exporter of custom-designed brushes including floor scrub, clean-up, fryers, nylon paddle scraper, grill, grease, glass and washing
Director Sales/Marketing: Christopher Meaney
General Manager: Robert Daley, Jr.
Estimated Sales: $200,000
Number Employees: 6
Square Footage: 16652
Type of Packaging: Food Service, Bulk
Brands:
Broiler Master
Galaxy
Hercules
Hi-Lo
Long Reach
Meteor
Venus

20265 Carlo Gavizzi
750 Hastings Dr
Buffalo Grove, IL 60089-6904 847-465-6100
Fax: 847-465-7373 sales@carlogavazzi.com
www.gavazzionline.com

Importer of solid-state relays, electronic plug-in control modules and sensors, digital electronic counters and meters
President: Fred Shirzadi
Estimated Sales: $10 - 20 Million
Number Employees: 20-49

20266 **Carlson Engineering**
505 NE 37th St
Fort Worth, TX 76106 817-877-3815
Fax: 817-335-4712
office@carlsonengineeringinc.com
www.carlsonengineeringinc.com
Software development and systems integration
President: John Carlson
Estimated Sales: Below $5 000,000
Number Employees: 10-19

20267 **Carlson Products**
4601 N Tyler Rd
P.O. Box 429
Maize, KS 67101 316-722-0265
Fax: 316-721-0158 800-234-1069
sales@carlsonproducts.com
www.carlsonproducts.com
Manufacturer and exporter of lightweight double-acting aluminum impact and sliding aluminum cooler and freezer doors; also pizza pans
President: Stuart Gribble
Sales Manager: Rich Dreiling
Estimated Sales: $5-10 Million
Number Employees: 50-99
Square Footage: 50000
Parent Co: Jay Ca

20268 **Carlton Industries**
PO Box 280
La Grange, TX 78945 979-242-5055
Fax: 800-231-5934 800-231-5988
sales@carltonusa.com www.carltonusa.com
Product identification labels, decals, tags, tapes, signs, placards, etc
President: Kay M Carlton
Vice President: Richard Carlton
Marketing Director: Colette Merchant
Estimated Sales: $5 - 10 Million
Number Employees: 20-49
Square Footage: 80000

20269 **Carlyle Compressor**
Carrier Parkway, TR-4
PO Box 4808
Syracuse, NY 13221 315-432-6000
Fax: 315-432-3274 800-462-2759
carlyle.compressor@carrier.utc.com
www.carlylecompressor.com
President: Richard Laubstein

20270 **Carman And Company**
12 Wilmington Rd
Burlington, MA 01803 781-221-3500
Fax: 781-221-3508
connie@carmanandcompany.com
www.carmanandcompany.com
Counter display cabinets
Owner: Dan Carman
Estimated Sales: $500,000-$1 Million
Number Employees: 5-9

20271 **Carman Industries**
PO Box 579
Jeffersonville, IN 47131 812-288-4700
Fax: 812-288-4707 800-456-7560
info@carmanindustries.com
www.carmanindustries.com
Vibratory material handling and fluid-bed drying equipment including conveyors, feeders, bin dischargers and spiral elevators
President: C James Hyslop
VP: Carl Porter
VP: Carl Porter
Estimated Sales: $2.5-5 Million
Number Employees: 50-99
Square Footage: 40000

20272 **Carman Industries**
P.O.Box 579
Jeffersonville, IN 47131 812-288-4700
Fax: 812-288-4707 800-456-7560
info@carmanindustries.com
www.carmanindustries.com
Bulk material handling and processing equipment including vibrating feeders, vibrating conveyors, vibrating spiral elevators, vibrating bin dischargers and fluid bed dryers, heaters and coolers
President: C James Hyslop
CFO: Jack Ising
Quality Control: Bill Whearthon
Estimated Sales: $2.5 - 5 000,000
Number Employees: 50-99

20273 **Carmel Engineering**
PO Box 67
Kirklin, IN 46050 317-896-9367
Fax: 765-896-5713 888-427-0497
sales@carmeleng.com
www.carmelengineering.com
Supplier of food processing equipment that include heat exchangers, product tubes, heat exchanger parts, resting tubes, dump tanks and accumulator tanks and convection systems
Owner: Randy Weaver
VP: Randy Weaver
Estimated Sales: $1.5 Million
Number Employees: 10-19

20274 **Carmel Engineering**
PO Box 67
Kirklin, IN 46050 317-896-9367
Fax: 765-896-5713 888-427-0497
sales@carmeleng.com
www.carmelengineering.com
Supplier of food processing equipment that include heat exchangers, product tubes, heat exchanger parts, resting tubes, dump tanks and accumulator tanks and convection systems
Owner: Randy Weaver
VP: Randy Weaver
Estimated Sales: $1.5 Million
Number Employees: 10-19

20275 **(HQ)Carmi Flavor & Fragrance Company**
6030 Scott Way
City of Commerce, CA 90040 323-888-9240
Fax: 323-888-9339 800-421-9647
sales@carmiflavors.com www.carmiflavors.com
High quality natural and artificial flavors in liquid or powder form; supplier of packaging products.
President: Eliot Carmi
CEO: Frank Carmi
Sales: Bruce Rutenburg
Plant Manager: Roger Speakman
Purchasing Director: Judy Montgomery
Estimated Sales: $12 Million
Number Employees: 40
Number of Brands: 1
Number of Products: 500
Square Footage: 30000
Type of Packaging: Private Label, Bulk
Other Locations:
Carmi Flavor & Fragrance
Port Coquitlam, Canada
Carmi Flavor & Fragrance
Waverly LA
Brands:
Carmi Flavors
Flavor Depot

20276 **Carmona Designs**
737 3rd Ave
Chula Vista, CA 91910-5827 619-425-2800
Fax: 619-425-0225 carmonadgs@aol.com
Design consultant specializing in restaurants
President: Armando Carmona
General Manager: Armando Carmona
Estimated Sales: $1 - 2.5 Million
Number Employees: 10-19

20277 **Carmun International**
702 San Fernando Street
San Antonio, TX 78207-5041 210-224-1781
Fax: 210-227-5332 800-531-7907
Stainless steel fittings, aluminum cold plates, CO2 regulators and bar guns
Bus. Dev. Manager: Joe King
General Manager: Luther Cowden
Estimated Sales: $20-50 Million
Number Employees: 250-499
Parent Co: IMI Cornelius

20278 **CarneTec**
1415 N Dayton St
Chicago, IL 60642-2643 312-266-3311
Fax: 312-266-3363 info@meatingplace.com
www.meatingplace.com
Computer systems and software, meat industry publications and information
President: Mark Lefens
Chairman: Jim Franklin
Vice President of Information Systems: Annica Burns
Director of Marketing: Laurie Hachmeister
Account Executive: Dave Lurie
Production Manager: Shirleen Kajiwara
Estimated Sales: $5 - 10 Million
Number Employees: 20-49

20279 **Carnegie Manufacturing Company**
20 Montesano Road
Fairfield, NJ 07004-3310 973-575-3449
Fax: 973-575-2575
Aluminum molds
President: Barbara Carnegie
Estimated Sales: $1-2.5 Million
Number Employees: 5-9

20280 **Carnegie Textile Company**
31100 Solon Rd Ste D
Solon, OH 44139 440-542-1180
Fax: 440-542-1188 800-633-4136
info@carnegietextile.com
www.carnegietextile.com
Terry cloth wipes, bar mops, tablecloths, napkins and uniforms
President: Al Kay
General Manager: Carren Kay
Estimated Sales: $10-20 Million
Number Employees: 10-19
Square Footage: 34000
Parent Co: Surgical Manufacturing Company
Type of Packaging: Bulk

20281 **Carnes Company**
448 South Main Street
Verona, WI 53593 608-845-6411
Fax: 608-845-6504 carnes@carnes.com
www.carnes.com
Carnes Company is a manufacturer of commercial HVAC equipment. Its product line offering includes registers, grilles, diffusers. terminal units, ventilation equipment, louvers, penthouses, fire and smoke dampers, steam humidifiers andenergy recovering ventilators. Carnes has been a supplier of HVAC equipment since 1939.
Marketing Manager: David Olsen
Estimated Sales: $50-100 Million
Number Employees: 300
Square Footage: 93000

20282 **Carolina Container Company**
PO Box 2166
High Point, NC 27261-2166 336-883-7146
Fax: 336-883-7576 800-627-0825
www.carolinacontainer.com
Corrugated containers
President: I Paul Ingle Jr
CEO: Ron Sessions
General Sales Manager: David Mitchell
Estimated Sales: $20 - 50 Million
Number Employees: 100-249

20283 **Carolina Cracker**
P.O.Box 374
Garner, NC 27529-0374 919-779-6899
Fax: 919-779-6899 www.carolinacracker.net
Nut crackers for soft shell nuts, shelled pecans in bulk
President: Dot Woodruff
CEO: Harold Woodruff
Estimated Sales: $1-2.5 Million
Number Employees: 10-19
Number of Brands: 3
Square Footage: 4
Type of Packaging: Bulk
Brands:
The Carolina Cracker

20284 **Carolina Glove**
116 MCLIN Creek Rd
PO Box 999
Conover, NC 28613 828-464-1132
Fax: 828-485-2416 800-335-1918
webmaster@carolinaglovecompany.com
www.carolinaglove.com
Gloves including plastic, rubber, leather, cotton and knit
President: Robert Abernethy
National Sales Director: Marshall Fisher
Manager: Fred Abernethy
Estimated Sales: $5 - 10 Million
Number Employees: 20-49
Brands:
Eagle
Golden Hawk
Master Rigger
Patriot
Tiger Tuff
Tuff-Dot
Warm Grip

20285 **Carolina Knife**
224 Mulvaney St
Asheville, NC 28803 828-253-6796
Fax: 828-258-0693 800-520-5030
info@cknife.com www.cknife.com
Manufacturer and exporter of machine knives
President: Walter Ashbrook
Sales Manager: Paul Turner
Technical Rep.: Bart Loudermilk
Estimated Sales: $2.5-5 Million
Number Employees: 20-49
Square Footage: 6000
Parent Co: Hamilton Industrial Knife & Machine

20286 **Carolina Mop Company**
PO Box 5072
819 Whitehall Road
Anderson, SC 29623 864-225-8351
Fax: 864-225-1917 800-845-9725
info@carolinamop.com www.carolinamop.com
Manufacturer, importer and exporter of dust mops, wet mops, brooms and broom handles
President: Pam Ritter
Estimated Sales: $5 - 10 Million
Number Employees: 10-19
Square Footage: 100000
Brands:
Camoco
Cotton Queen

20287 **Carometec**
8548 Kapp Dr
Peosta, IA 52068 563-582-4230
Fax: 563-582-4130 js@carometec.com
www.carometecusa.com
Food equipment for carcass grading and quality control
President: Henrrick Anderson
Sales: Jeb Supple
Estimated Sales: Under $500,000
Number Employees: 3
Parent Co: Carometec

20288 **Caron Products & Services**
27640 State Route 7
Marietta, OH 45750 740-373-6809
Fax: 740-374-3760 800-648-3042
sales@caronproducts.com
www.caronproducts.com
Test chambers, temperature/humidity,photostability chambers,and reach in CO_
Manager: Terry St Peter
CEO: Steve Keiser
R&D: David Figel
Estimated Sales: Below $5 Million
Number Employees: 10-19
Square Footage: 10000

20289 **Carotek**
P.O.Box 1395
Matthews, NC 28106 704-847-4406
Fax: 704-847-5101 terri.smedley@carotek.com
www.carotek.com
Positive displacement pumps including internal and external rotary gear, magnetic drive and rotary lobe. air-operated double diaphragm pumps and abrasives, solids, corrosives and aggressive materials
President: Daryl Bell
Sales Engineer: Mike Mercredy
Sales and Marketing Assistance: Terri Smedley
Quality Control: Mack A Stewart
Manager: Stephen Bell
Estimated Sales: $20 - 50 Million
Number Employees: 100-249

20290 **Carpenter Advanced Ceramics**
13395 New Airport Rd
Auburn, CA 95602 530-823-3401
Fax: 530-888-1087 800-288-8730
cacsales@cartech.com www.cartech.com
President: James West
Quality Control: Marc Fichou
Financial Controller: Sonia Souron
Estimated Sales: $20 - 30 Million
Number Employees: 100-249

20291 **Carpenter Emergency Lighting**
2 Marlen Drive
Hamilton, NJ 08691 609-689-3090
Fax: 609-689-3091 888-884-2270
sales@carpenterlighting.com
www.carpenterlighting.com
Manufacturer and exporter of emergency lighting equipment, emergency exit, portable and rechargeable lights
President: Avinash Diwan
National Sales Manager: Philip Salvatore

20292 **Carpenter-Hayes Paper Box Company**
8 Walnut Avenue
East Hampton, CT 06424-1222 203-267-4436
Fax: 203-425-1769
Folding paper cartons
President: Bill Salinsky
CFO: Bill Salinsky
R&D: Bill Salinsky
Quality Control: Bill Salinsky
Estimated Sales: $5 - 10 Million
Number Employees: 15

20293 **Carpet City Paper Box Company**
36 Finlay Street
Amsterdam, NY 12010 518-842-5430
Paper set-up boxes for ravioli and nonperishable food products
Owner: John Bogdan
Estimated Sales: Less than $500,000
Number Employees: 4
Square Footage: 4200

20294 **Carpigiani Corporation of America**
3760 Industrial Drive
Winston Salem, NC 27105 336-661-9893
Fax: 336-661-9895 800-648-4389
info@carpigiani-usa.com
www.carpigiani-usa.com
Manufacturer, importer and exporter of self serve frozen dessert and drink machines, whip cream dispensers and batch ice cream freezers
VP: Randy Karns
General Manager: Jim Hall
Sales Manager: Jim Marmion
Operations Manager: Bill Van Hine
National Sales Manager: Jerry Hoefer
Estimated Sales: $5-10 Million
Number Employees: 10-19
Square Footage: 80000
Parent Co: Carpigiani Viaemilia
Type of Packaging: Food Service
Other Locations:
Coldelite Corp. of America
Bologna
Brands:
Coldelite
Colore
Kwik Whipper

20295 **Carrageenan Company**
200 E 61st St Apt 27a
New York, NY 10065-8580
Fax: 714-850-9865
sales@carrageenancompany.com
www.carrageenanco.com
Processor, importer and exporter of gum and hydrocolloide blends; also, custom blending of carrageenan products for dairy, meat and poultry
President: Vincent Zaragoza
Executive Director: Javier Zaragoza
Marketing Director: Yolanda Zaragoza
Sales Director: Carla Gonzales
Public Relations: Cristina Gonzales
Managing Director: Vincente Zaragoza
Estimated Sales: Below $5 Million
Number Employees: 5-9
Type of Packaging: Private Label
Brands:
Carrabind
Carrafat
Carralite
Carralizer
Carraloc
Carravis

20296 **Carriage Works**
1877 Mallard Ln
Klamath Falls, OR 97601-5522 541-882-0700
Fax: 541-882-9661 info@carriageworks.com
www.carriageworks.com
Manufacturer, importer and exporter of food service and retail merchandising carts, in-line concepts, kiosks and machines including espresso, hot dog, ice cream and beverage
President: Barbara Evensizer
Estimated Sales: $5 - 10 Million
Number Employees: 20-49

20297 **Carrier Commercial Refrigeration**
Ste 301
3 Farm Glen Blvd
Farmington, CT 06032-1981 704-525-2644
Fax: 630-585-9450 www.carrier.com
Manufacturer and exporter of refrigerating units for delivery trucks, marine containers and commercial refrigeration equipment
Chairman: Jeff Rhodenbaugh
President: Rick Sanfrey
Senior VP Operations: Ted Amyuni
Estimated Sales: $8 Billion
Number Employees: 20-49
Parent Co: Carrier Corporation

20298 **Carrier Corporation**
1 Carrier Place
Farmington, CT 06034-4015 860-674-3000
Fax: 860-674-3139 800-227-7437
www.carrier.com
Manufacturer and exporter of refrigerating units for delivery trucks, marine containers and commercial refrigeration equipment
Chairman: Jeff Rhodenbaugh
Estimated Sales: $7.2 Billion
Number Employees: 44500

20299 **Carrier Rental Systems**
9655 Industrial Dr
Bridgeview, IL 60455-2323 847-847-2220
Fax: 847-847-7330 800-586-8336
info@nutemp.com www.nutemp.com
Refrigeration, chiller sales, rentals and investment recovery
Manager: Laurie Werner
Marketing Manager: David Brockemeyer
Estimated Sales: $5 -10 Million
Number Employees: 50-99

20300 **Carrier Transicold**
1 Carrier Place
Farmington, CT 06034-4015
800-227-7437
www.carrier.com
Manufacturer and exporter of refrigerating units for delivery trucks, marine containers and commercial refrigeration equipment
President: Geraud Darnis
Vp Marketing And Communications: Rajan Goel
Estimated Sales: $11.4 Billion
Number Employees: 45,000
Parent Co: United Technologies Corporation

20301 **Carrier Transicold**
700 Olympic Dr
Athens, GA 30601 706-546-6469
Fax: 706-546-5207
carrier.transicold@carrier.utc.com
www.transicold.carrier.com

Manufactures refridgerated units for trucks and trailers
President Carrier Transicold: Richard Laubenstein
Manager: Jim Ferguson
Plant Manager: Troy Rector
Estimated Sales: $100-500 Million
Number Employees: 500-999
Parent Co: Carrier Corporation

20302 **(HQ)Carrier Vibrating Equipment**
P.O.Box 37070
Louisville, KY 40233 502-969-3171
Fax: 502-969-3172 cve@carriervibrating.com
www.carriervibrating.com
Manufacturer and exporter of custom designed screening conveyor systems and feeders, bin dischargers, stainless steel dairy dryers, coolers and bulk handling vibrating equipment
CEO: Brian M Trudel
Sales Manager: Steve Baker
Estimated Sales: $30 Million
Number Employees: 100-249
Square Footage: 185000
Other Locations:
Carrier Europe
Nivelles, Belgium

20303 **Carroll Chair Company**
W6636 L B White Rd
Onalaska, WI 54650 608-779-7505
Fax: 608-779-7508 800-331-4707
info@carrollchair.com www.carrollchair.com
Bar, restaurant and lounge seating
Member of the Board: Anthony Wilson
General Manager: Keith Martin
Estimated Sales: $10 - 20 Million
Number Employees: 100-249
Parent Co: Hospitality International
Brands:
Carroll Chair

20304 **Carroll Company**
2900 W Kingsley Rd
Garland, TX 75041 972-278-1304
Fax: 972-840-0678 800-527-5722
info@carrollco.com www.carrollco.com
Manufacturer and exporter of soap, cleaners, disinfectants and germicides
President: Kyle Ogden
VP Technical: Ron Cramer
VP Sales: Craig Neely
Estimated Sales: $20-50 Million
Number Employees: 100-249
Square Footage: 220000

20305 **Carroll Manufacturing International**
23 Vreeland Rd
Florham Park, NJ 07932-1510 973-966-6000
Fax: 973-966-0315 800-444-9696
info@carrollmi.com www.carrollmi.com
Manufacturer and exporter of exhaust systems, fire protection equipment, heat reclaim units and utility distribution systems
Chairman of the Board: Barry J Carroll
VP Sales: Richard Moon
General Manager: Byron Read
Estimated Sales: $10 - 15 Million
Number Employees: 10-19
Square Footage: 75000
Parent Co: Carroll International Corporation
Brands:
Aquafire
Carroll
Environair
Hmr Merchandiser
Transporter
Udisco

20306 **Carroll Packaging**
PO Box 780
Dearborn, MI 48121-0780 313-584-0400
Fax: 313-584-2022
rmorelli@carrollpackaging.com
www.carrollpackaging.com
Plastic packaging equipment
President: Hazen Carroll
Estimated Sales: $10 - 20 Million
Number Employees: 50-99

20307 **Carroll Products**
2900 West Kingsley Road
Garland, TX 75041 586-254-6300
Fax: 586-254-9458 800-527-5722
www.carrollco.com
Plastic bags and rollstock; also, printing services available
President: Gene Stys
Sales Manager: Gary Denenak
Estimated Sales: $2.5-5 Million
Number Employees: 20-49

20308 **Carron Net Company**
1623 17th St
PO Box 177
Two Rivers, WI 54241 920-793-2217
Fax: 920-793-2122 800-558-7768
sales@carronnet.com www.carronnet.com
Manufacturer and exporter of hardware and netting for racks and conveyors
President: William Kiel Jr
VP: Donald Schweiger
Estimated Sales: $5-10 Million
Number Employees: 20-49
Type of Packaging: Bulk

20309 **Carrs Ice Cream & Storage**
1501 State St
Bridgeport, CT 06605-2010 203-384-0820
Fax: 203-336-3235
General Manager: Michael Carraro
Estimated Sales: $3 - 5 Million
Number Employees: 5-9

20310 **Carry All Canvas Bag Company**
1983 Coney Island Ave
Brooklyn, NY 11223 718-375-4230
Fax: 718-375-5154 888-425-5224
sales@carryallbag.com www.carryallbag.com
Advertising specialties, bags and aprons; importer of tote bags; logo imprinting services available
Owner: Mitchel Kraut
Estimated Sales: $2.5-5 Million
Number Employees: 5-9

20311 **Carson Industries**
801 Corporate Center Dr
Pomona, CA 91768 909-592-6272
Fax: 909-592-7971 800-735-5566
info@carsonind.com www.carsonind.com
Plastic bulk containers and pallets
President: Richard Gardner
CEO: Richard Gordinier
Sales Coordinator: Roscoe Bes
Estimated Sales: $20-50 Million
Number Employees: 20-49
Brands:
Titan I
Titan Ii

20312 **Carson Manufacturing Company**
PO Box 750338
Petaluma, CA 94975-0338 707-778-3141
Fax: 707-778-8691 800-423-2380
sales@carsonmanufacturing.com
www.carsonmfg.com
Manufacturer and exporter of vinyl aprons
President: Curtis Lang
Number Employees: 10-19
Type of Packaging: Private Label, Bulk

20313 **Cart Mart**
PO Box 686
Itasca, IL 60143-0686 630-628-6655
Fax: 630-628-6855 800-628-3183
Material handling products including pallet rack, carts and used equipment
Estimated Sales: $1-2.5 000,000
Number Employees: 1-4

20314 **Carter Day International, Inc.**
500 73rd Ave NE
Minneapolis, MN 55432-3271 763-571-1000
Fax: 763-571-3012 info@carterday.com
www.carterday.com
Manufacturer and exporter of grain cleaning and sizing equipment
President: Paul Ernst
Director International Agribusiness: Matthew Ernst
Estimated Sales: $10 - 20 Million
Number Employees: 50-99

20315 **Carter Products Company**
2871 Northridge Dr NW
Grand Rapids, MI 49544 616-647-3380
Fax: 616-647-3387 888-622-7837
sales@carterproducts.com
www.carterproducts.com
Manufacturer and exporter of guide line and inspection lights; also, bandsaw guides, wheels and tires
President: Peter Perez
VP: Terry Camp
Marketing Director: Kip Walworth
Operations Manager: Jeff Folkert
Purchasing Manager: Char Mooney
Estimated Sales: $3 - 5 Million
Number Employees: 10-19
Square Footage: 15000
Brands:
Carter
Flip-Pod
Guidall
Inspecto-Light
Laser
Laser Diode
Micro-Precision

20316 **Carter-Hoffman Corp LLC**
1551 McCormick Blvd
Mundelein, IL 60060 847-362-5500
Fax: 847-367-8981 800-323-9793
sales@carter-hoffmann.com
www.carter-hoffmann.com
Manufacturer and exporter of stainless steel food carts including refrigerator, banquet and heated holding/transport
President: Bob Fortmann
CFO: Jim Fagan
CEO: Robert Fortman
Research & Development: Jim Minard
Marketing Director: Kim Aaron
Sales Director: Mark Anderson
Production Manager: John Bartoski
Purchasing Manager: Vince Unger
Estimated Sales: $20-25 Million
Number Employees: 100-249
Number of Products: 300+
Brands:
Carter-Hoffmann

20317 **Carteret Coding**
1431 Raritan Rd
Clark, NJ 07066 732-574-0900
Fax: 732-574-9212 ccisales@carteretcoding.com
www.carteretcoding.com
Date and lot coding systems
Owner: Charles Vill
Number Employees: 10-19

20318 **Carthage Cup Company**
115 Kodak Blvd
Longview, TX 75602 903-238-9833
Plastic cups, plates, bowls, deli containers and portion cups; also, hotel/motel wrapped cups with printing capability available
President: C Mark Abernathy
VP Consumer Sales: William Tostlebe
VP Institutional Sales: Brent Abernathy
Number Employees: 1 to 4
Parent Co: John Waddington
Brands:
Carthage
Cool Cups
Holiday

20319 **Carton Closing Company**
P.O.Box 629
Butler, PA 16003-0629 724-287-7759
Fax: 724-287-2811 www.ismsys.com
Industrial staples and staplers for corrugated carton closing
Marketing Manager: Mary Lawler
Sales Manager: Robert McHugh
Purchasing Manager: Paul Lucas
Estimated Sales: $1 - 5 Million
Number Employees: 100-249

20320 **Carton Service**
PO Box 702
Shelby, OH 44875 419-342-5010
Fax: 419-342-4804 800-533-7744
www.cartonservice.com

Boxes and cartons; contract packaging services available
President: Bob Lederer
VP: Mike Robinette
Marketing/Sales: Scott Garverick
Estimated Sales: $20-50 Million
Number Employees: 250-499

20321 Cartonplast
609 Burton Blvd
De Forest, WI 53532-1289 608-846-2516
Fax: 608-849-4496 info@cartonplast.com
www.cartonplast.com
Plastic tier sheets, plastic layer pads, layer pad pool system
Estimated Sales: less than $500,000
Number Employees: 1-4

20322 Cartpac
9377 Grand Ave
Franklin Park, IL 60131 630-629-9900
Fax: 630-629-6575 sales@graingroup.com
www.fraingroup.com
Rebuilt cartoner and case filling equipment; repair services available
Manager: Mitch Budic
CEO: Rich Frain
CFO: Chris Hostert
Senior Engineer: Thomas Suchan
Sales Manager: Steve Norman
HR Director: Olga Sivek
General Manager: Kenneth Campbell
Manager Engineer: Len Thomsen
Estimated Sales: Below $5 Million
Number Employees: 10-19
Square Footage: 63000
Parent Co: Frain Industries

20323 Carts Food Equipment Corporation
113 8th St
Brooklyn, NY 11215-3115 718-788-5540
Fax: 718-788-4962 www.cartsfoodeqp.com
Sinks, reach-in and underbar refrigerators and marble top pizza and stainless steel work tables; exporter of mobile food vending carts
President: Sol Rosenberg
CFO: Florence Rosenberg
VP: Dave Nadler
Estimated Sales: $2.5-5 Million
Number Employees: 20-49
Square Footage: 120000

20324 Carts of Colorado
5420 S Quebec St
Suite 204
Greenwood Vlg, CO 80111-1902 303-329-0101
Fax: 303-329-6577 800-227-8634
carts@cartsofcolorado.com
www.cartsofcolorado.com
Manufacturer and exporter of mobile food carts, kiosks, and modular systems
President & CEO: Daniel Gallery
Accountant: Bill Sheakin
Research & Development: Craig Green
Quality Control Manager: Jeff Clonk
Sales Director: John Gallery
Operations Manager: Jim Covey
Purchasing Manager: Deborah Gallery
Estimated Sales: $500,000 - $1 Million
Number Employees: 10-19
Number of Brands: 4
Number of Products: 10
Square Footage: 240000
Brands:
Carts of Colorado
Mobile Merchandising Systems
Peckam Carts
Power Carts

20325 Casa Herrara
2655 Pine St
Pomona, CA 91767-2115 909-392-3930
Fax: 909-392-0231 800-624-3916
alfredoj@casaherrera.com www.casaherrera.com
Food processing machines for commercial and industrial food makers
President: Alfred Herrera
Manager: Christopher Herrera
Mngr.: Susana Herrera
Estimated Sales: $20-50 Million
Number Employees: 100-249

20326 Casa Herrera
2655 North Pine Street
Pomona, CA 91767-2115
Fax: 909-392-0231 800-624-3916
rudyh@casaherrera.com www.casaherrera.com
Manufacturer and exporter of tortilla and corn chip machinery including cookers, millers, sheeters, bakers, coolers, dividers, pressers, seasoners, etc
President: Alfred Herrera
CEO: Ron Meade
VP Sales: Christopher Herrera
Manager: Susana Herrera
Estimated Sales: $20-50 Million
Number Employees: 100-249
Square Footage: 100000

20327 Casabar
42 Court St
Morristown, NJ 07960-5199 973-605-8995
Fax: 973-401-1519 877-745-8700
sales@lorenz-son.com www.instantdip.com
Instant Dip silver cleaner and polishing cloths
President: Mel Appelbaum
Administrative Assistant: Irene Carpio
General Manager: Mel Sales
Estimated Sales: Less than $500,000
Number Employees: 1-4
Brands:
Instant Dip

20328 Cascade Earth Sciences
7150 Supra Dr SW
Albany, OR 97321 541-967-7616
Fax: 541-967-7619 albany@cascade-earth.com
www.cascade-earth.com
President: Perry Rahe
CEO: Steel Maloney
Estimated Sales: G
Number Employees: 5,000-9,999

20329 Cascade Signs & Neon
P.O.Box 7268
Salem, OR 97303-0054 503-378-0012
Fax: 503-362-8154 info@cascade-signs.com
www.cascade-signs.com
Electric neon signs
Owner: Jay Kinnee
Estimated Sales: $500,000-$1 Million
Number Employees: 5-9

20330 Cascade Wood Components
15 Herman Creek Road
Cascade Locks, OR 97014 541-374-8413
Fax: 541-374-9054
Wooden pallets
President: Gary Hegewald
Manager: Gene Shultz
Sales Manager: Tim Todd
Office Manager: Gene Hill
Estimated Sales: $10-20 Million
Number Employees: 10 to 19

20331 Case Lowe & Hart
2484 Washington Blvd
Suite 510
Ogden, UT 84401-2346 801-399-5821
Fax: 801-399-0728 kevinl@clhae.com
www.clhae.com
President: Kevin Lewis
Estimated Sales: $1 - 3 Million

20332 Case Manufacturing Company
14304 29th Rd
Flushing, NY 11354-2312 914-965-5100
Fax: 914-965-2362 casestaty@aol.com
Tea and coffee industry coffee canisters
President: Jerome Sudnow
Estimated Sales: $1 - 5 000,000
Number Employees: 10

20333 Caselites
PO Box 161000
Hialeah, FL 33016-0017 305-819-7766
Fax: 305-819-8198 www.caselites.com
Lighting for steam tables, and refrigerated/nonrefrigerated cases. Also special lighting for food equipment
President: Barry Spade
R & D: Fred Morgan
Estimated Sales: $50-100 Million
Number Employees: 10
Square Footage: 10000

20334 Casella Lighting Company
10183 Croydon Way
Suite C
Sacramento, CA 95827 888-252-7874
Fax: 888-489-9543 Info@CasellaLighting.com
www.casellalighting.com/
Manufacturer and exporter of portable floor and table lamps, wall scones, chandeliers and solid brass fixtures
President: Georgine Casella
Buyer: Margig Yaka
Office Manager: Ronda Simi
Estimated Sales: $5-10 Million
Number Employees: 20-49
Square Footage: 120000
Type of Packaging: Food Service
Brands:
Casella
Grag Studios

20335 Cash Caddy
PO Box 13770
Palm Desert, CA 92255-3770 760-772-8884
Fax: 760-772-8885 888-522-2221
cashcaddy@aol.com www.cashcaddy.com
Change, dinner check and tip trays
Sales Manager: Eddie Robinson
General Manager: Judy Wilkins
Number Employees: 30
Square Footage: 12000
Parent Co: Plastic By Design
Brands:
Cash Caddy
Dinner Check

20336 Cashco
607 W 15th St
Ellsworth, KS 67439 785-472-4461
Fax: 785-472-3539 sales@cashco.com
www.cashco.com
Regulators, control valves and sanitary biotechnological products for the food and pharmaceutical industry
President: Phillip Rogers
National Sales Manager: Robert Schroeder
Estimated Sales: $10-20 Million
Number Employees: 100-249

20337 Cass Saw & ToolSharpening
3916 N Cass Ave
Westmont, IL 60559-1103 630-968-1617
Fax: 630-968-7767
Saw and knife sharpeners, carbide retipping and chain and circular saws
Owner: Sam Robertson
Manager: Joseph Robertson
Estimated Sales: Less than $500,000
Number Employees: 1 to 4

20338 Cassel Box & Lumber Company
1100 Falls Rd
Grafton, WI 53024 262-377-4420
Fax: 262-377-4421 www.casselboxlumber.com
Wooden boxes, crates, skids and pallets
President: John Cassel
Manager: John Cassel
Estimated Sales: $500,000-$1 Million
Number Employees: 10-19

20339 Casso-Solar Corporation
230 Route 202
P.O. Box 163
Pomona, NY 10970 845-354-2500
Fax: 845-362-1856 800-988-4455
sales@cassosolar.com www.cassosolar.com
Manufacturer and exporter of dryers, ovens, and electric and gas conveyor systems
President: Doug Canfield
VP Finance: Harry Lyons
Quality Control Manager: Alex Mankiewicz
VP Sales/Marketing: Frank Lu
Plant Manager: Jan Michalski
Purchasing Manager: John Moles
Estimated Sales: $10 Million
Number Employees: 20-49
Number of Products: 100
Square Footage: 25000
Brands:
Solar Infrared Heater

20340 Cast Film Technology
7455 E Adamo Drive
Tampa, FL 33619-3433 847-487-8899
Fax: 847-487-7288 sales@cast-film.com
www.cast-film.com
Edible plastic films, customized films made with food ingredients for packaging and barrier uses
President: James Rossman
Vice President: Scott Schaneville
Research & Development: Caroline Decker
Estimated Sales: $8 Million
Number Employees: 50
Number of Products: 15
Square Footage: 80000

20341 Cast Nylons
4300 Hamann Pkwy
Willoughby, OH 44094 440-269-2300
Fax: 440-269-2323 800-543-3619
cnlmail@castnylon.com www.castnylon.com
Manufacuturer of cast nylon materials
President: Jack Thorp
CFO: Dan Welsh
VP: Steve Tischler
Quality Control: Tom Schaffer
Marketing Head: Shelly Pike
Sales: Traci Deiner
Estimated Sales: $10-20 000,000
Number Employees: 50-99
Type of Packaging: Bulk

20342 Castell Interlocks
150 N Michigan Avenue
Sutie 800
Chicago, IL 60601 312-360-1516
Fax: 312-268-5174 ussales@castell.com
www.castell.com
Dock locks
Manager: Bill Roth
Number Employees: 10-19

20343 Castella Imports
60 Davids Dr
Hauppauge, NY 11788 631-231-5500
Fax: 631-777-1022 866-227-8355
info@castellaimports.com
www.castellaimports.com
Castella Imports, Inc. is one of the country's largest importer, manufacturer and distributor of specailty foods; bringing gourmet flavor to your table from around the world. From cheeses and spices to olives and olive oils, CastellaImports offers only the best in quality, service and price. Through hard work and dedication, Castella is continually adding to and improving to this extensive line of quality products.
President: Andrew Benzoni
Sales Director: A. Laurino
Production Director: Bruce Leibowitz
Estimated Sales: $100+ Million
Number Employees: 100-249
Square Footage: 66000

20344 Castino Restaurant Equipment & Supply
50 Utility Ct
Rohnert Park, CA 94928 707-585-3566
Fax: 707-585-7306 800-238-0404
sales@castinocom.com
www.castinosolutions.com
Wholesaler/distributor of restaurant equipment, kitchen equipment, furniture, refrigeration hood systems, chinaware, glassware, pots, pans, etc
President/CEO: David Castino
Purchasing Manager: Ron Nasuti
Estimated Sales: $8 Million
Number Employees: 20-49
Square Footage: 30000
Parent Co: Castino Refrigeration Company

20345 Castle Bag Company
115 Valley Road
Wilmington, DE 19804 302-656-1001
Fax: 302-656-2830 castlebag@juno.com
www.castlebagcompany.com
Polyethylene bags
President/Owner: Harry B Russell
VP/Secretary: Christine Ditzler
Estimated Sales: $750 Million
Number Employees: 2
Square Footage: 6000
Type of Packaging: Consumer, Food Service, Private Label, Bulk
Brands:
Castle Bag

20346 Castleberry
1621 15th St
Augusta, GA 30901-3929 706-733-7765
Fax: 706-733-5079 castleby@casteberrys.com
www.castleberrys.com
Established co-pack and private label producer
Sales: Roy Bryant
Estimated Sales: $100 - 150 Million
Number Employees: 500-999
Type of Packaging: Private Label
Brands:
Castleberry
Snow's

20347 Castrol Industrial North America
201 N Webster St
White Cloud, MI 49349 231-689-0002
Fax: 231-689-0372 800-582-3266
lubeconcc@castrol.com www.lubecon.com
Lubrication equipment, conveyor cleaners, lubricants, machinery lubrication
BDM: Frank Langley
BDM: Ted Edwards
BDM: Jerry Robinson
Production Manager: Kathy Crickmore
Purchasing Manager: Chris Warren
Estimated Sales: $10-20 Million
Number Employees: 20-49
Square Footage: 10000

20348 Catalina Cylinders
7300 Anaconda Ave
Garden Grove, CA 92841 714-890-0999
Fax: 714-890-1744 sales@catalinacylinders.com
www.catalinacylinders.com
Empty aluminum high pressure CO2 cylinders aluminum cylinders to the compressed gas industry
President: Tom Newell
Quality Control: Ward Dekker
Sales Director: Michael Krupsky
Estimated Sales: $10-20 000,000
Number Employees: 100-249

20349 Catalyst International
8989 N Deerwood Dr
Milwaukee, WI 53223 414-362-6800
Fax: 414-362-6794 800-236-4600
info@catalystinternational.com
www.catalystinternational.com
Manufacturer and exporter of computer software for warehouse management
President: Bruce Cameron
CFO: David Jacobson
Quality Control: Alan Kreuser
Marketing Coordinator: Wendy Erwin
Number Employees: 70
Type of Packaging: Bulk

20350 Catalytic Products International
980 Ensell Rd
Hawthorn Wds, IL 60047 847-438-0334
Fax: 847-438-0944 info@cpilink.com
www.cpilink.com
Air pollution control equipment, baking oven emission control, catalytic and thermal oxidizers
President: Dennis Lincoln
Marketing Manager: Jan Carlson
Estimated Sales: $1 - 2.5 000,000
Number Employees: 10-19

20351 CaterMate
61 Brown Road
Ithaca, NY 14850-1247 800-486-2283
Fax: 607-257-1902 catermate@catermate.com
www.catermate.com
Software for catering and event management
President: John Alexander
VP: Tim Tighe
Marketing: Susie Stephnson
Sales Manager: Ron Prorus
Number Employees: 10-19
Parent Co: The CBORD Group, Inc.
Type of Packaging: Food Service
Brands:
Eventmaster

20352 Cates Mechanical Corporation
3901 Corporation Cir
Charlotte, NC 28216 704-394-6314
Fax: 704-392-8932
ernest.cates@catesmechanical.com
www.catesmechanical.com
Packaging machinery
President: Ernest W Cates
Estimated Sales: Below $5 000,000
Number Employees: 10-19

20353 Catskill Craftsmen
15 W End Ave
Stamford, NY 12167 607-652-7321
Fax: 607-652-7293 info@catskillcraftsmen.com
www.catskillcraftsmen.com
Manufacturer and exporter of butcher block tables, cutting boards, solid maple housewares and kitchen furniture and work counters
President: Duncan Axtel
Vice President: Kenneth Smith
Quality Control: John Locastro
VP Sales: Dick Carpenter
Purchasing Manager: Hank Cioccari
Estimated Sales: $5 - 10 Million
Number Employees: 50-99
Number of Products: 17
Square Footage: 104000
Type of Packaging: Consumer, Food Service, Private Label

20354 Cattron Group International
25 W Shenango St
Sharpsville, PA 16150-1123 724-962-1629
Fax: 724-962-4310 sales@cattrongroup.com
www.cattrongroup.com
Cattron Group International, including the Cattron, Remtron, Theimeg and Vectran brands, provides industrial radio remote control systems for overhead cranes, hoists, conveyors, yard locomotives, overhead doors, boom trucks, concretepumps or anywhere the operator of equipment can be moved to a safer, more efficient location.
President/CEO: John Paul
CFO: Mike Pearson
Marketing/Public Relations: Amanda Bailey
Sales: Jeremy Pearson
Production: Rich Patterson
Estimated Sales: $10-20 Million
Number Employees: 100-249
Number of Brands: 6
Parent Co: Cattron Group
Other Locations:
Cattron Group-Remtron
Escondido CA
Brands:
Cattron
Remtron
Theimeg
Vectran

20355 Catty Corporation
6111 White Oaks Rd
Harvard, IL 60033 815-943-2288
Fax: 815-943-4473 plawther@cattycorp.com
www.cattycorp.com
Manufacturer and exporter of flexible packaging including foil, foil/paper, poly structures, margarine and candy wraps and lidding
President: Bruce Scott
CFO: Bill Schmiederer
Marketing and Sales Coordinator: Kristen Dahm
Sales Manager: Sheri Morelli
Operations Manager: Chuck DiPietro
Vice President, Engineering: Ron Klint
Number Employees: 42
Square Footage: 135000

20356 Cavanna USA
2150 Northmont Parkway
Suite A
Duluth, GA 30096 770-688-1501
Fax: 973-383-0741
cavanna.usa@cavannagroup.com
www.cavanna.com
Wholesaler/distributor of horizontal flow wrapping machinery
President: William Stoebling
Estimated Sales: Below $5 Million
Number Employees: 6

20357 (HQ)Cavert Wire Company
620 Forum Pkwy
Rural Hall, NC 27045 336-969-2601
Fax: 336-969-2621 800-245-4042
cspittler@cavertwire.com www.cavertwire.com
Single loop wire bale ties used in supermarkets for waste corrugated boxes
CEO and President: William Spittler
CFO: Harry Sages
VP Sales: Ben Shifler

Estimated Sales: $20 - 50 Million
Number Employees: 20-49
Square Footage: 200000
Other Locations:
Cavert Wire Co.
Atlanta GA

20358 Cawley
1544 North Eighth Street
PO Box 2110
Manitowoc, WI 54221-2110 920-686-7000
Fax: 920-686-7080 800-822-9539
info@cawleyco.com www.cawleyco.com
Manufacturer and exporter of engravable badges, plates, plaques and awards; also, electronic personalization systems for do-it-yourself engraving
President/CEO: Jim Peterson
CFO: Jerry Harris
R & D: Jim Peterson
Quality Control: Paul Mueller
Marketing Director: Molly Peterson
Public Relations: Molly Peterson
Operations/Productions Manager: Paul Mueller
Plant Manager: Diane Fogltanz
Estimated Sales: Below $5 Million
Number Employees: 90
Square Footage: 112000
Parent Co: Contemporary
Brands:
Champ Awards
Chrom-A-Grav
Engravable Gifts

20359 Cayne Industrial Sales Corporation
429 Bruckner Blvd.
Bronx, NY 10455-5007 718-993-5800
Manufacturer and exporter of industrial racks, handling equipment and food lockers including custom plastic.
President: Steven Cayne
Manager: Hank Cayne
Estimated Sales: $1-2.5 Million
Number Employees: 1 to 4
Square Footage: 10000
Brands:
Uni-Steel Lockers

20360 Cbord
61 Brown Rd
Ithaca, NY 14850-1247 607-257-2410
Fax: 607-257-1902 800-982-4643
sales@cbord.com www.cbord.com
Manufacturer and exporter of computer software that generates LTC food service, tickets, nourishment labels, production tallies, recipes, inventory, nutritional analysis, etc
President: Max Steinhardt
Vice President of Client Support and Edu: Nancy Sullivan
Vice President of Human Resources: Lisa Patz
Executive Vice President: Bruce Lane
Director of Development, Odyssey Systems: Shane Boyer
VP, Marketing: Cindy McCall
VP, Sales: Read Winkelman
Director of Contract Administration: Chris Curkendall
Senior Director, Service Operations: Jodi Denman
Estimated Sales: Below $5 Million
Number Employees: 250-499
Parent Co: GeriMenu
Brands:
Gerimenu

20361 Cecor
102 Lincoln St
Verona, WI 53593 608-845-6771
Fax: 608-845-6792 800-356-9042
cecor@cecor.net www.cecor.net
Waste handling equipment including dumping containers, sump cleaners and filter units for separation of solids from liquids
President: Dennis Johnson
Production Manager: Paul Elmer
Estimated Sales: $2.5-5 Million
Number Employees: 5-9
Brands:
Cecor

20362 Cedar Box Company
2012 Cedar Ave S
Minneapolis, MN 55404 612-332-4287
Fax: 612-332-8619 sales@cedarboxcompany.com
www.cedarboxcompany.com
Corrugated and wooden boxes, wooden pallets skids, specialty wood bases, and specialty wood blocking
President: Michael Mintz
Owner: Jefferey Migershone
CFO: Michael Mintz
Purchasing Agent: C Skjeveland
Estimated Sales: $5-10 Million
Number Employees: 10-19
Square Footage: 15000

20363 Ceilcote Air Pollution Control
7251 Engle Rd Ste 300
Cleveland, OH 44130 440-243-0700
Fax: 440-243-9854 800-554-8673
sales@ceilcoteapc.com www.verantis.com
Manufacturer and exporter of air pollution control equipment including fans, tower packing, blowers, mist eliminators, resin systems and ionizing wet scrubbers, turn key systems, emergency vapor spill equipment
President: Larry Hein
CEO: Lars ÿButtkus
Sales: John Tonkewiciz
Engineering Director: Nat Dickinson
Number Employees: 20-49
Square Footage: 50000
Brands:
Duracor
Iws
Tellerette

20364 Celebrity Promotions
P.O.Box 200
Remsen, IA 51050 712-786-1100
Fax: 712-786-2900 800-332-6847
sewncm@midlands.net www.sewnusa.com
Aprons and re-usable cloth shopping bags inclduing washable and poly-cotton; screen printing and embroidery available
CFO: Connie Mueller
QC and R&D: Paul Mueller
VP Marketing: Mark Mueller
Estimated Sales: Below $5 Million
Number Employees: 20-49
Square Footage: 18000
Brands:
Celebrity Stars

20365 Celite Corporation
2500 San Miguelito Rd
Lompoc, CA 93436 805-736-1221
Fax: 805-736-1222 info@worldminerals.com
www.worldminerals.com
Manufacturer and exporter of diatomite filter aids and functional fillers; also, absorbents, synthetic calcium silicate and mineral fillers
CEO: John Oskam
Estimated Sales: $5 - 10 Million
Number Employees: 250-499

20366 Cell-O-Core Company
6935 Ridge Road
PO Box 342
Sharon Center, OH 44274-0342 330-239-4370
Fax: 330-239-4403 800-239-4370
cellocore@cellocore.com www.cellocore.com
Cocktail stirrers, straws and wooden and plastic toothpicks
President: Craig Cook
Quality Control: Damm Damwillan
R&D: Mathew Willam
CFO: Creak Cook
Director: Hugh Alpeter
Director: Jill Hoffman
(Ditributor Service): Dede Beynon
Estimated Sales: $5 - 10 Million
Number Employees: 20-49
Square Footage: 30000
Brands:
Cell-O-Core

20367 Cellier Corporation
135 Robert Treat Paine Drive
Taunton, MA 02780-7266 508-655-5906
Fax: 508-653-2508
Paper coatings and kitchen lube oil
Acting General Manager: Stephen Noworski
Number Employees: 10

20368 Cello Bag Company
123 Willamette Lane
Bowling Green, KY 42101-9170 800-347-0338
Fax: 270-782-7478
Packaging materials including plastic bags and film
Number Employees: 25

20369 Cello Pack Corporation
55 Innsbruck Dr
Cheektowaga, NY 14227 716-668-3111
Fax: 716-668-3816 800-778-3111
sbrown@cello-pack.com www.cello-pack.com
Flexible packaging, process printing and film laminations; exporter of printed laminated rollstock; also, slitting and bag making available
President: Richard Gioia
VP: Sam Brown
Operations: Compton Plummer
Purchasing Director: Tim Shiley
Estimated Sales: $20 - 50 Million
Number Employees: 100-249
Square Footage: 100000
Type of Packaging: Consumer, Food Service, Private Label, Bulk

20370 Cellofoam North America
1917 Rockdale Industrial Blvd
PO Box 406
Conyers, GA 30012 770-929-3688
Fax: 770-929-3608 800-241-3634
info@cellofoam.com www.cellofoam.com
Manufacturer and exporter of expanded polystyrene foam insulation
President: Steve Gardner
VP Sales/Marketing: Cliff Hanson
Estimated Sales: $10-20 Million
Number Employees: 100-249
Brands:
Cello Foam
Permafloat
Permaspan
Poly Shield
Super Sheath

20371 Cellotape
47623 Fremont Blvd
Fremont, CA 94538 510-651-5551
Fax: 510-651-8091 800-231-0608
sales@cellotape.com www.cellotape.com
Adhesive panels and pressure sensitive labels
President/Chief Executive Officer: Peter Offerman
Vice President, Sales: Steve Suppa
Estimated Sales: $50-100 Million
Number Employees: 100-249
Square Footage: 35000

20372 Cellox Corporation
1200 Industrial St
Reedsburg, WI 53959 608-524-2316
Fax: 608-524-2362 sales@cellox.com
www.cellox.com
Manufacturer and exporter of packaging supplies and plastic molding for advertising displays
Manager: Howard Phillips
Estimated Sales: $10 - 20 Million
Number Employees: 50-99

20373 (HQ)Cellucap
4626 North Fifteenth Street
Philadelphia, PA 19140 215-324-0213
Fax: 215-324-1290 800-523-3814
sales@cellucap.com www.cellucap.com
Personal protective apparel with a full range of headwear, disposable apparel, aprons and gloves
President: Jane Wagenfeld
Executive VP: Mark Davis
VP Sales: John Twamley
VP Sales: Nancy Lozoff
Operations Manager: David Richman
Estimated Sales: $2.5-5 Million
Number Employees: 20-49
Type of Packaging: Food Service

20374 Cellulo Company
81 M St
Fresno, CA 93721-3215 559-485-2692
Fax: 559-485-4254 866-213-1131
sales@gusmerenterprises.com
www.gusmerenterprises.com
Manufacturer and exporter of filter and fiber media for food and beverages
CEO: Marla Jeffrey
VP/Technical Sales: Phil Crantz

Estimated Sales: $5 - 10 Million
Number Employees: 50-99
Square Footage: 240000
Parent Co: Gusmer Enterprises
Other Locations:
Cellulo Co.
Crawford NJ
Brands:
Cellu Flo
Cellu Pore
Cellu Stacks
Kolor Fine
Oak Mor

20375 Celplast Metallized Products Limited
67 Commander Boulevard
Unit 4
Toronto, ON M1S-3M7 416-293-4330
Fax: 416-293-9198 800-866-0059
jim@celplast.com http://cmp.celplast.com
Producer and manufacturer of metallized films for the food industry.
President/Founder: Chuck Larsen
CEO: Dante Ferrari
Vice President: Bill Hellings
Technical Representative: Dante Ferrari
Technical Sales: Jim Lush
Account Manager: Naomi Panagrapka

20376 Celsis
400 W Erie St Ste 300
Chicago, IL 60654 312-476-1200
Fax: 312-476-1201 800-222-8260
info@celsis.com www.celsis.com
ATP bioluminescence end product screening systems
CEO: Jay Le Coque
Estimated Sales: $5-10 000,000
Number Employees: 5-9

20377 Celsis Laboratory Group
600 W. Chicago Avenue
Suite 625
Chicago, IL 60654-2822 312-476-1282
Fax: 312-476-1201 800-222-8260
RDinfo@celsis.com www.celsis.com
Consultant and independent testing laboratory specializing in microbiology, analytical chemistry and toxicology testing services
Chief Executive Officer: Jay Lecoque
Manager Marketing Development: Martin Gilman, Ph.D.
Associate Director: William Gilman
Estimated Sales: $5-10 Million
Number Employees: 50-99
Square Footage: 140000
Parent Co: Celsis Laboratory Group

20378 Centennial Molding LLC
P.O.Box 1007
1900 Summit Ave
Hastings, NE 68901 402-462-2189
Fax: 402-462-2900 888-883-2189
www.centennialmolding.com
Manufacturer and exporter of plastic tanks and drums
President: G Peter Konen
CEO: G Peter Konen
Sales Manager: Jeff Armstrong
Product Manager: Val Kopke
Plant Manager: Bob Shockey
Estimated Sales: $1 Million
Number Employees: 12
Number of Brands: 1
Number of Products: 3
Square Footage: 600000
Type of Packaging: Food Service, Private Label, Bulk
Brands:
Pure-Life

20379 Centennial Transportation Industries
P.O.Box 708
Columbus, GA 31902-0708 706-323-6446
Fax: 706-327-9921 www.newcentennial.com
Manager: Bob Hudak
Estimated Sales: $10 - 20 Million
Number Employees: 50-99

20380 Centent Company
3879 S Main St
Santa Ana, CA 92707-5710 714-979-6491
Fax: 714-979-4241 info@centent.com
www.centent.com
Manufacturer and exporter of industrial controls for factory automation including computer guided multiple axis positioning systems
President and CEO: Luke Freimanis
Estimated Sales: $2.5-5 Million
Number Employees: 10-19

20381 Center for Packaging Education
358 Route 202
Somers, NY 10589-3234 914-276-0425
Fax: 914-276-0428
Consultant and educators in packaging, provide expert testimony in legal conflicts
President: Dr. Robert Goldberg
Vice President: Mark Goldsberg
Estimated Sales: Less than $500,000
Number Employees: 1-4
Square Footage: 2000

20382 Centimark Corporation
401 Technology Dr Ste 2
Canonsburg, PA 15317 724-743-7039
Fax: 724-743-7770 jason.meyers@centimark.com
www.centimark.com
Cleaners, flooring, floor grating, floor and wall coating materials, paints and enamels
President: Timothy Dunlap
Estimated Sales: H
Number Employees: 1,000-4,999

20383 Central Bag & Burlap Company
5601 N Logan St
Denver, CO 80216 303-297-9955
Fax: 303-297-9960 800-783-1224
scarichcorp@aol.com www.centralbag.com
Manufacturer and wholesaler/distributor of packaging materials including paper and plastic bags, deli containers, cups and packaging for meats and seafood; also, custom printed and plain bags available
President: Esther Seaman
CFO: David Fine
Vice President: Morton Zussman
Operations Manager: David Zussman
Estimated Sales: $5 Million
Number Employees: 5-9
Square Footage: 35000
Parent Co: Al-AAction Bag Company
Type of Packaging: Consumer, Food Service, Private Label, Bulk

20384 Central Bag & Burlap Company
5601 N Logan St
Denver, CO 80216 303-297-9955
Fax: 303-297-9960 800-783-1224
searichcorp@aol.com www.centralbag.com
Manufacturer and exporter of bags including plastic, burlap and cotton; also, plastic film; importer of burlap and woven polypropylene bags
President: Esther Seaman
VP: Lewis Bradford
Sales Director: Morton Seaman
Estimated Sales: $500,000 - $1 Million
Number Employees: 5-9
Square Footage: 24000
Parent Co: Sea-Rich Corporation
Type of Packaging: Bulk

20385 Central Bag Company
4901 South 4th Street
Leavenworth, KS 66048 913-250-0325
Fax: 913-727-1760
sales@centralbagcompany.com
www.centralbagcompany.com
Bags including burlap, cotton and polypropylene multi-wall; also, shrink wrap
President: Christopher Klimek
Estimated Sales: $5-10 Million
Number Employees: 50-99

20386 Central Coated Products
2025 McCrea St
Alliance, OH 44601-2794 330-821-9830
Fax: 330-821-3114
www.centralcoatedproducts.com
Coated paper packaging materials
President: Thomas Tormey
VP: Steve Porter
Estimated Sales: $10 - 20 Million
Number Employees: 20-49

20387 Central Container Corporation
3901 85th Ave N
Minneapolis, MN 55443-1907 763-425-7444
Fax: 763-425-7917
customerservice@centralcontainer.com
www.centralcontainer.com
Manufacturer and wholesaler/distributor of corrugated boxes, cushion packaging, flexible films, litho labels and static control products
President: James E Haglund
Sales: Steve Braun
VP Sales/Marketing: Steve Braun
General Manager: Jerry Condon
Estimated Sales: $10-20 Million
Number Employees: 50-99
Square Footage: 150000

20388 Central Decal Company
6901 High Grove Blvd
Burr Ridge, IL 60527 630-325-9892
Fax: 630-325-9878 800-869-7654
info@centraldecal.com www.centraldecal.com
Manufacturer and exporter of flexible nameplates, pressure sensitive labels and decals
President: Bob Keflin
CFO: Jennifer Loconte
VP: Robert Kaplan
Sales Manager: George Labine
Estimated Sales: $10 - 20 Million
Number Employees: 50-99
Square Footage: 30000

20389 Central ElectropolishingCompany
124 N Lawrence Ave
Anthony, KS 67003 620-842-3701
Fax: 620-842-3208 877-200-5488
steve@celcoinc.com www.celcoinc.com
Electropolishing, passivation and oxygen cleaning of stainless steel and other alloys
President: Kenneth Bellesine
CFO: Kim Bell
Quality Control: Jerry Smith
Estimated Sales: $2.5-5 000,000
Number Employees: 20-49

20390 Central Fabricators
408 Poplar St
Cincinnati, OH 45214 513-621-1240
Fax: 513-621-1243 800-909-8265
info@centralfabricators.com
www.centralfabricators.com
Manufacturer and exporter of stainless and carbon steel pressure vessels, heat exchangers, storage tanks, condensers, cookers, evaporators and kettles; also, other alloys available
President: David Angner
CEO: Dave Angner
CFO: Dan Meade
Vice President: Tim Maly
Operations Manager: Troy Black
Estimated Sales: $3 - 5 Million
Number Employees: 20-49
Square Footage: 20000

20391 Central Fine Pack
7707 Vicksburg Pike
Fort Wayne, IN 46804 260-432-3027
Fax: 260-432-9275 www.cfine.com
Plastic disposable food packaging and trays
Director Sales/Marketing: David Brown
Plant Manager: Russ Stephens
Estimated Sales: $20-50 Million
Number Employees: 250-499

20392 Central Grocers, Inc.
2600 W Haven Ave
Joliet, IL 60433 815-553-8800
Fax: 815-553-8710 sales@central-grocers.com
www.central-grocers.com
Supplier/distributor of food items and general merchandise to retail grocery stores
President & CEO: James Denges
CFO: Tim Kubis
Director of Marketing: Mike Oneill
Director of Retail Sales: Drew Jackman
Director of Produce Operations: Joe Ahlbach
Estimated Sales: $1.8 Billion
Number Employees: 2300
Square Footage: 90000
Brands:
Centrella

20393 Central Ice Machine Company
6279 S 118th St
Omaha, NE 68137 402-731-4690
Fax: 402-731-0823 800-228-7213
customerservice@centralice.com
www.centralice.com
Compressors, control valves, hand valves, relief valves, condensers and evaporators, gauges, refrigeration controls, refrigeration pumps, purgers, X-pando pipe joint compound, MSA gas masks, sulphur sticks, litmus paper and neverseez
President: Don Erftmier
Number Employees: 5-9

20394 Central Missouri Sheltered Enterprises
PO Box 10147
Columbia, MO 65205-4002 573-442-6935
Fax: 573-499-0586 bruce@cmse.org
www.cmse.org
Promotional items and packaging for barbecue sauce and rice cakes
Executive Director: Bruce Young
Executive Director: Bruce Young
Estimated Sales: $20-50 Million
Number Employees: 100-249

20395 Central Ohio Bag & Burlap
1000 E, Fifth Ave
Columbus, OH 43203 614-294-4495
Fax: 614-294-4362 800-798-9405
info@centralohiobagandburlap.com
www.centralohiobagandburlap.com
Bags and packaging materials
President: James Stout
Estimated Sales: $1 - 3,000,000
Number Employees: 5-9

20396 Central Pallet Mills
PO Box 190
Central City, KY 42330 270-754-2900
Fax: 270-754-2902
Lift truck pallets
President: Jack Brewer
Estimated Sales: $20-50 Million
Number Employees: 20-49

20397 Central Paper Box
2911 Belleview Avenue
Kansas City, MO 64108-3538 816-753-3126
Fax: 816-753-6923
Paper boxes including candy, paper and set-up; also, folding cartons
General Manager: Lon Wilkerson
Estimated Sales: $20-50 Million
Number Employees: 50-100
Square Footage: 125000

20398 Central Plastics Corporation
39605 Independence
Shawnee, OK 74804
800-654-3872
www.centralplastics.com
Molded plastic boxes
Estimated Sales: $1 - 5 Million
Number Employees: 2

20399 Central Products Company
741 4th St
Menasha, WI 54952-2801 920-725-4335
Fax: 920-729-4118 800-558-5006
www.centralproducts.com
Manufacturer and exporter of printed and plain pressure sensitive and gummed tapes: kraft paper and reinforced carton sealing; pressure sensitive carton sealing machine systems
President: Dale McSween
Product Manager: Steve Pistro
Product Manager: Tom Zettler
Plant Manager: John Cullen
Estimated Sales: $2.5-5 Million
Number Employees: 250-499
Parent Co: Intertape Polymer Group

20400 Central Solutions
401 Funston Rd
Kansas City, KS 66115 913-621-6542
Fax: 913-621-7031 800-255-0662
markn@centralsolutions.com
www.centralsolutions.com
Disinfectants and cleaners; also, custom formulating available
President: Mark Nobrega
CEO: Mike Noberga
Estimated Sales: $10-20 Million
Number Employees: 20-49

20401 Central States Industrial Equipment & Services
2700 N Partnership Blvd
Springfield, MO 65803 417-831-1411
Fax: 417-831-5314 800-654-5635
sales@csidesigns.com www.csidesigns.com
Fluid handling systems for food process and CIP
President: Mark Cook
Estimated Sales: $10-20 000,000
Number Employees: 50-99

20402 Centredale Sign Company
221 Jefferson Blvd
Warwick, RI 02888-3818 401-231-1440
Fax: 401-231-1481 custserv@aathriftysign.com
Neon signs and awnings; installation services available
President: A J Steinlage
Operations Manager: Tom Grenga
Estimated Sales: $5 - 10 Million
Number Employees: 13
Square Footage: 10000

20403 Centrifuge Solutions
2232 S Main Street
Suite 357
Ann Arbor, MI 48103-6938 734-424-0713
Fax: 734-426-9016
sales@centrifugesolutions.com
www.centrifugesolutions.com
Custom blended seasonings.
President: Tom Czartoski
Sales: Ron Mederski

20404 Centrisys Corporation
9586 58th Pl
Kenosha, WI 53144 877-339-5496
Fax: 262-764-8705 info@centrisys.us
www.centrifuge-systems.com
Centrifuges and separators; also, centrifuge services available
President: Michael Copper
Marketing Manager: Michael Kopper
Estimated Sales: $2.5-5 Million
Number Employees: 20-49
Brands:
Centrisys

20405 Century 21 Manufacturing
8008 Harney Street
Omaha, NE 68114-4451 402-391-2104
High quality vending machines
President: R Lebron

20406 Century Box Company
2412 W Cermak Road
Chicago, IL 60608-3704 773-847-7070
Fax: 773-847-7868 info@centurybox.com
www.centurybox.com
Wooden boxes
President: Daniel Leon
Estimated Sales: Less than $500,000
Number Employees: 1-4
Square Footage: 25000

20407 Century Chemical Corporation
28790 County Road 20
PO Box 1442
Elkhart, IN 46515 574-293-9521
Fax: 574-522-5723 800-348-3505
sales@centurychemical.com
www.centurychemical.com
Manufacturer and exporter of industrial and household deodorants and sanitizers; also, nontoxic anti-freeze
President: Edward A Fetters
Office Manager: Bobbi Holdeman
Plant Manager: David Eller
Estimated Sales: $1-2.5 Million
Number Employees: 5-9
Brands:
Travel-Jon

20408 Century Crane & Hoist
210 Washington Ave
Dravosburg, PA 15034 412-466-6987
Fax: 412-469-0813 888-601-8801
info@centurysteel.com www.centurysteel.com
Energy absorbing bumpers, overhead electric cranes and hoists; also, repair services and OSHA inspections
President: Don Taylor
Sales Representative: Frank Marchese

20409 Century Extrusion
2412 W Aero Park Ct
Traverse City, MI 49686 231-947-6400
Fax: 231-947-8400 sales@centuryextrusion.com
www.centuryextrusion.com
Twin screw extrusion equipment, replacement parts and support services.
President: Robert Urtel
Regional Sales/Food Product Manager: Aaron Gordon
Estimated Sales: $950,000
Number Employees: 85
Square Footage: 13553

20410 Century Foods International
400 Century Ct
Sparta, WI 54656 608-269-1900
Fax: 608-269-1910 800-269-1901
info@centuryfoods.com www.centuryfoods.com
Century Foods International is a manufacturer of nutritional powders and ready-to-drink beverages under private label and contract manufacturing agreements for food, sports, health and nutritional supplement industries. Other servicesprovided include agglomeration, blending and instantizing, research and development, analytical testing, and packaging from bulk to consumer size.
President: Tom Miskowski
VP R&D: Julie Wagner
VP Sales/Marketing: Gene Quast
VP Operations: Wade Nolte
Number Employees: 250-499
Square Footage: 1680000
Parent Co: Hormel Foods Corporation
Type of Packaging: Private Label, Bulk
Brands:
Cenprem
Lacey Delite
Pizazz
Ready Cheese

20411 Century Glove
145 John Bankson Drive
Summerville, GA 30747 973-751-0300
Fax: 212-371-5407 centuryglove@445park.com
www.centuryglove.com
Manufacturer and importer of cotton work and uniform gloves
Manager: Mary Seiler
Sales: Mary Seiler
*Estimated Sales:*less than $500,000
Number Employees: 1-4

20412 Century Industries
PO Box C
Sellersburg, IN 47172 812-246-3371
Fax: 812-246-5446 800-248-3371
info@centuryindustries.com
www.centuryindustries.com
Manufacturer and exporter of mobile concession trailers and kitchens
President: Robert Uhl
VP: John Uhl
Sales Manager: Matt Gilland
Estimated Sales: $5-10 Million
Number Employees: 20-49
Type of Packaging: Food Service
Brands:
Goldrush

20413 Century Products
1 Doulton Place
Peabody, MA 01960-3817 978-535-9001
Fax: 978-535-9002 800-225-3472
info@poolcover.com www.poolcover.com
Air bubble cushioning materials and shipping bags
Estimated Sales: $10-20 Million
Number Employees: 100-249

20414 Century Refrigeration
P.O.Box 1206
Pryor, OK 74362-1206 918-825-6363
Fax: 918-825-0723 century@rae-corp.com
www.century-refigeration.com

Commercial and industrial refrigeration equipment including condensing units, unit coolers, product coolers and chillers
President/CEO: Eric Swank
VP/CTO: Vickie Stephens
VP/Engineering: Jay Kindle
Manager of Quality: John Martin
Manager Marketing: Lisa Schrader
VP/Sales: Kevin Trowhill
Marketing Specialist: Heather Grubb
Vp/Operations: Jerry Salcher
Purchasing Manager: Jerry Douglas
Estimated Sales: $50-100 Million
Number Employees: 275
Square Footage: 125000
Parent Co: RAE Corporation

20415 Century Rubber Stamp Company
121 Fulton St Fl 2
New York, NY 10038 212-962-6165
Numbering machinery, stamps, stencils, etc
Manager: Harry Gold
Estimated Sales: $500,000-$1 Million
Number Employees: 5-9

20416 Century Sign Company
1622 Main Ave # E
Fargo, ND 58103-1553 701-235-5323
Fax: 701-235-5325 dwalstad@cooksignco.com
www.cooksignco.com
Neon and plastic signs
President: Matt Brasel
CFO: Steven Fliflet
Estimated Sales: $5 - 10 Million
Number Employees: 20-49

20417 Cenveo, Inc.
3001 N Rockwell St
Chicago, IL 60618-7993 773-267-3600
Fax: 773-267-2440 800-388-8406
www.cenveo.com
Envelopes including advertising clasp, string, window, postage saver, pressure sensitive, billing, etc
President: Robert G. Burton Jr
Chairman, CEO: Robert G. Burton Sr.
CFO: Scott Goodwin
VP: Ian Scheinmann
Estimated Sales: $1-2.5 Million
Number Employees: 100-249
Square Footage: 1080000

20418 Ceramic Color & ChemicalManufacturing Company
PO Box 297
New Brighton, PA 15066 724-846-4000
Fax: 724-846-4123 cccmfg@ccia.com
Inorganic pigments
Owner: Bill Wenning
Sales Manager: Tom Knox
Sales/Shipping Coordinator: Sally Antonini
Estimated Sales: $20-50 Million
Number Employees: 20-49

20419 Ceramic Decorating Co.
4651 Sheila St
Commerce, CA 90040 323-268-5135
Fax: 323-268-5108
sales@ceramicdecoratingco.com
www.ceramicdecoratingco.com
Supplier of custom made packaging labels.
CEO: Chad Johnson

20420 Ceramica De Espana
7700 NW 54th St
Doral, FL 33166-4106 305-597-9161
Fax: 305-597-9161 sales@moniquecde.comm
www.moniquecde.com
Manufacturer and importer of ceramic tableware, vases and candlesticks, bathroom, table top, cookware, table accessories, pottery, garden pottery
President: Monica Ruiz
Estimated Sales: $5-10 Million
Number Employees: 5-9
Type of Packaging: Consumer, Food Service

20421 Cermex
5600 Sun Court
Norcross, GE 30092 678-221-3570
Fax: 678-221-3571 cermexinc.sales@sidel.com
www.cermexinc.com
Side loading case packer specifically developed for pharmaceutical industry, pick and place robot for plastic bottles, top loading machines, compact machine integrating case erection and high speed shrinkwrapping machine of cans andbottles
Manager: Marc Daniel

20422 Certain Teed Shade Systems
6317 Busch Blvd
Columbus, OH 43229 614-844-5990
Fax: 614-844-5991 800-894-3801
info@shadetreecanopies.com
www.shadetreecanopies.com
Manufacturer and exporter of retractable awnings
President: Marvin Williams
CFO: Richard O Keith
Quality Control: Ken Wagner
VP Marketing: Dwayne Williams
Sales: Don Preston
Estimated Sales: $2.5-5 Million
Number Employees: 10-19
Parent Co: Certain Teed
Brands:
Shade Tree

20423 Certified Grocers Midwest
1 Certified Dr
Hodgkins, IL 60525 708-579-2100
Fax: 708-354-7502 www.certisaver.com
Grocery supplier
President: James Bradley
CEO: Jim Denges
Number Employees: 100-249

20424 Certified Labortories
200 Express St
Plainview, NY 11803-2423 516-576-1400
Fax: 516-576-1410 800-237-8522
corp@800certlab.com www.800certlab.com
Full service laboratory
General Manager: Martin Mitchell
Estimated Sales: $10 - 20 Million
Number Employees: 50-99

20425 Certified Machinery
3175 Princeton Pike
Lawrenceville, NJ 08648-2308 609-912-0300
Fax: 609-912-0144 info@certifiedmachinery.com
www.certifiedmachinery.com
Inkjet and labeling product handling equipment including off line coding and labeling, base coding diverter, l-sealers and heat tunnels
President: Frank Rogers
Estimated Sales: Below $5 Million
Number Employees: 5-9
Square Footage: 50000

20426 Certified Piedmontese Beef
100 West Harvest Drive
PO Box 82545
Lincoln, NE 68521 402-458-4442
Fax: 402-458-4531 800-414-3487
info@piedmontese.com www.piedmontese.com
Prime cuts of beef
President: Billy Swain

20427 Cesco Magnetics
Po Box 6359
Santa Rosa, CA 95406 707-585-2402
Fax: 707-585-3886 877-624-8727
sales@cescomagnetics.com
www.cescomagnetics.com
Manufacture magnetic separation equipment and sanitary valves
Estimated Sales: $1 - 3 Million
Number Employees: 5-9
Brands:
Cesco

20428 Chad Company
19950 W 161st St Ste A
Olathe, KS 66062 913-764-0321
Fax: 913-764-0779 800-444-8360
mike@chadcompany.com
www.chadcompany.com
Manufacturer and exporter of automated washing and pasteurizing equipment for meat slaughtering operations
President: Mike Gangel
Estimated Sales: Below $5 Million
Number Employees: 10-19
Square Footage: 5200

20429 Chaffee Company
4111 Citrus Ave
#10
Rocklin, CA 95677 916-630-3980
Fax: 916-630-3987 chaffee@chaffeeco.com
www.chaffeeco.com
Barrier laminate, cellophane and polyethylene sealers, and sealer systems.
President: Charlie Harper
Estimated Sales: $2.5-5 Million
Number Employees: 5-9
Brands:
Chaffee

20430 Chain Restaurant Resolutions
Suite 5
Toronto, ON M5S 1T8
Canada 416-934-4334
Fax: 416-934-4333
Consultant providing physical and financial restructuring to the restaurant and fast food industries
Estimated Sales: $1 - 5,000,000
Number Employees: 2

20431 (HQ)Chain Store Graphics
2220 E Logan Street
Decatur, IL 62526-5133 217-428-4695
Fax: 217-423-4010 800-443-7446
Advertising materials including paper and plastic signs, sign kits and decals; also, OEM decals and fleet markings
VP: Scott Bowers
Estimated Sales: $500,000-$1 Million
Number Employees: 4
Square Footage: 25000

20432 (HQ)Chaircraft
P.O.Box 608
Hickory, NC 28603-0608 828-326-8458
Fax: 828-326-8447
scott-regenbogen@centuryfurniture.com
www.centuryfurniture.com
Chairs and bar stools
President: Cick Finch
Plant Manager: Kevin Boyle
Estimated Sales: $20 - 50 Million
Number Employees: 100-249
Parent Co: Century Furniture

20433 Challenge-RMF
4417 E 119th St
Grandview, MO 64030 816-765-0515
Fax: 816-765-4101 sales@rmfsteel.com
www.rmfsteel.com
Manufacturer and exporter of food processing equipment including flow-through massaging, marinating systems, deboning and portioning
President/CEO: Bruce Gould
Plant Manager: Terry Rozell
Estimated Sales: $1-2.5 Million
Number Employees: 1-4
Parent Co: Challenge-RMF
Other Locations:
Challenge-RMF
Belgium
Challenge-RMF
Tampa FL

20434 (HQ)Challenge-RMF
4417 E 119th St
Grandview, MO 64030 816-765-0515
Fax: 816-765-0067 info@challenge-rmf.com
www.rmfsteel.com
Manufacturer and exporter of food processing equipment including flow-thru massaging, marinating, deboning and portioning
President/CEO: Bruce Gould
Plant Manager: Terry Rozell
Estimated Sales: $50-100 Million
Number Employees: 50-99
Parent Co: RMF

20435 (HQ)Challenger Pallet & Supply
24 N 3210 E
Idaho Falls, ID 83401 208-523-1969
Fax: 208-523-1972 800-733-0205
lll777@ida.net www.challengerpallet.com
Pallets, stakes, wedges and saw dust
President: Tad Hegsted
R&D: Justin Hegsted
VP Operations: Kelly Bennion
Estimated Sales: $5 - 10 Million
Number Employees: 20-49
Square Footage: 30000

Other Locations:
Challenger Pallet & Supply
Midvale UT

20436 Chalmur Bag Company, LLC
1426 Frankford Avenue
Philadelphia, PA 19125 215-425-0400
Fax: 215-425-4749 800-349-2247
chalmurbag@msn.com
chalmurbag.homestead.com/
Printed bags including polyethylene, cellophane, mini-lock and pre-opened on rolls, extruded narrow width tubing and cellophane sheets; also, carton and drum lining
Manager: Bob Livingston
Sales Manager: John Yarris
Plant Manager: Jon Ashley
Estimated Sales: $5 - 10 Million
Number Employees: 10-19
Square Footage: 64000

20437 (HQ)Chamberland Engineering
PO Box 817
West Warwick, RI 02893 800-687-1136
Fax: 401-615-7758 vibrate020@aol.com
www.chamberlandengineering.com
Vibrating screens, vibrating separators, vibrating sieves, bin and hopper vibrators, point and strip samplers, rotary tray dryers, ball valves, dust collectors,cyclones, scrubbers, electromechanical feeders, dosing feeders, air sweeprssystems, weigh belt feeders, bulk bag unloaders, BIC bins, blenders and mixers, ingredient dispensing systems
President: David Chamberland
VP: Steven Chamberland
R & D: Albert Bleau
Estimated Sales: $3.5 Million
Number Employees: 4
Number of Brands: 5
Number of Products: 27
Square Footage: 40000
Type of Packaging: Food Service

20438 Chambers Container Company
145 Bluedevil Dr
Gastonia, NC 28056-8610 704-377-6317
Fax: 704-864-4022 scotc@earthlink.net
www.chamberscontainer.com
Corrugated boxes
Manager: Roger Powers
Controller: Beth Hudson
VP: Scott Chambers
Estimated Sales: $20-50 Million
Number Employees: 50-99
Square Footage: 54000

20439 Champaign Plastics Company
PO Box 6413
Champaign, IL 61822 217-359-3664
Fax: 217-359-0091 800-575-0170
products@champaignplastics.com
www.champaignplastics.com
Manufacturer and wholesaler/distributor of disposable aprons, gloves, boots, shoe covers, hats, beard restraints, sleeves, children's and adult bibs and banquet rolls
President: Donna Williams
Estimated Sales: Below $5,000,000
Number Employees: 1-4

20440 Champion Chemical Co.
PO Box 5429
Whittier, CA 90607
800-621-7868
service@championchemical.com
www.cleanthatpot.com
Manufacturer and exporter of carbon and grease removers
Estimated Sales: $1 - 5 Million
Number Employees: 5
Square Footage: 72000
Brands:
Sokoff

20441 Champion Industries
3765 Champion Blvd
Winston Salem, NC 27105 336-661-1556
Fax: 336-661-1979 800-532-8591
info@championindustries.com
www.championindustries.com
Manufacturer and exporter of commercial dishwashers, pot and pan washers and waste disposal systems
President: Dexter Laughlin III
Chairman of the Board: Luciano Berti
CEO: Hank Holt
CFO: Christa Miller
R & D: Perry Money
Director Sales: Pete Michailo
Advertising Manager: Patrick Elworth
Purchasing Manager: Donna Mealka
Estimated Sales: $20-50 Million
Number Employees: 100-249
Square Footage: 130000
Parent Co: Comenda-Alispa
Type of Packaging: Food Service
Brands:
Champion
Moyer Diebel

20442 Champion Plastics
220 Clifton Blvd
Clifton, NJ 07011-3645
Fax: 800-526-1238 800-526-1230
sales@championplastics.com
www.championplastics.com
Manufacturer and exporter of polyethylene bags and films
President: Melvin Fischman
General Manager: John Callaghan
Estimated Sales: $20 - 30 Million
Number Employees: 100-249
Square Footage: 96000
Parent Co: X-L Plastics
Brands:
Champtuf Polyethylene

20443 (HQ)Champion Trading Corporation
P.O.Box 227
Marlboro, NJ 07746 732-780-4200
Fax: 732-780-9839 info@champtrading.com
www.champtrading.com
Manufacturer and exporter of used and rebuilt processing and packaging machinery
Principal: David Matthews
Co-Owner: James Matthew
Co-Owner: Michael Matthews
Plant Manager: S Bassett
Estimated Sales: $1-2,500,000
Number Employees: 5-9
Square Footage: 50000

20444 Champlin Company
236 Hamilton St
Hartford, CT 06106 860-951-9217
Fax: 860-951-3464 800-458-5261
info@champlincompany.com
www.champlincompany.com
Wooden and corrugated boxes
President: Rory Poole
VP: W James Schumaker
Estimated Sales: $3 - 5 Million
Number Employees: 20-49

20445 Chandre Corporation
14 Catharine Street
Poughkeepsie, NY 12601-3104 845-473-8003
Fax: 845-473-8004 800-324-6252
sales@chandre.com www.chandre.com
Chocolate tempering machines
Estimated Sales: 700000
Number Employees: 10

20446 (HQ)Chaney Instrument
965 S Wells St
P.O. Box 70
Lake Geneva, WI 53147 877-221-1252
Fax: 262-248-8707 800-777-0565
info@chaney-inst.com
www.chaneyinstrument.com
Manufacturer and exporter of digital and analog kitchen thermometers, timers and clocks
President: John Billicki
National Sales Manager Food Service: Allan Ahrens
Number Employees: 100-249
Square Footage: 95000
Type of Packaging: Consumer, Food Service, Private Label, Bulk
Other Locations:
Chaney Instruments
Lake Geneva WI
Brands:
Acu-Rite
Chaney Instrument

20447 Change Parts
185 S Jebavy Dr
Ludington, MI 49431 231-845-5107
Fax: 231-843-4907 info@changeparts.com
www.changeparts.com
Custom designed changeover parts including fillers, cleaners, cappers, timing screws, stars and guides, nozzles, drive wheels and belts; also, remanufactured and used packaging equipment
President: Ronald D Sarto
CFO: Greg Simsa
VP: Greg Simsa
Marketing: Dori Bray
National Sales Manager: Jon Goad
Operations Manager: Andy Kmetz
Production: Andy Kmetz
Estimated Sales: $2.5-5 Million
Number Employees: 20-49
Square Footage: 45000

20448 Chantland-MHS Company
502 7th Street North
Dakota City, IA 50529 515-332-4045
Fax: 515-332-1502 chantland@chantland.com
www.chantland.com
Manufacturer and exporter of belt conveyors, bag filling equipment and bag palletizers
Manager: Harry Thomas
Principal: Carla Vonderhaar
Director, Finance: Carla Victor
Marketing Manager: Kim Wasilewski
Sales Manager: Scott Jorgensen
Purchasing Manager: Greg Reed
Estimated Sales: $33 Million
Number Employees: 200
Square Footage: 144500

20449 Chapman Corporation
3366 Tree Court Ind Blvd
Saint Louis, MO 63122-6688 636-225-5313
Fax: 636-825-2610 800-843-1404
sales@chapmanstl.com www.chapmanstl.com
Replacement knives, blades, slitters and perforators for processing and packaging equipment.
Executive VP: Mark Zumbehl
Estimated Sales: $2.5-5,000,000
Number Employees: 10-19

20450 Chapman Manufacturing Company
481 West Main Street
P.O. Box 359
Avon, MA 02322-0359 508-588-3200
Fax: 508-587-7592 hospitality@chapmanco.com
www.chapmanco.com
Manufacturer and exporter of lamps and lighting fixtures, encompasses table and floor lamps, chandeliers, sconces, accent furniture and decorative accessories. Authentic reproductions, traditional adaptations and transitional andoriginal contemporary designs
President: Thomas Ruskin
Estimated Sales: $10-20 Million
Number Employees: 50-99

20451 Chapman Sign
23253 Hoover Rd
Warren, MI 48089-1934 586-758-1600
Fax: 586-758-1610 chapmansigns@msn.com
Electric signs
Manager: Harold Chapman
*Estimated Sales:*less than $500,000
Number Employees: 5

20452 Charles Beck Machine Corporation
400 W Church Road
King of Prussia, PA 19406-3185 610-265-0500
Fax: 610-265-5627 beckmachine@verizon.net
www.beckmachine.com
Manufacturer and exporter of set-up box lidders and rotary shear sheet cutters
President: Arthur Beck
Manager Parts/Service: Robert Pickell
Estimated Sales: Below $5 Million
Number Employees: 10

20453 Charles Beseler Company
2018 West Main Street
Stroudsburg, PA 18360 800-237-3537
Fax: 800-966-4515 tech@beselerphoto.com
www.beseler.com

Shrink packaging
President: Hank Gasikowski
Estimated Sales: $300,000-500,000
Number Employees: 1-4

20454 Charles Beseler Corporation
R.D. #2 West Main Street
P.O. Box 431
Stroudsburg, PA 18360 570-517-0400
Fax: 800-966-4515 800-237-3537
vicki@beseler.com www.beseler.com
Manufacturer and exporter of shrink wrap machinery
President: Hank Gasikowski
Dealer Supprt. Spec.: Amelia Garcia
General Manager/VP: Joe Capp
Tech. Service: Rob Irvin
Estimated Sales: $100-500 Million
Number Employees: 1-4

20455 Charles Craft
P.O.Box 1049
Laurinburg, NC 28353 910-844-3521
Fax: 910-844-9846
cliftonbuie.charlescraft@earthlink.net
www.charlescraft.com
Towels including dish, pot holders and aprons
President: Charles G Buie Jr
President: Clifton Buie
Estimated Sales: $50-100 Million
Number Employees: 50-99
Brands:
Charles Craft

20456 Charles E. Roberts Company
539 Fairmont Rd
Wyckoff, NJ 07481-1318 973-345-3035
Fax: 973-345-8516 800-237-2684
Manufacturer and exporter of embossed ribbon for awards, badges, prizes, contests, emblems, fairs and conventions
Owner/President: Bernard Gallant
Estimated Sales: $5-10 Million
Number Employees: 10-19
Square Footage: 14000

20457 Charles Engineering & Service
1 Tye Green Paddoc
Belcamp, MD 21017-0428 410-272-1090
Temperature sensitive containers; custom design available
Sr. VP: Charles Furlong
Estimated Sales: $300,000-500,000
Number Employees: 7
Square Footage: 16000

20458 Charles Gratz Fire Protection
241 W Oxford St
Philadelphia, PA 19122-3798 215-235-5800
Fax: 215-236-2510
Manfacturer of fire alarm systems and fire extinguishers
Owner: Harry Gratz
Office Manager: Deborah DeSimone
Estimated Sales: Below $5 Million
Number Employees: 5 to 9

20459 Charles H. Baldwin & Sons
1 Center St
P.O.Box 372
West Stockbridge, MA 01266 413-232-7785
Fax: 413-232-0114 www.baldwinextracts.com
Flavoring extracts and flavors, maple table syrup and supplier of baking supplies.
Owner: Earl Moffatt
Estimated Sales: $500,000-$1 Million
Number Employees: 1-4
Brands:
Baldwin

20460 Charles Lapierre
56 Etna Road
Lebanon, NH 03766-1403
Canada 603-448-0300
Fax: 603-448-4810 800-432-2990
info@njmpackaging.com www.njmcli.com
President: Charles Lapierre
Vice President of Operations: Andre Caumartin
R&D: Louis Lasluer
Director of International Sales: Marc Lapierre
Number Employees: 25

20461 Charles Mayer Studios
105 E Market St
Suite 114
Akron, OH 44308-2037 330-535-6121
Fax: 330-434-2016
Manufacturer, exporter and importer of hotel and restaurant menu boards, white liquid chalk boards, bulletin boards, easels, trade show displays and today's specials boards, custom tables
Owner: Jeffrey Mayer
Executive VP: M Barton
Estimated Sales: $1-3 Million
Number Employees: 20-49
Square Footage: 105000
Type of Packaging: Food Service
Brands:
Mayer Hook N' Loop
Mayer Magna

20462 (HQ)Charles Ross & Son Company
710 Old Willets Path
Hauppauge, NY 11788 631-234-0500
Fax: 631-234-0691 800-243-7677
mail@mixers.com www.mixers.com
Manufacturer, importer and exporter of mixing, blending and dispersion equipment
President: Richard Ross
Executive VP: Bogard Lagman
Estimated Sales: $20-50 Million
Number Employees: 100-249
Square Footage: 150000
Other Locations:
Ross, Charles, & Son Co.
Savannah GA
Brands:
Double Planetary
Powermix
Ross
X-Series

20463 Charles Tirschman Company
1936 Graves Ct
Baltimore, MD 21222-5508 410-282-6199
Pallets and skids
Owner: Charles Tirschman
Estimated Sales: $500,000-$1 Million
Number Employees: 5-9

20464 Charlotte Tent & Awning
207 Lawton Road
Charlotte, NC 28216-3313 704-394-1616
Fax: 704-394-2725
www.charlottetentandawning.com
Commercial awnings
Estimated Sales: $1-2,500,000
Number Employees: 12

20465 Charlton & Hill
655 30th Street N
Lethbridge, AB T1H 5G5
Canada 403-328-3388
Fax: 403-328-3533 mfab@charltonandhill.com
www.charltonandhill.com
Conveyors; wholesaler/distributor of ranges, coolers and hot plates; serving the food service market; also, metal fabrication available
Sales Manager: Dwayne Huber
Estimated Sales: $1 - 5 Million
Number Employees: 100-250

20466 Charm Sciences
659 Andover St
Lawrence, MA 01843 978-683-6100
Fax: 978-687-9216 info@charm.com
www.charm.com
Manufacturer and exporter of food safety diagnostic instruments for antibiotic, aflatoxin and pesticide residues, ATP sanitation/hygiene, pasteurization efficiency and doneness in meat products
President: Dr Stanley Charm
VP Sales: Gerard Ruth
Estimated Sales: $25.7 Million
Number Employees: 100-249
Brands:
Chef Test
Cidelite
Paslite
Pathogel
Pocketswab
Sl Test

20467 Chart Applied Technologies
3505 County Road 42 W
Burnsville, MN 55306-3803 952-882-5000
Fax: 952-882-5172 888-877-3093
www.mve-inc.com
VP: Eric M Rottier
Estimated Sales: $1 - 5 Million
Number Employees: 250-499

20468 (HQ)Chart Industries - MVE Beverage Systems
1 Infinity Corp Ctr Dr Ste 300
Cleveland, OH 44125 440-753-1490
800-247-4446
mary.nelson@chart-ind.com www.chart-ind.com
Manufacturer and exporter of CO2 storage tanks used for carbonation in soda dispensing machines
President: John Wikstrom
VP: Eric M Rottier
Marketing Director: Mary Nelson
Sales Director: Dick Mich
Estimated Sales: $20-50 Million
Number Employees: 250-499
Type of Packaging: Food Service

20469 Charter House
500 E 8th St Ste 1000
Holland, MI 49423 616-399-6000
Fax: 616-399-8396 www.gotochi.com
Food service dining room furniture
President: Chuck Reid
Finance Executive: Jacob Burroughs
Director/Managing Engineer: Bill Regan
Plant Manager: Harriet Trethewey
Purchasing Manager: Bill Forslund
Estimated Sales: $10 - 20 Million
Number Employees: 50-99
Square Footage: 40000
Parent Co: Franke

20470 Chase Doors
10021 Commerce Park Dr.
Cincinnati, OH 45246 513-860-5565
Fax: 800-245-7045 800-543-4455
summeranderson@staples-stevens.com
www.staplesandstevens.com
Manual, electric sliding cold storage room, swing and vertical lift doors for walk-in coolers and freezers. Full line of parts. Commercial refrigeration sales, service, and installation
Owner: Jeff Staples
General Manager: David Canady
Estimated Sales: $2.5-5 Million
Number Employees: 1-4
Square Footage: 64000

20471 Chase Doors
10021 Commerce Park Dr
Cincinnati, OH 45246 513-860-5565
Fax: 800-245-7045 800-543-4455
info@chasedoors.com www.chasedoors.com
Impact traffic doors, service doors, flexible doors, security doors, corrosion resistant doors, fire and service doors, pharmaceutical doors, door operations, cold storage doors and dock seals and shelters
President: Jim Lindsay
CEO: Robert W Muir
Estimated Sales: $10-25 000,000
Number Employees: 100-249

20472 Chase Industries
1210 E 223rd St Ste 322
Carson, CA 90745 310-763-9900
Fax: 310-637-4506 info@chaseusa.com
www.chaseusa.com
Chase Industries, Inc. manufactures a full line of manual and semi-automatic L-Sealers, Shrink Tunnels, and Bar Sealers as well as fully automatic Sleeve Wrappers, Bundlers, Blister Sealers, Clam Shell Sealers, Curing Systems andFormfill equipment. Our goal as a manufacturer, is to provide top performance and top quality to the customer in as many combinations of size and options as possible. We like to work closely with our distributors and their customers for the bestpossible standards
CEO: Elizabeth Braslow
CEO: Jim Braslow
R&D: James Braslow
Purchasing: Jose Garcia

Estimated Sales: $5 - 10 Million
Number Employees: 10-19
Number of Brands: 10
Square Footage: 15000
Brands:
Chase
Cii
Ultrablister
Ultrasealer

20473 **(HQ)Chase-Doors**
10021 Commerce Park Dr
Cincinnati, OH 45246 513-860-5565
Fax: 513-245-7045 800-543-4455
www.chasedoors.com
Manufacturer and exporter of vinyl and roll up doors, fire and insulated doors, door operators and air curtains
President: Dan O'Connor
CEO: Dan O'Connor
CFO: Drew Bachman
CEO: Robert W Muir
R&D: Rory Falato
Marketing: Rory Falato
General Manager: Carl Johnson
Plant Manager: Rick Schweitzer
Purchasing Director: Diane Wells
Estimated Sales: $20 - 50 Million
Number Employees: 100-249
Number of Brands: 10
Number of Products: 35
Other Locations:
Chase-Durus
Memphis TN

20474 **Chase-Logeman Corporation**
303 Friendship Dr
Greensboro, NC 27409 336-665-0754
Fax: 336-665-0723 info@chaselogeman.com
www.chaselogeman.com
Manufacturer and exporter of liquid filling, plugging and screw capping machinery, tray loaders and unloaders, conveyors, unscramblers, rotary tables, accumulators and monoblocks; also, custom designing available
President: Douglas Lodgeman
Vice President: Joel Slazyk
Quality Control: Louis Stier
Plant Manager: Lew Stier
Estimated Sales: $1 Million
Number Employees: 20
Square Footage: 18000
Brands:
Chaselock

20475 **Chaska Chemical Company**
12502 Xenwood Ave
Savage, MN 55378 952-890-1820
Fax: 952-890-3844 800-788-7449
sales@chaskachem.com www.chaskachem.com
Industrial cleaners
President: Sean Teske
CEO: Paul Moe
General Manager: Monica Tucker
Director Production Deptartment: Jeff Gray
Plant Manager: Jeff Gray
Estimated Sales: Below $5 Million
Number Employees: 10-19

20476 **(HQ)Chaska Chocolate**
821 Oriole Lane
Chaska, MN 55318-1131 952-448-5699
Fax: 952-448-6719
Consultant for the oilseed extraction, fats and oils, chocolate and coffee industries; also, food technology research available
Estimated Sales: $1 - 5 Million
Number Employees: 2
Square Footage: 1100
Other Locations:
Chaska Chocolate
Chicago IL

20477 **Chatelain Plastics**
413 N Main St
Findlay, OH 45840-3541 419-422-4323
Fax: 419-422-1122 cp-signs@bright.net
Advertising signs
Owner: Tom Klein
President: Jim Chatelain
Estimated Sales: Below $5 Million
Number Employees: 5 to 9

20478 **(HQ)Chatfield & Woods Sack Company**
651 Enterprise Dr
Harrison, OH 45030-1691 513-202-9700
Fax: 513-202-0900
Paper sacks
President: Alan Bicknayer
General Manager: Mark Mitter
Number Employees: 5
Square Footage: 30000
Other Locations:
Chatfield & Woods Sack Co.
Harrison OH

20479 **Chatillon**
8600 Somerset Dr
Largo, FL 33773-2700 727-536-7831
Fax: 727-538-2400 chatillon.fl-lar@ametek.com
www.ametek.com
Mechanical and electronic calibration equipment for hydraulic, pneumatic, materials testers
Quality Control: Mike Guglicelli
Manager: Nick Hoiles
Estimated Sales: $10 - 20 Million
Number Employees: 50-99
Parent Co: Amatek

20480 **Chattanooga Labeling Systems**
P.O.Box 2492
Chattanooga, TN 37409-0492 423-825-2125
Fax: 423-825-2173 cls@cledeco.com
www.clsdeco.com
Pressure sensitive, heat transfer and shrink sleeve labels; glassware and plastic screen printing
President: Marvin Smith
CFO: Dave Houseman
Head Of Customer Service Dept.: Chris Gonzalez
Office Manager: Jenny Hughes
Production Manager: Don Gilbert
Estimated Sales: $20 - 30 Million
Number Employees: 20-49

20481 **Chattanooga Rubber Stamp& Stencil Works**
P.O.Box 443
Sale Creek, TN 37373-0443 423-894-1163
Fax: 423-894-1164 800-894-1164
crs4018@aol.com
Rubber stamps
President: John L McNair Jr
Estimated Sales: Less than $500,000
Number Employees: 3

20482 **Chattin Awning Company**
85 Newfield Ave
Edison, NJ 08837 732-225-8800
Fax: 732-225-2110 800-394-3500
mainattractions3500@gmail.com
www.mainattractions.com
Commercial awnings
President: Rocky Sconda
CEO: Kevin Bova
Operations Manager: Dean Dialfonso
Estimated Sales: $5 - 10 Million
Number Employees: 20-49

20483 **Chaucer Press**
535 Stewart Rd
Wilkies-Barre, PA 18706 570-825-2005
Fax: 570-825-0535 www.chaucerpress.com
Communnicone and Xtenda-cone collars for on-pack promotion, folding cartons, pressure-sensitive and cut labels, and other printed materials
CEO: Patricia A. Frances
COO: Frank A. Franzo
Plant Manager: Al Saldy
Estimated Sales: $2.5-5 000,000
Number Employees: 20-49

20484 **Check Savers**
PO Box 823389
Dallas, TX 75382-3389 972-272-7533
Fax: 972-276-8315
Checks
President: Rex McNabb
CEO: Bret Woods
National Sales Rep.: Mike Voight
Number Employees: 10

20485 **Checker Bag Company**
10655 Midwest Industrial Blvd
Saint Louis, MO 63132 314-423-3131
Fax: 314-423-1329 800-489-3130
www.checkerbag.com
Manufacturer, importer and exporter of polyethylene, polypropylene and cellophane bags including bakery, confection and gourmet
President: Robert Freund
VP: Al Stix
Number Employees: 10-19

20486 **Checker Engineering**
2701 Nevada Ave N
New Hope, MN 55427-2879 763-544-5000
Fax: 763-544-1272 888-800-5001
cm@checkermachine.com
www.checkermachine.com
Spiral conveyors, ovens and freezers
President: Steve Lipinski
CFO: John Ackerman
Vice President: Steve Lipinski
Sales/Marketing Manager: Don Hockman
Production Manager: Brad Schmitt
Plant Manager: Steve Lipinski
Estimated Sales: $5 - 10 Million
Number Employees: 20-49
Square Footage: 400000
Parent Co: Checker Machine
Brands:
Checker
Stein/Checker

20487 **Cheese Merchants of America**
248 Tubeway Dr
Carol Stream, IL 60188 630-768-0317
Fax: 630-221-0584 johnp@cheesemerchants.com
www.cheesemerchants.com
Processors of custom blends of Italian cheeses, converters of hard Italian cheeses to grated, shredded, and shaved.
EVP/Managing Partner: Robert Greco
Director Purchasing/Quality Assurance: Paul DelleGrazie
Central Regional Sales Manager: Mark Lewis
EVP Sales: Jim Smart
VP of Retail Sales: Tom DeSimone
Estimated Sales: $19.3 Million
Number Employees: 90
Square Footage: 105000
Type of Packaging: Consumer, Food Service, Bulk

20488 **Cheese Outlet Fresh Market**
400 Pine St
Burlington, VT 05401 802-863-3968
Fax: 802-865-1705 800-447-1205
info@freshmarketvt.com
www.freshmarketgourmetvt.com
Retail gourmet bakery of cheeses, produce and gourmet items, prepared foods, wine and Vermont products
President: Simon Pozirekides
Manager: Sherie Cyr
Estimated Sales: $5 - 10 Million
Number Employees: 20-49
Square Footage: 5000

20489 **Chef Revival**
555 Koopman Ln
Elkhorn, WI 53121 262-723-6133
Fax: 262-723-4204 800-248-9826
info@sjcr.com www.chefrevival.com
Manufacturer, importer and exporter of traditional and contemporary chef uniforms including jackets,aprons,pants, hats,clogs,as well as a full line of ladies and chilrens clothing.
President: Jerry Rosenblum
VP: Kim dela Villefromoy
Marketing Director: Kelly Gloor
Sales: Jack Kramer
Production: Louis Nardella
Plant Manager: Paul Brady
Number Employees: 20
Square Footage: 8000
Type of Packaging: Consumer, Food Service
Brands:
Chef Revival
Chefcare
Chefcutlery
Knife & Steel

20490 **Chef Specialties Company**
411 W Water St
Smethport, PA 16749 814-887-5652
Fax: 814-887-2021 800-440-2433
info@chefspecialties.com
www.chefspecialties.com

Manufacturer, exporter and importer of metal and wood kitchen specialties including peppermills, spice mills, salad bowls and cutting boards
President: John W Pierotti
Sales: Mike Wagner
Estimated Sales: $500,000-$1 Million
Number Employees: 5-9
Square Footage: 25000
Type of Packaging: Consumer, Food Service, Private Label, Bulk
Brands:
Chef

20491 **Chef's Choice Mesquite Charcoal**
1729 Ocean Oaks Rd
PO Box 707
Carpinteria, CA 93014-0707 805-684-8284
Fax: 805-684-8284
Manufacturer and importer of mesquite charcoal
Owner: Bill Lord Jr.
Number of Products: 2
Type of Packaging: Food Service
Brands:
Chef's Choice

20492 **Chefwear**
2300 W Windsor Ct Ste C
Addison, IL 60101 773-427-6700
Fax: 630-396-8391 800-568-2433
info@chefwear.com www.chefwear.com
Manufacturer and exporter of culinary apparel and accessories
President: Rochelle Huppin Fleck
CEO: Gary Fleck
Sales Director: Glenn Woerz
General Manager: Rob James
Estimated Sales: Less than $500,000
Number Employees: 1-4
Square Footage: 12000
Brands:
Chef-R-Alls
Chefwear
Pint Size Duds

20493 **Cheil Jedang Corporation**
105 Challenger Rd
Ridgefield Park, NJ 07660-2101 201-229-6050
Fax: 201-229-6058 annie@cheiljedang.com
www.ccaworld.com
Flavor enhancers
President: Ben Heo
Estimated Sales: $10 - 20 Million
Number Employees: 50-99

20494 **Chem Mark International**
635 E Chapman Ave
Orange, CA 92866-1604 714-633-8560
Fax: 310-557-1976
Broker of commercial dishwashing machines, chemicals, air purification equipment, bar glass washer and flying insect control products. Also exporter of commercial dishwashing machines
President: Darol Carlson
VP: Betty Carlson
Marketing Director: Jay Jaeger
Estimated Sales: $1-2.5 Million
Number Employees: 1 to4

20495 **Chem-Pack**
2261 Spring Grove Ave
Cincinnati, OH 45214 513-241-6616
Fax: 513-241-6664 800-421-2700
info@chem-pack.com www.chem-pack.com
Contract packager of multi-packaged food products, health and beauty aids, skin and blister packaging, shrink wrap, liquids, powders, etc.; also display assembly.
President: John Pierce
Estimated Sales: $1-2.5 Million
Number Employees: 20-49
Square Footage: 50000

20496 **Chem-Pruf Door Company**
PO Box 4560
Brownsville, TX 78523-4560 956-544-1000
Fax: 956-544-7943 800-444-6924
info@chem-pruf.com www.chem-pruf.com
Noncorrosive fiberglass doors and wall windows, louver systems and fiberglass frames; also, stainless steel hardware available
Owner: Tony Mc Dermid
CFO: Bill Stirling
Estimated Sales: $10 - 20 Million
Number Employees: 50-99
Square Footage: 40000
Type of Packaging: Food Service, Private Label
Brands:
Chem-Pruf

20497 **Chem-Tainer Industries**
361 Neptune Ave
West Babylon, NY 11704 631-661-8300
Fax: 631-661-8209 800-275-2436
sales@chemtainer.com www.chemtainer.com
Manufacturer and exporter of plastic tanks and containers
President: James Glen
VP Marketing: Tony Lamb
Estimated Sales: $5-10 Million
Number Employees: 50-99
Square Footage: 500000
Brands:
Haz Mat

20498 **Chem-Tainer Industries**
361 Neptune Ave
West Babylon, NY 11704 631-661-8300
Fax: 631-661-8209 800-938-8896
sales@chemtainer.com www.chemtainer.com
Manufacturer and exporter of plastic tanks, containers and material handling equipment
President: James Glen
Executive VP: A Lamb
Estimated Sales: $5-10,000,000
Number Employees: 50-99
Square Footage: 40000
Parent Co: Chem-Trainer Industries

20499 **(HQ)ChemIndustrial Systems**
PO Box 500
Cedarburg, WI 53012 262-375-8570
Fax: 262-375-8559 info@chemindustrial.com
www.chemindustrial.com
Manufacturers of pH control, neutralizing process systems and hydrocyclones.
Sales Manager: Michael Lloyd
Estimated Sales: $5-10 Million
Number Employees: 10
Square Footage: 6000
Brands:
Chemindustrial

20500 **ChemTran**
5634 Shirley Lane
Houston, TX 77032 281-590-9400
Fax: 763-476-8155 800-523-9033
info@ChemTranUSA.com www.chemtran.com
Specialize in packaging for shipment of infectious substances; suppliers of UN Performance-Oriented Packaging
President: Joe Goldman

20501 **ChemTreat, Inc.**
4461 Cox Rd
Glen Allen, VA 23060-3331 804-935-2000
Fax: 804-965-0154 800-648-4579
cs_orders@chemtreat.com www.chemtreat.com
Manufacturer and exporter of water treatment chemicals for boilers and cooler, cooker and waste water treatment and clarification systems
Manager,Food Industry Marketing: David Anthony
Dierctor Food Industry Division: Dennis Martin
Purchasing Manager: Steve Hemmis
Estimated Sales: $300,000-500,000
Number Employees: 1-4

20502 **Chemclean Corporation**
13045 180th St
Jamaica, NY 11434 718-525-2500
Fax: 718-481-6470 800-538-2436
info@chemclean.com www.chemclean.com
Manufacturer and exporter of industrial cleaners, degreasers, disinfectants, and deodorizers
President: Bernard Esquenet
CEO: Frank Bass
Manager: S Emil Johnsen
Estimated Sales: $20-50 Million
Number Employees: 20-49
Square Footage: 20000
Brands:
D-Carb 297
D-Scale
Multichlor
Neutraclean
Sparkleen 310

20503 **Chemco Products Company**
1349 Grand Oaks Dr.
Howell, MI 48843 517-546-7800
Fax: 517-546-5163 info@chemcoproducts.net
www.chemcoproducts.net
USDA sanitation chemicals, boiler, cooling tower and wastewater treatment; provides and installs related dispensing equipment, controllers, tanks, CIP systems, lube systems, pressure washers
President: Janis Utz
CFO: Elaine Cooper
CEO: Joe Mickunas
Quality Control: Elaine Cooper
VP Sales: Dave McCalo
Estimated Sales: $10 - 20 000,000
Number Employees: 50-99

20504 **Chemdet**
730 D Commerce Center Dr
Sebastian, FL 32958 772-388-2755
Fax: 772-388-8813 800-645-1510
info@chemdet.com www.chemdet.com
Manufacturer and exporter of stainless steel tank washers
President: Phillip Joachim
Estimated Sales: $2.5-5 Million
Number Employees: 1-4
Brands:
Chem Disc
Clip Disc
Fury
Rotaball
Spray Ball
Turbodisc

20505 **Chemetall**
675 Central Ave
New Providence, NJ 07974 908-464-6900
Fax: 908-464-4658 800-526-4473
mail@oakite.com www.oakite.com
President: Mark Bruner
Number Employees: 500-999

20506 **Chemex Division/International Housewares Corporation**
69 S Church St
Pittsfield, MA 01201 413-499-2370
Fax: 413-443-3546 800-243-6399
www.chemexcoffeemaker.com
Manufacturer, importer and exporter of drip coffee makers and filters
President: Eliza Grassy
Estimated Sales: $1 - 3 Million
Number Employees: 5-9
Type of Packaging: Consumer
Brands:
Chemex

20507 **Chemi-Graphic**
340 State St
PO Box 410
Ludlow, MA 01056 413-589-0151
Fax: 413-589-7448
customer.service@chemi-graphic.com
www.chemi-graphic.com
Etched, lithographed and silk screened name plates, dials and scales
President: Paul Pohl
Executive VP: Donald Devine
Estimated Sales: Below $5 Million
Number Employees: 50-99

20508 **Chemicolloid Laboratories, Inc.**
P.O.Box 251
New Hyde Park, NY 11040-0251 516-747-2666
Fax: 516-747-4888
customersupport@colloidmill.com
www.colloidmill.com
Manufacturer and exporter of colloid mills used in applications to process materials being dispersed, suspended, emulsified, homogenized or comminuted, and process equipment.
VP: Robert Best
Marketing: Susan Okeefe
Sales Director: George Ryder
Purchasing: Steve Best
Estimated Sales: $3 - 5 Million
Number Employees: 20-49
Square Footage: 144000
Brands:
Charlotte
Colloid Mills

20509 Chemifax
11641 Pike St
Santa Fe Springs, CA 90670 562-908-0405
Fax: 562-908-0077 800-527-5722
info@carrollco.com www.carrollco.com
Manufacturer and exporter of cleaning products including floor waxes, finishes, detergents, soaps and chemical specialties
Manager: Mohammed Nilchian
Sales Manager: Mike Greene
Sales Manager: Mike Meller
Estimated Sales: $20 - 50 Million
Number Employees: 50-99
Square Footage: 80000
Parent Co: Carroll Company
Brands:
Airx
Nature's Orange
Show Patrol
Shower Patrol Plus
Solar System
Trewax Hardware
Trewax Industrial
Trewax Janitorial

20510 Chemineer
P.O.Box 1123
Dayton, OH 45401-1123 937-454-3200
Fax: 937-454-3379 chemineer@nov.com
www.chemineer.com
Agitators and mixers
Manager: Patty Breig
Estimated Sales: $10 - 50 Million
Number Employees: 250-499

20511 Chemineer-Kenics/Greerco
125 Flagship Dr
North Andover, MA 01845-6119 978-687-0101
Fax: 978-687-8500 800-643-0641
inquiry@kenics.com www.chemineer.com
Processing equipment: static and high shear mixers and heat exchangers
Manager: Mark Raymond
Quality Control: John Cercone
Marketing Director: Dave Ryan
Purchasing Manager: Laura Parker
Estimated Sales: $20 - 50 Million
Number Employees: 20-49
Parent Co: Robbins & Meyers
Brands:
Greerco
Kenics

20512 Chemtreat
4461 Cox Rd # 106
Glen Allen, VA 23060-3331 804-935-2000
Fax: 804-965-6974 800-442-8292
michaelk@chemtreat.com www.chemtreat.com
Estimated Sales: $1 - 5 Million
Number Employees: 1-4

20513 Chemtura Corporation
199 Brenson Road
Middlebury, CT 06831-2560 203-573-2000
Fax: 607-754-7517 800-295-2392
www.chemtura.com
Estimated Sales: C
Number Employees: 1-4

20514 Cherry's Industrial Equipment Corporation
600 Morse Ave
Elk Grove Vlg, IL 60007 847-364-0200
Fax: 800-350-8454 800-350-0011
sales@cherrysind.com www.cherrysind.com
Manufacturer and exporter of aluminum shipping containers and pallet transfer machines, inverters and retrievers; importer of pallet inverters
President: Clerance Cherry
National Accounts Manager: James Woods III
Estimated Sales: $500,000-$750,000
Number Employees: 5-9
Square Footage: 30000

20515 Chesapeake Packaging
301 Green Ridge St
Scranton, PA 18509 570-342-9217
Fax: 570-342-8410 www.templeinland.com
Corrugated boxes and containers
VP Manufacturing: Don Hayhurst
Estimated Sales: $10-20 Million
Number Employees: 50-99
Parent Co: Chesapeake Corporation of VA

20516 Chesapeake Packaging Company
PO Box 1240
Binghamton, NY 13902-1240 607-775-1550
Fax: 607-775-2505 www.templeinland.com
Corrugated containers and displays
President: Thomas H Johnson
CFO: Andrew J Kohut
VP Marketing: David Davenport
Plant Manager: Gerry Hoover
Estimated Sales: $50-100 Million
Number Employees: 100-249
Parent Co: Chesapeake Packaging Company

20517 Chesapeake Spice Company
4613 Mercedes Drive
Belcamp, MD 21017 410-272-6100
Fax: 410-273-2122 csc@chesapeakespice.com
www.chesapeakespice.com
Processor and importers of spices and seasoning. including the following types of herbs..anise,cumin,sage and sage oil,black pepper,paprika,cinnamon,saffron ,thyme,and ginger.
President: Larry Lessans
Vice President: David Lessans
Estimated Sales: $5-10 Million
Number Employees: 20-49
Square Footage: 200000
Type of Packaging: Bulk

20518 Cheshire Signs
201 Old Homestead Highway
Keene, NH 03431-4441 603-352-5985
Neon and plastic signs
President: Anthony A Magaletta
Estimated Sales: $500,000-$1 Million
Number Employees: 1 to4

20519 Chesmont Engineering Company
619 Jeffers Cir
Exton, PA 19341 610-594-9200
Fax: 610-594-1909 heatpro@aol.com
www.chesmontengineering.com
Fume incinerators for volatile organic compounds and odors; also, process heating systems, fuel and propane standby systems and baking ovens
President: Christopher S Mohler
Office Administrator: Lois Lanza
VP: Christopher Mohler
Office Manager: Kathy Tiffany
Estimated Sales: Below $1Million
Number Employees: 1-4
Square Footage: 4000

20520 Chester Hoist
PO Box 449
Lisbon, OH 44432 330-424-7248
Fax: 330-424-3126 800-424-7248
sales@chesterhoist.com www.chesterhoist.com
Manufacturer and importer of hoists including manual chain, worm-drive and electrical low headroom; exporter of manual and electric chain hoists
Manager: Bob Burkey
Quality Control: Bob Eusanio
Sales Rep.: Chris Reynolds
Application Engineer: Vince Anderson
Product Manager: Joe Runyon
Estimated Sales: $10-20 Million
Number Employees: 50-99
Parent Co: Columbus McKinnon Corporation
Brands:
Chester
Model Am
Zephyr

20521 Chester Plastics
Highway 3
P.O. Box 460
Chester, NS B0J 1J0
Canada 902-275-3522
Fax: 902-275-5002
inquiries@chesterplastics.com
www.chesterplastics.com
Manufacturer and exporter of rigid plastic packaging and thermoformed plastic bottles; importer of plastic sheeting
President: George Nemskeri
General Manger: John Babiak
Marketing Manager: Ed Baker
General Manager: Michael Johnston
Number Employees: 90
Square Footage: 108000

20522 (HQ)Chester-Jensen Company,Inc.
PO Box 908
Chester, PA 19016-0908 610-876-6276
Fax: 610-876-0485 800-685-3750
htxchng@chester-jensen.com
www.chester-jensen.com
Stainless steel food processing equipment including beverage tanks and coolers, pasteurizers, regenerators, internal tube heaters, plate type heat exchangers, etc.; exporter of chillers and plate type heat exchangers
President: Richard Miller
CEO: Steven Miller
Sales Director: Robert Skoog
Estimated Sales: $10 - 20 Million
Number Employees: 50-99
Square Footage: 38000
Other Locations:
Chester-Jensen Company
Cattaraugus NY

20523 Chesterfield Awning Company
16999 Van Dam Rd
South Holland, IL 60473 312-666-0400
Fax: 708-596-9469 800-339-6522
david@chesterfieldawning.com
www.chesterfieldawning.com
Commercial awnings
President: Howard Ausema
Estimated Sales: $1-2,500,000
Number Employees: 1-4

20524 Chestnut Labs
3233 E. Chestnut Expressway
Springfield, MO 65802 417-829-3788
Fax: 417-829-3787
information@chestnutlabs.com
www.chestnutlabs.com
Laboratory testing for food microbiology pathogens such as Salmonella and Listeria testing, and water analysis testing.

20525 Chevron Global Lubricants
555 Market Street
San Francisco, CA 94105-2800 415-894-4646
Fax: 415-894-1297
Number Employees: 10,000 +

20526 Chicago Automated Labeling
44 N 450 E
Valparaiso, IN 46383 219-531-0646
Fax: 219-462-8315 info@chicagoautolabel.com
www.chicagoautolabel.com
Manufactueers of labeling equipment
Owner: Mark Walker
CEO: Ken Walker
Estimated Sales: $2 000,000
Number Employees: 10-19

20527 Chicago Conveyor Corporation
330 S La Londe Avenue
Addison, IL 60101-3309 630-543-6300
Fax: 630-543-2308 sales@chicagoconveyor.com
www.chicagoconveyor.com
Pneumatic conveying systems for powder or granular materials, storage spaces and related equipment, weighing bathcing and controls
VP Sales: Tom Hodanovac
Purchasing Manager: Keith Stark
Estimated Sales: $5-10 Million
Number Employees: 20
Square Footage: 60000

20528 Chicago Dowel Company
4700 W Grand Ave
Chicago, IL 60639 773-622-2000
Fax: 773-622-2047 800-333-6935
sales@chicagodowel.com
www.chicagodowel.com
Skewers for candy, apples, corn dogs and meat
President: Ralph Iacono
Sales Director: Jay Goodwin
Manager: George Iacono
Estimated Sales: $5 - 10 Million
Number Employees: 20-49
Square Footage: 50000

20529 Chicago Ink & Research Company
97 Ida Ave
Antioch, IL 60002-1836 847-395-1078
Fax: 847-395-3568

Industrial marking and rubber stamp inks
President: Charles Doty
General Manager: F Arthur Doty
Estimated Sales: $1-2.5 Million
Number Employees: 5 to 9
Square Footage: 8000

20530 Chicago Scale & Slicer Company
2359 Rose St
Franklin Park, IL 60131-3504 847-455-3400
Fax: 847-455-3450
Manufacturer, importer and exporter of hand operated and electric slicers; also, grinders and knives
Owner: Eugene Dee
Estimated Sales: $1 - 5 Million
Number Employees: 10 to 19
Square Footage: 14000
Parent Co: Lawndale Corporation
Brands:
Digi
Globe

20531 Chicago Show
851 Asbury Dr
Buffalo Grove, IL 60089 847-955-0200
Fax: 847-955-9996
jsnediker@chicagoshowinc.com
www.chicagoshow.com
Point of purchase advertising displays and signs; also, fixtures
CEO: James Snediker
CFO: B Fier
Estimated Sales: $5 - 10 Million
Number Employees: 50-99
Square Footage: 100000

20532 Chicago Stainless Equipment
1280 SW 34th St
Palm City, FL 34990 772-781-1441
Fax: 772-781-1488 800-927-8575
tfr@chicagostainless.com
www.chicagostainless.com
Since 1937, manufacturer of high quality sanitary pressure gauges, homogenizer gauges and digital thermometers
Manager: Jerry Williamson
VP of Marketing: Mark Mistarz
Sales Director: Jerry Williamson
Estimated Sales: $2.5-5 Million
Number Employees: 10-19
Brands:
Pharma-Flow
Sani-Flow

20533 Chicago Trashpacker Corporation
290 N Prospect St
Marengo, IL 60152-3235 815-568-5116
800-635-5745
info@chicagotrashpacker.com
www.chicagotrashpacker.com
Trash compactors, can and glass crushers
President/CEO: Fredrick Gohl
VP/R&D/Quality Control: Bill Phillips
Estimated Sales: Below $5 Million
Number Employees: 10
Number of Products: 12
Square Footage: 1000
Brands:
Trashpacker

20534 Chickadee Products
1208 N Swift Road
Addison, IL 60101-6104 773-523-7972
Fax: 773-523-9066 800-621-5046
donaldmk@aol.com www.kellyflour.com
Custom blending
Estimated Sales: $5-10 Million
Number Employees: 10-19

20535 Chickasaw Broom Manufacturing
7710 Jamison Road
Little Rock, AR 72209-5541 501-532-0311
Brooms and mops
CEO: Everette Hatcher
Number Employees: 25

20536 Chief Industries
PO Box 848
Kearney, NE 68848-0848 308-237-3186
Fax: 308-237-2650 800-359-8833
agri@chiefind.com www.chiefind.com
Manufacturer and exporter of grain drying and handling equipment; also, bins
President: Roger Townsend
Research & Development: Jim Moffit
Sales Director: Ed Benson
Plant Manager: Duene McCann
Purchasing Manager: Rob Morris
Estimated Sales: $20-50 Million
Number Employees: 100-249
Number of Brands: 3
Number of Products: 12
Square Footage: 90000
Parent Co: Chief Industries
Type of Packaging: Bulk
Brands:
Caldwell Manufacturing
Chief
York

20537 Chil-Con Products
PO Box 1385
Brantford, ON N3T 5T6
Canada 519-759-3010
Fax: 519-759-1611 800-263-0086
geninfo@henrytech.com www.henrytech.com
Manufacturer and exporter of pressure vessels, oil separators, condensers, process cooling heat exchangers, direct expansion and flooded chillers
General Manager: Scott Rahmel
President, Chief Executive Officer: Michael Giordano
Business Manager: Harry Stewart
Plant Manager: Myron Harasym
Number Employees: 95
Square Footage: 400000
Parent Co: Valve, Henry, Company

20538 Childres Custom Canvas
711 E. Hwy 67
P.O.Box 238
Duncanville, TX 75137 972-298-4943
Fax: 972-709-7453 info@childresproducts.com
www.childresproducts.com
Awnings
President: Gary D Childres
CFO: Linda Childres
Estimated Sales: $2,500,000
Number Employees: 20-49
Square Footage: 10000

20539 Chili Plastics
4 Pixley Industrial Pkwy
Rochester, NY 14624-2399 585-889-4680
Fax: 585-889-6199
Molded plastics including containers
Manager: Mike Curley
Estimated Sales: $.5 - 1 million
Number Employees: 1-4

20540 Chill Rite/Desco
P.O.Box 5566
Slidell, LA 70469 985-641-4865
Fax: 985-641-0183 800-256-2190
www.chillrite32.com
Beverage dispensing and delivery systems
President: Martin Abraham
Estimated Sales: $1 - 5 Million
Number Employees: 10-19
Brands:
Chill Rite
Desco

20541 Chilson's Shops
8 Industrial Pkwy
Easthampton, MA 01027 413-529-8062
Fax: 413-529-2022 chilsons@chilsons.com
www.chilsons.com
Commercial awnings
President and R&D and QC: Edward Ghareeb
Estimated Sales: $1 - 2,500,000
Number Employees: 10-19

20542 Chilton Consulting Group
PO Box 129
Rocky Face, GA 30740-0129 706-694-8325
Fax: 706-694-8316 info@chiltonconsulting.com
www.chiltonconsulting.com
Consulting firm providing HACCP development, validation and training, food safety and quality audits, crisis management, environmental sanitation audits, employee safety training, etc
President: Jeff Chilton
General Manager: Brentÿ Heldt
Associate Consultant: Wayne Wassner

20543 China D Food Service
2535 S Kessler Street
Wichita, KS 67217-1044 316-945-2323
Fax: 316-945-5557
Food service and management
Purchasing: Lisa Diez
Estimated Sales: $300,000-500,000
Number Employees: 1-4
Type of Packaging: Food Service

20544 China Lenox Incorporated
1414 Radcliffe Street
Bristol, PA 19007-5413 267-525-7800
www.lenox.com
Manufacturer and exporter of fine china dinnerware and giftware
Human Resources Manager: Jim Haddix
Estimated Sales: $91 Million
Number Employees: 1,500
Square Footage: 9774
Parent Co: Brown-Foreman
Type of Packaging: Food Service

20545 Chinet Company
722 Barrington Circle
Winter Springs, FL 32708-6117 407-365-5372
Fax: 407-359-8381 800-539-3726
julie.stoetzer@us.huhtamaki.com
www.mychinet.com
Biodegradable disposable tableware; serving the food service industry
District Sales Manager: Marvin Tolley

20546 Chinet Company
27601 Forbes Rd # 59
Laguna Niguel, CA 92677-1242 949-348-1711
Fax: 949-489-2043
Disposable plastic and paper tableware
Owner: Xiao Qiu
Regional Sales Manager: Ronald Shillings
Estimated Sales: Less than $500,000
Number Employees: 10-19
Brands:
Chinet

20547 Chino Works America
22301 S Western Ave
Sutie 105
Torrance, CA 90501-4155 310-787-8899
Fax: 310-787-8899 888-321-9118
info@chinoamerica.com www.chinoamerica.com
Recorders, controllers, infared technology (pyrometers) and noncontact moisture reading on line
President: Toshikazu Inden
Sales, OEM and Tech Support: Toshi Toshi
Sales Engineer: Mike Matsuno
Estimated Sales: $500,000-$1 Million
Number Employees: 5-9
Number of Products: 100

20548 Chip-Makers Tooling Supply
7352 Whittier Ave
Whittier, CA 90602-1131 562-698-5840
Fax: 562-698-5646 800-659-5840
chipmakerca@yahoo.com www.chip-makers.com
A major supplier of machines and parts to the food industry.
Manager: Patty Rivera
Office Manager/Purchasing Agent: Laura Kurbel
Estimated Sales: $3 - 5 Million
Number Employees: 10-19
Square Footage: 48000

20549 (HQ)Chiquita Brands International, Inc.
550 S. Caldwell Street
Charlotte, NC 28202 980-636-5000
800-438-0015
www.chiquita.com
Grower & processor of bananas, avocados, pineapples, crunchy fruit chips, snack bites, fresh salads
President Chief Executive Officer: Edward Lonergan
President, North America: Joe Huston
SVP & CFO: Rick Frier
SVP/Chief People Officer: Kevin Holland
SVP & COO: Brian Kocher
VP, Global Quality & Food Safety: Michael Burness
SVP/General Counsel/Secretary: James Thompson
Estimated Sales: $3 Billion
Number Employees: 21,000

Type of Packaging: Consumer, Food Service, Private Label, Bulk
Brands:
Chiquita
Fresh Express
Chiquita Juices
Chiquita Fruits

20550 **Chlorinators Inc**
P.O.Box 1518
Stuart, FL 34995 772-288-4854
Fax: 772-287-3238 800-327-9761
regal@regalchlorinators.com
www.regalchlorinators.com
Manufacturer and exporter of gas chlorinators, waste water treatment systems, sulphonators, dual cylinder scales, chlorine gas detectors, flow pacing control valves and vacuum monitors
President: Diane Haskett
Vice President: Chris Myers
Marketing Manager: Jill Majka
Operations Manager: John Hentz
Estimated Sales: $3 - 5 Million
Square Footage: 10000
Brands:
Regal

20551 **Chocolate Concepts**
114 S Prospect Ave
Hartville, OH 44632-1360 330-877-3322
Fax: 330-877-1100 cc@dmpweb.net
www.dmpweb.net/chocolateconcepts
Manufacturer, importer and exporter of chocolate equipment including tempering tanks, measuring pumps, vibrating tables, cooling conveying tunnels, coin machines and kettles; manufacturer and exporter of plastic standard and custommolds
Owner: Bob Barton Jr
Estimated Sales: $1 - 2.5 Million
Number Employees: 5-9
Number of Products: 55
Square Footage: 120000
Parent Co: LCF
Brands:
Chocolate Concepts

20552 **(HQ)Choctaw-Kaul Distribution Company**
540 Vinewood Avenue
Detroit, MI 48208 313-894-9494
Fax: 313-894-7977 jgreer@choctawkaul.com
www.choctawkaul.com
Gloves, personal protective equipment and safety related products
Estimated Sales: $21 Million
Number Employees: 125
Square Footage: 110000

20553 **Choklit Molds Ltd**
23 Carrington Street
Lincoln, RI 02865 401-725-7377
Fax: 401-724-7776 800-777-6653
info@choklitmolds.com www.choklitmolds.com
Manufacturer and exporter of reusable plastic chocolate molds. Wholesaler of packaging supplies for the candy retail.
President: Lea Goyette
CEO: Richard Goyette
VP/Treasurer: Lea Goyette
Plant Manager: Chris Mottram
Purchasing: Kelly Mottram
Number Employees: 1-4
Square Footage: 20000
Type of Packaging: Bulk

20554 **Chop-Rite Two, Inc.**
531 Old Skippack Road
Harleysville, PA 19438 215-256-4620
Fax: 215-256-4363 800-683-5858
info@chop-rite.com www.chop-rite.com
Meat grinders, cherry stoners and juice extractors
Owner: Nancy Saeger
Estimated Sales: $5 - 10 Million
Number Employees: 10-19

20555 **Chord Engineering**
P.O.Box 518
Niwot, CO 80544 303-449-5812
Fax: 303-546-6405 sales@chord.org
www.chord.org
On-line inspection equipment for cans
Estimated Sales: Below $500,000
Number Employees: 2

20556 **Chore-Boy Corporation**
411 E Water Street
Centerville, IN 47330 765-855-5434
Fax: 765-855-1311
Sanitary pumps
President: Ronald Napier
Estimated Sales: $500,000-$1 Million
Number Employees: 5-9
Square Footage: 7000
Brands:
Chore-Boy
Kleen-Flo

20557 **Chori America**
154 Veterans Drive
Northvale, NJ 07647-2302 201-750-7050
Fax: 201-750-7055 866-420-7050
info@choripkg.com www.choripkg.com
Flexible pouch filling and sealing equipment
Estimated Sales: $1 - 3 Million
Number Employees: 1-4
Brands:
Hisaka Works Ltd
Toyo Jidoki

20558 **Chr Hansen, Inc**
9015 W Maple St
Milwaukee, WI 53214 414-601-5700
Fax: 414-607-5959 800-558-0802
dkinfo@chr-hansen.com www.chr-hansen.com
President and CEO: David R. Carpenter
Human Resources: Chris Beaudry
Estimated Sales: $50 - 75 Million
Number Employees: 350

20559 **(HQ)Chr. Hansen Inc.**
9015 W Maple St
Milwaukee, WI 53214 414-607-5700
Fax: 414-607-5959 800-558-0802
usinfo@chr-hansen.com
www.ch-humanhealth.com
Dairy cultures, natural and artificial colors, enzymes, probiotics for human health
Region VP, North America: David Carpenter
Sales & Marketing Coordinator: Joan Miller
Director of Sales, North America: Jim Hollida
Estimated Sales: $66 Million
Number Employees: 250
Type of Packaging: Food Service, Bulk

20560 **Chr. Hansen, Inc.**
9015 W Maple St
Milwaukee, WI 53214 414-607-5700
Fax: 414-607-5959 800-558-0802
usinfo@chr-hansen.com www.chr-hansen.com
Manufacturer, researcher and developer specializing in dairy cultures, colors, enzymes and probiotics for both human and animal health and nutrition.
President/CEO: Cees De Jong
Executive VP: Klaus Pederson

20561 **(HQ)Christianson Systems**
20421 15th St SE
PO Box 138
Blomkest, MN 56216 320-995-6141
Fax: 320-995-6145 800-328-8896
info@christianson.com www.christianson.com
Manufacturer and exporter of pneumatic conveyors and ship and barge unloaders
President: Jim Gerhardt
Marketing Manager: Barbara Gilberts
Sales: Tim Flaan
Estimated Sales: $5-10 Million
Number Employees: 50-99
Square Footage: 85000
Brands:
Chem-Vac
Handlair
Push-Pac
Superportable
Supertower
Vac-U-Vator

20562 **Christman Screenprint**
2822 Wilbur St
Springfield, MI 49037-7954 269-964-4240
Fax: 269-962-9411 800-962-9330
dtc@christmanscreenprint.com
www.ad-wise.com
Decals, labels, signs, aprons, shirts, jackets and hats
President: David Christman
Secretary: Dana Christman
VP: Michael Christman
Estimated Sales: Less than $500,000
Number Employees: 1-4

20563 **Christy Industries**
1812 Bath Ave
Brooklyn, NY 11214-4547 718-236-0211
Fax: 718-259-3294 800-472-2078
www.christy-ind.com
Manufacturer and exporter of fire and burglar alarms; wholesaler/distributor of intercoms and television equipment including security and closed circuit
President: Thomas Principale
Estimated Sales: $1 - 3 Million
Number Employees: 5 to 9
Square Footage: 3000

20564 **Christy Machine Company**
118 Birchard Ave
P.O. Box 32
Fremont, OH 43420 419-332-6451
Fax: 419-332-8800 888-332-6451
sales@christymachine.com
www.christymachine.com
Manufacturer and exporter of conveyers; also, filling, icing and glazing machinery
President: E B Christy
Estimated Sales: $1 - 2.5 Million
Number Employees: 5-9

20565 **Chroma Tone**
P.O.Box 4
Saint Clair, PA 17970 214-321-8601
Fax: 214-320-3791 800-878-1552
www.chromatoneinc.com
Metal and plastic signs, decals, point of purchase displays and candy rail strips
President: Matthew Parulis
Marketing Director: Nan Merchant
Plant Manager: Jerry Watts
Estimated Sales: $2.5-5 Million
Number Employees: 20-49
Square Footage: 30000

20566 **Chromalox**
103 Gamma Drive
Pittsburgh, PA 15238 412-967-3800
Fax: 412-967-5148 800-443-2640
www.chromalox.com
Manufacturer and exporter of electric heating elements for commercial cooking equipment
Managing Director: Steve Valentino
Chief Financial Officer/Secretary: Edward Cumberledge
Vice President: Peter Ranalli
Vice President, Engineering: Roger Ormsby
Quality Manager: Jack Foster
Marketing Manager: Paul Skidmore
Senior Vice President, Sales: John Halloran
Facilities Manager: Roger Iverson
Procurement Manager: Kristina McCann
Estimated Sales: $161 Million
Number Employees: 80
Square Footage: 20259
Parent Co: Emerson Electric Company
Brands:
Chromalox

20567 **Chronos Richardson**
2 Stewart Place
Fairfield, NJ 07004-2202 973-227-3522
Fax: 973-227-8478 800-284-3644
info@bmhchronosrichardson.com
www.bmhchronosrichardson.com
Bags, batching systems, form, fill and seal, palletizing
Mktg. Manager: Mike Hudak
Number Employees: 415

20568 **Chroust Associates International**
22311 Ventura Boulevard
Suite 115
Woodland Hills, CA 91364-1555 818-348-1438
Fax: 818-348-1094 chroust@aol.com
www.members.aol.com/chroust/associates.html
Consultant specializing in engineering and design for restaurants, schools, hotels, casinos, schools and universities
Principal: Thomas Chroust FCSI
Product Manager: Ivan Benes
Number Employees: 3
Square Footage: 6000

20569 Chrysler & Koppin Company
7000 Intervale St
Detroit, MI 48238 313-491-7100
Fax: 313-491-8769 800-441-0038
dkoppin@aol.com www.chryslerkoppin.com
Pre-fabricated walk-in refrigerators and freezers
President: Douglas G Koppin
CEO: Dean Koppin
CFO: Karen Mac-Donell-Oakley
Estimated Sales: $5-10 Million
Number Employees: 20-49

20570 Chrysler Jeep Dodge Ramof Kirkland
12828 NE 124th Street
Kirkland, WA 98034 877-606-8196
www.eastsidecj.com
Manufacturer and exporter of checkstands and display fixtures
Owner: Jack Carroll
Director Sales: Ginny Hansen
Estimated Sales: $5-10 Million
Number Employees: 50-99
Square Footage: 680000

20571 Chu's Packaging
10011 Santa Fe Springs Rd
Santa Fe Springs, CA 90670-2921 562-944-6411
Fax: 562-944-7113 800-377-4754
sales@movingpads.com www.movingpads.com
President: Julie Chu
Estimated Sales: $10 - 20 Million
Number Employees: 10-19

20572 Chuppa Knife Manufacturing
133 N Conalco Drive
Jackson, TN 38301 731-424-1212
Fax: 731-424-8937 chuppak@aol.com
Manufacturer and exporter of stainless steel and aluminum handle cutlery
President: Elmer Rausch
Estimated Sales: $1 - 2.5 Million
Number Employees: 8
Number of Products: 350
Type of Packaging: Consumer, Food Service, Private Label

20573 (HQ)Church & Dwight Company
Princeton South Corporate Center
500 Charles Ewing Boulevard
Princeton, NJ 08628
800-833-9532
www.churchdwight.com
Largest US producer of sodium bicarbonate, which it sells together with other specialty inorganic chemicals for a variety of industrial, institutional, medical and food applications. Also sells specialty cleaning products.
Co-Founder: Austin Church
Chairman & CEO: James Craigie
Executive VP & CFO: Matthew Farrell
Co-Founder: John Dwight
Exec. VP, Global Research & Development: Paul Siracusa PhD
EVP, Global New Products Innovation: Steven Cugine
Executive VP & Chief Marketing Officer: Bruce Fleming
Executive VP, Domestic Consumer Sales: Louis Tursi Jr.
Executive VP, Human Resources: Jacquelin Brova
Executive VP, Global Operations: Mark Conish
Estimated Sales: $2.9 Billion
Number Employees: 4400
Type of Packaging: Consumer, Food Service, Bulk
Other Locations:
Lakewood NJ
London OH
Green River WY
Old Fort OH
Madera CA
Oskaloosa IA
Princeton NJ
Colonial Heights VA
North Brunswick NJ
Harrisonville MO
Brands:
Arm & Hammer®
Kaboom®

20574 Church Offset Printing Inc. & North American Label
1731 Margaretha Ave.
P.O. Box 988
Albert Lea, MN 56007 507-373-6485
Fax: 507-373-2716 800-345-2116
sales@churchoffsetprinting.com
www.churchoffsetprinting.com
Labels for automatic or hand application; also, specializing in flexographic printing
President, CEO: Micheal Kruse
Financial Manager: Dan Bodensteiner
Plant and Project Manager: Todd Hoenisch
Estimated Sales: Below $1 Million
Number Employees: 1-4

20575 (HQ)Cima-Pak Corporation
50 Lindsay? Avenue
Dorval, QC H9P 2T8?
Canada 514-631-6222
Fax: 514-631-7361 877-631-2462
info@cima-pak.com www.cima-pak.com
Shrink packaging machinery
President: Tim Dawson
Sales Manager: Todd Trudel
Other Locations:
Mississauga, ON
Mooers NY

20576 Cimino Box Company
8500 Clinton Rd # J
Cleveland, OH 44144-1000 216-961-7377
Fax: 216-961-4054
Pallets
Owner: Frank Ritson
VP: Frank Ritson
Estimated Sales: $500,000-$1 Million
Number Employees: 5 to 9

20577 Cin-Made Packaging Group
1780 Dreman Ave
Cincinnati, OH 45223-2456 513-681-3600
Fax: 513-541-5945 info@cin-made.com
www.cin-made.com
Manufacturer and exporter of paper composite cans and tubes for specialty markets including wine and spirits, fancy foods and teas.
Manager: Hartmut Geisselbrecht
CFO: John Ewalt
Quality Control: Erik Frey
Marketing Director: Hartmut Geisselbrecht
Sales Manager: Janet Pickerell
Plant Manager: Eric Frey
Purchasing Manager: Phyllis Dietrich
Estimated Sales: $10-20 Million
Number Employees: 20-49
Type of Packaging: Consumer, Private Label

20578 (HQ)Cincinnati Boss Company
2420 Z St
Omaha, NE 68107-4430 402-556-4070
Fax: 402-556-2927 sperlingboss@aol.com
www.sperlingind.com
Manufacturer and exporter of meat processing equipment including sausage makers, cookers, renderers, cutters, presses and grinders, as well as food processing machinery. Also material handlers and conveyors
President: Craig Ellett
Executive VP: C Schmidt
Estimated Sales: $3 - 5 Million
Number Employees: 10-19
Square Footage: 400000
Other Locations:
Cincinnati Boss Co.
Bellevue NE
Brands:
Boss
Chop Cut
Excoriator
Permeator

20579 Cincinnati Convertors
1730 Cleneay Ave
Cincinnati, OH 45212 513-731-6600
Fax: 513-731-6605
cincinnatconvertors@cincinnaticonvertors.com
www.cincinnaticonvertors.com
Up to 6 color printed and plain flexible packaging for food, pharmaceutical and chemical applications: cellophane bags, confectioners' bags, heat sealed bags, food bags, plastic packaging, thermoformed cups, pouch lidding materials andtea bag tags
President: Donald U Ellsworth Jr
VP: Donald Ellsworth, Jr.
Estimated Sales: $2.5 - 5 Million
Number Employees: 20-49

20580 Cincinnati Foam Products
3244 McGill Rd
Cincinnati, OH 45251 513-741-7722
Fax: 513-741-7723
info@cincinnatifoamproducts.com
www.cincinnatifoamproducts.com
Manufacture high quality foam shipping containers, protective packaging, molded EPS and fabricated foam.
Founder: Carl Welage
Plant Manager: John Shearer
Estimated Sales: Below $5 Million
Number Employees: 5-9
Square Footage: 10000
Type of Packaging: Consumer, Food Service, Private Label, Bulk

20581 Cincinnati Industrial Machinery
4600 N. Mason-Montgomery Rd.
Mason, OH 45040 513-923-5601
Fax: 513-923-5694 800-677-0076
sales@cinind.com www.afindustries.com
Warewashing equipment for bakeries, supermarkets, food processing, and institutions
Global Sales Director: George Shillcock
Estimated Sales: $5 - 10 Million
Number Employees: 50-99
Number of Brands: 2
Square Footage: 320000
Parent Co: The Armor Group, Inc
Type of Packaging: Food Service

20582 Cincinnati Industrial Machine
4600 N Mason Montgomery Rd
Mason, OH 45040 513-923-5669
Fax: 513-923-5694 800-677-0076
sales@cinind.com www.cinind.com
Manufacturer and exporter of baking ovens and can washing equipment; also turnkey finishing systems and cleaning/drying/curing systems
President: Dave Schmidt
Marketing Director: Liz Chamberlain
Public Relations: Liz Chamberlain
Operations Manager: Joe Bohlen
Estimated Sales: $20 - 25 Million
Number Employees: 100-249
Square Footage: 317000

20583 Cinelli Esperia
380 Chrislea Road
Woodbridge, ON L4L 8A8
Canada 905-856-1820
albert@cinelli.com
www.gcinelli-esperia.com
Manufacturer and exporter of spiral mixers, bagel and roll machinery, steam proofers, baguette and bread molders, automatic bun dividers, rounders, sheeters, etc.; importer of coffee machines and revolving rack and convection ovens
President: Guido Cinnelli
Sales/Marketing Manager: Albert Cinelli
Number Employees: 50
Square Footage: 160000
Brands:
G. Cinelli-Esperia Corp.

20584 (HQ)Cintas Corporation
PO Box 625737
6800 Cintas Blvd
Cincinnati, OH 45262-5737 513-459-1200
Fax: 513-573-4130 800-246-8271
info@cintas.com www.cintas.com
Business uniforms; also, rental uniform service available
President & Chief Operating Officer: J. Phillip Holloman
Chief Executive Officer: Scott Farmer
Senior VP & Chief Financial Officer: William Gale
Vice President & Treasurer: J. Michael Hansen
Estimated Sales: $4.1 Billion
Number Employees: 30,000

20585 Cintex of America
283 E Lies Rd
Carol Stream, IL 60188 630-588-0900
Fax: 425-962-4600 800-424-6839
info@cintex.com www.cintex.com
Manufacturer and exporter of metal detection check weighing equipment, x-ray inspection systems and vision systems
President: Anthony Divito
CEO: Simon Armstrong
CFO: Richard Harwood Smith
Marketing: Dan Izzard
Sales: Dan Izzaro
Production: Jeff Hoffman
Plant Manager: Jeff Hoffman
Purchasing: Sandy Sell
Estimated Sales: $10-20 Million
Number Employees: 50-99
Number of Brands: 10
Number of Products: 4
Square Footage: 30000
Brands:
Autosearch
Eclipse
Insight

20586 Cipriani Harrison Valves
30271 Tomas St
Rcho Sta Marg, CA 92688 949-589-3978
Fax: 949-589-3979
chris@cipriniharrisvalves.com
www.ciprianiharrisonvalves.com
Manufacturer, distributor and importer of hygienic stainless steel valves
President: Carlo Cipriani
CEO: Robert Moreno
Vice President: Maria Grazia Cipriani
Marketing/Sales VP: Carlo Cipriani
Estimated Sales: $1,000,000
Number Employees: 5-9
Square Footage: 3000

20587 Circle Packaging Machinery Inc
2020 American Blvd
De Pere, WI 54115 920-983-3420
Fax: 920-983-3421
dstelzer@circlepackaging.com
www.circlepackaging.com
Vertical and horizontal form/fill/seal machines. F/F/S machines can be used to package a wide verity of liquids, tablet, capsules and other food and beverage products.
President: John Dykema
VP Marketing & Sales: Don Stelzer
Product Manager: Craig Stelzer
Production Manager: Steve Joosten
Parts & Service Manager: Ralph Ruggiero
Estimated Sales: Less than $500,000
Number Employees: 20-49
Type of Packaging: Consumer

20588 Circuits & Systems
59 2nd St
East Rockaway, NY 11518 516-593-4465
Fax: 516-593-4607 800-645-4301
sales@arlynscales.com www.arlynscales.com
Manufacturer and exporter of electronic scales
President: Arnold Gordon
Estimated Sales: Below $5 Million
Number Employees: 20-49
Square Footage: 10000

20589 Cisco-Eagle
2120 Valley View Ln
Farmers Branch, TX 75234 972-406-9330
Fax: 972-406-9577 www.cisco-eagle.com
Carton erecting and sealing equipment; conveyors, conveyor systems, storage systems
President: Steve Strifler
Chairman the Board: Warren W Gandall
CEO: Warren W Gandall
Office Manager: Marc Dewall
Estimated Sales: $20 - 50 Million
Number Employees: 50-99
Type of Packaging: Bulk

20590 Citadel Computer Corporation
60A State Route 101A
Amherst, NH 03031-2213 603-672-5500
Fax: 603-672-5590 sales@citadelcompouter.com
www.citadelcomputer.com
Industrial computer systems for advanced information management and data collection applications in industrial warehousing, transportation and logistics-product configurations include integrated touchscreens and multilple displaysizes
President: Gregory Walker
CFO: Lesley Sillion
Manager: Andy Nacard
VP Sales: Brandy Herring
Estimated Sales: $10 - 25 Million
Number Employees: 2

20591 Citra-Tech
1757 Birchwood Loop
Lakeland, FL 33811 863-646-3868
Fax: 941-683-8483
Manufacturer and exporter of fruit handling and processing machinery; consultant specializing in the design and construction of fresh and citrus fruit processing facilities
President: P M Irby
VP: P Irby, Jr.
Number Employees: 25
Square Footage: 4000

20592 Citrus and Allied Essences
3000 Marcus Ave, Ste 3e11
New Hyde Park, NY 11042 516-354-1200
Fax: 516-354-1502 www.citrusandallied.com
Supplier of essential oils, oleoresins, aromatic chemicals and specialty flavor ingredients.
President/CEO/Owner: Richard Pisano Jr.
Executive Vice President: Stephen Pisano
Sales Manager: Ann Heller
Director Purchasing: Rob Haedrich
Number Employees: 100+
Type of Packaging: Food Service, Bulk

20593 City Box Company
4390 Liberty Street
Aurora, IL 60504-9502 773-277-5500
Fax: 773-277-9541 citybox@cityboxco.com
Corrugated cartons; also, inner packaging
Marketing/Sales: Mark Rosenhlatt
*Estimated Sales:*less than $500,000
Number Employees: 20
Square Footage: 89000

20594 City Canvas
750 W San Carlos St
San Jose, CA 95126 408-287-2688
Fax: 408-287-1727 info@citycanvas.com
www.citycanvas.com
Commercial awnings, canopies, backyard products, custom projects and yards. Also custom fabrication and installation of the finest commercial and residential retractable styles
President: Johnny Cerrito
Estimated Sales: $1-2,500,000
Number Employees: 10-19
Number of Brands: 25

20595 City Grafx
243 Grimes Street
Suite D
Eugene, OR 97402 541-345-1101
Fax: 541-345-1942 800-258-2489
info@citygrafx.com www.citygrafx.com
Manufacturer and exporter of tabletop signs, table numbers, specialty merchandising boards, custom signs, menu boards and dimensional graphics
President: Jeff Phoenix
VP: Mary Phoenix
Estimated Sales: Below $5 Million
Number Employees: 1-4
Square Footage: 16000

20596 City Neon Sign Company
3117 E Glass Ave Ste C
Spokane, WA 99217 509-483-5171
Advertising, neon, electric and plastic signs
Owner: Thomas Quigley
*Estimated Sales:*less than $500,000
Number Employees: 1-4

20597 City Sign Services
3914 Elm St
Dallas, TX 75226-1218 214-826-4475
Fax: 214-826-4722 css1956@aol.com
Signs including advertising, neon, painted, indoor and outdoor
President: Patsy Waits
CFO: Shelly Peters
Quality Control: Kenneth Waits
Estimated Sales: $2.5 - 5 Million
Number Employees: 20 to 49

20598 City Signs
65 Bonwood Dr
Jackson, TN 38301 731-424-5551
Fax: 731-427-9096 877-248-9744
sales2@citysigns.com www.citysigns.com
Electric, plastic and neon signs, billboards and electronic message centers
Owner: John Mc Caskill
Marketing Director: Paul Anderson
National Sales Manager: Scott Rogers
Estimated Sales: $2.5-5 Million
Number Employees: 10-19

20599 City Stamp & Seal Company
1308 W Anderson Ln # A
Austin, TX 78757-1467 512-452-2577
Fax: 512-452-2979 800-950-6074
Rubber stamps, badges, wall signs and embossing seals
Owner: Donald L Daniel
Office Manager: Sharon Smith
General Manager: Stacy Daniel
Estimated Sales: $1 - 2.5 Million
Number Employees: 5 to 9
Square Footage: 4200

20600 Claire Manufacturing Company
500 S Vista Ave
Addison, IL 60101 630-543-7600
Fax: 630-543-4310 800-252-4731
www.clairemfg.com
Cleaning compounds, glass cleaners, aerosols, disinfectants, polishers and insecticides
President: Tony Schwab
CFO: Roger Hayes
VP Sales/Marketing: Bob Potvin
Estimated Sales: G
Number Employees: 250-499
Square Footage: 85000
Parent Co: Oakite Products
Brands:
Dust Up
Fast Kill
Fly Jinx
Gleme
Mister Jinx

20601 Clamco Corporation
775 Berea Industrial Parkway
Berea, OH 44017 216-267-1911
Fax: 216-267-8713 info@clamcocorp.com
www.clamcocorp.com
Manufacturer and exporter of shrink packaging machinery and bag sealers
Owner: Serge Bergun
CEO: Mark Goldman
VP: Dennis McGrath
R&D: Rob Patton
Marketing: Dennis McGrath
Sales Director: Bruce Howell
General Manager: Larry Boyles
Purchasing: Bob Snyder
Estimated Sales: $5-10 Million
Number Employees: 40
Square Footage: 24000
Parent Co: PAC Machinery Group
Type of Packaging: Consumer, Food Service, Private Label, Bulk

20602 Clamp Swing Pricing Company
8386 Capwell Dr
Oakland, CA 94621 510-567-1600
Fax: 510-567-1830 800-227-7615
cspinfo@clampswing.com
www.clampswing.com
Manufacturer and exporter of pricing tags, sign holders, display hooks, hand trucks, handheld plastic shopping baskets, etc
President: Benjamin Garfinkle
Sales/Marketing Executive: Kamran Faizi
Purchasing Manager: Ron Coffman
Estimated Sales: $3 - 5 Million
Number Employees: 20-49
Brands:
Celographics
Deligraphics
Doubletalk
Frameworks
Fresh Facts
Kick-Off
Monorail

Spacesaver
Vari-Extenders
View-Lok

20603 Clanton & Company
2204 E Vista Canyon Rd
Orange, CA 92867 714-282-7980
Fax: 714-978-7103 fssearch@aol.com
Executive recruitment firm specializing in the placement of sales and management personnel within the food and disposable manufacturing industry
Owner: Diane Clanton
Estimated Sales: Less than $500,000
Number Employees: 1-4

20604 (HQ)Claridge Products & Equipment
601 US 32
Harrison, AR 72602
Fax: 870-743-1908 orders@claridgeproducts.com
www.claridgeproducts.com
Manufacturer and exporter of menu signs and boards, display cases and cabinets, easels, chalkboards, markerboards, etc.; importer of raw materials
President: Helen Clavey
CFO: Leslie Eddings
VP: Paul Clavey II
Purchasing Director: John Wilson
Number Employees: 250-499
Square Footage: 300000
Other Locations:
Claridge Products & Equipment
Mamaroneck NY
Claridge Products & Equipment
Palatine IL
South Central Claridge
Farmers Branch TX
Claridge Products & Equipment
San Leandro CA
Brands:
Claridge Cork
Fabricork
Lcs
Vitracite

20605 Clark Caster Company
7310 Roosevelt Rd
Forest Park, IL 60130-0073 708-366-1913
Fax: 708-366-5103 800-538-0765
info@clarkcaster.com www.clarkcaster.com
Casters, wheels
President: James Clark
Estimated Sales: $2.5 - 5 Million
Number Employees: 5-9
Square Footage: 6000

20606 Clark Stek-O Corporation
148 E 5th St
Bayonne, NJ 07002-4252 201-437-0770
Fax: 201-437-0664 www.muralo.com
Label pastes for glass, metal, wood, paper, etc.; also, adhesives
President: Jim Norton
Estimated Sales: $11.7 Million
Number Employees: 100
Parent Co: Norton & Son

20607 Clark-Cooper DivisionMagnatrol Valve Corporation
855 Industrial Highway
Unit 4
Cinnaminson, NJ 08077 856-829-4580
Fax: 856-829-7303
techsupport@clarkcooper.com
www.clarkcooper.com
Metering pumps and valves; exporter of pumps and skid systems
Manager: Brian White
CEO: Brian Hagan
CFO: Kevin Hagan
Plant Manager: John Chando
Estimated Sales: $3 - 5 Million
Number Employees: 10-19
Square Footage: 32000
Brands:
Chemtrol

20608 Clarke
14600 21st Avenue North
Plymouth, MN 55447
800-253-0367
chuck.ball@alto-us.com www.clarkeus.com
Floor maintenance equipment such as floor polishers, floor sanders, carpet extractors and vacuum cleaners
CEO: Mark Hefty
CFO: Niels Olsen
R&D: Tom Benton
Marketing: Rob Godlewski
Sales: John Castaldo
Estimated Sales: $10-20 Million
Number Employees: 300
Number of Products: 150
Square Footage: 250000
Parent Co: Incentive Group
Brands:
A.L. Cook Technology
American Sanders Technology
American-Lincoln Technology
Clarke Technology
Delco Technology
Kew Technology
Simpson Technology

20609 Clarkson Chemical Company
213 Main St
Williamsport, PA 17702-7312 570-916-1308
Fax: 570-286-6419 800-326-9457
clarksonmurphy@gmail.com
Warewashing and laundry washing products; also, chemicals for hydro-therapy equipment
President: Mike Stuempfle
Estimated Sales: $1-2.5 Million
Number Employees: 5-9

20610 Classic Signs
13 Columbia Dr Unit 16
Amherst, NH 03031 603-883-0384
Fax: 603-882-2962 800-734-7446
ptripp@classicsignsnh.com
www.classicsignsnh.com
Electric signs including interior, vehicle and changeable letter
President: Paul Tripp
Estimated Sales: Below $5 Million
Number Employees: 10-19

20611 Classico Seating
801 N Clay St
Peru, IN 46970 765-473-6691
Fax: 800-242-9787 800-968-6655
sales@classicoseating.com
www.classicoseating.com
Manufacturer and exporter of metal chairs, barstools, dinettes, tables and table bases
President: Kim Regan
CFO: Hank Richardson
Estimated Sales: $20 - 50 Million
Number Employees: 100-249
Square Footage: 125000
Type of Packaging: Consumer, Food Service
Brands:
Classico Seating

20612 Classy Basket
9275 Trade Place
San Diego, CA 92126-6318 858-274-4901
Fax: 858-274-0795 888-449-4901
info@patent.org www.classybasket.com
Novelty food gift baskets
Estimated Sales: $1 - 5 Million
Number Employees: 2

20613 Claude Neon Signs
1808 Cherry Hill Rd
Baltimore, MD 21230-3522 410-685-7575
Fax: 410-837-3154
Electric, neon and fluorescent signs, floodlights and bullet resistant protection equipment
President: Alan Nethen
Estimated Sales: $1 - 2.5 Million
Number Employees: 20-49
Square Footage: 8000

20614 Clauss Tools
60 Round Hill Road
Fairfield, CT 6824 877-412-7467
Fax: 419-332-8077 800-835-2263
orders@shopatron.com www.claussco.com
Hand tools: engonomic food processing shears
President: Scott Sprause
Marketing Director: William Miller
Sales Director: E Ted Miller
Estimated Sales: $5-10 Million
Number Employees: 10
Type of Packaging: Bulk

20615 Clawson Container Company
4545 Clawson Tank Dr
Clarkston, MI 48346 248-625-3921
Fax: 248-625-3066 800-325-8700
customerservice@clawsoncontainer.com
www.clawsoncontainer.com
Complete line of steel, composite, and rotationally and blow molded polyethylene intermediate bulk containers. Container management services include daily rental program and ReturnNet System for the Passport IBC, which picks upreconditions and recycles the container for the customer; ISO 9001:200 certified.
President: Dick Harding
VP: Robert Harding
Quality Control: Peter Ricketts
Marketing: Carol Abid
Sales: Dave McKenna
Public Relations: Mike Lehman
Estimated Sales: $20 - 50 Million
Number Employees: 20-49
Type of Packaging: Bulk
Brands:
Enviroclean Gold
Jumbo Bin

20616 Clawson Machine
12 Cork Hill Rd
Franklin, NJ 07416-1304 973-827-8209
Fax: 973-827-4613 800-828-4088
eclipse@nac.net www.clawsonmachine.com
Cole slaw cutters and ice crushers and shavers for sno-cones; exporter of ice crushers, ice shavers and slaw cutters
President: Ryan Barbulescu
Customer Service: Diane Olsen
Estimated Sales: $10 - 20 Million
Number Employees: 50-99
Square Footage: 10000
Parent Co: Technology General Corporation
Type of Packaging: Food Service
Brands:
Hail Queen
Plus Crusher
Princess Chipper
Snow Ball Ice Shavers

20617 Clayton & Lambert Manufacturing
3813 West Highway 146
Buckner, KY 40010 502-222-1411
Fax: 502-222-1415 800-626-5819
info@claytonlambert.com
www.claytonlambert.com
Manufacturer and exporter of galvanized and stainless steel tanks for storage
President: John Lambert
Estimated Sales: $2.5-5 Million
Number Employees: 10-19
Square Footage: 700000
Brands:
Herd King
Silver Shield

20618 Clayton Corporation
866 Horan Dr
Fenton, MO 63026 636-349-5333
Fax: 636-349-5335 800-729-8220
sales@claytoncorp.com www.claytoncorp.com
Manufacturer and exporter of aerosol valves and covers
President: Bryan Lapin
CEO: Barry Baker
VP Engineer: Joe Lott
Research & Development: Ken Rueschhoff
Quality Control: Dale Damron
Marketing Director: Stacy Thomas
Sales Manager: Ric Berger
Public Relations: Stacy Thomas
Operations Manager: Berry Baker
Plant Manager: Phil Birdstill
Purchasing Manager: Gene Lapin
Estimated Sales: $1 - 5 Million
Number Employees: 100-249
Type of Packaging: Bulk

20619 Clayton Industries
17477 Hurley St
City of Industry, CA 91744 626-435-1200
Fax: 626-435-0180 800-423-4585
sales@claytonindustries.com
www.claytonindustries.com

Manufacturer and exporter of steam generators
President: John Clayton
Chairman: William N
CFO: Boyd Calvin
Quality Control: Jess Alvear
Sales: Marsha Ashley
Plant Manager: Robin Pope
Purchasing Director: Maria Serna
Estimated Sales: $20-50 Million
Number Employees: 100-249

20620 Clayton L. Hagy & Son
5000 Paschall Ave
Philadelphia, PA 19143-5136 215-844-6470
Fax: 215-724-9983
Wiping cloths and cheesecloth
Owner: Andriea Bookbinder
Estimated Sales: $1 - 3 Million
Number Employees: 10 to 19
Parent Co: American By Products

20621 Clayton Manufacturing Company
7873 Catherine Street
Derby, NY 14047-9597 716-549-0392
Fax: 716-549-0392 claytonmfg@aol.com
Pie crimpers and cake slicers
President: John Clayton
Vice President: Jim Oetinger
Square Footage: 35000
Type of Packaging: Food Service

20622 Clean All
838 Erie Boulevard W
Syracuse, NY 13204-2214 315-472-9189
Fax: 315-472-3904 cleanallproducts@aol.com
Owner/President: Severino Gonnella
CEO/Finance Executive: August Gonnella
Sales Executive: August Gonnella
Estimated Sales: Below $5 Million
Number Employees: 25

20623 Clean Freak
3900 N Providence Avenue
Appleton, WI 54913 920-882-8453
Fax: 920-380-0878 888-722-5508
info@cleanfreak.com www.cleanfreak.com
Maufacturer and supplier of cleaning equipment and supplies

Parent Co: Packaging Tape Inc.

20624 Clean Room Products
1800 Ocean Ave
Ronkonkoma, NY 11779-6532 631-588-7000
Fax: 631-588-7863 800-777-2532
pjcarcara@knfcorporation.com
www.knfcorporation.com
Clean rooms and equipment, controls, energy controls, piping, fittings and tubing, sanitary, processing and packaging
President: Phil Cacara
Sales Manager: Lee Gordon
General Manager: John Stuerzel
Estimated Sales: $10-20 Million
Number Employees: 50-99

20625 Clean That Pot
PO Box 5429
Whittier, CA 90607 909-674-8332
Fax: 909-674-8395 800-621-7868
service@championchemical.com
www.cleanthatpot.com
Provides effective solutions for the coffee industry's toughest cleaning challenges.
President: Andrew Ellis
VP: Dennis Hall
Estimated Sales: $1.4 Million
Number Employees: 8
Square Footage: 32000

20626 Clean Water Systems International
2322 Marina Drive
PO Box 146
Klamath Falls, OR 97601-0008 541-882-9993
Fax: 541-882-9994 866-273-9993
info@cleanwatersysintl.com
www.cleanwatersysintl.com
Manufacturer and exporter of solid state ballasts, UV sensing, monitor and control system, ultraviolet water, and waste water treatment systems and air ozone units
President/CEO: Charles Romary
Estimated Sales: $500,000
Number Employees: 5-9
Square Footage: 6000
Parent Co: C G Romary & Son
Type of Packaging: Private Label
Brands:
Cws

20627 Clean Water Technologies
151 W 135th St
Los Angeles, CA 90061 310-380-4648
Fax: 310-380-4658 info@cleanwatertech.com
www.cleanwatertech.com
Solid/liquid separating machines in wastewater.
Parent Co: The Marvin Group

20628 Clear Lam Packaging
1950 Pratt Blvd
Elk Grove Village, IL 60007 847-439-8570
Fax: 847-439-8589 www.clearlam.com
Flexible and rigid packaging materials printed and laminated films for form/fill/seal and lidding.
President: James Sanfilippo
CMO: Roman Forowycz
Estimated Sales: $100-500 Million
Number Employees: 500-999

20629 Clear Pack Company
11610 Copenhagen Ct
Franklin Park, IL 60131 847-957-6282
Fax: 847-957-1529 info@clearpk.com
www.clearpk.com
Thermoformed plastic containers used in the frozen food industry
Manager: Art Hagg
VP Finances: R Sperl
Sales Manager: Dan Curtis
Estimated Sales: $20 - 50 Million
Number Employees: 100-249
Square Footage: 240000
Type of Packaging: Bulk

20630 (HQ)Clear View Bag Company
5 Burdick Dr
Albany, NY 12205 518-458-7153
Fax: 518-458-1401 800-458-7153
sales_info@clearviewbag.com
www.clearviewbag.com
Plastic bags
President: William Romer
CFO: Virginia Trimarchi
Quality Control: Todd Romer
Sales Manager: Trent Romer
General Manager: William Todd Romer
Estimated Sales: $10 Million
Number Employees: 50-99
Square Footage: 64000
Type of Packaging: Consumer, Food Service, Private Label, Bulk
Other Locations:
Clear View Bag Co.
Thomasville NC

20631 Clear View Bag Company
7137 Prospect Church RD
Thomasville, NC 27360-8839 336-885-8131
Fax: 336-885-1044
Plastic bags
VP: Joe Romer
Manager: Daniel A Jones
Estimated Sales: $5-10 Million
Number Employees: 50-99
Parent Co: Clear View Bag Company

20632 Clearbags
4949 Windplay Drive
Suite 100
El Dorado Hills, CA 95762 916-933-4700
Fax: 916-933-4717 800-233-2630
sales@clearbags.com www.clearbags.com
Accessories/supplies i.e picnic baskets, specialty food packaging i.e .gift wrap/labels/boxes/containers.
Marketing: Danielle Badeaux

20633 Clearly Natural Products
1560 Big Shanty Drive
Kennesaw, GA 30144-1115
800-451-7096
cnatu31927@aol.com
www.clearlynaturalsoaps.com
Fruit and vegetable wash, citrus based and glycerine hand soaps, air fresheners and cleaners
Owner: Robert Rice
Public Relations: Wat Bagley
Office Manager: Peggy Dunne
Estimated Sales: $10-20 Million
Number Employees: 20-49
Number of Brands: 5
Number of Products: 20
Square Footage: 26000
Parent Co: Beaumont Products, Inc.
Type of Packaging: Consumer, Private Label
Brands:
Clearly Natural

20634 Clearplass Containers
40 Powell Ln
Penn Yan, NY 14527-1072 315-536-5690
Fax: 315-536-5699
d.rockefeller@silganplastics.com
www.silganplastics.com
Plastic jars and bottles
CFO: Joe Polhein
Sales/Marketing Manager: Jim McCormick
Manager (Customer Service): Dianne Clark
Plant Manager: Joel Sieber
Estimated Sales: $100 - 500 Million
Number Employees: 10-19
Parent Co: Silgan Plastics

20635 Clearr Corporation
6325 Sandburg Rd
Minneapolis, MN 55427-3629 763-398-5400
Fax: 763-398-0134 800-548-3269
info@clearrcorp.com www.clearrcorp.com
Pop displays, signage, light boxes, poster frames
President/Owner: Andy Steinfeldt
VP: Pete Nelson
Marketing: Ryan Lester
Sales: Darryl Helleman
Estimated Sales: $10 Million
Number Employees: 50-99
Number of Products: 15
Square Footage: 40000
Parent Co: Stylmark
Brands:
Alcon Plus
Edge Lite
Luminate Ultra
Moving Pix
Pointframe
Stretch Frame
Tension
Triad
Triola

20636 Clearr Corporation
6325 Sandburg Rd
Minneapolis, MN 55427-3629 763-398-5400
Fax: 763-398-0134 800-548-3269
info@clearrcorp.com www.clearrcorp.com
Manufacturer and exporter of back-lit, edge-lit and nonlit graphic display products; also, static graphic display products, sequential image, programmable multi-image and scrolling units available.
President: Andy Steinfeldt
Number Employees: 50-99
Brands:
A-Frame
Edgelite
Graphic Revolutions
Impact Island
Litewall
Luminaire
Luminaire Ultra
Luminaire Ultra Ii
Movingpix
Neon Plus E
Print Frame
Stretchframe
Triad

20637 Cleartec Packaging
409 Parkway Dr
Park Hills, MO 63601-4435 314-543-4150
Fax: 314-543-4054 800-817-8967
sales@cleartecpackaging.com
www.cleartecpackaging.com
Sales Manager: Michael Wester
Estimated Sales: $1 - 5 Million

20638 **Clearwater Packaging**
615 Grand Central St Ste B
Clearwater, FL 33756 727-442-2596
Fax: 727-447-3587 800-299-2596
sales@clearwaterpackaging.com
www.clearwaterpackaging.com
Manufacturer and exporter of packaging machinery
President: John Hoover
Estimated Sales: $5 - 10 Million
Number Employees: 20-49

20639 **Clearwater Paper Corporation**
Suite 1100
Spokane, WA 99201 509-344-5900
877-847-7831
www.clearwaterpaper.com
Manufacturer and exporter of paper packaging products
President/CEO: Linda Massman
Chief Financial Officer/SVP: John Hertz
SVP/General Counsel/Corporate Secretary: Michael Gadd
SVP, Human Resources: Jackson Lynch
Facility Manager: Rick Tucker
Vice President, Procurement: Terry Borden
Estimated Sales: $1.87 Billion
Number Employees: 3,860
Parent Co: Bell Fibre Company
Type of Packaging: Consumer, Bulk
Brands:
Rap-In-Wax
Wax Tex

20640 **Cleasby Manufacturing Company**
1414 Bancroft Ave
PO Box 24132
San Francisco, CA 94124 415-822-6565
Fax: 415-822-1843 info@cleasby.com
www.cleasby.com
Tar buckets, kettles, dump trailers and hoisting equipment
President: John Cleasby
Estimated Sales: $10-20 Million
Number Employees: 20-49

20641 **Cleaver-Brooks**
11950 West Lake Park Drive
Milwaukee, WI 53224 414-359-0600
www.cleaverbrooks.com
Manufacturer and exporter of packaged steam and hot water boilers; applications include food processing, packaging, sterilization, heating/ventilation/air conditioning, etc
President/CEO: Welch Goggins
Jr. President, Chief Executive Officer,: Welch Goggins
CFO/VP: Jeff Beine
Vice President of Procurement: Dan Harris
Vice President of Sales: Mike Donahue
Senior Vice President of Operations: Brett Kieffer
Plant Manager: Ronald G Thimm
Estimated Sales: I
Number Employees: 1,000-4,999
Square Footage: 100000

20642 **Cleco Systems**
1395 S Marietta Pkwy SE
Bldg 750
Marietta, GA 30067-4440 770-392-0330
Fax: 770-795-8093 clecosales@fkilogistex.com
www.clecosys.com
President: Kenneth Matson
R&D: Percy Nay
Quality Control: Ban Sandlnato
Estimated Sales: $5 - 10 Million
Number Employees: 15

20643 **Cleland Manufacturing Company**
2125 Argonne Dr NE
Columbia Heights, MN 55421-1317 763-571-4606
Fax: 763-571-4606
clealandmanufacturing@tcq.net
Manufacturer and exporter of grain/seed cleaners and spiral separators
President: Robert Maxton
Quality Control: George Maxton
VP: Mary Maxton
Estimated Sales: Less than $500,000
Number Employees: 2
Square Footage: 3000
Brands:
Expert Line

20644 **(HQ)Cleland Sales Corporation**
11051 Via El Mercado
Los Alamitos, CA 90720 562-598-6616
Fax: 562-598-3858
sales@blizzardbeersystems.com
www.clelandsales.com
Manufacturer, importer and exporter of automatic refill devices, beer chillers and beverage and dry powder dispensers.
President: Arlene Cleland
Vice President: Jimmy Cleland
Sales Director: Mike Pollock
Estimated Sales: $1 - 3 Million
Number Employees: 5-9
Square Footage: 20000
Type of Packaging: Food Service
Other Locations:
Cleland Sales Corp.
Los Alamitos CA
Brands:
Automate
Automix
Blizzard Beer Systems
Choc-O-Lot
Dove
Starline

20645 **Clements Industries**
50 Ruta Ct
South Hackensack, NJ 07606 201-440-5500
Fax: 201-440-1455 800-222-5540
steven@tach-it.com www.tach-it.com
Tape and label dispensers, twist tie equipment and supplies
President: Alan Clements
CEO: Steven Clements
CFO: Steven Clements
Vice President: Steven Clements
Research & Development: Steven Clements
VP Marketing: Steven Clements
VP Sales: Steven Clements
Operations Manager: Steven Clements
Production Manager: Alan Clements
Plant Manager: Steven Clements
Purchasing: Marilyn Ring
Number Employees: 10-19
Parent Co: Tech-It

20646 **Clerestory**
1740 Ridge Avenue
Suite 117
Evanston, IL 60201 312-640-5777
Fax: 312-915-5933 www.clstory.com
Tea and coffee industry cans
Founding principal and managing partner: Linda Toops
Founding principal and partner: Michelle Kerr
Estimated Sales: Below $5 Million
Number Employees: 5-9

20647 **Cleveland Canvas Goods Manufacturing Company**
1960 E 57th St
Cleveland, OH 44103 216-361-4567
Fax: 216-361-1728 sales@clevelandcanvas.com
www.clevelandcanvas.com
Insulated carrying cases and filter bags
President: William Morton
Treasurer: W Morton III
VP Sales: M Howard
Estimated Sales: $2.5-5 Million
Number Employees: 20-49
Square Footage: 32000
Brands:
The Coldholder

20648 **Cleveland Menu Printing**
1441 E 17th St
Cleveland, OH 44114 216-241-5256
Fax: 216-241-5696 800-356-6368
web_sales@clevelandmenu.com
www.clevelandmenu.com
Manfacturer and exporter of menus and menu boards, covers, holders and displays
President: Tom Ramella
Estimated Sales: $2.5-5 Million
Number Employees: 20-49

20649 **Cleveland Metal StampingCompany**
1231 W Bagley Rd #1
Berea, OH 44017-2942 440-234-0010
Fax: 440-234-8050
Manufacturer and exporter of bottle openers, burner bowls for gas ranges and metal shelf extenders; also, barbecue utensils including spatulas and forks.
Manager: Frank Ghinga
CFO: Dorina Ghinga
VP: Pascu Ghinga
Estimated Sales: $1 - 3 Million
Number Employees: 50 to 99
Number of Products: 200
Square Footage: 43000
Type of Packaging: Private Label, Bulk

20650 **Cleveland Mop Manufacturing Company**
5261 W 161st St
Cleveland, OH 44142-1606 216-898-5866
Fax: 216-898-5867 800-767-9934
clevelandmop@hotmail.com
www.clevelandmop.com
Wet mop heads, mop head handles, dust and bowl mops, floor machine pads, push brooms and broom handles
Owner: David Rhodes
Estimated Sales: $5-10 Million
Number Employees: 1-4
Square Footage: 40000
Brands:
Dumor
Eagle
Kleen Mor

20651 **Cleveland Motion Controls**
7550 Hub Pkwy
Cleveland, OH 44125 216-524-8800
Fax: 216-642-2199 800-321-8072
literature@cmccontrols.com
www.cmccontrols.com
Electronic industrial controls and systems
President: E Wayne Foley
Marketing/Communications Director: Tim Schultz
Product Manager: Kenneth Bobick
Estimated Sales: $50 - 100 Million
Number Employees: 100-249
Parent Co: IMC

20652 **Cleveland Plastic Films**
41740 Schadden Road
Elyria, OH 44035-2294 440-324-2222
Fax: 440-324-2790 800-832-6799
info@cpfco.net www.clevelandplasticfilms.com
Polyethylene films and printed and plain polyethylene bags for poultry, meat and pastries
CFO: Thomas Tyler
Vice President: James Hendershot
Sales Director: Frank Szabo
Plant Manager: Dan McDonald
Purchasing Manager: Paul Mirka
Estimated Sales: $5 - 10 Million
Number Employees: 100
Square Footage: 240000
Parent Co: Global Film & Packaging Corporation
Type of Packaging: Food Service, Bulk

20653 **Cleveland Range Company**
1333 East 179th Street
Cleveland, OH 44110 216-481-4900
Fax: 216-481-3782 800-338-2204
www.clevelandrange.com
Manufacturer and exporter of steam cooking equipment including convection steamers, kettles, skillets, combi-ovens and cook-chill systems
Estimated Sales: $48 Million
Number Employees: 220
Square Footage: 150000
Parent Co: The Manitowac Company, Inc.
Type of Packaging: Food Service
Brands:
Cleveland
Combicraft
Spectrum
Steamcraft

20654 **(HQ)Cleveland Specialties Company**
6612 Miami Trails Dr
Loveland, OH 45140-8044 513-677-9787
Fax: 513-683-4132
Plastic closures, plastic shrink film, milk carton handles and polycoated paperboard products including folding boxes and cartons; importer of packaging products
President: Nancy Hartmann
Vice President: James Downing

Estimated Sales: $1-2.5 Million
Number Employees: 1 to4
Type of Packaging: Consumer, Food Service, Private Label, Bulk

20655 Cleveland Vibrator Company
2828 Clinton Ave
Cleveland, OH 44113 216-241-7157
Fax: 216-241-3480 800-221-3298
cvc@clevelandvibrator.com
www.clevelandvibrator.com
Industrial vibrators including air piston, air ball, electromagnetic and rotary electric; also, air and electric brute force feeders and screeners and vibratory tables and conveyors
President: William Lee Gardner
CFO: Mike Valore
VP: Glen Roberts
CEO: Jeff Chokel
Marketing: Susan Koblyski
Sales: Jack Steinbuch
Public Relations: Suasan Kobylski
Plant Manager: Mike Weisinger
Estimated Sales: Below $5 Million
Number Employees: 20-49
Square Footage: 28000
Type of Packaging: Bulk
Brands:
Hybrute
Vibra-Ball
Vibra-Might

20656 Cleveland Wire Cloth & Manufacturing Company
3573 E 78th St
Cleveland, OH 44105-1596 216-341-1832
Fax: 216-341-1876 800-321-3234
cleveland@wirecloth.com www.wirecloth.com
Manufacturer, importer and exporter of woven wire cloth and wire cloth products.
President: C Crone
CFO: Joe Sarasa
VP Marketing: Larry Schrader
Estimated Sales: $5 - 10 Million
Number Employees: 20-49
Square Footage: 100000

20657 Cleveland-Eastern Mixers
4 Heritage Park Rd
Clinton, CT 06413-1836 860-669-1199
Fax: 860-669-7461 800-243-1188
info@emimixers.com www.clevelandmixer.com
Manufacturer and exporter of industrial fluid mixers
President: James Donkin
Sales Director: Sean Donkin
Estimated Sales: $10 Million
Number Employees: 20-49
Number of Brands: 30
Number of Products: 2
Square Footage: 25000
Parent Co: EMI Inc Technology Group
Brands:
Cleveland
Eastern

20658 Clevenger Frable LaVallee
39 Westmoreland Ave Ste 114
White Plains, NY 10606 914-997-9660
Fax: 914-997-9671 CFL@CFLDESIGN.COM
www.cfldesign.com
Consultant specializing in the design of commercial food facilities
President: Foster Frable Jr
CFO: James Lavalle
VP: James LaVallee
Number Employees: 20-49
Square Footage: 4000

20659 Clextral, Inc
14450 Carlson Cir
Tampa, FL 33626 813-854-4434
Fax: 813-855-2269 clextralusa@clextralusa.com
www.clextral.com
Manufacturer and exporter of food processing machinery including twin screw extruders
President: Frank Campiglia
Finance Administration: C Travaglini
VP: Benoit DeLaual
Estimated Sales: Below $5 Million
Number Employees: 10-19
Parent Co: Framatome USA

20660 Climate Master
7300 SW 44th St
Oklahoma City, OK 73179 405-745-6000
Fax: 405-745-6058 877-436-0263
cyperry@climatemaster.com
www.climatemaster.com
Manufacturer and exporter of heat pumps, air conditioners, filters and controls
President: Daniel Ellis
Estimated Sales: H
Number Employees: 250-499
Parent Co: LSB Corporation
Brands:
Climate Master

20661 Climax Industries
11836 Judd Ct
Suite 320
Dallas, TX 75243 972-881-8860
Fax: 972-424-0293 800-854-5063
artwork@climax-industries.com
www.climax-industries.com
Estimated Sales: $1 - 3 Million
Number Employees: 5-9

20662 (HQ)Climax Manufacturing Company
7840 State Route 26
Lowville, NY 13367 315-376-8000
Fax: 315-376-2034 800-225-4629
corporate@climaxpkg.com www.climaxpkg.com
Paperboard boxes and cartons
President/Chief Executive Officer: Patrick Purdy
Chief Financial Officer: Mary Wuest
Executive Vice President: Sarah Miller
Marketing: Lynn Campany
Sales Manager: Peter Dawes
Chief Operating Officer: Lizbeth Hirschey
Purchasing Agent: Kenny Hayter
Estimated Sales: $31 Million
Number Employees: 360

20663 Climax Packaging Machinery
25 Standen Dr
Hamilton, OH 45015 513-874-1233
Fax: 513-874-3375 info@climaxpackaging.com
www.climaxpackaging.com
Manufacturer and exporter of uncasing and case packing equipment, bottle conveyors, lane dividers, tray stackers and carton and flap openers
President: William George
Marketing/Sales: Jack Bunce
Purchasing: Barb Ruthwell
Estimated Sales: $5 - 10 Million
Number Employees: 20-49
Square Footage: 20000
Parent Co: GL Industries
Brands:
Air Cush'n
Sof-Pac

20664 Clipco
5841 Melshire Drive
Dallas, TX 75230-2117 972-239-8028
Fax: 972-980-7552
Plastic containers

20665 Clippard Instrument Laboratory
7390 Colerain Ave
Cincinnati, OH 45239 513-521-4261
Fax: 513-521-4464 sales@clippard.com
www.clippard.com
President: William L Clippard Iii
R&D: Sid Hendry
Chairman of the Board: William L Clippard III
Estimated Sales: $20 - 50 Million
Number Employees: 100-249

20666 Clipper Belt Lacer Company
1995 Oak Industrial Dr NE
Grand Rapids, MI 49505 616-459-3196
Fax: 616-459-4976 info@flexco.com
www.flexco.com
Manufacturer and exporter of mechanical belt fastening systems for conveyors
Manager: Nancy Ayres
CFO: Lee Merys
Marketing Specialist: Beth Miller
Estimated Sales: $10-20 Million
Number Employees: 50-99
Square Footage: 152000
Parent Co: Flexco - Grand Rapids
Brands:
Baler Belt Lacer
Clipmark
Clipper
Microlacer
Roller Lacer
Unibar
Valulacer

20667 Clipper Products
675 Cincinnati Batavia Pike
Cincinnati, OH 45245 513-528-7676
Fax: 513-528-7676 800-543-0324
sales@clipperproducts.com
www.clipperproducts.com
Two-wheel portable hand carts
Owner: Paul Wilhelm
CFO: Rose Mappin
Marketing Director: Mark Glassmeyer
Estimated Sales: $10 - 20 Million
Number Employees: 20-49
Brands:
Caddy-All
Jet Set
Super Cart

20668 Clock Associates
1629 SE 11th Ave
Portland, OR 97214 503-234-0202
Fax: 503-238-0420 www.clockassociates.com
Manufactures food product machinery
President: Ken Clock
Estimated Sales: Less than $500,000
Number Employees: 1-4

20669 (HQ)Clofine Dairy & Food Products
PO Box 335
Linwood, NJ 08221 609-653-1000
Fax: 609-653-0127 800-441-1001
info@clofinedairy.com www.clofinedairy.com
Manufacturer and distributor of a full line of fluid and dried dairy products, proteins, cheeses, milk replacement blends, tofu and soymilk powders, vital wheat gluten, etc.
Chairman: Larry Clofine
President/CEO: Frederick Smith
Account Manager: Andri Kuswendra
Account Manager: Rob Bernisky
Marketing - Fluid Products: Dawn Sink
Director/Manufactured Products: Jennifer Ingram
Estimated Sales: $20-50 Million
Number Employees: 10-19
Number of Brands: 2
Number of Products: 100
Type of Packaging: Food Service, Private Label, Bulk
Brands:
Fine-Mix Dairy
Food Blends
Soy Products
Soyfine
Soymilk

20670 (HQ)Clorox Company
P.O.Box 24305
1221 Broadway
Oakland, CA 94623 510-271-7000
Fax: 510-832-1463 888-271-7000
clorox@casupport.com
www.thecloroxcompany.com
Dips, dip mixes, and bbq sauces, marinades
Chairman/CEO: Donald Knauss
Estimated Sales: $5.5 Billion
Number Employees: 8400
Brands:
Brita
Clorox
Glad Bags
Kitchen Bouquet
Hidden Valley
Masterpiece

20671 Closure Systems International
7702 Woodland Drive
Suite 200
Indianapolis, IN 46278 317-390-5000
Fax: 317-390-5079 800-311-2740
www.csiclosures.com

Suppliers of closures for carbonated soft drinks, bottled water, juice & isotonic, milk and dairy products, alcoholic beverages, packaged foods and wine.
President: Thomas Degnan
President: Ruth Mack
VP Finance: Robert Smith
EVP: Lawrence Purtell
Quality Manager: Praveen Mathur
VP Human Resources: Arrigo Bodda
Number Employees: 586
Square Footage: 64000
Parent Co: Rank Group Limited

20672 **Cloud Company**
4120 Horizon Ln Ste A
San Luis Obispo, CA 93401 805-549-8093
Fax: 805-549-0131 800-234-5650
gb@cloudinc.com www.cloudinc.com
Manufacturer and exporter of rotary tank cleaning machines
President: David Rucker
Product and Marketing Manager: Mike Kemp
Regional Sales Manager: Lee LaFond
Division Manager: Greg Boege
Job Shop Division Mgr.: Richard Riggs
Manufacturing Mngr.: Brad Erickson
Estimated Sales: $2.5-5 Million
Number Employees: 20-49
Brands:
Cloud

20673 **Cloud Corporation**
1938 S Wolf Rd
Des Plaines, IL 60018-1928 847-390-9410
Fax: 847-299-2821 mwerner@cloudps.com
www.cloudps.com
Contract packager of powdered foods; manufacturer and exporter of packaging machinery including flexible pouch
President: Kevin Fritzmeyer
CFO: Bryan Lobett
VP: Michael Lear
Quality Control: Mark Orrison
Sales Director: Tom Gresge
Estimated Sales: $20 - 50 Million
Number Employees: 100-249

20674 **Cloudy & Britton**
6202 214th St SW
Mountlake Ter, WA 98043-2097 425-775-7424
Fax: 425-775-1715 info@cbife.com
www.cbife.com
Refrigeration systems including industrial refrigerators, freezing tunnels and spiral and plate freezers
President: Edward Cloudy
Purchasing Agent: Gordon Derksema
Estimated Sales: $5-10 Million
Number Employees: 5-9
Brands:
Cloudy & Britton

20675 **Clymer Enterprises**
P.O.Box 266
Pandora, OH 45877 419-384-3212
Fax: 419-384-7239 800-448-0784
clymersales@clymer-rack.com
www.clymer-rack.com
Manufacturer and exporter of roll-formed pallet rack systems
National Sales Manager: David Johnstone
Estimated Sales: $10-20 Million
Number Employees: 50-99
Parent Co: Unarco Material Handling, Inc.
Type of Packaging: Bulk

20676 **Co-Rect Products**
7105 Medicine Lake Rd
Golden Valley, MN 55427 763-542-9200
Fax: 763-542-9205 800-328-5702
co-rect@co-rectproducts.com
www.co-rectproducts.com
Bar and restaurant supplies; serving the food service market
President: M Pierce
Sales Manager: Bryan Mattson
Accounts Representative: Brian Mattson
Estimated Sales: $10-20 Million
Number Employees: 20-49
Number of Brands: 20
Square Footage: 30000
Type of Packaging: Food Service, Private Label, Bulk

20677 **Coade**
12777 Jones Rd Ste 480
Houston, TX 77070 281-890-4566
Fax: 281-890-3301 800-899-8787
sales@coade.com www.coade.com
Estimated Sales: $5-10 000,000
Number Employees: 20-49

20678 **Coast Controls**
7500 Commerce Ct
Sarasota, FL 34243 941-355-7555
Fax: 941-359-2321 800-513-2345
sales@coastcontrols.com
www.coastcontrols.com
Industrial process controls
President: Thomas Marks
Vice President: Kyle Koontz
Contact-Marketing/Sales: Rodney Shrock
Estimated Sales: Below $5 000,000
Number Employees: 10-19

20679 **Coast Label Company**
17406 Mount Cliffwood Cir
Fountain Valley, CA 92708 714-426-1410
Fax: 714-426-1440 800-995-0483
sales@coastlabel.com www.coastlabel.com
Offset, letterpress, flexography and seal press printed labels
President: Craig Moreland
Chief Executive Officer: Craig Moreland
Quality Control: Dave Fox
VP Sales: Tom Miller
Estimated Sales: $1 - 2.5 Million
Number Employees: 20-49

20680 **Coast Packing Company**
3275 East Vernon Avenue
Vernon, CA 90058 323-277-7700
Fax: 323-277-7712 www.coastpacking.com
Quality shortening products for the restaurant, baking and food industries. A supplier of animal fat and vegetable oil shortenings.
President: Ronald Gustafson
Sales: Dieter Rehnberg
Type of Packaging: Consumer, Food Service
Brands:
Viva
Flavor King
Supreme
Gold Coast
Coast
Bakers Choice
Golden Bake
Bakers Satin Blend

20681 **Coast Paper Box Company**
205 S Frank Bland Drive
San Bernardino, CA 92408 909-382-3475
Fax: 909-382-3481
Folding paper boxes
Number Employees: 50-99

20682 **Coast Scientific**
P.O. Box 185
Rancho Santa Fe, CA 92067
Fax: 800-791-8999 800-445-1544
info@coastscientific.com
www.medcosupplies.com
Manufacturer and exporter of adhesive mats, aprons, polyethylene bags, bouffant caps, carts, shelving, latex and vinyl gloves, convection ovens and disposable wipers
Manager: Alex Sardarian
Director Operations: Stacy Camp
Estimated Sales: $2.5-5 Million
Number Employees: 10-19

20683 **Coast Signs & Graphics**
520 Cypress Ave
Hermosa Beach, CA 90254 310-379-9921
Fax: 310-372-2160 coastsigns@earthlink.net
www.coastsignsandgraphic.com
Banners and signs of all types; also, screen printing, graphi design, digital, large and small format available
President: Bill Febbo
Owner: William Febbo
Marketing Director: Linda Hopkins
Art Director: Wayne Morris
Estimated Sales: Less than $500,000
Number Employees: 1-4
Square Footage: 6

20684 **Coastal Canvas ProductsCompany**
73 Ross Rd.
P.O.Box 22834
Savannah, GA 31403 912-236-2416
Fax: 912-232-7884 800-476-5174
sales@coastalcanvas.net www.coastalcanvas.net
Commercial canvas awnings, roll curtains, storon protection machinery covers, sunscreens, and strip curtians
President: Glen C Wood
CFO: Marlene Wood
Vice President: Duane Wood
Estimated Sales: $2.5-5,000,000
Number Employees: 20-49

20685 **Coastal Mechanical Services**
33 Parker Ave
Stamford, CT 06906-1713 203-359-3070
Fax: 203-995-9129 coastalac@earthlink.net
Consultant specializing in design of HVAC and refrigeration systems; also, engineering and installation services available
President: David Besterfield
Estimated Sales: $1-2,500,000
Number Employees: 10-19

20686 **Coastal Pallet Corporation**
135 E Washington Ave
Bridgeport, CT 06604-3607 203-333-6222
Fax: 203-333-1892 www.coastalpallet.com
Wooden pallets and boxes
President: Peter G. Standish
Estimated Sales: $1-2.5 Million
Number Employees: 20 to 49

20687 **Coastal Products Company**
PO Box 208
Westbrook, ME 04098-0208 207-854-5616
Fax: 207-854-2118
Chemicals
President: Herb Pressman

20688 **Coastal Sleeve Label**
200 Indigo Dr
Brunswick, GA 31525-6864 912-466-9556
Fax: 912-466-9558 877-753-3837
csl@darientel.net www.fortdearborn.com
PVC tamper evident bands, body and polyethelene labels and combo packs for shrink applications
Manager: Allen Rigdon
VP Sales: Craig Clark
VP Operations: Harry Harriman
Estimated Sales: $20-50 Million
Number Employees: 50-99
Square Footage: 50000

20689 **Coastline Equipment**
2235 E Bakerview Rd
Bellingham, WA 98226 360-739-2480
Fax: 360-734-9321 coasteq@qwest.net
www.coastline-equipment.com
Designer and manufacturer of processing and handling equipment. A complete package from design to fabrication and start-up. Family owned for 30 years
President: Kurt Lunde
Sales Manager: Brian Claudon
Estimated Sales: $5 - 10 Million
Number Employees: 20-49
Square Footage: 128000

20690 **Coating Excellence International**
975 Broadway St
Wrightstown, WI 54180 920-996-1900
Fax: 920-996-1905 800-765-9283
tbauer@coating-excellence.com
www.coating-excellence.com
Estimated Sales: $50 - 75 Million
Number Employees: 100-250

20691 **Coating Technologies International**
805 Birch Street
Algonquin, IL 60102-2213 847-854-9620
Fax: 847-854-9621 mrgintl@aol.com
Lolipop processing equipment, pans and pan lids

20692 **Coats American**
3430 Toringdon Way # 301
Charlotte, NC 28277-2576 704-329-5800
Fax: 704-329-5820 800-631-0965
sales@coats.com www.coats.com

Thread
CFO: Donna Armstrong
CEO: Max Perks
CEO: Max Perks
Estimated Sales: $5 - 10 Million
Number Employees: 5,000-9,999

20693 Coats American Industrial
745 Gotham Pkwy
Carlstadt, NJ 07072-2413 201-935-0200
Fax: 201-804-9392
Tea and coffee industry packaging
Estimated Sales: $3 - 5 000,000
Number Employees: 5-9

20694 Cobatco
1327 NE Adams St
Peoria, IL 61603 309-676-2663
Fax: 309-676-2667 800-426-2282
www.cobatco.com
Manufacturer and exporter of specialty baking equipment for waffles, waffle cones, doughnuts, edible shells, etc.; also, mixes including vanilla and chocolate waffle cone, regular and multigrain waffle and vanilla and chocolatedoughnut
President: Donald Stephens
Estimated Sales: $2.5-5 Million
Number Employees: 10-19
Square Footage: 120000
Type of Packaging: Food Service
Brands:
Cobatco
Cobatco Olde Time

20695 Cobb & Zimmer
7900 Mack Avenue
Detroit, MI 48214-1766 313-923-0350
Fax: 313-923-1916
Bar fixtures, laminated counter and table tops and tables including wood and steel
Estimated Sales: $1 - 5 Million
Number Employees: 1
Square Footage: 15000

20696 Cobb Sign Company
528 Elmira St
Burlington, NC 27217-1382 336-227-0181
Fax: 336-227-0206
Neon and plastic signs
President: Kennith Speagle
President: Kenneth Speagle
Manager: Jody Speagle
Estimated Sales: $1-2.5 Million
Number Employees: 10-19

20697 Cober Electronics, Inc.
151 Woodward Ave
Norwalk, CT 06854-4721 203-855-8755
Fax: 203-855-7511 800-709-5948
sales@cober.com www.cober.com
Manufacturer and exporter of batch and continuous conveyorized microwave ovens for the food scientist and production floor; also, laboratory and pilot plant services, process development and engineering design
CEO: Bernard Krieger
President: Martin Yonnone
VP Engineering: Martin Yonnone
Estimated Sales: $30-50 Million
Number Employees: 20-49
Square Footage: 39000

20698 Cobitco, Inc
5301 Bannock St
Denver, CO 80216 303-296-8575
Fax: 303-297-3029 info@cobitco.com
www.cobitco.com
Cobitco is a private label and branded chemical solutions provider with 20+ years experience and over 10,000 product formulations. Markets include jan-san, automotive, industrial, bulk, health care and marine.
President: Cynthia Bitting
Marketing Director: Ray Harter
Sales Director: Greg Dauer
Number Employees: 100-249
Number of Brands: 10
Number of Products: 1200
Square Footage: 100000
Type of Packaging: Food Service, Private Label, Bulk
Brands:
Car Chem
Cobit+Care
Enviro~Chem
Enviro~Chem Gold
Norseman
Pressure Patch
Pro-Magic
Tidal Marine

20699 Coblentz Brothers
7101 S Kohler Rd
Apple Creek, OH 44606-9613 330-857-7211
Fax: 330-857-4966
Wooden pallets
President: Wayne Liechty
Business Manager: Don Yoder
Vice President: Jonas Coblentz
Estimated Sales: $2.5-5 Million
Number Employees: 28
Square Footage: 20000

20700 (HQ)Coburn Company
P.O.Box 147
Whitewater, WI 53190-0147 262-473-2822
Fax: 262-473-3522 800-776-7042
export@coburnco.com www.coburnco.com
Manufacturer and exporter of dairy equipment including milking and sanitation
President: Jim Coburn
CFO: David Granum
Marketing: Ginny Coburn
Sales & Marketing: Joe Coburn
Operations Manager: Thayer Coburn
Export Manager: Jack Kolo
Estimated Sales: $5-10 Million
Number Employees: 20-49
Type of Packaging: Bulk

20701 Coburn Graphic Films
1650 Corporate Rd W
Lakewood, NJ 08701 732-367-5511
Fax: 732-367-2908 coburn@aol.com
www.coburn.com
President: Roger Jacobs
Vice President: James Putvinski
Number Employees: 20-49

20702 (HQ)Coca-Cola Enterprises, Inc
2500 Windy Ridge Pkwy
Atlanta, GA 30339 770-989-3000
Fax: 770-989-3788 800-233-7210
www.cokecce.com
Third largest Coca-Cola bottler in the world, product portfolio encompasses a full range of beverage categories, including energy drinks, still and sparkling waters, juices, sports drinks, fruit drinks, coffe-based beverages and teas.Provides products and services that meet the beverage and business needs in other countries.
Chairman & CEO: John Brock
Executive VP & CFO: William Douglas III
Senior Vice President & CIO: Esat Sezer
VP/Deputy General Counsel: Suzanne Forlidas
VP Sales, Strategy & Marketing Innov.: Paul Gordon
Sr. VP Public Affairs & Communications: Laura Brightwell
General Manager: Stephen Moorhouse
Estimated Sales: $8.3 Billion
Number Employees: 13,250
Type of Packaging: Consumer, Food Service, Bulk
Brands:
5-Alive
Andina
Appollinaris
Aquana
Aquarius
Bacardi Mixers
Barq's
Beat
Bistrone
Body Style Water
Bonaqua
Bright & Early
Burn
Buzz
Campbell's V8
Canada Dry
Canning's
Caribou Coffee
Chaudfontaine
Cherry Coke
Coca-Cola
Crush
Dasani
Delaware Punch
Diet Coke
Dr Pepper
Earth & Sky
Enviga
Evian
Fanta
Far Coast
Fresca
Fruitopia
Full Throttle
Fuze
Galceau Fruit Water
Godiva Belgian Blends
Gold Peak
Hi-C
Kinley
Lift
Mello Yello
Minute Maid Juices
Monster
Mr Pibb
Nestea
Northern Neck
Nos
Odwalla
Powerade
Red Flash
Rehab
Seagram's
Simply Juices
Smartwater
Sprite
Super Caffeinated Canned Coffee
Super Caffeinated Coffee
The Wellness From Coca-Cola
Vitaminwater

20703 Coconut Code
4490 N Federal Hwy
Lighthouse Point, FL 33064 954-786-0252
Fax: 954-481-9360 www.coconutcode.com
Software for financial reporting, inventory control, product/menu analysis, time and attendance for food service operations
Chairman Of Board: Jack Abdo
CEO/President: Mark Wotell
President: Mark Woterl
VP/R&D: E Wotell
Estimated Sales: $5 - 10 Million
Number Employees: 50-99
Square Footage: 7000
Brands:
Coconut Code
Food Service Management Systems
Remotecontroller
Timeware

20704 Coddington Lumber Company
19501 Shaft Rd SW
Frostburg, MD 21532-3723 301-689-8816
Fax: 301-689-1629
Pallets
President: Carl Mazer
Estimated Sales: $2.5 - 5 Million
Number Employees: 5 to 9

20705 Codeck Manufacturing
PO Box 2940
Sausalito, CA 94966-2940 415-331-9509
Fax: 415-331-9469 800-878-5663
Manufactures coding equipment for various industries
Estimated Sales: $500,000-$1 000,000
Number Employees: 4

20706 Codema
11790 Troy Ln N
Maple Grove, MN 55369 763-428-2266
Fax: 763-428-4411 info@codemallc.com
www.codemainc.com
Manufacturer, importer and exporter of processing equipment; packaging systems. Also have reconditioned and used equipment.
President: Heinz Baecker
VP: Steve Parker
VP sales: Larry Yarger
VP Engineering: Rick Gilles
Estimated Sales: $1-2.5 Million
Number Employees: 5-9
Square Footage: 35000

20707 **Coe & Dru Inc.**
589 W Terrace Dr
San Dimas, CA 91773 909-599-5500
Fax: 909-599-2005 800-722-7538
inquiry@coedru.com www.coedru.com
Supplies baskets to those who make gift baskets.
President: Frank Chu
Sales Manager: Steve Wemane
Human Resources Manager: Lena Chu
Production Manager: Kwok Lai
Purchasing Manager: Kwonk Wong
Estimated Sales: $1.6 Million
Number Employees: 8

20708 **Coextruded Packaging Technologies**
3706 Enterprise Drive
Janesville, WI 53546 608-314-2020
Fax: 608-314-2021 info@cptplastics.com
www.cptplastics.com
Barrier foamed polypropylene trays
President: Linda Bracha
Estimated Sales: $5-10 Million
Number Employees: 20-49

20709 **Coffee Brothers**
1204 Via Roma
Colton, CA 92324 909-370-1100
Fax: 909-370-1101 888-443-5282
info@coffeebrothers.com
www.coffeebrothers.com
Coffee and espresso; importer and wholesaler/distributor of espresso machines
Owner: Cal Amodemo
General Manager: Max Amodeo
Estimated Sales: $2.5-5 Million
Number Employees: 1-4
Square Footage: 44000
Type of Packaging: Private Label, Bulk
Brands:
Coffee Brothers
Il Caffe
Sigma

20710 **Coffee Concepts**
10836 Grissom Lane
Suite 110
Dallas, TX 75229-3544 214-363-9331
Fax: 972-241-1619 espresso@ont.com
www.coffeeconcepts.com
Roaster of arabica coffees, flavor syrups, granita machines and mixes, espresso bar supplies, consulting, employee training, private labeling and unique customized signature blends
Estimated Sales: $1 - 5 Million
Number Employees: 20-49

20711 **Coffee Enterprises**
32 Lakeside Avenue
Burlington, VT 05401-8319 802-865-4480
Fax: 802-865-3364 800-375-3398
info@coffee-ent.com www.coffee-ent.com
Coffee extracts and chilled coffee-based beverage concentrates; laboratory specializing in the testing and analyzing services for coffee; consultant specializing in the marketing and promotion of coffee
Owner/President: Daniel C Cox
Administrative Assistant: Christine Hibma
Office Manager: Judy Mammorella
Estimated Sales: $1 - 3 Million
Number Employees: 10-19
Square Footage: 14000
Type of Packaging: Bulk

20712 **Coffee Express Company**
47722 Clipper St
Plymouth, MI 48170 734-459-4900
Fax: 734-459-5511 800-466-9000
info@coffeeexpressco.com
www.coffeeexpressco.com
Wholesaler roaster of specialty coffees; distributors of associated products.
President: Tom Isaia
Office Manager: Joyce Novak
Production: Scott Novak
Number Employees: 10-19
Number of Brands: 8
Number of Products: 20
Square Footage: 32000
Type of Packaging: Consumer, Food Service, Private Label, Bulk
Brands:
Coffee Express
Mountain Country

20713 **Coffee PER**
111 Freeport Circle
Fallon, NV 89406-2823 775-423-8857
Fax: 775-423-8859 866-957-9233
coffee@phonewave.net www.coffeeper.com
Roasting machines
President: Sherman Dodd
CFO: Phyliss Dodd
Estimated Sales: $1-5 Million
Number Employees: 5-9

20714 **Coffee Processing Systems**
3666 Swenson Avenue
3
St Charles, IL 60174-3442 630-443-0034
Fax: 630-443-0049 coffeepros@worldnet.att.net
www.coffeepros.net
Automatic controls, bin silo systems and storage, conveying equipment, elevators, machiners and buckets
Estimated Sales: Less than $500,000
Number Employees: 4

20715 **Coffee Sock Company**
PO Box 10023
Eugene, OR 97440-2023 541-344-7698
Fax: 541-344-7672 www.coffeesockcompany.com
Reusable cloth coffee filters and household storage products
Director Sales/Marketing: Robert Thomas
Estimated Sales: $5-10 Million
Number Employees: 5-9

20716 **Coffee-Inns of America**
3617 E La Salle St
Phoenix, AZ 85040 602-438-8286
Fax: 602-437-2270 800-528-0552
skaner@coffeeinns.com www.coffeeinns.com
Brewers
Owner: John Bergmann
Estimated Sales: $10-20 000,000
Number Employees: 100-249

20717 **Cog-Veyor Systems, Inc.**
371 Hanlan Road
Woodbridge, Ontario, ON L4L 3T1
Canada 416-798-7333
Fax: 416-743-7196 888-337-2358
frubino@ontariobelting.com
www.cog-veyor.com
Conveyor's designed for use in the food processing, canning and bottling industries.
Production Manager: Brian Kilbride

20718 **Cognitive**
4403 Table Mountain Dr Ste A
Golden, CO 80403 303-273-1400
Fax: 303-273-1414 800-765-6600
sales@cognitive.com www.cogsol.com
Labelers, label printing equipment and printing systems
VP: Arthu Kennedy
Marketing Manager: Vic Barezyk
Estimated Sales: $20-50 Million
Number Employees: 100-249
Parent Co: Axiohm Transaction Solutions

20719 **Colbert Packaging Corporation**
28355 N Bradley Rd
Lake Forest, IL 60045 847-367-5990
Fax: 847-367-4403 mbaker@colbertpkg.com
www.colbertpkg.com
Rigid paper heart-shaped candy boxes.
President: James Hamilton
Chairman: Nancy Colbert MacDougall
Sales Manager: Dave Sult
Sales Representative: Michael Baker
General Manager: Tim Price
Estimated Sales: $10 - 20 Million
Number Employees: 10-19
Square Footage: 115000
Type of Packaging: Consumer

20720 **Colbert Packaging Corporation**
28355 N Bradley Rd
Lake Forest, IL 60045 847-367-5990
Fax: 847-367-4403 jhamilton@colbertpkg.com
www.colbertpkg.com
Rigid paper heart-shaped candy boxes
President: Jim Hamilton
Sales Manager: Dave Sult
General Manager: Tim Price
Estimated Sales: $32 Million
Number Employees: 100-249
Square Footage: 115000
Parent Co: Colbert Packaging Corporation

20721 **Colbert Packaging Corporation**
28355 N Bradley Rd
Lake Forest, IL 60045 847-367-5990
Fax: 847-367-4403 info@colbertpkg.com
www.colbertpkg.com
Rigid paper heart-shaped candy boxes
President: James Hamilton
Sales Manager: Dave Sult
General Manager: Tim Price
Estimated Sales: $20 - 50 Million
Number Employees: 100-249
Square Footage: 115000
Parent Co: Colbert Packaging Corporation

20722 **Colborne Foodbotics**
28495 N Ballard Dr
Lake Forest, IL 60045-4510 847-371-0101
Fax: 847-371-0199 jenny@questequipment.co.uk
www.colborne.com
Cutting systems ideal for cutting sticky, fragile and difficult to cut products and bakery industry turnover systems
President: Richard Hoskins
Quality Control: Don Guther
Estimated Sales: $5 - 10 Million
Number Employees: 100-249

20723 **ColburnTreat**
276 E Allen St # 5
Winooski, VT 05404-1570 802-654-8603
Fax: 802-654-8618 877-877-1224
info@stellarfoodequipment.com
www.colburntreat.com
Manufacturer, boilerless atmospheric steamers in 4 and 6 pan sizes, stackable up to 12 pan configuration. convection fan and automatic waterfill makes steam convection and simple
President: Michael G Colburn
CFO: Bob McLaughlin
VP: Mary Treat
Quality Control: Stephen Bogner
Marketing: Mary Treat
Sales/Public Relations: Mary Esthertrout
Purchasing: Steve Bogner
Estimated Sales: Below $5 Million
Number Employees: 20-49
Number of Brands: 1
Number of Products: 3
Square Footage: 20000
Brands:
Steller Steam

20724 **Cold Chain Technologies**
29 Everett St
Holliston, MA 01746 508-429-1395
Fax: 508-429-9056 800-370-8566
info@coldchaintech.com
www.coldchaintech.com
Manufacturer and exporter of insulated shipping containers and refrigerant packs for perishable food shipments
President: Lawrence Gordon
VP, General Manager: Robert Bohne
VP Sales/Marketing: Donald Nolde
Number Employees: 100-249
Square Footage: 40000
Type of Packaging: Food Service, Private Label, Bulk
Brands:
Fdc
Koolit

20725 **Cold Jet**
455 Wards Corner Rd # 100
Loveland, OH 45140-9033 513-831-1835
Fax: 513-831-1209 800-337-9423
info@coldjet.com www.coldjet.com
Dry ice blast cleaning technology
President: Gene Cooke
CFO: Tom McIlvoy
Quality Control: Tony Lening
Marketing Director: Betsey Seibel
Sales Director: Brian Allen
Operations Manager: Bob Ooten
Number Employees: 100-249
Square Footage: 58400

20726 Cold Jet LLC
9370 7th Street
Unit E
Rancho Cucamonga, CA 91730-5509
Fax: 513-831-3672 800-777-9101
info@coldjet.com www.dryiceblasting.com
Manufacturer and exporter of dry ice blast cleaning systems
President: Scott Statford
Marketing Director: Ken Lay
Sales Director: Russ Lawler
Estimated Sales: $1-2.5 Million
Number Employees: 1-4
Parent Co: CAE Company

20727 Cold Storage Building Products
510 Turtle Cove Boulevard
Suite 100
Rockwall, TX 75087-5374 972-771-7824
Fax: 972-771-7822 888-544-4225
roger.csbp@rockwall.net
Estimated Sales: $3 - 5 Million
Number Employees: 1-4

20728 ColdZone
8101 E Kaiser Blvd Ste 110
Anaheim, CA 92808-2661
Fax: 714-529-8503 support@coldzone.com
www.coldzone.com
Manufacturer and exporter of refrigeration equipment including remote racks and fluid coolers
President: Jim Grob
VP: Ken Falk
National Sales Manager: R Echols
Product Manager: R Dotson
Estimated Sales: $20 - 50 Million
Number Employees: 100-249
Square Footage: 260000
Parent Co: Ardco
Type of Packaging: Food Service
Brands:
C/Z
Cold Saver
Enviro-Cool
Enviro-Therm
Fc-Pack
Mini-Pak
Parallel-Pak
Uni-Pak

20729 Colder Products Company
1001 Westgate Dr
Saint Paul, MN 55114 651-645-0091
Fax: 651-645-5404 800-444-2474
brad.ferstan@colder.com www.colder.com
Industrial connectors
President: Gary Rychley
Number Employees: 250

20730 Coldmatic Building Systems
8500 Keele Street
Concord, ON L4K 2A6
Canada 905-326-7600
Fax: 905-326-7600 800-668-4165
markgalea@rogers.com www.coldmatic.com
President: MARK GALEA
Sales Manager: DEREK FRANCIS
Estimated Sales: $1 - 5 Million

20731 Coldmatic Refrigeration
8500 Keel Street
Concord, ON L4K 2A6
Canada 905-326-7600
Fax: 905-326-7601 mark@summitproducts.com
www.coldmatic.com
Manufacturer and exporter of automatic and manual doors including cold storage, double acting, plastic and refrigerator
President: Mark Galea
CFO: Stafford Mass
VP: Rex Palmatier
Marketing Director: Dan Gregero II
Sales Manager- Ontario & Eastern Canada: Mike Robbie
Plant Manager: Derrick Lee
Estimated Sales: $1 - 3 Million
Number Employees: 5-9
Parent Co: Coldmatic Refrigeration

20732 Coldstream Products Corporation
10 McCool Crescent
P.O. Box 878
Crossfield, AB T0M 0S0
Canada 403-946-4097
Fax: 403-946-0148 888-946-4097
ken.savard@coldstreamproducts.com
www.coldstreamproducts.com
Manufacturer and exporter of coolers, freezers and display cases
President: George Zafir
VP: Trevor Rees
VP Marketing: Trevor Rees
Director of Sales: Ken Savard
Operations: Rick Lewis
Purchasing: Les Lewis
Number Employees: 100-249
Number of Brands: s
Number of Products: 75
Square Footage: 1000000
Parent Co: Coldmatic Group of Companies
Brands:
Cold Tech
Coldstream

20733 Cole-Parmer Instrument Company
625 Bunker Ct
Vernon Hills, IL 60061 847-549-7600
Fax: 847-247-2929 800-323-4340
info@coleparmer.com www.coleparmer.com
Centrifuges, meters, flow, piping, fittings and tubing, nonsanitary, sanitary
President: Andy Greenawalt
Quality Control: Robert Czapla
Estimated Sales: $20 - 50 Million
Number Employees: 250-499

20734 Colecraft Commercial Furnishings
1021 Allen Street
Jamestown, NY 14701 716-488-2810
Fax: 716-488-2824 800-622-2777
www.colecraftcf.com
Plastic laminated food service tables
Manager: Dave Messinger
CEO: Robert Benzel
Vice President: Peter Cardinale
Plant Manager: Neil Hergott
Purchasing Manager: Pat Cleary
Estimated Sales: $8 Million
Number Employees: 50-99
Square Footage: 400000
Parent Co: TR Manufacturing

20735 Coleman Manufacturing Company
48 Waters Ave
Everett, MA 02149-2011 617-389-0380
Fax: 617-389-0769 www.coleman.com
Manufacturer and exporter of hand cleaners
President: Richard Coleman
Estimated Sales: $1 - 2.5 Million
Number Employees: 5-9
Square Footage: 20000

20736 Coleman Resources
PO Box 8129
Greensboro, NC 27419-0129 336-852-4006
Fax: 336-854-8469 www.colemanresources.com
Business printed materials
Manager: Tom Byerly
Estimated Sales: Below $5 Million
Number Employees: 20-49

20737 Coleman Stamps, Signs &Recognition Products
171 Madison Avenue
Daytona Beach, FL 32114 386-253-1206
Fax: 386-257-5301
www.colemanrubberstamps.com
Rubber stamps, signs, seals, etc
President: Carole C Ford
VP: Carole Ford
Estimated Sales: $5 - 10 Million
Number Employees: 10-19

20738 Coley Industries
11885 Granger Road
Wayland, NY 14572-9745 716-728-2390
Woodenware, wooden and gourmet salad bowls, pepper grinders, salt and pepper shakers and mounted/unmounted time and hour glasses
President: John Coley

20739 Colgate-Palmolive
P.O.Box 1928
Morristown, NJ 07962 973-630-1500
Fax: 973-630-1476 800-432-8226
www.colpakcommercial.com
Manufacturer and exporter of cleaning supplies
CEO: Eian Cook
Director Marketing Services: Diane Suchosky
VP Sales: Gary Ponder
VP Marketing: Ed Gagliardi
Estimated Sales: $100-500 Million
Number Employees: 1,000-4,999
Brands:
Ajax
Menwen
Murphy
Palmolive

20740 Collector's Gallery
2601 E Main St
Saint Charles, IL 60174 630-584-5235
Fax: 630-584-1224 800-346-3063
cginfo@wpccg.com www.studiostyle.com
Extensive line of decorative boxes, bags and wraps
Executive Director: Kevin Hughes
Project Manager: Sandy Peterman

20741 Collegeville Flag & Manufacturing Company
24 W 4th Avenue
Collegeville, PA 19426-2601 610-489-4131
Fax: 610-489-4164 800-523-5630
In store displays, flags and banners including U.S., custom logo, advertising, etc.; also, poles and accessories
Chairman: Richard Doyle
Account Executive: Jennifer Engle
Estimated Sales: $10-20 Million
Number Employees: 50-99
Parent Co: Collegeville Flag & Banner

20742 Colliers International
3439 Brookside Rd
Suite 108
Stockton, CA 95219 209-475-5100
Fax: 209-475-5102 goleary@colliersparrish.com
www.colliersmn.com
Partner: Michael Goldstein
Senior Vice President: Lisa Hodgson
Vice President: Adam Lucatello
Operations Manager: Maria Marquez
Estimated Sales: Below $500,000
Number Employees: 10-19

20743 Collins & Aikman
1212 7th St SW
Canton, OH 44707 330-253-3826
Fax: 330-456-0849 800-321-0244
www.collinsaikman.com
Manufacturer and exporter of rubber and vinyl matting
Quality Control: Chris Carpenter
CEO: Mike Geaghan
VP Merchandising: Scot Landeis
Production Manager: Gary Taylor
Plant Manager: Todd Weber
Estimated Sales: $.5 - 1 million
Number Employees: 20-49
Type of Packaging: Food Service
Brands:
Aqua Trap
Cushion Ease

20744 Collins Manufacturing Company Ltd
9835 199 A Street
Langley, BC V1M 2X7
Canada 604-888-2812
Fax: 604-888-7689 800-663-6761
info@collinsmfg.com www.collinsmfg.com
Refrigerated and dry freight van-bodies and flat-decks ditributor of Maxon liftgates, Parco-Hesse beverage bodies and Utilimaster walk-in bodies
President: Michael Sondergaard
Controller: Lili Murphy
Account Manager: Brent Wilson
Plant Manager: Jerry Brownlee
Number Employees: 50-99
Brands:
Collins
Maxon
Parco-Hesse
Utilimaster

20745 **Collins Technical**
8330 Route a i a S
St Augustine, FL 32086 904-461-4546
Fax: 904-461-4539 jcllins@aug.com
Moulding equipment
Sales Manager: Jack Collins
Estimated Sales: $1 - 5 000,000
Number Employees: 6

20746 **Colloides Naturels**
15 Somerset St
Somerville, NJ 08876 908-707-9400
Fax: 908-707-9405 800-872-1850
cnaturels@cnius.com www.cniworld.com
Wholesaler/distributor and importer of food additives including gum acacia; serving the flavor and confectionery industries
President: Gontran Dondain
Manager Finance and Administration: Carol Rice
VP Sales/Marketing: Brent Lambert
Estimated Sales: $5-10 Million
Number Employees: 75
Parent Co: Collides Naturales
Type of Packaging: Bulk

20747 **Colmac Coil Manufactoring**
P.O.Box 571
Colville, WA 99114-0571 509-684-2595
Fax: 509-684-8331 800-845-6778
mail@colmaccoil.com www.colmaccoil.com
Sales Manager: Jeremy Olberding
Estimated Sales: $20 - 50 Million
Number Employees: 120
Square Footage: 225000

20748 **Colmar Storage Company**
6695 NW 36th Ave
Miami, FL 33147 305-696-1614
Fax: 305-836-5800
Storage of coffee (green coffee), samplers and weighers
manager: Robert Olmedo
Manager: Robert Olmedo
Estimated Sales: $2.5-5 000,000
Number Employees: 10-19
Type of Packaging: Private Label

20749 **Colonial Marketing Associates**
400 Broadway
Freehold, NJ 07728-1494 732-431-3419
Fax: 732-431-3419
Marketing consultant for the egg industry
Owner: Abe Opatut
Number Employees: 6

20750 **Colonial Paper Company**
P.O.Box 310
Silver Springs, FL 34489-0310 352-622-4171
Fax: 352-422-7247 cpcweb@aol.com
www.cpc4me.com
Paper goods, disposable tabletop items and janitorial, dishwashing and warewashing equipment and supplies
President: William H Tuck Sr
Estimated Sales: $10-20 Million
Number Employees: 20-49

20751 **Colonial Transparent Products Company**
870 S Oyster Bay Road
mail.com
Hicksville, NY 11801-3576 516-822-4430
Fax: 516-822-4292
Plastic films, sleeve labels and polyethylene bags; also, design, printing and converting available
President: L Goldstein
VP: E Goldstein
Office Manager: C Bland
Estimated Sales: $5-10 Million
Number Employees: 20-49
Square Footage: 25000

20752 **Color Ad Tech Signs**
6500 S Washington St
Amarillo, TX 79118-7817 806-374-8117
Advertising signs
Owner: Truet Cargill
Estimated Sales: $1 - 3 Million
Number Employees: 5-9
Square Footage: 7500

20753 **Color Box**
623 S G St
Richmond, IN 47374 765-966-7588
Fax: 765-962-5584 www.gp.com
Manufacturer and exporter of paper boxes and cartons
Manager: Jeff Pobanz
VP Sales: Frank Mazzei
VP Manufacturing: Mike Roark
Estimated Sales: $20-50 Million
Number Employees: 250-499
Parent Co: Georgia Pacific
Type of Packaging: Consumer, Bulk

20754 **Color Box**
1275 S Granada Dr
Madera, CA 93637-4803 559-674-1049
Fax: 559-674-1050
Wine industry bag, box and carton packaging
Manager: Tim McCoy
VP: Barbara Fox
Number Employees: 20-49

20755 **Color Carton**
341 Canal Pl
Bronx, NY 10451-6091 718-665-0840
Fax: 718-993-1776
customerservice@colorcarton.com
www.colorcarton.com
Folding paper boxes
President: Nicholas P Loprinzi
VP: Nicholas LoPrinzi
Treasurer: Vincent LoPrinzi
Estimated Sales: $5-10 Million
Number Employees: 20-49

20756 **Color Communications**
4000 W Fillmore St
Chicago, IL 60624 773-638-1400
Fax: 773-638-0887 www.ccicolor.com
Creates visual quality colors control standards and color tolerance to communicate your product
President: Steve Winter
VP: Steven Winter
General Manager: Harry Lerner
Marketing Director: Jill Goldstein
Estimated Sales: $50 - 100 Million
Number Employees: 250-499
Type of Packaging: Bulk

20757 **Color-Tec**
28 Center St Ste 1
Clinton, NJ 08809 908-735-2248
Fax: 908-236-7865 sales@color-tec.com
www.color-tec.com
Develops and markets technologically advanced PC software and color instruments for industrial applications and point-of-sale merchandising; delivering color measuring instruments and nutritional labeling software to the food andagriculture industry.
President: James Degroff
Vice President: C Womer
Estimated Sales: $1 - 3 Million
Number Employees: 5-9
Number of Brands: 3
Number of Products: 3

20758 **Colorado Nut Company**
2 Kalamath Street
Denver, CO 80223
800-876-1625
sales@coloradonutco.com
www.coloradonutco.com
Manufactures and Imports candies, chocolates, unique trail mixes, snack mixes, dried fruits and gift baskets for any occasion. Also roast nuts on site. Also offer products with private labeling and customized logos for a variety ofspecialized events.
President: Kathy Renaud
Owner: Roger Renaud
Type of Packaging: Consumer, Private Label

20759 **Colorcon**
275 Ruth Rd
Harleysville, PA 19438 215-256-7700
Fax: 215-256-7799 www.colorcon.com
Custom dispersed colorant systems, natural colorants, pearlescent color systems, barrier coatings, glazes, FD&C certified pigments, color blends and monogramming and nontoxic printing inks for food packaging applications; exporter offood colorants, coatings, inks, etc.
President: Kenneth Lord
Marketing Director: David Hibbs
Estimated Sales: $50-100 Million
Number Employees: 250-499
Parent Co: Berwind Pharmaceutical Services
Type of Packaging: Bulk

20760 **Colson Caster Corporation**
3700 Airport Rd
Jonesboro, AR 72401 870-932-4501
Fax: 870-932-1146 800-643-5515
info1@colsoncaster.com www.colsoncaster.com
Manufacturer and exporter of casters, wheels and bumpers
President: Chuck Bub
CEO: Jim Blankenship
Chairman the Board: Robert Pritzker
VP: Bill Blackley
Marketing: Cary Gillespie
Estimated Sales: $50 - 100 Million
Number Employees: 100-249

20761 **Colter & Peterson**
414 East 16th Street
Paterson, NJ 07514 973-684-0901
Fax: 973-684-0260 contact@colterpeterson.com
www.colter-peterson.com
New and rebuilt machinery for set-up, folding and corrugated boxes
Manager: Lawrence Harris
VP: Lawrence Harris
Assistant Manager: Jo Taylor
Estimated Sales: $1-2.5 Million
Number Employees: 5-9

20762 **Columbia Equipment & Finance**
586 Silver Lake Dr
Danville, CA 94526-6226 925-314-1242
Fax: 925-314-1240 800-733-3939
information@columbialeasing.com
www.columbialeasingusa.com
Equipment lease financing and small business loans
President: Stan Nathanson
Estimated Sales: $.5 - 1 million
Number Employees: 1-4

20763 **(HQ)Columbia Jet/JPL**
750 Almeda Genoa Road
Houston, TX 77047-4106 713-433-4511
Fax: 713-434-1397 800-876-4511
Lighting fixtures
Director Sales: Mack Pyle
Marketing Manager: Tom Scott
Sales Manager: Les Simpson
Estimated Sales: $1 - 5 Million

20764 **Columbia Labeling Machinery**
1580 Dale Ave
PO Box 5290
Benton City, WA 99320
Fax: 509-588-5080 888-791-9590
sales@rippedsheets.com
www.columbialabel.com
Manufacturer and exporter of automatic and semi-automatic labeling machines and supplies; also, bar code printing and labeling equipment
President: Raymond MacNeill
Sales: Catherine Bryson
Estimated Sales: $1-2.5 Million
Number Employees: 4
Square Footage: 100000

20765 **Columbia Lighting**
701 Millennium Blvd
Greenville, SC 29607 864-599-6000
Fax: 866-898-0131 www.columbialighting.com
Manufacturer and exporter of lighting fixtures including electric and fluorescent
Manager: Kevin Clark
Production Manager: Bruce Hemmelman
Estimated Sales: $100-500 Million
Number Employees: 500-999
Square Footage: 680000
Parent Co: Lighting Corporation of America
Brands:
Columbia

20766 **Columbia Machine**
P.O.Box 8950
Vancouver, WA 98668 360-694-1501
Fax: 360-695-7517 800-628-4065
pallsales@colmac.com www.colmac.com

Floor, high level and robotic palletizers for cases, bags, pails, bales and trays
President: Jerry Finolay
CFO: Winston Asai
CEO: Rick Goode
Sales Director: Richard Armstrong
Estimated Sales: $50 - 100 Million
Number Employees: 500-999
Square Footage: 186530

20767 Columbia Okura LLC
301 Grove St
Vancouver, WA 98661 360-735-1952
Fax: 360-905-1707 taygoo@colmac.com
www.columbiamachine.com
Robotic palletizing experts.
President: Rick Goode
Estimated Sales: $20 - 50 Million
Number Employees: 10-19

20768 Columbian TecTank
2101 S 21st St
Parsons, KS 67357 620-421-0200
Fax: 620-421-9122 800-421-2788
sales@columbiantectank.com
www.columbiantectank.com
Manufacturer and exporter of bolted and welded carbon steel, stainless steel and aluminum storage tanks and silos
Plant Manager: Steve Allen
Estimated Sales: $20 - 50 Million
Number Employees: 100-249
Brands:
Aquastore
Harvestove
Peabody Tectank
Seal Weld

20769 Columbus Container
3460 Commerce Drive
Columbus, IN 47201 812-376-9301
Fax: 812-376-9891 www.columbuscontainer.com
Corrugated boxes, displays and packaging
President: Bob Haddad
CEO: Bob Haddad Sr
Estimated Sales: $50-100 Million
Number Employees: 250-499
Square Footage: 248500

20770 Columbus Instruments
950 N Hague Ave
Columbus, OH 43204 614-276-0861
Fax: 614-276-0529 800-669-5011
sales@colinst.com www.colinst.com
Manufacturer and exporter of respirometers for measuring the sterility, bacterial and fungal growth, biodegradation and oxidation of fats; also, calorimeters, precision gas mixers and air dryers
President: Jan A Czekajewski
Estimated Sales: $2.5 - 5 Million
Number Employees: 20-49
Square Footage: 20000
Brands:
Micro-Oxymax
Oxymax

20771 Columbus McKinnon Corporation
140 John James Audubon Parkway
Amherst, NY 14228-1197 716-689-5400
800-888-0985
www.cmworks.com
Manufacturer and exporter of chains, hoists, forgings, lift tables, jib arms, manipulators and conveyors
Chairman: Ernest Verebelyi
President/CEO/Director: Timothy Tevens
Vice President, Finance/CFO: Gregory Rustowicz
Vice President: Jim Douglas
Vice President, Information Technology: Ed Sieler
Quality Assurance Manager: Peter Hogan
Director, Marketing Communications: Rob Beightol
Facilities Manager: Chris Czomdel
Estimated Sales: $597 Million
Number Employees: 2,578
Brands:
Big Orange
Cyclone
Herc-Alloy
Lodestar
Rigger

20772 Columbus McKinnon Corportion
140 John James Audubon Parkway
Amherst, NY 14228-1197 716-689-5400
Fax: 231-739-6408 800-888-0985
www.cmworks.com
Manufacturer and exporter of hoists
President: Timothy T Tevens
Chief Executing Officer: Timothy t Tevens
CFO: Gregory P rustowicz
Vice President: Gregory P Rustowicz
Chairman of the Board: James Needham
VP Marketing: Phil Betlejewski
Number Employees: 250-499
Parent Co: Columbus McKennan

20773 Columbus Paperbox Company
595 Van Buren Dr
Columbus, OH 43223 419-628-2381
Fax: 419-628-3105 800-968-0797
info@globusprinting.com
www.globusprinting.com/
Folding cartons and rigid set-up boxes
President: William Reiber
VP: Robert Reiber
VP Sales: Thomas Kasle
Estimated Sales: $5-10 Million
Number Employees: 20-49
Square Footage: 240000
Parent Co: Globus Printing & Packaging, Inc.
Brands:
Conoco Lubricants
Conoco/Andero
Hydroclear

20774 Com-Pac International
P.O.Box 2707
Carbondale, IL 62902-2707 618-529-2421
Fax: 618-529-2234 800-824-0817
compac@com-pac.com www.compac.com
Plastic bag machines and recloseable plastic bags with zippers
CEO: Greg Sprehe
Estimated Sales: $20-50 Million
Number Employees: 100-249
Brands:
Z Patch

20775 Com-Pac International
800 West Industrial Park Road
Carbondale, IL 62902 800-824-0817
Fax: 618-529-2234 888-297-2824
compac@com-pac.com www.com-pac.com
In-line reclosable zipper system with air-tight seal
President: Greg Sprehe
CEO: Don Wright
R&D: Chris Pemberton
Quality Control: Kendall Henkins
Marketing: Durrell McDannel
Sales: Darrell McDannel
Estimated Sales: Below $5 Million
Number Employees: 200
Number of Brands: 4
Number of Products: 20
Type of Packaging: Consumer, Food Service, Private Label
Brands:
Integra
Integra Cm
Integra T
Rtr 1000
Z Patch

20776 Com-Pak International
11615 Cardinal Circle
Garden Grove, CA 92843-3814 714-537-5772
Fax: 714-537-4326 compak@earthlink.net
www.compakintl.com
Wholesaler/distributor of food and chemical processing and packaging equipment
President: Billy Fielder
VP: David West
Estimated Sales: $1 - 3 Million
Number Employees: 7
Square Footage: 72000
Parent Co: Garden Grove
Other Locations:
Com-Pak International
Hemet CA

20777 Comalex
419-B Gordon Avenue
Van Buren, AR 72956
866-343-2594
renewberry@comalex.com www.comalex.com
Manufacturers computer software designed to automate Point-of-Sale (POS) food service operations in K-12 public and private schools and colleges
President: Richard Newberry
Number Employees: 16
Square Footage: 12400

20778 Comark Instruments
P.O.Box 9029
Everett, WA 98206-9029 360-435-5571
Fax: 360-403-4243 800-555-6658
sales@comarkusa.com global.bayliner.com
Supplier of electronic measurement instruments inculding food and industrial thermometers, thermocouples, temperature probes, data loggers, data management systems and timers plus humidity and pressure instruments.
President: Jeff Behan
Marketing Manager: Alan Mellinger
National Sales Manager: Bob Bader
Estimated Sales: $5-10 Million
Number Employees: 1,000-4,999
Number of Brands: 1
Number of Products: 200
Parent Co: Brunsik Corporation
Type of Packaging: Food Service
Brands:
Comark
Kane-May/Km

20779 Comasec Safety, Inc.
8 Niblick Road
Enfield, CT 06082 860-749-0506
Fax: 860-741-0881 800-333-0219
www.comasecsafety.com
Manufacturer and importer of gloves including PVC/nitrile, knit lined latex, plastic, cotton/mesh lined, heavy unlined rubber; exporter of knit lined latex gloves
General Manager: P Gelinas
Tecnical Manager: Joe Krocheski
Estimated Sales: $5-10 Million
Number Employees: 10-19
Brands:
Astroflex

20780 Comax Flavors
130 Baylis Rd
Melville, NY 11747-3808 631-249-0505
Fax: 631-249-9255 800-992-0629
info@comaxflavors.com
http://www.comaxflavors.com
Supplier of flavors
President: Peter Calabretta
CFO: Virginia Wyan
Vice President: Paul Calabretta
Research & Development: Agneta Weisz
Quality Control: Frank Vollaro
Marketing Director: Catherine Armstrong
Sales Director: Norman Katz
PR/Communications Manager: Laura Ferrante
Production Manager: Jorge Quintanilla
Plant Manager: Marion Cunningham
Purchasing Manager: Michael Keppel
Estimated Sales: $15 Million
Number Employees: 55

20781 Combake International
3050 Royal Boulevard S
Suite 150
Alpharetta, GA 30022-4454 770-667-4944
Fax: 770-677-3440 wpib@aol.com

20782 Combi Packaging Systems
5365 E Center Dr NE
Canton, OH 44721-3734 330-456-9333
Fax: 330-456-4644 800-521-9072
sales@combi.com www.combi.com
President/CEO: John Fisher
CFO: Barb Karch
Vice President of Sales: Mark Freidly
Marketing Manager: Sue Lewis
Sales Manager: Fred May
Estimated Sales: $10 - 20 Million
Number Employees: 50-99

20783 Combi Packaging Systems
5365 E Center Dr NE
PO Box 9326
Canton, OH 44721 330-456-9333
Fax: 330-456-4644 800-521-9072
sales@combi.com www.combi.com

30 year manufacturer of case erectors, case packers and case sealers, robotic pick and place pakcers with integrated case erectors; ergonomic hand packaging stations and drop packers with integrated case erectors.
President/CEO: John Fisher
CFO: Barb Karch
Research & Development: Bill Mitchell
Marketing Director: Sue Lewis
Sales Director: Mark Freidly
Plant Manager: Brian Miller
Estimated Sales: $10-20 Million
Number Employees: 100-249
Square Footage: 135000
Brands:
Combi America
Laser 2000
Z-Ez

20784 **Combined Computer Resource**
2777 N Stemmons Fwy Ste 1046
Dallas, TX 75207 214-267-1010
Fax: 214-267-1019 800-956-1866
paul@winocular.com www.winocular.com
Suppliers of management software solutions that solve problems with paper and electronic document movement,retrieval,storage and archival or retention
Owner: Nick Sanders
Quality Control: Kim Roberts
VP: Rocky Chesnutt
VP: Kim Roberts
Estimated Sales: $4 000,000
Number Employees: 10-19

20785 **Combustion Systems Sales**
12946 SE Kent Kangley Road
300
Kent, WA 98030-7940 206-623-1141
Fax: 501-556-4104
Roasters (machines), conveying equipment (elevators, machiners and buckets), repair services

20786 **Comco Signs**
1624 Toal St
Charlotte, NC 28206-1522 704-375-2338
Fax: 704-333-3335 john@comcosigns.com
www.comcosigns.com
Signs
President: John W Ulery
Estimated Sales: Below $5 Million
Number Employees: 20 to 49

20787 **Comet Neon Advertising Company**
235 W Turbo Dr
San Antonio, TX 78216-3313 210-341-7245
Fax: 210-341-7279 info@cometsigns.com
www.cometsigns.com
Indoor and outdoor signs including advertising and electric
President: Arthur Sitterle
VP: Pete Sitterle
Estimated Sales: $5-10 Million
Number Employees: 50-99

20788 **Comm-Pak**
2406 Frederick Rd
Opelika, AL 36801-7222 334-749-6201
Fax: 334-749-1948
Point of purchase displays and pressure sensitive decals and labels; also, custom printing of plastic drinkware available
President: Trey Gafford
Estimated Sales: $1-2.5 Million
Number Employees: 10 To 19
Square Footage: 18000

20789 **Command Belt Cleaning Systems**
8431 Parsons Blvd
Jamaica, NY 11432-1643 718-297-2800
Fax: 718-658-1949 800-433-7627
Automated conveyor belt cleaning systems
Operations Manager: Frank Pennino
General Manager: John Rice
Number Employees: 20-49
Square Footage: 10000
Parent Co: Pari Industries

20790 **Command Communications**
14510 E Fremont Ave
Centennial, CO 80112-4233 304-839-4051
Fax: 303-792-0899 800-288-3491
chibbard@commandcommunications.com
www.commandcommunicationsllc.com
Manufacturer and exporter of wireless, staff, guest, hostess and waitress paging systems. Also communication products designed to reduce the number of phone lines— saving monthly phone line expenses
President/CEO: Craig Hibbard
VP Operations: Mary Larson
Director of Communications/Online Mkting: Michael Rose
National Accounts Sales Manager: Charla Martin
Estimated Sales: $3 - 5 Million
Number Employees: 10-19
Number of Products: 10
Type of Packaging: Consumer, Food Service, Private Label, Bulk

20791 **Command Electronics**
15670 Morris Industrial Dr
Schoolcraft, MI 49087-9628 269-679-4011
Fax: 269-679-5410 sales@streetperformance.com
www.commandelectronics.com
Manufacturer and exporter of fluorescent and incandescent lighting
President: Cary Campagna
Vice President: Dan Campagna
Estimated Sales: $1 - 5 Million
Number Employees: 20-49
Square Footage: 26000
Brands:
Porta-Lamp

20792 **Command Line Corporation**
1090 Kng Geo Pst Rd Ste 802
Edison, NJ 08837 732-738-6500
Fax: 732-738-6504
commandlinecorp@worldnet.att.net
www.commandlinecorp.com
Customized purchasing, distribution and manufacturing management software systems for multi-site inventory control, requisitions, receiving, bar coding, A/P interfaces, warehouse locator systems, etc
President: Donald Staffin
Estimated Sales: $1-2.5 Million
Number Employees: 10-19

20793 **Command Packaging**
3840 E 26th St
Vernon, CA 90058 323-980-0918
Fax: 323-260-7047 800-996-2247
info@commandpackaging.com
www.commandpackaging.com
Elegant, upscale, and value added bags for retail stores including, bakeries and delies, restaurants, and grocery stores. We specialize in bags for restaurant carry out
President: Albert Halimi
CEO: Pete Grande
Marketing Director: Vicki Stiling
Operations Manager: Carol Bullock
Estimated Sales: $10 - 20 Million
Number Employees: 100-249
Square Footage: 100000
Type of Packaging: Food Service

20794 **(HQ)Commencement Bay Corrugated**
13414 142nd Ave E
Orting, WA 98360 253-845-3100
Fax: 253-445-0772 www.cbcbox.com
Manufacturer and exporter of corrugated paper boxes
Manager: Paul Winber
Sales Coordinator: James Kressler
General Manager: Joe McQuade
Plant Manager: Randy Snow
Estimated Sales: $20 - 50 Million
Number Employees: 100-249
Square Footage: 130000

20795 **Commercial Corrugated Corporation**
4101 Ashland Avenue
Baltimore, MD 21205-2924 410-522-0900
Fax: 410-522-6184 800-242-8861
jpauly@commercialcorrugated.com
Corrugated boxes and containers; also, point of purchase displays
President: John Pauley Sr
Estimated Sales: $10 - 20 Million
Number Employees: 15
Type of Packaging: Private Label, Bulk

20796 **Commercial Creamery Company**
159 South Cedar Street
Spokane, WA 99201 509-747-4131
Fax: 509-838-2271 salez@cheesepowder.com
www.cheesepowder.com
Dried cheese and yogurt powders; processor and exporter of snack seasoning and spray dried dairy flavors
President: Michael Gilmartin
Controller: David Foedisch
VP: Peter Gilmartin
Estimated Sales: $28 Million
Number Employees: 100

20797 **(HQ)Commercial Dehydrator Systems Inc**
256 Bethel Dr
Eugene, OR 97402 541-688-5281
Fax: 541-688-5989 800-369-4283
chuck@dryer.com www.dryer.com
Berry crate washers, insect sterilization chambers, roasters, cookers and dryers including continuous belt, bin and tray; exporter of dryers/roasters and sorting/grading belting.
President: Leroy Stone
Vice President: David Stone
Sales: Lee Luege
Field Representative: Darryl Hastings
Estimated Sales: $1-2.5 Million
Square Footage: 27000

20798 **Commercial Envelope Manufacturing Company**
350 Wireless Blvd Ste 102
Hauppauge, NY 11788-3947
Fax: 631-242-6935
www.commercial-envelope.com
Envelopes
President: Alan Kristel
Estimated Sales: $20-50 Million
Number Employees: 100-249

20799 **(HQ)Commercial Furniture Group**
810 W Highway 25 70
Newport, TN 37821 423-586-7000
Fax: 423-586-7000 800-873-3252
www.commercialfurnituregroup.com
Manufacturer and exporter of chairs, benches, booths and tables
Manager: Bob Branstetter
CFO: Neal Restivo
Marketing Specialist: Teri Winters
Number Employees: 9
Type of Packaging: Food Service
Brands:
Epic
Falcon
Howe
Shelby Williams
Thonet

20800 **Commercial Kitchen Company**
3219 W Washington Blvd
Los Angeles, CA 90018 323-732-2291
Fax: 323-732-2729 info@ckreps.com
www.commercialkitchenreps.com
Stainless steel hoods, tables and shelving
President: Gordon Zuckerman
Estimated Sales: $500,000-$1,000,000
Number Employees: 1-4

20801 **Commercial Lighting Design**
43 S Dudley St
Memphis, TN 38104 901-774-5771
Fax: 901-946-2478 800-774-5799
www.lumalier.com
Manufacturer and exporter of lighting fixtures
President: Charles Dunn
CEO: Charles Dunn, Sr.
VP: Charles Dunn, Jr.
Estimated Sales: $1-2,500,000
Number Employees: 10-19
Brands:
Lumalier

20802 **Commercial Manufacturing**
PO Box 947
Fresno, CA 93714-0947 559-237-1855
Fax: 559-266-5149 info@commercialmfg.com
www.commercialmfg.com

Food processing equipment for the fresh, frozen, canned and dehydrated food industries.
President: Larry Hagopian
Estimated Sales: $4 Million
Number Employees: 50-99
Type of Packaging: Food Service

20803 Commercial Manufacturing& Supply Company
P.O.Box 947
Fresno, CA 93714-0947 559-237-1855
Fax: 559-266-5149 info@commercialmfg.com
www.commercialmfg.com
Manufacturer and exporter of bin handling systems, conveyors, bucket elevators, air dryers, coolers and cleaners, washers, centrifuges, food pumps, graders and mix and blend systems
President: Larry Hagopian
Sales Manager: Jack Kraemer
Sales Engineer: Jim MacKenzie
Sales Engineer: Bob Peschel
Estimated Sales: $10-20 Million
Number Employees: 50-99

20804 Commercial Packaging
8425 Fairway Place
Middleton, WI 53562-2548 608-836-7181
Fax: 608-831-9632 800-500-9519
info@commercialpackaging.com
www.commercialpackaging.com
Packaging material
Manager: Bonnie Dahlk
VP: Aaron Egbers
Estimated Sales: $5 - 10 Million
Number Employees: 5-9
Parent Co: Commercial Packaging

20805 Commercial Printing Company
P.O.Box 10302
Birmingham, AL 35202-0302 205-251-9203
Fax: 205-251-6133 800-989-9203
www.commercialprinting.com
Manufacturers of printers and printing related services like scanning, digital and conventional stripping, multicolor printing, bindery, on demand printing and elkote finishing
President: Thomas Arledge
Executive Vice President: Mike Leathers
Account Executive: Alex Berger
Estimated Sales: $10-20 Million
Number Employees: 50-99

20806 Commercial Refrigeration Service, Inc.
2501 West Behrend Drive
Suite 39
Phoenix, AZ 85027-4148 623-869-8881
Fax: 623-869-8882 www.comrefsvc.com
Manufacturer and exporter of beverage dispensers
Estimated Sales: $1 - 5 Million
Number Employees: 100-250
Square Footage: 240000
Type of Packaging: Food Service
Brands:
Jet Spray

20807 Commercial Seating Specialist
481 Laurelwood Rd
Santa Clara, CA 95054 408-453-8983
Fax: 408-453-8986 www.comseat.com
Booths and table tops.
President: James Day
CEO: Patricia Day
Marketing Director: Rich Buchner
Sales Director: Mike Alexander
Purchasing Manager: Scott Wallace
Estimated Sales: $1-2.5 Million
Number Employees: 20-49

20808 Commercial Testing Lab
514 Main St
Colfax, WI 54730 715-962-3121
Fax: 715-962-4030 800-962-5227
ctlfoods@ctlcolfax.com www.ctlcolfax.com
President and CFO: Micheal F Bean
R&D: Cheryl Bean
Estimated Sales: $2.5 - 5 000,000
Number Employees: 20-49

20809 Commercial Textiles Corporation-Best Buy Uniforms
500 E 8th Ave
Homestead, PA 15120 412-461-4600
Fax: 412-461-4016 800-345-1924
customer-service@bestbuyuniforms.com
www.bestbuyuniforms.com
Manufacturer, wholesaler/distributor and importer of image apparel uniforms; also, custom T-shirts, table cloths, napkins and work uniforms; serving the food service market
Owner: David Frischman
CEO: Lester Frischman
Estimated Sales: $1 - 5 Million
Number Employees: 5-9
Square Footage: 12000
Type of Packaging: Food Service

20810 Commodity Traders International
101 E. Main Street
P.O. Box 6
Trilla, IL 62469-0006 217-235-4322
Fax: 217-235-3246 sales@commoditytraders.biz
www.commoditytraders.biz
Manufacturer and exporter of new and used milling, grain handling and seed processing machinery
Executive Trustee: Charles Stodden

20811 Common Sense Natural Soap & Bodycare Products
109 Lincoln Avenue
Rutland, VT 05701-3226 802-773-0582
Fax: 561-753-8207
Natural soap products
General Manager: Michael Delaney
Estimated Sales: $5-10 Million
Number Employees: 10-19

20812 Compacker Systems LLC
9104 N ZenithÿAvenueÿ
P.O. Box 2026
Davenport, IA 52806 563-391-2751
Fax: 563-391-8598 sales@compacker.com
www.compacker.com
Manufacturer and exporter of case packing and sealing equipment including case erectors, wrap-around and top and bottom sealers, traymakers, etc
President: Keith Tucker
Quality Control: Jane Bower
Marketing Manager: Michael Bower
General Manager: Keith Tucker
Estimated Sales: $5-10 Million
Number Employees: 10-19
Square Footage: 80000
Brands:
Bottom Line
Compacker Ii
Compacker Ii Abf-3
Compacker Iii
Endpacker
Rap-Up 90
Tm1000

20813 Compact Industries
3945 Ohio Ave
St Charles, IL 60174 630-513-9600
Fax: 630-513-9655 800-513-4262
www.compactind.com
Private label and contract packager: dry product packaging, in-house blending, formulating
President/CEO: Michael Brown
CFO: Steve Zaruba
VP Sales: Gary Johnson
Estimated Sales: $9 Million
Number Employees: 100-249
Square Footage: 150000
Type of Packaging: Consumer, Food Service, Private Label, Bulk
Brands:
Casa Verde
Cool Off
Geneva Freeze
John Foster Green

20814 Compact Mold
3436 Turfway Road
Erlanger, KY 41018-3169 859-371-3250
Fax: 859-371-2290
Blow molds
Estimated Sales: $1-5 000,000
Number Employees: 12

20815 Compactors
PO Box 3173
Hilton Head Island, SC 29928-3173 843-686-5503
Fax: 843-686-3290 800-423-4003
info@compactorsinc.com
www.compactorsinc.com
Manufacturer and exporter of can and bottle crushers, trash compactors and densifiers
President: Mike Pierson
VP: Bill Phillips
Estimated Sales: Below $5 Million
Number Employees: 10
Square Footage: 8000
Parent Co: Hilton Head SC
Brands:
Pac Crusher I

20816 Compatible Components Corporation
1213 West Loop North
Suite 180
Houston, TX 77055 713-688-2008
Fax: 713-688-2993 sales@cccmix.com
www.compatible-components.com
Mixing/blending products and separating/dewatering products
President: Gerald Lott

20817 Complete Automation
1776 W Clarkston Rd
Lake Orion, MI 48362 248-693-0500
Fax: 248-693-0503 marketing@completeco.com
www.completeco.com
Coolant filtration systems and filtration products.
President: Kenneth Matheis
Square Footage: 45000

20818 Complete Inspection Systems
334 4th Ave
Indialantic, FL 32903-4214 321-952-2490
Fax: 321-952-2475
sales@completeinspectionsystems.com
www.completeinspectionsystems.com
Complete Inspection Systems provides technology and products for automated inspection and anti-counterfeiting systems specializing in creating custom solutions for packaging medical devices and pharmaceuticals.
President: Gary Parish
Marketing: Angela Kirshon
Sales: Derek Ford
Estimated Sales: $1 - 3 Million
Number Employees: 5-9

20819 (HQ)Complete Packaging & Shipping Supplies
83 Bennington Ave
Freeport, NY 11520-3913 516-546-2100
Fax: 877-269-4346 877-269-3236
johnc@completepackage.com
www.completepackage.com
Corrugated boxes; exporter and importer of tapes, cartons, stretch film, impulse sealers and plastic strapping materials. 3000 box sizes in stock
Owner: Jeffery Berkowitz
Director Of Sales: Tom DiGiacomo
Estimated Sales: $10-20 Million
Number Employees: 10-19

20820 Complete Packaging Solutions & Systems
325 Curie Dr
Alpharetta, GA 30005 770-751-7400
Fax: 770-751-0706 800-417-3178
info@kallfass-us.com www.kallfass.com
Fully automatic l-sealer, side sealers and sleeve wrapper, shrink tunnels and semiautomatic l-sealer
President: Melanie Goepfert
Vice President: Bodo Goepfert
Marketing/Sales Manager: Cece Loft
Estimated Sales: $1-2.5 000,000
Number Employees: 5-9

20821 Complete Packaging Systems
2411 Loma Avenue
South El Monte, CA 91733-1415 626-579-4670
Fax: 626-579-2015 ndowd@pisc.com
Prints blister cards and thermoforms blisters
President: Bruce Romfo
Estimated Sales: $10-20 000,000
Number Employees: 100-249

20822 **Completely Fresh Foods**
1117 West Olympic Blvd
Montebello, CA 90640 323-722-9136
Fax: 323-722-9139
www.completelyfreshfoods.com
Processor and distributor of fresh and frozen beef, poultry, pork and seafood products
President: Josh Solovy
Vice President: Eric Litmanovich
COO: Shaun Oshita
Estimated Sales: $60 Million
Number Employees: 200

20823 **Complex Steel & Wire Corporation**
36254 Annapolis
Wayne, MI 48184 734-326-1600
Fax: 734-326-7421 www.complexsteel.com
Wire rack decking and partitions.
President: Vincent Fedell
Sales Manager: Gary Snarkas
Estimated Sales: $2.5 - 5 Million
Number Employees: 10-19

20824 **Compliance Control**
1595 Cabin Branch Dr
Hyattsville, MD 20785 301-773-7600
800-810-4000
info@hygenius.com www.hygenius.com
Manufacturer and exporter of handwashing verification systems
President: Noel Segal
Executive VP: Bill Karlin
Estimated Sales: $2.5-5 Million
Number Employees: 10-19
Type of Packaging: Food Service, Private Label
Brands:
Hygenius

20825 **(HQ)Component Hardware Group**
1890 Swarthmore Ave
Lakewood, NJ 08701 732-363-4700
Fax: 732-363-9864 800-526-3694
www.coponenthardware.com
Manufacturer, importer and exporter of food service equipment including beverage preparation and serving products, dispensers, faucets, spray washers, water stations, tables including legs and bases, drains, grease filters, castersetc
President: Alfred Klein
VP Marketing: William Matthaei
VP Sales: Pat Campbell
Estimated Sales: $30 - 50 Million
Number Employees: 50-99
Square Footage: 96000
Brands:
Encore
Standard-Keil

20826 **Composite Can & Tube Institute**
50 S Pickett St Ste 110
Alexandria, VA 22304 703-823-7234
Fax: 703-823-7237 ccti@cctiwdc.org
www.cctiwdc.org
VP: Kristine Garland
Estimated Sales: $2.5 - 5,000,000
Number Employees: 1-4

20827 **Composition Materials Company**
249 Pepes Farm Rd
Milford, CT 06460 203-874-6500
Fax: 203-874-6505 800-262-7763
info@compomat.com www.compomat.com
Plastic Blasting Media, a distributor of a multitude of filers and extenders, supplier of Walnut Shell grits and flours, and importer of birch wood flour from Sweden.
President: Alan K. Nudelman
Chairman: Theodore Diamond
Sales Representative: Steven D. Essex
Product Operations Manager: David M. Elster
Estimated Sales: $2.5-5 Million
Number Employees: 10-19
Square Footage: 10000
Brands:
Clear-Cut
Cob Dry
Plasti-Grit
Resistat

20828 **Compris Technologies**
2651 Satellite Blvd
Duluth, GA 30096-5810 770-418-4616
Fax: 770-795-3333 800-615-3301
info@compriscorp.com www.compristech.com
Manufacturer and exporter of computer software including point of sale, labor, inventory, scheduling, executive information and cash management
President: Alaa Pasha
Vice President, Development: Eric Kobres
Area VP Sales: Ron Small
Estimated Sales: $5 - 10 Million
Number Employees: 100-249

20829 **Computer Aid, Inc.**
1390 Ridgeview Dr.
Allentown, PA 22180 610-530-5000
Fax: 703-281-3461 800-327-4243
blake@computeraid-llc.com www.compaid.com
In-house payroll, automated time and attendance software
President: Joe Angronaco
Program System Analyst: Kyle Bonney
Estimated Sales: $3 - 5 Million
Number Employees: 20-49
Square Footage: 1500
Brands:
Pay Master
Pay Master Plus

20830 **Computer Aided Marketing**
PO Box 4990
Chapel Hill, NC 27515-4990 919-401-0996
Fax: 919-489-4980
Restaurant back office software for frequent diners
VP Sales/Marketing: Bill Ryan
Number Employees: 6
Brands:
Cam Frequent Diners

20831 **Computer Associates International**
2950 Express Dr S Ste 106
Central Islip, NY 11749 631-342-2984
Fax: 631-342-5329 800-225-5224
www.ca.com
Prepackaged software publishing
President: Sanjay Kumar
C.E.O: Sanjay Kumar
Quality Control: Douglas Robinson
C.T.O: Yogesh Gupta
G.M. Global Mkting.: Kenneth Fitzpatrick
Executive VP/GM: Stephen Richards
Exec. V.P. Administrative Services: Gary Quinn
Estimated Sales: $1 - 5 000,000
Number Employees: 1,000-4,999

20832 **Computer CommunicationsSpecialists**
2960 Shallowford Rd # 102
Marietta, GA 30066-3093 770-509-5321
888-231-4227
lnewby@epos.com
Designer and manufacturer of integrated information response systems
Manager: Andy Pereira
Marketing Specialist: David Gay
Estimated Sales: $10 - 20 Million
Number Employees: 1-4
Brands:
Acca
First Line

20833 **Computer Controlled Machines**
1 Magnuson Ave
Pueblo, CO 81001-4889 719-948-9500
Fax: 719-948-9540 sales@magnusoncorp.com
www.magnusoncorp.com
Manufacturer and exporter of vegetable processing equipment for sweet corn, green beans and peas
Owner: Bob Smith
VP/General Manager: Craig Furlo
Estimated Sales: $5 - 10 Million
Number Employees: 20-49
Parent Co: Atlas-Pacific Engineering

20834 **Computer Group**
4212 N Arlington Heights Rd
Arlington Hts, IL 60004-1372 847-818-9200
Fax: 847-818-9300 dsj@computer-group.com
Service computers and internet services
Owner: Dave Besser
Estimated Sales: $5-10 000,000
Number Employees: 10-19
Square Footage: 4500

20835 **(HQ)Computerized Machinery System**
11733 95th Ave N
Maple Grove, MN 55369-5551 763-493-0099
Fax: 763-493-0093 sales@cmsitechnologies.com
www.labelmart.com
Manufacturer and exporter of pressure sensitive labels; wholesaler/distributor and exporter of barcode printers, label scanners and applicators
Owner: Lee Sorenson
Sales: Eric Sorensen
Estimated Sales: Below $5 Million
Number Employees: 10-19
Brands:
Dura-Kote

20836 **Computerway Food Systems**
635 Southwest Street
High Point, NC 27260 336-841-7289
Fax: 336-841-2594 sales@mycfs.com
www.mycfs.com
President: William Altenpohl
Estimated Sales: $2.5-5 000,000
Number Employees: 20-49

20837 **Computrition**
19808 Nordhoff Pl
Chatsworth, CA 91311 818-701-5544
Fax: 818-701-1702 800-222-4488
info@computrition.com www.computrition.com
Offers completely integrated food service and nutrition care management software systems for operations of all size. Software features include diet order, recipe, menu and inventory management, online order entry and nutrientanalysis
President: Luros Luros-Elson RD
CEO: Scott Saklad
R&D: Joseph Bibbo
Manager, Marketing: Marty Yadrick, RD
Sales: Scott Saklad
Operations: Kim Goldberg
Estimated Sales: $20-50 Million
Number Employees: 50-99
Square Footage: 17000
Type of Packaging: Food Service
Brands:
Hospitality Suite

20838 **(HQ)Computype**
2285 County Road C W
Saint Paul, MN 55113 651-633-0633
Fax: 651-633-5580 800-328-0852
www.computype.com
Manufacturer and exporter of bar code labels, printers and applicators
President: R Huntsinger
VP: J Ammann
CEO: William Roche
Estimated Sales: $20-50 Million
Number Employees: 100-249
Other Locations:
Computype
Concord NH

20839 **Comstar Printing Solutions**
10175 Philipp Pkwy
Streetsboro, OH 44241-4706 330-528-2800
Fax: 330-528-2828 info@printpro.com
www.printpro.com
In-line and thermal transfer imprinters for in-line packaging and table top labeling systems
Executive Assistant: Sharon Spaeth
Production Manager: Jeff Burke

20840 **Comstock-Castle Stove Company**
119 W Washington St
Quincy, IL 62301 217-223-5070
Fax: 217-223-0007 800-637-9188
sales@castlestove.com www.castlestove.com
Manufacturer, importer and exporter of cooking equipment including gas broilers, deep fat fryers, ovens, griddles, ranges, hot plates, etc
President: John Spake
Vice President: Timothy Spake
Marketing/Sales: Curtis Spake
Purchasing Manager: Bob Speckhart
Estimated Sales: $5-10 Million
Number Employees: 20-49
Square Footage: 85000
Type of Packaging: Food Service, Private Label

Brands:
Castle
Economy

20841 Comtec Industries
10210 Werch Dr Ste 204
Suite 204
Woodridge, IL 60517 630-759-9000
Fax: 630-759-9009
feedback@comtecindustriesltd.com
www.comtecindustriesltd.com
Baking equipment and supplies including dough formers for pot pies, hors d'oeuvres and top/bottom crusts; also, dies and tooling for pies, tarts, cheese-cakes, etc.; exporter of dough presses
President: James Reilly
Estimated Sales: $1 - 3 Million
Number Employees: 10
Square Footage: 4000
Brands:
Comtec

20842 Comtek Systems
309 Breesport Street
San Antonio, TX 78216-2699 210-340-8253
Fax: 210-340-8255 comtek@texas.net
Point of sale systems
President: Thomas Hayes
Plant Manager: M Hayes
Number Employees: 5-9
Square Footage: 2500
Brands:
Comtek Supercharger

20843 Comtrex Systems Corporation
1247 N Church St Ste 7
Moorestown, NJ 08057 856-778-0090
Fax: 856-778-9322 800-220-2669
Sales@Comtrex.com www.comtrex.com
Manufacturer and exporter of point of sale terminals, peripherals and software
CEO: Jefferey C Rice
Estimated Sales: $1 - 3,000,000
Number Employees: 1-4
Type of Packaging: Food Service
Brands:
Comtrex
Pcs5000 System

20844 Comus Restaurant Systems
9667 Fleetwood Court
Frederick, MD 21701 301-698-6208
Manufacturer and exporter of point of sale and full back office software
Marketing: Fred Ihrer
Estimated Sales: $2.5-5 Million
Number Employees: 10
Square Footage: 4000
Parent Co: Comus Software
Brands:
Comus Restaurant Systems

20845 Con-tech/Conservation Technology
2783 Shermer Rd
Northbrook, IL 60062-7708 847-559-5505
Fax: 847-559-5505 800-728-0312
contech@con-techlighting.com
www.con-techlighting.com
Manufacturer, importer and exporter of lighting products and industrial fans
President: John Ranshaw
Secretary: Sandy Grossman
VP: John Ranshow
Sales/Marketing Executive: Olga Draqunsky
Purchasing Agent: Larry Sabatino
Estimated Sales: $20-50 Million
Number Employees: 20-49
Square Footage: 36000
Brands:
Con-Tech

20846 ConAgra Corn ProcessingCompany
16755 274th Rd
Atchison, KS 66002-9202 913-367-3251
Fax: 913-367-0734 800-541-2556
cwilson@bunge.com
www.bungenorthamerica.com
Dry corn milling
Manager: Bill Gross
Manager: Telly Irvin
Estimated Sales: $1 Billion+
Number Employees: 50-99

20847 ConAgra Food Lamb Weston
599 South Rivershore Lane
Eagle, ID 83616-4979 208-336-5355
Fax: 208-336-2282 800-766-7783
lwinfo@conagrafoods.com
www.lambweston.com
Frozen potato products, battered onion rings and vegetables, and appetizer products.
President/CEO: F. Gilbert Lamb
Regional Sales Manager: Jeff Herbst
Estimated Sales: $2.5-5 Million
Number Employees: 6,000
Parent Co: ConAgra Foods
Other Locations:
Lamb Weston Manufacturing Plant
Weston OR
Lamb Weston Manufacturing Plant
Kennewick WA
Lamb Weston Manufacturing Plant
Prosser WA
Lamb Weston Manufacturing Plant
Boise ID
Lamb Weston Manufacturing Plant
Alberta, Canada
Brands:
My Fries
Stealth Fries
Generation 7 Fries
Lw Private Reserve
Inland Valley
Lamb's Natural
Sweet Things
Tavern Traditions
Alexia
Tantalizers

20848 ConAgra Foods Inc.
1 Conagra Drive
Omaha, NE 68102-5001 402-240-4000
Fax: 402-240-4707 877-266-2472
www.conagrafoods.com
Consumer foods segment manufactures and markets leading branded products to retail and foodservice customers in the US and internationally. Commercial foods segment manufactures and sells a variety of specialty products to foodserviceand commercial customers worldwide. Major brands include Lam Weston, a leading producer of quality frozen potato products and ConAgra Mills, a top provicer of premium multi-use flours with the broadest portfolio of whole grain ingredients. Has 481plants worldwide.
President, Consumer Foods: Tom McGough
CEO: Gary Rodkin
Chief Financial Officer: John Gehring
President, Commercial Foods: Paul Maass
EVP, Research, Quality & Innovation: Al Bolles PhD
EVP/General Counsel/Corporate Secretary: Colleen Batcheler
Exec VP & Chief Marketing Officer: Joan Chow
President ConAgra Foods Sales: Doug Knudsen
Exec VP & Chief Administrative Officer: Brian Keck
Senior Vice President, Human Resources: Nicole Theophilus
Exec VP & Chief Strategy Officer: Andrew Ross
Estimated Sales: $12.4 Billion
Number Employees: 25,000
Number of Brands: 51
Square Footage: 11042
Type of Packaging: Consumer, Food Service, Bulk
Other Locations:
ConAgra Headquarters
Kennewick WA
ConAgra Headquarters
Naperville IL
Sales Office
Anaheim CA
Sales Office
Mesa AR
Sales Office
San Antonio TX
Sales Office
Plano TX
Sales Office
Tampa FL
Sales Office
Baltimore MD
Sales Office
Mason OH
Sales Office
Troy OH
Brands:
Banquet
Chef Boyardee
David Seeds
Egg Beaters
Healthy Choice
Hebrew National
Hunt's
Kid Cuisine
Marie Callender's
Orville Redenbacher's
Pam
Reddi-Wip
Slim Jim
Snack Pack
Wesson
Act Ii
Alexia
Andy Capp's
Banquet Brown 'n Serve
Blue Bonnet
Crunch 'n Munch
Dennison's
Fiddle Faddle
Fleischmann's
Gulden's
Jiffy Pop
La Choy
Libby's
Manwich
Parkay
Penrose
Peter Pan
Poppycock
Ranch Style
Ro*Tel
Rosarita
Swiss Miss
Van Camp's
Wolf Brand Chili
Conagra Mills
Lamb Weston
Spicetec Flavors & Seasonings
Ultra Grain
Angela Mia
Award Cuisine
Lamb Weston Inland Valley
Gebhardt
J. Hungerford Smith
J.M. Swank
The Max
Vogel Popcorn
Kangaroo
National Pretzel Company
Del Monte Canada
Odom's Tennessee Pride

20849 ConAgra Foods Inc.
2301 Washington Street
Hamburg, IA 51640 712-382-2634
Fax: 712-382-1357 800-831-5818
info@vogelpopcorn.com
www.vogelpopcorn.com
Popcorn and popcorn seeds
Operations Manager: Rodney Daiker
Plant Manager: Kelly Mag
Other Locations:
Manufacturing Plant
Lakeview IA
Manufacturing Plant
Brookston IN
Brands:
Orville Redenbacher

20850 Conam Inspection
192 Internationale Blvd
Glendale Heights, IL 60139-2094 630-681-0008
Fax: 630-681-0009
Consultant providing nondestructive testing laboratory services, lubricant and fuel analysis and chemical and environmental testing
President: Laurie Todd
Estimated Sales: $10-20 Million
Number Employees: 50-99

20851 Conatech Consulting Group, Inc
501 N Lindbergh Blvd Ste 105
Saint Louis, MO 63141 314-995-9767
Fax: 314-995-9766 rjbockserman@conatech.com
www.conatech.com
Consulting engineering firm, processing-packaging-distribution of food products. Product and package development, line integration, federal regulations, expert testimony trial, research and discovery; product liability, patentinfringement research and discovery, depositions, trial testimony
President: Robert Bockserman

Estimated Sales: $500,000-$1 Million
Number Employees: 42
Number of Products: 42

20852 Conax Buffalo Technologies
2300 Walden Ave
Buffalo, NY 14225-4779 716-684-4500
Fax: 716-684-7433 800-223-2389
conaxbuf@conaxbuffalo.com
www.conaxbuffalo.com
Manufacturer and exporter of measurement systems including temperature sensors, sealing devices and fiber optic systems
President: Robert Fox
Marketing Director: Richard Paluch
Director of Sales and Marketing: Michael Valachos
Purchasing: Joe Kelly
Estimated Sales: $10-20 Million
Number Employees: 50-99
Square Footage: 93000

20853 Conbraco Industries
P.O.Box 247
Matthews, NC 28106-0247 704-847-9191
Fax: 704-841-6021 www.conbraco.com
Water gauge valves
Manager: Melinda Courtney
CFO: Eric Miller
Estimated Sales: Below $5 Million
Number Employees: 250-499

20854 Concept Foods
141 Covington Dr
Bloomingdale, IL 60108-3107 630-539-3100
Fax: 630-539-3109 800-762-1734
President: Kenneth Rzeszutko
Estimated Sales: $20 - 50 Million
Number Employees: 20-49

20855 Concept Hospitality Group
325 Cutwater
Foster City, CA 94404 650-357-1224
Fax: 760-323-0170 tomkelley@juno.com
Consultant specializing in image enhancement, product marketing and promotion for the hospitality and service markets
Managing Partner: Tom Kelley
Number Employees: 5

20856 Concept Packaging Technologies
13 Carry Way
Carson City, NV 89706-7777 775-246-5977
Fax: 775-246-7169 800-796-2769
www.wspackaging.com
Manufacturer and exporter of automatic labeling equipment and bar code printers and scanners
Manager: Joel Smith
Estimated Sales: $1 - 3,000,000
Number Employees: 5-9
Square Footage: 10500
Brands:
Concept 100
Concept 1000
Concept 400pa
Concept 500pa
Concept Packaging

20857 Concepts & Design International, Ltd
203 Foxwood Road
West Nyack, NY 10994-2507 845-358-1558
Fax: 845-358-1558
Design and engineering consultant for food facilities including restaurants, schools and hotels.
President: Philip Amato
CFO: Adrienne Amato
Estimated Sales: $300,000-$500,000
Number Employees: 1
Square Footage: 156
Type of Packaging: Food Service

20858 Concord Chemical Company
1700 Federal St
Camden, NJ 08105 856-966-1526
Fax: 856-963-0246 800-282-2436
miguelcastillo@concordchemical.com
www.concordchemical.com
Producer of eco-friendly cleaners, soaps, lubricants, release agents, dust control products and more.
President/CEO: Miguel Castillo
VP Product Development: Jack Cram
VP Sales: Carol Griffiths
VP Purchasing: Lauren DeSilvio
Number Employees: 50-99
Square Footage: 60000
Parent Co: Seacord Corporation
Brands:
22 K Gold Finish
3-D Degreaser
Creamedic
Harley Activated Pine
Lemonee-8

20859 Conductive Containers, I
4500 Quebec Avenue North
New Hope, MN ÿ55428
Fax: 763-537-1738 800-327-2329
info@corstat.com www.corstat.com
Manufacturer and exporter of containers including conductive fiberboard, corrugated, chipboard and plastic
VP: Paul Granning
VP Operations/R&D: Robert Marlovits
Estimated Sales: $1-2.5 Million
Number Employees: 5-9
Square Footage: 100000
Brands:
Corstat

20860 ConeTech
1450 Airport Blvd Ste 180
Santa Rosa, CA 95403 707-577-7500
Fax: 707-577-7511 info@conetech.com
www.conetech.com
President: Anthony Dann
CFO: Robert E Williams
Estimated Sales: $1-2.5 000,000
Number Employees: 5-9

20861 Conesco Conveyor Corporation
953 Paulison Avenue
Clifton, NJ 07011-3641 973-365-1440
Fax: 973-365-1923 conesco@aol.com
www.consecoconveyors.com
Belt and chain conveyors
President: John Garratt
VP: Jim Garratt
Estimated Sales: Below $5 Million
Number Employees: 4
Square Footage: 40000

20862 Confection Art Inc
3636 North Williams Avenue
Portland, OR 97227 503-505-0481
info@chocolatecraftkits.com
www.chocolatecraftkits.com
Molded chocolates
President: Nancy Baggett
Master Pastry Chef: Pierre Herme
Number Employees: 8

20863 Conflex Incorporated
6637 N Sidney Pl
Germantown, WI 53022 262-512-2665
Fax: 262-512-1665 800-225-4296
jmorrissey@conflex.com www.conflex.com
President: Kevin Laird

20864 Conflex, Inc.
W130 N10751 Washington Drive
Germantown, WI 53022 262-512-2665
Fax: 262-512-1665 800-225-4296
info@conflex.com www.conflex.com
Manufacturer and exporter of shrink wrapping equipment
President: Bill Morrissey Jr
CEO: Joe Morrissey
CFO: Jim Benton
Research & Development: Mark Kubisiak
Tech Services: Kevin Thomas
Product Manager: Joe Morrissey
Purchasing Manager: Bill Morrissey, Jr.
Number Employees: 20-49
Square Footage: 320000
Type of Packaging: Consumer, Food Service, Bulk

20865 Conflow Technologies, Inc.
18 Regan Road
Units 28 & 29
Brampton, ON L7A 1C2
Canada 905-840-6800
Fax: 905-840-6799 800-275-9887
sales@conflow.ca www.conflow.ca
Manufacturer and importer of food processing machinery including certified milk reception and loadout systems, in-plant sanitary flow meters and calibration services and batch and blend control systems; also, transport custodydispensing systems
President: Gary Collins
CFO: Anna Lynn Wiebe
Vice President: Gerry Camirand
Research & Development: Anna Lynn
Quality Control: Gerry Camirand
Number Employees: 7
Square Footage: 2700
Brands:
Contrec
Flowdata, Inc.
Hoffer Flow Controls Inc.
Proces-Data

20866 Congent Technologies
11140 Luschek Drive
Cincinnati, OH 45241-2434 513-469-6800
Fax: 513-469-6811
Bioluminescence lighting system
President: Jim Leroy
Estimated Sales: $2.5-5 000,000
Number Employees: 5-9
Square Footage: 2000

20867 Conifer Paper Products
4911 Central Avenue
Richmond, CA 94804-5842 510-527-8222
Fax: 510-526-3376 www.conifercrent.com
Tea and coffee industry bags and packaging film supplies
Number Employees: 104

20868 Conimar Corporation
PO Box 1509
Ocala, FL 34478-1509 352-732-7235
Fax: 352-732-6888 800-874-9735
www.conimar.com
Beverage coaster, flexible cutting mats and bamboo cutting boards
President: Mr Crawford
CFO: Eric Robinson
VP: Ron Dampier
Marketing: Terry Putty
Estimated Sales: $10-15 Million
Number Employees: 50-99
Square Footage: 70000
Type of Packaging: Private Label

20869 (HQ)Connecticut Container Corporation
455 Sackett Point Rd
North Haven, CT 06473 203-248-2161
Fax: 203-248-0241 www.unicorr.com
Corrugated boxes, containers, displays, foam and plastic packaging
President: Harry Perkins
President: Lawrence Perkins
Sales Manager: B Etra
Estimated Sales: $20 - 50 Million
Number Employees: 100-249

20870 Connecticut Culinary Institute
230 Farmington Avenue
Suite 5
Farmington, CT 06032-1973 860-677-7869
Fax: 860-676-0679 ct.culinary.inst@snet.net
Consulting firm providing assistance for food service operators
President: David Tine
Number Employees: 20-49
Square Footage: 10000
Parent Co: Hartine Corporation

20871 Connecticut Laminating Company
162 James St
New Haven, CT 06513 203-787-2184
Fax: 203-787-4073 800-753-9119
info@ctlaminating.com www.ctlaminating.com
Manufacturer and exporter of plastic laminated advertising signs, place mats, tags, menus and cards
President: Henry Snow
VP: Steve Snow
Estimated Sales: $10 Million+
Number Employees: 100-249
Square Footage: 55000

20872 Connerton Company
1131 East Wakeham Avenue
Santa Ana, CA 92705-4145 714-547-9218
Fax: 714-547-1969
sales@connertoncompany.com
www.connertoncompany.com
Commercial gas cooking equipment including broilers, hot plates, griddles, stock pot stoves and over/under broilers
President: Connie Tyler
VP: Craig Reynolds
Number Employees: 10-19
Brands:
Connerton

20873 Conpac
131 Industrial Dr
Warminster, PA 18974 215-322-2755
Contract packaging
President: Sam Gerbino
Estimated Sales: Less than $500,000
Number Employees: 1-4

20874 Conquest International LLC
1108 SW 8th St
Plainville, KS 67663 785-434-2483
Fax: 785-434-2736 conquest@ruraltel.net
www.envirolyteconquestusa.com
Water treatment and purification systems, and bottled water plants
President: Ned Colburn
Estimated Sales: Under $300,000
Number Employees: 1-4
Square Footage: 40000
Brands:
Natural Pure

20875 Consolidated Baling Machine Company
P.O.Box 6922
Jacksonville, FL 32236-6922 904-358-3812
Fax: 904-358-7013 800-231-9286
sales@intl-baler.com www.intl-baler.com
Manufacturer and exporter of balers, compactors and drum crushers/packers
President: William Nielsen
CEO: Roger Griffin
Sales Manager: Jerry Wise
Estimated Sales: F
Number Employees: 50-99
Square Footage: 4000
Parent Co: Waste Technology Corporation
Brands:
Cmbc
Consolidated Baling Machine Co.
Ibc
Ips
International Baler Corp.
International Press & Shear
Wpc

20876 Consolidated Can
15725 Illinois Ave
Paramount, CA 90723 562-634-5245
Fax: 562-634-8689 888-793-2199
www.consolidatedcan.com
Manufacturer and exporter of tin cans; also, tops, bottoms, plugs and caps for containers
Owner: Doug Lampson
CFO: Doug Lampson
Estimated Sales: $1 - 2.5 Million
Number Employees: 1-4
Square Footage: 3000
Type of Packaging: Bulk

20877 Consolidated CommercialControls
200 International Way
Winsted, CT 06098 860-738-7112
Fax: 860-738-7140 800-332-2500
CustServ@AllPointsFPS.com
www.allpointsfps.com
Manufacturer and exporter of commercial cooking and refrigeration equipment parts; importer of cast iron parts and supplies.
CEO: John Hanby
CFO: Dan Cox
Vice President: Azie Kahn
Research & Development: Azie Kahn
Marketing Director: John McDermott
Sales Director: Phil Wisehart
Purchasing Manager: Linda Feichtl
Estimated Sales: $15-20 Million
Number Employees: 20-49
Square Footage: 45000
Type of Packaging: Food Service

20878 Consolidated Container Company
3101 Towercreek Parkway
Suite 300
Atlanta, GA 30339 678-742-4600
Fax: 678-742-4750 888-831-2184
www.ccllc.com
Blow molded plastic packaging for the dairy, water, beverage and food industries.
President/CEO/Director: Jeffrey Greene
CFO: Richard Sehring
EVP Sales/Market Development: Kenneth Branham
VP Human Resources: Bradley Newman
COO: Robert Walton
Number Employees: 55
Square Footage: 16000
Type of Packaging: Consumer, Food Service

20879 (HQ)Consolidated Container Company
3101 Towercreek Parkway
Suite 300
Atlanta, GA 30339 678-742-4600
Fax: 678-742-4750 888-831-2184
www.ccllc.com
Manufacturer and exporter of blow molded plastic bottles
President/Director/CEO: Jeffrey Greene
Vice President, Human Resources: Bradley Newman
Estimated Sales: $237 Million
Number Employees: 2,700
Square Footage: 16000
Parent Co: Bain Capital, LLC

20880 Consolidated Display Company
1210 US Highway 34
Oswego, IL 60543 630-851-8666
Fax: 630-851-8756 888-851-7669
buzzp@aol.com
www.letitsnow.com/contact.ivnu
Food props for displays
President: Sebastian Puccio
VP: Anthony Puccio
Estimated Sales: Below $5 Million
Number Employees: 10-19
Square Footage: 60000

20881 Consolidated Label Company
925 Florida Central Pkwy
Longwood, FL 32750 407-339-2626
Fax: 407-331-1711 800-475-2235
liz@consolidatedlabel.com
www.consolidatedlabel.com
Manufacturer and exporter of pressure sensitive labels and tags
President: Joel Carmany
National Sales Manager: Beau Bowman
Plant Manager: Dick St Hilaire
Estimated Sales: $20-50 Million
Number Employees: 50-99
Square Footage: 35000
Type of Packaging: Private Label, Bulk

20882 Consolidated Plastics
4700 Prosper Rd
Stow, OH 44224 800-362-1000
Fax: 800-858-5001 800-858-5001
Blow molded plastic bottles
Number Employees: 50-99

20883 Consolidated Thread Mills, Inc.
P.O. Box 1107
Fall River, MA 02722 508-672-0032
Fax: 508-674-3773 ctmills@meganet.net
www.consolidatedthreadmills.com
Manufacturer and exporter of bounded and waxed industrial twine including nylon, polyester, rayon and cotton
Owner: Colleen Pacheco
Estimated Sales: $1 - 5 Million
Number Employees: 5-9

20884 Constar International
1100 Northbrook Drive, 2nd Floor
Trevose, PA 19053 215-552-3700
constar@constar.net
www.constar.net
Plastic containers and bottles for soft drinks, mustard, edible oils, wine and liquors
President: Mike Hoffman
CFO: Bill Rymer
R&D: Don Deual
Production: Craig Renton
Estimated Sales: $2.5 - 5 Million
Number Employees: 20
Parent Co: Crown Cork & Seal

20885 Consulting Nutritional Services
26500 Agoura Road
Suite 210
Calabasas, CA 91302-3550 818-880-6774
Fax: 818-880-6797 cns@foodsafe.com
www.foodsafe.com

20886 Consumer Cap Corporation
PO Box 7259
New Castle, PA 16107-7259 724-657-9440
Fax: 724-654-8573 800-545-5504
www.consumercap.com
Plastic closures
Number Employees: 100

20887 Contact Industries
411 Wales Ave
Bronx, NY 10454-1719 908-351-5900
Fax: 908-351-6037 info@safegaurdchemical.com
www.contactind.com
Contract packager of aerosols, adhesives, cements, insecticides, room deodorants and oven cleaners
President: Edward Piranian
Quality Control: Leo Hu
Estimated Sales: $10 - 20 Million
Number Employees: 40
Parent Co: Safeguard Chemical Corporation
Type of Packaging: Food Service, Private Label

20888 Containair Packaging Corporation
37 E 6th St
Paterson, NJ 07524 973-523-1800
Fax: 973-523-1818 888-276-6500
www.containair.com
Manufacturer and exporter of semi-bulk containers for food ingredients; also, slotted cartons and graphic displays available
CEO/President: Lawrence Taylor
VP: Paul Davis
Plant Manager: Ken Kutner
Estimated Sales: $2.5-5 Million
Number Employees: 20-49
Square Footage: 47000
Brands:
K Box
Kl Box

20889 Container Handling Systems
621 E Plainfield Rd
Countryside, IL 60525 708-482-9900
Fax: 708-482-8960 sales@chsc1.com
www.containerhandlingsystems.com
Conveyors and conveyor systems
President: John Nalbach
R&D: David Haskell
Estimated Sales: $5 - 10 000,000
Number Employees: 50-99

20890 Container Machinery Corporation
1060 Broadway
Albany, NY 12204 518-694-3310
Fax: 608-719-8380 www.cmc-kuhnke.com
High speed notching presses; exporter of seam quality inspection and measuring systems; importer of can making machinery
Managing Director: Thomas Duve
VP: Alex Grossjohann
Technical Service Manager: Markus Kellner
Marketing Manager: Aura Marcks
Sales Manager Southeast Asia: Ning Qian
Customer Service Manager: Jose Rodriguez
Vice President, Managing Director: Alex Grossjohann
Estimated Sales: $1 - 3 Million
Number Employees: 5-9
Square Footage: 60000
Brands:
Bertil-Ohlsson
Imeta
Krupp (Sig Cantech)
Lanico
Mbt (Lubeca)
Mh Press Systems

Sanyu
Wegro Metal Crown

20891 Container Manufacturing
P.O.Box 428
Middlesex, NJ 08846 732-563-0100
Fax: 732-563-0704
www.containermanufacturing.com
Plastic containers
President: David Jennings
Estimated Sales: $5-10 000,000
Number Employees: 20-49

20892 Container Services Company
PO Box 1115
Warrenton, OR 97146-1115 503-861-3338
Fax: 503-861-0287 cscastoria@aol.com
www.containerserviceco.com
Estimated Sales: $1 - 5 Million

20893 Container Specialties
1950 N Mannheim Rd
Melrose Park, IL 60160 708-615-1400
Fax: 708-615-0381 800-548-7513
midwestcan@aol.com www.midwestcan.com
Plastic bottles and sanitary cans
Owner: John Trippi Sr
CFO: Janet Johnson
Quality Control: John Trippi Jr
Sales/Marketing: Alan Trippi
Estimated Sales: $10 - 20 Million
Number Employees: 20-49
Square Footage: 80000
Parent Co: Midwest Can Company

20894 Container Supply Company
12571 Western Ave
Garden Grove, CA 92841 714-891-4896
Fax: 714-892-3824
tbertoglio@containersupplycompany.com
www.containersupplycompany.com
Manufacturer and exporter of tin cans and plastic pails and containers
Owner: Robert Hurtt
Quality Control: C Bonnet
Regional Sales Manager: T Carlson
Director Sales: Tony Bertoglio
Export Sales: F Ceja
Estimated Sales: $20 - 50 Million
Number Employees: 100-249
Square Footage: 160000

20895 Container Testing Lab
607 Fayette Ave
Mamaroneck, NY 10543 914-381-2600
Fax: 914-381-0143 800-221-5170
assignments@containertechnologylabs.com
www.containertechnologylabs.com
Laboratory and consulting service specializing in container materials and systems including package engineering, related material handling and package testing certification
President: Vasilis Morfoupolous
Lab Manager: S Brooks
Technical Director: C Coleman, Ph.D.
Estimated Sales: Less than $500,000
Number Employees: 5 to 9
Square Footage: 14500

20896 Container-Quinn TestingLaboratories
170 Shepard Ave Ste A
Wheeling, IL 60090 847-537-9470
Fax: 847-537-9098
spowell@container-quinn.com
Consultant offering package testing, design development, engineering and systems services
President: Todd R Nelson
Lab Director: Stephen Powell
*Estimated Sales:*less than $500,000
Number Employees: 1 to 4

20897 (HQ)Containment Technology
1105 Highway 30
St Gabriel, LA 70776-5011 225-642-3963
Fax: 225-642-9629 800-388-2467
contectun.bin@aol.com
www.containmenttechnology.com
FDA approved steel containers for liquid and dry hazardous and nonhazardous materials
President: Robert Allen
Vice President: Sylvia Allen
Marketing: Roderick Franklin
VP Sales: Gerald Scruggs
Estimated Sales: $1-2.5 Million
Number Employees: 10-19
Square Footage: 40000
Type of Packaging: Bulk
Other Locations:
Material Containment
City of Commerce CA
Brands:
Blend Tanks
Fda Steel Container
Greane Bins

20898 Contech
314 Straight Ave SW
Grand Rapids, MI 49504-6485 616-459-4139
Fax: 616-459-4140 800-767-8658
info@contech-inc.com www.contech-inc.com
Manufacturer and exporter of pesticide-free insect trapping adhesives
President and CEO: Mark Grambart
VP of Sales and Marketing: Allen Spigelman
VP of Sales and Marketing: Allen Spigelman
VP of Operations: Bill Jones
Estimated Sales: $2.5 - 5 Million
Number Employees: 5-9
Square Footage: 80000
Type of Packaging: Private Label
Brands:
Tangle-Trap
Tanglefoot

20899 Contemporary Products Company
275 Hein Dr
Garner, NC 27529-7221 919-779-4228
Fax: 919-779-9734
Manufacturer and importer of award plaques and shields, trophies and cup bases
VP: David Hamilton
Manager: Joan Squillini
Estimated Sales: $1 - 5 Million
Number Employees: 1 to4

20900 (HQ)Contico Container
15510 Blackburn Ave
Norwalk, CA 90650 562-921-9967
Fax: 562-926-4979 www.contico.com
Manufacturer and exporter of polyethylene containers
Engineering-R&D: Michael Angelo
Estimated Sales: $20 - 50 Million
Number Employees: 100-249
Parent Co: Contico International

20901 Continental Cart by Kullman Industries
1 Kullman Corporate Campus Dr
Lebanon, NJ 08833-2163 908-236-0220
Fax: 908-236-0848 888-882-2278
gblackman@kullman.com www.kullman.com
Manufacturer and exporter of carts and kiosks; also, modular construction for diners, schools and correctional facilities
President: Amy Marks
CEO: Avi Telyas
Vice President of Operations: Michael Hathaway
Vice President of Production: Bobby Pohlman
Estimated Sales: $50 - 60 Million
Number Employees: 250-499

20902 Continental Commercial Products
305 Rock Industrial Park Dr.
Bridgeton, MO 63044 314-656-4301
Fax: 800-327-5492 800-325-1051
janics@contico.com
www.continentalcommercialproducts.com
Wastebaskets, recycle collection and trash receptacles, utility carts, liners, mopping equipment, squeegees, trigger sprayers, caution signs, plastic shelves, food service products and mobile equipment
President: Mike Boland
VP: Jim Dunn
Number Employees: 250-499
Square Footage: 12000000
Parent Co: Katy Industries
Brands:
Guardsboy
Guardsmen
Huskee
King Kan
Kleen Aire
Kleen Mist
Roun' Top
Snapoff
Steeline
Structolene
Swing Top
Tip Top
Wall Hugger

20903 Continental Custom Ingredients
1170 Invicta Drive
Oakville, ON L6H 6G1
Canada 905-815-8158
Fax: 905-815-9194 sales.support@cic-can.net
www.cci-can.net
Specializes in the design and application of stabilization, emulsification, and functional ingredient systems to impart the desired body and texture characteristics and self life stability to processed foods, beverage and dairyproducts.
Number Employees: 20-49
Type of Packaging: Private Label, Bulk
Brands:
Aquamin
Durafresh
Fargo

20904 Continental Disc Corporation
3160 W Heartland Dr
Liberty, MO 64068 816-792-1500
Fax: 816-792-2277 pressure@contdisc.com
www.contdisc.com
Food processing machinery parts including rupture discs for overpressure protection
President: Kenneth R Shaw
Estimated Sales: $20 - 50 Million
Number Employees: 100-249

20905 Continental Envelope Corporation
1700 Averill Rd
Geneva, IL 60134 630-262-8080
Fax: 630-262-1450 800-621-8155
sales@continentalenvelope.com
www.continentalenvelope.com
Custom made printed flexo and lithographed envelopes
President: Fred Margulies
Estimated Sales: $20 - 50 Million
Number Employees: 100-249
Square Footage: 120000

20906 Continental Equipment Corporation
P.O.Box 18662
6103 N. 76th Street
Milwaukee, WI 53218 414-463-0500
Fax: 414-463-3199
fred@continentalequipment.com
www.continentalequipment.com
Manufacturer and exporter of custom washing machinery
President: Fred Felder
VP Sales: Doug Piszczek
Engineer: Brennen Cullen
Estimated Sales: $3-5 Million
Number Employees: 20-49
Square Footage: 30000
Brands:
Aqucous Washing Systems

20907 Continental Extrusion Corporation
11 Cliffside Drive
Cedar Grove, NJ 07009-1234 973-239-4030
Fax: 973-239-9289 800-822-4748
Bags including specialty squared bottom HDPE and SOS style
VP Sales/Marketing: Ronald Basso
Estimated Sales: $10-20 Million
Number Employees: 100
Square Footage: 133
Brands:
Superbag
Superbag Jr.

20908 Continental Girbau
2500 State Road 44
Oshkosh, WI 54904 920-231-8222
Fax: 920-231-4666 800-256-1073
info@continentalgirbau.com
www.continentalgirbau.com
Manufacturer and exporter of commercial and industrial laundry equipment
President: Mike Floyd
Vice President: Joel Jorgensen
Public Relations: Amy Arnetveit
Number Employees: 20-49
Parent Co: Girbau S.A.

Brands:
Continental

20909 Continental Identification
140 E Averill St
Sparta, MI 49345-1516 616-887-7342
Fax: 616-887-0154 800-247-2499
www.continentalid.com
Manufacturer and exporter of counter mats, screen printed decals and cooler doors danglers
President: James Clay
Operations Manager: Dave Clay
Estimated Sales: $10 - 20 Million
Number Employees: 100-249
Parent Co: Celia Corporation

20910 Continental Industrial Supply
6935 Grande Vista Way S
South Pasadena, FL 33707-4702 727-341-1100
Fax: 727-343-3606
Flooring, trenchdrains, gratings and water conditioners and steamers (dry steamers)
Owner: Mike Marshall
Brands:
Kitchen Best
Never Scale
Polycast

20911 Continental Packaging Corporation
1327-29 Gateway Drive
Elgin, IL 60124 847-289-6400
Fax: 847-289-9048 info@continentalpkg.com
www.continentalpkg.com
Custom flexible packaging materials including bags and printed and plain overwrap
President: Rory Lent
CEO: Christian Krupsha
Estimated Sales: $5 Million
Number Employees: 20-50
Square Footage: 60000

20912 Continental Plastic Container
2515 McKinney Avenue
Suite 850
Dallas, TX 75201-7617 972-303-1825
Fax: 972-303-1829
Blow molded plastic bottles
Director Marketing: John Murphy
VP Sales/Marketing: John Roesch

20913 Continental Products
2000 W Boulevard St
Mexico, MO 65265 573-581-4128
Fax: 573-581-8711 800-325-0216
mail@adbags.com www.adbags.com
Plastic and cloth shopping bags
President: Carl Fuemmeler
National Sales Manager: Thad Fisher II
Estimated Sales: $1-2.5 Million
Number Employees: 5-9

20914 Continental Refrigerator
539 Dunksferry Rd
Bensalem, PA 19020 215-244-1400
Fax: 215-244-9579 800-523-7138
jjh@continental-refrig.com www.nrproducts.com
President: Brian Kelly
Estimated Sales: $50 - 100 Million
Number Employees: 100-249

20915 Continental Terminals
112 Port Jersey Blvd
Jersey, NJ 07305 973-578-2702
Fax: 973-578-2795
infonj@continentalterminals.com
www.continentalterminals.com
Tea and coffee industry reconditioners, samplers and weighers
Owner: Vito Difalco
Estimated Sales: Less than $500,000
Number Employees: 10-19

20916 Continental-Fremont
Airport Industrial Park 1685 S. County
PO Box 489
Tiffin, OH 44883 419-448-4045
Fax: 419-448-4048
www.senecaenvironmental.com
Manufacturer and exporter of carbon and stainless steel storage tanks, plating, bins, hoppers, and silos; sanitary and metal fabrication services available
President: C William Harple
CFO: Melissa Hoover
Quality Control: Ron Ranson
Marketing/Sales: Don Harple
Operations Manager: Ron Ransom
Estimated Sales: Below $5 Million
Number Employees: 20-49
Square Footage: 50000

20917 Contour Packaging
637 W Rockland St
Philadelphia, PA 19120 215-457-1600
Fax: 215-457-5040 www.contourpackaging.com
Manufacturer and exporter of stand-up pouches and blow molded plastic bottles and containers; also, screen printing and hot foil stamping services available
President: Stephen D Mannino
Sales Engineer: Mark Rysak
Estimated Sales: $10-20 Million
Number Employees: 50-99

20918 Contour Products
4001 Kaw Dr
Kansas City, KS 66102 913-321-4114
Fax: 913-321-8063 800-638-3626
contour@contourfoam.com
www.contourfoam.com
Molded foam
President: Richard Nickloy
Sales Manager: E Brandt
Estimated Sales: $2.5-5 Million
Number Employees: 1-4

20919 Contract Chemicals
201 Concourse Boulevard
Suite 102
Glen Allen, VA 23059-5640 804-967-9761
Fax: 804-967-9764 info@contractchemicals.com
www.contractchemicals.com
Specialty chemicals
Estimated Sales: $1-2.5 Million
Number Employees: 4

20920 Contract Comestibles
2004 Beulah Ave
East Troy, WI 53120 262-642-9400
Fax: 262-642-9404 www.contractcomestibles.com
Packagers
Owner: Matt Nitz
Purchasing: Matthew Nitz
Estimated Sales: $1-2,500,000
Number Employees: 10-19

20921 Contrex
8900 Zachary Ln N
Maple Grove, MN 55369 763-424-7800
Fax: 763-424-8734 info@contrexinc.com
www.contrexinc.com
Manufacturer and exporter of electronic controls including universal motor speed, universal motor synchronizing, rotary die/knife synchronizing, cut-to-length/indexing and digital DC motor
President: Gary C Hansen
VP: Glen Gauvin
Estimated Sales: $5-10 Million
Number Employees: 10-19
Brands:
M-Cut
M-Drive
M-Rotary
M-Shuttle
M-Track
M-Traverse
M-Trim

20922 Control & Metering
6500 Kestrel Road
Mississauga, ON L5T 1Z6
Canada 905-795-9696
Fax: 905-795-9654 800-736-5739
sales@candm.ca www.controlandmetering.com
Manufacturer and exporter of dry material handling equipment including bulk bag dischargers, fillers and controls
President: Chris Gadula
COO: Don Mackrill
Marketing Manager: Don Mackrill
Operationa Manager: Carmine Cacciarro
Number Employees: 15

20923 Control Beverage
PO Box 578
Adelanto, CA 92301-0578 330-549-5376
Fax: 330-549-9851 yrdsbna@aol.com
Manufacturer and exporter of drink dispensers including liquor and soft drink; also, portable bars
President: P Beeghly
VP/Division Manager: Glenn Lewis
Sales Director: Kenneth Wogberg
Manager Technical Services: Dan Pershing
Purchasing Manager: Glenn Lewis
Estimated Sales: $1-3 Million
Number Employees: 6
Square Footage: 5000
Parent Co: International Carbonic
Brands:
Bevcon

20924 Control Chief Corporation
PO Box 141
Bradford, PA 16701 814-362-6811
Fax: 814-368-4133 sales@controlchief.com
www.controlchief.com
Wireless industrial remote control manufacturer
President: Doug Bell
CFO: David Dedionisio
R&D: David Higgs
Quality Control: Christine Foster
Marketing Director: Allison Ambrose
Sales: Brian Landries
Operations: Paul McCord
Production: Jack Zelina
Purchasing Director: Dan Johnston
Estimated Sales: $10 - 20 Million
Number Employees: 50-99

20925 Control Concepts
1860 Lake Drive E
Chanhassen, MN 55317 952-474-6200
Fax: 952-474-6070 800-765-2799
www.ccipower.com
Manufacturer and exporter of electric temperature process controls
President: Gary Gretenhuis
CEO: Stan Kintigh
CEO: Stanley S Kintigh
Director Sales Support: William Rovick
Operations Manager: Don Christomer
Production Manager: Linh Nguyen
Number Employees: 20
Square Footage: 14000

20926 Control Instrument Service
3607 Ventura Drive E
Lakeland, FL 33811-1229 863-644-9838
Fax: 863-644-8608 800-644-9839
cinstser@gate.net www.cispuertorico.com
Instrumentation, valves, weighing equipment including temperature, pressure, level, flow and weight
Chairman: John Benedict
Estimated Sales: $1-2.5 Million
Number Employees: 9
Type of Packaging: Bulk

20927 Control Instruments Corporation
25 Law Dr # 1
Fairfield, NJ 07004-3295 973-575-9114
Fax: 973-575-0013 info@controlinstruments.com
www.controlinstruments.com
Manufacturer and exporter of hazardous gas detection systems
CEO: Chris Schaeffer
Marketing Manager: Patty Gardner
Sales Director: Debra Woods
Estimated Sales: $5-10 Million
Number Employees: 20-49
Type of Packaging: Private Label

20928 Control Module
89 Phoenix Ave
Enfield, CT 06082 860-745-2433
Fax: 860-741-6064 800-722-6654
info@controlmod.com www.controlmod.com
Manufacturer and exporter of bar code data collection equipment including label printers, laser scanners, data collection terminals and cluster buffers
President: James Bianco
VP: John Fahy
VP Marketing/Sales: James Bianco
Estimated Sales: $10-20 Million
Number Employees: 50-99
Square Footage: 40000
Brands:
Bioscan Ii

Linc
Savetime
Securcode Ii

20929 Control Pak International
11494 Delmer Drive
Suite #100
Fenton, MI 48430 810-735-2800
Fax: 734-761-2880 info@controlpak.com
www.controlpak.com
Manufacturer and exporter of energy management control systems for temperature, humidity and HVAC applications
President: Timothy Glinke
Office Manager: Julie Bodziak
Engineer: Len Poma
Estimated Sales: $1-2,500,000
Number Employees: 5-9

20930 Control Products
1724 Lake Dr W
Chanhassen, MN 55317 952-448-2217
Fax: 952-448-1606 800-947-9098
info@controlproductsinc.com
www.controlproductsinc.com
Digital electronic temperature, humidity and pressure controls including timers, alarms, indicators and controllers; also, custom design available
President: Chris Berghoff
VP Operations: Paul Carlson
Director Foodservice Industry: Jerry Brown
Marketing Manager: Mark Bjornstad
Business Development Manager: Jim Helgerson
National Sales Manager: Greg Colvin
Estimated Sales: $20 - 50 Million
Number Employees: 100-249

20931 Control Systems Design
PO Box 647
Forest Hill, MD 21050-0647 410-296-0466
Fax: 410-337-8360
Industrial control and data acquisition systems
President: Eldon Hiebert
Part Owner: Jay King
Estimated Sales: $1-2.5 Million
Number Employees: 9
Square Footage: 3000

20932 Control Techniques
12005 Technology Dr
Eden Prairie, MN 55344 952-995-8000
Fax: 952-995-8020 800-893-2321
info.cta@emerson.com
www.emersondrivesolutions.com
Supplier of intelligent drives for commercial and industrial motor control applications. Products help increase productivity, save energy and reduce operating costs.
CFO: Curt Eslinger
Marketing: Rob Kelly
Sales: Kurt Schmitz
Operations: Brad Schwartz
Estimated Sales: $110 Million
Number Employees: 100-249
Parent Co: Emerson
Other Locations:
Grand Island NY
York PA
Fort Meyers FL
Portland OR
Salt Lake City UT
Cleveland OH
Toronto, ON
Calagary AB Canada

20933 Control Technology Corporation
25 South St
Hopkinton, MA 01748 508-435-9596
Fax: 508-435-2373 800-282-5008
sales@ctc-control.com www.ctc-control.com
Designs, manufactures and markets products that enable electronic automation device to be controlled, configured, or reprogrammed over the internet and/or internets.
President: Thomas Schermerhorn
Controller: Lisa St George
Director of Research & Development: Kevin Halloran
Quality Control: Tim Leavitt
Sales Director: Karl Chambers
Operations Manager: Tim Leavitt
Estimated Sales: $4 - 5 Million
Other Locations:
Control Technology Corporation
Mequon WI

20934 Controls Unlimited
4823 N Ridge Rd
Perry, OH 44081 440-259-2500
Fax: 440-259-5015
mail@southshorecontrols.com
www.southshorecontrols.com
Manufacturer and exporter of controls and control panels for food processing equipment, material handling equipment, freezers, etc
President: Rick Stark
Sales Director: John Sauto, Jr.
Estimated Sales: $6 Million
Number Employees: 20-49
Square Footage: 29000

20935 Convay Systems
100 Carrier Drive
Etobicoke, ON M9W 5R1
Canada 905-279-9970
Fax: 416-675-6691 800-811-5511
convay@onramp.ca
Manufacturer and exporter of washing and drying systems, pasteurizers, coolers, warmers and dry trash removal systems for the food, beverage and dairy industries
President: Roger Potts
Controller: Carol Ruggiero
Engineering Manager: Michael Voss
Number Employees: 18
Square Footage: 14000

20936 Convectronics
111 Neck Rd
Haverhill, MA 01835 978-374-7714
Fax: 978-374-7794 800-633-0166
info@convectronics.com
www.convectronics.com
Manufacturer and exporter of electric air heaters and thermocouples
President: Philip G Aberizk Jr
VP/Quality Control: Steve Becker
R&D: Bryce Budrow
Sales: Leslie Woodfall
Estimated Sales: Below $5 Million
Number Employees: 10-19
Square Footage: 20000

20937 Convergent Label Technology
620 S Ware Blvd
Tampa, FL 33619 813-621-8128
Fax: 813-620-1206 800-252-6111
pnelson@convergentlabeltech.com
www.convergentlabeltech.com
Manufacturer and exporter of weigh price labeling equipment and labels
President: Graham Lloyd
Marketing Director: Paula Nelson
Sales/Marketing: Chris Walker
Purchasing Manager: Steve Halbrook
Estimated Sales: $60 Million
Number Employees: 100-249
Square Footage: 166000
Type of Packaging: Food Service

20938 Conveyance TechnologiesLLC
24803 Detroit Rd
Cleveland, OH 44145 440-899-7440
Fax: 440-835-3107 800-701-2278
billwalzer@conveyancecart.com
www.conveyancecart.com
Manufacturer, importer and exporter of material handling products including mobile loading docks, stocking systems, hydraulic lifts, nestable warehouse carts, stocking carts, conveyors, pallet carriers and platform trucks
President: William Walzer
Sales Manager: Sam Aquino
Estimated Sales: $1 - 2 Million
Number Employees: 20-49
Square Footage: 220000
Brands:
Roll-A-Bench
Thru-Put
Uni-Cart
Uni-Lift

20939 Conveying Industries
3795 Paris St
Denver, CO 80239 303-373-2035
Fax: 303-373-5149 877-600-4874
info@conveyind.com www.conveyind.com
Conveyors and palletizers
Manager: Don Simmonds
Sales Manager: Bob Carr
Estimated Sales: $5-10 Million
Number Employees: 10-19

20940 Conveyor Accessories
7013 High Grove Blvd
Burr Ridge, IL 60527 630-655-4205
Fax: 630-655-4209 800-323-7093
cai@conveyoraccessories.com
www.conveyoraccessories.com
Manufacturer and exporter of conveyor belt fasteners, tools and accessories
President: Thomas Richardson
Estimated Sales: $10-20 Million
Number Employees: 25
Square Footage: 30000

20941 Conveyor Components Company
PO Box 167
130 Seltzer Road
Croswell, MI 48422 810-679-4211
Fax: 810-679-4510 800-233-3233
info@conveyorcomponents.com
www.conveyorcomponents.com
Quality engineered conveyor accessories including emergency stop switches & pull cords, compact stop controls, belt mi-alignment switches, tripper position switches, bucket elevator alignment switches, damaged belt detectors, bulkmaterial flow switches, motion controls and zero speed switches, aeration pads, level controls including rotating paddles and tilt switches, skirtboard clamps, a rotary brush style belt cleaner as well as a wide variety of other conveyor beltcleaners.
President/CEO: Clint Stimpson
General Manager: Barb Stimpson
Sales Manager: Rich Washkevich
Purchasing Coordinator: Sandy VanBrande
Estimated Sales: $5-10 Million
Number Employees: 50-99
Square Footage: 80000
Brands:
Insul-Air
Insul-Glare

20942 Conveyor Dynamics Corporation
7000 W Geneva Drive
Saint Peters, MO 63376 636-279-1111
Fax: 636-279-1121
info@conveyordynamicscorp.com
www.conveyordynamicscorp.com
Manufacturer and exporter of vibratory processing machinery for bulk and material handling applications
President: Mike Didion
Engineer: Scott Milsark
Estimated Sales: $500,000 - $1,000,000
Number Employees: 1-4
Square Footage: 72000

20943 Conveyor Mart
3972 S Us Highway 45
Oshkosh, WI 54902-7351 920-233-2724
Fax: 920-233-3159 sales@conveyormart.com
www.conveyormart.com
On-line conveyors and conveyor parts
President: James L Nerenhausen
Quality Control: Kurt Frank
Estimated Sales: Below $5 Million
Number Employees: 50-99

20944 Conveyor Supply
1334 Dartmouth Ln
Deerfield, IL 60015 847-945-5670
Fax: 847-945-5676 conveyorsupply2@att.net
Conductors and conveyor systems
President: Walter Weiss
CEO: Keith Weiss
Number Employees: 5-9
Square Footage: 8000

20945 Conveyor Systems
21 Norman Ave
Delran, NJ 08075-1009 856-461-8084
Fax: 856-764-9367 info@conveyorsystems.com
www.conveyorsystems.com
Conveyors and conveyor systems
Owner: Thomas Mc Larney
Estimated Sales: $5-10 Million
Number Employees: 1-4

20946 Conveyor Technologies Intergraded
1001 W Waukau Ave
Oshkosh, WI 54902 920-233-2756
Fax: 920-233-3159
cti@conveyortechnologies.com
www.conveyortechnologies.com
Material handling equipment, packaging machinery, material handling and conveyor equipment
Number Employees: 5-9

20947 Conviron
572ÿSouth Fifth Street
Suite 2
Pembina, ND 58271-0347 204-786-6451
Fax: 204-786-7736 800-363-6451
sales@conviron.com www.conviron.com
Refrigerated structures, walk-in coolers and freezer building and construction consultants, meat distributing center
President: Steve J Kroft
Estimated Sales: $1-2.5 Million
Number Employees: 100-249

20948 Convoy
PO Box 8589
Canton, OH 44711 330-453-8163
Fax: 330-453-8181 800-899-1583
sales@convoycontainers.com
www.convoycontainers.com
Manufacturer and exporter of plastic collapsible containers and plastic tote boxes
President: Phillip Dannemiller
National Sales Manager: Daren Newman
Estimated Sales: $2.5 - 5 Million
Number Employees: 10-19
Type of Packaging: Bulk

20949 Conwed
2810 Weeks Ave SE
Minneapolis, MN 55414 630-293-3737
Fax: 800-426-0137 800-426-0149
contact@conwedplastics.com
www.conwedplastics.com
Netting
Manager: John Burke
Quality Control: Tim Downes
Estimated Sales: $5 - 10 Million
Number Employees: 50-99

20950 Conxall Corporation
601 E Wildwood Ave
Villa Park, IL 60181 630-834-7504
Fax: 630-834-8540 sales@conxall.com
www.conxall.com
Custom nonmetallic product connectors and cable assemblies for processing and controls
President: Keith Bandolik
CFO: Dave Bandolik
Quality Control: Jim Collado
Plant Manager: Rob Smith
Estimated Sales: $20 - 50 Million
Number Employees: 100-249
Square Footage: 45000
Brands:
Maxi-Con
Mega-Con
Micro-Con
Mil-E-Qual
Mini-Con
Multi-Con

20951 Cook & Beals
221 S 7th St
Loup City, NE 68853-8041 308-745-0154
Fax: 308-745-0154 www.cooknbeals.com
Manufacturer and exporter of honey processing equipment including rotary knife uncappers, spin float honey-wax separators, heat exchange units, honey pumps, wax melters, etc
President: Patrick Kuehl
Secretary: Carol Kuehl
VP: Lawrence Kuehl
Estimated Sales: $1-2.5 Million
Number Employees: 5 to 9

20952 Cook Associates
212 W Kinzie St
Chicago, IL 60654 312-329-0900
Fax: 312-329-1528 info@cookassociates.com
www.cookassociates.com
Executive search firm for the food and beverage industry
President: Arnie Kins
CEO: Mary Kier
VP: Jessica Gentile
Division Manager: Walter Rach
Estimated Sales: $2.5-5 Million
Number Employees: 50-99

20953 Cook King
22601 Allview Ter
Laguna Beach, CA 92651-1547 949-497-1235
Fax: 949-494-2625
Ovens, broilers, deep fat fryers, continuous oil filters and conveyor systems
President: Craig Miller
Executive VP: Dick Naess
Marketing Director: Coby Naess
Number Employees: 60
Square Footage: 55000

20954 Cook Neon Signs
5382 New Manchester Hwy
Tullahoma, TN 37388-6783 931-455-0944
Fax: 931-455-4536 rhonda@cookneon.com
www.cookneon.com
Internally illuminated signs
President: Sue Cook
Estimated Sales: Below $5 Million
Number Employees: 10-19

20955 CookTek
156 N. Jefferson Street
Suite 300
Chicago, IL 60661-1436 312-563-9600
Fax: 312-432-6220 888-266-5835
customerservice@cooktek.com
www.cooktek.com
Manufacturer and exporter of induction cooking systems
President: Robert Wolters
Quality Control: Robbe Gibb
Marketing Director: Tricia Cleary
Estimated Sales: $.5 - 1 million
Number Employees: 1-4
Number of Brands: 1
Number of Products: 5
Square Footage: 100000
Parent Co: Wolters Group International
Brands:
Cooktek

20956 Cooking Systems International
907 Honeyspot Road
Stratford, CT 06615-7140 203-377-4174
Fax: 203-377-8187 info@mysck.com
www.sck.com
Manufacturer and exporter of rethermalizing units for cook chill, sous vide, precooked and frozen food
Chairman: B Koether
Executive VP: Scott Wakeman
VP Sales/Marketing: George Koether
Estimated Sales: $10 - 20 Million
Number Employees: 25
Square Footage: 40000
Type of Packaging: Food Service
Brands:
Csi

20957 Cookshack
2304 North Ash Street
Ponca City, OK 74601-1100 580-765-3669
Fax: 580-765-2223 800-423-0698
info@cookshack.com www.cookshack.com
Sauces & spices, smoking wood accessories for better barbeque, Cookshack smoked foods cookbooks, electric smoker ovens, pellet fired smokes, charbroilers, pellet grills
President: Brent Matthews
VP: Edward Aguiar Jr
Marketing Coordinator: Cayley Armstrong
Finance/Marketing/Sales Manager: John Shiflet
General Manager: Stuart Powell
Production Manager: Jim Linnebur
Estimated Sales: $4 Million
Number Employees: 30
Number of Brands: 2
Number of Products: 1
Square Footage: 44000
Type of Packaging: Consumer, Food Service, Private Label, Bulk
Brands:
Fast Eddy's

20958 Cookson Plastic Molding
787 Watervliet Shaker Road
Latham, NY 12110-2285 518-951-1000
Fax: 518-783-0004 888-738-8800
pools@pacificpools.com www.pacificpools.com
President: Bruce Quay
Technical Services Manager: Peter Morgan

20959 Cool Care
4020 Thor Drive
Boynton Beach, FL 33426-8407 561-364-5711
Fax: 561-364-5766 mike.bianco@na.dole.com
www.coolcarehvac.com
Manufacturer, importer and exporter of ripening rooms for produce with cold storage and controlled atmosphere; also, vacuum coolers, ice injectors, etc.; installation services available
President: Mike Bianco
Director Sales: Ron Roberts
Engineering Manager: Bob Windecker
Number Employees: 20-49
Square Footage: 100000
Parent Co: Dole Food Company

20960 Cool Cargo
5324 Georgia Highway 85
Forest Park, GA 30297-2475 770-994-0338
Temperature control systems.
President: Burt Pedowitz

20961 Cool Curtain/CCI Industries
350-A Fischer Ave
Costa Mesa, CA 92626 714-662-3879
Fax: 714-662-0943 800-854-5719
www.coolcurtain.com
Freezer curtains, fly traps and broiler griddles
President: Michael Robinson
Sales Manager: Randy Wall
VP Production: Marion Mills
Estimated Sales: $5-10 Million
Number Employees: 20-49
Square Footage: 16000
Brands:
Clear Vu

20962 Cool-Pitch Company
5948 Rocky Mount Dr
Jacksonville, FL 32258-5415 904-260-1876
800-938-0128
Pitcher coolers
President: William Coker
Estimated Sales: $1 - 3,000,000
Number Employees: 5-9
Brands:
Cool-Pitch

20963 CoolBrands International
4175 Veterans Memorial Highway
3rd Floor
Ronkonkoma, NY 11779-7639 631-737-9700
Fax: 631-737-9792
info@coolbrandsinternational.com
www.eskimopie.com
Distributor of frozen desserts including ice cream, also flexible packaging
CFO: Gary Stevens
Estimated Sales: $35 Million
Number Employees: 35
Type of Packaging: Food Service, Bulk
Brands:
Breyers
Care Bears
Chipwich
Crayola
Disney
Dogsters
Eskimo Pie
Fruit a Freeze
Godiva Ice Cream
No Pudge
Snapple
The Sopranos
Trix
Tropicana
Wholefruit
Yoplait

20964 Cooling Products
PO Box 470523
Tulsa, OK 74147 918-251-8588
Fax: 918-251-8837 coolprod@gorilla.net
www.coolprod.com

Manufacturer and exporter of heat exchangers, radiators, finned tubes and condensers
Manager: Steve Chalmers
Production: Harold Gordon
Sales Manager: Stephen Chalmers
Estimated Sales: $20 - 50 Million
Number Employees: 50-99

20965 **Cooling Technology**
1800 Orr Industrial Ct.
Charlotte, NC 28213 704-596-4109
Fax: 704-597-8697 800-872-1448
info@coolingtechnology.com
www.coolingtechnology.com
Manufacturer and exporter of temperature controllers, chillers and evaporative cooling and pumping systems.
President: Pat Oza
Marketing Director: Chris Fore
Director of Sales and Marketing: Laura Walker
Operations Manager: Sheetal Desai
Estimated Sales: $3-5 Million
Number Employees: 20-49
Number of Products: 20
Square Footage: 40000

20966 **Cooling and Applied Technology**
PO Box 1279
Russellville, AR 72811 479-890-3433
Fax: 479-967-2651 888-890-3433
sales@gocatgo.biz www.gocatgo.biz
Supplier of chilling systems, whole muscle pumps, plant monitoring and weighing systems
CEO: Michael Miller
Principal: Dion Henson
Estimated Sales: $26 Million
Number Employees: 170

20967 **Cooper Crouse-Hinds, LLC**
Wolf & 7th North St.
Syracuse, NY 13208 315-477-7000
Fax: 315-477-5118
crousecustomerctr@crouse-hinds.com
www.coopercrouse-hinds.com
Manufacturer and exporter of outdoor and emergency lighting
Chairman & Chief Executive Officer: Alexander Cutler
Vice Chairman & Chief Financial Officer: Richard Fearon
Estimated Sales: $135.1 Million
Number Employees: 1300
Parent Co: Cooper Industries

20968 **Cooper Decoration Company**
PO Box 81
Weston, MA 02493-0005 315-475-1661
Fax: 315-475-1664 tsmallcoop@aol.com
Christmas lights and decorations; also, food show decorator
President: Jon Cooper
VP: Lou Galtieri
Operations Manager: Jim Cooper
Estimated Sales: $1-2.5 Million
Number Employees: 10
Parent Co: Cooper Drapery Company

20969 **Cooper Instrument Corporation**
P.O.Box 450
Middlefield, CT 06455-0450 860-349-3473
Fax: 860-349-8994 800-835-5011
sbennett@cooperinstrument.com
www.cooper-atkins.com
CEO: Carol P Wallace
Director of Marketing: Cherylann Hunt
Estimated Sales: $1 - 5 Million
Number Employees: 100-249

20970 **Cooper Instrument Corporation**
P.O.Box 450
Middlefield, CT 06455-0450 860-349-3473
Fax: 860-349-8994 800-835-5011
info@cooper-atkins.com
www.cooper-atkins.com
Manufacturer and exporter of temperature, time and humidity measuring instruments
President: Carol Wallace
Director of Marketing: Cherylann Hunt
Estimated Sales: $20-50 Million
Number Employees: 100-249
Square Footage: 40000

20971 **Cooper Lighting**
1121 Highway 74 South
Peachtree City, GA 30269 770-486-4800
www.cooperindustries.com
Manufacturer and exporter of emergency, indoor and outdoor lighting
Owner: Sam Wattar
CEO: H John Riley, Jr.
Estimated Sales: $99 Million
Number Employees: 1-4
Parent Co: Eaton

20972 **Cooper Turbocompressor**
3101 Broadway St
Buffalo, NY 14227-1034 716-896-0199
Fax: 716-896-1233 877-805-7911
info@turbocompressor.com
www.turbocompressor.com
Manufacturer and exporter of oil-free centrifugal compressors
President: Robert J Rajeski
CFO: Altamari Jeff
Executive Assistant: Nancy DiPirro
Estimated Sales: $100+ Million
Number Employees: 250-499
Square Footage: 200000
Brands:
Joy

20973 **Cooperheat/MQS**
P.O.Box 123
Alvin, TX 77512-0123 281-331-6154
Fax: 281-331-4107 800-526-4233
cooperheat-mqs@2isi.com
www.cooperheat-mqs.com
Manufacturer and exporter of heat treating equipment, accesories and services, heat tracing equipment and services; also, induction equipment and nondestructive testing
President: Kenneth Tholan
VP Sales: Charels Silver
VP International Sales: Jim Campbell
Number Employees: 20-49
Square Footage: 160000
Parent Co: International Industrial Services
Brands:
Eagle
Versatrace

20974 **Copack International**
1270 Belle Ave # 115
Winter Springs, FL 32708-1905 407-699-7507
Fax: 407-699-7543 padamission@copack.com
www.copack.com
Food packaging materials
President: Paul J Adamission
Estimated Sales: $4 Million
Number Employees: 50-99
Square Footage: 400000
Type of Packaging: Consumer, Food Service, Private Label, Bulk

20975 **Cope Plastics**
4441 Industrial Drive
Alton, IL 62002 262-650-0085
Fax: 262-650-0086 800-851-5510
mi@copeplastics.com www.copeplastics.com
FDA, 3A and USDA compliant plastic components
President & CEO: Jane Saale
VP of Finance: John Theen
Quality Manager: Mike Chism
Director of Marketing: Cindy Smalley
VP of Sales: John Lee
VP of Operations: Josh Kuhnash
Manufacturing Manager: Jerry Dunnagan
Estimated Sales: $1-2.5 Million
Number Employees: 5-9
Parent Co: Cope Plastics

20976 **Copeland Corporation**
1675 W Campbell Rd
Sidney, OH 45365 937-498-3011
Fax: 937-498-3203 www.copeland-corp.com
Manufacturer and exporter of compressors for air conditioning and refrigeration
President: Tom Bettcher
Number Employees: 1,000-4,999
Type of Packaging: Food Service
Brands:
Copeland

20977 **Coperion Corporation**
663 E Crescent Ave
Ramsey, NJ 07446 201-327-6300
Fax: 201-825-6494 info.cus@coperion.com
www.coperion.com
Manufacturer and exporter of twin screw extruders, kneaders, and turnkey systems
CEO: Daniel Mielcarek
CFO: Dieter Ohl
Public Relations: Paula Nurnberger
Estimated Sales: $50-100 Million
Number Employees: 100-249
Square Footage: 125000
Parent Co: Krupp USA

20978 **Copesan**
W175 N5711 Technology Drive
Menomonee Falls, WI 53051 262-783-6261
Fax: 262-783-6267 800-267-3726
info@copesan.com www.copesan.com
Provides effective pest management services for all your pest management needs, including insect, rodent stored product pest, bird and weed control, and fumigations
President: Deni Naumann
Vice President of Finance: Kevin Fixel
Vice President: Mike Campbell
Quality Control: Jim Snkiele
Technical Advisor: Jim Snkiele
Marketing Director: Elizabeth Johnson
VP, Sales: Aric Schroeder
Director, HR: Jessica Janiszewski
Operations Manager: Carl Griswold
Estimated Sales: $2.5 - 5 Million
Number Employees: 250

20979 **Copper Brite**
PO Box 50610
Santa Barbara, CA 93150-0610 805-565-1566
Fax: 805-565-1394 custsvc@copperbrite.com
www.copperbrite.com
Manufacturer and exporter of insecticides and wood rot fungicides; also, cleaner and polish for copper, brass and stainless steel
President/ CEO: Alan D. Brite
CFO: Alan Brite
Executive VP: Terry Brite
R&D: Alan Brite
Quality Control: Terry Brite
Estimated Sales: $2.5 - 5 Million
Number Employees: 1-4
Brands:
Copper Brite
Roach Prufe
Termite Prufe

20980 **Copper Clad Products**
600 S 9th St
Reading, PA 19602-2506 610-375-4596
Fax: 610-375-3557
Metal polish cleaners including silver, brass, copper and stainless steel
President: Thomas Ziemer
Estimated Sales: $10 - 20 Million
Number Employees: 10 to 19
Square Footage: 72000
Brands:
Farberware
Revere

20981 **Copper Hills Fruit Sales**
4337 N Golden State Boulevard
Suite 102
Fresno, CA 93722-3801 559-432-5400
Fax: 559-432-5620
Packers of peaches, plums, nectarines, apricots, pomegranates, and persimmons
Managing Member: Wilma J. Deniz

20982 **Copperwood InternationalInc**
9249 S Broadway
Unit 200-238
Highland Ranch, CO 80129-5692 303-683-1234
Fax: 303-683-0933 800-411-7887
copperwoodfoods@aol.com
Broker of a wide variety of closeout, excess and discounted food items
Sales Director: Michael Casey
Estimated Sales: $5,000,000
Number Employees: 4
Number of Brands: 76
Number of Products: 127
Square Footage: 50000

20983 Coral LLC
5576 Bighorn Dr.
Carson City, NV 89701 775-883-9854
Fax: 775-883-9858 800-882-9577
sales@coralcalcium.com www.corallc.com or www.coralcalcium.com
Natural minerals
Sales Director: Alberto Galdamez

20984 Corben Packaging & Display
976 Grand Street
Brooklyn, NY 11211-2707 718-388-7666
Fax: 718-388-6592 packitgood@aol.com
Full service contract packaging includes shrink wrapping, poly bagging, blister packaging, custom packaging, clam shells and folding boxes
Estimated Sales: $1-2.5 000,000
Number Employees: 12

20985 Corbett Package Company
1200 Castle Hayne Rd
Wilmington, NC 28401-8885 910-763-9991
Fax: 910-763-3426 800-334-0684
Wooden wirebound crates
President: Scott Corbett
Partner: William Corbett II
Sales Manager (Containers): Donald Williamson
Estimated Sales: $10-20 Million
Number Employees: 50 to 99
Square Footage: 150000

20986 Corby Hall
3 Emery Ave
Randolph, NJ 07869 973-366-8300
Fax: 973-366-9833 info@corbyhall.com
www.corbyhall.com
Manufacturer and exporter of stainless steel and silver plated flatware and hollowware; importer of flatware
President: Alan Millward
CFO: Alan Millward
Vice President: Adrian Millward
Quality Control: Andrew Millward
VP Marketing: Andrew Millward
Estimated Sales: $500,000 - $1 Million
Number Employees: 5-9
Square Footage: 15000
Type of Packaging: Food Service
Brands:
Algarve
Corby Hall
Riviera
St. Morirz

20987 Cord-Tex Company
136 Industrial Ave
Jefferson, LA 70121-2902 504-834-2862
Fax: 504-837-7645
Distributor, importer and exporter of manila, sisal and synthetic rope and twine
President: Carl Ruch
VP: Gerard Ruch
Estimated Sales: $1 - 3 Million
Number Employees: 1 to4

20988 Core Products Company
401 Industrial Park
PO Box 669
Canton, TX 75103 903-567-1341
Fax: 903-567-1346 800-825-2673
core@unbelievablebrand.com
www.coreproductsco.com
Manufacturer and exporter of odor control agents, carpet and upholstery cleaning products, stain and rust removers, degreasers and cleaners for tub, tile, glass, chrome and stainless steel
President: Ed Crawford
CFO: Debbie Crawford
VP: Debbie Crawford
Sales Manager: Brian Hawkins
Estimated Sales: $500,000-$1 Million
Number Employees: 10-19
Square Footage: 40000
Brands:
Believe It
Beta-Kleen
Bonnet Buff
De-Foamer
Hot Water Extract
Incredible Blue
Juice Out
Leather Magic
Mal-X
Perfect Image
Plus Ii
Preconditioner Traffic Lane
Rust Bust'r
Tann-X
Unbelievable Green
Unbelievable!

20989 Corenco
3275 Dutton Ave
Santa Rosa, CA 95407 707-824-9868
Fax: 707-824-9870 888-267-3626
sales@sizereduction.com
www.sizereduction.com
Manufactures size reduction equipment for the food processing industry.
President/CEO: Chris Cory
Corporate Secretary/Accounting: Saraj Cory
VP/COO: Jeff Boheim
Estimated Sales: $1-2.5 Million
Number Employees: 7
Number of Brands: 1
Number of Products: 14
Square Footage: 7000
Brands:
Corenco

20990 Corfab
6700 S Sayre Avenue
Chicago, IL 60638 708-458-8750
Corrugated paperboard partitions, boxes, file folders and displays
President: R Izenstark
VP: Sy Ginsberg
Plant Manager: Frank Fandl
Estimated Sales: $20-50 Million
Number Employees: 50-99

20991 Corinth Products
74 Hob Rd
Corinth, ME 04427 207-285-3387
Fax: 207-285-7738
Wooden pallets and boxes
President/CEO: Peter Higgins
Estimated Sales: Below $5 Million
Number Employees: 10

20992 Cork Specialties
1454 NW 78th Ave #305
Miami, FL 33126 305-477-1506
Fax: 305-591-0593 corkspec@aol.com
Manufacturer, importer and exporter of corks and plastic top stoppers
President: Rafael Figueroa
VP: Orlando Barranco
Estimated Sales: Below $5 Million
Number Employees: 5-9

20993 Corman & Associates
881 Floyd Dr
Lexington, KY 40505 859-233-0544
Fax: 859-253-0119 ted@cormans.com
www.cormans.com
Point of purchase displays and store fixtures
President: Ted Corman
Estimated Sales: $5-10 Million
Number Employees: 50-99
Square Footage: 110000

20994 Corn States Metal Fabricators
1323 Maple St
PO Box 65635
West Des Moines, IA 50265 515-225-7961
Fax: 515-225-9382 www.cornstates.com
Conveyors and elevators
President and CEO: Randall Golay
Estimated Sales: $5-10 Million
Number Employees: 20-49
Square Footage: 30000

20995 Cornelia Broom Company
756 Hoyt St
Cornelia, GA 30531 706-778-4434
Fax: 706-778-9814 800-228-2551
cbc1@alltel.net
Brushes, brooms, mops and handles
President: Joby Scroggs
Secretary: Fran Chastain
VP: Marcia Scroggs
Estimated Sales: $5 - 10 Million
Number Employees: 24
Square Footage: 20000

20996 Cornelius Wilshire Corporation
2401 N Palmer Dr
Schaumburg, IL 60196-0001 847-397-4600
Fax: 847-539-6960 mikes@cornelius.com
www.cornelius-usa.com
Ice makers and juice dispensers
President: Tim Hubbard
Sales/Marketing: Michael Orlando
Brands:
Wilshire

20997 Cornell Machine Company
45 Brown Ave
Springfield, NJ 07081-2992 973-379-6860
Fax: 973-379-6854 info@cornellmachine.com
www.cornellmachine.com
Manufacturer and exporter of food processing equipment including homogenizers, emulsifiers, mixers, oxygen removers, deaerators and defoaming equipment
President: Martin Huska
Estimated Sales: $1-2.5 Million
Number Employees: 5-9
Brands:
Cornell Versator

20998 Cornell Pump Company
P.O.Box 6334
Portland, OR 97228-6334 503-653-0330
Fax: 503-653-0338 info@cornellpump.com
www.cornellpump.com
Manufacturer, importer and exporter of pumps for food product handling, hot oil circulation, refrigeration and waste handling
President: Jeff Markham
Marketing: Brenda Case
Number Employees: 100-249
Parent Co: Roper Industries
Brands:
Cycloseal
Redi-Prime

20999 Cornerstone
750 Patrick Pl
Brownsburg, IN 46112-2211 317-852-6522
Fax: 317-852-6433 800-659-7699
info@cornerstoneflooring.com
www.cornerstoneflooring.com/industries/industries.shtml
Manufacturer and installer of high performance polymer flooring, lining and coating materials for a variety of industries including that of food and beverage.
President: Dann Hess
Sales Manager: Tracy Figley
Estimated Sales: $1 - 5 000,000
Number Employees: 20-49

21000 Corniani
501 Southlake Blvd
Richmond, VA 23236-3042 804-794-6688
Fax: 804-794-6187 corniani.usa@gid.it
www.gdpackagemachinery.com
President: Giuseppe Venturi
Number Employees: 100-249

21001 Corning Costar
45 Nagog Park
Acton, MA 01720-3413 978-635-2200
Fax: 978-635-2476 800-492-1110
www.corning.com
Manufacturer and exporter of molded plastic containers
President: Pierce Baker
Estimated Sales: $20-50 Million
Number Employees: 100-249
Parent Co: Corning

21002 (HQ)Corning Life Sciences
45 Nagog Park
Acton, MA 01720 978-635-2200
Fax: 978-635-2476 800-492-1110
clswebmail@corning.com www.corning.com
Pyrex Laboratory glassware, Corning brand instruments and equipment, and Cornin and Costar brand plasticware
Chairman/CEO: James R Houghton
President/COO: Wendell P Weeks
CFO: James B Flaws
Senior VP/GM Life Sciences: Pierce Baker III
Media Communications: Julie Eckmann
Estimated Sales: $1 Billion+
Number Employees: 100-249
Parent Co: Corning

Brands:
Checkmate
Checkmite
Corex Ii
Corning
Costar
Pyrex
Pyrex Plus
Scholar
Vycor

21003 Cornish Containers
205 W Sophia Street
Maumee, OH 43537-2166 419-893-7911
Fax: 419-893-5146
Chest and door type insulated and refrigerated containers
CEO: Jody Holbrook
Sales Director: Tim McNulty
Estimated Sales: $1-2.5 Million
Number Employees: 6
Square Footage: 25000
Brands:
Frigi-Top
Transafe

21004 Coronet Chandelier Originals
12 Grand Blvd # 16
Brentwood, NY 11717-5195 631-273-1177
Fax: 631-273-1247 coronetchandelier.com
www.coronetchandelier.com
Manufacturer and exporter of custom chandeliers; importer of chandelier crystals, wrought iron tables, wall solders, pendents
President: Irwin Goldberg
Estimated Sales: $1 - 3 Million
Number Employees: 10-19
Square Footage: 60000

21005 Corpak
PO Box 364747
San Juan, PR 00936-4747 787-787-9085
Fax: 787-740-5230
Paperboard boxes
VP Sales: Minerva Medina
Estimated Sales: $1 - 5 Million
Number Employees: 50-99

21006 Corporate Safe Specialists
14800 S McKinley Ave
Posen, IL 60469 708-385-4586
Fax: 708-371-3326 800-342-3033
curreyj@corporatesafe.com
www.corporatesafe.com
CSS is an industry leader providing innovative security solutions to the restaurant and retail industries globally. CSS safes, smart safes and kiosks can be configured to provide closed-loop cash management to deter armed robberyburglary and internal theft.
President: Edward McGunn
CEO: Ed McGunn
CFO: Lisa Marsh
Vice President: Rosemary Leonard
Marketing Director: Peter Muiznieks
Sales Director: James Currey
Operations Manager: Adam Saggese
Estimated Sales: $35 Million
Number Employees: 50-99
Square Footage: 60000
Brands:
Power Lever
Quik Lock Ii

21007 Corpus Christi Stamp Works
502 S Staples St
Corpus Christi, TX 78403 361-884-4801
Fax: 361-884-1038 800-322-4515
sales@ccstampworks.com
www.ccstampworks.com
Marking devices, rubber and pre-inked stamps and engraved signs and name badges
President: Harry Lee Chester
VP: Catherine Ray
Office Manager: Mildred Ashmore
Estimated Sales: $2.5-5 Million
Number Employees: 20-49
Square Footage: 5000

21008 Corr-Pak Corporation
8000 Joliet Rd Ste 100
Mc Cook, IL 60525-3256 708-442-7806
Fax: 708-442-0467
Corrugated boxes, containers and point of purchase displays; silk screen printing available
President: Henry Taylor III
Estimated Sales: Below $5 Million
Number Employees: 10

21009 Corrigan Corporation ofAmerica
104 Ambrogio Dr
Gurnee, IL 60031-3373 847-263-5955
Fax: 847-263-5944 800-462-6478
sales@corriganmist.com www.corriganmist.com
Produce misting, meat humidification and water filtration systems
Owner: J Michael Corrigan
Account Manager: Charles Noland
Estimated Sales: $3 - 5 Million
Number Employees: 10-19
Parent Co: Corrigan Corporation of America
Brands:
Hypersoft
Optimist
Ultramist
Vaporplus

21010 Corro-Shield International, Inc.
7059 Barry Street
Rosemont, IL 60018 847-298-7770
Fax: 847-298-7784 800-298-7637
csi@corroshield.com www.corroshield.com
Industrial floors and wall coatings.

21011 Corrobilt Container Company
7888 Marathon Dr
Livermore, CA 94550-9325 925-373-0880
Fax: 209-249-3130
Corrugated containers
President: Edward Childe
Number Employees: 5 to 9
Type of Packaging: Bulk

21012 Corrugated Inner-Pak Corporation
51 Washington Street
Conshohocken, PA 19428 610-825-0200
Fax: 610-828-0907
Corrugated paper and foam plastic packaging specialties and wooden boxes and crates; contract packaging available for the government and commercial industries
President: Robert E Doyoe
Treasurer: Ben Watson
VP: John McCarthy
Estimated Sales: Below $5 Million
Number Employees: 9
Parent Co: Inter-Pack Corporation

21013 Corrugated Packaging
1683 Cattlemen Rd
Sarasota, FL 34232 941-371-0000
Fax: 941-378-5637
Packaging materials including corrugated boxes, pads, folders and die cuts
Owner: Nancy James
President: Arthur James Jr
Marketing Director: Herbert Markham
Purchasing Manager: Robert Mecall
Estimated Sales: $2.5-5 Million
Number Employees: 10
Square Footage: 26500

21014 Corrugated Specialties
352 12th St # 2
Plainwell, MI 49080-1154 269-685-9821
Corrugated paper and boxes
Owner: Jim Skrobot
President: James Skrobot
Estimated Sales: $1-2.5 Million
Number Employees: 1 to4

21015 Corrugated Supplies
5043 West 67th Street
Chicago, IL 60638 708-458-5525
Fax: 708-458-0013 888-826-2738
customerservice@vancraft.com
www.csclive.com
Corrugated paper sheets/flexographic colors on demand for corrugated sheets- 98" web-inline process
Vice President, Finance: Mike Rubinstein
Operations Executive: John Schweiner
Estimated Sales: $21 Million
Number Employees: 100
Square Footage: 100000
Type of Packaging: Consumer, Food Service, Bulk

21016 Corrupad Protective Packaging
89 Oleary Dr
Bensenville, IL 60106-2270 630-238-8090
Fax: 630-238-8096 www.corrupadusa.com
Recycled paper packaging materials
President: Norman Lynn
Estimated Sales: $10-25 Million
Number Employees: 20-49

21017 Corsair Display Systems
5560 Airport Rd
Canandalgua, NY 14424 585-396-3480
Fax: 585-396-5953 800-347-5245
sales@corsairdisplay.com
www.corsairdisplay.com
Merchandising stations, pastry cases, carts, kiosks, menu systems and bulkhead signs
President: David Mansfield
Vice President: Alison Leet
Marketing/Sales: Bruce Meckling
Operations Manager: Cindy DeRycke
Purchasing Manager: Eric Rands
Estimated Sales: $3-5 Million
Number Employees: 20-49
Square Footage: 40000

21018 Corson Manufacturing Company
20 Michigan Street
24
Lockport, NY 14094-2628 716-434-8871
Fax: 716-434-8801
Paper boxes for cereal, snacks, cookies, etc
CEO: Anthony Gioia
Estimated Sales: $3 - 5 Million
Number Employees: 230

21019 Corson Rubber ProductsInc
P.O.Box 154
Clover, SC 29710 803-222-7779
Fax: 803-222-9022 info@corsonrubber.com
www.corsonrubber.com
Color coded sanitation was FDA compliant knobby mats.
President: Denis Garvey
Plant Manager: Terry Wallace
Estimated Sales: $9-15 Million
Type of Packaging: Consumer, Food Service, Private Label, Bulk
Brands:
Corson

21020 Cortec Corporation
4119 White Bear Parkway
St. Paul, MN 55110 651-429-1100
Fax: 651-429-1122 800-426-7832
info@cortecvci.com www.cortecvci.com
Polyethylene film and bags including plain and printed
General Manager: Usama Jacir
Vice President of Sales: Cliff Cracauer
Regional Sales Manager: Ashlee Meints
Plant Manager: Tim Bliss
Estimated Sales: $1 - 3 Million
Number Employees: 5-9
Square Footage: 106400

21021 Cortec Corporation
4119 White Bear Pkwy
Saint Paul, MN 55110 651-429-1100
Fax: 651-429-1122 800-426-7832
info@cortecvci.com www.corteccorp.com
Cortec Corporation is a pioneer of environmentally friendly, corrosion protection Vapor Phase Corrosion Inhibitors(VpCIin), a Migratory corrosion Inhibitors(MCI) Technologies for the packaging industry. ISO 9001:2000 & 14001Registered
President: Boris Miksic
Estimated Sales: $10 - 20 000,000
Number Employees: 50-99
Number of Brands: 5
Number of Products: 400+
Type of Packaging: Consumer, Food Service, Private Label, Bulk

21022 Cosco
P.O.Box 2609
Columbus, IN 47202-2609 812-372-0141
Fax: 812-372-0911 ddillman@coscoinc.com
www.coscoproducts.com
Manufacturer and exporter of high chairs
President: David Taylor
Estimated Sales: $100-500 Million
Number Employees: 1,000-4,999
Parent Co: Dorel Industries

Type of Packaging: Food Service
Brands:
Cosco

21023 Cosense Inc
155 Ricefield Ln
Hauppauge, NY 11788-2031 631-231-0735
Fax: 631-231-0838 sales@cosense.com
www.cosense.com
Designs and manufactures lliquid level sensors utilizing patented ultrasonic technology.
Owner: Naim Dam
Sales Director: Kevin Conlin
Estimated Sales: $5-10 Million
Number Employees: 20-49
Square Footage: 20000
Brands:
Millennuim
Pointsense
Sentio
Sonic Eye

21024 Cosgrove Enterprises
14300 Northwest 77th Court
Miami Lakes, FL 33016 305-623-6700
Fax: 305-820-9790 800-888-3396
orders@e-cosgrove.com
www.cosgroveenterprises.com
Manufacturer, exporter and importer of cleaning equipment and janitorial supplies including brooms, brushes and paper products
President: R Gregory Rogers
Quality Control: Louides Cohen
VP: Randy Shelton
Estimated Sales: $500,000 - $1 Million
Number Employees: 30
Square Footage: 220000

21025 Cosmic Company
151 A Haskins Way
South San Francisco, CA 94080 650-742-0888
Fax: 650-742-6777 cosmic@cosmicco.us
www.cosmicco.us
Boxes, thermal-formed trays, compartments, semi-rigid clear containers
VP: Agnes Cheung
Estimated Sales: $2.5-5 000,000
Number Employees: 10-19

21026 Cosmo/Kabar
140 Schmitt Blvd
Farmingdale, NY 11735-1461 631-694-6857
Fax: 631-694-6846 info@cosmos-kabar.com
www.cosmos-kabar.com
President: Bruce McKee
R&D: Bryan Matty
CFO: Bruce McKee
Estimated Sales: $2 Million
Number Employees: 20-49

21027 Cosmos International
PO Box 7740
Burbank, CA 91510-7740 626-330-8499
Fax: 626-333-4210
Canned fruit
Office Manager: Janet Muna

21028 Coss Engineering Sales Company
3943 S Creek Drive
Ts
Rochester Hills, MI 48306-4729 248-370-0707
Fax: 248-370-9211 800-446-1365
pneuconv@aol.com
Manufacturer and exporter of pneumatic conveying systems, surge hoppers and storage silos
CEO and President: Carter Coss
Estimated Sales: Less than $500,000
Number Employees: 4

21029 Costa Broom Works
3606 E 4th Ave
Tampa, FL 33605-5835 813-385-1722
Fax: 813-247-6060
Brooms, mops, mop heads and brushes; importer of related products for cleaning
Owner: Frank J Costa
Estimated Sales: $1-2.5 Million
Number Employees: 20-30
Type of Packaging: Food Service, Bulk

21030 Cott Technologies
14923 Proctor Ave
La Puente, CA 91746-3206 626-961-0370
Fax: 626-333-9307 www.cotttechnologies.com
Automated vacuum packaging machines and refrigerator display cases
Owner: Gilbert De Cardenas
Estimated Sales: $10 - 20 Million
Number Employees: 20-49
Brands:
Vari-Pack

21031 Cotter Corporation
8 Southside Rd
Danvers, MA 01923
Fax: 978-750-6219 info@cotterbrothers.com
www.cotterbrothers.com
High purity process piping and skid mounted systems; also, installation available
President: Ralph Cotter
VP: David Cotter
Domestic Sales Manager: William Fraga
Estimated Sales: $10-20 Million
Number Employees: 50-99

21032 Cotterman Company
130 Seltzer Rd
Croswell, MI 48422 810-679-4400
Fax: 810-679-4510 800-552-3337
info@cotterman.com www.cotterman.com
Manufacturer and exporter of rolling safety and fixed ladders including powder-coated and aluminum; also, portable elevating work platforms
President/CEO: C Stimpson
CFO: B Stimpson
Research & Development: J Kerr
Sales Manager: David Taylor
Manufacturing Manager: Robert Stimpson
Production Manager: L Higgins
Purchasing Manager: G Smith
Estimated Sales: $20-50 Million
Number Employees: 100-249
Square Footage: 60000
Parent Co: Material Control
Brands:
Maxi-Lift
Stockmaster
Tiltnroll
Workmaster

21033 (HQ)Cotton Goods Manufacturing Company
259 N California Ave
Chicago, IL 60612 773-265-0088
Fax: 773-265-0096 cotton2@earthlink.net
www.cottongoodsmfg.com
Manufacturer and exporter of table skirts and linens
President/CEO: Edward Lewis
Sales Manager: Kevin Higgins
Estimated Sales: $3 - 5 Million
Number Employees: 10-19
Square Footage: 10000
Brands:
Grip Clips

21034 Couch & Philippi
10680 Fern Avenue
PO Box A
Stanton, CA 90680 714-527-2261
Fax: 714-827-2077 800-854-3360
sales@couchandphilippi.com
www.couchandphilippi.com
Designing and producing innovative products for restaurants and beverage copmanies nationwide.
President: Steve Ellsworth
Estimated Sales: $5 - 10 Million
Number Employees: 50-99

21035 Country Save Corporation
19704 60th Ave NE
Arlington, WA 98223ÿ 360-435-9868
Fax: 360-435-0896 info@countrysave.com
www.countrysave.com
Manufacturer and exporter of phosphate-free laundry detergent and dishwashing powder; also, chlorine-free powdered bleach
President: Brink
Estimated Sales: $2.5-5 Million
Number Employees: 9
Brands:
Country Save

21036 County Neon Sign Corporation
PO Box 504
Plainview, NY 11803-0504 516-349-9550
Fax: 516-349-0090
Lighting fixtures and electric and neon signs
President: George Schneider
VP: Joe Miller
Estimated Sales: $2.5-5,000,000
Number Employees: 20-49

21037 Couprie Fenton
4282 Belair Frontage Rd
Suite 5
Augusta, GA 30909 706-650-7017
Fax: 706-868-1534
Crab, conch, crabmeat, dogfish, full line seafood, halibut, lobster, lobster meat
Manager: Yves Latremouille
Estimated Sales: $.5 - 1 million
Number Employees: 1-4

21038 Courtesy Sign Company
3101 S Fillmore St
Amarillo, TX 79110-1025 806-373-6609
Fax: 806-373-2953 courtesy@arn.net
www.courtesysigns.com
Window signs, over-the-wire banners, point of purchase markers, aisle product signs, pennant banners, flags, etc
Manager: Bruce Milton
CFO: Wesley Ninemire
Sales: Dixie Flaherty
Estimated Sales: Below $5 Million
Number Employees: 5-9
Square Footage: 148000

21039 Courtright Companies
26749 S. Governors Hwy.
Monee, IL 60449-8095 708-534-8400
Fax: 708-534-9140 sales@right-tape.com
www.right-tape.com
Manufacturer & exporter of reusable shipping containers, Teflon tapes, shellac adhesives, tensilized polypropylene and stretch film
Owner: Patricia Schoenbeck
Sales Director: Ted Bachand
Purchasing Manager: Ted Bachand
Estimated Sales: $3-5 Million
Number Employees: 6
Square Footage: 40000
Type of Packaging: Food Service, Private Label

21040 Cousins Packaging
105 Claireport Crescent
Etobicoke, ON M9V 6P7
Canada 416-743-1341
Fax: 416-743-1831 888-209-4344
info@cousinspackaging.com
www.cousinspackaging.com
Number Employees: 50

21041 Covance Laboratories
210 Carnegie Center
Princeton, NJ 08540-6233 609-452-4440
Fax: 609-452-9375 www.covance.com
Consultant/research laboratory offering sanitation testing and analysis
Chairman/CEO: Joseph Herring
Corporate SVP/Chief Financial Officer: Alison Cornell
Corporate VP, Business Development: Nigel Brown
Corporate SVP/Chief Information Officer: William Klitgaard
Corporate SVP/General Counsel/Secretary: James Lovett
Corporate SVP, Human Resources: Lisa Uthgenannt
Chief Commerical Officer/Corporate SVP: John Watson
EVP/Group President, R&D Laboratories: Deborah Keller
Purchasing Manager: Christopher Martino
Estimated Sales: $2 Billion
Number Employees: 11,790
Parent Co: Corning

21042 Covance Laboratories Inc.
3301 Kinsman Boulevard
Madison, WI 53704-2523 608-241-4471
Fax: 608-241-7227 info@covance.com
www.covance.com

Analytical testing services to the food, dietary supplement and biotechnology industries
Chairman of the Board/CEO: Joseph Herring
Corporate VP/Chief Financial Officer: Alison Cornell
Corporate VP: Honggang Bi Ph.D.
Group President, R&D Laboratories: Deborah Keller
Corporate SVP/Chief Information Officer: William Klitgaard
Corporate VP, Business Development: Nigel Brown
Estimated Sales: $277 Million
Number Employees: 1,800
Square Footage: 191000
Parent Co: Covance

21043 Cove Four Slide & Stamping Corporation
195 E Merrick Rd
Freeport, NY 11520 516-379-4232
Fax: 516-379-4563 jgentile@covefour.com
www.covefour.com
Wire products including corkscrews and custom; also, forming available
President: Barry Jaffe
VP Marketing: Bill Freedman
Estimated Sales: $10 - 20 Million
Number Employees: 50-99

21044 Cove Woodworking
743 Western Ave Ste 5
Gloucester, MA 01930 978-526-4755
Fax: 978-526-4188 800-273-0037
whit33@msn.com www.covewoodworking.com
Restaurant tables, bars, bar stools, booths, chairs, bases, built-ins and custom work.
President: Dennis Whittemore
CFO: Patty Kenaedy
Production Manager: Paul Hargreaves
Estimated Sales: $1 Million
Number Employees: 10-19
Square Footage: 8500
Type of Packaging: Food Service

21045 Coverall
50 Suffolk St # 1
Worcester, MA 01604-3792 508-754-9112
Fax: 508-754-9117 800-356-2961
info@coverallcovers.com
www.coverallcovers.com
Duty vinyl Rack Covers, Velcro Strip Doors, PVC Display Rack, Quality Controlled Anti-Bacterial Covers for Health Care Industry, Carts, Transport Bins, Racks & Equipment, Food Service Equipment, Covers for Slicers, Utility Carts, DishDollies, Mixers
Owner: George Najemy
CEO: George Najemy
Estimated Sales: $1 Million
Number Employees: 20-49
Square Footage: 60000
Type of Packaging: Bulk

21046 Covergent Label Technology
620 S Ware Boulevard
Tampa, FL 33619-4443 800-252-6111
Fax: 813-620-1206
sprice@convergentlabeltech.com
www.convergentlabeltech.com
Weighing and labeling systems
Estimated Sales: $20 - 25 Million
Number Employees: 100-250

21047 Coy Laboratory Products
14500 Coy Dr
Grass Lake, MI 49240 734-475-2200
Fax: 734-475-1846 sales@coylab.com
www.coylab.com
Glove boxes, anaerobic chambers, controlled environment
President: Richard Coy
Estimated Sales: $2.5 - 5 000,000
Number Employees: 10-19

21048 Coz Plastics
349 Lake Road
Dayville, CT 06241-1509 860-774-3770
Fax: 860-779-7320
customerservice@plasticscolor.com
www.plasticscolor.com
Color concentrates for thermoplastic, pre-colored, natural and clear materials
President: Douglas Borgsdorf
Controller: Clyde Smith
Vice President of Business Development: Tim Workman
Vice President of Sales and Marketing: Joe Byrne
Estimated Sales: $100 - 500 Million
Number Employees: 100
Square Footage: 250000
Parent Co: Plastics Color Corporation

21049 (HQ)Cozzini
4300 W Bryn Mawr Ave
Chicago, IL 60646 773-478-9700
Fax: 773-478-8689 sales@cozzini.com
www.cozzini.com
Manufacturer and exporter of meat processing equipment and blades
President: Ivo Cozzini
VP: Oscar Cozzini
R&D: Greg Grady
Quality Control: Mario Lucchesi
Catalog Sales Technical Assistance: Pete Pierazzi
Estimated Sales: $20 Million
Number Employees: 100-249
Square Footage: 65000
Other Locations:
Cozzini
Soucy
Brands:
Cozzini
Ergo
Primedge
Suspentec

21050 Cozzoli Machine Company
50 Schoolhouse Rd
Somerset, NJ 08873-1289 732-564-0400
Fax: 732-564-0444 sales@cozzoli.com
www.cozzoli.com
Estimated Sales: $10 - 20 Million
Number Employees: 50-99

21051 Cozzoli Machine Company
50 Schoolhouse Rd
Somerset, NJ 08873-1289 732-564-0400
Fax: 732-564-0444 sales@cozzoli.comm
www.mrmelgin.com
Designs and manufactures integrated precision packaging systems solutions.
President: Frank Cozzoli
General Manager: Fred Hart
Controller: Michael Shanker
Marketing Director: Crystal Basiluk
Sales: Bruce Teeling
Purchasing Manager: Steve Turkus
Estimated Sales: $10-20 Million
Number Employees: 100-249
Number of Brands: 2
Number of Products: 200
Square Footage: 90000
Parent Co: Cozzoli Machine Company
Type of Packaging: Food Service
Brands:
Inline Fill-To-Level Filler
Inline Piston Filler
Rotary Fill-To-Level Filler
Rotary Piston Filler
Versa-Cap
Versa-Fil

21052 Cr. Manufacturing
10240 Deer Park Rd
Waverly, NE 68462 402-786-2000
Fax: 402-786-2096 877-789-5844
info@crmfg.com www.crmfg.com
Plastic supplies and smallwares to the food service, food prep, bakery, restaurant, scoop and scoop accessories, specialty items, pourers and pourer accessories, bar supply and bar accessories markets
Customer Service: Gary Knaub
Marketing/Sales: Sheila Camprecht
National Sales: Scott Donalds
Plant Manager: Bob Cooper
Estimated Sales: $20 Million
Number Employees: 100-249
Number of Brands: 27
Number of Products: 29
Square Footage: 120000
Parent Co: PMC Group Companies
Type of Packaging: Food Service, Private Label, Bulk
Brands:
3-Cup Measurer
Betterway Pourers
Cr Scoops
Cr Food Baskets
Cake Comb
Crystal Shooter Tubes
Drip Catchers
Econo Pourer
Exacto-Pour Tester
Ezy-Way Pourer
Jigg-All
Jumbo Straws
Kover All Dust Cap
Lid-Off Pail Opener
Magic-Mesh
Marga-Ezy
Pizza Slicer
Polar Pitcher
Posi-Pour 2000 Pourer
Posi-Pour Pourer
Pour Mor
Pro-Flo Pourer
Roxi Rimming Supplies
Roxi Sugar and Salt Spices/Flavors
Shakers Prepackaged Accessories
Shotskies Gelatin Mixes
Steakmarkers
Super Slicer
Whisky Gate Pourer

21053 Craft Corrugated Box
4674 Acushnet Ave
New Bedford, MA 02745-4736 508-998-2115
Fax: 508-998-8112
Corrugated boxes and other corrugated products
President: Ronald Mardula
Estimated Sales: Below $5 Million
Number Employees: 5 to 9

21054 Craft Industries
26-35 47th Avenue
Long Island City, NY 11101 252-753-3152
Fax: 252-753-3154 sales@craftindustries.com
www.craftindustries.com
Portable LP gas cookers and trailers for caterers; also, custom made cookers and trailers available
President and CFO: Jim Craft Jr
VP Financing: Sylvia Craft
Estimated Sales: Below $5 Million
Number Employees: 1-4
Square Footage: 80000
Brands:
Craftmaster
Steelcraft

21055 Craig Manufacturing
30 Loretto St
Irvington, NJ 07111 973-923-3211
Fax: 973-923-1767 800-631-7936
buycraig@aol.com www.craigmfg.com
Deli cases, steam tables, back bars, refrigerators and sandwich units
President: Craig Dubov
Estimated Sales: $5 - 10 Million
Number Employees: 50-99
Square Footage: 75000
Type of Packaging: Food Service

21056 Crain Walnut Shelling, Inc.
10695 Decker Ave
Los Molinos, CA 96055 530-529-1585
Fax: 530-529-1458
crainwalnut@crainwalnut.com
www.crainwalnut.com
Shelled walnuts supplying industrial ingredient needs.
Owner: William Crain
Owner: Harold Crain
Vice President of Sales & Logistics: Vicki Lapera
Quality Assurance: Devan Wilson
Sales Administrator: Kimberly Gonsalves
Type of Packaging: Bulk

21057 Cramer
1222 Quebec St
Kansas City, MO 64116 816-471-4433
Fax: 816-471-7188 800-366-6700
information@cramerinc.com
www.cramerinc.com
Industrial steel seating, step stools and ladders
President: Nick Christianson
CEO: Jason Rann
Director Marketing: J Sanders
VP Sales/Marketing: Jeff Meyer
Director Product Development: Lee Denny

Estimated Sales: $10-20 Million
Number Employees: 1-4
Parent Co: Rotherwood Corporation

21058 Cramer Company
105 Nutmeg Rd S
South Windsor, CT 06074 877-684-6464
Fax: 860-610-0897
customer-service@mhrhodes.com
www.cramer-motors.com
Manufacturer and exporter of motors and timers for process control systems
President: Kenneth Mac Cormac
VP: Wayne Taylor
Director Operations: Frank Darmig
Estimated Sales: $3 - 5 Million
Number Employees: 5-9
Square Footage: 110000
Parent Co: Owosso Corporation
Type of Packaging: Bulk

21059 Cramer Products
381 Park Ave S
New York, NY 10016-8806 212-645-2368
Fax: 212-242-6799 www.abpaonline.org
Manufacturer and exporter of temperature controlled storage units, humidors, wire and wood storage racks and cooling panels for wine and cheese
President: Richard Rothschild
Treasurer: Valerie Tomaselli
Vice President: Nancy Hall
Estimated Sales: Less than $500,000
Number Employees: 1-4
Brands:
Cmc
Cool-Kit
Cool-Safe
Cramarc
Well Tempered

21060 Crandall Filling Machinery
80 Gruner Rd
Buffalo, NY 14227 716-897-3486
Fax: 716-897-3488 800-280-8551
infocrandall.com www.crandall.com
Manufacturer and exporter of filling, packaging and closing machinery
President: Heather Wood
Technician: Scott Reed
VP sales: Charles Wood
Estimated Sales: $1 - 3 Million
Number Employees: 1-4
Square Footage: 8000

21061 Crane Carton Corporation
555 N Tripp Avenue
Chicago, IL 60624-1079 773-722-0555
Fax: 773-722-3510
Folding paper boxes
Estimated Sales: $20 - 50 Million
Number Employees: 100-249

21062 Crane Composites Inc
23525 W Eames Street
Channahon, IL 60410-3220 815-467-8600
Fax: 815-467-8666 800-435-0080
sales@cranecomposites.com
www.cranecomposites.com
Fiber-reinforced composite materials.
President: Thomas Jeff Craney
VP of Building Products: Kelly Erdmann
Eastern Regional Sales Manager: Kevin Bellinger
Western Regional Sales Manager: Chris Schamer

21063 Crane Environmental
2650 Eisenhower Ave Ste 100a
Norristown, PA 19403 610-631-7700
Fax: 610-631-6800 800-633-7435
rburke@cranenv.com www.cranenv.com
Manufacturer and exporter of water treatment equipment including reverse osmosis, demineralizers, softeners, filters, CB pumps, deaerators and steam specialty items
Manager: Russ Burke
Marketing Manager: Russell Burke
Purchasing Agent: Sandra Bisci
Estimated Sales: $20-30 Million
Number Employees: 1-4
Square Footage: 100000
Parent Co: Crane Company
Brands:
Accu-Spray
Delta
Epro
Spiraflow
Uni-Mod
Uni-Pac

21064 Crane National Vendors
12955 Enterprise Way
Bridgeton, MO 63044 314-298-0055
Fax: 314-298-3534 www.cranems.com
Tea and coffee industry dispensers
President: Brad Ellis
Estimated Sales: $50 - 100 Million
Number Employees: 100-249

21065 (HQ)Crane Research & Engineering Company
617 Regional Dr
Hampton, VA 23661-1800 757-826-1707
Fax: 757-838-3728
Crab processing, picking and cleaning machinery
Owner: Danny Schrum
Plant Manager: Dan Schrum, Jr.
Estimated Sales: $5-10 Million
Number Employees: 20-49
Square Footage: 16500
Brands:
Quik-Pik

21066 Crate Ideas by Wilderness House
P.O.Box 675
Cave Junction, OR 97523-0675 541-592-2106
Fax: 541-592-6670 800-592-2206
sales@crateideas.com www.crateideas.com
Custom wooden and decorative gift crates
President: Eugene Schreiber
Sales Director: Sarah Peiffer
Estimated Sales: $1 - 3 Million
Number Employees: 10-19

21067 Crawford Packaging
1609 N Capitol Avenue
Indianapolis, IN 46202-1202 317-924-2494
Fax: 317-283-1817 rdcrawfo@in.net
Estimated Sales: $1 - 5 000,000
Number Employees: 20-49

21068 Crayex Corporation
1747 Commerce Dr
Piqua, OH 45356 937-773-7000
Fax: 770-957-6874 800-837-1747
crayex@crayex.com www.crayex.com
Low density polyethylene film and bags for shrink packaging and wrapping
Manager: Keith Killingsworth
CFO: Lori Webster
Quality Control: Jeff Gower
Manager: Keith Killingsworth
Estimated Sales: $10 - 20 Million
Number Employees: 20-49
Square Footage: 90000

21069 Crayex Corporation
1747 commerce drive
Piqua, OH 45356 937-773-7000
Fax: 770-957-6874 800-837-1747
crayex@crayex.com www.crayex.com
Low density polyethylene bags
Manager: Keith Killingsworth
CEO: Clifford R Alexander
Production Manager: Keith Killingsworth
Estimated Sales: $5-10 Million
Number Employees: 20-49
Parent Co: Crayex Corporation

21070 Cream of the Valley Plastics
5750 Lamar Street
Arvada, CO 80002 303-425-5499
Fax: 303-425-0734
Milk and juice containers
Plant Supervisor: Bart Hurley
Estimated Sales: $2.5-5 Million
Number Employees: 10-19
Parent Co: Southern Foods

21071 Creamery Plastics Products, Ltd
8989 Charles Street
Chilliwack, BC V2P 2V8
Canada 604-792-0232
Fax: 604-792-1890 info@creamercaddy.com
www.icechiller.net
Cream and condiment dispensers; also, buffet displays and ice chillers to keep foods & beverages chilled for many hours.
President: Lucy Vales
CEO: Tony Rapaz
Purchasing Agent: Tony Rapaz
Number Employees: 4

21072 Creative Automation
5404 Jedmed Court
Saint Louis, MO 63129-2221 800-745-9539
Fax: 314-845-7779
e-mail@creativeautomation.com
www.creativeautomation.com

21073 Creative Automation
61 Willet St Ste 3b
Passaic, NJ 07055 973-778-0061
Fax: 973-614-8336 info@creative-auto.com
www.creative-auto.com
Manufacturer and exporter of automatic feeders, bar code verification equipment, turnkey systems, leaflet inserters and outserters, vertical, form, fill and seal equipment
President: John Calabrese
CEO: John Bartlo
VP: John Calabrese
Estimated Sales: $1-2.5 Million
Number Employees: 1-4

21074 Creative Canopy Design
4272 Columbus Dr
Hernando Beach, FL 34607 866-970-5200
Fax: 303-424-0172 866-970-5200
laura@creative-canopy.com
www.creative-canopy.com
Portable canopies/shade structures, commercial tents, banner flags, screen printing and dyesub printing.
Owner: Laura Uribe

21075 Creative Coatings Corporation
28 Charron Avenue
1165
Nashua, NH 03063-1783 603-889-8040
Fax: 603-889-3780 800-229-1957
flocking@aol.com
www.flocking.thomasregister.com
Packaging materials including laminated vinyls, metallized barrier and pressure sensitive films, etc.; importer of bakery and confectionery mixers and homogenizers
President: Robert Borowski
CEO: Robert Borowski
Customer Service Manager: Barbara Landry
Number Employees: 5
Square Footage: 20000

21076 Creative Converting
255 Spring Street
Clintonville, WI 54929
Fax: 800-848-1421 800-826-0418
press@creativeconverting.com
www.creativeconverting.com
Paper table cloths, napkins, plates and cups
Estimated Sales: $50-100 Million
Number Employees: 100-249
Square Footage: 105000
Parent Co: Hoffmaster Group, Inc.
Brands:
Every Occasion

21077 Creative Cookie
8673 Commerce Dr
Suite 7
Easton, MD 21601 410-819-0091
Fax: 410-819-0255 800-451-4005
sales@creativecookieetc.com
www.creativecookieetc.com
Manufacturer and exporter of themed fortune cookies and candy boxes
Owner: Marty Schwartz
Vice President: Joan Schwartz
General Manager: Martin Schwartz
Estimated Sales: Less than $500,000
Number Employees: 1-4
Number of Products: 80
Type of Packaging: Consumer, Food Service, Private Label, Bulk
Brands:
A World of Good Fortune
Anniversary
Baseball Trivia
Bible Verse

Birthday
Calling Card
Christmas
Congratulations!
Doctor's
Easter
Executive
For Kid's Only
Get Well
Golfer's
Halloween
Holiday Greetings
Housewarming
Irish
It's a Baby!
Italian
Jewish
Millenium Message
Mother's Day
Movie Trivia
Naughty But Nice!
Over the Hill
Romantic
Sports Trivia
Teachers
Thank You
Trivia
Valentine
Wedding
Year 2000
You're the Greatest!

21078 Creative Enterprises
12 Rochelle Drive
Kendall Park, NJ 08824-1405 732-422-0300
Fax: 732-422-0008 creative@cre-8-tive.com
www.cre-8-tive.com
Platforms, point of purchase and store displays, dump tables and cabinets
President: S Y Goldberg
Estimated Sales: Below $5 Million
Number Employees: 2

21079 Creative Essentials
2155 5th Ave
Ronkonkoma, NY 11779-6908 631-467-8370
Fax: 631-467-4255 800-355-5891
sales@menudesigns.com www.menusasap.com
Manufacturer and exporter of menu covers, acrylic stands, placemats, recipe holders, menus and check presenters
President: Allen Fischer
Sales Manager: Jonathan Sunshine
Sales: Karen Chalson
Number Employees: 20-49
Square Footage: 64000

21080 Creative Foam Corporation
300 N Alloy Dr
Fenton, MI 48430 810-629-4149
Fax: 810-750-7613
psweinrauch@creativefoam.com
www.creativefoam.com
Manufacturer and exporter of packaging and material handling systems
President: Wayne Blessing
Sales Manager: David Rosser
Estimated Sales: $20 - 50 Million
Number Employees: 100-249
Type of Packaging: Bulk

21081 Creative Food Ingredients
4-3470 Laird Road
Mississauga, ON L5L 5Y4
Canada 905-828-8889
Fax: 905-828-6664 888-701-8888
jfox@creativefoods.com www.creativefoods.com
Manufacturer and marketer of baked ingredient products
President: A William O'Flaherty
Vice President: K Michael O'Flaherty
National Sales Manager: Mark Otis Humphrey

21082 Creative Forming
PO Box 128
Ripon, WI 54971-0128 920-748-7285
Fax: 920-748-9466 www.creativeforming.com
Manufacturer and exporter of thermoformed plastic trays
President: Glen Yurjevich
General Manager: John Beard
Estimated Sales: $20 - 50 Million
Number Employees: 100-249
Parent Co: Wellman

Type of Packaging: Consumer, Food Service, Bulk

21083 Creative Impressions
7697 9th St
Buena Park, CA 90621-2898 714-521-4441
Fax: 714-522-2733 800-524-5278
email@emenucovers.com
www.emenucovers.com
Clear and soft plastic menu covers in 30 colors and textures; also, inserts available
President: Marc Abbott
Estimated Sales: $5-10 Million
Number Employees: 20-49

21084 Creative Industries
1024 Western Dr
Indianapolis, IN 46241 317-247-4953
800-776-2068
cii@creativeind.com www.creativeind.com
Pass- and talk-thru, plastic laminated and bulletproof windows
President: Larry Clark
Estimated Sales: Below $5 Million
Number Employees: 10-19
Type of Packaging: Private Label

21085 Creative Label Designers
3890 SW Harbor Drive
Lees Summit, MO 64082-4679 816-537-8757
Fax: 816-537-8757
Pressure sensitive printed and thermal bar code labels
President: Dale G Wheat
Number Employees: 4
Square Footage: 4000

21086 Creative Menus
200 Lakewood Cir
Burr Ridge, IL 60527 630-734-3244
Menus
Owner: Rick Styfer
Estimated Sales: $500,000-$1 Million
Number Employees: 1-4

21087 Creative Mobile Systems
P.O.Box 8198
Manchester, CT 06040-0198 860-649-6272
Fax: 860-643-2830 800-646-8364
cms189@ntplx.net www.cmssystem.com
Catering trucks, hot dog carts and concession trailers
President: Edward Izzo
CFO: Mary Davis
VP: Richard Lumpkin
VP: Richard Lumpkin
Purchasing Manager: John Izzo
Estimated Sales: Below $5 Million
Number Employees: 5-9
Square Footage: 24000
Brands:
Cms, Inc.

21088 Creative Packaging Corporation
700 Corporate Grove Dr
Buffalo Grove, IL 60089 847-459-1001
Fax: 847-325-3919 sales@creativepkg.com
www.creativepkg.com
Manufacturer and exporter of dispensing closures
President: John Weeks
CFO: Mike Farreoo
Quality Control: Samantha Gibson
VP Sales/Marketing: Jeff Teth
Corporate Manager: Robert Giles
Estimated Sales: $50-75 Million
Number Employees: 10
Square Footage: 1100000
Parent Co: Courtesy Corporation
Brands:
Shear Pak
Sports Cap

21089 Creative Signage System
9101 51st Place
College Park, MD 20740 301-345-3700
Fax: 301-220-0289 800-220-7446
creative@creativesignage.com
www.creativesignage.com
Plastic signs
President: John Mayer
Sales: Peter Van Allen
Estimated Sales: $2.5 - 5 Million
Number Employees: 20-49

21090 Creative Storage Systems
2700 Barr Lks Blvd NW Ste 500
Kennesaw, GA 30144 770-514-0711
Fax: 770-514-0622 888-370-8810
marketing@creativestorage.com
www.creativestorage.com
High density dynamic warehouse storage systems, conveyors/gravity, flow-through pallet systems, pallets/racks, racks/storage, storage
President: Robert Lawless
Estimated Sales: $10-20 000,000
Number Employees: 20-49

21091 Creative Techniques
2441 N Opdyke Rd
Auburn Hills, MI 48326 248-373-3050
Fax: 248-373-3458 800-473-0284
www.creativetechniques.com
Manufacturer and exporter of packaging and material handling products
President: Richard Yeakey
Sales Manager: Stanley Shore
Estimated Sales: $20-50 Million
Number Employees: 100-249

21092 Creegan Animation Company
508 Washington St
Steubenville, OH 43952-2140 740-283-3708
Fax: 740-283-4117 creegans@weir.net
www.creegans.com
Manufacturer and exporter of animations, costume characters and audio-animatronics
Owner: George Creegan
Estimated Sales: $1 - 5 Million
Number Employees: 20-49

21093 Creekstone Farms Premium Beef
604 Goff Industrial Park Road
PO Box 869
Arkansas City, KS 67005 620-741-3366
Fax: 620-741-3353
angusinfo@creekstonefarms.com
www.creekstonefarms.com
Their own line of Creekstone Farms Natural and Premium Black Angus Beef marketed under the USDA Process-Verified Tender Beef label.
President: John Stewart
Genetics Division: Joe Bill Meng
Bull and Semen Sales: Danny Rankin
Feeder Calf Program: Ryan Meyer
Natural Beef Program: Matt Bode
Type of Packaging: Food Service

21094 Crepas & Associates
15w725 Virginia Lane
Elmhurst, IL 60126-1259 630-833-4880
Fax: 630-833-0580 kretebob@aol.com
eee.crepasassoc.com
Consultant providing structural engineering services for facility renovations new contruction renovation specialize in floors concrete and epoxy
President: Robert Crepas
Estimated Sales: Less than $500,000
Number Employees: 4

21095 Cres Cor
5925 Heisley Rd
Mentor, OH 44060 440-350-1100
Fax: 440-350-7267 877-273-7267
crescor@crescor.com www.crescor.com
A complete line of quality mobile food service equipment including hot cabinets, utility cabinets and racks, banquet cabinets, dish dollies, ovens and more. Since 1936...There is no equal.
President: Clifford D Baggott
VP: Rio DeGennaro
Director of Engineering: Heather Stewart
Sales/Marketing Director: Michael Capretta
Brands:
Cres Cor

21096 Cresco Food Technologies, LLC
717 2nd Ave SE
Cresco, IA 52136 563-547-4241
Fax: 563-547-4504 cft@iowatelecom.net
www.aveka.com
Nutraceutical and food processing facility.
Parent Co: Aveka, Inc.

21097 Crespac Incorporated
5032 N Royal Atlanta Drive
Tucker, GA 30084 770-938-1900
Fax: 770-939-4900 800-438-1900
info@crespac.com www.atp-plastic.com

Disposable thermoformed food trays and containers; exporter of produce and food containers
CEO: Jeff Moon
Estimated Sales: $5-10 Million
Number Employees: 50-99
Square Footage: 400000
Brands:
Big Green

21098 Cresset Chemical Company
One Cresset Center
PO Box 367
Weston, OH 43569 419-669-2041
Fax: 419-669-2200 800-367-2020
cresset@cresset.com www.cresset.com
Manufacturer and exporter of hand cleaners, release agents and admixtures
President: George F Baty
CFO: Roger Davis
Vice President: Mike Baty
Quality Control: Rick Reynolds
VP Sales: Skip Schenck
Estimated Sales: Below $5 Million
Number Employees: 10
Brands:
Crete-Lease
Crete-Trete
Han-D
Sol-Zol
Spatter-Cote
Super Strip
Super-Trete

21099 Crest Foods Company
905 Main Street
Ashton, IL 61006 815-453-7411
Fax: 815-453-2646 877-273-7893
www.crestfoods.com
Established in 1941. Processor of food ingredients including emulsifying agents, proteins, caseinates, whey, stabilizers and flavors for dips, bases and seasonings; contract packaging available
President: Jeff Meiners
CEO: Shirley Reif
VP Manufacturing: Mike Meiners
VP Corporate Sales: Steven Meiners
VP Manufacturing: Mike Meiners
Estimated Sales: $20-50 Million
Number Employees: 250-499
Type of Packaging: Consumer, Food Service, Private Label

21100 Cresthill Industries
196 Ashburton Ave
Yonkers, NY 10701-4001 914-965-9510
Fax: 914-965-9534 www.cresthillindustries.com
Manufacturer and exporter of bag closures
President: Christopher Rie
Treasurer: J Rie
Estimated Sales: $10-20 Million
Number Employees: 50-99
Parent Co: Cresthill Industries
Brands:
Kisco Bip

21101 Crestware
520 N Redwood Rd
PO Box 540210
North Salt Lake City, UT 84054-0210801-292-0656
Fax: 877-874-1784 800-345-0513
sales@crestware.com www.crestware.com
Manufacturer and importer of china, flatware, steamtable pans, chafers, pots, pans, smallwares, thermometers and scales
President: Hal Harrison
VP Marketing: Stephen Jordan
VP Operations: Greg Harrison
Estimated Sales: $10 - 20 Million
Number Employees: 2
Square Footage: 80000
Brands:
Crestware

21102 Cretel Food Equipment
303 Little Station Road
Holland, MI 49424-2618 616-786-3980
Fax: 616-786-0299 jim@smithassocs.com
www.smithassocs.com
Bags for beef, ham, bacon and sausage; films, laminates, flexible packages, vacuum packaging materials and equipment, processing equipment, skinning machines, fish processing equipment, plant layout and product flow
Owner: James Smith
Estimated Sales: $1 - 3 Million
Number Employees: 5
Number of Brands: 4
Number of Products: 10
Type of Packaging: Consumer, Food Service

21103 Cretorr
3243 N California Ave
Chicago, IL 60618-5890 773-588-1690
Fax: 773-588-2171 800-228-1885
marketing@cretors.com www.cretors.com
Popcorn machines
President: Charles D Cretors
Quality Control: Wally Krzak
Vice President of Sales and Marketing: Shelly Olesen
Estimated Sales: $10 - 20 Million
Number Employees: 100-249

21104 Crippen Manufacturing Company
ÿ400 Woodside Drive
St. Louis, MI 48880 989-681-4323
Fax: 989-681-3818 800-872-2474
dbjerke@crippenmfg.com www.crippenmfg.com
Grain separators, polishers and conveyors
President: Jim Gascho
System Technician: Daniel Kelley
CFO: Shane Gascho
V P/Sales: Douglas Clark
V P and Mktg: Kevin Kennedy
Conveying and Systems Product Mgr: Jerry Valch
Density Specialist: William Donnell
New Equipment Sales: Kevin Vogt
Customer Service: Kevin Vogt
Design Eng'r /Air Screen Equipment: James Strawder
Design Eng'r/Density Equipment: Robert Gilbert
Materials Mgr: Darren Losey
Product Specialist: Steve Galgoczi
Estimated Sales: $1-2.5 Million
Number Employees: 50-99
Square Footage: 260000

21105 Crisci Food Equipment Company
P.O.Box 8327
New Castle, PA 16107-8327 724-654-6609
Fax: 724-654-9266
Stainless steel food services equipment, ladders, step stools and conveyors
President: Sally Firmi
Estimated Sales: $2.5-5 000,000
Number Employees: 10-19

21106 Crispy Lite
10 Sunnen Drive
St. Louis, MO 63143-3800 775-689-5700
Fax: 314-781-5445 888-356-5362
clientcare@wellsbloomfield.com
www.wellsbloomfield.com
Manufacturer and exporter of display cases, filters, pressure fryers, fans, hoods and food warmers
Vice President, Sales/Marketing, Wells-B: Paul Angrick
VP Sales/Marketing: David Moore
Mngr.: D Joseph Lambert
Number Employees: 250-499
Square Footage: 248000
Parent Co: Wells Bloomfield Company
Type of Packaging: Food Service

21107 Critzas Industries
4041 Park Ave
St Louis, MO 63110-2391 314-773-8510
Fax: 314-773-4837 800-537-1418
goop@earthlink.net www.goophandcleaner.com
Manufacturer and exporter of premium waterless hand cleaner.
President/Treasurer: John Critzas
Estimated Sales: $10-20 Million
Number Employees: 10-19
Square Footage: 60000
Brands:
Goop

21108 Criveller East
6935 Oakwood Drive
Niagara Falls, ON L2E 6S5
Canada 905-357-2930
Fax: 905-374-2930 888-894-2266
info@criveller.com www.criveller.com
President: Mario Criiveller
CFO: Jim Farlane
Number Employees: 10

21109 Croll-Reynolds Company
6 Campus Dr Ste 1
Parsippany, NJ 07054 908-232-4200
Fax: 908-232-2146 www.croll.com
Manufacturer and exporter of food processing machinery including combined evactor/condenser/liquid ring vaccum, vapor recovery and vacuum cooling systems and ejectors
President/CEO: Samuel Croll III
CEO: James Reynolds
CEO: Samuel W Croll Iii
Division Manager: Henry Hage
Plant Manager: Ellis Production/Shipping
Estimated Sales: $5 - 10 Million
Number Employees: 20-49
Brands:
Chill-Vactor
Core-Chill
Evactor
Rotajector
Scrub-Vactor

21110 Croll-Reynolds Engineering Company
2400 Reservoir Ave
Trumbull, CT 06611-4793 203-371-1983
Fax: 203-371-0615 creco@att.net
Design and manufacture backwashable, liquid pressure, tubular element polishing type filters and strainers.
President/CEO: John Quinlan PE
Sales Manager: Louis Ancillai
Estimated Sales: $200,000
Number Employees: 3
Number of Brands: 3
Number of Products: 3
Square Footage: 5000
Brands:
Clarite
Flexodisc
Flexoleed

21111 (HQ)Crompton Corporation
One American Lane
Greenwich, CT 06831-2560 203-573-2000
Fax: 203-552-2010 800-295-2392
www.cromptoncorp.com
Chemical ingredients and food additives
Chairman/ President/ CEO: Craig A. Rogerson
CFO/ SVP: Stephen C. Forsyth
VP/ Corporate Controller/ Principal Acco: Laurence Orton
Global Market Manager: Bob Ruckle
Sales Director: Rick Beitel
Number Employees: 20-49
Other Locations:

21112 Crosfield Company
111 Ingalls Ave
Joliet, IL 60435-4373 815-727-3651
Fax: 815-774-2804 www.ineossilicas.com
Manufacturer and exporter of silicon dioxide gels and precipitates; also, silica hydrogel
Plant Manager: Pat Murphy
Estimated Sales: $1 - 5 Million
Number Employees: 100-249
Brands:
Gasil
Neosyl

21113 Crossroads Espresso
P.O.Box 23610
Eugene, OR 97402 541-344-4600
Fax: 541-344-8992
sales@crossroads-espresso.com
www.coffeestuff.com
Espresso parts and espresso machines
President: James Glang
Estimated Sales: $1-5 000,000
Number Employees: 10-19

21114 Crosswind Foods
P.O.Box 29
Sabetha, KS 66534 785-284-3462
Fax: 785-284-3940
crosswindfoods@crosswindindustries.com
www.crosswindindustries.com
Contract food manufacturing
President: Ken Matson
Vice President: Bob Niehues
Quality Control: Gary Lierz
Plant Manager: Chris Shelly
Estimated Sales: $5 - 10 000,000
Number Employees: 20-49

Type of Packaging: Consumer, Private Label, Bulk
Other Locations:
Crosswind Industries
Kansas City MO

21115 **Crouch Supply Company, Inc**
PO Box 163829
Ft. Worth, TX 76161-3829 865-522-2672
Fax: 865-522-2674 800-825-1110
k.kertis@crouchinc.com www.crouchinc.com
Distribution of process and refrigeration equipment, supplies and services
Sales: Karyn Kertis

21116 **Crouzet Corporation**
3237 Commander Drive
Carrollton, TX 75006-2506 972-620-7713
Fax: 972-250-3865 800-677-5311
tnuttall@messagerie.crouzet.com
www.crouzet.com
Manufacturer and exporter of OEM products for packaging and processing equipment: timers, proximity sensors, counters, control relays, solid state relays and temperature controllers
President: Gerald Vincent
VP Marketing: Phillipe Dubois
Estimated Sales: $20-50 Million
Number Employees: 100-249
Parent Co: Crouzet
Brands:
Crouzet
Gordos
Syrelec

21117 **Crowell Corporation**
1 Crowell Rd
Wilmington, DE 19804 302-998-0557
Fax: 302-998-0626 800-441-7525
sales@crowellcorp.com www.crowellcorp.com
Manufacturer and exporter of gummed tapes and cohesively coated cold seal packaging materials; importer of kraft paper; also, laminating, printing and coating of films, paper, board and foam available
President: Herbert Adelman
VP: Robert Adelman
Sales Director: Joel Steinbrunner
Purchasing Manager: Dottie Alexander
Estimated Sales: $50-100 Million
Number Employees: 100-249
Square Footage: 125000
Brands:
Cro-Nel
Newport
Nyvel
Samson
Tufftape

21118 **Crown Battery Manufacturing Company**
P.O.Box 990
Fremont, OH 43420-0990 419-334-7181
Fax: 419-334-7416 800-487-2879
info@crownbattery.com www.crownbattery.com
Manufacturer and exporter of industrial batteries used in lift trucks and food service equipment
President: Hal Hawk
CEO: Harold F Hawk Jr
Director Marketing: Mark Kelley
Estimated Sales: $20 - 50 Million
Number Employees: 250-499
Square Footage: 200000

21119 **Crown Chemical Products**
6125 Netherhart Road
Mississauga, ON L5T 1G5
Canada 905-564-0904
Fax: 905-564-0906
Sanitation and janitorial chemicals including hand cleaners, degreasers, disinfectants, deodorants, plumbing and carpet chemicals, etc.; custom blending available
President: Keith Chan
Quality Control: Annie Chan
Number Employees: 10
Square Footage: 15000
Type of Packaging: Food Service, Private Label

21120 **Crown Cork & Seal Company**
One Crown Way
Philadelphia, PA 19154-4599 215-698-5100
www.crowncork.com
Metal cans
Sales Department: Bill Keith

21121 **(HQ)Crown Cork & Seal Company**
One Crown Way
Philadelphia, PA 19154-4599 215-698-5100
ir@crowncork.com
www.crowncork.com
Manufacturer and exporter of bottle caps, can tops, crowns and cans including tin, beer and ale; also, bottling machinery
Chairman/Chief Executive Officer: John Conway
VP Purchasing: Edward Vesey
Estimated Sales: $613 Million
Number Employees: 4400
Other Locations:
Crown Cork & Seal Co.
Apopka FL

21122 **Crown Cork & Seal Company**
1 Crown Way
Philadelphia, PA 19154-4599 215-698-5100
Fax: 215-698-5206 www.crowncork.com
Packaging materials.
Chief Executive Officer: John Conway
Estimated Sales: $613 Million
Number Employees: 4400

21123 **Crown Custom Metal Spinning**
1-176 Creditstone Road
Concord, ON L4K 4H7
Canada 416-243-0112
Fax: 416-243-0112 800-750-1924
sales@crowncookware.ca
www.crowncookware.ca
Manufacturer and exporter of bakery racks and aluminum cookware including stockpots and cake and pizza pans; importer of stainless steel mixing bowls
President: David P Vella
CFO: Franco Mazzuca
Customer Service: Carmen D'Cruze
Administrator: Gilda Leib
Number Employees: 10
Square Footage: 80000
Type of Packaging: Consumer, Food Service, Bulk

21124 **Crown Equipment Corporation**
44 South Washington Street
New Bremen, OH 45869 419-629-2311
Fax: 419-629-2900 www.crown.com
Manufacturer and exporter of lift trucks
Chairman Emeritus: James Dicke
Chairman/Chief Executive Officer: James Dicke II
President: James Dicke III
Senior Vice President: David Besser
Senior Vice President: James Mozer
Senior Vice President: Timothy Quellhorst
Senior Vice President: John Tate
Vice President/Chief Financial Officer: Kent Spille
Vice President, Engineering: Steven Dues
Vice President, Design: Michael Gallagher
Vice President, Manufacturing Operations: David Beddow
Estimated Sales: $736 Million
Number Employees: 8500

21125 **Crown Holdings, Inc.**
One Crown Way
Philadelphia, PA 19154-4599 215-698-5100
Fax: 215-698-5201 ir@crowncork.com
www.crowncork.com
Manufacturer and exporter of spiral wound composite cans, paper and fiber tubes, easy open closures and specialties
Senior Vice President - Finance: Thomas A. Kelly
VP Investor Relations & Corporate Affair: Thomas T. Fischer
Marketing Manager: Melissa Quintana
Sales Manager: Renate Himmel
Estimated Sales: $5 - 10 Million
Number Employees: 250-499
Parent Co: Crown Cork & Seal
Type of Packaging: Bulk

21126 **Crown Holdings, Inc.**
1 Crown Way
Philadelphia, PA 19154-4599 215-698-5100
Fax: 215-698-5201
michael.dunleavy@crowncork.com
www.crowncork.com
Manufacturer and exporter of cans and plastic bottles
CEO: John W Conway
Marketing Manager: Melissa Quintana
Sales Manager: Renate Himmel
Parent Co: Crown Cork & Seal

21127 **Crown Industries**
155 N Park St
East Orange, NJ 07017 973-672-2277
Fax: 973-672-7536 877-747-2457
www.4rails.com
Furniture including railings and fittings: brass; also, crowd control stanchion and ropes; tables, easels and dance floors
President: Gene Loebner
VP: Mario Camerota
VP: Carmen Ware
Estimated Sales: $500,000-$1 Million
Number Employees: 5-9
Square Footage: 28000

21128 **(HQ)Crown Iron Works Company**
PO Box 1364
Minneapolis, MN 55440 651-639-8900
Fax: 651-639-8051 888-703-7500
sales@crowniron.com www.crowniron.com
Manufacturer and exporter of oil extractors, oil/fat processing systems and dryer/cooler systems including flash and spray
VP: Ralph Romano
VP Marketing/Sales: Jeffrey Scott
Product Sales Manager: Richard Ozer
VP Asian Operations: Dan Anderson
Estimated Sales: $1 - 5 Million
Number Employees: 50-99
Brands:
Crown
Wurster & Sanger

21129 **Crown Iron Works Company**
P.O.Box 1364
Minneapolis, MN 55440 651-639-8900
Fax: 651-639-8051 sales@crowniron.com
www.crowniron.com
Extractors and desolventization equipment
VP: Ralph Romano
Sales/Marketing: Jeff Scott
Estimated Sales: $20-50 Million
Number Employees: 50-99

21130 **Crown Jewels Marketing**
423 W Fallbrook Ave
Suite 204
Fresno, CA 93711 559-438-2335
Fax: 559-438-2341
mail@crownjewelsproduce.com
www.crownjewelsproduce.com
Owner: Steve Poindexter
Sales: Rob Mathias
Administration: Danell Wright
Estimated Sales: $5 - 10 Million
Number Employees: 20-49

21131 **Crown Label Company**
663 Young Street
Santa Ana, CA 92750 714-557-3830
Fax: 714-557-0401 800-422-3590
sales@crownlabel.com www.crownlabel.com
Labels, decals and tags; also, silk screening available
Owner: Gary Siposs
Estimated Sales: $1 - 2,500,000
Number Employees: 10-19

21132 **Crown Manufacturing Corporation**
147 Cross Rd
Waterford, CT 06385-1216 860-442-4325
Fax: 860-442-9658
Cabinets and boxes
President: David Parker
Estimated Sales: $1-2.5 Million
Number Employees: 5 to 9
Type of Packaging: Bulk

21133 **Crown Marking**
4270 Dahlberg Dr
Minneapolis, MN 55422 763-543-8243
Fax: 763-543-8244 800-305-5249
sales@crownmarking.com
www.crownmarking.com

Stamps, stamp pads and name plates, signs and ID badges
CEO: Gregg Prest
VP: Thomas Knauer
Estimated Sales: $1-2.5 Million
Number Employees: 5-9
Square Footage: 4600
Brands:
Bates
Cosco
X-Stamper

21134 (HQ)Crown Metal Manufacturing Company
9400 Baseline Rd
Alta Loma, CA 91701-5830 909-948-9300
Fax: 909-948-9402 glenn@computer-pals.com
www.crownmetal.com
Manufacturer and exporter of metal store fixtures, pegboard equipment and sign holders
Manager: Mike Volosin
Vice President: Glenn Dalglerish
Research & Development: Steve Varon
Sales Director: Scott Durham
Production Manager: Wayne Baker
Estimated Sales: $10-20 Million
Number Employees: 100-249
Number of Brands: 8
Number of Products: 500
Square Footage: 170000
Type of Packaging: Bulk
Other Locations:
Crown Metal Manufacturing Co.
Rancho Cucamonga CA

21135 Crown Metal Manufacturing Company
765 South State
Route 83
Elmhurst, IL 60126-4228 630-279-9800
Fax: 630-279-9807 ca-sales@crownmetal.com
www.crownmetal.com
Manufacturer and exporter of store fixtures including wall standards, brackets, showcase hardware and sign holders
Manager: Mike Volosin
Operations Manager: Mike Volosin
Estimated Sales: Less than $500,000
Number Employees: 1-4
Parent Co: Crown Metal

21136 Crown Packaging
17854 Chesterfield Airport Road
Chesterfield, MO 63005 636-681-8000
Fax: 636-681-9600 800-883-9400
www.crownpack.com
Wholesaler/distributor of packaging machinery and materials
Estimated Sales: $70 Million
Number Employees: 95
Square Footage: 18800
Other Locations:
Atlanta GA
Baltimore MD
Baton Rouge LA
Boston MA
Charlotte NC
Cincinnati OH
Cleveland OH
Dallas/Ft. Worth TX
Des Moines IA
Evansville IN
Indianapolis IN
Knoxville TN
Lenexa KS

21137 Crown Plastics
12615 16th Ave N
Plymouth, MN 55441 763-557-6000
Fax: 763-557-6638 800-423-2769
www.crownplasticsinc.com
Tea and coffee industry dispensers; whisper blend sound enclosures.
President: Tom Van Beusekom
CEO: Tom Van Beusekon
Estimated Sales: $2.5-5 000,000
Number Employees: 20-49
Number of Brands: 1
Number of Products: 1
Square Footage: 30000
Type of Packaging: Food Service, Bulk

21138 Crown Simplimatic Company
1320 Wards Ferry Rd
Lynchburg, VA 24502-2908 434-582-1200
Fax: 434-582-1284 rpeters@ambec.com
www.crown-simplimatic.com
Manufacturer and exporter of product handling equipment including tray film packaging systems, palletizers and de-palletizers, rinsers and conveyor systems
Executive VP: James Parker
Sales/Marketing Manager: Thonda Knight
Plant Manager: Bob Jones
Estimated Sales: $100+ Million
Number Employees: 250-499
Square Footage: 250000
Parent Co: Crown Cork & Seal
Brands:
Simpli-Clean
Simpli-Flex
Simpli-Pak
Simpli-Pal
Simpli-Snap
Sure-Grip

21139 Crown Steel Manufacturing
177 Newport Drive
San Marcos, CA 92069 760-471-1188
Fax: 760-471-1189 info@crownsteelmfg.net
www.crownsteelmfg.net
Kitchen and restaurant equipment including tables and sinks
President: John Carr
VP: David Carr
Estimated Sales: $3 - 5 Million
Number Employees: 20-49
Square Footage: 80000

21140 Crown Verity
37 Adams Boulevard
Brantford, ON N3S 7V8
Canada 519-751-1800
Fax: 519-751-1802 888-505-7240
info@crownverity.com www.crownverity.com
Manufacturer and exporter of stainless steel barbecues
President: William Verity
Founder: Bill Verity
CFO: Tracy McIngrrey
Quality Control: Allan Frennett
R & D: William Verity
Sales Manager: John Foulger
Number Employees: 10
Square Footage: 48000
Brands:
Chef's Choice

21141 Crown-Simplimatic
1200 S Newkirk Street
Baltimore, MD 21224-5308 410-563-6700
Fax: 410-563-6782

21142 Crown/Tonka Walk-Ins
15600 37th Ave N., Suite 100
Plymouth, MN 55446 763-541-1410
Fax: 763-541-1563 800-523-7337
sales@crowntonka.com www.crowntonka.com
Manufacturer and exporter of walk-in coolers and freezers
Senior Vice President Sales & Marketing: Greg Sullens
Estimated Sales: $5-10 Million
Number Employees: 20-49
Type of Packaging: Consumer, Food Service

21143 Crownlite ManufacturingCorporation
1546 Ocean Ave
Bohemia, NY 11716-1916 631-589-9100
Fax: 631-589-4584
Manufacturer and exporter of fluorescent and HID lighting fixtures and supplies; specializing in supermarket lighting
President: William Siegel
Sales Executive: Lois Carbonaro
Sales Manager: C Longo
Estimated Sales: $5 - 10 Million
Number Employees: 50 to 99

21144 Crucible Chemical Company
10 Crucible Ct
Greenville, SC 29605-5411 864-277-1284
Fax: 864-299-1192 800-845-8873
Food grade defoamers
President: Robert Wilson
Assistant to the President: Kathryn Stroud
Lab Manager: Danny Hawkins
Estimated Sales: $10-20 Million
Number Employees: 20 to 49
Brands:
Foamkill

21145 Crunch Time InformationSystems
129 Portland Street
Boston, MA 02114 857-202-3000
www.crunchtime.com
Purchasing and inventory control information systems
President: Bill Bellissimo
Chief Operating Officer: David Daugherty
Vice President of Client Services: Jean Fogarty
VP, Prodcut Development: James Krawcynski
Director of Marketing: Chris Bauer
Sales Manager: Michelle Bullock
Chief Operating Officer: David Daugherty
Estimated Sales: $500,000-$1 Million
Number Employees: 1-4

21146 Cruvinet Winebar Company
PO Box 10304
Reno, NV 89510-0304 775-827-4044
Fax: 800-873-7894 800-278-8463
info@cruvinetsys.com www.cruvinetsys.com
Manufacturer, importer and exporter of wine dispensing/preserving systems, nitrogen-based preserving systems and wine storage cases; also, service, repair and preventative maintenance for all makes and models of wine dispensing andcellaring systems
President/CEO: Matt Kuchnis
Vice President: Jennifer Kuchnis
Director of Sales: Matt Kuehnis
Production: Matt Kuehnis
Estimated Sales: $5-10 Million
Number Employees: 10-19
Square Footage: 19960
Brands:
Cruvinet Collector
Cruvinet Estate
Le Cavernet
Le Grand Cruvinet
Le Grand Cruvinet Mobile
Le Grand Cruvinet Premier
Le Sommelier
Petite Sommelier
Petite Sommelier Cruvinet
The Cruvinet
Ultra Cruvinet

21147 Cryochem
PO Box 20268
St Simons Island, GA 31522-8268 912-262-0033
Fax: 912-262-9990 800-237-4001
sales@cryochem.com www.cryochem.com
Manufacturer and exporter of cryogenic freezing and chilling equipment including single and tri-deck freezers, immersion and batch cabinets; also, custom-designed systems
Marketing Manager: Bryan Smith
General Manager: Frank Grillo
Estimated Sales: $1 - 5 Million
Number Employees: 18
Square Footage: 120000
Parent Co: Cryogenic Industries
Brands:
Kryospray

21148 Cryogenesis
2140 Scranton Rd
Cleveland, OH 44113 216-696-8797
Fax: 651-969-8794
jbecker@cryogenesis-usa.com
www.cryogenesis-usa.com
Manufacturer and exporter of dry ice blast cleaning equipment
President: James Becker
Sales Manager: John Whalen
Estimated Sales: $500,000-$1,000,000
Number Employees: 5-9
Brands:
Cryogenesis

21149 Cryogenic Systems Equipment
2363 136th St
Blue Island, IL 60406 708-385-4216
Fax: 708-385-4390 dsink@cryobrain.com
www.cryobrain.com

Cryogenic food processing equipment, exhaust, parts
President: Brian Sink
CFO: Devin Sink
Marketing Director: Todd Czernik
Sales Director: Brian Sink
Operations Manager: Peter Kruse
Purchasing Manager: Gary Magdziarz
Estimated Sales: $3.2 Million
Number Employees: 20-49
Number of Products: 15
Square Footage: 30

21150 Cryopak
6818 Jarry Street E
St. Leonard, QC H1P 1W3
Canada
514-324-4720
Fax: 514-324-9623 888-423-7251
bstapleton@cryopak.com www.cryopak.com
A wide range of gel packs and insulated containers for shipping perishables
President: Maurice Barakat
VP: Raj Gill
Marketing/Sales: Bruce Stapleton
Estimated Sales: $1 - 5 Million

21151 Cryovac
100 Rogers Bridge Rd
Duncan, SC 29334 864-433-2000
Fax: 864-433-2134 800-845-3456
cryovac.mkt@sealedair.com www.cryovac.com
Bonding material for conveyor use
President: Karl Deily
Quality Control: Mackey Cataenzano
R & D: Johnny Walters
Marketing Manager: John Gatch
Estimated Sales: K
Number Employees: 1,000-4,999
Parent Co: W.R. Grace

21152 Crystal Chem Inc.
1536 Brook Dr
Suite A
Downers Grove, IL 60515 630-889-9003
Fax: 630-889-9021 sales@crystalchem.com
www.crystalchem.com
Food allergen and vitamin kits for easy to use detection of allergens in both raw and processed food.
President: Priyavadan Shah
VP: Hema Shah
Safety Manager: Robert Kyle
Sales Manager: Sachin Shah
Estimated Sales: $3 Million

21153 Crystal Creative Products
PO Box 450
Middletown, OH 45042 513-423-0731
Fax: 513-423-0516 800-776-6762
Manufacturer, importer and exporter of tissue including wrapping and industrial
President: James Akers
Vice President: John Crider
Sales Director: Ed Miller
Purchasing Manager: Randy Clark
Estimated Sales: $20-50 Million
Number Employees: 100-249
Brands:
Crystal
Crystalized
Fantasy Wrap
Radiant Wrap
Tiara

21154 Crystal Lake Manufacturing
P.O.Box 159
Autaugaville, AL 36003 334-365-3342
Fax: 334-365-3332 800-633-8720
customerservice@crystallakemfg.com
www.crystallakemfg.com
Manufacturer and exporter of brooms, mops and handles
President: Edward Pearson
Chairman: Theresa Dunn
Chairman the Board: Theresa Dunn
Sales Director: Ron Poole
Estimated Sales: $10 - 20 Million
Number Employees: 100-249
Square Footage: 203000
Type of Packaging: Consumer, Food Service, Private Label, Bulk
Brands:
Crystal Lake

21155 Crystal-Flex Packaging Corporation
10 Oxford Road
Rockville Centre, NY 11570-2122 770-218-3556
Fax: 732-967-9839 888-246-7325
sales@crystalflex.com www.crystalflex.com
Manufacturer and exporter of polyethylene bags, plastic and barrier film, food packaging, pouches and laminations
President: Lesley Craig Litt
Number Employees: 6
Brands:
Flexbarrier
Oven Pak

21156 Crystal-Vision PackagingSystems
23870 Hawthorne Blvd
Torrance, CA 90505-5908 310-373-6057
Fax: 310-373-6157 800-331-3240
don@crystalvisionpkg.com
www.crystalvisionpkg.com
Shrink film; printed shrink labels; dry food weigh/fill machines; packaging machines and bag sealers; food bags; & printed stand-up food bags.
President/CEO/CFO: Donald Hilmer
Quality Control: Emilio Diaz
Sales: Karl Behrens
Public Relations: Patricia Hilmer
General Manager: Jeff Hilmer
Purchasing: Bernie Johnson
Estimated Sales: $5 Million
Number Employees: 11
Square Footage: 60000
Parent Co: AID Corporation
Brands:
Aie
Cal Vac
Crystal Vision
Curwood
Good Year
Multivac

21157 Cube Plastics
190 Maplecrete Road
Concord, Ontario, ON L4K 2B6
Canada 905-669-8669
Fax: 905-669-8646 877-260-2823
www.cubeplastics.com
Microwavable food containers in a variety of sizes.

21158 Cuerden Sign Company
1330 Mckay Ave
Conway, AR 72034-6535 501-329-6317
Fax: 501-327-3438 cuerden@swbell.net
www.cscsigns.com
Signs including interior, outdoor and electric
Owner: Jasper Burton
VP Sales: Jap Burton
Estimated Sales: $1-2.5 Million
Number Employees: 15
Square Footage: 10000

21159 Cugar Machine Company
3579 McCart Avenue
Fort Worth, TX 76110-4612 817-927-0411
Fax: 817-927-0473 www.cugarmachine.com
Food processing machinery including bin dumpers, trimlines, pivot conveyors, catwalks, washing systems, onion peelers, etc
President: Gary Greene
Estimated Sales: $1-2.5 Million
Number Employees: 5-9

21160 Culicover & Shapiro
220 S Fehrway
Bay Shore, NY 11706-1208 631-918-4560
Fax: 631-918-4561
Floor brooms and brushes
President: Richard Shapiro
Marketing: David Shaw
Estimated Sales: $500,000-$1 Million
Number Employees: 5 to 9
Square Footage: 8000

21161 Culinar
4945 Ontario Rue E
Montreal, QC H1V 1M2
Canada 514-255-2811
Fax: 514-251-2184
Consultant providing research and development for cookies
Director Sales: Daniel Merci
Estimated Sales: $1 - 5 Million
Parent Co: Culinar Canada

21162 Culinart
7609 Production Dr
Cincinnati, OH 45237 513-244-2999
Fax: 513-244-2555 800-333-5678
questions@culinart.net www.culinart.net
Tallow sculptures and specialty candles; also, bulk tallow in white, butter, cheddar and chocolate available
Founder: Dominic Palazzolo
Estimated Sales: $500,000 - $1 Million
Number Employees: 1-4
Type of Packaging: Bulk

21163 Culinary Papers
10 Maybrook Dr
Toronto, ON M1V 4B6 416-757-6768
Fax: 416-757-5183 eva@culinarypapers.com
www.culinarypapers.com
Accessories/supplies i.e. picnic baskets, cooking implements/housewares.
Marketing: Bill Benson

21164 Culligan Company
1 Culligan Parkway
Northbrook, IL 60062-6287 847-205-6000
Fax: 847-205-6030 800-527-8637
feedback@culligan.com www.culligan.com
Manufacturer and exporter of commercial/industrial water softeners, filters, deionizers, dealkalizers and reverse osmosis units
President: Tim Tousignant
Sales Director: Doug Dickinson
Estimated Sales: $35 - 40 Million
Number Employees: 250-500
Square Footage: 120000
Brands:
Bruner
Bruner-Matic
Iqs/3
Salt-Master

21165 Culmac
720 Hanford St # 2
Geneseo, IL 61254 309-944-6494
Fax: 309-944-6495 culmac@geneseo.com
Flexographic printing presses
President: Archie Cullen
Estimated Sales: $1-2.5 000,000
Number Employees: 10-19

21166 Cumberland Box & Mill Company
215 W Elder St
Cumberland, MD 21502-4606 301-724-1010
Fax: 301-777-0700
Wooden skids and lids
President: James L Ketterman
Estimated Sales: $1 - 2.5 Million
Number Employees: 5 to 9

21167 Cumberland Container Corporation
1027 N Chestnut St
PO Box 250
Monterey, TN 38574 931-839-2227
Fax: 931-839-3971
service@cumberlandcontainer.com
www.cumberlandcontainer.com
Corrugated containers
President: Eugene Jared
Computer: Randall Hardison
Plant Manager: Chris Landers
Estimated Sales: Less than $500,000
Number Employees: 100-249

21168 Cummings
PO Box 23194
Nashville, TN 37202-3194 615-673-8999
Fax: 615-782-6699
stacey.hawke@cummingssigns.com
www.cummingsstudyguides.net
Manufacturer and exporter of electric signs and marquees
President: Stephen R Kerr
Sr VP: Bruce Cornett
Executive VP National Accounts: Jerry Morrison
Estimated Sales: $20-50 Million
Number Employees: 50-99
Square Footage: 175000

21169 Cummins Label Company
2230 Glendenning Rd
Kalamazoo, MI 49001 269-345-3386
Fax: 269-345-6657 800-280-7589
lboekhoven@cumminslabel.com
www.cumminslabel.com
Pressure sensitive labels and seals
President: Phil Nagel
Vice President: Kevin Nagel
Chairman: Gordon Nagle
Marketing/Sales Executive: Len Boekhoven
Estimated Sales: $5 - 10 Million
Number Employees: 20-49
Type of Packaging: Private Label, Bulk

21170 Cummins Onan
1400 73rd Ave NE
Minneapolis, MN 55432 763-574-5000
Fax: 763-574-5298 ask.powergen@cummins.com
www.cumminsonan.com
Electric generators and engines
President: Livingston Satterthwaite
Managing Director: Neil Hill
Chief Financial Officer/Vice President: Patrick Ward
Vice President: Robert Verdurmen
Quality Control Assurance: Bill Schiro
Director, Marketing: Dennis Quinn
Director, Sales: Robert Marquardt
Plant Manager: Dave McKeeth
Director, Global Supply Chain: Samer Abughazaleh
Estimated Sales: $194 Million
Number Employees: 1,800

21171 Cunningham Field & Research
400 Carswell Ave
Daytona Beach, FL 32117-4400 386-677-8700
Fax: 386-677-5534
paul@cunninghamresearch.com
www.cunninghamresearch.com
Sensory research for the food industry
President: Mary R Cunningham
General Manager: Tom Brett
VP Corporate Operations: Frankie Tonelli
Number Employees: 20-49

21172 Cuno
400 Research Pkwy
Meriden, CT 06450 203-237-5541
Fax: 203-238-8977 800-243-6894
www.cuno.com
Manufacturer and exporter of water filtration products for food service equipment including ice and vending machines, carbonators, beverage dispensers, steamers and coffee makers. Designs, manufactures, and markets a comprehensive lineof filtration products for the separation, clarification, and purification of fluids and gasses
CFO: Frederick Flynn
Senior VP: Thomas J Hamlin
Marketing Manager: J Thompson
Estimated Sales: $243 Million
Number Employees: 1,000-4,999
Brands:
Cuno Foodservice
Cuno System One

21173 Cup Pac Contract Packagers Ltd
777 Progressive Ln
South Beloit, IL 61080 815-624-7060
Fax: 815-624-8170 info@cuppac.com
www.cuppac.com
President: Dennis James
Estimated Sales: $20 - 50 Million
Number Employees: 20-49

21174 Cup Pac Contract PackageRs
777 Progressive Ln
South Beloit, IL 61080 815-624-7060
Fax: 815-624-8170 877-347-9725
info@cuppac.com www.cuppac.com
Manufacturer and exporter of machinery for filling, tamper-evident sealing, lidding and code dating plastic cups; contract packaging available
President: Dennis James
VP Sales: Russell James
Estimated Sales: $4 Million
Number Employees: 5
Square Footage: 34000
Type of Packaging: Consumer, Food Service, Private Label, Bulk

21175 Currie Machinery Company
1150 Walsh Avenue
Santa Clara, CA 95050-2647 408-727-0424
Fax: 408-727-8892 currieco@aol.com
Manufacturer and exporter of material handling equipment including automatic palletizers, case elevators, beverage pallet stackers and powered discharge conveyors; also, dispensers including pallet, slip and tier sheet
President: Donald Currie
Marketing Director: Gerry Haase
Estimated Sales: $5-10 Million
Number Employees: 20-49
Square Footage: 80000

21176 Curry Enterprises
1248 Zonolite Road NE
Atlanta, GA 30306-2006 404-873-1163
800-241-7308
Screen printed point of purchase displays and merchandising systems
Sales Manager: Steve Cornett
Estimated Sales: $1 - 5 Million
Number Employees: 17

21177 (HQ)Curtainaire
6000-T S. Gramercy Place
Los Angeles, CA 90047 323-753-4266
Fax: 323-753-6460
Air curtains
President: Ken Burns
VP Sales: Gary Burns
Estimated Sales: $5-10 Million
Number Employees: 19
Square Footage: 32000
Brands:
Curtainaire

21178 Curtis 1000
1725 Breckinridge Parkway
Suite 500
Duluth, GA 30096 678-380-9095
877-287-8715
www.curtis1000.com
Labels; also, printing available
Estimated Sales: $50-75 Million
Number Employees: 50-99
Parent Co: American Business Products

21179 Curtis Packaging Corporation
44 Berkshire Road
Sandy Hook, CT 06482-1499 203-426-5861
Fax: 203-426-2684 www.curtispackaging.com
Manufacturer and exporter of folding paper boxes; also, hot stamping and UV coating available
Chairman/President/CEO: Donald Droppo Jr
Director: William Donston
Chief Financial Officer: Bob Johnson
Vice President: Jay Willie
Director, Quality Control: Catherine Gall
Operations Officer: Pamela Michel
Facilities Operations: David Rosato
Purchasing Manager: Louis Granata
Estimated Sales: $35 Million
Number Employees: 155
Square Footage: 150000
Parent Co: Curtis Corporation

21180 Curtis Restaurant Equipment
P.O.Box 7307
Springfield, OR 97401 541-746-7480
Fax: 541-746-7384 sales@curtisresteq.com
www.curtisresteq.com
Consultant specializing in design for the food service market; wholesaler/distributor of equipment and supplies; serving the food service market
President: Daniel Curtis
CEO: Daniel Curtis
Chief Financial Officer: Bill Kettas
Estimated Sales: $20-30 Million
Number Employees: 50-99
Square Footage: 38000

21181 Curtron Products
5350 Campbells Run Rd
Pittsburgh, PA 15205 412-787-9750
Fax: 412-787-3665 800-833-5005
info@curtronproducts.com
www.curtronproducts.com
A division of TMI, LLC and an industry leader in food service energy, traffic, and insect control solutions. Curtron Products manufactures PVC Strip Doors, Air Doors, Restaurant and Traffic Doors, Flexible PVC Swinging Doors, RackCovers, Curtains, Roll-Up Doors, and more.
President/CEO: Joe Peilert
Estimated Sales: $30 Million
Number Employees: 1-4
Square Footage: 65000
Parent Co: TMI, LLC
Brands:
Curtron
Insul-Cover
Milko Curtains
Protecto-Cover
Save-T
Save-T Air Doors

21182 Curtron Products
5350 Campbells Run Rd
Pittsburgh, PA 15205-9738 412-787-9750
Fax: 412-787-3665 800-833-5005
service@tmi-pvc.com www.bulkpvc.com
Manufacturer and exporter of leading food safety products such as strip doors, air doors, rack covers, swinging doors, hood enclosures, display cooler curtains, milk cooler curtains and eutectic packs
Manager: Joseph Klaynjans
Estimated Sales: $15 Million
Number Employees: 50-99
Square Footage: 50000
Parent Co: TMI
Brands:
Save-T

21183 Curwood
2200 Badger Ave
PO Box 2968
Oshkosh, WI 54903-2968 920-527-7300
Fax: 920-527-7309 800-544-4672
curwood@bemis.com www.curwood.com
A preferred supplier of innovative packaging materials and systems for food, beverage, household, industrial and personal care industries.
Number Employees: 1,000-4,999
Parent Co: Bemis Company
Type of Packaging: Consumer, Food Service, Private Label, Bulk

21184 Curwood, Inc.
2200 Badger Avenue
PO Box 2968
Oshkosh, WI 54903-2968 920-303-7300
Fax: 920-303-7309 800-544-4672
curwood@bemis.com www.curwood.com
Supplier of films, trays, lids and other packaging materials for the food and beverage industries.
Founder: Howard Curler
Founder: Bob Woods

21185 Curzon Promotional Graphics
1013 S 75th St
Omaha, NE 68114-4658 402-393-2020
Fax: 402-393-1502 800-769-7446
kirby@curzongraphics.com
www.curzongraphics.com
Banners, posters, decals and screen printed point of purchase displays
President: Kirby Smith
CFO: E J Stanek
Sales Manager: Bob Drake
Product Manager: Ray Serfass
Estimated Sales: $2.5 - 5 Million
Number Employees: 20-49
Square Footage: 40000

21186 Cush-Pak Container Corporation
904 State Highway 64 W
Henderson, TX 75652-5516 903-657-0555
Corrugated and wooden boxes and containers
Estimated Sales: $20-50 Million
Number Employees: 20-49

21187 Cusham Enterprises
441 Commonwealth Avenue
Erlanger, KY 41018-1425 859-727-9727
Fax: 859-727-9796
Buys and sells food equipment and companies and then resells their machinery and parts
Estimated Sales: $1 - 5 Million

21188 Custom Baking Products
111 Erick Street
Suite 129
Crystal Lake, IL 60014-1314 877-455-4938
Fax: 815-455-2735
info@custombakingproducts.com
www.custombakingproducts.com

21189 Custom Bottle of Connecticut
P.O.Box 979
Naugatuck, CT 06770-0979 203-723-6661
Fax: 203-723-6687 sales@bottles.com
www.custombottle.com
Plastic blow molded bottles and extruded containers
Vice President of Engineering: William Padgett
Vice President of Sales: Ed Jacquette
Executive Vice President, Chief Operatin: Richard Allen
Estimated Sales: $30 - 50 Million
Number Employees: 100-249
Square Footage: 75000

21190 Custom Brands Unlimited
PO Box 500
Solebury, PA 18963-0500 215-297-9842
Fax: 215-297-0161 customerbran@aol.com
Private-label gourmet mixes, candy, tea, snack items and fruit
Owner: David Vissor

21191 (HQ)Custom Business Interiors
1701 Athol Avenue
Henderson, NV 89011-4072 702-564-6661
Fax: 702-564-6767 cbilv@aol.com
www.architecturalmillwork.com
Store fixtures
General Manager: John Filar
Estimated Sales: $1 - 5 Million
Number Employees: 20
Other Locations:
Custom Business Interiors
Ventura CA

21192 Custom Business Solutions
12 Morgan
Irvine, CA 92618 949-380-7674
Fax: 949-380-7644 800-551-7674
info@cbsnorthstar.com www.cbsnorthstar.com
Point of sale hardware and software
Founder & CEO: Art Julian
Chief Financial Officer: Michael Block
VP, Software Development: Joseph Castillo
VP, Sales & Marketing: Gary Stotko
Inside Sales: Jason Perovich
Square Footage: 16528
Other Locations:
San Diego CA
Dallas TX

21193 Custom Card & Label Corporation
P.O.Box 433
Lincoln Park, NJ 07035-0433 973-492-0022
Fax: 973-492-0022
Pressure sensitive labels
Owner: John Miller
Sales Manager: John Miller
Estimated Sales: $1-2.5 Million
Number Employees: 1-4

21194 Custom Control Products
1300 N Memorial Dr
Racine, WI 53404 262-637-9225
Fax: 262-637-5728 800-279-9225
www.customcntl.com
Batch control systems, cleaning equipment, distributed control systems, expert systems, flow diverson stations, instruments/sensors, process control, process software, heat exchangers, plate, scraped surface, tubular
Estimated Sales: $1-5 000,000
Number Employees: 15

21195 Custom Conveyor & SupplyCorporation
PO Box 668
Racine, WI 53401-0668 262-634-4920
Fax: 262-634-1787
Manufacturer and designer of belt and chain conveyors and lifts
President: George Seater, Jr.
VP: Thomas Fountas
Estimated Sales: $1-2.5 Million
Number Employees: 9

21196 Custom Craft Laminates
4705 N Manhattan Ave
Tampa, FL 33614 813-870-0840
Fax: 813-877-5285 800-486-4367
mblanton@Humidorstore.com
www.humidorstore.com
Store fixtures
President: Jim Blanton
Estimated Sales: $5 - 10 Million
Number Employees: 20-49

21197 Custom Design InteriorsService & Manufacturing
2181 34th Way N.
Largo, FL 33771 727-536-2207
Fax: 727-536-2208 cdideb@juno.com
www.cdimfg.com
Manufacturer and exporter of booths, tables and bars; also, custom design services available.
President: David Goudy
VP: Deborah Goudy
Sales Director: David Goudy Jr
Estimated Sales: Less than $900,000
Number Employees: 1-10
Square Footage: 15200
Type of Packaging: Food Service, Private Label

21198 Custom DiamondInternational
895 Munck Avenue
Laval, QC H7S 1A9
Canada 450-668-0330
Fax: 450-662-1326 800-326-5926
www.diamondgroup.com
Smokers, ovens, combi-oven systems, food transport systems, heated and refrigerated stainless steel tables, counters, carts, dollies, feeding systems, etc.; exporter of food service equipment including ovens, prison food carts, andrethermalization food systems
President/CEO: Ron Diamond
CFO: D Bucci
Vice President: Allan Weber
R&D: Jason B
Marketing: Alex Malikian
Sales/Public Relations: Nick V
Production/Plant Manager: Paul Nesi
Plant Manager: H Diamond
Purchasing: George D
Square Footage: 204000
Type of Packaging: Bulk
Brands:
Brute
Custom
Diamond

21199 Custom Diamond International
895 Munck Avenue
Laval, QC H7S 1A9
Canada 450-668-0330
Fax: 450-662-1326 800-363-5926
info@diamond-group.com
www.diamond-group.com
Refrigerators, work tables, buffets, ovens, dispensers, glass washers, etc
President: Ron Diamond
CFO: Craig Aronoff
Quality Control: Hilly Diamond
Number Employees: 50
Parent Co: The Diamond Group

21200 (HQ)Custom Fabricating & Repair
1932 E 26th St
Marshfield, WI 54449 715-387-6598
Fax: 715-384-3768 800-236-8773
cfr.dawni@tznet.com www.gotocfr.com
Stainless steel filtration and cheese processing equipment; wholesaler/distributor of fittings, valves and pumps
President: Steve Mc Cullough
VP: Dawn Isenberg
Sales Director: Jay Moore
Estimated Sales: $7 Million
Number Employees: 50-99
Square Footage: 65000
Other Locations:
Custom Fabricating & Repair
Fridley MN
Brands:
Custom Fab

21201 Custom Foam Molders
122 Mulberry St
Foristell, MO 63348-0100 636-441-2307
Packaging including expandable polystyrene, food protective and thermal insulation
VP: Mike Loyet
Estimated Sales: $500,000-$1 Million
Number Employees: 1-4
Square Footage: 16000

21202 Custom Food Equipment
2266 South Walker Road
Cleveland, TX 77328-6336 281-593-1319
Fax: 281-593-2898 cfejck@aol.com
www.cheesemakers.com
General Manager: James Keliehor
Estimated Sales: $2.5-5 Million
Number Employees: 10-19

21203 (HQ)Custom Food Machinery
1881 E Market Street
Stockton, CA 95205-5673 209-463-4343
Fax: 209-463-3831
Rebuilder, importer and exporter of machinery including canning, beverage and beer bottling, fruit and vegetable, processing, filling, sterilization, can closing, packaging, cartoning, etc
President: Ron McNiel Sr
VP Sales/Advertising (Inventory): Richard Gomez-Stockton
VP Operations: Ron McNiel, Jr.
Estimated Sales: $10 - 20 Million
Number Employees: 50-99
Other Locations:
Custom Food Machinery
Sampron Nakornpathom

21204 Custom I.D.
3506 E Venice Ave
Venice, FL 34292 941-488-8430
Fax: 941-485-1969 800-242-8430
order@custom-id.com www.custom-id.com
Signs, displays and name badges
Quality Control: Jerry Barnes
Estimated Sales: Below $5 Million
Number Employees: 1-4

21205 Custom Lights & Iron
3101 Hoover Ave
National City, CA 91950-7221 619-474-8593
Fax: 619-474-8596
joe@customlightsandiron.com
www.customlightsandiron.com
Lighting fixtures
Owner: Paul Bell
Sales Manager: Joe Campbell
Estimated Sales: $20-50 Million
Number Employees: 20-49
Square Footage: 24000

21206 Custom Machining, Inc
1204 Hale Road
P.O. Box 192
Shelbyville, IN 46176-0192 317-392-2328
Fax: 317-398-8856 cmi@svs.net
www.custommachininginc.com
Pumpkin processing equipment, including washers, cutters, deseeders and dryers; tapered auger dryer, pork cutter depositor
Owner: Darrell Mollenkotpf
Estimated Sales: Less than $500,000
Number Employees: 20-49

21207 Custom Metal Designs
921 W Oakland Ave.
PO Box 783037
Oakland, FL 34778 407-656-7771
Fax: 407-656-6230 800-334-1777
sales@custommetaldesigns.com
www.custommetaldesigns.com
Manufacturer and exporter of material handling equipment including conveyors and systems, depalletizers, elevators, accumulators and bagging equipment and supplies
President: Steven Grimes
Estimated Sales: $10-20 Million
Number Employees: 50-99
Type of Packaging: Bulk

21208 Custom Metalcraft
PO Box 10587
Springfield, MO 65808-0587 417-862-0707
Fax: 417-864-7575
cmcsales@custom-metalcraft.com
www.custom-metalcraft.com

Process vessels and food processing equipment including material handling systems.
President: Dwayne Holden
CEO: Jerry Cowan
CFO: Sharon Saunders
Marketing Director: Nikki Holden
Sales Director: Drew Holden
Production Manager: Scott Higgins
Purchasing Manager: Tom Georges
Estimated Sales: $30 Million
Number Employees: 150
Number of Brands: 35
Square Footage: 125000
Brands:
Cm-L Lifters
Flex Bag
Invert-A-Bin
Transchem
Transitainer
Transtore
Voyager

21209 **Custom Metalcraft, Architectural Lighting**
65 Sprague Street
Boston, MA 02136 617-242-0868
Fax: 617-242-0743 info@custommetalcraft.com
www.custommetalcraft.com
Electric lighting fixtures
Owner: Mike Elson
Sales/ Quotations: Mike Elson
Estimated Sales: $1-2.5 Million
Number Employees: 5-9

21210 **Custom Millers Supply Company**
511 S 3rd St
Monmouth, IL 61462 309-734-6312
Fax: 309-734-7466
Grain processing equipment including corn cutters, hammer mills and trailers
President: L Howard White
Secretary: Wanda White
VP: Loran White
Estimated Sales: $1-2.5 Million
Number Employees: 5-9
Square Footage: 10000
Brands:
Big Chief
White

21211 **Custom Mobile Food Equipment**
275 South 2nd Road
Hammonton, NJ 08037-0635 609-561-6900
Fax: 609-567-9318 800-257-7855
info@foodcart.com
www.customsalesandservice.com
President: William Sikora
Estimated Sales: $5 - 10 Million
Number Employees: 100-249

21212 **(HQ)Custom Molders**
PO Box 7100
Rocky Mount, NC 27804-0100 919-688-8061
Fax: 919-688-8439 www.custommolders.com
Injection custom-molded plastics including trays
President/CEO: Hwa-Yong Jo
VP Manufacturing: Chung-Yong Jo
Estimated Sales: $20 - 30 Million
Number Employees: 100-250
Other Locations:
Custom Molders
Morrisville NC

21213 **Custom Pack**
650 Pennsylvania Dr
Exton, PA 19341 610-524-4222
Fax: 610-321-2526 800-722-7005
sales@custompackinc.com
www.custompackinc.com
Converter of plastic films, bags, and lidding stick
President: Frank Menichini
Estimated Sales: $6 Millon
Number Employees: 20-49
Square Footage: 27000
Brands:
Poleguards

21214 **Custom Packaging**
1003 Commerce Rd
Richmond, VA 23224-7007 804-232-3299
Fax: 804-232-6230 www.custompack.com
Manufacturer and exporter of corrugated boxes and point of purchase displays
President: Ed Beadels
VP: Jackie Cowden
VP Sales: Gary West
Estimated Sales: $20-50 Million
Number Employees: 10-19

21215 **Custom Packaging Systems**
200 W North Avenue
Northlake, IL 60164-2402 231-723-5211
Fax: 231-723-6301 800-968-5211
scholle@scholle.com www.scholle.com
Rhino spouted form-fit dry liners; multiply liquid liners; liquid squeeze bags for fill and discharge of highly viscous products; bulk bags; Rhino protecto tank and the Rhino mussle pack bag-in-box
President: Lee Lefleur
Estimated Sales: $10 - 20 Million
Number Employees: 150

21216 **Custom Paper Tubes**
15900 Industrial Pkwy
PO Box 35140
Cleveland, OH 44135 216-362-2964
Fax: 216-362-2980 800-343-8823
sales@custompapertubes.com
www.custompapertubes.com
Produce custom containers for the food industry. Samples available upon request
President: Jodi Lombardo
Founder: Luther Stevens
Sales Director: Phil VanDuyn
Vice President of Sales & Marketing: Kevin Kline
Marketing Manager: Emily Miller
Assistant Sales Manager: David Esper
Manufacturing Director: Paula Murad
Estimated Sales: Below $5 Million
Number Employees: 20-49
Square Footage: 30000
Type of Packaging: Consumer, Private Label

21217 **Custom Paper Tubes**
15900 Industrial Parkway
PO Box 35140
Cleveland, OH 44135 216-362-2964
Fax: 216-362-2980 800-343-8823
sales@custompapertubes.com
www.custompapertubes.com
Cosmetic pakaging, food grade packaging and see through packaging
Owner: Jodi Lombardo
Founder: Luther Stevens
Vice President of Sales/Marketing: Kevin Kline
Marketing Manager: Emily Miller
Assistant Sales Manager: David Esper
Manufacturing Director: Paula Murad

21218 **Custom Plastics**
250 Laredo Dr
Decatur, GA 30030 404-373-1691
Fax: 404-373-8605
sales@custom-plasticssinc.com
www.custom-plasticsinc.com
Acrylic sneeze guards for salad bars, indoor plastic signs and skylights; also, custom acrylic fabrication available
President: Scarlett Luke
Estimated Sales: $1-2.5 Million
Number Employees: 5-9
Square Footage: 12000

21219 **Custom Pools & Spas**
373 Shattuck Way
Newington, NH 03801-7870 603-431-7800
Fax: 603-431-5109 800-323-9509
info@custompools.com www.custompools.com
Manufacturer and wholesaler/distributor of ultraviolet disinfection equipment for opaque fluids, juices, etc
Founder: Gene Short
Vice President: Darrel Short
VP: David Short
Estimated Sales: $3 - 5 Million
Number Employees: 20-49

21220 **Custom Quality Products**
1645 Blue Rock St
Cincinnati, OH 45223 513-541-1191
Fax: 513-541-1192 800-477-4720
www.cqpinc.com
Temperature controls, cold storage doors and hardware
President: George White
Estimated Sales: $2.5-5 000,000
Number Employees: 20-49

21221 **Custom Rubber Stamp Company**
326 5th Street North East
Crosby, MN 55461 612-866-4977
Fax: 866-485-9205 888-606-4579
orders@crstamp.com www.crstamp.com
Manufacturer, exporter and importer of custom rubber stamps, self-inking and pre-inked stamps, embossers, engraved plastic signs, name tags and inks
President: James Grimes
Co-Owner: Jean Grimes
Employee: Paula Steigauf
Estimated Sales: Below $5 Million
Number Employees: 1-4
Square Footage: 4000
Brands:
2000 Plus
Aero
Albany
Base Lock
Brailltac
Brooklyn
Comet
Cooke
Cosco
Dapon
Eagle Zephyr
Imprintz
Quik
Rowmark
Triumph
X-Stamper

21222 **Custom Sales & Service Inc.**
275 South 2nd Road
Hammonton, NJ 08037 609-561-6900
Fax: 609-567-9318 800-257-7855
info@foodcart.com
www.customsalesandservice.com
Manufacturer and exporter of mobile food equipment including trucks, trailers, vans and cart systems
CEO: William Sikora
VP Sales/Marketing: Lynda Sikora
Estimated Sales: $5-10 Million
Number Employees: 100-249
Square Footage: 140000

21223 **(HQ)Custom Stamp Company**
37449 Regal Blue Trail
Anza, CA 92539-8806 323-292-0753
Fax: 323-292-0754
Manufacturer and exporter of pressure sensitive labels, rubber stamps, name plates, stencils, daters, marking products, metal tags and serial numbering on metal
President: Jack Coleman
Sales Manager: Steve Glass
Number Employees: 8
Square Footage: 3600
Type of Packaging: Food Service
Brands:
Cosco
Custom
Dymo
Garvey
Jrs
Melind
Roovers

21224 **(HQ)Custom Stamping & Manufacturing**
1340 SE 9th Ave
Portland, OR 97293-0340 503-238-3700
Fax: 503-238-3740
Custom metal stampers and foil food containers
Owner: Dave Stoudt
General Manager: D Stoudt
Engineer: D Marcotte
Estimated Sales: $10-20 Million
Number Employees: 50-99
Square Footage: 120000

21225 **Custom Systems Integration Company**
P.O.Box 130414
Carlsbad, CA 92013 760-635-1099
Fax: 760-766-3307 bill@csicinc.com
www.csicinc.com

Machinery and services for the packaging and automation industries serving the food and beverage markets. Including feeders, conveyors and custom automation
President: Bill Davis
Estimated Sales: $500,000-$1 Million
Number Employees: 1-4
Square Footage: 10000
Type of Packaging: Food Service, Private Label
Brands:
Archimedes

21226 Custom Table Pads
455 Hayward Ave N
St Paul, MN 55128-5374 651-714-5720
Fax: 651-501-9246 www.sentrytablepad.com
Table pads and cloths; also, place mats
Owner: Steve Mc Kay
Estimated Sales: $10 - 20 Million
Number Employees: 20-49

21227 Custom Tarpolin Products
8095 Southern Blvd
Youngstown, OH 44512-6336 330-758-1801
Fax: 330-758-9872 info@customtarpaulin.com
www.customtarpaulin.com
Commercial awnings
President: Gerald Robinson
Estimated Sales: $10-20 Million
Number Employees: 10-19

21228 CustomColor Corporation
14320 W 101st Terrace
Lenexa, KS 66215 913-730-3100
Fax: 913-730-9301 888-605-4050
info@customcolor.com www.customcolor.com
Menu boards
CEO: Matthew Keith
Director Strategic Marketing: Jan Ray
Corporate Sales Rep.: Joe Goodwin
Estimated Sales: $5-10 Million
Number Employees: 50-99

21229 Customized Equipment SE
4186 Railroad Ave
Tucker, GA 30084-4484 770-934-9300
Fax: 770-934-0610
service@teddybearsupply.com
www.teddybearsupply.com
Manufacturer and exporter of packaging machinery including automatic and semi-automatic baggers and sealers; also, random and fixed size carton taping machinery
President: Kermit Cooper
Sales Director: Bruce Cooper
Estimated Sales: $1 - 5 Million
Number Employees: 10 to 19
Square Footage: 20000

21230 Cutco Vector
P.O.Box 810
Olean, NY 14760-0810 716-373-6148
Fax: 716-790-7160 www.cutco.com
Manufacturer and exporter of knives, forks and spoons
President: Brent Driscoll
President: James Stitt
Executive Vice President of Eastern Regi: Amar Dave
President, Chief Operating Officer: John Whelpley
Estimated Sales: H
Number Employees: 500-999
Parent Co: Alcas-Cutco Corporation
Type of Packaging: Consumer

21231 (HQ)Cutler Brothers Box & Lumber Company
711 W Prospect Ave
PO Box 217
Fairview, NJ 07022 201-943-2535
Fax: 201-943-8532 cutler711@aol.com
www.cutlerpallets.com
Wooden and reconditioned pallets; also, scrap wood removal and pallet repair services available
Owner: Greg Cutler
VP: Greg Cutler
VP: Jed Cutler
Estimated Sales: $12 Million
Number Employees: 50-99
Square Footage: 30000
Other Locations:
Cutler Brothers Box & Lumber
Woodland PA

21232 Cutler Industries
8300 Austin Avenue
Morton Grove, IL 60053-3209 847-965-3700
Fax: 847-965-8585 800-458-5593
info@cutlerovens.com www.cutlerovens.com
Manufacturer and exporter of revolving tray, rack and utility ovens and under counter proofers
Director Marketing Support: Kathleen Casey
Estimated Sales: $1 - 5 Million
Number Employees: 50-99
Square Footage: 340000

21233 Cutler-Hammer
811 Green Crest Drive
Westerville, OH 43081-2838 614-882-3282
Fax: 614-895-7111 www.ch.cutler-hammer.com
Open control and automation solutions including software, logic products, operator interface, sensors, acuators, and industrial PC's
Estimated Sales: $30 - 50 Million
Number Employees: 250-500

21234 Cutrite Company
PO Box 851
Fremont, OH 43420-0851 419-332-1380
Fax: 419-334-2383 800-928-8748
sales@arius-eickert.com www.scissorguys.com
Manufacturer and exporter of cooking knives, poultry shears and meat processing specialty tools and utensils
Sales Manager: Ramon Eickert
General Manager: Becky Smith
Estimated Sales: $3-5 Million
Number Employees: 20-50
Square Footage: 100000
Parent Co: A. Eickert Company
Brands:
Arius-Eickert
Cutrite
Proline

21235 Cutter Lumber Products
10 Rickenbacker Cir
Livermore, CA 94550 925-443-5959
Fax: 925-443-0648 sales@cutterlumber.com
www.cutterlumber.com
Pallets and skids
President: Tony Palma
Sales Manager: Todd Samuels
Estimated Sales: $1-2.5 Million
Number Employees: 1-4
Other Locations:
Cutter Lumber Products
Willits CA

21236 Cuutom Poly Packaging
3216 Congressional Pkwy
Fort Wayne, IN 46808 260-483-4008
Fax: 260-484-5166 800-548-6603
info@custompoly.com www.custompoly.com
Polyethylene, polypropylene, trash, shopping and laboratory bags; importer of sample bags
Owner: Michael Carpenter
Estimated Sales: $2.5-5,000,000
Number Employees: 10-19
Square Footage: 13000

21237 CxR Company
2599 N Fox Farm Rd
PO Box 1114
Warsaw, IN 46581-1114 574-269-6020
Fax: 574-269-7140 800-817-5763
info@cxrcompany.com www.cxrcompany.com
Industrial x-ray machines; also, x-ray inspection services available
President: Cassandra Stewart
Vice President: Paula Zeigler
Research & Development: Tim Murphy
Sales Manager: Scott Stewart
Plant Manager: John Sherman
Estimated Sales: $5-10 Million
Number Employees: 10-19
Square Footage: 32000
Brands:
Accuvue

21238 CxR Company
2599 N Fox Farm Rodd
Warsaw, IN 46580 574-269-6020
Fax: 574-269-7140 800-817-5763
info@cxrcompany.com www.cxrcompany.com
Safety X-ray inspection for contaminants
President: Cassandra Stewart
CEO: Barb Colbes
Vice President: Paula Zeigler
Research/Development: Tim Murphy
Sales: Scott Stewart
Plant Manager: John Sherman
Estimated Sales: $5-10 Million
Number Employees: 10-19

21239 Cyborg Equipment Corporation
8 Graham St
Wareham, MA 02571 508-291-0999
Fax: 781-297-0097 cec-bz@cyborgeq.com
www.cyborgeq.com
Packaging, vacuum, tumblers, crede machine, form, fill and seal machines, temp monitoring device
Manager: Jennifer Lawrence
Estimated Sales: $1 - 2.5 000,000
Number Employees: 1-4

21240 Cyclamen Collection
2140 Livingston St
Oakland, CA 94606 510-434-7620
Fax: 510-434-7624 CYCLAMENCOLL@aol.com
www.cyclamencollection.com
Manufacturer and exporter of dinnerware, serveware, bakeware and vitrified stoneware, pitchers, vases, and lamps
Owner: Julie Sanders
Sales: Julie Sanders
Estimated Sales: $500,000-$1,000,000
Number Employees: 5-9
Number of Products: 200+
Type of Packaging: Bulk
Brands:
Calla
Cyclamen
Ergo
Fallingwater
Fiamma
Forma
Mosaica
Nelson
Nova
Patchwork
Stella

21241 Cycle Computer Consultants
95 Jerusalem Ave
Hicksville, NY 11801 516-733-1892
Fax: 516-935-0697 info@cyclecomputer.com
Consultant offering computer services for food distributors
Owner: Anthony Manzillilo
Marketing Manager: Frank Berelson
Number Employees: 10-19
Parent Co: Tomark-Cyber Associates

21242 Cyclonaire Corporation
P.O.Box 366
York, NE 68467 402-362-2000
Fax: 402-362-2001 800-445-0730
sales@cyclonaire.com www.cyclonaire.com
Manufacturer and exporter of pneumatic conveying equipment and accessories
President: Jerry Elfring
CEO: Don Baker
VP: Scott Schmidt
Sales: Joe Morris
Plant Manager: Deryl Kliewer
Purchasing: Sheila Miller
Estimated Sales: $10 - 20 Million
Number Employees: 20-49
Square Footage: 40000
Brands:
Cyclojet
Cyclolift
Cyclolok
Cyclonaire
Vibra Pad

21243 Cynter Con Technology Adviser
656 Quince Orchard Road
7th Floor
Gaithersburg, MD 20878-1409 301-208-3958
Fax: 301-990-3434 800-287-1811
info@cyntercon.com www.cyntercon.com
Consultant specializing in technology for the food service and retail industries
Business Development Manager: Francis Carmello
Number Employees: 12
Square Footage: 40000

21244 (HQ)Cyntergy Corporation
400 E Gude Dr
Rockville, MD 20850-1365 301-315-8610
Fax: 301-315-8611 800-825-5787
info@cyntergy.com www.cyntergy.com
Consultant specializing in project management, training, implementation/training and documentation for the food service and retail industries
President: Mitchell Rambler
Chairman/CEO: Rob Grimes
VP Sales/Marketing: Cort Grey
Estimated Sales: $5-10 Million
Number Employees: 50-99
Type of Packaging: Bulk

21245 Cyplex
6311 Primrose Ave Apt 18
Los Angeles, CA 90068-4413
Fax: 323-436-0190 cyplex@cyplex.net
www.cyplex.net
Developer of point of sale hardware and software
Estimated Sales: $1-2,500,000
Number Employees: 10-19
Brands:
Alliance

21246 Cypress Systems
40365 Brickyard Drive
Suite 101
Madera, CA 93636 559-229-7850
Fax: 559-225-9007 800-235-2436
info@cypresshome.com www.cypsystems.com
Electrochemical instrumentation
President: Dr Webser
Business Manager: Huei Chi Alice Sutherland
Estimated Sales: $500,000-$1 Million
Number Employees: 6

21247 Cyrk
14224 167th Avenue
Monroe, WA 98272
Fax: 800-545-8840 800-426-3125
www.cyrk.com
Manufacturer and exporter of advertising novelties including screen printed promotional materials
Sales Manager: Steve Paradiso
Estimated Sales: $40 Million
Number Employees: 250-500
Type of Packaging: Food Service

21248 Cyro Industries/Degussa
P.O.Box 677
Parsippany, NJ 07054-0677 973-541-8000
Fax: 973-541-8445 800-631-5384
cyro@degussa.com www.cyro.com
Manufacturer and exporter of molding and extrusion compounds for food bins and displays
President: Thomas Bates
Marketing Director: Cynthia Zey
Public Relations: Gail Wood
Number Employees: 500-999
Parent Co: Cytec Industries/Rohm GmbH
Brands:
Cyrolite G-20
Xt

21249 Cyvex Nutrition
1851 Kaiser Ave
Irvine, CA 92614 949-622-9030
Fax: 949-622-9033 888-992-9839
sales@cyvex.com www.cyvex.com
High quality, reliable and accurate refractometers and polarimeters for liquid concentration control
Director, Operations: Quang La
R&D: Denise Lam
Marketing: Charlene Lee
Number Employees: 5-9
Number of Brands: 1
Number of Products: 3
Square Footage: 15000
Brands:
Atago Brand

21250 D & F Equipment
8641 Highway 227 North
PO Box 275
Crossville, AL 35962 256-528-7842
Fax: 256-528-7171 800-282-7842
terrycleghorn@dfequip.com www.dfequip.com
Equipment and machinery for meat processing
Owner: Larry Fortenberry
Owner: Lynn Fortenberry
Owner: Dawn Knox
SVP: Greg Cagle
Director of Engineering: Gary Cambron
Corporate Purchasing/Marketing: Gene Pledger
Sales Manager: Terry Cleghorn
Human Resources Manager: Ricky Farmer
VP of Operations & Service: Joey Knott
Accounts Receivable: Cathy Sims
Accounts Payable: Towania Williams
Number Employees: 20

21251 D & L Manufacturing
1818 S 71st St
Milwaukee, WI 53214 414-256-8160
Fax: 414-476-0564 sales@kempsmith-dl.com
www.kempsmith-dl.com
Manufacturer and exporter of machinery including file folder, paper converting, cutting, creasing, folding carton, folding and glueing, laminating, printing, embossing and rotary die cutting
President: Brett Burris
CEO: Robert Burris
Sales Director: Judy Lewis
Estimated Sales: $10-20 Million
Number Employees: 20-49
Square Footage: 58000

21252 (HQ)D De Franco & Sons
1000 Lawrence St
Los Angeles, CA 90021 213-627-8575
Fax: 213-627-9837 800-992-3992
Defrancomp@aol.com
www.defrancoandsons.com
Manager: Paul De Franco
CEO: Paul DeFranco
CFO: Jerry De Franco
VP: Gerald DeFranco
R&D: Salvatore DeFranco
Estimated Sales: $15 Million
Number Employees: 20-49
Square Footage: 50000
Type of Packaging: Consumer, Food Service, Private Label, Bulk
Brands:
Sunripe

21253 D&D Sign Company
6232 Southwest Pkwy
Wichita Falls, TX 76308-0803 940-692-4643
Fax: 940-692-1344 ddsigns@nts-online.net
Metal, electric, neon, plexiglass and wooden signs; also, installation and services available
Co-Owner: Mark Patterson
Estimated Sales: $1-2.5 Million
Number Employees: 5-9

21254 D&L Manufacturing
1818 S 71st St
Milwaukee, WI 53214 414-256-8160
Fax: 414-476-0564 sales@kempsmith-dl.com
www.kempsmith-dl.com
Bottle washers and fillers
President: Les Johnson
CEO: Robert E Burris
Estimated Sales: $10 - 20 Million
Number Employees: 20-49

21255 D&M Pallet Company
118 Morris St
Neshkoro, WI 54960-9599 920-293-4616
Fax: 920-293-4660
Pallets, skids, crates and boxes
President: David Heinzelman
Estimated Sales: $500,000 - $1 Million
Number Employees: 1 to4

21256 D&M Products
2310 Michigan Avenue
Santa Monica, CA 90404 310-453-0485
Fax: 310-828-9670 800-245-0485
sales@dm-products.com www.dm-products.com
Hydro-air pressure guns for cold stream cleaning
President and CFO: Karl Hirzel
Estimated Sales: Below $5 Million
Number Employees: 1-4
Brands:
D&M

21257 D&S Manufacturing Company
14 Sword St Ste 4
Auburn, MA 01501-2171 508-799-7812
Fax: 508-753-3468
Knives; also, screens for granulators and choppers
President: Graham Scarsbrook
Estimated Sales: $1 - 2.5 Million
Number Employees: 5 to 9
Parent Co: L. Hardy

21258 D&W Fine Pack
800 Ela Road
Lake Zurich, IL 60047
Fax: 847-438-0369 800-323-0422
www.dwfinepack.com
Manufacturer and exporter of metal baking pans for muffins, cupcakes, breads, baguettes, pizza, cakes, pies, buns and rolls; also, aluminum foil containers, plastic domes, plastic containers, and plastic clamshells
President & CEO: Dave Randall
CFO, VP Finance: Tom Nickele
VP, CIO: Michael Casula
VP Sales Grocery & Processor: Rick Barton
SVP Operations: Jay DuBois
Number Employees: 310
Square Footage: 1200000
Type of Packaging: Consumer, Food Service, Private Label, Bulk
Brands:
Bakalon
Bake King
Chicago Metallic
Cm Packaging
Sure-Bake
Sure-Bake & Glaze
Ultraslik
Village Bakers

21259 D'Addario Design Associates
123 W 44th Street
New York, NY 10036-4000 212-302-0059
Fax: 212-764-7262
Design consultant specializing in labels, cartons, logos, wooden boxes and POS and merchandising aids
President: Thomas D'Addario
VP: Adam D'Addario
Estimated Sales: Less than $500,000
Number Employees: 1-4
Square Footage: 2000

21260 D'Lights
533 West Windsor Road
Glendale, CA 91204 818-956-5656
Fax: 818-956-2157 slsmgr@dlights.com
www.dlights.com
Manufacturer and exporter of lighting fixtures and food warmers
President: Kent Erle Sokolow
General Manager: Steve Sink
Estimated Sales: Below $5 Million
Number Employees: 10

21261 D. Henry & Sons
58480 Frudden Road
Bradley, CA 93426-9674 805-472-2600
Fax: 805-472-2626 800-752-7507
mark@dhenryandsons.com
www.dhenryandsons.com
Weight control systems, casing stuffer, extrudeers, ham stuffing equipment, sausage linkers, stuffers and accessories
CEO: David F Henry
Vice President: Mark Henry
Estimated Sales: $1.5 Million
Number Employees: 1-4

21262 D. Picking & Company
119 S Walnut St
Bucyrus, OH 44820 419-562-6891
Fax: 419-562-0078 www.dpicking.com
Copper kettles for use in the processing of apple butter and decorative items
Owner: Helen Picking-Neff
Office Manager: Steve Schifer
Director: Sylvia Cooper
Estimated Sales: $5-10 Million
Number Employees: 5-9

21263 D.A. Berther
9000 W Becher St
West Allis, WI 53227 414-328-1995
Fax: 414-328-1818 877-357-9622
info@daberther.com www.daberther.com

Stainless steel food equipment, supplies, tables and sinks
President/CEO: David A. Berther
CFO: David Berther
Vice President/Sales Consultant: Jeff Berther
Inside Sales/Rental Manager: Jim Lidwin
Estimated Sales: $1 - 2.5 Million
Number Employees: 10-19
Square Footage: 21000

21264 D.A. Colongeli & Sons
16 Pomeroy Street
Cortland, NY 13045-2241 607-753-0888
Fax: 607-756-2997 800-322-7687
dacsoup@odyssey.net
www.knorrinstitutionalfoodproducts.com
Established in 1970; purveyors of fine foods.
President: Donald Colongeli
Number Employees: 1
Square Footage: 4000
Type of Packaging: Food Service
Brands:
Fancy
Fine
Gourmet
Haco Foods
Knorr

21265 D.D. Bean & Sons Company
207 Peterborough St
Jaffrey, NH 03452 603-532-8311
Fax: 603-532-6001 800-326-8311
info@ddbean.com www.ddbean.com
Manufacturer and exporter of matchbooks
President: D Bean
VP: Peter Leach
Manager: Terry Fecto
Estimated Sales: $20-50 Million
Number Employees: 100-249
Square Footage: 100000
Type of Packaging: Food Service, Private Label

21266 D.D.& D. Machinery
7620 Seneca St
East Aurora, NY 14052-9457 716-652-4410
Fax: 716-652-0677 info@dddmachinery.com
www.dddmachinery.com
President: Norbert Gerhard
Estimated Sales: $3 - 5 Million
Number Employees: 1-4

21267 D.R. McClain & Son
7039 E Slauson Ave
Commerce, CA 90040-3620 323-722-7900
Fax: 323-726-4700 800-428-2263
dale@alfrescogrills.com www.acmemcclain.com
Bakery equipment including dough rollers, sheeters and molders
Owner: Jeff Branstein
National Sales Manager: Norm Gwinn
Estimated Sales: $1 - 5 Million
Number Employees: 50-99
Square Footage: 76000

21268 D.W. Davies & Company
3200 Phillips Ave
Racine, WI 53403 262-637-6133
Fax: 262-637-3933 800-888-6133
dwdavies@dwdavies.com www.dwdavies.com
Chemicals, cleaners, floor finishes, boiler compounds and dishwashing detergents.
CEO: David Davies
President: Daniel Davies
CFO: David Rubenstein
Estimated Sales: $10-20 Million
Number Employees: 50-99
Square Footage: 40000
Type of Packaging: Consumer, Private Label
Brands:
D.W. Concentrate

21269 DAC Lighting
420 Railroad Way
PO BOX 262
New York, NY 10543 914-698-5959
Fax: 914-698-6061 www.daclighting.com
Manufacturer and importer of lighting fixtures including electric and flourescent
Customer Service: Peggy Guglielmo
General Manager: Moshe Toledo
Estimated Sales: $1-2.5 Million
Number Employees: 6
Square Footage: 100000

21270 (HQ)DBE Inc
310 Rayette Road
Concord, ON L4K 2G5
Canada 905-738-0353
Fax: 905-738-7585 800-461-5313
marketing@poseidondbe.com
www.poseidondbe.com
Manufacturer, importer and exporter of seafood equipment including commercial fish/lobster tanks, electrical fish sealers, customized seafood tanks
President: Fima Dreff
Marketing Director: Lesya Sklyarenko
Sales Director: Joe Albis
Public Relations: Lesya Sklyarenko
Plant Manager: Jean-Pierre Paquette
Estimated Sales: $10 - 20 Million
Number Employees: 15
Number of Brands: 6
Square Footage: 50000
Other Locations:
DBE Food Equipment
Kyiv
Brands:
Dde

21271 DC Tech
619 East 19th Street
Kansas City, MO 64108-1743 816-842-9090
Fax: 816-842-4121 877-742-9090
sales@dctech-inc.com www.dctech-inc.com
Meat packing and food processing equipment including carts, tables, smokehouse trucks and vats. Manufacturer of grocery store and restaurant equipment, and custom stainless steel fabrication. Polished aluminum performance car partsbattery covers and turbo shields
President: William O Mitchum
Sales/Marketing Executive: Buddy Mitchum
Purchasing Manager: Robert Mitchum
Estimated Sales: $3 - 5 Million
Number Employees: 10-19
Square Footage: 148000

21272 (HQ)DCI
P.O.Box 1227
St Cloud, MN 56302-1227 320-252-8200
Fax: 320-252-0866 sales@dciinc.com
www.dciinc.com
Manufacturer and exporter of stainless steel processing and storage tanks as well as OEM components (tank heads, manways, mixers/agitators,parts). Also offering DCI Site-Fab (field fabrication of any size tank up to 500,00 gallons).
President/Owner: Jeffrey Keller
VP: Chuck Leonard
Estimated Sales: $20 - 50 Million
Number Employees: 100-249
Square Footage: 88000
Other Locations:
D C I
Cedar City UT

21273 DCM Tech
4455 Theurer Blvd
PO Box 1304
Winona, MN 55987 507-452-4043
Fax: 507-452-7970 800-533-5339
interest@dcm-tech.com www.dcm-tech.com
Supplier of metal cutting tools and machines
President/Owner: Don Arnold
Financial Controller: Jennifer Fruth
Technical Specialist: Mike Anderson
Engineering Manager: Jerry Lawson
Purchasing Manager: Denise Aitken
Estimated Sales: $4 Million
Number Employees: 39

21274 DCS IPAL Consultants
1043 Autoroute Chomedey
Laval, QC J7W 4V3
Canada 450-973-3338
Fax: 450-973-3339
arbour@mail.gebo-indust.com
www.sidel.com
Consultant specializing in packaging and process engineering
Engineering & Material Handling: Marc Aury
Controls and Automation Dir.: Franck Klotz
Director Operations: Alex Gieysztor
Number Employees: 250
Square Footage: 56000
Parent Co: Gebo Industries

21275 DCS Sanitation Management
7864 Camargo Rd
Cincinnati, OH 45243 513-271-9300
Fax: 513-271-5710 800-837-8737
lchapman@dcs.ms.com www.pssi.co
Consultants and sanitation programs for the meat industry; sanitation supplies and equipment, including cleaning compounds and solutions, cleaning and washing equipment and accessories, and sanitizers
President: Tom Murray
Estimated Sales: $1 - 5 Million
Number Employees: 1-4

21276 DCV BioNutritionals
3521 Silverside Road
Wilmington, DE 19810-4900 800-641-2001
Fax: 302-695-5188 800-641-2001
dcvfood@dcvinc.com
Microencapsulation of nutrition, baking and specialty food ingredients: choline and betaine salts
Estimated Sales: $50 - 100 Million
Number Employees: 50-99

21277 DD Williamson & Company
1901 Payne St
Louisville, KY 40206 502-895-2438
Fax: 502-895-7381 800-227-2635
info@ddwmson.com www.caramel.com
Liquid and powder caramel colorings for desserts and baked goods, beverages, cereals & snacks
President: Theodore Nixon
CEO: Sindy Nixon
VP R & D: Owen Parker
Estimated Sales: $20 - 50 Million
Number Employees: 50-99

21278 DECI Corporation
One Todd Drive
Burgettstown, PA 15021 724-947-3300
Fax: 724-947-3621 deci@decicorp.com
www.decicorp.com
Consultant specializing in food processing plant engineering and design
Vice President: Bruce Mahoney
Estimated Sales: $2.5-5 Million
Number Employees: 20-50
Square Footage: 29824

21279 DEFCO
165 Sawmill Road
Landenberg, PA 19350-9302 215-274-8245
Fax: 610-274-0342
Fiberglass reinforced thermoset plastic process equipment; also, installation and maintenance available
VP: John Field
Estimated Sales: $1-2.5 Million
Number Employees: 10-19
Square Footage: 16000

21280 DEMACO
411 S Ebenezer Road
Florence, SC 29501-7916 407-952-6600
Fax: 407-952-6683

21281 DF Ingredients, Inc
127 Elm Street
Suite 200
Washington, MO 63090 636-583-4801
Fax: 630-583-4877 888-583-0802
michael@dfingredients.com
www.dfingredients.com
Ingredients and dairy products
President: Michael Husmann
Vice President: Larry Rice
Sales Rep: Richard Kuddes
Sales Rep: Kenneth Johnson
Sales Rep: Jim Wesselschmidt

21282 DFL Laboratories
111 E. Wacker Dr.
Suite 2300
Chicago, IL 60601 312-938-5151
Fax: 209-521-1005 blagoyevich@worldnet.att.net
www.silliker.com
Consultant specializing in chemical and microbiological testing services
Manager: Stephanie Campbell
Estimated Sales: $10-20,000,000
Number Employees: 100-249

21283 **DH/Sureflow**
402 SE 31st Avenue
Portland, OR 97214-1929 503-236-9263
Fax: 503-236-9264 800-654-2548
sureflow@dhsales.com www.dhsales.com
Manufacturer and exporter of drain cleaning machinery and power snakes
Owner and President: Doug Hemenway
VP: Geoff Hemenway
Number Employees: 3
Square Footage: 10000
Brands:
Sureflow

21284 **DHM Adhesives**
P.O.Box 2418
Calhoun, GA 30703-2418 706-629-7960
Fax: 706-625-2819 800-745-1346
www.dhmadhesives.com
Pressure sensitive and hot melt adhesives
President: Matt Devine
CFO: Bill Matthews
Vice President of Procurement: Bob Goodman
Vice President of Sales and Marketing: Bob Shumaker
Plant Manager: David Chase
Purchasing Manager: Milton Bryson
Estimated Sales: $5 - 10 Million
Number Employees: 10-19

21285 **DHP**
1206 E 20th St
Farmington, NM 87401-4215 505-326-3431
Fax: 505-327-2934 877-711-4347
info@dhptraining.com www.dhptraining.com
Water treatment, training, products and service
President: David Paul
Vice President: Cal Tingy
Head of Marketing Department: Bruce Caris
Estimated Sales: $100-200 Million
Number Employees: 20-49

21286 **DI Engineering Corporation**
1658 Cole Blvd Ste 290
Lakewood, CO 80401 303-231-0045
Fax: 303-231-0050 www.diec-group.com
Export and import of cans and end making machinery, fill line equipment, spare parts, and associated technologies, equipment sales and service
VP: Patty Locke
Estimated Sales: $2.5-5 Million
Number Employees: 1-4

21287 **DI Manufacturing**
13335 C Street
Omaha, NE 68144 402-330-5650
info@dimanufacturing.com
www.dimanufacturing.com
Specialty food products including gluten free foods, garlic bread, wrapped breads, pizza, cookie dough
Type of Packaging: Food Service, Bulk

21288 **DIC International**
35 Waterview Blvd Ste 100
Parsippany, NJ 07054-1270
Fax: 201-836-4962 tomiyama@dica.com
www.dic.co.jp/eng/products/pps/global.html
Manufacturer, importer and exporter of a natural nontoxic chlorophyll colorant
President: Shintaro Asada
CFO: Yuzi Koike
Marketing Manager: Y Akiyama
Number Employees: 20-49
Parent Co: Dainippou Ink & Chemicals
Brands:
Co-Enzyme Q-10
Linablue A
Pantethine
Sqvalene

21289 **DIPIX Technologies**
1051 Baxter Road
Ottawa, ON K2C 3P2
Canada 613-596-4942
Fax: 613-596-4914 info@dipix.com
www.dipix.com
President: Anton Kitai
Director of Sales: Geoff Evans
Chief Operating Officer: Peter Wakeman
Estimated Sales: $1 - 5 Million
Number Employees: 20-50

21290 **DL Enterprises**
399 Cameron St
Etters, PA 17319-9775 717-938-1292
Fax: 717-938-5110 dlentp@paonline.com
www.panetwork.com/aisle-a-gator
Battery powered wet/dry vacuum cleaners for grocery warehouses, distribution centers, food processors, warehouses and retail stores
President: Dick Lewis
Estimated Sales: $300,000-500,000
Number Employees: 1-4
Square Footage: 10000
Brands:
The Aisle-A-Gator

21291 **DLX Industries**
1609 Roote 202
Pomona, NY 10970-2902 845-517-2200
www.dlxonline.com
Manufacturer and exporter of vinyl-imprinted advertising specialties and promotional items
Estimated Sales: $78,000
Number Employees: 2
Number of Products: 120
Square Footage: 12804
Parent Co: DLX

21292 **DM Sales & Engineering**
1325 Sunday Drive
Indianapolis, IN 46217-9334 317-783-5493
Fax: 317-787-5642 www.dmsales-eng.com
Decorative and thermoforming plastic molding and plastic packaging products
President: David D Mickel
Estimated Sales: $2.5-5 Million
Number Employees: 20-49

21293 **DMC-David ManufacturingCompany**
1600 12th Street NE
Mason City, IA 50401-2543 641-424-7010
Fax: 641-424-7017
Manufacturer and exporter of grain-handling equipment including cleaners and dryers; also, moisture sensing devices for flowing or moving material
CEO and President: Wes Cagle
Sales/Marketing Manager: Jim Balk
Estimated Sales: $20-50 Million
Number Employees: 100-249
Square Footage: 157000
Brands:
Cal-Cu-Dri
Calc-U-Dryer
Hi-Cap
Stirator

21294 **DMG Financial**
950 South Cherry St
Suite 424
Denver, CO 80246 303-756-1794
Fax: 303-756-9484 888-331-3882
info@dmgfinancial.com www.dmgfinancial.com
Management consultants specializing in management consulting, mergers and acquisitions, financial services
President: Karl Edmunds
Estimated Sales: $1-5 Million
Number Employees: 1-4

21295 **DMN Incorporated**
220 South Woods St.
West Memphi, AR 72301 870-733-9100
Fax: 870-733-9101 dmnfo@dmn-inc.com
www.dmn-inc.com
Rotary valves, diverter valves
President: Steve Bremmers
Estimated Sales: Below $5 Million
Number Employees: 5-9

21296 **DOWL HKM**
4041 B Street
Anchorage, AK 99503 907-562-2000
Fax: 907-563-3953 800-478-3695
info@dowlhkm.com www.dowlhkm.com
Glycine, chelating agents, surfactants, dispersing agents and emulsion polymers
Chairman: Gary R. Simonich
CEO: Andrew Liveris
Executive VP: Geoffery Merszel
Marketing Manager: Art Paulidis
Commercial Manager: Mark DeGeorge
Estimated Sales: $2.5-5 Million
Number Employees: 20-49

21297 **DPC**
21 W Fornance St # 150
Norristown, PA 19401-3300 610-277-3000
Fax: 610-277-1264 800-220-9473
marcaro@disposableproductsco.com
www.dpcllc.com
Disposable and nonwoven counter and table wipers in folded, roll and portion control dispenser box form
President: Jim Drucker
CFO: Daniel Chojnacki
VP: Jeff Berk
Director Marketing: D Bancroft
Estimated Sales: $1-2.5 Million
Number Employees: 50-99
Square Footage: 600000
Parent Co: RTR Industries
Other Locations:
D.P.C.
Greenville SC

21298 **DQB Industries**
32165 Schoolcraft Rd
Livonia, MI 48150 734-525-5660
Fax: 734-525-0437 800-722-3037
customerservice@dqb.com www.dqb.com
Manufacturer and exporter of brooms, brushes, dusters and mop heads
Owner: Donald Weinbaum
Sales Manager: John Avgoustis
Estimated Sales: $1 - 5 Million
Number Employees: 50-99
Type of Packaging: Consumer, Food Service

21299 **DQCI Services**
5205 Quincy St
Saint Paul, MN 55112-1400 763-785-0484
Fax: 763-785-0584 info@dcqi.com
www.dqci.com
Laboratory providing chemical analysis and testing services to the dairy industry; also, calibration standards
Owner: Tom Janas
Estimated Sales: $5 - 10,000,000
Number Employees: 20-49

21300 **DR McClain & Son**
PO Box 95
Pico Rivera, CA 90660-0095 562-699-4542
Fax: 562-692-0026 800-428-2263
Dough rollers and sheeters

21301 **DR Technology**
73 South St
Freehold, NJ 07728 732-780-4664
Fax: 732-780-1545
sales@DRTechnologyInc.com
www.drtechnologyinc.com
Manufacturer and exporter of wet scrubbers used to control atmospheric emissions in food manufacturing plants
President: Richard Schwartz
CEO: Doris Schwartz
Marketing Director: Debra Kruggen
Estimated Sales: $.5 - 1 million
Number Employees: 5-9
Square Footage: 2500

21302 **DRS Designs**
217 Greenwood Ave
Bethel, CT 06801 203-744-2858
Fax: 203-743-4389 888-792-3740
info@drs-designs.com www.drs-designs.com
Rubber stamps, engraved signs and pressure sensitive labels; also, general printing, laminating and hot stamping services available
Manager: Samantha Conrad
Estimated Sales: $500,000-$1 Million
Number Employees: 1-4
Square Footage: 1200

21303 **DSA-Software**
34 School St Ste 201
Foxboro, MA 02035 508-543-0400
Fax: 508-543-0856 sales@dsasoft.com
www.dsasoft.com
Warehouse management software
President: Lee Petri
Estimated Sales: Below $5 Million
Number Employees: 5-9
Brands:
Foxware Dc Label
Foxware Dc Manager
Foxware Edi Manager
Foxware Rf Manager

21304 **DSI**
15304 NE 95th St
Redmond, WA 98052 425-885-5223
Fax: 425-882-2025 rich_kish@fmc.com
Cutting, boning devices and processing equipment, defatting machines, trimming devices, dicers, and slicers
President: Jim Heber
Estimated Sales: $5-10 000,000
Number Employees: 20-49

21305 **DSI Data Specialists**
1021 Proctor Drive
Elkhorn, WI 53121-2027 262-723-5726
Fax: 262-723-5767 info@dataspecialists
www.dataspecialists.com
Process accountablity and reconciliatoin business software for food and dairy industry
President: Sherrie Mertes
Estimated Sales: $2.5-5 Million
Number Employees: 10-19

21306 **DSI Process Systems**
4630 W Florissant Ave
St Louis, MO 63115-2233 314-382-1525
Fax: 314-382-5234 800-342-5374
jack@dsiprocess.com www.dsiprocess.com
Conveyor systems, stainless steel food processing equipment, tanks, and sanitary piping
President: Jack W Luechtefeld
Marketing Contact: Jack Luechtefeld
Estimated Sales: $10 - 20 Million
Number Employees: 50-99

21307 **DSL Forming Collars**
6504 Mayfair St
Houston, TX 77087 713-645-9177
Fax: 713-645-9131 800-460-3164
sales@dslformers.com www.dslformers.com
Forming collars to fit draw bar, pull belt, vacuum pull belt and continuous motion baggers and packaging machinery
President: Louis Posada
R & D: Simon Gonales
Marketing Manager: Simon Gondales
Estimated Sales: Below $5 000,000
Number Employees: 10-19

21308 **DSM Nutritional Products**
45 Waterview Blvd
Parsippany, NJ 07054 973-316-1029
Fax: 973-257-8420 800-526-0189
webshop.dnpna@dsm.com
www.dsmnutritionalproducts.com
Supplier of vitamins, carotenoids and other fine chemicals to the feed, food, pharmaceutical and personal care industries.
President/CEO: Leendert Staal
President: Dr Chris Goppelsroeber
SVP Finance/Control & Info Management: Geert Mooren
Research & Development: Manfred Eggerersdorfer
COO: Bob Hartmayer
Global Marketing: Mauricio Adade
Account Manager: Matt Owca
SVP Human Resources: Jacoline van Blokland
SVP Operations: Mark Stock
Global Communications: Alex Filz
Estimated Sales: $1 - 5 Billion
Number Employees: 1,200
Type of Packaging: Bulk

21309 **DSO Fluid Handling Company**
300 McGaw Drive,
Raritan Center Edison
Irvington, NJ 08837 732-225-9100
Fax: 732-225-9101 1 8-0 5-7 68
info@dsofluid.com www.dsofluid.com
Owner: Darrin Oppenheim
Estimated Sales: $10-20 000,000
Number Employees: 10-19

21310 **DSR Enterprises**
38404 Hidden Creek Way
Mechanicsville, MD 20659 301-472-4990
Fax: 610-942-4273 800-238-0310
dsr@dsrenterprises.com www.dsrenterprises.com
Electrical panel management schedules and estimates loads
Partner: Randy Junkins
President: David Groh
Estimated Sales: Below $1 000,000
Number Employees: 4
Square Footage: 1500
Type of Packaging: Private Label

21311 **DSW Converting Knives**
1504 8th Avenue N
Birmingham, AL 35203 205-322-2021
Fax: 205-322-2576 sales@dswknives.com
www.dswknives.com
Manufacturer and exporter of machine knives
President: Chris Mc Ilvaine
Estimated Sales: Below $5 Million
Number Employees: 10-19
Type of Packaging: Bulk

21312 **DT Converting Technologies - Stokes**
207 Mill St
Bristol, PA 19007-4808 215-788-3500
Fax: 215-781-1122 800-635-0036
stokes-info@dtindustries.com
www.dtindustries.com
Manufacturer tablet presses, granulators, tablet deduster, tornado mills
President: Ken Peterson
Vice President: George Graff
Research & Development: Dave Breen
Marketing Director: Barb McDevitt
Sales Director: George Graff
Number Employees: 20-49
Parent Co: DT Industries
Brands:
Genesis Removable Head Press
Tablet Press 328
Valitah 3000

21313 **(HQ)DT Industries**
313 Mound St
Dayton, OH 45402 937-586-5600
Fax: 937-586-5601 kcook@dindustries.com
Manufacturer and exporter of packaging systems and equipment
Manager Marketing Communications: Kenneth Cook
Estimated Sales: $200 - 250 Million
Number Employees: 20-49

21314 **DT Packaging Systems**
18105 Trans Canada
Kirkland, QC H9J 3Z4
Canada 514-694-2390
Fax: 514-694-6552 888-384-3343
lvilleneuve@kalishdti.com
www.dtindustries.com

21315 **DT Packaging Systems**
7 New Lancaster Road
Leominster, MA 01453-5224 978-537-8534
Fax: 978-840-0730 800-851-1518
www.imanova.com
Line integration conveyors, online quality assurance, filling by count, bulk handling
President: Jim Ririe
Plant Manager: Stewart Harvey
Estimated Sales: $5-10 Million
Number Employees: 100-249

21316 **DUCTSOX**
9866 Kapp Court
Peosta, IA 52068 563-588-5300
Fax: 563-588-5330 866-563-7729
cpinkalla@ductsox.com www.ductsox.com
Fabric air dispersion systems
President: Cary Pinkalla
Key Person: Lou Wiegand
Number Employees: 100-249

21317 **DWL Industries Company**
65 Industrial Road
Lodi, NJ 07644 973-916-9958
Fax: 973-916-9959 888-946-2682
cs@wincous.com www.wincodwl.com
Wholesaler/distributor, importer and exporter of knives, utensils and tableware; serving the food service market
President: David Li
Officer: Jieyui Ding
VP Sales: Steve Chang
Number Employees: 15
Square Footage: 40000

21318 **DYCO**
50 Naus Way
Bloomsburg, PA 17815 570-752-2757
Fax: 570-752-7366 800-545-3926
sales@dyco-inc.com www.dyco-inc.com
Conveyers, bagger and debagger machines
Finance Executive: Dan Bierdziewski
Estimated Sales: $1 - 5 Million
Number Employees: 50-99

21319 **Dabrico**
1555 Commerce Dr
Bourbonnais, IL 60914 815-939-0580
Fax: 815-939-7798 888-439-0580
sales@dabrico.com www.dabrico.com
President: Efrain A Davila
Marketing Manager: Maria Carter
Director of Sales and Marketing: Chuck Goranson
Purchasing Manager: Mario Trevino
Estimated Sales: $3 - 5 Million
Number Employees: 10-19

21320 **Dacam Corporation**
PO Box 310
Madison Heights, VA 24572-0310 434-929-4001
Fax: 434-847-4487 www.dacammachinery.com
Manufacturer and exporter of packaging machinery
President: Ed Tolle
Sales And Marketing: Dean Hargis
Director Engineering: David Vaughan
Estimated Sales: $2.5-5 Million
Number Employees: 20-49
Square Footage: 80000
Brands:
Dacam

21321 **Dacam Machinery**
113 N Amherst Highway
Madison Heights, VA 24572 434-369-1259
Fax: 434-369-1949 www.dacammachinery.com
Produces high quality packaging and material handling equipment for the food and beverage industries.
Estimated Sales: $2.5-5 Million
Number Employees: 20-49

21322 **Daclabels**
10491 Brockwood Rd
Dallas, TX 75238 214-340-2055
Fax: 214-340-2272 800-483-1700
daclbl@aol.com www.daclabels.com
Printed labels and tags; wholesaler/distributor of thermal transfer printers and ribbons
President: Harlan Leeds
CEO: Jay Fair
R & D: Greg Swindle
VP: Judy Vinson
Marketing Manager: Greg Towers
Customer Support: Michelle Ywhite
Estimated Sales: $5 - 10 Million
Number Employees: 10-19

21323 **Dadant & Sons**
51 S 2nd St
Hamilton, IL 62341 217-847-3324
Fax: 217-847-3660 888-922-1293
dadant@dadant.com www.dadant.com
Injection molded hardware and honey handling and processing equipment; also, chocolate melters
President: Tim Dadant
CFO: Tom Ross
VP: T Ross
Quality Control: Gary Stanspery
Estimated Sales: $1-2.5 Million
Number Employees: 100-249

21324 **Dade Canvas Products Company**
12067 Tech Road
Silver Spring, MD 20904 301-680-2500
Fax: 301-680-0851 thomasawning@prodigy.net
www.thomasawning.com
Commercial awnings
Owner: Michael Riley
Estimated Sales: $1-2.5 Million
Number Employees: 1-4

21325 **Dade Engineering**
15150 Nighthawk Drive
Tampa, FL 33625 813-264-2273
Fax: 813-343-8117 800-321-2112
richard@starsouth.us www.daeco.net
Manufacturer and exporter of walk-in coolers and freezers and cold storage doors
President: Joanne Goodstein

Estimated Sales: $5 - 10 Million
Number Employees: 10-19
Square Footage: 80000
Brands:
Daeco

21326 **Daesang America**
1 University Plz Ste 407
Hackensack, NJ 07601 201-488-4010
Fax: 201-488-4625
President: David Park
Estimated Sales: $20 - 50 Million
Number Employees: 5-9

21327 **Daewoo Heavy IndustriesAmerica Corporation**
4350 Renaissance Pkwy
Cleveland, OH 44128-5793 216-595-1212
Fax: 216-595-1214 800-323-9662
tbaronch@dhiac.com www.doosanlift.com
Manufacturer, importer and exporter of industrial trucks
President: Mike Lavelle
VP Sales/Marketing: Michael Lavelle
Public Relations: Trudi Baronchuck
Estimated Sales: $1 Billion+
Number Employees: 20-49
Parent Co: Daewoo Heavy Industries

21328 **Daga Restaurant Ware**
500 Alakawa St Rm 220c
Honolulu, HI 96817 808-847-3100
Fax: 808-843-2977
Restaurant supplies
Owner: Noreen Quirk
Vice President: Alfred Coscina
Estimated Sales: $2.5-5 000,000
Number Employees: 1-4

21329 **Dagher Printing**
11775 Marco Beach Dr
Jacksonville, FL 32224 904-998-0911
Fax: 904-998-0921 www.dagher.com
Commercial printer of business stationery; color printing available
President: Joseph G Dagher
Treasurer: Mouma Khourly
VP: Sam Dagher
Estimated Sales: $1-2.5 Million
Number Employees: 10-19
Square Footage: 8000

21330 **Dahl Tech, Inc.**
5805 Saint Croix Trl N
Stillwater, MN 55082 651-439-2946
Fax: 651-439-2976 800-626-5812
daltechinc@qwestoffice.net
www.dahltechplastics.com
Custom blew molding company and manufacturer of plastic containers, devices, and hollow structures for the food packaging, chemical, automotive, agricultural, healthcare, recreational, and household products industries.
President/CEO: Mark Dahlke
Sales: Nichole Blekum
Plant Manager: Brian Hell
Estimated Sales: $5 Million
Number Employees: 50
Square Footage: 128000
Type of Packaging: Consumer, Food Service, Private Label, Bulk

21331 **Dahmes Stainless**
6300 County Road 40
New London, MN 56273 320-354-5711
Fax: 320-354-5712 info@dahmes.com
www.dahmes.com
President: Forrest Dahmes
CFO: Dan DeGeest
Sales Director: Steve Frank
Production Manager: Jeff Kampsen
Purchasing Manager: Brad Doyle
Estimated Sales: $5-10 000,000
Number Employees: 20-49
Type of Packaging: Consumer, Bulk

21332 **Daido Corporation**
1031 Fred White Boulevard
Portland, TN 37148 615-323-4020
Fax: 615-323-4015 866-219-9972
info@daidocorp.com www.daidocorp.com
President: Mike Kato
CEO: Steve Pudles
Sales Executive: Lee Carrier
Estimated Sales: $10 - 20 Million
Number Employees: 20-49

21333 **Daily Printing**
2333 Niagara Ln N
Plymouth, MN 55447 763-475-2333
Fax: 763-449-6320 800-622-6596
info@dailyprinting.com www.dailyprinting.com
Manufacturer and exporter of size reduction equipment for grinding, deagglomerating and pulverizing feeds, foods, spices, etc
President: Pete Jacobson
CFO: Ken Rein
Quality Control: Don Bergeron
Estimated Sales: $10 - 20 Million
Number Employees: 100-249
Square Footage: 100000

21334 **Dairy Concepts LP**
3253 E. Chestnut Expressway
Springfield, MO 65802 417-829-3400
Fax: 717-566-8466 877-596-4374
mwilliams@dairiconcepts.com
www.dairiconcepts.com

21335 **Dairy Concepts LP**
3253 E. Chestnut Expressway
Springfield, MO 65802 417-829-3400
Fax: 717-566-8466 877-596-4374
mwilliams@dairiconcepts.com
www.dairiconcepts.com

21336 **(HQ)Dairy Conveyor Corporation**
38 Mount Ebo Rd S
Brewster, NY 10509 845-278-7878
Fax: 845-278-7305 info@dairyconveyor.com
www.dairyconveyor.com
Manufacturer and exporter of material handling equipment for dairies and ice cream plants
President: Karl Kleinschrod
CEO: Karl Kleinsahrod
Southeast Regional Sales Manager: Greg Reid
Eastern Regional Sales Manager: Tony Gomez
Estimated Sales: $12 Million
Number Employees: 50-99
Square Footage: 12000

21337 **Dairy Foods**
1050 IL Route 83
Suite 200
Bensenville, IL 60106 630-694-4341
Fax: 630-227-0527 phillipsd@bnp.com
www.bnp.com
Market Analyst: Jerry Dryer
Estimated Sales: Below $5 Million
Number Employees: 10

21338 **Dairy Service & Manufacturing**
1818 Linn Street
North Cancas, MO 64116 816-472-0011
Fax: 816-472-7935 800-825-0011
dsikc@dsiprocess.com www.dsiprocess.com
Custom fabrication, processing and packaging
Owner: Jack W Luechtefeld
Controller: Charlie Siebert
Accounts Manager: Gordon Gosejohan
Vice President: Gary Rinck
Technical Sevices/Refrigeration Manager: Dave Smith
Customer service: Brandon Barr
Marketing Manager: Lori Collier
Inside Sales: Nicole Wohletz
Customer Service: Dawn Jinson
Operations Manager: Georgia Pilla
Project Engineer: Paul Wallace
Estimated Sales: $2.5 - 5 000,000
Number Employees: 50-99

21339 **Dairy Services, Inc.**
450 W Meadow Street
Stratford, WI 54484
800-221-3947
dsistratford@dairyservicesinc.com
www.dairyservicesinc.com
Majority Owner: Jerome Oelke
Number Employees: 11
Square Footage: 32000

21340 **Dairy Specialties**
8536 Cartney Ct
Dublin, OH 43017 614-764-1216
Fax: 614-855-3114 dsibrown@aol.com
Exporter, importer and wholesaler/distributor of milk proteins, flavor producing enzymes and dried dairy ingredients
President: David Brown
CEO: V Brown
Estimated Sales: $2 Million
Number Employees: 1-4
Square Footage: 3000
Type of Packaging: Bulk

21341 **Dairyland Plastics Company**
N 8986 County Rd
Colfax, WI 54730-4500 715-962-3425
Plastic bags
Owner: David Haugle

21342 **Dakota Corrugated Box**
4501 N 2nd Ave
Sioux Falls, SD 57104-0676 605-332-3501
Fax: 605-332-3496
Corrugated containers
President: Robert Bittner
CFO: Bob Bittner
Sales Manager: Mike Bartlett
General Manager: Mike Bartlett
Estimated Sales: $2.5 - 5 Million
Number Employees: 20 to 49

21343 **Dakota Valley Products,Inc.**
419 3rd St.
Willow Lake, SD 57278 605-625-2526
Fax: 605-352-0558
tim@dakotavalleyproducts.com
www.dakotafarms.com
Agricultural products marketing company
Estimated Sales: $1 - 5 Million
Number Employees: 4

21344 **Dalare Associates**
217 S 24th St
Philadelphia, PA 19103-5593 215-567-1953
Fax: 215-567-1168 info@dalarelab.com
www.dalarelab.com
Analytical and Environmental analysis through a full range of laboratory services.
President: Joseph J Strug Jr
Estimated Sales: $500,000-$1 Million
Number Employees: 5-9

21345 **Daleco**
1000 Wilmont Mews
5th Floor
West Chester, PA 19382 610-429-0181
Fax: 610-429-0818 info@dalecoresources.com
www.dalecoresources.com
Steamed cheeseburger making machines
President: Robert Gattilia
Estimated Sales: $.5 - 1 million
Number Employees: 1-4
Brands:
Burg'r Tend'r

21346 **Dalemark Industries**
575 Prospect St Ste 211
Lakewood, NJ 08701 732-367-3100
Fax: 732-367-7031 sales@dalemark.com
www.dalemark.com
Manufacturer and exporter of coding, imprinting and labeling equipment including thermal, hot stamp, ink jet and contact printers for web, sheets, flat products, containers and bulk packaging
President: Michael Delli Gatti
CFO: Kathy Scalzo
Research & Development: Thurman Becker
Marketing: Maria Rau
Sales: Maria Rau
Purchasing: Maria Rau
Estimated Sales: $2 Million
Number Employees: 10
Number of Brands: 15
Number of Products: 25
Square Footage: 12000
Type of Packaging: Food Service
Brands:
Codaire
Consecu-Printer
Handi-Coda
Htd
Inka-Rol
Jet Pen
Perma-Grip
Srr Roller

21347 (HQ)Dallas Container Corporation
8330 Endicott Ln
Dallas, TX 75227 214-381-7148
Fax: 214-381-8279 www.dallascontainer.com
Corrugated containers
President: Rod Turnipseed
Estimated Sales: $10-20 Million
Number Employees: 50-99
Other Locations:
Dallas Container Corp.
Albuquerque NM

21348 Dallas Group of America
374 Us Highway 22
Whitehouse, NJ 08888 908-534-7800
Fax: 908-534-0084 800-367-4188
info@dallasgrp.com www.dallasgrp.com
Magnesium silicate, frying oil purifiers, filter aids and absorbents; exporter of magnesium silicate
Owner: Bob Dallas Sr
Estimated Sales: $10-20,000,000
Number Employees: 50-99
Type of Packaging: Food Service, Bulk
Brands:
Dalsorb
Haze-Out
Magnesol
Xl

21349 Dallas Roth Young
100 N Cottonwood Drive
Suite 108
Richardson, TX 75080-4772 972-233-5000
Fax: 972-235-5210 rydallas@ix.netcom.com
Executive search firm specializing in selection and placement of food industry personnel
President: Ben Dickerson
Sales/Marketing Manager: Chad Dickerson
Number Employees: 3
Square Footage: 800
Parent Co: Winston Franchise Corporation

21350 Dalloz Safety
10 Thurber Blvd
Smithfield, RI 02917-1858 401-233-0333
Fax: 401-232-1830 800-977-9177
jwomer@dallozsafety.com www.cdalloz.com
Ear muffs, laser eyewear, safety spectacles, goggles and disposable and reusable respirators and ear plugs
Director Marketing Communication: Elizabeth Antry
Director Sales: Scott Walker
Estimated Sales: $50-100 Million
Number Employees: 10-19
Brands:
Bilsom
Gpt
Glendale

21351 Dalls Semiconductor
160 Rio Robles
San Jose, CA 95134 972-702-9250
Fax: 972-371-3748 888-629-4642
sales-us@maximintegrated.com
www.maxim-ic.com
President and Chief Executive Officer: Tun‡ Doluca
SVP and Chief Financial Officer: Bruce E. Kiddoo
President; Chief Executive Officer; Dire: Tunc Doluca
Vice President, Test Engineering: Rob Georges
Vice President, Quality: Bryan Preeshl
Vice President of Sales and Marketing: Walter Sangalli
Vice President of Human Resources: Steve Yamasaki
SVPof Manufacturing Operations: Vivek Jain
Estimated Sales: $1 - 5 Million
Parent Co: Maxim Integrated

21352 Dalmec
469 Fox Ct
Bloomingdale, IL 60108 630-307-8426
Fax: 630-307-8436 800-935-8686
sales@dalmecusa.com www.dalmec.com
Industrial manipulators for handling rolls, barrels, boxes, pails or custom product manufacture highly ergonomic manipulators, combined with bispoke tooling heads, custom-built to handle a specific product
Manager: Al Izzo
Sales Manager: Al Killian
Branch Manager: Allan Izzo
Estimated Sales: $2.5-5 000,000
Number Employees: 10-19

21353 Dalton Electric HeatingCompany
28 Hayward St
Ipswich, MA 01938 978-356-9844
Fax: 978-356-9846 dalton@daltonelectric.com
www.daltonelectric.com
Industrial heating products-Wall-Flex® Cartridge Heaters.
Sales: E W Whitney III
Plant Manager: Steve Lounes
Estimated Sales: $5-10 000,000
Number Employees: 41
Square Footage: 17000

21354 Damas Corporation
1977 N Olden Avenue Ext
Suite 289
Trenton, NJ 08618-2112 609-695-9121
Fax: 609-695-9225
Manufacturer and exporter of washing and drying equipment for laboratory glassware, trays, tote bins, tubs, pallets and carts
President: David M Smith
Engineer: Dave Smith
Estimated Sales: $1-2,500,000
Number Employees: 5-9
Brands:
Aquasan
Thermajet

21355 Damascus/Bishop Tube Company
795 Reynolds Industrial Park Road
Greenville, PA 16125-4203 724-646-1500
Fax: 724-646-1514
FDA approved steel stainless pipe and tubing for dairy processors
President: Brent Ward
Estimated Sales: $1 - 5 Million
Number Employees: 100-249

21356 Damon Industries
12435 Rockhill Avenue, NE
Alliance, OH 44601 330-821-5310
Fax: 330-821-6355 800-362-9850
info@damonq.com www.damonq.com
Manufacturer cleaning chemicals and disinfectants; consultant specializing in food safety and HACCP
President: Amy Damon
Administrative Vice President: Deborah Martin
Executive Vice President: R.C. Brumbaugh
Vice President, Sales: Scott Butterfield
Service Manager: Ken Hacker
Production Manager: Daryl Culler
Warehouse & Traffic Manager: William Davis
Estimated Sales: $50-100 Million
Number Employees: 100-249
Square Footage: 45000

21357 Damons Graoo
11 Green Pond Road
Rockaway, NJ 07866-2001 973-664-1000
Fax: 973-664-1305
Manufacture high pressure enjection molded products for food and agriculture
Estimated Sales: $300,000-500,000
Number Employees: 10

21358 Damp Rid
W.M. Barr
P.O. Box 1879
Memphis, TN 38101-6948 407-851-6230
Fax: 407-851-6246 888-326-7743
www.damprid.com
Manufacturer and exporter of mildew preventatives, moisture absorbers and odor eliminators
President: Darien Jalka
CFO: Ken Lasseter
Quality Control: Oliver Cunanan
Sales Director: Darin Galka
Purchasing Manager: Roy Rosado
Estimated Sales: $5-10 Million
Number Employees: 10
Square Footage: 288000
Parent Co: Tetra Technologies Incorporated
Type of Packaging: Consumer
Brands:
Damp Rid
Fresh-All
Magic Disk

21359 Damrow Company
894 S Military Rd
Fond Du Lac, WI 54935 920-922-1500
Fax: 920-922-1502 800-236-1501
info@damrow.com www.damrow.com
Dairy and food processing equipment including cheese making, automated control systems, process and storage tanks, evaporators, CIP systems and process piping; exporter of cheese making equipment
Manager: Gary Ring
Sales Director: Mark Steffens
Operations: Todd Martin
Estimated Sales: $10 - 20 Million
Number Employees: 5-9
Square Footage: 150000
Parent Co: Carlisle Process Systems

21360 Dan Mar Co
2131 N Collins St
B433-738
Arlington, TX 76011 817-822-5767
Fax: 218-338-5909 danmarco1@msn.com
www.danmarco.net
Supplier of products in antimicrobial control for beef, pork and poultry industries
President: Paul Edwards
Estimated Sales: Under $500,000
Number Employees: 1-4

21361 Dan-D Foods Ltd
11760 Machrina Way
Richmond, BC V7A 4V1
Canada 604-274-3263
Fax: 604-274-3268 800-633-4788
info@dan-dpak.com www.dan-d-pak.com
Fine food importer, manufacturer and distributor of cashews, dried fruits, rice crackers, snack foods, spices etc. from around the world.
Chairman/President/CEO/Founder: Dan On
Number Employees: 500
Type of Packaging: Food Service, Bulk

21362 (HQ)Dana Labels
7778 SW Nimbus Ave
Beaverton, OR 97008-6423 503-646-7933
Fax: 503-641-4728 800-255-1492
info@danalabels.net www.danalabels.net
Labels and labeling machines
Owner: Wilfredo Rabanal
Sales Manager: Dave Pancoast
Estimated Sales: $20 - 50 Million
Number Employees: 20-49
Brands:
Axcess

21363 Dana S. Oliver & Associates
21 Island Drive
Savannah, GA 31406-5238 912-354-1455
Fax: 912-354-2455 bigd1942@aol.com
Consultants for executive searches and placement in the food and beverage industry
President: Dana Oliver

21364 (HQ)Danafilms
5 Otis St
Westborough, MA 01581 508-366-8884
Fax: 508-898-0106 www.danafilms.com
Manufacturer and exporter of polyethylene films for packaging.
President: Sherman Olson
VP Sales: Bob Simoncini
Marketing Director: Steve Crimmin
Sales Manager: Steve Crimmin
General Manager: Alan Simoncini
Purchasing Manager: Alan Simoncini
Estimated Sales: $20-30 Million
Number Employees: 50-99
Square Footage: 40000
Type of Packaging: Consumer, Food Service, Private Label, Bulk
Other Locations:
Danafilms
Hopedale MA

21365 Danaher Controls
1675 N Delany Rd
Gurnee, IL 60031-1282 847-662-2666
Fax: 847-662-6633 800-873-8731
dancon@dancon.com www.dancon.com

Industrial controls, counters, encoders, tachometers, temperative controllers
President: Steve Boeitzka
VP: Susan Ottmann
Estimated Sales: $20 - 50 Million
Number Employees: 1,000-4,999
Number of Products: 8

21366 Danbury Plastics
239 Castleberry Industrial Dr
Cumming, GA 30040-9051 678-455-7391
Fax: 203-790-6801 info@danburyplastics.com
www.danburyplastics.com
Manufacturer, importer and exporter of compression and injection molded bottle caps as well as linings and gaskets
President: Michael Da Cruz
Quality Control: Diana Cepada
Sales: Donna Dyke
Plant Manager: Rocco Grosse III
Estimated Sales: $2.5-5 Million
Number Employees: 10-19
Square Footage: 18000
Type of Packaging: Consumer, Private Label

21367 Dandelion Chocolate
740 Valencia Street
San Francisco, CA 94110 415-349-0942
800-785-2301
info@dfandelionchocolate.com
www.dandelionchocolate.com
Chocolates
President: Cameron Ring
CEO: Todd Masonis

21368 (HQ)Danfoss
7941 Corporate Dr
Baltimore, MD 21236-4925 410-931-8250
Fax: 410-931-8256 baltimore@danfoss.com
www.acr.danfoss.com
Supplier of mechanical and electronic components for air conditioning and refrigeration systems
President: Peter Simson
Executive VP/CFO: Ole Steen Andersen
Executive VP/COO: Hans Kirk
Operations: Henrik Christensen
Estimated Sales: $100 Million+
Number Employees: 100-249
Square Footage: 47000
Parent Co: Danfoss A/S
Brands:
Adap-Kool
Akcess
Climatech
Danfoss
Ec 1000
Eci
Iris
No Sweat
Powerfocus
Rc 2000

21369 Danfoss Drives
2995 Eastrock Drive
Rockford, IL 61109-1737 815-398-2770
Fax: 815-398-2869 www.us.water.danfoss.com
President: Jergen Clausen
CEO: Jergen Clausen
Executive VP & CFO: Frederik Lotz
Estimated Sales: $1 - 5 Million

21370 Danfoss VLT Drives
4401 N Bell School Rd
Loves Park, IL 61111 815-639-8600
Fax: 815-639-8000 800-432-6367
salesinformation@danfoss.com
www.danfossdrives.com
Electronic AC motor controls
President: Arnaldo Ricca
Sales: Brian Kelly
Estimated Sales: $100 Million+
Number Employees: 10-19

21371 Danger Men Cooking
3 Lumen Ln
Highland, NY 12528-1903 845-691-7029
Fax: 845-691-2852
cowboypete@dangermencooking.com
www.dangermencooking.com
BBQ accesories and gear for men
President: Peter Rooney
Estimated Sales: $10 - 20 Million
Number Employees: 10-19
Brands:
Bbq Sauce
Danger Men Cooking
Hot Sauce
Ketchupepper
Steak Sauce
Tough Guy's
Wussy Hot Sauce

21372 Daniel Boone Lumber Industries
1375 Clearfork N
Morehead, KY 40351 606-784-7586
Fax: 606-783-1858
New and reconditioned wooden pallets and skids
President: Gail Lincoln
Regional Sales Manager: Mike Coburn
Sales Manager: Mike Coburn
Plant Supervisor: Elvis Middleton
Estimated Sales: Below $5 Million
Number Employees: 10-19
Square Footage: 25000

21373 Daniel J. Bloch & Company
PO Box 263
Essex, CT 06426-0263 860-767-8204
Fax: 860-767-8205 cofiman@aol.com
Roasters and roasting machines
Owner: Daniel Bloch

21374 Daniel Woodhead Company
3411 Woodhead Drive
Northbrook, IL 60062-1892 847-272-7990
Fax: 847-272-8133
General packing house electrical and safety equipment and devices; AC Waterlite plugs and connectors, quick disconnect molded control connectors, temporary lighting, portable outlet boxes, electric reels, wire mesh grips, DC batteryconnectors and push b
Estimated Sales: $2.5-5 000,000
Number Employees: 10-19

21375 Danieli Awnings
2530 Oak St
Napa, CA 94559-2227 707-257-6100
Fax: 707-257-0318 www.danieliawnings.com
Commercial awnings
President: Charles Gibson
Estimated Sales: $500,000-$1,000,000
Number Employees: 5-9

21376 Daniels Food Equipment
310 North Clayborn Ave
PO Box 341
Parkers Prairie, MN 56361 218-338-5000
Fax: 218-338-5909 danielsfood@midwestinfo.net
www.danielsfood.com
Supplier of stainless steel products for meat industry; including grinders, stuffers, grinders, mixers, etc
Owner: Keith Anderson
President: Marty Weibye
Estimated Sales: $2 Million
Number Employees: 15

21377 Danish Food Equipment
1633 E Madison St
Petaluma, CA 94954-2320 707-763-0110
Fax: 707-763-1303 maersk@dfeas.com
www.dfeas.com
Owner: Flemming Maersk
Vice President: Flemming Maersk
Estimated Sales: $1 - 5 Million

21378 Daniso USA
PO Box 653
Pine Brook, NJ 07058-0653 201-784-9300
Fax: 201-784-0604 infous@calchauvet.com
Estimated Sales: $1 - 5 Million

21379 Danlac
1917 Twilight Ln
Hudson, WI 54016-9271 715-381-5575
Fax: 715-381-5576
Butter processing and dairy equipment
Owner: Liane Niedermhoefer
Estimated Sales: less than $500,000
Number Employees: 1-4

21380 Danmark Packaging Systems
PO Box 560901
Lewisville, TX 75056-6901 972-625-8311
Fax: 972-370-9113
Shrink packaging machinery including semi and fully automatic L-sealers and shrink tunnel combinations, horizontal form, fill, seal machines and semi and fully automatic sleeve wrap and bundling systems with in-line and multi-packcollating capabilities

21381 Dansk International Designs
108 Corporate Park Drive
Suite 301
White Plains, NY 10604-3805 914-697-6400
Fax: 914-697-6464 www.dansk.com
China, crystal, housewares, tabletop items, giftware, etc
President: David Herman
VP Merchandising: Jeanne Allen
Estimated Sales: $1 - 5 Million
Number Employees: 250-500
Parent Co: Lenox

21382 Dap Technologies Corporation
8945 South Harl Avenue
Suite 112
Tempe, AR 85284 813-969-3271
Fax: 813-969-3334 800-229-2822
tpm@qbc.daptech.com www.daptech.com
Packaging equipment specializing in bar code scanner technology
President: Yzes Oaroctue
CEO: Michel Oatointe
Estimated Sales: $2.5-5 Million
Number Employees: 9

21383 Dapec
1000 Evenflo Dr
Ball Ground, GA 30107 770-345-2841
Fax: 770-345-5926 jimh@dapec.com
www.dapec.com
Processing equipment
President: Scott Russell
Chairman of the Board: Jack Hazenbroek
Estimated Sales: $20 - 50 Million
Number Employees: 20-49

21384 Dapec/Numafa
1000 Evenflo Dr
Ball Ground, GA 30107-4544 770-345-2841
Fax: 770-345-5926 scott@numafa.com
www.dapec.com
Conveyor systems and accessories, sanitation supplies, temperature control equipment
President: Scott Russell
Estimated Sales: $10-20 Million
Number Employees: 20-49

21385 Dar-B-Ques Barbecue Equipment
3631 Blecha Road
Imperial, MO 63052-1123 636-296-4408
Barbecue grills and pig roasters
President: Freddrew Freddrew
Estimated Sales: Below $5 Million
Number Employees: 1-4
Square Footage: 75000
Brands:
Dar-B-Ques

21386 Darcor Casters
7 Staffordshire Place
Toronto, ON M8W 1T1
Canada 416-255-8563
Fax: 416-251-6117 800-387-7206
casters@darcor.com www.darcor.com
Manufacturer and exporter of casters and wheels
President: Rob Hilborn
Controller: Dan Watson
Engineering Manager: Adrian Steenson
Director of Marketing: Kirk Tobias
Number Employees: 75
Square Footage: 320000
Parent Co: Darcor Casters
Brands:
Carpet Master
Cartwashable
Solid Elastomer

21387 Darcy Group
1350 Home Ave Ste L
Akron, OH 44310 330-633-4700
Fax: 330-633-8779 www.thedarcygroup.com
Manager: Jodi Westphal
Quality Control: Bob Tredd
Estimated Sales: $2.5 - 5 000,000
Number Employees: 50-99

21388 **Darifill, Inc.**
750 Green Crest Drive
Westerville, OH 43081 614-890-3274
Fax: 614-890-4230 info@darifill.com
www.darifill.com
Equipment that offers a variety of filling, packaging styles and sealing methods for the dairy and ice cream industries.

21389 **Darlington Dairy Supply**
17332 State Road 81
Darlington, WI 53530 608-776-4064
Fax: 608-776-4092 800-877-4064
daveg@ddsco.com www.ddsco.com
Heat exchangers, plate, tubular, process control
President: Mae Thuli
Marketing: Torry Thuli
Estimated Sales: $5-10 000,000
Number Employees: 10-19

21390 **Darmex Corporation**
71 Jane Street
Roslyn Heights, NY 11577-1359 516-621-3000
Fax: 516-621-3627 800-645-6368
info@fuchs.com www.darmex.com
Sanitary lubricants
Estimated Sales: $50-100 Million
Number Employees: 140

21391 **Darnell-Rose Corporation**
17915 Railroad St
City of Industry, CA 91748 626-912-1688
Fax: 626-912-3765 800-327-6355
www.darnellrose.com
Manufacturer and exporter of casters and wheels, including stainless steel models and other mobility products
President: Brent Bardar
Research & Development: Bob Siegried
Quality Control: Phil Mazzolini
Marketing Director: Brent Bargar
Sales Director: Bob Siegried
Operations Manager: Richard Martinez
Purchasing Manager: Robbie McCullah
Estimated Sales: $10-20 Million
Number Employees: 50-99
Square Footage: 85000
Type of Packaging: Food Service, Bulk

21392 **Darson Corporation**
7650 Chrysler Dr Ste 150
Detroit, MI 48211-1734 313-875-7781
Fax: 313-875-1666 800-783-7781
medarson@sbcglobalnet
www.thedarsoncorp.com
Screen printed decals, labels and name plates
President: Mary Ellen Darge
Controller: Shirley Lyle
Production Manager: David Breuhan
Estimated Sales: $1-2.5 Million
Number Employees: 5 to 9

21393 **Dart Container Corporation**
500 Hogsback Road
Mason, MI 48854
Fax: 517-676-3883 800-248-5960
sales@dart.biz www.dartcontainer.com
Manufacturer and exporter of disposable tabletop supplies including foam cups, containers and lids, plastic cups and lids, fusion cups, foam plastic dinnerware, foam hinged lid containers, clear containers, portion containers and lidsplastic cutlery
Chairman: William Dart
Chief Executive Officer: Robert Dart
Payroll Manager: Gene Rachon
Vice President: Peter Byron
Quality Control Manager: Leola Burks
Marketing Manager: Jeb Buterbaugh
Director, Sales: Robert Williams
Operations Manager: Fred Forrester
Production Manager: John Witmer
Plant Manager: Mike Kitchens
Purchasing Director: Charlie Witty
Estimated Sales: $847 Million
Number Employees: 7,650
Brands:
Clear Pac
Concorde
Dart
Famous Service
Horizon
Impulse
Quiet Classic
Select
Showtime

21394 **Dashco**
17 Westpark Drive
Gloucester, ON K1B 3G6
Canada 613-834-6825
Fax: 613-834-6826 cl666@freenet.carleton.ca
Manufacturer and exporter of degradable plastic carry-out/check-out bags
President: Dave Paul
Number Employees: 2
Brands:
Biosolo
Dashco

21395 **Data Compostition**
1099 Essex Avenue
Richmond, CA 94801-2112 800-227-2121
Fax: 510-235-2176 800-227-2121
www.www.datacomp.com
Wine industry UPC bar code labels
Estimated Sales: $1 - 5 Million

21396 **Data Consultants**
P.O.Box 180
Pleasant Hill, MO 64080 805-748-3427
Fax: 703-330-2436 info@dataconsultantsinc.com
www.dataconsultantsinc.com
PCs and management of and access to critical business information
Owner: Mike Mc Neall
Accountant and Public Relations: Shelly Haines
Marketing: Mark Frund

21397 **Data Consulting Associates**
18000 Coleman Valley Rd
Occidental, CA 95465-9236 707-874-3067
Fax: 707-874-3848 www.monitor.net
Wine industry computer software
Owner: Carey Dubbert
Estimated Sales: $1 - 3 Million
Number Employees: 1-4

21398 **Data Management**
3322 Loop 306
San Angelo, TX 76904 325-949-7856
Fax: 325-653-3597 800-749-8463
www.timeclockplus.com
Software for restaurants including programs for recording and calculating payroll hours, taking orders, customer service, P.O.S., delivery systems, time, attendance and scheduling packages
President: Jorge Ellis
Director Marketing: Scott Turner
Sales/Technical Manager: Mark Moorman
Estimated Sales: $1-2.5 Million
Number Employees: 10-19
Square Footage: 1700
Brands:
Timeclock Plus

21399 **Data Scale**
42430 Blacow Rd
Fremont, CA 94539 510-651-7350
Fax: 510-651-6343 800-651-7350
sales@datascale.com www.datascale.com
Liquid drum and pail filling systems
Owner: Terry B Lowe
Sales Director: Tim DuClos
Estimated Sales: $1-2,500,000
Number Employees: 10-19
Type of Packaging: Consumer, Food Service
Brands:
Data Scale

21400 **Data Specialist**
1021 Proctor Drive
Elkhorn, WI 53121 262-723-5726
Fax: 262-723-5767 800-211-1545
info@dataspecialist.com
www.dataspecialists.com
Manufacutrer of computers and software designed for the dairy industry including production, costing, inventory, distribution, payroll, etc.; installation and start-up services available
President: Sherrie Mertes
Estimated Sales: $2.5-5 Million
Number Employees: 10-19

21401 **Data Visible Corporation**
PO Box 7767
Charlottesville, VA 22906-7767 434-296-5608
Fax: 434-977-1076 800-368-3494
sales@datavisible.com www.datavisible.com
Quick reference cash register units, flip cards, job-aids for bulk pricing and instructions, color coded folders, labels, filing cabinets, etc
President: A Patton Janssen Jr
Executive VP: Gary Sloan
Number Employees: 10
Brands:
Data Visible
Dataflex

21402 **Datalogic ADC**
959 Terry Street
Eugene, OR 97402 541-349-8283
Fax: 541-687-7998 800-929-3221
info.adc.us@datalogic.com www.datalogic.com
Sensors, capacitive sensors, photoelectrics, linear transducers and identification for packaging and electronic sensors for automation manufacturer of both CCD and LASER bar code reading technologies
President: Darrell Owens
CFO: Mack Ruacker
Estimated Sales: $5 - 10 000,000
Number Employees: 20-49

21403 **(HQ)Datapaq**
187 Ballardvale St
Wilmington, MA 01887-1082 978-988-9000
Fax: 978-988-0666 800-326-5270
websales@datapaq.com www.datapaq.com
Monitors the temperature profiles of a food product as it passes through continuous cook, bake, chill, freeze, and fry processes. A Datapaq system is comprised of four major components: a data logger, a protective thermal barrier toprotect the logger, thermocouple probes, and easy-to-use software to analyze and store temperature data collected during a process. Detailed graphical information gives a complete picture of the continuous process
President: Michael E White
Marketing Director: Kathleen Higgins
Sales Director: Bill Adaschik
Estimated Sales: $5-10 Million
Number Employees: 10-19
Square Footage: 19200
Other Locations:
Datapaq
Cambridge
Brands:
Datapaq Multi-Tracker System

21404 **Datapax**
11225 North 28th Drive
Suite D-102
Phoenix, AZ 85029 602-212-9202
Fax: 602-274-1476 877-328-2729
contactus@GlobalBakeUSA.com
www.datapax.com
Computer programming, management systems and services for bakeries and food processing in modular and integrated system format
Owner: Tyson Philippi
Estimated Sales: $2.5-5 000,000
Number Employees: 5-9

21405 **Datu**
159 Maxwell Avenue
Geneva, NY 14456-1760 315-787-2288
Fax: 315-787-2284 tea2@cornell.com
www.nysaes.cornell.edu/datu
GCO systems for analysis of odors
President: Terry Accree
CEO: Stephen Wyckoff

21406 **Daubert Cromwell**
12701 S Ridgeway Ave
Alsip, IL 60803 708-293-7750
Fax: 708-293-7765 info@daubertcromwell.com
www.daubertvci.com
Rust inhibiting paper, film and paper converting
President: Francis Houlihan
CEO: Martin J Simpson
Estimated Sales: $5-10 000,000
Number Employees: 50-99

21407 **Daubert VCI**
1333 Burr Ridge Pkwy Ste 200
Burr Ridge, IL 60527 630-203-6800
Fax: 630-203-6900 800-535-3535
info@dayvertvci.com www.daubert.com
Corrosion-preventive packaging products paper, film, emitters
President: M Lawrence Garman
CFO: Peter Miehl

Estimated Sales: H
Number Employees: 100-249

21408 Dave's Imports
6824 N Main Street
Jacksonville, FL 32208-4726 904-764-6886
Fax: 904-764-7131 800-553-2837
service@davesimports.com
www.davesimports.com

Advertising specialties
Graphic Artist/Admin.: Kimberly Pratt
Estimated Sales: less than $500,000
Number Employees: 1

21409 Davenport Machine
301 Second St
PO Box 6635
Rock Island, IL 61201 309-786-1500
Fax: 309-786-0771 sales@davenportdryer.com
www.davenportdryer.com

Manufacturer and exporter of rotary dryers and coolers, foundry equipment and continuous dewatering presses
President: R Nixon Jr
General Sales Manager: Lauren Reimer
Chief Engineer: R Bateman
Estimated Sales: $5-10 Million
Number Employees: 20-50
Square Footage: 86000
Parent Co: Middle States Corporation

21410 David A. Lingle & Son Manufacturing Company
PO Box 519
Russellville, AR 72811 479-968-2500
Fax: 479-968-1998

Walk-in coolers and freezers, cold storage doors and insulated specialties
Owner/Partner: David Lingle
Partner: Larry Lingle
CFO: Jean Harbison
Estimated Sales: $1 - 3 Million
Number Employees: 5-9
Square Footage: 20000

21411 (HQ)David Dobbs Enterprise & Menu Design
4600 Us Highway 1 N
St Augustine, FL 32095-5701 904-824-6171
Fax: 904-824-9989 800-889-6368
sales@menudesigns.com
www.dobbsapparel.com

Vinyl and leather menu covers, wine lists and guest service directories; also, promotional items including hats, T-shirts, tote bags, aprons and pizza bags
President: David Dobbs
CFO: Peggy Dobbs
Executive VP: Jay Maguire
Quality Control: Terry Sechen
Sales Manager: J Michael Davis
Estimated Sales: $10-20 Million
Number Employees: 50-99

21412 David E. Moley & Associates
PO Box 920
Wrightsville Beach, NC 28480 910-256-3826
Fax: 910-256-8639 moleyusa@aol.com

Executive search consultant for food service manufacturers seeking sales and marketing executives
VP: Gloria Moley
Estimated Sales: less than $500,000
Number Employees: 5

21413 David's Goodbatter
PO Box 102
Bausman, PA 17504-0102 717-872-0652
Fax: 717-872-8152

Processor, packager and exporter of organic pancakes and baking mixes, pasta, couscous, Irish oatmeal, dried beans, bean blends and gluten-free and wheat-free foods; importer of maple candies and syrup; also, custom packaging andprivate labeling available
Owner: Jane David
Estimated Sales: $1-2.5 Million appx.
Number Employees: 1-4
Square Footage: 26000
Type of Packaging: Consumer, Food Service, Private Label, Bulk
Brands:
David's Goodbatter
Gabriel & Rose

21414 Davidson's Safest Choice Eggs
2963 Bernice Road
Lansing, IL 60438 708-418-8500
Fax: 708-418-1235 800-410-7619
info@safeeggs.com www.safeeggs.com

Pasteurized eggs
President: Greg West
CFO: Michael Smith

21415 Davis & Small Decor
1888 Clements Ferry Rd
Charleston, SC 29492 843-881-8990
Fax: 800-227-7398 800-849-5082
orders@dsdecor.com www.dsdecor.com

Manufacturer and exporter of decorative wall items for restaurants
President: Thomas M Davis
Estimated Sales: $3 - 5 Million
Number Employees: 20-49

21416 Davis Brothers Produce Boxes
8264 Haynes Lennon Highway
Evergreen, NC 28438-0069 910-654-4913

Packaging material including wooden containers and boxes
President: Bedford S David Jr
Estimated Sales: $1 - 5 Million
Number Employees: 20

21417 Davis Core & Pad Company
1140 Davis Rd SW
Cave Spring, GA 30124 706-777-3675
Fax: 706-777-8690 800-235-7483
sales@daviscore.com www.daviscore.com

Custom molded expanded polystyrene packaging materials, cold storage shipping containers and disposable shipping pallets; industrial sizes available
President: Joel Davis
Estimated Sales: $5 Million
Number Employees: 50-99
Square Footage: 30000
Brands:
Kol-Boy Products

21418 Davlynne International
3383 E Layton Ave Stop 3
Cudahy, WI 53110 414-481-1011
Fax: 414-481-3155 800-558-5208
davoyneintl@aol.com

Manufacturer and exporter of strip curtains and doors, custom cart covers and enclosures
President: Kristin Larson
CEO: Randall Larson
Marketing Director: Krista Larson
Estimated Sales: $2.5-5 Million
Number Employees: 7
Square Footage: 6500
Brands:
Glare-Eze
Inhibidor

21419 Davron Technologies
4563 Pinnacle Ln
Chattanooga, TN 37415-3811 423-870-1888
Fax: 423-870-1108 sales@davrontech.com
www.davrontech.com

Manufacturer and exporter of all types of custom process equipment including, but not limited to, ovens, conveying systems, washing systems and frying systems
President: Ronald Speicher
Director Sales/Marketing: Jimmy Evans
Customer Service: Linda Jones
Equipment Design Manager: David Craft
Estimated Sales: $10 - 20 Million
Number Employees: 50-99

21420 Dawn Equipment Company
3333 Sargent Rd
Jackson, MI 49201 517-789-4400
Fax: 517-789-4495 800-248-1844
rzieman@donfoods.com www.dawnfoods.com

Manufacturer and exporter of baking and frying equipment, glazers, icers, topping and filling machines
Manager: Ron Wilcox
General Manager: Bill Kirchen
Quality Control: Jim Sayles
Estimated Sales: $5 - 10 Million
Number Employees: 1-4
Square Footage: 15000
Parent Co: Dawn Food Products
Type of Packaging: Consumer

21421 Day & Zimmerman International
1500 Spring Garden Street
Philadelphia, PA 19130-4067 215-299-8000
Fax: 215-299-8344 800-523-0786
media.relations@dayzim.com www.dayzim.com

Electrical, electronic and construction engineering equipment and services for food and beverage industry
CEO: Harold Yoh III
Vice President: Anthony Bosco Jr.
Marketing Manager: Tamara Dean
Chief Operating Officer: Michael McAreavy
Number Employees: 500-999

21422 Day & Zimmermann International
610 Minuet Lane
Charlotte, NC 28217-2723 704-943-5007
Fax: 704-943-5112
tjeresa/amzelone@dayzim.com
www.dayzim.com

CEO: Harold Yoh III
Vice President And CIO: Anthony Bosco Jr.
Marketing Manager: Tamara Dean
Chief Operating Officer: Michael McAreavy

21423 Day Basket Factory
714 S Main St
North East, MD 21901 410-287-8100
Fax: 410-287-8835 www.daybasketfactory.com

Hand-made white oak baskets including grocery and shopping
Owner: Robert Fredrick
Estimated Sales: $500,000-$1 Million
Number Employees: 1-4
Type of Packaging: Private Label

21424 Day Lumber Company
34 South Broad Street
Westfield, MA 01085 413-568-3511
Fax: 413-568-6668 allen@daylumber.com
www.daylumber.com

Wooden skids and pallets; also, plywood containers
President: Arthur Grodd
VP Sales / General Manager: Allen Nadler
Operations Manager: Lee Krieg
Estimated Sales: $2.5-5 Million
Number Employees: 10-19

21425 Day Manufacturing Company
419 E Lamar St
Sherman, TX 75090 903-893-1138
Fax: 903-892-0218 www.daypackaging.net

Folding cartons
President: Herald W Totten
VP: Curry Vogelsang
Operations Manager: Rick Smith
Estimated Sales: $10-20 Million
Number Employees: 20-49
Square Footage: 53500
Parent Co: Washington Iron Works

21426 Day Mark/Food Safety Systems
12830 S Dixie Hwy
Bowling Green, OH 43402-9697 419-353-2458
Fax: 419-354-0514 corgan@daymarklabel.com
www.daymarksafety.com

Manufacturer, importer and exporter of dissolve-a-way food labels, coding, dating and marking equipment, label applicators and food rotation systems
VP/General Manager: Jeff Palmer
Estimated Sales: $1 - 3 Million
Number Employees: 1-4
Square Footage: 172000
Parent Co: CMC Group
Brands:
Daymark
Dissolve-A-Way

21427 Day Nite Neon Signs
PO Box 2716
Dartmouth, NS B3B 1E3
Canada 902-469-7095
Fax: 902-469-2124 info@daynite.ca
www.daynite.ca

Illuminated and architectural signs and interior graphics
President: Chris Boone Jr
CFO: Allen Fraser
Sales Director: Wayne Stewart
Number Employees: 10

21428 Day-O-Lite ManufacturingCompany
126 Chestnut St
Warwick, RI 02888-2104 401-808-6849
Fax: 401-941-2960 sales@dayolite.com
www.dayolite.com
Fluorescent lighting fixtures
Owner: Michael Coltta
Estimated Sales: $20-50 Million
Number Employees: 50-99
Square Footage: 4000

21429 Dayco
4681 107th Circle N
Clearwater, FL 33762-5006 727-573-9330
Fax: 727-573-2879 jashbaugh@daycousa.com
www.daycoindia.com
Stainless steel custom chef lines and tables
President: James Ashbaugh
Sales Director: Ron Rogers
Estimated Sales: $2.5-5 Million
Number Employees: 10
Square Footage: 60000

21430 Daydots
1801 Riverbend West Dr
Fort Worth, TX 76118 817-590-4500
Fax: 817-590-4501 800-321-3687
sales@daydots.com www.daydots.com
A goal of making the world a safer place to eat. Daydots offers more than 4,000 products and services including original day of the week food safety labels. Produce and distribute products for food rotation, temperture control;cross-contamination prevention; personal hygiene and sanitation and cleaning, employee safety and food safety education.
President/Owner: Mark Smith
Marketing: Paul McGinnis
Sales: Laura Manatis
Operations: Chad Logan
Number Employees: 50-99
Number of Products: 4000
Square Footage: 100000
Type of Packaging: Food Service, Private Label
Brands:
Coders
Daydots

21431 Daymark Food Safety System
12830 S Dixie Hwy
Bowling Green, OH 43402 419-353-2458
Fax: 419-354-0514 866-517-0490
international@daymarklabel.com
www.daymarkinternational.com
President: Jeff Palmer
Vice President: Tammy Corral
Director, Inside Sales: Heidi Chambers
Estimated Sales: $1 - 3 Million
Number Employees: 200

21432 Daystar
12530 Manor Road
Glen Arm, MD 21057-9503 410-592-3106
Fax: 410-592-3362 800-494-6537
sales@lenoxlaser.com www.lenoxlaser.com
Micro leaks for can and bag testing valves for gas handling, laser systems, rapid prototyping and small hole drilling services
Quality Control: John Whelan
General Manager: Gary Thornton
Number Employees: 10
Square Footage: 18000
Parent Co: Lenox Laser
Brands:
Microleak

21433 Daytech Limited
70 Disco Road
Toronto, ON M9W 1L9
Canada 416-675-1195
Fax: 416-675-7183 877-329-1907
info@daytechlimited.com
www.daytechlimited.com
Illuminated and nonilluminated signage shelters, parking lot kiosks, shopping cart corrals, smoking shelters and covered walkways
President, COO: Dion McGuire
VP Operations: Dave Bradley
Sales & Marketing Manager: John Duthie
Purchasing Manager: Rick Rankin
Estimated Sales: $5 - 10 Million
Number Employees: 25

21434 Dayton Bag & Burlap Company
322 Davis Ave
Dayton, OH 45403 937-258-8000
Fax: 937-258-0029 800-543-3400
info1@daybag.com www.daybag.com
Manufacturer and exporter of bags including burlap, feed, grain, greaseproof, paper, paper lined, plastic and polypropylene for shipping commodities
President: Samuel Lumby
VP Marketing: Sue Spiegel
Customer Service: Delilah Oda
Estimated Sales: $1 - 3 Million
Number Employees: 1-4
Square Footage: 75000
Type of Packaging: Bulk

21435 Dayton Marking Devices Company
1681 Ladera Trl
Dayton, OH 45459-1401 937-432-0285
Fax: 937-254-9638
Rubber stamps, printing dies, steel stamps and dies, engraved/etched nameplates, time equipment and signaling devices
Owner: Michael Dunham
Estimated Sales: Below $5 Million
Number Employees: 10

21436 Dayton Reliable Tool
618 Greenmount Blvd
Dayton, OH 45419 937-298-7391
Fax: 937-298-7190 postoffice@drtusa.com
www.drtusa.com
Specializes in the design of conversion systems for all types of easy-open end applications including SOT, ringpull and full aperture, spare parts tooling for all types of cans including conversion systems, shell systems and cuppers
President: Gary Van Gundy
CFO: James Sass
CEO: Gary L Vangundy
Quality Control: George Kloos
R & D: Paul Klips
Estimated Sales: $20-50 Million
Number Employees: 100-249

21437 De Felsko Corporation
802 Proctor Ave
Ogdensburg, NY 13669 800- 44- 383
Fax: 131- 39- 847 800-448-3835
techsale@defelsko.com www.defelsko.com
Automatic liquor pourers
President: Frank Koch
Estimated Sales: $5-10 Million
Number Employees: 20-49
Brands:
Accupour

21438 De Leone Corporation
1258 SW Lake Rd
Redmond, OR 97756 541-504-8311
Fax: 541-504-8411 sam@deleone.com
www.labelslabels.com
Labels and labeling material
President: Samuel A De Leone
Quality Control: David Hawes
Sales Representative: Diana Jibiden
Estimated Sales: $5-10 000,000
Number Employees: 20-49

21439 De Royal Textiles
100 E York St
Camden, SC 29020 803-432-1103
Fax: 803-425-4566 800-845-1062
customerservice@deroyal.com
www.deroyaltextiles.com
Wipers and cheesecloth
President: Steve Ward
Quality Control: John Getting
VP: E Steven Ward
Sales Manager: Jay Green
Plant Manager: John Gettys
Estimated Sales: Below $5 Million
Number Employees: 1-4
Square Footage: 275000
Brands:
Hermitex
Idealfold
Jiffy Roll

21440 De Ster Corporation
225 Peachtree Street
Suite 400
Atlanta, GA 30303-1727 404-659-9100
Fax: 404-659-5116 800-237-8270
info@dester.com www.dester.com
Manufacturer, importer and exporter of disposable and reusable trays, plates, flatware, containers, cups and cutlery
Executive VP: Gerrit de Kiewit
Director Marketing/Development: John Squire
Senior VP Sales: Dan Whitehead
Estimated Sales: $5-10 Million
Number Employees: 150-200
Square Footage: 640000
Parent Co: De Ster Holding BV
Type of Packaging: Consumer, Food Service, Private Label, Bulk
Brands:
Isobox
Microstar
Octaview

21441 DeLaval Cleaning Solutions
11100 North Congress Avenue
Kansas City, MO 64153-1296 816-891-1530
Fax: 816-891-1505
www.delavalcleaningsolutions.com
Manufacturer and suppliers of cleaning and sanitizing products for the dairy, food, and beverage processing industies.

21442 DeLeone Corporation
1258 SW Lake Rd
Redmond, OR 97756 541-504-8311
Fax: 541-504-8411 deleone@deleon.com
www.labelslabels.com
President: Samuel A De Leone
Estimated Sales: $5 - 10 Million
Number Employees: 20-49

21443 DeLeone Corporation
1258 SW Lake Rd
Redmond, OR 97756 541-504-8311
Fax: 541-504-8411 sam@deleone.com
www.labelslabels.com
Manufacturer and exporter of pressure sensitive and custom labels; wholesaler/distributor of label dispensers
President: Samuel A De Leone
General Manager: David Hawes
Sales Director: Diana Jibiden
Estimated Sales: $5-10 Million
Number Employees: 20-49

21444 DeLoach Industries
818 Cattlemen Road
Sarasota, FL 34232-2808 941-371-4995
Fax: 941-377-2649 www.deloachindustries.com
Water treatment aeration and degassing equipment; gravity filters
Owner: Anthony De Loach
VP: Laurie Deloach
Estimated Sales: $2.5 - 5 Million
Number Employees: 10-19

21445 DeVere Chemical Company
1923 Beloit Ave
Janesville, WI 53546-3028 608-752-0576
Fax: 608-752-6625 800-833-8373
www.deverechemical.com
Cleaning and sanitizing chemicals including dishwashing detergents
President: Cynthia Shackelford
VP: Frank Drew
Estimated Sales: Below $5 Million
Number Employees: 20-49
Square Footage: 26000

21446 Deadline Press
1652 N Roberts Road NW
Suite C-2
Kennesaw, GA 30144-3634 770-419-2232
Fax: 770-419-2933
Advertising specialties, flags, pennants, banners and labels
Owner: Susan Lester
Other Locations:
Deadline Press
Atlanta GA

21447 Dean Custom Awnings
529 Route 303
Orangeburg, NY 10962 845-425-1193
Fax: 845-425-6678
mail@deancustomawnings.com
www.deancustomawnings.com
Commercial awnings
President: Charles Collishaw
Estimated Sales: Less than $500,000
Number Employees: 1-4

21448 (HQ)Dean Foods Company
2711 N Haskell Ave
Suite 3400
Dallas, TX 75204 214-303-3400
Fax: 214-303-3499 800-431-9214
deanfoods@casupport.com www.deanfoods.com
Manufacturer and distributor of milk, dairy products, soy products, water, juices and drinks, ice cream and novelties, yogurt, cottage cheese, sour cream and dips.
Chief Executive Officer: Gregg Tanner
Estimated Sales: $11.46 Billion
Number Employees: 21915
Square Footage: 11027
Type of Packaging: Food Service
Brands:
Adohr Farms
Alta Dena
Barber's
Berkeley Farms
Borden
Broughton Foods
Brown's Dairy
Celta
Country Delite
Country Fresh
Creamland
Dairy
Dairy Ease
Dairy Fresh
Dean's
Foremost
Friendship Dairies
Gandy's
Garelick Farms
Land O' Lakes
Lehigh Valley Dairy Farms
Louis Trauth
Mayfield Dairy Farms
McArthur Dairy
Meadow Brook Dairy
Meadow Gold
Meadown Gold, Hawaii
Model Dairy
Oak Farms Dairy
Organic Cow
Pet Dairy
Price's Creameries
Purity Dairies
Reiter Dairy
Robinson Dairy
Schenkel's
Schepps Dairy
Silk Soymilk
Suiza
Swiss Tea
T.G. Lee Dairy
Tuscan Dairy
Ultra
Verifine
Wengert's Dairy

21449 Dean Industries
14501 S Broadway
Gardena, CA 90248 310-353-5000
Fax: 310-327-3343 800-995-1210
salesmkt@frymaster.com www.dean.welbilt.com
Manufacturer and exporter of fryer baskets and deep fat fryers
Owner: Jimmy Dean
General Manager: Al Cote
Estimated Sales: $300,000-500,000
Number Employees: 1-4
Parent Co: ENODIS

21450 Dearborn Mid-West Company
8245 Nieman Road
Lenexa, KS 66214 913-384-9950
www.dmwcc.com
Manufacturer and exporter of material handling systems including conveyors, palletizers and palletizing systems
President, CEO: Tony Rosati
EVP, General Manager: Sudy Vohra
Manager of Sales: Gerry Cohen

21451 Dearborn Mid-West Conveyor Company
20334 Superior Rd
Taylor, MI 48180 734-288-4400
Fax: 734-288-1914 jwp@dmwcc.com
www.dmwcc.com
Automated material handling systems
President: Tony Rosati
Controller: Sherry Gavito
VP: Jeff Homenik
Quality Control: Mark Duxter
Sales: John Confar
Human Resources: Kelly Schafer
Plant Manager: Bruce Mazarowski
Purchasing: Katarina Katsavrias
Estimated Sales: $500,000 - $1 Million
Number Employees: 5
Number of Products: 5

21452 Deb Canada
42 Thompson Rd W
Waterford, ON N0E 1Y0
Canada 519-443-8697
Fax: 519-443-5160 888-332-7627
debcanada@debcanada.com www.debgroup.com
Hand and body cleansers, protective creams, anti-bacterial, gel, heavy duty and waterless soaps and soap dispensers
Controller: Dan Balan
General Manager: Didier Bauton
Asst. to General Manager: Theresa Sulisz
Number Employees: 50-99
Square Footage: 40000
Parent Co: Deb Group
Type of Packaging: Private Label
Brands:
Debba
Ensuite
Florafree
Great White
Hands
Heiress
Hypor
Inhibit
Lanimol
Maxipor
Mitzi
Quick Shift
Sceptre
Suprega
Tiv Plus
Tuf'n Ega

21453 Debbie Wright Sales
5852 E Berry St
Fort Worth, TX 76119 817-429-8282
Fax: 817-429-8882 800-935-7883
dwsales@flash.net www.debbiewright.com
Manufacturer and wholesaler/distributor of stud welding equipment and supplies
Owner: Debbie Wright
Sls. Rep.: Allan Yarber
Estimated Sales: $1-2.5 Million
Number Employees: 20-49

21454 Debelak Technical Systems
W6390 Quality Drive
Greenville, WI 54942-8015 920-757-9980
Fax: 920-757-9987 800-888-4207
debelek@debtechsys.com www.debetech.com
Control systems including clean-in-place, instrument monitoring, pasteurization and temperature for the food and dairy industries
President: William Debelak
Production Manager: Lee Fintelmann
Estimated Sales: $5-10 Million
Number Employees: 10

21455 Debelis Corporation
5000 70th Ave
Kenosha, WI 53144 262-656-8320
Fax: 262-656-8326 800-472-7462
info@debelis.net www.debelis.net
R&D: Gloria Brandes
Quality Control: Eillen Walo
Manager: Benoit Keppenne
Estimated Sales: $10 - 20 Million
Number Employees: 20-49

21456 Deborah Sales, LLC
109 Meeker Ave
Newark, NJ 07114 973-344-8466
Fax: 973-344-3981 crei@deborahsales.us
www.deborahsales.us
Advertising specialties and premiums
President: Carlos Rei
Estimated Sales: $1-2.5 Million
Number Employees: 5-9

21457 Decade Products
3910 Plainfield Ave NE
Grand Rapids, MI 49525-1602 616-365-2887
Fax: 616-956-9492 www.decadeproducts.com
Owner: Cindy Douthett

21458 Decal Techniques
25 Mahan St Unit A
West Babylon, NY 11704 631-491-1800
Fax: 631-491-1816 800-735-3322
decalinfo@earthlink.net www.decaltech.com
Silk screened labels, posters, banners and displays
President: Eugene P Snyder
Estimated Sales: $1 - 2.5 Million
Number Employees: 10-19
Square Footage: 5000

21459 Decartes Systems Group
120 Randall Drive
Waterloo, ON N2V 1C6
Canada 519-746-8110
Fax: 519-747-0082 info@descartes.com
www.descartes.com
Computer accounting systems for the dairy, beverage and food industries
Executive Vice President of Information: Raimond Diederik
Regional Manager: Rick Spencer
Estimated Sales: $1 - 5 Million
Type of Packaging: Bulk

21460 Deccofelt Corporation
PO Box 156
555 S Vermont Ave
Glendora, CA 91741 626-963-8511
Fax: 626-914-2734 800-543-3226
sales@deccofelt.com www.deccofelt.com
Industrial tapes including adhesive coated, heat activated and laminated
Chairman: Edwin C Heinrich
Director Sales: Kathy Smith
Estimated Sales: $5-10 Million
Number Employees: 20-49
Square Footage: 120000

21461 (HQ)Decision Analyst
604 Avenue H E
Arlington, TX 76011 817-640-6166
Fax: 817-640-6567 800-262-5974
jthomas@decisionanalyst.com
www.decisionanalyst.com
Consultant performing consumer testing and advertising pre-testing; market researcher including new product development and strategy
President: Jerry Thomas
Vice President: Stan Hazen
Marketing Director: Cristi Johnson
Number Employees: 100-249
Square Footage: 50000
Brands:
Copytest
Optima

21462 Decker Tape Products Company
6 Stewart Pl
Fairfield, NJ 07004 973-227-5350
Fax: 973-808-9418 800-227-5252
jack.dtp@worldnet.att.net www.deckertape.com
Pressure sensitive tapes and stock labels and in-house converting services include custon imprinting 2-color, die cutting, spooling, laminating, sheeting, narrow width and long length rolls
Owner: Jack Decker
Estimated Sales: $20-50 Million
Number Employees: 50-99

21463 Decko Products
2105 Superior St
Sandusky, OH 44870 419-626-5757
Fax: 419-626-3135 800-537-6143
shumphrey@decko.com www.decko.com

Edible cake and candy decorations and packaged rings, gels
President: F William Niggemyer
Marketing Director: Sara Humphrey
Estimated Sales: $10 Million
Number Employees: 100-249
Square Footage: 35000
Type of Packaging: Private Label
Brands:
Royal Icing Decoration

21464 Deco Labels & Tags
28 Greensboro Drive
Toronto, ON M9W 1E1
Canada 416-247-7878
Fax: 416-247-9030 888-496-9029
www.decolabels.com
Pressure sensitive labels, shipping tags, stickers, decals and seals; also, silk screening, data processing and hot stamping available
President: Doug Ford
Quality Control: Brian Burke
General Manager: Douglas Ford
Assistant Manager: Robbie Ford
Number Employees: 10
Square Footage: 72000
Brands:
Data-Tabs
Hard-Tac
Sof-Tac

21465 DecoPac
3500 Thurston Ave
Anoka, MN 55303-4874 763-574-0091
Fax: 763-574-1060 tana.krona@decopac.com
www.decopac.com
President: Christine McKenna
CFO: Mike McGlynn
Quality Control: Kim Roy
Estimated Sales: $10 - 20 Million
Number Employees: 100-249

21466 Decolin
9150 Parc Avenue
Montreal, QC H2N 1Z2
Canada 514-384-2910
Fax: 514-382-1305 www.decolin.com
Table cloths and runners; also, place mats
President: Leonard Mendel
CFO: Alissa Ratpatort
Number Employees: 50

21467 Decorated Products Company
PO Box 580
Westfield, MA 01086-0580 413-568-0944
Fax: 413-568-1875 www.decorated.com
Labels including food product, carton and computer pin feed
President: Mike Goepfert
Sales Manager: Joe Menh
Operations Manager: Stafford Springs
Number Employees: 10
Square Footage: 180000

21468 Decoren Equipment
133 Chaucer Court
Willowbrook, IL 60527-8418 708-789-3367
Fax: 708-789-3367
Carts including specialty, china and plate
Marketing Manager (West): Howard Charles
Administrative Manager: Jule Arvans
Estimated Sales: $1 - 5 Million

21469 Dedert Corporation
20000 Governors Dr # 3
Olympia Fields, IL 60461-1034 708-747-7000
Fax: 708-755-8815 info@dedert.com
www.anhydro.com
Manufacturer and exporter of evaporators, filters, centrifuges and liquid/solid separation equipment; importer of filters, liquid/solid separation equipment and centrifuges
President: Guy Lonergan
Marketing Director: John Ruhl
Estimated Sales: $20-50 Million
Number Employees: 20-49
Brands:
Dedert
Lfc
Reineveld

21470 (HQ)Deep Rock Water Company
5660 New Northside Drive
Suite 500
Atlanta, GA 30328 303-292-2020
Fax: 303-296-8812 800-695-2020
questions@deeprockwater.com
www.deeprockwater.com
Bottled spring, artesian and distilled water
President: Pete MacLean
CEO: Tom Harrington
VP Sales & Marketing: Craig Dodd
Estimated Sales: $10-20 Million
Number Employees: 100-249
Type of Packaging: Consumer, Food Service
Brands:
Deep Rock

21471 Defontaine of America
16720 W Victor Rd
New Berlin, WI 53151 262-754-4665
Fax: 262-797-5735 sternw2@earthlink.net
www.definox.usa.com
Sanitary butterfly, check valves, air-operated valves, pigging systems, mixproof valves
President: William Stern
Marketing: Wayne Johnson
Estimated Sales: $1-2.5 000,000
Number Employees: 1-4

21472 Defreeze Corporation
PO Box 330
Southborough, MA 01772 508-485-8512
Fax: 508-481-1491 albezanson@defreeze.com
www.defreeze.com
Industrial microwave processing and frozen fish slicing equipment
President: Allan Bezanson
Estimated Sales: $1 - 3 Million
Number Employees: 1-4

21473 Degussa BioActives
P.O.Box 1609
Waukesha, WI 53187-1609 262-547-5531
Fax: 262-547-0587 800-342-5724
Estimated Sales: $1 - 5 Million
Number Employees: 50-99

21474 Degussa Corporation
379 Interpace Pkwy
Parsippany, NJ 07054 973-316-5804
Fax: 973-541-8013 www.degussa.com
Biocides, coloring chemicals, resins, fine chemicals, bleaching and water chemical, flavor and fruit extracts, aroma chemicals, super absorbants, high performance polymers, oil additives, wax modifier, hydrocollides, emulsifiersdietary supplements, acrylic sheets, moulding and extrusive compound, concrete additives, sealants, wall coatings, filings and filmed silica, carbon black, precipitated silica, monofides, silica olive silicas
President: Saldacore Saldacore
Quality Control: Cacherh Davison
Manager: Borys Schafran
Estimated Sales: $2.8 Billion
Number Employees: 10
Number of Products: 800

21475 Degussa Flavors
1000 Redna Ter
Cincinnati, OH 45215-1187 513-771-4682
Fax: 513-771-8748 888-771-2448
flavors.us@degussa.com
www.flavors-fruit-systems.com
Number Employees: 20-49

21476 Dehyco Company
1000 Kansas Street
Memphis, TN 38106-1925 901-774-3322
Fax: 901-774-2076
Manufacturer and exporter of hammer mills, custom grinders, pulverizers, separators and packaging machinery
President: Mike Broussard
VP: Albert Harris, Jr.
Estimated Sales: $10-20 Million
Number Employees: 20-49

21477 Dehydration & Environmental System
864 Saint Francis Way
Rio Vista, CA 94571-1250 707-374-7500
Fax: 707-374-7505 800-992-9113
sales@desllc.biz www.desllc.biz
Dewatering and drying equipment; by-product used to process both food and waste
President: Dan Simpson
Estimated Sales: $2.5-5 Million
Number Employees: 5-9

21478 Deibel Laboratories
103 S 2nd St
Madison, WI 53704 847-329-9900
Fax: 847-329-9903 madison@deibellabs.com
www.deibellabs.com
Analytical laboratory specializing in chemical and microbiological food testing including nutrition labeling, dietary fiber, cholesterol, sulfites, vitamins, trace minerals, sugar profiles, etc
President: Robert H Deibel
Plant Manager: Dan Coules
Estimated Sales: $3 - 5 Million
Number Employees: 25
Square Footage: 7000

21479 Deibel Laboratories
7165 Curtiss Ave
Sarasota, FL 34231 941-925-1579
Fax: 941-925-2130
SarasotaLab@DeibelLabs.com
www.deibellabs.com
Analytical laboratory specializing in chemical and microbiological food testing including nutrition labeling, dietary fiber, cholesterol, sulfites, vitamins, trace minerals, sugar profiles, etc
President: Robert H Deibel
Research & Development: Dr. Lawrence Rosner
Manager: Dean Reed
Plant Manager: Dan Coules
Estimated Sales: $300,000-500,000
Number Employees: 1-4
Square Footage: 7000

21480 Deibel Laboratories
7120 N Ridgeway Ave
Lincolnwood, IL 60712 847-329-9900
Fax: 847-329-9903
LincolnwoodLab@DeibelLabs.com
www.deibellabs.com
Analytical laboratory specializing in chemical and microbiological food testing including nutrition labeling, dietary fiber, cholesterol, sulfites, vitamins, trace minerals, sugar profiles, etc
President: Charles Deibel
Research & Development: Dr. Lawrence Rosner
Manager: Dean Reed
Plant Manager: Dan Coules
Estimated Sales: $1 - 3 Million
Number Employees: 10-19
Square Footage: 7000

21481 Deibel Laboratories
407 Cabot Rd
South San Francisco, CA 94080 650-952-4209
Fax: 650-952-4518 Sales@DeibelLabs.com
www.deibellabs.com
Analytical laboratory specializing in chemical and microbiological food testing including nutrition labeling, dietary fiber, cholesterol, sulfites, vitamins, trace minerals, sugar profiles, etc
President and CEO: Dr. Robert Deibel
Research & Development: Dr. Lawrence Rosner
Manager: Dean Reed
Plant Manager: Dan Coules
Number Employees: 10
Square Footage: 14000

21482 Deibel Laboratories
7120 N Ridgeway Ave
Lincolnwood, IL 60712 847-329-9900
Fax: 847-329-9903
LincolnwoodLab@DeibelLabs.com
www.deibellabs.com
Analytical laboratory specializing in chemical and microbiological food testing including nutrition labeling, dietary fiber, cholesterol, sulfites, vitamins, trace minerals, sugar profiles, etc
President and CEO: Dr. Robert Deibel
Research & Development: Dr. Lawrence Rosner
Manager: Dean Reed
Plant Manager: Dan Coules
Number Employees: 10
Square Footage: 14000

21483 Deibel Laboratories
3530 NW 97th Blvd
Gainesville, FL 32606 352-331-3313
Fax: 352-332-2050
GainsvilleLab@DeibelLabs.com
www.deibellabs.com

Analytical laboratory specializing in chemical and microbiological food testing including nutrition labeling, dietary fiber, cholesterol, sulfites, vitamins, trace minerals, sugar profiles, etc
Research & Development: Dr Lawrence Rosner
Manager: Kirsten Hunt
Manager: Dean Reed
Plant Manager: Dan Coules
Estimated Sales: $.5 - 1 million
Number Employees: 1-4
Square Footage: 7000

21484 Deitz Company
1750 Route 34
PO Box 1108
Wall, NJ 07719 732-681-0200
Fax: 732-681-8468 800-394-2709
contact-pharmafill@deitzco.com
www.deitzco.com

Machinery
President: James L Deitz
VP Engineering: John Deitz
Estimated Sales: $2.5 - 5 000,000
Number Employees: 10-19

21485 Deko International Co, Ltd
155 Clifton Blvd
Clifton, NJ 07011 973-778-0212
Fax: 973-778-0242 tracy@dekointl.com
www.dekointl.com

Supplier of ingredients
Account Manager: Tracy Yen
Other Locations:
Service Location
Earth City MO
Service Location
Rancho Cucamonga CA
Service Location
Norcross GA
Service Location
Houston TX

21486 Del Monte Fresh Produce
9880 S Dorchester Ave
Chicago, IL 60628 773-221-9480
Fax: 773-221-9388
contact-us-executive-office@freshdelmonte.com
www.freshdelmonte.com
Distribution center providing a variety of services including ripening, sorting, re-packing, fresh cut processing, and delivery of fruits and vegetables.
President/Chief Operating Officer: Hani El-Naffy
Chief Executive Officer/Chairman: Mohammad Abu-Ghazaleh
SVP/Chief Financial Officer: Richard Contreras
SVP/General Counsel & Secretary: Bruce Jordan
VP/Research-Development Agricultural Svs: Thomas Young Ph.D
SVP/North American Sales & Product Mgmt: Emanuel Lazopoulos
VP/Human Resources: Marissa Tenazas
SVP/North American Operations: Paul Rice
Parent Co: Del Monte Fresh Produce Company
Type of Packaging: Consumer, Food Service

21487 Del Monte Fresh Produce
2200 Westbelt Dr
Columbus, OH 43228-3820 614-527-7398
Fax: 614-527-8575 800-348-8878
contact-us-executive-office@freshdelmonte.com
www.freshdelmonte.com
Distribution center providing a variety of services including ripening, sorting, re-packing, fresh cut processing, and delivery of fruits and vegetables.
President: Andy Pschesang
Chief Executive Officer/Chairman: Mohammad Abu-Ghazaleh
SVP/Chief Financial Officer: Richard Contreras
SVP/General Counsel & Secretary: Bruce Jordan
VP/Research-Development Agricultural Svs: Thomas Young Ph.D
SVP/North American Sales & Product Mgmt: Emanuel Lazopoulos
VP/Human Resources: Marissa Tenazas
SVP/North American Operations: Paul Rice
Parent Co: Del Monte Fresh Produce Company
Type of Packaging: Consumer, Food Service

21488 Del Monte Fresh Produce
1400-1500 Parker St
Dallas, TX 75215 214-428-3600
Fax: 214-421-9502 800-428-3600
contact-us-executive-office@freshdelmonte.com
www.freshdelmonte.com
Distribution center providing a variety of services including ripening, sorting, re-packing, fresh cut processing, and delivery of fruits and vegetables.
President/Chief Operating Officer: Hani El-Naffy
Chief Executive Officer/Chairman: Mohammad Abu-Ghazaleh
SVP/Chief Financial Officer: Richard Contreras
CEO: Larry Crowley
VP/Research-Development Agricultural Svs: Thomas Young Ph.D
SVP/North American Sales & Product Mgmt: Emanuel Lazopoulos
VP/Human Resources: Marissa Tenazas
SVP/North American Operations: Paul Rice
Parent Co: Del Monte Fresh Produce Company
Type of Packaging: Consumer, Food Service

21489 Del Monte Fresh Produce
3101 SW 42nd St
Ft Lauderdale, FL 33312 954-791-4828
Fax: 954-791-2273
contact-us-executive-office@freshdelmonte.com
www.freshdelmonte.com
Distribution center providing a variety of services including ripening, sorting, re-packing, fresh cut processing, and delivery of fruits and vegetables.
President/Chief Operating Officer: Hani El-Naffy
Chief Executive Officer/Chairman: Mohammad Abu-Ghazaleh
SVP/Chief Financial Officer: Richard Contreras
SVP/General Counsel & Secretary: Bruce Jordan
VP/Research-Development Agricultural Svs: Thomas Young Ph.D
SVP/North American Sales & Product Mgmt: Emanuel Lazopoulos
VP/Human Resources: Marissa Tenazas
SVP/North American Operations: Paul Rice
Parent Co: Del Monte Fresh Produce Company
Type of Packaging: Consumer, Food Service

21490 Del Monte Fresh Produce
7780 Westside Industrial Drive
Unit 5
Jacksonville, FL 32219 904-378-0051
Fax: 904-378-0260
contact-us-executive-office@freshdelmonte.com
www.freshdelmonte.com
Distribution center providing a variety of services including ripening, sorting, re-packing, fresh cut processing, and delivery of fruits and vegetables.
President/Chief Operating Officer: Hani El-Naffy
Chief Executive Officer/Chairman: Mohammad Abu-Ghazaleh
SVP/Chief Financial Officer: Richard Contreras
SVP/General Counsel & Secretary: Bruce Jordan
VP/Research-Development Agricultural Svs: Thomas Young Ph.D
SVP/North American Sales & Product Mgmt: Emanuel Lazopoulos
VP/Human Resources: Marissa Tenazas
SVP/North American Operations: Paul Rice
Parent Co: Del Monte Fresh Produce Company
Type of Packaging: Consumer, Food Service

21491 Del Monte Fresh Produce
6311 Deramus Ave
Kansas City, MO 64120-1358 816-241-6242
Fax: 816-483-4050
contact-us-executive-office@freshdelmonte.com
www.freshdelmonte.com
Distribution center providing a variety of services including ripening, sorting, re-packing, fresh cut processing, and delivery of fruits and vegetables.
President/Chief Operating Officer: Hani El-Naffy
Chief Executive Officer/Chairman: Mohammad Abu-Ghazaleh
SVP/Chief Financial Officer: Richard Contreras
Human Resources: Angela Porter
VP/Research-Development Agricultural Svs: Thomas Young Ph.D
SVP/North American Sales & Product Mgmt: Emanuel Lazopoulos
VP/Human Resources: Marissa Tenazas
SVP/North American Operations: Paul Rice
Parent Co: Del Monte Fresh Produce Company
Type of Packaging: Consumer, Food Service

21492 Del Monte Fresh Produce
2825 East Cottonwood Parkway
Suite 575
Salt Lake City, UT 84121 801-990-3175
Fax: 801-990-3375
contact-us-executive-office@freshdelmonte.com
www.freshdelmonte.com
Distribution center providing a variety of services including ripening, sorting, re-packing, fresh cut processing, and delivery of fruits and vegetables.
President/Chief Operating Officer: Hani El-Naffy
Chief Executive Officer/Chairman: Mohammad Abu-Ghazaleh
SVP/Chief Financial Officer: Richard Contreras
SVP/General Counsel & Secretary: Bruce Jordan
VP/Research-Development Agricultural Svs: Thomas Young Ph.D
SVP/North American Sales & Product Mgmt: Emanuel Lazopoulos
VP/Human Resources: Marissa Tenazas
SVP/North American Operations: Paul Rice
Parent Co: Del Monte Fresh Produce Company
Type of Packaging: Consumer, Food Service

21493 Del Monte Fresh Produce
3151 Regatta Boulevard
Suite E
Richmond, CA 94804 510-236-2719
Fax: 510-236-2029
contact-us-executive-office@freshdelmonte.com
www.freshdelmonte.com
Distribution center providing a variety of services including ripening, sorting, re-packing, fresh cut processing, and delivery of fruits and vegetables.
President/Chief Operating Officer: Hani El-Naffy
Chief Executive Officer/Chairman: Mohammad Abu-Ghazaleh
SVP/Chief Financial Officer: Richard Contreras
SVP/General Counsel & Secretary: Bruce Jordan
VP/Research-Development Agricultural Svs: Thomas Young Ph.D
SVP/North American Sales & Product Mgmt: Emanuel Lazopoulos
VP/Human Resources: Marissa Tenazas
SVP/North American Operations: Paul Rice
Parent Co: Del Monte Fresh Produce Company
Type of Packaging: Consumer, Food Service

21494 Del Monte Fresh Produce
1001 Industrial Hwy
Building D
Eddystone, PA 19022 610-499-9049
Fax: 610-499-9042
contact-us-executive-office@freshdelmonte.com
www.freshdelmonte.com
Distribution center providing a variety of services including ripening, sorting, re-packing, fresh cut processing, and delivery of fruits and vegetables.
President/Chief Operating Officer: Hani El-Naffy
Chief Executive Officer/Chairman: Mohammad Abu-Ghazaleh
SVP/Chief Financial Officer: Richard Contreras
SVP/General Counsel & Secretary: Bruce Jordan
VP/Research-Development Agricultural Svs: Thomas Young Ph.D
SVP/North American Sales & Product Mgmt: Emanuel Lazopoulos
VP/Human Resources: Marissa Tenazas
SVP/North American Operations: Paul Rice
Parent Co: Del Monte Fresh Produce Company
Type of Packaging: Consumer, Food Service

21495 Del Monte Fresh Produce
3602 W Washington Street
Suite 1
Phoenix, AZ 85009 602-252-4758
Fax: 602-252-8265 800-226-4758
contact-us-executive-office@freshdelmonte.com
www.freshdelmonte.com
Distribution center providing a variety of services including ripening, sorting, re-packing, fresh cut processing, and delivery of fruits and vegetables.
President/Chief Operating Officer: Hani El-Naffy
Chief Executive Officer/Chairman: Mohammad Abu-Ghazaleh
SVP/Chief Financial Officer: Richard Contreras
VP/Research-Development Agricultural Svs: Thomas Young Ph.D
Sales: Lance Nichols
SVP/North American Sales & Product Mgmt: Emanuel Lazopoulos
VP/Human Resources: Marissa Tenazas
SVP/North American Operations: Paul Rice
Parent Co: Del Monte Fresh Produce Company

Type of Packaging: Consumer, Food Service

21496 Del Monte Fresh Produce
14550 West La Estrella
Goodyear, AZ 85338-3615 623-925-0900
Fax: 623-932-7999
contact-us-executive-office@freshdelmonte.com
www.freshdelmonte.com
Distribution center providing a variety of services including ripening, sorting, re-packing, fresh cut processing, and delivery of fruits and vegetables.
Chief Executive Officer/Chairman: Mohammad Abu-Ghazaleh
SVP/Chief Financial Officer: Richard Contreras
SVP/General Counsel & Secretary: Bruce Jordan
VP/Research-Development Agricultural Svs: Thomas Young Ph.D
SVP/North American Sales & Product Mgmt: Emanuel Lazopoulos
VP/Human Resources: Marissa Tenazas
SVP/North American Operations: Paul Rice
Manager: Norma Banda
Parent Co: Del Monte Fresh Produce Company
Type of Packaging: Consumer, Food Service

21497 Del Monte Fresh Produce
3306 Sydney Road
Plant City, FL 33566 813-752-5145
Fax: 813-759-8625
contact-us-executive-office@freshdelmonte.com
www.freshdelmonte.com
Distribution center providing a variety of services including ripening, sorting, re-packing, fresh cut processing, and delivery of fruits and vegetables.
President/Chief Operating Officer: Hani El-Naffy
Chief Executive Officer/Chairman: Mohammad Abu-Ghazaleh
SVP/Chief Financial Officer: Richard Contreras
SVP/General Counsel & Secretary: Bruce Jordan
VP/Research-Development Agricultural Svs: Thomas Young Ph.D
SVP/North American Sales & Product Mgmt: Emanuel Lazopoulos
VP/Human Resources: Marissa Tenazas
SVP/North American Operations: Paul Rice
Parent Co: Del Monte Fresh Produce Company
Type of Packaging: Consumer, Food Service

21498 Del Monte Fresh Produce
10730 Patterson Pl
Santa Fe Springs, CA 90670 562-777-1127
Fax: 562-777-9498
contact-us-executive-office@freshdelmonte.com
www.freshdelmonte.com
Distribution center providing a variety of services including ripening, sorting, re-packing, fresh cut processing, and delivery of fruits and vegetables.
Chief Executive Officer/Chairman: Mohammad Abu-Ghazaleh
SVP/Chief Financial Officer: Richard Contreras
SVP/General Counsel & Secretary: Bruce Jordan
VP/Research-Development Agricultural Svs: Thomas Young Ph.D
SVP/North American Sales & Product Mgmt: Emanuel Lazopoulos
VP/Human Resources: Marissa Tenazas
SVP/North American Operations: Paul Rice
Manager: Kevin Hopps
Parent Co: Del Monte Fresh Produce Company
Type of Packaging: Consumer, Food Service

21499 Del Monte Fresh Produce
504-42nd St NE
Suite 101
Auburn, WA 98002 253-850-3190
Fax: 253-850-3182
contact-us-executive-office@freshdelmonte.com
www.freshdelmonte.com
Distribution center providing a variety of services including ripening, sorting, re-packing, fresh cut processing, and delivery of fruits and vegetables.
Chief Executive Officer/Chairman: Mohammad Abu-Ghazaleh
SVP/Chief Financial Officer: Richard Contreras
SVP/General Counsel & Secretary: Bruce Jordan
VP/Research-Development Agricultural Svs: Thomas Young Ph.D
SVP/North American Sales & Product Mgmt: Emanuel Lazopoulos
VP/Human Resources: Marissa Tenazas
SVP/North American Operations: Paul Rice
Manager: Doug Robertson
Parent Co: Del Monte Fresh Produce Company
Type of Packaging: Consumer, Food Service

21500 Del Monte Fresh Produce
118-A Forest Pkwy
Forest Park, GA 30297 404-366-3699
Fax: 404-366-3996
contact-us-executive-office@freshdelmonte.com
www.freshdelmonte.com
Distribution center providing a variety of services including ripening, sorting, re-packing, fresh cut processing, and delivery of fruits and vegetables.
President: Mike Ford
Chief Executive Officer/Chairman: Mohammad Abu-Ghazaleh
SVP/Chief Financial Officer: Richard Contreras
SVP/General Counsel & Secretary: Bruce Jordan
VP/Research-Development Agricultural Svs: Thomas Young Ph.D
SVP/North American Sales & Product Mgmt: Emanuel Lazopoulos
VP/Human Resources: Marissa Tenazas
SVP/North American Operations: Paul Rice
Parent Co: Del Monte Fresh Produce Company
Type of Packaging: Consumer, Food Service

21501 Del Monte Fresh ProduceDC/Fresh Cut Operations
7970 Tarbay Dr
Jessup, MD 20794 410-799-4440
Fax: 410-799-3828
contact-us-executive-office@freshdelmonte.com
www.freshdelmonte.com
Distribution center providing a variety of services including ripening, sorting, re-packing, fresh cut processing, and delivery of fruits and vegetables.
Chief Executive Officer/Chairman: Mohammad Abu-Ghazaleh
SVP/Chief Financial Officer: Richard Contreras
SVP/General Counsel & Secretary: Bruce Jordan
VP/Research-Development Agricultural Svs: Thomas Young Ph.D
SVP/North American Sales & Product Mgmt: Emanuel Lazopoulos
VP/Human Resources: Marissa Tenazas
SVP/North American Operations: Paul Rice
Manager: Jack Scriber
Parent Co: Del Monte Fresh Produce Company
Type of Packaging: Consumer, Food Service

21502 Del Monte Fresh Produce
105 Shawmut Rd
Shamut Industrial Park
Canton, MA 02021-1438 781-830-2600
Fax: 781-830-2699
contact-us-executive-office@freshdelmonte.com
www.freshdelmonte.com
Distribution center providing a variety of services including ripening, sorting, re-packing, fresh cut processing, and delivery of fruits and vegetables.
President/Chief Operating Officer: Hani El-Naffy
Chief Executive Officer/Chairman: Mohammad Abu-Ghazaleh
SVP/Chief Financial Officer: Richard Contreras
SVP/General Counsel & Secretary: Bruce Jordan
VP/Research-Development Agricultural Svs: Thomas Young Ph.D
SVP/North American Sales & Product Mgmt: Emanuel Lazopoulos
VP/Human Resources: Marissa Tenazas
SVP/North American Operations: Paul Rice
Parent Co: Del Monte Fresh Produce Company
Type of Packaging: Consumer, Food Service

21503 Del Monte Fresh Produce
15845 E 32nd Ave
Suite D
Aurora, CO 80011-1570 720-857-9678
Fax: 720-857-9956
contact-us-executive-office@freshdelmonte.com
www.freshdelmonte.com
Distribution center providing a variety of services including ripening, sorting, re-packing, fresh cut processing, and delivery of fruits and vegetables.
President/Chief Operating Officer: Hani El-Naffy
Chief Executive Officer/Chairman: Mohammad Abu-Ghazaleh
SVP/Chief Financial Officer: Richard Contreras
SVP/General Counsel & Secretary: Bruce Jordan
VP/Research-Development Agricultural Svs: Thomas Young Ph.D
SVP/North American Sales & Product Mgmt: Emanuel Lazopoulos
VP/Human Resources: Marissa Tenazas
SVP/North American Operations: Paul Rice
Parent Co: Del Monte Fresh Produce Company
Type of Packaging: Consumer, Food Service

21504 Del Monte Fresh Produce
6532 Judge Adams Rd
Whitsett, NC 27377-9630 336-446-7408
Fax: 336-446-6590 800-455-3564
contact-us-executive-office@freshdelmonte.com
www.freshdelmonte.com
Distribution center providing a variety of services including ripening, sorting, re-packing, fresh cut processing, and delivery of fruits and vegetables.
President/Chief Operating Officer: Hani El-Naffy
Chief Executive Officer/Chairman: Mohammad Abu-Ghazaleh
SVP/Chief Financial Officer: Richard Contreras
SVP/General Counsel & Secretary: Bruce Jordan
VP/Research-Development Agricultural Svs: Thomas Young Ph.D
SVP/North American Sales & Product Mgmt: Emanuel Lazopoulos
VP/Human Resources: Marissa Tenazas
SVP/North American Operations: Paul Rice
Parent Co: Del Monte Fresh Produce Company
Type of Packaging: Consumer, Food Service

21505 Del Monte Fresh Produce
2500 Broadway Avenue
Drawer 24
Camden, NJ 08101 856-365-9200
Fax: 856-365-7389
contact-us-executive-office@freshdelmonte.com
www.freshdelmonte.com
Distribution center providing a variety of services including ripening, sorting, re-packing, fresh cut processing, and delivery of fruits and vegetables.
President/Chief Operating Officer: Hani El-Naffy
Chief Executive Officer/Chairman: Mohammad Abu-Ghazaleh
SVP/Chief Financial Officer: Richard Contreras
Human Resources: Angela Porter
VP/Research-Development Agricultural Svs: Thomas Young Ph.D
SVP/North American Sales & Product Mgmt: Emanuel Lazopoulos
VP/Human Resources: Marissa Tenazas
SVP/North American Operations: Paul Rice
Parent Co: Del Monte Fresh Produce Company
Type of Packaging: Consumer, Food Service

21506 Del Monte Fresh Produce
701 North Broadway
C/O Holt Marine Terminal
Gloucester City, NJ 08030 856-742-9202
Fax: 856-742-9209
contact-us-executive-office@freshdelmonte.com
www.freshdelmonte.com
Distribution center providing a variety of services including ripening, sorting, re-packing, fresh cut processing, and delivery of fruits and vegetables.
Chief Executive Officer/Chairman: Mohammad Abu-Ghazaleh
SVP/Chief Financial Officer: Richard Contreras
SVP/General Counsel & Secretary: Bruce Jordan
VP/Research-Development Agricultural Svs: Thomas Young Ph.D
SVP/North American Sales & Product Mgmt: Emanuel Lazopoulos
VP/Human Resources: Marissa Tenazas
SVP/North American Operations: Paul Rice
Manager: James Gagnon
Parent Co: Del Monte Fresh Produce Company
Type of Packaging: Consumer, Food Service

21507 Del Monte Fresh Produce
9243 N Rivergate Blvd
Portland, OR 97203-6615 503-285-0992
Fax: 503-285-1040
contact-us-executive-office@freshdelmonte.com
www.freshdelmonte.com
Distribution center providing a variety of services including ripening, sorting, re-packing, fresh cut processing, and delivery of fruits and vegetables.
President/Chief Operating Officer: Hani El-Naffy
Chief Executive Officer/Chairman: Mohammad Abu-Ghazaleh
SVP/Chief Financial Officer: Richard Contreras
SVP/General Counsel & Secretary: Bruce Jordan
VP/Research-Development Agricultural Svs: Thomas Young Ph.D
SVP/North American Sales & Product Mgmt: Emanuel Lazopoulos
VP/Human Resources: Marissa Tenazas
SVP/North American Operations: Paul Rice
Plant Manager: Philix Lopez
Parent Co: Del Monte Fresh Produce Company
Type of Packaging: Consumer, Food Service

21508 Del Monte Fresh Produce
1810 Academy Ave
Sanger, CA 93657 559-875-5000
Fax: 559-875-1301
contact-us-executive-office@freshdelmonte.com
www.freshdelmonte.com
Distribution center providing a variety of services including ripening, sorting, re-packing, fresh cut processing, and delivery of fruits and vegetables.
President/Chief Operating Officer: Hani El-Naffy
Chief Executive Officer/Chairman: Mohammad Abu-Ghazaleh
SVP/Chief Financial Officer: Richard Contreras
COO: Hector Calderon
VP/Research-Development Agricultural Svs: Thomas Young Ph.D
SVP/North American Sales & Product Mgmt: Emanuel Lazopoulos
VP/Human Resources: Marissa Tenazas
SVP/North American Operations: Paul Rice
Parent Co: Del Monte Fresh Produce Company
Type of Packaging: Consumer, Food Service

21509 Del Monte Fresh Produce
Pier 18
Galveston, TX 77550 409-762-4638
Fax: 409-762-5358
contact-us-executive-office@freshdelmonte.com
www.freshdelmonte.com
Distribution center/port providing a variety of services including ripening, sorting, re-packing, fresh cut processing, and delivery of fruits and vegetables.
President/Chief Operating Officer: Hani El-Naffy
EVP/Chief Financial Officer: John Inserra
SVP/General Counsel & Secretary: Bruce Jordan
VP/Research-Development Agricultural Svs: Thomas Young Ph.D
SVP/North American Sales & Product Mgmt: Emanuel Lazopoulos
VP/Human Resources: Marissa Tenazas
SVP/North American Operations: Paul Rice
Manager: Joseph Wiley
Parent Co: Del Monte Fresh Produce Company
Type of Packaging: Consumer, Food Service

21510 Del Monte Fresh Produce
300 Broadacres Drive
Suite 205
Bloomfield, NJ 07003 973-338-8591
Fax: 973-338-1523
contact-us-executive-office@freshdelmonte.com
www.freshdelmonte.com
Distribution center/port providing a variety of services including ripening, sorting, re-packing, fresh cut processing, and delivery of fruits and vegetables.
President/Chief Operating Officer: Hani El-Naffy
EVP/Chief Financial Officer: John Inserra
SVP/General Counsel & Secretary: Bruce Jordan
VP/Research-Development Agricultural Svs: Thomas Young Ph.D
SVP/North American Sales & Product Mgmt: Emanuel Lazopoulos
VP/Human Resources: Marissa Tenazas
SVP/North American Operations: Paul Rice
Manager: Todd Jetter
Parent Co: Del Monte Fresh Produce Company
Type of Packaging: Consumer, Food Service

21511 Del Monte Fresh Produce
Dock 1, Berth 3
Port Hueneme, CA 93041 805-488-0881
Fax: 805-488-2428
contact-us-executive-office@freshdelmonte.com
www.freshdelmonte.com
Distribution center/port providing a variety of services including ripening, sorting, re-packing, fresh cut processing, and delivery of fruits and vegetables.
President/Chief Operating Officer: Hani El-Naffy
EVP/Chief Financial Officer: John Inserra
SVP/General Counsel & Secretary: Bruce Jordan
VP/Research-Development Agricultural Svs: Thomas Young Ph.D
SVP/North American Sales & Product Mgmt: Emanuel Lazopoulos
VP/Human Resources: Marissa Tenazas
SVP/North American Operations: Paul Rice
Manager: Chuck Caulkins
Parent Co: Del Monte Fresh Produce Company
Type of Packaging: Consumer, Food Service

21512 Del Monte Fresh Produce
200 Delmonte Way
Palmetto, FL 34221-6609 941-722-3060
Fax: 941-722-7075
contact-us-executive-office@freshdelmonte.com
www.freshdelmonte.com
Distribution center/port providing a variety of services including ripening, sorting, re-packing, fresh cut processing, and delivery of fruits and vegetables.
President/Chief Operating Officer: Hani El-Naffy
EVP/Chief Financial Officer: John Inserra
SVP/General Counsel & Secretary: Bruce Jordan
VP/Research-Development Agricultural Svs: Thomas Young Ph.D
SVP/North American Sales & Product Mgmt: Emanuel Lazopoulos
VP/Human Resources: Marissa Tenazas
SVP/North American Operations: Paul Rice
Manager: Brian Giuliani
Parent Co: Del Monte Fresh Produce Company
Type of Packaging: Consumer, Food Service

21513 Del Packaging
18113 Telge Rd
Cypress, TX 77429 281-653-0099
Fax: 281-653-0077 sales@delpackaging.com
www.delpackaging.com
Packaging equipment
President: W Gordon Mylius
Quality Control: Paro Patrick
CFO: Patrick Paro
Estimated Sales: Below $5 000,000
Number Employees: 1-4

21514 Del-Tec Packaging
PO Box 6879
Greenville, SC 29606 864-288-7390
Fax: 864-288-7237 800-747-8683
sales@del-tec.com www.del-tec.com
Totes, bins, trays and vacuum and thermoformed plastic containers
Owner: Richard Lackey
VP Finance: Jere Davis
VP Sales: Bob Kocis
Customer Service: Joy McCullough
Plant Manager: Tim Shea
Estimated Sales: $1-2.5 Million
Number Employees: 20-49
Square Footage: 260000

21515 Delavan Spray Technologies
PO Box 969
Bamberg, SC 29003-0969 803-245-4347
Fax: 803-245-4146 800-982-6943
delavansales@goodrich.com
www.delavaninc.com
Manufacturer, importer and exporter of spray nozzles and accessories including flat spray, straight stream, hollow and solid cone, etc
EVP: Terrence G Linnert
Senior VP: Stephen R Huggins
VP: Joseph F Andolino
Plant Manager: Roger Young
Estimated Sales: $1 - 5 Million
Number Employees: 100-249

21516 Delavan Spray Technologies
2730 W Tyvola Rd # 600
Charlotte, NC 28217-4578 704-423-7000
Fax: 704-423-4098 www.goodrich.com
Manufacturer, importer and exporter of spray nozzles and accessories including flat spray, straight stream, hollow and solid cone, etc
President: Ray Davis
Division Controller: Carolin Kirsch
CEO: Marshall O Larsen
Executive Vice President of Operation: Jerry Witowski
Estimated Sales: $5-10 Million
Number Employees: 10,000
Parent Co: Coltec Industries
Brands:
Mini Sdx
Sdx
Sdx Iii

21517 Delavan-Delta
11 Rado Drive
Naugatuck, CT 06770-2220 203-720-5610
Fax: 203-720-5616
Manufacturer and exporter of level controls
Sales/Marketing Manager: Dean Cheramie
Number Employees: 65
Parent Co: Coltec Industries

21518 (HQ)Delco Tableware
19 Harbor Park Dr
Port Washington, NY 11050-4657 516-484-7965
Fax: 516-625-0859 800-221-9557
info@delcointl.com
Flatware, hollowware, steak knives and chinaware
Executive VP: Robert Delman
VP Distributor Sales: Holly Newme
Other Locations:
Delco Tableware
Port Washington NY
Brands:
Atlantic
Ceramicor
Delco
Hotel America
Table De France

21519 Delfield Company
980 S Isabella Rd
Mt Pleasant, MI 48858 989-773-7981
Fax: 800-669-0619 800-733-8821
www.delfield.com
Manufacturer and exporter of freezers and cabinets, display cases, cafeteria/restaurant serving counters, dispensers, ventilation systems, commercial refrigerators, mobile cafeteria systems, salad bars, pizza tables and stationary andmobile hot tables
Executive VP: Graham Tillotson
Manager (Eastern): Bill Hoffman
Manager (Western): Jeff Lucksted
Estimated Sales: $1 - 5 Million
Number Employees: 500-999
Square Footage: 535000
Parent Co: ENODIS
Brands:
Air Tech
Mark V
Shelleyglass
Shelleymatic

21520 Delfield Walk-Ins
980 South Isabella Rd
Mt. Pleasant, MI 48858 989-773-7981
Fax: 800-733-8821 800-669-0619
www.delfield.com
Parent Co: ENODIS

21521 Delfin Design & Manufacturing
23301 Antonio Pkwy
Rcho Sta Marg, CA 92688 949-888-4644
Fax: 949-888-4626 800-354-7919
john@delfinfs.com www.delfinfs.com
Manufacturer and exporter of plastic displayware including crocks, bowls, platters, trays, domes and covers
President: John Rief
VP Sales: Gary Mazzone
Estimated Sales: $2.5-5,000,000
Number Employees: 20-49
Square Footage: 25000

21522 Deli - Boy
100 Matthews Ave
Syracuse, NY 13209 315-488-4411
Fax: 315-488-4155 www.deli-boy.com
Owner: Lon Frocione
Estimated Sales: $20 - 50 Million
Number Employees: 50-99
Brands:
Grande
Premier/Nugget

21523 Delice Global Inc
150 Roosevelt Place
Palisades Park, NJ 07650 201-438-0300
Fax: 201-947-0320 info@deliceusa.com
www.deliceglobal.com
Baking equipment

21524 Deline Box Company
3700 Lima St
Denver, CO 80239 303-373-1430
Fax: 303-373-2325 webmaster@delinebox.com
www.delinebox.com
Corrugated boxes
President: Dade Deline
Sales Manager: Jim Davis
Estimated Sales: $10 - 20 Million
Number Employees: 100-249

21525 **Delkor Systems, Inc**
8700 Rendova St NE
Minneapolis, MN 55014 763-783-0855
Fax: 763-783-0875 800-328-5558
sales@delkorsystems.com
www.delkorsystems.com
Provides end-of-line packaging systems that deliver robust, innovative solutions for carton forming, loading, and closing, top load case and tray packing, flat pad shrink wrapping, and robotic palletizing. Delkor's packaging solutionsare engineered for maximum versatility and flexibility to help customers meet ever-changing market requirements while preserving their capital investments.
Owner: Dale Andersen
CFO: Terry Cook
Estimated Sales: $10 - 20 Million
Number Employees: 50-99

21526 **Dell Marking Systems**
721 Wanda St
Ferndale, MI 48220 248-547-7750
Fax: 248-544-9115 info@dellid.com
www.dellid.com
Marking and identification systems
President: Michael Grattan
Estimated Sales: $1-2.5 000,000
Number Employees: 10-19

21527 **Delphi International**
625 S Smith Rd
Suite 21
Tempe, AZ 85821-2967 480-483-8361
Fax: 480-483-8396
foodmachinery@delphifm.com
www.delphifm.com
Dealers of used processing equipment
Owner: Peter Yioulos
Estimated Sales: $.5 - 1 million
Number Employees: 1-4

21528 **Delran Label Corporation**
1829 Underwood Boulevard
Suite 10
Delran, NJ 08075-1241 856-764-1336
Fax: 856-764-3470
Wine industry labels

21529 **Delta Carbona**
376 Hollywood Ave # 208
Fairfield, NJ 07004-1807 973-808-6260
Fax: 973-808-5661 888-746-5599
www.carbona.com
Stain removers
President: Timothy Wells
Marketing Director: Sherry Polevoy
Purchasing Manager: Eileen Hirschfield
Estimated Sales: $1-2.5 Million
Number Employees: 5-9
Square Footage: 80000
Brands:
Carbona Cleanit! Oven Cleaner
Carpet Wizard
Color Run Remover
Pet Stain & Odor Remover
Stain Devils
Stain Stop
Stain Wizard
Stain Wizard Wipes

21530 **Delta Chemical Corporation**
P.O.Box 73054
Baltimore, MD 21273-3054 410-354-3253
Fax: 410-354-1021 800-282-5322
jack@deltachemical.com
www.deltachemical.com
Chlorine liquid bleaches
President: John Besson
CEO: Rebecca Besson
Director of Technology: Jim Dulko
Natl Sls Mgr: Jack Colgan
Director of Technology: Jim Dulko
Sales Manager (South): Joe Shemanski
Northern Regional Sales: Dan Moyer
Western/Caribbean Regional Sales Manager: Ed Penick
Vice President, Marketing & Sales: Terry Badwak
Estimated Sales: $20 - 50 Million
Number Employees: 100-249

21531 **Delta Container Corporation**
220 Plantation Rd
New Orleans, LA 70123-5312 504-733-7292
Fax: 504-734-8920 800-752-7292
www.prattindustries.com
Corrugated containers
President: Jim Hale
Chairman: Anthony PrattGlobal
CFO: Gary Byrd
Quality Control: Mark May
Estimated Sales: $10 - 20 Million
Number Employees: 50-99
Square Footage: 85000
Parent Co: Pratt Industries

21532 **Delta Cooling Towers**
41 Pine St Ste 103
Rockaway, NJ 07866 973-586-2201
Fax: 973-586-2243 800-289-3358
sales@deltacooling.com www.deltacooling.com
Polyethylene non-corroding cooling towers and air strippers
President: John Flaherty
Sales: David Jurgensen
Estimated Sales: Above $10MM
Number Employees: 10-19
Brands:
Paragon
Pioneer
Premier
Vanguard

21533 **Delta Cyklop Orga Pac**
2601 Westinghouse Blvd
Charlotte, NC 28273-6517 704-588-2510
Fax: 704-588-6838 800-446-4347
www.itwpbna.com
Polyester, steel, cord and polypropylene strapping; also, tape dispensers, strapping machines and elastic string tying equipment
VP Sales/Marketing: James Prieb
Estimated Sales: $10 - 20 Million
Number Employees: 20-49
Parent Co: Illinois Tool Works

21534 **Delta Engineering Corporation**
3 Freedom Way
Walpole, MA 02081 781-729-8650
Fax: 781-729-6149
info@deltaengineeringcorp.com
www.deltaengineeringcorp.com
Electronic counting and weighing systems, boxing and bagging equipment
Manager: Peter Knobel
R&D: Herb Mac Rae
Sales: Steve Hill
Production: Richard Pooler
Plant Manager: Pete Knobel
Estimated Sales: $2.5-5 000,000
Number Employees: 1-4
Number of Products: 25
Type of Packaging: Consumer, Food Service, Bulk

21535 **Delta F Corporation**
4 Constitution Way Ste I
Woburn, MA 01801 781-935-4600
Fax: 781-938-0531 www.delta-f.com
Oxygen analyzers
VP: John Swyers
Sales Manager: Margaret Lanoue
Estimated Sales: $50-100 Million
Number Employees: 50-99
Parent Co: TGE Group

21536 **Delta Foremost ChemicalCorporation**
3915 Air Park St
Memphis, TN 38118 901-363-4340
Fax: 800-238-5174 800-238-5150
sales@deltaforemost.com
www.deltaforemost.com
Cleaning compounds, insecticides, germicidal soap, aerosols, etc
President: Ronald Cooper
CFO: John Trobaugh
R & D: Steve Cooper
Quality Control: Charles Autks
Director Sales: George Foust
VP Sales Administrator: Steven Cole
Plant Manager: Tim Martin
Estimated Sales: $10-20 Million
Number Employees: 100-249
Square Footage: 100000

21537 **Delta Industrial Services**
11501 Eagle St NW
Coon Rapids, MN 55448 800-279-3358
Fax: 763-755-7799 800-279-3358
delta@deltaind.com www.deltaind.com
Narrow web converting, packaging
Estimated Sales: $1-5 000,000
Number Employees: 50-99

21538 **Delta Machine & Manufacturing**
137 Teal St
Saint Rose, LA 70087 504-949-8304
Fax: 504-467-0071 debra@deltamachinemfg.com
Manufacturer and exporter of bakery equipment including trough elevators
President/Owner: Dale Kessler
CEO: Andrew Kessler, Jr.
CFO: Debra Kessler
Estimated Sales: Below $1 Million
Number Employees: 5-9

21539 **Delta Plastics**
106 Delta Pl
Hot Springs, AR 71913 501-760-3000
Fax: 501-760-3005 sales@deltaplastics.com
www.deltaplastics.com
Packaging supplies for the food industry. Rexam PLC has now acquired the company as of September 2005
CEO: Lothar Schweigert
VP: Kurt Nyberg
VP Sales: Kurt Nyberg
Estimated Sales: $50 Million
Number Employees: 250-499
Parent Co: Rexam PLC
Type of Packaging: Food Service

21540 **Delta Pure Filtration**
11011 Richardson Rd
Ashland, VA 23005 804-798-2888
Fax: 804-798-3923 800-785-9450
tfurbee@deltapure.com www.deltapure.com
Manufacturer and exporter of active carbon cartridge filters for water, juice, vegetable oil, etc
Owner: Joseph Yack
Operations Manager: Frank Williams
Number Employees: 20-49
Square Footage: 18000
Type of Packaging: Bulk
Brands:
Aquatrust
Delta Pure

21541 **Delta Signs**
1802 Hickory Dr
Haltom City, TX 76117 817-838-0213
Fax: 817-665-0167 866-643-3582
deltasigns@delta-sign.com delta-sign.com
Electric signs and awnings; also, installation available with crane service
Owner: Steve Jessup
CEO: Sergio Contreras
CFO: Steve Jessup
Quality Control: N Cao
Estimated Sales: Below $5 Million
Number Employees: 5-9
Square Footage: 20800

21542 **Delta Systems**
535 West Dyke Road
Rogers, AR 72758 479-631-2210
Fax: 479-631-2217 800-631-2214
sales@delta-systems-inc.com
www.delta-systems-inc.com
Horizontal flow wrapping machinery, turnkey packaging systems, automatic feeding equipment, distribution equipment
President: Jake Bushey
Director of Sales: Liam Buckley
Estimated Sales: $5-10 Million
Number Employees: 20-49

21543 **Delta T Construction Company**
10838 Old Mill Rd Ste A
Omaha, NE 68154 402-333-0830
Fax: 402-333-6635 info@deltatconstruction.com
www.deltatconstruction.com
Cold storage doors and hardware, insulated building panels, insulation-floors, ceilings, and refrigerated structures
Manager: Ty Kestel
Estimated Sales: Less than $500,000
Number Employees: 1-4

21544 Delta Technology Corporation
1602 Townhurst Dr
Houston, TX 77043 713-464-7407
Fax: 713-461-6753 info@deltatechnology.com
www.deltatechnology.com
Electronic color sorting equipment
VP/Sales: Eduardo Libin
Estimated Sales: $5-10 Million
Number Employees: 10-19

21545 Delta Trak
PO Box 398
Pleasanton, CA 94566-0039 925-249-2250
Fax: 925-249-2251 800-962-6776
salesinfo@deltatrak.com www.deltatrak.com
Innovator of cold chain managament and food safety solutions. Product line includes a wide range of temperature, humidity, and pH monitoring and recodring devices such as data loggers, wireless systems, and a variety of professionalthermometers.
President/Founder: Fredrick Wu
R&D Director: George Krasten
Marketing/Business Development Director: Ray Caron
Operations Director: Steve Hibbs
Production Manager: Satwant Chand
Estimated Sales: $10-15 000,000
Number Employees: 70+
Number of Brands: 4
Number of Products: 220+
Square Footage: 6000
Brands:
Air Repair
Coldtrak
Flash Link
Temp Dot
Thermotrace

21546 Delta/Ducon
Three Tun Center
33 Sproul Road
Malvern, PA 19355 610-695-9700
Fax: 610-695-9724 800-238-2974
sales@deltaducon.com www.deltaducon.com
Pneumatic conveying equipment for flour, unloading rail cars, in-plant transfer and dust capture systems.
Manager: Gini Krisciunas
Sales Director: Ron Tempesta
Engineering: Dave Lizzi
Purchasing Manager: Cathy Heinser
Estimated Sales: $5 Million
Number Employees: 10-19
Brands:
Perma/Flo
Perma/Lok
Spira/Flo
Xl Airlock

21547 DeltaTrak
P.O.Box 398
Pleasanton, CA 94566 925-249-2250
Fax: 925-249-2251 800-962-6776
salesinfo@deltatrak.com www.deltatrak.com
DeltaTrak, Inc. is a leading innovator of cold chain management and temperature monitoring solutions. DeltaTrak offers a wide range of temperature and humidity data loggers and wireless systems. DeltaTrak develops and manufactures highquality portable test instruments that monitor/record temperature and humidity. DeltaTrak's comprehensive cold chain management systems also include professional digital probe and infrared thermometers.
Quality Assurance Manager: Tony Trapolino
VP Marketing & Business Development: Ray Carson
Director, Operations: Rick Delgado
Estimated Sales: $8,000,000
Number Employees: 250
Number of Brands: 20
Number of Products: 80+
Type of Packaging: Food Service, Private Label, Bulk
Brands:
Flash Link
Thermotrace

21548 Delux Manufacturing Company
4650 Airport Rd
PO Box 1027
Kearney, NE 68848-1027 308-237-2274
Fax: 308-234-3765 800-658-3240
info@deluxmfg.com www.deluxmfg.com
Manufacturer and exporter of grain dryers
President: Eric Michel
VP/Sales Manager: Bob Schultz
Estimated Sales: $2.5-5 Million
Number Employees: 20-49
Square Footage: 144000

21549 Deluxe Equipment Company
P.O.Box 11390
Bradenton, FL 34282-1390 941-753-4184
Fax: 941-753-4529 800-367-8931
deluxe@gte.net www.deluxeovens.com
Manufacturer and exporter of ovens, proofers, warmers.
President: Gib Smith
CFO: Sandra Smith
VP/Sales: Russ D'Aiuto
Estimated Sales: $2.5-5 Million
Number Employees: 10-19
Square Footage: 25000
Brands:
Convect a Ray
Deluxe

21550 (HQ)Dema Engineering Company
10020 Big Bend Rd
Saint Louis, MO 63122 314-966-3533
Fax: 314-965-8319 800-325-3362
jond@demaeng.com www.demaeng.com
Manufacturer and exporter of warewash, laundry and liquid soap dispensers including injectors, proportioning detergent feeders, rinse pumps and foamers
President: Carl Deutsch
Sales/Marketing Manager: Jonathan Deutsch
Purchasing Manager: David Deutsch
Estimated Sales: $10-20 Million
Number Employees: 20-49
Square Footage: 28000
Other Locations:
Dema Engineering Co.
Gerald MO

21551 Demaco
4645 Metropolitan Ave
Ridgewood, NY 11385
Fax: 718-417-9264
Manufacturer and exporter of pasta equipment
President: Leonard Defrancisci
VP: John Deluca
Mngr: Amy Casaburri
Estimated Sales: $10-20 Million
Number Employees: 20-49
Parent Co: Howden Food Equipment

21552 Demarle
8 Corporate Dr Ste 1
Cranbury, NJ 08512 609-395-0219
Fax: 609-395-1027 888-353-9726
info@demarleusa.com www.demarleusa.com
Silicone applied mold and trays for baking and freezing
President: Hatsuo Takeuchi
Sales Manager: Eliane Feiner
Estimated Sales: $5 - 10 000,000
Number Employees: 10-19
Brands:
Flexipan
Silform
Silpat

21553 Dematic Corp
507 Plymouth Ave NE
Grand Rapids, MI 49505 877-725-7500
Fax: 616-913-7701 877-725-7500
usinfo@dematic.com www.dematic.us
Material handling, systems and management.
CEO: John K Baysore
Number Employees: 770
Parent Co: Siemens Dematic AG
Brands:
Dematic
Direct It
Pick Director
Q-Can
Rapid Sort
Rapistan
Siplace
Sort Director
Staging Director

21554 Dembling & Dembling Architects
307 Washington Avenue
Albany, NY 12206 518-463-8066
Fax: 518-463-8610 daved@ddarch.com
www.ddarch.com
Consultant specializing in the design of food service and hospitality establishments
President: Daniel Dembling AIA
Partner: David Dembling
Estimated Sales: Below $5 Million
Number Employees: 10-19

21555 Demeyere Na, Llc
3 Dorchester Dr
Westport, CT 06880-4037 203-255-2402
Fax: 203-255-2406 800-338-7304
dem.breeden@prodigy.net
www.demeyerecookware.com
Commercial stainless steel cookware with seven ply construction, industry rated for all energy sources especially efficient induction
President: John Walters
Estimated Sales: $50 Million+
Number Employees: 1-4
Number of Brands: 11
Number of Products: 1700
Square Footage: 120000

21556 Dempster Systems
PO Box 1388
Toccoa, GA 30577-1424 706-886-2327
Fax: 706-886-0088
Manufacturer and exporter of refuse handling systems
President: John Boonstra
Estimated Sales: $20-50 Million
Number Employees: 100-249
Parent Co: Technology
Type of Packaging: Consumer, Food Service, Bulk

21557 Demptos Glass Corporation
2300 Cordelia Rd
Fairfield, CA 94534 707-422-9999
Fax: 707-422-1242 david@demptos.com
www.demptos.com
Manufacturers of wine bottles, champagne bottles, spirits bottles, beer bottles etc
Manager: John Symank
COO: Rob Belke
General Manager: John Symank
Estimated Sales: $20-50 Million
Number Employees: 50-99

21558 Den Ray Sign Company
1057 Whitehall St
Jackson, TN 38305 731-427-5466
Fax: 731-427-5473 800-530-7291
sales@denraysign.com www.denraysign.com
Plastic and neon signs; custom designs, service and maintenance available
President: Rhea Deming
Estimated Sales: $500,000-$1 Million
Number Employees: 10-19

21559 Denair Trailer Company
1195 W Glenwood Avenue
Turlock, CA 95380-5703 209-667-1551
Fax: 209-667-0414 800-533-5046
www.denair.com
Wine industry agricultural trailers
Estimated Sales: $100-500 Million
Number Employees: 20-49

21560 Denice & Filice PackingCompany
10001 Fairview Rd
Hollister, CA 95023-9209 831-636-0544
Fax: 831-637-4174
Estimated Sales: $20 - 50 Million
Number Employees: 20-49

21561 Denman Equipment
2020 Satinwood Dr
Memphis, TN 38119-5631 901-755-7135
Fax: 901-754-0105 dennydenman@comcast.net
www.denserv.com
Dealer of used and rebuilt food processing equipment for the meat and poultry industry
Owner: Pierce Denman
Estimated Sales: $.5 - 1 million
Number Employees: 1-4

21562 **(HQ)Denmar Corporation**
1005 Reed Rd
North Dartmouth, MA 02747-1567 508-999-3295
Fax: 508-999-6108 henrydenmar@corp.com
Stainless steel and wood tables including dish, work and steam; also, shelving and sinks
President: Henry Martin
Estimated Sales: $1 - 2.5 Million
Number Employees: 600
Other Locations:
Denmar Corp.
North Dartmouth MA
Brands:
Aqua-Vent
Denmar
Simplex

21563 **(HQ)Dennis Group**
1537 Main St Fl 2
Springfield, MA 01103 413-787-1785
Fax: 413-787-1786 mccreary@dennisgrp.com
www.dennisgrp.com
Full-Service architectural, engineering, process design and construction management firm providing total project solutions, from conception through start-up, exclusively to the food and beverags industries.
President: Thomas Dennis
Sales: Dan McCreary
Estimated Sales: $15-$25 Million
Number Employees: 100-249
Other Locations:
Salt Lake City UT
San Diego CA
Wheaton IL
Toronto, Canada

21564 **Denstor Mobile Storage Systems**
2966 Wilson Drive NW
Walker, MI 49534 616-735-9100
Fax: 616-988-4045 800-234-7477
sales@pippmobile.com www.denstor.com
High density mobile storage systems
President, CEO: Craig J. Umans
Chief Financial Officer: Keith Carpentier
Director of Retail Sales: Len Kowalski
Operations Manager: Tom French
Estimated Sales: $5 - 10 Million
Number Employees: 20
Parent Co: Pipp Mobile Storage Systems, Inc

21565 **DentalOne Partners**
17300 Dallas Parkway
Suite 1070
Dallas, TX 75248-7725 972-755-0800
Fax: 972-387-9774
dallas.office@dentalonepartners.com
www.dental-one.com
Printing materials, film coextruded, film laminated, film LLDPE, film LDPE, stand-up pouch, film stretch, film shrink, film oriented polxprotylene, film coated
CEO: R Kirk Huntsman
Estimated Sales: $3 - 5 Million
Number Employees: 20-49

21566 **Denver Instrument Company**
5 Orville Dr.
Bohemia, NY 11716 303-431-7255
Fax: 303-423-4831 800-321-1135
info@denverinstrument.com
www.denverinstrumentusa.com
Balances, multiple weighing units
Manager: Karen Ware
Estimated Sales: Below $5 Million
Number Employees: 10-19
Brands:
Apex

21567 **Denver Mixer Company**
6565 Vine Ct
Denver, CO 80229 303-287-0025
Fax: 303-287-0924
President: Chris Barnhill
Estimated Sales: $2.5-5 000,000
Number Employees: 5-9

21568 **Denver Reel & Pallet Company**
4600 Monaco Parkaway
Denver, CO 80216 303-321-1920
Fax: 303-321-1949 denverreel@aol.com
www.denverreelandpallet.com
Pallets, reels, skids, boxes and crates
President: Kurt Heimbrock
CFO: Kurt Heimbrock
VP: Darold Herrera
R&D: Kurt Heimbrock
Quality Control: Kurt Heimbrock
Estimated Sales: $2.5 - 5 Million
Number Employees: 20-49
Square Footage: 16000
Brands:
Dratco

21569 **Denver Sign Systems**
1701 31st St
Denver, CO 80216-5003 303-637-0287
Fax: 303-295-2093 888-295-7446
www.denversigns.com
Displays and signs including neon, lighted and nonilluminated; installation services available
President: Mike Nudd
VP: Jennifer Dent
Estimated Sales: Below $5 Million
Number Employees: 5 to 9

21570 **Depaul Industries**
4950 NE M L King Blvd
Portland, OR 97211 503-281-1289
Fax: 503-284-0548 800-518-6637
lfletcher@depaulindustries.com
www.depaulindustries.com
DePaul Industries provides food and consumer goods packaging services.
CEO: Bennett Johnson
Foods & Consumer Goods Packaging Manager: Chris Cusack
Business Development Manager: Lori Fletcher
Type of Packaging: Consumer

21571 **Dependable DistributionServices**
1301 Union Ave
Pennsauken, NJ 08110 856-665-1762
Fax: 856-488-6332
rmassman@dependableinc.com
Coffee blending and mixing equipment, cleaners (green coffee), weighing machines and augers
Owner: Harvey Weiner
Estimated Sales: $5 - 10 000,000
Number Employees: 20-49

21572 **Dependable Machine Company**
80 Pompton Ave
Verona, NJ 07044-2945 973-239-7800
Fax: 973-239-7855 800-356-3237
dependable_machine_co@att.net.net
Manufacturer, importer and exporter of screen and pad printing equipment, printing inks and accessories
President: Thomas Skeels
VP: Brett Skeels
Estimated Sales: $2.5 - 5 Million
Number Employees: 10-19
Square Footage: 20000

21573 **(HQ)Derse**
1234 N 62nd St
Milwaukee, WI 53213-2996 414-257-2000
Fax: 414-257-3798 800-562-2300
ezeum@derse.com www.derse.com
Custom exhibits and highway business signs
CEO: William Haney
President: Adam Beckett
VP Sales/Marketing: Kent Jones
Estimated Sales: $10-20 Million
Number Employees: 100-249
Other Locations:
Derse
Carrollton TX

21574 **Des Moines Stamp Manufacturing Company**
PO Box 1798
Des Moines, IA 50306-1798 515-288-7245
Fax: 515-288-0418 888-236-7739
info@dmstamp.com www.dmstamp.com
Rubber stamps, notary seals and stencils
President: Thomas Child
Estimated Sales: $2.5-5 Million
Number Employees: 20-49
Square Footage: 80000

21575 **Desco Equipment Corporation**
1903 Case Pkwy
Twinsburg, OH 44087-2343 330-405-1581
Fax: 330-405-1584 desco@descoequipment.com
www.descoequipment.com
Innovators of high quality, cost-efficient printing systems for the container and closure industry.
President: Leo Henry
Purchasing Manager: Dennis Sweeney
Estimated Sales: $3.7 Million
Number Employees: 26
Square Footage: 200000
Brands:
Desco

21576 **Descon EDM**
54 W Main St
PO Box 189
Brocton, NY 14716 716-792-9300
Fax: 716-792-9363 descon@cecomet.net
Manufacturer and exporter of material handling equipment including vibrating and belt conveyors, graders, etc
President: David Beehler
CEO: David Beehler
R&D: Christopher Beehler
General Manager: C Beehler
Estimated Sales: Below $5 Million
Number Employees: 1-4
Square Footage: 10000

21577 **Desert Box & Supply Corporation**
P.O.Box 281
Thermal, CA 92274-281 760-399-5161
Wooden boxes, packaging materials and corrugated boxes
President: Michael Wills
Co-Owner: Ann Wills
Estimated Sales: Less than $500,000
Number Employees: 10

21578 **Deshazo Crane Company**
P.O.Box 1450
Alabaster, AL 35007-2062 205-664-2006
Fax: 205-664-3668 contact@deshazo.com
www.deshazo.com
Manufacturer and exporter of cranes including overhead bridge, gantry and semi-gantry
CEO: Guy K Mitchell Jr
Estimated Sales: $20-50 Million
Number Employees: 100-249
Type of Packaging: Bulk

21579 **Desiccare**
10600 Shoemaker Avenue
Suite C
Santa Fe Springs, CA 90670-4073 888-932-0405
Fax: 562-903-2272 800-446-6650
desiccant@desiccare.com www.desiccare.com
Silica gel, clay, molecular sieve and activated carbon desiccants ranging in size from 0.25 grams to 2,500 grams
President: Ken Blankenhorn
Estimated Sales: $10-20 Million
Number Employees: 50-99

21580 **Design Group Inc**
1002 S Prospect Ave
Clearwater, FL 33756 727-441-2825
Fax: 727-446-0388
thedesigngroup@tampabay.rr.com
www.thedesigngroupincusa.com
Interior design services for hospitality - hotels and restaurants. Licensed in the state of Florida (ID - 0001657, IBC - 000317)
President: Jeanette Brewer
Vice President: Delayna Cowley Nestell
Marketing: Jeanetter Brewer
Sales: Delayna Nestell
Production: Irene Bishop
Purchasing Manager: Delayna Cowley Nestell
Estimated Sales: Less than $500,000
Number Employees: 4
Square Footage: 12000
Brands:
Daniel Paul
Flexsteel Contract
Lexmark Carpet
McI Group
Mtj Seating
Shelly Williams Seating

21581 Design Ideas
2521 Stockyard Road
P.O.Box 2967
Springfield, IL 62708-2967 217-525-8764
Fax: 217-753-3080 800-426-6394
designideas@designid.com www.designid.com
Containers, gift packaging, and candle holders
Owner: Andy Van Meter
Director Sales/Marketing: Christine Netznik
Number Employees: 100-249
Number of Products: 1500

21582 Design Label Manufacturing
7 Capitol Dr
East Lyme, CT 06333 860-739-6266
Fax: 860-739-7659 800-666-1575
customerservice@designlabel.com
www.designlabel.com
Pressure sensitive and promotional labels, clam shell and polystyrene inserts and coupons
President: Jeff P Dunphy
Controller: Kim Dunphy
Estimated Sales: $10-20 Million
Number Employees: 20-49

21583 Design Mark Corporation
3 Kendrick Rd
Wareham, MA 02571 508-295-9591
Fax: 508-295-6752 800-451-3275
support@design-mark.com
www.design-mark.com
Manufacturer and exporter of labels, nameplates and membrane switch panels
President: Carl Burquist
Quality Control: Jim Brawders
Operations: Jon Winzler
Marketing Director: Denise Shurtley
Estimated Sales: $14 Million
Number Employees: 50-99
Square Footage: 20000
Type of Packaging: Bulk

21584 Design Packaging Company
100 Hazel Ave
Glencoe, IL 60022-1731 773-486-8100
Fax: 773-486-2160 800-321-7659
Polypropylene and polyethylene bags and sheets; importer of polyethylene and polyproplyne bags; exporter of polyethylene sleeves and bags
President: Myron Horvitz
CFO: Greg Horvitz
VP: Randy Block
Sales Representative: Greg Horvitz
Purchasing Agent: Randy Block
Estimated Sales: $5 - 10 Million
Number Employees: 20-49
Square Footage: 40000
Brands:
Designbags
Foiltex
Kristalene

21585 Design Plastics
3550 Keystone Dr
Omaha, NE 68134 402-572-7177
Fax: 402-572-0500 800-491-0786
contactus@designplastics.com
www.designplastics.com
Plastic packaging and containers for dry and frozen foods
President: Rick Breden
Director Marketing: Sylvio Rebolloso
Estimated Sales: $10-20 Million
Number Employees: 100-249

21586 Design Specialties
1890 Dixwell Ave Ste 200
Hamden, CT 06514 203-288-3587
Fax: 203-288-3594 800-999-1584
design@duralux4you.com
www.designspecialties.org
Reusable plastic tableware including flatware, trays, dishes, tumblers, mugs and bowls; also, insulated trays and high temperature dishes available for cooking and chilling
Owner: Patricia Whitlock
VP: Patricia Whitlock
Estimated Sales: $5 - 10 Million
Number Employees: 5-9
Number of Brands: 1
Number of Products: 40
Brands:
Duralux

21587 Design Systems
38799 W 12 Mile Rd Ste 100
Farmington Hills, MI 48331 248-489-4300
Fax: 248-489-4321 800-660-4374
pmunzenberger@dsidsc.com www.dsidsc.com
Process engineering company specializing in lean manufacturing and controls integration, through put simulation
Manager: Steve Puranen
Sales Director: Paul Munzenberger
Estimated Sales: $35 Million
Number Employees: 250-499

21588 Design Technology Corporation
5 Suburban Park Drive
Billerica, MA 01821-3904 978-663-7000
Fax: 978-663-6841 info@designtechsales.com
www.design-technology.com
Custom designed and built food processing, material handling, packaging, inspection and assembly equipment
President: Marvin Menzin
Estimated Sales: $5-10 Million
Number Employees: 20-49
Square Footage: 120000

21589 Design Technology Corporation
26 Mason Street
Lexington, MA 02421 781-862-5107
Fax: 303-440-5127 800-597-7063
webinfo@design-technology.com
www.design-technology.com
Manufacturer and exporter of material handling equipment, food processing machinery and process control systems
President: Marvin Menzin
Estimated Sales: $1-2,500,000
Number Employees: 4

21590 Designer's Choice Stainless
7620 W Olive Ave
Peoria, AZ 85345-7102 623-878-7900
Fax: 623-878-7774 800-592-3274
Stainless steel, wooden and laminated food processing machinery, bar equipment, dining room seating, utensils, counters, etc.; also, turnkey packaging and installation available
President: Eric Wasserstrom
VP Finance and Administration: Robert Hudgins
Sales Manager: Mark Medonich
Plant Manager: Lou Weaver
Estimated Sales: $10 - 20 Million
Number Employees: 100-249
Square Footage: 87000
Parent Co: Wasserstrom Company

21591 Designers Plastics
4740 126th Ave N Ste A
Clearwater, FL 33762 727-573-1643
Fax: 727-572-7078 sales@designersplastics.com
www.designersplastics.com
Acrylic displays
President: Bruce Ely
CFO and Quality Controller: Penny Carrigan
Estimated Sales: $1 - 2.5 Million
Number Employees: 10-19

21592 Designers-Folding Box Corporation
84 Tennessee St
Buffalo, NY 14204 716-853-5141
Fax: 716-853-5149
sales@designersfoldingbox.com
www.designersfoldingbox.com
Folding paper boxes and carry-out trays and boxes; also, die cut inserts
President: Jeffrey Winney
CSR: Teri McAndrews
PA: Donald Rounds
Estimated Sales: $5-10 Million
Type of Packaging: Consumer, Food Service, Private Label, Bulk

21593 Designpro Engineering
20092 Edison Circle East
Clearwater, MN 55320 320-558-6000
Fax: 320-558-6110 800-221-4144
dpro@designproengineering.com
www.franklinoutdoor.com
Poultry cutting machinery
Owner: Keith Franklin
Director: John Boughner
Head Technical Department: Jon Boughner
Estimated Sales: $500,000-$1 Million
Number Employees: 1-4
Square Footage: 28000

21594 Despro Manufacturing
PO Box 2503
Cedar Grove, NJ 07009-2503 973-239-0202
Fax: 973-239-1595 800-292-9906
mailbox@emcoplastics.com
www.emcoplastics.com
Acrylic bulk food containers and bins, steel shelving, display racks, point of purchase displays, awnings and pastry cases
President: James Mc Namara
VP: Mark Mercadante
Estimated Sales: $20 - 50 Million
Number Employees: 100-249
Square Footage: 40000
Parent Co: Emco Industrial Plastics

21595 Detecto Scale
203 E Daugherty St
Webb City, MO 64870 417-673-4631
Fax: 417-673-5001 800-641-2008
detecto@cardet.com www.detecto.com
Weighing scales
President: David H Perry
Chief Financial Officer: Elise Crume
Vice President: Larry Hicks
Research/Development: Tony Herrin
Quality Control: Ginger Harper
Marketing: Jonathan Sabo
Sales: Fred Cox
Operations/Production: Matt Stovern
Estimated Sales: $45 Million
Number Employees: 350
Square Footage: 350000
Parent Co: Cardinal Scale Manufacturing Company

21596 Detecto Scale Company
203 E Daugherty St
Webb City, MO 64870 417-673-4631
Fax: 417-673-5001 800-641-2008
detecto@cardet.com www.cardet.com
Manufacturer and exporter of scales including portion control, top loading, price computing, bench, platform, counter, pre-packaging, hanging and receiving
President: David Perry
Chief Financial Officer: Elise Crume
Vice President: Larry Hicks
Research And Development: Tony Herrin
Quality Control: Ginger Harper
Marketing Director: Jonathan Sabo
Sales: Fred Cox
Advertising Manager: Jonathan Sabo
Estimated Sales: $50 - 60 Million
Number Employees: 350
Square Footage: 400000
Parent Co: Cardinal Scale Manufacturing Company
Type of Packaging: Food Service
Brands:
Cardinal
Detecto

21597 Detex Corporation
302 Detex Dr
New Braunfels, TX 78130 800-729-3839
Fax: 830-620-6711 detex@detex.com
www.detex.com
Security locks, alarms, panels, switches and electric and manual guard tour clocks
President: John Blodgett
Chairman of the Board: Philip Haselton
R & D: George Val
Director Sales/Marketing: Gary Hackney
National Accounts Sales Manager: Ken Khueler
Production Manager (Hardware): Greg Drake
Estimated Sales: $5-10 Million
Number Employees: 100-249

21598 Detroit Forming
19100 W 8 Mile Rd
Southfield, MI 48075 248-352-8108
Fax: 248-352-1566 sales@detroitforming.net
www.detroitforming.net
Manufacturer and exporter of plastic food trays for meat, produce, ice cream and cookies
President: Leigh Rodney
National Sales Manager: Ken Sherry
Estimated Sales: $10 - 20 Million
Number Employees: 100-249
Type of Packaging: Food Service

21599 **Detroit Marking Products**
15100 Castleton St
Detroit, MI 48227 313-838-9760
Fax: 800-831-4243 800-833-8222
dmp@dmpco.com www.dmpco.com
Rubber stamps
President: William Foerg
Estimated Sales: $1-2.5 Million
Number Employees: 10-19

21600 **Devar**
706 Bostwick Ave
Bridgeport, CT 06605 203-368-6751
Fax: 203-368-3747 800-566-6822
sales@devarinc.com www.devarinc.com
Process control instruments including indicators, data acquisition recorders and temperature transmitters, alarms and panel meters; also, pH analyzers and instrument calibrators
President: Tony Ruscito
VP Engineering: A Gura
VP Sales: Terry Tomasko
Estimated Sales: $2.5 - 5 Million
Number Employees: 20-49
Square Footage: 20000
Brands:
Smart Chart

21601 **Developak Corporation**
2525 Pioneer Ave
Vista, CA 92081-8419 760-598-7404
Fax: 760-598-7402
Custom packaging machinery
President: Brian Pike
Executive VP: Annette Watson
Estimated Sales: Less than $500,000
Number Employees: 1-4
Square Footage: 2000

21602 **Development Workshop**
555 W 25th St
Idaho Falls, ID 83402 208-524-1550
Fax: 208-523-3148 800-657-5597
ktg@dwinc.org www.dwinc.org
Plastic trash liners and specialty and grain bags; also, hand cleaners and wooden pallets
President: Dwight Whittaker
VP: Gerald Hodges
CFO: Bruce Cook
CEO: Michael O'Bleness
Mktg Mgr and Sales Mgr and Pub Relns Mgr: Gregg Katainen
Operations Mgr: Mike O'Bleness
Prodn Mgr: Joe Hodge
VP Operations: Gerry Hodges
VP Upper Valley Industries: Rose Murphy
Estimated Sales: $2.5-5 Million
Number Employees: 100-249

21603 **Deville Technologies**
8515 Bourassa West
St Laurent, QC 4Y5 1P7
Canada 514-366-4545
Fax: 514-366-9606 866-404-4545
info@devilletechnologies.com
www.devilletechnologies.com
Manufacturers of high capacity food reduction equipment such as shredders, graters, dicers, strip cutters
President: Angelo Penta
Marketing: Lou Penta
Sales: Terry Baggott
Number Employees: 15

21604 **Dewatering Equipment Company**
6002 SW Texas Court
Portland, OR 97219-1175 503-246-8899
Fax: 503-248-7016 800-426-1723
dewatering@attbi.com
www.dewateringequipment.com
Number Employees: 4

21605 **Dewey & Wilson Displays**
5635 Bancroft Avenue
Lincoln, NE 68506-4517 402-489-0868
Advertising signs, posters and emblems
President: Lynn Wilson
Estimated Sales: $500,000-$1 Million
Number Employees: 1-4

21606 **(HQ)Dewied International**
5010 East I H 10
San Antonio, TX 78219 210-661-6161
Fax: 210-662-6112 800-992-5600
hq@dewiedint.com www.dewied.com
Natural and synthetic sausage casings specializing in hog, sheep and beef casings
President/CEO: Howard Dewied
VP Sales: George Burt
Estimated Sales: $10-20 Million
Number Employees: 50-99
Brands:
Dewied

21607 **Dex-O-Tex Crossfield Products Corporation**
3000 E Harcourt St
Compton, CA 90221-5589 310-886-9100
Fax: 310-886-9119 jodih@cpcmail.net
www.crossfieldproducts.com
Seamless sanitary flooring
President/CEO: Bradford Watt
CFO: David Johnson
Marketing Director: Jodi Hood
Estimated Sales: $30 Million
Number Employees: 100-249
Number of Brands: 3
Number of Products: 25

21608 **Dexco**
104 N Maple Ave
Leola, PA 17540 717-656-2616
Fax: 717-656-3281 800-345-8170
tcrippen@rosstechnology.com
www.rosstechnology.com
Manufacturer and exporter of storage rack systems including pallet rack, drive-in, thru-flow and push back
Owner: Don Spicher
Sales Manager: Tom Crippen
Estimated Sales: $20-50 Million
Number Employees: 50-99
Square Footage: 54000
Type of Packaging: Bulk

21609 **Dexter Corporation**
2 Elm St
Windsor Locks, CT 06096 860-623-8234
Fax: 860-654-8301 ellen.miles@ahlstrom.com
www.dexternonwovens.com
Tea and coffee industry filters (paper), pouch materials (cellophane, paper, films), teabag paper
VP: Gary Dzioba
Number Employees: 5,000-9,999

21610 **Dexter-Russell**
44 River St
Southbridge, MA 01550 508-765-0201
Fax: 508-764-2897 sales@dexter-russell.com
www.dexter-russell.com
Manufacturer and exporter of knives, turners and spatulas
President: Alan Peppel
Sales: Kevin Clark
Estimated Sales: $10 - 20 Million
Number Employees: 250-499
Brands:
Connoisseur
Dexter Russell
Russell Green River
Russell International
Sani-Safe
Sofgrip

21611 **Diablo Products**
610 S 32nd St
Fort Dodge, IA 50501 515-576-4948
Fax: 515-955-4206 800-548-1385
sales@diablo-products.com
www.diablo-products.com
Manufacturer and exporter of soaps, detergent and oven cleaners
Estimated Sales: $500,000
Number Employees: 1-4
Brands:
Diablo

21612 **Diablo Valley Packaging**
2373 N Watney Way
Fairfield, CA 94533 707-422-4300
Fax: 707-422-4545 sales@dvpackaging.com
www.dvpackaging.com
Wine industry bottles and packaging
Owner: Jeffrey Jones
VP: William Bronson
Estimated Sales: $25 Million
Number Employees: 10-19

21613 **Diagraph Corporation**
1 Missouri Research Park Dr
St Charles, MO 63304-5685 636-300-2000
Fax: 636-300-2003 800-722-1125
info@diagraph.com www.diagraph.com
Automated coding and labeling systems for product identification, case marking, shipment addressing and barcoding
Manager: Cathie Windle
Marketing Director: Quentin Griesenauer
VP Slaes: John Campbell
Estimated Sales: $50-100 Million
Number Employees: 100-249

21614 **Dial Corporation**
19001 N Scottsdale Rd
Scottsdale, AZ 85255 480-754-3425
Fax: 480-754-1098 www.henkelna.com
Cleaning products including bath and liquid soaps, floor polish and detergents
President/Owner: Bradley Casper
Senior VP/Controller: Ian Parrish
Senior VP Research & Development: Richard Theiler
Senior VP Sales: Tracy VanBibber
Number Employees: 775
Parent Co: Henkel KGaA
Brands:
Armour Star Canned Foods

21615 **Diamond & Lappin**
20-21 Wagaraw Road
Bldg 30a
Fair Lawn, NJ 07410-1322 973-636-9550
Fax: 973-636-9590 877-527-7461
estimates@diamondlappin.com
www.diamondlappin.com
Consultant specializing in private label designing including photography, pre-press and print, digital and conventional production. Package design and manufacture, labeling
Estimated Sales: $1 - 5 Million
Number Employees: 5
Square Footage: 16000
Parent Co: Lappin Marketing Group

21616 **Diamond Automation**
23550 Haggerty Rd
Farmington Hills, MI 48335 248-426-9394
Fax: 248-476-0849
techinfo@diamondsystems.com
www.diamondsystems.com
Manufacturer and exporter of automated packaging equipment; also, egg production and processing equipment
President: Michel Defenbau
Estimated Sales: $20 - 50 Million
Number Employees: 1-4

21617 **Diamond Brands**
1800 Cloquet Ave
Cloquet, MN 55720 218-879-6700
Fax: 800-777-7943 diamondinfo@alltrista.com
www.diamondbrands.com
Matches, toothpicks, plastic cutlery, ice cream sticks, candles, etc
Estimated Sales: $20-50 Million
Number Employees: 250-499

21618 **Diamond Chain Company**
402 Kentucky Ave
Indianapolis, IN 46225 317-638-6431
Fax: 317-633-2243 800-872-4246
custsvc@diamondchain.com
www.diamondchain.com
Manufacturer and exporter of transmission chains and chain drives
President: Mike Fwiderski
VP Operations: Jerry Randich
CFO: Sheeley Faback
Quality Control: Joe Fossard
VP Sales/Marketing: Douglas Bademoch
VP Operations: Pat Taylor
Purchasing Manager: Barbara Heacock
Number Employees: 500-999
Parent Co: Amsted Industries

21619 Diamond Chemical & Supply Company
524 S Walnut St
Wilmington, DE 19801 302-656-7786
Fax: 302-656-3039 800-355-7786
sales@diamondchemical.com
www.diamondchemical.com
Wholesaler/distributor of paper products, commercial dishwashing and laundry chemicals, floor maintenance and janitorial equipment and insecticides
President: Richard Ventresca
CFO: Saeed Malik
VP: Richard Ventresca
Sales Manager: Gene Mirolli
Warehouse: Ryan Rynar
Estimated Sales: $5 Million
Number Employees: 20-49
Square Footage: 26000

21620 Diamond Chemical Company
P.O.Box 7428
East Rutherford, NJ 07073-7428 201-935-4300
Fax: 201-935-6997 800-654-7627
sales@diamondchem.com
www.diamondchem.com
Manufacturer and exporter of detergents and cleaners for meat and poultry plants; also, laundry detergent and bleach
President: Harold Diamond
CFO: R Diamond
Estimated Sales: $20 - 50 Million
Number Employees: 100-249
Square Footage: 137000
Brands:
Diamond

21621 Diamond Electronics
P.O.Box 415
Lancaster, OH 43130 740-687-4001
Fax: 740-756-4237 800-443-6680
consultation@diamondelectronics.com
www.diamondelectronics.com
Closed circuit camera and discreet dome surveillance systems
Director Marketing: Pat Kula
Customer Service Manager: Lee Montgomery
Estimated Sales: $1 - 5 Million

21622 Diamond Machining Technologies
85 Hayes Memorial Dr
Suite 1
Marlborough, MA 01752 508-481-5944
Fax: 508-485-3924 800-666-4368
dmtsharp@dmtsharp.com www.dmtsharp.com
Manufacturer and exporter of knife sharpeners
President: Christine Miller
Chairman: Elizabeth Powell
R&D: Stan Watson
Sales Manager: George Pettee
Estimated Sales: $1 - 2.5 Million
Number Employees: 40
Square Footage: 20000
Brands:
Diamond

21623 (HQ)Diamond Packaging
111 Commerce Drive
Rochester, NY 14623 585-334-8030
Fax: 585-334-9141 800-333-4079
sales@diamondpkg.com
www.diamondpackaging.com
Folding carton manufacturing and contract packaging services
President/Owner: Kirsten Werner
CEO/Owner: Karla Fichter
CFO: Keith Robinson
CEO: Karla Fichter
Research & Development: Dave Ziemba
Quality Control: Heidi Ingersol
Director of Marketing: Dennis Bacchetta
Director of Business Development: Sue Julien
Director of Business Development: Dave Semrau
Plant Manager: Dan Gurbacki
Estimated Sales: $20 - 50 Million
Number Employees: 225
Square Footage: 90000
Type of Packaging: Consumer, Private Label
Other Locations:
Diamond Packaging Company
Rochester NY

21624 Diamond Pheonix Corporation
P.O.Box 1608
Lewiston, ME 04241-1608 207-784-1381
Fax: 207-786-0271
dfrohlich@diamondphoenix.com
www.diamondphoenix.com
President: E Strayhorn
CFO: Peter Pacetti
President, Chief Executive Officer: Tom Coyne
Director of Sales: Dennis Duell
Estimated Sales: $20 - 50 Million
Number Employees: 50-99

21625 Diamond Roll-Up Door
P.O.Box 420
Upper Sandusky, OH 43351 419-294-3373
Fax: 419-294-3329
diamondinfo@australmonsoon.com
www.diamondrollupdoor.com
Tractor trailer and cargo van roll-up doors; industrial roll-up doors
President: Ray Van Gunten
Admin Manager: Sheri Gatchell
Estimated Sales: $10 - 20 000,000
Number Employees: 50-99

21626 Diamond Sign Company
2950 Airway Ave Ste D9
Costa Mesa, CA 92626 714-545-1440
Fax: 714-545-1449 diamondsignco@aol.com
Flags, pennants, banners, signs, displays and exhibits; screen printing service available
President: John Kasell
Partner: Nancy Gill
Estimated Sales: Below $5,000,000
Number Employees: 1-4
Square Footage: 3000

21627 Diamond Water Conditioning
PO Box 39
Hortonville, WI 54944-0039 920-779-9940
Fax: 920-779-9950 800-236-8931
info@diamondh2o.com www.diamondh2o.com
Water treatment and purification systems including filters, softeners, etc
President: Tom Griesbach
Sales Commercial/Industrial: Bill Calabria
Estimated Sales: Below $5 Million
Number Employees: 10
Square Footage: 20000

21628 Diamond Wipes International
4651 Schaefer Ave
Chino, CA 91710 909-230-9888
Fax: 909-230-9885 800-454-1077
info@diamondwipes.com
www.diamondwipes.com
Manufacturer and exporter of pre-moistened paper towels
President: Eve Yen
R&D: Map Taing
Quality Control: Anthony Castro
Marketing: Anthony Reyes
Estimated Sales: $5 - 10 Million
Number Employees: 50-99
Square Footage: 7500
Brands:
Diamond Wipes
La Fresh
With Our Compliment

21629 Diazteca Company
993 E Frontage Rd
Rio Rico, AZ 85648 520-281-4281
Fax: 520-281-1024 gabriela@diazteca.com
www.diazteca.com
Processor and distributor of Mexican fresh mangos, fresh hot peppers, granulated cane sugar, refrigerated and frozen lean beef, frozen shrimp, frozen IQF fruits and vegetables, aseptic fruit purees and other food products.
Owner/President: Ismael Diaz Jr
Vice President: Roderigo Diaz
Estimated Sales: $2.6 Million
Type of Packaging: Consumer, Private Label, Bulk

21630 Dibpack USA
196 Coolidge Avenue
Englewood, NJ 07631-4522 201-871-8787
Fax: 201-871-8908 800-990-3424
info@dibipack.com www.dibipack.com
Packaging, graphic and printing services
President: Ira Dermanski
CEO: Peter Quercia
CFO: Ira Dermanski
Number Employees: 20

21631 Dick's Packing Plant
7745 State Route 37 E
New Lexington, OH 43764-9512 740-342-4150
Fresh meats
Partner: Richard Knipe
Partner: Blanche Knipe
Partner: Rex Knipe
Estimated Sales: $320,000
Number Employees: 12
Square Footage: 3955
Type of Packaging: Consumer, Food Service, Bulk

21632 Dickey Manufacturing Company
1315 E Main St
St Charles, IL 60174 630-584-2918
Fax: 630-584-0261 info@securityseals.com
www.securityseals.com
Manufacturer and exporter of security and tamper proof seals for containers, rail cars, trucks, etc.; also, locking devices
Manager: Terry Mauger
Sales: Dan Bemis
General Manager: Terry Mauger
Estimated Sales: Below $5,000,000
Number Employees: 20-49
Square Footage: 40000

21633 (HQ)Dickler Chemical Labs
4201 Torresdale Ave
Philadelphia, PA 19124-4789 215-743-4201
Fax: 215-288-0847 800-426-1127
sales@dclsolutions.com www.dclsolutions.com
Manufacturer and exporter of floor finishes, strippers, oven/grill cleaners, hand soaps, degreasers and portion control water soluble packets
President: Laurence R Dickler
CFO: Bill Harry
VP: Bill Paris
Estimated Sales: $5 - 10 Million
Number Employees: 1 to4
Square Footage: 60000
Brands:
Chemical Service
Pak It
Vapguard

21634 Dickson
930 S Westwood Ave
Addison, IL 60101-4917 630-543-3747
Fax: 630-543-0498 800-757-3747
dicksoncsr@dicksondata.com
www.dicksondata.com
High temperature stainless steel data loggers for tracking, sterilization, pasteurization, autoclave and oven temperatures
President: Michael Unger
CFO: Mike Kohlmeier
Quality Control: Dan Gawel
Estimated Sales: Below $5 Million
Number Employees: 50-99

21635 Dickson Company
930 S Westwood Ave
Addison, IL 60101-4917 630-543-3747
Fax: 630-543-0498 800-757-3747
dicksoncsr@dicksondata.com
www.dicksondata.com
Data loggers, chart recorders and indicators.
President: Michael Unger
Marketing: Kathy Donovan
Estimated Sales: $5 - 10 Million
Number Employees: 50-99

21636 Die Cut Specialties
12543 Rhode Island Avenue
Savage, MN 55378-1136 952-890-7590
Fax: 952-890-7590
Manufacturer and exporter of packaging materials and bulk boxes for sugar, cocoa etc
President: Robert Jones
Plant Manager: Mike Jones
Estimated Sales: $500,000-$1 Million
Number Employees: 10
Square Footage: 10000
Type of Packaging: Bulk

21637 **DieQua Corporation**
180 Covington Dr
Bloomingdale, IL 60108 800-480-1095
Fax: 630-980-1232 info@diequa.com
www.diequa.com
Power transmission and drive components
President: Meikel Quaas
Estimated Sales: $10-20 000,000
Number Employees: 20-49

21638 **Diebel Manufacturing Company**
6505 Oakton Street
Morton Grove, IL 60053-2736 847-967-5678
Fax: 847-967-0655 jeffs@diebel.com
www.diebel.com
President and CEO: Richard H Schaefer Sr
Chief Executive Officer: Mike Chester
Quality Control: Victor Rivera
Estimated Sales: $10 - 20 Million
Number Employees: 40

21639 **Diebolt & Company**
100 Halls Rd
Old Lyme, CT 06371 860-434-2222
Fax: 860-434-0370 800-343-2658
sales@dieboltco.com www.heatedhose.com
Steam transfer and Teflon hoses for filtering cooking oil
President: Mark Diebolt
Sales Manager: Terrence Murphy
Estimated Sales: Below $5,000,000
Number Employees: 5-9
Brands:
Electroflo
Kleenflo
Steamflo

21640 **Diehl Food Ingredients**
136 Fox Run Dr
Defiance, OH 43512 419-782-5010
Fax: 419-783-4319 800-251-3033
diehl@bright.net www.diehlinc.com
Lactose free beverages, powdered fat, coffee creamers and whip topping bases.
President: Charles Nicolais
CFO: Darren Lane
CEO: Peter Diehl
Research & Development: Joan Hasselman
Quality Control: Kelly Roach
Marketing Director: Dennis Reid
Sales Director: Jim Holdrieth
Number Employees: 100-249
Parent Co: Diehl
Type of Packaging: Consumer, Food Service, Bulk
Brands:
Chocomite
Vitamite

21641 **Diequa Corporation**
180 Covington Dr
Bloomingdale, IL 60108-3105 630-980-1133
Fax: 630-980-1232 800-480-1095
info@diequa.com www.diequa.com
President: Meikel Quaas
CFO: Norman Quaas
Marketing Coordinator: Jeff Gibbons
Inside Sales Manager: Jeff White
Motion Products Manager: Tom Kahn
Number Employees: 20-49

21642 **Dietary Managers Association**
406 Surrey Woods Dr
St Charles, IL 60174 630-587-6336
Fax: 630-587-6308 800-323-1908
info@anfponline.org www.dmaonline.ggnet.net
President: William S St John
Quality Control: Pam Himrogh
Vice President of Development: Katherine Church
Marketing Manager: Kim Harden
Executive Vice President, Chief Operatin: Marla Isaacs
Estimated Sales: Below $5 Million
Number Employees: 20-49

21643 **Dietzco**
6 Bigelow St
Hudson, MA 01749-2697 508-481-4000
Fax: 508-481-4004 www.entwistleco.com
Spiral winding equipment for production of composite, paper and fiber cans; exporter of paper converting equipment
President: H Corkin
CEO: V Robinson
VP: R J Heidel
Estimated Sales: G
Number Employees: 100-249
Square Footage: 200000
Parent Co: Entwistle Company

21644 **Digatex**
4301 Westbank Drive
Suite B
Austin, TX 78746-4400 512-346-8090
Fax: 512-328-3556 800-285-1636
sales@digatex.com www.digatex.com
Complete route accounting software solutions for Direct Store Distribution companies. Includes accounting routing, production, sales, inventory and more!
Estimated Sales: $2.5-5 Million
Number Employees: 10-19

21645 **Digital Design**
67 Sand Park Rd
Cedar Grove, NJ 07009 973-857-9500
Fax: 973-857-9375 800-469-2205
edg@ddiworldwide.com www.omniprint.com
Marking devices
Manager: Richard Coventryu
Estimated Sales: $5-10 000,000
Number Employees: 20-49

21646 **Digital Dining/Menusoft**
7370 Steele Mill Dr
Springfield, VA 22150 703-912-3000
Fax: 703-912-4305 moconnor@menusoft.com
www.digitaldining.com
Point of sale software
Owner: Kay Branson
Estimated Sales: $5-10 Million
Number Employees: 20-49
Brands:
Digital Dining

21647 **Digital Dynamics**
5 Victor Sq
Scotts Valley, CA 95066 831-438-4444
Fax: 831-438-6825 800-765-1288
sales@digitaldynamics.com
www.digitaldynamics.com
Wash down safe industrial computers, and computer work stations
President: Daryl A. Gault
Vice President Engineering: Craig Nelson
Sales Manager: Steve Wait
Estimated Sales: $5 - 10 Million
Number Employees: 20-49
Number of Brands: 4
Square Footage: 200000

21648 **Digital Image & Sound Corporation**
11 Denonville Rdge
Rochester, NY 14625 585-381-0410
Fax: 585-381-0428 jfroom@aol.com
www.digimcorp.com
Computer hardware, software and systems for dairy and food processors; also, package design consultant
President: James Froom
Treasurer: Kathryn Froom
Sales Manager: Chris Ince
Estimated Sales: Less than $500,000

21649 **Dilley Manufacturing Company**
215 E 3rd St
Des Moines, IA 50309 515-288-7289
Fax: 515-288-4210 800-247-5087
www.dilleymfg.com
Menu covers
President: David Dilley
Estimated Sales: $5-10 Million
Number Employees: 20-49

21650 **Dillin Engineered Systems Corporation**
8030 Broadstone Rd
Perrysburg, OH 43551 419-666-6789
Fax: 419-666-4020 ldillin@dillin.com
www.dillin.com
Accumulators and conveyor systems; merge, divert, elevate and orientation equipment; caselifts; gripper lifts; air conveyor and accumulation
President: Larry Dillin
Estimated Sales: $10-20,000,000
Number Employees: 20-49
Square Footage: 40000
Brands:
Air Deck
Over-The-Top
Roe-Lift

21651 **Dillon Companies**
P.O.Box 1608
Hutchinson, KS 67504-1608 620-665-5511
Fax: 620-669-3167 www.dillons.com
Supermarket chain
President: John Bays
Plant Manager: Albert Garcia
Parent Co: Kroger

21652 **Dimension Graphics**
800 Burton St SE
Grand Rapids, MI 49507-3320 616-245-1447
Fax: 616-245-2899 855-476-1281
dime@dimensiongraphics.com
www.dimensiongraphics.com
Advertising signs including banners, point of purchase and silk-screened
President: Ken Blessing
Estimated Sales: $500,000 - $1 Million
Number Employees: 5-9

21653 **Dimension Industries**
3404 Iowa Street
Alexandria, MN 56308-3345 763-425-3955
Fax: 763-425-3641 info@douglas-machine.com
www.dimensionindustries.com
Standard, custom continuous and intermittent-motion cartoners, automatic placers, robotic palletizers, etc
President: Vernon Anderson
Marketing Director: Jon Ballone
Sales Director: Mike Huss
Operations Manager: Bill Lawrence
Estimated Sales: $20-50 Million
Number Employees: 50-99
Square Footage: 85000
Parent Co: Douglas Machine

21654 **Dimensional Insight**
111 S Bedford St Ste 206
Burlington, MA 01803 781-685-0481
Fax: 781-229-9113 info@dimins.com
www.dimensionalinsight.com
Integrated data visualization, analysis and reporting solution that delivers information with unparalleled speed and simplicity
President: Frederick A Powers
CFO: Cathy Sweet
R&D: Stan Zanarotti
Estimated Sales: $10 - 20 000,000
Number Employees: 1,000-4,999

21655 **Dimplex Thermal Solutions**
2625 Emerald Dr
Kalamazoo, MI 49001 269-373-7729
Fax: 269-349-8951 bbutch@dimplexthermal.com
www.dimplexthermal.com
Supplier of cooling solutions
President: Ola Wettergren
National Sales Manager: William Butch
Director of Operations: Mark Siegfried
Estimated Sales: $34 Million
Number Employees: 105

21656 **Dinex International**
4711 E. Hefner Rd
Oklahoma City, OK 73131 800-872-4701
Fax: 405-475-5600 800-654-8210
customerservice@carlislefsp.com
www.dinex.com
CEO: Kick Dzuvin
Chairman of the Board: Barry Taintor
VP: Jacqueline Gustafson
Quality Control: Marc Ginnett
Estimated Sales: $3 - 5 Million
Number Employees: 50-99

21657 **Dings Company/Magnetic Group**
4740 W Electric Ave
Milwaukee, WI 53219-1626 414-672-7830
Fax: 414-672-5354 magnets@dingsco.com
www.dingsco.com

Manufacturer and exporter of magnetic separators for the removal of ferrous metal contaminants from free-flowing powders and granular materials
President: Harold Bolstad
CEO: Brian Nahey
Estimated Sales: $10-20 Million
Number Employees: 50-99

21658 **Dinosaur Plastics**
2815 Gulf Fwy
Houston, TX 77003 713-923-2278
Fax: 713-923-4454 www.dinosaurplastics.com
Plastic signs, name badges and buttons, T-shirts, multi-color counter cards, window posters, pennants, banners, promotional products and give-aways; also, letters including plastic, metal and zip change
Owner: Jinny Stephens
Marketing: Chris Conrad
Estimated Sales: Less than $500,000
Number Employees: 5-9
Square Footage: 3000
Brands:
Gemini
Wagner

21659 **Dinovo Produce Company**
135 Wilson Street
Newark, OH 43055-4921 740-345-4025
Fax: 740-349-7276
Fruit and vegetables
President: Mark Dinovo
Estimated Sales: $2.5 - 5 000,000
Number Employees: 4
Type of Packaging: Private Label, Bulk

21660 **Dionex Corporation**
1228 Titan Way
Sunnyvale, CA 94085-3603 408-737-0700
Fax: 408-730-9403 www.dionex.com
Systems provide interference-free determination of inorganics, carbohydrates, organic acids, amines, proteins, flavors, pesticides and additives in foods and beverages
Chief Executive Officer: Frank Whitney
Estimated Sales: $173.30 Million
Number Employees: 1550

21661 **Dipix Technologies**
1051 Baxter Road
Ottawa, ON K2C 3P2
Canada 613-596-4942
Fax: 613-249-7341 info@dipix.com
www.dipix.com
Manufacturer and exporter of two dimensional and three dimensional vision inspection systems for the detection of defects in the color, size and shape of baked goods
President: Anton Kitai
Chairman And Acting CEO: Don Gibbs
VP Engineering: Andy Peters
VP Marketing/Sales: John Lawrence
Director of Sales: Geoff Evans
Chief Operating Officer: Peter Wakeman
Square Footage: 60000
Brands:
Dipix Vision Inspection Systems

21662 **Dipwell Company**
106 Industrial Dr
Northampton, MA 01060 413-587-4673
Fax: 413-587-4609 rinse@dipwell.com
www.dipwell.com
Manufacturer and exporter of food processing equipment including creamery, ice cream, mashed potatoes, butter, sour cream, cole slaw and peas; also, stainless steel running water wells to keep scoops sanitary
Owner: Maude Perry
President: Lynn Perry-Alstadt
VP: Fred Perry, Jr.
Number Employees: 7
Square Footage: 5000
Type of Packaging: Food Service
Brands:
Collar-Dip
Dipwell

21663 **Direct Fire Technical**
45 Bounty Road W
Benbrook, TX 76132-1043 817-568-8778
Fax: 817-568-8784 888-920-2468
jackgn1@airmail.net
Manufacturer and exporter of industrial hot water heaters and steam generators
President: J Baker
VP: Jack Nichols
Estimated Sales: $1-2,500,000
Number Employees: 20-49
Brands:
Dft Series
Direct Fire Technical, Inc.

21664 **Direct South**
P.O.Box 2445
Macon, GA 31203-2445 478-746-3518
Fax: 478-745-5668
info@restaurantandkitchensupply.com
www.directsouth.com
Food service equipment
Chairman of the Board: Danny Truelove
Estimated Sales: $5-10 Million
Number Employees: 20-49

21665 **Dirt Killer Pressure Washers, Inc**
1708 Whitehead Road
Baltimore, MD 21207 410-944-9966
Fax: 410-944-8866 800-544-1188
info@dirtkiller.com www.dirtkiller.com
Manufacturer and wholesaler/distributor of pressure washers, accessories and cleaning soaps
President: Jeffrey Paulding
Sales Director: Ken Rankin
Estimated Sales: $3 - 5 Million
Number Employees: 10
Square Footage: 60000
Brands:
China-Brite
Dirt Killer
Kranzle

21666 **Discovery Chemical**
2141 Carlyle Drive
Marietta, GA 30062-5836 770-973-5661
800-973-9881
Wastewater treatment chemicals, sanitizers, insecticides, degreasers, etc
Estimated Sales: $2.5-5,000,000
Number Employees: 2

21667 **Discovery Products Corporation**
13619 Mukilteo Speedway # 1180
Lynnwood, WA 98087-1626 425-267-9577
Fax: 425-267-9156 carbonoff@aol.com
www.discoveryproducts.com
President: Dennis A Clark
Vice President of Sales and Marketing: David Muir
Estimated Sales: $300,000-500,000
Number Employees: 1-4

21668 **Diskey Architectural Signage Inc.**
450 E. Brackenridge St.
Fort Wayne, IN 46802 260-424-0233
Fax: 260-424-0668 Orders@DiskeySign.com
www.diskeysign.com
Interior and exterior signs
President: Mike Butler
Estimated Sales: $1 - 3 Million
Number Employees: 10-19

21669 **Dispensa-Matic Label Dispense**
28220 Playmor Beach Road
Rocky Mount, MO 65072 573-392-7684
Fax: 573-392-1757 800-325-7303
info@dispensamatic.com
www.dispensamatic.com
Pressure sensitive label dispensers for roll labels and computer printouts
President: David Pocost
Marketing: Richard Shannon II
Sales Manager: Rich Laycob
Estimated Sales: $5 - 10 Million
Number Employees: 1-4
Parent Co: Commercial Mailing Accessories

21670 **Dispense Rite**
2205 Carlson Dr
Northbrook, IL 60062 847-753-9595
Fax: 847-753-9648 800-772-2877
sales@dispense-rite.com www.dispense-rite.com
Dispensing equipment for the foodservice industry
President: Robert Gapp
R&D: Robert Riley
Quality Control: Don Hitchcock
VP Marketing/Sales: Ronald Klein
Plant Manager: Don Hitchcok
Purchasing Agent: Robert Gapp
Estimated Sales: $3 - 5,000,000
Number Employees: 20-49
Number of Brands: 1
Number of Products: 250
Parent Co: Diversified Metal Products
Brands:
Dispense Rite

21671 **Display Concepts**
Rr 3
Trenton, ME 04605 207-667-3386
Fax: 207-667-4103 800-446-0033
www.displayconcepts.com
Store decor letters and signs including neon; also, aisle markers, trim and graphics
President: S Shelton
CEO: K Shelton
Number Employees: 20-49
Square Footage: 120000
Brands:
Iridescents
Neoneon

21672 **Display Craft Manufacturing Company**
3939 Washington Blvd
Halethorpe, MD 21227-4185 410-242-0400
Fax: 410-242-0475 sales@displaycraft.com
www.displaycraftmfg.com
Store fixtures
CEO: Ronald Weitzmann
CEO: Ronald Weitzman
Estimated Sales: $5-10 Million
Number Employees: 50-99

21673 **Display Creations**
PO Box 70449
Brooklyn, NY 11207-0449 718-257-2300
Fax: 718-257-2558 ron@displaycreations.com
www.displaycreations.com
Manfacturer of lucite displays, store fixtures and point of purchase displays
President: Ronald Newman
Sales Director: Michael Mathless
Purchasing Manager: Jeffry Baum
Estimated Sales: $5-10 Million
Number Employees: 50-99
Square Footage: 320000

21674 **Display One**
621 N Wacker Dr
Hartford, WI 53027-1001 262-673-5880
Fax: 262-670-2008 info@menasha.com
www.menasha.com
Corrugated boxes and containers including shipping and display
CFO: Arthur Huge
President, Chief Executive Officer: James Kotek
Vice President of Corporate Development: Evan Pritz
Sales Manager: Mike Waite
Estimated Sales: $20 - 50 Million
Number Employees: 100-249
Parent Co: Menasha Corporation

21675 **Display Pack**
1340 Monroe Ave NW Ste 1
Grand Rapids, MI 49505 616-451-3061
Fax: 616-451-8907 info@displaypack.com
www.dpiautomotive.com
Contract packaging and materials, vacuum and thermoformed plastics,printed packaging and phone-card packaging
President: Roger Hansen
Estimated Sales: $20-50 Million
Number Employees: 250-499
Square Footage: 400000
Type of Packaging: Private Label, Bulk

21676 **Display Specialties**
9 Beacon Dr
Wilder, KY 41076 859-781-7711
Fax: 859-572-4219 800-545-9362
foodservice@displayspecialties.com
www.shopdsi.com

In store merchandising and display accessories, including service case, signage and pricing systems, store decor and small wares. Best services equipment solutions
President: Douglas Bray
CFO: John Brooke
Vice President: Tom Frickman
R & D: Mike Augspack
Quality Control: Al Treatka
Marketing Director: Sheila Bray
Estimated Sales: $100-500 Million
Number Employees: 100-249
Number of Products: 3000
Square Footage: 120000

21677 Display Studios Inc.
5420 Kansas Ave
Kansas City, KS 66106 913-754-8900
Fax: 913-754-8901 800-648-8479
info@displaystudios.com
www.displaystudios.com
Manufacturer and exporter of displays and exhibits
President: John Mc Coy
Estimated Sales: $2.5 - 5 Million
Number Employees: 20-49

21678 Display Technologies
11101 14th Ave
Flushing, NY 11356 718-321-3100
Fax: 718-939-4034
info@display-technologies.com
www.display-technologies.com
Computer display, monitors and systems
President: Richard Jay
CFO: Leslie Tannenbaum
Estimated Sales: $30 - 50 Million
Number Employees: 50-99

21679 Display Tray
5475 Royalmount Avenue
Mont-Royal, QC H4P 1J3
Canada 514-735-2988
Fax: 514-735-8933 800-782-8861
displaytray@hotmail.com www.displaytray.com
Manufacturer and exporter of high impact styrene food display and market trays; also, plastic proof and bagel boards
President: Gail Cantor
CEO: Simy Oliel
Sales: Yoel Acoca
Number Employees: 4
Square Footage: 8000

21680 Dispoz-O Plastics
3736 Abercrombie Rd
Fountain Inn, SC 29644 864-862-4004
Fax: 864-862-4511 pgehrels@dispozo.com
www.dispozo.com
Plastic cutlery
President: Joseph D Lancia
CFO: Todd Linecerger
Estimated Sales: $75 - 100 Million
Number Employees: 500-999

21681 DistaView Corporation
121 E Wooster St # 201
Bowling Green, OH 43402 419-354-5087
Fax: 419-353-6080 800-795-9970
sales@distaview.com www.distaview.com
Manufacturer and exporter of liquid and material process controllers
President: Rick Kramer
Estimated Sales: $3 - 5 Million
Number Employees: 20-49
Square Footage: 27200
Brands:
2point
Levelair
Liquavision
Twoview
Vacview

21682 Distillata Company
1608 E 24th St
Cleveland, OH 44114 216-771-2900
Fax: 216-771-1672 800-999-2906
ClevelandCustomerService@Distillata.com
www.distillata.com
Bottler of spring and distilled water
Owner: Kevin Schroeder
Office Manager: Kelly Stewart
Estimated Sales: $10-20 Million
Number Employees: 100-249
Type of Packaging: Consumer, Food Service, Private Label, Bulk
Brands:
Distillata

21683 Distinctive Embedments
110 Kenyon Ave
Pawtucket, RI 02861 401-729-0770
Fax: 401-729-0772
Advertising novelites including key tags and paper weights
President: Mario Carosi
General Manager: Mario Carosi
Estimated Sales: $10 - 20 Million
Number Employees: 20 to 49

21684 Distributed Robotics
172 Lockrow Rd
Troy, NY 12180-9622 518-279-3419
Fax: 518-279-3611
derbys@distributedrobotics.com
www.distributedrobotics.com
President: Steven Derby
Estimated Sales: Below $5 Million
Number Employees: 5-9

21685 Distribution Results
900 Moe Dr
Akron, OH 44310-2519 330-633-0727
Fax: 330-633-0728 800-737-9671
sales@icsponge.com www.icsponge.com
Manufacturer, importer and exporter of cellulose sponges for the bakery, dairy and candy industries
Owner: Larry Rowlands
VP: Larry Rowlands
Research & Development: Jeff Shaffer
Quality Control: Carol Schaffer
Sales: Sherwood Shoemaker
Operations: Dotty Barrott
Estimated Sales: $1 Million
Number Employees: 10-19
Square Footage: 60000
Parent Co: Distribution Results

21686 Dito Dean Food Prep
4231 Pacific St Ste 27
Rocklin, CA 95677 916-652-5824
Fax: 916-652-4154 800-331-7958
dito-foodservice@electrolux.com
www.ditodean.com
Manufacturer and exporter of blenders, cheese shredding and cubing equipment, cutters, slicers, food and vegetable processors, salad dryers and verticle cutters and mixers
President: Gary Probert
Estimated Sales: $1-2.5 Million
Number Employees: 5-9
Parent Co: WCI
Type of Packaging: Food Service

21687 Ditting USA
1000 Air Way
Glendale, CA 91201-3030 818-247-9479
Fax: 818-247-9722 800-835-5992
info@ditting.com www.ditting.com
Manufacturer, importer and exporter of commercial coffee grinders
President: Albert Bezjian
CEO: Nancy Wideman
CFO: Mike Hatun
Estimated Sales: Below $5 Million
Number Employees: 5-9
Number of Brands: 1
Square Footage: 16000
Brands:
Ditting

21688 DiverseyLever NA Food Group
3630 E Kemper Road
Cincinnati, OH 45241-2011 513-956-4897
Fax: 513-956-4841
charlie.weber@diverseylever.com
www.johnsondiversey.com
Estimated Sales: $1 - 5 Million

21689 DiverseyLever North America
3630 E Kemper Rd
Cincinnati, OH 45241-2011 513-554-4200
Fax: 513-554-4330
Bill.Boylan@JohnsonDiversey.com
www.johnsondiversey.com
Supplier of cleaning and hygiene systems for dairy, beverage, brewing and food industries
Manager: Jim Walker
President/CEO: Gregory E Lawton
Managing Director/Regional President: Tom Gartland
Executive VP Corporate Development: Michael J Bailey
Estimated Sales: $2.6 Billion
Number Employees: 100-249
Parent Co: JohnsonDiversey

21690 Diversi-Plast Products
7425 Laurel Ave
Minneapolis, MN 55426 763-540-9700
Fax: 763-540-9709 800-828-6114
www.diversi-plast.com
Corrugated plastic sheets and containers
Manager: Lanny Jass
Estimated Sales: $2.5-5 000,000
Number Employees: 20-49

21691 Diversified Brands
101 Prospect Ave NW
Cleveland, OH 44115-1075 216-566-2000
Fax: 216-566-2947 800-247-3266
srupp@fulfillmentcenter.com www.sherwin.com
Food grade aerosol lubricants in silicone and nonsilicone formulations; also, nonozone depleting food grade mold releases
President: Richard Wilson
CEO: Christopher Connor
Director Sales: Jason Butler
Estimated Sales: K
Number Employees: 10,000
Parent Co: Sherwin-Williams Company

21692 Diversified Capping Equipment
8030 Broadstone Road
Perrysburg, OH 43551-4856 419-666-2566
Fax: 419-666-0275 sales@divcap.com
www.divcap.com
Manufacturer and exporter of closure application machines, cap sorters and cap conveying equipment
VP: Jack Weber
Engineering Manager: John Louy
Estimated Sales: $2.5-5 Million
Number Employees: 10-19
Square Footage: 128000
Brands:
Diversified (Dce)

21693 Diversified Label
136 Industrial Dr
Birmingham, AL 35211 205-942-4791
Fax: 205-942-4896 800-777-4791
www.diversifiedlabel.com
Point of sale for beer, beverage and snack industry; also labels
President: Jerry Shelly
Marketing Director: Jennifer Davis
Sales Director: Chad Johnson
Number Employees: 20-49

21694 Diversified Lighting Diffusers Inc
175-B Liberty St
Copiague, NY 11726 631-842-0099
Fax: 631-980-7668 800-234-5464
info@receilit.com www.1800ceiling.com
Manufacturer and distributor of fluorescent safety sleeves and vapor-tight lenses; also, custom fabrication of acrylic and lexan diffusers
Executive Director: Joe Broser
CEO: Joe Broser
COO: Colleen Baum
Estimated Sales: $1 - 3 Million
Number Employees: 5-9
Square Footage: 100000

21695 Diversified Metal Engineering
54 Hilstrom Ave.
PO Box 553
Charlottetown, PE C1E 2C6
Canada 902-628-6900
Fax: 902-628-1313 info@dmeinternational.com
www.dmeinternational.com

Manufacturer and exporter of washers, cookers, conveyors, graders and coolers for fish; also, brewery and dairy tanks, potato and vegetable shapers, turnkey microbrewery systems, portion packing equipment and piping systems andconveyors for dairy products, pressure vessels, complete skid systems and tanks.
President: Peter Toombs
VP Marketing/Sales: Barry MacLeod
Marketing Director: Kelly Lantz
Director of Sales and Marketing: David Campbell
Production Manager: Blair MacKinnon
Purchasing Manager: Ralph MacDonald
Estimated Sales: $7 Million
Number Employees: 50-99
Square Footage: 80000
Brands:
Dme

21696 Diversified Metal Manufacturing
2661 Alvarado St
San Leandro, CA 94577-4304 510-667-9900
Fax: 510-667-9700
Tea and coffee industry carts
Owner: Shawn O'Leary
Estimated Sales: Less than $500,000
Number Employees: 1-4

21697 Diversified Metal Products
2205 Carlson Dr
Northbrook, IL 60062 847-753-9595
Fax: 847-753-9648 800-772-2877
sales@dispense-rite.com www.dispense-rite.com
Dispensing equipment for the foodservice industry
President: Robert Gapp
CFO: Paul Gapp
R&D: Robert Riley
Quality Control: Don Hitchcok
Marketing Director: Ronald Klein
Sales Administration Manager: Ronald Klein
Plant Manager: Don Hitchcock
Purchasing Manager: Robert Gapp
Estimated Sales: $3 - 5 Million
Number Employees: 15
Number of Brands: 3
Number of Products: 350
Square Footage: 30000
Brands:
Dispense-Rite

21698 Diversified Panel Systems
2345 Statham Blvd
Oxnard, CA 93033 805-988-5070
Fax: 805-988-4630 www.dpspanels.com
President: Richard C Bell
Estimated Sales: $1 - 3 Million
Number Employees: 5-9

21699 Diversified Plastics
120 W Mount Vernon St
Nixa, MO 65714 417-725-2622
Fax: 417-725-5925 sales@dpcap.com
www.dpcap.com
Custom molded polystyrene packaging materials, plastic molding and foam fabricating
President: Kenny L Magers
Quality Control: Shane Boston
Estimated Sales: $20-50 Million
Number Employees: 250-499

21700 Diversified Products
1460 Kings Wood Lane
Eagan, MN 55122 651-269-9091
Fax: 651-454-8079 800-942-2282
sales@divprod.com www.divprod.com
Wine industry packaging
President: James Crea
Estimated Sales: $500,000-$1 Million
Number Employees: 1-4

21701 Dividella
14501 58th Street North
Clearwater, FL 33760 727-532-6509
Fax: 727-532-6537 info@kmedipak.com
www.dividella.com
Carton packaging for vials, ampoules, cartridges, syringes, tablet blisters, blistercards, sachets and similar products and automatic tray and carton loading systems for vials
Estimated Sales: $1 - 5 Million

21702 Dixie Canner Company
786 E Broad St
Athens, GA 30601-2827 706-549-1914
Fax: 706-549-0137 sales@dixiecanner.com
www.dixiecanner.com
Manufacturer and exporter of low-volume canning equipment including seamers, retorts, exhausters and vacuum closers; also, blanchers, pulpers/finishers and lye peelers
President: B Gentry
Chairman: W Stapleton Sr
VP Manufacturing: J Campbell
VP Sales: Parrish Stapleton
Estimated Sales: $1-2.5 Million
Number Employees: 5
Square Footage: 12000
Brands:
Dixie

21703 Dixie Flag ManufacturingCompany
1930 N Panam Expy
San Antonio, TX 78208 210-227-5039
Fax: 210-227-5920 800-356-4085
dixieflg@dixieflag.com www.dixieflag.com
Manufacturer and exporter of flags, street net banners and pennants
President: Henry P Van Deputte Jr
VP: Sally Van de Putte
VP: Glenda Krueger
Estimated Sales: $5 - 10 Million
Number Employees: 20-49

21704 Dixie Graphics
636 Grassmere Park
Nashville, TN 37211 615-832-7000
Fax: 615-832-7621 info@dixiegraphics.com
www.dixiegraphics.com
Rubber printing plates, photo engraving and color separations
President: James R Meadows
Estimated Sales: $10-20 000,000
Number Employees: 50-99

21705 Dixie Maid Ice Cream Company
206 E 2nd St
Deridder, LA 70634-5004 337-463-8835
Ice cream novelties
Owner: L C Kern
Estimated Sales: $5-10 Million
Number Employees: 7
Type of Packaging: Consumer

21706 Dixie Neon Company
3001 W Granada St
Tampa, FL 33629 813-248-2531
Fax: 813-247-6230
Signs including advertising, electric and plastic
Owner: Freddie Hevia Iii III
Estimated Sales: $1-2.5 Million
Number Employees: 5-9

21707 Dixie Poly Packaging
916 Tanner Road
Greenville, SC 29607-6036 864-268-3751
Fax: 864-268-0511
Polyethylene poultry bags
Owner: Whit Jordan
Estimated Sales: $5-10 Million
Number Employees: 20-49

21708 Dixie Printing & Packaging
7358 Baltimore Annapolis Blvd
Glen Burnie, MD 21061-3242 410-766-1944
Fax: 410-761-4032 800-433-4943
bill.linehan@dixiebox.com www.dixiebox.com
Folding paper boxes
Owner: A Newth Morris Iii III
VP Sales: Bill Linchan
General Manager: Raymond Bedell
Estimated Sales: $15 - 20 Million
Number Employees: 100-249
Square Footage: 67500
Type of Packaging: Consumer, Food Service, Private Label

21709 Dixie Rubber Stamp & Seal Company
PO Box 54616
Atlanta, GA 30308-0616 404-875-8883
Fax: 404-872-3504 plates@dixieseal.com
www.dixiseal.com
Rubber stamps and ink products
President: Jack Anders
Plant Manager: Brad Grice
Estimated Sales: $10 - 20 Million
Number Employees: 80

21710 Dixie Search Associates
3297 Hickory Bluff Dr
Marietta, GA 30062-4242 770-675-7300
Fax: 770-850-9295 dsa@dixiesearch.com
www.dixiesearch.com
Executive search agency specializing in supermarket, food sales/marketing, manufacturing and hospitality industries
President: Clifford G Fill
Senior VP: Ellyn Fill
Estimated Sales: $300,000-500,000
Number Employees: 10-19
Square Footage: 3000
Parent Co: Fill Corporation

21711 Dixie Signs
2930 Drane Field Rd
Lakeland, FL 33811 863-644-3521
Fax: 863-644-3524 ess@dixiesignsinc.com
www.dixiesignsinc.com
Interior and exterior signs and graphics
President: Roger Snyder
Estimated Sales: $2.5-5 Million
Number Employees: 20-49

21712 Dixon Lubricants & Specialty Pro Group
P.O.Box 144
Asbury, NJ 08802-0144 908-537-2155
Fax: 908-537-2908 sendinfo@asbury.com
www.asbury.com
Chief Executive Officer: Stephen Riddle
Vice President of Manufacturing: Gary Ziegler
Quality Manager: Ken Newton
Sales Manager: Debra Nowacki
Plant Manager: Michael Mares
Estimated Sales: $1 - 5 Million
Number Employees: 500-999

21713 Dize Company
1512 S Main Street
Winston Salem, NC 27127-2707 336-722-5181
Fax: 336-761-1334 dizeco@dizeco.com
www.dizeco.com
Commercial awnings, tarps, window coverings, and food cart covers
President: Cr Skidmore
CFO: Mike Durr
Marketing/Sales: Carl Livengood
Operations Manager: Jim Shaver
Estimated Sales: $10-20,000,000
Number Employees: 50-99
Square Footage: 80000
Type of Packaging: Bulk

21714 Do-It Corporation
1201 Blue Star Hwy
PO Box 592
South Haven, MI 49090-0592 269-639-2600
Fax: 269-637-7223 800-426-4822
sales@do-it.com www.do-it.com
Manufacturer, importer and exporter of self-adhesive plastic hangers and hang tabs; also, contract packaging available
President: Mark Mc Clendon
Director Marketing: John Deschaine
VP Sales: Chuck Miller
Estimated Sales: $5-10 Million
Number Employees: 50-99
Square Footage: 40000
Brands:
Do-It

21715 Dober Chemical Corporation
14461 S Waverly Ave
Midlothian, IL 60445 630-410-7300
Fax: 630-410-7444 800-323-4983
doberinfo@dober-group.com
www.dobergroup.com
Liquid and powdered soap; also, cleaning chemicals for metal finishing
President: John G Dobrez
VP Sales: Tom Blakmore
Estimated Sales: $10-20 Million
Number Employees: 50-99

21716 Doering Company
6343 River Rd SE
Clear Lake, MN 55319 320-743-2276
Fax: 320-743-3723 info@doering.com
www.doering.com
Stainless steel valves for high pressure directional control, manually operated stainless steel pumps for high pressure hydraulic service and manually activated hand wash water valves UHMW and stainless construction
President: Russ Doering
Sales Director: Kris King
Estimated Sales: $3 - 5 Million
Number Employees: 10-19
Square Footage: 10000
Brands:
Doering
Water Miser

21717 Doering Machines, Inc.
2121 Newcomb Avenue
San Francisco, CA 94124 415-526-2131
Fax: 415-526-2136 sales@doeringmachines.com
www.doeringmachines.com
Manufacturer and exporter of pumping, extruding, portioning, metering, cartoning and wrapping systems for high viscosity products including dough, butter, cheese and polymers
President: Richard Doering
CEO: Tim Doering
Estimated Sales: $2.5-5 Million
Number Employees: 3
Square Footage: 60000

21718 Dolco Packaging
2110 Patterson St
Decatur, IN 46733 260-422-0796
Fax: 260-728-9958
Manufacturer and exporter of polystyrene foam packaging
Vice President: Norm Patterson
Quality Control: Doug Keller
Marketing Director: Phil Laughlin
Public Relations: Amy Geradoj
Production Manager: Jeff Brown
Plant Manager: Roger Lichtle
Purchasing Manager: Terry Alberson
Estimated Sales: $20-50 Million
Number Employees: 100-249
Parent Co: Tekni Plex
Type of Packaging: Food Service

21719 (HQ)Dole Refrigerating Company
1420 Higgs Rd
Lewisburg, TN 37091-4402 931-359-6211
Fax: 931-359-8664 800-251-8990
sales@doleref.com www.doleref.com
Manufacturer and exporter of truck refrigeration units including eutectic plate and blower; also, quick freeze plates for food processing, double contact quick freezing freezers and fiberglass coolers
President: John Cook
CFO: Joe Mulliniks
Sales Manager: Bobby Dunnivant
Chief Engineer: Rod Hardy
Estimated Sales: $20 - 50 Million
Number Employees: 50-99
Square Footage: 55000
Brands:
Cold-Cel
Freze-Cel

21720 Dometic Mini Bar
P.O.Box 490
Elkhart, IN 46515-0490 574-294-2511
Fax: 574-293-9686 800-301-8118
In-room refreshment products including honor bars, automated systems, carts, safes, etc
CEO: John Waters
National Sales Manager: Tyler Ellendorff
General Manager: Hans Disch
Estimated Sales: F
Number Employees: 20-49
Parent Co: A.B. Electrolux

21721 Dominion I.P. Pasta Machines
2129 Harrison St
San Francisco, CA 94110-1321 415-621-1171
Fax: 415-621-4613 info@tmr9.com
Pasta machines
President: Paulo Tondo
Estimated Sales: $300,000-500,000
Number Employees: 1-4

21722 Dominion Pallet Company
9644 Cross County Rd
Mineral, VA 23117 540-894-5401
Fax: 540-894-0108 800-227-5321
info@dominionpallet.com
www.dominionpallet.com
Lift truck pallets
Owner: Dan Yancey
CFO: Bernon Aenos
Buyer (Lumber): Scott Walton
General Manager: Vernon Jones
Estimated Sales: $10 - 20 Million
Number Employees: 20-49

21723 Dominion Regala
4 Overlea Blvd
Toronto, ON M4H 1A4
Canada 416-752-9987
Fax: 416-752-9986 866-423-4086
info@dominionregalia.com
www.dominionregalia.com
Patio umbrellas, flags, banners and continously printed ribbons
President: Ross Chafe
Quality Control: Summer Zurawski
Director Marketing: Connie Murphy
Number Employees: 10

21724 Domino Amjet
1290 Lakeside Dr
Gurnee, IL 60031-2499 847-244-2501
Fax: 847-244-1421 800-444-4512
service@domino-na.com
www.domino-printing.com
Digital printing solutions used for date coding, product markings, serialization and variable printing.
President: Michael Brown
Chief Executive Officer: Brian McGarry
Chief Financial Officer: David Hollister
Chairman of the Board: Nigel Bond
Research & Development: Chris Gehring
Quality Assurance Manager: Barbara Diliberti
Vice President, Marketing: Carl Traynor
Vice President, Sales: David Ellen
Product Manager: Adem Kulauzovic
Estimated Sales: $39 Million
Number Employees: 200
Square Footage: 72000
Parent Co: Domino Printing Sciences PLC

21725 Domnick Hunter
5900 Nthwds Pkwy Ste B
Charlotte, NC 28269 704-921-9303
Fax: 704-921-1960 800-345-8462
www.domnickhunter.com
MAXIGAS Nitrogen Gas Generators which generate nitrogen gas on-site from compressed air. MAXIGAS eliminates all hassels of bottled nitrogen gas supply. Easy to install, operate and maintain, flow rates are available up to 10,000 scfheith nitrogen 97% to 99.999%. Domnick Hunter also manufacturers compressed air, liquid and gas filters, CO2 purifiers and industrial chillers for the food and beverage industry.
Manager: Nick Herrig
Estimated Sales: $150 Million
Number Employees: 50-99
Brands:
Maxigas Nitrogen Gas Generators
Pneudri Desiccant Air Dryers

21726 Don Lee
1991 Don Lee Place
Escondido, CA 92029-1130 760-745-0707
Fax: 760-746-2856 connieberry@aol.com
Dough cutters and dividers.
President: Lee Berry
CFO: Kim Key
Vice President: Connie Berry
Number Employees: 20-49
Number of Products: 2
Square Footage: 10000
Type of Packaging: Private Label
Brands:
Cloverleaf
Roll Former/Divider

21727 Don Walters Company
11630 Western Ave
Stanton, CA 90680 714-892-0275
Fax: 714-901-1852 donwaltersco@aol.com
www.donwaltersinc.com
Wholesaler/distributor of restaurant equipment; also, design consulting available
President/CEO: Roger Criswell
CFO/VP: Mindy Criswell
Estimated Sales: $1-2,500,000
Number Employees: 5-9
Type of Packaging: Food Service

21728 (HQ)Donahower & Company
15615 S Keeler Ter
Olathe, KS 66062-3509 913-829-2650
Fax: 913-829-5494
Manufacturer and exporter of conveyors including package handling, flat top chain and material handling; also, lidding and capping machinery and bottle rotators
President: Carol Brooks
Vice President: Ken Koelzer
Estimated Sales: $1-2.5 Million
Number Employees: 5-9
Square Footage: 5000

21729 Donalds & Associates
3900 Kilroy Airport Way # 190
Long Beach, CA 90806-6815 562-290-8440
Fax: 562-438-2668
Consultant specializing in restaurant conceptualization
President: Steve Donalds

21730 Donaldson Company
1400 W 94th St
Minneapolis, MN 55431 952-887-3131
Fax: 952-887-3155 800-767-0702
www.donaldson.com
Manufacturer, importer and exporter of dust control equipment
Chairman/President/CEO: Bill Cook
Marketing Manager: Jennifer Wilkinson
Estimated Sales: $2.5 Billion
Number Employees: 13,000
Parent Co: BTR Environmental
Brands:
Dce Dalamatic
Dce Siloair
Dce Sintamatic
Dce Unicell
Dce Unimaster

21731 Dongyu
2590 Main St
Irvine, CA 92614 949-251-9388
Fax: 949-251-8865 888-580-0088
info@dongyu.us www.dongyu.us
Manufacturer and distributor of L-Carnitine products, amino acids, vitamins, sweeteners, sports nutrition ingredients, food and beverage ingredients
Manager: Weili Zhang
Square Footage: 40000

21732 Donnelly Industries, Inc
557 Route 23 South
Wayne, NJ 07470 973-672-1800
Fax: 973-323-8699
info@donnellyconstruction.com
www.donnellyconstruction.com
Wooden boxes
President: Gerard J Donnelly Jr
CEO: Rod Donnelly
VP: Christopher Powers
Estimated Sales: $1 - 2.5 Million
Number Employees: 5-9

21733 Donnick Label Systems
1450 Lane Ave N
Jacksonville, FL 32254
Fax: 904-786-7301 800-334-7849
info@donnick.com www.donnick.com
Direct thermal scale and product labels, thermal printers and ribbons
President: Jerry Smith
Owner: Anne Smith
CFO: Anne Smith
Sales/Marketing: David Frederick
Estimated Sales: $.5 - 1 million
Number Employees: 5-9
Square Footage: 7000

21734 Donoco Industries
P.O. Box 3208
Huntington Beach, CA 92605 714-893-7889
Fax: 714-897-7968 888-822-8763
info@encoreplastics.com
www.encoreplastics.com

Manufacturer and exporter of plastic mugs and tumblers
President: Richard Harvey
Estimated Sales: $5 - 10 Million
Number Employees: 25
Brands:
Encore

21735 Donovan Enterprises
200 Lukken Industrial Dr E
Lagrange, GA 30241-5920 706-882-6343
Fax: 706-882-9536 800-233-6180
sales@itwip.com www.itwip.com
Manufacturer and exporter of insulated pallets covers, portable bulkheads, walkramps, pallet covers, plastic returning air bulkheads, curtains, and refrigeration chutes for food distribution
General Manager: Pam Ward
Sales Manager: Bonnie Schilling
Operations Manager: Dan Autry
Production Manager: Toby Clark
Estimated Sales: $100-500 Million
Number Employees: 20-49
Parent Co: Illinois Tool Works
Type of Packaging: Food Service, Private Label
Brands:
Centerline
Eliminator
Even Temp
Skinny Buns

21736 Dontech Industries/MicroPure
76 Center Drive
Gilberts, IL 60136-9712 847-428-8222
Fax: 847-428-6855 rap@micropure.com
www.dontechindustriesinc.com
Ultraviolet disinfection systems for food processing, sanitation, water and wastewater treatment
Owner: D L Catton
Estimated Sales: $1-2.5 Million
Number Employees: 5-9

21737 Dorado Carton Company
Carr 693
Dorado, PR 00646-0546 787-796-1670
Fax: 787-796-2988
Paper, pizza and food service boxes, doilies, place mats and shelf and wrapping paper; also, coated stock available
President: Keneth Schulman
VP F.C. Meyer Division: Paul Robinson
Business Manager: Nazira Wightman
Number Employees: 16
Square Footage: 22000
Parent Co: Frank C. Meyer Company/Mafcote Industries

21738 Doran Scales
1315 Paramount Pkwy
Batavia, IL 60510-1460 630-879-1200
Fax: 630-879-0073 800-365-0084
sales@doranscales.com www.doranscales.com
Stainless steel washdown safe scales.
Chairman/CEO: William Podl
CEO: William Podl
Marketing Coordinator: Mark Anderson
Applications Engineer: Mark Podl
Estimated Sales: $5 - 10 Million
Number Employees: 20-49
Square Footage: 80000
Brands:
Digibar

21739 Dordan Manufacturing Company
2025 Castle Rd
Woodstock, IL 60098 815-334-0087
Fax: 815-334-0089 800-663-5460
sales@dordan.com www.dordan.com
Heat sealing and plastic vacuum formed packaging products
President: Daniel Slavin
Estimated Sales: $2.5-5 Million
Number Employees: 20-49

21740 Dorden & Company
7446 Central St
Detroit, MI 48210 313-834-7910
Fax: 313-834-1178
All types of rubber floor and window squeegees
President: Bruce M Gale
CEO: Bruce M Gale
Public Relations: Bruce Gale
Purchasing: Bruce Gale
Estimated Sales: $.5 - 1 million
Number Employees: 1-4
Square Footage: 15000
Type of Packaging: Food Service, Private Label, Bulk

21741 (HQ)Dorell Equipment Inc
80 Veronica Ave # 60
Somerset, NJ 08873-3498 732-247-5400
Fax: 732-247-5700 sales@dorell.com
www.dorell.com/
Food and beverage packaging equipment including tray and case erectors, and loaders, shrink wrapping systems, collation and stacking systems.
Manager: Lu Mado
Vice President: Joseph Minond
Marketing/Sales: Jon Levin
Sales Representative: Eli Schloss
Plant Manager: Ray Jenito
Purchasing Manager: Tami Minond
Estimated Sales: $2.5-5 Million
Number Employees: 20-49
Type of Packaging: Bulk
Other Locations:
Dorell Equipment Company
Cincinati OH
Dorell Equipment Company
Atlanta GA
Brands:
Dorell

21742 Dormont Manufacturing Company
6015 Enterprise Dr
Export, PA 15632 724-733-4800
Fax: 724-733-4808 800-367-6668
info@dormont.com www.dormont.com
Safety system flexible stainless steel gas appliance connectors and gas connection accessories; also, pre-rinse assemblies and faucets
CEO: Evan Segal
VP: Mark Humenansky
Marketing Manager: Judi D'Amico
VP Sales: David Berstein
Purchasing Manager: Norman Czarnecki
Estimated Sales: H
Number Employees: 100-249
Square Footage: 70000
Parent Co: Watts Water Technologies
Type of Packaging: Food Service, Private Label, Bulk
Brands:
Cimfast
Hi-Psi-Flex(Water)
Power Force
Supr Swivel
Supr-Safe (Gas)

21743 Dorner Manufacturing Corporation
PO Box 20
Hartland, WI 53029 262-367-7600
Fax: 262-367-5827 800-397-8664
info@dorner.com www.dorner.com
Belt conveyors
President: Werner Dorner
President: Scott Lucas
CFO: Dale Visgar
Engineering Manager: Michael Hosch
Marketing Director: Gary Wemmert
Sales Director: Mark Wedell
Operations Manager: Randy Meis
Purchasing Manager: Greg Sipek
Estimated Sales: $10 - 20 Million
Number Employees: 100-249

21744 Dorpak
1780 Dreman Avenue
Cincinnati, OH 45223-2456 513-681-2323
Fax: 513-541-5945 info@cin-made.com
www.dorpak.com
High graphic, re-closable, rectangular paperboard drums
President: Robert Fry
CFO: John Ewalt
Quality Control: Brian Kilpatrick
Estimated Sales: Below $5 Million
Number Employees: 10

21745 Dorton Incorporated
3436 N Kennicott Ave
Arlington Hts, IL 60004-7814 847-577-8600
Fax: 847-392-6212 800-299-8600
dortoninc@juno.com www.dortongroup.com
President: Ed Collins
CFO: Al Nowak
VP: Marie Collins
R&D: Milt Lynn
Marketing: Micki Bagnuolo
Sales: Micki Bagnuolo
Public Relations: Ed Collins
Operations Manager: Michelle Gilbert
Production: M Levinberg
Purchasing: Cindy Byrne
Number Employees: 10-19
Number of Brands: 2
Number of Products: 12
Square Footage: 15200
Type of Packaging: Food Service
Brands:
Dor-Blend
Dor-Mixer
Dor-Opener
Dorton

21746 Dosatron
2090 Sunnydale Blvd
Clearwater, FL 33765-1201 727-443-5404
Fax: 727-447-0591 800-523-8499
mailbox@dosatronusa.com
www.dosatronusa.com
Distributor of Dosatron water powered chemical injectors used int he food processind sanitation process. They are easy to adjust and automatically compensate for changes in water pressure or flow, allowing for a fine tuned chemical mixthat provides improved results and reduced waste.
President: Edward Kelly

21747 Dot Packaging Group
1500 Paramount Pkwy
Batavia, IL 60510 630-879-0121
Fax: 630-879-7000 800-323-6160
info@dotpack.com www.dotpack.com
Blister card packaging and insert cards
President: Jim Shaw
President: Jon Quinn
CFO: Tim Hackman
Quality Control: Mike Wenzelman
Estimated Sales: $10 - 20 000,000
Number Employees: 100-249

21748 Dot-It Food Safety Products
2011 E Randol Mill Rd
Arlington, TX 76011 817-275-7714
Fax: 817-275-0122 800-642-3687
craftmk@flash.net www.magicmile.com
Labels and tags
Manager: Ben Nicholson
Director Sales: Robert Galan
General Manager: Sonya Peterson
Estimated Sales: $1 - 3 Million
Number Employees: 5-9
Square Footage: 72000
Parent Co: Craftmark Label Graphics

21749 Double E Company
319 Manley St Ste 5
West Bridgewater, MA 02379 508-588-8099
Fax: 508-580-2915 doublee@doubleusa.com
www.doubleeusa.com
Core chucks anad core shafts for packaging and paper, film and foil converting
President: Mark Fortin
CEO: Redward Flagg
Estimated Sales: $10 - 20 000,000
Number Employees: 100-249

21750 (HQ)Double Envelope Corporation
7702 Plantation Rd
Roanoke, VA 24019 540-362-3311
Fax: 540-366-8401 www.bscventures.com
Pressure sensitive labels, bind-in order forms and envelopes
Sales Manager: Jim Long
Estimated Sales: $20-50 Million
Number Employees: 100-249

21751 Double H Plastics
50 W Street Rd
Warminster, PA 18974 215-674-4100
Fax: 215-674-4109 800-523-3932
phaney@doublehplastics.com
www.doublehplastics.com
President: Harry J Harp Iii
Estimated Sales: $20-50 Million
Number Employees: 100-249

21752 Double R Enterprises
221 Grove St
New Castle, PA 16101 724-658-2477
Fax: 724-658-7427 www.ccclle.com
Plastic containers for liquids including orange juice and syrup
Sales Manager: John Wolfgang
General Manager: Joe Smarrelli
Plant Manager: Nick Shuler
Purchasing Manager: Bill Bullano
Estimated Sales: $20-50 Million
Number Employees: 50-99
Parent Co: Rostan Corporation

21753 Double Wrap Cup & Container
Po Box 5167
Buffalo Grove, IL 60089-5167 847-478-0184
Fax: 847-777-0586 www.comfortgripwrap.com
High quality,low cost insulated wrap for paper coffee cups.
CEO: Ted Alpert
VP: Ted Alpert
Marketing Director: Ted Alpert
Sales Director: Ted Alpert
Public Relations: Ted Alpert
Operations Manager: Ted Alpert
Estimated Sales: $3 - 5 Million
Number Employees: 10-19
Type of Packaging: Food Service

21754 Doucette Industries
20 Leigh Dr
York, PA 17406-8474 717-845-8746
Fax: 717-845-2864 800-445-7511
info@doucetteindustries.com
www.doucetteindustries.com
Manufacturer and exporter of suction line and vented double wall heat exchangers, CO2 Vaporizers, coaxial coils, counterflow condensers and vibration absorbers for air conditioning, refrigeration and hydronic applications
President: John Lebo
Number Employees: 20-49

21755 DoughXpress
1201 E 27th Terrace
Pittsburg, KS 66762 620-231-8568
Fax: 620-231-1598 800-835-0606
sales@hixcorp.com www.doughxpress.com
Bakery equipment including bread slicers, dough dividers, rounders, air compressors, release agents, storage carts, dough dockers, dual heated, presses, air automatic pizza presses, flat grills, and meat presses
President: Doug Condra
Chairman: Jack Deboer
Treasurer: Kay Stroud
Marketing & Product Manager: Tim McNally
Sales & Marketing Manager: Lorin Rigby
National Sales Manager: Willie Anderson
Human Resources Manager: Debbie Sloan
Plant Manager: Jim Mattson
Purchasing Manager: Dave Gromer
Estimated Sales: $8.2 Million
Number Employees: 60
Square Footage: 222000
Parent Co: Hix Corporation
Type of Packaging: Food Service, Bulk

21756 Doughmakers, LLC
PO Box 10034
Terre Haute, IN 47801 812-299-8750
Fax: 812-299-7788 888-386-8517
service@doughmakers.com
www.doughmakers.com
Manufacturer and distributor of bakeware pans, sheets, and tins
Quality Control: Tony Buck
Manager: Robert Bossar
Estimated Sales: $5 - 10 Million
Number Employees: 20-49

21757 Doughpro
20281 Harvill Ave
Perris, CA 92570 800-624-6717
Fax: 562-869-7715 800-594-5528
rfizer@doughpro.com www.doughpro.com
Pizza presses and wood fired ovens
President: Eugene Raio
Number Employees: 10

21758 Douglas Battery Manufacturing Company
500 Battery Dr
Winston Salem, NC 27107 336-650-7000
Fax: 336-650-7072 800-368-4527
info@douglasbattery.com
www.douglasbattery.com
CEO: Tom S Douglas Iii
Estimated Sales: $100+ Million
Number Employees: 500-999

21759 (HQ)Douglas Machine
3404 Iowa Street
Alexandria, MN 56308 320-763-6587
Fax: 320-763-5754 info@douglas-machine.com
www.douglas-machine.com
Manufacturer and exporter of packaging machinery including high speed continuous and multi-range intermittent motion case packers, case openers, bottom sealers, integrated conveyor systems, shrink wrappers, tray formers, palletizerssleevers, cartoners, multipackers and provide rebuild/conversion services
Chairman: Vernon Anderson
COO/President: Rick Paulsen
EVP: Paul Anderson
VP Manufacturing: Chris Haugen
Estimated Sales: $94 Million
Number Employees: 483
Square Footage: 218000
Parent Co: Douglas
Type of Packaging: Consumer, Food Service, Private Label, Bulk

21760 Douglas Machines Corporation
2101 Calumet St
Clearwater, FL 33765 727-461-3477
Fax: 727-449-0029 800-331-6870
info@dougmac.com www.dougmac.com
Manufacturer and exporter of automatic washing and sanitizing equipment including pan washers, rack washers, and tunnel washers for all containers, commonly found in the food processing industry.
President: David Ward
CFO: Susan Mader
Vice President: Kevin Lemen
Sales Manager: Marie Neven
Estimated Sales: $5-10 Million
Number Employees: 5-9
Number of Brands: 3
Number of Products: 40
Square Footage: 25000
Brands:
Douglas

21761 (HQ)Douglas Products & Packaging
1550 E Old State Route 210
Liberty, MO 64068 816-781-4250
Fax: 816-781-1043 800-223-3684
douglasproducts@douglasproducts.com
www.douglasproducts.com
Custom packager of liquid products
President: Jerry McCaslin
CEO: Bill R Fuller
General Manager: Jim Osment
Estimated Sales: $10-20 Million
Number Employees: 10-19
Square Footage: 55000
Type of Packaging: Private Label, Bulk

21762 Douglas Stephen Plastics
P.O.Box 2775
Paterson, NJ 07509-2775 973-523-3030
Fax: 973-523-0643
bmccullough@douglasstephen.com
www.douglasstephen.com
Plastic containers and trays
President and CFO: Stewart Graff
National Sales Manager: Brian McCullough
VP Operations: Doug Graff
Estimated Sales: $10 - 20 Million
Number Employees: 100-249

21763 Dove Screen Printing Company
18 Salem Rd
Royston, GA 30662 706-245-4975
Fax: 706-245-7500
www.dovescreenprinting.norwood.com
Manufacturer and exporter of advertising specialties, signs and restaurant aprons; importer of caps and coffee mugs
Owner: Ronny Dove
Estimated Sales: Less than $500,000
Number Employees: 1-4

21764 Dover Chemical Corporation
3676 Davis Rd NW
Dover, OH 44622-0040 330-343-7711
Fax: 330-364-1579 800-321-8805
dave.schlarb@doverchem.com
www.doverchem.com
Manufacturer and exporter of bleaches, muratic acids and antioxidants
President: Dwain S Colvin
CFO: Mike Caffrey
Quality Control: Dave Schlarb
Marketing Manager: Don Chapman
Purchasing Agent: Robert Ren
Number Employees: 100-249
Parent Co: ICC Industries
Brands:
Dover Phos Foods

21765 Dover Hospitality Consulting
6 Tallforest Crescent
Etobicoke, ON M9C 2X2
Canada 416-622-9294
Fax: 416-622-5944 bdover@idirect.com
Consultant specializing in chain restaurant marketing and operations
President: Bill Dover
Number Employees: 1

21766 Dover Industries
3005 Highland Parkway
Downers Grove, IL 60515 630-541-1540
Fax: 630-743-2671 www.doverind.com
President: Michael Zhang
President, Chief Executive Officer: Robert Livingston
CFO: Robert Scheuer
Vice President, Treasurer: Brian Moore
Operations Manager of Sales: Greg Smith
Estimated Sales: $1.2 Million
Number Employees: 1,000-4,999

21767 Dover Metals
4768 Hwy M-63
Coloma, MI 49038 269-849-1411
Fax: 269-849-2903 sales@dovermetals.com
www.dovermetals.com
Accessories and supplies for the food service and hospitality industry
President/Owner: Deborah Bedwell
VP: Nick Anders
Estimated Sales: $2.8 Million
Number Employees: 8

21768 Dover Parkersburg
PO Box 610
Follansbee, WV 26037-610
Fax: 304-485-3214 www.doverparkersburg.com
Manufacturer and importer of tinware including baking pans, garbage cans, buckets, tubs, wringers and mopping equipment
Sales: Donna Burns
Director Operations: William Cusack, Jr.
Estimated Sales: $10-20 Million
Number Employees: 50-99
Parent Co: Louis Berkman
Type of Packaging: Bulk

21769 Dover Products Company
607 W Jefferson St # 1
Bloomington, IL 61701-8208 309-821-1271
Fax: 502-633-3798 800-351-5582
dpi@ka.net
Grease, oil and tallow
President: Egerton M Dover
Plant Manager: Robert Kepfer
Estimated Sales: $500,000-$1 Million
Number Employees: 5 to 9

21770 Dow AgroSciences
450 1st St SW
Suite 2100
Calgary, AB T2P 5H1
Canada 403-735-8902
davandam@dow.com
www.omega-9oils.com
Omega-9 oils
President: Richard Smith
Manager: Pete Desai
Estimated Sales: $57.96 Million
Number Employees: 150
Type of Packaging: Food Service, Bulk

21771 **Dow Chemical Company**
727 Norristown Road
Spring House, PA 19477 215-619-5164
Fax: 215-619-1608 800-447-4369
dowcig@dow.com www.dow.com
Processor and exporter of food ingredients including gums, stabilizers and chelating agents; exporter of methylcellulose and hydroxypropyl methylcellulose.
President/CEO/Chairman: Andrew Liveris
Lead Technical Sales Manager: Jon Fisher
Estimated Sales: $49 Billion
Number Employees: 10,000
Brands:
Amplify
Blox
Briners Choice
Carbowax
Dow
Dowex
Dowflake
Dowtherm
Filmtec
Inspire
Instill
Liduidow
Methocel
Optim
Primacor
Saran
Styron
Ucon
Versene

21772 **(HQ)Dow Corning Corporation**
P.O.Box 994
2200 W. Salzburg Rd.
Midland, MI 48686-0994 989-496-4000
Fax: 989-496-6731 webmaster@dowcorning.com
www.dowcorning.com
Manufacturer, importer and exporter of ingredients and process aids including antifoamers, release agents and lubricants
President & Chief Executive Officer: Robert Hansen
EVP & Chief Financial Officer: J. Donald Sheets
VP & Chief Human Resouces Officer: Mike Conway
Estimated Sales: $6.5 Billion
Number Employees: 12000
Square Footage: 1000000
Type of Packaging: Food Service, Bulk
Other Locations:
Dow Corning Corp.
Midland MI
Brands:
Affinity Polyolefin Plastomers
Attane Copolymer
Blox Thermoplastic Resins
Calcium Chloride
Dow Corning
Dow Hdpe Copolymer
Dow Ldpe Copolymer
Dowex Ion Exchange Resins
Dowlex Copolymer
Dowtherm Heat Transfer Fluids
Elite Epw Copolymer
Epoxy Products and Intermediates
Filmtex Membrane Elements
Glycine
Lldpe Copolymer
Methoxwl Methyl Cellulose
Molykote
Optim and Dow Glycerine
Oxides and Glycols
Primacor Copolymer
Saran Barrier Films and Resins
Saran Wrap
Styron Polystyrene Resins
Syloff
Uldpe Copolymer
Versene Chelating Agents

21773 **Dow Cover Company**
373 Lexington Ave
New Haven, CT 06513 203-469-5394
Fax: 203-469-0742 800-735-8877
mark@dowcover.com www.dowcover.com
Canvas covers and aprons including custom logo, screenprint and embroidery
President: Mark Steinhardt
Estimated Sales: $5-10 Million
Number Employees: 50-99
Square Footage: 34000
Brands:
Dowsport America

21774 **Dow Fabricated Products**
P.O.Box 1206
Midland, MI 48641-1206 989-636-1000
Fax: 989-832-1465 800-441-4369
presidingdirector@dow.com www.dow.com
Polyethylene foam products for cushioning of high-value products and plank and sheet packaging products
President: William Stavropoulos
CEO: Mike Parker
President: Andrew N Liveris
CEO: Andrew N Liveris
CFO: J Pedro Reinhard
Estimated Sales: K
Number Employees: 10,000

21775 **Dow Industries**
271 Ballardvale St
Wilmington, MA 01887 978-988-8815
Fax: 978-658-2307 800-776-1201
sales@dowindustries.com
www.dowindutries.com
Manufacturer and exporter of pressure sensitive labels and automatic labeling equipment
President: Walter Dow
CEO: Andy Farquharson
CFO: John Morrison
Quality Control: Scott Boucher
Senior VP: Bill Donovan
Operations Manager: D Apgar
Estimated Sales: $20 Million
Number Employees: 64
Square Footage: 64000
Type of Packaging: Consumer, Private Label

21776 **DowElanco**
9330 Zionsville Road
Indianapolis, IN 46268-1053 317-337-3000
Fax: 317-337-4140 800-258-3033
www.dowagro.com
Wine industry vineyard chemicals
Director: Rogelio Lara
Estimated Sales: $1 - 5 Million
Number Employees: 1-4

21777 **Dowling Company**
1801 Princess Anne St
Fredericksburg, VA 22401 540-373-6675
Fax: 540-371-7543 800-572-2100
signsdsi@aol.com www.dowlingsignsinc.com
Signs specializing in ADA (American Disabilities Act) approved including illuminated and nonilluminated identification
President: Allen Malocha
Secretary and Treasurer: Susanne Bradley
General Manager: Allen Malocha
Production Manager: Charles Ward
Estimated Sales: $2.5-5 Million
Number Employees: 20-49
Square Footage: 30000

21778 **Downeast Chemical**
88 Scott Dr
Westbrook, ME 04092-1927 207-773-9668
Fax: 207-773-0832 800-287-2225
Detergents, degreasers and boiler treatment compounds; also, custom blending
President: Joseph Brita
VP: John Bowns
Customer Service: Heather Bowns
Estimated Sales: $1 - 3 Million
Number Employees: 9
Square Footage: 8400

21779 **Downs Crane & Hoist Company**
8827 Juniper St
Los Angeles, CA 90002 323-589-6061
Fax: 323-589-6066 800-748-5994
sales@downscrane.com www.downscrane.com
Manufacturer and exporter of lifting devices including grabs, tongs, spreaders, manipulators, hooks, cranes and crane wheels and assemblies
President: John W Downs Jr
Number Employees: 10-19
Type of Packaging: Bulk
Brands:
Grabmaster

21780 **Doyen Medipharm**
4030 S Pipkin Rd Ste 102
Lakeland, FL 33811 863-683-6335
Fax: 863-683-6857 info@doyennet.com
www.doyenmedipharm.com
Packaging machinery for food industry
President: Ray Johnson
VP: Martin Beriswill
Estimated Sales: $2.5-5 000,000
Number Employees: 20-49

21781 **Doyle Signs**
232 W Interstate Rd
Addison, IL 60101 630-543-9490
Fax: 630-543-9493 info@doylesigns.com
www.doylesigns.com
Interior and exterior electric identification signs; also, design, installation and maintenance services available
President: T Doyle
VP: P Doyle
Sales Director: J Doyle
Estimated Sales: $10 Million
Number Employees: 50-99
Square Footage: 37000

21782 **Doyon Equipment**
1255 Rue Principale
Liniere, QC G0M 1J0
Canada 418-685-3431
Fax: 418-685-3948 800-463-4273
doyon@doyon.qc.ca www.doyon.qc.ca
Doyon Equipment Inc has been a manufacturer of bakery and pizza ovens for more than 55 years. The Doyon trademark is recognized for its quality and service, its exports their products all over the world. This family owned is aworldwide leader providing solutions for all types of bake shops, pizzerias, hotels, cafes and various restaurants.
President: Karl Doyon
Research & Development: Pierre Poirier
Marketing Director: Jennifer Letourneau
Regional Sales Director: John Herbert
Regional Sales Director: Jim Markee
Estimated Sales: $10-20,000,000
Number Employees: 20
Brands:
Doyon
Jet Air

21783 **Drackett Professional**
8600 Governors Hill Drive
Cincinnati, OH 45249-1360 513-583-3900
Fax: 513-583-3968 sjmoser@jwp.com
www.drackett.com
Cleaners and mops
National Sales Director: Steve Moser
Director Advertising/PR: Diego Esquibel
General Manager: Terry Conlon
Number Employees: 20-49
Parent Co: S.C. Johnson Wax
Brands:
Beer Clean
Draino
Easy Paks
Glade
Ice-Foe
Raid
Windex

21784 **Draeger Safety**
101 Technology Dr
Pittsburgh, PA 15275 412-787-8383
Fax: 412-787-2207 800-922-5518
prodinfo@draeger.net www.draeger.com
Develops safety technology for manufacturing industry.
President: Ralf Drews
CFO: Graeme Roberts
Estimated Sales: $50 - 100 Million
Number Employees: 100-249

21785 **Draiswerke**
40 Whitney Rd
Mahwah, NJ 07430 201-847-0600
Fax: 201-847-0606 800-494-3151
salesinfo@draiswerke-inc.com
www.draiswerke-inc.com
Tea and coffee industry mills for micro wet grinding and dispersing, mixers, dryers, reactors, and compounding systems
President: Gisbert Schall
Estimated Sales: $10 - 20 000,000
Number Employees: 20-49

21786 **Drake Container Corporation**
1401 Greengrass Dr
Houston, TX 77008 713-869-9121
Fax: 713-869-3512 800-299-5644
www.drakecontainer.com
Manufacturer and exporter of corrugated boxes and lithographic displays
CEO: John Carrico
CEO: John Carrico
Sales/Service Manager: Kevin Fiedler
Estimated Sales: $1 - 5 Million
Number Employees: 100

21787 **Drapes 4 Show**
12811 Foothill Blvd
Sylmar, CA 91342-5316 818-838-0852
Fax: 818-222-7469 800-525-7469
staff@drapes.com www.drapes.com
Tabletop accessories including napkins, table skirting and table linens
President, Founder: Karen Honigberg
CEO: Karen Honigberg
Customer Service: Kathryn Pereyra
Estimated Sales: Below $5 Million
Number Employees: 20-49
Square Footage: 12800

21788 **Dreaco Products**
172 Reaser Court
Elyria, OH 44035-6285 440-366-7600
Fax: 440-365-5858 800-368-3267
www.dreaco.com
Manufacturer and exporter of exhaust hoods and fans; also, make-up air fans
Owner and President: Robert Gargasz
Sales/Marketing Executive: Karen Kauk
Purchasing Agent: Michael Gargasz
Estimated Sales: $2.5-5 Million
Number Employees: 20-49
Square Footage: 100000
Brands:
Dreaco

21789 **DreamPak LLC**
4717 Eisenhower Avenue
Alexandria, VA 22304 703-751-3511
877-687-4662
info@dreampak.com www.dreampak.com
On-the-go beverages
President/CEO: Dr. Aly Gamay
Executive Vice President: Terry Schneider
Vice President, Operations: Randy Cook
Brands:
Fruitslim
Soluflex
Dogflex
Trimma
Enhance To Go
Joker's Wild Energy
Chocolate Slim
Zeniht

21790 **Drehmann Paving & Flooring Company**
847 Bethel Ave
Pennsauken, NJ 08110-2605 856-486-0202
Fax: 856-486-0808 800-523-3800
bvarra@drehman.com
Manufacturer and exporter of brick floor coatings, plates and drains; installation services available
President: William Varra
VP: J Kline, Jr.
Executive VP: Horace Furman
Research & Development: M Bojesuk
Quality Control: S Furman
Estimated Sales: $5,000,000
Number Employees: 75-100
Number of Brands: 1
Number of Products: 10
Square Footage: 18000
Type of Packaging: Private Label

21791 **Drehmann Paving & Flooring Company**
2101 Byberry Road
Philadelphia, PA 19116-3017 215-464-7700
Fax: 215-673-9755 800-523-3800
www.drehmann.com
Industrial brick flooring, epoxy, joint materials, expansion joints,cast iron floor drains and stainless steel floor drains

21792 **Drescher Paper Box**
459 Broadway St
Buffalo, NY 14204 716-854-0288
Fax: 716-854-1920 jb@drescherpuzzle.com
www.drescherpuzzle.com
Rigid set-up paper boxes, jigsaw puzzles, board games
President: J Baird Langworthy
CEO: Joyce MacLeod
Estimated Sales: $10-20 Million
Number Employees: 10-19
Square Footage: 48000

21793 **Dresco Belting Company**
122 East St
East Weymouth, MA 02189 781-335-1350
Fax: 781-340-0500 sales@drescobelt.com
www.drescobelt.com
Manufacturer and exporter of conveyor and transmission belting
Owner: James Dresser
V.P.: Norman Dresser, Jr.
VP: James Dresser
Estimated Sales: $1-2.5 Million
Number Employees: 5-9
Square Footage: 20000

21794 **Dresser Industries Roots Division**
801 W Mount St
Connersville, IN 47331 765-827-9200
Fax: 765-827-9266 www.rootsblower.com
Rotary and centrifugal air and gas blowers, compressors, high vacuum and industrial compressor equipment
Manager: Gary Redelman
President: Andrew E Graves
Estimated Sales: $1 Billion
Number Employees: 100-249

21795 **Dresser Instruments**
250 E Main St
Stratford, CT 06614 203-378-8281
Fax: 203-385-0402 800-328-8258
info@ebro.com www.ebro.com;
www.dresserinstruments.com
Ebro instruments can be used for applications in the food and beverage industries. Ebro products are high-precision measuring instruments for use in applications where reliability and performance are required. Ebro instruments canmeasure and store temperature, pressure, humidity, pH, oil quality, current/voltage, salt and RPM, as well as other physical units.
Managing Director: Wolfgang Klun
General Sales Manager: Iven Kruse
Quality Manager: Thomas Koch
Sales Manager USA: Frank Crisafulli
Marketing Manager: Norbert Niggl
Number Employees: 500-999
Number of Brands: 2
Square Footage: 325000
Brands:
Ashcroft
Ebro

21796 **Dreumex USA**
3445 Board Rd
York, PA 17406-8409 717-767-6881
Fax: 717-767-6888 800-233-9382
dreumex@dreumex.com www.dreumex.com
Manufacturer and exporter of waterless gel and lotion hand cleaners and liquid soap; also, hand and multi-purpose wipes, dispensing systems, and car/truck wash
President/CEO: Jim Strickler
Research & Development: Gail Shermeyer
Quality Control: Gail Shermeyer
Marketing Director: Karen Hansen
Sales Director: Jim Strickler
Public Relations: Karen Hansen
Operations Manager: Jeff Strickler
Production Manager: Jim Mitzel
Plant Manager: Jim Mitzel
Purchasing Manager: Bob Keyser
Estimated Sales: $5 - 10 Million
Number Employees: 20-49
Number of Brands: 13
Number of Products: 13
Square Footage: 160000
Type of Packaging: Private Label
Brands:
Citrus
Gent-L-Kleen
Grime Grabber
Power Wipes Formula Z
Premium Blue
Pumicizied Advantage Plus
Skin Armor
Zapper

21797 **Dri Mark Products**
15 Harbor Park Dr
Port Washington, NY 11050 516-484-6200
Fax: 516-484-6279 800-645-9118
www.drimark.com
Manufacturer and exporter of pens including nylon, felt and plastic tip, ball point, roller ball and counterfeit detector; also, watercolor and permanent markers, highlighters and drawing sets
President: Charles Reichmann
CFO: Cathy Owens
VP Sales: Mark Dobbs
Purchasing Manager: Mickey Cirrani
Estimated Sales: $20 - 50 Million
Number Employees: 100-249
Square Footage: 70000
Brands:
Buffalo
Color Graphic
Communication
Mr. Doodler
Perma Graphic

21798 **DriAll**
P.O.Box 309
Attica, IN 47918 765-295-2255
Fax: 317-272-1097 driallusa@att.net
www.driallusa.com
Manufacturer and exporter of grain dryers and air curtain destructors for controlled open residue burning
Manager: Dave Scott
Estimated Sales: Less than $500,000
Number Employees: 1-4
Type of Packaging: Food Service, Bulk

21799 **Driam**
181 Access Road
Spartanburg, SC 29303 864-579-7850
Fax: 864-579-7852 info@driamusa.com
www.driamusa.com
Confectionary and candy sorting and inspection machinery. Coating equipment for the pharmeceutical and confectionary industry
Owner: Marilyn Drumm
Sales Manager: Hans Peter Schwendeler
Estimated Sales: Below $5 Million
Number Employees: 1-4
Parent Co: Driam

21800 **Dried Ingredients, LLC**
4256 NW 35th Court
Miami, FL 33142 786-999-8499
Fax: 888-893-5495 info@driedingredients.com
www.driedingredients.com
Teas, tea ingredients, herbs, spices, essential oils and air & freeze dried vegetables.
Chairman: Til Brautigam
Chairman: Jorn Burchard
VP Sales/Marketing: Armin Dilles
Parent Co: Dried Ingredients
Type of Packaging: Food Service, Bulk

21801 **Driscoll Label Company**
19 West Street
East Hanover, NJ 07936 973-585-7291
Fax: 973-585-7295 craguso@driscolllabel.com
www.driscolllabel.com
Wine industry pressure sensitive labels
President: John Riguso
Vice President: Patricia Biava
Sales Director: Patricia Vargas
Estimated Sales: $10-20 000,000
Number Employees: 20-49

21802 **Drives Incorporated**
901 19th Ave
Fulton, IL 61252 815-589-2211
Fax: 815-589-4420 custserv@drivesinc.com
www.drivesinc.com
Power transmission products, conveyor chain, screw conveyors
President: David J Vogel
CFO: Michael Landers

Estimated Sales: $50-100 Million
Number Employees: 250-499

21803 Drum-Mates Inc.
PO Box 636
Lumberton, NJ 08048-0636 609-261-1033
Fax: 609-261-1034 800-621-3786
info@drum mates.com www.drummates.com
Manufacturer and exporter of bung mounting, air operated and adjustable liquid food/beverage drum mixers, IBC blenders, hand dispensers, pumps, etc
Marketing Manager: David Marcmann
Estimated Sales: $1 - 5 Million
Number Employees: 20
Square Footage: 50000
Parent Co: Drum-Mates Pty.
Brands:
Drum-Mate
Quikmix
Threadconverter
Threadguard

21804 Drying Technology
P.O.Box 1635
Silsbee, TX 77656 409-385-6422
Fax: 409-385-6537
drying@moisturecontrols.com
www.moisturecontrols.com
Moisture controls
President: John W Robinson
Estimated Sales: Below $5 000,000
Number Employees: 1-4

21805 Dryomatic
7924 Reco Avenue
Frederick, MD 70814 301-668-8200
Fax: 225-612-7407 sales@dryomatic.com
www.dryomatic.com
Parent Co: Airflow Company

21806 Du-Good Chemical Laboratory & Manufacturing Company
1215 S Jefferson Ave
Saint Louis, MO 63104-1992 314-773-5007
Fax: 314-773-5007 dugood@stlnet.com
Dishwashing detergent and waterless hand cleaning products
President: Lincoln I Diuguid
VP: Lewis Diuguid
Manager: V Diuguid
Estimated Sales: $.5 - 1 million
Number Employees: 5 to 9
Square Footage: 6575
Brands:
Du-Good
Rainbow Delight

21807 DuBois Chemicals
3630 East Kemper Road
Sharonville, OH 45241-2011 513-762-6804
Fax: 800-543-1720 800-438-2647
cs@duboischemicals.com
www.duboischemicals.com
Sanitation and cleaning products including color-coded cleaners and sanitizers, can washing, CIP systems, ATP-based rapid tests for sanitation, wastewater treatment, food-grade lubricants, boiler and cooling water treatment andmonitoring and application
President: Tom Gartland
Vice President: Mark Greylak
Estimated Sales: $500,000-$1 Million
Number Employees: 4

21808 DuPont
1007 Market St
Wilmington, DE 19898 302-774-1000
Fax: 302-355-4013 800-441-7515
info@dupont.com www.dupont.com
Chemical supplies including emulsifying agents, bleaches, plastic films, etc
CFO: Gary M Pfeiffer
President: Wille Marcin
CEO: Ellen J Kullman
CEO: Charles O Holliday Jr
Estimated Sales: $2.5 - 5 Million
Number Employees: 10,000

21809 DuPont Packaging
222 Philadelphia Pike # 5
Wilmington, DE 19809-3166 302-761-4660
Fax: 302-999-4754 info@dupont.com
www.dupont.com
Nonstick coatings for commercial bakeware
Manager: Michelle Holmes
Estimated Sales: $1 - 5 Million
Number Employees: 5-9

21810 DuPont Packaging
222 Philadelphia Pike # 5
Wilmington, DE 19809-3166 302-761-4660
Fax: 302-999-4754 info@dupont.com
www.dupont.com
Non-stick coatings for commercial bakeware
Manager: Michelle Holmes
Business Develpment Manager: P Krishna Mohan
Estimated Sales: $1 - 5 Million
Number Employees: 5-9

21811 DuPont Packaging
222 Philadelphia Pike # 5
Wilmington, DE 19809-3166 302-761-4660
Fax: 302-999-4754 800-438-7225
info@dupont.com www.dupont.com
Chair of the Board & Chief Executive Off: Ellen Kullman
EVP and Chief Financial Officer: Nicholas C. Fanandakis
EVP and Chief Innovation Officer: Thomas M. Connelly, Jr.
VP - Safety, Health & Environment CSO: Linda J. Fisher
SVP - DuPont Human Resources: Benito Cachinero-S nchez
Estimated Sales: $1 - 5 Million
Number Employees: 5-9

21812 DuPont Packaging
1007 N Market St # D5000
Wilmington, DE 19898-0001 302-773-3061
Fax: 302-892-7321 800-438-7225
info@dupont.com www.packaging.dupont.com
Provider of technology solutions that streamline the design, construction, operation and maintenance of commercial building property
CEO: Charles Holliday
Vice President: James Borel
Number Employees: 1,000-4,999

21813 DualTemp Companies
4301 South Packers Avenue
Chicago, IL 60609 773-254-9800
Fax: 773-254-9840 800-255-9801
sales@dualtempcompanies.com
www.dualtempcompanies.com
President: Rolly Weinstein
Estimated Sales: $1 - 5 Million
Number Employees: 20-49

21814 Dualite Sales & Service
1 Dualite Ln
Williamsburg, OH 45176 513-724-7100
Fax: 513-724-9029 dualite@dualite.com
www.dualite.com
National account sign manufacturer
CEO/President: Greg Schube
Executive VP Administration: E Lynn Webb
R&D: Pat Seggerson
National Sales Manager: Robert Stephany
Plant Manager: Jerry Hinnenkamp
Purchasing: Greg Hoffer
Estimated Sales: $35-50 Million
Number Employees: 250-499
Square Footage: 600000
Parent Co: Dualite

21815 Dub Harris Corporation
2875 Metropolitan Place
Pomona, CA 91767 909-596-6300
Fax: 909-596-6336 dubharris@dubharris.com
www.dubharris.com
Plastic bags; wholesaler/distributor of corrugated boxes and packaging materials
President: Maurice Harris
Estimated Sales: $2.5-5 Million
Number Employees: 5-9

21816 Dubor GmbH
4801 Harbor Pointe Dr.
Suite 1305
North Myrtle Beach, SC 29016-9458 803-691-8941
Fax: 803-754-7755
benmuller@mullerinternational.com
www.mullerinternational.com

21817 Dubuit of America
70 Monaco Dr
Roselle, IL 60172 630-894-9500
Fax: 847-647-1796 www.dubuit.com
Printers and screen printing equipment
Estimated Sales: $3 000,000
Number Employees: 10-20

21818 Dubuque Steel Products Company
340 E 12th St
Dubuque, IA 52001 563-556-6288
Fax: 563-583-7365
sales@dubuquesteelproducts.com
www.dubuquesteelproducts.com
Stainless steel tubs, trucks, dollies, racks, drums and vats
President: Tom Geisler
CEO: Dave Geisler
Vice President: Todd Geisler
Estimated Sales: $2.5-5 Million
Number Employees: 5-9
Parent Co: Geisler Brothers Company

21819 Duck Waok
44535 Main Road
PO Box 962
Water Mill, NY 11976-0962 631-765-3500
Fax: 631-765-3509 www.duckwalk.com
Wines
Owner: Alexander Damianos
VP and General Manager: Alex Zamianos
Estimated Sales: Below $5 Million
Number Employees: 10-19

21820 Duda Farm Fresh Foods, Inc.
PO Box 620257
Oviedo, FL 32762-0257 407-365-2111
Fax: 407-365-2147 www.duda.com
Full-ervice grower, packer, shipper, marketer, importer and exporter of fresh fruits and vegetables and fresh-cut vegetables. Citrus, celery/fresh cut celery, broccoli, cauliflower, sweet corn, lettuce/leaf, onions and radishes.
Manager: Joseph Duda
Estimated Sales: $10-20 Million
Number Employees: 20-49
Parent Co: A. Duda & Sons
Type of Packaging: Consumer, Bulk
Brands:
Dandy®

21821 Dudson USA
5604 Departure Dr
Raleigh, NC 27616 919-877-0200
Fax: 919-877-0300 800-438-3766
thomsonc@dudsonusa.com www.dudsonusa.com
Importer and wholesaler/distributor of dinnerware including china; serving the food service market
President: Elmer Carr
VP: Lorraine Delois
VP Marketing/Sales: Joel DeNoble
VP Corporate Accounts: Maire-Anne Bassil
Estimated Sales: $1-2.5 Million
Number Employees: 10-19
Square Footage: 90000
Parent Co: Dudson Company
Type of Packaging: Food Service

21822 Duerr Packaging Company
892 Steubenville Pike
Burgettstown, PA 15021 724-947-1234
Fax: 724-947-4321 sales@duerrpack.com
www.duerrpack.com
Rigid paper boxes, transformed plastics
CEO: Samuel Duerr Jr
CFO: Wayne Albroght
VP: David Duerr
Estimated Sales: $2.5 - 5 Million
Number Employees: 20-49

21823 Dufeck Manufacturing Company
P.O.Box 428
210 Maple Street
Denmark, WI 54208 920-863-2354
Fax: 920-863-2054 888-603-9663
info@dufeckwood.com www.dufeckwood.com
Wooden cheese and wine boxes, custom display units, containers, gift boxes and baskets and wooden pallets
President: Paul Dufeck
R&D: Junette Dufeck
Plant Manager: Al Bouressa

Estimated Sales: $10 - 20 Million
Number Employees: 20-49
Square Footage: 20000

21824 Dugussa Texturant Systems
3582 McCall Pl
Atlanta, GA 30340-2802 770-455-3603
Fax: 770-986-6216 800-241-9485
texturants@degussa.com
www.texturantsystems.com

President: Ed Baranski
Number Employees: 50-99

21825 Dukane Corporation
2900 Dukane Dr
Saint Charles, IL 60174 630-584-2300
Fax: 630-797-4949 usservice@dukcorp.com
www.dukcorp.com

Ultrasonic food cutting
President: Jean Stone
CEO: Michael W Ritschdorff
Marketing Communications: Kathy Jensen
Sales Director: Joe Re
Estimated Sales: G
Number Employees: 100-249
Brands:
Ultrasonic Equipment

21826 Dukane Ultrasonics
2900 Dukane Dr # 1
St Charles, IL 60174-3395 630-584-5852
Fax: 630-797-4949 usuntl@dukane.com
www.dukane.com/us

CEO: Michael W Ritschdorff
Estimated Sales: $1 - 5 Million
Number Employees: 100-249

21827 Duke Manufacturing Company
2305 N Broadway
Saint Louis, MO 63102 314-231-1130
Fax: 314-231-5074 800-735-3853
customerservice@dukemfg.com
www.dukemfg.com

Manufacturer and exporter of ingredient bins, cabinets, sneeze guards, conveyors, counters, filters, freezers, ovens, steam tables, pans, racks, coolers, kiosks, fire extinguishing systems, sinks, carts, etc
President: John Hake
CFO: Larry Reader
Quality Control: Art Lamley
Estimated Sales: $20-50 Million
Number Employees: 250-499
Square Footage: 300000

21828 Duluth Sheet Metal
P.O.Box 16582
Duluth, MN 55816-0582 218-722-2613
Fax: 218-727-8870 info@duluthsheetmetal.com
www.duluthsheetmetal.com

Stainless steel tables, stands, shelves, counter tops, cabinets, sinks and vapor hoods; custom fabricator of conveyors, platforms, tanks, etc
President: Mark Jam
Estimated Sales: $1-2.5 Million
Number Employees: 10-19
Square Footage: 12000

21829 Dunbar Manufacturing Company
390 N Gilbert St
South Elgin, IL 60177 847-741-6394
Fax: 847-741-6394
www.dunbarmanufacturing.com

Manufacturer and exporter of caramel and regular popcorn equipment including mixers, tumblers, poppers and sprayers
President: Ray Goode Jr
Estimated Sales: Less than $500,000
Number Employees: 2
Number of Products: 40
Square Footage: 6000
Brands:
Popt-Rite

21830 Dunbar Systems
1186 Walter Street
Lemont, IL 60439-3993 630-257-2900
Fax: 630-257-3434 info@dunbarsystems.com
www.dunbarsystems.com

Bakery equipment
CEO: George Dunbar
Executive Vice President, Owner: Mark Dunbar
Vice President of Operations: James Diver
Estimated Sales: $5-10 Million
Number Employees: 10-19

21831 Dunbar Systems Inc.
186 Walter Street
Lemont, IL 60439-3993 630-257-2900
Fax: 630-257-3434 www.dunbarsystems.com

Automated serpentine baking systems for cookies, cakes, biscuits, bread, pies, pastries, muffins and puddings
Chief Executive Officer, Founder: George Dunbar
Executive Vice President, Owner: Mark Dunbar
Vice President of Operations: James Diver
Estimated Sales: $5 - 10 Million
Number Employees: 10-19

21832 Dunhill Food Equipment Corporation
PO Box 496
Armonk, NY 10504 718-625-4006
Fax: 718-625-0155 800-847-4206
sales@dunhill-esquire.net
www.dunhill-esquire.com

Manufacturer and exporter of cafeteria and kitchen equipment including cashier stands, serving counters, sinks, refrigerated display cases and tables
President: Geoffrey Thaw
VP: Larry Dubow
Estimated Sales: $5-10 Million
Number Employees: 10-19
Square Footage: 50000
Parent Co: Esquire Mechanical Group
Type of Packaging: Food Service
Brands:
Dunhill

21833 Dunkin Brands Inc.
130 Royall Street
Canton, MA 02021 781-737-3000
Fax: 781-737-4000 800-458-7731
www.dunkinbrands.com

Coffee, donuts, and ice cream
President, Dunkin Brands Int'l: Giorgio Minardi
CEO: Nigel Travis
CFO: Paul Carbone
SVP/General Counsel: Richard Emmett
SVP/Chief Brands Officer: Bill Mitchell
Chief Global Marketing & Innovation: John Costello
SVP/Chief Human Resources Officer: Ginger Gregory
SVP/Corporate Communications: Karen Raskopf
Chief Operating Officer: Paul Twohg
Estimated Sales: $8.3 Billion
Number Employees: 10,000+
Square Footage: 175000
Type of Packaging: Food Service
Brands:
Baskin Robbins
Dunkin Donuts

21834 Dunkley International
1910 Lake St
Kalamazoo, MI 49001-3274 269-343-5583
Fax: 269-343-5614 800-666-1264
info@dunkleyintl.com www.dunkleyintl.com

Manufacturer and exporter of pitters, de-stemmers and electronic sorters, inspection systems and conveyors
President: Richard L Bogard
General Manager: Ernest Kenneway
Plant Manager: Rob Prange
Estimated Sales: $1 - 3 Million
Number Employees: 10-19
Square Footage: 120000
Parent Co: Cherry Central

21835 Dunn Woodworks
536 S Main Street
Shrewsbury, PA 17361-1739 717-235-1144
Fax: 717-227-2828 877-835-8592
woodpilot@aol.com

Manufacturer, broker and wholesaler/distributor of custom designed displays, kiosks, racks, P.O.P, P.O.S. and merchandisers. Custom designed wine racks and display headers. Over ten thousand displays made annually
Owner: Henry Dunn
Estimated Sales: $1 - 3,000,000
Number Employees: 5
Square Footage: 10000

21836 Dunrite
3405 N Yager Rd
Fremont, NE 68025-7880 402-721-3061
Fax: 402-721-3040 800-782-3061
www.dunriteinc.com

Pneumatic grain conveyors, grain elevator vacuums and accessories including respirators, dust masks and duct tape
Manager: Leroy Klinzing
VP: Leroy Klinzing
Estimated Sales: $2.5-5 Million
Number Employees: 5-9
Brands:
Buckskin Bill
Harvestvac

21837 Duo-Aire
39 Third Street SW
Suite 606
Winter Haven, FL 33880 863-294-2272
Fax: 863-294-2704 info@duoaire.com
www.duoaire.com

Commercial kitchen ventilation systems
President: Gary Smith
Accounting: Jan Smith
Sales & Parts: Jody Reynolds
Estimated Sales: $470,000
Number Employees: 4
Square Footage: 14836
Parent Co: Ventilation Marketing Services

21838 Duplex Mill & Manufacturing Company
P.O.Box 1266
Springfield, OH 45501-1266 937-325-5555
Fax: 937-325-0859 www.dmmc.com

Diverter valves and mixing, blending, conveying, elevating, size reduction and slide gate machinery; exporter of mixers, conveyors and hammer mills
President: Eric Wise
CEO: Eric Wise Jr
Sales Manager: Eric Wise
Production Manager: Eric Brickson
Plant Manager: Eric Brickson
Estimated Sales: $2-3 Million
Number Employees: 10-19
Square Footage: 320000
Brands:
Kelly Duplex

21839 Dupont Liquid PackagingSystems
6950 Worthington Galena Rd
Worthington, OH 43085 614-888-9280
Fax: 614-888-0982 info@dupont.com
www.liquidpackaging.dupont.com

Supplier of liquid packaging system solutions for food and beverage companies
President: William White
CFO: Michael Oxley
CEO: Samuel B Davis
Director Research/Development: David Yake
Director Marketing/Sales: Colleen Brydon
Sales Manager: Wendy Andrushko
Operations Director: Glen Wood
Estimated Sales: $142 Million
Number Employees: 50-99
Type of Packaging: Private Label, Bulk

21840 Dupont Qualicon
ESL, Bldg 400
Rt 141 & Henry Clay Rd
Wilmington, DE 19880 302-695-5300
Fax: 302-695-6842
barbara.d.robleto@usa.dupont.com
www.qualicon.com

Supplies products to meet diagnostics needs of the food industry
CEO: Ellen Kullman
CFO: Nicholas Fanandakis
Estimated Sales: $1 Billion +
Number Employees: 6,000

21841 Dupps Company
P.O.Box 189
Germantown, OH 45327 937-855-6555
Fax: 937-855-6554 info@dupps.com
www.dupps.com

Manufacturer and exporter of process equipment and protein waste recovery systems including cookers and dryers; also, computerized control and information systems, screw presses, conveyor systems, high viscosity material pumps and sizereduction equipment
President: John A Dupps Jr
VP: Frank Dupps
Quality Control: Tim Seebach
Marketing Manager: Rich Hollmeyer

Estimated Sales: $20-50 Million
Number Employees: 100-249
Square Footage: 120000
Brands:
Equacookor
Precrushor
Pressor
Ring Dryer

21842 Dupuy Storage & Forwarding Corporation
P.O.Box 52381
New Orleans, LA 70152-2381 504-245-7600
Fax: 504-245-7643 www.dupuystorage.com
Tea and coffee industry bulk silo services, reconditioners, samplers and weighers
President: Allan B Colley
Estimated Sales: $50-100 Million
Number Employees: 1-4

21843 Dur A Flex
95 Goodwin St
East Hartford, CT 06108 860-528-9838
Fax: 860-528-2802 877-251-5418
contact_us@dur-a-flex.com www.dur-a-flex.com
Commercial and seemless industrial flooring systems and wall coatings and polymer components - epoxies, urethanes and methyl methacrylates (MMA) plus premium colored quartz aggregates.
Marketing: Mark Paggioli
Number Employees: 75
Square Footage: 130000
Brands:
Cryl-A-Chip
Cryl-A-Flex
Cryl-A-Floor
Cryl-A-Quartz
Poly-Crete

21844 Dur-Able Aluminum Corporation
1555 Barrington Rd
Hoffman Estates, IL 60169-1019 847-843-1100
Fax: 847-843-0764
Manufacturer and exporter of aluminum foil bakeware including pans, plates, trays and cooking and baking utensils
Estimated Sales: $20-50 Million
Number Employees: 1-4
Type of Packaging: Food Service, Bulk

21845 Dura Electric Lamp Company
64 E Bigelow Street
Newark, NJ 07114-1699 973-624-0014
Fax: 973-624-3945
Manufacturer and exporter of incandescent and fluorescent lamps and starters
President: Lawrence Portnow
General Manager: A Gross
Estimated Sales: $2.5-5 Million
Number Employees: 5-9
Square Footage: 40000
Brands:
Dura
Durelco

21846 (HQ)Dura-Ware Company of America
PO Box 53006
Oklahoma City, OK 73152-3006 405-475-5600
Fax: 405-475-5607 800-664-3872
customerservice@carlislefsp.com
www.carlislefsp.com
Manufacturer, importer and exporter of commercial cookware and servingware including stock pots, frying pans, sauce pans, pasta cookers, chafers, etc
President: David Shannon
VP Sales: David Wasserman
Estimated Sales: $20 - 50 Million
Number Employees: 50-99
Square Footage: 70000
Brands:
Celebration
Dura-Ware
Signature
Ssal
Symphony

21847 Durable Corporation
P.O.Box 290
Norwalk, OH 44857 419-668-8138
Fax: 419-668-8068 800-537-1603
sales@durablecorp.com www.durablecorp.com
Dock bumpers, wheel chocks and floor mats and matting
President: Thomas Secor
Sales Director: Phil Lorcher
Estimated Sales: $20-50 Million
Number Employees: 50-99
Type of Packaging: Private Label

21848 Durable Engravers
521 S County Line Rd
Franklin Park, IL 60131 773-467-8728
Fax: 630-766-0219 800-869-9565
durableengravers@sbcglobal.net.com
Manufacturer and exporter of steel and brass codes, logo blocks and holders for the food and pharmaceutical industries
CEO: Gary Berenger
VP: Jim Maybach
Estimated Sales: $1-2.5 Million
Number Employees: 20-49
Square Footage: 10000
Type of Packaging: Food Service, Bulk

21849 Durable Packaging Corporation
5117 Dansher Rd
Countryside, IL 60525-6905 708-387-2253
Fax: 708-387-2211 800-700-5677
dgrewe@durablepack.com www.okcorp.com
Case erectors and sealers
Manager: Adam Kwiek
Sales/Marketing Manager: Carol Crouse
General Information: Leslie Hickey
Estimated Sales: $5 - 10 Million
Number Employees: 10-19

21850 Duralam
2621 W Everett St
Appleton, WI 54914 920-734-6698
Fax: 920-831-3483 800-255-6698
quality@duralam.com www.curwood.com
Manager: Tom Van Handel

21851 Duralite
15 School St
Riverton, CT 06065 860-379-3113
Fax: 860-379-5879 888-432-8797
sales@duralite.com www.duralite.com
Manufacturer and exporter of quartz tubes for heating/cooking equipment with element enclosed is tube or wrapped around tube, also heating elements (electric) heating and cooking, coiled or not
President: Mark Jessen
CEO: Elliott Jessen
Chairman: Elliot Jessen
Sales Director: Barbara Asselin
Estimated Sales: $1 Million+
Number Employees: 10
Square Footage: 7500

21852 (HQ)Durand-Wayland, Inc.
PO Box 1404
Lagrange, GA 30241 706-882-8161
Fax: 706-882-0052 800-241-2308
sales@durand-wayland.com
www.durand-wayland.com
Manufacturer and exporter of fruit processing and packing machinery including conveyors, cleaners, sizers, sorters, blemish graders and sprayers
President: Brooks Lee
VP Sales: Ray Perry
Marketing Director: Ashley Scott
Sales Manager: Suzanne Bryan
Purchasing Manager: Savral Patel
Number Employees: 250-499
Other Locations:
Durand-Wayland
Reedley CA

21853 (HQ)Durango-Georgia Paper
4301 Anchor Plaza Parkway
Suite 360
Tampa, FL 33634 813-286-2718
Fax: 912-576-0713
Manufacturer and exporter of bleached boards for folding cartons; also, grease resistant decorative paper plates and lightweight cups, bleached and natural kraft paper
VP Marketing: Joseph Meighan
Estimated Sales: $1 - 5 Million
Parent Co: Corporation Durango.

21854 Durant Box Factory
916 Crooked Oak Dr
Durant, OK 74701-2218 580-924-4035
Fax: 580-924-7276
Hardwood pallets and skids
Estimated Sales: $1-2.5 Million
Number Employees: 20
Square Footage: 25000

21855 Durashield
601 W Cherry St
Sunbury, OH 43074-9333 740-965-3008
Fax: 740-965-4485
Non-stick coatings
Operations Manager: Brad Moore
Estimated Sales: $1 - 2.5 000,000
Number Employees: 10-19

21856 (HQ)Durasol Awnings
225 Tower Dr
Middletown, NY 10941 845-692-1100
Fax: 845-692-1101 800-444-6131
wdavidson@durasol.com www.durasol.com
Custom-made awnings and awning products
President: Rich Lemond
Estimated Sales: $50 - 100 Million
Number Employees: 50-99
Square Footage: 50000
Other Locations:
Durasol
Tolleson AZ

21857 Durastill
4200 NE Birmingham Rd
Kansas City, MO 64117 816-454-5260
Fax: 816-452-7581 800-449-5260
info@masterpitch.com www.durastill.com
Manufacturer and exporter of water distillation systems
President: Paul S Giovagnoli
Director Sales: Horace Mansfield
Sales: Jeff Thompson
Estimated Sales: $500,000-$1 Million
Number Employees: 10-19
Parent Co: Master Pitching Machine Company

21858 Durham Manufacturing Company
PO Box 230
Durham, CT 06422 413-781-7900
Fax: 860-349-8572 info@durhammfg.com
www.durhammfg.com
Manufacturer and exporter of metal storage cabinets, bins, security boxes, drawers and office products
President and CEO: Richard Patterson
Quality Control: Francis Korn
VP Marketing: Joseph Soja
Regional Manager: John Mansfield
Estimated Sales: $20-50 Million
Number Employees: 250-499

21859 Durham Manufacturing Company
201 Main Street
Duham, CT 06422 860-349-3427
Fax: 800-782-5499 800-243-3744
info@durhammfg.com www.frickgallagher.com
Manufacturer and exporter of pallet rack and industrial duty steel shelving
President: Paul H Frick Jr
Sales/Marketing Administrative Manager: David Massie
Estimated Sales: $2.5-5 Million
Number Employees: 20-49

21860 Duro Bag
1 Duro Way
Walton, KY 41094 859-485-6660
Fax: 859-485-4641 www.durobag.com
Tea and coffee industry bags (flexible)
President: Charles Shor
Estimated Sales: $20 - 50 Million
Number Employees: 100-249

21861 Duske Drying Systems
6901 Industrial Loop
Greendale, WI 53129 414-529-0240
Fax: 414-529-0362 www.duskedryingsystems.com
Drying systems
President: Mike Uzelac
Estimated Sales: $2.5 000,000

21862 Dusobox Company
233 Neck Rd
Haverhill, MA 01835-8029 978-372-7192
Fax: 978-372-7198
Corrugated boxes
Manager: Peter Grogan
General Manager: Peter Grogan

Estimated Sales: $2.5-5 Million
Number Employees: 10 to 19
Parent Co: Dusobox Company

21863 Dutchess Bakers' Machinery Company
302 Grand Ave
Superior, WI 54880-0039 715-394-2387
Fax: 715-394-2406 800-777-4498
sale@dutchessbakers.com
www.dutchessbakers.com
Dutchess Bakers' Machinery Company has been manufacturing high quality dough dividers and dough divider rounders for the foodservice industry since 1886! We are the originator and most respected & recognized name in the world for thiskind of equipment; also offers the bun & bagel slicer.
President: Kent Phillips
Marketing Director: Tony Marino
Plant Manager: John Skandel
Estimated Sales: $3 - 5 Million
Number Employees: 10-19
Square Footage: 60000
Parent Co: Superior-Lidgerwood-Mundy Corporation
Brands:
Dutchess

21864 Dutro Company
675 N 600 W Ste 2
Logan, UT 84321 435-752-3921
Fax: 800-875-7559 866-388-7660
dutro@dutro.com www.dutro.com
Manufacturer and exporter of carts, dollies and trucks
President: Bill Dutro
CEO: William Dutro
Estimated Sales: $17,483,702
Number Employees: 5-9
Number of Products: 16

21865 Duval Container Company
PO Box 41006
Jacksonville, FL 32203 904-355-0711
Fax: 904-350-9709 800-342-8194
www.duvalcontainer.com
Corrugated boxes; wholesaler/distributor of containers and packaging materials
President: Richard L Gills
CFO: Mary Geller
Estimated Sales: $10 - 20 Million
Number Employees: 20-49

21866 Dwinell's Central Neon
101 Butterfield Rd
Yakima, WA 98901-2008 509-248-3772
Fax: 509-457-8026 800-932-8832
norm@dwinells.com www.dwinells.com
Indoor and outdoor signs including advertising, electric, neon and painted
President: Chuck Colmenero
President: Glenn Terrell
Estimated Sales: $5 - 10 Million
Number Employees: 50-99

21867 Dwyer Instruments
P.O.Box 373
Michigan City, IN 46361-0373 219-879-8000
Fax: 219-872-9057 800-872-3141
info@dwyer-inst.com www.dwyer-inst.com
Manufacturer and exporter of HVAC instruments including air filter gauges, thermostats, air velocity transmitters, temperature and process controllers and mercury switches
President: Steve Clark
CFO: Tom Dhaeze
Quality Control: Don Goad
Purchasing Manager: Dave Pilarski
Estimated Sales: $50 - 100 Million
Number Employees: 100-249

21868 Dyco
6951 Naus Way
Bloomsburg, PA 17815 570-752-2757
Fax: 570-752-7366 800-545-3926
sales@dyco-inc.com www.dyco-inc.com
Provides custom engineered container handling solutions
President: Peter Yohe
Finance Executive: Dan Bierdziewski
Sales Manager: Kevin John
Operations Manager: John Wittman
Number Employees: 50-99

21869 Dylog USA Vanens
7213 Sandscove Court
Suite 5
Winter Park, FL 32792-6901 407-265-9385
Fax: 407-265-9003 rsvanens@earthlink.net

21870 Dyna-Veyor
10 Hudson St
Newark, NJ 07103-2804 973-484-1119
Fax: 973-484-7790 800-930-4760
dynaveyor@aol.com www.dyna-veyor.com
Manufacturer and exporter of plastic conveyor chain belting, sprockets, idlers and corner tracks for the food processing, beverage, canning, pharmaceutical, packaging and container industries
CEO: Beverly Ayre
Estimated Sales: $5-10 Million
Number Employees: 10-19

21871 Dynabilt Products
31 Industrial Drive
Readville, MA 02136-2355 617-364-1200
Fax: 617-364-7643 800-443-1008
http://dynabilt.com
Pallet racking and mezzanine systems, floor trucks and refuse and recycling containers
President: Charles Burtman
VP: Mark Goodman
National Sales Manager: Paul Venini
Estimated Sales: $10-20 Million
Number Employees: 50-99
Square Footage: 120000
Parent Co: Burtman Iron Works

21872 Dynablast Manufacturing
94 Riverside Drive
Mississauga, ON V5N 7K5
Canada 905-567-4126
Fax: 905-567-4330 888-242-8597
sales@dynablast.com www.dynablast.com
Gas fired pressure washers for kitchen degreasing and hot water and steam drain cleaning
President: Max Minkhorst
CFO: Don Kent
General Manager: William Duff
Purchasing Manager: Harry Bowker
Number Employees: 10
Square Footage: 340000
Brands:
Dynablast

21873 Dynaclear Packaging
500 West Main Street
Suite 12
Wyckoff, NJ 07481 201-337-1001
Fax: 201-337-5001 gerard@shrinkfilm.com
www.shrinkfilm.com
Manufacturer and supplier of packaging equipment and supplies.
Chairman/CEO: Peter Quercia
Manager: Jim Quercia
CFO: Barbara Kaywork
Manager of Sales: Michael Kintzley
Estimated Sales: $3.4 Million
Number Employees: 18
Other Locations:
Warehouse & Shipping
Wyckoff NJ

21874 Dynaco USA, Inc
935 Campus Drive
Mundelein, IL 60060 847-562-4910
Fax: 847-562-4917 800-459-1930
dynaco@dynacodoor.us www.dynacodoor.us
High performance roll-up doors.
President: Bryan Gregory
CEO: Dirk Wouters
Estimated Sales: Below $5 Million
Number Employees: 20-49

21875 Dynalon Labware
175 Humboldt St
Suite 300
Rochester, NY 14610 585-334-2064
Fax: 585-334-0241 800-334-7585
dynaloninfo@dyna-labware.com
www.dynalabcorp.com
Wholesaler and distributor of plastic lab supplies
President & CEO: Martin Davies
Data Processing: Brian Genter
Product Manager: Steve Yudicky
Human Resources Director: Patti Zimmer
Engineering Manager: William Potter
Manager: Christine Leskovar
Plant Manager: Robert Pfeil
Estimated Sales: $6.7 Million
Number Employees: 35
Square Footage: 100000
Brands:
Stuart
Ads Laminaire
Burkle
Kartell
Azlon
Baritainer ® Jerry Cans
Bio-Bin® Waste Disposal
Sterilin
Delrin®
Noryl®
Sintra®
Kydex®
Kynar®
Ultem®

21876 Dynamet
7687 N 6th St
Kalamazoo, MI 49009-8865 269-385-0006
Fax: 269-385-4750 dynamet@net-link.net
www.dynametconveyor.com
Specialty bulk material handling conveyors including flexible screw, tubular drag and oscillating; also, hydraulic dumpers
President: Robert Sutton
Estimated Sales: $1 - 3 Million
Number Employees: 10 to 19
Square Footage: 5000

21877 Dynamic Air
1125 Willow Lake Blvd
Saint Paul, MN 55110 651-484-2900
Fax: 651-484-7015 info@dynamicair.com
www.dynamicair.com
Pneumatic conveying of bulk solids for the processing industries.
President: James Steele
National Sales Manager: Tom Acheson
Estimated Sales: $20-50 Million
Number Employees: 100-249

21878 Dynamic Automation
4525 Runway St
Simi Valley, CA 93063 805-584-8476
Fax: 805-584-8479
info@dynamicautomation.com
www.dynamicautomation.com
Bottling, bag closing, food and dairy processing, packaging, material handling and conveyor systems and equipment
Owner: Marc Freedman
Sales Executive: Randy Gray
Estimated Sales: $2.5-5,000,000
Number Employees: 10-19

21879 Dynamic Coatings Inc
3315 W Sussex Way
Fresno, CA 93727-1320 559-225-4605
Fax: 559-225-4606 info@dynamiccoatingsinc.net
www.dynamiccoatingsinc.net
Product and service line is concrete restoration and protective coating products for floors and walls applications of which include that of food processing plants, kitchens, wineries, dairies, bakeries and breweries.
Owner: Jose A Gonzales
President: Scott Hamilton
Sales Representative: Jose Gonzalez
Estimated Sales: $857,000
Number Employees: 12

21880 Dynamic Cooking Systems
5900 Skylab Rd
Huntington Beach, CA 92647-2061 714-372-7000
Fax: 714-372-7096 800-433-8466
info@dcsappliances.com
www.dcsappliances.com
Manufacturer and exporter of ranges, broilers, counter equipment, drop-in-cook tops, wall and convection ovens, ventilation hoods, outdoor barbecues and patio heaters
President: Mike Goadby
President: Michael Markowich
VP: Randy Rummel
CFO: Jeff Elder
Quality Control: Chillie Waiemas
Marketing Manager: Scott Davies
Estimated Sales: $5 - 10 Million
Number Employees: 500-999
Square Footage: 66000

Brands:
Professional

21881 **Dynamic International**
PO Box 3322
Champlain, NY 12919-3322 514-956-0127
Fax: 877-668-6623 800-267-7794
info@dynamicmixers.com
www.dynamicmixers.com

21882 **Dynamic International**
N25 W23287 Paul Road
Pewaukee, WI 53072-4074 262-521-1100
Fax: 877-668-6623 800-267-7794
info@dynamicmixers.com
www.dynamicintl.com
Salad driers, juicers, hand-held immersion mixers, manual vegetable slicers, shredders and dicers
Manager: Tony Tisigortis
Eastern Region Sales Manager: Shaun McDonald
Marketing: Lance Brown
Operations Manager: Tony Tsirigotis
Number Employees: 10
Number of Brands: 1
Number of Products: 28
Square Footage: 64000
Type of Packaging: Food Service

21883 **Dynamic Packaging**
5725 International Pkwy
Minneapolis, MN 55428-3079 763-535-8669
Fax: 763-535-8768 800-878-9380
www.dynamicpkg.com
Printed and laminated flexible packaging films, roll stock and bags including simplex style and wicketed side-weld polyethylene; importer of polypropylene and polyester packaging films
Owner: George Butgusaim Sr
VP Sales: James Pater, Jr.
VP Production: Thoams Guerity
Estimated Sales: $1-2.5 Million
Number Employees: 10-19
Square Footage: 80000

21884 **Dynamic Pak**
102 W Division St
Suite 100
Syracuse, NY 13204-1428 315-474-8593
Fax: 315-474-8795
Thermoforming and contract packaging including labeling andpackaging.
President: William Birchenough Jr
Sales Executive: Herman Garcia
Estimated Sales: $1 - 3 Million
Number Employees: 5-9

21885 **Dynamic Storage SystemsInc.**
15315 Flight Path Dr.
Brooksville, FL 34604
Fax: 254-221-4106 800-974-8211
info@dynamicstorage.com www.hi-linerack.com
Sales storage and pallet racks, belt conveyors, cantilevers and guided rail entries
VP Sales: Robert Egner
Estimated Sales: $2.5-5 Million
Number Employees: 20-49
Brands:
Flexi-Guide
Gold Shield
Hi-Line
Hipir Kart

21886 **Dynaric**
5740 Bayside Rd
Virginia Beach, VA 23455 757-460-3725
Fax: 757-363-8016 800-526-0827
gd@d-y-c.com www.dynaric.com
Manufacturer and exporter of strapping machinery and nonmetallic strapping
President: Joseph Martinez
CEO: Mike Moses
CFO: John Guzdus
Plant Manager: Vernon Wilson
Assistant Marketing Manager: Brian Cosgrove
Plant Manager: Dennis Fuller
Number Employees: 100-249
Square Footage: 100000
Type of Packaging: Consumer, Food Service, Private Label, Bulk
Brands:
Durastrap
Dynaric
Dynastrap

21887 **Dynasys Technologies**
2106 Drew Street
Suite 104
Clearwater, FL 34698-7880 727-443-6600
Fax: 727-443-4390 800-867-5968
dynasys@dyna-sys.com www.dyna-sys.com
Products for automatic identification datacapture, temperature indicators, and other products
President: Robert Scher
CEO/owner: Bobby Burkett
Director of R&D/COO: Tomas Grajales
Estimated Sales: $5 - 10 Million
Number Employees: 20-49

21888 **Dynatek Dalta ScientificInstruments**
105 E 4th St
Galena, MO 65656 417-357-6155
Fax: 417-357-6327 800-325-8252
dynatek@dynatekdalta.com
www.dynatekdalta.com
Texture analysis and adhesive testing
President: Elaine R Strope
Estimated Sales: $1-5 000,000
Number Employees: 10-19

21889 **(HQ)Dynynstyl**
855 NW 17th Avenue
Suite A
Delray Beach, FL 33445-2520 561-547-5585
Fax: 561-547-0993 800-774-7895
dstyl@bellsouth.net www.ecofuel.org
Manufacturer and exporter of china, flatware, hollowware, chafing dishes, trays, buffetware, etc.; also, polishers, burnishers, silver cleaners and canned fuel for chafing dishes, etc.; silver and stainless steel repair servicesavailable
CEO: Dennis Paul
Vice President: Debra Cosner
Estimated Sales: $1 - 5 Million
Number Employees: 10
Brands:
Dynynstyl
Eco Lamp
Eco Pure Aqua Straw
Ecofuel
Emperor
Empress
Fold Flat

21890 **E & E Process Instrumentation**
4-40 North Rivermede Road
Concord, Ontario, ON L4K 2H3318
Canada 905-669-4857
Fax: 905-669-2158 info@eeprocess.com
www.eeprocess.com
Manufacturer, importer and exporter of thermometers, hygrometers and hydrometers. Instruments for quality control and research and development. Nist certification of test instruments for FDA & USDA compliance
President: Todd Teichert
Estimated Sales: $1-2.5 Million
Number Employees: 5-9
Square Footage: 16000
Parent Co: E & E Process Instrumentation
Brands:
Brooklyn

21891 **E A Bonelli & Associates**
8450 Edes Avenue
Oakland, CA 94621 510-740-0155
Fax: 510-740-0160 marco@eabonelli.com
www.eabonelli.com
President: Marco Di Gino
Estimated Sales: $3 - 5 Million
Number Employees: 20-49

21892 **E&M Electric & Machinery**
126 Mill St
Healdsburg, CA 95448 707-433-5578
Fax: 707-431-2558 www.enm.com
Wine industry machinery
President: Judith Deas
Estimated Sales: $20 - 50 Million
Number Employees: 50-99

21893 **E-Control Systems**
5170 Sepulveda Blvd
Suite 240
Sherman Oaks, CA 91403 818-783-5229
Fax: 818-783-5219 888-384-3274
sales@eControlSystems.com
www.econtrolsystems.com
President: Abraham Bernstein
CEO: Abraham Bernstein
Estimated Sales: $10 - 20 Million
Number Employees: 50-99

21894 **E-Cooler**
4320 S. Knox Avenue
Chicago, IL 80632 773-284-9975
Fax: 773-284-9973 866-955-3266
www.e-cooler.com
Supplier of corrugated boxes and custom designed boxes for the meat, seafood and produce industries.

21895 **E-J Industries Inc**
1275 S Campbell Ave
Chicago, IL 60608-1013 312-226-5023
Fax: 312-226-5976 www.ejindus.com
Manufacturers of contract commercial seating and cabinetry for the hospitality industry.
President: Leonard Weitzman
CEO/CFO: Keith Weitzman
VP: Keith Weitzman
Quality Control: W Nowak
Estimated Sales: $7 Million
Number Employees: 70-75
Square Footage: 120000

21896 **E-Lite Technologies**
2285 Reservoir Ave
Trumbull, CT 06611 203-371-2070
Fax: 203-371-2078 877-520-3951
sales@e-lite.com www.e-lite.com
Manufacturer and exporter of electroluminescent lamps
President: Mark Appelberg
President: Mark Appleberg
VP/COO: Mark Appelberg
Office Manager: Judith Sepelak
Estimated Sales: Below $5,000,000
Number Employees: 10-19
Brands:
Flatlite

21897 **E-Pak Machinery**
1555 S State Road 39
La Porte, IN 46350 219-393-5541
Fax: 219-324-2884 800-328-0466
sales@epakmachinery.com
www.epakmachinery.com
President: Lyle Lucas
CEO: Ron Sarto
Vice-President: Chris Ake
Purchasing Director: Susie Nehal
Estimated Sales: $10 - 20 Million
Number Employees: 50-99

21898 **E-Quip Manufacturing Company**
230 Industry Ave
Frankfort, IL 60423 815-464-0053
Fax: 815-464-0059 equipmfg@ix.netcom.com
www.e-quipmfg.com
OEM stainless steel equipment for food applications
President: Millard Minyard
CFO: Marge Minyard
Estimated Sales: $2.5-5 000,000
Number Employees: 20-49

21899 **E-Saeng Company**
17316 Edwards Rd # 240
Cerritos, CA 90703-2450 562-404-1844
Fax: 562-404-1774 esaeng@wcis.com
Plastic bottle, container and tray, multi-layer plastic sheet, flexible package, co-extruded
VP: K J Chang
Estimated Sales: $1 - 3 000,000
Number Employees: 1-4

21900 **E-Z Edge**
6119 Adams St
West New York, NJ 07093 201-295-1171
Fax: 201-295-1115 800-232-4470
order@e-zedge.com www.e-zedge.com
Manufacturer, exporter and importer of food processing equipment including shears, knives and grinders for meat, fish and poultry; importer of stainless steel fish shears, bowl cutter knives and cutlery
Owner: Michael Maffei
VP: Michael Maffei
Manager: Paul Povinelli
Estimated Sales: $2.5-5 Million
Number Employees: 1-4
Square Footage: 7500

Brands:
Finney
Giesser
Speco
Steffens
Triumph
Victorianox
Zico

21901 E-Z Shelving Systems
5538 Merriam Dr
Merriam, KS 66203 913-384-1331
Fax: 913-384-3399 800-353-1331
info@e-zshelving.com www.e-zshelving.com
Heavy duty cantilever shelving systems for walk-in coolers, back room storage and sales areas
President: R Johnson
Estimated Sales: $1-2.5 Million
Number Employees: 10-19
Square Footage: 8000
Type of Packaging: Consumer, Food Service, Private Label, Bulk

21902 E-ZLIFT Conveyors
2000 S Cherokee St
Denver, CO 80223-3917 303-733-5533
Fax: 303-733-5642 800-821-9966
ez@ezliftconveyors.com
www.ezliftconveyors.com
Manufacturer and exporter of lightweight conveyors for beans, fruits, nuts and vegetables including troughing belt, belt bucket, bottom dump car unloader and floor-to-floor
President: Kenneth B Drost
Estimated Sales: $1-2.5 Million
Number Employees: 5-9
Square Footage: 10000
Brands:
E-Z Lift

21903 E.C. Shaw Company
1242 Mehring Way
Cincinnati, OH 45203 513-721-6334
Fax: 513-721-6350 866-532-7429
johnpinkley@ecshaw.com www.ecshaw.com
Flexographic plates, marking devices, nameplates, brass dies and steel stamps
President: Joseph C Grome
Rubber Stamp Sales: Marilyn Schalk
Customer Service Manager: Diana Randolph
Plant Manager: Joe Moffitt
Estimated Sales: $3 - 5 Million
Number Employees: 20-49

21904 E.F. Bavis & AssociatesDrive-Thru
201 Grandin Rd
Maineville, OH 45039-9762 513-677-0500
Fax: 513-677-0552 info@bavis.com
www.bavis.com
Manufacturer and exporter of drive-thru and vertical conveyor systems including transaction cash drawers
President: William Sieber
R&D: Mike Brown
Director Marketing/Sales: Terry Roberts
Estimated Sales: $5 - 10 Million
Number Employees: 20-49
Number of Products: 2
Type of Packaging: Food Service
Brands:
Transaction Drawer
Vittleveyor

21905 E.F. Engineering
9710 Humboldt Ave S
Minneapolis, MN 55431 952-888-6596
Fax: 952-888-3619 sales@efengineering.com
www.efengineering.com
Owner: Eyal Fine

21906 E.G. Staats & Company
608 N Iris Rd
Mount Pleasant, IA 52641 319-385-2116
Fax: 319-385-2429 800-553-1853
info@staatsawards.com www.staatsawards.com
Custom award ribbons
General Manager: Robert Mendenhall
Manager: Andy Zinkle
Estimated Sales: $5 - 10 Million
Number Employees: 20-49
Parent Co: Midwest Publishing Company

21907 E.H. Wachs
600 Knightsbridge Pkwy
Lincolnshire, IL 60069 847-537-8800
Fax: 847-520-1147 800-323-8185
sales@ehwachs.com www.ehwachs.com
President: Ken Morency
VP Finance: Nate Drucker
Quality Control: Peter Mullally
Marketing: John Geis
Sales: Chris Bauer
Public Relations: John Geis
Plant Manager: Craig Lewandowski
Purchasing: Ken Jarasz
Estimated Sales: $10-20 000,000
Number Employees: 100-249

21908 E.K. Lay Company
3469 Belgrade St
Philadelphia, PA 19134 215-739-1141
Fax: 215-739-7470 800-523-3220
info@eklay.com www.eklay.com
Cultery, utensils, foam plates and hinge take-out containers and cups
President: Jim O'Brien
VP: James O'Brien
Sales: William Gallen
Estimated Sales: $10-20 Million
Number Employees: 10-19

21909 (HQ)E.L. Nickell Company
385 Centreville St
Constantine, MI 49042 269-435-2475
Fax: 616-435-8216 bhicks@elnickell.com
Manufacturer and exporter of pressure vessels and heat exchangers
President: Brian Hicks
Sales Manager: Roger Bainbridge
Estimated Sales: $5-10 Million
Number Employees: 20-49
Square Footage: 30000

21910 E.S. Robbins Corporation
2802 Avalon Ave
Muscle Shoals, AL 35661-3748 256-248-2400
Fax: 256-248-2410 800-800-2235
www.esrchairmats.com
Expandable and collapsible reusable beverage and food storage containers, plastic measuring caps and canisters
President: Edward Robbins III
CFO: Ron Mansel
CEO: Edward S Robbins Iii
VP Sales/Marketing: Steve Doerr
Purchasing Manager: Nancy Hamilton
Estimated Sales: $10 - 20 Million
Number Employees: 100-249
Parent Co: E.S. Robbins Corporation
Brands:
Flex-Flo
Kleer-Measure
Poptite

21911 E.T. Oakes Corporation
686 Old Willets Path
Hauppauge, NY 11788 631-232-0002
Fax: 631-232-0170 info@oakes.com
www.oakes.com
Food processing equipment including mixers, depositors, blenders, controllers, creme injectors, agitators, emulsifiers, extruders, homogenizers, fillers and lidders, and cake depositors
President: W Peter Oakes
Vice President: Bob Peck
Marketing Director: Karen Oakes
Sales Director: Chris Oakes
Estimated Sales: Below $5 Million
Number Employees: 20-49

21912 E2M
3300 Breckinridge Blvd
Duluth, GA 30096-8983 770-449-7383
Fax: 770-328-2880 800-622-4326
fskwira@e2m.com www.e2m.com
Specializing in the integration of people, machines, controls, procedures, materials and laytout into seamless highly efficient packaging systems
President: Waye Young
Vice President of Development: Don Baldwin
General Manager: Fran Skwira
Estimated Sales: $20-50 Million
Number Employees: 50-99

21913 EAM
19 Pomerleau St.
Biddeford, ME 04005 207-283-3001
Fax: 207-283-3023 info@eaminc.com
www.eaminc.com
President: Stephen G Swinburne
Outside Sales: Kevin Call
Estimated Sales: $3 - 5 Million
Number Employees: 10-19

21914 EB Box Company
20 Pollard Street
Unit #3
Richmond Hill, ON L4B 1C3
Canada 905-889-5600
Fax: 905-889-5602 800-513-2269
sales@ebbox.com www.ebbox.com
Paper boxes for fish and chips, Chinese food, doughnuts andpatties, auto parts, computer parts, health products, cosmetics, garments, innerboxes, trays and custom boxes
Number Employees: 5-9

21915 EB Eddy Paper
P.O. Box 5003
Port Huron, MI 48061-5003 810-982-0191
Fax: 810-982-4057 salbright@eddy.com
www.domtar.com
Manufacturer and exporter of packaging and specialty coated papers
Vice President: Mark Ushpol
Marketing Manager: Rob Belanger
Production Manager: David Rushton
Estimated Sales: $30 - 50 Million
Number Employees: 20-49
Parent Co: Domtar

21916 EB Metal Industries
Poultney St
Whitehall, NY 12887-0149 518-499-1222
Fax: 518-499-2220
Vending equipment, zinc die castings and sheet metal fabrication
Sales Director: Stu Tesser
Purchasing Director: Patti Abbott

21917 EBM Technology
641 Keeaumoku Street
Suite 5
Honolulu, HI 96814 330-929-8929
Fax: 808-945-3105 866-212-6127
info@ebmtech.com www.ebmtech.com
Fully automated, highspeed collating and packing system which will top load or side load with gantry robots, two axis robots or pushers
President: Martin Dannenberg
Number Employees: 5200

21918 EBS
14657 Pebble Bend Drive
Houston, TX 77068-2922 713-939-1000
Fax: 281-444-7900 www.ebs-next.com
Software for material handling systems
President: William H Jones Jr
VP: Don Beach
Estimated Sales: $1 - 3,000,000
Number Employees: 30

21919 ECOLAB
370 Wabasha St N # 100
St Paul, MN 55102-1390 651-293-2233
Fax: 651-293-2092 800-733-8705
debbie.tollofson@ecolab.com www.ecolab.com
Manufacturer and exporter of pesticides
CEO: Douglas M Baker Jr
Office Manager: Pat Hogan
Estimated Sales: $10-20 Million
Number Employees: 10,000
Square Footage: 110000
Parent Co: Ecolab

21920 (HQ)ECOLAB
370 N. Wabasha Street
St Paul, MN 55102-2233 651-293-2233
Fax: 651-293-2092 800-352-5326
debbie.tollofson@ecolab.com www.ecolab.com
Soap, disinfectants, sanitizers, floorcare products, air fresheners, etc.; also, pest elimination and water care services available
Chairman: Allan L Schuman
President/CEO: Douglas M Baker Jr
Executive VP/CFO: Steven L Fritze
CEO: Douglas M Baker Jr

Estimated Sales: Below $500,000
Number Employees: 10,000
Other Locations:
Ecolab
Danbury CT
Brands:
Aickem
Ecotemp
Erostar
Huntington
Jani Source
Monarch
Oasis
Quik Fill
Raburn
Simplex
Turbo

21921 ECOLAB Food & Beverage Engineering
4732 Prairie Hill Rd
South Beloit, IL 61080-2539 815-389-3441
Fax: 815-389-0611 www.ecolab.com
Chemical dispersion and control equipment; automation systems for cleaning and sanitation
manager: Robert Zoeller
Estimated Sales: $50-100 Million
Number Employees: 250-499
Brands:
Victory Fruit/Veg. Wash Solutions

21922 ECS Warehouse
2381 Fillmore Ave
Buffalo, NY 14214 716-829-7356
Fax: 716-210-8334 permerling@emerfood.com
www.ecswarehouse.com
A warehouse that understands your needs. Frozen, dry, refrigerated warehouse on Canadian border, within 500 miles of 70% of the entire Canadian population and 55% of the entire USA population. Services include: pick & pack, crossdocking, express service, repacking, distribution, TL & LTL, rail, consolidation, salvage, quick access to NYC, Boston, D.C., Cleveland, Buffalo, Toronto, Rockland, Syracuse, Detroit and Cincinnati. If you have special product needs, call us.
Manager: Peter Emerling
CEO: Peter Emerling
Square Footage: 500000
Type of Packaging: Bulk
Brands:
Chocolate Moose
Flathead Lake Monster Gourmet Soda
Havana Cappuccino
Hill-Tween Farms
Ocean Spray

21923 EDL Packaging Engineers
1260 Parkview Rd
Green Bay, WI 54304 920-336-7744
Fax: 920-336-8585 sales@edlpackaging.com
www.edlpackaging.com
Manufacturer and exporter of shrink and stretch bundling machinery
President: Ken Carter
Director Of Sales: Larry D Cozine
Product Manager/Bagged Product: Jariath Harkin
Estimated Sales: $5 - 10,000,000
Number Employees: 20-49
Number of Products: 4
Square Footage: 25000
Parent Co: EDL UK
Type of Packaging: Consumer, Food Service, Private Label, Bulk

21924 EDT Corporation
1006 NE 146th St Ste J
Vancouver, WA 98685 360-574-7294
Fax: 360-574-3834 edtsales@edtcorp.com
www.edtcorp.com
Sanitary bearings and bearings for extreme environments
President: Carl Klinge
Estimated Sales: $1 - 5 000,000
Number Employees: 10-19

21925 EFA Processing EquipmentCompany
13308 C St
Omaha, NE 68144-3602 402-592-9360
Fax: 402-592-9366
Cutters, boning devices and slaughtering equipment, skinning machines and stunning apparatus
Manager: Donald Novonty

Estimated Sales: $500,000-$1 000,000
Number Employees: 1-4

21926 EFCO Products
130 Smith St
Poughkeepsie, NY 12601 845-452-4715
Fax: 845-452-5607 800-284-3326
info@efcoproducts.com www.efcoproducts.com
Leading supplier of mixes, fruit and creme style fillings, jellies, jams and concentrated icing fruits to the baking industry.
President & CEO: Steven L. Effron
VP/Controller: Kevin Laffin
Culinary Innovation Manager: Matt Plaza
VP Sales & Marketing: David A. Miller
VP Operations: Andy Herzing
Director of Manufacturing Operations: Veronica Miller
Estimated Sales: $2.5-5 Million
Number Employees: 50-99

21927 EFP Corporation
223 Middleton Run Rd
Elkhart, IN 46516 574-295-4690
Fax: 574-295-6512 info@efpcorp.com
www.efpcorp.com
Molders and fabricators of expanded polystyrene for packing, insulation, flotation and foundry patterns
President: Bill B Flint
Estimated Sales: G
Number Employees: 50-99

21928 EG&G Instruments
100 Midland Rd
Oak Ridge, TN 37830
Fax: 865-483-0396 800-251-9750
info@signalrecovery.com www.ortec-online.com
Modular research instrumentation; gamma and alpha semiconductor detectors
VP: Jon P Kidder
Estimated Sales: $25-50 Million
Number Employees: 250-499

21929 EGA Products
4275 N 127th St
Brookfield, WI 53005 262-781-7899
Fax: 262-781-3586 johnk@egaproducts.com
www.egaproducts.com
Material handling equipment; also, cabinets, racks and containers
President: Dave Young
Marketing/Sales: John Kuhnz
Estimated Sales: $10 - 20 Million
Number Employees: 50-99

21930 EGS Electrical Group
7770 Frontage Rd
Skokie, IL 60077 847-679-7800
Fax: 847-268-6011 www.egseg.com
Manufacturer and exporter of electrical products including controls, switches and lighting fixtures
President: Eric Meyer
CFO: Michael Bryant
Quality Control: L Engler
Marketing Communication Manager: Michelle Miller
Estimated Sales: $20 - 50 Million
Number Employees: 100-249
Parent Co: EGS Electrical Group

21931 EGW Bradbury Enterprises
479 US Highway 1
PO Box 129
Bridgewater, ME 04735-0129 207-429-8141
Fax: 207-429-8188 800-332-6021
info@bradburybarrel.com
www.bradburybarrel.com
Manufacturer and exporter of tongue and groove white cedar barrels, tubs and barrelcraft and wooden display fixtures; also, custom wooden displays, fixtures and accessories
President/CEO: Adelle Bradbury
Sales/Marketing Manager: Wayne Bradbury
Office Manager: Jennifer Griffin
Estimated Sales: $5-10 Million
Number Employees: 20-49

21932 EIT
532 W Lake St
Elmhurst, IL 60126-1408 630-279-3400
Fax: 630-279-3420 eitpromo@aol.com

Manufacturer and exporter of flags and promotional products
Owner: Mark Tober
CFO: Lucille Tobor
VP: Mark Tobor
Quality Control: Beth Pirc
Chairman of the Board: Earl Tobor
Estimated Sales: Below $5 Million
Number Employees: 5 to 9
Square Footage: 16000

21933 EJ Brooks Company
8 Microlab Rd
Livingston, NJ 07039 973-597-2900
Fax: 973-597-2919 800-458-7325
usasales@ejbrooks.com www.ejbrooks.com
Security seals and locking devices.
President/CEO: John Roessner III
Sales Director: Paul Dietlin
Director Purchasing: George Weber
Estimated Sales: $5-10 Million
Number Employees: 250-499

21934 EKATO Corporation
700 C Lake St
St Ramsey, NJ 07436 201-825-4684
Fax: 201-825-9776 jerry.baresich@ekato.com
www.ekato-usa.com
Manufacturer and exporter of industrial mixers and agitators for fluids and solids
President: Paul Dwelle
Sales Director: Michael Starer
Estimated Sales: $5-10,000,000
Number Employees: 10-19
Parent Co: EKATO Ruhr Und Mischtechnik-GmbH
Brands:
Esd
Ekato
Fluid
Unimix

21935 ELAU-Elektronik Automatiions
4201 W Wrightwood Avenue
Chicago, IL 60639-2095 773-342-8400
Fax: 773-342-8404 sales@elau.com
www.elau.com
Motion control systems
President: Thomas Cord
CEO: Thomas Cord
Business Manager: Ronda Dade
Estimated Sales: $2.5-5 Million
Number Employees: 1-4
Parent Co: Elau Germany

21936 ELBA
4717 Sweden Road
Charlotte, NC 28273-5935 704-643-5777
Fax: 704-643-2010 sales@elbausa.com
Complete bag making systems, ice cube bags, systems for producing extruded netting and systems to produce mesh bags from extruded material
President: Carlo Louni
CFO: Angle Louni
Warehouse Manager: Bill Lebact
Estimated Sales: $3 - 5 000,000
Number Employees: 10

21937 ELF Machinery
1555 S State Road 39
La Porte, IN 46350-6301 219-325-3060
Fax: 219-324-2884 800-328-0466
sales@elfmachines.com www.elfmachines.com
Manufacturer and exporter of liquid packaging equipment including fillers, cappers, labelers, induction sealers, coders, bottle cleaners, unscramblers, conveyors, turntables, etc
President: Thomas Ake Reed
CEO: Ron Sarto
International Sales Manager: Eric Thorgren
Number Employees: 100-249
Square Footage: 320000
Type of Packaging: Food Service
Brands:
Elf

21938 ELISA Technologies
2501 NW 66th Ct
Gainesville, FL 32653 352-337-3929
Fax: 352-337-3928 info@elisa-tek.com
www.elisa-tek.com

Manufacturer, importer and exporter of test kits for antibiotic, food protein and raw and cooked meat speciation; also, testing, consulting and analytical services available
President: Bruce Ritter
Quality Control: Daniel McClenden
R & D: Ed Mason
Laboratory Director: Susan Knicker
Estimated Sales: $75-100 Million
Number Employees: 10-19
Brands:
Dtek
Elisa-Tek Microwell

21939 **EM Industries**
480 S Democrat Rd
Gibbstown, NJ 08027-1239 914-592-4660
Fax: 914-592-9469 www.emscience.com
Specialty chemicals
Estimated Sales: $10 - 15 Million
Number Employees: 50-99

21940 **EM Sergeant Pulp**
66 Brighton Rd
Clifton, NJ 07012-1600 973-472-9111
Fax: 973-472-5686
dchristman@sergeantchem.com
www.sergeantchem.com
President: A Reisch
Estimated Sales: $10 - 20 Million
Number Employees: 10-19

21941 **EMC Solutions, Inc**
302 S Ash St
Celina, OH 45822 419-586-2388
Fax: 419-586-3311 sales@emcconveyor.com
www.emcconveyor.com
Stainless steel and painted overhead trolley conveyors.
President: Jeff Hazel
Estimated Sales: Below $1 Million
Number Employees: 1-4
Square Footage: 10000
Type of Packaging: Food Service

21942 **EMCO**
170 Monarch Ln
Miamisburg, OH 45342 661-294-9966
Fax: 937-865-6605 800-722-3626
www.emcolabels.com
Manufacturer and exporter of code labelers and printers for price marking and UPC/EAN code printing
President: Robert H Hay
Sales Manager: Morris Bargorch
Estimated Sales: $5-10 Million
Number Employees: 10
Brands:
Coronet
Mark Ii
Medalist
Regal
Signet

21943 **EMD Chemicals Inc**
One International Plaza
Suite 300
Philadelphia, PA 19113 484-652-5749
888-367-3275
emdinfomerckgroup.com www.emd.us
Specialty testing products for the Food and Beverage industry including Microbiology Culture Media featuring granulated media for safety and convenience; the MAS-100 Eco, a lightweight, portable air sampling instrument; the HYLiTE 2system, a portable system for determining the cleanliness of surfaces and work spaces; and Test Strip Kits for rapid testing of Ions and pH measurement
President/CEO: Meiken Krebs
CFO: Klaus Rueth
Vice President: Octavio Diaz
Research & Development: Jim Morgera
Quality Control: Stephen Bates
Marketing Director: Ted Rothermich
Key Account Manager: Taina Franke
Public Relations: Rina Spatafore
Operations Manager: Thorsten Hartis
Production Manager: John Alestra
Plant Manager: Bob Jones
Purchasing Manager: Ron Wisda
Estimated Sales: $10-25 Million
Number Employees: 500-999
Parent Co: Merck KgaA Darmstadt

21944 **EMD Products**
33 Zarpa Way
Hot Springs Village, AR 71909-7108 847-549-8308
Fax: 501-922-4873 800-910-4000
emdproduct@aol.com www.emdproducts.com
Servo motion control products, single axis positioning brushless servo systems, multi-axis controllers and analog and digital brushless servo systems and software
Member: Ray Eimerman

21945 **EMED Company**
2491 Wehrle Dr
Buffalo, NY 14221 716-626-1616
Fax: 716-626-1630 800-442-3633
customerservice@emedco.com
www.emedco.com
Signs and marking and safety devices including warning flags, tags, convex mirrors and laminated metal and pressure sensitive labels
President: David Ewert
Quality Control: Bill Meehen
Marketing Director: Kathleen Brunner
Sales Manager: Joseph Reinhart
Estimated Sales: $10 - 20 Million
Number Employees: 100-249
Square Footage: 70000
Brands:
Economarks
Kwik-Koils

21946 **EMI**
4 Heritage Park Rd
Clinton, CT 06413 860-669-1199
Fax: 860-669-7461 800-243-1188
info@clevelandmixer.com www.emimixers.com
Fluid mixing and blending, wine industry tank mixers
President: Emmett Barker
Estimated Sales: $10-20 000,000
Number Employees: 20-49

21947 **ENJAY Converters Limited**
495 Ball Street
Cobourg, ON K9A 3J6
Canada 905-372-7373
Fax: 905-377-8066 800-427-5517
sales@enjay.com www.enjay.com
Manufactures complete line of laminated and grapped cake circles and sheets

21948 **ENM Company**
5617 N Northwest Hwy
Chicago, IL 60646-6135 773-775-8400
Fax: 773-775-5968 enmco@aol.com
www.enmco.com
Manufacturer and exporter of counting and number devices and hour meters; also, mechanical, electromechanical and electronic digital counters
Owner: Nicholas Polydoris
Sales Manager: Dale Hall
Sales Manager: Lee Bryant
Sales Engineer: Megan Fitzgerald
Estimated Sales: $20 - 50 Million
Number Employees: 100-249

21949 **ENSCO**
5400 Port Royal Rd
Springfield, VA 22151 703-321-9000
Fax: 703-321-4529 williams.susan@ensco.com
www.ensco.com
Vision based food product color verification inspection systems; instantaneous feedback process control for food processing applications
CEO: Paul W Broome Iii
Director Marketing: Tom Cirillo
Estimated Sales: $80 Million
Number Employees: 100-249

21950 **EPC International**
PO Box 160
Sierra Madre, CA 91025 626-355-5375
Fax: 949-660-9309
berkusd@epcinternational.com
www.epcinternational.com

21951 **EPCO**
P.O.Box 20428
Murfreesboro, TN 37129-0428 615-893-8432
Fax: 615-890-3196 800-251-3398
www.useco.com
Manufacturer and exporter of food service equipment including bun racks, heater/proofer cabinets, banquet carts, can racks and air curtain refrigerators
Controller: Philip Keller
VP/General Manager: Thomas Taylor
VP Sales/Marketing: James Jean
Number Employees: 10-19
Square Footage: 400000
Parent Co: Standex International Corporation
Type of Packaging: Food Service

21952 **EPD Technology Corporation**
14 Hayes St
Elmsford, NY 10523-2502 914-592-1233
Fax: 914-347-2181 800-892-8926
epd@epdtech.com www.epdtech.com
Steam management products, software and services; also, infrared thermometers and ultrasonic test instruments.
President: Gary Mohr
CEO: Helen Clint
VP Marketing: Alan Bardes
Estimated Sales: $5-10 Million
Number Employees: 20-49
Square Footage: 40000
Parent Co: UE Systems

21953 **EPI Labelers**
1145 E Wellspring Rd
New Freedom, PA 17349 717-235-8345
Fax: 717-235-0608 800-755-8344
sales@epilabelers.com www.epilabelers.com
Pressure sensitive label applicators and premium inserting equipment
President: Linda Erwin
Co-Owner: Lynn Vonderhorst
R&D: Linda Fulginiti
General Manager: Linda Fulginiti
Estimated Sales: $5 - 10 Million
Number Employees: 20-49

21954 **EPI World Graphics**
3824 147th St Ste F
Midlothian, IL 60445-3460 708-389-7500
Fax: 708-389-7522 epiworld@aol.com
Nameplates and labels; also, imprinting services available
President: Nancy Kolar
VP: Karen R Steffey
Purchasing: Chuck Tanner
Estimated Sales: $5-10 Million
Number Employees: 5 to 9
Square Footage: 25000

21955 **EPL Technologies**
2 International Plz Ste 245
Philadelphia, PA 19113-1505 610-521-5500
Fax: 610-521-5985 800-637-3743
wrromig@aol.com
Consultant providing technology, products and services to maintain the quality of fresh cut produce
VP Technology: William Romig
Commercial Manager: Lisa Herickhoff
Number Employees: 20-49

21956 **ERB/Ensign Ribbon Burner**
101 Secor Ln
Pelham, NY 10803-2791 914-738-0600
Fax: 914-738-0928 info@erbensign.com
www.ensignrb.com
Industrial gas burners
President: John F Cavallo
Estimated Sales: $2.5-5 Million
Number Employees: 10-19

21957 **ERC Parts**
4001 Cobb Intl Blvd NW
Kennesaw, GA 30152 770-984-0276
Fax: 770-951-1875 800-241-6880
marketing@erconline.com www.erconline.com
Drive-thru displays, recording devices and timers and battery chargers; importer of cash register parts; exporter of point of sale systems, parts and software; wholesaler/distributor of VAR products; serving the food service market
President: Charles Rollins
CFO: Stuart Dobson
Vice President: Charles Barnes
Research & Development: Timothy Adams
Marketing Director: Bryon Finkel
Parts/Manufacturing Division: Eric Hart
Purchasing Manager: Rob Haight

Estimated Sales: $1 - 2.5 Million
Number Employees: 50-99
Square Footage: 180000
Other Locations:
ERC Parts
Louisville KY
ERC Parts
Lexington KY
ERC Parts
Cleveland OH
ERC Parts
Las Vegas NV
ERC Parts
Baltimore MD
ERC Parts
Greensboro NC
ERC Parts
Raleigh NC

21958 ERO/Goodrich Forest Products
19255 SW 65th Ave # 110
Tualatin, OR 97062-9717 503-885-9414
Fax: 503-625-5825 800-458-5545
Manufacturer and exporter of plywood shipping containers and pallets
Manager: Elizabeth Brashear
Sales Manager: Harry Nelson
Estimated Sales: $1 - 5 Million
Number Employees: 16
Type of Packaging: Bulk

21959 ERS International
488 Main Avenue
Norwalk, CT 06851-1008 203-849-2500
Fax: 203-849-2501 800-377-4685
Electronic displays and shelf labels
CEO and President: Bruce Failing
Number Employees: 50-99
Square Footage: 10000
Brands:
Shelfnet

21960 ESA
22 Alpha Rd
Chelmsford, MA 01824-4123 978-250-7000
Fax: 978-250-7090 www.esainc.com
Manufacturer and exporter of food analysis instrumentation and HPLC systems. Contract Analytical services available.VitascCan - fat soluble vitamin analysis system
CEO: Walter DiGusto
CEO: Robert J Rosenthal
Marketing VP: John Christensen
Purchasing: Paul Todis
Estimated Sales: $10-20 Million
Number Employees: 100-249
Brands:
A.P.L.C.

21961 ESCO
5325 Glenmont
Suite C
Houston, TX 77081 713-777-8649
800-966-5514
www.escopro.com
Rebuilt and reconditioned food processing equipment, dashers, freezer barrels, thermometers, homo blockes, piston plungers, pumps, etc.; also, OEM, machining and grinding services available

21962 ESCO Manufacturing, Inc
2020 4th Ave SW
PO Box 1237
Watertown, SD 57201 605-886-4616
Fax: 605-886-5454 800-843-3726
wholesale@escomfg.com
www.escomanufacturing.com
Indoor and outdoor signs including neon, electric and painted
Owner: Mark Stein
Engineering Manager/Account Representati: Dave Bartels
Paint Supervisor: Jeremy Raap
Manufacturing Manager: Kevin Morris
Resources Manager: Laurie Gates
Senior Account Manager: Rob Fjerstad
*Estimated Sales:*less than $500,000
Number Employees: 100-249
Parent Co: Esco

21963 ESE, Inc
PO Box 1107
Marshfield, WI 54449-7107 715-387-4778
Fax: 715-387-0125 800-236-4778
sudat@ese1.com www.ese1.com
Process control systems; also, specialty applications and integration services available for PC based systems
President: Mark Weber
Director of Sales: Brandon Teachman
Director of Operations: Justin Hobson
Estimated Sales: $5-10 Million
Number Employees: 5-9
Square Footage: 68000

21964 ESE, Inc.
3600 Downwind Drive
Marshfield, WI 54449-7107 715-387-4778
Fax: 715-387-0125 800-236-4778
sudat@ese1.com www.ese1.com
Owner: Mark Weber
Director of Sales: Brandon Teachman
Director of Operations: Justin Hobson
Estimated Sales: $2.5 - 5 Million
Number Employees: 5-9

21965 ESI - Qual International
968 Washington Street
Stoughton, MA 02072 781-344-6344
Fax: 781-341-3978 800-443-0511
info@esiqual.com www.esiqual.com
Enviromental services and equipment, laboratory testing equipment, sanitation supplies and equipment, environmental, occupational, and food safety consultants.
President/CEO: Phil Ventresca
Vice President: Vince Vantresca
Estimated Sales: Below 1 Million
Number Employees: 5-9

21966 ESI Group USA
950 Walnut Ridge Drive
Hartland, WI 53029-9388 262-369-3535
Fax: 262-369-3536 866-369-3535
sales@esigroupusa.com www.esigroupusa.com
ESI is an industry leading design-build firm focused on the new construction, expansion and renovation of foodservice facilities. Our single source approach streamlines the building process allowing the team at ESI to remain focusedon the needs of the customer, the success of their project and their financial bottom line.
President: Brad Barke

21967 ESKAY Corporation
5202 D Corrigan Way Ste 100
Salt Lake City, UT 84116 801-363-6100
Fax: 801-359-9911 800-253-1003
info@eskay.com www.eskay.com
Designs, sells, installs, and supports a complete line of world-class logistics systems for automated material handling in factory, distribution, and cleanroom environments. Full range of advanced-technology products forrefrigerated/frozen food distribution includes conveyors, sortation systems, transport vehicles, order-picking systems, automated storage buffers, and real-time warehouse management software (WMS)
President: Itsud Oyamatsu

21968 ESS Technologies
3160 State Street
Blacksburg, VA 24060-6603 540-961-5716
Fax: 540-961-5721 info@esstechnologies.com
www.esstechnologies.com
Packaging equipment including overwrapping and bundling, shrinkwrapping, stretch banding, automatic cartoning and case packing, candy wrapping equipment, filling and packaging equipment and turnkey lines and integration services
President: Kevin Browne
Sales Manager: Michael Morgan
Estimated Sales: $1 - 2.5 Million
Number Employees: 10-19
Parent Co: Parent Company By Itself
Type of Packaging: Private Label, Bulk

21969 ESummits
PO BOX 27946
Scottsdale, AZ 90831-0002 562-983-8050
Fax: 562-983-8051 800-643-0797
info@esummits.com www.esummits.com
Marketing company, promote food products globally
Chief Executive Officer, Director: Paul Ortman
Estimated Sales: Below $500,000
Number Employees: 1-4

21970 ET International Technologies
3705 Kipling Street
Suite 103
Wheat Ridge, CO 80033 303-854-9087
Fax: 303-722-7379 855-412-5726
info@easytapperint.com www.easy-tapper.com
Manufacturer and exporter of hot tapping machines for the HVAC/R and piping industries
President: Greg Apple

21971 ET Oakes Corporation
686 Old Willets Path
Hauppauge, NY 11788-4102 631-232-0002
Fax: 631-232-0170 info@oakes.com
www.oakes.com
Agitators, blenders, chocolate equipment, aerators, depositors, chocolate, marshmallow cream, extruders, confectionery, continuous mixers, homogenizers, whippers, creme injectors, color mixes, enrobing and sandwiching equipment
Estimated Sales: $2.5-5 Million
Number Employees: 20-49

21972 ETS Laboratories
899 Adams St Ste A
Saint Helena, CA 94574 707-963-4806
Fax: 707-963-1054 info@etslabs.com
www.etslabs.com
Wine, beer, and spirits testing, ISO Guide 25 accredited
President: Gordon Burns
Estimated Sales: $1-2.5 000,000
Number Employees: 10-19

21973 EVAPCO
5151 Allendale Ln
Taneytown, MD 21787 410-756-2600
Fax: 410-756-6450 marketing@evapco.com
www.evapco.com
Manufacturer and exporter of industrial refrigeration equipment including evaporative condensers, cooling towers, evaporators, vessels, valves, recirculator packages, rooftop hygienic air systems, and closed curcuit coolers
President: Bill Bartley
CFO: Harold Walsh
VP: Joseph Mondato
VP Marketing/Sales: Dave Rule
Number Employees: 5-9
Square Footage: 180000

21974 EVAPCO
5151 Allendale Lane
Taneytown, MD 21787 410-756-2600
Fax: 410-756-6450 marketing@evapco.com
www.evapco.com
Evaporative condensors, refrigeration air units, refrigeration recirculators, critical process air systems, ice storage, non-chemical water treatment, closed circuit coolers, and cooling towers.
President: W.G. Bartley
CEO: W.G. Bartley
Senior Vice President: Harold Walsh
Sr Vice President: Joseph Mandato
Corporate QC Manager: Jason Shearer
Marketing: John Kollash
Production Manager: William Jones
Purchasing Manager: Kip Conner
Number Employees: 5-9

21975 EXE Technologies
8787 N Stemmons Fwy
Dallas, TX 75247 214-775-6000
Fax: 214-775-0900 800-393-8324
Warehouse management systems, supply chain distribution
CEO: Raymond Hood
Senior VP Professional Services/CFO: Michael Burstein
Director: Adam Belsky
Estimated Sales: $35 - 40 Million
Number Employees: 100

21976 EZ Edge
6119 Adam St
West New York, NJ 07093
Fax: 201-295-1115 800-232-4470
order@e-zedge.com www.e-zedge.com
Supplier of custom made blades and saws, injector needles, packing blades, bowl choppers, etc
Manager: April Carazani
Estimated Sales: $4.3 Million
Number Employees: 19

21977 **EZ-Tek Industries**
7041 Boone Avenue
Brooklyn Park, MN 55428 800-835-9344
Fax: 763-795-8867 800-796-3279
info@eztek.com www.eztek.com
Manufacturer and exporter of case sealers, tapers, material handling and packaging equipment; importer of case sealers, tapers and strappers
President: Bob Kops
CFO: Bob Kops
Estimated Sales: $1 Million
Number Employees: 4
Brands:
Easy Gluer
Easy Strapper
Easy Taper

21978 **Eagel-Picher Minerals**
9785 Gateway Dr # 1000
Reno, NV 89521-2991 775-824-7600
Fax: 775-824-7601
inquiry.minerals@eaglepicher.com
www.eaglepicher.com
Wine industry filter aids
President: Randy Moore
CEO: David Treadwell
Vice President of Technology: Greg Miller
Director of Quality Assurance: Forrest Reed
Estimated Sales: H
Number Employees: 20-49

21979 **Eagle Bakery Equipment**
9989 Lickinghole Road
Ashland, VA 23005 804-798-8920
Fax: 804-752-6828
support@eaglebakeryequipment.com
www.eaglebakeryequipment.com
Bun, bread make-up lines and equipment, dough pumps, tortillia and speciality equipment
Manager: Paul Peebles
CFO: Wd David Abbott
R&D: Howard Brandon
Quality Control: Howard Brandon
Sales: Mac Broddus
Estimated Sales: Below $5 000,000
Number Employees: 1-4

21980 **Eagle Box Company**
1 Adams Blvd Ste 1
Farmingdale, NY 11735 212-255-3860
Fax: 212-249-4517 info@eaglebox.com
www.eaglebox.com
Printed folding paperboard cartons
Owner: Jay Hoffman
Sales Director: Jim Fahlgren
Plant Manager: Steve Williamson
Estimated Sales: $10 Million
Number Employees: 20-49
Square Footage: 80000

21981 **Eagle FoodserviceEquipment**
100 Industrial Blvd
Clayton, DE 19938 302-653-3000
Fax: 302-653-2065 800-441-8440
answers@eaglegrp.com www.eaglegrp.com
Manufacturer and exporter of wire, solid and polymer shelving, work tables, sinks, handsinks, countertop equipment, underbar equipment, bun pans, as well as custom fabricated items
Owner: Larry N McAllister
Sales Director: Linda Donavon
Number Employees: 250-499
Type of Packaging: Food Service

21982 **Eagle Home Products**
1 Arnold Dr
Huntington, NY 11743
Fax: 631-435-3467
custerv@eaglehomeproducts.com
www.eaglehomeproducts.com
Manufacturer, importer and exporter of cleaning aids and rubber gloves
President: Albert Chemtob
Vice President: Andre Chemtob
Estimated Sales: $5-10 Million
Number Employees: 20-49
Square Footage: 100000
Brands:
Denta Brite
Diamond Brite
Diamond Grip
Eagle
Eagle Absolute
Soft Touch

21983 **Eagle Labeling**
1741 Industrial Dr
Sterling, IL 61081-9290 815-625-1858
Fax: 815-625-8554 800-527-7549
inquire@eagleauto.com www.eagleauto.com
Custom label applicators, labeling in-line, label dispensors, automation
Estimated Sales: Below $500,000
Number Employees: 5-9

21984 **Eagle Packaging Corporation**
2100 Dennison St
Oakland, CA 94606 510-533-3000
Fax: 510-534-3000 800-824-EAGL
pesales@parsons-eagle.com www.eaglepack.net
Estimated Sales: $20-50 Million
Number Employees: 20-49

21985 **Eagle Products Company**
P.O.Box 431601
Houston, TX 77243-1601 713-690-1161
Fax: 713-690-7661 info@eaglechair.com
www.eaglechair.com
Quality manufacturer and exporter of booths, chairs, bar stools, tabletops and bases
Executive Director: Maximillian Yurgulich
CEO: Natalia Jurcic-Koc
CFO: Nathalai Kac
Director of Operations: Max Yuglich
Estimated Sales: $5 - 10 Million
Number Employees: 10-19
Square Footage: 80000
Parent Co: Eagle Chair
Type of Packaging: Food Service
Brands:
Eagle Chair

21986 **Eagle Research**
2375 Bush St
San Francisco, CA 94115 415-495-3131
Fax: 415-441-6709 info@xeaglex.com
www.xeaglex.com
Custom software for any indsutry
President: E Allen Gleazer
Vice President: Nina Rosa carino
Vice President: Nina Carino
Estimated Sales: $1-5 000,000
Number Employees: 1-4

21987 **Eagle Wire Works**
3173 E 66th St
Cleveland, OH 44127 216-341-8550
Fax: 216-341-6460 info@eaglewireworks.com
www.hold-it-open.com
Refrigerator racks and stands and racks to hold plastic bags
President: James J Malik
Estimated Sales: $1-2.5 Million
Number Employees: 5-9

21988 **Eagle-Concordia Paper Corporation**
1 Adams Blvd
Farmingdale, NY 11735-6611 212-255-3860
Fax: 212-249-4530 info@eaglebox.com
www.eaglebox.com
Wholesaler/distributor of boxes, cartons, packaging tape, bubble wrap, etc.; also, package design services available
Owner: Michael Hoffman
Estimated Sales: $10-20 Million
Number Employees: 20-49

21989 **EaglePack Corporation**
2100 Dennison St
Oakland, CA 94606-5236 510-533-3000
Fax: 510-534-3000 800-824-3245
info@eaglepack.net www.eaglepack.net
President: Peter Hatchell
Product Manager: Jeff Reed
Vice President of Sales: Pete Butler
Estimated Sales: $10 Million
Number Employees: 20-49

21990 **Eagles Printing & LabelCo., Inc.**
1206 International Dr
Eau Claire, WI 54701 715-835-6631
Fax: 715-835-1601 eagles@eaglesprinting.com
www.eaglesprinting.com
Commercial printing and labels
President: Barb Sands
Estimated Sales: $1-2.5 Million
Number Employees: 20-49

21991 **Eagleware Manufacturing**
12683 Corral Pl
Santa Fe Springs, CA 90670 562-20 -100
Fax: 314-527-4314
Parent Co: Harold Leonard & Company

21992 **Eagleware Manufacturing**
2835 E Ana Street
Compton, CA 90221-5601 310-604-0404
Fax: 310-604-1748
Manufacturer and exporter of cookware
President: Jesse Gross
Vice President: Brett Gross
Estimated Sales: Below $5,000,000
Number Employees: 10
Square Footage: 70000
Parent Co: Harold Leonard & Company
Brands:
Eagleware

21993 **Eam-Mosca Corporation**
675 Jaycee Dr
Hazle Township, PA 18202 570-459-3426
Fax: 570-455-2442 info@eammosca.com
www.eammosca.com
Plastic strapping systems for pallets, off-line and in-line strappers, side-seal pallet strappers, drive-thru pallet strappers and horizontal pallet strapper
President: Daniel Dreher
Regional Sales Manager: Jim Gum
Sales Coordinator: Denise Casanova
Estimated Sales: $30 - 50 Million
Number Employees: 50-99

21994 **Earl Soesbe Company**
1347 Enterprise Drive
Romeoville, IL 60446-1015 219-866-4191
Fax: 219-866-7979
Bulk material handling equipment including self-dumping hoppers
President: Jerry Schlottmann
Sales Manager: Claas Schlottmann
Estimated Sales: $2.5-5 Million
Number Employees: 10-19
Square Footage: 53000

21995 **Earthstone Wood-Fire Ovens**
6717 San Fernando Rd
Glendale, CA 91201-1704 818-553-1134
Fax: 818-553-1133 800-840-4915
earthstone@earthlink.net
www.earthstoneovens.com
Manufacturer/exporter of wood and gas fire ovens including pre-assembled, commercial kit and residential; also, wood fire training available
President: Jean-Paul Sabbagh
Sales Director: Dennis Hahn
Estimated Sales: $3 - 5 Million
Number Employees: 10-19
Square Footage: 60000
Brands:
Earthstone

21996 **Earthy Delights**
1161 E Clark Road
Suite 260
Dewitt, MI 48820 517-668-2402
Fax: 517-668-1213 800-367-4709
info@earthy.com www.earthy.com
Specialty foods
President: Ed Baker
Marketing: Angie Padgett
Estimated Sales: $2.5 Million
Number Employees: 12

21997 **Eash Industries**
120 Rush Ct
Elkhart, IN 46516 574-295-4450
Fax: 574-389-1190
High gloss bar tops and tables; also, custom logos and inlaid graphics available
President: Todd Eash
Estimated Sales: $2.5-5,000,000
Number Employees: 5-9
Brands:
Diamond Clear

21998 **East Bay Fixture Company**
941 Aileen St
Oakland, CA 94608 510-652-4421
Fax: 510-652-5915 800-995-4521
rick@ebfc.com www.ebfc.com

Store fixtures
Owner: Richard Laible
Estimated Sales: $5-10 Million
Number Employees: 20-49

21999 East Coast Group New York
23209 Merrick Boulevard
Springfield Gardens, NY 11413-2116718-527-8464
Fax: 718-527-8498 eastcoastg@worldnet.att.net
Garbage, insulated, multi-wall and plastic bags and packaging materials
Sr Partner: Trevor Ford
Estimated Sales: $500,000-$1,000,000
Number Employees: 9
Brands:
East Coast

22000 East Coast Mold Manufacturing
30 Eastern Ave # 1
Deer Park, NY 11729-3100 631-253-2397
Fax: 631-254-6682 800-933-9533
Candy and confectionery equipment
President: Sebastian Piccione
Number Employees: 5-9

22001 East Coast RefrigeratedServices Corporation
215 N Mill Rd
Vineland, NJ 08360-3433 856-696-0055
Fax: 856-696-1451
Manager: Bob Bradway
Estimated Sales: $1 - 5 Million
Number Employees: 5-9

22002 East Memphis Rubber Stamp Company
6246 Acorn Dr
Bartlett, TN 38134-4608 901-384-0887
Fax: 901-384-3507 ermsco@cs.com
Rubber stamps
President: Buddy Good
VP Marketing: Buddy Good
Estimated Sales: Below $5 Million
Number Employees: 1 to4

22003 Easterday Belting Company
1400 E Touhy Ave # 409
Des Plaines, IL 60018-3341 847-297-8200
Fax: 847-803-9290
Thermal and solid color jet inks, for small character jet printers
Owner: Azam Nizamudiz
Estimated Sales: $5-10 000,000
Number Employees: 10-19

22004 Easterday Fluid Technologies
4343 S Kansas Ave
Saint Francis, WI 53235 414-482-4488
Fax: 414-482-3720
Supplies the food processing industry thermal sensitive coding links. Manufactures thermal sensitive, solid color, and UV jet inks for noncontact jet printers for tough, reliable product codes on retorted food containers andpasteurization processes of the beer and beverage industry
President: Max Baum
Director Operations: Lee Robbins
National/International Services Manager: Paul Oetlinger
Estimated Sales: $1-3 Million
Number Employees: 5-9
Square Footage: 6000
Brands:
Easterday

22005 Eastern Bakery
475 Stevens Rd
York Haven, PA 17370-9236 717-938-8278
Fax: 717-938-3060 ebeco1@paonline.com
Manufacturers of bakery equipment
President and R&D: Ken Johson
CFO: Cindy Ng
Quality Control: Jeff Love
Plant Manager: Jeff Love
Estimated Sales: Below $5 000,000
Number Employees: 10-19
Parent Co: Gemini Bakery Equipment Company

22006 Eastern Cap & Closure Company
726 N Kresson Street
Baltimore, MD 21205-2907 410-327-5640
Fax: 410-522-6068
Caps and closures for bottles and jars
Manager: John Lepus
Number Employees: 30
Square Footage: 49000
Parent Co: Penn Bottle & Supply Company

22007 Eastern Container Corporation
60 Maple St
Mansfield, MA 02048-1505 508-337-0400
Fax: 508-339-8493 www.smurfitstone.com
Corrugated shipping containers and displays
General Manager: Randy Thrasher
Estimated Sales: $5 - 10 Million
Number Employees: 250-499
Parent Co: Eastern Container
Brands:
Radio Pack

22008 Eastern Design & Development Corporation
PO Box 440
Hershey, PA 17033-0440 717-533-2452
Fax: 717-533-2036 eddco@aol.com
Confectionary and baking equipment
Estimated Sales: $1-2.5 000,000
Number Employees: 20-49

22009 Eastern Envelope
5 Laurel Dr
Flanders, NJ 07836-4701 973-584-3311
Fax: 973-584-4125
Envelopes
President: Jerome Kessler
Estimated Sales: $1-2.5 Million
Number Employees: 5-9

22010 Eastern Machine
80 Turnpike Dr # 2
Middlebury, CT 06762-1830 203-598-0066
Fax: 203-598-0068 info@perlpackaging.com
www.perlpackaging.com
Manufacturer and exporter of capping machinery for metal and plastic screw and snap caps; also, cap tighteners, fitment applicators and trigger sprayers
President: David Baker
Number Employees: 5-9
Square Footage: 20000

22011 Eastern Plastics
PO Box 1266
Pawtucket, RI 02862-1266 401-724-8050
Fax: 401-728-3770 800-442-8585
Clear acrylic products including bulk food bins, step up racks, product displays, bag holders, description holders, literature dispensers, recipe card holders, etc
President: Jim Rosenthal
Sales Representative: Irene Champagne
Number Employees: 20
Square Footage: 10000

22012 Eastern Poly PackagingCompany
53 Prospect Park W
Brooklyn, NY 11215-2629 718-788-4700
Fax: 718-788-5463 800-421-6006
www.easternpoly.com
Printed and plain bags including polypropylene and polyethylene
Owner: Stephen Somers
General Manager: Tran Van Lam
Director: Tran Minh Tam
Estimated Sales: $2.5-5 Million
Number Employees: 20-49
Parent Co: X

22013 Eastern Regional Research Center
600 E Mermaid Ln
Wyndmoor, PA 19038 215-233-6595
Fax: 215-233-6606 www.ars.usda.gov
Government research center for fresh and processed foods; food development services available
Manager: Wendy H Kramer
Technical Transfer Coordinator: C Crawford
Director: John Cherry
Number Employees: 250-499
Parent Co: Agricultural Research Service/US Department of Agriculture

22014 Eastern Silver TabletopManufacturing Company
445 Park Ave
Brooklyn, NY 11205-2735 718-522-4142
Fax: 718-522-4155 888-422-4142
sales@easterntabletop.com
www.easterntabletop.com
High quality silver plated and stainless steel food service equipment including chafing dishes, coffee urns, trays, serving and tabletop accessories, punchbowls and candelabras
President: Sol Basch
Estimated Sales: $10 - 20 Million
Number Employees: 10-19
Brands:
Eastern

22015 Eastey Enterprises
7041 Boone Avenue
Brooklyn Park, MN 55428 800-835-9344
Fax: 763-795-8867 800-835-9344
parts_eastey@dgi.net www.eastey.com
Electric or air operated L-sealers, shrink tunnels, high speed tunnels, banding tunnels, bundling tunnels and manual or automatic sleeve wrapping systems
President: Jeff Eastey
Estimated Sales: $4 Million
Number Employees: 20-49

22016 (HQ)Easy Up Storage Systems
18271 Andover Park West
Seattle, WA 98188 206-394-3330
Fax: 206-575-6829 800-426-9234
sales@easyupusa.com
easyupusa.theonlinecatalog.com
Boltless steel storage and shelving systems
President: Dave Saman
VP: Kyle Jones
VP/C-Store Manager: Ken Davis
Estimated Sales: $5-10 Million
Number Employees: 20-49
Square Footage: 56000
Brands:
Easy Up

22017 Easy-Care Environs
7002 Maplewood Court SW
Olympia, WA 98512-2031 360-754-1013
Fax: 360-754-1013 info@easycareenvirons.com
Specialty walls and ceilings (glass, FRP)

22018 Easybar Beverage Management Systems
19799 SW 95th Ave.
Suite A
Tualatin, OR 97062-7584 503-624-6744
Fax: 503-624-6741 888-294-7405
info@easybar.com www.easybar.com
Manufacturer and exporter of liquor, beer, wine and soda dispensers.
CEO: James Nicol
Marketing: Sarah Puglia
Sales: Margo Winquist
Estimated Sales: $5 - 10 Million
Number Employees: 20-49
Brands:
Easybar

22019 Eatec Corporation
1900 Powell St
Suite 230
Emeryville, CA 94608 510-594-9011
Fax: 510-549-1959 877-374-4783
info@agilysys.com www.agilysys.com
A provider of enterprise back-office software and services for the foodservice and hospitality industries. EatecNetX, Eatec's proven software solution, is recognized as a state-of-the-art foodservice management system that iscentralizzed, scalable, web-centric and user-friendly for food and beverage operators of every variety.
Manager: Jeff Gebhardt
Estimated Sales: $5 - 10 Million
Number Employees: 20-49
Brands:
Catertec
Clubtec
Eatec Netx
Eatec System

22020 Eatem Foods Company
1829 Gallagher Drive
Vineland, NJ 08360 856-692-1663
Fax: 856-692-0847 800-683-2836
sales@eatemfoods.com www.eatemfoods.com

Food base manufacturing; supplier of savory flavor systems, flavor concentrates, broth concentrates and seasoning bases.
President, CEO: Ron Savelli
Chief Technical Officer: John Randazzi
Chief Financial Officer: Danine Freeman
Vice President, Treasurer: Mario Riviello
Director, R&D: Bill Cawley
Marketing Manager: Gerrie Bouchard
Vice President, Sales: Don Witherspoon
Director of Operations: Jerry Santo
Estimated Sales: $14 Million
Number Employees: 80
Square Footage: 12916
Type of Packaging: Consumer, Food Service, Bulk
Brands:
Eatem

22021 Eaton Corporation
1111 Superior Ave E Fl 19
Cleveland, OH 44114 216-523-5000
Fax: 216-523-4787 800-386-1911
www.eaton.com
Noncontact sensors used in food processing, packaging and material handling equipment
CEO: Alexander M Cutler
Marketing Director: Steven Lefley
Estimated Sales: $5 - 10 Million
Number Employees: 10,000
Square Footage: 100000
Parent Co: Eaton Corporation
Brands:
Comet
Sn Series
Targetlock Perfect Prox
Iprox

22022 Eaton Equipment
5210 State Road 133
PO Box 55
Boscobel, WI 53805 608-375-2256
Fax: 608-375-2256 cqeaton@mchsi.com
Homoginizers, cheese equipment, custom fabrication, heat exchangers, plate, agitators, cookers, ford, hoop washers, hoops, knives, molds, automatic presses, manual presses, piping, fittings and sanitary tubing
President: Don Eaton
Estimated Sales: $500,000-$1 Million
Number Employees: 1-4

22023 Eaton Filtration, LLC
44 Apple Street
Tinton Falls, NJ 07724 732-212-4700
Fax: 952-906-3706 800-859-9212
info@rpaprocess.com www.eaton.com
Manufacturer and exporter of fluid filters and strainers
Chairman: Alexander M. Cutler
CEO: Alexander M. Cutler
CFO: Richard H. Fearon
Vice Chairman: Richard H. Fearon
SVP - Sales and Marketing: Steven M. Boccadoro
SVP - Public and Community Affairs: William B. Doggett
Vice Chairman/COO— Industrial Sector: Craig Arnold
Number Employees: 50-99
Brands:
Ronningen-Petter

22024 Eaton Filtration, LLC
44 Apple Street
Tinton Falls, NJ 07724 732-212-4700
Fax: 952-906-3706 800-859-9212
info@rpaprocess.com www.eaton.com
Uninterruptible power systems for computers and other critical loads; also, point of sale devices and power management software available
Chairman: Alexander M. Cutler
CEO: Alexander M. Cutler
CFO and Vice Chairman: Richard H. Fearon
SVP - Sales and Marketing: Steven M. Boccadoro
SVP - Public and Community Affairs: William B. Doggett
Vice Chairman/COO— Industrial Sector: Craig Arnold

22025 Eaton Manufacturing Company
PO Box 1607
Houston, TX 77251 713-223-2331
Fax: 713-223-2342 800-328-6610
www.eatonmfg.com
Manufacturer and exporter of labels, laminated films, cash control envelopes and bags including polyethylene, polypropylene and ice
President: Tom B Eaton Jr
General Manager: Joe Williams
Estimated Sales: $5-10 Million
Number Employees: 20-49
Square Footage: 100000

22026 (HQ)Eaton Sales & Service
PO Box 16405
Denver, CO 80216 303-296-4800
Fax: 303-296-5749 800-208-2657
sales@eatonmetal.com
www.eatonmetalsales.com
Atmospheric and pressure tanks; also, installation services available
President: Timothy J Travis
CFO: Dorothy Martin
General Manager Administration: Kirby Boutelle
Estimated Sales: $20 - 50 Million
Number Employees: 50-99

22027 Eaton-Quade Company
1116 W Main St
Oklahoma City, OK 73106 405-236-4475
Fax: 405-236-4520 doug@eatonquade.com
www.eatonquade.com
Custom formed plastics including sneeze protectors, displays, food display covers, etc
President: Doug Swindell
Estimated Sales: $1-2.5 Million
Number Employees: 5-9
Square Footage: 30000

22028 Eaton/Cutler-Hammer
P.O.Box 463
Milwaukee, WI 53201-0463 414-449-6207
Fax: 414-449-6760 800-354-7061
www.eaton.com
Controls and control systems
President: Bradley Morton
Senior Vice President: Barbara ODell
Estimated Sales: $50 - 100 Million
Number Employees: 250-499

22029 Ebel Tape & Label
1832 Westwood Ave
Cincinnati, OH 45214-1347 513-471-1067
Fax: 513-471-5657 ebellabel@suse.net
Tapes including gummed and pressure sensitive; also, pressure sensitive labels
President: Greg Dulle
CFO: James Dulle
Estimated Sales: Below $5 Million
Number Employees: 5 to 9

22030 Ebenezer Flag Company
64 Spring St
Newport, RI 02840-6803 401-846-1891
Fax: 401-849-1640
Flags and banners
President: Tina Croce
Estimated Sales: less than $500,000
Number Employees: 1 to4

22031 Eberbach Corporation
505 South Maple Rd
Ann Arbor, MI 48103 734-665-8877
Fax: 734-665-9099 800-422-2558
info@eberbachlabtools.com
www.eberbachlabtools.com
Laboratory and pilot-plant equipment, instruments, apparatus, shakers, mixers, homogenizers and blenders
President: Ralph O Boehnke Jr
CFO: Ralph O Boehnke Jr
R&D: Chris Boehnke Jr
Quality Control: Ralph O Boehnke Jr
Estimated Sales: Below $5 000,000
Number Employees: 10-19

22032 EcFood.Com
4655 Old Ironsides Dr
Santa Clara, CA 95054-1808 408-496-2900
Fax: 408-566-6148 877-532-7253
info@ecfood.com www.ecfood.com
Estimated Sales: $1 - 5 Million
Number Employees: 1-4

22033 EcFood.com
410 Jessie St
San Francisco, CA 94103-1834 415-869-6100
Fax: 415-869-6148 877-532-7253
info@ecmarkets.com www.ecmarkets.com
President: Dave Laukat
Estimated Sales: $10 - 20 Million
Number Employees: 20-49

22034 Echo
400 Oakwood Rd
Lake Zurich, IL 60047 847-540-8400
Fax: 847-540-8413
marketing@echoincorporated.com
www.echo-usa.com
Wine industry hoses and sprayers
President: Yasuhiko Kitazume
CEO: Dan Obringer
Estimated Sales: $220 Million
Number Employees: 500-999

22035 Eckels-Bilt, Inc
7700 Harwell St
Fort Worth, TX 76108 817-246-4555
Fax: 817-246-7139 800-343-9020
info@eckelsbilt.com www.eckelsbilt.com
Manufacturer and exporter of conveyor belt automatic tracking systems
President: John Mic Kunas
Sales Manager: Tony Keeton
Estimated Sales: $5-10 Million
Number Employees: 10-19
Square Footage: 7500
Brands:
True Tracker

22036 Ecklund-Harrison Technologies
11000 Metro Pkwy Ste 40
Fort Myers, FL 33966-1245 239-936-6032
Fax: 239-936-6327
debbie@ecklund-harrison.com
www.ecklund-harrison.com
Manufacturer and exporter of heat penetration equipment and pasteurization monitor computers
President: Daniel Highbaugh
Estimated Sales: $500,000
Number Employees: 5-9

22037 Eclectic Contract Furniture Industries
450 Fashion Avenue
Suite 2701
New York, NY 10123 212-967-5504
Fax: 212-760-8823 888-311-6272
eclecticinc@aol.com www.eclecticcontract.com
Tables, chairs, booths and barstools
President: Alex Marc
Estimated Sales: Less than $500,000
Number Employees: 1-4

22038 Eclipse Electric Manufacturing
6512 Walker St
St Louis Park, MN 55426 952-929-2500
Fax: 952-929-0024 emailchico@aol.com
www.eclipseelectric.us
Electric custom lighting fixtures
President: David Jenkins
VP Marketing: Dave Jenkins
Estimated Sales: $1-2.5 Million
Number Employees: 5-9
Square Footage: 20000

22039 Eclipse Espresso Systems
1733 Westlake Avenue N
Seattle, WA 98109-3014 206-587-3767
Fax: 206-587-0339
members.aol.com/eclsystm/parts.htm
Tea and coffee industry blending and mixing equipment, dryers and feeders, evaporators
Estimated Sales: $500,000-$1 Million
Number Employees: 5

22040 Eclipse Innovative Thermal Solutions
5040 Enterprise Blvd
Toledo, OH 43612 419-729-9726
Fax: 419-729-9705 800-662-3966
sales@exothermics.com www.eclipsenet.com
Industrial air-to-air heat exchangers and heat recovery equipment; exporter of industrial heat exchangers
Manager: Paul Wilde
R&D: Bob Shaffer
Number Employees: 20-49
Square Footage: 35000
Parent Co: Eclipse

22041 Eclipse Systems
943 Hanson Court
Milpitas, CA 95035 408-263-2201
Fax: 408-263-2206 www.eclipsesystem.com
Manufacturer and exporter of mixers including electric and pneumatic drive
President: Charles Fletcher
CFO: Helen Fletcher
Sales Director: Diane Olsen
Estimated Sales: $20-50 Million
Number Employees: 20-49
Square Footage: 30000
Parent Co: Technology General Corporation
Brands:
Pneumix

22042 Eco-Air Products
7466 Carroll Rd # 101
San Diego, CA 92121-2356 858-271-8111
Fax: 858-578-3816 800-284-8111
pcurrie@shoreline.com www.precisionaire.com
Manufacturer and exporter of air, rangehood and grease filters
President: Wesley Measamer
CFO: John Hodson
Vice President of Division: Charlie Kwiatkowski
Manager: Robert Jaquay
Quality Control: Bill Stevens
VP Marketing: Bill O'Brien
Director of Sales: Bill Cawley
Senior Vice President of Operations: Kirk Dominick
Estimated Sales: $30-50 Million
Number Employees: 20-49
Square Footage: 110000

22043 Eco-Bag Products
23-25 Spring St, #302
Ossining, NY 10562 914-944-4556
Fax: 914-271-4867 800-720-2247
sales@ecobags.com www.eco-bags.com
Manufacturer, importer and exporter of natural and organic cotton bags including shopping and promotional tote, lunch and produce; printing services available
President: Sharon Rowe
Marketing: Ellen Ornato
PR & Communications: Rob Bradey
Estimated Sales: Below $5 Million
Number Employees: 1-4
Type of Packaging: Consumer, Food Service, Bulk
Brands:
Eco-Bags

22044 Eco-Pak Products Engineering
P.O.Box 179
Fenton, MO 63026-0179 636-305-9800
Fax: 636-305-9800 info@ecopakproducts.com
www.eco-pakproducts.com
Multi-packaging for beverage and food products, customizing packaging with or without full color graphics
President: Helly Miller
Estimated Sales: Less than $500,000
Number Employees: 1-4

22045 EcoFish
340 Central Ave
Suite 305
Dover, NH 03820 603-834-6034
Fax: 603-430-9929 comments@ecofish.com
www.ecofish.com
Distributor and promoter of ecologically sound seafood
President: Henry Lovejoy
Manager: Hector Gudino
Estimated Sales: $1 - 3 Million
Number Employees: 5-9

22046 Ecodyne Water Treatment,LLC
1270 Frontenac Rd
Naperville, IL 60563 630-961-5043
Fax: 630-671-8846 800-228-9326
sales@ecodyneind.com www.ecodyneind.com
Manufacturer and exporter of water treatment equipment including softeners, filters and reverse osmosis systems
President: Patrick O'Neill
Finance Executive: Todd Mc Gee
Research & Development: Wayne Simpson
Quality Control: Mark Thenhaus
Sales Director: Patrick O'Neill
Public Relations: Patrick O'Neill
Operations Manager: Mark Thenhaus
Production Manager: Mark Thenhaus
Plant Manager: Mark Thenhaus
Purchasing Manager: Mark Thenhaus
Estimated Sales: $5 - 10,000,000
Number Employees: 20-49
Square Footage: 50000
Brands:
Red Line

22047 Ecolab
370 N. Wabasha Street
St. Paul, MN 55102-2233 651-293-2233
www.ecolab.com
Industrial cleaners and sanitation supplies
Chairman and Chief Executive Officer: Douglas M. Baker, Jr.
Chief Financial Officer: Daniel J. Schmechel
EVP & Chief Information Officer: Stewart H. McCutcheon
President and Chief Operating Officer: Thomas W. Handley
Number Employees: 500-999

22048 Ecolab, Inc
370 N Wabasha Street
St Paul, MN 55102-2233 651-293-2233
Fax: 651-293-2092 800-232-6522
www.ecolab.com
Cleaning and sanitizing products, equipment, systems and services for the agribusiness, beverage, brewery, pharmaceutical, dairy, meat, poultry and food processing industries.
Chairman/President/CEO: Douglas Baker Jr
CFO: Steven Fritze
VP/CIO: Robert Tabb
SVP Human Resources: Michael Meyer
Estimated Sales: $6 Billion
Number Employees: 1400
Square Footage: 24135
Type of Packaging: Food Service

22049 Ecolo Odor Control Systems Worldwide
59 Penn Drive
North York, ON M9L 2A6
Canada 416-740-3900
Fax: 416-740-3800 800-667-6355
info@ecolo.com www.ecolo.com
Manufacturer and exporter of odor control systems and air solutions to deodorize washrooms, garbage rooms, transfer stations, waste water treatment plants, etc
President: Calvin Sager
Vice President: Ian Howard
Marketing Director: Cindy Pickard
Director Manufacturing: John Linthwaite
Number Employees: 20
Square Footage: 60000
Parent Co: Sager Industries
Brands:
Air Solution
Ecolo

22050 Ecological Laboratories
P.O.Box 184
Malverne, NY 11565-0184 516-823-3441
Fax: 866-389-7776 800-645-2976
info@propump.com www.propump.com
Live bacterial cultures
President: Barry Richter
Estimated Sales: $5-10 Million
Number Employees: 20-49
Type of Packaging: Bulk

22051 Ecom Cocoa
17 State St
23rd Floor
New York, NY 10004 212-248-7475
Fax: 212-248-0143 ddomingo@ecomtrading.com
www.ecomtrading.com
Cocoa and cocoa products
Director: Andrew Halle
Vice Chairman: Jose Recolons
Vice Chairman: Jorge Recolons
Estimated Sales: $4 Billion
Type of Packaging: Consumer, Food Service, Private Label, Bulk

22052 Econo Equipment
PO Box 250
Westfield, WI 53964-0250 608-296-3646
Fax: 608-296-4029
Packaging equipment
President: Michael Johnson
Estimated Sales: $1-2.5 000,000
Number Employees: 19

22053 Econo Frost Night Covers
PO Box 40
Shawnigan Lake, BC V0R 2W0
Canada 250-743-1222
Fax: 250-743-1221 800-519-1222
info@econofrost.com www.mgvinc.com
Manufacturer, importer and exporter of color corrected lighting and night covers for refrigerated display cases
President: Mark Granfar
Marketing: Samantha Criddle
Sales: Trevor Brien
Number Employees: 20-49
Number of Products: 1
Square Footage: 3000
Parent Co: MGV Inc
Type of Packaging: Food Service
Brands:
Econofrost
Instamark
Mgv
Mr16
Multichrome
Promolux
Samark

22054 Econocorp
72 Pacella Park Dr
Randolph, MA 02368 781-986-7500
Fax: 781-986-1553 info@econcorp.com
www.econocorp.com
Manufacturer and exporter of carton sealing machinery
President: Wayne Goldberg
Quality Control: Richard Norton
VP: Mark Jacobson
Estimated Sales: $10 - 20 Million
Number Employees: 50-99
Square Footage: 21000
Brands:
Econoseal

22055 Econofrost Night Covers
Box 40
Shawnigan Lake, BC V0R 2W0
Canada 250-743-1222
Fax: 250-743-1221 800-519-1222
info@econofrost.com www.econofrost.com
Night covers for the refrigerated display cases in supermarkets.
President: Mark Granfar
Marketing: Lyn Rose
Sales: Trevor Brian
Sales: Scott Werhun
Sales: Jamie Farr
International Sales: Carlos Paniagua
Number Employees: 15
Number of Brands: 2
Square Footage: 3000
Type of Packaging: Private Label
Brands:
Econofrost

22056 Economic Sciences Corporation
1516 Le Roy Ave
Berkeley, CA 94708 510-841-6869
Fax: 510-644-1943 info@econsci.com
www.econsci.net
Computer software
President: B F Roberts
VP: Helen Chin
Estimated Sales: Below $5 Million
Number Employees: 1-4

22057 Economy Folding Box Corporation
2601 S La Salle St
Chicago, IL 60616 312-225-2000
Fax: 312-225-3082 800-771-1053
info@economyfoldingboxcorp.com
www.economyfoldingboxcorp.com

Manufacturer and exporter of paper boxes
President: Michael M Mitchel
CEO: Clifford Moos
VP/Treasurer: Michael Mitchel
Purchasing Officer: Marie Hernandez
Sales Manager: Joseph Moos
Estimated Sales: $10 - 20 Million
Number Employees: 50-99
Square Footage: 165000
Type of Packaging: Consumer, Food Service, Private Label

22058 Economy Label Sales Company
515 Carswell Ave
Daytona Beach, FL 32117-4411 386-253-4741
Fax: 386-238-0775 www.economylabel.com
Manufacturer and exporter of flexible plastic and vinyl labels including pressure sensitive, plain, hot-stamped and printed
Estimated Sales: $5-10 Million
Number Employees: 50-99
Parent Co: Meadow USA

22059 Economy Novelty & Printing Company
407 Park Ave S Apt 26a
Suite 26A
New York, NY 10016 212-481-3022
Fax: 212-481-4514 info@thinkideas.com
www.thinkideas.com
Manufacturer and importer of advertising specialties including badges, medals, decals and ribbons
President: Robert Becker
VP: Warren Becker
Estimated Sales: $500,000-$1,000,000
Number Employees: 5-9
Square Footage: 2000
Parent Co: Economy Novelty
Brands:
Thinkideas

22060 Economy Paper & Restaurant Supply Company
180 Broad St
Clifton, NJ 07013 973-279-5500
Fax: 973-279-4140 sales@economysupply.com
www.economysupply.com
Soaps, degreasers and custom fabricated equipment; wholesaler/distributor and exporter of food service equipment, disposables, janitorial supplies, smallwares, glassware, flatware and china; installation and consulting available
President: L J Konzelman
CFO: Susan Majors
VP: Micheal Konzelman
R&D: Alex Nasarone
Public Relations: Susan Majors
Purchasing: Kevin Konzelman
Estimated Sales: $3 - 5 Million
Number Employees: 10-19
Square Footage: 25000
Type of Packaging: Food Service
Brands:
Econo-Flash
Econo-Suds

22061 Economy Tent International
2995 NW 75th Street
Miami, FL 33147 305-835-7098
Fax: 305-835-7098 800-438-3226
sales@economytent.com www.economytent.com
Supplier and exporter of party tents for the food service industry
President: Hal Paul Lapping
VP Marketing: Hal Lapping
Estimated Sales: $1 - 2.5 Million
Number Employees: 20
Type of Packaging: Food Service

22062 Ecover
PO Box 911058
Los Angeles, CA 90091-1058 323-720-5730
Fax: 323-720-5732 ecover@pacbell.net
www.ecover.com
Natural bases, environmentally safe cleaning products.
CEO: Philip Malmberg
Sales Manager: Maureen Davis
Estimated Sales: $3 - 5 Million
Number Employees: 5-9

22063 Ed Smith's Stencil Works
4227 Bienville St
New Orleans, LA 70119 504-525-2128
Fax: 504-525-2157 sales@edsmiths.net
www.edsmiths.net
Marking devices, rubber stamps, checks, name badges, price markers, stencils and plastic signs
Owner: Michael Rowan
VP: Ronald Schaefer
Assistant Sales Manager: Michael Rowan
Estimated Sales: $1-2.5 Million
Number Employees: 20-49
Square Footage: 13584

22064 Edco Industries
203 Dekalb Ave
Bridgeport, CT 06607 203-333-8982
Fax: 203-333-7950 edcoindustries@sbcglobal.net
www.edcoindustries.com
Molded plastic products including housewares, ice buckets, tumblers, trays, coasters, etc.; also, hot stamping available
President: John Thomas Szalan
VP: Anna Marie Szalan
Plant Manager: Hector Mendez
Estimated Sales: $1 Million
Number Employees: 10-19
Square Footage: 13400

22065 Edco Supply Corporation
323 36th St
Brooklyn, NY 11232 718-788-8108
Fax: 718-788-7481 800-221-0918
info@edcosupply.com www.edcosupply.com
Antistatic packaging including antistatic bags, commercial translucent static shielding materials, desiccant, indicator cards, caution labels and VCI papers
President: Carl Freyer
Estimated Sales: $5 - 10 000,000
Number Employees: 20-49

22066 Ederback Corporation
505 South Maple Road
Ann Arbor, MI 48103 734-665-8877
Fax: 734-665-9099 800-422-2558
info@eberbachlabtools.com
www.eberbachlabtools.com
Manufacturer and exporter of laboratory equipment including shakers, mixers, homogenizers and blenders
President: Ralph Boehnke Jr
Estimated Sales: $3 - 5 Million
Number Employees: 10-19

22067 Ederer
3701 S Norfolk St Ste A
Seattle, WA 98118 206-622-4421
Fax: 206-623-8583 ederer@ederer.com
www.ederer.com
Manufacturer and exporter of cranes, hoists and crane controls
General Manager: Joe Hoff
VP: Neil Skogland
Director Sales/Marketing: Jaems Nelson
Estimated Sales: $10-20 Million
Number Employees: 1-4
Type of Packaging: Bulk

22068 Edge Paper Box Company
4916 Cecilia Street
Cudahy, CA 90201 323-771-7733
Fax: 323-562-0934
Rigid paper and plastic boxes
President: Joseph Erhardt
VP: Craig Harrison
Estimated Sales: $5-10 Million
Number Employees: 50-99
Square Footage: 70000
Parent Co: Pacific Paper Box Company

22069 Edge Resources
1 Menfi Way
Unit 20
Hopedale, MA 01747-1542 508-634-8214
Fax: 508-634-9888 888-849-0998
info@edgeresources.com
www.edgeresources.com
Manufacturer and importer of food service equipment and supplies; consultant specializing in marketing and sales services
President/CEO: Frank Curty
Estimated Sales: $500,000-$1 Million
Number Employees: 5-9
Square Footage: 16000

22070 EdgeCraft Corporation
825 Southwood Rd
Avondale, PA 19311 610-268-0500
Fax: 610-268-3545 800-342-3255
val.gleason@edgecraft.com www.edgecraft.com
Manufacturer and exporter of manual and power driven sharpeners slicer and cutlery
President: Sam Weiner
CEO: Daniel Friel Sr
Estimated Sales: G
Number Employees: 150
Brands:
Chef's Choice

22071 Edgemold Products
37031 E Wisconsin Ave
PO Box 88
Oconomowoc, WI 53066 262-567-9313
Fax: 262-567-4814 800-334-3665
info@edgemold.com www.fiberesin.com
Urethane-edged tables and tabletops
President: Larry Starkweather
National Sales Manager: Lonie Wise
Estimated Sales: $1 - 5 Million
Number Employees: 100-249
Parent Co: Fibersin Industries
Brands:
Edgemold

22072 Edgerton Corporation
22560 Lunn Rd
Strongsville, OH 44149 440-268-0000
Fax: 440-268-0300
information@edgertoncorp.com
www.edgerton.com
Computer systems for material handling
President: Bob Walters
CFO: Susan Sponsler
Executive VP: Barry Zimmerman
COO: Jed Cavadas
Estimated Sales: $10 - 20,000,000
Number Employees: 20-49

22073 Edhard Corporation
279 Blau Rd
Hackettstown, NJ 07840 908-850-8444
Fax: 908-850-8445 888-334-2731
meter@edhard.com www.edhard.com
Bakers' equipment and supplies including plastic injection molds and dies
President and R&D: Edgar Bars
CFO: Joe Englert
Sales Manager: Nancy Neri
Estimated Sales: $2.5 - 5 Million
Number Employees: 20-49
Brands:
Edhard Injectors & Depositors

22074 Edible Software
3603 Westcenter Dr
Suite 100
Houston, TX 77042 832-200-8322
Fax: 832-200-8001 sales@ediblesoftware.com
www.ediblesoftware.com
Accessories/supplies i.e. picnic baskets
President, Chief Executive Officer: Henri Morris
Senior Vice President: Trevor Morris

22075 Edison Price Lighting
41-50 22nd Street
Long Island City, NY 11101 718-685-0700
Fax: 718-786-8530 jlattanzio@epl.com
www.epl.com
Manufacturer and exporter of architectural, energy efficient, recessed and surface mounted lighting fixtures
President: Emma Price
Finance: MaryAnna Romano
R&D: Richard J. Shaver
Sales/Marketing: Joel Seigel
Sales Service: Joanie Lattanzio
Customer Service: Stephanie Smith
Administration: James D. Vizzini
purchasing/operations: George H. Closs
Number Employees: 130
Brands:
Anglux
Artima
Autotrak
Bablux

Duplux
Multipurpose
Sight Line
Simplux
Spredlite
Triples

22076 **Edlund Company Inc**
PO Box 929
Burlington, VT 05402-0929 802-862-9661
Fax: 802-862-4822 800-772-2126
scrane@edlundco.com www.edlundco.com
Develops and manufactures operator-oriented stainless steel equipment for the food service industry product line of which includes can crushers; manual, electric and air-powered can openers; high speed industrial systems; mechanicaland digital portion control scales; mechanical and digital receiving scales; knife sharpeners; knife racks; and tongs.
President: Willett S Foster Iv IV
Vice President: Peter Nordell
Vice President of Sales and Marketing: David Sebastianelli
Estimated Sales: $10-25 Million
Number Employees: 100-249
Brands:
Edlund

22077 **Edmeyer**
315 27th Ave NE
Minneapolis, MN 55418-2715 651-450-1210
Fax: 651-450-0003 edmeyer@edmeyerinc.com
www.edmeyerinc.com
Manufacturer and exporter of casers, conveyors, case packers and palletizers
President: Larry Smith
VP: Jerry Kisch
Sales Manager: Greg Reid
Estimated Sales: $20-50 Million
Number Employees: 20-49
Square Footage: 12000

22078 **Edson Packaging Machinery**
215 Hempstead Drive
Hamilton, ON L8V 4L5
Canada 905-385-3201
Fax: 905-385-8775 www.edson.com
Manufacturer and exporter of robotic top load packers, packaging machinery including case openers, robotic palletizers, stretch bundlers, sealers and automatic packers
CEO: Robert Hattin
Vice President, General Manager: Gary Evans
Engineering Manager: Bob Krouse
Quality Control: Bob Krause
Account Manager: Scott Killins
Estimated Sales: $10 Million
Number Employees: 70
Number of Brands: 5
Square Footage: 48300
Type of Packaging: Consumer, Food Service
Brands:
Edson

22079 **(HQ)Educational Products Company**
P.O. Box 295
Hope, NJ 07844 908-459-4220
Fax: 908-459-4770 800-272-3822
cookiecutters1947@hotmail.com
www.cookiecutters.com
3-D cookie cutters
President: Christopher Maier
Manager: Lucy Kise
Estimated Sales: $500,000 - $1 Million
Number Employees: 1-4
Brands:
Cookie Craft

22080 **Edward & Sons Trading Co**
PO Box 1326
Carpinteria, CA 93014 805-684-8500
Fax: 805-684-8220 www.edwardandsons.com
Innovative natural and organic vegetarian foods

22081 **Edwards Engineering Corporation**
101 Alexander Ave Unit 3
Pompton Plains, NJ 07444 973-835-2800
Fax: 973-835-3222 800-526-5201
rprol@edwards-eng.com www.edwards-eng.com
Manufacturer and exporter of heating/cooling equipment and products, control components, hydronic heating/cooling systems and vapor recovery units for pollution and process control; also, packaged industrial chillers
President: R Waldrop
VP Engineering: G Passaro
Plant Manager: Jose Mercedes
Estimated Sales: $40 Million
Number Employees: 50-99
Brands:
Box'fin
Quiet' Slide

22082 **Edwards Fiberglass**
P.O.Box 1252
Sedalia, MO 65302-1252 660-826-3915
Fax: 660-827-2793 www.edwardsfiberglass.com
Above and below ground fiberglass storage tanks
President: Robert L Edwards
VP: Shane Edwards
Sales: Donna Schoolman
Estimated Sales: $20 - 50 Million
Number Employees: 20-49
Square Footage: 31000

22083 **Edwards Products**
1223 Budd St
Cincinnati, OH 45203 513-851-3000
Fax: 513-851-9300 800-543-1835
info@edwardsproducts.com
www.edwardsproducts.com
Stock trucks and storage racks
President: Thomas Reilly
Quality Control: Kevin Reilly
General Manager: John Sloniker
Estimated Sales: $20 - 50 Million
Number Employees: 20-49
Square Footage: 30000

22084 **Efficient Frontiers**
2021 W.Las Positas Ct.Ste 127
Livermore, CA 94551 925-456-6700
Fax: 925-456-6701 888-433-4725
info@efficient-frontiers.com
www.efficient-frontiers.com
Automated software for event sales, dining reservations and club membership
Director Sales/Marketing: Beth Goodell
Brands:
Efficient Frontiers
Reserve

22085 **Eggboxes Inc**
PO Box 8651
Deerfield Beach, FL 33443 954-410-5565
Fax: 954-783-3456 800-326-6667
customerservice@eggboxes.com
www.eggboxes.com
Egg cartons, baskets, egg washing supplies, hatchery supplies, bird care, incubating trays, feeders, scales, and nest accessories
President: James Tongle

22086 **Ehmke Manufacturing Company**
4200 Macalester St
Philadelphia, PA 19124 215-324-4200
Fax: 215-324-4210
www.ehmkemanufacturing.com
Commercial awnings
President: Louis Verna
CEO: Bob Rosania
Manager, Quality Assurance: Richard Ludwig
Director, Sales & Marketing: Brad Milnes
Sales Manager: Brad Daniels

22087 **Ehrgott Rubber Stamp Company**
4615 E 10th St
Indianapolis, IN 46201-2823 317-353-2222
Fax: 317-357-7750 ehrgott@aol.com
www.ehrgott.com
Rubber stamps, engraved signs and name tags
President and CFO: Mary Clevenger
Estimated Sales: $500,000 - $1 Million
Number Employees: 1-4

22088 **Eichler Wood Products**
5477 Mauser Street
Laurys Station, PA 18059-1317 610-262-6749
Fax: 610-262-4454
Wooden pallets, boxes, crates and skids
Manager: Henry Taylor
Owner: Henry Taylor
Business Manager: Thomas R Nemeth
Estimated Sales: $1 - 3 Million
Number Employees: 30
Square Footage: 20000

22089 **Eide Industries**
16215 Piuma Ave
Cerritos, CA 90703 562-402-8335
Fax: 562-924-2233 800-422-6827
don@eideindustries.com
www.eideindustries.com
Manufacturer and exporter of commercial awnings, canopies, tension structures and custom fabric covers
President: Don Araiza
Secretary/VP Marketing: Joe Belli
VP Sales: Dan Neill
Production Coordinator: Ignacio Pellegrin
Chairman/VP Manufacturing: Jesse Borrego
Estimated Sales: $8 Million
Number Employees: 50-99
Square Footage: 41000

22090 **Einson Freeman**
240 Frisch Ct
Paramus, NJ 07652-5248 201-226-0300
Fax: 201-226-9262 cnichols@einson.com
www.cafsnj.org
Manufacturer and exporter of point of purchase displays, exhibits and sales promotion items
President: Jean Mojo
President, Chief Executive Officer: Robert Jones
Vice President of Development: Madinah Grier
Senior Project Manager: Jeff Shapiro
Estimated Sales: $10 - 20 Million
Number Employees: 50-99
Parent Co: WPP Group PLC

22091 **Eirich Machines**
4033 Ryan Rd
Gurnee, IL 60031 847-336-2444
Fax: 847-336-0914 eirich@eirichusa.com
www.eirich.com/en/eirich-machines
Manufacturer and exporter of high speed, ribbon, paddle, plow and fluidized zone mixers, finishers, bag dump work stations, viscous pumps, blenders and hoppers
Co-President: Paul Eirich
Sales: Richard Zak
VP Sales: Richard Zak
Estimated Sales: $10-20 Million
Number Employees: 50-99
Square Footage: 75000
Parent Co: Maschinenfabrik G. Eirich GmbH

22092 **Eisai**
3 University Plz
Hackensack, NJ 07601-6208 201-692-0999
Fax: 201-692-1972 eis@rocky.eisai.com
www.eisaiusa.com
Fully automated inspection machines for parenternal products
President: Micheal De La Montaign
Estimated Sales: $10 - 15 Million
Number Employees: 10-19

22093 **Eischen Enterprises**
10111 S Cedar Ave
Fresno, CA 93725 559-834-0013
Fax: 559-834-9183 veischen@aol.com
www.eischenenterprisesinc.com
Sell food processing equipment, used and reconditioned.
President: Virgil Eischen
Marketing: Janice Jepsen
Sales: Virgil Eischen

22094 **Eisenmann Corporation**
150 E Dartmoor Dr Ste 1
Crystal Lake, IL 60014 815-455-4100
Fax: 815-455-1018 craig.benner@eisenmann.com
www.eisenmann.com
Manufacturer and exporter of turnkey material handling systems including electrified monorail systems and belt, power, chain, overhead chain and free conveyors; system design services available
VP: Craig Benner
General Manager (General Industry): R Trenn
Estimated Sales: $50-100 Million
Number Employees: 250-499
Square Footage: 300
Parent Co: Eisenmann Corporation
Type of Packaging: Bulk

22095 **El Cerrito Steel**
1424 Kearney St
El Cerrito, CA 94530-2397 510-529-0370
Fax: 510-233-0116
Steel canning and preserving kettles
President: John Kim
Estimated Sales: $1-2.5 Million
Number Employees: 2

22096 **El Dorado Paper Bag Manufacturing Company**
PO Box 1585
El Dorado, AR 71731 870-862-4977
Fax: 870-862-8520
Manufacturer and exporter of paper bags
President: Louis Hall III
CEO: Louis T Hall Iii
Estimated Sales: $20 - 50 Million
Number Employees: 100-249
Type of Packaging: Consumer

22097 **Elan Chemical Company**
268 Doremus Ave
Newark, NJ 07105-4875 973-344-8014
Fax: 973-344-1948 sales@elan-chemical.com
www.elan-chemical.com
Manufacturer and exporter of organic kosher certified vanilla extract, flavoring and synthetic and natural aromatic chemicals
Director Of Chemical Sales: Isabel Couto
Compliance Manager: Ramona Kistler
National Sales Manager: Jeff Rakity
Sales Account Executive: Marcia Couto
International Sales: David Pimentel
Estimated Sales: $20-50 Million
Number Employees: 50-99
Type of Packaging: Bulk

22098 **Elanco Food Solutions**
2500 Innovation Way
PO Box 708
Greenfield, IN 46140 317-276-9846
800-428-4441
drcobb@lilly.com www.elanco.com
Food safety products and services
President: Jeff Simmons
Number Employees: 2,500

22099 **Elba Pallets Company**
PO Box 276
Elba, AL 36323-0276 334-897-6034
Fax: 334-897-6421
Wooden pallets
President: L Little
Estimated Sales: $5-10 Million
Number Employees: 19

22100 **Elberta Crate & Box Company**
231 W Main Street
Suite 207
Carpentersville, IL 60110-1769 847-426-3491
Fax: 847-426-3520 888-672-9260
eschbachw@aol.com
Manufacturer and exporter of wirebound boxes, crates and expendable pallets
CEO: Ramsay Simmons
Sales Director: Walter Eschenbach
Public Relations: Todd Mills
Estimated Sales: $1 - 5 Million
Number Employees: 1-4
Parent Co: Elberta Crate & Box Company
Type of Packaging: Food Service, Bulk
Brands:
Elberta
Skee
Woodkor

22101 **Eldetco**
20 Anson Road
Burlingame, CA 94010-7226 650-579-7655
Fax: 650-579-7650
Conveyors and conveying equipment
President: Don Lunghi
Estimated Sales: $1 000,000
Number Employees: 9

22102 **Eldorado Miranda Manufacturing Company**
1744 12th St SE Ofc
Largo, FL 33771 727-586-0707
Fax: 727-585-4797 800-330-0708
eldoradomfg@tampabay.rr.com
www.eldoradomfg.com
UL listed ventmatic hoods; also, stainless steel work tables, square corner sinks, shelving and commercial dishwasher tables
President: Andrew Miranda Jr
Quality Control: Cora Miranda
VP: Andrew Miranda III
Estimated Sales: Below $5 Million
Number Employees: 5-9
Square Footage: 45000
Brands:
Eldorado Miranda

22103 **Elecro-Craft/Rockwell Automation**
6950 Washington Ave S
Eden Prairie, MN 55344-3407 952-942-3600
Fax: 612-942-3636 800-752-6946
eesemea@ra.rockwell.com
www.electro-craft.com
Programmable limit switches and electornic rotary cam switches used to control food processing and packaging machinery
General Manager: Philip Martin
President, Chief Executive Officer: James Elsner
Senior VP: William Calisse
Vice President of Business Development: Rob Kerber
VP: David Dorgan
Vice President of Sales: Tom Ouellette
Plant Manager: Rick Roberts
Estimated Sales: $50 - 100 Million
Number Employees: 100-249
Number of Products: 4
Square Footage: 279000
Type of Packaging: Bulk

22104 **Electra-Gear**
1110 N Anaheim Boulevard
Anaheim, CA 92801-2502 714-535-6061
Fax: 714-535-2489 sales@electragear.com
www.electragear.com
Manager: Katherine Garrison
Human Resoures and Administration: Anna Alvarez
Estimated Sales: $3 - 5 Million
Number Employees: 1
Parent Co: Regal-Beloit Company

22105 **Electric City Signs & Neon Inc.**
701 US Hwy 28 By Pass
PO Box 656
Anderson, SC 29622 864-225-5351
Fax: 864-225-9050 800-270-5851
www.electriccitysigns.com
Plastic and neon signs
Owner: Darrell Ridgeway
Secretary and Treasurer: Patricia Ridgeway
Production Manager: Chris Bowser
Estimated Sales: $2 Million
Number Employees: 20-49
Square Footage: 60000

22106 **Electrical Engineering &Equipment Company**
1808 Delaware Ave
Des Moines, IA 50317-6341 515-266-8890
Fax: 515-266-1181 800-33 -722
www.3e-co.com
Conveyors, elevators, bins and other material handling systems
Owner: J D Pilmer
Controller: Jay Turner
Executive VP: J Pilmer
Estimated Sales: $10-20 Million
Number Employees: 50-99

22107 **Electro Alarms**
24 S Washington St
Tiffin, OH 44883 419-447-3062
800-261-9174
information@electroalarms.com
www.electroalarms.com
Broker of burglar and fire alarm systems. Repair and installation services available
Owner: Howard Beisner
Sales Director: Howard Beisner
Estimated Sales: $1-2.5 Million
Number Employees: 1-4

22108 **Electro Cam Corporation**
13647 Metric Rd
Roscoe, IL 61073 815-389-2620
Fax: 815-389-3304 800-228-5487
info@electrocam.com www.electrocam.com
Manufacturer and exporter of packaging and food processing controls and software including programmable and electric switches
President: Donald Davis
Quality Control: Mike Engevretson
Marketing Manager: Barbara Scheeberger
Sales Manager: John Straw
Estimated Sales: $5 - 10 Million
Number Employees: 20-49
Brands:
Plus
Plusnet
Slimline

22109 **Electro Freeze**
2116 8th Ave
East Moline, IL 61244 309-755-4553
Fax: 309-755-9858 sales@electrofreeze.com
www.hcduke.com
Manufacturer, importer and exporter of soft serve ice cream, slush, shake and frozen yogurt equipment
Marketing: Joe Clark
Estimated Sales: $20 - 50 Million
Number Employees: 100-249
Square Footage: 115000
Parent Co: H.C. Duke & Son

22110 **Electro Sensors**
6111 Blue Circle Dr
Minnetonka, MN 55343 952-945-2800
Fax: 952-930-0130 1 8-0 3-8 61
sales@electro-sensors.com
www.electro-sensors.com
Electro-Sensors, Inc. manufactures a complete line of motion monitoring and speed control systems for industrial machinery including: Speed Sensors, Speed Sensitive Switches, Tachometers, Counters, Speed to Analog Converters, DigitalPulse Generators, Closed Loop Motor Speed Control Systems, and Material Level Controls
President/CEO': Brad Slyle
CFO: Gloria Grundhoefer
Marketing/Sales: Philip Rae
Estimated Sales: $5-10 000,000
Number Employees: 20-49

22111 **Electro-Lite Signs**
9155 Archibald Ave Ste 303
Rancho Cucamonga, CA 91730 909-945-3555
Fax: 909-945-9805
Electric signs
Owner: Ken Brown
Estimated Sales: $500,000-$1,000,000
Number Employees: 5-9

22112 **Electro-Sensors**
6111 Blue Circle Dr
Minnetonka, MN 55343 952-945-2800
Fax: 952-930-0130 800-323-6170
sales@electro-sensors.com
www.electro-sensors.com
Speed monitoring systems, speed switches, tachometers, counters, speed to analog converters, ratemeters
CEO: Brad Flye
CEO: Bradley D Slye
Manager: Mike Kroening
Estimated Sales: E
Number Employees: 20-49
Number of Products: 14

22113 **Electro-Steam GeneratorCorporation**
50 Indel Avenue
PO Box 438
Rancocas, NJ 08073-0438 609-288-9071
Fax: 609-288-9078 866-617-0764
sales@electrosteam.com www.electrosteam.com
Manufacturer all-electric steam generators that are used in industry for ovens, proofers, kettles, and for cleaning, sanitizing, and heating
President: Robert Murnane
Quality Control: Barbara Aikens
Marketing/National Sales Manager: Jack Harlin
Operations: Jack Harlin
Manufacturing Executive: Sal Negro
Plant Manager: Barbara Aikens
Purchase Executive: Gary Lango
Estimated Sales: $1-3 Million
Number Employees: 10-19
Number of Brands: 4
Square Footage: 26000
Type of Packaging: Private Label
Brands:
Baby Giant

Little Giant
Low Boy
Space Savers

22114 (HQ)Electrodex
4554 19th St Ct E
Bradenton, FL 34203 941-753-5663
Fax: 941-753-7049 800-362-1972
mike@electrodex.com www.electrodex.com
Manufacturer and exporter of lighting fixtures
President: Mike Guritz
Sales Manager: Warren Dalton
Estimated Sales: $2.5-5 Million
Number Employees: 10-19
Type of Packaging: Food Service

22115 Electrol Specialties Company
441 Clark St
South Beloit, IL 61080 815-389-2291
Fax: 815-389-2294 esc@jvlnet.com
www.esc4cip.com
Clean-in-place, computer and control systems, sanitation equipment, transfer panels and tanks; custom fabrication services available
President: Frank Bazo
Quality Control: Roger Schwartz
VP/General Manager: John Franks
Senior Sales Engineer: Dick Gleed
Estimated Sales: $5 - 10,000,000
Number Employees: 50-99
Square Footage: 50000
Type of Packaging: Bulk

22116 Electrolift
204 Sargeant Ave
Clifton, NJ 07013-1932 973-471-0204
Fax: 973-471-2814 info2@electrolift.com
www.electrolift.com
Manufacturer and exporter of hoists for monorail, dual rail, hatchway or base-mounted applications
President: David Erenstoft
Estimated Sales: $5 - 10 Million
Number Employees: 20-49
Type of Packaging: Bulk

22117 Electron Machine Corporation
15824 County Road 450
P.O. Box 2349
Umatilla, FL 32784 352-669-3101
Fax: 352-669-1373 sales@electronmachine.com
www.electronmachine.com
Microprocessor refractometers
President: Carl A Vossberg Iii
Estimated Sales: $2.5-5 000,000
Number Employees: 20-49

22118 Electronic Development Labs
244 Oakland Drive
Danville, VA 24540 434-799-0807
Fax: 434-799-0847 800-342-5335
sales@edl-inc.com www.edl-inc.com
Provides products and service, the most reliable precision temperature meassuring sensors, equipment, accessories, and calibrators; customized to customer specifications as needed. EDL offers an extensive line of calibratorsthermocouples, RTD's, thermistors, wire, high temperature bore thru compression fittings, bimetals, lab thermometers, recorders, infrared, high temperature insulations, over 10,000 sensors, and a full range of precision handheld pyrometers.
President and CFO: Donald Polsky
Quality Control: Steve Winnes
Marketing: Kristen Gusler
Sales: Jean Moore
Sales: Danielle Polsky
Purchasing: Stephanie King
Number Employees: 35

22119 Electronic Filling Systems
574 Barrow Park Drive
Winder, GA 30680-3416 770-621-9200
Fax: 770-934-0959 sales@electronicfilling.com
In-line liquid filling systems including volumetric piston liquid fillers, stainless steel tabletop chain conveyors, rotary unscramblers and accumulators and ink jet imagers
Estimated Sales: $5-10 000,000
Number Employees: 10-19

22120 Electronic Liquid Fillers
P.O.Box 387
Kingsbury, IN 46345-0387 219-393-5571
Fax: 219-393-5283 800-328-0466
sales@elfmachines.com www.elfmachines.com
Owner: Mitch Juszkiewicz
CEO and CFO: Ronald Sarto
Number Employees: 50-99

22121 Electronic Machine Parts
400 Oser Ave # 2000
Hauppauge, NY 11788-3658 631-434-3700
Fax: 631-434-3718 sales.emp@attglobal.net
www.empregister.com
Registration controls, rebuilding labeling machines
President: Maureen Mc Adam
Estimated Sales: $10-20 Million
Number Employees: 10-19

22122 Electronic Weighing Systems
664 Fisherman Street
Opa Locka, FL 33054 305-685-8067
Fax: 305-685-2440 www.electronicweighing.com
Manufacturer and exporter of electronic scales for receiving, counter, heavy duty, warehouse and crane scale
VP: Victor Perez, Jr.
Estimated Sales: $2.5-5 Million
Number Employees: 7
Square Footage: 84000
Brands:
Ews

22123 Electrostatics
352 Godshall Dr Ste D
Harleysville, PA 19438-2017 215-513-0850
Fax: 215-513-0855 888-782-8427
sales@electrostatics.com
www.electrostatics.com
Static neutralizing-generating and related contamination control equipment including static measuring locator and meter, high and low pressure guns, nozzles and blowers, static neutralizing bars, power units, static inducingequipment
President: Peter Mariani
Marketing: Maryjane Vielhauer
Sales: Maryjane Vielhauer
Director Engineering: Bob Meyers
Production: Keri Farrington
Purchasing: Janet Benfield
Estimated Sales: $2.5-5 000,000
Number Employees: 10-19

22124 Electrotechnology Applications Center
3835 Green Pond Rd
Bethlehem, PA 18020 610-861-4552
Fax: 610-861-5060 877-862-3696
mule@etctr.com www.etctr.com
Infrared, ultraviolet, microwave, and radiofrequency energy to improve heating, drying, curing, and coating processes

Number Employees: 9

22125 Elegant Awnings
13831 Oaks Avenue
Chino, CA 91710-7009 626-575-3556
Fax: 626-575-3567 800-541-9011
mchiovare@elegantawnings.com
www.elegantawnings.com

Commercial awnings
President: Mike Chiovare
CFO: Tony Chiovare
sales manager: Mike Chiovare
Estimated Sales: Below $5 Million
Number Employees: 10-19

22126 Elegant Packaging
5253 West Roosevelt Road
Cicero, IL 60804 708-652-3400
Fax: 708-652-6444 800-367-5493
www.elegantpackaging.com
Manufacturer and designers of customized rigid specialty boxes, presentation binders, soft sewn packaging and compression thermal forming.
Estimated Sales: $11 Million
Number Employees: 80
Square Footage: 96000
Type of Packaging: Consumer, Food Service, Private Label, Bulk

22127 Elettric 80
8100 Monticello Avenue
Skokie, IL 60076 847-329-7717
Fax: 847-329-9923 usa@elettric80.it
www.elettric80.com
Robotic palletizers, laser-guided vehicle systems
President: Johan Castegren
Estimated Sales: Below $5 Million
Number Employees: 6

22128 Elgene
299 Welton St
Hamden, CT 06517-3938 203-562-9948
Fax: 203-562-2053 800-922-4623
answers@elgene.com www.chargar.com
Industrial cleaning compounds
President: Tim Reason
VP: Giulio Fraenza
Estimated Sales: $1 - 3 Million
Number Employees: 1-4
Number of Brands: 22
Number of Products: 22
Square Footage: 60000
Parent Co: Chargar Corporation
Brands:
Fabulene

22129 (HQ)Eliason Corporation
9229 Shaver Rd
Kalamazoo, MI 49024 269-327-7003
Fax: 269-327-7006 800-828-3655
doors@eliasoncorp.com www.eliasoncorp.com
Manufacturer and exporter of swing doors and night covers for open refrigerated cases and freezers.
Owner: Edwanda Eliason
Marketing Director: Michael Woolsey
Estimated Sales: $5 - 10 Million
Number Employees: 50-99
Square Footage: 175000
Other Locations:
Eliason Corporation
Woodland CA
Brands:
Easy Swing
Econo-Cover
Eliason

22130 Elisa Technologies
2501 NW 66th Court
Gainesville, FL 32653 352-337-3929
Fax: 352-337-3928 info@elisa-tek.com
www.elisa-tek.com
Food testing kits and lab services, meat species and food allergies
President: Bruce Ritter
Laboratory Scientist: James McIden
Estimated Sales: $500,000 - $1 Million
Number Employees: 10-19

22131 Elite Forming Design Solutions, Inc.
15 Commerce Court
Rome, GA 30161 706-232-3021
Fax: 706-232-3121 info@eliteforming.com
www.eliteforming.com
Manufacturer and supplier of OEM plates and parts.

22132 Elite Spice
7151 Montevideo Rd
Jessup, MD 20794 410-796-1900
Fax: 410-379-6933 800-232-3531
jbrandt@elitespice.com www.elitespice.com
Founded in 1988. Spice, seasoning, capsicum, oil & oleoresin, and dehydrated vegetable producer.
Owner/CEO: Isaac Samuel
CFO/Human Resources Director: Debbie Ingle
R&D Director: Leslie Krause
Quality Control Directory: Dave Anthony
Marketing Executive: Kathy Lyons
Sales Executive: Paul Kurpe
VP/Plant Manager: George Mayer
Purchasing Manager: Margie Schneidman
Estimated Sales: $20-50 Million
Number Employees: 260
Square Footage: 11000
Type of Packaging: Private Label

22133 Elite Trading Worldwide
P.O.Box 320688
Brooklyn, NY 11232-0688 718-369-3664
Fax: 718-369-7125 888-354-8388
sales@elite88.com www.elite88.com

Manufacturer and importer of beechwood and metal chairs and high chairs
Owner: Emanuel Toporowitz
Sales/Marketing Director: Ricky Wolbrom
Estimated Sales: $10-20 Million
Number Employees: 20-49
Square Footage: 50000

22134 **Elkay Plastics Company**
6000 Sheila St
Commerce, CA 90040 323-722-7073
Fax: 323-869-3911 800-809-8393
info@elkayplastics.com www.elkayplastics.com
Manufacturer and distributor of flexible polyethylene packaging
President: Louis Chertkow
CFO: Stuart Hortwiz
Quality Control: Christina Lucas
Estimated Sales: $20 - 50 Million
Number Employees: 5-9

22135 **Ellab**
1299 Del Mar Ave
San Jose, CA 95128-3548 408-938-0506
Fax: 408-280-0979 888-533-5588
sales@phfspec.com www.phfspec.com
Estimated Sales: $300,000-500,000
Number Employees: 1-4

22136 **Ellab**
Trollesmindealle 25
Hilleroed, DK 3400 454-452-0500
Fax: 454-453-0505 info@ellab.com
www.ellab.com
Temperature, pressure and relative humidity monitoring
Estimated Sales: $1-2.5 Million
Number Employees: 1-4

22137 **Ellay**
6900 Elm St
Commerce, CA 90040-2625 323-725-2974
Fax: 323-725-6466 mark.stern@solvay.com
www.renolit.com
Manufacturer and exporter of plastic materials including PVC films, compounds and roll stock for packaging and devices requiring food grade applications
President: Richard Sternthar
Finance Executive: Laurie Dunbar
VP Sales: Mark Stern
Estimated Sales: $10-20 Million
Number Employees: 100-249
Square Footage: 85000

22138 **Ellehammer Industries**
20146 100 A Avenue
Langley, BC V1M 3G2
Canada 604-882-9326
Fax: 604-882-9703 www.pliantcorp.com
Manufacturer and exporter of plastic bags and film
Quality Control: Jack Tucker
Plant Manager: Ralph Schnitzer
Number Employees: 50

22139 **Ellenco**
4419 41st Street
Brentwood, MD 20722-1515 301-927-4370
Fax: 301-927-4376 salesinfo@ellenco.com
www.ellenco.com
Manufacturer and exporter of fire alarm systems
VP: Bob Harding
Estimated Sales: $1 - 5 Million
Number Employees: 20-50

22140 **Ellett Industries**
1575 Kingsway Avenue
Port Coquitlam, BC V3C 4E5
Canada 604-941-8211
Fax: 604-941-6854 ellett@ellett.bc.ca
www.ellett.bc.ca
Manufacturer and exporter of fabricated alloy metal, tanks, stills, heat exchangers, vessels, stainless steel and titanium pipes and fittings
President/CEO: J Ellett
Vice President: Bob Gill
Sales Director: L Osberg
Production Manager: David Clift
Purchasing Manager: Don Young
Estimated Sales: $20 Million
Number Employees: 100-250
Square Footage: 120000

22141 **Ellingers**
PO Box 450
Sheboygan, WI 53082-0450 920-457-7746
Fax: 920-457-2972 888-287-8906
jenny@ellingerswoodproducts.com
www.agatized.com
Manufacturer and exporter of wood bowls, bar trays, cutting boards and wood bowl gift sets.
President: Willard Neese
Sales Director: Jennifer Stafford
Estimated Sales: $800,000
Number Employees: 15
Number of Products: 35
Square Footage: 25000
Type of Packaging: Consumer, Food Service

22142 **Elliot Horowitz Associates**
675 Third Avenue 23rd Floor
New York, NY 10017 212-972-7500
Fax: 212-972-7050 EHAreps4U@aol.com
www.elliothorowitz.com
Manufacturers' representative for food service equipment and supplies including smallwares and heavy cooking and freezing equipment
Owner: Elliot Horowitz
Estimated Sales: $.5 - 1 million
Number Employees: 1-4
Type of Packaging: Food Service
Brands:
Brewmatic
Doyen
Piper Industries

22143 **Elliot Lee**
445 Central Ave Unit 100
Cedarhurst, NY 11516 516-569-9595
Fax: 516-569-8088 sales@misterpromotion.com
www.misterpromotion.com
Manufacturer, importer and wholesaler/distributor of advertising specialties including sign holders, awards, badges, bags, cups, pens and plaques
President/CFO: Victor Deutsch
CFO: Elliot Deutsch
Marketing Director: Elliot Deutsch
Estimated Sales: Below $5 Million
Number Employees: 5-9

22144 **Elliott Bay Espresso**
950 NW Elford Drive
Seattle, WA 98177-4125 206-467-6838
Fax: 206-467-6819
Espresso machines and accessories

22145 **Elliott Manufacturing Company Inc.**
PO Box 11277
Fresno, CA 93772 559-233-6235
Fax: 559-233-9833 elliottmfg@elliott-mfg.com
www.elliott-mfg.com
Manufacturer and exporter of date and raisin processing machinery and olive, date and prune pitters; also, packaging machinery including erectors, sealers, cartoners and case packers
President, Chief Executive Officer: Terry Aluisi
National Sales Manager: John Rea
Estimated Sales: $1-5 Million
Square Footage: 120000

22146 **Elliott-Williams Company**
3500 E 20th St
Indianapolis, IN 46218 317-635-1660
Fax: 317-453-1977 800-428-9303
ew@elliott-williams.com
www.elliottwilliams.com
Manufacturer and exporter of blast chillers, walk-in coolers, freezers and refrigerators; also, pre-fabricated refrigerated warehouses
Owner: Stuart Mc Keehan
CFO: R Scott
Purchasing Manager: K McCoy
Estimated Sales: $20-50 Million
Number Employees: 100-249
Square Footage: 100000
Brands:
Correctchill
Faster Freezer

22147 **Elm Packaging Company**
5837 Distribution Dr
Memphis, TN 38141-8204 901-795-2711
Fax: 901-795-8035 www.tekni-plex.com
Foam carry out containers
President: Kenneth Baker
CFO: Glean Davis
Plant Manager: Rick Nelson
Estimated Sales: $20 - 30 Million
Number Employees: 100-249

22148 **Elmar Industries**
P.O.Box 245
Depew, NY 14043 716-681-5650
Fax: 716-681-4660 800-433-3562
elmar@worldnet.att.net
www.elmarworldwide.com
Filling machines: rotary piston (both rotary and vertical valve), bottom fill, gravity, true monoblock volumetric pocket, and vacuum syruper product fillers
President: Mark Dahlquist
Estimated Sales: $10-20 000,000
Number Employees: 50-99

22149 **Elmar Worldwide**
P.O.Box 245
Depew, NY 14043-0245 716-681-5650
Fax: 716-681-4660 800-433-3562
elmar@worldnet.att.net
www.elmarworldwide.com
Manufacturer, exporter and designer of rotary valve piston fillers, multi-flex particulate fillers, vacuum syrupers and monoblock systems; also, re-manufacturing, R&D, computer/electronic line control systems, product testing andflush-in place systems
President: Mark Dahlquist
CEO: Martin Jolden, Jr.
CFO: Linda Gregorio
Sales: Tom Depczynski
Estimated Sales: $10 - 20 Million
Number Employees: 50-99
Brands:
Elmar

22150 **Elmark Packaging**
901 S Bolmar St Bldg 1j
West Chester, PA 19382 610-692-2455
Fax: 610-692-8793 800-670-9688
sales@elmarkpkg.com www.elmarkpkg.com
Provider of equipment, products and knowledge to enable customers to add information to their products and packages in plant, on-line with self-adhesive labels and/or all forms of printing
President: Jeff Baughan
Estimated Sales: Below $5 Million
Number Employees: 5-9
Square Footage: 8200
Brands:
Mini-Pro

22151 **Elmeco SRL**
5700 Ferguson Road
Suite 8
Bartlett, TN 38134-4557 901-385-0490
Fax: 901-373-7091
Slush machines
President: David Roberts
Number Employees: 4

22152 **Elmo Rietschle - A Gardner Denver Product**
1800 Gardner Expressway
Qunicy, IL 62305 217-222-5400
Fax: 217-228-8243 www.elmo-rietschle.com
Compressors and pumps for the beverage and food production industries.
President & CEO: Barry Pennypacker
Chairman Board Of Directors: Frank Hansen

22153 **Elmwood Sensors**
500 Narragansett Park Dr
Pawtucket, RI 00861 401-727-1300
Fax: 401-728-5390 800-356-9663
linda.lundgren@invensys.com
www.elmwoodsensors.com
Manufacturer and exporter of thermostats and controls
VP/General Manager: Steven Fof
Estimated Sales: $50-100 Million
Number Employees: 100-250
Square Footage: 160000
Parent Co: Fasco

22154 **Elo Touch Systems**
301 Constitution Dr
Menlo Park, CA 94025-1110 650-361-4800
Fax: 650-361-4721 800-557-1458
eloinfo@elotouch.com www.elotouch.com

Manufacturer and exporter of operator interfaces and point of sale systems
General Manager: Mark Mendenhall
Chief Executive Officer: Craig Witsoe
CFO: Roxi Wen
Vice President, Chief Technical Officer: Brunó Thuillier
VP, Corporate Development: Sharon Segev
VP, Global Quality: Anita Chang
Manager of Marketing: Fumiko Sasaki
Vice President of Global Sales: Sean Miller
Vice President of Operations: Mike Moran
Number Employees: 500-999
Parent Co: Amp
Type of Packaging: Food Service
Brands:
Ad-Touch
Info Board
Smart Frame
Total Touch
Touch In a Box

22155 Elopak
30000 S Hill Rd
New Hudson, MI 48165 248-486-4600
Fax: 248-486-4601 hyengese@elopakus.com
www.elopak.com
Manufacturer and exporter of cartons, aseptic and plastic pouches, form/fill/seal systems and packaging equipment for paper and plastic; importer of filling machinery
Executive VP: Jorg Thiels
Marketing Director: Harold Engeset
Estimated Sales: $20-50 Million
Number Employees: 100-249
Square Footage: 175000
Parent Co: Elopak A/S
Brands:
Elopouch
Pure-Pak
Unifill

22156 Elreha Controls Corporation
2510 Terminal Drive South
St Petersburg, FL 33712 727-327-6236
Fax: 727-323-7336 sales@elreha.com
www.elreha.com
Electronic timers, cooking computers and thermometers
President: Abdul Hamadeh
General Manager: Bonnie DelGrosso
Estimated Sales: $5 - 10 Million
Number Employees: 100-249
Square Footage: 260000

22157 Elrene Home Fashions
261 5th Ave
New York, NY 10016-7794 212-213-0425
Fax: 212-481-1738 elrene@elrene.com
www.elrene.com
Place mats and tablecloths including plastic and fabric
President: Mark Siegel
CEO: Mark Siegel
CFO and QC: Ron Selber
Estimated Sales: $2.5 - 5 Million
Number Employees: 100-249
Parent Co: Elrene Manufacturing Company

22158 (HQ)Elro Sign Company
400 W Walnut St
Gardena, CA 90248 310-380-7444
Fax: 310-380-7452 800-927-4555
sales@elrosigns.com www.elrosigns.com
Electric, plastic, neon and metal signs; installation service available nationwide
President: Max Rhodes
VP: Frank Rhodes
Estimated Sales: $4 Million
Number Employees: 20-49
Square Footage: 72000
Other Locations:
Elro Sign Co.
Marietta GA

22159 Elwell Parker
4200 Casteel Drive
Coraopolis, PA 15108 216-432-0638
Fax: 216-881-7555 800-272-9953
nick@elwellparker.com www.elwellparker.com
Manufacturer and exporter of material handling equipment including rider style, electric fork and platform trucks
Sales and Marketing: Nick Marshall
VP Sales/Marketing: Jeff Leggett
Manager Sales/Parts/Service/Support: Curt Roupe
Estimated Sales: $3 - 5 Million
Number Employees: 5-9

22160 Elwood Safety Company
2180 Elmwood Ave
Buffalo, NY 14216 716-877-6622
Fax: 716-874-2110 866-326-6060
leslie@elwoodsafety.com
www.elwoodsafety.com
Manufacturer and exporter of protective clothing including aprons, coveralls, sweatbands, lab coats and flame retardant clothing; also, voltage testers, food and beverage coolers and filtration systems
Estimated Sales: $1 - 5 Million
Number Employees: 10-19
Square Footage: 15000

22161 Embee Sunshade Company
722 Metropolitan Ave # 1
Brooklyn, NY 11211-3722 718-387-8566
Fax: 718-782-2642 info@embeesunshade.com
www.embeesunshade.com
Umbrellas for carts and tables
Owner: Barnett S Brickner
Estimated Sales: $2.5-5 Million
Number Employees: 10-19
Square Footage: 48000

22162 Ember-Glo
4140 West Victoria Street
Chicago, IL 60646-6727 773-604-8714
Fax: 773-604-4070 866-705-0515
info@emberglo.com www.emberglo.com
Manufacturer and exporter of commercial cooking equipment including gas broilers and steam cookers
President: Teryl A Stanger
Marketing Director: J Kelderhouse
National Sales Manager: Karen Trice
Estimated Sales: $3,000,000
Number Employees: 100-249
Number of Brands: 1
Square Footage: 320000
Parent Co: Midco International
Type of Packaging: Food Service
Brands:
Ember-Glo

22163 Emblem & Badge
123 Dyer Street
Suite 2
Providence, RI 02903-3907 401-365-1265
Fax: 401-365-1263 800-875-5444
sales@recognition.com www.recognition.com
Manufacturer, importer and exporter of plaques, trophies, advertising novelties, name badges, desk sets, glassware, custom awards, etc
President: David Resnik
Vice President: Mike Hersherits
Sales: RI Johnston
Number Employees: 50-99
Square Footage: 100000
Type of Packaging: Bulk
Brands:
Awards America
Emblem & Badge

22164 Embro Manufacturing Company
400 Nassau Street E
East Canton, OH 44730-1330 330-489-3500
Fax: 330-488-3131
O.E.M. wire forms, point of purchase and displays
Customer Service: Joni Nelson
Production Manager: Gary Wilson
Estimated Sales: $2.5-5 Million
Number Employees: 20-49
Square Footage: 68000

22165 Emco Industrial Plastics
99 Commerce Rd
Cedar Grove, NJ 07009 973-239-0202
Fax: 973-239-1595 800-292-9906
mailbox@emcoplastics.com
www.emcoplastics.com
Supplier of plastic sheet, rod, tubing and films including plexiglass, cutting boards, and vinyl door strip. Manufacturer of plastic point of purchase displays including bulk food containers, bagel bins, pastry cases, candy binsframes, sign holders, and sneeze guards.
President: James Mc Namara
Vice President: Mark Mercadante
Sales Manager: Jim McNamara
Estimated Sales: $20-50 Million
Number Employees: 50-99
Square Footage: 50000
Type of Packaging: Food Service

22166 Emerald Packaging
33050 Western Ave
Union City, CA 94587 510-429-5700
Fax: 510-429-5715 fkevin@empack.com
www.empack.com
Polyethylene bags
President: Kevin Kelly
Estimated Sales: $20-50 Million
Number Employees: 100-249

22167 Emerling International Foods
2381 Fillmore Ave
Suite 1
Buffalo, NY 14214-2197 716-833-7381
Fax: 716-833-7386 pemerling@emerfood.com
www.emerlinginternational.com
We supply food manufacturers and food service customers worldwide (since 1988) with bulk ingredients including: Fruits & Vegetables; Juice Concentrates; Herbs & Spices; Oils & Vinegars; Flavors & Colors; Honey & Molasses. We alsoproduce PURE MAPLE SYRUP.
President: J P Emerling
Sales: Peter Emerling
Public Relations: Jenn Burke
Estimated Sales: $10-20 Million
Number Employees: 20-49
Square Footage: 250000

22168 Emerson Electronic Motion Controls
1365 Park Road
Chanhassen, MN 55317-9527 612-474-1116
Fax: 612-474-8711 800-397-3786
applener@minn.net www.emersonemc.com
Motion control applications for the packaging line process
President: Tim Erhart
Marketing Manager: Karl Meier
Number Employees: 100
Square Footage: 160000
Parent Co: Emerson Electric Company

22169 Emerson Electronic Motion Controls
12005 Technology Dr
Eden Prairie, MN 55344-3620 952-995-8000
Fax: 952-995-8020 800-397-3786
info@emersonct.com www.emersonct.com
Programmable motion controls
Estimated Sales: $20-50 Million
Number Employees: 100-249

22170 Emerson Motion Control
12005 Technology Dr
Eden Prairie, MN 55344 952-995-8000
Fax: 952-995-8020 800-893-2321
info@emersonct.com
www.emersondrivesolutions.com
Number Employees: 100-249

22171 Emerson Power Transmission
1248 E 2nd St
Maysville, KY 41056 606-564-2011
Fax: 606-564-2022 sdonovan@emerson-ept.com
www.emerson-ept.com
Conveying products: motorized and traditional conveyor pulleys, conveyor modules, module plastic belts, conveying chain. Bearing products: beverage bearings, high temperature bearings
President: Eugene Yarussi
Vice President: Ronald Barker
Estimated Sales: $164 Million
Number Employees: 1,000-4,999
Number of Brands: 8
Number of Products: 28

22172 Emery Thompson Machine &Supply Company
15350 Flight Path Drive
Brooksville, FL 34604-6861 718-588-7300
Fax: 352-796-0720
STEVE@EMERYTHOMPSON.COM
www.emerythompson.com
Manufacturer, importer and exporter of ice cream, Italian ice, frozen lemonade and frozen custard making machinery
President: Steve Thompson
CEO: Ted Thompson
Estimated Sales: $2.5-5 Million
Number Employees: 20-49
Square Footage: 180000

22173 Emery Winslow Scale Company
73 Cogwheel Ln
Seymour, CT 06483-3930 203-881-9333
Fax: 203-881-9477 sales@emerywinslow.com
www.emerywinslow.com
Industrial scale manufacturer
Owner/CEO: Walter Young
CFO/President: Bill Fischer
VP/Marketing: Rudi Baisch
Research & Development: Sam Sagarsee
Sales: David Young
Operations Manager: Bill Rosser
Plant Manager: Jim Evinger
Purchasing Manager: Jonathan Young
Estimated Sales: $20 Million+
Number Employees: 50-99
Number of Brands: 3
Square Footage: 120000
Other Locations:
Pennsylvania Scale Company
Lancaster PA
Brands:
Emery
Flattop
Genesis
Hydrostatics
Hytronics
Lifemount
Totalizer
Weighsquare
Winslow

22174 Emico
13570 Larwin Circle
Santa Fe Springs, CA 90670 562-926-9600
Fax: 562-926-9611 info@emicoinc.com
www.emicoinc.com
Magnetic pan indexer, dough maker, zig-zag board rotary and boards, bread moulder, up-down pan indexer, wet onion applicator, bread and bun cooler, and screw pan; parts and service
Estimated Sales: $1 - 5 Million

22175 Emiliomiti
219 9th St
San Francisco, CA 94103-3806 415-621-1909
Fax: 415-621-4613 866-867-2782
info@pastabiz.com www.pastabiz.com
Wholesaler/distributor of espresso coffee machines, pasta machines and wood burning brick pizza ovens; serving the food service market
Owner: Emilio Mitidieri
CEO: Emilio Mitidieri
Estimated Sales: 900000
Number Employees: 10-19
Number of Brands: 5
Number of Products: 16
Square Footage: 12000
Brands:
Capitani
Emiollomiti
Libitalia
Pastabiz
Technomachine

22176 Emjac Industries
1075 Hialeah Dr
Hialeah, FL 33010 305-883-2194
Fax: 305-883-2197
Walk-in coolers and freezers
President: David Dorta
Estimated Sales: $20 - 50 Million
Number Employees: 100-249

22177 Emmeti
101 Sherwood Drive
Boalsburg, PA 16827-1612 816-466-2781
Fax: 816-466-2782 emmeti@nauticom.net
www.emmeti-spa.com
Fully automatic, floor level, bulk palletizers, intelligent bottle stacker, automatic layer pad, top frame and empty pallet inserters
President: Kevin Zarnick
Marketing Manager/Owner: Fausto Savazzi
Sales Manager and PET Industry: Paolo Biondi
V P: Beth Zarnick-duffy
Sales Manager: Fabrizio Boschi
Technical Manager: Luis Garcia

22178 Emmeti USA
7320 East Fletcher Avenue
Tampa, FL 33637 813-490-6252
Fax: 813-490-6253 emmetiusa@emmetiusa.com
www.emmetiusa.com
President: Kevin Zarnick
Vice President: Fausto Savazzi
USA Sales Manager: Beth Zarnick-Duffy

22179 Emoshun
10022 6th Street
Rancho Cucamonga, CA 91730-5746909-484-9559
Fax: 909-484-9560
Insulated bags and bottles
Estimated Sales: $1 - 5 Million

22180 Empire Bakery Equipment
1 C Enterprise Place
Hicksville, NY 11801-5347 516-681-1510
Fax: 516-681-1510 800-878-4070
info@empirebake.com www.empirebake.com
Distributor of mixers, dough dividers, rounders, moulders, stampers, bagel machines, retarders, freezers, refrigerators, ovens, display cases, tables, slicers, etc
Owner: S Wechsler
VP: C Zarate
Estimated Sales: Below $8 Million
Number Employees: 20-49
Square Footage: 64000

22181 Empire Candle
2925 Fairfax Trfy
Kansas City, KS 66115 913-621-4555
Fax: 913-621-3444 800-231-9398
customerservice@empirecandle.com
www.empirecandle.com
Candles including scented and seasonal citronella
Owner: Rick Langley
CEO: Drummond Crews
CFO: Mick Buttress
Marketing: Brenda Cherpitel
Operations Manager: Eric Coulter
Purchasing: Larry Palmer
Estimated Sales: $10 - 20 Million
Number Employees: 50-99

22182 Empire Container Corporation
1161 E Walnut St
Carson, CA 90746-1382 323-537-8190
Fax: 323-604-4880 www.empirecontainercorp.com
Designer and manufacturer of corrugated packaging displays, industrial containers, cardboard counter displays, bulk boxes, cardboard sheets, marketing displays, pallet display, point of purchase displays, shipping containers, shippingboxes and custom consumer packaging.
President: Lewis Eagle
VP: Norman Eagle
Estimated Sales: $10 - 20 Million
Number Employees: 50-99
Type of Packaging: Consumer, Food Service, Private Label, Bulk

22183 Empire Safe Company
6 E 39th St
New York, NY 10016-0112 212-226-2255
Fax: 212-684-5550 info@empiresafe.com
www.empiresafe.com
Safes including burglar resistant and cash depositing
President: Richard Krasilovsky
CFO: Andy Genett
Director of Operations: Mark Rubin
Estimated Sales: $5-10 Million
Number Employees: 5-9
Square Footage: 80000

22184 Empire Screen Printing, Inc.
N5206 Marco Rd
Onalaska, WI 54650 608-783-3301
Fax: 608-783-3306 dougb@empierscreen.com
www.empirescreen.com
Empire is a leader in the latest printing processes including flexographic, screen & digital printing, as well as doming. Empire is a supplier to the appliance, retail, food, and beverage industries. Products include retail signagepackage labels, and marketing support items.
President: Johns Freismuth
CEO: James Brush
Vice President: James Schwinefus
Research & Development: Keith Cole
Quality Control: Steve Johnson
Marketing Director: Douglas Billings
Sales Director: Kathleen Cuellar
Public Relations: Douglas Billings
Operations Manager: John Johnsonth
Plant Manager: Lee Vieth
Purchasing Manager: Lori Taube
Estimated Sales: $25 Million
Number Employees: 265
Number of Brands: 2
Square Footage: 150000
Type of Packaging: Food Service, Private Label

22185 Empire Sweets Oswego Growers and Shippers
103 Gardenier Rd
Oswego, NY 13126-5741
Fax: 315-343-5371 info@blandfarms.com
www.empire-sweets.com
Empire Sweets Onions.
President: John Zappala
Vice President: Sam Zappala Jr
Vice President: Jim Zappala
Type of Packaging: Food Service

22186 Emtrol
425 E Berlin Rd
York, PA 17408-8810 717-846-4000
Fax: 717-846-3624 800-634-4927
cgales@emtrol.com
www.weldonmachinetool.com
Manufacturer, importer and exporter of material handling equipment and controls, plant automation equipment and custom warehouse/inventory software
President: George Sipe
Executive VP: Matthew Anater
VP Sales/Marketing: Nicholas Selch
Estimated Sales: $20-50 Million
Number Employees: 50-99
Square Footage: 52000

22187 Emulso Corporation
2750 Kenmore Ave
Tonawanda, NY 14150 716-854-2889
Fax: 716-854-2809 800-724-7667
info@emulso.com www.emulso.com
General and specialty cleaning compounds
President: James Minneci
VP: Marie Glenn
Estimated Sales: $5-10 Million
Number Employees: 5-9
Square Footage: 17000
Type of Packaging: Private Label, Bulk
Brands:
Emulso

22188 En-Hanced Products, Inc.
229 E Broadway Ave
Westerville, OH 43081 614-882-7400
Fax: 614-882-7549 800-783-7400
en-hancedproducts.com
Food grade elevators and conveyors; also, hand and power seed cleaners.
President: Jim Hance
Sales Director: Dennis James
Production Manager: Tim Woodruff
Purchasing Manager: Dennis James
Estimated Sales: $750,000
Number Employees: 7
Square Footage: 28000

22189 EnWave Corporation
1066 W Hastings Street
Suite 2000
Vancouver, BC V6E 3X2
Canada 604-822-4425
Fax: 604-806-6112 tdurance@enwave.net
www.enwave.net

Dehydration of food, live or active bulk liquids, and sensitive pharmaceuticals.
President/Co-CEO: John McNicol
Chairman/Co-CEO: Tim Durance
CFO: Salvador Miranda
EVP Sales: Beenu Anand
Estimated Sales: $127 Million
Number Employees: 5
Square Footage: 4736

22190 **Encapsulation Systems**
1489 Baltimore Pike
Suite 109
Springfield, PA 19064-3958 610-543-0800
Fax: 610-543-0688 www.encsys.com
Manufacturers of specially controlled release products for use in the pharmaceutical and medical-device field
President and CEO: Bruce Retting
Executive Vice President, Licensing: Cyril Burke
Number Employees: 10

22191 **Encompass Ind./Merch Services of Texas**
2425 Dillard Street
Grand Prairie, TX 75051-1004 972-730-3626
Fax: 972-352-5083 800-299-4824
joseph.ford@polkme.com www.encompass.com
Construction and design services
President: Ken Polk
CFO: Frank Dauglous
Quality Control: Gory Palito
Executive VP Marketing/Sales: Bill O'Dwyer
Estimated Sales: $250 Million
Number Employees: 1700

22192 **Encore Glass**
4345 Industrial Way
Benicia, CA 94510 707-745-4444
Fax: 707-748-4444 sales@Encoreglass.com
www.encoreglass.com
Wine industry recycled equipment
Sales Director: Dave Hammond
Estimated Sales: $5-10 000,000
Number Employees: 40

22193 **Encore Paper Company**
1 River Street
South Glens Falls, NY 12803-4790 800-362-6735
Fax: 518-793-2650
Napkins, paper towels and toilet paper
Director Marketing/National Accounts: Scott Milburn
Sr VP Sales/Marketing: Don Lewis
Estimated Sales: $50-100 Million
Number Employees: 250-499
Brands:
Ovation

22194 **Encore Plastics**
P.O.Box 3208
Huntington Beach, CA 92605 714-893-7889
Fax: 714-897-7968 888-822-8763
info@encoreplastics.com
www.encoreplastics.com
Manufacturer and exporter of beverageware and plastic stemware
President: Richard Harvey
Quality Control: David Martin
VP: Donald Okada
Estimated Sales: $500,000-$1 Million
Number Employees: 10
Parent Co: Donoco Industries

22195 **Endress & Hauser**
P.O.Box 246
Greenwood, IN 46142-0246 317-535-7138
Fax: 317-535-1489 800-428-4344
info@us.endress.com www.us.endress.com
Electronic process control instruments
Manager: Todd Lucey
VP Controller: Nancy Winter
Executive VP: Joseph Schaffer
VP Manufacturing: Phil Tumey
Estimated Sales: $20-50 Million
Number Employees: 250-499
Square Footage: 78000
Parent Co: Endress & Hauser Consult

22196 **Endurart**
20 W 22nd St
New York, NY 10010-5804 212-779-8522
Fax: 212-691-4751
Advertising novelties and specialties including awards, trophies, embedments and coins
Manager: William Kalsman
Estimated Sales: $5-10 Million
Number Employees: 20-49

22197 **Enercon Industries Corporation**
PO Box 773
Menomonee Falls, WI 53052 262-255-6070
Fax: 262-255-7784 info@enerconind.com
www.enerconind.com
Corona treaters and power supplies
Owner: Don Nimmer
CEO: Donald Nimmer
Estimated Sales: $10-20 000,000
Number Employees: 100-249

22198 **(HQ)Enercon Systems**
P.O.Box 4030
Elyria, OH 44036 440-323-7080
Fax: 440-323-5734 enercon@earthlink.net
www.enerconsystems.com
Manufacturer and exporter of process temperature control systems, fluid heat systems and incinerators
President: David Hoecke
Vice President: John Somodi
Estimated Sales: $3 Million
Number Employees: 20-49
Square Footage: 50000
Brands:
Conserthern
Super-Trol
Ventomatic

22199 **Enerfab, Inc.**
4955 Spring Grove Ave
Cincinnati, OH 45232 513-641-0500
Fax: 513-482-7767 www.enerfab.com
Stainless and carbon steel tanks, bulk aseptic storage systems, epoxy tank linings, sanitary manways and gasket materials
President & Chief Operating Officer: Jeffrey Hock
Executive Chairman & Chief Exec. Officer: Wendell Bell
Chief Financial Officer: Daniel Sillies
Estimated Sales: $251 Million
Number Employees: 2200
Square Footage: 250000
Brands:
Lastiglas/Munkadur

22200 **Energy Saving Devices**
1751 Highway 36 E
Saint Paul, MN 55109-2108 651-222-0849
Fax: 651-222-4626
Commercial and industrial fluorescent and vapor tight lighting fixtures
President: Kerry Petersen
VP: Mike Holder
Estimated Sales: Below $5 Million
Number Employees: 5 to 9

22201 **Energy Sciences**
42 Industrial Way
Wilmington, MA 01887-3471 978-694-9046
Fax: 978-694-9046 tmclaughlin@ebeam.com
www.ebean.com
Manufactures laser bean machinery that are used to make bags used in the food industry
President: Harvey Clough
CEO: Gsunio Kadayashi
Sales Director: Brian Sullivan
Estimated Sales: $50 - 100 Million
Number Employees: 50-99

22202 **Energy Sciences Inc.**
42 Industrial Way
Wilmington, MA 01887 978-694-9000
Fax: 978-694-9046 www.ebeam.com
Manufacturer and exporter of electron beam processing machinery used for drying and curing packaging materials, printed foil, etc
President: Tsuneo Kobayashi
Manager: Harvey Clough
Accounts: Sharon Lagos
Chief Operating Officer: Ed Maguire
Estimated Sales: $7 Million
Number Employees: 50
Square Footage: 52000
Parent Co: Iwasaki Electric

22203 **Energymaster**
105 Liberty St
Walled Lake, MI 48390 248-624-6900
Fax: 248-624-6975 www.energymasterusa.com
Manufacturer and exporter of energy conservation equipment for heating and cooling, summer/winter ventilation and make-up air
President: Erik Hall
Estimated Sales: $2.5 - 5 Million
Number Employees: 10-19
Square Footage: 3600
Type of Packaging: Consumer, Food Service
Brands:
Energymaster
Seasonmaster
Ventilation

22204 **Enerquip, LLC**
P.O.Box 467
611 North Road
Medford, WI 54451 715-748-5888
Fax: 715-748-6484 ronherman@enerquip.com
www.enerquip.com
Designer and fabricator of stainless steel shell and tube heat exchangers and custom components.
President & CEO: Jeannie Deml
Parts and Service: Sue Rhyner
Quality Control: John Barna
Director of Sales & Marketing: Ron Herman
Thermal Design and Inside Sales: Ron Herman
Number Employees: 41

22205 **Engineered Automation**
5134 W River Drive NE
Comstock Park, MI 49321-8522 616-784-4227
Fax: 616-784-6225 engaut@engaut.com
Packaging machinery including rotary lidders, puck inserters and removers and rotary overcappers
National Sales Manager: Suzanne Farrell
Number Employees: 20

22206 **Engineered Plastics**
211 Chase St
Gibsonville, NC 27249-0227 336-449-4121
Fax: 336-449-6352 800-711-1740
engplas@triad.rr.com www.engplas.com
Illuminated buffet and ice sculpture display equipment, acrylic serving bowls and trays and specialty display items
Sales Manager: Robert Ratliff
Food Service Manager: W Mottinger
Estimated Sales: $2.5-5 Million
Number Employees: 20-49
Square Footage: 75000
Brands:
Glo-Ice

22207 **Engineered Products**
12202 Missouri Bottom Rd
Hazelwood, MO 63042-2318 314-731-5744
Fax: 314-731-5744 800-474-1474
tdaugherty@enprod.com www.epico.com
President: Dave Wendel
Estimated Sales: $10 - 20 Million
Number Employees: 50-99

22208 **(HQ)Engineered Products**
12202 Missouri Bottom Rd
Hazelwood, MO 63042-2318 314-731-5744
Fax: 314-731-5744 www.epico.com
Custom plastic injection molding including containers
President: Dave Wendel
VP/General Manager: Ron McGee
Estimated Sales: $10-20 Million
Number Employees: 50-99
Square Footage: 48000
Other Locations:
Engineered Products
Dequeen AR

22209 **Engineered Products & Systems**
141 Ben Burton Cir
Bogart, GA 30622-1791 706-543-8101
Fax: 706-543-7934 mike@epsifillers.com
www.epsifillers.com
Executive Director: Mike Vandurnen
Estimated Sales: $1 - 3 Million
Number Employees: 5-9

22210 **Engineered Products Corporation**
355 Woodruff Rd Ste 204
Greenville, SC 29607 864-234-4888
Fax: 864-234-4860 800-868-0145
sales@engprod.com www.engprod.com

Manufacturer and exporter of pallet storage racks, gravity flow storage systems and conveyors; also, turnkey warehouse engineering services available
Manager: David Shupe
Sales/Marketing Executive: Charles Rouse
Purchasing Agent: Allen Griffith
Estimated Sales: $5-10 Million
Number Employees: 100-249
Square Footage: 200000
Parent Co: Gower
Brands:
Deepflo
Durabit
Pushbak Cart
Selectrak
Traytrak

22211 **Engineered Products Group**
P.O.Box 8050
Madison, WI 53708 608-222-3484
Fax: 608-222-9314 800-626-3111
www.boumatic.com
Manufacturer and exporter of heat transfer equipment, jacketed shells, troughs, baffles and tanks, plates for fluid bed coolers and heaters, process vessels and storage and mixing tanks; also, carbon steel, stainless stell, titaniumand other alloys available
Owner: John Kotts
Sales: R Albrecht
Estimated Sales: $1-2.5 Million
Number Employees: 250-499
Parent Co: DEC International

22212 **Engineered Security Systems**
1 Indian Ln
Towaco, NJ 07082 973-257-0555
Fax: 973-257-0550 800-742-1263
info@engineeredsecurity.com
www.engineeredsecurity.com
Manufacturer and exporter of computer based security systems; closed circuit TV monitoring available
ChairMan of the Board: Laurice R George
Estimated Sales: $20-50 Million
Number Employees: 50-99
Square Footage: 8500

22213 **Engineered Systems & Designs**
119 Sandy Dr # A
Newark, DE 19713-1148 302-456-0446
Fax: 302-456-0441 esd@esdinc.com
www.esdinc.com
Wine industry laboratory equipment
President: Robert Spring
Estimated Sales: Below $5 Million
Number Employees: 1-4

22214 **Engineered Textile Products, Inc.**
P.O.Box 7474
715 Loeffler Street
Mobile, AL 36670 251-476-8001
Fax: 251-476-0956 800-222-8277
ken@etpinfo.com www.etpinfo.com
Commercial awnings
President: John K Robinson Jr
Estimated Sales: $1-2.5 Million
Number Employees: 20-49
Brands:
Artcraft

22215 **Engineering & ManagementConsultants**
742 Butternut Dr
Franklin Lakes, NJ 07417-2243 201-847-0748
Fax: 201-847-0748 rhmeeremc@aol.com
Consultant specializing in plant operations, production and inventory control, laboratory and technical activities, marketing, regulatory and financial affairs, processing functions, certification, etc
President: Richard H Meer
Estimated Sales: $1 - 5,000,000
Number Employees: 1-4

22216 **England Logistics**
4701 West 2100 South
Salt Lake City, UT 84120 801-972-2712
Fax: 801-977-5795 800-887-0764
info@englandlogistics.com
www.englandlogistics.com
Transportation firm providing local, short and long haul trucking; also, contract warehousing available
President: Dan England
CEO: Dean England
Senior Vice President Chief Financial Of: Keith Wallace
Vice President: Brandon Harrison
Executive Vice President of Corporate Sa: David Kramer

22217 **Englander Container Company**
701 Texas Central Parkway
Waco, TX 76712 254-776-2360
Fax: 254-776-1213 888-314-5259
info@englanderdzp.com
www.englandercontainer.com
Corrugated boxes
Chairman of the Board: Louis Englander
Chief Executive Officer: Marty Englander
Chief Financial Officer: Hal Whitaker
Executive Vice President: Steve Hager
Executive Vice President: Carl Renner
Customer Service Director: Sydney Williams
Logistics Manager: Tim Luke
Estimated Sales: $23 Million
Number Employees: 160
Square Footage: 100000

22218 **English Manufacturing Inc**
11292 Sunrise Park Dr
Rancho Cordova, CA 95742-6599
Fax: 916-638-9961 800-651-2711
sales@englishmfg.com www.englishmfg.com
Stainless steel sneeze gaurds and food guards, glass racks and partition posts.
President: Doug English
CFO: Diana English
Vice President: Jennifer Kogler
Research & Development: Shawn Rice
Quality Control: A J Wells
Marketing Director: Andrew Nelson
Sales Director: Cindy Lucas
Public Relations: Tim Kelly
Operations Manager: Mike Richardson
Production Manager: Sara Stefanik
Estimated Sales: $5,000,000
Number Employees: 20-49
Number of Brands: 2
Number of Products: 12
Square Footage: 10000
Type of Packaging: Food Service, Private Label
Brands:
Matrix Sneezegaurd

22219 **Engraph Label Group**
1187 Industrial Rd
Cold Spring, KY 41076-8799 859-781-6161
Fax: 859-781-6339 800-422-6633
www.cclabel.com
Wine industry label printers
President: Eric Schaffer
Estimated Sales: $3 - 5 Million
Number Employees: 10-19

22220 **Engraving Services Co.**
818 Port Road
Woodville South, SA 05011
engrave@engravingservices.com.au
www.engravingservices.com.au
Manufacturer and exporter of labels, nameplates, decals and engraved plastic and electric signs
Sales/Marketing Director: Peter Vasic
Production Manager: Jamie Smale
Estimated Sales: $5-10 Million
Number Employees: 50-99
Type of Packaging: Bulk

22221 **Engraving Specialists**
503 N Washington Ave
Royal Oak, MI 48067 248-542-2244
Fax: 248-542-1847 engspec@comcast.net
www.engravingspecialist.com
Engraved promotional items, award plaques and name badges; also, signage including ADA, directional, label, vinyl letter and logo available
Owner: Marc Milosevich
VP/Secretary/Treasurer: Dick Lang
Estimated Sales: $500,000-$1 Million
Number Employees: 1-4
Square Footage: 2800

22222 **Enhance Packaging Technologies**
201 S Blair Street
Whitby, ON L1N 5S6
Canada 905-668-5811
Fax: 905-666-7005
Liquid pouch form/fill/seal equipment including pasteurized and aseptic fillers; also, films matched to application and equipment
Marketing Development Manager (US Dairy): Harry Akamphuber
Marketing Development: Wayne Naumowich
Marketing Development: Joe Shields
Parent Co: DuPont Canada
Brands:
Mini-Sip

22223 **Enjay Converters Ltd.**
495 Ball Street
Cobourg, ON K9A
Canada 905-372-7373
Fax: 905-377-8066 800-427-5517
sales@enjay.com www.enjay.com
Manufactures a complete line of laminated and wrapped cake circles and shieets
President: Jay Cassidy
Number Employees: 10

22224 **Ennio International**
1005 N. Commons Drive
Aurora, IL 60504-4100 630-851-5808
Fax: 630-851-7744 info@enniousa.com
www.enniousa.com
Manufacturer and supplier of high quality netting and casings for the meat and poultry industries.
Director Of Sales: Ralph Schuster

22225 **Ennis Inc.**
2241 Presidential Parkway
Midlothian, TX 76065 972-775-9801
Fax: 800-645-8339 800-972-1069
HOTLine@ennis.com www.ennis.com
Restaurant supplies including menus, place mats and paper items
Chairman/CEO/President: Keith Walters
Vice President, Finance/CFO: Richard Travis Jr
Executive Vice President/Secretary: Michael Magill
Chief Tecnhology Officer: Irshad Ahmad
Chief Technology Officer: Irshad Ahmad
Vice President, Administration: Ronald Graham
Plant Manager: Mike Allen
Estimated Sales: $533 Million
Number Employees: 5,818

22226 **Enotech Corporation**
PO Box 576
Palo Alto, CA 94302-0576 650-851-2040
Fax: 650-851-2034 info@enotechusa.com
Wine industry equipment

22227 **Enpoco**
4263 Carolina Avenue
Suite J
Richmond, VA 23222-1400 804-228-9934
Fax: 703-668-1400 800-338-2581
Grease interceptors
President: Patrick Okeefe
CEO: Patrick Okeefe
Interceptor Production Manager: Roy Hetzler
Estimated Sales: $2.5-5 Million
Number Employees: 10-19
Parent Co: Watts Industries

22228 **Enrick Company**
150 E 1st St
Zumbrota, MN 55992 507-732-5215
Fax: 507-625-6570 rollorkari@yahoo.com
www.enrickco.com
Manufacturer and exporter of hand trucks, dollies and carts
Owner: Vince Small
Estimated Sales: $1-2.5 Million
Number Employees: 5-9

22229 **Ensign Ribbon Burners**
101 Secor Ln
PO Box 8369
Pelham, NY 10803-8369 914-738-0600
Fax: 914-738-0928 info@erbensign.com
www.erbensign.com
President: John F Cavallo
Vice President: James Pezzuto
Director of Sales: Mario Anelich

Estimated Sales: $3 - 5 Million
Number Employees: 10-19

22230 **Ensinger Hyde Company**
1 Main St
Grenloch, NJ 08032-9007 856-227-0500
Fax: 856-232-1754 dguckin@alhyde.com
www.shopforplastics.com
Manufacturer and exporter of plastic packaging materials
Director Sales/Marketing: Bruce Dickinson
Technical Director: Ken Schwartz
Estimated Sales: $10 - 20 Million
Number Employees: 50-99
Parent Co: Dana Her Corporation
Type of Packaging: Bulk

22231 **Entech Systems Corporation**
607 Maria St
Kenner, LA 70062 504-469-6541
Fax: 504-465-9192 800-783-6561
entech@msn.com www.entech.cc
Manufacturer and exporter of automatic ULV insect fogging systems for killing crawling and flying insects; also, semi-automatic and portable systems, sanitation audits and insecticides
President and CFO: Robert Drudge
Corporate Secretary: Gail Stumpf
Purchasing Manager: Marcus Curtis
Estimated Sales: Below $5 Million
Number Employees: 5-9
Square Footage: 8000
Brands:
Auto Fog
Entech Fog

22232 **Entergy's Teamwork Louisiana**
4809 Jefferson Highway
Jefferson, LA 70121-3126 504-840-2562
Fax: 504-840-2512 800-968-8243
laed@entergy.com www.entergy.com
Chairman of the Board; Chief Executive O: Wayne Leonard
Senior Vice President: Donna Jacobs
Estimated Sales: $1 - 5 Million

22233 **Enterprise**
7800 Sovereign Row
Dallas, TX 75247-4887 214-688-5223
Fax: 214-638-2016 800-527-9431
Estimated Sales: $10-20 000,000
Number Employees: 5-9

22234 **Enterprise Box Company**
10 Burnside Street
Montclair, NJ 07043-1325 973-509-2200
Fax: 973-509-1910
Paper boxes and envelopes
VP: Lenore Klein
Estimated Sales: Less than $500,000
Number Employees: 1-4

22235 **Enterprise Company**
616 S Santa Fe St
Santa Ana, CA 92705 714-835-0541
Fax: 714-543-2856 www.enterpriseco.com
Manufacturer and exporter of baling presses
CFO: Daniel Gould
Marketing Director: John Gould
Estimated Sales: $2.5-5 Million
Number Employees: 50-99
Type of Packaging: Bulk

22236 **Enterprise Envelope Inc**
920 Kenosha Industrial Dr SE
Grand Rapids, MI 49508 616-247-1301
Fax: 616-247-1343 800-422-4255
orders@enterpriseenvelope.com
www.enterpriseenvelope.com
Envelopes including lithographed, commercial catalog, special size and window; up to four color process
President: Gary Helmholdt
Estimated Sales: $1-3 Million
Number Employees: 10-19
Square Footage: 42000

22237 **Enterprise Products**
6875 Suva St
Bell Gardens, CA 90201-1998 562-928-1918
Fax: 562-927-8413
Wire display racks and shelving; also, tubing goods and stampings
CEO: Ron Spicer
Estimated Sales: $20-50 Million
Number Employees: 100-249

22238 **Enting Water Conditiong**
3211 Dryden Rd
Dayton, OH 45439 937-294-5100
Fax: 937-294-5485 800-735-5100
sales@enting.com www.enting.com
Manufacturer and exporter of water treatment systems including softeners, reverse osmosis, cartridge filters and ultra-violet purifiers
President: Mel Entingh
President/COO: Dan Entingh
Estimated Sales: $5-10 Million
Number Employees: 20-49
Square Footage: 43400
Brands:
Aquamate
Enting
Kane
Watermate

22239 **Entoleter**
251 Welton St
Hamden, CT 06517 203-787-3575
Fax: 203-787-1492 800-729-3575
info@entoleter.com www.entoleter.com
Manufacturer, exporter of centrifugal impact mills, wet scrubbers and wet electrostatic precipitators
President: Woody Kokley
Sales Manager: Todd Gardner
Sales Manager: Dick Steinsuaag
Estimated Sales: $5-10 000,000
Number Employees: 20-49
Square Footage: 62000
Parent Co: Spinnaker Industries
Brands:
Centrified
Centrimil
Eid
Esa

22240 **Enviro Doors By ASI Technologies**
5848 N. 95th Court
Milwaukee, WI 53225-2613 414-464-6200
Fax: 414-464-9863 800-558-7068
sales@asidoors.com www.asidoors.com
President: George C Balbach
Estimated Sales: $6 Million
Number Employees: 100-249

22241 **Enviro-Clear Company, Inc**
152 Cregar Rd
High Bridge, NJ 08829 908-638-5507
Fax: 908-638-4636 info@enviro-clear.com
www.enviro-clear.com
Manufacturer and exporter of clarifiers and belt and pressure filters and separators
President: Joe Muldowney
VP Marketing: Cindy Meyer
Sales: James Grau
Estimated Sales: $3 - 5 Million
Number Employees: 5-9
Square Footage: 40000
Brands:
Enviro-Clear
Pronto

22242 **Enviro-Pak**
15450 SE For Mor Ct
PO Box 1569
Clackamas, OR 97015 503-655-7044
Fax: 503-655-6368 800-223-6836
sales@enviro-pak.com www.enviro-pak.com
Manufactures food processing ovens, smokers, dryers, steam cabinets and chillers for further processing of meat, fish and poultry. Products are also now being used in different industries such as pet foods, fruits, vegetables, tofubakery products, mushrooms, and more.
Owner: Gil Martini
Estimated Sales: $10 - 20 Million
Number Employees: 20-49

22243 **Enviro-Safety Products**
8248 West Doe Ave
Visalia, CA 93291-9263 559-625-5592
Fax: 559-651-1320 800-637-6606
info@envirosafetyproducts.com
www.envirosafetyproducts.com
Wine industry powdered spray and sulfur helmets, protective clothing, respirators of all types
Manager: Scott Newton
R & D: Peggy Dahlvang
Estimated Sales: $500,000
Number Employees: 20-49
Brands:
3m
Aearo/Peltor
Paulson
Sas

22244 **Enviro-Test/Perry Laboratories**
8102 Lemont Rd Ste 1500
Woodridge, IL 60517-7776 630-324-6685
Fax: 630-734-9534
Laboratory testing and analysis firm
President: Maria Lenos
VP Sales: Detrie Zacharias
Lab Director: George Lenos
Estimated Sales: Less than $500,000
Number Employees: 10 to 19
Square Footage: 3000

22245 **Enviro-Ware**
100 Sandusky Street
2nd Floor
Pittsburgh, PA 15212-5822 412-642-2222
Fax: 412-642-2223 888-233-7857
info@envirο-ware.com www.enviro-ware.com
Manufacturers of biodegradable dinnerware and packing
Estimated Sales: $1 - 5 Million
Brands:
Enviro-Ware

22246 **EnviroPAK Corporation**
4203 Shoreline Dr
Earth City, MO 63045 314-739-1202
Fax: 314-739-2422 sales@enviropak.com
www.enviropak.com
Pulp packaging for numerous industries including that of food and beverage.
President: John Wichlenski
Treasurer: Joseph Walsh
VP: Jon Smith
Vice President Sales & Marketing: Bill Noble
Sales Coordinator: Kay Walsh
Vice President Manufacturing: Rodney Heenan
Estimated Sales: $4 Million
Number Employees: 35
Square Footage: 40000

22247 **EnviroPak Corporation**
4203 Shoreline Dr
Earth City, MO 63045 314-739-1202
Fax: 314-739-2422 info@enviropak.com
www.enviropak.com
Molded pulp packaging
President: John Wichlenski
Estimated Sales: $5-10 000,000
Number Employees: 10-19

22248 **Envirolights Manufacturing**
50 Viceroy Road
Concord, ON L4K 2L8
Canada 905-738-0357
Fax: 905-738-0647
Pest and insect control systems and devices including industrial electrocution and glue board type insect light traps
President: Ken Nayler
VP: Douglas Nayler
Number Employees: 5-9
Parent Co: Envirolights Manufacturing
Brands:
Electri-Fly
Flintrol
The Flylight

22249 **Enviromental Structures**
950 Walnut Ridge Dr
Hartland, WI 53029-9388 262-369-3535
Fax: 262-369-3536
mlivesay@esidesignbuild.com
www.esidesignbuild.com
President: Brad Barke
Estimated Sales: $10 - 20 Million
Number Employees: 20-49

22250 **Environmental Consultants**
391 Newman Ave
Clarksville, IN 47129-3247 812-282-8481
Fax: 812-282-8554

Environmental consultants specializing in pollution control, testing and analysis
President: Robert Fuchs
Office Manager: Patti Kinchlow
Estimated Sales: $1-2.5 Million
Number Employees: 5 to 9

22251 **Environmental Express Inc.**
2345A Charleston Regional Pkwy
Charleston, SC 29492 843-881-6560
Fax: 843-881-3964 800-343-5319
suggestions@envexp.com www.envexp.com
Supplier of environmentally safer laboratory equipment for the food and beverage research & development industry.
CEO: Dennis Pope
Bookkeeper: Lourl Mastin
Vice President: Paul Strickler
Technical Sales Representative: Allison Ditullio
Manager: Paula Borgstedt
Estimated Sales: $5.2 Million
Number Employees: 40

22252 **Environmental Products**
730 Commerce Dr
Venice, FL 34292 941-486-1325
Fax: 941-480-9201 800-828-2447
ro@cranenv.com www.cranenv.com/index1
Reverse osmosis based water purification equipment, including pre-treatment and post-treatment systems
Estimated Sales: $10-20 000,000
Number Employees: 50-99

22253 **(HQ)Environmental Products Corporation**
99 Great Hill Rd
Naugatuck, CT 06770 203-720-4059
Fax: 203-720-9302 800-275-3861
www.envipco.com/usa-connecticut.asp
Reverse-vending machinery; also, container accounting and collection services available
President: Bhajun G Santchurn
CFO: Pilraj Chuwla
Marketing/Sales: Bill Donnelly
Operations Manager: Charles Ricey
Plant Manager: Harry Yerrick
Estimated Sales: $.5 - 1 million
Number Employees: 5-9
Square Footage: 80000
Other Locations:
Environmental Products Corp.
Fairfax VA

22254 **Environmental Products Company**
197 Poplar Place #3
North Aurora, IL 60542-8191 630-892-2414
Fax: 630-892-2467 800-677-8479
environmentalpds@sbcglobal.net
www.environmental-products.com
Manufacturer and exporter of polyvinyl chloride strip doors, heat recycling fans and welding screens
Manager: Kurt Pfoutz
Office Manager: Kurt Pfoutz
Estimated Sales: $5 - 10 Million
Number Employees: 10 to 19
Square Footage: 15000
Parent Co: Material Control

22255 **Environmental Systems Service**
218 N Main St
Culpeper, VA 22701 540-825-6660
Fax: 540-825-4961 800-541-2116
info@ess-services.com www.ess-services.com
Consultant specializing in dairy and sanitation testing, quality control and analysis including water, wastewater, microbiological and shelf-life
President: W Robert Jebson
VP: Donald Hearl
Estimated Sales: $5 - 10 Million
Number Employees: 20-49
Square Footage: 10000

22256 **Environmizer Systems Corporation**
25 W Highland Avenue
Atlantic Highlands, NJ 07716-2804 732-291-4700
Fax: 732-291-4720 drrex@injersey.com
Magnetic scale removal in evaporators, separators, pasteurizers
Estimated Sales: Less than $500,000
Number Employees: 4

22257 **Epcon Industrial Systems**
17777 I-45 South
Conroe, TX 77385 936-273-3300
Fax: 936-273-4600 800-447-7872
sales@epconlp.com www.epconlp.com
Manufacturer and exporter of air pollution control systems for enclosures, odor control systems and oxidizers; also, general bake ovens
President and R&D: Aziz Jamaluddin
CFO: Sunny Naidu
Quality Control: Mike Paddie
Sales Engineer: Brad Morello
Engineer Designer: Nedzad Hadzajlic
Estimated Sales: $5 - 10 Million
Number Employees: 50-99
Square Footage: 400000

22258 **Epic Industries**
1007 Jersey Ave
New Brunswick, NJ 08901 732-249-6867
Fax: 732-249-7683 800-221-3742
sales@epicindustries.com
www.epicindustries.com
Institutional and industrial cleaning
President and CFO: Ted Bustany
Quality Control: John Nelson
Director: Sam Levine
Estimated Sales: $1 - 2.5 000,000
Number Employees: 50-99
Square Footage: 55000

22259 **Epic Products**
2801 S Yale St
Santa Ana, CA 92704 714-641-8194
Fax: 714-641-8217 800-548-9791
info@epicproductsinc.com
www.epicproductsinc.com
Bar supplies including plastic wine glasses, acrylic glassware, servingware, wine racks, cork pullers and drink stirrers
Owner: Ardeen Dubow
VP: Matt DuBow
Estimated Sales: $5 - 10 Million
Number Employees: 20-49

22260 **Epsen Hilmer Graphics Company**
13748 F St.
Omaha, NE 68137 402-342-7000
Fax: 402-342-9284 800-228-9940
hg@.com www.ehg.net
Manufacturer and exporter of labels including pressure sensitive, glue applied litho, in-mold and PET beverage
President: Tom Helmer
VP Opers.: Thomas Hillmer
VP Sales/Marketing: R Craig Cunran
VP Operations: Thomas Hillmer
Estimated Sales: $.5 - 1 million
Number Employees: 1-4

22261 **Epsilon Industrial**
2215 Grand Avenue Pkwy
Austin, TX 78728 512-251-1500
Fax: 512-251-1593 info@epsilon-gms.com
www.epsilon-gms.com
Provides food technologists with instrumentation to perform multicomponent analysis on clear or cloudy liquids, slurries, powders, solids
Estimated Sales: $1-2.5 000,000
Number Employees: 5-9

22262 **Epsilon-Opti Films Corporation**
132 Case Dr
South Plainfield, NJ 07080-5109 908-791-1732
Fax: 908-791-1030 800-235-8383
epsilon@epsilonopti.com www.epsilonopti.com
Polyolefin shrink films
Number Employees: 20-49

22263 **Equichem International**
510 Tower Boulevard
Carol Stream, IL 60188-9426 630-784-0432
Fax: 630-784-0436 mail@equichem.com
www.equichem.com
Custom vitamin and mineral premixes and enzyme blends.
President: Luis C Lovis
Research/Development Director: Luis J Lovis
Sales Director: Anna Lovis
Type of Packaging: Bulk

22264 **Equilon Lubricants**
1111 Bagby Street
Houston, TX 77002-2551 713-752-6695
Fax: 713-752-4678 800-645-8237
www.shell-lubricants.com
Synthetic and mineral based fluids and greases for food or beverage processing plants
Chief Executive Officer: Peter Voser
Research & Development: Kris Kaushik
Marketing Director: David Rowe
Sales Director: Larry Cekella
Parent Co: Shell International Petroleum Company
Brands:
Cassida Fluids and Greasers
Cyenus Fluids and Greasers
Shell Fm Fluids and Greasers

22265 **Equipex Limited**
765 Westminster St
Providence, RI 02903 401-273-3300
Fax: 401-273-3328 800-649-7885
equipex@compuserve.com www.equipex.com
Manufacturer and exporter of ovens and restaurant equipment
President: Gary Licht
VP: Val Ginzburg
Sales/Marketing Division: Irina Mirsky-Zayas
Operations: Loretta Fortier
Estimated Sales: $2.5-5,000,000
Number Employees: 1-4

22266 **Equipment Design & Fabrication**
722 N Smith St
Charlotte, NC 28202 704-372-4513
Fax: 704-372-4514 800-949-0165
contact@equipmentdesignandfab.com
www.equipmentdesignandfab.com
Materials handling, railroad maintenance, textile & furniture manufacturing equipment
President: Terry D Miller
Purchasing Manager: Tony Walkins
Number Employees: 10-19

22267 **Equipment Distributing of America**
1776 Country Road M
PO Box 213
Wahoo, NE 68066 402-592-9360
Fax: 402-443-1384 efa.efa-usa@windstream.net
www.efa-germany.de
Supplier of meat processing machines and industrial tools
Manager: David Weinert
Estimated Sales: Under $500,000
Number Employees: 1-4
Parent Co: EFA Germany

22268 **Equipment Enterprises**
6670 E Harris Blvd
Charlotte, NC 28215-5101 704-568-3001
Fax: 704-536-3259 800-221-3681
sales@wardtank.com www.wardtank.com
Water treatment systems
President: Donald Ward
President, Chief Executive Officer: Jon Ward
President, Chief Executive Officer: Jon Ward
Operations Sales Manager: Rick Shepherd
Vice President of Operations: Bob Besh
Estimated Sales: $5 - 10 Million
Number Employees: 20-49
Square Footage: 64000
Parent Co: Ward Tank & Heat Exchanger

22269 **Equipment Enterprises**
1875 Graves Road
Norcross, GA 30093-1022 770-368-9789
Fax: 770-368-0587 800-221-3681
Water treatment systems including lime coagulation, direct filtraton, membranes, carbon purifiers, filters, ozanators, and ultraviolet units
Estimated Sales: $1-5 000,000
Number Employees: 9

22270 **Equipment Equities Corporation**
866 United Nations Plaza
Suite 440
New York, NY 10017-1838 212-688-8800
Fax: 212-688-0061
Estimated Sales: $3 - 5 Million
Number Employees: 1-4

22271 **Equipment Exchange Company**
10042 Keystone Drive
Lake City, PA 16423-1060 814-774-0888
Fax: 814-774-0880 info@eeclink.com
www.eeclink.com
Buyers and sellers of used food process machinery. Choppers, grinders, patty, meat forming and portion, smokehouses and accessories, seasonings, ingredients, batters and breading
President: Robert J Breakstone
Estimated Sales: $2.5 - 5 Million
Number Employees: 10-19
Square Footage: 120000

22272 **Equipment Express**
60 Wanless Court
Ayr, ON N0B 1E0 519-740-8008
Fax: 519-740-6297 800-387-9791
carrief@equipmentexpress.com
equipmentexpress.com
Unscramblers, air and wet bottle cleaners, conveyors, fillers, cappers, induction sealers, labelers, coders, tapers, case erectors, case packers, palletizer, bundlers, pallet warppers, turnkey bottled water plants, including watertreatment systems, specialty machines
President: Jeff Ake
VP Marketing: Liliana Ake
Production Manager: Kurt Organ
Plant Manager: John Naughton
Purchasing Manager: Teresa Mago
Estimated Sales: $1-4 Million
Number Employees: 20

22273 **Equipment Innovators**
800 Industrial Park Dr
Marietta, GA 30062 770-427-9467
Fax: 770-425-2350 800-733-3434
sales@equipmentinnovators.com
www.equipmentinnovators.com
President: Richard C McCamey
CEO: Joe Rubin
Estimated Sales: $10 - 20 Million
Number Employees: 20-49

22274 **Equipment Outlet**
199 N Linder Road
Meridian, ID 83642-2440 208-887-1472
Fax: 208-887-4874 smag@equipmentoutlet.com
www.equipmentoutlet.com
Supplier of packaging equipment materials
Salesman: Brian Maglecic
Estimated Sales: $1-2.5 Million
Number Employees: 10

22275 **Equipment Specialists**
310 Us Highway 17 92 W
Haines City, FL 33844 863-421-4567
Fax: 863-421-1010
sales@equipmentspecialists.com
www.equipmentspecialists.com
Manufacturer and exporter of new and used food processing and packaging equipment
President: Michael Gordon
CEO: Beverly Gordon
Vice President: Jeremy Gordon
Sales Director: Mariano Montealegre
Operations Manager: Jose Macy
Plant Manager: Reinaldo Mendoza
Purchasing Manager: Eric Ball
Estimated Sales: $10-20 Million
Number Employees: 20-49
Square Footage: 150000
Type of Packaging: Food Service

22276 **Equipment for Coffee**
71 Lost Lake Ln
Campbell, CA 95008-6642 650-259-7801
Fax: 650-259-7603
Tea and coffee industry colorimeters, pollution control equipment, vacuum packaging machinery
Plant Manager: Gordon McNeil
Estimated Sales: Less than $500,000
Number Employees: 1-4
Square Footage: 3000

22277 **Erb International**
290 Hamilton Road
New Hamburg, ON N3A 1A2
Canada 519-662-2710
Fax: 519-662-3316 800-665-2653
werb@erbgroup.com www.erbgroup.com
President: Vernon D Erb
CFO: Kevin Copper
Number Employees: 10

22278 **Erca-Formseal**
1210 Campus Dr
Morganville, NJ 07751-1262 732-536-8770
Fax: 732-536-8850 sales@hassiausa.com
www.oystarusa.com
President: Charles Ravalli
Estimated Sales: $3 - 5 Million
Number Employees: 10-19

22279 **Erell Manufacturing Company**
2678 Coyle Ave
Elk Grove Vlg, IL 60007 847-427-3000
800-622-6334
erell1@aol.com
Plastic aprons; exporter and manufacturer of vinyl industrial and promotional products
Estimated Sales: $1-2.5 Million
Number Employees: 10-19
Square Footage: 17000
Brands:
Plasti-Guard

22280 **Ergonomic Handling Systems**
PO Box 338
Line Lexington, PA 18932-0338 215-822-8778
Fax: 215-822-8088 800-223-6430
info@ergonomichandling.com
www.vacuhoist.com
General and CNC machining, drilling, boring, cutting and honing, general welding, fabricating and material handling
Sales Director: Tim Burns
Estimated Sales: $1-2.5 Million
Number Employees: 20-50

22281 **Erickson Industries**
717 Saint Croix St
River Falls, WI 54022 715-426-9700
Fax: 715-426-9701 800-729-9941
sales@erickson-industries.com
www.erickson-industries.com
Manufacturer and exporter of refrigerators, freezers, walk-in coolers and pre-fabricated cooling and freezing warehouses; also, manufacturer of tubular towers and planter grids
Owner: Paul Erickson
Sales: Debbie Huppert
Sales Engineering: Joel Johnson
Advertising Manager: H Walsh
Estimated Sales: $1-2.5 Million
Number Employees: 1-4
Square Footage: 40000
Brands:
Chill-Air
Erickson
Kool-Rite

22282 **Erie Container Corporation**
4700 Lorain Ave
Cleveland, OH 44102-3443 216-631-1650
Fax: 216-631-1249
Paper tubes and containers
President: Frank Lipinski
VP: Joseph Lipinski
Estimated Sales: $5 - 10 Million
Number Employees: 5 to 9

22283 **Erie Cotton Products Company**
1112 Bacon St
Erie, PA 16511 800-459-6644
Fax: 814-453-7816 800-289-4737
sales@eriecotton.com www.eriecotton.com
Towels including burlap, cheesecloth, nonwovens, dish, glass, bar and disposable; also, janitorial supplies, gloves, disposable aprons and hair caps
President: Gregory Rubin
CFO: Louise Clemens
General Manager: Rick Gore
Estimated Sales: $5 - 10 Million
Number Employees: 20-49

22284 **(HQ)Erie Foods International**
401 7th Ave
PO Box 648
Erie, IL 61250 309-659-2233
Fax: 309-659-2822 800-447-1887
glindsey@eriefoods.com www.eriefoods.com
Co-dried and concentrated milk proteins; also sodium, calcium, combination and acid-stable caseinates and dairy blends; importer of milk proteins
President/CEO: David Reisenbigler
CFO: Mark Delaney
Executive VP: Jim Klein
Technical Services Manager: Craig Air
Quality Assurance Manager: Jo Kelly
International General Manager: Ryan Tranel
Regional Sales Manager: Jake VanDeWostine
Process Development Manager: Jim Jacoby
Purchasing Manager: Shawn Larson
Estimated Sales: $1-2.5 Million
Square Footage: 120000
Parent Co: Erie Foods International Inc
Type of Packaging: Bulk
Other Locations:
Erie Foods International
Beenleigh QLD
Brands:
Ecco
Erie
Pro-Gim

22285 **Eriez Magnetics**
4700 W 23rd St
Erie, PA 16506
Fax: 814-838-4960 800-346-4946
eriez@eriez.com www.eriez.com
Manufacturer and exporter of vibratory feeders and conveyors, magnetic separators, metal detectors, vibratory and material-sizing screeners, lifting magnets and magnetic conveyors.
Chairman: R Merwin
President/CEO: Tim Shuttleworth
Treasurer: M Mandel
Quality Control: J Snyder
Marketing: K Jones
VP Sales/Marketing: C Ingram
VP Operations: M Mankosa
Plant Manager: J Kiehl
Estimated Sales: $50 - 100 Million
Number Employees: 250-499
Square Footage: 110000
Brands:
E-Z Tec
Hi-Vi
Metalarm
Safehold

22286 **Erika Record, LLC**
37 Atlantic Way
Clifton, NJ 07012 973-614-8500
Fax: 973-614-8503 800-682-8203
max@erikarecord.com www.erikarecord.com
Bun divider and rounder, bakery equipment
President: Max Oehler
Estimated Sales: Below $5 000,000
Number Employees: 1-4
Type of Packaging: Bulk

22287 **Ermanco**
6870 Grand Haven Rd
Norton Shores, MI 49456 231-798-4547
Fax: 231-798-8322 info@ermanco.com
www.ermanco.com
Manufacturer and exporter of conveyors including belt/live roller, lineshaft driven, belt driven and sortation; also, turnkey systems
President: Leon Kirschner
Quality Control: Bob Dorgan
VP of Marketing: Lee Schomberg
VP of Sales: Gordon Hellberg
Estimated Sales: $30 - 50 Million
Number Employees: 100-249
Square Footage: 100000
Parent Co: Paragon Technologies
Brands:
Accurol
Ers Sorter
Intellorol
Nbs Sorter
Swing Arm Diverter
Xenopressure Xenorol

22288 **Ernest F. Mariani Compan**
573 W. 2890 S.
Salt Lake City, UT 84115 801-531-9615
Fax: 801-531-9615 800-453-2927
sales@efmco.com www.efmco.com
Accumulating of bottling supplies and equipment
President: Wil Fiedler
Finance Manager: Clay Dalton

Estimated Sales: $5 - 10 Million
Number Employees: 10-19

22289 **Ernest F. Mariani Company**
573 W 2890 S
Salt Lake City, UT 84115 80- 4-3 29
Fax: 801-531-9615 sales@efmco.com
www.efmco.com
Accumulating conveyors, aseptic packaging systems and aseptic processing equipment, bottle supplies and equipment
President: Wil Fiedler
Finance Manager: Clay Dalton
Estimated Sales: $5-10 000,000
Number Employees: 10-19

22290 **Ernst Timing Screw Company**
1534 Bridgewater Rd
Bensalem, PA 19020 215-639-1438
Fax: 215-244-0166 ernstime@comcat.com
www.ernsttiming.com
Feed screws, change parts, star wheels, center guides
President: Suzanne Cannon
CEO: Lee Cannon
Estimated Sales: $1 - 2,500,000
Number Employees: 10-19

22291 **Ertel Alsop**
132 Flatbush Avenue
Kingston, NY 12401 845-331-4552
Fax: 845-853-1526 800-553-7835
sales@ertelalsop.com www.ertelalsop.com
Manufacturer and exporter of filtration equipment, filter media and mixers for liquids; also, glass crushing equipment
President: George Quigley
VP: George Quigley
Marketing Manager Food & Beverage: Mike Kelly
VP Sales/Marketing: William Kearney
Estimated Sales: $5 - 10 Million
Number Employees: 50-99
Brands:
Alpha-Media
Bottle-Buster
Micro-Deck
Micro-Media
Vapor-Master

22292 **Ertelalsop Inc.**
132 Flatbush Avenue
Kingston, NY 12401 845-331-4552
Fax: 845-853-1526 800-553-7835
sales@ertelalsop.com www.ertelalsop.com
Manufacturer and exporter of filtration equipment and filter media for food and beverage applications and manufacturing
President/Owner: George Quigley
Executive VP: William Kearney
Estimated Sales: $5 - 10 Million
Number Employees: 50-99
Brands:
Aquakv-Pak
Disc-Pak
Zeta-Pak

22293 **Erving Industries**
97 East Main Street
Erving, MA 01344 413-422-2700
Fax: 413-422-2710 www.ervingpaper.com
Custom printed and plain paper products including napkins, placemats, traycovers and table covers
Estimated Sales: $50-100 Million
Number Employees: 1-4
Square Footage: 130000
Brands:
Savlin

22294 **Erwin Food Service Equipment**
2915 Horton Rd
Fort Worth, TX 76119-5635 817-535-0021
Fax: 817-535-2999
Stainless steel cooking and heating equipment, tables, sinks, counters and hoods
President: Al Erwin
Office Manager: Barbara Vandever
Estimated Sales: $500,000-$1 Million
Number Employees: 1 to4
Square Footage: 10000

22295 **Erwyn Products Company**
200 Campus Dr Ste C
Morganville, NJ 07751 732-972-1440
Fax: 732-972-1263 800-331-9208
steve@erwyn.com www.erwyn.com
Manufacturer, importer and exporter of waste paper baskets and ice buckets
President: Randy Grant
Estimated Sales: $10 - 20 Million
Number Employees: 20-49

22296 **Esbelt of North America:Divison of ASGCO**
301 W Gordon Street
Allentown, PA 18102-3136 610-821-0216
Fax: 610-778-8991 rlehman@asgco.com
www.asgco.com
Heavyweight conveyor belts
Estimated Sales: $1 - 5 Million

22297 **Escher Mixers, USA**
2770 W Commerce Street
Suite 100
Dallas, TX 75212-4913 214-572-7777
Fax: 214-572-8888 usoffice@eschermixers.com

22298 **Esco Manufacturer**
PO Box 1237
Watertown, SD 57201-6237 605-886-9668
Fax: 605-886-5454 800-843-3726
wholesale@escomfg.com
www.escomanufacturing.com
Signs and displays
President: Mark Stein
Senior Account Manager of Sales: Rob Fjerstad
Manufacturing Manager: Kevin Morris
Resources Manager of Purchasing: Laurie Gates
Estimated Sales: $10-20 Million
Number Employees: 100-249

22299 **Esha Research**
4747 Skyline Rd S Ste 100
Salem, OR 97306 503-585-6242
Fax: 503-585-5543 800-659-3742
sales@esha.com www.esha.com
Software for formulation development and nutrition labeling; exporter of nutritional labeling software
CEO: Robert Geltz
Vice President: David Hands
Sales Director: Scott Hadsall
Estimated Sales: $2 Million
Number Employees: 22
Number of Brands: 6
Number of Products: 6
Square Footage: 500
Brands:
Genesis R&D

22300 **Eskay Metal FabricatingCompany**
83 Doat St
Buffalo, NY 14211 716-893-3100
Fax: 716-893-0443 800-836-8015
info@specialitystainless.com
www.specialtystainless.com
Food preparation equipment including sinks, chef's tables, restaurant, cafeteria, serving and specialty counters, etc.; also, cabinets, coolers and self contained mobile hot dog and display carts.
President: Jeff Subra
Public Relations: Kathy Bristol
Engineering Manager: Ken White
Estimated Sales: $1 Million
Number Employees: 5-9
Square Footage: 16000
Parent Co: Schuler-Subra
Brands:
Buffalo Grill

22301 **Esko Pallets**
805 Tall Pine Ln
Cloquet, MN 55720-3164 218-879-8553
Fax: 218-879-8560 pallets@frontiernet.net
Pallets
Owner: Al Raushel
Manager: Al Raushel
Estimated Sales: $1-2.5 Million
Number Employees: 10-19

22302 **Espresso Carts and Supplies**
429 United States Avenue
Lindenwold, NJ 08021-2658 856-782-1775
Fax: 856-782-1775 800-972-CART
74274.60@compuserve.com
www.espressocartsusa.com
Carts, espresso carts, espresso machines and accessories, bars, kiosks displays
Vie President of Sales/Marketing: Anthony Santangelo
Estimated Sales: 250000
Number Employees: 3
Type of Packaging: Bulk

22303 **Espresso Roma Corporation**
1310 65th St
Emeryville, CA 94608 510-420-8898
Fax: 510-420-8980 800-437-1668
sandydboyd@aol.com www.espresso-roma.com
Processor and wholesaler/distributor of roast coffee; manufacturer and wholesaler/distributor of espresso machines and restaurant equipment
President: Sandy Boyd
VP: Pat Weigt
Sales Manager: Sandy Boyd
Estimated Sales: $1-2.5 Million
Number Employees: 10-19

22304 **Esquire Mechanical Corp.**
PO Box 496
Armonk, NY 10504 718-625-4006
Fax: 718-625-0155 800-847-4206
sales@dunhill-esquire.net
www.dunhill-esquire.com
Manufacturer and exporter of cafeteria and kitchen equipment including cashier stands,serving counters,sinks,refrigerated display cases,tables and bbq and rotisserie machines.
President: Geoffrey Thaw
Estimated Sales: $1 - 5 Million
Number Employees: 10-19
Square Footage: 240000
Parent Co: Dunhill Food Equipment
Type of Packaging: Food Service

22305 **Esselte Meto**
1200t American Road
Morris Plains, NJ 07950-2453 973-359-0947
Fax: 201-455-7492 800-645-3290
Manufacturer and exporter of handheld labeling and merchandising systems, thermal and laser bar code printers and supplies, tags and labels
President: Travis Howe
VP Marketing: Bob Cantono
VP Sales: Bob Evans
Estimated Sales: $300,000-500,000
Number Employees: 50-99
Square Footage: 135000
Parent Co: Esselte AB
Type of Packaging: Consumer, Private Label
Brands:
Essette Meto
Laser-Link
Meto
Meto/Primark
Price Marquee
Take a Number
Turn-O-Matic

22306 **Essential Industries**
PO Box 12
28391 Essential Road
Merton, WI 53056-0012 262-538-1122
Fax: 262-538-1354 800-551-9679
sales@essind.com
www.essentialcontractmfg.com
Manufacturer and exporter of household and industrial hand, glass and window cleaners, liquid and powder dishwashing compounds and soap, detergents and floor polish
Chairman of the Board: James Wheeler Jr
Chief Executive Officer: Jim Coddington
Controller: Carol Sanchez
Senior Vice President: Nick Contos
Quality & Safety Regional Manager: Maureen Smith
Vice President, Sales & Marketing: Ed Zgrabik
Vice President, Operations: Thomas Gitzlaff
Production Manager: Brandon Coulter
Director, Purchasing: Kathleen Leemon
Estimated Sales: $15 Million
Number Employees: 85
Square Footage: 110000
Type of Packaging: Private Label, Bulk
Brands:
Durabrite
Silhouette
Sport Kote
Superbase
Trust

22307 **Essentra Packaging Inc.**
1625 Ashton Park Drive
Suite D
Colonial Heights, VA 23834-5908 804-518-1803
Fax: 804-518-1809 800-849-0633
info@essentrapackaging.com www.pppayne.com
Pressure sensitive tear tape
President: Bob Donnahoo
Estimated Sales: $5 - 10 Million
Number Employees: 30

22308 **Essex Plastics**
1531 NW 12th Ave
Pompano Beach, FL 33069 954-956-1100
Fax: 954-956-4200 800-231-4191
www.essexplastics.com
Plastic film and bags
CFO: David Schaefer
Number Employees: 250

22309 **Esstech**
13911 NW 3rd Court
Vancouver, WA 98685-5703 360-546-5662
Fax: 360-546-5664
Boxes, multi-wall and plastic bags designed to eliminate or reduce the use of banding and stretch wrapping without damaging package graphics or appearance
President: Paul Mazi
Estimated Sales: $500,000-$1 000,000
Number Employees: 1-4
Type of Packaging: Bulk

22310 **Ester International**
29 Junction Pond Lane
Monmouth Junction, NJ 08852-2924 732-967-0561
Fax: 732-967-0563 esterintl@aol.com
Plain, corona treated, chemically treated film, polyester film, milky white film, colored film and different types of polyester resins
General Manager: S Shridhar
Number Employees: 4
Number of Brands: 1

22311 **Esterle Mold & Machine Company**
1539 Commerce Dr
Stow, OH 44224-1783 330-686-1685
Fax: 330-686-9434 800-411-4086
info@esterle.com www.esterle.com
Peel boards made from 100% long-lasting high impact, virgin and prime rigid plastic; standard 18 in. x 26 in. and custom sizes. Hygienic and FDA approved; 100% recyclable
President: Richard Esterle
VP: Kathleen Sawyer
Vice President: Kathleen Sawyer
Chairman: Adam Esterle
Sales Director: Patrick Miller
Operations Manager: Mark Starnes
Purchasing Manager: Steve Staszak
Estimated Sales: Below $5 Million
Number Employees: 50-99
Square Footage: 120000

22312 **Etched Images**
1758 Industrial Way Ste 101
Napa, CA 94558 707-252-5450
Fax: 707-252-2666 info@etchedimages.com
www.etchedimages.com
Wine industry applications; bottle design
Owner: Stu Mc Farland
Estimated Sales: $20-50 Million
Number Employees: 20-49

22313 **Etna Sales**
1112 W Barkley Avenue
Orange, CA 92868-1213 714-520-5204
Fax: 714-563-0339
Brewing devices, coffee urn cleaners

22314 **Ettore Products Company**
2100 North Loop Road
Alameda, CA 94502 510-748-4130
Fax: 510-748-4146 info@ettore.com
www.ettore.com
Manufacturer and exporter of window and floor squeegees and window washing equipment
Chairman of the Board: Michael Smahlik
VP Sales/Marketing: Patrick Murphy
National Sales Manager: Herman Miron
Estimated Sales: $1 - 2.5 Million
Number Employees: 50-99
Type of Packaging: Consumer, Food Service, Bulk
Brands:
Ehore

22315 **Etube and Wire**
50 W. Clearview Dr.
Shrewsbury, PA 17361 717-227-8400
Fax: 717-428-2974 800-618-4720
sales@etubeandwire.com
www.etubeandwire.com
Wire fryer baskets, displays, hooks, hangers, rings, screens, grills, filters, guards, fan guards, and shelving
Owner: Glenn Eyster
General Manager: Larry Krumrine
Manager: Larry Krumrwe
Estimated Sales: $2.5 Million
Number Employees: 20-49
Square Footage: 120000

22316 **Euchner-USA**
6723 Lyons St
East Syracuse, NJ 13057 866-547-7206
Fax: 315-701-0319 info@euchner-usa.com
www.euchner-usa.com
Sensors for automation, safety and man-machine interface products including safety interlocking swithches, enabling switches, trip dogs and rails, encoders, read/write coding systems, read only identification systems, joysticks andoperator panels
President: Michel Ladd
Number Employees: 10

22317 **Eugene Welding Company**
2420 Wills St
Marysville, MI 48040 810-364-7421
Fax: 810-364-4347 spacerak@tir.com
www.spacerak.thomasregister.com
Manufacturer and exporter of racks including pallet storage, drive-in, push back and cantilever
President: Charles Vamella
CEO: Jim Bradshaw
Sales: Scott Samples
Public Relations: Dawne Kimberley
Plant Maanger: Wes Boyne
Purchasing: Dave Campa
Estimated Sales: $20-50 Million
Number Employees: 250-499
Square Footage: 120000
Parent Co: Eugene Welding Company
Brands:
Spacerak

22318 **Eureka Company**
807 N Main St
Bloomington, IL 61701 309-828-2367
Fax: 309-823-5335 800-282-2886
kathy.luedke@eureka.com www.eureka.com
Manufacturer and exporter of commercial vacuums including canisters, uprights, home cleaning, built-ins and rechargeable
President: John Case
CEO: Jan Wolansky
VP Advertising: Don Johnson
Quality Control: Steve Knuth
Number Employees: 250-499
Parent Co: White Consolidated Industries
Type of Packaging: Consumer
Brands:
Eureka

22319 **Eureka Door**
PO Box 276
Ballwin, MO 63022-0276 314-256-1949
800-673-8735
www.eurekadoor.com

22320 **Eureka Ice & Cold Storage Company**
12 Waterfront Dr
Eureka, CA 95501-0368 707-443-5663
Fax: 707-443-6481 eurekaice@att.net
http://eurekaice.com/index.html
Warehouse providing freezer and cooler storage and a manufacturer of ice. Eureka Ice also offers Blast Freezing, a quick freezing of up to 80 tons of product in a short time.
Manager: Tom Devere
Manager: Tom Devero
Estimated Sales: $2.5-5 Million
Number Employees: 5-9
Square Footage: 140000

22321 **(HQ)Eureka Paper Box Company**
PO Box 1476
Williamsport, PA 17703-1476 570-326-9147
Fax: 570-326-7239 mmertz@csrlink.net
www.eureka-box.com
Custom paper folding cartons
Co-Owner: Jim Waters
Co-Owner: John McInerney
CFO: Bob Bernaski
Production Manager: Joseph Cioffi
Estimated Sales: $5 - 10 Million
Number Employees: 80
Square Footage: 212000
Other Locations:
Eureka Paper Box Co.
Syracuse NY

22322 **Euro-Pol Bakery Equipment**
2770 W Commerce St
Dallas, TX 75212-4913 214-637-2253
Fax: 214-637-2257 europol@flash.net
President: Mariusz B. Bandurski

22323 **Eurobar Sales Corporation**
12b W Main Street
Elmsford, NY 10523-2401 914-592-5770
Fax: 914-592-6004
Espresso machines and accessories

22324 **Eurodib**
PO Box 1798
1320 State Route 9
Champlain, NY 12919 450-641-8700
Fax: 451-641-8705 888-956-6866
shaun@eurodib.com www.eurodib.com
Importer of citrus and centrifugal juicers, dispensers, coffee grinders, blenders, vegetable cutters, grills, mandolines, cookware, and dishwashers
President: Jean Yves Dumaine
VP: Shaun McDonald
Marketing: Shaun McDonald
Purchasing Manager: Robert Perrier
Number Employees: 14
Number of Brands: 15
Number of Products: 500
Square Footage: 176000

22325 **Eurodispenser**
6480 Majors Lane
Decatur, IL 62521-9697 217-864-4061
Fax: 217-864-6722 admin@veteranssupply.com
www.eurodispenser.com
Quality dispensing equipment including condiments, sauces, toppings, syrups, soap and cleaning compounds
Estimated Sales: $1-2.5 Million
Number Employees: 1-4

22326 **(HQ)Eurofins Scientific**
2200 Rittenhouse Street
Suite 150
Des Moines, IA 50321 515-280-8378
Fax: 515-280-7068 800-841-1110
info@eurofinsus.com www.eurofins.com
Laboratory offering nutrition labeling, food analysis, microbiology, nutritional bioassays, toxicology and independent testing
President: Gary Wnorowski
Quality Assurance Director: Rhonda Krick
VP Sales/Marketing: Michael Meyers
Client Services Representative: Sophies Holbrook
Account Manager: Charles Hecht
Estimated Sales: $5 - 10 Million
Number Employees: 20-49
Other Locations:
Eurofins Scientific
Teltow/Berlin

22327 **Eurofins Scientific**
2394 Us Highway 130 # E
Dayton, NJ 08810-1500 732-355-3270
Fax: 901-272-2926 800-880-1038
www.productsafetylabs.com
Laboratory specializing in nutrition analysis for amino acids, dietary fibers, microbiological, proximate and vitamins; also, pesticide and residue testing, mycotoxin screening, authenticity, and GMO/ONA testing
President: Gary Wnorowski
CFO: Jean-Denis Giraudet
Quality Assurance Director: Rhonda Krick
Marketing Director: Lori Overstreet
Sales Director: Jay Kurmaski
Estimated Sales: $1-2.5 Million
Number Employees: 5-9

22328 **Europa Company**
11289 Slater Ave
Fountain Valley, CA 92708-5421 714-432-0112
Fax: 714-432-7246 www.europa-co.com
Espresso machines and accessories, grinders
Estimated Sales: Less than $500,000
Number Employees: 1-4

22329 **European Gift & Hardware**
514 S 5th Ave
Mt Vernon, NY 10550-4408 914-664-3448
Fax: 914-664-3257 800-927-0277
sales@europeangift.com www.europeangift.com
Espresso machines and accessories.
President: Anjelo Forzano
Estimated Sales: $5 - 10 Million
Number Employees: 5-9

22330 **European Packaging Machinery**
PO Box 40
Tennent, NJ 07763-0040 732-845-3557
Fax: 732-845-3844 epm@monmouth.com
www.epmincorporated.com
Packaging form-fill-seal, fill-seal, filling, inspection equipment, special engineering and customized handling and assembling equipment
President: Klans Huenecke
Brands:
Asg
Alfa-Kortogleu
Deltamat
Siebler

22331 **Eurosicma**
36 Lake St
Wilmington, MA 01887-3708 978-657-8841
Fax: 978-657-8847 eurosicma@galactica.it
www.eurosicma.it
Pillow pack wrapping machine for hard boiled candy, chewing-gum balls, deposited candies and milk tablets
Estimated Sales: $1 - 5 Million
Number Employees: 1-4

22332 **Eurotherm Controls**
44621 Guilford Dr Ste 100
Ashburn, VA 20147 703-443-0000
Fax: 703-669-1300 info@eurotherm.com
www.eurotherm.com
Supplier of precision process and temperature control instrumentation including single and multiloop digital controllers, alarms and indicators.
President: John Searle
Executive: Dan Dudici
Marketing Director: Al Betz
Sales Director: Al Betz
Estimated Sales: $50 Million
Number Employees: 100-249
Number of Brands: 5
Number of Products: 1000
Parent Co: Invensys Intelligent Automation

22333 **Eutek Systems**
2925 NW Aloclek Drive Suite 140
Hillsboro, OR 97124 503-615-8130
Fax: 503-615-2906 info@eutek.com
www.eutek.com
Manufacturer and exporter of wastewater reclamation and reuse equipment; also, grit removers
Operations: Steve Tansley
Estimated Sales: $1-2.5 Million
Number Employees: 10-19

22334 **Eval Company of America**
1001 Warrenville Rd # 110
Lisle, IL 60532-1392 312-347-0126
Fax: 312-893-8510 800-423-9726
info@evalca.com www.evalca.com
Plastic containers for food applications like ketchup or juice, coextruded films for flexible packaging of food, coextruded plastic tubing, coated paperboard and films in both standard and biaxially oriented forms
Owner: Rodger Bloch
Vice President Of Sales: George Avdey
Director Of Sales: Jim Claggett
Estimated Sales: $20-50 Million
Number Employees: 10-19

22335 **Evans Adhesives Corporation**
925 Old Henderson Rd
Columbus, OH 43220-3779 614-451-2665
Fax: 614-451-1373 800-868-0925
orders@evansadhesive.com
www.evansadhesive.com
Packaging adhesives for all applications
President: Rusty Thompson
Estimated Sales: $10 Million
Number Employees: 1-4

22336 **Evanston Awning Company**
2801 Central St
Evanston, IL 60201 847-864-4520
Fax: 847-864-5886
awnings@evanstonawning.com
www.evanstonawning.com
Commercial awnings
President: Edward Hunzinger Jr
Estimated Sales: $1-2,500,000
Number Employees: 10-19

22337 **Evapco**
5151 Allendale Lane
Taneytown, MD 21787 410-756-2600
Fax: 410-756-6450 marketing@evapco.com
www.evapco.com
President/CEO: W. J. Bartley
Sr Vice President Finance: Harold Walsh
Sr Vice President: Joseph Mandato
Corporate QC Manager: Jason Shearer
Director of Marketing: John Kollasch
Number Employees: 5-9

22338 **Evaporator Dryer Technologies Inc**
1805 Ridgeway St
Hammond, WI 54015 715-796-2313
Fax: 715-796-2378 info@evapdryertech.com
www.evapdryertech.com
Engineering and supply of custom evaporators and spray drying systems, heat recovery, dust collection, and exclusive sanitary designed components: liquid-activated, retractable CIP spray nozzles and systems, fire suppression systemssanitary, heavy-duty manways and inspection ports
President: Jens Peter Jensen
Purchasing: Jeff Derrick
Estimated Sales: $3-10 Million
Square Footage: 13000
Other Locations:
Stainless Steel Machining Division
Fond du Lac WI

22339 **Ever Extruder**
7 Goodwin Dr
Festus, MO 63028 636-937-8830
Fax: 636-937-6111 www.everextruder.com
Custom designer & manufacturer of new extruder bases, power transmissions, barrel assemblies and dischargers to fit existing aftermarket extruder systems.
President: Ned Williams
Chief Engineer: Steve Stewart

22340 **(HQ)Everbrite**
4949 S. 110th Street
Greenfield, WI 53228 414-529-3500
Fax: 414-529-7191 800-558-3888
www.everbrite.com
Manufacturer and exporter of signs and displays including indoor, outdoor, neon and electric; also, menu boards
President: Bill Fritz
Chief Financial Officer: David Heger
Estimated Sales: $74.8 Million
Number Employees: 850
Square Footage: 1000000
Type of Packaging: Food Service

22341 **Everbrite LLC**
4949 S. 110th Street
Greenfield, WI 53228 414-529-3500
800-558-3888
sales@everbrite.com www.everbrite.com
Manufacturer and exporter of electric signs
Founder: Charles Wamser
General Manager: Keith Le Mere
Estimated Sales: $5-10 Million
Number Employees: 50-99
Type of Packaging: Food Service, Bulk

22342 **Everedy Automation**
345 Renninger Rd
Frederick, PA 19435 610-754-1775
Fax: 610-754-1108 www.everedyautomation.com
Manufacturer and exporter of bakery machinery for batter, scaling, cake cutting, icing, splitting, slicing, cake sandwich, pie, custard and fruit filling and meringue/cream topping; also, raisin cleaning and stemming equipmentavailable.
President: Irv Fisher
Sales Director: Irv Fisher
Number Employees: 2
Square Footage: 15600

22343 **Everest Interscience**
2102 N.Forbes Blvd.
Suite 107
Tucson, AZ 85705-6429
Fax: 520-792-4545 info@everestinterscience.com
www.everestinterscience.com
Wine industry infrared thermometers
President: Charles Everest
CFO: Marilin Everest
Estimated Sales: $1 - 5 000,000
Number Employees: 5-9

22344 **Everett Stamp Works**
2933 Wetmore Ave
Everett, WA 98201-4016 425-258-6747
Fax: 425-252-8858
Rubber stamps and plastic signs
Owner: Jeff Hathaway
Owner: Jeffrey Hathaway
Estimated Sales: Less than $500,000
Number Employees: 1 to4

22345 **Everfilt Corporation**
3167 Progress Cir
Mira Loma, CA 91752 951-360-8380
Fax: 951-360-8384 800-360-8380
everfilt@everfilt.com www.everfilt.com
Water and waste water filtration and separation equipment for food processing plants, packing houses, etc
Operations Manager: Brian Tolson
Estimated Sales: $2.5-5 Million
Number Employees: 10-19
Square Footage: 10600
Brands:
Everfilt

22346 **Evergreen Packaging Equipment**
2400 6th Street Southwest
Cedar Rapids, IA 52404
www.evergreenpackaging.com
Gable top packaging equipment and gable top cartons.
President/Chief Executive Officer: Malcolm Bundy
CEO/Chief Sales Officer: Gary Nissen
Vice President: John Roon
Chief Technology Officer: Peter Sobczynski
Vice President, Worldwide Sales: James Coe
Product Manager: Ramki Ptoehaplli
Plant Manager: Bob Fruth
Supply Chain Manager: Brad Johnson
Estimated Sales: $50-100 Million
Number Employees: 160
Square Footage: 26217
Parent Co: Rank Group Limited
Type of Packaging: Consumer, Food Service

22347 **Everpure, LLC**
1040 Muirfield Drive
Hanover Park, IL 60133 630-307-3000
Fax: 630-307-3030 info@everpure.com
www.everpure.com
Manufacturer and exporter of water filters
Estimated Sales: $35 - 40 Million
Number Employees: 1-4
Parent Co: Culligan International Company

22348 **Everson Spice Company**
2667 Gundry Ave
Signal Hill, CA 90755 562-988-1223
Fax: 562-988-0219 800-421-3753
customerservice@eversonspice.com
www.eversonspice.com
Seasonings, dry rubs, stuffing mixes and marinades
Chairman: Tom Everson
President: Ken Hopkins
CEO: Kim Everson
Estimated Sales: $2.5-5 Million
Number Employees: 20-49

Type of Packaging: Food Service

22349 **Evonik Corporation**
299 Jefferson Rd
Parsippany, NJ 07054 973-541-8000
Fax: 973-541-8013
www.north-america.evonik.com
Precipitated and fumed silica used to improve the flow properties of food products, prevent caking, transfer liquids into free-flowing powders, improve dispersability, and function as processing aids in spray drying and millingapplications.
CEO: Dr. Klaus Engel
CFO: Dr. Wolfgang Colberg
Chief Human Resources Officer: Thomas Wessel
Estimated Sales: $3.58 Billion
Number Employees: 3500
Other Locations:
Production/Health & Nutrition
Blair NE
Production/Inorganic Materials
Clavert City KY
Production/R&D
Chester PA
Production/Coatings & Additives
Deer Park TX
Production/Performance Polymers
Fortier LA
Production/Advanced Intermediates
Galena KS
Production/Consumer Specialties
Garyville LA
Production/R&D
Greensboro NC
Production/Coatings & Additives
Hopewell VA
Production/Coatings & Additives
Horsham PA
Production/Consumer Specialties
Janesville WI
Customer Services/Health/Nutrition
Kennesaw GA
Tippecanoe Laboratories
Lafayette IN

22350 **Ex-Cell Kaiser**
11240 Melrose Avenue
Franklin Park, IL 60131 847-451-0451
Fax: 847-261-9448 service@ex-cell.com
www.ex-cell.com
Manufacturer and exporter of metal check order rails, long handle dust pans, handheld dust pans, waste receptacles, bus tub and water carts, bar speed rails, bottlecap catchers, mobile coat racks, condiment trays, luggage racks, andluggage carriers
Director: Anna Cosentino
Managing Member: Janet Kaiser
Vice President/General Manager: Jeffrey Speizman
Human Resources/Purchasing: Elaine Abba
Estimated Sales: $8 Million
Number Employees: 40
Square Footage: 70000
Brands:
Banquet Series
Ex-Cell
Landscape Series
Note Minder
Quicksilver
Safeguard
Service Solutions Series

22351 **Ex-Tech Plastics**
11413 Burlington Road
PO Box 576ÿ
Richmond, IL 60071 847-829-8100
Fax: 847-829-8190 sales@extechplastics.com
www.extechplastics.com
Extruded, plastic film and sheet PVC, PET, COPP, HOPP, and PLA
President: Jeff Fidler
Marketing: Laura Pichon
Estimated Sales: $10 - 20 000,000
Number Employees: 50-99

22352 **Exact Equipment Corporation**
20 N Pennsylvania Ave
Morrisville, PA 19067-1110 215-295-2000
Fax: 215-295-2080 sales@exacteq.com
www.exactequipment.com
Automatic and manual wrapping equipment, indexer labelers, scales and printers
Manager: Rich Lee
National Sales Manager: F Basil
VP Operations: S Smith
Estimated Sales: $5 - 10 Million
Number Employees: 50-99
Brands:
Exact Weight
Power Pack
Pre-Pac
Speedmaster
Work Horse

22353 **Exact Mixing Systems**
4739 S Mendenhall Rd
Memphis, TN 38141-8202 901-362-8501
Fax: 901-362-5479 jwarren@exactmixing.com
www.readingbakery.com
Continuous dough mixers and ingredient metering systems
President: Jim Warren
CFO and Corporate Secretary: Cheryl Followell
Chairman/VP: Robert Followell
Estimated Sales: $2.5-5 Million
Number Employees: 5-9
Square Footage: 40000

22354 **Exact Packaging**
1145 E Wellspring Rd
New Freedom, PA 17349-8426 717-235-8345
Fax: 717-235-0608 800-755-8344
lfullginiti@epilabelers.com
www.exactpackaging.com
President: Randy Cotteleer

22355 **Exaxol Chemical Corporation**
14325 60th St N
Clearwater, FL 33760 727-524-7732
Fax: 727-532-8221 800-739-2965
info@exaxol.com www.exaxol.com
Manufacturer and exporter of food quality control laboratory chemicals
President: Joseph Papa
Estimated Sales: $1 - 2,500,000
Number Employees: 1-4

22356 **Excalibur Bagel & BakeryEquipment Company**
4-01 Banta Pl
Fair Lawn, NJ 07410 201-797-2788
Fax: 201-797-2711 excaliburequip@aol.com
www.excalibur-equipment.com
Manufacturing ovens, mixers (spiral), two-arm mixers, bagel machines
VP: Shelley Kuo
Estimated Sales: $1-2.5 000,000
Number Employees: 10-19

22357 **Excalibur Miretti Group**
285 Eldridge Road
Fairfield, NJ 07004-2508 973-808-8399
Fax: 973-808-8398 sales@exequipment.com
www.exequipment.com
Explosion-proof forklifts, electric and forklift trucks, exporter of forklifts
President: Angelo Miretti
Square Footage: 44000
Brands:
Go Getters
Gregory

22358 **Excalibur Seasoning Company**
1800 Riverway Drive
Pekin, IL 61554 309-347-1221
Fax: 309-347-9086 800-444-2169
sales@excaliburseasoning.com
www.excaliburseasoning.com
Seasoning
President: Jay Hall
Estimated Sales: $5 - 10 Million
Number Employees: 50-99

22359 **Excel**
P.O. Box 459
Lincolnton, NC 28093 704-735-6535
Fax: 704-735-4899 info@xl-inc.com
www.excelhandling.com
Manufacturer and exporter of industrial hand, flat deck, order picking and specially fabricated trucks. Also, material handling carts, dollies, pin trucks, and yarn and beam transports
President/CEO: Charles Eurey
VP Administration/Sales: Jim Eurey
Estimated Sales: $20-50 Million
Number Employees: 10-19
Square Footage: 65000

22360 **Excel Chemical Company**
2385 Corbett St
Jacksonville, FL 32204-1705 904-356-0446
Fax: 904-356-1906
Cleaning compounds
President: William D Gladney
Number Employees: 5 to 9

22361 **Excel Engineering**
100 Camelot Dr
Fond Du Lac, WI 54935 920-926-9800
Fax: 920-926-9801 info@excelengineer.com
www.excelengineer.com
Architectural design, surveyor and engineering resources
President: Jeff Quast
CEO: Steve Soodsma
Business Development Director: Tony LeShay

22362 **Excel-A-Tec**
3695 N 126th St
Brookfield, WI 53005 262-252-3600
Fax: 262-252-3664 excelatec@aol.com
www.excelatec.com
Heat recovery systems, homogenizers, aseptic processing equipment, cheese equipment, blenders, deactators, heat exchangers, piping, fittings and tubing, sanitary, process control, process software
President: Harve Bronnert
Vice President: Joan Bronnert
Estimated Sales: $5 - 10 Million
Number Employees: 10-19

22363 **Excell Products**
2500 Enterprise Blvd
Choctaw, OK 73020-8400 405-390-4491
Fax: 405-390-4493 800-633-7670
sales@excellproducts.com
www.excellproducts.com
Screen painting, offset painting, signing systems, aisle markers, plastic extruding, spiral painting systems
President and CFO: Merle Medcalf
Estimated Sales: $500,000 - $1 Million
Number Employees: 5-9

22364 **Excellence Commercial Products**
1750 N University Dr
Pompano Beach, FL 33071-8903 954-752-0010
Fax: 954-752-0080 800-441-4014
howard@stajac.com www.stajac.com
Wholesaler/distributor, importer and exporter of coolers, freezers and ice cream cabinets
President: Howard Noskowicz
Quality Control: Catherina Derr
Number Employees: 1-4
Parent Co: Stajac Industries

22365 **Excellent Bakery Equipment Company**
315 Fairfield Rd
Fairfield, NJ 07004 973-244-1664
Fax: 973-244-1696 888-BAG-ELS1
staff@excellent-bagels.com
www.excellent-bagels.com
Bakery machinery, graters and shredders, triple action mixers, spiral mixers, rack ovens, formers and dividers, removable owl and self tipping mixers, bagel ovens and kettles, deck ovens, and volumetric dough dividers
President: Karin Seruga
Estimated Sales: $5 - 10 000,000
Number Employees: 10-19

22366 **Excelsior Transparent Bag Manufacturing**
159 Alexander St
Yonkers, NY 10701-2520 914-968-1300
Fax: 914-968-6567 againes@excelsiorcorp.com
Printed flexible packaging and laminated materials, bags and envelopes
President: Arleen Neustein
CFO: Ron Shenesh
VP: Cynthia Gaines
Customer Service: Adam Gaines
Estimated Sales: $10 - 20 Million
Number Employees: 50 to 99

22367 **ExecuChef Software**
862 Sir Francis Drake Boulevard
Suite 282
San Anselmo, CA 94960-1914 415-488-9600
Fax: 415-488-9690 sales@execuchef.com

Computer software including back-of-the-house management, inventory, cost, etc
Brands:
Chef Apprentice
Chef Explosion
Execuchef Pro

22368 Executive Line
30 Church St
Chatham, NY 12037-0352 518-392-5761
Fax: 518-392-5156 800-333-5761
www.chatco.com
Advertising specialties including tags, badges, pins, magnets, name plates, calendars, rulers, etc
President: Danny Crellin
VP Finance: Bernie Rizzo
Sales Manager: Jane Ryan
Estimated Sales: $2.5-5 Million
Number Employees: 1 to49
Square Footage: 2500

22369 Executive Match
PO Box 693
Salem, OH 44460-0693 330-332-2674
Fax: 330-332-2673 800-860-2674
bpenfold@meatrecruiter.com
www.meatrecruiter.com
Estimated Sales: $1 - 5 Million
Number Employees: 1

22370 Executive Referral Services
5440 N Cumberland Ave
Chicago, IL 60656-1490 773-693-6622
Fax: 773-693-8466 866-466-3339
info@facilitec-sw.com www.facilitec-sw.com
International consultant specializing in operations and sales management positions for grocery, convenience store, retail, food service and manufacturing organizations
Owner: Bruce Freier
Vice President: Mark Gray
Accounting Executive: Garry Chesla
Estimated Sales: $1-2.5 Million
Number Employees: 5-9

22371 Exhausto
PO Box 720651
Atlanta, GA 30358-2651 770-587-3238
Fax: 770-587-4731 800-255-2923
steenh@exhausto.com www.exhausto.com
Manufacturer, importer and exporter of kitchen exhaust/grease fans
President: Steen Hagensen
Marketing Director: Kelly Johnson
Sales Director: Mark Sylvia
Purchasing Manager: Joan Chenier
Estimated Sales: $40 Million
Number Employees: 100
Number of Brands: 1
Square Footage: 18000
Parent Co: Exhausto A/S
Type of Packaging: Bulk
Brands:
Exhausto

22372 Exhibitron Corporation
505 SE H St
Grants Pass, OR 97526 541-471-7400
Fax: 541-471-7200 800-437-4571
info@exhibitroncorp.com
www.exhibitroncorp.com
Screen printing commercial signage, and decor products and garments, aisle markers for grocery and retail stores; also, general fabrication and screen printing available
Owner: Ken Northrup
CEO: Kenneth Northup
Vice President: Marlene King
Estimated Sales: Below $5 Million
Number Employees: 1-4
Square Footage: 6500

22373 Exhibits and More
7843 Goguen Drive
Liverpool, NY 13090 315-652-0383
Fax: 315-652-8020 888-326-9100
bobd@exhibitsandmore.com
www.exhibitsandmore.com
Store fixtures
President: Bob Davidson
CEO: Frank Carnovale
VP of Sales: Valerie Low
COO: Jeff Vandeyacht
Estimated Sales: $500,000-$1 Million
Number Employees: 9
Other Locations:
Victor NY

22374 (HQ)Eximco Manufacturing Company
5311 N Kedzie Ave
Chicago, IL 60625-4711 773-463-1470
Fax: 773-583-5131
Fluorescent lighting fixtures, light bulbs, energy-saving lighting, alkaline batteries and fluorescent ballasts; importer and exporter of lamps
President: R Ramsden
General Manager: John Perell
Estimated Sales: $2.5-5 Million
Number Employees: 20-49
Square Footage: 20000
Other Locations:
Eximco Manufacturing Co.
Chicago IL

22375 Exopack
501 Williams St
Tomah, WI 54660 608-372-2153
Fax: 608-372-5702 flex.pack@exopack.com
www.exopack.com
Manufacturer and exporter of polyethylene film and bags
Quality Control: Don Bergum
President: Stan Bikulege
Sales Manager: Bruce Baker
Plant Manager: Terry Smith
Estimated Sales: $20 - 50 Million
Number Employees: 250-499
Parent Co: Union Camp Corporation
Type of Packaging: Consumer, Bulk

22376 Exopack, LLC
P.O.Box 5497
Spartanburg, SC 29304 864-596-7300
Fax: 864-596-7150 877-447-3539
flex.pack@exopack.com www.exopack.com
Flexible packaging materials made from paper and/or plastic. Products include multi-wall bags, plastic shipping sacks, stand-up pouches, printed rollstock and printed shrink films
Manager: Alfred Mc Clellan
CEO: Patrick Woods
Marketing Director: Lani Craddock
Sales Director: Robert Laird
Estimated Sales: $400 - 500 Million
Number Employees: 1,000-4,999
Type of Packaging: Consumer, Food Service, Private Label, Bulk
Brands:
Aqua Crystal
Instabowl
Repellence
Safe-T-Strip
Serve-N-Seal
Slide-Rite

22377 Expanko Cork Company
180 Gordon Drive
Suite 113
Exton, PA 19341 610-380-0300
Fax: 610-363-0735 800-345-6202
sales@expanko.com www.expanko.com
Wine industry corks and closures
President: Rob Mc Kee
Estimated Sales: $2.5-5 000,000
Number Employees: 5-9

22378 Expert Industries
848 E 43rd St
Brooklyn, NY 11210 718-434-6060
Fax: 718-434-6174 www.rubiconhx.com
Custom fabricated ribbon blenders, tanks, hoppers, mixers, dispersers, agitators, batch containers, cooling towers, half pipe coils, reactors, polishing pans, liquid and powder transporting bins, etc
Manager: Matt Rubinderg
Sales: E Senatore
General Manager: M Sterling
Estimated Sales: $10-20,000,000
Number Employees: 20-49

22379 Expo Instruments
1122 Aster Ave Ste E
Sunnyvale, CA 94086 408-554-8822
Fax: 408-554-8822 408-775-EXPO
info@expoinstruments.com
www.expoinstruments.com
Custom liquid level sensors, moniters, controls
President: George Rauchwerger
Estimated Sales: Below $5 000,000
Number Employees: 1-4

22380 ExpoDisplays
3401 Mary Taylor Rd
Birmingham, AL 35235-3234 205-439-8284
Fax: 205-439-8201 800-747-3976
webuildimages@expodisplays.com
www.expodisplays.com
Manufacturer and exporter of portable and modular displays and exhibits for tradeshow exhibition and marketplace display
Owner: Jeff Culton
VP: David Holladay
Marketing: Sara Mathews
Public Relations: Jay Burkette
Estimated Sales: $10 - 20 Million
Number Employees: 50-99
Square Footage: 30000
Brands:
2001
Airlite
Eclipse
Expoaire
Expoframe
Odyssey
Quantum
Visions

22381 Express Card & Label Company
2012 NE Meriden Rd
Topeka, KS 66608 785-233-0369
Fax: 785-233-2763 absales@expresscl.com
www.expresscl.com
Labeling equipment
President: John George
CEO: Stephen Atha
CFO: Mark Tillings
Estimated Sales: $5 - 10 Million
Number Employees: 50-99

22382 Express Packaging
Highway 67
PO Box 1333
Pembroke, GA 31321 912-653-2800
Fax: 912-653-2801 info@expresspkg.com
www.expresspkg.com
President: John Reardon
Vice President/Sales Manager: Mike Reardon
Estimated Sales: $10 - 20 Million
Number Employees: 20-49

22383 Expresso Shoppe Inc
524 N York Rd
Bensenville, IL 60106 630-350-0066
Fax: 336-393-0295 info@expressoshoppe.com
www.expressoshoppe.com
Owner: David Dimbert
Estimated Sales: Below $5 Million
Number Employees: 1-4

22384 Expro Manufacturing
2800 Ayers Avenue
Vernon, CA 90058 323-415-8544
Fax: 323-268-4060 jernster@expromfg.com
www.expromfg.com
Manufacturer and packager of food ingredients, including custom dry powder blends
President: Peter Ernster
CEO: Douglas Kantner
R&D: Greg Rowland
VP Sales: Michele Mullen
Purchasing: James Ernster
Number Employees: 20

22385 Exquis Confections
17629 Wheat Fall Drive
Derwood, MD 20855-1151 301-926-7043
Fax: 301-926-6432

22386 Extech Instruments
285 Bear Hill Rd
Waltham, MA 02451 781-890-7440
Fax: 781-890-7864 extech@extech.com
www.extech.com
Test and measurement instruments
Marketing Coordinator: Tracy Milhomme
Number Employees: 50-99

22387 **Extrutech Plastics Inc.**
5902 W Custer St
Manitowoc, WI 54220 920-684-9650
Fax: 920-684-4344 888-818-0118
info@epiplastics.com www.epiplastics.com
Plastic panels that are lightweight and easy to install. Panels can be used both indoors and out for dairy barns, foodplants, car washes and will not rust, peel, rot or corrode and are very easy to clean.
President/CEO/CFO: Greg Sheehy
Research/Development: Mike Sheehy
Quality Control: Ashley Shulz
Marketing: Greg Sheehy
Sales Representative: Scott Charles
Senior Project Engineer: Chuck Grozis
Estimated Sales: $10 Million
Number Employees: 60

22388 **Exxon Chemical Company**
13501 Katy Fwy
Houston, TX 77079-1306 281-870-6000
Fax: 281-870-6661 800-231-6633
www.exxonmobilchemical.com
Inorganic chemicals and low and high density polyethylene
President: Stephen D Pryor
Chairman And CEO: Rex Tillerson
Senior Vice President: Mark Albers
Estimated Sales: $25 - 30 Million
Number Employees: 10,000

22389 **Exxon Company**
745 Highway 6 S
Houston, TX 77079 281-493-9409
Fax: 281-870-6661 800-443-9966
www.exxonmobilchemical.com
Industrial lubricants
President: Stephen D Pryor
Estimated Sales: $1 - 5 000,000
Number Employees: 10,000

22390 **Exxon Mobil Chemical Company**
729 State Route 31
Macedon, NY 14502 315-966-1000
Fax: 315-966-5033 800-868-9206
films.americas@exxonmobil.com
www.exxonmobilchemical.com
Pressure sensitive oriented polypropylene labels, roll stock cut and stack
President: Rex Tillerson
VP: Robert Dobies
Estimated Sales: $1 Billion+
Number Employees: 250-499
Brands:
Label-Lyte

22391 **ExxonMobil Lubricants And Petroleum Specialties**
4550 Dacoma St
Houston, TX 77092-8614 713-680-7993
www.exxonmobil.com
Chairman of the Board: R. W. Tillerson
Senior Vice President: M. W. Albers
Vice President-Human Resources: M. A. Farrant

22392 **Ez Box Machinery Company**
6126 Brookshire Blvd Ste E
Charlotte, NC 28216 704-399-0727
Fax: 704-393-3629 sales08@ezbox.com
www.ezbox.com
Box machines, slitters, corrugated boxes
President: Andrew Dunn
Sales Director: Johnnie Quinn
Number Employees: 1-4

22393 **Eze Lap Diamond Products**
3572 Arrowhead Dr
Carson City, NV 89706 775-888-9500
Fax: 775-888-9555 800-843-4815
sales@eze-lap.com www.eze-lap.com
Sharpeners and sharpening stones for knives, slicing wheels, saw chains and pizza cutters; also, grinding equipment
President: Jay Fletcher
Sales Coordinator: Donna Long
Office Manager: Lisa Fletcher
General Manager: Ralph Johnson
Estimated Sales: $1 - 20,000,000
Number Employees: 20-49
Brands:
Diamond

22394 **F & F and A. Jacobs & Sons, Inc.**
1100 Wicomico St
Baltimore, MD 21230 410-727-6397
Fax: 800-426-4595 www.rjuniform.com
Military, commercial and institutional uniforms
President: Robert Friedlander
Estimated Sales: $1 - 5 Million
Number Employees: 20-49

22395 **F&A Fabricating**
104 Arbor St
Battle Creek, MI 49015 269-965-3268
Fax: 269-965-8371 www.fa-fabricating.com
Manufacturer and exporter of stainless steel fabricated products including belt conveyors
President: Hiep Nguyen
Estimated Sales: $2.5-5 Million
Number Employees: 20-49
Type of Packaging: Food Service, Bulk

22396 **F&G Packaging**
US Highway 17
Yulee, FL 32097 904-225-5121
Fax: 904-225-9500
Paper bags
General Manager: Allan Young
Number Employees: 177
Parent Co: Stone Container

22397 **F&S Awning & Blind Company**
13 Coral St
Edison, NJ 08837-3242 732-738-4110
Fax: 732-738-7255 www.fsawning.com
Commercial awnings
Owner: Bob Trotte
Estimated Sales: $1-2,500,000
Number Employees: 10-19

22398 **F&S Engraving**
1620 W Central Rd
Mt Prospect, IL 60056 847-870-8400
Fax: 847-870-8414 fsengrav@aol.com
www.tmanet.com/fsengraving
Bronze rotary cookie and cracker molds, and steel dye engraving
President: Jim Fromm
Estimated Sales: $5 - 10 000,000
Number Employees: 20-49

22399 **F. Harold Haines Manufacturing**
243 Main St
Presque Isle, ME 04769-2858 207-762-1411
Fax: 207-762-1412
Potato handling equipment, sizers and washers
Owner: Harold F Haines
VP: Harold Haines
Estimated Sales: $2.5-5 Million
Number Employees: 10 to 19

22400 **F.B. Leopold**
227 S Division St
Zelienople, PA 16063 724-452-6300
Fax: 724-452-1377 sales@fbleopold.com
www.fbleopold.com
Wine industry filtration equipment
VP: Robert M Clements
Estimated Sales: $1 - 5 Million
Number Employees: 50-99

22401 **F.B. Pease Company**
1450 E Henrietta Road
Rochester, NY 14623-3184 585-475-1870
Fax: 716-475-9621 sales@fbpease.com
www.fbpease.com
Paring, coring, slicing and conveying machinery for apples, kiwifruit, potatoes, squash and eggplant; exporter of apple parers, corers and slicers
Chairman: Warren Pease
President: Dudley Pease
Export Manager: Vivian Bubel
Estimated Sales: $2.5-5 Million
Number Employees: 19
Square Footage: 88000
Parent Co: Pease Development Company

22402 **F.D.S.**
P.O.Box 3120
Pomona, CA 91769-3120 909-591-1733
Fax: 909-591-1571 custserv@fdsmfg.com
www.fdsmfg.com
Fruit and vegetable packaging
Chairman: Sameul Stevenson
Estimated Sales: $20 - 50 Million
Number Employees: 100-249

22403 **F.E. Wood & Sons**
5 Brown Road
PO Box 46
East Baldwin, ME 04091 207-286-5003
Fax: 207-787-2575 info@fewoodenergy.com
www.fewoodenergy.com
Wooden pallets, bins and skids
President: Dean Wood
VP: Anthony Wood
Estimated Sales: $1-2.5 Million
Number Employees: 20-49

22404 **F.M. Corporation**
1360 SW 32nd Way
Deerfield Beach, FL 33442-8110 954-570-9860
Fax: 954-570-9865
Manufacturer and exporter of kitchen ventilation equipment including oven hoods
Plant Manager: Twayn Katz
Estimated Sales: $1 - 5,000,000
Number Employees: 20-50
Parent Co: Hood Depot
Type of Packaging: Food Service

22405 **F.N. Sheppard & Company**
1261 Jamike Ave
Erlanger, KY 41018 859-525-2358
Fax: 859-525-8467 800-733-5773
beltinfo@fnsheppard.com www.fnsheppard.com
Manufacturer and exporter of industrial belting for packaging including custom, flat, surreys and power transmission; also, design assistance, custom fabrication, field service, splicing tools and equipment available
President: James Reilly
Vice President: Frank Klaene
R&D: Tim Reilly
Quality Control: Bob Black
Marketing Director: Flint Coltharp
Sales Director: Wayne Siemer
Manufacturing Executive: Dan Martin
Plant Manager: Jim Reilly, Jr.
Purchasing Manager: Jack Fassel
Estimated Sales: $10 - 20 Million
Number Employees: 50-99
Square Footage: 20000

22406 **F.N. Smith Corporation**
1200 S 2nd St
Oregon, IL 61061 815-732-2171
Fax: 815-732-6173 fnsmith@fnsmithcorp
www.fnsmithcorp.com
Bins, conveyors, packaging and extrusion equipment, knives, cartoning equipment and forming rolls for flaking/forming food; exporter of oat hullers and grain steamers
President: Ed Smith
CFO: Fred Smith
VP: Edward Smith
Estimated Sales: $2.5-5 Million
Number Employees: 20-49
Square Footage: 35000

22407 **F.O. Carlson Company**
3622 S Morgan
Chicago, IL 60609 773-847-6900
Fax: 773-847-6924 focarlson@interaccess.com
www.focarlson.com
Indoor advertising signs and graphics
Owner: Raul Correa
Quality Control: Earl Raas
VP: Douglas Carlson
Number Employees: 20-49

22408 **F.P. Smith Wire Cloth Company**
11700 W Grand Avenue
Northlake, IL 60164-1373 708-562-3344
Fax: 800-310-8999 800-323-6842
Manufacturer and exporter of woven and welded wire cloth
VP of Manufacturing: John Crupper
VP Sales: Ted Kapp
VP Manufacturing: Dr. John Crupper
Estimated Sales: $2.5-5 Million
Number Employees: 500
Square Footage: 57000
Brands:
Metaloom

22409 **F.R. Drake Company**
1410 Genicom Dr
Waynesboro, VA 22980-1956 540-949-6215
Fax: 540-949-8363 sales@drakeloader.com
www.drakeloader.com

Frankfurter loaders
President and CFO: Russ Martin
Vice President of Engineering: George Reed
R&D: George Reid
Sales Manager of North America: Tyrone Beatty
Estimated Sales: $10 - 20 Million
Number Employees: 50-99

22410 F/G Products
3000 Pioneer Ave
Rice Lake, WI 54868 715-234-2334
Fax: 715-234-6259 800-247-3854
info@fgproducts.com www.fgproducts.com
Insulated and return air bulkheads and center partition systems for the refrigerated transportation industry
President: Roger Nelson
Marketing Director: Matthew Nelson
Sales Manager: Ron Hagen
Estimated Sales: $10 - 20 Million
Number Employees: 50-99
Square Footage: 25000

22411 FABCO Technologies
11200 W Silver Spring Rd
Milwaukee, WI 53225 414-461-9100
Fax: 414-461-8899 sal@fabco.com
www.fabco.com
Disinfection of pumpable foods and drinking water
Estimated Sales: $500,000-$1 Million
Number Employees: 1-4

22412 FAN Separator
466 Randy Road
Carol Stream, IL 60188-2120 922-793-8400
Fax: 922-793-8444 800-451-8001
info@fan-separator.de www.fan-separator.de
Liquids, solid separation
President: Friedrich Wiegand
Estimated Sales: $1 - 2.5 Million
Number Employees: 2

22413 FARGO Electronics
6533 Flying Cloud Dr Ste 1000
Eden Prairie, MN 55344 952-941-9710
Fax: 952-941-7836 sales@fargo.com
www.fargo.com
ID CARD printers
President: Gary Holland
Quality Control: Jeff Sasse
VP: Thomas C Platner
CFO: Paul Stephenson
Sales Manager: Mark Anderson
Number Employees: 100-249

22414 FASTCORP LLC
22 Shelter Rock Lane
Danbury, CT 06810 973-455-0400
Fax: 973-455-7401 888-457-0716
fastcorp1@aol.com www.fastcorpvending.com
Estimated Sales: $3 - 5 Million
Number Employees: 20-49

22415 FBM/Baking Machines Inc
1 Corporate Drive
Cranbury, NJ 08512 800-449-0433
Fax: 609-860-0576 800-449-0433
info@fbmbakingmachines.com
www.fbmbakingmachines.com
Ovens and machines, VMI mixers, Panimatic retarders/proofers and ovens
President: Oliver Frot
CFO: Beatrice Harmett
Number Employees: 5-9

22416 FCD Tabletops
812 Snediker Ave
Brooklyn, NY 11207 718-649-1002
Fax: 800-938-0818 800-822-5399
Manufacturer and exporter of table, bar and counter tops
Sales Manager: Eric Grossman
VP Sales: Peter Stagg
Estimated Sales: $5-10,000,000
Number Employees: 20-49
Square Footage: 35000

22417 FCF Ginseng, LLC
3225 Halder Dr
Mosinee, WI 54455 715-693-3166
Fax: 715-693-5541 burgey@pcpros.com
www.fcfginseng.com
President: Lawrence Murray
CFO: Yvonne Murray
Estimated Sales: Below $5 Million
Number Employees: 1-4

22418 FCI Company
4661 Giles Rd
Cleveland, OH 44135-3756 216-251-5200
Fax: 216-251-5206 800-321-1032
fci@fci-usa.com www.fci-usa.com
Change parts for bottle fillers and cappers, replacement parts fore beverage equipment, vent tubes
President: Kenneth J Edgar
Operations Manager: Mike Peronek
Estimated Sales: $10-20 Million
Number Employees: 50-99

22419 FDL/Flair Designs
P.O.Box 606
Kokomo, IN 46903-0606 765-452-6000
Fax: 765-452-5882 glena@fdlinc.com
www.fdlinc.com
Chairs, cushions, pads and bar/counter stools
Estimated Sales: $1-2.5 Million
Number Employees: 20-49

22420 FDP
1330 N Dutton Avenue
Suite 100
Santa Rosa, CA 95401-4653 707-547-1776
Fax: 707-545-5270 sales@fdpusa.com
www.fdpusa.com
Founded in 1978. Manufacturer of dehydrated fruits and vegetables
President: Mark Martindill
Quality Control: Scott Klinger
National Sales Manager: Michael Bray
Sales: Nancy Costa
Procurement Manager: Andrew McCoy
Estimated Sales: $20-50 Million
Number Employees: 20-49
Parent Co: FDP GmbH
Brands:
Soubry Instant Pasta
Taura Urc

22421 FEC/Food Engineering Corporation
P.O.Box 29505
Raleigh, NC 27626-0505 919-851-2000
Fax: 919-851-6029 sales@aeroglide.com
www.aeroglide.com
Design and manufacture of custom industrial dryers, roasters, and coolers for food processing.
President: Fred Kelly Jr
CEO: J Fredrick Kelly Jr
Sales Director: Tom Barber
Number Employees: 100-249

22422 FECO/MOCO
1441 Chardon Road
Cleveland, OH 44117-1510 216-531-1599
Fax: 216-441-6529 sales@fecoweb.com
www.ajaxtocco.com
Custom designing and manufacturing industrial ovens and thermal processing equipment Engineering and design capabilities include the unique ability to combine heat-processing and curing technologies with material handling andconveying methods
President: Dave Ekers
Project Manager Conveyors: Jim Hercik
Project Manager Ovens: Alan Semetana
Purchasing Manager: Jack Specker
Estimated Sales: $10-20 Million
Number Employees: 10
Square Footage: 120000
Parent Co: Park Ohio Company

22423 FEI
934 S 5th Ave
Mansfield, TX 76063 817-473-3344
Fax: 817-473-3124 800-346-5908
sales@feiconveyors.com www.feiconveyors.com
Manufacturer and exporter of sanitary and anti-corrosive conveyors including gravity, powered and stainless steel skate wheels; also, conveyor components
President: Duane Murray
VP: David Murray
Estimated Sales: $5-10 Million
Number Employees: 20-49
Square Footage: 34000

22424 FEI Cold Storage
1125 Berryhill St
Harrisburg, PA 17104 717-232-1083
Fax: 888-381-6910 ftxrscac@aol.com
www.feicoldstorage.com
Warehouse providing cooler, freezer, humidity-controlled and dry storage
Manager: Greg Shipe
Estimated Sales: $1-2.5 Million
Number Employees: 10-19
Square Footage: 80000
Type of Packaging: Consumer, Food Service

22425 FEMC
22201 Aurora Rd
Cleveland, OH 44146-1273 216-663-1208
Fax: 216-663-9337 info@femc.com
www.femc.com
President: Bob Sauer
Estimated Sales: $5 - 10 Million
Number Employees: 20-49

22426 FES Systems
PO Box 2306
York, PA 17405-2306 717-767-6411
Fax: 717-764-3627 800-888-4337
www.fessystems.com
Processor and exporter of refrigeration equipment for food processing plants
President: Ronald Eberhard
VP Domestic Sales: Jeffrey Grady
International Sales: W Humm
Estimated Sales: $20-50 Million
Number Employees: 250-499
Square Footage: 73640
Parent Co: Thermo-Electron Corporation

22427 FES West
2617 Willowbrook Ln
Aptos, CA 95003-6022 831-462-6603
Fax: 831-462-9781 800-251-6603
feswst@aol.com www.r717.com
Wine industry refrigeration systems
Owner: Harold Paul
Estimated Sales: $1-2.5 Million
Number Employees: 1-4

22428 FETCO - Food Equipment Technologies Corporation
P.O.Box 429
Lake Zurich, IL 60047-0429 847-719-3000
Fax: 847-719-3001 800-338-2699
info@fetco.com www.fetco.com
Manufacturer, importer and exporter of food service equipment including coffee carts, tea brewing equipment servers, commissary systems and coffee and tea equipment
President: Zbigniew Lassota
CFO: Zeel Lasoda
VP: Christopher Nowak
VP of Marketing and Sales: Richard Baggett
Estimated Sales: $10 - 20 Million
Number Employees: 50-99

22429 (HQ)FFE Transportation Services
P.O.Box 655888
Dallas, TX 75265-5888
Fax: 214-819-5625 800-569-9200
ir@ffex.net www.ffex.net
To get to any information for the other FFE sites please visit the web address in this listing, transportation firm providing refrigerated local, long and short haul trucking and van service, LTL, and TL
CEO: Stoney M Stubbs Jr
Estimated Sales: D
Number Employees: 250-499
Other Locations:
FFE Transportation Services
Oakland CA

22430 FFI Corporation
P.O. Box 20
1004 East Illinois Street
Assumption, IL 62510 217-226-5100
www.fficorpo.com
Manufacturer and exporter of continuous flow commercial and industrial grain dryers
Estimated Sales: $50-100 Million
Number Employees: 250-499

22431 FIB-R-DOR
10021 Commerce Park Dr.
P.O.Box 13268
Cincinnati, OH 45246 501-758-9494
Fax: 501-758-9496 800-342-7367
fibrdor@fibrdor.com www.fibrdor.com
Manufacturer and exporter of fiberglass doors, etc.
President: Jason Dileo
Marketing Director: Wes Lacewell
Sales Director: Mike Ferrell
Estimated Sales: $2.5 Million
Number Employees: 10-19
Number of Products: 3
Square Footage: 50000
Parent Co: Advance Fiberglass
Type of Packaging: Bulk
Brands:
Fib-R-Dor

22432 FJC International
2418 Hilton Way
Gainesville, GA 30501 770-718-0100
Fax: 770-718-0909 info@fjcinternational.com
www.fjcinternational.com
Provides equipment and turnkey operations for poultry processing plants
President: Juan Chiarella
Estimated Sales: $1.3 Million
Number Employees: 8

22433 (HQ)FLEXcon Company
1 S Spencer Rd
Spencer, MA 01562 508-885-8200
Fax: 508-885-8400 www.flexcon.com
Pressure sensitive film and adhesive products
CEO: Neil McDonough
Number Employees: 1,000-4,999

22434 FMB Company
RR 1
Box 564
Broken Bow, OK 74728-9780 580-513-5309
Fax: 580-584-2971 fmbco@octm.com
www.fmbco.com
Consultant providing design and building services for food and industrial plants
President: Fred Bray
Director Marketing: Tonya Laffey
Estimated Sales: Below $5 Million
Number Employees: 1
Square Footage: 6400

22435 FMC Corporation
1735 Market Street
Philadelphia, PA 19103-7501 215-299-6000
Fax: 215-299-5998 800-346-7880
james.fitzwater@fmc.com www.fmc.com
Natural soda ash, sodium bicarbonate, sodium cyanide, sodium sesquicarbonate, caustic soda
President: William G Walter
Sales Manager: Osman Parlak
Number Employees: 100-249

22436 FMC Corporation Biopolymer
1735 Market St
Philadelphia, PA 19103-7597 215-299-6000
Fax: 215-299-6140 800-526-3649
olg-drebotij@fmc.com www.fmc.com
President: William G Walter
General Manager: Gerald Moss
Sales Manager: Osman Parlak
Estimated Sales: $200 Million
Number Employees: 5,000-9,999

22437 FMC Corporation Chemical Products
1735 Market St
Philadelphia, PA 19103-7597 215-299-6000
Fax: 215-299-6140 800-523-5005
shelley-woods@fmc.com www.fmc.com
Natural soda ash for sodium bicarbonate, sodium cyanide, sodium sesquicarbonate and caustic soda, hydrogen peroxide, active oxidants, phosphorus chemicals and phosphoric acid
Chairman/CEO: William Walter
Senior VP/CFO: W Kim Foster
Vice President: Andrea Utecht
VP Agricultural Products: Milton Steele
Sales Manager: Osman Parlak
Estimated Sales: K
Number Employees: 5,000-9,999

22438 FMC Fluid Control
2825 W Washington St
Stephenville, TX 76401 254-968-2181
Fax: 254-965-8256 800-772-8582
fluid.control@fmcti.com www.fmc.com
Manufacturer and exporter of flow and level control equipment, environmental analyzers and process control instrumentations including flow meters, level controls, valves, oil detectors, etc
Manager: Fernando Camuzzi
General Manager Fluid Control: Steve Barrett
Business Manager: Mark Earl
Plant Manager: John Moore
Estimated Sales: $5 Billion
Number Employees: 250-499
Square Footage: 268000
Brands:
Envirolert
Leveltronic

22439 FMC Fluid Control
103 E Maple Street
Hoopeston, IL 60942-1699 217-283-8300
Fax: 217-283-8424 www.fmcinvalco.com
Wine industry vineyard sprayers
Co- Owner: Thomas Hamilton
Chairman, President, Chief Executive Off: John Gremp
Vice President of Infrastructure: Barry Glickman
Regional Sales Manager: Ellen Hao
Estimated Sales: $10-20 Million
Number Employees: 50-99

22440 FMC FoodTech
400 Fairway Ave
Lakeland, FL 33801-2468 863-683-5411
Fax: 863-683-3677 citrus.info@fmcti.com
www.fmcfoodtech.com
Manufacturer and exporter of citrus fruit, noncitrus fruit and vegetable juicers for use in supermarkets, hotels, restaurants and food service operations
Customer Service Manager: Connie West
HR Manager: Leigh Marconi
Plant Manager: Richard Ballard
Estimated Sales: $5 Billion
Number Employees: 100-249
Square Footage: 150000
Parent Co: FMC Corporation
Brands:
Fresh 'n Squeeze

22441 FMC FoodTech
2300 W Industrial Ave
Madera, CA 93637-5210 559-673-2766
Fax: 703-548-6563 madera.fpsd@fmcti.com
www.fmcfoodtech.com
Food processing machinery including fruit and vegetable juice extractors, blanchers, freezers, can closers, corers, pitters, choppers, etc
Director Sales/Marketing: Ken Jones
Estimated Sales: $5 Billion
Number Employees: 100-249
Parent Co: FMC Corporation

22442 FMC Technologies
400 Highpoint Dr
Chalfont, PA 18914 215-822-6109
Fax: 215-822-4553 888-362-3622
sgv.sales@fmcti.com www.fmcsgvs.com
Automated guided vehicles
Manager: Barry Douglas
Advertising Manager: Amy Porter
Estimated Sales: $50 - 100 Million
Number Employees: 100-249

22443 FMI Display
360 Glen Way
Elkins Park, PA 19027-1740 215-663-1998
Fax: 215-763-7099
Wire display racks and point of purchase displays including paper and plastic; also, screen printing services available
President: Kenneth Hoffman
Number Employees: 10
Square Footage: 5000

22444 FMI Fluid Metering
5 Aerial Way
Suite 500
Syosset, NY 11791-5593 516-922-6050
Fax: 516-624-8261 800-223-3388
pumps@fmipump.com www.fmipump.com
Dispensers, ingredients, lubricant, ingredient feeders
President: Harry Pinkerton
Number Employees: 50-99

22445 FMS
328 Commerce Blvd # 8
Bogart, GA 30622-2200 706-549-2207
Fax: 706-548-1724 fmssales@fmsathens.com
www.fmsathens.com
Manager: Eric Gunderson
Estimated Sales: $10 - 20 Million
Number Employees: 20-49

22446 FMS Company
338 Alana Drive
New Lenox, IL 60451-1784 815-485-4955
Fax: 815-485-4011 800-992-2814
Wine industry financial software
Estimated Sales: $2.5-5 000,000
Number Employees: 1-4

22447 FONA International Inc.
1900 Averill Rd
Geneva, IL 60134 630-578-8600
www.fona.com
Flavoring extract and syrup
President/CEO: Joseph Slawek
CFO: James Evanoff
Purchasing Manager: Debbie Fleming
Estimated Sales: $50 Million
Number Employees: 100-249

22448 FOODesign Machinery & Systems, Inc.
29103 SW Kinsman Road
P.O.Box 2449
Wilsonville, OR 97070 503-685-5030
Fax: 503-685-5034 info@foodesign.com
www.foodesign.com
Commercial and industrial cooking/baking equipment, fryers, Cryo-Jet® cooling units, coating/seasoning equipment, food grade bulk packaging handling conveyers and specialty cooking equipment.
President: Joseph Mistretta
VP/Sales: Daniel Luna
Number Employees: 20

22449 FP Developments
402 South Main Street
Williamstown, NJ 08094-1729 856-875-7100
Fax: 856-875-6717 sales@fpdevelopments.com
www.fpdevelopments.com
Specialized packaging equipment
President: Fred Pfleger
Estimated Sales: $5-10 Million
Number Employees: 20-49

22450 FP International
1090 Mills Way
Redwood City, CA 94063 650-261-5300
Fax: 650-361-1713 800-866-9946
virginia.lyle@fpintl.com www.fpintl.com
Manufactures cushioning material for protective packaging
President: Arthur Graham
CFO: Dennis Fernandes
Marketing: Larry Lenhart
Estimated Sales: $30 - 50 Million
Number Employees: 5-9

22451 FP Packaging Company
193 Camino Dorado
Napa, CA 94558-6213 707-258-3940
Fax: 707-258-3949 www.collopack.com
Wine industry packaging and wine corks
President: Gregory Fulford
CEO: Gregory Fulford
Founder, Executive Vice President Sales: Phil Giacalone
Founder, Vice President of Sales: Joe Mironicki
Estimated Sales: $10 - 20 Million
Number Employees: 10-19
Type of Packaging: Bulk

22452 FPC Corporation
355 Hollow Hill Rd
Wauconda, IL 60084 847-487-4583
Fax: 847-487-0174 sales@surebonder.com
www.surebonder.com
Glue sticks, staples and staple guns
President: M Bernard Kamins
CFO: Patrick Kamins
Quality Control: M Bernard Kamins
Estimated Sales: $10-20 000,000
Number Employees: 20-49

22453 FPEC
2216 Ford Ave
Springdale, AR 479-751-93 479-751-9399
Fax: 479-751-9399 salesark@fpec.com
www.fpec.com
Processing equipment for beef, chicken, sausage, fish and ham
President: Alan Davison
Estimated Sales: $5-10 Million
Number Employees: 20-49

22454 FPEC Corporation
13623 Pumice St
Santa Fe Springs, CA 90670-5105 562-802-3727
Fax: 562-802-8621 salescal@fpec.com
www.fpec.com
Manufacturer and exporter of food processing equipment including blenders, conveyors and vacuum tumblers
President: Alan Davison
Plant Manager: Dwayne Lee
Estimated Sales: $5 - 10 Million
Number Employees: 20-49
Square Footage: 212000
Brands:
Fpec

22455 FR Drake Company
1410 Genicom Drive
Waynesboro, VA 22980-1956 540-451-2790
Fax: 540-942-2649 sales@drakeloader.com
www.drakeloader.com
Designs and manufactures automatic loading systems for cylindrical products and frozen patties. Frankfurters and other cylindrical products are loaded into packages at speeds up to 1,800 pieces per minute
President: Russ Martin
Vice President of Engineering: George Reed
Sales Manager of North America: Tyrone Beatty
Number Employees: 50-99
Type of Packaging: Food Service, Bulk

22456 FRC Environmental
1635 Oakbrook Dr
Gainesville, GA 30507 770-534-3681
Fax: 770-535-1887 sales@frcenvironmental.com
www.frcenvironmental.com
Manufacturer and exporter of stainless steel waste water treatment equipment and systems
President: Lonnie Finley
Estimated Sales: $2,600,000
Number Employees: 25
Square Footage: 36000
Type of Packaging: Bulk

22457 FRC Systems International
1770 Ridgefield Drive
Roswell, GA 30075 770-534-3681
Fax: 770-992-2289 info@FRCsystems.com
www.frcsystems.com
Water and wastewater treatment systems for the dairy, poultry, meat & seafood processing industries.

22458 FRICK by Johnson Controls
100 C V Avenue
Waynesboro, PA 17268-0997 717-762-2121
Fax: 717-762-1305 john.h.gay@jci.com
www.jci.com/frick
Industrial refrigeration, food and beverage, petrochemical, oil and gas extraction
CEO: James Furlong
R&D: Joe Pillis
Marketing Manager: John Gay
Sales: John Ferguson
Estimated Sales: $100-500 Million
Number Employees: 500
Parent Co: Johnson Controls

22459 FRS Industries
64 4th St N
Fargo, ND 58102 701-235-5347
Fax: 701-235-0753 800-747-4795
info@frsind.com www.frsind.com
Advertising novelties and specialites including award ribbons, rosettes, trophies, promotional buttons, imprinted T-shirts, jackets, caps, etc
Owner: Sheri Larson
Controller: Timothy Dockter
Sales Manager: Sheri Larson
Estimated Sales: $5-10 Million
Number Employees: 20-49

22460 FSFG Capital
814 Fontana Avenue
Richardson, TX 75080-3002 972-783-0611
Fax: 972-235-5310
Investment firm for food companies
Vice President: Richard Harju

22461 FSI Technologies, Inc.
668 E Western Ave
Lombard, IL 60148-2097 630-932-9380
Fax: 630-932-0016 800-468-6009
info@fsinet.com www.fsinet.com
Machine vision and systems, automatic inspection systems, rotary shaft encoders, electronic counters and displays for motion variables, specialized photoelectric sensors.
President: Scott Tobey
VP: Fred Turek
Sales: Kim Jackson
Estimated Sales: $2.5-5 Million
Number Employees: 20-49
Brands:
Checker Vision System
Cirrus
Defender
Ese
Hde
Indicoder
Pulsar
Rse
Tuff-Coder

22462 FTC International Consulting
19021 Mitchell Road
Pitt Meadows, BC V3Y 1Y1
Canada 604-288-2719
Fax: 604-288-8565 contact@ftcinternational.com
www.ftcinternational.com
Consulting: product development, nutrition analysis, regulatory consulting, quality programs
President: Walter Dullemond
Operations Manager: Eva Savova

22463 FTI International Automation Systems
10914 N 2nd Street
Machesney Park, IL 61115-1400 815-877-4080
Fax: 815-877-0073 sales@ftii.com
www.ftiautomationsystems.com

22464 FTL/Happold Tensil Structure Design & Engineering
44 East 32nd Street
3rd Floor
New York, NY 10016 212-732-4691
Fax: 212-385-1025 ngoldsmith@ftlstudio.com
www.ftlstudio.com
Commercial tents, fabric structures
Owner: Todd Dalland
Genetics Department: Andre Chaszar
Engineer: Wayne Rendeley
Estimated Sales: $1 - 5 Million
Number Employees: 20-49
Parent Co: Buro Happold

22465 FTR Processing EquipmentCompany
2101 Troy Ave
South El Monte, CA 91733 626-452-1870
Fax: 626-452-1857 ftrequipment@yahoo.com
ftrequipment.com
Packaging, processing and slaughtering equipment
Owner: Francisco Prejo
Vice President: Gloria Trejo
Sales Director: Jair Trejo
Estimated Sales: Below $5 000,000
Number Employees: 20-49
Number of Brands: 55

22466 FWE/Food Warming Equipment Company, Inc
338 Memorial Dr. Suite 300
Crystal Lake, IL 60014 815-459-7500
Fax: 815-459-7989 800-222-4393
sales@fweco.com www.fweco.com
Manufacturer and exporter of stainless steel heated and refrigerated utility carts and mobile cabinets
President: Richard Klemm
CEO: Deron Lichte
CFO: Chris Huffman
VP Marketing/Sales: Curt Benson
Estimated Sales: $5 - 10 Million
Number Employees: 50-99
Square Footage: 280000
Brands:
Prm-Ii (Prime Rib Master)
Weather-All Bars

22467 FX Technology & Products
900 Factory Rd
PO Box 547
Fremont, NE 68026 402-727-5222
Fax: 402-721-5154 866-938-8388
info@fibrimex.com www.fibrimex.com
Proteins
Regional Sales Manager: Rick Young
Office Manager: Debbie Vacha
Estimated Sales: Under $500,000
Number Employees: 10-19

22468 FX-Lab Company
725 Lehigh Avenue
Union, NJ 07083-7642 908-810-1212
Fax: 908-810-1630
Manufacturer and exporter of beneficial bacterial cleaning compounds and liquefiers for septic tanks and cesspools
President: George Weinik
Number Employees: 5
Square Footage: 2400

22469 FYH Bearing Units USA
285 Industrial Dr
Wauconda, IL 60084 847-487-9111
Fax: 847-882-5360 fyhusa@aol.com
www.fyhusa.com
Mounted bearing units and insert bearings; inch and metric shaft sizes, heavy duty, medium duty, standard duty, and light duty units; specialty series include solid stainless steel, bright white thermoplstic, clean series, taper borelocking UK-series
Manager: J Frasor
CFO: Rodney Jones
Executive VP: Tohru Yamashita
General Manager: Charles Horwitz
Estimated Sales: $10 - 20 000,000
Number Employees: 5-9
Type of Packaging: Private Label

22470 Fab-X/Metals
PO Box 1903
Washington, NC 27889-1903 252-977-3229
Fax: 252-977-6605 800-677-3229
sales@fabxmetals.com www.fabxmetals.com
Manufacturer and wholesaler/distributor of chairs, ovens, sinks, spoons, tables, etc.; also, supermarket equipment including store fixtures and racks; serving the food service market
President: Jonathan Turner
COO: Cyrus Watson
Quality Control: Carol Causeway
Estimated Sales: $10-20 Million
Number Employees: 10
Square Footage: 100000

22471 FabOhio
521 E 7th St
Uhrichsville, OH 44683 740-922-4233
Fax: 740-922-4785 fabohio@tusco.net
www.fabohio.com
Manufacturer and exporter of protective clothing and products including drum liners, meat cutters' aprons and smocks and shoe covers. Also custom fabrication available.
President: Dave Shelley
CEO: Kurt Shelley
CFO: Kurt Shelley
Purchasing Manager: Dennis Sautters
Estimated Sales: $1-3 Million
Number Employees: 20-49
Square Footage: 25000

22472 FabWright, Inc
13912 Enterprise Dr
Garden Grove, CA 92843 714-554-5544
Fax: 714-554-5545 800-854-6464
jamesc@fabwrightinc.com
www.fabwrightinc.com
Manufacturer and exporter of custom stainless steel kitchen equipment fabrication; complete line of commercial food waste disposers
President/CEO: R Wright
Vice President: J Wright
Purchasing Manager: D Yeardley
Number Employees: 20-49

Type of Packaging: Food Service

22473 Fabco Equipment
P.O.Box 754
Albertville, AL 35950-0012 256-878-5010
Fax: 256-878-7879 www.fabcoinc.com
CEO: Rocky Frazier
Director of Sales: Stephen Frazier
Manufacturing Manager: Phillip Murphree
Estimated Sales: $20-50 Million
Number Employees: 50-99

22474 Fabreeka International
696 W Amity Rd
Boise, ID 83705-5401 208-342-4681
Fax: 208-343-8043 800-423-4469
farbo@cybergateway.net www.beltservice.com
Manufacturer and exporter of lightweight custom conveyor belting including food grade, food grade incline, special profile, harvester, PVC and polyurethane
Branch Manager: Bob Holda
General manager: Toby Grindstaff
Division Manager: Toby Grindstaff
Assistant Division Manager: Mitz Pellicciotta
Estimated Sales: Below $5 Million
Number Employees: 10-19
Square Footage: 400000
Parent Co: Fabreeka International
Other Locations:
Fabreeka International
Oakville ON
Brands:
Fablene
Fablon
Fabreeka
Fabsyn

22475 Fabreeka International
1023 Turnpike St
Stoughton, MA 02072 781-341-3655
Fax: 781-341-3983 800-322-7352
info@fabreeka.com www.fabreeka.com
Integrally molded cleated and special profile rubber belting and European style thermoplastics belting
President: Pat Norton
Estimated Sales: $25 - 30 Million
Number Employees: 100-249

22476 Fabri-Form Company
10501 Burt St
Byesville, OH 43723 740-685-0424
Fax: 740-685-6211 jbrandts@socplas.org
www.fabri-form.com
Material handling equipment including trays, pallets and covers; exporter of electrical components
Director: John W Knight
VP Sales: Larry Howard
Manager Customer Service: Dennis Hardin
Plant Manager: Jerry Andrech
Number Employees: 50-99

22477 Fabri-Kal Corporation
600 Plastics Pl
Kalamazoo, MI 49001 269-385-5050
Fax: 269-385-0197 800-888-5054
info@f-k.com www.fabri-kal.com
Thermoformed plastic containers and cups including custom designed, prototype, production, stock food service line, clear or colored and FDA certified
CEO: Robert P Kittredge
Marketing Manager: Scott Tindall
Estimated Sales: $10-20 Million
Number Employees: 50-99
Brands:
Kal-Tainer

22478 Fabricated Components
2018 West Main Street
PO Box 431
Stroudsburg, PA 18360-0431 570-421-4110
Fax: 570-421-2553 800-233-8163
info@fabricatedcomponents.com
www.fabricatedcomponents.com
Manufacturer and exporter of pallets, dollies, carts, cabinetry and containers
President: Bob Deinarowicz
Estimated Sales: $2.5-5 Million
Number Employees: 20-49
Square Footage: 100000
Type of Packaging: Private Label

22479 Fabricating & Welding Corporation
12246 S Halsted St
Chicago, IL 60628 773-928-2050
Fax: 773-928-4950
bobdelcotto@fabricatingandwelding.com
www.fabricatingandwelding.com
Steel skids, base plates and motor bases
President: Pasquale Del Cotto
CFO: Elizabeth Pecora
Research & Development: Steven Samecak
Production Manager: Jim Foley
Purchasing Manager: Robert Del Cotto
Estimated Sales: $5 - 10 Million
Number Employees: 20-49
Square Footage: 30000

22480 Fabrication SpecialtiesCorporation
2898 Crestridge Dr
Centerville, TN 37033-5941 931-729-2283
Fax: 931-729-2585
Wood pallets and shipping skids
Owner: Mike Goodpasture
VP: William Goodpasture
Estimated Sales: $2.5-5 Million
Number Employees: 20 to 49
Square Footage: 20000

22481 Fabrichem
2226 Black Rock Tpke Ste 206
Fairfield, CT 06825 203-366-1820
Fax: 203-366-1850 sales@fabricheminc.com
www.fabricheminc.com
Aspartame, amino acids, L-Tyrosine, botanical extracts, L-theanine, Lutein, D-Glucuronolactone
President: Jacob Eallthra
Estimated Sales: $5-10 000,000
Number Employees: 10
Number of Brands: 4
Number of Products: 50

22482 Fabricon Products
PO Box 18358
River Rouge, MI 48218 313-841-8200
Fax: 313-841-4819
bsmith@fabriconproducts.com
www.fabriconproducts.com
Manufacturer, importer and exporter of flexible packaging materials including printed waxed and coated paper, films, frozen/novelty food packaging and wrapping, preformed paper bags and film laminated pouches; also, package designservices available
President: Bruce Dinda
CFO: Roland David
Sales Director: Jim Nolan
Production Manager: Mike Aslanian
Plant Manager: John Kuzawinski
Purchasing Manager: Colleen Loweifer
Estimated Sales: $9 Million
Number Employees: 50-99
Square Footage: 151000
Type of Packaging: Consumer, Food Service, Private Label, Bulk

22483 Fabriko
P.O.Box 67
Altavista, VA 24517-0067 434-369-1170
Fax: 434-369-1169 888-203-8098
afbriko@voyager.net www.fabriko.com
Manufacturer and importer of barbecue and waist aprons, coolers and bags including lunch, grocery and shopping
Owner: Ranata Allbeck
Sales Manager: Jerry Fischer
Estimated Sales: $3 - 5 Million
Number Employees: 10-19

22484 Facilitec
73 S Riverside Dr
Elgin, IL 60120-6425 847-931-9500
Fax: 847-931-9629 jjodoin@faciliteccorp.com
www.faciliteccorp.com
Estimated Sales: $1 - 5 Million
Parent Co: Ecolab

22485 Facilities Design
100 Brubaker Road
Lititz, PA 17543-8662 717-285-9442
Fax: 717-285-3102 info@facilitiesdesign.com
www.facilitiesdesign.com
Full-service design capabilities including construction services with special expertise in cold storage warehousing and food processing facilities, complete architectural engineering and materials handling design
President: Joe Shaffer
Marketing Director: Jack Stone
Estimated Sales: $5 - 10 Million
Number Employees: 9

22486 Facility Group
2233 Lake Park Dr SE Ste 100
Smyrna, GA 30080 770-437-2700
Fax: 770-437-3900 info@fdgatlanta.com
www.facilitygroup.com
Fully integrated planning, engineering and construction management firm specializing in turn-key services for the food processing and distribution industries. Refrigeration engineering and insulation technology, materials handlingequipment selection
CEO: Ennis Parker
Estimated Sales: $50
Number Employees: 250-499

22487 Faciltec Corporation
73 S Riverside Dr
Elgin, IL 60120-6425 847-931-9500
Fax: 847-931-9629 800-284-8273
smacky@faciltec-corp.com
www.faciltec-corp.com
Manufacturer and exporter of a rooftop grease containment system for food service and industrial markets; also, cleaning services available
Executive VP: Christopher Barry
National Sales/Service Manager: Patrick Molloy
Estimated Sales: $1 - 5 Million
Number Employees: 50-99
Square Footage: 104000
Type of Packaging: Food Service
Brands:
Afc
G2 Grease Guard
Grease Guard

22488 Factory Cat
1509 Rapids Drive
Racine, WI 53404-2383 262-681-3583
Fax: 262-632-3335 800-634-4060
www.factorycat.com
Industrial, walk-behind and rider sweepers and scrubbers

22489 Fair Publishing House
15 Schauss Ave
PO Box 350
Norwalk, OH 44857 800-824-3247
Fax: 800-340-9988 info@fairsupplies.com
www.fairpublishing.com
Manufacturer and exporter of award ribbons, tickets and signs including advertising
President: Kevin Doyle
Sales Director: Charles Doyle
Production Manager: Kenneth Kosie
Estimated Sales: $3 - 5 Million
Number Employees: 20-49
Square Footage: 25000
Parent Co: Rotary Printing Company
Other Locations:
Fair Publishing House
Norwalk OH

22490 Fairbanks Scales
821 Locust Street
Kansas City, MO 64106 816-471-0231
Fax: 816-471-0241 800-451-4107
www.fairbanks.com
Manufacturer and exporter of stainless steel hostile environment scales including bench, unirail, omnicells, digital indicators, bench and portable scales, and bar code dataprinter
President: Richard Norden
Chairman: F.A. Norden
Chief Financial Officer: Steve Wurtzler
Vice President, Engineering: Tom Luke
Quality Assurance Manager: Craig Schnepf
Vice President, Sales & Marketing: Bob Jozwiak
Director, Product Development: Derrick Mashaney
Plant Manager: Wayne Gaboriault
Purchasing Manager: Keith George
Estimated Sales: $81 Million
Number Employees: 656
Square Footage: 12000
Parent Co: Fancor, Inc.

22491 Fairborn
P.O.Box 151
Upper Sandusky, OH 43351-0151 419-294-4987
Fax: 419-294-4980 800-262-1188
info@fairbornusa.com www.fairbornusa.com
Manufacturer and exporter of truck and rail loading dock enclosures
President: Mark Dillon
General Manager: Mark Dillon
Number Employees: 50-99

22492 Fairchester Snacks Corporation
100 Lafayette Ave
White Plains, NY 10603 914-761-2824
Salty biscuts
Owner: John Barisano
Estimated Sales: $300,000-500,000
Number Employees: 1-4

22493 Fairchild Industrial Products Company
3920 Westpoint Blvd
Winston Salem, NC 27103 336-659-3400
Fax: 336-659-9323 800-334-8422
sales@fairchildproducts.com
www.fairchildproducts.com
Manufacturer and exporter of industrial controls including electro-pneumatic transducers and pneumatic pressure regulators; also, mechanical power transmission equipment including differential and draw transmissions
President: Mark Cuthbert
CFO: Todd Bergstrom
VP Industrial Controls: Thomas McNichol
Quality Control: Greg Argrabright
R&D: Andy Askew
VP Power Transportation Equipment: Jack Dunivant
Estimated Sales: $10 - 20 Million
Number Employees: 100-249
Square Footage: 88000
Brands:
Cubic
Fairchild
Harmonic
Specon
Vari-Chain

22494 Fairfield Line Inc
605 W Stone Ave
PO Box 500
Fairfield, IA 52556 641-472-3191
Fax: 641-472-3194 800-423-7437
www.fairfieldlineinc.com
Manufacturer, importer and exporter of work gloves including cotton, leather, leather-palm, coated and string knits
President: Fred B Hunt
VP: Larry Sheffler
Sales Manager: Larry Ray Sheffler
Estimated Sales: $5 - 10 Million
Number Employees: 20-49
Parent Co: Fairfield Line

22495 Falco
1245 Industrielle Street
La Prairie, CA J5R 2E4 450-444-0566
Fax: 450-444-2227 info@berliefalco.com
www.berliefalco.com
Manufacturer and exporter of food processing, dairy and brewery equipment, stainless steel silos and tanks
Co-President: Bertrand Blanchette
VP: Louis Penta
Vice President of Sales and Marketing: Stephane Audy
Estimated Sales: $500,000-$1 Million
Number Employees: 5-9
Parent Co: A&B Process

22496 Falco Technologies
1245 Rue Industrielle
La Prairie, QC J5R 2E4
Canada 450-444-0566
Fax: 450-444-2227 info@falcotechnologies.com
www.falcotechnologies.com
Manufacturer and exporter of stainless steel food processing equipment including silos, tanks, hoppers, mixing kettles, wine storage units, brewery machinery, dairy processing equipment and custom fabrication turn key solutions tosimple and complex problems - from tank installation to complete process
Co-President: Bertrand Blanchette
Co-President: Marc Regnaud
Quality Control: Andre Pichette
Marketing/Sales: Nicolas Courchesne
Vice President of Sales and Marketing: Stephane Audy
Production/Plant Manager: Jonathan Gingras
Purchasing: Susan Hynes
Estimated Sales: $10 Million
Number Employees: 75
Square Footage: 65000
Parent Co: Falco
Brands:
Falco

22497 Falcon Belting
8338 SW 15th Street
Oklahoma City, OK 73128-9594 405-495-7563
Fax: 405-495-7911 800-922-0878
falcon@iamerica.net
Plastic belts
Estimated Sales: $5-10 000,000
Number Employees: 60

22498 Falcon Fabricators
422 Allied Dr
Nashville, TN 37211-3304 615-832-0027
Fax: 615-832-0048 www.falconnashville.com
Stainless steel work tables, hot fat filters, chicken marinators, etc.; also, replacement parts available
President: Gary Heckle
President: Gary Heckle
Account Manager: Jan Wilson
Estimated Sales: $20-50 Million
Number Employees: 50-99
Square Footage: 50000
Parent Co: Trendco

22499 Falkenberg
P.O.Box 656
Hubbard, OR 97032-0656 503-656-9511
Fax: 503-981-9143 garyf@hydrobrush.com
High pressure pumps, nozzles and accessories
President: Gary Falkenberg
Estimated Sales: $2.5-5 000,000
Number Employees: 10-19

22500 Fallas Automation
7000 Imperial Dr
PO Box 20354
Waco, TX 76702 254-772-9524
Fax: 254-751-1242 sales@fallasautomation.com
www.fallasautomation.com
Manufacturer and exporter of automatic packaging machinery
President and CFO: David Fallas
Vice President: Mark McAninch
Sales Manager: Crese Calebrese
Estimated Sales: $10 - 20 Million
Number Employees: 20-49
Square Footage: 65000

22501 Falls Chemical Products
123 Caldwell Ave
Oconto Falls, WI 54154 920-846-3561
Fax: 920-846-4830 fallschemical@ez-net.com
Cleaners, sanitizers, soaps and dish washing detergent for restaurant, bar and janitorial services; also, dairy chemicals
Owner/President: Sam Scimemi
Number Employees: 2

22502 Fallshaw Wheels & Casters
6848 Moorhen Place
Oceanside, CA 92009 760-476-9713
Fax: 760-476-9714 jdavitt@fallshaw.com.au
www.fallshaw.com
Estimated Sales: $1 Million
Number Employees: 1

22503 Fallwood Corp
75 South Broadway, Ste 494
White Plains, NY 10601 914-304-4065
Fax: 914-304-4063 ana@fallwoodcorp.com
www.fallwoodcorp.com
Manufacturer and supplier of all natural nutraceutical ingredients and raw materials. All glanulars - Bovine and Porcine Enzymes
President/CEO: Jorge Millan
Vice President: Graciela Rocchia
Sales: Wayne Battenfield
Adminstration: Anne Marie Rodriguez
Estimated Sales: Under $500,000
Number Employees: 4
Parent Co: Loboratorio Opoterapico Argentino

22504 Famco Automatic SausageLinkers
P. O. Box 8647
Pittsburgh, PA 15221 412-241-6410
Fax: 412-242-8877 info@famcousa.com
www.famcousa.com
Linking machines for sausage and frankfurter production
President: Charles Allen
Vice President: R. Robert Allen
Sales: Dick Carson

22505 Famco Sausage Linking Machines
421 N Braddock Ave
Pittsburgh, PA 15208-2514 412-241-6410
Fax: 412-242-8877 info@famcousa.com
www.famcousa.com
Sausage linkers
Owner: Bob Allen
VP: R Robert Allen
Estimated Sales: $1 - 5 Million
Number Employees: 20-49

22506 Family Tree Farms
41646 Road 62
Reedley, CA 93654 559-591-6280
Fax: 559-595-7795 866-352-8671
www.familytreefarms.com
Manufacturer, packer, shipper, exporter, and distributor of fresh fruit such as plumcots, apricots, yellow flesh peaches, blueberries, cherries, white flesh peaches, citrus, plums, and apriums.
President: David Jackson
CFO: Dan Clenney
Quality Control: Mary Ortiz
Estimated Sales: $20 - 50 Million
Number Employees: 250-499
Brands:
Eat Smart
Great Whites
Flavor Safari
Farmers Market
Summerripe
River Run

22507 Famous Software
8080 North Palm Avenue
Suite 210
Fresno, CA 93711 559-438-3600
Fax: 559-447-6338 800-444-8301
support@FamousSoftware.com
www.famoussoftware.com
Accounting, sales, purchase order, invoicing, and inventory software
President: Keith Paris
CFO: Rick Befford
R & D: Doug Rosenfold
Number Employees: 10

22508 Fan Bag Company
4307 W Division St
Chicago, IL 60651-1714 773-342-2752
Fax: 773-342-4413
Plastic bags
CEO: Florian Nocek
VP Marketing: Carl Nocek
Estimated Sales: $5 - 10 Million
Number Employees: 25

22509 Fantapak International
12150 Merriman Rd.
Livonia, MI 48150 734-838-1300
Fax: 248-743-2970 800-856-3803
sales@fantapak.com
www.fantapakinternational.com
President: Chia Hsiang Chang
Estimated Sales: $5 - 10 Million
Number Employees: 20-49

22510 Faraday
805 S Maumee St
Tecumseh, MI 49286-2053 517-423-2111
Fax: 517-423-2320 castleberry@siemens.com
www.faraday.com

Manufacturer and exporter of fire alarm systems
Manager: Tim Wertz
Estimated Sales: $20 - 50 Million
Number Employees: 100-249
Parent Co: Cerberus Pryotronics
Brands:
Faraday

22511 Fargo Automation
969 34th St N
Fargo, ND 58102 701-232-1780
Fax: 701-232-1929 888-616-0188
sales@fargoautomation.com
www.fargoautomation.com
Owner: Kevin Biffert
Estimated Sales: $20 - 50 Million
Number Employees: 20-49

22512 (HQ)Faribault Foods, Inc.
Campbell Mithun Tower
Suite 3380
Minneapolis, MN 55402 612-333-6461
ConsumeResponse@faribaultfoods.com
www.faribaultfoods.com
Canned vegetables, sauced beans, refried beans, baked beans, kids' and family style pasta, soup, chili, and organic and Mexican specialties. Specialists in creating private label products that are a match for the leading nationalbrands. Also providing contract manufacturing for all product categories, copacking leading branded products. All can sizes available, also pop top lids, microwaveable bowls and stand up pouches for beverage products.
President & CEO: Reid MacDonald
CFO: Mark Hentges
Executive VP: Gary Kindseth
Executive VP Innovation & Technology: James Nelson
Executive VP Sales & Marketing: Frank Lynch
VP of Branded Sales: Jim Noonan
VP Private Label & New Bus. Development: Mike Gilbertson
Executive VP of Operations: Scott King
Estimated Sales: $164 Million
Number Employees: 5
Number of Brands: 8
Type of Packaging: Consumer, Private Label, Bulk
Other Locations:
Faribault Foods Distribution
Faribault MN
Faribault Foods Plant
Cokato MN
Brands:
BUTTER KERNEL
CHILLIMAN
KUNER'S
KUNER'S SOUTHWESTERN
MRS. GRIMES
PASTA SELECT
PRIDE
S & W BEANS

22513 Faribo Manufacturing Company
820 20th St NW
Faribault, MN 55021 507-334-4377
Fax: 507-334-0674 800-447-6043
tcook.sales@faribomfg.com www.faribomfg.com
Plastic light globes, food containers, dunnage racks and ingredient bins; also, custom roto molded components available.
President: Timothy Hoschette
National Sales/Marketing Manager: Tom Cook
Purchasing Manager: Tim Hoschette
Estimated Sales: $2.5-5 Million
Number Employees: 27
Number of Brands: 2
Number of Products: 150+
Square Footage: 54000
Parent Co: Hoschette Enterprises

22514 Farmer Brothers Company
13131 Broadway Extension
Oklahoma City, OK 73114-2246 405-511-2188
800-735-2878
info@farmerbroscousa.com
www.farmerbroscousa.com
Blending and Packaging spices, also a distributor.
President, CEO & Director: Michael Keown
Chairman of the Board: Guenter Berger
CFO & Treasurer: Jeffrey Wahba
Vice President & Controller: Hortensia Gomez
Secretary: John Anglin
General Counsel & Asst Corp Secretary: Larry Garrett
Sr Vice President of Route Sales: Thomas Mortensen
Sr Vice President of Operations: Mark Harding
Square Footage: 19700
Parent Co: Farmer Brothers Company
Type of Packaging: Food Service, Bulk

22515 (HQ)Farmer Brothers Company
777 E. Vilas Road
Central Point, OR 97502-3269 541-772-9305
Fax: 541-770-5917 800-735-2878
info@farmerbroscousa.com
www.farmerbroscousa.com
Purchasing, roasting, and packaging coffee plant, also distributor
President, CEO & Director: Michael Keown
Chairman of the Board: Guenter Berger
CFO & Treasurer: Jeffrey Wahba
Vice President & Controller: Hortensia Gomez
Secretary: John Anglin
General Counsel & Asst Corp Secretary: Larry Garrett
Sr Vice President of Route Sales: Thomas Mortensen
Sr Vice President of Operations: Mark Harding
Square Footage: 20296
Parent Co: Farmer Brothers Company
Type of Packaging: Food Service, Bulk

22516 (HQ)Farmer Brothers Company
11519 S Petropark Drive
Houston, TX 77041-4921 713-937-3400
800-735-2878
info@farmerbroscousa.com
www.farmerbroscousa.com
Purchasing, roasting, and packaging coffee plant, also distributor
President, CEO & Director: Michael Keown
Chairman of the Board: Guenter Berger
CFO & Treasurer: Jeffrey Wahba
Vice President & Controller: Hortensia Gomez
Secretary: John Anglin
General Counsel & Asst Corp Secretary: Larry Garrett
Sr Vice President of Route Sales: Thomas Mortensen
Sr Vice President of Operations: Mark Harding
Square Footage: 19700
Parent Co: Farmer Brothers Company
Type of Packaging: Food Service, Bulk

22517 Farmer Direct Foods, Inc
PO Box 326
511 Commercia
Atchison, KA 66002 913-367-4422
Fax: 913-367-4443 800-372-4422
info@farmerdirectfoods.com
www.farmerdirectfoods.com
President: Tony Plunkett
Director: Dave Pfefer
Estimated Sales: $2.5 - 5 Million
Number Employees: 20-49

22518 Farmers Co-op Elevator Co.
3302 Prospect St
P.O. Box 219
Hudsonville, MI 49426 616-669-9596
Fax: 616-669-0490 800-439-9859
info@fcelevator.com www.fcelevator.com
Corrugated cartons and wooden shipping crates, boxes and baskets
Manager: Larry Roelofs
General Manager: Jim Roskam
Estimated Sales: $1 - 5 Million
Parent Co: Farmer's Cooperative Elevator Co., Inc.

22519 Farmland Industries
103 W 26th Ave
Kansas City, MO 64116 816-713-0000
Fax: 816-713-6323 info@farmland.com
Offset printing and typesetting; glue, side wire and saddle stitch binding
President: Robert Terry
VP and CFO: John Berardi
VP Human Resources: Holly McCoy
VP Administration: Drue Sander
Estimated Sales: $100-500 Million
Number Employees: 100-249

22520 Farnell Packaging
30 Ilsley Avenue
Dartmouth, NS B3B 1L3
Canada 902-468-9378
Fax: 902-468-3192 800-565-9378
sales@farnell.ns.ca www.farnell.ns.ca
Flexible packaging, plastic films and pressure sensitive labels
President: Donald Farnell
CFO: Bill Morash
Quality Control: Danny Christianson
Sales/Marketing Manager: D Stanfield
General Manager: H Christianson
Number Employees: 160
Square Footage: 75000

22521 Fas-Co Coders
422 Thornton Rd # 103
Lithia Springs, GA 30122-1581 770-739-7798
Fax: 480-545-1998 800-478-0685
danp@fas-cocoders.com
Manufacturer and exporter of coding and marking equipment
Owner: Victor Er
CFO: Roger Van Steenkiste
VP: Dan Piercy
Quality Control: Ty Martin
Estimated Sales: $6,000,000
Number Employees: 20-49
Square Footage: 15000

22522 Fashion Industries
1120 Everee Inn Rd
Griffin, GA 30224 770-412-9214
Fax: 770-412-1124
Table cloths
CEO: William Shapard
Estimated Sales: $50-100 Million
Number Employees: 250-499

22523 Fashion Seal Uniforms
PO Box 4002
Seminole, FL 33775 727-397-9611
Fax: 727-391-5401
worklon@superioruniformgroup.com
www.superioruniformgroup.com
Manufacturer and exporter of aprons, restaurant smocks, sheeting, knit shirts, hats and cloth bags
Executive VP: Peter Benstock
President: Alan Schwarcz
CEO: Michael Benstock
Marketing: Glenn Fasani
Sales: Kurt Schaver
Estimated Sales: I
Number Employees: 500-999
Square Footage: 60000
Parent Co: Superior Surgical Manufacturing Company

22524 Fasson Company
250 Chester St
Painesville, OH 44077-4141 440-358-3000
Fax: 440-358-6164
Wine industry labeling equipment
Estimated Sales: $500,000 - $1 000,000
Number Employees: 10-19

22525 Fast Bags
2501 Ludelle Street
Fort Worth, TX 76105-1036 817-534-9950
Fax: 817-534-1771 800-321-3687
Paper and plastic bags and labels
Estimated Sales: $1 - 5,000,000
Parent Co: Daydots International

22526 Fast Industries
1850 NW 49th St
Fort Lauderdale, FL 33309-3304 954-776-0066
Fax: 954-776-5387 800-775-5345
info@fastindustries.com www.fastindustries.com
Manufacturer and exporter of label placement systems, sign holders and merchandising aids; also, cleaning supplies including stain, laundry, rust and odor removers
President: Jacob Fast
Market Manager: Mike Brinkman
Estimated Sales: $10 - 15 Million
Number Employees: 100 to 249
Square Footage: 95000
Brands:
Carpet Gun

Ez View
Frontrunner
One Drop
One Spray
Rust Gun
Sell Strip
Smoking Gun
Stain Gun

22527 Fast Stuff Packaging
2 Village Road
Suite 10
Horsham, PA 19044-3816 877-388-3278
Fax: 215-830-9332
Void fill packaging system

22528 Fastcorp
1 Cory Road
Morristown, NJ 07960-3103 973-455-0400
Fax: 201-939-0255
Estimated Sales: $500,000-$1 000,000
Number Employees: 5-9

22529 Fasteners for Retail
P.O.Box 635696
Cincinnati, OH 45263-5696 440-505-6919
Fax: 440-505-6900 800-422-2547
info@ffr.com www.ffr.com
Since 1962, has been developing innovative merchandising systems and accesories to effectively position brands at retail. Offers custom design services and fullfillment
President/CEO: Donald Kimmel
CFO: Nathaniel Smith
CEO: Stanley Burson
Research & Development: Daniel Kump
Marketing Director: Paul Bloom
Sales Director: Michael DeJohn
Operations Manager: Drew Phillips
Estimated Sales: $50 - 100 Million
Number Employees: 100-249
Number of Brands: 40
Number of Products: 1700
Square Footage: 100000

22530 Fata Automation
6050 19 Mile Rd
Sterling Heights, MI 48314 586-323-9400
Fax: 248-553-6013 info@fatainc.com
www.fatainc.com
Conveyors, integrated systems and controls
President: Piero Bugnone
Sales Manager: Ron Benish
Estimated Sales: $75 Million
Number Employees: 100
Square Footage: 65000
Parent Co: Fata Automation Group

22531 Fato Fiberglass Company
462 S 5000w Rd
Kankakee, IL 60901 815-932-3015
Fax: 815-932-9839 fatoindustries@gmail.com
www.fato-industries.com
Fiberglass and polyethylene tanks, covers, trays and totes
President: Thomas Fato
CFO: Chris Fato
Quality Control: Tom Fato
R&D: Tom Fato
Estimated Sales: Below $5,000,000
Number Employees: 1-4
Square Footage: 10000

22532 Faubion Central States Tank Company
P.O.Box 26085
Shawnee Mission, KS 66225-6085 913-681-0069
Fax: 913-681-0150 800-450-8265
dfaubion@faubiontank.com
www.faubiontank.com
Food grade and heated stainless steel storage tanks
Owner: Dan Faubion
VP: Tom Thompson
Plant Manager: Dave Hill
Estimated Sales: $1-2.5 Million
Number Employees: 5-9
Square Footage: 160000

22533 Faultless Caster
1421 N Garvin Street
Evansville, IN 47711-4687 866-316-2163
Fax: 800-322-9329 800-322-7359
fcaster@faultlesscaster.com
www.faultlesscaster.com
Casters and wheels
Sales Manager: Matt Olson
Manager (Industrial Distribution): Brian Robb
Sales/Production Manager: Denny Garness
Number Employees: 250-499
Parent Co: FKI Industries
Brands:
Dynatred
Heavy Metal
K-Wheel
Rt

22534 Favorite Foods
29 Interstate Drive
Somersworth, NH 3878 603-692-4990
Fax: 603-692-4993 800-NUT-S4YO
favorite99@aol.com www.favoritefoods.com
Vertical mixers, moulding and nut processing equipment
Owner: Fred Lewin
CEO: Chris Barstow
VP: Tom Myers
Estimated Sales: $2.5-5 Million
Number Employees: 10-19

22535 Fawema Packaging Machinery
1701 Desoto Road
Palmetto, FL 34221-3066 941-351-9597
Fax: 941-351-4673 fawema@worldnet.att.net
www.fawema.com
Manufacturer, importer and exporter of bag packaging systems including formers, fillers and closers; also, control modules, checkweighers and hot melt glue applicators
Customer Service Manager: Frank Potvin
Estimated Sales: $1-2.5 Million
Number Employees: 1-4
Square Footage: 20000
Parent Co: Fawema Maschinenfabrik GmbH
Brands:
Allen Bradley
Electro Cam
Emerson
Hi-Speed
Nordson

22536 Fax Foods
1205 Activity Dr
Vista, CA 92081-8510 760-599-6030
Fax: 760-599-6040 sales@faxfoods.com
www.faxfoods.com
Manufacturer and exporter of plastic food replica.
Owner: Judy Preston
Square Footage: 60000
Parent Co: Fax Plastics
Type of Packaging: Food Service
Brands:
Foodart By Francesco
Replikale

22537 Fay Paper Products
124 Washington St # 101
Foxboro, MA 02035-1368 781-769-4620
Fax: 781-769-8522 800-765-4620
paper@aol.com www.faypaper.com
Manufacturer and exporter of cash register rolls and stationery items
President: Gregory Steele
VP: Peter Steele
Estimated Sales: $5-10 Million
Number Employees: 20-49
Brands:
Fay-Vo-Rite

22538 Feather Duster Corporation
10 Park St
Amsterdam, NY 12010-4214 518-842-3690
Fax: 518-842-3754 800-967-8659
duster@dustwiththebestltd.com
www.dustwiththebestltd.com
Manufacturer, importer and exporter of dusters including ostrich feather and wool; also, applicator pads
President and CFO: Neil Stravitz
Quality Control: Susan Spagnola
Plant Manager: Susan Spagnola
Estimated Sales: Below $5 Million
Number Employees: 5-9
Square Footage: 20000

22539 Federal Industries
215 Federal Ave
Belleville, WI 53508 608-424-3331
Fax: 608-424-3234 800-356-4206
geninfo@federalind.com www.federalind.com
Refrigerated and nonrefrigerated display cases for bakery and deli products
National Sales Manager (Food Service): Bill Rice
Plant Manager: Gary Hamburg
Estimated Sales: $20-50 Million
Number Employees: 100-249
Parent Co: Standex International Corporation

22540 Federal Industries Corporation
2550 Niagara Ln N
Minneapolis, MN 55447 763-476-1500
Fax: 763-476-8155 800-523-9033
chemtran@aol.com www.chemtran.com
Shipping systems for hazardous materials
President: Joe Goldman
Estimated Sales: $1-2.5 000,000
Number Employees: 1-4

22541 Federal Label Systems
7920 Barnwell Avenue
Elmhurst, NY 11373-3727 718-899-2233
Fax: 718-397-1921 800-238-0015
Product merchandising tags, pressure sensitive labels, on-product coupons, display and card packaging
President: Alan Rothchild
Co-Chairman: Herbert Rothchild
Executive VP: Paul Rothchild
Estimated Sales: $10-20 Million
Number Employees: 100-249
Square Footage: 45000
Parent Co: Rothchild Printing Group

22542 Federal Machines
8040 University Blvd.
Des Moines, IA 50325 515-274-3641
Fax: 515-274-5180 800-247-2446
info@federal.com www.fawnvendors.com
Manufacturer and exporter of vending machines for snacks, candy, pastries, milk, canned drinks, gum, mints, hot beverages, frozen foods and ice cream; also machine parts (full line vending equipment manufacturing company).
President/CEO: John Bruntz
CFO: Ray Lantz
CEO: F A Wittern Jr
Sales: Gary Bahr
Director Operations: Gary Bahr
Estimated Sales: $5-10 Million
Number Employees: 250-499
Number of Brands: 10
Number of Products: 20
Square Footage: 1400000
Type of Packaging: Food Service, Private Label
Brands:
Fs1
Us1

22543 Federal Mfg Co
201 West Walker Street
Milwaukee, WI 53204 414-384-3200
Fax: 414-384-8704 www.federalmfg.com
Designers and Manufacturers of bottle filling and capping systems and specialty products for the Dairy, Juice, Water, Food, and Pharmaceutical Industries.
President: Otis Cobb
CEO: Marjorie Fee
Estimated Sales: $5-10 Million
Number Employees: 50-99
Square Footage: 240000

22544 Federal Sign
160 W Carmel Dr
Suite 236
Carmel, IN 46032 317-581-7790
Fax: 317-581-7783 800-527-9495
Marketing@federalheath.com
www.federalheath.com
Manufacturer and exporter of custom interior and exterior signs including plastic and metal; also, installation and maintenance available
Account Executive: Randy Cearlock
Estimated Sales: $1-2.5 Million
Number Employees: 5-9
Square Footage: 150000
Parent Co: Federal Signal Corporation

22545 Federal Sign of Rhode Island
135 Dean St
Providence, RI 02903-1603 401-421-3400
Fax: 401-351-2233 www.federalsigns.net
Advertising signs including electric, luminous and billboards.
Manager: Frank Benell
VP: William Benell II
Estimated Sales: $500,000-$1 Million
Number Employees: 5-9
Square Footage: 30000
Parent Co: Hub Sign Company

22546 Federal Stamp & Seal Manufacturing Company
2210 Marietta Blvd NW
Atlanta, GA 30318-2020 404-525-6103
Fax: 404-525-3320 800-333-7726
info@fessco.net www.fessco.net
Pre-inked and self-inking rubber stamps; also, engraved signs, seals, numbering machines, ink and ink pads
President: Don Bradshaw
Plant Manager: Gary D'Andrea
Purchasing Manager: Mick Mortensen
Number Employees: 20-49

22547 Federated Mills
3620 Tamiami Trl N
Naples, FL 34103-3705 239-659-5450
Fax: 518-734-5805 888-692-6226
fedmills@mhcable.com www.federatedmills.com
Mold inhibitors for mycoban calcium propionate, mycoban sodium propionate, supreme brand dykon (sodium diacetate), potassium sorbate, sorbic acid, sodium citrate, sodium benzoate, xanthan gum, citric acid
VP: Douglas Sweet
VP: Doug Sweet
Estimated Sales: Below $5 Million
Number Employees: 1-4

22548 Feedback Plus
5757 Alpha Rd Ste 100
Dallas, TX 75240 972-661-8989
Fax: 972-661-5414 800-882-7467
feedback@feedbackplusinc.com
www.feedbackplusinc.com
Consulant offering market research
CEO: Vickie Henry
VP Marketing: Bill Waston
Food Service Sales Representative: Kelly Heatly
VP Of Store Operations: Monica Rattay
Estimated Sales: $2.5-5,000,000
Number Employees: 10-19

22549 Fehlig Brothers Box & Lumber Company
1909 Cole St.
St Louis, MO 63106 314-241-6900
Fax: 314-436-0315 fehligbrothers@sbcglobal.net
www.fehligbrotherslumber.com
Custom made wooden crates, boxes and pallets
President: John O'Leary
Treasurer: Tim O'Leary
Estimated Sales: Below $5 Million
Number Employees: 20-49
Square Footage: 152000

22550 Felco Bag & Burlap Company
4001 E Baltimore St
Baltimore, MD 21224-1544 410-276-2389
Fax: 410-276-2367 800-673-8488
www.felcopackaging.com
Manufacturer, importer and exporter of corrugated boxes, tapes, burlap, canvas, pallets, paper products and bags
President: Jeffrey Feldman
Controller: Sherry Feldman
Estimated Sales: $5 - 10 Million
Number Employees: 1 to 4
Square Footage: 75000

22551 (HQ)Feldmeier Equipment
6800 Townline Rd
Syracuse, NY 13211 315-454-8608
Fax: 315-454-3701 sstanks@feldmeier.com
www.feldmeier.com
Manufacturer and exporter of heat exchangers, pasteurizers, stainless steel tanks, processing vessels, strainers, and stainless steel ice builders
President: John Feldmeier
CEO: Robert Feldmeier
CFO: Margaret Feldmeier
VP: Robert Feldmeier
Estimated Sales: $40 Million
Number Employees: 250-499
Other Locations:
Feldmeier Equipment
Little Falls NY
Feldmeier Equipment
Reno NV
Feldmeier Equipment
Cedar Falls IA
Brands:
Across-The-Line
Feldmeier
Torpedo

22552 Felins U.S.A Incorporated
8306 W Parkland Ct
Milwaukee, WI 53223 414-355-7747
Fax: 414-355-7559 800-843-5667
sales@felins.com www.felins.com
Estimated Sales: $10 - 20 Million
Number Employees: 20-49

22553 Felins USA
8306 W Parkland Ct
Milwaukee, WI 53223 414-355-7747
Fax: 414-355-7559 800-336-3220
salesteam@felins.com www.felins.com
Manufacturer, importer and exporter of manual and automatic bundling, tying, wrapping, strapping and banding equipment; also, automated banding systems for multi-packing food products
Manager: Bruce Bartelt
Owner: James Chisholm
CFO: Ron Kuzia
Marketing: Peter Chapman
Sales: Mark Meyer
Public Relations: Neal Donding
Production: Bruce Lanham
Estimated Sales: $8.5 Million
Number Employees: 20-49
Square Footage: 25000
Brands:
Flexstrap
Loop Plus
Pak Tyer 2000

22554 Felix Storch
770 Garrison Ave
Bronx, NY 10474 718-328-8101
Fax: 718-842-3093 800-932-4267
sales@summitappliance.com
www.summitappliance.com
Manufacturer and exporter of sliding glass-top, solid-top and upright freezers, beverage coolers, beer taps and wine cellars; importer of freezers, beverage coolers, compact refrigerators and mini bars
President: Felix Stroch
Marketing Manager: Allan Cohen
VP Sales/Marketing: Steve Ross
Purchasing Manager: Paul Storch
Estimated Sales: $50-100 Million
Number Employees: 50-99
Square Footage: 150000
Brands:
Summit

22555 Fell & Company International
3266 Winbrook Drive
Memphis, TN 38116 901-332-6669
Fax: 901-332-6433 800-356-8588
info@fellcoinc.com www.fellcoinc.com
Cocoa and chocolate preparation equipment including batch kneaders, block shavers, conches, enrobing, refiners, cooling equipment and cooling tunnels, cream machines, depositors and nut processing equipment, bean cleaners, roasterswinnowers, liquor grinders, cocoa powder systems, mixer/kneaders, pre-refiners, continuous conches, storage and pumps/piping, moulding machine
President/CEO/CFO: Marc Fell
Sales Manager: Mike Dunn
Sales/ Operations Manager: Marc Fell
Estimated Sales: $1-2.5 Million
Square Footage: 48000

22556 Fenco
P.O.Box 428
Three Lakes, WI 54562-0428 715-546-8077
Fax: 715-546-3561
Conveyor components, plastic conveyor belt, and wearstrips
Estimated Sales: less than $500,000
Number Employees: 1-4

22557 Fenner Drives
311 W Stiegel St
Manheim, PA 17545 717-665-2421
Fax: 717-665-2649 800-243-3374
info@fennerdrives.com www.fennerdrives.com
Industrial transmission conveyor belts
CEO: Nick Hobson
Marketing Director: Robin Palmer
Sales Director: Craig Harris
Estimated Sales: $50+ Million
Number Employees: 10-19
Type of Packaging: Private Label, Bulk
Brands:
Orange Belt

22558 Fenner Drives
311 W Stiegel St
Manheim, PA 17545 717-665-2421
Fax: 717-665-2649 800-327-2288
info@fennerdrives.com www.fennerdrives.com
Industrial belting, power transmission and motion control components, maintains extensive engineering, development, and testing facilities
CEO: Nick Hobson
Marketing Director: Robin Palmer
Sales Director: Craig Harris
Estimated Sales: $30 - 50 Million
Number Employees: 250-499
Number of Products: +0
Type of Packaging: Bulk
Brands:
Clear - Go
Minikeeper
Orange - Go
Powertwist
Quik - Go
Red - Go
Torquekeeper
Trantorque
Veelos

22559 Fenner Dunlop Engineered Conveyer Solutions
1000 Omega Drive, Suite 1400
Pittsburgh, PA 15205 412-249-0700
Fax: 412-249-0701
www.fennerdunlopamericas.com
Conveyors and elevator belting
President: Cassandra Pan
Chief Financial Officer: William Mooney
Chief Operating Officer: Mark Hardwick
Estimated Sales: $1 - 5 Million
Number Employees: 100-249
Brands:
Duratrax

22560 Fenster Consulting
29 Davis Rd
Port Washington, NY 11050 516-944-7108
Fax: 516-944-7953 fred@fensterconsulting.com
www.fensterconsulting.com
Consultant specializing in factory, warehouse and material handling, packaging and storage system design
President: Fred Fenster
Vice President: Linda Necroto
Sales Director: Jordan Fenster
Purchasing Manager: Sandra Lee
Number Employees: 5-9
Square Footage: 20000

22561 Fenton Art Glass Company
700 Elizabeth St
Williamstown, WV 26187 304-375-6122
Fax: 304-375-7833 800-933-6766
askfenton@fentonartglass.com
www.fentonartglass.com

Manufacturer and exporter of decorative glassware and lamps
President: George Fenton
CFO: Stan Van Lanqingham
VP: Tom Fenton
R&D: Nancy Fenton
Quality Control: Tom Bobbitt
Sales VP: Scott Fenton
Public Relations: Terry Nutter
Purchasing Director: Mike Fenton
Estimated Sales: $25-30 Million
Number Employees: 250-499
Type of Packaging: Consumer, Bulk
Brands:
Fenton Art Glass

22562 **Ferguson Containers**
20 Industrial Rd
Phillipsburg, NJ 08865 908-454-9755
Fax: 908-454-7144 fergusoncontainers@nni.com
www.fergusoncontainers.com
Corrugated boxes and containers
Owner: Stuart Ferguson
General Manager: Ed Reichard
Estimated Sales: $5 Million
Number Employees: 20-49
Square Footage: 21000

22563 **Ferm-Rite Equipment**
PO Box 1233
Woodbridge, CA 95258-1233 209-794-2700
Fax: 209-794-8164 ferm-rite@softcom.net
www.m.farm-riteequipment.com
Wine industry bungs
President: Martyn Nastasian
Bookkeeper: Jil Nastasian
Number Employees: 2

22564 **Fermpro Manufacturing**
P.O.Box 5000
Kingstree, SC 29556-1000 843-382-8485
Fax: 843-382-8676 800-898-0891
info@fermpro.com www.martek.com
Contract manufacturing facility for large-scale fermentation and downstream processing
President: Barney Easterling
Human Resources: Brian Lee
Mngr.: Ronald Easler
Estimated Sales: $50-100 Million
Number Employees: 50-99
Square Footage: 21780000

22565 **Fernholtz Engineering**
15471 Victory Boulevard
Van Nuys, CA 91406-6241 818-785-5800
Fax: 818-785-8406
Manufacturer and exporter of mills, sifting and screening machinery, wet and dry magnetic separators, mixers, blenders and agitators
President: Vivian Fernholtz
VP: Frank Fernholtz
Estimated Sales: $500,000-$1 Million
Number Employees: 1-4

22566 **Fernqvist Labeling Solutions**
2544 Leghorn
Mountain View, CA 94043-1451 650-428-0330
Fax: 650-428-1615 800-426-8215
sales@fernqvist.com www.fernqvist.com
Digital and flexo labels provided nationally, thermal transfer printers, labling software, TT ribbons, and other labling supplies.
President: Per Fernqvist
Operations/Production Officer: Richard Hernandez
Estimated Sales: $3 - 5 Million
Number Employees: 22

22567 **Fernqvist Labeling Solutions**
1245 Space Park Way
Suite C
Mountain View, CA 94043 650-428-0330
Fax: 650-428-1615 800-426-8215
sales@fernqvist.com www.fernqvist.com
Label and bar code printing systems, labels, thermal transfer ribbons, dispensers, bar code verifiers, scanners, etc
President: Per Fernqvist
VP: Bill Goodman
Manufacturing Manager: Richard Hernandez
Estimated Sales: Below $5 Million
Number Employees: 20-49
Square Footage: 3500
Brands:
Fernqvist Prodigy Max

22568 **Ferrell-Ross**
PO Box 50669
Amarillo, TX 79159 806-359-9051
Fax: 806-359-9064 800-299-9051
info@ferrellross.com www.ferrellross.com
Manufacturer and exporter of grinding and flaking mills for breakfast cereals, spices and snack foods; also, grain and cereal blenders, grain and seed cleaning machinery
President: David Ibach
Vice President: Philip Petrakos
Sales Director: Clay Gerber
Estimated Sales: $10 - 20 Million
Number Employees: 10
Square Footage: 25000
Parent Co: Bluffton Agri Industrial Corporation
Other Locations:
Ferrell-Ross
Bluffton IN
Brands:
Clipper Precision
Ferrell-Ross

22569 **Ferrer Corporation**
415 Calle San Claudio
San Juan, PR 00926-4206 787-761-5151
Fax: 787-755-0450 info@rotulosferrer.com
www.rotulosferrer.com
Manufacturer and exporter of interior and exterior signs including electric, metal, neon and plastic
President: Juan Ferrer Davila
Controller: Jose Vazquez
Sales Manager: Enid Cintron
Number Employees: 50
Square Footage: 80000
Brands:
Rotulos Ferrer

22570 **Ferrite Company**
165 Ledge St
Nashua, NH 03060-3061 603-881-5234
Fax: 603-881-5406 info@ferriteinc.com
www.ferriteinc.com
President: Richard Wolfe
Quality Control: Bill Tabonnu
Estimated Sales: $50 - 100 Million
Number Employees: 100-249

22571 **Ferro Corporation**
1315 Main St
Pittsburgh, PA 15215-2501 412-781-7519
Fax: 412-781-1152 www.ferro.com
Manufacturer and exporter of printing inks, labels and label supplies
Owner: Frank Ferra
CFO: Thomas M Gannon
Corporate VP: James C Bays
VP Specialty Plastics: John Comanita
VP Color/Glass: Celeste Beeks Mastin
General Manager: Cliff Ruderer
Estimated Sales: $1.6 Billion
Number Employees: 20-49
Parent Co: Ferro Corporation

22572 **Festo Corporation**
395 Moreland Rd
Hauppauge, NY 11788 631-435-0800
Fax: 631-435-8026 800-99F-ESTO
info@festo-usa.com www.festo-usa.com
Offers one of the largest selections of pneumatic components and controls available from a single source. Select from over 90 product families, including pneumatic valves, cylinders and controls. Festo has the engineering expertiseto design and build
President: Hans Zobel
Estimated Sales: $20 - 50 Million
Number Employees: 250-499

22573 **Fettig Laboratories**
900 Godfrey Ave SW
Grand Rapids, MI 49503 616-245-3000
Fax: 616-245-3299 radonman01@aol.com
Laboratory providing nutritional analysis and labeling, bacteriological testing, QC/QA program design and management, shelf life testing, contamination/adulteration identification and witness service
President: Patricia Fettig
Marketing Director: Gregory Painter
Estimated Sales: $500,000-$1 Million
Number Employees: 5-9

22574 **Fetzer Vineyards**
PO Box 611
Hopland, CA 95449 707-744-7600
Fax: 707-744-7605 800-846-8637
Fernando.Avalos@fetzer.com
www.bonterra.com
Manufacturer and exporter of table wines, barrels and corks
Head Operations: Pat Voss
Manager: Tim Nall
Director Winemaking: Dennis Martin
Estimated Sales: $19.2 Million
Number Employees: 100-249
Parent Co: Brown-Forman Corporation
Type of Packaging: Consumer, Food Service, Private Label, Bulk
Brands:
Bel Arbors
Bon Terra
Fetzer

22575 **Fiber Does**
1470 N 4th Street
San Jose, CA 95112-4715 408-453-5533
Fax: 408-453-9303 fdi@fiberdoes.com
www.corporationwiki.com
Manufacturer and exporter of fiber optic lighted signs including indoor, outdoor and window display
CEO: Song Lee
Sales/Customer Service Manager: Rick Perez
Estimated Sales: $3,000,000
Number Employees: 20-50
Brands:
Fiberpro
Optickles

22576 **Fibercel Corporation**
46 Brooklyn St
Portville, NY 14770 716-933-8703
Fax: 716-933-6948 800-545-8546
bcarrow@fibercel.net www.fibercel.com
Bulk packaging
General Manager: Mitch Gray
Sales Administrator: Geoff Buckner
Estimated Sales: $20 - 50 Million
Number Employees: 100-249

22577 **Fibergate Composite Structures**
5151 Beltline Rd
Suite 1212
Dallas, TX 75254-7028 972-250-1633
Fax: 972-250-1530 800-527-4043
info@fibergate.com www.fibergrate.com
President: Marshall Liverman
CFO: Travis Kirsch
Quality Control: Ray Blackshear
Number Employees: 200

22578 **Fibergrate CompositeStructures**
5151 Belt Line Rd Ste 1212
Dallas, TX 75254 972-250-1633
Fax: 972-250-1530 800-527-4043
info@fibergrate.com www.fibergrate.com
Manufacture fiberglass, reinforced plastic, gratings and products for the food and beverage industry
President: Eric Breiner
CFO: Sean Lovison
Operations Manager: Wendell Hollingsworth
Estimated Sales: $10-25 Million
Number Employees: 20-49
Brands:
Chemgrate
Fibergrate
Rigirtex0

22579 **Fiberich Technologies**
3280 Gorham Ave Ste 202
St Louis Park, MN 55426 952-920-8054
Fax: 952-920-8056 buzzbeverley@msn.com
Pea fiber, vegetable fiber, bean and lentil precooked whole and powders
President: Edward Schmidt
Estimated Sales: $1-2.5 000,000
Number Employees: 1-4
Type of Packaging: Bulk

22580 **Fiberich Technologies**
3280 Gorham Ave
Suite 202
St Louis Park, MN 55426 952-920-8054
Fax: 952-920-8056 fiberichtech@popp.net
Processes and markets peas, beans and lentil based ingredients
President: Ed Schmidt

Type of Packaging: Consumer, Bulk

22581 Fibertech
11744 Blue Bell Rd
Elberfeld, IN 47613 812-983-2642
Fax: 812-983-4953 800-304-4600
jluttrell@fibertechnic.net www.fibertechinc.net
President: William Scott
Estimated Sales: Below $5 Million
Number Employees: 10-19

22582 Fibertech
11744 Blue Bell Rd
Elberfel, IN 47613 812-983-2642
Fax: 812-983-4953 800-304-6400
nyoug@fibertechinc.net www.fibertechinc.net
Supplies fiber materials used in food industry manufacturing
Number Employees: 45

22583 Fibre Containers Company
15250 Don Julian Rd
City of Industry, CA 91745-1031 626-968-5897
Fax: 626-330-0870 sales@fibrecontainers.com
www.fibrecontainers.com
Corrugated shipping containers
President: Tony Pietrangelo
Director Sales: Lloyd Kennedy
Estimated Sales: $20-50 Million
Number Employees: 250-499

22584 Fibre Converters
1 Industrial Park Dr
PO Box 130
Constantine, MI 49042 269-279-1700
jamey.southland@fibreconverters.com
www.fibreconverters.com
Manufacturer and exporter of die cut slip sheets for replacement of pallets as well as special laminated or solid fibre paperboard
President and CEO: James Stuck
Chairman: David T Stuck
Operations Manager: Stephen Reed
Estimated Sales: $25 Million
Number Employees: 100
Square Footage: 160000
Brands:
Fiber-Pul
Fico
Valdor

22585 Fibre Leather Manufacturing Company
686 Belleville Avenue
New Bedford, MA 02745-6093 508-997-4557
Fax: 508-997-7268 800-358-6012
fibreleather@earthlink.net
Manufacturer and exporter of latex-impregnated and coated paper for box coverings; also, base stock for pressure sensitive tapes and jean label stock.
President: Daniel Finger
VP: Louis Finger
Production Manager: Ellen Hull
Shipping Manager: Charles Hull
Estimated Sales: $10-20 Million
Number Employees: 50-99
Square Footage: 200000

22586 Fibreform
N115w19255 Edison Dr
Germantown, WI 53022-3092 262-251-1901
Fax: 262-251-1941
customersupport@fibreforminc.com
www.fibreforminc.com
Model pulp protective packaging
President: Edward Gratz
Estimated Sales: $20 - 50 Million
Number Employees: 20-49

22587 (HQ)Fiebing Company
PO Box 694
Milwaukee, WI 53201-0694 414-271-5011
Fax: 414-271-3769 800-558-1033
custserv@fiebing.com www.fiebing.com
Manufacturer and exporter of soap and waterproofers
President: Richard Chase
R&D: Mansur Abul
VP: Dennis Kendall
Estimated Sales: $10 - 20 Million
Number Employees: 20-49
Square Footage: 70000
Brands:
Fiebing
Kelly
Snow Proof

22588 Fiedler Technology
84 Malmo Court
Units 13-15
Maple, ON L6A 1R4
Canada 905-832-0493
Primary and secondary packaging machinery for nonstandard packages
President: Edgar Fiedler
Number Employees: 5-9
Square Footage: 6000

22589 Field Container Company
1500 Nicholas Blvd
Elk Grove Vlg, IL 60007-5516 847-437-1700
Fax: 847-956-9250 www.fieldcontainer.com
Manufacturer and exporter of folding cartons
President: Larry Field
Number Employees: 10-19

22590 Field Manufacturing Corporation
2750 Oregon Court
Suite M8
Torrance, CA 90503-2636 310-781-9292
Fax: 310-781-9386 mcwilliams@fieldmfg.com
www.fieldmfg.com
Plastic molded store fixtures
President: Steven Fields
Vice President: Mary McWilliams
Research & Development: Omar Balley
Estimated Sales: $5 - 10 Million
Number Employees: 100

22591 Fife Corporation
P.O.Box 26508
Oklahoma City, OK 73126-0508 405-755-1600
Fax: 405-755-8425 800-639-3433
fife@fife.com www.fife.com
Automatic process controls
President: Terry Brookes
CEO: Bruce Ryan
CEO: Bruce E Ryan
Estimated Sales: $20 - 50 Million
Number Employees: 100-249

22592 Filet Menu
P.O.Box 352161
Los Angeles, CA 90035 310-202-8000
Fax: 310-559-0917
Manufacturer and designer of menus, point of purchase displays, table cards, dinner napkins, place mats, etc
Owner: Michael Le Vine
Marketing: Marcia Petersen
Estimated Sales: $2.5-5,000,000
Number Employees: 20-49
Type of Packaging: Food Service

22593 Filler Specialties
440 100th Ave
Zeeland, MI 49464 616-772-9235
Fax: 616-772-4544 filler@filler-specialties.com
www.filler-specialties.com
Manufacturer and exporter of capping and closing equipment, conveyor systems and fillers and filling equipment
President: Vernon Slagh
Sales Manager: Jim Grant
Estimated Sales: $5-10,000,000
Number Employees: 20-49

22594 Filling Equipment Company
15-39 130th St
Flushing, NY 11356 718-445-2111
Fax: 718-463-6034 800-247-7127
filling@fillingequipment.com
www.fillingequipment.com
Manufacturer and exporter of packaging equipment, tables, conveyors, automatic cap tighteners, etc
President: Robert Hampton
Sales: G Hite
Sales: J Popper
Estimated Sales: $1-2.5 Million
Number Employees: 10-19

22595 Fillit
18105 Trans Canada Highway
Kirkland, QC H9J 3Z4
Canada 514-694-2390
Fax: 514-694-6552 rzajko@kalishdti.com
www.fillitindia.com
Manufacturer and exporter of conveying, filling, capping and counting equipment
President/Owner: ý
Production Manager: Richard Zajko
Number Employees: 100-249
Brands:
Fillit
Fillkit
Kapit
Power Fillit
Torquit

22596 Film X
20 Louisa Viens Dr
Dayville, CT 06241 860-779-3403
Fax: 860-779-3406 800-628-6128
sales@primastrip.com www.filmxinc.com
Packaging materials including film; also, extrusion coating and slitting services available
Manager: Michael Quarry
Sr. Account Manager: Peter Hendrickson
General Manager: Jon Pluff
Estimated Sales: $5 - 10 Million
Number Employees: 1-4
Parent Co: Web Industries

22597 Film-Pak
201 S Magnolia Street
Crowley, TX 76036-3110 817-297-4341
Fax: 817-572-7568 800-526-1838
robertr@film-pak.com www.film-pak.com
Film and plain and printed bags
President: Rossi Callender
Sales Manager: Chris Walters
Estimated Sales: $5-10 Million
Number Employees: 20-49
Square Footage: 16000

22598 Filmco
1450 S Chillicothe Rd
Aurora, OH 44202 330-562-6111
Fax: 330-562-2740 800-545-8457
www.linpac.com
Manufacturer and exporter of PVC film
President: Rolland Castellanos
Customer Service: Marianne Martone
General Manager: Richard Pohland
Purchasing Manager: Susan Burkholder
Estimated Sales: $20-50 Million
Number Employees: 10
Parent Co: Linpac Plastics Inc.
Brands:
Britepak
Crustpak

22599 (HQ)Filmpack Plastic Corporation
266 Ridge Rd
Dayton, NJ 08810 732-329-6523
Fax: 732-329-8543
company@filmpackplastic.com
Plastic translucent polystyrene cold drinking cups
President: Morris Herman
VP: Moric O'Streicher
Estimated Sales: $5-10 Million
Number Employees: 20-49

22600 Filter Equipment Company
1440 State Route 34
Wall Township, NJ 07753 732-938-7440
Fax: 800-777-3477 800-445-9775
sales@filter-equipment.com
www.filter-equipment.com
Filtration equipment
VP: Scott Groh
Estimated Sales: $5 - 10 000,000
Number Employees: 20-49

22601 Filter Products
8314 Tiogawoods Dr
Sacramento, CA 95828 916-689-2328
Fax: 916-689-1035 j.teshera@fpifilters.com
www.fpifilters.com
Wine industry filtration equipment
President: Paris Rivera
Estimated Sales: $5 - 10 000,000
Number Employees: 20-49

22602 Filtercarb LLC/ Filtercorp
9805 NE 116th St
Suite A-200
Kirkland, WA 98034-4245 425-820-4850
Fax: 425-820-2816 800-473-4526
rbernard@filtercorp.com www.filtercorp.com

President: Robin Bernard
Estimated Sales: $5-10 Million
Number Employees: 10-19

22603 **Filtercold Corporation**
1840 E University Drive
Suite 2
Tempe, AZ 85281-7760 800-442-2941
Tea and coffee industry filtration equipment

22604 **(HQ)Filtercorp**
2585 S Sarah Street
Fresno, CA 93706-5034 559-495-3140
Fax: 559-495-3145 800-473-4526
www.filtercorp.com
Manufacturer, importer and exporter of nonwoven cellulose fiber filter pads used for cooking fats and oils
President: Don Eskes
Estimated Sales: $500,000-$1 Million
Number Employees: 4
Square Footage: 24000
Brands:
Supersorb
Unifit

22605 **Filtration Engineering Company**
12255 Ensign Ave N
Champlin, MN 55316 763-421-2721
Fax: 763-421-1988 800-553-4457
thutson@filtrationeng.com
www.filtrationeng.com
Reverse osmosis, ultra-osmosis, ultrafiltration, and microfiltration systems, also a complete line of replacement membranes, engineering for system expansion, water purification, and waste treatment
Owner: George Hutson
Sales Manager: Todd Hutson
Estimated Sales: $2.5-5 000,000
Number Employees: 20-49
Type of Packaging: Bulk

22606 **Filtration Systems**
10304 NW 50th St
Sunrise, FL 33351-8007 954-572-2700
Fax: 954-572-3401 service@filtsys.com
www.filtrationsystems.com
Liquid filters, pressure vessels and filter media
President: Sidney Goldman
VP: Michael Goldman
Estimated Sales: $2.5-5 Million
Number Employees: 10-19
Parent Co: Mechanical Manufacturing Corporation

22607 **Filtration Systems Products**
6662 Olive Boulevard
Saint Louis, MO 63130-2644 314-802-2153
Fax: 314-721-4519 800-444-4720
OEM filter products including cartridges, bags, paper rolls, pressure plates, HVAC and frame sheets.
President: Robin Vance
VP: David Harrell
Research & Development: Andy Burns
Sales Director: Dave Kassabaum
Production: Russell Brown
Estimated Sales: $5 - 10 Million
Number Employees: 20-49
Square Footage: 50000

22608 **Filtrine Manufacturing Company**
15 Kit St
Keene, NH 03431 603-352-5500
Fax: 603-352-0330 thanslet@filtrine.com
www.filtrinemfg.com
Water filtration systems and ingredient water coolers for baked goods, confections, brewing, etc
Chairman: John Hansel
President: Peter Hansel
Sales: Philip Tussing
Estimated Sales: $10 - 20 Million
Number Employees: 50-99
Square Footage: 250000
Brands:
Filtrine
Larco
Steri-Flo
Taste Master

22609 **Final Filtration**
139 Columbia Dr.
Williamsville, NY 14221 716-568-8080
Fax: 716-568-8079 800-454-2357
info@cleanerpools.net www.cleanerpools.net
Filtration for wine and beverages
President: David Privitera
Estimated Sales: $500,000 - $1 Million
Number Employees: 5-9

22610 **Fine Foods International**
9907 Baptist Church Rd
St Louis, MO 63123-4903 314-842-4473
Fax: 314-843-8846 ffinylp@aol.com
Tea and coffee industry bags (brick packs), coffee and cappuccino mixes
Manager: Carole Garnett
VP: Keith Sheller
Operations: Carole Garnett
Estimated Sales: Less than $500,000
Number Employees: 1-4
Type of Packaging: Bulk

22611 **Fine Woods Manufacturing**
2413 East Jones
Phoenix, AZ 85040 602-258-3868
Fax: 602-258-3868 800-279-2871
info@finewoodsmfg.com
www.finewoodsmfg.com
Store fixtures including steel, wood and laminate cabinet displays
President: Dennis Thomas
Estimated Sales: $5 - 10,000,000
Number Employees: 20-49

22612 **Finger Lakes Construction**
10269 Old Route 31
Clyde, NY 14433 315-923-7777
Fax: 315-923-9158 800-328-3522
www.fingerlakesconstruction.com
Winery construction
President: Robert Brisky
Estimated Sales: $50-100 Million
Number Employees: 100-249

22613 **Finn & Son's Metal Spinning Specialists**
PO Box 72
South Lebanon, OH 45065-0072 513-494-2898
Fax: 513-494-2885
Metal spun professional bowls and pans
Estimated Sales: $500,000-$1,000,000
Number Employees: 3
Square Footage: 5000

22614 **Finn Industries**
1921 S Business Pkwy
Ontario, CA 91761 909-930-1500
Fax: 909-930-1510 www.finnindustriesinc.com
PVC containers, folding cartons and rigid boxes
President: William Finn
Estimated Sales: $5-10,000,000
Number Employees: 20-49

22615 **Fiore Di Pasta, Inc.**
4776 East Jensen Avenue
Fresno, CA 93725 559-457-0431
Fax: 559-457-0164 info@fioredipasta.com
www.fioredipasta.com
Fresh and frozen organic pastas, sauces, and entrees
President/CEO: Panfilo Primavera
Chief Operating Officer: Benedetta Primavera
Vice President: Anthony Primavera
Purchasing Director: John Day
Number Employees: 175
Square Footage: 120000

22616 **Fioriware**
333 Market Street
Zanesville, OH 43701-3429 740-454-7400
Fax: 740-454-7790 info@fioriware.com
www.fioriware.com
Flatware
President: Howard Peller
Estimated Sales: $.5 - 1 million
Number Employees: 10
Brands:
Fioriware

22617 **Fire & Flavor Grilling**
375 B Commerce Blvd
Bogart, GA 30622 706-369-9466
Fax: 706-369-9468 866-728-8332
info@fireandflavor.com www.fireandflavor.com
Grilling planks, grilling papers, brine mixes, rubs & sals, skewers & spice
CEO: Genevieve Knox
CFO: Davis Knox
Estimated Sales: $1.5 Million
Number Employees: 11

22618 **Fire Protection Industries**
1765 Woodhaven Dr Ste B
Bensalem, PA 19020-7107 215-245-1830
Fax: 215-245-8819 ausmfpi@cswebmail.com
www.fireproind.com
Fire sprinkler systems; installation available
President: Aus Marburger
Sales Manager: Galen Young
Estimated Sales: $5-10 Million
Number Employees: 100-249
Parent Co: Williard Company

22619 **(HQ)Firematic Sprinkler Devices**
900 Boston Turnpike
Shrewsbury, MA 01545 508-845-2121
Fax: 508-842-3523
Manufacturer and exporter of fire protection devices and control valves
Sales Manager: Greta Heath
Estimated Sales: $10-20 Million
Number Employees: 20-49

22620 **Firl Industries**
P.O.Box 1045
Fond Du Lac, WI 54936-1045 920-921-6942
Fax: 920-921-7329 800-558-4890
info@firlindustries.com www.firlindustries.com
Manufacturer and exporter of doors and accessories including vinyl strip-traffic.
President: John Buser
Estimated Sales: $1-2.5 Million
Number Employees: 12
Brands:
Roll-Up

22621 **Firmenich Incorporated**
250 Plainsboro Rd
Plainsboro, NJ 08536 609-452-1000
Fax: 609-452-6077 www.firmenich.com
Flavors and fragrances
President: Hans Peter Van Houte
General Director: David Sisgy
Vice President, Finance: David Shipman
Vice President: Eric Wallborsky
President, Marketing: Patrick Firmenich
Vice President, Sales: Joy Atkinson
Vice President, Communications: Karen Saddler
Maintenance Facilities Management: Scot Bishop
Estimated Sales: $500 Million +
Number Employees: 5,680
Square Footage: 15000
Other Locations:
Firmenich Chemical Plant
Newark NJ
Fermenich Citrus Center
Safety Harbor FL

22622 **First Bank of Highland P**
633 Skokie Blvd
3rd Floor
Northbrook, IL 60062-2871 847-272-1300
Fax: 847-562-2000 www.firstbankhp.com
Consultant specializing in market research, strategic planning, direct marketing and point of sale merchandising; manufacturer of food display magnetic base counter signs
President: Randy L. Green
Chief Executive Officer: Randy L. Green
Estimated Sales: $.5 - 1 million
Number Employees: 1-4
Square Footage: 3200

22623 **First Brands Corporation**
1221 Broadway
Oakland, CA 94612-1837 203-731-2427
Fax: 203-731-2097
Plastic wrap and bags
President/CEO: W Stephenson
Sales: Julie Mays
Number Employees: 100-249
Parent Co: Clorox Company
Brands:
Glad Bags
Glad Wrap

22624 **First Choice Sign & Lighting**
610 Rock Springs Rd
Escondido, CA 92025-1623 760-746-5069
Fax: 760-746-5393 800-659-0629

Neon lighting, channel letters and architectural and electrical monument signs
Owner: Noel Johnson
Manager: Robby Seeds
Estimated Sales: Less than $500,000
Number Employees: 1-4

22625 First DataBank
1111 Bayhill Dr # 350
San Bruno, CA 94066-3056 650-827-4555
Fax: 650-588-6867 800-633-3453
cs@firstdatabank.com www.firstdatabank.com
Software programs for analyzing diets, menus, formulations and individual food items for nutrient content
President: Joe Hirshman
VP Sales/Marketing: Jim Wilson
Sales Representative: Michele O'Reilly-Kim
Production Manager: Judy Lichtman
Estimated Sales: $20 - 50 Million
Number Employees: 100-249
Parent Co: Hearst Corporation/First Data Bank
Brands:
Nutritionist Iv

22626 First Midwest of Iowa Corporation
616 10th Street
Des Moines, IA 50309-2621 515-243-0768
Fax: 515-243-8103 800-247-8411
Multi-wall paper bags
Estimated Sales: $2.5-5 Million
Number Employees: 50-99
Square Footage: 55000

22627 Fischbein Company
151 Walker Rd
Statesville, NC 28625 704-871-1159
Fax: 704-872-3303 sales@fischbein.com
www.fischbein.com
Manufacturer and exporter of bag closing equipment including bag closing, sealing and flexible material handling
President: Jeff Reed
VP Of Sales/Marketing: Lee Thompson
Manager: Mike Hersey
VP Sales/Marketing: Sean O'Flynn
Sales Development Manager: Tom Conroy
Operations Manager: Lynn McDonald
Purchasing Manager: Curt Poppe
Estimated Sales: $5,000,000
Number Employees: 50-99
Number of Brands: 3
Number of Products: 21
Square Footage: 56000
Parent Co: AXIA
Brands:
Fischbein
Inglett
Saxon

22628 Fischer Paper Products
179 Ida Ave
Antioch, IL 60002 847-395-6060
Fax: 847-395-8619 800-323-9093
bags@fischerpaperproducts.com www.fppi.net
Specialty paper bags for foodservice, prescription, merchandise and industrial applications.
President: Benno Fischer
Vice President: William Fischer
VP Sales: William Fischer
Estimated Sales: $10-15 Million
Number Employees: 50-99
Square Footage: 70000
Type of Packaging: Food Service

22629 Fish Oven & Equipment Corporation
120 W. Kent Ave
PO Box 875
Wauconda, IL 60084 847-526-8686
Fax: 847-526-7447 877-526-8720
info@fishoven.com www.fishoven.com
Manufacturer and exporter of mechanical revolving tray, rotating rack, and woodburning ovens for baking, roasting, supermarket, food service and institutions.
President: James M Campbell III
Sales Manager: Sandra Bradley
Estimated Sales: $2.5-5 Million
Number Employees: 20-49
Square Footage: 160000
Parent Co: Campbell International

22630 Fisher Manufacturing Company
1900 South O Street
PO Box 60
Tulare, CA 93275-0060 559-685-5200
Fax: 559-685-5222 800-421-6162
info1@fisher-mfg.com www.fisher-mfg.com
Manufacturer and exporter of stainless steel faucets, spray washers and water stations
President: Ray Fisher Jr
Quality Control: Delbert Poole
CFO: Rudy Fernandes
Estimated Sales: $10 - 20 Million
Number Employees: 50-99
Type of Packaging: Food Service

22631 Fisher Scientific Company
2000 Park Lane Dr
Pittsburgh, PA 15275-1104 412-490-8300
Fax: 412-490-8759 www.fishersci.com
Manufacturer and exporter of food grade laboratory chemicals
Estimated Sales: $50-100 Million
Number Employees: 500-999
Parent Co: Fisher Scientific International

22632 Fisher Scientific Company
2844 Soquel Ave
Santa Cruz, CA 95062-1411 831-425-7240
Fax: 800-926-1166 800-766-7000
www.fisherscientific.com
Wine industry laboratory equipment
Owner: William Fisher
Estimated Sales: $.5 - 1 million
Number Employees: 1-4

22633 Fishers Investment
8950 Rossash Road
Cincinnati, OH 45236-1210 513-731-3400
Fax: 513-731-8113 800-833-5916
www.texo.com
Manufacturer and exporter of cleaning equipment and supplies including glass cleaners, hand soap, dishwashing and washing compounds
Number Employees: 10
Type of Packaging: Food Service, Private Label

22634 Fishmore
1231 East New Haven Avenue
PO Box 24018
Melbourne,, FL 32901
Canada 321-723-4751
Fax: 321-726-0939 info@fishmore.on.ca
www.fishmore.com
Manufacturer, exporter and importer of custom fish processing equipment including automatic scaling, heading and gutting machines, glazers, conveyors, cutting tables etc
President: Al Sebastian
VP: Tim Cojocari
Estimated Sales: $300,000-500,000
Number Employees: 4
Square Footage: 12000
Brands:
Simor

22635 Fiskars Brands Inc.
PO Box 320
Baldwinsville, NY 13027-0320 315-635-9911
Fax: 315-635-1089 consumeraffairs@fiskars.com
www.fiskars.com
Manufacturer and exporter of casual resin and aluminum furniture for restaurants and cafes; also, clocks, plaques and wall mirrors
President: Ray Carrock
R&D: Melisa Rader
CFO: Michael Read
Quality Control: Tom Norgrack
Number Employees: 250-499

22636 Fiske Brothers Refining
129 Lockwood St
Newark, NJ 07105-4782 973-578-2692
Fax: 973-589-4432 800-733-4755
info@lubriplate.com www.lubriplate.com
USDA H-1/H-2/FDA lubricants for use in food and beverage processing, petroleum-based and synthetic lubricants
President: Richard McCouskey
CEO: Richard T Mc Cluskey
Sales/Marketing: James Girarg
Estimated Sales: G
Number Employees: 50-99
Brands:
Lubriplate

22637 Fitec International
3525 Ridge Meadow Pkwy
Suite 200
Memphis, TN 38115 901-366-9144
Fax: 901-366-9446 800-332-6387
www.fitecgroup.com
Manufacturer, importer and exporter of cotton and nylon mesh bags; also, netting, twine and rope
President: Joe Amore
Sales: Mark Hall
Estimated Sales: $5 - 10 Million
Number Employees: 5-9
Type of Packaging: Bulk

22638 Fittings
3300 Fisher Ave
Fort Worth, TX 76111 817-332-3300
Fax: 817-332-5102 800-473-3301
sales@fitandcp.com www.fitandcp.com
Stainless steel fittings and cold plates for premix and postmix dispensing equipment
Owner: Mark Gannon
Estimated Sales: $5-10 000,000
Number Employees: 50-99

22639 Fitzpatrick Brothers
10700 88th Ave
Pleasant Prairie, WI 53158 773-722-3100
Fax: 773-722-5133 800-233-8064
boconnor@oldsfitz.com
Manufacturer and exporter of scouring powders, cleansers and detergents
General Manager/VP: Odie Ramien
VP: William O'Connor
VP: Tim McAvoy
Plant Manager: Vic Luburich
Estimated Sales: $.5 - 1 million
Number Employees: 1-4
Parent Co: Olds Products Company
Brands:
Babo
Kitchen Klenzer
Old Dutch
Tip Top

22640 Fitzpatrick Company
832 N Industrial Dr
Elmhurst, IL 60126 630-530-3333
Fax: 630-530-0832 info@fitzmill.com
www.fitzmill.com
Manufacturer and exporter of grinder and hammer mills, fluid bed dryers, roll compactors and continuous mixers
President: Scott Patterson
Quality Control: Jose Molimar
CFO: Gary Minta
R&D: Scott Waemmnerstrun
Director Development/Marketing: Scott Wennerstrum
Manager, Sales: Tom Kendrick
Plant Manager: Al Cedno
Estimated Sales: $20 - 50 Million
Number Employees: 100-249
Square Footage: 150000
Brands:
Chilsonator
Fitzmill
Guiloriver
Malaxator

22641 Fitzpatrick Container Company
800 E Walnut St
North Wales, PA 19454 215-699-3515
Fax: 215-699-7603 contain@fitzbox.com
www.fitzbox.com
Corrugated containers and point of purchase displays
President: Thomas J Shallow Jr
VP: Thomas Shallow
Estimated Sales: $2.5-5 Million
Number Employees: 50-99

22642 Five Continents
P.O.Box 2134
Darien, IL 60561-7134 773-927-0100
Fax: 773-927-5113 support@fivecontinents.com
www.fivecontinents.com
Marketing Manager: Marilyn Mara
Estimated Sales: $30 - 35 Million
Number Employees: 100-250

22643 Five-M Plastics Company
178 N State Street
Marion, OH 43302-3065 740-383-6246

Manufacturer and instalation, indoor/outdoor signs and displays
Owner: John Chapman
Sales Manager: Phil George
Estimated Sales: $500,000-$1 Million
Number Employees: 9

22644 Fixtur-World
P.O.Box 6002
Cookeville, TN 38502-6002 931-528-7259
Fax: 931-528-9214 800-634-9887
nallison@fixturworld.com www.fixturworld.com
Manufacturer and exporter of wooden and stainless steel furniture including stands, benches, booths, chairs, cushions, pads, counters/tabletops and hot food tables; custom fabrications available
President: Horace Burks
Sales Director: Bobby Hull
General Manager: Al Paker
Estimated Sales: $10-20 Million
Number Employees: 1-4
Square Footage: 120000

22645 Fixtures Furniture
4121 Rushton Street
Florence, AL 35630 855-321-4999
Fax: 800-831-9821 icare@izzyplus.com
www.izzyplus.com
Tables, stools and benches
Founder/CEO: Chuck Saylor
Estimated Sales: $2.5 - 5 Million
Number Employees: 50
Parent Co: JSJ Corp.
Brands:
Albi
Astro
Baby Bola
Bola
D Chair
Encore
Jazz
Ole
Romo

22646 Flair Electronics
212 Mercury Circle
Pomona, CA 91768
Fax: 909-568-0151 800-532-3492
www.flairsecurity.com
Glass break detectors, water sensors and door annunciators and contacts
Estimated Sales: $1 - 2.5 Million
Number Employees: 10-19
Type of Packaging: Bulk

22647 Flair Flexible PackagingCorporation
2605 S Lakeland Dr
Appleton, WI 54915-4193 920-574-3121
Fax: 920-574-3122
marketing@flairpackaging.com
www.flairpackaging.com/
Flair Flexible Packaging is a fully integrated packaging solutions company providing complete in-house services within the United States and Canada since 1992. Product line includes printing and manufacturing of rolls and bags:multilayer lamination; dry lamination; extrusion lamination and tandem extrusion lamination.
Director/Operations: Cheryl Miller Balster
Type of Packaging: Consumer

22648 Flakice Corporation
60 Liberty Street
Metuchen, NJ 08840-1237 732-494-1070
Fax: 908-686-3430 800-654-4630
Manufacturer and exporter of fluid chillers and industrial ice machines
President: Antoine Hajjar
Vice President: Robert Butler
Chairman: William Adelman
Number Employees: 25
Square Footage: 25000
Brands:
Flakice
Instant-Ice
Liquid Freeze

22649 Flambeau Commercial Marketing Group
100 Grace Drive
Weldon, NC 27890-1200 252-536-2171
Fax: 252-536-2201 800-344-5716
info@flambeau.com www.flambeau.com
Plastic blow molded and injection molded packaging
Plant Manager: David Burke
Estimated Sales: $1 - 5 Million
Number Employees: 100-249
Square Footage: 5600000

22650 Flame Gard
1890 Swarthmore Avenue
PO Box 2020
Lakewood, NJ 08701 800-526-3694
Fax: 732-364-8110 sales@flamegard.com
www.flamegard.com
Manufacturer and exporter of UL classified and commercial grease extracting filters, baffles for kitchen exhaust hoods and grease containment products
President: Lawrence Capalbo
CFO: Gary Barros
VP: Gary Barros
Estimated Sales: Below $5 Million
Number Employees: 20-49
Square Footage: 48000
Parent Co: Component Hardware Group, Inc.
Brands:
Flame Gard
Flame Gard Iii

22651 Flamingo Food Service Products
3095 E 11th Ave
Hialeah, FL 33013 305-691-4641
Fax: 305-696-7342 800-432-8269
info@flamingopaper.com
www.flamingopaper.com
Manufacturer and exporter of paper napkins
President: Tonny Arias
Operations Manager: Evelyn Hernandez
Estimated Sales: $1 - 5 Million
Number Employees: 10-19
Type of Packaging: Consumer, Food Service

22652 Flanders Corporation
531 Flanders Filters Road
Washington, NC 27889 813-286-4767
Fax: 813-286-4769 800-637-2803
customerservice@flanderscorp.com
www.flanderscorp.com
Air filters for heating, air conditioning and ventilation systems
Chief Executive Officer: Harry L. Smith, Jr.
SVP: Charlie Kwiatkowski
Senior Vice President of Sales: Travis Stephenson
Number Employees: 50-99

22653 FlashBake Ovens Food Service
47817 Fremont Boulevard
Fremont, CA 94538-6506 510-498-4200
Fax: 510-498-4224 800-843-6836
Cooking and heating equipment including visible light wave ovens
Director Sales/Marketing: Nora Romo
VP Sales: Rick Schoenberg
Estimated Sales: $300,000-500,000
Number Employees: 1-4
Parent Co: Quadlux

22654 Flashfold Carton
1140 Hayden St
Fort Wayne, IN 46803-2040 260-423-9431
Fax: 260-423-4351 www.flashfold.com
Folding cartons
Estimated Sales: $20-50 Million
Number Employees: 100-249

22655 Flat Plate
2161 Pennsylvania Avenue
York, PA 17404-1793 717-767-9060
Fax: 717-767-9160 888-854-2500
apps@flatplate.com www.flatplate.com
Manufacturer and exporter of brazed plate heat exchangers
President: Steve Wand
CEO: Charles Schmidt
CFO: Mike Losties
Quality Control: Brian Emery
R&D: Brian Emery
Marketing Head: Steve Wand
Estimated Sales: $10 - 20 Million
Number Employees: 20-49

22656 Flatten-O-Matic: Universal Concepts
1147 SW 1st Way
Deerfield Beach, FL 33441-6640 954-327-0194
Fax: 954-792-4502 flattenomatic@aol.com

22657 Flavor Burst Company
499 Commerce Dr
Danville, IN 46122 317-745-2952
Fax: 317-745-2377 800-264-3528
support@flavorburst.com www.flavorburst.com
Owner: Ernie Gerber
Estimated Sales: $5 - 10 Million
Number Employees: 10-19

22658 Flavor Dynamics
640 Montrose Ave
South Plainfield, NJ 07080 908-822-8855
Fax: 908-822-8547 888-271-8424
customercare@flavordynamics.com
www.flavordynamics.com
Food and beverage flavors
President: Dolf DeRovira
Vice President: Marilyn DeRovira
Quality Control Director: Dolf DeRovira Jr.
Sales Director: Colleen Roberts
Plant Manager: Ken Warren
Purchasing: Kristy Callari
Estimated Sales: H
Number Employees: 26
Square Footage: 29000
Type of Packaging: Food Service, Private Label, Bulk
Other Locations:
Flavor Dynamics
Glenview IL
Flavor Dynamics
Corona Del Mar CA
Flavor Dynamics
Cape Charles VA

22659 Flavor House
9516 Commerce Way
Adelanto, CA 92301 760-246-9131
Fax: 760-246-8431 flavorhouse@msn.com
President and CFO: Richard Staley
Quality Control: Debbie Anderson
Sales: Debbie Anderson
Manager: Mike Jastrab
Production: Xavier Rodriguez
Estimated Sales: $20 - 50 Million
Number Employees: 40
Type of Packaging: Bulk

22660 Flavor Wear
28425 Cole Grade Road
Valley Center, CA 92082-6572 760-749-1332
Fax: 760-749-6164 800-647-8372
flavorwr@ix.netcom.com www.flavorwear.com
Manufacturer and exporter of uniform accessories including ties, vests, hair accessories, hats, suspenders, bows, shirts and aprons
President: Lawrence Schleif
Owner/CEO: Martin Anthony
Vice President: Annie Smith
Estimated Sales: $2 Million
Number Employees: 23
Number of Brands: 2
Number of Products: 50
Square Footage: 40000
Parent Co: Anthony Enterprises
Type of Packaging: Food Service, Private Label
Brands:
Designs By Anthony
Flavor Classics
Flavor Touch
Flavor Trim
Flavor Wear
Flavor Weave

22661 Flavors of North America
1900 Averill Rd
Geneva, IL 60134-1601 630-578-8600
Fax: 630-578-8601 800-308-3662
info@fona.com www.fonaflavors.com
Flavors, creation and manufacture of confection flavors, beverage flavors, cereal flavors, snack flavors, bakery flavors, dessert flavors, dairy flavors and flavors for use in functional food, prepared food and animal foodindustries.creates and manufactures a full line of quality flavors for the food, beverage, pharmaceutical and nutraceutical industries
President: Robert Allen
CEO: Joseph J Slawek
R&D: Sue Johnson
Quality Control: Carol Lund
Marketing: Tracy Bergfeld
Sales: TJ Widuch
Purchasing: Terry Emmel

Estimated Sales: $50-100 Million
Number Employees: 100-249

22662 Flavorseal
35179 Avon Commerce Pkwy
Avon, OH 44011 440-937-3900
Fax: 440-937-3901 877-827-5962
info@flavorseal.com www.flavorseal.com
Supplies shring bags, cooking bags, netting, casings and other accessories
Principal: Ron Mitchell
Estimated Sales: $1-2.5 Million
Number Employees: 50-99
Square Footage: 133
Parent Co: Carroll Manufacturing and Sales

22663 Flavourtech Americas
9505 N. Congress Ave
Kansas City, MO 64153-1811 816-880-9321
Fax: 707-829-6211 mail@scanamcorp.com
www.flavourtech.com
President: Anthony Dann
Number Employees: 19

22664 Fleet Wood Goldco Wyard
10615 Beaver Dam Rd
Cockeysville, MD 21030-2204 410-785-1934
Fax: 410-785-2909 service@fgwa.com
www.barrywehmiller.com
Manufacturer and exporter of mechanical conveyors and low pressure accumulating conveying and blending systems; also, package line engineering and integration of systems
President: Tom Spangenberg
VP: John Molite
R&D: Tom Spangenberg
Marketing: Dee Yakel
Sales: Michael Tymowezak
Operations: Bob Jones
Estimated Sales: $30 Million
Number Employees: 20-49
Square Footage: 50000
Type of Packaging: Consumer, Food Service, Private Label, Bulk
Brands:
Air Flow
Ambec 10
Ambec 10r
Can Jet
Double Density Miniroller
Isometric
Lite Touch
Ring Jet

22665 (HQ)Fleetwood
1305 Lakeview Dr
Romeoville, IL 60446 630-759-6800
Fax: 630-759-2299 sales@fleetinc.com
www.barry-wehmillerco.com
Manufacturer and exporter of magnetic and specialized food handling and processing equipment including conveyors, capping, sealing, seaming, canning and food packing
Chairman of the Board: Robert H Chapman
CFO: David Brown
CEO: Phil Ostapowicz
VP Sales: Neil McConnellogue
Estimated Sales: $20 - 50 Million
Number Employees: 100-249
Square Footage: 200000
Parent Co: Barry-Wehmiller
Other Locations:
Fleetwood Systems
Orlando FL

22666 Fleetwood InternationalPaper
2721 E 45th Street
Vernon, CA 90058-2301 323-588-7121
Fax: 323-588-9219
Corrugated cartons and displays
Marketing Manager: Clive Costa
Estimated Sales: $20-50 Million
Number Employees: 100-249

22667 Fleetwood Systems
1264 La Quinta Dr
Orlando, FL 32809-7724 407-855-0230
Fax: 407-857-3792
Material handling systems and components including conveyor belts, chains, vacuums, elevators and lowerators
Sales Applications: Norman Nissen
General Manager: Gerald Janesek
Number Employees: 50-99
Square Footage: 60000
Parent Co: Fleetwood Systems
Type of Packaging: Private Label, Bulk

22668 FleetwoodGoldcoWyard
1305 Lakeview Dr
Romeoville, IL 60446 630-759-6800
Fax: 630-759-2299 www.fgwa.com
Manufacturer and exporter of depalletizers, brewery pasteurizers, warmers, coolers, complete turnkeys, conveyors and rinsers; also, engineering and installation services available
President: David Brown
CEO: Phil Ostapowicz
R&D: Neil McConnellogue
Chairman of the Board: Robert Chapman
General Sales Manager: Richard Witte
Number Employees: 100-249
Square Footage: 200000
Parent Co: Barry-Wehmiller Co.
Brands:
Ez-Just

22669 Fleming Packaging Corporation
411 Hamilton Blvd # 1518
Peoria, IL 61602-1185 309-676-7657
Fax: 309-676-8776
Partner: John Fleming
CEO: Ken Lyons
CFO: Paul Wayvon
General Manager: J Willard Briggs
Estimated Sales: $1 - 3 Million
Square Footage: 82000

22670 Flex Products
PO Box 188
Carlstadt, NJ 07072-0188 201-933-3030
Fax: 201-933-2396 800-526-6273
info@flex-products.com www.flex-products.com
Manufacturer and exporter of plastic extruded tube containers, closures and caps
President: Ed Friedhoff
Vice President: Bill Rooney
Sales Director: Darby Rosa
Plant Manager: Chris Smolar
Estimated Sales: $5-10 Million
Number Employees: 50-99
Square Footage: 65000
Brands:
Flexshape

22671 Flex Sol Packaging
1531 NW 12th Ave
Pompano Beach, FL 33069-1730 800-325-7740
Fax: 800-828-0530 877-353-9765
www.flexsolpackaging.com
Custom industrial extruder of flexible packaging film and bag
President: Brian Stevenson
Estimated Sales: $43 Million
Number Employees: 600
Type of Packaging: Food Service, Bulk
Other Locations:
Flex Sol Packaging
Chicago IL
Flex Sol Packaging
Newark NJ
Flex Sol Packaging
Nashville TN
Flex Sol Packaging
Marshville NC

22672 Flex-Hose Company
6801 Crossbow Dr
East Syracuse, NY 13057 315-437-1611
Fax: 315-437-1903 sales@flexhose.com
www.flexhose.com
Manufacturer and exporter of hoses including Teflon, stainless steel and rubber flexible; also, couplings and expansion joints
President: Philip Argersinger
VP: Philip Argersinger
Operations Coordinator: Charles Phillips
Estimated Sales: Below $5 Million
Number Employees: 10-19
Square Footage: 10000
Brands:
Flexzorber
Guideline
Pumpsaver
Te-Flex
Tri-Flex Loop

22673 Flex-O-Glass
1100 N Cicero Ave Ste 1
Chicago, IL 60651 773-379-7878
Fax: 773-261-5204 www.flexoglass.com
Ionomer skin packaging film
Owner: Harold Warp
Estimated Sales: $10-20 000,000
Number Employees: 10-19

22674 FlexBarrier Products
5350 Campbells Run Road
Pittsburgh, PA 15205 412-787-9750
Fax: 412-787-3665 800-888-9750
www.flexbarrier.com
Manager: Rick M Rochelle
Estimated Sales: $1 - 3 Million
Number Employees: 5-9
Parent Co: TMI, LLC

22675 Flexco
2525 Wisconsin Avenue
Downers Grove, IL 60515 630-971-0150
Fax: 630-971-1180 800-541-8028
info@flexco.com www.flexco.com
Fasteners for conveyor belts, endless splicing products and other products that improve conveyor productivity.
President: Richard White
EVP: Tom Wujek
VP Marketing: Michael Stein
Sales Manager: Richard Reynolds
PR Specialist: Kelly Clancy
Estimated Sales: $20-50 Million
Number Employees: 500
Other Locations:
Grand Rapids MI

22676 Flexco
2525 Wisconsin Ave
Downers Grove, IL 60515 630-971-0105
Fax: 630-971-1180 800-323-3444
info@flexco.com www.flexco.com
Supplier of belt conveyor products
Number Employees: 800

22677 Flexco
2525 Wisconsin Ave
Downers Grove, IL 60515-4241 630-971-0150
Fax: 630-971-1180 800-323-3444
info@flexco.com www.flexco.com
Single source for light-duty endless and mechanical belt splicing solutions.
President/CEO: Richard White
CFO: Glen Paradise
EVP/COO: Tom Wujek
Marketing: Mike Stein
Sales: Dick Reynolds
Public Relations: Kelly Clancy
Estimated Sales: $20-50 Million
Number Employees: 250-499
Square Footage: 175000
Other Locations:
Australia
Chile
China
England
Germany
Mexico
India
Singapore
South Africa
Brands:
Alligator
Clipper
Flexco
Novitool

22678 (HQ)Flexible Foam Products
1900 W Lusher Ave
Elkhart, IN 46517 574-294-7694
Fax: 574-522-4823 800-678-3626
Foamed polyurethane plastic products including containers; also, custom cutting to specific shapes available
General Manager: Jerry Egan
Chemist: Karl Baier
Plant Manager: John Noble
Estimated Sales: $20-50 Million
Number Employees: 100-249

22679 Flexible Material Handling
410 Horizon Dr Ste 200
Suwanee, GA 30024 216-587-1575
Fax: 216-587-2833 800-669-1501
soflynn@fischbein.com www.flexmh.com

Conveyors including portable, flexible gravity and powered; also, portable storage racks
Sales Administration: Nancy Stohlman
Sales/Marketing Manager: Karl Dearnley
Estimated Sales: $20-50 Million
Number Employees: 50-99
Parent Co: Axia

22680 Flexible Products Company
1881 W Oak Pkwy
Marietta, GA 30062-2230 770-419-4503
Fax: 770-421-3216 800-659-3270
info@flexpro.com www.flexibleproducts.com
Polyurethane compounds, foam and chemicals
CEO: Pete Henson
Global VP: Bob Wood
Chief Technical Officer: William Banholzer
Estimated Sales: $50-100 Million
Number Employees: 250-499

22681 Flexible Tape & Label Company
243 Jefferson Ave
Memphis, TN 38103 901-522-1410
Fax: 901-523-0073 art@flexiblelabel.com
www.flexiblelabel.com
Printed pressure sensitive labels
President: E Alan Magnus
VP: Melanie Magnus
Estimated Sales: $1-2.5 Million
Number Employees: 5-9

22682 Flexicell
10463 Wilden Dr
Ashland, VA 23005 804-550-7300
Fax: 804-222-1496 webinfo@flexicell.com
www.flexicell.com
Manufacturer and exporter of robotic packaging machinery for case packing, collating, palletizing and conveying
President: Hans Dekoning
R & D: Jack Morris
VP of Sales: Hans Schouten
Plant Manager: John Architzel
Purchasing Manager: Jim Golob
Estimated Sales: Below $5 Million
Number Employees: 20-49
Square Footage: 24000
Brands:
Flexi-1850
Flexi-Cell
Flexilinear
Flexiloader

22683 Flexicon
165 Chicago St
Cary, IL 60013 847-639-3530
Fax: 847-639-6828 custservice@flexiconinc.net
www.flexiconinc.net
Flexible packaging materials for the food and pharmaceuticalical industries, supplied in rollstock for thermoforming, lidding, and form fill and seal applications. Preformed pouches are also supplied. Specializing in rollstock orpouches for boil and freeze applications.
President: Robert Biddle
CEO: Greg Baron
Estimated Sales: $20 Million
Number Employees: 50-99
Type of Packaging: Consumer, Food Service, Private Label

22684 (HQ)Flexicon Corporation
2400 Emrick Blvd
Bethlehem, PA 18020-8006 610-814-2400
Fax: 610-814-0600 sales@flexicon.com
www.flexicon.com
Manufacturer and exporter of flexible screw conveyor systems, bulk bag dischargers, weigh batching systems and bulk handling systems with automated controls
CEO: William S Gill
Number Employees: 50-99
Other Locations:
Flexicon Corporation
Kent
Brands:
Batch-Con
Bev-Con
Flow-Flexer
Pop-Top

22685 Flexlink Systems
6580 Snowdrift Rd Ste 200
Allentown, PA 18106 610-973-8200
Fax: 610-973-8345 800-782-1399
us1.marketing@flexlink.com www.flexlink.com
Plastic chain conveyor systems and automation components
President: Dave Clark
CFO: Nino Dipietrroo
Estimated Sales: $20-50 Million
Number Employees: 5-9

22686 Flexlume Sign Corporation
1464 Main Street
Buffalo, NY 14209 716-884-2020
Fax: 716-881-0361 info@flexlume.com
www.flexlume.com
Indoor and outdoor signs
President: Alfred P Rowell Jr
Estimated Sales: Below $5 Million
Number Employees: 5-9

22687 Flexo Graphics
900 S Georgia St
Amarillo, TX 79102-1204 806-374-5363
Fax: 806-371-7104 866-533-5396
info@grandoldflagshop.com www.mwickett.com
Labels including die-cut and pressure sensitive
Owner: Kevin Ahrens
Sales: Ray Clark
Office Manager: Dylan Clark
Estimated Sales: $500,000-$1 Million
Number Employees: 1 to 4
Square Footage: 3500

22688 Flexo Transparent
28 Wasson St
Buffalo, NY 14210 716-825-7710
Fax: 716-825-0139 877-993-5396
mbarrile@flexotransparent.com
www.flexotransparent.com
Flexographic printer, manufacturer and exporter of custom designed and printed plastic films up to ten colors including process print. Flexible packaging materials including: bags, rollstock, bottle sleeves, sheeting, reclosablezipper, resealable tape, pallet covers, specialty prepared foods totes, custom shaped packaging, etc. EDI and VMI capable; Just in Time Deliveries; Fast turnaround shipments.
President: Ronald Mabry
Sales: Mark Barrile
Estimated Sales: $20-50 Million
Number Employees: 50-99
Number of Brands: 4
Square Footage: 84000
Type of Packaging: Consumer, Food Service, Private Label, Bulk
Brands:
Chicken Keeper
Crispy Keeper
Rotisserie Keeper
Safti Keeper

22689 Flexo-Printing EquipmentCorporation
416 Hayward Ave N
Saint Paul, MN 55128 651-731-9499
Fax: 651-731-0525 www.flexo-siat.com
Die cutting and slitting capability for tape and labels
President: Wynn Lidell
Estimated Sales: Below $5 000,000
Number Employees: 1-4

22690 (HQ)Flexpak Corporation
3720 W Washington St
Phoenix, AZ 85009 602-269-7648
Fax: 602-269-7640
drichardson@flexpakcorp.com
www.flexpakcorp.com
Thermoformed products including shelf organizers, freezer trays, point of purchase displays and shipping and handling trays; also, contract packaging including club packs, assembly, shrink packaging, display packout, bagging andlabeling
President: Donald Bond
CFO: Steve Merray
Quality Control: Carlos Pineda
Marketing Director: Don Richardson
Operations Manager: Rick Colton
Purchasing Manager: Jim Boley
Estimated Sales: $20 - 50 Million
Number Employees: 100-249
Square Footage: 82000
Type of Packaging: Consumer, Food Service, Private Label, Bulk

22691 (HQ)Flint Boxmakers
2490 E Bristol Road
Burton, MI 48529-1391 810-743-0400
Fax: 810-743-9577 www.michiganmall.com
Corrugated boxes
President: Thomas Landaal

22692 Flint Rubber Stamp Works
3518 Fenton Rd
Flint, MI 48507 810-235-2341
Fax: 810-235-3919 rodzinaind@aol.com
www.gy.com
Marking and coding devices including rubber stamps
President: Robert Cross Jr
Estimated Sales: $500,000-$1 Million
Number Employees: 5-9
Parent Co: Rodzina Industries

22693 Flo-Cold
29290 Wall St,
PO Box 930317
Wixom, MI 48393 248-348-6666
Fax: 248-348-6667
Coolers, freezers and racked modular refrigeration systems
President: Dean M Koppin
Engineer: Albert Durand
Estimated Sales: $2.5 - 5 Million
Number Employees: 60
Parent Co: Chrysler & Koppin Company
Brands:
Flo-Cold

22694 Flo-Matic Corporation
1982t Belford North Drive
Belvidere, IL 61008-8565 815-547-5650
Fax: 815-544-2287 800-959-1179
Manufacturer and exporter of washers and washing systems
Chief Engineer: Edward Herman
Estimated Sales: $1 - 5,000,000

22695 Floaire
1730 Walton Road
Suite # 203
Blue Bell, PA 19422-1230 610-239-8405
Fax: 610-239-8941 800-726-5623
sales@floaire.com www.floaire.com
Ventilation equipment and commercial cookware
President: Clark S Fuller
Marketing Administration: Dawn Kearny
VP Sales Food Service: Richard Kinzler
Estimated Sales: $1 - 5 Million
Number Employees: 5-9
Parent Co: Ralph Kearney & Sons

22696 Flodin
PO Box 1578
Moses Lake, WA 98837-0245 509-766-2996
Fax: 509-766-0157 sales@flodin-inc.com
www.flodin.com
Manufacturer and exporter of potato processing equipment including conveyors, dumpers, friers, dryers and frozen concertrate, thawing and breaker systems, etc
Sales Executive: Bill Flodin
Purchasing Agent: Rod Wright
Estimated Sales: $2.5-5 Million
Number Employees: 10-19
Square Footage: 92000
Brands:
Flodin

22697 Flojet
20 Icon
Foothill Ranch, CA 92610-3000 949-859-4945
Fax: 949-859-1153 800-235-6538
www.flojet.com
Manufacturer, importer and exporter of bag-in-box packaging pumps, motor pump units and power sprayers for soda, beer, cider, wine, condiments and water
President: Russ Davis
Marketing Director: Brud LeTourneav
Sales Director: Jon Byrd
Estimated Sales: $50 - 100 Million
Number Employees: 250

22698 **Flomatic International**
12990 SE Highway 212
Clackamas, OR 97015-9004 503-775-2550
Fax: 503-771-0068 800-435-2550
csd@gflomaticintl.com
Manufacturer and exporter of post-mix soft drink dispensing valves
VP: John Cochran
Estimated Sales: $10-20 Million
Number Employees: 20-49
Square Footage: 21600
Parent Co: Manitowoc Foodservice Group
Brands:
Flomatic

22699 **Floormaster**
1157 Hooker Road
Chattanooga, TN 37407-3248 423-867-4525
Fax: 423-867-4563 floormaster@gateway.net
Floor sweeping compounds
President: Johnny Bailey
Estimated Sales: $2.5-5 Million
Number Employees: 10 to 19
Square Footage: 10000

22700 **Florart Flock Process**
13870 W Dixie Hwy
North Miami, FL 33161-3343 305-643-3900
Fax: 305-981-9929 800-292-3524
flags4u@mindspring.com www.flagusa.com
Manufacturer and exporter of flags, flagpoles, pennants, indoor flag sets and banners
Owner: Barbara Dabney
CEO: Stephanie Ledlow
Number Employees: 5-9
Square Footage: 20800
Brands:
Annin
Cf
Eder
Valley Forge

22701 **Florida Knife Company**
1735 Apex Rd
Sarasota, FL 34240 941-371-2104
Fax: 941-378-9427 800-966-5643
sales@florida-knife.com www.florida-knife.com
Manufacturer and exporter of knives for ice, candy and packaging; also, food processing machine knife blades
President: Tom Johanning
Sales: Tom Johanning Jr
Personnel: Debbie Dean
Estimated Sales: $2.5-5 Million
Number Employees: 20-49
Square Footage: 24000

22702 **Florida Plastics International**
10200 S Kedzie Ave
Evergreen Park, IL 60805-3735 708-499-0400
Fax: 708-499-4620 mail@keyserind.com
www.keyserind.com
Manufacturer and exporter of point of purchase displays, signs and menu boards
President: Bill Keyser
CEO: Donald Keyser
Quality Control: Tom Page
Estimated Sales: $10 - 20 Million
Number Employees: 50-99
Square Footage: 60000
Type of Packaging: Food Service

22703 **Florida Seating**
6100 Mears Court
Clearwater, FL 33760 727-540-9802
Fax: 727-540-9403 www.floridaseating.com
Manager: Jeremy Williams
Estimated Sales: $1 - 5 Million
Number Employees: 5-9

22704 **Florin Box & Lumber Company**
PO Box 292338
Sacramento, CA 95829-2338 916-383-2675
Fax: 916-383-1397 800-767-2675
florinbox@aol.com
Wine industry gift boxes, packaging, wood crates
Estimated Sales: $5-10 000,000
Number Employees: 20-49

22705 **Flour City Press-Pack Company**
P.O.Box 398198
Minneapolis, MN 55439-8198 952-831-1265
Fax: 612-378-9441
Paper boxes including set-up and folding
Owner: Gene N Fuller
Quality Control: Richard Hall
Estimated Sales: $300,000-500,000
Number Employees: 1-4

22706 **Flow Autoclave Systems**
3721 Corporate Dr
Columbus, OH 43231 614-891-2732
Fax: 614-891-4568 kbrowning@flowae.com
www.flowae.com
Manufacturer and exporter of high pressure processing equipment to eliminate microorganisms, inactivate enzymes, extend shelf life and retain vitamin levels and natural flavor
Manager: Melanie Harter
Sales Director: David Peltier
Operations Manager: Terry Lansing
Estimated Sales: $70 Million
Number Employees: 20-49
Square Footage: 16000

22707 **(HQ)Flow International Corporation**
23500 64th Ave South
Kent, WA 98032-2305 253-850-3500
Fax: 253-813-9377 800-610-1798
info@flowcorp.com www.flowcorp.com
Manufacturer and exporter of food processing and high-pressure waterjet cutting and cleaning equipment
President: Pat Adams
CFO: Steve Reichenbach
CEO: Charlie Brown
Quality Control: Chris Bohnen
R & D: Felix Sciulli
Marketing: Camille Roskamp
Vice President of Global Sales: Dick LeBlanc
Estimated Sales: $200 Million
Number Employees: 250-499
Square Footage: 150000
Brands:
Fresher Under Pressure

22708 **Flow Robotics**
1635 Production Dr
Jeffersonville, IN 47130-9624 812-283-7888
Fax: 812-284-3281 www.flowcorp.com
Manufacturer and exporter of positioning systems for waterjet cutting pick and place robots
Manager: Anthony Neeley
Vice President of Global Sales: Dick LeBlanc
General Manager: Gerald Malmrose
Chief Engineer: Mark Saberton
Estimated Sales: $1 - 5 Million
Number Employees: 50-99
Square Footage: 108000
Parent Co: Flow International

22709 **Flow Technology**
P.O.Box 52103
Phoenix, AZ 85072-2103 480-240-3400
Fax: 480-240-3401 800-528-4225
ftimarket@ftimeters.com www.ftimeters.com
Instrumetation and controls, flow meters
President: Alan Eschbach
Quality Control: Randy Larrison
Estimated Sales: $10 - 20 Million
Number Employees: 50-99

22710 **Flow of Solids**
1 Technology Park Drive
Westford, MA 01886-3139 978-392-0300
Fax: 978-392-9980 mail@jenike.com
www.jenike.com
Portable and stationery containers including silos, bins, hoppers, feeders, tumble blenders, chutes, solid pumps and slide gates
Director Sales/Marketing: Roderick Hossfeld
National Sales Manager: Brian Pittenger
Estimated Sales: $3 - 5 Million
Number Employees: 20-49
Parent Co: Jenike & Johanson

22711 **Flow-Turn, Inc.**
1050 Commerce Avenue
Union, NJ 07083 908-687-3225
Fax: 908-687-1715 sales@flow-turn.com
www.flow-turn.com
Manufacturer, importer and exporter of USDA listed powered belt curve and custom straight conveyors
President: Herman Migdel
Product Manager: J Grabowski
Operations Manager: Dan Otero
Estimated Sales: $2.5-5 Million
Number Employees: 12
Square Footage: 144000
Brands:
Floturn

22712 **Flowdata**
8930 South Beck Ave
Suite #107
Tempe, AZ 85284 602-437-1315
Fax: 972-907-8016 800-833-2448
ftimarket@ftimeters.com www.flowdata.com
Positive displacement and turbine flow meters
President: C Foran, Jr.
Number Employees: 20
Square Footage: 60000
Brands:
Decathlon Series
Exact Series

22713 **Fluid Air**
2580 Diehl Road, Unit E
Aurora, IL 60502 630-665-5001
Fax: 630-665-5981 fluidairinfo@spray.com
www.fluidairinc.com
Manufacturer and exporter of milling equipment for fine grinding and dryers/agglomerators for drying, agglomerating, coating and encapsulating foods and flavors
President: Martin Bender
CEO: Thomas Tappen
Director Process Development: Donald Verbarg
Estimated Sales: $5 - 10 Million
Number Employees: 20-49
Square Footage: 64000
Parent Co: Spraying Systems Company

22714 **Fluid Energy Processingand Equipment Company**
2629 Penn Avenue
Hatfield, PA 19440 215-368-2510
Fax: 215-368-6235 sales@fluidenergype.com
www.fluidenergype.com
Manufacturer and exporter of jet/micronizing grinding mills, pulverizers and flash drying equipment
Estimated Sales: $5 - 10 Million
Number Employees: 50-99
Brands:
Jet-O-Mizer
Micro-Jet
Roto-Jet
Roto-Sizer
Thermajet

22715 **Fluid Metering**
5 Aerial Way Ste 500
Syosset, NY 11791 516-922-6050
Fax: 516-624-8261 800-223-3388
pumps@fmipump.com www.fmipump.com
Manufacturer and exporter of metering pumps, dispensers and accessories including valveless and variable positive displacement piston pumps
President: Harry Pinkerton III
Marketing Manager: Herb Werner
VP Sales: David Peled
Purchasing Director: Anthony Mennella
Estimated Sales: $10-20 Million
Number Employees: 50-99
Square Footage: 12000
Brands:
Fmi
Micro-Petter
Ratiomatic

22716 **Fluid Systems**
10054 Old Grove Rd
San Diego, CA 92131 858-695-3840
Fax: 858-695-2176 800-525-4369
trubyr@kochind.com www.fluid-systems.com
Crossflow membrane filtration processes and systems for the industrial, good, water, chemical, and biotechnology markets
CFO: William Colins

22717 **Fluid Transfer**
50 West Pine St
Philipsburg, PA 16866 814-342-0902
Fax: 814-342-5660 sales@leeind.com
www.leeind.com

Manufacturer and exporter of sanitary flush bottom and in-line ball valves
Owner & President/CEO: Robert Montler
Owner & VP Of Finance And Operations: Joshua Montler
VP, Sales: Greg Wharton
Advertising Manager: John Weaver
Estimated Sales: $5-50 Million
Number Employees: 250-499
Parent Co: Lee Industries
Brands:
Fluid Flow

22718 **Fluted Partition**
850 Union Ave
Bridgeport, CT 06607 203-368-2548
Fax: 203-367-5266 flutedpartition@aol.com
www.valleycontainer.com
Fluted partitions, corrugated and solid fiber boxes
Owner: Arthur W Vietze Jr
VP: Richard Jackson
Estimated Sales: $5-10 000,000
Number Employees: 20-49
Number of Products: 1
Type of Packaging: Private Label, Bulk

22719 **Flux Pumps Corporation**
4330 Commerce Cir SW
Atlanta, GA 30336 404-691-6010
Fax: 404-691-6314 800-367-3589
contact-flux-usa@flux-pumpen.de
www.flux-pumps.com
Manufacturer and exporter of pumps including centrifugal, pneumatic, positive displacement, progressive cavity and sanitary
President: L G Eastman
Vice President: Mike O'Toole
Estimated Sales: $1-2.5,000,000
Number Employees: 5-9
Parent Co: Flux Pumps Corporation
Type of Packaging: Bulk

22720 **Flynn Burner Corporation**
425 5th Ave
New Rochelle, NY 10801 914-636-1320
Fax: 914-636-3751 800-643-8910
webmaster@adpositive.com
www.flynnburner.com
Industrial gas burners for baking and surface treating (3D and flat web), paper, plastic
CEO: Edward S Flynn
Number Employees: 50-99
Type of Packaging: Food Service, Private Label

22721 **Foam Concepts**
27 Mendon St
PO Box 410
Uxbridge, MA 01569 508-278-7255
Fax: 508-278-3623 sales@foamconcepts.com
www.foamconcepts.com
Manufacturer and exporter of custom molded insulated foam shipping containers and custom packaging for perishables
Owner: Mark Villamaino
VP Sales: Philip Michaelson III
Estimated Sales: $5 - 10 Million
Number Employees: 20-49
Square Footage: 80000

22722 **Foam Fabrications**
8722 E San Alberto Dr # 200
Scottsdale, AZ 85258-4353 480-607-7330
Fax: 480-607-7333
scottsdale@foamfabricatorsinc.com
www.foamfabricatorsinc.com
Custom molded polystyrene packaging materials, expanded polystyrene, expanded polypropylene, expanded polyethylene
President: James Hughes
CFO: James Hughes
Estimated Sales: $5 - 10 Million
Number Employees: 10-19

22723 **Foam Pack Industries**
72 Fadem Rd
Springfield, NJ 07081-3116 973-376-3700
Fax: 973-467-9850 foampack@verizon.net
www.foampackindustries.com
Polystyrene packaging materials and containers; also, ice packs
President: Harvey Goodstein
CFO: David Goodstein
Sales Manager: Lacy Seabrook
Estimated Sales: $5 - 10 Million
Number Employees: 5-9

22724 **Foam Packaging**
106 Commercial Drive
Footsville, WI 53537 608-876-4217
Fax: 601-636-2655 info@foampackaging.com
www.foam-packaging.com
Manufacturer and exporter of food service trays and insulated food containers for eggs, poultry and produce
President: Ray B English
Estimated Sales: $1-2.5 Million
Number Employees: 1-4

22725 **Foamex**
18801 Old Statesville Rd
Cornelius, NC 28031-9306 704-892-8081
Fax: 704-892-0409 www.foamex.com
Polyurethane foam
General Manager: Fran Conard
Finance Executive: Jennifer Hughes
Manager of Laminated Products: L Peterson
Estimated Sales: $20-50 Million
Number Employees: 100-249

22726 **Foamold Corporation**
34 Birchwood Dr
PO Box 95
Oneida, NY 13421-0095 315-363-5350
Fax: 315-363-4518
Foam packaging materials
Plant Manager: Jay Reinhardt
Plant Manager: Jay Rheinhardt

22727 **Focke & Company**
5730 Millstream Rd
Whitsett, NC 27377 336-449-7200
Fax: 336-449-5444 sales@fockegso.com
www.focke.com
Packaging machinery
President: Juergen Focke
Financial Controller: Alec Pratto
VP: Johann Betschart
Estimated Sales: $10 - 20 000,000
Number Employees: 50-99

22728 **Focus**
2852 Anthony Ln S
Minneapolis, MN 55418-3233 612-706-4444
Fax: 612-706-0544
food@focusexecutivesearch.com
www.focusexecutivesearch.com
Executive search firm specializing in personnel for general management, sales, research and development, operations, production and administration positions
President: Tim Mc Lafferty
CFO: Gayle Hope
Vice President: Tim Schultz
R & D: Nicholas Kallenbach
Sales Director: Tony Misum
Public Relations: Gayle Holt
Estimated Sales: Below $5 Million
Number Employees: 5-9
Square Footage: 400000

22729 **Fogel Group**
44 W Flagler St # 350
Miami, FL 33130-6813 305-577-4905
Fax: 305-372-0936
Commercial refrigerators specifically designed for beverage and beer industries
Estimated Sales: $300,000-500,000
Number Employees: 1-4

22730 **(HQ)Fogel Jordon CommercialRefrigeration Company**
2501 Grant Avenue
Philadelphia, PA 19114-2307 215-535-8300
Fax: 215-289-1597 800-523-0171
Manufacturer and exporter of refrigerators, walk-in cabinets, refrigerated display cases, beverage coolers, cooling rooms, etc
Secretary/Treasurer: Gene Sterner
Sales Manager: Howard Smith
Estimated Sales: $20-50 Million
Number Employees: 50-99
Square Footage: 200000
Type of Packaging: Consumer, Bulk
Brands:
Fogel
Jordon
Jordon Scientific

22731 **Fogg Company**
3455 John F Donnelly Drive
Holland, MI 49424-9207 616-786-3644
Fax: 616-786-0350 info@foggfiller.com
www.foggfiller.com
Manufacturer and exporter of packaging machinery including bottle fillers and cappers, and rinsers for flowable liquid, and noncarbonated products
President: Mike Fogg
Vice President: Al Nienhuis
Marketing Director: Susan Lamar
Sales Director: Ben Fogg
Plant Manager: Randy Dewaard
Estimated Sales: $10-20 Million
Number Employees: 50-99
Square Footage: 40000
Type of Packaging: Consumer, Food Service, Private Label, Bulk
Brands:
Clip Go Valve
Easi-63
Filt Pro 5000
Ventraflow

22732 **Foilmark**
5 Malcolm Hoyt Dr
Newburyport, MA 01950 978-462-7300
Fax: 978-462-0831 sales@itwfoilmark.com
www.foilmark.com
Wine industry fillers
President: Joe Olsen
Estimated Sales: $50-100 Million
Number Employees: 100-249

22733 **(HQ)Fold-Pak Corporation**
Van Buren Street
Newark, NY 14513 315-331-3159
Fax: 315-331-0093
Manufacturer and exporter of folding ice cream and carry out food cartons
President/CEO: Karl De May
Senior VP Sales/Marketing: Robert Mullally
VP Sales: Max Richter
Estimated Sales: $50-100 Million
Number Employees: 100-249
Type of Packaging: Consumer, Private Label
Other Locations:
Fold-Pak Corp.
Hazleton PA

22734 **Fold-Pak South**
3961 Cusseta Rd
Columbus, GA 31903-2045 706-689-2924
Fax: 706-689-2308 www.gsdpackaging.com
Manufacturer and exporter of food trays, soup containers and wire-handled food pails including Oriental and microwaveable; available with or without pagoda design
Quality Control: Coral Vessel
Plant Manager: Carl Vessell
Estimated Sales: $10 - 20 Million
Number Employees: 20-49
Type of Packaging: Food Service
Brands:
Bio-Pak

22735 **Folding Carton/FlexiblePackaging**
12323 Sherman Way
North Hollywood, CA 91605-5517 818-896-3449
Fax: 818-982-9039
Paper boxes, cartons, blister cards and skin sheets
General Manager: Tom Hiraishi
Number Employees: 60
Parent Co: Marfred Industries

22736 **Folding Guard Company**
2101 S Carpenter Street
Chicago, IL 60608-4597 312-829-3500
Fax: 312-829-8338 www.foldingguard.com
Manufacturer and exporter of partitions, gates and lockers
Operations Manager: Keith Stadwick
Estimated Sales: $10-20 Million
Number Employees: 50-99
Type of Packaging: Bulk
Brands:
Quik-Fence

22737 Foley Sign Company
572 Mercer St
Seattle, WA 98109 206-324-3040
Fax: 206-328-4953 5999markmetcalf@qwest.net
www.foleysign.com

Manufacturer and exporter of signs
Owner: Mark Metcalf
Estimated Sales: $1-2.5 Million
Number Employees: 10-19

22738 Foley's Famous Aprons
3441 Filbert St
Wayne, MI 48184-1974 734-641-9507
Fax: 734-721-8426 800-634-3245
Work cloths, caps and aprons
Owner: Terrence Foley
Secretary: Kevin Foley
VP: Tom Foley
Estimated Sales: $300,000-500,000
Number Employees: 1-4
Square Footage: 5000

22739 Follett Corporation
801 Church Ln
Easton, PA 18040 610-252-7301
Fax: 610-250-0696 800-523-9361
info@folletice.com www.follettice.com
Manufacturer and exporter of high quality, innovative ice storage bins, ice storage and transport systems, ice and water dispensers, ice and beverage dispensers, and Chewblet® ice nugget ice machines
President/CEO: Steven Follett
CFO: Thomas Rohrbach
Executive VP: Robert Bryson
Marketing Director: Lois Schneck
VP Sales: Ed Barr
Manager, Marketing Services: Robin Porter
VP Operations: David Tumbusch
Manager, Materials: Jeff Craig
Type of Packaging: Food Service

22740 Fonda Group
P.O.Box 2038
Oshkosh, WI 54903 920-235-9330
Fax: 920-235-1642 800-367-2877
info@solocup.com www.fondagroup.com
Institutional and consumer food service items: baking, eclair, portion, burger cups; hot dog trays; pan liners; bath mats/car mats; doilies; lace and linen placemats, printed and custom designed placemats; plain and printed napkins;tray sovers and table covers
President: Robert Korzenski
CEO: Dennis Mehiel
CFO: Haris Heinsen
VP Operations: Bryan Hollenbach
Marketing Director: Beth Dahlke
Sales Director: John Lewchenko
Public Relations: Jenny Leichtfuss
Plant Manager: Tom Glaeser
Purchasing Manager: Mike Marquardt
Number Employees: 500-999
Number of Brands: 9
Square Footage: 485000
Parent Co: SF Holdings Group
Other Locations:
Fonda Group
Lakeland FL
Fonda Group
Goshen IA
Fonda Group
Glens Falls NY
Fonda Group
Williamsberg PA
Fonda Group
St. Albans VT
Fonda Group
Appleton WI
Fonda Group
Augusta GA
Fonda Group
Indianapolis IA
Brands:
American
Budgetware
Dollarwise
Firmware
Fonda
Hoffmaster
Linen-Like
Sensations
Smartware

22741 Fonda Group
PO Box 2038
Oshkosh, WI 54903 920-235-9330
Fax: 920-235-1642 800-558-9300
www.fondagroup.com
Disposable tableware including plates, napkins, table covers, cups, bowls, trays, take-out containers, etc
President: Robert Korzenski
Marketing Director: Beth Dahlke
Procurement Director: Mike Marquardt
Estimated Sales: $100-500 Million
Number Employees: 500-999
Parent Co: Fonda Group
Brands:
Budgetware
Classic
Lifestyle
Rave
Smartware

22742 Fonda Group
PO Box 519
Goshen, IN 46527-0519 574-534-2515
Fax: 574-533-6330
Paper plates
President: William Lester
Principal: Meg Amadeo
Number Employees: 50

22743 Food & Agrosystems
1289 Mandarin Drive
Sunnyvale, CA 94087-2028 408-245-8450
Fax: 408-748-1826 fasi@foodagrosys.com
www.foodagrosys.com
Consultant specializing in process engineering, product/process development, plant/process layout, equipment design, feasibility analysis, production problem-solving, management assistance, etc
President: Thomas Parks
VP Marketing: Robert Marquardt
Estimated Sales: $1-2.5 Million
Number Employees: 10

22744 Food & Beverage Consultants
1260 Oaklawn Ave
Cranston, RI 02920 401-463-5784
Fax: 401-463-7931
Consultant specializing in food and beverage development, flavor modification, food service and institutional consulting, recipe and menu development, quality control, food labeling, sensory evaluation and training programs
President: Demetri Kazantzis
Estimated Sales: $.5 - 1 million
Number Employees: 1-4

22745 Food Automation ServiceTechniques
905 Honeyspot Road
Stratford, CT 06615-7147 203-377-4414
Fax: 203-377-8187 800-327-8766
sales@fastinc.com www.fastinc.com
Manufacturer and exporter of appliance timers and controls for frying, cooking, roasting, proofing, retarder-proofing, baking, etc.; also, portable shortening filter machines and software systems for appliance diagnostics
Chairman: Bernard G Koether
President: George F Koether
CEO: Seth Lukash
Sales Operations Manager: Sherry Kraynak
Estimated Sales: $10 - 20 Million
Number Employees: 130
Brands:
Fastfilter
Fastimer
Fastpak
Fastron
Sck

22746 Food Automation ServiceTechniques
905 Honeyspot Road
Stratford, CT 06615-7147 203-377-4414
Fax: 203-377-8187 800-327-8766
sales@fastinc.com www.fastinc.com
Food processing appliance controls
Chairman: Bernard G Koether
Sales Operations Manager: Sherry Kraynak
Estimated Sales: $10-20 Million
Number Employees: 100-250

22747 (HQ)Food Business Associates
PO Box J
Temple, ME 04984-0539 207-778-2251
Fax: 207-778-5097
Consultant and market development specialist providing growth strategy planning and consumer and trade acceptance research; also, supermarket supervisor training services available
President: Robert Bull
VP: Stephen Bull
Estimated Sales: Less than $500,000
Number Employees: 4

22748 Food Consulting Company
13724 Recuerdo Drive
Del Mar, CA 92014-3430 858-793-4658
Fax: 800-522-3545 800-793-2844
info@foodlabels.com www.foodlabels.com
Consultant specializing in nutrition analysis and food labeling
Estimated Sales: Below $500,000
Number Employees: 1

22749 Food Development Centre
PO Box 1240
Portage La Prairie, NB R1N 3J9
Canada 306-933-7555
Fax: 306-933-7208 800-870-1044
ÿinfo@foodcentre.sk.ca www.foodcentre.sk.ca
Consultant specializing in product development, packaging, equipment, food analyses, nutritional profiles, QC programs, food research and development, food processing, process engineering, etc.; full service food science and technologylibrary in house; also, seminars available
CEO: Dave Donaghy
Research & Development: AlPhonSus Utioh
Marketing Director: Markus Schmulgen
Number Employees: 25
Square Footage: 80000
Parent Co: Manitoba Agriculture & Food

22750 Food Engineering Network
1050 Il Route 83
Bensenville, IL 60106-1049 630-616-0200
Fax: 630-227-0204 whalenn@bnp.com
www.bnpmedia.com
CEO: Jim Henderson
Estimated Sales: $1 - 5 000,000

22751 Food Engineering Unlimited
1501 N Harbor Blvd Ste 103
Fullerton, CA 92835 714-879-8762
Fax: 714-773-0911 feu@earthlink.net
www.food-eng.com
Conveyors,material handling systems, bakery ovens, mixers and spiral freezers; also, installation services available
President: Russ Juergens
Estimated Sales: $1-2,500,000
Number Employees: 1-4

22752 Food Equipment BrokerageInc
PO Box 6541
Key West, FL 33041
800-968-8881
febinc@mo.net www.febinc.com
We do turn key c-stores across the United States and Canada. We also export to Asia
CEO: Michael Hesse
Marketing: J R Kim
Sales: Dave Schuller
Number Employees: 110
Number of Brands: 400
Type of Packaging: Food Service, Private Label

22753 Food Equipment Manufacturing Company
22201 Aurora Rd
Bedford Heights, OH 44146 216-663-1208
Fax: 216-663-9337 info@femc.com
www.femc.com
Manufacturer and exporter of packaging machinery including fillers, de-stackers, sealers and slicers
President: Robert Sauer
CFO: Obert Sauer
VP: Joseph Lukes
Sales Manager: Daniel Auvil
Estimated Sales: $5-10 Million
Number Employees: 20-49
Square Footage: 60000

22754 Food Executives Network
10415 West Michigan Street
Milwaukee, WI 53226 414-962-7684
Fax: 414-962-6261
careers@foodexecsnetwork.com
www.rothyoungmilwaukee.com
Search firm speacializing in the selection and placement of executive, managerial and technical professionals.
President and CEO: Thomas Brenneman
VP: Kay Boxer
Business Manager: Christine Brennemen
Director of BD, SE Office: Kay Boxer
Business Manager, Milwaukee Office: Christine Brenneman
Estimated Sales: $300,000-500,000
Number Employees: 1-4
Square Footage: 6000
Parent Co: Winston Franchise Corporation

22755 Food Handling Systems
8948 SW Barbur Boulevard
Suite 720
Portland, OR 97219-4047 877-266-6972
Fax: 503-691-0917 foodhdlsys@aol.com
Gentle food handling, horizontal motion conveyors and vibratory equipment
Chairman: Richard Frank
President/CEO: Trevor Fagerskog
CFO: Steven Reiss
VP Sales/Marketing: Karen Orton Katz
Type of Packaging: Bulk

22756 (HQ)Food Industry ConsultingGroup
21050 SW 93rd Lane Road
Dunnellon, FL 34431-5802 352-489-8919
Fax: 352-489-8919 800-443-5820
fISgroup@ARTDDC.NET
Consultant specializing food service systems especially food procruement productivity in food preperation and service
CEO: J Hill
Operations: James Mixon
Estimated Sales: $1 - 5 Million
Number Employees: 6
Square Footage: 2500
Other Locations:
Food Industry Consulting Group
Silver Spring MD

22757 Food Industry Equipment
1121 W 14th Street
Lorain, OH 44052-3800 440-246-3150
Fax: 440-246-1739 fiezsales@erienet.net
Defattting machines, skinnning machines and accessories and trimming devices, deboning equipment/meat, knives/powered, sharpening systems, boning machines, meat and poultry, cutters/knives, cutters/trimmers, consultants/processingequipment and consultants/processing equipment
Manager Customer Support: Pam Agocki

22758 Food Insights
1100 Connecticut Avenue NW
Suite 430
Washington, DC 20036 202-296-6540
Fax: 901-755-1006 info@foodinsight.org
www.foodinsight.org
Consultant specializing in marketing research, operating systems and management strategy services, customer relationship management
President: Judy Patton
CEO: Judy Patton
Marketing: Carolyn Thomas
Operations: Sandy Brickley
Purchasing: Larry Ruggles
Estimated Sales: $300,000-500,000
Number Employees: 1-4

22759 Food Instrument Corporation
115 Academy Ave
Federalsburg, MD 21632 410-754-5714
Fax: 410-754-8796 800-542-5688
kickout@verizon.net
www.foodinstrumentcorporation.com
Manufacturer, wholesaler/distributor and exporter of microprocessor based quality control instrumentation including closure seal testers, rejectors, data analyzers, can orienters and diverters
President: Richard V Kudlich
Sales Director: James Boehm
Estimated Sales: $1-5 Million
Number Employees: 10-19
Number of Brands: 1
Number of Products: 6
Square Footage: 40000
Brands:
Adr
Das Ii
Div-10
Vrr

22760 Food Machinery Sales
328 Commerce Blvd # 8
Bogart, GA 30622-2200 706-549-2207
Fax: 706-548-1724 fmssales@fmsathens.com
www.fmsathens.com
Manufacturer and exporter of product handling and packaging machinery for the biscuit and cracker industries
Manager: Eric Gunderson
Estimated Sales: $10-20 Million
Number Employees: 20-49

22761 Food Machinery of America
3115 Pepper Mill Court
Mississauga,, ON L5L 4X5
Canada 905-823-5522
Fax: 905-607-0234 800-465-0234
sales@omcan.com www.omcan.com
Estimated Sales: $1 - 5 Million

22762 Food Management Search
235 State Street
Suite 326
Springfield, MA 01103 413-732-2666
Fax: 413-732-6466
recruiters@foodmanagementsearch.com
www.foodmanagementsearch.com
Contingency firm specializing in recruiting food industry career professionals in the areas of food production, supermarket and distribution, food service, restaurant, culinary, hotel food and beverage and sales and marketingnationwide. Position salaries range between $40K and $150K
Number Employees: 5-9

22763 (HQ)Food Pak Corporation
2300 Palm Ave
San Mateo, CA 94403-1817 650-341-6559
Fax: 650-341-2110
Chili seasonings, board and food coatings; manufacturer and exporter of custom packaging products including flexible X-ray film, insulated and sandwich bags, containers, folding cartons, shopping bags, flexible packaging bags, paper &foil bags
CEO: Steve Kanaga
CEO: Stephen Kanaga
Estimated Sales: Below $5 Million
Number Employees: 1 to 4
Square Footage: 7000
Type of Packaging: Food Service, Private Label, Bulk
Brands:
A.B. Curry's
Hyfroydol
Safety Pak
Scoop It
Sta-Hot
Zest

22764 Food Plant Companies
15945 N 76th Street
Scottsdale, AZ 85260-1781 480-991-6534
Fax: 480-991-1243

22765 Food Plant Engineering
PO Box 9906
Yakima, WA 98909-0906 509-248-5530
Fax: 509-453-3008
Meat industry services: architects and engineers, building and construction consultants, temperature controls, refrigerated structures and refrigeration systems

22766 Food Plant Engineering
10816 Millington Ct # 110
Cincinnati, OH 45242-4025 513-488-8888
Fax: 513-641-0057
mail@foodplantengineering.com
www.foodplantengineering.com
We specialize in facility design, engineering, architectural and construction management services for expansions, renovations and new construction. We provide master planning, production capacity studies, plant flow investigationprocess and equipment layouts, process design, lean manufacturing principle implementation and process simulation analysis. We offer a variety of project formats including competitive bidding, construction management and design build
President: Mark Redmond
Marketing Director: Jennifer Redmond
Project Manager: Michael Cowgill
Estimated Sales: D
Number Employees: 10-19

22767 Food Processing Concepts
4212 Happy Valley Cir
Newnan, GA 30263 628-478-4700
davidmckinney@mindspring.com
www.foodprocessingconcepts.com
Equipment for food industry used in the production process
Sales: David McKinney

22768 Food Processing Equipment Company
13623 Pumice St
Santa Fe Springs, CA 90670 479-751-9392
Fax: 479-751-9399 salesark@fpec.com
www.fpec.com
Manufacturer and exporter of food processing and material handling equipment including vacuum tumblers, blenders and mixers, chilled massage blenders, conveyors, dumpers, screw conveyors, cart lifts, screw loaders, vacuum hoppers, openblenders and mixers, etc
Owner: Alan Davison
Sales Manager: Larry Butler
Estimated Sales: $5 - 10 Million
Number Employees: 20-49
Square Footage: 36000

22769 Food Processors Institute
1350 I St NW Ste 300
Washington, DC 20005 202-393-0890
Fax: 202-639-5932 800-355-0983
fpi@nfpa-food.org www.fpi-food.org
Non-profit association that provides education for food processors and affiliated industries
CEO: Cal Dooley
Executive Director: Lisa Weddnig
Number Employees: 1-4

22770 Food Products Lab
12003 NE Ainsworth Cir # 105
Portland, OR 97220-9034 503-253-9136
Fax: 503-253-9019 800-375-9555
www.fplabs.com
Manager: Nidel Kahl
Quality Control: Nadil Kahl
Estimated Sales: $3 - 5 Million
Number Employees: 20-49

22771 Food Quality Lab
6305 Rosewood St Ste B
Lake Oswego, OR 97035-5388
Fax: 503-297-3738 800-977-3636
ken@foodqualitylabs.com
www.foodqualitylabs.com
Food analyst consultant that determines cleanliness and nutritional value
VP: Ken Ayers
Estimated Sales: Below $5 Million
Number Employees: 5-9
Square Footage: 1800

22772 Food Resources International
504 W Olive Avenue
Redlands, CA 92373-5166 714-299-8829
Fax: 714-299-8115 office@foodsource.ae
Manufacturer and exporter of food processing equipment including dairy machinery, membrane systems and spray dryers; also, reconditioned equipment available; importer of casein and whey and milk protein concentrates
President: Jon Chesnut
VP: Karen Chesnut
Number Employees: 10-19

22773 **Food Safety Net Services**
199 W Rhapsody Dr
San Antonio, TX 78216 210-477-3626
Fax: 210-525-1702 888-525-9788
tcornett@food-safetynet.com
www.food-safetynet.com
Laboratory specializing in microbiological, nutritional, and chemical analysis, consulting and auditing, education and training
President: Gina R. Bellinger
CEO: John W. Bellinger
CFO/COO: Alan W. Uecker
VP of Operations: Dr. Randal Garrett
Quality Control: Micheal Devine
Marketing Director: Tesa Cornett
Business Development Manager: Tim Deary
Business Development Manager: Tony Nguyen
Lead Special Scientist: Amit Morey PhD
Estimated Sales: Below $5 Million
Number Employees: 5-9
Square Footage: 24000
Type of Packaging: Food Service
Other Locations:
Food Safety Net Services
Richardson TX

22774 **Food Sanitation Consultant Service**
64 Fulton St # 702
New York, NY 10038 212-732-9540
Fax: 212-608-7862 www.foodsanitation.net
Consultant specializing in food sanitation and safety
President: Barbara Kleiner
CEO: Martin Muchanic
CFO: Barbara Kleiner
Estimated Sales: $1-2.5 Million
Number Employees: 10 to 19

22775 **Food Scene**
P.O.Box 459
Colts Neck, NJ 07722 732-431-1132
Fax: 732-577-8445 bkahn@foodscene.com
www.foodscene.com
Owner: Barry Kahn
Estimated Sales: $20-50 Million
Number Employees: 10-19

22776 **Food Science Associates**
PO Box 525
Crugers, NY 10521-0525 914-739-7541
Fax: 914-739-7541
sierrasunset-mchang@worldnet.att.net
www.foodconsult.com
Consultant providing product development, nutritional labeling, culinary assistance, regulatory compliance, etc
VP: Frank del Valle
Estimated Sales: $1 - 5 Million
Number Employees: 14

22777 **Food Science Consulting**
PO Box 30992
Walnut Creek, CA 94598-7992 925-947-6785
Fax: 925-947-2811 bkeefer42@worldnet.att.net
www.foodonline.com
Consultant for product formulation and development, process development, plant implementation, recipe development, food styling and commercialization of recipes
President: Dorothy Keefer
Number Employees: 1

22778 **Food Service Equipment Corporation**
727 Del Prado Boulevard N
Cape Coral, FL 33909-2254 941-574-7767
New and used hotel restaurant, deli, cafeteria equipment and heavy duty equipment and small wares
President: J Furdell
Estimated Sales: $500,000-$1 Million
Number Employees: 4

22779 **Food Tech Structures LLC**
10 Crescent Rd
Riverside, CT 06878 203-637-2471
Fax: 203-637-2527 800-880-0118
mgolden@foodtechstructures.com
www.foodtechstructures.com

22780 **Food Technologies**
10001 Wayzata Boulevard
Golden Valley, MN 55405 763-544-8586
Fax: 763-544-0999
Consultant specializing in food product development, program design and marketing for food processors
President: William Drier, Ph.D.
Marketer: C Carroll Hicks
Production Developer: Gene Monroe
Number Employees: 3
Square Footage: 2000

22781 **Food Technology Corporation**
45921 Maries Rd # 120
Sterling, VA 20166-9278 703-444-1870
Fax: 703-444-9860 info@foodtechcorp.com
www.foodtechcorp.com
Manufacturer and exporter of food texture testing systems and measurement equipment including texture profile analysis, pea tenderometers, peak force measurement systems, and kramer shear press
President: Shirl Lakeway
Estimated Sales: $3 Million
Number Employees: 5
Square Footage: 3000
Brands:
Kramer Shear Press
Tenderometers
Tenore Measurement Equipment

22782 **Food Tools**
315 Laguna St
Santa Barbara, CA 93101 805-962-8383
Fax: 805-966-3614 877-836-6386
mail@foodtools.com www.foodtools.com
Owner: Marty Grano
Chairman of the Board: Martin Grano
Estimated Sales: $5-10 Million
Number Employees: 20-49

22783 **Food and Dairy ResearchAssociates**
107 Homer St
Commerce, GA 30529-1859 706-335-9703
Fax: 706-335-9704
Owner: Steve Green
Estimated Sales: $.5 - 1 000,000
Number Employees: 5-9

22784 **Food-Tek**
9 Whippany Rd Bldg C-2
Whippany, NJ 07981 973-257-4000
Fax: 973-257-5555 800-648-8114
info@foodtek.com www.foodtek.com
Consultant specializing in product development services for food manufacturers
President: Gilbert Finkel
CFO: Gilbert Finkel
Vice President: Victor Davila
R&D: Gilbert Finkel
Quality Control: Gilbert Finkel
Estimated Sales: $5 - 10 Million
Number Employees: 5-9
Square Footage: 5000

22785 **FoodHandler**
2301 Lunt Avenue
Elk Grove Village, IL 60007 516-338-4433
Fax: 516-338-4405 800-338-4433
www.foodhandler.com
Disposable gloves, aprons, hair restraints, bibs, worker protection and food safety training
Number Employees: 20-49

22786 **FoodTools**
315 Laguna St
Santa Barbara, CA 93101-1716 805-962-8383
Fax: 805-966-3614 877-836-6386
mail@foodtools.com www.foodtools.com
Manufacturer and exporter of de-panners, cake slabbers, crumb spreaders and ultrasonic slicers and mechanical slicers
Owner: Marty Grano
Vice President: Mike Christenson
Vice President: Doug Petrovich
VP of Engineering: Matt Browne
VP of Production: Gary Grand
Estimated Sales: $5 - 10 Million
Number Employees: 20-49
Square Footage: 78000

22787 **Foodchek Systems**
1414 8 St SW
Suite 450
Calgary, AB T2R 1J6 403-269-9424
Fax: 403-263-6357 877-298-0208
info@foodcheksystems.com
www.foodcheksystems.com
Supplier of food safety pathogen tests
President: William Hogan
Estimated Sales: $500,000- 1 Million
Number Employees: 8

22788 **Foodesign Machinery & Systems**
29103 SW Kinsman Rd
Wilsonville, OR 97070 503-685-5030
Fax: 503-685-5034 sales@foodesign.com
www.foodesign.com
President: Joseph Mistretta
Estimated Sales: $5 - 10 Million
Number Employees: 20-49

22789 **Foodesign Machinery & Systems**
29103 SW Kinsman Road
PO Box 2449
Wilsonville, OR 97070 503-685-5030
Fax: 503-685-5034 sales@foodesign.com
www.foodesign.com
Supplier of heavy-duty precision built cooking and processing machines
President: Joe Mistretta
Sales Executive: Daniel Luna
Number Employees: 26

22790 **(HQ)Foodpro International**
P.O.Box 53110
San Jose, CA 95153 408-227-2332
Fax: 408-227-4908 bwashburn@foodpro.net
www.foodpro.net
Consultant provides engineering services including studies, plans and specifications development, construction and equipment installation management; exporter of fruit fly extermination systems
President: M W Washburn
CEO: M Wm Washburn
CFO: Lou Kong
Research & Development: Olga Osipova
Marketing Director: Richard Jennings
Branch Manager: Alex Tarasov
Estimated Sales: $1 - 3 Million
Number Employees: 12

22791 **Foods Research Laboratories**
130 Newmarket Sq Ste 3
Boston, MA 02118 617-442-3322
Fax: 617-442-2013
Laboratory providing microbiological and chemical analysis of food and nutrition labeling; also, consultant services include plant sanitation, quality control and HACCP audits and verifications
Owner: Andrea Fontaine
Lab Director: Andrea Fontaine
Chemist: Regina Pierce
Estimated Sales: Less than $500,000
Number Employees: 1 to 4

22792 **Foodservice Design Associates**
10207 General Dr
Orlando, FL 32824-8529 407-896-4115
Fax: 407-895-7022
p.bean@foodservice-design.com
www.foodservice-design.com
Consultant specializing in architectural design and specification services for the food service industry
Principal: Philip Bean
Estimated Sales: $150,000
Number Employees: 1-4

22793 **Foodservice East**
197 Eighth St., No. 728
Charlestown, MA 02129-4234 617-242-2217
Fax: 617-742-5938 800-852-5212
susan@foodserviceeast.com
www.foodserviceeast.com

22794 **Foodservice Equipment &pplie**
110 Schiller
Suite 312
Elmhurst, IL 60126 847-390-2010
Fax: 800-630-4169 800-630-4168
maureen@zoombagroup.com www.fesmag.com

22795 **Foodservice Equipment Distributors Association**
2250 Point Boulevard
Suite 200
Elgin, IL 60123 224-293-6500
Fax: 224-293-6505 feda@feda.com
www.feda.com
President: Brad Pierce
Executive Vice President: Raymond W. Herrick
Secretary: Jay Ringelheim
Number Employees: 5-9

22796 **Foodservice Innovation Network**
335 North River Street
Batavia, IL 60510 630-879-3006
Fax: 630-879-3014 info@airesconsulting.com

22797 **Foodworks**
400 N 4th Street
La Grange, KY 40031-1512 502-222-0135
Fax: 502-222-0135 easyhaccp@aol.com
Consultant providing HACCP training, food safety seminars, food plant sanitation and food safety auditing
President: Dotty Heady
Executive VP: Kazmer Wolkensperg
Number Employees: 4

22798 **Foote & Jenks Corporation**
1420 Crestmont Ave
Camden, NJ 08103 856-966-0700
Fax: 856-966-6137
Estimated Sales: $20-50 Million
Number Employees: 10-19

22799 **Foran Spice Company**
7616 S 6th St
P.O. Box 109
Oak Creek, WI 53154 414-764-1220
Fax: 414-764-8803 800-558-6030
customerservice@foranspice.com
www.foranspice.com
Re-cleaned and sterilized spices, custom engineered seasonings, and value-added food products
President: Patty Goto
CFO: Andy Gitter
Vice President: Joy Hauser
VP Sales: Paul Duddleston
Engineer: Alan Goto
Estimated Sales: $19 Million
Number Employees: 128
Square Footage: 71000
Type of Packaging: Food Service, Private Label, Bulk

22800 **Forbes Industries**
1933 E Locust St
Ontario, CA 91761 909-923-4559
Fax: 909-923-1969 sales@forbesindustries.com
www.forbesindustries.com
Manufacturer and exporter of banquet cabinets and carts, tables, sign stands, boards, easels, bins, carts, menus, etc.; also, bars including salad, soup and portable.
President: Tim Sweetland
Estimated Sales: $50-100 Million
Number Employees: 250-499

22801 **Forbes Products**
45 High Tech Dr
Rush, NY 14543
Fax: 585-334-6180 800-316-5235
www.forbesproducts.com
Customized vinyl office products and promotional items including pocket planners, binders, desk and carrying portfolios, proposal covers, clear envelopes and business card holders
President: Mark McDermott
VP Sales: Rick Blowers
Estimated Sales: $2.5-5 Million
Number Employees: 20-49
Square Footage: 300000

22802 **(HQ)Forbo Siegling LLC**
12201 Vanstory Dr
Huntersville, NC 28078 704-948-0800
Fax: 704-948-0995 800-255-5581
siegling.us@forbo.com www.forbo-siegling.us
Transilon conveyor belts, extremultus flat transmission belts, transfer conveyor belting, prolink plastic modular belts, proposition high-efficiency timing belts and other related products specifically designed for the food andbeverage industry.
President: Wayne Hoffman
VP Sales/Marketing: John Casal
Research & Development: Jay Leighton
Quality Control: Natalie Deal
Marketing Director: Kitty Spence
National Sales Manager: Dany Bearden
VP Production: Chris Flannigan
Number Employees: 250-499
Square Footage: 100000
Other Locations:
Siegling America
Wood Dale IL
Siegling America
Englewood NJ
Siegling America
Fullerton CA
Siegling America
Manteca CA
Siegling America
Kansas City MO
Siegling America
Mobile AL
Siegling America
Stone Mountain GA
Siegling America
Mansfield TX
Brands:
Extremultus
Transilon
Transtex

22803 **Foreign Candy Company**
1 Foreign Candy Dr
Hull, IA 51239-7499 712-439-1496
Fax: 712-439-3207 800-831-8541
jc.reichter@foreigncandy.com
www.foreigncandy.com
Distributors of confectionery
CEO/President/Owner: Peter DeYager
VP Marketing: Art Zito
VP Sales: Jim Finelli
Estimated Sales: $5-10 Million
Number Employees: 50-99
Type of Packaging: Private Label
Brands:
Mega Warheads
Rips Toll

22804 **Foremost Machine Builders**
23 Spielman Road
Fairfield, NJ 07004-6155 973-227-0700
Fax: 973-227-7307 sales@foremostmachine.com
www.foremostmachine.com
Manufacturer and exporter of plastic scrap recovery and bulk material handling systems
President: Marlene Heydenreich
VP/General Manager: Clifford Weinpel
Assistant Sales Manager: Drew Schmid
Estimated Sales: $10 - 20 Million
Number Employees: 50-99
Square Footage: 55000

22805 **Forest Manufacturing Company**
1665 Enterprise Pkwy
Twinsburg, OH 44087 330-425-3805
Fax: 330-425-9604 info@forestcorporation.com
www.forestcorporation.com
Manufacturer/exporter of flags, pennants, banners, pressure-sensitive product markings and decals
President: Reynold E Bookman
CFO: Bob Briggs
Sales Manager: Dick Dragonnette
General Manager: John Hammons
Estimated Sales: $20 - 30 Million
Number Employees: 100-249
Square Footage: 135000

22806 **Forlife**
1811 W Mahalo Place
Compton, CA 90220-5429 310-638-6386
Fax: 310-638-6305 info@forlifedesign.com
www.forlifedesign.com
Accessories/suplies i.e. picnic baskets, cooking implements,/housewares.

22807 **FormFlex**
PO Box 218
Bloomingdale, IN 47832-0218 765-498-8900
Fax: 765-498-5200 800-255-7659
www.formflexproducts.com
Manufacturer and exporter of polyolefin sheets, signs, and packaging
CEO: Brent Thompson
Marketing Director: David Elliott
Sales Director: Brent Thompson
Public Relations: Janice Stewart
Estimated Sales: $10-20 Million
Number Employees: 250-499
Square Footage: 30000
Parent Co: Futurex Industries
Type of Packaging: Bulk
Brands:
Formflex

22808 **Formaticum**
165 Court Street
Apt 104
Brooklyn, NY 11201 503-922-3866
Fax: 503-389-7675 800-830-0317
mark@formaticum.com www.formaticum.com
Accessories/supplies i.e. picninc baskets, cooking implements/housewares, dispaly fixtures, specialty food packaging i.e. gift wrap/labels/boxes/containers.
Marketing: Mark Goldman

22809 **Formax/Provisur Technologies**
9150 191st Street
Mokena, IL 60448 708-479-3500
Fax: 708-479-3598 marketing@formaxinc.com
www.formaxinc.com
Advanced forming and slicing systems for the food processing industry. Also provide tooling, filling systems and packaging supplies.
VP N. American Sales/Marketing/Service: Kevin Howard

22810 **Formax/Provisur Technologies**
9150 W 191st Street
Mokena, IL 60448 708-479-3500
Fax: 708-479-3598 815-485-4400
info@provisur.com www.provisur.com
Food processing equipment: forming machines, multi-loaf slicers and automatic transport equipment
Number Employees: 250-499

22811 **Formel Industries**
2355 25th Ave
Franklin Park, IL 60131 847-455-3300
Fax: 847-928-9655 800-373-3300
www.formelinc.com
Cellophane bags
Owner: Don O' Malley
Estimated Sales: $5 - 10 Million
Number Employees: 20-49

22812 **Former Tech**
9367 Winkler Drive
Houston, TX 77017-5915 713-944-5336
Fax: 713-944-2194 800-843-8914
www.formertech.com
President and CEO: Ron Hokanson
Estimated Sales: $5 - 10 Million
Number Employees: 25

22813 **Formers By Ernie**
7905 Almeda Genoa
Suite B
Houston, TX 77075 713-991-3455
Fax: 713-991-0048 866-991-3455
sales@formingcollars.com
www.formersbyernie.net
Metal and aluminum bag formers and packaging machinery equipment
President: Ernie Sanchez
CFO: Terry Sanchez
Quality Control: Ernie Jr Sanchez
R&D: Dennis Kokkins
Estimated Sales: $2 000,000
Number Employees: 10-19

22814 **Formers of Houston**
3533 Preston Ave
Pasadena, TX 77505 281-998-9570
Fax: 281-998-9692 800-468-5224
info@formers.com www.formers.com
Packaging machinery parts
President: John Dominguez Jr
Vice President: John Dominguez III
Quality Control: Chico Marquez
Sales Director: Patty O'Neal
Production Manager: Ben Dominguez

Estimated Sales: $5 - 10 000,000
Number Employees: 20-49
Square Footage: 9500
Type of Packaging: Consumer

22815 Formost Packaging Machines
19211 144th Ave NE
Woodinville, WA 98072 425-483-9090
Fax: 425-486-5656 sales@formostpkg.com
www.formostpkg.com
Manufacturer and exporter of high-speed automated horizontal and vertical bagging and wrapping machines including formers/fillers/sealers
President: Norm Formo
CFO: Dan Semanskee
Executive VP: Norm Formo
VP Sales: Dennis Gunnell
Plant Manager: Al Shelton
Purchasing Manager: Michelle Richards
Number Employees: 50-99
Type of Packaging: Consumer, Food Service, Private Label, Bulk

22816 Formula Espresso
65 Commerce Street
Brooklyn, NY 11231-1642 718-834-8724
Fax: 718-834-9022 info@espressosystems.com
www.espressosystems.com
Manufacturer and exporter of commercial stainless steel espresso equipment
Owner: George Ilardo
Estimated Sales: $1-2.5 Million
Number Employees: 5-9
Type of Packaging: Food Service
Brands:
Formula

22817 Formulator Software,LLC
28 Center St
Clinton, NJ 08809-2635 908-735-2248
Fax: 908-236-7865 jdegroff@formulatorus.com
www.formulatorus.com
Offering barcode solutions and products including route accounting softwareand implementation, warehouse management software and wireless integration.
Managing Partner: James Degroff
Technical Manager: C Womer
Research & Development: C Longfield
Estimated Sales: $1 - 3 Million
Number Employees: 12
Number of Brands: 20
Number of Products: 8000
Brands:
Eltron
Hhp
Symbol
Zebra

22818 Forpack
16905 Neill Path
Hastings, MN 55033-8743 651-438-2115
Fax: 651-437-8755 dlange@forpakinc.com
President: Loyd Lowweden
CFO: Loyd Lowweden
Quality Control: Dave Lege
Estimated Sales: $3 - 5 Million
Number Employees: 10

22819 Forpak
16901 Neill Path
Hastings, MN 55033-8743 651-438-2115
Fax: 651-437-8755 mmaher@forpakinc.com
President: Lloyd Lodewegen
CFO: Suzanne Lloyd
Estimated Sales: $1 - 2.5 000,000
Number Employees: 7

22820 Forrest Engraving Company
92 1st St
New Rochelle, NY 10801-6121 914-632-9892
Fax: 914-632-7416
Manufacturer and exporter of plastic and metal nameplates and signs
President: Thomas Giordano
Manager: Tom Giordano
Estimated Sales: $500,000-$1 Million
Number Employees: 5 to 9

22821 Forster & Son
1900 B St
Ada, OK 74820-2831 580-332-6020
Fax: 580-332-6021 jforster@wilnet1.com
Flour and feed mill machinery; also, custom steel fabrication, steel perforation and mining equipment
Owner: John Forster
Estimated Sales: Less than $500,000
Number Employees: 1 to 4

22822 (HQ)Fort Dearborn Company
6035 W Gross Point Rd
Niles, IL 60714 773-774-4321
Fax: 773-774-9105 info@fortdearborn.com
www.fortdearborn.com
Manufacturer and exporter of stack labels including paper, metalized paper, PET substrates, film laminate and pressure sensitive; also, film labels
Estimated Sales: $20-50 Million
Number Employees: 100-249
Square Footage: 500000
Other Locations:
Fort Dearborn Co.
Elk Grove Vlg IL

22823 Fort Dearborn Flexible Packaging
1530 Morse Ave
Elk Grove Village, IL 60007 847-357-9500
Fax: 847-357-8726 info@fortdearborn.com
www.fortdearborn.com
President: Ed Heil
CEO: Mike Anderson
Director Marketing: Suzanne Maicke
Estimated Sales: $10 000,000
Number Employees: 500-999

22824 Fort Hill Sign Products, Inc.
13 Airport Rd.
Hopedale, MA 01747 508-381-0357
Fax: 508-381-3784 fh@forthillsigns.com
www.forthillsigns.com
Plastic cut letters and logos, name plates and signs
Owner: Michael Dolan
Estimated Sales: $3 - 5 Million
Number Employees: 10-19

22825 Fort James Canada
137 Bentworth Avenue
Toronto, ON M6A 1P6
Canada 416-784-1621
Fax: 416-789-0170
Disposable cups including paper, plastic and foam
National Sales Manager: Phil Wahl
Number Employees: 500-999
Parent Co: James River Corporation

22826 Fort James Corporation
P.O.Box 6000
Norwalk, CT 06856-6000 203-854-2000
Fax: 203-854-2420 800-257-9744
www.gp.com
Disposable tabletop supplies including napkins, plates, cups, cutlery, towels, tissues and soap for washrooms
President: Brent Paugh
Executive Vice President: Christian Fischer
VP Sales/Marketing: Joe Neil
VP Sales: Gary Simons
Executive Vice President of Operations: Wesley Jones
Number Employees: 10-19
Parent Co: James River Corporation
Brands:
Dixie
Executive

22827 Fort James Corporation
1650 Lake Cook Rd Ste 150
Deerfield, IL 60015 847-317-5000
Fax: 847-317-3755
larryhoward@fortjamesmail.com
www.fortjames.com
Paper
Owner: James Fort
Estimated Sales: $7 Billion
Number Employees: 10,000

22828 Fort Lock Corporation
3000 River Road
River Grove, IL 60171-1097 708-456-1100
Fax: 708-456-9476
Manufacturing, electronic and mechanical locks for the vending industry
President: Jay Fine
VP: Gary Myers
Estimated Sales: $10 - 20 000,000
Number Employees: 3

22829 Forte Technology
58 Norfolk Ave.
Suite 4
South Easton, MA 02375-1055 508-297-2363
Fax: 508-297-2314 info@forte-tec.com
www.forte-tec.com
Manufacturer and exporter of electronic moisture measurement systems
President: Patricia White
Plant Manager: Mark Donohowski
Estimated Sales: $2.5-5 Million
Number Employees: 5-9
Square Footage: 28000
Brands:
Forte

22830 Fortenberry's Ice
3128 Fortenberry Rd
Kodak, TN 37764-2020 865-933-2568
Fax: 865-933-2568
Ice
President: Arvil Fortenberry
Estimated Sales: Below $5,000,000
Number Employees: 5-9

22831 Fortifiber Corporation
300 Industrial Dr
Fernley, NV 89408 775-575-5557
Fax: 775-575-4995 www.fortifiber.com
Paper bags, building papers and linings
Manager: Bill Rieger
Plant Manager: Greg Hobbs
Estimated Sales: $5-10 Million
Number Employees: 20-49
Brands:
Fibreen Economy
Super Bar

22832 Fortress Technology
51 Grand Marshall Drive
Scarborough, ON M1B 5N6
Canada 416-754-2898
Fax: 416-754-2976 888-220-8737
sales@fortresstechnology.com
www.fortresstechnology.com
Fortress Technology is a world leader in the design and manufacture of the highest quality metal detector systems for the food processing, material handling and packaging operations.
President: Steve Gidman
Marketing Director: Adam Lang
Sales Director: Steve Mason
Number Employees: 60
Number of Brands: 4
Number of Products: 20

22833 Fortress Technology
51 Grand Marshall Dr
Toronto, ON M1B 5N6 416-754-2898
Fax: 416-754-2976 888-220-8737
info@fortresstechnology.com
www.fortresstechnology.com
Food safety detector equipment

22834 (HQ)Fortune Plastics
5160 W Missouri Ave
Glendale, AZ 85301-6002 623-842-2236
Fax: 623-930-9406 800-243-0306
amiles@fortuneplastics.com
www.fortuneplastics.com
Polyethylene food and utility bags, printed bags, trash can liners, sleeves, tubing, interfold and sheeting
Manager: Ron Shaw
VP Sales/Marketing: Ed Gillespie
Estimated Sales: $20-50 Million
Number Employees: 20-49
Other Locations:
Fortune Plastics
Phoenix AZ
Brands:
Duraliner
Dynaplas
Enviroplas
Hid-Tuff

22835 Fortune Plastics, Inc
P.O Box 637
Williams Ln.
Old Saybrook, CT 06475
Fax: 860-388-9930 800-243-0306
www.fortuneplastics.com

Manufacturer and exporter of plastic bags
Estimated Sales: $5 - 10 Million
Number Employees: 20-49
Parent Co: Hilex Poly Co. LLC

22836 Fortune Products
2010A Windy Terrace
Cedar Park, TX 78613 800-742-7797
Fax: 800-600-5373 contact@accusharp.com
www.accusharp.com
Manufacturer and exporter of manually operated knife and scissor sharpeners
President: Jay Cavanaugh
VP: Dale Fortenberry Jr
Operations: Randy Fortenberry
Estimated Sales: $1-2.5 Million
Number Employees: 5-9
Square Footage: 6500
Type of Packaging: Consumer, Food Service, Private Label, Bulk
Brands:
Accusharp
Sharp 'n' Easy
Shear Sharp

22837 Forum Lighting
900 Old Freeport Rd
Pittsburgh, PA 15238-3130 412-781-5970
Fax: 412-244-9032 joe@forumlighting.com
www.forumlighting.com
Manufacturer and exporter of fluorescent and HID linear lighting; custom designs available
Special Projects: Paula Garret
Controller: Julie McElhattan
Senior VP: Jonathan Garret
Special Projects: Paula Garret
Vice President of Sales: Steve Seligman
Plant Manager: Bill Dapper
Estimated Sales: $20-50 Million
Number Employees: 20-49
Square Footage: 70000

22838 Foster Forbes Glass
E Charles St
Marion, IN 46952 765-668-1200
Fax: 765-668-1389 www.sgcontainers.com
Glass containers
Sr. VP Sales/Marketing: R Deneau
VP Operations/Service: J Fordham
Manager of Purchasing: T Moreland
Estimated Sales: $1-2.5 Million
Number Employees: 5-9
Parent Co: American National Can Company

22839 (HQ)Foster Poultry Farms
1000 Davis St
Livingston, CA 95334-1526 209-267-1121
Fax: 209-394-6342 800-255-7227
comments@fosterfarms.com
www.fosterfarms.com
Poultry products.
CEO: Ron Foster
Senior Vice President & CFO: John Landis
Director of Quality Control: Tony Melo
Senior VP Marketing: Bob Wangerien
Senior VP Retail Sales: Bob Kellert
Manager Consumer Affairs: Teresa Lenz
Sr. VP Live Poultry Operations: Mike Pruitt
Plant Manager: Ron O'Bara
Estimated Sales: $2.3 Billion
Number Employees: 10,500
Square Footage: 40000
Type of Packaging: Consumer, Food Service, Private Label, Bulk
Other Locations:
Foster Farms
Porterville CA
Brands:
Fircrest Farms
Foster Farms
Foster Farms Dairy Products
Foster Farms Deli Meat
Foster Farms Poultry
Valchris Farms
Foster Farms Frozen Chicken

22840 Foster Refrigerator Corporation
PO Box 718
Kinderhook, NY 12106 518-828-3311
Fax: 518-828-3315 888-828-3311
fosterusa@yahoo.com www.foster-us.com
Manufacturer and exporter of commercial refrigerators, freezers, coolers and ovens
Owner: James Dinardi
Estimated Sales: $1 - 5 Million
Number Employees: 1-4
Square Footage: 100000
Type of Packaging: Food Service
Brands:
Fosters

22841 Foster-Forbes Glass Company
4855 E 52nd Pl
Vernon, CA 90058 323-562-5100
Fax: 323-560-4165 800-767-4527
www.sgcontainers.com
Glass bottles
Plant Manager: Art Jones
Estimated Sales: $1 - 5 Million
Number Employees: 250-499
Parent Co: Sant' Gobian

22842 Foster-Miller
350 2nd Ave
Waltham, MA 02451-1196 781-890-3200
Fax: 781-290-0693 pdebakker@foster-miller.com
www.foster-miller.com
Custom food processing and vending equipment; design services available engineering and R&D services from 200+ engineers and sciencists
President: Michael G. Stolarik
CEO: Duane P. Andrews
Sr. Vice President: John Lambeth
Marketing: Peter Debakker
Number Employees: 325
Square Footage: 190000

22843 Fotel
1125 E St Charles Rd Ste 100
Lombard, IL 60148-2085 630-932-7520
Fax: 630-932-7610 800-834-4920
www.fotel.com
Bar code film masters, pre-printed bar code labels and equipment, RFID systems for manufacturing bar code verifiers.
President: John Nachtries
CEO: John Nachtrieb
Marketing Director: Beverly Nachtries
Operations Manager: Kevin Sousa
Plant Manager: Cathy Letza
Estimated Sales: $2.5-5 Million
Number Employees: 20-49
Square Footage: 20000

22844 Foth & Van Dyke
P.O.Box 19012
Green Bay, WI 54307-9012 920-497-2500
Fax: 920-497-8516 foth@foth.com
www.foth.com
Consultant for custom machine development and design, packaging line layout and design and modifications and upgrades to lines and equipment
CEO: Tim Weyenberg
CEO: Tim Weyenberg
Estimated Sales: $50 Million
Number Employees: 250-499

22845 Fountainhead
1726 Woodhaven Drive
Bensalem, PA 19020-7108 215-638-4240
Fax: 215-638-1617 800-326-8998
Manufacturer and exporter of stainless steel beverage dispensers, fountains, hoods and fans
General Manager: Ralph Kearney
Number Employees: 50-99
Parent Co: Floaire

22846 Four Corners Ice
801 W Arrington St
Farmington, NM 87401-5530 505-325-3813
Ice
Owner: Shirley Whipple
Estimated Sales: $500,000-$1 Million
Number Employees: 5 to 9

22847 Four Corporation
1015 Centennial St
Green Bay, WI 54304-5597 920-336-0621
Fax: 920-336-0089 john.ruppell@fourcorp.com
www.fourcorp.com
Manufacturer and exporter of ASME certified process vessels
President: Paul Meeuwsen
Marketing/Sales: John Ruppel
Estimated Sales: $10-20 Million
Number Employees: 20-49
Square Footage: 110000

22848 Four M Manufacturing Group
210 San Jose Avenue
San Jose, CA 95125-1033 408-998-1141
www. four m manufacturing.com
Paper products including plates, cups, partitions and corrugated cardboard boxes
President: Dennis Mechiel
Owner: Frank Martinez
Executive VP: Peter Mechiel
Estimated Sales: Less than $500,000
Number Employees: 4

22849 Four Seasons Produce, Inc
400 Wabash Road
PO Box 788
Ephrata, PA 17522-0788 717-721-2800
Fax: 717-721-2597 800-422-8384
sales@fsproduce.com www.fsproduce.com
Fruits and vegetables
President/CEO: Ron Carkoski
VP Finance: Loretta Radanovic
Quality Manager: Daniel Oloro
National Sales Manager: Stan Paluszewski
VP/General Manager: Rob Kurtz
Number Employees: 423
Square Footage: 261000

22850 Fowler Products Company
150 Collins Industrial Blvd
Athens, GA 30601 706-549-3300
Fax: 706-548-1278 877-549-3301
sales@fowlerproducts.com
www.fowlerproducts.com
Manufacturer and exporter of bottling, capping and packaging machinery
President: Don Cotney
VP Sales: Andy Monroe
Estimated Sales: $10-20 Million
Number Employees: 10-19
Square Footage: 75000

22851 Fox Brush Company
29 Tiger Hill Road
Oxford, ME 04270 207-539-2208
Fax: 207-539-2208 tcushman@cros.net
Wholesaler/distributor of corn, road, push and street sweeper brooms and brushes; manufacturer of specialty brushes
Owner: Linda Cushman
Manager: Thomas Cushman
Estimated Sales: Below $5 Million
Number Employees: 1

22852 Fox Stamp, Sign & Specialty
618 Airport Rd
Menasha, WI 54952 800-236-3699
Fax: 800-236-2037 office@foxstamp.com
www.foxstamp.com
Rubber and pre-inked stamps, daters, stamp pads, inks, engraved signs and badges, notary and other embossers; also, advertising and political buttons
Owner: Jon Ceninger
Sales Director: Steve Kryscio
Production Manager: Jason Burmeister
Purchasing Manager: Deb Zuck
Estimated Sales: Below $5 Million
Number Employees: 10-19
Square Footage: 2200
Parent Co: Fox Stamp, Sign & Specialty

22853 Fox Valley Wood Products
W811 State Highway 96
Kaukauna, WI 54130 920-766-4069
Fax: 920-766-1220 jeff@foxvalleyproducts.com
www.foxvalleyproducts.com
Pallets, crates and boxes
President: Don Van Zeeland
VP: Dale Van Zeeland
Estimated Sales: $1-2.5 Million
Number Employees: 20-49

22854 Fox-Morris Associates
9140 Arrow Point Boulevard
Suite 380
Charlotte, NC 28273-8140 704-522-8244
Fax: 704-529-1465 800-777-6503
gberman@fox-morris.com
Executive search firm specializing in the bakery and food industry
VP Executive Search: Toni Marie
Estimated Sales: $500,000-$1,000,000
Number Employees: 5-9

22855 **FoxJet**
P.O.Box 83
South Canaan, PA 18459-0083 570-937-4921
Fax: 570-937-3229 800-572-3434
info@loveshaw.com www.loveshaw.com
Marking and coding equipment and barcodes/labeling equipment
Marketing Director: Mark Gilvey
Plant Manager: Mark Gilvy
Estimated Sales: $10-20 Million
Number Employees: 100-249
Parent Co: Illinois Tool Works
Brands:
Foxjet
Lablex
System Master
Waxjet

22856 **Foxboro Company**
33 Commercial St
Foxboro, MA 02035 508-543-8750
Fax: 508-543-8764 888-369-2676
ips.csc@invensys.com www.foxboro.com
Manufacturer and exporter of microprocessor based enterprise network systems, instruments and controls
President: Mike Caliel
Industry Consultant: John Blanchard
VP: Ken Brown
Manager: Joe Fillion
Number Employees: 6000
Parent Co: Siebe

22857 **Foxcroft Equipment & Service Company**
2101 Creek Rd
Glenmoore, PA 19343 610-942-2888
Fax: 610-942-2769 800-874-0590
sales@foxcroft.com www.foxcroft.com
Chlorine control equipment, on-line analyzers, gas pacing valves, loop (set point) controllers and toxic gas detectors
Owner: Roger W Irey Jr
General Manager: Sandra Moriarity
Estimated Sales: $2.5-5 000,000
Number Employees: 10-19

22858 **Foxfire Marketing Solutions**
750 Dawson Drive
Newark, DE 19713 302-533-2240
Fax: 302-533-2241 800-497-0512
info@foxfiresigns.com
www.foxfiremarketingsolutions.com
Point of purchase displays and sales aids including tissue decor kits, special event cards, contest boxes and parking lot pennants.
President: Gerry Senker
Marketing Director: Jeanne Nooney
Sales Director: Bob Wegbreit
Estimated Sales: $5-10 Million
Number Employees: 50-99

22859 **Foxjet**
2016 E Randol Mill Road
Suite 409
Arlington, TX 76011-8223 817-795-6056
Fax: 817-795-7101 800-369-5384
ssingleton@foxjet.com www.foxjet.com
Marketing Manager: Dina Garland
Sales Director: Steve Shoup

22860 **Foxon Company**
235 W Park St
Providence, RI 02908-4851 401-421-2386
Fax: 401-421-8996 800-556-6943
Manufacturer and exporter of pressure sensitive, flexible and embossed/debossed foil and paper labels
President: William Ewing
Estimated Sales: $10-20 Million
Number Employees: 20 to 49

22861 **Frain Industries**
9377 Grand Ave
Franklin Park, IL 60131 630-629-9900
Fax: 630-629-6575 847-629-6575
sales@fraingroup.com www.fraingroup.com
Wholesaler/distributor of used packaging and processing equipment; rental/leasing services
Owner: Richard Frain
CEO: David Eggleston
Marketing Director: Suzanne Eaton
Estimated Sales: $14 Million
Number Employees: 20-49
Square Footage: 175000

22862 **Framarx/Waxstar**
3224 Butler St
S Chicago Hts, IL 60411-5505 708-755-3530
Fax: 708-755-3617 800-336-3936
saus@framarx.com www.framarx.com
Manufacturer and exporter of waxed and coated papers
President: Lawrence Czaszwicz
Vice President: Cindy Cofran
Marketing Coordinator: Julia Saeid
Sales: Deborah M
Operations Manager: Christopher Czaszwicz
Production Manager: Jim Merrell
Estimated Sales: $20 - 50 Million
Number Employees: 20-49
Type of Packaging: Food Service, Private Label, Bulk

22863 **FranRica Systems**
PO Box 30127
Stockton, CA 95213-0127 209-948-2811
Fax: 209-948-5198 www.fmcfoodtech.com
Food processing and filling equipment, including heat exchangers (tubular, scraped surface, aseptic flash cooling, steam injection), hot break systems, evaporators, control panels, pre-made aseptic bag fillers, aseptic bulk storagesystems, complete syst
President: Eric Kurtz
CFO: Marty Menz
R&D: Bill Kreaner
Estimated Sales: $20 - 30 Million
Number Employees: 125

22864 **France Personalized Signs**
1559 E 17th St
Cleveland, OH 44114-2921 216-241-2198
Fax: 216-771-5111
Signs, banners, decals, interior graphics and displays
President: Stephen Treitinick Jr
Estimated Sales: less than $500,000
Number Employees: 1-4

22865 **(HQ)Francis & Lusky Company**
1437 Donelson Pike
Nashville, TN 37217-2957 615-242-0501
Fax: 615-256-0862 800-251-3711
fl@4fl.com www.promoville.com
Manufacturer, importer and exporter of advertising calendars; distributor of promotional products
President: Richard Francis
VP Marketing: Eric Wittel
VP Sales: Jeff Brown
Estimated Sales: $20 - 50 Million
Number Employees: 20-49

22866 **(HQ)Francorp**
20200 Governors Dr
Suite 300
Olympia Fields, IL 60461 708-481-2900
Fax: 708-481-5885 800-327-6244
info@francorp.com www.francorp.com
Management consulting firm specializing in franchise development providing legal, financial, operational and marketing services
CEO: Donald Boroian
President: L Patrick Callaway
Executive VP/COO: Mary Kennedy
COO: Mary Kennedy
Estimated Sales: $10-15 Million
Number Employees: 20-49
Square Footage: 13000
Other Locations:
Francorp
Seville

22867 **Frank B. Ross Company**
970 New Brunswick Ave Ste H
Rahway, NJ 07065 732-669-0810
Fax: 732-669-0814 techinfo@rosswaxes.com
www.frankbross.com
Natural waxes and wax blends
President: Larry Powell
VP: Donald Ayerlee
Estimated Sales: $1 - 5 Million
Number Employees: 16
Square Footage: 80000

22868 **Frank Haile & Associates**
2650 Freewood Dr
Dallas, TX 75220 214-357-6659
Fax: 214-357-9321 800-544-2511
n4fh@aol.com www.fha-usa.com
Bulk and minor ingredients handling systems
President/CEO: Frank Haile Jr
CFO: Dale Fehlman
Vice President: Elaine Cook
Estimated Sales: $2.5 000,000
Number Employees: 10-19
Square Footage: 6400

22869 **Frank Torrone & Sons**
400 Broadway
Staten Island, NY 10310-2096 718-273-7600
Fax: 718-447-5103 atorrone@aol.com
Electric signs
Owner: Arthur Torrone
Estimated Sales: $1-2.5 Million
Number Employees: 10-19

22870 **Franke**
305 Tech Park Dr
La Vergne, TN 37086-3632 615-287-8200
Fax: 615-287-8250 888-437-2653
tom.campion@franke.com www.franke.com
CEO: Tom Campion
Estimated Sales: $50 Million
Number Employees: 250-499

22871 **Franke Commercial Systems**
3050 Campus Dr.
Suite 500
Hatfield, PA 19440 615-793-5990
Fax: 615-793-5940 800-626-5771
jack.wilson@franke.com www.franke.com
Appliances, refrigerator and prep tables, cutlery and glassware
President: Jack Wilson
Sales: Nancy Dutton
Estimated Sales: $1 - 5,000,000
Number Employees: 250-499
Parent Co: Franke

22872 **Franke Contract USA Group**
305 Tech Park Dr
La Vergne, TN 37086-3632 615-287-8200
Fax: 615-287-8250 888-437-2653
northamericacontact@franke.com
www.franke.com
CEO: Tom Campion
Estimated Sales: $1 - 5 Million
Number Employees: 250-499
Parent Co: Franke

22873 **Franklin Automation**
1981 Bucktail Lane
Sugar Grove, IL 60554-9609 630-466-1900
Fax: 630-466-1902 info@franklinautomation.com
www.franklinautomation.com
Form, fill and seal machine for packaging small consumer products
President: Frank Kigyos
Estimated Sales: $3 - 5 Million
Number Employees: 10-19

22874 **Franklin Crates**
P.O.Box 279
Micanopy, FL 32667 352-466-3141
Fax: 352-466-0708 fcrates@bellsouth.net
www.franklincrates.com
Fruit and vegetable wirebound crates
President: Ben O Franklin Iii III
Secretary: W Davis
Estimated Sales: $5-10 Million
Number Employees: 50-99

22875 **Franklin Equipment**
P.O.Box 8246
Greenville, TX 75404-8246 903-883-2002
Fax: 903-883-3210 800-356-7591
sales@thg1.com www.thehenrygroup.com
Food plant construction services, stainless fabrication services, matching of replacement part for food equipment
President, Chief Executive Officer, Owne: Troy Henry
Estimated Sales: $10-25 Million
Number Employees: 100-249

22876 **Franklin Machine Products**
PO Box 992
Marlton, NJ 08053-0992 856-983-2500
Fax: 800-255-9866 800-257-7737
sales@fmponline.com www.fmponline.com
Wholesaler/distributor of parts and accessories: serving the food service market
CEO: Carol Adams
Vice President: Michael Conte, Sr.

Estimated Sales: $20-50 Million
Number Employees: 100-249
Square Footage: 50000

22877 Franklin Rubber Stamp Company
301 West 8th Street
Wilmington, DE 19801 302-654-8841
Fax: 302-654-8860 orders@franklinstamps.com
www.franklinstamps.com
Rubber stamps and magnetic and engraved plastic signs
President: Tom Tanzilli
Manager: Russell Protas
Estimated Sales: $1-2.5 Million
Number Employees: 10-19

22878 Franklin Uniform Corporation
3946 Cloverhill Rd
Baltimore, MD 21218-1707 410-235-8151
Fax: 410-347-7607 www.paulaannefranklin.com
Uniforms and special clothing
Owner: Paula A Franklin
Estimated Sales: $1-2.5 Million
Number Employees: 1-4

22879 Frankston Paper Box Company of Texas
699 N Frankston Hwy
Frankston, TX 75763 903-876-2550
Fax: 903-876-4458
admin@frankstonpackaging.com
www.frankstonpackaging.com
Rigid set-up, paper, plastic and folding boxes
Owner: Norm Bollock
CFO: Norm Bullock
Quality Control: Edwin Adcock
Sales: D'Wayne Odom
Production Manager: Charles Montrose
Plant Manager: Bill McHam
Estimated Sales: $20 - 50 Million
Number Employees: 50-99
Square Footage: 45000

22880 Franmara
P.O.Box 2139
Salinas, CA 93902-2139 831-422-4000
Fax: 831-422-7000 800-423-5855
franksr@franmara.com www.franmara.com
Wine industry tasting room supplies
President: Frank Pat Chiorazzi
Estimated Sales: $10 - 20 Million
Number Employees: 20-49
Number of Products: 19

22881 Franrica Systems
PO Box 30127
Stockton, CA 95213-0127 209-948-2811
Fax: 209-948-5198
Manufacturer, importer and exporter of aseptic fillers, heat exchangers, tanks, pumps, evaporators, flash coolers, tomato paste processing plants, etc
Director: Eric Curtz
Controller: Marty Menz
Estimated Sales: $20 - 30 Million
Number Employees: 125
Square Footage: 70000
Parent Co: FMC Technologies
Brands:
Franrica

22882 Frantz Company
P.O.Box 344
Butler, WI 53007-0344 414-462-8700
Fax: 414-462-6655 inform@frantzcompany.com
www.frantzcompany.com
Smokehouse sawdust
President: Steve Frantz
CFO: John Tesensky
Estimated Sales: $5-10 Million
Number Employees: 10-19

22883 Franz Haas Machinery ofAmerica
6207 Settler Rd
Richmond, VA 23231-6044 804-222-6022
Fax: 804-222-0217 sales@haasusa.com
www.haasusa.com
Bakery machinery including ovens
Manager: Michael Fleetwood
Director Sales/Marketing: M Fleetwood
General Manager: Michael Fleetwood
Application Engineer: Bill Redden
Estimated Sales: $10-20 Million
Number Employees: 20-49
Parent Co: Franz Haas Machinery of America

22884 Fraser Stamp & Seal
215 N. Des Plaines St. 2N
Chicago, IL 60661 312-922-4970
Fax: 312-922-2692 800-540-8565
fraserstamp@aol.com www.fraserstamp.com
Sealing stamps, stamp pad inks and marking stencils
President: Ray Fraser
Estimated Sales: $1-2.5 Million
Number Employees: 19

22885 Frazier & Son
P.O.Box 2847
Conroe, TX 77305 936-494-4040
Fax: 936-494-4045 800-365-5438
info@frazierandson.com
www.frazierandson.com
Manufacturer and exporter of power operated packaging machinery including fillers for frozen food; also, bucket elevators
Owner: Mark Frazier
Sales/Engineer: Robert Gennario
Estimated Sales: $2.5 - 5 Million
Number Employees: 1-4
Square Footage: 10000
Brands:
Whiz-Lifter

22886 Frazier Industrial Company
91 Fairview Ave
Long Valley, NJ 07853 908-876-3001
Fax: 908-876-3615 800-859-1342
frazier@frazier.com www.frazier.com
Structural steel pallet rack systems
President: Bill Maschorka
CEO: William L Mascharka
CEO: William Mascharka
Marketing Director: Jessica Hoagiend
Estimated Sales: $50 - 100 Million
Number Employees: 100-249

22887 Frazier Precision Instrument Company
925 Sweeney Dr
Hagerstown, MD 21740 301-790-2585
Fax: 301-790-2589 info@frazierinstrument.com
www.frazierinstrument.com
Manufacturer and exporter of test instruments and measuring equipment
President: Thomas F Scrivener
Estimated Sales: $1 - 2.5 Million
Number Employees: 5-9

22888 Frazier Signs
1304 N 20th St
Decatur, IL 62521 217-429-2349
Fax: 217-429-2340
Signs including neon, plastic, metal, magnetic, vinyl and pressure sensitive; also, maintainenance, installation and repair services available
Manager (Vinyl Graphics): Robert Frazier
Estimated Sales: less than $500,000
Number Employees: 1-4
Square Footage: 6000

22889 Fred Beesley's Booth & Upholstery
264 Brookfield Ln
Centerville, UT 84014-1474 801-364-8189
Restaurant booths, counters and tables
President: Fred Beesley
Marketing Director: Fred Beesley
Estimated Sales: Below $5 Million
Number Employees: 10

22890 (HQ)Fred D. Pfening Company
1075 W 5th Ave
Columbus, OH 43212-2691 614-294-1633
Fax: 614-294-1633 sales@pfening.com
www.pfening.com
Manufacturer and exporter of bakers' machinery including proof boxes, sifters and water metering devices; also, material handling equipment
President: Fred Pfening III
VP of Sales/Marketing: Norm Meulenberg
Purchasing Agent: Patrick Inskeep
Estimated Sales: $10 - 20 Million
Number Employees: 50-99
Square Footage: 75000
Brands:
Wat-A-Mat

22891 Fredman Bag Company
5801 W Bender Ct
Milwaukee, WI 53218 414-462-9400
Fax: 414-462-9409 800-945-5686
www.fredmanbag.com
Printed packaging materials including recloseable polyethylene bags and breathable films
President: Tim Fredman
Executive VP: Tim Fredman, Jr.
Number Employees: 62
Square Footage: 25000

22892 Fredrick Ramond Company
PO Box 4318
Cerritos, CA 90703-4318 562-926-1361
Fax: 562-926-1015 800-743-7266
www.fredrickramond.com
Manufacturer, importer and exporter of decorative light fixtures
President: Fredrick Glassman
National Sales Manager: Alan Dubrow
Inside Sales: David Brusius
Support Manager: Carol Romero
Estimated Sales: $10-20 Million
Number Employees: 100-249
Brands:
F. Ramond
Palm Springs

22893 Free Flow Packaging Corporation
1090 Mills Way
Redwood City, CA 94063 650-261-5300
Fax: 650-361-1713 800-888-3725
vlyle@ix.netcom.com www.free-flow.com
Interior cushioning material for protective packaging; also, dispersing systems for loose-fill cushioning materials
President: Arthur Graham
Marketing Manager: Jim Jensen
National Sales Manager: Harry Reynolds
Number Employees: 350
Brands:
Flo-Pak
Flo-Pak Bio 8

22894 Freedom Press Packaging
195 Aviation Way Ste 201
Watsonville, CA 95076 831-722-3565
Fax: 831-724-0995
laura@freedomfromstress.com
www.freedompackaging.com
Packaging supplies for frozen foods
Owner: Tom Prague
Owner/CEO: Thomas Sprague
CEO: Thomas Sprague
Estimated Sales: $3 - 5,000,000
Number Employees: 1-4

22895 Freely Display
12401 Euclid Ave
Cleveland, OH 44106-4314 216-721-6056
Fax: 216-721-6081 freely@ix.netcom.com
www.freelydisplay.com
Manufacturer and exporter of wood store fixtures and displays
Controller: Bernadette Gello
Operations Manager: Thomas Olechiw
Estimated Sales: $2.5-5 Million
Number Employees: 5-9

22896 Freeman Company
911 Graham Drive
Fremont, OH 43420 419-334-9709
Fax: 859-525-0992 800-223-7788
info@freemancompany.com
www.freemancompany.com
Cutting equipment, presses, dies, tooling
President: Greg Defisher
CEO: Louis G Freeman III
CFO: Scott Clifford
Estimated Sales: $2.5-5 Million
Number Employees: 10

22897 Freeman Electric Company
534 Oak Ave
Panama City, FL 32401 850-785-7448
Fax: 850-747-1162
73699freemanelectric@mindspring.com
Plastic and neon signs
President: Tommy Duncan
Estimated Sales: $1-2.5 Million
Number Employees: 1-4

22898 **FreesTech**
P.O. Box 2156
Sinking Spring, PA 19608 717-560-7560
Fax: 717-560-7587 info@freestech.com
www.freestech.com
Manufacturer and exporter of palletizers, freezing and cooling systems, conveyors and storage and retrieval machines for warehouse applications
Estimated Sales: $500 Million-1Billion
Number Employees: 10
Brands:
Auto-Pal
Fusion Cell
Milk-Stor
Tri-Flow
Tri-Stacker
Tri-Tray

22899 **Frelco**
PO Box 316
Stephenville, NL A2N 2Z5
Canada 709-643-5668
Fax: 709-643-3046 frelco@nf.sympatico.ca
Manufacturer, importer and exporter of conveyors, hoppers, tables and cabinets

22900 **Frem Corporation**
60 Webster Place
Worcester, MA 01603-1920 508-791-3152
Fax: 508-791-7969
Manufacturer and exporter of injection molded plastic housewares including food storage bins, crates and waste baskets
CEO: M.L. Sherman
CFO: D.A. Denovellis
Vice President: J.J. Althoff
Manager: Tim Eunice
Parent Co: Ekco Group

22901 **Fremont Die Cut Products**
3177 E State St
Fremont, OH 43420 419-334-2626
Fax: 419-334-3327 800-223-3177
Tonyae@northamericancontainer.com
www.northamericancontainer.com
Corrugated plastic products including bulk and sleeve packs, sheets and containers
President: Les Mintz
Estimated Sales: $1 - 5 Million
Number Employees: 20-49
Square Footage: 320000

22902 **French Awning & Screen Company**
4514 South McRaven Rd
Jackson, MS 39204 601-922-1132
Fax: 601-922-9671 800-898-1132
kerry@frenchcanvasawnings.com
www.frenchcanvasawnings.com
Commercial awnings
President: Kerry French
Estimated Sales: $500,000-$1 Million
Number Employees: 5-9

22903 **French Oil Mill Machinery Company**
1035 W Greene St
Piqua, OH 45356 937-773-3420
Fax: 937-773-3424 sales@frenchoil.com
www.frenchoil.com
Manufacturer and exporter of vegetable oilseed processing equipment including cracking and flaking mills, conditioners, full, extruder and pre-presses, dewatering and drying presses, liquid-solid separation equipment and hydraulicpresses
President: Daniel French
CFO: Dennis Bratton
CEO: Jason P McDaniel
Quality Control: Jason McDaniel
Sales Director: James King
Public Relations: Eric Brockman
Estimated Sales: $10 - 20 Million
Number Employees: 50-99
Square Footage: 225000

22904 **Fres-Co System**
3005 State Rd
Telford, PA 18969-1021 215-256-4172
Fax: 215-721-0747 contact@fresco.com
www.fresco.com
Tea and coffee industry bag formers/fillers/sealers, bagging machines, bags and packaging film supplies, espresso pod machines, foil laminates, machinery for coffee roasters, packaging (flexible), vacuum packaging machinery, scalesteabag machinery, pac
President: Tullio Vigano
Estimated Sales: $20-50 Million
Number Employees: 250-499

22905 **Fresh Express, Inc.**
950 E. Blanco Rd.
Salinas, CA 93901-4419 831-775-2300
www.freshexpress.com
Certified organic salads and lettuce, cole slaw & shreds, delicious kits, flavorful spinach, gourmet cafe salads, harvest originals, refreshing mixes, tasty greens mixes, and tender leaf mixes.
President: Tanios Viviani
Chairman & CEO: Jim Lugg
Vice President: Bob Warnock
Estimated Sales: $368.3 Million
Number Employees: 3349
Square Footage: 20000
Parent Co: Chiquita Brands International, Inc
Type of Packaging: Bulk
Brands:
Fresh Express

22906 **Fresh Mark**
1888 Southway SW
Massillon, OH 44646 330-832-7491
www.freshmark.com
Bacon, ham, weiners, deli and luncheon meats, dry sausage and other specialty meat items.
Estimated Sales: $219 Million
Number Employees: 1600
Square Footage: 80000
Type of Packaging: Consumer, Food Service, Private Label

22907 **Freshloc Technologies**
15443 Knoll Trail Dr
Suite 100
Dallas, TX 75248 972-759-0111
Fax: 972-759-0090 888-225-9458
sales@freshloc.com www.freshloc.com
President/CEO: Alan C Heller
Founder: Richard G. Fettig
Vice President of Sales & Operations: JD Donnelly
Sales Director: Donna Fettig
Estimated Sales: $2.5 - 5 Million
Number Employees: 10-19

22908 **Freshway Distributors**
50 Ludy St
Hicksville, NY 11801-5115 516-870-3333
www.freshway.com
Refrigerating company and also offers transportation services

22909 **Fresno Neon Sign Company**
5901 E Clinton Ave
Fresno, CA 93727 559-292-2944
Fax: 559-292-2980 www.fresnoneon.com
Signs including point of purchase, neon luminous tube and plastic
Owner: Bill Kratt
Manager: Bill Kratt
Estimated Sales: $1-2.5 Million
Number Employees: 10-19

22910 **Fresno Pallet, Inc.**
PO Box 268
Sultana, CA 93666 559-591-4111
Fax: 559-591-6116 Info@FresnoPallet.Com
www.fresnopallet.com
Fencing, skids, plywood bins and wooden and plastic pallets; also, rail and truck unloading services available
Owner: Steven Johnson
Sales Manager: Steve Johnson
Operations Manager: Michael Johnson
Estimated Sales: $2.5-5 Million
Number Employees: 10-19

22911 **Fresno Tent & Awning Company**
100 M St
Fresno, CA 93721-3117 559-264-4771
Fax: 559-485-5629
Commercial awnings
President: Margaret Mingle
Estimated Sales: $2.5 - 5,000,000
Number Employees: 1-4

22912 **Freudenberg Nonwovens**
2975 Pembroke Road
Hopkinsville, KY 42240 270-887-5115
Fax: 270-886-5069
HVAC@freudenberg-filter.com
www.freudenberg-filter.com
Manufacturer and importer of air and liquid filters; also, filtration media
Estimated Sales: $50-100 Million
Number Employees: 100-249
Brands:
Micronair
Viledon

22913 **Frick by JohnsonControls**
5757 N. Green Bay Ave.
PO Box 591ÿ
Milwaukee, WI 53201 414-524-1200
Fax: 717-762-8624 john.h.gay@jci.com
www.johnsoncontrols.com
Industrial refrigeration equipment
CFO: Steve Bixler
VP: Jim Furlong
Number Employees: 500-999
Parent Co: Johnson Controls
Brands:
Acuair
Frick
Power Pac
Powerflow

22914 **(HQ)Friedman Bag Company**
865 Manhattan Beach Boulevard
Suite 204
Manhattan Beach, CA 90266-4955 213-628-2341
Fax: 213-687-9772
Manufacturer and exporter of burlap, cotton, polyethylene, open mesh bags; wholesaler/distributor of paper bags, cartons and packaging supplies
President: Al Lanfeld
VP/Operations Manager: David Friedman
Sales/Service: Diane Dal Porto
Estimated Sales: $20-50 Million
Number Employees: 250-499
Square Footage: 400000

22915 **Friedr Dick Corporation**
33 Allen Blvd
Farmingdale, NY 11735 800-554-3425
Fax: 631-454-6184 800-554-3425
customerservice@fdick.us www.fdick.com
Manufacturer and distributor of cutlery
Sales: Morgan
Operations: Scott Belovin
Number Employees: 5-9
Number of Brands: 7
Number of Products: 600
Square Footage: 5000
Type of Packaging: Consumer, Food Service, Bulk
Brands:
Friedr. Dick

22916 **Friedrich Metal ProductsCompany**
6204 Technology Dr
Browns Summit, NC 27214 336-375-3067
Fax: 336-621-7901 800-772-0326
info@friedrichproducts.com
www.friedrichmetalproducts.com
Manufacturer and exporter of smokehouses, bakery ovens, smokers, deli equipment, etc
President: Laura Friedrich-Bargebuhr
CFO: Jennefer Friedrich
Vice President: Laura Friedrich-Bargebuhr
Quality Control: Axel Dender
Estimated Sales: $1 - 3 Million
Number Employees: 20
Square Footage: 30000

22917 **Friend Box Company**
90 High St
Danvers, MA 01923 978-774-0240
Fax: 978-777-7921 service@friendbox.com
www.friendbox.com
Boxes including rigid paper and loose wrap candy
President and CFO: Charles J Fox
Quality Control: Rich Lombardo
CEO: Charlie Walker
VP Sales: Fran Dollard
VP Operations: Larry Comeau

Estimated Sales: $5 - 10 Million
Number Employees: 50-99

22918 Friendly City Box Company
520 Oakridge Dr
Johnstown, PA 15904-6915 814-266-6287
Fax: 814-266-9757
Folding paper cartons
President: Larry Blackburn
Estimated Sales: $1-2.5 Million
Number Employees: 10-19

22919 Frigid Coil
13711 Freeway Drive
Santa Fe Springs, CA 90670-5688 562-921-4310
Fax: 562-921-6412 www.yorkinternational.com
Manufactures refrigeration and air conditioning equipment for commercial use
President: David Myers
Quality Control: Thomas Serry
R & D: Gary Price
Estimated Sales: $1-2.5 Million
Number Employees: 10

22920 Frigidaire
701 33rd Ave N
St Cloud, MN 56303-3040 320-253-1212
Fax: 320-240-3498 www.frigidaire.com
Freezers
General Manager: Kyle Chown
Plant Manager: Shawn Anderson
Estimated Sales: $100-500 Million
Number Employees: 1,000-4,999
Parent Co: Electrolux
Brands:
Gibson
Kelvinator
White Westinghouse

22921 Frigoscandia
9577 153rd Ave NE
Redmond, WA 98052-2513 425-883-2244
Fax: 425-882-0948 800-423-1743
dave_faires@fmc.com www.frigoscandia.com
Freezing/refrigeration equipment including in-line quick freezing and spiral freezers, freezer control systems and pre-packaged refrigeration systems; also, steam pasteurization systems for carcasses
Vice President: Charlie Cannon
Director Sales: Mike Kish
Number Employees: 20-49
Parent Co: FMC Corporation
Brands:
Flofreeze
Frigopak
Gyrocompact
Gyrostack
Lewis Iqf
Sps

22922 Frigoscandia Equipment
1700 Cannon Road
Northfield, MN 55057-1680 507-645-9546
Fax: 507-645-6148 800-426-1283
fmcfoodtech.info@fmcti.com
www.fmctechnologies.com
Manufacturers inline spiral freezer for food processing industry
President: Simoau Jeff
Quality Control: Chucks Moder
Regional Sales Manager: Ellen Hao
Estimated Sales: $20 - 50 Million
Number Employees: 100

22923 Frigoscandia Equipment
1700 Cannon Road
Northfield, MN 55057-1680 507-645-9546
Fax: 507-645-6148 800-426-1283
info@northfieldfreezing.com
www.frigoscandia-equipment.com
Freezing systems, specializing in in-process line freezers, chillers, coolers, bakery proofers, dehydrators, bottle elevators, conveyors, fluidized belt freezers, trolley freezers
President: Joseph Northerland
Marketing Manager: Larry DeBoer
Estimated Sales: $20 - 50 Million
Number Employees: 75

22924 Frisk Design
PO Box 504
Saint Helena, CA 94574-5004 707-944-1655
Fax: 707-944-1655
Wine industry bottle etching and design

22925 (HQ)Friskem Infinetics
PO Box 2330
Wilmington, DE 19899 302-658-2471
Fax: 302-658-2475 fkmii@juno.com
Manufacturer and exporter of detectors including metal, pilferage, passive magnetometer and active field
President: M Schwartz
CEO: M Schwartz
Brands:
Friskem
Friskem-Af
Tellem

22926 Fristam Pumps
2410 Parview Rd
Middleton, WI 53562 608-831-5001
Fax: 608-831-8467 800-841-5001
fristam@fristampumps.com
www.fristam.com/usa
Manufacturer and exporter of stainless steel, centrifugal and positive displacement pumps, blenders and mixers.
President: Pete Herb
CEO: Wolfgang Stamp
VP: Pete Skora
Quality Control/Operations: Duane Ehlke
Marketing Supervisor: Dan Funk
Sales Director: Larry Cook
Public Relations: Wendy Andrew
Number Employees: 50-99
Number of Products: 80
Brands:
Fristam

22927 Fristam Pumps, USA, Ltd.Partnership
2410 Parview Road
Middleton, WI 53562-0065 608-831-5001
Fax: 608-831-8467 sales@fristampumps.com
www.fristam.com
Centrifugal pumps, shear pumps, powder mixers and positive displacement pumps

22928 Fritsch
921 Proton Rd
San Antonio, TX 78258-4203 210-227-2726
Fax: 210-227-5550 fritschsales@aol.com
Industrial bakery equipment (sheeting equipment) roll-fix USA (retail reversible sheeters)
President: Claus Fritsch
General Manager: Danny Kelly
Off. Mngr.: Joseph Mouyer
Estimated Sales: $300,000-500,000
Number Employees: 1-4

22929 Frobisher Industries
6260 Rte 105
Waterborough, NB E4C 2Y4
Canada 506-362-2198
Fax: 506-362-9090
Manufacturer and exporter of hamper baskets, veneer and wooden boxes for fruits and vegetables
President: George Staples
CFO: George Lorriaine
Number Employees: 10
Square Footage: 24000

22930 (HQ)Frohling Sign Company
419 E Route 59
Nanuet, NY 10954 845-623-2258
Fax: 845-623-2799 bocfrohlingsign@aol.com
Plastic, wood, interior, exterior, neon and metal signs; also, plaques
President: Brian O'Connor
Estimated Sales: $1-2.5 Million
Number Employees: 5-9

22931 Frommelt Safety Products& Ductsox Corporation
4343 Chavenelle Rd
Dubuque, IA 52002-2653 563-556-2020
Fax: 563-589-2776 800-553-5560
www.ritehite.com
Fabric air dispersion products for open ceiling architecture
President: Cary Pinkalla
Sr. Sales Promotion Specialist: Mary Jo Kluesner
Plant Manager: Lou Wiegand
Estimated Sales: $2 million
Number Employees: 5-9

22932 Frontier Bag Company
2420 Grant Street
Omaha, NE 68111 402-342-0992
Fax: 402-342-2107 800-278-2247
www.frontierbagco.com
Burlap and cotton bags; wholesaler/distributor of paper and plastic bags; serving the food service market
President: Judy Pearl-Lee
Sales Manager: Judy Pearl-Lee
Estimated Sales: $1-2.5 Million
Number Employees: 10-19

22933 Frontier Bag Company
PO Box 200
Grandview, MO 64030-0200 816-765-4811
Fax: 816-765-6603 www@frontierbag.com
www.frontierbag.net
Plastic, shrink and meat bags, polyethylene bag liners, pallet covers and sheeting; exporter of plastic bags; importer of polyethylene raw materials bager plain and printed
President: Mark Gurley
Owner: Ron Gurley
VP Sales: Tom Hauser
VP Production: Ron Avery
Estimated Sales: $20-50 Million
Number Employees: 50-99
Square Footage: 90000

22934 Frontier Packaging Company
1938 Occidental Avenue S
Seattle, WA 98134-1413 206-682-7800
Fax: 206-682-1669 800-737-7333
Wine industry packaging
Estimated Sales: $1-2.5 000,000
Number Employees: 19

22935 Frost Food Handling Products
2020 Bristol Ave NW
Grand Rapids, MI 49504-1494 616-453-7781
Fax: 616-453-2161 frost@frostinc.com
www.frostinc.com
Conveying components for food handling applications
Owner: Chad Frost
CEO: Chad Frost
CFO: Fred Sytsma
Sales Director: Joe Jakeway
Estimated Sales: $10-20 Million
Number Employees: 50-99
Square Footage: 60000
Parent Co: Frost Industries
Brands:
Attachments
Blue Poly Trolleys
Sani-Link Chain
Sani-Trolley
Sani-Wheel
Stainless Steel Bearings
Stainless Steel Trolleys
Stainless Steel X-Chain
X-Chain

22936 Frost Manufacturing Corporation
173 Grove Street
Worcester, MA 01605 508-756-4685
Fax: 508-757-5604 800-462-0216
info@frostmanufacturing.com
www.frostmanufacturing.com
Rubber stamps, signs, name plates, stencils, menu boards, inks, labels, banners and name badges
President: Douglas Frost
VP Marketing: Julieane Frost
Estimated Sales: $1 - 2.5 Million
Number Employees: 5-9

22937 Frost, Inc.
2020 Bristol Ave NW
Grand Rapids, MI 49504 616-453-7781
Fax: 616-453-2161 800-253-9382
frost.sales@frostinc.com www.frostinc.com
Overhead, inverted and converyor trolleys, guide rollers, conveyor roll bearings, and food processing components.

22938 Frosty Factory of America
2301 S Farmerville St
Ruston, LA 71270 318-255-1162
Fax: 318-255-1170 800-544-4071
dolph@frostyfactory.com
www.frostyfactory.com

Manufacturer and exporter of frozen beverage, soft serve ice cream and shake machines
President: Heath Williams
Finance Executive: Penny Taylor
Sales/Marketing: Craig Moss
Sales Executive: Christopher Williams
Engineer: Ralph Pettijohn
Purchasing Manager: Ralph Pettijohn
Estimated Sales: $5 Million
Number Employees: 20-49
Square Footage: 40000
Brands:
Petite Sorbeteer
Soft-Serve Ice Cream
Sorbeteer

22939 Frozen Specialties Inc.
8600 South Wilkinson Way
Suite G
Perrysburg, OH 43551 419-867-2005
www.frozenspecialties.com
Private label pizza and pizza bites, a multi-line supplier
Director: J Hall
Controller: Ken Nixon
Chief Information Officer: Doug Kulwicki
Quality Assurance Manager: Bill Steadman
Vice President, Marketing: Patrick Koralewski
Vice President, Sales: Rick Hicks
Human Resources Manager: Luann Hakka
Production Supervisor: Keith Traver
Plant Manager: Steve Dominick
Purchasing Manager: Jeff Miller
Estimated Sales: $56 Million
Number Employees: 140
Number of Brands: 1
Number of Products: 6
Square Footage: 13395
Type of Packaging: Consumer, Private Label, Bulk
Brands:
Mr. P'S

22940 Fru-Con Construction LLC
4310 Prince William Pkwy
Suite 200
Woodbridge, VA 22192-5199 703-586-6100
Fax: 703-586-6101 www.frucon.com
Packaging engineering and construction, maintenance and start-up services
President/Chief Executive Officer: Ray Bond
Controller: Eric Anderson
Vice President: Michael Fischer
Estimated Sales: $500 Million
Number Employees: 500-999

22941 Fruehauf Trailer Services
12813 Flushing Meadows Dr
St Louis, MO 63131-1835 314-822-1113
Refrigerated trailers; service available
CEO: Derek Nagle
Director Marketing/Advertising: Steve Havens
Number Employees: 10-19
Parent Co: Wabash National Company
Brands:
Fruehauf

22942 Fruit Growers Package Company
4693 Wilson Avenue SW
Suite H
Grandville, MI 49418-8762 616-724-1400
Manufacturer and exporter of wood veneer products, craft baskets and wooden shipping crates for berries
President: Diane Taylor
VP: Dennis Palasek
Estimated Sales: $600,000
Number Employees: 10
Square Footage: 80000
Type of Packaging: Consumer, Bulk

22943 Fruit Patch Sales
38773 Road 48
Dinuba, CA 93618 559-591-1170
Fax: 559-591-3604 julian@fruitpatch.net
www.fruitpatch.net
President: Glen McClaran
Estimated Sales: $100+ Million
Number Employees: 500-999

22944 Fruitcrown Products Corporation
250 Adams Blvd
Farmingdale, NY 11735 631-694-5800
Fax: 631-694-6467 800-441-3210
info@fruitcrown.com www.fruitcrown.com
Aseptic fruit flavors and bases for beverage, dairy and baking industries
President: Robert Jagenburg
Number Employees: 50-99
Type of Packaging: Bulk
Brands:
Asp
Exquizita
Fruitcrown
Huntingcastle

22945 Fruition Northwest LLC
29345 NW W Union Rd
PO Box 130
North Plains, OR 97133 503-880-5193
bobvaughan@fruitionnw.com
www.fruitionnorthwest.com
High-quality infused-dehydrated berry fruits to the wholesale market.
Owner: Alan Krassowski
Estimated Sales: $210 Thousand
Type of Packaging: Bulk

22946 Fruvemex
2420 M.L. King Suite B
Calexico, CA 92231 760-203-1896
Fax: 760-203-2389 fcaballero@fruvemex.com
www.fruvemex.com
Refrigerated and frozen fruit and vegetable products
President: Gustavo Caballero
VP Sales/Marketing: Yvonne Brewer
Number Employees: 85
Square Footage: 180000
Type of Packaging: Bulk

22947 Fry Tech Corporation
4430 Dodge Street
Dubuque, IA 52003-2600 319-583-1559
Fax: 319-557-8602 frytech@mwci.net
Fryers including ventless counter-top and auto-lift fryers with built-in air filtration and fire suppression systems
Owner: Rod Christ
VP: Donna Christ
Number Employees: 2
Square Footage: 3500
Brands:
Alpaire
Fan-C-Fry
U-Fry-It

22948 Frye's Measure Mill
12 Frye Mill Rd
Wilton, NH 03086 603-654-6581
Fax: 603-654-6103 www.fryesmeasuremill.com
Manufacturer and exporter of wooden dry measures, specialty packaging, veneer containers, colonial pantry and shaker boxes
President: Harley Savage
Quality Control: Harley Savage
Estimated Sales: Below $5 Million
Number Employees: 5-9
Brands:
Frye's Measure Mill
Old Tyme

22949 Frymaster, LLC.
8700 Line Ave
Shreveport, LA 71106 318-865-1711
Fax: 318-868-5987 800-221-4583
webmaster@frymaster.com www.frymaster.com
Supplier of commercial fryers, frying systems, water-bath rethermalizers, pasta cookers, and of the equipment related to these technologies.
President: Gene Baugh
Vice President & General Manager: Todd Phillips
Estimated Sales: $60 Million
Number Employees: 587
Square Footage: 180000
Parent Co: ENODIS
Type of Packaging: Food Service
Brands:
Frymaster
Master Jet

22950 Ft. Wayne Awning Company
7105 Ardmore Ave
Fort Wayne, IN 46809-9541 260-478-1636
Fax: 260-747-0466 www.fortwayneawning.com
Commercial awnings
Owner: Mel Mc Clain
Estimated Sales: Below $5,000,000
Number Employees: 10-19

22951 Fuji Health Science
3 Terri Lane
Unit 12
Burlington, NJ 08016 609-386-3030
Fax: 609-386-3033
contact@fujihealthscience.com
www.fujihealthscience.com
Markets and manufacturers natural specialty food ingredient, AstaReal astaxanthin, a powerful anti-oxidant
National Sales Manager: Joe Kuncewitch
Estimated Sales: Under $500,000
Number Employees: 10

22952 Fuji Labeling Systems
2025 S Arl Hts Rd Ste 100
Arlington Heights, IL 60005 847-690-1725
Fax: 847-690-1734 fujiusa@aol.com
Standard series labels
Estimated Sales: $300,000-500,000
Number Employees: 1-4

22953 Fujitso Transaction Solutions
11085 N Torrey Pines Road
La Jolla, CA 92037-1015 858-457-9900
Fax: 858-457-2701 800-340-4425
aselich@fjicl.com www.fjicl.com
Lightweight and rugged pen-based hand-held computers, route accounting, distributing
President: Hiroaki Kurokawa
Marketing Manager: Sandy Watts
Estimated Sales: $20 - 50 Million
Number Employees: 50

22954 Ful-Flav-R Foods
P.O.Box 82
Alamo, CA 94507 925-838-0300
Fax: 925-838-0310
customerservice@ffrfoods.com
www.fulflavr.com
Premium Ground Garlic, Minced Garlic (in oil & water), Ground and Minced Ginger, Ground Roasted Garlic, Ground Onion, diced Sweet Bell Peppers, Ground and Diced Jalepeno's, Fire Roasted Anaheim chili's, Ground Chili-Garlic Blends andother unique custom formulated blends. All of our products are pasteurized and pH controlled.
President: Joseph Farrell
Chief Operations Officer: Glen Farrell
Director Sales/Marketing: Steve Linzmeyer
Plant Manager: John Small
Estimated Sales: $1-2.5 Million
Number Employees: 5-9
Type of Packaging: Food Service, Bulk
Brands:
Ful-Flav-R

22955 Full-View Display Case
PO Box 79200
Fort Worth, TX 76179-0200 817-847-0775
Fax: 817-232-0214 800-252-1667
fullview@ev1.net www.fullviewdisplays.com
Refrigerated and nonrefrigerated display cases for the gourmet candy and bakery industries
Estimated Sales: $1-2.5 Million
Number Employees: 10-19

22956 Fuller Box Company
PO Box 9
North Attleboro, MA 02761-0009 508-695-2525
Fax: 508-695-2187 www.fullerbox.com
Cardboard and steel packaging and packaging machinery; also, metal stamping machinery
President: P Fuller
CFO: John Backner
Vice President: A Fuller
Sales/Marketing Executive: Thomas Mercer
Estimated Sales: $10 - 20 Million
Number Employees: 100-249
Square Footage: 97000
Parent Co: Fuller Companies

22957 Fuller Brush Company
One Fuller Way
Great Bend, KS 67530 620-792-1711
Fax: 620-792-1906 800-522-0499
info@fuller.com www.fuller.com
Manufacturer and exporter of detergents, mops, floor polish, brooms and plastic bottles
President: G Robert Gey
VP: Lewis L Gray
VP Sales: Dolores McConnaughy
VP Sales: Bill McCoy

Number Employees: 250-499
Square Footage: 500000

22958 Fuller Flag Company
1092 Main Street
Holden, MA 01520-1247 508-829-6016
Fax: 508-829-7767 800-348-6723
tjaitken@earthling.net
Flags and pennants, retail and wholesale flags
Sales Manager: Samantha McDonald
Office Manager: Samatha McDonald
Estimated Sales: $300,000-500,000
Number Employees: 1-4

22959 Fuller Packaging
1152 High St
Central Falls, RI 02863 401-725-4300
Fax: 401-726-8050 Sales@FullerBox.com
www.fullerbox.com
Manufacturer, importer and exporter of boxes including paper and counter display
President: Peter Fuller
Product Development Manager: Alvin Fuller
Estimated Sales: $10-20 Million
Number Employees: 100-249
Square Footage: 77000

22960 Fuller Ultraviolet CorpoRation
9416 Gulf Stream Road
Frankfort, IL 60423 815-469-3301
Fax: 815-469-1438 contact@fulleruv.com
www.fulleruv.com
Liquid sweetener tank storage, water purification
President: Kay Eckstrom
Number Employees: 20-49
Number of Brands: 1
Number of Products: 12
Square Footage: 16000

22961 Fuller Weighing Systems
1600 Georgesville Road
Columbus, OH 43228-3616 614-882-8121
Fax: 614-882-9594
Manufacturer and exporter of bulk weighing systems, feeders and automatic net-weigh container filling systems for liquids and dry materials
VP Sales: Tim Schultz
General Manager: Karl Hedderich
Production: David Patterson
Number Employees: 50
Square Footage: 30000
Parent Co: Cardinal Scale Manufacturing Company

22962 Fulton Boiler Works
3981 Port St
Pulaski, NY 13142 315-298-5121
Fax: 315-298-6390 service@fulton.com
www.fulton.com
Process, heat, steam for baking, cooking, frying
President: Ronald B Palm
Chairman: Ronald B Palm
Estimated Sales: $20 Million
Number Employees: 100-249

22963 (HQ)Fulton-Denver Company
3500 Wynkoop St
Denver, CO 80216-3650 303-294-9292
Fax: 303-292-9470 800-776-6715
Bags including burlap, mesh, poly, paper, bulk, cotton, vexar and wool; also, cartons, wrap, sheets, twine and thread
Manager: Steve Potter
President: Rhett Schuller
Estimated Sales: $5 - 10 Million
Number Employees: 1 to 4

22964 Fun City Popcorn
3211 Sunrise Ave
Las Vegas, NV 89101 702-367-2676
Fax: 702-876-1099 800-423-1710
www.funcitypopcorn.com
Caramel, cheese and butter popcorn; manufacturer of popcorn processing machinery
President/CEO: Richard Falk
CFO: Maryann Talavera
Estimated Sales: $1-3 Million
Number Employees: 5-9
Square Footage: 20000
Type of Packaging: Consumer, Food Service, Private Label, Bulk

22965 Fun-Time International
413 N 4th St
Philadelphia, PA 19123 215-925-1450
Fax: 215-925-1884 800-776-4386
orders@krazystraws.com www.krazystraws.com
Manufacturer and exporter of novelty drinking straws, eating utensils and drinking containers; also, novelty candy items
President: Stephanie Shepard
CFO: Stephanie Shepaid
VP: Stephanie Shepard
R&D: Stephanie Shepaid
Quality Control: Stephanie Shepaid
National Sales Manager: Richard Spector
Estimated Sales: $3 - 5 Million
Number Employees: 10-19
Square Footage: 1000
Brands:
Candy Bracelets
Connecter
Crazy Glasses
Funstraws
Krazy Koolers
Krazy Strawston
Krazy Utensils
Spookyware

22966 Funke Filters
P.O.Box 30097
Cincinnati, OH 45230-0097 513-528-5535
Fax: 513-528-5575 800-543-7070
mcox@fuse.net
Filters and filtration equipment
President: William F Funke
Estimated Sales: Below $5 000,000
Number Employees: 1-4

22967 Furgale Industries Ltd.
324 Lizzie Street
Winnipeg, NB R3A 0Y7
Canada
204-949-4200
Fax: 204-943-3191 800-665-0506
info@broom.com www.broom.com
Provider of cleaning tools to the north american market - tools include: brooms, mops & brushes
President: Jim Furgale
VP: Terry Gibb
Customer Service: Kate Furgale
Number Employees: 70
Number of Brands: 10
Number of Products: 250
Square Footage: 280000
Type of Packaging: Consumer, Private Label
Brands:
Furgale
Home Commercial
No Name
Northwest Co
Pro Seris
Shop Master
Western Family

22968 Furnace Belt Company
2316 Delaware Avenue
Suite 217
Buffalo, NY 14216
Canada
Fax: 800-354-7215 800-354-7213
fbc@furnacebeltco.com www.furnacebeltco.com
Manufacturer and exporter of wire processing belts for heat treating, brazing, annealing, sintering, quenching, freezing and baking
President: J Tatone
Number Employees: 40
Square Footage: 90000

22969 Furniture Lab
106 S Greensboro St Ste E
Carrboro, NC 27510 919-913-0270
Fax: 919-913-0271 800-449-8677
sales@furniturelab.com www.furniturelab.com
Manufacturer and exporter of wood and laminated tables, tabletops, chairs and bases
Marketing: Courtney Smith
Sales Director: Nathan Bearman
Estimated Sales: $1 - 3 Million
Number Employees: 25
Square Footage: 7000

22970 Futura 2000 Corporation
8861 SW 132nd Street
31
Miami, FL 33176-5926 305-256-5877
Fax: 718-349-2485
Menu boards and systems and point of purchase signage; also, retrofitting services available
VP: Diana Amengual
Sales Manager: Rocco Colafrancesco
Estimated Sales: $300,000-500,000
Number Employees: 1-4

22971 Futura Coatings
6614 Grant Road
Houston, TX 77066 281-397-0033
Fax: 281-397-6512 futra@inlink.com
www.futuracoatings.com
Wine industry tank linings and coating
CFO: David Wicks
Estimated Sales: $5-10 000,000
Number Employees: 50-99

22972 Futura Equipment Corporation
460 McLaughlin Rd
Yakima, WA 98908-9659 509-972-3300
Fax: 509-972-3377 888-886-2233
sales@futurequip.com www.futurequip.com
President: Andy Briesmeister
Estimated Sales: $1 - 3 Million
Number Employees: 5-9

22973 Future Commodities/Bestpack
10676 Fulton Ct
Rancho Cucamonga, CA 91730-4848 909-987-4258
Fax: 909-987-5189 888-588-2378
sales@bestpack.com www.bestpack.com
Manufacturer and exporter of carton sealers, erectors and end line packaging machinery
President: David Lim
VP: Chery Lim
Sales Manager: Patrick Brennan
Estimated Sales: $5 - 10 Million
Number Employees: 10-19
Square Footage: 108000
Parent Co: Future Commodities International
Brands:
Bestpack

22974 Future Foods
945 W. Fulton Marke
Chicago, IL 60607 312-987-9342
Fax: 773-561-0307 enquiries@futurefoods.com
www.motorestaurant.com
Consultant providing marketing services to the food service industry; also, product development available
President: Andrew Patterson
VP Sales: Ron Gulyas
Estimated Sales: $.5 - 1,000,000
Number Employees: 1-4

22975 Futures
P.O.Box 60
Barrington, NH 03825-0060 603-664-5811
Fax: 603-664-5864 info@futuressearch.com
www.cri-mms.com
Executive search firm specializing in food service sales and marketing
Manager: Peter Dutton
VP: Richard Mazzola
Estimated Sales: $500,000-$1 Million
Number Employees: 5-9
Square Footage: 8000

22976 Fygir Logistic Information Systems
25 Mall Road
Suite 300
Burlington, MA 01803-4144 781-270-0683
Fax: 781-238-6725
Production planning for developing and monitoring production resources
Estimated Sales: Under $500,000

22977 G E T Enterprises
1515 W Sam Houston Pkwy N.
Houston, TX 77043-3112 713-467-9394
Fax: 713-467-9396 800-727-4500
info@get-melamine.com
www.get-melamine.com
Importer and wholesaler/distributor of dinnerware, high chairs, tray stands, tumblers, platters and soup and coffee mugs; serving the food service market
President: Glen Hou
VP Sales/Marketing: Eve Hou
Estimated Sales: $5-10 Million
Number Employees: 20-49
Square Footage: 40000

22978 **G Lighting**
9777 Reavis Park Dr
St Louis, MO 63123 314-631-6000
Fax: 314-631-7800 800-331-2425
sales@glighting.com www.glighting.com
Designer and manufacturer of decorative commercial lighting fixtures
President: Nichols Gross
CEO: Robert Gross
Executive Vice President: Linton Gross
Marketing/R&D: Brent Paiva
Marketing/R&D: Brent Paiva
President, Sales Manager: Nick Gross
Customer Service: Kara Gross
Office Manager, Purchasing Manager: Jenny Cole
Production Manager: Dan Dickinson
Office Manager, Purchasing Manager: Jenny Cole
Estimated Sales: $5 - 10 Million
Number Employees: 20-49
Square Footage: 16000

22979 **(HQ)G&C Packing Company**
240 S 21st Street
Colorado Springs, CO 80904 719-634-1587
Fax: 719-636-1038
Supplier of slaughtering services only
Chairman: Frank Grindinger Sr
President: Frank Grindinger Jr
Estimated Sales: $7.6 Million
Number Employees: 20-49
Square Footage: 7950
Type of Packaging: Consumer, Food Service, Bulk

22980 **G&D America**
45925 Horseshoe Dr Ste 100
Sterling, VA 20166 703-480-2000
Fax: 703-480-2060 800-856-7712
info@gdai.com www.gdai.com
Manufacturer and exporter of high speed currency counters, dispensers and endorsers
President: Steve Reber
Director Distribution: Bill Chamberlain
Estimated Sales: $50-100 Million
Number Employees: 250-499
Parent Co: G&D America

22981 **G&D Chillers**
3498 W 1st Ave Ste 1
Eugene, OR 97402 541-345-3903
Fax: 541-345-8835 800-555-0973
dan@gdchillers.com www.gdchillers.com
Wine industry, glycol and process chiller
President and CFO: Dan Smith
VP: Ray Tatum
Estimated Sales: Below $5 000,000
Number Employees: 5-9

22982 **G&F Manufacturing Company**
5555 W 109th St
Oak Lawn, IL 60453-5070 708-424-4170
Fax: 708-424-4922 800-282-1574
gandf@gandf.com www.gandf.com
Designing and manufacturing high quality chemical resistant, durable and rugged Stainless steel products such as steel tanks, filling machines, piston filters, cappers, and labeling.
President: Ron Bais
Purchasing Manager: Ron Bais
Number Employees: 10-19
Square Footage: 15000
Type of Packaging: Food Service

22983 **G&H Enterprises**
344 McLaws Cir
Williamsburg, VA 23185-5648 757-258-1230
Fax: 757-258-1231 ghentinc@pilot.infi.net
Case packaging machinery, case packing, box erection, top sealing custom automated machinery and components
Estimated Sales: $1-2.5 000,000
Number Employees: 10-19

22984 **G&J Awning & Canvas**
1260 10th St N
Sauk Rapids, MN 56379 320-255-1733
Fax: 320-255-0130 800-467-1744
info@gjawning.com www.gjawning.com
Commercial awnings including interior and exterior
Owner: Gary Buermann
CEO: Janice Buermann
CFO: Janice Beurmann
Vice President: Janice Buermann
Estimated Sales: Below $5,000,000
Number Employees: 20-49
Square Footage: 9900

22985 **G&K Vijuk Intern. Corp**
715 Church Rd
Elmhurst, IL 60126 630-530-2203
Fax: 630-530-2245 info@guk-vijuk.com
www.vijukequip.com
Bindery finishing equipment, miniature folders
President: Joseph Vijuk
Estimated Sales: $10-20 Million
Number Employees: 35

22986 **G&R Graphics**
303 Irvington Ave
South Orange, NJ 07079 973-313-2200
Fax: 973-313-2211 813-503-8592
agonza8@verizon.net www.grgraphicsinc.com
Manufacturer and exporter of rubber printing plates, corporate seals, rubber stamps, inks and pads
President: David Gonzalez
Estimated Sales: $1 - 5 Million
Number Employees: 5-9
Square Footage: 4000

22987 **(HQ)G&S Metal Products Company**
3330 East 79th Street
Cleveland, OH 44127 216-441-0700
Fax: 216-441-0736 www.gsmetal.com
Aluminum and steel bakeware and housewares including pans
Estimated Sales: $50-100 Million
Number Employees: 250-499
Brands:
Baker-Eze
Black Beauty
Ez Baker
Silverstone

22988 **G.C. Evans**
3300 S Woodrow St
Little Rock, AR 72204-6550 501-664-5095
Fax: 501-663-8690 800-382-6720
sales@gcevans.com www.gcevans.com
Cooling tunnels, warmers and pasteurizers
President: Gerald McNamer
Sales/Marketing: Mark McNamer
Operations/Production: David McNamer
Estimated Sales: $5-10 000,000
Number Employees: 45
Square Footage: 50000

22989 **G.F. Frank & Sons**
9075 Le Saint Dr
Fairfield, OH 45014 513-870-9075
Fax: 513-870-0579 john@GFFrankAndSons.com
www.gffrankandsons.com
Manufacturer and exporter of meat hooks, skewers, trolleys and smokehouse shelving
President: George Frank
Vice President: John Frank
Estimated Sales: $10-20 Million
Number Employees: 10-19

22990 **G.G. Greene Enterprises**
2790 Pennsylvania Avenue
Warren, PA 16365 814-723-5700
Fax: 814-723-3037
awillingham@greenegroup.com
www.greenegroup.com
Manufactures guns, howitzers, mortars & related equipment; manufactures small arms ammunition; manufactures stamped or pressed metal machine parts; plate metal fabricator
Manager: Brent Long
Estimated Sales: $4,500,000
Number Employees: 20-49
Square Footage: 425000
Type of Packaging: Consumer, Food Service

22991 **G.L. Mezzetta Inc**
105 Mezzetta Ct
American Canyon, CA 94503 707-648-1050
Fax: 707-648-1060 800-941-7044
info@mezetta.com www.mezzetta.com
Glass-packed peppers and olives
President: Jeff Mezzetta
Founder: Giuseppe Luigi Mezzetta
General Manager: Ronald Mezzetta
Estimated Sales: $12.3 Million
Number Employees: 80

22992 **(HQ)G.S. Blodgett Corporation**
44 Lakeside Ave
Burlington, VT 05401 802-860-3700
Fax: 802-864-0183 800-331-5842
literature@blodgett.com www.blodgett.com
Manufacturer and exporter of ovens including convection, range, deck, pizza and conveyor; also, steamers, fryers, kettles, grills, mobile food carts, charbroilers, catering equipment and filtering systems
President: Gary Mick
CFO: Gary Mick
VP Sales/Marketing: Lance Servais
Director Corporate Communications: Ann Williams
Number Employees: 250-499
Parent Co: Maytag Corporation
Brands:
Blodgett
Blodgett Combi
Magikitch'n
Pitco Frialator

22993 **G.S. Laboratory Equipment**
275 Aiken Rd
Asheville, NC 28804-8740 828-658-2711
Fax: 828-645-2593 800-252-7100
www.thermofisher.com
Manufacturer and exporter of freezers; also, steel and plastic storage containers
Manager: Jeff Powers
Estimated Sales: $100+ Million
Number Employees: 250-499

22994 **G.V. Aikman Company**
6312 Southeastern Avenue
Indianapolis, IN 46203-5828 317-353-8181
Fax: 317-352-7695 800-886-4029
Designer of commercial kitchens for schools, institutions, etc
Estimated Sales: $2.5-5,000,000
Number Employees: 20-49

22995 **G.W. Berkheimer Company**
1011 E Wallace St
Fort Wayne, IN 46803 800-535-6696
Fax: 260-456-2177 www.gwberkheimer.com
Heating equipment
Manager: Chris Wansley
Branch Manager: Curt Rees
Estimated Sales: $10-20,000,000
Number Employees: 20-49
Parent Co: G.W. Berkheimer Company

22996 **G.W. Dahl Company**
8439 Triad Dr
Greensboro, NC 27409-9018 336-668-4444
Fax: 336-668-4452 800-852-4449
info@purolator-facet.com
www.purolator-facet.com
Filters including water, oil and air; also, I/P transducers, P/I transmitters and pneumatic relays
President: Bruss Stellfox
Quality Control: Stlee Bigary
Marketing Manager: John Mello
Sales Administration: Debbie Froelich
Number Employees: 100-249
Square Footage: 340000
Parent Co: Purolator Products Company

22997 **GA Design Menu Company**
28710 Wall Street
Wixom, MI 48393-3516 313-561-2530
Fax: 313-561-1049
Laminated menus including inserts and covers
Owner: Gary Anoshka
Number Employees: 3
Square Footage: 3000

22998 **GA Systems**
17872 Gothard St.
Huntington Beach, CA 92647 714-848-7529
Fax: 714-841-2356 sales@gasystemsmfg.com
www.gasystemsmfg.com
Stainless steel food service equipment and display cabinets
President: Steve Anderson
Founder: Gordon Anderson
Chief Financial Officer: Pat Devalle
Vice President: Steven Anderson
Sales: Virginia Anderson
Estimated Sales: $2.5-5 Million
Number Employees: 10-19
Square Footage: 64000

22999 GBN Machine & Engineering Corporation
17073 Bull Church Road
Woodford, VA 22580 804-448-2033
Fax: 804-448-2684 800-446-9871
gbnmach@verizon.net www.nailerman.com
Manufacturer and exporter of pallet assembly systems, lumber stackers and conveyors
President: Raj Nainani
VP: Paul Bailey
VP: Paul Bailey
Estimated Sales: Below $5 Million
Number Employees: 10-19

23000 GBS Corporate
7233 Freedom Ave. NW
North Canton, OH 44720 330-494-5330
800-552-2427
marketing@gbscorp.com www.gbscorp.com
Manufacturer and exporter of plastic film, pressure sensitive labels and tags
VP: Jim Lee
VP/General Manager: James Lee
Marketing Director: Jackie Davidson
Plant Manager: Bruce Budney
Estimated Sales: $4 Million
Number Employees: 20-49
Square Footage: 120000

23001 GBS Foodservice Equipment, Inc.
951 Matheson Boulevard E
Mississauga, ON L4W 2R7
Canada 905-897-2333
Fax: 905-897-2334 888-402-1242
pdouglas@gbscooks.com www.gbscooks.com
Distributor of foodservice equipment including; combi-ovens, open well fryers, rotisseries, blast chillers, for hot & cold merchandisers
General Manager: S Jaffer
Estimated Sales: $1 - 5 Million
Number Employees: 10-20

23002 GC Evans Sales & Manufacturing Company
3300 S Woodrow St
Little Rock, AR 72204 501-664-5095
Fax: 501-663-8690 800-382-6720
sales@gcevans.com www.gcevans.com
Accumulating conveyors
President: Gerald Mc Namer
Estimated Sales: $5-10 000,000
Number Employees: 20-49

23003 GCA Bar Code Specialist
5122 Bolsa Ave # 104
Huntington Beach, CA 92649-1050 714-379-4911
Fax: 714-379-4913 julie@gcalabels.com
www.gcalabels.com
Bar code equipment and supplies, labels, packaging, printers, software and marking devices; laser marking service available
President: Julie Grabel
Office Manager: Kim Benudict
Estimated Sales: $300,000-500,000
Number Employees: 1-4
Brands:
Loftware
Monarch

23004 GCJ Mattei Company
927 E Madison St
Louisville, KY 40204 502-583-4774
Fax: 502-583-4776
Displays
Owner: Louis Mattei
Estimated Sales: $500,000-$1 Million
Number Employees: 1-4
Square Footage: 12000

23005 GD Packaging Machinery
501 Southlake Blvd
Richmond, VA 23236-3078 804-794-9777
Fax: 804-794-6187 paul_smith@gidi.it
www.gdpackagemachinery.com
CFO: Lich Polchinski
Marketing: Glen Coater
Number Employees: 250-499

23006 GDM Concepts
15330 Texaco Ave
Paramount, CA 90723 562-633-0195
Fax: 562-633-1561 www.gdmconcepts.com
Store fixtures
President: George Myers
Estimated Sales: $10-20,000,000
Number Employees: 20-49

23007 GE Betz
4636 Somerton Road
Trevose, PA 19053-6742 215-355-3300
Fax: 215-953-5524 www.gewater.com
Chemicals for controlling sealing, corrosion and microbiological growth in pasteurizers, sterilizers, hydrostatic cookers and other process equipment. Also manaufactures chemicals for odor control.
President & CEO: Heiner Markhoff
CEO: Jeff Garwood
Engineered Systems Leader: Yuvbir Singh
Number Employees: 500-999
Parent Co: BetzDearborn
Other Locations:
BetzDearborn
Horsham PA
Brands:
Aquafloc
Bio Scan
Ferroquest
Polymate
Polyquest
Sterisafe

23008 GE Company
3135 Easton Tpke
Fairfield, CT 06828-0001 203-373-2211
Fax: 203-373-3131 800-626-2004
gary.sheffer@ge.com www.ge.com
General Manager: Gary Sheffer
Vice President of Legal: Alex Dimitrief
Vice President of Research: Mark Little
Estimated Sales: $100 - 150 Million
Number Employees: 10,000

23009 GE Distributed Power
1 River Road Bldg
Schenectady, NY 12345-6000 518-385-2211
Fax: 518-385-7045 800-560-3902
GEDistributedPower@ps.ge.com
Markets midrange power generation equipment, replacement parts and services
CEO: John G Rice
Estimated Sales: $1 - 5 Million
Number Employees: 1,000-4,999

23010 GE Interlogix Industrial
12345 SW Leveton Dr
Tualatin, OR 97062-6001 503-692-4052
Fax: 503-691-7377 800-247-9447
geraldine.williams@ge.com www.sentrol.com
Manufacturer and exporter of noncontract safety switches, position sensors and safety relays
President: Greg Burge
Estimated Sales: $50-100 Million
Number Employees: 500-999
Square Footage: 140000
Parent Co: Interlogix
Brands:
Failsafe Guardswitch
Guardswitch

23011 (HQ)GE Lighting
1975 Noble Rd
Cleveland, OH 44112 216-266-2121
Fax: 216-266-2510 800-435-4448
kim_freeman@ge.com www.gelighting.com
Lighting and lighting fixtures including incandescent, flourescent, HID, outdoor and mercury
CEO: Michael Petras
Marketing Development: Shawn Toney
Estimated Sales: $1 - 5,000,000
Number Employees: 1,000-4,999
Other Locations:
GE Lighting
Elmwood Park NJ

23012 GE Water & Process TechnOlogies
4636 Somerton Rd
Feasterville Trevose, PA 19053 215-355-3300
Fax: 215-953-5524 www.gewater.com
CEO: Jeff Garwood
Number Employees: 500-999

23013 GE Water & Process Technologies
4636 Somerton Road
Trevose, PA 19053 866-439-2837
Fax: 602-931-7727 800-446-8004
osmonics@worldnet.att.net www.osmonics.com
Fillers, ceramic
President & CEO: Heiner Markhoff
Engineered Systems Leader: Yuvbir Singh

23014 GEA Evaporation Technologies LLC
9165 Rumsey Rd
Columbia, MD 21045-1929 410-997-8700
Fax: 410-997-5021 info@evaptec.com
www.evaptec.com
President: Eric Bryars
Estimated Sales: $20 Million
Number Employees: 100-249

23015 GEA FES, Inc.
3475 Board Road
York, PA 17406 717-767-6411
Fax: 717-764-3627 800-888-4337
sales.fes@geagroup.com www.geafes.com
Industrial refrigeration equipment for the food and beverage industry.
President: John Ansbro
Vice President Of Finance: Glenn Miller
Quality Control Manager: Jeff Hoch
Vice President Of Marketing: Dennis Halsey
Vice President Int'l Sales/Marketing: Johann Waplinger
Vice President Of Manufacturing: Steve Bennis
Vice President Standard Product Sales: Gary Schrift
Vice President Of Engineering: Greg Kildonas
Number Employees: 20000

23016 GEA FES, Inc.
44840 Les SoriniŠres
York, PA 17406 025-119-1051
Fax: 024-005-7381 geneglace@gea.com
www.geneglace.fr
Industrial refrigeration components.
President: John Ansbro
Service Manager: Randy Keefer

23017 GEA Filtration
1600 Okeefe Rd
Hudson, WI 54016-2290 715-386-9371
Fax: 715-386-9376 info@geafiltration.com
www.geafiltration.com
President: Steve Kathleen
VP: Eric Bryars
Manufacturing Manager: Gerry Nelson
Sales: Bob Keefe
Estimated Sales: $20 - 50 Million
Number Employees: 100-249

23018 GEA Niro Soavi North America
10 Commerce Park North
Building 7
Bedford, NH 03110 603-606-4060
Fax: 603-606-4065 info@niro-soavi.com
www.nirosoavi.com
Manufacturer and supplier of high pressure pumps and homoginizers for the food industry.

23019 GEA PHE Systems NorthAmerica, Inc.
100 Gea Drive
York, PA 17406-8469 717-268-6200
Fax: 717-268-6162 800-774-0474
info.phe-systems.usa@gea.com
www.geaphena.com
Heat exchangers, industrial evaporating equipment, spray dryers
Manager: Steve Lovell
VP Sales: Clemens Starzinski
Estimated Sales: $7 Million
Number Employees: 5-9

23020 GEA Process Engineering,Inc.
9165 Rumsey Road
Columbia, MD 21045 410-997-8700
Fax: 410-997-5021 gea-pe.us@gea.com
www.evaptec.com
Liquid and powder processing equipment for the dairy and food and beverage industries.
President: Eric Bryars

23021 GEA Procomac
1600 O'Keefe Road
Hudson, WI 54016 715-386-9371
Fax: 715-386-9376 800-376-6476
pierpaolo.mattana@niroinc.com
www.niroinc.com

Powder and liquid processing equipment for the dairy and food & beverage industries.

23022 **GEA Refrigeration NorthAmerica, Inc.**
3475 Board Road
York, PA 17406 717-767-6411
Fax: 717-764-3627 800-888-433
sales.gearna@gea.com www.geafes.com
Aseptic processing equipment, pilot plants, batch control systems
President: Ronald Eberhard
Estimated Sales: $1-5 Million
Number Employees: 20

23023 **GEA Refrigeration NorthAmerica, Inc.**
3475 Board Road
York, PA 17406 717-767-6411
Fax: 717-764-3627 800-888-4337
sales.gearna@gea.com www.fessystems.com
Industrial refrigeration equipment
President: Ronald Eberhard
CFO: John Lutz
Quality Control: Jim Mesbitt
VP: Dennis Halsey
Marketing Manager: Teresa Sauble
Sales: John Miranda
Estimated Sales: $500,000 - $1 Million
Number Employees: 250-499

23024 **GEA Tuchenhagen North America, USA, LLC**
90 Evergreen Drive
Portland, ME 04103 207-797-9500
Fax: 207-878-7914 info.TNA@geagroup.com
www.tuchenhagen.us
Process components for the milk processing and beverage industries.
President: David Medlar
Sales Manager: Ulf Thiessen

23025 **GEBO Corporation**
6015 31st Street E
Bradenton, FL 34203-5382 941-727-1400
Fax: 941-727-1200 maury@gebousa.com
www.infogebousa.com
Packaging machinery
Marketing Director: George Rouli
Estimated Sales: $20-50 Million
Number Employees: 100-250

23026 **GED, LLC**
28107 Beaver Dam Branch Rd
Box 140
Laurel, DE 19956-9801 302-856-1756
Fax: 302-856-9888 gedllc@yahoo.com
Importers and exporters of cans, plus dealers of food processing machines and parts
Estimated Sales: $1 - 5 Million
Number Employees: 3

23027 **GEE Manufacturing**
2200 S Golden State Blvd
P.O. Box 397
Fowler, CA 93625 559-834-2929
Fax: 559-834-1715 800-433-1620
info@geemanufacturing.com
www.geemanufacturing.com
Wine industry stainless steel tanks
President and Owner: Glen Gee
Estimated Sales: $5-10 000,000
Number Employees: 20-49

23028 **GEI Autowrappers**
700 Pennsylvania Drive
Exton, PA 19341-1129 610-321-1115
Fax: 610-321-1199
Manufacturer and exporter of electronic flow wrappers
Sales Manager: Richard Landers
Number Employees: 120
Square Footage: 80000
Parent Co: GEI International

23029 **GEI International**
100 Ball Street
East Syracuse, NY 13057 315-463-9261
Fax: 315-463-9034 800-345-1308
info@geionline.com www.geionline.com
Complete food processing and packaging systems
Estimated Sales: $1 - 5 Million

23030 **GEI PPM**
569 W Uwchlan Ave
Exton, PA 19341-1563 610-524-7178
Fax: 610-321-1199 800-345-1308
sales@mateerburt.com www.matberburt.com
Manufacturer and exporter of pressure sensitive and multi-head/in-line rotary labelers
Owner: Jin Guo
Estimated Sales: $1 - 5 Million
Number Employees: 1-4
Square Footage: 320000
Parent Co: GEI International

23031 **GEI Turbo**
700 Pennsylvania Drive
Exton, PA 19341-1129 610-321-1100
Fax: 610-321-1199 800-345-1308
110146.132@compuserve.com
www.mateerburt.com
Manufacturer and exporter of hand-held and automatic high and low temperature filling equipment
Estimated Sales: $1 - 5 Million
Parent Co: GEI International

23032 **GEM Equipment**
2150 Progress Way
P.O.Box 2449
Woodburn, OR 97071-0359 503-982-9902
Fax: 503-981-6316 gem@gemequipment.com
www.gemequipment.com
President: Edward T McKenney
CEO: Steve Ross
Vice President, Sales: Jerry Bell
R&D: Dill Larson
Quality Control: Tony Meehl
Technical Sales: Jim Caughlin
Estimated Sales: $10 - 20 Million
Number Employees: 50-99

23033 **GEMS Sensors & Controls**
1 Cowles Rd
Plainville, CT 06062 860-747-3000
Fax: 860-747-4244 800-378-1600
info@gemsensors.com www.gemssensors.com
Designs and manufacturers a broad portfolio of liquid level, flow and pressure sensors, miniature solenoid valves, and pre-assembled fluidic systems to exact customer application and manufacturing requirements.
President: Alex Joseph
Estimated Sales: H
Number Employees: 250-499

23034 **GEMTEK Products, LLC**
3808 North 28th Avenue
Phoenix, AZ 85107 602-265-8586
Fax: 602-265-7241 800-331-7022
info@gemtek.com www.gemtek.com
Manufacturer and supplier of safe solvents, cleaners, and lubrications
President: Kim Kristoff
Other Locations:
Manufacturing Plant
Hayward CA
Manufacturing Plant
Mecedonia OH

23035 **GEO Graphics-Spegram**
PO Box 305
Mystic, CT 06355-0305 860-572-8507
Fax: 860-536-3961 gspmystic@gsptoday.com
www.gsptoday.com
Wine industry labelers
CEO: Erik H Ljungberg
Estimated Sales: $10-20 Million
Number Employees: 10-19

23036 **GERM-O-RAY**
1641 Lewis Way
Stone Mountain, GA 30083-1107 770-939-2835
Fax: 770-621-0100 800-966-8480
sales@insect-o-cutor.com
www.insect-o-cutor.com
Manufacturer and exporter of air disinfection fixtures and germicidal fluorescent, UV and UVC lamps; available in in-room, in-duct and custom styles
CEO: Bill Harris
Marketing Director: J Harris
Advertising: D Johnson
Systems Engineer: J Baum
Estimated Sales: $1 - 3 Million
Number Employees: 10-19
Brands:
Germ-O-Ray

23037 **GFI Stainless**
2084 Lapham Drive
Building A
Modesto, CA 95354-3909 209-571-1684
Fax: 209-571-2445 800-221-2652
sales@gfistainless.com www.gfistainless.com
Wine industry fluid handling products
President: Gordon Fluker
Vice President: Fred Elwood
Estimated Sales: $1-2.5 Million
Number Employees: 20-49

23038 **(HQ)GHM Industries**
100 Sturbridge Road
Charlton, MA 01507 508-248-3941
Fax: 508-792-0716 800-793-7013
info@millerproducts.net www.millerproducts.net
Manufacturer and exporter of textile machinery including automatic roll wrappers and polywraps
President: Paul Jankovic
Estimated Sales: $2.5-5 Million
Number Employees: 20-49

23039 **GJ Glass Company**
1019 Lincoln Street
Cedar Falls, IA 50613-3248 319-266-4444
Fax: 319-266-2041 800-422-8807

23040 **GKI Foods**
7926 Lochlin Road
Brighton, MI 48116 248-486-0055
Fax: 248-486-9135 chuck@gkifoods.com
www.gkifoods.com
Milk chocolate, sugar free chocolate, yogurt and cards products, panned and enrobed, bulk or packaged. Also produces custom granola (all natural, highly nutritional, low in fat and fat free), trail mixes, etc. Custom formulation. Aidcertified, GMP and HACCP accreditation.
President: Sue Wilts
General Manager: Jim Frazier
Number Employees: 20-49
Square Footage: 30000
Type of Packaging: Consumer, Private Label, Bulk

23041 **GKL**
20910 PeachTree Road
Dickerson, MD 20842-9159 301-948-5538
Fax: 301-972-7641 GKandL@aol.com
www.gkandl.com
Grease interceptors, floor sinks and solid strainers for restaurants
Owner: Gene Wilkes
Estimated Sales: $1-2.5 Million
Number Employees: 1-4
Brands:
Renn

23042 **GL Packaging Products**
1135 Carolina Dr
West Chicago, IL 60185 630-231-5440
Fax: 630-231-5447 866-935-8755
info@glpackaging.com www.glpackaging.com
Corrugated and wooden pallets
President: Todd Tomala
Sales Director: Len Kats
Operations Manager: Dale Komarek
Estimated Sales: $5 - 10 Million
Number Employees: 20-49
Square Footage: 160000

23043 **GLG Life Tech Corporation**
999 Canada Place
Suite 519 World Trade Centre
Vancouver, BC V6C 3E1 604-641-1368
Fax: 604-844-2830 info@glglifetech.com
www.glglifetech.com
Manufacturers all-natural sweetener, stevia extract
President: Brian Palmieri
CEO: Luke Zhang
Estimated Sales: $58 Million
Number Employees: 50-99

23044 **(HQ)GM Nameplate**
2040 15th Ave W
Seattle, WA 98119 206-284-2200
Fax: 206-284-3705 800-366-7668
webnet@gmnameplate.com
www.gmnameplate.com

Manufacturer and exporter of nameplates, labels, membrane switches, injection and compression molding.
President: Brad Root
Chairman & CEO: Donald Root
New Product Manager: Dennis Cook
Research & Development: Debbie Anderson
Marketing Manager: Shannon Kirk
VP Sales & Marketing: Gerry Gallagher
Operations Executive: Mark Samuel
Plant/Production Manager: Marc Doan
Purchasing Agent: Jim Davis
Square Footage: 560000
Other Locations:
Elite Plastics Division
Beaverton OR
Canada Division
Surrey BC
California Division
San Jose CA
North Carolina Division
Monroe NC
SuperGraphics Division
Seattle WA
Brands:
Color Cal
Mark Cal
Poly Cal

23045 GMF
9201 NW 78th
St Weatherby Lake, MO 64152 816-505-9900
Fax: 816-505-9995 mark.mckee@andritz.com
www.andritzgouda.com
GMF-Gouda supplies specialized machinery to the chemical and food industries.
President: Mark Mc Kee
Estimated Sales: $.5 - 1 million
Number Employees: 170
Parent Co: ANDRITZ Separation

23046 GN Thermoforming Equipment
345 Old Trunk 3
PO Box 710
Chester, NS B0J 1J0
Canada 902-275-3571
Fax: 902-275-3100 gn@gncanada.com
www.gnplastics.com
President: Georg Nemeskeri
Quality Manager: Curtis Dowe
Marketing Manager: Jerome Romkey
Sales Representative: Colin MacDonald
Number Employees: 100+

23047 GNT USA
660 White Plains Rd
Tarrytown, NY 10591 914-332-6663
Fax: 914-524-0681 877-468-8727
info@gntusa.com www.gnt-group.com
GNT manufactures Exberry natural colors and Nutrifood fuit and vegetable extracts.
President and CEO: Stefan Hake
Marketing: Jeannette O'Brien
Parent Co: GNT International B.V.
Type of Packaging: Food Service, Private Label, Bulk

23048 GOE/Avins Fabricating Company
60 John Glenn Dr
Amherst, NY 14228-2118 716-691-7012
Fax: 716-691-8202 info@goe-spray.com
www.avinsfab.com
President: Gerald Bogdan
Estimated Sales: $100+ Million
Number Employees: 20-49

23049 GP 50
2770 Long Rd
Grand Island, NY 14072 716-773-9300
Fax: 716-773-5019 meltsales@gp50.com
www.gp50.com
Controls: transducers and transmitters
President: Donald Less
Vice President: Ken Brodie
Director: Bob Atwood
Director: Bob Atwood
Estimated Sales: $10-20 000,000
Number Employees: 50-99
Square Footage: 30000

23050 GP Plastics Corporation
8900 NW 77th Court
Medley, FL 33166-2102 305-888-3555
Fax: 305-885-4204
Extruded polyethylene products including trash and produce bags
Division Manager: Pam Hauserman
Manager (Southeast): Elaine Kurau
Plant Manager: Bob Riber
Estimated Sales: $20-50 Million
Number Employees: 100-249

23051 GPI USA LLC.
10062 190th Place
Suite 107
Mokena, IL 60448 706-850-7826
Fax: 708-785-0608 800-929-4248
karen.haley@foodgums.com www.gpiglobal.net
Specialize in carageenan used for stabilization and as an additive for both dairy products and in the red meat and poultry industries.

23052 GSC Blending
3600 Atl Ind Pkwy NW
Atlanta, GA 30331 404-696-6200
Fax: 404-696-4546 800-453-9997
SShapiro@gaspiceco.com www.gaspiceco.com
President/Owner: Selma Shapiro
President: Robert S Shapiro
Estimated Sales: $10 - 20 Million
Number Employees: 16

23053 GSC Packaging
3715 Atlanta Industrial Pkwy
Atlanta, GA 30331-1049 404-505-9925
Fax: 404-696-2667 800-453-9997
gaspice1@aol.com www.gscpackaging.com
President and CEO: Robert Shapiro
Estimated Sales: $10 - 20 Million
Number Employees: 20-49

23054 GSMA Division of SWF Co
1949 E. Manning Avenue
Suite 5
Reedley, CA 93654 559-638-8484
Fax: 559-38 -478 800-344-8951
info@swfcompanies.com
www.swfcompanies.com
Automated robotics, barcode scanners, proofreaders
President: Roland Parker
Vice President / General Manager: Ed Suarez
Product Manager - Robotics: Matt Garcia
AMP Manager: Mark Freitas
Product Manager: Craig Friesen
General Manager: Mark Senti
Estimated Sales: $1-5 Million
Number Employees: 10

23055 GSW Jackes-Evans Manufacturing Company
4427 Geraldine Avenue
Saint Louis, MO 63115-1217 314-385-4132
Fax: 314-385-0802 800-325-6173
Manufacturer, importer and exporter of barbecue equipment and accessories
President: Rob Harris
BBQ Products: Joe Fernandez
Director Sales (Heating Products): Ron Bailey
Number Employees: 200
Square Footage: 250000
Parent Co: GSW
Type of Packaging: Consumer, Private Label, Bulk
Brands:
Chef Shop
E-Z Fit Barbecue
Party Chef
Super Chef

23056 GT International
1400 Post Oak Boulevard
Suite 270
Houston, TX 77056-3008 713-494-8779
Fax: 713-629-8908
Plasic pallets, plastic crates, bottled water
Estimated Sales: $500,000-$1 000,000
Number Employees: 1-4

23057 GTCO CalComp
14557 N. 82nd Street
Scottsdale, AZ 85260 410-381-3450
Fax: 480-948-5508 800-856-0732
calcomp.sales@gtcocalcomp.com
www.calcomp.com
Manufacturer and exporter of wide-format graphic printers and tablets
Sales Director: Kim Plasterer
VP Sales: Don Lightfoot
Number Employees: 1,000-4,999
Parent Co: eInstruction
Type of Packaging: Food Service

23058 GTI
12650 W 64th Ave # F
Arvada, CO 80004-3887 303-420-6699
Fax: 303-420-6699 gbott@sofseam.com
www.greatclips.com
Manufacturer and exporter of seamers
President: Charlie Simpson
Chairman of the Board: Ray Barton
Vice President: Michelle Sack
Senior Vice President of Operations: Steve Hockett
Estimated Sales: $1 - 5 Million
Brands:
Ease Out

23059 GW&E Global Water & Energy
2404 Rutland Drive
Austin, TX 78758 512-697-1930
Fax: 512-697-1931 info@gwaterenergy.com
www.gwaterenergy.com
Supplier of wastewater treatment and bio-waste-to-energy solutions with sludge management, scrubbing & utilizations sytems, reuse/reclaim water systems, and biological treatments.

23060 Gabriel Container Company
PO Box 3188
Santa Fe Springs, CA 90670 562-699-1051
Fax: 323-699-3284
Corrugated containers
President: Ronald Gabriel
Estimated Sales: $20-50 Million
Number Employees: 100-249

23061 Gabriella Imports
5100 Prospect Ave
Cleveland, OH 44103 216-432-3651
Fax: 216-432-3654 800-544-8117
info@gabimports.com www.gabimports.com
Manufacturer, importer and exporter of automatic espresso equipment and granita machines and products
Estimated Sales: $500,000-$1 Million
Number Employees: 35
Brands:
Gabriella

23062 Gadren Machine Company
PO Box 117
Mount Ephraim, NJ 08059-0117 856-456-4329
Fax: 856-456-2238 800-822-4233
gadreninfo@comcast.net
www.gadrenmachine.com
Wine industry valves and fittings
Estimated Sales: $3 Million
Number Employees: 20

23063 Gaetano America
9460 Telstar Ave
El Monte, CA 91731-2904 626-442-2858
Fax: 626-401-1988 gaetanorf@aol.com
Manufacturer and exporter of ceramic bowls, platters, serving pieces and dinnerware
Owner: Irving Chait
VP Sales/Marketing: Rick Frovich

23064 Gafco-Worldwide
6302 Harrison Avenue
Suite 5
Cincinnati, OH 45247-6413 513-574-2257
Fax: 513-574-2362 gafcoww@aol.com
Accumulating conveyors and bar code scanners, spare parts, export management brewery and soft drink applications
President: Frank May
Estimated Sales: $5-10 000,000
Number Employees: 9

23065 Gage Industries
P.O.Box 1318
Lake Oswego, OR 97035 503-639-2177
Fax: 503-624-1070 800-443-4243
sales@gageindustries.com
www.gageindustries.com
Manufacturer and exporter of plastic thermoformed packaging products including freezable and dual-ovenable food trays, cutting trays, totes, plastic containers, etc
President: Jeff Gage
Executive VP: Lizbeth Gage
Sales: Scott Tullis

Estimated Sales: $50 - 100 Million
Number Employees: 250-499
Number of Brands: 3
Number of Products: 70
Square Footage: 200000
Type of Packaging: Consumer, Food Service, Private Label, Bulk
Brands:
Gage

23066 **Gainco, Inc.**
1635 Oakbrook Dr
Gainesville, GA 30507 770-534-0703
Fax: 770-534-1865 800-467-2828
Sales@gainco.com www.gainco.com
Portion sizing and distribution equipment, sorting, counting, weighing, and bagging systems, as well as bench and floor scales for the poultry, meat and food processing industries.

23067 **Gainesville Neon & Signs**
618 S Main St
Gainesville, FL 32601 352-376-2750
Fax: 352-373-5734 800-852-1407
sales@gainesvilleneon.com
www.gainesvilleneon.com
Lighted signs including neon, wooden, vinyl, luminous tube and billboard
Owner: Daryl Tomlinson
General Manager: Robert Jammer
Estimated Sales: Below $5 Million
Number Employees: 10-19
Square Footage: 20000

23068 **Gainesville Welding & Rendering Equipment**
37 Henry Grady Hwy
Dawsonville, GA 30534-5717 706-216-2666
Fax: 706-216-4282 gwrendering@syclone.net
www.gwrendering.com
Cookers, dryers, prebakers, presses, tanks and storage units
Owner: Terry Stephens
Estimated Sales: $500,000-$1 000,000
Number Employees: 10-19
Type of Packaging: Bulk

23069 **Galaxy Chemical Corporation**
2041 Whitfield Park Ave
Sarasota, FL 34243-4085 941-755-8545
Fax: 941-751-9412 gccgps@aol.com
Manufacturer and exporter of hand cleaners
Owner: Allan M Sanger
Manager: Tim San
Estimated Sales: $5 - 10 Million
Number Employees: 10 to 19

23070 **Galbraith Laboratories**
2323 Sycamore Drive
Knoxville, TN 37921-1750 865-546-1335
Fax: 865-546-7209 877-449-8797
labinfo@galbraith.com www.galbraith.com
Consultant specializing in chemical microanalyses and analyses for all elements including trace analyses, TOX, ION chromatography, ICP metal scans and molecular weights
President: Brenda Saylor Thornburgh
CFO: Jim Cunnings
Senior VP: Lee Bates
Quality Control: Robert Logan
Estimated Sales: $10 - 20 Million
Number Employees: 50-99
Square Footage: 17000

23071 **(HQ)Galbreath LLC**
461 East Rosser Road
Winamac, IN 46996 574-946-6631
sales@wastequip.com
www.galbreath-inc.com
Manufacturer and exporter of detachable container systems, roll-off hoists and recycling containers, lugger boxes, self-dumping hoppers, dock carts, material-handling equipment, compactors, utility, trailers and balers
Chief Technology Officer: Lbehny Podell
Estimated Sales: $10 Million
Number Employees: 75
Square Footage: 250000
Parent Co: Wastequip, Inc.
Other Locations:
Galbreath
Ider AL
Brands:
Combo-Pack
Pack-Man
Super Pack-Man

23072 **Gallard-Schlesinger Industries**
245 Newtown Road
Plainview, NY 11803-4316 516-683-6900
Fax: 516-683-6990 800-645-3044
info@gallard.com www.gallard.com
Chemicals for food products
President: Karl Dorn
CFO: Jelle Westra
Quality Control: Henry Medello
Estimated Sales: $20 - 50 Million
Number Employees: 40

23073 **Galley**
50 South US Highway One
Jupiter, FL 33477-5107 561-748-5200
Fax: 561-748-5250 800-537-2772
galley@galleyline.com www.galleyline.com
Manufacturer and exporter of modular and mobile cafeteria and buffet equipment, salad bars, hot food tables and portable freezers
President: Alice Spritzer
CEO: Larry Spritzer
Estimated Sales: $500,000-$1 Million
Number Employees: 1-4
Square Footage: 11000
Brands:
Galley
Galley Line
Mate-Lock

23074 **Gallimore Industries**
PO Box 158
Lake Villa, IL 60046 847-356-3331
Fax: 847-356-6224 800-927-8020
mark@gallimoreinc.com
www.gallimoreindustriesinc.com
Manufacturer and exporter of in-pack coupons and coupon inserters
President: Claris Gallimore
CEO: C Clay Gallimore
Quality Control: Mark Gallimore
Equip. VP/Production Manager: Kent Gallimore
Print VP/Production Manager: Mark Gallimore
Estimated Sales: Below $5 Million
Number Employees: 10-19
Square Footage: 21000

23075 **Gallo Manufacturing Company**
3600 S Memorial Dr
Racine, WI 53403 262-752-9950
Fax: 262-752-9951 info@gallomfg.com
www.gallomfg.com
Manufacturer and exporter of resealable plastic bag sealers
President: Mary Sollman
VP: Thomas Sollman
Estimated Sales: $1 - 2.5 Million
Number Employees: 10-19
Square Footage: 16000
Brands:
Easy-Lock

23076 **Galvinell Meat Co., Inc.**
461 Ragan Rd
Conowingo, MD 21918 410-378-3032
galvinell@zoominternet.net
www.galvinell.com
Custom meat processor, also cooker services and products and private label, custom slaughtering, and party platters, salads, charcoal and ice also available. Beef, pork, goat, and lamb.
President: Dennis Welsh
Estimated Sales: $730 Thousand
Number Employees: 12
Type of Packaging: Consumer, Food Service, Private Label, Bulk

23077 **Gamajet Cleaning Systems**
604 Jeffers Circle
Exton, PA 19341-2524 610-408-9940
Fax: 610-408-9945 800-289-5387
sales@gamajet.com www.gamajet.com
Manufacturer and exporter of tank cleaning equipment and CIP systems for fermenters, reactors, tank trucks, storage tanks and industrial process vessels
Chairman of the board: Robert E Delaney
Chairman: Robert Delaney
Sales/Customer Service: Linda Chappell
Estimated Sales: $1-2.5 Million
Number Employees: 10-19
Square Footage: 19200
Parent Co: Alfa Laval Group
Brands:
Gamajet

23078 **Game Cock Chemical Company**
23 Plowden Mill Rd
Sumter, SC 29153-8909 803-773-7391
Fax: 803-775-8362
Sweeping compounds
Owner: George Self Jr
General Manager: Tommy Self
Estimated Sales: $1-2.5 Million
Number Employees: 5-9
Square Footage: 9500

23079 **Gamewell Corporation**
251 Crawford Street
Northborough, MA 01532-1234 508-231-1400
Fax: 508-231-0900 888-347-3269
gamewellco@aol.com www.gamewell.com
Manufacturer and exporter of fire alarm systems
President: Bill Abraham
Estimated Sales: $20-50 Million
Number Employees: 50-99

23080 **Gamse Lithographing Company**
7413 Pulaski Hwy
Baltimore, MD 21237 410-866-4700
Fax: 410-866-5672 gamse@gamse.com
www.gamse.com
Wine industry label design
President: Daniel Canzoniero
CFO: Shelly Welling
Vice President: Ivan Sigris
Marketing Director: Joan Ziegler
Production Manager: Bob Markel
Estimated Sales: $20 - 50 Million
Number Employees: 100-249

23081 **Ganau America**
21900 Carneros Oak Lane
Sonoma, CA 95476 707-939-1774
Fax: 707-939-0671 800-694-CORK
carla@italcork.com www.ganauamerica.com
Wine industry corks and cork stoppers
President: Marella Ganau
Sales Consultant: Kerry Smith
Accounting Manager: Gina Isi
Estimated Sales: $1-2.5 Million
Number Employees: 10-19

23082 **Ganeden Biotech**
5915 Landerbrook Dr
Suite 304
Mayfield Hts, OH 44124 440-229-5200
Fax: 440-229-5240 info@ganedenlabs.com
www.ganedenlabs.com
Probiotic ingredients.
Chairman: Ken Alibek
CEO: Andy Lefkowitz
VP Finance: Louise Hansbury
COO: Victor Peroni
VP of Business Development: Michael Bush
VP of Marketing: Marshall Fong
Sales Manager: Sherrie Mandanhall
Public Relations Manager: Gail Fein
Operations Director: David Maske
Estimated Sales: $15 Million

23083 **Gann Manufacturing**
1607 Wicomico St
Baltimore, MD 21230-1705 410-752-5040
Fax: 410-727-3521 800-922-9832
ganncorp@erols.com www.safetysupply.com
Safety products including gloves, liners, rainwear, boots and disposable clothing
CEO: Stuart Levin
Exec. Sales: Grace Gracey
Estimated Sales: $2.5-5 Million
Number Employees: 1-4

23084 **Gannett Outdoor of New J**
185 Us Highway 46
Fairfield, NJ 07004-2321 973-575-6900
Fax: 973-808-8316
george.gross@viacomoutdoor.com
www.viacomoutdoor.com
Outdoor advertising items including bulletins, posters and backlights
VP: George Gross
Local Sales Manager: Gerald Allen
VP/General Sales Manager: Seth Bosin

Estimated Sales: $1 - 5 Million
Number Employees: 100-249
Parent Co: Gannett Company

23085 Ganz Brothers
12 Mulberry Ct
Paramus, NJ 07652 201-845-6010
Fax: 201-384-1329 staff@ganzbrothers.com
Manufacturer and exporter of wrapping machinery including high speed, paperboard, multipack and shrink film for cans, bottles, cups and tubs
President: Christopher Ganz
VP: Jay Ganz
VP: Jay Ganz
Manager: Lisa Noch
Estimated Sales: $2.5-5 Million
Number Employees: 19
Square Footage: 12000

23086 Gar Products
170 Lehigh Ave
Lakewood, NJ 08701 732-364-2100
Fax: 732-370-5021 800-424-2477
elliotb@garproducts.com www.garproducts.com
Manufacturer and exporter of indoor and outdoor barstools, chairs, tables and bases; importer of chair frames and table base castings
President: Jay Garfunkel
Vice President: Ellen Garfunkle
Quality Control: Sam Garfunkle
Sales Director: Elliot Bass
Operations Manager: Sam Garfunkle
Plant Manager: Jose Lopez
Purchasing Manager: Daniel Hyams
Number Employees: 100-249
Square Footage: 150000

23087 Garb-El Products Company
240 Michigan St
Lockport, NY 14094 716-434-6010
Fax: 716-434-9148 800-242-7235
jcarbonejr@garb-el.com www.garb-el.com
Manufacturer and exporter of food waste disposal equipment and prep stations
VP: Deborah Carbone
Estimated Sales: $1-2.5 Million
Number Employees: 10-19
Square Footage: 15000
Brands:
Garb-El

23088 Gardenville Signs
4622 Hazelwood Ave
Baltimore, MD 21206-2812 410-485-4800
Fax: 410-485-4805 www.gardenvillesigns.com
Electric signs
Owner: Conley D Reems
Marketing: Conley Reams
Estimated Sales: $500,000-$1 Million
Number Employees: 5 to 9

23089 Gardiner Paperboard
721 Water Street
Gardiner, ME 04345-2013 207-582-3230
Fax: 207-582-8207
Paper board
CEO: Jeffrey Hinderliter
Estimated Sales: $20-50 Million
Number Employees: 50-99
Parent Co: Newark Group

23090 Gardner Denver Inc.
2150 Islington Avenue
Suite 207
Toronto, ON M9P 3V4
Canada 416-763-4681
Fax: 416-763-0440 www.gardnerdenver.com
Manufacturer and exporter of centrifugal blowers, stationary vacuum cleaners and can and bottle dryers
VP: R Mears
VP and General Manager: Robert Mears
Number Employees: 3

23091 Gardner Denver Inc.
2150 Islington Avenue
Suite 207
Toronto, ON M9P 3V4 416-763-4681
Fax: 416-763-0440 www.gardnerdenver.com
Manufacturer and exporter of industrial vacuum cleaners, blowers, exhausters, continuous cleaning filtration and pneumatic conveyor systems, etc
VP: R Mears
VP and General Manager: Robert Mears

Estimated Sales: $5-10 Million
Number Employees: 20-49
Square Footage: 168000
Brands:
Turbo Clean
Turbo Flow

23092 Gardner Manufacturing Company
1201 West Lake Street
Horicon, WI 53032 920-485-4303
Fax: 920-485-4370 800-242-5513
edm@gardnermfg.com www.gardnermfg.com
Manufacturer and exporter of insect electrocuting systems, traps and lamps
Owner: John S Jones
Quality Control: Mark Sullivan
Sales Division: Robert Marschke
Estimated Sales: $10 - 20 Million
Number Employees: 100-249
Square Footage: 95000
Brands:
Zap

23093 Garland Commercial Ranges Ltd.
1177 Kamato Road
Mississauga, ON L4W 1X4 905-624-0260
info@garland-group.com
www.garland-group.com
Manufacturer and exporter of commercial cooking equipment including ranges, ovens, gas and electric broilers and griddles; custom cooking equipment available
CFO: Angelo Ascidne
CEO: Dale Kostick
Senior VP: Dale Kostick
Regional Manager: Jeff McGowan
Number Employees: 250-499
Number of Brands: 2
Number of Products: 1005
Square Footage: 904000
Parent Co: ENODIS

23094 Garland Commercial Ranges
1177 Kamato Road
Mississauga, ON L4W 1X4
Canada 905-624-0260
Fax: 905-624-5669 keith@garland-group.com
www.garland-group.com
Commercial holding, warming and cooking equipment including ranges, ovens, gas and electric broilers, griddles, steam cookers and fryers; also, warming and ventilation equipment
President: Jack Seguin
CFO: Angelo Ascione
Quality Control: Keith Milmine
Group VP Sales/Marketing: Ian Osborne
Regional Manager: Jeff McGowan
Number Employees: 300
Parent Co: Welbilt Corporation

23095 Garland Floor Company
4500 Willow Pkwy
Cleveland, OH 44125-1042 216-883-4100
Fax: 216-883-9076 800-321-2395
intl@garlandfloor.com www.garlandfloor.com
Industrial flooring, thermal-shock/chemical resistant flooring systems
CEO: Byron Smith
Estimated Sales: $10-20 Million
Number Employees: 20-49

23096 Garland Truffles, Inc.
3020 Ode Turner Rd
Hillsborough, NC 27278 919-732-3041
Fax: 919-732-6037 sheila@garlandtruffles.com
www.garlandtruffles.com
Mushrooms including rare truffle mushrooms, also, truffle tree nursery
Estimated Sales: $1.6 Million
Number Employees: 11
Type of Packaging: Food Service

23097 Garland Writing Instruments
1 S Main St
Coventry, RI 02816-5757 401-821-1450
Fax: 401-823-7460 sales@garlandpen.com
www.garlandpen.com
Quality writing instruments and accessories. USA-made writing collections offer a full color logo top. All writing instruments and accessories can be customized
President: Louise Lanoie
VP: Kevin Bittle

Estimated Sales: $10 - 20 Million
Number Employees: 20-49
Number of Brands: 1
Square Footage: 65000

23098 Garman Company
401 Marshall Rd
Valley Park, MO 63088-1817 636-923-2121
Fax: 636-923-2144 800-466-5150
nancyl@vapcoproducts.com
www.vapcoproducts.com
Ice machine cleaners.
President: Scott Garner
Research & Development: Dr Joseph Raible
Marketing Director: Nancy Leppo
Sales Director: Bill Taylor
Estimated Sales: $2.5-5 Million
Number Employees: 10 to 19
Type of Packaging: Private Label
Brands:
Blow Out
Foaming Coil

23099 Garrity Equipment Compan
31 Georgia Trl
Medford, NJ 08055-8938 609-953-0007
Fax: 609-953-0022 markg8@yahoo.com
Dryers, drum, fluid bed, roller, spray, tunner, fillers, filtration equipment, heat exchangers, homogenizers, ice cream equipment, margarine processing equipment, custom fabrication, distributed control systems, processing andpackaging, pilot plants
Estimated Sales: $500,000-$1 000,000
Number Employees: 1

23100 Garroutte
830 NE Loop 410 # 203
San Antonio, TX 78209-1207 210-826-2321
Fax: 210-824-5253 888-457-4997
sales@garroutte.com www.garroutte.com
Manufacturer and exporter of custom designed food processing equipment
President: Bob Garrett
Sales Support Manager: Richard Knappen
International Rep.: John Wurster
Operations Manager: Dan Southwood
Estimated Sales: $5-10 Million
Number Employees: 5-9
Square Footage: 120000
Brands:
Waterfall Hydrochiller

23101 Garver Manufacturing
224 1/2 N Columbia St
PO Box 306
Union City, IN 47390 765-964-5828
Fax: 765-964-5828 sales@garvermfg.com
www.garvermfg.com
Manufacture a wide variety of industrial centrifuges, bottle shakers, and bottle washers as well as custom equipment.
President: Michael Read
Estimated Sales: $.5 - 1 million
Number Employees: 1-4
Number of Brands: 2
Number of Products: 5
Square Footage: 8000

23102 Garvey Corporation
208 S Route 73
Hammonton, NJ 08037 609-561-2450
Fax: 609-561-2328 800-257-8581
garvey@garvey.com www.garvey.com
Conveyors and accumulators; exporter of conveyor systems and components; also, installation and start-up services available
President: Mark Garvey
VP: William Garvey
Sales: Michael Earling
Estimated Sales: $20 - 50 Million
Number Employees: 50-99
Type of Packaging: Bulk

23103 Garvey Products
871 Redna Terrace
Cincinnati, OH 45215-1174 513-771-8710
Fax: 513-771-5108 info@garveyproducts.com
www.garveyproducts.com

Price marking equipment, pressure sensitive labels, ink cutters, blades and express baskets
President: Rick Gmoch
Quality Control: Dave Ramey
VP: Dennis Feltner
R&D: Dave Ramey
Marketing Director: Dan Cork
Estimated Sales: $5 - 10 Million
Number Employees: 60
Parent Co: Cosco Industries

23104 Garvey Products
5428 Duff Drive
West Chester, OH 45246 513-771-8710
800-543-1908
garveycares@garveyproducts.com
www.garveyproducts.com
Manufacturer and exporter of labeling machinery, marking devices, plastic bags, wire store fixtures, box cutters, machine ribbons, price marking guns and labels
President: Rick Gmoch
Director Sales: James Markham
Estimated Sales: $500,000 - $1 Million
Number Employees: 5-9
Parent Co: Cosco Industries
Brands:
Garvey

23105 Garvis Manufacturing Company
212 E 3rd Street
Des Moines, IA 50309-2006 515-243-8054
Fax: 515-243-1488
Steam cookers
President/Co-Owner: Robert Williams
VP/Co-Owner: Phillip Williams
Estimated Sales: Less than $500,000
Number Employees: 1-4
Parent Co: Fabricon

23106 Gary Manufacturing Company
1124 Bay Blvd Ste A
Chula Vista, CA 91911 619-429-4479
Fax: 619-429-4810 800-775-0804
sales@garymanco.com
www.garymanufacturing.com
Manufacturer and exporter of plastic and fabric table covers, aprons and napkins
Co-Owner: Helen Smith
Estimated Sales: $2.5-5 Million
Number Employees: 5-9
Square Footage: 10000

23107 Gary Plastic Packaging Corporation
3539 Tiemann Ave
Bronx, NY 10469-1636 718-231-4285
Fax: 203-629-1160 800-221-8151
sales@plasticboxes.com www.plasticboxes.com
Manufacturer and exporter of plastic boxes, containers and packaging materials; also, package design service available
Owner: Valerie A Gray
Sales: Rich Satone
Estimated Sales: 25-50 Million
Number Employees: 1-4

23108 Gary Plastic Packaging Corporation
3539 Tiemann Ave
Bronx, NY 10469-1636 718-231-4285
Fax: 203-629-1160 800-227-4279
sales@plasticboxes.com www.plasticboxes.com
Advertising specialties, plastic packaging and candy boxes; exporter of packaging products
Owner: Valerie A Gray
VP: Marilyn Hellinger
Sales: Rich Satone
Estimated Sales: $24 Million
Number Employees: 1-4
Square Footage: 4000
Brands:
Garyline

23109 Gary Sign Company
3289 E 83rd Pl
Merrillville, IN 46410-6542 219-942-3191
Fax: 219-942-3077
Signs and advertising displays
Owner: Paul Grochowski
Estimated Sales: $1-2.5 Million
Number Employees: 5 to 9

23110 Gary W. Pritchard Engineer
5082 Bolsa Ave Ste 112
Huntington Beach, CA 92649 714-893-5441
Fax: 714-893-8405
Food processing machinery and sanitary fittings
President: Gary Pritchard
Sales Manager: Lisa Carlson
Estimated Sales: $1-2,500,000
Number Employees: 19

23111 Gasser Chair Company
4136 Logan Way
Youngstown, OH 44505-1797 330-759-2234
Fax: 330-759-9844 800-323-2234
sales@gasserchair.com www.gasserchair.com
Wood and metal chairs, barstools and tables
President: Gary Gasser
CEO: George Gasser
President: Mark Gasser
VP Sales/Marketing: Cindy Gasser
Estimated Sales: $10-20 Million
Number Employees: 100
Square Footage: 150000

23112 (HQ)Gaston County Dyeing Machine Company
PO Box 308
Stanley, NC 28164 704-822-5000
Fax: 704-827-0476 info@gaston-county.com
www.gaston-county.com
Heat exchangers, pressure vessels, tanks, dryers and electronic assemblies
President: Hubert Craig
CEO: Joseph Mahoney
Advertising Manager: Sally Davis
Operations: Scott Davis
Purchasing: Scott Jonas
Estimated Sales: $20-50 Million
Number Employees: 500-999
Square Footage: 370000

23113 Gastro-Gnomes
22 Brightview Drive
West Hartford, CT 06117-2001 860-236-0225
Fax: 860-236-7967 800-747-4666
gastrognomes@ntalx.net
www.gastrognomes.com
Manufacturer and exporter of plastic and thematic menu stands, menus and pop-out menu inserts
President: Allan Grody
Vice President: Marjorie Grody
Number Employees: 4

23114 Gates
PO Box 90
West Peterborough, NH 03468-0090 603-924-3394
Fax: 603-924-9677 888-543-6316
gatescases@aol.com
Wooden boxes
President: Mike Herz
Marketing Manager: John Naylor
Estimated Sales: $1-2.5 Million
Number Employees: 10-19

23115 Gates Manufacturing Company
6924 Smiley Avenue
Saint Louis, MO 63139 314-647-5662
Fax: 314-645-7003 800-237-9226
bmartin@gatesmfg.com www.gatesmfg.com
Custom commercial kitchen equipment including bins, conveyors, dish tables, refrigerators and tray make-up systems
President: Earl Gates Jr Jr
Marketing/Sales: Robert Martin
Estimated Sales: $5-10 Million
Number Employees: 50

23116 Gates Mectrol
9 Northwestern Dr
Salem, NH 03079 603-890-1515
Fax: 603-890-1616 800-394-4844
contact@gatesmectrol.com
www.gatesmectrol.com
Timing pulleys and polymer based automation components and synchronous timing belts.

23117 Gates Rubber Company
P.O.Box 5887
Denver, CO 80217 303-744-1911
Fax: 303-744-4443 www.gates.com
Wine industry transfer hoses
President: John Bohenick
Estimated Sales: $1 - 2 Billion
Number Employees: 10,000

23118 Gateway Packaging Company
5910 Winner Rd
Kansas City, MO 64125 816-483-9800
Fax: 816-483-4169
marketing@gatewaypackaging.com
Multiwall, small and specialty paper bags
Owner: Roger Miller
VP/CFO: Judy Samayda
Estimated Sales: $1 - 5 Million
Number Employees: 100-249
Square Footage: 150000

23119 Gateway Packaging Corporation
P.O.Box 33
Murrysville, PA 15668 412-241-7278
Fax: 724-325-7447 888-289-2693
sales@gatepack.com www.gatepack.com
Corrugated boxes
President: Benjamin Getty
VP: Thomas Gill
General Manager: Scott Getty
Estimated Sales: $10-20 Million
Number Employees: 50-99
Square Footage: 98000

23120 Gateway Plastics
5650 W County Line Rd
Mequon, WI 53092 262-242-2020
Fax: 262-242-7262 www.gatewayplastics.com
Plastic caps and closures, custom plastic packaging
President: Carl Vogel
Marketing/Sales: Bob Proudfoot
Estimated Sales: $20+ Million
Number Employees: 100-249
Number of Brands: 2
Square Footage: 200000
Type of Packaging: Consumer, Food Service, Private Label, Bulk
Brands:
Gateway Closures
Gateway Plastics

23121 Gateway Printing Company
3425 N Ridge Avenue
Arlington Heights, IL 60004-1496 847-394-0625
Fax: 847-727-1200 www.gateway-printing.com
Printing on skin and blister packaging board
General Manager: Bill Waters
CEO: John Rohrer
Estimated Sales: $10-20 Million
Number Employees: 50-99

23122 (HQ)Gatewood Products LLC
814 Jeanette St
3001 Gateman Drive
Parkersburg, WV 26101 304-422-5461
Fax: 304-485-2714 800-827-5461
custserv@gatewoodproducts.com
www.gatewoodproducts.com/
Wood and wood-and-metal containers, pallets, skid shocks and wire-bounds; also, dry warehousing and transportation service available
President/CEO/Vice Chairman: Perry Smith
Estimated Sales: $20-50 Million
Number Employees: 20-49
Square Footage: 1150000

23123 Gavco Plastics
9840 S 219th East Ave
Broken Arrow, OK 74014 918-455-7888
Fax: 918-455-3695 info@GavcoPlastics.com
www.gavcoplastics.com
President: Randall Gavlik
Estimated Sales: $1 - 5 Million
Number Employees: 50-99

23124 Gaychrome Division of CSL
220 Exchange Dr # D
Crystal Lake, IL 60014-6282 815-459-6000
Fax: 815-459-6105 800-873-4370
gaychrome@csltd.com www.csltd.com
Tray stands, high chairs, etc., for the hospitality and food service industries.
President: Jay Maher
Director Sales: Rus Budde
Plant Manager: Joe Mancuso
Purchasing Manager: Sharri Kapaldo
Estimated Sales: $10-20 Million
Number Employees: 20-49
Type of Packaging: Consumer, Food Service, Private Label

23125 **Gaylord Container Corporation**
8700 Adamo Dr
Tampa, FL 33619-3524 813-621-3591
Fax: 813-621-3318 www.templeinland.com
Manufacturer and exporter of corrugated shipping containers, boxes and cartons
Manager: Wayne Parker
Controller: P Wilkins
General Manager: John Thrift
Production Supervisor: R Piepenbring
Estimated Sales: $20-50 Million
Number Employees: 100-249

23126 **Gaylord Container Corporation**
2301 Wilbur Ave
Antioch, CA 94509 925-779-3200
Fax: 925-779-4960 800-727-2699
Wine industry packaging
President: Michael Keough
CEO: Marvin Pomerantz
CFO: Daniel Casey
Senior VP: Lawrence Rogna

23127 **Gaylord Industries**
10900 SW Avery St
Tualatin, OR 97062 503-691-2010
Fax: 503-692-6048 800-547-9696
info@gaylordusa.com www.gaylordusa.com
or more than 75 years, Gaylord's ventilation systems have been known for durability, dependability, and meticulous attention to detail. They continue to revolutionize the industry with groundbreaking new designs as well as aninnovative approach to solving the two main priorities facing foodservice operators: enrg savings and labor optimization.
President: Dan Shoop
CFO: Jeana Randall
R&D: Biucazx Lukins
Estimated Sales: $10 - 20 Million
Number Employees: 100-249
Square Footage: 75000
Brands:
Gaylord

23128 **Gaynes Labs**
9708 Industrial Dr
Bridgeview, IL 60455 708-233-6655
Fax: 708-233-6985 gayneslabs@aol.com
www.gaynestesting.com
Consultant and testing laboratory for packaging materials
President: Yury Beyderman
Estimated Sales: $1-2.5 Million
Number Employees: 10 to 19
Square Footage: 11000

23129 **Ge-No's Nursery**
12285 Road 25
Madera, CA 93637-9013 559-674-4752
Fax: 559-674-3724
Grapevines for wine industry
Manager: Martin Nonin
Estimated Sales: Below $5 000,000
Number Employees: 10-19

23130 **Gea Intec, Llc**
4319 S Alston Ave
Suite 105
Durham, NC 27713 919-433-0131
Fax: 919-433-0140 sales@intecvrt.com
www.intecvrt.com
Single and variable retention time freezers/chillers for the food and beverage industries.
Parent Co: Intec USA

23131 **Geac Computers**
175 Ledge St
Nashua, NH 03060-3107 603-889-5152
Fax: 603-889-7538 rsdinfo@geac.com
www.rsd.geac.com
Point of sales equipment including cash registers
Quality Control: Erwin Yaffie
R&D: Andy Tims
General Manager: David Poole
Purchasing Manager: Michael Wickstrom
Estimated Sales: $20 - 50 Million
Number Employees: 100-249
Parent Co: Geac Computers

23132 **Gebo Conveyors, Consultants & Systems**
1045 Autoroute Chomedey
Laval, QC H7W 4V3
Canada 450-973-3337
Fax: 450-973-3336 aury@gebo-indust.com
www.sidel.com
Manufacturer and exporter of stainless steel tabletop conveying systems and equipment including package line controls, pressure-free combiners, packer infeed systems and line audits
President: Mark Aury
Sales Manager: Jean Dion
Project Director: Mike De Cotiis
Number Employees: 250
Square Footage: 260000
Parent Co: Gebo Industries
Brands:
Gebo

23133 **Gebo Corporation**
6015 31st Street E
Bradenton, FL 34203-5382 941-727-1400
Fax: 941-727-1200 maury@gebousa.com
Manufacturer, importer and exporter of conveyors including air trans and cap feeder
President: Mark Aury
Marketing Director: George Louli
General Manager: Christian Fitsch-Mouras
Estimated Sales: $20-50 Million
Number Employees: 100-249
Square Footage: 40000
Parent Co: Sidel Corporation
Brands:
Flat Top
Garro
Magneroll
Uf Feeder

23134 **Gecko Electronics**
Riedtlistrasse 72
CH-8006
Zurich, SW G2E 5W6
Canada 418-872-4411
Fax: 418-872-0920 contact@gecko-research.com
www.gecko-research.com
President: Michel Authier
R&D: Bemoit Laslamme
Number Employees: 350

23135 **Geerpres**
PO Box 658
Muskegon, MI 49443-0658 231-773-3211
Fax: 231-773-8263 sales@geerpres.com
www.geerpres.com
Manufactures cleaning tools for the maintenance supply industry in a business-to-business environment: steel, stainless steel, plastic, microfiber and metal components.
President: Michael Gluhanich
CFO: Bryan Depree
R&D: Joe Fodrocy
Quality Control: Jeff Kulbe
Marketing Director: Megan Schihl
Sales Director: Ted Moon
Purchasing Manager: Barb McAttnen
Estimated Sales: Below $5 Million
Number Employees: 20-49
Square Footage: 340000

23136 **Gehnrich Oven Sales Company**
PO Box 601
Smithtown, NY 11787-0601 631-585-8787
Fax: 631-585-9285 gehnrich@aol.com
www.gehnrich.thomasregister.com
Manufacturer and exporter of convection baking and cooking ovens
President: Richard Gehnrich
Treasurer: Leon Pedigo, Jr.
VP: Wayne Pedigo
Estimated Sales: $1-2.5 Million
Number Employees: 20-49
Square Footage: 22500
Parent Co: Nevo Corporation

23137 **Geiger**
PO Box 1609
Lewiston, ME 04241 215-672-8782
Fax: 215-773-8336 geigerorders@geiger.com
www.geiger.com
Manufacturer and exporter of advertising specialties
Regional VP East: Fred Snyder
Owner, CEO: Gene Geiger
CFO: Bob Blaisdell
Owner, Executive Vice President: Peter Geiger
V.P. Marketing: Gary Biron
V.P. Sales & Marketing: Jim Habzda
Vice President of Operations: Sheila Olson
Estimated Sales: $500,000 - $1 Million
Number Employees: 1-4
Square Footage: 40000
Brands:
Farmer's Almanac
Time By Design

23138 **Gelberg Signs**
6511 Chillum Pl NW
Washington, DC 20012 202-882-7733
Fax: 202-882-1580 800-443-5237
sales@gelbergsigns.com www.gelbergsigns.com
Menu boards, signs and point of purchase displays
President: Neil A Brami
CFO: Dave Elmore
VP: Neil Brami
Production Manager: Mark McCluney
Estimated Sales: Below $5 Million
Number Employees: 20-49
Square Footage: 25000

23139 **Gem Electric Manufacturing Company**
20 Commerce Dr
Hauppauge, NY 11788-3910 631-273-2230
Fax: 631-273-9876 800-275-4361
Electrical wiring devices and electrical lighting accessories
President: Harvey Cooper
Vice President: Peter Massa
Marketing Director: Neal Massa
Plant Manager: Andy Aqkr
Estimated Sales: Over $10 Million
Number Employees: 30
Number of Brands: 1
Number of Products: 8000
Square Footage: 70000
Parent Co: Gem Electric Manufacturing Company
Type of Packaging: Consumer, Private Label

23140 **Gem Equipment of Oregon**
PO Box 359
Woodburn, OR 97071-0359 503-982-9902
Fax: 503-981-6316 gem@gemequipment.com
www.gemequipment.com
Manufacturer and exporter of blanchers, conveyor systems and components, fryers, dumpers, mixers, preheaters and batter mix systems
President: Edward McKenney
COO: Steve Ross
Vice President of Sales: Jerry Bell
Plant Manager: Ray Rowe
Purchasing Manager: Ray Rowe
Estimated Sales: $20-50 Million
Number Employees: 100-249
Square Footage: 100000

23141 **Gem Refrigerator Company**
7340 Milnor St
Philadelphia, PA 19136-4211 215-426-8700
Fax: 215-426-8731
support@gemrefrigeratorcompany.com
www.gemrefrigeratorcompany.com
Refrigerators and freezers including walk-in and reach-in, also custom boxes
President: Bruce Gruhler
Sales: John Greenwood
Plant Manager/Sales: Tony Iacono
Estimated Sales: $5 - 10 Million
Number Employees: 20 to 49
Square Footage: 40000

23142 **Gemini Bakery EquipmentCompany**
9991 Global Rd
Philadelphia, PA 19115 215-673-3520
Fax: 215-673-3944 800-468-9046
sales@geminibe.com www.geminibe.com
Manufacturer and importer of bakery equipment
President: Mark Rosenberg
Marketing Coordinator: Laura Albright
Estimated Sales: $10-20 Million
Number Employees: 50-99

23143 Gemini Data Loggers
3685 Lakeside Drive
Suite A
Reno, NV 89509-4850 877-799-5199
Fax: 877-799-5198
sales@geminidataloggers.com
www.geminidataloggers.com

23144 Gemini Plastic Films Corporation
535 Midland Ave
Garfield, NJ 07026 973-340-0700
Fax: 973-340-1045 800-789-4732
www.geminiplasticfilms.com
FDA/USDA approved plastic bags, sheeting, tubing, pallet covers and film
President: Richard Hulbert Jr
Marketing/Sales: Frank Fusaro
Maintenance Manager: Pasquale Pavillo
Traffic Manager: Arthur Pirvirotto
Production Manager: Jack Pezdic
Purchasing Manager: Richard Primo
Estimated Sales: $5-10 Million
Number Employees: 20-49
Square Footage: 50000
Type of Packaging: Consumer, Food Service, Private Label, Bulk

23145 Gems Sensors
1 Cowles Rd
Plainville, CT 06062 860-747-3000
Fax: 860-747-4244 www.gemssensors.com
Manufacturer and exporter of conductance actuated liquid level controls including sanitary probes and fittings; also, underground leak detection services available
President: Alex Joseph
Marketing Specialist: Tony Mancin
Estimated Sales: H
Number Employees: 250-499
Square Footage: 29000
Parent Co: Danaher Corporation

23146 Genarom International
41 Mountain Blvd
Warren, NJ 07059-2630 908-753-8484
Fax: 908-753-9635 800-352-8672
dhiller@crfc.com
Owner: Kenny Woo

23147 Gene K. Nelson
12786 Old Redwood Hwy
Healdsburg, CA 95448 707-433-5138
Fax: 707-433-9214
Wine industry wood bungs
Owner: Gene Nelson
*Estimated Sales:*less than $500,000
Number Employees: 1-4

23148 Genecor International
925 Page Mill Road
Palo Alto, CA 94304 650-846-7500
Fax: 585-256-6952 800-847-5311
www.genencor.com
Enzymes, such as amylases, cellulases, xylanases, glucose-oxidase, catalase and proteases
Number Employees: 73

23149 Genemco
4455 Carter Creek Pkwy.
Bryan, TX 77802 979-268-7447
Fax: 979-268-0102 877-268-5865
sales@genemco.com www.genemco.com
Agitation systems, milk and tank, cheese equipment, vacuum chambers, centrifuges, chillers, dryers, drum, fluid bed, roller, spray, tunnel, homogenizers, ice equipment, ingredient feeders, fillers, air gravity, milk, steam, filtrationequipment, flow div
manager: Arnold Amador
Estimated Sales: $500,000-$1 Million
Number Employees: 1-4

23150 General Analysis Corporation
PO Box 528
Norwalk, CT 06856-0528 203-852-8999
Fax: 203-838-1551
Diet and carbonation monitors for soft drink, beer, tea, and juice lines; lab testers for measuring CO2 in packaged beverage products
Estimated Sales: $1 - 5 000,000
Number Employees: 20-50

23151 General Bag Corporation
3368 W 137th St
Cleveland, OH 44111 216-941-1190
Fax: 216-476-3401 800-837-9396
generalbag@aol.com www.generalbag.com
Manufacturer and distributor of all packaging materials paper bags, poly, mesh. Boxes all sizes, bulk and waxed produce cartons; also packaging machinery
President: Rob Sprosty
Sales Manager: Dan Juba
Sales Representative: Larry Sprosty
Estimated Sales: $5 - 10 Million
Number Employees: 20-49
Square Footage: 80000

23152 General Body Manufacturing Company of Texas
7110 Jensen Dr
Houston, TX 77093-8703 713-692-5177
Fax: 713-692-0700 800-395-8585
sales@generalbody.com www.generalbody.com
Truck bodies including van, slide-ins, cold plates and refrigerated
CEO: Barbara Paull
Sales: Clayton Price
Plant Manager: Tollan Maxwell
Estimated Sales: $10 - 20 Million
Number Employees: 50-99

23153 General Cage
238 N 29th St
Elwood, IN 46036-1702 765-552-5039
Fax: 765-552-6962 800-428-6403
www.generalcage.com
Manufacturer and exporter of wire products including forms, specialties, cages, display racks, partitions, grills, etc
Member: Bruce D Cook
Estimated Sales: $10-20 Million
Number Employees: 100-249
Square Footage: 108000

23154 General Chemical Corporation
90 E Halsey Rd Ste 301
Parsippany, NJ 07054 973-515-0900
Fax: 973-515-3232 info@genchemcorp.com
www.gentek-global.com
Industrial specialty and fine chemicals
CEO: William E Redmond Jr
Estimated Sales: G
Number Employees: 1,000-4,999

23155 General Conveyor Company
245 Industrial Parkway South
Auroua, ON L4G 4J9
Canada 905-727-7922
Fax: 905-841-1056 gcc@gccl.com
www.gccl.com
Design and manufacture a wide range of standard and customized conveyors, accumulators, end-of-line automation and custom machinery. Our primary focus is in the food, personal care, pharamceutical, beverage, irrafiation and plasticsmarkets.

23156 General Corrugated Machinery Company
269 Commercial Avenue
Palisades Park, NJ 07650-1154 201-944-0644
Fax: 201-944-7858
70451.2363@compuserve.com
Manufacturer and exporter of corrugated box formers; also, case formers, sealers, case packers and palletizers
Sales Manager: John Lavin
Estimated Sales: $1 - 5 Million
Brands:
Galaxy
Model Cf
Nova

23157 General Cutlery
1918 N County Road 232
Fremont, OH 43420-9595 419-332-2316
Fax: 419-334-7119
Cutlery including knives
President: David Reitz
VP: David Reitz
Estimated Sales: Below $5 Million
Number Employees: 10 to 19
Square Footage: 20000
Brands:
Hard-Edge

23158 General Data Company
P.O.Box 541165
Cincinnati, OH 45254 513-752-7978
Fax: 513-752-6947
mschwietering@general-data.com
www.general-data.com
President: Peter Wenzel
Quality Control: Marsha Doon
Estimated Sales: $20-30 Million
Number Employees: 100-249

23159 General Electric Company
3135 Easton Turnpike
Fairfield, CT 06828 203-373-2211
www.geconsumerandindustrial.com
Household appliances including freezers and garbage disposal units
President & Chief Executive Officer: Ferdinando Beccalli-Falco
CEO: Jeff Immelt
CEO: James P Campbell
VP Marketing: Bruce Albertsons
Estimated Sales: $500,000-$1 Million
Number Employees: 10,000

23160 General Electric Company
Appliance Park
Louisville, KY 40225-0001 502-452-4311
Fax: 502-452-0944
www.geconsumerandindustrial.com
Thermoplastics used in material handling, packaging and logistics systems
CEO: James P Campbell
New Business Development Manager: Bill Featherstone
Estimated Sales: $1 - 5 Million
Number Employees: 10,000

23161 General Equipment & Machinery Company
1617 NW 79th Avenue
Doral, FL 33126-1105 305-471-0802
Fax: 305-471-6196 info@genequipment.com
www.genequipment.com
Machinery for PET stretch blow molding, form-fill seal, injection molding and film shrink wrap packing
Estimated Sales: $2.5-5 Million
Number Employees: 8

23162 General Espresso Equipment Corporation
7912 Industrial Village Rd
Greensboro, NC 27409 336-393-0224
Fax: 336-393-0295 info@geec.com
www.geec.com
Espresso machine cleaners, espresso machines/accessories, espresso pod machines
Owner: Roberto Daltio
Estimated Sales: $500,000-$1 000,000
Number Employees: 5-9

23163 General Films
645 S High St
Covington, OH 45318 937-473-2051
Fax: 937-473-2403 888-436-3456
johnannarino@generalfilms.com
www.generalfilms.com
Manufacturer and exporter of plastic bags, packaging coextruded films and bag-in-box bulk liquid packaging
Chairman of the Board: Roy Weikert
Quality Control: Norman Slade
Sales (Food Pkg.): Linda Lyons
Sales Manager (Industrial Pkg.): Howard Stutzman
Sales (Bag-in-Box): Cindy Grogean
Estimated Sales: $20 - 50 Million
Number Employees: 50-99
Square Footage: 60000
Brands:
Duratuf

23164 General Floor Craft
4 Heights Ter
Little Silver, NJ 07739-1323 973-742-7400
Fax: 973-742-0004 genfloor@juno.com
www.generalfloorcraft.com
Manufacturer and exporter of vacuums and carpet cleaning machinery
Owner: Barry Gore
VP: Jeff Gore
Estimated Sales: $2.5-5 Million
Number Employees: 20-49
Square Footage: 27000

23165 (HQ)General Foam Plastics Corporation
3321 E Princess Anne Rd
Norfolk, VA 23502 757-857-0153
Fax: 757-857-0033 sales@genfoam.com
www.genfoam.com
Styrofoam coolers and plastic novelties
President: George Dieffenbach
Sales: B Andrews
Estimated Sales: $100-500 Million
Number Employees: 500-999
Other Locations:
General Foam Plastics Corp.
San Bernandino IN

23166 General Formulations
309 S Union St
Sparta, MI 49345 616-887-7387
Fax: 616-887-0537 800-253-3664
mclay@generalformulations.com
www.generalformulations.com
Manufacturer and exporter of self-adhesive and floor advertising films
CEO: James Clay
Marketing Manager: Mike Clay
Regional Sales Manager: Jeff Balasko
Estimated Sales: $20-50 Million
Number Employees: 100-249
Square Footage: 100000
Brands:
Permalar
Traffic Graffic

23167 (HQ)General Grinding
801 51st Ave
Oakland, CA 94601 510-261-5557
Fax: 510-261-5567 800-806-6037
ggrind@aol.com www.generalgrindinginc.com
Knife sharpeners; also, replacement parts for machinery including curling and beading rings; repair services available
President: Michael Bardon
Sales Manager: Daniel Bardon
Estimated Sales: $5-10 Million
Number Employees: 20-49
Square Footage: 21000

23168 General Industries
3048 Thoroghfare Road
PO Box 1279
Goldsboro, NC 27533 919-751-1791
Fax: 919-751-8186 888-735-2882
tanks@gitank.com www.gitank.com
Vaulted tire rated, mix/process, above ground and underground steel storage tanks and oil/water separators also carbon steel and stainless steel
President: John Wiggins
Sales Marketing: Nancy Lilly
Purchasing Manager: Jody Vernon
Estimated Sales: $6 Million
Number Employees: 20-49
Square Footage: 80000
Brands:
Fireguard
Permatank

23169 General Machinery Corporation
1831 N 18th Street
PO Box 717
Sheboygan, WI 53082-0717 920-458-2189
Fax: 920-458-8316 888-243-6622
sales@genmac.com www.genmac.com
Manufacturer and exporter of meat and cheese processing equipment including meat flakers, slicers, dicers, mechanical tenderizers, grinders, pork rind chippers and cheese cutters; also, cake and bun slabbers, pan washers and beltconveyors.
President: Michael Horwitz
CFO: Marsha Binversie
VP Operations: Robert Jeske
Production Manager: Gary Mueller
Estimated Sales: $2.5-5 Million
Number Employees: 10-19
Brands:
Cannon
Hydraucuber Super Slicer
Hydrauflakers
M-8 Slitter
Multislicer
Rotary Dicer
S/M Flaker
Sp-250 Flattener
Tenderit
Tu-Way

23170 General Magnaplate Corporation
1331 W Edgar Rd
Linden, NJ 07036 908-862-6200
Fax: 908-862-6110 800-852-3301
info@magnaplate.com www.magnaplate.com
Metal finishing, surface enhancement coatings for food and drug processing and packaging equipment, wear and corrosion resistant coatings for metal parts.
President: Candida Aversenti
CEO: Candida Aversenti
Estimated Sales: $12 Million
Number Employees: 100-249

23171 General Methods Corporation
3012 SW Adams Street
Peoria, IL 61602 309-497-3344
Fax: 309-497-3345 gemco@mtco.com
Manufacturer and exporter of coupon and premium dispensers; also, contract thermoform packaging and seal integrity verification equipment
President: Dale Kuykendall
Chief Tech.: Ken Brackett
Estimated Sales: Less than $500,000
Number Employees: 3
Square Footage: 13000

23172 General Neon Sign Company
900 Buena Vista St
San Antonio, TX 78207-4308 210-227-1203
Fax: 210-227-0067 jk@general-neon.com
www.general-neon.com
Signs including neon, plastic, vinyl, advertising, electric, etc.; also, installation and repair services available
President: Dianna Kaupert
Quality Control: Jason Kaupert
Estimated Sales: Below $5 Million
Number Employees: 10 to 19

23173 General Packaging Equipment Company
6048 Westview Dr
Houston, TX 77055 713-686-4331
Fax: 713-683-3967
gpeinfo@generalpackaging.com
www.generalpackaging.com
Manufacturer and exporter of packaging machinery including bag forming and net weighers
President: Robert C Kelly
Sales: Thomas L Wilson
Estimated Sales: $5-10 Million
Number Employees: 20-49
Square Footage: 33000
Type of Packaging: Consumer, Food Service, Private Label
Brands:
General Packager
Hydrafeed

23174 General Packaging Products
1700 S Canal St
Chicago, IL 60616-1108 312-226-8380
Fax: 312-226-4027 800-621-1921
info@generalpk.com www.generalpk.com
Wrappers and protective packages for food industry
President: William K Kellogg III
CFO: Tom Woods
CEO: William Kellogg
Quality Control: Eric Courtney
Sales (Central Region): Tim Schoolman
VPO: Volney Bunch
Plant Manager: Joe Bunch
Estimated Sales: $10-25 Million
Number Employees: 100-249
Type of Packaging: Private Label

23175 General Packaging Service
43 Samworth Rd
Clifton, NJ 07012-1714 973-472-4900
Fax: 973-471-7579 www.caraustar.com
Contract packager
Manager: Mike Carollo
VP: Jim Walden
Estimated Sales: $20 - 50 Million
Number Employees: 250-499
Square Footage: 90000
Parent Co: Caraustar Industries

23176 General Press Corporation
110 Allegheny Drive
PO Box 316
Natrona Heights, PA 15065-0316 724-224-3500
Fax: 724-224-3934 genpress@generalpress.com
www.generalpress.com
Manufacturer and exporter of die cut paper labels for food and beverage containers; also, heat seal foil lids for single serve jelly cups, injection mold labels and lightweight plastic labels.
President: James Wolff
Sales Manager: David Wolff
VP Operations: T Conroy
Estimated Sales: $5-10 Million
Number Employees: 50-99
Square Footage: 60000

23177 General Processing Systems
12838 Stainless Drive
Holland, MI 49424 616-399-2220
Fax: 616-399-7365 800-547-9370
jswiatlo@nbe-inc.com www.productsaver.com
Manufacturer and exporter of bag opening equipment and custom designed product recovery systems.
President: Ed Swiatlo
Sales Manager: Jeff Swiatlo
Estimated Sales: $3 - 5 Million
Number Employees: 10-19
Square Footage: 40000
Parent Co: General Processing Systems

23178 General Resource Corporation
P.O.Box 470
Dassel, MN 55325-0470 952-933-7474
Fax: 952-933-9777 generalresource@uswest.net
www.generalresourcecorp.com
Airlock, gates, air slides
President: Joseph Pausch
VP: Jim Masterman
Estimated Sales: $1 - 3 Million
Number Employees: 1-4

23179 General Sign Company
2723 North Jackson Highway
Sheffield, AL 35660 256-383-3176
gensign@hiwaay.net
www.generalsignco.com
Identification and deco electrical signage
General Manager: Ted Martin
CEO/President: Lenn Scheibal
Controller: Kris Sneed
Engineer: Dean Precival
Sales Director: Kim Underwood
Estimated Sales: $5-10 Million
Number Employees: 50-99
Square Footage: 280000
Type of Packaging: Bulk

23180 General Sign Company
2723 North Jackson Highway
Sheffield, AL 35660 256-383-3176
gensign@hiwaay.net
www.generalsignco.com
Signs including neon, plastic, porcelain and electric
General Manager: Ted Martin
CFO: Kris Sneed
Sales Contact: Kim Underwood
Estimated Sales: $1 - 2.5 Million
Number Employees: 50-99

23181 General Steel Fabricators
927 S Schifferdecker Ave
Joplin, MO 64801-3528 417-623-2224
Fax: 417-623-2204 800-820-8644
srife2@doanepetcare.com
www.generalsteelfabricators.com
Tanks, bucket elevators and dust and cyclone collectors
Manager: Stan Rife
General Manager: Stan Rife
Assistant General Manager: Paul Howey
Purchasing Manager: Jim Cruzan
Estimated Sales: $10 - 20 Million
Number Employees: 50-99
Square Footage: 40200
Parent Co: Doane Pet Care

23182 General Tank
328 West Front Street
P O Box 488
Berwick, PA 18603-2138 570-752-4528
Fax: 570-752-6121 800-435-8265
ssfab@generaltank.com www.generaltank.com
Conveyors, fittings, pumps, valves, tanks, washers and control systems
President: Dan Bower
Estimated Sales: Below 1 Million
Number Employees: 1-4

23183 **General Tape & Supply**
28505 Automation Blvd
Wixom, MI 48393-3154 248-357-2744
Fax: 248-357-2749 800-490-3633
jhooker@gentape.com www.gentape.com
Manufacturer and exporter of pressure sensitive labels
President: Mary Raden
COO: Jack Hooker
Research & Development: Debbie Wojcik
Sales Director: Julie Stallings
Estimated Sales: $2.5 - 5 Million
Number Employees: 30

23184 **General Trade Mark Labelcraft**
55 Lasalle St
Staten Island, NY 10303 718-448-9800
Fax: 718-448-9808 gtm@bigfoot.com
www.incrediblelabels.com
Embossed and printed labels, price tag seals and stickers; exporter of printed labels
Owner: Richard Capuozzo
CEO: V Kruse
Estimated Sales: $10 - 20 Million
Number Employees: 20-49
Square Footage: 20000
Brands:
Sure-Stik

23185 **General Wax & Candle Company**
6863 Beck Ave
North Hollywood, CA 91605 818-765-5800
Fax: 818-765-0555 800-929-7867
www.genwax.com
Manufacturer and exporter of candles
VP: Mike Tapp
Estimated Sales: $10 - 15 Million
Number Employees: 50-99
Type of Packaging: Food Service

23186 **General, Inc**
3355 Enterprise Ave.
Suite 160
Weston, FL 33331 954-202-7419
Fax: 954-202-7337 info@generalfoodservice.com
www.generalfoodservice.com
Manufacturer, importer and exporter of slicers, grinders and mixers; manufacturer of food and organic waste disposers
President: John Westbrook
VP Sales/Marketing: Harry Ristan
Purchasing Manager: Dean Council
Estimated Sales: $5-10 Million
Number Employees: 100-249
Square Footage: 80000
Parent Co: Standex International Corporation
Type of Packaging: Food Service
Brands:
General Slicing

23187 **Genesee Corrugated**
PO Box 7716
Flint, MI 48507-0716 810-235-6120
Fax: 810-235-0350
Manufacturer and exporter of corrugated shipping containers and interior packing materials
President: Willie Artis
Material Control: Bobbi Jackson
Estimated Sales: $23.1 Million
Number Employees: 325
Type of Packaging: Bulk

23188 **Genesis Machinery Products**
400 Eagleview Blvd Ste 100
Exton, PA 19341 610-458-4900
Fax: 610-458-4939 800-552-9980
gmp@genesismachinery.com
www.genesismachinery.com
President: Bruce Smith
CFO: Bill Seiler
Estimated Sales: $5 - 10 000,000
Number Employees: 20-49

23189 **Genesis Total Solutions**
3524 Decatur Highway
Suite 104
Fultondale, AL 35209-8314 205-877-3228
Fax: 205-877-3224 gts@gts-genesis.com
www.genesis.com
rovides quality software solutions to the Food & Beverage Industry for over 35 years. We have users located throughout the United States, in Canada and overseas. Our applications include Accounting, Distribution, Production, and OrderFulfillment. All of our applications were developed by, and are supported through our staff of responsive professionals. Our solutions were designed to address the specific requirements of the F/B industry and an be used by both large and smallbusinesses.
President and Owner: Bill Miller
Vice President: Chris Miller
Technical Director: Camille Bourque
Estimated Sales: Below $5 Million
Number Employees: 4
Square Footage: 6000

23190 **Genesta Manufacturing**
1850 Interstate 30
Rockwall, TX 75087
Canada 972-771-1653
Fax: 972-722-1179 info@genesta.com
www.genesta.com
Extruded formed fluorescent lighting fixtures and vacuum formed display components
VP: Merv Schwantz

23191 **Geneva Awning & Tent Works Inc**
96 Lewis St
Geneva, NY 14456 315-789-3151
Fax: 315-789-2695 800-789-3151
tgenevaa@rochester.rr.com
www.genevatent.com
Commercial awnings and tents,also rental and sales
Owner: Sam Heakel
VP: Dan Warder
Estimated Sales: $1 - 2.5 Million
Number Employees: 5-9

23192 **Geneva Lakes Cold Storage**
PO Box 39
Darien, WI 53114-0039 262-724-3295
Fax: 262-724-4200 hoptim@genlak.com
www.genevalakescoldstorage.com
Warehouse offering cooler, freezer and dry storage for frozen, refrigerated and nonperishable food items; transportation firm providing refrigerated truck and van services including local, short and long haul
Number Employees: 1-4

23193 **Genflex Roofing Systems**
250 West
96th Street
Indianapolis, IN 46260 972-233-4100
Fax: 817-588-3099 800-443-4272
info@fbpe.be www.genflex.com
Partner: Rick L Cohen
Sales Manager: Bob Marini
QBS Regional Manager: Brian Stevenson
Sales Manager: Tim Creagan
Sales Manager: Mike Melito
Customer Service Representative: Linda Monroe
Estimated Sales: $1 - 3 000,000
Number Employees: 5-9

23194 **Genlyte Thomas Group**
3 Burlington Woods
Suite 3
Burlington, MA 01803-4514 662-842-7212
Fax: 662-680-6619
capriomega@capriomegalighting.com
www.nitebrites.com
Indoor and outdoor lighting including fluorescent lamps, HID and exit signs
Manager: Clifford Jackson
Estimated Sales: $470.2 Million
Number Employees: 4070
Square Footage: 550000
Parent Co: Genlyte Thomas Group

23195 **Genpak**
25 Aylmer Street
P O Box 209
Peterborough, ON K9J 6Y8
Canada 705-743-4733
Fax: 705-743-4798 800-461-1995
info@genpak.com www.genpakca.com
Manufacturer and exporter of plastic containers, cups and lids; also, single-serve packaging machinery for butter, margarine, creamers, etc
Quality Control: Jennifer Seeley
R&D: Jennifer Seeley
National Sales Manager: Kevin Callahan
Production Manager: Bernie Logan
Plant Manager: Brian May
Number Employees: 60
Type of Packaging: Bulk
Brands:
Purity Pat
Sealcup

23196 **Genpak**
P.O.Box 727
Glens Falls, NY 12801 518-798-9511
Fax: 518-798-0834 800-626-6695
info@genpak.com www.genpak.com
Manufacturer and exporter of plastic and styrofoam take out containers including plates, bowls and take-out containers. Dual oven meal solutions and bakery trays in opet plastic for retail packs. Packaging for processor, food serviceand retail applications
President: James Reilly
CEO: Tawn Whittemore
CFO: Jeff Cole
Marketing Coordinator: Michele Quirk
Estimated Sales: $100-500 Million
Number Employees: 1,000-4,999

23197 **Genpak LLC**
8235 220th St. West
Lakeville, MN 55044 952-881-8673
Fax: 952-881-9617 800-328-4556
www.genpak.com
Plain and printed new and recycled polyethylene bags and film, flexible packaging, laminations and pouches for various food and snack food applications.
President: Kim Lenhardt
Sales: Kevin Callahan
Plant Manager: Russ Snyder
Estimated Sales: $20 - 50 Million
Number Employees: 100-249
Number of Products: 100+
Square Footage: 140000
Parent Co: Jim Pattison Group
Other Locations:
Strout Plastics
Lakeville MN
Brands:
Bags Again
Flip & Grip
Mr. Neat
Value Tough

23198 **Gensaco Marketing**
1751 2nd Ave
New York, NY 10128-5388 212-876-1020
Fax: 212-876-1003 800-506-1935
espmachine@aol.com www.giannasca.com
Coffee bars, espresso and cappuccino machines; importer of grinders; exporter of espresso machines, ice cream machines - restaurant equipment
Partner: Edward V Giannasca
CEO: Al Elvino
VP Sales: Lawrence Coal
VP Purchasing: Carbone Lorenzo
Estimated Sales: $1 Million
Number Employees: 5-9
Square Footage: 34000
Parent Co: Gensaco
Brands:
Gensaco

23199 **Gentile Packaging Machinery**
8300 Boettner Rd
Saline, MI 48176 734-429-1177
Fax: 734-429-4714 info@gentilemachinery.com
www.gentilemachinery.com
Packaging machinery
President: Aliseo Gentile
Vice President: Anthony Gentile
Plant Manager: Rob Wilkerson
Estimated Sales: $1 - 2.5 000,000
Number Employees: 1-4

23200 **Genysis Nutritional Labs**
391 S Orange St
Salt Lake City, UT 84104 801-973-8824
Fax: 801-973-8807 sales@gnlabs.net
www.gnlabs.net

Testing services offered for chemical and microbiological nutraceutical and food needs.
Managing Partner: Jeff Reynolds
Technical Account Manager: Melissa Robbins
Business Development: Rachelle Maass
On-Staff Physician: Joe Giacalone MD
Sr Laboratory Manager: Edgar Grigorian
Microbiology Manager: Scott Larsen

23201 Geo. Olcott Company
PO Box 267
Scottsboro, AL 35768-0267 256-259-4937
Fax: 256-259-4942 800-634-2769
Manufacturer and exporter of glass bead blast-cleaning cabinets, degreasing tanks, magnetic detectors and jet spray washers
President: Richard Olcott
Vice President: Marilyn Olcott
Estimated Sales: $1-2.5 Million
Number Employees: 9
Square Footage: 8400
Brands:
Olcott

23202 Georg Fischer Disa PipeTools
PO Box 40
Holly, MI 48442-0040 248-634-8251
Fax: 248-634-2507 gfpipe@gfdisaholly.com
www.georgefischer.com
Pipe cutting and beveling equipment
CEO: Kurt Stirnemann
Estimated Sales: $20-50 Million
Number Employees: 100-249

23203 George Basch Company
PO Box 188
Freeport, NY 11520 516-378-8100
Fax: 516-378-8140 info@nevrdull.com
www.nevrdull.com
Metal cleaners and polishes
President: Laurie Basch-Levy
Vice President: Mark Ax
Estimated Sales: $5-10 Million
Number Employees: 10-19
Number of Brands: 1
Number of Products: 1
Brands:
Nevr-Dull Polish

23204 George G. Giddings
61 Beech Road
Randolph, NJ 07869-4548 973-361-4687
Fax: 973-887-1476
Consultant for food processing preservation
Consultant: George Giddings, Ph.D.
Number Employees: 1

23205 George Glove Company, Inc
301 Greenwood Ave
Midland Park, NJ 07432 201-251-1200
Fax: 201-251-8431 800-631-4292
steve@georgeglove.com www.georgeglove.com
Importer of white gloves
President/CEO: Andrew Wilson
CFO: Andrew Wilson
Marketing Director: Roy Miller
Sales: Roy Miller
Operations Manager: Juan Mino
Estimated Sales: $2 Million
Number Employees: 7
Square Footage: 48000
Brands:
Beauty
Dermal
While-U-Color

23206 George Gordon Associates
12 Continental Blvd
Merrimack, NH 03054 603-424-5204
Fax: 603-424-9031 sales@ggapack.com
www.ggapack.com
Packaging machinery, kits packaging, pouching systems, case/carton/gaylord loaders
President: Don Blanger
VP Sales/Marketing: Ron Downing
Purchasing Manager: Maurice Demarais
Estimated Sales: $10-20 000,000
Number Employees: 20-49

23207 George Lapgley Enterprises
4988 E Rolling Glen Drive
Pipersville, PA 18947 267-221-2426
Fax: 215-766-1687 info@getfoodhelp.com
www.getfoodhelp.net
Specialist in food safety & security consulting. Liason with regulatory agencies. Production, retail, food service, HACCP Plans, food safety training, expert testimony, food safety audits

23208 George Lauterer Corporation
310 S. Racine Ave.
6th Floor North
Chicago, IL 60607 312-913-1881
Fax: 312-913-1811 sales@lauterer.com
www.lauterer.com
Advertising novelties and specialties including flags, banners, badges and buttons
Owner: Earl Joyce
VP Marketing: John Joyce
Estimated Sales: $2.5-5 Million
Number Employees: 20-49

23209 George Risk Industries
802 S Elm St
GRI Plaza
Kimball, NE 69145 308-235-4645
Fax: 308-235-3561 800-523-1227
gri@megavision.com www.grisk.com
Reed-type panel mount pushbutton switches, burglar alarms, door, window and keyboard switches, alphanumeric keyboards and proximity systems
CEO/Chairman: Ken R Risk
CFO: Stephanie Risk
VP Sales: Mary Ann Brothers
Quality Control: Bonnie Heaton
Sales Administration: Sharon Westby
Estimated Sales: F
Number Employees: 100-249

23210 George's Bakery Equipment
1525 Macarthur Boulevard
Suite 4
Costa Mesa, CA 92626-1413 714-437-7143
Fax: 714-437-1016 gbakequip@aol.com
Owner: George Grezaud
Estimated Sales: $3 - 5 Million
Number Employees: 5-9

23211 (HQ)Georgia Duck & Cordage Mill
21 Laredo Drive
Scottdale, GA 30079 404-297-3170
Fax: 404-296-5165 sales@gaduck.com
www.gd-enerka.com
Manufacturer and exporter of conveyor and elevator belting including vinyl, rubber and urethane
President: Raymond Willoch
VP Sales/Marketing: Ken Dangelo
Sales Manager/National Accounts: Jim Hinson
Sales Manager: Jim Panter
Number Employees: 490

23212 Georgia Pacific
P.O.Box 19130
Green Bay, WI 54307 920-435-8821
Fax: 920-496-9445 darin.pekarek@gapac.com
www.gp.com
Facial tissue, hand towels, napkins, wipers, dispensing systems and printed specialty products
VP: Russ Mc Collister
Sr. VP Sales: George Hartmann
VP Sales: Paul Farren
Estimated Sales: $1 - 5 Million
Number Employees: 1,000-4,999
Brands:
Adnaps
Belnap
Bevnaps
Bi-Tex
Billow
Commander Ii
Dari-Dri
Dine-A-Wipe
Dine-A-Wipe Plus
Drize
Dust 'n Clean
Elfin
Essence
Fornap
Fort Howard
Generation Ii
Handifold
Hy-Tex
Hynap
Miltex
Mini-Mornap
Mornap
Mynap
Nornap Jr.
Nu-Nap
Pom
Palmer
Paperlux
Perfection
Plyfold
Pom-Etts
Prim
Pul-A-Nap
Ritenap
Selford
Shur-Wipe
Sirnap
So-Dri
Sof-Knit
Soft 'n Fresh
Soft 'n Gentle
Spread
Staynap
Studio Colors
Stylene
Texnap
Tidynap Jr.
Twin-Tex
Ultra Wipe
Wipe Away

23213 Georgia Tent & Awning
1356 English St NW
Atlanta, GA 30318 404-523-7551
Fax: 404-525-0601 800-252-2391
www.georgiatent.com
Commercial awnings
President: Ken Spooner
Quality Control: Mike Hill
VP: Bob Spooner
CFO: Gary Meacher
Chairman of the Board: Robert Spooner
Estimated Sales: $5 - 10,000,000
Number Employees: 50-99

23214 Georgia-Pacific LLC
133 Peachtree St. NE
Atlanta, GA 30303 404-652-4000
Fax: 404-749-2454 www.gp.com
Manufacturer and exporter of corrugated shipping cases
President/Chief Executive Officer: James Hannan
SVP/Chief Financial Officer: Tyler Woolson
SVP/Communications, Gov't & Pub. Affairs: Sheila Weidman
EVP/Operations Excellence & Compliance: W. Wesley Jones
Estimated Sales: $17 Billion
Number Employees: 45,000
Square Footage: 350000

23215 Gerber Innovations
24 Industrial Park Rd W
Tolland, CT 06084
Fax: 978-657-7977 800-331-5797
sales@data-technology.com
www.gerberinnovations.com
Manufacturer and exporter of computer plotters and sample makers for packaging design
President: Steven Gore
Director of Sales & Marketing: Don Skenderian
Vice President, Business Development: Mark Bibo
Technical Manager: Ken Hooks
Director of International Sales: Francisco Javier Sole
General Manager: W Staniewicz
Estimated Sales: $10 - 20 Million
Number Employees: 50-99
Parent Co: Data Technology

23216 Gerber Legendary Blades
14200 SW 72nd Ave
Portland, OR 97224 503-639-6161
Fax: 503-684-7008 sales@gerberblades.com
www.gerberblades.com
Culinary knives including steak, carving, slicing, etc
President: Wayne Fethke
Chief Executive Officer: Robert Bascom
Estimated Sales: $37.4 Million
Number Employees: 260
Parent Co: Fiskars

23217 Germantown Milling Company
6098 Brooksville Germantown Rd
Germantown, KY 41044-9060 606-728-5857
Fax: 606-883-3172 cstrickland@ekns.net

Feed
President: Jack Myrick
Estimated Sales: Below $5 Million
Number Employees: 2
Square Footage: 300000

23218 Gerrity Industries
PO Box 121
Monmouth, ME 04259 207-933-2804
Fax: 207-933-1081 877-933-2804
info@gerrityindustries.com
www.gerrityindustries.com
Pallets and skids
President: Peter Gerrity
Sales: Leo Moody
Estimated Sales: Below $5 Million
Number Employees: 20-49
Square Footage: 120000

23219 Gerstel
701 Digital Dr Ste J
Linthicum Hts, MD 21090 410-247-5885
Fax: 410-247-5887 800-413-8160
info@gerstelus.com www.gerstelus.com
Gas chromatographic systems for analysis of complex samples in the flavoring and food additive business including thermal desorption, static headspace, fraction collectors and multi-column switching systems
President: Bob Collins
CFO: Robert Collins
Vice President: Robert Collins
R&D: Ed Pfannkoch
Estimated Sales: Below $5 Million
Number Employees: 10-19
Parent Co: Gerstel GmbH
Brands:
Gerstel

23220 Gervasi Wood Products
2611 W Beltline Highway
Madison, WI 53713-2349 608-274-6752
Counters
Estimated Sales: $500,000-$1 Million
Number Employees: 5-9

23221 Gessner Products Company
241 North Main Street
PO Box 389
Ambler, PA 19002-0389 215-646-7667
Fax: 215-646-6222 800-874-7808
sales@gessnerproducts.com
www.gessnerproducts.com
Manufacturer and exporter of plastic ashtrays, credit card trays, coasters, signs, condiment jars, sugar caddies and restaurant smallwares
President: Edward H Gessner
Controller: Neo Brown
Executive VP: Geoffrey Ries
Quality Control: Steve Fuhrmeister
National Sales Manager: Michael Salemi
Production Manager: Chuck Denoncour
Estimated Sales: $5 - 10 Million
Number Employees: 100-249

23222 Geyersville Printing Company
21001 Geyersville Avenue
Geyserville, CA 95441 707-857-1704
Fax: 707-857-1705
Wine industry labels
Estimated Sales: less than $500,000
Number Employees: 6

23223 Ghibli North American
14 Germay Drive
Wilmington, DE 19804 302-654-5908
Fax: 302-652-7159 ghibli@frontiernet.net
Manufacturer and exporter of high pressure and hot water cleaning equipment
General Manager: Gordon Thomas
Estimated Sales: $1 - 5 Million
Number Employees: 5 to 9
Brands:
Ghibli

23224 Ghirardelli Chocolate Company
1111 139th Ave
San Leandro, CA 94578 510-483-6970
Fax: 510-297-2649 800-877-9338
www.ghirardelli.com
Chocolate
President/CEO: Fabrizio Parini
CFO: Jurgen Auerbach
VP Sales/Marketing: Marty Thompson
Estimated Sales: $100-500 Million
Number Employees: 250-499
Type of Packaging: Private Label
Brands:
Ghirardelli

23225 Gianco
1635 Oakbrook Drive
Gainesville, GA 30507-8492 770-534-0703
Fax: 770-534-1865 800-467-2828
Sales@gainco.com www.gainco.com
Automated weighing and sorting systems for the meat and poultry industry
Manager: Gene Parets
Number Employees: 20-49
Parent Co: Bettcher Industries

23226 (HQ)Giant Gumball Machine Company
200 Macarthur Blvd
Grand Prairie, TX 75050-4739 972-262-2234
Fax: 972-262-3167
Manufacturer and exporter of vending machines
President: Dan Clemson
National Sales Manager: Bob Rogers
National Sales Manager: Dan Wright
Estimated Sales: $300,000-500,000
Number Employees: 1-4

23227 Giant Packaging Corporation
545 W Lambert Road
Suite F
Brea, CA 92821-3916 714-256-8498
Fax: 714-256-8499 giant@gus.net
Strapping and wrapping machines, carton sealers, impulse sealers, and strapping hand tools
Estimated Sales: $2.5-5 000,000
Number Employees: 1-4

23228 Gibbs Brothers Cooperage Company
PO Box 20848
Hot Springs, AR 71903 501-623-8881
Fax: 501-623-9610 gibbsbro@swbell.net
www.gibbsbrothers.com
White oak wooden kegs and barrels
President: James Gibbs Sr
Manager: Jay Gibbs
Estimated Sales: $1-2.5 Million
Number Employees: 5-9
Square Footage: 48000

23229 (HQ)Gibraltar Packaging Group
2000 Summit Ave
Hastings, NE 68901 402-463-1366
Fax: 402-463-2467
investorrelations@gibpack.com
www.gibpack.com
Folding cartons, litho-laminated cartons, regular and corrugated cartons and flexible packaging including converted bags and rollstock
President and COO: Richard Hinrichs
CEO: Walter E Rose
Chairman of the Board: Walter E Rose
VP Sales: Mark Lessor
Corporate Marketing/Investor Rel. Mgr: Leslie Schroeder
Estimated Sales: Below $5,000,000
Number Employees: 250-499
Other Locations:
Gibraltar Packaging Group
Mount Gilead NC

23230 Giddings & Lewis
P.O.Box 1960
Fond Du Lac, WI 54936-1960 920-921-7100
Fax: 920-906-7669 800-558-4808
mwl@giddings.com www.danahermotion.com
Automotion controls, measurement, sensing
Manager: Pete Winkelmann
President, Chief Executive Officer: Lawrence Culp
Estimated Sales: $50 - 100 Million
Number Employees: 100-249

23231 Giffin International
1900 Brown Rd
Auburn Hills, MI 48326-1701
Fax: 248-478-1321 info@giffinusa.com
www.giffinusa.com
Cooking and chilling systems; smoke houses, air chillers, batch and continuous systems
Owner: Donald Giffin Sr
Estimated Sales: $20-50 Million
Number Employees: 20-49

23232 Gilbert Industries, Inc
5611 Krueger Drive
Jonesboro, AR 72401-6818 870-932-6070
Fax: 870-932-5609 800-643-0400
mailbox@gilbertinc.com www.gilbertinc.com
Electronic wall-mounted flytraps
President: David Gilbert
Sales: Stephen Goad
Sales: Libby Mackey
Estimated Sales: $1 - 5 Million

23233 Gilbert Insect Light Traps
5611 Krueger Dr
Jonesboro, AR 72401-6818 870-932-6070
Fax: 870-932-5609 800-643-0400
mailbox@gilbertinc.com www.gilbertinc.com
Manufacturer and exporter of professional flytraps, emergency lighting and LED exit signs; also, consultant on flying insect control
President/ILT Research/Customer Service: David Gilbert
ILT Sales/Customer Service: Stephen Goad
Executive Administrator/Customer Service: Libby Mackey
Estimated Sales: $1 - 3 Million
Number Employees: 20-49
Number of Brands: 2
Number of Products: 15
Square Footage: 152000
Parent Co: Gilbert Industries
Brands:
Gilbert

23234 Gilchrist Bag Company
PO Box 189
Camden, AR 71711 870-836-6416
Fax: 870-836-8379 800-643-1513
sales@gilchristbag.com www.gilchristbag.com
Manufacturer and exporters of a wide variety of quality paper bags, sacks and specialty supplies used by a variety of markets.
President: Leslie Gilchrist Jr
Director Operations Marketing: Randy Robertson
Plant/Production Manager: Larry Starnes
Plant Manager: Louis Hammond
Estimated Sales: $5-10,000,000
Number Employees: 40
Square Footage: 175000
Type of Packaging: Consumer, Food Service, Private Label

23235 (HQ)Giles Enterprises
P.O.Box 210247
Montgomery, AL 36121-0247 334-272-1457
Fax: 334-272-3561 800-288-1555
intsales@gilesent.com www.chesterfried.com
Manufacturer and exporter of kitchen and deli equipment including ventless hood fryers
President: Ted Giles
Financial Director: Ken Robinson
Quality Control: Sheila Munday
VP Sales: David Byrd
Estimated Sales: $10 - 20 Million
Number Employees: 100-249
Square Footage: 80000
Brands:
Chester Fried
Giles

23236 Gillis Associated Industries
750 Pinecrest Dr
Prospect Heights, IL 60070-1806 847-541-6500
Fax: 847-541-0858 info@gillisindustries.com
www.gillisindustries.com
Wire systems for shelving, carts, palletainer stacking wire containers, rack decking, high-density mobile storage and rivet rack with wire decking
President: Harvey Baker
President, Chief Executive Officer: Steven DarnelL
Vice President of Business Development: Dave Mack
VP Sales: Mark Jones
Vice President of Operations: Bob Buehler
Estimated Sales: $5-10 Million
Number Employees: 20-49

23237 Gilson Company Incorporated
P.O.Box 200
Lewis Center, OH 43035 740-548-7298
Fax: 740-548-5314 800-444-1508
customerservice@gilson.com
www.globalgilson.com
Liquid handling
President: Trent Smith
CEO: Robert H Smith
Marketing Director: Carl Kramer
Technical Development Manager: Jim Bibler
Estimated Sales: $12-20 Million
Number Employees: 50-99
Brands:
Fristch Mills
Gilsonic Autosiever
Ultra Siever

23238 Giltron
104 Adams St
PO Box 187
Medfield, MA 02052 508-359-4310
Fax: 508-359-4317 sales@giltron.com
www.giltron.com
Induction heat cap foil sealers for bottles and jars
President: Fred Giltron
CFO: A Stanley Pittman
Quality Control: Bruce Green
R & D: Mike Sievert
Service Manager: William Koivu
VP Operations: Fred Pittman
Estimated Sales: Below $5 Million
Number Employees: 5-9
Square Footage: 7000
Brands:
Giltron Foilsealer

23239 Ginnie Nichols Graphic Design
780 W Napa St
Sonoma, CA 95476-6452 707-996-0164
Fax: 707-938-3855 800-399-7890
ginnie16@comcast.net
www.nicholsarchitects.com
Package design
President: Jenny Nichols
Estimated Sales: $300,000-500,000
Number Employees: 1-4

23240 Gintzler Graphics
100 Lawrence Bell Dr
Williamsville, NY 14221 716-631-9700
Fax: 716-631-0075 sales@gintzler.com
www.gintzler.com
Pressure sensitive labels
President: Frank Nice
Sales Manager: James Calamita
Estimated Sales: $20-50 Million
Number Employees: 50-99

23241 Girard Spring Water
1100 Mineral Spring Ave
North Providence, RI 02904-4104 401-725-7298
Fax: 401-725-7913 800-477-9287
Spring water and water coolers
President: John Ponton
Estimated Sales: $500,000-$1 Million
Number Employees: 1 to 4
Square Footage: 2500
Type of Packaging: Consumer, Private Label, Bulk

23242 Girard Wood Products
PO Box 830
Puyallup, WA 98371-0075 253-845-0505
Fax: 253-845-5463
greg@girardwoodproducts.com
www.girardwoodproducts.com
Wooden pallets and skids; also, pallet recycling services including retrieval, repair and disposal available
President: Steve Vipond
VP of Sales: Greg Vipond
Sales Director: Dave Loden
Operations Manager: Scott Vipond
Plant Manager: Virgil Vwngwirth
Purchasing Manager: Stan Henry
Estimated Sales: $10 - 20 Million
Number Employees: 20-49

23243 Girton Manufacturing Company, Inc.
PO Box 900
Millville, PA 17846 570-458-5521
Fax: 570-458-5589 info@girton.com
www.girton.com
Manufactures stainless steel washing equipment for the Food & Dairy Processing Industries, including COP tanks, bin and tub washing systems for pallets, drums, cases, etc. Girton MFG co Inc also manufactures King Zeero Ice Builders.
President: Dean Girton
Sales: Wm Bruce Michael
Plant Manager: Jim Eves
Purchasing Director: Donna Bender
Estimated Sales: $10 - 20 Million
Number Employees: 100-249
Square Footage: 45000
Brands:
Girton King Zeero

23244 Giunta Brothers
2612 S 17th St
Philadelphia, PA 19145-4502 215-389-9670
Culinary strainers and graters
Owner: Anthony P Giunta
Estimated Sales: less than $500,000
Number Employees: 1 to 4

23245 Glamorgan Bakery
3919 Richmond Rd SW
Building 19
Calgary, AB T3E 4P2
Canada 403-232-2800
glamorganbakery@gmail.com
www.glamorganbakery.com
Freshly baked goods
President/Owner: Douwe Nauta
General Manager: Don Nauta
Sales/Customer Service: Jeremy Nauta
Number Employees: 8

23246 Glaro
735 Calebs Path
Hauppauge, NY 11788 631-234-1717
Fax: 631-234-9510 info@glaro.com
www.glaro.com
Manufacturer and exporter of waste containers, engraved signs, aluminum tray stand equipment, crowd control stanchions, planters, coat racks, etc
CEO: Michael Glass
VP: Robert Betensky
Estimated Sales: $20-50 Million
Number Employees: 5-9
Square Footage: 50000

23247 Glasko Plastics
3123 W Alpine St
Santa Ana, CA 92704 714-751-7830
Fax: 714-751-4039
Plastic containers
Estimated Sales: $2.5-5 Million
Number Employees: 20-49

23248 Glass Industries
340 Quinnipiac St Unit 5
Wallingford, CT 06492 203-269-6700
Fax: 203-269-8782
Manufacturer and exporter of lighting fixtures including bent and decorated glassware
Owner: George Sutherland
Manager: Jack Jackson
Estimated Sales: $2.5-5 Million
Number Employees: 10-19
Parent Co: L.D. Kichler

23249 Glass Pro
2300 W Windsor Ct
Addison, IL 60101-1491 630-268-9494
Fax: 800-875-6243 888-641-8919
glasspro@imaxx.net www.glass-pro.com
Manufacturer and exporter of glass washing machinery, sanitizers and accessories
President: Robert Joesel
CEO: Evelyn Joesel
R&D: Robert Joesel
Quality Control: Robert Joesel
Estimated Sales: Below $5 Million
Number Employees: 5-9
Number of Brands: 4
Number of Products: 3
Square Footage: 12000
Type of Packaging: Food Service, Private Label
Brands:
Brush-Rite
Glass Maid
Glass Pro

23250 Glass Tech
23780 NW Huffman St Ste 101
Hillsboro, OR 97124 888-284-7934
Fax: 503-626-2890 sales@glasstechweb.com
www.glasstechweb.com
Wine industry tasting room supplies
Estimated Sales: $1-2.5 000,000
Number Employees: 10-19

23251 Glassline System Packaging
P.O.Box 147
Perrysburg, OH 43552-0147 419-666-5942
Fax: 419-666-1549 www.glassline.com
Hot and cold seal packaging machinery
Owner: Tom Ziems
Estimated Sales: $10-20 Million
Number Employees: 5-9

23252 Glastender
5400 N Michigan Rd
Saginaw, MI 48604 989-752-4275
Fax: 989-752-4444 800-748-0423
info@glastender.com www.glastender.com
Manufacturer and exporter of bar and restaurant equipment including glass washers, cocktail stations, underbar and refrigerated backbar equipment, mug frosters, beer and soda line chillers, ice cream freezers and coolers
President: Todd Hall
CFO: Jamie Rievert
VP Admin: Kim Norris
Quality Control: David Burk
VP Operations: Mark Norris
Plant Manager: Mark Norris
Purchasing Manager: Zoa May
Estimated Sales: $10 - 20 Million
Number Employees: 50-99
Square Footage: 100000

23253 Glatech Productions
325 2nd St
Lakewood, NJ 08701 732-364-8700
Fax: 732-370-0877 info@kosherGELATIN.com
www.koshergelatin.com
Producer of Kolatin® Kosher gelatin and Elyon® kosher confectionery products.
CEO: Moshe Eider
Marketing: Chez Eider
Estimated Sales: $1 - 5 Million
Number Employees: 5-9
Number of Brands: 2
Type of Packaging: Bulk
Brands:
Elyon
Kolatin

23254 Glatfelter
96 S George St
Suite 500
York, PA 17401 717-225-4711
Fax: 717-846-7208 866-744-7680
info@glatfelter.com www.glatfelter.com
Teabag paper, bags and packaging film supplies, coffeebag paper, coffeebag paper (metallized)
CEO: George Glatfelter
CFO: John Jacunski

23255 Glatt Air Techniques
20 Spear Rd
Ramsey, NJ 07446 201-825-8700
Fax: 201-825-0389 info@glattair.com
www.glattair.com
Process controls, material handling equipment, coaters, fluid bed dryers, granulators, etc
EVP: Stephen Sirabian
General Manager Sales: John Carey
Director Business Development: Ted Wisniewski
VP Sales/Technical Operations: Stephen Sirabian
Estimated Sales: $30 - 50 Million
Number Employees: 100-249
Square Footage: 60000
Parent Co: Glatt GmbH
Other Locations:
Glatt Air Techniques
San Leandro CA

23256 Glawe Manufacturing Company
851 Zapata Dr
Fairborn, OH 45324-5165 937-754-0064
Fax: 937-754-1780 800-434-8368
bhughes@glaweawning.com
www.glaweawning.com
Commercial awnings
CEO: L Vernon Schaefer

Estimated Sales: $2.5-5 Million
Number Employees: 20-49

23257 Gleason Industries
3013 Douglas Boulevard
Suite 230
Roseville, CA 95661-3847 916-784-1302
Fax: 310-679-5581
CSLosAngeles@GleasonIndustries.com
www.gleasonindustries.com
Converting box boards and layerboards for the candy and bakery industries
President: Michael Richards
CEO: Mike Richards
VP Finance: John Mahar
Sales Director: Carlene Milligan
Plant Manager: Tony Concad
Estimated Sales: $1 - 3 Million
Number Employees: 85
Other Locations:
Gleason Industries
Sacramento CA
Gleason Industries
Summer WA
Gleason Industries
Millwaukie OR
Gleason Industries
West Valley City UT
Gleason Industries
Rancho Cocamonca CA

23258 Gleeson Constructors
2015 E 7th Street
P.O.Box 625
Sioux City, IA 51102-0625 712-258-9300
Fax: 712-277-5300 www.gleesonllc.com
Specializes in the construction of food processing facilities, freezers, cold storage facilities and distribution centers.
President: Harlan Vandezandschul

23259 Glen Mills, Inc.
220 Delawanna Ave
Clifton, NJ 07014 973-777-0777
Fax: 973-777-0070 staff@glenmills.com
www.glenmills.com
Markets a line of laboratory and small-scale production equipment: the Turbula® Shaker-Mixer and dyna-MIX® for 3D mixing without cleanl-up: various mills for grinding coarse, fine, fibrous, wet or dry materials; sample dividersfor exact representation; sifters and sieves for accurate size cuts and Grinding media in all materials
President: Stanley Goldberg
Sales Manager: E. Szwerc
Public Relations: D. Ahrens
Operations: S Goldberg
Purchasing: A Ahrens
Estimated Sales: $2.5-5 Million
Number Employees: 10
Square Footage: 48000

23260 Glen Raven Custom Fabrics, LLC
1831 N Park Avenue
Glen Raven, NC 27217-1100 336-227-6211
Fax: 336-226-8133 oford@glenraven.com
www.sunbrella.com
Solutions dyed acrylic fabrics for awnings and umbrellas
President: Allen E Gant Jr
CFO: Garry Smith
R&D: John Coates
Sales/Marketing Administration: Harry Gobble
National Sales Manager: Ocie Ford
Number Employees: 1,000-4,999
Parent Co: Glen Raven Custom Fabrics LLC
Type of Packaging: Food Service

23261 Glenmarc Manufacturing
2001 S.Blue Island Ave.
Chicago, IL 60608 312-243-0800
Fax: 312-243-4670 800-323-5350
glenmarc@aol.com www.aleri.com
Manufacturer and exporter of adhesive dispensing equipment. Also 304/316 stainless steel pressure tanks
President: John Sims
Chairman, Chief Executive Officer: John Chen
CEO: Don Deloach
Senior Vice President of Operations: Billy Ho
Purchasing Manager: Steve Eichele
Estimated Sales: Below $500,000
Number Employees: 5-9
Square Footage: 26000

23262 (HQ)Glenro
39 McBride Ave
Paterson, NJ 07501 973-279-5900
Fax: 973-279-9103 800-922-0106
info@glenro.com www.glenro.com
Hot air and infrared ovens for food packaging
President: Gary Van Denend
Vice President: Jim Karrett
Sales Director: Jim Karrett
Estimated Sales: $10-15 Million
Number Employees: 50-99

23263 Glenroy
1437 Wells Dr
Bensalem, PA 19020 215-245-3575
Fax: 215-245-3589 800-441-2230
plarkin@glenroylabels.com
www.glenroylabels.com
Labeling technologies, bar code scanners
Owner: Patrick Larkin Jr
Vice President: Terry la Ruffa
CFO: Vince Laruffa
Estimated Sales: $5-10 000,000
Number Employees: 20-49

23264 Glit Microtron
305 Rock Industrial Park Dr
Bridgetown, MO 63044
Fax: 800-327-5492 800-325-1051
janics@contico.com
www.continentalcommercialproducts.com
Abrasive coated synthetic sponge, scour pads and scrub sponges
President: Gordan Kirsch
Research Manager: Alan Christopher
Number Employees: 250-499
Parent Co: Katy Industries

23265 Glit/Disco
13330 Lakefront Drive
Earth City, MO 63045-1513 314-770-9919
Fax: 800-327-5492 contmfg@contico.com
www.continental-mfg.com
Estimated Sales: $1 - 5 Million
Parent Co: Katy Company

23266 Glo Germ Company
P.O. Box 189
Moab, UT 84532 435-259-6034
Fax: 435-259-5930 800-842-6622
info@glogerm.com www.glogerm.com
Handwashing training
President: Joe D Kingsley
Estimated Sales: $1 000,000
Number Employees: 5-9
Type of Packaging: Consumer, Bulk
Brands:
Superior Systems

23267 Glo-Quartz Electric Heater Company
7084 Maple Street
Mentor, OH 44060 440-255-9701
Fax: 440-255-7852 800-321-3574
tstrokes@gloquartz.com www.gloquartz.com
Electric immersion heaters and tubular metal and quartz heating elements for food processing and packaging; also, temperature controls; exporter of electric heaters
President: George Strokes
VP: Thomas Strokes
Sales: John Paglia
Plant Manager: Jeff Payne
Estimated Sales: $3 - 5 Million
Number Employees: 20-49
Square Footage: 88000
Brands:
Glo-Quartz

23268 Global Carts and Equipment
640 Herman Road
Suite 2
Jackson, NJ 08527-3068 732-899-9555
Fax: 732-899-1719 800-653-0881
dogwagon1@aol.com www.globalcarts.com
Hot dog carts, soup carts, food merchandiser
VP: Mary Doumas
Marketing Director: Salvatore Badalamente
Sales Coordinator: Bessie Kent
Plant Manager: Dawn Gerom
Purchasing Manager: Gregory Christon
Estimated Sales: $2.5-5 Million
Number Employees: 5-9
Square Footage: 104000

23269 Global Environmental Packaging
221 3rd Street
Newport, RI 02840-1087 401-847-4603
Fax: 401-847-4654 800-729-4210
jharris@mtg.saic.com

23270 Global Equipment Company
11 Harbor Park Drive
Port Washington, NY 11050 516-608-7000
Fax: 888-381-2868 888-628-3466
www.globalindustrial.com
Manufacturer, exporter and importer of steel bins, benches, wire shelving and material handling equipment
Chairman of the Board: Richard Leeds
Chief Financial Officer: Lawrence Reinhold
Vice President: Bruce Leeds
Quality Control Assurance: Paul Betzold
Marketing Manager: Maureen Cronin
Director, Sales: Steve McNamara
Operations: Jack Kaserow
Product Manager: Elise Wong
Purchasing Manager: Eric Bertel
Estimated Sales: $28 Million
Number Employees: 400
Square Footage: 85000
Parent Co: Systemax

23271 Global Manufacturing
1801 E 22nd St
Little Rock, AR 72206 501-374-7416
Fax: 501-376-7147 800-551-3569
info@globalmanufacturing.com
www.globalmanufacturing.com
Manufacturer and exporter of vibrators including hydraulic, pneumatic, electric, air blasters and turbine
President: Catherine Janosky
Quality Control: Wilfred Coney
Marketing: April Crocker
Sales: Perry Schnebelen
Operations: Tom Janosky
Production: Stan Kligman
Plant Manager: Rod Treat
Purchasing Director: Howard Stewart
Estimated Sales: $3 - 5,000,000
Number Employees: 50-99
Brands:
Quiet Thunder
Silver Sonic
Yellow Jacket

23272 Global New Products DataBase
333 West Wacker Drive
Suite 1100
Chicago, IL 60606 312-932-0400
Fax: 312-932-0469 helpdesk@mintel.com
www.gnpd.com
Comprehensive database that monitors worldwide product innovation in consumer packaged goods markets
Manager: Jon Butcher
CFO: John Weeks
Estimated Sales: $5 - 10 Million
Number Employees: 20-49

23273 Global Organics
339 Massachusetts Ave
PO Box 272
Arlington, MA 02474 781-648-8844
Fax: 781-648-0774
amy.dinsmore@global-organics.com
www.global-organics.com
Supplier of certified organic ingredients
President: Dave Alexander
Vice President: Roland Hoch
Account Manager: Dino Scarsella
Sales and Marketing Coordinator: Ravi Arori
Estimated Sales: Under $500,000
Number Employees: 25

23274 Global Packaging Machinery Company
1500 Cardinal Drive
Little Falls, NJ 07424 973-450-4601
Fax: 973-450-4603
global@globalpackmachinery.com
www.globalpackmachinery.com
President: Daniel Waldron
R & D: Mike Kurgyla
Vice President/Mechanical Engineer: Herman Andrade
Estimated Sales: Below $5 Million
Number Employees: 10

23275 **Global Payment Technologies**
170 Wilbur Place
Bohemia, NY 11716 631-563-2500
Fax: 631-563-2630 robertdunn@gpt-europe.com
www.gptx.com
Paper currency validators, lockable stackers for use in the gaming, beverage and vending industries
President: Thomas Oliveri
R & D: Tom Madowiesky
Quality Control: Dede Lisa
Sales Director: Mary Russell
Number Employees: 10

23276 **Global Sticks, Inc.**
13555-23A Avenue
Surrey, BC V4A 9V1
Canada 604-535-7748
Fax: 604-535-7749 866-433-5770
rn@global-sticks.com www.global-sticks.net
Wooden ice cream spoons & sticks, corn dog sticks & coffee stirrers.
President: Reggie Nukovic
General Manager: Earl Metcalf

23277 **Global USA**
1990 M St. NW
Washington, DC 20036 202-296-2400
Fax: 817-568-1327 info@globalusainc.com
www.globalusainc.com
Chairman and Chief Executive Officer: Dr. Bo Denysyk
Senior Vice President: David C. Fine
Director - Research and Analysis: Viktor Sulzynsky

23278 **Global Water & Energy**
2404 Rutland Dr
Suite 200
Austin, TX 78758 512-697-1930
Fax: 512-697-1931 mail.usa@globalwe.com
www.globalwaterengineering.com
Industrial wastewater treatment and bio-waste-to-energy solution provider for food industries
Chairman/CEO: Jean-Pierre Ombregt
Controller: Mike Herbert
Estimated Sales: $1 Million
Number Employees: 5
Parent Co: GLV

23279 **Global Water Group**
8601 Sovereign Row
Dallas, TX 75247 214-678-9866
Fax: 214-678-9811 info@globalwater.com
www.globalwater.com
Mobile, self-contained and fixed based water purification systems, wastewater processing equipment, and gray water recycling equipment
Chairman: Alan M Weiss
COO: Rick Stafford
CFO: Rd Stafford
Vice President: N Kanmer
Research & Development: Jacob Kupersztoch
Quality Control: Thomas Boutwell
Public Relations: Cherie Weiss
Estimated Sales: $10 Million
Number Employees: 10-19
Number of Brands: 6
Number of Products: 50
Square Footage: 20000

23280 **Globe Canvas Products Company**
5000 Paschall Avenue
Philadelphia, PA 19143 610-622-7211
Fax: 610-284-4323
kanvasking@globecanvas.com
www.globecanvas.com
Wholesale manufacturer and distributor, with a diverse product mix comprised of 60% awning, 25% athletic pads for track and field, 10% industrial covers and 5% bags.
President: Kevin Kelly
Estimated Sales: $1-2.5 Million
Number Employees: 1-4
Square Footage: 72000

23281 **(HQ)Globe Fire Sprinkler Corporation**
4077 Airpark Dr
Standish, MI 48658 989-846-4583
Fax: 989-846-9231 800-248-0278
globe_man@msn.com www.globesprinkler.com
Manufacturer, importer and exporter of commercial, industrial and residential fire sprinklers, deluge/preaction, alarm, dry pipe and check valves, water motor alarms and accessories for sprinkler systems
President: Robert Worthington Sr
VP Sales/Marketing: Robert Worthington, Jr.
VP Engineering: Brian Hoening
Estimated Sales: $10-20 Million
Number Employees: 100-249
Square Footage: 40000
Brands:
Globe
Kennedy
System Sensor

23282 **Globe Food Equipment Company**
2153 Dryden Rd
Dayton, OH 45439 937-299-5493
Fax: 937-299-8623 800-347-5423
globeinfo@globeslicers.com
www.globeslicers.com
Manufactures slicers, vegetable cutters, mixers, choppers and scales
President: Hilton Gardner
Marketing: Alicia Sanders
Sales: Bob Adams
Number Employees: 20-49
Brands:
Chefmate
Globe
Protech

23283 **Globe International**
902 E E St
Tacoma, WA 98421 253-572-9637
Fax: 253-572-9672 800-523-6575
sales@globemachine.com
www.globemachine.com
Manufacturer and exporter of material handling equipment including hydraulic lift tables, conveyors, personnel carriers, tilters, dumpers and transfer cars
Special Projects Manager: Mark Allen
Operations Manager: Michael Natucci
Estimated Sales: $20 - 50 Million
Number Employees: 100-249
Square Footage: 225000
Parent Co: Globe Machine Manufacturing Company

23284 **Globe Packaging**
368 Paterson Plank Rd
Carlstadt, NJ 07072 201-939-3335
Fax: 201-939-3325 888-221-0989
sales@globecasing.com www.globecasing.com
Natural casing for meat industries
Owner: Israel Bank
VP: David Knoebel
Estimated Sales: $2 Million
Number Employees: 8

23285 **(HQ)Globe Ticket & Label Company**
300 Constance Dr
Warminster, PA 18974 215-443-7960
Fax: 215-956-2493 800-523-5968
rpuleo@globeticket.com www.globeticket.com
Tickets, coupons and labels including heat seal, pressure sensitive and EDP
COO: Randy Hicks
CFO: Don Schilling
Treasurer: Maddalena Krause
Estimated Sales: $20-50 Million
Number Employees: 100-249
Brands:
Tak-A-Number

23286 **Glolite**
2250 E Devon Ave # 349
Des Plaines, IL 60018-4507 847-803-4500
Fax: 847-803-4584 sales@nudell.com
www.posterframescentral.com
Electric blackboards and signs, point of purchase displays, easels, rope lights, changeable message and marker boards and other indoor signage
Owner: David Block
Sales Director: Mari Carmona
Customer Service: Janis Vazquez
Estimated Sales: $10 - 20 Million
Number Employees: 5-9
Parent Co: Nu-Dell Manufacturing Company
Type of Packaging: Food Service
Brands:
Ad-Lite
Glo-Glaze
Glo-Ons
Glolite

23287 **Glopak**
4755 Boulevard De Grandes Prairies
St Leonard, QC H1R 1A6
Canada 514-323-4510
Fax: 514-323-5999 800-361-6994
glopak@glopak.com www.glopak.com
Manufacturer and exporter of packaging equipment and supplies including bags, fillers, filling equipment, films, flexible packaging, pouches and wrapping material
President: Ritchie Baird
CEO: Harold Martin
CFO: John Mireault
Quality Control: Hens Pohl
R&D: Eves Quiten
Number Employees: 130
Type of Packaging: Bulk

23288 **Glover Latex**
PO Box 167
Anaheim, CA 92815 714-535-8920
Fax: 714-535-3635 800-243-5110
Plastic, rubber and protective gloves
President: Paul Babcock
CEO: Sandra Robles
Sales Director: R Fisher
Estimated Sales: $2.5-5 Million
Number Employees: 20-49
Square Footage: 17000
Type of Packaging: Consumer, Food Service, Private Label, Bulk

23289 **Glover Rubber Stamp Corporation**
1015 Goodnight Blvd
Wills Point, TX 75169 214-824-6900
Fax: 214-824-6906 glover@gloverstamp.com
www.gloverstamp.com
Rubber stamps and signs
Manager: Anna Prile
Estimated Sales: $500,000 - $1 Million
Number Employees: 5-9

23290 **Glowmaster Corporation**
312 Lexington Ave
Clifton, NJ 07011-2366 973-772-1112
Fax: 973-772-4040 800-272-7008
sales@glowmaster.com
www.e-hospitality.com/storefronts/glowmaster.html
Manufacturer and importer of cooking and heating equipment including portable tabletop butane stoves and fuel, chafers, griddles, service carts and induction cooking systems; exporter of portable butane stoves
Owner: Juan Travezano
CFO: Linda Smith
Director Sales: Frank Palatiello
Number Employees: 10-19
Square Footage: 28000
Brands:
Chafermate
Glowmaster

23291 **Gluefast Company**
3535 State Route 66 # 1
Neptune, NJ 07753-2623 732-918-4600
Fax: 732-918-4646 800-242-7318
info@gluefast.com www.gluefast.com
Adhesives and applicators used for packaging, labeling, palletizing, gluing and hot melts
President: Lester Mallet
Vice President: Amy Altman
Estimated Sales: $2.8 Million
Number Employees: 10-19
Square Footage: 68000

23292 **Gluefast Company, Inc**
3535 State Route 66 # 1
Neptune, NJ 07753-2623 732-918-4600
Fax: 732-918-4646 800-242-7318
info@gluefast.com www.gluefast.com
Pressure sensitive adhesives, packaging adhesive, adhesive applicators, faux finish texture coating/texturizing products, hot melt glue systems, coating and laminating equipment, palletizing glue, mountin and laminating products andmuch more.
President: Lester Mallet
General Manager: Joe Benenati
Vice President: Amy Altman

Estimated Sales: $5 - 10 Million
Number Employees: 10-19

23293 Gluemaster
12620 Wilmot Rd
Kenosha, WI 53142-7360 262-857-7212
Fax: 262-857-7430
Labeling and packaging machinery
President: Darlene Sanew
Estimated Sales: $1 - 2.5 Million
Number Employees: 5-9

23294 Go-Jo Industries
PO Box 991
Akron, OH 44309-0991 330-255-6000
Fax: 330-255-6119 800-321-9647
www.gojo.com
Manufacturer and exporter of hand cleaners and soap dispensers
President/Chief Operating Officer: Mark Lerner
Chief Executive Officer: Joe Kanfer
Managing Director: Adrian Coombes
Vice Chair: Marcella Rolnick
Research & Development: Thales De Nardo
Quality Control Assurance: Susan Jack
Vice President, Sales & Marketing: Jeff Buysse
Vice President, Sales: Greg Conner
Product Manager: Aaron Conrow
Lab Manager: Dan Willis
Purchasing: Debbie Topliff
Estimated Sales: $75 Million
Number Employees: 550
Square Footage: 500000
Brands:
Derma-Pro
Go-Jo

23295 Godshall Paper Box Company
146 Algoma Boulevard
Oshkosh, WI 54901 920-235-4040
Fax: 920-235-2326
Candy boxes for chocolate candy manufacturers and cheese manufacturers
President: Patrick Kogutkiewiez
CEO: Terry Tormoen
Estimated Sales: $2.5 - 5 Million
Number Employees: 15
Square Footage: 21000

23296 Goe/Avins Fabricating
60 John Glenn Dr
Amherst, NY 14228-2118 716-691-7012
Fax: 716-691-8202 888-735-6907
info@goe-avins.com www.avinsfab.com
President: Gerald Bogdan
Estimated Sales: $3 - 5 Million
Number Employees: 10-19

23297 Goebel Fixture Company
528 Dale St SW
Hutchinson, MN 55350 320-587-2112
Fax: 320-587-2378 888-339-0509
gfinfo@gf.com www.gf.com
Wooden and plastic cutting boards and knife storage blocks
President: Bob Croatt
VP: Richard Goebel
General Manager: Bob Croatt
Department Manager: Brian Koehler
Estimated Sales: $10 - 20 Million
Number Employees: 100-249
Square Footage: 100000

23298 (HQ)Goeman's Wood Products
PO Box 270240
Hartford, WI 53027-0240 262-673-6090
Fax: 262-673-6459 info@gwp-inc.com
www.gwp-inc.com
Shipping crates, pallets and skids
President: Danny Guzman
Controller: Rich Blair
CEO: Danny Goeman
General Manager: Don Woods
Purchasing: Gary Hyber
Estimated Sales: $10-20 Million
Number Employees: 50-99
Square Footage: 40000
Other Locations:
Goeman's Wood Products
Hartford WI

23299 Goergen-Mackwirth Company
P.O.Box 750
Buffalo, NY 14207 716-874-4800
Fax: 716-874-4715 sales@gomac.com
www.gomac.com
Stainless steel and aluminum custom metal bins; also, conveyors
President: Wayne Mertz
Project Manager: Paul Kruger
Estimated Sales: $5 - 10 Million
Number Employees: 20-49
Square Footage: 24000

23300 Goex Corporation
2532 Foster Ave
Janesville, WI 53545 608-754-3303
Fax: 608-754-8976 goex@goex.com
www.goex.com
Manufacturer and exporter of packaging materials including rigid plastic sheet products
President: Joshua D Gray
Sales Manager: Richard Hamlin
Estimated Sales: $50-100 Million
Number Employees: 50-99

23301 Gold Bond
5485 Hixson Pike
Hixson, TN 37343 423-842-5844
Fax: 423-842-7934 lisan@goldbondinc.com
www.goldbondinc.com
Advertising novelties including pencils, pens, rulers and wooden nickels; also, custom plastic injection molding available
CEO: Donald W Godsey
Estimated Sales: $20-50 Million
Number Employees: 250-499

23302 Gold Coast Ingredients
2429 Yates Ave
Commerce, CA 90040 323-724-8935
Fax: 323-724-9354 800-352-8673
info@goldcoastinc.com www.goldcoastinc.com
A wholesale manufacturer of flavors and colors selling only to the wholsale segment of the food industry.
CEO: Chuck Brasher
Vice President: Laurie Goddard
Estimated Sales: $12 Million
Number Employees: 8
Type of Packaging: Private Label, Bulk

23303 Gold Medal Products Company
10700 Medallion Dr
Cincinnati, OH 45241 800-543-0862
Fax: 513-769-8500 800-543-0862
info@gmpopcorn.com www.gmpopcorn.com
Manufacturer and exporter of food products and concession equipment including popcorn machines, supplies and staging cabinets, butter dispensers, caramel, kettle and cheese corn, cotton candy machines and supplies, shave ice & sno-conemachines, drinks and frozen beverages, fried foods & bakers, nachos & cheese dispensers, hot dog grills & cookers, candy & caramel apples, whiz bang carnival games and more.
President: Dan Kroeger
Senior VP: John Evans
National Sales: Chris Petroff
International Sales: David Garretson
Estimated Sales: $20 - 50 Million
Number Employees: 250-499
Square Footage: 325000
Type of Packaging: Consumer, Food Service, Private Label, Bulk
Brands:
Love My Popper

23304 Gold Star Products
21680 Coolidge Hwy
Oak Park, MI 48237 248-548-9840
Fax: 248-548-9844 800-800-0205
info@goldstarmail.com
www.goldstarproducts.com
Restaurant equipment including refrigerators, stoves, freezers, etc.; also, trays, forks, napkins, etc
President: Jeffrey Applebaum
Estimated Sales: $5-10,000,000
Number Employees: 1-4

23305 (HQ)Goldco Industries
5605 Goldco Dr
Loveland, CO 80538 970-278-4400
Fax: 970-663-7212
info@goldcointernational.com
www.goldcointernational.com
Manufacturer and exporter of container and material handling equipment including depalletizers, palletizers and container, case and pallet handling systems
President: Richard Vander Meer
Marketing: Jim Parker
Sales: Jim Parker
Estimated Sales: $1 - 3 Million
Number Employees: 5-9
Square Footage: 100000
Other Locations:
Goldco Industries
Appleton WI

23306 Golden Eagle Extrusions
1762 State Route 131
Milford, OH 45150 513-248-8292
Fax: 513-248-8300 800-634-3355
info@goldeneagleextrusions.com
www.goldeneagleextrusions.com
President: Dave Eagle
CEO: Jenny Eagle
CFO: Jenney Dunkin
Product Development: Pat Delany
Plant Supervisor: Joe Herzog
Estimated Sales: $3 - 5 Million
Number Employees: 10-19

23307 Golden Needles Knitting& Glove Company
1300 Walnut Street
Coshocton, OH 43812-2262 919-667-5102
Fax: 919-838-2753 www.ansell.com
Manufacturer and exporter of protective gloves
Managing Director, Chief Executive Offic: Magnus Nicolin
Senior Vice President, Director of Asia: Denis Gallant
Communications Director: Wouter Piepers
Senior Vice President of Operations: Steve Genzer
Estimated Sales: $1 - 5 Million
Number Employees: 1000
Type of Packaging: Consumer, Food Service, Private Label, Bulk
Brands:
Hotpan'zers
Polar Bear

23308 (HQ)Golden Star
PO Box 12539
N Kansas City, MO 64116 816-842-0233
Fax: 816-842-1129 800-821-2792
goldenstar@goldenstar.com
www.goldenstar.com
Manufacturer and exporter of floor and furniture polish, mops, dry carpet cleaner solvent, mats and mattings
President: Gary Gradinger
Executive VP: Bill Gradinger
National Sales Manager: Steve Lewis
Estimated Sales: $20-50 Million
Number Employees: 20-49
Square Footage: 350000
Type of Packaging: Consumer, Food Service, Private Label
Brands:
Admiral
Barricade
Clencher
Comet Blend
Disposo-Treet
Dus-Trol
Golden Star
Healthcare
Infinity Twist
King
Performer
Quality
Quik-Change
Set-O-Swiv
Sno-White
Soil Sorb
Sta-Flat
Starborne
Wearever

23309 **Golden State Citrus Packers**
PO Box 697
Woodlake, CA 93286 559-564-3351
Fax: 559-564-3865 vcpg@vcpg.com
www.vcpg.com
Golden State Citrus Packers is a licensed commercial shipper of citrus products for Sunkist Growers, Inc.
President: George Lambeth
Office Manager: Judith Jenkins
Plant Manager: Raul Gamez
Parent Co: Visalia Citrus Packing Group
Type of Packaging: Food Service

23310 **Golden State Herbs**
60125 Polk St
Thermal, CA 92274 760-399-1133
Fax: 760-399-1555 800-730-3575
tony@goldenstateherbs.com
www.goldenstateherbs.com
Herbs whole and ground including sweet basil, dill weed, cilantro, marjoram, greek oregano, italian parsley, savory, spearmint, tarragon, thyme, and organic versions of each as well. Available as large, coarse, medium, fine andground.
Owner: Sam Vince
Secretary/Treasurer: Jack Vince
Sales Manager: Tony Griffin
VP of Operations: Curtis Vince
Estimated Sales: $3.4 Million
Number Employees: 50
Square Footage: 100000

23311 **Golden West Packaging Concept**
24342 Muirlands Blvd
Lake Forest, CA 92630-3679 949-855-9646
Fax: 949-645-7043
Custom and stock plastic packaging
General Manager: Connie Nash
Number Employees: 5-9
Square Footage: 5000

23312 **Golden West Sales**
16730 Gridley Rd
Cerritos, CA 90703-1730 562-924-7909
Fax: 562-924-7930 800-827-6175
info@gwsales.com www.gwsales.com
Manufacturer and exporter of tote boxes, magnetic flatware retriever systems and cutlery bins, covers, and rapid cooling flash chill bottles
Owner: Jitu Patel
Treasurer: Estee Edwards
Estimated Sales: $.5 - 1 million
Square Footage: 60000
Brands:
The Chute
Tough Guy Totes

23313 **Goldman Manufacturing Company**
13697 Elmira St
Detroit, MI 48227-3015 313-834-5535
Fax: 313-834-0496
Cardboard boxes, box partitions and separator pads; also, die cutting services available
Owner: Cherrie L Goldman
Office Manager: Elaine Patterson
Estimated Sales: $2.5-5 Million
Number Employees: 10 to 19

23314 **Goldmax Industries**
17747 Railroad St
City of Industry, CA 91748 626-964-8820
Fax: 626-964-6629 sales@goldmax.com
www.goldmax.com
Manufacturer and importer of wooden and bamboo toothpicks, chopsticks, stirrers, plastic bags, glove dispensers, skewers, disposable gloves and aprons; also, cocktail and party straws and picks
President: Paul Cheng
COO: Marcelo Mancilla
Sales Director: David Wang
Production: Manuel De La Roja
Purchasing Manager: William Hsing
Estimated Sales: $1 - 2.5 Million
Number Employees: 15
Type of Packaging: Food Service

23315 **(HQ)Gonterman & Associates**
5411 S Grand Blvd
Saint Louis, MO 63111 314-771-0600
Fax: 314-771-0610
Manufacturer and exporter of custom calendars and other advertising specialties
Estimated Sales: $1 - 5 Million
Number Employees: 5
Square Footage: 3000000
Brands:
S-Line

23316 **Good Idea**
351 Pleasant St
PMB 224
Northampton, MA 01060 413-586-4000
Fax: 413-585-0101 800-462-9237
info@larien.com www.larien.com
Manufacturer and exporter of bagel slicers and replacement blades.
President: Rick Ricard
Sales/Marketing Executive: Jim Dodge
Estimated Sales: $1 - 3 Million
Number Employees: 1-4
Brands:
Bagel Biter
Smartblade

23317 **Good Pack**
500 E Plume Street
Suite 509
Norfolk, VA 23510-2312 757-627-8889
Fax: 757-627-8989 gpusa@norfolk.infi.net
Steel cargo carrier shipping baskets
Estimated Sales: $1-5 000,000
Number Employees: 10

23318 **Goodall Rubber Company**
Quakerbridge Executive Drive
Lawrenceville, NJ 08648 609-799-2000
Fax: 609-799-4582 800-524-2650
Wine industry transfer and washing hoses
Estimated Sales: $1 - 5 000,000

23319 **Goodell Tools**
9440 Science Center Dr
New Hope, MN 55428-3624 763-531-0053
Fax: 763-531-0252 800-542-3906
info@goodelltools.com www.goodelltools.com
Manufacturer and exporter of grill scrapers and ice picks
Owner: Rick Garon
Marketing/Sales: Linda Alexander
Estimated Sales: $5 - 10 Million
Number Employees: 20-49
Square Footage: 88000
Type of Packaging: Private Label, Bulk
Brands:
Goodell

23320 **Goodman & Company**
401 Cooper Street
Camden, NJ 8102 856-225-6070
Fax: 856-225-6559 sales@goodmanfiltration.com
www.cgoodman.com
Filter cloths for filter presses, centrifuges, others
President: Arnold H Goodman
Estimated Sales: $5 - 10 Million
Number Employees: 50

23321 **Goodman Wiper & Paper**
PO Box 136
Auburn, ME 04212-0136 207-784-5779
Fax: 207-777-1717 800-439-9473
ken@goodmanwiper.com
www.goodmanwiper.com
New and recycled wiping cloths; distributor of paper towels, towel systems, trash liners, linen and terry towels, cleaners, gloves, oil absorbent pads and compounds.
President: Joel Goodman
CFO: Ken Goodman
VP/Plant Manager: Steve Goodman
Sales/Purchasing Director: Ken Goodman
Plant Manager: Steven Goodman
Estimated Sales: $10 - 20 Million
Number Employees: 10-19
Square Footage: 6000
Type of Packaging: Consumer, Food Service, Private Label

23322 **Goodnature Products**
3860 California Rd
Orchard Park, NY 14127 716-855-3325
Fax: 716-855-3328 800-875-3381
sales@goodnature.com www.goodnature.com
Manufacturer and exporter of food and juice processing equipment
President/Treasurer: Dale Wettlaufer
President: Diane Massett
Marketing: Angela Dedlin
Operations: Diane Massett
Estimated Sales: $3.5 Million
Number Employees: 20-49
Number of Brands: 1
Number of Products: 21
Brands:
Cmp Pasteurizer
Juice-It
Maximizer
Squeezebox
X-1

23323 **Goodway Industries**
175 Orville Drive
Bohemia, NY 11716-2503 631-567-2929
Fax: 631-567-2423 800-943-4501
info@goodwaysales.com
Manufacturer, importer and exporter of batch mixers, emulsifiers, dispersers, homogenizers, foamers, injectors, fillers, toppers and depositors
Director Sales/Marketing: Phillip Branning
Estimated Sales: $1 - 3,000,000
Number Employees: 23

23324 **Goodway Technologies Corporation**
420 West Ave
Stamford, CT 06902-6384 203-359-4708
Fax: 203-359-9601 800-333-7467
goodway@goodway.com www.goodway.com
Manufacturer and exporter of tube cleaning equipment, vacuums and pressure washers
President: Per Reichdlin
CFO: David Lobelson
CEO: Per K Reichborn
Director Marketing: Chris Van Name
Estimated Sales: $10 - 20,000,000
Number Employees: 50-99
Square Footage: 35000
Brands:
Awt-100
Jet Cleaner
Rea-A-Matic
Soot-A-Matic
Soot-Vac

23325 **(HQ)Goodwin Company**
12102 Industry St
Garden Grove, CA 92841 714-894-0531
Fax: 714-897-7673 www.goodwininc.com
Manufacturer and exporter of detergents
President: Tom Goodwin
General Manager: Rusty Peters
Estimated Sales: $20 - 50 Million
Number Employees: 50-99

23326 **Goodwin-Cole Company**
8320 Belvedere Ave
Sacramento, CA 95826 916-381-8888
Fax: 916-383-3499 800-752-4477
info@goodwincole.com www.goodwincole.com
Commercial awnings, party tents and flags
President: Roger Gilleland
Estimated Sales: $1-2,500,000
Number Employees: 10-19

23327 **Goodwrappers/J.C. Parry& Sons Company**
1920 Halethorpe Farms Rd
Halethorpe, MD 21227-4501 410-536-0400
Fax: 410-536-0484 800-638-1127
www.goodwrappers.com
Manufacturer and exporter of pallet stretch wrapping systems, printed stretch and black, red, orange, green, blue and white opaque and color tinted films and stretch netting
President: Bea Parry
CEO: John Parry
VP Marketing: David Parry
Estimated Sales: $10-20 Million
Number Employees: 20-49
Brands:
Goodwrappers Handwrappers
Goodwrappers Identi-Wrap

23328 Goodyear Tire & Rubber Company
P.O.Box 3531
Akron, OH 44309-3531 330-796-2121
Fax: 330-796-2222 www.goodyear.com
Tires for most applications.
President/CEO: Richard Kramer
Vice President: Darren Wells
Research/Development: Jean-Claude Kihn
Marketing: Scott Rogers
Public Relations: Ed Markey
Operations: Greg Smith
Purchasing: Mark Purtilar
Estimated Sales: $22.8 Billion
Number Employees: 72,000

23329 Goodyear Tire & Rubber Company
P.O.Box 83248
Lincoln, NE 68501-3248 402-466-8311
Fax: 402-467-8175 800-235-4632
hydraulics@goodyear.com www.goodyear.com
Wine industry hoses
VP E-Commerce: Eric Berg
President, Latin America Region: Christopher Clark
Senior VP Global Product Supply: Vernon Dunckel
Senior VP Tech./Global Prdts Planning: Joseph Gingo
VP Human Resources Planning Development: Donald Harper
VP Government Relations: Isabel Jasinowski
VP Purchasing: Gary Miller
Plant Manager: Dan Granatowicz
VP Global Prodt Marketing/Tech. Planning: William Hopkins
Estimated Sales: $100-500 Million
Number Employees: 250-499
Type of Packaging: Private Label

23330 Gorbel
P.O.Box 593
Fishers, NY 14453-0593 585-924-6262
Fax: 585-924-6273 www.gorbel.com
Manufacturer and exporter of aluminum and steel track cranes
President: David Reh
VP: David Butwid
Estimated Sales: $20.9 Million
Number Employees: 100-249
Parent Co: Raytek Group

23331 Gordon Food Service
1300 Gezon Parkway SW
Wyoming, MI 49509 616-530-7000
Fax: 616-717-7600 888-437-3663
info@gfs.com www.gfs.com
Distributor of food, beverages, and supply items to the food service industry
Parent Co: Gordon Food Service

23332 Gordon Graphics
15 Digital Drive
Suite A
Novato, CA 94949-5792 415-883-0455
Fax: 415-883-5124 charlie@gordongraphics.com
www.gordongraphics.com
Wine industry labels
President: Gordon Lindstron
Estimated Sales: $5-10 Millon
Number Employees: 10

23333 Gordon Sign Company
2930 W 9th Ave
Denver, CO 80204 303-629-6121
Fax: 303-629-1024 sales@gordonsign.com
www.gordonsign.com
Electrical advertising displays, signs and menu boards
President: James Skagen
Shop Manager: Bob Abeyta
Director Sales/Marketing: Harry Grass
Estimated Sales: $10-20 Million
Number Employees: 1-4
Square Footage: 100000
Parent Co: C.G. Industries

23334 Gorilla Label
7466 E Monte Cristo Avenue
Scottsdale, AZ 85260-1208 480-443-0303
Fax: 480-368-7923 800-615-7277
info@gorillalabel.com www.gorillalabel.com

23335 Goring Kerr
642 Blackhawk Dr
Westmont, IL 60559-1116 847-842-2397
Fax: 630-734-1497 866-269-0070
sales@goringkerr.com www.goring-kerr.com
Manager: Aaron Soto
Estimated Sales: $1 - 5 Million
Number Employees: 1-4
Parent Co: Thermo Fisher Scientific Inc

23336 Gortons Inc
128 Rogers Street
Gloucester, MA 01930 978-283-3000
Fax: 978-281-7949 800-321-7009
www.gortons.com
Manager: Karen Carter
Estimated Sales: C

23337 Gotham Pen & Pencil Company
1827 Washington Ave # 29
Bronx, NY 10457-6203 718-294-6699
Fax: 718-294-9044 800-334-7970
gothampen@aol.com www.gothamline.com
Pens and pencils; also, custom imprinting services available
Owner: Marshall Sutterman
Estimated Sales: $2.5-5 Million
Number Employees: 20-49

23338 Gough Econ, Inc.
PO Box 668583
Charlotte, NC 28266-8583 704-399-4501
Fax: 704-392-8706 800-204-6844
sales@goughecon.com www.goughecon.com
Bucket elevator and conveyor systems; exporter of bucket elevator systems; also, multiple discharges available. Also manufacturer of complete line of vibratory conveyors, feeders, screens and belt conveyors
President: David Risley
CEO: David Risley
VP: Don Calvert
Marketing: Angela Gallagher
Sales: Andrew Leitch
Estimated Sales: $5-10 Million
Number Employees: 20-49
Square Footage: 160000

23339 Gourmet Coffee Roasters
46956 Liberty Dr
Wixom, MI 48393 248-669-1060
Fax: 248-669-1111 866-933-6300
info@javamasters.com www.javamasters.com
In-store coffee roasters
Owner: Richard Sewell
Estimated Sales: $10-20,000,000
Number Employees: 5-9
Square Footage: 17000

23340 Gourmet Display
6040 S 194th Street
Suite 102
Kent, WA 98032-1191 206-764-6094
Fax: 206-767-4711 800-767-4711
info@gourmetdisplay.com
www.gourmetdisplay.com
Mirrored and marble serving equipment for buffets and banquets
National Sales Manager: Howard Michaelson
Vice President: Mark Vollmar
Marketing Manager: T Ecker
Sales Manager: Julien Chomette
General Manager: T Schueler
Estimated Sales: $2.5-5 Million
Number Employees: 20-50
Parent Co: Plastic Dynamics
Brands:
Riser Rims
Serving Stone
Texture Tone

23341 Gourmet Gear
1413 Westwood Blvd
Los Angeles, CA 90024-4911 310-268-2222
Fax: 310-301-4115 800-682-4635
sales@gourmet-gear.com www.gourmetgear.com
Culinary apparel
Owner: Farhad Besharati
CEO: Newton Katz
Director Marketing: Marcee Katz
Estimated Sales: $500,000-$1 Million
Number Employees: 1-4

23342 Gourmet Tableskirts
9415 West Bellfort Street
Houston, TX 77031-2308 713-666-0602
Fax: 713-666-0627 800-527-0440
gkammerman@gourmet-table-skirts.com
www.tableskirts.com
Manufacturer and exporter of table cloths, skirts and runners, napkins, place mats and aprons
President: Glen Kammerman
Estimated Sales: $2.5-5 Million
Number Employees: 20-49
Square Footage: 64000
Type of Packaging: Consumer, Food Service
Brands:
Permalux
Permanent Press
Polytwill
Visa

23343 Governair Corporation
4841 N Sewell Ave
Oklahoma City, OK 73118 405-525-6546
Fax: 405-528-4724 info@governair.com
www.governair.com
Manufacturer and exporter of air handling units, evaporative condensing package water chillers, etc
President: Jim Durr
General Manager: Jim Durr
Quality Control: Bill Taylor
R & D: Mark Sly
Marketing: Mark Fly
Sales: Buddy Cross
Plant Manager: Brad Campbell
Purchasing: Vickey Hopper
Estimated Sales: $20-30 Million
Number Employees: 100-249
Square Footage: 150000
Parent Co: Nortek
Brands:
Governair

23344 Government Food Service
P.O.Box 1500
Westbury, NY 11590-0812 516-334-3030
Fax: 516-334-3059 ebm-mail@ebmpubs.com
www.ebmpubs.com
President: Murry Greenwald
R & D: Fred Shaen
Estimated Sales: $10 - 20 Million
Number Employees: 20-49

23345 Goya Foods of Florida
13300 NW 25th Street
Miami, FL 33182 305-592-3150
Fax: 305-592-4202 info@goya.com
www.goyafoods.com
Founded in 1936. Wholesaler/distributor of Hispanic and Latin foods including olive oil, olives, beans, rice, fish preserves, canned meats, frozen foods, etc.
President: Mary Unanue
Controller: Raul Zabala
VP: Uben Chavez
Human Resource Manager: Maria Banos
Purchasing Director: Luis Olarte
Estimated Sales: $20 - 50 Million
Number Employees: 100
Square Footage: 26541
Parent Co: Goya Foods
Brands:
Goya Seasonings
Goya Foods

23346 (HQ)GraLab Corporation
900 Dimco Way
Centerville, OH 45458-2710 937-433-7600
Fax: 937-433-0520 800-876-8353
glsales@gralab.com www.gralab.com
Electromechanical and electronic timing devices for commercial cooking and baking applications, food testing laboratories, process control systems and sanitation; also, thermoset and thermoplastic compression and injection moldedproducts.
President & CEO: Michael Sieron
Treasurer: Terry Tate
Quality Control: Lyle Crum
Sales & Marketing Manager: Linda Raisch
Production: James Daulton
Number of Brands: 1
Number of Products: 20
Parent Co: Dimco-Gray Corporation

23347 **Grace-Lee Products**
2450 2nd Street NE
Minneapolis, MN 55418 612-379-2711
Fax: 763-789-6263
Detergents and institutional cleaning products
President: Barry Graceman
Executive VP: Sherman Gleekel
Institutional Sales Manager: Tom Pross
Number Employees: 75
Square Footage: 55000

23348 **Gracey Instrument Corporation**
PO Box 231591
Encinitas, CA 92023-1591 760-436-8070
Fax: 760-436-8073 800-304-5859
www.graceyinstrument.com
Manufacturer and importer of thermometers including bi-metal, digital, pocket test, vapor tension dial, refrigeration, oven, barbecue grill and deep fry
President: Michelle J. Gracy
Marketing Manager: Michelle Dahm
Estimated Sales: $1 - 5 Million

23349 **(HQ)Graco**
P.O.Box 1441
Minneapolis, MN 55440-1441 612-623-6000
Fax: 612-378-3505 877-844-7226
info@graco.com www.graco.com
Manufacturer and exporter of industrial and portable cleaners, sanitary pumps and dispensers.
Chairman/President/CEO: David Roberts
Chief Administrative Officer: Mark Sheahan
Chief Financial Officer/Treasurer: James Graner
CEO: Patrick J McHale
Sales & Marketing Director: Rick Berkbigler
Vice President Operations: Charles Rescoria
Estimated Sales: $7 Million
Number Employees: 1,000-4,999
Brands:
Graco, Inc.

23350 **Graff Tank Erection**
RR 1
Box 246
Harrisville, PA 16038-9511 814-385-6671
Fax: 814-385-6657 grafftank@grafftankinc.com
www.grafftankinc.com
Above-ground steel storage tanks, bins and hoppers; field based erection and repair services available
Owner: William Graff
Controller: Rose Graff
Quality Control: Rose Graff
President: William Graff
Engineer Manager: Raymond Graff
Estimated Sales: $500,000 - $1 Million
Number Employees: 10
Square Footage: 32000

23351 **Grafoplast Wiremakers**
6875 E 48th Ave
Denver, CO 80216-5310 303-321-5995
Fax: 303-399-5054 800-864-3874
sales@grafoplast.com www.grafoplast.com
Markers for terminal blocks, relays, wire, and cable
Manager: Maureen Wilkins
Estimated Sales: $1-2.5 Million
Number Employees: 1-4

23352 **Grafoplast Wiremarkers**
6875 E 48th Ave
Denver, CO 80216 303-321-5995
Fax: 303-399-5054 800-864-3874
sales@graoplast.com www.grafoplast.com
Estimated Sales: $3 - 5 Million
Number Employees: 1-4

23353 **(HQ)Graham Engineering Corporation**
1203 Eden Rd
York, PA 17402 717-848-3755
Fax: 717-846-1931 www.grahamengineering.com
Manufacturer and exporter of blow-molded plastic bottles and containers
President: Steven F Wood
VP: Joe Spohr
CEO: Wolfgang Liebertz
CFO: Rich Rutkowski
VP Sales/Marketing: F White
Estimated Sales: $20 - 50 Million
Number Employees: 100-249

23354 **Graham Ice & Locker Plant**
328 Elm Street
Graham, TX 76450-2514 940-549-1975
Ice; slaughterer, processor and wholesaler/distributor of deer
Owner: James Black
Estimated Sales: Less than $500,000
Number Employees: 1 to 4
Type of Packaging: Consumer

23355 **Graham Pallet Company**
3234 Celina Rd
Tompkinsville, KY 42167 270-487-6609
Fax: 270-487-9420 888-525-0694
Wooden pallets and skids
President: Rick Miller
Sales Manager: Mike Scoby
Production Manager: Carolyn Grove
Plant Manager: J Stewart
Estimated Sales: $5 - 10 Million
Number Employees: 50-99
Square Footage: 50000

23356 **Grain Machinery Manufacturing Corporation**
1130 NW 163rd Dr
Miami, FL 33169 305-620-2525
Fax: 305-620-2551 grainman@bellsouth.net
www.grainman.com
Manufacturer and exporter of grain elevators, dryers, graders, cleaners, pea and bean hullers, casting and rice machinery, bagging scales and conveyor belts; importer of casting and rice machinery
Owner: Manny Diaz
Treasurer: Librada Dieguez
Vice President: Cary Dieguez
Sales Director: Jose Martinez
Purchasing Manager: Brissa Pichardo
Estimated Sales: $3 - 5 Million
Number Employees: 10-19
Square Footage: 86000
Brands:
Cell-O-Matic
Grainman
Rimac

23357 **Grain Processing Corporation**
1600 Oregon St
Muscatine, IA 52761 563-264-4727
Fax: 563-264-4289 800-448-4472
sales@grainprocessing.com
www.grainprocessing.com
Manufacturer and worldwide marketer of corn-based products.
President: Doyle Tubandt
CEO: Gage Kent
VP: Brian Tompoles
R&D: Frank Barresi
Quality Control: Rani Thomas
Marketing/Public Relations: Diane Rieke
Technical Sales: Charles Lambert
Operations: Ron Zitzow
Purchasing: Brian Hasser
Number Employees: 656
Square Footage: 300000
Parent Co: Muscatine Foods Corporation
Brands:
Incosity
Instant Pure-Cote
Maltrin
Maltrin Qd
Pure-Bind
Pure-Cote
Pure-Dent
Pure-Gel

23358 **(HQ)Gram Equipment of America**
1212 N 39th St Ste 438
Tampa, FL 33605 813-248-1978
Fax: 813-248-2314 sales@gramequipment.com
www.gram-equipment.com
Box/carton formers, ice cream makers, feeders, freezers and heat exchangers
Owner: Hans Gram
Number Employees: 5-9
Type of Packaging: Food Service, Bulk

23359 **GranPac**
4709 39th Avenue
Wetaskiwin, AB T9A 2J4
Canada 780-352-3324
Fax: 780-352-3387
Polyethylene plastic food containers
Sales Manager: G Jacobson
Managing Director: J Patel
Estimated Sales: $1 - 5 Million
Number Employees: 20-50
Square Footage: 40000

23360 **Granco Pumps**
2010 Crow Canyon Place
Suite 100
San Ramon, CA 94583 925-359-3290
Fax: 925-359-3291 info@grancopump.com
www.grancopump.com
Manufacturer and exporter of hydraulically driven and low shear pumping systems; also, rotary positive pumps for displacement of viscous liquids.
President: Ivan Dimcheff
CEO: Michael Alessandro
Operations: Ivan Dimcheff
Production Manager: David Kenzler
Estimated Sales: $.5 - 1 million
Number Employees: 5-9
Square Footage: 64000
Parent Co: Challenge Manufacturing Company
Type of Packaging: Private Label
Brands:
Grandco
Hy-Drive Systems

23361 **Grand Rapids Label Company**
2351 Oak Industrial Dr NE
Grand Rapids, MI 49505-6017 616-459-8134
Fax: 616-459-4543 grlabel@grlabel.com
www.grlabel.com
Manufacturer and exporter of pressure sensitive and heat seal labels including advertising and supermarket
President: W W Muir
CFO: John Laninga
R&D: Tony Maravalo
Quality Control: Christine Howlett
VP Sales: Tom Topel
Estimated Sales: $10 - 20 Million
Number Employees: 50-99
Type of Packaging: Bulk

23362 **Grand Silver Company**
289 Morris Avenue
Bronx, NY 10451-6198 718-585-1930
Fax: 718-402-4724 grandsilve@aol.com
www.grandsilver.net
Silver plated hollowware, coffee pots, sugar bowls and creamers; also, repairing and replating services available
CEO: Barry Kostrinsky
Estimated Sales: $2.5-5 Million
Number Employees: 20-49

23363 **Grand Valley Labels**
4417 Broadmoor Ave SE
Grand Rapids, MI 49512-5367
Fax: 616-784-2915
Pressure sensitive labels, tags, envelopes, bar codes, label printing systems, packaging, etc.
Estimated Sales: $5-10 Million
Number Employees: 1-4
Square Footage: 5000

23364 **Grande Chef Company**
21 Stewart Court
Orangeville, ON L9W 3Z9
Canada 519-942-4470
Fax: 519-942-4440 www.grande-chef.ca
Manufacturer, importer and exporter of stainless steel cooking equipment including cookers, kettles, ovens and broilers
President: Frank Edmonstone
Sales/Marketing Executive: Lisa Ashton
Sales/Marketing Executive: Alex Mackay
Operations Manager: Lisa Ashton
Purchasing Manager: Frank Edmonstone
Number Employees: 5-9
Brands:
Grande Chef

23365 **Grande Custom Ingredients Group**
Dairy Rd
Brownsville, WI 53006-0067 920-269-7200
Fax: 920-269-7124 800-678-3122
gcig@grande.com www.grande.com

Processor and exporter of specialty whey products and lactose
CEO: Wayne Matzke
CEO: Wayne Matzke
R&D: Michelle Ludtke
Marketing Director: Stephen Dott
Operations: Mike Nelson
Purchasing Director: Kevin Hampton
Estimated Sales: $25 Million
Number Employees: 5-9
Square Footage: 10000
Parent Co: Grande Cheese Company
Type of Packaging: Bulk
Brands:
Grande Bravo Whey Protein
Grande Gusto Natural Flavor
Grande Ultra Nutritional Whey Prot.

23366 **Grande Ronde Sign Company**
2302 Cove Avenue
La Grande, OR 97850-3907 541-963-5841
Fax: 541-963-4337 grsignco@eoni.com
Signs including neon, wood, plastic and vinyl
President: Mat Barber
Office Manager: Jenne O'Daol
Estimated Sales: Below $5 Million
Number Employees: 1 to 4

23367 **Granite State Stamps, Inc.**
PO Box 5252
Manchester, NH 03108-5252 603-669-9322
Fax: 603-669-5182 800-937-3736
sales@granitestatestamps.com
www.granitestatestamps.com
Engraved name pins and rubber stamps
President: Lynn A Hale
VP Sales: Lynn Hale
Estimated Sales: $1-2.5 Million
Number Employees: 10-19
Square Footage: 20000

23368 **Grant Chemicals**
PO Box 13
New Hope, PA 18938-0013 215-331-3350
Fax: 215-331-2394
Wine industry chemicals

23369 **Grant Laboratories**
14688 Washington Ave
San Leandro, CA 94578-4218 510-483-6070
Fax: 510-483-9846 skip81445@aol.com
Insecticides including ant and insect granular
CEO: William E Brown
COO: Louis Antonali
COO: Quazui Iqbal
Sales Director: Brian Bate
Estimated Sales: $5-10 Million
Number Employees: 5 to 9
Square Footage: 26000
Parent Co: Central Garden & Pet
Type of Packaging: Consumer
Brands:
Grants Kill Ants

23370 **Grant-Letchworth**
110 Mullen Street
Tonawanda, NY 14150-5424 716-692-1000
Fax: 716-692-3638 response@letchworth.com
www.letchworth.com
Grinders, mixers and stuffers
President: W Keith Jackson
Sales Manager: James Smith
Estimated Sales: $1-2.5 Million
Number Employees: 4

23371 **Granville ManufacturingCompany**
P.O.Box 15
Granville, VT 05747 802-767-4747
Fax: 802-767-3107 800-828-1005
bowlmill@madriver.com www.bowlmill.com
One piece wooden bowls made from premium hardwoods in Vermont
President: Robert Fuller
Marketing Director: Cindy Fuller
Purchasing Manager: Cindy Fuller
Estimated Sales: $1,000,000
Number Employees: 10-19
Square Footage: 10000

23372 **Graphic Apparel**
2365 Industrial Park Road
Inniasfil, ON L9S 3W1
Canada 705-436-6137
Fax: 705-436-6139 800-757-4867
sales@graphicapparel.on.ca
www.graphic-apparel.ca
Distributor of career apparel and promotions
President: Werner Syndikus
Sales Manager: Mitch Dawkins
Number Employees: 10
Square Footage: 32000
Type of Packaging: Food Service

23373 **Graphic Arts Center**
709 Silver Palm Ave
Suite H
Melbourne, FL 32901 321-725-0710
Fax: 321-984-3783 888-345-7436
gac@yourlink.net www.graphicartscenter.net
Graphic designer of packages, labels, advertising materials, cartons, displays, literature and trade show displays
Owner: D D Rhem
Estimated Sales: $500,000-$1 Million
Number Employees: 1-4
Square Footage: 4800
Parent Co: Rhem Group
Type of Packaging: Consumer, Food Service, Private Label, Bulk

23374 **Graphic Calculator Company**
234 James Street
Barrington, IL 60010-3388 847-381-4480
Fax: 847-381-5370 info@slide-chart.com
www.slide-chart.com
Manufacturer and exporter of advertising novelties including slide rules, printed calculators and feature demonstrators
President: Capron Gulbronsen
VP: Lorraine Gorski
Estimated Sales: $5 - 10 Million
Number Employees: 10

23375 **Graphic Impressions of Illinois**
8538 Grand Ave
River Grove, IL 60171 708-453-1100
Fax: 708-453-1169
graphicimpressions@prodigy.net
Quality flexographic labels and printing plates. Custom labels priced by specification. Complete design for flexible packaging. ValueStar certified. A family owned business since 1956
Estimated Sales: $1-2,500,000
Number Employees: 5-9

23376 **Graphic Packaging Corporation**
4455 Table Mountain Drive
Golden, CO 80403 720-497-4724
Fax: 303-273-2935 800-677-2886
info@graphicpkg.com www.graphicpkg.com
Labels, bottle carriers and beverage and carrier cartons
Chairman/ President/ CEO: David W. Scheible
CFO/ SVP: Daniel J. Blount
SVP, Flexible Division: R. Allen Ennis
Plant Manager: Jeffrey Coors
Estimated Sales: $1 - 5 Million
Number Employees: 100-249
Parent Co: Graphic Packaging Corporation

23377 **Graphic Packaging Holding Company**
814 Livingston Court
Marietta, GA 30067 770-644-3000
www.graphicpkg.com
Paperboard containers
President: John Pfeifle
CEO: Mike Doss
Sales/Marketing Executive: David Frambach
VP Manufacturing: Mike Doff
Estimated Sales: $4.34 Billion
Number Employees: 13900
Parent Co: Graphic Pakaging Corporation

23378 **(HQ)Graphic Promotions**
7418 SW 23rd Court
Topeka, KS 66614-6079 785-234-6684
Fax: 785-354-1519 gpromotion@aol.com
Consultant specializing in promotional services and support including point of purchase signage, labels, specialty items, fulfillment, creative art/graphics, design, inventory manangement and printing
VP: Kurt Oswald
Number Employees: 100-249
Square Footage: 72000
Other Locations:
Graphic Promotions
Topeka KS

23379 **Graphic Technology**
301 Gardner Dr
New Century, KS 66031 913-764-5550
Fax: 913-764-0320 800-767-9920
marketing@graphic-tech.com
www.graphic-tech.com
Manufacturer, exporter and importer of bar coded and nonbar coded shelf labels for product unit pricing; bar code printers and software; also, picking labels
VP Sales/Marketing: Tom Pooton
Estimated Sales: $1 - 5 Million
Number Employees: 500-999
Square Footage: 250000
Parent Co: Nitto Denko Corporation

23380 **Graphics Unlimited**
10477 Roselle St Ste B
San Diego, CA 92121 858-453-4031
Fax: 858-453-5337 guinc@cts.com
Decals, name plates and banners; also, screen printing available
Owner: Les Burge
Estimated Sales: $1-2,500,000
Number Employees: 5-9

23381 **Graphite Metallizing Corporation**
1050 Nepperhan Ave
Yonkers, NY 10703 914-968-8400
Fax: 914-968-8468 sales@graphalloy.com
www.graphalloy.com
Manufacturer and exporter of graphalloy high-temperature self-lubricating bearings for ovens
President: Eben Walker
Quality Control: Mohmed Youssef
Director Marketing: Eric Ford
Estimated Sales: $10 - 20 Million
Number Employees: 50-99
Square Footage: 50000
Brands:
Graphalloy
Graphilm

23382 **Grasselli SSI**
410 Charles St
Throop, PA 18512 570-489-8001
Fax: 570-485-8005 800-789-4353
info@grasselli-ssi.com www.grasselli-ssi.com
Processing equipment for meat and fish industries; slicing and skinning
President: David Atcherley
Vice President: Helga Harrington
Estimated Sales: $8 Million
Number Employees: 12

23383 **Grasselli SSI**
410 Charles St
Throop, PA 18512-0379 570-489-8001
Fax: 570-489-8005 800-789-4353
info@skinnersystems.com
www.skinnersystems.com
Defatting machines, skinning machines, slicing blades
VP: Helga Harrington
Number Employees: 5-9

23384 **Grasso**
1101 N Governor Street
Evansville, IN 47711-5069 812-465-6600
Fax: 812-465-6610 800-821-3486
grasso@fessystems.com www.grasso.nl
Industrial reciprocating and screw refrigeration compressors, custom-built refrigeration packages for any refrigerant including ammonia; self-limiting automatic purgers for refrigeration systems
President: Jake Grifford
Manager of Quality: Harald Wilke
Marketing Manager: Martina Chao
Manager of International Sales: Siegfried Pitsch
Estimated Sales: $20-50 Million
Number Employees: 10

23385 Grating Pacific/Ross Technology Corporation
3651 Sausalito St
Los Alamitos, CA 90720-2436 562-598-4314
Fax: 562-598-2740 800-321-4314
sales@gratingpacific.com
www.gratingpacific.com
Founded in 1971. Distributor of industrial flooring.
President: Ron Robertson
Estimated Sales: $20 - 30 Million
Number Employees: 50-99

23386 Graver Technologies
200 Lake Dr
Glasgow, DE 19702 302-731-1700
Fax: 302-731-1707 800-249-1990
info@gravertech.com www.hydroglobe.com
Microfiltration membranes
President: John McPeak
VP Finance and Administration: Sharon Gatta
VP and General Manager Liquid Filters: Bill Cummings
Product Manager: Scott Wittwer
Number Employees: 50-99

23387 Gray Woodproducts
297 Swetts Pond Rd
Orrington, ME 04474-3706 207-825-3578
Fax: 207-825-3200
Pallets and skids
Treasurer: Patricia Gray, Jr.
Vice President: W Douglas Gray, Jr.
Estimated Sales: $500,000-$1 Million
Number Employees: 1-4

23388 Graybill Machines
221 W Lexington Rd Ste 1
Lititz, PA 17543 717-626-5221
Fax: 717-626-1886 info@graybillmachines.com
www.graybillmachines.com
Designs and builds custom food machinery, specializing in finishing systems, product registration/handling, process machinery and specialized packaging
President: David Fyock
Marketing Director: Matthew Randolph
Sales Director: John Stough
Estimated Sales: $2.5-$5 Million
Number Employees: 10-19
Square Footage: 22000

23389 Grayco Products Sales
100 Tec Street
Hicksville, NY 11801-3650 516-997-9200
Fax: 516-870-0510
Wholesaler/distributor and exporter of paper and disposable products including tabletop and industrial equipment, packaging and printing supplies
Owner: Helen Kushner
CEO: Adrienne Kushner
Vice President: Alan Kushner
Operations Manager: D Pascale
Estimated Sales: $1 - 5 Million
Number Employees: 2
Square Footage: 5000
Parent Co: ASK Sales

23390 Graydon Lettercraft
81 Cuttermill Rd
Great Neck, NY 11021-3153 516-482-0531
Fax: 516-482-5632
Advertising specialties and custom printed brochures and stationery
Owner: Pasquale Riccardi
VP: Ruth Theobald
Estimated Sales: $300,000-500,000
Number Employees: 1-4

23391 Grayline Housewares
455 Kehoe Blvd
Suite 105
Carol Stream, IL 60188-5203 630-682-3330
Fax: 630-682-3363 800-222-7388
Coated-wire space savers and organizers including bag and pot holders, bars, wall grids and racks including can, kitchen and wire
President: Fred Rosen
Director: Paul Nearpass
Estimated Sales: $500,000-$1 Million
Number Employees: 10

23392 Grayling Industries
1008 Branch Dr
Alpharetta, GA 30004 770-751-9095
Fax: 770-751-3710 800-635-1551
raymond.joyner@graylingmail.com
www.graylingindustries.com
Director of Sales: Raymond Joyner
Estimated Sales: $16 Million
Number Employees: 10-19
Parent Co: ILC Dover
Type of Packaging: Food Service, Bulk

23393 Grays Harbor Stamp Works
110 N G St
Aberdeen, WA 98520 360-533-3830
Fax: 360-533-3210 800-894-3830
graysharborstamp@olynet.com
www.graysharborstamp.com
Promotional buttons, engraved signage and rubber stamps
Partner: Ronald Windell
Partner: Ron Windell
Partner: Kenneth Windell
Estimated Sales: $2.5-5 Million
Number Employees: 5-9

23394 Graytech Carbonic
9460 230th Street E
Lakeville, MN 55044-8137 952-461-8020
Fax: 952-461-8022
Estimated Sales: $1-2.5 000,000
Number Employees: 1-4

23395 Grease Master
608 Matthews-Mint Hill Rd.
Suite 105
Matthews, NC 28105-0309 704-844-6907
Fax: 704-844-8013 info@greasemaster.com
www.greasemaster.com
Kitchen ventilation systems including wall mounted and exhaust only canopies
Division Manager: David Breidt
Sales Quotations Design: Harvey Worrell
Division Manager: David Breidt
Plant Manager: Nick Nakos
Estimated Sales: $1 - 5 Million
Number Employees: 20-49
Square Footage: 92000
Parent Co: Custom Industries
Brands:
Grease Master

23396 Great Dane Trailers, Inc.
602 E. Lathrop Ave.
Savannah, GA 31415-1062 912-232-4471
Fax: 912-233-8334 www.greatdanetrailers.com
Refrigerated tractor trailers
President: Christopher Hammond
Estimated Sales: $257.6 Million
Number Employees: 4320
Brands:
Great Dane

23397 Great Lakes Brush
6859 Audrain Road #9139
Centralia, MO 65240 573-682-2128
Fax: 573-682-2121 sales@greatlakesbrush.com
www.greatlakesbrush.com
Manufacturer and importer of brushes and wire drawn products
President: Matthew Kallas
Estimated Sales: $500,000-$1 Million
Number Employees: 1-4
Square Footage: 4000

23398 Great Lakes Corrugated
1400 Matzinger Rd
Toledo, OH 43612-3827 419-726-3491
Fax: 419-726-2703 www.greif.com
Bulk boxes, die cuts and curtain contained corrugated shipping containers
Manager: George Petzelt
VP Sales/Marketing: Dan Lautermilch
Sales Representative: David Mackson
Number Employees: 100-249

23399 Great Lakes Scientific
2847 Lawrence St
Stevensville, MI 49127 269-429-1000
Fax: 269-429-1550 gls@glslab.com
www.glslab.com
An independent laboratory offering confidental testing services for food, water and environmental samples. A USDA recognized (microbiology) and accredited (chemistry) laboratory.
President: Wayne Gleiber
Estimated Sales: $1-2.5 Million
Number Employees: 20-49
Square Footage: 5000

23400 Great Lakes Software ofMichigan
P.O.Box 2222
Howell, MI 48844 517-548-4333
Fax: 517-548-4433
sales@greatlakessoftware.com
www.greatlakessoftware.com
C.I.M.S.(computerized inventory and logistic management system) designed for beverage industry manufacturing, distribution, warehousing and sales
Owner: Gene Chandler
Estimated Sales: $1 - 2.5 000,000
Number Employees: 1-4

23401 Great Lakes-Triad Package Corporation
3939 36th Street
Grand Rapids, MI 49512 616-241-6441
Fax: 616-241-4145 www.gltpackaging.com
Corrugated boxes and containers
Estimated Sales: $50-100 Million
Number Employees: 50-99

23402 Great Northern Corporation
PO Box 939
Appleton, WI 54912 920-739-3671
Fax: 920-739-7096 800-236-3671
webgnc@greatnortherncorp.com
www.gnc-net.com
Manufacturer and exporter of expandable polystyrene plastic packaging products including boxes and containers
President: John Davis
CEO: William Raaths
CFO: Terry Abrahim
Quality Control: Stacey Lipperg
Marketing Director: Brien Fiebig
Estimated Sales: $100-500 Million
Number Employees: 500-999
Type of Packaging: Bulk
Brands:
Rollguard

23403 Great Northern Corporation
1800 South Street
Racine, WI 53404 262-639-4700
800-558-4711
www.greatnortherncorp.com
Corrugated boxes
Estimated Sales: $50-100 Million
Number Employees: 191
Square Footage: 70058
Parent Co: Great Northern Corporation
Type of Packaging: Bulk

23404 Great Plains Beef
PO Box 82545
Lincoln, NE 68501 800-544-1359
Fax: 402-458-4531 info@piedmontese.com
www.greatplainsbeef.com
High quality beef
President: Billy Swain
Brands:
Lone Creek Cattle Company
Great Plains
Certified Piedmontese

23405 Great Plains Software
1 Lone Tree Road S
Fargo, ND 58104-3911 701-281-0550
Fax: 701-282-9243 800-456-0025
info@greatplains.com www.greatplains.com
Backoffice accounting software
Sr. VP (Marketing Communications): Michael Olsen
Franchise Marketing Manager: Judy Felch

23406 Great Southern Corporation
3595 Regal Blvd
Memphis, TN 38118 901-365-1611
Fax: 901-365-4498 800-421-7802
sales@greatsoutherncorp.com
www.greatsoutherncorp.com

Manufacturer, importer and exporter of licensed gloves consisting of leather, cotton, plastic and rubber gloves; also, rubber bands
President: Scott Vaught
Chairman: C Vaught
Estimated Sales: $20 - 50 Million
Square Footage: 48000
Parent Co: Great Southern Corporation
Brands:
Sirco

23407 Great Southern Industries
PO Box 5325
Jackson, MS 39296-5325 601-948-5700
Fax: 601-355-3214 gsibox@netdoor.com
www.gsi.com
Corrugated shipping containers
President: Charles Ellis
President, Chief Executive Officer: Tom Tiernan
CFO: Nancy Hocutt
Executive Vice President, General Manage: Michael Elia
Production Manager: Bill Dahlman
Estimated Sales: $10-20 Million
Number Employees: 100-249

23408 Great Western Chemical Company
5200 SW Macadam Ave # 200
Portland, OR 97239-3800 503-228-2600
Fax: 503-228-8471 800-547-1400
www.greatwesterninorganics.com
Manufacturer and wholesaler/distributor of cleaning and sanitation chemicals and food ingredients including acidulants, preservatives, etc
Manager: Jason Keyes
Bus. Mgr.: Tom Cervenka
Bus. Mgr.: Andy Pollard
VP Marketing: Tami Mainero
Estimated Sales: $50-100 Million
Number Employees: 5-9

23409 Great Western Manufacturing Company
2017 So. 4th Floor
PO Box 149
Leavenworth, KS 66048 913-682-2291
Fax: 913-682-1431 800-682-3121
sifter@gwmfg.com www.gwmfg.com
Screening machines, shakers, sifters, screens and sieves.
CFO: Michael Bell
General Manager: Robert Ricklefs
Sales, Services & Applications Engineeri: Bob Recklifs
Production Manager: Steve Wood
Purchasing Manager: Michael Glassford
Estimated Sales: $5-10 Million
Number Employees: 10
Type of Packaging: Food Service
Brands:
Hs
Tru Balance

23410 Great Western Products
1929 S Campus Ave
Ontario, CA 91761-5410 909-923-9258
Fax: 909-923-9228 888-598-5588
info@knl-international.com
www.knl-international.com
Manufacturer, Importer and Exporter of chopsticks, toothpicks, guest checks, napkins, plastic T-Shirt bags, bamboo skewers, matches, sushi containers, wood sushi plates, wood sushi boats (bridge), swirl bowls, dried seaweed, eel(unagi), wasabi powder and soybean (edamame).
President: David Kao
VP: Susan Lin
Marketing Director: Richard Yeang
Manager: May Lin
Estimated Sales: $5 - 10 Million
Number Employees: 5-9
Number of Products: 20
Square Footage: 100000
Type of Packaging: Food Service, Private Label

23411 Great Western Products Company
30290 Us Highway 72
Hollywood, AL 35752 256-259-3578
Fax: 256-259-2939 800-239-2143
info@gwproducts.com. www.gwproducts.com
Manufacturer and exporter of high quality concession supplies and concession equipment including popcorn, popping oils, popcorn topping, cotton candy, sno-cone syrups, candy apple coatings, funnel cakes, waffle cones, corn dog mixetc
President: Larry Jones
VP: Ralph Ferber-Theatus
R&D: Gerald Scott
Sales: M Hamilton
Purchasing Director: Rocky Franklin
Estimated Sales: $10-20 Million
Square Footage: 48000
Type of Packaging: Consumer, Food Service, Private Label, Bulk
Brands:
Great Western
S.T. Echols
Senor Carlos
Sunglo

23412 Great Western Products Company
30290 US Highway 72
Hollywood, AL 35752 256-259-3578
Fax: 573-734-6454 info@ghproudct.com
www.gwproducts.com
Processor and exporter of popcorn, popping corn oil, cotton candy, sno-cone syrup, candy apple coatings, funnel cakes, waffle cones, corn dog mix, etc.; manufacturer of concession equipment including corn poppers
Manager: Marvin Scott
Estimated Sales: $500,000-$1,000,000
Number Employees: 5-9
Type of Packaging: Consumer, Food Service, Private Label, Bulk

23413 Great Western Products Company
2047 E 1350 North Rd
Assumption, IL 62510 217-226-3241
Fax: 217-226-3569
Processor and exporter of popcorn, popping corn oil, cotton candy, sno-cone syrup, candy apple coatings, funnel cakes, waffle cones, corn dog mix, etc.
General Manager: Mike Calcara
Estimated Sales: $10-20,000,000
Number Employees: 40
Type of Packaging: Consumer, Food Service, Private Label, Bulk

23414 Grecon, Inc.
15875 SW 74th Ave
Suite 100
Tigard, OR 97224 503-641-7731
Fax: 503-641-7508 sales@grecon-us.com
www.grecon-us.com
Spark detection and extinguishing systems, as well as quality assurance measuring systems.

23415 Greeley Tent & Awning
2209 9th St
P.O.Box 571
Greeley, CO 80632-0571 970-352-0253
Fax: 970-352-2013 info@greeleytadirect.com
www.greeleytadirect.com
Commercial awnings
Owner: Julie Heyer
CFO: Barbara Hendricks
Estimated Sales: Less than $500,000
Number Employees: 1-4

23416 Green & Black's OrganicChocolate
PO Box 259011
Plano, TX 75025 973-909-3900
Fax: 973-909-3930 877-299-1254
greenandblacks@cohnwolfe.com
www.greenandblacks.com/us
Organic choclate
President/Owner: Neil Turpin
CFO: James Reed
Number Employees: 8

23417 Green Bag America Inc.
15430 Cabrito Road
Unit 1
Van Nuys, CA 91406 818-787-6223
Fax: 818-453-0316 877-224-2299
sales@greenbagamerica.com
www.greenbagamerica.com
Accesories/supplies i.e. picninc baskets, display fixtures, specialty food packaging i.e. gift wrap/labels/boxes/containers.
Marketing: Tom Maor

23418 Green Bay Machinery
P.O. Box 19010
Green Bay, WI 54307 920-455-6749
Fax: 920-455-2203 info@gbm-co.com
www.gbm-co.com
Estimated Sales: $2.5-5 000,000
Number Employees: 250-499

23419 (HQ)Green Bay Packaging
1700 North Webster Court
Green Bay, WI 54307-9017 920-433-5111
Fax: 920-433-5471 www.gbp.com
Manufacturer and exporter of corrugated shipping containers and labels including coated and stock
Chairman: James Kress
VP, Finance: Carter Moore
Senior VP/General Counsel: Scott Wochos
Director, Quality Management: William Kelley
Marketing Manager: Patricia Mulvey
Sales Manager: Matt Chesser
Operations Executive: Steve Lewins
Plant Manager: Matt Malesa
Purchasing Manager: Sherri Kratz
Estimated Sales: $850 Million
Number Employees: 2,902
Type of Packaging: Consumer, Food Service, Private Label, Bulk

23420 Green Bay Packaging
555 87th Ln NW
Coon Rapids, MN 55433 763-786-7446
Fax: 763-786-5101 www.gbp.com
Corrugated shipping containers
President: Will Kareff
Sales and Marketing Manager: John Powle
General Manager: Irwin Hess
Plant Manager: Pete Nelson
Estimated Sales: $20 - 50 Million
Number Employees: 50-99

23421 Green Bay Packaging
555 87th Ln NW
Coon Rapids, MN 55433 763-786-7446
Fax: 763-786-5101 www.gbp.com
Printed and plain corrugated shipping containers
President: Will Kress
Quality Control: Tom Merrill
General Manager: John Towle
Sales Manager: Dave Veenhuis
Plant Manager: Pete Nelson
Estimated Sales: $20 - 30 Million
Number Employees: 50-99
Square Footage: 312000
Parent Co: Green Bay Packaging

23422 Green Bay Packaging
6106 W 68th St
Tulsa, OK 74131 918-446-3341
Fax: 918-446-5266 jfowler@gbp.com
www.gbp.com
Corrugated boxes
President: Will Kress
Manager: Ryan Boega
VP/General Manager: Jim Young
Sales Manager: Jim Fowler
Plant Manager: Robert Price
Estimated Sales: $20-50 Million
Number Employees: 100-249
Parent Co: Green Bay Packaging

23423 Green Bay Packaging
555 87th Ln NW
Coon Rapids, MN 55433 763-786-7446
Fax: 763-786-5101 800-236-6456
www.gbp.com
Corrugated boxes and displays; also, recycled materials available
sales and marketing manager: Erwin Hess
General Manager: Neil Slamka
Plant Manager: Pete Nelson
Estimated Sales: $20-50 Million
Number Employees: 50-99
Parent Co: Green Bay Packaging

23424 Green Brothers
43 Massasoit Avenue
Barrington, RI 02806 401-245-9043
Steel rule dies and paper boxes
President: James McClelland
Estimated Sales: $1-2.5 Million
Number Employees: 19

23425 **Green Earth Bags**
815C Tecumseh
Point-Claire, QC H9R 4B1 514-694-9440
Fax: 514-694-6311
keberwein@fiberlinkstextiles.com
www.fiberlinkstextiles.com
Accessories/supplies i.e. picninc baskets, specialty food packaging i.e. gift wrsp/labels/boxes/containers.
Marketing: Kassandra Eberwein

23426 **Green Metal Fabricated Company**
536 Houston St Ste A
West Sacramento, CA 95691-2253 916-371-0192
Fax: 916-371-7541
Sheet metal and stainless steel fabrications for use in restaurants
Owner: Harry Green Jr
Estimated Sales: Below $5 Million
Number Employees: 8

23427 **Green Mountain Awning Company**
36 Marble Street
West Rutland, VT 05777 802-438-2951
Fax: 802-438-2951 800-479-2951
info@greenmountainawning.com
www.greenmountainawning.com
Flags, pennants and banners
President: Robert Pearo Sr
Vice President: Robert Pearo, Jr.
Marketing Director: Robert Pearo, Jr.
Estimated Sales: Below $5 Million
Number Employees: 1-4

23428 **Green Mountain Coffee Roasters, Inc.**
33 Coffee Ln
Waterbury, VT 05676 802-244-5621
Fax: 802-244-5436 888-879-4627
customercare@gmcr.com
www.greenmountaincoffee.com
Coffee beans, supplier of coffee machines, filters, and other coffee making accessories
President, CEO & Director: Lawrence Blanford
CFO, Secretary & Treasurer: Frances Rathke
VP & CEO: James Prevo
VP Development: Stephen Sabol
Quality Assurance: Linda Schliebus
Director Public Relations: Sandy Yusen
Estimated Sales: $2.65 Billion
Number Employees: 5600
Type of Packaging: Consumer, Food Service, Bulk
Brands:
Green Mountain Coffee
Tully's Coffee
Barista Prima
Bigelow
Brew Over Ice
Cafe' Escapes
Caribou
Celestial Seasonings
Coffee People
Diedrich Coffee
Donut House
Donut Shop Coffee
Gloria Jean's Coffee
Green Mountain Natural
Kahlua
Newman's Own Organics
Revv
Timothy's
Vitamin Burst
Swiss Miss

23429 **Green Mountain Graphics**
P.O.Box 1417
Long Island City, NY 11101 718-472-3377
Fax: 718-472-4040 sales@signsandimprints.com
www.gm-graphics.com
Manufacturer and wholesaler/distributor of signs, awards and promotional products
President: Eric Greenberg
VP Sales: Steve Goldman
Estimated Sales: $1 - 2,500,000
Number Employees: 10-19
Square Footage: 6000
Parent Co: Eastern Concepts

23430 **Green Seams**
11605 100th Avenue N
Maple Grove, MN 55369-3203 612-929-3213
Fax: 612-929-3027
Totes, bags, uniforms and promotional garments
Owner: Francis Green

23431 **Green Spot Packaging**
100 S Cambridge Ave
Claremont, CA 91711 909-625-8771
Fax: 909-621-4634 800-456-3210
www.greenspotusa.com
Processor, importer and exporter of juices, juice concentrates, drinks, flavors and fragrances; aseptic packaging services available
CEO: John Tsu
Finance Executive: Don Koury
Sales Executive: Greg Faust
Chief Operating Officer: Dana Staal
Plant Manager: Roy Cooley
Estimated Sales: $6.5 Million
Number Employees: 20-49
Square Footage: 100000
Type of Packaging: Consumer, Food Service, Private Label, Bulk
Brands:
Action Ade
Apple Delight
Apple Royal
Awesome Orange
Black Cherry Royal
Citrus Royal
Galactic Grape
Good Buddies
Green Spot
Peach Royal
Superstar Strawberry
Tropical Royal

23432 **Green Sustainable Solutions**
1624 Staunton Avenue
Parkersburg, WV 26101 304-422-5461
Fax: 304-428-7530 800-827-5461
custserv@gssllc.us.com www.gssllcus.com
CEO: Perry D. Smith
Marketing: Eric Watkins
Estimated Sales: $1 - 5 Million
Number Employees: 5-9

23433 **Green-Tek**
3708 Enterprise Dr
Janesville, WI 53546 608-884-9454
Fax: 608-884-9459 800-747-6440
greentek@green-tek.com www.green-tek.com
Plastic pallets and trays for oven use and manual heat sealers to package meals for ovens and microwaves. Manufacturer of disposable, dual-ovenable and microwavable food trays and lids
President: Linda Bracha
CFO: Sandy Boyer
Sales Representative: Steve Guertin
General Manager: Paul Jacobson
Estimated Sales: $20 - 50 Million
Number Employees: 20-49
Square Footage: 10000
Brands:
Green-Tek
Polyziv
Seal N' Serve

23434 **Greenbelt Industries**
45 Comet Ave
Buffalo, NY 14216 716-873-6923
Fax: 905-564-6709 800-668-1114
www.greenbelting.com
Manufacturer and exporter of Teflon-coated conveyor belting for baking pans and trays
Manager: Gail Lipka
Marketing Director: Joe Smith
Operations Manager: Scott O Hearn
Purchasing Manager: Jennifer White
Estimated Sales: $5-10 Million
Number Employees: 50-99
Square Footage: 200000

23435 **Greenbush Tape & Label,Inc.**
40 Broadway
PO Box 1488
Albany, NY 12201 518-465-2389
Fax: 518-465-5781
stickybiz@greenbushlabel.com
www.greenbushlabel.com
Manufacturer and exporter of pressure sensitive tapes and labels
President: Alfred Chenot
VP: James Chenot
VP: James Chenot
Estimated Sales: Below $5 Million
Number Employees: 22
Type of Packaging: Consumer, Food Service, Private Label, Bulk

23436 **Greene Brothers**
134 Broadway
Brooklyn, NY 11211-6031 718-388-6800
Fax: 718-782-4123
Manufacturer and exporter of lighting fixtures
Fmn.: Matthew Santoro
Number Employees: 5-9
Parent Co: Greene's Lighting Fixtures

23437 **Greene Industries**
65 Rocky Hollow Road
East Greenwich, RI 02818 401-884-7530
Fax: 401-885-9370 rallengreene@aol.com
Plywood and fiberboard cases and wooden shipping crates
President: R Allen Greene
Estimated Sales: Below $5 Million
Number Employees: 5-9

23438 **Greener Corporation**
4 Helmly St
Bayville, NJ 08721 732-341-3880
Fax: 732-286-7842 800-634-9933
custserve@greencorp.com
www.greenercorp.com
Bag and pouch sealers, closing equipment: bag closure, heat seal
President: Ted Wojtech
R&D: Matt Wojtech
Estimated Sales: Below $5 000,000
Number Employees: 20-49

23439 **Greenfield Disston**
7345 W Friendly Ave # G
Greensboro, NC 27410-6252 336-855-4200
Fax: 336-299-0616
Industrial cutting tools including machine knives
CEO: Henry Libby
Marketing Manager: Holly Oakley
Estimated Sales: $3 - 5 Million
Number Employees: 10-19
Square Footage: 8000
Parent Co: Rule Industries

23440 **Greenfield Packaging**
39 Westmoreland Avenue
White Plains, NY 10606-1937 914-993-0233
Fax: 203-934-7172 gpind@aol.com
We sell stock and custom plastic, glass and aluminum bottles, jars and caps; also, print logos, hex-packs and drums available
President: Debra Greenfield
Executive VP: Barbara Greenfield
Estimated Sales: $1 - 5,000,000

23441 **Greenfield Paper Box Company**
55 Pierce St
Greenfield, MA 01301 413-773-9414
Fax: 413-774-5134 www.greenfieldpaperbox.com
Manufacturer and designer of set-up and folding boxes for candy, cookies, cereal, etc
President: Brian T Lowell
VP Marketing: Brian Lowell
VP Manufacturing: Robert Fischlein
Production Manager: Roger Phillips
Estimated Sales: $2.5 - 5 Million
Number Employees: 20-49
Square Footage: 20000
Type of Packaging: Private Label

23442 **Greenheck Fan Corporation**
1100 Greenheck Dr.
Schofield, WI 54476 715-359-6171
Fax: 715-355-2444 info@greenheck.com
www.greenheck.com
Manufacturer and exporter of kitchen ventilation equipment including exhaust and supply fans, air units and exhaust hoods; also, pre-piped fire suppression systems including wet chemical and water spray
Chairman: Dwight David
Chief Executive Officer & Director: James McIntyre
Estimated Sales: $203.7 Million
Number Employees: 1282
Square Footage: 1000000
Brands:
Greenheck

23443 Greenline Corporation
200 Forsyth Hall Dr
Charlotte, NC 28273 704-333-3377
Fax: 704-334-6146 800-331-5312
info@icb-usa.com www.icb-usa.com
Manufacturer and exporter of overhead conveyors for poultry and meat processing
Director: Darlene Rockwell
Manager: Iris Chasteen
Estimated Sales: $5.6 Million
Number Employees: 11
Square Footage: 100000
Brands:
Dura-Plate
Greenline

23444 Greensburg ManufacturingCompany
513 N Depot Street
Greensburg, KY 42743-1300 270-932-5511
Fax: 270-932-7866
Cutting boards and butcher blocks with lacquer finishes
General Manager: Daryl Parnell
Estimated Sales: $1 - 3 Million
Number Employees: 160
Parent Co: Kimball International

23445 Greenville Awning Company
325 New Neely Ferry Rd
Mauldin, SC 29662 864-288-0063
Fax: 864-288-3683
support@greenvilleawning.com
www.greenvilleawning.com
Commercial awnings
President: Gerhard Kuhn
Estimated Sales: $10-20,000,000
Number Employees: 20-49

23446 Greenwood Mop & Broom
312 Palmer Street
Greenwood, SC 29646 864-227-8411
Fax: 864-227-3200 800-635-6849
gmb@emeraldis.com
www.greenwoodmopandbroom.com
Brooms, dry and wet mops, handles and brushes
President: Henry E Bonds
CEO: Henry Bonds
VP: Freida Bonds
VP Sales/Marketing: Sid Johnston
Estimated Sales: $10-20 Million
Number Employees: 50-99
Square Footage: 157000

23447 (HQ)Greer's Ferry Glass Work
PO Box 797
Dubuque, IA 52004-0797 501-589-2947
Fax: 800-310-0525 gfgw@hotmail.com
www.gfglass.com
Manufacturer and exporter of thermometers, refractometers and hydrometers for testing salt, alcohol, sugar, etc
Sales: Brenda Marler
Operations: Bob Mallis
Estimated Sales: $1-2.5 Million
Number Employees: 5-9
Other Locations:
Greer's Ferry Glass Works
West Paterson NJ
Brands:
Brix
Salometers

23448 Greerco High Shear Mixers
125 Flagship Dr
North Andover, MA 01845-6119 978-687-0101
Fax: 978-687-8500 800-643-0641
inquiry@kenics.com www.chemineer.com
Homogenizers, colloid mills, laboratory homogenizers, self contained systems and high shear mixers
Manager: Mark Raymond
Estimated Sales: $20 - 50 Million
Number Employees: 20-49

23449 Grefco
23705 Crenshaw Blvd
Torrance, CA 90505-5236 310-660-8840
Fax: 213-517-0794 www.grefco-industry.com
Wine industry filter acids
Estimated Sales: $2.5-5 Million
Number Employees: 10-19

23450 Gregg
5048 Vienna Dr
Waunakee, WI 53597-9746 608-846-5143
Fax: 608-846-5143 greggind@gregginc.com
www.greggind.com
Smokers, parts, and equipments
President: Wesley Gillespie
Estimated Sales: $300,000-500,000
Number Employees: 1-4

23451 Gregg Industries
5048 Vienna Dr
Waunakee, WI 53597 608-846-5143
Fax: 608-846-5143 greggind@gregginc.com
www.smokehouseparts.com
Industrial equipment for meat industries; smokehouse door air seals, wet bulb socks and silicone gasket
President: Wesley Gillespie
Vice President: Kathleen Triggs
Estimated Sales: Under $500,000
Number Employees: 1-4

23452 Gregor Jonsson, Inc
13822 W Laurel Dr
Lake Forest, IL 60045 847-831-2030
Fax: 847-247-4272 sales@jonsson.com
www.jonsson.com
Manufacturer and exporter of shrimp peeling systems
President: Frank Heurich
Vice President: Beth Dancy
Computer Support/Database Design: Ann Curry
Operations Manager: Scott Heurich
Operations Manager: Scott Heurich
Estimated Sales: $10 - 20 Million
Number Employees: 20-49
Square Footage: 40000

23453 Greif Brothers Corporation
3113 W 110th Street
Cleveland, OH 44111-2753 216-941-2021
Fax: 216-476-8209 800-424-0342
www.greif.com
Corrugated cartons
Product Manager: Rick Volker
Sales Manager: Michael Blatt
Plant Manager: Bob Dozer
Estimated Sales: $20-50 Million
Number Employees: 100-249

23454 Greif Inc.
425 Winter Road
Delaware, OH 43015 216-941-2021
Fax: 216-476-8209 800-476-1635
www.greif.com
Specialty packaging, signage and displays including point of purchase
President, Chief Executive Officer: David B. Fischer
EVP: Gary R. Martz
COO: Peter G. Watson
Number Employees: 40
Square Footage: 260000

23455 Greig Filters
412 High Meadows Blvd., 70507
P.O.Box 91675
Lafayette, LA 70509-1675 337-237-3355
Fax: 337-233-9263 800-456-0177
gfi@greigfilters.com www.greigfilters.com
Manufacturer and exporter of filtration systems for cooking oil and beverages
Owner: Alan Greig
Office Manager: Tammy Roy
Engineer: Shane Hulin
Estimated Sales: $1-2.5 Million
Number Employees: 10-19
Square Footage: 40000
Brands:
Greig Filters
Pressure Leaf Filter
Purifry

23456 Greitzer
P.O.Box 2008
Elizabeth City, NC 27906-2008 252-338-4000
Fax: 252-338-5445 kevin@greitzer.com
www.greitzer.net
Conveyors and ventilators
Owner: Kevin Gilroy
Estimated Sales: $300,000-500,000
Number Employees: 1-4

23457 Greydon
391 Greendale Rd Ste 2
York, PA 17403 717-848-3875
Fax: 717-843-6435 info@greydon.com
www.greydon.com
Inline printing for packaging
President: Gregory Rochon
Vice President: John Rochon
Sales Director: Leo Zitella
Plant Manager: Jim Buchmver
Purchasing Manager: Brian Newman
Estimated Sales: $2.5-5 000,000
Number Employees: 20-49

23458 Gribble Stamp & StencilCompany
121 Saint Emanuel Street
Houston, TX 77002 713-228-5358
Fax: 713-228-2127 sales@gribblestamp.com
www.gribblestamp.com
Rubber and steel stamps, stencils, engraved signs, security seals and plaques
President: C W Gribble
President: C Gribble
Number Employees: 1-4

23459 Gridpath, Inc.
328 Glover Road
Stony Creek, ON L8E 5M3
Canada 905-643-0955
Fax: 905-643-6718 info@gridpathinc.com
www.gridpathinc.com
High pressure processing equipment for non-thermal pasteurization and packaging for the food processing industry.
President: Rick Marshall

23460 Grief Brothers Corporation
425 Winter Rd
Delaware, OH 43015 740-549-6000
Fax: 740-549-6100 www.greif.com
Fiber and plastic packaging, steel drums, corrugated containers, etc
CFO: Donald S Huml
CEO: Michael J Gasser
Product Manager: Rick Volker
Estimated Sales: $1 - 5 Million
Number Employees: 10,000

23461 Griffin Automation
240 Westminster Rd
Buffalo, NY 14224 716-674-2300
Fax: 716-674-2309 sales@griffinautomation.com
www.griffinautomation.com
Design adn build automation machinery
CEO: Gerald Bidlack
VP Finance: John Shepherd
VP Engineering: Robert Kern
Sales: Richard Hacker
Plant Manager: Mike Baines
Purchasing Manager: Chuck Peskir
Estimated Sales: $5-10 000,000
Number Employees: 30
Number of Products: 20
Square Footage: 40000
Type of Packaging: Private Label

23462 (HQ)Griffin Brothers
3033 Industrial Way N.E.
Salem, OR 97303 503-540-7886
Fax: 503-540-7929 800-456-4743
griffinbros1@yahoo.com
www.jadcochemical.com
Manufacturer and exporter of disinfectants, polymer floor finish, etc
President: Ryan Kelly
Estimated Sales: $1 - 3 Million
Number Employees: 5-9
Type of Packaging: Consumer, Food Service

23463 (HQ)Griffin Cardwell, Ltd
330 Boxley Avenue
Louisville, KY 40209 502-636-1374
Fax: 502-636-0125 www.gchintl.com
Manufacturer and exporter of surge bins, vibrating sizing conveyors, enrobers and separators; also, freezers including spiral, tunnel and trolley
Chief Operating Officer: Haldun Turgay
VP Business Development: Edward Ward
Sales Manager Food: Thomas Fahed
Estimated Sales: $1-2.5 Million
Number Employees: 19-Oct
Square Footage: 360000
Parent Co: GCH International

Other Locations:
Cardwell Machine Co.
Farnborough NH
Brands:
Spiro-Freeze
Trolly-Freeze
Uni-Freeze
Vibe-O-Bin
Vibe-O-Vey

23464 Griffin Products
P.O.Box 90
Wills Point, TX 75169 903-873-6388
Fax: 903-873-6389 800-379-9709
sales@griffinproducts.com
www.griffinproducts.com
Stainless steel sinks and tables including work and dish
President: Shane Griffin
CFO: Kenneth Fratcher
Sales: Janet Griffen
Sales: Mike Whitus
Estimated Sales: $2.5 - 5,000,000
Number Employees: 20-49

23465 Griffin-Rutgers Company
1170-12 Lincoln Avenue
Holbrook, NY 117741 631-981-4141
Fax: 631-981-4171 800-237-6713
custserv@griffin-rutgers.com
www.griffin-rutgers.com
Supplying printing
President: James B Umbdenstock
Estimated Sales: $1-2.5 Million
Number Employees: 5-9

23466 (HQ)Griffith Laboratories,Inc.
1 Griffith Ctr
Alsip, IL 60803 708-371-0900
Fax: 708-389-4055 900-346-9494
www.griffithlaboratories.com
protein seasonings for fresh, cooked and dried sausages & patties, inject, tumble, and static marinades for whole muscle and formed products, glazes, rubs, sprinkle-ons, cures, side-dish seasonings, snack seasonings, sauces, graviessoups mixes, salsa & condiments, texture systems, bakery & dough blends, custom culinary
President & Chief Executive Officer: Herve de la Vauvre
Executive VP & Chief Financial Officer: Joseph Maslick
Estimated Sales: $286.8 Million
Number Employees: 2500
Square Footage: 250000
Type of Packaging: Food Service, Private Label, Bulk

23467 Grigsby Brothers Paper Box Manufacturers
817 NE Madrona Street
PO Box 11189
Portland, OR 97211 503-285-8341
Fax: 503-285-3334 866-233-4690
inquiry@grigsbypaperbox.com
www.grigsbypaperbox.com
And folding cartons; package design and full service printing available
President: Terry Grigsby
CFO: Jane Hewitt
VP: Terry Grigsby
R&D: Todd Grigsby
Estimated Sales: $2.5 - 5 Million
Number Employees: 10-19

23468 Gril-Del
400 Southbrook Circle
Mankato, MN 56001-4782 507-776-8275
Fax: 507-776-8276 800-782-7320
Manufacturer and exporter of outdoor cooking utensils for the barbecue grill including spatulas, tongs and knives; also, aprons, salt and pepper shakers, handmade baskets, mitts and meat platters
President: Steven Saggau
VP: Connie Saggau
Number Employees: 10
Square Footage: 6000
Type of Packaging: Consumer, Food Service, Private Label, Bulk
Brands:
Gril-Classics
Gril-Del

23469 Grill Greats
PO Box 568
Saxonburg, PA 16056-0568 724-352-1511
Fax: 724-352-1266 sales@du.co.com
www.du-co.com
Manufacturer and exporter of ceramic briquettes for barbecue grills
President: Tom Arbanas
Quality Control: Paul Sekeras
Sales: Mike Carson
Estimated Sales: $50 - 100 Million
Number Employees: 100-249
Square Footage: 150000
Type of Packaging: Private Label, Bulk
Brands:
Grill Greats

23470 Grillco
1775 Mallette Rd
Aurora, IL 60505 630-906-0290
Fax: 630-906-0289 800-644-0067
sales@grillcoinc.com www.grillcoinc.com
Portable grills including charcoal, gas and pit barbecue; also, rotisseries, hoods, shelves and racks
Sales Director: Brian Ruseitti
Number Employees: 10-19
Brands:
Grillco, Inc.

23471 Grills to Go
5659 W San Madele Avenue
Fresno, CA 93722-5066 559-645-8089
Fax: 559-645-8088 877-869-2253
info@grillstogo.com www.grillstogo.com
Manufacturer, Distributor and Exporter of commerical barbecue equipment, smoker ovens, Southern Pride brand ovens and Rotisseries and supplies
President: Michael Hall
CEO: Nora Hall
Estimated Sales: $1-2.5 Million
Number Employees: 1-4
Square Footage: 12000
Brands:
Grills To Go

23472 Grimes Packaging Materials
600 North Ellis Road
Jacksonville, FL 32254 904-786-5711
Fax: 904-786-7805 800-474-6378
gpmesales@aol.com www.grimespackaging.com
Heat sealers, tong welders, impulse sealers, impulse bar sealers, and rotary hospital sealers
Estimated Sales: Less than $500,000
Number Employees: 1-4

23473 (HQ)Grindmaster Corporation
4003 Collins Ln
Louisville, KY 40254 502-425-4776
Fax: 502-425-4664 800-695-4500
info@gmcw.com www.grindmaster.com
Manufacturers of a complete line of hot, cold and frozen beverage dispensing equipment.
CEO: Tom McDonald
Plant Manager: Jim Howell
Estimated Sales: $5 - 10 Million
Number Employees: 5-9
Brands:
American Metal Ware
Crathco
Espressimo
Grindmaster
Wilch

23474 Grindmaster-Cecilware Corporation
4003 Collins Lane
Louisville, KY 40245 502-425-4776
Fax: 502-425-4664 800-695-4500
info@gmcw.com www.grindmaster.com
Manufacturer and exporter of stainless steel coffee urns, freeze dried coffee and tea brewers, hot chocolate, hot water, coffee and iced tea dispensers
Vice President of Domestic Sales: Frank Coronado
Plant Manager: Rich Perillo
Estimated Sales: $5-10 Million
Number Employees: 20-49
Square Footage: 200000
Parent Co: Grindmaster
Type of Packaging: Food Service
Brands:
American Metalware

23475 Grindmaster-Cecilware Co
4003 Collins Lane
Louisville, KY 40245 502-425-4776
Fax: 502-425-4664 800-695-4500
info@gmcw.com www.gmcw.com
Brewers coffee warmers, decanters, carafes, grinders
President: Richard Moore
Vice President, Sales: Keith Enscoe
Estimated Sales: $10-20 000,000
Number Employees: 250-499

23476 Grinnell Fire ProtectionSystems Company
4985 Quail Rd NE
Sauk Rapids, MN 56379 320-253-8665
Fax: 320-253-4540 www.simplexgrinnell.com
Fire protection and sprinkling systems
Branch Manager: Harry Ramler
Estimated Sales: $10 - 20 Million
Number Employees: 100
Parent Co: TYCO International Company

23477 Grinnell Fire ProtectionSystems Company
4985 Quail Rd NE
Sauk Rapids, MN 56379 320-253-8665
Fax: 320-253-4540 888-870-6894
www.simplexgrinnell.com
Fire extinguishers and kitchen hood systems
Regional Manager: Don Molloy
Estimated Sales: $10 - 20,000,000
Number Employees: 250
Parent Co: TYCO International Company

23478 Grocery Products Distribution Services
14 Ridgedale Ave Ste 106
Cedar Knolls, NJ 07927 973-538-1035
Fax: 973-538-0944 richgpds@aol.com
Consultant specializing in distribution marketing services for public grocery distribution centers
President: W Richards
VP: Florence Richards
Staff Assistant: Barbara Brown
Estimated Sales: $.5 - 1 million
Number Employees: 5-9

23479 Groen
1055 Mendell Davis Dr
Jackson, MS 39272-9788 888-994-7636
Fax: 888-864-7636
webmaster@unifiedbrands.net
www.unifiedbrands.net
President: Bill Strenglis
CFO: Scott Stevenson
R&D: Pam Holmes
Quality Control: Mike Blackwell
V.P. of Sales and Marketing: Blair Alfdord
Estimated Sales: $10 - 20 Million
Number Employees: 500-999

23480 Groen
1055 Mendell Davis Dr
Byram, MS 39272-9788 601-371-4417
Fax: 601-373-9587 800-676-9040
info@groen.com www.groen.com
Manufacturers of steam jacketed kettles, braising pans, convection steamers, combi ovens, cook-chill and continuous processing systems for food service operators and industrial processors worldwide
President: Bill Strenglis
CFO: Scott Stevenson
R&D: Pam Holmes
Quality Control: Mike Blackwell
Sales/Marketing: Clay Thames
Estimated Sales: $10 - 20 Million
Number Employees: 500-999
Parent Co: Dover Industries

23481 Groen Process Equipment
271 Country Commons Rd
Trout Valley, IL 60013-2543 847-462-1865
Fax: 847-462-1950 info@groen.com
www.groen.com
Manager: Frank Lobes
Estimated Sales: Below $5 Million
Number Employees: 1-4

23482 Grosfillex Contract Furniture
230 Old West Penn Avenue
Robesonia, PA 19551 610-693-5835
Fax: 610-693-5414 800-233-3186
info@grosfillexfurniture.com
www.grosfillexfurniture.com
Supplier, importer and exporter of commercial outdoor resin furniture
Estimated Sales: $50-100 Million
Number Employees: 100-249
Parent Co: Grosfillex SARL
Other Locations:
Grosfillex Contract Furniture
Chino CA
Brands:
Grosfillex

23483 Gross Company
1208 Sunset Street
Middletown, OH 45042 513-424-6035
Fax: 330-686-9262 salesfrgross@newcas.com
www.grossinc.com
Chill rolls, hearto rolls and process water systems
Chairman of the board: Robert Paul
Estimated Sales: $5-10 Million
Number Employees: 20-49

23484 Grote Company
1160 Gahanna Pkwy
Columbus, OH 43230-6616 614-868-8414
Fax: 614-863-1647 888-534-7683
sales@grotecompany.com
www.grotecompany.com
Manufacturer and exporter of food processing equipment including high yield slicer applicators, multi-purpose slicers, cheese shredders, pizza topping lines and paper sheeter systems
President: Jelff Rawef
CEO: Bruce Hohl
Chairman: James Grote
Quality Control: Jon Feifeit
Marketing Communication/Sales Coord.: Terri Hoover
National Sales Director: Tony Ceritelli
Estimated Sales: $10 - 20 Million
Number Employees: 100-249
Square Footage: 70000
Brands:
Grote

23485 Groth International
13650 N. Promenade Blvd
Stafford, TX 77477 281-295-6800
Fax: 281-295-699 800-354-7684
ÿsales@grothcorp.comÿ www.grothcorp.com
Consultant specializing in sales and marketing for U.S. companies overseas through exclusive distributorships and joint venture arrangements
Managing Director: Helen Groth
Estimated Sales: $1 - 5 Million
Number Employees: 2
Square Footage: 300

23486 Group One
21 W 3rd St
South Boston, MA 02127 617-268-7000
Fax: 617-268-0209 info@grouponeinc.com
www.grouponeinc.com
Consultant specializing in food service design for facilities including kitchens and restaurants; also, food service programming and interior design
President: Harry Wheeler
Principal: Kevin Mullin
Principal: Harry Wheeler
Director Food Service Design: William Stenstrom
Estimated Sales: $1 - 2.5 Million
Number Employees: 20-49

23487 Gruenewald ManufacturingCompany
100 Ferncroft Rd Ste 204
Danvers, MA 01923 978-777-0200
Fax: 978-777-9432 800-229-9447
info@whipcream.com www.whipcream.com
Manufacturer, importer and exporter of dispensers for food products, including ice cream and whipped cream
Owner: Fredrick Gruenewald
Sales/Marketing: Kevin Muldoon
VP Sales: Thomas Muldoon
Sales: Joseph Ransom
Estimated Sales: $10-20 Million
Number Employees: 10-19
Square Footage: 15000
Type of Packaging: Food Service
Brands:
Refillo
River of Cream
Rocket

23488 Grueny's Rubber Stamps
210 S Gaines St
Little Rock, AR 72201-2218 501-376-0393
Fax: 501-376-6327
Price markers and rubber stanps
President and CFO: John Ward Jr
Quality Control: Bob Pinkerton
Sales Manager: Brit Wood
Estimated Sales: Less than $500,000
Number Employees: 1 to 4

23489 Guardsman/Valspar Corp
4999 36th St SE
Grand Rapids, MI 49512-2005 616-940-2900
Fax: 616-285-7870 sbrogger@valspar.com
www.guardsman.com
Carpet and fabric cleaners, degreasers and adhesive removers
Manager: Kate Bass
New Business Development Manager: Sandi Brogger
Estimated Sales: $10 - 20 Million
Number Employees: 50-99
Parent Co: Lilly Industries
Brands:
Afta
Carpet Guard
Goof Off
One-Wipe

23490 Guest Supply
P.O.Box 902
Monmouth Jct, NJ 08852 609-514-9696
Fax: 609-514-2692 800-448-3787
eservice@guestsupply.com
www.guestsupply.com
Cleaning equipment and chemicals
President: Clifford Stanley
Number Employees: 100

23491 Gulf Arizona Packaging
7720 FM 1960 East
Humble, TX 77346 281-582-6700
Fax: 281-852-1590 800-364-3887
consumerservicehumble@gulfpackaging.com
www.gulfazpackaging.com
Manufacturer and wholesaler/distributor of packaging equipment and materials including bags, containers, closures, conveyors, labels, linings, tapes, ties, etc
Manager: Paul Corley
General Manager: Paul Corley
General Manager: Jay Crabb
Estimated Sales: $5 - 10 Million
Number Employees: 5-9
Parent Co: Gulf Systems

23492 Gulf Coast Plastics
9314 Princess Palm Ave
Tampa, FL 33619 813-621-8098
Fax: 813-623-1408 800-277-7491
sales@gulfcoastplastics.com
www.gulfcoastplastics.com
Manufacturer and exporter of anti-static plastic bags
President: Tom Coryn
CFO: Tom Coryn
Quality Control: Tom Coryn
Manager: Thomas Coryn
Estimated Sales: Below $5 Million
Number Employees: 20-49
Square Footage: 12000
Parent Co: Dairy Mix
Type of Packaging: Consumer, Food Service, Bulk

23493 Gulf Coast Sign Company
380 Clematis Street
Pensacola, FL 32503-2839 850-438-2131
Fax: 850-432-6367 800-768-3549
gulfcoastsign@hotmail.com
www.gulfcoastsign.com
U.L. approved neon, plastic, electric and sandblasted signs; also, maintenance, repair and erection services
President: William Terry
CEO: William Terry
Estimated Sales: $1-2.5 Million
Number Employees: 19
Square Footage: 40000

23494 Gulf Packaging Company
323 9th Avenue N
Safety Harbor, FL 34695 727-725-4424
Fax: 727-725-2885 800-749-3466
Folding, paper, set-up and transparent boxes; also, blister and skin cards
President: Jeffrey A Herran
Chairman: F Edward Herran
Chairman: F Edward Herran
Plant Manager: Patrick Herran
Estimated Sales: $2.5 - 5 Million
Number Employees: 20
Square Footage: 16000

23495 (HQ)Gulf States Paper Corporation
P.O. Box 48999
Tuscaloosa, AL 35404 205-562-5000
Fax: 205-562-5012 www.westerveltcompany.com
Custom printed, die-cut and glued folding cartons, solid bleached sulphate paperboard for food contact use and line of dual paperboard packaging
President/Chief Executive Officer: Michael Case
Vice President, Natural Resources: Jim King
Vice President, Finance: Gary Dailey
Vice President, Business Development: Alicia Cramer
Vice President, Lumber: Joe Patton
Vice President/Secretary/General Counsel: Ray Robbins
Estimated Sales: $67 Million
Number Employees: 650
Square Footage: 90000
Brands:
E-Z Serve
Heritage

23496 Gulf Systems
3815 N Santa Fe Ave
Oklahoma City, OK 73118-8528 405-528-2293
Wholesaler/distributor of packaging equipment and materials
Customer Service Representative: Cathy Wyatt
Estimated Sales: $2.5-5,000,000
Number Employees: 5-9
Parent Co: Gulf Systems

23497 Gulf Systems
3815 N Santa Fe Ave
Oklahoma City, OK 73118-8528 405-528-2293
Wholesaler/distributor of packaging equipment and materials
Customer Service Representative: Cathy Wyatt
Estimated Sales: $1 - 5,000,000
Number Employees: 5-9
Parent Co: Gulf Systems

23498 Gulf Systems
801 E Fronton St
Brownsville, TX 78520 800-217-4853
Fax: 956-504-9800 www.gulfpackaging.com
Wholesaler/distributor of packaging equipment and materials
Manager: Blanca Puga
CFO: Debby Malone
Customer Service Representative: Cathy Wyatt
Estimated Sales: Below $5,000,000
Number Employees: 5-9
Parent Co: Gulf Systems

23499 Gulf Systems
3815 N Santa Fe Ave
Oklahoma City, OK 73108 800-364-3887
Fax: 405-557-0903
Wholesaler/distributor of packaging equipment and materials
Customer Service Representative: Cathy Wyatt
Estimated Sales: $5-10,000,000
Number Employees: 5-9
Parent Co: Gulf Systems

23500 Gulf Systems
2109 Exchange Dr
Arlington, TX 76011 817-261-1915
Fax: 817-861-0092 tlanter@gulfpackaging.com
www.gulfpackaging.com
Wholesaler/distributor of packaging equipment and materials
Manager: Denise Stiger
Customer Service Representative: Cathy Wyatt
Estimated Sales: $20 - 50 Million
Number Employees: 20-49
Parent Co: Gulf Systems

23501 **Guth Lighting**
PO Box 7079
Saint Louis, MO 63177 314-533-3200
Fax: 314-533-9127
customerservice@guthlighting.com
www.guth.com
Manufacturer and exporter of sealed and gasketed fluorescent and high-intensity discharge lighting equipment for use in water wash down and corrosive environments
Manager: Robert Catone
VP and Controller: Sue Pries
VP/General Manager: Robert Catone
Research & Development: Mike Kurtz
Estimated Sales: $20 - 50 Million
Number Employees: 50-99
Square Footage: 100000
Parent Co: JJI
Brands:
Duraclamp
Enviroguard
Kleenseal
Plascolume
Railtite
Steeltite

23502 **H A Stiles**
PO Box 779
Westbrook, ME 04098 207-854-8454
Fax: 207-854-3863 800-447-8537
askhastiles@hastiles.com www.hastiles.com
Manufacturer and exporter of wooden kitchen utensils and bread and cake boards; also, toothpicks
President: Ambrose Berry
Estimated Sales: $500,000-$1 Million
Number Employees: 5-9

23503 **H&H Lumber Company**
11100 SE 3rd Ave
Amarillo, TX 79118 806-335-1813
Fax: 806-335-3734
Wooden pallets
Owner: Doyle Herring
Estimated Sales: Less than $500,000
Number Employees: 1-4
Square Footage: 12000

23504 **H&H Metal Fabrications**
3066 Faulkner Rd
PO Box 1505
Belden, MS 38826 662-489-4626
Fax: 662-489-4626 www.hhmetalfab.com
Manufactures electrical enclosures & panels; residential & commercial fluorescent light fixtures; steel sheet metal fabricating; punch press work & welding
Administrator: Christi Huey
Number Employees: 10-19

23505 **(HQ)H&H Wood Products**
5600 Camp Rd
Hamburg, NY 14075 716-648-5600
Fax: 716-648-3246 hhwood1@aol.com
Wooden pallets; heat treating service
President: William Heussler
Production Coordinator: Richard Perez
Estimated Sales: $3 Million
Number Employees: 20-49
Square Footage: 26000
Type of Packaging: Bulk
Other Locations:
H&H Wood Products
Hamburg NY

23506 **H&H of the Americas**
225 W 34th Street
Suite 1310
New York, NY 10122-1310 212-695-4980
Fax: 212-695-7153 johntripas@msn.com
Processing equipment for the meat industry
President: Barbara Negron
CFO: Barbara Negron
Estimated Sales: Below $5 000,000
Number Employees: 6

23507 **H&M Bay**
P.O.Box 280
Federalsburg, MD 21632 410-754-8001
Fax: 410-754-3495 800-932-7521
information@hmbayinc.net www.hmbayinc.net
Warehouse offering cooler and freezer storage of seafood; transportation firm providing refrigerated trucking services including local, short and long haul
Co-Owner: Walter Messick
CFO: Al Nulph
Marketing And Sales Manager: Scott Steinhardt
COO: Michael Ryan
Number Employees: 50-99

23508 **H&N Packaging**
92 County Line Rd
Colmar, PA 18915-9606 215-997-6222
Fax: 215-997-3976 info12@hnpack.com
www.hnpack.com
Manufacturer and exporter of foil, juice and yogurt lids, butter wrappers, etc
CEO: Jerry Decker
Estimated Sales: $50-100 Million
Number Employees: 50-99
Parent Co: H&N Packaging
Type of Packaging: Bulk

23509 **H&N Packaging**
92 County Line Rd
Colmar, PA 18915-9606 215-997-6222
Fax: 215-997-3976 info12@hnpack.com
www.hnpack.com
CEO: Jerry Decker
Estimated Sales: $20 - 50 Million
Number Employees: 50-99

23510 **H&R Industries**
30553 S Dixie Hwy
Beecher, IL 60401 708-946-3244
Fax: 708-946-0991 800-526-3244
info@hrind.com www.thermosafe.com
Insulated containers
Manager: Paul Wiechen
Marketing: Jeff Smith
Estimated Sales: $5-10 Million
Number Employees: 19
Square Footage: 46000

23511 **H. Arnold Wood Turning**
220 White Plains Road
Suite 245
Tarrytown, NY 10591 914-381-0801
Fax: 914-381-0804 888-314-0088
staff@arnoldwood.com www.arnoldwood.com
Wooden items including mini crates and boxes, broom and mop handles, turned handles, rolling pins, flag poles, skewers and dowels; importer of broom and mop handles and dowels
VP: Johnathan Arnold
VP Sales: Jonathan Arnold
Estimated Sales: $500,000-$1 Million
Number Employees: 5-9

23512 **H. Gartenberg & Company**
260 Blackthorn Drive
Buffalo Grove, IL 60089-6341 847-821-7590
Fax: 773-268-6402 melgart@aol.com
Commercial drying, pulverizing and blending equipment for dried egg processing; also, dehydration services available
President: Melvin Gartenberg
Estimated Sales: $2.5-5 Million
Number Employees: 10
Square Footage: 30000
Type of Packaging: Bulk

23513 **H. Reisman Corporation**
377 Crane St
Orange, NJ 07050 973-677-9200
Fax: 973-675-2766 800-631-3424
sales@hreisman.com www.hreisman.com
President: David Holmes
Sales/Marketing Manager: Dillon McLellan
Estimated Sales: $5 - 10 000,000
Number Employees: 20-49

23514 **H. Yamamoto**
8 Hickory Road
Port Washington, NY 11050-1504 718-821-7700
Fax: 718-366-1619
Zinc and aluminum die castings

23515 **H.A. Phillips & Company**
770 Enterprise Avenue
DeKalb, IL 60115 630-377-0050
Fax: 630-377-2706 info@haphillips.com
www.haphillips.com
Manufacturer and exporter of float controls, valves and pressure vessels for ammonia refrigeration systems; wholesaler/distributor and importer of pressure regulating and solenoid valves
President/Chief Executive Officer: Michael R. Ryan
Executive Director: John Schroeder
Vice-President of Finance: Janet L. Jones
Vice-President of Engineering: Steve L. . Yagla, P.E
R&D/Quality Control: Mike Ryan
Sales/Marketing: Ed Murziuski
Corporate Sales Manager: Thomas W. Herman
Secretary/Vice President of Human Resour: Mary Wright
Operations Manager: Andrew McCullough
Vice President of Manufacturing: Brian J. Youssi
Plant Manager: David Williams
Purchasing Manager: Rou Coleman
Estimated Sales: $4.2 Million
Number Employees: 20-49
Square Footage: 30000
Brands:
Dump Trap
Live Brine
Phillips
Phillips Level-Edge

23516 **H.A. Sparke Company**
1032 Texas Ave
PO Box 674
Shreveport, LA 71162-0674 318-222-0927
Fax: 318-222-2731 info@hasparke.com
www.hasparke.com
Manufacturer and exporter of restaurant fixtures including pot, pan and utensil racks; also, guest check handling equipment
President: Richard W Sparke
Estimated Sales: $1-2.5 Million
Number Employees: 5-9
Square Footage: 7000

23517 **H.B. Fuller Company**
1200 Willow Lake Blvd
St Paul, MN 55110-5101 651-236-5900
www.hbfuller.com
Adhesives including hot melt, palletizing and low temperature application
President & Chief Executive Officer: Jim Owens
Senior VP & Chief Financial Officer: James Giertz
Senior Vice President Market Development: Pat Trippel
Vice President Human Resources: Ann Parriott
Vice President Global Operations: Kevin Gilligan
Estimated Sales: $1.9 Billion
Number Employees: 3700
Brands:
Adventra
H.B. Fuller
Palletite
Potimelt

23518 **H.B. Wall & Sons**
1744 E Trafficway St
P.O.Box 1416
Springfield, MO 65802-1416 417-869-0791
Fax: 417-869-6053
Commercial awnings
Owner: Greg Casey
Estimated Sales: Below $5,000,000
Number Employees: 10-19

23519 **H.C. Bainbridge, Inc**
718 North Salina Street
Syracuse, NY 13208 315-475-5313
Fax: 315-475-5469
bainbridgeflags@twcny.rr.com
www.bainbridgeflags.com/
Flags, flag poles and banners
President: Marilyn Swetland
Estimated Sales: Less than $500,000
Number Employees: 1-4
Square Footage: 8000

23520 **H.C. Duke & Son**
2116 8th Ave
East Moline, IL 61244-1800 309-755-4553
Fax: 309-755-9858 sales@electrofreeze.com
www.hcduke.com
Manufacturer and exporter of soft serve ice cream machines
Marketing: Joe Clark
VP Sales: Jim Duke

Estimated Sales: $20-50 Million
Number Employees: 100-249
Square Footage: 115000
Type of Packaging: Food Service
Brands:
Electro Freeze
H.C. Duke & Son

23521 H.F. Coors China Company

PO Box 59
New Albany, MS 38652-0059 310-338-8921
Fax: 310-641-9429 800-782-6677
customer_service@coorschina.com
www.coorschina.com
Manufacturer and exporter of cookware and tableware including high strength china, health care service dishes, cups and mugs; also, custom decorated, colored, decal and banding available
Controller: George Holzheimer
General VP: Robert Gasbarro
Ceramics Engineer: Leo Suzuki
Number Employees: 50-99
Square Footage: 400000
Parent Co: Standex International Corporation
Type of Packaging: Food Service, Private Label, Bulk
Brands:
Alox
Chefsware
Roca Beige

23522 H.F. Staples & Company

9 Webb Dr.
PO Box 956
Merrimack, NH 03054 603-889-8600
Fax: 603-883-9409 800-682-0034
info@hfstaples.com www.hfstaples.com
Manufacturer and exporter of wood filler, wax and ladder accessories. Contract private label tube filling of viscous products
President: James Stratton
Vice President: Thomas Stratton
Estimated Sales: $5 - 10 Million
Number Employees: 5-9
Square Footage: 26000
Type of Packaging: Private Label

23523 H.G. Weber & Company

725 Fremont St
Kiel, WI 53042 920-894-2221
Fax: 920-894-3786 info@hgweber.com
www.hgweber.com
Manufacturer and exporter of paper and film bag machinery, flexographic printers and vertical case conveyors
President and CEO: John Koehn
CFO: John Smith
Senior VP: Donald Ludwig
Marketing Director: Jeff Vogel
Sales Director: Brian Niemuth
Estimated Sales: $20 - 50 Million
Number Employees: 100-249
Square Footage: 130
Brands:
Presto Flex
Upender
Weber-Univers

23524 H.H. Franz Company

3201 Fallscliff Rd
Baltimore, MD 21211 410-889-2975
Fax: 410-889-2160 800-731-3309
franz@qis.net www.hhfranzco.com
Food processing equipment
President: Bob Mintiens Jr
Estimated Sales: $1 - 2.5 000,000
Number Employees: 10-19

23525 H.J. Jones & Sons

1155 Dundas Street
London, ON N5W 3A9
Canada 519-451-5250
Fax: 519-451-0545 800-667-0476
jonesy@farmline.com
Packaging materials including stretch pak and blister cards and folding cartons
President: Michael Jones
Controller: Scott Switzer
Vice President: Doug Jones
Marketing Director: Les Meeneil
Purchasing Manager: Glen Davies
Number Employees: 50

23526 H.K. Systems

P.O.Box 1512
Milwaukee, WI 53201-1512 262-860-7000
Fax: 262-860-7010 800-424-7365
lonnie.watkins@hksystems.com
www.hksystems.com
Manufacturer and exporter of sorting equipment, conveyors, automated storage retrieval systems, palletizers, software and controls.
CEO: Michael Gonzalez
Account Executive: Lonnie Watkins
Estimated Sales: $100-500 Million
Number Employees: 500-999
Square Footage: 175000
Parent Co: H.K. Systems
Type of Packaging: Bulk

23527 (HQ)H.L. Diehl Company

9 Babcock Hill Rd
South Windham, CT 06266 860-423-7741
Fax: 860-423-2654 info@giant-vac.com
www.giant-vac.com
Manufacturer and exporter of power cleaning equipment including industrial vacuum cleaners
President: Anton Janiak
VP: Gail Marie Diehl
Estimated Sales: $10 - 20 Million
Number Employees: 50-99

23528 H.P. Neun

75 N Main St
Fairport, NY 14450 585-388-1360
Fax: 585-388-0184
Manufacturer and exporter of foam products and paper boxes including corrugated, folding, candy, set-up and fancy.
President: Mike Hanna
Estimated Sales: $20-50 Million
Number Employees: 100-249

23529 H.S. Crocker Company

12100 Smith Dr
Huntley, IL 60142-9618 847-669-3600
Fax: 847-669-1170 lmsulma@hscrocker.com
www.hscrocker.com
Cartons, foil lids, paper labels
CFO: John Dai
CEO: Ron Giordano
Chairman and CEO: Ron Giordano
Estimated Sales: $10 - 20 Million
Number Employees: 50-99

23530 HABCO Beverage Systems

501 Gordon Baker Road
Toronto, ON M2H 2S6
Canada 416-491-6008
Fax: 416-491-6982 800-448-0244
info@habcotech.com www.habcotech.com
Manufacturer and exporter of reach-in refrigerators, freezers, and merchandisers.
Vice President/Marketing: Scott Brown
EVP/Sales: Jim Maynard
Number Employees: 100
Number of Brands: 2
Number of Products: 27
Brands:
Cold Space
Habco
Signature Series

23531 HAMBA USA, Inc

2050 Trade Center Dr E
Saint Peters, MO 63376
Fax: 636-281-1503 gpyles@hambausa.com
www.hambausa.com
Filler for still beverages and almost any liquid or pasty product
President: Gary Pyles
VP: Ken Hicks
Number Employees: 10-19

23532 HATCO Corporation

635 S 28th St
Milwaukee, WI 53215 414-671-6350
Fax: 414-615-1226 800-558-0607
www.hatcocorp.com
Manufacturer and exporter of heating, warming, toasting, cooking and equipment including display warmers, holding cabinets, low temperature and slow cookers and booster and sink heaters for hot water, toasters, etc
Founder/President: Gordon Hatch
Co-Founder: Lareine Hatch
Vice President - Sales: Michael Whiteley
National Sales Manager: Mark Pumphret
Number Employees: 250-499
Type of Packaging: Food Service
Brands:
Chef System
Flav-R-Fresh
Flav-R-Savor
Glo-Ray
Hatco
Toast King
Toast Rite
Toast-Qwik

23533 HB Fuller Company

P.O.Box 64683
St Paul, MN 55164-0683 651-236-5900
Fax: 651-236-5161 800-426-1803
www.hbfuller.com
Hot melt adhesive-coated strings and tapes for reinforcing critical stress areas and for creating tear tape opening systems in corrugated and folding carton packaging
CEO: Michele Volpi
VP Operations: Stephen Large
Sr.VP/Performance Products: Alan Longstreet
Estimated Sales: $20-50 Million
Number Employees: 1,000-4,999

23534 (HQ)HBD Industries

PO Box 948
Salisbury, NC 28145 704-636-0121
Fax: 704-633-3880 800-438-2312
info@hbdthermoid.com www.hbdthermoid.com
Industrial hoses for nondairy or alcoholic applications
President: Robert Lyons
Manager: David Dockins
Customer Service Manager: Pat Stubbs
General Manager: Lou Smith
Plant Manager: Dave Dockins
Estimated Sales: $20-50 Million
Number Employees: 100-249
Square Footage: 300000

23535 HBD/Thermoid, Inc

1301 W. Sandusky Avenue
Bellefontaine, OH 43311 937-593-5010
Fax: 937-593-4354 800-543-8070
info@hbdthermoid.com www.hbdthermoid.com
The Thermoidid brand manufactured by HBD/Ttermoid inc. has set the standard for reliable industrial rubber products.hbd/thermoid produces standard and custom -designed hose(aviation,automotive,hand-built,industrial,marine andpetroleum.)conveyor belting.power transmission.v-belt/ timing belts, rubber roll coverings,contend rubber fabrics,backing strips and rubber bands.
Ceo: Randy Greely
Cfo: Mark Pyll
Quality Control: Dan Green
Director/Sales/Marketing: David Schempp
Sales Director: Ed Bookwalter
Operations Manager: Dan Atwood
Production Manager: Ken Harriger
Plant Manager: Ken Harriger
Estimated Sales: $1 - 5 Million
Number Employees: 250-499

23536 HCI Corporation

28 S 5th St
Geneva, IL 60134 630-208-3100
Fax: 630-208-3111 www.hci-search.com
Executive search and placement firm
President: Frank Cianchetti
Estimated Sales: $500,000 - $1 000,000
Number Employees: 5-9

23537 HCR

Highway 87 West
Lewistown, MT 59457 406-538-7781
Fax: 406-538-5506 800-326-7700
contact@hcrdoors.com www.hcr-inc.com
President: Peter Smith
Estimated Sales: $10 - 20 Million
Number Employees: 20-49
Parent Co: The Jamison Door Company

23538 **HD Electric Company**
1475 Lakeside Dr
Waukegan, IL 60085 847-473-4980
Fax: 847-473-4981 www.hdelectriccompany.com
Manufacturer and exporter of electrical test equipment and portable/emergency lighting products
CEO: M Hoffman
Marketing Manager: Kimberly Higgins
Sales: Berstrom
Estimated Sales: $2.5-5 Million
Number Employees: 20-49
Brands:
Digivolt
Halo
Mark
Quickcheck
Versa-Lite

23539 **HDT Manufacturing**
RR 9
Salem, OH 44460 330-337-8565
Fax: 330-337-8576 800-968-7438
Manufacturer and exporter of industrial trailers and trucks
President: Dave Lawless
VP: Shawn Lawless
Purchasing Manager: Don Souce

23540 **HEMCO Corporation**
711 S Powell Rd
Independence, MO 64056 816-796-2900
Fax: 816-796-3333 800-779-4362
info@hemcocorp.com www.hemcocorp.com
Complete line of laboratory fume hoods, lab furniture, countertops, sinks, and fixture plumbing options. Large floor mount hoods, ventilation equipment, emergency shower decontamination booths, and Modular Clearn Labs class1,000-100,000.
President: Ron Hill
Vice President: David Campbell
VP Sales: David Campbell
Estimated Sales: 3 Million
Number Employees: 20-49
Square Footage: 60000
Brands:
Enviromax
Microflow I
Microflow Ii
Uniflow
Unilab
Unimax

23541 **HG Weber & Company**
725 Fremont St
Kiel, WI 53042 920-894-2574
Fax: 920-894-3786 info@hgweber.com
www.hgweber.com
Bag making machines
President: John Koehn
Estimated Sales: $20-50 Million
Number Employees: 100-249

23542 **HH Controls Company**
6 Frost Street
Arlington, MA 02474-1012 781-646-2626
Heat storage/exchange devices for full size convection ovens
Estimated Sales: Less than $500,000
Number Employees: 1-4

23543 **HH Franz Company**
3201 Fallscliff Rd
Baltimore, MD 21211 410-889-2975
Fax: 410-889-2160 www.hhfranzco.com
Packaging, bottle fillers
President: Bob Mintiens Jr
Estimated Sales: $1-2.5 000,000
Number Employees: 10-19

23544 **(HQ)HHP**
14 Buxton Industrial Drive
PO Box 489
Henniker, NH 03242-0489 603-428-3298
Fax: 603-428-3448 hhp@conknet.com
www.hhp-inc.com
Manufacturer and exporter of wooden pallets; also, saw mill
President: Ross D Elia
Estimated Sales: $5-10 Million
Number Employees: 20-49

23545 **HI-TECH Filter**
80 Myrtle Street
North Quincy, MA 02171-1728 617-328-7756
Fax: 617-773-4192 800-448-3249
Air filters

23546 **HK Systems**
2855 S James Dr
New Berlin, WI 53151 262-860-7000
Fax: 262-860-7010 800-424-7365
cheryl.falk@hksystems.com
www.hksystems.com
Chairman of the Board: John Splude
Vice President and CFO: James P Purko
Vice President, Corporate Marketing: Cheryl Falk
Estimated Sales: $20 - 30 Million
Number Employees: 500-999

23547 **HMC Corporation**
284 Maple St
Hopkinton, NH 03229 603-746-4691
Fax: 603-746-4819 petertaylor@hmccorp.com
www.hmccorp.com
Manufacturer and exporter of saw mill conveyors
President: Peter Taylor
Estimated Sales: $20-50 Million
Number Employees: 50-99

23548 **HMG Worldwide**
8710 Ferris Avenue
Morton Grove, IL 60053-2841 847-965-7100
Fax: 947-965-7141 www.hmgworldwide.com
Custom and stock in-store marketing programs and displays
President: Stephen Dopp
Number Employees: 50
Parent Co: Howard Marlboro Group

23549 **(HQ)HMG Worldwide In-Store Marketing**
371 7th Ave
New York, NY 10001-3984 212-736-2300
Fax: 212-564-3395 www.hmgworldwide.com OR
www.egomedia.com OR www.zeffdesign.com
Manufacturer and exporter of point-of-sale displays, integrated merchandising systems and interactive electronics; also, in-store related research, market planning, package design and space management services available
CEO Director: Andrew Wahl
CEO: Michael Lipman
Estimated Sales: $1 - 5 Million
Number Employees: 5-9
Square Footage: 1200000
Other Locations:
HMG Worldwide In-Store Market
Chicago IL

23550 **HONIRON Corporation**
400 S. Canal Street
Jeanerette, LA 70544 337-276-6314
Fax: 337-276-3614 sales@honiron.com
www.honiron.com
Manufacturer and exporter of sugar machinery
Owner: John Deere
Estimated Sales: $1 - 5 Million
Number Employees: 50-99
Type of Packaging: Bulk

23551 **HP Manufacturing**
3705 Carnegie Ave
Cleveland, OH 44115 216-361-6500
Fax: 216-361-6508 info@hpmanufacturing.com
www.hpmfg.com
Plastic items including sheets, rods and tubes
President: John Melchiorre
CFO: Ken Lutke
Quality Control: Paul Glozer
Chairman of the Board: Terry Poltorek
VP Sales/Marketing: Bob Roman
Estimated Sales: $5 - 10 Million
Number Employees: 50-99

23552 **HPI North America/Plastics**
900 Apollo Rd
Eagan, MN 55121-2477 651-454-2520
Fax: 651-229-5470 800-752-7462
plastics-inc@pi.hpii.com www.plastics-inc.com
Disposable plastic dinnerware including plates, tumblers, trays, coffee cups, barware, etc
Estimated Sales: $1 - 5 Million
Number Employees: 250-499
Parent Co: Newell Companies

23553 **HPI North America/Plastics**
4501 W 47th St
PO Box 2830
Saint Paul, MN 55102-0830 651-229-5300
Fax: 651-229-5470 800-752-7462
Disposable plastic tableware and drinkware
President: Frank Biller
VP Merchandising: Jim Schmidt
Number Employees: 500-999
Parent Co: Newell Companies
Brands:
Beverageware
Dinnerware
Flip-N-Fresh
Gourmet To Go
Hi-Heat
Legacy
Microproof
Microware
Pop-Tops
Prestige
Scrollware
Stow Away
Swirl

23554 **HS**
1301 W Sheridan Ave
Oklahoma City, OK 73106 405-239-6864
Fax: 405-239-2242 800-238-1240
sales@hsfoodservers.com
www.hsfoodservers.com
Thermal food containers for tabletop service
President: Esther Feiler
Owner: Ester Stephenson
Sales Manager: Sue Garcia
Estimated Sales: $2.5-5 Million
Number Employees: 10-19
Parent Co: ACO

23555 **HS Crocker Company**
12100 Smith Dr
Huntley, IL 60142-9618 847-669-3600
Fax: 847-669-1170 www.hscrocker.com
Specialty, gravure, flexographic and letterpress printing; paper and pressure sensitive labels; tickets; pharmaceutical, portion pack, foil, juice and yogurt lids
CFO: John Dai
CFO: John Dai
CEO: Ron Giordano
Marketing Manager: Ron Giordano
Estimated Sales: $20 - 30 Million
Number Employees: 50-99

23556 **HSI**
9977 North 90th Street
Suite 300
Scottsdale, AZ 85258 480-596-5456
Fax: 480-707-6223 info@hsi-solutions.com
www.hsi-solutions.com
Hospitality application software
Controller: Ron McNamee
General Manager And VP: Cyndi Shepley
Director of Operations: Norbert Holzmann
Purchasing Director: Jim Nicholas
Number Employees: 100-249

23557 **HSI Company**
3002 Hempland Rd
Lancaster, PA 17601-1992 717-392-2987
Fax: 717-392-0723 info@hsico.com
Ice cream hardening machinery and warehouse storage systems
Estimated Sales: $10-25 000,000
Number Employees: 10-19

23558 **HTI Filteration**
30241 Tomas
Rancho Santa Margarita, CA 92688 949-546-0809
Fax: 949-269-6438 877-404-9372
info@htifiltration.com www.htifiltration.com
Manufacturer and exporter of filtration equipment including oil, and hydraulic, specializing in water removal from oils
CEO: Steven Parker
VP: Steve Parker
Sales: Steve Parker
Technical Service: Ron Hart
Estimated Sales: $1 - 5 Million
Number Employees: 1-4
Square Footage: 40000
Parent Co: Temcor
Type of Packaging: Private Label

Brands:
H-F 201
H-F 211
H-S 410
Hydra-Supreme
Hydro-Fil

23559 HTM Electronics Industries
8651 Buffalo Avenue
Niagara Falls, NY 14304-4382 716-283-8748
Fax: 716-283-2127 800-644-1756
service@htmsensors.com www.htmsensors.com
Supplier of sensing devices
Owner: Bob Hooper
Vice President: Arthur Ramsay
Estimated Sales: $1-2.5 Million
Number Employees: 5-9

23560 HUBCO Inc.
215 South Poplar
PO Box 1286
Hutchinson, KS 67504-1286 620-663-8301
Fax: 620-663-5053 800-563-1867
hubcoinc@mindspring.com www.hubcoinc.com
Manufacturer, importer and exporter of bags including drawstring, cotton, flannel, polypropylene and burlap for flour, rice, popcorn, nuts, etc.; also, specialty food packaging available
President: Merlin Prehein
VP: Trey McPherson
VP: Jim Schmidt
Plant Manager: Fred Moore
Estimated Sales: $5 - 10 Million
Number Employees: 50-99
Square Footage: 284000
Brands:
Protexo
Sentry
Sentry Ii

23561 HW Theller Engineering
1540 Crown Rd
Petaluma, CA 94954-1487 707-762-3820
Fax: 707-769-0874 hut@theller.com
www.theller.com
Hot tack heatsealer tester, mini tensile tester, precision heatsealer tester
Estimated Sales: $1-2.5 Million
Number Employees: 5-9

23562 Haabtec
116 Bohannon Park
Shacklefords, VA 23156 804-785-4408
Fax: 804-785-3208 sales@haabtec.com
www.haabtec.com
Packaging equipment
President: Bobby Haab
Estimated Sales: $5-10 000,000
Number Employees: 10-19

23563 Haake
33 N Century Rd
Paramus, NJ 07652-2810 201-262-3628
Fax: 201-265-1977 800-631-1369
info@haake.usa.com www.haake.usa.com
Rheological instrumentation including viscometers, rheometers, thermal analyzers and circulators/water baths
Sales Director: Stephen Dieter
Estimated Sales: $1 - 5 Million
Number Employees: 1-4
Brands:
Minilab Micro Compouuder
Polylab
Rheostress Rs1
Rheostress Rs300
Rheostress Rv1
Rheostress Rs150
Vt-550

23564 Haas Tailoring Company
3425 Sinclair Ln
Baltimore, MD 21213-2030 410-732-3804
Fax: 410-732-9310
Clothes and service uniforms
Comptroller: Mark McLean
President Of Sales: Matthew Haas
Estimated Sales: $5-10 Million
Number Employees: 100-249

23565 Haban Saw Company
9301 Watson Industrial Park
St.Louis, MO 63126 314-968-3991
Fax: 314-968-1240 info@habansaw.com
www.habansaw.com
Manufacturer and exporter of butcher handsaws and blades
Estimated Sales: $1-2.5 Million
Number Employees: 4

23566 Habasit America
805 Satellite Blvd
Suwanee, GA 30024-7124 678-288-3600
Fax: 800-422-2748 800-458-6431
info.america@us.habasit.com
www.habasitamerica.com
Manufacturer, importer and exporter of belting
Chairman: Thomas Habegger
CEO: Andrea Volpi
CFO: Beat Stebler
Vice Chairman: Alice Habegger
R&D: Bill Humsby
Marketing: Allison Cox
National Sales Manager: Bert Fliegi
Segment Manager: Mike Creo
Head of Product Division Fabrics: Maarten Aarts
Estimated Sales: $5 - 10 Million
Number Employees: 100
Parent Co: Habasit-AG
Type of Packaging: Bulk

23567 Habasit Belting
3453 Pierce Drive NE
Chamblee, GA 30341-2496 770-458-6431
Fax: 770-454-6164 800-458-6431
hbi.habasit@us.habasit.com
www.habasitusa.com
Industrial flat belting
President: Harry Cardillo
Estimated Sales: $10-25 Million
Number Employees: 115

23568 Habasit Canada Limited
2275 Bristol Circle
Oakville, ON L6H 6P8
Canada 905-827-4131
Fax: 905-825-2612
Canada.CustomerCare@habasit.com
www.habasit.ca
Food handling conveyor belts, modular belts and flat power transmission belts.
President: John Visser
Plant Manager: Marty Ahearn
Number Employees: 30
Square Footage: 100000
Parent Co: Habasit AG

23569 Habco
1262 Windermere Way
Concord, CA 94521-3344 925-682-6203
Fax: 925-686-2036
heidiplinder@mindspring.com
Custom kitchen and galley equipment including steam tables, cabinets, counters and foodstands
Owner: Heidi Linder
CEO: Sarah Trissel
Estimated Sales: 500000
Number Employees: 1-4
Number of Brands: 50
Number of Products: 100
Square Footage: 1200

23570 Hach Co.
PO Box 608
Loveland, CO 80539-0389 970-669-3050
Fax: 970-669-2932 800-227-4224
techhelp@hach.com www.hach.com
Manufacturer of oxygen sensors and water analysis products for the beverage and water bottling industries. Also manufactures, designs, and distributes test kits for testing the quality of water in food industry applications.

23571 Hach Company
PO Box 389
Loveland, CO 80539 800-227-4224
Fax: 970-669-2932 800-227-4224
www.techhelp@hach.com
Manufacturer and exporter of waste water samplers and flow meters for use in water quality monitoring in food processing plants, tools and components and process/environmental controls
President: Jon Clark
VP: Donald Miller
Marketing: Diane Wood
Estimated Sales: $1 - 5 Million
Number Employees: 1,000-4,999
Square Footage: 62000

23572 Hach Company
P.O. Box 389
Loveland, CO 80539 970-669-3050
Fax: 970-669-2932 800-227-4224
httc@hach.com www.hach.com
Supplier of water and wastewater analysis equipment, including products for laboratory and microbiology testing, on-line analysis, and flow and sampling measurement equipment
President: Jon Clark
CFO: Jary Dreher
Number Employees: 1,000-4,999

23573 Hach Company
P.O. Box 389
Loveland, CO 80539-0389 414-355-3601
Fax: 970-669-2932 800-227-4224
info@gliint.com www.gliint.com
Wine industry flow and level gauges
Owner: Kathryn Hach

23574 Hackney Brothers
911 West 5th Street
Box 880
Washington, NC 27889 252-946-6521
Fax: 252-975-8340 800-763-0700
kgodley@vthackney.com
www.hackneyinternational.com
Manufacturer and exporter of refrigerated truck bodies and trailers; also, refrigeration systems and ice cream vending carts
President/Chief Executive Officer: Michael Tucker
Managing Director: Leandro Rodriguez
President, International Division: R. Hodges Hackney
Estimated Sales: $50-100 Million
Number Employees: 100-249
Square Footage: 220000
Type of Packaging: Food Service
Brands:
Hackney
Hackney Champion
Hackney Classic
Short Stop
Sno Van
Starlite
Vari-Temp

23575 Haden Signs of Texas
1102 30th St
Lubbock, TX 79411 806-744-4404
Fax: 806-744-1327 hadensigns@nts-online.net
www.hadensigns.com
Illuminated and nonilluminated signs including neon, plexiglass, metal and vinyl; also, electronic message centers; service and installation available
President: Curt Jones
CFO: Delwin Jones
Estimated Sales: Below $5 Million
Number Employees: 5-9

23576 Hager Containers
1015 Hayden Dr
Carrollton, TX 75006 972-417-7660
Fax: 972-417-8875 hasales@hagercontainers.com
www.hagercontainers.com
Corrugated boxes, partitions, point of purchase displays and value added packaging
President: Carl Renner
VP/General Manager: Carl Renner
Sales/Marketing Manager: Steve Main
Estimated Sales: $10-20 Million
Number Employees: 50-99

23577 Hahn Laboratories
1111 Flora Street
Columbia, SC 29201-4569 803-799-1614
Fax: 803-256-1417 hahnlab@flash.net
Consultant and chemical analyst providing agricultural and food service testing
Owner: Frank Hahn
Lab Manager: Frank Hahn

Estimated Sales: $500,000-$1 Million
Number Employees: 5 to 9

23578 Haier American Trading
1356 Broadway
New York, NY 10018-7300 212-594-3330
Fax: 212-594-3434 vcefalu@haieramerica.com
www.haieramerica.com
Owner: Michael Jamal
Estimated Sales: $1 - 5 Million
Number Employees: 5-9

23579 Haifa Chemicals
6800 Jericho Tpke
Suite 216w
Syosset, NY 11791-4488 516-921-0044
Fax: 516-921-0228 800-404-2368
marie@haifachemusa.com www.haifachem.co.il
Sales Manager: JoAnn Sprung
Estimated Sales: $2.5-5 Million
Number Employees: 9

23580 Haines Packing Company
5 1/2 Mile Mud Bay Rd
PO Box 930
Haines, AK 99827 907-766-2828
www.hainespacking.com
Five salmon species including; sockeye, king, coho, chum, and pink salmon. Products offered include; headed & gutted, fresh or vacuum packed and frozen, fillets, steaks, portions, hot smoked fillets & portions, and cold smoked fillets& portions, salmon caviar, halibut, and custom processing also available
President & CEO: William Weisfield
CFO & Controller: Bob Hall
Vice President & Owner: Jan Supler
Estimated Sales: 100 Million
Number Employees: 40
Square Footage: 5963
Type of Packaging: Consumer, Food Service, Bulk
Other Locations:
Ward Cove Packing Co.
Seattle WA
Brands:
Northern Pride
Pirate

23581 Hairnet Corporation of America
151 W 26th St # 2
New York, NY 10001-6810 212-675-5840
Fax: 212-685-6225
Manufacturer and exporter of hairnets
President: E Gard
Secretary: M Moron
VP: T Persad
Estimated Sales: $2.5-5 Million
Number Employees: 1-4
Square Footage: 1750
Brands:
Jac-O-Net
Lady Swiss
Mirage

23582 Hal Mather & Sons
11803 Il Route 120
Woodstock, IL 60098-1900 815-338-4000
Fax: 815-338-3003 800-338-4007
sales@mather-dataforms.com
www.mather-dataforms.com
Tags, labels and tickets
President: Douglas Mather
CFO: Paul Weathersby
VP: Jim Mather
General Manager: David Diverde
Estimated Sales: $5 - 10 Million
Number Employees: 1-4

23583 Hal-One Plastics
801 E Highway 56
Olathe, KS 66061-4999 913-782-3535
Fax: 913-764-7369 800-626-5784
Manufacturer and wholesaler/distributor of reusable plastic tableware and trays
President and CEO: Joyce Stawarz
CEO: Joyce Stawarz
1st Executive VP Sales: Galen Soule
Estimated Sales: $10 - 20 Million
Number Employees: 50-99
Square Footage: 30000

23584 Hall China Company
1 Anna St
East Liverpool, OH 43920 330-385-2900
Fax: 330-385-6185 800-445-4255
custserv@hallchina.com www.hallchina.com
Chinaware
President: Rick Shepperd
National Sales Manager: Jim Clunk
National Distributor Account Manager: Joe Owen
National Chain Account Manager: Joe Brice
Estimated Sales: $20 - 50 Million
Number Employees: 100-249

23585 Hall Manufacturing Company
1321 Industrial Drive
Henderson, TX 75652-5019 903-657-4501
Fax: 903-657-4502
Tote bags
Estimated Sales: $1-2.5 Million
Number Employees: 5-9

23586 Hall Manufacturing Corporation
297 Margaret King Ave
Ringwood, NJ 07456 973-962-6022
Fax: 973-962-7652
kerry@hallmanufacturing.com
www.hallmanufacturing.com
Manufacturer and exporter of extruded plastic tracks for refrigeration industry; also, co-extrusions and tubing
President: Mike Goceljak
Sales Manager: Kerry Goceljak
Estimated Sales: $2.5-5 Million
Number Employees: 20-49
Square Footage: 21000

23587 Hall's Safety Apparel
1020 W 1st Street
Uhrichsville, OH 44683-2210 740-922-3671
Fax: 740-922-4880 800-232-3671
Protective Clothin Manufacturing; Supplier, Importer and Exporter
Owner: Gregory Schneider
VP: Delores Schneider
Public Relations: Arnold Ziffel
Estimated Sales: $1-3 Million
Number Employees: 5 to 9
Square Footage: 21000
Parent Co: Schneider Enterprises USA
Type of Packaging: Food Service, Private Label, Bulk
Brands:
Polytex
Solvaseal

23588 Hall-Woolford Tank Company
5500 N Water St
Philadelphia, PA 19120 215-329-9022
Fax: 215-329-1177 woodtanks@aol.com
www.woodtank.com
Manufacturer and exporter of noncorrosive wood tanks, vats and tubs; wholesaler/distributor of flexible tank liners; industrial wood products; all products FDA approved. Also industrial wood products
General Manager: Jack Hillman
Sales Manager: Jack Hillman
Operations Manager: Robert Riepen
Estimated Sales: $1 - 3 Million
Number Employees: 5-9
Square Footage: 19000

23589 Hallams
5204 N 10th Ave
Ozark, MO 65721 417-581-3786
Fax: 417-581-3786 rzkozark@yahoo.com
www.hallamsfoods.com
Owner: Robert Zoppelt
Vice President: Katherine Zoppelt
Marketing Director: Robert Zoppelt
Estimated Sales: 300000
Number Employees: 1-4
Number of Brands: 1
Square Footage: 1800
Type of Packaging: Private Label

23590 Hallberg Manufacturing Corporation
PO Box 23985
Tampa, FL 33623-3985 800-633-7627
Fax: 800-253-7323
Manufacturer and exporter of industrial hand soap
President: Charles Hallberg
VP: Linda Werlein
Estimated Sales: $300,000-500,000
Square Footage: 10000
Brands:
Aloe Jell Water Less
Citra Jell
Pumice Jell
Surety Pwd Hand Soap

23591 Hallmark Equipment
11040 Monterey Rd
Morgan Hill, CA 95037-9362 408-782-2600
Fax: 408-782-2605 hallmark@heiusa.com
www.heiusa.com
Supplier of used packaging and food processing equipment
President: Ronald Wilson
Estimated Sales: $1 - 3 Million
Number Employees: 5-9

23592 Hallock Fabricating Corporation
324 Doctors Path
Riverhead, NY 11901-1509 631-727-2441
Fax: 631-369-6021
Stainless steel and carbon steel exhaust hoods and countertops; also, custom metal fabrication
Owner: Cory Hallock
Estimated Sales: $1 - 5 Million
Number Employees: 1 to 4
Square Footage: 9200

23593 Halmark Systems, Inc
354 Page Street
Stoughton, MA 02072 781-344-8616
Fax: 781-341-4505 800-225-5823
sales@halmarksystems.net
www.halmarksystems.net
Price marking equipment, custom-printed labels, and date marking equipment
President: Mark Crean
Operations: Lisa Allen
Estimated Sales: $5-10 Million
Number Employees: 10-19

23594 Halpak Plastics
10 Burt Dr
Deer Park, NY 11729-5702 631-242-1100
Fax: 631-242-6150 800-442-5725
hal@halpak.com www.halpak.com
Shrink bands and labels
Marketing Director: Sande Kaplan
Estimated Sales: $5-10 Million
Number Employees: 20-49

23595 Halton Company
101 Industrial Dr
Scottsville, KY 42164 270-237-5600
Fax: 270-237-5700 800-442-5866
info@haltoncompany.com
www.haltoncompany.com
Manufacturer and exporter of stainless steel hoods, filters and fans; also, fire suppression and ventilation systems
President: Rick Bagwell
R&D: Andre Livchak
Controller: Chris Gentry
National Sales Manager: Rich Catan
Plant Manager: Phil Meredith
Purchasing Manager: Eric Key
Estimated Sales: $10 - 20 Million
Number Employees: 50-99
Square Footage: 50000
Parent Co: Halton O.Y.
Brands:
Capture Jet
Capture Rey

23596 Halton Packaging Systems
1045 S Service Road W
Oakville, ON L6L 6K3
Canada 905-847-9141
Fax: 905-847-9145 info@haltonpackaging.com
www.haltonpackaging.com
Manufacturer and exporter of pallet packaging machinery including stretch wrapping, conveyors, and pallet handling machinery
President: Peter Hughes
Estimated Sales: $2 Million
Number Employees: 10-19
Square Footage: 120000
Brands:
Halton

23597 Hamer
14650 28th Ave N
Plymouth, MN 55447 763-231-0100
Fax: 763-231-0101 800-927-4674
packaging@hamerinc.com www.hamerinc.com

Form-fill-seal systems, bag closers, bag fillers, balers
President: Roger Breisch
Sales Manager: Jerome Eller
Estimated Sales: $5-10 Million
Number Employees: 20-49

23598 Hamilton
1637 Dixie Hwy
Hamilton, OH 45011-4087 513-863-3300
Fax: 513-863-5508 888-699-7164
info@hamiltoncaster.com
www.hamiltoncaster.com
Manufacturer and exporter of nonpowered material handling carts, hand trucks, trailers, industrial casters and wheels
President: David Lippert
Executive VP: Steven Lippert
Quality Control: Mary Latimer
Marketing Director: Mark Lippert
Sales Director: James Lippert
Estimated Sales: $10 - 20 Million
Number Employees: 50-99
Brands:
Ace-Tuf
Aqualite
Bondalast
Cush-N-Aire
Cush-N-Flex
Cush-N-Tuf
Duralast
Ebonite
Eleva-Truck
Flexonite
Freightainer
Hi-Lo
Instoematic
Job-Built
Leader
Lite-N-Tuff
Lube-Gard
Maxi-Duty
Nu-Flex
Nu-Last
Plastex
Poly-Tech
Roll Models
Roll-N-Stor
Stack-N-Roll
Steeltest
Super-Flex
Superlast
Ultra-Lite
Unilast
Versa-Tech
Vulcalite

23599 Hamilton Awning Company
469 Market St
Beaver, PA 15009 724-774-7644
Fax: 724-775-4221
Commercial awnings
Owner: Dave Mulcahy
Estimated Sales: $1-2,500,000
Number Employees: 10-19

23600 Hamilton Beach/Proctor-Silex
261 Yadkin Road
Southern Pines, NC 28387 804-273-9777
Fax: 804-527-7142 800-711-6100
salessupportA@hamiltonbeach.com
www.hamiltonbeach.com
Foodservice equipment for restaurant, bars, nursing homes, healthcare facilities, hotels, and more
CEO: Michael J Morecroft
Sales Director: Steve Sarfaty
Public Relations: Kirby Kriz
Estimated Sales: $1 - 5 Million
Number Employees: 5,000-9,999
Parent Co: Nacco Industries
Type of Packaging: Food Service
Brands:
Hamilton Beach
Proctor Silex

23601 Hamilton Kettles
2898 Birch Drive
Weirton, WV 26062-5142 304-794-9400
Fax: 304-794-9430 800-535-1882
sales@hamiltonkettles.com
www.hamiltonkettles.com
Manufacturer and exporter of sanitary stainless steel and steam jacketed kettles, mix-cookers, pressure cookers, agitators, vacuum kettles and custom designed processing kettles and mixers
President: Charles Friend
Quality Control: Ed Henderson
VP/General Manager: George Gruner
R&D: Ed Henderson
Sales Director: Peggy Miller
Production Manager: Kenneth Henderson
Estimated Sales: $5 - 10 Million
Number Employees: 25
Square Footage: 128000
Parent Co: Allegheny Hancock Corporation

23602 Hamilton Manufacturing Corporation
1026 Hamilton Dr
Holland, OH 43528 419-867-4858
Fax: 419-867-4850 www.hamiltonmfg.com
Currency validators and changemakers
President: Robin Ritz
Estimated Sales: $10-20 Million
Number Employees: 100-249

23603 Hamilton Soap & Oil Products
51 Bleeker Street
Paterson, NJ 07524 973-225-1031
Fax: 973-225-0268
Soap and detergent; also, private label and contract packaging services available
Estimated Sales: $1 - 5 Million

23604 Hammar & Sons Sign Company
71 Bridge St
PO Box 184
Pelham, NH 03076-0184 603-635-2292
Fax: 603-635-7904 800-527-7446
info@hammarandsons.com
www.signsnownh.com
Signs including neon, wood, sandblasted window, in-store and aisle markers; also, banners and posters; installation and repair services available
Owner: Al Hammar
VP: Mike Hammar
Estimated Sales: $1-2.5 Million
Number Employees: 20-49
Square Footage: 12000
Brands:
Hammar

23605 Hammer Packaging
200 Lucius Gordon Drive
PO Box 22678
Rochester, NY 14692-2678 585-424-3880
Fax: 585-424-3886
contactus@hammerpackaging.com
www.hammerlitho.com
Hammer Packaging is a multicolor packaging printer of sheet-fed cut and stack labels, box-wraps and premium packets, along with roll fed UV and water base flexo-graphic pressure sensitive labels, wrap labels and form/fill labels forconsumer products.
President/CEO: Jim Hammer
President, Chief Executive Officer: James Hammer
Sales Manager: Ed Nugent

23606 (HQ)Hammer Packaging Corporation
P.O.Box 22678
Rochester, NY 14692-2678 585-424-3880
Fax: 585-424-3886
contactus@hammerpackaging.com
www.hammerpackaging.com
Labels for the food and beverage industry; holticulture, wine and spirits and household products
President: James Hammer
CFO: Christopher Wieser
Research & Development: Hart Swisher
Quality Control: Charles Fowler
Marketing/Sales: Louis Iovoli
Operations/Production/Plant Manager: Marty Karpie
Purchasing Manager: Jim Peabody
Estimated Sales: $100 Million
Number Employees: 450
Square Footage: 92000
Type of Packaging: Consumer, Food Service, Private Label

23607 Hammerstahl Cutlery
3232 Woodsmill Drive
Melbourne, FL 32934 561-373-1925
Fax: 321-253-0737 felipe.florida@netzero.com
www.hammerstahl.com

23608 Hampden Papers
PO Box 149
Holyoke, MA 01041-0149 413-536-1000
Fax: 413-532-9161 www.hampdenpapers.com
Embossed and plain foil and glazed, laminated and gift wrapping paper, packaging components, FDA compliant
President/COO: Richard Wells
CEO: Robert Fowler
Vice President of Sales and Marketing: Bob Adams
VP Operations: Michael Archambeault
Estimated Sales: $33 Million
Number Employees: 100-249
Square Footage: 400000

23609 Hampel Corporation
W194n11551 McCormick Dr
Germantown, WI 53022 262-255-4540
Fax: 262-255-9731 800-494-4762
sales@hampelcorp.com www.hampelcorp.com
Manufacturer and exporter of plastic pallets including rugged light weight, steel reinforced, thermoformed, nestable, standard and custom interlocking sleeve pack and double decker
President: Lance Hampel
Estimated Sales: $10 - 20 Million
Number Employees: 53
Brands:
Calf-Tel
Intrustor
Pallid

23610 Hampton Roads Box Company
619 E Pinner St
Suffolk, VA 23434 757-934-2355
Fax: 757-539-4918
Manufacturer and exporter of pallets, wooden boxes and shipping crates
President: Mark Sullivan
Estimated Sales: $1.2 Million
Number Employees: 5-9

23611 Hampton-Tilley Associates
740 Goddard Ave
Chesterfield, MO 63005 636-537-3353
Fax: 636-536-4114 sales@stl.hamptontilley.com
www.htdcr.com
Consultant specializing in automation and engineering services; designer of software for recipes, cooking, processing, packaging and quality control/validation
Manager: Pat Finefield
VP: C Tilley
Estimated Sales: $5 - 10 Million
Number Employees: 10-19
Square Footage: 21000

23612 Hamrick Manufacturing &Service
1436 Martin Rd
Mogadore, OH 44260 330-628-4877
Fax: 330-628-2180 800-321-9590
hmspkg@aol.com www.hamrickmfg.com
Manufacturer and exporter of packaging machinery including case packers, case sealers, bottled water case packers, lock tab pullers/breakers, liter tray packers, four flap openers, uncasers, etc.; custom built machinery available
President: Gene Hamrick
CEO: Luther Hamrick
VP Sales: Tom Hamrick
VP of Production: Phil Hamrick
Purchasing Director: Kurt Kothmayer
Estimated Sales: $5-10 Million
Number Employees: 20-49
Number of Products: 18
Square Footage: 28000
Brands:
Hms

23613 Hanco Manufacturing Company
1301 Heistan Place
Memphis, TN 38104 901-725-7364
Fax: 901-726-5899 800-530-7364
Disinfectants, insecticides, cleaners and degreasers
VP: Scott Hanover

Estimated Sales: $1-2.5 Million
Number Employees: 19
Square Footage: 30000
Brands:
Hanco

23614 Hancock Gourmet LobsterCompany
46 Park Dr
Topsham, ME 04086 207-725-1855
Fax: 207-725-1856
cal@hancockgourmetlobster.com
www.hancockgourmetlobster.com
Gourmet lobster and other seafood specialty products including appetizers, soups, entrees, sweets, samplers and more
Founder & President: Cal Hancock
VP: Jack Rosberg
Executive Chef: Kevin Messier
Wholesale Sales Manager: Laura Meier
Director of Operations & Marketing: Amber Pelletier
Estimated Sales: $1.3 Million
Number Employees: 6
Type of Packaging: Consumer, Food Service, Bulk

23615 Hand Made Lollies
465 S Orlando Avenue
Suite 205
Maitland, FL 32751 877-784-2724
Fax: 877-249-6419 info@handmadelollies.com
www.handmadelollies.com
Handmade and personalized lollipops
President: Timothy Lang

23616 Handgards
901 Hawkins Blvd
El Paso, TX 79915 915-779-6606
Fax: 915-779-1312 800-351-8161
sales@handgards.com www.handgards.com
Manufacturer and exporter of disposable plastic gloves, aprons and bags; importer of latex and PVC gloves
CEO: Bob McLellan
Estimated Sales: $500,000-$1,000,000
Number Employees: 250-499
Square Footage: 140000
Type of Packaging: Food Service, Private Label
Brands:
Handgards
Neatgards
Tuffgards
Valugards
Zipgards

23617 Handicap Sign
1142 Wealthy St SE
Grand Rapids, MI 49506 616-454-9416
Fax: 616-454-4999 800-690-4888
handicapsign@gmail.com www.hsisign.com
Custom screen printing, vinyl graphics and hand lettering for decals, signs, posters, banners and P.O.P displays
VP: Kim Tasma
Estimated Sales: $500,000-$1 Million
Number Employees: 5-9
Square Footage: 7500

23618 Handling Specialty
PO Box 279
Niagara Falls, NY 14304-0279 716-694-6333
Fax: 716-694-6903 800-559-8366
info@handling.com www.handling.com
Manufacturer and exporter of material handling equipment including lifting systems for very hot or cold environments, tilters, rotators, fork truck service lifts and robotic indexing tables
President: Thomas Beach
Marketing Director: Lydia Macugajlo
Direct Sales: Mike Roper
Estimated Sales: C
Number Employees: 10-19
Parent Co: Handling Specialty
Brands:
Forklevator

23619 Handtmann
28690 N.
Ballard Drive
Lake Forest, IL 60045 847-808-1100
Fax: 847-808-1106 800-477-3585
www.handtmann.com
Vacuum fillers with in-line grinders, and high speed clipping machines
President: Steve Tennis
Sales Director: Robert Kors
Estimated Sales: $5 - 10 000,000
Number Employees: 20-49

23620 Handtmann, Inc.
28690 N. Ballard Drive
Lake Forest, IL 60045 847-808-1100
Fax: 847-808-1106 800-477-3585
info@handtmann.com www.handtmann.com
Filling, portioning and linking machines for the sausage and meat industries. Also manufacture deli product systems and grinding machines.

23621 Handy Roll Company
1236 Anna Lane
San Marcos, CA 92069-2160 760-471-6214
Carton cutters
Co-Owner: Glenn Spear
Co-Owner: Margaret Spear
Number Employees: 1
Brands:
Handy Blade

23622 Handy Store Fixtures
337 Sherman Ave
Newark, NJ 07114
Fax: 973-642-6222 800-631-4280
www.handystorefixtures.com
Manufacturer and exporter of store and wall fixtures, show cases, gondolas and shelving units
President: Marc Kurland
CFO: Scott McClymont
Executive VP: Richard Kurland
VP Sales: Walter Pincus
Number Employees: 250-499
Square Footage: 1200000
Type of Packaging: Food Service

23623 (HQ)Handy Wacks Corporation
100 E Averill St
Sparta, MI 49345 616-887-8268
Fax: 616-887-6110 800-445-4434
customerserv@handywacks.com
www.handywacks.com
Manufacturer, exporter and importer of waxed packaging products including sandwich and interfolded high density polyethylene wrap, baking cups, hot dog trays, and steak, freezer, locker, delicatessen and bakery tissue and paper
President: H B Fairchild Iii III
Cfo: Fran Brant
Director Of Sales: George Siwik
Production Manager: Mike Moberly
Purchasing Manager: Mike Moberly
Estimated Sales: $20-25 Million
Number Employees: 50-99
Number of Brands: 12
Number of Products: 225
Square Footage: 90000
Type of Packaging: Food Service
Brands:
Handy Wacks

23624 Hanel Storage Systems
121 Industry Dr
Pittsburgh, PA 15275 412-787-3444
Fax: 412-787-3744 info@hanel.us
www.hanelus.com
Manufacturer, importer and exporter of vertical storage systems
President: Joachim Hanel
Vice President: Brian Cohen
VP: Brian Cohen
Sales Director: Michael Fanning
Estimated Sales: $5-10 Million
Number Employees: 10-19
Parent Co: Hanel GmbH
Brands:
Hanel Lean-Lift
Hanel Vertical Carousels

23625 Hangzhou Sanhe USA Inc.
20536 Carrey Rd
Walnut, CA 91789 909-869-6016
Fax: 909-869-6015 sales@sanheinc.com
www.sanheinc.com
Food ingredients and additives.
President: Aili Chen
Estimated Sales: $1 Million
Type of Packaging: Bulk

23626 Hank Rivera Associates
13600 W Warren Ave
Dearborn, MI 48126-1421 313-581-8300
Manufacturer and exporter of uniforms, aprons and pizza delivery equipment including heat retention/insulated food bags, nylon pan pullers, beverage carriers and pizza lid supports
President: Dante Rivera
Secretary/Treasurer: Hank Rivera
Number Employees: 10-19
Square Footage: 12500
Brands:
Hank's

23627 Hankin Specialty Equipment
3237 Fitzgerald Road
Rancho Cordova, CA 95742 916-381-2400
Fax: 916-381-2481 800-831-8395
info@hankinspecialty.com
www.hankinspecialty.com
Wine industry pallet postitioners
President and QC: Neil Hankin
CFO: Mike Seebode
Estimated Sales: $5 - 10 Million
Number Employees: 10-19

23628 Hankison International
1000 Philadelphia St
Canonsburg, PA 15317-1777 724-746-1100
Fax: 724-745-6040
inquiry@airtreatment.spx.com
www.spxdehydration.com
Manufacturer and exporter of compressed air dryers, filters, condensate drains and air purifiers
Manager: Neal Horrigan
Marketing: Bill Kennedy
Sales: Rod Smith
Estimated Sales: $5-10 Million
Number Employees: 50-99
Square Footage: 808000
Parent Co: Hansen

23629 Hanley Sign Company
26 Sicker Rd
Latham, NY 12110 518-783-6183
Fax: 518-783-0128 ltymchyn@hanleysign.com
www.hanleysign.com
Signs and advertising displays
President: Lisa Tymchyn
Quality Control: Lisa Tymchyn
Estimated Sales: Below $5 Million
Number Employees: 20-49
Square Footage: 8000

23630 Hanna Instruments
584 Park East Dr
Woonsocket, RI 02895 401-765-7500
Fax: 401-765-7575 800-426-6287
sales@hannainst.com www.hannainst.com
Manufacturer and exporter of electro-analytical instruments including sodium chloride and chlorine analyzers, conductivity, pH and relative humidity meters, temperature recorders and thermo hygrometers
President: Martino Nardo
VP: Jim McKenzie
VP Sales & Marketing: Peter Hail
General Manager: Harry Lau
Estimated Sales: $100 Million
Number Employees: 59
Square Footage: 26000
Type of Packaging: Consumer, Food Service, Bulk
Brands:
Agricare
Bravo
Champ
Checker
Checktemp
Conmet
Elth
Food Care
Hydrocheck
Key
Micro Phep
Phandy
Phep
Piccolo
Temp Care
Temp Check

23631 **Hannan Products Corporation**
220 N Smith Ave
Corona, CA 92880 951-735-1587
Fax: 951-735-0827 800-954-4266
sales@hannanpak.com www.hannanpak.com
Manufacturer and exporter of machinery and materials for skin and blister packaging; also, for die cutting
President: Henry H Jenkins
CFO and QC and R&D: Alfred Ramos
Sales Manager: Lawrence Jenkins
Estimated Sales: $5 - 10 Million
Number Employees: 20-49

23632 **Hannay Reels**
P.O.Box 159
553 State Route 143
Westerlo, NY 12193 518-797-3791
Fax: 518-797-3259 877-467-3357
reels@hannay.com www.hannay.com
Metal reels for hose & cable, water, washdown, fluid handling
COB: Roger Hannay
COO: Elaine Gruener
Quality Control: Ken Fritz
Marketing Manager: Jennifer Wing
Sales Manager: Mark Saker
Public Relations: Maureen Bagshaw
President/CEO: Eric Hannay
Production: Mike Ferguson
Facilities Manager: Walt Scram
Materials Manager: Dick Storm
Estimated Sales: $25-50 Million
Number Employees: 140
Square Footage: 118612

23633 **Hannic Freight Forwarders, Inc**
16214 S Lincoln Hwy
PO Box 445
Plainfield, IL 60586-5146 815-436-4521
Fax: 815-436-1734 800-786-4521
sales@hffi.net www.hffi.net
President: Debbie Maass
Vice President: Hans Maass
Estimated Sales: $.5 - 1 million
Number Employees: 5-9

23634 **Hano Business Forms**
PO Box 275
Wilbraham, MA 01095-0275 413-781-7800
Fax: 413-781-7808 www.hano.com
Printed documents
CEO and President: John Sindstorm
VP: Jim Michill
Number Employees: 50

23635 **Hansaloy Corporation**
820 W 35th St
Davenport, IA 52806 563-386-1131
Fax: 563-386-7707 800-553-4992
sales@hansaloy.com www.hansaloy.com
Manufacturer and exporter of blades including slicing/dicing, band and reciprocating with scalloped and straight edges for slicing bread and boneless meat
President: Stephen Wright
CEO: Howard H Cherry Iii
Quality Control: Stephen Wright
VP Sales/Marketing: K Brenner
Customer Service Manager: Fran Draude
Estimated Sales: $5 - 10 Million
Number Employees: 50-99
Square Footage: 40000

23636 **Hansen Beverage Company**
1010 Railroad Street
Corona, CA 92882 714-634-4200
Fax: 714-634-4272 800-426-7367
Estimated Sales: $1 - 3 000,000
Number Employees: 5-9

23637 **Hansen Technologies Corporation**
400 Quadrangle Dr Ste F
Bolingbrook, IL 60440 630-325-1565
Fax: 630-325-1572 800-426-7368
info@hantech.com www.hantech.com
Hansen Technologies Corporation offers an extensive line of components for industrial refrigeration systems including sealed motor valves, control valves, shut-off valves, pressure-relief valves, refrigerant pumps, air purgers, defrostcontrols, and liquid level controls
President: Jeffrey Nank
CEO: Jeff Markham
CFO: Mark Sebben
R&D: John Yencho
Marketing Manager: Denise Ernst
Sales: Harold Streicher
Operations: Jim Flurry
Purchasing Director: Joe Reicher
Estimated Sales: $20 - 50 Million
Number Employees: 100-249
Number of Brands: 3
Number of Products: 300

23638 **Hansen's Laboratory**
N67w33880 Loghouse Ct
Oconomowoc, WI 53066-1936 262-966-4952
Fax: 414-607-5959
Culture research
Owner: Marsha Hanson
Estimated Sales: $1 - 3 000,000
Number Employees: 5-9

23639 **Hanset Stainless**
P.O.Box 11350
Portland, OR 97211 503-283-8822
Fax: 503-283-8875 800-360-7030
info@hansetstainless.com
www.hansetstainless.com
Custom stainless steel food service equipment
President: Jim Hanset
Estimated Sales: $20-50 Million
Number Employees: 50-99
Square Footage: 25000

23640 **Hanson Box & Lumber Company**
12 New Salem Street
Wakefield, MA 01880-1979 617-245-0358
Fax: 781-245-8043
Plywood and pine boxes, shipping containers, pallets and skids
President: Kirk Hanson

23641 **Hanson Brass**
7530 San Fernando Road
Sun Valley, CA 91352-4344 818-767-3501
Fax: 818-767-7891 888-841-3773
info@hansonbrass.com www.hansonbrass.com
President: Tom Hanson Jr
CEO: Jim Hanson
CFO: Tom Hanson Sr
VP: Robert Hanson
Plant Manager: Mark Denny
Number Employees: 5-9

23642 **Hanson Lab Furniture**
814 Mitchell Rd
Newbury Park, CA 91320 805-498-3121
Fax: 805-498-1855 info@hansonlab.com
www.hansonlab.com
Manufacturer and exporter of laboratory furniture, fume hoods and accessories; also, installation and lab planning services available
VP: Mike Hanson
Estimated Sales: $5 - 10 Million
Number Employees: 20-50
Parent Co: Norlab

23643 **(HQ)Hantover**
P.O.Box 410646
Kansas City, MO 64141-0646 816-761-7800
Fax: 816-761-0044 800-821-7849
contactus@hantover.com www.hantover.com
Manufacturer and exporter of vacuum packaging machinery and stainless steel cutlery and utensils
Chairman: Bernard Huff
General Manager: David Philgreen
Estimated Sales: $20 - 50 Million
Number Employees: 100-249
Type of Packaging: Food Service
Other Locations:
Hantover
Kansas City MO

23644 **Hapco/Leister**
390 Portage Blvd
Kent, OH 44240-7283 330-678-9353
Fax: 330-677-8282 800-345-9553
gary@hapcoinc.com www.hapcoinc.com
Owner: Harold Neidlinger
Estimated Sales: $10 - 20 Million
Number Employees: 20-49

23645 **Hapco/Leister**
390 Portage Blvd
Kent, OH 44240-7283 330-678-9353
Fax: 330-677-8282 800-345-9353
www.hapcoinc.com
Hot air tools, sealing equipment
Owner: Harold Neidlinger
VP: Mike Harrison
Estimated Sales: $10-20 Million
Number Employees: 20-49

23646 **Hapman Conveyors**
6002 E N Ave
Kalamazoo, MI 49048 269-343-1675
Fax: 269-349-2477 800-968-7722
info@hapman.com www.hapman.com
Manufacturer and exporter of flexible screw, pneumatic and tubular drag conveyors, bulk bag unloaders, manual bag dump stations, batch weigh equipment and silo dischargers
President: Edward Thompson
Quality Control: Randy McBroom
Marketing: Greg Nowak
Estimated Sales: $20 - 50 Million
Number Employees: 50-99
Square Footage: 100000
Parent Co: Prab
Brands:
Helix
Mini-Vac

23647 **Happy Chef**
22 Park Place
Suite 2
Butler, NJ 07405 973-492-2525
Fax: 973-492-0303 800-347-0288
info@happychefuniforms.com
www.happychefuniforms.com
Manufacturer and wholesaler/distributor of uniforms and table linens for kitchen and waiter/waitress personnel. Serving the food service market
President: James Nadler
VP: Howard Curtin
VP, Sales/Marketing: Howard Curtin
Estimated Sales: $10 Million
Number Employees: 20-49
Square Footage: 15000
Type of Packaging: Private Label

23648 **Happy Ice**
625 Henry Avenue
Winnepeg, MB R3A 0V1 888-573-9237
Fax: 204-783-9857 info@arcticglacier.com
www.arcticglacier.com
The largest manufacturer of bagged ice
President/CEO: Keith McMahon
EVP/Chief Financial Officer: Doug Bailey
Estimated Sales: $233 Million
Number Employees: 20-49

23649 **Harbor Pallet Company**
301 W Imperial Hwy
Anaheim, CA 90631 714-533-4940
Fax: 714-535-2175 pomonabox@att.net
www.harborpallet.com
Wooden and plastic pallets and skids and wooden boxes and containers
President: Ross Gilroy
Estimated Sales: $2.5-5 Million
Number Employees: 5-9

23650 **Harborlite Corporation**
PO Box 519
Lompoc, CA 93438-0519 800-342-8667
Fax: 805-735-5699 info@worldminerals.com
www.worldminerals.com
Manufacturer and exporter of perlite filter aids and functional fillers
Type of Packaging: Food Service, Bulk

23651 **Harborlite Corporation**
P.O.Box 462908
Escondido, CA 92046-2908 760-745-5900
Fax: 760-745-6349
lemmonse@worldminerals.com
www.worldminerals.com
Wine industry filtration and wastewater systems
Manager: Darin Jackman
Estimated Sales: $2.5-5 Million
Number Employees: 10-19

23652 Harbour House Bar Crafting
737 Canal Street
Bldg 16
Stamford, CT 06902-5930 203-348-6906
Fax: 203-348-6190 800-755-1227
bigbars@snet.net www.harbourhouse.com
Manufacturer solid wooden bars, tables, booths and carts
President: Steven Kline
VP: Jeff Watkins
Estimated Sales: $1-2.5 Million
Number Employees: 10
Type of Packaging: Food Service

23653 Harbour House Furniture
37 Canal Street
Bldg 16
Stamford, CT 06902-5930 203-348-6906
Fax: 203-348-6190 bigbars@snet.net
www.harbourhouse.com
President: Steven Kline

23654 Harbro Packaging
2635 N Kildare Ave
Chicago, IL 60639 773-489-6520
Fax: 773-489-6584 877-428-5812
www.harbro.net
Distributor of tabletop and stand - alone vacuum machines
Owner: Susan Thomas
CFO: Susan Thomas
Quality Control: Rand Thomas
Estimated Sales: $5 - 10 Million
Number Employees: 20-49

23655 Harco Enterprises
675 the Parkway
Peterborough, ON K9J 7K2
Canada 705-743-5361
Fax: 705-743-4312 800-361-5361
sales@harco.on.ca www.harco.on.ca
Manufacturer, wholesaler/distributor and exporter of promotional items including hot stamping, pad printing, multi-color imprints, glow-in-the-dark custom products, coasters, swizzle sticks, toys, flyers, key tags, spoons, etc; servingthe food service market. Supplier of spare parts to the dairy and food industries
President: Ray Harris
VP Finance: Kathy Perry
VP: Terry Harris
VP Marketing: Kathy Perry
VP Administration: Joan Harris
Number Employees: 10
Square Footage: 64000
Type of Packaging: Food Service

23656 Harcros Chemicals
5200 Speaker Road
Kansas City, KS 66110-2930 913-321-3131
Fax: 913-621-7718 KansasCityCS@harcros.com
www.harcroschem.com
Surface active agents and medicinal chemicals
President, Chief Executive Officer: Kevin Mirner
Vice President: Dan Larsen
Director of Operations: Dan Johnson
Number Employees: 250-499

23657 Hardi-Tainer
P.O.Box 201
South Deerfield, MA 01373-0201 413-665-2163
Fax: 413-665-4801 800-882-9878
hardiggacct@hardigg.com www.hardigg.com
Returnable and reusable intermediate bulk containers with wide mouth openings
President, Chief Executive Officer: Lyndon Faulkner
CEO: James S Hardigg
Vice President of Research: Kevin Deighton
Vice President of Sales: Mark Rolfes
Estimated Sales: $20 - 50 Million
Number Employees: 250-499
Square Footage: 100000
Parent Co: Hardigg Industries
Brands:
Hardi-Tainer

23658 Hardin Signs
3663 N Meadowbrook Rd
Peoria, IL 61604 309-688-4111
Fax: 309-688-3217 www.hardinsigns.com
Signs including neon plastic; also, lettering, installation and maintenance services available
President: William Hardin
CFO: Marian Hardin
VP: James Hardin
Estimated Sales: $2.2 Million
Number Employees: 14
Square Footage: 48000
Type of Packaging: Bulk

23659 Hardt Equipment Manufacturing
1756 50th Avenue
Lachine, QC H8T 2V5
Canada
888-848-4408
www.hardt.ca
Designer and manufacturer of food service equipment including commercial rotisseries, heated merchandisers, counter-top healted display cases and a cleaning apparatus for cookin utensils and accessories.
Purchasing Manager: Tony Morrone
Number Employees: 75
Square Footage: 112000
Brands:
Inferno
Snack Zone
The Cleaning Solution
Zone

23660 Hardware-Components
1021 Park Avenue
New Matamoras, OH 45767 740-865-2424
Fax: 740-865-2534
hci@hardwarecomponents.com
www.hardwarecomponents.com
Manufacturer and importer of ferrous and nonferrous castings, stampings, forgings, furniture and cabinets
President: Robert Robinson
VP/General Manager: Danny Gautschi
VP Sales: Chris Dickinson
Estimated Sales: $5 - 10,000,000
Number Employees: 10-19

23661 Hardwood Products Company
PO Box 149
Guilford, ME 04443 207-876-3312
Fax: 207-876-3704 800-289-3340
info@hwppuritan.com www.hwpuritan.com
Manufacturer and exporter of wooden ice cream sticks and spoons, stir sticks and skewers; also, industrial cleaning swabs, cocktail forks, cocktail spears, corn dog sticks, flag sticks, fan paddles, dawels
Chief Finacial Officer: Scott Welman
Quality Control: William Young
Sales Manager: Ann Erickson
Sales Manager: Charles Martell
CSR Rep: Jessica Brown
VP of Operations: James Cartwright
Plant Manager: Bruce Jones
Purchasing Agent: Joseph Cartwright
Estimated Sales: $20-50 Million
Number Employees: 250-499
Square Footage: 600000
Type of Packaging: Consumer, Food Service, Private Label, Bulk
Brands:
Gold Bond
Puritan
Purswab
Trophy

23662 Hardy Diagnostics
1430 W McCoy Ln
Santa Maria, CA 93455 805-346-2766
Fax: 805-346-2760 800-266-2222
techservice@hardydiagnostics.com
www.hardydiagnostics.com
President: Jay R Hardy
CFO: Nathaniel Gragssle
Estimated Sales: $10-20 000,000
Number Employees: 10-19

23663 Hardy Instruments
9440 Carroll Park Dr # 150
San Diego, CA 92121-5201
Fax: 858-278-6700 800-821-5831
hardyinfo@hardyinst.com www.hardyinst.com
Designer and manufacturer of process weighin, tension control and vibration monitoring equipment serving the food, chemical, petrochemical, pharameutical, feed and grain, mining and metal, pulp and paper, oil and gas, and generalautomation industries.
Manager: Jim Ephraim
Sales: Jerry Samaniego
Number Employees: 100-249

23664 Hardy Systems Corporation
610 Anthony Trl
Northbrook, IL 60062 847-272-4400
Fax: 847-272-4471 800-927-3956
thardy@hardysystems.com
www.hardysystems.com
Manufacturer and exporter of bins, batching scales, conveying systems and flow control panels
President: Richard Walter
Sales Manager: J Soling
Head Engineer: D Acker
Estimated Sales: Below $5,000,000
Number Employees: 5-9

23665 Hardy-Graham
P.O.Box 487
Ambler, PA 19002 215-699-6111
Fax: 215-699-6106 800-445-4271
sales@hardy-builtfastner.com
www.hardy-builtfastener.com
Knock-down, returnable, reusable crates and containers made of wood, metal, plastic
President: A Stuart Graham
CFO: A Stuart Graham
Estimated Sales: Below $5 Million
Number Employees: 5-9

23666 Harford Duracool LLC
P.O.Box 1026
Aberdeen, MD 21001-6026 410-272-9999
Fax: 410-272-8508 sales@harfordduracool.com
www.harfordduracool.com
Walk-in coolers
President: Arley Mead
Operations: Charles Mike
Sales Manager: Scott Smith
Number Employees: 50-99
Parent Co: IPC Industries
Brands:
Harford Duracool

23667 Harford Glen Water
PO Box 214
Harford, NY 00001-2838 607-844-8351
Fax: 607-844-8351 866-844-8351
daniel.correll@verizon.net
www.harfordglenwater.com
Company is a supplier of natural spring water.
President/CEO: Edmund McHale
CFO/VP: Lura McHale
Number Employees: 6
Number of Brands: 2
Number of Products: 5
Square Footage: 6000
Type of Packaging: Food Service, Private Label

23668 Harford Systems
PO Box 700
Aberdeen, MD 21001-0700 410-272-3400
Fax: 410-273-7892 800-638-7620
pwatson@harfordsystems.com
www.harfordsystems.com
Manufacturer and exporter of alarm systems and refrigeration equipment and machinery
President: Ralph Ahrens
VP: George Gabriel
HR Manager: Kate Pelonquin
Estimated Sales: $20-50 Million
Number Employees: 100-249
Parent Co: Bio Medic Corporation
Brands:
Duracool

23669 Harlan Laws Corporation
304 Muldee Street
Durham, NC 27703 919-596-2124
Fax: 919-596-0421 800-596-7602
sales@harlanlaws.com www.harlanlaws.com
Signs including electric and neon
Owner: Steven Laws
VP: Gary Hester
Estimated Sales: $10-20 Million
Number Employees: 50-99
Square Footage: 50000

23670 **Harland America**
1803 Underwood Blvd
Delran, NJ 08075 856-764-9622
Fax: 856-764-9615
us.enquiries@harland-hms.com
www.harlandamerica.com

Manager: John Lyall
Estimated Sales: $2.5 - 5 Million
Number Employees: 10-19

23671 **Harland Simon Control Systems USA**
Windsor Office Plaza
210 West 22nd Street, Suite 138
Oakbrook, IL 60523 630-572-7650
Fax: 630-572-7653 sales@harlandsimon.com
www.harlandsimon.com
Manufacturer and exporter of control systems including drive systems
Systems Sales Manager: Robert Picknell
National Sales Support Manager: Scott Mincher
Number Employees: 70
Square Footage: 164000
Parent Co: Monotype Systems
Brands:
Micropower
Micropower Ac
Symtec

23672 **Harmar Products**
2075 47th St
Sarasota, FL 34234-3109 941-351-2776
Fax: 941-351-5801 800-833-0478
garys@harmar.com www.harmar.com
Custom wire displays and wire forms; also, bending spot welding and coated parts available
President: Robert Williams
Founder, President, Chief Executive Offi: Chad Williams
Vice President of Sales: Paul Johnson
Vice President of Operations: Todd Walters
Estimated Sales: $10-20 Million
Number Employees: 20-49
Square Footage: 45000

23673 **Harmony Enterprises**
704 Main Avenue North
Harmony, MN 55939 507-886-6666
Fax: 507-886-6706 800-658-2320
info@harmony1.com www.harmony1.com
Manufacturer and exporter of waste handling and recycling equipment including inside compactors and vertical balers
President: Steve Cremer
Vice President/Sales: Brent Christiansen
Sales/Operations: Chris Cremer
Production: Steve Johnson
Estimated Sales: $5-10 Million
Number Employees: 20-49
Brands:
Gpi

23674 **Harold Import Company**
747 Vassar Ave
Lakewood, NJ 08701 732-367-2800
Fax: 732-364-3253 800-526-2163
info@haroldskitchen.com
www.haroldimport.com
Paper, brewers (tea), filters (cloth, cotton), grinders.
President: Mildred Laub Polansky
Estimated Sales: $50 - 100 Million
Number Employees: 50-99

23675 **Harold Leonard SouthwestCorporation**
1812 Brittmoore Road
Suite 230
Houston, TX 77043-2216 713-467-8105
Fax: 713-467-0072 800-245-8105
Manufacturer and wholesaler/distrbutor of smallwares
President: Carl Marcus
CEO: Herb Kelleher
Marketing Director: Roger Randall
Sales Representative: Jerry Williams
Estimated Sales: $1-2.5 Million
Number Employees: 6
Square Footage: 50000
Parent Co: Harold Leonard & Company
Brands:
Eagleware

23676 **Harold Wainess & Associates**
2045 N Dunhill Court N
Arlington Heights, IL 60004 847-259-6400
Fax: 847-259-6460 847-722-8744
hwainess@aol.com www.haroldwainess.com
Food safety consultant providing audits, food equipment evaluations and testing
President: Kenneth Anderson
V.P.: Kenneth Anderson
R&D: Erickson
Estimated Sales: Below $5 Million
Number Employees: 4

23677 **Harpak-Ulma**
175 John Quincy Adams Rd
Taunton, MA 02780 508-884-2500
Fax: 508-884-2501 800-813-6644
info@harpak-ULMA.com
www.harpak-ulma.com
Distributor of tray sealing, filling and meal assembly equipment. Manufacturer and designer of packaging equipment and systems.
President: Linda Harlfinger
Treasurer/Controller: Heidi Harlfinger
VP: Jim Ryan
Regional Sales Manager: Kevin Kennedy
Admin.: Richard Rogan
Estimated Sales: $24 Million
Number Employees: 75
Brands:
Rama

23678 **Harper Associates**
31000 Northwestern Hwy Ste 240
Farmington Hills, MI 48334 248-932-1170
Fax: 248-932-1214 Info@HarperJobs.com
www.harperjobs.com
Personnel placement specialist for the hospitality industry
President: Ben Schwartz
Vice President: Cindy Kramer
CEO: Ben Schwartz
Estimated Sales: $500,000 - $1 Million
Number Employees: 5-9

23679 **Harper Brush Works**
400 N 2nd St
Fairfield, IA 52556 641-472-5186
Fax: 641-472-3187 800-223-7894
info@harperbrush.com www.harperbrush.com
Manufacturer and exporter of brooms, brushes, mops and squeegees
President: Barry Harper
CEO: Barry Harper
Marketing: Pat Adam
Sales: Jerry Armstrong
Public Relations: Pat Adam
Operations: Don Sander
Purchasing Director: Randy Rhoads
Estimated Sales: $20 - 50 Million
Number Employees: 100-249
Type of Packaging: Consumer, Food Service, Bulk

23680 **Harper Trucks**
P.O.Box 12330
Wichita, KS 67277-2330 316-942-1381
Fax: 316-942-8508 800-835-4099
j.darnell@harpertrucks.com
www.harpertrucks.com
Manufacturer and exporter of industrial trucks
President: Phillip G Ruffin
CFO: Phillip Ruffin
Vice President: Gary Leiker
Marketing Director: David Rife
Sales Director: Judy Darnell
Plant Manager: Hugh Sales
Purchasing Manager: Sonya Kellogg
Estimated Sales: $20 Million
Number Employees: 100-249
Number of Brands: 1
Square Footage: 350000

23681 **Harrington Equipment Company**
475 Orchard Rd
Fairfield, PA 17320 717-642-6001
Fax: 302-422-7149 800-468-8467
RSH5@live.com
www.harringtonsequipment.com
Dealer of rebuilt can seamers, replacement parts and change parts
President: Thomas H Harrington Jr

23682 **Harrington Hoists**
401 W End Ave
Manheim, PA 17545 717-665-2000
Fax: 717-665-2861 800-233-3010
www.harringtonhoists.com
Material handling equipment including hoists, lever pullers and cranes
President: Ned Hunter
National Sales Manager: W David Merkel, Jr.
Estimated Sales: $10-20 Million
Number Employees: 50-99
Parent Co: Kito Corporation

23683 **Harris & Company**
980 Salem Pkwy
Salem, OH 44460 330-332-4127
Fax: 330-332-9627 info@harrisandcompany.com
www.harrislabel.com
CIS labels, self adhesive labels in sheets, coated paper and printed boards
President: David E Ritchie
VP (Pre-Press): George Ritchie
VP Sales: Norm Ritchie
Estimated Sales: $1 Million
Number Employees: 5-9
Square Footage: 11000

23684 **Harris Equipment**
2040 N Hawthorne Ave
Melrose Park, IL 60160 708-343-0866
Fax: 708-343-0995 800-365-0315
customer_service@harrisequipment.com
www.harrisequipment.com
Heat exchangers; wholesaler/distributor of oil free air compressors and compressed air filtration equipment, oil flooded compresser air dryers, stainless steel vavles, filter regulated lubricators
President: Gary Pollack
VP: John Pearson
Marketing: Tony Beaman
Purchasing Manager: Humer Lovett
Estimated Sales: $10-20 Million
Number Employees: 20-49
Square Footage: 28000

23685 **Harris Specialty Chemicals**
P.O.Box 2789
Jacksonville, FL 32203-2789 904-598-9808
Fax: 904-598-9833 800-537-4722
hsc@hsc-ss.com www.hsc-ss.com
Polymer floor systems
CEO: Ellen Harris
Estimated Sales: $1 - 5 Million
Number Employees: 5-9

23686 **Harrison Electropolishing**
13002 Brittmoore Park Drive
Houston, TX 77041 832-467-3100
Fax: 832-467-3111 info@harrisonep.com
www.harrisonep.com
Specializes in mechanical, electropolishing and passivation for brew kettles, fermenters and lagering tanks.
President: Tom Harrison

23687 **Harrison of Texas**
7142 Siena Vista Dr
Houston, TX 77083-2938 281-498-8206
Fax: 713-981-9589 800-245-5707
tomh@harrisonoftexasep.com
www.harrisontexasep.com
Electropolishing and mechanical polishing service for stainless steel food processing equipment; also, oxygen cleaning and mil-spec passivation services available
President: Tom Harrison
Office Manager: Patricia Bays
Operations Manager: Matt Buck
Estimated Sales: $300,000-500,000
Number Employees: 1-4
Square Footage: 60000

23688 **Harry Davis & Company**
1725 Blvd of the Allies
Pittsburgh, PA 15219 412-765-1170
Fax: 412-765-0910 800-775-2289
sales@harrydavis.com www.harrydavis.com
CEO: Martin Davis
Estimated Sales: $20 - 50 Million
Number Employees: 100-249

23689 **(HQ)Hart Associates**
PO Box 1387
Ruston, LA 71273-1387 318-255-8328
Fax: 318-255-8328 800-592-3500
www.hart-associates.net
Electric lighting fixtures
President: Charles Hart
CEO: Charles Hart
Quality Control: Sandra Hart
Sales: Amy Foster
Estimated Sales: $20 - 50 Million
Number Employees: 50-99

23690 **(HQ)Hart Design & Manufacturing**
1940 Radisson St
Green Bay, WI 54302-2037 920-468-5927
Fax: 920-468-5888 hartdesn@netnet.net
www.hartdesign.com
Designs and constructs specialty, standard and proprietary equipment for use in the Food and Dairy industry. Our packaging machinery includes process cheese wrappers, automatic puching, filling and sealing lines for process and creamcheese, a ribbon cheese casting, slitting, slice stacking equipment, automatic product feeders, and portion cutting equipment for block and barrel cheese.
President: John Adams
CEO: John Adams
Marketing Manager: Dennis Adelmeyer
Sales Manager: Dennis Adelmeyer
Estimated Sales: $4 Million
Number Employees: 20 to 49
Square Footage: 40000
Brands:
Hart

23691 **Hartel International LLC**
W7603 Koshkonong Mounds Road
Fort Atkinson, WI 53538 920-563-6597
Fax: 920-563-7515 doughartel@gmail.com
www.hartelinternational.com
Manufacturer, importer and exporter of process control systems including blending, processing, clean-in-place, refrigeration, level, load cell, metering, proportioning and packaging.
President: Douglas Hartel
Estimated Sales: $300,000-500,000
Number Employees: 2
Square Footage: 5332

23692 **Hartford Containers**
PO Box 399
Terryville, CT 06786-0399 860-584-1194
Fax: 860-582-5051
Corrugated containers
President: Bob Braverman
Estimated Sales: $20 - 50 Million
Number Employees: 50-99

23693 **Hartford Plastics**
10861 Mill Valley Rd
Omaha, NE 68154
Fax: 860-683-8484
Manufacturer and exporter of plastic bottles and containers; also, custom blow molding, labeling, hot stamping and silk screening available
VP Marketing: Anthony Roncaioli
Estimated Sales: $10-20 Million
Number Employees: 50-99
Parent Co: Comtrol

23694 **Hartford Stamp Works**
201 Locust Street
Hartford, CT 06114 860-249-6205
Fax: 860-409-4110
Rubber stamps, name plates, seals, name pins, self-inking stamps, etc.; also, inks
CEO: Ramani Ayer
Office Manager: Sandy Williams
Estimated Sales: $1-2.5 Million
Number Employees: 10-19
Square Footage: 7500

23695 **Harting Graphics**
111 N Cleveland Ave
Wilmington, DE 19805-1714 302-622-8911
Fax: 302-622-8909 800-848-1373
harting1876@fcc.net www.hartinggraphics.com
Advertising signs and point of purchase posters and banners
President: Theodore Harting
Sales/Marketing Executive: Susan Cuttance
Purchasing Agent: Kim Livermore
Estimated Sales: Below $5 Million
Number Employees: 5-9
Square Footage: 40000

23696 **Hartness International**
1200 Garlington Road
P.O. Box 26509
Greenville, SC 26509 864-297-1200
Fax: 864-297-4486 800-845-8791
www.hartness.com
Manufacturer and exporter of packaging equipment and machinery including case packers, decasers, single filers/laners and conveyor and mass product flow systems
Managing Director: Jim Gordon
Chief Executive Officer: Bernard McPheely
Chief Financial Officer: Lamar Jordan
Vice President: Sean Hartness
Marketing Manager: Anne Elmerick
Vice President, Sales & Marketing: Scott Smith
Product Manager: Bill Gemmell
Director, Procurement: Dianne Hall
Estimated Sales: $50-75 Million
Number Employees: 250-499
Brands:
Dynac

23697 **Hartstone**
1719 Dearborn St
Zanesville, OH 43701-5299 740-452-9999
Fax: 800-506-9627 www.hartstonepottery.com
Manufacturer, importer and exporter of stoneware, dinnerware, cookware, bakeware, tabletop accessories, oven dishwashers and microwave safe cookie molds
Manager: Wess Foltz
VP/General Manager: Patrick Hart
Sales Manager: Mike Flynn
Operations Manager: Shawn McGee
Estimated Sales: $7 Million
Number Employees: 1-4
Square Footage: 400000
Parent Co: Carlisle Companies
Type of Packaging: Consumer, Food Service
Brands:
Hartstone
The Original Cookie & Shortbread
The Wine Tote

23698 **Hartzell Fan**
910 S Downing St
Piqua, OH 45356-3824 937-773-8494
Fax: 937-773-8994 800-336-3267
info@hartzellfan.com www.hartzellfan.com
Manufacturer and exporter of general and process ventilation fans and centrifugal fans and blowers
President: George D Atkinson
Sales: George Atkins
Operations Manager: R Wallace
Estimated Sales: $20-50 Million
Number Employees: 100-249
Brands:
Duct Axial

23699 **Harvard Folding Box Company**
71 Linden St
Lynn, MA 01905 781-598-1600
Fax: 781-598-2950 www.idealboxmakers.com
Manufacturer and exporter of folding paper boxes
President: Leon Simkins
General Manager: George Lenesak
Plant Manager: Jimmy Mc Gee
Estimated Sales: $10 - 20 Million
Number Employees: 100-249
Parent Co: Simkins Industries

23700 **Harvest Innovations**
1210 North 14th Street
Indianola, IA 50125 515-962-5063
info@harvest-innovations.com
www.harvest-innovations.com
Natural ingredients such as legumes, soy & multigrain flours, cereal grains and oilseeds for the food industry.
President: Barry Nadler
Director Of Research: Dr. Noel Rudie
Product Development & Quality Assurance: Regena Butler
VP Sales/Marketing: Nicole Tomba
Innovation and Sales: Giovanni Santi
Director Food Technology: Dr. Wilmot Wijeratne

23701 **Harvey W. Hottel**
18900 Woodfield Rd Ste A
Gaithersburg, MD 20879 301-921-9599
Fax: 301-948-1892 jhottel@harveyhottel.com
www.harveyhottel.com
Air conditioning, heating and refrigeration items, financing, food service, HVAC, plumbing, design/build case study
President: Richard Hottel
VP: Jeff Hottel
VP Sales: Bernard Mejean
Estimated Sales: $10 - 20 Million
Number Employees: 100-249
Square Footage: 10000

23702 **Harvey's Groves**
P.O.Box 560700
Rockledge, FL 32956 321-636-6072
Fax: 321-633-4132 800-327-9312
support@harveysgroves.com
www.harveysgroves.com
Fruit gift baskets
President: Jim Harvey
Manager: Ann Manerino
Estimated Sales: $2.5-5 Million
Number Employees: 20-49

23703 **Harwil Corporation**
541 Kinetic Dr
Oxnard, CA 93030 805-988-6800
Fax: 805-988-6804 800-562-2447
harwil@harwil.com www.harwil.com
Manufacturer and exporter of bag closing machinery, heat sealers and flow and liquid level switches. Also manufature fluid liquid level switches, liquid level pumpup/plumpdown controlles, pump emergency shutdown controllers andachemical feed pump interface module
VP: Bruce Bowman
Number Employees: 20-49

23704 **Hasco Electric Corporation**
84 S Water St Ste 1
Greenwich, CT 06830 203-531-9400
Fax: 203-531-9408
Lighting fixtures
Owner: Donna Sagona
VP: Brad Sagona
Estimated Sales: $5-10,000,000
Number Employees: 20-49
Square Footage: 58000

23705 **Hassia USA**
1210 Campus Dr
Morganville, NJ 07751-1262 732-536-8770
Fax: 732-536-8850 sales@hassiausa.com
www.oystarusa.com
President: Charles Ravalli
Estimated Sales: $3 - 5 Million
Number Employees: 10-19

23706 **Hastings Lighting Company**
1206 Long Beach Ave
Los Angeles, CA 90021 213-622-2009
Fax: 213-622-9157 www.hastingslighting.com
Fluorescent showcase lighting fixtures for use in show cases
President: Jim Culbertson
VP: Jeffrey Colby
Office Manager: Joan Culbertson
Estimated Sales: $1-2.5 Million
Number Employees: 1-4
Square Footage: 4800

23707 **Hasty-Bake**
1313 S. Lewis
Tulsa, OK 74104 918-665-8220
Fax: 918-665-8225 800-426-6836
info@hastybake.com www.hastybake.com
Charcoal ovens and barbecue accessories
Estimated Sales: $2.5-5 Million
Number Employees: 10-19

23708 **Hathaway Stamp Company**
635 Main St Ste 1
Cincinnati, OH 45202 513-621-1052
Fax: 513-621-7339
contact@hathawaystamps.com
www.hathawaystamps.com
Rubber stamps
Manager: Larry Schultz
VP: Robert Ruwe
Estimated Sales: $1 - 2.5 Million
Number Employees: 5-9

Square Footage: 4000
Parent Co: Volk Corporation

23709 Hatteras Packaging Systems
8753 S Highway A1a
Melbourne Beach, FL 32951-4008 321-728-0908
Fax: 321-984-7252 hatteraspk@aol.com
Number Employees: 10

23710 Haumiller Engineering
445 Renner Dr
Elgin, IL 60123 847-695-9111
Fax: 847-695-2092 sales@haumiller.com
www.haumiller.com
Manufacturer and exporter of high-speed automatic custom assembly machines, flip top closure closing machines, cappers, spray tip and fitment applicators, reducer plug inserters and collar placers
President: Russ Holmer
VP Sales: John Giacopelli
Estimated Sales: $5-10 Million
Number Employees: 50-99
Square Footage: 45000

23711 Hauser Packaging
44 Exchange Street
Suite 202
Portland, ME 04101-5018 207-899-3306
Fax: 207-899-3970 888-600-2671
info@hauserpack.com www.hauserpack.com
Wine industry bottles

23712 Hautly Cheese Company
251 Axminister Dr
St. Louis, MO 630266 653-533-4400
Fax: 653-533-4401 info@hautly.com
www.hautlycheese.com
Cheese, cheese products
Owner: Craig Chettle
Estimated Sales: Less than $500,000
Number Employees: 5-9

23713 Have Our Plastic Inc
6990 Creditview Road
Unit 4
Mississauga, ON L5N 8R9
Canada 905-821-7550
Fax: 905-821-7553 800-263-5995
sales@hop.ca www.hop.ca
Manufacture and distrubute synthetic paper, plastic and wire binding products, laminating equipment and supplies, other equipment and supplies, restaurant menu covers, display and merchandising products and PVC.
Estimated Sales: $5,000,000
Number Employees: 16
Number of Brands: 1
Square Footage: 96000
Type of Packaging: Private Label, Bulk
Brands:
E-Binder
H.O.P.
Hop-Syn
Print Protector
The Menu Roll

23714 Haviland Products Company
421 Ann St NW
Grand Rapids, MI 49504 616-361-6691
Fax: 616-361-9772 800-456-1134
www.havilandusa.com
Industrial, food grade and U.S.P. specialty cleaners and wastewater treatment chemicals; wholesaler/distributor of various food grade and U.S.P. process chemicals
President: E Bernard Haviland
CFO: Tom Simmons
Quality Control: Terry Schoew
Sales/Marketing Manager: Eric Earl
Estimated Sales: $20 - 50 Million
Number Employees: 100-249
Square Footage: 185000

23715 Haward Corporation
29 Porete Ave
North Arlington, NJ 07031 201-991-8777
Fax: 201-991-1903 800-342-9041
sales@haward.com www.haward.com
Metal finisher whose services include teflon and plastic coating and electropolishing of stainless steel
President: Dean Ward
Vice President: Dean Ward, Jr.
Sales Director: Gary Horman
Estimated Sales: $5-10 Million
Number Employees: 20-49
Square Footage: 30000

23716 Hawkeye Corrugated Box Company
725 Ida St
Cedar Falls, IA 50613 319-268-0407
Fax: 319-268-0057 www.hawkeyebox.com
Corrugated boxes
President: Scott Bittner
Estimated Sales: $20-50 Million
Number Employees: 20-49

23717 Hawkeye Pallet Company
6055 NW Beaver Dr
Johnston, IA 50131-1349 515-276-0409
Wooden pallets
Owner: Bill Haller
Estimated Sales: Less than $500,000
Number Employees: 1 to 4

23718 Hawkins Inc
3100 E Hennepin Ave
Minneapolis, MN 55413 612-617-8572
Fax: 612-331-5304 800-328-5460
fritz.wagner@hawkinsinc.com
www.hawkinsinc.com
Food ingredients; including phosphates, sodium lactate and custom blends
President: Patrick Hawkins
VP Operations: Mark Beyer
Estimated Sales: $297 Million
Number Employees: 120

23719 Hayes & Stolz IndustrialManufacturing Company
3521 Hemphill St
PO Box 11217
Fort Worth, TX 76110 817-926-3391
Fax: 817-926-4133 800-725-7272
sales@hayes-stolz.com www.hayes-stolz.com
Manufacturer and exporter of batch mixers, continuous blenders, liquid coaters, bucket elevators, valves and rotary screeners
President: B J Masters
VP: Mark Hayes
Chairman of the Board: Vernon Hayes
Sales Engineer: Duane Chambers
Sales Engineer: Kris Helsley
Estimated Sales: $10 - 20 Million
Number Employees: 100-249

23720 Hayes Machine Company
3434 106th Cir
Des Moines, IA 50322 515-252-1216
Fax: 515-252-1316 800-860-6224
aandersen@hayesmachine.com
www.hayesmachine.com
Packaging and cartoning machines
President: Luca Berrone
CFO: John Stone
R & D: Allan Anderson
Inside Sales Manager: Julie Reincke
Plant Manager: Allan Anderson
Estimated Sales: Below $5 Million
Number Employees: 20-49
Square Footage: 16000
Parent Co: Gram Equipment of America

23721 Haynes Manufacturing Company
24142 Detroit Rd
Cleveland, OH 44145 440-871-2188
Fax: 440-871-0855 800-992-2166
info@haynesmfg.com www.haynesmfg.com
Manufacturer and exporter of food grade lubricants
Owner: Beth Kloos
Sales and Marketing Coordinator: Tammy Doctor
Estimated Sales: $20-50 Million
Type of Packaging: Food Service, Private Label, Bulk
Brands:
Haynes

23722 (HQ)Hayon Manufacturing & Engineering Corporation
9682 Borgata Bay Blvd
Las Vegas, NV 89147 702-562-3377
Fax: 702-562-3351 hayonmfg@aol.com
Manufacturer and exporter of bakery machinery including automatic pan greasers and coaters, egg washers and icing/glaze applicators
Owner: Z Hayon
VP: Ziona Hayon
Estimated Sales: Below $500,000
Number Employees: 1-4
Brands:
Hayon Select-A-Spray

23723 Hayssen
225 Spartangreen Blvd
Duncan, SC 29334-9400 864-486-4000
Fax: 864-486-4333 sales@hayssen.com
www.hayssen.com
Manufacturer and exporter of horizontal flow wrapping and horizontal and vertical form/fill/seal machinery
President: Daniel L Jones
Vice President of Sales and Marketing: Dan Minor
Estimated Sales: $50 Million
Number Employees: 250-499
Parent Co: Barry Wehmiller Companies
Brands:
Edge
Rt
Servo Ii
Turbo
Ultima
Ultra

23724 HayssenSandiacre
225 Spartangreen Blvd
Duncan, SC 29334 864-486-4000
Fax: 717-239-5084 sandiacre.usa@molins.com
www.sandiacre.com
Packaging machinery and machinery parts, vertical form fill and seal bagmakers and horzaontal flow wrappers
Founder: Herman Hayssen
General Manager: Troy Snader
Vice President of Sales and Marketing: Dan Minor
Estimated Sales: $8-10 Million
Number Employees: 5-9
Parent Co: Molins Richmond

23725 Hayward Gordon
6660 Campobello Road
Mississauga, ON L5N 2L9
Canada 905-567-6116
Fax: 905-567-1706 info@haywardgordon.com
www.haywardgordon.com
President: John Hayward
CFO: Jeanne Gray
Number Employees: 10

23726 Hayward Industrial Products
One Hayward Industrial Drive
Clemmons, NC 27102 908-355-7995
Fax: 908-351-7893 www.hayward-pool.com
Manufacturer and exporter of cartridge filters, pipeline strainers, gas/liquid separators, plastic valves and flow meters
President: Robert Davis
Marketing Communication Manager: D Treslan
Number Employees: 250-499
Brands:
Flosite
Loeffler
Qic
Strainomatic
Wright-Austin

23727 Hazen Paper Company
PO Box 189
Holyoke, MA 01041-0189 413-538-8204
Fax: 413-533-1420 customerservice@hazen.com
www.hazen.com
Paper including foil and metallized film laminations, heat sealing, fancy, printed and embossed paper
President: John Hazen
Quality Control: Alfred Zuffoletti
R&D: Kyle Parent
VP Sales: Steve Smith
Purchasing Manager: Larry Hoague
Estimated Sales: $20 - 50 Million
Number Employees: 100-249

23728 Healdsburg Machine Company
2584 Rim Rock Way
Santa Rosa, CA 95404-1819 707-433-3348
Fax: 707-433-3340

Manufacturer and exporter of grape crushing and stemming machinery; also, special pumps for the canning industry
President: Arthur Rafanelli
VP: Ron Rafanelli
Marketing: Ron Rafanelli
Estimated Sales: $1-2.5 Million
Number Employees: 10
Square Footage: 90000
Parent Co: Healdsburg Machine Company

23729 Health Star
80 Pacella Dr
Randolph, MA 02368 781-961-5400
Fax: 781-961-5456 800-545-3639
info@HealthStaronline.com
www.healthstaronline.com
New, and rebuilt processing and packaging machinery including liquid fillers
Marketing Manager: Bonnie Cote
Sales: Patl Lais
Estimated Sales: $2.5-5 Million
Number Employees: 50-99
Brands:
Level Star Ls Level Sensing Fillers
Purecop
Purefil

23730 HealthFocus
1140 Hightower Trail
Suite 201
Atlanta, GA 30350-2988 770-645-1999
Fax: 770-518-0630 hfocus@bellsouth.net
www.healthfocus.net
Market research firm specializing in consumer health and nutrition trends
Marketing Director: Julie Johnson
Estimated Sales: $500,000-$1 Million
Number Employees: 1
Square Footage: 8000

23731 Healthline Products
100 N Santa Fe Avenue
Los Angeles, CA 90012-4021 213-620-8600
Fax: 213-620-8636 800-473-4003
info@healthlineproducts.com
Pot holders, gloves, towels, uniforms, etc
President: Courtney Sapin
National Sales Manager: Trina Brown
Customer Service: Rita Recio
Estimated Sales: $5-10,000,000
Number Employees: 19
Square Footage: 15000

23732 Healthstar
1 Randolph Road
Randolph, MA 02368-4321 781-961-5400
Fax: 781-961-5456 800-LIK-ENEW
info@healthstaronline.com
www.healthstaronline.com
Pre-owned, rebuilt, and new processing and packaging equipment
President: William Graboswki
CFO: Scott Johnson
Estimated Sales: $10 - 20 Million
Number Employees: 60

23733 Healthy Dining
4849 Ronson Ct Ste 115
San Diego, CA 92111 858-541-2049
Fax: 858-541-0508 800-266-2049
erica@healthy-dining.com
www.healthydiningfinder.com
Consultant specializing in marketing and promoting healthy restaurant menu items; also, computerized nutrition analysis of menu items available
President: Anita Jones
VP: Erica Bohm
Regional Director: Erica Bohm
Estimated Sales: Below $5,000,000
Number Employees: 5-9

23734 Heart Smart International
6702 E Clinton St
Scottsdale, AZ 85254-5254 480-948-7631
Fax: 480-948-9834 800-762-7819
www.heartsmartinternational.net
Consultant specializing in the computer analysis of menu items, product marketing and nutritional training assistance
Owner: Jay Philips
Director Customer Relations: Judy Peters
Production Manager: Joe Cox

Estimated Sales: less than $500,000
Number Employees: 1-4
Square Footage: 1000
Parent Co: Best of Taste

23735 Hearthside Food Solutions LLC
3250 Lacey Road
Suite 200
Downers Grove, IL 60515 630-967-3600
info@hearthsidefoods.com
www.hearthsidefoods.com
Exporter and contract packager of cereals and snack foods. Ryt-way Food Products Company is one of the largest contract packagers of its kind in the United States today
Chairman, CEO & Co-Founder: Rich Scalise
Chief Financial Officer: James Wojciechowski
Senior Vice President Human Resources: Steve England
Number Employees: 500-999
Square Footage: 800000
Type of Packaging: Private Label

23736 Heartland Farms Dairy & Food Products, LLC
3668 South Geyer Road
Suite 205
St. Louis, MO 63127 314-965-1110
Fax: 314-965-1118 888-633-6455
info@heartlandfarmsdairy.com
www.heartlandfarmsdairy.com
Dairy products
President: Tom Jacoby
Marketing Assistant: Pat Hittmeier
Sales of Dry Products: Tim Fann
Sales & marketing of Fluid Products: Tom Jacoby, Jr.
Weights and Tests: Jenn Jacoby
Type of Packaging: Consumer, Bulk

23737 Heartland Ingredients LLC
802 West College Street
Troy, MO 63379
Fax: 877-841-2067 800-557-2621
contactus@heartlandingredients.net
www.heartlandingredients.net
Ingredients, food and technical grade chemicals and colors, dairy products, meat products, sugar, artifical sweeteners, close dated finished products.

23738 Heartwood Cabinets
5063 Arrow Hwy
Montclair, CA 91763 909-626-8104
Fax: 909-626-7636
Solid surfacing materials and store fixtures
Estimated Sales: Less than $500,000
Number Employees: 1-4

23739 Heat Seal
4580 E 71st St
Cleveland, OH 44125-1048 216-341-2022
Fax: 216-341-2163 800-342-6329
custserv@heatsealco.com www.heatsealco.com
Horizontal form/fill/seal machines, shrink packaging systems, rotary blister packaging machinery, high speed shrink tunnels and vertical L-sealer bagger
Owner: Ron Skalsky
Estimated Sales: $20-50 Million
Number Employees: 100-249

23740 Heat-It Manufacturing
12050 Crownpoint Dr
San Antonio, TX 78233-5362 210-650-9112
Fax: 210-967-8345 800-323-9336
marketing@heat-it.com www.heat-it.com
Manufacturer and exporter of canned heating fuels for buffets, catering, camping and emergencies
Manager: Lisa Garza
General Manager: Georgina Yoast
Estimated Sales: $.5 - 1 million
Number Employees: 1-4
Square Footage: 60000
Brands:
Heat-It

23741 Heatcraft
2175 W Park Place Blvd
Stone Mountain, GA 30087 770-465-5600
Fax: 770-465-5990
hrrdp.feedback@heatcraftrpd.com
www.heatcraftrpd.com

Manufacturer and exporter of commercial refrigeration equipment
VP: Ken Rothgeb
Director Marketing: Jeff Almond
Director Sales: Mark Westphal
General Manager: J Jones
Estimated Sales: $10-20,000,000
Number Employees: 100-249
Square Footage: 140000
Parent Co: Lennox International
Brands:
Bohn
Chandler
Climate Control
Larkin

23742 Heatec
P.O.Box 72760
Chattanooga, TN 37407 423-821-5200
Fax: 423-821-7673 800-235-5200
heatec@heatec.com www.heatec.com
Heaters, storage tanks and related products
President: Richard Dorris
VP/Marketing: Tom Wilkey
Sales: Jerry Vautrease
Parent Co: Astec Industries

23743 Heath & Company
3411 Johnson Ferry Road
Roswell, GA 30075-5205 770-650-2724
info@heathandco.com
www.heathandco.com
Signs including advertising, changeable letter, electric, luminous tube, etc
Manager: Ken Plass
Number Employees: 150
Parent Co: Jim Patterson Group

23744 Heath & Company
2121 Orange Street
Alhambra, CA 91803-1419 626-457-3000
Fax: 626-457-3016 800-421-9069
rsmith@heathsign.com
Signs including electric advertising, plastic and luminous tube
Operation Manager: Ray Smith
Estimated Sales: $1-2.5 Million
Number Employees: 10
Parent Co: Heath Sign Inc

23745 Heath Signs
278 Hillcrest Dr
Reno, NV 89509-3705 775-359-9007
Fax: 775-359-2527
Neon signs
President: Steve Scharfe
Secretary: Cathleen Wallman
Estimated Sales: Less than $500,000
Number Employees: 10

23746 Heatrex
P.O.Box 515
Meadville, PA 16335-0515 814-724-1800
Fax: 814-333-6580 800-394-6589
sales@heatrex.com www.heatrex.com
Manufacturer and exporter of heaters including tubular/finned tubular, flanged/screw plug immersion, circulation, defrost, high temperature duct, infrared and radiant process; also, heater controls
Owner: Fred O'Polka
CFO: Fred O Polka
R&D: Larry Clever
Quality Control: Kim Lenhart
Marketing: Earl Pifer
Sales: Earl Pifer
Operations Manager: Earl Pifer
Plant Manager: Kim Lenhart
Estimated Sales: $10 - 20 Million
Number Employees: 50-99
Brands:
Heatzone
Quartzone

23747 Heatron
3000 Wilson Ave
Leavenworth, KS 66048 913-946-1394
Fax: 913-651-5352 chrisk@heatron.com
www.heatron.com
Custom designers and manufacturers of patented non-stick cartridge heaters, Max2000 mica band and strip heater, Ceramix ceramic bands, Extruheat tubular channel bands, aluminum and bronze cast in heaters, flexible silicone rubberetched-foil
CEO: Michael W Keenan

Estimated Sales: $5-10 000,000
Number Employees: 100-249

23748 (HQ)Hebeler Corporation
2000 Military Road
Tonawanda, NY 14150 716-873-9300
Fax: 716-873-7538 800-486-4709
info@hebeler.com www.hebeler.com
Stainless steel food processing machinery including bakers' mixers, candy, syrup and beverage coolers, food dryers, deaerators, distillation units, evaporative condensers, separators, heat exchangers and preheaters
President: Brian Sullivan
Chairman: John Coleman
Vice President, Finance: James Breyer
Information Technology Manager: Dan Emma
Quality Assurance Manager: Lisa Glass
Vice President, Sales & Marketing: Cody Pinelli
Chief Operating Officer: Kristina Leibring
Production Supervisor: Christine Hockenberry
Purchasing: Lori Neidlinger
Estimated Sales: $25 Million
Number Employees: 140
Square Footage: 100000
Other Locations:
Hebeler Corp.
Vicksburg MS

23749 Hebenstreit GmbH
2465 Byron Station Dr. SW,
Suite B
Byron Center, MI 49315 616-583-1458
Fax: 616-583-1646 bryan@bainbridge-assoc.com
www.hebenstreit.de
Representative: Ross Brainbridge

23750 Hector Delorme & Sons
1631 Route 235
Farnham, QC J2N 2R2
Canada 450-293-5310
Fax: 450-293-5319
High pressure washers
President: Yves Cloutier
Number Employees: 5
Brands:
Cyclone

23751 Hectronic
4300 Highline Blvd # 300
Oklahoma City, OK 73108-1843 405-946-3574
Fax: 405-946-3564 info@hetronic.com
www.hetronic.com
Manufacturer and exporter of material handling equipment including remote control systems
President: Dave Krueger
Executive VP: Torsten Rempe
VP: Torsten Rempe
Marketing: Laurel Benjamin
Sales: Bob Peddycoart
Estimated Sales: $5 - 10 Million
Number Employees: 20-49
Parent Co: Hectronic

23752 Hedges Neon Sales
616 Reynolds St
Salina, KS 67401 785-827-9341
Fax: 785-827-1411
Signs including luminous tube, painted, wooden, etc
President: Nancy Hedges
Estimated Sales: $.5 - 1 million
Number Employees: 1-4

23753 Hedgetree Chemical Manufacturing
119 Prosperity Drive
Savannah, GA 31408-9551 912-691-0408
Fax: 912-692-0440
Organic and biodegradable household and industrial cleaning compounds; also, freezer, food and meat processing equipment cleaners
President: Larry Skinner Sr
Sales/Marketing: James Wallace
Estimated Sales: $1 - 2.5 Million
Number Employees: 7
Square Footage: 13600
Brands:
U.N.L.O.C.C.

23754 Hedland Flow Meters
PO Box 081580
Racine, WI 53408 262-639-6770
Fax: 262-639-2267 800-433-5263
hedlandsales@racinefed.com www.hedland.com
President: John Erksine
Sales Manager: Mark Leveille
Estimated Sales: $10 - 20 Million
Number Employees: 100-249

23755 Hedstrom Corporation
1401 Jacobson Ave
Ashland, OH 44805 419-289-9310
Fax: 419-281-3371 700-765-9665
ggretchko@wyselandau.com www.hedstrom.com
Rotationally molded polyethylene and vinyl bins, material handling containers, hoppers, etc
President: Jim Braeunit
VP: James Braeunig
VP (Industrial Sales): Marty Fickenscher
Sales Manager (Technical): Jim Cotter
VP Operations: James Braeunig
Estimated Sales: $20 - 50 Million
Number Employees: 100-249
Square Footage: 300000
Parent Co: GAI Partners

23756 Hedwin Corporation
1600 Roland Heights Ave
Baltimore, MD 21211 410-889-5189
Fax: 410-889-5189 800-638-1012
sales@hedwin.net www.hedwin.com
Manufacturer and exporter of plastic products including containers, film bags, shipping trays and drum protector lids; also, dispensing systems, drum and film liners, pails and flexible packaging
President: David E Rubley
Sales Service Manager: Wayne Deal
Number Employees: 500-999
Parent Co: A. Solvay America Company
Brands:
Cubitainer
Ecoset
Hedliner
Hedpak
Payliner
Topliner
Winliner
Winpak

23757 Heely-Brown Company/Leister
1280 Chattahoochee Ave NW
Atlanta, GA 30318-3683 404-917-8762
Fax: 404-350-2693 800-241-4628
info@heely-brown.com www.heelybrown.com
President: Bill Brown
CFO: Mike Spencer
Estimated Sales: $20 - 50 Million
Number Employees: 50-99

23758 Hefferman Interactive
1196 Easton Road
Horsham, PA 19044-1405 610-517-2877
Fax: 215-441-5292
Estimated Sales: $500,000-$1 000,000
Number Employees: 1-4

23759 Heico Chemicals
P.O.Box 730
Delaware Wtr Gap, PA 18327-0730 570-420-3900
Fax: 570-421-9012 800-344-3426
jdoherty@cambrex.com www.cambrex.com
Organic and inorganic fine chemicals and organic performance chemicals
Vice President of Business Development: Dan Giambattisto
Manager of Corporate Sales: Joshua Kley
Estimated Sales: $10-25 Million
Number Employees: 20-49

23760 Heimann Systems Corporation
3203 Regal Dr
Alcoa, TN 37701 865-379-1670
Fax: 865-379-1677
mail.pid@smiths-heimann.com
www.heimannsystems.com
President: Brad Mueller
Estimated Sales: $20 - 50 Million
Number Employees: 50-99

23761 Heinlin Packaging Service
3121 South Ave
Toledo, OH 43609 419-385-2681
Industrial and food packaging machinery
Manager: John Heinlin
VP: John Heinlin
Estimated Sales: $1-2.5 000,000
Number Employees: 5-9
Square Footage: 25000

23762 Heinrich Envelope Corporation
925 Zane Ave N
Minneapolis, MN 55422 763-544-3571
Fax: 763-544-6287 800-346-7957
information@heinrichenvelope.com
www.heinrichenvelope.com
Envelopes
President: Bill Berkner
Sales Manager: Don Schindle
Estimated Sales: $10 - 20 Million
Number Employees: 50-99
Parent Co: Taylor Corporation

23763 Heinzen Sales International
405 Mayock Rd
Gilroy, CA 95020-7040 408-842-7233
Fax: 408-842-6678 hmisales@heinzen.com
www.heinzen.com/heinzen
Manufacturer and exporter of food processing equipment including fruit peelers, dryers, dumpers, trim lines and conveyors with complete engineering service for new plant layout and equipment
President: Allan Heinzen
Sales: Gary M Hertzog
Estimated Sales: $10-20 Million
Number Employees: 50-99
Square Footage: 44000

23764 Heisler Industries, Inc
224 Passaic Ave
Fairfield, NJ 07004 973-227-6300
Fax: 973-227-7627 heislersales@heislerind.com
www.heislerind.com
Packaging equipment amd 5 gallon pail handling equipment; denesters, lid placers, lid closers, labelers, palletizers, case packers, gray packers, lipstackers, line integration, pail orientation, bail-o-matic,spcialty equipment.
President: Richard Heisler
VP Sales: James Lamb
Sales Administrator: Judy Vinson
Estimated Sales: $3 - 5 Million
Number Employees: 50-99
Number of Products: 12
Square Footage: 100000
Type of Packaging: Food Service, Bulk
Brands:
Casettraypackers
Denester
Lid Placers
Lid Press

23765 Helken Equipment Company
171 Erick Street, Unit Q1
Crystal Lake, IL 60014 847-697-3690
Fax: 847-697-3692 info@helkenequipment.com
www.helken.com
Used and rebuilt food processing equipment
Owner: Bob Henry
Estimated Sales: $1-2.5 Million
Number Employees: 1-4
Square Footage: 14800

23766 (HQ)Heller Seasonings
150 S Wacker Dr Ste 3200
Chicago, IL 60606 312-546-6800
Fax: 312-346-3140 800-323-2726
Seasonings
VP Finance: Allen Marshall
CEO: John Heller
President: Roger Maehler
VP Finance: Allen Marshall
Estimated Sales: $5 - 10,000,000
Number Employees: 5-9

23767 Heller Truck Body Corporation
138 Us Highway 22
Hillside, NJ 07205-1888 973-923-9200
Fax: 973-923-9269 800-229-4148
dnovak2491@hotmail.com www.hellertruck.com
Truck bodies, trailers, cargo containers, service and repair all major brands of liftgates.
President: D Novak
Estimated Sales: $1-2.5 Million
Number Employees: 5-9

23768 Helm Software
4722 N 24th Street
Suite 225
Phoenix, AZ 85016-9140 602-522-2999
Fax: 602-522-8046 info@helmsoftware.com
www.helmsoftware.com

Provide trade spending and equipment program software to food service manufacturing
President: Daniel Buckstaff
Executive VP: Doug McFetters
Quality Control: Douglas McFetters
Estimated Sales: Below $5 Million
Number Employees: 15

23769 Helman International
4196 Suffolk Way
Pleasanton, CA 94588-4119 925-484-5000
Fax: 925-484-5007 pahelman@attb.com
www.aimblending.com
Ribbon blenders
President: Phil Helman
Estimated Sales: $2.5-5 Million
Number Employees: 20-49

23770 Helmer
14395 Bergen Blvd.
Noblesville, IN 46060 317-773-9073
Fax: 800-743-5637 317-773-9082
sales@helmerinc.com www.helmerinc.com
Refrigerators and freezers.
President: David Helmer
Market Integration Manager: Ann Marie Rohe

23771 Hench Control, Inc.
3701 Collins Avenue
Suite 8C
Richmond, CA 94806 510-741-8100
Fax: 510-307-9804 sales@henchcontrol.com
www.henchcontrol.com
Efficiently controlling compressors , condensers, evaporaters, vessels, heat exchangers, pumps and total alarms.
Chief Executive Officer: Alex Daneman

23772 Hendee Enterprises
P.O.Box 4289
Houston, TX 77210-4289 713-796-2322
Fax: 713-796-0494 800-323-3641
sales@hendee.com www.hendee.com
Commercial awnings
President: Chuck Hendee
Quality Control: Buddy Tearifon
CEO: John Macfarlane
Sales: Kathy Davis
Estimated Sales: $10 - 20 Million
Number Employees: 100-249

23773 Henkel Adhesives
1345 Gasket Dr
Elgin, IL 60120 847-468-9200
Fax: 847-468-9819
dave.millar@henkel-americas.com
www.henkel.com
Sales and Marketing manager: Steve Roseti
Executive VP Finance CFO: Dr. Lothar Steinebach
Plant Manager: Paul Grala
Estimated Sales: $100+ Million
Number Employees: 100-249

23774 Henkel Consumer Adhesive
32150 Just Imagine Dr
Avon, OH 44011 440-937-7000
Fax: 440-937-7077 800-321-0253
ask.a.duck@us.henkel.com
www.henkelcamsds.com
Manufacturer and exporter of pressure sensitive tapes including masking, strapping, packaging, identification, cloth, foil, electrical and specialty
President: Jack Kahle
CEO: John Kahle
Number Employees: 250-499
Type of Packaging: Consumer, Food Service

23775 Henkel Corporation
PO Box 628
Mauldin, SC 29662-0628 864-963-4031
Fax: 864-967-5156 www.cognis.com
Emulsifying agents including sorbitan oleates, stearates, esters and surfactants
Executive Vice President, President of B: Beate Ehle
Plant Manager: Raymond Mockridge
Estimated Sales: $20 - 50 Million
Number Employees: 50-99

23776 (HQ)Henley Paper Company
4229 Beechwood Dr
Greensboro, NC 27410-8108 336-668-0081
Fax: 336-605-9366 www.atlanticpkg.com
Manufacturer and wholesaler/distributor of die cutting, hosiery inserts, slitting, rewinding, sheeting, transfer tissue, electrical insulator paper
VP Sales/Marketin: Bill Parks
Estimated Sales: $10 - 20 Million
Number Employees: 50-99

23777 Henny Penny, Inc.
1561 Adelaide St.
Suite 1
Detroit, MI 48207-4545 313-877-9550
www.hennypenny.com
Manufacturer and exporter of pressure and open fryers, heated holding equipment, combination convection and steamer ovens, rotisseries, filters, etc.
President: Elias Zedan
Manager: Kay Lee
Purchasing: Simon Zodan
Estimated Sales: $2.00 Million
Number Employees: 5
Square Footage: 400000
Brands:
Climaplus
Hot N' Tender
Sure Chef
Sure Chef Climaplus Combi

23778 Henry Group
P.O.Box 8246
Greenville, TX 75404-8246 903-883-2002
Fax: 903-883-3210 sales@thg1.com
www.henrygroupny.com
Custom food processing equipment and food plant reconstruction services
Owner: Troy Henry
VP Business Development: Darren Jackson
Estimated Sales: $5 - 10 Million
Number Employees: 50-99

23779 Henry Hanger & Fixture Corporation of America
450 Seventh Ave 23rd Floor
New York City, NY 10123 212-279-0852
Fax: 212-594-7302 877-279-0852
www.henryhanger.com
Manufacturer and exporter of store fixtures and garment hangers
Estimated Sales: $5-10 Million
Number Employees: 50-99

23780 Henry Molded Products
71 N 16th St
Lebanon, PA 17042 717-273-3714
Fax: 717-274-3743 henry@henry-molded.com
www.henry-molded.com
Pressed and molded pulp goods, fiber containers and custom packaging service, including pharmaceutical and wine bottles, etc
President: Douglas Henry
CEO: Sue Wymann
CFO: Susan Weiman
Estimated Sales: $20-50 Million
Number Employees: 50-99
Brands:
Stakker

23781 Henschel Coating & Laminating
15805 W Overland Dr
New Berlin, WI 53151 262-786-1750
Fax: 262-786-3852 warren@henschelcoating.com
www.henschelcoating.com
Coated and laminated paper
President: Warren Henschel
R & D: Brian Lemke
VP: Warren Henschel
Estimated Sales: Below $5 Million
Number Employees: 20-49

23782 Herbert Miller
1548 Old Skokie Rd
Highland Park, IL 60035-2704 847-831-2083
Fax: 847-831-2193 hminc427@prodigy.net
Aseptic processing systems, including packaging and all forms of processing equipment
Owner: Herb Miller
Estimated Sales: Less than $500,000
Number Employees: 1-4

23783 Herche Warehouse
4735 Leyden Street
Denver, CO 80216-3301 303-371-8186
Manufacturer and wholesaler/distributor of packaging equipment and materials including bags, containers, closures, conveyors, labels, linings, tapes, ties, etc
Customer Service Representative: Cathy Wyatt
Estimated Sales: $1 - 5,000,000
Parent Co: Gulf Systems

23784 Herculean Equipment
4917 Encinita Ave
Temple City, CA 91780 626-286-7057
Fax: 626-286-7922 800-441-3455
Owner: Steven Law
Estimated Sales: $300,000-500,000
Number Employees: 1-4

23785 Hercules Food Equipment
145 Millwick Drive
Weston, ON M9L 1Y7
Canada 416-742-9673
Fax: 416-742-6486 hercules@interlog.com
Custom stainless steel sinks, counters and exhaust canopies; also, refrigerated and heated display units, barbecue ovens and Chinese cooking equipment; wholesaler/distributor of food service equipment; serving the food servicemarket
President: R Barron
CEO: M Lepage
Number Employees: 20-49
Square Footage: 17000

23786 Herdell Printing Company
340 McCormick St
Saint Helena, CA 94574 707-963-3634
Fax: 707-963-5002 866-963-3634
info@herdellprinting.com
www.herdellprinting.com
Wine industry labels
CEO: Ardis Herdell
VP: Michael Herdell
Quality Control: Steve Herdell
Estimated Sales: $2.5-5 000,000
Number Employees: 20-49

23787 Heritage Bag Company
1648 Diplomat Dr
Carrollton, TX 75006-6847 972-241-5525
Fax: 972-241-5543 pebbert@heritage-bag.com
www.heritage-bag.com
Plastic trash bags
CEO: Carl Allen Jr
Estimated Sales: $10-20 Million
Number Employees: 50-99

23788 Heritage Corrugated BoxCorporation
454 Livonia Ave
Brooklyn, NY 11207 718-495-1500
Fax: 718-922-9553
Manufactures corrugated & solid fiber boxes
President: Jeff Schatz
Estimated Sales: $5.2 Million
Number Employees: 50-99
Type of Packaging: Bulk

23789 Heritage Equipment Company
9000 Heritage Dr
Plain City, OH 43064 614-873-3941
Fax: 614-873-3549 800-282-7961
eric@heritage-equipment.com
www.heritage-equipment.com
President: Eric Zwirner
VP: Lisa Zwirner
Ops Mgr: Lou Costillo
Estimated Sales: $5 - 10 Million
Number Employees: 20-49

23790 Heritage Packaging
625 Fishers Run
Victor, NY 14564 585-742-3310
Fax: 978-682-2572 sales@heritagepackaging.com
www.heritagepackaging.com
Manufacturer and exporter of shipping containers and packaging for equipment
President: Philip M Defusco
Estimated Sales: $1-2.5 Million
Number Employees: 10-19

23791 Herkimer Pallet & Wood Products Company
Arthur Street Extension
Herkimer, NY 13350-1440 315-866-4591
Fax: 315-866-4591

Wooden crates, boxes, pallets, etc
President: Michael Lennon
CFO: Karen Dass
VP Marketing: Dave Bass
Manager: Karen Bass
Estimated Sales: Below $5 Million
Number Employees: 1 to 4

23792 Hermann Ultrasonics Inc
1261 Hardt Cir
Bartlett, IL 60103 630-736-7400
Fax: 630-626-1627
info@hermannultrasonics.com
www.hermannultrasonics.com
Ultrasonic packaging sealing equipment
President: Thomas Hermann
Marketing Director: Emily Rutkoske

23793 Hersey Measurement Company
PO Box 4585
Spartanburg, SC 29305-4585 864-574-8964
Fax: 864-578-7308 800-845-2102
hersey@worldnet.att.net
Batch control systems
Estimated Sales: $20-50 Million
Number Employees: 100-249

23794 (HQ)Hershey Company
100 Crystal A Drive
Hershey, PA 17033 717-534-4200
800-468-1714
www.thehersheycompany.com
Quality chocolate and non-chocolate confectionery and chocolate-related grocery products. The company also is a leader in the gum and mint category.
President & CEO: John Bilbrey
Exec VP, CFO, & Chief Admin Officer: Humberto Alfonso
Sr VP, Chief Human Resources Officer: Kevin Walling
Sr Vice President of Global Operations: Terence O'Day
Estimated Sales: $6.08 Billion
Number Employees: 13080
Square Footage: 15803
Type of Packaging: Consumer, Food Service, Private Label
Brands:
Hershey®'s
Dagoba
5th Avenue
Almond Joy
Breathsavers
Bubble Yum
Cadbury
Good & Plenty
Heath
Ice Breakers
Jolly Rancher
Kit Kat
Mauna Loa
Milk Duds
Mounds
Mr. Goodbar
Scharffen Berger
Payday
Reese's
Rolo
Skor
Take 5
Twizzlers
Whatchamacallit
Whoppers
York
Young & Smylie
Zagnut
Zero
Hershey Kisses
Hershey Bliss
Reese's Pieces
Ice Breakers Frost
Ice Breakers Ice Cubes
Pot of Gold
Symphony

23795 Hess Machine International
PO Box 639
Ephrata, PA 17522-0639 717-733-0005
Fax: 717-733-2255 800-735-4377
ozone@hessmachine.com
www.hessmachine.com
Manufacturer and exporter of water treatment equipment including ozone analyzers, ozone generators and filteration equipment.
President: Richard Hess
Marketing Director: Lynn Martin
Plant Manager: Calburn McEllheauey
Estimated Sales: $.5 - 1 million
Number Employees: 5-9

23796 Heuft
2820 Thatcher Rd
Downers Grove, IL 60515-4051 630-968-9011
Fax: 630-968-8767 edi.e.gilich@heuft.com
www.heuft.com
Container inspection equipment including online empty and full container inspectors, valve monitors and bottle sorting equipment
General Manager: Carl Bonnan
Marketing Manager: Bob Klien
Sales Manager: Carl Bonnan
Administrative Manager: Edi Gilch
Estimated Sales: $10-20 Million
Number Employees: 20-49
Parent Co: Heuft SystemTechnik GmbH

23797 Hevi-Haul International
P.O.Box 580
Menomonee Falls, WI 53052 262-502-0333
Fax: 262-502-0260 800-558-0577
info@havihaul.com www.hevihaul.com
Manufacturer and exporter of rollers and material handling equipment
President: Daniel Knaebe
VP: S Knaebe
Sales/Marketing Executive: M Knaebe
Purchasing Agent: M Knaebe
Estimated Sales: $1-2.5 Million
Number Employees: 5-9

23798 Hewitt Manufacturing Company
P.O.Box 262
Waldron, IN 46182 765-525-9829
Fax: 765-525-7185 hewittmfg@tds.net
www.hewittmfg.com
Wire goods including display and refrigerator racks
President: Donald Hewitt
Estimated Sales: $1-2.5 Million
Number Employees: 5-9

23799 Hewitt Soap Company
654 Residenz Pkwy # H
Dayton, OH 45429-6290 937-293-2697
Fax: 937-258-3123 800-543-2245
contact@hewittsoap.com www.hewittsoap.com
Manufacturer and exporter of bar soap
Vice President of Marketing: Deb McDonough
Estimated Sales: $33.9 Million
Number Employees: 1-4
Square Footage: 400000
Parent Co: ASR

23800 Hewlett-Packard Company
1000 NE Circle Blvd
Corvallis, OR 97330 541-757-2000
Fax: 541-715-6925 www.hp.com
Printers, computers, desktops, laptops, printer ink
Estimated Sales: $20-50 Million
Number Employees: 5,000-9,999

23801 Hi Roller Enclosed BeltConveyors
5100 W 12th St
Sioux Falls, SD 57107-0551 605-332-3200
Fax: 605-332-1107 800-328-1785
sales@hiroller.com www.hiroller.com
Manufacturer and exporter of enclosed belt conveyors and related accessories
Owner: Philip Clark
Controller: Sally Dieltz
Sales Manager: Mike Spillum
General Manager: John Nelson
General Manager: Steve Tweet
Estimated Sales: $10 - 20 Million
Number Employees: 20-49
Square Footage: 60000
Parent Co: Hansen Manufacturing Corporation
Brands:
Hi Roller

23802 Hi-Tech Packaging
One Bruce Avenue
Stratford, CT 06645 203-378-2700
Fax: 314-381-7412 sales@hitechpackaging.net
www.hitechpackaging.com
Packaging machinery
Estimated Sales: $1-5 000,000
Number Employees: 12

23803 Hi-Temp
820 Mississippi St
PO Box 478
Tuscumbia, AL 35674 256-383-5066
Fax: 256-383-5175 800-239-5066
hitemp@hitemp.net www.hitemp.biz
Check and plug valves, pump impellers, valve stems, plastic mallets, rubber pipe grommets, gaskets, dies and floor drains
President: Billy Rumbley Jr
CEO: Billy Rumbley
Plant Manager: Randy Inman
Estimated Sales: $5-10 Million
Number Employees: 10-19
Square Footage: 38100

23804 HiTec Food Equipment
818 Lively Blvd
Wood Dale, IL 60191 630-521-9460
Fax: 630-521-9466 information@hitec-usa.com
www.hitech-usa.com
President: Tatsuo Nakamura
CFO: Takeshi Kojima
Estimated Sales: Below $5 000,000
Number Employees: 1-4

23805 HiTech Manufacturing Solutions, Inc
825 Ontario Rd
Green Bay, WI 54311 920-465-4600
Fax: 920-465-4601 hitech@hitech-inc.com
www.hitech-inc.com
Control systems integration, design and build custom automation machinery and control panels
Number Employees: 50-99

23806 Hibco Plastics
1820 US Hwy 601 South
PO Box 157
Yadkinville, NC 27055 336-463-2391
Fax: 336-463-5591 800-849-8683
webpage@hibco.com www.hibco.com
Plastic foam
President: Mark Pavlansky
Quality Control: Landon Hardy
Estimated Sales: $10 - 20 Million
Number Employees: 50-99
Square Footage: 120000

23807 Hibrett Puratex
7001 Westfield Avenue
Pennsauken, NJ 08110 856-662-1717
Fax: 856-662-0550 800-260-5124
Manufacturer and wholesaler/distributor of compound cleaning chemicals and water treatment products
CEO: Jerome Ellerbee
Sales: Nelissa Abreu
Number Employees: 20
Number of Products: 1000
Square Footage: 21000
Parent Co: Hibrett Puratex
Type of Packaging: Private Label

23808 Hickory Industries
4900 W Side Ave
North Bergen, NJ 00047 201-223-4382
Fax: 201-223-0950 800-732-9153
bbqs@worldnet.att.net www.hickorybbq.com
Manufacturer and exporter of cooking equipment including grills, warmers, ovens and rotisseries; also, barbecue machinery and accessories
President: Steven Maroti
VP Sales/Marketing: Joe Slusz
Estimated Sales: $20 - 50 Million
Number Employees: 100-249
Square Footage: 50000
Brands:
Hickory
Old Hickory

23809 Hickory Zesti Smoked Specialties
783 Old Hickory Boulevard
Suite 300
Brentwood, TN 37027-4508 615-373-8838
Fax: 615-371-1780 800-251-2076
info@hickoryspecialties.com
www.hickoryspecialties.com
Liquid smoke products
President: Pat Moeller

Estimated Sales: $5 - 10 Million
Number Employees: 110

23810 Hiclay Studios
3015 Locust Street
St Louis, MO 63103-1328 314-533-8393
Fax: 314-533-8397

Displays and signs
President: Harold A Lutz Jr
Estimated Sales: $1-2.5 Million
Number Employees: 1-4

23811 High Ground of Texas
401 N. 3rd Street
PO Box 716
Stratford, TX 79084-0716 806-366-7510
Fax: 806-366-7511 information@highground.org
www.highground.org
Estimated Sales: Below $500,000
Number Employees: 1-4

23812 High-Purity Standards
7221 Investment Drive
North Charleston, SC 29418 843-767-7900
Fax: 843-767-7906 866-767-4771
dwy@hps.net www.highpuritystandards.com
Manufactures single and multielement standards of extremely high purity for the calibration of analytical instruments such as the AAS, ICP, ICP-MS and IC.
President: Theodore Rains PhD
CEO: Connie Hayes
Estimated Sales: $1,904,757
Number Employees: 20-49
Square Footage: 40000

23813 Highland Plastics
3650 Dulles Dr
Mira Loma, CA 91752 951-360-9587
Fax: 951-360-9465 800-368-0491
mmurphy@hiplas.com www.hiplas.com
Lid capping equipment and containers, cups and closures; also, custom printing and labeling available
CEO: James Nelson
Marketing Director: Mark Murphy
Estimated Sales: $10-20 Million
Number Employees: 50-99
Square Footage: 81000

23814 Highland Sugarworks, Inc
49 Parker Road
Wilson Industrial Park, Po Box 58
Websterville, VT 05678 615-274-3959
Fax: 802-479-1737 800-452-4012
jclose@highlandsugarworks.com
www.highlandsugarworks.com
Pure maple syrup and pancake mixes including apple cinnamon,buttermilk and blueberry; also, gift packs available
President: Jim Mac Isaac
Sales/Marketing: Jim Close
Operations: Deb Frimodig
Estimated Sales: $500,000-$1 Million
Number Employees: 10-19
Square Footage: 60000
Type of Packaging: Consumer, Food Service, Private Label, Bulk
Brands:
Highland Sugarworks

23815 Highland Supply Company
1111 6th St
Highland, IL 62249 618-654-2161
Fax: 618-654-3911 800-472-3645
orderdesk@highlandsupply.com
www.highlandsupply.com
Converted printed, tinted and clear film; also, shredded material and pre-cut covers
President: Donald Weder
Sales Service Manager: Scott Greathouse
Estimated Sales: $20 - 50 Million
Number Employees: 250-499
Brands:
Speed Cover

23816 Highlight Industries
2694 Prairie St SW
Wyoming, MI 49519 616-531-2464
Fax: 616-531-0506 800-531-2465
info@highlightindustries.com
www.highlightindustries.com
Manufacturer and exporter of stretch wrapping machinery, case sealing, case strapping, and shrink wrap machinery
Owner: Kurt Riemenschneide
Estimated Sales: $10-20 Million
Number Employees: 50-99
Square Footage: 60000
Brands:
Freedom
Poly Packer
Revolver
Synergy

23817 Hilden Halifax
1044 Commerce Lane
P.O.Box 1098
South Boston, VA 24592-1098 434-572-3965
Fax: 434-572-4781 800-431-2514
sales@hildenhalifax.com
www.hildenamerica.com
Manufacturer, importer and exporter of table linens and kitchen textiles
President: Russell Basch
Vice President of Sales: Tom Hall
Sales: Sharlene Gulley
Estimated Sales: $2.5-5 Million
Number Employees: 20-49
Square Footage: 160000
Parent Co: Hilden Manufacturing Company
Brands:
Village Square

23818 Hilderth Wood Products
825 Mt Vernon Rd
Wadesboro, NC 28170 704-826-8326
Fax: 704-826-8097
hildrethwoodproducts@windtream.net
www.hidrethwoodproducts.com
Wooden pallets and skids
Owner: Blake E Hildreth Jr
General Manager: Leon Hildreth
Estimated Sales: $3 - 5 Million
Number Employees: 20-49

23819 Hilex Company
990 Apollo Rd # A
Eagan, MN 55121-2390 651-454-1160
Fax: 651-454-2507
Bleaches, sanitizers and disinfectants
President: Tom Gates
COO: Ray Lee
Estimated Sales: $5-10 Million
Number Employees: 20 to 49
Square Footage: 60000
Brands:
Hilex 6-40

23820 Hill Brush, Inc.
811 Rolyn Ave
Baltimore, MD 21237 410-325-7000
Fax: 410-325-6477 800-998-1515
info@hillbrushinc.com
www.hillbrushinc.com/index.htm
Cleaning systems for hygienically sensitive areas within food and beverage production facilities, restaurants & kitchens, catering, dairies and hospitals. Color coded manual cleaning tools.
President: Philip Coward
Manager: Ernest Atkinson
VP: Peter Coward
National Sales Director: James Sokaitis
Manager: Margie Gessinger
Estimated Sales: $600 Thousand
Type of Packaging: Food Service, Bulk

23821 Hill Manufacturing Company
1500 Jonesboro Rd SE
Atlanta, GA 30315 404-522-8364
Fax: 404-522-9694 sales@soap.com
www.soap.com
Manufacturer, importer and exporter of USDA cleaning products including hand cleaners, liquid washing and industrial cleaning compounds, germicide disinfectants and floor polish
President: Stewart Hillman
VP: Jack Hillman
Estimated Sales: $20-50 Million
Number Employees: 100-249
Square Footage: 110000
Type of Packaging: Bulk
Brands:
Hilco

23822 Hill Parts
211 Hogan Pond Ln
Ball Ground, GA 30107 770-735-4199
Fax: 770-735-4494 800-241-4003
sales@hillparts.com www.hillparts.com
Equipment and parts for poultry processing
Owner: Donald Hill
Chief Executive: Billy Hill
Account Manager: Marty Lee
Number Employees: 103
Parent Co: Cooperatieve Meyn

23823 Hilliard Corporation
100 W 4th St
Elmira, NY 14901 607-733-7121
Fax: 607-737-1108 hilliard@hilliardcorp.com
www.hilliardcorp.com
Motion control products, oil filtration and reclaiming equipment, starters for industrial gas, diesel engines and gas turbines, and plate and frame filter presses used in the food and beverage industry.
President: Paul Webb
CEO: Nelson Mooers Van Den
CEO: Nelson Mooers Van Den Blink
Regional Sales Manager: Gerry Lachut
Estimated Sales: $50 - 75 Million
Number Employees: 500-999

23824 Hilliard's Chocolate System
275 E Center Street
West Bridgewater, MA 02379-1813 508-587-3666
Fax: 508-587-3735 800-258-1530
sales@hilliardschocolate.com
www.hilliardschocolate.com
Candymaking utensils and manufacturers of chocolate machinery
President: James S Bourne
Estimated Sales: $1 Million
Number Employees: 5-9
Type of Packaging: Bulk
Brands:
Hilliard

23825 Hillside Metal Ware Company
1060 Commerce Ave
Union, NJ 07083-5026 908-964-3080
Fax: 908-964-3082 www.hillware.com
Manufacturer and exporter of aluminum cookware and bakeware including molds, black steel pizza, springform and cake pans
Estimated Sales: $2 Million
Number Employees: 20-49
Square Footage: 120000
Brands:
Hillware

23826 Hilltop Services LLC
6616 Fribay Road
Byron, IL 61010 815-234-8600
Fax: 815-234-3028 mmhilltop@verizon.net
Supplies prep equipment/machinery
President: Michael Lingel
CFO: Mary Lingel
Sales/PR: Mike Lingel

23827 Hillyard
302 North 4th Street
P.O. Box 909
Saint Joseph, MO 64501 816-233-1321
Fax: 800-861-0256 800-365-1555
www.hillyard.com
Manufacturer and exporter of floor seals, finishes, waxes, polishes and cleaners
President: Robert Roth
Chief Financial Officer: Neil Ambrose
Executive Vice President: Scott Hillyard
Vice President, R&D: Stuart Hughes
Vice President, Sales: David Schauer
Operations Manager: Jon Gottlieb
Product Manager: Blake Roth
Purchasing Manager: Tom Armstrong
Estimated Sales: $66 Million
Number Employees: 800
Square Footage: 325600

23828 Hilter Stainless
614 Eau Placine Street
Stratford, WI 54484 715-387-8260
Fax: 715-387-0148 hilter@tznet.com
Estimated Sales: $1-2.5 Million
Number Employees: 15

23829 **Himolene**
1648 Diplomat Drive
Carrollton, TX 75006-6847 203-731-3600
Fax: 203-731-3620 800-777-4411
High density industrial can liners
VP/General Manager: Paul Hart
Marketing Manager: Dave Shewmaker
Estimated Sales: $1-2.5 Million
Number Employees: 5-9
Parent Co: First Brands Corporation
Brands:
Stick 'n Stay
Tie-Tie

23830 **(HQ)Hinchcliff Products Company**
13477 Prospect Road
Strongsville, OH 44149 440-238-5200
Fax: 440-238-5202
sales@hinchcliffproducts.com
www.hinchcliffproducts.com
Manufacturer and exporter of wooden pallets, skids, boxes, crates and containers
President: Jay D Phillips
VP of Sales: Don Phillips
Purchasing Manager: Scott Phillips
Estimated Sales: $500,000-$1 Million
Number Employees: 1-4
Number of Products: 3
Square Footage: 100000

23831 **Hinds-Bock Corporation**
2122 222nd St SE
Bothell, WA 98021-4430 425-885-1183
Fax: 425-885-1492 garyh@hinds-bock.com
www.hinds-bock.com
Manufacturer and exporter of standard and custom piston filling machines, depositors and transfer pumps for liquids and viscous products with delicate particulates
President: Gary Hinds
CFO: John Davis
VP Sales/Marketing: Lance Aasness
Estimated Sales: $5 - 10 Million
Number Employees: 20-49
Square Footage: 96000

23832 **Hines III**
1650 Art Museum Dr
Suite 18
Jacksonville, FL 32207-2188 904-398-5110
Fax: 904-396-1867
Fiberglass, steel and wood benches/seats; also, planters, ash and trash receptacles, tables, table tops and planter/bench combinations
President: Samuel J Hines
CEO: Samuel Hines
Estimated Sales: Below $5 Million
Number Employees: 1-4
Square Footage: 32000

23833 **Hinkle Manufacturing**
5th & D Streets Ampoint Industrial Park
Perrysburg, OH 43551 419-666-5550
Fax: 419-666-5367 klembke@hinklemfg.com
www.hinklemfg.com
Corrugated boxes and recyclable plastic and foam packaging
Mnager: Taber Hinkle
VP Marketing: Malcolm Eddy
General Manager: John Mayland
Estimated Sales: $10-20 Million
Number Employees: 50-99

23834 **Hino Diesel Trucks**
41180 Bridge Street
Novi, MI 48375 248-699-9300
Fax: 248-699-9310 daniels@hino.com
www.hino.com
VP: Francis Merz
IT Manager: Brad Czischke
VP Marketing and Dealer Operations: Glenn Ellis
SM, Human Resources and Administration: Joseph Whalen
VP of Service Operations: George M. Daniels

23835 **Hishi Plastics**
600 Ryerson Road
Lincoln Park, NJ 07035-2057 973-633-1230
Fax: 973-872-8381
customerservice@hishiplastics.com
www.hishiplastics.com
Food and HBA packaging materials
President: Shawn Kawazato
Estimated Sales: $5-10 Million
Number Employees: 50-99

23836 **Hiss Stamp Company**
100 N Grant Ave
Columbus, OH 43215-5119 614-224-5119
Fax: 614-224-0464
Manufacturer and wholesaler/distributor of stamps and FDA approved inks
Manager: Michael Gaborcik
Estimated Sales: Less than $500,000
Number Employees: 4
Square Footage: 3500
Parent Co: Cosco Industries

23837 **Hitachi Maxco**
1630 Cobb Intl Blvd NW
Kennesaw, GA 30152 770-424-9350
Fax: 770-424-9145 800-241-8209
twalker@hitmax.com www.hitmax.com
President: Martin Bando
CFO: Douglas Roberts
Number Employees: 20-49

23838 **Hitec Food Equip. Inc.**
818 Lively Blvd
Wood Dale, IL 60191 630-521-9460
Fax: 630-521-9466 information@hitec-usa.com
www.hitec-usa.com
Food processing machines for the ham and sausage industry.
President: Tatsuo Nakamura

23839 **Hiwin Technologies Corporation**
520 E Business Center Drive
Mt Prospect, IL 60056-2186 847-827-2270
Fax: 847-827-2291 info@hiwin.com
www.hiwin.com.tw
High quality linear motion products
President: Joe Jou
Sales Engineer: Fred Chevalau
Sales Engineer: Joe Long
Sales Engineer: Chuck Haas
Accounting Dept.: Geneva Wang
Inventory Control: Andrew Choi
Estimated Sales: $5 - 10 Million
Number Employees: 30

23840 **Hixson Architects & Engineers**
659 Van Meter Street
Cincinnati, OH 45202-1568 513-241-1230
Fax: 513-241-1287 info@hixson-inc.com
www.hixson-inc.com
Hixson provides engineering and design solutions that enable food and beverage processors to increase production speed and thoughput, improve product quality and consistency, reduce costs, and deliver capital projects more effectively.Design capabilities include process, packaging, material handling, automation, electrical, HVAC, plumbing, refrigeration, civil and structural engineering, architecture, environmental, health and safety compliance, project management, constructionadministration.
President & CEO: J Wickliffe Ach
Sales: Jim Rivard
Sales: Mike Steur
Estimated Sales: $20 - 30 Million
Number Employees: 125+

23841 **Hixson Architects and Engineers**
659 Van Meter Street
Cincinnati, OH 45202-1566 513-241-1230
Fax: 513-241-1287 info@hixson-inc.com
www.hixson-inc.com
Engineering and design solutions that enable food and beverage processors to increase production speed and through-put, improve product quality and consistency, reduce costs, and deliver capital projects more effectively. Designcapabilities include process, packaging, material handling, automation, electrical, HVAC, plumbing, refridgeration, civil and structural. Hixson assists companies with renovations, expansion, site selection, master planning, utility improvements andmore.
President/CEO: J Wickliffe Ach
Chief Financial Officer: Thomas Banker
Vice President: William Sander NCARB
Marketing/Sales: Mike Steur
Sales: Jim Rivard
Public Relations: Patricia Helmbrook
Estimated Sales: $20-30 Million
Number Employees: 120

23842 **Hoarel Sign Company**
819 NE 7th Ave
Amarillo, TX 79107 806-373-2175
Fax: 806-373-2329 www.hoarelsign.com
Point of purchase displays and signs including advertising, changeable letter, electric, interchangeable, luminous tube and plastic
President: Gary Cox
Secretary and Treasurer: Linda Cox
VP: Ray Cox
Estimated Sales: $1-2.5 Million
Number Employees: 10-19
Square Footage: 16000

23843 **Hobart Corporation**
701 S Ridge Ave
Troy, OH 45374-0001 937-332-3000
Fax: 937-332-2852 888-446-2278
www.hobart.com
Manufacturer and exporter of mixers, slicers, dishwashers and refrigerators; also, cooking and bakery equipment
President: Ken Lee
CFO: Ken Kessler
Director Training/Communication: Dean Landeche
VP Sales/Marketing: John McDonough
Estimated Sales: $100 - 250 Million
Number Employees: 1,000-4,999
Parent Co: Illinois Tool Works
Type of Packaging: Food Service
Brands:
Hobart

23844 **Hobart Corporation**
701 S. Ridge Ave.
Troy, OH 45374 937-332-3000
Fax: 937-332-2852 888-446-2278
www.hobartcorp.com
Mixers, grinders, freezers, dishwashers and warewashers
Manager: David Higgins
Manager: Charles Rodriguez
Estimated Sales: $5-10 Million
Number Employees: 20-49
Parent Co: Hobart Corporation

23845 **Hobart Corporation**
701 S. Ridge Ave.
Troy, OH 45374 937-332-3000
Fax: 937-332-2852 888-446-2278
www.hobartcorp.com
Dishwashers, warewashers, freezers, mixes and grinders
Manager: David Higgins
Manager: Harry Harrington
Estimated Sales: $10-20 Million
Number Employees: 20-49
Parent Co: Hobart Corporation

23846 **Hobart Corporation**
701 S. Ridge Ave.
Troy, OH 45374 937-332-3000
Fax: 937-332-2852 888-446-2278
www.hobartcorp.com
Commercial slicers, grinders and mixers
Manager: David Higgins
Manager: Brian Hallman
Estimated Sales: $10-20 Million
Number Employees: 20-49
Parent Co: Hobart Corporation

23847 **Hobart Food Equipment**
701 S Ridge Ave
Troy, OH 45374-0001 937-332-3000
Fax: 937-332-2852 www.hobart.com
Bakery machinery and equipment
President: Ken Lee
CFO: Ken Kessler
Estimated Sales: Above $5 Billion
Number Employees: 1,000-4,999

23848 **Hodge Design**
22 Chestnut Street
Evansville, IN 47713 812-422-2558
Fax: 812-422-3337 info@hodgestructural.com
www.hodgestructural.com
Wine industry label design
Owner: Steve Hodge
Estimated Sales: $1 - 5 000,000
Number Employees: 1

23849 **Hodge Manufacturing Company**
55 Fisk Ave
Springfield, MA 01107 413-781-6800
Fax: 413-349-8235 800-262-4634
hodgemfg@javanet.com www.durhammfg.com
Steel work benches, carts, platforms, shelf and hand trucks, recycle receptacles, waste material containers, shelving racks, hook-on bins, storage cabinets, safety equipment, wire carts, etc
Manager: Bob Hall
Estimated Sales: $10-20,000,000
Number Employees: 50-99
Square Footage: 50000

23850 **Hodges**
PO Box 187
Vienna, IL 62995-0187 618-658-9070
Fax: 773-379-8102 800-444-0011
info@lpstorage.com
Racks, shelving, casters, dolly trucks, utilty carts and mobile storage equipment
National Sales Manager: Chris Geurden
Estimated Sales: $1 - 5,000,000
Number Employees: 100-249
Square Footage: 240000
Parent Co: Leggett & Platt Storage Products Group
Brands:
Postmaster

23851 **Hoegger Alpina**
PO Box 175918
Covington, KY 41017-5918 865-344-8642
Fax: 865-344-8743
Commerical meat processing machines, choppers, stuffers, and chip machines

23852 **Hoegger Food TechnologyInc.**
3555 Holly Lane N
Suite 10
Minneapolis, MN 55447 763-233-6930
Fax: 802-223-5499 877-789-5400
info.usa@hoegger.com www.hoegger.com
Meat presses for bacon, pork and strip steaks, as well as post packaging pasteurization products for hams, sausage and other meat products as well as pasta and vegetables.

23853 **Hoffer Flow Controls**
P.O.Box 2145
Elizabeth City, NC 27906 252-331-1997
Fax: 252-331-2886 800-628-4584
info@hofferflow.com www.hofferflow.com
Manufacturer and exporter of sanitary turbine flowmeters for batch controlling, flow rate indication and totalization.
President: Bob Carrell
CEO: Ken Hoffer
CEO: Sandra Kelly
Quality Control: Wendy Brabble
Marketing Manager: Janna Critcher
Sales: Linda Markham
Production Manager: Deborah Blakeney
Purchasing: Melissa Stallings
Estimated Sales: $5-10 Million
Number Employees: 90
Square Footage: 40000
Brands:
Hoffer

23854 **Hoffman Company**
PO Box 893
Corpus Christi, TX 78403-0893 262-391-8664
sales@hoffman-co.com
www.hoffman-co.com
Doors, cabinets and store fixtures
President: Bryan Hoffman
Marketing Manager: Brian Hoffman
Estimated Sales: $5-10 Million
Number Employees: 20-49

23855 **Hoffmann-La Roche**
340 Kingsland St
Nutley, NJ 07110 973-235-5000
Fax: 973-235-7605 800-526-6367
www.rocheusa.com
President: George B Abercrombie
Chief Financial Officer: Ivor MacLeod
Number Employees: 1,000-4,999
Parent Co: Roche Group

23856 **Hoffmeyer Company**
1600 Factor Ave
San Leandro, CA 94577 510-895-9955
Fax: 510-895-9014 800-350-2358
sales@hoffmeyerco.com www.hoffmeyerco.com
Manufacturer and fabricator of conveyor belting, gaskets, seals, hoses, fittings and assemblies
Owner: Frederick O Shay
Chairman Board/CEO: Frederick Oshay
Chairman: Frederick Oshay
Estimated Sales: $5 - 10 Million
Number Employees: 10-19
Square Footage: 17000

23857 **Hofmann & Leavy/Tasseldepot**
3251 SW 13th Dr
Deerfield Beach, FL 33442-8166 954-698-0001
Fax: 954-698-0009 info@tasseldepot.com
www.tasseldepot.com
Manufacturer and exporter of napkin rings and decorative items including tassles and chair tie-backs
President: Roger Leavy
Marketing/Design: April Leavy
Estimated Sales: $1-2.5 Million
Number Employees: 20-49
Square Footage: 23000

23858 **Hoge Brush Company**
701 S Main Street
State Route 29
New Knoxville, OH 45871 419-753-2351
Fax: 419-753-2893 800-494-4643
info@hoge.com www.hoge.com
Counter dusters, dairy, floor, sweeping, garage and window brushes, street brooms, etc
President: John Hoge
Sales/Marketing Executive: David Zwiep
Production Manager: Ray Slone
Plant Manager: Dave Zwiep
Purchasing Manager: David Zwiep
Estimated Sales: $1 - 3 Million
Number Employees: 5-9
Square Footage: 35742
Parent Co: Hoge Lumber Company
Brands:
Hoge

23859 **Hogshire Industries**
2401 Hampton Blvd
Norfolk, VA 23517 757-877-2297
Fax: 757-624-2328 www.hogshire.com
Commercial awnings
Estimated Sales: $1-2,500,000
Number Employees: 20-49

23860 **Hogtown Brewing Company**
2351 Royal Windsor Drive
Unit 6
Mississauga, ON L5J 4S7
Canada 905-855-9065
Fax: 905-822-0990 hogman@infinity.net
www.hogtownbrewers.org
Beer; also, bottling services available
President: Maria Lopez
General Manager: Peter Lazaro
Number Employees: 5-9
Type of Packaging: Consumer, Food Service

23861 **Hohn Manufacturing Company**
200 Sun Valley Cir
Fenton, MO 63026 636-349-1400
Fax: 636-349-1440 800-878-1440
hohnmfginc@toast.net
Manufacturer and exporter of furniture polishes, cleaning compounds, soaps, detergents, tablets, etc
President: Larry Harrington
Estimated Sales: $1-4 Million
Number Employees: 5-9
Square Footage: 72000
Type of Packaging: Private Label
Brands:
Vita Lustre

23862 **Hohner Corporation**
PO Box 3004
Beamsville, ON L0R 1B3
Canada 905-563-4924
Fax: 905-563-7209 800-295-5693
hohner@hohner.com www.hohner.com
President: Walter Bloechle
Number Employees: 10

23863 **(HQ)Holcor**
13603 S Halsted Street
Riverdale, IL 60827-1163 708-841-3800
Fax: 708-841-3941
Fluorescent, incandescent and mercury lighting
President: S Larson
Estimated Sales: $20-50 Million
Number Employees: 50-99
Square Footage: 5000

23864 **(HQ)Holden Graphic Services**
607 Washington Ave N
Minneapolis, MN 55401-1220 612-339-0241
Fax: 612-349-0433 holden@usinternet.com
www.holdengraphicservices.com
Printed cash register tapes, coupons and business forms
President: George T Holden
CFO: Gary Plager
CFO: Gary Plager
Sales Manager: Dave Brow
Estimated Sales: $5-10 Million
Number Employees: 20-49
Other Locations:
Holden Graphic Services
Minneapolis MN

23865 **Holland Applied Technologies**
7050 High Grove Blvd
Burr Ridge, IL 60527 630-325-5130
Fax: 630-654-2518 information@hollandapt.com
www.hollandapt.com
Packaging equipment and materials, clean-in-place systems, filters, gauges, heat exchangers and valves
President: Dave Cheney
VP: Fred Kramer
Estimated Sales: $25 Million
Number Employees: 50-99

23866 **Holland Chemicals Company**
4590 Rhodes Drive
Windsor, ON N8W 5C2
Canada 519-948-4373
Fax: 519-945-2256 info@hollandcleaning.com
www.hollandcleaning.com
Floor finishes and detergents
Manager: Mike Shalub

23867 **Holland Company**
153 Howland Ave
Adams, MA 01220-1199 413-743-1292
Fax: 413-743-1298 800-639-9602
info@hollandcompany.com
www.hollandcompany.com
Manufacturer and exporter of food grade additives including ammonium, potassium and iron-free aluminum sulfates
President: Daniel J Holland
Estimated Sales: $10-20,000,000
Number Employees: 20-49

23868 **Holland Manufacturing Company**
P.O.Box 404
Succasunna, NJ 07876 973-584-8141
Fax: 973-584-6845 hollandmfg@earthlink.net
www.hollandmfg.com
Converted paper products and packaging tapes
President: Jack Holland
CFO: Mitch Cantor
R&D: Donald Thoren
Estimated Sales: $20 - 50 Million
Number Employees: 50-99

23869 **Hollander Horizon International**
16 Wall St
Princeton, NJ 08540-1513 609-924-7577
Fax: 609-924-8626 www.hhisearch.com
Hollander Horizon International is the premier executive search firm specializing in the technical sector of the food and consumer products industry. The areas we serve are: research and development, manufacturing and engineeringquality control, and quality assurance.
East Coast Senior Partner: Michael Hollander
West Coast Senior Partner: Arnold Zimmerman
Estimated Sales: $300,000-500,000
Number Employees: 5-9
Parent Co: Hollander Horizon International

23870 **Hollandia Bakeries Limited**
PO Box 100
Mt Brydges, ON N0L 1W0
Canada 519-264-1020
800-265-3480
www.hollandiacookies.com

Cookies
President: Joop De Voest Jr
Controller: Rick Bannister
Quality Control: Mike Hobley
VP Sales: Doug Smith
Brands:
Kerleens
Sugar Free Cookies
Hard Cookies
Soft Cookies
Gourmet Specialty Cookies
Mini Tubs
Red Label

23871 Hollingsworth Custom Wood Products
284 N Street
Sault Ste. Marie, ON P6A 7B8
Canada 705-759-1756
Fax: 705-759-0275
info@maplewoodproducts.com
www.maplewoodproducts.com
Manufacturer and exporter of butchers' blocks, cutting boards and wooden bakers' tops
Marketing Director: Paul Hollingsworth
Customer Service: Ruth Bradley
General Manager: Jim Webb
Estimated Sales: $1 - 5 Million
Number Employees: 15
Parent Co: Soo Mill Lumber
Brands:
Woodwelded

23872 Hollowell Products Corporation
570 Central St
Wyandotte, MI 48192-7123 734-282-8200
Fax: 734-282-0678 mail@elephant-vac.com
www.elephant-vac.com
Industrial vacuum cleaners including mobile, gas and electric powered
President: John F Hollowell
Estimated Sales: Below $5 Million
Number Employees: 5-9

23873 Hollowick
PO Box 305
Manlius, NY 13104 315-682-2163
Fax: 315-682-6948 800-367-3015
info@hollowick.com www.hollowick.com
Manufacturer and exporter of liquid candle lamps, lamp fuel, wax candles, chafing fuel and silk flowers ceramic vases
President: Alan Menter
CFO: Eugene Duffy
Marketing: Mike Cleveland
Sales: Mike Cleveland
Plant Manager: Tom Palmeter
Estimated Sales: $5-10 Million
Number Employees: 20-49
Brands:
Easy Florals
Easy Heat
Select Wax

23874 Hollymatic Corporation
600 E Plainfield Rd
Countryside, IL 60525 708-579-3700
Fax: 708-579-1057 hollyinfo@hollymatic.com
www.hollymatic.com
Manufacturer, exporter and importer of food processing equipment and supplies including tenderizers, grinders, mixers/grinders/ patty machines, meat saws, etc.
President: James Azzar
R&D: Hardev Somal
Marketing Manager: Rob Kovack
Estimated Sales: $5 - 10 Million
Number Employees: 50-99
Type of Packaging: Food Service
Brands:
Hollymatic

23875 Hollywood Banners
539 Oak St
Copiague, NY 11726 631-842-3000
Fax: 631-842-3148 800-691-5652
info@hollywoodbanners.com
www.hollywoodbanners.com
Manufacturer and exporter of indoor and outdoor banners including plastic and cloth
President: Daniel F Mahoney
VP Sales: Timothy Cox
Production Manager: Hugo Canedo

Estimated Sales: $1-3 Million
Number Employees: 20-49
Square Footage: 100000

23876 Holm Dietz Computer Systems
8080 North Palm Avenue
Suite 210
Fresno, CA 93711-5797 559-438-3600
Fax: 559-447-6338
support@FamousSoftware.com
www.famoussoftware.com
Wine industry computer systems
President: Kirk Parrish
CFO: Rick Desehr
Estimated Sales: $5 - 10 Million
Number Employees: 50-99

23877 Holman Boiler Works
1956 Singleton Blvd
Dallas, TX 75212 214-637-0020
Fax: 214-637-2539 800-331-1956
dal-sales@holmanboiler.com
www.holmanboiler.com
Manufacturer and exporter of watertube and firetube boilers; also, burners
President: John Campollo
CEO: Richard Maxson
Quality Control: Greg Martinez
Manager Business Development: Gary Perskhini
Estimated Sales: $50 - 100 Million
Number Employees: 50-99
Parent Co: Copes-Vulcan
Brands:
E.D.G.E.

23878 Holman Cooking Equipment
10 Sunnen Dr
Saint Louis, MO 63143-3800 888-356-5362
Fax: 800-264-6666 info@holmancooking.com
www.holmancooking.com
Food service equipment including conveyor toasters, conveyor ovens and specialty/finishing ovens
CFO: Mike Barber
CEO: Frank Ricchio
VP Engineering: Doug Vogt
Marketing Manager: Candi Benz
Number Employees: 100-249
Square Footage: 40000
Parent Co: Star Manufacturing International

23879 Holmco Container Manufacturing, LTD
1501 TR 183
Baltic, OH 43804-9677 330-897-4503
Fax: 330-698-3200
Manufacturer and exporter of stainless steel milk containers.
Owner: Eli Troyer
Number Employees: 2
Square Footage: 38400
Type of Packaging: Food Service

23880 Holo-Source Corporation
12060 Hubbard St
Livonia, MI 48150 734-427-1530
Fax: 734-525-8520 sales@holo-source.com
www.holo-source.com
President: Deryl C Lacey
Estimated Sales: $100 - 250 Million
Number Employees: 10-19

23881 Holophane
P.O.Box 3004
Newark, OH 43058-3004 740-587-7218
Fax: 740-349-4451 sbacklund@holophane.com
www.holophane.com
Lighting and control equipment, glass reflectors and HID lighting fixtures, emergency lighting systems, and back-up power supplies
President: Crawford Lipsey
CFO: Daren Cox
Vice President: Bob Petro
Quality Control: Lowry Pierce
Manufacturing Director: Kim Lombardi
Estimated Sales: $50 - 100 Million
Number Employees: 10-19

23882 Holsman Sign Services
15002 Woodworth Rd
Cleveland, OH 44110-3310 216-761-4433
Fax: 216-761-4439
Signs including neon, electric, plastic, wood, vinyl, metal, etc.; also, service and installation available
Branch Manager: J Burge

Estimated Sales: $1 - 5 Million
Number Employees: 10 to 19
Square Footage: 60000
Parent Co: Identitek

23883 Holstein Manufacturing
5368 110th St
Holstein, IA 51025-9539 712-368-4342
Fax: 712-368-2351 800-368-4342
hmi@pionet.net www.holsteinmfg.com
Barbecue equipment, portable grills and flatbed, livestock and concession trailers
VP: Darrin Schmidt
Estimated Sales: $1-2.5 Million
Number Employees: 5-9

23884 Home City Ice
P.O. Box 111116
Cincinnati, OH 45211 513-598-3000
Fax: 513-574-5409 800-759-4411
www.homecityice.com
Packaged and block ice
Manager: Robert Everly
Estimated Sales: $1-2.5 Million
Number Employees: 5-9

23885 Home Plastics
5250 NE 17th St
Des Moines, IA 50313 515-265-2562
Fax: 515-265-8872 info@homeplastics.com
www.homeplastics.com
Manufacturer and exporter of polyethylene heat sealed bags, tubes and liners; also, plastic film and plain and printed slip-on sleeve labels, political signs
President and QC: Samuel Siegel
Estimated Sales: $20 - 50 Million
Number Employees: 100-249
Type of Packaging: Consumer, Food Service, Private Label, Bulk

23886 Home Rubber Company
PO Box 878
Trenton, NJ 08605-0878 609-394-1176
Fax: 609-396-1985 800-257-9441
www.homerubber.com
Manufacturer and exporter of industrial rubber food and milk unloading hoses, belting, molded goods and sheet rubber
President: Richard Balka
VP: Stephen Kelley
Estimated Sales: $10-20 Million
Number Employees: 50-99
Brands:
Sterling

23887 (HQ)Homer Laughlin China Company
672 Fiesta Dr
Newell, WV 26050 304-387-1300
Fax: 304-387-0593 800-452-4462
hlc@hlchina.com www.hlchina.com
Manufacturer and exporter of dinnerware china
CFO: William Danley
CEO: Joseph Wells III
CEO: Joseph M Wells Iii
Marketing Director: Kimberly Faloon
Production Manager: Wilbur Waigoneer
Plant Manager: John Bennley
Purchasing Manager: Otto Jirianni
Estimated Sales: $20-50 Million
Number Employees: 1,000-4,999
Square Footage: 1700000
Brands:
Ameriwhite
Best China
Fiesta
Gothic
Lyrica
Milford
Pristine
Seville

23888 Honeywell
101 Columbia Road
Mailstop M6/LM
Morristown, NJ 07962
877-841-2840
info@corp.honeywell.com
www.yourhomeexpert.com

Manufacturer and exporter of fire alarm systems and controls
Chairman and CEO: David M Cote
Vice Chairman: Andreas Kramvis
Senior VP/Chief Financial Officer: Tom Szlosek
Vice Chairman: Roger Fradin
Senior VP/General Counsel: Katherine Adams
Senior VP, Engineering Operations & IT: Krishna Mikkilneni
Cheif Strategy & Marketing Officer: Rhonda Germany
SVP, HR, Procurement & Communications: Mike James
Estimated Sales: $37 Billion
Number Employees: 132,000
Square Footage: 15803

23889 Honeywell
1100 Virginia Dr
Fort Washington, PA 19034 215-641-4300
Fax: 215-641-3513
virgus.l.volertas@honeywell.com
www.honeywell.com
Industrial process controllers, recorders, programmers, industrial actuators, flame safeguard controls; complete line of analytical instruments consisting of sanitary durafet PH electrode, conductivity and resistivity analyzer anddewpoint transmitter
Manager: Stephen Bilo
Estimated Sales: $50 - 100 Million
Number Employees: 250-499

23890 Honeywell International
25 E. Algonquin Road
P.O. Box 5017
Des Plaines, IL 60017-5017 847-391-2000
Fax: 847-391-3804 800-877-6184
foodaux@uop.com www.uop.com
Food antioxidants and immobilized enzymes
Estimated Sales: $1 - 5 Million
Number Employees: 1000-4999

23891 Honeywell's
11 W Spring St
Freeport, IL 61032-4316 815-235-5500
Fax: 815-235-5574 800-537-6945
info.sc@honeywell.com www.honeywell.com
Manufacturer and exporter of switches and sensors for packaging lines (smart distributed systems): photoelectric, proximity, pressure, cuttent and ultrasonic
President: Roger Fradin
Vice President, Chief Information Office: Mike Lang
VP: Tim Mickle
VP Marketing: Ron Sieck
Senior Vice President of Operations: Larry Kittelberger
Estimated Sales: $500 Million to $1 Billion
Number Employees: 1,000-4,999
Parent Co: Honeywell

23892 Hood Flexible Packaging
1887 Gateway Blvd
St Paul, MN 55112-2770 651-636-2500
Fax: 651-636-0663 800-448-0682
pdinneen@hoodpackaging.com
www.hoodpackaging.com
Plastic bags for frozen and nonfrozen foods
Manager: Steve Hendrickson
Quality Control: Demetrius Ward
Chairman of the Board: Warren A Hood Jr
Director: Kevin McCarthy
Estimated Sales: $100 - 250 Million
Number Employees: 100-249
Parent Co: Southern Bag Corporation

23893 Hood Packaging
2380 McDowell Road
Burlington, ON L7R 4A1
Canada 905-637-5611
Fax: 905-637-9954 877-637-5066
www.hoodpkg.com
Paper and plastic packaging supplies
President: John McCade
Director Sales/Marketing: Robert Morris
Estimated Sales: $250 - 500 Million
Number Employees: 250

23894 Hoover Company
4211 Shuffel St NW
North Canton, OH 44720 330-499-9200
Fax: 330-966-5448 www.hoovercompany.com
Manufacturer and exporter of extractors, vacuum cleaners and supplies including bags, belts, air freshener tablets and steamvac cleaning solutions
Director Special Markets: Brad Nyholm
Estimated Sales: $350 - 400 Million
Number Employees: 1,000-4,999
Square Footage: 527000
Parent Co: Maytag Corporation

23895 Hoover Materials Handling Group
6875 Shiloh Road E
Alpharetta, GA 30005-8372 770-664-4047
Fax: 770-664-2850 800-391-3561
www.hooveribcs.com
Manufacturer and exporter of containers and tanks
President: Ernie Mathia
Chairman, Chief Executive Officer: Donald Young
Estimated Sales: $115 Million
Number Employees: 450
Parent Co: Hoover Group
Brands:
Apr
Bdi
Bdii
Bdiii
Liquitote
Mamor
Suredrain

23896 Hope Chemical Corporation
PO Box 908
Pawtucket, RI 02862 401-724-8000
Fax: 401-724-8076
Industrial cleaning compounds
President: R Bernstein
Number Employees: 50

23897 Hope Industrial SystemsInc.
1325 Northmeadow Pkwy
Suite 100
Roswell, GA 30076 678-762-9790
Fax: 678-762-9789 877-762-9790
sales@hopeindustrial.com
www.hopeindustrial.com
Flat panel touchscreens and monitors for the food processing and dairy industries.

23898 Hope Paper Box Company
33 India Street
Pawtucket, RI 02860-5510 401-724-5700
Corrugated paper boxes and partitions
President: Timothy H Hayes
VP: Gregory Yates
Estimated Sales: $2.5-5 Million
Number Employees: 20-49

23899 Hopp Companies
815 2nd Ave
New Hyde Park, NY 11040 516-358-4170
Fax: 516-358-4178 800-889-8425
hoppco1@aol.com www.hoppcompanies.com
Plastic chips, strips, restocking tags, label backers and covers used as label holders, overlays and decorative coverings for shelf moldings
President: Lani Hopp
CEO: Cani Hopp
CEO: Bob Hopp
Estimated Sales: $2.5-5 Million
Number Employees: 1-4
Number of Brands: 1

23900 Hoppmann Corporation
13129 Airpark Dr # 120
Elkwood, VA 22718-1761 540-825-2899
Fax: 540-829-1724 800-368-3582
sales@ShibuyaHoppmann.com
www.shibuyahoppmann.com
Manufacturer and exporter of assembly packaging systems including feeders, pre-feeders, conveyors, turnkey systems, etc.; also, integration services available
President: Mark Flanagan
CEO: Peter Hoppmann
CEO: Peter Hoppmann
Executive Vice President: Kazuhiro Miyamae
VP Finance: Maryanne Flusher
Product Manager: Chad Roberts
Sales Director: Dave Martin
Number Employees: 100-249

23901 Horix Manufacturing Company
1384 Island Ave
Mc Kees Rocks, PA 15136 412-771-1111
Fax: 412-331-8599 info@horix.net
www.horixmfg.com
Manufacturer, importer and exporter of liquid filling, capping, labeling and rinsing machinery for cans and bottles
President: Linda Fzramowski
Plant Manager: Felgon Robert
Research & Development: Russell Myers
CEO: Linda M Szramowski
Sales Director: David Becki
Plant Manager: Robert Feltop
Purchasing Manager: Brad Barber
Estimated Sales: $5 - 10 Million
Number Employees: 25
Square Footage: 60000
Brands:
Dura-Base
Flo-Fil
Hytamatic
Posi-Sync
Screen-Flo
Ultra-Fil
Var-I-Vol
Volufil
Weigh-Master

23902 Horizon Plastics
Northam Industrial Park, Bldg 3
PO Box 474
Cobourg, ON K9A5V7 905-372-2291
Fax: 905-372-9397 855-467-4066
info@horizonplastics.com
www.horizonplastics.com

23903 Horizon Software International
2915 Premiere Parkway
Suite 300
Duluth, GA 30097 770-554-6353
Fax: 770-554-6331 800-741-7100
sales@horizon-boss.com www.horizon-boss.com
Point of sale and back office solutions for all your food service management needs
President: Randy Eckels
VP/Finance: Jason Hayes
Senior VP/R&D: Robbie Payne
VP/Sales: Sharon McGuire
VP/Customer Experience: Andrew Eggleston
Estimated Sales: $10 - 20 Million
Number Employees: 50-99
Brands:
Fast Lane 2000
Visual Boss

23904 Hormann Flexan Llc
20a Avenue C
Leetsdale, PA 15056-1305 412-749-0400
Fax: 412-749-0410 800-365-3667
sales@flexoninc.com www.flexoninc.com
Manufacturer and exporter of industrial/commercial doors and loading dock equipment including delivery truck ramps.
President: Christoph Hormann
CEO: Charles A De La Porte
VP: Patrick Boyle
Marketing: Alic Permigiani
Public Relations: Alice Permigiani
Plant Manager: Mark Permigiani
Purchasing: David Palmosina
Estimated Sales: $10 - 20 Million
Number Employees: 20-49
Square Footage: 90000
Parent Co: Hexon
Brands:
Easy Hinge
Flexidoor
Weathershield

23905 (HQ)Hormel Foods Corporation
One Hormel Place
Austin, MN 55912 507-437-5611
Fax: 507-437-5129 800-523-4635
info@hormelfoods.com www.hormelfoods.com

Established in 1891. Processor of soups, entrees, desserts, broths, puddings, sauces and meats including ham, sausage, bacon, turkey, pre-packaged chicken and deli items.
Chairman/President/CEO: Jeffrey Ettinger
EVP/Corporate Strategy: Ronald Fielding
SVP/CFO: Jody Feragen
EVP/Refigerated Products: Steven Binder
Group VP/Hormel Foods International: Richard Bross
Group VP/Foodservice: Thomas Day
Group VP/Grocery Products: James Splinter
Group VP/Specialty Foods: Michael Tolbert
Group Vp/Consumer Products Sales: Larry Vorpahl
SVP/Supply Chain: William Snyder
VP/Corporate Innovation: Deanna Brady
VP/Corporate Communications: Julie Craven
VP/Operations, Grocery Products: Michael Devine
Estimated Sales: $8 Billion
Number Employees: 19,700
Type of Packaging: Consumer, Food Service, Private Label
Other Locations:
Manufacturing Facility
Austin MN
Manufacturing Facility
Algona IA
Manufacturing Facility
Alma KS
Manufacturing Facility
Atlanta GA
Manufacturing Facility
Aurora IL
Manufacturing Facility
Barron WI
Manufacturing Facility
Beloit WI
Manufacturing Facility
Bondurant IA
Manufacturing Facility
Bremin GA
Manufacturing Facility
Browerville MN
Manufacturing Facility
Dayton OH
Manufacturing Facility
Dubuque IA
Manufacturing Facility
Eldridge IA
Brands:
Chi-Chi's Salsa
Di Lusso
Dinty Moore
Farmer John
Herb-Ox
Herdez
Hormel
Hormel Natural Choice
Jennie-O
Lloyd's Barbeque
Megamex
Not-So-Sloppy-Joe
Saag's Sausages
Spam
Stagg Chili
Valley Fresh
World Food
Marrakesh Express Couscous

23906 Horn & Todak
10505 Judicial Dr # 101
Fairfax, VA 22030-5157 703-352-7330
Fax: 703-352-6940 billhorn@ineva.net
Partner: Bob Horan
Estimated Sales: Below $5 Million
Number Employees: 5-9

23907 (HQ)Horn Packaging Corporation
580 Fort Pond Road
Lancaster, MA 01523 800-832-7020
Fax: 978-772-4611 horn@horninternational.com
www.hornpackaging.com
Paper, wooden and corrugated boxes and wooden skids and crates; also, plastic foam fabricating and molding
President: David Walsh
CEO: Peter Hamilton
Estimated Sales: $10 - 20 Million
Number Employees: 50-99

23908 Horner International
5304 Emerson Drive
Raleigh, NC 27609 919-787-3112
Fax: 919-787-4272 sales@hornerintl.com
www.hornerinternational.com
Supplier of natural exracts and flavors
Parent Co: Horner International

23909 Hosch Company
1002 International Dr
Oakdale, PA 15071-9226 724-695-3002
Fax: 724-695-3603 800-695-3310
hosch@hoschusa.com www.hoschusa.com
Scrapers for conveyor belt cleaning.
Owner: Hans Otto Schwarze
Operations: Grace Barkhurst
Estimated Sales: $5-10 Million
Number Employees: 20-49

23910 Hose Master
1233 E 222nd St
Cleveland, OH 44117 216-481-2020
Fax: 216-481-7557 info@hosemaster.com
www.hosemaster.com
Manufacturer and exporter of gas, steam and water connectors
President: Sam Foti Jr
CEO: Sam Foti
Quality Control: Mike Thompson
CEO: Sam J Foti
Estimated Sales: $20 - 50 Million
Number Employees: 100-249
Square Footage: 130000
Brands:
Live Link
Smart

23911 Hoshizaki
530 Lakeview Plaza Blvd # F
Worthington, OH 43085-4710 614-848-7702
Fax: 614-848-7706 800-642-1140
www.hoshizaki.com
VP: Gary Peffly
Estimated Sales: $1 - 5 Million
Number Employees: 5-9

23912 Hoshizaki America
618 Highway 74 S
Peachtree City, GA 30269 770-487-2331
Fax: 770-487-1325 800-438-6087
marketing@hoshizaki.com www.hoshizaki.com
Commercial ice machines and refrigeration equipment.
President: Youki Suzuki
CEO: Youki Suzuki
Executive VP: Mark McClanahan
Quality Control: Carter Davis
Marketing Director: Carter Davis
Operations Manager: Jim Procuro
Production Manager: Jim Procuro
Plant Manager: Jim Procuro
Number Employees: 500-999
Parent Co: Hoshizaki Electric Company
Brands:
Cleancycle 12
Cyclesaver
Evercheck
Hoshizaki America
Temp Guard

23913 Hosokawa Confectionery &Bakery Technology and Systems
10 Chatham Rd
Summit, NJ 07901-1310 908-273-6360
Fax: 908-273-7432 info@hms.hosokawa.com
www.hosokawa.com
Agglomeration, size reduction, compaction/briquetting, mixing/blending, thermal reactors, disintegrators and drying and cooling machinery; consultant for process designs, engineering, research, testing, istallation, etc. available.Small scale food grade production agreements, AIG certified
Manager: Rob Vorhees
CEO: Masuo Hosokawa
Estimated Sales: $5 - 10 Million
Number Employees: 1,000-4,999
Parent Co: Hosokawa Micron Corporation

23914 Hosokawa Micron Powder System
10 Chatham Rd
Summit, NJ 07901-1310 908-273-6360
Fax: 908-273-7432 800-526-4491
info@hmps.hosokawa.com www.hosokawa.com
Weighing machines and augers, blending and mixing equipment (coffee), brewing devices (urns, cleaners, coffeemakers), bulk silo services (green coffee), dryers, feeders, grinders, agglomeration, size reduction, compaction, thermalreactors and packaging
Manager: Rob Vorhees
Estimated Sales: $10-25 Million
Number Employees: 1,000-4,999

23915 Hosokawa/Bepex Corporation
PO Box 880
Santa Rosa, CA 95402-0880 707-586-6000
Fax: 707-585-2325 info@hmfg.hosokawa.com
www.hosokawamicron.com
Food processing equipment including size reduction, liquid/solid separation, mixing/blending and thermal processing
President: Masuo Hosokawa
CEO: Masuo Hosokawa
Vice President And COO: Kiyomi Miyata
Estimated Sales: $1 - 5 Million
Number Employees: 100-249
Brands:
Rietz
Strong-Scott

23916 Hospitality International
W6636 L B White Rd
Onalaska, WI 54650 608-783-2800
Fax: 608-783-6115 info@carrollchair.com
www.hospitalityinternational.com
President: Anthony Wilson
Vice President of Development: Ron Provus
Estimated Sales: $10 - 20 Million
Number Employees: 100-249

23917 Hot Food Boxes
451 East County Line Road
Mooresville, IN 46158 317-831-7030
Fax: 317-831-7036 800-733-8073
schirico@theramp.net www.secoselect.com
Manufacturer and exporter of insulated stainless steel and aluminum equipment for hot and cold foods; also, steam tables and heated bulk food carts for banquet service.
President: John Schirico
Vice President: Pat Darre
Estimated Sales: $2.5-5 Million
Number Employees: 20-49
Square Footage: 50000
Brands:
Piper
Road Warrior

23918 Hot Shot Delivery Systems
155 Covington Dr
Bloomingdale, IL 60108-3107 630-924-8817
Fax: 630-924-8819 sales@deliveryconcepts.com
www.hotshotdeliverysystems.com
Mobile vending trucks for hot, cold and refrigerated foods
Owner: Bernard Pfeiffer
General Sales Manager: Nick Prestia
Estimated Sales: $10 - 20 Million
Number Employees: 5-9

23919 Hotset Corporation
1045 Harts Lake Rd
Battle Creek, MI 49037 269-964-4600
Fax: 269-964-4526 800-937-4681
sales@hotset.com www.hotset.com
Cartridge, coil, band, strip and tubular heaters, temperature controls, thermocouples, connectors
President: Srekumar Bandyopadhyay
Estimated Sales: $5-10 000,000
Number Employees: 20-49

23920 Hotsy Corporation
10099 Ridgegate Pkwy # 280
Lone Tree, CO 80124-5534 303-792-5200
Fax: 303-792-0547 800-525-1976
info@hotsy.com www.hotsy.com
Pressure washers
Vice President Of Sales: Frank Rotondi
Estimated Sales: $1 - 5 Million
Number Employees: 50-99

23921 Houdini
4225 N Palm St
Fullerton, CA 92835 714-525-0325
Fax: 714-996-9605 rritts@houdini.com
www.houdiniinc.com

Manufacturer, importer and exporter of food and wine; manufacturer of gift baskets
President: Timothy Dean
Estimated Sales: $500,000 - $1 Million
Number Employees: 50-99
Brands:
California Pantry
Wine Country

23922 **House Stamp Works**
107 W Van Buren St
Chicago, IL 60605 312-939-7177
Fax: 312-939-8520 info@housestampworks.com
www.housestampworks.com
Stamps, dies, seals, etc
President: Edward Leppert
Estimated Sales: Less than $500,000
Number Employees: 1-4

23923 **House of Webster**
1013 North Second Street
Po Box 1988
Rogers, AR 72756 479-636-4640
Fax: 479-636-2974 800-369-4641
www.houseofwebster.com
Apple butter, jelly, salsa, barbecue sauce and preserves, ice cream toppings, ham, bacon and sausage, candy and cheese, pancake mix and assorted gifts.
Owner/CEO: John Griffin
CFO: Nate Burden
Executive VP/COO: Craig Castrellon
Quality Control: Will West
Marketing Director: Michael Kelleysley
Sales Manager: Patrick Thompson
Director of Operations: Craig Ducan
Plant Manager: Bobby Scott
Purchasing: Deann Brown
Estimated Sales: $6.7 Million
Number Employees: 65
Square Footage: 392000
Type of Packaging: Consumer, Private Label
Brands:
Webster's

23924 **Houser Neon Sign Company**
6411 Airline Dr
Houston, TX 77076-3507 713-691-5765
Lighted signs
Owner: Kimberly Mallett
Division Manager: Robert Betz
Estimated Sales: Less than $500,000
Number Employees: 1-4
Parent Co: Southwest Neon Signs

23925 **Houston Atlas**
1201 N Velasco Street
Angleton, TX 77515-3009 409-849-2344
Fax: 409-849-2166 sales@onixpa.com
Analytical instrumentation
President: Hammond Rood
Estimated Sales: $5-10 000,000
Number Employees: 50

23926 **Houston Label**
909 Shaver Street
Pasadena, TX 77506 713-477-6995
Fax: 713-477-0023 800-477-6995
sales@houstonlabel.com www.houstonlabel.com
Manufacturer and exporter of labels including pressure sensitive, printed, unprinted, color processed, UPC and inventory automatic labeling equipment
President: Hans Ryholt
Executive VP: Hans Ryholt
Outside Sales Manager: Willie Hager
Estimated Sales: $5-10 Million
Number Employees: 1-4
Square Footage: 92000
Type of Packaging: Consumer, Food Service, Private Label, Bulk
Other Locations:
Houston Tape & Label Co.
Pasadena TX
Brands:
3m
Fasson
Mactac
Technicote

23927 **Houston Stamp & StencilCompany**
601 Jackson Hill St
Houston, TX 77007 713-869-4337
Fax: 713-869-4339 sales@houstonstamp.com
www.houstonstamp.com
Plastic signs, rubber stamps, nameplates and marking dies
President: Bruce La Roche
Estimated Sales: $1 - 5 Million
Number Employees: 5-9

23928 **Houston Wire Works, Inc.**
1007 Kentucky
South Houston, TX 77587 713-946-2920
Fax: 713-946-3579 800-468-9477
info@houstonwire.com www.houstonwire.com
Manufacturer and exporter of water bottle display, refrigerator, wine and wire racks; also, steel platform ladders and hand carts; exporter of storage racks
President: Ken Legler
CEO: Barbara Leagler
VP Sales/Marketing: Steve Foster
Sales Director: Melanie Houser
Sales Manager: Bill Watkins
Purchasing Manager: Raquel Garza
Estimated Sales: $3 - 5 Million
Number Employees: 45
Square Footage: 280000
Type of Packaging: Food Service
Brands:
Hww
Space-Saver

23929 **Hovair Systems Inc**
6912 S 220th St
Kent, WA 98032 253-872-0405
Fax: 253-872-0406 800-237-4518
info@hovair.com www.hovair.com
Manufacturer and exporter of air film material handling equipment. Manufactures air bearing systems and air film products for a wide variety of applications, with particular emphasis on the movement of heavy loads and equipment withintoday's industry.
Manager: Betty Roberts
Marketing: Betty Roberts
Operations: Betty Roberts
Plant Manager: Jeff Grow
Estimated Sales: $3 - 5 Million
Number Employees: 5-9

23930 **Hovus Incorporated**
272 Brodhead Rd Ste 200
Bethlehem, PA 18017 610-997-8800
Fax: 610-997-0485 sales@hovus.com
www.hovus.com
HOVUS Incorporated is a flexible packaging consultation and sales organization that is focused on the needs of wholesale food manufacturer's in the private, public and not-for-profit sectors.
Owner: Alfred Haus

23931 **Howard Fabrication**
PO Box 90550
City of Industry, CA 91715-0550 626-961-0114
Fax: 626-961-8533 john@howardfab.com
www.howardfab.com
Custom stainless steel mixing and storage tanks for food, pharmaceutical and dairy products
President: John Gill
Sales Manager: Ron Reed
Estimated Sales: Below $5 Million
Number Employees: 10
Square Footage: 160000

23932 **Howard Imprinting Machine Company**
5013 Tampa West Blvd
PO Box 15027
Tampa, FL 33634 813-884-2398
Fax: 813-881-1554 800-334-6943
howard.imprinting@gte.net
www.howardimprinting.com
Manufacturer and exporter of hot stamp imprinting machinery
President: James Wrobbel
Estimated Sales: $3 - 5 Million
Number Employees: 5-9

23933 **(HQ)Howard McCray**
831 E Cayuga St
Philadelphia, PA 19124 215-464-6800
Fax: 215-969-4890 800-344-8222
sales@howardmccray.com
www.howardmccray.com
Manufacturer and exporter of commercial refrigerators and freezers, open merchandisers; deli, fish, poultry and red meat service cases; produce cases; bakery display, proofers, retarders; glass door; step in and reach in units. Alsodistribute beer frosters, bottle coolers, beer dispensers, under counter coolers, and prep tables.
Owner: Chris Scott
CFO: Marie Ginon
Marketing Director: Diane Scott
Plant Manager: Brian Tyndall
Estimated Sales: $1 - 10 Million
Number Employees: 100-249
Number of Products: 60
Square Footage: 460000
Parent Co: HMC Enterprises,LLC

23934 **Howard Overman & Sons**
517 N Bradford Street
Baltimore, MD 21205-2403 410-276-8445
Fax: 410-254-6358
Household and commercial brooms
Estimated Sales: Less than $500,000
Number Employees: 4

23935 **Howard/McCray Refridgerator Company**
831 E Cayuga St
Philadelphia, PA 19124-3815 215-464-6800
Fax: 215-969-4890 hmccray850@aol.com
www.howardmccray.com
President: Chris Scott
Estimated Sales: $10 - 20 Million
Number Employees: 100-249

23936 **Howe Corporation**
1650 N Elston Ave
Chicago, IL 60642 773-235-0200
Fax: 773-235-1530 webinfo@howecorp.com
www.howecorp.com
Specialty refrigeration equipment including flake ice manchines, bin transport systems, packaged refrigeration systems, compressors and pressure vessels
President: Mary C Howe
CFO: M Aguilar
Senior VP: Kevin McCool
Research & Development: A Ahuja
Marketing Director: K McCool
VP Sales: A Ortman
Director Sales/Marketing: Chuck Janovsky
Production Manager: Steve Bokor
Plant Manager: John Myrda
Purchasing Manager: Bob Dondzik
Estimated Sales: $20-50 Million
Number Employees: 20-49
Square Footage: 65000
Brands:
Conditionaire
Rapid Freeze

23937 **Howell Brothers ChemicalLaboratories**
5007 Overbrook Ave
Philadelphia, PA 19131-1402 215-477-0260
Manufacturer and exporter of glass cleaners and hair products
President: Douglas C Howell
Manager: David Hart
Production Manager: Charles Thomson
Estimated Sales: $2.5-5 Million
Number Employees: 7
Square Footage: 12000
Type of Packaging: Consumer, Private Label

23938 **Howell Consulting**
1611-A South Melrose Dr
211
Vista, CA 92081 760-536-3456
Fax: 760-536-3457
inquiry@HowellConsultingGroup.com
www.howellconsultingGroup.com
Control systems, design assembly, installation and service. Consultant and systems integrator for process control systems
Owner: Rodney A Howell
Estimated Sales: Below $5 000,000
Number Employees: 10

23939 **Hoyer**
753 Geneva Pkwy N
Lake Geneva, WI 53147-4579 262-249-7400
Fax: 262-249-7500 info@stanpacnet.com
www.tetrapakhoyer.com

Ice cream processing equipment
President: Gustav Korsholm
Estimated Sales: $5-10 Million
Number Employees: 20-49

23940 (HQ)Hoyt Corporation
251 Forge Rd
Westport, MA 02790 508-636-8811
Fax: 508-636-2088 hoytinc@hoytinc.com
www.hoytcorp.com
Manufacturer and exporter of vapor recovery systems and dry cleaning equipment including commercial washer extracts, laundry dryers and extractors
Chairman: Jean H Olinger
VP Marketing: Pat King
Estimated Sales: $10-20 Million
Number Employees: 10-19
Brands:
Petro-Miser
Sniff-O-Miser
Solvo-Miser

23941 Huard Packaging
685 Discovery Bay Boulevard
Discovery Bay, CA 94514-9443 650-857-1501
Fax: 650-852-8138 800-752-0900

23942 Hub City Brush
PO Box 503
Petal, MS 39465 601-544-6206
Fax: 601-544-2600 800-278-7452
hubcitybrush@hubcitybrush.com
www.hubcity.arrayi.com
Commercial brooms, mops and brushes
Owner: Robert Sedotal
VP: Cecil Cedotal
Quality Control: Russel Herrin
Estimated Sales: $5 - 10Million
Number Employees: 10-19
Square Footage: 18360

23943 Hub Electric Company
6207 Commercial Rd
Crystal Lake, IL 60014 815-455-4400
Fax: 815-455-1499
richardvaralightinc@juno.com
Manufacturer and exporter of dimming systems and special lighting equipment
President and CFO: Richard Latronica
VP: Kenneth Hansen
Estimated Sales: Below $1 Million
Number Employees: 5-9

23944 Hub Folding Box Company
774 Norfolk St
Mansfield, MA 02048 508-339-0005
Fax: 508-339-0102 hubbox@ici.net
Paper folding boxes
Owner: Fred Di Rico
Sales Manager: Lucy Gilligan
Estimated Sales: $20-50 Million
Number Employees: 100-249

23945 Hub Labels
18223 Shawley Dr
Hagerstown, MD 21740 301-790-1660
Fax: 301-745-3646 800-433-4532
jdoyle@hublabels.com www.hublabels.com
Adhesive and pressure sensitive labels
CEO: Abbud S Dahbura
Sales/Marketing: Anton Dahbura
General Manager: Mary Dahbura
Estimated Sales: $10 Million
Number Employees: 100-249
Square Footage: 16000

23946 Hub Pen Company
230 Quincy Avenue
Quincy, MA 02169-6741 617-471-9900
Fax: 617-471-2990 www.hubpen.com
Manufacturer and exporter of felt tip markers, pens, pencils, etc
President: Helen Fleming
Quality Control: Howard Ernest
Sales Manager: Robert McGaughey
Estimated Sales: $10 - 20 Million
Number Employees: 65
Square Footage: 10000
Brands:
Hub Pen

23947 Hub-Federal Signs
135 Dean St
Providence, RI 02903-1603 401-421-9643
Fax: 401-351-2233 fedrosigns@juno.com
Manufacturer, designer and installer of electrical signs
President: Frank Benell Jr
VP: William Benell II
Estimated Sales: Below $5 Million
Number Employees: 6
Square Footage: 17000
Parent Co: Federal Sign Company

23948 Hubbell Electric HeaterCompany
45 Seymour Street
PO Box 288
Stratford, CT 06615-0288 203-378-2659
Fax: 203-378-3593 800-647-3165
info@hubbellheaters.com
www.hubbellheaters.com
Manufacturer and exporter of electric hot water booster heaters for sanitizing water
President: William E Newbauler
Head of Quality Control: Clifford Dineson
Sales Director: Sean Clarker
Estimated Sales: $5 - 10 Million
Number Employees: 30
Brands:
Hubbell

23949 Hubbell Lighting
701 Millenium Blvd
Greenville, SC 29607 540-382-6111
Fax: 540-382-1526 www.hubbelllighting.com
Manufacturer and exporter of industrial, commercial, emergency, exit, recessed and track lighting
President: Vincent Petrecca
VP: Scott Veil
VP Sales/Marketing: Richard Barrett
VP Sales: James O'Hargan
Number Employees: 500-999
Parent Co: Hubbell

23950 (HQ)Huber Technology
9735 Northcross Center Ct Ste A
Huntersville, NC 28078-7331 704-949-1010
Fax: 704-949-1020 huber@hhusa.net
www.huber-technology.com
Huber Technology offers different treatment systems to provide clean and healthy drinking water in order to meet the requirements of different surface water qualities and customer preferences. The systems process includes: coarsematerial separation; oxygenation; fine material separation: flocculation and sedimentation; filtration; oxidation and disinfection; absorption; network protection and water storage.
President: Forstner Gerhard
CEO: Mr. Dana Hicks III
Marketing: T.R. Gregg
Number Employees: 35
Square Footage: 96000
Parent Co: Hans Huber AG

23951 Huck Store Fixture Company
1100 N 28th St
Quincy, IL 62301-3447 217-222-0713
Fax: 217-222-0751 800-680-4823
huck@huck-fyc.com www.huckfixtures.com
Store fixtures
VP: Mark Flegel
Purchase: Cory Phipps Phipps
Sales and Marketing: Romhamann Hamann
Marketing Director: Christopher Peters
VP Production: Ron Hamann
Number Employees: 250-499
Square Footage: 1208000

23952 Hudson Belting & ServiceCompany
85 E Worcester St
Worcester, MA 01604-3649 508-756-0090
Fax: 508-753-6844
Manufacturer and wholesaler/distributor of food grade belting including leather, rubber, conveyor and timing; installation services available
President: Tom Jennette
Plant Manager: John Whitney
Estimated Sales: Below $5 Million
Number Employees: 5 to 9
Square Footage: 7500
Type of Packaging: Consumer, Food Service

23953 Hudson Control Group
10 Stern Ave
Springfield, NJ 07081-2905 973-376-7400
Fax: 973-376-8265 info@hudsoncontrol.com
www.hudsoncontrol.com
Manufacturer and exporter of custom designed and integrated robotic automation systems including case packers/unpackers; also, software
President: Phil Farrelly
CSO: Cliff Olson, Ph.D.
VP Sales/Marketing: Tom Gilman
Estimated Sales: $1 - 2.5 Million
Number Employees: 20-49
Square Footage: 6000
Brands:
Hudson's Total Control For Windows
Packit

23954 Hudson Poly Bag
578 Main St
Hudson, MA 01749 978-562-7566
Fax: 978-568-0797 800-229-7566
sales@hudsonpoly.com www.hudsonpoly.com
Plain and printed polyethylene and poly propylene bags and sheets, film and narrow width tubing.
President: William Renwick
CEO: Richard Renwick
Marketing/General Manager: Jim Chapman
Estimated Sales: $5 - 10 Million
Number Employees: 20-49
Square Footage: 17500
Type of Packaging: Consumer, Food Service, Private Label, Bulk

23955 Hudson-Sharp Machine Company
P.O.Box 13397
Green Bay, WI 54307-3397 920-494-4571
Fax: 920-496-1322 sales@hudsonsharp.com
www.hudsonsharp.com
Manufacturer and exporter of converting and pouch and plastic bag making equipment
President: Peter Hatchell
CFO: Gary Reinert
CEO: Rod Drummond
Research & Development: Danford Anderson
Marketing Director: Mark Smith
Sales Director: Paul Staab
Operations Manager: Scott Romenesko
Estimated Sales: $50-100 Million
Number Employees: 50-99

23956 Hueck Foils LLC
1955 State Route 34
Suite 2
Wall, NJ 07719-9703 732-974-4100
Fax: 732-974-4111 info@hueckfoils.com
www.hueckfoils.com
Hueck ia a foil converter supplying flexible packaging materials for the food and pharmecutical industries
Quality Control: Rosalyn White
Marketing: Angela Boggenhofer
Sales: Kevin Judd
Plant Manager: Manfred Rauer
Estimated Sales: $3 - 5 Million
Number Employees: 5-9
Parent Co: Hueck Folien

23957 Huettinger Electronic
4000 Burton Dr
Santa Clara, CA 95054-1509 408-454-1180
Fax: 408-454-1181 800-910-0035
info-us@huettinger.com www.huettinger.com
Induction cap sealing equipment and power supplies
President: Juergen Mertens
VP Sales: Paul Oranges
Estimated Sales: $3 - 5 000,000
Number Employees: 5-9

23958 Hughes Equipment Company LLC
1200 W James St
Columbus, WI 53925 920-623-2000
Fax: 920-623-4098 866-535-9303
hughes@hughesequipment.com
www.hughesequipment.com
Food processing equipment
President/CEO: Ross Lund
Sales Manager: Tracey Lange
Sales Manager: Ryan Metzdorf
Director of Engineering: Todd Belz
Plant Manager: Bill Wandersee
Estimated Sales: $10 - 20 Million
Brands:
Digisort
Hughes

23959 **Hughes Manufacturing Company**
2301 W Highway 290
Giddings, TX 78942 979-542-0333
Fax: 979-542-0335 800-414-0765
www.hughesmanufacturing.com
Manufacturer and exporter of nylon and plastic flags, pennants and banners
Manager: Lisa Marek
Operations Manager: Larry Conlee
Operations Manager: Larry Conlee
Estimated Sales: Below $5 Million
Number Employees: 10-19
Square Footage: 20000

23960 **Hughson Nut Company**
1825 Verduga Road
Hughson, CA 95326 209-883-0403
Fax: 209-883-2973 info@hughsonnut.com
www.hughsonnut.com
Almond nuts diced, sliced, slivered, milled, blanched and dry toasted
President: Martin Pohl
Estimated Sales: $2.5-5 Million
Number Employees: 10-19
Number of Brands: 1
Square Footage: 300000
Type of Packaging: Consumer, Private Label, Bulk

23961 **Huhtamaki Food Service Plastics**
100 N Field Drive
Suite 300
Lake Forest, IL 60045-2520 847-295-6100
Fax: 847-295-9862 800-244-6382

23962 **Huhtamaki, Inc.**
9201 Packaging Drive
De Soto, KS 66018 913-583-3025
Fax: 913-583-8756 800-255-4243
info.hq@fi.huhtamaki.com www.huhtamaki.com
President: Clay Dunn
Chief Executive Officer: Jukka Moisio
Estimated Sales: $50 - 100 Million
Number Employees: 3,300

23963 **Huls America**
220 Davidson Avenue
Somerset, NJ 08873-4149 732-980-6800
Fax: 732-980-6970
Wine industry enzymes
President: Joseph Fuhrman
CEO: Joseph Fuhrman
Marketing Manager: Tom Wickett
Number Employees: 1000

23964 **Hungerford & Terry**
226 Atlantic Ave
PO Box 650
Clayton, NJ 08312 856-881-3200
Fax: 856-881-6859 sales@hungerfordterry.com
www.hungerfordterry.com
Manufacturer and exporter of water treatment systems including filters, softeners, demineralizers and reverse osmosis
President: Allen Davis
Executive VP: Vernon Dawson
VP Sales: Kenneth Sayell
Estimated Sales: $10-20 Million
Number Employees: 50-99
Square Footage: 20000
Brands:
Ferrofilt
Ferrosand
H&T
Hungerford & Terry
Invercab

23965 **Hunt Midwest**
8300 NE Underground Drive
Kansas City, MO 64161 816-455-2500
Fax: 816-455-2890
mediacontact@huntmidwest.com
www.huntmidwest.com
President: Ora Reynolds
Chairman of the Board: Jim Holland
Vice President and CFO: Don Hagan
Assistant General Manager of Sales: Dick Ringer
Number Employees: 50-99

23966 **Hunter Fan Company**
7130 Goodlett Frm Pkwy Ste 400
Cordova, TN 38016 901-743-1360
Fax: 901-248-2258 techsupport@hunterfan.com
www.hunterfan.com
Ceiling fans, programmable thermostats, air purifiers and humidifiers
President: Robert Beasley
Director Sales/Special Markets: Rick Neuman
VP Sales: Brennon Byrney
Estimated Sales: $50-100 Million
Number Employees: 250-499

23967 **Hunter Graphics**
140 N Orlando Avenue
Suite 140
Umatilla, FL 32784 407-644-2060
Fax: 407-644-0957
huntergraphics@sprintmail.com
www.huntergraphics.com
Consultant specializing in the design of packaging and labels; support services available
President: Brian Hunter
Estimated Sales: Below $500,000
Number Employees: 1
Square Footage: 14000
Parent Co: Optimal Graphics

23968 **Hunter Packaging Corporation**
865 Commerce Drive
South Elgin, IL 60177-2633 847-741-4747
Fax: 847-741-1100 800-428-4747
infodesk@hunterpackaging.com
Corrugated boxes and displays
Vice President: Tom Pabelick
Office Manager: Susan Brown
Estimated Sales: $3-5 Million
Number Employees: 31
Square Footage: 70000

23969 **Hunter Woodworks**
21038 S Wilmington Ave
Carson, CA 90810 310-835-5671
Fax: 323-775-2540 800-966-4751
bruce@hunterpallets.com
www.hunterpallets.com
Wooden pallets, boxes and crates
General Manager: Bruce Benton
CEO: Bill Hunter
Sales Manager: Frank Gower
General Manager: Bruce Benton
Number Employees: 100-249
Square Footage: 500000

23970 **Hunterlab**
11491 Sunset Hills Rd
Reston, VA 20190-5264 703-471-1920
Fax: 703-471-4237 sales@hunterlab.com
www.hunterlab.com
Manufacturer and exporter of color measurement systems
President: Philip Hunter
CFO: Teresa Demangos
R & D: Jim Freal
Quality Control: Ambur Daley
Estimated Sales: $10-20 Million
Number Employees: 100-249
Square Footage: 70000
Brands:
Colortrend Ht

23971 **Huntington Foam Corporation**
101 N. 4th Street
Jeannette, PA 15644 724-522-5144
Fax: 814-265-8627 www.huntingtonfoam.com
Construction and packaging foam
President: Gary B. McLaughlin
CFO: Tom Kuehl
Director of Sales & Enginnering: Ed Flynn
Director of Operations: Benjamin Raygoza
Estimated Sales: $5-10 000,000
Number Employees: 20-49

23972 **Huntington Park Rubber Stamp Company**
2761 E Slauson Ave
PO Box 519
Huntington Park, CA 90255 323-582-6461
Fax: 323-582-8046 800-882-0029
hprubberstamp@pacbell.net
www.hprubberstamp.com
Marking devices including rubber stamps
President: Marry Barlam
Sales Manager: Robert Barlam
Estimated Sales: $1 - 2.5 Million
Number Employees: 10-19
Square Footage: 6250

23973 **Huntsman Packaging**
PO Box 97
South Deerfield, MA 01373-0097 413-665-2145
Fax: 413-665-4854 www.pliantcorp.com
Manufacturer and exporter of co-extruded polyethylene packaging film
VP Finance: Peter Dube
Chairman: Charles Barker
Plant Manager: Clark Sylvester
Estimated Sales: $50-100 Million
Number Employees: 100-249
Square Footage: 100000
Brands:
Strata

23974 **Huntsman Packaging Corporation**
PO Box 11085
Birmingham, Bi 35202-1085 205-328-4720
Fax: 205-322-2505
Plastic film
President: John Huntsman
President/CEO: John Huntsman
Controller: John Clark
Production Manager: Pete Lenzer
Plant Manager: Larry Bearden

23975 **Hurlingham Company**
1158 W 11th Street
Apt F
San Pedro, CA 90731-3479 310-538-0236
Fax: 310-538-4436 michelead@earthlink.net
Store fixtures
President: Eusebio Espejo
VP Sales: Michele Duston
Estimated Sales: Below $5,000,000
Number Employees: 30
Square Footage: 25000

23976 **Hurri-Kleen Corporation**
6000 Southern Industrial Dr
Birmingham, AL 35235 205-655-8808
Fax: 205-655-5392 800-455-8265
dgillespie@hurrikleencorp.com
Manufacturer and dirtributor of intermediate bulk containers and related parts and accessories
Estimated Sales: $1-5,000,000
Number Employees: 1-4
Square Footage: 100000
Brands:
Hurri-Kleen

23977 **Hurst Corporation**
PO Box 737
Devon, PA 19333 610-687-2404
Fax: 610-687-7860 sales@hurstcorp.com
www.hurstcorp.com
De-labeling machinery
Owner: Richard Hurst
Estimated Sales: $5-10 Million
Number Employees: 20-49

23978 **Hurst Labeling Systems**
20747 Dearborn St
PO Box 5169
Chatsworth, CA 91311 818-701-0710
Fax: 818-701-8747 800-969-1705
info@hurstinternational.net
www.hurstinternational.net
Manufacturer and exporter of pressure sensitive labels and label application equipment
President: Aron Lichtenberg
CFO: Rita Rebera
Quality Control: Rick Aranbul
Sales Representative: Melody Nichols
Sales Representative: Chaylon Holland
Estimated Sales: $3 - 5 Million
Number Employees: 10-19
Square Footage: 13000

23979 **Hurt Conveyor EquipmentCompany**
6615 8th Ave
Los Angeles, CA 90043-4353 323-541-0433
Fax: 323-541-0442 hurt@pcmagic.net
Belt and chain conveyors
President: Ramesh Soni
VP: Saroj Soni
Number Employees: 7
Type of Packaging: Private Label

23980 (HQ)Huskey Specialty Lubricants
1580 Industrial Ave
Norco, CA 92860-2946 951-340-4000
Fax: 951-340-4011 888-448-7539
mmontgomery@huskey.com www.huskey.com
Manufacturer and exporter of food grade grease and lubricating oils for food processing machinery
President: Sheldy Huskey
R&D: Jim Landry
Vice President: Mike Montgomery
Research & Development: Hugh Woodworth
Foreign Sales Manager: Denis Alonso
Plant Manager: Chris Kimball
Purchasing Manager: Cathy Merlo
Estimated Sales: $10 - 20 Million
Number Employees: 30
Square Footage: 60000
Type of Packaging: Private Label, Bulk
Other Locations:
Huskey Specialty Lubricants
Twinsburg OH
Brands:
Huskey

23981 Hussmann International
12999 Saint Charles Rock Road
Bridgeton, MO 63044-2483 314-291-2000
Fax: 314-298-4756 info@hussman.com
www.hussmann.com
Commercial and display refrigerators and coolers
President: John Gialouris
VP Finance/Corporate Controller: T G Korte
Vice President: G E Swimmer
Chief Marketing Officer: Shelley Minardo
Director of Sales: Rod Widman
Plant Manager: Greg Whitton
Estimated Sales: $1 Billion
Number Employees: 9,100
Brands:
Impact
Protocol

23982 Hutchison-Hayes International
P.O.Box 2965
Houston, TX 77252-2965 713-455-9600
Fax: 713-455-7753 800-984-3397
sales@hutch-hayes.com www.hutchhayes.com
Centrifuges
Owner: Richard Parks
Quality Control and R&D: Lee Hilpert
Chairman: John Joplin
Estimated Sales: $10 - 20 Million
Number Employees: 50-99

23983 Huther Brothers
1290 University Avenue
Rochester, NY 14607-1674 585-473-9462
Fax: 585-473-9476 800-334-1115
ghuther1@rochester.r..com
Manufacturer and exporter of industrial food processing cutting blades and circular, straight and specialty knives
President: George W Huther Iii III
CFO: James Aldridge
Bookkeeper: Margie Campaigne
Foreman: Eric Nash
Estimated Sales: $3 - 5 Million
Number Employees: 10-19
Square Footage: 19000

23984 Hutz Sign & Awning
2415 Hubbard Rd
Youngstown, OH 44505 330-743-5168
Fax: 330-743-2319 hutzsigns@worldnet.att.net
Advertising signs
President: Tom Kling
VP: David Hutz
Estimated Sales: $3 - 5 Million
Number Employees: 10-19

23985 Hy-Ko Enviro-MaintenanceProducts
PO Box 26116
Salt Lake City, UT 84126-0116 801-973-6099
Fax: 801-973-9746 sales@hyko.com
www.hyko.com
Cleaners including hand, dairy, glass, household and industrial, pipe, toilet bowl and window; also, washing compounds, disinfectants and floor polishes
President: Ron Starr
CFO: Ron C Starr Sr
Sales Manager: John Hille
Estimated Sales: $10 - 20 Million
Number Employees: 20-49

23986 Hy-Ten Plastics
38 Powers St
Milford, NH 03055 603-673-1611
Fax: 603-673-0970 sales@hy-ten.com
www.hy-ten.com
Designer of custom injection molded products
Chairman: Udo Fritsch
Sales/Engineer: Peter Fritsch
VP Operations: Mike McGown
Estimated Sales: $10-20 Million
Number Employees: 50-99
Square Footage: 30000

23987 Hy-Trous/Flash Sales
3R-T Green Street
Woburn, MA 01801 781-933-5772
Hand soaps and cleaning compounds
Estimated Sales: $1 - 5 Million
Number Employees: 5
Square Footage: 15000
Parent Co: Hy-Trous Corporation
Brands:
Flash
Hy-Trous Plant Foods
Skat

23988 Hyatt Industries Limited
1572 West 4th Avenue
Vancouver, BC V6J 1L7
Canada 604-736-7301
Fax: 604-736-7305 800-482-7446
sales@hyatt-ind.com www.hyatt-ind.com
President: Lindsay Lawrence
Number Employees: 10

23989 Hybrinetics
225 Sutton Pl
Santa Rosa, CA 95407 707-585-0333
Fax: 707-585-7313 800-247-6900
hybrinet@voltagevalet.com
www.voltagevalet.com
Manufacturer and exporter of dimmer controls for incandescent and fluorescent lighting
President: Rick Rosa
Estimated Sales: $20 - 50 Million
Number Employees: 100-249
Brands:
Aladdin Products
Star Controls

23990 Hycor Corporation
562 E Bunker Court
Vernon Hills, IL 60061-1831 847-473-3700
Fax: 847-473-0477 technology@parkson.com
www.parkson.com
Wine industry wastewater treatment
President: Zain Mahmood
CEO: Zain Mahmood
Estimated Sales: $10-25 Million
Number Employees: 250-499

23991 Hyder North America
270 Granite Run Dr
Lancaster, PA 17601-6804 717-569-7021
Fax: 717-560-0577 info@thearrogroup.com
www.thearrogroup.com
Water and wastewater treatment, total outsourcing solutions
President: G Matthew Brown
CFO: Susan L Long
Estimated Sales: $10 - 20 Million
Number Employees: 50-99

23992 Hydra-Flex
32975 Industrial Rd
Livonia, MI 48150 734-522-9090
Fax: 734-522-9579 800-234-0832
customerservice@hydra-flex.com
www.hydra-flex.com
Manufacturer and wholesaler/distributor of hoses, valves, fittings, tubing, etc
President: Charley Blank
R&D: Jim Poole
VP: Bill Berlin
Sales Manager: Bill Berlin
Warehouse Manager: Jason Pinard
Estimated Sales: $10 - 20 Million
Number Employees: 10-19

23993 Hydrel Corporation
12881 Bradley Ave
Sylmar, CA 91342-3828 818-362-9465
Fax: 818-362-6548 www.hydrel.com
Manufacturer and exporter of outdoor lighting fixtures including flood, ingrade and underwater; also, custom environment fixtures
President: Craig Jennings
VP: Dwight Hochstein
VP: Mark Blackford
CFO: John Gay
VP Marketing: Hal Madsen
Sales Manager: Dan Roth
Estimated Sales: $20 - 50 Million
Number Employees: 100-249
Parent Co: GTY Industries
Brands:
9000 Series
Hypak
Sunlite

23994 Hydrite Chemical Co
300 N Patrick Blvd
Brookfield, WI 53045-5831 262-792-1450
Fax: 414-792-8721 800-543-4560
milwaukee.orders@hydrite.com.
www.hydrite.com
Sodium hypochlorite, sulfur dioxide, bisulfite aqua ammonia and food processing cleaners
CEO: John Honkamp
Sales Manager: Richtar Michael
Number Employees: 1,000-4,999

23995 Hydrite Chemical Company
300 N Patrick Blvd
Brookfield, WI 53045 262-792-1450
Fax: 414-792-8721 sales@hydrite.com
www.hydrite.com
Manufacturer and wholesaler/distributor of industrial cleaning, sanitaring ingredients and water treatment chemicals
CEO: John Honkamp
Sales Director: Rob Adams
Sales Director (Special Chemicals): Rich Carmichael
Purchasing Manager: Chuck Krior
Number Employees: 1,000-4,999

23996 Hydro Life
503 Maple St
Bristol, IN 46507 574-848-1661
Fax: 574-848-1400 800-626-7130
sales@hydrolife.com www.hydrolife.com
President: La Von Troyer
Sales: Roger Egli
Estimated Sales: $1 - 3 Million
Number Employees: 5-9

23997 Hydro Power
3601 N Fruitridge Ave
Terre Haute, IN 47804-1756 812-232-0156
Fax: 812-232-8068 hydrpwr@aol.com
www.otpnet.com
Manufacturer and exporter of overhead bridge cranes, wire rope winches, conveyors and reciprocating feeders
Manager: Walt Tompkins
CEO/Engineer: Steve White
CFO: Jim Bennett
Vice President: Joe Goda
Marketing Director: Dave Parks
Sales Director: Tom Bland
Public Relations: Tom Bland
Plant Manager: Steve Rowe
Purchasing Manager: Jerry Taylor
Estimated Sales: $16.5 Million
Number Employees: 10-19
Square Footage: 20000

23998 Hydro Seal Coatings Company
12151 Madera Way
Riverside, CA 92503-4849 760-723-8992
Fax: 760-723-7206 www.hydrosealpolymers.com
Wine industry coatings
Vice President of Technology: Sergio Franyutti

23999 Hydro-Miser
906 Boardwalk # B
San Marcos, CA 92069-4071 442-744-5083
Fax: 442-744-5031 800-736-5083
info@hydromiser.com www.hydromiser.com
Manufacturer and exporter of portable and thermal storage chillers and cooling towers and systems; also, food processing equipment and supplies
President/CEO: Kimberly Howard
Estimated Sales: $1-2.5 Million
Number Employees: 1-4
Parent Co: Applied Thermal Technologies

Brands:
Copeland
Gould

24000 Hydro-Tech EnvironmentalSystems
410 Petaluma Blvd S # A
Petaluma, CA 94952-4278 707-769-9247
Fax: 707-769-9140 800-559-3102
info@htes.com www.htes.com
Wastewater treatment, bad reduction, product recovery, product concentration
Manager: Susan Stone
CFO and CTO: Aron Lavner
Estimated Sales: $.5 - 1 million
Number Employees: 5-9
Square Footage: 6800

24001 Hydro-Thermal
400 Pilot Ct
Waukesha, WI 53188 262-548-8900
Fax: 262-548-8908 800-952-0121
info@hydro-thermal.com
www.hydro-thermal.com
Direct contact steam injection heaters and heat exchangers for liquids and slurries for both industrial and 3A applications
President: Gary Zaiser
VP: John Warne
Marketing: Kristie Anderson
Estimated Sales: $5-10 Million
Number Employees: 20-49
Brands:
Hydrohelix
Hydroheater

24002 HydroCal
23011 Moulton Parkway
ÿSuite G5
Laguna Hills, CA 92653-1263 949-455-0765
Fax: 949-455-0764 800-877-0765
ollieb@hydrocal.com www.hydrocal.com
President: Donald Meylor
Estimated Sales: $1,000,000 - $3,000,000
Number Employees: 5-9

24003 HydroCal
22732 Granite Way Ste A
Laguna Hills, CA 92653 949-455-0765
Fax: 949-455-0764 800-877-0765
don@hydrocal.com www.hydrocal.com
Wastewater treatment equipment
President: Donald Meylor
VP: Oilie Breen
Director Marketing/Operationss: Jorge Funez
Sales: Ollie Breen
Sales: Donald Meylor
Estimated Sales: $500,000-$1 000,000
Number Employees: 5-9
Number of Products: 8

24004 HydroMax
P.O.Box 1207
Emmitsburg, MD 21727 301-447-3800
Fax: 301-668-3700 800-326-0602
info@hydromax.net www.hydromax.net
Manufacturer and exporter of water filtration and purification equipment including reverse osmosis, ultraviolet, ozone and filtration technologies
President: Frederick N Reidenbach
Estimated Sales: $1-2.5 Million
Number Employees: 20-49

24005 Hydropure Water Treatment Company
5727 NW 46th Dr
Coral Springs, FL 33067 954-971-7593
Fax: 954-971-0801 800-753-1547
Exporter of rotary vane pumps and water filtration, purification and reverse osmosis systems.
President: Vittorio Sordi
VP: Susan Shasser
Estimated Sales: $1.6 Million
Number Employees: 10-19
Number of Brands: 4
Number of Products: 78
Type of Packaging: Consumer, Food Service
Brands:
Carbonetor Pumps
Hydropure Pumps

24006 Hygenic Fabrics & Filters
118 South Broad Street
P.O.Box 34
Lanark, IL 61046-0034 815-493-2502
Fax: 815-493-1098 sales@hyfab.com
www.hyfab.com
Cheese equipment, firesavers, bandages, fillers, milk
Manager: Shirley Gothard Jr
Vice President: Thomas Laiken
Production Supervisor: Kelly Leicht
Plant Manager: Shirley Gothard
Estimated Sales: $1,981,533
Number Employees: 5-9

24007 Hygiene-Technik
4743 Christie Drive
Beamsville, ON L0R 1B4
Canada 905-563-4987
Fax: 905-563-6266 info@gotoHTI.com
www.gotoHTI.com
Specializing in the design, development and manufacturing of proprietary dispensing systems.
President: Heiner Ophardt
VP/General Manager: Tony Kortleve-Snider
Business Development Manager: Marina Nava
Number Employees: 50
Square Footage: 180000
Brands:
Ingo-Man
Ingo-Top

24008 Hygrade Gloves
30 Warsoff Pl
Brooklyn, NY 11205 718-488-9000
Fax: 718-694-9500 800-233-8100
hygrade@mindspring.com
www.hygradesafety.com
Manufacturer, importer and exporter of protective and disposable clothing including gloves, aprons, goggles, hair nets, uniforms, boots and dust masks
President: Lazar Follman
Estimated Sales: $1 - 5 Million
Number Employees: 20-49
Square Footage: 440000
Parent Co: LDF Industries
Brands:
American Optical
Comfiwear

24009 Hypro Corporation
375 5th Ave NW
New Brighton, MN 55112 651-766-6300
Fax: 651-766-6600 800-424-9776
mattc@hypropumps.com www.hypropumps.com
Wine industry pumps, fluid handling products for the agricultural, pressure cleaning, fire services, industrial, semiconductor equipment and marine markets
President: Donald Jorgensen
CFO: Steve Dickhaus
CEO: Paul Meschke
R&D: Bruce Maki
Executive Assistant: Myrna Press
Estimated Sales: $75 - 100 Million
Number Employees: 100-249

24010 Hyster Company
7227 Carroll Rd
San Diego, CA 92121 858-566-4181
Fax: 858-578-6165 800-437-8371
www.hyster.com
CFO: Kevin Kelley
Vice President/GM: David Ohm
General Sales Manager: Bob Pilon
Manager: Scott Stearne
General manager: Steve Smith
Number Employees: 10-19
Parent Co: Hyster-Yale Materials Handling

24011 Hyster Company
7227 Carroll Rd
San Diego, CA 92121 855-804-2118
Fax: 858-578-6165 www.johnson-lift.com
Manufacturer and exporter of automatic storage and handling systems and industrial trucks; also, service and rental available
Manager: Scott Stearne
Service Manager: Steve Lacroix
Estimated Sales: $5-10 Million
Number Employees: 10-19
Parent Co: Johnson Machinery
Brands:
Hyster

24012 Hytrol Conveyor Company
2020 Hytrol St
Jonesboro, AR 72401 870-935-3700
Fax: 800-852-3233 info@hytrol.com
www.hytrol.com
President: Gregg Goodner
VP of Business Operations: Bob West
VP of Manufactoring Operations: Don Wilson
Estimated Sales: $80 Million
Number Employees: 500-999

24013 I. Fm Usa Inc.
9490 Franklin Ave
Franklin Park, IL 60131 847-288-9500
Fax: 847-288-9501 866-643-6872
info@ifmusa.com www.sirman.com
Slicers, panini grills, meat & food processors and bar equipment.

24014 I.C. Technologies
613 W Manlius St
East Syracuse, NY 13057 315-423-5051
Fax: 315-423-0086 800-554-2832
sra@blistertech.com www.blistertech.com
Estimated Sales: $1,000,000 - $5,000,000

24015 I.H. McBride Sign Company
PO Box 622
Lynchburg, VA 24505 434-847-4151
Fax: 434-845-6980 info@mcbridesigns.com
www.mcbridesigns.com
Signs including advertising, changeable letter, electric, interchangeable, luminous tube, plastic and point of purchase; also, installation and service available
Owner: Tony Mc Bride
General Manager: Lawrence Bryant
Vice President: Tony McBride
Estimated Sales: $1.25 Million
Number Employees: 10-19
Square Footage: 89000
Type of Packaging: Private Label

24016 I.J. White Corporation
20 Executive Blvd
Farmingdale, NY 11735 631-293-2211
Fax: 631-293-3788 sales@ijwhite.com
www.ijwhite.com
Spiral conveyors and belts
President: Peter J. White
CFO: Lou Goldman
Estimated Sales: $5-10 Million
Number Employees: 50-99
Square Footage: 42
Brands:
Blast Freezers
Multi-Path Systems
Pure-Air
Spiraland Conveyor Systems
Thremal-Pak
Veras-Pak

24017 I.W. Tremont Company
79 4th Ave
Hawthorne, NJ 07506 973-427-3800
Fax: 973-427-3778 www.iwtremont.com
Manufacturer and exporter of filter media including inspection, analysis, sampling and testing systems
President: Sal Averso
CFO: Andrew Averso
Production Manager: Andrew Averso
Production Manager: James Averso
Estimated Sales: $20 - 50 Million
Number Employees: 10-19
Square Footage: 10000

24018 IABM Bakery Systems
48 Prospect Park SW
Brooklyn, NY 11215 718-499-6200
Fax: 718-499-8040
iabmbakerysystems@compuserve.com
Vice President: Alvin Mintz
Estimated Sales: $3 - 5 Million
Number Employees: 5-9

24019 IABN Bakery Systems
48 Prospect Park SW
Brooklyn, NY 11215-5915 718-499-6200
Fax: 718-499-8040
Suppliers of bakery equipment
President: Leann Angel
Estimated Sales: $1-2.5 000,000
Number Employees: 1-4

24020 **IAFIS Dairy Products Evaluation Contest**
1451 Dolley Madison Boulevard Suite 10
Mc Lean, VA 22101-3847 703-761-2600
Fax: 703-761-4334 info@iafis.org
www.fpsa.org
President, Chief Executive Officer: David Seckman
Vice President of Development: Andy Drennan
Director of Sales: Grace Yee
Number Employees: 20-49

24021 **IAS Corporation**
17 Research Drive
Hampton, VA 23666 757-766-7520
Fax: 757-766-7505 800-916-4272
sales@iascorp.net www.iascorp.net
Manufacturer and exporter of analog chart recorder
Owner: Kathy Burton
Marketing Supervisor: Don Crawford
Estimated Sales: $1-2.5 Million
Number Employees: 10-19
Brands:
Pricorder

24022 **IASE Company**
161 Industrial Pkwy
Branchburg, NJ 08876 908-218-1104
Fax: 908-218-1337 info@iase.net
www.iase.net
Robotic packaging equipment
President: Michael Degidio
Estimated Sales: $2.5-5 Million
Number Employees: 20-49

24023 **IB Concepts**
657 Dowd Avenue
Elizabeth, NJ 07201-2116 215-739-9960
Fax: 215-739-9963 888-671-0800
celwaconcepts@att.net www.celwa.com
Manufacturer and exporter of printed, embossed and molded crepe wadding inserts and liners; also, absorbent cellulose doilies, pulpboard coasters, die cut polyester discs, and die cut foam
General Manager: Robert Pettus
Operations Manager: Michael Hersh
Number Employees: 25
Square Footage: 80000

24024 **IBA**
P.O.Box 37
Florham Park, NJ 07932-0037 973-660-9334
Fax: 908-647-6560 pastoretec@aol.com
www.iba.be
Estimated Sales: $1 - 5 Million
Number Employees: 1-4

24025 **IBA Food Safety**
6000 Poplar Avenue
Suite 426
Memphis, TN 38119-3981 901-681-9006
Fax: 901-681-9007 800-777-9012
cphillips@iba-group.com
Sterilization, gamma irradiation, electron beam radiation and microorganism reduction systems; materials processing services and installation available
President: Rick Doscher
VP Perishable Foods: Chip Colonna
Number Employees: 1300
Parent Co: IBA Chemin Du Cyclotron
Brands:
Sterigenics

24026 **IBC ""Creative Packaging**
2249 Davis Ct
Hayward, CA 94545 510-785-6500
Fax: 510-785-6349 info@industrialboxboard.com
www.ibccreativepackaging.com
Wooden crates and containers including corrugated, foam, urethane and styrofoam
President: John T Hunter
General Manager: J Hunter
Estimated Sales: $5-10 Million
Number Employees: 10-19
Square Footage: 95000

24027 **IBC/Shell Containers**
1981 Marcus Ave
New Hyde Park, NY 11042-1038 516-352-4505
Fax: 516-352-3084 info@ibcshell.com
www.shellcontainers.com
Custom packaging, display boxes and point of purchase displays for specialty foods
Chief Executive Officer, Chief Creative: Norman Kay
Sr VP: Phillip Schoonmaker
VP Sales: Michael Morano
Estimated Sales: $20-50 Million
Number Employees: 250-499
Parent Co: Shell Group

24028 **ICI Surfactants**
Strawinskylaan 2555
Amsterdam, ZZ 1077 302-762-0555
Fax: 302-762-4750 800-424-3696
www.ici.com
Food surfactants for bakery, edible oil, dairy, confectionery, and miscellaneous food processors
Manager: Amber Prichett
CFO: Alan Brown
Technical Manager: Wei Shi
Estimated Sales: $.5 - 1 million
Number Employees: 1-4

24029 **ICM Controls**
6333 Daedalus Road
Cicero, NY 13039-8889 315-233-5266
Fax: 315-233-5276 800-411-4270
dhamilton@icmcontrols.com
www.icmcontrols.com
HVAC controls
President: Ronald Kadah
CFO: Lauri Kadah
Estimated Sales: $100-500 Million
Number Employees: 10

24030 **ICOA Corporation**
111 Airport Rd
Warwick, RI 02889 401-648-0690
Fax: 401-648-0699 888-408-0600
sales@icoacorp.com www.icoacorp.com
Wireless internet services (design, deployment management)
Chairman/CEO: George Strouthopoulos
Director/CFO: Erwin Vahlsing
Sales Director: Joe Farrugla
Operations Manager: Chris Browne
Estimated Sales: $4 Million
Number Employees: 20-49
Number of Brands: 7
Brands:
Airport Network Solutions
Authdirect
Cafe.Com
Linkspot
Toll Booth
Webcenter
Wisezone
Idockusa

24031 **ID Images**
2991 Interstate Pkwy
Brunswick, OH 44212 330-220-7300
Fax: 330-220-3838 866-516-7300
customerservice@idimages.com
www.idimages.com
Baggers and printers
Marketing Director: Lisa Stang
Estimated Sales: $500,000-$1,000,000
Number Employees: 5
Brands:
Pack Star
Park Star Plus
Versa Color

24032 **ID Technology**
2051 Franklin Dr
Fort Worth, TX 76106 817-626-7779
Fax: 817-626-0553 888-438-3242
marketing@idtechnology.com
www.idtechnology.com
Labeling, coding and marking equipment
President: Robert Zuilhof
CEO/CFO: Tina Millwood
VP: Alan Shipman
R&D: Mark Snedecor
Marketing: Hillary Taylor
Sales: Alan Shipman
Public Relations: Hillary Taylor
Plant Manager: Kim Pulliam
Purchasing: Kim Pulliam
Estimated Sales: $50 Million
Number Employees: 100
Parent Co: Pro Mach Inc

24033 **ID Technology**
2051 Franklin Dr
Fort Worth, TX 76106 817-626-7779
Fax: 817-626-0553 888-438-3242
marketing@idtechnology.com
www.idtechnology.com
Labels, label printer/applicators, label applicators, laser marketing, inkjet coding, thermal transfer overprinting
CFO: Tina Millwood
VP: Alan Shipman
Marketing: Hilary Taylor
Estimated Sales: $75 Million
Number Employees: 120
Other Locations:
Pewaukee WI
Fresno CA

24034 **IDC Food Division**
1879 Capital Cir NE
Tallahassee, FL 32308-4598 850-656-5600
Fax: 850-656-3032 800-831-6340
info@idcfcp.com
Estimated Sales: $1 - 5 Million

24035 **IDESCO Corporation**
37 W 26th St
New York, NY 10010 212-889-2530
Fax: 212-889-7033 800-336-1383
info@idesco.com www.idesco.com
Manufacturer and exporter of integrated security systems
President: Andrew Schonzeit
CFO: Ray O' Connor
Vice President of Strategic Sales: Andrew Goldstone
VP Sales: Andy Goldstone
Operations Manager: Brian Simpson
Estimated Sales: $10-20 Million
Number Employees: 20-49
Square Footage: 10000
Brands:
Vita

24036 **IDEX Corporation**
1925 West Field Court
Suite 200
Lake Forest, IL 60045-4824 847-498-7070
Fax: 724-387-1774 800-843-8210
hmitts@idexcorp.com www.idexcorp.com
Chairman and Chief Executive Officer: Andrew Silvernail
Senior Vice President-Chief Financial Of: Heath Mitts
Vice President, Tax and International Fi: Gerald Carter
Senior Vice President, Fluid & Metering: Brett Finley
Senior Vice President-Health, Science &: Eric Ashleman
Senior Vice President-Chief Human Resour: Jeffrey Bucklew
COO: James W Patterson
Estimated Sales: 2,024,130
Number Employees: 6,787

24037 **IDL**
4250 Old William Penn Hwy
Monroeville, PA 15146-1626 724-733-2234
Fax: 724-327-6420 dball@idlpop.com
www.idlpop.com
Advertising decals including pressure sensitive and reflective
Sales Manager: Jim Krentz
Estimated Sales: $20-50 Million
Number Employees: 100-249

24038 **IEW**
49 W Federal Street
Niles, OH 44446 330-652-0113
Manufacturer and exporter of industrial electronic weighing devices and scales for mobile material handling equipment
Estimated Sales: $1 - 5 Million
Brands:
Criterion
Sos

24039 **IFC Disposables**
P.O.Box 469
Brownsville, TN 38012-0469 731-779-0959
Fax: 731-772-2282 800-432-9473
info@cascades.com www.ifcdisposables.com

Nonwoven wiping towels and tissue products
President and CFO: Robert E Briggs
Marketing: Laura Brooks
Purchasing Agent: Sherry Elliot
Estimated Sales: $10 - 20 Million
Number Employees: 50-99
Parent Co: Wyant Corporation
Brands:
Busboy
Dusterz

24040 IFP
2125 Airport Dr
Faribault, MN 55021-7798
Fax: 507-334-7969 800-997-4437
sales@ifpinc.biz www.ifp-inc.com
Custom manufacturing services including agglomeration, encapsulation, and packaging for food and beverage powders
Marketing Director: Anna Batsakes
Sales Director: Scott Sijan
Estimated Sales: $23.4 Million
Number Employees: 180

24041 IFS North America
5451 E Williams Blvd Ste 181
Tucson, AZ 85711 520-512-2000
Fax: 520-512-2001 info@ifsna.com
www.ifsna.com
President: Theresa Sheridan
CFO: Mitch Dwight
R&D: William Grant
Estimated Sales: $20 - 50 Million
Number Employees: 100-249

24042 IGEN
16020 Industrial Dr
Gaithersburg, MD 20877 301-208-3784
Fax: 301-947-6990
Laboratory testing equipment and kits; safety equipment

24043 IGEN International
16020 Industrial Dr
Gaithersburg, MD 20877-1414 301-208-3784
Fax: 301-947-6990 800-336-4436
m-series@igen.com www.igeninternational.com
Provides biotechnical services to the food and beverage industry
President: Samuel Wohlstadter
Number Employees: 100-249

24044 IGS Store Fixtures
58 Pulaski St
Peabody, MA 01960-1800 978-532-0010
Fax: 617-569-0201 www.igsfixtures.com
Store fixtures and counters
CFO: Harvey Gordon
Estimated Sales: $10-20 Million
Number Employees: 100-249
Square Footage: 48000
Brands:
Jahbo Showcases
Lozier

24045 IHS Heath Information
15 Inverness Way E
Englewood, CO 80112-5710 800-716-3447
Fax: 800-716-6447 800-525-5539
info@ihs.com www.ihsparts.com
Meat industry services (computer systems and software, importing-exporting, publications and information, nutrition labeling, quality control instruments, sanitation programs); seasonings and ingredients; meat products

24046 IJ White Corporation
20 Executive Blvd
Farmingdale, NY 11735 631-293-2211
Fax: 631-293-3788 info@ijwhite.com
www.ijwhite.com
Spiral systems for both the food processing and bakery industries: blast freezing, refrigerated cooling, proofing, elevating, accumulating, drying, and pasteurizing
President: Peter J. White
Estimated Sales: $5-10 Million
Number Employees: 50-99

24047 IKA Works
2635 Northchase Pkwy SE
Wilmington, NC 28405 910-452-7059
Fax: 910-452-7693 800-733-3037
process@ikausa.com www.ikausa.com
Laboratory, pilot plant and processing equipment including particle size reducers, dispersers and homogenizers; also, continuous and vertical kneaders, overhead stirring motors and magnetic stirrers; sanitary design servicesavailable
Vice President: Robert Hardin
Sales Director: Davis Thompson
Number Employees: 50-99
Square Footage: 30000
Parent Co: IKA Werke
Brands:
Conterna
Dispax Reactor
Eurostar
Ikamag
Planetron
Ultra-Turrax

24048 IKG Industries
1801 Forrest Park Dr
Garrett, IN 46738 260-357-0005
Fax: 615-254-4363 800-467-2345
salesikg@harsco.com www.ikgindustries.com
Manufacturer and exporter of fiberglass grating used for flooring in food processing plants
Marketing Manager: Tom Toler
VP Sales/Marketing: Ray Palombi
Estimated Sales: $1 - 5 Million

24049 ILC Dover
1 Moonwalker Rd
Frederica, DE 19946-2080 302-335-3911
Fax: 302-335-0762 800-631-9567
customer_service@ilcdover.com
www.ilcdover.com
Frozen keg jackets
Data Processing: Arthur Hunt
Estimated Sales: $100-500 Million
Number Employees: 250-499
Square Footage: 225000
Brands:
Keg Wrap

24050 IMA North America
7 New Lancaster Rd
Leominster, MA 01453-5224
Fax: 215-826-0400 toddima@aol.com
www.ima.it
Bag formers/fillers/sealers, carton machines (folding, lining, filling, closing), pouch machines, shrink wrap machine, teabag machinery, wrapping machines, blister machines
President: Warren Roman
CEO: Krouchiek
CFO: Jerry Krouchick
Estimated Sales: $20 - 50 Million
Number Employees: 50-99
Parent Co: IMA North America

24051 IMAS Corporation
2905 Brittany Court
St. Charles, IL 60175 630-584-7011
847-274-9383
sphelps@IMASLtd.com www.xspec.com
Software for specification management; also, information management consulting available
Vice President: Steven Meier
Estimated Sales: $2.5-5 Million
Number Employees: 20-49
Brands:
Winspex
Xspec

24052 IMC Instruments
N60w 14434 Kaul Avenue
Menomonee Falls, WI 53051 262-252-4620
Fax: 262-252-4623 sales@imcinstruments.com
www.imcinstruments.com
Instrumentation for temperature, pressure, humidity, vacuum and air flow measurement
President: Louis Frias
VP: Ronald Frias
Estimated Sales: $2.5-5 Million
Number Employees: 10
Square Footage: 32000

24053 IMC Teddy Food Service Equipment
50 Ranick Drive East
PO Box 338
Amityville, NY 11701
Fax: 631-789-3633 800-221-5644
imcteddy@aol.com www.imcteddy.com
Stainless steel shelving, floor troughs and gratings, sinks, can washers, counter tops, floor drains, tables and cabinets
Partner and President: Asit Majundar
Marketing Manager: Suzane Girrsoli
General Sales Manager: Joe Campbell
Customer Service: Joan Brent
Purchasing Manager: Madelin Fernandez
Estimated Sales: $5 - 10 Million
Number Employees: 50-99
Square Footage: 10000

24054 IMI Cornelius
101 Broadway Street W.
Osseo, MN 55369 763-488-8200
Fax: 763-488-4298 800-838-3600
info@cornelius.com www.cornelius.com
Manufacturer and exporter of beverage dispensing and ice making equipment
President: David Storey
CFO: Clayton Jacoby
Estimated Sales: $241.8 Million
Number Employees: 2000
Number of Brands: 5
Number of Products: 6
Parent Co: IMI
Type of Packaging: Food Service
Other Locations:
IMI Cornelius
Norwood MA
Brands:
Cornelius
Jet Spray
Rencor
Wilshire

24055 IMI Cornelius
2401 N Palmer Dr
Schaumburg, IL 60196-0001 847-397-4600
Fax: 847-539-6960 800-323-4789
www.cornelius.com
Manufacturer and exporter of ice making and dispensing equipment including beverage, ice, juice and beer
President: Tim Hubbard
Executive VP Sales/Marketing: Joseph Asfoud
President (Wilshire Canada): David Noble
Estimated Sales: $1 - 5 Million
Number Employees: 250-499
Parent Co: IMI Cornelius

24056 IMI Cornelius
1210 Maben Ave
Garner, IA 50438 641-424-6150
Fax: 641-424-3601 www.cornelius.com
Manufacturer and exporter of ice makers and dispensers
VP Operations: Craig Draves
Estimated Sales: $100+ Million
Number Employees: 350
Parent Co: IMI Cornelius
Type of Packaging: Food Service

24057 IMI Norgren
325 Carr Dr
Brookville, OH 45309-1929 937-833-4033
Fax: 937-833-4205 www.norgren.com
Pneumatic components for the packaging industry including aluminum and steel NFPA interchangeable cylinders, rodless cylinders, small bore cylinders and directional control valves
President: Peter Wallace
Quality Control: John Campbell
Senior VP: Patty Lynch
Technical Marketing Manager (Actuators): Douglas Kelly
Estimated Sales: $20 - 50 Million
Number Employees: 100-249
Square Footage: 47000
Parent Co: IMI Norgren
Brands:
Airserv
Airswitch
Decel-Air
Fast/Bak
Pak-Lap
Tiny Tim

24058 IMO Foods
P.O.Box 236
Yarmouth, NS B5A 4B2
Canada 902-742-3519
Fax: 902-742-0908 imofoods@ns.sympatico.ca
www.imofoods.com

Processor and exporter of canned fish including herring, mackerel, sardines, skinless/boneless salmon and herring roe.
President: Sidney Hughes
Executive VP/General Manager: Phillip Le Blanc
Director Marketing: David Jollimore
Number Employees: 100-249
Parent Co: IMO Foods
Type of Packaging: Consumer, Food Service, Private Label
Other Locations:
Brands:
Golden Treasure
Kersen
West Island

24059 **IMTEC**
49036 Milmont Drive
Fremont, CA 94538 802-463-9502
Fax: 802-463-4334 800-854-6832
sales@imtec.com www.imtecacculine.com
High preformance automated identification systems
CEO: Tim Thompson

24060 **(HQ)INDEECO**
425 Hanley Industrial Ct
St Louis, MO 63144-1511 314-644-4300
Fax: 314-644-5332 800-243-8162
sales@indeeco.com www.indeeco.com
Electric heating elements and systems including heat transfer systems, circulation and pipeline impedance; exporter of electric heaters and controls
President: Fred Epstein
CEO: John Eulich
Research & Development: Steve Links
Quality Control: Jana Jensen
Marketing Director: Kevin Healy
Operations Manager: Ron Kohlman
Production Manager: Cathy Luster
Purchasing Manager: John ie Harrington
Estimated Sales: $50 - 100 Million
Number Employees: 250-499
Square Footage: 200000
Other Locations:
INDEECO
Saint Louis MO
Brands:
Hynes

24061 **INOVAR Packaging Group**
602 Magic Mile St
Arlington, TX 76011 817-277-6666
Fax: 817-275-2770 800-285-2235
sales@inovarpkg.com www.inovarpkg.com
Custom printed labels, tags and decals. Also, distribute label applicators and packaging equipment.
President: Gary Cooper
CFO: Kyle Dailey
Research & Development: Alton Berry
Quality Control: Sonya Ayers
Marketing/Sales: Steve Nevil
Operations Manager: Darryl Parham
Purchasing Manager: Mark Ingus
Estimated Sales: $15,000,000
Number Employees: 50-99
Square Footage: 53000
Parent Co: Conti Industries
Type of Packaging: Consumer, Food Service, Private Label, Bulk
Brands:
Kraftmark

24062 **INTEC Video Systems**
23301 Vista Grande Dr
Laguna Hills, CA 92653 949-859-3800
Fax: 949-859-3178 800-468-3254
info@intecvideo.com www.intecvideo.com
Rear vision cameras systems
President: Don Nama
Marketing Director: Manuel Mendez
Sales Director: Roy Barbatti
Estimated Sales: $12 000,000
Number Employees: 20-49

24063 **IPEC**
185 Northgate Circle
New Castle, PA 16105 800-377-4732
Fax: 724-658-3054 pkossack@silganipec.com
www.ipec.com
Plastic closures and capping equipment
President: Charles Long Jr
CEO: Joseph Giordano Jr
CFO/Secretary/Treasurer: Shawn Fabry
VP Operations: Jay Martin
Number Employees: 75
Square Footage: 12922

24064 **IPG International Packaging Group**
5611 Foxwood Drive
Apt B
Agoura Hills, CA 91377-3982 818-865-1428
Fax: 818-889-9691 ahsipg@jps.net
www.ipgweb.com
Consultant specializing in product marketing and packaging design including structural and graphic for the consumer market; importer of finished printed packages
Design: Debbiz Zakrzeudski
Design: Tyson Marquardt
Estimated Sales: Less than $500,000
Number Employees: 4
Type of Packaging: Consumer

24065 **(HQ)IPL Inc**
140 Commerciale
Saint-Damien, QC GOR-2Y0
Canada 418-789-2880
Fax: 418-789-3153 800-463-4755
info-ipl@ipl-plastics.com www.ipl-plastics.com
Producer of molded plastic products through injection and extrusion for various industrial sectors, specially food
President: Julien M,Tivier
CEO: Serge Bragdon
Estimated Sales: $10-$20 Million
Number Employees: 10-19
Type of Packaging: Consumer, Food Service, Private Label

24066 **IPL Plastics**
20 Boyd St
Edmundston, NB E3V 4H4
Canada 506-739-9559
Fax: 506-739-1028 800-739-9595
ipl@commercial.nbnet.nb.ca
Manufacturer and exporter of thin wall plastic food containers; also, molding and printing services available
Sales Manager: Pierre Boilard
Administrative Services: Claude Nadeau
Operations Manager: Mario Gaudieauit
Number Employees: 100
Square Footage: 90000
Parent Co: IPL

24067 **IPM Coffee InnovationsLLC**
1130 Springtown Road
Suite A
Alpha, NJ 08865 610-865-1900
Fax: 888-762-2173 ipmcoffee@gmail.com
www.ipmcoffee.com
Cappuccino machines
Owner & President: George Strysky
Owner & Office Manager: Lela Evans Strysky

24068 **IPS International**
20124 Broadway Ave
Snohomish, WA 98296 360-668-5050
Fax: 360-415-9056 info@ipsintl.com
www.independentpetsupply.com
Manufacturer and exporter of thermal and insulated handling and shipping containers
Estimated Sales: less than $500,000
Number Employees: 1
Brands:
Pal Pac
Sof-Pak
Speedwall

24069 **IQ Scientific Instruments**
2075 Corte Del Nogal # E
Carlsbad, CA 92011-1414 760-930-6501
Fax: 760-930-0615 techsupport@phmeters.com
www.phmeters.com
Manufacturer and exporter of pH meters
President: Malcolm Mitchell
Marketing Director: Kate Roberts
Sales Director: Rod Stark
Estimated Sales: $10 - 20 Million
Number Employees: 10-19
Brands:
Iq120 Minilab
Iq125 Minilab
Iq150
Iq240
Minilab

24070 **IR Systems**
725 N Highway A1a
Jupiter, FL 33477-4571 561-743-7171
Fax: 561-743-2121 800-893-7540
info@infrared-systems.com
www.infrared-systems.com
Infrared and conveyorized oven systems
Owner: J J Cunningham
Estimated Sales: less than $500,000
Number Employees: 1-4
Square Footage: 8800

24071 **IRM Corporation**
2300 W Pecan Ave
Madera, CA 93637 559-673-4764
Fax: 559-673-4716 CustServe@IRM-CORP.Com
www.irm-corp.com
Sales and marketing information systems to food and beverage manufacturers, distributors and brokers.
President: Dean Abrams
CEO: Art Harding
Sales: Tim Shine
Other Locations:
IRM Corporation
Dallas TX
Brands:
Compass Forecast System
Discovery System
Promo Assist

24072 **ISM Carton**
PO Box 629
Butler, PA 16003-0629 800-378-3430
Fax: 800-827-4762 800-378-3430
www.ismsys.com
Quality products for construction, industrial and packaging applications
CEO: Mark Kania
CEO: Steve Macefe
Director Operations: Luciano Aldeghi
Estimated Sales: $50-100 Million
Number Employees: 100-249
Type of Packaging: Private Label, Bulk

24073 **ISS/GEBA/AFOS**
23 Water St
PO Box 480
Ashburnham, MA 01430-1258 978-827-3160
Fax: 978-827-3162 800-269-2367
sales@intlsmokingsystems.com
www.intlsmokingsystems.com
Vacuum packaging equipment, slicers, smokehouses
President: Mark Carlisle
Estimated Sales: $5-10 Million
Number Employees: 1-4

24074 **ISi North America**
175 Route 46 West
Fairfield, NJ 07004-7316 973-227-2426
Fax: 973-227-4520 800-447-2426
customerservice@isinorthamerica.com
www.isinorthamerica.com
Hand held whippers and soda siphons.
President: Richard W Agresta
Estimated Sales: $5 - 10 Million
Number Employees: 10-19
Brands:
Espuma

24075 **(HQ)ITC Systems**
49 Railside Road
Unit 63
Toronto, ON M1H 2X1
Canada 416-289-2344
Fax: 416-289-4790 877-482-8326
sales@itcsystems.com www.itcsystems.com
Manufacturer, importer and exporter of cash card systems hardware and software for prepaid services at vending machines and manual food operations; manufacturer of photo identification cards with on-line debit/credit balances
Chief Executive Officer, President: Cam Richardson
Vice President of Business Development: Dan Bodolai
Director Sales: David Hulbert
Purchasing Manager: Janet Exconde
Number Employees: 10
Square Footage: 44000
Other Locations:
ITC Systems
Longwood FL

24076 **ITC Systems**
49 Railside Road
Toronto, ON M3A 1B3
Canada 416-289-2344
Fax: 416-289-4790 877-482-8326
service@itcsystems.com www.itcsystems.com
Manufacturer, importer and exporter of cash card systems hardware and software for prepaid services at vending machines and manual food operations; manufacturer of photo identification cards with on-line debit/credit balances
Chief Executive Officer, President: Cam Richardson
R&D: Igor Irlin
Director of Sales: Dave Hulbert
Director Sales: David Hulbert
Plant Manager: Bryan Bull
Purchasing Manager: Janet Exconde
Number Employees: 25
Square Footage: 22000
Parent Co: ITC Systems

24077 **ITS/ETL Testing Laboratories**
27611 La Paz Rd # C
Laguna Niguel, CA 92677-3938 949-448-4100
Fax: 949-448-4111 www.itsqs.com
Laboratory specializing in microbiological and chemical testing; also, sanitation and electrical inspection
Manager: Bill Bocchini
Estimated Sales: $5-10 Million
Number Employees: 1-4

24078 **ITT Industries**
33 Centerville Road
Lancaster, PA 17603 717-509-2200
Fax: 717-509-2336 800-366-1111
engvavlescustserve@fluids.ittind.com
www.engvalves.com
Valves: Cam-Line, Cam-Tite, Dia-Flo, Pure-Flo, Fabri-Valve, Skotch, Richter products
Estimated Sales: $2.5-5 Million
Number Employees: 5-9

24079 **ITT Jabsco**
1485 Dale Way
Foothill Ranch, CA 92610 949-609-5106
Fax: 949-853-1254 gary.cragin@flojet.ittind.com
www.jabsco.com
Manufactures food and dairy products pumps
President: Russ David
VP: Oliver Dupre
R&D: Scott Shimer
Quality Control: John Ebeling
Sales Manager: David Farrer
Estimated Sales: $20 - 50 Million
Number Employees: 250

24080 **ITW Angleboard**
113 Censors Road
Villa Rica, GA 30180-2120 770-459-5747
Fax: 770-459-1305 www.itw.com
Manufacturer and exporter of protective packaging profiles for shipping, unitizing and palletization
CEO: David Speer
CFO: James Wooten Jr.
Investor Relations: John Brooklier
Estimated Sales: $1 - 5 Million
Brands:
Edgeboard

24081 **ITW Auto-Sleeve**
2003 Case Pkwy S
Suite 3
Twinsburg, OH 44087 330-487-2200
Fax: 330-487-3700 800-852-4571
sales@itw-autosleeve.com
www.itw-autosleeve.com
CFO: Roy Marschke
Estimated Sales: Below $5 Million
Number Employees: 10-19

24082 **ITW Coding Products**
111 W Park Dr
Kalkaska, MI 49646 231-258-5521
Fax: 231-258-6120 800-748-0525
hssales@codingproducts.com
www.codingproducts.com
Hot stamp ribbons, thermal transfer ribbons, inks and hot ink rollers for packaging applications
Sales Executive: Rob Fickling
Plant Manager: Ron Maxey
Estimated Sales: $50-100 Million
Number Employees: 50-99
Parent Co: Illinois Tool Works

24083 **ITW Dymon**
805 E Old 56 Highway
Olathe, KS 66061 913-829-6296
Fax: 913-397-8707 800-443-9536
cservice@dymon.com www.dymon.com
Cleaning supplies including disinfectants, hand sanitizer wipes and polishing clothes
R&D: Jason McCauley
Quality Control: David Madsen
General Manager: Paul Taylor
Marketing Manager: Andrew Bolin
National Sales Manager: Alan Smith
General Manager: Paull Taylor
Estimated Sales: Below $5,000,000
Number Employees: 50-99
Parent Co: Illinois Tool Works
Brands:
Antimicrobial Sanitizer Scrubs
Lemon Glo
Metal Polish Scrubs
Scrubs In-A-Bucket

24084 **ITW Dynatec**
31 Volunteer Drive
Hendersonville, TN 37075-3156 615-824-3634
Fax: 615-264-5248 info@itwdynatec.comÿ
www.itwdynatec.com
Hot melt glue systems
President: Zent Myer
CFO: Doug Betew
CFO: Doug Detew
R & D: Marie McLain
Number Employees: 100-249

24085 **ITW Foamseal**
2425 N Lapeer Rd
Oxford, MI 48371-2425 248-628-2587
Fax: 248-628-7136 info@ironout.com
www.itwfoamseal.com
Manufacturer and exporter of polyurea elastomeric coatings, urethane foam systems, application equipment and set-up processing stations. ITW Foamseal is currently supplying a wide range of urethane products for many uses in theautomotive, manufactured housing, fenestration, furniture, sports equipment, recreational vehicle, medical, tolling and infrastructure markets
General Manager: Ted Stolz
Business Manager: Tim Walsh
Estimated Sales: $20-50 Million
Number Employees: 5-9
Square Footage: 50000
Parent Co: Illinois Tool Works
Type of Packaging: Private Label
Brands:
Infraseal

24086 **ITW Hi-Cone**
1140 W Bryn Mawr Ave
Itasca, IL 60143 630-438-5300
Fax: 630-438-5315 www.hi-cone.com
Multi-pack plastic ring carriers for cans and bottles of beverages,vegetables,fruits, pasta and soup.
President: Tim Gardner
VP Sales: Steve Henn
Estimated Sales: $5-10 Million
Number Employees: 100-249
Parent Co: Illinois Tool Works
Brands:
Hi-Cone

24087 **ITW Minigrip/Zip-Pak**
1800 W Sycamore Rd
Manteno, IL 60950 815-468-6500
Fax: 815-468-6550 800-488-6973
info@zippak.com www.zippak.com
Reclosable and reusable polyethylene bags with plastic zippers
Finance Executive/Controller: Roger Geckner
Bruiness Unit Manager: Stephen Schaller
Estimated Sales: $10 - 20 Million
Number Employees: 50-99
Parent Co: Illinois Tool Works

24088 **ITW Plastic Packaging**
4950 Colorado Blvd
Denver, CO 80216 303-316-6816
info@itwplastics.com
www.itwplastics.com
Plastic transport packaging products: slip sheets, tier sheets, EZ Grab LoadLoc, pallets, top frams, DuraSheets and Replastec Separators, pallets

24089 **ITW Stretch Packaging System**
3700 W Lake Ave
Glenview, IL 60026 847-657-4444
Fax: 847-657-7764 itwmima@itwmima.com
www.itw.com
Stretch wrap and film machinery
President: Jim Chase
CEO: William Aldinger
Marketing: Bonnie Lipner
Sales: Pat McCormick
Number Employees: 5-9
Parent Co: Illinois Tool Works
Brands:
Accustretch
Accuwrap
Cobra
Mimawrap

24090 **IVEK Corporation**
10 Fairbanks Rd
N Springfield, VT 05150 802-886-2238
Fax: 802-886-8274 800-356-4746
ivek@ivek.com www.ivek.com
Precision small volume liquid dispensing and metering systems
President: Mark Tanny
CFO: Dennis Crowley
Vice President: Frank DiMaggio
Research & Development: Mark Tanny
Quality Control: Ken Neal
Marketing Director: Tracey Tanny
Sales Director: Frank DiMaggio
Public Relations: Pauline Asselin
Operations Manager: Gary Blake
Production Manager: Tara Curtis
Plant Manager: Brad Deedy
Purchasing Manager: Wade McAllister
Estimated Sales: Below $5 Million
Number Employees: 60

24091 **IWS Scales**
9885 Mesa Rim Road
Suite 128
San Diego, CA 92191
Fax: 858-784-0542 800-881-9755
info@internationalweighingsystems.com
iwsscales.com
Manufacturer, importer and exporter of mechanical and electronic scales including platform, receiving, portion, racking, computing, etc
Estimated Sales: $1 - 3 Million
Number Employees: 50
Square Footage: 40000
Parent Co: Western Scale
Brands:
Airway
West Weigh

24092 **Ice-Cap**
P.O.Box 292
Piermont, NY 10968-292 718-729-7000
Fax: 718-392-4193 888-423-2270
www.icecap.com
Manufacturer and exporter of air conditioners
CEO: Mo Siegel
CFO: Mo Siegel
Estimated Sales: $20 - 50 Million
Number Employees: 10

24093 **Ice-O-Matic**
11100 E 45th Ave
Denver, CO 80239 303-371-3737
Fax: 303-371-6296 800-423-3367
customer.service@iceomatic.com
www.iceomatic.com
Parent Co: ENODIS

24094 **Ice-O-Matic**
11100 E 45th Ave
Denver, CO 80239 303-371-3737
Fax: 303-371-6296 800-423-3367
customer.service@iceomatic.com
www.iceomatic.com

Ice making equipment since 1952 including cubers, flakers, dispensers, bins and accessories. Provides equipment for restaurants, bars, hotels/motels, hospitals, etc
President: Kevin Fink
CFO: Dave Weller
Quality Control: David Spiciarich
Marketing Director: Keith Kelly
Public Relations: Linda Gleeson
Plant Manager: Randy Karas
Number Employees: 250-499
Brands:
Ice-O-Matic Ice Machines

24095 Icee-USA Corporation
4701 E Airport Dr
Ontario, CA 91761-7817 909-390-4233
Fax: 909-390-4260 800-426-4233
www.icee.com
Manufacturer and exporter of frozen carbonated beverage dispensers; also, point of sale signs and displays available
President: Dan Fachner
CFO: Kent Galloway
VP: Rod Sexton
Estimated Sales: $5 - 10 Million
Number Employees: 100-249
Square Footage: 88000
Parent Co: J&J Snack Foods Company

24096 Ickler Machine Company
2832 First Street South
Saint Cloud, MN 56301 320-251-8282
Fax: 320-251-8389 800-243-8382
ickler@ickler.com www.ickler.com
Machine shop services, custom fabrication, and retail bearing sales
Owner: Todd McGonagle
Estimated Sales: $600,000-$700,000
Number Employees: 10-19

24097 Iconics
100 Foxboro Blvd Ste 130
Foxborough, MA 02035 508-543-8600
Fax: 508-543-1503 800-946-9679
us@iconics.com www.iconics.com
ICONICS is the lead supplier of HMI SCADA, Energy Management, and Productivity Analytics software solutions to the Food and Beverage Industry. ICONICS GENISIS64 HMI/SCADA and Analytix software improves operational performance andproductivity by providing 360 degrees of visibility and real time control for business and production systems.
President, Founder: Russell Agrusa
CEO: Russell Agrusa
VP Finance/Administration, CFO: Paula Agrusa
VP Worldwide Sales: Chris Volpe
Business Development Manager for Buildin: Oliver Gruner
VP Product Marketing: Gary F. Kohrt
VP, Worldwide Sales: Mark Hepburn
Estimated Sales: E
Number Employees: 50-99
Square Footage: 96000
Brands:
Alarmwork Multimedia
Genesis32 Enterprise Edition
Genesis For Windows
Pocket Genesis
Winworx
Winworx Open Series

24098 Idaho Steel Products Company
255 E Anderson St
Idaho Falls, ID 83401 208-522-1275
Fax: 208-522-6041 sales@idahosteel.com
www.idahosteel.com
Manufacturer and exporter of food processing equipment including blanchers, cookers, coolers, drum dryers and complete processing lines
President: Lynn Bradshaw
CFO: Craig Parker
Engineering Manager: Alan Bradshaw
Marketing/Public Relations: Davis Christiansen
Sales Director: Bruce Ball
Operations Manager: D Bradshaw
Purchasing Manager: Adam French
Estimated Sales: $10 - 20 Million
Number Employees: 50-99
Square Footage: 50000

24099 Ideal Office Supply & Rubber Stamp Company
222 E Center Street
Kingsport, TN 37662-0935 423-246-7371
Fax: 423-246-3535
Office supplies including rubber stamps and plastic signs
President: Cynthia Culberton
Number Employees: 12

24100 Ideal Packaging Systems
1662 Broughton Court
Atlanta, GA 30338-4633 770-352-0210
Fax: 770-352-0106 ioealvr@yahoo.com
Pallet stretch wrapping and bundle shrink wrapping equipment
Estimated Sales: $10-20 Million
Number Employees: 5

24101 Ideal Sleeves, International
182 Courtright Street
Wilkes Barre, PA 18702-1802 570-823-8456
Fax: 570-823-8458 sales@integrityseal.com
www.idealsleeves.com
Tamper evident shrink seals, multipak, sleeves, shrink labels, preforms, seamed and seamless materials including PVC and Pet-G
Manager: Dave Frable
Chief Executive Officer, President: James Dwyer
G.M.: Arlene Warnuck
Estimated Sales: $5 - 10 Million
Number Employees: 20-49

24102 Ideal Stencil Machine &Tape Company
5307 Meadowland Parkway
Marion, IL 62959-5893 618-233-0162
Fax: 618-233-5091 800-388-0162
sales@idealstencil.com www.idealstencil.com
Manufacturer and exporter of ink including meat branding, hog tattoo, coding and jet printer; also, fountain brushes, conveyor line coders, ink applicators, metal markers and electronic stencil and embossing machines
Sales Manager: Jim Boyd
Executive VP Operations: Marco Ziniti
Estimated Sales: $2.5-5 Million
Number Employees: 20-49
Square Footage: 240000
Brands:
Handy A&C
Ht80
Ideal Mark
Ideco
M074
Meat Marking
Roll-Eze
Speedry

24103 Ideal Wire Works
820 S Date Ave
Alhambra, CA 91803 626-282-1302
Fax: 626-282-2674 www.idealwireworks.com
Manufacturer and exporter of custom wire display racks, rings and parts in steel or stainless steel
President: Andrew Wren
VP: Jim Freitag
Estimated Sales: $2.5 - 5 Million
Number Employees: 20-49
Square Footage: 20000

24104 Ideal Wrapping Machine Company
81 Sprague Avenue
89
Middletown, NY 10940-5223 845-343-7700
Fax: 845-344-4248
Manufacturer and exporter of forming, cutting and wrapping machinery for caramel, nougat and toffee candies
President: Lee Quality Tire
General Manager: Jim Horton
Number Employees: 5-9

24105 Ideal of America
205 Regency Executive Park Drive
Suite 309
Charlotte, NC 28217-3989 704-523-1604
Fax: 704-523-1635
Packaging equipment including bundlers, shrink wrappers and automatic baggers
VP: David Katz
Sales Manager: Lana Taylor
Estimated Sales: $1 - 5 Million
Number Employees: 100-250
Square Footage: 40000

24106 Ideal of America/ValleyRio Enterprise
1662 Broughton Court
Atlanta, GA 30338-4633 770-352-0210
Fax: 770-352-0106 idealvr@yahoo.com
www.idealvr.com
Manufacturer and exporter of stainless steel packaging equipment including fully automated shrink and stretch wrappers
Vice President: Alan Pullock
Estimated Sales: $10 Million
Number Employees: 100-250
Square Footage: 105000
Parent Co: Ideal of America
Brands:
Ideal

24107 Ideal-Pak Incorporated
4607 Dovetail Dr
Madison, WI 53704 608-241-1118
Fax: 608-241-4448 800-383-1128
sales@ideal-pak.com www.ideal-pak.com
Industrial liquid filling and closing equipment
President/CEO: Steve Bethke
Sales & Marketing Director: Russell Schlager
Vice President: Bruce Bierman
Marketing Manager: Steven Meyer
National Sales Manager: Robert D. Whetstone
Regional Sales Manager: Kevin Sam
Operations Manager: Bruce Bierman
Purchasing Manager: Aric Riley
Estimated Sales: $1 Million +
Number Employees: 20-49
Number of Brands: 3
Square Footage: 30000
Type of Packaging: Food Service, Private Label, Bulk

24108 Ideas Etc
8305 Dawson Hill Rd
Louisville, KY 40299 502-231-4303
Fax: 502-239-0555 800-733-0337
ideasetc@msn.com www.idea-etc.com
Manufacturer and exporter of shot and martini glasses, beverage containers and 4-necker T-shirts; importer of martini glasses. Designers and printers of food service calendars and planners
President: Jerry Griggs
Estimated Sales: $500,000+
Number Employees: 1-4
Brands:
Palm Tree Cooler
Splitshot
Yardski

24109 Ideas in Motion
P.O.Box 8504
New Castle, PA 16107-8504 724-924-9680
Fax: 724-924-9665 800-367-3535
sales@iim-inc.com www.iim-inc.com
Owner: Brian Crisci
Estimated Sales: $1-2.5 Million
Number Employees: 20-49

24110 Idec Corporation
1175 Elko Dr
Sunnyvale, CA 94089 408-747-0550
Fax: 408-744-9055 800-262-IDEC
opencontact@idec.com www.idec.com
Control components, switches, pushbuttons, sensors and relays
Chairman of the Board: Toshiyuki Funaki
VP: Sada O'Hara
Estimated Sales: $50 - 100 Million
Number Employees: 100-249
Number of Products: 5500

24111 IdentaBadge
3219 Johnston St
Lafayette, LA 70503 337-984-8888
Fax: 337-984-1666 800-325-8247
badgepro@identabadge.com
www.identabadge.com
Name badges, directional signs and advertising specialties and awards
Owner: D A Savoie
CEO: Dale Savoie
VP: Sidney Savoie
Sales: Dottie Blanchard
Public Relations: Dottie Blanchard

Estimated Sales: $5 - 10 Million
Number Employees: 5-9
Number of Brands: 1
Number of Products: 25
Square Footage: 5500
Parent Co: Trophyland
Type of Packaging: Bulk

24112 Idexx Laboratories
1 Idexx Dr
Westbrook, ME 04092 207-856-0300
Fax: 207-856-4346 800-321-0207
investorrelations@idexx.com www.idexx.com
Manufacturer and exporter of cleaning and validation systems including testing kits for salmonella, coliforms/E coli in water, residues in milk and microbiological; also, dehydrated culture media
President: Jonathan Ayres
CEO: Jonathan W Ayers
Estimated Sales: K
Number Employees: 1,000-4,999
Brands:
Acumedia
Bind
Colilert
Lightning
Simplate
Snap

24113 Ifm Efector
782 Springdale Dr
Exton, PA 19341-2850 610-524-2000
Fax: 610-524-2020 800-441-8246
customer_service@ifmefector.com
www.ifmefector.com
Industrial sensors including capacitive, inductive and plug-connector type proximity switches, photoelectric controls, flow monitor switches, pressure switches, and temperature sensors
Estimated Sales: $70 Million
Number Employees: 100-249

24114 Igloo Products
777 Igloo Rd.
Katy, TX 77494 713-584-6800
Fax: 713-465-2009 800-364-5566
www.igloocoolers.com
Ice chest coolers, insulated catering chests, softside catering carriers and beverage and cup dispensers
Chairman & Chief Executive Officer: Gary Kiedaisch
Estimated Sales: $108.90 Million
Number Employees: 1000
Square Footage: 1400000
Type of Packaging: Food Service
Brands:
Igloo
Igloo 2go
Igloo Stralth

24115 Igus Inc
P.O.Box 14349
East Providence, RI 02914-0349 401-438-2200
Fax: 401-438-7270 800-521-2747
sales@igus.com www.igus.com
Packaging machinery components, cable carriers, high flex cables, bearings and linear guides
VP: Carsten Blase
Number Employees: 160
Square Footage: 352000
Parent Co: Igus GmbH

24116 Ilapak
105 Pheasant Run
Newtown, PA 18940 215-579-2900
Fax: 215-579-9959 marketing@ilapak.com
www.ilapak.com
Flexible horizontal and vertical packaging machinery including fin seal and shrink wrappers, vertical form/fill/seal, four-side seal pouch, horizontal modified atmosphere, etc
President: Andrew G Axberg
CFO: Frank Zellucci
VP Sales: Randy Rice
Estimated Sales: $10 - 20 Million
Number Employees: 20-49
Square Footage: 18000
Parent Co: Ilapak Holding
Brands:
Alfa
Carrera 1000 M
Carrera 1000 Pc
Carrera 2000 Pc
Carrera 500 M
Cougar
Delta
Delta 3000 D-Cam
Delta 3000 Ld
Delta 3000 Sb
Indy
Rose Forgrove
Sandiacre
Vegatronic 3000
Vegatronic 1000
Vegatronic 2000
Vegatronic 3000

24117 Ilapak Inc
105 Pheasant Run
Newtown, PA 18940 215-579-2900
Fax: 215-579-9959 cpaczkowski@ilapakusa.com
www.ilapak.com
Supplier of industrial wrapping machinery for food industry
CEO: Andrew Axberg
Office Manager: Claire Paczkowski
Number Employees: 31

24118 Illinois Lock Company
301 W Hintz Rd
Wheeling, IL 60090-5754 847-537-1800
Fax: 847-537-1881 800-733-3907
sales@illinoislock.com www.illinoislock.com
Producers of custom engineered key locks, keyless locks, electric switch locks, high - security locks, and wire harness lock assemblies
Manager: Len Samela
Estimated Sales: $10-20 Million
Number Employees: 50-99
Parent Co: Eastern Company

24119 Illinois Range Company
9555 Ainslie St
Schiller Park, IL 60176-1115 847-928-2490
Fax: 847-928-2782 800-535-7041
www.illinoisrange.com
Custom stainless steel kitchen equipment including counters, hoods, ranges, ovens, smallwares, etc
President: John Domdek
Estimated Sales: Below $5 Million
Number Employees: 1-4
Square Footage: 504000

24120 Illinois Valley Container Corporation
2 Terminal Rd
Peru, IL 61354-3700 815-223-7200
ivcbox@ivnet.com
Corrugated containers
President: Timothy Alter
General Manager: Jim Ewert
Estimated Sales: $5-10 Million
Number Employees: 20 to 49

24121 Illinois Wholesale CashRegister Corporation
2790 Pinnacle Dr
Elgin, IL 60124-7943 847-310-4200
Fax: 847-310-8490 800-544-5493
info@illinoiswholesale.com
www.illinoiswholesale.com
Refurbished point of sale equipment
President: Al Moorhouse
Vice President of Accounting: Bob Tracy
Chief Operating Officer, Vice President: Darin Moorhouse
Operations Manager: Jeff Burton
Estimated Sales: $10 - 20 Million
Number Employees: 50-99

24122 Illuma Display
P.O.Box 1531
Brookfield, WI 53008-1531 262-446-9220
Fax: 262-446-9260 800-501-0128
info@illuminadisplay.com
www.illumadisplay.com
Manufacturer and exporter of curved light boxes, graphic stands and backlit displays
President: Joe Galati
VP: Tony Galati
Estimated Sales: Less than $500,000
Number Employees: 1-4

24123 Illumination Products
175 Frederico Costas Street
Tres Monjitas Park
San Juan, PR 00918 787-754-7193
Fax: 787-250-7813
www.illuminationproductsinc.com
Fluorescent light fixtures and lamps
President: Robert Santiago
Quality Control: Raul Millan
Estimated Sales: Below $5 Million
Number Employees: 25

24124 Illy Espresso of the Americas
15455 N Greenway Hayden Loop
Scottsdale, AZ 85260-1611 480-951-4074
Fax: 480-483-8631 800-872-4559
info@illyusa.com www.illyusa.com
Espresso pods
Estimated Sales: $20-50 Million
Number Employees: 20-49

24125 Ilsemann Corp.
398 Circle of Progress
Suite 102
Pottstown, PA 19464 610-323-4143
Fax: 610-323-4709 sales@ilsemannusa.com
www.ilsemann.com/index.php?id= company&L= 1
Estimated Sales: $1,000,000 - $3,000,000
Number Employees: 5-9
Parent Co: Heino Ilsemann GmbH

24126 Image Development
PO Box 218
Plymouth, CA 95669-0218 209-267-1850
Fax: 209-267-1850 id@bauerengraving.com
Chocolate coin imprinting, dies, candy
President: William Bratt
Number Employees: 2

24127 Image Experts Uniforms
1623 Eastern Pkwy
Schenectady, NY 12309 518-377-4523
Fax: 518-374-1236 800-789-2433
sales@chefdirect.com www.imageexperts.com
Manufacturer and exporter of uniforms
CEO: Thomas J Salamone
Estimated Sales: $1-2.5 Million
Number Employees: 20-49
Square Footage: 8000
Parent Co: Image Experts Uniforms
Brands:
Chef Direct
Really Cookin' Chef Gear

24128 Image Fillers
735 Fox Chase
Suite 111
Coatesville, PA 19320 610-466-1440
Fax: 610-466-0116
imagefillers@imagefillers.com
www.imagefillers.com

24129 Image National
16265 Star Road
Nampa, ID 83687 208-345-4020
Fax: 208-336-9886 jcarico@imagenational.com
www.imagenational.com
Manufacturer and exporter of electric signs, store fronts and interior graphics
President: Brent Lloyd
Service Install Manager: Jeff Carico
Sales Manager: Tony Adams
General Manager: Doug Bender
Estimated Sales: $5 - 10 Million
Number Employees: 130
Parent Co: Futura Corporation

24130 Image Plastics
5919 Jessamine Street
Houston, TX 77081-6506 713-772-2811
Fax: 713-772-6445 800-289-2811
Insulated and noninsulated plastic drinkware
VP: Jim Houseal
Director Marketing: Gary Opperman
Director Sales: Mike Barrow
Estimated Sales: $20-50 Million
Number Employees: 100-249
Brands:
Automug
Sportsmate

24131 Imaging Technologies
445 Universal Drive
Cookeville, TN 38506-4603 931-432-4191
Fax: 931-432-4199 800-488-2804
iti@multipro.com www.icglink.com
Manufacturer and exporter of high resolution ink jet printing systems for printing bar codes, alphanumerics and graphics on porous surfaces
President: Loyd Tarver
Controller: Ted Bonnay
Vice President of Marketing: Chris Jones
Marketing Manager: Steve Shoup
Number Employees: 30
Square Footage: 24000
Brands:
Iti
Kd Jet Streamer
Marksman
Porelon

24132 Imaje
1650 Airport Rd NW
Kennesaw, GA 30144-7039 770-421-7700
Fax: 770-421-7702 coding@imajeamericas.com
www.imaje.com
Coding, dating and marking equipment, barcoding systems and inks for food packaging; importer of ink jet coders; exporter of ink jet coders, inks and additives
Manager: Linda Kaimesher
CFO: Steve Wakeford
Marketing Director: Alisha Curd
Sales Director: Tim Sines
Purchasing Manager: Norm Coon
Estimated Sales: G
Number Employees: 50-99
Parent Co: Dover Technologies
Brands:
Crayon
Crayon Z-Tra
Imaje 7s
Lightjet
Lightjet Vector
McP
McP Barcode
McP Series
Prima
Pulsar
S8 1p65
S8 Classic
S8 Contrast
S8 Master

24133 Iman Pack
5762 E Executive Dr
Westland, MI 48185-9125 734-467-9016
Fax: 734-467-8642 800-810-4626
sales@imanpack.com www.imanpack.com
Manufacturer and importer of automatic packaging equipment including horizontal and vertical form/fill/seal machinery, shrink wrappers, counting and weighing scales, case packers, palletizers, etc
President: Antonio Bonotto
Sales/Marketing: Lori Scheinman
National Sales Director: Fred Barbarotto
Estimated Sales: $1 - 3 Million
Number Employees: 5-9
Parent Co: Iman Pack SRL
Brands:
Gianopac
Ultravert

24134 Iman Pack
5762 E Executive Dr
Westland, MI 48185-9125 734-467-9016
Fax: 734-467-8642 sales@imanpack.com
www.imanpack.it
Packaging equipment including vertical form, fill and seal baggers
President: Antonio Bonotto
VP: Giovanni Bonotto
Estimated Sales: $1 - 3 Million
Number Employees: 5-9
Parent Co: Imanpak

24135 Iman Pack Sigma System
5762 E Executive Dr
Westland, MI 48185 734-467-9016
Fax: 734-467-8642 sales@imanpack.com
www.imanpack.com
President: Antonio Bonotto
VP Sales: Massimo Denipoti
Estimated Sales: $1 - 5 Million
Number Employees: 5-9

24136 Imar
2301 Collins Avenue
Miami Beach, FL 33139-1639 305-531-5757
Fax: 305-538-2957
113634.3075@compuserve.com
www.imar-mv.com
Manufacturer, importer and exporter of packaging machinery for pouches
CEO: Thomas Tennant
Parent Co: Imar
Brands:
Imar

24137 Imdec
2061 Freeway Dr
Suite E
Woodland, CA 95776 530-661-9091
Fax: 530-661-9206 glenl@imdecinc.com
www.imdecinc.com
Tomato and fruit processing equipment
President: Glen Langstaff
Estimated Sales: $1 - 2.5 Million
Number Employees: 9

24138 Imeco
3820 S Il Route 26
Polo, IL 61064 815-946-2351
Fax: 815-946-3409 stencel@york.com
www.frickcold.com
Manufacturer and exporter of refrigeration equipment including prime surface evaporative condensers and sub-zero blast freezers
President: Mark Stencel
General Manager: Ian McGavisk
Quality Controller: Mark Smith
Director Operations: Colin McDonough
Estimated Sales: $50-100 Million
Number Employees: 100-249
Square Footage: 135000
Parent Co: York International

24139 Imex Vinyl Packaging
2559 Plantation Center Drive
Matthews, NC 28105 704-815-4600
Fax: 704-815-4601 800-938-4639
sales@imexvp.com www.imexpackaging.com
Clear vinyl bags and packaging.
President & Owner: Steve Jefferey
Operations Manager: Danny Love
Number Employees: 10
Type of Packaging: Consumer, Private Label, Bulk

24140 Impact Awards & Promotions
748 Us Highway 27 N
Avon Park, FL 33825-2639 561-394-8002
Fax: 561-394-9002 888-203-4225
www.impactpromotions.com
Signs, trophies, awards, nameplates and name tags
Owner: Doug Singletary
Marketing: Doug Singletary
Estimated Sales: Less than $500,000
Number Employees: 1-4
Square Footage: 3000

24141 Impact Products
2840 Centennial Road
Toledo, OH 43617-1898 419-841-2891
Fax: 419-841-7861 800-333-1541
custserv@impact-products.com
www.impact-products.com
Wholesaler/distributor of toilet bowl mops, soap dispensers, dust pans, plastic pumps, disposable plastic gloves and washroom accessories
President/Chairman: John Harbal
Founder: James Findlay
Quality Assurance Manager: Carolyn Helminiak
Vice President, Marketing: Jeannie McCarthy
Sales & Marketing Executive: Kaiko Laser
Vice President, Operations: Brian Paul
Procurement Manager: James Knechtges
Estimated Sales: $29 Million
Number Employees: 151
Square Footage: 155000

24142 Impaxx Machines
550 Burning Tree Rd
Fullerton, CA 92833-1400 714-449-5155
Fax: 714-526-0300 info@label-aire.com
www.label-aire.com
Provides advanced and reliable pressure-sensitive labeling machinery to blue-chips firms world over
V P: Stuart Moss
CEO: Ken Phillips

Estimated Sales: $20 - 50 Million
Number Employees: 100-249

24143 Imperial
303 Paterson Plank Road
Carlstadt, NJ 07072
Fax: 201-288-8990 800-526-6261
imperial@imperialusa.com
www.imperialusa.com
Bar stools
Estimated Sales: $1 - 5 Million
Number Employees: 15

24144 Imperial
6300 W Howard St
Niles, IL 60714 847-581-3300
Fax: 847-647-3105 800-967-4442
www.imperialbakingcompany.com
Wholesale bakery
President: Betty Dworkin
Estimated Sales: $2.5-5 000,000
Number Employees: 20-49

24145 Imperial Broom Company
PO Box 8018
Richmond, VA 23223-0018 804-648-7840
Fax: 804-648-0113 888-353-7840
www.imperialbroom.com
Brooms
Owner: Matthew J Robinson Jr
General Manager: Carlton Robinson
Estimated Sales: less than $500,000
Number Employees: 1-4
Square Footage: 20800

24146 Imperial Commercial Cooking Equipment
1128 Sherborn Street
Corona, CA 92879-2089 951-281-1830
Fax: 951-281-1879 800-343-7790
imperialsales@imperialrange.com
www.imperialrange.com
Ranges, convection ovens, fryers and filter systems, char-broilers, hot plates, griddles, roasters, cheesemelters and griddles/broilers
Sales Manager (Eastern): Daniel Monfort
Brands:
Elite

24147 Imperial Containers
13400 Nelson Ave
City of Industry, CA 91746 626-333-6363
Fax: 714-630-2737
Corrugated containers and inner packing
Estimated Sales: $10-20 Million
Number Employees: 20-49
Parent Co: Orange County Container

24148 Imperial Industries Inc
P.O.Box 1685
Wausau, WI 54402-1685 715-359-0200
Fax: 715-355-5349 800-558-2945
indsales@imperialind.com
www.imperialind.com
Bulk storage silos and tanks, liquid waste tanks both self-contained and truck mounted, portable toilets, wash sinks and barricades. Also Asme certified tanks and DOT 407/412 truck mounted tanks.
President: Russ Putnam
Reaserch/Development: Rial Potter
Quality Control: Doug Hagen
Marketing/Sales Manager: T Aerts
Plant Manager: K Mannel
Purchasing Director: Lisa Schultz
Number Employees: 135
Square Footage: 75000
Parent Co: Wausau Tile
Type of Packaging: Bulk

24149 Imperial Packaging Corporation
1 Campbell Street
PO Box 2383
Pawtucket, RI 02861 401-753-7778
Fax: 401-765-5537 info@imperialpkg.com
www.imperialpkg.com
Paper folding boxes
VP: Steven Felici
VP Sales/Marketing: Stevem Felici
General Manager: Robert Gilmore
Estimated Sales: $10 - 20 Million
Number Employees: 20-49

24150 **Imperial Plastics**
21320 Hamburg Ave
PO Box 907
Lakeville, MN 55044 952-469-4951
Fax: 952-469-4724 www.imperialplastics.com
Plastic signs, trays and boxes
President: Norman Oberto
Number Employees: 100-249

24151 **Imperial Plastics**
21320 Hamburg Ave
PO Box 907
Lakeville, MN 55044 952-469-4951
Fax: 952-469-4724 www.imperialplastics.com
Manufacturer and exporter of plastic stoppers and advertising novelties
President: Norman Oberto
Number Employees: 100-249
Type of Packaging: Private Label

24152 **Imperial Schrade Corporation**
7 Schrade Ct
Ellenville, NY 12428 212-210-8600
Fax: 845-210-8671 info@schradeknives.com
www.schradeknives.com
Knive sharpeners, forks, spoons, fish splitting and stainless knives, shears, etc
Marketing Manager: Rick Marchlik
VP Sales: Jim Strathis
Estimated Sales: $75 Million
Number Employees: 500

24153 **Imperial Signs & Manufacturing**
924 Eglin St
Rapid City, SD 57701-9525 605-348-2511
Fax: 605-399-2705 www.bigsurwaterbeds.com
Signs including neon, plastic and painted
Estimated Sales: $1-2.5 Million
Number Employees: 10-19

24154 **Importers Service Corporation**
65 Brunswick Ave
Edison, NJ 08817-2512
Fax: 201-332-4152 iscgums@iscgums.com
www.iscgums.com
Manufacturers of gum arabic, gum acacia, gum karaya, gum tragacanth and gum ghatti
President: Eric Berliner
Plant Engineer: Chris Berliner
Quality Control: David Hulmes
Product Manager: David Hulmes
Director Sales: Robert Vilim
Office Manager: Nancy Meurer
Plant Manager: Henry Schleckser
Estimated Sales: $20-50 Million
Number Employees: 10
Square Footage: 70000
Type of Packaging: Private Label, Bulk

24155 **Impress Industries**
PO Box 477
Emmaus, PA 18049-0477 610-967-6027
Fax: 610-844-9521 www.impresspkg.com
Corrugated boxes for cakes, candy, etc
President: Thomas Galiardo
Controller: Debbie White
Sales Manager: Peter Tisi
Estimated Sales: $20-50 Million
Number Employees: 100-249
Square Footage: 81000

24156 **Impress USA**
936 Barracuda St
San Pedro, CA 90731 310-519-2400
Fax: 310-519-2281 www.impressgroup.com
Manufacture metal packaging for food industry
Plant Manager: Michael Borne
Estimated Sales: $100+ Million
Number Employees: 100-249

24157 **Imprinting Systems**
803 Pressley Rd # 104
Charlotte, NC 28217 704-527-4545
Fax: 704-527-4546 800-497-1403
issilbl@beusouth.net
Pressure-sensitive labels
President: Glenn E Randolph
Marketing Manager: Mark Kessler
Estimated Sales: $500,000-$1 Million
Number Employees: 5-9

24158 **Improved Blow Molding**
27 Hillside Dr
Hollis, NH 03049-6158 603-465-6190
Fax: 603-465-6190 800-256-1766
Manufacturer and exporter of plastic blow molding machinery for food packaging
Owner: Ron Beaulieu
VP Marketing: H Lance Goldberg
VP Engineering: Ronald Beaulieu
Estimated Sales: $500,000-$1 Million
Number Employees: 1-4
Square Footage: 70000
Parent Co: Goodman Equipment Company
Brands:
Automa
Impco

24159 **Impulse Signs**
25 Advance Road
Toronto, ON M8Z 2S6
Canada 416-231-3391
Fax: 416-236-2116 866-636-8273
mgisborne@impulsesigns.com
www.impulsesigns.com
Manufacturer and exporter of menu boards and table signs
President/General Manager: Alex Cachia
Director, Marketing: Ron Wynne
VP, Sales: Carole Lynch
Estimated Sales: $1 - 5 Million
Number Employees: 20-50
Square Footage: 96000
Brands:
Impulse

24160 **In the Bag**
1540 19th St N
St Petersburg, FL 33713 727-894-6797
Fax: 727-894-6734 800-330-2247
www.bagmasters.com
Converted and printed poly food and plastic bags
Owner: Eric Johannsen
VP: Sandra Johannsen
General Manager: Eric Johannsen, Jr.
Estimated Sales: $1-2.5 Million
Number Employees: 10-19
Square Footage: 60000

24161 **In-Line Corporation**
11121 Excelsior Blvd
Hopkins, MN 55343-3434 952-938-0046
Fax: 952-938-0046 info@inlinecorporation.com
www.inlinecorporation.com
Wrappers and skin packaging and premium and promotional packaging
Sales Manager: Chris Thornby
Operations Manager: Don Steen
Estimated Sales: $5-10 Million
Number Employees: 50-99
Square Footage: 340000
Type of Packaging: Bulk

24162 **In-Line Labeling Equipment**
7282 Spa Road
North Charleston, SC 29418-8437 843-569-2530
Fax: 843-569-2531 800-465-4630
info@labeling.net www.labeling.net
Pressure sensitive labellers and cold glue labellers
President: Greg L Brandon
CFO: Greg L Brandon
Estimated Sales: $2.5 - 5 Million
Number Employees: 10-19
Square Footage: 80000

24163 **In-Sink-Erator**
4700 21st St
Racine, WI 53406 262-554-5432
Fax: 262-554-3530 800-558-5700
jack.backstrom@insinkerator.com
www.insinkerator.com
Garbage disposal units and hot water dispensers
President: Jerry Ryder
CFO: William Ivy
Secretary and Marketing: Cathy Davis
Number Employees: 1,000-4,999
Parent Co: Emerson Electric Company
Brands:
In-Sink-Erator

24164 **In-Touch Products**
555 W 1100 N
North Salt Lake, UT 84054 801-298-4466
Fax: 801-298-1955
Custom thermoformed trays, blisters, clam shells and other packaging supplies
President: Tim Keniewfki
Sales Representative: Douglas Johnson
Operations: Curtis Reeves
Estimated Sales: $5-10 Million
Number Employees: 10

24165 **InFood Corporation**
1575 Oak Avenue
Evanston, IL 60201-4274 773-338-8485
Software for food processors including inventory, nutritional analysis/labeling, formulations/BOM, costing, lot tracking, production planning/scheduling, work orders, yield analysis, QC/statistical sampling, etc
Estimated Sales: $1 - 5 Million
Number Employees: 4

24166 **Ina Company**
837 Industrial Rd # G
San Carlos, CA 94070-3333 650-631-7066
Fax: 650-873-4729
Importer of china and plastic bags and garbage bags
Owner: Philip Wong
Estimated Sales: Less than $500,000
Number Employees: 1-4
Brands:
Ina

24167 **Incinerator International**
2702 N Main Street
Houston, TX 77009 713-227-1466
Fax: 713-227-0884 sales@incinerators.com
www.incinerators.com
Manufacturer and importer of material handling equipment including incinerators, balers, compactors, containers, crushers, trucks, hoppers and environmental; exporter of incinerators
Owner: Tom Leervig
Estimated Sales: $2.5-5 Million
Number Employees: 5-9
Square Footage: 5000
Parent Co: International Environmental Equipment Company
Brands:
Iii

24168 **Incinerator Specialty Company**
6018 Golden Forest Dr
Houston, TX 77092-2360 713-681-4207
Manufacturer and exporter of destructors, afterburners and incinerators including pathological, garbage, waste, burners and parts
President: Mick Kromer
Estimated Sales: $1-2.5 Million
Number Employees: 4

24169 **Incomec-Cerex Industries**
1515 Black Rope Type
Fairfield, CT 06432 203-335-1050
Fax: 203-366-7305 cerexpro@aol.com
www.incomec-cerex.com
Manufacturer and exporter of grain processing equipment, flavoring spray booths, puffing guns, drying and infrared toasting ovens and continuous popcorn popping and caramelizing coating systems
President: Stephan Vandenberghe
Executive Vice President: Dennis Norberg
Market Development: Jeff Norberg
Estimated Sales: $25 Million
Number Employees: 60
Number of Brands: 5
Number of Products: 34
Square Footage: 300000

24170 **Incredible Logistics Sol**
112 W Boca Raton Road
Phoenix, AZ 85023-6249 602-548-1295
Fax: 602-548-0322 je_elenteny@msn.com

24171 **Indco**
PO Box 589
New Albany, IN 47151-0589 812-945-4383
Fax: 812-944-9742 800-942-4383
info@indco.com www.indco.com
Industrial mixers
President: Mark Hennis
CFO: J T Sims
Vice President: Kris Wilberding
Estimated Sales: $5 - 10 Million
Number Employees: 30

24172 Indeco Products
P.O.Box 865
San Marcos, TX 78667 512-396-5814
Fax: 512-396-5890 info@indecoproducts.com
www.indecoproducts.com
Plastic strapping and packaging systems and polyester meat slings
President: Daniel R Springs
R & D: Jesse Hinojosa
General Manager: David Behal
Estimated Sales: $2-5 Million
Number Employees: 20-49
Square Footage: 17000
Brands:
Linear
Net-Rap
Polychem

24173 Indemax
1 Industrial Dr
Vernon, NJ 07462 973-209-2424
Fax: 973-209-2644 800-345-7185
sales@indemax.com www.indemax.com
Manufacturer and exporter of parts for hot melt equipment
President: A Infurna
Vice President: P Infurna
Quality Control: P Infurna
Sales Director: R Infurna
Plant Manager: C Peterson
Purchasing Manager: J Tapscnyi
Estimated Sales: $5-10 Million
Number Employees: 5-9

24174 Independent Can
2040 S Lynx Ave
Ontario, CA 91761 909-923-6150
Fax: 909-923-6052 Ryan@independentcan.com
www.westernspecialty.com
Wine industry packaging
President: Rick Huether
VP: John Thompson
Manager: Joyce Sutton
Estimated Sales: $1-5 Million
Number Employees: 5-9

24175 (HQ)Independent Can Company
1300 Brass Mill Road
Po Box 370
Belcamp, MD 21017 909-923-6150
Fax: 909-923-6052
salesdept@independentcan.com
www.independentcan.com
Manufacturer, importer and exporter of decorative tin containers for coffee, peanuts, cookies, cakes, popcorn, candies, ice cream, etc
Manager: Cathy Mc Clelland
Marketing: Neil Defrancisco
Sales: Frank Shriver
Public Relations: George R McClelland
Opertaions: G William Goodwin
Plant Manager: Frank Currens
Purchasing: Page Edwards
Estimated Sales: $20-50 Million
Number Employees: 100-249
Square Footage: 360000
Type of Packaging: Consumer, Private Label
Other Locations:
Independent Can Co.
Ontario CA

24176 Independent Can Company:Western Specialty Division
2040 S Lynx Ave
Ontario, CA 91761-8010 909-923-6150
Fax: 909-923-6052 johnt@westernspecialty.com
www.westernspecialty.com
Owner: John Thompson
VP: John Thompson
Estimated Sales: $3 - 5 Million
Number Employees: 5-9

24177 Independent Dealers Advantage
780 Buford Highway Bldg
C-100
Suwanee, GA 30024 678-720-0555
Fax: 678-720-0650 bob.settle@dvtsensors.com
www.idallc.com
Packaging inspection, robotic positioning, 2D datamatrix code reading
President: Larry Pierson
CEO: Dr. Robert Shillman
CFO: Richard Morin
Senior Vice President: Richard Morin
Estimated Sales: $5-10 000,000
Number Employees: 50-99

24178 Independent Energy
42 Ladd Street
Suite 6
E Greenwich, RI 02818-4358 401-884-6990
Fax: 401-885-1500 800-343-0826
info@IndependentEnergyLLC.com
www.independentenergyllc.com
Wine industry temperature controls
Estimated Sales: $2.5-5 Million
Number Employees: 20-49

24179 Independent Ink
13700 Gramercy Pl
Gardena, CA 90249 310-523-4657
Fax: 310-329-5366 800-446-5538
inkinquiries@independentink.com
www.independentink.com
Marking machines and coding and ink jet inks; exporter of inks and solutions
Owner: Barry Brucker
Executive VP/COO: Randa Nathan
International Sales: Nora Valdez
Estimated Sales: $5-10 Million
Number Employees: 20-49
Square Footage: 25000
Type of Packaging: Consumer, Private Label

24180 Indian Valley Industries
PO Box 810
Johnson City, NY 13790-0810 607-729-5111
Fax: 607-729-5158 800-659-5111
custserv@ivindustries.com
www.iviindustries.com
Manufacturer and exporter of burlap and textile bags; also manufacturers and supplies products relating to environmental protection, erosion control, and the containment of both air and waterborn pollutants.
President: Wayne Rozen
CEO: Nilton Rozen
VP Marketing: Phil March
Estimated Sales: $10 - 20 Million
Number Employees: 10-19

24181 Indiana Bottle CompanyInc.
300 W Lovers Ln
Scottsburg, IN 47170-6729 812-752-8700
Fax: 812-752-8702 800-752-8702
mccarty@indianabottle.com
www.indianabottle.com
Custom blow molded, high and low density polyethylene and polypropylene bottles; also, screen printing services available
President: David Keener
Sales Manager: Mike McCarty
General Manager: David Baker Jr
Estimated Sales: $3.9 Million
Number Employees: 43
Square Footage: 25000

24182 Indiana Box Company
2200 Royal Dr
Greenfield, IN 46140 317-462-7743
Fax: 317-462-6412 www.royalbox.com
Corrugated containers, boxes and crates; also, die cuts available
President: Jay King
Marketing Director: Doug Holizllan
Purchasing Manager: Karen Hutinson
Estimated Sales: $5-10 Million
Number Employees: 20-49
Square Footage: 90000

24183 Indiana Carton Company
1721 W Bike St
PO Box 68
Bremen, IN 46506 574-546-3848
Fax: 574-546-5953 800-348-2390
salesservice@indianacarton.com
www.indianacarton.com
Manufacturer and exporter of boxes and cartons
President: David Petty
Chairman of the Board: Kenneth Petty
Estimated Sales: $10-20 Million
Number Employees: 50-99

24184 Indiana Cash Drawer Company
PO Box 236g
Shelbyville, IN 46176-0236 317-398-6643
Fax: 317-392-0958 800-227-4379
cshergi@icdpos.com www.icdpos.com
Manufacturer, importer and exporter of wood and steel undercounter and electronic cash drawers; serving the food service market
VP: Randal Boone
Marketing/Sales: Catherine Shergi
Estimated Sales: $20 - 50 Million
Number Employees: 50-99
Square Footage: 60000
Type of Packaging: Consumer
Brands:
Cherry
Indiana Cash Drawer
Ithaca Peripherals
Metrologic
Psc
Poshoe
Sld
Star Micronics

24185 Indiana Glass Company
37 West Broad Street
Columbus, OH 43215 513-563-6789
Fax: 513-563-9639 800-543-0357
www.lancastercolony.com
Manufacturer and exporter of housewares including candleholders, glasses and other beverage containers
Human Resources: Cathy Durham
VP/Marketing: Jerry Vanden Eynden
National Sales Manager: Mark Cunningham
International Sales Manager: Alex Morroni
Estimated Sales: $1 - 5 Million
Number Employees: 500-999
Parent Co: Lancaster Colony Corporation
Type of Packaging: Bulk

24186 Indiana Supply Company
7710 Freedom Way
Fort Wayne, IN 46818 260-497-0533
Fax: 260-497-0420 president@indianasupply.com
www.indianasupply.com
Heating equipment
Manager: Mike Spaulding
Branch Manager: John Hirsch
Estimated Sales: $2.5-5,000,000
Number Employees: 20-49
Parent Co: Indiana Supply Company

24187 Indiana Vac-Form
2030 N Boeing Rd
Warsaw, IN 46582 574-269-1725
Fax: 574-269-2723 bret@invacform.com
www.invacform.com
Manufacturer and exporter of custom plastic vacuum and thermoformed products including containers and refrigerator liners
Owner: Donald Robinson
Operations Manager: Roy Szymanski
Production Manager: Bob Stevents
Estimated Sales: $2.5-5 Million
Number Employees: 20-49
Square Footage: 45000
Type of Packaging: Food Service

24188 Indiana Wiping Cloth
2340 Schumacher Dr
Mishawaka, IN 46545 574-255-9666
Fax: 574-255-9676 800-446-9645
www.indianawipingcloth.com
Wiping cloths and absorbent products
Manager: Darren Sauer
Estimated Sales: $5-10 Million
Number Employees: 10-19

24189 Indiana Wire Company
803 S Reed Rd
PO Box 947
Fremont, IN 46737 260-495-1231
Fax: 260-495-0087 877-786-6883
iwsales@gte.net www.indianawireco.com
Wire mesh decking, shelving, baking equipment and wire products
Sales Manager: Jackie Masternik
Sales Manager: Greg Bosk
Plant Manager: Jeremy Breen
Estimated Sales: $5-10,000,000
Number Employees: 50-99
Parent Co: Indiana Wire Company
Brands:
Indiana Wire

24190 **Indianapolis Container Company**
PO Box 40006
Indianapolis, IN 46240 317-580-5000
Fax: 800-760-3319 800-760-3318
sales@containerworks.com
www.containerworks.com
Plastic and glass bottles and jars; also, pails
Manager: Stephen Roco
CFO: Nancy Heidt
VP: Nancy Lilly
Owner: Tom Asher
Estimated Sales: Below $5 Million
Number Employees: 10-19
Square Footage: 56000

24191 **Industrial Air Conditioning Systems**
1883 W Fullerton Avenue
Chicago, IL 60614-1923 773-486-4236
Fax: 773-486-4238
Proof boxes, dough rooms, bread and cake coolers and stainless steel sanitary pan trucks
VP: Albert Wentzel
Estimated Sales: $2.5-5 Million
Number Employees: 5-9
Square Footage: 15000

24192 **Industrial Automation Systems**
28440 Redwood Canyon Place
Santa Clarita, CA 91390-5724 661-257-3482
Fax: 661-257-7627 888-484-4427
iasmag@earthlink.net
www.industrialautomation.org
Bag making and closing, food processing, labeling and packaging machinery; also, material handling equipment and conveyor systems
Manager: Peter Adams
Manager: Guido Pydde
Estimated Sales: Less than $500,000
Number Employees: 1-4

24193 **Industrial Brush Corporation**
P.O.Box 2608
Pomona, CA 91769-2608 909-591-9341
Fax: 909-627-8916 800-228-6146
ibcsales@industrial-brush.com
www.industrialbrush.com
Brushes for industry and food processing
President: John Cottam
Vice Presient: Greg Tripp
Estimated Sales: $10 - 25 Million
Number Employees: 50-99
Square Footage: 360000

24194 **Industrial Ceramic Products**
14401 Suntra Way
Marysville, OH 43040 937-642-3897
Fax: 937-644-2646 800-427-2278
sales@industrialceramic.com
www.industrialceramic.com
Manufacturer and exporter of ceramic pizza stones
President: R C Oberst
Estimated Sales: $5 - 10 Million
Number Employees: 20-49
Square Footage: 50000

24195 **Industrial Chemical**
136 Long Ridge Rd
Bedford, NY 10506 914-234-9303
Fax: 914-234-9305 800-431-1075
sales@industrialchemicaldiv.com
www.industrialchemicaldiv.com
Natural fast deodorization and organic waste digestion
Director of Sales: Andy Sinclair
Estimated Sales: $1-2.5 Million
Number Employees: 10-19

24196 **Industrial Chemicals**
P.O.Box 660688
Vestavia Hills, AL 35266 205-823-7330
Fax: 205-978-0485 800-476-2042
sales_marketing@industrialchem.com
www.industrialchem.com
Ingredients to water and wastewater treatment chemistry
President: Bill Welsch
Sales Manager: L Pickens
Estimated Sales: $20-50 Million
Number Employees: 100-249

24197 **Industrial Consortium**
110 Gilmer St
Sulphur Springs, TX 75482-2703 903-885-6610
Fax: 903-885-6701 cdq@icthruput.com
www.icthruput.com
Consultant providing engineering services for packaging companies
President: Dale Stephens
Estimated Sales: $10 Million
Number Employees: 5-9

24198 **Industrial Container Corporation**
107 Motsinger St
High Point, NC 27260 336-886-7031
Fax: 336-886-2044 ccpkg.com
Plain, printed and wax corrugated boxes
President: Bernard Rosinsky
General Manager: Ron Horney
Number Employees: 10

24199 **Industrial Contracting &Rigging Company**
41 Ramapo Valley Rd
Mahwah, NJ 07430 201-529-5111
Fax: 201-529-3754 888-427-7444
info@icrnj.com www.icrnj.com
Trucking, rigging, crating & storage machinery
Owner: Joseph Sensale
Engineer: James Certaro
VP Marketing: Joseph Sensale
Estimated Sales: $1-2.5 Million
Number Employees: 10-19

24200 **(HQ)Industrial Crating & Packing, Inc.**
PO Box 88299
Seattle, WA 98138 425-226-9200
Fax: 425-226-9205 800-942-0499
sales@indcrate.com www.indcrate.com
Corrugated boxes and wooden shipping crates
President: Tom Kalil
Estimated Sales: $1-2.5 Million
Number Employees: 10-19

24201 **Industrial Custom Products**
2801 37th Ave NE
Minneapolis, MN 55421-4217 612-781-2255
Fax: 612-781-1144 877-784-2415
icp@industrialcustom.com
www.industrialcustom.com
Specialists in forming heavy-gauge plastics for OEM and material-handling applications. The company specializes in custom applications and is experienced in die-cutting and fabricating a broad range of
President: Herb Houndt
Estimated Sales: $10-20 Million
Number Employees: 5-9

24202 **Industrial Design Corporation**
2020 SW 4th Ave
Portland, OR 97201-4953 503-224-6040
Fax: 503-223-1494 800-224-0707
info@www.idc.ch2m.com www.idc.ch2m.com
Facility services including planning, site selection, environmental/permitting, facility design and engineering, industrial engineering, system integration, waste treatment, construction management, commissioning/startup andoperations/maintenance
President: George Lemmon
Corporate Management: Sue King
Vice President: Jim Hall
Marketing Director: Jeff Cross
Purchasing Manager: Mark Varon
Number Employees: 250-499

24203 **Industrial Design Fabrication & Installation, Inc.**
2501 Murray Street
Suite A
Sioux City, IA 51111 712-224-5600
Fax: 712-224-5604 877-873-5858
info@idfi.com www.idfi.com
Designer and manufacturer of conveyor systems for the food industry.

24204 **Industrial Devices Corporation**
3925 Cypress Drive
Petaluma, CA 94954-5695 707-789-1000
Fax: 707-789-0175 sales@idcmotion.com
www.idcmation.com
Electric linear actuators, servo controls and positioning systems for packaging equipment
VP Sales/Marketing: Al Statz
Customer Service Manager: Joe Ording
Estimated Sales: $10-20 Million
Number Employees: 50-99

24205 **(HQ)Industrial Dynamics Company**
3100 Fujita Street
Torrance, CA 90505 310-325-5633
Fax: 310-530-1000 888-434-5832
www.filtec.com
Manufacturer and exporter of automatic inspection systems for empty bottles, cases, missing caps, labels, filler/seamer monitors and packaging line detectors
President/Chief Executive Officer: Steve Calhoun
Managing Director: Reginaldo Pereira
Chief Financial Officer: Dan Leo
Manager, Research & Development: Kendall Hudson
Vice President, Sales & Marketing: Joanie Natisin
Chief Operating Officer: Bob Catalanotti
Purchasing Agent: Bill Herich
Estimated Sales: $44 Million
Number Employees: 216
Square Footage: 155000
Type of Packaging: Food Service
Other Locations:
Industrial Dynamics Co.Ltd.
Hamburg 30, West
Brands:
Dairyvision
Ebi-Ultraline
Ft-50
Omnivision 1200
Omnivision 900

24206 **Industrial EnvironmentalPollution Control**
127 Bruckner Boulevard
Bronx, NY 10454-4698 718-585-2410
Fax: 718-292-8353 info@foamatic.com
www.foamatic.com
Air pollution control, bacteria control equipment, cleaning and washing equipment and accessories, detergent dipensing systems, drain and sewer cleaning compounds, floor scrubbers and sweepers, odor control equipment, pan, vat and moldwashing, pressure
Manager: James Albanese
Vice President: Mike Mouracade
Food Safety Specialist: Alex Mouracade
Estimated Sales: $1-5 Million
Number Employees: 10-19
Brands:
Foamatic

24207 **Industrial Equipment Company**
35 Maple St
Suite 2
Derry, NH 03038 603-432-2037
Fax: 603-437-7539
Hand and electric power trucks and fork-lifts
President/CFO: Robert Shaver
Manager: Bob Shaver
Estimated Sales: $2 - 3 Million
Number Employees: 1-4

24208 **Industrial Grinding Inc**
2306 Ontario Ave
Dayton, OH 45414 937-277-6579
Fax: 937-277-4536 888-322-6579
sales@industrialgrinding.com
www.industrialgrinding.com
President: J M Welch
CFO: Sabrina Welch
Estimated Sales: $1 - 2.5 Million
Number Employees: 10-19

24209 **(HQ)Industrial Hardwood**
521 F St
Perrysburg, OH 43551 419-666-2503
Wooden boxes, pallets and skids
Owner: Ashvin Shah
General Manager: William Eckel
Estimated Sales: $2.5-5 Million
Number Employees: 1-4
Square Footage: 7500
Other Locations:
Industrial Hardwood
Oak Harbor OH

24210 **Industrial Hoist Service**
21525 N Highway 288b
Angleton, TX 77515-4888 979-798-7077
Fax: 979-798-1963 800-766-7077
apiwonka@nesrentals.com
www.industrialhoist.com

Air chain hoists
Manager: James Kowalk
Chief Executive Officer: Kevin Rodgers
Senior Vice President, General Manager o: James Kowalik
Vice President of Sales, Division I: Anthony Piwonka
Vice President of Sales: Kurt Charpentier
President, Chief Operating Officer: Mitch Hausman
Vice President of Purchasing: Tony DAmico
Estimated Sales: $20-50 Million
Number Employees: 50-99
Number of Brands: 3
Square Footage: 130000

24211 **Industrial Information Systems**
393 Cumberland St
Memphis, TN 38112-2712 901-324-5535
Fax: 901-324-0104 800-494-7916
INDINFO@BELLSOUTH.NET
www.infosnh3.com

Developer of training software for ammonia refrigeration operating engineers
President: Hanns Wittjen
Estimated Sales: $500,000 - $1 Million
Number Employees: 5-9

24212 **(HQ)Industrial Kinetics**
2535 Curtiss St
Downers Grove, IL 60515 630-655-0300
Fax: 630-655-1720 800-655-0306
ikiinfo@iki.com www.iki.com

Manufacturer and exporter of material handling and conveyor systems
Owner: George Huber Jr.
Marketing/Sales: Dwight Pentzien
Operations Manager: Dennis Harsnbarger
Production Manager: John Zienda
Plant Manager: John Zienda
Estimated Sales: $10-20 Million
Number Employees: 50-99
Square Footage: 90000
Other Locations:
Industrial Kinetics
Atlanta GA
Brands:
Olson Conveyors
Pallet-Pro

24213 **Industrial Laboratories**
4046 Youngfield St
Wheat Ridge, CO 80033 303-287-9691
Fax: 303-287-0964 800-456-5288
www.industriallabs.net

Full service analytical support to the food industry, dietary and sports supplements, veterinary regulatory and therapeutic monitoring. Analytical support includes food chemistry, food safety monitoring, nutritional analyses, andtesting for other potential contaminants. Provides BAX analyses fo E. coli 0157:H7, Salmonella and Listeria, food safety monitoring
President: Seth Wong
Business Development Manager: Larisa Moore
Lab Manager: Mike Gross
Estimated Sales: $2.5-5 Million
Number Employees: 20-49
Square Footage: 12000

24214 **Industrial Laboratory Equipment**
3210 Piper Lane
PO Box 220245
Charlotte, NC 28222 704-357-3930
Fax: 704-357-3940 ile@ile-textiles.com
www.ile-textiles.com

Manufacturer and exporter of industrial testing equipment including custom, food and portion scales for analytical, counting and inventory use
President: William B Floyd
VP: Harry Simmons
Estimated Sales: $1-2.5 Million
Number Employees: 1-4
Square Footage: 10000
Brands:
Ile
Multi-Scale
Ohaus

24215 **Industrial Labsales**
PO Box 30628
Portland, OR 97294-3628 800-524-8224
Fax: 503-255-8367

24216 **Industrial Lumber & Packaging**
925 W Savidge St
Spring Lake, MI 49409 616-842-1457
Fax: 616-842-9352

Pallets, skids and wooden boxes and shipping crates
Owner: Jim Walsh
Number Employees: 7
Square Footage: 14800

24217 **Industrial Machine Manufacturing**
8140 Virginia Pine Ct
Richmond, VA 23237 804-271-6979
Fax: 804-275-0813 sales@uniflow1.com
www.uniflow1.com

Customized hot melt dispensing machinery
President: Marvin Garrett
R & D: Leo Moore
VP Marketing: Leo Moore
Estimated Sales: $1-2.5 Million
Number Employees: 10-19

24218 **Industrial Magnetics**
1385 S M 75
Boyne City, MI 49712 231-582-3100
Fax: 231-582-0622 800-662-4638
imi@magnetics.com www.magnetics.com

Manufacturer and exporter of magnetic separation devices for the removal of ferrous and metals.
President/CEO: Walter Shear III
CFO: Robin Wottowa
CEO: Walter J Shear III
R&D: Dan Allore
Sales/Marketing Director: Dennis O'Leary
Public Relations: Dennis O'Leary
Production: Jeff Veryser
Plant Manager: Jeff Veryser
Purchasing: Deb Knutson
Estimated Sales: $10-15 Million
Number of Brands: 3
Number of Products: 2000
Square Footage: 38000
Brands:
Bullet

24219 **Industrial Marking Equipment**
4152 Lazy Hammock Road
Palm Beach Gardens, FL 33410-6114561-845-2828
Fax: 561-848-8930

Custom printing systems, printing attachments for converting and packaging applications
Estimated Sales: $1-2.5 Million
Number Employees: 5-9

24220 **Industrial Nameplates**
29 Indian Dr
Ivyland, PA 18974 215-322-1111
Fax: 215-953-1161 800-878-6263
info@industrialnameplates.com
www.industrialnameplate.com

Labels, tapes, tags, folding paper boxes, point of purchase displays, shelf talkers, styrene cards, etc
President: David Stitzer
Manager Marketing: Fred Knup
Estimated Sales: $2.5 - 5 Million
Number Employees: 20-49
Square Footage: 14000

24221 **Industrial Neon Sign Corporation**
6223 Saint Augustine St
Houston, TX 77021 713-748-6600
Fax: 713-748-6621 info@ins-corp.com
www.ins-corp.com

Architectural, electrical, magnetic, metal, neon, painted, plastic, silk screen, vinyl lettering & wooden signs
Owner: Sarah Joans Jr
Estimated Sales: $470,000
Number Employees: 10-19

24222 **Industrial Netting**
7681 Setzler Pkwy N
Minneapolis, MN 55445 763-496-6355
Fax: 763-496-6356 800-328-8456
info@industrialnetting.net
www.industrialnetting.com

Plastic netting for meat racks, separators, bird netting and fencing
Owner: Greg Frandsen
Vice President: David Brentz
Sales: Karen Slater
Estimated Sales: $72,000
Number Employees: 32

24223 **(HQ)Industrial Piping**
800 Culp Rd
PO Box 518
Pineville, NC 28134 704-588-1100
Fax: 704-588-5614 800-951-0988
sales@goipi.com www.goipi.com

Manufacturers and exporter of custom fabricated process equipment including coils, columns, condensers, exchangers, mix tanks, piping systems, pressure vessels, reactors and towers
President: Robert Jones
VP: Michael Roberts PE
Quality Control: Ron Miller
Business Development: Earl Dowdy
Estimated Sales: $10-20 Million
Number Employees: 50-99
Square Footage: 68000

24224 **Industrial Plastics Company**
8307 Ball Rd
Fort Smith, AR 72908-8435 479-646-8293
Fax: 479-646-6020 800-850-0916
vision@alltrista.com
www.jardenplasticsolutions.com

VP: Jim Rahn
Manager: Kyle Dejaeger
Estimated Sales: $20 - 50 Million
Number Employees: 100-249
Parent Co: Jarden Corporation

24225 **Industrial Products Corporation**
1 Hollywood Ave
Suite 30
Ho Ho Kus, NJ 07423 201-652-5913
Fax: 201-652-2494 800-472-5913

Manufacturer and exporter of standard and custom industrial blades for food processing machinery for pasta, pretzel and baked goods
Owner: Ken Dohner
Estimated Sales: $500,000-$1 Million
Number Employees: 1-4
Square Footage: 8100

24226 **Industrial Pumps Sales Company**
37 Williams S. Canning Blvd.
Tiverton, RI 2878 888-322-2926
Fax: 401-624-3373 sales@ipspump.com
www.ipspump.com

Pumps and mixers
Estimated Sales: $3-5 Million
Number Employees: 8

24227 **Industrial Razor Blade Company**
575 Nassau St
Orange, NJ 07050-1262 973-673-4286
Fax: 973-673-7165 ÿsales@industrialrazor.com
www.industrialrazor.com

Knives and blades specializing in strip ground blades; custom manufacturing available
President: John J Florey
VP: Francis Florey
Estimated Sales: Less than $500,000
Number Employees: 1-4
Square Footage: 5000

24228 **Industrial RefrigerationServices**
403 Dividend Drive
Hampton, GA 30228 770-946-9235
Fax: 770-946-3115 800-334-0273

C.E.O: Terry Childers

24229 **Industrial Screw Conveyors**
4133 Conveyor Drive
Burleson, TX 76028 817-641-0691
Fax: 817-556-0224 800-426-4669
sales@screwconveyors.com
www.screwconveyors.com

Dedicated to the design, engineering, and fabrication of helical flighting, helical screw assemblies, and helical screw conveyors using helical flighting.
President: Ralph Jones
Estimated Sales: $5,000,000
Number Employees: 50
Square Footage: 480000

24230 **Industrial Sheet Metal**
1457 E 39th Street
Cleveland, OH 44114-4198 216-431-9650
Fax: 216-431-6650 ismine@worldnet.att.com
Sheet metal and stainless steel custom restaurant equipment including cooking, heating and food processing; also, store fixtures.
Owner: Milan Suka
Secretary/Treasurer: Donna Sens
Vice President: Jeff Dixon
Operations Manager: Guy DiSiena
Plant Manager: Guy DiSiena
Estimated Sales: $1-2.5 Million
Number Employees: 10-19
Square Footage: 12000

24231 **Industrial Sign Company**
9635 Klingerman Street
South El Monte, CA 91733-1726 562-602-2420
Fax: 562-602-2599 800-596-3720
www.southeimotte.com
Point of purchase displays, flags, pennants, banners and electric signs
Owner: Maria Saavetra
Estimated Sales: $1-2,500,000
Number Employees: 20-49

24232 **Industrial Signs**
5501 Jefferson Hwy
Suite A
New Orleans, LA 70123 504-736-0600
Fax: 504-736-9285 sales@industrialsigns.net
www.industrialsigns.net
Signs including electrical, neon, industrial, etc
President: William F Hunter
Estimated Sales: $2.5 - 5 Million
Number Employees: 20-49

24233 **Industrial Systems Group**
5140 Moundview Drive
Red Wing, MN 55066-1100 651-388-2267
Fax: 651-385-2279 800-ROB-OTIC
Estimated Sales: $1 - 5 Million

24234 **Industrial Test Systems**
1875 Langston Street
Rock Hill, SC 29730 803-392-9712
Fax: 803-329-9743 800-861-9712
its@sensafe.com www.sensafe.com
Tests for water quality parameters.
Owner: Ivars Jaunakais
VP: Lea Jaunakais
Marketing: Mike McBride
Sales: George Bailey
Plant Manager: Angelo Perry
Estimated Sales: $5-10 Million
Number Employees: 40

24235 **Industrial Washing Machine Corporation**
PO Box 1509
Jackson, NJ 08527-0266 732-304-9203
Fax: 732-286-0862 inwamacorp@yahoo.com
Pot and pan washers.
President: Joseph Gangi
Number Employees: 10-19
Square Footage: 20000
Brands:
Industrial

24236 **Industrial Washing Machine Corporation**
PO Box 506
Matawan, NJ 07747-0506 732-566-4660
Fax: 732-566-2201
Pot and pan washers
President: Joseph Gangi
Estimated Sales: $1-3 Million
Number Employees: 19
Square Footage: 20000
Brands:
Industrial

24237 **Industrial WoodFab & Packaging Company**
18620 Fort St
Riverview, MI 48193 734-284-4808
Fax: 734-284-5308 www.industrialwoodfab.com
Wooden crates, boxes and pallets
President: Richard E Ott
Engineer: Tom DeFeyten
Manager: Frank Nicnski
Estimated Sales: $1-2.5 Million
Number Employees: 10-19
Square Footage: 65000

24238 **Industries for the Blind**
445 S Curtis Rd
West Allis, WI 53214-1016 414-778-3040
Fax: 414-933-4316 sales@ibmilw.com
www.industriesoftheblind.com
Manufacturer and exporter of household cleaning supplies including plastic window brushes and brooms
President: Charles Lange
VP: Karen Walls
Manager: Lee Kaboski
Estimated Sales: $10-20 Million
Number Employees: 50-99
Parent Co: Industries For The Blind
Type of Packaging: Consumer, Food Service, Bulk

24239 **Industries of the Blind**
920 West Lee Street
Greensboro, NC 27403 336-274-1591
Fax: 336-544-3739 info@iob-gso.com
www.industriesoftheblind.com
Mops including cotton, rayon, wet and dry; also, brooms, wooden mop handles, clipboards and pens
Executive Director: Mike Burge
Director Human Resources: Don Bassett
General Manager: Derek Davis
Plant Manager: Jack Permer
Purchasing Manager: Bob Gwyn
Estimated Sales: $10 - 20 Million
Number Employees: 100-249
Square Footage: 130000
Type of Packaging: Consumer

24240 **Industrious Software Solutions**
500 W Florence Ave
Inglewood, CA 90301 310-672-8700
Fax: 310-419-6000 800-351-4225
info@2000accounting.com
www.2000accounting.com
Developer of operations management software for wholesalers/distributors, manufacturers, exporters and importers
President: Stephen Ryza
Quality Control: Gary Zenun
Estimated Sales: $10-20 Million
Number Employees: 20-49

24241 **Industronics Service Company**
489 Sullivan Ave
PO Box 649
South Windsor, CT 06074 860-289-1551
Fax: 860-289-3526 800-878-1551
service@industronics.com
www.industronics.com
Incinerators and commercial furnaces and ovens
President: James Wyse
VP: Dean Hills
Estimated Sales: Below $5 Million
Number Employees: 20-49
Brands:
Consertherm

24242 **Indy Lighting**
12001 Exit 5 Pkwy
Fishers, IN 46037 317-849-1233
Fax: 317-576-8006
Incandescent, compact fluorescent, recessed, surface and track lighting fixtures
VP Sales: Steve Fetter
VP Marketing: Barry Hindman
Manager: Kevin Fagan
Estimated Sales: $10 - 20 Million
Number Employees: 50-99
Square Footage: 125000
Parent Co: Juno Lighting

24243 **Infanti International**
3075 Richmond Terrace
Staten Island, NY 10303-1300 718-447-5632
Fax: 718-447-5667 800-874-8590
www.infanti.com
Manufacturer and exporter of serving carts and chairs
Estimated Sales: $3 - 5 Million
Number Employees: 20-49
Type of Packaging: Food Service

24244 **Inficon**
2 Technology Pl
East Syracuse, NY 13057 315-434-1100
Fax: 315-437-3803 reachus@inficon.com
www.inficon.com
VP: Gary W Lewis
Estimated Sales: I
Number Employees: 100-249

24245 **Infitec**
P.O.Box 2956
Syracuse, NY 13220 315-433-1150
Fax: 315-433-1521 800-334-0837
sales@infitec.com www.infitec.com
Timing controls (industrial/time delay), speed controls, flashers, and custom controls.
CEO/CFO/President: George Ehegartner, Sr Sr
Quality Control/Marketing: George Ehegartner, Jr Jr
VP Sales: David Lawrie
Estimated Sales: $10-20 Million
Number Employees: 32
Square Footage: 25000
Type of Packaging: Bulk
Brands:
Inc
Infitec

24246 **Inflatable Packaging**
P.O.Box 40
Newtown, CT 06470-0040 203-426-2900
Fax: 203-426-6976 800-520-3383
sales@inflatablepackaging.com
www.inflatablepackaging.com
Air bag dunnage system for internal packaging designed to replace peanuts, compressed paper, expansion foam and air bubble materials. Manufacture Void-Fill Bags, En-Cap Sleeves, and Waffle-Paks in various sizes to meet your shippingrequirements
President: Michell Tschantz
Estimated Sales: $1 - 3 Million
Number Employees: 5-9

24247 **Infometrix**
11807 North Creek Parkway South
Suite B-111
Bothell, WA 98011 425-402-1450
Fax: 425-402-1040 info@infometrix.com
www.infometrix.com
Analyses for quality control, online monitoring of processes, sensory evaluation and research in the food and beverage industries
President: Brian Rohrback
Sales/Marketing Manager: Paul Bailey
Estimated Sales: Below $5 Million
Number Employees: 10-19
Brands:
Biocount
Ein Sight
Pirouette

24248 **Infopro, Inc.**
2920 Norwalk Court
Aurora, IL 60502-1310 630-978-9231
Fax: 734-638-6139 info@sysmaker.com
www.sysmaker.com/infopro
Menuing and application development systems
President: Sue Graham
CEO: Sue Graham
Vice President And CFO: Eileen Anderson
Executive Vice President And COO: Greg Capella
Administrative Manager: Susan Boarden
Estimated Sales: $500,000-$1 Million
Number Employees: 5
Brands:
Guidemaker
Systemaker

24249 **Information Access**
8801 E Pleasant Valley Rd
Cleveland, OH 44131-5599 216-328-0100
Fax: 216-328-0913 info@infoaccess.net
www.infoaccess.net
Software for food brokers
CEO: Edward Schnell
National Sales Manager: James Garskie
Estimated Sales: $10-20 Million
Number Employees: 1-4

24250 Information Resources
150 N Clinton St
Chicago, IL 60661 312-726-0005
888-262-5973
www.symphonyiri.com
Supplier of market content, analytic services, and business performance management solutions.
Chairman: Romesh Wadwani
CEO: John Freeland
CFO: Michael Duffy
CEO: John Freeland
Grp President/International Operations: Mark Tims
CTO/CIO: Marshall Gibbs
Estimated Sales: $554 Million
Number Employees: 1,000-4,999
Other Locations:
Information Resources
LK, Bel
Information Resources - UK
Berkshire, GBR
IRI Hellas
New Ionia, Athens
IRI France
Chambourcy, France
IRI USA
Waltham MA

24251 Informed Beverage Management
420 Minuet Ln
Charlotte, NC 28217 704-527-1709
Fax: 704-527-8509 800-438-5058
sales@informedbeverage.com
www.highjump.com
Computer software and hardware
Manager: Pel Dael
Manager: Jerry Morrow
Manager: Ed Browning
Estimated Sales: $5-10 Million
Number Employees: 10-19

24252 Infra Corporation
5454 Dixie Hwy
P.O. Box 300997
Waterford, MI 48330 248-623-0400
Fax: 248-623-1766 888-434-6372
sales@infracorporation.com
www.infracorporation.com
Bar and restaurant equipment, stainless and brass small wares
President: Bryan A Mc Graw
Estimated Sales: $1 - 3 Million
Number Employees: 5-9
Square Footage: 48000

24253 InfraTech Corporation
939 N Vernon Avenue
Azusa, CA 91702-2202 626-331-9400
Fax: 626-858-1951 800-955-2476
joe@infratech-usa.com
Comfort heat for patios
President/CEO: Sam Longo Jr.
Research & Development: Joe Petro
Marketing Director: Joe Petro
Sales Manager: Joseph Petro
Estimated Sales: $.5 - 1 million
Number Employees: 90
Square Footage: 75000

24254 Ingersoll Rand
1467 Rte 31 S
PO Box 970
Annandale, NJ 08801
800-376-8665
www.ingersollrandproducts.com
Oil-free rotary screw and centrifugal compressors for reducing the risk of food and beverage contamination and also reducing energy consumption.
President, Industrial Tech Sector: Robert Zafari
Chairman & CEO: Michael Lamach
SVP & CFO: Steven Shawley
SVP: John Conover IV
SVP Innovation/Technology: Paul Camuti
SVP Human Resourcees & Communications: Marcia Avedon
SVP Global Operations: Todd Wyman
Estimated Sales: $14.78 Billion
Number Employees: 150
Parent Co: Ingersoll-Rand

24255 Ingles Markets
2913 US Highway 70 W
Black Mountain, NC 28711-9103 828-669-2941
Fax: 828-669-3678
customerservice@ingles-markets.com
www.ingles-markets.com
Dairy and beverages
President/COO/Director: James Lanning
Chairman/CEO: Robert Ingle
CFO/Director/VP Media Relations: Ronald Freeman
Estimated Sales: $31.7 Million
Number Employees: 16,000
Other Locations:
Dairy Manufacturing
Asheville NC
Brands:
Milko
Sealtest

24256 Inglett & Company
151 Walker Road
Statesville, NC 28625-2535 706-738-1488
Fax: 706-736-5416 tFspitzer@hotmail.com
Automatic packaging machinery
Estimated Sales: $5-10 Million
Number Employees: 20-50

24257 Ingman Laboratories
2945 34th Avenue S
Minneapolis, MN 55406-1707 612-724-0121
Fax: 612-724-0603 adkb@mci2000.com
http://inglabs.pconline.com
Consultant specializing in product development, food labeling and laboratory services including chemical and microbiological analysis for the food and agricultural industries
President: Pete Meland
Public Relations: Kipp Barksdale
Office Manager: Dick Davidson
Chief Chemist: Glenn Kyle
Number Employees: 24
Square Footage: 40000

24258 Ingredient Masters
1080 Nimitzview Dr
Suite 302
Cincinnati, OH 45230 513-231-7432
Fax: 513-231-3104 sales@ingredientmasters.com
www.ingredientmasters.com
Custom-designing bulk dry ingredient and dispensing systems
President: Scott Culshaw
Estimated Sales: Below $5 Million
Number Employees: 1-4

24259 (HQ)Ingredients Solutions
631 Moosehead Trail
Waldo, ME 04915 207-722-4172
Fax: 207-722-4271 800-628-3166
info@ingredientssolutions.com
www.ingredientssolutions.com
Independent supplier of Carrageenan. Offers a full range of Natural and Organic allowed products including Xanthan Gums, Sodium Alginates and Carrageenans for use in dairy, meat & poultry, sauces & dressings, bakery, confections, petfood, pharmaceuticals and personal-care applications.
President & COO: Donna Ravin
CEO: Scott Rangus
CFO: Janine Mehuren
Lab Manager: Kevin Johndro
Purchasing: Kristin Grover
Number Employees: 10
Type of Packaging: Bulk

24260 (HQ)Ingredion Incorporated
5 Westbrook Corporate Ctr
Westchester, IL 60154 708-551-2600
www.ingredion.com
Makers of food ingredients and industrial products from corn and other starch-based raw materials. Produces sweetners like high-fructose corn syrup, starch, corn oil and corn gluten.
Chairman, President & CEO: Ilene Gordon
SVP/General Counsel/CCO/Corporate Sec.: Christine Castellano
SVP/Chief Innovation Officer: Anthony Delio
Executive Vice President/CFO: Jack Fortnum
SVP, Human Resources: Diane Frisch
VP/Corporate Controller: Matthew Galvanoni
SVP, Corporate Strategy: John Saucier
SVP, Operations Excellence & EHS&S: Robert Stefansic
VP/Corporate Treasurer: Kevin Wilson
EVP, Global Specialties: James Zallie
Estimated Sales: $6.87 Billion
Number Employees: 12,100
Type of Packaging: Bulk
Other Locations:
Corn Products International
Etobicoke ON
Brands:
Abc Carrier
Brewer's Crystals
Buffalo
Cerelose
Enzose
Fiberbond
Globe
Globe Plus
Invertose Hfcs
Proferm
Royal
Royal-T
Stablebond
Surebond
Ultrabond
Unidex

24261 Inject Star of America
355 Industrial Road
Mountain View, AR 72650 203-740-8441
Fax: 203-740-8331 800-253-6475
info@injectstar.com www.injectstar.com
Meat processing equipment and food packaging equipment
President: Larry Jacobson
Estimated Sales: Below $5 Million
Number Employees: 7

24262 Inksolv 30, LLC.
2495 N Ave
PO Box 66
Emerson, NE 68733 515-537-5344
info@inksolv30.com
www.inksolv30.com
Manufacturer and exporter of powdered hand soap
President: Kevin Wilson
Estimated Sales: $2.5-5 Million
Number Employees: 1-4

24263 Inland Consumer Packaging
17507 S Dupont Hwy
Harrington, DE 19952-2370 302-398-4211
Fax: 302-398-1422 www.gp.com
Folding paper boxes
President: Brent Paugh
Executive Vice President: Christian Fischer
Executive Vice President of Operations: Wesley Jones
Estimated Sales: $20 - 50 Million
Number Employees: 100-249

24264 Inland Label and Marketing Services, LLC
2009 W Avenue South
La Crosse, WI 54601 608-788-5800
800-657-4413
info@inlandlabel.com www.inlandlabel.com
Labels
Owner: Steve Winterfield
Director of Sales: Don Iverson
Number Employees: 70
Square Footage: 41138

24265 Inland Paper Board & Packaging
1500 W Elk Ave
Elizabethton, TN 37643-2873 423-542-2112
Fax: 423-542-8739 thoover@iccnet.com
www.templeinland.com

Manufacturer and exporter of corrugated boxes
COO: Steve Sliva
Sales Manager: Bob Mavity
General Manager: Tim Hoover
Estimated Sales: $100-500 Million
Number Employees: 50-99
Parent Co: Temple Inland

24266 **Inland Paperboard & Packaging**
210 Mount Phillips Street
Rock Hill, SC 29730-3340 803-366-4103
Fax: 803-366-1648
Corrugated containers, boxes and sheets
CEO: Dale Stahl
Sales Manager: Mannonum Heller
General Manager: George Hare
Estimated Sales: $20-50 Million
Number Employees: 100-249
Parent Co: Temple Inland Company

24267 **Inland Paperboard & Packaging**
P.O.Box 40
Austin, TX 78767-0040 512-434-5800
Fax: 512-434-3750 www.templeinland.com
Manufacturer and exporter of corrugated shipping containers
President: Sarilee Norton
CEO: Doyle R Simons
VP Public Affairs: J Areddy
Estimated Sales: K
Number Employees: 10,000
Parent Co: Temple Inland

24268 **Inland Showcase & Fixture Company**
1473 N Thesta St
Fresno, CA 93703-3791 559-237-4158
Fax: 559-237-7238 inlandshowcase@qnis.net
www.inlandshowcase.tripod.com
Restaurant and store fixtures including plastic counters
Purchasing Manager: Richard Bertad
Estimated Sales: $10-20 Million
Number Employees: 50-99
Square Footage: 30000

24269 **Inline Automation**
14758 Bluebird St NW
Anoka, MN 55304 763-434-2828
Fax: 763-755-5757 websales@intelligentline.com
President: Gerald Jilts
Number Employees: 10

24270 **Inline Filling Systems**
216 Seaboard Ave
Venice, FL 34285 941-486-8800
Fax: 941-486-0077 sales101@fillers.com
www.fillers.com
Manufacturer and exporter of liquid filling equipment, capping machinery, conveyors and unscramblers
President: Sam Lubus
R&D: Jay Carlson
VP Sales: Joe Schemenauer
Estimated Sales: $10,000,000
Number Employees: 1-4
Square Footage: 20000
Brands:
Levelhead 2

24271 **Inline Plastics Corporation**
42 Canal St
Shelton, CT 06484 203-924-2015
Fax: 203-924-0370 800-826-5567
sales@inlineplastics.com
www.inlineplastics.com
Thermoformed plastic packaging including trays
CEO: Thomas Orkisz
Estimated Sales: $5-10 Million
Number Employees: 250-499
Square Footage: 315000

24272 **Inline Services**
27731 Commercial Park Ln
Tomball, TX 77375 281-401-8142
Fax: 281-401-8147 888-973-0079
inline@flash.net www.inlineservices.com

Pigging systems for product displacement and batching pipe cleaning
President: Gary Smith
Financial Director: Deanne Schillaci
Vice President: Harvey Diehl
Sales: Jessica Nichols
General Manager: Rick Meade
Warehouse: Russell Williams
Accounts Payable: Susan Thomas
Estimated Sales: $1.5 Million
Number Employees: 5-9

24273 **Inman Foodservices Group**
3807 Charlotte Ave
Nashville, TN 37209 615-321-5591
Fax: 615-321-5689
foodservicedesign@inman-inc.com
www.inman-inc.com
Consultant specializing in food service facility planning and design
President: Bill Inman
Vice President: Brandi Hale
Estimated Sales: $5-10 Million
Number Employees: 20-49

24274 **Inmotion Technologies**
211 Overlook Dr
Sewickley, PA 15143-2459 412-749-0710
Fax: 412-749-0705 info_us@inmotech.com
www.danahermotion.com
Multi-axis motion control systems for advanced packaging and printing featuring accurate coordination and synchronization functions
President, Chief Executive Officer: Lawrence Culp
Estimated Sales: $1 - 5 Million
Number Employees: 5-9

24275 **InnaVision Global Marketing Consultants**
1615 Count Turf Ln
Racine, WI 53402-2058 262-633-1000
www.innavision.com
Marketing consultant for equipment manufacturers, distributors and representatives
Managing Member: Charles Allison
Estimated Sales: $190,000
Number Employees: 2

24276 **Innerspace Design Concepts**
16015 Van Aken Boulevard
Apt 104
Shaker Heights, OH 44120-5345 216-295-1589
Fax: 216-295-1593 innerspace@stratos.net
Complete design services for restaurants and stores
President: Steven Goldschel
CEO: Steven Goldschel
Number Employees: 12
Square Footage: 3500

24277 **Inno Seal Systems**
10900 S Commerce Blvd Ste B
Charlotte, NC 28273 704-521-6068
Fax: 704-521-6038 sales@innoseal.com
www.innoseal.com
President: Jeff Rebh
Parent Co: Twinseal Systems B.V.

24278 **Innophos Holdings, Inc.**
259 Prospect Plains Road
Cranbury, NJ 08512 609-495-2495
Fax: 609-860-0138 www.innophos.com
Producer of specialty grade phosphate products
Chairman/CEO/President/Director: Randolph Gress
CFO/Vice President: Neil Salmon
Vice President, Speciality Phosphates: Joseph Golowski
Senior Director, Human Resources: Gail Holler
Vice President, Operations: Louis Calvarin
Plant Manager: Susan Turner
Director, Purchasing: Denis Lapointe
Estimated Sales: $862 Million
Number Employees: 1,290

24279 **Innova Envelopes**
7213 Rue Cordner
La Salle, QC H8N 2J7
Canada 514-595-0555
Fax: 514-595-1112 supremex@supremex.ca
www.supremex.com

Manufacturer and exporter of envelopes
President: Gilles Cyrcs
CFO: Stephan Lavigne
VP/General Manager: Gilles Cyr
R&D: Alain Tremblay
Estimated Sales: $30 - 50 Million
Number Employees: 200
Parent Co: Supremex

24280 **Innova-Tech**
1500 E Lancaster Ave # 100
Paoli, PA 19301-1500 610-640-9350
Fax: 610-640-2670 800-523-7299
www.innovatechnologies.in
Wastewater treatment equipment and dissolved air flotation units
President: John Murphy
Chief Engineer: Greg Laurent
Number Employees: 1-4
Square Footage: 54600

24281 **Innovations Expressed LLC**
Po Box 1823
Sparta, NJ 07871-3850 201-452-0557
info@perfectlyexpressed.com
www.perfectlyexpressed.com
Specialty food packaging i.e. gift wrap/labels/boxes/containers.
Marketing: Jody Shampton-Moore

24282 **Innovations by Design**
19 Foothill Path
Chadds Ford, PA 19317-9146 610-558-0160
Fax: 610-558-1960 morganel@erols.com
Consultant specializing in food service design, cad layouts and project administration for cafeterias, prisons, schools, hospitals, sports arenas, etc
President & CEO: Jon Shaw
President & CEO: Jon Shaw
VP Of Operations: John Fogleman
Director Of Marketing: Scott Huggins
Director Of Sales: Allen Wells

24283 **Innovative Ceramic Corp.**
432 Walnut St
East Liverpool, OH 43920-3130 330-385-6515
Fax: 330-385-6510 info@innovativeceramic.com
www.innovativeceramic.com
Rubber stamps and high temperature inks
President: Orville Steininger
Estimated Sales: Below $5 Million
Square Footage: 20000

24284 **Innovative Components**
P.O.Box 294
Southington, CT 06489-0294 860-621-7220
Fax: 860-620-0288 800-789-2851
info@liquidlevel.com www.liquidlevel.com
Manufacturer and exporter of sanitary liquid level instrumentation for level indication, alarms and controls
Owner: Pete Meade
Sales: Pete Meade
Production: Joe Kubisek
Estimated Sales: $1-2.5 Million
Number Employees: 5-9
Square Footage: 10000

24285 **Innovative Controls Corp**
1354 E Broadway St
Toledo, OH 43605 419-691-6684
Fax: 419-691-0170
sales@innovativecontrolscorp.com
www.innovativecontrolscorp.com
Provides the following services to the food & beverage industry: packaging integration; packaging machine rebuilds and retrofits; automated process control panels; conveyor systems; bar coding; verticle form fill seal bagging machines;cup feeders - auger and filling; rebuilds and retrofits of processing equipment; transfer feeds; materials handling distribution; mills - sugar, flour & meal; process controls for weighing, blending, & batching; PLC controlled robotics. Individualconsulting.
President & CEO: Louis Soltis
Marketing Director: Angela Hitchens
Sales Director: Michael Hitchens
Director of Operations: Robert Simon
Estimated Sales: $5-7 Million
Number Employees: 20-49
Square Footage: 70000

24286 Innovative Energy Inc
10653 West 181st Avenue
Lowell, IN 46356 219-696-3639
Fax: 219-696-5220 info@insul.net
www.insul.net

Specialty food packaging i.e. gift wrap/labels/boxes/containers.
President: Robert Wadsworth
Marketing: Tammy Snyder

24287 Innovative Folding Carton Company
901 Durham Ave
South Plainfield, NJ 07080 908-757-0205
Fax: 908-757-6464 linde@innovativecps.com
www.theinnovativepkg.com

Folding cartons and pressure sensitive labels
President: Shawn Smith
CFO: Bob Sgaitierri
CFO: Robert S Pierre
Quality Control: Will Suton
VP Sales: Shawn Smith
VP Operations: Ray Karst
Estimated Sales: $20-50 Million
Number Employees: 100-249
Square Footage: 100000
Parent Co: Impaxx

24288 Innovative Food Solutions LLC
4516 Kenny Road
Suite 320
Columbus, OH 43220-3711 614-326-1421
Fax: 614-326-1443 800-884-3314
jliebrec@columbus.rr.com
www.innovativefoodsolutions.com

Consulting firm ready to assist you to quickly launch new food products and manufacturing processes, new food industry ingredients, perform technical troubleshooting and produce prototype samples for trade shows and market researchstudies. Areas of experience include organic, natural and nutraceutical/functional food products, including aseptic and retort liquids, and spray dried powders.
President: Jeff Liebrecht
R&D: Jeff Liebrecht

24289 Innovative Foods, Inc.
338 N Canal
Suite 20
South San Francisco, CA 94080 650-871-8912
Fax: 650-871-0837 ed@innovativefoods.org
www.innovativefoods.org

Infused foods, including using product forming, flavoring, coloring and value added to underutilized raw materials.
Owner: Gilbert Lee
VP/Secretary & Treasurer: Fay Hirschberg
Research & Development: Edward Hirschberg
Estimated Sales: $190 Thousand
Square Footage: 74000

24290 Innovative Marketing
6595 Edenvale Blvd Ste 160
Eden Prairie, MN 55346-2567 952-392-2280
Fax: 952-949-8865 800-438-4627
info@innovamarketing.com
www.innovamarketing.com

Manufacturer and exporter of lid openers for plastic containers
President: Brad Pappas
Operations Manager: Amy Vinar
Estimated Sales: 150000
Number Employees: 1-4
Square Footage: 20000
Brands:
Pco
The Lid Cutter

24291 Innovative Molding
6775 McKinley Ave
Sebastopol, CA 95472 707-829-2666
Fax: 707-829-5212
whunt@innovativemolding.com
www.innovativemolding.com

Manufacturer and exporter of threaded plastic caps and lids for jars and bottles.
Administrator: Alan Williams
Vice President: Ron Cook
Operations Manager: Warren Hunt
Estimated Sales: $5-10 Million
Number Employees: 50-99
Square Footage: 28000

24292 Innovative Moving Systems, Inc.
310 S 10th St
P.O. Box 700169
Oostburg, WI 53070 920-564-6272
Fax: 920-564-2322 800-619-0625
president@lectrotruck.com www.lectrotruck.com

USA manufacturer of the ORIGINAL battery operated stail climbing hand truck for over 40 years. Safely move heavy loads from 600lbs/272kg to 1500lbs/680kg in less time. All models include free battery, battery charger, strap bar(s), 2year motor warranty and a 1year entire unit warranty.
President: Kevin Peters
Sales/Marketing Executive: Jason Tagel
Estimated Sales: Below $5 Million
Number Employees: 5
Square Footage: 34000
Brands:
Lectro Truck

24293 Innovative Packaging Solution
1692 12th Street
Martin, MI 49070-8745 616-656-2100
Fax: 616-656-2101

Litho cut and stack labels, seals, stickers, label application equipment and computerized artwork
CEO: James Rand
Sr VP: Jim English
Communications Director: Kate Hunter
Estimated Sales: $20-50 Million
Number Employees: 100-249
Square Footage: 30000
Parent Co: Excellence Group

24294 Innovative Plastech
1260 Kingsland Dr
Batavia, IL 60510 630-232-1808
Fax: 630-232-1978 ghernandez@inplas.com
www.inplas.com

Custom thermoforming, tool and package designing, plastic trays
President: Jim Gustafson
CFO: Jake Clever
VP: Edward Gustafson
R&D: Denny Bahl
Quality Control: Girish Raval
Sales: Dave Lyons
Production: Martine Del Toro
Plant Manager: John Martinez
Purchasing: Larry Rosales
Estimated Sales: $15 Million
Number Employees: 64
Square Footage: 90000
Type of Packaging: Consumer, Private Label

24295 Innovative Plastics Corporation
400 Route 303
Orangeburg, NY 10962 845-359-7500
Fax: 845-359-0237
service@innovative-plastics.com
www.innovative-plastics.com

Thermoformed plastics packaging and contract packaging services
President: Judith Hershaft
VP: Bud Macfarlane
Estimated Sales: $35 - 40 Million
Number Employees: 100-249
Square Footage: 60000
Type of Packaging: Consumer
Other Locations:
Innovative Plastics Corporation
Nashville TN

24296 Innovative Space Management
2645 Brooklyn Queens Expressway
Woodside, NY 11377-7826 718-278-4300
Fax: 718-274-0973 contact@ny.diam-int.com

Manufacturer, exporter and designer of shelf management systems and point of purchase displays
VP/General Manager (ISM Division): Bryan Yablans
VP Sales: Winn Esterline
VP Operations: Valerie Vignola
Number Employees: 850
Square Footage: 150000
Parent Co: POP Displays

24297 Inovatech
3911 Mount Lehman Road
Abbotsford, BC V4X 2N1
Canada 604-857-9080
Fax: 604-857-0843 info@inovatech.com
www.inovatech.com

Number Employees: 10

24298 Inovpack Vector
40 Vreeland Avenue
Suite 107
Providence, RI 888-227-4647
Fax: 203-852-0136

Casings

24299 Inpaco Corporation
PO Box 286
Nazareth, PA 18064-0286 610-759-8544
Fax: 610-759-9021

Wine industry bags

24300 Inpak Systems Inc
540 Tasman Street
Madison, WI 53714 608-221-8180
Fax: 608-221-4473 sales@inpaksystems.com
www.inpaksystems.com

Distributor of industrial packaging equipment
President: Gerald Hoagne
VP: Ronn Ferrell
Marketing: Tom McDonnell
Sales: Dennis Murphy
Operations: Mike Kennedy
Estimated Sales: $3-4 Million
Number Employees: 7
Square Footage: 8000
Type of Packaging: Bulk

24301 Inprint Systems
208 Spring Dr
Saint Charles, MO 63303 636-946-2439
Fax: 636-724-4670 888-ETL-ABEL
sales@inprint-americas.com www.cclabel.com

Computerized numbering and bar coding devices; pressure sensitive labels
President: Brian Madden
CEO: Chuck Jongeward
R & D: John Dultz
Quality Control: Steve Harding
Human Resources: Sheila Eicheo
Office Manager: Jeanne Hodges
Estimated Sales: $5-10 Million
Number Employees: 50-99

24302 Inscale
1607 Maple Ave
Terre Haute, IN 47804-3234 812-232-0893
Fax: 812-232-6876 855-839-9147
incell@inscale-incell.com
www.bestbuyscale.com

Checkweighing devices, weight control systems, scales
Owner: Fred Herrmann
General Manager: Paul Herrmann
Estimated Sales: $5-10 Million
Number Employees: 20-49
Square Footage: 140000
Type of Packaging: Bulk

24303 Insect-O-Cutor
1641 Lewis Way
Stone Mountain, GA 30083 770-939-2835
Fax: 142-386-3497 800-988-5359
info@pandlesystems.com
www.insect-o-cutor.com

Industrial commercial grade insect light traps; 110 volt, 220 volt, stainless steel, scatterproof, energy-efficient
President: W A Harris
Type of Packaging: Private Label
Brands:
Germ-O-Ray
Guardian
Insect-O-Cutor

24304 Insects
16950 Westfield Park Rd
Westfield, IN 46074 317-896-9300
Fax: 317-867-5757 800-992-1991
insectsltd@aol.com www.insectslimited.com

Manufacturer, exporter and wholesaler/distributor of pest control systems including traps, lures, insect monitoring and detection devices, fumigation products, etc.; importer of cigarette beetle pheromone traps; also, pest controlaudits and seminars available
President: David Mueller
CFO: Barbara Bass
VP: John Mueller
General Manager: Patrick Kelley
Estimated Sales: $1 Million
Number Employees: 10-19
Square Footage: 3000

Brands:
Bullet Lure
Lasio
No Survivor
Serrico
Storgard

24305 **Insight Distribution Systems**
222 Schilling Cir
Suite 275
Hunt Valley, MD 21031-8638 410-403-1100
Fax: 410-329-1114 800-310-3548
info@routescape.com www.routescape.com
Beverage distribution software, specilizing in mobile computers, route accounting, inventory, financials, account management software
President: Bob Jenkin
Estimated Sales: $10-20 Million
Number Employees: 10

24306 **Insight Packaging**
1000 Muirfield Drive
Hanover Park, IL 60133-5468 630-980-4314
Fax: 630-980-4316 info@insightpack.com
www.insightpack.com
Package food items for other companies
President: Gregory Batton
Estimated Sales: $10 - 20 Million
Number Employees: 10

24307 **Insignia Systems**
8799 Brooklyn Boulevard
Minneapolis, MN 55445 763-392-6200
Fax: 763-392-6222 800-874-4648
info@insigniasystems.com
www.insigniasystems.com
Manufacturer and exporter of promotional items including signage and software for bar coding and large format printing
President/CEO: Glen P. Dall
VP, Finance: John C. Gonsior
CFO: John C. Gonsior
Quality Control: Bob Norman
VP Marketing: Scott Simcox
Number Employees: 80
Brands:
Insignia Pops
Stylus

24308 **(HQ)Insinger Machine Company**
6245 State Rd
Philadelphia, PA 19135-2966 215-624-4800
Fax: 215-624-6966 800-344-4802
sales@insingermachine.com
www.insingermachine.com
Manufacturer and exporter of commercial dishwashers potato peelers, garbage disposal units, french fry cutters, tray washers and driers and dish, glass, pot and pan washers
President: John Stern
CEO: Robert Cantor
VP Sales/Marketing: Ari Cantor
Chief Engineer: Jim Bittner
Quality Control: Kris Hogan
Marketing Director: Annemarie Fisher
Regional Sales Manager: Don Gazzillo
Vice President of Operations: Kristine Hogan
Purchasing Manager: Kristine Hogan
Estimated Sales: $10 - 20 Million
Number Employees: 50-99
Square Footage: 65000

24309 **Insinger Machine Company**
6245 State Rd
Philadelphia, PA 19135-2966 800-344-4802
Fax: 215-624-6966 800-344-4802
rcantor@insingermachine.com
www.insingermachine.com
Manufacturer and exporter of dishwashers
President: John Stern
CEO: Robert A. Cantor
Vice President-Sales & Service: Ari Cantor
Chief Engineer: Jim Bittner
Quality Control: Kristine Hogan
National Marketing Representative/Govern: Sandy Diamond
Regional Sales Manager: Don Gazzillo
Customer Service Engineer: Chris Monteith
Vice President of Operations: Kristine Hogan
Manager (Parts): Mary McWilliams
Estimated Sales: $10 - 20 Million
Number Employees: 50-99
Parent Co: Insinger Machine Company

24310 **Inspired Automation**
5321 Derry Ave Ste D
Agoura Hills, CA 91301 818-991-4598
Fax: 818-597-4820
info@inspiredautomation.com
www.inspiredautomation.com
Automatic net weighing, counting, in-line batching and filling machinery; exporter of automatic net weighing, in-line batching and counting machinery
President: Robert Homes
Sales: Buzz Holmes
Plant Manager: Joesph Gonzales
Estimated Sales: $3 - 5 Million
Number Employees: 5-9
Number of Brands: 1
Number of Products: 22
Square Footage: 2000
Type of Packaging: Consumer, Food Service, Private Label, Bulk

24311 **Insta Pro International**
10104 Douglas Ave
Des Moines, IA 50322-2007 515-254-1260
Fax: 515-276-5749 800-383-4524
triplef@fff.com www.insta-pro.com
Manufacturer and exporter of processing equipment for textured soy products
President, Chief Executive Officer: Kevin Kacere
R&D: Wilmot Wijeratne
VP: Karl Arnold
Chairman: Wayne Fox
VP International Marketing: Tom Welby
Vice President of Operations: Hennie Pieterse
Estimated Sales: $5 - 10 Million
Number Employees: 10-19
Parent Co: Triple F
Brands:
Express
Insta-Pro

24312 **Instabox**
1139 40th Avenue North East
Calgary, AB T2E 6M9
Canada 403-250-9217
Fax: 403-250-8075 800-482-6173
info@instabox.com www.instabox.com
Corrugated cardboard boxes and shipping supplies
President: Jim Mace
CFO: Greg Mace
CEO: Greg Mace
Office Manager: Linda Burgher
Manager: Richard Bain
Order Desk: Dale Beck
Number Employees: 40

24313 **(HQ)Instacomm Canada**
Unit 1, Suite 376
Oakville, ON L6M 2Y1
Canada 905-465-1266
Fax: 905-465-0644 877-426-2783
info@instacomm.com www.instacomm.com
Distributor of guest and server oaging systems
Estimated Sales: $1 - 5 Million
Number Employees: 1-4
Other Locations:
Instacomm Canada
Creedmoor NC

24314 **Institute of Packaging Professionals**
1833 Centre Point Circle
Suite 123
Naperville, IL 60563 630-544-5050
Fax: 630-544-5055 info@iopp.org
www.iopp.org
Association for packaging professionals
Religious Leader: Paul Kim
Number Employees: 10-19

24315 **Institutional & Supermarket Equipment**
7362 NW 5th St
PO Box 17440
Plantation, FL 33317 954-584-3100
Fax: 954-584-5591 info@iseinc.org
www.iseinc.org
Industrial food serving equipment
Executive Director: Philip Polunsky
Estimated Sales: $1-2.5 Million
Number Employees: 10-19

24316 **Institutional Equipment**
704 Veterans Pkwy # B
Bolingbrook, IL 60440-4612 630-771-0990
Fax: 630-771-0994 iei@kwom.com
www.ieiusa.net
Stainless steel counters, shelving and tables including steam
President: Frank Fiene
VP Manufacturing: Don Wasielweski
Estimated Sales: $5-10 Million
Number Employees: 20-49
Square Footage: 160000

24317 **Instron Corporation**
825 University Ave
Norwood, MA 02062 781-828-2500
Fax: 800-877-6674 info@instron.com
www.instron.com
Materials and structural testing systems, SW, and accessories used to evaluate the mechanical properties and performance of various materials, components and structures
President: James Garrison
Estimated Sales: I
Number Employees: 1,000-4,999

24318 **Instrumented Sensor Technology**
4704 Moore St
Okemos, MI 48864 517-349-8487
Fax: 517-349-8469 info@isthq.com
www.isthq.com
President/CEO: Gregory Hoshal
Estimated Sales: $1 - 3 Million
Number Employees: 5-9

24319 **Insulair**
35275 S Welty Rd
Vernalis, CA 95385-9733 209-839-0911
Fax: 209-839-1353 800-343-3402
info@insulair.com www.insulair.com
Manufacturer and exporter of insulated triple-wall paper cups and plastic lids
President: Claus Sadlier
CFO: Larry Nally
Quality Control: Dale Houglant
Sales Director: Frank Gavin
Estimated Sales: $5 - 10 Million
Number Employees: 5-9
Brands:
Insulair

24320 **Intech Enterprises**
3825 Grant St
Washougal, WA 98671 360-835-8785
Fax: 360-835-5144 info@intechenterprises.com
www.intechenterprises.com
President: Tom Cunning
Estimated Sales: Below $5 Million
Number Employees: 10-19

24321 **Intedge Manufacturing**
1875 Chumley Road
Woodruff, SC 29388-8561 864-969-9601
Fax: 864-969-9604 866-969-9605
customer.service@intedge.com
www.intedge.com
Food service equipment including textiles, smallware, baking supplies, timers, thermometers, utensils, and much more.
Plant Manager: Debi Collier
Number Employees: 50-99
Type of Packaging: Food Service, Private Label
Brands:
Intedge
Metalwash

24322 **Integrated Barcode Solutions**
856 3rd St NW
Valley City, ND 58072
Fax: 530-273-4725 ibsed@inreach.com
www.home.inreach.com/ibsed
Portable terminal or fixed station data capture applications that employ bar code technology
*Estimated Sales:*less than $500,000
Number Employees: 1

24323 **Integrated Distribution**
2110 S 169th Plz # 200
Omaha, NE 68130-4650 402-397-8757
Fax: 402-397-8451 www.retalix.com

Computer software for food distribution
General Manager: Dror Kalush
Vice President of Information Technology: Bob Mawyer
Head of Marketing: Oren Betzaleli
Executive Vice President of Retail Sales: Mike Todd
Estimated Sales: $10 - 20 Million
Number Employees: 50-99

24324 Integrated Packaging Systems
3 Luger Rd
Suite 5
Denville, NJ 07834 973-664-0020
Fax: 973-263-2992 bfields@ipsnj.com
www.ipsnj.com
Tablet counting and liquid filling
President: Robert W Fields
Vice President: Michael McNeila
Technical Manager: Michael Frusteri
Sales Director: Marianne Mooney
General Manager: Phil DePalma
Estimated Sales: $4-5 Million
Number Employees: 5-9
Brands:
Procount Salt Counter
Versaflow Liquid Filler

24325 Integrated Restaurant Software/RMS Touch
9 West Ridgely Road
Timonium, MD 21093 201-461-9096
Fax: 410-902-5468 DARYL@rmstouch.com
www.rmstouch.com
Manufacturer and exporter of P.O.S. touch screen software for restaurants, bars, cafeterias, etc
President: Richard Adler
VP Sales: Peter Polizanno
Estimated Sales: $2.5 - 5 Million
Number Employees: 10-19
Square Footage: 12000

24326 Integrated Systems
1904 SE Ochoco Street
Portland, OR 97222-7315 503-654-7886
Fax: 503-654-7868 800-705-6401
packexpo@intsystem.com
Palletizers and depalletizers available in high or low level infeed with rates up to five layers a minute, options include depalletizing, pallet dispensers, tie sheets and fully automated multi-palletizer cells
Estimated Sales: $1 - 5 Million

24327 Intelligent Controls
PO Box 638
Saco, ME 04072 207-283-0156
Fax: 207-283-0158 800-872-3455
webadmin@incon.com www.incon.com
Manufacturer and exporter of microprocessor and programmable controls including liquid level measurement and process multiplexing systems, supervisory control and data acquisition systems
CEO: Scott Tremble
Director Marketing: John Eastman
VP: Dean Richards
Estimated Sales: F
Number Employees: 1,000-4,999
Square Footage: 14000
Parent Co: Franklin Fueling Systems

24328 Intellution
325 Foxboro Blvd
Foxboro, MA 02035-2879 508-698-7400
Fax: 508-698-6915 800-526-3486
mmoschetto@intellution.com
www.intellution.com
Intellution provides an industry-standard software platform that collects, distributes, controls and manages information from the plant floor throughout the enterprise, supplying customers with scalable solutions that deliver increasedproductivity and return on investment
VP Global Marketing: Harry Merkin
Chief Executive Officer: Maryrose Sylvester
VP Human Resources: Michael Jacobi
Senior VP Engineering: Bev Shultz
VP Customer Services: Sheila Kester
Estimated Sales: $20 - 50 Million
Number Employees: 100-249

24329 Intelplex
9607 Dielmn Rck Islnd Ind Dr
Olivette, MO 63132 314-983-9996
Fax: 314-983-9989 intouch@intelplex.com
www.intelplex.com
Consultant specializing in the design of restaurant equipment
Owner: Alan Sherman
Estimated Sales: $1-2.5 Million
Number Employees: 1-4

24330 Intentia Americas
1700 E Golf Rd # 9
Schaumburg, IL 60173-5816 847-762-0900
Fax: 847-762-0901 800-796-6839
moreinfo@intentia.com www.lawson.com
Managing Director, Intentia Australia/Ne: Linus Parker
Chief Executive Officer, President: Harry Debes
Vice President of Sales: Mikael Anden
Estimated Sales: $10 - 20 Million
Number Employees: 20-49

24331 (HQ)Inteplast Bags & Films Corporation
7503 Vantage Pl.
Delta, BC V4G 1A5 604-946-5431
Fax: 604-946-5343
Polyethylene produce bags, film, trash can liners and corrugated sheets
President: John Young
Estimated Sales: $12.4 Million
Number Employees: 90

24332 Inteplast Group, LTD
9 Peach Tree Hill Rd
Livingston, NJ 07039 973-994-8000
Fax: 973-994-8028 info@inteplast.com
www.inteplast.com
BOPP films, stretch wrap, and plastic concentrates and compounds.
President: John Young
Number Employees: 1,000-4,999

24333 Inter Tape Pharma
741 4th St
Menasha, WI 54952-2801 920-725-4335
Fax: 920-729-4118 800-626-2626
www.intertapepolymer.com
Carton-sealing machines including water-activated carbon sealers, carton sealing tapes both pressure sensitive and water-activated
Plant Manager: John Cullen
Purchasing Manager: Sandy Cordle
Estimated Sales: $100+ Million
Number Employees: 250-499

24334 Inter-Access
100 Carrier Drive
Etobicoke, ON M9W 5R1
Canada 514-744-6262
Fax: 514-744-3176
Executive search firm; also, consultant providing company re-engineering, manufacturing automation, ISO quality implementation, business planning and market surveys
President: Mohamed Geledi-Nami
VP: Edith Chandonnet
Senior Consultant: Tom Schopflocher
Number Employees: 5-9
Square Footage: 1000
Parent Co: Le Groupe Consortium Canada

24335 Inter-City Welding & Manufacturing
10058 E Wilson Rd
Independence, MO 64053-1541 816-252-1770
Fax: 816-252-8321
Industrial belt conveyors
Manager: Mary Robinett
Estimated Sales: $500,000-$1 Million
Number Employees: 1-4

24336 (HQ)Inter-Pack Corporation
PO Box 691
Monroe, MI 48161-0691 734-242-7755
Fax: 734-242-7756 www.interpackgroup.com
Manufacturer and exporter of corrugated paper and foam plastic; contract packaging services available
Manager: Frank Calandra
Estimated Sales: $20 - 50 Million
Number Employees: 20-49

24337 InterBio
P.O.Box 130549
The Woodlands, TX 77393-0549 281-298-9410
Fax: 281-298-9411 888-876-2844
pvoisinet@interbio.com
www.interlabsupply.com
Manufacturer and exporter of microbial products for drain maintenance, odor control, septic systems, etc.; also, in-house and field technical support available
President: Peter Perez
Estimated Sales: $3 - 5 Million
Number Employees: 5-9
Square Footage: 28400
Brands:
Bio Free Trap Clear
Biofree Septic Clear

24338 InterMetro Industries Corporation
651 N Washington St
Wilkes Barre, PA 18705 570-825-2197
Fax: 570-823-0250 800-441-2714
moreinfo-cp@intermetro.com
www.intermetro.com
Bins and storage identification tags
President: John Mackley
CFO: Don McAlonan
CEO: John Nackley
Quality Control: Wayne Scott
Estimated Sales: I
Number Employees: 1,000-4,999
Parent Co: Emerson

24339 InterXchange Market Network
32 Laurens Street
Charleston, SC 29401-1565 803-577-4794
Fax: 803-577-4794 800-577-4794
rrabago@halcyon.com
Brokers and commodity exchanges, computer systems and software
Number Employees: 45

24340 Interactive Sales Solutions
P.O.Box 1183
Coppell, TX 75019-1183 214-352-9575
Fax: 214-352-5729 800-352-9575
Sales@ISSI-IVR.com www.issi-ivr.com
Sales force automation software utilizing touch-tone phones for consumer sales, food service and retail food broker operations
President: William Godbey
VP: Dean Schenkel
Operations Manager: John Williamson II
Estimated Sales: $500,000-$1 Million
Number Employees: 5-9
Square Footage: 8000
Type of Packaging: Bulk
Brands:
Interactive Sales Manager

24341 Interactive Services Group
600 Delran Pkwy # C
Delran, NJ 08075-1268 856-824-9401
Fax: 856-824-9415 800-566-3310
jbdickinson@isg-service.com
www.ist.service.com
Hand-held computer system maintenance and support. Specialize in supporting Intermec and Symbols systems. Company also has priority software applications for route accounting industry
Owner: Igor Lukov
CEO: J Dickinson
Director Human Resources: Michele Galan
Estimated Sales: $4 Million
Number Employees: 20-49
Square Footage: 36000

24342 Interamerican Coffee
19500 State Hwy 249 # 255
Houston, TX 77070 713-462-2671
Fax: 713-912-7072 800-346-2810
traders@iaccoffee.com www.iaccoffee.com
Green coffee importer and distributer
President: Guy Burdett
Controller: Samantha Marino
Vice President of Operations: John Mason
Estimated Sales: $5-10 Million
Number Employees: 20-49

24343 **Interbake Foods**
3951 Westerre Parkway
Suite 200
Richmond, VA 23233 804-755-7107
Fax: 804-755-7173 inquiries@interbake.com
www.interbake.com
Crackers and cookies
President/CEO: Ray Baxter
SVP/CFO: Donald Niemeyer
Estimated Sales: $5-10 Million
Number Employees: 1,000-4,999
Type of Packaging: Consumer, Food Service, Private Label, Bulk
Other Locations:
Interbake Foods
Green Bay WI

24344 **Interbrand Corporation**
555 Market Street
Suite 900
San Francisco, CA 94105 347-334-3502
Fax: 415-593-2250 877-692-7263
inquiries@interbrand.com www.interbrand.com
Consultant for brand logos, packaging, identification and naming
Global CEO: Jez Frampton
Global Chief Creative Officer: Andy Payne
Global CFO & COO: Kelly Gall
Global Chief Strategy Officer: Leslie Butterfield
Office Manager: Paige Casamjor
Director of Operations: Michael Levtchenko
Estimated Sales: $5 - 10 Million
Number Employees: 20-49
Parent Co: Omnicom
Other Locations:
Interbrand Corp.
Chicago IL

24345 **Intercard**
1884 Lackland Hill Pkwy # 1
St Louis, MO 63146-3569 314-275-8066
Fax: 314-275-4998 info@intercardinc.com
www.intercardinc.com
Manufacturer and exporter of credit and debit card systems
President: Ray Sherrod
CEO: Ray Sherrod
CFO: Gerry Schmidt
Quality Control: Lynn Soreden
Estimated Sales: $10 - 20 Million
Number Employees: 20-49

24346 **Intercomp Company**
3839 County Road 116
Hamel, MN 55340 763-476-2531
Fax: 763-476-2613 800-328-3336
info@intercompcompany.com
www.intercompco.com
Manufacturer and exporter of electronic scales including crane, platform, pallet and portable truck, floor, bench and hanging
Owner: Robert Kroll
Quality Control: Mark Browne
Plant Manager: Jeff Weyandt
Estimated Sales: $20 Million
Number Employees: 50-99
Square Footage: 90000
Brands:
Cs 750
Cw 250
Cw 500
Pw 800
Pw 850

24347 **Interfood Ingredients**
60 Hickory Drive
Waltham, MA 02451 781-370-9983
Fax: 781-370-9997 info@interfoodinc.com
www.interfoodingredients.com
Supplier of dairy ingredients
President: Ferry Veen
Vice President: Jack Engels
Estimated Sales: $235 Million
Number Employees: 18
Parent Co: Interfood Holding

24348 **Interior Systems**
241 N Broadway
Suite 600
Milwaukee, WI 53202 414-224-0957
Fax: 414-224-0972 800-837-8373
info@isiamerica.com www.isiamerica.com
Food service fixtures, furniture, play equipment, artwork and signage
President/CEO: Tony Lutz
Chairman: Lindsey Bovinet
CFO: Bill Stoll
Vice President - Fulfillment: Mark Huck
IT Manager: Robert Graf
Director Of Sales: Jason Fredrickson
Director - Human Resources: Jim Carlson
Director of Operations: Darin Grobe
Creative Director: Tony Pagliuca
Controller: Zach Schaefer
Estimated Sales: $5 - 10 Million
Number Employees: 50-99

24349 **Interlake Material Handling**
1230 E Diehl Rd # 400
Naperville, IL 60563-7810 630-245-8800
Fax: 630-245-8906 800-468-3752
contactus@interlake.com www.ikcorp.com
Storage racks, conveyor systems and order picking software and controls; exporter of storage racks
CEO: Dan Wilson
VP Sales: Mike O'Reilly
Estimated Sales: $111 Million
Number Employees: 500-999

24350 **Interliance**
200 E Sandpointe Ave 510
Santa Ana, CA 92707 714-540-8889
Fax: 714-540-6113 800-540-7917
info@interliance.com www.interliance.com
Consultant providing performance improvement, process improvement, quality strategies, policies and procedures, regulatory compliance programs, site specific training, etc
President: Brad Kemp
CFO: Brad Kamth
Quality Control: Brad Kamth
Estimated Sales: $5 - 10,000,000
Number Employees: 1-4

24351 **Intermec Systems & Solutions**
6001 36th Avenue West
Everett, WA 98203-1264 425-348-2600
Fax: 425-355-9551 800-755-5505
www.intermec.com
Manufacturer and exporter of computer hardware and software systems including route accounting systems
President: Tom Miller
Interim President, Chief Executive Offic: Allen Lauer
Senior Vice President of Solutions: Earl Thompson
Chief Technical Officer: Arvin Danielson
Director Marketing: Betty Damisch
Senior Vice President of Sales and Marke: James McDonnell
Senior Vice President of Operations: Dennis Faerber
Estimated Sales: $1 - 5 Million
Number Employees: 250-499

24352 **Intermec Technologies Corporation**
6001 36th Ave West
Everett, WA 98203-1264 425-348-2600
Fax: 425-355-9551 800-755-5505
www.intermec.com
Designer, manufacturer and exporter of fully integrated data collection hardware, software, services and supplies including bar code devices, mobile computers, interactive reader language, thermal transfer ribbon printers, labels andtags
Interim President/CEO: Allen Lauer
SVP/Chief Financial Officer: Robert Driessnack
SVP, Global Operations: Dennis Faerber
Chief Technology Officer: Arvin Danielson
SVP/General Counsel/Corporate Secretary: Yukio Morikubo
SVP, Global Sales & Marketing: James McDonnell
General Manager: Ron Kubera
VP, Human Resources: Jeanne Lyon
Senior Buyer/Program Specialist: Sandra Ripley
Estimated Sales: $140 Million
Number Employees: 1,745
Square Footage: 312000
Parent Co: Honeywell
Other Locations:
Intermec Technologies Corp.
Dublin
Brands:
Crossbar
Duratherm
Irl
Janus
Ttr
Trakker

24353 **Intermec Technologies Corporation**
6001 36th Ave W
Everett, WA 98203-1264 425-348-2600
Fax: 425-267-2983 info@intermec.com
www.unova.com
Labels and tags
President: Tom Miller
CEO: Patrick J Byrne
Chief Technical Officer: Arvin Danielson
Chairman: Larry D Brady
Senior Vice President of Sales and Marke: James McDonnell
Senior Vice President of Operations: Dennis Faerber
Estimated Sales: $50-100 Million
Number Employees: 1,000-4,999
Parent Co: Intermec

24354 **Intermec/Norand Mobile Systems**
6001 36th Avenue West
Everett, WA 98203 - 12 425-348-2600
Fax: 425-355-9551 800-755-5505
info@intermec.com www.intermec.com
President: Tom Miller
Interim President, Chief Executive Offic: Allen Lauer
Senior Vice President of Solutions: Earl Thompson
Chief Technical Officer: Arvin Danielson
Senior Vice President of Sales and Marke: James McDonnell
Senior Vice President of Operations: Dennis Faerber
Estimated Sales: $1 - 5 Million
Number Employees: 250-499

24355 **Intermex Products USA**
1375 Ave S.
Suite 300
Grand Prairie, TX 75050 972-988-1333
Fax: 972-660-5941 800-508-8475
ravera@cydsa.com www.intermexproducts.com
Cydsa, cellophane, bi-oriented polypropylene, coextrusions, printed and laminated plastic films
Estimated Sales: $5-10 Million
Number Employees: 5-9
Parent Co: La Torre

24356 **Intermold Corporation**
30 Old Mill Rd
Greenville, SC 29607 864-627-0300
Fax: 864-627-0005 sales@.intermoldcorp.com
www.intermoldcorp.com
Manufacturer and exporter of plastic injection molding products including bakery proofer cups; custom molding for the baking industry available
President: Alan Butcher
VP: Jane Butcher
Estimated Sales: $1-2.5 Million
Number Employees: 10-19
Square Footage: 32000

24357 **International Approval Services**
8501 East Pleasant Valley Road
Cleveland, OH 44131-5516 216-524-4990
Fax: 216-642-3463 877-235-9791
info@csa-international.org
www.csa-international.org
Testing service for gas powered cooking equipment
President & CEO: Ash Sahi
EVP, Finance & Administration: Esteban De Bernardis
Regional Vice President, U.S. & Mexico: Rich Weiser
EVP, Science & Engineering: Helene Vaillancourt
Chief Operating Officer: Magali Depras
Estimated Sales: $1 - 5 Million
Number Employees: 100-249
Parent Co: CSA

24358 **International Automation**
332 Ramapo Valley Road
Oakland, NJ 7004 201-651-0500
Fax: 201-760-9960 info@iaiusa.com
www.iaiusa.com

Checkweighers
President: Mark Schultz
Estimated Sales: $.5 - 1 million
Number Employees: 5-9

24359 **International Carbonic**
P.O.Box 578
Adelanto, CA 92301 760-246-3900
Fax: 760-246-4044 Info@BeverageWorld.com.
www.ici.us
Carbonated beverage dispensing equipment, including carbonators, valves, fittings and systems; complete sheet metal facility
President: Joe Suarez
Estimated Sales: $20-50 Million
Number Employees: 20-49

24360 **International Coatings**
2925 Lucy Ln
Franklin Park, IL 60131 847-451-0279
Fax: 847-451-0379 800-624-8919
custserv@icocoat.com
www.internationalcoatings.com
Flooring, coatings
President: Mike Kramer
Marketing Director: Raymond Hurley
Estimated Sales: $10 - 20 Million
Number Employees: 10-19

24361 **International Cold Storage**
215 E 13th St
Andover, KS 67002 316-733-1385
Fax: 316-733-2434 800-835-0001
sales@icsco.com www.icsco.com
Walk-in coolers and freezers; exporter of walk-in coolers
President: Matt Madeksza
CFO: Dean McSpadden
Sales Manager: Dave Konecny
Plant Manager: Jay Risley
Estimated Sales: $10 - 20 Million
Number Employees: 100-249
Square Footage: 80000
Parent Co: Tyler Refrigeration Company

24362 **International ContainerSystems**
5401 W Kennedy Boulevard
Suite 711
Tampa, FL 33609-2447 813-287-8940
Fax: 813-286-2070 800-444-4274
Carton and container systems
Estimated Sales: $1-2.5 Million
Number Employees: 5-9

24363 **International Cooling Systems**
300 Granton Drive
Richmond Hill, ON L4B 1H7
Canada 416-213-5566
Fax: 416-213-9666 888-213-5566
sales@intlcoolingsystems.com
www.intlcoolingsystems.com
Manufacturer, importer and exporter of turnkey process cooling systems, cooling towers, chillers, flake and pumpable flow ice machines and water/fluid recirculation stations
President: Victor Gardiman
VP: Otto Novak
Plant Manager: Steve Novak
Number Employees: 10-19
Square Footage: 96000

24364 **International Envelope Company**
2 Tabas Ln
Exton, PA 19341 610-363-0900
Fax: 610-363-2999 www.goiec.com
Specialty mailing envelopes and filing products
CEO: Sandy Moyer
VP Marketing: Sandy Moyer
Estimated Sales: $1 - 5 Million
Number Employees: 250-499
Square Footage: 150000
Parent Co: American Business Products

24365 **International Environmental Solutions**
6860 Gulfport Blvd S.
Suite 131
South Pasadena, FL 33707-2108 727-573-1676
Fax: 727-573-0747 800-972-8348
davidleeti@aol.com www.drycamping.com
Automatic faucet controls
President: Steve Gordon
Estimated Sales: Less than $500,000
Number Employees: 20-49
Square Footage: 16000
Brands:
Ez Flo
Med Flo
Quik Flo
Sani-Flow

24366 **International EquipmentTrading**
960 Woodlands Parkway
Vernon Hills, IL 60061-3103 847-913-0777
Fax: 847-913-0785 800-438-4522
info@ietltd.com www.ietltd.com
Buy, lease, rent, trade, sell refurbished analytical isntruments
President: Turgay Kaya
Estimated Sales: $3 - 5 Million
Number Employees: 5-9

24367 **(HQ)International Flavors &Fragrances, Inc.**
521 W 57th St
New York, NY 10019-2960 212-765-5500
Fax: 212-708-7132 iffusaflavors@iff.com
www.iff.com
Flavors for beverages, sweet goods, savory and dairy products
President, Flavors Division: Hernan Vaisman
CEO & Chairman: Douglas Tough
EVP & CFO: Kevin Berryman
SVP Research & Development: Ahmet Baydar
SVP Human Resources: Angelica Cantlon
SVP Operations: Francisco Fortanet
Estimated Sales: $2.79 Billion
Number Employees: 5600
Square Footage: 100000
Type of Packaging: Bulk

24368 **International Flavors &Fragrances, Inc.**
3005 International Blvd
Augusta, GA 30906 706-796-2800
Fax: 706-560-3640 iffusaflavors@iff.com
www.iff.com
Flavors for beverages, sweet goods, savory and dairy products
Parent Co: International Flavors & Fragrances, Inc.
Type of Packaging: Bulk

24369 **International Flavors &Fragrances, Inc.**
1620 West Crosby
Carrolton, TX 75006-6656 972-245-2117
Fax: 972-242-2966 iffusaflavors@iff.com
www.iff.com
Flavors for beverages, sweet goods, savory and dairy products
Parent Co: International Flavors & Fragrances, Inc.
Type of Packaging: Bulk

24370 **International Flavors &Fragrances, Inc.**
600 Highway 36
Hazlet, NJ 07730 732-264-4500
Fax: 732-335-2551 iffusaflavors@iff.com
www.iff.com
Flavors for beverages, sweet goods, savory and dairy products
Parent Co: International Flavors & Fragrances, Inc.
Type of Packaging: Bulk

24371 **International Flavors &Fragrances, Inc.**
2051 North Lane Avenue
Jacksonville, FL 32254 904-783-2180
Fax: 904-695-4616 iffusaflavors@iff.com
www.iff.com
Flavors for beverages, sweet goods, savory and dairy products
Parent Co: International Flavors & Fragrances, Inc.
Type of Packaging: Bulk

24372 **International Flavors &Fragrances, Inc.**
1515 State Highway #36
Union Beach, NJ 07735 732-264-4500
Fax: 732-335-2591 iffusaflavors@iff.com
www.iff.com
Flavors for beverages, sweet goods, savory and dairy products
Parent Co: International Flavors & Fragrances, Inc.
Type of Packaging: Bulk

24373 **International Flavors &Fragrances, Inc.**
521 West 57th Street
New York, NY 10019 212-765-5500
Fax: 212-708-7132 iffusafragrances@iff.com
www.iff.com
Flavors for beverages, sweet goods, savory and dairy products
Parent Co: International Flavors & Fragrances, Inc.
Type of Packaging: Bulk

24374 **International Group**
2875 N Main St
Oshkosh, WI 54901 920-233-5500
Fax: 920-233-4345 www.igivax.com
Petroleum wax and wax blends, hot melt coatings and cheese wax
Manager: Gary Fraaza
General Manager: Gary Fraaza
Production Manager: Tom Brunner
Number Employees: 20-49
Square Footage: 60000

24375 **International Ingredients Corporation**
4240 Utah Street
Saint Louis, MO 63116-1820 314-776-2700
Fax: 314-776-3395 iicag@iicag.com
www.iicag.com
Processing of food plant waste
President: Bill Holtgrieve
Chairman: Fred E Brown Jr
Estimated Sales: $30 - 50 Million
Number Employees: 130

24376 **International Knife & Saw**
1435 N Cashua Dr
Florence, SC 29501-6950 843-662-6345
Fax: 843-664-1103 800-354-9872
iks@iksinc.com www.iksinc.com
Manufacturer and exporter of fruit and vegetable slicing machinery; also, machine knives
President: Don Weeks
Vice President of Division: Terry Isaacs
Vice President, Metal & Printing Divisio: Jim Ranson
Sales: Warren Balderson
Vice President, Finance & Manufacturing: Mike Gray
Purchasing Manager of Materials: Sarah Strother
Estimated Sales: $60 Million
Number Employees: 100-249

24377 **International Kosher Supervision**
351 Keller E Price Street
Suite 200
Keller, TX 76248 817-337-4700
Fax: 817-337-4901 www.ikckosher.com
Kosher food certification agency with rabbinical staff
Rabbinical Administration: Rabbi Dovid Jenkins
General Manager: Jerry Dillig
Parent Co: Texas K International

24378 **International MachineryExchange**
PO Box 438
Deerfield, WI 53531-0438 608-764-5481
Fax: 608-764-8240 800-279-0191
sales@imexchange.com www.imexchange.com
Manufacturer and exporter of re-manufactured machinery including refrigeration, cheese making, centrifuges, compressors and heat exchangers; also, tanks and custom control systems
President: Greg Mergen
Sales Director: George Bamman
Estimated Sales: $5-10 Million
Number Employees: 10-19
Square Footage: 40000

24379 International Meat Inspection Consultants
P.O.Box 264
Germantown, MD 20875-0264 301-570-1058
Fax: 240-821-5939 imic@thefoodtrainer.com
www.thefoodtrainer.com
Consultants, importing/exporting, label expediting
President: Barbara Bennett
CFO: John Cucl
Estimated Sales: $.5 - 1 million
Number Employees: 1-4

24380 International Media & Cultures
1250 South Parker Road Ste. 203
Denver, CO 80231 303-337-4028
Fax: 303-337-5140 mantha@earthnet.net
www.askimac.com
Cheese anti-caking agent and starter media
President: Malireddy Reddy
Plant Manager: Ed Price
Estimated Sales: $5 - 10 Million
Number Employees: 10-19

24381 International Molded Packaging Corporation
206 Central Main Street
Central City, SD 57754-2070 605-578-2500
Fax: 605-578-3933 800-307-2194
sales@impakcorp.com www.impakcorp.com
President and CEO: Rod Galland
Estimated Sales: Below $5,000,000
Number Employees: 10

24382 International Omni-Pac Corporation
2079 Wright Ave
La Verne, CA 91750-5822 909-593-2833
Fax: 909-593-2829 bobdavis@omni-pac.com
www.omni-pac.com
Manufacturer and exporter of packaging systems and juice and soft drink bottle carriers
President: Richard Erickson
Sales Manager: Bob Davis
Estimated Sales: Below $5 Million
Number Employees: 5-9
Square Footage: 40000

24383 International PackagingMachinery
PO Box 8597
Naples, FL 34101-8597 941-643-2020
Fax: 941-643-2708 800-237-6496
Manufacturer and exporter of stretch wrapping machinery including film tensioners and stretch film delivery systems
Estimated Sales: $5-10 Million
Number Employees: 20-49
Square Footage: 21000
Brands:
Ipm
Roller-Brake
Uni-Tension

24384 International PackagingNetwork
409 N Jefferson Street
Kearney, MO 64060-8379 816-628-3002
Fax: 800-247-4904 800-932-3597
jerryflxar@aol.com
High performance and flexibility polyolefin film
Estimated Sales: $500,000-$1 Million
Number Employees: 1-4

24385 International Paper
2400 Shamrock Ave
Fort Worth, TX 76107 817-338-4000
Fax: 817-877-3761 www.internationalpaper.com
Corrugated shipping containers
President: W O'Grady
VP: M O'Grady
VP: W Poteet
Manager: Chris Harding
Plant Manager: Val Miranda
Estimated Sales: $20 - 50 Million
Number Employees: 100-249

24386 International Paper Beverage
6400 Poplar Ave
Memphis, TN 38197-0198 901-419-7000
Fax: 901-419-4439 comm@ipaper.com
www.internationalpaper.com
Aseptic beverage packaging
CEO: John V Faraci
Estimated Sales: K
Number Employees: 10,000

24387 (HQ)International Paper BoxMachine Company
PO Box 787
Nashua, NH 03061-0787 603-889-6651
Fax: 603-882-2865
Manufacturer, exporter and importer of carton folding and gluing machinery; also, corrugated converters including liquid-tight packaging
President: Hugh McAdam
Marketing Manager: Larry Macko
Marketing Communications Manager: Michael Sutcliffe
Estimated Sales: $20-50 Million
Number Employees: 100-249
Square Footage: 165000

24388 International Paper Co.
6400 Poplar Avenue
Memphis, TN 38197
800-207-4003
internationalpaper.comm@ipaper.com
www.ipaper.com
Boxes including printed and windowed for bakeries; also, bottles, paper cups and straight lined and right angled glue
President/Chief Operating Officer: Mark Sutton
Chairman/Chief Executive Officer: John Faraci
SVP, Corporate Development: C. Cato Ealy
SVP, Industrial Packaging Group: William Hoel
SVP, Manufacturing & Technology: Tommy Joseph
SVP, Human Resources & Communications: Paul Karre
SVP/General Counsel/Corporate Secretary: Sharon Ryan
SVP/Chief Financial Officer: Carol Roberts
Estimated Sales: $27.83 Billion
Number Employees: 70000

24389 International Paper Company
2 Manhattanville Rd
Suite 401
Purchase, NY 10577 914-397-4057
Fax: 914-397-1650 800-223-1268
comm@ipaper.com www.internationalpaper.com
Packaging, distribution, papers, forrest products, chemical products, forrest resources, branigar, pulp
Chairman/CEO: John Faraci
CFO: Christopher Liddell
Executive VP: David Oskin
Executive VP: C Wesley Smith
Executive VP Papers: Robert Amen
Senior VP Marketing/Sales: Michael Balduino
Senior VP Consumer Packaging: Thomas Gestrich
Senior VP Building Materials: Manco Snapp
Senior VP Distribution: Thomas Costello
Estimated Sales: $500,000-$1 Million
Number Employees: 20-49
Number of Brands: 9

24390 International Paper Container
801 Fountain Ave
Lancaster, PA 17601-4532 717-397-3741
Fax: 717-393-5130
lancaster.customerservice@ipaper.com
www.ipaper.com
Fiber board and packing machinery
Manager: James Bonifas
Estimated Sales: $20-50 Million
Number Employees: 50-99

24391 International Paper Packaging
6400 Poplar Ave
Memphis, TN 38197 901-419-9000
internationalpaper.comm@ipaper.com
www.ipaper.com
Containerboard and corrugated boxes, bleached board, folding cartons, liquid packaging, specialty industrial papers
Chairman/Chief Executive Officer: John Faraci
Managing Director: Jeff Metzgar
Senior Vice President/CFO: Carol Roberts
Senior Vice President/CIO: John Balboni
Quality Control Manager: Tim Brinker
Director, Marketing: Marilyn Link
Sales Manager: Blake Asbury
Vice-Chief Operating Officer: Lawrence Beck
Plant Manager: Dru Kraus
Supply Chain Manager: Libby Johnson
Estimated Sales: $27.8 Billion
Number Employees: 70,000
Square Footage: 17780

24392 International Patterns,Inc.
50 Inez Dr
Bay Shore, NY 11706-2238 631-952-2000
Fax: 516-938-1215
sales@internationalpatterns.com
www.internationalpatterns.com
Manufacturer and exporter of illuminated and nonilluminated menu, changeable letter and write-on boards, nonneon signs, banners, point of purchase displays, tray stands, ice-free wine coolers and youth chairs
President: Shelley Beckwith
CFO: Shelly Beckwi
Vice President: Shellay Beckwith
R & D: Paul Kaplan
VP Marketing: Murray Gottieb
VP Sales: Andrew Replan
Production Manager: Ran Alvaeri
Purchasing Manager: Nancy St. Nicholas
Estimated Sales: $5-10 Million
Number Employees: 50-99
Number of Brands: 1
Number of Products: 50
Square Footage: 140000
Type of Packaging: Food Service
Brands:
City Lites
Comet
Grandstand
Lite Writer
Magnetic Menumaster
Menu Master
Menu Master

24393 (HQ)International Plastics &Equipment Corporation
185 Northgate Cir
New Castle, PA 16105-5537 724-658-3004
Fax: 724-658-5138 www.ipec.biz
Manufacturer and supplier of plastic closures and capping equipment
President: Joseph Giordano
Sales Manager: Robert Harding
Estimated Sales: $8-$10 Million
Number Employees: 50-99
Square Footage: 340000
Other Locations:
Brewton AL

24394 International Polymers Corporation
426 S Aubrey St
Allentown, PA 18109-2769 610-437-5463
Fax: 610-437-1799 800-526-0953
ipc@fast.net www.ipc.org.nz
Reprocessed polyethylene, polypropylene and polystyrene
President: David Bates
CFO: Frank Pope
Marketing: Bob Barette
VP Production: Blair Manning
Estimated Sales: $20 - 50 Million
Number Employees: 20-49

24395 International Process Plants-IPP
17 Marlen Drive
Hamilton, NJ 08691-1634 609-586-8004
Fax: 609-586-0002 michaelj@ippe.com
www.ippe.com
Buyers and sellers of new, rebuilt and used process equipment and plants worldwide. Has an inventory of over 20,000 items that allow them to offer on-time and on-budget process solutions
President: Ronald Gale
Executive VP: Jan Gale
VP Sales: Michael Joachim
Number Employees: 500-999

24396 (HQ)International ProcessingCorporation
1100 Enterprise Dr
Winchester, KY 40391-9668 859-745-2200
Fax: 859-745-6636 pts@cardinal.com
www.catalent.com

Consultant offering agglomeration, instantizing, encapsulation and solids drying services
President: David Heyens
President, Chief Executive Officer: John Chiminski
Vice President of Audit: Charles Silvey
Senior Vice President of Quality: Sharon Johnson
Senior Vice President of Sales and Marke: Will Downie
VP Business Development: Michael Valazza
Estimated Sales: $19.7 Million
Number Employees: 250-499
Square Footage: 100000
Other Locations:
International Processing Corp
Ramsey NJ

24397 **International Reserve Equipment Corporation**
46 Chestnut Avenue
Clarendon Hills, IL 60514-1238 708-531-0680
Fax: 630-325-7045 ireserve@cs.com
www.internationalreserveequip.com
Manufacturer, importer and exporter of food processing equipment including centrifuges, separators, dryers, screeners, mills, filters, mixers and blenders; also, pollution control, wastewater treatment and sludge de-wateringequipment
Owner: Robert Mertz
Marketing Manager: Thomas Mertz
Estimated Sales: $1 - 5 Million
Number Employees: 2
Brands:
Centrifuges
Dewater Equipment
Filtration Equipment
Screeners
Separators

24398 **International Roasting Systems**
3450 N State St
Ukiah, CA 95482 707-462-6164
Fax: 707-462-5258
Cleaners, blending and mixing equipment (coffee), afterburners, automatic controls, grinders, bin silo systems and storage, bin vibrators, bulk silo services, roasters, smoke control equipment and afterburners, quality controlinstruments and conveying equipment
Owner: Steve Pardini
Management Consultant: Jane Pfeiffer
Estimated Sales: $500,000-$1 Million
Number Employees: 5-9

24399 **International Smoking Systems**
23 Water St
PO Box 480
Ashburnham, MA 01430 978-827-3160
Fax: 978-827-3162 800-269-2367
markhcarlisle@cs.com
www.intlsmokingsystems.com
Provides smoking and defrosting kilns for salmon and fish processing needs
President: Mark Carlisle
Estimated Sales: Under $500,000
Number Employees: 2

24400 **International Supply**
820 E 20th St
Cookeville, TN 38501-1451 931-526-1106
Fax: 931-526-8338 bob@sproutnet.com
www.sproutnet.com
President: Robert Rust
Estimated Sales: Below $5 Million
Number Employees: 20-49

24401 **International Tank & Pipe Co**
PO Box 590
Clackamas, OR 97015-0590 503-288-0011
Fax: 503-493-0372 888-988-0011
Info@WoodTankandPipe.com
woodtankandpipe.com
Manufacture wood stove tanks and pipe. Install new wood stove tanks and pipe and repair existing tanks and pipe.
President/CEO: Michael Bye
CFO: Jacqueline Bye
R&D/Purchasing Director: Kent Huschka
Quality Control: Matthew Bye
Marketing/Sales/Production: Michael Bye
Estimated Sales: $2-4 Million
Number Employees: 12
Number of Brands: 2
Square Footage: 40000
Type of Packaging: Consumer
Other Locations:
Portland OR
Brands:
International Tank & Pipe
National Tank & Pipe

24402 **International Tape Company**
6 Industrial Drive
PO Box 240
Windham, NH 03087 603-893-1894
Fax: 603-898-9025 800-253-4450
sales@itctapes.com www.itctapes.com
Manifactures a complete line of double coated, single-coated, transfer tapes, bag sealing, foam and high tack/low tack products along with a wide range of coating and converting capabilities.
Manager: Dennis Salois
Estimated Sales: $5 - 10 Million
Number Employees: 20-49

24403 **International Thermal Dispensers**
67 Batterymarch St # 600
Boston, MA 02110-3211 617-239-3600
Fax: 617-239-3650 www.atlanticretail.com
Espresso, hot and cold food vending carts and concession equipment
Managing Partner: Bryan W. Anderson
Partner: Brian Mc Donaldÿ
Partner: Ben Starr
Broker: James C. Bagleyÿ
ÿBroker: Adam Cirelÿ
ÿBroker: Tom Sibleyÿ
ÿBroker: Brian Roacheÿ
Sales Manager: Anne McCormick
Estimated Sales: $300,000-500,000
Number Employees: 5-9

24404 **International Tray Pads& Packaging, Inc.**
3299 NC 5 Highway
P.O. Box 307
Aberdeen, NC 28315 910-944-1800
Fax: 910-944-7356 www.traypads.com
Manufacturer and supplier of tray pads for meats and case liners for produce and dairy products.

24405 **International Wax Refining Company**
3 Mountain Blvd
Warren, NJ 07059-5613 908-561-2500
Fax: 908-561-7411 www.villagetravel.com
Bee's wax
President: J D Panella
Executive VP: L Powell
Number Employees: 10-19

24406 **International Wood Industries**
PO Box 399
Snohomish, WA 98291-0399 509-966-4610
Fax: 509-965-6141 800-922-6141
harry@intlwoodind.com www.nepapallet.com
Manufacturer and exporter of skids, wooden pallets and bins, couch boxes, baggage boxes, household goods
President: Denton Sherry
General Manager: Joe Carlos
Estimated Sales: $10-20 Million
Number Employees: 100-249
Parent Co: International Wood Industries

24407 **(HQ)Interplast**
1400 Lytle Road
Troy, OH 45373-9401 937-332-1110
Fax: 937-332-0672
Manufacturer and exporter of plastic custom-injection moldings
Sales Manager: Bob Garton
Estimated Sales: $5-10 Million
Number Employees: 50-99

24408 **Interroll Corporation**
3000 Corporate Dr
Wilmington, NC 28405 910-799-1100
Fax: 910-392-3822 800-830-9680
usa-sales@interroll.com www.interroll.com
President: Tim McGill
VP: Richard Keely
Estimated Sales: $20 Million
Number Employees: 100-249

24409 **Interroll Corporation**
3000 Corporate Dr
Wilmington, NC 28405 910-799-1100
Fax: 910-392-3822 800-830-9680
usa-sales@interroll.com www.interroll.com
Manufacturer and exporter of conveyor components and flow storage systems
VP: Kim Byriel
VP: Richard Keely
VP Sales/Marketing: Steve Vineis
Estimated Sales: $20-50 Million
Number Employees: 100-249
Square Footage: 250
Parent Co: Interroll Holding AG
Brands:
Driveroll
Joki
Logix
Taperhex Gold

24410 **Interstate Monroe Machinery**
2230 1st Avenue S
Seattle, WA 98134-1408 206-682-4870
Fax: 313-891-5449
Manufacturer and exporter of controls and instrumentation equipment
General Manager: Larry Gruendike
Estimated Sales: $1-2.5 Million
Number Employees: 9
Square Footage: 15000
Parent Co: Statco Engineering & Fabrication

24411 **Interstate Packaging**
PO Box 789
White Bluff, TN 37187 615-797-9000
Fax: 615-797-9411 800-251-1072
ldoochin@interstatepkg.com
www.interstatepkg.com
Manufacturer and exporter of pressure sensitive labels and poly bags; manufacturer of printed flexible films
President: Gerald Doochin
Sales Manager: Lawrence Doochin
Customer Service Representative: Robert Garlock
Purchasing Manager: Liz Gilliam
Estimated Sales: $20-50 Million
Number Employees: 100-249
Square Footage: 100000
Type of Packaging: Consumer

24412 **Interstate Showcase & Fixture Company**
PO Box 402
West Orange, NJ 07052-0402 973-483-5555
Fax: 973-669-0200
Store fixtures, showcases, wallcases and refrigerated candy cases
CEO: L Miller
Estimated Sales: Less than $500,000
Number Employees: 1-4
Square Footage: 25000

24413 **Interstates Electric**
P.O.Box 260
Sioux Center, IA 51250-0260 712-722-1664
Fax: 712-722-1667 bdev@interstates.com
www.interstates.com
Electrical engineering, electrical construction and automation
Chairman of the Board: Larry Den Herder
CFO: Scott Peterson
Estimated Sales: $40 - 60 Million
Number Employees: 100-249
Number of Brands: 4

24414 **Intertape Polymer Group**
3647 Cortez Rd W
Bradenton, FL 34210-3169 941-753-6738
Fax: 941-753-8560 877-318-5752
info@itape.com www.intertapepolymer.com
Hot melt, pressure sensitive, acrylic and gummed tape including light, medium, heavy duty and reinforced
CEO: Mel Yull
Sales Manager: W Troup
Estimated Sales: $20-50 Million
Number Employees: 20-49
Square Footage: 151100
Brands:
Carton Master
Classic
Convoy
Tru-Test

24415 **(HQ)Intertech Corporation**
PO Box 14690
Greensboro, NC 27415 336-621-1891
Fax: 336-621-1893 800-364-2255
www.intertechcorp.com
Plastic bottles
President: Jack Worsham
VP: Leon Worsham
VP: Jim Sitton
Estimated Sales: $5-10 Million
Number Employees: 50-99
Square Footage: 232000

24416 **(HQ)Intertek Testing ServiceETL SEMKO**
70 Codman Hill Road
Boxborough, MA 01719-1737 978-263-2662
Fax: 978-264-9403 800-967-5352
icenter@intertek.com
www.intertek-etlsemko.com
Laboratory specializing in the testing of food service equipment
President: Greegg Tiemann
Chief Executive Officer: Wolfhart Hauser
Division Executive Vice President: Andrew Swift
Marketing Director: Erik Holladay
Business Development Manager: Carlos Velasco
Estimated Sales: $30 - 50 Million
Number Employees: 800
Square Footage: 150000
Other Locations:
Intertak Testing Services
Cortland NY

24417 **Intralox**
P.O.Box 50699
New Orleans, LA 70150-0699 504-733-0463
Fax: 504-734-0063 800-535-8848
msantana@intralox.com www.intralox.com
Manufacturer and exporter of USDA accepted and FDA compliant modular plastic screw conveyors and conveyor belting
President: James Lapeyre Jr
Marketing Manager: Michelle Waite
National Sales Manager: Da Waters
Number Employees: 500-999
Parent Co: Laitram Corporation
Brands:
Intralox, Inc.

24418 **Intralox, L.L.C., USA**
301 Plantation Road
Harahan, LA 70123 504-733-0463
Fax: 504-734-0063 www.intralox.com
Designers and manufacturers of conveyor belt systems for the meat, poultry, seafood and beverage industries.

24419 **Intralytix Inc**
701 E Pratt St
Rm 4036
Baltimore, MD 21202 410-625-3813
Fax: 410-625-2506 877-489-7424
info@intralytix.com www.intralytix.com
Produces bacteriophage-based products to control bacterial pathogens in food processing

24420 **Intrex**
149 Grassy Plain St
Bethel, CT 06801-2851 203-792-7400
Fax: 203-778-3991 info@asi-intrex.com
www.asi-intrex.com
Waste receptacles, smoking urns and planters; custom design available
President: Steven Decker
CEO: Mary Edgerton
Quality Control: Jim Patnaude
Chairman: Philip Feinman
Estimated Sales: Below $5 Million
Number Employees: 20-49

24421 **Introdel Products**
1339 Industrial Drive
PO Box 723
Itasca, IL 60143-1847 630-773-4250
Fax: 907-562-8517 800-323-4772
Water conditioning and filtration products including nonchemical cartridges for use in steamers, combi ovens, warewashing equipment, ice machines, water wash hoods, coffee and tea equipment, post mix applications, etc
Estimated Sales: $500,000-$1,000,000
Number Employees: 19

24422 **Invensys APV Products**
10900 Equity Drive
Houston, TX 77041 713-329-1600
Fax: 920-648-1441 apvproducts.us@apv.com
www.apv.invensys.com
Supplier of a wide range of pumps, valves, heat exchangers and homogenisers designed for use in the food, dairy and brewing industries
Executive Director: Jim Keene
Marketing Communications Manager: Antonella Crimi
Parent Co: Invensys Limited
Type of Packaging: Food Service, Bulk

24423 **Invensys Process Systems**
5100 River Road
3rd Floor
Schiller Park, IL 60176-1058 847-678-4300
Fax: 847-678-4300 888-278-9087
answers@apv.com www.apv.com
Project Sales Manager: Enrique Hinojosa

24424 **Invictus Systems Corporation**
5505 Seminary Rd Apt 2210n
Suite 202
Falls Church, VA 22041-3544
Fax: 703-503-8064 web@invictus63.com
www.govcon.com/storefronts/invictus
Manufacturer and exporter of custom computer software for the food industry including facts panel creation, nutrition calculators, formula costing, time to market analysis and operations planning. Our services include custom websoftware for both internal and external use
President: Anthony Latta
CFO: Kim Witney
Chief Scientist: Kenneth Latta
Quality Control: Benson Wetta
Business Developer: Scott Weaver
Estimated Sales: Below $5 Million
Number Employees: 20-49
Number of Products: 3
Square Footage: 15000
Type of Packaging: Bulk

24425 **Invitrogen Corporation**
P.O.Box 6482
Carlsbad, CA 92018 760-603-7200
Fax: 760-774-3157 800-767-8786
www.invitrogen.com
Polymer technology: adhesives, encapsulants, and coating systems, electronic materials, semicondutor materials, printed wiring board products, and magnetic technologies and polymer systems
CEO: Gregory T Lucier
Estimated Sales: K
Number Employees: 1,000-4,999

24426 **Iowa Rotocast Plastics**
1712 Moellers Dr
Decorah, IA 52101 563-382-9636
Fax: 563-382-3016 800-553-0050
irp@irpinc.com www.irpinc.com
Portable bars, special event carts and super coolers
President: Floyd Mount
VP Sales: Steve Rolfs
Estimated Sales: $10 Million
Number Employees: 100-249

24427 **(HQ)Ipec**
185 Northgate Circle
New Castle, PA 16105 800-377-4732
Fax: 724-658-3054 info@ipec.com
www.ipec.biz
Supplier of plastic closures and capping equipment
President: Joseph Giordano Jr
Sales Manager: Robert Harding
Estimated Sales: $22 Million
Number Employees: 75

24428 **Ira L Henry Company, Inc**
PO Box 157
Watertown, WI 53098 920-261-0648
Fax: 920-261-3525 info@irabox.com
www.iralhenry.com
Custom set-up paper boxes and gameboards
Owner: Gregoory Farado
Sales Director: Keith Thomas
Customer Service Manager: Joanne Duckworth
Design & Production Manager: Clark Farago
Plant Manager: Bob Wolfram
Estimated Sales: $1-3 Million
Number Employees: 20-49

24429 **Irby**
2913 S Church St
Rocky Mount, NC 27803 252-442-0154
Fax: 252-442-4909 wiggins@irby.com
www.irby.com
Custom fabricated metal food service equipment including conveyors, racks, stampers, welders, parts, etc
President: Mike Wigton
Chief Financial Officer: John Honigfort
Vice President of Supply Chain: Dave Armstrong
Vice President of Sales: Chad Cravens
Chief Operating Officer: Andy Waring
Plant Manager: Tony Whitley
Estimated Sales: $.5 - 1 million
Number Employees: 1-4
Square Footage: 112000

24430 **Iron Out**
7201 Engle Road
Fort Wayne, IN 46804-2228 260-483-2519
Fax: 260-483-2277 888-476-6688
info@summitbrands.com
www.summitbrands.com
Cleaning products
Owner: Joel Harter
Executive VP: Stan Stuart
Estimated Sales: $5-10 Million
Number Employees: 20-49
Brands:
All Out
Drain Out
Super Iron Out
Super Iron Out Dignio
Yellow Out

24431 **Ironwood Displays**
PO Box 632
Niles, MI 49120-0632 231-683-8500
Fax: 231-683-6803
Store fixtures and wooden and plexiglass display racks
Director Marketing: Judy Truesdell
Number Employees: 25

24432 **Irresistible Cookie Jar**
PO Box 3230
Hayden Lake, ID 83835-3230 208-664-1261
Fax: 208-667-1347
service@irresistiblecookiejar.com
www.irresistiblecookiejar.com
Cookie and muffin mixes, cookie cutters and decorations
President: Wanda Hall
Estimated Sales: $300,000-500,000
Number Employees: 10
Brands:
Boyds' Kissa Bearhugs
Mimi's Muffins
Susan Winget

24433 **Irvine Analytical Labs**
10 Vanderbilt
Irvine, CA 92618 949-951-4425
Fax: 949-951-4909 info@ialab.com
www.ialab.com
Laboratory offering chemical and microbiological analysis for food and food supplements
President: Iassad Kazeminy
Lab Director: Assad Kazeminy
Regional Sales Representative: JoAnne Nordel
Business Development Manager: Rambod Omid
Estimated Sales: Less than $500,000
Number Employees: 50-99
Square Footage: 25000
Parent Co: Irvine Analytical Labs

24434 **Irvine Pharmaceutical Services**
10 Vanderbilt
Irvine, CA 92618 949-951-4425
Fax: 949-951-4909 877-445-6554
custserv@irvinepharma.com
www.irvinepharma.com
Contract laboratory, chemical and microbiological testing services
President: Iassad Kazeminy
Laboratory Director: Abbass Kamalizad
Business Development Manager: Gregory McLaughlin
Estimated Sales: $10 - 20 Million
Number Employees: 50-99

24435 **Irwin Research & Development Inc**
P.O.Box 10668
Yakima, WA 98909-1668 509-248-0194
Fax: 509-248-3503
crichardson@irwinresearch.com
www.irwinresearch.com
Thermoforming equipment, tooling and granulators.
President: Jere Irwin
Sales and Marketing Representative: Craig Richardson
Estimated Sales: $10-20 Million
Number Employees: 250-499

24436 **Isbre Holding Corporation**
225 Glen Rd
Woodcliff Lake, NJ 07677 201-802-0005
Fax: 201-802-0006 info@isbre.com
www.isbre.com
Bottled spring drinking water.
President: Stevan A Sandberg
Regional Director of Sales: Rene Skanning

24437 **Isco**
P.O.Box 82531
Lincoln, NE 68501-2531 402-464-0231
Fax: 402-465-3064 800-228-4373
info@isco.com www.joeselfinc.com
Instruments for rapid fat/oil analysis, wastewater monitoring
VP: Vikas V Padhye
Estimated Sales: $50 Million
Number Employees: 5,000-9,999

24438 **Island Delights, Inc.**
5104 Greenwich Road
Seville, OH 44273 330-769-2800
Fax: 330-769-3935 866-877-4100
acrall@islanddelights.com
www.islanddelights.com
Coconut candies
Sales: Ann Crall
Sales: Greg Miller
Estimated Sales: $5-10 Million
Number Employees: 15

24439 **Island Poly**
514 Grand Blvd
Westbury, NY 11590-4712 516-338-4433
Fax: 516-338-4405 800-338-4433
Gloves including vinyl, natural latex, poly and cut resistant; also, natural rubber nitrile, neoprene and poly aprons, bouffant head caps and beard covers
President: Dan Grinberg
Controller: Denise Ramo
Director Marketing: Jane Donnelly
Estimated Sales: $2.5 - 5 Million
Number Employees: 20-49
Brands:
Foodhandler
Jobhandler

24440 **Isotherm**
7401 Commercial Blvd E
Arlington, TX 76001 817-472-9922
Fax: 817-472-5878 info@iso-therm.com
www.iso-therm.com
President: Zahid Ayub
Engineering Manager: Adnan Ayub
Production Manager: Al Faisal
Estimated Sales: $5 - 10 Million
Number Employees: 10-19

24441 **It's A Corker**
P.O.Box 11549
Chattanooga, TN 37401-2549 423-756-1200
Fax: 423-266-5913 info@corkergroup.com
www.lukenholdings.com
Wine industry closures
President: Robert P Corker
Executive Assistant, Chief Executive Off: Carolyn Stringer
Controller: Beth Robertson
CEO: Kim Hudson White
Estimated Sales: $.5 - 1 million
Number Employees: 5-9

24442 **Itac Label**
179 Lexington Ave
Brooklyn, NY 11216-1114 718-625-2148
Fax: 718-625-3806
Manufacturer and exporter of labels including pressure sensitive, magnetic, shipping, bar code and file folder; also, tags and decals
CEO: James H C Tao
Estimated Sales: $5-10 Million
Number Employees: 10-19
Square Footage: 14000
Brands:
Ul

24443 **Italtech**
3425 NW 112 STREET
Miami, FL 33167 305-256-9651
Fax: 305-685-0990 800-547-5075
pasta@italtech.net www.italtech.net
Pasta and noodle equipment, extruders, dryers, mixers, dies, pasteurizers, noodle cutters, sheeters, Italian equipment for confectionery industry
Engineering Director: Romolo Battistini
Estimated Sales: $2.5-5 Million
Number Employees: 1-4

24444 **Item Products**
16111 Park Entry Drive
Suite 100
Houston, TX 77041-4077 281-893-0100
Fax: 281-893-4836 800-333-4932
sales@item-products.com
Manufacturer and exporter of carts and storage racks; also, consultant specializing in the design of custom machinery
Marketing Coordinator: Claudia Sears
National Marketing Manager: Jim Boyd
Estimated Sales: $10-20,000,000
Number Employees: 20-49
Square Footage: 30000

24445 **Ito En Ltd**
20 Jay Street
Suite 530
Brooklyn, NY 11201 718-250-4000
Fax: 718-246-1325 888-832-7832
customerservice@itoen.com www.itoen.com
Supplier of green tea
Marketing: Yoshie Yano-Pennings
Public Relations: Rona Tison

24446 **Ito Packing Company**
707 W South Ave
Reedley, CA 93654 559-638-2531
Fax: 559-638-2282 craigi@itopack.com
www.itopack.com
Packs and ships fruit
President: Craig Ito
Estimated Sales: $45 Million
Number Employees: 1,000-4,999
Brands:
Red Jim
Ufo

24447 **Iug Business Solutions**
132 Nassau Street
Room 1402
New York, NY 10038-2424 212-404-6168
Fax: 212-404-6180 dphelps@iug.net
www.iug.net
Accessories/supplies i.e. picnic baskets, display fixtures.
Marketing: Edward Ip
Chief Operating Officer: Michael Lazarus

24448 **Ivarson**
3100 W Green Tree Rd
Milwaukee, WI 53209 414-351-0700
Fax: 414-351-4551 cellingson@ivarsoninc.com
www.ivarsoninc.com
Brining systems, butter processing equipment, cheese equipment, custom fabrication, cutting equipment, heat exchangers, scraped surface, margarine processing equipment, piping, fittings and tubing
President and R&D: Glenn Ivarson
CFO: Lennie Ivarson
Estimated Sales: $20 - 50 Million
Number Employees: 50-99

24449 **Ivek Corporation**
10 Fairbanks Rd
N Springfield, VT 05150 802-886-2238
Fax: 802-886-8274 800-356-4746
ivek@ivek.com www.ivek.com
Precision liquid metering and dispensing systems.
President, CEO & R&D: Mark Tanny
CFO: Dennis Crowley
VP, Sales: Frank Dimaggio
Quality Control: Ed Lawrence
Marketing: Tracey Tanny
Public Relations: Pauline Asselin
Operations: Gary Blake
Production: Brad Doody
Plant Manager: Gary Blake
Purchasing: Wade McAllister
Estimated Sales: $3 - 5 Million
Number Employees: 66
Square Footage: 68000
Brands:
Digispense 2000
Digispense 700
Digispense 800
Microspense Ap
Multiplex
Multispense
Ox/Digifeeder
Sanitary Split Case Pump
Syncrospense

24450 **Ives-Way Products**
2030 N Nicole Ln
Round Lake Beach, IL 60073 847-740-0658
Manufacturer and exporter of automatic can sealers for food, giftware or other sealed shipping containers
VP: Laura Ours
Estimated Sales: Less than $500,000
Number Employees: 1-4
Square Footage: 2000

24451 **Iwatani International Corporation of America**
2200 Post oak Blvd.
Suite 1150
Houston, TX 77056 713-965-9970
Fax: 713-963-8497 800-775-5506
christopher@iwatani.com www.iwatani.com
Manufacturer and importer of portable butane stoves and induction cookers.
Regional Sales Manager: Karen Buquicchio
National Sales Manager: Gary Rodgers
Estimated Sales: $5-10 Million
Number Employees: 5-9
Parent Co: Iwatani International
Brands:
Cassette Feu

24452 **Izabel Lam International**
204 Van Dyke Street
Brooklyn, NY 11231-1038 718-797-3983
Fax: 718-797-0030 info@izabellam.com
www.izabellam.com
Manufacturer and exporter of tabletop products including cutlery, dinnerware and drinkware
Estimated Sales: $500,000-$1 Million
Number Employees: 1-4
Square Footage: 112000
Type of Packaging: Consumer, Food Service
Brands:
Glacier
Golden Wind
Morning Tide
Mt. Rainbow Series
Pale Wind
Rushing Tide
Sphere
Splash
Wind Over Water

24453 **J W Hulme Company**
678 7th St W
Saint Paul, MN 55102 651-222-7359
Fax: 651-228-1181 800-442-8212
sales@jwhulmeco.com www.jwhulmeco.com
Sport bags, gun cases, duffles, breifcases and luggage.
Manager: Dwayne Carlin Jr
Estimated Sales: $500,000-1,000,000
Number Employees: 20-49

24454 **J&J Corrugated Box Corporation**
210 Grove St
Franklin, MA 02038-3119 508-528-6200
Fax: 508-528-2316
Corrugated boxes
Manager: Dan McKinney
General Manager: Richard Koestner

Estimated Sales: $20-50 Million
Number Employees: 100-249
Parent Co: Georgia-Pacific

24455 J&J Industries
107 Gateway Rd
Bensenville, IL 60106-1950 630-595-8878
Fax: 630-595-9010
Nonmetallic die cut parts including gaskets and noise control materials
Owner: Jerry Haug
General Manager: Grant Cramer
Estimated Sales: $1-2.5 Million
Number Employees: 5-9

24456 J&J Mid-South ContainerCorporation
1745 Doug Barnard Pkwy
Augusta, GA 30906-9277 706-798-7420
Fax: 706-793-6947 800-395-1025
www.georgiapacific.com
Corrugated shipping containers
President: Brent Paugh
Chief Executive Officer, President: James Hannan
Executive Vice President: Christian Fischer
Executive Vice President of Operations: Wesley Jones
Estimated Sales: $20-50 Million
Number Employees: 100-249
Parent Co: Georgia-Pacific Corporation

24457 J&J Sliding & Windows SaInc
600 CEPI Drive
Chesterfield, MO 63005 636-532-3320
www.jandjslidingandwindows.com
Commercial awnings
Estimated Sales: $500,000-$1 Million
Number Employees: 9

24458 J&M Industries
300 Ponchatoula Pkwy
Ponchatoula, LA 70454 985-386-6000
Fax: 985-386-9066 800-989-1002
www.JM-ind.com
Packaging supplies
President & CFO: Maurice Gaudet IV
Quality Control: Tim Sanders
Marketing Director: Ricky Brossard
Sales Manager: Mark Arnold
Plant Manager: Lance Powers
Plant Manager: Lance Powers
Purchasing: Ruth Sweeney
Estimated Sales: $20 - 50 Million
Number Employees: 105

24459 J&M Laboratories
12 Nordson Dr
Dawsonville, GA 30534 706-216-1520
Fax: 706-216-1517 www.nordson.com
Tea and coffee industry filters
VP: George Porter
Estimated Sales: $30 - 50 Million
Number Employees: 100-249

24460 J&R Manufacturing
820 W. Kearney
Mesquite, TX 75149 972-289-0801
Fax: 972-288-9488 800-527-4831
sales@jrmanufacturing.com
www.jrmanufacturing.com
Manufacturer and exporter of barbecue pits, broilers, grills, rotisseries and combo broiler/rotisseries
VP: Larry Bellows
Estimated Sales: $5 - 10 Million
Number Employees: 20-49
Square Footage: 30000
Brands:
Combo
Fabuloso
Little Red Smokehouse
Oyler
Smoke-Master
Spinnin' Spits
Wood Show

24461 J. James
723 Lorimer Street
Brooklyn, NY 11211-1311 718-384-6144
Fax: 718-384-6112
Place mats and tray covers
*Estimated Sales:*less than $500,000
Number Employees: 1-4

24462 J. Scott Company
175 Barneveld Ave
San Francisco, CA 94124 415-824-1743
Fax: 415-824-5849 888-OIL-LUBE
jscottco@aol.com
Oils and lubricants
Manager: John Scott
Estimated Sales: Below $5 Million
Number Employees: 5-9

24463 J.A. Thurston Company
Route 2
Rumford, ME 04276 207-364-7921
Fax: 207-369-9903 sales@jathurston.com
www.jathurston.com
Manufacturer and exporter of chairs and stools
VP: John Thurston
Sales: Cindy Giroux
Estimated Sales: $5 - 10 Million
Number Employees: 5-9

24464 J.C. Ford Company
901 Leslie St
La Habra, CA 90631 714-871-7361
Fax: 714-773-5827 info@jcford.com
www.jcford.com
Manufacturer and exporter of cooling conveyors, corn masa feeders, tamale steamers and extruders, tortilla and chip ovens, tortilla sheeter and corn cookers and grinders
Sales: Scott Ruhe
Engineer: Thomas Dosch
Estimated Sales: $5-10 Million
Number Employees: 5-9
Square Footage: 20000
Brands:
J.C. Ford Co.

24465 J.C. Products Inc.
66 Ranger Rd
Haddam, CT 06438 860-267-5516
Fax: 860-267-5519 jcproducts1@juno.com
www.jcproductsinc.com
Wire products including displays, racks and bread, roll and rotisserie baskets
Owner: Charles Helenek
Estimated Sales: $2.5-5 Million
Number Employees: 10-19

24466 (HQ)J.C. Whitlam Manufacturing Co.
PO Box 380
Wadsworth, OH 44282-0380 330-334-2524
Fax: 330-334-3005 800-321-8358
www.jcwhitlam.com
Manufacturer and exporter of refrigeration chemicals, waterless hand cleaners and other cleaning chemicals
President: Jack Whitlam
CFO: Doug Whitlam
Senior VP: Doug Whitlam
VP Operations: Steve Carey
Estimated Sales: $5-10 Million
Number Employees: 20-49
Square Footage: 280000

24467 J.E. Roy
60 Boulevard Begin
St Claire, QC G0R 2V0
Canada 418-883-2711
Fax: 418-838-8008 jeroyplast@bellnet.ca
Manufacturer, importer and exporter of plastic bottles and bottle nasal plugs
President: Ronald Leclair
Quality Control: Nicoles Mertileau
VP Sales: Sylvie Lefevbre
Number Employees: 55
Square Footage: 9000
Type of Packaging: Consumer, Food Service, Private Label
Brands:
Roy
Ropak

24468 J.G. Machine Works
2182 Route 35 South
Holmdel, NJ 07733 732-203-2077
Fax: 732-203-2078 sales@jgmachine.com
www.jgmachine.com
Rotary fillers
Manager: Don Nelson
National Sales Manager: John McArdle
Number Employees: 20-49

24469 J.H. Carr & Sons
37 S Hudson Street
Seattle, WA 98134-2416 206-763-1937
Fax: 206-763-7033 800-523-8842
jerryacarr@msn.com www.jhcarr.com
Bars, tables and bases, chairs, booths, barstools and service cabinets
VP Marketing/General Manager: Jerry Carr
Sales Manager: Wayne Muliner
Estimated Sales: $5 Million
Number Employees: 25-49
Square Footage: 200000

24470 J.H. Thornton Company
879 N Jan Mar Ct
Olathe, KS 66061 913-764-6550
Fax: 913-764-1314 thornton@tfs.net
Manufacturer, exporter and wholesaler/distributor of conveyor systems; installation services available
President: Douglas Metcalf
Estimated Sales: $3 - 5 Million
Number Employees: 10

24471 J.I. Holcomb Manufacturing
6400 Rockside Road
Independence, OH 44131-2309 800-458-3222
Fax: 216-524-4381 www.premierind.com
Cleaners including hand, toilet and bowl, dishwashing and washing compounds, mops, brooms, floor polish, soap, insecticides, etc
President: David Stanic
CEO: Shawn Dunmire
Estimated Sales: $52 Million
Number Employees: 500
Number of Products: 1600
Parent Co: Premier Industrial Corporation

24472 J.K. Harman, Inc.
1139 Dixwell Ave
Hamden, CT 06514 203-777-9726
Fax: 203-782-6575 800-248-1627
www.jkharman.com
Custom store fixtures
President: D Harman
Estimated Sales: $5-10 Million
Number Employees: 10-19

24473 J.L. Analytical Services
P.O.Box 576185
Modesto, CA 95357-6185 209-538-8111
Fax: 209-538-3966 www.jlanalytical.com
Laboratory specializing in food analysis and water testing
President: Mary Jacobs
CEO: Richard Jacobs, Ph.D.
VP: Mark Jacobs
Estimated Sales: $5 - 10 Million
Number Employees: 20-49

24474 J.L. Becker Company
41150 Joy Rd
Plymouth, MI 48170 734-656-2000
Fax: 734-656-2009 800-837-4328
www.jlbecker.com
Manufacturer and exporter of heat treating furnaces and conveyor belts including wire mesh and flat wire
Owner: John Becker
CEO: Wayne Webbe
CFO: Ellen Beckor
Vice President: John Beckor
Sales Manager: David Peterson
Estimated Sales: $10-20 Million
Number Employees: 50-99
Type of Packaging: Bulk

24475 J.L. Clark
923 23rd Ave
Rockford, IL 61104 815-962-8861
Fax: 815-966-5862 info@jlclark.com
www.jlclark.com
Manufacturer and exporter of decorative tin cans and injection molded plastic dispensing closures
President: Phil Baerenwald
CFO: Bill Holiday
Vice President/General Manager: Walt Pietruch
R&D: Ron Axon
Sales: Mike Tolluer
Public Relations: Luanna Grimes
Purchasing: George Mastromatteo
Estimated Sales: H
Number Employees: 250-499
Parent Co: Clarcor Consumer Products

Type of Packaging: Consumer, Food Service, Private Label

24476 J.L. Honing Company
4150 South Nevada Avenue
milwaukee, WI 53235-4515 414-744-9500
Fax: 414-744-9515 800-747-9501
contact@jlhoning.com www.jlhoning.com
Sanitary finishing for stainless steel tubing; also, ID polishing and honing of tubing and piping available
Owner: Timothy Putney
VP: David Putney
Operations Manager: Dana Felske
Estimated Sales: Below $5 Million
Number Employees: 10-19
Square Footage: 60000

24477 J.L. Industries
4450 W 78th Street Cir
Minneapolis, MN 55435 952-835-6850
Fax: 952-835-2218 800-554-6077
nmpeterson@jlindustries.com
www.jlindustries.com
Manufacturer, exporter and importer of fire extinguishers and cabinets, other fire and emergency AED cabinets, metal access panels and roof hatches, dirt control floor mats and gratings, and detention specialties.
President: Kirby Bayerle
Marketing: Nona Peterson
Estimated Sales: $10 - 20 Million
Number Employees: 50-99
Square Footage: 58000
Parent Co: Activar

24478 J.Leek Associates
145 Peanut Dr
Edenton, NC 27932 252-482-4456
Fax: 252-482-5370 info@pert-labs.com
www.jleek.com
Laboratory providing aflatoxin, microbiological, pesticide residue and chemical/physical analyses of food and feed products; services also include product development, packaging, shelf life and sensory studies, etc
Manager: Mike Jackson
Manager Analytical Services: Mike Jackson
Manager: Mike Jackson
Estimated Sales: $1-2.5 Million
Number Employees: 10-19
Square Footage: 7200
Parent Co: Seabrook Enterprises

24479 J.M. Packaging/Detroit Tape & Label
26300 Bunert Rd
Warren, MI 48089-3639 586-771-7800
Fax: 586-771-5440 www.jmindustries.com
Manufacturer and exporter of printed tapes and labels; contract packaging available
Owner: Kris Moulds
VP: Michael Jones
Estimated Sales: $5-10 Million
Number Employees: 50-99
Type of Packaging: Bulk

24480 J.M. Rogers & Sons
PO Box 8725
Moss Point, MS 39562-0011 228-475-7584
Pallets, drag line mats, skids, lumber, etc.; exporter of pallets
Owner: Louis Rogers
Number Employees: 50

24481 J.M. Swank Company
520 W Penn St
North Liberty, IA 52317-9775 319-626-3683
Fax: 319-626-3662 800-567-9265
www.jmswank.com
Ingredient blending, label and special palletizing, inventory management, quality control and freight consolidation
President: Taylor Strubell
VP: Ron Pardekooper
Estimated Sales: $29.5 Million
Number Employees: 175

24482 J.R. McCullough Company
1980 Old Philadelphia Pike
Rte 340
Lancaster, PA 17602 717-735-8772
Fax: 717-735-8774 trish@jrmccullough.com
www.jrmccullough.com
Commercial awnings
Estimated Sales: $500,000-$1,000,000
Number Employees: 5-9

24483 J.R. Ralph Marketing Company
4317 E Genesee Street
Suite 210
Syracuse, NY 13214-2114 315-445-0255
Fax: 315-445-0245
Consultant specializing in the introduction and expansion of products to the food industry
Partner: Chris Ralph
Estimated Sales: $1-2.5 Million
Number Employees: 1-4

24484 J.R. Short Milling Company
1580 Grinnell Road
Kankakee, IL 60901 815-937-2635
Fax: 815-937-3989 800-544-8734
jrshort@shortmill.com www.shortmill.com
Founded in 1910. A bakery ingredient supplier company that transforms natural grains into functional foods.
Founder: J.R. Short
Estimated Sales: $10-20 Million
Number Employees: 10

24485 (HQ)J.R. Simplot Company
999 W Main Street
Suite 1300
Boise, ID 83702 208-336-2110
Fax: 208-389-7515 jrs_info@simplot.com
www.simplotfoods.com
Potatoes and potato products, also, avocados, dehydrated products, frozen potatoes, fruits, roasted products, specialty, sweet potatoes, and vegetables.
President, CEO & Director: William Whitacre
Manager, Focus Marketing, Food Products: Meghan Swan
Manager of Public Relations: David Cuoio
Estimated Sales: $5.8 Billion
Number Employees: 10000
Square Footage: 30000
Type of Packaging: Consumer, Food Service, Private Label
Other Locations:
J.R. Simplot Potato Processing
Aberdeen ID
J.R. Simplot Potato Processing
Caldwell ID
J.R. Simplot Potato Processing
Grand Forks ND
J.R. Simplot Potato Processing
Moses Lake WA
J.R. Simplot Potato Processing
Nampa ID
J.R. Simplot Potato Processing
Othello WA
J.R. Simplot Vegetable Processing
West Memphis AR
Brands:
Chef's Choice
Conquest®
Culinary Select™
Dehydrofrozen
Fiesta
Freezerfridge®
Glori Fri®
Grand Valley®
Harvest Supreme™
Idahoan®
Infinity®
Jr Buffalo®
Krunchie Wedges®
Mariner®
Megacrunch®
Naturalcrisp®
Old Fashioned Way®
Pancake Pods®
Payette Farms®
Plate-Perfect®
Quickmash®
Recipe Quick®
Roastworks®
Savory
Seasonedcrisp®
Select Recipe®
Simplot®
Simplot® Culinary Fresh™
Skincredibles®
Skincredibles® Plus
Sour Cream & Chive
Spudsters®
Sun Crop®
Tastee Spud™
Tater Pals®
Top Cat®
Traditional
True Recipe®
Ultra Clear®
Upsides®
Wonder Fry

24486 J.S. Alberici Construction Company
8800 Page Avenue
Saint Louis, MO 63114 314-733-2000
Fax: 314-733-2001 800-261-2611
gkozicz@alberici.com www.alberici.com
President/CEO: Gregory J. Kozicz
Vice President: Mark W. Okroy
Quality Control: Ron Rogge
Marketing Leader: Donald C. Oberlies
Estimated Sales: $.5 - 1 million
Number Employees: 10

24487 J.V. Reed & Company
1939 Goldsmith Ln
Suite 121
Louisville, KY 40218-3175 502-454-4455
Fax: 502-587-6025 877-258-7333
ablieden@jvreed.com
Manufacturer and exporter of dust pans, metal waste baskets, signs, tabs, labels, burner covers, hot pads, stove and counter mats, canister sets, etc
Owner: Jean Reid
Chairman Board: Marc Ray
Estimated Sales: $10-20 Million
Number Employees: 1-4
Square Footage: 80000

24488 J/W Design Associates
401 Terry Francois St
Suite 212
San Francisco, CA 94158 415-546-7707
Fax: 415-546-4004 info@webbdesign.com
www.webbdesign.com
Design consultant for restaurants, hotels and resorts
Owner: Kim Webb
Designer: Jack Donald Webb
Estimated Sales: $1 - 3 Million
Number Employees: 10-19

24489 JA Emilius Sons, Inc
537 Woodland Avenue
Cheltenham, PA 19012-2195 215-379-6162
Fax: 215-663-8985 800-224-6162
sales@emilius.com www.emilius.com
Machine shop, conveyors, conveyor belt, confectionery equipment confectionery, bakery, food process equipment
Owner: Carl A Emilius Iii
CFO: Beth Emilius
Sales: Vince McCabe
Estimated Sales: $1 - 2.5 Million
Number Employees: 20-49
Number of Brands: 4

24490 JAS Manufacturing Company
3228 Skylane Dr
PO Box 702041
Carrollton, TX 75370-2041 972-380-1150
Fax: 972-931-6218 jastrack@swbell.net
Dust and mist collectors and bakery equipment
Director Production: Jim Singleton
Estimated Sales: $2.5-5 Million
Number Employees: 20-49

24491 JAX/USA
W134n5373 Campbell Dr
Menomonee Falls, WI 53051-7023 262-781-8850
Fax: 262-781-3906 800-782-8850
info@jax.com www.jax.com
Food grade lubricants including antiwear food grade greases, hydraulic oils and gear oils, food grade airline oils, chain and conveyor lubricants and extreme temperature lubricants
President: Eric J Peter
Estimated Sales: $10 - 20 Million
Number Employees: 20-49

24492 JBA International
3701 Algonquin Road
Rolling Meadows, IL 60008-3127 847-590-0299
Fax: 847-590-0394 800-522-4685
jcrawford@jbaintl.com

Wine industry computer software

24493 JBC Plastics
2239 Gravois Ave
St Louis, MO 63104-2852 314-771-2279
Fax: 314-771-0910 877-834-5526
mail@jbcplastic.com www.jbcplastic.com
Displays, napkin holders and signs
Owner: Cheryl Mc Grath
Customer Service: Jennifer Ward
Estimated Sales: $.5 - 1 million
Number Employees: 1-4

24494 JBT Foodtech
1622 First St
Sandusky, OH 44870 419-626-0304
Fax: 419-626-9560 800-408-7788
frigostein.info@jbtc.com www.jbtfoodtech.com
Provides equipment solutions for fruits and vegetable processing, tuna processing, freezing and chilling, etc
President: Steve Smith
Chairman: Charles H. Cannon, Jr
Vice President/CFO: Ronald D. Mambu
Vice President and Division Manager: John Lee
Number Employees: 260
Parent Co: John Bean Technologies

24495 JC Industries
89 Eads St
West Babylon, NY 11704-1186 631-420-1920
Fax: 631-420-0467 800-322-1189
www.jcpenney.com
Refuse handling equipment
President: Joseph Celano
Estimated Sales: $3 - 5 Million

24496 JCB Enterprises
P.O.Box 209
Liverpool, NY 13088-0209 315-451-2770
Fax: 315-451-8503 jgb2@ix.netcom.com
www.jgbhose.com
Hose assemblies
President: J Bernhardt
Quality Control: Glenn Beede
CFO: Bod Zywicki
Estimated Sales: $50 - 100 Million
Number Employees: 100-249

24497 JCH International
978 E Hermitage Rd NE
Rome, GA 30161 706-295-4111
Fax: 706-295-4114 800-328-9203
info@jchinternational.com
www.jchinternational.com
Manufacturer and exporter of industrial and commercial mats and matting for entrance, meat cutting and produce areas; also, specialty flooring available; importer of heavy duty carpets
President: John Hoglund
Number Employees: 5-9
Type of Packaging: Food Service
Brands:
Champions Sports Tile
Drainthru
Floorsaver
Locktile

24498 JCS Controls, Inc.
460 Buffalo Road
Suite 200
Rochester, NY 14611-2020 585-227-5910
Fax: 585-723-3213 sales@jcs.com
www.jcs.com
JCS has strong core competence in product development (R&D), Aseptic Processing, Mass Balanced Digital In-Line Blending Application, S88 Compliant Batching Systems, and many advanced technology processing systems such as EvaporationSpray Drying, Cheese VAT control, Membrane Processes, and more.
Founder: Philip Frechette
VP: Don Frechette
Operations: Rob Frechette
Estimated Sales: $3.7 Million
Number Employees: 20
Other Locations:

24499 JDG Consulting
3800 N Lake Shore Drive
8c
Chicago, IL 60613-3301 312-621-8900
Fax: 312-621-0162 800-243-7037
jdryer@dairymarketanalyst.com
Consultant providing market research and communications
VP: Alan Levitt
Administrative Assistant: Ann Marie Alanes
Number Employees: 3

24500 JDO/LNR Lighting
7980 Pat Booker Road
Suite A1
Live Oak, TX 78233-2603 210-637-6244
Fax: 210-637-6910 800-597-1570
Electric lighting fixtures
VP Marketing: Bob Windro
Manager: Leonard Almendarez
Number Employees: 30

24501 JEM Wire Products
2303 South Main Street
PO Box 2606
Middletown, CT 06457 860-347-0447
Fax: 860-347-9743 ed@jemwireproducts.com
www.jemwireproducts.com
Wire products for baskets, displays, racks and shelves; also, custom wire forming and spot welding services available
President: Edward Muzik
Vice President: Tom Muzik
Marketing/Sales: Yale Gordon
Estimated Sales: $2.5-5 Million
Number Employees: 10-19

24502 JH Display & Fixture
P.O.Box 432
Greenwood, IN 46142 317-888-0631
Fax: 317-888-0671 jon@jhdisplay.com
www.jhdisplay.com
Manufacturer, importer and exporter of wood, acrylic, metal and glass fixtures. Also custom shelving and tables available. Antique and vintage decorative props for all types of settings
Owner: John Holbrook
VP/Owner: Trudy Holbrook
Estimated Sales: $1-2.5 Million
Number Employees: 5-9

24503 JHRG LLC
303 S Pine St
Spring Hope, NC 27882 252-478-4997
Fax: 252-478-4998 800-849-4997
info@hsarmor.com jhrgllc.com
Owner: John Holland
Estimated Sales: $1 - 5 Million

24504 JIT Manufacturing & Technology
4101 Stuart Andrew Boulevard
Suite D
Charlotte, NC 28217-1580 800-804-3910
Fax: 704-522-1603 jitchar@mindspring.com
Art patented print and apply equipment, bar coding systems, distribution programming, labeling and inventory control

24505 JJ Rios Farm Services
4890 E Acampo Rd
Acampo, CA 95220 209-333-7467
Fax: 209-333-3715
Wine industry vineyard services
Owner: Jose Rios
Estimated Sales: $1-2.5 Million
Number Employees: 10-19

24506 JJI Lighting Group, Inc.
11500 Melrose Ave.
Franklin Park, IL 60131-1334 847-451-0700
www.jjilightinggroup.com
Manufacturer, importer and exporter of lighting fixtures and systems
CEO: Robert Haidinger
Estimated Sales: $55 Million
Number Employees: 650
Number of Products: 15
Type of Packaging: Private Label, Bulk

24507 (HQ)JM Canty, Inc.
6100 Donner Rd
Buffalo, NY 14094-9227 716-625-4227
Fax: 716-625-4228 sales@jmcanty.com
www.jmcanty.com
Manufacturer and exporter of fiber optic lighting, image processing and inspection and color analysis
President: Thomas Canty
Quality Control: Dan Raby
VP: Tod Canty
Estimated Sales: $5 - 10 Million
Number Employees: 20-49
Square Footage: 152000
Other Locations:
Canty
Dublin, Ireland
Brands:
Canty

24508 JM Huber Chemical Corporation
907 Revolution St
Havre De Grace, MD 21078-3723 410-939-3500
Fax: 410-939-7302 hubermaterials@huber.com
www.huber.com
Industrial inorganic chemicals
President: Tom Lamb
President, Chief Executive Officer: Michael Marberry
R&D: John Clrnelius
Vice President of Environmental: Andrew Miles
Quality Control: Matt Hall
Vice President of Public Affairs: Robert Currie
Plant Manager: Pat Jackson
Estimated Sales: $20 - 30 Million
Number Employees: 100-249

24509 JM Swank Company
395 Herky St
North Liberty, IA 52317
Fax: 402-516-0585 800-593-6375
bill.burgeson@conagrafoods.com
www.jmswank.com
Food ingredients for the dairy, beverage, meat, bakery, snack, confection, ethnic and prepared food industries
Vice President/General Manager: Shawn Meany
Quality Control: Laura McCurdy
Sales: Bill Burgusen
Estimated Sales: $400 Million
Number Employees: 155
Parent Co: ConAgra

24510 JMA
658 Blue Point Road
Holtsville, NY 11742-1848 631-475-0023
Fax: 631-475-0549 800-428-8377
info@crazyhatter.com www.crazyhatter.com
Wine industry bottles
Owner: Jeffery Leibowitz
Estimated Sales: $1 - 3 Million
Number Employees: 10-19

24511 JMC Packaging Equipment
3470 Mainway Drive
Burlington, ON L7M 1A8
Canada 905-335-4196
Fax: 905-335-4201 800-263-5252
davidk@jmcpackaging.com
www.jmcpackaging.com
Manufacturer and exporter of bagging and bag sealing machinery
Sales Manager: David Kay
Office Manager: Linda Campbell
Number Employees: 10-19
Type of Packaging: Consumer, Food Service, Private Label, Bulk

24512 JMS Packaging Consultants
10 Lenbar Cir
New City, NY 10956-4908 845-708-0701
Fax: 845-708-0702
jstrassman@jmspackaging.com
www.jmspackaging.com
Custom gift packaging, plastic set-up and folding boxes
CEO: Joel Strassnan
Number Employees: 1

24513 JP Plastics, Inc.
67 Green Street
Foxboro, MA 02035 508-203-2420
Fax: 508-203-2401 sales@jp-plastics.com
www.jp-plastics.com
Custom vacuum formed packaging products
President: John P Cheever
Estimated Sales: Below 1 Million
Number Employees: 7
Square Footage: 64000

24514 JPS Packaging Company
1972 Akron Peninsula Rd
Akron, OH 44313-4810 330-923-5281
Fax: 330-923-9637 www.jpsp.com

Manufacturer and converter of flexible packaging and label products for use by customers in the food and beverage industry and other niche markets
Plant Manager: Anthony Oakes
Estimated Sales: $1 - 5 Million
Number Employees: 100-249

24515 JR Mats
1519 McDaniel Dr
West Chester, PA 19380-7037 610-692-0280
Fax: 610-696-6760 800-526-7763
justrightmats@aol.com www.jrmats.com
Manufacturer and distributor of quality entry matting, kitchen matting and antifatigue matting. Custom logo mats
Manager: Joela Powell
Sales/Marketing: Jay McGrath
General Manager: Jeri Delahanty
Estimated Sales: $1 Million
Number Employees: 5-9
Number of Brands: 10
Number of Products: 25
Square Footage: 116000
Type of Packaging: Consumer, Food Service, Private Label, Bulk
Brands:
Silver Streak

24516 JS Giles Inc
8810 Emmott Street
Suite 400
Houston, TX 77040-3592 713-690-3333
Fax: 713-690-3353 800-254-0709
sales@jfgilesinc.com www.jfgilesinc.com
Medium intensity horizontal and vertical mixers
President: John Giles
R & D: Peter Foxon
Estimated Sales: Below $5 Million
Number Employees: 5-9

24517 JVC Rubber Stamp Company
PO Box 2338
Elkhart, IN 46515 574-293-0113
Fax: 574-293-0113
Rubber stamps
Owner: Ron Cataldo
Estimated Sales: Less than $500,000
Number Employees: 1-4

24518 JVM Sales Corp.
3401 A Tremley Point Rd
Linden, NJ 07036 908-862-4866
Fax: 908-862-4867 anthony@jvmsalescorp.com
jvmsales.com
Italian grated cheeses including parmesan, romano, asiago, parmesan & romano blend, grated three cheese blend, and also custom blends.
President & CEO: Mary Beth Tomasino
VP of Sales & Marketing: Anthony Caliendo
Estimated Sales: $2-4 Million
Square Footage: 150000
Type of Packaging: Consumer, Food Service, Private Label, Bulk
Other Locations:
JVM Sales South
Delray Beach FL

24519 JVNW
390 S Redwood St
Canby, OR 97013 503-263-2858
Fax: 503-263-2868 800-331-5869
tanks@jvnw.com www.jvnw.com
Brewing vessels
President: Donald Jones
CFO: Donald Jones
Estimated Sales: $5 - 10 Million
Number Employees: 100-249

24520 JVR/Sipromac
100 W Drullard Ave
Lancaster, NY 14086-1670 716-206-2500
Fax: 716-897-4731 www.jvrinc.com
Vacuum packaging, processing equipment
President: John Radziwon
Parts & Service Manager: Kevin Monk
Estimated Sales: $2.5 Million
Number Employees: 5-9

24521 JW Leser Company
4408 W Jefferson Blvd
Los Angeles, CA 90016-4090 323-731-4173
Fax: 323-731-4175 ray@jwleserco.com
www.jwleserco.com
Sell and manufacture fillers, pumps, homogenizers, tanks, mixers, and filters
President: Ray Leser
Number Employees: 1-4
Brands:
Alesco
In-Shear

24522 JWC Environmental
290 Paularino Ave
Costa Mesa, CA 92626 949-833-3888
Fax: 949-833-8858 800-331-2277
jwce@jwce.com www.jwce.com
Heavy duty solids reduction grinders, screening, and dewatering equipment
President: Ron Duecker
CFO: John Harrison
Marketing Director: Fritz Egger
Sales Director: Pete Garcia
Estimated Sales: $20 - 30 Million
Number Employees: 100-249
Square Footage: 55000
Parent Co: JWC International
Brands:
Auger Monster
Channel Monster
Muffin Monster

24523 Jack Langston Manufacturing Company
3700 Elm Street
Dallas, TX 75226-1214 214-821-9844
Fax: 214-824-5777
Commercial refrigerators and walk-in coolers and freezers
President: Olden Phil Paul
Chairman Board: J Langston, Jr.
Plant Manager: David Cormican
Number Employees: 25
Parent Co: Camp Langston

24524 Jack Stone Lighting & Electrical
3131 Pennsy Dr
Landover, MD 20785 301-322-3323
Fax: 301-322-8407 service@jackstone.net
www.jackstone.net
Electrical signs
President: Trevor Stone
Operations Manager: Spencer Stone
Estimated Sales: $5-10 Million
Number Employees: 50-99

24525 Jack the Ripper Table Skirting
4003 Greenbriar Drive
Suite A
Stafford, TX 77477 281-240-1024
Fax: 281-240-0343 800-331-7831
sales@tableskirting.com www.tableskirting.com
Manufacturer and exporter of table skirting, table cloths, napkins, place mats and tray stand covers
Director Sales: Erik Dean
Customer Service: Jessie Carpenter
Estimated Sales: $1 Million
Number Employees: 20-50

24526 Jacks Manufacturing Company
PO Box 50695
Mendota, MN 55150-0695 651-452-1474
Fax: 651-452-1477 800-821-2089
jack@jacks-mfg.com
Manufacturer and exporter of boiler compounds and carpet and upholstery cleaners
Chairman Board: C Nimis
Director: S Nimis
Office Manager: Sharon Bruesile
Estimated Sales: $2.5-5 Million
Number Employees: 1-4

24527 Jackson Corrugated Container
225 River Rd
Middletown, CT 06457 860-346-9671
Fax: 860-346-9320 info@jacksonbox.com
www.jacksonbox.com
Supplier of corrugated packaging.
President: William P Herlihy
Estimated Sales: $5.2 Million
Number Employees: 20-49

24528 Jackson MSC
P.O.Box 1060
Barbourville, KY 40906-5060 606-523-9795
Fax: 606-523-9196 888-800-5672
jcwilliams@jacksonmsc.com
www.jacksonmsc.com
Commercial dishwashers and ovens
President: David Crane
VP Sales/Marketing: Mark Whalen
Production/Inventory Control Manager: Teresa Doan
Purchasing Manager: Sheila Reeder
Estimated Sales: $5-10 Million
Number Employees: 10-19
Square Footage: 436000
Parent Co: ENODIS

24529 Jackson Restaurant Supply
1119 S Us Highway 45 Byp
Jackson, TN 38301-3277 731-664-5100
Fax: 731-664-0978 800-424-8943
usamfg@usamanufacturing.com
www.usamanufacturing.com
Automatic barbecue cookers
President: James Griffith
Estimated Sales: $5-10 Million
Number Employees: 20-49
Square Footage: 64000
Brands:
Hickory Creek Bar-B-Q Cooker

24530 Jacksonville Box & Woodwork Company
PO Box 3447
Jacksonville, FL 32206 904-354-1441
Fax: 904-354-6088 800-683-2699
jaxbox@jaxbox.com www.jaxbox.com
Packaging products including wooden bins for juice, fruit, egg and vegetable boxes, collapsible pallet mats for melons and wooden shipping crates
President: Jennings B King
Vice President: J King, Jr.
Sales: Tom More
Estimated Sales: $5-10 Million
Number Employees: 10-19

24531 Jackstack
221 Sheridan Blvd
Inwood, NY 11096-1226 325-062-1020
Fax: 325-061-5757 800-999-9840
info@jackstack.com www.jackstack.com
Manufacturer and importer of mobile plate racks
Manager: Tom Staub
Managing Director: Tom Staub
Sales Manager: John Falzarano
Sales Manager: Pascale Steingueldoir
Estimated Sales: Less than $500,000
Number Employees: 5-9
Parent Co: Jackstack International

24532 Jacob Holtz Co.
10 Industrial HWY MS-6 Airport Business
Lester, PA 19029 215-423-2800
Fax: 215-634-7454 800-445-4337
info@jacobholtz.com www.onthelevel.net
Supplier and exporter of self-adjusting table glides
Estimated Sales: Below $5 Million
Number Employees: 3
Square Footage: 9600
Brands:
Superlevel

24533 Jacob Tubing LP
3948 Willow Lake Blvd
Memphis, TN 38118 901-566-1110
Fax: 901-566-1910 info@jacob-tubing.com
www.jacob-tubing.com
Primary supplier of modular tubing systems with pull ring connections to major industries worldwide.
Manager: Volker Eynck
Number Employees: 10-19
Parent Co: Jacob Soehne

24534 Jacob White Packaging
12720 Pennridge Drive
Bridgeton, MO 63044-1235 314-791-6448
Fax: 314-291-6913 800-248-6448
www.jacobwhite.com
Fully automatic horizontal end load cartoner
Estimated Sales: $1 - 3 Million
Number Employees: 10

24535 Jacobi-Lewis Company
622 South Front St
PO Box 1289
Wilmington, NC 28401 910-763-6201
Fax: 910-763-5610 800-763-2433
jl@jacobi-lewis.com www.jacobi-lewis.com

Wholesaler/distributor of equipment, supplies, furniture, etc.; serving the food service market
President: Greg Lewis
Chairman: French Lewis
Vice President: Gloria Ludewic
Marketing/Sales: Chris Gannon
Purchasing Manager: Wilson Horton
Estimated Sales: $7 Million
Number Employees: 20-49
Number of Brands: 700
Square Footage: 22500

24536 Jade Range
2650 Orbiter Street
Brea, CA 92821 714-961-2400
800-884-5233
dpack@maytag.com www.jaderange.com
OEM equipment including commercial cooking ranges and refrigerators
President: Ray Williams
VP Sales: Lex Poulos
Customer Service Manager: Susan Hopkins
Production Engineering Manager: Peng Wang
Estimated Sales: $2.5-5 Million
Number Employees: 100-250
Parent Co: Maytag Corporation
Brands:
Dynasty
Jade Range
Jade Refrigeration
Utility Refrigeration

24537 Jagenberg
PO Box 1229
Enfield, CT 06083-1229 860-741-2501
Fax: 860-741-2508 lemo@jagenberginc.com
www.jagenberg.com
Automatic folding carton gluers and packers
VP: C Himmelsbach
VP Converting Gruop: A Groat
Estimated Sales: $20-50 Million
Number Employees: 100-249
Parent Co: Jagenberg-Werke AG
Brands:
Jagenberg Diana

24538 Jagla Machinery Company
26 Woodland Ave
San Rafael, CA 94901 415-457-7672
Fax: 415-457-1143
Wine industry equipment fabricators
President: Lee Jagla
Estimated Sales: Below $5 Million
Number Employees: 5-9
Square Footage: 5000

24539 James Austin Company
115 Downieville Road
P.O. Box 827
Mars, PA 16046 724-625-1535
Fax: 724-625-3288 www.jamesaustin.com
Household chlorine bleaches, laundry and dishwashing detergents, disinfectants, ammonia, pines oil cleaners, windshield washer fluid, fabric softeners and glass cleaners
Chairman of the Board: John Austin Sr
Managing Director: Kristie Kollinger
Chief Information Officer: Adam Barnard
Director, Human Resources: Patti Harpster
Purchasing Manager: Frank Bjalobok
Estimated Sales: $52 Million
Number Employees: 215
Number of Brands: 10
Number of Products: 30
Square Footage: 180000
Type of Packaging: Consumer, Food Service, Private Label
Brands:
101
A-1
Austin
Snoee
Wipe Away

24540 James River Canada
137 Bentworth Avenue
North York, ON M6A 1T6
Canada 416-789-5151
Fax: 416-789-3590
Disposable cups, plates and cutlery
Estimated Sales: $1 - 5,000,000
Number Employees: 250
Parent Co: James River Corporation

24541 (HQ)James Thompson & Company
381 Park Ave S
Rm 718
New York, NY 10016 212-686-4242
Fax: 212-686-9528 inquiry@jamesthompson.com
www.jamesthompson.com
Manufacturer and exporter of buckrams, netting, cotton goods, burlap, cheesecloth, etc
President: Robert B Judell
Treasurer: Barry Garr
Vice President, Sales/Marketing: Marc Bieler
Vice President, Manufacturing: Steve Luchansky
Merchandise Manager: Gail Boyle
Estimated Sales: $300,000-500,000
Number Employees: 1-4

24542 James V. Hurson Associates
200 N. Glebe Road
Suite 321
Arlington, VA 22203-3755 703-524-8200
Fax: 703-525-8451 800-642-6564
info@hurson.com www.hurson.com
Consultant specializing in food labeling, trademarks and patents
President: James Hurson
Manager: J Hurson
Estimated Sales: $2.5 - 5 Million
Number Employees: 20-49

24543 James Varley & Sons
1200 Switzer Ave
Saint Louis, MO 63147 314-383-4372
Fax: 314-383-4379 800-325-3303
customerservice@daleyinternational.com
www.daleyinternational.com
General purpose and meat room cleaners, degreasers, sanitizers, housekeeping chemicals, floor polish and hand soap
President: John Daley
CEO: Jack Daley
Estimated Sales: $5-10 Million
Number Employees: 20-49
Parent Co: Daley International, Ltd
Brands:
Everwear
Med-I-San

24544 Jamestown Awning
289 Steele St
Jamestown, NY 14701-6287 716-483-1435
Fax: 716-483-3995 jhwawn@alltell.net
www.jamestownawning.com
Commercial awnings
President: Mark Saxton
Estimated Sales: $1 - 2,500,000
Number Employees: 10-19

24545 Jamestown Container Corporation
8146 Bavaria Road
Macedonia, OH 44056 216-831-3700
Fax: 216-831-3709 800-247-1033
www.jamestowncontainer.com
Corrugated cartons
President: Larry Hudson
Sales Manager: Jeffrey Davidson
General Manager: Louis Petitti
Plant Manager: Joseph Palmeri
Estimated Sales: $10-20 Million
Number Employees: 50-99
Parent Co: Willamette Industries

24546 Jamison Door Company
P.O. Box 70
Hagerstown, MD 21740
Fax: 240-329-5155 800-532-3667
www.jamisondoor.com
Cold storage refrigerator and freezer doors.
Purchasing: Don Wilson
Number of Brands: 3

24547 Jamison Door Company
P.O.Box 70
Hagerstown, MD 21741-0070 301-733-3100
Fax: 301-733-7339 800-532-3667
contact@jamisondoor.com
www.jamisondoor.com
Manufacturer and exporter of cold storage, sound reduction, blast and clean room doors
Chairman: John Williams
Executive VP: Thomas Johnson
Marketing Manager: George Hamilton
VP Sales/Marketing: Dwight Clark
Estimated Sales: $20-50 Million
Number Employees: 10-19
Brands:
Jamisonic
Jamoclear
Jamolite
Jamotuf
Mark Iv
Plyfoam

24548 Jamison Plastic Corporation
5001 Crackersport Rd
Allentown, PA 18104 610-391-1400
Fax: 610-391-1414
Manufacturer and designer of custom and plastic injection molded products
President: Marc Solda
Estimated Sales: $10-20 Million
Number Employees: 50-99
Square Footage: 105000

24549 JanTec
1777 Northern Star Dr
Traverse City, MI 49696-9244 231-941-4339
Fax: 231-941-1460 800-992-3303
accounting@jantec.com www.jantec.com
Manufacturer and exporter of belt, angle-edge and spiral conveyors; also, power turns and specialty stainless steel conveying equipment for food and washdown applications
Owner: Ronald Sommerfield
Number Employees: 20-49

24550 Janedy Sign Company
27 Carter St
Everett, MA 02149 617-776-5700
Fax: 617-387-5822
Signs
Owner: William Penney
Estimated Sales: $500,000-$1 Million
Number Employees: 5-9

24551 Janows Design Associates
5323 W Pratt Avenue
Lincolnwood, IL 60712-3121 847-763-0620
Fax: 847-763-0621
Consultant specializing in engineering and design of commercial food service equipment
President: Quintilla Janows
Principal: Sherwin Janows
Estimated Sales: $500,000-$1 Million
Number Employees: 5-9

24552 January & Wood Company
PO Box 308
Maysville, KY 41056-0308 606-564-3301
Fax: 606-564-8425
Cotton and cotton/polyester twine
Estimated Sales: $5-10 Million
Number Employees: 50-99

24553 Jarboe Equipment
411 N Bedford St
Georgetown, DE 19947-2197 302-856-7988
Fax: 302-856-7408 800-699-7988
www.jarboeequipment.com
Dealer of new and used food processing equipment
Owner: Ronald Snyder
Estimated Sales: $1 - 5 Million
Number Employees: 1-4

24554 Jarchem Industries
414 Wilson Ave
Newark, NJ 07105 973-578-4560
Fax: 973-344-5743 info@jarchem.com
www.jarchem.com
Acetates and chlorides
VP: Arthur Hein
CEO: Arnold Stern
Sales Manager: Steve Yonder
Estimated Sales: $20-50 Million
Number Employees: 1-4

24555 Jarden Home Brands
14611 W. Commerce Road
P.O Box 529
Daleville, IN 47334 800-392-2575
Fax: 765-557-3250 info@jardenhomebrands.com
www.diamondbrands.com
Cocktail forks, toothpicks, corn-on-the-cob holders, skewers, candy sticks, spoons, etc; exporter of woodware and cutlery; importer of toothpicks and candy apple sticks
Sales Manager: Phil Dvorak

Brands:
Diamond
Forster
Permaware
Universal

24556 **Jarisch Paper Box Company**
1560 Curran Highway
North Adams, MA 01247-3900 413-663-5396
Fax: 413-664-4889
Boxes including set-up paper and plastic; also, partitions
General Manager: Gary Mallows
Number Employees: 45

24557 **Jarke Corporation**
750 Pinecrest Dr
Prospect Hts, IL 60070 847-541-6500
Fax: 847-541-0858 800-722-5255
customerservice@jarke.com
www.gillisindustries.com
Steel pallets and skids; also, racks including portable stacking, pallet storage and cantilever; nonpowered trucks and carts for warehouse coolers and freezers available
President: Harvey Baker
Marketing Director: Liz Cheevers
Sales: George Luft
Estimated Sales: $10-20 Million
Number Employees: 20-49
Square Footage: 120000
Brands:
Airector
Button-On
Cupl-Up
Hi-Drum
Mini-Module
Minitree
Quiktree
Steeltree
Tri-Drum
Utilitier

24558 **Jarlan Manufacturing Company**
8701 Avalon Blvd
Los Angeles, CA 90003 323-752-1211
Fax: 323-752-2037
Bar tops and ice bins
President: Craig Malburg
Estimated Sales: $500,000-$1 Million
Number Employees: 5-9

24559 **Jarvis Caster Company**
881 Lower Brownsville Rd
Jackson, TN 38301-9667 731-554-2138
800-995-9876
inof@jarviscaster.com www.jarviscaster.com
Manufacturer and exporter of industrial casters and wheels
President: Rodney Brooks
CFO: Ronnie Fondrun
Vice President: Scott Lackey
Research & Development: Harry Green
Marketing Director: Cary Gillespie
Sales Director: Scott Lackey
Operations Manager: Harold Clark
Purchasing Manager: Tracy Hall
Number Employees: 100-249
Square Footage: 800000
Parent Co: Standex International Corporation
Type of Packaging: Bulk
Other Locations:
Jarvis East
Mississauga ON

24560 **(HQ)Jarvis Products Corporation**
33 Anderson Rd
Middletown, CT 06457 860-347-7271
Fax: 860-347-9905 sales@jarvisproducts.com
www.jarvisproducts.com
Meat and poultry processing equipment.
President: Vincent Volpe
Estimated Sales: $14.8 Million
Number Employees: 100-249
Square Footage: 12000
Brands:
Jarvis

24561 **Jarvis-Cutter Company**
184 Bremen Street
Boston, MA 02128-1738 617-567-7532
Fax: 617-567-5644
General, infectious and pathological waste incinerators and heat recovery boilers
Estimated Sales: $.5 - 1 million
Number Employees: 6
Parent Co: Jarvis-Cutter

24562 **Jasper Seating Company**
P.O.Box 231
Jasper, IN 47547-0231 812-481-9259
Fax: 812-482-1548 blish@jasperseating.com
www.jasperseating.com
Technical Services Manager: Amilcar Ubiera
Sales Territory Manager: Jimi Barreiro
Estimated Sales: $10 - 20 Million
Number Employees: 100-249

24563 **Java Jackets**
910 NE 57th Ave # 300
Portland, OR 97213 503-281-6240
Fax: 503-281-6462 800-208-4128
info@javajacket.com www.javajacket.com
Manufacturer and exporter of hot and cold paper cup coffee sleeves, joe to go boxes and custom sized sleeves.
President: Jay Sorensen
CEO: Colleen Sorensen
Estimated Sales: $500,000-$1 Million
Number Employees: 5-9
Brands:
Java Jacket

24564 **Jax, Inc**
W134n5373 Campbell Dr
Menomonee Falls, WI 53051-7023 262-781-8850
Fax: 262-781-3906 800-782-8850
info@jax.com www.jax.com
Jax INC is a manufacturer of high technology, industrial, synthetic and food grade lubricants. Founded in 1955, JAX produces conventional and extreme performance synthetic lubricants for food processing and numerous other industrysegments. JAX lubrication products are distributed worldwide.
President/CEO: Eric Peter
CFO: Steve Matiacci
Vice President: Carter Anderson
Marketing Director: Tracey Huebner
Estimated Sales: $10-20 Million
Number Employees: 20-49
Parent Co: Pressure-Lube
Type of Packaging: Private Label, Bulk
Other Locations:
Benhkle Lubricants/Western Regional
Sacramento CA
Brands:
Jax Lubricants

24565 **Jay Bee Manufacturing**
PO Box 986
Tyler, TX 75710 903-597-9343
Fax: 903-593-8725 800-445-0610
jaybeemfg@suddenlinkmail.com
www.jaybeehammermills.com
Manufacturer and exporter of stainless steel hammer mills for particle reduction of fruits, rice cakes and spices
President: Edwina Granberry
Estimated Sales: $1-2.5 Million
Number Employees: 5-9
Square Footage: 140000
Brands:
Jay Bee

24566 **Jay Packaging Group**
100 Warwick Industrial Dr
Warwick, RI 02886 401-739-7200
Fax: 401-738-0137 siteadmin@jaypack.com
www.jaypack.com
Manufacturer and exporter of displays, blister cards, skin sheets and thermoformed trays and blisters
President: Richard E Kelly
CFO: Fernando Lemos
CFO: Fernando Lemos
VP Sales: Jim Nattiucci
Estimated Sales: $20 - 50 Million
Number Employees: 100-249

24567 **Jay R. Smith Manufacturing Company**
P.O.Box 3237
Montgomery, AL 36109-0237 334-277-8520
Fax: 334-272-7396 sales@jrsmith.com
www.jrsmith.com
Grease remediation systems and grease intercepters
CFO: Dale Evans
CEO: Jay Smith
CEO: Jay L Smith
Marketing: Charles White
Vice President of Domestic Sales: John Roberts
Plant Manager: Jeff Cannon
Purchasing Director: Bruce Tomlinson
Estimated Sales: $40 Million
Number Employees: 250-499
Number of Products: 200
Square Footage: 250000
Parent Co: Smith Industries

24568 **Jayhawk Boxes**
1150 South Union
Fremont, NE 68025
800-642-8363
jaystevr@lpco.net www.lpco.net
Corrugated shipping boxes
Estimated Sales: $20 Million
Number Employees: 65
Parent Co: Lawrence Paper Company

24569 **Jayhawk Manufacturing Company, Inc.**
PO Box 313
1426 North Grand Street
Hutchinson, KS 67501 620-669-8269
Fax: 620-669-9815 866-886-8269
info@jayhawkmills.com www.jayhawkmills.com
Manufacturer and exporter of wet process, stone grinding and colloid mills used primarily in the production of condiments
President: Merle Starr
Estimated Sales: $500,000-$1 Million
Number Employees: 1-4
Brands:
Jayhawk Mills

24570 **Jeb Plastics**
3519 Silverside Rd Ste 106
Wilmington, DE 19810 302-479-9223
Fax: 302-479-9227 800-556-2247
info@jebplastics.com www.jebplastics.com
Wholesaler/distributor/broker of poly bags, vinyl bags, heat sealers and packaging supplies
Owner: Sherri Lindner
Estimated Sales: Below $500,000
Number Employees: 1-4
Square Footage: 4000

24571 **Jeco Plastic Products**
885 Andico Rd
Plainfield, IN 46168 317-839-4943
Fax: 317-839-1209 800-593-5326
kimk@jecoplastics.com www.jecoplastics.com
FDA approved plastic pallet and containers
President/CEO: Craig Carson
CFO: Sherry Arndt
R & D: Roger Streling
Sales: Paul Koehl
Sales/Customer support: Ann Carson
Plant Manager: Don Andrews
Estimated Sales: Below $5 Million
Number Employees: 20-49
Square Footage: 37000
Type of Packaging: Bulk
Brands:
Perfect Pallet

24572 **Jedwards International,Inc.**
141 Campanelli Dr.
Braintree, MA 02184 617-472-9300
Fax: 617-472-9359 sales@bulknaturaloils.com
www.bulknaturaloils.com
Manufacturer and supplier of organic and conventional specialty oils, essential oils, butters, waxes, and botanicals

24573 **Jeffcoat Signs**
1611 S Main St
Gainesville, FL 32601 352-377-2322
Fax: 352-377-4249 877-377-4248
info@jeffcoatsigns.com www.jeffcoatsigns.com
Signs including plastic, neon and painted; installation services available
President: Kevin Jeffers
Estimated Sales: $1-2.5 Million
Number Employees: 5-9
Square Footage: 45000

24574 Jefferson Packing Company
765 Marlene Drive
Gretna, LA 70056-7639 504-366-4451
Fax: 504-366-9382
Packaging solutions
President: William Marciante

24575 Jefferson Smurfit Corporation
1228 Tower Rd
Schaumburg, IL 60173-4308 847-884-1200
Fax: 847-884-7206 supplierzone@smurfit.com
www.jefferson-smurfit.com
Flexible packaging
President: Gary Mc Daniel
VP: Mark A Polivka
Estimated Sales: $20 - 50 Million
Number Employees: 100-249

24576 Jel-Sert Company
Rte. 59 and Conde St.
West Chicago, IL 60185 630-876-4838
Fax: 630-231-3993 800-323-2592
www.jelsert.com
Frozen juice pops, juice beverages and mixes
President: Kenneth Wegner
CFO: Tony D'Anna
Research & Development Director: John Dobrozsi
Quality Assurance Manager: Erika Scherer
Director of Marketing: Tracie Rodriguez
Vice President of Sales & Marketing: Robert Clements
Director of Human Resources: Juan Chavez
Project Manager: Alan Sherman
Engineer & Plant Manager: Simon Richards
Estimated Sales: $5.7 Million
Number Employees: 225
Number of Brands: 14
Square Footage: 1600000
Type of Packaging: Consumer, Food Service, Bulk
Brands:
Pop Ice
Fla-Vor-Ice
Otter Pops
Mr. Freeze
Frootee Ice
Kool Pops
Wyler's Italian Ice
Bolis
Wyler's Light
Flavor Aid
Wyler's
Royal
My't'fine
Mondo

24577 Jel-Sert Company
Route 59 & Conde Street
West Chicago, IL 60185 630-231-0500
Fax: 630-231-5342 800-323-2592
www.jelsert.com
Distribution center and warehouse for Jel-Sert
President: Kenneth Wegner
CFO: Tony D'Anna
Research & Development Director: John Dobrozsi
Quality Assurance Manager: Erika Scherer
Director of Marketing: Tracie Rodriguez
Vice President of Sales & Marketing: Robert Clements
Director of Human Resources: Juan Chavez
Project Manager: Alan Sherman
Engineer & Plant Manager: Simon Richards
Number of Brands: 14
Square Footage: 13982
Type of Packaging: Consumer, Food Service, Bulk

24578 Jem Laboratory Services
P.O.Box 1634
Rome, GA 30162-1634 706-232-1709
Fax: 706-802-1175 sales@jemsalesinc.com
www.jemsalesinc.com
Water pollution treatment and monitoring, analytical laboratory services
Owner: Chris Mauer
Estimated Sales: $2.5-5 Million
Number Employees: 20-49

24579 Jemolo Enterprises
100 S Westwood Street
Spc 126
Porterville, CA 93257-7708 559-784-5566
Fax: 209-823-2506 jemoloente@aol.com
www.jemolo.en.ec21.com
Manufacturer and exporter of environmental technological building systems including water purification and waste water and sanitation treatment; also, reverse osmosis water treatment systems
President: Fred Niswonger

24580 Jen-Coat, Inc.
132 North Elm Street
PO Box 274
Westfield, MA 01086 877-536-2628
Fax: 413-562-8771 info@jencoat.com
www.jencoat.com
Manufacturer and exporter of plastic coated paper
President: James Kauffman
Estimated Sales: $1 - 5 Million
Number Employees: 250-499
Parent Co: Ana Business Products

24581 Jenco Fan
6393 Powers Ave
Jacksonville, FL 32217-2217 904-731-4711
Fax: 904-737-8322 e-mail@jencofan.com
www.breidert.com
Owner: Patrick M Williams Sr
Estimated Sales: $20 - 50 Million
Number Employees: 100-249
Parent Co: Breidert Air Products

24582 (HQ)Jenike & Johanson
400 Business Park Dr
Tyngsboro, MA 01879-1077 978-649-3300
Fax: 978-392-9980 mail@jenike.com
www.jenike.com
Manufacturer, design engineer and consultant for bulk solid handling equipment including portable and stationary containers, hoppers, bins and silos
President: John Carson
V.P. of Technology: T Anthony Royal
Marketing Director: Rod Hossefeld
Sales Director: Brian Pittenger
Estimated Sales: $2.5-5 Million
Number Employees: 20-49
Type of Packaging: Bulk
Other Locations:
Jenike & Johanson
Westford MA
Brands:
Binsert

24583 Jenkins Sign Company
1400 Mahoning Ave
Youngstown, OH 44509 330-799-3205
Fax: 330-799-3024 jenkinsadmin@neo.rr.com
Plastic, metal and neon signs
President: Joseph Jenkins
Administrative Assistant: Sue Kaden
Estimated Sales: $3 - 5 Million
Number Employees: 20-49

24584 JennFan
6393 Powers Ave
Jacksonville, FL 32217-2217 904-731-4711
Fax: 904-737-8322 e-mail@jencofan.com
www.breidert.com
Manufacturer and exporter of commercial restaurant exhaust fans and ventilation equipment
Owner: Patrick M Williams Sr III
VP Sales: Mike Wanek
Manufacturing/Product Manager: Jim Webster
Estimated Sales: $10-20 Million
Number Employees: 100-249
Square Footage: 75000
Parent Co: Breidert Air Products
Type of Packaging: Consumer, Food Service, Private Label, Bulk
Brands:
Breidert Air
Jennfan
Stanley

24585 Jensen Fittings Corporation
107 Goundry Street
111
North Tonawanda, NY 14120-5998 800-255-4111
Fax: 800-523-4165 800-255-4111
sales@jensenfittings.com
www.jensenfittings.com
Sanitary stainless steel valves, pumps, and fittings
Estimated Sales: $10-20 Million
Number Employees: 19

24586 Jensen Luhr & Sons
PO Box 297
Hood River, OR 97031-0065 541-386-3811
Fax: 541-386-4917 info@luhrjensen.com
www.luhrjensen.com
Sausage and brine mixes and seasonings and spices; also, sausage making kits, electric smokers and wood flavor fuels
President: Philip Jensen
Customer Service: Linda Gordon
Estimated Sales: $10-20 Million
Number Employees: 250-499
Square Footage: 50000

24587 Jentek
PO Box 809
North Branford, CT 06471-0809 203-488-5334
Fax: 203-481-9006
Dry coating equipment for ice cream sticks
President: Susanna Jensen
Plant Manager: Christian Jensen
Estimated Sales: $500,000-$1 Million
Number Employees: 1-4

24588 Jergens
15700 S Waterloo Rd
Cleveland, OH 44110 216-486-2100
Fax: 216-481-6193 800-537-4367
info@jergensinc.com www.jergensinc.com
Knobs and handles, cranks, threaded inserts, quick change devices and hardware, automated tape dispensing equipment, toggle clamps, grippers, slides, vacuum generators, rotary actuators, pick-n-place, and remote IO transmissiondevices
President: Jack Schron
CFO: W Howard
Quality Control: J Klindenerg
Estimated Sales: $20 - 50 Million
Number Employees: 100-249

24589 Jersey Shore Steel Company
70 Maryland Ave.
Avis, PA 17740 570-753-3000
Fax: 570-753-3782 800-833-0277
sales@jssteel.com www.jssteel.com
Wine industry metal grape stakes
Owner: John Schultz
Estimated Sales: $63.40 Million
Number Employees: 400

24590 (HQ)Jervis B. Webb Company
34375 W 12 Mile Rd
Farmington Hills, MI 48331 248-553-1000
Fax: 248-553-1228 info@jervisbwebb.com
www.jervisbwebb.com
Manufacturer and exporter of conveyor and integrated material handling systems
President: Susan Webb
CFO: John Ball
CEO: Ryuichi Kitaguchi
Marketing Director: Sarah Carlson
Estimated Sales: $100-250 Million
Number Employees: 1,000-4,999
Other Locations:
Webb, Jervis B., Co.
Chardon OH

24591 Jesco Industries, Inc.
PO Box 388
Litchfield, MI 49252-0388 517-542-2903
Fax: 517-542-2501 800-455-0019
www.jescoonline.com
Manufacturer, importer and exporter of hoppers, dumpers, security trucks, carts, dollies, baskets, wire mesh partitions, security cages, window guards and enclosures, etc
President: Bonny Desjardin
VP: B Desjardin
Marketing Director: Bonny DesJardin
Sales Engineer: Phil Risedorph
Estimated Sales: $8 Million
Number Employees: 70
Square Footage: 360000
Brands:
Jesco
Wipco

24592 (HQ)Jescorp
300 E Touhy Avenue
Suite C
Des Plaines, IL 60018-2669 847-299-7800
Fax: 847-299-7822 www.jescorp.com

Manufacturer and exporter of thermoformed and laminated containers and films, integrated gas flushing systems, gas flush tray sealers and vacuum seamers
VP Direct Sales: Jim Sanfilippo
Number Employees: 64
Square Footage: 280000
Brands:
Belt-Vac
Map-Fresh
Map-Seal
Ms-1400
Ms-25
Ms-55
Ms-700
Nitro-Flush
Vbt-1100
Vbt-250
Vbt-550

24593 Jess Jones Farms
6496 Jones Ln
Dixon, CA 95620 503-304-3806
Fax: 707-678-3898 jessjonesvineyard.com
Processor, packer and exporter of popcorn
President: Jess Jones
CEO: Mary Ellen Jones
Estimated Sales: $700,000
Number Employees: 1-4
Square Footage: 10000
Type of Packaging: Consumer, Bulk
Brands:
California Golden Pop
Customer's Bags
Jess Jones Farms

24594 Jesse Jones Box Corporation
499 E Erie Avenue
Philadelphia, PA 19134-1104 215-425-6600
Fax: 215-425-4705 bill@styledpackaging.com
Set-up and folding boxes, specialty containers and point of purchase displays
Director Sales: Harvey Brenner
Production Manager: Joseph Pomray
Estimated Sales: $3-5 Million
Number Employees: 50-75
Square Footage: 45000
Parent Co: Jesse Jones Industries
Type of Packaging: Bulk

24595 Jessup Paper Box
211 S Railroad St
Brookston, IN 47923 765-490-9043
Fax: 765-563-3424 troxler@jessuppaperbox.com
www.jessuppaperbox.com
Paper boxes and novelties
President: Butch Huber
CFO: Butch Huber
General Manager: Donald Winship
Plant Manager: Donald Cross
Purchasing Manager: Peggy Ruckdeschel
Estimated Sales: Below $5 Million
Number Employees: 20-49

24596 Jet Age Containers Company
5555 W 73rd St
Chicago, IL 60638-6505 708-594-5260
Fax: 708-594-5263 info@jetagellc.com
www.fieldpackaginggroup.com
Corrugated boxes
Owner: Martin Field
General Manager: Ben Gercone
Estimated Sales: $10-20 Million
Number Employees: 50-99

24597 Jet Box Company
1822 Thunderbird
Troy, MI 48084 248-362-1260
Fax: 248-362-2736
Corrugated boxes
Chairman of the Board: Lynda K Zardus
Estimated Sales: Below $5 Million
Number Employees: 20-49

24598 Jet Lite Products
PO Box 279
Highland, IL 62249 618-654-2217
Fax: 618-654-2217
Lighting fixtures and neon signs
President: John D Kutz Jr
Vice President: Roger Huber
Plant Manager: Joe Kutz
Estimated Sales: Below $5 Million
Number Employees: 10-19
Square Footage: 12000

24599 Jet Plastica Industries
1100 Schwab Rd
Hatfield, PA 19440
www.dwfinepack.com
Manufacturer and exporter of molded plastics including packaging kits, tumblers, cutlery and straws
Estimated Sales: $43 Million
Number Employees: 600
Square Footage: 300000
Parent Co: D&W Fine Pack

24600 JetNet Corporation
505 North Drive
79 North Industrial Park
Sewickley, PA 15143-2339 412-741-0100
Fax: 412-741-0140 800-245-1036
info@jetnetcorp.com www.jetnetcorp.com
Cutting and boning devices, general packinghouse equipment, uniforms, aprons and clothing; processing equipment, netting and tying machines
President: Donald Sartore
Estimated Sales: $5-10 Million
Number Employees: 50-99

24601 Jetstream Systems
4690 Joliet Street
Denver, CO 80239-2922 303-371-9002
Fax: 303-371-9012
jetstream.sls@worldnet.att.net
Manufacturer and exporter of mechanical and air conveyors, palletizers and depalletizers, bottle and can fillers and rinsers
Director Sales: Neal McConnellogue
Director Applications: Vince Jones
Number Employees: 153
Square Footage: 132000
Parent Co: Barry-Wehmiller Company

24602 Jewel Case Corporation
110 Dupont Dr
Providence, RI 02907 401-943-1400
Fax: 401-943-1426 800-441-4447
contact@jewelcase.com www.jewelcase.com
Manufacturer and exporter of gift and promotional packaging for candy, confections, gourmet foods and cutlery/tableware
President: Donald Wolfe
Controller: Terry Eisen
Marketing Manager: Lynn Johnson
Estimated Sales: $10 - 20 Million
Number Employees: 100-249
Square Footage: 100000
Type of Packaging: Consumer, Private Label, Bulk

24603 Jewell Bag Company
228 Yorktown St
Suite B
Dallas, TX 75208-2045 214-749-1223
Fax: 214-749-1226
FDA approved polyethylene bags
President: Michael Smith
Estimated Sales: $1-2.5 Million
Number Employees: 1-4

24604 (HQ)Jif-Pak Manufacturing
1451 Engineer St Ste A
Vista, CA 92081 760-597-2665
Fax: 760-597-2667 800-777-6613
info@jifpak.com www.jifpak.com
Manufacturer and exporter of elastic and nonelastic nettings, stockinettes, stuffing horns, semi and automatic netting machines and elastic trussing loops
President: Joe Mc Closkey
Marketing Executive: John Connelly
Operations Ex: Lee Jared
Estimated Sales: $1 - 5 Million
Brands:
Casing-Net
Jif-Pak

24605 Jiffy Mixer Company
1691 California Ave
Corona, CA 92881 951-272-0838
Fax: 951-279-7651 jiffymixer@earthlink.net
www.jiffymixer.com
Nonelectric mixers including portable and heavy duty
President: Jeff Johnson
Production Manager: Douglas Kaus
Office Manager: Al Measham
Estimated Sales: Below $5 Million
Number Employees: 5-9
Square Footage: 6000

24606 Jilson Group
20 Industrial Rd
Lodi, NJ 07644 973-471-2400
Fax: 973-471-3993 800-969-5400
heretohelp@jilson.com www.jilson.com
Manufacturer and importer of casters, wheels, noncorrosive bearings and bearing housings as well as plastic packaging ties.
Chief Financial Officer: Pete Rennard
VP: David Baughn
Products Manager: Steven Becher
Vice President Sales: David Baughn
Purchasing Manager: Tony Alfano
Estimated Sales: $2.5-5 Million
Number Employees: 10-19
Square Footage: 20000
Brands:
Steinco Casters

24607 Jim Did It Sign Company
PO Box 17
Allston, MA 02134 617-782-2410
Fax: 781-782-5433
Manufacturer and exporter of commercial signs for supermarkets and other businesses
Owner: Robert Thompson
Estimated Sales: $500,000-$1 Million
Number Employees: 5-9

24608 Jim Lake Companies
1350 Manufacturing St # 101
Dallas, TX 75207 214-741-5018
Fax: 214-741-5020 info@jimlakeco.com
www.jimlakeco.com
Rubber stamps and seals
Founder: Jim Lake
Marketing Coordinator: Monica Diodati
Estimated Sales: $500,000-$1 Million
Number Employees: 10-19

24609 Jim Scharf Holdings
PO Box 305
Perdue, SK S0K 3C0
Canada 306-237-4365
Fax: 306-237-4362 800-667-9727
jim@ezeewrap.com www.ezeewrap.com
Manufacturer and exporter of plastic wrap dispensers, process refrigerator/freezer odor absorbers, shopping bag handles, bagel cutters and lettuce knives; processor of instant lentils
President: Bruna Scharf
Marketing: Leanna Carr
Plant Manager: Mary Ann Cotterill
Estimated Sales: Below $5,000,000
Number Employees: 10
Square Footage: 12000
Brands:
Bagel Buddy
Bakeware Buddy
E-Zee Wrap
Grocery Grip
Heavenly Fresh
Kitchen Buddy
The Lettuce Knife

24610 Jimbo's Jumbos
PO Box 465
185 Peanut Drive
Edenton, NC 27932 252-482-2193
Fax: 252-482-7857 800-334-4771
www.jimbosjumbos.com
Snacks and peanuts, custom formulation is available
Manager: Hal Burns
Number Employees: 100-249
Type of Packaging: Private Label

24611 Jogue
14731 Helm Court
Plymouth, MI 48170 734-207-0100
Fax: 734-207-0200 800-521-3888
sales@foodfront.com www.jogue.com
Flavor development
President: Dattu Sastry
Estimated Sales: $5 Million
Number Employees: 20-49
Type of Packaging: Food Service, Private Label

24612 Jogue/Northville Laboratories
P.O.Box 190
Northville, MI 48167-0190 248-349-1500
Fax: 248-349-1505 sales@jogue.com
www.jogue.com
Flavors
President: Dattu Sastry
Estimated Sales: $10-20 Million
Number Employees: 20-49

24613 Johanson TransportationsServices
5583 E Olive Ave
Fresno, CA 93727 559-458-2200
800-742-2053
LJohanson@johansontrans.com
www.johansontrans.com
Transporters of dry and temperature controlled freight.
President: Larry Johanson
CFO: Janice Spicer
Vice President: Craig Johanson
Chief Operations Officer: Jerry Beckstead
Corporate Accounting & Administration Ma: Becky Martin

24614 John A. Vassilaros & Son
2905 120th St
Flushing, NY 11354 718-886-4140
Fax: 718-463-5037 sales@vassilaroscoffee.com
www.vassilaroscoffee.com
Coffee and tea
President: John Vassilaros
Director: Ann Vassilaros
Estimated Sales: $10-20 Million
Number Employees: 20-49
Type of Packaging: Private Label

24615 (HQ)John Boos & Company
315 S 1st St
Effingham, IL 62401 217-347-7701
Fax: 217-347-7705 sales@johnboos.com
www.johnboos.com
Manufacturer and exporter of cutting boards, butchers' blocks, dining room tables and chairs and stainless steel work tables and sinks
President: Joseph Emmerich
VP Sales: Eric Johnson
Estimated Sales: $10-20 Million
Number Employees: 100-249
Square Footage: 130000
Other Locations:
John Boos & Co.
Philipsburg PA
Brands:
Cucina Americana
Pro Bowl
Pro Chef
Stallion
The Table Tailors

24616 John Burton Machine Corporation
3251 John Muir Pkwy
Rodeo, CA 94572 510-799-5000
Fax: 510-799-5003 800-664-4178
info@johnburton.com www.johnburton.com
Packaging machines and case conveyor, case conveyors for cardboard boxes and tote boxes
President: Burton Rice
Sales Director: Burton Rice
Estimated Sales: Below $5 Million
Number Employees: 1-4
Brands:
Chain-In-Channel

24617 John Crane Mechanical Sealing Devices
6400 Oakton St
Morton Grove, IL 60053-2725 847-967-2400
Fax: 847-967-3915 800-732-5464
seal@johncrane.com www.johncrane.com
Manufacturer and exporter of mechanical seals, bearing isolators, couplings, lubrication systems, heat exchangers and pressure reservoirs
President: Bob Wasson
Estimated Sales: $200 Million
Number Employees: 5,000-9,999
Square Footage: 9000
Parent Co: TI Group

24618 John Dusenbery Company
80 E State Rt 4
Suite 290
Paramus, NJ 07652 973-366-7500
Fax: 973-366-7453 info@dusenbery.com
www.deluk.com
Manufacturer and exporter of converting equipment for food packaging
CEO: John Wilkes
Estimated Sales: $10-20 Million
Number Employees: 50-99

24619 John E. Ruggles & Company
PO Box 8179
New Bedford, MA 02742-8179 508-992-9766
Fax: 508-992-9734 chinyawa@mediaone.net
www.123sawtooth.com
Manufacturer, importer and exporter of varietal fiber regular and dyed rope, twine and braid
President: John Ruggles
Estimated Sales: $5-10 Million
Number Employees: 50-99
Square Footage: 100000

24620 John Henry Packaging
10005 Main St
Penngrove, CA 94951 707-664-8018
Fax: 707-762-1253 800-327-5997
sales@jhpwest.com www.jhpwest.com
Producer of digital, flexo, embossed, screened labels and cartons
Owner: John Herpeck
Digital Print Manager/Marketing Director: Dan Welty
Number Employees: 5-9
Number of Brands: 30
Square Footage: 8000
Parent Co: John Henry Company
Type of Packaging: Consumer, Food Service, Private Label, Bulk

24621 John I. Nissly Company
PO Box 633
Lancaster, PA 17608-0633 717-393-3841
Fax: 717-397-6239
Signs; also, industrial finishing and silk screen printing available
President: Andrew Nissly
General Manager: Andrew Nissley
Estimated Sales: $500,000-$1 Million
Number Employees: 5-9

24622 John J. Adams Die Corporation
10 Nebraska St
Worcester, MA 01604-3628 508-757-3894
Fax: 508-753-8016 jadamsdie@aol.com
Knives; exporter of cutting dies
President and CFO: Richard Adams
General Manager: John J Adams II
Marketing: John Adams
Estimated Sales: $2.5 - 5 Million
Number Employees: 1-4
Square Footage: 20000

24623 John L. Denning & Company
330 N Washington St
Wichita, KS 67202 316-264-2357
Fax: 316-264-3521
Brooms
President: Ed Collins
Number Employees: 4

24624 John Larkin and Company
96 Ford Rd # 15
Denville, NJ 07834-1359 973-627-7779
Fax: 973-627-7809 john.larkin@verizon.net
www.johnlarkinandcompany.com
Tea and coffee industry repair service
President: John J Larkin
Estimated Sales: $1 - 2.5 Million
Number Employees: 1-4

24625 John Morrell & Company
P.O. Box 405020
Cincinnati, OH 45240-5020
800-722-1127
www.johnmorrell.com
Wholesaler/distributor of an assortment of meat products including; ham and turkey, bacon, hot dogs, smoked sausage, lunchmeat, and special reserve hams
President & CEO: Joseph Sebring
Vice President: Steve Crim Sr.
Executive Vice President/CIO: Scott Saunders
Quality Assurance Manager: Nancy Kent
Vice President, Marketing: Mark Dietz
Operations Manager: Mike Phillips
Plant Manager: Dennis Hamm
Purchasing Manager: Benjamin Flottman
Estimated Sales: $886 Million
Number Employees: 6565
Type of Packaging: Consumer, Food Service, Private Label, Bulk
Brands:
John Morrell
Armour
Eckrich
Margherita
Carando
Patrick Cudahy
Curly's
Healthy Ones
Kretschmar
Krakus
Active Packs

24626 John Plant Company
P.O.Box 527
Ramseur, NC 27316 336-824-2366
Fax: 336-824-3177 800-334-2711
gloves@johnplant.com www.johnplant.com
Manufacturer and importer of gloves and safety supplies
President: Robert Jarman
CEO: Ron Tesh
Estimated Sales: $2.5 - 5 Million
Number Employees: 20-49
Square Footage: 24000
Parent Co: John Plant Company

24627 John Rock Inc
500 Independence Way
Coatesville, PA 19320 610-857-8080
Fax: 610-857-4809 jrock@johnrock.com
www.johnrock.com
Recycled wooden pallets
President: Bill Mac Cauley
Finance: Steve Hedrick
Lumber: Penn Cooper
Sales: Mike Veneziale
Customer Service: Jeanne Ryan
Operations: Ed Healy
Administration: Robyn Stoltzfus
Facilities/Fleet: Steve Marrs
Estimated Sales: $5 - 10 Million
Number Employees: 50-99
Square Footage: 100000

24628 John Rohrer ContractingCompany
2820 Roe Ln
Kansas City, KS 66103-1594 913-236-5005
Fax: 913-236-7291
www.johnrohrercontracting.com
Manufacturer and exporter of concrete floors
President: John W Rohrer
Sr VP: Bill Henry
Estimated Sales: $1-2.5 Million
Number Employees: 10-19

24629 Johnson & Sons Manufacturing
534-D West 2nd St.
Elgin, TX 78261 512-285-2462
Fax: 512-285-2464
info@johnsonbaggingequipment.com
www.johnsonbaggingequipment.com
Estimated Sales: $300,000 - $500,000
Number Employees: 1-4

24630 Johnson & Wales University
8 Abbott Park Pl
Providence, RI 02903 401-598-1000
Fax: 401-598-2880 800-342-5598
pvd.admissions@jwu.edu www.jwu.edu
President: John J Bowen
Number Employees: 1,000-4,999

24631 **Johnson Associates**
600 W Roosevelt Road
Unit B-2
Wheaton, IL 60187 630-690-9200
Fax: 630-690-9910 sjohnson@jasearch.com
www.jasearch.com
Recruiter specializing in the placement of mid and senior level management in food and beverage manufacturing, distribution, and processing.
President: Scott Johnson
VP: Mary Johnson
Estimated Sales: Below $5 Million
Number Employees: 1-4

24632 **Johnson Brothers Manufacturing Company**
412 W 3rd Street
Elgin, TX 78621-2117 512-285-2462
Fax: 512-285-2464
Bagging scales
Estimated Sales: $1 - 5 Million
Number Employees: 1-4

24633 **Johnson Brothers Sign Company**
307 S. State St.
PO Box 345
South Whitley, IN 46787-0345 260-723-5161
Fax: 260-723-6778 800-477-7516
info@johnsonbros-sign.com
www.johnsonbros-sign.com
Electric, neon and plastic signs
President: Bill Howard
Estimated Sales: $1-2.5 Million
Number Employees: 20-49
Square Footage: 37600

24634 **Johnson Controls**
5757 N. Green Bay Ave.
P.O. Box 591
Milwaukee, WI 53201 800-950-7539
www.johnsoncontrols.com
Gas and electronic and electromechanical refrigeration controls, HVAC/refrigeration/lighting store management systems
President: David Myers
Number Employees: 1,000-4,999

24635 **Johnson Corrugated Products Corporation**
PO Box 246
Thompson, CT 06277 860-923-9563
Fax: 860-923-2531
Corrugated packaging materials inlcuding corrugated and paper boxes; also, cake and pizza circles
Manager: Andrew Baumont
General Manager: Dick Clark
Estimated Sales: $20-50 Million
Number Employees: 10-19

24636 **Johnson Diversey**
8310 16th St
Sturtevant, WI 53177 262-631-4001
Fax: 262-631-4282 www.johnsondiversey.com
Floor finishes, cleaners, disinfectants and carpet cleaners
President: Paul McLaughlin
CEO: Edward F Lonergan
VP Sales: William Taylor
Estimated Sales: $20-50 Million
Number Employees: 10,000
Brands:
Butcher's

24637 **Johnson Diversified Products**
1408 Northland Dr
Suite 406
Mendota Heights, MN 55120-1013 651-688-0014
Fax: 952-686-7670 800-676-8488
info@jdpinc.com www.jdpinc.com
Wholesaler/distributor of food service equipment, and HACCP related instruments, tools and systems; serving the food service market
President: Thomas Johnson
CEO: Thomas Johnson
Vice President: Paul Johnson
Estimated Sales: $5 - 10 Million
Number Employees: 5-9

24638 **(HQ)Johnson Food Equipment**
2955 Fairfax Trfy
Kansas City, KS 66115 913-621-3366
Fax: 913-621-1729 800-288-3434
sales@baader-johnson.com
www.baader-johnson.com
Poultry processing equipment
President: Andy Miller
CFO: Shawn Nicholas
Sr VP: David Crawford
General Sales Manager: Steve Abram
Sales Manager (Food Systems): Bruce Sterling
Estimated Sales: $20 - 50 Million
Number Employees: 100-249
Square Footage: 70000
Other Locations:
Johnson Food Equipment
Kitchener ON

24639 **Johnson Industries**
6391 Lake Rd
Windsor, WI 53598 608-846-4499
Fax: 608-846-7195 info@johnsonindint.com
www.johnsonindint.com
Manufacturer cheese processing equipment
President/ Co - Owner: Grant Nesheim
Owner and Cheese Industry Expert: Peter Nelles
Sales Director: Todd Martin
Plant Manager: Eric Severson
Director Purchasing: Scott Peterson
Number of Brands: 4
Square Footage: 200000

24640 **Johnson Industries International, Inc.**
6391 Lake Road
Windsor, WI 53598 608-846-4499
Fax: 608-846-7195 info@johnsonindint.com
www.johnsonindint.com
Manufacturer and exporter of mozzarella cheese making machinery
Estimated Sales: $5 - 10 Million
Number Employees: 20-49
Square Footage: 77408
Brands:
Supreme

24641 **Johnson International Materials**
2908 Boca Chica Blvd
Brownsville, TX 78521-3506 956-541-6364
Fax: 956-541-1446
Manufacturer and exporter of wiping rags
President: Jim Johnson
VP Marketing: Bob Ewing
Estimated Sales: $20-50 Million
Number Employees: 100-249

24642 **Johnson Pumps of America**
1625 Hunter Rd
Hanover Park, IL 60133 847-671-7867
Fax: 847-671-7909
customerservice@johnsonpumpchi.com
www.johnson-pump.com
Positive displacement rotary lobe pumps
CEO: Jerry Assessor
VP Sales: Mitch Pixley
Production Manager: Tony Wuethrich
Estimated Sales: $20 - 50 Million
Number Employees: 50-99
Parent Co: Johnson Pumps of America
Brands:
Albin

24643 **(HQ)Johnson Refrigerated Truck Bodies**
215 E Allen St
Rice Lake, WI 54868-2203 715-234-7071
Fax: 715-234-4628 800-922-8360
jtbsales@johnsontruckbodies.com
www.johnsontruckbodies.com
Manufacturer and exporter of fiberglass composite plastic refrigerated truck bodies and trailers, and all-electric truck refrigeration systems.
President: Ron Ricci
VP Sales/Marketing: Mayo Rude
Public Relations: Nicole King
VP Operations: Chris Olson
Square Footage: 134000
Type of Packaging: Food Service

24644 **Johnson Starch Molding**
13549 W Greenview Drive
Wadsworth, IL 60083-9309 847-872-1989
Fax: 847-872-1988
Boards, starch, conveyors, cooling equipment, cooling tunnels, elevators, bucket, feeder belts
Estimated Sales: $1 - 5 Million
Number Employees: 4

24645 **Johnson-Rose Corporation**
5303 Crown Dr
Lockport, NY 14095-0447 716-434-2711
Fax: 716-434-2762 800-456-2055
info@johnsonrose.com www.johnsonrose.com
Aluminum cookware and bakeware; importer and exporter of commercial kitchen utensils including ladles, spoons, tongs, mixing bowls, collanders, steam pans, etc
President: Ernie Berman
CFO: Viola Wilson
Director of Marketing: Mark Kuligowski
Operations Manager: D Kuligowski
Inventory Control: Darrell Szyprygada
Estimated Sales: $2.5-5 Million
Number Employees: 20-49
Square Footage: 41000
Parent Co: Johnson-Rose

24646 **Johnston Boiler Company**
300 Pine St
Ferrysburg, MI 49409 616-842-5050
Fax: 616-842-1854 info@johnstonboiler.com
www.johnstonboiler.com
Boilers, generators, heat recovery systems, burners, energy savings, JBC engineering, emission data, JBC specifications, driving directions
President: R Kim Black
Director: Pat Baker
Estimated Sales: $5 - 10 Million
Number Employees: 50-99

24647 **Johnston Equipment**
#105-581 Chester Road
Annacis Island
Delta, BC V3M 6G7
Canada 604-524-0361
Fax: 604-524-8961 800-237-5159
couttsd@johnstonequipment.com
www.johnstonequipment.com
Manufacturer, wholesaler/distributor and exporter of material handling equipment including electric forklifts and pallet racking/shelving systems
President & CEO: Michael Marcotte
Regional Sales Manager: John Binns
Sales Manager: Curt Snigol
Estimated Sales: $1 - 5 Million
Number Employees: 50-99
Square Footage: 66000
Brands:
Pacific Westeel
Serco

24648 **Johnstown Manufacturing**
1055 S Hamilton Rd
Columbus, OH 43227-1309 614-236-8853
Fax: 614-876-6797
Plastic straws and stirrers
Manager: John Scott
Number Employees: 50-99

24649 **Jokamsco Group**
18 Hudson St
Mechanicville, NY 12118-1927 518-237-6416
Fax: 518-233-7203
Gears and machine replacement parts for the food and beverage industry; also, industrial knife grinding available
President: Colleen Swedish
Estimated Sales: $300,000-500,000
Number Employees: 1-4
Square Footage: 5000

24650 **Jomac Products**
7525 N Oak Park Avenue
Niles, IL 60714-3819 215-343-0800
Fax: 215-343-0912 800-566-2289
gloves@jomac.com
Manufacturer and exporter of terrycloth, cut-resistant and nomex gloves, mitts, aprons, pads and sleeves
Marketing Manager: Charlie Lake
Sales Manager: Jim Podall
Number Employees: 499
Type of Packaging: Food Service, Bulk
Brands:
Cool Blues
Pott Holdr
The Shield

24651 **Jomar Corporation**
PO Box 1020
Pleasantville, NJ 08232 609-646-8000
Fax: 609-645-9166 jomarsales@worldnet.att.net
www.jomarcorp.com
Manufacturer and exporter of plastic injection blow molding machinery and plastic molds and dies
President: William Petrino
Senior VP: Walter Priest
Estimated Sales: $10-20 Million
Number Employees: 50-99
Square Footage: 45000
Parent Co: Inductotherm Industries
Brands:
Aquatral
Jomar

24652 **Jomar Plastics Industry**
1304 Shoemaker St
Nanty Glo, PA 15943-1255 814-749-9131
Fax: 814-749-8079 800-681-4039
jomar@floodcity.net www.jomarplastics.com
Plastic bags for bakery, meat and poultry
President: Pam Harkcom
VP: Susan Ott
Estimated Sales: $500,000-$1 Million
Number Employees: 1-4
Square Footage: 5000

24653 **Joneca Corporation**
4332 E La Palma Avenue
Anaheim, CA 92807 714-993-5997
Fax: 714-993-2126 info@joneca.com
www.joneca.com
Manufacturer and exporter of dehydrators and waste reduction and water purification systems
President: Edward E Chavez
Estimated Sales: Below $5 Million
Number Employees: 10
Parent Co: Anaheim Marketing International
Brands:
Aquacare
Commodore
Compacta
Mr. Scrapy

24654 **Jones Automation Company**
11838 W Carroll Rd
Beloit, WI 53511 608-879-9307
Fax: 608-879-2266 information@jacsite.com
www.jacsite.com
Forming, filling and sealing equipment, stacking and interleaving equipment, vacuum packaging equipment, wrapping and overwrap machines, slicers and weigh-convey systems
Estimated Sales: $1-5 Million
Number Employees: 10

24655 **Jones Environmental**
2404 Rutland Dr Ste 200
Austin, TX 78758-5249 512-834-6040
Fax: 512-834-6039 website@enviroquip.com
www.enviroquip.com
Waste treatment plants capable of anaerobic and aerobic processes for the food and beverage industries; custom design services available
President: Jim Porteous
CEO: Dick Johnson
CFO: Nelda Tallman
Chairman: Richard Johnson
Marketing Assistant: Ann Perry
Production: Arthur Shaffer
Estimated Sales: Less than $500,000
Number Employees: 20-49

24656 **Jones Packaging Machinery**
8005 Wolftever Dr
Ooltewah, TN 37363 423-238-4558
Fax: 423-238-6018
Packaging machinery
President: Charles Abernathy
CFO: Charles Abernathy
Quality Control: Jeff Smith
Plant Manager: James Dillard
Estimated Sales: Below $5 Million
Number Employees: 10
Square Footage: 12000

24657 **Jones-Hamilton**
30354 Tracy Rd
Walbridge, OH 43465 419-666-9838
Fax: 419-666-1817 info@jones-hamilton.com
www.jones-hamilton.com
Industrial inorganic chemicals
CFO: Brian Brooks
EVP: Bernard Murphy
Plant Manager: Chuck Almroth
Estimated Sales: $64 Million
Number Employees: 50

24658 **Jones-Zylon Company**
P.O.Box 149
West Lafayette, OH 43845 740-545-6341
Fax: 740-545-6671 800-848-8160
miker@joneszylon.com www.joneszylon.com
Institutional tableware, compartments and serving trays, tumblers, cups, bowls, plates and reusable plastic flatware; exporter of dinnerware and flatware
President: Todd Kohl
Quality Control: Chuck Laney
Sales (Mid Atlantic): Mike Robertson
Sales (West): Myron Vile
Chairperson: Marion Mulligan-Sutton
Estimated Sales: $5 - 10 Million
Number Employees: 10-19
Square Footage: 40800
Parent Co: Jones Metal Products Company
Brands:
Jones Zylon

24659 **Jonessco Enterprises**
2801 Regal Road
Suite 103
Plano, TX 75075-6315 972-985-7961
Fax: 972-612-1741
Consultant specializing in food technology, marketing and promotion for the supermarket and food service industries
President: Buck Jones
CFO: Buck Jones
R&D: Bill Jacob
Estimated Sales: Below $5 Million
Number Employees: 5
Type of Packaging: Bulk

24660 **Jordan Box Company**
140 Dickerson Street
PO Box 1054
Syracuse, NY 13201 315-422-3419
Fax: 315-422-0318 sales@JordanBoxCo.com
www.jordanboxco.com
Paper boxes
President: Richard M Casper
Estimated Sales: $1-2.5 Million
Number Employees: 10-19

24661 **Jordan Paper Box Company**
5045 W Lake St
Chicago, IL 60644 773-287-5362
Fax: 773-287-5362
Manufacturer, importer and exporter of paper boxes
President/CFO: John Jordan
President: Jam Jordan
Estimated Sales: $1 - 2.5 Million
Number Employees: 5-9
Square Footage: 30000
Type of Packaging: Bulk

24662 **Jordan Specialty Company**
129 13th St
Brooklyn, NY 11215-4603
Fax: 718-238-3221 877-567-3265
jordanspecialty@mindspring.com
www.jordanspecialty.com
Transparent card cases, covers, holders and menu covers
Manager: Joshua Handler
Manager: Soul Handler
Estimated Sales: $1-2.5 Million
Number Employees: 20-49
Square Footage: 25000
Brands:
Bondstar

24663 **Jordon Commercial Refrigerator**
2200 Kennedy Street
Philadelphia, PA 19137-1820 215-535-8300
Fax: 215-289-1597 800-523-0171
Manufacturer, importer and exporter of refrigerators and freezers
President: Gene Sterner
VP, Sales: Jim Duff
Purchasing Manager: Jerry Joyce
Number Employees: 100-249
Square Footage: 148000
Parent Co: Jordon/Fleetwood/Fogel, LLC
Other Locations:
Jordon Commercial Refrigerato
Fleetwood PA
Brands:
Fleetwood
Fogel
Jordon

24664 **Jordon-Fleetwood Commercial Refrigerator Company**
2200 Kennedy Street
Philadelphia, PA 19137-1820 215-535-8300
Fax: 215-289-1597 www.keepitcool.com

24665 **(HQ)Josam Company**
P.O.Box T
Michigan City, IN 46361-0360 219-872-5531
Fax: 219-874-9539 800-365-6726
www.josam.com
Drains, interceptors, backwater valves, carriers, hydrants and water hammer arrestors
President: Barry Hodgkins
President, Chief Executive Officer: Scott Holloway
CFO: David Szerencse
Vice President of Sales and Marketing: Paula Bowe
Chief Operating Officer: Barry Hodgekins
Estimated Sales: $20 - 50 Million
Number Employees: 100-249

24666 **Josef Kihlberg of America**
2400 Galvin Dr
Elgin, IL 60124
Fax: 315-452-9597 800-437-9818
reception@khilberg.se www.kihlberg.us
Stapling and strapping tools and fasteners
Estimated Sales: $1 - 3 Million
Number Employees: 10-19

24667 **Joseph Manufacturing Company**
5011 Antioch Road
Overland Park, KS 66203-1314 913-677-1660
Fax: 913-677-1658 800-373-6671
josephmfg@worldnet.att.net
Automated and manual label dispensing and applying equipment
V.P.: Shawn Hornung
Estimated Sales: $5-10 Million
Number Employees: 19

24668 **Joseph Struhl Company**
195 Atlantic Ave
PO Box N
Garden City Park, NY 11040 516-741-3660
Fax: 516-742-3617 800-552-0023
info@magicmaster.com www.magicmaster.com
Manufacturer and exporter of signs including open/closed self-adhesive reusable and removable static vinyl and stock and custom using static cling vinyl
Managing Director: Cliff Stevens
Sales Manager: H Green
Manager: Cliff Stevens
Estimated Sales: $1 - 2.5 Million
Number Employees: 10-19
Brands:
Design Master
Magic Master
Ready Made
Super Moderna

24669 **Joseph Titone & Sons**
1006 Jacksonville Rd
Burlington, NJ 08016-3802
Fax: 609-386-8978 800-220-4102
titone@pics.com www.metrolace.com
Nets and hair nets for food handlers
President: Alfred Titone
CFO/Attorney: John Titone
V.P.: Edward Dormand
Number Employees: 20-49
Square Footage: 55000

24670 **Joul, Engineering StaffiSolutions**
110 Fieldcrest Avenue
Raritan Plaza 1
Edison, NJ 08837 732-548-1069
Fax: 732-632-9795 877-494-8835
www.jouleinc.com
Consultant of custom design plant modernization and automation equipment
Senior VP: Howard Moseman

Estimated Sales: $1 - 5 Million
Number Employees: 50-99
Parent Co: Joule

24671 Jowat Adhesives
6058 Lois Ln
Archdale, NC 27263-8588 336-434-9000
Fax: 336-434-9019 800-322-4583
info@jowat.com www.jowat.com
Packaging hot melts, anti-slip hot melts, casein glues, pressure sensitives, dextrins, water-based dispersions
President: Rainhard Kramme
Estimated Sales: $10-25 Million
Number Employees: 100-249

24672 Jowat Corporation
6058 Lois Ln
Archdale, NC 27263-8588 336-434-9000
Fax: 336-434-9019 800-322-4583
info@jowat.com www.jowat.com
President: Rainhard Kramme
Estimated Sales: $100+ Million
Number Employees: 100-249

24673 Joyce Engraving Company, Inc.
1262 Round Table Dr
Dallas, TX 75247 214-638-1262
Fax: 214-638-5432 sales@joyceengraving.com
www.joyceengraving.com
Steel stamps, stencils and branding equipment including burning, meat and tire
VP: Rick Joyce
VP: R Joyce
Estimated Sales: Below $5 Million
Number Employees: 5-9
Square Footage: 40000

24674 Joyce/Dayton Corporation
3300 South Dixie Drive
Kettering, OH 45439 937-294-6261
Fax: 937-297-7173 sales@joycedayton.com
www.joycedayton.com
Lifts including hydraulic and mechanical powered
President: Tim Gockel
CFO: Kim Gockal
Director Sales: Warren Webster
Estimated Sales: $10 - 20,000,000
Number Employees: 50-99

24675 Joylin Food Equipment Corporation
51 Chestnut Ln
Woodbury, NY 11797-1918
Fax: 516-742-2123 800-456-9546
joylin1961@aol.com
Manufacturers' representative for food service equipment
President: Rich Kirsner
Marketing Director: Tom Pitts
Sales Director: M Kohn
Operations Manager: Tom DiRusso
Purchasing Manager: Yvette Western
Estimated Sales: $20-50 Million
Number Employees: 21
Number of Brands: 16
Square Footage: 12000

24676 Judel Products
45 Knollwood Road
Suite 24
Elmsford, NY 10523-2822 914-592-6200
Fax: 914-592-1216 800-583-3526
Manufacturer, importer and exporter of glassware
President: Mel Schulweis
VP: John Rufus
Sales Director: Stven Fox
Office Manager: Dorothy See
Estimated Sales: $500,000 - $1 Million
Number Employees: 1-4
Parent Co: Tiffany & Company
Type of Packaging: Food Service
Brands:
Durobor
Judel
Opticrystal
Vintner's Ii
Vintner's Selection

24677 Judge
300 Conshohocken State Rd #300
W Conshohocken, PA 19428-3820 610-667-7700
Fax: 610-667-1058 888-228-7162
wgladstone@judge.com www.judgeinc.com
Executive search agency specializing in operations and distribution management
President: Michael F Ferreri
CEO: Martin Judge, Jr.
Estimated Sales: $1 - 5 Million
Number Employees: 20-49
Parent Co: Judge Group

24678 Judith Quick & Associates
13944 Roberts Rd
Hancock, MD 21750-1620 301-678-5737
Fax: 301-678-5730 jnichols@nfis.com
Consulting firm specializing in regulatory and quality control, labeling, etc
President: Judith Quick
Estimated Sales: Below $5 Million
Number Employees: 1-4
Square Footage: 400

24679 Juice Merchandising Corporation
9237 Ward Parkway
Suite 104
Kansas City, MO 64114 816-361-5343
Fax: 816-361-2033 800-950-1998
kcjmc@haotmail.com
Plastic juice bottles as well as wholesaler/distributor of juice processing equipment
President and CFO: Robert Bushman
CEO: Helen Bushman
Manager, Operations: Bill Young
Estimated Sales: Below $5 Million
Number Employees: 1-4
Square Footage: 4000
Type of Packaging: Private Label

24680 Juice Tree
10861 Mill Valley Road
Omaha, NE 68154-3975 714-891-4425
Fax: 714-892-3699
harrietadams@reidplastics.com
www.reidplastics.com
Manufacturer and exporter of citrus juice extractors, pineapple peelers, mobile ice display tables for fresh fruit products and capped plastic containers for juice
President: James Beck
Plant Administrator: B Copeland
Estimated Sales: $1-2.5 Million
Number Employees: 19
Brands:
Juice Tree

24681 Juicy Whip
1668 Curtiss Ct
La Verne, CA 91750 909-392-7500
Fax: 626-814-8016 www.juicywhip.com
Hispanic bottled and bag-in-the-box concentrates.
President/CEO: Gus Stratton
Purchasing: Craig Allen
Estimated Sales: $4 Million
Number Employees: 25
Square Footage: 88000
Brands:
Juicy Whip

24682 Jumo Process Control Incc
6733 Myers Road
East Syracuse, NY 13057 315-697-5866
Fax: 315-437-5860 800-554-5866
info@jumoplus.com www.jumoplus.com
Meat thermometers, temperature control probes and refrigeration controllers.
President: Carsten Juchheim
CEO: Bernhard Juchheim

24683 Junction Solutions
9785 Maroon Cir
Suite 410
Englewood, CO 80112 877-502-6355
Fax: 303-327-8804
webinfo@junctionsolutions.com
www.junctionsolutions.com
Advanced enterprise software that allows food and beverage processors to improve control over operations, quality, and compliance
CEO/President: Jeff Grell
CFO: Jeff Allen
Product Marketing: George Casey
VP Sales: Michael Frauenhoffer
COO: Jeff Grell
VP Product Development: Greg Penn

24684 Jupiter Mills Corporation
20 Walnut Dr
Roslyn, NY 11576 516-484-1166
Fax: 516-484-1242 800-853-5121
info@jupitermillscorp.com
www.jupitermillscorp.com
Manufacturer and exporter of bags, barrels, drums, bottles, boxes, cans, cartons, cases, containers, foam, packaging materials, paper, partitions, tapes and tubes
President: Fred Fisher
Customer Service: Harvey Chestman
Office Manager: Pat Fisher
Estimated Sales: $5,000,000
Number Employees: 20-49
Square Footage: 2000

24685 Jurra Capresso
81 Ruckman Rd
PO Box 775
Closter, NJ 07624 201-767-3999
Fax: 20- 7-7 96 800-767-3554
contact@capresso.com www.capresso.com
Espresso machines and accessories, coffee makers, coffee grinders, coffee/espresso centers and toasters.
President: Michael Kramm
Estimated Sales: $10 - 20 000,000
Number Employees: 10-19
Type of Packaging: Bulk

24686 Just Plastics
250 Dyckman St
New York, NY 10034 212-569-8500
Fax: 212-569-6970 info@justplastics.com
www.justplastics.com
Manufacturer and exporter of custom acrylic point of purchase displays, signs, sneeze guards, menu holders, tent card holders and containers
President: Robert Vermann
VP: Lois Vermann
Sales Associate: Tommy de Los Angeles
VP: Robert Vermann
Estimated Sales: $20 - 50 Million
Number Employees: 20-49
Square Footage: 15000

24687 Justman Brush Company
828 Crown Point Ave
Omaha, NE 68110 402-451-4420
Fax: 402-451-1473 800-800-6940
justman@radiks.net www.justmanbrush.com
Manufacturer and exporter of twisted-in-wire brushes including bottle, toilet bowl, hospital and laboratory
Owner: John Matthews
Estimated Sales: $1-2.5 Million
Number Employees: 20-49
Square Footage: 12000

24688 Justrite Rubber Stamp &Seal Company
1701 Locust St
Kansas City, MO 64108 816-421-5010
Fax: 816-421-1939 800-229-5010
sales@justriterubberstamp.com
www.justriterubberstamp.com
Rubber stamps, daters, self-inking and pre-inked, custom logos and kits.
President: John Thomas
CFO/R&D: Paul Thomas
Estimated Sales: $1 - 2.5 Million
Number Employees: 5-9
Square Footage: 10000

24689 Jutras Signs
711 Mast Rd # 1
Manchester, NH 03102-1409 603-622-2341
Fax: 603-623-3562 800-924-3524
graphics@jutrassigns.com www.jutrassigns.com
Signs including interior and exterior illuminated, billboards and neon and electronic message centers; also, flagpoles and accessories available
President: Cathy Champagne
General Manager: Joe Champagne
Estimated Sales: $2.5 - 5 Million
Number Employees: 20-49
Square Footage: 40000

24690 Juvenal Direct
PO Box 5449
Napa, CA 94581-0449 707-254-2000
Fax: 707-642-2288 888-254-2060
juvenaldirect@juvenaldirect.com
www.juvenaldirect.com

Grape presses, membrane presses and wine corks
CEO: Manuel Santiago
Number Employees: 8

24691 **(HQ)K Katen & Company**
65 E Cherry Street
Rahway, NJ 07065-4011 732-381-0220
Manufacturer and importer of linen goods including tablecloths, napkins, pillowcases and kitchen towels
VP: Pauline Katen
Manager: Benny Yabut
Manager: Steven Richards
Number Employees: 3
Square Footage: 2000
Type of Packaging: Consumer
Brands:
Keepsake Table Fashions

24692 **K Trader Inc.**
1452 W. 9th Street
Suite D
Upland, CA ÿ91786ÿ 909-949-0327
Fax: 909-992-3471 sales@ktraderinc.com
www.ktraderinc.com
Exporter of fresh fruits, vegetables and meats to overseas markets.
President: Robert Amakasu
Manager: Kay Shimivu
Estimated Sales: $1 Million
Number Employees: 10

24693 **K&H Container**
126 S Turnpike Road
Wallingford, CT 06492-4371 203-265-1547
Fax: 203-269-6837
Corrugated shipping containers
VP/General Manager: Steve Wasko
Customer Service Manager: Lou Carigliano
Plant Manager: Mark Andres
Estimated Sales: $5-10 Million
Number Employees: 20-49
Square Footage: 35000
Parent Co: K&H Corrugated Case Company

24694 **K&H Corrugated Case Company**
330 Lake Osiris Rd
Walden, NY 12586 845-778-1631
Fax: 845-778-7417 www.unicorr.com
Corrugated boxes
Manager: Mark Andrews
Estimated Sales: $20-50 Million
Number Employees: 20-49
Parent Co: K&H Corrugated Case Corporation

24695 **K&I Creative Plastics**
582 Nixon St
Jacksonville, FL 32204-3010 904-387-0438
Fax: 904-387-0430 projr@prodigy.net
www.kicreativeplastics.net
Displays, sneeze guards, engraved signs, food bins and condiment trays; also, metal engraved signs, custom plastic fabricating available, and point of purchase displays
Owner: Bonnie Osterman
Estimated Sales: $1 - 3 Million
Number Employees: 5-9
Square Footage: 12000

24696 **K&M International**
1955 Midway Dr Ste A
Twinsburg, OH 44087 330-425-2550
Fax: 330-425-3777 www.kmtoys.com
LED signs for display
President: G Pillai
CFO: G Pillai
Sales Manager: Marianne Zmyslinski
Estimated Sales: $20 - 50 Million
Number Employees: 20-49

24697 **K&R Equipment**
2033 Gateway Place
Suite 500
San Jose, CA 95110 408-573-6427
Fax: 408-573-6471 sales@kandrequip.com
www.kandrequip.com
Case forming, poly bag insertion, decuffing, case sealing
President: Owen Kellep
CFO: Adam Kwiek
VP: Richard Lee
Marketing/Sales: Dennis Alexander
Plant Manager: Fred Kruger
Estimated Sales: Below $5 Million
Number Employees: 20-49

Number of Products: 15
Square Footage: 30000

24698 **K-C Products Company**
16780 Stagg Street
Van Nuys, CA 91406-1635 818-267-1600
Fax: 323-261-5882 info@kcprodco.com
Plastic bags and covers; also, vinyl and fabric table cloths, chair pads, place mats, appliance covers, etc
VP: Ingrid Albrechtson
Operations Manager: George Chamberlain
Estimated Sales: $1 - 5 Million
Number Employees: 1-4

24699 **K-Patents, Inc**
1804 Centre Point Cir # 106
Naperville, IL 60563-1492 630-955-1545
Fax: 630-955-1585 info@kpatents-usa.com
www.kpatents.com
Process refractometer for in-line liquid concentration measurement
Estimated Sales: $1 - 3 Million
Number Employees: 5-9
Parent Co: K-Patents OY

24700 **K-Tron**
PO Box
Salina, KS 67402-0017 785-825-1611
Fax: 785-825-8759 info@ktron.com
www.ktron.com
Manufacturer and exporter of pneumatic conveying and feeding systems
General Manager: Todd Smith
Estimated Sales: $20-50 Million
Number Employees: 100-249
Square Footage: 115000
Parent Co: K-Tron America

24701 **K-Tron International**
Routes 55 and 553
P.O. Box 888
Pitman, NJ 08071-0888 856-589-0500
Fax: 856-256-3281 800-203-4130
www.ktron.com
Maqnufacture feeders for low to high feed rate applications, precision feeding and material control with complete PLC-DCS system integration, vacuum loaders and receivers. Offer volumetric screw feeders, weighbelt feeders, vibratingfeeders, etc
President: Kevin Bowen
Estimated Sales: $77.50 Million
Number Employees: 727
Square Footage: 92000
Parent Co: K-Tron International
Brands:
Digi-Drive
K-Commander
K-Link
K-Modular
K-Tron Soder
K10s
K2-Modular
Smart Flow Meter
Smart Force Transducer

24702 **K-Way Products**
759 W Commercial St
Mount Carroll, IL 61053-9762 815-244-2800
Fax: 815-244-2799 800-622-9163
kway@internetni.com
Manufacturer and exporter of soda, juice, beer and coffee dispensing equipment including pre and post-mix ice chests, carbonator/chiller dry refrigerated systems and soda and liquor guns
VP Marketing: Gene Deleeuw
VP Sales: John Hiney
Estimated Sales: $5-10 Million
Number Employees: 20-49
Square Footage: 38000
Type of Packaging: Food Service
Brands:
Bar-O-Matic
K-Way

24703 **K.F. Logistics**
10045 International Boulevard
Cincinnati, OH 45246-4845 513-874-0788
Fax: 513-881-5383 800-347-9100
www.buschman.com
Manufacturer and exporter of case conveyors and sortation products
CFO and Sr VP Finance: Robert Duplain
Sr VP Sales/Marketing: Lawrence Frey

Number Employees: 10
Square Footage: 1200000

24704 **KAPCO**
1000 Cherry Street
PO Box 626
Kent, OH 44240 330-678-1626
Fax: 330-678-3922 800-843-5368
converting@kapco.com www.kapco.com
Manufacturer and exporter of coated and converted pressure sensitive flexible materials, labels, tapes and paper
President: Edward Small
Operations Manager: Phil Zavracky
Estimated Sales: $10 - 20 Million
Number Employees: 50-99
Square Footage: 90000

24705 **KB Systems Baking Machinery Design Company**
90 Jacktown Rd
Bangor, PA 18013 610-588-7788
Fax: 610-588-7785 sales@kbsysteminc.com
www.kbsysteminc.com
Material hadling systems flour/sugar; roll, pita bread and tortilla equipment
Estimated Sales: $5-10 Million
Number Employees: 20-49

24706 **KC Automation**
7741 Whitepine Rd
Richmond, VA 23237 804-743-7790
Fax: 804-275-9070 davidb@kc-automation.com
www.kc-automation.com
Wine industry pH valves and manufactures of machinery for tobacco industry
Managing Director: Shawn Maxwell
Estimated Sales: $2.5-5 Million
Number Employees: 1-4

24707 **KC Booth Company**
1760 Burlington St
Kansas City, MO 64116 816-471-1921
Fax: 816-471-2461 800-866-5226
info@kcbooth.com www.kcbooth.com
Manufacturer and exporter of benches, front-end booths, tables and chairs
Owner: John Buddemeyer
VP: Scott Neuman
Operations Manager: Jack Buddemeyer
Estimated Sales: $5-10 Million
Number Employees: 20-49
Type of Packaging: Food Service

24708 **KCL Corporation**
PO Box 629
Shelbyville, IN 46176-0629 317-392-2521
Fax: 317-392-4772 sales@kclcorp.com
www.kclcorp.com
Reclosable poly zipper packaging
Estimated Sales: $20-50 Million
Number Employees: 100-249

24709 **KD Kanopy**
3755 W 69th Pl
Westminster, CO 80030 303-650-1310
Fax: 303-650-5093 800-432-4435
askme@kdkanopy.com www.kdkanopy.com
Manufacturer and exporter of instant set-up canopies, tents and banners; also, customized graphics available
President: John T Matthews
CFO: John T Matthews
Director Marketing: Helene Schmid
Sales: Scott Rudin
Sales: Matt Lehman
Estimated Sales: $1 - 2.5 Million
Number Employees: 20-49
Square Footage: 20000
Brands:
Kd Bannerpole
Kd Majestic
Kd Party Shade
Kd Starshade
Kd Starstage

24710 **(HQ)KEMCO**
8 Thatcher Lane
Wareham, MA 02571-1076 508-295-5959
Fax: 508-291-2364 800-231-5955

New and used stainless steel fabrications including sinks, tables, push and tow along carts, exhaust hoods, walk-in coolers and freezers and food service equipment
Owner and President: John Limpus
Purchasing/AR/AP: Beverly Limpus
Number Employees: 17
Square Footage: 40000

24711 **KES Science & Technology, Inc.**
3625 Kennesaw N Ind Pkwy
Kennesaw, GA 30144 770-427-6500
Fax: 770-425-0837 800-627-4913
info@kesair.com www.kesair.com
Food safety air sanitation system for maximum shelf/storage life, optimum product integrity and reduced food spoilage
President: John Hayman III
Marketing Manager: Kristi George
National Sales Manager: Jimmy Lee
Billing Contact: Scott Hayman
Estimated Sales: $8 Million

24712 **KHL Engineered Packaging**
1640 S Greenwood Ave
Montebello, CA 90640 323-721-5300
Fax: 323-725-0312 www.khlengpkg.com
Manufacturer and wholesaler/distributor of flexible packaging equipment and materials including shrink and stretch film, tape, poly and corrugated boxes, chipboard, skin film and poly bags
VP: Jed Wockensuss
General Sales Manager: Bill Browne
Estimated Sales: $5-10 Million
Number Employees: 1,000-4,999
Square Footage: 50000

24713 **KHM Plastics**
4090 Ryan Rd # B
Gurnee, IL 60031-1201 847-249-4910
Fax: 847-249-4976 dankay@khmplastics.com
www.khmplastics.com
Custom bulk acrylic food bins; importer of acrylic sign holders. Custom displays for food service
President: Dan Kloczkowski
Marketing Director: Dan Kay
Sales Director: Glenn Murphy
Operations Manager: Dan Bunting
Estimated Sales: $2.5-5 Million
Number Employees: 20-49
Square Footage: 200000
Brands:
Photo-Mates

24714 **KHS**
PO Box 1508
Waukesha, WI 53187-1508 262-798-1102
Fax: 262-797-2045 khs@khs-inc.com
www.khs-inc.com
Designs, manufactures and supports filling and capping systems, process equipment, and pasteurizers
President: Mark Arrant
CFO: Jim Elliot
Plant Manager: Jeffrey Czarnecki
Estimated Sales: $20 - 50 Million
Number Employees: 100-249
Square Footage: 250000
Parent Co: Kloeckner Capital Corporation

24715 **(HQ)KHS Company**
25 Fox Den Road
West Simsbury, CT 06092-2219 860-658-9454
Printed tags and labels
Sales Manager: Kerwin Spangler
Number Employees: 2

24716 **KHS Process Systems Division**
880 Bahcall Ct
Waukesha, WI 53186-1801 262-797-7210
Fax: 262-797-7219
Stainless steel commercial food processing and beverage bottling machinery, processing, continual mixing and blending, rinsing, filling, capping, net weight fillers, aseptic fillers, labels
President: Mark Arrant
CEO: Mark Arrant
CFO: Jim Elliott
Executive Director of Sales: Jeffrey Tietz
Plant Manager: Randy Uebler
Estimated Sales: $1-5 Million
Number Employees: 20-49
Parent Co: KHS

24717 **KIK Custom Products**
101 MacIntosh Boulevard
Concord, ON L4K 4R5
Canada 905-660-0444
Fax: 905-660-9310 800-479-6603
www.kikcorp.com
Contract packager of aerosols, liquids and sticks
President/Chief Executive Officer: Jeffrey Nodland
EVP, Finance/Chief Financial Officer: Ben Kaak
EVP, Legal Affairs/Corporate Secretary: Mark Halperin
Purchasing Agent: Dave Reeves
Estimated Sales: $50-100 Million
Number Employees: 500-999
Parent Co: CPC International

24718 **KIRKCO**
P.O.Box 509
Monroe, NC 28111 704-289-7090
Fax: 704-289-7091 sales@kirkcocorp.com
www.kirkcocorp.com
Food processing, packaging, code dating and case sealing machinery
President: T W Kirkpatrick
Estimated Sales: $1-2,500,000
Number Employees: 5-9

24719 **KISS Packaging Systems**
1399 Specialty Drive
Vista, CA 92081-8521 760-714-4177
Fax: 760-714-4188 888-522-3538
sales@kisspkg.com www.kisspkg.com
Manufacturer and exporter of liquid fillers, cappers, conveyors, turntables, feeders/orienters, labelers and integrated packaging systems
Estimated Sales: $2.5-5 Million
Number Employees: 19
Square Footage: 34000

24720 **KISS Packaging Systems**
1399 Specialty Drive
Vista, CA 92081-8521 760-714-4177
Fax: 760-714-4188 sales@kisspkg.com
www.kisspkg.biz
Packaging machinery
Estimated Sales: $2.5-5 Million
Number Employees: 19

24721 **KL Products, Ltd.**
234 Exeter Road
London, ON, ON N6L 1A3
Canada 519-652-1070
Fax: 519-652-1071 800-388-5744
kadmin@klproducts.com www.klproducts.com
Automated food processing equipment. Poultry and hatchery equipment and washing systems.
President: Patrick Poulin
Vice President, Sales & Marketing: Rick Bennett

24722 **KLLM Transport Services**
135 Riverview Dr
Richland, MS 39218 601-932-8616
Fax: 601-936-5449 800-925-1000
lpurvis@kllm.com www.kllm.com
President/CEO: James M. Richards, Jr.
Chairman of the Board: William J. Liles III
CFO: Terry Thornton
Vice President - Strategic Partnerships: Milton Tallant, Jr
V.P. of Sales and Marketing: Moe Shroter
Vice President of Human Resources: Steve SzaboVP of Operations: Greg Carpenter
Estimated Sales: $1 - 5 Million
Number Employees: 1,000-4,999

24723 **KLR Machines**
350 Morris St
Suite E
Sebastopol, CA 95472 707-823-2883
Fax: 707-823-6954 klrmach@pacbell.net
Winery equipment, fruit and vegetable juice processing
VP: Mike Haswell
Estimated Sales: $5 - 10 Million
Number Employees: 5-9

24724 **KLS Lubriquip**
P.O.Box 1441
Minneapolis, MN 55440-1441 612-623-6000
Fax: 612-378-3590 info.lubriquip@idexcorp.com
www.lubriquip.com
Manufacturer and exporter of conveyor lubrication equipment and specialty lubricants
HR Manager: Kathy Buechel
Vice President, General Counsel, Secreta: Karen Gallivan
Service Manager: Gary Knutson
Plant Manager: Ryan Eidenschink
Estimated Sales: $10 - 20 Million
Number Employees: 1,000-4,999
Parent Co: IDEX

24725 **KM International**
320 N Main St
Kenton, TN 38233 731-749-8700
Fax: 256-539-9799 kevin@kminternational.com
www.kminternational.com
Manufacturer, importer and exporter of plastic bags and film
President: Kourosh Vakili
CEO: Kevin Vakili
Estimated Sales: $20 - 50 Million
Number Employees: 35

24726 **KNF Flexpak Corporation**
Rr 3 Box 6b
Tamaqua, PA 18252 570-386-3550
Fax: 570-386-3703 800-823-7786
pfloro@knfcorporation.com
www.knfcorporation.com
Nylon, polyethylene, pan liners, co-extrusion, oven bags, cook chill, cashings and vacuum bags
Sales Director: David Dunphy
Estimated Sales: $12 Million
Number Employees: 50-99
Number of Brands: 4
Number of Products: 250
Square Footage: 28000
Type of Packaging: Consumer, Food Service, Private Label, Bulk

24727 **KOCH Supplies Inc.**
1414 West 29th Street
Kansas City, MO 64108-3604 816-753-2150
Fax: 816-753-4976 800-456-5624
info@kochequipment.com
www.kochequipment.com
President: Steve Kingeter
CEO and Chairman of the Board: John D. Starr
Estimated Sales: $50 - 100 Million
Number Employees: 250-499

24728 **KOF-K Kosher Supervision**
201 the Plz
Teaneck, NJ 07666 201-837-0500
Fax: 201-837-0126 info@kof-k.org
www.kof-k.org
Consultant specializing in kosher certification
CEO: Rabbi Dr Zecharia Senter
Public Relations: Yehudis Zidele
Number Employees: 100-249
Square Footage: 5000

24729 **KOFAB**
300 Kofab Dr
Algona, IA 50511 515-295-7265
Fax: 515-295-7268 sales@kofab.com
www.kofab.com
Custom food processing equipment and stainless steel conveyor belt pulleys
Owner: Brian Schiltz
Vice President: Bill Schiltz
Plant Manager: Gray Schiltz
Estimated Sales: $1 - 3 Million
Number Employees: 10-19
Square Footage: 42000

24730 **KP Aerofill**
P.O.Box 3848
Davenport, IA 52808-3848 563-391-1100
Fax: 563-391-4951 800-257-5622
sales@packt.com www.kpaerofill.com
CEO: Barry Shoulders

24731 **KSW Corporation**
1731 Guthrie Ave
PO Box 3224
Des Moines, IA 50316 515-265-5269
Fax: 515-265-9072 kswborp@aol.com
www.kswcorporation.com
Manufacturer and exporter of mechanical blades and knives
President: Paul Naylor
National Sales Manager: Michelle Struble

Estimated Sales: $3 - 5 Million
Number Employees: 10-19
Type of Packaging: Consumer, Food Service

24732 **KT Industries**
3925 Ardmore Ave
Fort Wayne, IN 46802-4237 260-432-0027
Fax: 260-436-2195 800-366-4584
jand@ktindustriesinc.com
www.webindustries.com
Insulating tape and textile converting
Manager: Dan Alt
CEO: Don Romine
Chief Financial Officer: Carl Rubin
Executive Vice President: Dennis Latimer
Vice President Sales And Marketing: Tom Burns
Estimated Sales: $20-50 Million
Number Employees: 20-49
Square Footage: 110000

24733 **KTG**
11353 Reed Hartman Hwy
Cincinnati, OH 45241-2443 513-793-5366
Fax: 866-533-6950 888-533-6900
katchall@aol.com www.kigsolutions.com
Wireless temperature tracking computer software
CEO: Jim Flood
VP: Jack Kennamer
VP Sales: Jeff Carletti
VP Operations: Susan Payne
Estimated Sales: $10-20 Million
Number Employees: 5-9
Square Footage: 100000
Brands:
Bladerunner
Board-Mate
Code Red Kit
Cook-Eze
Disposer Saver
Fridgekare
K-Mars
Katchall
Kleen-Cup
Kleen-Pail
Kolor Cut
Kool-Tek
Kwik-Flo
Linen-Saver
Magnetic Scrap Board
N'Ice Ties
Poly-Roll
Poly-Slice
Polyliner
Rapi-Kool
Safetywrap
Sat-T-Ice
Sat-T-Mop
Side Swipe Spatula
Tableware Retrievers
Traysaver
Tuff-Cut
Whizard Gloves

24734 **KTI-Keene Technology**
14357 Commercial Parkway
South Beloit, IL 61080-2621 815-624-8989
Fax: 815-624-4223 info@keenetech.com
www.keenetech.com
Automatic zero speed splicers, rewinders, web tension controls, infeeds, unwind/rewind stands and related web handling equipment.
President: John Keene
Sales Manager: Darrel Spors
Plant Manager: Bill Carpenter
Estimated Sales: $5-10 Million
Number Employees: 50-99
Square Footage: 260000

24735 **KTR Corporation**
P.O.Box 9065
Michigan City, IN 46360 219-872-9100
Fax: 219-872-9150 ktr-us@ktr.com
www.ktrcorp.com
Shaft couplings
CFO: Tedd Slesinsky
Marketing Director: Marshall Marcos
Estimated Sales: $5-10 Million
Number Employees: 20-49

24736 **KTech by Muckler**
1190 Meramac Road
Suite 207
Manchester, MO 63021 314-631-7616
Fax: 314-631-7409 800-952-0241
ktechinfo@mucklerktech.com
www.mucklerktech.com

24737 **KVP Falcon Plastic Belting**
825 Morgantown Rd
Reading, PA 19607-9533 610-373-1400
Fax: 610-373-7448 800-445-7898
info@kvpfalcon.com www.kvp-inc.com
Manufacturers of modualar plastic conveyor belts, chains and flat top chains
President: Christopher Nigon
VP Marketing/Sales: Joe Gianfalla
Marketing: Galina Rodzirosky
Estimated Sales: F
Number Employees: 500-999
Type of Packaging: Bulk

24738 **KWS Manufacturing Company**
3041 Conveyor Dr
Burleson, TX 76028 817-295-2247
Fax: 817-447-8528 800-543-6558
sales@kwsmfg.com www.kwsmfg.com
Manufacturer and exporter of bulk elevators and conveyors including belt and screw; also, spare parts and repair services available. Installation and field service available
President: Mark Osbron
CEO: Tim Harris
CFO: Olin Miller
Marketing Director: Bill Porterfield
Plant Manager: Joe Radloff
Purchasing Manager: Eddie Maxwell
Estimated Sales: $10 - 20 Million
Number Employees: 100-249
Square Footage: 125000
Parent Co: J.B. Poindexter & Co., Inc.
Type of Packaging: Bulk

24739 **Kadon Corporation**
55 W Techne Center Drive
Milford, OH 45150-8901 937-299-0088
Fax: 513-831-5474
Manufacturer and exporter of plastic pallets, tote boxes, storage containers and wash baskets; OEM services available
Sales Manager: Chuck Acton
Administrative Assistant: Linda Brandeburg
Type of Packaging: Bulk

24740 **Kady International**
P.O.Box 847
Scarborough, ME 04070-0847 207-883-4141
Fax: 207-883-8241 800-367-5239
kady@kadyinternational.com
www.kadyinternational.com
Manufacturer and exporter of high speed dispersion mills for mixing, blending, dispersing, emulsifying and cooking
President: Robert Kritzer
VP: Todd Kritzer
Sales: Todd Kritler
Estimated Sales: $5-10 Million
Number Employees: 10-19
Square Footage: 200000
Brands:
Kady
Kadyzolvers

24741 **Kaeser Compressors**
P.O.Box 946
Fredericksburg, VA 22404 540-898-3087
Fax: 540-898-5520 info.usa@kaeser.com
www.kaeser.com
Rotary screw compressors, SmartPipe, Rotary screw vacuum packages, Rotary lobe blowers, portable compressors.
President: Reiner Mueller
Number Employees: 100-249

24742 **Kafko International Ltd.**
3555 West Howard Street
Skokie, IL 60076 847-763-0333
Fax: 847-763-0334 800-528-0334
sales@oileater.com www.oileater.com
Manufacturer and supplier of cleaning products
Sales Manager: Jack Freeman

24743 **Kagetec**
309 Elm Avenue SW
Montgomery, MN 56069 612-435-7640
Fax: 612-435-7641 kagetecusa@gmail.com
www.kagetec.com
Industrial flooring for the dairy, food and brewery industries.

24744 **KaiRak**
500 S State College Blvd
Fullerton, CA 92831-5114 714-870-8661
Fax: 714-870-6473 sales@kairak.com
www.kairak.com
Manufacturer and exporter of remote refrigeration systems, pan chillers and sandwich and pizza prep tables
President/General Manager: Mark Curran
VP Sales & Marketing: Steve Asay
National Sales Manager: Steve Asay
Administrative Assistant: Susie Parodi
Estimated Sales: $15 Million
Number Employees: 20-49
Square Footage: 80000
Parent Co: Hobart Corporation
Type of Packaging: Consumer, Food Service
Other Locations:
KaiRak
Gardena CA
Brands:
Advantage Rak
Pan Chillers

24745 **Kaines West Michigan Company**
211 E Dowland St
Ludington, MI 49431 231-845-1281
Fax: 231-843-2259 kwmco@aol.com
www.kwmco.com
Custom welded wire products including racks, trays, refrigerator/freezer shelving, etc
President: John Kaines
CEO: Les Kaines
Engineering: Mike Felty
Human Resources: Jody Stewart
Materials Management: Jim Negele
Shipping Manager: Kevin Marcoux
Ordering Department: Nancy Van Liere
Estimated Sales: $5 - 10 Million
Number Employees: 50-99
Square Footage: 48000

24746 **Kal Pac Corporation**
207 Wembly Rd
New Windsor, NY 12553-5537 845-567-0095
Fax: 845-567-0199 www.kalpac.com
Manufacturer, importer and exporter of plastic take out bags
Owner: Mike Nozawa
CEO: Mike Nozawa
Sales Representative: Henry Meola
Estimated Sales: $10-20 Million
Number Employees: 20-49
Square Footage: 30000
Type of Packaging: Food Service

24747 **Kalco Enterprises**
443 Park Avenue South
New York, NY 10016-7322 212-627-5311
Fax: 212-627-3323 800-396-6600
kalconet@aol.com www.kalconet.com
Handmade food packaging products.
President: Ariel Kalaty
Sales Manager: Silverio Baranda
Type of Packaging: Consumer, Private Label, Bulk

24748 **Kalix DT Industries**
36 4th Street
Somerville, NJ 08876-3206 514-694-2390
Fax: 514-694-6552 rzajko@kalishoti.com
Filling machines, conveyors, cappers

24749 **Kalle USA**
5750 Centerpoint Ct Ste B
Gurnee, IL 60031 847-775-0781
Fax: 847-775-0782 www.kalle.de
Sausage casings
Sales Manager: John Lample
Brands:
Pullulan
Sunmalt
Trehalose

24750 Kalman Floor Company
1202 Bergen Pkwy
Suite 110
Evergreen, CO 80439-9559 303-674-2290
Fax: 303-674-1238 866-266-7146
Karl.Johnson@kalmanfloor.com
www.kalmanfloor.com
Seamless industrial concrete floors suitable for the food and beverage industries.
President: Donald Ytterberg
Sales Engineer: Karl Johnson
Sales Engineer: Jeffrey Brown

24751 Kalsec
PO Box 50511
Kalamazoo, MI 49005-0511 269-349-9711
Fax: 269-382-3060 800-323-9320
info@kalsec.com www.kalsec.com
Processor and exporter of natural flavors, colors, extracts, spice oleoresins and essential oils
President: George Todd
Treasurer: Don Baird
Research & Development: Don Berdahl
Marketing Director: Bill Goodrich
VP Sales: Gary Hainrihar
Plant Manager: Harry Todd
Purchasing Manager: Walt Bower
Estimated Sales: $3 - 5 Million
Number Employees: 5-9
Parent Co: Kalamazoo Holdings
Type of Packaging: Food Service, Bulk
Brands:
Aquaresin Spices
Aquaresins
Durabrite
Durabrite Colors
Duralox
Duralox Blends
Herbalox
Herbalox Seasonings
Hexahydrolone
Hexalone
Hop Oil
Hoppy Drops
Hydraisolone
Hydrolone
Isolone
Kalsec
Kettle Aroma Extract
Strolone
Tetrahydrolone
Tetralone
Vegetone
Vegetone Colors

24752 Kama Corporation
600 Dietrich Ave
Hazleton, PA 18201 570-455-0958
Fax: 570-455-0178 kamaadmin@kamacorp.com
www.kamacorp.com
Manufacturer and exporter of transparent biaxially oriented polystyrene sheets used for pressure and vacuum forming
VP/General Manager: Eugene Whitacre
Plant Manager: Juan Escobar
Estimated Sales: $20-50 Million
Number Employees: 100-249

24753 Kamflex Corporation
1321 West 119th Street
Suite C
Chicago, IL 60643 630-682-1555
Fax: 630-682-9312 800-323-2440
kamflex@kamflex.com www.kamflex.com
Conveyors and stainless steel conveyors for bakeries and cereal companies, as well as for the dairy, poultry, seafood, meat, frozen foods and beverage industries.
Square Footage: 40000

24754 Kamflex Corporation
1321 West 119th Street
Chicago, IL 60643 630-682-1555
Fax: 630-682-9312 800-323-2440
kamflex@kamflex.com www.kamflex.com
Manufacturer and exporter of FDA and USDA approved stainless steel conveyors and systems with fabric, plastic or steel belts, rotary turntables, air operations, etc
President: Kirit Kamdar
Marketing Director: John Tomaka
Operations Manager: Dave Matan
Estimated Sales: $5 - 10 Million
Number Employees: 10
Square Footage: 35000
Brands:
Elevair

24755 Kammann Machine
235 Heritage Ave
Portsmouth, NH 03801 978-463-0050
Fax: 630-377-7759
sales@kammannmachines.com
www.kammannmachines.com
Printing machinery for packaging.
Vice President of Sales and Marketing: Steve Gilbertson
Sales Manager: Barney Hanrahan
Estimated Sales: $2.5-5 Million
Number Employees: 5-9
Square Footage: 400000
Brands:
K-14

24756 Kamran & Company
411 E Montecito St
Santa Barbara, CA 93101 805-963-3016
Fax: 805-962-5915 800-480-9418
webinfo@kamranco www.kamranco.com
Preparation tables
President: Faye Amiri
Estimated Sales: $5 - 10 Million
Number Employees: 20-49
Square Footage: 55200
Type of Packaging: Private Label, Bulk

24757 Kane Bag Supply Company
1200 S East Ave
Baltimore, MD 21224-5099 410-732-5800
Fax: 410-675-0079
Plastic bags
Owner: Karen Kane
VP: Karen Kane
Estimated Sales: $1-2.5 Million
Number Employees: 10-19
Square Footage: 20000

24758 (HQ)KapStone Paper and Packaging Corporation
1101 Skokie Boulevard
Sutie 300
Northbrook, IL 60062-4124 847-239-8800
Fax: 847-205-7551 www.longviewfibre.com
Producer of unbleached Kraft paper and corrugated products.
President/COO/Director: Matt Kaplan
Chairman/Chief Executive Officer: Roger Stone
Vice President/Chief Financial Officer: Andrea Tarbox
Senior Buyer: Brenda Carr
Estimated Sales: J
Number Employees: 1,000-4,999
Other Locations:
Longview Fibre Co.
Rockford IL

24759 Kapak Corporation
5305 Parkdale Dr
Minneapolis, MN 55416 952-541-0730
Fax: 952-541-0735 info@kapak.com
www.kapak.com
Flexible high barrier packaging and sealing equipment; also, rollstock retort films, preformed pouches, die cuts, handles and closures
CEO: Gary Bell
Sales: Craig Rutman
National Sales Manager: Brian Bell
Director Manufacturing: Kathy Cyracks
Estimated Sales: $20-50 Million
Number Employees: 50-99
Brands:
Coffee-Pak
Kap-Pak
Stan-Pak

24760 Kaps-All Packaging Systems
200 Mill Road
Riverhead, NY 11901-3125 631-727-0300
Fax: 631-369-3903 www.kapsall.com
Manufacturer and exporter of packaging machinery including fluid filling, bottle capping, bottle orienting and bottle cleaning; also, unscramblers, torque meters cap sealers and conveyor systems
President: Kenneth Herzog
Packaging Solutions: Michael Herzog
Estimated Sales: $500 Million to $1 Billion
Number Employees: 1,000-4,999
Square Footage: 65000
Brands:
Filz-All
Kaps-All
Orientainer
Torq-All

24761 Karl Schnell
P.O.Box 49
New London, WI 54961 920-982-9974
Fax: 920-982-0580 sales@karlschnell.com
www.karlschnell.com
Food pumps, emulsifiers, mixers/blenders, cookers, etc
Manager: John Mauthe
Estimated Sales: $2.5-5,000,000
Number Employees: 10-19
Square Footage: 10000
Parent Co: Karl Schnell Gmbh
Brands:
Karl Schnell

24762 Karma
PO Box 433
Watertown, WI 53094 920-262-8688
Fax: 920-261-3302 800-558-9565
karma@karma-inc.com www.karma-inc.com
Manufacturer and exporter of hot and cold beverage and mashed potato dispensers; also, warmers including hot fudge
President: Chris Gorski
Vice President: Jerry Scheiber
Marketing VP: Elizabeth Brennecke
VP Sales: Jeremy Scheiber
Estimated Sales: $10-20 Million
Number Employees: 20-49
Square Footage: 60000
Brands:
Cafe-Matic
Choco-Matic
Drink-Master
Insti-Mash
Juice-Master
Tea-Master
Whip-Master

24763 Karolina Polymers
1508 S Center Street
Hickory, NC 28602-5220 828-328-2247
Fax: 828-322-3674
Plastic film
President: Paul Kolis
VP: Jim Koshinski
Estimated Sales: $5-10 Million
Number Employees: 20-49
Type of Packaging: Bulk

24764 Karyall-Telday
8221 Clinton Rd
Cleveland, OH 44144-1008 216-281-4063
Fax: 216-281-5428 karyall@core.com
www.karyalltelday.com
Shop pans and tote boxes including aluminum, steel and stainless steel
President: James Mindek
Estimated Sales: $10-20,000,000
Number Employees: 20-49

24765 Kasco Sharptech Corporation
1569 Tower Grove Ave
Saint Louis, MO 63110 314-771-5162
Fax: 314-771-5162 800-325-8940
service@kascocorp.com
www.kascosharptech.com
Seasonings and ingredients, knives, chopper plates, grinder plates and other meat processing equipment
President: Brian Turner
CEO: Tom Orelup
Manufacturing Director: Bill McGuire
R & D: Jerry Peterson
Sales: Mark Dobson
Public Relations: David Neu
Production: Larry Jones
Plant Manager: Bill McGuire
Purchasing: Jerry Brooks
Estimated Sales: $10-25 Million
Number Employees: 50-99

24766 **Kase Equipment Corporation**
7400 Hub Pkwy
Cleveland, OH 44125 216-642-9040
Fax: 216-986-0678 info@plastechnic.com
www.kaseequip.com
Manufacturer and exporter of printers for cups, pails, lids and closures
President: Patrick Hawkins
CEO: Edward Thomas
Estimated Sales: $50 - 100 Million
Number Employees: 50-99
Type of Packaging: Consumer, Food Service, Private Label

24767 **Kasel Associated Industries**
3315 Walnut St
Denver, CO 80205-2429 303-296-4417
Fax: 303-293-9825 800-218-4417
kasel@kasel.net www.kasel.net
Manufacturer and exporter of meat slicers, conveyors and automatic loaders
President: Raymond Kasel
Sls./Mktg. Mgr.: Jon Toby
Quality Control: Galana Kasel
Estimated Sales: $32 Million
Number Employees: 5-9

24768 **Kasel Engineering**
5911 Wolf Creek Pike
Dayton, OH 45426 937-854-8875
Fax: 937-854-8875 don@kaselengineering.com
www.kaselengineering.com
Bacon equipment, slicing machines and scales.
Owner: Donald Kasel
Estimated Sales: A
Number Employees: 8

24769 **Kasel Industries**
3315 Walnut St
Denver, CO 80205 303-296-4417
Fax: 303-293-9825 800-218-4417
sales@kasel.net kasel.net
Slicers
President: Raymond J Kasel
CFO: Oigita Jrausau
Quality Control: Galinajasto Kasel
Estimated Sales: $2.5 - 5 Million
Number Employees: 5-9

24770 **Kashrus Technical Consultants**
PO Box 172
Lakewood, NJ 08701-0172 732-364-8046
Fax: 732-363-5451 kashrusy@aol.com
www.kosherconsumer.org
Consultant specializing in the kosher food industry
Owner: Yehuda Shan
Number Employees: 10
Type of Packaging: Consumer, Food Service

24771 **Kason Central**
7099 Huntley Road
Columbus, OH 43229-1073 614-885-1992
Fax: 614-888-1771
Manufacturer, exporter and wholesaler/distributor of refrigerator latches and hinges, strip curtains, hood lights, grease filters, gaskets, stainless steel food service hardware, thermometers for ovens and refrigerators and plumbingfixtures
Manager: David Katz
Sales Representative: Rich Kaiser
Office Manager: Greg Murray
General Manager: David Katz
Estimated Sales: $1-2.5 Million
Number Employees: 5-9
Square Footage: 4000
Parent Co: Kason Industries
Type of Packaging: Consumer, Food Service, Private Label

24772 **Kason Industries**
140 Herring Road
Newnan, GA 30265 770-254-0553
Fax: 770-253-3370 vinyl@kasonind.com
www.kasonind.com
Commercial food service equipment hardware and accessories including hinges, latches, feet, legs, door closers, panel fasteners, sliding door ware, vinyl strip doors, heated vents, grease extracting filters, etc
Estimated Sales: $50-100 Million
Number Employees: 8
Number of Products: 400
Square Footage: 6572
Parent Co: Kason Industries
Other Locations:
Kason Industries
Forest Hills NY
Brands:
Doorware
Easimount
Panelock
Safeguard
Thermal Flex
Trapper

24773 **Kason Industries, Inc.**
8889 Whitney Drive
Lewis Center, OH 43035 740-549-2100
Fax: 740-549-0701 Central@kasonind.com
www.kasonind.com
Food bins, bumper systems for walls and strip doors; wholesaler/distributor of commercial refrigeration hardware and bulk food merchandisers
Estimated Sales: $1 - 5 Million
Number Employees: 3

24774 **Kason Vinyl Products**
57 Amlajack Blvd
Newnan, GA 30265-1093 770-251-1422
Fax: 770-253-3370 800-472-7450
www.kasonind.com
Vinyl strip curtains and swing doors for refrigeration and storage
President: Peter Katz
National Sales Manager: Larry Crabtree
Estimated Sales: $50-100 Million
Number Employees: 250-499
Parent Co: Kason Industries
Brands:
Easimount
Maximount
Thermal Flex

24775 **Kastalon**
4100 W 124th Pl
Alsip, IL 60803 708-389-2210
Fax: 708-389-0432 800-527-8566
sales@kastalon.com www.kastalon.com
Owner: Bruce Dement
Estimated Sales: $100+ Million
Number Employees: 100-249

24776 **Kathabar Dehumidification Systems**
1 Executive Drive
Suite 410
Somerset, NJ 08873 732-356-6000
Fax: 732-356-0643 888-952-8422
sales@kathabar.com www.kathabar.com
Dehumidification for all food processing, baking candy, enrobing, freeze drying, coating, drying, spraying, dehydration, packaging, etc.
President: Pedro Correa
Global Sales Director: Nick Honko
Vice President: Bill Szabo
Sales Director: Stephen Constant
Product Manager: Michael Harvey
Estimated Sales: $5-10 Million
Number Employees: 30
Number of Brands: 1
Number of Products: 24

24777 **Katz Marketing Solutions**
295 S Dawson Ave
Columbus, OH 43209-1736 614-252-7824
Fax: 614-252-6113
info@katzmarketingsolutions.com
www.katzmarketingsolutions.com
A marketing and brand management consulting firm specializing in consumer products and food beverage marketing
CEO: Tammy Katz
CEO: Tammy Katz
Type of Packaging: Consumer
Brands:
Boost
Borden
Dearfoams
Enfamil
Frito Lay
Miller Lite
Mount Vernon Mantel Company
Pathlire
Rice Select
Scotts
Sopakco
Titebond

24778 **Kaufman Engineered Systems**
1260 Waterville Monclova Rd
Waterville, OH 43566 419-878-9727
Fax: 419-878-9726 info@kaufmanengsys.com
www.kaufmanengsys.com
Industrial stretch wrappers, conveyor systems, pick and place machinery, palletizers and stackers
President: Charlie Kaufman
VP: Bob Kaufman
Estimated Sales: $20-50 Million
Number Employees: 50-99

24779 **Kaufman Paper Box Company**
187 N Main St
Providence, RI 02903-1220 401-272-7508
Fax: 401-272-9738
Set-up boxes for candy and other related products
Owner: Arnold Kaufman
Estimated Sales: $1-2.5 Million
Number Employees: 5-9
Square Footage: 12000
Type of Packaging: Private Label, Bulk

24780 **Kauling Wood Products Company**
15735 Old Us Hwy 50
Beckemeyer, IL 62219 618-594-2901
Fax: 618-594-4218
www.woodfibre.com/trade/aa009934.html
Material handling equipment including hardwood pallets and skids; also, pallet mattes/tops
General Manager: Jim Kauling
Estimated Sales: $1 - 5 Million
Number Employees: 1-4

24781 **Kay Home Products**
90 McMillen Rd
Antioch, IL 60002 847-395-3300
Fax: 847-395-3305 800-600-7009
info@kayhomeproducts.com
www.kayhomeproducts.com
Manufacturer and exporter of patio and tray tables, lap trays, barbecue grills, etc
Chairman: Edward Crawford
CEO: Jack Murray
Estimated Sales: $1 - 5 Million
Number Employees: 5-9
Square Footage: 300000
Parent Co: Park-Ohio Industries
Brands:
Marshallan
Quaker

24782 **Kaydon/Electro-Tec**
1501 N Main Street
Blacksburg, VA 24060-2523 540-522-2111
Fax: 540-951-3832 800-382-5366
sales@electro-tec.com www.kaydon.com
Sliprings
Estimated Sales: $50-100 Million
Number Employees: 250-499

24783 **Kaye Instruments**
101 Billerica Avenue
Suite 7
N Billerica, MA 01862-1256 978-262-0273
Fax: 978-439-8181 800-343-4624
kaye@ge.com www.kayeinstruments.com
Manufacturer and exporter of data acquisition systems for process monitoring, controlling, archiving and reporting
President: Kenneth B Hurley
CEO: Ken Hurley
CFO: Al Parenteau
VP Sales/Marketing: Karen Huffman
Number Employees: 120
Square Footage: 240000
Brands:
Autograph
Dialog
Digi-Link
Digistrip
Fix Dmacs
Netpac

24784 **Keating of Chicago**
8901 W 50th St
Mc Cook, IL 60525 708-246-3000
Fax: 708-246-3100 800-532-8464
keating@keatingofchicago.com
www.keatingofchicago.com

Manufacturer and exporter of fryers, frying baskets, serving equipment, griddles, griddle brushes, pasta cookers, food warmers, hot plates, salting/bagging stations and grease/oil filtration systems.
Owner: Eliza Moravec
Estimated Sales: $2.5-5 Million
Number Employees: 20-49
Brands:
Instant Recovery Fryer
Keating's Incredible Frying Machine
Miraclean Griddle
Pasta Plus System

24785 **Kedco Wine Storage Systems**
564 Smith St
Farmingdale, NY 11735
Fax: 516-454-4876 800-654-9988
Manufacturer and importer of store fixtures, glass doors, temperature-controlled wine storage equipment, display cabinets and refrigeration and wine racks
VP: David Windt
VP: Ken Windt
Estimated Sales: $1-2.5 Million
Number Employees: 1-4
Square Footage: 25000

24786 **Keen Kutter**
20608 Earl St
Torrance, CA 90503 310-370-6941
Fax: 310-370-3851 rshaver814@aol.com
www.shaverengines.com
Manufacturer and exporter of vegetable cutters
President: George W Shaver
Manager: Scott Shaver
Estimated Sales: $2.5-5 Million
Number Employees: 20-49
Brands:
Keen' Kutter

24787 **Keena Corporation**
25 Lenglen Road
Suite 4
Newton, MA 02458-1420 617-244-9800
Fax: 617-527-0056 keena@keenatape.com
www.keenatape.com
Reinforced gummed paper, fiberglass, gummed tape
President: Harvey Epstein
Business Manager: Leslie Kent
Estimated Sales: $5 Million
Number Employees: 19-Oct
Square Footage: 80000

24788 **Keene Technology**
14357 Commercial Pkwy
South Beloit, IL 61080 815-624-8989
Fax: 815-624-4223 info@keenetech.com
www.keenetech.com
Automatic film splicer
President: Terry Keene
Sales Manger: Darrel Spors
Machine Shop Manager: Mark Sweet
Purchasing: Mike Wolfe
Estimated Sales: $5-10 Million
Number Employees: 50-99

24789 **Keenline Conveyor Systems**
1936 Chase Dr
Omro, WI 54963 920-685-0365
Fax: 920-685-0506 mail@keenline.com
www.keenline.com
Manufacturer and exporter of conveying equipment including tabletop chain, belt and case conveyors, accumulators, indexers, pushers, counters, clamps, mergers, dividers, combiners and gripper elevators/de-elevators
President: David Kersztyn
Vice President: Ed Gamoke
Estimated Sales: $5 - 10 Million
Number Employees: 20-49
Square Footage: 30000
Brands:
Keenline

24790 **Keeper Thermal Bag Company**
93 Berkshire Dr Ste E
Crystal Lake, IL 60014 815-479-0125
Fax: 815-479-0225 800-765-9244
keepertb@sbcglobal.net
www.keeperthermalbags.com
Manufacturer and exporter of insulated bags including food, pizza and catering; also, beverage carriers
Owner: Mike Leel
Manager: Mike Leel

Estimated Sales: $1 - 3 Million
Number Employees: 5-9
Brands:
Kee-Per

24791 **(HQ)Kehr-Buffalo Wire FrameCompany**
PO Box 806
Grand Island, NY 14072-0806 716-893-4276
Fax: 716-897-2389 800-875-4212
sales@kbwf.net www.kbwf.net
Manufacturer and exporter of custom fabricated store fixtures and point of purchase displays for baked goods, produce and beverage products
Owner: James A Rogers Jr
CFO: James Rogers
Research & Development: James Rogers
Quality Control: James Rogers
Sales Director: George Rogers
Estimated Sales: $3 - 5 Million
Number Employees: 10-19
Square Footage: 25000
Type of Packaging: Bulk

24792 **Keith Machinery Corportion**
34 Gear Ave
Lindenhurst, NY 11757 631-957-1200
Fax: 631-957-9264 sales@keithmachinery.com
www.keithmachinery.com
Agitators, attritors, autoclaves, bag filling and sealing machines, bag labeling equipment, blenders, bundling machines, carton machines: closing, filling, sealing, checkweighers
VP: John Hatz
VP: John Hatz
Estimated Sales: $10-20 Million
Number Employees: 50-99

24793 **Kell Container Corporation**
421 Palmer St
Chippewa Falls, WI 54729 715-723-1801
Fax: 715-723-7744 800-472-1800
sales@kellcc.com www.kellcc.com
Corrugated shipping containers, inner packaging partitions and point of purchase displays
CEO: John Kell
CEO: John Kell
Plant Production Manager: Rick Gates
Estimated Sales: $30 - 50 Million
Number Employees: 100-249
Square Footage: 250000

24794 **Keller-Charles**
P.O.Box 3993
Philadelphia, PA 19146-0293 215-732-2614
Fax: 215-732-4327 www.kellercharles.com
Tea and coffee industry cans
Owner: Peggy Fields
Estimated Sales: $20-50 Million
Number Employees: 20-49

24795 **Kelley Advisory Services**
PO Box 2193
Northbrook, IL 60065-2193 847-412-9234
Fax: 847-412-9235
Consultant specializing in industrial ingredients, finished products, marketing, sales and distribution
President: H Kelley
VP: M Kelley
Customer Service: Karen Bass
Number Employees: 5
Square Footage: 10000

24796 **Kelley Company**
1612 Hutton Drive
Suite 140
Carrollton, TX 75006 972-462-5800
Fax: 972-389-4752 800-558-6960
sales@kelleycompany.com
www.kelley.4frontes.com

CEO: Anthony J Parella
Estimated Sales: I
Number Employees: 1,000-4,999

24797 **Kelley Company**
1612 Hutton Drive
Suite 140
Carrollton, TX 75006
Fax: 972-389-4752 800-558-6960
www.kelleycompany.com
Hydraulic, mechanical and air-powered dock levelers, restraints, controls and seals for loading dock shelters.

24798 **Kelley Supply**
P.O.Box 100
Abbotsford, WI 54405-0100 715-223-3614
Fax: 800-338-0754 800-782-8573
info@kelleysupply.com www.kelleysupply.com
Cheese equipment, defoamers, dispensers, lubricant
President: Bernard Alberts
Estimated Sales: $5 - 10 Million
Number Employees: 20-49

24799 **Kelley Wood Products**
85 River St
Fitchburg, MA 01420 978-345-7531
Fax: 978-343-3070 kwpmainoffice@cc.com
www.kelleywoodpro.com
Wooden skids, boxes, shooks and pallets
President: Michael Kelley
VP: John Kelley
Estimated Sales: $1 - 2.5 Million
Number Employees: 10-19

24800 **Kelly Box & Packaging Corporation**
2801 Covington Rd
Fort Wayne, IN 46802 260-432-4570
Fax: 260-432-2042 dcope@kellybox.com
www.kellybox.com
Corrugated cartons and corrugated and wooden boxes
CEO: Thomas J Kelly Jr
Sales Manager: Doug Cope
Customer Service Manager / Estimator: Chris Dowty
Estimated Sales: $5-10 Million
Number Employees: 100-249

24801 **Kelly Dock Systems**
6720 N Teutonia Avenue
Milwaukee, WI 53209-3119 414-352-1000
Fax: 414-352-2093
Manufacturer and exporter of dock equipment including levers and restraints
Sales/Marketing Manager: Steve Sprunger
Estimated Sales: $20-50 Million
Number Employees: 100-249

24802 **Kelman Bottles**
1101 William Flynn Highway
Glenshaw, PA 15116 412-486-9100
Fax: 412-486-6087 kelmanbottles.com
Formerly Glenshaw Galss Company, producers of glass containers for the food and beverage industry in the US, Canada and Mexico
President: William Kelman
Sales: Richard Hensler
Operations Manager: John Lilley
Plant Manager: Dawn Dietz
Estimated Sales: $660 Thousand
Number Employees: 7
Square Footage: 3829

24803 **Kelmin Products**
P. O. Box 1108
Plymouth, FL 32768 407-886-6079
Fax: 407-886-6579 kelminwik@aol.com
www.kelminproductsinc.com
Chafing fuel, chafing heaters, wick, chafin dish fuel, diethylenol glycol
President: Robert Jankun
CEO: Betty J Jankun
Estimated Sales: $1 - 3 Million
Number Employees: 10-19
Number of Brands: 1
Number of Products: 3
Square Footage: 28000
Type of Packaging: Food Service, Private Label, Bulk
Brands:
Ultra Pumps
Witte Pumps

24804 **Kem-A-Trix**
PO Box 580
Champlain, NY 12919 206-764-4668
Fax: 206-764-7213 888-215-8237
mpenton@kematrix.com www.kem-a-trix.com
Specialty lubricants manufacturer as well as sealants for pumps and valves
President: Norman Katz
Marketing: Jeffrey Katz

Number Employees: 49
Number of Products: 34
Type of Packaging: Consumer, Food Service, Private Label, Bulk

24805 Kemco Systems
11500 47th St N
Clearwater, FL 33762 727-573-2323
Fax: 727-573-2346 800-633-7055
sales@kemcosystems.com
www.kemcosystems.com
System equipment for meat and poultry industry, heaters-water, heat reclaiming systems, water pollution treatment and monitoring, total plant sanitation and waste water treatment systems
President: Carol Gorrel
CEO: Lee Kesbering
VP: Gerald Van Gils
R & D: Gerald Van Gils
Marketing: Bernie Weintraub
VP Sales: Al Jenneman
Plant Manager: David Gregg
Purchasing: Rod Kummer
Estimated Sales: $10-25 Million
Number Employees: 100-249
Number of Brands: 18
Square Footage: 60000

24806 Kemex Meat Brands
2400 T Street NE
Washington, DC 20002-1919 301-277-2444
Fax: 301-277-0235
Manufacturer and exporter of USDA inspection legend insert labels
Owner: Mary Ellen Campbell
Estimated Sales: Less than $500,000
Number Employees: 4

24807 Kemin Industries, Inc.
2100 Maury Street
P.O. Box 70
Des Moines, IA 50317 515-559-5100
Fax: 515-559-5232 800-777-8307
kftcs.am@kemin.com www.kemin.com
Liquid products which help to enhance the shelf life of food items.
Co- Founder: Mary Nelson

24808 Kemper Bakery Systems
300 Forge Way
Rockaway, NJ 07866-2032 973-625-1566
Fax: 973-586-2091 info@kemperusa.com
www.kemerusa.com

24809 Kemutec Group
130 Wharton Rd # A
Keystone Industrial Park
Bristol, PA 19007-1685 215-788-8013
Fax: 215-788-5113 sales@kemutecusa.com
www.kemutecusa.com
Manufacturer, importer and exporter of blenders, mixers, centrifugal sifters, grinding mills and valves
President: Rob Dallow
Director of Marketing: Kathy Moncur
Estimated Sales: $5-10 Million
Number Employees: 5-9
Square Footage: 40000
Brands:
Kek
Mucon

24810 Kemwall Distributors
250 Avenue W
Brooklyn, NY 11223 718-372-0486
Fax: 718-372-3421 fldwr@msn.com
Estimated Sales: $1 - 3 Million
Number Employees: 5-9

24811 Ken Coat
P.O.Box 575
Bardstown, KY 40004-575
Fax: 270-259-9858 888-536-2628
info@kencoat.com www.kencoat.com
Manufacturer and exporter of plastisol-coated, metal outdoor furniture including tables, benches, chairs, etc.; also, trash receptacles
President: J R Davis
Sls.: Philip Clemens
Estimated Sales: $5-10 Million
Number Employees: 10-19
Square Footage: 37500

24812 Kendall Frozen Fruits, Inc.
9777 Wilshire Blvd
Suite 818
Beverly Hills, CA 90212-1908 310-288-9920
Fax: 310-288-9913 susan@kendallfruit.com
www.kendallfruit.com
Frozen fruits including dried, juice concentrates, purees, freeze dried fruit, fruit powders, vegetable products, chocolate covered dried fruit, and yogurt covered dried fruit
President: Susan Kendall
Manager/Berkeley: Deborah Kendall
Manager/Littleton: Larry Kendall
VP Finance: Debra Olk
VP: Mike Daems
VP: Frank Abarca
VP: Kelly Marks
Estimated Sales: $3.6 Million
Number Employees: 14

24813 Kendall Packaging Corporation
633 W Wisconsin Ave
Milwaukee, WI 53203-1918 414-276-4770
Fax: 414-276-5668 800-237-0951
www.kendallpkg.com
Flexible, food, and industrial packaging
President and COO: Eric Erickson
VP Marketing/Sales: Stuart Zeisse
Manager: Randy Mjelde
Estimated Sales: $10-20 Million
Number Employees: 20-49

24814 Kendel
5320 Dansher Rd
Countryside, IL 60525-3124 708-813-1520
Fax: 708-813-1539 800-323-1100
www.welchpkg.com
Folding paper boxes; flexo printing and structural and graphic designing services available
Manager: Ian Mercer
VP: Gary Davidson
Manager Account Services: Rick Berg
Estimated Sales: $10-20 Million
Number Employees: 50-99
Square Footage: 140000

24815 Kendon Candies Inc
460 Perrymont Avenue
San Jose, CA 95125 408-297-6133
Fax: 408-297-4008 800-332-2639
sales@kendoncandies.com
www.kendoncandies.com
Varieties of hand made lollipops
President: Kate Glass

24816 Kendrick Johnson & Associates
9609 Girard Avenue South
Bloomington, MN 55431-2619 952-888-2847
Fax: 952-888-8336 800-826-1271
sales@kendrick-johnson.com
www.kendrick-johnson.com
Plastic dish covers, trays, plates, tumblers, cups and soup and cereal bowls
President: Byron C Hamilton
Vice President: Nancy Hamilton
Sales Director: Lori Green
Estimated Sales: Less than $500,000
Number Employees: 1-4

24817 Kennedy Enterprises
4910 Rent Worth Dr
Lincoln, NE 68516 402-423-3210
Fax: 402-423-5129 800-228-0072
shanekei@windstream.net
www.kennedyenterprisesinc.com
Greases and oils, accessory equipment, forming, filling and sealing equipment, vacuum packaging equipment
President: Rick Kennedy
Chairman: Maxine Kennedy
Estimated Sales: $1 - 2.5 Million
Number Employees: 10-19

24818 Kennedy Group
38601 Kennedy Pkwy
Willoughby, OH 44094 440-951-7660
Fax: 440-951-3253
kennedygroup1@kennedygrp.com
www.clearlabel.com
Developer and manufacturer of labeling, packaging, promotional labels, and identification systems. Manufactures prime labels, clear labels, booklets, coupons, blister cards, instant digital labels, case pack labels, versa-cards, tab-onads, shrink labels, etc
President: Michael Kennedy
Marketing/Sales: Patrick Kennedy
Operations Manager: Todd Kennedy
Estimated Sales: $10 - 20 Million
Number Employees: 50-99
Square Footage: 80000
Type of Packaging: Consumer, Food Service, Private Label, Bulk

24819 Kennedy's Specialty Sewing
Box 250
Erin, ON N0B 1T0
Canada 519-833-9306
Fax: 519-833-2357
Flags, canvas goods, coffee filters and aprons
President: Brenda Broughton
Number Employees: 10-19

24820 Kenray Associates
11576 Hwy. 150
Greenville, IN 47124 812-923-9884
Fax: 812-923-2820 sales@kenray.com
www.kenray.com
Data processing systems for brokers, distributors and manufacturers including multi-office capability, hardware/software training, integrated e-commerce, EDI and support
President: Kenneth Mcgee Sr
Estimated Sales: $1-2.5 Million
Number Employees: 5-9

24821 Kenro
200 Industrial Dr
Fredonia, WI 53021 262-692-2411
Fax: 262-692-9141 www.kenro.com
Plasticware including trays, dishes and dinnerware
Estimated Sales: $20-50 Million
Number Employees: 100-249
Parent Co: Carlisle Company

24822 Kensington Lighting
593 Rugh St
Greensburg, PA 15601-5637 724-850-2433
Fax: 724-837-8087
Manufacturer and exporter of energy efficient lighting fixtures and flourescent lighting
Owner: Gary Whiteknight
Estimated Sales: $500,000-$1 Million
Number Employees: 5-9
Parent Co: Adience Equities
Type of Packaging: Consumer, Food Service

24823 Kent Company, Inc.
PO Box 610102
Miami, FL 33261 305-944-4041
Fax: 305-944-1106 800-521-4886
kentcomp@aol.com www.kent-company.com
Rubber de-feathering fingers for use in chicken or turkey processing machines.
Sales: Dolly Tomlinson
Technical: Edd Woike

24824 Kent Corporation
PO Box 170399
Birmingham, AL 35217-0399 205-853-3420
Fax: 205-856-3622 800-252-5368
sales@kentcorp.com www.kentcorp.com
Manufacturer and exporter of store fixtures including modular steel display shelving
President: M A Oztenkin
CEO: V Albano
CFO: Sharron Harbison
Sales Director: Allan Solomon
Estimated Sales: $20 - 50 Million
Number Employees: 100-249
Square Footage: 250000

24825 Kent District Library
814 West River Center Dr. NE
Comstock Park, NE 49321 616-784-2007
lwerner@kdl.org
www.kdl.org
Material handling equipment including skids and factory trucks
Chairman: Charles R. Myers
Treasurer: Scott Petersen
Technology Director: Mike Carpenter
Plant Supervisor: John McKay

Number Employees: 20-49
Square Footage: 40000
Brands:
Globe
Wheel-Ezy

24826 **Kent R Hedman & Associates**
3312 Woodford Dr # 200
Arlington, TX 76013-1139 817-277-0888
hedman@onramp.com
Executive search firm
Owner: Kent Hedman
Principal: K Dunbar
Estimated Sales: Less than $500,000
Number Employees: 1-4

24827 **Kentfield's**
180 Nadina Way
Greenbrae, CA 94904 415-461-7454
Fax: 415-461-5553 888-461-7454
kentfield2000@aol.com
21tchen towels, canvas aprons, canvas totes, cocktails napkins
Owner: Donna Vanmalder
CFO: Donna Vanmalder
Estimated Sales: Below $5 Million
Number Employees: 4

24828 **Kentmaster ManufacturingCompany**
1801 S Mountain Ave
Monrovia, CA 91016 626-359-8888
Fax: 626-303-5151 800-421-1477
sales@kentmaster.com www.kentmaster.com
Manufacturer and exporter of portable power beef and hog slaughtering equipment
Owner: Ralph Karubian
Sls./Svce. Mgr.: Joe Leamen
Estimated Sales: $5-10 Million
Number Employees: 50-99

24829 **Kentwood Spring Water Company**
100 Stable Drive
Patterson, LA 70392-0743 985-395-9313
Fax: 985-395-2148
Coffee service filtration systems; also, bottled and distilled spring water
Branch Mgr.: Scott Coy
Branch Manager: Dwayne Duplantis
Estimated Sales: $500,000-$1 Million
Number Employees: 9
Parent Co: Syntori
Type of Packaging: Consumer

24830 **Kenyon Press**
2850 Walnut Street
Signal Hill, CA 90755 562-424-6600
Fax: 562-424-7599 800-752-9395
sales@kenyonpress.com www.kenyonpress.com
Menus; custom designing available
President: F O'Neill Taylor
Sls.: Dan Reed
Estimated Sales: Below $5,000,000
Number Employees: 20-49

24831 **Kepes**
9016 58th Pl
Suite 600
Kenosha, WI 53144 262-652-7889
Fax: 262-652-7787 800-345-3653
inquire@kepes.com www.kepes.com
Carton glue erectors, semiautomatic carton gluing machines, hot melt glue application equipment, unit rate and totalizing counters, rubber and urethane covered machine components and permalube lubrication system
President: Wayne Pagel Jr
Estimated Sales: $10-20 Million
Number Employees: 20-49

24832 **Keplinger & Son**
2789 Egypt Rd
Eagleville, PA 19403-2254 610-666-6191
Fax: 610-666-6215
Flags, banners and flagpoles
Owner: John W Keplinger
Estimated Sales: Less than $500,000
Number Employees: 1-4

24833 **Kerian Machines**
PO Box 311
Grafton, ND 58237-0311 701-352-0480
Fax: 701-352-3776 sales@Kerian.com
www.kerian.com
Manufacturer and exporter of fruit and vegetable graders and sizers
President: John Kerian
CEO: James Kerian
Estimated Sales: $1-2.5 Million
Brands:
Kerian Sizer

24834 **Kerr/Sun Coast Food & Beverage**
7350 26th Ct E
Sarasota, FL 34243-3947 941-355-7166
Fax: 941-351-2464 800-237-9107
corporate_mail@kerrgroup.com
www.kerrgroup.com
Senior-friendly, child-resistant closures and tamper-evident and wide-mouth closures for food and beverages
Plant manager: John Rogers
Sls Mngr: Tom Sweeney
Controller: Boyd Truelove
VP: Steve Elllis
Estimated Sales: $20 - 50 Million
Number Employees: 100-249

24835 **Kerrigan Paper Products**
PO Box 510
Haverhill, MA 01831 978-374-4797
Fax: 978-521-4067
Corrugated boxes
President: William Law
Estimated Sales: $1 - 2.5 Million
Number Employees: 5-9

24836 **Kesry Corporation**
16133 W 45th Dr
Golden, CO 80403-1791 303-271-9300
Fax: 303-271-3645 garyg@kevry.com
www.kevey.com
President: Tom Kissinger
Estimated Sales: $5 - 10 Million
Number Employees: 5-9

24837 **Kess Industries Inc**
130 37th St NE
Auburn, WA 98002 253-735-5700
Fax: 253-735-2851 800-578-5564
ray@kessind.com www.kessind.com
Kess Industries produces an extensive array of standard and custom equipment for accumulating, chilling, coating, depositing, distributing, drying, dumping, metering, pasteurizing, transferring, washing and weighing products. Allequipment designs are acc
President: K Jell Fogelgren
Sales and Estimating: Ray Cassingham
Estimated Sales: Below $5 Million
Number Employees: 10-19
Square Footage: 48000

24838 **Kessenich's Restaurant Supplies**
131 S Fair Oaks Ave
Madison, WI 53704 608-249-5391
Fax: 608-249-1628 800-248-0555
www.kessenich.com
Restaurant equipment
President: Robert Kessenich
CEO: Cheri Martin
Estimated Sales: $2.5 - 5 Million
Number Employees: 20-49

24839 **Kessler Sign Company**
2669 National Rd
Zanesville, OH 43701 740-453-0669
Fax: 740-453-5301 800-686-1870
info@kesslersignco.com www.kesslersignco.com
Signs and awnings
President/CEO: Bob Kessler
Service Director: Mike Taylor
VP: Rodger Kessler
Vice President-Operations: David Kessler
Account Executive: Doug Gabriel
Estimated Sales: $5 - 10 Million
Number Employees: 50-99

24840 **Ketch**
1006 E Waterman St
Wichita, KS 67211 316-383-8700
Fax: 316-383-8715 800-766-3777
rpasmore@ketch.org www.ketch.org
Electrical extension cords, wooden pallets, shipping boxes and air filters; contract packaging services available
President/CEO: Ron Pasmore
Chairman: Fred Badders
CFO: Coral Houdyshell
Vice President of Finance: Sheila Brown
R&D: Pattie Knauff
Vice President of Quality Assurance: Sallie Jensen
Vice President of Human Resources: Pattie Knauff
Estimated Sales: Less than $500,000
Number Employees: 250-499
Square Footage: 60000

24841 **Kett**
9581 Featherhill Dr
Villa Park, CA 92861 714-779-8400
Fax: 714-693-2923 800-438-5388
sales@kett.com www.kett.com
Our focus is moisture and organic composition analysis, coating thickness measurement, friction, wear, peel, adhesion and other surface property analyses, rice quality instrumentation and other agricultural test instruments for thegrain and seed marketplace.
Owner: Bob Clark

24842 **Kew Cleaning Systems**
1500 N Belcher Road
Clearwater, FL 33765-1301 800-942-1690
High pressure washers and waste water treatment systems
G.M.: Ed Hilfretz
Number Employees: 12
Brands:
Kew

24843 **Kewanee Washer Corporaton**
3209 Saint Andrews Court
Findlay, OH 45840-2948 419-435-8269
Fax: 419-425-0512
Commercial pot and pan washing units
Owner: Judith White
GM: C Paul White
Estimated Sales: Less than $500,000
Number Employees: 1-4
Square Footage: 8
Brands:
Kewanee K99

24844 **Key Automation**
1301 Corporate Center Drive
Suite 113
Eagan, MN 55121-1259 651-455-0547
Fax: 651-686-5232 tgriffith@keyauto.com
Standard and custom designed packaging machinery including cartoners and case packers for pouches and bags; also, product handling, orienting and feeding systems
Sls.: David Olson
Estimated Sales: $1 - 5 Million
Number Employees: 8
Square Footage: 4000
Brands:
Ccl

24845 **Key Container Company**
PO Box 71
South Gate, CA 90280 323-564-4211
Fax: 323-564-5127 custsvc@keycontainer.com
www.keycontainer.com
Shipping containers
President: Robert J Watts
Estimated Sales: $20-50 Million
Number Employees: 100-249

24846 **Key Industrial**
997 Enterprise Way
Napa, CA 94558-6209 707-252-1205
Fax: 707-252-9054 800-812-5258
keyindust@interx.net www.keyindustrial.com
Wine industry equipment
President: Stan Boyanich
Estimated Sales: $5 - 10 Million
Number Employees: 10-19

24847 **(HQ)Key Industries**
400 Marble Road
Fort Scott, KS 66701
800-835-0365
customerservice@keyapparel.com
www.keyindustriesinc.com

Manufacturer and exporter of clothing and uniforms
President/Chief Executive Officer: Chris Barnes
Chairman: William Pollock
Controller: Julian McPharson
Senior Vice President: Mike Johnson
Information Technology Manager: Jeff Sweetser
Director, Marketing: Mike Hughey
Estimated Sales: $9 Million
Number Employees: 45
Square Footage: 130000

24848 **Key International**
4 Corporate Dr
Suite A
Cranbury, NJ 0512-3613 609-619-3685
Fax: 732-972-2630 kevin@keyinternational.com
www.keyinternational.com
Packaging and processing equipment
President: Kevin Beenders
CEO: Valerie Ianieri
CEO: Primo Ianieri
VP Sales: Kevin Beenders
Purchasing: Bill Howard
Estimated Sales: $5-10 Million
Number Employees: 10-19

24849 **Key Material Handling**
4790 Alamo St
Simi Valley, CA 93063 805-539-7225
Fax: 805-520-3007 800-539-7225
sales@keymaterial.com www.keymaterial.com
Stainless steel and aluminum material handling equipment, racks, containers, conveyors, lifts, scales, shelving, tables and trucks; custom fabrication available
Owner: Rick Galbraith
Sls.: John Galbraith
Estimated Sales: $1 - 5 Million
Number Employees: 10-19
Square Footage: 40000
Brands:
Interlake
Keyrack
Rapid Rack

24850 **Key Packaging Company**
15th Street East
Sarasota, FL 34243 941-355-2728
Fax: 941-351-8708 webinfo@keypackaging.com
www.keypackaging.com
Manufacturer and exporter of thermoformed plastic packaging, containers, food trays and blister packs
President: Earl Smith
Quality Control: Gifford Quast
Sales Coordinator: Gene Donohue
Sales Director: Karlson Strouse
Manager: Karlson Strouse
Purchasing Manager: Chris Rathbun
Estimated Sales: $10-20 Million
Number Employees: 50-99
Square Footage: 52000
Type of Packaging: Consumer, Food Service, Bulk

24851 **(HQ)Key Technology**
150 Avery St
Walla Walla, WA 99362 509-529-2161
Fax: 509-527-1331 product.info@key.net
www.key.net
Design, manufacture and market process automation systems for food and other industries. This technology integrates automated optical inspection systems, specialized conveyor systems, and processing/preparation systems, as well asresearch, development, and world-class engineering.
President & CEO: John Ehren
VP Research & Development: Michael Nichols PhD
VP Sales: Stephen Pellegrino
SVP Global Operations: Louis Vintro PhD
Estimated Sales: $116.33 Million
Number Employees: 556
Square Footage: 173000
Other Locations:
Redmond OR
Brands:
Veo™
Manta®
Tegra®
Optyx®
Iso-Flo®
Horizon™
Impulse™
Spiral-Flo™
Symetix®
Remotemd™
Adr®
Smart Shaker®
Tobacco Sorter™ 3
Oncore®
Veg-Mix™
Turbo-Flo®

24852 **(HQ)Key-Pak Machines**
1221 Us Highway 22
Suite 1
Lebanon, NJ 08833 908-236-2111
Fax: 908-236-7013 sales@key-pak.com
www.key-pak.com
An extension of the specialized packaging equipment manufactured by Research & Development Packaging Corp. Specializing in vertical form/fill/seal machines, Key-Pak has consistently expanded its machinery portfolio over the years byadding combinational net-weigh scales, cup indexing system, piston liquid fillers and even conveyors.
President: Donald Bogut
CEO: Donald Bogut
Vice President: Chris Wanthouse
Research & Development: Don Bogut
Marketing Director: Christopher Wanthouse
Sales Director: Christopher Wanthouse
Operations Manager: Stan Florey
Estimated Sales: $1 - 3 Million
Number Employees: 5-9
Number of Brands: 1
Square Footage: 8500
Brands:
Key-Pak

24853 **Key-Pak Machines**
1221 Us Highway 22
Suite 1
Lebanon, NJ 08833 908-236-2111
Fax: 908-236-7013 keypak@worldnet.att.net
www.key-pak.com
Vertical form fill seal machines, net weight scale systems
President: Donald Bogut
Principal: Arthur Bogut
Estimated Sales: $1 - 3 Million
Number Employees: 5-9

24854 **Keystone Adjustable CapCompany**
1591 Hylton Road
Pennsauken, NJ 08110 856-663-5740
Fax: 856-663-6075 800-663-5439
info@keystonecap.com www.keystonecap.com
Disposable sanitary headwear including paper and cloth chef hats, overseas caps and bouffants, beard covers, hair nets, etc.; also, aprons, shoe covers, nonwoven coveralls and sleeves; exporter of overseas caps, chef hats and hairnets
Estimated Sales: $50-100 Million
Number Employees: 100-249
Number of Brands: 1
Number of Products: 400
Square Footage: 95000
Type of Packaging: Consumer, Food Service, Private Label, Bulk
Brands:
Classy Caps
Cordon Bleu Chef Hats

24855 **Keystone Adjustable Cap**
1591 Hylton Road
Pennsauken, NJ 08110 856-663-5740
Fax: 856-663-6075 800-663-5439
info@keystonecap.com www.keystonecap.com
Tin and aluminum continuous thread caps for glass and plastic containers
President: Dorothy Lynch
Secy.: Marie Forman
Plant Manager: Rodger Rohebach
Estimated Sales: $2.5-5 Million
Number Employees: 5-9
Square Footage: 9000

24856 **Keystone Manufacturing**
668 Cleveland St.
Rochester, PA 15074-0270 724-775-2227
Fax: 724-775-2739 800-446-7205
sales@keystonemfg.com www.keystonemfg.com
Metal conveyor belting
President: Richard Elste
CFO: Richard Elste
Quality Control: Drew Elste
Estimated Sales: $2.5 - 5 Million
Number Employees: 20-49
Number of Products: 7-10

24857 **Keystone Packaging Service**
555 Warren St
Phillipsburg, NJ 08865 908-454-8567
Fax: 908-454-7173 800-473-8567
Polyethylene plastic for packaging, printed and unprinted rolls, sheets and bags
President: John R Schoeneck
Estimated Sales: $2.5-5 Million
Number Employees: 10-19
Square Footage: 74000

24858 **Keystone Process Equipment**
PO Box 446
Philipsburg, PA 16866-446 814-684-5500
Fax: 814-684-7475 sales@keystoneprocess.com
www.keystoneprocess.com
Agitation systems, curd, tank, aseptic processing system, custom fabrication, processing and packaging
Manager: Greg Kearney
Estimated Sales: $1 - 3 Million
Number Employees: 1-4

24859 **Keystone Rubber Corporation**
PO Box 9
Greenbackville, VA 23356 717-235-6863
Fax: 717-235-9681 800-394-5661
www.keystonerubber.com
Manufacturer and exporter of conveyor belting, rubber sheeting hoses, rubber gaskets and fittings; FDA approved materials
President: Gloria Lawson
Sales: Mary Baley
Estimated Sales: $5 - 10 Million
Number Employees: 10-19
Parent Co: Maryland Rubber Corporation

24860 **Keystone Universal**
18400 Rialto St
Melvindale, MI 48122 313-388-0063
Fax: 313-388-6495 ebonex@flash.net
www.keystoneuniversal.com
Ammonium carbonate lump, chip powder
President: Michelle Toenniges
President: Michelle Toenniges
Estimated Sales: $1 - 5 Million
Number Employees: 10-19

24861 **Keystone Valve**
9100 W Gulf Bank Road
Houston, TX 77240 713-937-5375
Fax: 713-937-5478 www.tyclvalves.com
Wine industry valves

24862 **Kidde Fire Systems**
400 Main St
Ashland, MA 01721 508-881-2000
Fax: 508-881-6134 info@kiddefiresystems.com
www.kiddefiresystems.com
Fire protection products including clean agent suppression systems, pre-engineered systems, high sensitivity smoke detection devices, alarm and suppression control units, conventional/intelligent fire sensors, alarm devices and specialhazard fire and overheat detection
President: John Sullivan
CFO: Michael Cousindau
Quality Control: Robert Lovell
Number Employees: 250-499

24863 **Kidde Safety Products**
1016 Corporate Park Drive
Mebane, NC 27302 919-563-5911
Fax: 919-563-3954 www.kiddie.com
Manufacturer and exporter of portable and hand-held fire extinguishers
Number Employees: 250-499
Parent Co: William Holdings
Type of Packaging: Consumer, Food Service, Private Label, Bulk

24864 **Kidron**
P.O.Box 17
Kidron, OH 44636 330-857-3011
Fax: 330-857-8451 800-321-5421
ksales@kidron.com www.kidron.com
Manufacturer and exporter of refrigerated truck bodies and trailers
President: Mike Tucker
Executive VP: John Sommer

Estimated Sales: $5-10 Million
Number Employees: 100-249
Parent Co: TTI
Type of Packaging: Food Service
Brands:
Glacieruan
Hackney Ultimate
Polauan
Ultra

24865 Kiefel Technologies
5 Merrill Industrial Dr # -B
Hampton, NH 03842-1963 603-929-3900
Fax: 603-926-1387 info@kiefeltech.com
www.kiefeltech.com
Thermoforming and heat sealing equipment
President: Alfred Rak
Estimated Sales: $10-20 Million
Number Employees: 20-49

24866 Kiefer Brushes, Inc
15 Park Dr
Franklin, NJ 07416
Fax: 888-239-1986 800-526-2905
support@kieferbrushes.com
www.kieferbrushes.com
Manufacturer, exporter and importer of brushes including oven, floor, window and counter; also, broom and wax applicators, squeegee mop handles, paint rollers and brushes
President and CFO: Edward F Boscia
CEO: Gregory Kiefer
Number Employees: 20-49
Square Footage: 100000
Brands:
Dispose a Scrub
Easy Sweep
Lil Wunder-Miniature Scrub
Lok-Tight Handle
Rid-A-Gum

24867 Kiefer Industries
400 Industrial Dr
Random Lake, WI 53075-1653 920-994-2332
Fax: 920-994-4005
Food service equipment including stainless steel tables
Owner: James Eischen
Estimated Sales: $1-2.5 Million
Number Employees: 10-19

24868 Kikkoman International
50 California St Ste 3600
San Francisco, CA 94111 415-956-7750
Fax: 415-956-7760 dac@kikkoman.com
www.kikkomanusa.com
Chairman of the Board: Yuzaburo Mogi
Estimated Sales: I
Number Employees: 100-249

24869 Kilcher Company
1308 Pasadena Avenue S
Apt 11
South Pasadena, FL 33707-3754 727-367-5839
Fax: 727-363-1959
Consultant specializing in sales and marketing for the barbecue industry
Pres.: James Kilcher
Number Employees: 16

24870 Kildon Manufacturing
192 Thomas Street
Ingersoll, ON N5C 267
Canada 519-485-1593
Fax: 519-485-1084 800-485-4930
thunt@town.ingersoll.on.ca
www.town.ingersoll.on.ca
Hand cleaners including waterless, lotion and liquid soap
President: Paul White
Secy./Treas.: Nelda Rumble
Quality Control: Donald Parker
Estimated Sales: Below $5 Million
Number Employees: 3

24871 Kilgore Chemical Corporation
880 Heritage Park Boulevard
Suite 200
Layton, UT 84041-5680 801-546-9909
Fax: 801-775-9468
Environmentally-safe cleaning chemicals
Estimated Sales: $5 - 10,000,000
Number Employees: 5-9
Brands:
Natural Solutions

24872 Killington Wood ProductsCompany
PO Box 696
Rutland, VT 05702-0696 802-773-9111
Fax: 802-770-3551 www.carris.net
Wooden pallets and boxes
President: William H Carris
Opers. Mgr.: Boris Serkalow
Estimated Sales: $1-2.5 Million
Number Employees: 250-499
Parent Co: Carris Reels

24873 Killion Industries
1380 Poinsettia Ave
Vista, CA 92081 760-727-5107
Fax: 760-599-1612 800-421-5352
sales@killionindustries.com
www.killionindustries.com
Manufacturer and exporter of checkstands, and refrigerated fixtures
President: Richard W Killion
Estimated Sales: $20-50 Million
Number Employees: 100-249
Square Footage: 200000

24874 Kim Lighting
PO Box 60080
City of Industry, CA 91716-0080 626-968-5666
Fax: 626-369-2695 sales@kimlighting.com
www.kimlighting.com
Manufacturer and exporter of lighting fixtures
President: Bill Foley
Regional Sales Manager: Debbie Bell
Estimated Sales: $20-50 Million
Number Employees: 250-499
Parent Co: US Industries

24875 Kimball Companies
75 N Main St
East Longmeadow, MA 01028-2358 413-525-1881
Fax: 413-525-2668 kimball@kimballco.com
Wood, corrugated and plastic boxes, bulk containers, foam pads, plastic skids and collapsible storage bins
VP: David Kimball
VP: D Michael Killoran
Manager: Jeanne Matty
Estimated Sales: Below $5 Million
Number Employees: 5-9
Square Footage: 200000
Type of Packaging: Bulk

24876 Kimberly-Clark Corporation
P.O. Box 2020
Neenah, WI 54957-2020
888-525-8388
www.kimberly-clark.com
Manufacturer and exporter of toilet paper, paper towels, diapers, feminie products, tissues.
Chief Executive Officer/Chairman: Thomas Falk
Estimated Sales: $21 Billion
Number Employees: 58,000
Type of Packaging: Consumer, Food Service, Private Label, Bulk

24877 Kimberly-Clark Corporation
1400 Holcomb Bridge Rd
Roswell, GA 30076 770-587-8000
Fax: 770-587-8840 888-525-8388
kcpinfo@kcc.com www.kimberly-clark.com
Paper and nonwoven products including facial and bath tissues, hand towels, disposable wipers and protective garments; also, hand towel dispensers and bath tissue systems
President: J Bauer
Estimated Sales: $500,000-$1 Million
Number Employees: 1,000-4,999
Parent Co: Kimberly-Clark Corporation
Brands:
Kimtex
Kleenex
Kleenguard
Profile
Regard
Surpass
Teri
Workhorse

24878 Kincaid Enterprises
PO Box 549
Nitro, WV 25143 304-755-3377
Fax: 304-755-4547 800-951-3377
Manufacturer and exporter of insecticides and other agricultural chemicals
President: R E Kincaid
VP Production: Brian Kincaid
Estimated Sales: $5 - 10 Million
Number Employees: 5-9
Brands:
Chloroneb
Marlate
Terraneb

24879 Kinematics & Controls Corporation
14 Burt Drive
Deer Park, NY 11729-5752 631-595-1803
Fax: 631-595-1523 800-833-8103
Manufacturer and exporter of liquid level sensors and liquid/powder filling machines
President: John Rakucewicz
Number Employees: 10
Square Footage: 4000

24880 Kinergy Corporation
7310 Grade Ln
Louisville, KY 40219 502-366-5685
Fax: 502-366-3701 kinergy@kinergy.com
www.kinergy.com
Manufacturer, designer, importer and exporter of bulk solid material handling equipment including bin and container activators, storage pile and rail car dischargers, rail car shakers, feeders, conveyors, deliquefying and desliming screens and fluid bed coolers
President: George Dumbaugh
CEO: Scott Greenwell
CFO: Charles Hays
Estimated Sales: $10-20 Million
Number Employees: 20-49
Square Footage: 25000

24881 Kinetic Company
6775 W Loomis Rd
Greendale, WI 53129-2700 414-425-8221
Fax: 414-425-7927
joseph.masters@knifemaker.com
www.knifemaker.com
Manufacturer and exporter of perforating blades, machine and packaging knives and slitters
President: J0Seph Masters
Sales Manager: Dermot OFarrell
Estimated Sales: $10 - 20 Million
Number Employees: 100-249
Type of Packaging: Food Service

24882 Kinetic Equipment Company
2146 W Pershing Street
Appleton, WI 54914-6074 806-293-4471
Fax: 806-293-1103
Cooling, food processing and material handling equipment and machinery including pump feeders, blenders, dumpers, mixers, conveyors; also, replacement parts
Owner: Joe Offield
V.P.: Susan Stevenson
Purch. Agt.: Herb Chaney
Estimated Sales: $10 - 20 Million
Number Employees: 5
Brands:
Cryojet
Kec I

24883 Kinetico
10845 Kinsman Rd
Newbury, OH 44065 440-564-9111
Fax: 440-564-9541 custserv@kinetico.com
www.kinetico.com
Manufacturer and exporter of water conditioners, purifiers and filters. Systems are utilized in a wide variety of residential and commercial applications that include restaurants, hotels, carwashes, hospitals and others
President: Keith Tompkins
Commercial Sls. Mgr.: George Hohman
CFO: Trevor Wilson
CEO: Shamus Hurley
R&D: Keith Brown
VP Industrial: Chris Hanson
Estimated Sales: $20 - 50 Million
Number Employees: 100-249
Type of Packaging: Bulk
Brands:
Kinetico

24884 **King 888 Company**
PO BOX 51360
Sparks, NV 89436 775-530-5718
Fax: 800-785-3674 800-785-3674
info@king888.com www.king888.com
Manufacturers an energy drink that is available in Silver Label (citrus blend flavor), Original Gold (ginger/lemon flavor) and Authentic Cola (natural cola flavor).
Sales Representative: Gary Larson
Type of Packaging: Food Service

24885 **King Arthur**
646 Shelton Ave
Statesville, NC 28677-6104 704-873-0300
Fax: 704-872-4194 800-257-7244
karthur@i-america.net
Manufacturer and exporter of room service carts, furniture, sternos, chafers and serving equipment
V.P. Sls./Mktg.: Greg Holroyd
Estimated Sales: $10-20,000,000
Number Employees: 1-4
Parent Co: Falcon Products
Brands:
Sterno

24886 **King Badge & Button Company**
17792 Metzler Ln
Suite A
Huntingtn Bch, CA 92647 714-847-3060
Fax: 714-841-3380 kingbadge@earthlink.net
home.earthlink.net/~kingbadge
Promotional products including badges and buttons. Available with graphic arts engraving
CEO: Dick Dusterhoft
Manager: Mike Kuskie
Estimated Sales: $300,000+
Number Employees: 1-4
Square Footage: 2200

24887 **King Bag & Manufacturing Company**
1500 Spring Lawn Ave
Cincinnati, OH 45223 513-541-5440
Fax: 513-541-6555 800-444-5464
mike@kingbag.com www.kingbag.com
Manufacturer, importer and exporter of bulk handling bags, filters bags and curtains, crumb belts
President: Ronald A Kirsch Sr
VP: Ron Kirsch Jr
Marketing: Connie McCuan
Sales: Mike Jennings
Production: Chris Miller
Estimated Sales: $2.5-5 Million
Square Footage: 40000

24888 **King Company**
4830 Transport Drive
Dallas, TX 75247-6310 507-451-3770
Fax: 507-455-7400 king@kingcompany.com
www.kingcompany.com
Manufacturer and exporter of air curtains, process air conditioning, filtration systems and finned coils
Sls. Mgr.: Thomas Heisler
Marketing Manager: Mike Kaler
Sales Manager: Bruce Glover
Estimated Sales: $1 - 5 Million
Number Employees: 100-249
Square Footage: 240000
Parent Co: United Dominion Industries
Brands:
National

24889 **King Electric Sign Co**
PO Box 1884
Nampa, ID 83653-1884 208-466-2000
Fax: 208-468-0546
kingelectricsigns@hotmail.com
Neon and plastic signs
President: Ron Harrold
Estimated Sales: Less than $500,000
Number Employees: 10

24890 **King Engineering - King-Gage**
8019 Ohio River Boulevard
Newell, WV 26050
800-242-8871
www.King-Gage.com
Level measurement systems and compressed air filters
President: Steve Lefevre
Estimated Sales: Below $5 Million
Number Employees: 20-49
Square Footage: 28000
Type of Packaging: Bulk
Brands:
King Filters
King-Gage Systems

24891 **King Packaging Corporation**
708 Kings Rd
Schenectady, NY 12304-3665 518-370-5464
Fax: 518-393-5464
kingspackaging@nycap.rr.com
www.kingpackagingcorp.com
Contract packaging of cat litter, ice melt products and decorative landscape stone.
President: W Venezio
Plant Manager: Anthony Farone
Estimated Sales: $5-10 Million
Number Employees: 10
Number of Brands: 6
Number of Products: 24
Square Footage: 240000
Type of Packaging: Consumer, Private Label

24892 **King Plastics**
1100 N. Toledo Blade Blvd.
North Port, FL 34288-8694 941-493-5502
Fax: 941-497-3274 llathrum@kingplastics.com
www.kingplastic.com
Manufacturer and exporter of tamper-resistant plastic containers including cups
President: Phillip Lathrum
VP: Robert King
Marketing Manager: Marjorie Williamson
Sales Manager: Larry Lathrum
Estimated Sales: $10 - 20 Million
Number Employees: 50-99
Square Footage: 100000
Type of Packaging: Bulk
Brands:
Seal-Top
Tamp-R-Saf

24893 **King Products**
1435 Bonhill Road
Unit 25
Mississauga, ON L5T 1V2
Canada 866-454-6757
Fax: 416-850-9828 sales@mzero.com
www.kingproducts.com
Manufacturer and exporter of outdoor plastic signs, point of purchase displays and furniture
President: Philippe Moulin
CFO: Roger Whitzel
Number Employees: 90
Parent Co: Meridian Kiosks

24894 **King Research Laboratory**
PO Box 700
Maywood, IL 60153-0700 708-344-7877
Alarm systems including early warning sonic bug that detects shoplifting, gun shots and break-ins through any solid material
President/Inventor: John King
Estimated Sales: Less than $500,000
Number Employees: 4

24895 **King Sales & EngineeringCompany**
2965 Gatlin Road
Placerville, CA 95667-5116 888-546-4725
Fax: 530-644-8279 888-546-4725
snowline@directcon.net
www.directcon.net/kingsales
Wine industry labelers, label gluers, parts and repair
Estimated Sales: $1-2.5 Million
Number Employees: 10-19

24896 **King Sign Company**
355 W Thornton St
Akron, OH 44307 330-762-7421
Fax: 330-762-7422
Plastic, wood, metal and cast aluminum signs
President: Wayne V King
Estimated Sales: $500,000-$1 Million
Number Employees: 1-4

24897 **(HQ)King of All Manufacturing**
PO Box 178
Clio, MI 48420-0178 810-564-0139
Fax: 810-232-6698
Drain/sewer and septic tank cleaners, dishwashing machine detergents and restaurant cleaners
Estimated Sales: $1-2.5 Million
Number Employees: 5-9
Square Footage: 16000
Brands:
King of All

24898 **Kingery & Associates**
P.O.Box 428
Carmi, IL 62821-0428 618-382-3347
Fax: 618-382-3611 888-844-1665
www.grocerytraders.com
Grocery, meat, produce and HBC
President: Ron Kingery
VP: Woodie Pontey
President: Ron Kingery
Public Relations: Bob Estes
Operations: Steve Kemer
Estimated Sales: $10 - 20 Million
Number Employees: 5-9
Square Footage: 33300
Type of Packaging: Consumer, Food Service, Private Label, Bulk

24899 **Kings River Casting**
1350 North Ave
Sanger, CA 93657 559-875-8250
Fax: 559-875-1491 888-545-5157
kingsrivercasting@verizon.net
www.kingsrivercasting.com
Manufacturer and exporter of tables, chairs and barstools
President/CEO: Pat Henry
Vice President: Dale Monteleone
Estimated Sales: Below $5 Million
Number Employees: 10-19
Square Footage: 27000
Parent Co: Kings River Casting
Type of Packaging: Food Service

24900 **Kingspan Insulated Panels, Ltd.**
Langley Office
5202-272nd Street
Langley, BC, BC
Canada 604-607-1101
877-638-3266
www.kingspanpanels.com
Cold storage and blast freezer doors, as well as controlled environment and low temperature doors for the food and beverage industry. Also a manufacturer of paneling and roof panels for industrial buildings.

24901 **Kingston McKnight**
419 Avenue Del Ora
Redwood City, CA 94062 650-462-4900
Fax: 650-462-4906 800-900-0463
jeff@kmshoes.com www.kmshoes.com
Manufacturer, importer and exporter of slip-resistant safety shoes serving the hospitality industry
Owner: Jeff Mc Knight
VP: Terry Kingston
Estimated Sales: $1,000,000
Number Employees: 1-4
Square Footage: 5000
Other Locations:
Kingston McKnight
Las Vegas NV
Brands:
Kingston McKnight

24902 **Kinsa Group**
9779 S Franklin Dr Ste 200
Franklin, WI 53132 414-421-2000
Fax: 414-421-6000 recruiter@kimsa.com
www.kinsa.com
Full-service recruiting firm in the food and beverage industry
Owner: Chuck Nolan
Vice President: Michelle Nolan
Estimated Sales: $1-2.5 000,000
Number Employees: 10-19

24903 **Kinsley Inc**
901 Crosskeys Dr
Doylestown, PA 18902 215-348-7723
Fax: 215-348-7724 800-414-6664
info@kinsleyinc.com www.kinsleyinc.com
Manufacturer and exporter of bottle sorters and unscramblers, capping and filling machinery, bottle conveyors and timing screws.
President/Owner: Tim Mc Carthy
R&D: James Malloy
Quality Control: James Malloy
Sales: Brandon Concannon
Engineering Manager: David Hansen
Plant Manager: Dan Froehlich
Estimated Sales: Below $5 Million
Number Employees: 5-9

Brands:
Kinsley Timing Screw
Roll-Tite

24904 **Kinsley-Omni**
901 Crosskeys Drive
Doylestown, PA 18902-1025 215-348-7723
Fax: 215-348-7724 800-414-6664
www.kinsleyinc.com
Container feed machinery, line combiners, dividers, cap elevator feeders, screw cap tighteners, custom changing parts
President: T Mc Carthy
Senior Engineer: Dave Hanson
Plant Manager: Dan Froehlich
Estimated Sales: $2.5-5 Million
Number Employees: 5-9

24905 **Kisco Manufacturing**
5520 Blackburn Rd
Greendale, BC V3W 7X4
Canada 604-823-7456
Fax: 866-860-6619 www.kiscomanufacturing.com
Manufacturer and exporter of flour silos and scales, conveyor systems and water meters
Pres.: Svend Kuhr
Svce. Mgr.: Peter Kuhr
Number Employees: 5
Square Footage: 7000
Parent Co: Kisco Foods
Brands:
Kimac
Kisco
Mix Master

24906 **Kiss International/Di-tech Systems**
965 Park Center Drive
Vista, CA 92081-8312 800-527-5477
Fax: 760-599-0207 800-527-5477
info@kissintl.com www.kissintl.com
Manufacturer and exporter of reverse osmosis water purification systems; also, components and filter cartridges
VP/General Manager: Theresa Hawks
Sales/Customer Service: Becky Rivera
Sales/Customer Service: Kerri Rivera
Number Employees: 22
Square Footage: 80000
Parent Co: Aqua Care Corporation
Brands:
Di-Tech

24907 **Kisters Kayat**
5501 N Washington Boulevard
Sarasota, FL 34243-2249 386-424-0101
Fax: 386-424-0266 parts@kkiusa.com
www.kkiusa.com
Manufacturer, importer and exporter of high speed tray and wraparound packers, shrink wrappers, tray stackers and turners and case sealers
VP Finance: Peter Welen
VP Engineering: Gary Hunt
Number Employees: 90
Square Footage: 144000
Parent Co: Kisters Maschinenbau GmbH

24908 **Kistler-Morse Corporation**
150 Venture Blvd
Spartanburg, SC 29306 864-574-2763
Fax: 864-574-8063 800-426-9010
sales@kistlermorse.com www.venturemeas.com
Manufacturer and exporter of level measurement, weight and batching instrumentation for tanks, silos and hoppers; also, PC based bulk inventory monitoring software
President: Mark Earl
Quality Control: Bennett Connvlly
R&D: Joe Dejuzman
CFO: Mick Hallinan
Marketing: Jamie Ives
Estimated Sales: $5 - 10 Million
Number Employees: 20-49
Brands:
Ld Blous
Ldbxi
Load Disk Ii
Microcell
Multi-Vessel System
Orb
Ou
Rope
Sonocell
Ultracell
Ultrasonic Sensor
Ultraware

24909 **Kitchen Equipment Fabricating Company**
PO Box 14129
Houston, TX 77221 713-747-3611
Fax: 713-747-1892
Stainless steel sinks, tables and counters
President: Lloyd Hartsfield
Estimated Sales: $5 - 10 Million
Number Employees: 20-49

24910 **KitchenRus**
1006 S. Milpitas Blvd
Milpitas, CA 95035 408-262-1898
Fax: 408-262-1890 800-796-7797
service@kitchenrus.com www.kitchenrus.com
Cutelry; spreader, salad server set, pepper mill, kitchen utensils, flatware
Estimated Sales: $500,000-$1 Million
Number Employees: 9

24911 **Kitchener Plastics**
962 Guelph Street
Kitchener, ON N2H 5Z6
Canada 519-742-0752
Fax: 519-742-9247 800-429-5633
Manufacturer and exporter of plastic signs
President: Gabrielle Wolf
Estimated Sales: Below $5 Million
Number Employees: 4

24912 **Kitcor Corporation**
9959 Glenoaks Blvd
Sun Valley, CA 91352 818-767-4800
www.kitcor.com
Custom made stainless steel food processing equipment for hotels, schools, restaurants and hospitals
President: Kent Kitchen
Vice President: James Kitchen
Purchasing: Kathleen Anderson
Estimated Sales: $5 Million
Number Employees: 20-49
Type of Packaging: Food Service

24913 **Kiva Designs**
1350 Hayes St
Suite C-16
Benicia, CA 94510-2945 707-748-1614
Fax: 707-748-1621 jerica@kivadesigns.com
www.kivadesigns.com

24914 **Kiwi Coders Corporation**
265 E. Messner Dr
Wheeling, IL 60090 847-541-4511
Fax: 847-541-6332 info@kiwicoders.com
www.kiwicoders.com
Marking and coding equipment
President: Allen McKay
Estimated Sales: $2.5-5 Million
Number Employees: 20-49

24915 **Kleen Products**
PO Box 75223
Oklahoma City, OK 73147 405-495-1168
Fax: 405-495-1175 800-392-1792
ken@joeshandcleaner.com
www.joeshandcleaner.com
Manufacturer and exporter of hand, glass and floor cleaners
President: Kenneth Newman
CEO: Kenneth Newman
CFO: Kenneth Newman
Vice President: Michael Newman
R&D: Kenneth Newman
Quality Control: Joe Brantley
Estimated Sales: $1.5 Million
Number Employees: 5-9
Type of Packaging: Private Label

24916 **Kleenline Corporation**
7 Opportunity Way
Newburyport, MA 01950-4044 978-352-6737
Fax: 978-463-0847 800-259-5973
info@kleenline.com www.kleenline.com
Stainless steel conveyors, wash-down duty, custom conveyors, single units, complete systems. Manufacturer and system integrator of custom stainless steel sanitary conveyors and equipment, including controls and automation. Engineeringand consulting services available for material handling requirements.
President: James Laverdiere
Sales: Stuart Olsen
Plant Manager: Scott Fallovollita
Estimated Sales: $1-5 Million
Number Employees: 20-49

24917 **Kleer Pak Mfg**
320 S Lalonde Ave
Addison, IL 60101 630-543-0208
Fax: 630-543-0811 888-550-2247
sales@kleerpak.com www.kleerpak.com
Custom bags/pouches for the packaging industry.
Owner: Kam Patel
Vice President: Kenneth Johnson
Estimated Sales: $3 Million
Number Employees: 20

24918 **Klever Kuvers**
2889 San Pasqual Street
Pasadena, CA 91107-5364 626-355-8441
Fax: 626-355-1331
kleverkuvers100@earthlink.net
Indoor and outdoor vinyl table cloths and vinyl aprons
Owner: Mary Ann Froede
CEO: Ruth Breslow
Estimated Sales: $100,000
Number of Brands: 1
Number of Products: 3-5
Type of Packaging: Consumer, Food Service, Private Label, Bulk
Brands:
Klever Kuvers

24919 **(HQ)Kliklok-Woodman**
5224 Snapfinger Woods Dr
Decatur, GA 30035 770-981-5200
Fax: 770-987-7160 sales@kliklok-woodman.com
www.kliklok-woodman.com
Manufacturer and exporter of paperboard packaging equipment
President: Peter Black
CFO: Peter Black
CEO: William Crist
Marketing Service Manager: Curt Kuhr
Estimated Sales: $20 - 50 Million
Number Employees: 250-499
Square Footage: 220000

24920 **Kliklok-Woodman**
5224 Snapfinger Woods Dr
Decatur, GA 30035 770-981-5200
Fax: 770-987-7160 sales@kliklok-woodman.com
www.kliklok-woodman.com
Manufacturer and exporter of flexible packaging machinery for the snack food, confectionery, nut and baking industries including fillers, sealers, weighers, loaders, closers, etc
President: Peter Black
CEO: William Crist
Sales Director: T Long
Public Relations: C Kuhr
Estimated Sales: $45 Million
Number Employees: 250-499
Number of Brands: 5
Number of Products: 50
Square Footage: 220000
Parent Co: Kliklok Corporation
Brands:
Captain
Certipack
Clipper
Concorde
Cyclone
Gemini
Pacer
Polaris
Woodman

24921 **Kline Process Systems**
625 Spring Street
Suite 200
Reading, PA 19610-1771 610-371-0200
Fax: 610-371-0300 information@kpsnet.com
www.kpsnet.com

Batch control systems, custom fabrication and process control systems for the food and dairy industry
Owner/President: Robert Kline
Number Employees: 10-19

24922 Klinger Constructors LLC
P.O.Box 90850
Albuquerque, NM 87199-0850 505-822-9990
Fax: 505-821-0439 www.klingerllc.com
Offers extensive construction and design-build services in commercial, industrial and institutional markets
President: John Gleeson
CEO: Tom Novak
Business Development Manager: Shirley Anderson
Estimated Sales: $30 Million
Number Employees: 100-249
Parent Co: Klinger Company

24923 Klippenstein Corporation
5399 S Villa Ave
Fresno, CA 93725 559-834-4258
Fax: 559-834-4263 888-834-4258
sales@klippenstein.com www.klippenstein.com
Case sealers, formers and material handling, packaging and conveyor systems
President: Ken Klippenstein
President: Richard Klippenstein
General Manager: Ken Klippenstein
Estimated Sales: $1 - 3,000,000
Number Employees: 5-9
Square Footage: 10000

24924 Klockner Bartelt
5501 N Washington Blvd
Sarasota, FL 34243 941-359-4000
Fax: 941-359-4086 877-227-8358
info@barteltinc.com www.barteltinc.com
Packaging and special machinery including bag and carton filling and shrink-banding
President: Reno Cruz
Executive: Paul Rosile
Estimated Sales: $5 - 10 Million
Number Employees: 50-99
Brands:
Bartelt
Weco

24925 Klockner Filter Products
8314 Tiogawoods Dr
Sacramento, CA 95828-5048 916-689-2328
Fax: 916-689-1035 jteshera@fpifilters.com
www.fpifilters.com
Wine industry filtration systems, laboratory instruments and supplies
President: Paris Rivera
Estimated Sales: $1 - 5 Million
Number Employees: 20-49

24926 Klockner Medipak
14501 58th St N
Clearwater, FL 33760 727-538-4644
Fax: 727-532-6521 info@kpafilms.com
www.kloeckner-medipak.com
Specialty molds, dies and packaging machinery
Estimated Sales: $10-25 Million
Number Employees: 20-49

24927 Klockner Packaging Machinery
6767 Forest Hill Avenue
Suite 305
Richmond, VA 23225 804-560-7767
Fax: 804-560-7752 browch@klockner.com

24928 Klockner Pentaplast of America
P.O.Box 500
Gordonsville, VA 22942 540-832-3600
Fax: 540-832-5656 info@kpafilms.com
www.klockner.com
Manufacturer and exporter of rigid vinyl, polyester and barex films for form/fill/seal, hot fill, trays, cups, portion packs, rounds, clamshells and modified atmospheric packaging of food and full body shrink sleeves for beverages
President: Michael Tubridy
Vice President: Michael Tubridy
Research & Development: Dean Inman
Marketing Director: Michael Ryan
Sales Director: Bobby Nolan
Communications Manager: Nancy Ryan
Number Employees: 500-999
Number of Brands: 17
Type of Packaging: Consumer, Food Service
Brands:
Pentafood

24929 Kloppenberg & Company
2627 W Oxford Ave
Englewood, CO 80110 303-761-1615
Fax: 303-789-1741 800-346-3246
klopco@kloppenberg.com
www.kloppenberg.com
Ice storage, handling, carting, dispensing and bagging equipment
President: Joseph R Kloppenberg
Estimated Sales: Below $5 Million
Number Employees: 50-99
Square Footage: 120000

24930 Kluber Lubication NorthAmerica
32 Industrial Dr
Londonderry, NH 03053-2008 603-434-7704
Fax: 603-647-4106 kevin.wylie@us.kluber.com
www.kluber.com
CEO: Wolfgang Christandl
Estimated Sales: $20 Million
Number Employees: 50-99

24931 (HQ)Kluber Lubrication NorthAmerica LP
32 Industrial Dr
Londonderry, NH 03053 603-647-4104
Fax: 603-647-4106 800-447-2238
kevin.wylie@us.kluber.com www.kluber.com
Specialty lubricants designed for extreme conditions and environments in canning, baking, beverage, confectionery and pasta plants. Kluber offers a full range of products conforming to USDA H1 and H2 requirements. The stringent qualityassurance in components and production makes Kluber the food and beverage industry's partner for healthier and safer world
EVP/General Manager: Glenn Boyle
CEO: Wolfgang Christandl
North America Marketing Manager: James Sellect, Jr.
Estimated Sales: $20 Million
Number Employees: 20-49

24932 Knapp Container
17 Old Turnpike Rd
Beacon Falls, CT 06403 203-888-0511
Fax: 203-881-1817
Corrugated boxes and containers
Owner: George A Meder
Estimated Sales: $10-20 Million
Number Employees: 10-19

24933 Knapp Logistics & Automation
2124 Barrett Park Drive
Suite 100
Kennesaw, GA 30144-3607 678-388-2880
Fax: 678-388-2893 sales.us@knapp.com
www.knapp.com
Owner: Ingomar Penz

24934 Knapp Manufacturing
5227 E Pine Ave
Fresno, CA 93727 559-251-8254
Fax: 559-251-8224 sriley@knappmfg.com
www.knappmfg.com
Household and industrial cleaners, laundry detergents, disinfectants, germicides and floor polish
President: Mike Knapp
Technical Director: Doug Banta
G.M.: Sandra Christino
Estimated Sales: $2.5-5 Million
Number Employees: 5-9
Square Footage: 29000
Parent Co: BouMatic, LLC

24935 Knapp Shoes
2469 State Route 54a
Penn Yan, NY 14527
Fax: 315-536-6909
Slip-resistant and steel toe footwear
Pres./COO: Willie Taaffe
Number Employees: 25
Parent Co: Iron Age Corporation

24936 Knechtel Laboratories
7341 Hamlin Ave
Skokie, IL 60076 847-673-4477
Fax: 847-673-4487 info@knechtel.com
www.knechtel.com
Confectionery, pharmaceutical and foods development, troubleshooting and pilot plant operations support
President: Robert Boutin
CFO: Robert Boutin
Estimated Sales: $1 - 2.5 Million
Number Employees: 10-19
Square Footage: 108000
Type of Packaging: Consumer, Food Service, Private Label, Bulk

24937 Knight Equipment Canada
Unit 6
Mississauga, ON L5N 7X8
Canada 949-595-4800
Fax: 905-542-1536 800-854-3764
cs.knight@idexcorp.com www.knightequip.com
Chemical dispensing equipment and dishwashing machines
Number Employees: 7
Parent Co: Knight Equipment

24938 Knight Equipment International
20531 Crescent Bay Dr
Lake Forest, CA 92630-8825 949-595-4800
Fax: 949-595-4801 800-854-3764
info.knightus@idexcorp.com
www.knightequip.com
Manufacturer and exporter of low energy dish washing machines; also, pumps, controls and dispensers
President: George Noa
Pres.: Paul Beldham
Sales/Mktg: George Noa
Estimated Sales: $20-50 Million
Number Employees: 1,000-4,999
Brands:
Ultra Wash

24939 Knight Industries
1140 Centre Rd
Auburn Hills, MI 48326-2602 248-377-4950
Fax: 248-377-2135 literature@knight-ind.com
www.knight-ind.com
Air powered positioning equipment and ergonomic lifting equipment
CEO: James Zaguroli Jr
Estimated Sales: $20-50 Million
Number Employees: 100-249

24940 Knight Paper Box Company
4651 W 72nd St
Chicago, IL 60629-5882 773-585-2035
Fax: 773-585-3824 www.knightpaperbox.com
Paper folding boxes
Estimated Sales: $10-20 Million
Number Employees: 50-99
Square Footage: 85000

24941 Knight's Electric
11410 Old Redwood Hwy
Windsor, CA 95492 707-433-6931
Fax: 707-431-2342 info@knightselectric.com
www.knightselectric.com
Wine industry service and repair
CFO: Barbara Ragstale
Administrator: Barbara Ragsdale
Estimated Sales: $5 - 10 Million
Number Employees: 20-49

24942 Knobs Unlimited
13350 Bishop Rd
Bowling Green, OH 43402 419-353-8215
Fax: 419-353-8325 knobsinc@dacor.net
www.knobsunlimitedinc.com
Manufacturer and exporter of plastic replacement knobs for appliances
Owner/Plt. Mgr.: John Cardenas
R & D: William Anderson
R & D: John Cardinas
Estimated Sales: Below $5 Million
Number Employees: 5-9
Square Footage: 8500

24943 Knott Slicers
290 Pine Street
Canton, MA 02021-3353 781-821-0925
Fax: 781-821-0768 www.knottslicers.com

Manufacturer and exporter of slicing machinery for potato chips, yams, plantains, yuccas, bananas, taro roots, beets, potatoes, tomatoes and bagel sticks
President: Alan Burgess
VP: Steve Burgess
Quality Control: Doug Merrill
Marketing/Sales: Alan Burgess
Operations: Jim Stratis
Estimated Sales: $10-15 Million
Number Employees: 50-99
Number of Products: 5
Square Footage: 60000
Parent Co: Burgess Brothers
Type of Packaging: Food Service

24944 Knox Stove Works
PO Box 751
Knoxville, TN 37901 865-524-4113
Fax: 865-637-2461 Knoxstoveworks@aol.com
www.knoxstove.com

Coal and wood cooking ranges
Acct.: David Oglesby
Estimated Sales: $10-20 Million
Number Employees: 5-9
Square Footage: 21000

24945 Koch Container Corporation
797 Old Dutch Rd
Victor, NY 14564 585-924-1600
Fax: 585-924-7040 koch1@frontiernet.net
www.kochcontainer.com
Corrugated boxes and displays; wholesaler/distributor of corner boards, edge protectors, plastic bags and fiber tubes
President: Bob Harris
Mgr. Cust. Svce.: Cheryl Wessells
Estimated Sales: $20 - 50 Million
Number Employees: 50-99
Parent Co: Buckeye Corrugated

24946 (HQ)Koch Equipment
1414 W 29th St
Kansas City, MO 64108-3604 816-753-2150
Fax: 816-753-4976 info@kochequipment.com
www.kochequipment.com
Manufacturer and distributor of processing, packaging and labeling equipment to the meat, poultry, seafood and general food manufacturing markets
Owner: John Starr
CEO: John Starr
Estimated Sales: $38 Million
Number Employees: 50-99
Number of Brands: 10
Number of Products: 30
Square Footage: 180000
Type of Packaging: Consumer, Food Service, Private Label, Bulk
Brands:
Cook Master
Crossweb
Grand Prize
Injectamatic
Intact
Kats
Koch
Market Master
Portion Master
Ultravac

24947 Koch Membrane Systems, Inc.
850 Main St
Wilmington, MA 01887-3388 978-694-7000
Fax: 978-657-5208 888-677-5624
info@kochmembrane.com
www.kochmembrane.com
Developer and manufacturer of innovative membrane filtration systems.
President: David Koch
Number Employees: 250-499

24948 Kochman Consultants Limited
5545 Lincoln Avenue
Morton Grove, IL 60053-3430 847-470-1195
Fax: 847-470-1189 info@kclcad.com
www.kclcad.com
Designer and exporter computer software for the food service industry
President: Ronald Kochman
R & D: Kevin Kochman
Vice President: Kevin Kochman
Estimated Sales: Below $5 Million
Number Employees: 5-9
Square Footage: 8000
Type of Packaging: Food Service
Brands:
Kcl Cad Foodservice
The Kcl Cadalog

24949 Kodex Inc
160 Park Ave Ste 8
Nutley, NJ 07110 973-235-0606
Fax: 973-235-0132 800-325-6339
sales@kodexray.com www.securitydefense.com
Manufacturer, importer and exporter of x-ray inspection systems for detection of contaminants in packaged and fresh food products
President: Donna Korkala
General Manager: Don Airey
VP: Gary Korkala
Quality Control: Garrett Sollitto
Sales: Richard Zieminski
Estimated Sales: $3-4 Million
Number Employees: 2
Square Footage: 8800
Brands:
Imagex
Rapiscan
Scanvision

24950 Koehler Gibson Marking &Graphics
875 Englewood Ave
Buffalo, NY 14223 716-838-5960
Fax: 716-838-6859 800-875-1562
sales@kgco.com www.kgco.com
Manufacturer and exporter of marking devices, steel stamps, embossing dies, stencils, etc.; also, printing plates and cutting dies for plastic and corrugated packaging
Owner: David Koehler
Estimated Sales: $2.5-5 Million
Number Employees: 20-49
Square Footage: 14000

24951 Koehler Instrument Company
1595 Sycamore Ave
Bohemia, NY 11716 631-589-3800
Fax: 631-589-3815 800-878-9070
sales@koehlerinstrument.com
www.koehlerinstrument.com

Manufacturer and exporter of lubricant, grease and viscosity testing equipment
President: Roy Westerhaus
CFO: Peter Brey
R&D: Dr Raj Shah
Marketing: Dr Wayne Goldenberg
Sales: Atul Gautama
Production: Joseph Russo
Estimated Sales: $10-20,000,000
Number Employees: 20-49
Number of Brands: 2
Number of Products: 200
Square Footage: 35000
Brands:
Okzdata
Ruler

24952 Koflo Corporation
309 Cary Point Drive
Cary, IL 60013 847-516-3700
Fax: 847-516-3724 800-782-8427
info@koflo.com www.koflo.com
Static mixers, calibration columns and injection quills.
President: James Federighi
VP: Anthony Federighi
Estimated Sales: $5-10 Million
Brands:
Calibration Columns
Injection Quills
Static Mixers

24953 Kohlenberger AssociatesConsulting Engineering
611 S Euclid St
Fullerton, CA 92838 714-738-7733
Fax: 714-738-3905
kohlenberger@kaceenergy.com
www.kaceenergy.com

Design and engineering consultant specializing in food processing plants and systems, refrigeration and freezing systems and cold storage warehouses
President: M Kohlenberger
CFO: Karl Kohlenberger
Vice President: Ted Kohlenberger
Estimated Sales: $500,000-$1 Million
Number Employees: 1-4
Square Footage: 8800

24954 Kohler Awning
2600 Walden Ave
Cheektowaga, NY 14225 716-685-3333
Fax: 716-685-0126 sales@kohlerawning.com
www.kohlerawning.com

Commercial awnings
President: John Martin Kohler Sr
Estimated Sales: $10 - 20,000,000
Number Employees: 50-99

24955 Kohler Industries
4925 N 56th Street
Lincoln, NE 68504 402-465-8845
Fax: 402-465-8847 800-365-6708
info@kohlerequip.com www.kohlerequip.com
Food processing and packaging equipment
President: Jim Kohler
Sales Director: Norm Pavlish
Estimated Sales: $3 - 5 Million
Number Employees: 10-19
Square Footage: 18000
Parent Co: Kohler Industries

24956 Kohler Industries, Inc.
4925 North 56th Street
PO Box 29496
Lincoln, NE 68504 402-465-8845
Fax: 402-465-8847 800-365-6708
info@kohlerequip.com www.kohlerequip.com
Manufacturer and distributor of freezers, conveyors, bagging equipment and mixers.
President/Owner: Jim Kohler
IT: Scott Jaquez
Sales: Norm Pavlish
Office Mgr./ Inventory Control: Dave Bonczynski

24957 Koke
582 Queensbury Ave
Queensbury, NY 12804
Fax: 888-231-5521 800-535-5303
kokeinc@capital.net www.kokeinc.com
Material handling equipment including pallet jacks, dock boards and levelers and fork lifts
Pres.: John Koke
CEO: John Koke
Estimated Sales: Below $5,000,000
Number Employees: 20-49
Square Footage: 30000

24958 Kold Pack
5014 Page Ave
Jackson, MI 49201 517-764-1550
Fax: 517-764-1195 800-824-2661
sales@koldpack.com www.koldpack.com
Coolers and freezers
President: Glen Stuard
Marketing Manager: Ed Sayles
Purchasing Manager: Kim LaSerra
Estimated Sales: $5 - 10 Million
Number Employees: 10-19
Brands:
Copeland
Heatcraft
Russell
Tecumseh

24959 Kold-Draft
1525 E Lake Rd
Erie, PA 16511-1088 814-453-6761
Fax: 814-455-6336 tomm@kold-draft.com
www.kolddraft.com

CEO: John Brigham
Estimated Sales: $5 - 10 Million
Number Employees: 20-49
Parent Co: Uniflow Manufacturing

24960 Kold-Hold
P.O.Box 570
Edgefield, SC 29824-0570 803-637-3166
Fax: 803-637-3046 sellis@edgefield.tranter.com
www.tranterradiators.com
Manufacturer and exporter of cold plates for refrigeration trucks; used in short delivery
President: Paul Cooper
G.M.: Dave Stasktlunas
Number Employees: 100-249
Square Footage: 440000
Parent Co: Tranter
Brands:
Kold-Hold

24961 Kole Industries
PO Box 20152
Miami, FL 33102 305-633-2556
Fax: 305-638-5821
Manufacturer and exporter of corrugated parts, bins and mailing and shipping room supplies
President: Arthur Kaplan
Estimated Sales: $5 - 10 Million
Number Employees: 15
Parent Co: National Lithographers

24962 Kolinahr Systems
6840 Ashfield Dr
Blue Ash, OH 45242 513-745-9401
Fax: 513-794-3240 sales@geneng.com
www.geneng.cc
Pallet labeling and pallet load stacking equipment
President: Gary Jenkins
Marketing Director: Bill Walker
Estimated Sales: $2 Million
Number Employees: 10-19
Number of Products: 9

24963 Kolpak
2915 Tennessee Ave N
Parsons, TN 38363 731-847-6361
Fax: 731-847-5387 800-826-7036
www.kolpak.com
Manufacturer and exporter of walk-in coolers and freezers
General Manager: Gerry Senion
VP: Jack Antell
Estimated Sales: $50-100 Million
Number Employees: 100-249
Type of Packaging: Food Service

24964 Kolpak Walk-ins
P.O.Box 550
Parsons, TN 38363-0550 731-847-6361
Fax: 731-847-5387 800-826-7036
pmaxwell@kolpak.com www.kolpak.com
Manufacturer and exporter of walk-in coolers, freezers and refrigeration systems
Quality Control: Barry Autry
CFO: Tonny Jordan
VP: Jack Antell
Research & Development: Richard Fahey
Marketing Director: Stephanie Ferrell
Plant Manager: Steve Clayton
Estimated Sales: $50 - 75 Million
Number Employees: 20-49
Parent Co: Manitowoc Foodservice Group
Brands:
Expresso
Kolpake
Polar-Chill
Polar-Pak

24965 Komatsu Forklift
1701 W. Golf Rd.
PO Box 5049
Rolling Meadows, IL 60008 847-437-5800
Fax: 770-784-0700
forkliftmarketing@komatsuna.com
www.komatsuforkliftusa.com
Fork lift trucks
President: Motohisa Kai
CFO: David Adea
Estimated Sales: $5 - 10 Million
Number Employees: 100-249
Square Footage: 125000

24966 Komax Systems
15301 Graham ST
Huntington Beach, CA 92649 800-826-0760
Fax: 310-830-4320 800-826-0760
info@komax.com www.komax.com
Owner: Richard Carlson
Estimated Sales: $3,000,000 - $5,000,000
Number Employees: 10-19

24967 Komline-Sanderson
12 Holland Avenue
Peapack, NJ 07977-0257 908-234-1000
Fax: 908-234-9487 800-225-5457
info@komline.com www.komline.com
Paddle Dryer/Processor for drying, crystallizing, calcining, tooling, heating, reacting, sterilization. Liquid solid separation filters, filtration with cake washing and clarification, vacuum filtration products. Pumps, wastewatertreatment sludge by-product dewatering and drying.
CEO: Russell Komline
Vice President: Christopher Komline
Purchasing Manager: W Tiger
Estimated Sales: $35-40 Million
Number Employees: 100-249
Square Footage: 85000

24968 Konica Minolta Corporation
101 Williams Dr
Ramsey, NJ 07446 201-825-4001
Fax: 201-825-7567 888-473-3637
isdcolor@minolta.com www.konicaminolta.com
Manufacturer and exporter of color measuring instrumentation including spectrophotometers, colorimeters, light meters, etc.; also, computer software for color formulation and quality control
CEO: Jun Haraguchi
Marketing Director: Maria Repici
Number Employees: 10,000

24969 Kontane
1000 Charleston Regional Pkwy
Charleston, SC 29492 843-352-0011
Fax: 828-397-3683 info@kontanelogistics.com
www.kontane.com
Manufacturer and exporter of containers: heavy duty wooden, household storage and custom built; also, pallet and export boxes and cleated plywood
President: Ed Byrd
VP: Jason Essenberg
COO: Rusty Byrd
Estimated Sales: $2.5-5 Million
Number Employees: 100-249

24970 Konz Wood Products
616 N Perkins St
Appleton, WI 54912 920-734-7770
Fax: 920-734-4811 877-610-5145
info@konzwoodproducts.com
www.konzwoodproducts.com
Pallets, skids and wooden shipping crates
Owner: Lawrence Konz Jr
Quality Control: Lawrence A Konz
Estimated Sales: $2.5 - 5 Million
Number Employees: 50-99
Parent Co: Appleton Lumber Company

24971 Koolant Koolers
2625 Emerald Dr
Kalamazoo, MI 49001 269-349-6800
Fax: 269-349-8951 800-968-5665
sales@koolant.com www.dimplexthermal.com
Custom and standard liquid coolers and water chillers for the removal of heat from industrial and continuous processes
President: Mark Rostagno
CEO: Mark Rostagno
VP: Spencer Malcolm
Sales Manager: Kristen Ulsh
Vice President Of Operations: Spencer Malcom
Estimated Sales: $20 - 50 Million
Number Employees: 50-99
Square Footage: 60000
Brands:
Koolant Koolers

24972 Kopykake Enterprises
3699 W. 240th Street
Torrance, CA 90505-6087 310-373-8906
Fax: 310-375-5275 800-999-5253
sales@kopykake.com www.kopykake.com
Manufacturer and exporter of computerized cake photo printing, edible frosting sheets and edible ink. kartriges, cake decorating equipment and supplies, including drawing projectors, airbrushes and compressors, food colors, disposabledecorating bags, etc
President: Gerry Mayer
Vice President: Greg Mayer
Sales Director: Rudy Arce
Estimated Sales: $1-2.5 Million
Number Employees: 20-49
Square Footage: 80000
Type of Packaging: Food Service
Brands:
Airmaster
Kobra
Kopykake
Kopyrite
Kroma Jet
Kroma Kolor

24973 Korab Engineering Company
7727 Beland Avenue
Los Angeles, CA 90045-1128 310-670-7710
Fax: 310-670-7710 korab2@ix.netcom.com
Manufacturer, exporter and importer of packaging machinery including liquid fillers, monoblock machinery, automation systems, vertical form fillers, seal machinery, horizontal thermoforming equipment, tray makers, pick and placeequipment, etc
Pres./G.M.: Jacek Zdzienicki
Shop Mgr.: Eric Zuber
Cust. Rel.: Janine Luciano
Number Employees: 5-9
Square Footage: 8000

24974 Kord Products Inc.
325B West Street #200
PO Box 265
Brantford, ON N3T 5M8
Canada
Fax: 519-753-2667 800-452-9070
www.kord.ca
Manufacturer and exporter of plastic injection molded products including blisters, clamshells and fiber protective packaging, custom molded products
President: Don Gayford
CEO: Gerry Docksteader
Research & Development: David Penkmann
Marketing Director: Jon Hensen
Plant Manager: Brock Howes
Purchasing Manager: Rachel St. Laurent
Number Employees: 200

24975 Kornylak Corporation
400 Heaton Street
Hamilton, OH 45011 513-863-1277
Fax: 513-863-7644 800-837-5676
kornylak@kornylak.com www.kornylak.com
Manufacturer and exporter of material handling equipment including conveyors, multi-directional and plastic skate wheels and gravity controlled live storage systems
President: Thomas Kornylak
Staff, Engineering Department: Richard Kornylak
Marketing/Sales Manager: Anne McAdams
Purchasing Director: Ginger Vizedom
Estimated Sales: $5 Million
Number Employees: 20-49
Square Footage: 400000
Brands:
Ags 100
Armorbelt
Mini-Wheel
Palletflo
Superwheel
Transwheel
Ts Conveyor
Zipflo

24976 Kosempel Manufacturing Company
3760 M Street
Philadelphia, PA 19124-5538 215-533-7110
Fax: 215-744-5220 800-733-7122
Custom metal products including bowls, funnels, hoppers and coating pans
Sls.: Rob Borst
Estimated Sales: $5-10 Million
Number Employees: 50-99
Square Footage: 60000

24977 (HQ)Koser Iron Works
PO Box 133
Barron, WI 54812 715-537-5654
bill@poweram.com
www.koserironworks.com
Storage racks; also, custom stainless steel fabrication available
President: Willian E Koser
Production Manager: David Fall
Purchasing Manager: David Fall
Estimated Sales: Below $5 Million
Number Employees: 20-49
Square Footage: 30400

24978 Kotoff & Company
324 N San Dimas Ave
San Dimas, CA 91773-2601 626-443-7115
Fax: 626-443-7110

Standard and custom plated wire shelving
President: James Kotoff
VP: Mary Ann Kotoff
Manager: Dean Miller
Estimated Sales: $1-2.5 Million
Number Employees: 5-9
Square Footage: 12500

24979 Koza's
2910 S Main Street
Pearland, TX 77581 281-485-1462
Fax: 281-485-8000 800-594-5555
sales@kozas.com www.kozas.com
Manufacturer and exporter of advertising novelties including caps and hats; also, custom cresting available
Owner: Joseph Koza Jr
Estimated Sales: $6 Million
Number Employees: 50
Square Footage: 40000

24980 Kraissl Company
299 Williams Ave
Hackensack, NJ 07601-5225 201-342-0008
Fax: 201-342-0025 800-572-4775
kraissl@aol.com www.strainers.com
Strainers, filters, valves for pipelink service
President/CEO: Richard Michel
Foreman: Winston Philips
Chairman of the Board: Richard Michel
Tech Sales: Bill Henderson
Office Supervisor: Barbara Punthsecca
Estimated Sales: Below $5,000,000
Number Employees: 20-49
Square Footage: 14000
Type of Packaging: Bulk
Brands:
Kraissl
Sea-View

24981 Kramer
125 Clairemont Ave
Suite 330
Decatur, GA 30030-2551 404-371-1835
Fax: 404-892-8881
Owner: Myron N Kramer
Estimated Sales: $.5 - 1 million
Number Employees: 5-9

24982 Kraus & Sons
215 W 35th St
Suite 300
New York, NY 10001 212-620-0408
Fax: 212-924-4081 info@krausbanners.com
www.krausbanners.com
Manufacturer and exporter of badges, buttons, flags, banners and awnings
Owner: Paul Schneider
Estimated Sales: Below 1 Million
Number Employees: 5-9
Type of Packaging: Food Service

24983 Kreative Koncepts
154 W Washington Street
Marquette, MI 49855-4320 906-228-9354
Fax: 906-228-8918 800-638-2019
kki@kreativekoncepts.com
www.kreativekoncepts.com
Microwave accessories
President: Robert Green
Brands:
Rib Chef
Souper 1 Step

24984 Kreissle Forge Inc
7947 N Tamiami Trl
Sarasota, FL 34243-1999 941-355-6795
Fax: 941-351-3213
Ornamental iron fixtures
President: Martin Haas
VP: Joey Kreissle
Estimated Sales: $500,000-$1 Million
Number Employees: 1-4

24985 Krewson Enterprises
855 Canterbury Rd
Cleveland, OH 44145-1420 440-871-8780
Fax: 440-871-5127 800-521-2282
airtools@superiorpneumatic.com
www.superiorpneumatic.com
Manufacturer and exporter of adjustable freezer and cooler alarms
President: Bradley Krewson
Estimated Sales: $5-10 Million
Number Employees: 5-9
Square Footage: 10000
Parent Co: Superior Pneumatic & Manufacturing
Brands:
Protecto-Freeze
Protecto-Temp

24986 Krimstock Enterprises
1426 Union Ave
Pennsauken, NJ 08110 856-665-3676
Fax: 856-662-8083 krim@bellatlantic.net
Advertising specialties, signs, displays and exhibits; cutting and engraving services available
Owner: Joseph Crew
Estimated Sales: $1 - 5,000,000
Number Employees: 5-9
Square Footage: 7000

24987 Krispy Kist Company
120 S Halsted Street
Department R8
Chicago, IL 60661-3508 312-733-0900
Fax: 312-733-3508
Manufacturer and exporter of snack food processing machinery including extruders, fryers, kettles, coating tumblers, mixers, ovens and peanut roasters
Sales/Operations: J Geiersbach
Office Mgr.: Kevin Coster
Estimated Sales: $1-5 Million
Number Employees: 8
Square Footage: 10000
Type of Packaging: Food Service
Brands:
Krispy
Krispy Kist

24988 Krogh Pump Company
251 W Channel Rd
Benicia, CA 94510 707-747-7585
Fax: 707-747-7599 800-225-7644
sales@kroghpump.com www.kroghpump.com
Manufacturer and exporter of horizontal and vertical centrifugal pumps for abrasive, corrosive, food and sewage services
Owner: Charles O' Brian
Estimated Sales: $2.5-5 Million
Number Employees: 10-19
Square Footage: 15000
Type of Packaging: Food Service, Private Label

24989 Krohne Inc
4100 N. Sam Houston Parkway W
Building C - Suite 220
Houston, TX 77086 281-598-0050
Fax: 281-598-0051 866-689-1250
oilandgas@krohne.com us.krohne.com
Flow meters
Marketing: Joe Incontri
Number Employees: 50-99

24990 Krones
PO Box 321801
9600 S. 58th Street
Franklin, WI 53132-6241 414-409-4000
Fax: 414-409-4140 salesusa@kronesusa.com
www.kronesusa.com
Manufacturer and exporter of food processing and packaging machinery including blenders, fillers, labelers, bottle washers and rinsers, palletizers, depalletizers, pasteurizers, etc
Chairman: Volker Kronseder
Finances & Accounting: Christopher Klenk
Estimated Sales: $52.6 Million
Number Employees: 469
Square Footage: 232000
Parent Co: Krones AG Hermann Kronseder Maschinenfabrik

24991 Krowne Metal Corporation
100 Haul Rd
Wayne, NJ 07470 973-305-8300
Fax: 973-485-1424 800-631-0442
customerservice@krowne.com
www.krowne.com
Manufacturer and exporter of bar equipment, hand sinks and faucets
Exec. V.P.: Roger Forman
Estimated Sales: $5-10,000,000
Number Employees: 20-49
Square Footage: 80000

24992 Krueger Food Laboratories
21 Alpha Road
Suite D
Chelmsford, MA 01824 978-256-1220
Fax: 978-256-1222 dkrueger@kfl.com
www.kfl.com
Analytical testing service for pesticide residues and nutritional labeling; also, microbiology, consultation and sampling
President: Dana Krueger
Lab Mgr.: Jeanne Maciel
Office Mgr.: Sherida George
Estimated Sales: $5-10 Million
Number Employees: 10
Square Footage: 16000

24993 (HQ)Krueger International
1330 Bellevue Street
Green Bay, WI 54308
Fax: 920-468-2270 800-424-2432
consultki@ki.com www.ki.com
Manufacturer and exporter of tables, stools and chairs
President/CEO: Richard Resch
Senior Vice President: Brian Krenke
Quality Engineer: Susan Kehoe
Vice President, Marketing: Tom Abrahamson
Vice President, Sales: Richard Butrym
Operations Executive: Paul Schueller
Product Manager, Movable Walls: Rob Wittl
Estimated Sales: $650 Million
Number Employees: 2,300
Square Footage: 250000

24994 Krusoe Sign Company
5365 Canal Rd
Cleveland, OH 44125 216-447-1177
Fax: 216-447-1516 46694krusoesign@aol.com
Signs including advertising and plastic
President: Dale Krusoe
Estimated Sales: Less than $500,000
Number Employees: 1-4

24995 Krystal Holographics
555 W 57th St
New York, NY 10019-2925 212-261-0400
Fax: 212-262-0414 800-998-5775
info@krystaltech.com
Suppliers of semi-conductors, electro mechanical components
Owner: Azi Lezi
CEO: Dan Toben
Estimated Sales: $5 - 10 Million
Number Employees: 50-99

24996 Krystatite Films
PO Box 89
Mar Lin, PA 17951-0089 570-621-6097
Fax: 570-622-1037 vcfilm@monmouth.com
Flat, centerfolded and tube PVC shrink film for overwrapping and bundling
Estimated Sales: $1 - 5 Million

24997 Kuecker Equipment Company
801 W Markey Rd
Belton, MO 64012 816-331-7070
Fax: 816-331-7888 info@kuecker.com
www.kuecker.com
President: Stanley Kuecker
CEO: Mike Langdom
CFO: Alice Kuecker
VP Sales: Jim Kuecker
System Sales: Dan Bingaman
Estimated Sales: Below $5 Million
Number Employees: 10-19

24998 Kuehne Chemical Company
86 North Hackensack Avenue
Kearny, NJ 07032 973-589-0700
Fax: 973-589-4866 info@kuehnecompany.com
www.kuehnecompany.com
Industrial strength bleach including sodium hypochlorite; wholesaler/distributor of caustic soda, caustic potash, chlorine and sulfur
Estimated Sales: $61 Million
Number Employees: 200
Square Footage: 10000

24999 Kuepper Favor Company, Celebrate Line
P.O.Box 428
Peru, IN 46970-0428 765-473-5586
Fax: 765-472-7247 800-321-5823
www.partydirect.com

Manufacturer and importer of paper party favors, favor goodie bags, custom imprinted lite-up favors and novelties.
President: Mike Kuepper
VP: Douglas Kuepper
Head Of Marketing Department: Jane Grund
Number Employees: 50-99
Type of Packaging: Consumer, Private Label, Bulk
Brands:
Celebrate Line
K Line
Party Direct

25000 Kuest Enterprise
PO Box 110
Filer, ID 83328-0110 208-326-4084
Fax: 208-326-6604
goldengraingrinder@hotmail.com
www.goldengraingrinder.com
Manufacturer and exporter of grain grinders
Founder: Johnnie Kuest
Estimated Sales: $500,000 - $1 Million
Number Employees: 1-4

25001 Kuhl Corporation
39 Kuhl Rd
PO Box 26
Flemington, NJ 08822 908-782-5696
Fax: 908-782-2751 khk@kuhlcorp.com
www.kuhlcorp.com
Industrial washing machines for the food industry
President: Henry Kuhl
CEO: Kevin Kuhl
CFO: Rick Kuhl
Marketing/Public Relations: Michael Vella
Operations Manager: John Pichell
Plant Manager: Al Fisher
Estimated Sales: $12 Million
Number Employees: 70
Square Footage: 20000

25002 Kuriyama of America
360 E State Pkwy
Schaumburg, IL 60173 847-755-0360
Fax: 847-885-0996 800-800-0320
www.kuriyama.com
Thermoplastic, rubber and metal hose products and accessories including couplings and fittings for use in industrial and commerical applications
Marketing: Gary Kammes
Estimated Sales: $70+ Million
Number Employees: 20-49
Type of Packaging: Private Label, Bulk
Other Locations:
Houston TX
Santa Fe Springs CA
Kennesaw GA
New Egypt NJ
Mexico

25003 Kurtz Food Brokers
1333 Johnson Avenue
San Luis Obispo, CA 93401 805-543-3727
Fax: 866-633-2140 800-696-7423
kevin@kurtzinc.net www.kurtzfoodbrokers.com
Broker of confectionery products, industrial ingredients, rice, rice crackers, raisins, nuts, etc.
President: Ed Kurtz
Diretor Sales/Marketing: Kevin Magon
Sales Coordinator: Vicki Crawford
Estimated Sales: $280
Number Employees: 3
Square Footage: 1500

25004 Kurtz Oil Company
3305 Healy Dr
Winston Salem, NC 27103-1406 336-768-1515
Fax: 336-722-4634
Industrial lubricants
President: Anne Kiger
Estimated Sales: $1 - 2.5 Million
Number Employees: 1-4
Brands:
Pilot

25005 Kurz Transfer Products
3200 Woodpark Boulevard
Charlotte, NC 28206 704-927-3700
Fax: 704-927-3701 800-333-2306
sales@kurzusa.com www.kurzusa.com
Metalized and coated films, hot stamping foils and plastic printing machinery
Estimated Sales: $28 Million
Number Employees: 190
Square Footage: 60000

25006 Kusel Equipment Company
PO Box 87
Watertown, WI 53094-0087 920-261-4112
Fax: 920-261-3151 sales@kuselequipment.com
www.kuselequipment.com
Manufactures stainless steel drainage systems and cheese equipment.
President: Dave Smith
Estimated Sales: $10 Million
Number Employees: 1-4

25007 Kwasny/Sanicrete
24535 Hallwood Court
Farmington Hills, MI 48335 248-893-1000
Fax: 248-893-1000 amyk@sanicrete.com
www.sanicrete.com
Designer of sanitary floor and lining systems for the food and beverage industries.
Number Employees: 40

25008 Kwik Lok Corporation
P.O.Box 9548
Yakima, WA 98909-0548 509-248-4770
Fax: 509-457-6531 800-688-5945
websales@kwiklok.com www.kwiklok.com
President: Jerre Paxton
VP: Hal Miller
VP Sales: James Forsthe
Estimated Sales: $20 - 50 Million
Number Employees: 50-99

25009 Kwik-Lok Corporation
PO Box 9548
Yakima, WA 98909-0548 509-248-4770
Fax: 509-457-6531 800-688-5945
sales@kwiklok.com www.kwiklok.com
Manufacturer and exporter of bag closures and bag closing machinery using plastic clips and labels
President: Jerre Paxton
VP: Hal Miller
Quality Control: Jim Paxton
Sales: Rich Zaremba
Public Relations: Bill Klancke
Purchasing Director: Kohen Kelly
Estimated Sales: $10-20 Million
Brands:
Kwik Lok
Striplok

25010 Kwikprint ManufacturingCompany, Inc.
4868 Victor St
Jacksonville, FL 32207 904-737-3755
Fax: 904-730-0349 800-940-5945
info@kwikprint.net www.kwik-print.com
Manufacturer and exporter of foil, gold and hot stamping equipment; also, custom stamping dies and foils; wholesaler/distributor of advertising specialties and promotional items
President and CFO: Jay D Cann Jr
V.P.: Lynn Cann
Estimated Sales: Below $5 Million
Number Employees: 10-19
Square Footage: 48000
Type of Packaging: Food Service, Private Label, Bulk
Brands:
Kwikprint

25011 Kysor Panel Systems
4201 N Beach St
Fort Worth, TX 76137 817-230-8703
Fax: 817-281-5521 800-633-3426
jburke@kysorpanel.com www.kysorpanel.com
Manufacturer and exporter of refrigerated walk-in coolers
President: David Frase
Quotations: Gary Holloway
Estimated Sales: $20-50 Million
Number Employees: 100-249
Square Footage: 300000
Parent Co: Scotsman Industries
Other Locations:
Kysor Panel Systems
Goodyear AZ

25012 Kysor/Kalt
7320 NE 55th Ave
Portland, OR 97214-2138 503-235-0776
Fax: 503-249-8452
Walk-in coolers and freezers
Owner: Kevin Kayser
Estimated Sales: $1 - 3 Million
Number Employees: 1-4
Parent Co: Kysor Industrial Corporation

25013 Kysor/Warren
5201 Transport Boulevard
Columbus, GA 31907 800-866-5596
Fax: 706-568-8990 800-866-5596
marietta.oneill@heatcraftrpd.com
www.kysorwarren.com
Manufacturer and exporter of refrigerated display fixtures, walk-in coolers/freezers and refrigeration systems
President: Ralph Schmitt
Director of Sales-Eastern U.S. & Canada: Larry Norton
Director of Sales-Western U.S.: Robert Greene
Executive VP: Cliff Hill
Sales Manager: Brian Eddins
Dealer Development Manager: Oscar Stuart
Estimated Sales: $1 - 5 Million
Number Employees: 1-4
Square Footage: 490000
Parent Co: Heatcraft Worldwide Refrigeration
Brands:
Dual Jet
Kysor/Warren

25014 Kyung Il Industrial Company
10771 El Caballo Avenue
San Diego, CA 92127-3311 858-673-1211
Fax: 858-673-5311 sales@kyungilind.com
www.kyungilind.com
Rotogravure printing, laminated rolls on pouches, flat standup zipper
President: Lee Sung Ho
CEO: Kyo Sun Kim
Quality Control: Sunyu Kim
Partner: Kyosun Kim
Estimated Sales: Below $5 Million
Number Employees: 4

25015 L ChemCo Distribution
3230 Commerce Center Place
Louisville, KY 40211-1900 502-775-8387
Fax: 502-775-5981 800-292-1977
lchemco@bellsouth.net
Wholesale distributor of commercial and industrial janitorial cleaning supplies and equipment; also including sell of pesticides, weedicides and herbicides
Estimated Sales: $1.5 Million
Number Employees: 9
Square Footage: 14000

25016 L&A Engineering and Equipment
PO Box 2997
Turlock, CA 95381-2997 209-668-8107
Fax: 209-668-0636
Wine industry processing equipment
Estimated Sales: $1-5 Million
Number Employees: 3

25017 L&A Process Systems
1704 Reliance St
Modesto, CA 95358 209-581-0205
Fax: 209-581-0194 landaprocess@aol.com
Manufacturer and exporter of evaporators, distilleries, rotary coil vessels for jam and jelly production, ceramic cross flow micro-filtration and essence/aroma recovery systems
CEO: Don Carter
Estimated Sales: $1-2.5 Million
Number Employees: 5-9

25018 L&C Plastic Bags
500 Dick Minnich Dr
Covington, OH 45318 937-473-2968
Fax: 937-473-5334 sales@LCPlastics.com
www.lcplastics.com
Plastic and polyethylene bags
President: Rodney Sprenkel
Estimated Sales: Below $5 Million
Number Employees: 10-19

25019 L&H Wood Manufacturing Company
PO Box 441
Farmington, MI 48332-0441 248-474-9000
Fax: 248-474-0269 lhwoodmfg@aol.com
New and used pallets, skids, wood and wirebound boxes, stretch film and machines, steel and synthetic strapping and strapping machines
Sales Manager: Bill Lindbert
Controller: Kris Lindbert

Estimated Sales: $5-10 Million
Number Employees: 10-19
Square Footage: 30000

25020 L&L Engraving Company
40 Old Lake Shore Road
Gilford, NH 03249-6522 603-524-3032
Fax: 603-524-6106 888-524-3032
info@llengraving.com www.llengraving.com
Manufacture of stamps, rubber stamps, dating and numbering, coding, dating and marking equipment, advertising signs, plastic signs, plastic and metal fabricators
CEO: Melanie Burgess
Estimated Sales: less than $500,000
Number Employees: 1-4

25021 L&L Reps
4630 200th Street SW
Lynnwood, WA 98036-6608 425-778-9536
Fax: 425-778-6071 tltayne@landrets.com
Brewing devices (urns, cleaners, coffeemakers), coffee filters, dispensing equipment, filtration equipment
President: Tracy Tayne
Estimated Sales: $5 - 10 Million
Number Employees: 3

25022 L&M Chemicals
5018 Trenton Street
Tampa, FL 33619-6832 813-247-6007
Fax: 813-247-6473 800-362-3331
lmccbill@gmail.com www.lmcc.com
Industrial chemicals including disinfectants, detergents and hand cleaners
Owner: Robert Pasciuta
Estimated Sales: Less than $500,000
Number Employees: 4
Parent Co: Gator Supply

25023 L&M Foodservice
885 Airpark Dr
Bullhead City, AZ 86429-5886 928-754-3241
Fax: 928-754-2241 info@lmfoodservice.com
www.lmfoodservice.com
Wholesaler/distributor of equipment and fixtures and general merchandise including paper, janitorial and bar supplies; serving the food service market
President: Ron Laughlin
CEO: Andy Roesch
Vice President: Judy Laughlin
Plant Manager: Tom Watkins
Purchasing Manager: Dick Motsinger
Estimated Sales: $14 Million
Number Employees: 20-49
Square Footage: 50000

25024 L&N Label Company
2051 Sunnydale Blvd
Clearwater, FL 33765 727-442-5400
Fax: 727-442-8915 800-944-5401
customerservice@lnlabel.com
www.LNlabel.com
Manufacturer and exporter of die cut pressure sensitive labels; blank and printed types and roll, sheet, long and short runs available. Four color process labels, up to 8 colors.
President: Steve Sabadosh
Vice President: Julee Sabadosh
Sales Director: Reyna Martin
Production Manager: Curtis Booth
Plant Manager: Dave Gioia
Estimated Sales: $4-5 Million
Number Employees: 2
Square Footage: 80000
Type of Packaging: Private Label

25025 L&S Pallet Company
15150 Middlebrook Drive
Houston, TX 77058-1210 281-443-6537
Wooden pallets
Secretary/Treasurer: Allan Findley
Estimated Sales: $1-2.5 Million
Number Employees: 5-9

25026 L&S Products
422 Jay St
Coldwater, MI 49036-2112 517-279-9526
Fax: 517-278-8648 info@lsproducts.com
Store fixtures including garment and display racks and steel tubing products
President: Mark Neesley
CEO: Mark Neesley
CFO: Shanayne Neesley
R&D: Shanayne Neesley
Estimated Sales: Below $5 Million
Number Employees: 1-4
Square Footage: 60000

25027 L. Stocker & Sons
34 Suydam Lane
Bayport, NY 11705-2198 631-472-1881
Fax: 631-472-8069 www.stockerandsons.com
German made slicing blades and chopping knives for the food processing industry
Owner: Lee Stocker
Estimated Sales: $1-2.5 Million
Number Employees: 1-4

25028 L.A. Darling Company
1401 Highway 49b
Paragould, AR 72450 870-239-9564
Fax: 870-239-6427 800-643-3499
www.ladarling.com
Modular merchandising systems, store fixtures, gondolas and shelving systems, gourmet racks, checkouts, service desks and P.O.P. displays, gondolas, specialty wood and metal fixtures
President: Tom Weiss
Estimated Sales: $110.8 Million
Number Employees: 1500
Square Footage: 3000

25029 L.C. Thompson Company
1303 43rd St.
Kenosha, WI 53140 262-652-3662
Fax: 262-652-3526 800-558-4018
www.lcthomsen.com
Manufacturer, importer and exporter of dairy processing machinery including control systems, filters, gaskets, hoses, pumps, strainers, thermometers, tubing and valves
President: Wayne Borne
Sls. Mgr.: Mike Dyutka
Service Manager: Mike Dyutka
Sales: Joyce Saftig
Number Employees: 20-49
Square Footage: 48000

25030 L.F. Pease Company
21 Massasoit Ave
East Providence, RI 02914 401-438-2850
Fax: 401-434-6520 president@necpa.org
www.peasecompany.com
Commercial awnings; also, installation services available
President: Ted Franklin
VP: Donald Franklin
Purchasing Manager: Edwin Franklin
Estimated Sales: $1 - 5 Million
Number Employees: 1-4
Square Footage: 84000

25031 LA Cabinet & Finishing Company
810 E Jefferson Blvd
Los Angeles, CA 90011-2593 323-233-7245
Fax: 323-233-7248 www.lacabinetco.com
Store fixtures
President: Mark Klein
VP: Mark Klein
Estimated Sales: $1-2.5 Million
Number Employees: 10-19

25032 LA Dreyfus
3775 Park Avenue
Edison, NJ 08820-2595 732-549-1600
Fax: 732-549-1685 ddiaz@ladreyfus.com
www.ladreyfus.com
Chewing gum base
Estimated Sales: $15 - 20 Million
Number Employees: 100-249
Square Footage: 500000

25033 LA Graphics
15 Ellwood Court
Greenville, SC 29607-5340 864-297-1111
Fax: 864-987-9920 lagraphics@la-graphics.com
Commercial awnings
Corperate Manager: Nancy Keller
Quality Control: Larry Boeller
Estimated Sales: Below $5,000,000
Number Employees: 50

25034 LAB Equipment
1326 New Seneca Tpke
Skaneateles, NY 13152 315-685-5781
Fax: 315-685-8106 800-522-5781
service@labequipment.com
www.labequipment.com
Shock, vibration, compression and incline impact test systems, as well as test data acquisition systems
President: Robert Noonan
Sales Director: Thomas Dunne
Estimated Sales: $1 - 5 Million
Number Employees: 20

25035 LABLynx
PO Box 724207
Atlanta, GA 31139 770-859-1992
Fax: 678-391-6982 800-585-5969
sales@lablynx.com www.lablynx.com
President: John H Jones
Number Employees: 8

25036 LAKOS
1365 N Clovis Ave
Fresno, CA 93727 559-255-1601
Fax: 559-255-8093 800-344-7205
info@lakos.com www.lakos.com
Fluid handling systems
Owner: Claude Laval
Estimated Sales: $10-20 000,000
Number Employees: 50-99

25037 LB Furniture Industries
99 S 3rd St
Hudson, NY 12534 518-828-1501
Fax: 518-828-3219 800-221-8752
sales@lbfurnitureind.com
www.lbfurnitureind.com
Manufacturer and exporter of tables, chairs and booths
President: Les Lak
Estimated Sales: $1-2.5 Million
Number Employees: 10-19
Square Footage: 325000

25038 (HQ)LBL Lighting
7400 Linder Ave
Skokie, IL 60077 708-755-2100
Fax: 847-626-6350 800-323-3226
lblcseast@lbllighting.com www.lbllighting.com
Manufacturer, importer and exporter of lighting fixtures
President/Owner: Steve Harriott
Sales: Krista Fischer
Plant Manager: Don Clark
Purchasing Director: Cathy Santiago
Square Footage: 70000
Parent Co: Encompass Lighting

25039 LBP Manufacturing
1325 S Cicero Ave
Cicero, IL 60804-1404 708-652-5600
Fax: 708-652-5537 sales@lbpmfg.com
www.lbpmfg.com
Manufacturer and exporter of hot cup sleeves, take-out containers and acrylic displays and dispensers
President: Barry Silverstein
Pricing Manager: Mary Lou Medina
CFO: Mike Schaechter
VP: Matthew Cook
R&D and QC: Barry M
Estimated Sales: $10 - 20 Million
Number Employees: 10-19
Parent Co: Terrace Paper Company
Brands:
Coffee Clutch
Coffee on the Move
Safepak

25040 LCI Corporation
P.O.Box 16364
Charlotte, NC 28297-6364 704-393-0220
Fax: 704-393-7091 info@lcicorp.com
www.watsonelec.com
Thin-film evaporation systems, agglomeration systems, pelleting presses and feeder equipment manufactures
Manager: Scott Meyers
President: Lacey Hayes
Estimated Sales: $20 - 50 Million
Number Employees: 100-249
Parent Co: Bacon Industrial Manufacturing

25041 **LDC Analytical**
28271 Leticia
Mission Viejo, CA 92692-2329 949-586-5340
Fax: 949-586-9373
Wine industry probers and meters

25042 **LDI Manufacturing Company**
417 North St Rm 104
Logansport, IN 46947-2775 574-722-3124
Fax: 574-722-7213 800-366-2001
ldihvac@mindspring.com
Manufacturer and exporter of exhaust ventilation equipment including commercial exhaust hoods and fans. Distribution of complete, pre-engineered heating and air conditioningequipment system. Custom stainless steel and metalfabrication. Indoor environment air quality equipment systems
Manager: Susan Begley
VP Finance: Camille Hall
Marketing Director: Susan Erny
VP Customer Services: Susan Erny
Estimated Sales: $5-10 Million
Number Employees: 19
Square Footage: 50000
Type of Packaging: Food Service
Brands:
Greese Gobler
Magic Wash
Smart Hood
Sup-Ex
Top Sergent

25043 **LDJ Electronics**
1280 E Big Beaver
PO Box 219
Troy, MI 48083-0219 248-528-2202
Fax: 248-689-2525 info@ldj-electronics.com
Process control, monitoring and line monitoring systems; also, computer software systems and services
Public Relations: Derrick Peterman
Estimated Sales: $5-10,000,000
Number Employees: 20-49

25044 **LDS Corporation**
7900 E Union Ave
Suite 1007
Denver, CO 80237 303-928-1124
Fax: 303-217-7050 866-25 -ARDE
www.ldsinc.com/www.cadretech.com
President/CEO: Joe Caston
VP of Finance/CFO: John C. Frank
Estimated Sales: $10 - 20 Million
Number Employees: 20-49

25045 **LECO Corporation**
3000 Lakeview Ave
Saint Joseph, MI 49085 269-985-5496
Fax: 269-982-8977 800-292-6141
info@leco.com www.leco.com
Analytical instrumentation
President: Robert J Warren
Number Employees: 1,000-4,999

25046 **LEE Industries**
50 W Pine St
P.O. Box 687
Philipsburg, PA 16866-2430 814-342-0461
Fax: 814-342-5660 lee@leeind.com
www.leeind.com
President, CEO: Robert W. Montler
Vice President of Operations: Josh Montler
Estimated Sales: $25 Milion
Number Employees: 250-499

25047 **LEE Industries**
50 W Pine St
P.O. Box 687
Philipsburg, PA 16866-2430 814-342-0461
Fax: 814-342-5660 lee@leeind.com
www.leeind.com
Custom sanitary process equipment
President/CEO: Robert W. Montler
Vice President: Bruce Kephart
Quality Control: Bruce Kephart
Plant Manager: Joe Bordack
Estimated Sales: $100+ Million
Number Employees: 250-499

25048 **LEE Industries**
50 W Pine St
Philipsburg, PA 16866-2430 814-342-0461
Fax: 814-342-5660 lee@leeind.com
www.leeind.com
Sanitary process equipment, agitated kettles and tanks, sanitary vaves and storage tanks
President: Robert Montler
R&D: Jim Demchak
CFO: John Horon
Vice President of Operations: Josh Montler
Estimated Sales: $20 - 50 Million
Number Employees: 100-249

25049 **LEESON Electric Corporation**
2100 Washington St
Grafton, WI 53024 262-377-8810
Fax: 262-377-9025 leeson@leeson.com
www.leeson.com
Manufacturer and exporter of electric motors, gears and drives for food processing machinery.
CEO: Henry Knueppel
CFO: Dave Barta
VP: Bud Pritchard
Marketing: Philippe De Gail
Sales: Mike Catania
COO: Mark Gliebe
Number Employees: 500-999
Brands:
Leeson
Speedmaster
Washguard

25050 **LEWA Inc**
PO Box 6820
Holliston, MA 01746-6820 508-429-7403
Fax: 508-429-8615 888-539-2123
sales@amlewa.com www.lewa-inc.com
Manufacturer and exporter of precision metering and mixing pumps and systems for blending and proportioning all liquids; also, seal-less controlled volume pumps for process services and moderate high pressures
President/Owner: Lee Bollow
Marketing: Marlis Morse
Estimated Sales: $10 - 20 Million
Parent Co: LEWA GmbH

25051 **LEWCO**
706 Lane St
Sandusky, OH 44870 419-625-4014
Fax: 419-625-1247 sales@lewcoinc.com
www.lewcoinc.com
Conveyor systems including belt, bottle and chain, stainless steel, gravity and powered roller. Also industrial ovens for drum heating and general thermal processing applications
President: Ronald Guerra
CFO: Jim Chapman
VP Oven Products: Ron Guerra
Quality Control: Andrews Smith
VP Conveyor Products: Jerry Guerra
Estimated Sales: $10 - 20 Million
Number Employees: 100-249
Square Footage: 135000
Brands:
Heat-Pro

25052 **LGInternational, Inc.**
6700 SW Bradbury Ct
Portland, OR 97224 503-620-0520
Fax: 503-620-3296 800-345-0534
sales.usa@lgintl.com www.lgintl.com
Manufacturer and exporter of pressure sensitive, front panel, bar code and clean room labels
President: Michael Martin
International Sales: Greg Jarmin
Sales Manager: Dale Gremaux
Estimated Sales: $1 - 5 Million
Number Employees: 50-99
Square Footage: 172000

25053 **LIS Warehouse Systems**
9201 Southern Pine Boulevard
Suite E
Charlotte, NC 28273-5537 704-926-1700
Fax: 704-926-1799 888-547-9670
info@rp-mail.com www.redprairie.com
Software for warehousing, inventory management, material handling and control
Chairman of the Board: Alok Singh
Senior Vice President, Director of Accou: Andrew Kirkwood
VP Sales/Marketing: Bob Carver
Number Employees: 25
Parent Co: LIS

25054 **LIST**
42 Nagog Park
Acton, MA 01720-3445 978-635-9521
Fax: 978-263-0570 sales@list.us
Food processing machinery for viscous, sticky and crust forming materials including mixers, kneaders, dryers, heaters, melters, coolers, etc
CEO: Klaus List
VP Sales: Hefunt Schildknecht
Estimated Sales: $1-5 Million
Number Employees: 20
Square Footage: 9000
Parent Co: LIST AG

25055 **LMC International**
893 N Industrial Dr
Elmhurst, IL 60126 630-834-7789
Fax: 630-834-4322 info@Latiniusa.com
www.lmcinternational.com
Equipment for the confectionery and bakery industries
Sales/Marketing: Pat Kiel
Sales Director: Roger Hohberger
Sales: Daniel Herman
Estimated Sales: $15 000,000
Number Employees: 50
Number of Brands: 2
Number of Products: 50
Square Footage: 30000
Brands:
Hohberger Products
Latini Products

25056 **LMCO**
4705 Highway 36 S
Suite 1
Rosenberg, TX 77471-9254 281-342-8888
Fax: 832-595-5000
Brooms, mops and handles
President: Leslie Moore
Estimated Sales: $500,000-$1 Million
Number Employees: 5-9
Square Footage: 9000

25057 **LMH**
1714 Colfax St
Suite E
Concord, CA 94520 925-686-6400
Fax: 925-686-3836 800-531-6782
gmccann@lmh-eqp.com
Wine industry pumps, mixers, tanks and process equipment; local service, fabrication and equipment repair
Estimated Sales: $5-10 Million
Number Employees: 10-19

25058 **LMI Packaging Solution**
8911 102nd Street
Pleasant Prairie, WI 53158-2212 262-947-3300
Fax: 262-947-3301 800-208-3331
info@labelmakers.com www.lmipackaging.com
Manufacturer and exporter of heat sealing lidding, flexible packaging solutions, daisychain, rollstock & die cut lidding
Owner: Virginia Moran
CEO: Jean Moran
Vice President of Business Development: Randall Troutman
Vp R&D: Mike Gorzynski
Director of Marketing: Lea Connelly
National Accounts Manager: Gary Morrison
Vp Operations: Vince Incandela
Estimated Sales: $5-10 Million
Number Employees: 20-49

25059 **LMK Containers**
PO Box 1001
Centerville, UT 84014-5001 626-821-9984
Manufacturer, importer and exporter of glass and plastic bottles, jars, caps and containers
Purchasing Director: Robert Frome
Type of Packaging: Consumer, Food Service, Private Label, Bulk
Brands:
Aastro

25060 **LPA Software**
400 Linden Oaks
Suite 140
Rochester, NY 14625
866-783-9900
info@lpa.com www.lpa.com

Prepackaged software, software development and consulting for a variety of business applications including supply chain, semiconductor, internet and client server systems
President: Donald Soule
Vice President: Katrina Adams
Estimated Sales: $300,000-500,000
Number Employees: 120

25061 **LPACK - Loersch Corporation**
1530 E Race Sreet
Allentown, PA 18109 610-264-5641
Fax: 610-266-0330 info@lpack.com
www.lpack.com
Manager: Robert Kreger
Estimated Sales: $1,000,000 - $3,000,000
Number Employees: 5-9

25062 **LPI Imports**
901 N Kilpatrick Avenue
Chicago, IL 60651-3326 877-389-6563
Fax: 773-379-5616
joanne.ramsay@lpstorage.com
Shelving, shelf ledges, shelf dividers, posts and casters; also, labels
General Manager: Alan Kaplan
Parent Co: Leggett & Platt
Brands:
Snake Shelving

25063 **LPI Information Systems**
10020 Fontana
Overland Park, KS 66207 913-381-9118
Fax: 913-381-9118 888-729-2020
www.datasmithpayroll.com
Manufacturer and exporter of payroll software and tax forms
President: David Land
Number Employees: 5-9
Brands:
Datacheck
Datasmith

25064 **LPI, Legacy Plastics**
1116 5th St
Henderson, KY 42420 270-827-1318
Fax: 270-831-6510
SCourtney@LegacyPlastics.com
www.lpilegacy.com
A custom thermoplastic Profile extrusion company offering products such as signage, price channels, dividers, extrusions and plastic components made from materials such as: styrene, acrylic, ABS, PVC, polycarbonate, etc; as well asflexible tubing products.
President: Roger Courtney
CEO: Doug Bray
CFO: John Brooks
Sales Director: Tom Simmering
Production Manager: Sharon Courtney
Purchasing Manager: Barb Claridge
Estimated Sales: $1.5 Million
Number Employees: 10-19
Number of Products: 100+
Square Footage: 40000
Parent Co: Display Specialties

25065 **LPS Industries**
10 Caesar Pl
Moonachie, NJ 07074 201-438-3515
Fax: 201-438-1326 800-275-4577
info@lpsind.com www.lpsind.com
Flexible packaging including stand up pouches, reclosable polyethylene and 3D barrier bags; coated products including pressure sensitive envelopes, blank stock direct thermal and transfer labels, ribbons, printers; general packagingsystems and ID products.
President/CEO: Madeleine Robinson
Research & Development: Tony Russo
Marketing Director: Ann McHenry
Sales Director: Jack Cunneen
Estimated Sales: $50-100 Million
Number Employees: 100-249
Square Footage: 250000

25066 **LPS Technology**
1009 McAlpin Court
Grafton, OH 44044-1322 440-355-6992
Fax: 440-355-6998 800-586-1410
Manufacturer and exporter of washers, ovens, compressed air systems, conveyors and air vacuums
President: Dean Burke
General Manager: Dave Bobak
Estimated Sales: $1-2,500,000
Number Employees: 10-19
Parent Co: Eton Fab Company

25067 **LRM Packaging**
41 James St
South Hackensack, NJ 07606 201-342-2530
Fax: 201-342-4351 info@lrmpackaging.com
www.lrmpackaging.com
Contract packager of snack and dry foods, etc
President: John Natali Jr
Director Sales: John Natali, Jr.
Production Manager: Mike Hoskins
Estimated Sales: Below $5,000,000
Number Employees: 1-4
Square Footage: 100000

25068 **LSI Industries**
10000 Alliance Road
PO Box 42728
Cincinnati, OH 45242-0728 513-651-3550
Fax: 513-984-1335 800-436-7600
www.lsi-industries.com
Manufacturer and exporter of electric lighting fixtures
VP Marketing (C&I Lighting Group): Wayne Peppercorn
Marketing Manager: Carl Miller
Estimated Sales: $1 - 5 Million
Number Employees: 1500
Parent Co: LSI Industries

25069 **LSI Industries Inc.**
10000 Alliance Road
Cincinnati, OH 45242 513-793-3200
www.lsi-industries.com
Visual merchandising displays and pressure sensitive signs
President: David McCauley
Quality Control: Bruce Soleinger
VP Sales/Marketing: Robert Lux
National Sales Manager: Todd Blandford
Estimated Sales: $1 - 3 Million
Number Employees: 5-9

25070 **LT Industries**
811 Russell Ave
Suite 302
Gaithersburg, MD 20879 301-990-4050
Fax: 301-990-7525 sales@ltindustries.com
www.ltindustries.com
Manufacturer and exporter of control systems and instrumentation for quality control measurements in labs and on line, including, liquid, solid, powders, pellets, etc.
President: Aviva Landa
Marketing Director: Aviva Landa
Estimated Sales: $1-5 Million
Number Employees: 10-19

25071 **LTG Technologies**
105 Corporate Dr
Spartanburg, SC 29303-5045 864-599-6340
Fax: 414-672-8800 sales@itsllcusa.com
www.itsllcusa.com
Manufacturer and exporter of controlled heat processing systems for the metal container industry
President: Gerhard Seyffer
General Manager: Bill Lawrence
VP: Brian Schofield
Estimated Sales: $20 - 50 Million
Number Employees: 100-249
Square Footage: 180000

25072 **LTI Printing**
518 N Centerville Rd
Sturgis, MI 49091 269-651-7574
Fax: 269-651-3262 www.ltiprinting.com
Manufacturer and exporter of labels and offset cartons
President: Don Frost
Estimated Sales: $20-50 Million
Number Employees: 50-99
Type of Packaging: Consumer, Food Service, Bulk

25073 **LVO Manufacturing**
P.O.Box 188
Rock Rapids, IA 51246-0188 712-472-3734
Fax: 712-472-2203 marilyn_lvo@yahoo.com
www.lvomfg.com
Bakery equipment
President: Marilyn Mammenga
CFO: Lambert Benno
Estimated Sales: $5 - 10 Million
Number Employees: 20-49

25074 **LXE**
P.O.Box 926000
Norcross, GA 30010-6000 770-447-4224
Fax: 770-447-4405 info@lxe.com
www.lxe.com
RF computer network systems, logistics, transportation, health care
President: Jim Childress
CEO: Alfred Hansen
CEO: Paul B Domorski
VP Sales: B Johnson
Estimated Sales: $50 - 100 Million
Number Employees: 250-499
Parent Co: EMS technologies

25075 **La Creme Coffee & Tea**
438 W Mockingbird Lane
Dallas, TX 75247 214-352-8190
Fax: 214-352-8173 877-493-2326
info@lacremecoffeeandtea.com
www.lacremecoffeeandtea.com
Tea and coffee brewers
Estimated Sales: $500,000-$1 Million
Number Employees: 9

25076 **La Crosse**
W6636 L B White Rd
Onalaska, WI 54650 608-783-2800
Fax: 608-783-6115 800-345-0018
mail@lacrossecooler.com
www.hospitalityinternational.com
Manufacturer and exporter of underbar items including sinks, drain boards, ice chests, cocktail stations and storage units; also, portable bars
Owner: Tony Wilson
CEO: Tony Wilson
CFO: Jack Lauer
Vice President of Development: Ron Provus
Marketing Director: Bridget Crave
Sales Director: Della Indahl
Estimated Sales: $50 - 100 Million
Number Employees: 100-249
Parent Co: Hospitality International
Brands:
La Crosse
Stowaway

25077 **La Crosse Milling Company**
105 Hwy 35
Cochrane, WI 54622 608-248-2222
Fax: 608-248-2221
ghartzell@lacrossemilling.com
www.lacrossemilling.com
Whole grain, organic and Kosher grain ingredients including oats, barley and wheat, products include conventional and organic oat flakes, oat flour, oat bran, oat fiber, pearled barley, barley flakes, barley flour, rolled wheat andother specialty milled grains.
President: Dan Ward
Director: William Ziegler
Manager: Jim Backus
Lab Manager: Bryan Hoch
Quality Assurance Manager: Wendy Biesterveld
Food Sales Assistant: Michelle Kosidowski
VP of Sales: Glen Hartzell
Research & Development Director: William Bruegger
Buyer Manager: Dale Peterson
Estimated Sales: $48.56 Million
Number Employees: 95
Type of Packaging: Bulk

25078 **La Marche ManufacturingCompany**
106 Bradrock Dr
Des Plaines, IL 60018 847-299-1188
Fax: 847-299-3061 www.lamarchemfg.com
Manufacturer and exporter of battery chargers for forklift trucks and vehicles
President: Rick Rutkowski
EVP: Raj Dhiman
CFO: Rick Rutkowski
Vice President: J. Vargas
Research & Development: Vance Pearson
Quality Control: Bert Watson
Marketing Director: S. Burg
Sales Director: John Pawula
Public Relations: R. Dhiman
Director Purchasing: Bob Lewinski

Estimated Sales: $10-20 Million
Number Employees: 1-4
Square Footage: 85000

25079 La Menuiserie East Angus
25 Rue Willard
East Angus, QC J0B 1R0
Canada 819-832-2746
Fax: 819-832-3474
Wooden pallets
President/CFO: Robert La Pointe
Quality Control/R&D: Robert Lapointe
Estimated Sales: Below $5 Million
Number Employees: 40

25080 La Poblana Food Machines
5952 East Nance Street
Mesa, AZ 85215 480-258-2091
Fax: 480-452-0538
sherrie.soria@lapoblanafoodmachines.com
www.lapoblanafoodmachines.com
La Poblana Food Machines LLC offers sales and service of commercial-grade tortilla-making equipment. Manufacture their lines as well as custom machinery.
President: Sherrie Soria

25081 La Rinascente Macaroni Company
41 James St
South Hackensack, NJ 07606 201-342-2500
Fax: 201-342-4351 info@lrmpack.com
www.lrmpackaging.com
Macaroni, flour and packaged food products
President: John Natali Jr Sr
COO: John Hoskins
VP: Mike Hoskins
Sales: John Natali Jr
Estimated Sales: $2738540
Number Employees: 1-4
Square Footage: 48000
Type of Packaging: Consumer, Food Service, Private Label, Bulk
Brands:
La Rinascente Pasta Products

25082 LaCrosse Safety and Industrial
18550 NE Riverside Parkway
Portland, OR 97230-4975 503-766-1010
Fax: 800-558-0188 800-557-7246
www.lacrosse-industrial.com
Manufacturer and importer of waterproof protective clothing and footwear including vulcanized double coated rubber aprons
President: John McGinnis
Manager: Tammy Woolrage
Sales Director: Ken Furtech
Number Employees: 100-249
Number of Products: 600
Parent Co: Standalone

25083 LaGrou Distribution
3514 S. Kostner Avenue
Chicago, IL 60632-3818 847-298-8195
Fax: 847-298-8196 SSchuldt@lagrou.com
www.lagrou.com
Public warehousing and trucking company for the food industry
President: Donald Schimmek
C.E.O: Donald E. Schimek
V.P. Finance: Steve Schuldt
Estimated Sales: $.5 - 1 million
Number Employees: 20

25084 LaMonica Fine Foods
48 Gorton Rd.
PO Box 309
Millville, NJ 08332-0309 856-825-8111
Fax: 856-825-9354 info@lamonicafinefoods.com
www.lamonicafinefoods.com
Surf clams and ocean clams from US certified waters, serving the fresh, canned and frozen markets.
Owner: Danny La Vecchia
Founder: Peter LaMonica
CFO: Jack Pipala
VP Operations: Michael LaVecchia
Square Footage: 360000
Type of Packaging: Consumer, Food Service, Private Label, Bulk
Brands:
Cape May
Lamonica
Maryland House
Ocean Chef
Sea Kove

25085 LaRos Equipment Company
8278 Shaver Rd
Portage, MI 49024-5440 269-323-1441
Fax: 269-323-0456 laros@globalcrossing.net
www.laros.com
Manufacturer and exporter of conveyor systems
President: G R Laure
Estimated Sales: $10-20 Million
Number Employees: 20-49
Parent Co: George R. Laure Enterprises

25086 LaRosa Refrigeration & Equipment Company
19191 Filer Avenue
Detroit, MI 48234-2807 313-368-6620
Fax: 313-368-1317 800-527-6723
info@larosaequip.com www.larosaequip.com
Commercial refrigeration equipment including freezers; also, liquid and portable bars, holding cabinets, holding and warming equipment and steam tables
Owner, President: Sebastiano Grillo
Vice President: Jerry Grillo
Marketing, Administrations: Chelsea Van Hazenbrouck
Sales and Design Manager: Dan Gudenau
Estimated Sales: $2.5-5 Million
Number Employees: 20-49

25087 LaVazza Premium Coffee
3 Park Ave Fl 35
New York, NY 10016 212-725-8800
Fax: 212-725-9475 info@lavazza.it
www.lavazzausa.com
Manufacturer and importer of Italian coffee and espresso machines
VP: Ennio Ranaboldo
Estimated Sales: $10-20 Million
Number Employees: 20-49
Parent Co: LaVazza Premium Coffee
Type of Packaging: Consumer, Food Service

25088 Lab-Tech Industries
7707 Lyndon St
Detroit, MI 48238-2465 313-862-1737
Fax: 313-862-1131 800-525-8667
Industrial cleaners and specialty chemicals
President/Co-Owner: Corey Bryce
Co-Owner: Dennis Bryce
Estimated Sales: Less than $500,000
Number Employees: 10-19

25089 LabVantage Solutions
1160 Us Highway 22 Ste 200
Bridgewater, NJ 00807
Fax: 908-707-1179 888-346-5467
nasales@labvantage.com www.labvantage.com
Developer of laboratory information management systems for sample forecasting, scheduling and login, data calculations, product specification checks, quality control and reporting
Manager: Deborah Washington
Marketing Manager: Heather Maguire
VP Sales/Marketing: Don Seitz
Estimated Sales: $10 - 15 Million
Number Employees: 10
Brands:
Labmaestro
Labmaestro Chrom Perfect
Labmaestro Ensemble
Labvantage
Pro-Lims
Seedpak
Trace

25090 Labconco Corporation
8811 Prospect Ave
Kansas City, MO 64132 816-333-8811
Fax: 816-363-0130 800-821-5525
labconco@labconco.com www.labconco.com
Manufacturer and exporter of scientific laboratory equipment and apparatus including chloride instruments, Kjeldahl nitrogen determination apparatus and fat and fiber apparatus
President: Stephen Gound
Executive VP: Mark Weber
VP Marketing: Debbie Kenny
National Sales Manager: Tom Schwaller
Estimated Sales: $30 Million
Number Employees: 100-249
Brands:
Centrivap
Flaskscrubber
Freezone
Paramount
Protector
Purifier
Rapidvap
Steamscrubber
Waterpro

25091 Label Aire
550 Burning Tree Rd
Fullerton, CA 92833 714-441-0700
Fax: 714-526-0300 info@label-aire.com
www.label-aire.com
Manufacturer and exporter of pressure-sensitive label applicators and rotary and incline systems
President: George Allen
Marketing Manager: William Claproth
Sales: Steve Winders
Operations: Gene Bukovi
Estimated Sales: $20 - 50 Million
Number Employees: 100-249
Square Footage: 60000
Parent Co: Impaxx
Type of Packaging: Consumer, Food Service, Private Label, Bulk

25092 Label Art
2278 Brockett Rd
Tucker, GA 30084 770-939-6960
Fax: 770-939-6960 800-652-1072
Manufacturer and exporter of grocery shelf marking products, warehouse picking labels and continuous and sheet fed laser printer products
National Sales Manager: Deborah Goss
Sales Representative: Lisa Wood
Estimated Sales: $20-50 Million
Number Employees: 100-249
Square Footage: 30000

25093 Label Express
1305 S 630 E
American Fork, UT 84003-3375 801-772-0677
Fax: 801-642-3510 877-639-8600
info@labelexp.com www.labelexpress.com
Labels, shrink bands and folding cartons
CFO: Jeff Sinclair
R&D: Carlene West
General Manager: Mike Kekeegan
Marketing Manager: Derick Sims
Estimated Sales: $20 - 50 Million
Number Employees: 50-99
Parent Co: Impaxx

25094 Label Graphix
1720 James Pkwy
Heath, OH 43056 740-929-2210
Fax: 740-929-2734 ghild@lginc.com
www.wspackaging.com
Pressure sensitive labels
President: David Ghiloni
VP Finances: Lori Harvey
Sr. VP: George Ware
Quality Control: Bill Tracey
Estimated Sales: $10 - 20 Million
Number Employees: 50-99
Square Footage: 49000
Parent Co: WL Group

25095 Label House
503 S Raymond Ave
Fullerton, CA 92831-5026 714-449-0632
Fax: 714-441-0698 800-499-5858
sales@labelhouse.com www.labelhouse.net
Pressure sensitive labels and tags; wholesaler/distributor of label dispensers and applicators, thermal transfer ribbons, case coders, bar code printers and software
Owner: Al Jiacomin
owner: Karen Freeman
VP Sales: Leone Grant
Estimated Sales: $1 - 2.5 Million
Number Employees: 10-19

25096 Label Impressiosn
1831 W Sequoia Ave
Orange, CA 92686 714-634-3466
Fax: 714-634-3468 info@labelimpressions.com
www.labelimpressions.com

High quality customer labels, tags and flexible packaging. Recognized as a quality, green technology manufacturer.
President: Jeff Salisbury
CEO: Ted Salisbury
CFO: Carolyn Deyse
VP Sales & Sustainability: Jeff Morrow
R&D: Marie Graham
Quality Assurance: Steve Smith
Operations: Rick Ybarra
Estimated Sales: $8 Million
Number Employees: 35
Number of Products: 1000
Square Footage: 40000
Type of Packaging: Consumer, Food Service, Private Label, Bulk

25097 Label Makers
8911 102nd St
Pleasant Prairie, WI 53158-2212 262-947-3300
Fax: 262-947-3301 800-208-3331
www.lmipackaging.com
Manufacturer and exporter of heat seal lidding, flexible packaging solutions, daisychain, rollstock & die cut lidding
Owner: Virginia Moran
CEO: Jean Moran
Vice President of Business Development: Randall Troutman
VP Research & Development: Mike Gorzynski
Director of Marketing: Lea Connelly
National Accounts Manager: Gary Morrison
VP Operations: Vince Incandela
Number Employees: 20-49

25098 Label Mill
2416 Jackson Street
Savanna, IL 61074-2836 815-273-4707
Fax: 815-273-7074 800-273-4707
pmills@labelmill.com www.labelmill.com
Standard and custom label applicators
Owner: Andy Mills
Estimated Sales: $1 - 3 Million
Number Employees: 5-9

25099 Label Products
10525 Hampshire Avenue S
Suite 300
Bloomington, MN 55438-2690 952-996-0909
Fax: 952-996-0202 877-370-0688
sales@labelproducts.com
www.labelproducts.com
Labels including pressure sensitive, UPC and bar code; also, embossed, holographic and computer designed available
President and CFO: Ed Christenson
Product Manager: Stu Knilons
Sales Manager: Kevin Peterson
Operations Manager: Kevin Peterson
Production Manager: Stu Knilons
Plant Manager: Kevin Peterson
Estimated Sales: $10 - 20 Million
Number Employees: 20
Square Footage: 14500

25100 Label Solutions
151 W. Passaic St.
2nd Floor
Rochelle Park, NJ 07662 201-599-0909
Fax: 201-599-9888 ilana@labelsolutions.net
www.labelsolutions.net
Wine industry pressure sensitive labels
President: Ilana Weiss
Estimated Sales: Below $5 Million
Number Employees: 1-4

25101 Label Specialties
704 Dunn Way
Placentia, CA 92870 714-961-8074
Fax: 714-961-8276 800-635-2386
sales@labelspecs.com www.labelspec.com
Labels including scale printer, ingredient printer, bar code, plain, pressure sensitive, stock and custom; also, transfer ribbons
Owner: Micheal Gyure
VP: Thomas Wetterhus
Estimated Sales: $1-2.5 Million
Number Employees: 10-19
Square Footage: 9000

25102 Label Systems
1150 Kerrisdale Blvd.
Unit 2
Newmarket, ON L3Y 8Z9
Canada 905-836-7844
Fax: 905-853-9357 m.kirby@label-systems.com
www.label-systems.com
Manufacturer and exporter of pressure sensitive label machinery and equipment.
Sales Director: Matthew Kirby
Number Employees: 5
Square Footage: 44000

25103 Label Systems
56 Cherry St
Bridgeport, CT 06605 203-333-5503
Fax: 203-336-8570 www.lsauthentication.com
Labels including pressure sensitive, imprintable and holographic for shelf marking applications
President: Michael Zubretsky
Quality Control: Howard Sands
R&D: George Houston
VP: Rich Zucker
Estimated Sales: $10 - 20 Million
Number Employees: 100-249
Parent Co: Bridgestone Company

25104 Label Systems & Solutions
1430 Church St
Bohemia, NY 11716-5028 631-563-4549
Fax: 631-567-4338 800-811-2560
www.labelsystems.com
Badges, printers, advertising specialties, labels, tags and tapes; also, art production services available
Sales Manager: Stacy Moller
Estimated Sales: $500,000-$1 Million
Number Employees: 5-9

25105 Label Technology
2050 Wardrobe Ave
Merced, CA 95341 209-384-1000
Fax: 209-384-0322 800-388-1990
info@labeltech.com www.labeltech.com
Pressure sensitive labels, tags and flexible packaging; also, label imprinters and applicators
President: John Bankson
VP Product Development: Dennis Deisenroth
VP Sales: Phil Henderson
Estimated Sales: $2.5-5,000,000
Number Employees: 50-99
Square Footage: 63000

25106 Label World
29 Jet View Dr
Rochester, NY 14624 585-235-0200
Fax: 585-235-0398 800-836-8186
sales@laborworldinc.com
www.labelworldinc.com
Prime labels
President/CEO: John McDermott
CEO: Janet Allardice
VP Sales & Marketing: Skylar Rote
Estimated Sales: $10-20 Million
Number Employees: 50-99

25107 LabelPrint Corporation
8 Opportunity Way
Newburyport, MA 01950-4043 978-463-4004
Fax: 978-463-9748
accounting@labelprintamerica.com
www.labelprintamerica.com
Labels, decals, tags, pressure sensitive labeling equipment and thermal imprinters
President: Antonio Yemma
President Marketing: Tony Yemma
VP Operations: Bob Haley
Estimated Sales: $2.5 - 5 Million
Number Employees: 20-49
Square Footage: 84000

25108 LabelQuest
493 W Fullerton Ave
Elmhurst, IL 60126 630-833-9400
Fax: 630-833-9421 800-999-5301
lblqst@inil.com
Manufacturer and exporter of labels, decals and heat transfers
President: Pat Vandenberg
Sales Manager: Neil Vandenberg
Estimated Sales: $2.5 - 5 Million
Number Employees: 50-99
Square Footage: 5000

25109 Labelette Company
1237 Circle Avenue
Forest Park, IL 60130-2416 708-366-2010
Fax: 708-366-0226 sales@labelette.com
www.labelette.com
Manufacturer and exporter of semi-automatic and automatic labeling machinery
Estimated Sales: $5 - 10 Million
Number Employees: 20-49
Square Footage: 40000
Brands:
Labelette

25110 Labeling Systems
32 Spruce St
Oakland, NJ 07436 201-405-0767
Fax: 201-405-1179 888-405-4574
lsi@labelingsystems.com
www.labelingsystems.com
Labeling machinery
President: Theodore Zaccheo
Estimated Sales: $5 - 10 Million
Number Employees: 20-49

25111 Labeling Systems Clearwater
PO Box 1955
Largo, FL 33779-1955 727-539-7784
Fax: 727-538-5626 800-749-1057
Supplies for DSD route sales, handheld labelers for price marking, promotional labeling, date coding
Estimated Sales: $1-2.5 Million
Number Employees: 5-9

25112 Labelmart
11733 95th Ave N
Maple Grove, MN 55369 763-493-0099
Fax: 763-493-0093 888-577-0141
info@cmsitechnologies.com
www.cmsitechnologies.com
Pressure sensitive labels and tags including die cut blank and printed; also, thermal transfer ribbons and printers
Owner: Lee Sorenson
Estimated Sales: $5-10 Million
Number Employees: 10-19
Parent Co: Computerized Machinery Systems

25113 Labelmax
1209 San Dario Avenue
Laredo, TX 78040-4515 956-722-6493
Pressure sensitive labels and thermal transfer and laser sheet; consultant specializing in bar coding services
CEO: Jorge Martinez
Finance Manager: Edgar Martinez
Estimated Sales: $3 - 5,000,000
Number Employees: 80

25114 Labels & Decals International
300 Frontier Way
Bensenville, IL 60106 630-227-0500
Fax: 630-227-1016 info@labels-decals.com
www.labels-decals.com
Pressure sensitive labels and decals
Owner: Cliff Bode
Estimated Sales: $2.5-5 Million
Number Employees: 10-19

25115 Labels By Pulizzi
3325 Wahoo Dr
Williamsport, PA 17701 570-326-1244
Fax: 570-326-3453 www.labelsbypulizzi.com
Customized pressure sensitive labels for food products
President: Charline Pulizzi
R&D: Joseph Pulizzi
VP: Joseph Pulizzi, Jr.
Manager: Mark Porter
Purchasing Executive: Dalbys Kreisher
Estimated Sales: $10 - 20 Million
Number Employees: 50-99
Square Footage: 200000

25116 Labels Plus
2407 106th St SW
Everett, WA 98204-3628 425-745-4592
Fax: 425-523-1973 800-275-7587
sales@labelsplus.com www.labelsplus.com
Custom printed pressure sensitive labels
President: Eric C Phillips
Accountant: James Peterson
Estimated Sales: $10 - 20 Million
Number Employees: 20-49

25117 Labels Systems, Inc
4111 Lindbergh Dr.
Addison, TX 75001-4345 972-387-4512
Fax: 972-387-4935 800-220-9552
sales@labelsystemsinc.com
www.labelsystemsinc.com
Labels including custom designed, pressure sensitive, plain, printed, die cut on rolls and sheeted; also, decals and metal name plates
Owner: John Van Brunt
VP: Amy Van Brunt
Quality Control: Marcia Macias
Sales: Rick Brown
Public Relations: Sue Van Brunt
Operations/Production: Bruno Contreaus
Purchasing: Yivan Chenn
Estimated Sales: $2.5-5 Million
Number Employees: 20-49
Number of Products: 150

25118 Laboratory Devices
PO Box 6402
Holliston, MA 01746-6402 508-429-1716
Fax: 508-429-6583
Manufacturer and exporter of laboratory instruments
Estimated Sales: $1 - 5 Million
Number Employees: 5

25119 Labpride Chemicals
2281 Light St
Bronx, NY 10466-6136 718-547-5757
Fax: 718-994-0494 800-467-1255
www.jennyexhaust.com
Heavy duty degreasers, disinfectants, sanitizers, detergents, brooms, mops, sponges, squeegees, brushes and cleaners including glass, oven, walls, bathrooms, etc
Owner: Ralph Derose
VP: Domenick DeRose
Operations Manager: James Lanfear
Estimated Sales: $5 - 10 Million
Number Employees: 20-49
Square Footage: 8000

25120 Labvantage Solutions
200 Broadway
Troy, NY 12180-3289 518-274-1990
Fax: 518-274-7824 www.labvantage.com
Laboratory Information Management Systems (LIMS), chromatography and a broad spectrum of other applications
Chief Executive Officer: Jeff Ferguson
Vice President of Professional Services: Anuj Uppal
Vice President of Quality: Fernando Casanova
Business Director: Anneli Friberg
Estimated Sales: $1 - 5 Million

25121 Laciny Brothers
6622 Vernon Ave
Saint Louis, MO 63130 314-862-8330
Fax: 314-862-8332 julz@lacinybros.com
www.lacinybros.com
Custom fabricated food processing equipment.
President/CEO/CFO: Robert Laciny
Marketing/Sales/Public Relations: John Ulz
Operations/Production: Rick Gratza
Plant Manager: Don Fitzgerald
Purchasing Manager: Terry Brown
Estimated Sales: $2.5-5 Million
Number Employees: 20-49
Square Footage: 62000

25122 Lacroix Packaging
77 De l'Eglise Street
St-Placide, Quebec, QC J0V 2B0
Canada 450-258-2262
Fax: 450-258-3345
cbouveret@emballagelacroix.com
www.emballagelacroix.com
Customized packaging and labels.

25123 Lacrosse-Rainfair SafetyProducts
3600 S Memorial Dr
Racine, WI 53403-3822 262-554-7000
Fax: 414-554-6619 800-558-5990
info@lacrossesafety.com
Manufactures protective outerware, footwear, aprons and insulated clothing
CEO: Joe Schneider
CFO: Bruce Bartelt
Vice President: Gregg Liederbach
Public Relations: Anna Gardner
Plant Manager: John Schleicher
Purchasing Manager: Cindy Krause
Estimated Sales: $44 Million
Number Employees: 100-249

25124 Ladder Works
1125 E Saint Charles Rd
Lombard, IL 60148-2085 630-629-7154
Fax: 630-268-9655 800-419-5880
Manufacturer and exporter of flag poles and flags
Owner: Ed Reeder
Inside Sales Manager: Lisa Simpson
Estimated Sales: $10-20,000,000
Number Employees: 20-49
Parent Co: Uncommon USA

25125 (HQ)Lady Mary
126 Lady Mary Lane
PO Box 157
Rockingham, NC 28379-4965 910-997-7321
Fax: 910-997-7324 ladymaryinc@etinternet.net
www.ladymaryinc.com
Round, rectangular, round/square, moisture/grease proof and recyclable disposable cake boards
President: Mary Stanley
Estimated Sales: $2.5-5 Million
Number Employees: 10-19
Square Footage: 80000
Other Locations:
Lady Mary
Rockingham NC
Brands:
Dainty Boards
Party Plates
Tuftboard

25126 Lafayette Sign Company
47 Sindle Ave
Little Falls, NJ 07424-1650 973-812-5000
Fax: 973-812-8222 800-343-5366
pad@lafayettesign.com www.lafayettesign.com
Plastic and neon signs
President: John Scott
Permit Coordinator: Gerald Koczot
Estimated Sales: $1-2.5 Million
Number Employees: 10-19

25127 Lafayette Tent & AwningCompany
125 S 5th St
Lafayette, IN 47901 765-742-4277
Fax: 765-742-4462 800-458-2955
lta@lafayettent.com www.lafayettetent.com
Commercial awnings and rental tents/full line special event rental firm.
President: Henry Ebershoff
CEO: Craig Ebershoff
CFO: Craig Ebershoff
Vice President: Craig Ebershoff
Research & Development: Craig Ebershoff
Quality Control: Craig Ebershoff
Marketing Director: Craig Ebershoff
Sales Director: Craig Ebershoff
Public Relations: Craig Ebershoff
Operations Manager: Craig Ebershoff
Production Manager: Craig Ebershoff
Plant Manager: Craig Ebershoff
Purchasing Manager: Craig Ebershoff
Estimated Sales: $5-10,000,000
Number Employees: 20-49

25128 Lafitte Cork & Capsule
45 Executive Court
Napa, CA 94558-6267 707-258-2675
Fax: 707-258-0558 800-343-2675
info@lafitte-usa.com www.lafitte-usa.com
Wine industry corks and capsules
President: David Hanson
VP: Barry Rucker
Estimated Sales: $1-2.5 Million
Number Employees: 10-19

25129 Laggren's
P.O.Box 7173
Monroe Township, NJ 08831 908-756-1948
Fax: 908-756-7560 dlasser@comcast.net
Commercial awnings, window treatments, canopies, custom draperies, flags, flagpoles, banners, and radiator covers and enclosures.
President: David Lasser
Estimated Sales: $1-2,500,000
Number Employees: 10-19
Square Footage: 7000

25130 Laidig Industrial Systems
14535 Dragoon Trl
Mishawaka, IN 46544 574-256-0204
Fax: 574-256-5575 sales@laidig.com
www.laidig.com
Manufacturer and exporter of bulk material steel storage structures and handling systems including conveyors
President: Wyn Laidig
SVP: Tom J Lindenman
Vice President Marketing/Information: Daniel Laidig
Vice President Sales: Mike Laidig
VP, Manufacturing: Dan Collins
Estimated Sales: $5-10 Million
Number Employees: 50-99
Parent Co: LIS Corporation

25131 Lail Design Group
1505 Main St
Saint Helena, CA 94574 707-963-1565
Fax: 707-963-4509 info@laildesign.com
www.laildesign.com
Facility planning and design
Principal Architect: S Doug Osborn
Principal Architect: Paul Kelley
Marketing Director: Tim Martin
Manager: Doug Osborn
Estimated Sales: $1.6 Million
Number Employees: 10-19

25132 Laitram Machinery
220 Laitram Ln.
Harahan, LA 70123-5308 504-733-6000
Fax: 504-733-6111 800-533-8253
www.laitrammachinery.com
Manufactures high-quality, stainless steel equipment for the seafood processing industry. Product line includes shrimp peeling systems, shrimp grading systems, shrimp deveiners, and seafood steam cookers and chillers
President: Paul Gariepy
Marketing Director: Albert Esparza
Operations Manager: Albert Wilson
Estimated Sales: $8.7 Million
Number Employees: 81
Parent Co: Laitram Corporation

25133 Lake City Signs
604 Avenue C
Boulder City, NV 89005-2738 702-293-5805
Fax: 705-293-0624
Electric signs, pennants and banners; also, lettering service available
Co-Owner: Denise Henderson

25134 Lake Eyelet Manufacturing Company
123 Old Canal Way
Weatogue, CT 06089-9688 860-628-5543
Fax: 860-628-4899
Eyelet machinery products including bottle capping, ferrules, shells and stampings
Sales Manager: Joseph Ciriello
Estimated Sales: $2.5-5 Million
Number Employees: 50-100

25135 Lake Michigan Hardwood Company
PO Box 265
Leland, MI 49654-0265 231-256-9811
Wooden pallets
Estimated Sales: $2.5-5 Million
Number Employees: 19

25136 Lake Process Systems
27930 W Commercial Ave
Lake Barrington, IL 60010-2442 847-381-7663
Fax: 847-381-7688 800-331-9260
paul@lakeprocess.com www.lakeprocess.com
Cleaning and sanitizing systems, fittings, CIP and COP units, skid systems and sanitary heat exchangers; also, design and installation of process and CIP systems available
President: Paul Harris
Secretary/Treasurer: Rebecca Harris

Estimated Sales: $1-2.5 Million
Number Employees: 10-19

25137 Lake Shore Industries
1817 Poplar St
Erie, PA 16512 814-456-4277
Fax: 814-453-4293 800-458-0463
info@lsisigns.com www.lsisigns.com
Interior and exterior signage; exporter of signs and markers
President: Leo Bruno
Estimated Sales: $2.5 - 5 Million
Number Employees: 10-19
Square Footage: 19240
Brands:
Lashimar
Letter-Lites

25138 Lakeland Rubber Stamp Company
PO Box 372
Lakeland, FL 33802-0372 863-682-5111
Fax: 863-682-5114 www.holmesstamp.com
Rubber stamps
President: James Bronson
Quality Control: Hood Thom
VP Marketing: Thomas Hood
Estimated Sales: $10-20 Million
Number Employees: 5-9

25139 Lakeside Container Corporation
299 Arizona Ave
Plattsburgh, NY 12903 518-561-6150
Fax: 518-561-4449 www.lakesidecontainer.com
Corrugated boxes and pads
President: George Bouyea
CFO: Paige Raville
Plant Manager: Tom Vaughan
Estimated Sales: $1 - 2.5 Million
Number Employees: 10-19

25140 (HQ)Lakeside Manufacturing
4900 W Electric Ave
Milwaukee, WI 53219 414-902-6400
Fax: 414-902-6545 888-558-8574
info@elakeside.com www.elakeside.com
Manufacturer and exporter of mobile material handling and food service equipment including carts, racks, containers, dispensers, portable beverage bars, etc
President: Joe Carlson
Chairman/CEO: Lawrence Moon
Chairman of the Board: Lawrence Moon
VP Sales: Alex Carayannopoulos
Estimated Sales: $10 - 20 Million
Number Employees: 100-249
Brands:
Adjust-A-Fit
Aris
Condi Express
Creation Station
Ergo-One
Extreme Duty
Lakeside
Party Pleaser
Serv 'n Express

25141 Lakeside-Aris Manufacturing
1977 S Allis Street
Milwaukee, WI 53207-1248 414-481-3900
Fax: 414-481-9313 800-558-8565
lakeside@corrections.com www.earis.com
Manufacturer and exporter of serving carts and culinary display trays
VP: Jon Carlson
VP Sales: Alex Carayannopoulos
Estimated Sales: $10-20 Million
Number Employees: 100-249
Parent Co: Lakeside Manufacturing
Type of Packaging: Consumer, Food Service

25142 Lakeview Rubber Stamp Company
4316 N Lincoln Ave
Chicago, IL 60618 773-539-1525
Fax: 773-539-2718
Rubber stamps
Owner: Terry Lange
*Estimated Sales:*less than $500,000
Number Employees: 1-4
Square Footage: 1100

25143 Lakewood Engineering & Manufacturing Company
501 N Sacramento Blvd
Chicago, IL 60612-1099 773-722-4300
Fax: 773-722-1541 800-621-4277
custserv@lakewoodeng.com
www.lakewoodeng.com
Industrial and portable electric fans and heaters; also, heavy-duty and ball-bearing swivels, plastic and metal christmas tree stands
President: David Hirschfield
VP Marketing: Charles Herndon
Sales/Marketing Executive: Chip Herndon
National Sales Manager: Dennis McCarthy
Purchasing Agent: Lou Petrrica
Purchasing Agent: John Sharkey
Estimated Sales: $80 Million
Number Employees: 500-999
Square Footage: 750000

25144 Lakewood Processing Machinery
875 Brooks Ave
Holland, MI 49423-5338
Fax: 616-392-8977 800-366-6705
info@lakewoodpm.com www.lakewoodpm.com
Sizers, netweight fillers, checkweighers, washers, volumetric fillers, color sorters
President: Mike Miedema
VP Sales & Marketing: Denny Schepel
R & D: Dale Miedima
Estimated Sales: $5-10 Million
Number Employees: 10-19

25145 Lako Tool & Manufacturing
7400 Ponderosa Road
P.O.Box 425
Perrysburg, OH 43552 419-662-5256
Fax: 419-874-4992 800-228-2982
lsmith@lakotool.com www.lakotool.com
Sealing, cutting and punching devices
President: Larry Smith
Sales Manager: Jo Montano
Estimated Sales: $2.5-5 Million
Number Employees: 10-19

25146 Lamar
405 Country Place Pkwy
Pearl, MS 39208 601-948-3443
Fax: 601-355-6255 800-893-2560
twall@lamar.com www.lamar.com
Outdoor advertising signs
Manager: Marty Elrod
CEO: Kevin Reilly Jr.
CFO: Keith Istre
Executive Vice Prsident: Brent McCoy
Chief Marketing Officer: Thomas Teepell
Vice President, Director of National Sal: John Miller
Vice President of Operations: Robert Switzer
Estimated Sales: $5 - 10 Million
Number Employees: 20-49

25147 Lamar Advertising Co
5321 Corporate Blvd.
Baton Rouge, LA 70808 225-926-1000
www.lamar.com
Advertising signs including outdoor, painted and poster panel
CEO: Kevin Reilly
CFO: Keith Istre
Executive Vice President: Brent McCoy
Chief Marketing Officer: Thomas Teepell
Vice President, Director of National Sal: John Miller
Vice President of Operations: Robert Switzer
Estimated Sales: $2.5-5 Million
Number Employees: 10-19

25148 Lamb Sign
11979 Falling Creek Dr
Manassas, VA 20112 703-791-7960
Fax: 703-263-1761 lambsign@aol.com
www.lambsign.com
Building identification and marking devices including metal letters, directory and bulletin boards and signs
President: Robert W Schneider
VP: R Wiesheier
Estimated Sales: Below $5 Million
Number Employees: 1-4
Square Footage: 61200

25149 Lambert Company
PO Box 740
Chillicothe, MO 64601-0740 660-646-2150
Fax: 660-646-2152 800-821-7667
Manufacturer and exporter of work gloves and headwear
President: James Lambert
CFO: James Lambert
Estimated Sales: $5 - 10 Million
Number Employees: 6
Type of Packaging: Consumer, Food Service, Private Label

25150 (HQ)Lambert Material Handling
6581 Townline Rd
Syracuse, NY 13206 315-471-5103
Fax: 315-478-2804 800-253-5103
www.lambertpalletizers.com
Palletizers and conveyor systems
Purchasing: Wendy Lewke
Number Employees: 10-19
Type of Packaging: Consumer
Other Locations:
Lambert Material Handling
Baldwinsville NY

25151 Lambertson Industries
1335 Alexandria Ct
Sparks, NV 89434 775-857-1100
Fax: 775-857-3289 800-548-3324
sales@lamberston.com www.lambertson.com
Stainless steel manufacturing
President: Theodore Lambertson
Marketing Director: Justin Pecot
Sales Manager: Ken Hewson
Operations Manager: Joseph McCaslin
Production Manager: Oswaldo Garcia
Estimated Sales: $1.5-3,500,000
Number Employees: 20-49
Square Footage: 30000
Brands:
L.I. Industries

25152 Lambeth Band Corporation
PO Box 50490
New Bedford, MA 02745-0017 508-984-4700
Fax: 508-984-4780 lambeth@tiac.net
lambethbandsbelts.com
Manufacturer and exporter of belting including nylon and urethane elastic bands.
President: Braley Gray
CEO: Lisa Larsen
Estimated Sales: $3 - 5 Million
Number Employees: 5-9
Square Footage: 14000
Brands:
Lambeth Band

25153 Lamco Chemical Company
212 Arlington St
Chelsea, MA 02150-2313 617-884-8470
Fax: 617-889-4207
Floor wax and cleaner
President: Jim Lam
Estimated Sales: $1 - 3 Million
Number Employees: 1-4

25154 Lamcor
8025 South Willow Street
Unit 109
Minneapolis, NH 3103 603-647-6386
Fax: 603-647-6388 info@Lamcor.com
www.lamcor.com
Tea and coffee industry packaging materials
Estimated Sales: $5-10 Million
Number Employees: 45

25155 Lamcraft
4131 NE Port Dr
Lees Summit, MO 64064 816-795-5505
Fax: 816-795-8310 800-821-1333
customer-service@lamcraft.com
www.lamcraft.com
Laminating equipment and supplies including plastic laminates; also, plastic and paper laminating services for menus, price lists, recipe cards, table tents, etc
Owner: Bob Sabin
Finance Executive: Darlene Rose
Estimated Sales: $10-20 Million
Number Employees: 20-49

25156 Laminated Paper Products
14491 Wyrick Ave
San Jose, CA 95124-3533 408-888-0880
sales@laminatedpaperproducts.com
www.laminatedpaperproducts.com
Folding cartons
Owner: P Drake
Estimated Sales: less than $500,000
Number Employees: 1-4

25157 Laminated Papers
PO Box 351
Holyoke, MA 01041-0351 413-533-3906
Fax: 413-533-2709
Laminated waterproof paper
President: Bernard Adams
Estimated Sales: $20-50 Million
Number Employees: 50-99

25158 Laminating TechnologiesIndustries
291 N Industrial Way
Canton, GA 30115 770-704-9992
Fax: 770-704-9992 866-704-9992
pstoker@bakenship.com www.bakenship.com
Containers for hot and cold food products
Owner: Pat Haddon
Estimated Sales: $1-5 Million
Number Employees: 20-49

25159 Laminations
PO Box 8033
Appleton, WI 54912 920-831-0596
Fax: 920-831-0612 800-925-2626
webgnc@greatnortherncorp.com
www.laminationsonline.com
Uboard edge protectors
President: Richard C Detienne
Estimated Sales: $10-20 Million
Number Employees: 50-99

25160 Lamotte Company
P.O.Box 329
Chestertown, MD 21620-0329 410-778-3100
Fax: 410-778-6394 800-344-3100
mkt@lamotte.com www.lamotte.com
Kits, test strips and meters for water analysis, monitoring sanitizer and caustic or acid cleaner concentrations, process or waste waters and boiler and cooling tower waters
President: David Lamotte
CFO: Roland Willis
Quality Control: Susan Franklin
Marketing Director: Sue Byerly
VP Sales: Richard Lamotte
Estimated Sales: $50 - 100 Million
Number Employees: 100-249

25161 Lamports Filter Media
777 E 82nd St
Cleveland, OH 44103-1817 216-881-2050
Fax: 216-881-8957 info@lamports.com
www.lamports.com
Manufacturer and exporter of fabricated textiles for air and liquid filtration
President: Walter Senney
Customer Service: Jennifer Geraci
Estimated Sales: $5 - 10 Million
Number Employees: 20-49
Square Footage: 120000

25162 Lampson Tractor Equipment
P.O.Box 85
Geyserville, CA 95441-0085 707-967-3554
Fax: 707-967-3575 jmarcust@sbcglobal.net
www.lampsontractor.com
Power equipment
Manager: Mark Terrell
Estimated Sales: $5-10 Million
Number Employees: 10-19

25163 Lamson & Goodnow Manufacturing Company
45 Conway St
Shelburne Falls, MA 01370 413-625-0201
Fax: 413-625-9816 800-872-6564
info@lamsonsharp.com www.lamsonsharp.com
Manufacturer and exporter of culinary knives including butchers' cleavers, bread, cheese and steak
President: Ross Anderson
CFO: David Dunn
Marketing: Kurt Saunders
Sales Manager: Kurt Zanner
Plant Manager: Fran Gipe
Estimated Sales: $10 - 20 Million
Number Employees: 50-99
Type of Packaging: Consumer, Food Service, Private Label, Bulk
Brands:
Lamson
Lamson Sharp

25164 Lancaster ColonyCorporation
37 West Broad Street
Columbus, OH 43215 614-224-7141
Fax: 614-469-8219 www.lancastercolony.com
Litho paper labels and laminations; commercial printing available
Chairman/ President/ CEO & Director: John B. Gerlach, Jr.
VP/ CFO/ Treasurer/ Asst. Secretary & Di: John L. Boylan
Vice President: Bruce L. Rosa
General Manager: Kevin Haitt
Estimated Sales: Below $5 Million
Number Employees: 1,000-4,999
Parent Co: Lancaster Colony Corporation

25165 Lancaster Colony Commercial Products
2353 Westbrooke Drive
Columbus, OH 43228 614-876-1026
Fax: 614-876-1276 800-528-2278
info@lccpinc.com www.lccpinc.com
Glassware, cookware, rubber floor matting and coffee urns; importer of glassware; exporter of coffee urns and ice molds
President: Ken Evans
Executive VP: Ken Evans
Vice President: Thomas Deschler
Research & Development: Lou Lemoine
VP Marketing: Dick Anderson
VP Grocery Sales: Gary Thompson
Technical Director: Paul Pratt
Operations Manager: Watts Patterson
Purchasing Manager: Tom Kellett
Estimated Sales: $5 - 9.9 Million
Number Employees: 10-19
Parent Co: Lancaster Colony Corporation
Other Locations:
Lancaster Colony Commercial P
Cincinnati OH
Brands:
Candle-Lite
Cardini
Chatham Village Foods
Colony
Girard's Dressings
Girard's Mr. Marinade
Indiana Glass
Inn Maid Premium Egg Noodles
Jack Daniels Mustard
Marzetti
Mountain Top
Ny Hearth Baked Frozen Breads
Nyracord
Pfeiffer Salad Dressing
Reames Frozen Pasta
Romanoff Caviar
Texas Best Barbecue Sauce
Texas Best Steak Sauce
Texas Garlic Toast

25166 Lancaster Colony Corporation
P.O.Box 630
37 West Broad St.
Columbus, OH 43216-0630 614-224-7141
Fax: 614-469-8219 800-292-7260
www.lancastercolony.com
Manufacturer and exporter of amenities including glassware, ice and food molds, iced tea dispensers, wood grain serving trays, ice buckets, aluminum cookware and commercial coffee urns, candles and matting
Chairman/CEO/President/Director: John Gerlach Jr.
Vice President/CFO/Treasurer: John Boylan
Estimated Sales: $1.13 Billion
Number Employees: 3100
Square Footage: 223000

25167 Lancaster Laboratories
PO Box 12425
Lancaster, PA 17605 717-656-2300
Fax: 717-656-2681 env@lancasterlabs.com
www.lancasterlabs.com
Analytical laboratory providing comprehensive sanitation and pollution testing, microbiology, method development and validation/quality control services
President: J Wilson Hershey
Manager: Art Pezzica
Directory Contact: Anne Osborn
Estimated Sales: $20-50 Million
Number Employees: 500-999
Square Footage: 175000

25168 (HQ)Lancer Corporation
6655 Lancer Blvd
San Antonio, TX 78219 210-310-7000
Fax: 210-310-7088 800-729-1565
www.lancercorp.com
Manufacturer and exporter of soft drink dispensing equipment
President: Luis Alvarez
Estimated Sales: $52 Million
Number Employees: 515
Square Footage: 1000000
Type of Packaging: Food Service
Other Locations:
Lancer Corp.
Beverley

25169 Land O'Lakes
4001 Lexington Ave N.
Arden Hills, MN 55126-2998 651-481-2222
Fax: 651-481-2000 800-328-9680
www.landolakesinc.com
Dairy-based food products for consumers, foodservice professionals and food manufacturers. Butter and deli cheese.
President/CEO: Christopher Policinsky
Exec VP & CFO: Dan Knutson
Chief Marketing Officer: Barry Wolfish
Sr. VP & Chief Human Resources Officer: Loren Heeringa
Exec VP, Chief Supply Chain & Operations: Beth Ford
Estimated Sales: $12.85 Million
Number Employees: 9,000
Number of Products: 300+
Square Footage: 275000
Type of Packaging: Consumer, Food Service, Private Label, Bulk
Other Locations:
Land O'Lakes
Gustine CA
Brands:
Land O Lakes
Purina Feed
Winfield Solutions

25170 Landau Uniforms
8410 W Sandidge Rd
Olive Branch, MS 38654 662-895-7200
Fax: 662-895-5099 800-238-7513
sales@landau.com www.landau.com
Manufacturer, importer and exporter of aprons, shirts and fast-food uniforms
President: Nat Landau
CEO: Bruce Landau
CFO: Nancy Russell
Vice President: Gregg Landau
Quality Control: Dale Scott
Estimated Sales: $20 - 50 Million
Number Employees: 250-499
Type of Packaging: Food Service
Brands:
Landau

25171 Landen Strapping Company
5050 Prince George Dr
Prince George, VA 23875 804-452-0011
Fax: 804-452-2011 landenservice@gmail.com
plasticstrappingmachines.com
Owner: Margaret Spencer

25172 Landis Plastics
5750 W 118th St
Alsip, IL 60803-6012 708-396-1470
Fax: 708-824-3722 berryplastics.com
Manufacturer and exporter of injected molded plastic packaging supplies including can lids, jar caps, containers, scoops and pails; exporter of containers and lids
Manager: H R Landis
Vice President: Jennifer Bjerga
Purchasing: Tim Brenner
Estimated Sales: $50-100 Million
Number Employees: 300
Square Footage: 102063
Parent Co: Berry Plastics Group, Inc.

25173 Landmark Kitchen Design
1900 W. Chandler Blvd.
Phoenix, AZ 85224 602-443-0344
Fax: 623-846-6877 866-621-3192
sean@landmarkphx.com www.landmarkphx.com
Principal: Sean Kellenbarger
Vice President: Sean Kellenbarger
VP R&D: John Andrews
Project Coordinator: Sean P Kellenbarger
Estimated Sales: Below $5 Million
Number Employees: 1-4

25174 Landoll Corporation
P.O.Box 111
Marysville, KS 66508 785-562-5381
Fax: 785-562-4891 mhpsales@landoll.com
www.landoll.com
Manufacturer and exporter of articulated front-wheel steered forklifts and electric forklift trucks for narrow aisle storage applications
President: Donald Landoll
CEO: Ron Otten
CFO: Dan Caffrry
R&D: Dave Kongs
Quality Control: Henk Crucker
Sales Director: Alan Laney
Estimated Sales: $30 - 50 Million
Number Employees: 500-999
Number of Brands: 2
Number of Products: 1
Square Footage: 350000
Type of Packaging: Bulk
Brands:
Bendi
Pivotmast

25175 Landoo Corporation
331 Maple Avenue
Horsham, PA 19044-2139 785-562-5381
Fax: 785-562-4853 kfox@drexeltrucks.com
www.drexeltrucks.com
Manufacturer and exporter of lift trucks
President: Jon Landoo
CFO: Dan Caffrey
Quality Control: Hank Burker
R & D: Dave Kongs
Marketing Supporting Manager: Jennifer Reynolds
VP Sales Manager: Kim Wanamaker
Export Sales Manager: Dave Pederson
Estimated Sales: $20-50 Million
Number Employees: 10
Square Footage: 65000

25176 Landsman Foodservice Net
2403 Logan Road
Owing Mills, MD 21117 410-363-7038
Fax: 301-330-4299 jeff@ifsn.com
Employment agency/executive search firm specializing in selection and placement of food service industry personnel
President: Jeffrey Landsman
Estimated Sales: Less than $500,000
Number Employees: 4
Parent Co: Winston Franchise Corporation

25177 Lane Award Manufacturing
1118 S Central Ave
Phoenix, AZ 85004-2734 602-258-8505
Fax: 602-254-5489 800-843-2581
info@laneaward.com www.laneaward.com
Corporate and personal awards, business gifts, advertising and promotional items
President: John Luvisi
National Sales Manager: David Norgord
General Manager: Mack Gleekel
Purchasing Manager: Mike Abril
Estimated Sales: Below $5 Million
Number Employees: 20-49
Square Footage: 80000

25178 Lang Manufacturing Company
6500 Merrill Creek Pkwy
Everett, WA 98203-5860 425-349-2400
Fax: 425-349-2733 800-882-6368
info@langworld.com www.langworld.com
Offer a quality line of innovative gas and electric commercial cooking equipment to the commercial, retail, marine, correctional, and government foodservice inductries
CEO: Tracy Olson
Executive VP: Steve Hegge
Manager of Marketing: Annette Steinbach
Vice President of Sales and Marketing: Jim Baxter
Purchasing Manager: Mark Johnston
Estimated Sales: $20-50 Million
Number Employees: 100
Square Footage: 90000
Type of Packaging: Food Service
Brands:
Pane Bella

25179 (HQ)Langen Packaging
6154 Kestrel Road
Mississauga, ON L5T 1Z2
Canada 905-670-7200
Fax: 905-670-5291 sales@langeninc.com
www.langeninc.com
Manufacturer and exporter of packaging machinery and carton and case packers
President: Stuart Cooper
CFO: Alan Makhan
VP Marketing/Sales: Kevin Walsh
VP Engineering: Peter Guttinger
Purchasing Manager: Elinor Workman
Estimated Sales: $20 - 30 Million
Number Employees: 100
Square Footage: 80000

25180 (HQ)Langer Manufacturing Company
1025 7th Street SW
Cedar Rapids, IA 52404-1918 319-362-1481
Fax: 319-364-7131 800-728-6445
langermfg@aol.com
Manufacturer and exporter of wire products including milk bottle crates, bakery racks, partitioned cases, custom baskets and display racks
President: John R Langer
CEO: James M Langer
Sales: John Langer
Operations: James Langer
Estimated Sales: $2.5 Million
Number Employees: 20-49
Number of Products: 150
Square Footage: 40000

25181 Langer Manufacturing Company
1025 7th Street SW
Cedar Rapids, IA 52404-1918 319-362-1481
Fax: 319-364-7131 800-728-6445
langermfg@aol.com
Carriers, racks, P.O.P. displays
President: John R Langer
Estimated Sales: $2 Million
Number Employees: 55

25182 Langsenkamp Manufacturing
1699 South 8th St
Indianapolis, IN 46060 317-773-2100
Fax: 317-585-1715 877-585-1950
rogerm@warnerbodies.com
www.warnerbodies.com
Manufacturer and exporter of canning and food processing machinery including pumps, finishers, tanks, can openers and crushers, etc
President: Rick Manasek
Sales: Roger McNew
Controller: Bryan Lindsay
Estimated Sales: $2.5-5 Million
Number Employees: 18-25
Number of Brands: 1
Number of Products: 10
Square Footage: 31000

25183 (HQ)Langston Bag Company
PO Box 60
Memphis, TN 38101-0060 901-774-4440
Fax: 901-942-5402 lango@bellsouth.net
www.langstonbag.com
Manufacturer and exporter of bags including burlap, produce and multi-wall paper
CEO: Robert Langston
Production Manager: Steve Winston
Estimated Sales: $20-50 Million
Number Employees: 50-99

25184 Lanly Company
26201 Tungsten Rd
Cleveland, OH 44132-2997 216-731-1115
Fax: 216-731-7900 sales@lanly.com
www.lanly.com
Designs and builds custom heat processing equipment for an extensive range of industries.
President: Dennis Hill
Sales Director: Ed Chapman
Plant Manager: Tim Brooks
Estimated Sales: $5-10 Million
Number Employees: 20-49
Square Footage: 68000

25185 Lanly Company
26201 Tungsten Rd
Cleveland, OH 44132 216-731-1115
Fax: 216-731-7900 lanly@lanly.com
www.lanly.com
Custom heat process equipment: dryers, ovens, material handling equipment and controls
VP: Dennis Hill
Plant Manager: Tim Brooks
Estimated Sales: $5-10 Million
Number Employees: 20-49

25186 Lanmar
3160 Doolittle Drive
Northbrook, IL 60062 847-564-5520
Fax: 847-564-4682 800-233-5520
ptfe@lanmarinc.com www.lanmarinc.com
PTFE tapes, PTFE fabrics, custom PTFE belts.
President: Martin Jacobs
Sales Director: Paul Siegal
Production: Logan Jacobs
Estimated Sales: $1-2.5 Million
Number Employees: 1-4
Type of Packaging: Food Service, Private Label

25187 Lansing Corrugated Products
16248 S Lowell Rd
Lansing, MI 48906-9324 517-323-2752
Fax: 517-323-9322
Corrugated and fiber boxes

25188 Lansmont CorporationRyan Ranch Research Park
17 Mandeville Court
Monterey, CA 93940-5745 831-655-6600
Fax: 831-655-6606 sales@lansmont.com
www.lansmont.com
Shock, drop, field data recorders, vibration, compression, data acquisition systems.
President: Joe Driscoll
CFO: Patti Monahan
VP: Peter Brown
Vice President Marketing/Business Dvlpmt: Eric Joneson
Customer Support Manager: Eric Whitfield
Customer Support Specialist: Aaron Brown
Estimated Sales: $5 - 10 Million
Number Employees: 50-99

25189 Lantech
11000 Bluegrass Pkwy
Jeffersontown, KY 40299-2399 502-267-4200
Fax: 502-266-5031 800-866-0322
jerryt@lantech.com www.lantech.com
Stretch wrappers, palletizers, conveyor systems
President: Jim Lancaster
Estimated Sales: $50 - 75 Million
Number Employees: 250-499

25190 Larco
210 10th Ave NE
Brainerd, MN 56401 218-829-9797
Fax: 218-829-0139 800-523-6996
sales@larcomfg.com www.larcomfg.com
Manufacturer and exporter of switch mats and controls for machine guarding safety
President: Jim Bartel
Sales Manager: Joe Schultz
Estimated Sales: $2.5-5 Million
Number Employees: 20-49
Parent Co: Acrometal Companies

25191 Larien Products
351 Pleasant St
PMB 224
Northampton, MA 01060 413-586-4000
Fax: 413-585-0101 800-462-9237
lsmith@larien.com www.larien.com

Larien is noted for a patented bagel slicing design that safely isolates the user from the slicing action. We manufacture a consumer model and a commercial model
President: Rick Ricard
CEO: Lois Smith
National Sales Manager: Jim Dodge
Operations: Elizabeth DiVito
Estimated Sales: $1 Million
Number Employees: 1-4
Number of Brands: 4
Number of Products: 4
Type of Packaging: Consumer, Food Service
Brands:
Bagel Biter
Bagel Butler
Commerical Bagel Biter
Original Bagel Guillotine
Original Bigfoot Bottle Inversion

25192 **Larkin Industries**
114 David Green Rd
Birmingham, AL 35244 205-987-1535
Fax: 205-987-0583 800-322-4036
Ventilation systems including exhaust hoods and fans, supply fans, heated make-up air units, duct work and roof curbs
Owner: Larkin Strong
VP: Stephen Ridlespurge
Sales: Thomas Renfroe
Estimated Sales: $2.5 - 5 Million
Number Employees: 20-49
Square Footage: 40000

25193 **Larose & Fils Lt^e**
2255 Industrial Boulevard
Laval, QC H7S 1P8
Canada 514-382-7000
Fax: 450-667-8515 877-382-7001
info@larose.ca www.larose.ca
Cleaning equipment and supplies including sweepers, pressure washers, germicides, disinfectants, drain openers, etc.; industrial floor polishers and waxstrippers; importer of vacuum cleaners
President: Jean Larose
CEO: Manon Larose
CFO: Richard Colerette
VP: Pierre Larose
Research & Development: Andr^ Foisy
Quality Control: Yves Lafrances
Marketing Director: France Morin
Sales Director: Andr^ Foisy
Public Relations: France Morin
Operations Manager: Manon Larose
Purchasing Manager: Anick Murray
Number Employees: 40
Square Footage: 120000
Parent Co: Labchem
Type of Packaging: Consumer, Food Service, Private Label
Brands:
Indo
Rare
Sensas
Sublime

25194 **Larry B. Newman PrintingCompany**
2010 Middlebrook Pike
Knoxville, TN 37921 865-524-1338
Fax: 865-524-1377 888-835-4566
info@larrynewmanprinting.com
larrynewmanprinting.com
Mounted and unmounted rubber stamps; also, engraved stationery
President: Larry Newman
Manager: Brian McMillan
Estimated Sales: Below $5 Million
Number Employees: 1-4
Square Footage: 21600
Type of Packaging: Consumer, Private Label, Bulk

25195 **Larson Pallet Company**
W4995 Bjorklund Rd
Ogema, WI 54459 715-767-5131
Fax: 715-767-5888
Pallets
President: Gerald Larson
Secretary: Gerald Larson
Estimated Sales: $1-2.5 Million
Number Employees: 20-49

25196 **Laschober & Sovich**
20301 Ventura Blvd
Suite 338
Woodland Hills, CA 91364-0949 818-713-9011
Fax: 818-713-1104 llanier@laschobersovich.com
www.laschobersovich.com
Consultant specializing in commercial kitchen design for quick serve restaurants, hotels and casinos, institutional facilities, prisons, hospitals, schools, etc
President: Larry Lanier
VP, Global Ideation: Klaus Mager
Project Manager: Jonathan Turnbull
VP, Global Ideation: Joy Shelter
Business Development: Carolyn Nott
Estimated Sales: $1 - 3 Million
Number Employees: 5-9

25197 **Lasco Composites**
8015 Dixon Dr
Florence, KY 41042 859-371-7720
Fax: 859-371-8466 kemlitesales@kemlite.com
www.kemlite.com
Composite fiberglass reinforced wall/ceiling panels
Executive VP, Business Development: Jim Simmons
Vice President Of Sales: Jack Stambaugh
Plant Manager: Jeff Rasmussen
Estimated Sales: $15 - 20 Million
Number Employees: 100-249

25198 **Lasermation**
2629 N 15th St
Philadelphia, PA 19132-3904 215-228-7900
Fax: 215-225-1593 800-523-2759
laser66555@aol.com www.lasermation.com
Manufacturer and exporter of brass and mylar stencils, awards, wine holders, pepper grinding mills and wooden back bar displays. Signs, executive gifts and awards
President: Joseph Molines
Estimated Sales: $1-3 Million
Number Employees: 10-19
Square Footage: 25000
Type of Packaging: Private Label

25199 **Lasertechnics**
80 Colonnade Rd
Nepean, OC K2E 7L2 613-749-4895
Fax: 613-749-8179
webinquiry@lightmachinery.com
www.lasertechnics.com
CEO: Martin Janiak

25200 **Lasertechnics Marking Corporation**
80 Colonnade Road
Nepean, ON K2E 7L2 613-749-4895
Fax: 613-749-8179
webinquiry@lightmachinery.com
www.lasertechnics.com
Manufacturer and exporter of laser code markers and date/code marking equipment
CEO: Martin Janiak
Sales/Marketing: Bob Michael
Director Sales Administration: Bob Baker
Estimated Sales: $2.5-5 Million
Number Employees: 20-49
Square Footage: 96000
Parent Co: Quantrad Sensor
Brands:
Blazer

25201 **Lask Seating Company**
3700 S Iron Street
Chicago, IL 60609-2118 773-254-3448
Fax: 773-254-1373 888-573-2846
stoolsandchairs@aol.com
www.stoolsandchairs.com
Wooden and metal chairs, stools, tabletops and bases
President and CFO: David Prawer
CEO: David Prawer
CFO: Judith Friedman
R&D: Howia Prawer
Estimated Sales: $3 - 5 Million
Number Employees: 25
Square Footage: 168000

25202 **Latendorf Corporation**
PO Box 205
Brielle, NJ 08730-0205 732-528-0180
Fax: 732-528-6804 800-526-4057
Manufacturer, importer and exporter of bakery machinery
Owner: Malcolm Latendorf
Estimated Sales: $1 - 5 Million
Number Employees: 50-99
Square Footage: 60000

25203 **Latendorf Corporation**
PO Box 205
Brielle, NJ 08730-0205 732-528-0180
Fax: 732-528-6804
Conveyor systems
Estimated Sales: $10-25 Million
Number Employees: 73

25204 **Laticrete International**
91 Amity Rd
Bethany, CT 06524 203-393-0010
Fax: 203-393-1684 800-243-4788
support@laticrete.com www.laticrete.com
President: David Rothbert
CFO: Jim Walker
CEO: David Rothberg
R&D: Clodio Nicolini
Quality Control: Dilsa Hawkins
Estimated Sales: $50 - 100 Million
Number Employees: 100-249

25205 **Latini Products Company**
893 Industrial Drive
Elmhurst, IL 60126-1117 630-834-7789
Fax: 630-834-4322 sales@latini-hohberger.com
www.latini-hohberger.com
Flat and ball lollipop machines, formers and wrapers
Director: Roger Hohberger
Estimated Sales: $3 - 5 Million
Number Employees: 10-19

25206 **Latter Packaging Equipment**
3206 W Jefferson Blvd
Los Angeles, CA 90018 323-737-0440
Fax: 323-737-4867 800-582-7711
info@latter.com www.latter.com
Modular shrink packaging systems including mini L-sealer shrink tunnel systems, one arm bar sealer systems, shrink band tunnels and conveyors and easy open shrink film tab system
President: Melvin Latter
CFO: Melvin Latter
R&D: Melvin Latter
Estimated Sales: $5 - 10 Million
Number Employees: 10-19

25207 **Laub/Hunt Packaging Systems**
13547 Excelsior Dr
Norwalk, CA 90650 562-802-9591
Fax: 562-802-8183 888-671-9338
info@laubhunt.com www.laubhunt.com
Manufacturer and exporter of liquid fillers
President: Edward Hunt
Quality Control: E J Daniel
Vice President: Jeff Hunt
Marketing Director: Jean Pei
Estimated Sales: Below $5 Million
Number Employees: 5-9
Square Footage: 10000

25208 **Laucks' Testing Laboratories**
940 S Harney St
Seattle, WA 98108 206-767-5060
Fax: 206-767-5063 info@laucksiabs.com
www.laucksiabs.com
Laboratory providing nutrient labeling and chemical and microbiological analyses.and mainly testing labs
President: Mike Owens
Technical Director: Mike Nelson
CFO: Jeff Owens
Chairman: James Owens
Lab Director: Kathy Kreps
Marketing/Sales: Mike Owens
Sr. Project Manager: Hugh Prentice
Estimated Sales: $5 - 10 Million
Number Employees: 55
Square Footage: 25000

25209 **Laughlin Corporation**
PO Box 163873
Fort Worth, TX 76161 817-625-7756
Fax: 817-625-0687
sales@laughlincorporation.com
www.laughlinconveyor.com
Manufacturer and exporter of conveyor systems including metal belt, chain, vibrating, magnetic, roller, etc.; also, custom designing available
President: Matt Laughlin Jr
VP Engineering/Manufacturing: David Laughlin
Sales Manager: Gene Fields

Estimated Sales: $1 - 2.5 Million
Number Employees: 10
Square Footage: 200000

25210 **Lauhoff Corporation**
241 Chene St
Detroit, MI 48207 313-259-0027
Fax: 313-259-2652 lauhoff@concentric.net
Cereal flaking mills and cookers, lab equipment and special process machinery
CEO: George H Lauhoff
President: Charles Lauhoff
VP: Greg Brecht
Estimated Sales: $20-30 Million
Number Employees: 10-19
Square Footage: 20000

25211 **Laundry Aids**
602 Washington Ave # A
Carlstadt, NJ 07072-2902 201-933-3500
Fax: 201-933-5193 nrosa@la-mp.com
Cleaning supplies including ammonia, fabric softener and laundry and dish detergent; contract packager of liquids in plastic bottles
President: R A Yaffa
VP Sales: Ved Sing
Purchasing Agent: Lou Gagliano
Estimated Sales: $40-60 Million
Number Employees: 250-499
Square Footage: 200000
Brands:
Fast'n Easy
Sea Mist

25212 **Laundrylux**
461 Doughty Boulevard
Inwood, NY 11096 516-371-4400
Fax: 516-371-4204 800-645-2205
info@laundrylux.com www.laundrylux.com
Commercial front load washers, dryers and dry cleaning equipment
Estimated Sales: $9 Million
Number Employees: 50
Square Footage: 80000

25213 **Laurel Awning Company**
1573 Hancock Ave
Apollo, PA 15613-8404 724-567-5689
Fax: 724-568-3152 888-567-5689
sales@laurelawnings.com
www.laurelawnings.com
Commercial awnings
Manager: Greg Schmieler
Co-Ownr.: Bonnie Schuster
Estimated Sales: $2.5-5 Million
Number Employees: 20-49

25214 **Lauritzen & Makin**
101 W Felix St
Fort Worth, TX 76115 817-921-0218
Fax: 817-921-3963 info@lmakin.com
www.lmakin.com
Custom restaurant fixtures, bars, hostess stands, serving lines, benches, stations, cabinets and table tops
President: J Hatcher James Iii
VP: Bruce Barker
Marketing/Sales Director: Georgia Clarke
General Manager: Robin Irvine
Estimated Sales: $1-2.5 Million
Number Employees: 20-49
Parent Co: Liberty Company

25215 **Laval Paper Box**
118 Hymus
Pointe Claire, QC H9R 1E8
Canada 450-669-3551
Fax: 514-694-5636
Manufacturer and exporter of cardboard boxes
President: Frank Carbone
Number Employees: 200
Type of Packaging: Bulk

25216 **Lavi Industries**
27810 Avenue Hopkins
Valencia, CA 91355-3409 661-257-9856
Fax: 661-257-4938 800-624-6225
sales@lavi.com www.lavi.com
Manufacturers of Architectural Metals, Public Guidance Systems,Hospitality Fixtures, Traditional Portable Post for Hospitality, Rope Ends & Snaps, Beltrac Series in many lengths, colors and widths, Sign Frames, Graphics, Sneeze GuardsStemware Racks, Bellman Carts, Trucks, Specialty Hardware Products and much more
President: Gavriel Lavi
Director Sales: Edward Bradford
Estimated Sales: $20 - 50 Million
Number Employees: 100-249
Square Footage: 75000
Type of Packaging: Food Service
Brands:
Beltrac

25217 **Lavo Company**
4829 W Mill Rd
Milwaukee, WI 53218-1407 414-353-2140
Fax: 414-353-4917 sales@palmerinc.com
www.palmerinc.com
Distributor of liquid soap; also, liquid and paste floor polish
Manager: Wendy Maus
Estimated Sales: $1 - 2.5 Million
Number Employees: 1-4
Parent Co: Palmer

25218 **Lawless Link**
7215 Westboro Pl # 100
San Antonio, TX 78229-4178
Fax: 210-342-8844 lawlessgrp@aol.com
Recruiter specializing in nationwide placement of mid-level and executive personnel for the food industry
President: Kathleen Lawless
CEO: John Lawless
CFO: J P Lawless
Estimated Sales: Below $5,000,000
Number Employees: 5-9

25219 **Lawrence Equipment**
2034 Peck Rd
South El Monte, CA 91733-3727 626-442-2894
Fax: 626-350-5181 800-423-4500
mteague@lawrenceequipment.com
www.lawrenceequipment.com
Manufacturer and exporter of food processing machinery including corn and flour tortilla systems, corn based snack lines and pizza forming lines; importer of dough processing equipment
President: John Lawrence
Vice President: Glenn Shelton
International Sales: Dan Woodward
Estimated Sales: $10-20 Million
Number Employees: 100-249
Square Footage: 86000

25220 **Lawrence Equipment**
2034 Peck Rd
South El Monte, CA 91733-3727 626-442-2894
Fax: 626-350-5181
mteague@lawrenceequipment.com
www.lawrenceequipment.com
Machinery for tortillas, pizzas and other flat breads
President: John Lawrence
VP: Glenn Shelton
Estimated Sales: $10-20 Million
Number Employees: 100-249

25221 **Lawrence Fabric Structures**
3509 Tree Court Ind Blvd
Saint Louis, MO 63122 636-861-0100
Fax: 636-861-0100 800-527-3840
sales@lawrencefabric.com
www.lawrencefabric.com
Commercial awnings and canopies
President: Jerel Grimaud
Vice President: Jerry Grimand
Plant Manager: John Hinckley
Purchasing Manager: Matt Roslawski
Estimated Sales: $5-10,000,000
Number Employees: 50-99

25222 **Lawrence Glaser Associates**
505 S Lenola Rd Ste 202
Moorestown, NJ 08057 856-778-9500
Fax: 856-778-4390 larryg@lgasearch.com
www.lgasearch.com
Executive search firm specializing in the selection of sales and marketing managers
President: Lawrence Glaser
Estimated Sales: Less than $500,000
Number Employees: 5-9
Square Footage: 1000

25223 **Lawrence Metal Products**
260 Spur Dr S
Bay Shore, NY 11706 800-441-0019
Fax: 631-666-0336 800-441-0019
sales@lawrencemetal.com
www.lawrencemetal.com
Manufacturer and exporter of brass, chrome and stainless steel bar railings; also, glass racks, food shields and crowd control
President: David Lawrence
CEO: Jeremy Williman
Marketing: Suzanne De Angelo
Director Sales/Marketing: Betty Castro
Estimated Sales: $10-20 Million
Number Employees: 1-4
Square Footage: 80000
Brands:
Lawrence
Tensabarrier

25224 **(HQ)Lawrence Paper Company**
PO Box 887
Lawrence, KS 66044-0887 785-843-8111
Fax: 785-749-3904 sales@lpco.net
www.lpco.net
Corrugated boxes
President: Justin Hill
Sales Manager: Mike Sullivan
Estimated Sales: $20-50 Million
Number Employees: 1-4
Square Footage: 230000

25225 **Lawrence Schiff Silk Mills**
1385 Broadway
Suite 914
New York, NY 10018 212-679-2185
Fax: 212-696-4565 800-272-4433
weborders@schiffribbons.com
www.schiffribbons.com
Manufacturer and exporter of ribbons, tapes, bindings, webbings and trims
President/CEO: Richard J. Schiff
CFO: Bruce Ershler
VP Sales/Marketing: Nancy Sherman
Estimated Sales: $5 - 10 Million
Number Employees: 10-19

25226 **Lawrence Signs**
945 Pierce Butler Rte
St Paul, MN 55104 651-488-6711
Fax: 651-488-6715 800-998-8901
info@lawrencesign.com www.lawrencesign.com
Signs and advertising displays
CEO: Rob Walker
CFO: Susan Joos
Sr. Vice President of Sales: Steve Hirtz
General Manager: Shannon King
Vice President of Sales & Marketing: Chuck Hesse
Office Manager: Brenda Aschoff
Production Manager: Joe Longtin
Estimated Sales: $2.5 - 5 Million
Number Employees: 20-49

25227 **Lawrence-Allen Group**
2031 Fairmont Drive
San Mateo, CA 94402-3925 650-345-2909
800-609-2909
info@nutrilabel.com www.nutrilabel.com
Consultant specializing in food product nutrition analysis and services for food processors and the food service market
Food Technologist: Karen Stiles
Estimated Sales: Below $500,000
Number Employees: 1

25228 **Lawson Industries**
1320 NW Us Highway 50
Holden, MO 64040-9497 816-732-4347
Crates and pallets
Owner: Donald Lawson
Estimated Sales: $500,000-$1 Million
Number Employees: 1-4

25229 **Lawson Mardon**
707 Skokie Boulevard
Suite 350
Northbrook, IL 60062-2892 847-498-7600
Fax: 847-498-7630
ezra.bowen@lawsonmardon.com

Flexible packaging
Marketing Director: Ezra Bowen
Estimated Sales: $1 - 5 Million
Number Employees: 20-50

25230 Lawson Mardon Flexible
5303 Saint Charles Rd
Bellwood, IL 60104-1048 708-544-1600
Fax: 708-649-3888 www.alcan.com
Flexible packaging including film, paper and foil
Manager: John Webster
VP Sales: Tom Grey
Director Marketing: David Stacey
Sales Manager (Food): Mitch Mekaelian
Estimated Sales: $100-500 Million
Number Employees: 100-249
Parent Co: Alusuisse-Lonza Holding Company
Brands:
Form Pack
Peelex

25231 Lawson Mardon Flexible Labels
130 Arrow Road
Weston, ON M9M 2M1
Canada 416-742-8910
Fax: 416-259-3058 www.lawsonmardon.com
Labels including rotogravure printed paper, embossed, die cut and metallized for beer and other beverages
Business Unit Director: Ray Brunelle
Parent Co: Lawson Mardon Group

25232 Lawson Mardon Packaging
PO Box O
New Hyde Park, NY 11042-0225 516-775-8000
Fax: 516-775-8723 david.pastrich@alcan.com
www.alcanpackaging.com
Manufacturer and exporter of roll labels for bottles
Mngr.: Tom Decolsmacker
Estimated Sales: $20-50 Million
Number Employees: 100-249

25233 Lawson Mardon Packaging
12500 Vulcan Way Richmond
Burnaby, BC V6V 1J9
Canada 604-278-9511
Fax: 604-439-0986 800-721-8211
www.lawsonmardon.com
Lithographic labels; also, embossing, foil stamping and bronzing available
Estimated Sales: $1 - 5 Million
Number Employees: 25-49
Parent Co: Lawson Mardon Packaging

25234 Lawson Mardon Packaging
5303 Saint Charles Rd
Bellwood, IL 60104-1048 708-544-1600
Fax: 708-649-3888 www.alcan.com
Aseptic packaging systems
Manager: John Webster
Estimated Sales: $10-25 Million
Number Employees: 100-249

25235 Lawson Mardon Radisson
8800 Sixty Rd
Baldwinsville, NY 13027-1235 315-638-4355
Fax: 315-638-8421 800-847-5677
www.radissoncommunity.com
High barrier rotogravure printed folding cartons made from recycled boxboard; also, can and bottle carriers
CEO: Carlton Highsmith
Logistics: Leo Basciano
Manufacturing: Robert Derby
Plant Manager: Leo Basciano
Estimated Sales: $50 - 100 Million
Number Employees: 100-249
Parent Co: Lawson Mardon Group

25236 Lawson Mardon Thermaplate Corporation
995 Merrimac Cir
Naperville, IL 60540-7149 630-548-0217
Fax: 630-548-0218
chalres.lu@lawsonmardon.com
www.larsonmardon.com
Plastic trays
Manager: Paul Vandenheuvel
Estimated Sales: $1 - 5 Million
Number Employees: 1-4

25237 Lawson Mardon Wheaton Company
5176 Harding Highway
Mays Landing, NJ 08330-2239 609-625-2291
Fax: 609-625-7173
Glass safety coated and aerosol containers
Customer Service: Antoinette Mazzoli
Manager Lab Services: Wendy Moore
Estimated Sales: $5 - 10 Million
Number Employees: 75
Parent Co: Lawson Mardon Wheaton

25238 Laydon Company
PO Box 69
Brown City, MI 48416-0069 810-346-2952
Fax: 810-346-2900 laydonco@greatlakes.net
www.laydoncompany.com
Manufacturer and exporter of precision custom plastic injection molding including long and short run
VP: Sandy Fuller
Sales Manager: Connie Dixon
Estimated Sales: $10-20 Million
Number Employees: 50-99
Square Footage: 35000

25239 Layflat Products
901 Tatum St
Shreveport, LA 71107 318-222-6141
Fax: 318-424-2949 800-551-8515
www.layflat.com
Manufacturer and exporter of screw-type wet mops, mop heads and handles
Owner: James Beadles
National Sales Manager: Bill Hill
Director Operations: Steve Williams
Estimated Sales: $3 - 5 Million
Number Employees: 20-49
Square Footage: 25000
Type of Packaging: Consumer, Food Service, Private Label
Brands:
Layflat

25240 Lazer Images
33664 5 Mile Road
Livonia, MI 48154-2866 734-427-4141
Fax: 734-531-2377 800-875-7446
custserv@laserimages.com
www.lazerimages.com
P.O.P. sign making equipment including custom signage onto blank or pre-printed stock banners
President: David Berger
Sales/Marketing: Chris Crews
Estimated Sales: $500,000-$1 Million
Number Employees: 1-4

25241 Lazy-Man
616 Hardwick St
PO Box 327
Belvidere, NJ 07823 908-475-5315
Fax: 908-475-3165 800-475-1950
www.lazyman.com
Commercial and domestic gas-fired barbecue equipment and cast iron burners for urns, steam tables, water heaters, hot dog carts, etc
President: G D Mc Glaughlin
CEO: D Nawrocki
Sales Manager: G Williams
Marketing Director: Garland Williams
Sales Director: Garland Williams
Estimated Sales: Below $5 Million
Number Employees: 6
Square Footage: 20000
Brands:
Ccc Burners
Lazy-Man
Minute Glow

25242 Lazzari Fuel Company
P.O. Box 34051
San Francisco, CA 94134 415-467-2970
Fax: 415-468-2298 800-242-7265
info@Lazzari.com www.lazzari.com
Mesquite lump charcoal and wood chips; importer and exporter of mesquite lump charcoal
Owner: Johnson Lazaro
CEO: Richard Morgan
Estimated Sales: $1 - 3 Million
Number Employees: 5-9
Square Footage: 74000
Type of Packaging: Consumer, Food Service, Private Label, Bulk
Brands:
Lazzari

25243 Le Claire Packaging Corporation
PO Box 293
Ixonia, WI 53036 920-206-9902
Fax: 920-206-9904 stucl@aol.com
Corrugated containers and packaging materials
President: Daniel Steuber
CEO: Daniel Steuber, Jr.
Vice President: James Steuber
Estimated Sales: Below $5 Million
Number Employees: 5-9
Number of Products: 3
Square Footage: 18000
Type of Packaging: Bulk

25244 Le Fiell Company, Inc.
5601 Echo Ave
Reno, NV 89506-3201 775-677-5300
Fax: 775-677-5319 meatsys@lefiellco.com
www.lefiellco.com
Manufacturer and exporter of conveyors, meat packing and slaughter house machinery, trolley and trucks, meat house, engineering and overhead track switches, hide pullers and dehairers and restrainers for custom installation
President: David Gomes
CEO: Brandon Camp
COO: Joe Gonzales
Plant Manager: Dave Gomes
Estimated Sales: $2.5 Million
Number Employees: 20-49
Square Footage: 100000
Brands:
Le Fiell

25245 Le Smoker
321 Park Avenue
Salisbury, MD 21801-4208 410-677-3233
Fax: 410-677-3234 richard@lesmoker.com
www.le-smoker.com
Stainless steel smokers, fire place, grills, wood chips, chunks and charcoal; exporter of smokers
President: Richard Isaacs
VP: Dominique Isaacs
Number of Brands: 3
Square Footage: 12000
Type of Packaging: Food Service
Brands:
Le Smoker

25246 (HQ)Le Sueur Cheese Company
719 N Main St
Le Sueur, MN 56058 507-665-3353
Fax: 507-665-2820 800-757-7611
info@daviscofoods.com www.daviscofoods.com
Variety of cheese including low-fat, no-fat, enzyme-modified cheeses and other customer specified varieties
President: Mark Davis
Vice President: Jim Ward
Production Manager: Roger Schroder
Purchasing Manager: Gregory Bush
Estimated Sales: $14.9
Number Employees: 120
Square Footage: 4000
Parent Co: Davisco Foods International, Inc.
Other Locations:
Le Sueur Cheese Plant
Jerome ID

25247 (HQ)Le-Jo Enterprises
765 Pike Springs Rd
Phoenixville, PA 19460 484-921-9000
Fax: 484-296-7993 ccurtin@lejo.com
www.lejo.com
Manual food preparation machines, grill maintenance tools, safety table lamps and chafing fuel
President: Dominic D'Ambro Sr
CFO: Lauras Hasan
Quality Control: Rudy Sciubba
VP Sales: Jack Kelly
Estimated Sales: $20 - 50 Million
Number Employees: 100-249
Other Locations:
Le-Jo Enterprises
Malvern PA
Brands:
Diablo
Dine Aglow

25248 LeFiell Company
5601 Echo Avenue
Reno, NV 89506-3201 775-677-5300
Fax: 775-677-5319 meatsys@lefiellco.com
www.lefiellco.com

President/Owner: Baldwin S. Schmidt
Senior Vice President/Co-Owner: Kathlene M. Schmidt
Estimated Sales: $5 - 10 Million
Number Employees: 5-9

25249 LeMatic
2410 W Main St
Jackson, MI 49203-1099 517-787-3301
Fax: 517-782-1033 sales@lematic.com
www.lematic.com
Manufacturer and exporter of bulk packaging, bagging machinery and dry pan cleaners; also, bakery equipment including garlic and French bread makers and slicers for buns, bagels, croissants, etc
CEO: Dale LeCrone
Director Sales: George Arnold
Estimated Sales: $5-10 Million
Number Employees: 20-49
Square Footage: 30000

25250 Leader Corporation
3205 Bishop Dr 105
Arlington, TX 76010 817-640-4610
Fax: 817-649-4182 leader@leadecorp.com
Estimated Sales: $3 - 5 Million
Number Employees: 10-19

25251 Leader Engineering-Fabrication
695 Independence Drive
PO Box 670
Napoleon, OH 43545 419-592-0008
Fax: 419-592-0340 leadengr@bright.net
www.leaderengineeringfabrication.com
Filling systems, peelers, peel eliminators and can unscramblers; also, custom design and fabrication available
President: Charles B Leader Jr
CFO: Charles B Leader Jr
R&D: Charles B Leader Jr
Quality Control: Charles B Leader Jr
Plant Manager: John Hill
Estimated Sales: $5 - 10 Million
Number Employees: 50-99
Square Footage: 24000
Brands:
Leader/Fox

25252 Leading Industry
1151 Pacific Ave
Oxnard, CA 93033 805-385-4100
Fax: 805-981-0444 www.ldind.com
Custom thermoformed blisters, clamshells and trays; also, cups and cookie containers
President: Samuel Hong
General Manager: Brian Yamaguchi
VP Operations: Sam Hong
Estimated Sales: $20 - 50 Million
Number Employees: 100-249
Square Footage: 43000

25253 Leal True Form Corporation
248 Buffalo Ave
Freeport, NY 11520 516-379-2008
Fax: 516-623-8011 franklintoribio@aol.com
lealplastics.com
Vacuum formed blisters and trays
Owner: Arnulfo Toribio
Estimated Sales: $1-2.5 Million
Number Employees: 10-19

25254 Leaman Container
5701 E Rosedale St # B
Fort Worth, TX 76112-7732 817-429-2660
Fax: 817-429-2839
customerservice@leamancontainer.com
www.leamancontainer.com
Corrugated boxes
Owner: Steve Leaman
VP Marketing: Perry Haynes
Estimated Sales: $20-50 Million
Number Employees: 50-99

25255 Lear Romec
PO Box 4014
Elyria, OH 44036 440-323-3211
Fax: 440-322-3378
chapman@craneaerospace.com
www.learromec.com
Pumps and fluid handling systems
Director Marketing: Seamus O'Brien
Number Employees: 100-249
Parent Co: Crane Company

25256 Least Cost Formulations
824 Timberlake Dr
Virginia Beach, VA 23464-3239 757-467-0954
Fax: 757-467-2947 sales@lcfltd.com
www.lcfltd.com
Manufacturer and exporter of material requirement planning and technical software for the blending industry
Owner: Robert Labudde
VP Marketing: Joy LaBudde
Estimated Sales: $1 Million
Number Employees: 1-4
Brands:
Least Cost Formulator
Market Forecaster
Qc Assistant
Qc Database Manager

25257 (HQ)Leathertone
2040 Industrial Dr.
Findlay, OH 45840 419-429-0188
Fax: 419-425-2927 sales@leathertone.com
www.leathertone.com
Plastic labels and signs
President: James Rubenstein
VP: Howard Rubenstein
Estimated Sales: $2.5-5 Million
Number Employees: 10-19

25258 Leaves Pure Teas
1392 Lowrie Avenue
South San Francisco, CA 94080-6402650-583-1157
Fax: 650-583-1163 pureteas@leaves.com
www.leaves.com
Retail and wholesale premium teas in teabags and loose for grocery, food service and specialty retailers
Estimated Sales: $1 - 5 Million

25259 Leavitt & Parris
256 Read St
Portland, ME 04103 207-797-0100
Fax: 207-797-4194 800-833-6679
ileavitt@maine.rr.com www.leavittandparris.com
Awnings; rental company of tents, chairs, tables, etc
President: John Hutchins
Estimated Sales: Below $5,000,000
Number Employees: 20-49

25260 Lebensmittel Consulting
10760 West County Road 18
Fostoria, OH 44830-9623 419-435-2774
Fax: 419-435-9139
webmaster@lebensmittelconsulting.com
www.labensmittelconsulting.com
Consultant offering laboratory, product development, process development, food testing and genetic engineering services
Owner: Richard Basel
VP: Margaret Basel
Research & Development: Richard Basel PhD
Quality Control: Richard Basel PhD
Number Employees: 10
Square Footage: 20000

25261 Lechler
445 Kautz Rd
St Charles, IL 60174 630-377-6611
Fax: 630-377-6657 800-777-2926
karenberker@lechlerusa.com
www.lechlerusa.com
We are one of the largest manufacturers of spray nozzles, accessories and headers. We produce these products in various alloys and plastics to serve a wide variety of fluid applications. From tank washing nozzles and machines which canclean tanks of all sizes to air atomizing nozzles which can coat food or lubricate equipment to standard flat fan and full cone nozzles which can wash food or mix fluids. We have the spraying application products for the food processing industry
President/CEO: Ralph Fish
Marketing/Sales: Karen Berker
Estimated Sales: $10-20,000,000
Number Employees: 50-99
Square Footage: 45000
Parent Co: Lechler GMBH
Brands:
Lechler
Spraco
Tank Cleaning Systems

25262 Leclerc Foods USA
44 Park Drive
Montgomery, PA 17752-8534 570-547-6295
Fax: 570-547-6719 www.leclerc.com
Cookies, snack bars, crackers, cereals and chocolate
Estimated Sales: $8.2 Million
Number Employees: 74

25263 Leco Corporation
3000 Lakeview Ave
Saint Joseph, MI 49085 269-985-5496
Fax: 269-982-8977 800-292-6141
info@leco.com www.leco.com
Analytical instrumentation for primary and secondary analyses of food, ingredients and flavors
President: Robert J Warren
Number Employees: 1,000-4,999

25264 Leco Plastics
130 Gamewell St
Hackensack, NJ 07601 201-343-3330
Fax: 201-343-0558 info@lecoplastics.com
www.lecoplastics.com
Bag and bundle tie, pack handles, die cutting, plastic ties
Owner: Barry Schwartz
Production: Burton Schwartz
Estimated Sales: $1-2.5 Million
Number Employees: 10-19
Square Footage: 14000
Type of Packaging: Bulk

25265 Leco Plastics
130 Gamewell St
Hackensack, NJ 07601 201-343-3330
Fax: 201-343-0558 info@lecoplastics.com
www.lecoplastics.com
Extruded and molded plastics, die cutting, plastic corrugated box handles, ties and plastic stampings
President: Barry Schwartz
Estimated Sales: $1-2.5 Million
Number Employees: 10-19

25266 Lee Engineering Company
505 Narragansett Park Drive
Pawtucket, RI 02861-1970 401-725-6100
Fax: 401-728-7840 sales@lee-presto.com
Material handling equipment including pallet stackers and scissor and dock lifts
CEO/President: Bill Sample
Estimated Sales: $10,000,000 - $25,000,000
Number Employees: 100-249
Parent Co: Long Reach Holdings

25267 Lee Financial Corporation
8350 N. Central Expressway
Suite 1800
Dallas, TX 75206 972-960-1001
Fax: 972-404-1123 Info@Leefin.com
www.leefin.com
Manufacturer and exporter of corn cutters, pea shellers and electric nutcrackers
President: Dana Pingenot
CEO & Founder: Richard Lee
CFO: Blake Decker
VP: Teresa Quinn
COO & Director of Human Resources: Jeff Ramsey
Estimated Sales: Below $5 Million
Number Employees: 20-49
Square Footage: 14000

25268 Lee IndustriesFluid Transfer
Po Box 471
Philipsburg, PA 16866-0471 814-342-0802
Fax: 814-342-5660 sales@leeind.com
www.leeind.com
Lee designs and manufactures stainless alloy process vessels and sanitary ball valves.
President: Robert Montler
CFO: John Horon
Vice President: Greg Wharton
Marketing Director: Ken Winters
Sales Director: Ken Winters
Vice President of Operations: Josh Montler
Estimated Sales: $21-$22 Million
Number Employees: 200-230
Square Footage: 120000

25269 Lee Products Company
800 E 80th St
Bloomington, MN 55420 952-854-3544
Fax: 952-854-7177 info@leeproducts.com
www.leeproducts.com

Hand cleaning pads
President: John Houle
CFO: Rey Lee
Estimated Sales: $5-10 Million
Number Employees: 20-49

25270 Lee Soap Company
6620 E 49th Ave
Commerce City, CO 80022 303-289-9041
Fax: 303-289-9042 800-888-1896
orders@leesoap.com www.leesoap.com
Janitorial supplies including compounders, laundry detergent and soap
Owner: Carl Kelley
Sales Manager: Jim Sumner
Estimated Sales: $5-10 Million
Number Employees: 10-19

25271 Leedal Avant
3453 Commercial Ave
Northbrook, IL 60062-1818 847-498-0111
Fax: 847-498-0198 www.leedal.com
Stainless steel equipment, custom fabrication, steam tables, sinks, and tanks
President: Sheldon Levin
Vice President: A Levin
Sales Director: Josie Negron
Estimated Sales: $10 - 20 Million
Number Employees: 20-49
Square Footage: 14000
Type of Packaging: Consumer, Food Service, Private Label, Bulk

25272 Leedal Inc
3453 Commercial Ave
Northbrook, IL 60062 847-498-0111
Fax: 847-498-0198 sink@leedal.com
www.leedal.com
Manufacturer, importer and exporter of pot and pan washers, disposers, power scrubbers, wire shelfing, hot dog cookers, and steam tables
President: Sheldon Levin
CFO: Sheldon Levin
Vice President: A Levin
Quality Control: Levin
Sales Director: Josie Negron
Estimated Sales: $5 - 10 Million
Square Footage: 14000
Type of Packaging: Consumer, Food Service, Private Label, Bulk

25273 Leeds Conveyor Manufacturer Company
PO Box 383
Guilford, CT 06437 203-453-5277
Fax: 203-453-6329 800-724-1088
info@leedsconveyor.com
www.leedsconveyor.com
Conveyor systems including chain and roller in mild and stainless steel, belt conveyors and mesh chain in metal and plastic; also, accumulators and unscramblers
President: Paul Nangle
CFO: Debbie Nancy Nangle
Manufacturing Manager: Sean LeTarte
Number Employees: 10
Square Footage: 64000

25274 Leeman Labs
6 Wentworth Dr
Hudson, NH 03051-4918 603-886-8400
Fax: 603-886-4322 salesinfo@leemanlabs.com
www.leemanlabs.com
Analytical instrumentation including coupled plasma spectrometers, metal alloy, cyanide and mercury analyzers and prep systems
CEO: John Leeman
Director Sales Marketing: Bill Driscoll
Director International Operations: Paul Maaskant
Estimated Sales: $10-20 Million
Number Employees: 20-49
Square Footage: 50000
Brands:
A30
Ap/Ps 1214
Ap/Ps200 Ii
Dre (Direct Reading Echelle Icp)
Plasma-Pure

25275 Leer Limited Partnership
206 Leer St
New Lisbon, WI 53950 608-562-3161
Fax: 608-562-6022 800-766-5337
info@leerlp.com www.leerlp.com
Manufacturer and exporter of bins, coolers, freezers, ice makers and other refrigeration equipment
Owner: Steven Dolezeo
Sales/Marketing Manager: Howard Farkash
Estimated Sales: $20 - 50 Million
Number Employees: 100-249
Type of Packaging: Food Service
Brands:
Leer

25276 Leer, Inc.
206 Leer Street
New Lisbon, WI 53950 813-882-3616
Fax: 813-882-3702 800-237-8350
info@leerlp.com www.leerinc.com
Manufacturer and exporter of self-service ice merchandising equipment and block ice-makers
VP: Charlotte Maginnis
CEO and Owner and President: Steve Dolenzel
Estimated Sales: $500,000 - $1 Million
Number Employees: 4
Square Footage: 320000
Parent Co: Leer Manufacturing Partner
Type of Packaging: Bulk
Other Locations:
Star/Starrett
Dumas AZ
Brands:
Leer
Star
Starrett

25277 Leeson Electric Corporation
1051 Cheyenne Avenue
PO Box 241
Grafton, WI 53024-0241 262-377-8810
Fax: 262-377-9025 leeson@leeson.com
www.leeson.com
Motors, gear motor's and drives.

25278 Legal Seafoods
1 Seafood Way
Boston, MA 02210-2702 617-783-8084
Fax: 617-782-4479 www.legalseafoods.com
President: Roger Berkowitz
CFO: Mark Synott
Quality Control: Steve Martinello
Estimated Sales: $10 - 100 Million
Number Employees: 1100

25279 Legge & Associates
PO Box 599
Rockwood, ON N0B 2K0
Canada 519-856-0444
Fax: 519-856-0555 scott@legge-fcsi.com
Consultant specializing in the design of food service and hospitality facilities
Principal: Scott Legge

25280 Leggett & Platt StorageP
11230 Harland Driveÿ
Vernon Hills, IL 60061-1547 847-816-6246
Fax: 847-968-3899 info@lpstorage.com
www.focuspg.com
Manufacturer and exporter of cabinets, racks, mobile storage equipment, shelving, carts, servingware, buffetware, utensils, utility trucks, dollies and tote/bus boxes
President: Keith Jaffee
Number Employees: 10-19
Square Footage: 2000000
Parent Co: SPG International, LLC
Other Locations:
Leggett & Platt
Charlotte NC

25281 Leggett and Platt, Inc.
P.O. Box 757
1 Leggett Road
Carthage, MO 64836 417-358-8131
Fax: 417-358-2171 www.leggett.com
Manufacturer and exporter of store fixtures including bakery showcases, cash register stands and checkouts, bulk shelving and storage units and custom wood display equipment
President/Director/CEO: David Haffner
Chairman: Richard Fisher
Senior VP/Chief Financial Officer: Matthew Flanigan
EVP/Chief Operating Officer: Karl Glassman
Director, Quality Assurance: Brad Richards
Marketing Manager: John Patrick
Director, Sales: Diane Holman
Operations Manager: Hal Gimmer
Plant Manager: Jim Winters
Director, Procurement: Jeff Mitchell
Estimated Sales: $3.7 Billion
Number Employees: 600
Square Footage: 15491
Parent Co: Reflector Hardware Corporation
Type of Packaging: Consumer, Food Service, Bulk
Other Locations:
Goer Manufacturing Co.
Union MO

25282 Legible Signs
2221 Nimtz Road
Loves Park, IL 61111-3928 815-654-7323
Fax: 815-654-9679 800-435-4177
info@legiblesigns.com www.legiblesigns.com
Polyethylene safety signs, aluminum name plates, custom decals and menu covers
Customer Service: Trina Bentley
Estimated Sales: $1-2.5 Million
Number Employees: 10-19

25283 Legion Industries
PO Box 728
Waynesboro, GA 30830 706-554-4411
Fax: 706-554-2035 800-887-1988
CORPORATE@LEGIONINDUSTRIES.COM
www.legionindustries.com
Food service equipment including steam equipment, kettles, ovens and braising pans
Manager: Susan Riggs
Estimated Sales: Below $5,000,000
Number Employees: 50-99
Square Footage: 2500

25284 Legion Lighting Company
221 Glenmore Ave
Brooklyn, NY 11207 718-498-1770
Fax: 718-498-0128 800-453-4466
sales@legionlighting.com
www.legionlighting.com
Manufacturer and exporter of architecturally engineered fluorescent lighting equipment
President: Michael Bellovin
VP Sales: Michael Bellovin
Engineering: Wayne Cowell
Sales: Evan Bellovin
Accountant: Gia Carla Rodriguez
Estimated Sales: $5-10 Million
Number Employees: 50-99
Square Footage: 6000
Brands:
Circledome
Comfort-Lume
Compact Cube
Contempo
Corritempo
Drum-Plex
Excelon
Gemini
Legion-Aire
Lytegress
Mod-Plex
Mod-U-Beam
My-T-Lite
Panelume
Paralume
Prismalier
Securlume
Skylume
Teg-U-Lume
Trimlume
Vandalex
Vaportron

25285 Legumex Walker, Inc.
1345 Kenaston Blvd
Winnipeg, MB R6W 4B3
Canada 204-808-0448
info@legumexwalker.com
www.legumexwalker.com

Grains
Investor & Media Relations: Marin Landis

25286 **Lehi Roller Mills**
833 E Main St
Lehi, UT 84043 801-768-4401
Fax: 801-768-4557 800-660-4346
sdejohn@lehirollermills.com
www.lehirollermill.com
Founded in 1906. Processor of flour, feed and meal; also, pancake mixes, cookie mixes, and muffin mixes.
President: Sherm Robinson
COO: Brock Knight
CFO: Kevin David
Estimated Sales: $20-50 Million
Number Employees: 20-49
Type of Packaging: Private Label
Brands:
Peacock
Turkey

25287 **Lehigh Safety Shoe Company**
39 East Canal Street
Nelsonville, OH 45764
866-442-5429
clientservices@lehighoutfitters.com
www.lehighsafetyshoes.com
Shoes including steel toe, nonsteel toe and nonslip
Brands:
Lehigh

25288 **Lehman Sales Associates**
3025 Saddle Brook Trl
Sun Prairie, WI 53590 608-575-7712
Fax: 608-837-8421 bob@lehmanequip.com
www.lehmanequip.com
Manufacturer and exporter of used and rebuilt food processing and packaging equipment
President: Richard Lehman
Estimated Sales: $1 - 2.5 Million
Number Employees: 1-4

25289 **Leibinger-USA**
2702-B Buell Drive
East Troy, WI 53120 262-642-4030
Fax: 262-642-4033 info@leibinger-group.com
www.leibingerusa.com
A family owned business since 1948 and a premier manufacturer of security, industrial and commerical printing solutions, introduces the Jet2 Printer-the only low maintenance continuous in jet (CIJ) printer on the market today. The Jet2features a retractable gutter which creates an air tight seal over the nozzle eliminating ink from drying in the nozzle. This revolutionary design is far superior to traditional flush nozzle systems.
President: Gunter Leibinger
Vice President: Steve Talbot
Sales Director: Alexander Deuchert
Number of Products: 3
Type of Packaging: Consumer, Food Service, Private Label, Bulk

25290 **Leica Microsystems**
3362 Walden Ave
Depew, NY 14043 716-686-3000
Fax: 716-686-3085 800-346-4560
analytical@leica-microsystems.com
www.analytical-refractometers.com
Refractometers, microscopes and colony counters
Marketing Director: Thomas Ryan
Sales Director: Terry Grant
Estimated Sales: $2.5-5 Million
Number Employees: 20-49
Parent Co: Leica AG
Brands:
Ar200
Ar600
Arias500
Auto Abbe
Brix 15hp
Brix 30
Brix 35hp
Brix 50
Brix 65hp
Brix 90
Brix 90hp
Leica
Mark Ii
Mark Ii Plus
Oe200

25291 **Leichtman Ice Cream Company**
175 N Vine St Apt 3b
Hazleton, PA 18201 570-454-2428
Fax: 570-454-2540 800-735-4379
icecream@intergrafix.net
www.leichtmanicecream.com
Ice Cream Distributors
Estimated Sales: $5-10 000,000
Number Employees: 15

25292 **Leister/Heely-Brown Company**
1139 Goodwin Rd NE
Atlanta, GA 30324-2715 404-846-0401
Fax: 404-350-2696 800-241-4628
info@heely-brown.com www.heely-brown.com
Hot air tools provide solutions for customers' packaging, shrinking, drying, heating, forming, staking,curing, plastic welding, prototyping, soldering and de-soldering and activating applications
Manager: Nancy Chambers
CFO: Michael Spencer
Estimated Sales: $20 - 50 Million
Number Employees: 1-4

25293 **Leister/Malcom Company**
207 High Point Avenue
Unit 7B
Portsmouth, RI 2871 401-683-3199
Fax: 401-683-3177 800-289-7505
malcom@tiac.net www.malcom.com
Hot air equipment for various packaging applications including hand-held heat guns and pallet shrink guns to large process heaters
Chairman: George Bixby
President: Jonathan Bixby
Sales/Marketing Administrator: Sheila Carpenter
President: Jonathan Bixby
Sales/Technical Support: Mary Bass
Application Engineer: Steve Robertson
Chairman: George Bixby
Estimated Sales: $1 - 3 Million
Number Employees: 1-4

25294 **Leister/Uneco Systems**
8412 Autumn Drive
Woodridge, IL 60517 630-972-0500
Fax: 630-910-0558 800-700-6894
junewitz@att.net www.heatgun.com
Plastic weld, packaging, roofing, process heat, drying SMT electronics, Leister hot air tools and blowers
President: John A Unewitz
CFO: John A Unewitz
Sales Director: John Unewitz
Estimated Sales: $1 - 3 Million
Number Employees: 1-4
Brands:
Leister Heat Guns

25295 **Leland**
2614 S Clinton Ave
South Plainfield, NJ 07080 908-668-1008
Fax: 908-668-7716 sales@lelandltd.com
www.lelandltd.com
Manufacturer and exporter of food mixing equipment
Owner: Leland Stanford
Engineer: P Bowlin
Customer Service: R Callaway
Estimated Sales: $5-10 Million
Number Employees: 10-19
Brands:
Leland Southwest

25296 **Leland**
2614 S Clinton Ave
South Plainfield, NJ 07080 908-668-1008
Fax: 908-668-7716 800-984-9793
sales@lelandltd.com www.lelandltd.com
Manufacturer, importer and exporter of whipped cream machinery and soda syphons
Owner: Leland Stanford
Estimated Sales: $5,000,000
Number Employees: 10-19
Square Footage: 15000
Type of Packaging: Food Service
Brands:
Leland
Mr. Fizz

25297 **Len E. Ivarson**
3100 W Green Tree Rd
Milwaukee, WI 53209-2535 414-351-0700
Fax: 414-351-4551 sales@ivarsoninc.com
www.ivarsoninc.com
Manufacturer and exporter of process and packaging equipment and parts for butter, cheese and margarine industries; also, set-up boxes
President: Glenn Ivarson
Engineering Manager: Chuck Ellingson
Manager Technical Services: Jim Wycklendt
Sales Director: Mark Mullinix
Estimated Sales: $10 - 20 Million
Number Employees: 50-99
Square Footage: 50100

25298 **Lengsfield Brothers**
PO Box 50020
New Orleans, LA 70150-0020 504-529-2235
Fax: 504-524-9281 mail@packagingfinder.com
Manufacturer and exporter of candy boxes

25299 **Lenkay Sani Products Corporation**
473 Wortman Ave
Brooklyn, NY 11208 718-927-9260
Fax: 718-257-0461
Custom packaging
President: Frank Drayer
Estimated Sales: Below $5 Million
Number Employees: 5-9
Square Footage: 12000

25300 **Lenox**
P.O. Box 735
Bristol, PA 19007-0735 609-896-2800
Fax: 609-896-1805 800-223-4311
lenox@lenox.com www.lenox.com
Manufacturer and exporter of chinaware, stemware, silverplated hollowware, crystal gifts and flatware including stainless and sterling
Manager: Mark Smith
CFO: James Burwitt
Quality Control: Dave Summers
Number Employees: 250-499
Parent Co: Brown-Foreman
Type of Packaging: Food Service

25301 **Lenox Locker Company**
PO Box 317
Dunmore, PA 18512-0317 740-375-0730
Fax: 717-222-4141
Sanitation supplies and equipment

25302 **Lenser Filtration**
1750 Oak St
Lakewood, NJ 08701 732-370-1600
Fax: 732-370-8411 mailbox@lenserusa.com
www.lenserusa.com
Polypropylene and other thermoplastic filter elements for use in solids and liquid seperation
Sales: Robert Iovino
Production: Tom Van Leet
Estimated Sales: $5 - 10 Million
Number Employees: 20-49

25303 **Lentia Enterprises Ltd.**
17733-66th Ave
Surrey, BC V3S 7X1
Canada 604-576-8838
Fax: 604-576-1064 888-768-7368
infovancouver@lentia.com www.lentia.com
Naturally fermented, dehydrated sourdoughs from both wheat and rye flours, specialty malted products such as whole malted rye kernels, aroma malts, colouring malts and clean label bread mixes.
President/Board Member: Karl Eibensteiner
Director: Gertrude Eibensteiner
Estimated Sales: $4.08 Million
Number Employees: 23

25304 **Lentz Milling Company**
P.O.Box 13159
Reading, PA 19612 610-921-0666
Fax: 610-929-3682 800-523-8132
www.lentzmilling.com
President: Edward A Lentz
Sales/Accounts Supervisor: Jane Adams
Estimated Sales: $50-100 Million
Number Employees: 100-249

25305 Leon Bush Manufacturer
1870 Elmdale Avenue
Glenview, IL 60026-1356 847-657-8888
Fax: 847-657-9710
Plastic injection molding for wedding cake plates and ornaments; also, industrial baking utensils and deli trays
Sales Manager: David Drew
Estimated Sales: $500,000-$1 Million
Number Employees: 5-9

25306 Leon C. Osborn Company
1020 Bay Area Blvd
Suite 120
Houston, TX 77289-0014 281-488-0755
Fax: 281-480-9739 dave@leoncosborn.com
www.leoncosborn.com
Washers for fresh pack pickles, brine stock, beets, potatoes, carrots, squash, and other vegetables
President: David S Osborn
Estimated Sales: $.5 - 1 million
Number Employees: 1-4

25307 Leotta Designers
800 Brickell Ave
Ste 602
Miami, FL 33131 305-371-4949
Fax: 305-371-2844 johnk@leottadesigners.com
www.leottadesigners.com
Interior designer; services include space planning, corporate interior design, site selection and lease negotiation
President: Marc J Leotta
VP: J Kalbach
Estimated Sales: $500,000 - $1 Million
Number Employees: 5-9

25308 Lepel Corporation
W227n937 Westmound Dr
Waukesha, WI 53186 262-782-0450
Fax: 262-782-3299 800-231-6008
sales@cap-sealing.com www.lepel.com
Process control systems features motion, linear, alignment and cap height detectors, along with idle control and Windows-compatible software for process control, induction cap sealing
Vice President: Al Peters
Sales Coordinator: Bonnie Leivenger
Manager: Bonnie Leitinger
Estimated Sales: $2.5 - 5 Million
Number Employees: 1-4
Square Footage: 2500
Parent Co: Lepel Corporation
Brands:
Cspiust Capsealing System
Lepakjr Capsealing System

25309 (HQ)Leprino Foods Company
1830 W 38th Ave
Denver, CO 80211 303-480-2600
Fax: 303-480-2605 800-537-7466
www.leprinofoods.com
Mozzarella cheese, cheese blends, and pizza cheese made especially for pizzeria and foodservice operators, frozen food manufacturers and private label cheese packagers.
Chairman: James Leprino
Vice President, Finance: Paul Adams
Senior Vice President, Global Business: Kevin Burke
Chief Information Officer: Adkins Mark
Vice President, Information Systems: Dwight Gibson
Vice President, Sales & Marketing: Bradley Olsen
Senior Sales Director: Scott Marshall
Vice President, Personnel: Tom Deany
Senior Vice President, Human Resources: Rob Schwartz
Vice President, Production Operations: Dan Vecchiarelli
Plant Manager: Phil Conrad
Purchasing Directors: Rich Collins
Estimated Sales: $899 Million
Number Employees: 3700
Square Footage: 60000
Type of Packaging: Food Service, Bulk
Other Locations:
Leprino Foods
Allendale MI
Leprino Foods
Fort Morgan CO
Leprino Foods
Ravenna NE
Leprino Foods
Remus MI
Leprino Foods
Roswell NM
Leprino Foods
Waverly NY

25310 Lermer Packaging
202 Washington Avenue
Carlstadt, NJ 07072-3001 908-789-0900
Fax: 908-789-0235
Wine industry packaging
Estimated Sales: $10-20 Million
Number Employees: 20-49

25311 Leroy Signs, Inc.
6325 Welcome Ave N
Brooklyn Park, MN 55429 763-535-0080
Fax: 763-533-2593 info@leroysigns.com
www.leroysigns.com
Plastic and neon signs
Owner: Leroy Reiter
Estimated Sales: $2.5-5 Million
Number Employees: 20-49

25312 Leroy's Restaurant Supply
1306 S Grant Ave
Odessa, TX 79761 432-333-2621
Fax: 915-333-2621 reedbbq@aol.com
Wholesaler/distributor of new and used food service equipment; serving the food service market
Owner: Marvin Reed
Estimated Sales: Less than $500,000
Number Employees: 19

25313 (HQ)Les Industries Touch Inc
4025 Lesage
Sherbrooke, QC J1L 2Z9
Canada 819-822-4140
Fax: 819-822-2904 800-267-4140
info@industriestouch.com
www.industriestouch.com
Manufacturer and exporter of toothpicks, skewers, plastic cutlery, straws etc.
President: Gervais Morier
Sales Director: Gerald Bouchard
Operations Manager: Jean-Yves Blouin
Estimated Sales: $10-20 Million
Number Employees: 50-99
Number of Products: 300+
Square Footage: 45000
Type of Packaging: Consumer, Food Service, Private Label, Bulk
Brands:
Touch

25314 Lesco Design & Manufacturing Company
1120 Fort Pickens Rd
La Grange, KY 40031 502-222-7101
Fax: 502-222-5508 sales@lesco-design.com
www.lescodesign.com
Conveyor belts
President: Lance Kaufman
CFO: Steve Herald
VP: Lance Kaufman
VP Sales: Dick Wilder
Estimated Sales: $20-50 Million
Number Employees: 100-249
Square Footage: 115000

25315 Lester Box & Manufacturing
1470 Seabright Ave
Long Beach, CA 90813-1152 562-437-5123
Fax: 562-436-1437 sales@lesterbox.com
www.lesterbox.com
Manufacturer and exporter of wooden boxes and crates, pallets, skids and foam inserts
Manager: Steve Amato
Estimated Sales: $1-2.5 Million
Number Employees: 10-19
Square Footage: 60000

25316 Letica Corporation
P.O.Box 5005
Rochester, MI 48308-5005 248-652-0557
Fax: 248-608-2153 800-538-4221
www.letica.com
Manufacturer and exporter of plastic shipping containers, paper and plastic cups and containers for cultured dairy products and freight lines
CEO: Ilija Letica
Sales Director: David Bradwell
Public Relations: David Schueler
Estimated Sales: $5 - 10 Million
Number Employees: 50-99
Brands:
Letica
Maui Cup

25317 Letraw Manufacturing Company
200 Quaker Rd
Box 2
Rockford, IL 61104 815-987-9670
Fax: 815-987-9830 rwartell@letraw.com
www.letraw.com
Cleaning supplies including metal scrubbers and scouring cloths; importer of Mexican vanilla extract
Partner: Ralph Wartell
Estimated Sales: less than $500,000
Number Employees: 5
Square Footage: 4000
Type of Packaging: Consumer, Food Service

25318 Leuze-Lumiflex
55395 Lyon Industrial Drive
New Hudson, MI 48165-8545 973-586-0100
Fax: 973-586-1590 info@leuze-lumiflex.com
www.leuze-lumiflex.com
Opto-sensors and work safety products including bar code readers, clear media detection sensors, clear and opaque label detection sensors, cap orientation detection sensors, fork sensors, luminescence sensors, laser distance sensingdevices and safety li
President: Vincent Orrico
Estimated Sales: $20 - 50 Million
Number Employees: 300

25319 Levelmatic
1135 NW 159th Dr
Miami, FL 33169-5882 305-625-2451
Fax: 305-623-0475 800-762-7565
sales@atlasfoodserv.com
www.atlasfoodserv.com
Self leveling dispensers for plates, bowls, racks, trays, etc
President: David Meade
VP Sales: Howard Bolnar
VP Manufacturing: Mark Siegfriedt
Estimated Sales: $10 - 20 Million
Number Employees: 100-249
Parent Co: Atlas Metal Industries

25320 Levin Brothers Paper
1325 S Cicero Ave
Cicero, IL 60804-1404 708-652-5600
Fax: 708-652-5537 800-666-8484
clutch@idt.net www.lbpmfg.com
Corrugated boxes, tape and packaging materials; wholesaler/distributor of paper products and restaurant supplies
President: Barry Silverstein
CFO: Mike Schaechter
VP: Matthew Cook
Quality Control: Larry Rosenberg
Estimated Sales: $10-20 Million
Number Employees: 10-19
Square Footage: 125000
Brands:
Safe-Pack

25321 Lewis Label Products Corporation
2300 Race St
Fort Worth, TX 76111 817-834-7334
Fax: 817-834-2210 800-772-7728
cmorvan@lewislabel.com www.lewislabel.com
Pressure sensitive labels
Owner: Gibson Lewis
CFO: Gibson Lewis
VP Sales: George Noah
Manager: Cole Morvan
Estimated Sales: $10 - 20 Million
Number Employees: 20-49

25322 Lewis M. Carter Manufacturing Company
PO Box 428
Donalsonville, GA 39845-0428 229-524-2197
Fax: 229-524-2531 sales@lmcarter.com
www.lmcarter.com
Manufacturer and exporter of peanut shellers, cleaners, vibratory conveyors, elevators, sizing shakers, reclaimers, stoners, gravity separators, belt sizers, bean polishers, blanchers and bean ladders. Also air pollution controlequipment
President: Lewis Carter Jr
Sales Representative: David Sandlin
Sales Manager: Jack Williams, Jr.

Estimated Sales: $10 - 20 Million
Number Employees: 150
Square Footage: 200000
Brands:
Lmc

25323 Lewis Packing Company
17480 Shelley Ave
Sandy, OR 97055-8055 503-668-8122
Packaging
Owner: Kris Jones
Estimated Sales: Under $500,000
Number Employees: 1-4

25324 Lewis Steel Works
613 S Main St
Wrens, GA 30833 706-547-6561
Fax: 706-547-3020 800-521-5239
lewisteel@bellsouth.net
www.lewissteelworks.com
Refuse containers
Owner/President: Brian Lewis
Chairman of the Board: R A Lewis
Estimated Sales: $10 - 20 Million
Number Employees: 50-99

25325 Lewisburg Container Company
275 Clay Street
P.O. Box 39
Lewisburg, OH 45338 937-962-2681
Fax: 937-962-4504
salesdept@lewisburgcontainer.com
www.lewisburgcontainer.com
Corrugated containers
President: Randy Love
Controller: Walter Locker
Vice President: David McKinney
Director, Quality Control: Robert Long MD
Chief Marketing Officer: Tami Meeks
Vice President, Sales & Marketing: David Dennis
Plant Manager: Michael Day
Procurement Manager: Dave McClellan
Estimated Sales: $39 Million
Number Employees: 250
Square Footage: 384000
Parent Co: Pratt Properties, Inc.

25326 Lewisburg PrintingCompany
PO Box 2608
170 Woodside Avenue
Lewisburg, TN 37091 931-359-1526
Fax: 931-359-1562 800-559-1526
info@lpcink.com www.lewisburgprinting.com
Manufacturer and exporter of litho sheet labels, point of purchase advertising brochures, posters and manuals
President: Seawell Brandau
CEO: Thomas Hale Hawkins, IV
CEO: Hale Hawkins
VP Sales: Kirk Kelso
Director Of Operations: Brian Tankersley
Estimated Sales: $5-10 Million
Number Employees: 20-49

25327 (HQ)Lewtan Industries Corporation
PO Box 2049
Hartford, CT 06145-2049 860-278-9800
Fax: 860-278-9019 lewtan@snet.net
www.lewtan8.com
Manufacturer and exporter of advertising specialties and promotional products including coasters, mighty grips, skimmers, clips, emblems, tape measures, mouse pads, calendars, etc
President: Douglas Lewtan
Estimated Sales: $10 Million
Number Employees: 20-49
Square Footage: 37000

25328 Lexel
2901 Shamrock Avenue
Fort Worth, TX 76107-1314 817-332-4061
lexel@flash.net
Wooden containers for shipping and storage
President: Pat Alexander
VP/Manager: Lee Ray Davis
Estimated Sales: $500,000-$1 Million
Number Employees: 4

25329 Lexidyne of Pennsylvania
PO Box 5372
Pittsburgh, PA 15206-0372 412-661-4526
Fax: 858-815-7346 800-543-2233
lexidyne@juno.com

General Manager: Rick Simoni
Number Employees: 10-19

25330 Ley Norback & Associates
3022 Woodland Trail
Middleton, WI 53562 608-233-3814
Fax: 608-233-3895 nla@norbackley.com
www.norbackley.com
Manufacturer and exporter of food safety, HACCP and thermal processing software in English, Spanish, French, and Japanese
Co-Owner: Kathleen Ley
Chief Executive Officer: Sebastian Norback
CFO: Kathryn Olszewski
Estimated Sales: $1-2.5 Million
Number Employees: 5-9
Number of Brands: 9
Number of Products: 14
Brands:
Aprenda Haccp
Do Haccp
Do Sop
Learn Haccp
Record Haccp
Tform
Tpro

25331 Leybold Vacuum
5700 Mellon Rd
Export, PA 15632-8900 724-327-5700
Fax: 724-325-3577 info@leyboldvacuum.com
www.leyboldvacuum.com
Manufacturer, importer and exporter of vacuum pumps and systems
Chief Executive Officer: Andreas Widl
Vice President: P Albert
Manager of Technical Services: Joachim GstAhl
Marketing Director: M Vitale
Head of Sales: Werner SchAdler
Chief Operating Officer, Chief Operating: Wolfgang Ehrk
Plant Manager: Dennis Pellegrino
Number Employees: 250-499
Square Footage: 596000
Parent Co: Leybold AG
Brands:
Sogevac

25332 (HQ)Leyman ManufacturingCorporation
10900 Kenwood Rd
Cincinnati, OH 45242 513-891-6210
Fax: 513-891-4901 866-539-6261
www.leymanlift.com
Manufacturer, importer and exporter of trailer and truck loading and unloading equipment, hydraulic lifts, elevators, tailgates, platforms, carts, dollies and van bodies
President: John McHenry
Marketing: Joann Russo
VP Sales: Chip Drews
Estimated Sales: $20-50 Million
Number Employees: 50-99
Type of Packaging: Food Service
Other Locations:
Leyman Manufacturing Corp.
Cincinnati OH

25333 (HQ)Libbey
PO Box 10060
Toledo, OH 43699-0060
www.libbey.com
Manufacturer and exporter of table glassware
Chairman: William Foley
CEO/Director: Stephanie Streeter
CFO/Vice President: Sherry Buck
Vice President/Treasurer: Kenneth Boerger
Marketing Manager: Elizabeth Geronimo
Sales Manager: Bernie Coaxum
Production Supervisor: Paul Kortier
Plant Manager: Frank Russell
Procurement Manager: Jennifer Butler
Estimated Sales: $828 Million
Number Employees: 6,663
Brands:
Libbey

25334 Libby Canada
Unit 26
Mississauga, ON L5L 4M1
Canada 905-607-8280
Fax: 905-607-8130 www.libbey.com
China, glassware, flatware and hollowware
CEO: John Mayer
National Accounts Manager: Giulio Accardi
Number Employees: 10
Square Footage: 10400
Parent Co: Libby
Brands:
Syracuse

25335 Libenn Aroma
375 Klug Cir
Corona, 92880-5408 909-738-0077
Fax: 909-738-0076 888-454-2366
libennchi@msn.com
Flavors for all uses
Estimated Sales: $14 Million
Number Employees: 20-50

25336 Liberty Carton Company
870 Louisiana Ave S
Minneapolis, MN 55426 763-540-9529
Fax: 763-540-9522 800-818-2698
customerservice@presentationpackaging.com
www.presentationpackaging.com
Specialty packaging, displays, promotional items, and gifts
General Manager: Michael Fiterman
Estimated Sales: $100 Million
Number Employees: 150
Parent Co: Liberty Diversified Industries

25337 Liberty Distributing, Inc.
909 Valley Ave NW
Puyallup, WA 98371 253-922-8506
Fax: 253-922-9507 888-882-8506
www.libertydistributing.com
Distributor of dairy for wholesalers including; milk, cottage cheese, butter, sour cream, ice cream, non-dairy sour cream, cheese, margarine, eggs, yogurt, creamers, chocolate milk & syrups, apple, orange & grape juices, organic milkssoft serve, flavored milk powders, ice cream topper sauces, buttermilk, tea, bread & buns, ice
Estimated Sales: $430,000
Type of Packaging: Consumer, Food Service, Private Label, Bulk

25338 Liberty Engineering Company
10567 Main St
Roscoe, IL 61073 815-623-7677
Fax: 815-623-7050 877-623-9065
info@libertyengineering.com
www.libertyengineering.com
Manufacturer and exporter of rotary dies, candy molds, starch molding processing equipment and depositing pumps
President: Brian Belardi
Engineering Manager: John Micinski
Quality Control: Rob Klein
Plant Manager: John Akelaitis
Estimated Sales: Below $5 Million
Number Employees: 10-19
Square Footage: 20000
Parent Co: Libco Industries

25339 Liberty Food Service
1410 Michigan St
Storm Lake, IA 50588-1961 712-732-3040
Fax: 713-732-3325 800-425-1088
www.libertyfoodservice.com
Owner: Connie Ellesson
Corporate Finance Manager: Liza Gunnerson
Sales/Customer Service Manager: Cindi Daufeldt
Estimated Sales: $5-10 Million
Number Employees: 5-9

25340 Liberty Labels, LLC
101 W Shrader Street
Liberty, MO 64068-2447
Fax: 620-223-2201 800-783-5285
sales@libertylabelsinc.com
www.libertylabelsinc.com
Pressure sensitive labels
Estimated Sales: $500,000-$1 Million
Number Employees: 5-9

25341 Liberty Machine Company
125 Derry Court
York, PA 17406-8405 717-848-1493
Fax: 800-745-8150 800-745-8152

Manufacturer and exporter of wire racks and grilles for refrigerators, ovens, etc.; also, wire material handling equipment
President: Brad Stump
Secretary/Treasurer: Patti Miller
Estimated Sales: $3 - 5 Million
Number Employees: 20
Square Footage: 18000
Type of Packaging: Food Service

25342 Libertyware
PO Box 160450
Clearfield, UT 84016 801-825-5885
Fax: 801-825-5875 888-500-5885
bbbrisko@aol.com www.libertywareusa.com
Manufacturer, importer and exporter of frying and stock pans, flatware, thermometers, disposable gloves and aprons, tongs, ladles, salt and pepper shakers and portion control equipment
President: Bob Brisko
Estimated Sales: $1 - 2,500,000
Number Employees: 10-19
Brands:
Libertyware

25343 Libman Company
220 N Sheldon St
Arcola, IL 61910 217-268-4200
Fax: 217-268-4168 877-818-3380
info@libman.com libman.com
Cleaning supplies including brushes, brooms, mops, scrubbers, etc
President: Robert Libman
CFO: William Libman
VP Sales/Marketing: Kim Spafford
Treasurer: William Libman
Estimated Sales: $1 - 2.5 Million
Number Employees: 1-4
Brands:
Libman

25344 (HQ)Libra Laboratories Inc
101 Liberty St
Metuchen, NJ 08840-1215 732-321-5200
Fax: 732-321-5203 asklibra@llbralabs.com
www.libralabs.com
Consulting R&D and analytical laboratories providing analyses/testing; problem-solving, on-site and remote consultation including expert witness services; shelf life studies; flavor, fat, oil and lipid analysis; refining and processingof ingredients; packaging material compatibility; chocolate analysis; and related. Wide variety of equipment available for advanced studies, e.g., digital scanning microscopy, texture analyzer, complete lab for deep-frying studies at severalscales
Senior Partner: Michael Blumenthal
VP: Trean Blumenthal
Estimated Sales: $1 - 3 Million
Number Employees: 5-9
Number of Brands: 3
Type of Packaging: Food Service
Brands:
Gitic
Veri-Fry
Veri-Fry Pro

25345 (HQ)Libra Technical Center
101 Liberty St
Metuchen, NJ 08840 732-321-5487
Fax: 732-321-1660 asktkt@libralabs.com
www.libralabs.com
Manufacturer and marketer of propietary, patented tests for estimation and measurement of chemical characteristics of fats and oils, especially with regard to degradation during deep-fat frying. Kits are correlated with OfficialMethods and are available for measurement fo Total Polar Materials, Free Fatty Acids, and ppm alkaline surfactants/soaps (Water Emulsion Titratables)
President: Michael Blumenthal PhD
Executive VP: Trean Blumenthal
Marketing/Sales: Ken Salzinger
Estimated Sales: $.5 - 1 million
Number Employees: 1-4
Number of Brands: 1
Type of Packaging: Food Service
Other Locations:
Libra Technologies
Metuchen NJ
Brands:
Veri-Fry
Veri-Fry Pro

25346 Liburdi Group of Companies
2599 Charlotte Highway
Mooresville, NC 28117 704-230-2510
Fax: 704-230-2555 800-533-9353
info@liburdidimetrics.com www.liburdi.com
Orbital welding equipment for tubes and pipes
President: Joe Liburdi
Estimated Sales: $3 Million
Number Employees: 20-49

25347 License Ad Plate Company
13110 Enterprise Ave
Cleveland, OH 44135 216-265-4200
Fax: 216-265-4203 lapco@stratos.net
Metal and plastic signs, pressure sensitive and thermal die cut decals, vinyls, mylars, scotchlite, frames, etc
President: Richard Russell
Estimated Sales: Below $5 Million
Number Employees: 10-19
Square Footage: 6000

25348 Licker Candy Company
1600 E Second Street
Winslow, AZ 86047-4456 520-289-4815
Fax: 520-289-9415

25349 Lido Roasters
3215 Brooklawn Ter
Chevy Chase, MD 20815-3936 301-718-9719
Fax: 301-718-9735
Tea and coffee roasters

25350 Life Spice Ingredients LLC
216 West Chicago Avenue
Chicago, IL 60654 312-274-0073
Fax: 312-274-2381
pgarvy@lifespiceingreients.com
www.lifespiceingredients.com
Spices
President: Peter Garvy
Vice President of Sales & Marketing: Lisa Stern
Vice President of Operations: Holland Schlutz
Estimated Sales: $25 Million
Number Employees: 50

25351 LifeLines Technology
116 American Rd
Morris Plains, NJ 07950-2443 973-984-0525
Fax: 973-984-1520 info@temptimecorp.com
www.lifelinestechnology.com
Self-adhesive time/temperature indicator labels that monitor the cummulative effect of heat over time
Chairman: Jean-Paul Martin
VP: Ted Prusik
Estimated Sales: $2.5-5 Million
Number Employees: 20-49
Number of Brands: 2
Number of Products: 2
Square Footage: 80000
Type of Packaging: Consumer, Food Service, Private Label, Bulk
Brands:
Fresh-Check
Fresh-Scan
Heatmaker Uvm

25352 (HQ)Lifetime Hoan Corporation
1000 Stewart Ave
Garden City, NY 11530 516-683-6000
Fax: 516-683-6161
questions@lifetimebrands.com
www.lifetimebrands.com
Exporter, importer and manufacturer of cutlery and gadgets
President: Steven Lizak
Chairman of the Board: Jeffrey Siegel
CFO: Rob Roknznally
VP: Bruce Cohen
VP: Larry Sklute
Number Employees: 50-99
Square Footage: 400
Brands:
Armstrong Forge
Avanti
Barclay Geneve
Carver Aid
Color Brights
Color Charms
Colorgems
Cordon Bleu
Country Christmas
Golden Barclay Geneve
Heartland
Jet Cut
L C Germain
Marmalade
Old Homestead
Paris Splendor
Pierre Santini
Pro/Star
Rack-The-Knife
Santa Fe
Southwest
Sugar Plum
Tristar
Welcome Home
Windy

25353 Lift Rite
5975 Falbourne Street - Unit 3
Mississauga, ON L5R 3L8
Canada 905-456-2603
Fax: 905-456-1383 infol@liftrite.com
www.liftrite.com
Manufacturer and exporter of stackers, pallet trucks, easy lifts and hi-lifters
President: Mel Griffin
Number Employees: 90

25354 Liftomatic Material Handling
700 Dartmouth Ln
Buffalo Grove, IL 60089 847-325-2930
Fax: 847-325-2959 800-837-6540
info@liftomatic.com www.liftomatic.com
Manufacturer and exporter of drum handlers, lift truck attachments and lifting equipment
President: Todd Berg
Sales Manager: E Darren Berg
Inside Sales: Angela Foster
Estimated Sales: $3-5,000,000
Number Employees: 1-4
Square Footage: 17000
Brands:
Ergo-Matic
Parrot-Beak

25355 Light Waves Concept
The Esquire Building 41st St
4100 1st Ave 3rd Floor North
Brooklyn, NY 11232 212-677-5230
Fax: 347-416-6201 800-670-8137
customerservice@lightwavesconcept.com
www.lightwavesconcept.com
Manufacturer, importer and exporter of lighting fixtures and low voltage track lighting
President: Joel Slavis
Estimated Sales: Below $5 Million
Number Employees: 10-19
Square Footage: 12000
Brands:
Lightwaves

25356 Lighthouse for the Blindin New Orleans
123 State St
New Orleans, LA 70118 504-899-4501
Fax: 504-895-4162 clee@lhb.org
www.lhb.org
Brooms, brushes, cotton and rayon mops, scrubbers and household textile items; also, remanufactured laser printer cartridges
President: Bill Crist
CEO: Bill Price
Controller: Ron Wattigny
Estimated Sales: $10 - 20 Million
Number Employees: 50-99
Square Footage: 400000
Brands:
Lighthouse
Skilcraft

25357 Lightnin Mixers
135 Mount Read Blvd
Rochester, NY 14611 585-436-5550
Fax: 585-436-5589 888-649-2377
www.lightninmixers.com
Mixers and impeller systems for industrial water and wastewater treatment.
Parent Co: SPX

25358 Lightolier
45 Industrial Way
Wilmington, MA 01887 978-657-7600
Fax: 978-988-3893 www.lightolier.com
Lighting fixtures
Controller: Bobbi McCoy
Director Marketing: Bill Bbri

Estimated Sales: $100-500 Million
Number Employees: 250-499
Parent Co: Gem Lyte Company

25359 Lights On
1960 Central Park Ave
Yonkers, NY 10710 914-961-0588
Fax: 914-961-0589 lights@liteson.com
www.liteson.com

Manufacturer, importer and exporter of lighting fixtures
Manager: Glenn Aroni
Estimated Sales: Less than $500,000
Number Employees: 10-19
Square Footage: 6000

25360 Lignetics of Missouri
P.O.Box 1706
Sandpoint, ID 83864-0901 208-263-0564
Fax: 208-263-9292 800-544-3834
info@lignetics.com www.lignetics.com

Barbecue pellets for pellet grills and flavor enhancers for charcoal
President: Ken Tucker
General Manager: Lyle Wiese
Regional Manager: Kevin Schaper
VP Sales/Marketing: Bob Wilson
Sales/Traffic Coordinator: Lindsay Turner
Estimated Sales: $2 Million
Number Employees: 20-49
Parent Co: Lignetics
Brands:
Bbq Pellets
Grill Master

25361 Lil' Orbits
2850 Vicksburg Ln N
Minneapolis, MN 55447 763-559-7505
Fax: 763-559-7545 800-228-8305
contact@lilorbits.com www.lilorbits.com

Manufacturer and exporter of vending carts, displays and automatic doughnut and crepe/pancake machines and accessories
Founder: Ed Anderson
President: Charlie Anderson
Vice President: Brian OGara
Marketing: Mike Foster
Sales: Brian O'Gara
Office Manager: Sue Larson
Service Production Manager: Terry OGara
Purchasing: Terry O'Gara
Estimated Sales: $3 - 5 Million
Number Employees: 10-19
Number of Brands: 2
Number of Products: 10
Square Footage: 100000
Brands:
Lil' Orbits
Orbie
Uni-Matic

25362 Lillsun Manufacturing
1350 Harris St.
PO Box 767
Huntington, IN 46750 260-356-6514
Fax: 260-356-8337 mail@lillsun.com
www.lillsun.com

Baker's woodenware; pizza and oven peels
CEO: Gregory Williams
VP: Carrie Williams
Estimated Sales: $1-2.5 Million
Number Employees: 5-9

25363 Lillsun Manufacturing Company, Inc.
1350 Harris St.
PO Box 767
Huntington, IN 46750 260-356-6514
Fax: 260-356-8337 mail@lillsun.com
www.lillsun.com

Manufacturer and exporter of bakers' woodenware including pizza and oven peels, paddles and proofing boards
President: Bill Sundermann
VP: W Sunderman
Estimated Sales: $1-2.5 Million
Number Employees: 5-9

25364 Lima Barrel & Drum Company
1140 Franklin St
Lima, OH 45804 419-224-8916
Fax: 419-227-3424

New and reconditioned steel drums, barrels and containers
President: Randy Hersh
Estimated Sales: $5 - 10 Million
Number Employees: 10-19

25365 Lima Sheet Metal
1001 Bowman Rd
Lima, OH 45804 419-229-1161
Fax: 419-229-8538
limasheetmetal@embarqmail.com
www.limasheetmetal.com

Food processing and canning equipment; also, safety guards, ladders and platforms; repair service available
President: James Emerick
Vice President and Senior Fabricator: Tom Emerick
Office Manager: Anne Emerick
Estimated Sales: $1-2.5 Million
Number Employees: 20-49
Square Footage: 44000

25366 Limoneria Company
1141 Cummings Rd
Santa Paula, CA 93060-9709 805-525-5541
Fax: 805-525-8761 info@limoneira.com
www.limoneira.com

Packing house for Sunkist Growers, Inc. citrus fruit.
President/CEO: Harold Edwards
VP/Finance & Administration: Don Delmatoff
Senior Vice President: Alex Teague
Business Development Manager: David McCoy
Marketing Director: John Chamberlain
Director Packing & Sales: Tomas Gonzales
Director Information Systems: Eric Tovias
Agritourism Operations Manager: Ryan Nasalroad
Estimated Sales: $20 Million
Type of Packaging: Food Service

25367 Lin Engineering
16245 Vineyard Blvd
Morgan Hill, CA 95037 408-919-0200
Fax: 408-919-0201 sales@linengineering.com
www.linengineering.com

Supplier of stepping moulder
President: Ted Lin
Accounting: Emma Lin
Quality Control: Rob Carl
Estimated Sales: $1 - 2.5 Million
Number Employees: 5-9

25368 (HQ)Lin Pac Plastics
200 Windrift Court
3
Roswell, GA 30076-3727 770-751-6006
Fax: 770-751-7154

Manufacturer and exporter of plastic egg cartons and food service packaging containers; also, processing and packaging trays
Sales/Marketing Manager: James Gullo
Other Locations:
Lin Pac Plastics
Sebring FL

25369 LinPac
6842 Templin Ct
San Angelo, TX 76904-4112 325-651-7378
Fax: 325-651-7482 800-453-7393
www.complete-packaging.com

Manufacturer and exporter of corrugated boxes and other packaging materials
President: Robert Hanton
Quality Control: Alvin Kennedy
R&D: Sal Flores
President: Nigel Roe
Plant Manager: Danny Lopez
Estimated Sales: $10 - 20 Million
Number Employees: 20-49
Square Footage: 50000
Parent Co: LinPac

25370 Lincoln
One Lincoln Way
St Louis, MO 63120 314-679-4200
Fax: 314-679-4359 www.lincolnindustrial.com

World leader in the manufacturer and sale of lubrication systems and industrial pumping equipment for industry
President: Bart Aitke
Number Employees: 500-999

25371 Lincoln Coders
2815 Independence Drive
PO Box 8009
Fort Wayne, IN 46808 260-482-8493
Fax: 260-483-2407 800-248-4452
sales@lincolncoders.com
www.lincolncoders.com

Carton coders and rubber type and ink rolls
President: Robert Beaver
Estimated Sales: $1-2.5 Million
Number Employees: 10-19

25372 Lincoln Foodservice
1333 East 179th Street
Cleveland, OH 44110 260-459-8200
Fax: 800-285-9511 800-374-3004
www.lincolnfp.com

Designs, manufactures, and markets commercial and institutional foodservice cooking equipment, serving systems, and utensils. The company also manufactures and markets a line of electric Fresh-O-Matic food steamers.
President: Charlie Kingdon
Plant Manager: Jim Muston
Purchasing Manager: Tom Hengy
Number Employees: 250-499
Brands:
Centurion
Fresh-O-Matic
Impinger
Impinger a La Carte
Redco
Traditionalware
Wear-Ever

25373 Lincoln Suppliers
1225 County Road 45 North
Owatonna, MN 55060 507-451-7410
Fax: 507-451-2968 800-622-8425
lincolnsuppliers@worldnet.att.net
www.lincolnsuppliers.com

Agitation systems, milk, silo, tank, aseptic processing equipment, batch control systems, cheese equipment, washer and drier chillers, fillers, milk, steam, heat exchangers, plate, scraped surface, homogenizers, margarine processingequipment, piping, fi
President: Michael Grunwald
Estimated Sales: $5 - 10 Million
Number Employees: 20-49

25374 Lincoln Tent & Awning
3900 Cornhusker Hwy
Suite 1
Lincoln, NE 68504 402-467-4559
Fax: 402-467-4907 800-567-4559
inquiries@lincolntent.com www.lincolntent.com
Commercial awnings
President: Thomas M Miller
Estimated Sales: $2.5 - 5 Million
Number Employees: 20-49

25375 Linde
575 Mountain Avenue
Murray Hill, NJ 07974 908-464-8100
800-755-9277
www.linde.com

Manufacturer and distributor of food freezing and chilling equipment.

25376 Linde Gas LLC
P.O.Box 94737
Cleveland, OH 44101 216-642-6600
Fax: 216-642-6625 800-983-5615
www.airgas.com

Gases and whole industrial welding equipment
President/CEO: Patrick Murphy
Applications Engineer: Michael Abshire
Estimated Sales: $250 Million
Number Employees: 100-249

25377 Linde Material HandlingNorth America Corporation
1056 Drop Off Dr
Summerville, SC 29483 843-871-0312
Fax: 843-875-8329 trucksales@lindelifttruck.com
www.lmh-na.com

Supplier of industrial lift trucks; which include both electric and internal combustion (IC) forklifts, sideloaders or container handlers, order pickers, tow tractors, high-level stackers, and reach trucks.
President: Brian Butler
Marketing Communications Manager: Meg Merritt

Estimated Sales: $50 - 100 Million
Number Employees: 100-249
Square Footage: 250000
Parent Co: Linde Material Handling
Brands:
Linde

25378 Line of Snacks Consultants
13220 Castleton Dr
Dallas, TX 75234-5113 972-484-1155
Fax: 972-243-3974
info@donpettyenterprises.com
www.donpettyenterprises.com/lineofsnacks
Consultant providing services to the snack industry worldwide for processing, technology, management, marketing, distribution and new product development
President: Donald Petty
Estimated Sales: Below $5 Million
Number Employees: 1-4
Square Footage: 2800

25379 Line-Master Products
PO Box 407
Cocolalla, ID 83813-0407 208-265-4743
Fax: 208-265-9393 lmprod@sandpoint.net
Manufacturer and exporter of work benches, push carts and fixed and mobile material handling racks
President: Jackie Warren
Estimated Sales: $1-2.5 Million
Number Employees: 5-9
Parent Co: Sandefur Engineering Company

25380 LineSource
600 Berkshire Avenue
Springfield, MA 01109-1052 413-747-9488
Fax: 413-746-4498 info@linesource.com
Food processing equipment; custom design services available
President: William Stotler
Vice President: Ken Bonardi
Sales/Marketing: Les Parkos
Estimated Sales: $1 - 3,000,000
Number Employees: 5-9
Type of Packaging: Consumer, Food Service, Private Label

25381 (HQ)Linear Lighting Corporation
3130 Hunters Point Ave
Long Island City, NY 11101 718-361-7552
Fax: 718-937-2747 mike@linearltg.com
www.linearltg.com
Manufacturer and exporter of lighting fixtures
President: Stanley Deutsch
CFO: Lois Shorr
R&D: Kewin Ehrhardt
Estimated Sales: $20 - 50 Million
Number Employees: 100-249

25382 Linett Company
390 Fountain St
Blawnox, PA 15238 412-826-8531
Fax: 800-530-8329 800-565-2165
eric@trl-arc.com
Strapping dispensers, castered stocking ladders, oily waste cans, special access ladders, crossovers and carts
President: Fred Schwartz
Vice President: Melvin Solomon
Marketing Director: Ronald Schwartz
Manager Operations: Nick Valore
Purchasing Manager: Chris Gianfrancesco
Estimated Sales: $10-20 Million
Number Employees: 130
Square Footage: 325000
Brands:
Castered Safety
Conveyor Crossovers
Ladder Crossovers
Tri-Arc Manufacturing

25383 Linette
PO Box 212
Womelsdorf, PA 19567-0212 610-589-4526
Fax: 610-589-2706
VP: James P Linette
Number Employees: 100-249

25384 Linker Equipment Corporation
5 Evans Terminal
Hillside, NJ 07205 908-353-0700
Fax: 908-353-1621 yaron@linkercorp.com
www.linkercorp.com
Owner, President: David Linker
Regional Manager: Rungkun Roeksangsri
Estimated Sales: $10,000,000 - $25,000,000
Number Employees: 100 - 250

25385 Linker Machines
20 Pine St
Rockaway, NJ 07866 973-983-0001
Fax: 973-983-0011 sales@linkermachines.com
www.linkermachines.com
Manufacturer and exporter of automatic sausage linking and peeling machinery; also, general purpose grease
Owner: Jean Hebrank
VP: R Hebrank
General Manager: Rob Hebrank, Jr.
Estimated Sales: $2.5-5 Million
Number Employees: 1-4
Square Footage: 4000
Brands:
Linkerlube
Ty-Linker
Ty-Peeler

25386 Linne's Candy & Cake Supplies
4149 Karg Industrial Pkwy
Kent, OH 44240-6425 330-678-7112
Fax: 330-678-7133
Candy and cake supplies
President: Christopher Romocean
Estimated Sales: $5 - 10 Million
Number Employees: 10-19

25387 Linnea's Candy & Cake Supplies
975 Oak Street
San Bernardino, CA 92410-2424 909-885-1446
Fax: 909-383-7201 sales@linneasinc.com
www.linneasinc.com
Candy, cake supplies, candy boxes, molds and all ingredients needed for cake and candy manufacturing
Manager: Mike Peterson
CFO: Polly Holman
Manager: Mike Peterson
Quality Control: Frank Romocean
Estimated Sales: Below $5 Million
Number Employees: 5-9
Parent Co: Linnea's Candy & Cake Supplies

25388 Linpac Materials Handling
3626 N Hall Street
Suite 729
Dallas, TX 75219-5127 214-599-9023
Fax: 214-599-9024 www.linpac.com
Supplier of reusable food containers to the supermarket industry

25389 Linpac Plastics
600 Corporate Drive
Suite 450
Fort Lauderdale, FL 33334-3606 954-492-5481
Fax: 954-489-0512 darin_gregg@linpac.com
www.linpac.com
Vice President of Marketing: Adam Barnett
Number Employees: 9

25390 Linvar
237 Hamilton St
Suite 202
Hartford, CT 06106 860-951-3818
Fax: 860-951-3547 800-282-5288
Manufacturer and exporter of metal shelving systems and plastic containers
Vice President: John Ramondetta
General Manager: John Ahern
Estimated Sales: $5 - 10 Million
Number Employees: 10-19
Square Footage: 25000
Brands:
Linbin's
Linshelf

25391 Linx Xymark
16 Lakeside Drive
Marlton, NJ 08053-2705 856-988-7125
Fax: 856-988-7126 info@linx-us.com
Estimated Sales: $1 - 5 Million

25392 (HQ)Linzer Products Corporation
248 Wyandanch Ave
W Babylon, NY 11704 718-961-0900
Fax: 718-358-0551 800-423-3254
info@linzerproducts.com www.arroworthy.com
Manufacturer and exporter of confectioners' and bakers' brushes and rollers
President: Alan Benson
VP Sales: Brent Swenson
VP Production: Sidney Zichvin
Number Employees: 300
Type of Packaging: Consumer

25393 Lion Apparel
7200 Poe Avenue
Suite 400
Dayton, OH 45414 937-898-1949
Fax: 937-898-2848 800-548-6614
www.lionapparel.com
Uniforms including work clothing, shirts, trousers, outerwear, cashiers' aprons and smocks
Executive Director: Bill Claire
CEO/Chief Marketing Officer: Stephen Schwartz
Chief Financial Officer: Jim Disanto
Senior Vice President: Terry Smith
Research & Development: Donald Aldridge
Director, Marketing: Hayley Fudge
Sales Manager: Jerry Loran
Director, Operations: Gary Lee
Estimated Sales: $66 Million
Number Employees: 760
Square Footage: 37000
Parent Co: Lion Apparel

25394 Lion Circle
4600 W 72nd St
Chicago, IL 60629-5810 773-582-5481
Fax: 773-284-3654 info@lioncircle.com
www.lioncircle.com
Advertising novelties and specialties including buttons, balloons, key tags, etc.
Sales/Marketing Executive: Rich Carollo
Purchasing Agent: Mike Webber
Estimated Sales: $1 - 5 Million
Number Employees: 50-99
Square Footage: 180000

25395 Lion Labels
15 Hampden Dr
South Easton, MA 02375 508-230-8211
Fax: 508-230-8116 800-875-5300
epage@lionlabels.com www.lionlabels.com
Manufacturer and exporter of signage, pressure sensitive labels and decals
President: Jerome M Berke
CEO: Michael Berke
CFO: Nina Berke
Sales Director: Moe Decelles
Operations Manager: Ed Page
Production Manager: Bruce Boteliao
Estimated Sales: $4.7 Million
Number Employees: 20-49
Square Footage: 29000
Type of Packaging: Consumer, Food Service, Private Label, Bulk

25396 Lion Laboratories
139 Mill Rock Road E
Old Saybrook, CT 06475-4217 860-388-6911
Fax: 860-388-6216
lion.laboratories@worldnet.att.net
Non-invasive authenticity testing

25397 Liqui-Box
1690 E Race St
Allentown, PA 18109 610-264-5420
Fax: 614-888-0982 liquibox@liquibox.com
www.liquibox.com
Manufacturer and exporter of form, fill and seal pouch packaging machinery; also, bag-in-box, retort and dispenser systems
Plant Manager: Barry Pritchard
Estimated Sales: $5-10 Million
Number Employees: 20-49
Parent Co: Liqui-Box Corporation

25398 (HQ)Liqui-Box Corporation
6950 Worthington Galena Rd.
Worthington, OH 43096-2360 614-888-9280
Fax: 614-888-0982 liquibox@liquibox.com
Manufacturer and exporter of food and industrial plastic packaging and packaging systems
Chief Executive Officer: Ash Sahi
Chief Financial Officer: Karen Conner
Chief Operating Officer: Stewart Graves
Estimated Sales: $128.6 Million
Number Employees: 1100

25399 **Liquid Air Engineering Corporation**
PO Box 460068
Houston, TX 77056 713-624-8000
Fax: 713-624-8794 www.airliquide.com
Wine gases
VP: Gregg Alexander
Estimated Sales: $1 - 5 Million
Number Employees: 1,000-4,999

25400 **Liquid Assets**
1421 Grove Street
Healdsburg, CA 95448-4711 707-527-9308
Fax: 707-527-9306 800-730-1030
Wine industry stainless steel tanks

25401 **Liquid Controls**
105 Albrecht Drive
Lake Bluff, IL 60044 847-295-1050
Fax: 847-295-8252 800-458-5262
lc-info.lcmeter@idexcorp.com www.lcmeter.com
Blending and batching equipment, flow meters and process control instrumentation
President: Matt Stillings
General Manager: Fred Niemeier
Global VP Sales & Marketing: John Thompson
VP Sales: Royal Wollberg
Number Employees: 250-499
Parent Co: IDEX Corporation

25402 **Liquid Sampling SystemsLLC**
P.O.Box 165
Cedar Rapids, IA 52406 319-365-2259
Fax: 319-365-2259 rob@pro-rata.com
www.pro-rata.com
Fluid sampling instrument sales and manufacturing
Owner: Robert Johnson
Estimated Sales: Below $5 Million
Number Employees: 1-4

25403 **Liquid Scale**
2033 Old Highway 8 NW
New Brighton, MN 55112 651-633-2969
Fax: 651-633-2969 888-633-2969
dtilden@isd.net
Manufacturer and exporter of milk silo air agitators, liquid level gauges and controls and needlepoint dividers
Estimated Sales: Under$300,000
Number Employees: 1-4
Square Footage: 3000
Brands:
Liquid Scale
Shimp

25404 **Liquid Scale**
2033 Old Highway 8 NW
New Brighton, MN 55112 651-633-2969
Fax: 651-633-2969 888-633-2969
www.liquidscale.com
Liquid level gauges
President: Dale J Tilden
Estimated Sales: Less than $500,000
Number Employees: 1-4

25405 **(HQ)Liquid Solids Control**
P.O.Box 259
Upton, MA 01568 508-529-3377
Fax: 508-529-6591
paulb@liquidsolidscontrol.com
www.liquidsolidscontrol.com
Manufacturer and exporter of in-line process control refractomers for continuous measurement and production; also, quality assurance of dissolved food solids available
President: Paul R Bonneau
CFO: Paul R Bonneau
VP: Gordon Vandenburg
Estimated Sales: $10 - 20 Million
Number Employees: 25
Square Footage: 25000
Other Locations:
Liquid Solids Control
Victoria BC
Brands:
Lsc Model 614
Lsc Model 725

25406 **Liquitane**
910 7th Ave
Berwick, PA 18603-1127 570-759-6200
Fax: 570-759-6254 www.ccclc.com
Plastic bottles and containers
Plant Manager: Bryan Statskey
Estimated Sales: $20-50 Million
Number Employees: 100-249
Parent Co: Liquitane

25407 **Lista International Corporation**
106 Lowland St
Holliston, MA 01746 508-429-1350
Fax: 508-626-0353 800-722-3020
sales@listaintl.com www.listaintl.com
Storage and workbench products.
President: Peter Lariviere
CFO: David Gavlik
Vice President: John Alfieri
Marketing: Anne Swagoriusky
Sales: John Alfieri
Estimated Sales: $50-100 Million
Number Employees: 225
Number of Brands: 2
Square Footage: 225000
Parent Co: Stanley Black & Decker
Brands:
Storage Wall

25408 **Listo Pencil Corporation**
1925 Union St
Alameda, CA 94501 510-522-2910
Fax: 510-522-3798 800-547-8648
sales@listo.com www.listo.com
Manufacturer and exporter of mechanical marking pencils, carton openers and industrial razor blades
President: Rick Stuart
VP: Rick Stuart
Estimated Sales: $2.5-5 Million
Number Employees: 5-9
Square Footage: 17000
Brands:
Listo

25409 **Litchfield Packaging Machinery Corporation**
71 Benedict Road
Morris, CT 06763 860-567-2011
Fax: 860-567-2012 imp@litchfieldpacking.com
www.litchfieldpackaging.com
Beverage packaging equipment
President: Ric Edwards
Estimated Sales: Below $5 Million
Number Employees: 4
Type of Packaging: Bulk

25410 **Litco International**
P.O. Box 150
Vienna, OH 44473-0150 330-539-5433
Fax: 330-539-5388 800-236-1903
info@litco.com www.litco.com
Supplier of export pallets, seperator sheets and air bags for the food industry also a supplier of export and domestic pallet solutions and load securement products.
President: Gary Trebilcock
CEO: Lionel Trebilcock
VP Sales: Gary Sharon
Estimated Sales: $5 Million

25411 **Lite-Weight Tool Manufacturing Company**
8621 San Fernando Rd
Sun Valley, CA 91352-3104 818-767-7901
Fax: 818-767-0010 800-859-3529
info@liteweighttool.com
www.liteweighttool.com
Manufacturer and exporter of squeegees including emulsion spreading, handheld and floor
President: C Brunson
VP: Andy Brunson
Estimated Sales: $500,000
Number Employees: 1-4
Square Footage: 5000

25412 **Litecontrol Corporation**
65 Spring St
Plympton, MA 02367 781-294-0100
Fax: 781-293-2849 info@litecontrol.com
www.litecontrol.com
Manufacturer and exporter of lighting fixtures
President/CEO: Brian Golden
Senior Accountant: Kristen Woods
VP/Sales: Vince Santini
R&D: Paul Duane
Quality Control: James Pierce
Marketing Manager: Cory Passerello
Project Manager: Barbara Goodwin
Estimated Sales: $5 - 10 Million
Number Employees: 100-249

25413 **Lithibar Matik**
13521 Quality Drive
Holland, MI 49424-8465 616-399-5215
Fax: 616-399-4026 800-626-0415
sales@besser.com www.lithibar-matik.com
Bag and case pallets
Estimated Sales: $10 - 15 Million
Number Employees: 50-100

25414 **Lithonia Lighting**
PO Box A
Conyers, GA 30012 770-922-9000
Fax: 770-483-2635 comments@lithonia.com
www.lithonia.com
Manufacturer and exporter of electric and fluorescent lighting fixtures
President: Vern Nagel
R&D: Ken Morgan
Number Employees: 1,000-4,999

25415 **Little Giant Pump Company**
PO Box 12010
Oklahoma City, OK 73157 405-947-2511
Fax: 405-947-8720
customerservice@littlegiant.com
www.littlegiant.com
Manufacturer and exporter of decorative and outdoor lighting fixtures; also, water removal and transfer pumps
President: Todd Strupp
R&D: Randy Karbs
Quality Assurance Manager: Charles Lamar
CEO: Todd Herrick
VP Sales/Marketing: Lynn McVay
Graphic Design Specialist: Brian Blake
Estimated Sales: I
Number Employees: 500-999
Square Footage: 270000
Parent Co: Tecumseh Products Company

25416 **Little Rock Broom Works**
7710 Jamison Rd
Little Rock, AR 72209 501-562-0311
Fax: 501-562-3887
House and whisk brooms; also, mop heads and sticks
Owner: Harold W Hatcher
Estimated Sales: $2.5-5 Million
Number Employees: 20-49

25417 **Little Rock Crate & Basket Company**
1623 E 14th St
Little Rock, AR 72202 501-376-6961
Fax: 501-372-6252 800-223-7823
www.lrbaskets.com
Fruit and vegetable shipping containers, wire bound crates for shrimp, fish and vegetables and veneer and novelty fruit baskets
President: Dudley Swann Jr
Estimated Sales: $10 - 20 Million
Number Employees: 50-99
Parent Co: Little Rock Crate & Basket Company

25418 **Little Rock Sign**
1117 Highway 365 S
Conway, AR 72032 501-327-4166
Fax: 501-327-4337
bob@littlerockconwaysign.com
www.littlerockconwaysign.com
Advertising, electric and plastic signs
President: Danny Glover
General Manager: Laverne Anderson
Estimated Sales: $1 - 2.5 Million
Number Employees: 10-19

25419 **Little Squirt**
10 Compass Court
Toronto, ON M1S 5R3
Canada 416-665-6605
Fax: 416-665-5631 info@opal.on.ca
www.opal.on.ca
Portion controlled and refrigerated cream/milk dispensers
President: Garnet Rich
R&D: Bryan Symonds
Number Employees: 40
Brands:
Little Squirt

25420 **Littleford Day**
PO Box 128
Florence, KY 41022-0128 859-525-7600
Fax: 859-525-1446 800-365-8555
sales@littleford.com www.littleford.com
Food processing equipment including mixers, granulators, sterilizers, agglomerators, vacuum dryers, liquid dispensers and pressure cookers; importer and exporter of mixers, dryers and sterilizers
President & CEO: Charles Kroeger
Research & Development: Glen Vice
Marketing & Sales: William R Barker
Estimated Sales: $50-100 Million
Number Employees: 100-249
Number of Brands: 10
Number of Products: 10
Type of Packaging: Food Service, Private Label

25421 **Live Floor Systems**
1076 Harrisburg Pike
Carlisle, PA 17013-1615 717-243-6644
Fax: 717-243-9926
Manufacturers ofautomated loading and unloading systems
Director Sales: Norm Fortney
Number Employees: 20

25422 **Livingston-Wilbor Corporation**
PO Box 496
Edison, NJ 08818-496 908-322-8403
Fax: 908-322-9230 livwil@cybernex.net
Manufacturer and exporter of labeler change parts
Purchasing Agent: Chris Haigh
Estimated Sales: $1-2.5 Million
Number Employees: 10-19
Square Footage: 12000
Type of Packaging: Consumer, Food Service, Private Label

25423 **Lixi**
11980 Oak Creek Pkwy
Huntley, IL 60142 847-961-6666
Fax: 847-961-6667 lixi@lixi.com
www.lixi.com
Manufacturer and exporter of inspection systems specializing in automatic detection of defects and rejection from conveyors
President: Brent Burns
Sales Manager: Joseph Plevak
Production: Ken Belzey
Estimated Sales: $2.5-5 Million
Number Employees: 5-9
Square Footage: 10000

25424 **Lixi, Inc.**
11980 Oak Creek Pkwy
Huntley, IL 60142 847-961-6666
Fax: 847-961-6667 lixi@lixi.com
www.lixi.com
Small x-ray imaging systems used for monitoring quality assurance, product malfunctions and fault analysis, security inspection and product tampering.

25425 **Lloyd Disher Company**
5 Powers Lane Place
Decatur, IL 62522-3287 217-429-0593
Fax: 217-423-2611
Manufacturer and exporter of aluminum alloy Teflon coated ice cream scoops
President: Gordan Lloyd
Sales Manager: Lucy Murphy
Estimated Sales: $1 - 5 Million
Number Employees: 1-4
Square Footage: 5000
Brands:
Lloyd

25426 **Lloyd's Register QualityAssurance**
1330 Enclave Pkwy
Suite 200
Houston, TX 77077 281-578-7995
Fax: 281-398-7337 888-877-8001
info-usa@lrqa.com www.lrqausa.com
Company providing quality system certification; serving the food and dairy industries
President: Paul Huber
CFO: Beverly Simmons
Quality Control: Atul Puri
Estimated Sales: $5-10 Million
Number Employees: 1-4

25427 **Lloyd's of Millville**
102 S 8th St # B
Millville, NJ 08332-3415 856-825-0345
Fax: 856-825-7666
Commercial awnings
President: Benjamin Lloyd Jr
VP: Rick Lioyd
Estimated Sales: Below $5,000,000
Number Employees: 1-4

25428 **LoTech Industries**
12136 W Bayaud Ave Ste 120
Lakewood, CO 80228 303-202-6337
Fax: 303-202-9252 800-295-0199
bev@lotechinc.com www.lotechinc.com
Manufacturer and exporter of catering and food service custom imprinted utensils including plastic spoons, tongs, cake servers, pizza cutters, ladles, spatulas, and pasta forks
Vice President: Bev Whiteside
Estimated Sales: $2 Million
Number Employees: 3
Type of Packaging: Consumer, Food Service, Private Label, Bulk
Brands:
Lotech

25429 **Load King ManufacturingCompany**
1357 W Beaver St
Jacksonville, FL 32209 904-354-8882
Fax: 904-353-1984 800-531-4975
sales@loadking.com www.loadking.com
Manufacturer and exporter of garbage and waste compactors, cardboard recycling balers, stainless steel tables, sinks, wire racks, carts, salad bars, checkout counters, etc. Manufactures fixtures and equipment worldwide to thesupermarket, restaurant and retail industries
President: Charles Chupp
CEO: Charlie Chupp Jr
VP Sales: Charles Chupp
Estimated Sales: $10 - 20 Million
Number Employees: 250-499
Square Footage: 300000
Type of Packaging: Consumer, Food Service

25430 **LoadBank International**
4654 35th St
Orlando, FL 32811-6521 407-957-4000
Fax: 407-957-4175 800-458-9010
m.willett@loadbank.com www.loadbank.com
Manufacturer and exporter of material handling and distribution equipment including dock staging and cross-docking systems
President: Doug Hughes
Vice President: Mike Willett
Sales Director: Mike Willett
Operations Manager: John Veitch
Estimated Sales: $1-2.5 Million
Number Employees: 20-49
Number of Brands: 12
Number of Products: 12
Brands:
Air-Trax
Dock Xpress
Loadbank
Xpresslane

25431 **Lobsters Alive Company**
3200 N Richmond Rd
Johnsburg, IL 60051 708-562-7837
Fax: 815-344-4479
Wholesaler/distributor of lobster tank supplies and parts; also, sales and service of new and reconditioned lobster tanks available; design consultant specializing in large holding systems
General Manager: Joann Baureis
Equipment Specialist: Dennis Baureis
Estimated Sales: $500,000-$1 Million
Number Employees: 1-4
Square Footage: 2000

25432 **Lobues Rubber Stamp Company**
1228 McGowan St
Houston, TX 77052 713-652-0031
Fax: 713-652-0511 lobuestamp@earthlink.net
www.lobuesrubberstampco.com
Rubber stamps
President: Grant Gaumer
Estimated Sales: $1-2.5 Million
Number Employees: 1-4

25433 **Location Georgia**
245 Peachtree Center Avenue NE
Atlanta, GA 30303-1222 800-946-4642
Fax: 404-302-8333
locationgeorgia@meagpower.org
www.meagpower.org
President, Chief Executive Officer: Robert Johnston
Sr. Vice President, Chief Administrative: Scott Jones
Sr. Vice President, Chief Operating Offi: Steven Jackson

25434 **Lock Inspection Systems**
207 Authority Drive
Fitchburg, MA 01420-6094 978-343-3716
Fax: 978-343-6278 800-227-5539
sales@lockinspection.com
www.lockinspection.com
Manufacturer, importer and exporter of advanced quality control detection systems including metal detectors, checkweighers and conveyors for the packaging and processing industries
President: Mark D'Onofrio
Marketing Director: Michelle Contois
VP of Sales & Marketing: David Arseneault
Public Relations: Michelle Contois
Production Manager: Brian Clough
Purchasing Manager: John Parker
Estimated Sales: $5-10 Million
Number Employees: 20-49
Square Footage: 120000
Parent Co: Transfer Technology Group PLC

25435 **Lockheed Martin Postal Technology**
6201 E 43rd St
Tulsa, OK 74135-6562 918-622-2697
Fax: 918-622-2697
Manual, advanced and multiline bar coding and mail sorting machines
President: Bill Dobbs
Estimated Sales: $10-20 Million
Number Employees: 5-9
Parent Co: Lockheed Martin

25436 **Locknane**
720 132nd St SW
Suite 207
Everett, WA 98204-9359 425-742-5187
Fax: 425-745-0277 800-848-9854
Manufacturer and exporter of nylon apparel and vinyl aprons; also, jackets
President: Duane Locknane
Marketing Director: Brent Locknane
Purchasing Manager: Tami Matuizek
Estimated Sales: $3 - 5 Million
Number Employees: 25
Square Footage: 7000
Type of Packaging: Food Service
Brands:
Jo-Lock

25437 **Locknetics**
11819 N Pennsylvania St
Carmel, IN 46032-4555
Fax: 860-584-2136 www.lockneticsonboard.com
Manufacturer and exporter of electro-magnetic locking systems
Finance Executive: Robert Zdanowski
Sales Manager: George Nortonen
Estimated Sales: $20 - 50 Million
Number Employees: 100-249
Parent Co: Ingersoll-Rand.

25438 **Lockwood Greene Engineers**
303 Perimeter Ctr N Ste 800
Atlanta, GA 30346 770-829-6500
Fax: 770-818-8100 lockwood@lg.com
www.lg.com
Consultant and designer providing plant and production line layout, process and packaging engineering, automation and control systems and environmental services
Manager: Angela Davis
Manager: Barry Hall
Sr. VP: Bill Leslie
VP: Fizool Israel
Estimated Sales: $50 - 100 Million
Number Employees: 250-499
Parent Co: Lockwood Greene Engineers

25439 **Lockwood Greene Engineers**
1450 Greene St Ste 200
Augusta, GA 30901 706-724-8225
Fax: 706-724-8422 lockwood@lg.com
www.lg.com
Consultant and designer providing plant and production line layout, process and packaging engineering, automation and control systems and environmental services
Manager: Tom Sickling
Project Manager: Bob Grahl
Estimated Sales: $10-20 Million
Number Employees: 50-99
Square Footage: 6000
Parent Co: Lockwood Greene Engineers

25440 **Lockwood Greene Engineers**
270 Davidson Ave # 4
Somerset, NJ 08873-4140 732-560-5700
Fax: 732-868-2300 lockwood@lg.com
www.lg.com
Consultant and designer providing plant and production line layout, process and packaging engineering, automation and control systems and environmental services
Manager: Sherman Schwartz
Project Director: Tom Geffert
Senior Vice President, Chief Human Resou: Don-Hyung Kang
President, Chief Operating Officer: Jong-Sik Kim
Estimated Sales: $20-50 Million
Number Employees: 100-249
Parent Co: Lockwood Greene Engineers

25441 **Lockwood Greene Engineers**
4201 Spring Valley Road
Suite 1500
Dallas, TX 75244-3669 972-991-5505
Fax: 972-960-2070 lockwood@lg.com
www.lg.com
Consultant and designer providing plant and production line layout, process and packaging engineering, automation and control systems and environmental services
President/COO: Lee McInitre
CEO: Ralph Peterson
Chief Financial Officer: Samuel Iapalucci
Senior Vice President, Chief Human Resou: Don-Hyung Kang
President, Chief Operating Officer: Jong-Sik Kim
Estimated Sales: $20 - 50 Million
Number Employees: 60
Parent Co: Lockwood Greene Engineers

25442 **Lockwood Greene Engineers**
2035 Lakeside Center Way
Suite 200
Knoxville, TN 37922-6595 256-533-9907
Fax: 256-533-7476
Consultant and designer providing plant and production line layout, process and packaging engineering, automation and control systems, environmental services and architectural engineering support
Office Manager: Tom Glazener
Estimated Sales: $1-2.5 Million
Number Employees: 19
Parent Co: Lockwood Greene Engineers

25443 **Lockwood Greene Engineers**
130 Concord Rd
Knoxville, TN 37934-2901 865-218-5377
Fax: 865-777-3834 www.lg.com
Consultant and designer providing plant and production line layout, process and packaging engineering, automation and control systems and environmental services
President: Cathy Neubert
CEO: Ralph Peterson
Senior Vice President, Chief Human Resou: Don-Hyung Kang
President, Chief Operating Officer: Jong-Sik Kim
Estimated Sales: $10-20 Million
Number Employees: 10-19
Parent Co: Lockwood Greene Engineers

25444 **Lockwood Greene Engineers**
2035 Lakeside Center Way
Suite 200
Knoxville, TN 37922-6595 251-476-2400
Fax: 251-344-7400
Consultant and designer providing plant and production line layout, process and packaging engineering, automation and control systems and environmental services
Office Manager: David Holland
Estimated Sales: $.5 - 1 million
Number Employees: 5-9
Parent Co: Lockwood Greene Engineers

25445 **Lockwood Greene Engineers**
7101 Executive Center Drive
Suite 297
Brentwood, TN 37027-3239 615-221-5031
Fax: 615-221-5078 scrady@lg.com
www.lg.com
Consultant and designer providing plant and production line layout, process and packaging engineering, materials handling, automation and control systems and environmental services
President: Lee McIntire
CEO: Ralph Peterson
Senior Vice President, Chief Human Resou: Don-Hyung Kang
President, Chief Operating Officer: Jong-Sik Kim
Estimated Sales: $1-2.5 Million
Number Employees: 19
Parent Co: Lockwood Greene Engineers

25446 **Lockwood Greene Engineers**
270 Davidson Ave # 4
Somerset, NJ 08873-4140 732-560-5700
Fax: 732-868-2300 www.lg.com
Consultant and designer providing plant and production line layout, process and packaging engineering, automation and control systems and environmental services
Manager: Sherman Schwartz
Senior Vice President, Chief Human Resou: Don-Hyung Kang
President, Chief Operating Officer: Jong-Sik Kim
Estimated Sales: $20 - 50 Million
Number Employees: 100-249
Parent Co: Lockwood Greene Engineers

25447 **Lockwood Greene Engineers**
165 Road Km 10 Pueblo Viejo
Guaynabo, PR 00968 787-781-9050
Fax: 787-781-0177 mayra.rodriguez@lg.com
www.lg.com
Consultant and designer providing plant and production line layout, process, packaging, engineering, automation and control systems, construction management, environmental services and validation services.
Office Manager: Gene Scott
Director Projects: Jorge Alvarez
Senior Vice President, Chief Human Resou: Don-Hyung Kang
Marketing Director: Mayra Rodriguez
Validations Manager: Victor Batista
Estimated Sales: $64 Million
Number Employees: 178
Square Footage: 13000
Parent Co: Lockwood Greene Engineers

25448 **Lockwood Greene Engineers**
1000 Towne Center Blvd
Pooler, GA 31322-4052 912-330-3000
Fax: 912-330-9025 www.lg.com
Consultant and designer providing plant/production line layout, process and packaging engineering, automation and control systems and environmental services.
President: Tom Hixson
CEO: Ralph Peterson
Senior Vice President, Chief Human Resou: Don-Hyung Kang
President, Chief Operating Officer: Jong-Sik Kim
Estimated Sales: $2.5-5 Million
Number Employees: 50-99
Parent Co: Lockwood Greene Engineers

25449 **Lockwood Greene Engineers**
1500 International Dr
Spartanburg, SC 29303 864-578-2000
Fax: 864-599-4117 tmaloney@lg.com
www.lg.com
Number Employees: 250-499

25450 **Lockwood Greene Technologies**
1450 Greene St Ste 200
Augusta, GA 30901 505-889-3831
Fax: 505-889-3842
Consultant and designer providing plant and production line layout, process and packaging engineering, automation and control systems and environmental services
Estimated Sales: $2.5-5 Million
Number Employees: 19
Parent Co: Lockwood Greene Engineers

25451 **Lockwood Manufacturing**
31251 Industrial Road
Livonia, MI 48150 734-425-5330
Fax: 734-427-5650 800-521-0238
customerservice@lockwoodusa.com
www.lockwoodusa.com
Wine racks, wine storage coolers, and food service equipment.
President: David Lamson
TBA Sales: David Lawrence
TBA Sales: Chad Buckles

25452 **Lockwood Packaging**
271 Salem Street
Unit G
Woburn, MA 01801-2004 781-938-1500
Fax: 781-938-7536 800-641-3100
Manufacturer and exporter of automatic weighing and bagging equipment and supplies; also, repair and operating services available
President: Richard Gold
VP: Thomas Gold
VP: Hans Van Der Sande
Estimated Sales: $.5 - 1 million
Number Employees: 20-49

25453 **Lodal**
620 N Hooper
Kingsford, MI 49802-2315 906-779-1700
Fax: 906-779-1160 800-435-3500
sales@lodal.com www.lodal.com
Manufacturer and exporter of refuse removal systems
President/Owner: Bernard Leger
CFO: Bernard Leger
Director Marketing: Darren Tavonatti
Estimated Sales: $10 - 20 Million
Number Employees: 10-19

25454 **Lodge Manufacturing Company**
503 S Cedar Ave
South Pittsburg, TN 37380 423-837-5919
Fax: 423-837-8279 lodges1@cdc.com
www.lodgemfg.com
Manufacturer, importer and exporter of cast iron cookware, bakeware and servingware
President: Henry Lodge
CEO: Bob Kellermann
CEO: Robert F Kellermann
R&D: Jeanne Scholze
Quality Control: Lou Zarzaur
VP Sales: Gray Bekurs
VP Production: Mike Whitfield
Estimated Sales: $20 - 50 Million
Number Employees: 100-249
Type of Packaging: Consumer, Food Service

25455 **Lodi Metal Tech**
P.O.Box 967
Lodi, CA 95241-0967 209-334-2500
Fax: 209-334-1259 800-359-5999
lmtracks@lodinet.com
Manufacturer and exporter of racks
Manager: Dean Bender
Estimated Sales: $10-20,000,000
Number Employees: 50-99
Square Footage: 155000

25456 **Loeb Equipment & Appraisal Company**
4131 S State Street
Chicago, IL 60609 773-548-4131
Fax: 773-548-2608 Sales@loebequipment.com
www.loebequipment.com
Wholesaler/distributor of used packaging and processing equipment.
President/CEO: Howard Newman
Marketing Director: Sara Bogin Sr
Sales Manager: Tom Larson
Number Employees: 25
Square Footage: 600000

25457 **Loeb Equipment & Appraisal Company**
4131 S State Street
Chicago, IL 60609-2942 773-548-4131
Fax: 773-548-2608 800-560-5632
sales@loebequipement.com
www.loebequipment.com
Buy and sell packaging and processing equipment to food industry. Also specialize in certified appraisels, asset managment and liquidators
President: Howard Newman
Vice President: John Hagist
Marketing Director: Sara Bogin
Sales Manager: Tom Larson
Type of Packaging: Food Service, Private Label

25458 **Loewenstein**
206 E Frazier Ave
Liberty, NC 27298-7211 336-622-2201
Fax: 954-960-0409 800-327-2548
info@loewensteininc.com
www.loewnsteininc.com
Chairs, stools, tables and table bases
President: Bruce Albertson
CFO: Winson Tortorici
Quality Control: Beata Kaminiski
VP Operations: David Biancofiore
Number Employees: 60
Square Footage: 165000

25459 **Logemann Brothers Company**
3150 W Burleigh St
Milwaukee, WI 53210 414-445-2700
Fax: 414-445-1460 logemannbalers@aol.com
www.logemannbalers.com
Manufacturer and exporter of scrap-metal, liber and refuse bales, also, alligator shears, briquettes and guillotines
Owner: Carl Dieterle
General Sales Manager: Robert Pichta
Estimated Sales: $2.5 Million

25460 **Logility**
470 E Paces Ferry Rd NE
Atlanta, GA 30305 404-261-9777
Fax: 404-264-5206 800-762-5207
ask@logility.com www.logility.com
President and CEO: J. Michael Edenfield
CFO: Vincent Klinges
VP of Research and Development: Mark A. Balte
Vice President of Marketing: Karin L. Bursa
Estimated Sales: $20 - 25 Million
Number Employees: 100-249

25461 **Logility TransportationGroup**
1011 East Touhy Avenue
Suite 315
Des Plaines, IL 60018 847-699-6620
Fax: 847-699-6671 www.logility.com
Software for routing, carrier selection, freight audit, order consolidation, freight accounting and transportation management; also, integrated and proven solutions
President, CEO: J. Michael Edenfield
CFO: Vincent Klinges
EVP Sales and Marketing: H. Allan Dow
Vice President of Research and Developme: Mark A. Balte
VP Marketing: Karin L. Bursa
Vice President of Customer Service: Donald L. Thomas
Estimated Sales: $2.5-5 Million
Number Employees: 20-49
Square Footage: 36800
Parent Co: Logility
Brands:
Base Rate
Carrier Select
Dsi Escort
Match Pay
Preshipment Planning
Ship Wise

25462 **Logix**
10518 NE 68th St
Suite 103
Kirkland, WA 98033-7003 425-828-4149
Fax: 425-828-9682 800-275-8112
info@logix-controls.com
www.logix-controls.com
Industrial refrigeration control system for the food, beverage and cold storage industries providing management and facility wide system tracking and reporting. Special fermentation controls available for wineries and alliedindustries
President: Jim Conant
CFO: Jim Conant
VP: Micheal Ghan
Sales: Stephen Bowers
Operations: Scott Gillette
Production: Thomas Kulin
Estimated Sales: $2.5 - 5 Million
Number Employees: 5-9
Number of Brands: 2
Number of Products: 6
Square Footage: 1000
Brands:
Logix

25463 **Logo Specialty Advertising Tems**
PO Box 270544
Tampa, FL 33688-0544 561-429-4725
800-704-0094
roz@everythinglogo.com
www.logospecialtyadvertisingitems.com
Specialty advertising items
Co-Owner: Roz Kodish
*Estimated Sales:*less than $500,000
Number Employees: 1-4

25464 **Logotech**
18 Madison Road
Fairfield, NJ 07004 973-882-9595
Fax: 973-882-0902 800-988-5646
sales@logotec-inc.com www.logotech-inc.com
Pressure sensitive label manufacturer
President: Leslie Gurland
CFO: Rodney Schundler
Research & Development: Jamie Fedor
Quality Control: Bruce Wade
Sales: Halley Mechanic
Estimated Sales: $5,000,000 -$15,000,000
Number Employees: 44
Square Footage: 56000

25465 **Lohall Enterprises**
6755 N Range Line Road
Milwaukee, WI 53209-3209 414-351-1270
Fax: 414-351-4531 lohall@execpc.com
Wrapping paper, wet waxed paper roll and sheet
Vice President: Arnold Garber
Purchasing Manager: Mary Anne Garber
Estimated Sales: $1 Million+
Number Employees: 3

25466 **Loma International**
283 E Lies Rd
Carol Stream, IL 60188-9421 630-588-0900
Fax: 630-588-1394 800-872-5662
tracey.hartje@loma.com www.loma.com
Manufacturer, exporter and importer of metal detectors and weighing equipment
President: Gary Wilson
CFO: Hary Pommier
Technical Director: Mike Nevin
Manager of IT: Brooke Kruger
Marketing Manager: James Chrismas
Sales Manager: Andrey Ivanov
Sales: Sandy Stillmaker
Estimated Sales: $20 - 50 Million
Number Employees: 50-99
Square Footage: 21000

25467 **Loma Systems**
283 E Lies Rd
Carol Stream, IL 60188 630-588-0900
800-872-5662
www.loma.com
Inspection systems-metal detectors, check weighess, x-ray inspection systems.
President: Martin Lymn
CFO: Harold Pommier
Sales: Sandy Stillmaker
Operations: Craig Scachitti
Estimated Sales: $20-$50 Million
Number Employees: 80

25468 **Lomont IMT**
1516 E. Mapleleaf Drive
Mt. Pleasant, IA 52641 319-385-1528
Fax: 319-385-1533 800-776-0380
info@lomont.com www.lomontimt.com
Industrial safety signs, equipment tags and labels.
Number Employees: 150
Square Footage: 200000

25469 **Lone Peak Labeling Systems**
1272 West 2240 South
Suite B
Salt Lake City, UT 84119 801-975-1818
Fax: 801-975-1865 800-658-8599
chrisa@lonepeaklabeling.com
www.lonepeaklabeling.com
Labels
President/Owner: Chris Appelbaum
Operations: Jason Halling
Estimated Sales: $3.5 Million
Number Employees: 20

25470 **Lone Star Banners and Flags**
212 South Main Street
Fort Worth, TX 76104 817-335-2548
800-288-9625
www.abcflag.com
Flags, banners, outdoor advertising displays and pennants; exporter of flags
President: James Eggleston
VP Marketing: Pam Engelhardt
Estimated Sales: $5-10 Million
Number Employees: 20-49
Square Footage: 80000

25471 **Lone Star Container Corporation**
700 N Wildwood Dr
Irving, TX 75061 972-579-1551
Fax: 972-554-6081 800-552-6937
jphipps@lonestarbox.com
www.lonestargraphic.com
Manufacturer and exporter of corrugated boxes
CEO: John McLeod
Manager: Joe Phipps
Estimated Sales: $500,000-$1 Million
Number Employees: 100-249

25472 **Long Company**
20 N. Wacker Drive
Suite 1010
Chicago, IL 60606-2901 312-726-4606
Fax: 312-726-4625 800-400-8615
info@thelongco.com www.thelongco.com
President: Bill Zimmerman
CEO: Roger Masa
V.P. Operations - Consulting Services: Gary Swymeler
Director of Quality, R & D: Albert Bachman
Director of Manufacturing Services: Duane Bull
Purchasing Director: Larry Devereux

25473 **Long Food Industries**
709 Rock Beauty Road
Fripp Island, SC 29920-7344 843-838-3205
Fax: 843-838-3918 longfood@isle.net
www.longfoodindustries.com
Shrimp, cooked/diced chicken, clam (meat and broth), beef (diced/cooked), lobster, fish and pork
President: Leon Long
Estimated Sales: $10-20 Million
Number Employees: 1
Type of Packaging: Food Service

25474 **Long Island Stamp Corporation**
5431 Myrtle Ave
Flushing, NY 11385 718-628-8550
Fax: 718-628-8560 800-547-8267
yona@longislandstamp.com
Rubber stamps, signs, labels, daters and seals
Owner: Harriet Pollak
VP: Harry Pollak
Estimated Sales: $1-2.5 Million
Number Employees: 10-19
Square Footage: 4500

25475 **Long Range Systems**
4550 Excel Pkwy Ste 200
Suite 200
Addison, TX 75001 214-553-5308
Fax: 214-221-0160 800-577-8101
info@pager.net www.pager.net

A leading innovator of guest and staff paging and management systems for 14 years. We invented the popular coaster pager and now offer more pagers than anyone else. We have over 35 products designed to help you streamline operationsimprove service and increase sales every day. We provide the highest quality, most durable products on the market, plus we offer exclusive products and services no other company can.
Owner: Ken Lovgren
Marketing Director: Kevin Hosey
Sales Director: Jim Livingston
Number Employees: 20-49
Brands:
Adverteaser
Coaster Call
Cool Blue
Keycall
Lobster Call
Star Pager
The Butler
The Informant
Total Control

25476 **Long Reach ManufacturingCompany**
136 Main Street
Suite 4
Westport, CT 06880-3304 713-434-3400
Fax: 713-433-9710 800-285-7000
sales@longreach.com www.longreach.com
Manufacturer and exporter of lift truck attachments and pallet trucks
Chief Executive Officer: William Masson
Chief Financial Officer: William Masson
Vice President: Pat Poyton
Estimated Sales: $33 Million
Number Employees: 142
Brands:
Rol-Lift

25477 **Longaberger Basket Company**
P.O. Box 3400
Newark, OH 43055 740-322-7800
Fax: 740-322-5022 info@longaberger.com
www.longaberger.com
Fruit and vegetable baskets
Chairman/Chief Executive Officer: Tami Longaberger
Estimated Sales: $50-100 Million
Number Employees: 6,390
Square Footage: 180000
Parent Co: J.W. Longaberger Basket Company

25478 **Longford Equipment International**
41 Lamont Avenue
Toronto, ON M1S 1A8
Canada 416-298-6622
Fax: 416-298-6627 888-298-2900
longford@longfordint.com
www.longfordint.com
Estimated Sales: $15 Million
Number Employees: 100

25479 **Longford Equipment US**
938 Manchester Rd
Glastonbury, CT 06033-2629 860-659-0762
Fax: 860-633-8207 feederpro@aol.com
Coupon and leaflet feeding machinery. Also turnkeys attaching to packaging lines available
Owner: Guy Sanderson
Manager: Guy Sanderson
Estimated Sales: $1-2.5 Million
Number Employees: 1-4

25480 **Longhorn Imports**
2202 E Union Bower Rd
Irving, TX 75061 972-721-9102
Fax: 972-579-4890 800-641-8348
info@longhornimports.com
www.longhornimports.com
Baskets, gift boxes, specialty containers, glassware, seasonal items and packaging products
President/Owner: Bruce Adoo
VP/VP Finance: Carol Adoo
Marketing: Wendy Mawhee
Estimated Sales: $3.1 Million
Number Employees: 17

25481 **Longhorn Packaging**
110 Pierce Ave
San Antonio, TX 78208 210-222-9686
Fax: 210-226-7511 800-433-7974
package1@aol.com
www.longhornpackaging.com
Manufacturer and exporter of converted flexible packaging film and vertical form/fill/seal packaging machinery; also, contract packaging available
President: Joe Carinhas
VP: Bill Green
VP Production: Harold Smith
Estimated Sales: $20-50 Million
Number Employees: 50-99
Square Footage: 40000

25482 **Longview Fibre Company**
300 Fibre Way
Longview, WA 98632 360-425-1550
Fax: 360-575-5934 800-929-8111
info@longfibre.com www.longviewfibre.com
Paper, corrugated and fibre containers, cushioning materials and corrugated pallets
Chairman of the Board: Richard Wollenberg
CEO: Frank V McShane
Sales Manager: Fran Goetz
Plant Manager: Harry Johnson
Estimated Sales: $20 - 50 Million
Number Employees: 1,000-4,999
Square Footage: 400000

25483 **Longview Fibre Company**
8705 SW Nimbus Ave
Beaverton, OR 97008-4000 503-350-1600
Fax: 323-725-6341 degroves@longfibre.com
www.longviewfibre.com
Manufacturer and exporter of disposable liquid bulk bins
Sales Manager: Dennis Dorgan
Vice President of Sales and Marketing: Lou Loosbrock
Sales Bulk Liquid Packaging: Paul Hansen
Estimated Sales: $1 - 3 Million
Number Employees: 5-9
Type of Packaging: Bulk
Brands:
Drumplex
Liquiplex

25484 **Longview Fibre Company**
P.O.Box 106
Oakland, CA 94604 510-569-2616
Fax: 510-569-4141 www.longviewfibre.com
Wine industry packaging and design
Vice President of Sales and Marketing: Lou Loosbrock
Plant Manager: Nathan Dyke
Estimated Sales: $10-20 Million
Number Employees: 50-99
Parent Co: Longview Fibre

25485 **Lonza Group**
17-17 State Route 208
Fair Lawn, NJ 07410-2820 201-794-6162
Fax: 201-794-2515 800-777-1875
techsery@lonza-us.com www.lonza.com
Supplier of l-Carnitine
CEO: Markus Germuend
VP Sales/Marketing: John Dobol
Communication Manager: Maureen Matson
Estimated Sales: $350 Million
Number Employees: 1000
Number of Products: 100

25486 **Loos Machine & Automation**
205 W. Washington Street
Colby, WI 54421 715-223-2844
Fax: 715-223-6140 www.loosmachine.com
Custom designed automated food processing equipment for the dairy, meat and poultry industries.

25487 **Loprest Water TreatmentCompany**
2825 Franklin Canyon Rd
Rodeo, CA 94572-2195 510-799-3101
Fax: 510-799-7433 888-228-5982
sales@loprest.com www.loprest.com
Water treatment equipment, ion exchange equipment and resin
President: Randy Richey
CFO: Randy Richey
Estimated Sales: $1 - 2.5 Million
Number Employees: 10-19

25488 **Lorac/Union Tool Company**
97 Johnson St
Providence, RI 02905-4518 401-781-3330
Fax: 401-941-7717 888-680-3236
lorac@loracunion.com www.loracunion.com
Manufacturer and exporter of point of purchase displays and sign holders
President: Richard Carroll
Estimated Sales: $5 - 10 Million
Number Employees: 20-49
Square Footage: 204000
Parent Co: Lorac Company
Brands:
Sava-Klip

25489 **Lorann Oils**
4518 Aurelius Road
Lansing, MI 48910 517-882-0215
Fax: 517-882-0507 800-862-8620
customercare@lorannoils.com
www.lorannoils.com
Coffee flavors, cocoa butter, flavoring oils, vanilla extracts, food colorings, fountain syrups, candy making molds and supplies, industrial ingredients, etc
CEO: John Grettenberger
COO: Carl Thelen
E-Commerce Director: Sandy Grettenberger
National Sales Manager: Troy Sprague
International Sales Manager: Joseph Lothamer
Estimated Sales: $2.6 Million
Number Employees: 17
Square Footage: 60000
Type of Packaging: Consumer, Food Service, Bulk
Brands:
Lorann Gourmet
Lorann International

25490 **Lord Label Group**
2980 Planters Place
Charlotte, NC 28216-4149 704-394-9171
Fax: 704-394-0641 800-341-5225
info@lordlabel.net
Manufacturer and exporter of labels and labeling equipment
Director Marketing: George McCrary
VP Sales Eastern Region: Jim Prendergast
Sales Manager Western Region: Tom Deegan
Number Employees: 250
Parent Co: Mail-Well
Other Locations:
Lord Label Group
Arlington TX

25491 **Lord Label Group**
1102 Jefferson Street
Algoma, WI 54201-1712 847-673-0039
Fax: 847-673-0632 800-341-5225
lordlabl@lordlabel.com
Labeling solutions, ranging from prime label and equipment to promotional coupons, screen labels and unsupported film labels for the beverage industry
Estimated Sales: $1 - 5 Million

25492 **Lord Label Machine Systems**
10350A Nations Food Road
Charlotte, NC 28273 704-644-1650
Fax: 704-664-1662 satosales@satoamerica.com
www.satoamerica.com
Manufacturer and exporter of label applicators
General Manager: Les Roisum
Number Employees: 20-49
Square Footage: 72000
Parent Co: Mail Well
Brands:
Label Robotix
Predator 1500-3000
Tr 1000-2000

25493 **(HQ)Loren Cook Company**
2015 E. Dale St.
Springfield, MO 65803-4637 417-869-6474
Fax: 417-862-3820 800-289-3267
info@lorencook.com www.lorencook.com
Manufacturer and exporter of fans, blowers and ventilators
President: Gerald Cook
Estimated Sales: $77 Million
Number Employees: 700
Other Locations:
Loren Cook Co.
Ashville NC

25494 **Lorenz Couplings**
PO Box 1002
Cobourg, ON K9A 4K2
Canada 905-372-2240
Fax: 905-372-4456 800-263-7782
www.lorenz.ca
Manufacturer and exporter of stainless steel gasket couplings for connection of pipe and tube in bulk handling conveying and vacuum systems
President: Peter Lorenz
CEO: Stacy Warner
Estimated Sales: Below $5 Million
Number Employees: 30
Square Footage: 80000

25495 **Lorenzen's Cookie Cutters**
2080 Maple Street
Wantagh, NY 11793-4108 516-781-7116
Fax: 516-781-1110 fclorenzen@aol.com
Custom stainless steel cookie cutters
CEO: Margaret Lorenzen
Estimated Sales: $1 - 5 Million
Number Employees: 2
Square Footage: 875

25496 **Lorrich & Associates**
11310 Ganesta Road
San Diego, CA 92126-1643 858-586-0823
Fax: 858-586-6210 lorrichusa@aol.com
www.lorrichusa.com
Consultant specializing in design, marketing and promotion for the restaurant industry
President: Richard Bartole
VP: Lorraine Bartole
Estimated Sales: Less than $500,000
Number Employees: 1-4

25497 **Los Angeles Label Company**
6141 Sheila St
Commerce, CA 90040-2406 323-720-1200
Fax: 323-724-1024 800-606-5223
info@lalabel.com www.lalabel.com
Prime labels, tickets, coupons, variable printing on tag stock and pressure sensitive materials
Manager: Bruce Frost
President, Chief Executive Officer: Thomas Waechter
Vice President: John Redgrave
Estimated Sales: $10 - 20 Million
Number Employees: 50-99
Square Footage: 30000

25498 **Los Angeles Paper Box &Board Mills**
PO Box 60830
Los Angeles, CA 90060-0830 323-685-8900
Fax: 323-724-2181 bill@lapb.com
www.lapb.com
Chip board and boxes including rigid, folding, set up, etc
President: William H Kewell Iii
CFO: Knita Chau
VP Sales: Robert Appoloney
Estimated Sales: $20 - 50 Million
Number Employees: 20-49

25499 **Louie's Finer Meats**
Highway 63 North
2025 Superior Avenue
Cumberland, WI 54829 715-822-4728
Fax: 715-822-3150 800-270-4297
lfm@louiesfinermeats.net
www.louiesfinermeats.com
Smoked sausages
Owner/President: Louie Muench Sr
VP: Louie Muench Jr
Number Employees: 4

25500 **Louis A Roser Company**
608 W 700 S
Salt Lake City, UT 84104 801-363-8849
Fax: 801-328-9670 800-324-6864
roserinfo@laroser.com www.laroser.com
President: Roy Iversen
Estimated Sales: $5 - 10 Million
Number Employees: 10-19

25501 **(HQ)Louis Baldinger & Sons**
875 3rd Ave Fl 9
New York, NY 10022-0123 718-204-5700
Fax: 718-721-4986
Manufacturer and exporter of decorative and custom lighting fixtures
President: Howard Baldinger
Chairman of the board: Daniel Baldinger
Quality Control: Shankar Balmick
VP Sales/Marketing: Linda Senter
Estimated Sales: $10-20 Million
Number Employees: 120
Type of Packaging: Consumer

25502 **Louis Jacobs & Son**
161 N 4th St
Brooklyn, NY 11211-3279 718-782-3500
Fax: 718-384-1167
Paper table covers, plain, embossed and creped, sheets and rolls
CEO: Abram Cohen
Estimated Sales: $10 - 20 Million
Number Employees: 5-9
Square Footage: 18000
Type of Packaging: Food Service, Private Label, Bulk
Brands:
Clothsaver Paper Tabl-Mats
Duo-Stress Place Mats

25503 **Louis Roesch Company**
289 Foster City Blvd
Suite B
Foster City, CA 94404-1100 415-621-4700
Fax: 415-621-1152 lroesch@pacbell.net
Paper labels; also, label printing services available
President: Michael A Davos
CFO: Mike Davos
Sales Manager: Bob Davos
Pur Mgr: Jason Hong
Estimated Sales: $10-20 Million
Number Employees: 10

25504 **Louisville Bedding Company**
10400 Bunsen Way
Jeffersontown, KY 40299 502-491-3370
Fax: 502-495-5346 custserv@loubed.com
www.loubed.com
Chair pads, table cloths and place mats
CFO: Maryjo Kissel
CEO: Steve Elias
R&D: Dede Gay
Quality Control: Robien Owens
Director Sales: John Glaser
Estimated Sales: I
Number Employees: 500-999

25505 **Louisville Container Company**
4401 W 62nd Street
Indianapolis, IN 46268-4829 502-361-5300
Fax: 317-297-5019 888-539-7225
Plastic and glass bottles and jars; also pails
President: Steve Heidt
Marketing Director: Nancy Heidt
Estimated Sales: $1 Million
Number Employees: 3
Square Footage: 7400

25506 **Louisville Dryer Company**
1100 Industrial Boulevrd
Louisville, KY 40219 502-969-3535
Fax: 502-962-2888 800-735-3613
mail@louisvilledryer.com
www.louisvilledryer.com
Manufacturer and exporter of rotary drying and cooling equipment, distillation columns, heat exchangers, pressure vessels and conveyors
VP Sales: Robin Henry
Process Engineer: John Robertson
Plant Manager: Gary Billion
Estimated Sales: $5-10 Million
Number Employees: 20-49

25507 **Louisville Lamp Company**
3316 Gilmore Industrial Blvd
Louisville, KY 40213 502-964-4094
Fax: 502-964-0167
customerservice@louisvillelamp.com
www.louisvillelamp.com
Custom fluorescent lighting fixtures
President: Rick Buehner
National Accounts: Mike Davidson
Estimated Sales: $1 - 2.5 Million
Number Employees: 5-9

25508 **Love Box Company**
PO Box 546
Wichita, KS 67201-0546 316-838-0851
Fax: 316-832-3269 www.lovebox.com
Corrugated boxes and wooden pallets
Chairman: Robert D Love
Estimated Sales: $168 Million
Number Employees: 500-999
Brands:
Love Box

25509 **Love Controls Division**
P.O.Box 373
Michigan City, IN 46361-0373 219-879-8000
Fax: 219-872-9057 800-828-4588
love@love-controls.com www.dwyer-inst.com
Manufacturer, distributor and exporter of temperature and process control instrumentation and associated products
President: Stephen Clark
Estimated Sales: $75 Million - 1 Billion
Number Employees: 100-249
Square Footage: 50000
Parent Co: Dwyer Instruments

25510 **Love and Quiches Desserts**
178 Hanse Ave
Freeport, NY 11520 516-623-8800
Fax: 516-623-8817 mgahn@loveandquiches.com
www.loveandquiches.com
Desserts and cakes manufacturer
CEO: Irwin Axelrod
Estimated Sales: $50 - 100 Million
Number Employees: 250-499
Type of Packaging: Food Service

25511 **Loveshaw**
2206 Easton Turnpike
PO Box 83
South Canaan, PA 18459 570-937-4921
Fax: 570-937-3229 800-572-3434
info@loveshaw.com www.loveshaw.com
Manufacturer and exporter of packaging machinery including case sealers and formers; also, ink jet printers, labeling equipment
President: Doug Henry-Om
VP: Mark Craddick
Marketing Manager: Valerie Burke
Sales: Chet Metcalf
Estimated Sales: $10-24 Million
Number Employees: 100-249
Parent Co: ITW
Brands:
Little David

25512 **Low Humidity Systems**
8425 Hazelbrand Road NE
Covington, GA 30014 770-788-6744
Fax: 770-788-6745 Info@dehumidifiers.com
www.dehumidifiers.com
Manufacturer and exporter of desiccant dehumidifiers
Sales Manager: Debra Adams
Estimated Sales: $2.5-5 Million
Number Employees: 10-19
Square Footage: 60000

25513 **(HQ)Low Temp Industries**
PO Box 795
Jonesboro, GA 30237-0795 770-478-8803
Fax: 770-471-3715 lt@lowtempind.com
www.lowtempind.com
Manufacturer and exporter of stainless steel, fiberglass and wood-free standing and hot food counters. Custom stainless steel kitchen equipment, serving lines, buffets and salad bars, portable hot and cold carts and custom millwork
CEO: William Casey
VP Sales: Steve Ballard
Director Purchasing: Dan Casey
Estimated Sales: $10-20 Million
Number Employees: 100-249
Square Footage: 250000
Type of Packaging: Food Service
Brands:
Cara
Colorpoint
Low Temp

25514 **Lowe Industries**
3575 3rd Ave
Marion, IA 52302 319-447-9724
Fax: 319-377-1204 sales@loweindustries.com
www.lowemixers.com

Manufacturer and exporter of mixing and blending equipment including ribbon, paddle and V-cone blenders and bag dump dust hoods
President: Doug Grunder
CFO: Doug Grunder
R&D: Doug Grunder
Quality Control: Doug Grunder
Sales Engineer: Bill Noonan
VP Operations: Doug Grunder
Estimated Sales: $1 - 5 Billion
Number Employees: 20-49
Brands:
Challenger

25515 Lowe Refrigeration
105 Cecil Ct
Fayetteville, GA 30214-7906 770-461-9001
Fax: 770-461-8020 info@lowerefrigeration.com
www.loweusa.com
President: Jerry Lowe
VP: Richard Epton
Estimated Sales: $1 - 3 Million
Number Employees: 10-19

25516 Lowell Packing Company
125 Harper Court
Fitzgerald, GA 31750 229-423-2051
Fax: 229-423-6601 800-342-0313
Meat slaughtering, smoking and packing meats and sausages; also storage and handling equipment and supplies
President: Morris Downing
VP: Scott Downing
Estimated Sales: $20 Million
Number Employees: 100-249
Square Footage: 48000
Type of Packaging: Consumer, Food Service
Brands:
Colony City
Georgia Star
Lowell

25517 Lowell Paper Box Company
23 Dumaine Ave
Nashua, NH 03063-4070 603-595-0700
Fax: 603-595-6337 www.lowellpaperbox.com
Paper folding cartons
President: Paul Connolly
CEO: Mark Dirico
Estimated Sales: $10-20 Million
Number Employees: 100-249

25518 Lowen Color Graphics
PO Box 1528
Hutchinson, KS 67504-1528 620-663-2161
Fax: 620-663-1429 800-545-5505
elainem@lowen.com www.lowencg.com
Point of sale vinyl graphics for floors and fleet and interior store graphics
Vice President of Sales & Marketing: Darren Keller
Estimated Sales: $20 - 25 Million
Number Employees: 100-249

25519 Lowery's Premium Roast Gourmet Coffee
P.O.Box 1858
Snohomish, WA 98291 360-668-4545
Fax: 360-863-9742 800-767-1783
jzimm@loweryscoffee.com
www.loweryscoffee.com
Coffee and wholesale and custom roasters, espresso machines, espresso accessories
President: Donald Lowery
CFO: Jeanette Zimmerman
Marketing: Mike Lowery
Roast/Operations Manager: Jerry Lowery
Estimated Sales: Below $5 Million
Number Employees: 20-49
Number of Brands: 2
Number of Products: 100
Square Footage: 20000
Type of Packaging: Private Label
Brands:
Lowery's Coffee
Pasano's Syrups

25520 Lowry Computer Products
1607 9th St
White Bear Lake, MN 55110 651-429-7722
Fax: 651-429-6006 800-429-7722
www.lowrycomputer.com
Manager: Karla Bridgeman
Estimated Sales: $20 - 50 Million
Number Employees: 50-99

25521 (HQ)Loy-Lange Box Company
222 Russell Blvd
Saint Louis, MO 63104 314-776-4712
Fax: 314-776-2810 800-886-4712
info@loylangebox.com www.loylangebox.com
Corrugated shipping containers and point of purchase displays
President: Larry McMahon
Chairman: C McMahon
VP: J Cochran
Estimated Sales: $2.5 - 5 Million
Number Employees: 50-99
Square Footage: 96000
Other Locations:
Loy-Lange Box Co.
Belle MO

25522 Loyal Manufacturing Corporation
1121 S Shortridge Rd
Indianapolis, IN 46239 317-359-3185
Fax: 317-353-9284 jan@loyalmfg.com
www.loyalmfg.com
Custom fabricated metal products including storage cabinets, shelving racks, etc.; also, cash drawers, point of sale components and security items
President: Ronald Lambert
Estimated Sales: $2.5-5 Million
Number Employees: 20-49
Square Footage: 13000
Brands:
Loyal

25523 Lozier Corporation
6336 Pershing Dr
Omaha, NE 68110 402-457-8000
Fax: 402-457-8478 800-228-9882
www.lozier.com
Manufacturer and exporter of store fixtures
CEO: Allan G Lozier
Estimated Sales: $500,000-$1 Million
Number Employees: 1,000-4,999
Parent Co: Lozier Corporation

25524 Lubar Chemical
1208 Iron Street
Kansas City, MO 64116-4009 816-471-2560
Fax: 816-421-2426 terryh@lubarchem.com
www.lubarchem.com
Institutional and industrial chemicals including cleaners, degreasers, detergents, floor care products, disinfectants and deodorants; custom blending and private labeling available
Estimated Sales: $5-10 Million
Number Employees: 20-49

25525 Lubriplate Lubricants
129 Lockwood St
Newark, NJ 07105 973-589-9150
Fax: 973-589-4432 800-733-4755
richardm@lubriplate.com www.lubriplate.com
Manufacturer and exporter of food grade lubricating oils and grease
President: Richard Mc Cluskey
Vice President, General Manager, Chief M: Jim Girard
Number Employees: 100-249
Parent Co: Fisk Brothers

25526 Lubriquip
P.O.Box 1441
Minneapolis, MN 55440-1441 612-623-6000
Fax: 612-378-3590 800-USA-LUBE
info.lubriquip@idexcorp.com
www.lubriquip.com
Automatic lubrication systems for food processing machinery and equipment, stainless steel injectors and feeder assemblies, single point centralized lubrication systems and conveyor systems
President: Rick Morgan
Quality Control: Jack Gacka
Vice President, General Counsel, Secreta: Karen Gallivan
Plant Manager: Ryan Eidenschink
Estimated Sales: G
Number Employees: 1,000-4,999

25527 Lucas Industrial
1445 American Way
PO Box 293
Cedar Hill, TX 75104 972-291-6400
Fax: 972-291-6447 800-877-1720
sales@lucasindustrial.com
www.lucasindustrial.com
Manufacturer, importer and wholesaler/distributor of power transmission products including steel and stainless steel shaft and split collars, linear bearing and shaftings, roller chains and mounted bearing
Owner: Michael Lucas
Sales Manager: Bobby Swann
Estimated Sales: Below $5 Million
Number Employees: 5-9

25528 Luce Corporation
336 Putnam Ave
Hamden, CT 06517-2744 203-787-0281
Fax: 203-230-2753 800-344-6966
Kitchen canisters with moisture absorbing knobs
President: Timothy Pagnam
Estimated Sales: $1 - 3 Million
Number Employees: 5-9
Brands:
Blue Magic
Krispy Kan

25529 Luciano Packaging Technologies
29 County Line Rd
Somerville, NJ 08876 908-722-3222
Fax: 908-722-5005 lpt@lucianopackaging.com
www.lucianopackaging.com
President: Lawrence W. Luciano
Estimated Sales: $3 - 5 Million
Number Employees: 20-49

25530 Lucie Sable Imports
3349 Howard St
Skokie, IL 60076-4010 847-677-2867
Fax: 847-677-2018 800-582-4326
luciesable@aol.com www.luciesableimports.com
Owner: Lucie Sable
CFO: Mike Kacyn
R & D: Madelaine Brown
Estimated Sales: $2.5-5 Million
Number Employees: 5-9

25531 Lucille Farms
PO Box 517
Montville, NJ 07045-0517 973-334-6030
Fax: 973-402-6361 800-654-6844
info@lucille-farms.com www.lucille-farms.com
Cheeses
President: Al Falivene
CEO: Jay Rosengarten
Number Employees: 90

25532 Luckner Steel Shelving
5454 43rd St
Maspeth, NY 11378 718-714-2105
Fax: 718-784-9169 800-888-4212
info@karpinc.com www.karpinc.com
Manufacturer and exporter of wire shelving
President: Burt Gold
CFO: Ron Peterson
Marketing: Claudia Holtz
Sales: Chantale Laraque
Estimated Sales: $5 - 10,000,000
Number Employees: 20-49
Square Footage: 45000
Parent Co: Karp Associates
Brands:
Penco

25533 Lucks Food Equipment Company
21112 72nd Avenue S
Kent, WA 98032-1339 253-872-2180
Fax: 253-872-2013 811-824-0696
info@lucks.com www.lucks.com
Rack ovens, proof boxes, dividers and rounders, revolving tray ovens, spiral mixers, sheeters and moulders
President: Rick Ellison
Chief Financial Officer: Carl Lucks
Senior Vice President Of Operations: Dan Elliott
VP Marketing: Kurt Lucks
Estimated Sales: $20-50 Million
Number Employees: 100-250

25534 **(HQ)Luco Mop Company**
3345 Morganford Rd
St Louis, MO 63116 314-772-5656
Fax: 314-772-5826 800-522-5826
www.lucomop.com
Mops, brooms and accessories
President: Dennis Shalhoub
Estimated Sales: $1-2.5 Million
Number Employees: 20-49

25535 **Ludeca**
1425 NW 88th Ave
Doral, FL 33172 305-591-8935
Fax: 305-591-1537 info@ludeca.com
www.ludeca.com
Laser tools for machinery alignment and instruments for machine condition monitoring
Manager: Frank Heilemann
Quality Control: Armando Martinez
Estimated Sales: $2.5-5 Million
Number Employees: 20-49

25536 **Ludell Ellis Corporation**
1400 W Bryn Mawr Ave
Itasca, IL 60143-1384 630-250-9222
Fax: 630-250-9241 800-611-6806
ksiriano@elliscorp.com www.elliscorp.com
Chief Executive Officer: Bob Fesmire
CEO: Robert H Fesmire
Estimated Sales: $10-20 Million
Number Employees: 50-99

25537 **Ludell Manufacturing Company**
5200 W State St
Milwaukee, WI 53208 414-476-9934
Fax: 414-476-9864 800-558-0800
sales@ludellmfg.com
www.ludellmanufacturing.com
Manufacturer and exporter of ASME certified heat exchangers, custom engineered wastewater heat recovery systems, direct contact water heaters, and boiler feedwater systems, replacement storage tanks and boiler stack economizers
President: Robert Fesmire Sr
Chief Executive Officer: Bob Fesmire Jr
CFO: David Arthur
Quality Control: Richard Ogren
Vice President: Robert Fesmire Jr
Sales Director: Greg Thorn
Plant Manager: Gary Nance
Purchasing Manager: Mark Grosskreutz
Estimated Sales: $8.5 Million
Number Employees: 50-99
Number of Brands: 6
Number of Products: 2
Square Footage: 200000

25538 **Luetzow Industries**
1105 Davis Ave
South Milwaukee, WI 53172 414-762-0410
Fax: 414-762-0943 800-558-6055
info@luetzow.cc www.luetzow.cc
Manufacturer and exporter of polyethylene bags and film, and sheating
President: Albert Luetzow
VP: Brent Luetzow
Estimated Sales: $10 - 20 Million
Number Employees: 60
Square Footage: 80000
Type of Packaging: Consumer, Private Label, Bulk
Brands:
Luetzow
Sir Flip Flop

25539 **Luke's Almond Acres**
11281 S Lac Jac Ave
Reedley, CA 93654 559-638-3483
Fax: 559-637-7788 www.lukesalmondacres.com
Wooden crates and gift boxes; packer of dried fruit and nuts
Owner: Ed Esajin
Owner: Lucas Nersesian
Estimated Sales: less than $500,000
Number Employees: 1-4
Square Footage: 5000
Brands:
Luke's Almond Acres

25540 **LumaSense Technologies**
3301 Leonard Ct
Santa Clara, CA 95054-2054
Fax: 408-727-1677 800-631-0176
info@lumasenseinc.com www.lumsenseinc.com
Temperature monitoring sensors used in microwave food processing development and gas monitoring systems.
CEO: Vivek Joshi
Marketing Director: Mark Reis
Public Relations: Judi Seavers
Estimated Sales: $10-20 Million
Number Employees: 50-99
Square Footage: 37000

25541 **Lumaco**
9-11 E Broadway
Hackensack, NJ 07601-6821 201-342-5119
Fax: 201-342-8898 800-735-8258
valvinfo@lumaco.com www.lumaco.com
Stainless steel manual and pneumatic valves
Owner: Anita Buxbaum
Sales Manager: Don Kiefer
Estimated Sales: $2.5-5 Million
Number Employees: 5-9
Square Footage: 5000

25542 **Lumaco Sanitary Valves**
9-11 East Broadway
Hackensack, NJ 07601-6821 201-342-5119
Fax: 201-342-8898 800-735-8258
valvinfo@lumaco.com www.lumaco.com
Sanitary stainless steel valves
Owner: Anita Buxbaum
Estimated Sales: $2.5-5 Million
Number Employees: 5-9
Square Footage: 10000
Brands:
Lumaco

25543 **Lumax Industries**
301 Chestnut Ave
Altoona, PA 16603 814-944-2537
Fax: 814-944-6413 sales@lumaxlighting.com
www.lumaxlighting.com
Manufacturer and exporter of lighting fixtures and H.I.D. luminares including commercial, industrial and custom
CEO: Donald E Snyder
National Sales Manager: Randy Solliday
VP Operations: Ken Merritts
Estimated Sales: $10-20 Million
Number Employees: 100-249
Square Footage: 160000
Type of Packaging: Consumer, Food Service, Private Label
Brands:
Light Forms

25544 **Lumber & Things**
PO Box 386
Keyser, WV 26726 304-788-5600
Fax: 304-788-7823 800-296-5656
info@lumberandthings
www.lumberandthings.com
We have been in business for over 30 years. Our customers depend on the standards that we build on: Honesty-Quality-Service. We produce: Reconditioned, Remanufacture and New pallets; Reconditioned, Remanufactured and Recycled tier/slipsheets; Reconditioned, Remanufactured and New top frames; Reconditioned and New can and glass bulk pallets. With an attendant standing by our 24 hour hotline we can provide your company with delivery within 24 hours of your phone call.
President: Jack Amoruso
National Accounts Manager: Victor Knight
Customer Service Specialist: Patricia Davis
Plant Manager: Jack Amoruso
Purchasing Director: Ken Winter
Number Employees: 100-249
Square Footage: 150000
Type of Packaging: Consumer, Food Service, Private Label, Bulk

25545 **Lumenite Control Technology**
2331 N 17th ave
Franklin Park, IL 60131 847-455-1450
Fax: 847-455-0127 800-323-8510
customerservice@lumenite.com
www.lumenite.com
Manufacturer, importer and exporter of blending and batching equipment, flow meters, level detectors and temperature indicators and controllers
Owner: Ron Calabrese
Office Manager: Craig Meixner
V.P. Engineering: Ronald Calabrese
Sales manager: David Calabrese
Advertising Manager: Carol Calabrese
Service Representative: Rosa Furio
Estimated Sales: $2.5-5 Million
Number Employees: 10-19
Square Footage: 40000
Brands:
Industrialeveline
Paneleveline

25546 **Luminiere Corporation**
4269 Park Ave
Bronx, NY 10457-4207 718-295-5450
Fax: 718-295-5451
Manufacturer, importer and exporter of crystal and bronze chandeliers, electric lamps, lighting fixtures and display lighting
Owner: Herbert Leggan
VP: A Langsam
VP: N Gussack
Estimated Sales: $3 - 5 Million
Number Employees: 5-9
Square Footage: 50000

25547 **Lumsden Corporation**
PO Box 4647
Lancaster, PA 17604 717-394-6871
Fax: 717-394-1640 800-367-3664
sales@lumsdencorp.com www.lumsdencorp.com
CEO: Glenn Farrell
Estimated Sales: $10-20 Million
Number Employees: 20-49

25548 **Lumsden Flexx Flow**
10 Abraso St
Lancaster, PA 17601-3104 717-394-6871
Fax: 717-394-1640 800-367-3664
sales@lumsdencorp.com www.lumsdencorp.com
Wire and mesh conveyor belting, chain driven belts, positive drive pin rolls, furnace curtains and wire straightening devices; exporter of conveyor belting
President: Glenn Farrell
Quality Control: Glenn Farrell
Sales Manager: Pete Moore
Estimated Sales: Below $15 Million
Number Employees: 20-49
Brands:
Flexx Flow

25549 **Lunn Industries**
1 Garvies Point Road
Glen Cove, NY 11542-2821 516-671-9000
Fax: 516-671-9005 dtrachte@lunnindustries.com
Fiberglass and reinforced plastic containers
President: Bob Robinson
Sales Manager: Don Trachta Reda
Number Employees: 10

25550 **Luseaux Laboratories Inc**
16816 South Gramercy Place
Gardena, CA 90247
Fax: 310-538-3889 800-266-1555
detergents@luseaux.com www.luseaux.com
Manufacturer, importer and exporter of cleaners, sanitizers and detergents including liquid and powder
President: Marjorie Duffy
Chief Information Officer: Charles Edwards
Office Manager: Kathleen Kalohi
Estimated Sales: $810,000
Number Employees: 5
Square Footage: 180000
Type of Packaging: Food Service, Private Label, Bulk
Other Locations:
Kingman AZ
Brands:
Luseaux

25551 **Lustre-Cal Nameplate Corporation**
715 S Guild Ave
Lodi, CA 95240 209-370-1600
Fax: 209-334-2610 800-234-6264
rbeckler@lustrecal.com www.lustrecal.com

Manufacturer and exporter of color anodized and etched aluminum nameplates and labels
Estimated Sales: $20-50 Million
Number Employees: 100-249

25552 Luthi Machinery Company, Inc.
1 Magnuson Avenue
Pueblo, CO 81001 719-948-1110
Fax: 719-948-9540 sales@atlaspacific.com
www.luthi.com
Manufacturer and exporter of can filling and dicing machinery for tuna, salmon, chicken, turkey, pork and beef
President: Erik Teranchi
CFO/VP: Don Freeman
V.P. & General Manager: Craig Furlo
Marketing/Sales: Robb Morris
Sales: Gini Fisher
Production: Vern Brown
Number Employees: 50
Square Footage: 136000

25553 Luxfer Gas Cylinders
3016 Kansas Ave
Riverside, CA 92507-3489 951-684-5110
Fax: 951-328-1117 www.luxfercylinders.com
President: John Rhodes
CFO: Micheal Edwards
R&D: Hendy Holrowd
Quality Control: Rick Willson
Estimated Sales: $20 - 50 Million
Number Employees: 250-499

25554 Luxo Corporation
Ste 105
5 Westchester Plz
Elmsford, NY 10523-1645 914-937-4433
Fax: 914-937-7016 800-222-5896
office@luxous.com www.luxous.com
Manufacturer and importer of magnification, ambient and task lighting fixtures
Regional Sales Manager: Doug Benway
Estimated Sales: $10-20 Million
Number Employees: 50-99
Square Footage: 60000
Parent Co: Luxo ASA
Type of Packaging: Food Service

25555 Lyco Manufacturing
PO Box 2022
Wausau, WI 54402-2022 715-845-7867
Fax: 715-842-8228 info@lycowausau.com
www.lycowausau.com
Stainless steel liquid ring vacuum pumps for food, pharmaceutical, chemical, medical, laboratory and general industrial applications where corrosion resistance is beneficial.
President: Thomas Frane
Number Employees: 50-99

25556 Lyco Manufacturing
115 Commercial Dr
Columbus, WI 53925 920-623-4152
Fax: 920-623-3780 sales@lycomfg.com
www.lycomfg.com
Commercial food processing equipment manufacturer specializing in the areas of heating/cooling, liquid/solid separation, root crop preparation and snap bean processing equipment
CEO: Steve Hughes
Estimated Sales: $4.5 Million
Number Employees: 50-99

25557 Lyco Wausau
P.O.Box 2022
Wausau, WI 54402-2022 715-845-7867
Fax: 715-842-8228 info@lycowausau
www.lycowausau.com
Manufacturer and exporter of stainless steel liquid ring vacuum pumps and systems for filling, deaerating, cooking, dewatering, conveying, evaporating and packaging
President: Thomas Frane
Estimated Sales: $3 - 5 Million
Brands:
Lyco
Vaqmer

25558 Lydall
PO Box 2002
Doswell, VA 23047-2002 804-266-9611
www.lydall.com
Packaging products and wooden pallet replacements
President, CEO: Dale G. Barnhart
EVP, CFO: Robert K. Julian
Vice President, Chief Accounting Officer: James V. Laughlan
VP Sales: P Mullins
Vice President, Human Resources: William M. Lachenmeyer
Plant Manager: E Smith
Estimated Sales: $1 - 5 Million
Number Employees: 100
Parent Co: Lydall

25559 (HQ)Lynch Corporation
140 Greenwich Avenue
Suite 4
Greenwich, CT 06830-6560 203-622-1150
Fax: 401-453-2009
richard.mcgrail@lynch-mail.com
www.lynchgraycorp.com
Manufacturer and exporter of glass forming and packaging machines
President: Richard E McGrail
CFO: Raymond Keller
Estimated Sales: $20 - 30 Million
Number Employees: 4

25560 Lynch-Jamentz Company
5150 Candlewood Street
Lakewood, CA 90712-1925 562-630-6798
Fax: 562-630-5901 800-828-6217
rtrepte@treptewire.com www.lynch-jamentz.com
Skewers, hot pan grips, spoons and racks including roasting, baking and broiling
Owner: Ron Trepte Sr
CEO: Ron Trepte, Sr.
Marketing Director: Ron Trepte, Sr.
Secretary: E Trepte
Purchasing Manager: Ron Trepte, Sr.
Estimated Sales: $1-2.5 Million
Number Employees: 10
Square Footage: 48000
Parent Co: Trepte's Wire & Metal Works

25561 Lynden Meat Company
1936 Front St
Lynden, WA 98264 360-354-2449
Fax: 360-354-7687
Livestock slaughtering services, herd managemnt, livestock breeding and grooming, livestock management, livestock selection, ice cube makers, ice block makers, industrial freezers.
Owner: Rick Biesheuvel
Estimated Sales: $3 - 5 Million
Number Employees: 5-9
Type of Packaging: Consumer

25562 (HQ)Lynn Sign
8 Gleason St
Andover, MA 01810 978-470-1194
Fax: 978-346-8197 800-225-5764
lynnsign@aol.com
Manufacturer and exporter of changeable plastic letters and signs, menu boards, building directories, bulletin boards, display cases, engraving stock and sign holders
Public Relations: Darlene Reiss
Manager: Lynn Sullivan
Estimated Sales: $300,000-500,000
Number Employees: 1-4
Number of Brands: 1
Square Footage: 17000
Type of Packaging: Bulk
Brands:
Lynnply

25563 Lyon Metal Products
P.O.Box 671
Aurora, IL 60507-0671 630-892-8941
Fax: 630-892-8966 lyon@lyon-metal.com
www.lyonworkspace.com
Manufacturer and exporter of metal storage equipment including shelving, cabinets, etc
CEO: R Peter Washington
Marketing Director: Robert Bell
Estimated Sales: $50-100 Million
Number Employees: 500-999

25564 Lyons Falls Pulp & Paper
77 E Crystal Lake Avenue
Crystal Lake, IL 60014-6171 815-455-0981
Fax: 815-455-0997
Tea and coffee industry pouch materials (cellophane, paper, films)
Estimated Sales: $1-2.5 Million
Number Employees: 1-4

25565 M & M Poultry Equipment
296 Carlton Rd
Hollister, MO 65672 417-297-0607
Fax: 417-334-6684 800-872-9687
drew.horst@mandmpoultry.com
www.mandmpoultry.com
Poultry processing equipment, overhead conveyor chain, picking fingers, misc, spare parts, and feather picker.
Executive Vice President: Drew Horst
Marketing: Larry McGriff
Sales: Sloan Houston
Production: Jason Burkett

25566 M & S Automated FeedingSystems
1194 Cliff Road East
Burnsville, MN 55337 952-894-3263
Fax: 952-895-9910 masafs@msautomated.com
www.msautomated.com
President: Mark Grinager
Estimated Sales: $3,000,000 - $5,000,000
Number Employees: 20-49

25567 M S Willett Inc
220 Cockeysville Rd
Cockeysville, MD 21030 410-771-0460
Fax: 410-771-6972 info@mswillett.com
www.mswillett.com
Manufacturer and exporter of precision equipment to produce stamped and formed metal food, shallow drawn and specialty containers and easy open can ends
President: James Lekin
R&D: Gary Ruby
Quality Control: Robert Burns
Sales Director: Gary Ruby
Public Relations: Linda Ambrose
Plant Manager: Larry Felty
Purchasing Director: Jack Kersch
Estimated Sales: $5 Million
Number Employees: 35
Square Footage: 240000

25568 M&C Sweeteners
650 Industrial Road
Blair, NE 68008-2649 402-533-1843
Fax: 402-433-1831

25569 M&D Specialties
17301 NW Oak Ridge Rd
Yamhill, OR 97148-8119 503-662-4516
Fax: 503-662-3629
Wine industry labelers, pumps
Estimated Sales: $500,000-$1 Million
Number Employees: 1-4

25570 M&E Manufacturing Company
PO Box 1548
Kingston, NY 12402-1548 845-331-2110
Fax: 845-331-4143
customerservice@zframerack.com
www.zframerack.com
Manufacturer and exporter of shelving, racks, tables, cutting boards, trucks, platters, dollies and carts
President: Jeffrey Weinberger
Executive VP: Don Hall
Estimated Sales: $20 - 50 Million
Number Employees: 100-249
Square Footage: 40000
Brands:
Butcher Buddy
Deli Buddy

25571 M&G Packaging Corporation
22610 Jamaica Ave
Floral Park, NY 11001 516-352-3100
Fax: 516-488-3181 800-240-5288
charles@mgpackaging.com
www.mgpackaging.com
Boxes, cartons, foam, packaging material and plastic bags
President: Charles Rick
VP: Charles Rick
Estimated Sales: $20-50 Million
Number Employees: 20-49
Brands:
Avi

25572 **M&H Crates**
4022 Fm 347 N
Jacksonville, TX 75766-6696 903-683-5351
Fax: 903-683-9593 m&hcrates@tyler.net
www.ckswireless.com
Wooden pallets and shipping crates
CEO: Davy Sanders
Supervisor: Andy McCown
Estimated Sales: $10-20 Million
Number Employees: 50-99
Square Footage: 20000

25573 **M&L Plastics**
150 Pleasant St
Easthampton, MA 01027-1887 413-527-1330
Fax: 413-527-8621
Manufacturer and exporter of plastic display containers
Number Employees: 10-19
Parent Co: Paragon Rubber Corporation

25574 **M&M Displays**
7700 Brewster Ave
Philadelphia, PA 19153 215-365-5200
Fax: 215-365-5610 800-874-7171
bobdigiorgio@mmdisplays.com
www.mmdisplays.com
Screen printing, digital printing, p.o.p. displays, metal sign frames, banners, decals, interior graphics, and several patented items including nozzle talkers brand
CEO: Michael Sell
Sales Director: Bob Schneider
Production Manager: Chris Mace
Purchasing Manager: William Gonzacez
Estimated Sales: $11 Million
Number Employees: 50-99
Square Footage: 80000

25575 **M&M Equipment Corporation**
7355 Monticello Ave
Skokie, IL 60076 847-673-0300
Fax: 847-673-0350 sales@mmequip.com
www.mmequip.com
Cutting and boning devices, slaughtering equipment
Owner: Marc Newman
Estimated Sales: $1 - 2.5 Million
Number Employees: 5-9

25576 **M&M Industries Inc**
316 Corporate Place
Chattanooga, TN 37419 423-821-3302
Fax: 423-821-9017 800-331-5305
cstone@mmcontainer.com
www.mmcontainer.com/
Life Latch plastic pails suitable for a variety of purposes including the food industry. Uses include livestock feed and grains; pet food storage; seeds; vitamin supplements, etc.
VP: Glenn H Morris Jr
Regional Accounts Manager: Rae Green
Regional Accounts Manager: Cindy Stone
Regional Accounts Manager: Tiffany King
Regional Accounts Manager: Janet Rogers
Estimated Sales: $10-25 Million
Number Employees: 25

25577 **M&O Perry Industries**
412 N Smith Ave
Corona, CA 92880 951-734-9838
Fax: 951-734-2454 sales@moperry.com
www.moperry.com
Filling equipment for the animal health, biotech, diagnostic, medical device, ophthalmic and pharmaceutical markets. liquid and powder filling technologies
President: Joseph Osterhaus
Estimated Sales: $5-10 Million
Number Employees: 20-49

25578 **M&Q Packaging Corporation**
1120 Welsh Rd
North Wales, PA 19454-3794 267-498-4000
Fax: 267-498-0030 info@mqplastics.com
www.pansaver.com
High quality plastic products.
President: David Carlin
Estimated Sales: $26 Million
Number Employees: 10-19
Parent Co: M&Q Plastics Products
Type of Packaging: Food Service

25579 **M&Q Plastic Products**
1120 Welsh Rd
Suite 170
North Wales, PA 19454 267-498-4000
Fax: 267-498-0030 877-726-7287
mallozzi@mqplasticproducts.com
www.mqplasticproducts.com
High Temperture flexible, packaging products ideal for use in oven, microwave, and steamtable applications
Director Sales/Marketing: Tim Blucher
Product Manager: George Schmidt
Estimated Sales: $2.5-5 Million
Number Employees: 75
Square Footage: 80000
Brands:
Monolyn
Pansaver

25580 **M&R Flexible Packaging**
PO Box 907
Springboro, OH 45066-0907 937-298-7272
Fax: 937-298-7388 800-543-3380
morris_co@msn.com
Manufacturer, importer and exporter of plastic bags, industrial packaging materials, plastics and shipping room supplies
President/Owner: Ronald Morris Sr
Estimated Sales: $2.5-5,000,000
Number Employees: 10-19

25581 **M&R Sales & Service, Inc**
1n372 Main St
Glen Ellyn, IL 60137 630-858-6101
Fax: 630-858-6134 800-736-6431
www.mrprint.com
Manufacturer and exporter of belting, switches, etc
CEO: Richard Hoffman
Estimated Sales: $1-2.5 Million
Number Employees: 250-499
Parent Co: M&R Printing Equipment

25582 **M&S Manufacturing**
3728 Telegraph Rd
Arnold, MO 63010 636-464-2739
Fax: 636-464-5923 www.m-smanufacturing.com
Hot food wells, refrigerated bases, hoods, walk-in coolers and tables including steam, salad, dish and soil
Owner: Darlene Spink
VP Secretary: Darline Spink
Estimated Sales: $500,000-$1 Million
Number Employees: 5-9
Square Footage: 2800

25583 **M&S Miltenberg & Samton**
2 Hollyhock Road
Wilton, CT 06897-4438 203-834-0002
Fax: 203-834-1002 miltsam@earthlink.net
www.miltsam.com
Carton machines: closing, filling, handling, sealing; coaters, cooling equipment: cooling tunnels, tables; cut and wrap equipment, extruders: chewing gum, coconut candy, confectionery; feeder belts, automatic, batch, rope, screw;feeding and placement system; flow-pack machines, glazing machines, gum sanders, kettles, licorice machines
Estimated Sales: $2.5-5 Million
Number Employees: 5-9

25584 **M&W Protective Coating Company**
2239 16 3/4 Ave
Rice Lake, WI 54868 715-234-2251
Protective coating
Manager: Douglas Winkel
Estimated Sales: $500,000-$1 Million
Number Employees: 5-9

25585 **M-E-C Company**
P.O.Box 330
Neodesha, KS 66757-0330 620-325-2673
Fax: 620-325-2678 mec@m-e-c.com
www.m-e-c.com
Manufacturer and exporter of dryer systems for nonedible biological materials and foodwastes including convection, total, rotary, and flash tube
CFO: Jerry Creekmore
R&D: Mike Hudson
Quality Control: Kent Shields
Sales Manager: Gary Follmer
Purchasing: John George
Estimated Sales: $20 - 50 Million
Number Employees: 100-249
Square Footage: 170000

25586 **M-One Specialties Inc**
974 W 100 S
Salt Lake City, UT 84104 801-596-2500
Fax: 801-521-6502 800-525-9223
mone@moneplumbing.com
www.monespecialties.com
Faucet and plumbing repair and replacement parts-bathroom hardware and ada parts
President/Owner: George Mattena
Estimated Sales: $5 - 10,000,000
Number Employees: 10
Number of Brands: 164
Number of Products: 2800
Type of Packaging: Bulk

25587 **M-TEK Inc**
1675 Todd Farm Dr
Elgin, IL 60123 847-741-3500
Fax: 847-741-3569 847-741-3500
mtek@mtekcorp.com www.mtekcorp.com
Vacuum packaging machinery
President: Richard Maskell
VP Marketing/Sales: Rick Tkaczyk
Operations Manager: Alan Wojak
Production Manager: Mark Evans
Purchasing Manager: Jason Aleo
Estimated Sales: $5-10 Million
Number Employees: 20-49
Number of Brands: 2
Type of Packaging: Consumer, Food Service, Private Label, Bulk

25588 **M-Tech & Associates**
4323 Stonewall Avenue
Downers Grove, IL 60515-2654 630-810-9714
Fax: 630-810-9712 tech_associates@msn.com
Consultant specializing in implementing MRP scheduling, training, production and process monitoring
Number Employees: 5
Square Footage: 1000

25589 **M-Vac Systems**
14621 S 800 W
Suite 100
Bluffdale, UT 84065 801-523-3962
www.m-vac.com
The m-vac is a dry or wet vacuuming collection/containment device used to detect and recover surface pathogens.
Owner: Dr. Bruce Bradley
Parent Co: MSI

25590 **(HQ)M.E. Heuck Company**
1111 Western Row Road
Mason, OH 45040-2649 513-681-1774
Fax: 513-681-2329 800-359-3200
Manufacturer, importer, exporter of kitchen utensils including barbecue tools, nut crackers, shellfish crackers, etc
President: Ramesh Malhotra
CFO: Tim Omelia
VP: Bill Dickmann
R&D: Tim Omelia
Manager: Linda Brandt
Estimated Sales: $20 - 50 Million
Number Employees: 30
Square Footage: 90000
Brands:
Burpee
H.M. Quackenbush
Mr. Food

25591 **M.G. Newell**
301 Citation Ct
Greensboro, NC 27409 336-393-0100
Fax: 336-393-0140 800-334-0231
sales@mgnewell.com www.mgnewell.com

We provide equipment and engineered solutions in automation and control, CIP and custom washing systems, field service, calibration, maintenance, repair, fluid handling, heat exchange, installation, material handling, mixing andblending, process design, skidded system fabrication
President: John Sherrill
CFO: Julie Hart
Vice President: Julie Hart
VP Engineering: Tony Saenz
Marketing Director: Gray Sherrill
Human Resources: Deb Gaither
VP/Chief Operating Officer: Michael Sherrill
Estimated Sales: $10 - 20 Million

25592 M.H. Rhodes Cramer
105 Nutmeg Rd S
South Windsor, CT 06074 860-291-8402
Fax: 860-610-0120 877-684-6464
customer-service@mhrhodes.com
www.mhrhodes.com
Manufacturer, importer and exporter of timers including audible signal and electronic as well as mechanical timers/time switches for OEM's
President: Ken Mac Cormac
Founder: Mark Rhodes, Sr.
Manager Sales: Jim Kline
Customer Service: Bernie Rodrigues
Purchasing Manager: Jeff Carlson
Estimated Sales: $10-20 Million
Number Employees: 100-249
Square Footage: 85000
Type of Packaging: Consumer, Food Service, Private Label, Bulk
Brands:
Mark-Time

25593 MAC Equipment
7901 NW 107th Ter
Kansas City, MO 64153-1910 816-891-9300
Fax: 816-891-8336 sales@macequipment.com
www.macequipment.com
President: Jay Brown
Estimated Sales: Below $5 Million
Number Employees: 250-499

25594 MAC Equipment
7901 NW 107th Ter
Kansas City, MO 64153-1910 816-891-9300
Fax: 816-891-8336 800-821-2476
sales@macequipment.com
www.macequipment.com
Equipment: pneumatic conveying and dust collection
President: Jay Brown
Food Group Manager: Stuart Carrico
Estimated Sales: $10-20 Million

25595 MAC Paper Converters
8370 Philips Hwy
Jacksonville, FL 32256 904-733-9660
Fax: 904-733-9622 800-334-7026
Envelopes and die cut paper
Manager: Bob Tees
Plant Manager: Ted Towner
Estimated Sales: $20-50 Million
Number Employees: 100-249
Parent Co: MAC Paper

25596 MAF Industries
36470 Highway 99
PO Box 218
Traver, CA 93673 559-897-2905
Fax: 559-897-3422 mafusa@aol.com
www.mafindustries.com
Manufacturer, importer and exporter of packaging equipment including sizers, color sorters, box fillers, robotic bin dumpers, washers, waxers, etc
CEO: Jack Kraemer
CFO/Controller: Raul Mejia
Sales Manager: Leendert Van Der Tas
Estimated Sales: $10-20 Million
Number Employees: 50-99
Square Footage: 50000
Parent Co: SMCM
Brands:
Agrobotic Technology

25597 MAK Wood, Inc.
1235 Dakota Dr
Unit E
Grafton, WI 53074 262-387-1200
Fax: 262-387-1400 info@makwood.com
www.makwood.com
Novelty sugars, cranberry, probiotics, lactobacillus and bifidobacterium. Supplier of L-arabinose, L-fucose, L-rhamnose, lactates, and of other probiotics.
Owner/President: Carol Brudnak
Secretary/Treasurer: Joseph Brudnak
Sr Executive VP: Mark Brudnak
Manager, Technical Sales Services: Eric Baer
Estimated Sales: $380,000
Type of Packaging: Private Label, Bulk

25598 MALO
12111 E 51st St
Suite 106
Tulsa, OK 74146 918-583-2743
Fax: 918-583-6208 sales@maloinc.com
www.maloinc.com
President: Chuck Clugston
Estimated Sales: $3 - 5 Million
Number Employees: 10-19

25599 MAP Systems International
300 E Touhy Avenue
Des Plaines, IL 60018-2669 847-299-7800
Fax: 847-299-8330 www.mapsystems.cc
Modified atmospheric packaging, vacuum packaging equipment, blenders, choppers, smokehouses, stuffers, slicers and plant supplies. Products and services for" industrial food processing equipment; industrial food packaging equipment;grocery and restauran equipment; and also butcher supplies and food processing supplies.
Number Employees: 30

25600 MAPS Software
P.O.Box 821
Columbus, MS 39703-0821 662-328-6110
Fax: 662-329-9799
Computer software including point of sale, free and reduced application, purchasing and financial
President: Victor Fuqua
CFO: Sandy David
Representative: Jenny Taylor
Office Manager: Sandy Robinson
Estimated Sales: Below $5 Million
Number Employees: 4

25601 MARQ Packaging Systems
3801 W Washington Ave
Yakima, WA 98903 509-966-4300
Fax: 509-452-3307 800-998-4301
info@marq.net www.marq.net
Wine industry Bag in Box, case sealing
President: Rocky Marquis
CEO: Ted Marquis Sr
CFO: Dyan Curtis
Chairman of the Board: Theodore Marquis Sr
Number Employees: 20-49

25602 MBC Food Machinery Corporation
78 McKinley St
Hackensack, NJ 07601 201-489-7000
Fax: 201-489-0614
jbattaglia@mbcfoodmachinery.com
www.mbcfoodmachinery.com
Manufacturer and exporter of filling pumps and automatic frozen pasta processing machinery including ravioli, manicotti and cavatelli
President and CFO: John Battaglia
Estimated Sales: Less than $500,000
Number Employees: 5-9

25603 MBX Packaging
PO Box 929
Wausau, WI 54402-0929 715-845-1171
Fax: 715-848-1054 randy@mbxpkg.com
www.mbxpkg.com
Recycled plastic pallets in custom sizes and styles
President: Harvey Scholfield
CEO: Harvey H Scholfield Jr
VP Sales: Randy Haupt
Estimated Sales: $10-20 Million
Number Employees: 100-249
Square Footage: 100000
Parent Co: MBX Packaging
Other Locations:
MBX Packaging
Beloit WI
Brands:
Enviro-Board

25604 MC Creation
1550 Bryant Street
Suite 760
San Francisco, CA 94103-4877 415-775-1135
Consultant specializing in home meal replacement concepts and food culture development promoting sushi
Estimated Sales: $300,000-500,000
Number Employees: 1-4

25605 MCD Technologies
2515 South Tacoma Way
Tacoma, WA 98409-7527 253-476-0968
Fax: 253-476-0974
info@mcdtechnologiesinc.com
www.mcdtechnologiesinc.com
Manufacturer and exporter of food dryers and evaporators; also, contract toll drying
President: Karin Bolland
VP: Richard Magoon
Marketing: Leo Schultz
Estimated Sales: $1-2.5 Million
Number Employees: 10-19
Square Footage: 18000
Brands:
Refractance Window

25606 MCM Fixture Company
21306 John R Rd
Hazel Park, MI 48030 248-547-9280
Fax: 248-547-9270 tawny@mcmstainless.com
www.mcmstainless.com
Stainless steel food service equipment including cafeteria counters, sinks, tables, hoods and refrigerators; custom fabrication available, custom wall panels, both smooth and quilted, as well as corner guards in all sizes to order.
Vice President: Eric Brown
Estimated Sales: $1-2.5 Million
Number Employees: 10-19

25607 MCR Technologies Group
13420 Galt Rd
PO Box 1016
Sterling, IL 61081 815-622-3181
Fax: 815-622-0819 877-622-3181
sales@weighshark.com
www.mcrtechnologiesgroup.com
Metal detectors
President: Mark Humphreys
Estimated Sales: $1.5 Million+
Number Employees: 1-4
Number of Brands: 4
Number of Products: 9
Square Footage: 4000
Type of Packaging: Food Service

25608 MDE Corporation
11965 Brookfield St
Livonia, MI 48150 734-744-5480
Fax: 734-744-5485 800-482-3393
mielsen@mdecorp.com www.mdecorp.com
Fillers, air, milk, filtration equipment, heat exchangers, plate, scraped surface, homogenizers, ice and ice cream equipment, ingredient feeders, meters, flow, milk, solids, aseptic processing equipment, batch control systems, andcentrifuges
President: Robert I Nielsen
VP: Robert Nielson Jr
Estimated Sales: $5-10 Million
Number Employees: 20-49

25609 MDH Packaging Corporation
101 Miller Drive
Crittenden, KY 41030-7560 859-746-0993
Fax: 859-746-0933 mdh@ripnzip.com
www.ripnzip.com
Estimated Sales: $3,000,000 - $5,000,000
Number Employees: 10-19

25610 MDI WorldWide
38271 W Twelve Mile Road
Farmington Hills, MI 48331 248-553-1900
Fax: 248-488-5700 800-228-8925
sales@mdiworldwide.com
www.mdiworldwide.com
Designs and manufactures marketing displays, retail displays, commercial sign holders, POP displays and merchandising displays
President: Robert Sarkisian
Number Employees: 100-249
Type of Packaging: Food Service

Brands:
Postergrip
Storeworks

25611 **MDR International**
14861 NE 20th Ave
North Miami, FL 33181 305-944-5019
Fax: 305-949-4136 mdrinc@bellsouth.com
www.mdrinternational.com
Glassware, hurricane glasses, plastic beer mugs, tumblers and mason jar mugs
Owner: Bernard Ghelbendorf
VP Marketing: Gary Fein
Estimated Sales: $2.5-5,000,000
Number Employees: 10-19

25612 **MDS**
3429 Stearns Rd
Valrico, FL 33596-6450 813-653-1180
Fax: 813-684-5953 tbattle@mdsincorporated.com
www.mdsvet.com
Manufacturer and exporter of scopes used to check bacteria in pipes and tubes
President: Paul Butler
Director Marketing: Trudi Battle
Estimated Sales: Less than $500,000
Number Employees: 5-9

25613 **MDS Nordion**
447 March Road
Ottawa, ON K2K 1X8
Canada 613-592-2790
Fax: 613-592-6937 800-465-3666
info@mds.nordion www.mds.nordion.com
Supplies patented food irradiation solutions for the meat, poultry and produce industry. Our equipment and process eliminates food-borne pathogens such as E. coli, Salmonella and Listeria from food, prolongs shelf life and treatsproduct for quarantine and bio-security after harvest
President: Steve West
CFO: Micheal Thomas
Senior Vice President, General Counsel,: Andrew Foti
Product Manager Food and Radiation: Joseph Borsa Ph D
R&D and Director: Pierre Lahaie
Marketing Director: Carolin Vandenberg
Senior Vice President of Sales and Marke: Kevin Brooks
Number Employees: 800
Parent Co: MDS
Brands:
Centurion

25614 **MDT**
971 Dogwood Trl
Tyrone, GA 30290 770-631-9074
Fax: 770-486-9903 info.us@mdt-tex.com
Shades,structures and umbrellas for commercial purposes
Estimated Sales: $1-2.5 Million
Number Employees: 5-9

25615 **MEGTEC Systems**
P.O.Box 5030
De Pere, WI 54115 920-336-5715
Fax: 920-336-3404 info@megtec.com
www.megtec.com
President: Mohit Uberoi
R&D: Steve Zager
CFO: Greg Lienn
Estimated Sales: I
Number Employees: 500-999

25616 **MEPACO**
200 Industrial Drive
PO Box 538
Beaver Dam, WI 53916-0538 920-356-9900
Fax: 920-887-0206 800-444-0398
dennis.buehring@mepaco.net www.mepaco.net
President: Duane Foulkes
V.P. of Sales & Marketing: Dennis Buehring
Estimated Sales: $5 - 10 Million
Number Employees: 160

25617 **MEPSCO**
1888 E Fabyan Pkwy
Batavia, IL 60510-1498
Fax: 630-231-9372 800-323-8535
info@mepsco.com www.mepsco.com
Estimated Sales: $9 Million
Number Employees: 20-49

25618 **METKO**
1301 Milwaukee Dr
New Holstein, WI 53061 920-898-4221
Fax: 920-898-1389 metko@metko.com
www.metko.com
President: Michael Mc Carthy
CEO: David McCarthy
Marketing: Jim Kreger
Sales: Jim Kreger
Public Relations: Jim Kreger
Human Resources: Diane McCarthy
Production: Mike Lider
Plant Manager: Mike Lider
Purchasing: Scott Lynch
Estimated Sales: $5-10 Million
Number Employees: 50-99
Square Footage: 21000
Brands:
Custom Metal Fabricator

25619 **METRO Material Handling& Storage Products**
P.O.Box A
Wilkes Barre, PA 18705-0557 570-825-2741
Fax: 570-823-0250 800-433-2232
www.intermetro.com
Manufacturer and exporter of modular and high density storage, material handling and hi-rise shelving systems; also, mobile workstations, storage and utility carts, mobile racks and merchandising and dispenser racks
President: John Nackley
CFO: Don McAlonan
Production VP: J Welsch
Estimated Sales: I
Number Employees: 1,000-4,999
Parent Co: Emerson Electric
Brands:
Metromax
Super Adjustable
Super Erecta

25620 **MF&B Restaurant Systems**
133 ICMI Road
Dunbar, PA 15431 724-628-3050
Fax: 724-626-0247 mike@ovenguys.com
www.ovenguys.com
Remanufacture conveyor pizza ovens, sell new and used parts
Owner: Mike French
Vice President: Michael French
Estimated Sales: $400,000
Number Employees: 1-4
Number of Brands: 5
Square Footage: 24000
Brands:
Lincoln Ovens
Middleby Marshall Ovens

25621 **MFG**
5620 19th Ave
Kenosha, WI 53140 262-652-3336
Fax: 262-652-3322 mfgincorp@aol.com
www.mfginc.info
Packaging machinery
President: George Roders
Estimated Sales: $1-5 Million
Number Employees: 5-9

25622 **MG America**
31 Kulick Road
Fairfield, NJ 07004-3307 973-808-8185
Fax: 973-808-8421 cradossi@mgamerica.com
www.mgamerica.com
Capsule fillers, liquid and powder fillers, tube fillers, capsule checkweighers, cartoners, case packers and palletizers
President: Fabio Trippodo
Estimated Sales: $2.5 - 5 Million
Number Employees: 10-19

25623 **MGF.com**
2700 Cumberland Parkway
Suite 500
Atlanta, GA 30339
Canada 770-444-9686
www.zep.mfg.com
Cleaning compounds, detergents and disinfectants
Founder, CEO: Mitch Free
Number Employees: 20
Square Footage: 60000

25624 **MGM Instruments, Inc**
925 Sherman Ave
Hamden, CT 06514-1150 203-288-3523
Fax: 203-288-2621 800-551-1415
sales@mgminstruments.com
www.mgminstruments.com
Analyzes and tests plant operations, wastewater
President: Patrick Harewood
Chairman and CEO: George Mismas
Number Employees: 20-49

25625 **MGS Machine Corporation**
9900 85th Ave N
Maple Grove, MN 55369 763-425-8808
Fax: 763-493-8818 800-790-0627
info@mgsmachine.com www.mgsmachine.com
Packaging machinery manufacturing; feeding and cartoning
President: Richard Bahr
Estimated Sales: $10-20 Million
Number Employees: 50-99

25626 **MGS Machine Corporation**
9900 85th Avenue North
Maple Grove, MN 55369-6801 763-425-8808
Fax: 763-493-8818 800-790-0627
info@mgsmachine.com www.mgsmachine.com
Vibratory feeders, centrifugal feed systems
President: Richard Bahr
Estimated Sales: $1-5 Million
Number Employees: 50-99

25627 **MIFAB Manufacturing**
1321 West 119th Street
Chicago, IL 60643 773-341-3030
Fax: 773-341-3047 800-465-2736
sales@mifab.com www.mifab.com
Manufacturer, importer and exporter of grease traps, oil, sediment and lint interceptors, floor drains, access doors, etc
President: Jim Whiteside
Accounting Manager: Daniel ODekirk
Vice President of Division: Paul Lacourciere
Engineering Manager: Jason Gremchuk
Quality Control Manager: John Murphy
National Sales Manager: Andrew Haines
Purchasing Manager: Alice OConnor
Number Employees: 20-49
Square Footage: 180000
Brands:
Mifab

25628 **MISCO Refractometer**
3401 Virginia Road
Cleveland, OH 44122 216-831-1000
Fax: 216-831-1195 866-831-1999
www.misco.com
Manufacturer and exporter of digital hand-held abbe/labprator, inline/process refractometers. Established in 1949 in Cleveland, Ohio and is recognized as a world leader in the refractometer industry.
CEO: Michael Rainer
Number Employees: 10-19
Type of Packaging: Food Service, Bulk
Brands:
Abbe

25629 **MIT Poly-Cart Corporation**
211 Central Park W
New York, NY 10024 212-724-7290
Fax: 212-721-9022 800-234-7659
info@mitpolycart.com www.mitpolycart.com
Industrial polyethylene hand carts and trucks
President: Daniel Moss
Vice President: Isaac Rinkewick
Research & Development: Isaac Rinkewick
Marketing Director: Sandy Divack
Sales Director: Marty Winnick
Customer Service: Marty Winnick
Estimated Sales: $1-2.5 Million
Number Employees: 10-19
Number of Brands: 1
Number of Products: 50
Type of Packaging: Bulk

25630 **MIWE USA**
54 Jamestown Road
Belle Mead, NJ 08502-5222 908-904-0221
Fax: 908-904-0241 miweusa@aol.com
www.miwe.de
President: Hary Jacoby
CFO: Hary Jacoby
Quality Control: Hary Jacoby
R&D: Hary Jacoby

Estimated Sales: $5 - 10 Million
Number Employees: 4

25631 MJD Trucking
2055 Demarco Dr
Vineland, NJ 08360 856-205-9490
Fax: 856-205-9491 800-458-0439
diane@mjdtrucking.com www.mjdtrucking.net
Owner: John Davey
Estimated Sales: $3 - 5 Million
Number Employees: 10-19

25632 MLP Seating
950 Pratt Blvd
Elk Grove Vlg, IL 60007 847-956-1700
Fax: 847-956-1776 800-723-3030
sales@mlpseating.com www.mlpseating.com
Manufacturer and exporter of chairs, tables and bar stools
President: Ralph D Samuel
R&D: Ralph D Samuel
Quality Control: Goerge Stembridge
Sales: Steven Seres
Estimated Sales: $5 - 10 Million
Number Employees: 20-49

25633 MLS Signs
25733 Dhondt Ct
Chesterfield, MI 48051 586-948-0200
Fax: 586-948-0300 www.mlssigns.com
Neon, acrylic, metal and vinyl letters, illuminated signs and cake stands; also, crane truck service and installation available
President: William Siewert
Estimated Sales: $1-2.5 Million
Number Employees: 10-19
Square Footage: 4000

25634 MM Industries
36135 Salem Grange Road
P.O. Box 720
Salem, OH 44460-0720 330-332-4958
Fax: 330-332-1543 800-227-7487
info@vorti-siv.com www.vorti-siv.com
Serving and filtration equipment. Manufacturer of sieving, straining and self-cleaning in-line filtration systems. Commonly used for ingredient sifting; particle separation and classification; liquid/solid separation and liquidfiltration
President: Barbara Maroscher
VP: Vic Maroscher
Public Relations: Dennis Ulrich
Estimated Sales: $2.5 - 5 Million
Number Employees: 10-19
Square Footage: 160000

25635 MMLC
12403 Wellington Park
Houston, TX 77072-3954 281-983-0315
Fax: 713-868-8041 800-727-5700
info@mmldesign.com www.mmldesign.com
President: Jerry Lecontte
Quality Control: Ray Nevill
Estimated Sales: $300,000-500,000
Number Employees: 1-4

25636 MMR Technologies
1400 N Shoreline Blvd Ste A5
Mountain View, CA 94043-1346 650-962-9620
Fax: 650-962-9647 855-962-9620
sales@mmr-tech.com www.mmr-tech.com
Manufacturer and exporter of microminiature refrigeration equipment for materials research
CEO: William Little
Sales VP: Robert Paugh
Estimated Sales: $2.5-5 Million
Number Employees: 10-19
Square Footage: 36000

25637 MNC Stribbons
1545 North West 165 Street
Miami, FL 33169 305-621-6022
Fax: 305-621-6109 info@mncstribbons.com
www.mncstribbons.com
Gift packs, accessories/supplies i.e. picnic paskets, specialty food packaging i.e. giftwrap/labels/boxes/containers.
Marketing: Michael Flynn

25638 MO Industries
9 Whippany Rd
Unit B1-2
Whippany, NJ 07981-1540 973-386-9228
Fax: 973-428-0221 sales@moindustries.com
www.moindustries.com
Manufacturer importer and exporter of movable and stationary drum lifters/positioners; also, dust control blending, crushing and milling size reducers, pallets, stainless steel funnels, quick-release valves, viscous materialdischargers, and stainless steel drums
President/CFO: Alex Maier
Estimated Sales: $4 Million
Number Employees: 5-9
Brands:
M.O.-Lift
Robusto
Vispro

25639 MOCAP
409 Parkway Dr
Park Hills, MO 63601 314-543-4000
Fax: 314-543-4111 800-633-6775
sales@mocap.com www.mocap.com
Transparent tubing
President: Joseph Miller
Estimated Sales: $10-20 Million
Number Employees: 50-99

25640 MOCON
7500 Boone Ave N Ste 110
Minneapolis, MN 55428 763-493-6370
Fax: 763-493-6358 info@mocon.com
www.mocon.com
Manufacturer and exporter of instrumentation, consulting, and laboratory services to medical, pharmaceutical, food and other industries worldwide. Develops and manufactures high technology instrumentation and provides consulting andanalytical service to research laboratories, manufacturers and quality control departments in the life sciences, food/beverage, polymer/adhesives, electronic and other industries
President: Robert Demorest
CEO: Robert Demorest
CFO: Darrell Lee
VP: Doug Lindemann
Research And Development: Dan Mayer
Marketing: Guy Wray
Sales: Betty Kauffman
Public Relations: Sophia Dilberakis
Production: Tim Ascheman
Estimated Sales: $25 Million
Number Employees: 120
Square Footage: 50000
Brands:
Gsa
Oxtran
Pac Check
Pac Guard
Permatran
Profiler
Skye

25641 MOOG
PO Box 18
East Aurora, NY 14052 716-652-2000
Fax: 716-655-2065 800-272-6664
www.moog.com
Brushless servo motors and drives
President/COO/CEO: John Scannell
Chairman: Robert T. Brady
CFO: Donald Fishback
Manager: Kelly Lalley
Estimated Sales: $.5 - 1 million
Number Employees: 10-19

25642 MPBS Industries
2820 E Washington Blvd
Los Angeles, CA 90023 323-268-8514
Fax: 323-268-6305 800-421-6265
info@mpbs.com www.mpbs.com
Modified atmospheric packaging, vacuum packaging equipment, blenders, choppers, smokehouses, stuffers, slicers and plant supplies. Products and services for: industrial food processing equipment; industrial food packaging equipment;grocery and restaurant equipment; and also butcher supplies and food processing supplies.
President: Michael Dernburg
Estimated Sales: $2.5 - 5 Million
Number Employees: 10-19

25643 MPE Group
6981 N Park Drive
Pennsauken, NJ 08109-4205 856-317-9960
Fax: 856-317-9963 info@mpegroupusa.com
www.mpe.nl
Scraped surface heat exchangers, unique bottom driven processing vessels, crystallization tanks, complete processing systems, aseptic processing systems, vacuum gas packaging systems, vacuum drying
Estimated Sales: $55 Million
Number Employees: 275

25644 MPI Label Systems
450 Courtney Rd
Sebring, OH 44672 330-938-2134
Fax: 330-938-9878 800-837-2134
info@mpilabels.com www.mpilabels.com
Pressure sensitive labels- film and paper, tags, instant redeemable coupons, clean-release cards, folded labels, etc. Distributor of thermal transfer printers, ribbons, automatic and semi-automatic label applicators
President: Rany Kocher
CFO: David Jonson
General manager: Joe Oyster
Marketing: Linda Buttermore
Production: Joe Oyster
Estimated Sales: $20 - 50 Million
Number Employees: 100-249
Square Footage: 110000
Parent Co: Miller Products
Brands:
Anchorseal
Mpi 90
Mpi-L
Prime Label
Prime Plus Irc
Scannable Bar Code Hologram

25645 MPI Simgraph
210 Meijer Dr
Suite B
Lafayette, IN 47905-4694 765-449-4100
Fax: 765-449-1703 info@mpimes.com
Visual packaging software products including Leapfrog graphic database manager, Imagepak for creating visual packaging instruction sheets and Iconworker for creating visual assembly and process instruction sheets
Estimated Sales: $1 - 5 Million

25646 MPS North America, Inc.
8236 Nieman Road
Lenexa, KS 66214 913-310-0055
Fax: 913-310-0088
s.knowlton@mps-northamerica.com
www.mps-group.nl
Food products machinery
President: Serge Cramer
VP: Jerry Frizzell
Operations Manager: John Estrada
Estimated Sales: $2 Million
Number Employees: 1-4
Parent Co: MPS meat processing systems

25647 MRC Bearing Services
1510 Gehman Rd
Harleysville, PA 19438 215-513-4400
Fax: 215-513-4736 800-672-7000
mrcinfo@skf.com www.mrcbearingservices.com
Bearings for the food industry
President: Don Poland
Sales Director: Jay Carlson
Public Relations: Wendy Garle
Estimated Sales: $1 - 5 Million

25648 MRC Bearing Services
1510 Gehman Road
Kulpsville, PA 19443 215-513-4726
Fax: 888-322-4672 800-672-7000
www.mrcbearingservices.com
Bearings
President: Tom Johnstone
Number Employees: 10

25649 MRI Flexible Packaging
122 Penns Trl
Newtown, PA 18940 215-860-7676
Fax: 215-860-6170 800-448-8183
info@mriflex.com www.mriflex.com
Polyethylene sleeve labels, specialty bags and roll stock; also, polypropylene roll feed labels
COO: Gney Lane
Marketing VP/Sales: Art Bucci
Estimated Sales: $30 Million
Number Employees: 100-249

25650 MRI Flexible Packaging
122 Penns Trl
Newtown, PA 18940 215-860-7676
Fax: 215-860-6170 800-448-8183
info@mriflex.com www.mriflex.com
Polyethylene stretch sleeve labels, oriented polypropylene roll-fed labels, shrink sleeves, and shrink roll-fed labels.
Sales: Jennifer Hirsch
Estimated Sales: $15 Million
Number Employees: 100-249
Type of Packaging: Private Label

25651 MS Plastics & PackagingCompany
10 Park Pl
Building 2-1A2
Butler, NJ 07405 973-492-2400
Fax: 973-492-7801 800-593-1802
web@msplastics.com www.msplastics.com
Polyethylene bags, liners, sheets, stretch wrap, printed bags, tubing, stretch and shrink film and bands; importer of plastic shrink films and bands
President: Al Saraisky
CFO: Al Saraisky
Estimated Sales: $3 - 5 Million
Number Employees: 10-19
Brands:
Banderwrapper
Disposawrapper
Freightwrap
Polybander

25652 MS Willett Inc
220 Cockeysville Road
Cockeysville, MD 21030 410-771-0460
Fax: 410-771-6972 info@mswillett.com
www.mswillett.com
Turnkey systems and tooling for the production of light metal packaging components, easy open ends, shallow drawn cans and food tray, hinge cover boxes, and small deep drawn parts
President: James Lekin
Engineering, Development & Sales: Gary Ruby
Quality & Safety: Robert Burns
Public Relations: Linda Ambrose
Manager Manufacturing Serv.: Jack Kersch
T&D Manager: Larry Felty
Estimated Sales: $5-10 Million
Number Employees: 35
Square Footage: 292000

25653 MSK Covertech
4170 Jvl Industrial Park Dr
Marietta, GA 30066 770-928-1099
Fax: 770-928-3849 info@msk.us
www.mskcovertech.com
Packaging machinery
Marketing: Marcela Leano
General Manager: Braden Camp
Estimated Sales: $1-5 Million
Number Employees: 8
Parent Co: MSK Covertech Group
Brands:
Econotech
Powertech
Recotech

25654 MSSH
901 N Carver St
Greensburg, IN 47240-1014 812-663-2180
Fax: 812-663-5405 ashleymachine@yahoo.com
Manufacturer and exporter of eviscerating tables, poultry pickers and scalders
Manager: Jim Israel
CFO: Jim Israel
Estimated Sales: $30-50 Million
Number Employees: 5-9
Square Footage: 8000

25655 MTC Food Equipment
17708 Widme Road
Unit D
Poulsbo, WA 98370 360-697-6319
Fax: 360-697-6738 mtc@mtcfoodequipment.com
www.mtcfoodequipment.com
De-boning machines, bowl choppers, vacuum packers, slicers, grinders, meat saws, ice machines, stuffing machines, freezing equipment, smokehouses, filleting machines, skinning machines, and many other types of food processmachinery.
Owner: Todd Comstock
Estimated Sales: $500,000
Number Employees: 3
Square Footage: 2367

25656 MTL Etching Industries
861 Fiske St
Woodmere, NY 11598-2429 516-295-9733
Fax: 516-295-9733
Manufacturer and exporter of advertising specialties, nameplates, dials, scales, rulers, etc
CEO: Alan Stern
Estimated Sales: $1 - 3 Million
Number Employees: 10-19

25657 MTP Custom Machinery Corporation
3857 Hyde Park Boulevard
Niagara Falls, NY 14305-1701 716-282-5705
Fax: 716-282-5741 mtpcorp@aol.com
Accumulating conveyors
Estimated Sales: $1-5 Million
Number Employees: 29

25658 MTS Seating
7100 Industrial Dr
Temperance, MI 48182 734-847-3875
Fax: 734-847-0993 info@mtsseating.com
www.mtsseating.com
Manufacturer and exporter of metal stack chairs, bar stools, pedestal tables and bases and a complete line of hospitality and food service seating
President: Bart Kulish
Marketing Manager: Eric Foster
Sales VP: Greg Piper
Estimated Sales: $20 - 50 Million
Number Employees: 250-499
Square Footage: 200000
Parent Co: Michigan Tube Swagers Fabricators
Type of Packaging: Food Service

25659 MacDonald Steel Ltd
200 Avenue Road
Cambridge, ON N1R 8H5
Canada 519-620-0400
Fax: 519-621-4995 800-563-8247
Sales@HDPCANADA.COM
www.hdpcanada.com
Number Employees: 10
Parent Co: HDP

25660 MacDonald's Magnetic Signs
PO Box 486
Alamo, TX 78516-0486 956-787-0016
Fax: 956-787-8466
Magnetic signs
Owner: Bill Mac Donald
Estimated Sales: Less than $500,000
Number Employees: 1-4

25661 MacKenzie Creamery
PO Box 325
Hiram, OH 44234 440-226-0772
Fax: 330-569-3387
info@mackenziecreamery.com
www.mackenziecreamery.com
Organic Artisan goat cheeses
Founder/President: Jean Mackenzie

25662 MacKinlay Teas
1289 Waterways Dr
Ann Arbor, MI 48108-2783 734-846-0966
Fax: 734-747-9193 sales@mackinlay.com
www.mackinlay.com
Teas
President: Davinder Singh
Estimated Sales: $2.9 Million
Number Employees: 1-4
Type of Packaging: Private Label
Brands:
Mackinlay Tea's
Queen Jasmine
White Tiger Rice
Wild Blend Rice

25663 MacMillan Bloedel Packaging
4001 Carmichael Rd
Montgomery, AL 36106-3613 334-244-0562
Fax: 334-213-6199 800-239-4464
Manufacturer and exporter of corrugated shipping containers
VP: J Tignor
Director Marketing: Stewart Williams

25664 Mace/Osmonics
5951 Clearwater Dr
Hopkins, MN 55343-8990 952-933-2277
Fax: 952-988-6060 800-334-2770
www.osmonics.com
Meters, flow
President: Edward J Fierko
CFO: Juan Carlos Monschein
Estimated Sales: $100+ Million
Number Employees: 500-999

25665 Machanix Fabrication
13929 Magnolia Ave
Chino, CA 91710 909-590-9700
Fax: 909-590-3932 800-700-9701
www.webflyer.machanixfab.com
Food processing equipment and supplies including blenders, mixers, slicers, toasters, etc
President: Craig Broswell
CEO: Craig Broswell
Estimated Sales: Below $5,000,000
Number Employees: 1-4
Square Footage: 12000

25666 (HQ)Machem Industries
1607 Derwent Way
Delta, BC V3M 6K8
Canada 604-526-5655
Fax: 604-526-1618 info@mchem.com
Manufacturer and exporter of alkaline, acid and specialty cleaners, sanitizers, chain lubes, defoamers, descalers and chlorine dioxide
General Manager: Paul Grehen
Other Locations:
Machem Industries
Regina SK
Brands:
Dairi-San
Kloriclean
Optimum
Orbit
Progress
Rinsol
Topsan
Tuff Stuff

25667 Machine Applications Corporation
3410 Tiffin Ave
Sandusky, OH 44870-9752 419-621-2322
Fax: 419-621-2321 info@macinstruments.com
www.macinstruments.com
Steam flow meters and high temperature humidity analyzers
President: Jim Weit
Sales Manager: Janet Jarrett
Estimated Sales: Below $5 Million
Number Employees: 5-9
Square Footage: 16000

25668 Machine Builders & Design
806 N Post Rd
Shelby, NC 28150 704-482-3456
Fax: 704-482-3000
mbdusa@machinebuilders.com
www.machinebuilders.com
Bakery equipment
President: Darryl Mims
Finance Manager: Steve Hyde
Vice President: Brad Hogan
Sales Manager: Rick McDaniel
Service Manager: Phillip Cannon
Estimated Sales: $5-10 Million
Number Employees: 20-49
Type of Packaging: Bulk

25669 Machine Builders and Design
806 N Post Rd
Shelby, NC 28150 704-482-3456
Fax: 704-482-3000 mbdusa@machinebuilders.net
www.machinebuilders.com
Manufacturer and exporter of cookie packaging machinery
President/Owner: Darryl Mims
Finance Manager: Steve Hyde
Vice President: Brad Hogan
Service Manager: Phillip Cannon
Sales Manager: Rick MaDaniel
Engineering Manager: Eric Grayson
Estimated Sales: $5-10,000,000
Number Employees: 20-49

25670 **Machine Electronics Company**
9 Devoe St
Brooklyn, NY 11211 718-384-3211
Manufacturer and exporter of packaging, wrapping and bag filling machinery
Manager: Tom Costello
Number Employees: 44

25671 **Machine Ice Company, Inc**
8915A Sweetwater Lane
Houston, TX 77037 713-868-1300
Fax: 713-868-4424 800-423-8822
info@machineice.com www.machineice.com
Wholesaler/distributor and exporter of mobile ice centers, ice plants, ice machines and refrigeration equipment; also, walk-in and reach-in coolers, cold storage facilities, ice cream makers, etc.; serving the food service market
President: Dan Celli
Sales Manager: Walter Felix
Number Employees: 15
Square Footage: 88000

25672 **Machine Ice Company, Inc**
8915A Sweetwater Lane
Houston, TX 77037 713-868-1300
Fax: 713-868-4424 800-423-8822
info@machineice.com www.machineice.com
Manufacturer and exporter of ice equipment including automatic ice cube makers, dispensers, crushers and storage bins; also, air conditioning units
President: Dan Celli
Sales Manager: Walter Felix
Estimated Sales: $2.5-5 Million
Number Employees: 20-49
Square Footage: 200000

25673 **Machinery & Equipment Company, Inc.**
PO Box 7632
San Francisco, CA 94120 415-467-3400
Fax: 415-467-2639 800-227-4544
info@machineryandequipment.com
www.machineryandequipment.com
President: Mike Ebert
CFO: Bryan Caston
Estimated Sales: E
Number Employees: 20

25674 **Machinery & Equipment Company**
3401 Bayshore Blvd
Brisbane, CA 94005-1498 415-467-3400
Fax: 415-467-2639 800-227-4544
info@machineryandequipment.com
www.machineryandequipment.com
Buy and sell used processing and packaging equipment. Manufacture sanitary ribbon mixes and sell new dicers
President: Mike Ebert
CFO: Bryant Caston
Food Division Manager: Don Riochet
Estimated Sales: $4 Million
Number Employees: 20-49

25675 **Machinery Corporation ofAmerica**
4401 Capitola Road
Suite 3
Capitola, CA 95010-3572 831-479-9901
Fax: 831-479-4443 capitola@mca-america.com
www.mca-america.com
Supplier of rebuilt food processing equipment
Estimated Sales: $1 Million
Number Employees: 5

25676 **Machinery Engineering Technology**
2629 E County Road O
Janesville, WI 53546 608-758-0506
Fax: 608-758-1343 877-758-0506
met-llc@execpc.com
Stainless steel equipment for food filling, sealing and lidding
Estimated Sales: $3 Million
Number Employees: 5-9

25677 **Mack-Chicago Corporation**
2555 S Leavitt St
Chicago, IL 60608-5202 773-376-8100
Fax: 773-376-0883 800-992-6225
www.waveflute.com
Point-of-purchase displays, gift boxes and corrugated shipping containers; also, fire retardant and corrugated disposable chafing dishes available
President: Alwin J Kolb
CFO: Alwin J Kolb
Quality Control: Jerry Santeford
Sales Manager: Dale Arnold
General Manager: Ron Praun
Plant Manager: Ken Kruger
Estimated Sales: $20 - 50 Million
Number Employees: 100-249
Square Footage: 425000
Parent Co: Mack Packaging Group

25678 **Mackie International. Inc.**
719 Palmyrita Avenue
Riverside, CA 92507 951-346-0530
Fax: 951-346-0541
carmel@mackieinternational.net
www.mackieinternational.net
Stabilizers
President: Ernesto U Dacay
Estimated Sales: $1 Million
Number Employees: 50-99

25679 **Maco Bag Corporation**
412 Van Buren St
Newark, NY 14513 315-226-1000
Fax: 315-226-1050 sales@macobag.com
www.macobag.com
Plastic bags and barrier packaging
CEO: J Scott Miller
Number Employees: 50-99
Square Footage: 50000
Type of Packaging: Consumer, Food Service, Private Label, Bulk

25680 **Macon Tent & Awning Company**
230 South Street
Macon, GA 31202 478-743-2684
www.macontentandawning.com
Commercial awnings
President: David B Redding Jr
Estimated Sales: $1-2.5 Million
Number Employees: 10-19

25681 **Macrie Brothers**
750 S 1st Rd
Hammonton, NJ 08037-8407 609-561-6822
Fax: 609-561-6296 bluebuck@bellatlantic.net
www.blueblueberries.com
Blueberries
Owner/CEO: Paul Macrie III
Superviser: Al Macrie
Operations: Nicholas Macrie
Production: Michael Macrie
Estimated Sales: Below $5 Million
Number Employees: 5
Square Footage: 120000
Type of Packaging: Consumer, Food Service, Private Label, Bulk
Brands:
Blue Buck

25682 **Macro Plastics**
2250 Huntington Dr
Fairfield, CA 94533 707-437-1200
Fax: 707-437-1201 800-845-6555
info@macroplastics.com
www.macroplastics.com
Manufacturer high pressure injection molded products for food and agriculture
CEO: Pat Brandt
Estimated Sales: $10 - 20 Million
Number Employees: 50-99

25683 **Mactac**
4560 Darrow Rd
Stow, OH 44224 330-688-1111
Fax: 330-688-2540 800-233-4291
mactac.americas@mactac.com www.mactac.com
Manufacturer and exporter of pressure sensitive paper, film and foil products
President: Jim Peruzzi
Executive VP: Robert Hawthorne
Purchasing Agent: Hank Cardarelli
Number Employees: 500-999
Parent Co: Bemls Company
Brands:
Copyback
Durascan
Eze-Gloss
Eze-Therm
Mac-Copy
Mac-Gloss
Mac-Jet
Optichrome
Opticlear
Optiscan
Pharmaclear
Pharmalite
Pharmasoft
Polyfilm
Trans Label
Ultrascan

25684 **Maddox/Adams International**
1421 SW 107th Ave
Suite 213
Miami, FL 33174 305-592-3337
Fax: 305-591-2591 alina@maddoxadams.com
www.maddoxmetalworks.com
Food processing equipment for snack foods including tortillas, corn chips and popcorn; also, bake and fry extrusion equipment and nut roasters
Sales: Alina Del Rivero
Estimated Sales: $300,000-500,000
Number Employees: 1-4
Parent Co: Beatrice Companies

25685 **MadgeTech, Inc.**
879 Maple Street
Contoocook, NH 03229 603-456-2011
Fax: 603-456-2012 info@madgetech.com
www.madgetech.com
Data logging instrumentation used for reading and monitoring temperatures both during and after the cooking process.

25686 **Madison County Wood Products**
3311 Chouteau Ave
Saint Louis, MO 63103-2911 314-772-1722
Fax: 314-772-1733 www.mcwp.com
New and used hard and soft wood pallets
President: James Kesting
Controller: William Brynda
Vice President: Douglas Gaines
Estimated Sales: $12 Million
Number Employees: 115
Square Footage: 50000

25687 **Madix**
1537 S Main St
Goodwater, AL 35072-6620 256-839-6354
Fax: 256-839-5608 www.madixinc.com
Supermarket fixtures and food service showcases
CFO/Senior VP/Chief Information Officer: David Satterfield
Vice President, Sales: Marcy Stephens
Operations Manager: Jay Dowdle
Plant Manager: Phillip Whitley
Purchasing Director: Kim Wright
Estimated Sales: $50-100 Million
Number Employees: 250-499
Square Footage: 91730

25688 **Madix, Inc.**
500 Airport Rd.
Terrell, TX 75160 214-515-5400
800-776-2349
www.madixinc.com
Manufacturer and exporter of retail display shelving, storage, wire and wood display systems
President: T. Satterfield
Estimated Sales: $56 Million
Number Employees: 784
Square Footage: 1070000
Brands:
Maximum Merchandiser
Multiple Media Fixture
Omega

25689 **Madsen Wire Products**
101 Madsen St
Orland, IN 46776 260-829-6561
Fax: 260-829-6652 bsnyder@madsenwire.com
www.madsenwire.com
Manufacturer and designer of wire baskets, bases, containers, carts, displays, grids, stands, trays, fan and clamp guards, shelving, cages, etc. Constructed out of cold roll steel or stainless steel
President: Steve Cochran
Estimator/Customer Service: Gwen Wheaton
Account Manager: Kim Straley
Estimated Sales: $10-20 Million
Number Employees: 50-99
Square Footage: 42000

Type of Packaging: Food Service, Private Label, Bulk

25690 **Magic American Corporation**
23700 Mercantile Road
Cleveland, OH 44122-5900 216-464-2353
Fax: 216-464-5895 800-321-6330
mail@magicamerican.com
www.magicamerican.com
Manufacturer and exporter of household cleaning products including stain removers and floor polish
President: Ross Chawson
VP: Scott Zeilinger
Sales Manager: Bob Beebe
Estimated Sales: $10 - 20 Million
Number Employees: 50
Square Footage: 55000
Brands:
Goo Gone
Magic

25691 **Magic Seasoning Blends**
720 Distributors Row
Po Box 23342
New Orleans, LA 70183 504-731-3578
Fax: 504-731-3576 800-457-2857
jmcmbride@chefpaul.com www.chefpaul.com
Dry spices, rubs, bottled sauces and marinades.
Owner: Paul Prudhomme
President/CEO: Shawn McBride
CFO: Paula LaCour
R&D Director: Sean O'Meara
VP Sales/Marketing: John McBride
Director of Sales and Marketing: Anna Zuniga
Human Resources Director: Naomi Roundtree
Director of Operations: Joey Duplechain
Vice President of Manufacturing: David Hickey
Purchasing Director: Patricia Cantrelle
Estimated Sales: $9.6 Million
Number Employees: 85
Number of Brands: 3
Number of Products: 29
Square Footage: 130000
Type of Packaging: Consumer, Food Service, Private Label, Bulk
Brands:
Barbecue Magic
Blackened Redfish Magic
Blackened Steak Magic
Breading Magic
Gravy & Gumbo Magic
Magic Pepper Sauce
Magic Sauce & Marinades
Meat Magic
Pizza & Pasta Magic
Pork & Veal Magic
Poultry Magic
Salmon Magic
Seafood Magic
Shrimp Magic
Sweetfree Magic
Vegetable Magic

25692 **Magikitch'n**
PO Box 501
Concord, NH 03302-0501 603-225-6684
Fax: 603-230-5548 800-441-1492
sales@pitco.com www.magikitchn.com
Manufacturer and exporter of commercial cooking equipment including mobile outdoor units and gas, electric and charcoal broilers; also, broiler-griddles including mesquite and charcoal
President: Paul Angrick
CFO: Bob Granger
Vice President, General Manager: Greg Moyer
VP: George McMahon
Quality Control: Ray Amitrano
Senior Manager of Sales: Bonnie Bolster
Public Relations: Thomas Cassin
VP Operations: Robert Granger
Vice President of Operations: Steve Reale
Purchasing Manager: Terri Miller
Estimated Sales: $30 - 50 Million
Number Employees: 10-19
Parent Co: Middleby Corporation
Type of Packaging: Food Service
Brands:
Magicater
Magikitch'n

25693 **Magline**
503 S Mercer St
Pinconning, MI 48650-9310 989-879-2411
Fax: 989-879-5399 800-624-5463
info@magliner.com www.magliner.com
Aluminum material handling equipment including 2 and 4 wheel hand trucks and delivery ramps; also, dock equipment
CEO: D Brian Law
Marketing: Carol Sundeck
Sales Manager: Joe Howeth
Number Employees: 100-249
Brands:
Brake
Equalizer
Gemini

25694 **Magna Industries**
1825 Swarthmore Ave
Suite 1
Lakewood, NJ 08701 732-905-0957
Fax: 732-367-2989 800-510-9856
sales@magnaindustries.com
www.magnaindustries.com
Racks and carts for bakery and food industries
Owner: Walter Ostricki
Estimated Sales: $10-20 Million
Number Employees: 20-49

25695 **Magna Machine Co.**
11180 Southland Rd.
Cincinnati, OH 45240 513-851-6900
Fax: 513-851-6904 800-448-3475
sales@magna-machine.com
www.magna-machine.com
Bakery machinery including horizontal mixers and depositors
President: Paul Kramer
VP: Rob Baur
Estimated Sales: $2.5-5 Million
Number Employees: 5-9

25696 **Magna Mixer Company**
11180 Southland Road
Cincinnati, OH 45240-0810 513-851-6900
Fax: 513-851-6904 800-448-3475
sales@magna-machine.com
www.magna-machine.com
Horizontal, batch, dough, bakery, adhesives, high viscosity, paint color dye, vacuum and pharmaceutical chemical mixers
President: Paul L Kramer
VP: Baur
CFO: Windy Willey
Estimated Sales: $2.5 - 5 Million
Number Employees: 5-9

25697 **Magna Power Controls**
P.O.Box 13615
Milwaukee, WI 53213-0615 262-783-3500
Fax: 262-783-3510 800-288-8178
lbostrom@magnetek.com www.magnetek.com
Manufacturer and exporter of material handling equipment including control, electrification and automation
President: Andy Glass
CFO: Ryan Gyle
CEO: Peter M McCormick
Quality Control: Mark Logic
R & D: Ban Beilfuss
Marketing/Sales: Perry Pabich
Estimated Sales: $20 - 50 Million
Number Employees: 250-499
Type of Packaging: Bulk

25698 **Magnaform Corporation**
2685 S 4th Street
Van Buren, AR 72956 479-474-7569
Fax: 479-474-2641 magnfrm@attg.net
www.magnaform.com
President: Ed Boyd
Estimated Sales: $1 - 3 Million
Number Employees: 20-49

25699 **Magnatech**
6 Kripes Rd
East Granby, CT 06026 514-393-3609
Fax: 514-393-9432 888-393-3602
info@magnatechllc.com www.magnatech.com
Sanitary processing tubes and fittings for food processing and dairy industries.

25700 **MagneTek**
16555 W Ryerson Rd
New Berlin, WI 53151-3633 262-782-0200
Fax: 262-782-1283 www.yaskawa.com
Fractional and integral horsepower AC/DC motors and speed controls
President & COO, Drives & Motion Divisio: Mike Knapek
President & COO, Drives & Motion Divisio: Mike Knapek
Estimated Sales: $50 - 100 Million
Number Employees: 100-249

25701 **Magnetic Products**
683 Town Center Dr.
Highland, MI 48357 248-887-5600
Fax: 248-887-6100 800-544-5930
info@mpimagnet.com www.mpimagnet.com
Magnetic separators, metal detectors and check weighers
R&D: Ron Kwaz
Marketing: Ellen Kominars
Sales: Del Butler
Estimated Sales: $6 Million
Number Employees: 100
Square Footage: 160000

25702 **Magnetic Technologies**
43 Town Forest Road
P.O. Box 257
Oxford, MA 01540 508-987-3303
Fax: 508-987-2875 sales@magnetictech.com
www.magnetictech.com
Magnetic clutches for bottle capping
President: John Deluca
VP: Greg Podstanka
Sales: Howard Schwerdlin
Estimated Sales: $1,000,000 - $5,000,000
Number Employees: 25

25703 **Magnetool**
505 Elmwood Dr
Troy, MI 48083 248-588-5400
Fax: 248-588-5710 sales@magnetoolinc.com
www.magnetoolinc.com
Manufacturer and exporter of magnetic separation equipment
President: Albert Churchill
Engineer: Mike Wright
VP: C Sulisz
Estimated Sales: $20 - 50 Million
Number Employees: 20-49
Square Footage: 40000

25704 **Magnum Coffee Packaging**
16800 Java Boulevard
Nunica, MI 49448 616-837-0333
Fax: 616-837-0777 www.magnumcoffee.com
Tea and coffee industry packaging materials and machines
Owner: Kevin Kihnke
Estimated Sales: $2.5 - 5 Million
Number Employees: 20-49

25705 **Magnum Custom Trailer &BBQ Pits**
10806 Ranch Road 620 N
Austin, TX 78726-1709 512-258-4101
Fax: 512-258-2701 800-662-4686
info@magnumtrailers.com
www.magnumtrailers.com
Manufacturer and exporter of barbecue and catering trailers, custom kitchens and mobile concession stands
President: Charles Mc Lemore
Sales: Todd McLemore
Sales: Richard Westlund
Plat Manager: Jeff Israel
Estimated Sales: $15 Million
Number Employees: 50-99
Square Footage: 100000
Brands:
Magnum

25706 **Magnum Systems**
1250 Seminary Street
Kansas City, KS 66103-2515 913-362-1710
Fax: 913-362-7863 800-748-7000
sales@smootco.com www.taylorproducts.com
Automated packaging machinery
President: Brian Klughardt

Estimated Sales: $500,000-$1 Million
Number Employees: 1-4
Parent Co: Taylor Products

25707 Magnuson Corporation
1 Magnuson Ave
Pueblo, CO 81003 719-948-9500
Fax: 719-948-9540 sales@magnusoncorp.com
www.magnusoncorp.com
Manufacturer and exporter of processing and packaging machinery including vegetable cutters and peelers, washers and feeders; also, full can palletizers
Owner: Bob Smith
VP/General Manager: Craig Furlo
Estimated Sales: $2.5-5 Million
Number Employees: 20-49
Parent Co: Atlas Pacific Engineering

25708 Magnuson Industries
3005 Kishwaukee Street
Rockford, IL 61109 815-229-2970
Fax: 815-229-2978 800-435-2816
ppsales@posi-pour.com www.posi-pour.com
Manufacturer, importer and exporter of portion control liquor pourers and bar supplies
VP: Stewart Magnuson
Director Sales: Robert Gough
Estimated Sales: $5-10 Million
Number Employees: 10-19
Square Footage: 80000
Brands:
Posi-Pour

25709 Magnuson Products
66 Brighton Rd
Clifton, NJ 07012 973-472-9292
Fax: 973-472-5686
Industrial cleaning compounds for bottles, dairy, glass, pipes, dishwashers, etc
President: Al Reisch
Estimated Sales: $10 - 20 Million
Number Employees: 10-19

25710 Magpowr
1626 Manufacturers Dr
Fenton, MO 63026-2839 636-343-5550
Fax: 636-326-0608 800-624-7697
magpowr@magpowr.com www.magpowr.com
Equipment components, tension and torque control and capping clutches
Owner: Benson Portnoy
VP: Jeff Hutchings
CEO: Bruce Ryen
Estimated Sales: $10 - 20 Million
Number Employees: 50-99
Brands:
Magpowr

25711 Magsys
4144 S 112th St
Milwaukee, WI 53228 414-543-2177
Fax: 414-541-9203
Manufacturer and exporter of stainless steel magnetic conveyor equipment for transport of ferrous crowns, caps and closures
President: Rudy Zwiebel
Estimated Sales: Below $5 Million
Number Employees: 1-4
Square Footage: 5000
Brands:
Magsys

25712 Mahaffy & Harder Engineering Company
140 Clinton Road
Fairfield, NJ 07004-0002 973-227-4004
Fax: 973-227-3634 sales@mahaffy-harder.com
www.mahaffy-harder.com
President: A Mahaffy-Berman
Vice President of Engineering: Henry Nixon
Vice President of Sales/Marketing: Russ Garofalo
Vice President of Operations: Mike Summersett
Estimated Sales: $5 - 10 Million
Number Employees: 50-99

25713 (HQ)Mahoney Environmental
712 Essigton Rd
Joliet, IL 60435 815-730-2080
Fax: 815-730-2087 800-892-9392
info@mahoneyenvironmental.com
www.mahoneyenvironmental.com
Grease handling equipment; also, grease collection, recycling and rendering services available
President: John Mahoney
Partner: John Mahoney
VP Marketing: Brad Schofield
Equipment Sales Manager: Kyle Taylor
Estimated Sales: $2.5 - 5,000,000
Number Employees: 50-99
Other Locations:
Mahoney Environmental
Mendota IL
Brands:
The Recycler

25714 Maier Sign Systems
515 Victor Street
Saddle Brook, NJ 07663-6118 201-845-7555
Fax: 201-845-3336 maiersign@aol.com
Manufacturer and exporter of bulletin and menu boards, directories, awnings and signs including plastic, metal and neon
President/CEO: Stuart Brown
Estimated Sales: Less than $500,000
Number Employees: 4
Square Footage: 16000
Parent Co: Elms Industries

25715 Mail-Well Label
295 Lillard Dr
Sparks, NV 89434-8902 775-359-1703
Fax: 775-359-1736 www.renaissancemark.com
Glue-applied paper and metallized and foil labels for wine, beer, beverage products, canned vegetables, fruit and seafood
CEO: John Brandoff
Site Manager: John Brandoff
VP: Cameron Beddome
Estimated Sales: $50-100 Million
Number Employees: 100-249
Parent Co: Lawson Mardon Group

25716 Mail-Well Label
6901 Rolling Mill Road
Baltimore, MD 21224-2030 410-282-4500
Fax: 410-288-3509 800-637-4879
Paper labels including litho-printed, square or die cut, high gloss and product resistant; also, aqueous coated laminates for corrugated containers
Community Manager: Richard Dix
General Manager: Russell Hoffman
Operations Manager: John Rixham
Estimated Sales: $20-50 Million
Number Employees: 250-499
Square Footage: 85000
Parent Co: Lawson Mardon Packaging

25717 Main Course Consultants
8629 Avers Avenue
Skokie, IL 60076-2201 847-869-7633
Fax: 847-866-0898 tana24@earthlink.net
Consultant specializing in concept and menu development for restaurants; also, cost analysis, business plans and mystery shopping services available
President: Lee Michaels
Number Employees: 27

25718 Main Lamp Corporation
1073 39th St
Brooklyn, NY 11219 718-436-2207
Fax: 718-438-6836
price@nationwidelighting.com
www.lampwarehouse.net
Lighting fixtures, table lamps and ceiling fans
President: William Ain
CFO: Misses Ains
Salesperson: J Piccozino
Manager Operations: R Dabideen
Estimated Sales: $2.5 - 5 Million
Number Employees: 10-19
Square Footage: 100000
Brands:
Casablanca
Stiffel
Weinstock

25719 (HQ)Main Street Gourmet
170 Muffin Lane
Cuyahoga Falls, OH 44223 330-929-0000
Fax: 330-920-8329 800-533-6246
snatoli@mainstreetgourmet.com
www.mainstreetmuffins.com
Gourmet frozen bakery items including an extensive selection of muffins and muffin batter, cookies, brownies and bars, granola, loaf cakes, cakes and baked goods, toppings
President/CEO: Steven Marks
President/CEO: Harvey Nelson
Quality Control: Angela Stoughton
Marketing: Joe Schaefer
Sales: Keith Kropp
Plant Manager/Operations: Mike Braun
Production: Tommie Smith
Production: Bryan Smith
Purchasing Director: Jim Braun
Estimated Sales: $15 Million
Number Employees: 100-249
Number of Brands: 6
Number of Products: 158
Square Footage: 65000
Type of Packaging: Consumer, Food Service, Private Label, Bulk
Other Locations:
Main Street Muffins
La Crosse WI
Main Street Cambritt Cookies
Cuyahoga Falls OH
Main Street Custom Foods
Cuyahoga Falls OH
Main Street Fund Raising
Cuyahoga Falls OH
Isabella's
Lacrosse WI
Brands:
Cambritt Cookies
Isabella's Extraordinary Muffins
Main Street Muffins
More Than Moist Muffins
The Softer Biscotti
Wild Fudge Brownies

25720 Main Street Gourmet
170 Muffin Ln
Cuyahoga Falls, OH 44223-3358 330-929-0000
Fax: 330-920-8329 800-533-6246
snatoli@mainstreetgourmet.com
www.mainstreetgourmet.com
Proprietary products including frozen dough, batter, and thaw and serve products
President/CEO: Steven Marks
President/CEO: Harvey Nelson
R&D: Dan Maurer
Quality Control: Angela Stoughton
Marketing: Brett Boyer
Sales: Nate Searles
Operations/Production: Mike Braun
Purchasing Director: Dan Wilson
Estimated Sales: $15 Million
Number Employees: 100
Number of Products: Cust
Square Footage: 65000
Parent Co: Main Street Gourmet, LLC
Type of Packaging: Consumer, Food Service, Private Label, Bulk

25721 Mainca USA
411 Eichelberger St
St Louis, MO 63111 314-351-4677
Fax: 314-353-6655 877-677-7761
maincausa@maincausa.com
www.maincausa.com
Meat processing equipment; including: mixers, choppers, saws, grinders, moulders and sausage stuffers
President: Dale Schmidt
Estimated Sales: Under $500,000
Number Employees: 1-4

25722 Maine Industrial Plastics & Rubber Corporation
21 Teague Street
P.O.Box 381
Newcastle, ME 04553 207-563-5532
Fax: 207-563-8457 800-540-1846
hgl@tidewater.net www.miprcorp.com
Conveyor belting, rubber and plastic sheet
President: Henry Lee
Vice President: Whitney Lee
Estimated Sales: $1 - 3 Million
Number Employees: 9
Square Footage: 48000
Parent Co: Maine Industrial Corp.

25723 Maine Poly Aquisition
PO Box 1385
Windham, ME 04062-1385 207-946-7440
Fax: 207-946-5102

Plastic bags
President: Kimball H Dunton
CFO: Jackie Coutier
Public Relations: Steve Spencer
Estimated Sales: $10-20 Million
Number Employees: 10

25724 Mainline Industries
1 Allen St
Suite 1
Springfield, MA 01108 413-733-5771
Fax: 413-733-5929 800-527-7917
customerservice@mainlineind.com
www.mainlineind.com
Manufacturer and exporter of disposable wipers, cleaning towels and scuff pads
President: Paul Motter
VP: Carlo Rovelli
Quality Control: Angie Smith
Marketing Support: Lee Albert
Estimated Sales: $2.5-5 Million
Number Employees: 5-9
Brands:
Aquawipes
Hydroscrubs
Hydrowype

25725 Mainstreet Menu Systems
1375 N Barker Rd
Brookfield, WI 53045 262-782-6000
Fax: 262-782-6515 800-782-6222
info@mainstreetmenus.com
www.mainstreetmenus.com
Manufacturer and exporter of point of purchase displays, menu boards and order racks. Design, engineer, produce & install menu boards, graphics & displays.
President/COO: Douglas Watson
CFO: Bill Hintz
Research & Development: Paul Steinbrenner
Marketing: Angie Herrmann
Estimated Sales: $10 - 20 Million
Parent Co: Howard Company
Type of Packaging: Food Service
Brands:
Mainstreet

25726 Maja Equipment Company
6005 N 9th Street
Omaha, NE 68110-1121 402-346-6252
Fax: 402-346-6953 jlong@majausa.com
www.majausa.com
Skinning and derinding machinery for fish, poultry, pork and beef; also, rotating evaporators
Product Manager: Steven Lemke
Sales: Kent Rounds
Sales: Aaron Borns
Estimated Sales: $1 - 5 Million
Number Employees: 20-50

25727 Majestic
60 Cherry Street
Bridgeport, CT 06605-2395 203-367-7900
Fax: 203-335-6973
Manufacturer, importer and exporter of plastic serving and tabletop accessories including beverage glasses, pitchers, bowls, mugs, stemware, ice buckets, plates, trays and coasters; manufacturer of electric lamps and plastic kitchentools and gadgets
Estimated Sales: $2.5-5 Million
Number Employees: 10-19
Parent Co: Zivco
Brands:
Basket Weave
Chroma Lamps
Diner Mug
Facets
Ice-Stir-Cools
Koziol
Seaglass
Transitions

25728 Majestic Coffee & Tea
3870 Charter Park Dr
San Jose, CA 95136-1388 408-448-6370
Fax: 408-448-8537 bobgard@gardfoods.com
www.gardfoods.com
Brewing devices, roasting machines
*Estimated Sales:*less than $500,000
Number Employees: 1-4

25729 Majestic Flex Pac
3337 Grapevine Street
Mira Loma, CA 91752 951-361-0247
Fax: 951-361-0260 sales@majesticflexpac.com
www.majesticflexpac.com/
Majestic Flex PAC is a manufacturer and supplier of shrink sleeves, pouches, laminations, and custom bags to numerous industries including that of food and beverage, dairy, bakery and snack, candy and confection.
President: Leonardo Gutierrez
Type of Packaging: Consumer

25730 Majestic Industries, Inc
15378 Hallmark Ct.
Macomb, MI 48042 586-786-9100
Fax: 586-786-9105 web@majesticind.net
www.majesticind.net
Manufacturer and exporter of treated dusting cloths and wet and dust mops
Owner: Alan Green
CEO: Gary Potashnick
Estimated Sales: $1 - 3 Million
Number Employees: 5-9
Number of Brands: 10
Number of Products: 250
Square Footage: 128000
Type of Packaging: Consumer, Food Service, Private Label, Bulk
Brands:
Monarch
Sir Dust-A-Lot
Sweeping Beauty
Velva-Sheen

25731 Makat
500 Tillessen Boulevard
Ridgeway, SC 29130-8543 803-337-4700
Fax: 803-337-4701 makatusa@infoave.net
Extruding and depositing machines for confectionery and baking industries, starch and starchless moulded goods as well as center-in-shell, nougat, fondant, fudge, truffles, chocolate, hard candy, and caramel products
Estimated Sales: $2.5-5 Million
Number Employees: 5-9

25732 Mako Services
4297 Buford Dr
Suite 2A
Buford, GA 30518-3400 770-932-3292
Fax: 770-932-3290
Full line seafood, meats
Owner: Joe Connor
Estimated Sales: $10 - 20 Million
Number Employees: 10-19

25733 Malco Manufacturing Corporation
13917 S Main St
Los Angeles, CA 90061 310-366-7696
Fax: 310-366-7694 866-477-7267
info@malcomfg.com www.malcomfg.com
Bun and pie pans, foil containers and aluminum bakery racks
VP: Steve Goodman
Estimated Sales: $5 Million
Number Employees: 5-9

25734 Malcolm Stogo Associates
41 Tudor Lane
Scarsdale, NY 10583-4909 914-472-7255
Fax: 914-472-8861 www.malcomstogo.com
International dairy and food consultant specializing in ice cream product development and marketing concept strategies
President: Malcolm Stogo
VP/Treasurer: Barbara Stogo
Number Employees: 7
Square Footage: 6000

25735 Mali's All Natural Barbecue Supply Company
161 Bramblewood Ln
East Amherst, NY 14051-1417 716-688-2210
Fax: 716-688-2795 800-289-6254
buymali@localnet.com
Manufacturer, importer and exporter of lump charcoal, briquettes and wood for smoking and cooking; also, grilling woods
President: James Maliszewski
CEO: Frances Maliszewski
Estimated Sales: $1 - 3 Million
Number Employees: 1-4
Number of Brands: 1
Brands:
Mali's

25736 Mall City Containers
2710 N Pitcher St
Kalamazoo, MI 49004 269-381-2706
Fax: 269-381-7878 800-643-6721
info@mallcitycontainers.com
www.mallcitycontainers.com
Corrugated boxes and point of purchase displays
Owner: Ben Boeresma
CEO: Ben Boersma
Sales Manager: Tom Vandenberg
Estimated Sales: $10 - 15 Million
Number Employees: 50-99

25737 Mallet & Company
51 Arch Street
PO Box 474
Carnegie, PA 15106-2022 412-276-9000
Fax: 412-276-9002 800-245-2757
sales@malletoil.com www.malletoil.com
Food grade release compounds, edible oils and specialty blends, emulsifiers and icing stabilizers, bread pan oilers, cake pan greasers, and machinery for the baking and food processing industries.
President & CEO: Robert Mallet
Director of Accounting/Treasurer: James Gaetano
Quality Control Manager: Nicole Anesetti
Marketing Mnaager: Mary Nicholson
Director of Sales: Jeff Reichel
Maintenance Manager: Roger Broz
Engineering Manager: Don Huber
Engineering Director: Bob Wilhelm
Plant Manager: James Baumgarten
Estimated Sales: $8.6 Million
Number Employees: 64
Square Footage: 32292
Type of Packaging: Consumer, Food Service, Private Label
Brands:
Everite
Fry Well
Fry'n Gold
Hiflex
Kake Mate
Mello Gold
Pan & Griddle Gold
Pic 77
Prime Fry
Satin Donut Fry
Satin Fry
Satin Glo
Satin Plus
Sparkle
Sunny Gold
Sunshine
Thriftee Gold
Touch O'Gold
Vegalube

25738 (HQ)Malnove Packaging Systems
13434 F St
Omaha, NE 68137 402-330-1100
Fax: 402-330-2941 800-228-9877
packaging.systems@malnove.com
www.malnove.com
Manufacturer and exporter of folding paperboard cartons
President, CEO: Paul Malnove
CFO: Jim Belcher
VP: Dick Lawson
VP Sales: Michael Querry
Operations: Steve Maynar
Plant Manager: Craig Beaber
Estimated Sales: B
Number Employees: 100-249
Square Footage: 800000
Type of Packaging: Consumer, Food Service, Private Label

25739 Malo/Loveless Manufacturing
12111 E 51st St # 106
Tulsa, OK 74146-6005 918-583-2743
Fax: 918-583-6208 sales@maloinc.com
www.maloinc.com

Manufacturer and exporter of crateless and overpressure retort systems for low-acid foods in metal and flexible containers
President: C Clugston
VP: Allen Stucky
Marketing/Sales: Rick Holsted
Estimated Sales: $2.5-5 Million
Number Employees: 10-19
Square Footage: 80000
Brands:
Malo

25740 **Malpack Polybag**
120 Fuller Rd
Ajax, ON L1S3R2
Canada 905-428-3751
Fax: 416-297-9874
Low and high density polyethylene t-shut carry-out sacks and bread and bagel bags
President: Guy DiPietro
General Manager: Jim Leo
Secretary: Joe Galea
Number Employees: 210
Square Footage: 120000
Parent Co: Malkpack
Other Locations:
Malpack Polybag
Ajax ON

25741 **Maltese Signs**
5550 Peachtree Industrial Blvd
Norcross, GA 30071-1450 770-368-0911
Fax: 770-454-7383 email@maltesesigns.com
www.maltesesigns.com
Signs
President: Eloi Duguay
CFO: Rejean Pelletiar
VP: Michael Maltese
Estimated Sales: $10 Million
Number Employees: 100-249
Square Footage: 65000

25742 **Malteurop North America, Inc.**
3830 W Grant Street
Milwaukee, WI 53215-2355 414-643-5984
www.malteurop.com
Processor and exporter of malt, also offers several modes of commercial collaboration, as well as consulting, engineering, and training services.
President: Alain Le Floch
Vice President: Chris Mulder
Chief Marketing Officer: Rick Barney
Plant Manager: Rick Slotness
Estimated Sales: $31.5 Million
Number Employees: 150
Parent Co: Malteurop
Type of Packaging: Food Service, Bulk

25743 **Malthus Diagnostics**
35888 Centre Ridge Road
North Ridgeville, OH 44039 440-327-2585
Fax: 440-327-7286 800-346-7202
malthususa@alltel.net
Automated microbiological analyzers; manufacturer, importer and exporter of incubators and growth media
Director Marketing/Sales: Joseph Carney
Director US Operations: Joseph Carney
Estimated Sales: $1-2.5 Million
Number Employees: 25
Square Footage: 1000
Parent Co: IDG
Brands:
Lab M Media
Malthus System V

25744 **Man-O Products**
811 Ridgeway Ave
Cincinnati, OH 45229 513-281-5959
Fax: 513-936-6555 888-210-6266
mano@manoproducts.com
www.manoproducts.com
Manufacturer and exporter of protective hand creams and soap products
President: Steve Seltzer
Quality Control: Andy Joseph
Sales Manager: Tom Joseph
Estimated Sales: $5 - 10 Million
Number Employees: 5-9

25745 **Man-Tech Associates**
600 Main St
Tonawanda, NY 14150-3723 716-743-1320
Fax: 519-763-2205 800-206-8116
literature@mantech.ca www.mantech.ca
Laboratory and analytical equipment including PC controlled automated ion analysis and titration systems
President: Edward Godman
Marketing Supervisor: Richard Veilans
Estimated Sales: Less than $500,000
Number Employees: 1-4

25746 **Manabo**
501 Main Street
Platte City, MO 64079-8460 816-431-3948
Fax: 816-431-3951
Cutting and boning equipment, sharpening machines and services; safety apparel; sanitation supplies and equipment

25747 **(HQ)Management Insight**
33 Boston Post Road West
Malborough, MA 01752 508-485-2100
Fax: 508-485-1388
michalski@foodserviceinsight.com
www.mgtinsight.com
Restaurant and food service consultant providing stratigic planning, facility programming, pre-opening planning, market and financial feasibilty studies, audits, menu development, and restaurant revitalization
President/CEO: Jack Mandelbaum
Vice President: Elizabeth Michalski
Estimated Sales: $.5 - 1 million
Number Employees: 3
Square Footage: 1575

25748 **Management Recruiters**
3645 Cortez Rd W Ste 140
Bradenton, FL 34210 941-756-3001
Fax: 941-756-0027 admin@mriflorida.com
www.mriflorida.com
Consultant specializing in employment search and recruitment
President: R Rush Oster
General Manager: Robert Boal
Estimated Sales: less than $500,000
Number Employees: 1-4
Parent Co: Management Recruiters International

25749 **Management Tech of America**
8233 Paseo Del N
Suite C-100
Scottsdale, AZ 85261 480-998-0200
Fax: 480-951-1458 sales@mtanet.com
www.mtanet.com
Manufacturer and exporter of software for the control of material handling systems
Estimated Sales: $10-20 Million
Number Employees: 50-99

25750 **Manchester Tool & Die**
601 S Wabash Rd
Manchester, IN 46962 260-982-8524
Fax: 260-982-4575
www.manchestertoolanddie.com
Manufacturer and exporter of packaging equipment and machinery; also, prototype development available
Sales/Supervisor: Robin Brubaker
Plant Manager: Josh Berry
Estimated Sales: $2.5-5 Million
Number Employees: 10-19
Square Footage: 17000

25751 **Mancini Packing Company**
PO Box 157
Zolfo Springs, FL 33890 863-735-2000
Fax: 863-735-1172 rmancini@mancinifoods.com
www.mancinifoods.com
Peppers and olive oil
Chairman/President: Frank Mancini
VP: Alan Mancini
Estimated Sales: $11 Million
Number Employees: 100-249
Type of Packaging: Consumer, Food Service, Private Label, Bulk
Brands:
Mancini

25752 **Mandarin Soy Sauce**
4 Sands Station Rd
Middletown, NY 10940 845-343-1505
Fax: 845-343-0731 info@wanjashan.com
www.wanjashan.com
Soy sauce, asian sauce, rice and vinegar
President: Michael Wu
VP: Mike Shapiro
Estimated Sales: $165 Million
Number Employees: 25
Square Footage: 85000
Brands:
Wan Ja Shan

25753 **Mandeville Company**
2800 Washington Ave N
Minneapolis, MN 55411-1683 612-521-3671
Fax: 612-521-3673 800-328-8490
dick@mandevilleco.com
www.mandevillecompany.com
Manufacturer and wholesaler/distributor of equipment for meat processors, delis and restaurants including saws, grinders, mixers, tumblers, marinators, knives, scales, juicers and slicers; also, reconditioned equipment; serving thefood service market
President: Julie Lane
Secretary: Phyllis Stellmaker
Estimated Sales: $2.5-5 Million
Number Employees: 10-19
Square Footage: 20000

25754 **Mane Inc.**
999 Tech Dr
Milford, OH 45150-9535 513-248-9876
Fax: 513-248-8808 requests@mane.com
www.mane.com
Founded in 1871. Manufacturer of flavors and seasoning blend
President/CEO: Jean Mane
President: Michell Mane
Executive Vice President: Kent Hunter
Estimated Sales: 20-50 Million
Number Employees: 50-99
Square Footage: 65000

25755 **Manitowoc Foodservice**
2100 Future Drive
Sellersburg, IN 47172 818-637-7200
Fax: 818-637-7222 800-367-4233
www.manitowocbeverage.com
Manufacturer, importer and exporter of automatic ice transportation systems, beverage and ice dispensers, faucets, fluid control devices, pumps, timers, bar guns and carbonators
Manager: Andrew Nelson
CEO: G McCann
Estimated Sales: $3 - 5 Million
Number Employees: 5-9
Square Footage: 480000

25756 **Manitowoc Foodservice Companies, Inc.**
2227 Welbilt Boulevard
New Port Richey, FL 34655 727-375-7010
Fax: 727-375-0472 877-375-9300
info@manitowocice.com
manitowocfoodservice.com
President: Tim Kraus
VP: Dan Brandl
Public Relations: Linda Johnson
Estimated Sales: $138 Million
Number Employees: 1500
Number of Brands: 6
Square Footage: 14120
Other Locations:
Manitowoc Ice
Franklin TN
Manitowoc Company
Manitowoc WI

25757 **Manitowoc Ice**
2110 South 26th Street
Manitowoc, WI 54220 920-682-0161
Fax: 920-683-7589 800-545-5720
info@manitowocice.com
www.manitowocice.com
Manufacturer and exporter of ice machines, ice storage bins and reach-in refrigerators and freezers
President: Mike Kachmer
Executive Vice President: Larry Bryce
Vice President of Sales: Kevin Clark
VP International Operations: Mark Kreple
Estimated Sales: $1 - 5 Million
Number Employees: 250-499
Square Footage: 365000
Parent Co: Manitowoc Foodservice Group

25758 **Mankato Tent & Awning Company**
1021 Range St
North Mankato, MN 56003 507-625-5115
Fax: 507-625-5111 866-747-3524
customercare@ripflag.com
www.mankatotent.com
Industrial curtains
President: Charles D Gasswint
Sales/Marketing Executive: Devin Gasswint
Purchasing Manager: Jesse Spiess
Estimated Sales: $1-2,500,000
Number Employees: 5-9
Square Footage: 10000
Type of Packaging: Consumer, Food Service

25759 **Mankuta Brothers RubberStamp Company, Inc.**
1395 Lakeland Ave., Unit 16
PO Box 240
Bohemia, NY 11716 516-694-6880
Fax: 516-694-6063 800-223-4481
info@mankuta.com www.mankuta.com
Rubber stamps and engraved signs; wholesaler/distributor of marking devices and pre-inked stamps; embossers; seals; time stamps; etc
President: Fred Mankuta
Co-Owner: Fred Mankuta
Estimated Sales: Less than $500,000
Number Employees: 1-4
Square Footage: 6000
Brands:
Justrite

25760 **Mannesmann Dematic Corporation**
29201 Aurora Rd
Solon, OH 44139 440-248-2400
Fax: 440-248-3086
Manufacturer and exporter of cranes and hoists
President: John Paxton
Administrative Assistant: Maureen Tilly
Estimated Sales: H
Number Employees: 250-499
Parent Co: Demag Material Handling

25761 **Mannhardt Inc**
3209 S. 32nd Street
Sheboygan Falls, WI 53082 920-467-1027
Fax: 773-625-5639 800-423-2327
mannhardt1@aol.com mannhardtice.com
Ice storage dispensers and bagging equipment
President: John Williams
Sales: Lori Justinger
Number Employees: 10-19

25762 **Mannhart**
4401 Blue Mound Rd
Fort Worth, TX 76106 817-421-0100
Fax: 817-421-0246 cm@mannhart.com
www.mannhart.com
Commercial vegetable cutters and salad dryers.
President: Edwin Mannhart
Marketing: Christa Mannhart
Sales: Christa Mannhart
Purchasing: Pat Mannhart
Estimated Sales: $3 - 5 Million
Number Employees: 10-19
Number of Brands: 1
Number of Products: 2
Square Footage: 15000
Brands:
Mannhart

25763 **(HQ)Manning Lighting**
PO Box 1063
Sheboygan, WI 53082-1063 920-458-2184
Fax: 920-458-2491 info@manningltg.com
www.manningltg.com
Manufacturer and exporter of lighting equipment including institutional decorative chandeliers
President: Lisette Manning
Controller: Mary Kuhfuss
Sales: Liz Manning
Estimated Sales: $10 - 20 Million
Number Employees: 50-99
Type of Packaging: Food Service

25764 **Manning Systems**
405 Barclay Blvd
Lincolnshire, IL 60069 913-712-5576
Fax: 913-712-5580 800-444-9935
manning@honeywell.com
www.manningsystems.com
Portion control trays, polysheets, poly bags
National Sales Manager: Chuck Linn
Estimated Sales: $1-$3 Million
Number Employees: 5-9
Parent Co: Honeywell

25765 **Mannkraft Corporation**
100 Frontage Rd
Newark, NJ 07114 973-589-7400
Fax: 973-465-6851
Corrugated boxes and point of purchase displays
President: Dennis Mehiel
Marketing Executive: John Prentiss
Sales Manager: Mark Taylor
Estimated Sales: $20-50 Million
Number Employees: 100-249

25766 **Mansfield Rubber Stamp**
174 S Mulberry St
Mansfield, OH 44902 419-524-1442
Fax: 419-524-7083 stamp174@aol.com
www.mansfieldrubberstamp.com
Rubber and pre-inked stamps, engraved plastic and wood signs and magnetic signs
Owner: Jerry Parrella
Estimated Sales: Less than $500,000
Number Employees: 1-4

25767 **Manta Ray**
N60w14551 Kaul Avenue
Menomonee Falls, WI 53051-5907 888-931-2207
Fax: 262-252-4382 info@mantaray.net
Carton taping, randon carton sealers

25768 **Manufacturers Agents forthe Foodservice Industry**
1199 Euclid Ave
Atlanta, GA 30307 404-214-9474
Fax: 770-433-2450 info@mafsi.org
www.mafsi.org
VP: M Jeffrey Hessel
Number Employees: 1-4

25769 **Manufacturers CorrugatedBox Company**
5830 57th St
Flushing, NY 11378-3110 718-894-7200
Fax: 718-894-2567
Corrugated boxes
Manager: Sheldon Baim
Manager: Steven Etra
Plant Manager: Curatola
Estimated Sales: $20 - 50 Million
Number Employees: 5-9

25770 **Manufacturers Railway Company**
One Arsenal Street
Saint Louis, MO 63118 314-577-1775
Fax: 314-577-1810
amund.whittley@anheuser-busch.com
www.trainweb.org
Provides terminal rail-switching services to industries in St. Louis over 42 miles of track and repairs and rebuilds locomotives for the railroad industry. Insulated beverage and hopper railcars. Its two trucking subsidaries, with afleet of 170 specialty designed trailers, furnish cartage and warehousing services at four locations to serve Anheuser-Busch and other beverage container customers
President: Kurt Andrew
Number Employees: 100-249
Parent Co: Anheuser-Busch Companies

25771 **(HQ)Manufacturers Wood Supply Company**
1936 Scranton Road
Cleveland, OH 44113-2429 216-771-7848
Fax: 216-771-7848
Manufacturer, importer and exporter of specialty and industrial wood products including plywood and masonite boxes, packaging inserts and basket bases; custom sizing available
Plant Manager: Joseph Rielinger
Estimated Sales: $1-2.5 Million
Number Employees: 6
Square Footage: 20000

25772 **Manufacturing Business Systems**
100 N Brand Blvd Ste 600
Glendale, CA 91203 818-551-1758
Fax: 253-399-6201 info@formulas.com
www.formulas.com
Wholesaler/distributor of process manufacturing software
President: Herbert Molano
Estimated Sales: $500,000 - $1,000,000
Number Employees: 5-9

25773 **Manufacturing Warehouse**
110 NW 24th Avenue
Miami, FL 33125-5260 305-635-8886
Fax: 305-633-2266
Manufacturer and exporter of freezers including walk-in, ice cream and quick freezing; also, walk-in coolers and doors: strip, supermarket and cold storage
Estimated Sales: $1 - 5 Million
Number Employees: 4
Square Footage: 10000

25774 **MapFresh**
20 Palmetto Pkwy
Suite F
Hilton Head Isle, SC 29926-2459 843-681-5900
Fax: 843-681-5924
Modified atmospheric packaging, trays, conveyor merge units and accessories, gas packaging equipment, vacuum packaging equipment
Estimated Sales: $1 - 5 Million

25775 **Maple Hill Farms**
12 Burr Rd
PO Box 767
Bloomfield, CT 06002 860-242-9689
Fax: 860-243-2490 800-842-7304
www.mhfct.com
Milk and ice cream vending machines
President: William Miller
General Manager: Edward Jones
Estimated Sales: $5-10 Million
Number Employees: 20-49

25776 **Maple Leaf Canvas Company**
8100 Warden Road
P.O.Box 6987
Sherwood, AR 72120 501-834-8891
Fax: 501-834-5397 800-947-4233
awnings@mapleleafcanvas.com
www.mapleleafcanvas.com
Commercial awnings
Owner: Jim Wilson
Estimated Sales: $1-2,500,000
Number Employees: 5-9
Parent Co: Custom Canvas Products
Brands:
Maple Leaf

25777 **Maptech Packaging Inc.**
145 Dillon Road
Hilton Head Island, SC 29925-4127 843-342-5900
Fax: 843-342-5924
gfoulke@maptechpackaging.com
www.maptechpackaging.com
Gas sensors that monitors the intake of ammonia, carbon monoxide, chlorine, chlorine dioxide, hydrogen sulfide, hydrogen, oxygen, etc.
President & CEO: Gary Bert
Estimated Sales: $1 - 3 Million
Number Employees: 5-9

25778 **Maptech Packaging Inc.**
145 Dillon Road
Hilton Head Island, SC 29925-4127 843-342-5900
Fax: 843-342-5924
gfoulke@maptechpackaging.com
www.maptechpackaging.com
President & CEO: Gary Bert
Estimated Sales: $1 - 3 Million
Number Employees: 10-19

25779 **Mar-Boro Printing & Advertising Specialties**
1219 Gravesend Neck Rd
Brooklyn, NY 11229-4209 718-336-4051
Fax: 718-336-7996
Advertising specialties, labels, boxes and bags; also, business cards, commercial printing and typesetting services available
VP: James Bruno
Estimated Sales: $500,000-$1,000,000
Number Employees: 5-9

25780 Mar-Con Wire Belt
2431 Vauxhall Place
Richmond, BC V6V 1Z5
Canada 604-278-8922
Fax: 604-278-8938 877-962-7266
www.metalbelt.com
Manufacturer and exporter of wire mesh conveyor belting, food processing equipment, conveyors and sheet metal fabrications including stamping
President: Michael Chiu
CFO: Michael Chiu
R&D: Michael Chiu
Sales Director: Krey Miller
Production/Purchasing: Nathan Chiu
Estimated Sales: $5 Million
Number Employees: 25
Square Footage: 10000
Brands:
Mar-Con

25781 Mar-Khem Industries
PO Box 2266
Cinnaminson, NJ 08077
Fax: 856-829-9203 tony@mar-khem.com
www.mar-khem.com
Supplier, exporter of closeouts; also, investment recovery and used equipment available
President: Anthony Corradetti
Number Employees: 5-9
Number of Brands: 200
Number of Products: 800
Square Footage: 250000
Type of Packaging: Consumer, Food Service, Private Label, Bulk

25782 Mar-Len Supply
23159 Kidder St
Hayward, CA 94545 510-782-3555
Fax: 510-782-2032 mark@marlensupply.com
www.marlensupply.com
Manufacturer and exporter of biodegradable oil and grease dispersing and removing compounds
Owner/President/office Manager: Shirley Winter
Technical Director: Frank Winter
Production/Sales Manager: Mark Wieland
Production Engineer: Curt Winter
Estimated Sales: $500,000-$1 Million
Number Employees: 1-4

25783 Marathon Equipment Company
PO Box 1798
950 County Hwy. 9 S.
Vernon, AL 35592-1798 205-695-9105
Fax: 205-695-8813 800-633-8974
marketing@marathonequipment.com
www.marathonequipment.com
Manufacturer and exporter of commercial waste and recycling equipment including balers and self-contained and stationary compactors
President: Gordon Shaw
Vice President Finance: Carolyn Ofeery
Estimated Sales: $47 Million
Number Employees: 540
Parent Co: Dover Corporation
Brands:
Bale Tech
Eliminator
Jobmaster
Ram-Jet
Rampro

25784 Marathon Products
627 McCormick Street
San Leandro, CA 94577-1109 510-562-6450
Fax: 510-562-6408 800-858-6872
marathon@marathonproducts.com
www.marathonproducts.com
Environmental monitors
Founder, President: Jon Nakagawa
CEO: Jon Nakagawa
Executive Vice President: Kevin Flynn

25785 Marble Manor
37231 SE Loudon Rd
Corbett, OR 97019 503-695-5531
Fax: 503-695-5534 www.marblemanor.com
Owner: William Marble
Number Employees: 10

25786 Marburg Industries
1207 Activity Dr
Vista, CA 92081-8510 760-727-3762
Fax: 760-727-5502 marburgind@aol.com
www.marburgind.com
Manufacturer and exporter of tamper evident packaging machinery
VP Marketing: Barbara Paschal
Manager: Barbara Paschal
Estimated Sales: $1-2.5 Million
Number Employees: 10-19
Square Footage: 10000
Type of Packaging: Food Service, Private Label, Bulk
Brands:
Autocapsealer

25787 Marc Refrigeration
7453 NW 32nd Ave
Miami, FL 33147-5877 305-691-0500
Fax: 305-691-1212 info@marcrefrigeration.com
www.marcrefrigeration.com
Manufacturer and exporter of commercial refrigerators and ice cream freezers
President: Hy Widel
Treasurer: Hal Videlitz
Secretary: Robert Gordon
Estimated Sales: $5-10 Million
Number Employees: 20-49
Square Footage: 228000
Type of Packaging: Food Service

25788 (HQ)Marcal Paper Mills
1 Market St
Elmwood Park, NJ 07407 201-796-4000
Fax: 201-796-0470 800-631-8451
www.marcalsmallsteps.com
Tissues, napkins and towels made from recycled paper
Chief Executive Officer: Tim Spring
Estimated Sales: $80 Million
Number Employees: 800
Other Locations:
Marcal Paper Mills
Augusta GA
Brands:
Aspen
Bella
Fluff Out
Sst
Sani-Hanks
Snowlily
Sunrise

25789 Marcam Solutions
95 Wells Avenue
Suite 1-1
Newton, MA 02459-3216 617-965-0220
Fax: 617-965-7273 800-962-7226
marcam.info@marcam.com www.marcam.com
Process focused MRP/ERP software
President: Duncan Angove
Chief Executive Officer: Charles Phillips
Senior Vice President: Ali Shadman
Vice President of Sales: Jean-Benoit Nonque
Chief Technical Officer: Michael Ehrenberg
Estimated Sales: $125 Million
Number Employees: 500-999
Brands:
Avantis
Prism
Protean

25790 Marcam Solutions
95 Wells Avenue
Suite 1-1
Newton, MA 02459-3216 617-965-0220
Fax: 617-965-7273 charlotte.locke@marcam.com
www.marcam.com
Software for process industries: ERP and EAM software for meat, poultry and beverage processing; software for safety, cost containment, inventory
President: Duncan Angove
Chief Executive Officer: Charles Phillips
Senior Vice President: Ali Shadman
Vice President of Sales: Jean-Benoit Nonque
Estimated Sales: $120 Million
Number Employees: 700

25791 Marcel S. Garrigues Company
560 3rd St
San Francisco, CA 94107 415-421-0371
Fax: 415-957-2638
Tea and coffee industry reconditioners, samplers and weighers
Manager: Lana Jow
Estimated Sales: $500,000-$1 Million
Number Employees: 5-9

25792 Marchant Schmidt
24 W Larsen Dr
Fond Du Lac, WI 54935 920-921-4760
Fax: 920-921-9640 sales@marchantschmidt.com
www.marchantschmidt.com
Manufacturers stainless steel products and equipment for the food and dairy industry
CEO: Myleen Schmidt
Vice President: Lyle Schmidt
Sales Director: Jeno Thuecks
Estimated Sales: $11 Million
Number Employees: 70
Square Footage: 48000

25793 Marchesini Packaging Machinery
43 Fairfield Pl
West Caldwell, NJ 07006 973-575-7445
Fax: 973-575-4051 info@marchesiniusa.com
www.marchesiniusa.com
Bag filling and sealing machines, bag forming machines, bundling machines, carton machines: closing, filling, handling, sealing, casing equipment: packers
President: Roger Toll
Controller: Elaine Miller
Estimated Sales: $2.5 - 5 Million
Number Employees: 10-19

25794 Marco Products
923 S Main St
Adrian, MI 49221-3709 517-265-3333
Fax: 517-265-3650
Plastic containers
Manager: Norman Double
Estimated Sales: $2.5-5 Million
Number Employees: 10-19
Square Footage: 54000

25795 Marconi Data Systems
1500 N Mittel Blvd
Wood Dale, IL 60191 630-860-7300
Fax: 630-616-3657 800-843-3610
www.videojet.com
President: Matt Trerotola
Estimated Sales: $1 - 5 Million
Number Employees: 1,000-4,999

25796 Marcus Carton Company
324 S Service Rd
Melville, NY 11747-3270 631-752-4200
Fax: 631-752-0022
Folding paper boxes
Vice President: Nancy Simon
Director Marketing: Douglas Campbell
Estimated Sales: $1 - 5 Million
Number Employees: 10-19
Square Footage: 37000

25797 Marden Edwards
1866 Verne Roberts Cir
Antioch, CA 94509 925-777-1403
Fax: 925-777-1406 800-332-1838
usasales@mardenedwards.com
www.mardenedwards.com
Packaging
Estimated Sales: Below 1 Million
Number Employees: 1-4

25798 Marel Food Systems, Inc.
8145 Flint Street
Lenexa, KS 66214 913-888-9110
Fax: 913-888-9124 info@marel.com
www.marel.com
Manufacturer of meat hoppers, checkweighers, scales and end line scales. Also manufacture batter mixers, flour and bread applicators, spiral and linear ovens and steam cookers.
CEO: Theo Hoen
CFO: Eric Kaman
Regional Sales Manager: David Bertelsen

25799 Marel Stork Poultry Processing
PO Box 1258
Gainesville, GA 30503 770-532-7041
Fax: 770-532-5672 800-247-8609
info.us@marel.com/poultry
www.marel.com/poultry
Poultry processing equipment
President: Theo Hoen
Director: Bob Conklin
Number Employees: 220
Parent Co: Marel

25800 Marel Townsend
2425 Hubbell Ave
Des Moines, IA 50317 515-265-8181
Fax: 515-263-3333 800-247-8609
info.townsendusa@stork.com www.marel.com
Processing equipment for meat processing; including single scales, production lines and turnkey systems
Parent Co: Marel

25801 Marel USA
9745 Widmer Road
Lenexa, KS 66215-1260 913-888-9110
Fax: 913-888-9124 888-888-9107
info@marelusa.com www.marel.com
Complete range of super fast scales, software, monitoring equipment intelligent portioning, grading modules, intergrated systems, flatteners, shish-kebab machines and service contracts
President: Noel Whitten
CFO: Noel Whitten
VP Service: Petur Petursson
Marketing Director: Heather MacKenzie
VP Sales: Larry Campbell
Public Relations: Heather Mackenzie
Estimated Sales: $2.5 - 5 Million
Number Employees: 35
Square Footage: 41600
Parent Co: Marel Hf.

25802 Maren Engineering Corporation
111 W Taft Dr
South Holland, IL 60473 708-333-6250
Fax: 708-333-7507 800-875-1038
sales@marenengineering.com
www.marenengineering.com
Manufacturer and exporter of vertical and horizontal balers for corrugated paper and other applications; also, shredders, drum crushers and packers
CFO: Lee Norbeck
Vice President: Charles Brown
R & D: David Rudofski
Manager: Greg Hermdon
Estimated Sales: $5-10 Million
Number Employees: 20-49
Parent Co: Kine Corporation

25803 (HQ)Marfred Industries
12708 Bradford St
Sun Valley, CA 91353 818-896-3449
Fax: 818-889-4239 800-529-5156
info@marfred.com www.marfred.com
Corrugated boxes and folding cartons
President: Marvin Fenster
CFO: Marc Fenster
Quality Control: John Ramirez
Marketing: Brian Mallay
Sales/Marketing Manager: Chris Gaff
Operations: Marc Fenster
Plant Manager: Randy Phares
Estimated Sales: $500,000-$1 Million
Number Employees: 100-249
Number of Brands: 50
Number of Products: 5000
Square Footage: 465000
Type of Packaging: Consumer, Food Service, Private Label, Bulk

25804 Margia Floors
270 Bellevue Ave.
Newport, RI 2840 401-489-7805
Fax: 228-822-0096 info@margiafloors.com
www.margiafloors.com
Floor and wall coating materials, flooring, floor grating, building and construction consultants
Estimated Sales: $1 - 5 Million
Number Employees: 2

25805 Marietta Corporation
37 Huntington Street
Cortland, NY 13045
Fax: 607-756-0658 800-950-7772
info@mariettacorp.com www.mariettacorp.com
Contract packager of food products, toiletries and detergents
Chief Executive Officer: Donald Sturdivant
Chief Financial Officer: Perry Morgan
SVP, Quality & Regulatory Affairs: Chris Calhoun
SVP, Business Development: David Hempson
SVP, Human Resources: Beth Corl
Plant Manager: Carol Gherardi
Estimated Sales: $163 Million
Number Employees: 1,500
Square Footage: 450000
Type of Packaging: Bulk

25806 Marin Cleaning Systems
3239 Monier Cir
Suite 1
Rancho Cordova, CA 95742-6833 916-635-6861
Wine industry tank cleaners
Owner: Nathan Bari
Estimated Sales: $300,000-500,000
Number Employees: 1-4

25807 Marineland Commercial Aquariums
3001 Commerce St.
Blacksburg, VA 24060-6671 805-529-0083
Fax: 805-529-0852 800-322-1266
consumersupport@unitedpetgroup.com
www.marineland.com
Manufacturer and exporter of display tanks for lobsters and fish
President: Gary Smith
CFO: John McGreevy
Vice President: Bill Sheweloff
Quality Control: Fred Bohmour
Sales Manager (West Coast): Jay Dersahagian
Director Export Sales: Don Sonderling
Estimated Sales: $5 - 10 Million
Number Employees: 250-499

25808 Marion Body Works
211 W Ramsdell St
Marion, WI 54950-0500 715-754-5261
Fax: 715-754-5776 contactus@marionbody.com
www.marionbody.com
Dry, refrigerated and curtainside vans; also, structural platforms and glasshaulers
President: James Simpson
Sales Manager: Mike Foley
Production Manager: Kent Cournoyer
Estimated Sales: $10 - 20 Million
Number Employees: 100-249
Square Footage: 120000
Brands:
Marion

25809 Marion Mixers
3575 3rd Ave
Marion, IA 52302 319-377-6371
Fax: 319-377-1204 sales@marionmixers.com
www.marionmixers.com
Manufacturer and exporter of horizontal batching and continuous mixers; also, paddle and ribbon designs available
Owner: John R Winistorfer
Sales Director: John Winistorter
VP Operations: Doug Grunder
Production: John Meeker
Estimated Sales: $5-10 Million
Number Employees: 20-49
Square Footage: 20000
Brands:
Marion

25810 Marion Pallet Company
281 Copeland Ave
Marion, OH 43302 740-382-5063
Fax: 740-387-9478 800-432-4117
New and rebuilt wooden pallets
Owner: Devin Needles
Estimated Sales: $10-20 Million
Number Employees: 10-19
Square Footage: 10000

25811 Marion Paper Box Company
600 E 18th St
Marion, IN 46953 765-664-6435
Fax: 765-664-6440 sales@marionbox.com
marionpaperboxco.com
Manufacturer and exporter of folding and set-up paper boxes; also, die cutting and partitions available. Also manufactures pads
President: David Wilson
Sales: Jason Priest
Manager Operations: David Wilson
Estimated Sales: $2.5 - 5 Million
Number Employees: 5-9
Square Footage: 15000

25812 Mark Container Corporation
1899 Marina Blvd
San Leandro, CA 94577-4225 510-483-4440
Fax: 510-352-1524 www.wellsfargo.com
Manufacturer and exporter of corrugated boxes
Manager: Shuzair Malik
Estimated Sales: $10-20 Million
Number Employees: 10-19

25813 Mark Products Company
46 Rainbow Trl
Denville, NJ 07834 973-983-8818
Fax: 973-627-6273 schwcses@cs.com
Manufacturer and exporter of packaging equipment and materials including shrink and pallet wrappers and wrapping films; importer of shrink PVC films
President: Doug Mark
VP: Charles Scweizer
Number Employees: 1-4
Number of Brands: 1
Number of Products: 10
Square Footage: 2000
Type of Packaging: Food Service, Bulk

25814 Mark Slade ManufacturingCompany
PO Box 325
Seymour, WI 54165-0325 920-833-6557
Fax: 920-833-7456 drhandles@new.rr.com
Wood dowels, core plugs, cant hooks, pallets and displays
*Estimated Sales:*less than $300,000
Number Employees: 2
Square Footage: 10050

25815 Mark-It Rubber Stamp & Label Company
912 Hope St
Stamford, CT 06907-0031 203-348-3204
Fax: 203-323-7846
Manufacturer and converter of self-stick labels, rubber stamps and marking devices
President: Archie Dean
Executive VP: Archie Dean
Quality Control: Archie Dean
Sales Manager: Jack O'Neil
Estimated Sales: Below $5 Million
Number Employees: 5-9

25816 MarkeTeam
Corporate Office
PO Box 850
Vancouver, WA 98666 360-696-3984
Fax: 360-693-0192 info@marketeamnw.com
www.marketeamnw.com
Manufacturers' representative for food service equipment including supplies and furniture
President: Daniel Miles
CEO: Jim Mincks
CFO: David Mincks
VP: William Kelly
Estimated Sales: Below $5 Million
Number Employees: 10-19

25817 Market Forge Industries
35 Garvey St
Everett, MA 02149-4403 617-387-4100
Fax: 617-387-4456 866-698-3188
custserv@mfii.com www.mfii.com
Comerical food service equipment
President: Jeffrey Leckel
Chief Financial Officer: Dave Zappala
Vice President: Robert Stefka
Chief Information Officer: Nancy Murphy
Vice President, Sales & Marketing: Peter Kelley
Sales Manager: Kelly Powers
Vice President, Operations: William McGourty
Production Manager: Hal Hamilton
Facilities Manager: Fred Bartlett
Estimated Sales: $13 Million
Number Employees: 75
Square Footage: 14859
Type of Packaging: Food Service

25818 Market Sales Company
PO Box 590639
Newton, MA 02459-0639 617-232-0239
Fax: 617-232-0239
marketsalescompany@comcast.net
www.marketsalescompany.com
Vacuum packaging equipment, vaccum bags and films.
Vice President: Linda Pollino
Sales Manager: Edward Pollino

25819 Market Sign Systems
75 W Commercial St
Portland, ME 04101-4797 207-773-7585
Fax: 207-773-3151 800-421-1799
info@nimlok-maine.com
Point of purchase aluminum sign holders
Owner: Ken Janson
VP: Marc Breton
Number Employees: 1-4
Square Footage: 1200
Brands:
Casemate

25820 Marketing & Technology Group
1415 N Dayton St
Suite 115
Chicago, IL 60642 312-266-3311
Fax: 312-266-3363 amcguire@meatingplace.com
www.meatingplace.com
Computer systems and software, meat industry publications and information, sales and advertising promotions and materials
Owner: Mark Lefens
VP Editorial: Bill McDowell
Circulation/Marketing Manager: Steve Gardberg
Sales Manager: Mary Lea
Chairman Operations: Jim Franklin
Production Manager: Bernie Schlameuss
Estimated Sales: $5-10 Million
Number Employees: 20-49
Parent Co: Marketing & Technology Group

25821 Marketing Concepts
34 Hinda Blvd
Riverhead, NY 11901-4804 631-727-8886
Fax: 631-369-3903 www.auto-matetech.com
Tea and coffee industry conveying equipment (elevators, machiners and buckets), cappers, cleaners and closers (for coffee jars)
Owner: Kenneth Herzog
Estimated Sales: $10 - 20 Million
Number Employees: 20-49

25822 Marketing Management
4717 Fletcher Ave
Fort Worth, TX 76107-6899 817-731-4176
Fax: 817-732-5610 800-433-2004
jgrulke@mmimail.com www.mmi-home.com
Retail & merchadising marketing, brand development, quality assurance, consumer research, consumer response, procurement, inventory management, category development, package design, information technology, networking and e-commercemulti media and more
President: H L Pease Jr
CEO: Herb Pease Jr
CFO: Ted Wilson
CEO: Herbert Pease Sr
R&D: Bill Bradshaw
Marketing Director: Bill Bradshaw
Sales: Bill Bradshaw
Public Relations: Joni Grulke
Operations: H Pease Jr
Estimated Sales: $10 - 20 Million
Number Employees: 50-99
Square Footage: 65000

25823 Marking Devices
3110 Payne Ave
Cleveland, OH 44114 216-861-4498
Fax: 216-241-1479 mdinc@en.com
www.realtyappreciation.com
Manufacturer and exporter of rubber and polymer printing plates and rubber and steel stamps
Owner: T Cutts
Sales Manager: Dave Tully
Estimated Sales: $2.5-5 Million
Number Employees: 20-49
Square Footage: 11000

25824 Marking Methods
301 S Raymond Ave
Alhambra, CA 91803 626-282-8823
Fax: 626-576-7564
experts@markingmethods.com
www.markingmethods.com
Permanent stress-free marking equipment including electro-chemical hot stamping for plastics, laser, dot peen for metal parts and equipment; exporter of electro-chemical marking equipment, etc
President: Charles Nichols
CEO: A Bennett
CFO: Susan Chu
Sales Director: Victor Amorim
Estimated Sales: Below $5 Million
Number Employees: 20-49
Square Footage: 20000
Brands:
Mark-300a
Marking Methods, Inc.

25825 Marklite Line
34 Davis Dr
Bellwood, IL 60104-1047 708-668-4900
Fax: 630-668-4906
Advertising and pressure sensitive tapes and labels; also, custom printing available
Customer Service: Agnes Vincenzo
Advertising: Maryann Mueller
Estimated Sales: $3 - 5 Million
Number Employees: 10-19

25826 Marko
1310 Southport Rd
Spartanburg, SC 29306 864-585-2259
866-466-2726
rmeehan@markoinc.com www.markoinc.com
Janitorial cleaners, disinfectants and waxes; wholesaler/distributor of paper supplies and janitorial equipment including aerosols and mops
Owner: Anne Meehan
CEO: Ann Meehan
VP Marketing: Richard Meehan, Jr.
Purchasing Manager: Melanie Meehan
Estimated Sales: 800000
Number Employees: 5-9
Number of Brands: 10
Number of Products: 450
Square Footage: 12000
Type of Packaging: Private Label
Brands:
Marko

25827 Marko
1310 Southport Rd
Spartanburg, SC 29306 864-585-2259
Fax: 312-829-8812 866-466-2756
rmeehan@markoinc.com www.markoinc.com
Manufacturer and exporter of table cloths and skirting; also, napkins, aprons and place mats
Owner: Anne Meehan
VP Sales/Marketing: Tony La Porte
VP Manufacturing: Rob James
Estimated Sales: $10-20 Million
Number Employees: 5-9
Type of Packaging: Food Service
Brands:
Marko Intl.
Markoated
Midwest Marko

25828 Markwell Manufacturing Company
692 Pleasant St
Norwood, MA 02062 781-769-6610
Fax: 781-769-7060 800-666-1123
info@mrkwll.com www.mrkwll.com
Manufacturer, importer and exporter of plier, box and hand, foot and air operated staplers, tackers and carton sealers; also, staples, collated nails, marking crayons, tapes, strech-wrap, and spray ashesives
President: Sam Opland
Estimated Sales: $1-2.5 Million
Number Employees: 5-9
Square Footage: 13500
Brands:
Markwell
Sta-Plyer
Tackmaster

25829 Marland Clutch Products
PO Box 308
La Grange, IL 60525-0308 708-352-3330
Fax: 877-216-3001 800-216-3515
info@marland.com www.marland.com
Heavy duty, industrial free wheeling clutches and conveyor back stops
President: Charlie Nins
CFO: John Young
Estimated Sales: $5 - 10 Million
Number Employees: 3

25830 Marlen
4780 NW 41st Street
Ste 100
Riverside, MO 64150 913-888-3333
Fax: 913-888-5471 www.marlen.com
Portioning and forming equipment, in-line grinders, pumping equipment and material handling products.
President: Richard Schneider
CEO: Jim Anderson
Regional Sales Manager: Fernando Casado

25831 Marlen International
9202 Barton St
Overland Park, KS 66214 913-888-3333
Fax: 913-888-6440 800-862-7536
jarrod.mccarroll@marlen.com
www.marleninternational.com
Food processing equipment, including: pumps, portioners, formers and in-line grinders
Vice President: Bill Faivre
Sales Manager: Jarrod McCarroll
Estimated Sales: $35 Million
Number Employees: 85
Parent Co: Pfingsten Partners

25832 Marlen International
441 30th St
Astoria, OR 97103-2807 503-861-2273
Fax: 913-888-5471 800-862-7536
sales@marlen.com www.marlen.com
Continuous flow slicers, dicers, strip cutters, shredders, volumetric rotary/piston fillers, pak-shapers, specialty conveyors, etc
Manager: Pete Johnson
CFO: Irene Codonau
Vice President: Jarrod McCarroll
Research & Development: Robert Zschoche
Quality Control: David Bogih
Marketing/Sales: Pete Johnson
Sales Manager: Brian Owen
Public Relations: Jack Walls
Inside Sales: Jack Walls
Production Manager: David Bogh
Plant Manager: Rusty Price
Purchasing Manager: Mark Ross
Estimated Sales: $10-20 Million
Number Employees: 20-49
Square Footage: 60000
Brands:
Auto-Logger
Auto-Shredder
Auto-Slicer
Automated Boxing Line
Home-Style
Mega-Slicer
Nu-Pak Performance F-Series
Nu-Pak Portion
Pak-Shaper
Pathfinder
Performance
Q-Ber
Table Top

25833 Marlen International
441 30th St
Astoria, OR 97103-2807 800-862-7536
Fax: 913-888-5471 sales@marlen.com
www.marlen.com
Manufactures dicing, filling, slicers and shredding machinery
Vice President: Jarrod McCarroll
Estimated Sales: $10-20 000,000
Number Employees: 20-49

25834 Marlen Research
P.O.Box 457
Hutchinson, KS 67504-457 316-683-6542
Fax: 316-665-6793 www.marlen.com
Elevators, loaders, lifters, dumpers, tubs, drums, tanks, vats and buckets for materials handling, processing equipment includes ham presses, molds and accessories, temperature controls, contact plate and belt freezers
Estimated Sales: $10-20 Million
Number Employees: 50-99
Parent Co: Marlen Research Corporation

25835 Marlen Research Corporation
9202 Barton St
Shawnee Mission, KS 66214 913-888-3333
Fax: 913-888-6440 sales@marlen.com
www.marlen.com

Designer and manufacturer of food processing equipment such as pump/vacuumizer, sizers, grinders, exact weight portioners, product racks, dumpers, vats, continous mold systems, thermal processing equipment and custom designed tanks andhoppers
President: Adam Anderson
VP: Bill Faivre
Marketing/Sales: Teresa Kem
Sales Manager: Fernando Casado
Estimated Sales: $6-$7 Million
Number Employees: 50-99
Square Footage: 40000
Brands:
Gbc
Marlen
Reno

25836 **Marlen Research Corporation**
9202 Barton St
Shawnee Mission, KS 66214 913-888-3333
Fax: 913-888-5471 800-862-7536
sales@marlen.com www.marlen.com
President: Adam Anderson
CFO: Larry Dearnond
Estimated Sales: $20 - 50 Million
Number Employees: 50-99

25837 **Marley Engineered Products**
470 Beauty Spot Road East
Bennettsville, SC 29512-2770 843-479-4006
Fax: 843-479-5205 800-327-4328
meptechsupport@marleymep.spx.com
www.marleymep.com
Blowers and fans
President: Dennis K Porzio
Estimated Sales: $5-10 Million
Number Employees: 10,000

25838 **Marlin Steel Wire Products**
2640 Merchant Dr
Baltimore, MD 21230 410-644-7456
Fax: 410-644-7457 877-762-7546
sales@marlinwire.com www.marlinwire.com
Steel wire shelving and racks
President: Drew Greenblatt
CFO: Susan Fuller
Estimated Sales: $20 - 50 Million
Number Employees: 20-49
Number of Products: 450
Square Footage: 25000

25839 **Marlite**
202 Harger Street
Dover, OH 44622
800-377-1221
www.marlite.com
Manufacturer and exporter of sanitary wall and ceiling panel systems, decorative wall panel systems, doors/frames, restroom partitions, korelock panels, retail merchandising display systems, etc
President/Chief Executive Officer: John Popa
Chief Financial Officer: Kimberly McBridge
Vice President, Sales & Marketing: Gregory Triplett
Senior Buyer: Larry Branham
Estimated Sales: $21 Million
Number Employees: 320
Square Footage: 450000
Brands:
Accents Frp
Borders
Displawall
Firetest
Korelock
Marlite
Marlite Brand Frp
Marlite Modules
Plank
Surface Systems
Symmetrix Frp

25840 **Marlo Manufacturing Company**
301 Division St
Boonton, NJ 07005 973-423-0226
Fax: 973-423-1638 800-222-0450
info@marlomfg.com www.marlomfg.com
Manufacturer, importer and exporter of stainless steel food service equipment
Founder: Sal Pirruccio
Owner/VP: Dino Tommasi
VP Sales & Marketing: Larry Dubov
Sales/Marketing: Dino Tommasi
Operations/Production: Paul Tommasi
Plant Manager: Paul Pirruccio
Estimated Sales: $4-6 Million
Number Employees: 20-49
Square Footage: 30000
Type of Packaging: Food Service

25841 **Maro Paper Products Company**
333 31st Ave
Bellwood, IL 60104-1527 708-649-9982
Fax: 708-649-9986 www.marocarton.com
Folding cartons and blister cards
Owner: Joseph Maro
VP: J Maro III
Estimated Sales: $5-10 Million
Number Employees: 100-249

25842 **(HQ)Marpac Industries**
PO Box 784
Philmont, NY 12565-0784 845-336-8100
Fax: 845-336-5006 888-462-7722
sales@marpac-kny.com www.marpac-kny.com
Plastic bottles and containers
VP Sales: B Williams
Operations: Gen Gendrow
Estimated Sales: $10-20 Million
Number Employees: 50-99
Square Footage: 34000
Type of Packaging: Consumer, Food Service
Other Locations:
Marpac Industries
Kingston NY
Brands:
E-Z Access

25843 **(HQ)Marq Packaging Systems**
3801 W Washington Ave
Yakima, WA 98903 509-966-4300
Fax: 509-452-3307 800-998-4301
info@marq.net www.marq.net
Case sealers, product settling & sealing, tray formers and case erector bottom sealers.
President: Rocky Marquis
VP: Kelli Barton
Sales Co-ordinator: Jim Hansen
Operations: G W Walker
Estimated Sales: $5-10 Million
Number Employees: 100+
Square Footage: 67500
Type of Packaging: Food Service, Bulk

25844 **MarquipWard United**
1300 N Airport Rd
Phillips, WI 54555-1527 715-339-2191
Fax: 715-339-4469 www.marquipwardunited.com
Manufacturer and exporter of packaging and stacking machinery
President/CEO: Timothy Sullivan
VP Sales: Randy Lorenz
Purchasing: Charles Kraiss
Estimated Sales: $100 - 500 Million
Number Employees: 500-999
Parent Co: Barry Wehmiller Companies

25845 **MarquipWardUnited**
1300 N. Airport Road
Phillips, WI 54555 715-339-2191
www.marquipwardunited.com
Machinery for corrugated containers
Estimated Sales: $1 - 5 Million
Number Employees: 250-500
Parent Co: Barry-Wehmiller

25846 **Marquis Products**
91 Pipin Road
Concord, ON L4K 4J9
Canada 905-738-2082
Fax: 905-738-2417 800-268-1282
Refrigeration equipment including walk-in, reach-in coolers, sliding and glass doors and freezers
President: Vincent Melfi
Number Employees: 30

25847 **Marriott Walker Corporation**
925 E Maple Rd
Bingham Farms, MI 48009 248-644-6868
Fax: 248-642-1213 mwc@marriottwalker.com
www.marriottwalker.com
Manufacturer and exporter of evaporators, spray dryers, etc
President: Winthrop Walker
VP Engineering: Mark Price
Estimated Sales: $1-2.5 Million
Number Employees: 5-9
Square Footage: 13200
Brands:
Marriott Walker

25848 **Marron Foods**
327 Woodlands
Box15
Harrison, NY 10528-0015 914-967-2442
Fax: 914-967-2220 888-464-7433
info@marronfoods.com www.marronfoods.com
Agglomeration/instantizing ,spray drying, blending, industrial, food serice, consumer pouch/canister packaging
Number Employees: 100

25849 **(HQ)Mars Air Systems**
14716 South Broadway
Gardena, CA 90248-1814 310-532-1555
Fax: 310-324-3030 800-421-1266
info@marsair.com www.marsair.com
Manufacturer and exporter of air purifiers and heated and unheated air curtains in electric, gas, steam and hot water for insect control and environmental separation; also, packaged make-up air, cooling, heating and ventilatingsystems
President: Martin Smilo
Vice President: Steve Rosol
Quality Control: Michael Goldman
Marketing Director: Dana Agens
Plant Manager/Purchasing Director: Frank Cuaderno
Estimated Sales: Below $5 Million
Number Employees: 50-99
Square Footage: 392000
Brands:
Ares
Combi
Mars
Whispurr Air
Windguard

25850 **Mars Systems**
1140 Empire Central Dr
Dallas, TX 75247-4322 214-634-7441
Fax: 972-252-9566 info@marssystems.com
www.marssystems.com
Restaurant entertainment systems
Owner: Robert Morris
Account Executive: Sheila Bellucci
Estimated Sales: $500,000-$1 Million
Number Employees: 5-9

25851 **Marsch Pacific Cork & Foil**
2427 Pratt Avenue
Hayward, CA 94544-7829 510-429-3200
Fax: 510-429-3200
Wine industry cork and capsule supplies
Estimated Sales: $5-10 Million
Number Employees: 10-19

25852 **(HQ)Marsh Company**
PO Box 388
Belleville, IL 62222-0388 618-234-1122
Fax: 618-234-1529 800-527-6275
marshco@marshco.com www.marshco.com
Manufacturer, exporter and importer of large and small character ink jet coding systems, marking and sealing machines and supplies
President: Robret Willett
CEO/Chairman: John Marsh
CFO: Mark Kuhn
Quality Control: Mark Wilmsen
R&D: Jerry Robortson
VP Sales/Marketing: P Wagner
Estimated Sales: $20 - 50 Million
Number Employees: 500
Other Locations:
Marsh Co.
S.A, Geneva
Brands:
Contact Marking
Dial Taper
Lcp/Dl
Lcp/Ml8
Mini-Mark
Symbol Jet
Touch Taper
Twin Taper
Ultra Taper
Unicorn

25853 **Marshakk Smoked Fish Company**
6980 75th St
Flushing, NY 11379-2531 718-326-2170
Fax: 718-384-6661

Specialty foods
President: Marie Cook
Vice President: Gary Cook
Sales Director: Sean Cook
Estimated Sales: $10-24.9 000,000
Number Employees: 50-99
Type of Packaging: Private Label
Brands:
Almondina
Aunt Jenny's
Babcock
Boone Maman
Bovril
Breadshop
Brianna's
Carapelli
Carr's
Celestial
Coco Pazzo
Colavita
Consorzio
Dececco
Del Verde
Dell Amore's
Delouis
Dessvilie
Dickinson
Droste
Dutch Gold
Eden
El Paso
Finncrisp
French Market
Green Mountain
Grielle
Guiltless Gourmet
Hero
Highland Sugar Vermont
Holgrain
Illy
Knorr
Konriko
La Marne Champ
La Posada
La Preferida
Langnese
Lindt
Maille
Marmite
McCann's
Melba
Melitta
Monnini
New York Flatbread
Old Monk
Poell
Pommery
Pritikin
Qugg
Rao's
Romanoff
Spice Hunter
Spice Island
St. Dalfour
Sunbrand
Texmati
Timpone's
Tip Tree
Tropical Bee
Twinings

25854 Marshall Air Systems
419 Peachtree Dr S
Charlotte, NC 28217-2098 704-525-6230
Fax: 704-525-6229 800-722-3474
customerservice@marshallair.com
www.marshallair.com

Manufacturer and exporter of food warming and conveyorized cooking systems including broilers; also, ventilation systems including hoods and fans
Chairman: Robert Stuck
Estimated Sales: $20-50 Million
Number Employees: 50-99
Type of Packaging: Food Service
Brands:
Autobake
Autobroil
Autobroil Omni
Autogrill
Automelt
Autoroast
Thermoglo

25855 (HQ)Marshall Boxes
715 Lexington Ave
Rochester, NY 14613-1807 585-458-7432
Fax: 585-458-6302 info@marshallboxes.com
www.marshallboxes.com

Wooden boxes, pallets and plywood parts
President: John Skuse
Estimated Sales: $2.5-5 Million
Number Employees: 10-19
Square Footage: 22000
Other Locations:
Marshall Boxes
Rancho Cucomonga CA

25856 Marshall Ingredients
5740 Limekiln Rd
Wolcott, NY 14590 800-796-9353
cbones@marshallingredients.com
www.marshallingredients.com

Fruits and vegetables in different forms such as fiber, pellet, whole, diced, sliced, powder, seeds, pomace
National Sales Manager: Casey Koehnlein
Type of Packaging: Bulk

25857 Marshall Instruments
2930 E La Cresta Ave
Anaheim, CA 92806 714-632-8565
Fax: 714-666-2326 800-222-8476
info@marshallinstruments.com
www.marshallinstruments.com

Bi-metallic dial thermometers, distributor of high performance shock proof pressure gauges
President: Nancy Lynch
VP: Nancy Lynch
Product Manager: Tim Bowers
Estimated Sales: $2.5-5 Million
Number Employees: 20-49
Square Footage: 12000

25858 (HQ)Marshall Paper Products
PO Box 267
East Norwich, NY 11732
Fax: 718-821-5779

Corrugated paper
VP: Brian Sadowsky
Estimated Sales: $1-2.5 Million
Number Employees: 5

25859 Marshall Plastic Film
904 E Allegan St
Martin, MI 49070 269-672-5511
Fax: 269-672-5035 mplasticf@aol.com
www.marshallplastic.com

Manufacturer and exporter of form, fill, seal and shrink plastic films and bags
President: John Roggow
VP: Casey McCarthy
Customer Service: William Rackley
Customer Service: Sylvia Davis
Estimated Sales: $20-50 Million
Number Employees: 50-99
Square Footage: 45500
Brands:
Marshall Blue
Marshall Pink Under the Sink

25860 Marshfield Food Safety
1100 N. Oak Avenue
Marshfield, WI 54449
888-780-9897
www.marshfieldfoodsafetyllc.com

Food safety testing facility.
Quality Manager: Debbie Chilson
Marketing: Marsha Barwick
Chief Scientific Officer: Roy Radcliff

25861 (HQ)Marston Manufacturing
13700 Broadway Ave
Cleveland, OH 44125-1945 216-587-3400
Fax: 216-587-0733 aavant@tomlinsonind.com
www.tomlinsonind.com

Wooden tray stands and oak chairs including high and booster; also, condiment holders, cast iron cookware, bread boards, sandwich tartans and underliners
President: H Meyer
CEO: Mike Figas
CFO: Don Calkins
Sales: John DiNapoli
Estimated Sales: $2.5-5 Million
Number Employees: 100-249
Square Footage: 160000
Other Locations:
Marston Manufacturing
Richmond VA

25862 Martco Engravers
792 Main Street
Fremont, NH 03044-3506 603-895-3561
Fax: 603-895-3717

Badges, ribbons, plaques, awards, trophies and rubber stamps
Partner: Arthur Courteau
Estimated Sales: Less than $500,000
Number Employees: 4

25863 Martech Research LLC
15 Myrtle Drive
Bishopville, SC 29010 803-428-2000
Fax: 803-428-1598
bmaresca@martechresearch.com
www.martechresearch.com

Custom manufacturing, formulation, private labeling and toll blending. Shelf life extension products for fruits, vegetables, oils and beverages.
Founder & President: Amie Maresca
Manager: Benny Maresca
Estimated Sales: $3.7 Million
Number Employees: 23
Square Footage: 84000
Type of Packaging: Consumer, Private Label, Bulk

25864 Martek Biosciences Corporation
6480 Dobbin Rd
Columbia, MD 21045 410-740-0081
Fax: 443-740-2985 info@martekbio.com
www.martek.com

CEO: Henry Radmer Ph.D
CFO: Peter Buzy
CEO: Steve Dubin
Operations Manager: Thomas Fisher
Estimated Sales: I
Number Employees: 500-999

25865 Martin Brothers
3057 Cajun Dr
Winnsboro, LA 71295 318-435-4581
Fax: 318-435-4581 800-652-2532
kmartin@teammartinbrothers.com
www.teammartinbrothers.com

Heat exchangers, ice cream equipment, ingredient feeders, piping, fittings and tubing, sanitary
Owner: Kelly Martin
VP Sales & Marketing: Conrad L. Gaither
Sales: Lamar Johnson
Sales: Kelly Martin
Sales: Dwayne Long
Estimated Sales: $5-10 Million
Number Employees: 10-19

25866 Martin Cab
7108 Madison Ave
Cleveland, OH 44102-4093 216-651-3882
Fax: 216-651-2079 www.martincab.com

Manufacturer and exporter of cab enclosures, including freezer cabs
President: James Martin
CFO: Jim Markin
Chairman: Pauline Martin
VP Sales/Marketing: James Girard
Estimated Sales: $20 - 50 Million
Number Employees: 50-99
Parent Co: Martin Sheet Metal

25867 Martin Control Systems Inc
5955 Wilcox Pl
Suite B
Dublin, OH 43016 614-761-5600
Fax: 614-761-5601 SalesEng@MartinCSI.com
www.martincsi.com

Designs, executes and completes industrial control system and data collection projects to automate manufacturing and process facilities.
President/Owner: Joe Martin
Principal Project Engineer: Rick Derthick
Marketing & Sales Manager: James Sellitto

25868 (HQ)Martin Engineering
1 Martin Pl
Neponset, IL 61345 309-594-2384
Fax: 309-594-2432 800-766-2786
info@martin-eng.com www.martin-eng.com

Manufacturer and exporter of belt conveyors and cleaners, transfer point skirting systems and electric, hydraulic and pneumatic vibrators; importer of electric vibrators
Owner: E H Peterson
CEO: Scott Hutter
CFO: Ron Vick
CTO: R Todd Swinderman
VP: Jim Turner
Public Relations: AD Marti
Estimated Sales: $20 - 50 Million
Number Employees: 175
Square Footage: 130000
Other Locations:
Martin Engineering
Walluf
Brands:
Durt Howg
Durt Tracker
Martin

25869 **Martin Engineering**
One Martin Place
Neponset, IL 61345-9766 309-852-2384
Fax: 800-814-1553 800-544-2947
info@martin-eng.com www.martin-eng.com
Vibration systems and solutions to boost material flow, linear and rotary vibrators keep material moving while reducing noise and air consumption, includes vibratory feeders, conveyors and compaction tables for metering transportingand compacting powder.vibrators in pneumatic, electric and hydraulic power
President: Scott Hutter
Chief Executive Officer: R Todd Swinderman
Vice President of Sales and Marketing: James Turner
Vice President of Operations: Robert Nogaj

25870 **Martin Laboratories**
PO Box 1873
Owensboro, KY 42302-1873 270-685-4441
Fax: 270-684-7859 800-345-9352
comments@m30.com www.m30.com
Manufacturer and exporter of hand cleaners and soaps including liquid and waterless
President: Harold C Martin
National Sales Manager: Art Wilbert
Customer Service: Stacia Jarvis
Estimated Sales: $10-20 Million
Number Employees: 5-9
Square Footage: 30000
Brands:
M30

25871 **Martin Sprocket and Gear**
3100 Sprocket Dr
Arlington, TX 76015 817-258-3000
Fax: 817-258-3333 mail@martinsprocket.com
www.martinsprocket.com
Wine industry conveyors and screws, power transmission and bulk material handling products, sprockets, sheaves, gears, couplings, timing pulleys, interchangeable bushings, screw conveyers (steel and plastic), bucket elevators, verticalscrew elevators
CEO: Gary Martin
CEO: Joseph R Martin Jr
Estimated Sales: $50-100 Million
Number Employees: 1,000-4,999

25872 **Martin Vibration Systems**
990 Degurse Ave
Marine City, MI 48039 810-765-7460
Fax: 810-765-7461 800-474-4538
felcom@pobox.com www.shake-it.com
Feeders, vibrators, dry bulk material handling equipment
President: Mike Lindbeck
Public Relations: Rick Felde
Type of Packaging: Food Service, Bulk

25873 **Martin's Ice**
280 Pleasant Valley Rd
Ephrata, PA 17522 717-733-7968
Fax: 717-733-1981 800-713-7968
office@martinsice.com?subject=
www.martinsice.com
Ice
Owner: Isaac Martin
Sales Manager: Randy Martin
Manager: Jerry Martin
Estimated Sales: $500,000-$1 Million
Number Employees: 5-9
Square Footage: 8400

25874 **Martin/Baron**
5454 2nd St
Irwindale, CA 91706-2000 626-960-5153
Fax: 626-962-1280 www.mbicryo.com
Manufacturer and exporter of food processing equipment, stainless steel conveying systems, cryogenic and mechanical coolers and freezers, steam and radiant heat cookers, spirals, tunnels, cabinets for heat transfer and vertical pizzaovens
President: Jonathan Martin
VP: David Baron
Sales: Allan Weiner
Operations: Carl Gumber
Estimated Sales: $3 - 5 Million
Number Employees: 10-19
Square Footage: 48000
Brands:
Mbi
Martin/Baron

25875 **Martingale Paper Company**
3022 N 16th St
Philadelphia, PA 19132 215-225-7070
Fax: 215-660-0822
Paperboard boxes and paper stationery products
Owner: Martin Grossman
Estimated Sales: $5-10 Million
Number Employees: 5-9

25876 **Martini SRL**
20 Industrial Street W
Clifton, NJ 07012-1712 973-778-4927
Fax: 973-778-9820 sales@frazierandson.com
Estimated Sales: Below 1 Million
Number Employees: 10

25877 **Marubeni America Corporation**
375 Lexington Ave
New York, NY 10017 212-450-0563
Fax: 212-450-0733 gendi-s@marubeni-usa.com
www.marubeni-usa.com
Oilseeds production (canola, rapeseed and soybean)
President: Koichi Mochizuki
Manager: Sherif Gendi
Estimated Sales: 1 Billion +
Number Employees: 100-249
Parent Co: Marubeni

25878 **Marv Holland Industries**
10939-120 Street
Edmonton, AB T5H 3R3
Canada 780-453-5044
Fax: 800-361-0263 800-661-7269
custserv@marvholland.com
www.marvholland.com
Manufacturer and distributor of apparel such as business uniforms and flame resistant safety wear for industry and casual clothing.
President: Gene Fyzenky
Number Employees: 100-249

25879 **Marvell Packaging Company**
490 Us Highway 46
Fairfield, NJ 07004-1906 973-822-9339
Fax: 973-575-6637 800-445-8947
Contract packaging service
Vice President: Barry Berman
Estimated Sales: $10 Million
Number Employees: 50-99
Number of Products: 20
Square Footage: 65000
Type of Packaging: Private Label

25880 **Maryland Packaging Corporation**
1822 Worcester St
Baltimore, MD 21230 410-347-0365
Fax: 410-347-7636 mdpackaging@aol.com
Manufacturer and exporter of shrink wrapping, sleeve bundling, horizontal form/fill/seal, overwrapping and horizontal bagging machinery, also have a contract packaging division
President: John Voneiff II
CEO: Marwan Moheyeldien
Sales Director: Jay Gibson
Estimated Sales: $5 - 10,000,000
Number Employees: 60
Square Footage: 25000
Type of Packaging: Consumer, Food Service, Private Label, Bulk
Brands:
Tpa

25881 **Maryland Plastics, Inc.**
251 E. Central Avenue
Federalsburg, MD 21632 410-754-5566
Fax: 800-544-5582 800-544-5582
sales@marylandplastics.com
www.marylandplastics.com
Accessories/supplies i.e. picnic baskets, cooking implements/housewares.
President: Allen Penrod
Marketing: John Bucchioni
Manager: Jerry Dickerson
Number Employees: 290

25882 **Maryland Wire Belts**
1001 Goodwill Ave
Cambridge, MD 21613 410-228-7900
Fax: 410-228-1647 800-677-2358
BW@CambridgeIntl.com
www.cambridgeintl.com
Manufacturer and Exporter of conveyor belting, conveyors and conveyor services
President: William Weber
CEO: Duane Marshall
CEO: Bill Colson
Number Employees: 100-249
Square Footage: 200000
Brands:
Bfs
Curve Flex
Curve Mesh
Elevayor
Flat Seat
Obfs
Pactite
Pos-A-Trak
Precision Belt Series
Shove-It Rods
Spun Head

25883 **(HQ)Maselli Measurements**
7746 Lorraine Ave Ste 201
Stockton, CA 95210 209-474-9178
Fax: 209-474-9241 800-964-9600
daveodum@maselli.com www.maselli.com
Process & laboratory refractometers
President/Owner: Antonio Maselli
Quality Control: Mario Maselli
Sales: Dave Odum
Estimated Sales: $2.5-5 Million
Number Employees: 5-9
Number of Brands: 1
Number of Products: 10
Other Locations:
Maselli Measurements
Leon, GTO
Brands:
Lr01 Laboratory Refractometer
Ur20 Process Refractometer

25884 **Maselli Measurements Inc.**
7746 Lorraine Ave Ste 201
Stockton, CA 95210 209-474-9178
Fax: 209-474-9241 800-964-9600
daveodum@maselli.com www.maselli.com
Liquid analysis machines such as carbonated beverage analysis systems, automatic and in-line refractometers.
President, CEO: Antonio Maselli
Sales Manager: Dave Odum

25885 **Mason Candlelight Company**
PO Box 59
New Albany, MS 38652-0059 310-338-6987
Fax: 310-348-0135 800-556-2766
customer_service@masoncandle.com
www.masoncandle.com
Manufacturer and exporter of tabletop lighting including lamps and candles
VP/General Manager: Robert Gasbarro
Plant Supervisor: Robert Bacher
Estimated Sales: $2.5-5 Million
Number Employees: 9
Square Footage: 180000
Parent Co: Standex International Corporation

25886 **Mason City Tent & AwningCompany**
408 S Federal Ave
Mason City, IA 50401 641-423-0044
Fax: 507-625-5111 customercare@ripflag.com
www.repflag.com
Commercial awnings and industrial curtains
Manager: Russalyn Davis

Estimated Sales: Below $5,000,000
Number Employees: 1-4
Square Footage: 10000
Parent Co: ITF Industries

25887 (HQ)Mason Transparent Package Company
PO Box 852
Armonk, NY 10504-0852 718-792-6000
Fax: 718-823-7279 info@masontransparent.com
www.masontransparent.com
Printed and converted films and bags including polyethylene, clysar, polypropylene, linear low density, co-extruded, etc.; importer of film
President: Richard Cole
VP: Kevin O'Connell
Estimated Sales: $2.5 - 5 Million
Number Employees: 10-19
Square Footage: 100000

25888 Mason Ways Indestructible Plastics
580 Village Blvd
West Palm Beach, FL 33409-1904 ÿ56- 47- 883
Fax: 800-693-7745 800-837-2881
amason@masonways.com www.masonways.com
Materials handling equipment; pallets and accessories, tubs, drums, tanks, vats, buckets
Owner: Judd Ettinger
CEO: Allen Mason
Marketing Director: Ira Brichta
Operations Manager: Debbie Shrake
Estimated Sales: $1 - 5 Million
Number Employees: 1-4
Number of Brands: 6
Number of Products: 60
Type of Packaging: Food Service, Private Label, Bulk

25889 Massachusetts ContainerCorporation
300 Cedar Hill St
Marlborough, MA 01752 508-481-1100
Fax: 508-481-9029 www.unicorr.com
Corrugated boxes
VP: Jack Aundre
Estimated Sales: $10-20 Million
Number Employees: 100-249
Parent Co: Connecticut Container Corporation
Other Locations:
Massachusetts ContainerCorp.
Sharon VT

25890 Massillon Container Company
49 Ohio St SW
Navarre, OH 44662 330-879-5653
Fax: 330-879-2772 benv@vailpkg.com
www.vailpkg.com
Corrugated shipping containers
President: Robert F Vail Jr
Quality Control: Cliff Robertson
Accounting: Donna Winter
Estimated Sales: $9 Million
Number Employees: 20-49
Parent Co: Vail Industries

25891 Master Air
415 S Grant St
Lebanon, IN 46052-3605 317-375-7600
Fax: 317-375-7607 800-248-8368
loren@master-air.com www.master-air.com
Manufacturer and exporter of commercial kitchen ventilation equipment including hood systems and fan controls
President: Loren Gard
Sales Engineer: Jim Rader
Office Manager: Sharon Amack
Engineer: Kevin Blandford
Estimated Sales: $2.5-5 Million
Number Employees: 20-49
Square Footage: 118000
Brands:
Mastertech
Mastertech Direct Fired

25892 Master Containers
209 SW Phosphate Blvd
Mulberry, FL 33860 863-425-5571
Fax: 978-964-1552 800-881-6847
sales@mastercontainers.com
www.mastercontainers.com
Foam cups and containers
President: Thomas Lyons
VP: Richard Lyone
Marketing Manager: Rachael Pantely
Sales Manager: Elaine Karau
Estimated Sales: $10 - 20 Million
Number Employees: 50-99

25893 Master Disposers
PO Box 27186
Cincinnati, OH 45227-0186 513-271-1861
Fax: 513-271-1867 sales@masterdisposers.com
www.masterdisposers.com
President: Mary Grogan
R&D: Rich Grogan
Estimated Sales: $3 - 5 Million
Number Employees: 10

25894 Master Magnetics
747 South Gilbert Street
Castle Rock, CO 80104 303-688-3966
Fax: 303-688-5303 800-525-3536
magnet@magnetsource.com
www.magnetsource.com
Magnetic products for food purification systems including ceramic plate, permanent pulleys and hopper grates; also, shelf marking systems
President: John E Nellessen
Marketing Manager: Jennifer Brown
General Manager: Pat Orcutt
Estimated Sales: $3 - 5 Million
Number Employees: 7
Square Footage: 44350

25895 Master Package Corporation
200 Madsen St
Owen, WI 54460 715-229-2156
Fax: 715-229-2689 800-396-8425
mpabich@masterpackage.com
www.masterpackage.com
Fiber board, cylindrical and metal bound containers
President: Mark Pabich
Office Manager: Carole Buss
Estimated Sales: $5-10 Million
Number Employees: 20-49

25896 Master Paper Box Company
3641 S Iron St
Chicago, IL 60609 773-927-0252
Fax: 773-927-8086 877-927-0252
musser@masterpaperbox.com
www.masterpaperbox.com
Set-up and heart paper boxes
Owner: Bill Farago
VP/ Sales: Michael Musser
Operations Manager: Bill Farago Jr.
Secretary/Treasurer: Angela Sears
Estimated Sales: $2.5-5 Million
Number Employees: 20-49
Square Footage: 110000

25897 Master Piece Crystal
PO Box 848
Jane Lew, WV 26378-0848 304-884-7841
Fax: 304-884-7842 deba@access.mountain.net
www.masterpiececrystal.com
Hand blown table and glassware
Owner: Bill Hogan
Marketing Director: William Hogan
Sales Manager/Customer Service: Debbie Bailey
Estimated Sales: $5-10 Million
Number Employees: 20-49

25898 Master Printers
308 Main St
Canon City, CO 81212-3732 719-275-8608
Fax: 719-275-8106 masterprinters@bresnan.net
www.masterprinters.net
Advertising signs
Owner: Susie Pacheco
VP: Susie Pacheco
Estimated Sales: $500,000-$1 Million
Number Employees: 1-4

25899 Master Signs
5545 Parkdale Dr
Dallas, TX 75227 214-338-4727
Fax: 214-381-1090
Plastic, electric, fluorescent and neon signs; also, illuminated awnings and interior graphics
President: Robert Green
CFO: Brenda Green
Estimated Sales: $1 - 2.5 Million
Number Employees: 10-19
Parent Co: Masterco

25900 Master Tape Printers, Inc.
4517 N Elston Ave
Chicago, IL 60630-4420 773-685-4100
Fax: 773-685-1555 800-621-5801
www.mastertapeprinters.com
Adhesive, gummed, marking and pressure sensitive tapes and labels
President: Robert Grant
CEO: Melcon Grant
CFO: Malcolm Grant
VP: Andy Casey
Quality Control: Robert Wren
Marketing Director: Bob Wern
Estimated Sales: Below $5 Million
Number Employees: 20-49

25901 Master-Bilt
908 Highway 15 North
New Albany, MS 38652 662-534-9061
Fax: 662-534-6049 800-647-1284
sales@master-bilt.com www.master-bilt.com
Manufacturer and exporter of commercial refrigeration products including refrigeration and freezer cabinets, walk-in and reach-in units, etc; also, merchandising units for dairy items and deli cabinets
President: David Parks
Chief Financial Officer: Edward Jacobs
Vice President, Sales & Marketing: Bill Huffman
Vice President, Operations: Eddie Carr
Purchasing: Larry Fry
Estimated Sales: $50-100 Million
Number Employees: 350
Square Footage: 64006
Parent Co: Standex International Corporation

25902 (HQ)Masterbuilt Manufacturing
7 Masterbuilt Ct
Columbus, GA 31907 800-489-1581
Fax: 706-660-8022
customerservice@masterbuilt.com
www.masterbuilt.com
Grills, smokers, fryers, spices, marinades, wheel free cargo carriers, and bike carriers
President: John McLemore
VP Sales/Marketing: Ben Garnto
Estimated Sales: $10 - 20,000,000
Number Employees: 50-99
Number of Brands: 4
Type of Packaging: Consumer, Food Service, Private Label

25903 Mastercraft
234 W Northland Ave
Appleton, WI 54911 920-739-7682
Fax: 920-739-3208 800-242-6602
Paper products including menus, place mats, menu covers and presentation folders
General Manager: Rick Kerr
Estimated Sales: $1-2.5 Million
Number Employees: 10-19
Square Footage: 12800

25904 Mastercraft Industries
777 South St
Newburgh, NY 12550 845-565-8850
Fax: 845-565-9392 800-835-7812
tfir@floorcare.com www.mastercraftusa.com
Manufacturer, importer and exporter of industrial vacuum cleaners, parts, floor machines, carpet extractors, automatic scrubbers, steamers, marble/stone maintenance equipment and chemicals
President: Howard Goldberg
Community Director: Jay Goldberg
Executive VP: Carol Andreasian
Quality Control: Jay Goldberg
Estimated Sales: $10 - 20 Million
Number Employees: 50-99
Square Footage: 100000
Brands:
Dynavac
Quarrymaster
Sootmaster

25905 Mastercraft International
PO Box 668407
Charlotte, NC 28266-8407 704-392-7436
Fax: 704-395-1600

Manufacturer and exporter of packaging machinery including vertical and horizontal cartoners
President: Dan Rothwell
Engineer: A Christopher
Estimated Sales: $1 - 2.5 Million
Number Employees: 9
Square Footage: 20000
Brands:
Mastercraft International
Memco

25906 **Mastercraft Manufacturing Company**
3715 11th St # B1
Long Island City, NY 11101-6006 718-729-5620
Fax: 718-729-5620
Awards, badges, medals, incentives, premiums and plaques; exporter of badges; importer of pins and patches
Owner: Murray Wiener
General Manager: Peter Borsits
General Manager: Peter Borsits
Estimated Sales: $500,000 - $1,000,000
Number Employees: 5-9
Square Footage: 2000

25907 **Mastermark**
19017 62nd Ave S
Kent, WA 98032 206-762-9610
Fax: 206-763-8492
customerservice@mastermark.net
www.mastermark.net
Food packaging, rubber pre-ink and self-inking stampss, interior and exterior architecural signage, printing coder dies and stencils products
President: Cindy Hutter
CFO: C G
Marketing/Sales: Brian Carter
Operations: CG Gambling
Production: CG Gambling
Estimated Sales: Below $5 Million
Number Employees: 1-4
Square Footage: 100000
Type of Packaging: Consumer, Private Label, Bulk
Brands:
Mastermark

25908 **Masternet, Ltd**
690 Gana Court
Mississauga, ON L5S 1P2
Canada 905-295-0005
Fax: 905-795-9293 800-216-2536
info@masternetltd.com www.masternetltd.com
Plastic net, nettingon rolls, net bags, mesh liners, packaging products, wattle nets, protection packaging.
VP: Linda Hartman
Number Employees: 40
Square Footage: 240000

25909 **Mastex Industries**
2035 Factory Ln
Petersburg, VA 23803 804-732-8300
Fax: 804-732-8395 www.mastex.com
Manufacturer and exporter of electric and thermostatically controlled dish warmers and cooking utensils
President: Frank Mast
National Sales Manager: Paul Christian
Estimated Sales: $1 - 5 Million
Number Employees: 10-19
Square Footage: 50000
Type of Packaging: Consumer

25910 **Mastio & Company**
2921 N. Belt Hwy
Suite M-14
Saint Joseph, MO 64506 816-364-6200
Fax: 816-364-3606 info@mastio.com
www.mastio.com
Consultant for the packaging industry providing market research and information, customer satisfaction benchmarking, databases and re-engineering solutions
Owner: Bart Thedinger
Sales/Marketing Executive: Bart Thedinger
MIS Manager: Steve Nash
Estimated Sales: Below $5 Million
Number Employees: 5-9
Square Footage: 17000

25911 **Matcon USA**
832 Industrial Drive
Elmhurst, IL 60126 856-256-1330
Fax: 856-256-1329 druble@idexcorp.com
www.matconibc.com
Matcon are specialists in providing 'Lean' systems for handling dry solids based around portable containers (Intermediate Bulk Containers or IBSs) for batch powder processes in the manufacturing industries, including foodpharmaceutical, chemical and metal powders. Our main business philosophy is to help our customers reap the benefits of Make to Order Production and Eliminating waste.
Vice President, Sales & Marketing: Dan Ruble
Commercial Operations: Phil Spuler
Estimated Sales: $5-10 Million
Number Employees: 5
Square Footage: 11000
Parent Co: Matcon Ltd.

25912 **Mateer Burt**
700 Pennsylvania Drive
Exton, PA 19341-1129 610-321-1100
Fax: 610-321-1199 800-345-1308
sales@mateerburt.com www.mateerburt.com
Manufacturer and exporter of filling and labeling machinery and parts; installation available
Marketing Manager: April Koss
Estimated Sales: $1 - 5 Million
Number Employees: 50-99
Number of Brands: 7
Number of Products: 4
Square Footage: 320000

25913 **(HQ)Material Control**
P.O.Box 308
North Aurora, IL 60542 630-892-4274
Fax: 630-892-4931 800-926-0376
sales@materialcontrolplus.com
www.materialcontrolinc.com
Conveyor safety stop switches, belt cleaners and hood covers, bin aerators; distributor of plastic bins and totes, shelving, cabinets, mats, matting, fans, measurement and gas monitoring instruments and ventilation equipment
Manager: Jack Pierce
Sales Director: Bob Hutchins
Plant Manager: Jim Pierce
Estimated Sales: $3 - 5,000,000
Number Employees: 5-9
Other Locations:
Material Control
Aurora IL

25914 **Material Handling Technology, Inc**
113 International Drive
Morrisville, NC 27560 919-388-0050
Fax: 919-388-0051 800-779-2475
mht@mht1.com materialhandlingtech.com
Conveyors, material handling equipment, sortation equipment

25915 **Material Storage Systems**
PO Box 1010
Gadsden, AL 35902 256-543-2467
Fax: 256-547-6725 877-543-2467
sales@mssistorage.com www.mssistorage.com
Exclusive rights to the Lemanco product line. Major products are modular bolted storage bins, welded silos and refuse containers. Many accessory items are also available
President: Barney Leach
CFO: Cindi Graves
Vice President: Craig Graves
R&D: Randall Wright
Quality Control: Robert Bellow
Marketing Director: Dawn Howell
VP Sales: Craig Graves
Operations Manager: Paul Allen
Production Manager: Paul Allen
Plant Manager: Randal Wright
Purchasing Manager: Robert Bellew
Estimated Sales: $1 Million
Number Employees: 30
Number of Brands: 1
Number of Products: 3
Square Footage: 45000
Brands:
Lamanco

25916 **Material Storage Systems**
8827 Will Clayton Parkway
Humble, TX 77338 281-446-7144
Fax: 281-446-7391 800-881-6750
info@msshouston.com www.msshouston.com
Manufacturer and exporter of storage and material handling equipment
Owner: Mike Gonzales
Plant Manager: Paul Eye
Estimated Sales: $1 - 2.5 Million
Number Employees: 10-19
Brands:
Webblock

25917 **Material Systems Engineering**
P O Box 115
Stilesville, IN 46180 317-745-7263
Fax: 317-203-0748 800-634-0904
sales@materialsystemsengineering.com
www.materialsystemsengineering.com
Bulk conveying systems including pneumatic dust collecting and drag chain; also, designing, engineering and fabrication services available
Owner: George Mc Comb
Purchasing/Office Manager: Rona Campbell
Estimated Sales: $1-2.5 Million
Number Employees: 5-9
Square Footage: 11600

25918 **Materials Handling Equipment Company**
3800 Quentin St
Denver, CO 80239 303-573-5333
Fax: 303-893-3854 gmoore@mheco.com
www.materials-handling-eqp.com
Wholesaler/distributor of material handling equipment
Manager: Jenett Garcia
CFO: Ron Conrad
Estimated Sales: $50 - 100 Million
Number Employees: 100-249
Square Footage: 60000

25919 **Materials Handling Systems**
20763 Bollman Place
Savage, MD 20763 410-379-0070
Fax: 410-379-0037 MHSUSA@aol.com
www.mhs-usa.com
Conveyors, hand trucks, casters and materials handling equipment
Estimated Sales: $10-20 Million
Number Employees: 50-99

25920 **Materials Storage Systems**
PO Box 1010
Gadsden, AL 35902-1010 256-543-2467
Fax: 256-547-6725 877-543-2467
sales@mssistorage.com www.mssistorage.com
Bolted nuts
Estimated Sales: $2.5-5 Million
Number Employees: 20-49

25921 **Materials TransportationCompany**
1408 S Commerce
PO Box 1358
Temple, TX 76503 254-298-2900
Fax: 254-771-0287 800-433-3110
info@mtcworldwide.com
www.mtcworldwide.com
Manufacturer and exporter of food processing equipment, cookers, dumpers, blenders and screw and belt conveyors
President & CEO: Jim Granfor
VP Sales: Stephen Hicks
Estimated Sales: $23.4 Million
Number Employees: 160
Number of Brands: 6
Number of Products: 6

25922 **Matfer**
16300 Stagg St
Van Nuys, CA 91406 818-782-0792
Fax: 818-782-0799 800-766-0333
matfercontact@matfer.com
www.matferbourgeatusa.com

Manufacturer, importer and exporter of kitchen and bakery utensils including molds, nonstick baking sheets, pastry bags, thermometers, food mills, juicers, casserole dishes, commercial mixers, mandolines, saute pans, etc
Manager: Jean Paul Riou
CEO: Jean Paul Rio
VP: Pierre Perisot
National Sales Manager: Dominique Besson
Estimated Sales: $8 Million
Number Employees: 10-19
Square Footage: 15000
Parent Co: Matfer France

25923 Mathason Industries
6659 Sanzon Rd
Baltimore, MD 21209 410-484-5935
Fax: 410-484-0334 imathason@hotmail.com
Supplier of bakery equipment
President: Susan Mathason
Comptroller: I Mathason
Sales Director: I Mathason
Estimated Sales: $250000
Number Employees: 1-4

25924 Mathews Conveyor
1524 Lebanon Rd
Danville, KY 40422-9601 859-236-9400
Fax: 859-238-7443 800-628-4397
crodgers@mathewsconveyor.com
www.fkilogistex.com
Conveyor systems and palletizers
President: Chuck Waddle
Chief Executive Officer: Chris Cole
CFO: Bob Duplain
Vice President of Project Management: Alfred Rebello
Chief Technical Officer: Ray Neiser
Marketing Coordinator: Beverly Cooper
Senior Vice President of Sales and Marke: Jim McKnight
Vice President of Operations: Chris Arnold
Purchasing Agent: Anna McClellan
Estimated Sales: $85 Million
Number Employees: 250-499
Square Footage: 300000
Parent Co: FKI Logistex

25925 Matik Inc.
33 Brook Street
West Hartford, CT 06110 860-232-2323
Fax: 860-233-0162 sales@matik.com
www.matik.com
President: Peter Schrobenhauser
Estimated Sales: $3 - 5 Million
Number Employees: 10-19

25926 Matiss
8800 25th Avenue
St Georges, QC G6A 1K5
Canada 418-227-9141
Fax: 418-227-9144 888-562-8477
doris.boily@matiss.com www.matiss.com
Manufacturer and exporter of bakery processing equipment including greasers, depositors, fillers, cutting and batching systems; also, snack food and pizza processing and packaging equipment; laboratory testing available
President: Jacques Martel
CFO: Pierre Martel
Sales Manager: Francois Henault
Sales Engineer: Patrice Painchaud
General Manager: Jacques Martel
Estimated Sales: Below $5 Million
Number Employees: 90
Square Footage: 80000

25927 Matot - Commercial GradeLift Solutions
2501 Van Buren
Bellwood, IL 60104-2459 708-547-1888
Fax: 708-547-1608 800-369-1070
sales@matot.com www.matot.com
Manufacturer and exporter of electric dumbwaiters
Co-President/ Owner: Anne B. Matot
Co-President: Cathryn Matot
Executive Vice President: Jim Piper
Senior Vice President, Sales: Jim Peskuski
Estimated Sales: $1-2.5 Million
Number Employees: 5-9
Square Footage: 32000

25928 Matrix Engineering
P.O.Box 650728
Vero Beach, FL 32965-0728 772-461-2156
Fax: 772-461-7185 800-926-0528
griprock@gate.net www.griprock.com
Manufacturer and exporter of safety and slip resistant floor mats and flooring
President: Thomas Hayes
CEO: Edward Saylor
Vice President: Thomas Hayes
Operations Manager: Randi McManus
Number Employees: 19
Number of Brands: 4
Number of Products: 4
Square Footage: 40000
Brands:
Grip Rock
Matrix
Super G

25929 Matrix Group Inc
16 Yantecaw Avenue
Bloomfield, NJ 07003 973-338-5638
Fax: 973-338-0164 info@m8trix.com
www.m8trix.com
Consulting to natural foods marketplace; master broker
President: Ray Wolfson
VP: Irene Sherman
Sales: Ray Wolfson
Estimated Sales: $2.5-5 Million
Number Employees: 5
Number of Brands: 3-6

25930 Matrix Packaging Machinery
650 Dekora Woods Blvd
Saukville, WI 53080 262-268-8300
Fax: 262-268-8301 sales@matrixpm.com
www.matrixpm.com
Manufacturer and exporter of vertical form/fill/seal machinery
Gen Mgr/R&D/Quality Control: Marc Willden
Marketing: Lori Stein
Sales: Ship Simenz
Public Relations: John LaBouve
Operations: Jane Barnett
Production/Plant Manager: Tim Marchant
Purchasing: Lori Klandrud
Estimated Sales: $15-20 Million
Number Employees: 60+
Square Footage: 40000
Parent Co: Pro Mach Inc
Brands:
Matrix 916
Matrix1000

25931 Matson, LLC
PO Box 1820
North Bend, WA 98045 425-888-6212
Fax: 425-888-6216 800-308-3723
www.corrys.com
Manufacturer and exporter of insecticides
President: Ken Matson
Sales Representative: Dave Grasmann
Estimated Sales: $5 - 10 Million
Number Employees: 5-9

25932 Matsutani America, Inc.
951 Bunker Lane
Duncan Fader, IL 62526-9317 630-329-2886
Fax: 217-875-9821
bheard@matsutaniamerica.com
www.matsutaniamerica.com
CEO: Bob Heard
President: Bob Heard
Number Employees: 3
Parent Co: Matsutani Chemical Insdustry Company
Brands:
Fibersol 2

25933 Mattec Corporation
1301 Mattec Dr
Loveland, OH 45140 513-683-1802
Fax: 513-683-1619 800-966-1301
info@mattec.com www.mattec.com
Control systems. manufacturers of blow molding, extrusion, blown film applications and related plastic processes. Printing, metal stamping, packaging, assembly and secondary operations
President: Mick Thiel
VP Sales/Marketing: David Monroe
Estimated Sales: $10-20 Million
Number Employees: 50-99

25934 Matthews International Corporation
6515 Penn Ave
Pittsburgh, PA 15206 412-665-3640
Fax: 412-665-2550 info@matw.com
www.matw.com
Manufacturer and exporter of marking equipment for identification of products and packaging; also, turnkey systems available
President: Brian Dunn
Vice President: Peter Hart
Marketing Director: Michelle Staulding
Estimated Sales: $10-20 Million
Number Employees: 100-249
Parent Co: Matthew International Corporation
Other Locations:
Matthews International Corp.
10156 Torino
Brands:
Indent-A-Mark
Jet-A-Mark
Jet-A-Mark/Linx
Print-A-Mark

25935 Matthiesen Equipment Company
566 N W.W. White Rd
San Antonio, TX 78219-2898 210-333-1510
Fax: 210-333-1563 800-624-8635
ctorres@matthiesenequipment.com
www.matthiesenequipment.com
Manufacturer and exporter of material handling processing machinery for ice including bins, baggers, belt and screw conveyors, crushers, bag closers, drying belts, etc.; exporter and wholesaler/distributor of ice machinery
Office Manager: Claudia Torres
Research & Development: Stephen Niestroy
National Sales Manager: Diane Hardekopf
Sales Engineer: Jerry Bosma
Production Manager: Pete Ruiz
Purchasing: John Barratachea
Estimated Sales: $2.5-5 Million
Number Employees: 20-49
Square Footage: 80000
Parent Co: Tour Ice National
Brands:
Arrow
Clinebell
Hamer
Kasten/Kamco
Mgr
Mannhardt
Matthiesen
Turbo
Vogt

25936 (HQ)Maugus Manufacturing Company
PO Box 4096
Lancaster, PA 17604-4096 717-299-5681
Fax: 717-397-0991 www.nnbc-pa.com
Manufacturer and exporter of brushes, applicators and metal screw caps
President: Richard Seavey
CFO: Bryan Howett
Quality Control: Sandy Donley
Sales Manager: Ronald Vellucci
Customer Service: Marianne Walsh
Estimated Sales: $20 - 50 Million
Number Employees: 100-249

25937 Maui Wowi Fresh HawaiinBlends
5445 DTC Parkway
Suite 1050
Greenwood Village, CO 80111-3142 303-781-7800
Fax: 303-781-2438 877-849-6992
hula@mauiwowi.com www.mauiwowi.com
A Entrepreneur 500 ranked gourmet smoothie and espresso cart franchise.
President: Mark Challis
CEO: Michael Haith
CEO: Michael Haith
Estimated Sales: $1 - 3 Million
Number Employees: 20-49
Number of Brands: 1
Number of Products: 3
Square Footage: 20000
Type of Packaging: Food Service

25938 Maull-Baker Box Company
16685 Lower Valley Ridge Drive
Brookfield, WI 53005-5557 414-463-1290
Fax: 414-463-5975

Manufacturer and exporter of wooden boxes, crates, pallets and skids
President: Jerry Maull
Estimated Sales: $2.5-5 Million
Number Employees: 9

25939 **Maurer North America**
6324 N Chatham Avenue
Kansas City, MO 64151-2473 816-914-3518
Fax: 816-746-5011 maurerna@aol.com
Manufacturer and importer of food processing equipment
President: Rolf Hammann
Parent Co: A.G. Maurer
Brands:
Atmos
Maurer

25940 **Mauser, Schindler & Wagner**
3102 Wilderness Boulevard E
Parrish, FL 34219-8419 941-776-2230
Fax: 941-776-2239 ken@mauserinc.com
www.schiwa.de/en/international
Weight control systems, slicers
President: Kem Mauser
CFO: Linda Mauser
VP: Linda Mauser
Number Employees: 4
Square Footage: 4800

25941 **Maverick Enterprises**
751 East Gobbi Street
Ukiah, CA 95482-6205 707-463-5591
Fax: 707-463-0188 maverick@saber.net
www.maverickcaps.com
Wine closures and caps
President: Steve Otterbeck
Executive Vice President of Business Dev: Jon Henderson
Vice President of Operations: Fred Koeppel
Estimated Sales: $5-10 Million
Number Employees: 100-249

25942 **Maves International Software Corp.**
100 York Boulevard
Suite 404
Richond Hill, ON L4B 1J8 905-882-8300
Fax: 905-882-1550 humanresources@maves.com
www.maves.com
President: Aaron Laird
CFO: Audrey Badb
Estimated Sales: C
Number Employees: 60

25943 **Max Packaging Company**
109 6th Ave NW
Attalla, AL 35954 256-538-5439
Fax: 256-538-1929 800-543-5369
info@maxpackaging.com
www.maxpackaging.com
Manufacturer and contract packager of disposable plastic cutlery
General Manager: D McFarland
Plant Manager: Jay Bailey
Estimated Sales: $5-10 Million
Number Employees: 250-499
Square Footage: 20000
Parent Co: Gadsen Coffee Company

25944 **Maxco Supply**
605 S Zediker Ave
Parlier, CA 93648 559-646-6700
Fax: 559-646-6710 markf@mx2co.com
www.maxcopackaging.com
Case erectors and tray and bliss box formers for corrugated boxes
President: Max Flaming
CFO: David Bryant
Sales Manager: Paul Flaming
Estimated Sales: $20 - 50 Million
Number Employees: 250-499

25945 **Maxi-Vac Inc.**
PO Box 688
Dundee, IL 60118 855-629-4538
sales@maxi-vac.com
www.maxi-vac.com
Manufacturer and exporter of pressure washers and steam cleaning equipment
President: Jim Nolan
Secretary and Treasurer: Janice Nolan
Estimated Sales: $1-2.5 Million
Number Employees: 1-4

Brands:
Jet Streamer

25946 **Maximicer**
4175 Country Road 280
Georgetown, TX 78628 512-259-0500
Fax: 512-258-8804 800-289-9098
info@Maximicer.com www.maximicer.com
Manufacturer and exporter of optimizers for ice making machinery
President: J L Love
Estimated Sales: $1 - 3,000,000
Number Employees: 1-4
Type of Packaging: Food Service, Private Label
Brands:
Maximicer

25947 **Maxitrol Company**
P.O.Box 2230
Southfield, MI 48037-2230 248-356-1401
Fax: 248-356-0829 info@maxitrol.com
www.maxitrol.com
Owner: Bonnie Kern-Koskela
CFO: Christopher Kelly
Estimated Sales: $20 - 50 Million
Number Employees: 50-99

25948 **May-Wes Manufacturing**
120 Eastgate Dr SE
Hutchinson, MN 55350 320-587-2322
Fax: 320-587-6112 800-788-6483
techsupport@maywes.com www.maywes.com
Grain hoppers and crop dividers; also, plastic combine skids
VP: Mark Bruns
Manager: Connie Lindbeck
Estimated Sales: $2.5-5 Million
Number Employees: 10-19

25949 **Maya Overseas Foods Inc.**
48-85 Maspeth Ave
Maspeth, NY 11378 718-894-5145
Fax: 718-894-5178 888-289-6292
maya.foods@verizon.net www.mayafoods.com
Supplier of South East Asian groceries to retail stores, restaurants and distributors throughout America.
President/Owner: Umesh Mody
Estimated Sales: $17.4 Million
Number Employees: 28

25950 **Mayco**
2811 Mican Dr
Dallas, TX 75212 214-638-4848
Fax: 214-638-4850 david@maycopallet.com
www.maycopallet.com
Wooden pallets
President: David Gwinn
Office Manager: Melba Gwinn
Corporate Controller: Ricky Thomason
Estimated Sales: Below $5 Million
Number Employees: 10-19
Square Footage: 60000

25951 **Mayekawa USA, Inc.**
8750 West Bryn Mawr Avenue
Suite 190
Chicago, IL 60631 773-516-5070
sales@mayekawausa.com
www.mayekawausa.com
Freezing, thawing and heating units.

25952 **Maypak**
5 Mansard Court
Wayne, NJ 07470 973-696-0780
Fax: 973-633-8621 info@maypakinc.com
www.maypakinc.com
Fabricated polyethylene, expanded polystyrene and polyurethane foam; also, wooden boxes and fiberboard cartons, cooler packs, die cutting, insulated containers, custom designed cases and inserts.
President: Paul Palombi
Number Employees: 10-19

25953 **Mayr Corporation**
4 North St
Suite 300
Waldwick, NJ 07463 201-445-7210
Fax: 201-445-8019 800-465-6297
info@mayrcorp.com www.mayrcorp.com
Real-time production and process monitoring systems, plant scheduling systems, full bar coding and product traceability and genealogy systems
President: Augie Mustardo
CFO: August Mustardo

Estimated Sales: Below $5 Million
Number Employees: 10-19

25954 **Mays Chemical Company**
5611 E 71st Street
Indianapolis, IN 46220 317-842-8722
Fax: 317-558-2267 info@mayschem.com
www.mayschem.com
Chemical ingredients and related products
President: William Mays
CFO: Deric Gillispie
Quality Control: Phill Poehler
Marketing Representative: Gloria Yuan
Estimated Sales: $.5 - 1 million
Number Employees: 1-4

25955 **Maytag Corporation**
553 Benson Road
Benton Harbor, MI 49022
800-344-1274
www.maytag.com
Manufacturer and exporter of ranges and stoves
President: Arthur Learmonth
Chief Financial Officer/EVP: George Moore
VP/Secretary/Deputy General Counsel: Patricia Martin
Head of Special Projects: Christopher Wignall
Estimated Sales: $500 Million - $1 Billion
Number Employees: 1500
Square Footage: 116393
Parent Co: May Tag Corporation
Brands:
Admiral
Hardwick
Jennair
Magic Chef
Maytag

25956 **Maywood Furniture Corporation**
23 W Howcroft Rd
Maywood, NJ 07607 201-845-6517
Fax: 201-845-4586 800-238-6797
sales@maywood.com www.maywood.com
President: Tom McMullen
CEO: Bill DeSaussure
CFO: Barbara Jenkins
Operations Manager: Jack DeSaussure
Plant Engineer: Toni Ljekocevic
Estimated Sales: $10 - 20 Million
Number Employees: 50-99

25957 **Mayworth Showcase Works**
1711 W State St
Tampa, FL 33606 813-251-1558
Fax: 813-251-1558
Display cases
Owner: Jack Mayworth
Estimated Sales: $1 - 3 Million
Number Employees: 5-9

25958 **Mba Suppliers Inc.**
1000 Fort Crook Rd N
Suite 100
Bellevue, NE 68005-4573 402-597-5777
Fax: 402-597-2444 800-467-1201
www.mbasuppliers.com
New, reconditioned, used and pre-owned food processing and meat equipment and supplies.

25959 **(HQ)McBrady Engineering**
PO Box 2549
Joliet, IL 60434 815-744-8900
Fax: 815-744-8901 mcbrady@sbcgloabl.net
www.mcbradyengineering.com
Manufacturer and exporter of container cleaning equipment
President: William J Mc Brady
Vice President: Garrett McBrady
Sales: David Anderson
Estimated Sales: $2 Million
Number of Brands: 7
Number of Products: 3
Square Footage: 30000
Brands:
Bottle Air
Bottle Duster
Orbit
Vial Washer-Dryer

25960 **McBrady Engineering Inc**
1251 S Larkin Ave
PO Box 2549
Violet, IL 60434 815-744-8900
Fax: 815-744-8901 mcbrady@sbcglobal.net
www.mcbradyengineering.com
Bottle cleaning machinery
President: Garrett McBrady
Sales: David Anderson
Purchasing: Gina Wharrie
Number Employees: 18
Type of Packaging: Consumer, Food Service
Brands:
Duster
Gripper
Model #10
Orbit
Unscrambler
Vial Washer

25961 **McCain Produce Inc.**
8800 Main Street
Florenceville, NB E7L 1B2
Canada 506-392-5541
contactus@mccain.com
www.mccain.com
Potato growers and processor
President & CEO: Dirk Van de Put
Chief Financial Officer: Max Koeune
Chief Science & Technology Officer: Theo Lioutas
Parent Co: McCain Foods Limited
Type of Packaging: Consumer, Food Service

25962 **McCall Refrigeration**
P.O.Box 550
Parsons, TN 38363 731-847-6251
Fax: 731-847-9012 888-732-2446
anorthcutt@mccallrefrigeration.com
www.mccallrefrigeration.com
Manufacturer and exporter of reach-in and under-counter refrigerators, deli cases, display merchandisers, dough retarders, freezers and holding cabinets
President: Tim Krause
CEO: Terry Wolcock
President: Tim Krause
Quality Control: Chuck Stangler
Estimated Sales: $100 - 500 Million
Number Employees: 100-249
Parent Co: Manitowoc Foodservice Group
Type of Packaging: Food Service

25963 **McCarter Corporation**
PO Box 351
Norristown, PA 19404-0351 610-272-3203
Fax: 610-275-5120
Manufacturer and exporter of paste and confectionery mixing equipment
President: H Craig McCarter
Number Employees: 17
Square Footage: 75000

25964 **McClancy Seasoning Company**
One Spice Road
Fort Mill, SC 29707 803-548-2366
Fax: 803-548-2379 800-843-1968
info@mcclancy.com www.mcclancy.com
Processor and exporter of spices, seasonings and dry food mixes including salad dressing, dips, breadings, batters, gravies, soups, sauces and meat marinades, snack food seasonings, nut and pretzel coatings, whole and ground spices;custom blending available.
President: F Reid Wilkerson III
Director: Charlie Czagas
VP: Allen Davis
VP Sales: Chuck Wiley
Estimated Sales: $21.2 Million
Number Employees: 100-249
Type of Packaging: Consumer, Food Service, Private Label, Bulk

25965 **McClier**
401 E Illinois St # 2
Chicago, IL 60611-4319 312-321-8900
Fax: 312-755-2750 mcclier@mcclier.com
www.mcclier.com
Architects and engineers, building and construction consultants
President: Kenneth Terpin
CFO: Nino Conti
CEO: Daniel McLean
Estimated Sales: $20 - 50 Million
Number Employees: 250-499

25966 **McCormack ManufacturingCompany**
PO Box 1727
Lake Oswego, OR 97035 503-639-2137
Fax: 503-639-1800 800-395-1593
mail@mmccoil.com www.mmccoil.com
Manufacturer and exporter of industrial refrigeration equipment including quick freezing and sub-zero freezers
CEO: Gary Montgomery
VP Engineering: Tom Resseler
Estimated Sales: $10-20 Million
Number Employees: 1-4
Square Footage: 25000

25967 **(HQ)McCormick Enterprises**
729 S Grove St
Delton, MI 49046 269-623-2582
Fax: 269-623-8087 800-223-3683
Processing and conveying equipment; installation services available
Owner: Bill Mc Cormick
CEO: B McCormick
CFO: C Palanca
Estimated Sales: $10-20 Million
Number Employees: 50-99
Other Locations:
McCormick Enterprises
Delton MI

25968 **McCormick SupHerb Farms**
P.O.Box 610
Turlock, CA 95381-0610 209-633-3600
Fax: 209-633-3644 800-787-4372
custserv@supherbfarms.com
www.supherbfarms.com
Processors and marketers of culinary herbs and specialty products the selection of which includes fresh, frozen and freeze-dried varieties.
President: Mike Brem
EVP/Strategic Planning & CFO: Francis Contino
SVP/General Counsel & Secretary: Robert Skelton
VP/Human Relations: Cecile Perich
Parent Co: McCormick & Company Inc

25969 **McCourt Label Company**
20 Egbert Ln
Lewis Run, PA 16738 814-362-3851
Fax: 814-362-4156 800-458-2390
mccourt@mccourtlabel.com
www.mccourtlabel.com
Pressure sensitive labels for thermal and laser imprinting
President: David G Ferguson
Quality Control: June Wegner
Operations Manager: Bert Clark
Estimated Sales: $10-20 Million
Number Employees: 50-99
Square Footage: 43000

25970 **McCrone Associates**
850 Pasquinelli Dr
Westmont, IL 60559 630-887-7100
Fax: 630-887-7764 info@mccrone.com
www.mccrone.com
Consultant providing microscopy and ultramicro-analytical services including materials analysis, characterization and identification; wholesaler/distributor of microscopes and microscopy supplies
CEO/President: Donald Brooks
VP: Richard Bisbing
VP/Director Operations: Bonnie Betty
Estimated Sales: $5-10 Million
Number Employees: 20-49
Square Footage: 25000
Parent Co: McCrone Group

25971 **McCullough Industries**
13047 County Road 175
P.O.Box 222
Kenton, OH 43326 800-245-9490
Fax: 419-673-8176 800-245-9490
sales@mcculloughind.com
www.mcculloughind.com
Manufacturer and exporter of self dumping hoppers
Owner: S McCullough
Owner: W McCullough
Number Employees: 100

25972 **McDowell Industries**
PO Box 2087
Memphis, TN 38101-2087 901-527-6596
Fax: 901-525-6596 800-622-3695
Manufacturer and importer of textile bags for vegetables and grain
Manager Customer Service: Scott Feuer
Plant Superintendent: Rod Johnston
Number Employees: 100-249
Square Footage: 250000
Type of Packaging: Consumer, Food Service, Private Label, Bulk
Brands:
McKnit
Softweve McKnit

25973 **McGaughlin Oil Company**
3750 E Livingston Ave
Columbus, OH 43227-2246 614-231-2518
Fax: 614-231-7431 800-839-6589
teresa@mcglaughlinoil.com
www.mcglaughlinoil.com
Lubricants food grade
President: Steve Theodor
CEO: Steve Theodor
Vice President: Dick Green
Sales Director: Dick Green
Estimated Sales: $5-10 Million
Number Employees: 100-249
Type of Packaging: Consumer, Food Service, Private Label, Bulk

25974 **McGraw Box Company**
PO Box 652
Mc Graw, NY 13101-0652 607-836-6465
Fax: 607-836-6413
Silverware chests and wooden boxes
Owner: Harold J Ousby Iii
Number Employees: 100-249

25975 **McGraw Hill/London House**
1030 Higgins Rd
Suite 205
Park Ridge, IL 60068-5760 847-292-1900
Fax: 847-292-1906 800-221-8378
Personnel service providing human resource testing and evaluation programs
President: Sam Maurice
Parent Co: MacMillan/McGraw Hill Educational Publishing Company

25976 **McGuckin & Pyle**
227 Brandywine Ave.
Downingtown, PA 19335-0220 610-269-9770
Fax: 800-220-1417 DConnolly@mcg-pyle.com
www.mcg-pyle.com
Packaging and process equipment
President: Keith Connolly
Chief Executive Officer: Dennis Connolly
Research: Brian Sproul
Operations: Tom Blam
Estimated Sales: $5-10 Million
Number Employees: 35

25977 **McGunn Safe Company**
29 S La Salle St # 425
Chicago, IL 60603-1599 312-782-3668
Fax: 312-782-4502 800-621-2816
alanh@mcgunnsafe.com
Manufacturer and exporter of safes and other security devices
Partner: Maureen J Mc Gann
Sales/Marketing: Pat McGunn
Estimated Sales: $.5 - 1 million
Number Employees: 1-4
Square Footage: 50000
Brands:
Cash Handler
Quick Drop
Smart Lock
Smart Safe 2000

25978 **McIlhenny Company**
General Delivery
Avery Island, LA 70513-9999 337-365-8173
Fax: 337-369-6326 877-964-1533
adschaub@tabasco.com www.tabasco.com
CEO: Paul C P McIlhenny
Estimated Sales: $20 - 30 Million
Number Employees: 100-249

25979 McIntosh Box & Pallet Company
5864 Pyle Dr
East Syracuse, NY 13057-9459 315-446-9350
Fax: 315-446-5427 800-219-9552
info@mcintoshbox.com www.mcintoshbox.com
Wooden boxes, pallets and skids
President: Rich Huftalen
Accounts Manager/Sales: Brian Hotchkin
Estimated Sales: $2.5-5 Million
Number Employees: 20-49
Square Footage: 100000

25980 McKearnan Packaging
PO Box 7281
Reno, NV 89510-7281 775-356-6111
Fax: 775-356-2181 800-787-7857
surplus@mckernan.com www.mckernan.com
Surplus packaging components
General Manager: Maurice Oschlog
Chief Operating Officer: Frank Maggio

25981 McKernan Packaging Clearing House
800 S Rock Blvd
Reno, NV 89502-4122 775-356-6111
Fax: 775-356-2181 800-787-7587
surplus@mckernan.com www.mckernan.com
President: Timothy Mc Kernan
Chief Operating Officer: Frank Maggio
Estimated Sales: $20 - 50 Million
Number Employees: 20-49

25982 McKey Perforating Company
3033 South 166th Street
New Berlin, WI 53151-3555 262-786-2700
Fax: 262-786-7673 800-345-7373
jmckey@mckey.com www.mckey.com
Manufacturer and exporter of component parts for food handling equipment and perforated metals and plastics
President/CEO: Jean Mc Key
General Manager: Don Pirlot
Product Development Manager: Tony Elsinger
VP Marketing: Jim Thurman
VP, Sales: Jim Thurman
Director of Operations: James Kuehn
Purchasing Manager: Wayne Schowalter
Estimated Sales: $4700000
Number Employees: 50-99
Square Footage: 280000

25983 (HQ)McLaughlin Gormley KingCompany
8810 10th Ave N
Golden Valley, MN 55427-4372 763-544-0341
Fax: 763-544-6437 800-645-6466
info@pyganic.com www.mgk.com
Manufacturer and exporter of insecticide concentrates and repellents
President: William D Gullickson Jr
CFO: Tom Majpor
Quality Control: Michael Lunch
Director Marketing: Dan Untiedt
Production Manager: Don Sundquist
Estimated Sales: $20-50 Million
Number Employees: 20-49
Square Footage: 100000
Other Locations:
McLaughlin Gormley KingCo.
Baltimore MD

25984 McLaughlin Paper Company
61 Progress Ave
West Springfield, MA 01089 413-732-7485
Fax: 413-730-6604 800-842-6656
sales@mclaughlinpaper.com
www.mclaughlin-paper.com
Paper, paper board, specialty grades: tissue, foils, metallized paper, release papers, foil board, holographic, heat seal, laminates, velours, papefilm, imports, folding cartons, rigid boxes, corrugated laminates, gift wrap, retail orprivate label, pict
Owner: Daniel Mc Laughlin
Estimated Sales: $1-2.5 Million
Number Employees: 10-19

25985 McLean Packaging Corporation
1504 Glen Ave
Moorestown, NJ 08057 215-423-7800
Fax: 856-359-2910 800-923-7801
dave@mcleanpackaging.com
www.mcleanpackaging.com
Manufacturers of Corrugated displays,containers, mini flute single face laminated boxes, vinyl and set-up rigid paper boxes, plastic folding boxes, transperent boxes and cylinders, vacuum forming
President Of Corrugated Division: Stuart Fenkel
Estimated Sales: $30 - 50 Million
Number Employees: 5-9
Square Footage: 400000

25986 McMahon's Farm Inc
305 Jackson Rd
Hopewell Junction, NY 12533 845-227-0120
Fax: 845-227-9282 orders@mcmahonsfarm.com
www.mcmahonsfarm.com
Wholesale distributor of organic, natural and specialty foods as well as eggs, dairy and other food products
Owner: Tom McMahon
Owner: Colette McMahon

25987 McMillin Manufacturing Corporation
2835 E Washington Blvd
Los Angeles, CA 90023 323-268-1900
Fax: 323-262-5144 www.mcmillinwire.com
Wire products including display and bakery racks and shelving
President: Bruce Goodman
Quality Control: Bell Harmon
Estimated Sales: Below $5 Million
Number Employees: 20-49
Square Footage: 120000
Brands:
McMillin Wire

25988 McNab
383 E 29th St
Suite 2
Buena Vista, VA 24416-1293 540-261-1045
Fax: 540-261-1268 info@themcnab.com
www.themcnab.com
President: H A Teass Jr
Quality Control: Brad Witt
Estimated Sales: $3 - 5 Million
Number Employees: 20-49

25989 McNairn Packaging
6 Elise St
Westfield, MA 01085 413-568-1989
Fax: 413-562-1903 800-867-1898
sales@mcnairnpackaging.com
www.mcnairnpackaging.com
Packaging paper for the food industry
President: Ken Miller
CFO: Dennis Czosnek
COO: Bart Gogarty
Estimated Sales: $19 Million
Number Employees: 110

25990 McNeil Food Machinery
1881 E Market Street
Stockton, CA 95205-5673 209-463-4343
Fax: 785-874-4241
tulio@mcnielfoodmachinery.com
Dealer and autioner of used food processing and packaging equipment
Estimated Sales: $10 - 20 Million
Number Employees: 50-99

25991 McNeil Nutritionals
7050 Camp Hill Rd
Fort Washington, PA 19034 215-273-7000
Fax: 908-874-1120 www.splenda.com
Artificial sweetners
President: Peter Luther
Vice President: Sheila Bergey
Estimated Sales: $10-20 Million
Parent Co: Johnson & Johnson

25992 McNeil Specialty Products Company
PO Box 2400
501 George St.
New Brunswick, NJ 08903-2400 732-524-3799
Fax: 732-524-3303
artifical sweetners.such as sucralose.
President: Stephen Fanning
Director Sales (North America): Jim Thornton
Director International Sales: Joseph Zannoni
Estimated Sales: $10-25million
Number Employees: 20-49
Parent Co: Johnson & Johnson

25993 McNeill Signs
555 S Dixie Hwy E
Pompano Beach, FL 33060 954-946-3474
Fax: 954-946-8051 sales@mcneillsigns.com
www.mcneillsigns.com
Signs including plastic, neon and metal
President: J R Mc Neill
CFO: Jay R McNeill
R&D: Jay R McNeill
Quality Control: Jay R McNeill
Estimated Sales: $1 - 2.5 Million
Number Employees: 20-49

25994 McNeilly Wood Products,Inc.
120 Neelytown Rd
Campbell Hall, NY 10916 845-457-9651
Fax: 845-457-4220
dan@mcneillywoodproducts.com
www.mcneillywoodproducts.com
Wooden and used pallets and skids
Owner: Timothy Mc Neilly
Vice President: Dan McNeilly
President: Tim McNeilly
Estimated Sales: $5-10 Million
Number Employees: 20-49
Square Footage: 40000

25995 McNew & Associates, William B.
225 San Marino Drive
San Rafael, CA 94901-1583 415-457-3940
Fax: 415-457-3142 mcnew@netiz.net
Wine industry tank vents
Owner: William McMill
Sales Engineer: Kevin McMill
Estimated Sales: $1-2.5 Million
Number Employees: 1-4
Square Footage: 2000
Type of Packaging: Private Label

25996 McNichols Company
251 Wille Rd # C
Des Plaines, IL 60018-1861 847-376-5848
Fax: 847-635-1115 800-237-3820
www.mcnichols.com
Grip strut safety grating, grate lock grating, fiberglass grating, safety flooring, bar grating, perforated metal and screens, decorative perforated patterns, wire cloth and screens, filter cloth, testing sieves, hardware cloth andsecurity screens
Manager: Kevin Shrout
Estimated Sales: Below $5 Million
Number Employees: 20-49

25997 McNichols Conveyor Company
21411 Civic Center Drive
Suite 204
Southfield, MI 48076 248-357-6077
Fax: 248-357-6078 800-331-1926
sales@mcnicholsconveyor.com
www.mcnicholsconveyor.com
Manufacturer, exporter and designer of conveyors including power roller, gravity roller and belt
President: Robert Iwrey
General Manager: Vince Giannone
Estimated Sales: $2.5-5 Million
Number Employees: 5-9
Brands:
F.E.I., Inc.
Gregory-Adams
New London Engineering
Omni-Metalcraft
Rapid Flex
Roach

25998 McQueen Sign & Lighting
1017 12th Street NE
Canton, OH 44704-1398 330-452-5769
Fax: 330-452-5792 68262mcqsign@cannet.com
Signs including neon, plastic, interchangeable and illuminated letters; also, interior graphics available
Estimated Sales: $500,000-$1 Million
Number Employees: 5-9

25999 McRoyal Industries
1421 Lilac St
Youngstown, OH 44502 330-747-8655
Fax: 330-747-3331 800-785-2556
www.mcroyal.com
Manufacturer and exporter of laminated restaurant fixtures including counters, booths, tables, kiosks, etc.; also, point of purchase displays
President: John K Lallo
CEO: John N Lallo
Purchasing Agent: Don Ceo

Estimated Sales: $2.5-5 Million
Number Employees: 10-19
Square Footage: 56000
Brands:
Formica
Nevamar
Pionite
Wilson Art

26000 MeGa Industries
5109 Harvester Road, Unit 3Aÿ
Burlington, ON L7L 5Y9
Canada 905-631-6342
Fax: 905-631-6341 800-665-6342
sales@megaindustries.com
www.megaindustries.com
Manufacturer, importer, exporter and wholesaler/distributor of material and bulk handling equipment including vibrating tables, conveyors, bins, feeders, vibrators and bin level controls and indicators
President: Mel Gallagher
Sales: Steve Atkinson
Number Employees: 5-9
Square Footage: 12000
Brands:
Dynapac

26001 Mead & Hunt
6501 Watts Rd
Madison, WI 53719 608-273-6380
Fax: 608-273-6391 888-364-7272
madison@meadhunt.com www.meadhunt.com
Consultant specializing in the design of plant layouts, processing, refrigeration, wastewater treatment and environmental systems; also, cold storage and warehouse and office/labs facilities
President: Rajan Sheth
Quality Control: Carry Rossa
Vice President: Doug Green
Marketing Director: Mike Pankratz
Food/Dairy Facilities Manager: Scott Freye
Estimated Sales: $20 - 50 Million
Number Employees: 100-249
Parent Co: Mead & Hunt
Other Locations:
Mead & Hunt
Modesto CA

26002 Mead Coated Board
PO Box 520
Phenix City, AL 36868-0520
Canada 334-448-6323
Fax: 334-448-6508 800-334-1476
nem@meadwestvaco.com
www.meadcoatedboard.com
President: Jack Goldfrenk
R&D: Alan Sheldon
CEO: John Luke
VP sales: Greg Chillemi
Number Employees: 80

26003 Mead Packaging International
1040 W. Marietta St. NW
Atlanta, GA 30318-5218 404-875-2711
Fax: 404-897-7922 www.meadwestvaco.com
Paperboard converters, packaging machinery systems, display racks and film
VP Technology: Mark Watkins
CEO: Jerome Tatar
CFO: Timothy McLevish
VP: William Cecil
VP Human Resources: A Robert Rosenberger
Estimated Sales: $130 Million
Number Employees: 125
Parent Co: Mead Corporation
Brands:
Bottle Master
Cluster-Pak
Duodozen
Yogo Pak

26004 MeadWestvaco Corporation
501 South 5th Street
Richmond, VA 23219-0501 203-461-7400
Fax: 843-745-3028 804-444-1000
www.mwv.com
Manufacturer and exporter of kraft paper
Chairman and Chief Executive Officer: John A. Luke, Jr.
SVP and Chief Financial Officer: E. Mark Rajkowski
Chief Marketing & Innovation Officer: Diane Teer
EVP, Global Operations: Robert A. Feeser
Estimated Sales: $5-10 Million
Number Employees: 10-19
Type of Packaging: Consumer, Food Service, Private Label, Bulk

26005 (HQ)Meadows Mills, Inc.
1352 West D Street
PO Box 1288
North Wilkesboro, NC 28659 336-838-2282
Fax: 336-667-6501 800-626-2282
sales@meadowsmills.com
www.meadowsmills.com
Manufacturer and exporter of stone burr and hammer mills, grits separators, bolters, eccentric sifters, elevating fans, collectors, elbows, piping, self rising corn meal mixer, and hand boggers, christmas tree palletizers
President: Robert Hege Iii
CFO: June Hege
Senior VP: Corey Sheets
VP Sales/Marketing: Brian Hege
VP Product Engineering: Robert Miller
Purchasing: Corey Sheets
Estimated Sales: $5 Million
Number Employees: 30
Number of Brands: 4
Square Footage: 210000
Type of Packaging: Consumer, Food Service, Private Label, Bulk
Other Locations:
Meadows Mills
Tynda, Amur
Brands:
Meadows
Stone Burr Mills

26006 Measurement Systems International
14240 Interurban Ave S
Tukwila, WA 98168 206-433-0199
Fax: 206-244-8470 800-874-4320
info@msiscales.com www.msiscales.com
Manufactures and markets integrated systems solutions for industrial wieghing and process control
President: Ronald A Wenzel
CFO: Ronald Wenzel
Quality Control: Rodney Rodems
Product Marketing Manager: Jeff Brandt
Sales Director: Tim Carroll
Purchasing Manager: David Bannister
Estimated Sales: $5 - 10 Million
Number Employees: 20-49
Brands:
Cellscale
Check-Weigh
Dyna-Link
Msi-6000
Msi-9000
Port-A-Weigh
Porta-Weigh-Plus

26007 Measurex/S&L Plastics
2860 Bath Pike
Nazareth, PA 18064-8898 610-759-0280
Fax: 610-759-0650 800-752-0650
mktg@slpinc.cc www.slpinc.cc
Plastic measuring scoops, plastic apothecary jars and clear plastic cubes
President: John Bungert
Marketing/Sales: Denise Yonney
Purchasing Manager: Ron Timura
Estimated Sales: $10-20 Million
Number Employees: 100-249
Square Footage: 190000
Brands:
Dynagro
Measurex

26008 Meat & Livestock Australia
1401 K Street NW, Ste 602
Washington DC, DC 20005 202-521-2555
Fax: 202-521-2699 sedwards@mlana.com
www.australian-meat.com
Beef, lamb and goatmeat
Regional Manager: Stephen Edwards
Marketing: Elise Garling
Retail Development: Linden Cowper
Estimated Sales: $4 Million
Number Employees: 5

26009 Meat Marketing & Technology
1415 N Dayton St
Chicago, IL 60642-2643 312-266-3311
Fax: 312-266-3363 www.meatingplace.com
Computer systems and software, meat industry publications and information, sales and advertising promotions and materials
President: Mark Lefens
Chairman: Jim Franklin
Vice President of Information Systems: Annica Burns
Director of Marketing: Laurie Hachmeister
Account Executive: Dave Lurie
Production Manager: Shirleen Kajiwara
Estimated Sales: $5 - 10 Million
Number Employees: 20-49

26010 Meat Quality
713 W Prospect Avenue
Springfield, IL 62704-5026 217-744-0150
Fax: 217-744-0630 agmed@msn.com
Quality control instruments, analyzing fat testing
Estimated Sales: $1 - 5 Million

26011 Meatlonn
2035 Lemoine Avenue
2nd Floor
Fort Lee, NJ 07024-5704 201-944-6814
Fax: 888-510-2350 800-965-5144
info@meatlonn.com www.taikoh-usa.com
Casings
President: Masaki Nomura
Estimated Sales: $5 - 10 Million
Number Employees: 1-4

26012 Mecco Marking & Traceability
290 Executive Drive
PO Box 307
Cranberry Township, PA 16066 724-779-9555
Fax: 724-779-9556 888-369-9190
info@mecco.com www.mecco.com
For over 100 years MECCO Marking Systems has partnered with a variety of industries for permanent marking solutions. Products range from high quality hand - held marking devices, portable marking tools, and computer - controlledmarking systems. The lates technology of bumpy barcode marking systems enhance MECCO's position as an industry leader and innovator for marking solutions
President: Dean Frenz
CEO: Dean Frenz
CFO: Christine Grabowski
R&D: Eric McElnoy
Marketing: Todd Hockenberry
VP Sales: Todd Hockenberry
Purchasing: Frank Zowojski
Estimated Sales: $3 - 5 Million
Number Employees: 20-49
Brands:
Code-A-Can
Code-A-Plas
Code-A-Top

26013 Mechtronics International
705 Old Westtown Rd
Suite E
West Chester, PA 19382-4988 610-431-3655
Fax: 610-431-3774
info@mechtronicsinternational.com
www.mechtronicsinternational.com
Waxed paper-single ply and 2-ply rollstock and cut sheets, bacon layout paper, bakery and cheese interleaf papers, polypropylene film, high density polyethylene film and pasta interleaf.
President: Jonathan Kent
VP: Karen Kent
Estimated Sales: Below $5 Million
Number Employees: 10-19
Type of Packaging: Consumer, Food Service, Private Label, Bulk

26014 Mechtronics Paper Corporation
1504 McDaniel Dr
West Chester, PA 19380 610-429-9860
Fax: 610-429-9864 ericrich1@aol.com
Interleaf paper and film waxed papers, grease proof, grease-resistant, patty paper, film, no-zorb moisture and grease resistant paper, 2 ply waxed paper
President/Owner: Eric Osner
Vice President: Karen Kent
Sales/Marketing Director: Karen Kent
Purchasing: Eric Osner
Estimated Sales: $1-2.5 Million
Number Employees: 1-4
Type of Packaging: Consumer, Food Service, Private Label, Bulk

26015 **Mectra USA**
P.O.Box 350
Bloomfield, IN 47424-0350 812-384-3521
Fax: 812-384-8518 mectralabs@mectralabs.com
www.mectralabs.com
Fully automatic, floor level, bulk palletizer for round and nonround containers, intelligent bottle stacker, automatic layer pad, top frame and empty pallet inserters
President: Tom Clement
Estimated Sales: $1 - 3 Million
Number Employees: 10-19

26016 **Mectrol Corporation**
9 Northwestern Dr
Salem, NH 03079 603-890-1515
Fax: 603-890-1616 800-394-4844
contact@mectrol.com www.gatesmectrol.com
Urethane timing belts, speed reducers and motion controle components
President: Bret Morrison
Estimated Sales: $20-50 Million
Number Employees: 100-249
Square Footage: 45000

26017 **Medallion Laboratories**
9000 Plymouth Ave N
Minneapolis, MN 55427 763-764-4453
Fax: 763-764-4010 800-245-5615
info@medlabs.com www.medlabs.com
Testing laboratory providing analytical and microbiological services to the food industry including nutrition labeling support, physical testing, shelf life studies, pesticides and special projects
President: Mike Baim
Marketing Director: Dereen Rief
Sales Director: Ann Diesen
Operations Manager: Barb Beckman
Estimated Sales: Less than $500,000
Number Employees: 30
Parent Co: General Mills

26018 **Medallion Labs**
9000 Plymouth Avenue N.
Minneapolis, MN 55427 763-764-4453
Fax: 763-764-4010 800-245-5615
info@medlabs.com www.tpclabs.com
Chemical, physical and microbiological testing
General Manager: Petros Levis
Technical Manager: David Plank
Business Development Manager: Lisa Povolny
Operations Manager: Kelly Schwenn
Number Employees: 20

26019 **Medical Packaging Corporation**
941 Avenida Acaso
Camarillo, CA 93012-8755 805-388-2383
Fax: 805-388-5531 info@medicalpackaging.com
www.medicalpackaging.com
Industrial and medical device manufacturer specializing in specimen collection and test devices
Owner: Fred Nason
Estimated Sales: $10-20 Million
Number Employees: 50-99

26020 **(HQ)Mednik Wiping MaterialsCompany**
4245 Forest Park Avenue
Saint Louis, MO 63108-2810 314-535-9090
Fax: 314-535-6828 800-325-7193
www.riverbendtextiles.com
Cheesecloths, dish and dusting cloths and paper towels; also, disposable nonwoven and paper wipers
President: James Mednik
Secretary: Nancy Mednik
VP: Richard Wolf
Estimated Sales: $10-20 Million
Number Employees: 10

26021 **Mee Industries**
204 W Pomona Ave
Monrovia, CA 91016-4526 626-359-4550
Fax: 626-359-4660 info@meefog.com
www.meefog.com
Wine industry fog humidifers
CEO: Thomas Mee Iii
Estimated Sales: $20-50 Million
Number Employees: 50-99

26022 **Meech Static Eliminators**
2915 Newpark Dr
Norton, OH 44203 330-564-2000
Fax: 330-564-2005 800-232-4210
info@meech.com www.meech.com
Static control equipment for the packaging industry
VP: Matt Fyffe
Estimated Sales: $2.5-5 Million
Number Employees: 20-49

26023 **Meguiar's**
17991 Mitchell S
Irvine, CA 92614 949-752-8000
Fax: 949-752-5784 jlakkis@meguiars.com
www.meguiars.com
Manufacturer and exporter of furniture and floor cleaning products including polish
CEO: Barry Meguiar
CEO: Barry Meguiar
Estimated Sales: $20 - 50 Million
Number Employees: 100-249
Brands:
Meguiar's
Meguiar's Mirror Glaze

26024 **Meheen Manufacturing**
325 N. Oregon Avenue
Pasco, WA 99301-4236 509-547-7029
Fax: 509-547-0939 meheen@owt.com
www.meheen-mfg.com
Computer automated carbonated beverage bottling machines
President: Dave Meheen
CFO: Dave Meheen
Quality Control: Dave Meheen
R&D: Dave Meheen
Estimated Sales: Below $5 Million
Number Employees: 1-4
Square Footage: 10000

26025 **Meil Electric Fixture Manufacturing Company**
1045 W Glenwood Ave
Philadelphia, PA 19133 215-228-8528
Fax: 215-228-3898
Fluorescent lighting fixtures
President: Stephen Dinerman
CFO: Stanley Neil
Estimated Sales: $1 - 2.5 Million
Number Employees: 5-9

26026 **Meilahn Manufacturing Company**
5900 W 65th St
Chicago, IL 60638 773-581-5204
Fax: 773-581-5404 info@meilahnmfg.com
www.meilahnmfg.com
Furniture, custom cabinetry and point of purchase displays
President: Gary Clarin
VP: Dave Sawyer
Estimated Sales: $5-10 Million
Number Employees: 10-19
Square Footage: 22000

26027 **Melcher Manufacturing Company**
PO Box 11857
Spokane Valley, WA 99211-1857 509-535-7626
Fax: 509-536-3931 800-541-4227
sales@melcher-ramps.com
www.melcher-ramps.com
Manufacturer and exporter of fiberglass truck-loading ramps
President: Wayne Hardan
Sales Manager: Wendell Anglesey
Plant Manager: Dick Colby
Estimated Sales: Below $5 Million
Number Employees: 1-4

26028 **Melco Steel**
1100 W Foothill Blvd
Azusa, CA 91702 626-334-7875
Fax: 626-334-6799 melcosteel@earthlink.net
www.melcosteel.com
Canned food sterilizing and cooking equipment including pressure vessels, retorts, quick opening doors, reaction chambers; manufacturer and exporter of autoclaves
President: Michel Kashou
VP: Joe Varela
Chief Engineer: Jeff Cowan
Estimated Sales: $2.5-5 Million
Number Employees: 20-49
Square Footage: 25000
Brands:
Harris

26029 **Melitta Canada**
10-6201 Highway #7
Vaughan, ON L4H 0K7
Canada 416-243-8979
Fax: 416-243-1808 800-565-4882
mjohnston@melitta.ca www.melitta.ca
Coffee filters; processor of coffee
Estimated Sales: $1 - 5 Million
Number Employees: 10-20
Parent Co: Melitta North America
Type of Packaging: Consumer

26030 **Melitta USA**
13925 58th St N
Clearwater, FL 33760-3721 727-535-2111
888-635-4880
consumerrelations@melitta.com
www.melitta.com
Processor, importer and exporter of coffee; also, coffee machines and filters
President & CEO: Martin Miller
Senior Product Manager: Kerrie Tobin
Quality Assurance Manager: Mark Kiczalis
Marketing Director: Chris Hillman
VP Sales: Edward Mitchell
National Sales Manager: Thomas Best
Plant Manager: Matthias Bloedorn
Estimated Sales: $27 Million
Number Employees: 150
Square Footage: 104000
Type of Packaging: Consumer, Food Service
Brands:
Melitta

26031 **Mell & Company**
6700 W Touhy Ave
Niles, IL 60714
Canada 847-470-0587
Fax: 847-470-0581 800-262-6355
customerservice@restaurantdiscountwarehouse.co
m www.mellandcompany.com
Sherbrooke OEM Ltd is an innovative company specializing in the design, fabrication and installation of bulk handling equipment for various industries
President: Art Kessler
Owner: Doug Warshauer
Marketing: Doug McCreight
Estimated Sales: $6.5 Million
Brands:
Sherbrooke Oem

26032 **Mello Smello**
6010 Earle Brown Dr Ste 100
Minneapolis, MN 55430 763-504-5400
Fax: 763-504-5493 888-574-2964
www.mellosmello.com
Mealbags, trayliners and kids premiums, stickers, tattoo's, static cling
President: Mark Miner
Estimated Sales: $24.4 Million
Number Employees: 180
Square Footage: 70000
Parent Co: Miner Group International
Type of Packaging: Food Service, Private Label
Brands:
Pizza Pozze

26033 **Melmat, Inc.**
5333 Industrial Dr
Huntington Beach, CA 92649 714-379-4555
Fax: 714-379-4554 800-635-6289
info@melmat.com www.melmat.com
Manufacturer and wholesaler/distributor of plastic, bulk and custom molded containers, tote boxes, tubs, tanks and insulated and single-wall bins
President: John Mellott
CEO: Laura Kreisberg
CFO: Vera Moeder
Vice President: David Kriegt
Estimated Sales: $1-2.5 Million
Number Employees: 10-19
Square Footage: 44000
Brands:
Kudl-Pak
Space Case

26034 **Melrose Displays**
2 Brighton Avenue
Passaic, NJ 07055-2002 973-471-7700
Fax: 973-471-6885

Custom point-of-purchase displays and store fixtures in wire, wood, metal, tubing and plastic; also, front end check out fixtures
President: Richard Cohen
CEO: Melvin Cohen
Sr. VP: Gerry Turk
Estimated Sales: $10 - 20 Million
Number Employees: 150
Square Footage: 225000
Brands:
Quick Step...The Produce Manager

26035 Melsur Corporation
7752 Us Route 5
Westminster, VT 05158-9683 802-463-3969
Fax: 802-463-1353 dgilkenson@venmed.com
www.melsur.com

26036 Melton Hot Melt Applications
745 West Winder Industrial Pkwy
Winder, GA 30680 770-307-0942
Fax: 770-307-0955 888-357-9317
sales@meltonus.com www.meltonus.com
Owner: Tony Laniewicz
Estimated Sales: Below $5 Million
Number Employees: 5-9

26037 Meltric Corporation
4640 W Ironwood Dr
Franklin, WI 53132 414-817-6160
Fax: 414-817-6161 800-824-4031
mail@meltric.com www.meltric.com
Switch related plugs and receptacles that ensures electrical safety
CEO: Paul Barnhill
Manager: Mark Rasmussen

26038 Melville Plastics
943 Trollingwood Rd
Haw River, NC 27258-8757 336-578-5800
Fax: 336-578-5402
customers@ckspackaging.com
www.ckspackaging.com
Plastic containers for dairy products
Operations Manager: Ken Pierceson
Plant Manager: Dave Sebastian
Estimated Sales: $20 - 50 Million
Number Employees: 100-249

26039 Melvina Can Machinery Company
30 Casey Rd
Hudson Falls, NY 12839 518-743-0606
Fax: 631-391-9039
Manufacturer, importer and exporter of compound liners, can machinery and oil filter equipment, including can seamers and closers
President: Thomas Cahill
Estimated Sales: $5-10 Million
Number Employees: 10-19
Parent Co: Can Industries

26040 Membrane Process & Controls
922 N 3rd Ave
Edgar, WI 54426 715-352-3206
Fax: 715-352-2194 jstencil@membranepc.com
www.membranepc.com
Membrane filtration, instrumentation and control engineering for the food and dairy industry
President: Joel Stencil
Process/Control Engineer: Joel Stencil
Estimated Sales: $500,000-$1 Million
Number Employees: 20-49

26041 Membrane System Specialists
1430 Second Street North
PO Box 998
Wisconsin Rapids, WI 54495-0998 715-421-2333
Fax: 715-423-6181
membrane@mssincorporated.com
www.mssincorporated.com
Manufacturer and exporter of brine and control systems, evaporators, condensers, filtration and membrane processing equipment, separators, clarifiers, waste water treatment systems and whey processing equipment for dairy industry
Owner: Greg Pesko
Regional Sales Manager: Marian Oehme
Production Manager: Derek Hibbard
Estimated Sales: Below $5 Million
Number Employees: 5-9
Square Footage: 20840

26042 Memor/Memtec America Corporation
2118 Greenspring Dr
Timonium, MD 21093-3112 410-252-0800
Fax: 410-560-2857 www.pall.com
Wine industry filtration equipment
President, Life Sciences: Yves Baratelli
Chairman & Chief Executive Officer: Lawrence D. Kingsley
Chief Financial Officer: Akhil Johri
Senior Vice President, Operations: Richard Jackson
Chief Technology Officer: Michael Egholm, Ph.D.
Estimated Sales: $1 - 5 Million
Number Employees: 250-499

26043 Memphis Delta Tent & Awning Company
296 East Street
Memphis, TN 38126 901-522-1238
Fax: 901-522-1241 mdtna.com
Aluminum and canvas awnings, tarpaulins and tents; also, bags including canvas, cotton duck, vinyl, nonwoven and filter
Owner: Chuck Cross
Owner & Sales Manager: Paul Gatti
Estimated Sales: $500,000-$1 Million
Number Employees: 10-19
Brands:
Delta

26044 Menasha Corporation
1645 Bergstrom Road
Neenah, WI 54956 920-751-1000
800-558-5073
info@menasha.com www.menasha.com
Corrugated containers
President/CEO: James Kotek
SVP/Chief Financial Officer: Thomas Rettler
VP/General Counsel/Corporate Secretary: Mark Fogarty
Vice President, Human Resources: Rick Fantini
Vice President, Corporate Development: Evan Pritz
Vice President/Corporate Controller: Shannon Van Dyke
Purchasing Manager: Don Feldman
Estimated Sales: $1 Billion
Number Employees: 3,800
Square Footage: 12523

26045 Menasha Corporation
1055 Corporate Center Dr
Oconomowoc, WI 53066 262-560-0228
Fax: 262-560-5841 info@orbiscorporation.com
www.orbis-menasha.com
Plastic pallets and containers
Sales Manager: Jo Ann Bahling
Sales Manager: Sherri Brigowatz
Sales Manager: Sally Meyers
Estimated Sales: $20-50 Million
Number Employees: 100-249
Parent Co: Menasha Corporation Convoy Plastic Pallets

26046 Menasha Packaging Company, LLC
1645 Bergstrom Road
Neehan, WI 54956 412-766-1234
Fax: 412-766-6335 877-818-2016
info@menasha.com
www.menashapackaging.com
Food packaging, packaging for in-store supermarket bakeries
CEO: Michael K Waite
Sales Director: Scott Sanders
Estimated Sales: $10 - 25 Million
Number Employees: 85
Parent Co: Menasha Corporation
Type of Packaging: Consumer, Food Service, Private Label, Bulk
Brands:
The Sunbrite Line

26047 Mengibar Automation
103 Steam Whistle Dr
Ivyland, PA 18974 215-396-2200
Fax: 215-396-6774 info@penntech-corp.com
www.penntech-corp.com
Manufacturers of packaging machinery for the pharmceutical industry
President: Ger Smit
General Manager: David Mohl
Estimated Sales: $10-20 Million
Number Employees: 1-4
Square Footage: 10000

26048 Menke Marking Devices
13253 Alondra Blvd
Santa Fe Springs, CA 90670 562-921-1380
Fax: 562-921-1184 800-231-6023
sales@menkemarking.com
www.menkemarking.com
Manufacturer and exporter of large and small character ink jet printers, roller coders and rubber and steel codes
President: Stephen Menke
VP: Rocco Falatico
Sales Manager: Paul Carrocino
Estimated Sales: $1-2.5 Million
Number Employees: 10-19
Square Footage: 10500

26049 Mennekes Electrical Products
277 Fairfield Rd
Fairfield, NJ 07004-1900 973-882-8333
Fax: 973-882-5585 800-882-7584
info@mennekes.com www.mennekes.com
20A - 100A power plugs, cord drop connectors for portable equipment applications, HP rated NEMA 4X motor disconnects and receptacles with interlocking for OSHA lockout, tagout requirements
President: Walter Mennekes
VP: Thomas Bodnar
Vice President of Sales and Marketing: Paul DiAntonio
Vice President of Operations: AnnaMarie Fusaro
Estimated Sales: $20 - 50 Million

26050 Mennel Milling Company
128 West Crocker Street
PO Box 806
Fostoria, OH 44830 419-435-8151
Fax: 419-436-5150 800-688-8151
info@mennel.com www.mennel.com
Founded in 1886. Processor of flour used in cake mixes, cookies, snack crackers, breadings, batters, gravies, soups, ice cream cones, pretzels and oriental noodles.
President: D. Ford Mennel
Controller: Lori A. Kitchen
Vice President of Grain: Rick D. Longbrake
VP R&D and Quality Assurance: C J Lin
Director Food Safety: Janice M. Levenhagen
VP Sales: Dave L. Braun
Vice President of Operations: David L. Marty
Corp Milling Engineer: Joel R. Hoffa
Estimated Sales: Below $5 Million
Number Employees: 100-249
Type of Packaging: Bulk

26051 Menu Graphics
PO Box 38397
Olmsted Falls, OH 44138-0397 216-696-1460
Fax: 216-696-1463
Manufacturer and designer of menus and menu accessories
Director: Felicia West
Estimated Sales: $1-2.5 Million
Number Employees: 10-19
Parent Co: AD Art Litho

26052 Menu Men
PO Box 1172
Palm Harbor, FL 34682-1172 727-934-7191
Fax: 727-937-0267
Menus and menu boards, covers, holders and displays
Number Employees: 1-4
Parent Co: Menu Men

26053 Menu Promotions
4510 White Plains Road
Bronx, NY 10470-1609 718-324-3800
Fax: 718-324-5598 sales@menupromotions.com
www.menupromotions.com
Menu covers
Estimated Sales: Less than $500,000
Number Employees: 5-9
Parent Co: Mona Slide Fasteners

26054 **Menu Solutions Company**
4510 White Plains Rd
Bronx, NY 10470 718-994-9049
Fax: 718-994-6913 800-567-6368
sales@menucovers.biz www.menucovers.biz
Owner: Joel Varrocas
Estimated Sales: $5 - 10 Million
Number Employees: 20-49

26055 **MenuLink Computer Solutions**
7777 Center Ave Ste 600
Huntington Beach, CA 92647 714-934-6368
Fax: 714-895-2332 menulink2004@menulink.net
www.menulink.net
Computer software including food cost, inventory, human resources, accounting and labor scheduling
Manager: Bob Thomas
CFO: Ronald Whitaker
Estimated Sales: $5 - 10 Million
Number Employees: 20-49
Brands:
Back Office Assistant
Menulink

26056 **MenuMark Systems**
5700 W Bender Court
Milwaukee, WI 53218-1608 414-228-4350
Fax: 414-228-4373 armour@dcim.com
www.menumarksystemsinc.com

26057 **Mepsco**
1888 E Fabyan Pkwy
Batavia, IL 60510-1498 630-231-4130
Fax: 630-231-9372 800-323-8535
info@mepsco.com www.mepsco.com
Manufacturer and exporter of mechanical tenderizers and pickle injector machinery for the curing of pork and beef, marinating of chicken and the basting of turkey
President: Robert Benton
Estimated Sales: $9000000
Number Employees: 20-49
Square Footage: 16000
Brands:
Mepsco

26058 **Meraz & Associates**
198 E 11th Street
Suite 6
Chico, CA 95928-5749 530-343-0830
Fax: 530-343-0751 888-244-4463
corian@eraz.com www.eraz.com
Design and manufacturing of Corian cutting boards.
Estimated Sales: $250 Million
Number Employees: 5
Number of Brands: 1
Number of Products: 35
Square Footage: 3000
Type of Packaging: Food Service, Bulk

26059 **Merchandising Frontiers**
1300 E Buchanan St
Winterset, IA 50273 515-462-4965
Fax: 515-462-4962 800-421-2278
sales@mfi4u.com www.mfi4u.com
Manufacturer and exporter of indoor/outdoor carts, displays and kiosks
Co-Owner And President: Jerry Mayer
Co-Owner And CEO: Janet Mayer
Estimated Sales: $2.5-5,000,000
Number Employees: 10-19
Square Footage: 62000

26060 **Merchandising Inventives**
1665 S Waukegan Rd
Waukegan, IL 60085 847-688-0591
Fax: 847-688-0748 800-367-5653
www.merchinv.com
Manufacturer and exporter of point of purchase advertising display hardware components including mobile kits, ceiling fixtures, pole displays, banner hangers, shelf fixtures, display fasteners, etc
President: Ethan Berger
CEO: Ethan Berger
CFO: Diane Johnson
Vice President: Dan Jezierny
Quality Control: Aier Torres
Public Relations: Kay Berger
Operations Manager: Dan Jezierny
Production Manager: Jose Gayton
Plant Manager: Sue Kradwitz
Purchasing Manager: Sue Kradwitz
Estimated Sales: $12 Million
Number Employees: 20-49
Number of Products: 2000
Square Footage: 45000
Parent Co: DisplaWerks

26061 **Merchandising Systems Manufacturing**
2951 Whipple Rd
Union City, CA 94587-1207 650-324-8324
Fax: 650-324-4584 800-523-1468
www.msmdisplays.com
Manufacturer and exporter of store displays and fixtures
President: Kyle Robinson
President: Kyle Robinson
National Account Manager: Carol Sauceda
Estimated Sales: $5 - 10 Million
Number Employees: 20-49
Square Footage: 176000

26062 **Merchants Publishing Company**
20 Mills St
Kalamazoo, MI 49048 269-345-1175
Fax: 269-345-6999 www.merchpub.com
Labels, tags and folding cartons
President: M Jack Fleming
CFO: Dick Nagle
VP Sales / Marketing: Ben Behrman
National Sales Manager (Label Division): Frank Brady
Estimated Sales: $10-20 Million
Number Employees: 50-99

26063 **Merco/Savory**
980 South Isabella R
Mt. Pleasant, MI 48858 989-773-7981
Fax: 800-669-0619 800-733-8821
mgilbert@lincolnfp.com www.mercosavory.com
Manufacturer and exporter of rotisseries, broilers, toasters, hot dog grilling systems, convection, pizza and cookie ovens, heated display cases and food warmers
President: Stephen Whiteley
COO: Marion Antonini
Director Marketing: Barbara Wolf
Director Sales: Alan Oates
Number Employees: 250-499
Square Footage: 30000
Parent Co: ENODIS
Type of Packaging: Food Service

26064 **Mercury Equipment Company**
15023 Sierra Bonita Lane
Chino, CA 91710-8902 909-606-8884
Fax: 909-606-8885 800-273-6688
donutequip@aol.com
Manufacturer and exporter of doughnut making equipment and bakery display cases and fixtures
President: Mike Campbell
Vice President: Joe Campbell
Estimated Sales: $1 - 3 Million
Number Employees: 6
Square Footage: 10000
Brands:
Belshaw
Dca
Mercury

26065 **Mercury Floor Machines**
110 S Van Brunt St
Englewood, NJ 07631 201-568-4606
Fax: 201-568-7962 888-568-4606
mrbill@mercuryfloormachines.com
www.mercuryfloormachines.com
Floor scrubbers, vacuums and carpet extractors
President/CEO: William Allen
Quality Control: William Parker
General Manager: Bill Bacich
Estimated Sales: $2.5-5 Million
Number Employees: 10
Square Footage: 8000

26066 **Mercury Plastic Bag Company**
168 7th St
Passaic, NJ 07055 973-778-7200
Fax: 973-778-0549
Polyethylene and polypropylene packaging bags
President: Marvin Rosen
VP Sales: Stuart Rosen
Estimated Sales: $5-10 Million
Number Employees: 20-49

26067 **Meriden Box Company**
321 Blue Hills Drive
Southington, CT 06489-4605 860-621-7141
Fax: 860-621-7141
Hard and soft wood boxes and pallets

26068 **Meritech**
600 Corporate Circle
Suite H
Golden, CO 80401-5643 303-790-4670
Fax: 303-790-4859 800-932-7707
cleantech@meritech.com www.meritech.com
No-touch automated hygiene equipment to the food processing, food service, medical, cleanroom, daycare, school and prison industries.
President/CEO: Jim Glenn
Sales: Michele Colbert
Estimated Sales: $5-10 Million
Number Employees: 10-19
Square Footage: 40000
Type of Packaging: Food Service
Brands:
Chg 2%
Chg 4%
Machine Mochers
Quat E-2
Quat F-5
Shelf Clean A-1

26069 **Meriwether Industries**
12 Prospect St
Bloomfield, NJ 07003 973-743-0463
Fax: 973-743-0614 800-332-2358
Power transmission and conveyor belts
President: Samuel Wolosin
CFO: Samuel Wolosin
Estimated Sales: $1 - 2.5 Million
Number Employees: 3
Square Footage: 3000
Brands:
Extremultus
Transilon

26070 **Merix Chemical Company**
230 W Superior St
Chicago, IL 60654-3595 312-573-1400
Fax: 773-221-3047 www.marxsaunders.com
Manufacturer and exporter of anti-static coatings for polyethylene films; also, anti-fog coatings to prevent moisture and condensation on food display cases
Owner: Bonnie Marx
Manager: Z Blowert
Estimated Sales: $1 - 5 Million
Number Employees: 5-9
Square Footage: 6000
Brands:
Merix

26071 **Merlin Development, Inc**
181 Cheshire Ln N Ste 500
Plymouth, MN 55441 763-475-0224
Fax: 763-475-1626 merlin@merlindev.com
www.merlindevelopment.com
Consultant providing contract research and product development services to the food industry
President: Paul Thompson
General Manager: Paul Thompson
Estimated Sales: $3 - 5 Million
Number Employees: 10-19
Square Footage: 8940

26072 **Merlin Process Equipment**
700 Louisiana St
Houston, TX 77002-2700 713-221-1651
Fax: 713-690-3353 sales@merlinmixers.com
www.merlinmixers.com
Manufacturer and exporter of mixers
Estimated Sales: $300,000-500,000
Number Employees: 1-4

26073 **Merric**
4742 Earth City Expy
Bridgeton, MO 63044 314-770-9944
Fax: 314-770-1440 info@merric.com
www.merric.com

Tabletops, booths, cabinets and point of sale counters
President: Steve Rosen
Administration: Tricia Weiss
Accounts Manager: Karrie Dyas
AutoCAD Engineer: Greg Koets
Engineer/IT: Aaron Pattillo
Sr. Project Manager: Amy DeVries
VP Operations: Tom Boylan
Project Manager: Chris Robertson
Estimated Sales: $2.5-5,000,000
Number Employees: 20-49

26074 Merrick Industries
10 Arthur Dr
Lynn Haven, FL 32444 850-265-3611
Fax: 850-265-9768 800-271-7834
info@merrick-inc.com www.merrick-inc.com
Manufacturer and exporter of process weighing and control equipment, belt feeders and loss-in-weight feeders
CEO: Joe K Tannehill Sr
Purchasing Manager: Steve Rhinehart
Estimated Sales: $10-20,000,000
Number Employees: 100-249
Square Footage: 55000
Brands:
Gravimerik
Mc2
Mc3
Superbridge

26075 Merrill Distributing, In
1301 N Memorial Dr
Merrill, WI 54452-3188 715-536-6322
Fax: 715-536-5757 800-677-6320
MerrillDistributing.com
www.merrilldistributing.com
Food service distributor
President: John Schewe
Estimated Sales: Below $5 Million
Number Employees: 50-99

26076 Merrillville Awning
1420 E 91st Dr
Merrillville, IN 46410 219-736-9800
Fax: 219-736-9100 800-781-6100
info@awningguys.com www.awningguy.com
Commercial awnings
Owner: Mike Blessing
Estimated Sales: $2.5-5,000,000
Number Employees: 10-19

26077 Merryweather Foam
1212 Wynette Rd
Sylacauga, AL 35151 256-249-8546
Fax: 256-249-8548 sales@merryweather.com
www.merryweather.com
Plastic foam parts and pressure-sensitive tapes
General manager: Bellaire Riley
Plant Manager: Cliff Shelnut
Estimated Sales: $5-10 Million
Number Employees: 20-49
Parent Co: Merryweather Foam

26078 (HQ)Merryweather Foam
1212 Wynette Rd
Sylacauga, AL 35151 256-249-8546
Fax: 256-249-8548 bellaire@merryweather.com
www.merryweather.com
Plastic foam parts; fabricator/convertor of polyurethane and polyethylene foams with and without pressure sensitive adhesives and coatings
Director Sales/Marketing: Don Sweigert
Sales Administrator: Tina Rockhold
Customer Service Manager: Theresa Karabinus
Manager: Bellaire Riley
General manager: Bellaire Riley
Estimated Sales: $10 - 20 Million
Number Employees: 20-49
Square Footage: 100000
Other Locations:
Merryweather Foam
Sylacauga AL

26079 Mertz L. Carlton Company
6147 W 65th Street
Bedford Park, IL 60638-5303 708-594-1050
Fax: 716-626-1616
Cleaning compounds
Estimated Sales: $2.5-5 Million
Number Employees: 10-19

26080 Mesa Laboratories
12100 W 6th Ave
Lakewood, CO 80228 303-987-8000
Fax: 303-987-8989 800-525-1215
datatracesales@mesalabs.com
www.mesalabs.com
Manufacturer, importer and exporter of temperature, pressure and humidity monitoring products for processing, distribution and transportation; also, ultrasonic composition analyzers and flow meters
President: Luke Schmieder
CFO: Steven Peterson
CEO: John J Sullivan
Research And Development: Preston Graves
Quality Control: Jeff Zepp
Marketing: David Price
Sales: Owen Israelsen
Operations: Clint Englehart
Production: Rex Trout
Estimated Sales: $9 Million
Number Employees: 100-249
Number of Brands: 7
Square Footage: 39616
Parent Co: Mesa Laboratories
Brands:
Datatrace

26081 Mesler Group
3725 Okemos Road
Okemos, MI 48864-3929 517-349-7066
Fax: 517-349-7069 mgi@voyager.net
Consulting for the food ingredient industry
President: Fred Mesler

26082 Messina Brothers Manufacturing Company
1065 Shepherd Avenue
Brooklyn, NY 11208-5713 718-345-9800
Fax: 718-345-2441 800-924-6454
Manufacturer, importer and wholesaler/distributor of mops, brooms and brushes
Sales Representative: Robert Messina
General Manager: Lawrence Mirro
Number Employees: 15
Square Footage: 45000
Parent Co: Howard Berger Company

26083 Met-Pro Corporation
1550 Industrial Dr
Owosso, MI 48867-9799 989-725-8184
Fax: 989-725-8188 info@dualldiv.com
www.dualldiv.com
Air pollution controls for food processing plants
Controller: Dave Mogg
Sales Manager: Rob Teich
Estimated Sales: $5 - 10 Million
Number Employees: 50-99
Square Footage: 240000
Parent Co: Met-Pro Corporation

26084 Met-Pro Environmental Air Solutions
1550 Industrial Dr
Owosso, MI 48867 989-725-8184
Fax: 989-725-8188 800-392-7621
info@mpeas.com www.mpeas.com
Pumps including fiber glass reinforced, vinyl ester, epoxy and chemical process
Controller: Dave Mogg
VP/General Manager: R De Hont
Sales/Marketing Manager: E Murphy
Engineering Manager: R Petersen
Estimated Sales: $5 Million
Number Employees: 50-99
Square Footage: 200000

26085 Met-Speed Label
6300 MacPherson Ave
PO Box 850
Levittown, PA 19058 215-946-7200
Fax: 215-946-7201 888-886-0638
info@metspeedlabel.com
www.metspeedlabel.com
Pressure sensitive tags and labels
VP: Joe Felix
Marketing: Bob Reeder
Estimated Sales: $2.3 Million
Number Employees: 20

26086 Metal Container Corporation
3636 S Geyer Rd # 400
St Louis, MO 63127-1218 314-957-9500
Fax: 314-957-9515 www.budlight.com
More than 20 billion cans and 20 billion lids annually at its 11 can and lid manufacturing facilities. Supplies about 60% of Anheuser-Bussch's container and lid requirements and is a signifcant supplier to the US soft-drink containermarket
CEO: Joe Eseloinger
President: Tony Bhalla
CEO: Joe Sellinger
Number Employees: 100-249
Parent Co: Anheuser-Busch Companies

26087 Metal Equipment Company
600 Dover Center Rd
Cleveland, OH 44140-3310 440-835-3100
Fax: 440-835-1780 800-700-6326
Manufacturer, importer and exporter of custom metal industrial carts, storage racks, industrial bottle washers, waste management tanks, guards, platform trucks and pallet carriers
Manager: Bill Reilly
General Manager: Paul Drda
VP: Robert Walzer
Estimated Sales: Below $5 Million
Number Employees: 5-9
Square Footage: 55000

26088 Metal Equipment Fabricators
PO Box 9607
Columbia, SC 29209-0607 803-776-9250
Fax: 803-776-9610
Restaurant equipment including metal sinks and tables
President: Frances Smoak
Estimated Sales: Below $5 Million
Number Employees: 5-9
Square Footage: 60000

26089 Metal Kitchen Fabricators
5121 April Ln
Houston, TX 77092 713-683-8375
Fax: 713-683-8378
www.metalkitchenfbcglobal.net
Custom manufacturer of food service equipment including stainless steel shelves, countertops and sinks
President: Bobby Propes
Estimated Sales: Below $5 Million
Number Employees: 10-19

26090 Metal Master
3262 E 45th Street
Tucson, AZ 85713-5211 520-325-3059
Fax: 520-325-6776 800-488-8729
metlmstr@flash.net
Manufacturer and exporter of food processing equipment and parts, cabinets, hoods, trays, tables, sinks, carts, tableware, canopies, fixtures, art metal, serving lines, bartops and countertops, etc
President: John Richards
VP: Bob Lonrod
Estimated Sales: $2.5 - 5 Million
Number Employees: 20-49
Square Footage: 52000
Parent Co: Richards Manufacturing & Services Corporation
Brands:
Biltrite
Caterware

26091 Metal Masters Food Service Equipment Company
100 Industrial Blvd
Clayton, DE 19938-8900 302-653-3000
Fax: 302-653-2065 800-441-8440
customerservice@eaglegrp.com
www.eaglegrp.com
Manufacturer and exporter of stainless steel food service equipment including shelving, sinks, tables, cookers, warmers and bar equipment
Owner: Larry Mc Allister
Sales: Linda Donavon
Estimated Sales: $50 - 75 Million
Number Employees: 250-499
Parent Co: Eagle Group
Brands:
Lifestore
Panco

26092 Metal Masters Northwest
20926 63rd Ave W
Lynnwood, WA 98036 425-775-4481
Fax: 425-775-2618 www.metalmastersnw.com

Custom fabricated stainless steel restaurant products including cooking, heating and serving equipment
Owner: Craig Jeppesen
VP: Timothy Eaves
Estimated Sales: $1-2.5 Million
Number Employees: 10-19
Square Footage: 10000

26093 **Metalcretye Manufacturing Company**
4133 Payne Ave
Cleveland, OH 44103-2324 440-526-5600
Fax: 440-526-5601 800-526-5602
sales@metalcreteindustries.com
www.metalcreteindustries.com
Owner: Ron Stankie
Estimated Sales: $3 - 5 Million
Number Employees: 10-19

26094 **Metaline Products Company**
101 N Feltus St
South Amboy, NJ 08879 732-721-1373
Fax: 732-727-0272 sales@metalineproducts.com
www.metalineproducts.com
Manufacturer and exporter of wood, wire, plastic and corrugated display racks, shelving and point of purchase displays
President: August J Zilincar Iii
VP: August Zilincar III
Estimated Sales: $2.5-5 Million
Number Employees: 20-49
Square Footage: 25000

26095 **Metalloid Corporation**
504 Jackson St
Huntington, IN 46750 260-356-3200
Fax: 260-356-3201 sales@metalloidcorp.com
www.metalloidcorp.com
Manufacturer and exporter of cutting fluids, tapping compounds and hand cleaners
President: Fred Edwards
VP Marketing: William Fair
Estimated Sales: $2.5-5 Million
Number Employees: 5-9

26096 **Metcalf & Eddy**
701 Edgewater Dr Ste 200
Wakefield, MA 01880 781-246-5200
Fax: 781-245-6293 me.info2@m-e.com
www.m-e.com
Consultant providing water and wastewater treatment services; also, engineering, design, construction, operations and maintenance available
President: Micheal S Burke
Chairman/CEO: John M Dionisio
Number Employees: 20-49
Parent Co: Air & Water Technology

26097 **Metcraft**
13910 Kessler Drive
Grandview, MO 64030-5312 816-761-3250
Fax: 816-761-0544 800-444-9624
info@powersoak.com www.metcraft.com
Stainless steel custom fabricated food processing equipment, plumbing fixtures and power soak pot washing systems
President: John Cantrell
President: John Cantrell
Vice President of Distribution: Barry Bergstein
Marketing Director: Virginia Black
President: John Cantrell
Vice President of Operations: John McCreight
Manufacturing Manager: Monty Patton
Estimated Sales: $5 - 10 Million
Number Employees: 60
Square Footage: 60000
Parent Co: Emco
Brands:
Power Soak

26098 **Metl-Span I Ltd**
1720 Lakepointe Drive
Suite #101
Lewisville, TX 75057-2650 972-221-6656
Fax: 972-420-9382 877-585-9969
www.metalspan.com
CEO: Karl F Hielscher
Estimated Sales: $5 - 10 Million
Number Employees: 100-249

26099 **Metlar LLC**
East 2248 Roanoke Ave
Riverhead, NC 11901 631-252-5574
Fax: 828-253-7773 seymourpt@usfilter.com
www.metlar-us.com
Manufacturer, importer and exporter of fine pore filters
Office Manager: Anne Ogg
Estimated Sales: $1 - 5 Million
Number Employees: 1-4
Parent Co: US Filter/Schumacher

26100 **Meto**
P.O.Box 518
Morris Plains, NJ 07950-0518 973-606-5660
Fax: 973-606-5661 800-645-3290
jeff.adams@checkpt.com www.meto.com
Barcode printers, applicators, labels
Manager: William E Staehle
Estimated Sales: $5 - 10 Million
Number Employees: 20-49

26101 **Metro Corporation**
P.O.Box A
Wilkes Barre, PA 18705-0557 570-825-2741
Fax: 570-823-0250 800-433-2233
moreinfo-cp@intermetro.com
www.intermetro.com
Supplier of food service storage, warehandling and transport solutions. The complete range of Metro products puts space to work in virtually avery area - cooler, freezer, dry storage, food preparation, catering and front of house.Flexible solutions for an industry that thrives on change
CEO: John Nackley
CEO: John Nackley
Marketing Director: Mike Ward
VP Sales: Bill O'Donoghue
Public Relations: Stacy Smulgwitz
Estimated Sales: I
Number Employees: 1,000-4,999
Type of Packaging: Food Service
Brands:
Flavor Lock
Metromax
Metromax Q
Sani-Stack
Smart Single
Smart Track
Smart Wall
Super Adjustable Super Erecta
Super Erecta
Top Truck

26102 **Metro Signs**
4224 Losee Road
Suite J
N Las Vegas, NV 89030 702-649-9333
Fax: 702-649-9336 www.sbn.com
Signs; lettering service available
President: Frank Gaskill
Estimated Sales: Less than $500,000
Number Employees: 4

26103 **Metron Instruments, Inc**
Dock 3 or 4
23103 Miles Road
Cleveland, OH 44128 216-332-0592
Fax: 216-274-9262
sanderson@metroninstruments.com
www.metroninstruments.com
Heat exchangers, plate, centrifuges, milk tester, milk standardizer
Owner: Robert P Carter
Estimated Sales: $1-2.5 Million
Number Employees: 5-9

26104 **Metroplex Corporation**
14423 Cornerstone Village Dr
Houston, TX 77014-1206 281-586-0559
Fax: 281-444-3376
horwitch@metroplexcore.com
www.metroplex-inc.com
Consultant for corporate and private outplacement including professional services
President: Willard Jackson
Principal: Reid Matthews
CFO: Bob Stevens
CEO: Zia Qureshi
R & D: Howard Davis
Estimated Sales: $10 - 20 Million
Number Employees: 50-99

26105 **Metropolitan Flag Company**
3237 Amber St # 5
Philadelphia, PA 19134 215-426-2775
Fax: 215-426-5106 Sales@metflag.com
www.metflag.com
Flags and banners
President: Robert Snyder
CFO: Robert Snyder
Quality Control: Robert Snyder
R&D: Robert Snyder
Estimated Sales: Below $5 Million
Number Employees: 10-19

26106 **Metrovock Snacks**
6116 Walker Avenue
Maywood, CA 90270-3447 323-771-3221
Fax: 323-771-2429 800-428-0522
paulpopcon@giftbasketsupplies.con
www.giftbasketsupplies.com
Themed gift baskets
President and QC: Paul Popcorn
Estimated Sales: $500,000 - $1 Million
Number Employees: 20

26107 **Metsys Engineering**
9855 W 78th Street
Suite 10
Eden Prairie, MN 55344-8003 952-944-1081
Fax: 952-944-1431 sales@metsyseng.com
Solutions to consumer product manufacturers through system engineering, development of operating documentation and technical training
Sales/Marketing Administrator: Mary Sandler
Estimated Sales: $2.5-5 Million
Number Employees: 20-49

26108 **Mettler Toldeo Safeline**
6005 Benjamin Rd
Tampa, FL 33634-5145 813-889-9500
Fax: 813-881-0840 800-447-4439
safeline.marketing@mt.com
www.mt.com/safelineus
Metal detectors and xray equipment for food products (including bulk, pakced, liquid, slurry and powder) and for pharmaceutical products.
President: Viggo Nielsen
Marketing: Joseph Gianfalla
Sales: Oscar Jeter
Public Relations: Sarrina Crowley
Estimated Sales: $5 Million
Number Employees: 100-249
Square Footage: 276000
Brands:
Safeline

26109 **Mettler Toledo-Rainin**
Rainin Road
Woburn, MA 01801 800-662-7027
Fax: 510-564-1733 mtprous@mt.com
www.mt.com/pro
Manufacturer, importer and exporter of process measurement equipment including pH and dissolved oxygen probes, transmitters and head space analyzers
Marketing Especialist: Janna Erickson
Estimated Sales: $10-20 Million
Number Employees: 50-99
Square Footage: 20000
Parent Co: Mettler-Toledo
Brands:
Infit
Ingold
Inpro
Intrac
Xerolyt

26110 **Mettler-Toledo**
1900 Polaris Pkwy
Columbus, OH 43240-4035 614-438-4511
Fax: 614-438-4646 800-523-5123
www.mt.com
Manufacturer and exporter of stainless steel scales and printing devices for processing applications including portion control, sorting, box weighing, shipping/receiving and in-motion weighing
Chief Executive Officer: Olivier Filliol
Chief Financial Officer: William Donnelly
Head of Human Resources: Christian Magloth
Estimated Sales: $2.34 Billion
Number Employees: 12400
Parent Co: AEA

26111 Mettley-Toledo Hi-Speed
5 Barr Rd
Ithaca, NY 14850-9117 607-257-6000
Fax: 607-257-5232 800-836-0836
hispeed@mt.com www.mt.com/hi-speed
Checkweighers, weighing and material handling
General Manager: Gerald Lisowski
Marketing Manager: Kyle Thomas
Sales: John Fletcher
Estimated Sales: $20 - 50 Million
Number Employees: 100-249
Type of Packaging: Food Service, Bulk

26112 Metz Premiums
250 W 57th St # 25
New York, NY 10107-0001 212-315-4660
Fax: 212-541-4559 metzpremiums@yahoo.com
Manufacturer and importer of uniforms; also advertising specialties including metal pins and key rings, tote bags, picture frames and ceramic products
VP Sales: Laurie Zelen
Purchasing Manager: Gerry Kroll
*Estimated Sales:*less than $500,000
Number Employees: 1-4

26113 Metzgar Conveyor Company
901 Metzgar Dr NW
Comstock Park, MI 49321 616-784-0930
Fax: 616-784-4100 888-266-8390
info@metzgarconveyors.com
www.metzgarconveyors.com
Manufacturer and exporter of conveyors and package and pallet handling systems
Chairman: D Robert Metzgar
VP: Roger Scholten
R & D: Tom Dewey
Marketing: Roger Schotten
Production: Jon Goeman
Purchasing Manager: David Stevens
Estimated Sales: $10 Million
Square Footage: 50000

26114 Mex-Char
1119 E 10th St
Douglas, AZ 85607-2301 520-364-2138
Fax: 520-364-2138
105456.3374@compuserve.com
Mesquite, horticultural, avicultural, industrial and granulated charcoal
Owner: Oscar Teran
Estimated Sales: $1 - 5 Million
Number Employees: 1-4
Square Footage: 40000
Type of Packaging: Bulk

26115 Meyer & Garroutte Systems
P.O.Box 5460
San Antonio, TX 78201-0460 210-736-1811
Fax: 210-736-9452
jlassiter@meyer-indusries.com
www.meyer-industries.com
CEO: Eugene W Teeter
Estimated Sales: $10 - 20 Million
Number Employees: 50-99

26116 Meyer Industries
3528 Fredericksburg Rd
San Antonio, TX 78201-0460 210-736-1811
Fax: 210-736-4662 sales@meyer-industries.com
www.meyer-industries.com
Food processing equipment
CEO: Eugene Teeter
CFO: Larry Marek
Number Employees: 70

26117 Meyer Label Company
15143 Winkler Rd
Fort Myers, FL 33919 239-489-0342
Fax: 201-894-8867 sales@meyerlabel.com
Manufacturer and exporter of pressure sensitive and roll labels
Owner: Kurt Meyer
VP Sales: Bob Reineke
Estimated Sales: $2.5-5 Million
Number Employees: 1-4
Square Footage: 25000

26118 Meyer Machine & Garroutte Products
P.O.Box 5460
San Antonio, TX 78201-0460 210-736-1811
Fax: 210-736-9452 Sales@meyer-industries.com
www.meyer-industries.com
Manufacturer and exporter of belt and vibratory conveyors and feeders, pivoting bucket elevators, spiral lowerators, fryers, broilers, ovens, live bottom and bin storage and food seasoning equipment.
President: Eugene Teeter
Quality Control and CFO: Larry Marek
North & South Central Regional Sales Mgr: Roland Metivier
Northeast/Southeast Regional Sales Mgr: Scott Carter
Western Regional Sales Mgr: Jim Lassiter
VP Manufacturing: Carroll Fries
Estimated Sales: $10 - 20 Million
Number Employees: 50-99
Square Footage: 100000
Parent Co: Meyer Industries
Other Locations:
Meyer Machine Co.
West Midlands
Brands:
Dynaflex
Magneflex
Simplex
Vibraflex

26119 Meyer Packaging
PO Box 232
Palmyra, PA 17078-0232 717-838-6300
sales@meyerpackaging.com
www.meyerpackaging.com
Set-up paper boxes
VP: Stephen Meyer
Estimated Sales: $10 - 15 Million
Number Employees: 50-100
Square Footage: 100000

26120 Meyers Corbox Co, Inc.
6701 Hubbard Ave
Cleveland, OH 44127-1475 216-441-0150
Fax: 216-441-4213 800-321-7286
info@corbox.com www.corbox.com
Shipping containers, bins and storage boxes
Owner: Kathy Zenisek
VP: Clyde Zenisek
Estimated Sales: $1-2.5 Million
Number Employees: 5-9
Square Footage: 96000
Parent Co: Corbox

26121 (HQ)Meyers Printing Company
7277 Boone Avenue North
Minneapolis, MN 55428 763-533-9730
Fax: 763-531-5771 info@meyers.com
www.meyers.com
Pressure sensitive and roll labels; lithographic, large format printing and printing on plastics available
Estimated Sales: $50-100 Million
Number Employees: 250-499

26122 Meyhen International
556 Industrial Way West
Eatontown, NJ 07724 732-363-2333
Fax: 732-905-7696 www.meyhenfingers.com
Food Processing equipment; rubber products
Owner: Meir Toshav
CEO: Henry Stern
Number Employees: 30

26123 Meyn America, LLC
1000 Evenflo Dr
Ball Ground, GA 30107 770-967-0532
Fax: 770-967-1318 888-881-6396
sales.usa@meyn.net www.meyn.com
Meat industry processing equipment
President: Scott Russel
Principal: David McNeal
Sales Director: Rick Boze
Number Employees: 150
Parent Co: Cooperatieve Meyn

26124 Mezza
222 E Wisconsin Avenue
Suite 300
Lake Forest, IL 60045-1723 847-735-2516
Fax: 415-727-4471 888-206-6054
sales@emezza.com
Suppliers to the finest kitchens in America with a worldwide selection of gourmet pantry items
Type of Packaging: Food Service, Private Label

26125 Mia Rose Products
177 Riverside Ave Ste F
Newport Beach, CA 92663 714-662-5465
Fax: 714-662-5891 800-292-6339
info@miarose.com www.miarose.com
Manufacturer and exporter of natural, biodegradable air fresheners, deodorizing mists and home cleaners made with real citrus
President/CEO: Mia Rose
Marketing/Sales: Carolena Hidalgo
Estimated Sales: $2 Million
Number Employees: 10-19
Square Footage: 4000
Type of Packaging: Consumer, Private Label
Brands:
Air Therapy
Citri-Glow
Pet Air

26126 Miami Beach Awning Company
3905 NW 31st Ave
Miami, FL 33142 305-576-2029
Fax: 305-576-0514 800-576-0222
sales@miamiawning.com
www.miamiawning.com
Commercial awnings
Manager: Joan Garvey
Estimated Sales: $5-10,000,000
Number Employees: 50-99

26127 Miami Metal
255 NW 25th Street
Miami, FL 33127-4329 305-576-3600
Fax: 305-576-2339 pompeii@worldnet.att.net
www.miamimetalfence.com
Manufacturer and exporter of chairs, cushions, pads, table legs and bases and booths
Sales Manager: Carol Sieger
Estimated Sales: $20-50 Million
Number Employees: 100-249
Type of Packaging: Food Service
Brands:
Pompeii Furniture

26128 Miami Systems Corporation
10001 Alliance Rd
Blue Ash, OH 45242 513-793-0110
Fax: 513-793-1140 800-543-4540
info@miamisystems.com
www.miamisystems.com
Business forms, salesbooks, cut sheets, unitsets, continuous register forms, mailers, cardsets, ATM forms, envelopes, checks, guest checks, gift certificates, labels, etc
President: Samuel Peters
CFO: Jim Enright
Executive VP: Henry Peters
VP Sales/Marketing: Tim Scully
Estimated Sales: $18 Million
Number Employees: 1,000-4,999

26129 (HQ)Mic-Ellen Associates
1173 Collegeville Rd
Collegeville, PA 19426 610-454-1582
Fax: 610-454-1583 800-872-1252
www.micellen.com
Consultant specializing in marketing natural products to the health food industry
President: Michael Molyneaux
Number Employees: 5-9
Square Footage: 12000

26130 Micelli Chocolate Mold Company
135 Dale St
West Babylon, NY 11704 631-752-2888
Fax: 631-752-2885 micelliusa@aol.com
www.micelli.com
Manufacturer and exporter of plastic and metal molds for chocolate products
President: Joseph Micelli
Vice President: John Micelli
Sales Director: John Micelli
Plant Manager: John Micelli
Estimated Sales: $3-5 Million
Number Employees: 10-19
Square Footage: 10000

26131 Michael Blackman & Associates
1106 Broadway
Santa Monica, CA 90401 310-709-7763
Fax: 310-393-9397 800-889-4925
michael@mbaassoc.com
www.therestaurantdesigngroup.com
Consultant providing design services
President: Micheal Blackman
Estimated Sales: $12,000,000 - $15,000,000
Number Employees: 17
Square Footage: 8000

26132 **Michael Distributor Inc**
PO Box 8681
Fountain Valley, CA 92728-8681
Fax: 714-966-1361 michaeldistinc@sbcglobal.net
www.michaeldistributor.com
Food distributor and related products provider - grocery, cooking oil, meat, sugar, canned foods, produce, dairy, candy & paper goods. Services to Food service and retail industries.
President: Miguel Ortega
Estimated Sales: $8 Million
Type of Packaging: Food Service, Private Label

26133 **Michael G. Brown & Associates**
311 Society Pl
Newtown, PA 18940 215-860-4540
Fax: 215-579-7355
Texture analyzers
Estimated Sales: $1 - 5 Million

26134 **Michael Leson Dinnerware**
P.O.Box 5368
Youngstown, OH 44514 330-726-4788
Fax: 330-726-2274 800-821-3541
www.americanrails.com
Manufacturer, exporter and importer of dinnerware, flatware, glassware, mugs, plate covers, platters, premiums, incentives, salt and pepper shakers, etc
Owner: Michael Leson
CEO: Michael Leson
Estimated Sales: $500,000-$1,000,000
Number Employees: 1-4
Parent Co: MLD Group

26135 **Michaelo Espresso**
309 S Cloverdale St
Ste D22
Seattle, WA 98108 206-695-4970
Fax: 206-695-4951 800-545-2883
info@michaelo.com www.michaelo.com
Kiosks, carts and vending equipment; importer and wholesaler/distributor of espresso and granita machinery and panini grills; serving the food service market
Owner: Mike Meyers
General Manager: Russ Myers
National Sales Manager: Douglas Pratt
Estimated Sales: $5-10 Million
Number Employees: 20-49
Square Footage: 40000
Type of Packaging: Food Service

26136 **Michelman**
9080 Shell Rd
Blue Ash, OH 45236 513-793-7766
Fax: 513-793-2504 800-333-1723
general@michem.com www.michem.com
Water-based performance coatings and coating application equipment for the corrugated and paper-converting industries,including floor polishes,inks,fibre glass,snack food packing
President: Steven Shifman
Vice President: Bob Poletti
Estimated Sales: $20 - 50 Million
Number Employees: 100-249
Parent Co: Michelman World
Type of Packaging: Bulk

26137 **Michelson Laboratories**
6280 Chalet Drive
Commerce, CA 90040 562-928-0553
Fax: 562-927-6625 888-941-5050
info@michelsonlab.com www.michelsonlab.com
Testing and analysis including microbiological analysis, pesticide residues, nutritionals, herbal analysis, vitamins, FDA import alert analysis, drinking water, wastewater and HACCP audits,meat processing, seafood, poultry, dairyproduce, bakery, spices and seasonings, wastewater and effluent
President: Grant Michealson
Laboratory Director: Stephen Roesch
Instrumentation Manager: Maria Lopez
Chemistry Operations Manager: Roy Lung
Microbiology Asst Manager: Nolberto Colon-Droz
Estimated Sales: $5-10 Million
Number Employees: 50-99
Square Footage: 80000

26138 **(HQ)Michiana Box & Crate**
2193 Industrial Dr
Niles, MI 49120-1254 269-683-6372
Fax: 269-684-7860 800-677-6372
lswlniles@aol.com www.kampsinc.com
GMA and can pallets, bulk bins, export boxes, crates and skids; exporter of bulk bins
President: Gary Cehovic
CEO: Thomas Kiehl
CFO: Dan Searfoss
Production Manager: Bog Modlin
Estimated Sales: $27 Million
Number Employees: 100-249
Number of Products: 205
Square Footage: 76000
Type of Packaging: Bulk

26139 **Michiana Corrugated Products**
PO Box 790
Sturgis, MI 49091-0790 269-651-5225
Fax: 269-651-5799 www.michianacorrugated.com
Corrugated and die cut boxes; also, pads, partitions and chipboard
President: Eric Jones
Sales Service: Patricia Vanzile
Estimated Sales: $20-50 Million
Number Employees: 20-49
Square Footage: 40000

26140 **Michigan Agricultural Cooperative Marketing Association**
P.O.Box 30960
Lansing, MI 48909-8460 517-323-7000
Fax: 517-323-6793 800-824-3779
www.michiganfarmbureau.com
Consultant for apple, cherry, asparagus and plum processors
President: Wayne Wood
Div. Manager: Jerry Campbell
CFO: John Vancermolen
Vice President: Mike Fusilier
Number Employees: 100-249
Parent Co: Michigan Farm Bureau Family of Companies

26141 **(HQ)Michigan Box Company**
1910 Trombly St
Detroit, MI 48211 313-873-9500
Fax: 313-873-8084 888-642-4269
info@michiganbox.com www.michiganbox.com
Manufacturer and exporter of corrugated and pizza boxes, point of purchase displays, crates and pallets; also, custom printed and corrugated carry-out food containers available
President: Elaine Fontana
Sales Manager: Scott Keech
Operations: Ralph Betzler
Estimated Sales: $10-20 Million
Number Employees: 50-99
Square Footage: 200000
Other Locations:
Michigan Box Co.
Detroit MI

26142 **Michigan Brush Manufacturing Company, Inc.**
7446 Central St
Detroit, MI 48210 313-834-1070
Fax: 313-834-1178 800-642-7874
sales@mi-brush.com www.mi-brush.com
Manufacturer and exporter of brushes, brooms, mops, and paint rollers, also squeegees for food processing and food services.
President: Bruce Gale
CFO: Bruse Gale
Estimated Sales: $1 - 3 Million
Number Employees: 10-19
Number of Brands: 4
Number of Products: 1001
Square Footage: 220000
Type of Packaging: Private Label, Bulk
Brands:
Dorden
Mibco
Mibrush
Rol-Brush

26143 **Michigan Dessert Corporation**
10750 Capital St
Oak Park, MI 48237-3134 248-544-4574
Fax: 248-544-4384 800-328-8632
sales@midasfoods.com www.midasfoods.com
Sweet dry mix items
President: Richard Elias
Sr VP Sales/Marketing: Gary Freeman
Estimated Sales: $7 Million
Number Employees: 20-49
Square Footage: 180000
Parent Co: Midas Foods India
Type of Packaging: Consumer, Food Service, Private Label, Bulk
Brands:
American Savory
Michigan Dessert
Sin Fill

26144 **Michigan Food Equipment**
8155 Fieldcrest Dr
Brighton, MI 48116-8316 810-231-5132
Fax: 810-231-5132
Shrink tunnels, bacon processing equipment and accessories, blenders, frozen meat slicers, flakers and breakers, grinders, stuffers and accessories
Owner: Gary Radtke
Estimated Sales: $1 - 2.5 Million
Number Employees: 1-4

26145 **Michigan Industrial Belting**
31617 Glendale St
Livonia, MI 48150 734-427-7700
Fax: 734-427-0788 800-778-1650
marty@mibelting.com www.mibelting.com
Conveyor belts and power transmission conveyor systems; wholesaler/distributor of conveyor belts, bearings, motors and controls
President: Willard J Kohler
Estimated Sales: Below $5 Million
Number Employees: 10-19
Square Footage: 120000

26146 **Michigan Maple Block Company**
1420 Standish Ave
Petoskey, MI 49770 231-347-4170
Fax: 231-347-7975 800-447-7975
mmb@mapleblock.com www.mapleblock.com
Manufacturer, importer and exporter of cutting boards, tabletops, carving boards and preparation and bakery tables
President: James Reichart
VP Sales & Marketing: Pat Stanley
VP Sales/Marketing: Russell Foth
Estimated Sales: $5-10 Million
Number Employees: 50-99
Parent Co: Bally Block Company
Type of Packaging: Food Service
Brands:
Wood Welded

26147 **Micor Company**
3232 N 31st St
Milwaukee, WI 53216 414-873-2071
Fax: 414-873-3904 800-284-4308
micorox@execpc.com www.micorco.com
Floors, floor sealers, protective coatings, epoxy floors, floor resurfacers
President: Barbara Greenberg
Estimated Sales: $1-2.5 Million
Number Employees: 5-9

26148 **Micro Affiliates**
3986 Ballynahown Cir
Fairfax, VA 22030-2497 301-881-4115
Fax: 301-881-0340 800-430-1099
Four-way security door viewers
Estimated Sales: $1 - 5 Million
Brands:
Door Spy

26149 **Micro Filtration Systems**
PO Box 367
Elon College, NC 27244-0367 336-570-1933
Fax: 336-570-1933
Wine industry laboratory equipment

26150 **Micro Flex**
P.O.Box 32000
Reno, NV 89533-2000 775-746-6600
Fax: 775-787-4600 800-876-6866
jfarris@microflex.com www.microflex.com
Food handling gloves
President: Mike Mattos
CEO: Lloyd Rogers
Director Sales: Chris Verhulst
Manager West Coast Food Service: Karen Baum
Manager Industrial Division: Mike Williamson
Estimated Sales: $20 - 50 Million
Number Employees: 50-99
Brands:
Micro Flex

26151 **Micro Matic**
19761 Bahama St
Northridge, CA 91324 818-701-9765
Fax: 818-341-9501 sac@micro-matic.com
www.micro-matics.com

Manufactures liquid transfer valves and related equipment
President: Peter Muzzonigro
CFO: Jim Motush
Sales Manager: Barry Broughton
Sales Manager: Bryan Gran
Estimated Sales: $20 - 50 Million
Number Employees: 50-99
Parent Co: Micro Matic AIS
Type of Packaging: Bulk

26152 **Micro Motion**
7070 Winchester Cir
Boulder, CO 80301-3566 303-530-8400
Fax: 303-530-8459 800-760-8119
micromotione@abtrack.com
www.micromotion.com

Transmitter electronics for control of flow measurement
VP: Gene Shanahan
Marketing: Glenn Cruger
Sales: Don Fragelette
Estimated Sales: $50 - 75 Million
Number Employees: 1,000-4,999
Parent Co: Micro Motion

26153 **Micro Motion**
7070 Winchester Circle
Boulder, CO 80301 303-530-8400
Fax: 303-530-8459 www.micromotion.com
Measurement and process controls for the food and beverage industry, as well as solutions for water and wastewater treatments.

26154 **Micro Qwik**
1017 Park St
Cross Plains, WI 53528-9631 608-798-3071
Fax: 608-798-4452
webmaster@plasticingenuity.com
www.plasticingenuity.com

Dual-ovenable plastic containers
President: Thomas Kuehn
Sales Manager: Denny McGuigan
Sales: Janet Erdman
Estimated Sales: $20 - 50 Million
Number Employees: 250-499
Parent Co: Plastic Ingenuity

26155 **Micro Solutions Enterprises**
8201 Woodley Avenue
Van Nuys, CA 91406 818-407-7500
Fax: 818-407-7575 800-673-4968
info@mse.com www.mse.com
Packaging equipment including specialties, metal parts, cartoners, conveyors, collators and assembly equipment
President: Martha Sherman
CEO: John Sherman
VP: Scott Sherman
Marketing Manager: Scott Sherman
Estimated Sales: $1-2.5 Million
Number Employees: 10-19
Square Footage: 100000

26156 **Micro Thermics**
3216-B Wellington Ct.
Raleigh, NC 27615 919-878-8076
Fax: 919-878-8032 info@microthermics.com
www.microthermics.com
Specializes in the simulation, scale up, and scale down of UHT, HTST, Aseptic, continuos cooking and hot-fill process
President: John Miles Ph.D
Vice President: David Miles
Regional Technical Sales Manager: Edgardo Vega
Estimated Sales: $1 - 3 Million
Number Employees: 10-19

26157 **Micro Wire Products Inc.**
PO Box 4440
Brockton, MA 02303-4440 508-584-0200
Fax: 508-584-1188 jwmwp@aol.com
www.microwire-products.com
Manufacturer and importer of welded wire baskets, store diplays and fixtures and dishwasher and tray racks
President: Jeffrey Weafer
Controller: Linda Weaver
Treasurer: Arnold Wilson
Estimated Sales: $5 - 10 Million
Number Employees: 20-30
Square Footage: 280000

26158 **Micro-Blend**
2550 4th Street
Ingleside, TX 78362-5911 361-776-0179
Fax: 361-776-3787 microblend@aol.com
Number Employees: 80

26159 **Micro-Brush Pro Soap**
1830 E Interstate 30
Rockwall, TX 75087-6241 972-722-1161
Fax: 972-722-1584 800-776-7627
scott@prosoap.com www.prosoap.com
Manufacturer and exporter of hand cleaning scrubs and pastes for removing inks, food coloring and food odors; also, soap dispensers
President: Scott L Self
VP Operations: James Wilkins, III
Estimated Sales: $10-20 Million
Number Employees: 5-9
Square Footage: 18000
Parent Co: Texas Nova-Chem Corporation
Type of Packaging: Food Service
Brands:
Micro-Brush
Pro Soap

26160 **Micro-Chem Laboratory**
Building A, Unit 16
Mississauga, ON L5T 2L5
Canada 905-795-0490
Fax: 905-795-0491 info@micro-chem.com
www.micro-chem.com
Consulting laboratory providing microbiological, nutritional and product development services
President: Ash Mathur
Lab Manager: Nancy Reynolds
Number Employees: 10
Square Footage: 20000

26161 **Micro-Strain**
291 Stony Run Rd
Spring City, PA 19475 610-948-4550
Manufacturer and exporter of digital and analog electronic measuring systems and devices including scales and weighing systems
President: Rolf Jespersen
Estimated Sales: Less than $500,000
Number Employees: 1-4
Square Footage: 5000

26162 **MicroAnalytics**
4500 140th Avenue
Ste. 101
Clearwater, FL 33762 727-483-5562
Fax: 727-538-4237 info@mapmechanics.com
www.bestroutes.com
Computer software, routing and scheduling software distribution planning and translation Of distribution logistics
President: J Michael Hooban
Director Sales: Ted Hooban
Estimated Sales: Below $5 Million
Number Employees: 10-19
Brands:
Bustops
Truckstop

26163 **MicroBioLogics**
200 Cooper Avenue North
Saint Cloud, MN 56303 320-253-7400
Fax: 320-253-6250 800-599-2847
info@microbiologics.com
www.microbiologics.com
CEO: Robert Corborn
National Sales Manager: Julie Sundgaard
Estimated Sales: $1 - 5 Million
Number Employees: 20-49

26164 **MicroCool**
30670 Hill Street
Thousand Palms, CA 92276-2618 760-322-1111
Fax: 760-343-1820 800-322-4364
info@microcool.com www.microcool.com
Wine industry temperature and humidity control systems, patio misting and cooling
Owner: Mike Lemche
Marketing: Mark Stanley
Sales: Jim Murphy
Estimated Sales: $3 - 5 Million
Number Employees: 5-9

26165 **MicroFlo Company**
530 Oak Court Dr # 100
Memphis, TN 38117-3722 901-432-5000
Fax: 901-432-5100 sales@microflocompany.com
www.arysta-na.com
Wine industry pheromones
VP: John Reid
Estimated Sales: $20-50 Million
Number Employees: 20-49

26166 **MicroPure Filtration**
1100 Game Farm Cir
Mound, MN 55364 952-472-2323
Fax: 952-472-0105 800-654-7873
tsenney@micropure.com www.micropure.com
Manufacturer, importer and exporter of food and beverage filtration and regulating devices including segmented stainless steel, cartridge, air, processing, sampler, trap filter removers and air filters, culinary steam.
President: Trey Senney
Estimated Sales: $685,789
Number Employees: 2
Square Footage: 4000
Brands:
Glas-Flo
Mem-Pure
Micro-Pure
Pro-Flo
Segma-Flo
Segma-Pure

26167 **Microbac Laboratories**
100 Barber Avenue
Worcester, MA 01606 508-595-0010
Fax: 508-595-0008 866-515-4668
micro_bacinfo@microbac.com
www.microbac.com
Consultant/laboratory firm providing environmental air, water and waste testing for EPA and OSHA compliance; also, food testing for nutritional value, bacteria, quality control, etc
President/CEO: J Trevor Boyce
Chairman: A Warne Boyce
Executive Vice President: Warne Boyce
Technical Director: Bryan Hauger
Chief Operating Officer: Sean Hyde
Estimated Sales: $10-20 Million
Number Employees: 10
Square Footage: 10000
Parent Co: Microbac Laboratories

26168 **Microbac Laboratories**
101 Bellevue Road
Suite 301
Pittsburgh, PA 15229-2132 412-459-1060
Fax: 866-515-4668
microbac_info@microbac.com
www.microbac.com
Laboratory consultant providing nutritional labeling, sanitation inspections, plastic container/wrap analysis, shelf-life studies and pathogen testing services
Chairman, President & CEO: J. Trevor Boyce
Senior Vice President: Robert S. Crookston
Technical Director: Bryan Hauger
Chief Operating Officer: Sean Hyde
Estimated Sales: $500,000 - $1 Million
Number Employees: 5-9
Parent Co: Microbac Laboratories

26169 **Microbac Laboratories**
2000 Corporate Drive
Wexford, PA 15090-7611 724-934-5030
Fax: 724-934-5088 cearle@microbac.com
www.microbac.com
Analytical services and consulting
Executive Vice President: Warne Boyce
Technical Director: Bryan Hauger
Technical Service/Market Development: Thomas Zierenberg
Chief Operating Officer: Sean Hyde
Estimated Sales: $10-20 Million
Number Employees: 250-499

26170 Microbest Products
670 Captain Neville Drive
Waterbury, CT 06705 203-597-0355
Fax: 561-995-7117 800-426-4246
breslinb@microbest.net www.microbest.com
Manufacturer and exporter of cleaning supplies and equipment including microbial floor cleaners, degreasers, treatment products, etc
CEO: Michael Troup
VP Sales/Marketing: Gary Garavaglin
Estimated Sales: $1 - 5 Million
Number Employees: 8
Brands:
Bio Cleansing Systems
Microbest, Inc.

26171 Microbiology International
5111 Pegasus Ct
Suite H
Frederick, MD 21704-8318 301-662-6835
Fax: 301-662-8096 800-396-4276
info@800ezmicro.com www.800ezmicro.com
Supply systems that automate sample preparation, bacterial enumeration and media preparation/plate and tube filling; provides complete media preparation services
Owner: Kevin Klink
Product Manager: Bill Richman
Estimated Sales: Below $5 Million
Number Employees: 10-19

26172 Microcheck Solutions
9777 West Gulf Bank Ste C-5
PO Box 984
Humble, TX 77347 713-856-9801
Fax: 713-460-0240 800-647-4524
info@microchecksolutions.com
www.microchecksystems.com
Point of sale equipment
Marketing Manager: Barbara Collins
Sales Manager: Barbara Collins
Estimated Sales: $1 - 3 Million
Number Employees: 1-4
Square Footage: 10000

26173 Microdry
5901 W Highway 22
Crestwood, KY 40014 502-241-8933
Fax: 502-241-8648 engineering@microdry.com
www.microdry.com
Manufacturer and exporter of industrial microwaves
Owner: Peter Nemeth
Systems Specialist: Mark Isgryg
Plant Manager: Herb Bullis
Estimated Sales: $2.5-5 Million
Number Employees: 10-19
Square Footage: 50000

26174 Microfluidics International Corporation
30 Ossipee Rd
Newton, MA 02464 617-969-5452
Fax: 617-965-1213 800-370-5452
mixinginfo@mfies.com
www.microfluidscorp.com
Manufacturer and exporter of high pressure mixing equipment for processing emulsions, dispersions, liposomes, particle size reduction, deagglomeration, high end food, flavorings and colorants
President: Robert Bruno
CEO: Irwin Gruverman
Controller: Dennis Riordan
Marketing Communications Manager: Wendy Rogalinski
Number Employees: 20-49
Square Footage: 30000
Brands:
Microfluidizer Pro.Equipment

26175 Micromeritics
4356 Communications Dr
Norcross, GA 30093-2901 770-662-3620
Fax: 770-662-3696 serv@micrometrics.com
www.micromeritics.com
Manufacturer and exporter of analytical instruments for production and process control application
President: Preston Hendrix
Estimated Sales: $20-50 Million
Number Employees: 100-249
Type of Packaging: Bulk

26176 Micron Automation
4516 W North a St
Tampa, FL 33609-2039 813-637-8810
Fax: 813-637-8819 info@pharmaworks.us
www.morrisautomation.com
President: Peter Buczynsky
Vice President Technical Operations: Ingo Federle
Vice President Sales And Service: Ben Brower

26177 Micron Separations
135 Flanders Rd
Westborough, MA 01581-1031 508-366-8212
Fax: 508-366-5840 800-444-8212
osmonics@worldnet.att.net www.msifilters.com
Wine industry filtration equipment
Estimated Sales: $5-10 Million
Number Employees: 50-99

26178 Microplas Industries
2364 Brookhurst Dr
Dunwoody, GA 30338 770-234-0600
Fax: 770-234-0601 800-952-4528
info@microplasa.com
Manufacturer and importer of polyethylene shrink film and black conductive and antistat LDPE and HDPE bags
President: John J Cawley
Estimated Sales: Below $500,000
Number Employees: 1-4
Square Footage: 5000
Brands:
Hi Shrink
Micorduct
Microstat

26179 Micropoint
1077 Independence Ave # B
Mountain View, CA 94043-1601 650-969-3097
Fax: 650-969-2067 www.microfit.com
Manufacturer, importer and exporter of writing and marking pens
President: Paul Vodak
Estimated Sales: less than $500,000
Number Employees: 1-4
Brands:
Art-Stik
Color Brush
Color-Craft
Facts Finder
Fine-Stik
Fits All
Gripper
Ink Stik
Ink-Stik 'n' Holder
Micro-Mini
Mustang
Perma-Mark
Phone Pen
Pinto
Premier
Super Marker
Unimark
White Board Marker
Wik Stik
Win Pen

26180 Micropub Systems International
10 Milford Rd
Rochester, NY 14625 585-385-3990
Fax: 585-654-8594 sales@micrpub.com
www.micropub.com
Manufacturer and exporter of beer brewing systems; processor of brewing ingredients
Manager: Barb Smith
Estimated Sales: Below $500,000
Number Employees: 10-19
Square Footage: 40000
Brands:
Micropub

26181 (HQ)Micros Systems/Fidelio Software Company
7031 Columbia Gateway Dr
Columbia, MD 21046-2583 443-285-6000
Fax: 443-285-0650 800-638-0985
info@micros.com www.micros.com
Manufacturer and exporter of management system software for hospitality, food and beverage, table seating for hotels, motels, casinos and other leisure and entertainment businesses
CEO: Al Giannopoulos
Marketing Director: Louisa Cassamanto
Sales Director: Alan Heyman
Public Relations: Louisa Cassamanto
Plant Manager: Donna Barron
Purchasing Manager: Connie Capel
Estimated Sales: $360 Million
Number Employees: 1,000-4,999
Square Footage: 250000
Parent Co: Micros Systems
Type of Packaging: Food Service
Other Locations:
Micros Systems/Fidelio Softwa
Elk Grove Village IL
Brands:
Fidelio
Micros

26182 Microscan Systems
700 SW 39th Street,Ste 100
Renton, WA 98057 425-226-5700
Fax: 425-226-8250 800-762-1149
info@microscan.com www.microscan.com
Bar code scanning equipment
President: Dennis Kaill
CFO: Mark Milburn
Marketing Director: Laura Hoffman
Sales Director: Bill Westgate
Public Relations: Susan Snyder
Operations Manager: Jerry Naumcheff
Production Manager: Jim Murray
Purchasing Manager: Mike Moritz
Estimated Sales: $10-20,000,000
Number Employees: 100-249
Number of Brands: 1
Number of Products: 9
Type of Packaging: Private Label
Brands:
Microscan

26183 Microtechnologies
123 Whiting St. Ste 1A
P.O.Box 7068
Plainville, CT 06062 860-829-2710
Fax: 860-829-2712 888-248-7103
sales@temperatureguard.com
www.temperatureguard.com
Manufacturer and exporter of HVAC controls
President: Frank Geissler
Estimated Sales: Below $5,000,000
Number Employees: 5-9
Square Footage: 4000

26184 Microthermics
3216-B Wellington Ct Ste 102
Raleigh, NC 27615 919-878-8045
Fax: 919-878-8032 info@microthermics.com
www.microthermics.com
Manufacturer and exporter of laboratory and food processing equipment for pasteurization and aseptic purposes
President: John Miles
VP Sales/Marketing/Business Operations: David Miles
Technical Manager Sales: Ron Seeley
Technical Sales Engineer: David Dickerson
Process Technologist: Titus Porter
Estimated Sales: $500,000-$1 Million
Number Employees: 10-19

26185 Microtouch Systems
501 Griffin Brook Dr
Methuen, MA 01844 978-851-9939
Fax: 978-659-9100 touch@mmm.com
www.solutions.3m.com
Point of sale touch screen systems
Number Employees: 500-999
Brands:
Microtouch

26186 Microtron Abrasives
10424 Rodney St
Pineville, NC 28134 704-889-7256
Fax: 704-889-5102 800-476-7237
www.glit-microtron.com
Abrasive and nonabrasive handpads, metal sponges, cellulose sponge products, griddle screens, soap impregnated abrasive pads, nonwoven floor maintenance pads and related accessories
Manager: Jeff Dean
VP/COO: Robert Quigley

Estimated Sales: $20-50 Million
Number Employees: 5-9
Square Footage: 100000
Parent Co: Katy Industries
Brands:
Hef-T-Clean
Jif-Y-Clean
Pot-N-Pan Handler
Soap-N-Scrub

26187 Microwave Research Center
3856 Princeton Cir
Eagan, MN 55123-1520 651-456-9190
Fax: 651-454-6480 info@rubbright.com
Consultants specializing in microwave technology, products and strategies; also, development of single and 2-mode applicators and related switch-mode power supplies
Project Director: Jan Claesson
VP: Per Risman
Estimated Sales: $.5 - 1 million
Number Employees: 1-4
Square Footage: 5000
Parent Co: Rubbright Group
Brands:
Microduction
Thermalizer

26188 Microworks POS Solutions
2112 Empire Blvd
Suite 2A
Webster, NY 14580 585-787-1090
Fax: 585-787-2289 800-787-2068
support@microworkspos.com
www.microworks.com
Point of sale hardware and software for dine-in, carry out and delivery restaurants,prism for windows,prism classictouch,prism classiclite
Estimated Sales: Less than $500,000
Number Employees: 1-4

26189 Mid Cities Paper Box Company
7661 Fostoria Street
Downey, CA 90241-3240 562-927-1431
Fax: 562-927-3271 877-277-6272
Paper boxes, folding cartons, laminate, foil stamp, window in-house and displays
President/CEO: Ken Sipple
Owner: Norm Sipple
Marketing Director: Angie Saavedra
Sales Director: Mike Sipple
Purchasing Manager: Letha Lands
Estimated Sales: $12 Million
Number Employees: 85
Square Footage: 110000
Type of Packaging: Consumer, Food Service, Private Label

26190 Mid South Graphics
PO Box 110889
Nashville, TN 37222-0889 615-331-4210
Fax: 615-331-4367
mdavenport@midsouthgraphics.com
www.midsouthgraphics.com
Pressure sensitive labels and tags
Customer Service Manager: Patricia Davenport
Estimated Sales: $4 Million
Number Employees: 20-50
Square Footage: 60000

26191 Mid State Awning & PatioCompany
113 Musser Ln
Bellefonte, PA 16823 814-355-8979
Fax: 814-355-1405 tepawning@aol.com
www.midstateawning.com
Commercial awnings
President: Terry Phillips
Estimated Sales: $400,000
Number Employees: 5-9

26192 Mid-Atlantic Packaging
14 Starlifter Ave
Dover, DE 19901-9200 302-734-8833
Fax: 302-734-8698 800-284-1332
sales@midatlanticpackaging.com
www.midatlanticpackaging.com
Bags, boxes, fill material, labels, ribbons and bows
President: Herbert Glanden
Marketing: Don Glanden
Sales Director: Donald Glanden
Estimated Sales: $3-7 Million
Number Employees: 20-49
Number of Brands: 50
Number of Products: 25
Square Footage: 30000

26193 Mid-Lands Chemical Company
6929 N 16th Street
Omaha, NE 68112-3456 402-455-9975
Fax: 402-455-9976 hayescpa@radiks.net
Manufacturer and exporter of ice packs
Account Manager: Brian Plautz
Operations Manager: Matt Sutej
Estimated Sales: $1-2,500,000
Number Employees: 10-19
Type of Packaging: Food Service, Private Label
Brands:
Polar Pack

26194 Mid-Southwest Marketing
3900 S Broadway
Edmond, OK 73013-4115 405-341-3962
Fax: 405-359-9043
Bubble gum dispensers; also, maintenance available
Manager: Teresa Brown
Estimated Sales: Less than $500,000
Number Employees: 1-4

26195 Mid-State Metal Casting& Manufacturing
2689 S 10th St
Fresno, CA 93725-2088 559-445-1974
Fax: 559-445-1320
Aluminum casters
President: Dave Pittman
Estimated Sales: $1-2.5 Million
Number Employees: 5-9

26196 Mid-States Manufacturing & Engineering
509 E Maple
PO Box 100
Milton, IA 52570 641-656-4271
Fax: 641-656-4225 800-346-1792
www.mid-states1.com
Manufacturer and exporter of steel shipping containers, hand and platform trucks and nonpowered material handling equipment
COO: Kevin Early
Purchasing Director: Suzie Lister
Estimated Sales: $5 Million
Number Employees: 50-99
Square Footage: 280000
Type of Packaging: Bulk

26197 Mid-West Wire Products, Inc
800 Woodward Hts
Ferndale, MI 48220-1488 248-399-5100
Fax: 248-542-7104 800-989-9881
schargo@midwestwire.com
www.midwestwire.com
Manufacturer and exporter of wire baskets and specialties including display, transporter and merchandising trays
President: Richard Geralds
VP: Steven Chargo
VP Sales: Steven Chargo
VP Manufacturing: William Klein
Estimated Sales: $5 - 10 Million
Number Employees: 20-49

26198 Mid-West Wire Specialties
4545 W Cortland Avenue
Chicago, IL 60639
Fax: 773-292-6304 800-238-0228
info@midwestwirechicago.com
www.midwestwirechicago.com
Custom point of purchase displays, material handling and filter baskets, guards, wire forms, oven racks and smoke sticks
Estimated Sales: $50-100 Million
Number Employees: 50-99
Square Footage: 55000

26199 Mid-Western Research & Supply
3639 N Comotara St
Wichita, KS 67226 316-262-0651
Fax: 316-262-5136 800-835-2832
sales@midwesternresearch.com
www.midwesternresearch.com
Manufacturer and exporter of brine pumps; wholesaler/distributor of meat processing equipment and butchers' supplies including saws, slicers and tenderizers, vacuum machines and bags and smokehouses
Owner: Don Walton
CEO: Brett Walton
Sales Director: Kurt Carter
Sales: Mark Schrag
Operations Manager: Brett Walton
Production Manager: Tim Fox
Purchasing Manager: Brett Walton
Estimated Sales: $1.8 Million
Number Employees: 10-19
Number of Brands: 25
Number of Products: 200
Square Footage: 71000
Type of Packaging: Food Service
Brands:
Double J

26200 Midbrook
P.O.Box 867
Jackson, MI 49204-0867 517-787-3481
Fax: 517-787-2349 800-966-9274
sales@midbrook.com www.midbrook.com
Manufacturer and exporter of washing, drying and wastewater treatment equipment
CEO: Mick Lutz
Manufacturing Manager: E Houghton
Estimated Sales: $20-50 Million
Number Employees: 100-249
Brands:
Hurricane Systems

26201 Midcal Packaging Technologies
500 S Santa Rosa Ave
Modesto, CA 95354-3717 209-341-4100
Fax: 209-341-3034 888-264-3225
sales@midcalusa.com www.g-3enterprises.com
Wine, Champagne, Beer, Soda, Water and Sake industries. Aluminum screw caps, corks, capsules
President, Chief Executive Officer: Robert Lubeck
Director Marketing/Sales: Lee McDonald
Customer Care Specialist: Jack Leguria
Estimated Sales: $20-50 Million
Number Employees: 100-249

26202 Midco Plastics
800 S Bluff St
Enterprise, KS 67441 785-263-8999
Fax: 785-263-8231 800-235-2729
jjahn@midcoplastics.com
www.midcoplastics.com
Plastic bags, covers and linings including printed or plain
President: Mike Carney
General Manager/VP: Michael Carney
Treasurer: Jeff Jahn
Estimated Sales: $10-20 Million
Number Employees: 50-99
Square Footage: 27000

26203 (HQ)Middleby Corporation
1400 Toastmaster Dr
Elgin, IL 60120 847-741-3300
Fax: 847-741-0015 www.middleby.com
Manufacturer, importer and exporter of conveyor and convection ovens, ranges, fryers, toasters and steamers
Chairman & Chief Executive Officer: Seli, Bassoul
Vice President & Chief Financial Officer: Timothy Fitzgerald
Estimated Sales: $1.04 Billion
Number Employees: 2300
Other Locations:
Middleby Corp.
Miramar FL
Brands:
Middlebe Marshal
Rofry
South Bend
Toast Master

26204 Middleby Marshall
1400 Toastmaster Dr
Elgin, IL 60120 847-741-3300
Fax: 847-741-0015 eheina@middleby.com
www.middleby.com

Bakery and cooking equipment, gas and electric ovens
President: Mark Sieron
VP: Sam Sidani
Sales Manager: Cindy Franz
Estimated Sales: $50 - 75 Million
Number Employees: 250-499
Type of Packaging: Bulk

26205 **Middleby Marshall, CTX**
1400 Toastmaster Dr
Elgin, IL 60120-9272 847-741-3300
Fax: 847-741-0015 800-323-5575
webmaster@middleby.com www.middleby.com
Manufacturer and exporter of high speed conveyor ovens for pizza, bagels, pretzels and full service restaurants; also, ranges, broilers, combi ovens, toasters, hot food warmers and steam equipment
President: Mark Sieron
CEO: Selinn Bassoul
Vice President: Mark Sleron
Marketing Director: Cyndy Franz
Sales Director: John Babila
Sales: Kevin Clark
Operations Manager: Sam Sidani
Production Manager: Rich Sadowski
Parts/Service: Don Johnson
Purchasing Manager: Jacob Joseph
Estimated Sales: $50 - 75 Million
Number Employees: 250-499
Square Footage: 285000
Parent Co: Middleby Corporation
Type of Packaging: Food Service
Other Locations:
Middleby Marshall, CTX
Elgin IL
Brands:
Ctx
Middleby Marshall
Southbend
Toastmaster

26206 **Middleby Worldwide**
1400 Toastmaster Dr
Elgin, IL 60120-9272 847-468-6068
Fax: 847-741-0015 lnowosad@middleby.com
www.middleby.com
Manufacturer, importer and exporter of equipment including food preparation, refrigeration, cooling, storage and material handling, serving, warewashing, etc
CEO: Selim A Bassoul
Estimated Sales: $200 - 500 Million
Number Employees: 1,000-4,999
Parent Co: Middleby Corporation

26207 **Middleton Printing**
200 32nd St SE
Grand Rapids, MI 49548 616-247-8742
Fax: 616-247-1352 800-952-0076
www.gomiddleton.com
Pressure sensitive roll and sheet labels, tags, name plates, commerical printing, booklets, forms, custom laser labels, etc.
President: Steven Middleton
Estimated Sales: $1-3 Million
Number Employees: 10-19
Square Footage: 40000

26208 **Middough Consulting Inc**
1901 E 13th St
Suite 400
Cleveland, OH 44114 216-367-6000
Fax: 216-367-6020 contactus@middough.com
www.middough.com
Middough's full service, single-source organization, provides food processors and distributors with professionals versed in HACCP, FDA, GMP, AIB, BISSIC, USDA, 3A Dairy and cGMP, as well as state-of-the-art technology, sanitary andsafety design practices for civil, structural, mechanical, electrical and controls. Applicable products in the food industry includes that of commodities/ingredients; processed foods and beverages.
President/CEO: Ronald Ledin PE
VP: Paul W. Jahn
Business Development Director: James Bingham

26209 **Midland Manufacturing Company**
101 E County Line Rd
Monroe, IA 50170 641-259-2625
Fax: 641-259-3216 800-394-2625
marianne@midlandmfgco.com
www.midlandmfgco.com
Blow molded plastic containers
President: Terry Vriezelaar
Vice President: Jeff Vriezelaar
Estimated Sales: $5 Million
Number Employees: 50-99
Square Footage: 50000

26210 **Midland Research Labratories**
851 N Martway Drive
Olathe, KS 66061-7053 913-888-0560
Fax: 913-492-7860
headquarters@midlandresearchlabsinc.com
Boiler water and cooling water treatment, food process chemicals for prevention of can corrosion and spotting plus chlorine dioxide
President: John Opelka
R & D: James Rauh
Quality Control: Fred Hopkins
Estimated Sales: $5-10 Million
Number Employees: 10

26211 **Midlands Packaging Corporation**
4641 N 56th St
Lincoln, NE 68504 402-464-9124
Fax: 402-464-6720
midlandspkg@midlandspkg.com
www.midlandspkg.com
Folding cartons, corrugated containers, and thermoformed plastics.
President: Steven Warman
Quality Assurance Manager: Pat Moser
Production Services Manager: Doug Smith
Plant Manager: Gary Riecke
Estimated Sales: $20-25 Million
Number Employees: 100-249
Square Footage: 235000

26212 **Midmac Systems**
590 Hale Ave N
Saint Paul, MN 55128 651-739-1700
Fax: 651-739-1777 info@midmac.com
www.midmac.com
Custom machinery, robotics, systems integration, automatic assembly
Estimated Sales: $10-20 Million
Number Employees: 50-99

26213 **Midvale Paper Box Corporation**
19 Bailey St
Wilkes Barre, PA 18705-1907 570-824-3577
Fax: 570-824-4639 midvalebox@hotmail.com
www.midvalebox.com
Set-up and folding boxes including pizza boxes, bakery boxes, frozen food boxes, beer 6-packs and 4-packs. stadium trays and meat boxes
President: David Frank
Estimated Sales: Below $5 Million
Number Employees: 5-9
Number of Products: 150
Square Footage: 200000

26214 **Midwest Aircraft Products Company**
125 S Mill St
Mansfield, OH 44904 419-522-2231
Fax: 419-522-4634 mapcosale@kosinet.com
www.midwestaircraft.com
Manufacturer and exporter of food handling equipment including liquid containers, ice drawers, oven racks and beverage drawers and carts for airline food services
Owner: Jerry Miller
CFO: Gayle Gorman Freeman
CEO: Gayle Gorman Freeman
Sales: Richard Baker
Manufacturing: Lee Craii
Production: Gene Wheitner
Estimated Sales: $10 - 20 Million
Number Employees: 20-49
Square Footage: 13000

26215 **Midwest Badge & Novelty Company Inc**
3337 Republic Ave
Minneapolis, MN 55426 952-927-9901
Fax: 952-927-9903
Manufacturer, importer and wholesaler/distributor of name badges, buttons and advertising specialties
President/CEO: Mark Joseph Saba
Estimated Sales: Less than $500,000
Number Employees: 3
Square Footage: 16000
Type of Packaging: Consumer, Private Label, Bulk

26216 **Midwest Box Company**
9801 Walford Ave
Suite C
Cleveland, OH 44102 216-281-3980
Fax: 216-281-5707 www.midwestboxco.com
Corrugated containers
Owner: Suzy Remer
Estimated Sales: $10 - 20 Million
Number Employees: 10-19

26217 **Midwest Fibre Products**
2819 95th Ave
Viola, IL 61486 309-596-2955
Fax: 309-596-2901
www.midwestfibreproducts.com
Boxes including corrugated and folding
Owner: Domenico Dulio
Estimated Sales: $5-10 Million
Number Employees: 20-49

26218 **Midwest Folding Products**
1414 S Western Ave
Chicago, IL 60608 312-666-3366
Fax: 312-666-2606 800-344-2864
sales@midwestfolding.com
www.midwestfolding.com
Banquet and meeting room tables in lighwieght plastic, steel edge plywood and high-pressure plastic laminate with plywood core tops. Comfort Leg meeting room tables afford your guests unobstructed knee space and increase seatingcapacity, dual-height cocktail tables, table storage and handling systems are also available
President: Darryl Rosser
CEO: Darryl Rossen
CFO: Len Farrell
Vice President: Chuck Pineau
Marketing Director: Ken Hufstater
Sales Director: Bob Bishop
Plant Manager: Sam Thomas
Purchasing Manager: Oscar Ortiz
Estimated Sales: $35 Million
Number Employees: 100-249
Number of Brands: 1
Square Footage: 200000
Type of Packaging: Bulk
Brands:
Midwest

26219 **Midwest Grain Products**
PO Box 130
Atchison, KS 66002
Fax: 913-367-0192 800-255-0302
selmak@mgpingredients.com
www.midwestgrain.com

26220 **Midwest Industrial Packaging**
PO Box 1927
Spartanburg, SC 29304-1927 864-503-2200
Fax: 864-503-2430 800-910-5592
millichem@milliken.com
www.millikenchemical.com
Packaging tools
President: Thomas J Malone
Estimated Sales: $5-10 Million
Number Employees: 50

26221 **Midwest Juice and SyrupCompany**
3993 Roger B Chaffee SE
Suite F
Grand Rapids, MI 49548 616-774-6832
Fax: 616-774-0373 877-265-8243
info@midwestjuice.com www.midwestjuice.com
Beverages, coffee dispensers, aseptic portion cups
Owner: Mike Luhn
Owner: Noel Luhn
Number Employees: 5-9
Type of Packaging: Food Service, Private Label, Bulk
Brands:
Triarc Beverages
Veryfine

26222 **Midwest Laboratories**
13611 B St
Omaha, NE 68144 402-334-7770
Fax: 402-334-9121 sue_ann@midwestlabs.com
www.midwestlabs.com

Laboratory specializing in the testing of food and agricultural products; also complete nutritional labeling, environmental and microbiological services available
President: Ken Pohlman
CEO: Ken Pohlman
Finance Ex: Laura Honeycutt
Quality Control: Jerry King
Marketing: Brent Pohlman
Estimated Sales: $5-10 Million
Number Employees: 50-99
Square Footage: 65000

26223 **Midwest Labs**
13611 B Street
Omaha, NE 68144 402-334-7770
Fax: 262-790-7011 www.midwestlabs.com
Consultant specializing in sanitation, analysis and testing services
President: Ken Pohlman
Estimated Sales: $500,000-$1 Million
Number Employees: 5-9

26224 **Midwest Metalcraft & Equipment**
200 Industrial Dr
Windsor, MO 65360 660-647-3167
Fax: 660-647-5580 800-647-3167
sales@4mmc.com www.4mmc.com
Stainless steel food processing equipment including vats, hoppers, screw conveyors, dumpers, mixers, blenders, liquid chilling systems, bel conveyors, spiral ham slicers an multi-blade band saw.
President: Dennis Brown
General Manager: Jay Warren
Production Manager: Alan Cooper
Estimated Sales: $5-10 Million
Number Employees: 20-49
Number of Brands: 1
Number of Products: 10
Square Footage: 28000

26225 **Midwest Paper Products Company**
1237 S 11th St
Louisville, KY 40210 502-636-2741
Corrugated boxes
Sales Manager: Woody Heckenkomp
Estimated Sales: $20-50 Million
Number Employees: 20-49
Square Footage: 50000

26226 **Midwest Paper Tube & CanCorporation**
2800 S 163rd St
New Berlin, WI 53151 262-782-7300
Fax: 262-782-7330
Paper cans and tubes
Owner: Ron Karani
CFO/QC: Sharon Mahoney
Estimated Sales: $5 - 10 Million
Number Employees: 10-19

26227 **Midwest Promotional Group**
2011 S Frontage Rd
Summit, IL 60527 708-563-0600
Fax: 708-563-0603 800-305-3388
sales@midwestgrp.com www.midwestgrp.com
Manufacturer and wholesaler/distributor of advertising calendars, embroidered aprons, uniforms, shirts, etc.; also, silk screening available
President: Dave Lewandowski
CEO: Don Lewandowski
VP: Keith Vacey
Sales Director: Rick Dignault
Operations Manager: Roger Wilson
Accounting Executive: Jeff Feichtinger
Estimated Sales: $5-10 Million
Number Employees: 50-99
Square Footage: 16500

26228 **Midwest Quality Gloves**
835 Industrial Rd
Chillicothe, MO 64601 660-646-2165
Fax: 660-646-6933 800-821-3028
ccarlton@midwestglove.com
www.midwestglove.com
Manufacturer and exporter of work, garden and sports protective gloves
Chairman of the Board: Stephen Franke
Marketing Manager: Shirley Fisher
Sales Manager: Clark Carlton
Estimated Sales: $20-50 Million
Number Employees: 100-249
Brands:
Smart Hands
Wolverine

26229 **(HQ)Midwest Rubber & SupplyCompany**
4980 Oneida St
Commerce City, CO 80022-4706 303-289-2800
Fax: 303-227-3241 800-537-7457
Standard conveyor belts, cleated flexible vanner edges, center guides and die cut rubber collapsible containers; also, custom fabrication, design and field vulcanizing available
Owner: Kathy Kroah
Inside Sales Manager: Dave Newell
Purchasing Agent: Todd Winn
Estimated Sales: $300,000-500,000
Number Employees: 1-4
Square Footage: 60000

26230 **Midwest Stainless**
408 3M Drive NE Suite B
Menomonie, WI 54751 715-235-5472
Fax: 715-235-5484 www.midweststainless.com
Manufacturer and exporter of dairy tanks, CIP systems, heat exchangers, cheese presses, pumps, valves, fittings and complete turn-key process systems for the food, dairy and biotechnical industries
VP: Robert Lechner
Sales Engineer: Tim Jenneman
Estimated Sales: $10-20 Million
Number Employees: 20-49
Square Footage: 19000

26231 **Midwest Wire Products**
649 S Lansing Ave
Sturgeon Bay, WI 54235 920-743-6591
Fax: 920-743-3777 800-445-0225
mwp@wireforming.com www.wireforming.com
Wire forms, grills, racks, shelves, baskets, etc.; contact services available
President: Eric Vollrath
CFO: Judy Weber
Engineering: John Buhk
Quality Control: Wendy Woodgate
Marketing/Sales: Dirk Huenink
Production Manager: Mike Noble
Plant Manager: Steve Culver
Purchasing Manager: Judy Weber
Estimated Sales: $7 Million
Number Employees: 50-99
Square Footage: 85000

26232 **Midwestern Bulk Bag**
3230 Monroe St
Toledo, OH 43607-0453 419-241-9955
Fax: 419-241-0080 800-448-6494
New and reconditioned bulk bags, standard and custom made containment racks , polyethylene bags
CEO: Tony O'Neal
VP: Paula Lalor
Production Manager: T King
Estimated Sales: $2.5-5 Million
Number Employees: 20-49
Square Footage: 45000

26233 **Midwestern Industries**
915 Oberlin Road SW
Massillon, OH 44648-0810 330-837-4203
Fax: 330-837-4210 info@midwesternind.com
www.midwesternind.com
Round and rectangular vibrating screening equipment, replacements parts and screens, electric screen heating products for rectangular vibrating machines
President: Barbara Sylvester
Estimated Sales: $10 - 20 Million
Number Employees: 50-99

26234 **Mies Products**
505 Commerce Street
West Bend, WI 53090 262-338-0676
Fax: 262-338-1244 800-480-6437
info@miesproducts.com www.miesproducts.com
Processor and exporter of breading for chicken, fish, meats and vegetables; also, holding and display warmers and electric pressure fryers and filter machines for fats and oils
President: David Mies
VP: Mike Mies
Sales: Mark Mey
Purchasing Director: Ed Casey
Estimated Sales: $3 - 5 Million
Number Employees: 10-19
Number of Brands: 1
Number of Products: 10
Square Footage: 135040
Type of Packaging: Food Service, Private Label
Brands:
Karbonaid Xx
Mies

26235 **Migali Industries**
516 Lansdowne Ave
Camden, NJ 08104-1198 856-963-3600
Fax: 856-963-3604 800-852-5292
contact@migali.com www.migali.com
Manufactures a complete line of G3 reach-in refrigerators and freezers, glass door merchandisers, sandwich tables, pizza preparation tables, and beer equipment. Also distributes Brema Ice Cream Makers, high quality machines inclusingundercounter and modular cubes and flakers.
President: Ernest Migali
Estimated Sales: $5-10 Million
Number Employees: 20-49

26236 **Migatron Corporation**
935 Dieckman St
Suite A
Woodstock, IL 60098 815-338-5800
Fax: 815-338-5803 info@migatron.com
www.migatron.com
Manufacturer, exporter and importer of ultrasonic sensors
President: Frank Wroga
Estimated Sales: $2.5 - 5 Million
Number Employees: 10-19
Brands:
Tubular Sonics

26237 **Mikasa Hotelware**
1 Mikasa Drive
Secaucus, NJ 07094-2581 201-867-9210
Fax: 201-867-2385 866-645-2721
gwen_opfell@mikasa.com www.mikasa.com
Manufacturer, exporter and importer of china, dinnerware and crystal
VP: Neil Orzeck
Number Employees: 100-249

26238 **Miken Cosmpanies**
PO Box 178
Buffalo, NY 14231-0178 716-668-6311
Fax: 716-668-7630
Packaging machinery including pressure sensitive label, adhesive coating, die cutting and foil stamping
President: Michael Bolas
President: M Bolas
Estimated Sales: $20 - 50 Million
Number Employees: 100-249
Other Locations:
Miken Cos.
Buffalo NY

26239 **Mil-Du-Gas Company/StarBrite**
4041 SW 47th Ave
Fort Lauderdale, FL 33314-4031 954-587-6280
Fax: 954-587-2813 800-327-8583
peter@starbrite.com www.starbrite.com
Manufacturer and exporter of mildew preventers with air fresheners and maintenance and cleaning chemicals
President: Peter Dornau
CEO: Peter Dornau
CFO: Jeff Barocas
Executive Vice President: Gregor Dornau
Vice President, Technology: Justin Gould
VP of Marketing / Art Dept & Literature: Bill Lindsey
Senior Vice President, Sales: Marc Emmi
Vice President, Sales: Dennis Torok
Vice President, Operations/Manufacturing: Will Dudman
Number Employees: 20-49
Square Footage: 560000
Parent Co: Ocean Bio-Chem
Other Locations:
Mil-Du-Gas Co./Star Brite
Montgomery AL
Brands:
Extend-A-Brush
M-D-G Formula-2
Star Brite

26240 **Milan Box Corporation**
2090 W Van Hook St
Milan, TN 38358 731-686-3338
Fax: 731-686-3330 800-225-8057
tony@milanbox.com www.milanbox.com

Plywood pallet boxes, crates and wirebound and wooden boxes; exporter of wirebound boxes
President: Franklin Dedmon
Finance Manager: Donna Hardy
VP: Susanne Dedmon
President/Head Sales/Marketing: Franklin Dedmon
Head of Operations: Freddy McCartney
Head of Production: Rudy Graves
Estimated Sales: $10 - 20 Million
Number Employees: 50-99
Brands:
Mylanbox Ibc

26241 Milani Gourmet
2150 N 15th Avenue
Melrose Park, IL 60160-1410 708-216-0704
Fax: 708-216-0709 800-333-0003
www.milanifoods.com
Seasonings, salad dressings, sugar replacements, salt substitutes and base mixes
Manager of Milani Foods: Linda Fortino
Number Employees: 1-4
Parent Co: Precision Foods
Type of Packaging: Food Service, Bulk
Brands:
Bakers Joy
Charcol-It
Milani
Molly McButter
Mrs Dash Salt Free Seasoning
Sugartwin

26242 Milburn Company
520 Bellevue Street
Detroit, MI 48207-3733 313-259-3410
Fax: 313-259-3415 frantatmilburn@aol
Manufacturer and exporter of soap and soap dispensers, manufacturing, skincreams and lotions
VP/Marketing: Frank Newman
Estimated Sales: Less than $500,000
Number Employees: 1-4
Square Footage: 10000
Brands:
Ply Skin Cream

26243 Mile Hi Express
1335 40th St
Denver, CO 80205 303-296-8465
Fax: 303-296-8468 800-332-2064
brit@milehiexpress.com
www.milehiexpress.com
President: Brit Schabacker
Comptroller/Operations: Diana Troute
Estimated Sales: $3 - 5 Million
Number Employees: 20-49

26244 Miles Willard Technologies
655 W Sunnyside Rd
Idaho Falls, ID 83402 208-523-4741
Fax: 208-529-8236 mwt@snackteam.com
www.snackteam.com
Research and development consultant for snack foods and potato processing
Managing Partner: Randy Kern
Research Manager: Veldon Hix
Estimated Sales: $10-20 Million
Number Employees: 10-19
Square Footage: 20000

26245 Military Club & Hospitality
825 Old Country Rd
Westbury, NY 11590-5501 516-334-3030
Fax: 516-334-3059 ebm-mail@ebmpubs.com
www.ebmpubs.com
President: Murry Greenwald
Estimated Sales: $10 - 20 Million
Number Employees: 20-49

26246 Miljoco Corporation
200 Elizabeth St
Mount Clemens, MI 48043-1643 586-777-4280
Fax: 586-777-7891 888-888-1498
info@mijoco.com www.miljoco.com
President: Howard M Trerice
Reaserch Development: Heath Trerice
Quality Control: Bruce Trerice
Marketing: Mike Mroz
Sales: Tom Adams
Public Relations: Mike Mroz
Plant Manager: Alex Jakob
Purchasing: Kimberly Trerice
Estimated Sales: $10-20 Million
Number Employees: 20-49
Square Footage: 47000
Brands:
Miljoco

26247 Mill Engineering & Machinery Company
727 66th Avenue
Oakland, CA 94621-3713 510-562-1832
Barley grain roller mills
Estimated Sales: $500,000-$1 Million
Number Employees: 4

26248 Mill Equipment Company
124 S Dodge St
Burlington, WI 53105-1900 262-763-9101
Fax: 262-763-9102 800-551-9101
skippercad@aol.com
Bins: bulk storage, hoppers; bulk handling systems: conveying, conveyor accessories, conveyor componenets, conveyors, feeder belts
Estimated Sales: $500,000-$1 Million
Number Employees: 1-4

26249 Mill Wiping Rags/The Rag Factory
1656 E 233rd St
Bronx, NY 10466-3306 718-994-7100
Fax: 718-994-1973 ragmaster67@optonline.net
www.misterrags123.com
Manufacturer and exporter of wiping rags, cheese-cloth and paper wipes, bar towels
President: F Scifo
Quality Control: A Pimento
Marketing Director: Eric Saltzman
Sales Director: Eric Saltzman
Plant Manager: F Scifo
Purchasing Manager: Eric Saltzman
Estimated Sales: $2 Million
Number Employees: 50-99
Number of Brands: 3
Number of Products: 100
Parent Co: D. Benedetto
Type of Packaging: Private Label, Bulk

26250 Mill-Rose Company
7995 Tyler Blvd
Mentor, OH 44060 440-255-9171
Fax: 440-255-5039 800-321-3598
info@cleannfit.com www.millrose.com
Manufacturer and exporter of grill and basting brushes
President: Paul Miller
CFO: Vincent Pona
Sales Manager: Gregory Miller
Purchasing Manager: Susan Stallknict
Estimated Sales: $20 Million
Number Employees: 195
Brands:
Clean Fit

26251 Millard Manufacturing Corporation
10602 Olive St
La Vista, NE 68128 402-331-8010
Fax: 402-331-0909 800-662-4263
sales@millardmfg.com www.millardmfg.com
Conveyors and food processing equipment for canners, poultry and frozen food processors; also, walk surfaces available
President/CFO: Ronald K Parks
VP: Mike Price
VP Administration: Mike Price
VP Sales: Harold Ellis
Purchasing Agent: Lynn Hedell
Estimated Sales: $5 - 10 Million
Number Employees: 50-99
Square Footage: 65000
Brands:
Optigrip

26252 Millenia Corporation
P.O.Box 953909
Lake Mary, FL 32795-3909 407-804-1193
Fax: 407-804-1934
frankbenevento@milleiaindustries.com
www.milleniaindustries.com
Manager: Frank Benevento
Estimated Sales: $1 - 3 Million
Number Employees: 10-19

26253 Miller Hofft Brands
PO Box 1323
Indianapolis, IN 46206-1323 317-638-6576
Fax: 317-638-9438
Conveying systems, bulk material bins, hoppers and screw conveyors
President: James Kuester
Estimated Sales: $1 - 5,000,000

26254 Miller Manufacturing
PO Box 337
Turlock, CA 95381-0337 209-632-3846
Fax: 209-632-1369 miller@thevision.net
www.millermanufacturing.com
Recycling machines
President: Richard Veeck
R&D: George Lazich
Estimated Sales: Below $5 Million
Number Employees: 5-9

26255 Miller Metal Fabricators
345 National Ave
Staunton, VA 24401 540-886-5575
U.S.D.A. approved conveyors, poultry chill tanks and hand carts; also, parts available
President: H D Thompson
VP: H Thompson
Estimated Sales: $5 Million
Number Employees: 20-49

26256 Miller Multiplex Displays Fixtures
1610 Design Way
Dupo, IL 62239-1820 636-343-5700
Fax: 636-326-1716 800-325-3350
info@miller-group.com
www.multiplexdisplays.com
Manufacturer and exporter of store fixtures and display systems including point of purchase
President: Tom Wollangk
CFO: Roger Lovejoy
Director Marketing: Tony Evans
Marketing: Catherine Lafarth
Marketing Services: Cathy Berding
Estimated Sales: $10 - 20 Million
Number Employees: 100-249
Square Footage: 40000
Parent Co: Miller Multiplex
Brands:
Multiplex

26257 (HQ)Miller Products, Inc
734 Fair Ave. NW
PO Box 997
New Philadelphia, OH 44663 330-339-1100
Fax: 330-339-4379 800-332-0050
dgray@miller-studio.com
www.miller-studio.com
Manufacturer and exporter of pressure sensitive double-coated tape for decorative trim, mounting, fastening, etc.; also, adhesive systems
President: John Basiletti
Purchasing Manager: Tina Schlemmer
Sales: Mark Gazdik
Estimated Sales: $5 - 10 Million
Number Employees: 50-99
Type of Packaging: Consumer
Brands:
Magic-Mounts

26258 Miller's Technical Service
7444 Haggerty Road
Canton, MI 48187 734-738-1970
Fax: 734-738-1975 millerstec@cs.com
www.mtsmius.com
Manufacturer and exporter of rebuilt and used packaging and food processing equipment; also, machinery parts; repair and rebuilding services available
President: James Miller
Estimated Sales: $.5 - 1 million
Number Employees: 15
Square Footage: 3000
Type of Packaging: Food Service

26259 Millerbernd Process Sytems
330 6th Street
P.O. Box 37
Winsted, MN 55395 320-485-2685
Fax: 320-485-3900 www.millerbernd.com

Design, manufacture and install processing equipment for the dairy and cheese industries such as pasteurization and heat transfer units, controls and automation systems, agitating tanks, batching/blending and barrel handlingsystems.
President: Brad Millerbernd
VP: Terry Voight
National Sales Manager: Lisa Stanger
Product Manager: Frank Bruggman
Purchasing: Sam Zimmerman

26260 Millhiser
1125 Commerce Road
Richmond, VA 23224-7505 804-233-9886
Fax: 804-233-1931 800-446-2247
millbag@worldnet.att.net
Plastic and cloth bags
President: Willard Foster
VP Sales/Marketing: James Bledsoe
Estimated Sales: $10-20,000,000
Number Employees: 100-249

26261 Milligan & Higgins
100 Maple Ave
PO Box 506
Johnstown, NY 12095-1041 518-762-4638
Fax: 518-762-7039 info@milligan1868.com
www.milligan1868.com
Founded in 1868. Manufacturer, importer and exporter of kosher edible and technical gelatins; protein factory providing gelatin blending and analytical and microbiological laboratories available
President: Lee Kornbluh
Technical Director: Jacob Utzig
Estimated Sales: $20-50 Million
Number Employees: 20-49
Parent Co: Hudson Industries Corporation
Type of Packaging: Bulk

26262 Milliken & Company
P.O.Box 1926
Spartanburg, SC 29304-1926 864-503-2020
Fax: 864-503-2100
mark.blackmon@milliken.com
www.millikencarpet.com
Aprons, table cloths and skirting and place mats
CFO: Ashley Alan
CEO: Joseph Salley
Sales (Hospitality): Steve Bobo
Estimated Sales: K
Number Employees: 10,000
Brands:
Ambassador
Embassy
Visa

26263 Milliken Chemical
P.O.Box 1926
Spartanburg, SC 29304-1926 706-880-5511
Fax: 864-250-5317 800-241-4826
millichem@milliken.com
www.millikencarpet.com
Unique, nonparticulate colorants and clarifying agents for polypropylene used in applications including injection molding, TWIM, blow molding and thermoforming
President and CFO: Ashley Allen
Plant Manager: Kevin Brown
Number Employees: 1,000-4,999

26264 Milliken Industries
101 South McCall Road
Englewood, FL 34223-3227 941-474-0223
Fax: 941-473-8804 800-255-0094
sales@millikenindustries.com
www.millikendistribution.com
Commercial awnings
President: Shawn Milliken
Estimated Sales: $1-2.5 Million
Number Employees: 20-49

26265 Milliken Packaging
P.O.Box 1926
Spartanburg, SC 29304-1926 864-598-0100
Fax: 864-598-0101 jessie_west@milliken.com
www.milliken.com
Tamper-evident and sanitary packaging materials for portion packed syrup, sour cream, frozen juice bars, juice drinks, etc
President: Roger Milliken
CFO: Ashley Allen
Plant Manager: Kevin Hazen
Marketing Manager: J West
Plant Manager: Elaine Strum

Estimated Sales: $10 - 20 Million
Number Employees: 20-49
Brands:
K-Pak
M-Pak

26266 Millipore Corporation
290 Concord Road
Billerica, MA 01821 970-715-4321
Fax: 781-533-3110 www.millipore.com
Wine and food industry filtration equipment. Multiscreen filter plates, Montage Plasmid Miniprep kit, Opticap Gamma sterilizable capsules, Ezpak membranes and membrane dispenser
Chairman: Fran Lunger
Number Employees: 500-999

26267 Milltronics
734 W North Carrier Pkwy
Grand Prairie, TX 75050-1001 817-277-3543
Fax: 817-277-3894 info@pointeck.com
www.milltronics.com
Wine industry measuring devices
Estimated Sales: $10-20 Million
Number Employees: 50-99

26268 Milprint
PO Box 2968
Oshkosh, WI 54903-2968 920-303-8600
Fax: 920-303-8610 milprint@bemis.com
www.milprint.com
Printed flexible packaging materials for the confectionery industry, including coatings, laminations, films and adhesives for foil, cellophane, glassine and paper
President: Robert Hawthorne
Alliance Manager: Karen Cverko
CFO: Stephanie Rucinski
Quality Control: Dennis Howard
Marketing Manager: Mike Miller
Estimated Sales: $10-20 Million
Number Employees: 10
Parent Co: Bemis Company

26269 Milsek Furniture PolishInc.
5525 E Pine Lake Rd
North Lima, OH 44452 330-542-2700
Fax: 330-542-1059 www.milsek.com
Manufacturer, exporter and wholesaler/distributor of furniture polish and cleaner
President: Jean Hamilton
VP: Susan Bender
Estimated Sales: Under $1 Million
Number Employees: 5-9
Number of Brands: 1
Number of Products: 2
Square Footage: 108000
Brands:
Milsek

26270 Miltenberg & Samton
4 High Street
Suite 7
Stamford, CT 06902-4923 203-834-0002
Fax: 203-321-1348 miltsan@milt.com
High speed flow wrapper, confectionery wrapping machinery, extruders and cooling tunnels for cut and wrap products, complete infeed and discharge systems, flexible packaging films
President: Ronald Kehle
Estimated Sales: $3 - 5 Million
Number Employees: 8
Square Footage: 200

26271 Milton Can Company
PO Box 1100
Elizabeth, NJ 07207-1100 908-289-8100
Fax: 908-355-2397
Tea and coffee cans, papers (electrolytic)
Estimated Sales: $25-50 Million
Number Employees: 70

26272 Milton Can Company
8200 Broadwell Rd
Cincinnati, OH 45244 513-388-2200
Fax: 513-388-2215 sales@bwaycorp.com
www.bwaycorp.com

Custom and generic aerosol cans for food and nonfood applications,custom metal services, coil cutting, sheet coating, decorative lithography
Manager: Dan Chance
VP Information Technology Services: Patrick Hodges
Executive VP: Ken Roessler
Executive VP: Ken Roessler
VP Manufacturing/Engineering: Tom Eagleson
Estimated Sales: $100-500 Million
Number Employees: 5-9
Parent Co: Bway Corporation

26273 Milvan Food Equipment Manufacturing
Units #1-3
Rexdale, ON M9W 5S5
Canada 416-674-3456
Fax: 416-674-2386
Commerical kitchen equipment including tables, exhaust canopies and back bars
President: Rocco Mazziotta
Number Employees: 10

26274 Milwaukee Dustless BrushCompany
1632 Hobbs Drive, Unit C
Delavan, WI 53115 800-632-3220
Fax: 323-724-1111
sales@milwaukeedustless.com
www.milwaukeedustless.com
Manufacturer, importer and exporter of floor brushes, squeegees, sponge mops, utility brushes and related janitorial maintenance tools
National Sales Manager: Jeff Feder
Estimated Sales: $5-10 Million
Number Employees: 50-99
Brands:
Speed Squeegy
Speed Sweep
Speedy Mop

26275 Milwaukee Sign Company
2076 1st Ave
Grafton, WI 53024 262-375-5740
Fax: 262-376-1686 mkesign@aol.com
Manufacturer and exporter of internally illuminated signs and menu systems
President: Kevin Sutherby
R&D: Rick Richards
Estimated Sales: $20 - 30 Million
Number Employees: 100-249
Type of Packaging: Food Service, Bulk

26276 Milwaukee Tool & MachineCompany
PO Box 94
Okauchee, WI 53069-0094 262-821-0160
Fax: 262-821-0162 mtmco@execpc.com
www.milwaukeetoolmachine.com
Manufacturer and exporter of packaging machinery
President: Richard Mumper
VP: Ralph Mumper
Estimated Sales: $5-10 Million
Number Employees: 10

26277 Mimi et Cie
P.O.Box 80157
Seattle, WA 98108-0157 206-545-1850
Fax: 800-284-3834 info@mimietcie.com
www.mimietcie.com
Manufacturer, importer and exporter of decorative packaging including shrink and printed basket wrap and food bags for cookies, candy, etc. Also waxed tissue paper, food containers and custom products including bags, totes andribbons
President: Mark Revere
Estimated Sales: $1-2.5 Million
Number Employees: 50-99
Square Footage: 80000
Type of Packaging: Consumer, Food Service, Private Label, Bulk
Brands:
Bagskets
Blooming Bags
Goodie Bags
Shimmer

26278 Minarik Corporation
905 East Thompson Avenue
Glendale, CA 91201 800-646-2745
Fax: 800-394-6334 888-646-2745
info@minarikcorp.com www.minarikcorp.com

Parent Co: Kaman Corporation

26279 Mince Master
6530 W Dakin St
Chicago, IL 60634 773-282-0722
Fax: 773-282-9744 888-646-2362
tech@mincemaster.com www.mincemaster.com
Emulsifiers, accessories, grinder plates and knives
Owner: Mike Mihailovic
Estimated Sales: $1 - 3 Million
Number Employees: 10-19

26280 Minges Printing & Advertising Specialties
323 S Chestnut St
Gastonia, NC 28054 704-867-6791
Fax: 704-867-3596 mingesco@belsouth.net
www.mingesprinting.com
Advertising specialties
President: Gene Minges Sr
Estimated Sales: $500,000 - $1 Million
Number Employees: 5-9
Square Footage: 6000

26281 Mini-Bag Company
83 Rome Street
Farmingdale, NY 11735-6699 631-694-3325
FDA approved polyethylene and plastic bags
Estimated Sales: $1-2.5 Million
Number Employees: 4

26282 Minigrip/Zip-Pak
1800 W Sycamore Rd
Manteno, IL 60950-9369 815-468-6500
Fax: 815-468-6550 800-488-6973
info@zippak.com www.zippak.com
Resealable zippered packaging
Finance Executive: Roger Geckner
Estimated Sales: $10 - 20 Million
Number Employees: 50-99

26283 Minipack
1832 N Glassell Sreet
Orange, CA 92865 714-283-4200
Fax: 714-283-4268 minipack@spm.it
www.minipack-america.com
Owner: Joe Sielski
Member: Joseph Sielski
Estimated Sales: $1 - 3 Million
Number Employees: 5-9

26284 Minners DesignsInc.
7 W 34th St
Suite 929
New York, NY 10001-8100 212-688-7441
Fax: 212-980-6309 info@minners.com
www.minners.com
Glassware and chinaware for the food service market
President: Maureen K Cole
Director Sales: Bernard Durkin
Director Purchasing: Maureen Cole
Estimated Sales: $1 - 2.5 Million
Number Employees: 5-9

26285 Minnesota Automation
975 3rd St SW
Crosby, MN 56441 218-546-2222
Fax: 218-546-2104 888-800-6861
suzanne.johnson@graphicpkg.com
www.minnesotaautomation.com
Packaging machinery, pick and place machines
Manager: Greg Mangan
Marketing/Sales: Ken Campbell
Plant Manager: Greg Maegan
Estimated Sales: $25-50 Million
Number Employees: 100-249
Parent Co: Riverwood International Corporation
Brands:
Minnesota Automation

26286 (HQ)Minnesota Valley Engineering
407 7th Street NW
New Prague, MN 56071-1000 952-758-4400
Fax: 952-758-8225 800-428-3777
aconrade@mve-inc.com www.mve-inc.com
Turnkey liquid nitrogen systems for food freezing, turnkey liquid nitrogen injection systems for still product manufacturing and bulk carbon dioxide systems for beverage carbonation
VP Industrial Gases Marketing: Ron' Stark
VP Technical Engineering: Jon Wikstrom
VP Restaurant Products: Paul Plooster
Number Employees: 900
Square Footage: 844000
Other Locations:
Minnesota Valley Engineering
Canton GA

26287 Minnesota Valley TestingLaboratories
1126 N Front St
New Ulm, MN 56073 507-354-8517
Fax: 507-359-2890 800-782-3557
crc@mtvl.com www.mvtl.com
Turnkey liquid nitrogen systems
Owner/CEO/President: Tom Berg
Marketing: Rob True
Sales: John Gray
Estimated Sales: $10-20 Million
Number Employees: 10 to 19
Square Footage: 26000

26288 Minnesuing Acres
8084 South Minnesuing Acres Drive
Lake Nebagamon, WI 54849 715-374-2262
Fax: 715-374-2118 jpolinsky@radisson.com
www.minnesuingacres.com
Consultant providing loyalty reward programs including electronic card and data based marketing, trading stamps, controlled markdowns, sweepstakes and related services
General Manager: Jim Polinsky
CFO: Tim Hennessy
VP/General Manager: Steve Aase
Director Marketing: Curt Lund
National Sales Manager: Brent Christiansen
Estimated Sales: $3 - 5 Million
Number Employees: 20-49

26289 Minsa Southwest Corporation
P.O.Box 484
Muleshoe, TX 79347-0484 806-272-5923
Fax: 806-272-5135 services@minsa.com.mx
www.minsa.com
Products for preparation of hot rack table tortillas, fresh or refrigerated, frozen tortilla or enchilada, hand feed tacos, in-line tacos and tortilla chips, extruded corn chips, tamales, and taquitos and/or enchiladas
President: Jose Cacho
President: Jorge Arturo
CFO: Teresa Sitz
R&D: Jim Barne
Quality Control: Veronica Arroyo
Customer Service Head: Gina Smith
Estimated Sales: $5 - 10 Million
Number Employees: 100-249

26290 Minster Machine Company
240 W 5th St
Minster, OH 45865 419-628-2331
Fax: 419-628-3517 service@minster.com
www.minster.com
Presses for production of food and beverage cans, ends, and easy open ends
President: John J Winch
Estimated Sales: $100-500 Million
Number Employees: 500-999

26291 Minuteman Power Boss
175 Anderson St
Aberdeen, NC 28315 314-283-7304
Fax: 910-944-7409 800-323-9420
info@minutemanintl.com www.powerboss.com
Manufacturer and exporter of power sweepers and scrubbers
President: Greg Rau
VP: Gregory Rau
Advertising Manager: Krista Harris
Estimated Sales: $5 - 10 Million
Number Employees: 100-249
Square Footage: 100000
Parent Co: Minuteman International
Other Locations:
Minuteman PowerBoss
Villa Park IL
Brands:
Armadillo
Badger
Otter
Prowler

26292 Minuteman Power Box Inc
175 Anderson Street
Aberdeen, NC 800-323-94 910-944-2105
Fax: 910-944-7409 info@minutemanintl.com
www.powerboss.com
CEO: Greg Rau
Number Employees: 100-249

26293 Mione Manufacturing Company
51 Democrat Rd
Mickleton, NJ 08056 856-423-1374
Fax: 856-423-6522 800-257-0497
Industrial and consumer use hand soap and laundry detergent
Manager: Benny Sorbello
Estimated Sales: $500,000-$1 Million
Number Employees: 1-4
Square Footage: 12000
Brands:
Mione W P-1

26294 Miracle Exclusives
PO Box 2508
Danbury, CT 06813-2508 203-796-5493
Fax: 203-648-4871 info@miracleexclusives.com
www.miracleexclusives.com
Home applicance pressure cooker
Vice President: Burn Wick
Estimated Sales: $500,000-$1 Million
Number Employees: 5

26295 Miroil
602 Tacoma St
Allentown, PA 18109-8103 610-437-4618
Fax: 610-437-3377 800-523-9844
hgos1946@gmail.com www.miroil.com
Manufacturer and exporter of frying oil stabilizer, filter aids and clean and reusable filters for fryers; also, testing for polar and alkaline contaminants
President: Bernard Friedman
Manager: J Wessner
Estimated Sales: $5 - 10 Million
Number Employees: 1-4
Square Footage: 140000
Brands:
Ez Flow
Frypowder
Miroil

26296 Miron Construction Co., Inc.
P.O.Box 509
Neenah, WI 54957 920-969-7000
Fax: 920-969-7393
businessdevelopment@miron-construction.com
www.miron-construction.com
Miron provides innovative pre-construction, construction management, design-build, general construction and industrial services to numerous markets, including the food processing industry where Miron has completed work on productionfacilities, complete food processing lines, freezers, coolers, warehouses and offices.
President/CEO: David G Voss Jr
Vice President/COO: Tim Kippenhan Jr
Secretary/Treasurer & CFO: Dean Basten
VP of Business Development: Corey Brumbaugh
Director/Marketing: Jen Bauer
Estimated Sales: $500 Million
Number Employees: 1200
Square Footage: 112000

26297 Mirro Company
1115 W 5th Ave
Lancaster, OH 43130 800-848-7200
Fax: 920-684-1929
Cookware, bakeware, tools and gadgets
Owner: Dave Moore
Estimated Sales: $1 - 5 Million
Number Employees: 1-4
Parent Co: Newell Companies
Type of Packaging: Food Service
Brands:
Mirro Foley
Rema
Wearever

26298 Mirro Products Company
PO Box 2243
High Point, NC 27261 336-885-4166
Fax: 336-885-1066 info@mirroproducts.com
www.mirroproducts.com
Plastic displays, vacuum-formed snack racks, plastic and electric signs
President: David Horney

Estimated Sales: $5 - 10 Million
Number Employees: 10-19

26299 Mirror Polishing & Plating Company Inc
346 Huntingdon Ave
Waterbury, CT 06708 203-574-5400
Fax: 203-597-9448 chromerolls@mpp.net
www.mpp.net
Chromium roll fabricating and surface finishing company that provides rebuilding, grinding, plating and finishing services for all web processing applications used in the manufacturing of plastic sheet & film, paper, non-woven fabricsand food processing industries.
President: Gary Nalband
Vice President Sales & Marketing: Rimas Kozica
Operations Manager: Carlos Pacheco
Plant Manager: Richard Hall

26300 Mirror-Tech
286 Nepperhan Ave
Yonkers, NY 10701-3403 914-423-1600
Fax: 914-423-1667 mirrortech@verizon.net
www.mirror-tech.com
Glass, metal and acrylic observation convex mirrors
President: Richard Cleary
Treasurer and CFO: D Barnett
Quality Control: Frank Serine
Estimated Sales: Below $5 Million
Number Employees: 10-19
Square Footage: 28000

26301 Mission Laboratories
2433 Birkdale St
Los Angeles, CA 90031 323-223-1405
Fax: 323-223-9968 888-201-8866
srose@missionlabs.net www.missionlabs.net
Commercial and household cleaning and sanitary supplies including floor finish and strippers, carpet cleaners, disinfectants, hand soaps, heavy duty cleaners/degreasers, sweeping compounds, etc. Supplier to the food industry andsuppliers to food service
President: Robert Rosenbaum
CFO: Robert Rosenbaum
Quality Control: David Schultz
Executive VP Sales/Marketing: Jim Ryan
Estimated Sales: $20 - 50 Million
Number Employees: 20-49
Square Footage: 75000
Type of Packaging: Consumer, Food Service, Private Label, Bulk

26302 Missouri Equipment Company
2222 N 9th St
St Louis, MO 63102 314-621-0144
Fax: 314-621-4170 800-727-6326
meco2222@sbcglobal.net
hstrial-meco.homestead.com
Sink tops, counters and tables
President: Greg Klapp
VP: C Klapp
Estimated Sales: $5 Million
Number Employees: 35
Square Footage: 120000

26303 Mister Label, Inc
PO Box 326
Bluffton, SC 29910 843-815-2222
Fax: 843-815-5488 800-732-0439
misterlabel@msn.com www.misterlabel.com
Manufacturer and exporter of labels including pressure sensitive, heat seal, gummed, tyvek and tag-stock
President: Todd Elliot
Chief Operating Officer: Kelly Elliot
Estimated Sales: $5-10 Million
Number Employees: 11
Square Footage: 30000
Type of Packaging: Food Service, Private Label, Bulk

26304 Mitec
2445 Meadowbrook Parkway
Duluth, GA 30096 770-813-5959
Fax: 319-286-2988 888-854-1851
brian@mitecinc.com www.mitecnet.com
Manufacturers of insulated metal panels for commercial, industrial and cold storage buildings.
President: Bryan A. Shaver
Estimated Sales: $1 - 5 Million
Number Employees: 1-4

26305 Mitsubishi CaterpillarFork
2121 W Sam Houston Pkwy N
Houston, TX 77043-2305 713-365-1000
Fax: 713-365-1441 800-228-5438
info@cat-lift.com www.mcfa.com
Lift trucks and tires
CEO: Shigeru Tanemura
Mktg Head: Jennifer Evans
Estimated Sales: $3 - 5 Million
Number Employees: 1-4

26306 Mitsubishi Fuso Track ofAmerica
2015 Center Square Rd
Swedesboro, NJ 08085-1683 856-467-4500
Fax: 856-467-4695 877-829-3876
www.mitsufuso.com
R&D: Jim Peary
CEO: Bob Mc Dowell
Estimated Sales: $10 - 20 Million
Number Employees: 100-249

26307 Mitsubishi Gas ChemicalAmerica
655 Third Avenue
24th Floor
New York, NY 10017 212-687-9030
Fax: 212-687-2812 888-330-6422
contact@mgc-a.com www.mgc-a.com
Estimated Sales: C
Number Employees: 250-499

26308 (HQ)Mitsubishi InternationalCorporation
520 Madison Avenue
Floor 18
New York, NY 10022-4327 212-759-5605
Fax: 212-605-1810 800-442-6266
inquire@mitsubishicorp.com www.micusa.com
Food commodities: coffee, cocoa, dairy products, fruits, vegetables and frozen juice concentrates. Food ingredients, enzymes, emulsifiers, baking agents.
President: James Brumm
CFO: Yasuyuki Sugiura
Executive VP/COO: Yoshihiko Kawamura
Sales/Purchasing Representative: Patrick Welch
Number Employees: 250-499
Other Locations:
Seattle WA

26309 Mitsubishi Polyester Film, Inc.
2001 Hood Road
PO Box 1400
Greer, SC 29652 864-879-5000
Fax: 864-879-5006 contact@m-petfilm.com
www.m-petfilm.com
Manufacturer, importer and exporter of biaxially oriented polyester films, and copolyester shrink sleeve film
President/COO/CEO: Dennis Trice
Chief Financial Officer: Dave Etherington
Vice President: William Radlein
Quality Assurance Director: Amy Lister
Sales & Marketing Director: Bill Wells
Logistics Manager: Colette Bright
Plant Manager: Joel Gilliam
Director, Purchasing: Patricia Knighting
Estimated Sales: $61 Million
Number Employees: 600
Number of Brands: 3
Number of Products: 100
Square Footage: 24239
Parent Co: Mitsubishi Chemical Corporation
Brands:
Diafoil
Hostaphan

26310 Mity-Lite
1301 West 400 North
Orem, UT 84057-4442 801-224-0589
Fax: 801-224-6191 800-909-8034
info@mitylite.com www.mitylite.com
Lightweight and durable folding tables, folding chairs, stacking chairs, carts, lecterns, portable partitions and portable dance floors.
CEO: Randi Hales
CEO: Brad Nielson
Marketing Manager: Michael Peterson
Sales/Marketing Director: Kevin Stoker
Number Employees: 250-499
Square Footage: 108850
Brands:
Myti Host Chair
Myti Lite Tables
Myti Taff Chair
Summit Lectern
Swift Set Folding Chairs

26311 (HQ)Miura Boiler Inc
1900 The Exchange
Suite 330
Atlanta, GA 30339
Canada 770-916-1695
Fax: 770-916-1858 atlanta@miuraz.com
www.miuraboiler.com
Steam and hot water boilers for the food processing plant.
President: Masashi Hirose
President: Mark Utzinger
Sales: Mike Mazzei
Estimated Sales: $1-$2.5 Million
Number Employees: 8

26312 Mobern Electric Corporation
9731 Washington Blvd N
Laurel, MD 20723 301-725-3030
Fax: 301-953-9310 800-444-9288
sales@mobern.com www.mobern.com
Lighting fixtures
Estimated Sales: $5-10 Million
Number Employees: 50-99

26313 Mobil Composite Products
PO Box 5445
Norwalk, CT 06856-5445 203-831-4200
Fax: 203-831-4222 800-BUY-TREX

26314 Mocon
7500 Mendelssohn Ave N
Minneapolis, MN 55428 763-493-6370
Fax: 763-493-6358 sales@mocon.com
www.mocon.com
Scientific testing and equipment, permeation, leak detection, headspace, weighing,testing
President/CEO: Robert Demorest
Estimated Sales: $37 Million
Number Employees: 150

26315 Mod-Pac Corporation
1801 Elmwood Ave
Buffalo, NY 14207 716-898-8480
Fax: 716-447-9201 800-637-2536
sales@modpac.com www.modpac.com
Specialty paperboard folding cartons, grease-proof cookie boxes, large takeout tote, upscale valentines' day designs and gift basket box
President/CEO: Daniel C. Keane
CFO: David B. Lupp
VP & Finance: Daniel Geary
Marketing Manager: Chuck Littlecom
VP & Sales: Phillip C. Rechin
Estimated Sales: $10-25 Million
Number Employees: 250-499
Number of Products: 500
Square Footage: 300000
Type of Packaging: Consumer, Food Service, Private Label
Brands:
Fashionglo

26316 Modagrafics
5300 Newport Drive
Rolling Meadows, IL 60008 847-392-3980
marketing@modagrafics.com
www.modagrafics.com
Manufacturer and exporter of graphics for food stores and truck fleets
President/Chief Executive Officer: Carlson Lennard
Vice President/Chief Financial Officer: Jack Masters
Executive Vice President: Robert Jurgens
Chief Information Officer/IT Director: Betsy Carlson
Marketing Department: Kate Kummer
Vice President, Operations: Howard Baden
Production Manager: Marty Dorner
Plant Engineering Manager: Salvatore Geraci
Director, Purchasing: Marty Anderson
Estimated Sales: $12 Million
Number Employees: 100
Square Footage: 80000

26317 Modar
1394 Empire Ave
Benton Harbor, MI 49022 269-925-0671
Fax: 269-925-0020 800-253-6186
modar@qtm.net www.modarinc.com

Manufacturer and exporter of ready-to-assemble store fixtures, shelving, point-of-purchase displays, furniture and storage cabinets; also, particle board laminating services available
President: Dennis Rousseau
Sales Manager: Gary Cichon
Inside Sales Manager: Jim Hendrix
Estimated Sales: $12.7 Million
Number Employees: 90
Square Footage: 150000
Other Locations:
Warehousing
Bridgman MI
Sales, Marketing, Design
Middletown CT

26318 Modern Brewing & Design
3171 Guerneville Road
Santa Rosa, CA 95401-4028 707-542-6620
Fax: 707-542-3147 mdrnbrew12@aol.com
Manufacturer and exporter of barrel microbrewing and brewpub equipment; also, support tanks and stainless steel wine storage vessels
President: Daniel Shulte
Secretary: Russell Kargell
VP: Robert Kral
Number Employees: 32

26319 Modern Electronics
PO Box 817
Mansfield, LA 71052-0817 318-872-4764
Fax: 318-872-4768
Pecan processing equipment
President: Richard M Oliver
Quality Control: Richard Oliver
Estimated Sales: $1 - 2.5 Million
Number Employees: 5-9

26320 Modern Metalcraft
1257 E Wackerly Rd
Midland, MI 48642 989-835-3291
Fax: 989-835-8431 800-948-3182
jdmcpeak@modernmetalcraft.com
www.modernmetalcraft.com
Metal products including displays
President: John McPeak
Product Group Manager: Frank Robison
Estimated Sales: Below $5 Million
Number Employees: 10-19
Square Footage: 30000

26321 Modern Metals Industries
128 Sierra St
El Segundo, CA 90245 310-516-0851
Fax: 310-322-8617 800-437-6633
www.mmimedcarts.com
Metal cabinets, industrial carts and material handling equipment
VP: Robert Lee Sherrill
Estimated Sales: $1-2,500,000
Number Employees: 19

26322 Modern Packaging
505 Acorn St
Deer Park, NY 11729 631-595-2437
Fax: 631-595-2742
info@modernpackaginginc.com
www.modernpackaginginc.com
Designs and manufactures precision packaging systems for the food, dairy, cosmetic and drug industries
President: Zaki Hossain
Estimated Sales: $7.9 Million
Number Employees: 50-99
Square Footage: 60000

26323 Modern Packaging
3245 N Berkeley Lake Rd NW
Duluth, GA 30096 770-622-1500
Fax: 770-814-0046
www.modernpackaginginc.com
Contract packager of condiments and liquid food items; warehouse providing dry, cooler and humidity-controlled storage of foodstuffs, liquid packaging products and seasonal sales items; also, pick and pack and rail siding available
President: Herb Sodel
VP: Nancy Sodel
Estimated Sales: $3.6 Million
Number Employees: 50-99
Square Footage: 400000

26324 Modern Paper Box Company
166 Valley Street
Bldg 3
Providence, RI 02909-2458 401-861-7357
Fax: 401-272-2040 11162@polygon.net
Paper boxes
Number Employees: 10

26325 Modern Plastics
706 Howard Ave
Bridgeport, CT 06605 203-333-3128
Fax: 203-333-4625 800-243-9696
customerservice@modernplastics.com
www.modernplastics.com
Plastic films.distributors of plastic sheets, tubes and films,provide custom fabrication. brands - ABS, Acetal, Ardel, Arlon, Acetron, Acculum, Acrylic, Benelex, ceanese, celazole PBI, Ensitep, hyzod sheets, isoplat, kel-F, Kydexkynar, lexan, MD nylon, Macrolux, Merlon, nylon, PAS, Peek, PCTFE, Phenolics, PET, PVDF, Radel, PVC, Rexolite, Rulon, Sanalite, Sintra, Sintimid, Surlyn, Teflon, Torlon, TPX, Valox, Victrex, Vespel, Warps, Xenoy, Zelux, Zytel
President: Bing Carbone
CEO: James Carborne
CFO: Patrick Roderick
Corporate VP: Robert Carbone
Quality Control: Daryl Guberman
Distribution Plastic Sales: Raymond Aneiro
VP Operations: Patrick Roderick
Fabrication/Production: Mark Moriarty
Corporate Purchasing Manager: John Fucci
Estimated Sales: $2.5-5 Million
Number Employees: 20-49

26326 Modern Process Equipment
3125 S Kolin Ave
Chicago, IL 60623 773-254-3929
Fax: 773-254-3935 solutions@mpechicago.com
www.mpechicago.com
Manufacture and market size reduction equipment for the coffee, food, chemical, mineral and pharmaceutical industry
President: Daniel Ephraim
Vice President: Phil Ephraim
Sales Director: Scott Will
Estimated Sales: $5-10 Million
Number Employees: 20-49

26327 Modern Stamp Company
1305 Saint Paul St
Baltimore, MD 21201 410-685-0505
Fax: 410-727-2146 800-727-3029
baumstamps@aol.com
Stamps, checks, seals, stencils, signs, trophies, awards, badges, labels, inks, printing dies, date and lot coding equipment and ink jet coders
Sales Manager: Dennis Burns
Manager: George Pagels
Estimated Sales: $1-2.5 Million
Number Employees: 5-9
Square Footage: 10000

26328 Modern Store Fixtures Company
2505 N Stemmons Fwy
Dallas, TX 75207 214-634-2505
Fax: 214-634-2543 800-634-7777
sales@modernstore.com www.modernstore.com
Glass display cases and store fixtures
VP: Lillian Knopf
General Manager: Bruce Meltzer
Estimated Sales: $5-10 Million
Number Employees: 10-19
Square Footage: 31000

26329 Modesto Tent & Awning
4448 Sisk Rd
Modesto, CA 95356 209-545-6150
Fax: 209-545-6158
signs1@modestotentandawning.com
www.modestotentandawning.com
Awnings, canopies, tarps and tents
President: Robert Valk
Secretary and Treasurer: Leonard Rigg
VP: Barney Valk
Estimated Sales: $1-2,500,000
Number Employees: 10-19
Square Footage: 18000

26330 Modular King Packaging Systems
6 Aspen Dr
Randolph, NJ 07869 973-970-9393
Fax: 973-970-9388
customer.services@modularpackaging.com
www.modularpackaging.com
Packaging machinery including unscrambler desiccant feeders, shrink bundlers, cottoners, blister and case packers, cappers, etc.; importer of cartoners, case and blister packers, counters, etc.; exporter of liquid fillers, tube fillersand cottoners
President: Clifford Smith
Vice President: Bradford Smith
Estimated Sales: $3 - 5,000,000
Number Employees: 10-19
Square Footage: 18000
Brands:
Eclipse
Modular Kt
Omega

26331 Modular Packaging System
6 Aspen Dr
Randolph, NJ 07869-1103 973-970-9393
Fax: 973-970-9388
customer.service@modularpackaging.com
www.modularpackaging.com
Packaging line design, integration and service support, liquid filling lines, filling, blister packaging, closing and labeling machines
President: Clifford Smith
Estimated Sales: $3 - 5 Million
Number Employees: 10-19

26332 Modular Panel Company
63 David Street
New Bedford, MA 02744-2320 508-993-9955
Fax: 508-993-9957
Manufacturer and exporter of insulated panels for freezers and coolers
President: James Chadwick
Drafting Engineer: Pasquale Sbardella
Estimated Sales: Below $5 Million
Number Employees: 10

26333 Modularm Corporation
61 Mall Dr
Commack, NY 11725 631-864-3860
Fax: 631-864-3863 info@modularm.com
www.modularm.com
A temperature and refrigeration monitoring systems manufacturer with innovative products designed to protect perishables, save energy and increase operator safety.
President: Donald Olsen
Marketing Director: Bryan Barash
Sales Director: Marci Norwood

26334 Modulighter
246 E 58th St
New York, NY 10022 212-371-0336
Fax: 212-371-0335
product.sales@modulator.com
www.modulightor.com
Manufacturer, importer and wholesaler/distributor of lighting fixtures
Owner: Ernst Wagner
Estimated Sales: $1-2.5 Million
Number Employees: 5-9
Square Footage: 26000
Brands:
Modulator

26335 Modutank
41-04 35th Avenue
Long Island City, NY 11101 718-392-1112
Fax: 718-786-1008 800-245-6964
info@modutank.com www.modutank.com
Above-ground, modular bolted steel tanks, liquid storage tanks, settling tanks, containment for earthen materials and slurries as well as a wide range of secondary containment systems for sanitary applications, tanker trucks andwheeled vehicles.
President: Reed Margulis
Estimated Sales: $1 - 5 Million
Number Employees: 10-19
Number of Products: 10

26336 Moeller Electric
4140 World Houstn Pkwy Ste 100
Houston, TX 77032 832-613-6250
Fax: 832-613-6225 800-394-5687
info@moellerusa.net www.moellerusa.net

Motor controls, miniature and standard circuit breakers and custom control panels; also, switches including cam, PLC, pushbutton and safety limit
President: John Hamm
VP Marketing: Tom Thornton
Estimated Sales: $20-50 Million
Number Employees: 5-9

26337 Moen Industries
10330 Pioneer Blvd
Suite 230
Santa Fe Springs, CA 90670 562-946-6381
Fax: 562-946-3200 800-732-7766
rstorms@moenindustries.com
www.moenindustries.com
Manufacturer and exporter of corrugated box forming and sealing equipment
Owner: Carl Moen
Sales Co-ordinator: Iris Walker
Purchasing Manager: Lori Maxey
Estimated Sales: $5-10 Million
Number Employees: 50-99
Square Footage: 38000
Brands:
Blissmaster
Lamo-Bliss
Lamo-Tray

26338 Moffat
12000 Crownpoint Drive
Suite 100
San Antonio, TX 78233-5360 210-590-9381
Fax: 210-590-9479 800-551-8795
stu_tex@sprynet.com
Half and full size electric and gas infrared convection ovens; also, proofers
Estimated Sales: $1 - 5 Million
Number Employees: 15
Parent Co: Moffat
Brands:
Bakbar
Turbofan

26339 Mohawk Northern Plastics
PO Box 583
Auburn, WA 98071 253-939-8206
Fax: 253-939-4015 800-426-1100
www.mohawkplastics.com
Extruded and printed flexible polyethylene packaging including bags and film
President: Dan Mc Farland
CFO: Dan McFarlan
Sales Manager: Tom Couples
Estimated Sales: $20-50 Million
Number Employees: 100-249

26340 Mohawk Paper Mills
1400 Crescent Vischer Ferry Road
Clifton Park, NY 12065 518-371-6700
info@mohawkpaper.com
www.mohawkterrace.com
Coated and uncoated printing paper
Estimated Sales: $50-100 Million
Number Employees: 250-499

26341 Mohawk Western Plastic
1496 Arrow Hwy
La Verne, CA 91750 909-593-7547
Fax: 909-596-8691
jhenderson@mohawkwestern.com
www.mohawkwestern.com
Polyethylene bags
President: Chris Mordoff
Estimated Sales: $5-10 Million
Number Employees: 20-49

26342 Moisture Register Products
9567 Arrow Route Suite#E
Rancho Cucamonga, CA 91730 909-941-7776
Fax: 909-941-1830 800-966-4788
sales@aquameasure.com
www.moistureregisterproducts.com
Manufacturer and exporter of computers for measuring moisture content in solids for the food processing industry
Owner: John Lundstrom
Sales: Gabriel Cote Jr
Estimated Sales: $3 - 5 Million
Number Employees: 10-19
Parent Co: Aqua Measure Instrument Company
Brands:
Bsp901
Smart Ii

26343 Mol Belting Company
2532 Waldorf Ct NW
Grand Rapids, MI 49544-1472 616-453-2484
Fax: 616-453-2008 800-729-2358
sales@molbelting.com www.molindustries.com
Materials handling equipment, conveyors and accessories
President: Edward Mol
Estimated Sales: $10-20 Million
Number Employees: 50-99

26344 Molded Container Corporation
1622 N Lombard St
Portland, OR 97217-5534 503-233-8601
Fax: 503-233-0621
Plastic containers and lids
Manager: Rick Copes
Estimated Sales: $16 Million
Number Employees: 100-249
Square Footage: 80000

26345 Molded Fiber Glass TrayCompany
6175 Highway 6
Linesville, PA 16424 814-683-4500
Fax: 814-683-4504 800-458-6050
info@mfgtray.com www.mfgtray.com
Manufactures reinforced composite trays, containers, and flats used in the confectionery, bakery, food service, pharmaceutical, and electronics industries as well as many other markets for in-process handling of goods.
Manager: Ron Orr
Estimated Sales: $20-50 Million
Number Employees: 100-249

26346 Molded Materials
44650 Helm Ct
Plymouth, MI 48170 734-459-5955
Fax: 734-459-6325 800-825-2566
info@moldedmaterials.com
www.moldedmaterials.com
Manufacturer and exporter of custom molded totes and trays for processing and shipping
Manager: Mike Wolf
COO: R Campbell
VP Engineering: T Elkington
Estimated Sales: Below $5 Million
Number Employees: 50-99
Square Footage: 80000

26347 Molded Pulp Products
1780 Dreman Avenue
Cincinnati, OH 45223-2456 513-681-3016
Fax: 513-681-5121 support@moldedpulp.com
Custom molded products
Estimated Sales: $20-50 Million
Number Employees: 50-99

26348 Molding Automation Concepts
1760 Kilkenny Ct
Woodstock, IL 60098 815-337-3000
Fax: 815-337-3020 800-435-6979
sales@macautomation.com
www.macautomation.com
Manufacturer and exporter of horizontal, incline and elevator belt conveyors for automatic box, tote bag and tray filling systems
President: Frank Altvedt
R&D: Frank Altvedt
Sales Manager: Randy Artheid
Estimated Sales: $10 - 20,000,000
Number Employees: 50-99
Type of Packaging: Bulk

26349 Moli-International
1150 W Virginia Ave
Denver, CO 80223 303-777-0364
Fax: 303-777-0658 800-525-8468
sales@moliinternational.com
www.moliinternational.com
Manufacturer and exporter of displays, sampling and merchandising covers, pans, trays, clear plexiglass, service carts, ice bins, water stations, sinks and sneeze guards
Owner: Van Larson
Secretary/Treasurer: Larry Larson
Estimated Sales: $500,000-$1 Million
Number Employees: 5-9
Square Footage: 12500
Type of Packaging: Food Service
Brands:
Merchant & Moli-Shields

26350 Moli-Tron Company
1457 Ammons St Ste 211
Lakewood, CO 80214 303-969-8888
Fax: 303-969-8110 800-525-9494
cleanair@moli-tron.com www.moli-tron.com
Manufactures complete line of commercial kitchen exhaust equipment including restaurant wet scrubbers, water scrubbing ventilators and restaurant odor control systems for restaurants and other commercial kitchens.
President: Arlen Gallagher
Estimated Sales: $500,000-$1 Million
Number Employees: 1-4
Brands:
Moli-Tron

26351 Moline Machinery
PO Box 16308
Duluth, MN 55816-0308 218-624-5734
Fax: 218-628-3853 800-767-5734
sales@moline.com www.moline.com
Manufacturer and exporter of proofing, frying and dough processing systems for doughnuts, specialty breads, snack foods and yeast raised products
President: Gary Moline
Sales Manager: Terry King
Engineering Director: Larry Meyer
Estimated Sales: $10-20 Million
Number Employees: 50-99
Square Footage: 95000
Brands:
Moline

26352 Molins/Sandiacre Richmond
8191 Brook Rd # G
Richmond, VA 23227-1334 804-421-8795
Fax: 804-421-8798 sandiacre.usa@molins.com
www.sandiacre.com
Manufacturer, importer and exporter of packaging machinery
Founder: Herman Hayssen
Vice President of Sales and Marketing: Dan Minor
Estimated Sales: $10 - 20 Million
Number Employees: 1-4

26353 Mollenberg-Betz
300 Scott St
Buffalo, NY 14204 716-614-7473
Fax: 716-614-7465
vmollen@mollenbergbetz.com
www.mollenbergbetz.com
Cold storage facilities, freezers, refrigeration equipment and parts; also, design and installation services available. Design and installation of refrigeration systems, suppliers of refrigeration equipment and parts-service
President: H Van Mollenberg
Quality Control: John Paytash
Executive VP: Joe Kilijanski
Purchasing: Gene Kaderbeck
Estimated Sales: $30 Million
Number Employees: 100-249
Square Footage: 30000

26354 Mollers North America
5215 52nd St SE
Grand Rapids, MI 49512 616-942-6504
Fax: 616-942-8825 mnagr@aol.com
www.mollersna.com
Designers and manufacturers of valve packing equipment, bag handling conveyors, automatic bag palletizers, pallet handling conveyors, stretch-hooders and shrinkwrapping systems
Executive VP: Tom Wagner
Executive VP: Carlos Saenz
Estimated Sales: $10 Million
Number Employees: 50-99
Square Footage: 100000
Parent Co: Maschinenfabrik Mollers GmbHu Company

26355 Moly-XL Company
Ih 295 Business Ctr
Westville, NJ 08093 856-848-2880
Fax: 856-848-2799
Industrial greases, oils and lubricants
President: Frank Iacovone
VP: Kenneth Kunz
Number Employees: 5-9
Square Footage: 10000
Parent Co: Master Lubricants Company
Brands:
Moly-Xl

26356 Momar
1830 Ellsworth Industrial Drive NW
Atlanta, GA 30318-3746
800-556-3967
info@momar.com www.momar.com
Manufacturer and exporter of industrial maintenance chemicals, water treatment products, lubricants and cleaning chemicals for the food processing industry
Estimated Sales: $34 Million
Number Employees: 300
Square Footage: 50000
Brands:
Aquatrol
Lubest
Mochem
Momarket

26357 Momence Pallet Corporation
PO Box 708
Momence, IL 60954 815-472-6451
Fax: 815-472-6453
Wooden pallets
President: Andrew Cryer
Secretary/Treasurer: Norm Cryer
Estimated Sales: $2.5-5 Million
Number Employees: 20-49
Square Footage: 50000

26358 Monadnock Paper Mills
117 Antrim Road
Bennington, NH 03442-4205 603-588-3311
Fax: 603-588-6289 www.mpm.com
Manufacturer and exporter of paper including uncoated cover, text, technical specialty and converting, nonwovens
President/Chairman/CEO: Richard Verney
Managing Director: Keith Hayward
Vice President/CFO/Treasurer: Andrew Manns
Vice President: Julie Hughes
Director, Information Technology: Joseph Gleason
Quality Control Manager: Richard Beahm
Vice President, Sales: James Clemente
Plant Manager: Dave Burnham
Purchasing Manager: Denise Long
Estimated Sales: $68 Million
Number Employees: 235
Square Footage: 300000

26359 Monarch Analytical Laboratories
349 Tomahawk Dr
Maumee, OH 43537 419-897-9000
Fax: 419-897-9111 testing@monarchlab.com
www.monarchlab.com
Laboratory providing analysis of packaging materials, raw materials and problems such as foreign materials, package failure, etc
Manager: Diane Paskiet
Manager (Inorganic): James Hojuicki
Estimated Sales: $2.5-5 Million
Number Employees: 20-49
Square Footage: 12000

26360 Monarch-McLaren
329 Deerhide Crescent
Weston, ON M9M 2Z2
Canada 416-741-9675
Fax: 416-741-2873
customerservice@monarch-mclaren.ca
www.monarch-mclaren.ca
Manufacturer, importer and wholesaler/distributor of conveyor and transmission belting, V-belts, timing belts, variable speed belts, hoses, pulleys, chains, sprockets, bearings, speed reducers, casters, motors, couplings, belt lacingleather packings, etc
President: Terence Whitfield
Sales Manager: Brian Flint
Estimated Sales: Below $5 Million
Number Employees: 10
Square Footage: 72400
Brands:
Monarch-Mclaren
Polyplast
Yorkcord
Yorkedge
Yorkflex
Yorkgrip
Yorklink
Yorklon
Yorkmate
Yorkpack
Yorktex
Yorktex Leather

26361 Monastary Mustard
840 South Main Street
Angel, OR 97362 503-949-6321
Info@MonasteryMustard.com
monasterymustard.com
Mustard
Mustard Flavor Creator: Sister Terry Hall

26362 Monitor Company
P.O.Box 4411
Modesto, CA 95352-4411 209-523-0500
Fax: 209-523-4267 800-537-3201
nick@monitorco.com www.monitorco.com
Manufacturer and exporter of temperature recorders
Estimated Sales: $1 - 5 Million
Number Employees: 15
Brands:
Temprecord

26363 Monitor Technologies
44W320 Keslinger Rd
Elburn, IL 60119 630-365-9403
Fax: 630-365-5646 800-601-6319
monitor@monitortech.com
www.monitortech.com
Manufacturer and exporter of level and flow monitoring products for powder and bulk solids
President/Owner: Craig Russell
Product Manager: Greg DeRudder
Marketing Director: Chris Otte
Director of Sales: Scott Bonine
Estimated Sales: $2.5-5 Million
Number Employees: 20-49
Type of Packaging: Private Label
Brands:
Bulksonics
Dustalarm

26364 Monoflo International
PO Box 2797
Winchester, VA 22604 540-771-3077
Fax: 540-665-0010 800-446-6693
sales@miworldwide.com
www.miworldwide.com
Collapsible plastic containers
Owner: Gus Nusu
Estimated Sales: $10-20 Million
Number Employees: 100-249

26365 Monon Process EquipmentCompany
6289 N 150 E
Monon, IN 47959-8010 219-253-7777
Fax: 219-253-8580 monopro@urher.net
www.mononprocess.com
President and CEO: Troy Paluchniak
Estimated Sales: Below $5 Million
Number Employees: 1-4

26366 Monroe Environmental Corporation
810 W Front St
Monroe, MI 48161 734-242-7654
Fax: 734-242-5275 800-992-7707
sales@monroeenvironmental.com
www.mon-env.com
Manufacturer oil mist, smoke and vapor collectors, venturi scrubbers, dust collectors, water & wastewater clarifiers.
Owner: Gary Pashaian
Sales Manager: Adam Pashaian
Operations Manager: Rob Cardella
Estimated Sales: $15 Million
Number Employees: 45
Square Footage: 35000

26367 (HQ)Monroe Kitchen Equipment
105 Dodge St
Rochester, NY 14606 585-235-3310
Fax: 585-235-7312 tcurtain@monroekitchen.com
monroekitchen.com
Custom stainless steel kitchen equipment: sinks, tables and hoods
President: Thomas Curtin
Sales: Anthony Salemme
Plant Manager: Craig Mackey
Purchasing: Adam Curtain
Estimated Sales: Below $5 Million
Number Employees: 45
Square Footage: 25000
Other Locations:
Monroe Kitchen Equipment
Rochester NY

26368 Monsol
1701 County Line Road
Portage, IN 46368-1234 219-762-3165
Fax: 219-763-4477 800-237-9552
info@monosol.com www.monosol.com
Packaging water soluble film
General Manager: P Scott Bening
Product Development Manager: Jonathan Gallagher
Customer Service Representative: Tracee Hatch
Clerk: Darlene Taylor
Estimated Sales: $1 - 5 Million
Number Employees: 50-99

26369 Montague Company
1830 Stearman Ave
Hayward, CA 94545 510-785-8822
Fax: 510-785-3342 800-345-1830
www.montaguecompany.com
Manufacturer and exporter of commercial gas and electric cooking equipment. Products include convection ovens, deluxe griddles, heavy duty & medium duty ranges, counter equipment, fryers, over-fired and under-fired broilers, deckovens, chinese ranges, induction cooking equipment, under-counter refrigeration, and custom island suites.
President: Thomas Whalen
VP Finance: R Erickson
VP Sales/Marketing: Gary Rupp
Purchasing: Lisa Catanzano
Estimated Sales: $30-30 Million
Number Employees: 100-249
Type of Packaging: Food Service
Brands:
Grizzly
Hearthbake
Legend
Vectaire

26370 Montalbano Development
3275 Veterans Hwy Ste B15
Ronkonkoma, NY 11779 631-467-8686
Fax: 631-467-1035 800-739-9152
j.montalbano@earthlink.net
www.montalbanoinc.com
Provider of computer services for the food industry including
Owner: Chris Montalbano
VP: Chris Montalbano
Manager: Steghen Naroney
Estimated Sales: $2.5-5,000,000
Number Employees: 10-19

26371 Montana Coffee Traders
5810 US Highway 93 South
Whitefish, MT 59937 406-862-7633
Fax: 406-862-7680 800-345-5282
traders@coffeetraders.com
www.coffeetraders.com
Founded in 1981. Producer of flavored coffees and teas
Owner: R C Beal
R&D: Heather Verintes
Estimated Sales: Below $5 Million
Number Employees: 50-99

26372 Monte Glove Company
1208 Industrial Park Road
Wilkesboro, NC 28697-8490 662-263-5353
Fax: 662-263-5771 monteglove@telepack.net
Work gloves, oven mitts, hand pads, sleeves
President: Glenn Clarke
Sales Manager: Theresa Lewis
Production: John Hall
Estimated Sales: $10-20 Million
Number Employees: 50-99
Parent Co: Golden Needles Knitting
Type of Packaging: Food Service, Private Label

26373 Monte Package Company
3752 Riverside Road
Riverside, MI 49084 269-849-1722
Fax: 269-849-0185 800-653-2807
sales@montepkg.com www.montepkg.com
Packaging materials including boxes
President: Salvatore P Monte
Owner: Sam Monte
Estimated Sales: $10-20 Million
Number Employees: 40

26374 **Montebello Container Corporation**
14333 Macaw St
La Mirada, CA 90638 714-994-2351
Fax: 714-994-3875 sales@montcc.com
www.montcc.com

Corrugated containers
President: R. Anthony Salcido
Vice President: John Salcido
Production Superintendent: Roger Esquer
Estimated Sales: $5-10 Million
Number Employees: 100-249

26375 **Montebello Packaging**
1036 Aberdeen St
Hawkesbury, ON K6A 1K5
Canada 613-632-7096
Fax: 613-632-9638 www.montebellopkg.com
Aluminum aerosol cans & aluminum/laminate tubes
President: Betty Pilon
Quality Control: Doug Bailey
Vice President: Douglas Stewart
VP Sales: Alex Paignareul
Plant Manager: Dan Blakeman
Estimated Sales: $70 Million
Number Employees: 400
Parent Co: The Jim Pattison Group
Brands:
M-Bond
M-Purity Ring
M-Purity Seal

26376 **Montello**
6106 E 32nd Pl
Suite 100
Tulsa, OK 74135 918-665-1170
Fax: 918-665-1480 800-331-4628
paulmontello@inc.com www.montelloinc.com
Specialty industrial chemicals
President: Aloen Johnson
Estimated Sales: $2.5 Million
Number Employees: 5-9

26377 **Monterey Bay Food Group**
661 Meadow Rd
Aptos, CA 95003-9786 831-685-8600
Fax: 831-685-8656 contact@mbfoodgroup.com
www.montereybaycorporatedevelopment.com
Consultant providing strategic planning, marketing and product management; also, assessment of products and business opportunities
Market Research Manager: Amy Seibert
Operations Manager: Lora Keyte
Estimated Sales: $1-2.5 Million
Number Employees: 5-9

26378 **Monument Industries**
159 Phyllis Ln
Bennington, VT 05201 802-442-8187
Fax: 802-442-8188
Manufacturer and exporter of polyethylene bags
President: Lawrence Amos
VP: Jay L Whitten
Estimated Sales: $5-10 Million
Number Employees: 20-49

26379 **Moody Dunbar**
PO Box 6048
Johnson City, TN 37602-6048 423-952-0100
Fax: 423-952-0289 800-257-2111
esimerly@moodydunbar.com
www.moodydunbar.com

Owner: Stanley Dunbar
Estimated Sales: $10 - 20 Million
Number Employees: 20-49

26380 **Moon Valley Circuits**
12350 Maple Glen Rd
Glen Ellen, CA 95442-7705 707-996-4157
jill@moonvalleycircuits.com
www.moonvalleycircuits.com
Wine industry temperature controls
President: Michael Miller
Quality Control: Michael Miller
CFO: Michael Miller
R&D: Michael Miller
Estimated Sales: $250,000
Number Employees: 1-4

26381 **Moore Efficient Communication Aids**
PO Box 11023
Denver, CO 80211 303-433-8456
Fax: 303-433-8450
Marking devices, rubber stamps and sign systems
Owner: Ed Moore
Executive Secretary: Pam Craig
Production Manager: Leroy Eddy
Estimated Sales: $1-2.5 Million
Number Employees: 5-9
Square Footage: 15000
Type of Packaging: Private Label, Bulk
Brands:
Lifetime
Trodat
X Stamper

26382 **Moore Paper Boxes**
2916 Boulder Ave
Dayton, OH 45414 937-278-7327
Fax: 937-278-5932
Manufacturer and exporter of paper boxes
President: Charles Moore
Estimated Sales: $10-20 Million
Number Employees: 20-49

26383 **Moore Production Tool Specialties**
37531 Grand River Ave
Farmington Hills, MI 48335-2879 248-476-1200
Fax: 248-476-6887 mpts@compuserve.com
Manufacturer and exporter of sealing jaws, knives, anvils and packaging tooling
President: Durk Moore
CEO: Richard Moore
President: Richard Moore
Sales: Brian Carfango
Estimated Sales: $2.5-5 Million
Number Employees: 20-49
Square Footage: 28000

26384 **Moore Push-Pin Company**
1300 E Mermaid Ln
Glenside, PA 19038 215-233-5700
Fax: 215-233-0660 info@invis-a-link.com
www.invis-a-link.com
Converting and batching equipment, specialty fasteners
President: George W Samson
Estimated Sales: $5-10 Million
Number Employees: 50-99

26385 **Moorecraft Box & Crate**
PO Box 1528
Tarboro, NC 27886-1528 252-823-2510
Fax: 252-823-2228 steve@moorecraft.com
www.moorecraft.com
Wood and plywood shipping boxes and crates and custom pallets
Owner: Stephen Redhage
VP: Sharon Redhage
Estimated Sales: $1-2.5 Million
Number Employees: 50-99
Square Footage: 4500

26386 **Moran Canvas Products**
8135 Center St
La Mesa, CA 91942 619-462-7778
Fax: 619-462-7776 800-515-1130
morancanvas@sbcglobal.net
www.morancanvas.com
Commercial awnings
President: Michael Moran
CFO: Paulette Moran
Sales Manager: Roger Smith
Estimated Sales: Below $5,000,000
Number Employees: 10-19

26387 **(HQ)Morgan Brothers Bag Company**
PO Box 25577
Richmond, VA 23260-5577 804-355-9107
Fax: 804-355-9100
customerservice@morganbrosbag.com
www.morganbrosbag.com
Textile bags for hams, peanuts, citrus fruits, scallops and crops
Owner: Jim Edge
VP: Annabel Lewis
Estimated Sales: $20-50 Million
Number Employees: 50-99
Square Footage: 37800

26388 **Morgan Corporation**
111 Morgan Way
PO Box 588
Morgantown, PA 19543 610-286-5025
Fax: 610-286-2246 800-666-7426
info@morgancorp.com www.morgancorp.com
President: Norb Markert
Estimated Sales: $1 - 5 Million
Number Employees: 1,000-4,999
Parent Co: J.B. Poindexter & Co

26389 **Morning Star Coffee, Inc.**
207 Carter Dr Ste E
West Chester, PA 19382-4506 610-701-7022
Fax: 610-701-7032 888-854-2233
antonio.sordi@morningstarcoffee.us
www.morningstarcoffee.us

Specialty coffee roasters
President: Thomas Gaspar
VP, Operations: Antonio Sordi
Estimated Sales: $75 - 100 Million
Number Employees: 5-9

26390 **Morning Star Foods**
8 Joanna Court
East Brunswick, NJ 08816-2108 800-237-5320
Fax: 732-432-3928
Manufacturer and marketer of consumer packaged goods
President/CEO: Herman Graffinder
CFO: Craig Miller
Sr. VP Marketing: Toby Purdy
Sr. VP Operations: Samuel Hillin
Parent Co: Dean Foods Company
Type of Packaging: Private Label, Bulk

26391 **Morphy Container Company**
17 Woodyatt Drive
Brantford, ON N3R 7K3
Canada 519-752-5428
Fax: 519-752-2260
Packaging containers including corrugated boxes
Office Manager: Barbara Shaw
Production Manager: Peter Hird
Square Footage: 6000

26392 **Morris & Associates**
803 Morris Dr
Garner, NC 27529 919-582-9200
Fax: 919-582-9100 info@morris-associates.com
www.morris-associates.com
Custom refrigeration equipment for the foodprocessing industry. Specializing in industrial ice makers and storage and delivery systems.
President: Bill Morris III
CEO: Bill Morris III
CEO: Bill Morris Iii
Research & Development: John Shell
Marketing Director: Virginia Arello
Sales Director: Bobby Cathey
Operations Manager: David Maw
Production Manager: Ron Correia
Purchasing Manager: Tomc Patterson
Estimated Sales: $5 - 10 Million
Number Employees: 10-19
Number of Products: 20+
Square Footage: 50000
Brands:
Chill Master
Ice Master

26393 **Morris Industries**
8130 Cryden Way
Forestville, MD 20747 301-568-5005
Fax: 301-420-4140 davem@morrisindustries.com
Pressure sensitive labels
President: Dave Morris
CEO: Dave Shotland
Estimated Sales: $3 - 5 Million
Number Employees: 10-19
Square Footage: 9000

26394 **Morris Transparent Box Company**
945 Warren Ave
East Providence, RI 02914 401-438-6116
Fax: 401-434-9779
Plastic wedding cake boxes and covers
President: Alfred T Morris Jr
VP: Jean Morris
Estimated Sales: $2.5-5 Million
Number Employees: 20-49

26395 **Morrison Timing Screw Company**
335 W 194th St
Glenwood, IL 60425-1501 708-331-6600
Fax: 708-756-6620 timingscr@aol.com
www.morrison-chs.com

Manufacturer and exporter of timing screws and automatic can opening systems
President: Nick Wilson
Vice President: Lois Hayworth
Vice President of Operations: Chris Wilson
Estimated Sales: $10-20 Million
Number Employees: 20-49

26396 **Morrison Weighing Systems**
7605 50th St
Milan, IL 61264 309-799-7311
Fax: 309-799-7313 info@morrison-weighing.com
www.morrison-weighing.com
Checkweighing devices, weight control systems, scales, weigh-convey systems
President: Donald G Morrison
Estimated Sales: $1-2.5 Million
Number Employees: 5-9

26397 **Morrissey Displays & Models**
20 Beverly Rd
Port Washington, NY 11050 516-883-6944
Fax: 516-767-2379
Manufacturer and exporter of display booths
Owner: Stuart Morrissey
Estimated Sales: $500,000-$1 Million
Number Employees: 1-4

26398 **Morrow Technologies Corporation**
12000 28th Streett North
St Petersburg, FL 33716 727-531-4000
Fax: 727-531-3531 877-526-8711
sales@janusdisplays.com
www.janusdisplays.com
Manufacturer and exporter of interior electronic signs including Leo, LCD and Plasma
Owner: Sharon Morrow
CEO: John Morrow
Controller: Kathy Naranjo
Marketing: Rhonda Candreva
Sales Manager: Steve Asbrand
Number Employees: 20-49
Brands:
Janus

26399 **Morse Manufacturing Company**
727 W Manlius St
East Syracuse, NY 13057 315-437-8475
Fax: 315-437-1029 inquiry@morsedrum.com
www.morsedrum.com
Drum handling equipment, fork attachments for drum moving and drum mixers; exporter of drum handling equipment including rotators, handlers and tumblers
President: Nate Andrews
Chairman Of the Board: Robert Andrews
Marketing: Ralph Phillips
Sales Manager: Phil Mulpagano
Number Employees: 20-49
Number of Brands: 1
Number of Products: 100

26400 **Mortec Industries**
29240 Country Rd R
Brush, CO 80723 970-842-5063
Fax: 970-842-5061 800-541-9983
joe@mortecscales.com mortecscales.com
Manufacturer and exporter of electronic weighing scales; wholesaler/distributor of computer hardware and software; serving the food service market
Owner: Evelyn Kral
Estimated Sales: $1-2.5 Million
Number Employees: 5-9
Type of Packaging: Consumer, Food Service

26401 **(HQ)Moseley Corporation**
31 Hayward St Ste 2a
Franklin, MA 02038 508-541-1300
Fax: 508-520-6915 800-667-3539
info@moseleycorp.com www.moseleycorp.com
Modular merchandising systems including carts, kiosks, point of purchase displays and store systems; also, design and architectural consulting services available
President: Thomas C Moseley Jr
COO: Richard Kerley
Sr. VP: Christine Milloff
Estimated Sales: $10 - 20 Million
Number Employees: 40
Square Footage: 50000
Other Locations:
Moseley Corp.
Dallas TX

26402 **Moser Bag & Paper Company**
32485 Creekside Drive
Cleveland, OH 44124-5221 216-341-4111
Fax: 216-341-6507 800-433-6638
Specialty bags including paper, glassine and kraft
President: Ted Welles
Estimated Sales: $5-10 Million
Number Employees: 20-49
Type of Packaging: Food Service
Brands:
Stubby Clear-Vue
Stubby Less Crush

26403 **Moss Printing**
2600 Elmhurst Rd
Elk Grove Village, IL 60007-6312
800-341-1557
www.mossinc.com
Custom labels including pressure sensitive, multi-panel and on-pack for recipes, coupons, product information, etc
President and CEO: Dan Patterson
EVP and CFO: Mark Ollinger
Executive Vice President of Research and: Bob Frey
Executive Vice President of Operations: Vince Marler
VP Production Logistics: Joe Donley
Number Employees: 268
Brands:
Fix-A-Form

26404 **Mosshaim Innovations**
13901 Sutton Park Drive S
Suite 120
Jacksonville, FL 32224-0229 614-985-3000
Fax: 614-985-0703 888-995-7775
jsarvadi@mosshaim.com www.mosshaim.com
Portable, 120 volt, vitro ceramic glass stovetops. Also produces 120 volt drop-in stovetops. Patented technology will replace gas and induction portables
President: James Sarvadi
Quality Control: Tom Dorothy
R & D: James Sarvadi
VP Marketing: Donald Lewis
VP Operations: James Sarvadi
Estimated Sales: Below $5 Million
Number Employees: 10
Number of Brands: 2
Square Footage: 40000
Parent Co: Mosshaim Innovations
Brands:
Le Gourmates
Series S

26405 **Mosuki**
105 Bridge Road
Islandia, NY 11749-5207 631-234-4111
Fax: 631-234-2940 varduino@aol.com
Espresso machines/accessories

26406 **Motion Industries**
1605 Alton Road
Birmingham, AL 35210 205-956-1122
Fax: 205-951-1179 877-609-7975
coby.carmicheal@motion-ind.com
www.motionindustries.com
Equipment parts and supplies.
Manager: Matt McComb

26407 **Motion Technology**
10 Forbes Rd
Northborough, MA 01532 508-460-9800
Fax: 508-460-5090 800-468-2976
mberrios@mtiproducts.com www.autofry.com
Ventless, enclosed, automated deep fryers
Sales: Jamie Fisher
National Sales Manager: James Hall
Estimated Sales: $2.5-5 Million
Number Employees: 5-9
Square Footage: 8500
Brands:
Autofry

26408 **Motom Corporation**
631 Il Route 83
Suite 180
Bensenville, IL 60106-1342 630-787-1995
Fax: 630-787-1795 motomas@enteraccess.com
www.motom.com
Manufacturer and exporter of drying and baking ovens, cleaning and automated material handling equipment
President: T Teshigawara
VP: W Kojima
Number Employees: 16
Parent Co: Tsukamoto Industrial Trading Company

26409 **Motoman**
805 Liberty Ln
West Carrollton, OH 45449 937-847-6200
Fax: 937-847-6277
customerservice@motoman.com
www.motoman.com
Robotic automation including packaging and palletizing
President: Steve Barhorst
Estimated Sales: $45 Million
Number Employees: 250-499
Square Footage: 182000
Parent Co: Yaskawa Company
Type of Packaging: Consumer, Food Service
Brands:
Motoman

26410 **Motomco**
3699 Kinsman Blvd
Madison, WI 53704 608-244-2904
Fax: 608-241-9631 800-418-9242
kgutzmer@motomco.com www.motomco.com
Rodent control products including rodenticides, liquid bait and glue boards
President: Linda Hughes
Marketing Director: Todd Butzon
National Accounts Manager: Todd Mikkelsen
Estimated Sales: $500,000-$1 Million
Number Employees: 1-4
Brands:
Hawk
Pmp
Rampage
Tomcat
Trapper

26411 **Mouli Manufacturing Corporation**
1 Montgomery Street
Belleville, NJ 07109-1305 201-751-6900
Fax: 201-751-0345 800-789-8285
moulimfg@aol.com
Manufacturer, importer and exporter of stainless steel food service equipment including cheese shredders, choppers, cutter, peelers, pots, pans and vegetable processors, etc
VP: P Varkala
Sales: Chris Varkala
Estimated Sales: $1 - 5 Million
Number Employees: 5-9
Square Footage: 30000
Brands:
Mouli

26412 **Mound Tool Company**
9301 Watson Industrial Park
Saint Louis, MO 63126 314-968-3991
Fax: 314-968-1240 info@moundtool.com
www.moundtool.com/index.html
President: R Osborne
Estimated Sales: Below $5 Million
Number Employees: 10-19

26413 **Mount Hope Machinery Company**
1 Technology Dr
Westborough, MA 01581-1786 508-616-9458
Fax: 508-616-9479
Web control equipment for textiles, paper, plastics, film and foil
President: Bertram Staudenmaier
President: Doug Milner
Director Applications: Carl Wertz
Sales Director: Kevin Frank
Customer Service Support Manager: Ed Gaudette
Estimated Sales: $10 - 20 Million
Number Employees: 50-99
Parent Co: BTR Paper Group

26414 **Mount Vernon Packaging**
135 Progress Dr
Mount Vernon, OH 43050 740-397-3221
Fax: 740-393-2002 888-397-3221
mvpkg@vcr.net mountvernonpackaging.com
Paper boxes
President: Donald Nuce

Estimated Sales: $5-10 Million
Number Employees: 5-9

26415 Mount Vernon Plastics
460 Ogden Ave
Mamaroneck, NY 10543-2225 914-698-1122
Fax: 914-698-1707
Plastic bags
Manager: Michael Dino
Estimated Sales: $2.5-5 Million
Number Employees: 10-19

26416 Mountain Pacific Machinery
11705 SW 68th Ave
Portland, OR 97223 503-639-7635
Fax: 503-639-7707 877-466-9031
parts@mountpac.com www.mountpac.com
Dealers of food processing, packaging and material handling equipment
President: Dean Smith
Sales: Josh Wiechman
Estimated Sales: $3 - 5 Million
Number Employees: 5-9

26417 Mountain Pacific Machinery
515 S 9th St
Boise, ID 83702 208-345-9033
Fax: 208-345-9037 877-466-9031
parts@mountpac.com www.mountpac.com
Dealers of food processing, packaging and material handling equipment
Sales: Josh Wiechman
Manager: Jeff Wiechman
Estimated Sales: $10-20 Million
Number Employees: 1-4

26418 Mountain Pride
421 Bell Drive
PO Box 6077
Ketchum, ID 83340 208-725-5600
Fax: 208-725-5601
President: Stuart Siderman
Estimated Sales: $.5 - 1 million
Number Employees: 1-4

26419 Mountain Safety Research
3800 1st Ave S
Seattle, WA 98134-2235 206-624-8573
Fax: 206-682-4184 800-877-9677
info@msrgear.com www.cascadedesigns.com
Manufacturer, importer, and exporter of camp stoves, fuel bottles, water filtration products and cook sets
President: Joe Mc Sweeney
Research & Development: Kevin Gallagher
Manager Marketing/Sales: Michael Glavin
VP Operations/Engineering: R Michael Ligrano
Manager Product: Gail Snyder
Estimated Sales: $10-20 Million
Number Employees: 1-4
Number of Brands: 1
Number of Products: 250
Square Footage: 80000
Parent Co: Recreational Equipment
Type of Packaging: Consumer
Brands:
Alpine/Xpd
Cloudliner
Denali
Msr
Msr Carabiners
Miniworks
Rapid Fire
Superfly
Water Works
Whisperlite
X-Gk

26420 Mountain Secure Systems
1350 Kansas Avenue
Longmont, CO 80501-6546 303-678-9898
Fax: 303-651-7171 800-MSI-PEAK
info@mountainsystems.com
www.mountainsecuresystems.com
Software MES, specification
Estimated Sales: $5-10 Million
Number Employees: 20-49

26421 Mountain States Processing & Rendering Equipment
1293 Denver Avenue
Fort Lupton, CO 80621 303-857-1060
mtnstatespr@aol.com
Industrial equipment and machinery
President: David Morgan
Estimated Sales: $1 Million
Number Employees: 6
Square Footage: 12000

26422 Mountain Valley Farms &Lumber Products, Inc.
1240 Nawakwa Rd
Biglerville, PA 17307-9728 717-677-6166
Fax: 717-677-9283 admin@mtvalleyfarms.com
www.mtvalleyfarms.com
Hardwood bins, skids and pallets; also, sawdust
President: H Taylor
CFO: Patrick McCreary
VP/Operations: H Michael Taylor
R & D: Jemay Lua
Estimated Sales: Below $5 Million
Number Employees: 50-99
Square Footage: 208000
Other Locations:
Mountain Valley Farms &Lumbe
Biglerville PA
Brands:
Enviro-Logs

26423 Mountaingate Engineering
540 Division Street
Campbell, CA 95008-6906 408-866-5100
Fax: 408-866-8896 mtgate@mtgate.com
Can and end drying, curing and sterilizing systems
Estimated Sales: $1 - 5 Million
Parent Co: Nordson Corporation Container Systems

26424 (HQ)Mouron & Company
1025 Western Dr
Indianapolis, IN 46241 317-243-7955
Fax: 317-243-2514 info@mouronandco.com
www.mouronstainless.com
Stainless steel tables and counters
President: Thomas Mouron
VP: G Mouron
Engineer: P Skrojane
Sales Manager: Phil Skorjanc
Accounting: Mark Bryant
Estimated Sales: $2.5-5 Million
Number Employees: 10-19

26425 MovinCool/Denso Sales ofCalifornia
3900 Via Oro Ave
Long Beach, CA 90810-1868 310-834-6352
Fax: 310-513-7319 info2@movincool.com
www.densocorp-na-dsca.com
Portable spot air conditioning
President: Yoshihiko Yamada
Marketing Director: Eddie Stevenson
Estimated Sales: $50 - 75 Million
Number Employees: 100-249
Brands:
Movincool

26426 Moyer Packing Company
741 Souder Road
Elroy, PA 18964
Fax: 970-336-5582 800-967-8325
www.mopac.com
Boxed and ground beef; exporter of fresh and frozen boxed beef
Estimated Sales: $0.5 Billion
Number Employees: 1600+
Square Footage: 85000
Parent Co: Smithfield Foods
Type of Packaging: Consumer, Private Label, Bulk
Brands:
Mopac

26427 Moyer-Diebel
3765 Champion Blvd
Winston Salem, NC 27105 336-661-1992
Fax: 336-661-1979 info@moyerdiebel.com
www.moyerdiebel.com
Manufacturer and exporter of commercial dishwashers
President: Erik Nommsen
Sales Associate: Robert Croker
Estimated Sales: $20-50 Million
Number Employees: 100-249

26428 Moyno
PO Box 960
Springfield, OH 45501 937-327-3111
Fax: 937-327-3177 mipinfo@moyno.com
www.moyno.com
Manufacturer and exporter of progressing cavity pumps and pinch valves
VP Operations: Norman Shearer
Product Manager: Andy Kosiak
VP Sales: Bob Lepera
Engineering Manager: Dale Parrett
Plant Manager: Todd Brown
Estimated Sales: $20-30 Million
Number Employees: 250-499
Square Footage: 240000
Parent Co: National Oilwell Varco
Brands:
Moyno
R&M

26429 Mp Equip. Co.
4305 Hamilton Mill Rd
Suite 400
Buford, GA 30518 770-614-5355
Fax: 770-614-5303 www.mpequipment.com
Designer and manufacturer of new equipment for the poultry, meat and seafood industries. Also sell pre-owned equipment such as batter mixers and applicators, frying systems, breaders, ovens, formers and reject conveyors.
President: Jerrill Sprinkle
General Manager: Jeff Sprinkle

26430 Mr. Bar-B-Q
445 Winding Rd
Old Bethpage, NY 11804 516-752-0670
Fax: 516-752-0683 800-333-2124
mzemel@mrbarbq.com www.mrbarbq.com
Manufacturer and importer of portable butane stoves, lighters, cookers and buffet and omelet stations
President/CEO: Marc Zemel
Senior VP: Adam Schillen
Director - Sales & Marketing: Wendy Sender
Senior VP -Sales: Jeff Lynch
VP operations: Michael Guadagno
Estimated Sales: $10 - 20 Million
Number Employees: 20-49
Square Footage: 34000
Brands:
Chef Master

26431 Mr. Bar-B-Q
445 Winding Rd
Old Bethpage, NY 11804 516-752-0670
Fax: 516-752-0683 800-333-2124
mzemel@mrbarbq.com www.mrbarbq.com
Designer, manufacturer, importer and distributor of BBQ's tools, accessories and parts
President: Al Zemel
COO: Lu Soguero
VP Sales/Marketing: Marc Zemel
Sales Director: Jeff Lynch
Purchasing Manager: Vera Hora
Estimated Sales: Less than $500,000
Number Employees: 10-19
Square Footage: 4200
Type of Packaging: Consumer, Food Service
Brands:
J B Bar-B-Q
Mr. Bar-B-Q

26432 (HQ)Mr. Ice Bucket
345 Sandford St
New Brunswick, NJ 08901 732-545-0420
Fax: 732-846-3383 sales@mistericebucket.com
www.mricebucket.com
Manufacturer and exporter of vinyl ice buckets and plastic trays and tumblers
President: Fred Haleluk
Information Systems Manager: Elaine Herman
Sales Manager: Sudesh Rajpal
Estimated Sales: $1-2.5 Million
Number Employees: 5-9
Square Footage: 20000
Brands:
Mr. Ice Bucket

26433 (HQ)Mrs. Clark's Foods
740 SE Dalbey Drive
Ankeny, IA 50021 828-685-8821
Fax: 828-685-8495 800-736-5674
info@mrsclarks.com www.mrsclarks.com
Shelf-stable beverages, sauces and dressings
President: Ron Kahrer
QC: Ned Williams
Sales: Julie Southwick
Plant Manager: John Weber
Purchasing: Ron Mathis

Estimated Sales: $450,000
Number of Brands: 12
Number of Products: 50
Square Footage: 240000
Parent Co: AGRI Industries
Type of Packaging: Consumer, Food Service, Private Label
Brands:
Alljuice
Nature's Choice

26434 Mrs. Smiths Bakeries
201 South St
Pottstown, PA 19464 610-326-2600
Fax: 610-327-5221
Manufactures foil baking pans
President: John Feeney
Vice President: Andy Platt
VP Marketing: Tim Vanecourt
Marketing Director: Mark Woepse
General Sales Manager: Jack McDonald
VP Technical Services: Harold Gobble
Purchasing Manager: Hunter Matthews
Estimated Sales: $100-500 Million
Number Employees: 500-999
Parent Co: Mrs. Smiths Bakeries

26435 Mt. Lebanon Awning & Tent Company
P.O.Box 27
Presto, PA 15142 412-221-2233
Fax: 412-221-0204 info@mtlebanonawning.com
www.mtlebanonawning.com
Commercial awnings
President: Robert Campbell
Estimated Sales: $1-2,500,000
Number Employees: 10-19

26436 Mt. Vernon Neon Company
1 Neon Dr
Mt Vernon, IL 62864-6723 618-242-0645
Fax: 618-244-6926 www.everbrite.com
Neon signs
Founder: Charles Wamser
Plant Manager: Steve Porter
Estimated Sales: $10-20 Million
Number Employees: 100-249
Parent Co: Everbright Electric Signs

26437 Muckler Industries, Inc
355 Leesmeadow Rd.
Suite 207
Saint Louis, MO 63125 314-631-7616
Fax: 314-631-7409 800-444-0283
ktechinfo@mucklerktech.com
Manufacturer and exporter of commercial kitchen hoods, baffle filters, waterwash and grease extractors, engineered commercial ventilation and utility distribution systems
National Sales Manager: Douglas Muckler
Sales: Sean Wood
Estimated Sales: $2.5-5 Million
Number Employees: 10
Square Footage: 30000
Type of Packaging: Food Service
Brands:
Challenger
Contender
Edc
Finalist
Performer

26438 (HQ)Muellermist Irrigation Company
2620 S 9th Ave
Broadview, IL 60155 708-450-9595
Fax: 708-450-1403 muellermist@comcast.net
www.muellermist.com
Manufacturer and exporter of underground lawn sprinkling and solar roof cooling systems
President: Tammy Boralli
Estimated Sales: $10 - 20 Million
Number Employees: 50-99
Square Footage: 18000
Type of Packaging: Bulk
Brands:
Fanjet

26439 Mugnaini Imports
11 Hangar Way
Watsonville, CA 95076 831-761-1767
Fax: 831-728-5570 888-887-7206
mugnaini@mugnaini.com www.mugnaini.com
Supplier and importer of wood burning ovens and gas fire
Owner: Andrea Smith
Manager: Ken Belardi
Estimated Sales: Less than $500,000
Number Employees: 1-4

26440 Mulholland
P.O.Box 727
Fort Worth, TX 76101 817-624-1153
Fax: 817-624-1445 www.mulhollands.com
Plastic signs and nameplates
Manager: Dean Brown
Marketing Manager: Sonny Muholland
Estimated Sales: $10-20 Million
Number Employees: 20-49

26441 Mulholland-Harper Company
PO Box C
Denton, MD 21629-0298 410-479-1300
Fax: 410-479-0207 800-882-3052
sales@mulhollandharper.com
www.mulhollandharper.com
Manufacturer and exporter of electric fixtures and signs including electric, plastic, metal and outdoor and exterior identification
President: Patrick Hanrahan
Manufacturing Manager: Michael Conner
Estimated Sales: $5-10 Million
Number Employees: 50-99
Square Footage: 100000

26442 Mulligan Associates
286 Barbados Dr
Mequon, WI 53092 262-242-3911
Fax: 262-242-3944 800-627-2886
gene@mulliganassociates.com
www.mulliganassociates.com
Manufacturer, importer and exporter of high and low volume citric and noncitric juicers, fruit and vegetable peelers, water vending machines and sugar cane and wheat grass extractors
President: Gene Mulligan
CFO: Gene Mulligan
Quality Control: Gene Mulligan
Marketing: Gene Mulligan
Sales Director: Gene Mulligan
General Manager: Bonnie Mulligan
Estimated Sales: $2 Million
Number Employees: 50-99
Square Footage: 15000
Parent Co: AOJ Manufacturing
Type of Packaging: Food Service

26443 Mulligan Sales
P.O.Box 90008
City of Industry, CA 91715-0008 626-968-9621
Fax: 626-369-8452 www.instantmilk.com
Dairy, preservatives, acids, bakery, gums, stabilizers, dehydrated fruits and vegetables
President: Jeff Mulligan
Sales Manager: Dean Lenz
Estimated Sales: $20-50 Million
Number Employees: 10-19
Square Footage: 30000

26444 Mullinix Packages
3511 Engle Rd
Fort Wayne, IN 46809-1194 260-747-3149
Fax: 260-747-1598
bschmitz@mullinixpackages.com
www.mullinixpackages.com
Plastic containers for frozen foods, prepared salads and fresh, refrigerated and controlled atmosphere products
President: Tom Feichter
President, Chief Executive Officer: Gene Gentili
VP Sales/Marketing: Tim Love
Regional Sales Manager, Central US: Brian Schmitz
Operations Manager: Carey Edwards
Estimated Sales: $20-50 Million
Number Employees: 500-999
Square Footage: 118000

26445 Multi-Fill Inc
4343 W 7800 S Ste B
West Jordan, UT 84088 801-280-1570
Fax: 801-280-4341 info@multi-fill.com
www.multi-fill.com
Volumetric filling equipment for the food processor. Line configurations for cooked rice, short/long pasta, vegetables, fruits, ready-to-eat salads (cut, sliced, IQF, blanched, or raw). New technology for the MPF fillers allows forfaster changeover, tighter accuracy's, increased cleanliness of fill, and results in less down time.
President: Richard Price
Sales Director: Bill Allred
Estimated Sales: Below $5 Million
Number Employees: 10-19
Square Footage: 11000

26446 Multi-Kem Corporation
P.O.Box 538
Ridgefield, NJ 07657-0538 201-941-4520
Fax: 201-941-5239 800-462-4425
multikem@mindspring.com www.multikem.com
President: Larry Muhlberg
Estimated Sales: $5 - 10 Million
Number Employees: 250-499

26447 Multi-Pak Corporation
180 Atlantic St
Hackensack, NJ 07601 201-342-7474
Fax: 201-342-6525 sales@multipakcorp.com
www.multipakcorp.com
Manufacturer and exporter of refuse compactors for multi-dwelling units, hotels, hospitals and restaurants; also, attaching containers, odor control equipment and other collection systems. Hopper door repairs, chute cleaning, recyclingsystem
President/QC: Phil Cahill
Chairman of the Board/CFO/R&D: Niel Cavanaugh
Estimated Sales: $2.5 - 5 Million
Number Employees: 20-49
Square Footage: 12000

26448 Multi-Panel Display Corporation
107 Georgia Ave
Brooklyn, NY 11207-2401 718-495-3800
Fax: 718-346-0871 800-439-0879
info@multi-display-panel.com
www.multi-display-panel.com
Display racks and swing type display boards and panels; exporter of display units
President: Tommy Weber
VP: Zipora Weber
Estimated Sales: Less than $500,000
Number Employees: 5-9
Square Footage: 40000

26449 Multi-Vac
21209 Durand Ave
Union Grove, WI 53182-9711 262-878-0366
Fax: 262-878-0368 800-640-4213
www.multivacinc.com
Stainless steel material handling equipment; also, industrial vacuum equipment and dust collectors
President: Wally Haag
V.P.: Margaret Haag
Plant Manager: Dwane Hartlage
Estimated Sales: Below $5 Million
Number Employees: 10-19
Square Footage: 60000
Parent Co: M&W Shops

26450 MultiFab Plastics
60B Tenean Street
Boston, MA 02122-2738 617-287-1411
Fax: 617-287-0299 888-293-5754
info@multifab.com www.multifab.com
Bagel and bulk food bins, acrylic displays, cases, table tents and sign holders
President: Stan Lisowski
Vice President: David Lisowski
Estimated Sales: $1-2.5 Million
Number Employees: 10-19

26451 MultiMedia Electronic Displays
11370 Sunrise Park Dr
Rancho Cordova, CA 95742-6542 916-852-4220
Fax: 916-852-8325 800-888-3007
info@multimedialed.com
www.multimedialed.com
Manufacturer and exporter of programmable electronic signs
President: William Y Hall
CEO: Rex Williams
Marketing Director: Karen Klueh
Operations Manager: Paul Selems
Plant Manager: George Pappas

Estimated Sales: $5 - 10 Million
Number Employees: 20-49
Number of Brands: 5
Number of Products: 200
Parent Co: SignUp
Type of Packaging: Food Service

26452 Multibulk Systems International
6 W 3rd Street
Wendell, NC 27591-8086 919-366-2100
Fax: 919-676-7716
Manufacturer and exporter of bulk bag flexible containers
Sales Manager: John Watson
Estimated Sales: $500,000-$1,000,000
Number Employees: 5-9
Type of Packaging: Private Label
Brands:
Multibulk

26453 Multifeeder Technology
4821 White Bear Pkwy
Saint Paul, MN 55110 651-407-3100
Fax: 651-407-3199 info@multifeeder.com
www.multifeeder.com
Friction Feeders
President: Neal Nordling
Estimated Sales: $.5 - 1 million
Number Employees: 1-4

26454 Multifilm Packaging Corporation
1040 N McLean Blvd
Elgin, IL 60123-1709 847-695-7600
Fax: 847-695-7645 800-837-9727
info@multifilm.com www.multifilm.com
Constantia Multifilm is an integrated manufacturer of flexible packaging solutions for the food, beverage, and confectionery industries.
President/CEO: Olle Mannertorp
Vice President Finance: Robert Tate
Graphics Manager: Terry Piatkowski
New Business Development Manager: Marcus Magnusson
Vice President Sales and Marketing: Chris Rogers
Customer Service: Nancy Jung
Production Manager: Mike Huey
Plant Manager: Dave Rohrschneider
Estimated Sales: Below $5 Million
Number Employees: 10-19
Type of Packaging: Consumer

26455 Multigrains Bakery
117 Water Street
Lawrence, MA 01841 978-691-6100
tom@multigrainbakeries.com
www.multigrainsbakeries.com
Multigrain breads
President/CEO: Joe Faro
EVP/Director R&D: Chuck Brandano
Director of Quality: Adam Gabour
Director of Purchasing: Darren Gaiero

26456 Multiplex Company, Inc.
2100 Future Drive
Sellersburg, IN 4717-1874 812-246-7000
Fax: 636-527-4313 800-787-8880
info@multiplex-beverage.com
www.multiplex-beverage.com
High capacity dispensing systems for beverages including beer; also, water filtration systems
President & Chief Operating Officer: J. Kisling III
Chief Executive Officer: Terry Growcock
Estimated Sales: $34.6 Million
Number Employees: 198
Square Footage: 10000000
Parent Co: Manitowoc Foodservice Group
Brands:
Beermaster
Computap
Intercept
Pr/O-Rox
Re-Fresh

26457 Multipond America
2301 Hutson Road
Green Bay, WI 54303 920-490-8249
Fax: 920-490-8482 sales-us@multipond.com
www.multipond.com
Multipond America Inc, is a wholly owned subsidiary of Multipond, Germany which is the sales and service division of the German based manufacturing company ATOMA. Mutlipond Weighing Technology and mutlihead weigher systems for thepackaging industry stands for the maximum accuaracy, performance, and reliability. We work closely with our customers on continuous improvement in all aspects of our design. We develop and produce customized multihead weigher systems for ourcustomers.
Controller: Paul Plutz
Project Manager: Keven Diederich
Research/Development: John Tuchscherer
VP Sales/Marketing: Frederick Horn
Technical Sales Engineer: Jerry Van Lannen
Estimated Sales: $10 Million
Number Employees: 12

26458 Multisorb Technologies
325 Harlem Road
Buffalo, NY 14224 716-824-8900
Fax: 716-24 -128 info@multisorb.com
www.multisorb.com
Estimated Sales: $1 - 3 Million
Number Employees: 5-9

26459 (HQ)Multisorb Technologies
325 Harlem Rd
West Seneca, NY 14224 716-824-8900
Fax: 716-824-4128 800-445-9890
www.multisorb.com
Manufacturer and exporter of active packaging technologies for food packaging, including odor absorbers, desiccants, and moisture regulators, and odor and other volatile absorbers.
Marketing: Tom Powers
Marketing Communications Coordinator: Kay Krause
Number Employees: 250-499
Square Footage: 170000
Other Locations:
Multisorb Technologies
Orchard Park NY
Brands:
Freshmax
Freshpax
Minipax
Natrasorb
Sorbicap

26460 Multivac
11021 N Pomona Ave
Kansas City, MO 64153 816-891-0555
Fax: 816-891-0622 800-800-8552
muinc@multivac.com www.multivac.com
Wholesaler/distributor, importer and exporter of thermoform, fill and seal packaging equipment; also, tray sealers, chamber vacuum packaging and labeling equipment; sales support services available
President: Michel Defenbau
CEO: Jan Erik Kuhlmann
CFO: Danny Liker
Sales Director: Norm Winkel
Estimated Sales: $50 - 60Million
Number Employees: 100-249
Square Footage: 60000
Parent Co: Multivac Export AG

26461 Mumper Machine Corporation
5081 N 124th St
Butler, WI 53007 262-781-8908
Fax: 262-781-1253
Manufacturer and exporter of vegetable topping and conveying equipment
President: Jordy Mumper
Estimated Sales: $500,000-$1 Million
Number Employees: 5-9

26462 Munck Automation Technology
161 Enterprise Drive
Newport News, VA 23603-1369 757-887-0485
Fax: 757-887-5588 800-777-6862
www.munck.com
Manufacturer and exporter of integrated and automated material handling software and equipment
President: Karl Puehringer
Chief Executive Officer: Remo Brunschwiler
Sr. VP Marketing: Brad Moore
Estimated Sales: $20-50 Million
Number Employees: 10
Square Footage: 50000
Parent Co: Swisslog

26463 Mundial
63 Broadway # 1
Norwood, MA 02062-3558 781-762-0053
Fax: 781-762-0364 800-487-2224
info@mundial-usa.com www.mundialusa.com
Manufacturer, importer and exporter of knives, scissors and shears
President: Adilson Delatorre
CFO: John Keese
Sales VP: Rich Zirpolo
Estimated Sales: $1-2.5 Million
Number Employees: 1-4
Square Footage: 200000
Parent Co: Zivi-Hercules
Type of Packaging: Consumer, Food Service, Bulk

26464 Munson Machinery Company
210 Seward Ave
PO Box 855
Utica, NY 13502 315-797-0090
Fax: 315-797-5582 800-944-6644
info@munsonmachinery.com
www.munsonmachinery.com
Mixers, blenders and size reduction equipment for bulk solid materials.
Partner/VP/COO: Thomas Dalton III
Marketing Manager: Charles Divine
Regional Sales Manager: Darren Woods
Estimated Sales: $5 - 10 Million
Number Employees: 40
Square Footage: 45000

26465 Munters Corporation
79 Monroe St
Amesbury, MA 01913 978-241-1100
Fax: 978-241-1219 800-843-5360
info@munters.us www.munters.com
Manufacturer and exporter of continuous desiccant dehumidification systems
President: Mike Mc Donald
Estimated Sales: $20-50 Million
Number Employees: 250-499
Square Footage: 175000
Parent Co: Munters Corporation

26466 Murata Automated Systems
PO Box 667609
2120 Queen City Drive
Charlotte, NC 28266 704-573-2250
Fax: 704-394-2001 800-428-8469
info@muratec-usa.com www.muratec-usa.com
Automated material handling and control systems including storage and retrieval, guided vehicles, conveyors, monorails, etc.; also, software
President: Masaharu Nishio
Manager Projects: Masato Ohzawa
CFO: Dale Mitchell
Quality Control: Gary Reynoles
Estimated Sales: $.5 - 1 million
Number Employees: 100
Parent Co: Murato Machinery

26467 Murk Brush Company
P.O.Box 726
New Britain, CT 06050-0726 860-249-2550
Fax: 860-249-2550 info@mbcbrush.com
www.mbcbrush.com
Brushes for the food and beverage industry, FDA approved brush construction; specialist in OEM Brush Design
Sales: Dave Hames
Estimated Sales: 500000
Number Employees: 1-4
Number of Products: 2600
Square Footage: 28000
Type of Packaging: Bulk

26468 Murnane Packaging Corporation
607 Northwest Ave
Northlake, IL 60164 708-449-1200
Fax: 708-449-1231
fjmsr@murnanecompanies.com
www.murnanecompanies.com
Packaging materials and paperboard boxes
President: Frank J Murnane Jr
Estimated Sales: $20-50 Million
Number Employees: 50-99

26469 Murnell Wax Company
237 Memorial Drive
Springfield, MA 01104-3228 781-395-1323
Fax: 781-395-8160

Floor polish and cleaners
Estimated Sales: $1-2.5 Million
Number Employees: 6

26470 Murotech Corporation
23820 Hawthorne Boulevard
Torrance, CA 90505-5926 310-791-1776
Fax: 310-791-7252 800-565-6876
muropeeler@aol.com
Manufacturer, exporter and importer of semi-automatic peeling machines for fruits and vegetables including oranges, apples, mangos, cantaloupes and rutabegas
President: Tamotsu Shimizu
Estimated Sales: $500,000-$1 Million
Number Employees: 1-4
Square Footage: 2000
Parent Co: Muro Corporation
Brands:
Muro

26471 (HQ)Murray Envelope Corporation
1500 N Main St
Suite C
Hattiesburg, MS 39401-1911 601-583-8292
Fax: 800-423-7589 murray@netdoor.com
Manufacturer and exporter of filing folders and envelopes
Owner: Marvin Murry
CFO: Joae Comprtallo
R & D: Lenda Wisa
Estimated Sales: Below $5 Million
Number Employees: 1-4

26472 Murray Runin
531 Cascade Court
Mahwah, NJ 07430-2750 201-512-3885
Fax: 201-512-3850 consultrun@aol.com
Management consultant specializing in operational and distribution problem solving
Owner: Murray Runin

26473 Murtech Manufacturing
835 Fairfield Avenue
Kenilworth, NJ 07033-2059 908-245-1556
Fax: 908-245-8707
Grids for bottle tanking
Owner: Mike Blazinsky
Estimated Sales: Less than $500,000
Number Employees: 4

26474 (HQ)Murzan
2909 Langford Rd
Rd. 1-700
Norcross, GA 30071 770-448-0583
Fax: 770-448-0967 murzan@murzan.com
www.murzan.com
Manufacturer and exporter of food processing pumps and drum unloading, turnkey and bag-in-box blending/batching systems
CEO: Alberto Bazan
Estimated Sales: $2,600,000
Number Employees: 20-49

26475 Music City Metals
2633 Grandview Ave
Nashville, TN 37211 615-255-4481
Fax: 615-255-4482 800-251-2674
musiccitymetals@musiccitymetals.net
www.musiccitymetals.net
Cast iron hot plates, gas burners, cooking grids, cast iron and stainless steel burners, grids and grates for gas grills.
President: Bo Richardson
Estimated Sales: $1 - 2.5 Million
Number Employees: 5-9
Brands:
Kings Kooker

26476 Muskegon Awning & Fabrication
2333 Henry St
Muskegon, MI 49441-3097 231-759-0911
Fax: 231-759-3200 800-968-3686
mailman@muskegonawning.com
www.muskegonawning.com
Awnings and canvas related products
President: David Bayne
CEO: Gordon Moen
President: Lora Davis
Sr. Sales Representative: Peter Yonkavit
Estimated Sales: Below $5 Million
Number Employees: 20-49
Square Footage: 57200

26477 Muskogee Rubber Stamp &Seal Company
23549 S 450 Rd
Fort Gibson, OK 74434 918-478-3046
www.muskogeerubberstamp.com
Seals, daters, magnetic signs, price marking inks and rubber stamps
Owner: Sarah Turner
Owner: Paul Owen
Estimated Sales: Less than $500,000
Number Employees: 1-4

26478 Musson Rubber Company
1320 E Archwood Ave
PO Box 7038
Akron, OH 44306 330-773-7651
Fax: 330-773-3254 800-321-2381
info@mussonrubber.com
www.mussonrubber.com
Floor mats
President: Ben Segers
Vice President: Robert Segers
Research & Development: Joe Kostko
Estimated Sales: $5-10 Million
Number Employees: 20-49

26479 Mutual Stamping Manufacturing Company
655 Plains Road
P.O.Box 5060
Milford, CT 06460-1460 203-877-3933
Fax: 203-877-1822 800-735-3933
info@drumsofsteel.com www.drumsofsteel.com
Wine industry stainless steel barrels
President: Jacob Fox
Estimated Sales: $500,000 - $1 Million
Number Employees: 5-9

26480 My Serenity Pond
15009 Held Cir
Cold Spring, MN 56320 320-363-0411
Fax: 320-363-0339 www.myserenitypond.com
Identification products including nameplates, and stamp business forms
President: Marlin Boeckmann
Estimated Sales: $300,000-500,000
Number Employees: 1-4
Square Footage: 40000

26481 My Style
614 NW Street
Raleigh, NC 27603 919-832-2526
Fax: 919-832-1546 800-524-8269
mystylepatio@bellsouth.net
Wholesaler/distributor, importer and exporter of teak, cast aluminum, stainless steel and hardwood outdoor furniture; also, wooden and market umbrellas
Director: Ward Usmar
Owner: Klaus Weihe
Owner: Eik Niemann
Marketing Administrator: Ceri Usmar
Number Employees: 1-4
Square Footage: 6750
Brands:
Caribbean Shade Market Umbrellas
Lingot Stainless & Hardwood Floors
Siesta Shade Market Umbrellas
Teake Furniture

26482 Mycom Group
110-6620 McMillan Way
Richmond, BC V6W 1J7
Canada 604-270-1544
Fax: 604-270-9870 www.mycomcanada.com
Refrigeration equipment and supplies
President: Yasushi Sasaki

26483 Mycom Sales
210 Summit Ave
Suite C12
Montvale, NJ 07645 201-307-9199
Fax: 201-307-1566
Estimated Sales: $1 - 3 Million
Number Employees: 1-4

26484 Mycom/Mayekawa Manfacturing
16825 Ih 35 N
Selma, TX 78154-1223 210-599-4536
Fax: 210-599-4538 www.mycomus.com
Manager: Pete Valdez
Estimated Sales: $1 - 3 Million
Number Employees: 1-4

26485 Myers Container Corporation
21301 Cloud Way
Hayward, CA 94545-1216 510-652-6847
Fax: 510-271-6215 jcutt@myerscontainer.com
www.myerscontainer.com
Manufacturer, exporter and reconditioner of steel drums including aseptic, hot pack food, conical and vegetable oil
President: John Cutt
Chief Executive Officer: Kyle Stavig
CFO: Thomas Holmes
Quality Control: Dana Zanone
Manager Food Sales: Roger Thornton
Estimated Sales: $50-100 Million
Number Employees: 10
Square Footage: 500000
Parent Co: IMACC Corporation
Brands:
Pureliner
Purestack
Purevac

26486 Myers Ice Company
102 N 9th St
Garden City, KS 67846-5350 620-275-5751
Fax: 620-275-8574 800-767-5751
Ice
Co-Owner: Craig Myers
Co-Owner: Carl Myers
Estimated Sales: $1-2.5 Million
Number Employees: 10-19
Brands:
Myers Ice Co.

26487 Myers Restaurant Supply
1599 Cleveland Ave
Santa Rosa, CA 95401 707-570-1200
Fax: 707-542-0350 800-219-9426
brett@myersrestaurantsupply.com
www.myersrestaurantsupply.com
Wholesaler/distributor of restaurant and bar equipment and supplies; serving the food service market
Owner: Rob Myers
CEO: Jon Myers
CFO: Brett Livingstone
Estimated Sales: $2.5 - 5 Million
Number Employees: 20-49
Square Footage: 22000

26488 N&A Manufacturing Spraymatic Sprayers
203 Inman St
Mallard, IA 50562-0064 712-425-3512
Fax: 712-425-3308 spraymatic@iowatelecom.net
Agricultural high pressure hot and cold washers, power scrapers and accessories for high pressure washer systems
President: Virgil Auten
Sales Manager: Troy Auten
Estimated Sales: $1 - 2.5 Million
Number Employees: 5-9
Square Footage: 6700
Brands:
Spraymatic
Vibramatic

26489 N. Wasserstrom & Sons
477 S Front St
Columbus, OH 43215-5677 614-228-6525
Fax: 614-228-8776 800-999-9277
admin@wasserstrom.com www.wasserstrom.com
Manufacturer and exporter of stainless steel, wooden dish and hot food tables and display cases; also, back bar refrigerators, sandwich and salad units, stainless steel steam tables and soda fountain equipment
President: Alan Wasserstrom
Estimated Sales: $50-100 Million
Number Employees: 250-499
Parent Co: Wasserstrom Company
Brands:
Aqua Scrubber

26490 N.A. Krups
7 Reuten Dr
Closter, NJ 07624-2120 201-767-5500
Fax: 201-784-3710 www.krupsusa.com
Brewing devices
President: Mark Navarre
Estimated Sales: $10-20 Million
Number Employees: 50-99

26491 N.G. Slater Corporation
42 W 38th St Rm 200
Suite 1002
New York, NY 10018 212-768-9434
Fax: 212-869-7368 800-848-4621
info@ngslater.com www.ngslater.com
Manufacturer and distributors of custom imprinted and specialties, badges, buttons and emblems
Owner: Robert Slater
VP: Alan Slater
Estimated Sales: $1 - 3,000,000
Number Employees: 5-9

26492 NACCO Materials HandlingGroup
4000 NE Blue Lake Road
Fairview, OR 97024-8710 503-721-6205
Fax: 503-721-1364 www.hysterusa.com
Manufacturer and exporter of forklift trucks
Engineering Manager: Darrel Libby
Estimated Sales: $50-100 Million
Number Employees: 141
Square Footage: 68384
Parent Co: NACCO Industries

26493 NAP Industries
667 Kent Ave
Brooklyn, NY 11211 718-625-4948
Fax: 718-596-4342 877-635-4948
info@napind.com www.napind.com
Manufacturer and exporter of bags including heat sealed, meat, plastic, polyethylene and shopping; also, pressure sensitive tapes
President: Leo Lowy
Estimated Sales: $5-10 Million
Number Employees: 20-49

26494 NAPCO Security Systems
333 Bayview Avenue
Amityville, NY 11701 631-842-9400
Fax: 631-789-9292 salesinfo@napcosecurity.com
www.napcosecurity.com
Manufacturer and exporter of electronic security systems and accessories including control panels
President/Chairman/Secretary: Richard Soloway
SVP, Operations & Finance/Director: Kevin Buchel
SVP, Engineering Development: Michael Carrieri
SVP Corporate Sales & Marketing: Jorge Hevia
Vice President, Sales: Scott Schramme
Purchasing: Edward Daber
Estimated Sales: $71 Million
Number Employees: 957
Square Footage: 90000
Brands:
Magnum Alert

26495 NB Corporation of America
46750 Lakerville Blvd.
Fremont, CA 94538 510-490-1420
Fax: 510-490-1733 888-562-4175
info@nbcorporation.com
www.nbcorporation.com
President: Toru Yamazaki
Estimated Sales: $3 - 5 Million
Number Employees: 10-19

26496 NCR Corporation
3097 Satellite Blvd.
Duluth, GA 3096-5810 937-445-5000
Fax: 937-445-1238 800-225-5627
www.ncr.com
Business forms, bar coded guest checks, folios, ink jet media, printer ribbons, thermal transfer ribbons and paper roll including custom printed and stock
President, Chairman, CEO: William Nuti
Estimated Sales: $5.7 Billion
Number Employees: 25,700

26497 NDC Infrared EngineeringInc
5314 Irwindale Ave
Irwindale, CA 91706 626-960-3300
Fax: 626-939-3870 info@ndcinfrared.com
www.ndcinfrared.com
Manufacturer and exporter of on-line instrumentation for measurement of moisture, fat/oil, protein and caffeine including testers and analyzers
President: Bromley Beadle
Marketing Manager: Raymond Shead
Sales/Marketing Executive: Bill Diltz
Estimated Sales: $20 - 50 Million
Number Employees: 50-99
Square Footage: 50000
Parent Co: Fairey Group

Brands:
Mm710
Tm710

26498 NDS
1740 Joyce Avenue
Columbus, OH 43216 614-294-4931
Fax: 614-299-0538 inforequest@norse.com
www.norse.com
Manufacturer and exporter of ice cream machinery for cups, cones and tubes
CEO: Scot Fulbright
Number Employees: 250-499

26499 NECO
9364 N 45th St
Omaha, NE 68152 402-453-6912
Fax: 402-453-0471 sales@necousa.com
www.necousa.com
Manufacturer and exporter of grain processing and handling equipment including cleaners, augers, spreaders, conveyors, dryers and aeration fans
President: Steve Campbell
VP: Bryan Hayes
Marketing Director: Steve Campbell
Sales Manager: Pat Mcarthy
Manager: William Hiltgen
Plant Manager: Rick Wulf
Purchase Head: Rick Wuls
Estimated Sales: Below $5 Million
Number Employees: 50-99
Square Footage: 150000
Parent Co: GLOBAL Industries

26500 NETZSCH
119 Pickering Way
Exton, PA 19341-1393 610-363-8010
Fax: 610-363-0971 netzsch@netzschusa.com
www.netzschusa.com
Manufacturer and exporter of pumps, filter presses and grinding mills
President: Dr Tilo Stahl
CEO: Dr Tilo Stahl
CFO: Mark Vitcov
VP: John Maguire
R&D: Harry Way
Quality Control: Bill Pye
Marketing: Kelly Rismiller
Public Relations: Kelly Rismiller
Production: Bob Hopple
Plant Manager: Bob Maxwell
Purchasing: Bob Hoffman
Estimated Sales: $30 Million
Number Employees: 100-249
Square Footage: 85000
Parent Co: Netzsch

26501 NHS Labs, Inc
11665 West State St
Star, ID 83669 208-898-4183
Fax: 208-939-5100 888-546-8694
info@nutritionmanufacturer.com
www.nutritionmanufacturer.com
Private label sports drinks, supplements, and energy drinks
CEO: Larry Leach
Square Footage: 74000

26502 NIMCO Corporation
1000 Nimco Drive
Crystal Lake, IL 60014 815-459-4200
Fax: 815-459-8119 info@nimco.com
www.nimco.com
Manufacturer, exporter and importer of gable-top carton packaging machinery for the filling of dairy and food products into environmentally-safe paperboard containers; also, food processing equipment
CEO: Larry G Bachner
CEO: Larry Bachner
Estimated Sales: $5-10 Million
Number Employees: 20-49
Square Footage: 160000
Type of Packaging: Consumer
Brands:
Cap-Pac
Inside-Out Spout
Nimco

26503 NIMCO Corporation
1000 NiMCO Drive
Crystal Lake, IL 60014 815-459-4200
Fax: 815-459-8119 info@nimco.com
www.nimco.com
Form, fill seal for gable-top cartons
CEO: Larry G Bachner
Estimated Sales: $5-10 Million
Number Employees: 20-49

26504 NJM Packaging
56 Etna Rd
Lebanon, NH 03766-1403 603-448-0300
Fax: 603-448-4810 800-432-2990
info@njmpackaging.com
www.njmpackaging.com
Packaging equipment and labeling equipment
President/CEO: Michel Lapierre
Director International Sales: Marc Lapierre
CFO: James Moretti
Vice President Operations Finances: Andre Caumartin
Vice President: Daniel Lapierre
Marketing Director: Marla Stallmann
VP Sales: Mark LaRoche
Human Resources: Todd Savage
Number Employees: 100-249

26505 NJM Packaging
56 Etna Road
Lebanon, NH 03766-1403 603-448-0300
Fax: 603-448-4810 800-432-2990
info@njmpackaging.com
www.njmpackaging.com
Wine industry labeling equipment
President & CEO: Michel Lapierre
CFO: James Moretti
VP: Daniel Lapierre
Marketing: Marla Stallman
Director International Sales: Marc Lapierre
Estimated Sales: $5-10 Million
Number Employees: 20-49

26506 NJM/CLI
8 Plateau Street
Pointe Claire, QC H9R 5W2
Canada 514-630-6990
Fax: 514-695-0801 info@njmcli.com
www.njmcli.com
Manufacturer, exporter and importer of packaging machinery including fillers, cappers, labelers, tablet and capsule counters, etc
President: Michel LaPierre
Director: Charles Lapierre
VP: Dan Lapierre
Marketing: Louise Lafleur
VP Sales: Mark Laroche
Number Employees: 150
Square Footage: 80000
Parent Co: NJM/CLI Packaging Systems International
Brands:
Blipack
Cli
Cremer
New Jersey Machine

26507 NORIT Americas
P.O. Box 790
Marshall, TX 75671 903-923-1000
Fax: 903-938-9701 800-641-9245
mark@norit-americas.com www.norit.com
Activated carbon
Number Employees: 20

26508 NPC Display Group
105 Avenue L
Newark, NJ 07105 973-589-2155
Fax: 973-589-2414 www.onentc.com
Containers including paper, corrugated and solid fiber
President: Dennis Mehiel
CFO: Allen Edelman
Number Employees: 100-249

26509 NRD
2937 Alt Boulevard
PO Box 310
Grand Island, NY 14072-0310 716-773-7634
Fax: 716-773-7744 800-525-8076
sales@nrdinc.com www.nrdstaticcontrol.com
Self-powered static control equipment for labeling, printing, coating and converting
President: Doug Fiegel
Marketing Manager: Colleen Coancy-O'Donnell
Sales Manager: Mike Grimaldi
Number Employees: 50-99

26510 NRD Advanced Static Control Solutions
2937 Alt Boulevard
P.O.Box 310
Grand Island, NY 14072-0310 716-773-7634
Fax: 716-773-7744 800-525-8076
sales@nrdinc.com www.nrdinc.com
President: Doug Fiegel
Number Employees: 50-99

26511 NRD LLC
2937 Alt Boulevard
P.O.Box 310
Grand Island, NY 14072 716-773-7634
Fax: 716-773-7744 800-525-8076
sales@nrdinc.com www.nrdinc.com
Manufacturer and exporter of static control products to increase safety, productivity and product quality including ionizers.
President: Doug Fiegel
Chairman: Sal Alfiero
Director Sales & Marketing: Greg Gumkowski
Production Manager: Kathleen Kowalik
Purchasing Manager: Jim Zoldowski
Number Employees: 50-99
Type of Packaging: Bulk

26512 NS International
800 Kirts Blvd # 300
Troy, MI 48084-4880 248-362-8570
Fax: 248-352-9125 george@nsusa.com
www.ns-international.net
High speed, vertical 3 or 4 sided fill and seal machine for liquids and paste with multi-task programmable control
President: Arthur McMillen
Estimated Sales: $20-50 Million
Number Employees: 1,000-4,999

26513 NSF International
789 N Dixboro Rd
Ann Arbor, MI 48105 734-769-8010
Fax: 734-769-0109 800-673-6275
info@nsf.org www.nsf.org
For 50 years, food safety, facility audits and sanitation conformity assessment programs. ANSI/NSF sampling, testing, labeling certification programs. On site, in-house
President: Kevan P Lawlor
CFO: Kevan Lawlor
General Manager Food Equipment: Joe Phillips
Estimated Sales: $50 - 100 Million
Number Employees: 250-499

26514 NST Metals
723 E Main St
Louisville, KY 40202 502-584-5846
Fax: 502-584-3481 sales@nstmetals.com
www.nstmetals.com
Manufacturer and exporter of food processing equipment, pressure vessels, hoppers, bins and silos
President: Joe Harvey
VP: Kenneth Harvey
VP: Brian Harvey
Estimated Sales: $1-2.5 Million
Number Employees: 5-9
Square Footage: 14000
Type of Packaging: Consumer, Bulk

26515 NSW Corporation
530 Gregory Ave NE
Roanoke, VA 24016 540-981-0362
Fax: 540-345-8421 800-368-3610
netting@nswplastics.com
www.conwedplastics.com
Manufacturer and exporter of bags including vented plastic netting and netting header, onion netting, mesh linings and netting pallet wrap for fruits, vegetables and meats; also, fruit and vegetable juice filter support cartridges
President: Lawrance Ptaschek
Sales Manager: Michael Woldanski
Controller: Del Ramsey
Plant Manager: Charlie Boxler
Estimated Sales: $10 - 20 Million
Number Employees: 50-99
Parent Co: Siemens Corporation
Brands:
Polynet

26516 NSW Corporation
530 Gregory Ave NE
Roanoke, VA 24016 540-981-0362
Fax: 540-345-8421 800-368-3610
netting@nswplastics.com
www.conwedplastics.com
Plastic netting, tower packing, filter tubes and plastic belts
President: Lawrance Ptaschek
CFO: Robert Savage
Quality Control: Daniel Clark
Plant Manager: Charlie Boxler
Estimated Sales: $10 - 20 Million
Number Employees: 50-99

26517 NT Industries
3700 Sandra Street
Franklin Park, IL 60131-1114 773-276-3250
Fax: 773-276-5580 847-451-6500
Manufacturer and designer of fluorescent lighting fixtures, backlighted menu display systems and transparency illuminators

Estimated Sales: $1 - 5 Million
Number Employees: 14

26518 NTN Wireless
6080 Northbelt Dr.
Norcross, GA 30071 770-277-2760
Fax: 770-277-2765 800-637-8639
james.frakes@ntn.com www.cynergyhitech.com
Manufacturer and exporter of wireless server call systems and in-house server, guest and table ready paging systems
President: Mark Degortor
Number Employees: 20-49
Square Footage: 16000
Parent Co: Hysen Technologies
Brands:
Beck 'n Call
Economy Pager
Perfect Pager
Serv 'r Call
Table Turner

26519 NTS
126 Peach State Court
Suite A-C
Tyrone, GA 30290-2744 770-631-0203
Fax: 770-631-0718 nts.inc@netra-systems.com
www.netra-systems.com
CFO: Philippe Jafflin
Estimated Sales: $10 - 20 Million
Number Employees: 20-49

26520 (HQ)NU-Trend Plastic/Corrigan & Company
119 Sewald St
Jacksonville, FL 32204-1731 904-353-5936
Fax: 904-353-2035
Manufacturer and exporter of thermoformed plastic containers, trays and inserts
Owner: Michael Corrigan
CEO: Michael Corrigan Jr
CFO: Mike Corrigan
Estimated Sales: $2-2.5 Million
Number Employees: 7
Square Footage: 15000
Type of Packaging: Consumer, Food Service, Private Label

26521 NYP Corporation
10 Site Rd
Leola, PA 17540 717-656-0299
Fax: 717-656-0350 800-541-0961
padiv@nyp-corp.com www.nyp-corp.com
Plain and printed bags including multi-wall, paper, polyethylene, woven polypropylene, burlap, cotton and mesh; importer of woven polypropylene bags
VP: Christopher LaBelle
VP Sales: Gerald LaBelle
Sales/Customer Service: Don Ament
Manager: Beverley Campbell
Division Manager: Robert Ellis
Purchasing Manager: Katie Gorsuch
Estimated Sales: less than $500,000
Number Employees: 1-4
Square Footage: 15000
Parent Co: NYP Corporation
Type of Packaging: Private Label, Bulk

26522 NYP Corporation
10 Site Rd
Leola, PA 17540 717-656-0299
Fax: 717-656-0350 800-524-1052
padiv@nyp-corp.com www.nyp-corp.com
Manufacturer, exporter and importer of burlap, cotton, woven, polypropylene, paper and plastic bags
Manager: Beverley Campbell
Sales Director: J LaBelle
Purchasing Manager: Katie Gorsuch
Estimated Sales: $5 - 10,000,000
Number Employees: 1-4
Type of Packaging: Consumer, Private Label, Bulk

26523 Nagel Paper & Box Company
3286 Industral Dr
Saginaw, MI 48601 989-753-4405
Fax: 989-753-2493 800-292-3654
info@nagelpaper.com www.nagelpaper.com
Fiber tubes, caps and plugs
Estimated Sales: $1 - 3 Million
Number Employees: 18
Square Footage: 40000
Type of Packaging: Food Service

26524 Nalbach Engineering Company, Inc.
621 E Plainfield Rd
Countryside, IL 60525 708-579-9100
Fax: 708-579-0122 neco@nalbach.com
www.nalbach.com
Manufacturer and exporter of high speed powder fillers for instant coffee, ground coffee and drink mixes; also, plastic bottle unscramblers, container orientors and aerosol filling lines.
President: Matthew Nalbach
CEO: John Nalbach
VP Engineering: David Nowaczyk
VP Marketing: Edward Atwell
VP Sales: Gary Lange
VP Manufacturing: Phil Testa
Estimated Sales: $5 - 10 Million
Number Employees: 51
Square Footage: 280000

26525 Nalge Process Technologies Group
75 Panorama Creek Dr
Rochester, NY 14625-2385 585-586-8800
Fax: 585-586-8431 nnitech@nalgenunc.com
www.nalgenunc.com
Manufacturer and exporter of blowers, fans, fittings, hoses, liquid mixers, pipe tube and hose clamps, safety equipment and tanks
Marketing: Karen Dally
Sales Manager: John Cooling
Product Manager: Greg Felosky
Number Employees: 500-999
Parent Co: Sybron Corporation

26526 Nalge Process Technologies Group
29 Brookfield Drive
Lafayette, NJ 07848-2006 973-579-1313
Fax: 973-579-3908 800-988-4876
Bins
Estimated Sales: $5-10 Million
Number Employees: 38

26527 Naltex
220 E Saint Elmo Rd
Austin, TX 78745 512-447-7000
Fax: 512-447-7444 800-531-5112
sales@naltex.com www.delstarinc.com
Manufacturer and exporter of plastic mesh, heat sealing and header bags; also, case liners
Marketing: Marjorie Wilcox
Product Manager: Susan Emory
Plant Manager: Scott Mc Henry
Estimated Sales: $20-50 Million
Number Employees: 100-249
Square Footage: 110000
Brands:
Flex Net
Mari-Net
Naltex
Shur-Grip
Softliner
Texliner

26528 Naman Marketing
9870 Pineview Avenue
Theodore, AL 36582-7403 251-438-2617
Fax: 251-433-5032
President: George Naman

26529 Namco Controls Corporation
760 Beta Dr # F
Cleveland, OH 44143-2334 440-460-1360
Fax: 440-460-3800 800-626-8324
www.namcocontrols.com
Manufacturer and exporter of packaging and material handling presence and position sensors including photoelectric, laser scanner, rotary cam switch and proximity
President: Alex Joseph
Marketing Manager: Chuck Juda
VP Sales/Marketing: Bob Joyce
Plant Manager: Jamy Robins
Number Employees: 1-4
Parent Co: Danaher Corporation
Other Locations:
Namco Controls Corp.
Herzhorn
Brands:
Cylindicator
Lasernet
Namco
Snap-Lock

26530 Namco Machinery
5421 73rd Pl
Maspeth, NY 11378
Fax: 718-803-0165
Manufacturer and exporter of bottle washing machinery for laboratory glassware
President: Manning E Cole
Sales Manager: R Jackson
Estimated Sales: $3 - 5 Million
Number Employees: 5-9

26531 Nameplates
87 Empire Dr
St Paul, MN 55103-1856 651-228-1522
Fax: 651-228-1314
Badges, medals, name plates, signs, stamps, tags and labels
President: Gerald Mellgren
Estimated Sales: $2.5-5 Million
Number Employees: 50-99
Parent Co: St. Paul Stamp Works

26532 Napa Fermentation Supplies
P.O.Box 5839
Napa, CA 94581-0839 707-255-6372
Fax: 707-255-6462 napafermentation@aol.com
www.napafermentation.com
Wine industry fermentation supplies
Owner: Pat Watkins
*Estimated Sales:*less than $500,000
Number Employees: 1-4

26533 Napa Valley Bung Works
151 Camino Dorado
Napa, CA 94558-6213 707-963-0241
Fax: 707-963-0241
Bung hole stoppers
Estimated Sales: $1 - 5 Million
Number Employees: 5-9

26534 Napa Wooden Boxes
P.O.Box 850
Napa, CA 94559-0850 707-224-6400
Fax: 707-224-1613 sales@napawoodenbox.com
www.napawoodenbox.com
Wooden gift boxes, wooden specialty packaging, wooden displays
President: Greg Chase
Estimated Sales: $5-10 Million
Number Employees: 20-49

26535 Napco Graphics Corporation
200 Covington Drive
Bloomingdale, IL 60108-3105 630-529-2900
Fax: 630-529-4395 ngsales@napcographics.com
www.napco.com
Flexographic printing, four-color process labels, thermal labels, thermal ribbons, custom pressure-sensitive labels
President: Geno Napolitano
Estimated Sales: $10-20 Million
Number Employees: 50-99

26536 Napoleon Appliance Corporation
214 Bayview Drive
Barrie, ON L4N 4Y8
Canada 705-726-4278
Fax: 705-725-2564 866-820-8686
wecare@napoleonproducts.com
www.napoleongrills.com
Manufacturer and exporter of gas grills
President: Wolfgang Schroeter
VP: Ingrid Schroeter
Research & Development: Steve Schwartz
Quality Control: Steve Taylor
Marketing/Sales: David Blain
Plant Manager: Michael Pulfer
Purchasing Manager: Lynda Allen
Number Employees: 100
Number of Brands: 11
Square Footage: 600000
Parent Co: Wolf Steel
Brands:
Elegance
Emerald
Horizon
Lifestyle
Napoleon
Premiere
Prestige
Signature
Ultrachef

26537 NaraKom
PO Box 368
Peapack, NJ 07977-0368 908-234-1776
Fax: 908-234-0964 info@narakom.com
www.narakom.com
Distributor of Nara milling, sizing, coating, and powder surface modification technology in the Americas
President: C Komline
Number Employees: 20-49
Parent Co: Komline-Sanderson Engineering Corporation

26538 Nashua Corporation
44 Franklin Street
Nashua, NH 03064-2665 603-661-2004
Fax: 603-880-5671 info@amstock.com
www.nashua.com
Manufacturer and exporter of industrial tape and labels
President: Andrew Albert
CFO: John Petenaude

26539 Nashua Corporation
3838 S 108th St
Omaha, NE 68144 402-397-3600
Fax: 402-392-6080 800-662-7482
mjarrett@nashualabel.com www.nashua.com
Manufacturer and exporter of computer and pressure sensitive labels
President: Andrew Albert
CFO: John Patenaude
VP: Michael Jarrett
VP: Mike Jarrutt
Number Employees: 100-249

26540 Nashville Display Manufacturing Company
1415 Elm Hill Pike
Nashville, TN 37210-4532 615-743-2900
Fax: 615-244-4368 800-251-1150
dissales@nashvillewire.com
www.nashvilledisplay.com
Manufacturer and exporter of displays and merchandisers for retail products
President: David L Rollins
CFO: Jeff McCeann
VP: E White
Quality Control: Charles Brittain
R & D: Juris Leikartt
Sales Manager: Richard Hornsay
Office Manager: Jere Lane
Estimated Sales: $10-20 Million
Number Employees: 20-49
Square Footage: 800000

26541 Nashville Wire Products
295 Driftwood St
Nashville, TN 37210 615-743-2480
Fax: 615-255-8349 oemsales@nashvillewire.com
www.nashvillewire.com
Wire oven and warming racks and barbecue grids
President: David L Rollins
Shipping Manager: Levon Mathis
Division Manager: Steven Rollins
Plant Manager: Roy Binkley
Estimated Sales: $20-50 Million
Number Employees: 10-19
Square Footage: 140000
Parent Co: Nashville Wire Products Manufacturing Company

26542 Nashville Wraps
242 Molly Walton Dr
Hendersonville, TN 37075 615-338-3200
Fax: 800-646-0046 800-547-9727
info@nashvillewraps.com
www.nashvillewraps.com
Bags and bows, gift wrap, tissue paper, ribbon, candy boxes, food packaging, custom printing and eco-friendly retail packaging
Marketing Director: James Meadows
Estimated Sales: $40 Million
Number Employees: 38

26543 Natale Machine & Tool Company
339 13th St
Carlstadt, NJ 07072 201-933-5500
Fax: 201-933-8146 800-883-8382
info@circle-d.com www.circle-d.com
Manufacturer and exporter of emergency lighting including flash, flood and spot lights; also, HID, quartz and commercial lighting available
President: Dominick Natale
CEO: Dominick Natale
VP: Lynn Natale
Sales: John Cocozzo
Production/Plant Manager/Purchasing: John Cocozzo
Estimated Sales: $3 - 5 Million
Number Employees: 10-19
Square Footage: 15000
Brands:
Circle D Lights
Streamlight

26544 Nation/Ruskin
206 Progress Dr
Montgomeryville, PA 18936 267-654-4000
Fax: 267-654-4010 800-523-2489
Barbara.Freed@nationruskin.com
www.nationruskin.com
Natural and synthetic sponges; also, cloths and brushes
President: Raymond Adolf
VP Sales: John Holcombe
VP Sales: Stan Ruskin
Estimated Sales: $1 - 3 Million
Number Employees: 10-19
Brands:
Ez-One

26545 National Air Vibrator Company
11929 Brittmoore Park Dr
Houston, TX 77041-7226 832-467-3636
Fax: 832-467-3800 800-231-0164
sales@navco.us www.navco.us
Manufacturer and exporter of material handling equipment including pneumatic and electric vibrators
President: Mark Neundorfer
Marketing Manager: Ben Snider
Number Employees: 20-49

26546 National Band Saw Company
25322 Avenue Stanford
Santa Clarita, CA 91355 661-294-9552
Fax: 661-294-9554 800-851-5050
harley@nbsparts.com www.nbsparts.com
Manufacturer, exporter and wholesaler/distributor of replacement parts for meat slicing and cutting machinery; importer of slicing knives, tenderizers and bread slicing and patty-making machines; wholesaler/distributor of office andshipping supplies
President: Harley Frank
VP: Chris Tuttle
R & D: Ron Voytek
Director of IT Computer Services: Jason Jasperson
Production: Ron Voytek
Estimated Sales: Below $5 Million
Number Employees: 17
Square Footage: 12200
Type of Packaging: Consumer, Food Service, Private Label, Bulk

26547 National Bar Systems
16571 Burke Ln
Huntington Beach, CA 92647-4537 714-848-1688
Fax: 714-848-2788 info@nbsmfg.
www.nbsmfg.com

Manufacturer and exporter of stainless steel under-bar equipment including sinks, work tables and ice storage equipment
President: Johnny Lee
VP: John Ashkarian
CFO: Joe Kim
Estimated Sales: $5 - 10 Million
Number Employees: 5-9

26548 National Cart Company
3125 Boschertown Rd
Saint Charles, MO 63301 636-947-3800
Fax: 636-723-4477 sales@nationalcart.com
www.nationalcart.com
Manufacturer and exporter of oven racks, bun pans and pan tray carts
CEO: Robert Unnerstall
Estimated Sales: $20-50 Million
Number Employees: 100-249
Square Footage: 100000

26549 National Chemicals
105 Liberty St
PO Box 32
Winona, MN 55987 507-454-5640
Fax: 877-858-4141 800-533-0027
info@natlchem.com
www.nationalchemicals.com
Detergents, sanitizers and cleaners for food service use
Chairman of the Board: Louis Landman
Estimated Sales: $10-20 Million
Number Employees: 10-19
Number of Brands: 21
Number of Products: 46

26550 National Companies
15505 Cornet St
Santa Fe Springs, CA 90670-5511 562-926-4511
Fax: 562-926-0222 800-221-9149
markm@natcos.com www.natcos.com
President: Gregory Mitchell
Estimated Sales: $5 - 10 Million
Number Employees: 20-49

26551 National Computer Corporation
211 Century Drive
Suite 100-B
Greenville, SC 29607 866-944-5164
Fax: 864-235-7688 sales@nccusa.com
www.nccusa.com
Manufacturer, importer and exporter of point of sale systems
President: Douglas Harris Jr
Estimated Sales: $5 - 10,000,000
Number Employees: 10-19

26552 National Construction Services
PO Box 820
Frazer, PA 19355 610-647-8050
Fax: 610-647-8540 800-557-8050
www.ncscos.com
President: Lee Krow
CFO: Lee Krow
R&D: Lee Krow
Quality Control: Lee Krow
Estimated Sales: $5 - 10 Million
Number Employees: 10-19

26553 National Construction Technologies Group
4967 Kensington Gate
Excelsior, MN 55331-9345 952-474-7126
Fax: 952-474-7370 info@nctg.org
www.nctg.org
Specialized concrete surfaces including surface preparation, surface coatings, concrete construction
Estimated Sales: $1 - 5 Million

26554 National Controls Corporation
1725 Western Dr
West Chicago, IL 60185-1880 630-231-5900
Fax: 630-231-1377 800-323-5293
webmaster@ametek.com
www.nationalcontrols.com
Manufacturer and exporter of cooking computers, electronic timers and thermometers
VP: Tim Croal
General Manager: Nick Hoilds
Sales/Marketing Executive: John Meggesin
Sales Manager: Gerald Brown
Purchasing Manager: Cathy Porch
Number Employees: 30
Parent Co: Ametek

Brands:
Ncc

26555 (HQ)National Conveyor Corporation
2250 Yates Ave
Commerce, CA 90040 323-725-0355
Fax: 323-725-1440 info@natconcorp.com
www.natconcorp.com
Manufacturer and exporter of utensil washers, conveyor equipment, dish handling systems and waste reduction systems
President: Jared Ufland
Customer Service Manager: Luis Vargas
Engineer Manager: Joseph Marin
Estimated Sales: $2.5 - 5 Million
Number Employees: 10-19
Square Footage: 30000
Type of Packaging: Food Service
Brands:
Power Dishtable
Roto-Stak
Uni-Band

26556 National Datacomputer
900 Middlesex Tpke
Suite 5-1
Billerica, MA 01821 978-663-7677
Fax: 978-667-1869 sales@ndcomputer.com
ww2.ndcomputer.com
Computer systems: handheld systems, route accounting, sales automation
CEO: William B Berens
Estimated Sales: $10-25 Million
Number Employees: 5-9

26557 National Discount Textiles
2210 Defoor Hills Road NW
Atlanta, GA 30318 404-351-1630
Fax: 800-433-9562 textilemfg@aol.com
Owner: Murray Shelton

26558 National Distributor Services
3033 S Parker Road
Suite 400
Aurora, CO 80014-2921 303-755-4411
Fax: 303-755-4545 www.ndscompanies.com
Manufacturer and exporter of forklifts
President: B Anthony Reed
CEO: Tony Reed
Number Employees: 50

26559 National Drying Machinery Company
2190 Hornig Rd
Philadelphia, PA 19116 215-464-6070
Fax: 215-464-4096 info@nationaldrying.com
www.nationaldrying.com
Manufacturer and exporter of thermal processing equipment including dehydrators, dryers, ovens, roasters, blanchers, coolers and multi-tier and multi-pass conveyor systems and feeders
President: Richard Parkes
Director Marketing/Sales: Paul Branson
Director: Richard Eckard
Estimated Sales: $20-50 Million
Number Employees: 100-249
Square Footage: 80000
Parent Co: Apollo Sheet Metal

26560 National Emblem
PO Box 5325
Carson, CA 90749-5325 310-515-5055
Fax: 310-515-5966 800-877-5325
national1@aol.com www.nationalemblem.com
Embroidered and screen printed emblems, caps, keyrings and woven labels
President: Milton Lubin Sr
CFO: Alicia Bsiez-Sounds
National Sales Manager: Marvin Grimm
Sales Director: Milton Lobin, Jr.
Estimated Sales: $20 - 50 Million
Number Employees: 250-499

26561 National Embroidery Service
3390 E Main Rd
Portsmouth, RI 02871 401-683-4724
Fax: 401-683-0012 800-227-1451
sales@nationalembroidery.com
www.nationalembroidery.com

Custom embroidered uniforms, hats, shirts, vests, chef coats and aprons
President and R&D: Dale Wood
Quality Control: Eileen Wood
CEO and CFO: Dale B Wood
Estimated Sales: Less than $500,000
Number Employees: 45
Square Footage: 5000

26562 National Energy Team
P.O. Box 562
Cedar Falls, IA 50613 319-231-0857
Fax: 877-553-0187 888-841-6987
info@nationalenergyconsultants.com
www.nationalenergyconsultants.com
Energy consulting, procurement, management and consolidated billing capabilities

26563 (HQ)National Equipment Corporation
801 E 141st St
Bronx, NY 10454 718-585-0200
Fax: 718-993-2650 800-237-8873
sales@unionmachinery.com
www.unionmachinery.com
Manufacturer, importer and exporter of used and reconditioned food processing and packaging equipment
VP: Arthur Greenberg
VP: Richard Greenberg
VP: Charles Greenberg
Number Employees: 20-49
Square Footage: 1800000
Other Locations:
National Equipment Corp.
Naucalpan

26564 National FABCO Manufacturing
12927 Gravois Rd
St Louis, MO 63127-1714 314-842-4571
Fax: 314-842-8088
Custom designed food serving equipment including counters, sinks, refrigerated carts, hoods, countertops and tables
President: John Gates
VP: Frank Ruggeri
Estimated Sales: $10 - 20 Million
Number Employees: 20-49
Square Footage: 5500
Type of Packaging: Food Service, Private Label
Brands:
Cleveland
Groen
Hatc
Hubort
Southbend
Thermobend
Traulsen
Victory

26565 National Foam
180 Sheree Blvd # 3900
Exton, PA 19341-1272 610-363-1400
Fax: 610-524-9073 webmaster@kidde-fire.com
www.kidde-fire.com
Manufacturer and exporter of foam fire extinguishing chemicals and equipment
Manager: Bobby Nelson
CFO: Larry Mansfield
Estimated Sales: $20 - 50 Million
Number Employees: 100-249
Parent Co: Racal-Chubb

26566 National Food Laboratory
2441 Constitution Drive
Livermore, CA 94551 925-551-4209
Fax: 925-243-0112 hillj@thenfl.com
www.thenfl.com
Consulting laboratory specializing in market research, sensory analysis, process and product development, analytical services and pilot plant services
President: Kevin Buck
VP Chemistry: Julie Hill
Division Manager: Rupinder Jaura
Estimated Sales: $10 - 20 Million
Number Employees: 50-99
Square Footage: 60000
Parent Co: National Food Processors Association

26567 **National Food ProcessorsAssociation**
1350 i St NW Ste 300
Washington, DC 20005 800-355-0983
Fax: 202-639-5932 fpi@nfpa-food.org
www.nfpa-food.org
President: John Cady
CEO: Cal Dooley
Estimated Sales: $5 - 10 Million
Number Employees: 1-4

26568 **National Food Product Research Corporation**
318 Main Street
P.O.Box 419
West Newbury, MA 01985-0519 978-363-2144
Fax: 978-363-2073 800-363-2144
info@nfpresearch.com www.nfpresearch.com
Consultant providing marketing research for food, products, equipment and services
Owner: John Sibley
Executive VP: John Sibley
Estimated Sales: Below $5 Million
Number Employees: 10-19

26569 **National Hotpack**
3538 Main Street
Stone Ridge, NY 12484 845-255-5000
Fax: 845-687-7481 800-431-8232
hotpack@spindustries.com www.hotpack.com
Hotpack manufactures and sells enviromental rooms and chambers, stability rooms and chambers, humidity rooms and chambers, glassware washers and dryers, vacuum ovens, sterilizers and autoclaves, C-O2 incubators, general purposeincubators, ovens, refrigerators, freezers
President/CEO: Bill Downs
CFO: Michael Bonner
Marketing: Shireen Scott
Sales: James Shiever
Estimated Sales: $65 Million
Number Employees: 100-249
Square Footage: 70000
Parent Co: SP Industries
Brands:
Heinicke
Hotpack
National Labortory Products
Oem Products

26570 **National Instrument Company**
4119 Fordleigh Rd
Baltimore, MD 21215 410-764-0900
Fax: 410-951-2093 800-526-1301
jrosen@filamatic.com www.filamatic.com
Manufacturer and exporter of liquid filling, capping and turnkey packaging equipment
CEO: Robert Rosen
VP Marketing/Sales: Jim Striese
Estimated Sales: $10-20 Million
Number Employees: 50-99
Brands:
Capamatic
Dial-A-Fill
Econofil
Filamatic
Synchromat

26571 **National Interchem Corporation**
13750 Chatham Street
Blue Island, IL 60406-3218 773-638-5100
Fax: 773-638-8769 800-638-6688
nicorp@msn.com
Manufacturer and exporter of industrial cleaning and maintenance chemicals
Director Sales: Greg Fishman
Estimated Sales: $2.5-5 Million
Number Employees: 10-19

26572 **National Label Company**
2025 Joshua Rd
Lafayette Hill, PA 19444 610-825-3250
Fax: 610-834-8854 www.nationallabel.com
Manufacturer and exporter of pressure sensitive labeling equipment and labels
CEO: James H Shacklett Iii
Estimated Sales: $50-100 Million
Number Employees: 250-499
Type of Packaging: Bulk

26573 **National Manufacturing Company**
507 J St
Lincoln, NE 68508 402-475-3400
Fax: 402-742-2234
gwyn.childress@tmcousa.com
www.tmco-usa.com
Cereal chemists' laboratory equipment
Presiden/CFO: Roland Temme
Quality Control/R&D: John Alberf
Manager: John Albers
Estimated Sales: $10 - 20 Million
Number Employees: 50-99
Parent Co: TMCO
Brands:
Mixograph

26574 **National Manufacturing Company**
507 J St
Lincoln, NE 68508 402-475-3400
Fax: 402-742-2234
gwyn.childress@tmcousa.com
www.tmco-usa.com
Manufacturer and exporter of displays
President: Roland Temme
VP Manufacturing: Joe Smith
Estimated Sales: $10-20 Million
Number Employees: 50-99

26575 **National Marker Company**
100 Providence Pike
North Smithfield, RI 02896 401-762-9700
Fax: 401-762-1010 800-453-2727
sales@nationalmarker.com
www.nationalmarker.com
Plastic safety signs
President: Michael Black
Marketing Director: Patricia O'Hara
Estimated Sales: $5 - 10 Million
Number Employees: 20-49

26576 **National Marking Products, Inc.**
5606 Greendale Road
Richmond, VA 23228 804-266-7691
Fax: 804-266-6110 800-482-1553
info@nationalmarkingproducts.com
www.nationalmarkingproducts.com
Promotional items including rubber stamps, plastic signs, shipping supplies, bronze tablets, labels, tags and awards
President: Rick Reinhard
President: Richard Reinhard
Manager: Brenda Puryear
Estimated Sales: Below $5 Million
Number Employees: 20-49
Square Footage: 30000

26577 **National Measures Polymers**
7920 W. 215th Street
Lakeville, MN 55044-9015 952-469-4977
Fax: 952-469-2051 800-328-4577
scoops@nationalmeasures.com
www.nationalmeasures.com
Plastic measures for powdered and liquid products
President: Dennis Anderson
CFO: Mac Moore
Sales Manager: Mac Moore
Production/Advertising: Wes Anderson
Number Employees: 50-99
Type of Packaging: Bulk

26578 **National Menuboard**
4302 B St NW # D
Auburn, WA 98001 253-859-6068
Fax: 253-859-8412 800-800-5237
sales@nationalmenuboard.com
www.nationalmenuboard.com
Menu boards including illuminated, nonilluminated, indoor and outdoor
President: Dave Medzegian
Sales Representative: Wendi Adsley
Estimated Sales: Below $5 Million
Number Employees: 5-9
Square Footage: 40000

26579 **National Metal Industries**
203 Circuit Avenue
West Springfield, MA 01089-4016 413-785-5861
Fax: 413-737-2309 800-628-8850
Manufacturer and exporter of metal stamps and parts for food processing equipment
Sales Manager: Bryan Costello
Estimated Sales: $10-20 Million
Number Employees: 50-99
Parent Co: Standex International Corporation

26580 **National Package SealingCompany**
10791 SE Skyline Drive
Santa Ana, CA 92705-7413 714-630-1505
Fax: 714-632-3217 custserv@npsdispensers.com
www.npsdispensers.com
Manufacturer and exporter of electric and manual dispensers for gummed carton sealing tapes and labels
President: William Amneus
Marketing Director: Fay Amneus
Estimated Sales: $2.5-5 Million
Number Employees: 19
Square Footage: 80000

26581 **National Packaging**
PO Box 4798
Rumford, RI 02916-0798 401-434-1070
Fax: 401-438-5203 nationalpkg@ids.net
www.multiwall.com
Manufacturer and exporter of cloth winding reels and single faced corrugated paper
President: Charles M Dunn
Estimated Sales: $20-50 Million
Number Employees: 10-19
Parent Co: Real Reel Corporation

26582 **(HQ)National Pen Corporation**
12121 Scripps Summit Dr.
San Diego, CA 92131 858-675-3000
info@nationalpen.com
www.nationalpen.com
Ink pens
Chief Executive Officer: Dave Thompson
Chief Financial Officer: Rich Obrigawitch
SVP, North America Direct: Ron Childs
Number Employees: 250-499

26583 **National Plastic Companyof California**
15505 Cornet St
Santa Fe Springs, CA 90670-5511 562-926-4511
Fax: 562-926-0222 800-221-9149
mra@natcos.com
Menu covers, loose leaf binders, wine lists, check presenters, transparent price card holders and pad holders; exporter of menu covers
President: Gregory Mitchell
Marketing Director: Mark Anderson
Sales Director: Brian Bromm
Office Manager: Bryan Carr
Plant Manager: Benjamin Jimenez
Estimated Sales: $5-10 Million
Number Employees: 20-49
Square Footage: 18000
Parent Co: National Plastic Company of California

26584 **National Poly Bag Manufacturing Corporation**
220 West Street
Brooklyn, NY 11222-1350 718-629-9800
Fax: 718-629-0265
Plastic bags and film
Estimated Sales: $1 - 5 Million
Number Employees: 12

26585 **National Printing Converters**
4310 Bonavita Dr
Encino, CA 91436 818-906-7936
jobs@ncplabels.com
Manufacturer and exporter of data processing printed, pressure sensitive, laser, on-line pattern adhesive and vinyl shelf marking labels and shelf talkers
President: Brain Buckley
Chairman: Robert Buckley
Operations Manager: Richard Atkins
Estimated Sales: $.5 - 1 million
Number Employees: 1-4
Square Footage: 55000
Brands:
Label Data-Set

26586 **National Provisioner**
7300 N. Linder Ave.
Skokie, IL 60077-3217 847-763-9534
Fax: 847-763-9538 NP@halldata.com
www.provisioneronline.com

26587 (HQ)National Refrigeration
539 Dunksferry Rd
Bensalem, PA 19020-5908 215-244-1400
Fax: 215-244-9579 800-523-7138
tam@continental-refrig.com
www.nrproducts.com
Refrigeration and air conditioning equipment
CEO: Brian Kelly
Marketing Director: Tara Montvydas
Sales Manager: Mike Coyle
Operations Manager: Ed Carruthers
Purchasing Manager: Amy Ahern
Estimated Sales: $50-100 Million
Number Employees: 100-249
Square Footage: 87000
Brands:
Continental Refrigerator
Hvac

26588 National Restaurant Supply Company
2513 Comanche Rd NE
Albuquerque, NM 87107 505-883-1999
Fax: 505-884-3549 800-351-0094
tboyden@nrsupply.com www.nrsupply.com
Wholesaler/distributor of restaurant supplies and equipment; serving the food service market
Sales Director: Russell Shupe
Operations Manager: Rick Levis
Manager: Rick Levis
Purchasing Manager: Phillip Zamora
Estimated Sales: $10 - 20 Million
Number Employees: 20-49

26589 National Scoop & Equipment Company
PO Box 325
Spring House, PA 19477-0325 215-646-2040
Manufacturer, wholesaler/distributor and importer of pails, buckets, scales, scoops, skimmers, dippers, disposable paper clothing, sinks and trucks
Manager: Ken Johnson

26590 National Sign Corporation
1255 Westlake Ave N
Seattle, WA 98109 206-282-0700
Fax: 206-285-3091
contacts@nationalsigncorp.com
www.nationalsigncorp.com
Plastic and neon signs; also, installation and maintenance services available
President: Timothy Zamberlin
Estimated Sales: $5-10 Million
Number Employees: 20-49
Square Footage: 30000

26591 National Sign Systems
4200 Lyman Ct
Hilliard, OH 43026 614-850-2540
Fax: 614-850-2552 800-544-6726
sales@natsignsys.com
www.nationalsignsystems.com
Signs, menu systems, copy strips and HVAC equipment screens
President: James Cullinan
CFO: Paul Saokendach
VP Sales/Marketing: Paul Falkenbach
Estimated Sales: $10 - 20,000,000
Number Employees: 100-249
Square Footage: 155460

26592 National Stabilizers
1846 Business Center Dr
Duarte, CA 91010-2997 626-359-4584
Fax: 626-359-4586 natstab@earthlink.com
Stabilizers
President: Robert Burger
Quality Control: Raivo Partma
VP Sales: Robert Burger
Sales/Purchasing: Tomas Martinez
Estimated Sales: $2.5-5 Million
Number Employees: 5 to 9
Brands:
Stabak
Stacol

26593 National Steel Corporation
100 Quality Drive
Ecorse, MI 48229-1850 734-953-3603
Fax: 734-953-3601
Tin plate and chromium coated steel for production of containers, ends, closures and crowns

26594 National Stock Sign Company
1040 El Dorado Ave
Santa Cruz, CA 95062 831-476-2020
Fax: 831-476-1734 800-462-7726
nationalstock@sbcglobal.net
www.nationalstocksign.com
Safety, parking and no smoking signs
President: Henrietta Cooper
Marketing Manager: Lorraine Kirkpatrick
General Manager: Joel Kirkpatrick
Estimated Sales: $1 - 3 Million
Number Employees: 10-19
Square Footage: 15000
Brands:
Nassco

26595 National Tape Corporation
5128 Storey Street
New Orleans, LA 70123-5320 504-733-8020
Fax: 504-734-8751 800-535-8846
natape@aol.com www.nationaltape.com
Manufacturer and exporter of pressure sensitive labels and tapes including masking, duct, electrical, pressure sensitive and marking
VP Sales: Joel Teachworth
VP: Robert Wiswall
Number Employees: 100
Square Footage: 520000

26596 National Time RecordingEquipment Company
64 Reade St
New York, NY 10007 212-227-3310
Fax: 212-227-5353 info@nationaltime.net
www.nationaltime.net
Manufacturer and exporter of time clocks, time stamps and thermometers
VP: K Kelly
Estimated Sales: $5-10 Million
Number Employees: 10-19

26597 National Towelette Company
1726 Woodhaven Drive
Bensalem, PA 19020 215-245-7300
Fax: 215-245-7390 info@towelettes.com
www.towelettes.com
Individually wrapped moist towelettes
President: Tim Brock
CFO: Tim Bro
Number Employees: 10-19
Square Footage: 25000

26598 National Velour
36 Bellair Ave
Warwick, RI 02886 401-737-8300
Fax: 401-738-7418 service@nationalvelour.com
www.nationalvelour.com
Manufacturer and exporter of flock for packaging and displays; also, custom flocking and stock lines available
President: Oscar Der Manouelian
Estimated Sales: $5-10 Million
Number Employees: 20-49

26599 National-Purity
6840 Shingle Creek Pkwy Ste 23
Brooklyn Center, MN 55430 612-672-0022
Fax: 612-672-0027
Soaps, detergents, cleaning agents and soap based industrial lubricants
President: John Spillane
National Account Manager: Bill Stark
Field Account Manager: Sean Spillane
Estimated Sales: $20-50 Million
Number Employees: 20-49
Square Footage: 52000

26600 Nationwide Boiler Incorporated
42400 Christy Street
Fremont, CA 94538 510-490-7100
Fax: 510-490-0571 800-227-1966
info@nationwideboiler.com
www.nationwideboiler.com
President: Jeffrey Shallcross
Chairman Of The Board: Richard Bliss
Estimated Sales: $5 - 10 Million
Number Employees: 20-49

26601 Nationwide Pennant & Flag Manufacturing
7325 Reindeer Trl
San Antonio, TX 78238-1214 210-684-3524
Fax: 210-680-2329 800-383-3524
sales@napmfg.com www.napmfg.com
Manufacturer and exporter of pennants, flags, flagpoles, banners and decals
President: Donald Engelhardt
CEO: Rick Sutton
Sales: Joe Pyland
Estimated Sales: $10-20 Million
Number Employees: 100-249
Square Footage: 60000

26602 Nationwide Wire & BrushManufacturing
411 Evergreen Drive
Lodi, CA 95242-4629 209-334-9660
Fax: 209-334-9432 nwwb@inreach.com
www.nationwidebrush.com
Power brooms and brushes for the food industry
President: Richard Savage
Sales Manager: Jim Olvera
Estimated Sales: Below $5 Million
Number Employees: 35

26603 Native Lumber Company
8 N Branford Road
Wallingford, CT 06492-2712 203-269-2625
Wooden pallets
Co-Owner: Dick Smith
Estimated Sales: $2.5-5 Million
Number Employees: 9

26604 Natural Marketing Institute
272 Ruth Rd
Harleysville, PA 19438 215-513-7300
Fax: 215-513-1713 steve@nmisolutions.com
www.nmisolutions.com
Consultant to food industry specializing in consumer research, market analysis and brand and product development.
President: Mary Ellen Molyneaux
Managing Partner: Steve French
Number Employees: 30
Square Footage: 10000
Parent Co: Mic-Ellen Associates

26605 Nature Most Laboratories
Trigo Business Park
60 Trigo Drive
Middletown, CT 06457-6157 860-346-8991
Fax: 860-347-3312 800-234-2112
sales@naturemost.com www.naturemost.com
Manufacturer, importer and exporter of products, vitamins, oils, minerals, herbal supplements
President: Robert Trigo
Marketing: Sam Schwartz
Sales: Donna Platnum
Operations: Fred Wuschner
Estimated Sales: $5 - 10 Million
Number Employees: 20-49
Number of Brands: 3
Number of Products: 300
Square Footage: 80000
Type of Packaging: Consumer, Private Label
Brands:
Naturemost Labs
Trigo Labs

26606 Nature Soy, Inc.
713 N 10th Street
Philadelphia, PA 19123 215-765-8889
support@naturesoy.com
www.naturesoy.com
Manufacturer/supplier of healthy soy and vegetarian products to the ethnic market
President: Yat Wen
CEO: Gene He
EVP: Fenjin He
Estimated Sales: $2.4 Million
Number Employees: 17
Square Footage: 35000

26607 Nature's Own
11 Fred Roddy Avenue
Attleboro, MA 02703 508-399-8690
Fax: 508-399-8693 130- 13- 612
www.naturesown.com.au

Natural hardwood charcoal and grilling/smoking woods; importer of herbwoods; exporter of hardwood charcoal
President/Owner: Don Hysko
VP: Holly Hysko
Sales Manager: Dana Bracket
Estimated Sales: $2.5-5 Million
Number Employees: 5-9
Square Footage: 25000
Brands:
Loon
Nature's Own
Pfb (Produits Forresters Baasques)
Treestock

26608 Naughton Equipment Company
P.O.Box 525
1203 Madison Street
Fort Calhoun, NE 68023 402-468-4682
Fax: 402-468-4683 866-858-4682
sales@naughtonequipment.com
www.naughtonequipment.com
Foof processing equipment for the meat, poultry, and fisch industries
President: Daniel Naughton
VP: Kathy Naughton
R & D: Ed Kermeen
Marketing: Jerry Naughton
Estimated Sales: $1 - 3 Million
Number Employees: 1-4
Square Footage: 60000
Brands:
Carcos Splutting Saw
Ez Splitter Ii

26609 Naughton Equipment Company
P.O.Box 525
1203 Madison Street
Fort Calhoun, NE 68023 402-468-4682
Fax: 402-468-4683
sales@naughtonequipment.com
www.naughtonequipment.com
President and CFO: Daniel Naughton
Estimated Sales: $1 - 3 Million
Number Employees: 5-9

26610 Navy Brand ManufacturingCompany
3670 Scarlet Oak Blvd
St Louis, MO 63122 636-861-5500
Fax: 636-861-5509 800-325-3312
navybrand@navybrand.com
www.navybrand.com
Manufacturer and wholesaler/distributor of industrial degreasers, cleaners and water treatment systems for boilers and cooling towers
President: Ed Schooling
CEO: Edwin Schooling
Director Sales: Jack Julier
Estimated Sales: $1.5 Million
Number Employees: 20-49
Square Footage: 200000

26611 Neal Walters Poster Corporation
PO Box 480
Bentonville, AR 72712-0480 501-273-2489
Fax: 501-271-2132
Manufacturer and exporter of billboard and point of purchase posters, product markings, decals, bar code and pressure sensitive labels, business and computer forms, etc
President: James Walters
Secy./Treas.: Thomas Walters
V.P.: John Walters
Estimated Sales: $500,000-$1 Million
Number Employees: 9
Square Footage: 30000

26612 Nebraska Neon Sign Company
1140 N 21st Street
Lincoln, NE 68503 402-476-6563
Fax: 402-476-3461 nesignco@gmail.com
www.nebraskaneonsign.com
Signs including neon, wooden, illuminated, etc
President: Robert Norris
Estimated Sales: $2.5-5 Million
Number Employees: 20-49

26613 Nebraska Popcorn
85824 519th Ave
Clearwater, NE 68726 402-887-5335
Fax: 402-887-4709 800-253-6502
popcorn@nebraskapopcorn.com
www.nebraskapopcorn.com
Experienced grower, processor and packager of quality popcorn. The fully integrated operation offers microwave, bulk, private label and poly bags of popcorn
President: Frank Morrison
VP: Brett Morrison
Sales: Michelle Steskal
Estimated Sales: $10 - 20 Million
Number Employees: 20-49
Number of Brands: 1
Square Footage: 5000
Type of Packaging: Consumer, Food Service, Private Label, Bulk
Brands:
Morrison Farms

26614 Necedah Pallet Company
703 N Harvey St
Necedah, WI 54646 608-565-2619
Fax: 608-565-2979 800-672-5538
necedahpallet@tds.net
www.northernpalletsupply.com
Wooden pallets and skids
Sales/Marketing: Steve Schultz
Manager: Terry Hess
General Manager: Terry Hess
Estimated Sales: $2.5-5 Million
Number Employees: 20-49
Square Footage: 20000
Parent Co: Northern Pallet & Supply
Type of Packaging: Bulk

26615 Nederman, LLC
102 Transit Avenue
Thomasville, NC 27361 734-729-3344
Fax: 734-729-3358 800-533-5286
info@nedermanusa.com www.nedermanusa.com
Nederman LLC is a leading manufacturer of state of the art Dust, Fume, and Mist Collection Systems for the paper industry and recycling processes. Our products deliver consistent reliability, low energy consumption and compliance withOSHA and NFPA combustible dust requirements. Our experience and proven techniques have allowed us to save customers up to 80 percent on their energy costs.
President: Thomas Ballus
Sales: Rob Williamson
Estimated Sales: $3 - 5 Million
Number Employees: 20-49

26616 Nefab
850 Mark Street
EGV, IL 60007 630-451-5300
lori.brownstein@nefab.com
www.nefab.us
Plywood, no-nail, foldable and reusable packaging systems for transport, storage and internal distribution
President, Chief Executive Officer: David MArk
Executive Vice President: Anders M"rk
Estimated Sales: $2.5-5 Million
Number Employees: 2
Parent Co: Nefab A.B.
Brands:
Repak

26617 Nefab
204 Airline Drive
Suite 600
Coppell, TX 75019ÿ 469-444-5320
Fax: 847-985-3200 800-536-7261
lori.brownstein@nefab.com www.nefab.com
No-nail, lightweight, collapsible export containers made from plywood and steel
President: Lars-ake Rydh
President, Chief Executive Officer: David MArk
Executive Vice President: Anders M"rk
Estimated Sales: $2.5-5 Million
Number Employees: 5-9

26618 Nefab
850 Mark Streetÿ
Elk Grove Village, IL 60007 ÿ 630-451-5300
Fax: 847-985-3200 800-536-7261
lori.brownstein@nefab.com www.nefab.com
No-nail, collapsible, export and reusable containers, easy to assemble and available in custom and stock sizes - made from a combination of plywood and steelContainers are delivered flat and designed to customer's specification.providing packaging solutions.cost effective transport containers
President, Chief Executive Officer: David MArk
Executive Vice President: Anders M"rk
Sales Director: Lori Brownstein
Estimated Sales: $2.5-5 Million
Number Employees: 2
Type of Packaging: Consumer

26619 (HQ)Nefab Packaging Inc.
204 Airline Dr
Suite 100
Coppell, TX 75019
Fax: 469-444-5308 800-322-4425
www.nefab.com
Industrial crates material handling products including pallets
Estimated Sales: $5 - 10 Million
Number Employees: 10
Square Footage: 92000

26620 Nefab Packaging, Inc.
204 Airline Drive
Suite 100
Coppell, TX 75019 469-444-5308
Fax: 603-367-4329 800-322-4425
sales@chickpackaging.com www.nefab.us
Manufacturer and exporter of wooden industrial packaging and distribution equipment including pallets, skids, crates and boxes; also, milling services available
Director of Global Business Development: Ken Wilson
Chief Executive Officer: Brian Bulatao
VP: Andi Wilson
Executive Vice President: Eric Howe
Number Employees: 400

26621 Neff Packaging Solutions
4700 Duke Dr
Suite 100
Mason, OH 45040 937-233-3333
Fax: 937-233-0238 800-445-4383
info@neffpackaging.com
www.neffpackaging.com
Folding paper boxes and cartons
Owner: Robert D Neff
Marketing Director: R Neff
Estimated Sales: $1-2.5 Million
Number Employees: 10-19
Parent Co: Neff Courier Group

26622 Negus Container & Packaging
114 N Bedford Street
Madison, WI 53703-2610 608-251-2533
Fax: 608-256-2604 888-241-7482
contact.negus@negusboxnbag.com
www.negusboxnbag.com
Manufacturer and exporter of corrugated ice cream containers; wholesaler/distributor and exporter of packaging supplies including bags
President: Rod Shaughnessy
Sales: Greg Koch
Operations: Al Baler
Estimated Sales: $1-5 Million
Number Employees: 5-9
Square Footage: 40000
Parent Co: Phoenix Industries Corporation
Brands:
Negus Octapak
Negus Square Pak

26623 Neil Fisk Advanced Company
14600 21st Ave N
Plymouth, MN 55447-4648 763-745-3500
Fax: 763-745-3718
info-plymouth@mn.nilfisk-advance.com
www.mn.nilfisk-advance.com
Vacuum cleaners, carpet shampoo and floor sweeping equipment
General Secretary: Gene Phares
Executive Vice President of Americas: Christian Cornelius
Estimated Sales: $100-500 Million
Number Employees: 500-999

26624 Neilson Canvas Company
715 W Washington St
Sandusky, OH 44870-2334 419-625-0581
Fax: 419-625-4315 nielsencan@aol.com
Commercial awnings
President: Robert Nielsen
VP: Darcy Neilson
Estimated Sales: $1-2,500,000
Number Employees: 10-19

26625 **Nelles Automation**
7000 Hollister St
Houston, TX 77040-5617 713-939-9399
Fax: 713-939-0393
tom.christopher@telvent.abengoa.com
www.telvent.com
Manufacturer and exporter of automated control systems and circuit boards for electric utility
President: Dave Jardine
CFO: Manuel Fanchez
VP: Tom Christopher
Estimated Sales: $1 - 3 Million
Number Employees: 5-9
Parent Co: Valmet

26626 **Nelson & Associates Recruiting**
PO Box 2686
Kirkland, WA 98083 425-823-0956
Fax: 425-820-4541 nelson@foodrecruiter.com
www.foodrecruiter.com
Personnel recruiter specializing in executive, managerial and technical food industry positions
President: Kenneth Nelson
Estimated Sales: Below $5 Million
Number Employees: 1-4

26627 **Nelson Company**
2116 Sparrows Point Rd
Baltimore, MD 21219-1798 410-477-3000
Fax: 410-388-0246 info@nelsoncompany.com
www.nelsoncompany.com
Wooden pallets and skids; wholesaler/distributor of plastic and metal pallets, shrink and stretch wraps, angleboards and void fillers
President: Arthur Caltrider
Estimated Sales: $5 - 10 Million
Number Employees: 50-99
Parent Co: Nelson Company

26628 **Nelson Company**
2116 Sparrows Point Rd
Baltimore, MD 21219-1798 410-477-3000
Fax: 410-388-0246 info@nelsoncompany.com
www.nelsoncompany.com
Bins, crates and pallets including wood, plywood, plastic and corrugated; also, unit load consulting available
President: Arthur Caltrider
CFO: Arthur Caltrider
VP: Jack Williams
Director Marketing Development: Marc Ottinger
Estimated Sales: $5 - 10 Million
Number Employees: 50-99
Square Footage: 100000
Brands:
Payload

26629 **Nelson Container Corporation**
W180n11921 River Ln
Germantown, WI 53022 262-250-5000
Fax: 262-250-5015 contact@nelsoncontainer.com
www.nelsoncontainer.com
Containers and corrugated boxes
President: Thomas C Nelson
President: Tom Nelson
Estimated Sales: $20-50 Million
Number Employees: 20-49

26630 **Nelson Custom Signs**
1199 S Sheldon Rd
Plymouth, MI 48170-2192 734-455-0500
Fax: 734-455-0800
Signs including neon, painted, wooden, etc
Manager: Pete Nelson
Estimated Sales: Less than $500,000
Number Employees: 1-4

26631 **Nelson-Jameson**
P.O.Box 647
Marshfield, WI 54449 715-387-1151
Fax: 715-387-8746 800-826-8302
sales@nelsonjameson.com
www.nelsonjameson.com
Wholesale distributor serving food and beverage processors. Wide-line distributor of sanitation, maintenance, laboratory, processing and flow control, personnel and safety supplies
President: Jerome Lippert
CEO: John Nelson
CEO: Bruce Lautenschlager
Estimated Sales: $50 - 75 Million
Number Employees: 50-99
Number of Brands: 750+
Other Locations:
Nelson-Jameson
Twin Falls ID
Nelson-Jameson
Turlock CA

26632 **Nemco Electric Company**
207 S Horton St
Seattle, WA 98134-1929 206-622-1551
Fax: 206-622-4449 pdowns@spectrum-mpi.com
Lighting equipment including custom chandeliers for hotel lobbies and banquet rooms and portable fluorescent work lights; also, custom lighting fixtures available
President: Arnold Larson
VP: Judy Larson
Estimated Sales: $1-2.5 Million
Number Employees: 1-4
Square Footage: 40000

26633 **Nemco Food Equipment**
301 Meuse Argonne St
PO Box 305
Hicksville, OH 43526 419-542-7751
Fax: 419-542-6690 800-782-6761
mwibel@nemcofoodequip.com
www.nemcofoodequip.com
Manufacturer and exporter of vegetable slicers and cutters
President: Stan Guilliam
Estimated Sales: $10-20 Million
Number Employees: 50-99
Type of Packaging: Food Service

26634 **Nemeth Engineering Associates**
5901 W Highway 22
Crestwood, KY 40014 502-241-1502
Fax: 502-241-5907
info@nemeth-engineering.com
www.nemeth-engineering.com
Manufacturer and exporter of radio frequency heating systems for drying, baking, moisture leveling, proofing, thawing, tempering and deinfestation
President: Peter Nemeth
Sales Manager: Ned Snow
Sales Associate: Bobbie Gardner
Estimated Sales: $5-10 Million
Number Employees: 20-49
Square Footage: 75000

26635 **Neo-Image Candle Light**
1331 Blundell Road
Mississauga, ON L4Y 1M6
Canada 905-273-3020
Fax: 905-273-6905 800-375-8023
info@candlesjustonline.com
www.neo-image.com
Candles and accessories
Sales Manager: Ric Jones
General Manager: Steve Stratakos
Estimated Sales: $15 Million
Number Employees: 25-49
Parent Co: North America Candle
Brands:
Neo-Image

26636 **(HQ)Neo-Kraft Signs**
686 Main St
Lewiston, ME 04240 207-782-9654
Fax: 207-782-0009 800-339-2258
info@neokraft.com www.neokraft.com
Aluminum, neon and plastic signs; also wide format digital thermal printing
President: Peter Murphy
VP: Phil Bolduc
Marketing Director: Paul Lessard
Estimated Sales: Below $5 Million
Number Employees: 20-49
Square Footage: 10000

26637 **Neo-Ray Products**
537 Johnson Avenue
Brooklyn, NY 11237-1304 718-456-7400
Fax: 718-456-5492 800-221-0946
info@neoray.com www.neoray.com
Manufacturer and exporter of architectural grade fluorescent lighting systems
National Sales Manager: Andrew Gross
Estimated Sales: $20-50 Million
Number Employees: 100-249

26638 **(HQ)Neogen Corporation**
620 Lesher Pl
Lansing, MI 48912 517-372-9200
Fax: 517-372-2006 800-234-5333
foodsafety@neogen.com www.neogen.com
Manufacturer and exporter of testing kits for natural and chemical residues affecting food quality and safety
President: James Herbert
CFO: Richard Current
VP: Paul Satoh
VP Sales/Marketing: Ed Bradley
Public Relations: Rod Poland
Operations Manager: Lon Bohannon
Production Manager: David Wall
Estimated Sales: $35 Million
Number Employees: 250-499
Square Footage: 60000
Other Locations:
Neogen Corp.
Lexington KY
Brands:
Acumedia
Hygicult
Isogrid
Pro-Tect
Reveal
Uni-Lite Xcel

26639 **Neogen Gene-Trak Systems**
620 Lesher Place
Lansing, MI 48912-1595 517-372-9200
Fax: 517-372-2006 800-234-5333
foodsafety@neogen.com www.neogen.com
Manufacturer, importer and exporter of food pathogen testing kits
CEO: James L Herbert
Marketing Manager: Margaret Cyr
General Manager: Mark Mozola
Estimated Sales: $2.5-5 Million
Number Employees: 250-499
Parent Co: Vysis
Brands:
Gene-Trak

26640 **(HQ)Neon Design-a-Sign**
26022 Cape Dr Bldg H
Laguna Niguel, CA 92677 949-348-9223
Fax: 949-348-1736 888-636-6327
sales@neon-das.com www.neon-das.com
Manufacturer and exporter of signs including changeable, fiber-optic neon and programmable LED message displays. Also have a full line of LED lighting.
President: Timothy Piper
CEO: Christine Busnardo
Estimated Sales: $600,000
Number Employees: 1-4
Square Footage: 8000
Brands:
Logo River
Neon Design-A-Sign
Neon Light Pegs

26641 **Neonetics**
900 S Main St
Hampstead, MD 21074 410-374-8057
Fax: 410-374-8056 AlanObligin@yahoo.com
www.neonetics.com
Manufacturer, importer and exporter of neon signs
Owner: Allen Obligen
CFO: Brad Sogollss
VP: Brad Sotoloff
Estimated Sales: Below $5,000,000
Number Employees: 1-4
Brands:
Ne-On the Wall
Neonetics

26642 **Neos**
12797 Meadowvale Road NW
Suite B
Elk River, MN 55330-1171 763-441-0705
Fax: 763-441-0706 888-441-6367
neosinc@att.net www.neos-server.org
Manufacturer and exporter of packaging machinery for rigid plastic containers; also, burrito and sliced bread dispensers, conveyors with filler depositers, folding tables for assembly and fillers
President: Jack T Mowry
CFO: Greg Erlandson
National Sales Manager: Joe Gibbs

Estimated Sales: $1-2.5 Million
Number Employees: 5-9
Square Footage: 48000

26643 Nepa Pallet & ContainerCompany
PO Box 399
Snohomish, WA 98290-399 360-568-3185
Fax: 360-568-9135 pjsherry@nepapallet.com
www.nepapallet.com
Manufacturer and exporter of pallets and bins
President: Denton Sherry
Estimated Sales: $5 - 10 Million
Number Employees: 50-99

26644 Nepcco
495 Oak Rd
Ocala, FL 34472-3005 352-867-7482
Fax: 352-867-1320 800-277-3279
info@waste2water.com www.nepcco.com
Manufacturer and exporter of water treatment equipment
Manager: Kevin Hawkins
Estimated Sales: $2.5-5 Million
Number Employees: 20-49
Square Footage: 100000
Parent Co: Zentox
Brands:
Cascade

26645 (HQ)Nercon Engineering & Manufacturing
PO Box 2288
Oshkosh, WI 54903-2288 920-233-3268
Fax: 920-233-3159 www.nercon.com
Manufacturer and exporter of table top, belt and case conveyors, bi-directional tables, vertical accumulators, label removers, twist rinsers, bottle emptiers, can coolers, etc
President: Jim Nerenhausen
CEO: Jay Nerenhausen
Marketing: Jim Streblow
Estimated Sales: $10 - 20 Million
Number Employees: 100-249
Square Footage: 166500
Other Locations:
Nercon Engineering & Manufact
Oconto WI
Brands:
Easy-Rol

26646 Net Material Handling
1300 W Fond Du Lac Ave
Milwaukee, WI 53205 414-263-1300
Fax: 414-263-7544 800-558-7260
Two and four-wheel hand trucks, two-wheel electric trucks, dollies, carts, ramps, etc
President: Wendy Alzell
VP: Wayne Kappel
Estimated Sales: $1-2.5 Million
Number Employees: 1-4
Square Footage: 14000
Brands:
Escalera
Magline
Yeats

26647 Net Pack Systems
36 Oak Street
Oakland, ME 04963-5019 207-465-4531
Fax: 207-465-9662
Bags including netting, open mesh, heat sealed, plastic and polyethylene for cooking, fruits, vegetables, poultry, meat and refrigeration
President: Edward Johnson
Operations Manager: Douglas Johnson
General Manager: Edward Johnson
Estimated Sales: $1 - 2.5 Million
Number Employees: 5-9

26648 Neugart
3047 Industrial Blvd # 12
Bethel Park, PA 15102-2537 412-835-4154
Fax: 412-835-4194 sales@neugartusa.com
www.neugartusa.com
Planetary gearboxes, angle gearboxes, custom made gears, honing, motor mounting
President: Gerhard Antony
VP sales: Tim Francis
Estimated Sales: $1 - 3 Million
Number Employees: 5-9

26649 Neupak
4607 Dovetail Drive
Madison, WI 53704 608-241-1118
Fax: 608-241-4448 800-383-1128
sales@ideal-pak.com www.neupak.com
Manufacture liquid filling machines
President, Chief Executive Officer: Steve Bethke
Vice President: Bruce Bierman
Marketing Manager: Steven Meyer
National Sales Manager: Robert Whetstone
Estimated Sales: $1 - 5 Million
Number Employees: 17

26650 Neupak
4607 Dovetail Drive
Madison, WI 53704-6302 608-241-1118
Fax: 608-241-4448 800-383-1128
sales@ideal-pak.com www.neupak.com
New weight and volumetric filling systems, automatic and semi-automatic machines for filling drums, totes, pails, can and jugs with foaming and nonfoaming products
President, Chief Executive Officer: Steve Bethke
Vice President: Bruce Bierman
Sales & Marketing Director: Russell Schlager
National Sales Manager: Robert D. Whetstone
Estimated Sales: $1-5 Million
Number Employees: 17

26651 Nevlen Co. 2, Inc.
96 Audubon Road
Wakefield, MA 01880-1200 978-462-7777
Fax: 978-462-7774 800-562-7225
nevlen@nevlen.com www.nevlen.com
Manufacturer and exporter of van equipment including roof racks, shelving, drawer units and partitions
VP: James Capomaccio
VP: M Nickerson
Executive VP/Treasurer: J Capomaccio
Estimated Sales: $2.5-5 Million
Number Employees: 20-49
Square Footage: 208000
Brands:
Nevlen

26652 (HQ)Nevo Corporation
50 Hayney Ct
PO Box 601
Ronkonkoma, NY 11779-7220 631-585-8787
Fax: 631-585-9285 sales@gehnrich.com
www.gehnrich.com
Manufacturer and exporter of roll-in and rotating rack convection ovens
President: Richard Gehnrich
Treasurer: Leon Pedigo
VP: Wayne Pedigo
Estimated Sales: $1 - 3 Million
Number Employees: 20-49
Square Footage: 23000

26653 New Age Industrial Corporation
16788 E Highway 36
PO Box 520
Norton, KS 67654 800-255-0104
Fax: 785-877-2616 800-255-0104
janet@newageindustrial.com
www.newageindustrial.com
Manufacturer and exporter of aluminum backroom equipment including mobile platters, lug carts, racks, shelving, dollies and tables
President: Larry Nelson
VP: Tom Sharo
Sales Director: Allen Hasken
Estimated Sales: $10 - 20 Million
Number Employees: 100-249
Type of Packaging: Food Service

26654 New Attitude Beverage Corporation
PO Box 117385
Burlingame, CA 94011-7385 310-414-6501
Fax: 310-414-6547 newattbev@aol.com
Unique package designs and products beverages for the industry
Estimated Sales: $2 Million
Number Employees: 22
Type of Packaging: Consumer, Food Service

26655 New Brunswick International
76 Veronica Ave
Somerset, NJ 08873 732-828-3633
Fax: 732-828-4884 marketing@nbidigi.com
www.nbidigi.net
Scales, labels, wrapping and overwrap machines
President: John Baumann
CFO: Victor Liras
R & D: Ed Hearon
Estimated Sales: $5-10 Million
Number Employees: 20-49

26656 New Brunswick ScientificCompany
175 Freshwater Boulevard
Enfield, CT 06082-4444
800-645-3050
info@eppendorf.com
www.newbrunswick.eppendorf.com
Laboratory equipment including biological shakers, media preparation equipment and fermentors
Estimated Sales: $47 Million
Number Employees: 437
Square Footage: 243000
Parent Co: Eppendorf, Inc.

26657 New Carbon Company
PO Box 71
Buchanan, MI 49107-0071 574-247-2270
Fax: 574-247-2280 newcarbon@qtm.net
www.goldenmalted.com
This company has 4 separate entries all of which are duplicates. Three of the entries are to be deleted and only one kept.

26658 New Castle Machinery
1399 Countyline Road
New Castle, PA 16101 724-656-5600
Fax: 724-656-5620 800-897-2830
info@nordsonxaloy.com www.xaloy.com
CEO: Walter Cox
Estimated Sales: $1 - 5 Million
Number Employees: 100-249
Parent Co: Nordson XALOY Incorporated

26659 New Centennial
P.O.Box 708
Columbus, GA 31902-0708 706-323-6446
Fax: 706-327-9921 800-241-7541
info@newcentennial.com
www.newcentennial.com
Non-refrigerated and refrigerated side and rear-access truck bodies and trailers for the beverage and food distribution industry
Manager: Bob Hudak
Marketing Director: Wes Hauglie
Sales Director: Dan Burt
Plant Manager: Bob Hudak
Purchasing Manager: Tim Fitzpatrick
Estimated Sales: $10-20 Million
Number Employees: 50-99

26660 New Chef Fashion
3223 E 46th St
Vernon, CA 90058-2407 323-581-0300
Fax: 213-489-1745 www.newchef.com
Manufacturer and exporter of aprons, uniforms and chef hats
Owner: Lucien Salama
Estimated Sales: $10-20 Million
Number Employees: 1-4
Type of Packaging: Food Service

26661 New Court
3200 Court St
Texarkana, TX 75501-6619 903-838-0521
Fax: 903-838-9452 www.newcourtinc.com
Laminated sanitary insulated and noninsulated wall and ceiling panels including fiberglass, painted aluminum and stainless steel
President: Calvin Court
VP Marketing: Melvin Court
Sales Director: Jodi Shewmaker
Estimated Sales: $20 - 50 Million
Number Employees: 100-249
Brands:
New-Glass
Poly-Liner

26662 New Data Systems
19 Claremont Ln
Suffern, NY 10901 845-357-7744
Fax: 845-357-7933 cats@catsnds.com
www.catstoday.com
Accounting and trading position software for importers, exporters and commodity traders
Owner: Peter Bellin
Estimated Sales: $1-2.5 Million
Number Employees: 1-4

26663 New England Cheese Making Supply Company
54 Whately Rd
Suite B
South Deerfield, MA 01373 413-397-2012
Fax: 413-397-2014 info@cheesemaking.com
www.cheesemaking.com
Ingredients and supplies for cheesemaking and home dairy needs
Owner: Ricki Carroll
Estimated Sales: Below $5 Million
Number Employees: 1-4

26664 New England Label
1213 US Route 302
Barre, VT 05641 802-476-6393
Fax: 802-476-7159 800-368-3932
salesoffice@wnpinc.com www.wnpinc.com
Pressure sensitive labels
Sales Representative: Vicki Adams
General Manager: Jim Veness
Production Manager: Chris Rivers
Estimated Sales: $500,000-$1 Million
Number Employees: 5-9
Square Footage: 3813
Parent Co: Willington Company

26665 New England Machinery Inc
2820 62nd Ave E
Bradenton, FL 34203 941-755-5550
Fax: 941-751-6281 info@neminc.com
www.neminc.com
Manufacturer and exporter of hopper/elevators and bottling machinery including unscramblers, orienters, cappers, lidders, puckers, de-puckers, gap transfers and more
President/CEO: Judith Bankuty Nickse
Director Sales/Marketing: Marge Bonura
VP Manufacturing: Geza Bankuty
Square Footage: 160000
Brands:
N.E.M.

26666 New England Overshoe Company
1193 S Brownell Rd
Williston, VT 05495-7416 802-846-8880
Fax: 802-863-6888 888-289-6367
Neos@overshoe.com www.overshoe.com
Footwear for the food and pharmaceutical industry, soles that keep particles from being spread, a Poly Urethane Upper that does not harbor bacteria and can be cleaned both inside and out reducing biohazard contamination
President: Scott Hardy
Marketing Coordinator: Robyn Terranova
Estimated Sales: $2.4 Million
Number Employees: 5-9
Parent Co: Linckia Development

26667 New England Pallets & Skids
250 West St
Ludlow, MA 01056-1248 413-583-6628
Fax: 413-583-5187 info@nepallets.com
www.nepallets.com
Wooden pallets
President: Cynthia Kawie
Estimated Sales: $1-2.5 Million
Number Employees: 10-19
Square Footage: 200000
Type of Packaging: Consumer, Food Service

26668 (HQ)New England Wooden WareCorporation
205 School St
Suite 201
Gardner, MA 01440 978-632-3600
Fax: 978-630-1513 800-252-9214
www.newoodenware.com
Manufacturer, importer and exporter of corrugated paper boxes
President: David Urquhart
VP Sales: R Goguen
Quality Control Manager: Don Broderick
Sales Manager: Mark Salisbury
Customer Service Manager: Jodi Womble
VP Production: D Urquhart
Estimated Sales: $10-20 Million
Number Employees: 100-249
Square Footage: 193000
Other Locations:
New England Wooden WareCorp.
Fitchburg MA

26669 New Era Label Corporation
51 Valley St
Belleville, NJ 07109-3011 973-759-2444
Fax: 973-759-2993
Seals, stickers and labels including paper, pressure sensitive, spot carbon, carbon interleaved and consecutively numbered
Sales: Fred Iannone
Manager: Tom Savano
Estimated Sales: $1 - 5 Million
Number Employees: 10-19

26670 New Generation Software
3835 N Freeway Blvd
Suite 200
Sacramento, CA 95834 916-920-2200
Fax: 916-920-1380 800-824-1220
admin@ngsi.com www.ngsi.com
Financial, distribution and business intelligence software solutions
President: Bernard B Gough
Estimated Sales: $10 - 20 Million
Number Employees: 50-99

26671 New Hatchwear Company
Bay 104, 4711
13th Street N.E.
Calgary, AB T2E 6M3
Canada 403-291-2525
Fax: 403-291-2521 800-661-9249
service@newhatchwear.com
www.newhatchwear.com
Uniform apparel including skirts, blouses, dresses, aprons, tunics, slacks, smocks, vests, jackets, tailored blazers, formals, kitchen whites, service coats, industrial clothing and outerwear, security, law enforcement and military.
Purchasing Manager: Sandra Dimitrijevic
Number Employees: 50-99
Type of Packaging: Consumer, Food Service, Private Label

26672 New Haven Awning Company
178 Chapel St
New Haven, CT 06513 203-562-7232
Fax: 203-624-4124 800-560-5650
info@nhawning.com www.nhawning.com
Commercial awnings
President: Dan Barnick
Partner: Tom Gumkowski
Estimated Sales: $5-10,000,000
Number Employees: 5-9

26673 New High Glass
12713 SW 125th Ave
Miami, FL 33186 305-232-0840
Fax: 305-251-7622 800-GLA-SSUS
sales@newhigh.com www.newhighglass.net
Wine industry bottles and closures
President: Enrico Raccah
Estimated Sales: $10-20 Million
Number Employees: 20-49

26674 New Hope Natural Media
1401 Pearl Street
Suite 200
Boulder, CO 80302 303-939-8440
Fax: 303-998-9020 info@newhope.com
www.newhope360.com
Supplements and ingredients
Executive Director: Len Monheit
Sr Marketing Manager: Brad Mastrine
Sales: Kim Merselis
Estimated Sales: $25 Million
Number Employees: 45
Square Footage: 60000

26675 New Horizon Foods
33440 Western Ave
Union City, CA 94587 510-489-8600
Fax: 510-489-9797 www.tovaindustries.com
Dough conditioners, bread bases, natural mixes, beverage, cake, muffin, pudding, meat spices, spice blends, snack and chip seasonings, custard, ice cream, waffle cone and sauce mixes and bases; exporter of dough conditioners and cakeand muffin mixes
President: Zach Melzer
Senior Vice President: Yael Melzer
Number Employees: 10-19
Parent Co: Tova Industries
Type of Packaging: Consumer, Food Service, Private Label, Bulk

26676 New Horizon Technologies
3100 Geo Washntn Way
Richland, WA 99354 509-372-4868
Fax: 509-372-4869 newhorizon@urx.com
Food irradiation processing facility specializing in fresh fruits and vegetable, poultry, meat and seafood for R&D applications
CEO: Michael Brown
VP Market Development: Carl Holder
VP Operations: Dave Eakin
Estimated Sales: $500,000-$1,000,000
Number Employees: 1-4

26677 New Jersey Wire Stitching Machine Company
1841 Old Cuthbert Road
Cherry Hill, NJ 08034 856-428-2572
Fax: 856-428-3069 sales@newjerseywire.com
www.newjerseywire.com
Manual and auto bag closers for poly, mesh and drawstring bags at high speeds; also, wire stitchers for fiber and corrugated containers, trays, metals, display boxes and plastics
Manager: Mike Menaquala
CEO: Fred Rexon
General Manager: Michael Menaquale
Estimated Sales: $500,000-$1 Million
Number Employees: 1-4
Square Footage: 40000
Parent Co: Precision Automation Company

26678 New Klix Corporation
551 Railroad Avenue
South San Francisco, CA 94080-3450650-761-0622
Fax: 650-589-6735 800-522-5544
newklix@aol.com
Manufacturer and exporter of warewash, laundry detergents and cleaning compounds
President: Rodrigo Ortiz
VP: Lautaro Ortiz
Estimated Sales: $2.5-5 Million
Number Employees: 19
Square Footage: 55000
Type of Packaging: Food Service, Private Label
Brands:
Klix

26679 New Lisbon Wood ProductsManufacturing Company
1127 S Adams St
New Lisbon, WI 53950 608-562-3122
Fax: 608-562-3221
acewoodproducts@excite.com
www.acewoodproducts.com
Custom wooden pallets, skids and crates
Owner: David Brinkman
Marketing: Linda Brinkman
Sales: Sonya Brach
Plant Manager: Dan Batten
Estimated Sales: $1-2.5 Million
Number Employees: 10-19
Square Footage: 20000
Parent Co: Ace Wood

26680 New London Engineering
1700 Division St
New London, WI 54961 920-982-4030
Fax: 920-982-6800 800-437-1994
nlesales@nleco.com www.nleco.com
Conveyors including line and table top chain
President: Martin Bonneson
CEO: Frank Ferdon
Quality Control: Dale Turdell
Director Sales/Marketing: Dale Trudell
Estimated Sales: $10 - 20 Million
Number Employees: 50-99
Square Footage: 50000
Parent Co: Bonntech International

26681 New Mexico Products
503 Vineyard Rd NE
Albuquerque, NM 87113 505-345-7864
Fax: 505-344-2581 877-345-7864
nmp@flash.net www.industrialcrating.net
Wooden boxes, crates and custom pallets including softwood only
President: David St John
Sales Director: Matt Walker
Office Manager: Stella Torres
Estimated Sales: Below $5 Million
Number Employees: 7
Square Footage: 6000

26682 New Pig Corporation
1 Pork Ave
PO Box 304
Tipton, PA 16684 814-684-0101
Fax: 814-684-0608 800-468-4647
salesdept@newpig.com www.newpig.com
Industrial leak, spill, safety, maintenance, storage, handling and repair products
President: Nino Vella
CFO: Jim Crlin
Executive VP: Doug Hershey
Quality Control: Steve Klling
R & D: Mark Woytowich
Director of Public Relations: Carl DeCaspers
Purchasing Manager: Bill Lidwell
Estimated Sales: Below $5 Million
Number Employees: 250-499

26683 New Resina Corporation
27455 Bostik Court
Temecula, CA 92590 951-296-6585
Fax: 951-296-5018 800-207-4804
sales@resina.com www.resina.com
President: Michael Tom
CEO: Andy Lask
Number Employees: 10-19

26684 New South Lumber Company
3700 Clay Pond Road
Myrtle Beach, SC 29579 843-236-9399
Fax: 843-236-9454 www.canfor.com
Wooden pallets
President/Chief Executive Officer: Don Kayne
SVP, Corporate & Legal Affairs: David Calabrigo
SVP, Finance/Chief Financial Officer: Alan Nicholl
Vice President/Treasurer: Patrick Elliott
SVP, Sales & Marketing: Wayne Guthrie
Vice President, Human Resources: Onkar Athwal
Estimated Sales: $50-100 Million
Number Employees: 100
Square Footage: 49705
Parent Co: Canfor Corporation

26685 New Tiger International
117 State Street,
Westbury, NY 11590 516-942-9312
Fax: 516-942-9306 newtiger6688@yahoo.com
www.greatporcini.com
Dried, frozen, fresh and canned mushrooms
Marketing: Richard Lin

26686 New Wave Enviro Water Products
P.O.Box 4146
Englewood, CO 80155 303-221-3232
Fax: 303-221-3233 800-592-8371
customerservice@newwaveenviro.com
www.newwaveenviro.com
Water filtration systems and accessories
President: Virgil Archer
Estimated Sales: $1 - 3 Million
Number Employees: 10-19

26687 New Way Packaging Machinery
PO Box 467
Hanover, PA 17331 717-637-2133
Fax: 717-637-2966 800-522-3537
sales@labeler.com www.labeler.com
Manufacturer and exporter of labeling machinery
President: Edward Abendschein
Estimated Sales: $10-20 Million
Number Employees: 5-9

26688 New York Corrugated BoxCompany
239 Lindbergh Pl
Paterson, NJ 07503 973-742-5000
Fax: 718-388-0557 www.nycorrugatedbox.net
Corrugated cartons and inserts
President: Robert Rosner
General Manager: Robert Rosner
Estimated Sales: $2.5-5 Million
Number Employees: 5-9
Square Footage: 28000

26689 New York Folding Box Company
129 Christie Street
Newark, NJ 07105-3915 973-589-0654
Fax: 973-344-6896
Folding boxes
President: Harry Kaplan
Chairman of the Board: Jerome Joseph Kaplan
VP: Robert Kaplan
Estimated Sales: $5-10 Million
Number Employees: 20-49

26690 New York State Electric& Gas Corpration
P.O.Box 5224
Binghamton, NY 13902-5224 607-762-7200
Fax: 607-762-8614 800-572-1111
custserv@nyseg.com www.nyseg.com
President: Jim Laurito
Estimated Sales: $1 - 5 Million
Number Employees: 1,000-4,999

26691 New-Ma Co. Llc
4618 44th St SE
Grand Rapids, MI 49512 616-942-5500
Fax: 616-942-5511 www.newma.it
Horizontal and vertical packaging machines, counting and weighing systems.

26692 NewTech
11 Hedding Dr
Randolph, VT 05060 802-728-9170
Fax: 802-728-9163 800-210-2361
dewater91@msn.com
www.aboutnewtechinc.com
Manufactures dewatering systems for wastewater
President: Robert Dimmick
Estimated Sales: $3 Million
Number Employees: 10-19

26693 Newark Wire Cloth Company
160 Fornelius Ave
Clifton, NJ 07013 973-778-4478
Fax: 973-778-4481 800-221-0392
info@newarkwire.com www.newarkwire.com
Manufacturer, exporter and importer of wire cloth, filters, strainers, testing sieves, etc. Manufacturers of the Sani Cloan Strainer product line. Consisting of: inline, side inlet, and hi-capacity basket strainers. Custom fabricationsare a specialty.
President/Owner: Richard Campbell
Estimated Sales: $5 - 10 Million
Number Employees: 29
Square Footage: 120000
Type of Packaging: Food Service

26694 Newcastle Company, Inc.
3812 Wilmington Rd
New Castle, PA 16105 724-658-4516
Fax: 724-658-5100 ncco@newcastleco.com
www.newcastleco.com
Manufacturer and integrator of load transfer systems, palletizers, pallet dispensers, sheet dispensers, and conveyors.
Owner: Dennis Alduk
Number Employees: 50-99
Brands:
Floor Level
Palavator

26695 Newco
PO Box 836
Butler, NJ 07405-836 973-383-0393
Fax: 973-383-0506
Decorative facing for paneling and wall coverings
President: James Berezny
Estimated Sales: $20-50 Million
Number Employees: 10

26696 Newco Enterprises
3650 New Town Blvd
Saint Charles, MO 63302 636-925-1202
Fax: 636-925-0029 800-325-7867
pat@newcocoffee.com www.newcocoffee.com
Coffee and tea brewing equipment and water treatment systems; exporter of commercial coffee brewers
President: Joseph P Webster
CFO: Mcenke Karen
VP Marketing: Anthony Westcott
VP Sales: Steve Hyde
Estimated Sales: $10 - 20 Million
Number Employees: 100-249
Square Footage: 80000

26697 Newcourt, Inc.
PO Box 182
Madison, IN 47250-0182 800-933-0006
Fax: 812-265-6455
Composite laminated floorings for mezzanines
Sales Director: John Gramke
Number Employees: 2

26698 Newlands Systems
602-30731 Simpson Road
Abbotsford, BC V2T 6Y7 604-855-4890
Fax: 604-855-8826 mail@nsibrew.com
www.nsibrew.com
Manufacturer and exporter of brewing equipment and machinery
President: Brad McQuhae
Director Marketing: Loch McJannett
Number Employees: 10
Square Footage: 80000
Type of Packaging: Food Service

26699 (HQ)Newly Weds Foods
2501 N Keeler Ave
Chicago, IL 60639 773-489-7000
Fax: 773-489-2799 800-621-7521
nwfnorthamerica@newlywedsfoods.com
www.newlywedsfoods.com
Processor and exporter of breadings, batters, seasoning blends, marinades, glazes and capsicum products
President: Charles T. Angell
CFO: Brian Johnson
SVP Sales & Marketing: Bruce Leshinski
R&D: Jim Klein
Sales Director: Jim Chin
VP Manufacturing: Mike Hopp
Plant Manager: Leo Vogler
Director of Purchasing: Tom Lisack
Estimated Sales: $959 Million
Number Employees: 2431
Square Footage: 1500000
Other Locations:
Newly Weds Foods
Bethleham PA
Newly Weds Foods
Chicago IL
Newly Weds Foods
Cleveland TN
Newly Weds Foods
Watertown MA
Newly Weds Foods
Yorkville IL
Newly Weds Foods
Horn Lake MS
Newly Weds Foods
Edmonton AB
Newly Weds Foods
Montreal QC
Newly Weds Foods
Toronto ON
Brands:
Batter Blends
Blended Breaders
Newly Weds

26700 Newman Labeling Systems
4400 Route 9 South
Suite 1000
Freehold, NJ 07728 609-597-8722
Fax: 609-597-8755 newmanmps@aol.com
www.newmanlabeling.com
President: John W Clayton
Vice President Operations: Michael Semiraro
Estimated Sales: $1 - 5 Million
Number Employees: 10-19

26701 Newman Sanitary Gasket Company
P.O.Box 222
Lebanon, OH 45036 513-932-7379
Fax: 513-932-4493
customer@newmangasket.com
www.newmangasket.com
Manufacturer and exporter of foodgrade sanitary process piping gaskets, seals and F.D.A. O-rings. Also custom molded rubber parts
President: David W Newman
CEO: Tom Moore
Marketing Director: Larry Hensel
Plant Manager: Matt Agricola
Estimated Sales: $1-5,000,000
Number Employees: 20-49
Square Footage: 32500
Type of Packaging: Private Label, Bulk
Brands:
Newman

26702 Newmarket International
135 Commerce Way
Portsmouth, NH 03801-3262 603-436-7500
Fax: 603-436-1826 888-829-8871
salesinfo@newsoft.com www.newmarketinc.com

Windows based sales, marketing and catering software
CEO: Sean O Neill
CFO: Ken Smaha
Estimated Sales: $33.4 Million
Number Employees: 380
Square Footage: 27000
Brands:
Breeze
Ccbreeze
Cvbreeze
Delphi
Delphi 7.0
Global Sfa
Regional Delphi

26703 Newstamp Lighting Corp.
227 Bay Road
P.O. Box 189
North Easton, MA 02356-0189 508-238-7071
Fax: 508-230-8312 www.newstamplighting.com
Wall and ceiling lights
Owner: Robert Zeitsiff
VP Marketing: Charles Edwards
Estimated Sales: $1-2.5 Million
Number Employees: 10-19

26704 Newstamp Lighting Corp.
227 Bay Road
PO Box 189
North Easton, MA 02356-0189 508-238-7071
Fax: 508-230-8312 info@newstamplighting.com
www.newstamplighting.com
Electric lighting fixtures, metal stamping equipment, plumbing products and security windows; exporter of electric lighting fixtures
President: Robert Zeitsiff
VP: Sandra Zeitstiff
Clerk: Charlotte Zeitsiff
Estimated Sales: $2.5-5 Million
Number Employees: 10-19
Square Footage: 68000

26705 Newton Broom Company
1508 W Jourdan St
PO Box 358
Newton, IL 62448 618-783-4424
Fax: 618-783-2442 sales@newtonbroom.com
www.newtonbroom.com
Brooms, mops and staple brushes
Manager: Becky Shamhart
Estimated Sales: Below $5 Million
Number Employees: 20-49

26706 Nexel Industries
11 Harbor Park Dr
Port Washington, NY 11050-4656 516-484-5225
Fax: 516-625-0084 800-245-6682
nexelinfo@nexelwire.com www.nexelwire.com
Manufacturer, importer and exporter of material handling and storage systems including solid steel and wire shelving, trucks and carts
VP: John Svitek
Inside Sales Manager: Howard Ziporkin
National Sales Manager: Jerry Mark
Number Employees: 100-249
Square Footage: 2400000
Type of Packaging: Food Service, Private Label
Brands:
Loadmaster
Nexel
Nexelite
Nexelon
Poly-Z-Brite
Space-Trac

26707 Nexen Group
560 Oak Grove Pkwy
Vadnais Heights, MN 55127 651-484-5900
Fax: 651-286-1099 800-843-7445
info@nexengroup.com www.nexengroup.com
Owner: Hutch Schilling
Estimated Sales: $20 - 50 Million
Number Employees: 50-99

26708 Nexen Group
560 Oak Grove Pkwy
Vadnais Heights, MN 55127 651-484-5900
Fax: 651-286-1099 800-843-7445
info@nexengroup.com www.nexengroup.com
Industrial clutches, brakes, web guides, tension and registration controls rollstand pneumatic
Owner: Hutch Schilling
Director Marketing/Communications: Scott Carson
Estimated Sales: $20 - 50 Million
Number Employees: 50-99

26709 Nexira, Inc.
15 Somerset St
Somerville, NJ 08876 908-707-9400
Fax: 908-707-9405 info-usa@nexira.com
www.nexira.com
Acacia gum and supplier/importer of natural ingredients including emulsifiers, texturizers, coating agents, encapsulation carriers along with innovative ingredients. Nexira Health focuses on original actives for weight-managementjoint-health, antioxidant, anti-stress and a large number of botanical extracts
President: Stefane Dondain
Director: Michael Skubienski
Exhibit Manager: Barbara Archiello
Junior Manager: Karen Paulino
Estimated Sales: $14 Million
Type of Packaging: Bulk

26710 Ni Energy Services
801 E. 86th Avenue
Merrillville, IN 46410-6271 219-647-5990
Fax: 219-853-5161 www.nisource.com
Air pollution control, chilling units, heating systems, recording and monitoring devices and controls
Chairman of the Board: Gary L Neale
CEO: Eileen O Odum
Estimated Sales: $5-10 Million
Number Employees: 5-9

26711 Niagara Blower Company
673 Ontario St
Buffalo, NY 14207 716-875-2000
Fax: 716-875-1077 800-426-5169
sales@niagarablower.com
www.niagarablower.com
Manufacturer and exporter of custom refrigeration systems including bacteria-free, frost-free moisture management, evaporators, condensers and dehumidification
President: Peter Demakos
Marketing Assistant: Jen Dorman
Sales Manager: Phil Rowland
COO: Peter Demakos
Estimated Sales: $10 - 20 Million
Number Employees: 50-99
Square Footage: 100000
Brands:
Aero Heat Exchanger
Hygrol
No Frost

26712 Niantic Awning Company
193 Pennsylvania Ave
Niantic, CT 06357 860-739-0161
Fax: 860-739-0168 sailawn@aol.com
www.necpa.org
Commercial awnings
President: Scott Massey
Vice President: Cheryl Yennaco
Vice President: Mike Cornell
Estimated Sales: Less than $500,000
Number Employees: 5-9

26713 (HQ)Nice-Pak Products
2 Nice Pak Park
Orangeburg, NY 10962 800-999-6423
Fax: 845-365-1729 800-999-6423
nicepak@nicepak.com www.nicepak.com
Manufacturer and exporter of cleaning and sanitizing supplies including moist towelettes, disposable wash cloths, surface disinfectants and hand sanitizers
President: Robert Julius
CEO: Ron Gordon
CFO: Peter Giallorenzo
VP: Zachary Julius
R&D: Anand Bhate
Quality Control: Jeffrey Jackowski
Marketing: Joann Reilly
Sales: Mark Aylmore
Production: Mike Sarnto
Purchasing: Doreen Abramcheck
Estimated Sales: $165.5 Million
Number Employees: 1000
Square Footage: 325000
Type of Packaging: Consumer, Food Service, Private Label
Brands:
Alcohol Prep Pads 100's
Nice-N-Clean
Pdi
Rub a Dubs
Sani-Cloth
Sani-Hands
Sani-Wipe
Wet-Nap 1000-Pak

26714 Nicholas Machine and Grinding
7500 San Felipe St
Suite 600
Houston, TX 77063-1790 713-914-8077
Fax: 713-972-1164 800-747-1256
Owner: James Nail

26715 Nicholas Marketing Associates
179 Larch Ave
Bogota, NJ 07603-1222 201-343-9414
Fax: 201-343-3256
Consultant specializing in marketing and promotion
Director: Gary Fermature
Managing Director: Nicholas Zampetti, Jr.
Estimated Sales: $1-2.5 Million
Number Employees: 2

26716 Nichols Specialty Products
10 Parker Street
Southborough, MA 01772-1949 508-481-4367
Fax: 508-481-7806
Manufacturer and exporter of bottle and can capping machinery
President: Larry Quinlan
CEO: Janet Wellman
CFO: Shannon Quinlan
Number Employees: 10
Brands:
Kinex

26717 Nichols Wire
1547 Helton Dr
Florence, AL 35630 256-764-4271
Fax: 256-767-5152 www.nicholswire.com
Teabag wire
President: Earl D Thomason
Estimated Sales: $25 - 50 Million
Number Employees: 100-249

26718 Nicol Scales
7239 Envoy Ct.
Dallas, TX 75247 214-428-8181
Fax: 214-428-8127 800-225-8181
sales@nicolscales.com www.nicolscales.com
Manufacturer and exporter of industrial scales and force measuring equipment; also, leasing available
President, CEO: Ted Tabolka
Director of Finance: Oliver Jackson
Vice President, Service: Steve Ford
Director of Sales and Marketing: Jim Budke
Estimated Sales: $5 - 10 Million
Number Employees: 10-19

26719 Nicomac
80 Oak Street
Norwood, NJ 07648 201-768-9501
Fax: 201-768-9504 800-628-0006
sales@nicosgroup.com www.nicomac.com
Autoclaves, coaters, ceiling grid systems, ceiling panels, coatings, tabletaquous, design services, doors, automatic and manual, floor finishes, modular rooms, ovens, steam generators, sterilizers, autoclave, stopper sterilizing tablet hoppers
President: Francesco Nigris
Manager: Rosanne Cangialosi
Estimated Sales: $5 Million
Number Employees: 5

26720 (HQ)Nicosia Creative Expresso
355 W 52nd St Fl 8
New York, NY 10019 212-515-6600
Fax: 212-265-5422 info@niceltd.com
www.niceltd.com
Consultant to the food industry; packaging design services available
President: Davide Nicosia
Estimated Sales: Below $5,000,000
Number Employees: 20-49
Square Footage: 8000
Type of Packaging: Consumer, Food Service, Private Label, Bulk

Other Locations:
Nicosia Creative Expresso
Madrid

26721 Nieco Corporation
7950 Cameron Dr
Windsor, CA 95492 707-284-7100
Fax: 707-284-7430 800-643-2656
sales@nieco.com www.nieco.com
Manufacturer and exporter of automatic bun grilling and meat broiling machines for hamburgers, steaks, chicken and fish
President: Ed Baker
Executive VP: John Brown
Estimated Sales: $10-20 Million
Number Employees: 50-99
Square Footage: 75000
Type of Packaging: Food Service

26722 Nifty Products
4 Jocama Blvd
Old Bridge, NJ 08857 732-591-1140
Fax: 732-591-8477 800-631-2172
contactus@niftypack.com www.niftypack.com
Shipping room products, tape, tape and label dispensers, stretch film, strapping and tools and envelopes
President: Norman Ferber
Estimated Sales: $10-20 Million
Number Employees: 20-49

26723 Nigrelli Systems Inc
16024 County Road X
Kiel, WI 53042 920-693-3161
Fax: 920-693-3634 sales@nigrelli.com
www.aquamasterfountains.com
Manufacturer and exporter of continuous motion case and tray packing systems, tray formers, plastic tray denesting systems, bulk container and bottled water packers, wrap around packers and shrinkwrapping equipment
President: Nicholas Nigrelli
VP Sales: David O'Keefe
Estimated Sales: $10 - 20 Million
Number Employees: 50-99

26724 Nijal USA
1920 S 1st St
Minneapolis, MN 55454-1055 651-353-6702
Fax: 612-395-5257 sales@nijalusa.com
www.nijalusa.com
Meat and bakery processing equipment
President: Michael Halbaut

26725 Nijhuis Water Technology North America
560 West Washington Blvd
Unit 320
Chicago, IL 60661
Canada 312-300-4103
Fax: 312-300-4105 info@nijhuis-water.com
www.nijhuis-water.nl
Provides complete wastewater treatment systems and installation services
Vice President: Adriaan Van Der Beck
Parent Co: Nijhuis Water Technology B.V.

26726 Nikka Densok
610 Garrison St # D
Lakewood, CO 80215-5882 303-202-6190
Fax: 303-202-6195 800-806-4587
sales@nikkadensok.com www.nikkadensok.com
Leak detection systems for food product packaging
President: Brian Ball
Estimated Sales: $5 - 10 Million
Number Employees: 5-9
Parent Co: Nikka Densok

26727 Nilfisk-Advance America, Inc.
Sognevej 25
Broendby, DK 2605 445-323-8100
Fax: 454-343-7700 800-645-3475
questions@nilfisk-advance.com
www.nilfisk-advance.com
Powered cleaning equipment
Finance Manager: Gabe Digiacomo
Marketing Manager: Jessica Letscher
Estimated Sales: $5.1 Million
Number Employees: 25
Square Footage: 100000
Parent Co: NKT Holding

26728 Nimbus Water Systems
41840 McAlby Ct # A
Murrieta, CA 92562-7080 951-894-2800
Fax: 760-591-0106 800-451-9343
salesinfo@nimbuswater.com
www.nimbuswater.com
Manufacturer and exporter of water treatment equipment; also, consultant providing water and water recycle systems design services
Founder: Donald Bray
CEO: Mike Faulkner
VP Marketing/Sales: Tony Pagliano
Purchasing Manager: Bree Ann Plange
Estimated Sales: $2.5-5 Million
Number Employees: 1-4
Number of Products: 50
Square Footage: 140000
Brands:
Nimbus Cs
Nimbus Fs
Nimbus N
Nimbus Sierra
Nimbus Watermaker

26729 Nina Mauritz Design Service
603 W Park Avenue
Libertyville, IL 60048-2664 847-968-4438
Fax: 847-816-8618
Consultant specializing in space allocation, traffic flow, design and specification of food service equipment and interior finishes for commercial kitchens, cafeterias and dining areas
Principal: Nina Mauritz

26730 Niro
1600 Okeefe Rd
Hudson, WI 54016 715-386-9371
Fax: 715-386-9376 info@niroinc.com
www.niroinc.com
Custom fabrication, filtration equipment, aseptic processing equipment, heat recovery systems, deaerators, dryers, fluid bed, spray, pilot plants, process control, high pressure pumps and homogenizers
President: Steve Kaplan
VP: Eric Bryars
VP: Christian Svensgaard
Marketing Coordinator: Heather Szymanski
Sales Engineer: D Pai
Manager Food/Dairy Evaporators: Bo Bjarekull
Estimated Sales: $20 - 50 Million
Number Employees: 100-249
Parent Co: GEA Group
Other Locations:
Niro
Columbia MD

26731 Niro Inc
1600 Okeefe Rd
Hudson, WI 54016 715-386-9371
Fax: 715-386-9376 www.niroinc.com
Powder handling and packing systems
VP: Eric Bryars
Estimated Sales: $20 - 50 Million
Number Employees: 100-249

26732 Niroflex, USA
PO Box 90
Deerfield, IL 60015 847-400-2638
Fax: 847-919-3809 metalmesh@niroflex.com
www.niroflex.com
Maker of stainless steel mesh gloves and apparel that is designed to protect workers in the meat and poultry food processing industry.
Vice President: Loren Rivkin

26733 Nirsystems
12101 Tech Rd
Silver Spring, MD 20904-1915 301-680-0252
Fax: 301-236-0134 info@foss-nirsystems.com
www.foss-nirsystems.com
Manufacturer and exporter of rapid quality control analysis equipment including moisture, fat, protein and sugar for laboratory and in-plant application using near infrared technology
Estimated Sales: $20 Million
Number Employees: 1-4

26734 Nissan Forklift Corporation of North America
240 N Prospect St
Marengo, IL 60152-3235 815-568-0061
Fax: 815-568-0179 800-871-5438
nfcsales@nfcna.com www.barrett-trucks.com
Industrial gas, lp and electric forklift, walkie and reach trucks
President: Takanobu Tokugawa
Director Marketing: Keith Allmandinger
Manager Media Marketing: Tim Haley
Number Employees: 500-999
Square Footage: 1400000
Parent Co: Nissan Motor Company

26735 Nita Crisp Crackers LLC
454 S. Link Lane
Fort Collins, CO 80524 970-482-9090
Fax: 970-482-1043 866-493-4609
www.nitacrisp.com
Artisan flatbreats in small batches or in bulk to natural grocers, specialty food stores, and restaurants from coast to coast
Managing Partner: Steve Landry
CEO: Paul Pellegrino
Customer Service / Sales: Michele Hattman
Estimated Sales: $170,000
Number of Products: 1
Square Footage: 5614
Type of Packaging: Consumer, Food Service, Bulk
Brands:
Nita Crisp

26736 Nitech
911 23rd St. East
P.O.Box 1023
Columbus, NE 68602 402-564-3188
Fax: 402-563-2792 800-397-1100
sales@nitechindustries.com
www.nitechindustries.com
Turntables and stretch wrapping equipment
Owner: Roger Bettenhousen
Sales Director: Chris Bettenhausen
Estimated Sales: $2.5-5,000,000
Number Employees: 20-49
Type of Packaging: Bulk

26737 Nitsch Tool Company
1715 Grant Blvd
Syracuse, NY 13208 315-472-4044
Fax: 315-472-4051
Manufacturer and exporter of machine knives for baking
President: J Leonard Nitsch
Estimated Sales: Less than $500,000
Number Employees: 5-9

26738 Nitta Corporation of America
7605 Nitta Drive
Suwanee, GA 30024 770-497-0212
Fax: 770-623-1398 800-221-3689
aballard@nitta.com www.nitta.com
Urethane and PVC conveyor belts, rubber covered, leather power transmission belts
VP: Tracy Mc Soley
Marketing/Sales: Bruce Cooper
VP Operations: Kim Millsaps
Estimated Sales: $5-10 Million
Number Employees: 20-49

26739 Nolon Industries
PO Box T
Mantua, OH 44255 330-274-2283
Fax: 330-274-2283
Manufacturer and exporter of fiberglass reinforced plastic boxes
President: Nick Nicolanti
Type of Packaging: Bulk

26740 Nolu Plastics
30152 Aventura
Rancho Santa Margarita, CA 92688-2060 949-765-8744
Fax: 866-447-6587 800-346-7822
solusteam@solusii.com www.solusii.com
Plastic conveyor components, guide rails, chain supports, PVC conveyor rollers
Inside Sales: Kathy Yakas
District Manager: Kevin Dahill
Number Employees: 35
Number of Products: 15

26741 Nomaco
501 Nmc Dr
Zebulon, NC 27597 919-269-6500
Fax: 919-269-7936 info@nomaco.com
www.nomaco.com
Plastic foam extrusions
President: Julian Young
CEO: Mick Dannin

Estimated Sales: $10 - 20 Million
Number Employees: 250-499

26742 Nomafa
975 Old Norcross Rd # A
Lawrenceville, GA 30045-4321 770-338-5000
Fax: 770-338-5024 sales.ads.us@albint.com
www.albanydoorsystems.com
Plant Manager: Dan Garrau
Estimated Sales: $20 - 50 Million
Number Employees: 100-249
Parent Co: Albany International

26743 Nook Industries
4950 E 49th St
Cleveland, OH 44125-1016 216-271-7900
Fax: 216-271-7020 800-321-7800
www.nookindustries.com
Ball bearing screws, thread screw products, worm gear actuators, splines and mechanical power jacks
President: Ronald Domeck
CEO: Joe Mac, Jr.
CFO: Jack Schiffer
CEO: Joseph H Nook Jr
Chairman: Joseph H Nook Jr
Estimated Sales: $10 - 25 Million
Number Employees: 100-249

26744 Nor-Cal Beverage Company
2286 Stone Blvd
West Sacramento, CA 95691 916-372-0600
Fax: 916-374-2605 www.ncbev.com
Producer and wholesaler/distributor of beers, hard ciders, and nonalcoholic beverages. Also contract manufacturing and equipment solutions
President & CEO: Shannon Deary-Bell
CFO: Michael Motroni
EVP, Marketing & External Affairs: Roy Grant Deary III
EVP, Beer Sales & Distribution: Timothy Deary
Director of Sales & Marketing: Shelley Deary
Sales & Marketing Manager: Michael Deary
Estimated Sales: $36.7 Million
Number Employees: 574
Square Footage: 152000
Type of Packaging: Consumer, Food Service, Bulk
Brands:
Anheuser-Busch Inbev®
Activate Drinks
Alaskan® Brewing Company
Arizona Iced Tea
Arrowhead Spring Water
Black Diamond Brewing Company®
Calistoga Water
Crispin® Cider
Crown Imports®
Firestone Walker Brewery™
Fox Barrell Hard Cider®
Go Girl Energy Drink
Icelandic Spring Water
Illy Chilled Coffee
Nestle Nesquick
Rogue® Brewery
Sierra Nevada®
Speed Energy Drink
Wyders® Cider
Budweiser®
Busch®
Natural Light®
O'Doul's®
Michelob Light®
Hurricane®
King Cobra®
Rolling Rock®
Shock Top Belgian White™
Jack's Pumpkin Spice™
Beach Bum Blonde Ale™
Dominion
Fordham
Goose Island Honker's Ale
Kona Pale Ale
Redhook Esb
Starr Hill Amber Ale
Widmer Hefeweizen
Ziegenbock®
Land Shark Lager™
Redbridge™
Wild Blue™
Stella Artois
Bass
Beck's
Boddingtons Pub Ale
Hoegaarden
Leffe Blonde
Czechvar Lager
Kokanee®
Kirin Ichiban
Margaritaville Paradise Key Teas
Lost Energy®
Monster Energy®
Rumba™ Energy Juice
Unbound Energy
Icelandic Glacial Water
Bacardi Silver™
Tilt®

26745 (HQ)Nor-Lake
11 Keewaydin Drive
Salem, NH 03079 603-893-9701
Fax: 603-893-7324 www.norlake.com
Refrigeration systems including walk-in coolers, walk0in freezers, milk coolers, ice cream freezers, environmental rooms, plasma refrigerators and chromatography refrigerators.
Chairman of the Board: Roger Fix
President/Chief Executive Officer: David Dunbar
VP/Chief Legal Officer/Secretary: Deborah Rosen
Chief Financial Officer: Thomas DeByle
Chief Accounting Officer: Sean Valashinas
Group VP, Food Service Group: John Abbott
Warehouse Supervisor: Cory Schlosser
Procurement Manager: Terry Clay
Estimated Sales: $26 Million
Number Employees: 300
Square Footage: 20000
Parent Co: Standex International Corporation
Type of Packaging: Food Service
Brands:
Barrier
Classic
Fineline
Foodbank
Kold Locker
Nova Ii
Thermo Flow

26746 NorCrest Consulting
2044 County Road 512
Divide, CO 80814 719-687-7635
drsmonroe@netzero.net
Consultant specializing in business management and technical information on fermentation, yeast products and genetic engineering for the food ingredient and biotechnology industries
President: John Norell
VP: Beverly Norell
Number Employees: 14
Square Footage: 4000

26747 (HQ)Noral
88 Pleasant Street S.,
Natick, MA ÿ01760-563 508-653-5574
Fax: 508-653-1828 800-348-2345
sales@noral.com www.noral.com
Manufacturer and exporter of portable digital thermometers and probes including temperature measurement griddle probes, insertion, handheld and compact
President: Albert Ladanyi
CEO: Dr Deszo Ladanyi
VP Sales: Vincent Passiatore
Operations: Dave Gilgenback
Purchasing Director: Mark O'Malley
Estimated Sales: $1-2.5 Million
Number Employees: 20
Square Footage: 80000

26748 Norandal
801 Crescent Centre Drive
Suite 600
Franklin, TX 37067 615-771-5700
Fax: 615-771-5701 investrel@noralinc.com
www.norandaaluminum.com
Manufacturer and exporter of laminated foil and aluminum foil pie plates
VP, Communication & Investor Relations: John Parker
Estimated Sales: $97 Million
Number Employees: 820
Parent Co: Noranda
Type of Packaging: Private Label, Bulk

26749 Norback, Ley & Associates LLC
3022 Woodland Trail
Middleton, WI 53562 608-233-3814
Fax: 608-233-3895 nla@norbackley.com
www.norbackley.com
Provider of software tools for the food safety industry
President: Kathleen Ley
CFO: John Norback
R&D: John Norback
Quality Control: Kathleen Ley
Estimated Sales: $1 - 3 Million
Number Employees: 5-9

26750 Norden
230 Industrial Pkwy
Branchburg, NJ 08876-3580 908-252-9483
Fax: 908-707-0073 sales@norden-pac.se
www.norden-pac.com
Tube filling and cartoning machinery; also, automatic tube feeders
President: Scott Winfield
Sales Director: Fredrik Nusson
Estimated Sales: $5 - 10 Million
Number Employees: 20-49
Parent Co: Norden Pac International AB

26751 Nordfab Systems
PO Box 429
Thomasville, NC 27361-0429 336-889-5599
Fax: 336-889-7873 800-533-5286
Manufacturer and importer of dust collection filters, cyclones, grinders, pipe clamps and ducts
President: Niels Pedersen
Marketing Director: Tarey Cullen
VP Sales: Steve McDaniel
Estimated Sales: $20-50 Million
Number Employees: 100-249
Brands:
Clean-Sweep
Quick-Fit
Vortex

26752 Nordic Doors
PO Box 20
Dumas, AR 71639-0020 800-827-0326
Fax: 870-382-6140

26753 Nordic Printing & Packaging
5017 Boone Ave N
New Hope, MN 55428 763-535-6440
Fax: 763-535-1821
briananderson@marcomnordic.com
moneta.lv
Lithopraphic printed and folding cartons
Owner: Dee Dee Foster
CFO: Dee Dee Faster
Quality Control: Mary Rubink
Sales Director: Rick Parkin
Office Manager: Lee Thomson
Purchasing Manager: Jeff Vander Plaats
Estimated Sales: $10 - 20 Million
Number Employees: 50-99
Type of Packaging: Consumer, Food Service, Private Label, Bulk

26754 Nordson Corporation
11475 Lakefield Dr
Duluth, GA 30097 770-497-3400
Fax: 866-667-3329 800-683-2314
pkgwebcontacts@nordson.com
www.nordson.com
Manufacturer and exporter of adhesive dispensers and applicators, adhesives, coatings, heat sealers and coating, gluing, labeling and packaging machinery
President: John Raven
VP: John Keane
Manager Marketing Communication: Dave Grgetic
Business Developmental Specialist: Salieta Stone
Estimated Sales: $20-50 Million
Number Employees: 250-499

26755 Noren Products
1010 Obrien Dr
Menlo Park, CA 94025 650-322-9500
Fax: 650-324-1348 866-936-6736
sales@norenproducts.com
www.norenproducts.com
Manufacturer and exporter of heat pipes, compact cabinet coolers, thermal pins, AcoustiLock, and HyTec Coolers.
Owner: Kimberely Dawn
Estimated Sales: $10-20,000,000
Number Employees: 100-249
Brands:
Compact

26756 Norgren
5400 S Delaware St
Littleton, CO 80120 303-794-2611
Fax: 303-798-4856 kathleenb@usa.norgren.com
www.norgren.com

Pneumatic filters, regulators, lubricators, valves, actuators, push-in fittings and accessories
President Airline Division: William Wolsky
CEO: Jim Mannebach
VP Marketing: Terry Weeber
Estimated Sales: $100 - 200 Million
Number Employees: 5,000-9,999
Parent Co: IMI

26757 Norgren-KIP Fluid Controls
72 Spring Ln
Farmington, CT 06032 860-677-0272
Fax: 860-677-4999 800-722-5547
sales@kipinc.com www.kipinc.com

Solenoid valves, liquid level controls, pressure switches
Executive Director: Gary Fett
Quality Control: Ned Lanfranco
Marketing: Karen Markie
Operations: Gary Fett
Purchasing: Dave Simons
Estimated Sales: $10-20 Million
Number Employees: 100-249
Parent Co: IMI Norgren

26758 Norgus Silk Screen Company
58 Sylvan Ave
Clifton, NJ 07011 973-365-0600
Fax: 973-365-2749

Shelf tackers, dividers, point of purchase signs, window banners and signage
President: Sanjay Thakker
Estimated Sales: $30-50 Million
Number Employees: 1-4
Square Footage: 8000

26759 Norland International
PO Box 67189
Lincoln, NE 68506 402-441-3737
Fax: 402-441-3735 bk@norlandintl.com
www.norland-intl.com

Bottled water plants, water distillation systems, small bottle filler options, ozone generating systems, pre-treatment systems, blow molding equipment
Owner: Mike Mc Farland
Estimated Sales: $1 - 2.5 Million
Number Employees: 20-49

26760 Norman International
4501 S Santa Fe Ave
Vernon, CA 90058-2129 323-582-7132
Fax: 323-582-3464 800-289-8644
un4g@yahoo.com
www.normaninternational.com

Manufactures vinyl radio frequency heat seald bags, is also an importer of vinyl zipper bags for retail packaging.
President: Norman Levine
Estimated Sales: $20-50 Million
Number Employees: 20-49

26761 Norman N. Axelrod Associates
445 E 86th St
New York, NY 10028 212-741-6302
naxelrod@ix.netcom.com
www.axelrodassociates.com

Manufacturer and exporter of optical sensing and vision systems for automated quality and process control systems for food processing and packaging. Consultant, market studies on optical sensing and control technologies
President: Norman N Axelrod, Phd
Manager of Systems Integration: C Chang
Manager Software Development: R Rolle
Estimated Sales: Below 1 Million
Number Employees: 10-19

26762 Normandie Metal Fabricators
55 Channel Drive
Port Washington, NY 11050-2216 516-944-9141
Fax: 516-944-3670 800-221-2398

Cabinets, carts, dollies, racks, tables, pizza ovens and transport equipment
VP Sales: Jordan Klein
VP Operations: Bill Koines
Number Employees: 20-49

26763 Norpak Corporation
70 Blanchard St
Newark, NJ 07105 973-589-4200
Fax: 973-578-8845 800-631-6970
sales@norpak.net www.norpak.net

Manufacturer, importer and exporter of plain and printed food wrap including foil laminated, waxed and freezer paper; also, baking pan liners and interfolded deli sheets
President: Anthony Coraci
CFO: Lidia Gelasmagas
VP/General Manager: Robert Godown
Sales Manager: Michael Pacyna
Estimated Sales: $20 - 30 Million
Number Employees: 50-99
Square Footage: 100000
Brands:
Delwrap
Lightning Wrap
Meat Pak
Mica Wax
Nuparch
War Wrap

26764 Norris Dispenser Company
1600 Xenium Ln N
Minneapolis, MN 55441-3706 763-923-2441
Fax: 763-553-1209 800-252-5561
info@stevens-lee.com www.silverking.com

Refrigerated bulk milk dispensers
President: Corey Kohl
Executive VP: Benjuman Rubin
Marketing Head: Benjuman Rubin
Estimated Sales: $15 - 20 Million
Number Employees: 100-249
Parent Co: Prince Castle
Brands:
Norris
Silver King

26765 Norristown Box Company
PO Box 377
Norristown, PA 19404-0377 610-275-5540
Fax: 610-275-6585

Set-up and folding paper boxes for pharmaceutical, glass, confectionery and industrial instruments
President: John P Eliff
Office Manager: S Fryer
Estimated Sales: $2.5-5 Million
Number Employees: 5-9
Brands:
Norrbox

26766 Norristown Box Company
PO Box 377
Norristown, PA 19404-0377 610-275-5540
Fax: 610-275-6585

Posters, paperboard, folding and set-up boxes
President: John P Eliff
Estimated Sales: $2.5-5 Million
Number Employees: 5-9

26767 Norse Dairy Systems
PO Box 1869
Columbus, OH 43216 614-294-4931
Fax: 614-299-0538 800-338-7465
kmcgrath@norse.com www.norse.com

Filling equipment for the ice cream industry; also, ice cream cones and push-up tubes
President: Scott Fullbright
CFO: Randy Harvey
R & D: Gunther Brinkman
Director Operations: John Deininger
Estimated Sales: $1 million
Number Employees: 2

26768 Norse Dairy Systems
1740 Joyce Avenue
Columbus, OH 43216 614-294-4931
Fax: 614-299-0538 inforequest@norse.com
www.norse.com

Ice cream cones
President: Scott Fullbright
R&D: Gunther Brinkman
CFO: Randy Harvey
Estimated Sales: $1 million
Number Employees: 1-4

26769 North American ContainerCorporation
1811 West Oak Park
Suite D
Maretta, GA 30062 770-431-4858
Fax: 770-431-6957 800-929-0610
www.nacontainer.com

Custom manufactured bulk boxes and fibercore wood replacement material
Estimated Sales: $10-20,000,000
Number Employees: 50-99
Type of Packaging: Bulk

26770 North American PackagingCorporation
140 E 30th St
New York, NY 10016 212-213-4141
Fax: 212-213-4145 800-499-3521
info@packagingonline.com
www.packagingonline.com

Manufacturer and importer of shopping, paper and plastic bags, gift boxes and stationery including letterhead, business cards, gift certificates, roll and sheet labels, press kits, catalogs, fliers, etc
Manager: John Destefano
Manager: John DeStefano
Estimated Sales: Below $5,000,000
Number Employees: 1-4

26771 North American Plastic Manufacturing Company
8 Park Lawn Dr
Bethel, CT 06801 203-577-4042
Fax: 203-598-0068 800-934-7752
perl@napcomfg.com www.napcomfg.com

Self-adhesive plastic hangers, hang tabs and point of purchase hangstrip systems for display packaging
Owner: Robert Laperriere
Sales Manager: Dean Kyburz
Estimated Sales: $1 - 5 Million
Number Employees: 1-4
Square Footage: 9000
Brands:
Pop Strip

26772 North American Roller Products, Inc
P.O.Box 2142
Glen Ellyn, IL 60138-2142 630-858-9161
Fax: 630-858-9103 info@narp-trapo.com
www.narp-trapo.com

Conveyor rollers and specialty conveyors
President: Jerry Miller
General Manager: Jerry Miller
Estimated Sales: Less than $500,000
Number Employees: 5-9

26773 (HQ)North American Salt Company
9900 W 109th St Ste 600
Overland Park, KS 66210 913-344-9100
Fax: 913-344-9314 www.compassminerals.com

Full-line salt manufacturer, products include agricultural, water softeners, consumer ice melters, industrial applications, food grade, and rock salt
CFO: Rodney Underdown
CEO: Angelo Brisimitzakis
Sales Director: Nathan Herrman
Estimated Sales: $100+ Million
Number Employees: 100-249
Other Locations:
Ogden UT
Lyons KS
Unity, Saskatchewan
Kenosha WI
Cote Blanche LA
Amherst, Nova Scotia
Goderich, Ontario

26774 North American Signs
PO Box 30
South Bend, IN 46624-0030 574-234-5252
Fax: 574-237-6166 800-348-5000
POBox30@northamericansigns.com
www.northamericansigns.com

Electric and neon signs
President: John Yarger
CEO: Noel Yarger
CFO: Tom Yarger
Production Manager: Doug McCoigge
Estimated Sales: $10-20 Million
Number Employees: 50-99

26775 North Atlantic EquipmentSales
Route 376
Hopewell Jct, NY 12533 845-221-2201
Fax: 845-227-7795 naes@vh.net
Analyzes and tests plant operations, infrared, total solids, fat, protein, process control
President: Varick Stringham
CFO: Varick Stringham
R&D: Varick Stringham
Quality Control: Varick Stringham
Estimated Sales: $500,000 - $1 Million
Number Employees: 1-4

26776 North Carolina Box
5620 Departure Dr
Raleigh, NC 27616 919-872-3007
Fax: 919-850-9353 www.prattindustries.com
Corrugated boxes
Manager: Pam Blackwell
Quality Control: Ed Allen
Sales Manager: Rick White
Estimated Sales: $20-50 Million
Number Employees: 50-99
Parent Co: Pratt Industries

26777 North Carolina's Southeast
707 West Broad Street
P.O.Box 2556
Elizabethtown, NC 28337 800-787-1333
Fax: 910-862-1482 locate@ncse.org
www.ncse.org
President: Steve Yost
Finance and Office Manager: Tammy Etheridge
Director: Paul G Butler Jr
Director of Business Development: Joe Melvin
Plant Manager: Derek Pringle
Estimated Sales: $1 - 3 Million
Number Employees: 5-9

26778 North Company
E1683 Larson Road
Waupaca, WI 54981-8734 715-258-6104
Fax: 715-258-4986 foodjobs@execpc.com
www.execpc.com/foodjobs
Executive search firm specializing in research and development
Executive Recruiter: Henry Warmbier, Ph.D.
Recruiter: Lori Warmbier
Number Employees: 2

26779 North Fork Welding
PO Box 547
Greenport, NY 11944 631-477-0671
Fax: 631-477-0702 sales@nfwss.com
www.nfwss.com
Wine industry netting reels
President: Joseph Schoenstein
VP: Fred Shonestein
Estimated Sales: $1-2.5 Million
Number Employees: 10-19

26780 North Side Packaging Corporation
2200 Rivers Edge Dr
Arnold, PA 15068-4540 724-335-5800
Fax: 724-335-2249
customerservice@northsidefoods.com
www.emberfarms.com
Processing
President: Robert G Hofmann Ii
CFO: Robert Muhl
R&D: Paula McDaniel
Quality Control: John Stavencon John
Estimated Sales: H
Number Employees: 250-499

26781 North Star
2120 Hewitt Avenue
Everett, WA 98201-3616 425-252-9600
Fax: 425-252-7598 amy@northstarinc.com
www.northstarinc.com
Espresso carts, coffee grinders
President: Craig Bunney
Estimated Sales: $1-2.5 Million
Number Employees: 5-9

26782 North Star Engineered Prduct
P.O.Box 1141
Perrysburg, OH 43552-1141 419-726-2645
Fax: 419-726-8583 sales@bockengineered.com
www.northstarengineered.com
Manufactures equipment to process fresh cut vegetables and fruit, including fruit processing centrifuges
Owner: Tom Ziems
CFO: John K Clement
Sales Manager: Joe Moroni
Technical Services: Buddy Santus
Estimated Sales: $2.5 - 5 Million
Number Employees: 10-19
Type of Packaging: Bulk
Brands:
Helical
Mini Brute
Six Shooter
Tornado

26783 North Star Ice EquipmentCorporation
8151 Occidental Ave S
PO Box 80227
Seattle, WA 98108 206-763-7300
Fax: 206-763-7323 800-321-1381
info@northstarice.com www.northstarice.com
Manufacturer and exporter of industrial ice makers and related handling equipment
President: Jonathan Deex
Chairman: Leland Shepardson
CFO: Alan Smyth
R&D: Lenny Kaplan
Marketing Director: Tom Crawford
Sales Manager: Larry Hunhoff
Estimated Sales: $10 - 20 Million
Number Employees: 20-49
Square Footage: 30000
Brands:
Cold Spell
Coldisc

26784 NorthStar Print Group
1222 Perry Way
Watertown, WI 53094 920-206-8626
Fax: 920-262-8582 labelsales@nspq.com
www.multicolorcorp.com
Label production
President: Richard Gasper
CEO: Richard Gasper
CFO: Jim Gombar
R&D: Jerry Fowler
Quality Control: Grieg Petere
Marketing: Terry Fowler
Sr. VP Manufacturing: Andy Walker
Plant Manager: Greg Petre
Estimated Sales: $60 Million
Number Employees: 100-249
Parent Co: Journal Communications

26785 Northbrook Laboratories
1818 Skokie Boulevard
Northbrook, IL 60062-4106 847-272-8700
Fax: 847-272-2348 877-366-3522
djalw@northlandlabs.com
www.northlandlabs.com
Laboratory analysis for food, feed and environmental applications
President: Jamal Alwattar
Estimated Sales: $5 - 10 Million
Number Employees: 50-99

26786 Northcoast Woodworks
381 Buffalo Street
Conneaut, OH 44030-2451 440-593-6249
Fax: 440-593-6249
Wine industry wooden gift boxes

26787 Northeast Box Company
PO Box 370
Ashtabula, OH 44005-0370 440-992-5500
Fax: 440-992-7820 800-362-8100
www.northeastbox.com
Corrugated boxes, shipping containers and point of purchase displays; consultant specializing in J.I.T. warehousing manufactured to specifications
President: Ronald Marchewka
CFO: Peter Adano
VP/Secretary/Treasurer: Paul Seibert
General Manager: Billy Powers
Estimated Sales: $20-50 Million
Number Employees: 50-99
Square Footage: 60000

26788 Northeast Container Corporation
125 Washington Ave
Dumont, NJ 07628-3066 201-385-6200
Fax: 201-385-7356
Corrugated shipping containers
President: John Payne
Estimated Sales: $8-9 Million
Number Employees: 50-99
Square Footage: 65000

26789 Northeast Distributors
210 Essex St
Suite 3
Whitman, MA 02382 781-447-0073
Fax: 781-447-6337 sales@nedinc.com
www.nedinc.com
Ice equipment, piping, fittings and tubing
CEO: Kenneth G Peterson
Quality Control: Linda Mahoney
Estimated Sales: Below $5 Million
Number Employees: 20-49

26790 Northeast Laboratory Services
PO Box 788
Waterville, ME 04903-0788 207-873-7711
Fax: 207-873-7022 866-591-7120
bmears@binax.com www.nelabservices.com
Food technology laboratory service specializing in USDA certified listeria-salmonella and KAB/nutritional analysis and food-born illness investigations; also, product development and shelf life determination
President & CEO: Rodney Mears
Production Planning Manager: Eva Chase
Administration Manager: Vicki Massey
Lab Manager: Pam Doughty
Estimated Sales: $6-8 Million
Number Employees: 50-99
Square Footage: 108000
Parent Co: BINAX
Type of Packaging: Consumer, Food Service, Private Label, Bulk

26791 Northeast Packaging Company
875 Skyway Street
Presque Isle, ME 04769 207-764-6271
Fax: 207-764-1957 www.nepcobags.com
Paper and poly bags
President: Robert Umphrey
Sales Representative: Ken Joy
General Manager: Chris Burtchell
Production Manager: Jesse Harris
Number Employees: 20-49
Type of Packaging: Consumer, Private Label

26792 Northeast Packaging Materials
20 Robert Pitt Dr Ste 202
Monsey, NY 10952 845-426-2900
Fax: 845-426-3700 sbraun@nepack.com
www.nepack1.com
Manufacturer and exporter of barrier films; available in roll stock and pouches
President and QC: Stewart Braun
Estimated Sales: Below $5,000,000
Number Employees: 1-4

26793 Northeastern Products Corporation
115 Sweet Road
PO Box 98
Warrensburg, NY 12885 518-623-3161
Fax: 518-623-3803 800-873-8233
info@nep-co.com www.nep-co.com
Manufacturer and exporter of meat smoking sawdust including hickory, maple, cherry and alder
President: Gary Shiavi
CEO: Paul Schiavi
Marketing Director: Richard Morgan
Estimated Sales: Below $5 Million
Number Employees: 50-99
Square Footage: 40000

26794 Northern Berkshire Manufacturing Company
121 Union St
North Adams, MA 01247-3533 413-663-9204
Marking devices, rubber stamps, pads, ink, decals, engraved nameplates,architectural signs,etc
President: John Luczynsky
Estimated Sales: $300,000-500,000
Number Employees: 1-4
Parent Co: JPDS

26795 Northern Box Company
PO Box 985
Elkhart, IN 46515-0985 574-264-2161
Fax: 574-262-8943

Corrugated shipping boxes
President: Heidi Linder
VP: Tina Linder
Estimated Sales: $5-10 Million
Number Employees: 20-49

26796 Northern Metals & Supply
2100 Llano Rd
Santa Rosa, CA 95407-6430 707-575-0555
Fax: 707-575-4088
Wine and food industry stainless sanitary fittings, butterfly valve, ball valves, stainless pipe and tubing, pipe fittings, and stainless and aluminum raw material
President: Thomas F Obuchowski
Estimated Sales: $5-10 Million
Number Employees: 5-9

26797 Northern Package Corporation
201 W 86th Street
Minneapolis, MN 55420-2784 952-881-5861
Fax: 952-881-6758
Corrugated paper boxes
General Manager: Joe Gerow
Number Employees: 55
Parent Co: Liberty Diversified Industries

26798 Northern Stainless Fabricating
P.O.Box 6715
Traverse City, MI 49696-6715 231-947-4580
Fax: 231-947-9074 mike@nsfi.com
www.nsfi.com
Manufacturer and exporter of custom made stainless steel kitchen equipment for food service and institutional use including salad bars, dish tables and prep tables
President: Mike Fisher
Chief Estimator: Harry Muse
CFO: Michael J Fisher
VP Production: Bruce Muzzarelli
Estimated Sales: $10-20 Million
Number Employees: 50-99
Square Footage: 30000

26799 Northern Wire Products
PO Box 70
St Cloud, MN 56302-0070 320-252-3442
Fax: 320-252-2832 800-458-5549
info@norwire.com www.norwire.com
Wire and tubing point of purchase merchandising displays and fixtures
President: Larry Leutt
CEO and President: Larry Lautt
Sr. Sales Engineering: Chuck Lauer
General Manager: Marc Illies
Estimated Sales: $10 - 20 Million
Number Employees: 100-249
Square Footage: 150000
Parent Co: St. Cloud Industry

26800 Northfield Freezing Systems
PO Box 98
Northfield, MN 55057-0098 507-645-9546
Fax: 507-645-6148 800-426-1283
info@northfieldfreezing.com
www.northfieldfreezing.com
Manufacturer and exporter of freezers, coolers, chillers, hardeners and spiral conveying freezing systems
President: Tim Colies
Sales/Marketing Executive: Larry Deboer
Purchasing Agent: Bill Westby
Estimated Sales: $20 - 50 Million
Number Employees: 120
Parent Co: Frigo Schndia

26801 Northland Consultants
3741 Highway 556
RR2
Sault Ste. Marie, ON P6A 5K7 705-541-8490
www.northlandconsultants.ca
Marketing consultant specializing in brand development for food products
Managing Partner: Marko Koskenoja
Estimated Sales: Less than $500,000
Number Employees: 1-4

26802 Northland Corporation
1260 E Van Deinse St
Greenville, MI 48838 616-754-5601
Fax: 616-754-0970 800-223-3900
customerservice@northlandnka.net
www.northlandnka.com
President: Gordon Stauffer
CFO: Brad Stauffer
R & D: Jim Holland
Quality Control: Jim Nielsen
Plant Manager: Kent Coon
Estimated Sales: Below $5 Million
Number Employees: 100-249
Parent Co: Aga Rangemaster Group

26803 Northland Laboratories
1818 Skokie Blvd
Northbrook, IL 60062-4106 847-412-6490
Fax: 847-272-2348 800-366-3522
djalw@northlandlabs.com
www.northlandlabs.com
Consultant specializing in food testing and analysis services for microbiological contamination, chemical analysis/composition and nutritional labeling
President: Jamal Alwattar
General Manager: D Alwatter
Estimated Sales: $1 - 5 Million
Number Employees: 50-99
Square Footage: 14000

26804 Northland Process Piping
1662 320th Ave
Isle, MN 56342 320-679-2119
Fax: 320-679-2785 mnoffice@nppmn.com
www.nppmn.com
Brine and clean-in place systems, floor plates and drains, platforms, walkways and stairs, pumps, tanks, tubing and valves
Owner: Dan Tramm
CFO: Kathy Tramm
Project Sales/Customer Service: Dan Tramm
Foreman: Eirik Andersen
Purchasing/Customer Service: Bruce Richards
Number Employees: 50-99
Other Locations:
Roswell GA
Lemoore CA
Horseheads NY

26805 Northland RefrigerationCompany
P.O.Box 400
Greenville, MI 48838-0400 616-754-5601
Fax: 616-754-0970 800-223-3900
www.northlandnka.com
Custom refrigeration, commercial and residential
President: Mike Bufton
CFO: Karen Braund
Vice President: Brad Stauffer
Research & Development: Jim Holland
Quality Control: Rick Waldorf
Marketing Director: Gerry Reda
Public Relations: Sindy Angi
Operations/Plant Manager: Kent Coon
Plant Manager: Kent Coon
Purchasing Manager: Richard Burns
Estimated Sales: $10 - 20 Million
Number Employees: 100-249
Square Footage: 220000
Parent Co: AGA Food Service Group
Brands:
Imperial

26806 Northland Stainless
1119A Bridge Street
PO Box 100
Tomahawk, WI 54487 715-453-5326
Fax: 715-453-5357 info@northlandstainless.com
www.samuelpressurevesselgroup.com
Fabricator of custom designed screw conveyors, heat exchangers, sanitary tanks, pressure vessels from stainless steel and other high alloy metals with sanitary finish
President: Barry Berquist
Quality Control: Gary Anderson
Sales Director: Robert Eaton
Plant Manager: Lenny Bartz
Purchasing Manager: Ann Kelash
Estimated Sales: $10 Million
Number Employees: 50-99
Square Footage: 65000
Parent Co: The Samuel Pressure Vessel Group

26807 Northstar Print Group
1836 Sal St
Green Bay, WI 54302-2114 920-468-1614
Fax: 920-468-6793 800-236-8208
labelsales@nspg.com www.multicolorcorp.com
Labels including flexo, pressure sensitive and glue applied; also, pressure sensitive films and tags
President: Andrew Walker
CFO: James Gombar
Operations: Gary Karnopp
Quality Control: Greg Liplante
Estimated Sales: $10 - 20 Million
Number Employees: 50-99
Square Footage: 40000
Parent Co: NorthStar Print Group

26808 Northview Laboratories
616 Heathrow Dr
Lincolnshire, IL 60069 847-564-8181
Fax: 847-564-8269 nvl@northviewlabs.com
www.us.sgs.com
Independent testing laboratory offering microbiological, sterility assurance, chemistry & toxicology services. Specialized services including water system validation and monitoring, environmental chamber storage and feeding studies
Manager: Martin Spalding
Quality Control: Leonart Wojtowicz
CEO: Martin J Spalding Sr
Marketing Director: Laura Ritter
Sales Director: Trisha Daugherty
Plant Manager: Richard Harrington
Estimated Sales: $20 - 50 Million
Number Employees: 100-249
Square Footage: 23000

26809 Northview Laboratories
106 Venture Boulevard
Spartanburg, SC 29306-3805 864-574-7728
Fax: 864-574-7873 nva@northviewlabs.com
www.northviewlabs.com
Independent testing laboratory offering microbiological, sterility assurance, chemistry and toxicology services
President: Delores Bruce
CFO: Ed Kelley
Vice President of Leasing: David Happ
Chief Operating Officer: Rolland Baribeau
Estimated Sales: $1 - 2.5 Million
Number Employees: 15
Square Footage: 92000
Other Locations:
Northview Laboratories
Spartanburg SC
Northview Laboratories
Hercules CA

26810 (HQ)Northview Pacific Laboratories
551 Linus Pauling Dr
Hercules, CA 94547 510-741-3744
Fax: 510-964-0551 nvp@northviewlabs.com
www.northviewlabs.com
Consultant offering food testing services
Manager: Mario Sotelo
Quality Control: Sarah Khan
VP: Thomas Spalding
R & D: Lonny Barish
Estimated Sales: $10-20 Million
Number Employees: 50-99
Parent Co: Northview Labs
Other Locations:

26811 Northwest Analytical
111 SW 5th Ave Ste 800
Portland, OR 97204-3606 503-224-7727
Fax: 503-224-5236 888-692-7638
nwa@nwasoft.com www.nwasoft.com
Manufacturer and exporter of SPC charting workstation and statistical quality control (SQC) software for control charting, process capability analysis and plant floor data collection
CEO: Cliff Vee
CFO: David Bundy
VP: Jeff Cawley
R&D: Louis Halvorsen
Marketing Director: Jennifer Anderson
Corporate Account Manager: Shawn McTimpeny
Estimated Sales: $10-20,000,000
Number Employees: 30

26812 Northwest Laboratories of Seattle
241 S Holden St
Seattle, WA 98108 206-763-6252
Fax: 206-763-3949 postmaster@nwlabs1896.com
www.nwlabs1896.com

Consultant offering analysis, testing and food research services
President: Richard Schefsky
CEO: Richard Schefsky II
Estimated Sales: $1 - 3 Million
Number Employees: 5-9
Square Footage: 21000

26813 Northwest Molded Products Classic Line
4915 21st Street
Racine, WI 53406-5028 262-554-4412
Fax: 262-554-8370 nwest@clawsonibcs.com
www.classicboxes.com
Small, rigid molded plastic boxes, hot stamp decorating, foam inserts and custom molding
Estimated Sales: $5-10 Million
Number Employees: 20-49

26814 Northwest Products
600 Oak St
Archbold, OH 43502 419-445-1950
Fax: 419-446-2984
Wooden pallets
COO: Philip Zuver
Executive Director: Bruce Abell
Sales Representative: John Miller
Executive Director: Phillip Zuver
Estimated Sales: $20 - 50 Million
Number Employees: 100-249
Parent Co: Quadco Rehabilitation Center

26815 Northwestern
15054 Oxnard St
Van Nuys, CA 91411 818-786-1581
Fax: 818-786-5063
russbrown@northwestern.com
Display cases and store fixtures
President: C Wayne Noecker
CFO: Rughann Etz
VP: Douglas Noecker
Estimated Sales: $10 - 20 Million
Number Employees: 50-99

26816 Northwestern Corporation
922 Armstrong St
PO Box 490
Morris, IL 60450 815-942-1300
Fax: 815-942-4417 800-942-1316
sales@nwcorp.com www.nwcorp.com
Manufacturer and exporter of vending machinery
President: Richard Bolen
CFO: Angie Stropel
R&D: Angie Stropel
Quality Control: Angie Stropel
Sales Director: Diane Olson
Estimated Sales: $10 - 20 Million
Number Employees: 50-99
Square Footage: 50000

26817 Northwind
13300 Maple Hill Rd
Alpena, AR 72611 870-437-2585
Fax: 870-437-2595 nw@northwindinc.com
www.northwindinc.com
Sanitary conveyors, wash stations, meat hoppers, tanks, catwalks and support equipment
President: Mark Ogier
Quality Control: Tim Ogier
Secretary: Tim Ogier
Estimated Sales: Below $5,000,000
Number Employees: 10-19

26818 Norton Performance Plastics
150 Dey Rd
Wayne, NJ 07470 973-696-4700
Fax: 973-696-4056 www.plastics.saint-gobain.com
Manufacturer and exporter of food tubing, operating pressures and dispensing tank samples; also, laboratory R&D available
President: Tom Kinisky
VP Fluid Systems: John Ekstrom
VP Marketing: K Sidman
Estimated Sales: $200 - 500 Million
Number Employees: 250-499
Parent Co: Saint-Gobain Corporation
Brands:
Norwell
Tygon

26819 Norvell Company
4002 Liberty Bell Rd
Fort Scott, KS 66701 620-223-3110
Fax: 620-223-3115 800-653-3147
sales@norvllco.com www.norvellco.com
Manufacturer and exporter of flour mill sifters for the processing of flour, spices, cereals, etc.; also, agitators for blending
Office Manager: Barbara Fitts
General Manager: Mark Shank
Manager: Mark Shank
Estimated Sales: $5-10 Million
Number Employees: 20-49
Square Footage: 40000
Type of Packaging: Food Service
Brands:
Jet Sifter
Santare
Super Drive Sifter

26820 Norwalt Design Inc.
961 State Route 10 # 2a
Randolph, NJ 07869 973-927-3200
Fax: 973-927-2841 norwalt@norwalt.com
www.norwalt.com
Bottle capping and plugging equipment, rotary disc and parts feeders, unscramblers, elevator hoppers and assembly machines
President: Walter McDonald
Director Marketing: Anthony Conte
Estimated Sales: $2.5 - 5 Million
Number Employees: 20-49
Square Footage: 60000

26821 Norwood Marking Systems
2538 Wisconsin Ave
Downers Grove, IL 60515 630-968-0646
Fax: 630-968-7672 800-626-3464
info@itw-norwood.com www.itw-norwood.com
Manufacturer and exporter of coding systems and accessories including hot stamp imprinters, thermal transfer printers, embossers, hot stamp and thermal transfer ribbon supplies and steel type
Manager: Larry Kulik
General Manager: Larry Kulik
Sales Director: Cliff Vanwey
Estimated Sales: $20-50 Million
Number Employees: 50-99
Parent Co: Illinois Tool Works

26822 Norwood Paper
7001 W 60th Stÿÿ
Chicago, IL 60638 773-788-1508
Fax: 708-656-5310 sales@norwoodpaper.com
www.norwoodpaper.com
Paper boards, box fillers and layering sheets
Sales Manager: Darin Rakowsky
Sales Manager: Matt Zeman
Estimated Sales: $10-20,000,000
Number Employees: 10

26823 Nosaj Disposables
PO Box 1290
Paterson, NJ 07509 973-279-4190
Fax: 973-279-6929 800-631-3809
nj@nosj.net www.ndiproducts.com
Trash liners, hand cleaners, disposable industrial paper towels and cloth wipers
President: Stanley Slosberg
Sales Director: Harold Gelvan
Estimated Sales: $5 - 10 Million
Number Employees: 10-19
Square Footage: 40000

26824 Nosco
651 S Martin Luther King Jr
Waukegan, IL 60085-7500 847-360-4806
Fax: 847-360-4924 rxquality@nosco.com
www.nosco.com
Folding cartons and labels including roll and cut; also, instructional enclosures and printing of promotional literature available
President: Russell Haraf
CFO: Michael Biesboar
Estimated Sales: $20 - 50 Million
Number Employees: 250-499
Square Footage: 200000

26825 Noteworthy Company
100 Church St
Amsterdam, NY 12010 800-696-7849
Fax: 518-842-8317 www.noteworthy.com
Bags including polyethylene, take home, patch, soft loop and molded handle, etc.; also, holiday
Owner: Carol Constigino
CFO: John Cloanglo
Estimated Sales: $10 - 20 Million
Number Employees: 250-499

26826 Nothum Food Processing Systems
631 S Kansas Ave
Springfield, MO 65802 417-831-2816
Fax: 417-866-4781 800-435-1297
nothum@nothum.com www.nothum.com
Manufacturer and exporter of batter applicators, breaders, pre-dusters, fryers, shuttle conveyors, char markers, coaters, blanchers, filters, ovens, polar therm and stack freezers, etc.
President/Chief Executive Officer: Robert Nothum
Sales & Marketing: Robert Nothum
Number Employees: 30

26827 Nottingham-Spirk DesignAssociates
2200 Overlook Rd
Cleveland, OH 44106 216-231-7830
Fax: 216-231-6275 www.nottinghamspirk.com
Custom designed packaging and displays
President: John Nottingham
Manager: Jeff Kalman
Estimated Sales: $5-10 Million
Number Employees: 50-99

26828 Nova Hand Dryers
12801 Worldgate Drive
Suite 500
Herndon, VA 20170
Canada 703-615-3636
Fax: 877-385-1291
mcohen@novahanddryers.com
www.nova-intl.com
Manufacturer and exporter of warm air hand dryers
Sales Manager: Maurine Cohen
Number Employees: 45
Parent Co: Avmor
Brands:
Nova

26829 Nova Industries
999 Montague St
San Leandro, CA 94577 510-357-0171
Fax: 510-357-3832 www.bordenlighting.com
Manufacturer and exporter of glare control devices and lighting fixtures including custom made and incandescent
President: James Borden
VP: Floyd Shreeve
Estimated Sales: $2.5-5 Million
Number Employees: 20-49
Square Footage: 14000

26830 Novacart U.S.A.
512 West Ohio Avenue
Richmond, CA 94804 510-215-8999
Fax: 510-215-9175 877-896-6682
info@novacartusa.com www.novacartusa.com
President: Giorgio Anghileri
Estimated Sales: $3 - 5 Million
Number Employees: 5-9
Parent Co: Novacart Italy

26831 Novamex
500 W Overland Ave
Suite 300
El Paso, TX 79901-1086 915-594-1618
Fax: 915-590-1225
raymundo.gomez@novamex.com
www.novamex.com
Founded in 1987. Markets and exports a variety of foods and beverages from Mexico.
Owner: Luis Fernandez
Executive Vice President: Sanford Gross
Sales Support Manager: Raymundo Gomez
Estimated Sales: $150,000,000
Type of Packaging: Food Service
Brands:
Cholula Hot Sauce
D'Gari Gelatin

26832 Novar
6060 Rockside Woods Blvd.
Suite 400
Cleveland, OH 44131
Fax: 216-682-1614 800-348-1235
customerservice@novar.com www.novar.com

Computerized control systems for rack and case refrigeration, store heating and cooling
President: James Ott
VP: Dean Lindstorm
Executive VP: David Weber
Number Employees: 230
Square Footage: 280000
Brands:
Spectrum

26833 **Novax Group/Point of Sales**
42 Broadway
New York, NY 10004-1617 212-684-1244
Fax: 212-684-2337 www.itsxchange.com
Point of sale systems and software
Manager: Reggie Menof
Manager: Charles Chen
Estimated Sales: $1-2.5 Million
Number Employees: 5-9
Parent Co: POS Technology

26834 **Novelis Foil Products**
1706 Shorewood Dr
Lagrange, GA 30240 706-812-2000
Fax: 706-812-2039 800-776-8701
www.novelis.com
Aluminum foil, rolls, sheets and disposable containers
Manager: Charlie Aheran
Marketing Director: Beverly Duncan
Sales Director: Charlie Ahern
Controller: Ed McGee
Number Employees: 10-19
Type of Packaging: Consumer, Food Service, Private Label, Bulk
Brands:
Alcan

26835 **(HQ)Novelty Advertising Company**
1148 Walnut St
Coshocton, OH 43812 740-622-3113
Fax: 740-622-5286 800-848-9163
www.noveltyadv.com
Manufacturer and exporter of calendars and advertising specialties
President: Robert Coffman
Owner: Greg Coffman
Owner: Thad Coffman
VP: Jim McConnell
Estimated Sales: $5-10 Million
Number Employees: 20-49
Type of Packaging: Consumer, Food Service, Bulk

26836 **Novelty Baskets**
PO Box 1481
Hurst, TX 76053-1481 817-268-5426
Fax: 817-423-6693 info@noveltybasket.com
www.noveltybasket.com
A manufacturer of wire basket displays for use in ice cream convenience stores
Owner: Ken Miller
Operations Manager: Ken Miller
Number Employees: 10

26837 **Novelty Crystal Corporation**
3015 48th Ave
Long Island City, NY 11101 718-786-5759
Fax: 718-458-9408 800-622-0250
joe@noveltycrystal.com
www.noveltycrystal.com
Plastic caterware which includes; plastic serving trays, plastic bowls, plastic bowls, plastic tumblers, plastic pitchers, plastic stemware and plastic serving accessories.
President: Rivka Michaeli
VP: Asher Michaeli
VP: Joseph Michaeli
CFO: Ashur Michaeli
Estimated Sales: $2.5 - 5 Million
Number Employees: 20-49
Square Footage: 120000
Type of Packaging: Consumer, Food Service

26838 **Novelty Crystal Corporation**
21005 Obrien Rd
Groveland, FL 34736 352-429-9036
Fax: 352-429-9039 novelty@aol.com
www.noveltycrystal.com
Hotel and restaurant supplies including catering and buffet trays, plastic drinkware, pitchers, bowls and serving utensils
President: Rivka Michaeli
CEO: Asher Michaeli
CFO: Joe Michaeli
VP: Sara Coslett
R&D: Joe Michaeli
Marketing: Ed Coslett
Sales Manager: Ed Coslett
Public Relations: Sara Coslett
Manager: Sara Michaeli
Plant Manager: Paul Patin
Estimated Sales: $1-2.5 Million
Number Employees: 20-49
Square Footage: 62500
Parent Co: Novelty Crystal Corporation
Type of Packaging: Food Service

26839 **Noveon**
9911 Brecksville Rd
Cleveland, OH 44141 216-447-5000
Fax: 216-447-5740 www.noveoninc.com
Piping components for touch industrial fluid applications and a superior balance of properties that provide longer service in hot corrosive environments
President: Stephen Kirk
Estimated Sales: $500,000-$1 000,000
Number Employees: 1,000-4,999

26840 **Novus**
12800 Highway 13 S
Suite 500
Savage, MN 55378 952-944-8000
Fax: 952-944-2542 800-328-1117
www.novusglass.com
Manufacturer and exporter of plastic polish and scratch remover and auto glass replacement products
President: Keith Beverige
Number Employees: 1,000-4,999
Square Footage: 20000
Parent Co: TCG International
Type of Packaging: Consumer
Brands:
Novus Plastic

26841 **Now Plastics**
136 Denslow Rd
East Longmeadow, MA 01028 413-525-1010
Fax: 413-525-8951 info@nowplastics.com
www.nowplastics.com
NOW Plastics offers an extensive line of high performance film sustracts including but not limited to; PET, BOPP, CPP, PVC, MOPP, FOPP, OPS, Nylon, Non Woven, Synthetic Paper, Skin Film, Retort films and Co-extrusions. AdditionallyNOW Plastics supplies various types of micro-perforated, laser perforated or high clarity bags and films for bakery and produce packaging.
President: Oded Edan
CEO: Larry Silverstein
Estimated Sales: $10 - 20,000,000
Number Employees: 10-19
Square Footage: 20000
Type of Packaging: Bulk

26842 **Nowakowski**
9909 S 57th St
Franklin, WI 53132-8685 414-423-9900
Fax: 414-423-6300 800-394-5866
nowar@exeupc.com
Stainless steel fabricated food processing equipment and other metal products
President: Jeff Nowakowski
Vice President: James Nowakowski, Sr.
Sales Director: Bill Redmond
Plant Manager: James Nowakowski, Jr.
Estimated Sales: $2-5 Million
Number Employees: 20-49
Square Footage: 37300

26843 **Nozzle Nolen**
3975 Coconut Rd
Palm Springs, FL 33461 561-964-6200
Fax: 561-272-2623 www.nozzlenolen.com
Pest control systems
Manager: Mike Antropoli
Estimated Sales: $1 - 2.5,000,000
Number Employees: 20-49
Parent Co: Nozzle Nolen

26844 **Nu-Con Equipment**
1610 Lake Dr W
Chanhassen, MN 55317 952-279-5205
Fax: 952-279-5206 877-939-0510
sales@nucon.com www.nucon.com
Turnkey sanitary process, conveying, and packaging solutions from raw material handling to consumer packaged goods. Sanitary and USDA approved process equipment and systems with easy to clean features
President: Marv Deam
Vice President: Mike Salvador
Marketing/Sales Executive: Marvin Deam
Purchasing Manager: Tom Haider
Estimated Sales: $20 - 50 Million
Number Employees: 20-49
Square Footage: 30000
Parent Co: Nu-Con

26845 **Nu-Meat Technology**
PO Box 599
Scotch Plains, NJ 07076-0599 908-232-7342
Fax: 908-232-5534
Choppers, chub separators, massagers and tumblers, meat tenderizers, mechanical, pickle injectors, slicers
Estimated Sales: $20-50 Million
Number Employees: 20-49

26846 **Nu-Star**
1425 Stagecoach Rd
Shakopee, MN 55379 952-445-8295
Fax: 952-445-0231 jadams@nustarinc.com
www.newstarinc.com
Manufacturer and exporter of carts for lifting, pushing and pulling
President: Scott Lorch
CFO: James Coan
VP Power Pusher Division: Scott Lorch
Estimated Sales: $5 - 10,000,000
Number Employees: 20-49
Type of Packaging: Bulk

26847 **Nu-Tex Styles, Inc.**
285 Davidson Ave # 104
Somerset, NJ 08873 732-485-5456
Fax: 732-873-0854 info@nu-tex.com
www.nu-tex.com
Manufacturer, importer and exporter of industrial fabrics and wiping rags including cheesecloth and dusting cloth
President: Howard Bromwich
Estimated Sales: $1-2.5 Million
Number Employees: 1-4
Number of Brands: 3
Number of Products: 57
Square Footage: 360000

26848 **Nu-Towel Company**
208 Bennington Ave
Kansas City, MO 64123 816-842-2909
Fax: 816-842-8679 800-800-7247
Disposable wipers, towels and rags
President: Dennis Wacknov
CEO: Paul Wacknov
Quality Control: Jason Wacknov
Director Operations: Pat Isbell
Estimated Sales: $1-2.5 Million
Number Employees: 20-49
Square Footage: 70000
Parent Co: American Textile Mills
Brands:
Alabama Rag
Arkansas Rag
California Rag
Carolina Rag
Colorado Rag
Georgia Rag
Illinois Rag
Indiana Rag
Iowa Rag
Kansas City Rag
Kansas Rag
Kentucky Rag
Louisiana Rag
Michigan Rag
Minnesota Rag
Mississippi Rag
Missouri Rag
Nebraska Rag
New Mexico Rag
Ohio Rag
Oklahoma Rag

Pennsylvania Rag
Tennessee Rag

26849 Nu-Vu
5600 13th St
Menominee, MI 49858-1029 906-863-4401
Fax: 906-863-5889 sales@nu-vu.com
www.nu-vu.com

Manager: Majib Maalouf
CFO: John McLaughin
Quality Control: Gary Hahn
Estimated Sales: $20 - 50 Million
Number Employees: 100-249
Parent Co: Win-Holt Equipment Group

26850 Nu-Vu Food Service Systems
5600 13th Street
Menominee, MI 49858 906-863-4401
Fax: 906-863-5889 800-338-9886
sales@nu-vu.com www.nu-vu.com
Ovens,proofers, oven/proofers, carts,racks,and roll-in rack ovens.
President: Najib Maalouf
Research & Development: Matt Deming
Sales Director: Reza McDaniel
Director Of Purchasing: Wendy Swanson
Estimated Sales: $1 - 5 Million
Number Employees: 100-249

26851 NuCO2
2800 SE Market Pl
Stuart, FL 34997-4965 772-221-1754
Fax: 772-221-1690 corporate@nuco2.com
www.nuco2.com
CO2 systems for fountains; also, service available
CFO and EVP: Robert Galvin
CEO: Michael E Dedomenico
Chairman of the Board: Michael Dedomenico
VP Sales: Randy Gold
Estimated Sales: I
Number Employees: 500-999
Brands:
Nuco2

26852 NuTEC Maufacturing
908 Garnet Ct
New Lenox, IL 60451-3569 815-722-2800
Fax: 815-722-2831 suggestions@nutecmfg.com
www.nutecmfg.com
Food forming and depositing equipment
President: Ken Sandberg
Estimated Sales: $10 - 20 Million
Number Employees: 10-19

26853 NuTec Manufacturing
908 Garnet Ct
New Lenox, IL 60451 815-722-2800
Fax: 815-722-2831 815-722-5348
sales@nutecmfg.com www.nutecmfg.com
Manufacturer, importer and exporter of food forming equipment including patties formers, cubers and conveyors
President: Ken Sandberg
CEO: Zibe Gibson
Vice President: Mike Barnett
Research & Development: Bob Nard
Marketing Director: Mike Barnett
Sales Director: Mike Barnett
Operations Manager: Roy French
Production Manager: John Goetzinger
Plant Manager: Ken Galloy
Purchasing: John Goetzinger
Estimated Sales: $2.5-5 Million
Number Employees: 10-19
Square Footage: 10000
Brands:
Nutec
Provatec

26854 NuTone
9825 Kenwood Rd
Suite 301
Cincinnati, OH 45242 513-527-5100
Fax: 513-527-5177 888-336-3948
www.nutone.com
Manufacturer and exporter of range hoods, exhaust fans, heaters, central cleaning systems, etc.
CEO: David Pringle
CFO: Bill Kissell
Quality Control: Gloria Wrenn
Manager: Fabio Fronda
Number Employees: 500-999
Parent Co: Nortek

26855 Nuance Solutions
1140 E 103rd St
Chicago, IL 60628 773-785-2300
Fax: 800-621-1276 800-621-8553
cjh@nuancesol.com
Manufacturer and exporter of liquid and jelly hand soap, degreasers, disinfectants, pine oil germicide, sanitizers and hard surface cleaners
VP Marketing: Neil Houtsma
Estimated Sales: $20 - 50 Million
Number Employees: 80
Square Footage: 150000
Parent Co: Bullen Metawest
Type of Packaging: Bulk

26856 Nucon Corporation
111 S Pfingsten Ste 100
Deerfield, IL 60015 847-564-3505
Fax: 847-509-0011 877-545-0070
awasserman@nucconet.com
www.brightsparktravel.com
Manufacturer and exporter of plastic pallets
Owner: Mitchell Slotnick
VP Sales/Marketing: Allan Wasserman
Estimated Sales: $2.5-5,000,000
Number Employees: 20-49

26857 Nulco Lighting
123 Dyer St
Suite 2
Providence, RI 02903 401-728-5200
Fax: 401-728-8210 kdownes@nulcolighting.com
www.nulcolighting.com
Decorative electric lighting fixtures
President: Kent Nulman
CEO: Robert Delogo
CFO: Robert Geloge
R & D: Richard Ruggeri
Quality Control: Joe Lenk
National Sales Manager: Stephen Rice
Estimated Sales: $5-10 Million
Number Employees: 100-249

26858 Numatics
46280 Dylan Dr
Novi, MI 48377-4906 248-596-3200
Fax: 248-596-3201 insidesales@numatics.com
www.numatics.com
VP: David K Dodds
Estimated Sales: $1 - 5 Million
Number Employees: 500-999

26859 Numeric Computer Systems
275 Oser Ave
Hauppauge, NY 11788 631-486-9000
Fax: 631-486-9032 800-321-7822
ward.irvin@ncsuite.com www.ncsuite.com
President / CEO: Robert Hochberg
Managing Director: Pedro Toro
CFO: Wayne Hochberg
Executive VP-Strategy and Business Devel: Allen Dickason
COO: Mark Hochberg
Estimated Sales: $5 - 10 Million
Number Employees: 10-19

26860 Nuova Distribution Centre
6940 Salashan Pkwy
Bldg - A
Ferndale, WA 98248-8314 360-366-2226
Fax: 360-366-4015 info@nuovadistribution.com
www.nuovadistribution.com
Manufacturer and importer of coffee and espresso grinders, sandwich grills and espresso, cappuccino and Italian slush/granita machines
President: Roberto Bresciani
Coordinator: Vic Bialas
Estimated Sales: $1 - 3 Million
Number Employees: 10-19
Brands:
Nuova Simonelli

26861 Nuova Simonelli
1915 1st Ave.
South Seattle, WA 98134 206-223-6150
Fax: 206-223-5525 info@nuovadistribution.com
www.nuovadistribution.com
Espresso machines and accessories, grinders
President: Roberto Bresciani
Member: Robert Bresciani
Estimated Sales: $1 - 3 Million
Number Employees: 10-19

26862 Nutec Manufacturing
908 Garnet Ct
New Lenox, IL 60451 815-722-2800
Fax: 815-722-2831 sales@nutecmfg.com
www.nutecmfg.com
Food processing equipment
President: Ken Sandberg
Estimated Sales: $5-10 Million
Number Employees: 10-19

26863 Nutra Food Ingredients,LLC
3631 44th Street SE
Suite D
Kentwood, MI 49512 616-656-9928
Fax: 419-730-3685
sales@nutrafoodingredients.com
www.nutrafoodingredients.com
Protein, gelatin/collagen, polyols, intensive sweetener, fiber, flavors and organic ingredients
Member: Bryon Yang
CEO: Mariann Davey
Director of New Business Development: Tim Wolffis
Estimated Sales: Under $500,000
Number Employees: 1-4

26864 Nutraceutical Corporation
1400 Kearns Blvd
2nd Floor
Park City, UT 84060 800-579-4665
Fax: 800-767-8514 800-669-8877
info@nutraceutical.com www.nutraceutical.com
Supplements
President: Bruce Hough
Chairman, Director & CEO: Frank Gay II
Vice President & CFO: Cory McQueen
Executive Vice President: Gary Hume
Executive VP, COO & Secretary: Jeffrey Hinrichs
Asst VP & Controller: Andrew Seelos
VP of Marketing & Sales: Christopher Neuberger
Estimated Sales: $188.07 Million
Number Employees: 803
Square Footage: 6103
Type of Packaging: Consumer, Food Service, Bulk
Brands:
Solaray®
Kal®
Nature's Life®
Natural Balance®
Naturalmax®
Veglife®
Premier One®
Pioneer®
Sunny Green®
Zand®
Natra-Bio®
Bioallers®
Herbs For Kids®
Naturalcare®
Natural Sport®
Supplement Training Systems™
Funfresh Foods™
Actipet®
Action Labs®
Thompson®
Montana Big Sky™
Living Flower Essences®
Life-Flo®
Larenim®
Monarch Nutritional Laboratories

26865 Nutri-Bake Inc
1208 Rue Bergar
Laval, QC H7L 5A2
Canada 450-933-5936
Fax: 888-263-3208 info@nutri-bake.com
www.organic-baked-goods.com
Manufacturer and wholesaler of baked goods
President: Peter Tsatoumas

26866 Nutricap Laboratories
70 Carolyn Boulevard
Farmingdale, NY 11735 631-247-0600
800-494-6154
info@nutricaplabs.com www.nutricaplabs.com
Sports drinks and supplements
President/Founder: Jason Provenzano
Chief Executive Officer: Jonathan Greenhut
Estimated Sales: $45 Million
Number Employees: 40

26867 Nutrifaster
209 S Bennett St
Seattle, WA 98108 206-767-5054
Fax: 206-762-2209 800-800-2641
Sales@Nutrifaster.com www.nutrifaster.com
Manufacturer and exporter of centrifugal juice extractors
President: Bert Robins
Sales/Service: Fred Davies
Estimated Sales: Less than $500,000
Number Employees: 5-9
Type of Packaging: Food Service
Brands:
Nutrifaster N-350

26868 Nutrin Distribution Company
1627 Connecticut Ave NW
Suite 3
Washington, DC 20009
Fax: 815-301-9184 888-718-3235
adam@nutrin.com www.nutrin.com
Supplier of peanut products, importer with just-in-time deliver in the US and Canada. Products include peanut flour, butter, oil, extract, and essence as well as roasted and chopped peanuts.
President: Adam Benado

26869 Nutrinfo Corporation
108 Water Street
Watertown, MA 02472-4696 617-923-2377
Fax: 617-926-6360 800-676-6686
Consultant to the U.S. food and dietary supplement industries providing services including design, food technology, marketing, promotion, sanitation, testing, nutritional analysis and international food labeling
President: Richard Litner
VP: Sanjeev Mohanti
Director Science: Thomas Hansen
Number Employees: 11
Square Footage: 3000

26870 Nutrinova
1601 Lbj Fwy
Dallas, TX 75234-6034 972-443-4000
Fax: 972-443-4994 800-786-3883
info@nutrinova-na.com www.nutrinova.com
A global technology and specialty materials company that engineers and manufacturers a wide variety of products essential to everyday living.
President: Graham Hall
Chairman, Chief Executive Officer: Mark Rohr
Vice President: Jiro Okada
Marketing Manager North America: Patricia Hanley
Chief Operating Officer: Doug Madden
Number Employees: 5-9
Parent Co: Nutrinova Nutrition Specialists & Food Ingredients GmbH

26871 Nutrition & Food Associates
PO Box 47007
Minneapolis, MN 55447 763-550-9475
Fax: 763-559-3675 info@nutriform.com
www.nutriform.com
Manufacturer and exporter of computer software for product development, nutrition labeling, recipe and menu analysis
President: Patricia Godfrey
Estimated Sales: Below $5 Million
Number Employees: 1-4
Type of Packaging: Food Service
Brands:
Nutriform

26872 Nutrition Network
4199 Campus Drive
Suite 550
Irvine, CA 92612-4694 949-753-7998
Fax: 949-497-8991 crainey@home.com
Nutrition support consultant providing services to food producers, dietitians and consumers
CEO: Charlene Rainey
Director Technical Services: Leslie Nyquist
Estimated Sales: $500,000-$1 Million
Number Employees: 5-9
Square Footage: 3000

26873 Nutrition Research
PO Box 971
Livingston, MT 59047-0971 406-686-4915
Research and development firm offering turnkey assistance in the design and processing of natural foods, vitamin, mineral and herbal supplements, etc
President: Lee Dreyer

26874 Nutty Bavarian
305 Hickman Drive
Sanford, FL 32771-6905 407-444-6322
Fax: 407-444-6335 800-382-4788
bruno@nuttyb.com www.nuttyb.com
Cinnamon nut glaze syrup and fresh roasted gourmet nuts; Manufacturer of nut roasting carts and warmers as well as paper and plastic cones and gift tins for nuts
President: David Brent
Customer Service Manager: Amber Stefanisko
Controller: Keya Morgan
Vice President of Sales: David Zangenberg
Production Manager: Ed Conrado
Estimated Sales: $500,000-$1 Million
Number Employees: 10-19
Square Footage: 28800
Type of Packaging: Consumer, Bulk
Brands:
Nbr 2000
Nutty Bavarian

26875 Nyco Products Company
5332 Dansher Rd
Countryside, IL 60525 855-426-6926
Fax: 708-579-9898 800-752-4754
bstahurski@nycoproducts.com
www.nycoproducts.com
Cleaning and sanitation supplies including deodorants, detergents, emulsifying agents, metal polish and glass, pipe, toilet bowl and drain cleaners
President: Robert Stahurski
VP Sales: John Wunderlich
VP Operations: Robert Houston
Estimated Sales: $5-10 Million
Number Employees: 20-49
Square Footage: 75000
Parent Co: NYCO Products Company

26876 Nydree Flooring
1115 Vista Park Dr.
Ste D
Forest, VA 24551 434-525-5252
Fax: 434-525-7437 800-682-5698
www.nydreeflooring.com
Commercial flooring
Owner: Barry Brubaker
VP Radiation: James Myron
Estimated Sales: $500,000-$1 Million
Number Employees: 20-49
Square Footage: 72000
Parent Co: Appliant Radian Energy Corporation
Brands:
Packing House

26877 Nylonge Company
1301 Lowell St
Elyria, OH 44035 440-323-6161
Fax: 440-323-6166
Manufacturer and exporter of cellulose sponges, sponge scrubbers, soap pads and sponge cloths
President: George Hrabik
VP: George Hrabik
Sales Manager: Jon Miller
Estimated Sales: $10-20 Million
Number Employees: 100-249
Type of Packaging: Consumer, Private Label, Bulk
Brands:
Nylonge

26878 Nyman Manufacturing Company
275 Ferris Ave
Rumford, RI 02916-1033 401-438-3410
Fax: 401-438-5975
Manufacturer and exporter of plastic cups, dinnerware, lids, caps and covers; also, paper cups
Marketing Director: Laura Coupal
General Manager (Paper): Walter Bennett
General Manager (Plastic): Al Domenici
Type of Packaging: Food Service
Brands:
First Choice
Natural Choice
Popular Choice

26879 O C Lugo Company
15 Third Street
New City, NY 10956 845-480-5121
Fax: 845-480-5122 info@oclugo.com
www.oclugo.com
Supplier of chemicals, vitamins, minerals, gelatins and food ingredients. OC Lugo's other division is Critical Filtration supplies
President: Richard Lugo
Estimated Sales: $830,000
Number Employees: 5-9

26880 O Chili Frozen Foods Inc
3634 Indian Wells Ln
Northbrook, IL 60062-3102 847-562-1991
Fax: 847-562-1822
Processed frozen meats including cooked pizza toppings, chopped and formed beef, veal, pork and poultry, breaded products, entrees, etc.;
Owner: J Rothschild
Number Employees: 20-49
Type of Packaging: Consumer, Food Service, Private Label, Bulk
Brands:
Chilli-O

26881 O'Brian Tarping Systems
2330 Womble Brooks Rd
Wilson, NC 27893 252-291-2141
Fax: 252-291-1416 800-334-8277
sales@obriantarping.com
www.obriantarping.com
Commercial awnings, unautomatic tarting systems
President: Woody O'Brian
Estimated Sales: $3 - 5 Million
Number Employees: 20-49

26882 O'Brien Brothers
51 Doty Cir
West Springfield, MA 01089 413-734-7121
Fax: 413-737-1642 800-343-0949
joeobrien@obrienbrothersinc.com
www.obrienbrothersinc.com
Locks and locksmith supplies
President: Joseph O'Brien
Estimated Sales: $.5 - 1 million
Number Employees: 1-4

26883 O'Brien Installations
4435 Corporate Drive
Burlington
Ontario, CA L7L 5T9
Canada 905-336-8245
Fax: 905-331-6494 info@obrieninstall.com
www.obrieninstall.com
Manufacturer and exporter of cranes
President: George O'Brien
Marketing Coordinator: John Marchetti
Sales Director: Wayne Davis
Production Manager: Randy Mullin
Purchasing Manager: Krys Klain
Estimated Sales: $1-10 Million
Number Employees: 50-99
Square Footage: 80000
Parent Co: O'Brien Material Handling
Other Locations:
O'Brien Material Handling
Memramock, NB

26884 O'Dell Corporation
PO Box 540
Ware Shoals, SC 29692 864-861-2222
Fax: 864-861-3171 800-342-2843
odellcorp@aol.com www.odellcorp.com
Manufacturer, importer and exporter of household and janitorial mops, brooms, brushes and handles
CEO: Wh O'Dell
VP: Paul O'Dell
Customer Service: Gayle O'Dell
Estimated Sales: $10-20 Million
Number Employees: 50-99
Square Footage: 85000
Brands:
Kitchen Queen

26885 O-Cedar
2188 Diehl Road
Aurora, IL 60502 217-379-2377
Fax: 217-379-9901 800-543-8105
www.ocedar.com
Brooms including corn, rattan, bamboo, etc
President: Stanley Koschnick
General Manager: Stanley Kochnick

Estimated Sales: $1 - 5 Million
Number Employees: 50-99
Parent Co: Freudenberg Household Products LP

26886 O-Cedar
2188 Diehl Road
Aurora, IL 60502 219-726-8128
800-543-8105
www.ocedar.com
Manufacturer and exporter of industrial brooms and brushes
Plant Manager: Mike White
Parent Co: O'Cedar Vining

26887 O-I
One Michael Owens Way
Perrysburg, OH 43551
glass@o-i.com
www.o-i.com
Manufacturer and exporter of plastic bottles, containers, closures and carriers including HDPE, PVC, PET, LDPE, multilayer and barex
Chairman and Chief Executive Officer: Al Stroucken
SVP and CFO: Steve Bramlage
SVP and General Counsel: Jim Baehren
SVP and Chief Administrative Officer: Paul Jarrell
Number Employees: 10

26888 O.A. Newton & Son Company
PO Box 397
16356 Sussex Hwy
Bridgeville, DE 19933-0397 302-337-8211
Fax: 302-337-3780 800-726-5745
solutions@oanewton.com www.oanewton.com
Manufacturer and exporter of weighing equipment and pneumatic and mechanical material handling systems including dust collection
President: Rob F Rider Jr
Number Employees: 50-99

26889 O.B.S. Trading
2370 N High
Suite 3
Jackson, MO 63755 573-243-6999
Fax: 573-243-8723 bollerslev@atprs.net
www.obstrading.com
Planning and designing to finding the best machines for meat processing
President: Henning Bollerslev

26890 (HQ)O.C. Adhesives Corporation
PO Box 3058
Ridgefield, NJ 07657-3058 973-279-8134
Fax: 973-279-0338 800-662-1595
Industrial water based adhesives for plastic film laminating, bottle labeling and difficult to stick surfaces and UV coated stock
President: Stanley Meyers Phd
Technology Director: Leonard Gross
Director Marketing: Sy Eckstein
Estimated Sales: $2.5-5 Million
Number Employees: 10-19
Square Footage: 25000

26891 O.D. Kurtz Associates
242 Hurst Road NE
Palm Bay, FL 32907-1566 321-723-0135
Fax: 321-723-0151 odklab@aol.com
www.odk.com
Laboratory specializing in extraneous analysis, sanitation appraisals and AOAC food testing
Estimated Sales: $500,000-$1 Million
Number Employees: 5-9

26892 O.I. Analytical
P.O.Box 9010
College Station, TX 77842 979-690-1711
Fax: 979-690-0400 oimail@oico.com
www.oico.com
CEO: J Bruce Lancaster
Estimated Sales: G
Number Employees: 100-249

26893 O.K. Marking Devices
1358 Cornwall Street
Regina, SK S4R 2H5
Canada 306-522-2856
Fax: 306-569-3566 rubberstamps@acesscomm.ca
Stencils, engraved signs, tags, corporation seals and rubber and photopolymer stamps
President: Fl Clark

Estimated Sales: Below $5 Million
Number Employees: 7
Square Footage: 2000

26894 O/K International Corporation
73 Bartlett Street
Marlborough, MA 01752-3071 508-303-8286
Fax: 508-303-8207 800-521-2908
sales@okcorp.com www.okcorp.com
Hot-air sealers, case erectors, case liners and conveyor systems, strech wrappers
Marketing Director: Ann Marie Kellett
Plant Manager: Hans Mentink
Estimated Sales: $5 - 10 Million
Number Employees: 25-49
Type of Packaging: Consumer, Bulk

26895 OA Newton
16356 Sussex Hwy
PO Box 397
Bridgeville, DE 19933 302-337-8211
Fax: 302-337-3780 800-726-5745
solutions@oanewton.com www.oanewton.com
Materials handling and control, feed and grain handling, irrigation
President: Rob F Rider Jr
Chairman of the Board: Robert Rider
Estimated Sales: $10 - 20 Million
Number Employees: 50-99

26896 (HQ)OCC Systems
1330 Hilton Rd
Ferndale, MI 48220-2898 248-547-3800
Fax: 248-547-8344 800-396-2554
cathyn@occ-conveyor.com
www.occ-conveyor.com
Supplier/mfg of material handling (conveyor) systems and (spurgeon) stacking machines for non-ferrous metals
President: Thomas Woodbeck
CEO: M Woodbeck Jr
Marketing & Sales Manager: Catherine Nall
Estimated Sales: $10-30 Million
Number Employees: 50-99
Square Footage: 100000
Parent Co: Spurgeon Company

26897 OCS Checkweighers Inc
2350 Hewatt Road
Snellville, GA 30039 678-344-8300
Fax: 678-344-8030 info.usa@ocs-cw.com
www.ocs-cw.com
Packaging machinery
President: Ingolf Latz
CEO/CFO: Theo Dueppre
Sales Manager: Rachel Edwards
Estimated Sales: $1.5 Million
Number Employees: 13

26898 OK Kosher Certification
391 Troy Avenue
Brooklyn, NY 11213-5322 718-756-7500
Fax: 718-756-7503 info@ok.org
www.ok.org
Manufacturers and suppliers of Kosher food, wine and utensils
President: Don Yoel Levy
Estimated Sales: $2.5 - 5 Million
Number Employees: 20-49

26899 OK Labs Kosher Certification
391 Troy Avenue
Brooklyn, NY 11213-5322 718-756-7500
Fax: 718-756-7503 info@ok.org
www.ok.org
Consultant specializing in kosher certification services
President: Don Yoel Levy
Chief Customer Relations Officer: Eli Lando
CFO: Thelma Lezy
Manager: Levi Marmulsteyn
R&D: Rikal Fogelman
Director: Chaim Fogelman
Operations Manager: Rikal Fogelman
Estimated Sales: $2.5 - 5 Million
Number Employees: 20-49

26900 OK Manufacturing
2340 S 900 W
Salt Lake City, UT 84119 801-974-9116
Fax: 801-974-5458 800-748-5480
okmfgsales@gmail.com www.okmfg.net
Bubble gum and novelty vending equipment and plush cranes
President: Jeff Ostler
Owner/Sales: Kurt Ostler
Owner/Production: Jeff Ostler
Estimated Sales: $5-10 Million
Number Employees: 50-99
Square Footage: 208000
Brands:
Ok

26901 OK Stamp & Seal Company
1608 Linwood Blvd
Oklahoma City, OK 73106-5052 405-235-7853
Fax: 405-232-4139
Rubber stamps
President: Steve Fagundes
Estimated Sales: Less than $500,000
Number Employees: 1-4

26902 OK Uniform Company
253 Church Street
New York, NY 10013 212-791-9789
Fax: 212-791-9795 866-700-5765
eliatry@aol.com www.okuniform.com
Manufacturer and exporter of uniforms including restaurant wear, formal wear and work/industrial wear; a complete line of anywhere shoes/clogs; full line of tuxedos and formal wear for men and women. We also carry disposable uniformscoveralls, etc
CEO: Ellie Cohen
CFO: Ezra Cohen
Sales Manager: Ivan Cohen
Public Relations: Taimara K
Manager: George Gross
Estimated Sales: $1-2.5 Million
Number Employees: 5-9
Number of Brands: 4
Brands:
Big Ben
Car Hartt
Dickies
Red Kap

26903 OMNOVA Solutions
175 Ghent Road
Fairlawn, OH 44333 330-869-4200
www.omnova.com
Plastic, calendered, plain and printed vinyl film
Chairman/President/CEO: Kevin McMullen
Senior Vice President/CFO: Michael Hicks
Senior VP/Chief Information Officer: Douglas Wenger
Director, Marketing Paper Products: Robin McCann
Director, National Sales: Dan Fox
Chief Administrative Officer: Michael Curran
Plant Manager: Lee Szwast
Purchasing Director: Robert Culp
Estimated Sales: $1.13 Billion
Number Employees: 2,390
Square Footage: 10124
Parent Co: GenCorp

26904 OMYA, Inc.
9987 Carver Rd
Suite 300
Cincinnati, OH 45242 513-387-4600
800-749-6692
eva.jimenez@omya.com www.omya.com
Fillers and pigments from calcium carbonate and dolomite, and distributor of chemical products.
President: Anthony Colak
CFO: Michael Phillips
Secretary: Leonard Eisenberg
Asst Sec: Patricia Kirkendall
Manager Technology Services: Michael Roussel
Sales Manager: Maria Burt
Manager: Scott McCalla
Manager Projects Engineering: Scott Schaffner
Director of Engineering: Rob Tikoft
Director Purchasing: Derrell Riley
Estimated Sales: $4.3 Million
Other Locations:
Proctor VT
Cincinnati OH
Woodland WA
Kingsport TN
Lucerne Valley CA
Johnsonburg PA
Florence VT
Hawesville KY
Sylacauga AL
Superior AZ
Long Beach CA

26905 ONGUARD Industries
1850 Clark Rd
Havre De Grace, MD 21078 410-272-2000
Fax: 410-272-3346 800-365-2282
sales@onguardindustries.com
www.onguardindustries.com
CEO/Chairman: Douglas Ramer
Chief Financial Officer: Dennis Wessel
CEO: Chris Maistros
Quality Coordinator: Jim Gorham
VP Operations: Chris Maistros
Number Employees: 10-19

26906 ORB Weaver Farm
3406 Lime Kiln Road
New Haven, VT 05472 802-877-3755
marjorie@orbweaverfarm.com
www.orbweaverfarm.com
Fresh fruits and vegetables, and fine cheeses
President: Marjorie Susman

26907 ORBIS
1055 Corporate Center Drive
PO Box 389
Oconomowoc, WI 53066 262-560-5000
800-890-7292
info@orbiscorporation.com
www.orbiscorporation.com
Provides reusable packaging for the bakery, dairy, beverage, red meat/poultry and general food processing industry.
President/Principal: Dave Schopp
VP Finance: Mark Gorzek
VP Marketing/Sales: James Solum
VP Sales: Tim Henkel
VP Human Resources: Tom Bissell
VP Operations: Mike McKay
Number Employees: 150
Square Footage: 15011
Parent Co: Menasha Corporation

26908 ORBIS Corporation
1055 Corporate Center Dr
Oconomowoc, WI 53066 800-890-7292
Fax: 262-560-5841 800-890-7292
info@orbiscorporation.com
www.orbiscorporation.com
Plastic containers, hand-held and bulk and pallets
President: Jim Kotek
CEO: Jim Kotek
Marketing Director: Pete Budney
Public Relations: Samantha Goetz
Purchasing Manager: Robert Kroening
Number Employees: 1,000-4,999
Parent Co: Menasha Corporation
Type of Packaging: Food Service, Bulk

26909 ORBIS RPM
5250 E Terrace Drive
Suite 106
Madison, WI 53718 608-852-8840
Fax: 608-237-8162 www.corbiplastics.com
Packaging materials including plastic reusable pallets, divider sheets/layer pads and top frames.
President: Jack Graham
General Manager: Chad Feehan
Parent Co: Menasha Corporation
Type of Packaging: Food Service

26910 (HQ)OSF
650 Barmac Drive
Toronto, ON M9L 2X8
Canada 416-749-7700
Fax: 416-740-6365 800-465-4000
marketing@osfinc.com www.osfinc.com
Manufacturer and exporter of store fixtures, showcases and displays; also, steel shelving
CEO: Harry Shier
Co-Chairman: Milton Shier
Number Employees: 2100
Square Footage: 8800000
Other Locations:
OSF
Blackstone VA
Brands:
Century Line
Tufkote
Vista Classic Line

26911 OSRAM SYLVANIA
100 Endicott Street
Danvers, MA 01923 978-777-1900
Fax: 978-750-2152 800-544-4828
www.sylvania.com
President: Charles Jerabeck
President, Chief Executive Officer: Rick Leaman
Manager of Corporate Communications: Anne Guertin
Number Employees: 10,000

26912 OSSID LLC
4000 College Road
PO Drawer 1968
Rocky Mount, NC 27809 252-446-6177
Fax: 252-442-7694 800-334-8369
sales@ossid.com www.ossid.com
Food packaging equipment.
Owner/President: Bud Lane
Principal/VP Finance: Kim Brewer
VP/General Manager: Ernie Newell
Sales Director: Jason Angel
Number Employees: 80
Square Footage: 80000

26913 OTD Corporation
P.O.Box 510
Hinsdale, IL 60522-0510 630-321-9232
Fax: 574-254-5092 info@otdcorp.com
www.otdcorp.com
Manufacturer and exporter of aluminum containers, racks and pallets
President: James Ogle
Controller: Jean Chatman
Estimated Sales: $20-30 Million
Number Employees: 1-4

26914 (HQ)OWD
PO Box 1260
Tupper Lake, NY 12986-0260 518-359-2944
Fax: 518-359-2994 800-836-1693
rjsull@owdinc.com
www.jarden.com/phoenix.zhtml?c= 72395&p= irol...ID.
Manufacturer and exporter of plastic spoons, forks, knives, straws, cups and plates
CEO: James E. Lillie
CFO: John Breshahan
Vice President: Mark Yamrick
VP Sales: Al Huggins
Estimated Sales: Less than $500,000
Number Employees: 100-249
Square Footage: 130000
Parent Co: Jarden Corporation
Other Locations:
O.W.D.
La Fayette GA
Brands:
Lady Dianne

26915 OXBO International Corporation
100 Bean St
Clear Lake, WI 54005 715-263-2112
Fax: 715-263-3324 800-628-6196
atalbott@oxbocorp.com www.oxbocorp.com
Manufacturer and exporter of pea, bean and sweet and seed corn harvesting machinery and vibratory sorting tables
President: Andy Tallobt
VP Sales: Andrew Talbott
Inside Sales: Doug Ahrens
Human Resources: Deborah Arcand
Estimated Sales: $10 - 20 Million
Number Employees: 50-99
Square Footage: 110000
Brands:
One Row Trac-Pix
Pixall Big Jack Mark Ii
Pixall Corn Puller
Pixall Cornstalker Db18
Pixall Cornstalker El20
Pixall One-Row Pull-Pix
Pixall Super Jack
Pixall Vst

26916 Oak Barrel Winecraft
1443 San Pablo Ave
Berkeley, CA 94702 510-849-0400
Fax: 510-528-6543 info@oakbarrel.com
www.oakbarrel.com
Oak barrels for wine and beer making, bottles and stoppers for wine, vinegar starter culture and bottling and brewery machinery; importer of wine presses, crushers and barrels; also, wholesaler/distributor of vinegar starter cultureand barrels
President and CFO: Bernard Rooney
Vice President: Homer Smith
Estimated Sales: $5 - 10 Million
Number Employees: 5-9
Square Footage: 12000

26917 Oak Creek Pallet Company
5059 N 119th Street
Milwaukee, WI 53225-3607 414-762-7170
Fax: 414-762-3070
Wooden pallets, boxes and crates
President: Gary LaMaster
Number Employees: 90

26918 Oak International
1160 White St
Sturgis, MI 49091 269-651-9790
Fax: 269-651-7849
oakhelp@oakinternational.com
www.cimcool.com
Manufacturer and exporter of FDA approved cutting, stamping and drawing oils; also, grinding coolants and cleaners
Sr. VP Sales/Operations: F Edwards
Plant Manager: Jim Phillips
Estimated Sales: $5 - 10 Million
Number Employees: 10-19
Square Footage: 26000
Brands:
Oak Draw
Oak Kleen
Oak Kool
Oak Kote
Oak Protect
Oil Rids

26919 Oakes & Burger
PO Box 665
Niles, OH 44446-0665 800-321-0106
Fax: 330-652-2617
Aseptic processing equipment, batch control systems, chillers, clean rooms and equipment, custom fabrication, deaerators, homogenizers, ice equipment, ingredient feeders, meters, expert systems, filters

26920 Oakes Carton Company
5575 Collingwood
Kalamazoo, MI 49004 269-381-6022
Fax: 269-381-2948
oakescartoncompany@worldnet.att.net
www.oakescarton.com
Paper folding cartons
President: James Oakes
VP Sales Manager: James Savage
Customer Service: Oakes Carton
Office Manager / Accounting / Human Reso: Judee Buckhout
Estimated Sales: $2.5-5 Million
Number Employees: 20-49

26921 Oakite Products
P.O.Box 7
New Providence, NJ 07974-0007 908-464-6900
Fax: 908-464-5354 800-526-4473
ceasternbranch@chemetall.com www.oakite.com
Developer. manufacturer and supplier of state-of-the-art specialty chemical products.
President: Don LeBart
CEO: Ron Felber
Estimated Sales: $75-$80 Million
Number Employees: 50-99

26922 Oaklee International
125 Raynor Avenue
Ronkonkoma, NY 11779 631-436-7900
Fax: 631-436-7985 800-333-7250
service@oaklee.com www.oaklee.com
Executive Director: Alice Zebrowski
Estimated Sales: $5 - 10 Million
Number Employees: 100-249

26923 Oaklee International
125 Raynor Ave
Ronkonkoma, NY 11779 631-436-7900
Fax: 631-436-7985 800-333-7250
service@oaklee.com www.oaklee.com
Shrink film, sleeve labels, promotional packaging, protective packaging
Executive Director: Alice Zebrowski

26924 Oakton Instruments
PO Box 5136
Vernon Hills, IL 60061-5136 888-462-5866
Fax: 847-247-2984 888-462-5866
info@4oakton.com www.4oakton.com

Provides pH, ORP, conductivity/TDS, dissolved oxygen, relative humity, time, temperature, and barometric pressure instrumentation, baths, ovens, vacuum pumps, desiccators, clamps and magnifiers
Marketing Director: Bob Langie
Estimated Sales: $1 - 5 Million
Brands:
Oakton

26925 **Oates Flag Company**
10951 Electron Dr
Louisville, KY 40299 502-267-8200
Fax: 502-267-8246 sales@oatesflag.com
www.oatesflag.com
Flags and pennants; silk screening, athletic lettering and embroidery available
Owner: C R Oates
Marketing Director: Reggie Oates
Estimated Sales: Below $5 Million
Number Employees: 10-19

26926 **Obergurg Engineering**
1814 Empire Industrial Court
Suite G
Santa Rosa, CA 95403-1946 707-542-4153
Fax: 707-542-4152
Wine industry label design
Manager: Joan Murphy
Number Employees: 7

26927 **Occidental Chemical Corporation**
5005 L B J Fwy
Suite 2200
Dallas, TX 75244 972-404-3800
Fax: 972-448-6631 800-733-3665
info@oxychem.com www.oxychem.com
Basic chemicals concentrated in the chloro-vinyls including chlorine, caustic soda, ethylene dichloride and polyvinylchloride
President: James Lienert
CFO: Dennis Blake
Site Manager: Rick Zelley
Number Employees: 3000
Parent Co: Occidental Petroleum Corporation

26928 **Occidental Chemical Corporation**
56 Street & Energy Boulevard
Niagara Falls, NY 14302 716-278-7027
Fax: 716-278-7880 www.oxy.com
Chemicals including bottle cleaning compounds; processor of soda for carbonated soft drinks
Plant Manager: Candace Jaunzemis
Director Purchasing: Tony Orbegoso
Estimated Sales: $.5 - 1 million
Number Employees: 1-4
Parent Co: Occidental Petroleum

26929 **(HQ)Ockerlund Industries**
7725 Van Buren St
Forest Park, IL 60130-1816 708-771-7707
Fax: 708-771-0614 guyo@ockerlund.com
www.ockerlund.com
Corrugated, plastic and wooden boxes
President: Stan Joray
CEO: Guy Ockerlund
Estimated Sales: $10 - 20 Million
Number Employees: 100-249

26930 **Ocme America Corporation**
2200 N Susquehanna Trail
York, PA 17404-1652 717-843-6263
Fax: 717-843-6748 tsnelbaker@ocmeusa.com
www.ocme.it
Packaging machinery including fillers, depalletizers, wrap-around case packers, shrink wrap machines and palletizers
President: Emmanuel Gattescht
President: Tony Introna
R&D: Anthony Trona
Sales Coordinator: Thelma Snelbaker
Estimated Sales: $5 - 10 Million
Number Employees: 10
Square Footage: 16000
Parent Co: Ocme SRL

26931 **Ocs Checkweighers, Inc.**
2350 Hewatt Rd
Snellville, GA 30039 678-344-8030
Fax: 678-344-8030 info.usa@ocs-cw.com
www.ocs-cw.com
High-speed weighing systems.

26932 **Oden Corporation**
199 Fire Tower Dr
Tonawanda, NY 14150 716-874-3000
Fax: 716-874-1589 800-658-3622
sales@odencorp.com www.odencorp.com
Manufacturer and exporter of volumetric and net weight filling machinery for liquid and semi-l;iquid products.
President/CEO: Iver Phallen
Marketing Director: Phyllis Phallen
Sales Director: Gary Laidman
Number Employees: 20-49
Brands:
Grav/Tronic
Mega/Fill
Net/Mass
Pro/Fill
Pro/Matic
Servo/Fill

26933 **Odenberg Engineering**
4038 Seaport Blvd
West Sacramento, CA 95691 916-371-0700
Fax: 916-371-5471 800-688-8396
sales@odenberg.com www.odenberg.com
Manufacturer and exporter of batch steam peelers, chillers/freezers and sorters
President: Maurice Moynihan
VP: Ashley Hunter
Production Sales Manager: Diamond Meagher
Estimated Sales: $10 - 20,000,000
Number Employees: 20-49
Parent Co: Odenberg Engineering

26934 **Odessa Packaging Services**
202 N Bassett St
Clayton, DE 19938 302-653-8474
Fax: 302-653-8612 800-633-7726
smallpak@smallpak.net www.smallpak.net

26935 **Odor Management**
One Corporate Drive
Suite 100
Long Grove, IL 60047 847-304-9111
Fax: 847-304-0989 800-662-6367
ecosorb@odormanagement.com
www.odormanagement.com
President: Phillip Coffey
Lead Scientist, Research and Development: Laura Haupert
Director of Marketing and Brand Developm: Melinda Adamec
National Sales Director: Tom Minett
Chief Operating Officer and Director of: Charles Timcik
Director of Operations: Stephen Lattis
Estimated Sales: $3 - 5 Million
Number Employees: 20-49

26936 **Oenophilia**
1713 Legion Road
Chapel Hill, NC 27517-2359 919-942-1250
Fax: 919-942-5718
Wine and bar accessories

26937 **Oerlikon Balzers**
1181 Jansen Farm Court
Rogers Business Park
Elgin, IL 60123 847-695-5200
Fax: 847-695-4051 info.balzers.us@oerlikon.com
www.oerlikon.com/balzers/us
President: Kristen Kunz
CEO: Hans Br,,ndle
CFO: Volker Dostmann

26938 **Oerlikon Leybold VacuumUSA Inc**
5700 Mellon Road
Export, PA 15632 800-764-5369
Fax: 800-215-7782
info@vacuum.ex@oerlikon.com
www.oerlikon.com
Packaging machinery
Owner: Lori Arola
VP: Maura Powers
Marketing Director: Mario Vitale
Human Resources Manager: Valerie Mooney
Estimated Sales: $60 Million
Number Employees: 90
Square Footage: 62000

26939 **Oetiker Inc**
P.O.Box 217
Marlette, MI 48453 989-635-3621
Fax: 989-635-2157 800-959-0398
info@us.oetiker.com www.oetiker.com
Supplier of hose clamps and rings
CEO: Chris Parker
Quality Control: Dan Roche
Marketing Coordinator: Christine Lowe
Sales Director: Brian Milek
Account Manager: Brent Christenen
Production Manager: Bruce Christensen
Purchasing Manager: Shelly Davies
Estimated Sales: $10 - 20 Million
Number Employees: 100
Parent Co: Hans Oetiker AG

26940 **Ogden Manufacturing Company**
103 Gamma Drive
Pittsburgh, PA 15238 412-967-3906
Fax: 412-967-3930 cs@ogdenmfg.com
www.ogdenmfg.com
Manufacturer and exporter of electric heating elements and microprocessor-based temperature controls
VP: Randy Lee
Marketing Manager: Gordon Hollander
Estimated Sales: $5-10 Million
Number Employees: 150-250
Square Footage: 130000
Brands:
Etr
Mighty Blade

26941 **Ohaus Corporation**
7 Campus Dr Ste 300
Parsippany, NJ 07054 973-377-9000
Fax: 973-593-0359 800-672-7722
marla.bormann@ohaus.com www.ohaus.com
Manufacturer and exporter of electronic, analytical, precision top loading and moisture balances; also, portable and bench scales
President: Ted Xia
CFO: Peter Minder
Estimated Sales: $25 - 50 Million
Number Employees: 250-499
Brands:
Ohaus

26942 **Ohio Conveyor & Supply**
PO Box 678
Findlay, OH 45839 419-422-3825
Fax: 419-422-4490 ohioconv@bright.net
www.ohioconv.com
Conveyors and wholesaler/distributor of conveyor belts
President: John R Snyder
Estimated Sales: $1 - 2.5 Million
Number Employees: 5-9

26943 **Ohio Magnetics-Stearns Magnetics**
5400 Dunham Rd
Cleveland, OH 44137-3653 216-662-8484
Fax: 216-662-2911 800-486-6446
salesohiomag1@quest.net
www.ohiomagnetics.com
Manufacturer and exporter of magnetic separators, metal detectors and conveyors
Manager: John Wohlgemuph
Sales Manager: Ken Richendollar
General Manager: John Wohlgemuth
Plant Manager: Tim Essick
Purchasing: Bob Zajc
Estimated Sales: $10-20 Million
Number Employees: 50-99
Square Footage: 144000
Parent Co: Ohio Magnetics
Brands:
Stearns

26944 **Ohio Rack**
1405 S Liberty Ave
PO Box 3517
Alliance, OH 44601 330-823-8200
Fax: 330-823-8136 800-344-4164
ohiorack@cannet.com www.ohiorack.com
Wholesaler/distributor of used portable stack racks and pallet rack systems; manufacturer of new portable stack racks
President: George Pilla
Estimated Sales: Below $5,000,000
Number Employees: 5-9

26945 Ohio Soap Products Company
1340 E 289th St
Wickliffe, OH 44092 440-585-1100
Fax: 216-341-9900
customerservice@diamondshine.com
www.diamondshine.com
Industrial soap
VP Sales: Scott Soble
Estimated Sales: $10-20 Million
Number Employees: 19
Brands:
Ohio

26946 Ohlson Packaging
490 Constitution Dr
Taunton, MA 02780 508-977-0004
Fax: 508-977-0007 sales@ohlsonpack.com
www.ohlsonpack.com
Manufacturer and exporter of automatic stainless steel weighing machinery for bagging or boxing pasta, frozen foods, candy, produce, etc
Owner: John Ohlson Jr
Vice President: John Ohlson
Estimated Sales: $7 Million
Number Employees: 10-19

26947 Ohly Americas
35 Adams St NE
Hutchinson, MN 55350-2689 320-587-2481
Fax: 320-234-4186 www.ohly.com
Manager: Chad Gunderson
Sales Director: Jay Wickeham
Estimated Sales: $100 - 200 Million
Number Employees: 20-49

26948 Ohmart/VEGA
4241 Allendorf Dr
Cincinnati, OH 45209-1599 513-272-0131
Fax: 513-272-0133 800-367-5383
mail@ohmartvega.com www.ohmartvega.com
Manufacturer and exporter of sensors and gauges
President: Joe Stigler
CFO: Ken Seldmenn
Quality Control: Matt Phomas
Advertising Manager: Patrick Schreiber
Estimated Sales: $20 - 50 Million
Number Employees: 100-249
Type of Packaging: Bulk
Brands:
Densart
Levelart
Moistart
Weighart

26949 Oil Skimmers
12800 York Road
Cleveland, OH 44133 440-237-4600
Fax: 440-582-2759 800-200-4603
info@oilskim.com www.oilskim.com
Waste oil removal
President: Mike Gaudiani
President/CEO: William Townsend
VP: Jim Petrucci
Marketing Director: Mary Petit
CIO/Sales Manager: Rob Fiorilli
Estimated Sales: $2.7 Million
Number Employees: 22
Square Footage: 100000

26950 Oil-Dri Corporation of America
410 N Michigan Ave
Suite 400
Chicago, IL 60611-4213 312-321-1515
Fax: 312-321-1271 800-621-7191
www.oildri.com
Developer of products for consumer, industrial and automotive, agricultural, sports fields and fluids purification markets.
CEO: Daniel Jefrey
President: Daniel Jefrey
CEO: Daniel S Jaffee
Estimated Sales: I
Number Employees: 500-999
Brands:
Oil-Dri

26951 Oklabs
921 NW 72nd Street
Oklahoma City, OK 73116-7107 405-843-6832
Fax: 405-843-6832 oklabs@ilinkusa.net
www.ok-labs.com
Laboratory providing microbiological, protein, fat, moisture and salt analysis; consultant specializing in product and process development
President: Walter Seideman
Estimated Sales: $500,000-$1 Million
Number Employees: 5-9

26952 Oklahoma Neon
6550 E Independence Street
Tulsa, OK 74115-7861 918-835-1548
Fax: 918-835-0528 888-707-6366
okneon@okneon.com www.okneon.com
Awnings, channel letters and architectural, plastic, neon and electric signs; also, service and installation
President: Randy Olmstead
Vice President: Gene Russell
Estimated Sales: $5-10 Million
Number Employees: 50-99

26953 Okura USA
9970 Lakeview Ave
Shawnee Mission, KS 66219 913-599-1111
Fax: 913-599-0096 800-772-1187
mike.coyle@okura-usa.com www.okurausa.com
Manufacturer and importer of polyolefin heat shrinkable packaging films
President: John Campbell
Sales Manager: Mike Coyle
Sales Manager: Bill Filer
Estimated Sales: $1 - 2.5 Million
Number Employees: 5-9
Square Footage: 25000
Parent Co: Okura Industrial Company

26954 Olam Americas
25 Union Pl
Suite 3
Summit, NJ 07901 908-988-1960
ir@olamnet.com
www.olamonline.com
Cocoa, coffee, cashew, sesame and rice products including almonds, cashews, peanuts, hazelnuts, dairy, grains, packaged foods, palm, sugar, dehydrated vegetables, spices, tomatoes, specialty vegetables and sesame
President: John Gibbons
Manager: Pallavi Shah
Estimated Sales: $15.7 Billion
Number Employees: 17000+
Type of Packaging: Bulk

26955 Olcott Plastics
95 N 17th Street
Saint Charles, IL 60174 630-584-0555
Fax: 630-584-5655 888-313-5277
sales@olcottplastics.com
www.olcottplastics.com
Manufacturer, importer and exporter of plastic containers, jars and jar closures.
Owner/President/VP Operations: John Brodner
CFO: Mark Herzog
Quality Manager: Perry Norsworthy
Sales Manager: Troy Rusch
Human Resources Director: Sandy Allen
Purchasing: Teresa Casey
Estimated Sales: $12.6 Million
Number Employees: 95
Square Footage: 60000
Type of Packaging: Consumer, Private Label, Bulk

26956 (HQ)Old Dominion Box Company
186 Dillard Rd
Madison Heights, VA 24572 434-929-6701
Fax: 434-929-6354 www.duckheadshoes.com
Boxes, cartons and containers
Owner: Malcolm Sydnor
VP Marketing/Sales: Amy Buhler-Scott
General Manager: William Hutter
Estimated Sales: $50-100 Million
Number Employees: 20-49

26957 Old Dominion Box Company
PO Box 77
Burlington, NC 27216-0077 336-226-4491
Fax: 336-570-1217
Manufacturer and exporter of small paper and set-up boxes
Estimated Sales: $500,000-$1 Million
Number Employees: 4
Parent Co: Mark IV Industries

26958 Old Dominion Wood Products
800 Craddock St
PO Box 11226
Lynchburg, VA 24501 434-845-5511
Fax: 434-846-1213 800-245-6382
csodwp@att.net www.olddominionwood.net
Manufacturer, importer and exporter of chairs, tray stands, laminated trash receptacles, booths, tabletops and table bases
Owner: George R Harris
Sales Director: Dennis Hunt
Estimated Sales: $3 - 5 Million
Number Employees: 10-19
Number of Products: 1000
Square Footage: 60000

26959 Old English Printing & Label Company
13661 Sandy Malibu Pt
Delray Beach, FL 33446 561-997-9990
Fax: 610-668-7920 oepbc@aol.com
Labels and forms; also, printing services available
President: H Brooks
Estimated Sales: $1-2.5 Million
Number Employees: 1-4

26960 Old Mansion Foods
PO Box 1838
3811 Corporate Rd
Petersburg, VA 23805-0838 804-862-9889
Fax: 804-861-8816 800-476-1877
elaina-t@oldmansion.com www.oldmansion.com
Quality spices, seasonings, coffee and teas
President: Dale Patton
Sales: Tom Mullen
Plant Manager: Kevin Laffoon
Purchasing Director: Wendy Bryant
Number Employees: 20-49
Type of Packaging: Consumer, Food Service, Private Label, Bulk
Brands:
Festiva
Grill Select
Old Mansion
Southern Classic

26961 Olde Country Reproductions
145 N Hartley St
York, PA 17401 717-843-8989
Fax: 717-845-7129 800-358-3997
pewtarex@epix.net www.pewtarex.com
Manufacturer and exporter of pewter plates, mugs, goblets, trays, skillets, platters, bowls, servers, candle sticks, ice coolers, ladles, pans and kettles
President: W Swartz
VP Sales: Chris Kiehl
Estimated Sales: $20 - 50 Million
Number Employees: 20-49
Number of Brands: 2
Number of Products: 2000
Square Footage: 50000
Type of Packaging: Bulk
Brands:
Pewtarex
York Pewter

26962 Olde Thompson/Leeds Engineering Corporation
3250 Camino Del Sol
Oxnard, CA 93030 805-983-0388
Fax: 805-604-9079 800-827-1565
jshumway@oldethompson.com
www.oldethompson.com
Wood, metal and plastic kitchenware; also, aluminum platters and peppermills
VP: Jeff Shumway
Contact: Anne Kerwien
Estimated Sales: $5-10 Million
Number Employees: 50-99
Brands:
Olde Thompson

26963 Ole Hickory Pits
333 N Main St
Cape Girardeau, MO 63701-7205 573-334-3377
Fax: 573-334-3377 800-223-9667
main@olehickorypits.com
www.olehickorypits.com
Manufacturer and exporter of commercial barbecue pits
President: David Knight
CFO: David Scherer
Sales Coordinator: Margaret Wiggins

Estimated Sales: Below $5 Million
Number Employees: 20-49
Square Footage: 40000
Type of Packaging: Consumer, Food Service, Private Label, Bulk
Brands:
Ole Hickory Pits

26964 Oles of Puerto Rico
350 Calle D
Bayamon, PR 00959-1907 787-786-1700
Fax: 787-740-3222 oles@poque.com
Envelopes and continous forms
President: John R Young
CFO: Moreno
Quality Control: Megiul Medina
General Manager: Raphael Moreno
Director Manufacturing: Roberto Soltero
Plant Manager: Miguel Medina
Estimated Sales: $5 - 10 Million
Number Employees: 85
Parent Co: Oles Envelope Corporation

26965 Olive Can Company
1111 Bowes Rd
Elgin, IL 60123 847-468-7474
Fax: 847-468-7695 cwisniewski@uscanco.com
www.olivecan.com
Manufacturer and exporter of decorative custom tins and trays
Executive VP/General Manager: Virginia Price
National Sales Manager: Tom Doyle
Trade Show Manager: Carolyn Wisniewski
Number Employees: 125
Square Footage: 144000

26966 Oliver Bentley's, LLC
13 W. York Street
Savannah, GA 31401 877-395-2275
Fax: 877-395-7335 ollieb@oliverbentleys.com
www.oliverbentleys.com
Maker of dog treats.

26967 Oliver Manufacturing Company
17777 Us Highway 50
Rocky Ford, CO 81067 719-254-7813
Fax: 719-254-6371 888-254-7813
contactus@olivermanufacturing.com
www.olivermanufacturing.com
Cleaners (green coffee), graders (automatic and pneumatic), reclaiming machinery
President/CEO: Brian Burney
Chief Engineer: Shane Pritchard
Director of Sales/ Marketing: Jon Moreland
Sales Director: Thomas Helman
Chief Operating Officer: Joe Pentlicki
Material Control Manager: Jeffrey Fawcett
Estimated Sales: $5-10 Million
Number Employees: 20-49
Square Footage: 60000
Brands:
Fluid Dryer
Hi-Cap
Linear Separator
Maxi-Cap

26968 Oliver Products Company
511 6th St NW
Grand Rapids, MI 49504 616-456-5290
Fax: 616-456-5820 ddebri@oliverproducts.com
www.oliverproducts.com
President: John R Green
CFO: Jim Johnson
R&D: Jack Knodlauch
Quality Control: Loura Keena
Estimated Sales: $50 - 100 Million
Number Employees: 100-249

26969 Olivina. LLC
4555 Arroyo Road
Livermere, CA 94550 925-455-7810
charles@theolivina.com
www.theolivina.com
Olive oils
President/Owner/CEO: Charles Crohare
General Manager: Alice Crohare
Estimated Sales: $25 Million
Number Employees: 20

26970 Olmarc Packaging Company
Ste 1100
350 N La Salle Dr
Chicago, IL 60654-5131 708-562-2000
Fax: 708-562-9044
Packaging service
President: Cain Olmarc
VP: Mark Olmarc
CEO: Kenneth Marchetti
Estimated Sales: $20 - 50 Million
Number Employees: 900

26971 Olney Machinery
9057 Dopp Hill Road
PO Box 280
Westernville, NY 13486 315-827-4208
Fax: 315-827-4249 info@olneymachinery.com
www.olneymachinery.com
Manufacturer, importer and exporter of canning and food packing machinery
President: W Floyd Olney
Secretary and Treasurer: J Olney
Estimated Sales: $2.5-5 Million
Number Employees: 20-49

26972 Olson Manufacturing/V-RAM Solids
620 S Broadway Ave
PO Box 289
Albert Lea, MN 56007 507-373-3996
Fax: 507-373-5937 888-373-3996
sales@vram.com www.vram.com
Manufacturer, importer and exporter of solids handling pumps for waste/rendering
President: David A Olson
Sales Director: Jeff Hall
Purchasing Manager: Rose Modderman
Estimated Sales: $3 - 5 Million
Number Employees: 5-9
Brands:
V-Ram

26973 Olson Wire Products Company
4100 Benson Ave
Halethorpe, MD 21227 410-242-1945
Fax: 410-247-4206
randy@olsonwireproducts.com
www.olsonwireproducts.com
Racks including bakery, bottle, display, refrigerator and wire. Also refrigerator shelves and trays
President: Randy Olson
Estimated Sales: $20-50 Million
Number Employees: 50-99

26974 Olympia International
4203 Pan American Blvd
P.O. Box 6836
Laredo, TX 78042-6836 956-725-8555
Fax: 956-723-6968 www.olympiaintl.com
Tea and coffee samplers and weighers
President: Sergio Velasquez
Vice President: Patsy Gonzalez
Estimated Sales: $1-2.5 Million
Number Employees: 10-19

26975 Olympus America
3500 Corporate Pkwy
Center Valley, PA 18034 484-896-5000
Fax: 631-844-5620 800-446-5260
info@olympusipg.com
www.olympusamerica.com
Testing and inspection equipment: industrial videoscopes, fiberscopes and rigid boroscopes, video cameras, packaging and assembly line equipment
President: Mark Gumz
CFO: Harryirnob Kawamata
Quality Control: Timothy Sullivan
Estimated Sales: C
Number Employees: 1,000-4,999

26976 Omaha Fixture International
10320 J Street
Omaha, NE 68127 402-592-3720
Fax: 402-593-5716 800-637-2257
Service@OmahaFixture.com
www.omahafixture.com
Store fixtures
Sales Manager: Dan Gould
Catalog Sales Manager: Roger King
Number Employees: 10

26977 Omaha Neon Sign Co, Inc.
1120 N 18th St
Omaha, NE 68102-4108 402-341-6077
Fax: 402-341-7654 800-786-6366
sales@omahaneon.com www.omahaneon.com
Signs including changeable letter, electric, luminous tube, neon and plastic
President: Samuel J Marchese
Estimated Sales: $5-10 Million
Number Employees: 50-99

26978 Omar Canvas & Awning Company
202 Wesley St
Johnson City, TN 37601 423-282-9180
Fax: 423-282-3970 800-274-6627
info@omarawning.com www.omarawning.com
Commercial awnings
President: Susan Snowden
Owner: Susan Snowden
Production Manager: Bobenn Ette
Estimated Sales: $1-2,500,000
Number Employees: 20-49

26979 Omcan Inc.
3115 Pepper Mill Court
Mississauga, ON L5L 4X5 800-465-0234
Fax: 905-607-0234 sales@omcan.com
www.omcan.com
Manufacturer and importer of food processing machinery
Estimated Sales: $500,000 - $1 Million
Number Employees: 1-4
Square Footage: 600000

26980 Omcan Manufacturing & Distributing Company
3115 Pepper Mill Court
Mississauga, ON L5L 4X5
Canada 905-607-0234
Fax: 905-828-0897 800-465-0234
sales@omcan.com www.omcan.com
Manufacturer and exporter of butcher knives; personalized knives available; wholesaler/distributor of food service equipment and supplies including cutters, slicers, choppers, bowls, vegetable processors, mixers, etc.; serving the foodservice market
Owner: Tar Nella
General Manager: Tarcisio Nella
Number Employees: 30
Square Footage: 600000

26981 Omega Company
P.O.Box 4047
Stamford, CT 06907-0047 203-359-1660
Fax: 203-359-7700 800-848-4286
www.omega.com
Consultant providing food process, architectural design and engineering services
Estimated Sales: $1-2.5 Million
Number Employees: 2
Type of Packaging: Bulk

26982 Omega Design Corporation
211 Philips Rd
Exton, PA 19341 610-363-6555
Fax: 610-524-7398 800-346-0191
sales1@omegadesign.com
www.omegadesign.com
Manufacturer and exporter of secondary orienters, desiccant feeders, plastic bottle unscramblers, wrap around case packers and shrink bundling, tray loading and wrapping equipment; importer of wrap around case packers and tray loadingand wrapping equipment
President: Glen Siegele
VP Sales/Marketing Manager: Randy Caspersen
International Sales Manager: Niall McDermott
Food/Beverage Manager: Paul Sherman
Estimated Sales: $10 - 20 Million
Number Employees: 50-99
Square Footage: 45000

26983 Omega Industrial Products
795 N Progress Dr
Saukville, WI 53080 262-284-4184
Fax: 262-284-4199 800-279-6634
omega@omegaindl.com www.omega.com
Manufacturer and exporter of conveyor and wall guards, handrails and steel safety barriers stairs
President: John Weber
CFO: John Weber
Operations Manager: James Pautmann
Number Employees: 5-9
Square Footage: 27000
Brands:
Omega Protective Systems
Quick-Step Stair Systems
Trak-Shield

26984 Omega Industries
1011 Hanley Industrial Ct
St Louis, MO 63144-1907 314-961-1668
Fax: 314-961-8172 omegaiijtm@msn.com
www.omegaindinc.com
Acrylic food bins, oak and plastic bakery racks, floor and counter bakery bins, vacuum formed trays and wood, wire and plastic point of purchase displays
President: Joseph T Mort
Vice President: Linda Mort
Quality Control: Adam Mort
Sales Director: Jackie Williams
Production Manager: Joseph Howard
Plant Manager: Danny Astroth
Estimated Sales: $1-2 Million
Number Employees: 5-9
Square Footage: 50000
Type of Packaging: Consumer, Bulk

26985 Omega Products
6291 Lyters Ln
Harrisburg, PA 17111-4622 717-561-1105
Fax: 717-561-1298 800-633-3401
omega@omegajuicers.com
www.omegajuicers.com
Manufacturer and exporter of fruit and vegetable juice extractors
Founder: Robert Leo
VP Sales: James Pascotti
Estimated Sales: $1600000
Number Employees: 5-9
Square Footage: 80000
Brands:
Omega

26986 Omega Thermo Products
PO Box 141
Stratford, WI 54484
Fax: 715-687-8053 800-470-1126
omega@laser-plate.com
www.omegathermoproducts.com
President: Phillip Kraft
Insider Sales Manager: Chuck Knetter
Engineering Manager: Don Hessefort
Plant Manager: Patrick Jenkins
Purchasing Agent: Matt Mackie
Estimated Sales: Below $5 Million
Number Employees: 10-19

26987 Omicron Steel Products Company
11701 Park Lane S
Jamaica, NY 11418-1014 718-805-3400
Fax: 718-805-3401
Manufacturer, importer and exporter of shelving, worktables, benches, counters, racks, storage cabinets, carts, hand trucks, conveyors, store fixtures, chairs and stools
Sales Manager: Jerry Czajowski
Estimated Sales: $1 - 5 Million
Number Employees: 6
Parent Co: Omicron Group

26988 Omni Apparel Inc.
113 Kingsbridge Dr
Carrollton, GA 30117 770-838-1008
Fax: 770-838-1038 oapparel@bellsouth.com
www.omniapparel.com
Butcher frocks, aprons, sweatshirts, t-shirts, golf shirts and hats which can be custom embroidered with your company logo.

26989 Omni Controls
5309 Technology Dr
Tampa, FL 33647 813-971-5001
Fax: 813-960-4779 800-783-6664
sales@omnicontrols.com
www.omnicontrols.com
Manufacturer and exporter of pressure, flow, temperature and sanitary transmitters
President: Robert F Lamb
Accountant: Dianne Delarenzo
Sales Director: Frank Most
Estimated Sales: $2.5-5 Million
Number Employees: 10-19
Square Footage: 1000
Brands:
Omni Controls

26990 Omni Facility Resources
2105 W Belmont Avenue
Chicago, IL 60618-6413 800-905-5061
Fax: 773-248-9791
Plant sanitation services

26991 Omni International
935-C Cobb Place Blvd. NWỳ
Kennesaw, GA 20187-3934 770-421-0058
Fax: 770-421-0206 800-776-4431
omni@omni-inc.com www.omni-inc.com
Manufacturer and exporter of mechanical shear homogenizers and dispersers suited for R/D, QA/QC, content analysis, fat replacement, beverages, dairy, etc
President: Karl Jahn
Vice President: James Partridge
Quality Control: Eric Ruwe
Manufacturing Manager: Pete Tortorelli
Estimated Sales: Below $5 Million
Number Employees: 15
Square Footage: 40000
Type of Packaging: Food Service, Private Label
Brands:
Omni-Glh
Omni-Macro
Omni-Mixer
Omni-Th
Omni-Uh
Shear Flow

26992 Omni Metalcraft Corporation
4040 Us Highway 23 N
Alpena, MI 49707 989-358-7000
Fax: 989-358-7020 info@omni.com
www.omni.com
Manufacturer and exporter of skatewheel, belt, roller, vertical and chain conveyors
Chairman of the Board: Ronald W Winter
VP Sales/Marketing: Paul Diamond
Estimated Sales: $20-50 Million
Number Employees: 50-99
Square Footage: 130000

26993 Omni Technologies
779 Rudolph Way
Greendale, IN 47025 812-539-4144
Fax: 812-539-4437 info@omnitechnologies.com
www.omnitechnologies.com
Packaging machinery, custom compression molded polyurethane parts and small quantities, runs of injection molded parts
President: Don Culbertson
Estimated Sales: $4 Million
Number Employees: 50-99

26994 Omni-Lift
1485 S 300 W
Salt Lake City, UT 84115 801-486-3776
Fax: 801-486-3780 omnibelt@aol.com
www.omni-lift.com
Conveyor belts and belt cleaners
Manager: Jim Gillett
VP Operations: Jim Gilett
Estimated Sales: $500,000-$1,000,000
Number Employees: 5-9

26995 Omnicraft, Inc.
5640 Feltl Rd
Minnetonka, MN 55343 952-988-9944
Fax: 952-938-2035 dhause@omnicraft.com
www.omnicraft.com
Manufacturer, exporter and designer of exhibits and displays
Estimated Sales: $1 - 5 Million
Number Employees: 20-50
Square Footage: 120000
Type of Packaging: Consumer, Food Service

26996 Omnimark Instrument Corporation
1320 S Priest Dr # 4
Tempe, AZ 85281-6959 480-784-2200
Fax: 480-784-4738 800-835-3211
info@omniwww.com www.omniwww.com
Moisture analyzers
President: Brian Taylor
Estimated Sales: $2.5 - 5 Million
Number Employees: 10-19

26997 Omnion
185 Plain St Rockland
Rockland, MA 02370-0614 781-878-7200
Fax: 781-878-7465 omnion@world.std.com
Manufacturer and exporter of oxidative stability analytical instrumentation for the food industry
President: Frank Mcgovern McGovern
Technical Specialist: Cheryl Porter
Estimated Sales: $1 - 3,000,000
Number Employees: 9-May
Type of Packaging: Bulk

26998 Omnipak Import
2916 120th St
Flushing, NY 11354-2506 718-353-3741
Fax: 718-353-3741 800-348-6664
info@omnipakimport.com
www.omnipakimport.com
Coffee, espresso coffee, espresso equipment, spring water, espresso bar furniture, espresso machine parts
Owner: Gregory Di Mattino
CEO: Kathy Tuschetpa
Estimated Sales: $10 - 20 Million
Number Employees: 10-19

26999 Omnitech International
2715 Ashman Street
Midland, MI 48640 989-631-3377
Fax: 989-631-0812 info@omnitechintl.com
www.omnitechintl.com
Manufacturer and exporter of turnkey can and can end systems for domestic and international installation
President: Lee Rouse
CEO: Lee Rouse
Vice President/Business Manager, Plastic: Phil Sarnacke
Operations Manager/Controller: Carolyn Owen
Estimated Sales: $5 - 10 Million
Number Employees: 10-19
Square Footage: 24000

27000 Omnitemp Refrigeration
9300 Hall Road
Downey, CA 90241-5309 562-923-9660
Fax: 562-862-7466 800-423-9660
omnitempdrafting@worldnet.att.net
www.omniteaminc.com
Manufacturer and exporter of display cases and heat recovery and refrigeration equipment
Owner: Don Hyatt
CEO, President: Mr. Haasis
Plant Manager: Jess McKeoun
Estimated Sales: $1 - 5 Million
Number Employees: 50-99
Type of Packaging: Food Service

27001 Omron Electronics
55 Commerce Dr
Schaumburg, IL 60173 847-882-2288
Fax: 847-884-1866 800-556-6766
omroninfo@omron.com www.omron.com
Instrumentation and control products including PLCs, sensors and temperature controllers
President: Craig Bauer
CEO: Tastu Goto
Estimated Sales: $4.6 Million
Number Employees: 100-249
Square Footage: 15000
Parent Co: Omron Corporation
Brands:
Smart Factory

27002 Omron Health Care
1200 Lakeside Dr
Bannockburn, IL 60015-1243 847-680-6200
Fax: 847-680-6269 800-323-1482
info@omron.com www.omronhealthcare.com
Latex gloves
President: Frank Zorn
Chairman: Kazuo Saito
CEO: Isao Ogino
Quality Control: Edward McGinnis
Sr. VP Sales/Marketing: Ed Siemens
Estimated Sales: $100-200 Million
Number Employees: 1,000-4,999

27003 Omron Systems
55 Commerce Dr
Schaumburg, IL 60173-5302 847-519-9465
Fax: 847-843-7686 www.omron.com
Electronic cash registers with software for fast food, fine dining and cafeteria markets; also, touch screen systems for restaurants and hospitality
Founder: Kazuma Tateisi
President, Chief Executive Officer: Yoshihito Yamada
Director, Vice President: Yoshinobu Morishita
Estimated Sales: $15 - 20 Million
Number Employees: 100-249

27004 On Site Gas Systems Inc
35 Budney Rd
Newington, CT 06111 860-667-8888
Fax: 860-667-2222 888-748-3429
info@onsitegas.com www.onsitegas.com
On Site Gas designs and manufacturers PSA, membrane and combustion based oxygen and nitrogen gas generation systems. Applications within the food industry utilizing food and beverage nitrogen include that of: beveragemixing/dispensing; coffee producers/packers; fruit orchards/storage; perishable transportation; winemakers; and kiln/grain drying. Snack food packaging.
President/Founder: Frank Hursey
CEO: Guy Hatch
Chief Engineer: Sanh Phan
Vice President Sales: Bob Wolff
PR: Maylin O Conner
Vice President Manufacturing: Sean Haggerty

27005 On-Campus Hospitality
P.O.Box 1500
Westbury, NY 11590-0812 516-334-3030
Fax: 516-334-3059 ebm-mail@ebmpubs.com
www.ebmpubs.com
President: Murry Greenwald
Estimated Sales: $10 - 20 Million
Number Employees: 20-49

27006 On-Hand Adhesives
940 Telser Road
Lake Zurich, IL 60047 847-437-7773
Fax: 847-437-8006 800-323-5158
gluguru@on-hand.com www.gluguru.com
Hot melt equipment and adhesives for case sealing and palletizing rebuilding machinery
Owner, President & Secretary: Mike Cooper
Chairman, Treasurer: George Cooper
Vice President: Lin Sliwa
Vice President: Margaret Cooper
Estimated Sales: $2.5 - 5 Million
Number Employees: 10-19
Square Footage: 27600

27007 OnTrack Automation Inc
592 Colby Drive
Waterloo, ON N2V 1A2
Canada 519-886-9090
Fax: 519-886-9306 ontrack@psangelus.com
www.ontrack-inc.com
Manufacturer and exporter of bottling machinery including orienters line conveyors, labeling change parts, feedscrews
President: Ward Flannery
Plant Manager: Ed Gardiner
Purchasing Manager: Daren Ste. Marie
Number Employees: 20-49
Parent Co: Joseph E. Seagram & Sons

27008 Ondeo Nalco Company
1601 W Diehl Rd
Naperville, IL 60563-1198 630-305-1000
Fax: 630-305-2900 webmaster@ondeo-nalco.com
www.nalco.com
Process chemicals, water treatment, waste water treatment
President: Bill Joyce
CEO: Jerik Frywald
Estimated Sales: K
Number Employees: 10,000

27009 (HQ)OneVision Corporation
5805A Chandler Court
Westerville, OH 43082 614-794-1144
Fax: 614-794-3366 neil@onevisioncorp.com
www.onevisioncorp.com
Can inspection systems
President: Neil Morris
Quality Control: Matt Allaire
Director Sales: Mike Raczynski
Estimated Sales: Below $5 Million
Number Employees: 9
Square Footage: 9000
Other Locations:
OneVision Corp.
Riverside CA

27010 Oneida Canada, Limited
163 Kenwood Ave
Oneida, NY 13421
Canada 905-356-9691
888-263-7195
sales@oneida.com www.oneida.com
Distrubutor of tabletop supplies including flatware, china, glassware and hollowware
Sales Manager: Frank Fan
Number Employees: 32
Number of Brands: 15
Number of Products: 8000
Square Footage: 400000
Parent Co: Oneida
Type of Packaging: Food Service
Brands:
D.J.
Delco Buffalo
Oneida
Rego
Sant Andrea
Schonwald
Schott Zwiesel

27011 Oneida Food Service
P.O.Box 1
Oneida, NY 13421-1001 315-361-3000
Fax: 315-361-3700 sales@oneida.com
www.oneida.com
Manufacturer, importer and exporter of stainless steel and silver plated hollowware and flatware; also, dinnerware, glassware, crystal and china
Chairman: Peter Kallet
CEO: James E Joseph
Sales Manager: Frank Fan
Estimated Sales: I
Number Employees: 1,000-4,999
Square Footage: 1500000
Parent Co: Oneida
Brands:
Buffalo
Calp
D.J.
Noritake
Oneida
Rego
Sant' Andrea
Schonwald
Schott

27012 Onguard Industries
1850 Clark Rd
Havre De Grace, MD 21078 410-272-2000
Fax: 410-272-3346 800-304-2282
sales@onguardindustries.com
www.onguardindustries.com
Protective clothing and non-slip boots.

27013 Onset Computer Corporation
470 Macarthur Blvd
Buzzards Bay, MA 02532 800-564-4377
Fax: 508-759-9100 800-564-4377
sales@onsetcomp.com www.onsetcomp.com
Design and manufacturing of miniature, battery-powered data loggers
President: Jack Sample
Product Application Specialist: Herman Gustafson
Estimated Sales: $13 Million
Number Employees: 90
Square Footage: 40000

27014 Onsite Sycom Energy Corporation
1010 Wisconsin Avenue NW
Suite 340
Washington, DC 20007-3680 202-625-4126
Fax: 202-625-1067

27015 Ontario Glove and Safety Products
5 Washburn Drive
Kitchener, ON N2R 1S1
Canada 519-886-3590
Fax: 519-886-3597 800-265-4554
sales@ontarioglove.com www.ontarioglove.com
Manufacturer and importer of gloves including PVC, cotton, latex and neoprene; wholesaler/distributor and exporter of leather and synthetic aprons
President: John McCarthy
CFO: Randell Moore
Quality Control: Truedy Henric
Number Employees: 10

27016 Ontario Neon Company
P.O.Box 9297
303 W Main Street
Ontario, CA 91762-3843 909-986-4632
Fax: 909-988-6376 mark@ontarioneon.com
www.encoreimage.com
Exterior and interior electric and neon signs; also, menus and awnings
Chairman of the Board: Terry Wilkins
VP Sales: Corey Northncott
Estimated Sales: $3-4,000,000
Number Employees: 20-49
Square Footage: 15000

27017 (HQ)Opal Manufacturing Ltd
10 Compass Court
Toronto, ON M1S 5R3
Canada 416-646-5232
Fax: 416-646-5242 rosa@nrttech.com
www.customvendingmachines.com
Manufacturer and exporter of custom vending machines and refrigerated liquid portion control cream dispensers
Sales: Brian Simon
Number Employees: 10
Brands:
Little Squirt
Opal

27018 Open Date Systems
PO Box 538
Georges Mills, NH 03751 603-763-3444
Fax: 603-763-4222 877-673-6328
info@opendate.com www.opendate.com
Coding systems including hot stamp, thermal transfer and fully and semi-automatic carton; feeding systems
President/CEO: Thierry Brousse
CFO: Nikki MacLennan
Vice President: Rick Berquist
Marketing/Sales: Don Morong
Production Manager: Terry Bartlett
Purchasing: Marcia Crawford
Estimated Sales: $3,000,000
Square Footage: 3000
Parent Co: Open Date Equipment
Brands:
Eurocode
Printmaster
Sprint
Thermocode

27019 Opie Brush Company
16400 E Truman Rd
Independence, MO 64050-4161 816-246-6767
Fax: 816-833-8955 800-877-6743
opiebrush@sbcglobal.net
www.opiebrushcompany.com
Manufacturer and exporter of custom made and industrial brushes including flour milling
Marketing: Connie Dulin
General Manager: Connie Dulin
Plant Manager: James Dulin
Estimated Sales: $500,000-$1 Million
Number Employees: 5-9
Number of Brands: 1
Square Footage: 24000

27020 Optek
5229 Cheshire Rd
Galena, OH 43021 740-548-4700
Fax: 740-548-4999 800-533-8400
wtkavage@optek-inc.com www.optek-inc.com
Manufacturer and exporter of volume flow measurement systems for belt conveyors, tablet counting systems and control systems including moisture, temperature and fill level
President/CFO: Dr. Marvin E. Monroe
VP: William Kavage
Estimated Sales: Below $5 Million
Number Employees: 1-4
Square Footage: 15000
Brands:
Check Fill

27021 Optek-Danulat, Inc
N118w18748 Bunsen Dr
Germantown, WI 53022 262-437-3600
Fax: 262-437-3699 888-551-4288
info@optek.com www.optek.com
High performance inline photometric analyzers for industrial liquid and gas processing applications, and photemetric measuring systems
CEO: Juergen Danulat
VP: Rik Meyer
Number Employees: 100-249
Number of Products: 50
Square Footage: 27000

27022 **Optel Vision**
2680 Boul Du Parc Technologique
Quebec, QC G1P 4S6
Canada 418-688-0334
Fax: 418-688-9397 866-688-0334
info@optelvision.com www.optelvision.com
Packaging line inspection systems. Label inspector, barcode inspector, date code inspector, blister pack inspector
President: Louis Roy
CFO: Nancy Houley
Vice President: Jean Lafortune
R&D: Mathew Kowalcyk
Marketing/Public Relations: Jenny Normandeau
Sales Director: Pierre Turcotte
Estimated Sales: Below $5 Million
Number Employees: 40
Square Footage: 12000

27023 **Optex**
13661 Benson Ave
Chino, CA 91710 909-993-5770
Fax: 310-533-5910 800-966-7839
jkessel@optexamerica.com
www.optexamerica.com
Manufacturer and exporter of alarm systems and sensors
President: Robert Blair
VP Marketing/Sales: Jay Kessel
Estimated Sales: $20 - 50 Million
Number Employees: 25-30
Parent Co: Optex
Brands:
Morse
Optex

27024 **Optical Security Group**
1932 Valley View Lane
Dallas, TX 75234 972-247-1288
Fax: 303-534-1010 osllc@sbcglobal.net
www.opticalsecurityllc.com
Manufactures lenticular products
President: Mark Turange
CEO: Mark Turnage
Estimated Sales: $1-5 Million
Number Employees: 50-99

27025 **Optima International**
10601 Jefferson Chemical Rd
Conroe, TX 77301 936-441-1333
Fax: 936-760-1141
info@optima-international.co.uk
www.optima-international.com
President: Simon Spiller
Quality Control: Christie Coites
Number Employees: 10

27026 **Optima Machinery Corporation**
1330 Contract Drive
Green Bay, WI 54304 920-339-2222
Fax: 920-339-2233 info@optima-usa.com
www.optima-usa.com
Filling and packaging machines
President: Thomas Seifert
Marketing Director: Cathy Hendricks
Estimated Sales: $5 - 10 Million
Number Employees: 20-49
Parent Co: Optima Packaging Group

27027 **Optipure**
2605 Technology Drive
Bldg 300
Plano, TX 75074 972-422-1212
Fax: 972-422-6262 kaldstadt@filterxpress.com
www.procamcontrols.com
Water filters and water filtration equipment; full line of filtration products for foodservice applications (ice machines, steam equipment, coffee./tea, espresso, balers, fountain, beverages).
Owner: Roy Sebert
Director Sales/Marketing: Keefe Aldstadt
Estimated Sales: $2.5-5 Million
Number Employees: 10-19
Number of Brands: 1
Number of Products: 50+
Parent Co: Procam Controls Inc
Type of Packaging: Consumer, Food Service, Private Label, Bulk
Brands:
Opti Pure

27028 **Oracle Packaging**
4949 Stickney Avenue
Toledo, OH 43612-3716 419-729-9771
Fax: 419-729-9055 800-952-9536
www.oraclepackaging.com
Folding cartons for the dairy industry
President: Ted McLaren
Plant Manager: Berkley Cooke
VP: Lou Carozza
Estimated Sales: $10-20 Million
Number Employees: 50-99
Square Footage: 55000

27029 **Orange Plastics**
1825 S Acacia Ave
Compton, CA 90220 310-609-2121
Stretch film, pallet wrap and produce and grocery bags
National Sales Manager: Michael Kopulsky
Estimated Sales: $20-50 Million
Number Employees: 100-249

27030 **Orangex**
104 E 40th Street
New York, NY 10016-1801 212-986-9353
Fax: 212-986-9357 sales@orangex.com
www.orangex.net

27031 **Oration Rubber Stamp Company**
RR 94
Columbus, NJ 08022 908-496-4161
Fax: 908-496-4989
Rubber stamps for food packaging
Customer Representative: Carole Vorhis
Manager: Chris Baier
Parent Co: Cosco

27032 **Orber Manufacturing Company**
1655 Elmwood Ave # 30
Cranston, RI 02910-4933 401-781-0050
Fax: 401-781-7720 800-761-4059
sales@orber.com www.orber.com
Metal specialties including badges, medals, emblems and key chains
Vice President: Larry Shwartz
Estimated Sales: $1 - 3 Million
Number Employees: 10-19

27033 **Orbis Corp.**
39 Westmore Drive
Rexdale, ON M9V 4Y6
Canada 416-745-6980
Fax: 416-745-1874 800-890-7292
info@orbiscorporation.com
www.orbiscorporation.com
Injection moulding
President: Howard Walton
Sales: Relph Kert
Number Employees: 250-499
Brands:
Norseman

27034 **Orbis/Menasha Corporation**
P.O.Box 389
Oconomowoc, WI 53066-0389 262-560-5000
Fax: 262-560-5841 800-999-8683
info@orbiscorporation.com
www.orbiscorporation.com
Total returnable packaging systems, containers, pallets, interiors
President: Jim Kotek
CEO: Dave Schopp
Estimated Sales: $20-50 million
Number Employees: 100-249

27035 **Orbisphere Laboratories**
3 W Main St
Buford, GA 30518 770-932-1400
Fax: 770-932-1230 gthomas@hachultra.com
www.hachultra.com
Gas analyzers for in-lines process and laboratory use
Estimated Sales: $500,000-$1 Million
Number Employees: 1-4

27036 **Orca**
199 Whiting St # 5
New Britain, CT 06051-3163 860-223-4180
Fax: 860-826-1729 cathysantiago@orce-mfg.com
www.orca-mfg.com
Manufacturer and exporter of custom caps including can, glass and screw neck ends
Owner: Greg Goguen
Estimated Sales: $5-10 Million
Number Employees: 20-49
Square Footage: 60000

27037 **Orchard Gold**
1762 Hester Avenue
PO Box 28481
San Jose, CA 95159 408-279-8822
Fax: 209-835-2044
President: Ron Ruscigno
Brands:
Corral Hollow Ranch
Orchard

27038 **Orchem Corporation**
4293 Mulhauser Rd
Fairfield, OH 45014 513-874-9700
Fax: 513-874-3624
craig.feltner@orchemcorp.com
www.orchem.com
Food and beverage cleaning and sanitation.
President: Oscar Robertson
General Manager: Craig Feltner
Estimated Sales: $5-10 Million
Number Employees: 20-49

27039 **Order-Matic Corporation**
PO Box 25463
Oklahoma City, OK 73125-0463 405-672-1487
Fax: 405-672-5349 800-767-6733
info@ordermatic.com www.ordermatic.com
Electronic restaurant equipment including communication systems and POS systems for fast food and drive-thru restaurants
President: William B Cunningham
CFO: Dan Webb
Vice President: Greg Cunningham
National Sales Manager: Paul Barron
Estimated Sales: $20-50 Million
Number Employees: 100-249

27040 **(HQ)Ore-Cal Corporation**
634 South Crocker St.
Los Angeles, CA 90021-1002 213-680-9540
Fax: 213-228-6557 800-827-7474
CustomerService@ore-cal.com www.ore-cal.com
Shrimp, pangasius, mahi mahi, swordfish, calamari, breaded shrimp, and ready mixed entree dishes such as; shrimp scampi, seafood gumbo, cioppino, shrimp pad thai, and shrimp torn kha soup.
President: William Shinbane
Human Resources: Josephine Davif
Controller/Vice President Finance: Mark Feldstein
Vice President: Mark Shinbane
Lab Director: Avito Moniz
Human Resources Compliance & Regulatory: Wendy Gomez
Manager of National Sales: Shelley Gee
Manufacturing Supervisor: Rick Kanase
Estimated Sales: $10.9 Million
Number Employees: 55
Number of Brands: 1
Number of Products: 11+
Square Footage: 80000
Type of Packaging: Consumer, Food Service, Private Label, Bulk
Brands:
Harvest of the Sea®

27041 **Oreck Corporation**
1400 Salem Road
Cookeville, TN 38506 504-733-8761
Fax: 504-733-6709 800-989-3535
ddesporte@oreck.com www.oreck.com
Industrial vacuum cleaners
President: Thomas A Oreck
CEO: David Oreck
CFO: San Eilers
Quality Control: Scott Dessen
Marketing Director: Nancy Willy
Number Employees: 1,000-4,999
Brands:
Oreck

27042 **Oregon Pacific Bottling**
93487 Sixes River Road
Sixes, OR 97476-9713 541-332-7307
Fax: 541-332-1603 info@oregon-pacific.com
Bottling,labeling
Number Employees: 10

27043 **(HQ)Oregon Potato Company**
650 E Columbia Ave.
PO Box 169
Boardman, OR 97818 541-481-2715
Fax: 513-481-3443 800-336-6311
cuatomerservice@oregonpotato.com
www.oregonpotato.com
Processor and exporter of frozen roasted potatoes, seasoned potatoes, IQF frozen potatoes, wedges, slices, diced, shredded, and whole baked potatoe
Grower & President: Frank Tiegs
CEO: Hal Neiman
Marketing/Sales: Don Smith
Director of Sales: Barry Stice
Number Employees: 5-9
Square Footage: 6000
Type of Packaging: Consumer, Food Service, Private Label, Bulk
Other Locations:
NorSun Food Group
Rexburg ID

27044 **Organic Products Company**
PO Box 560625
Dallas, TX 75356-0625 972-438-7321
Fax: 972-438-7321 ink@opcompany.com
www.opcompany.com
Marking inks
General Manager: Arthur Botvin
Estimated Sales: $1-2.5 Million
Number Employees: 10-19
Brands:
Opco
Organic Products
Sentry Seal
Torgue Seal

27045 **Organon Teknika Corporation**
100 Rodolphe St
Durham, NC 27712 919-620-2000
Fax: 800-968-9494 800-682-2666
dkafader@cybernetics.com
www.biomerieux-usa.com
Manufacturer and exporter of food processing equipment including aseptic, bacterial detection and microbiological
President: Robert Timmins
CFO: Brian Armstrong
CEO: Mark Mackowiak
R&D: Brian Daniel
Quality Control: Katie Foushee
VP Sales: Harry Schrick
Estimated Sales: $5 - 10,000,000
Number Employees: 1,000-4,999
Parent Co: Azko Nobel

27046 **Orics Industries**
240 Smith St
Farmingdale, NY 11735 718-461-8613
Fax: 718-461-4719 info@orics.com
www.orics.com
Manufacturer and exporter of tray sealers for vacuum gas flush map packaging
Owner: Ori Cohen
Number Employees: 20-49

27047 **Oriental Motor USA Corporation**
2580 W 237th Street
Torrance, CA 90505-5217 310-325-0040
Fax: 310-257-0297 800-816-6867
techsupport@orientalmotor.com
www.orientalmotor.com
President: Manatoshi Yamauchi
Estimated Sales: $20 - 50 Million
Number Employees: 80

27048 **(HQ)Original Bradford Soap Works**
200 Providence St
West Warwick, RI 02893 401-821-2141
Fax: 401-821-1660 info@bradfordsoap.com
www.bradfordsoap.com
Manufacturer and exporter of cake soap and industrial detergents
CEO: John H Howland
VP Sales: Ed Windsor
Estimated Sales: $20-50 Million
Number Employees: 250-499
Type of Packaging: Private Label

27049 **Original Packaging & Display Company**
4161 Beck Avenue
Saint Louis, MO 63116-2632 314-772-7797
Fax: 314-772-7271
Solid and set-up paper boxes
Member: Herbert J Strather
Sales Director: Ken Monschein
General Manager: Ed Taylor
Plant Manager: Mark Nehhans
Purchasing Manager: Todd Brock
Estimated Sales: $300,000-500,000
Number Employees: 20
Type of Packaging: Consumer, Food Service

27050 **Orion Packaging Systems**
4750 County Road 13 NE
Alexandria, MN 56308 901-888-4170
Fax: 901-365-1071 800-333-6556
sales@orionpackaging.com
www.orionpackaging.com
Manufacturers a wide range of high-quality stretch wrapping machines for virtually any pallet load of product unitizing application. Machines ore available in rotary tower, turntable or orbital ring styles. Orion equipment features allstructural steel construction, high-efficiency powered prestretch film delivery with easy threading, and the best warrenty in the industry
Manager: Glenn Greene
CFO: Marsha Greene
Advertising Manager: Peter Vilardi
Operations Manager: Glenn Greene
Plant Manager: Andre LaVigne
Estimated Sales: $5 - 10,000,000
Number Employees: 20-49
Number of Brands: 10
Number of Products: 34
Square Footage: 100000
Parent Co: Pro Mach
Other Locations:
Orion
Laval Quebec, Canada

27051 **Orion Research**
100 Cummings Ctr # 106n
Beverly, MA 01915-6105 978-524-8501
Fax: 978-524-8502 800-225-1480
info@thermoorion.com
www.orionresearchinc.com
Manufacturer and exporter of analytical instruments for the measurement of sodium, pH chemical species in solutions and moisture in foods
Owner: Michael O Brien
Director Marketing: David Ingalls
VP Marketing: Tom Paquette
Estimated Sales: $100-500 Million
Number Employees: 1-4
Parent Co: Thermedics Detection
Brands:
Orion
Perphect
Ross

27052 **Orkin Commercial Services**
1521 W. Broadway Ave.
Anaheim, CA 92802 877-250-1652
Fax: 714-630-0562 866-949-6098
www.orkin.com
Exterminators
President/CEO/COO: Glen Rollins
VP/CFO: Harry Cynkus
VP Publc Relations: Martha Craft
Number Employees: 4000
Square Footage: 120000
Parent Co: Rollins Inc

27053 **Orkin Pest Control**
P.O.Box 647
Atlanta, GA 30301-0647 404-888-2000
Fax: 404-888-2012 www.orkin.com
Pest control, fly control, rodent control, bird control, odor control
President: Glen W Rollins
Estimated Sales: I
Number Employees: 5,000-9,999

27054 **Ortemp**
11889 Creek Hollow Rd
Healdsburg, CA 95448 707-433-4459
Fax: 707-433-4450
Wine industry temperature warning devices

27055 **Orthodox Union**
11 Broadway
New York, NY 10004-1307 212-563-4000
Fax: 212-564-9058 koegelp@ou.org
www.oukosher.org
World's largest and most respected kosher certification, over 400,000 products.
CEO: Eli Edelman
Marketing: Phyllis Koegel

27056 **(HQ)Ortmayer Materials Handling Inc**
926 Bedford Ave
Brooklyn, NY 11205 718-875-7995
Fax: 718-875-6385 info@ortmayer.com
www.ortmayer.com
Material handling equipment including hand carts, semi line skids, stock trucks, lockers and shelving, also distributors of Magline and B&P alum hand trucks
President: Mendel Gross
Vice President: Noson Schelhter
Estimated Sales: $4 Million
Number Employees: 10-19
Square Footage: 10000

27057 **Orwak**
10820 Normandale Boulevard
Minneapolis, MN 55437-3112 612-881-9200
Fax: 612-881-8578 800-747-0449
orwak@wwz.com www.orwak.us
Manufacturer and exporter of trash compactors and recycling balers
Estimated Sales: $500,000-$1 Million
Number Employees: 4
Brands:
Orwak

27058 **Osage Food Products**
120 West Main St
Washington, MO 63090 636-390-9477
Fax: 636-390-9485 sales@osagefood.com
www.osagefood.com
Osage is a multi-dimensional company supplying ingredients and food products. Our ingredients for manufacturing. Our packaged goods division supplies national brands and private label products for food service and retail. Our specialtyproducts division works with manufacturers, marketing residual ingredients and finished goods that are needed to sell
President: William Dickinson
Estimated Sales: $2.5 - 5,000,000
Number Employees: 5-9
Type of Packaging: Consumer, Food Service, Private Label, Bulk
Brands:
Central Volky
Oven Gem

27059 **Oscartielle Equipment Company**
855 Mahler Road
Burlingame, CA 94010-1603 650-827-3510
Fax: 650-827-3511 800-672-2784
info@otl-usa.com www.oscartielle-usa.com
Gelato and ice cream displays
President: Rabih S Ballout
Number Employees: 10

27060 **Osgood Industries**
601 Burbank Rd
Oldsmar, FL 34677 813-855-7337
Fax: 813-855-3068 sales@osgoodinc.com
www.osgoodinc.com
Fillers and heat sealers for containers
President: Martin Mueller
Executive VP: Richard Mueller
Estimated Sales: $20-50 Million
Number Employees: 100-249
Type of Packaging: Food Service, Private Label, Bulk

27061 **Osgood Industries Inc.**
601 Burbank Rd
Oldsmar, FL 34677 813-855-7337
Fax: 813-855-3068 www.osgoodinc.com

Manufactureer of trays, containers and packaging for the dairy and food industries.

27062 Oshikiri Corporation ofAmerica
10425 Drummond Rd
Philadelphia, PA 19154-3898 215-637-6005
Fax: 215-637-6041
oshikiri-production@msn.com
www.oshikiri.com
Bakery mixers, molders and proofers
Estimated Sales: $2.5-5 Million
Number Employees: 20-49

27063 Osmonics, Inc.
5951 Clearwater Dr
Hopkins, MN 55343-8995 952-933-2277
Fax: 952-933-0141 www.osmonics.com
Filtration and sepatation components, reverse osmisis and ultrafiltration technologies, valves and flow control components, equipment and systems, instrumentation and controls and laboratory products
President: Edward J Fierko
Estimated Sales: $207.44 Million
Number Employees: 1318

27064 Osram Sylvania
100 Endicott St # 1
Danvers, MA 01923 978-777-1900
Fax: 978-750-2152 800-544-4828
communications@sylvania.com
www.sylvania.com
Lamps and ballasts
President: Charles Jerabeck
President, Chief Executive Officer: Rick Leaman
CFO: Martin Goetzeler
Quality Control: Russell Liddle
R&D and Executive Director: John Gustafson
Manager Sales/Marketing: Bob Nigrello
Manager of Corporate Communications: Anne Guertin
Number Employees: 10,000
Brands:
Capsylite
Dulux
Lumalux
Metalarc
Octron

27065 Osram Sylvania Products
129 Portsmouth Ave
Exeter, NH 03833-2105 603-772-4331
Fax: 603-772-1072 www.sylvania.com
Quartz tubing, sockets, infrared heaters
President: Charles Jerabek
President, Chief Executive Officer: Rick Leaman
Quality Control: Lake Patterson
Manager of Corporate Communications: Anne Guertin
Plant Manager: Michael Huelsemann
Estimated Sales: $25 - 50 Million
Number Employees: 250-499

27066 Oss Food Plant Sanitation Services
1050 Tower Lane
Bensenville, IL 60106
Fax: 630-521-0092 800-905-5061
jlyman@ossfoodplantsanitation.com
www.ossfoodplantsanitation.com
Sanitation cleaning, environmental cleaning, staffing for maintenance and operation

27067 (HQ)Osterneck Company
Highway 72 E
Lumberton, NC 28358 910-738-2416
Fax: 910-739-2881 800-682-2416
Manufacturer and exporter of plastic bags and woven polypropylene products
Vice President: Leroy Freeman
Estimated Sales: $1 - 5 Million
Number Employees: 50-99
Square Footage: 200000
Brands:
O-Tex

27068 Ostrem Chemical Co. Ltd
2310-80 Avenue
Edmonton, AB T6P 1N2
Canada 780-440-1911
Fax: 780-440-1241 inquiries@ostrem.com
www.ostrem.com
Industrial cleaning compounds
President: Roar Tungland
CFO: Ben Tungland
Marketing Director: Ken Sagan
Number Employees: 40
Square Footage: 160000
Type of Packaging: Private Label

27069 Ott Packagings
719 Route 522
Selinsgrove, PA 17870-1298 570-374-2811
Fax: 570-374-2891 ottpkg@ttt.net
Set-up boxes
Chairman of the Board: Robert McNeil
Quality Control Manager: Bob Vanhorn
Sales Manager: Steve Stancaco
Operations Manager: Wes Craig
Purchasing Mgr: John Clark
Estimated Sales: $5-10 Million
Number Employees: 50-99

27070 Ottenheimer Equipment Company
PO Box 4395
Lutherville Timonium, MD 21094-4395 410-597-9700
Fax: 410-252-7775 ottco@comcast.net
Wholesaler/distributor of food service equipment; serving the food service market; also, consultant for the design of food facilities
Estimated Sales: $.5 - 1 million
Number Employees: 1-4

27071 Otterbine Barebo
3840 Main Rd E
Emmaus, PA 18049 610-965-6018
Fax: 610-965-6050 800-237-8837
info@otterbine.com www.otterbine.com
Water aeration systems
Owner: Charles Barebo
Estimated Sales: $1 - 3 Million
Number Employees: 20-49
Brands:
Concep2

27072 Otto Braun Bakery Equipment
115 Dingens Street
Buffalo, NY 14206-2304 716-824-1252
Fax: 716-824-6076
Bakery racks, proofers, coaters, frying screens, doughnut fryers and hand trucks
President: Rudolph Hug
Secretary/Treasurer: Arthur Karneth
Estimated Sales: $1-2.5 Million
Number Employees: 4

27073 Otto Material Handling
14609 Sorrel Ct
Charlotte, NC 28278-8322 704-587-1055
Fax: 704-587-9368 800-942-2758
info@otto-usa.com www.reottoandsons.com
Plastic waste containers
President: R Otto
Sales/Marketing Coordinator: Meredith Burris
Estimated Sales: $10-20 Million
Number Employees: 10-19

27074 Ottumwa Tent & Awning Company
635 W 2nd St
P.O.Box 494
Ottumwa, IA 52501 641-682-2257
Fax: 641-682-4357
www.ottumwatentandawning.com
Commercial awnings
President: Michael Swallow
Estimated Sales: $1 - 2,500,000
Number Employees: 5-9

27075 Ouachita Packaging Machinery
120 N Hilton St
West Monroe, LA 71291-7499 318-396-1468
Fax: 318-396-1668 omworks@yu.com
Manufacturer and exporter of packaging machinery including automatic and stretch balers
President: Jimmy Dulaney
CFO: Jimmy Dulaney
R&D: Don Hudson
Quality Control: Jimmy Dulaney
Estimated Sales: Below $5 Million
Number Employees: 20-49
Parent Co: Ouachita Machine Works

27076 Ouellette Machinery Systems
1761 Chase Drive
Fenton, MO 63026-2037 636-343-7200
Fax: 636-343-6615 800-545-7619
sales@omsinc.net www.omsinc.net
Bulk palletizers and depalletizers; case, drum, pail palletizers; pallet and container conveyors, pallet stackers and unstackers, sheet stackers and unstackers
President: Joseph Ouellette
VP Design: Richard Ouellette
Purchasing: Robert Del Pietro
Estimated Sales: $10-20 Million
Number Employees: 50-99
Square Footage: 73230

27077 Our Name is Mud
224 W 29th St
New York, NY 10001-5204 212-244-4711
Fax: 800-972-9982 877-683-7867
wholesale@ournameismud.com
www.ournameismud.com
Emphasizing engineering for bulk material handling, process, bag opening and disposal systems
Owner: Lorrie Veasey
CEO: Kip Veasey
CFO: John Nelsen
Marketing: Victoria Compton-Jorasch
Sales: Jill Bukzin
Public Relations: Victoria Compton-Jorasch
Estimated Sales: $3 - 5 Million
Type of Packaging: Bulk

27078 Outlook Packaging
PO Box 775
Neenah, WI 54957-0775 920-722-1666
Fax: 920-722-0008
Manufacturer, importer and exporter of flexible packaging materials for meat, cheese, candy, frozen food, fish, poultry and other various industrial applications
President: Joe Baksha
Contact: Dennis Grabski
Estimated Sales: G
Number Employees: 250-499
Square Footage: 83000
Parent Co: Flexible Technology
Type of Packaging: Bulk

27079 Outotec
8280 Stayton Drive
Suite M
Jessup, ID 20794 301-543-1200
Fax: 301-543-0002 www.energyproducts.com
Manufacturer and exporter of energy recovery systems including waste incinerators and waste disposal equipment; also, fluidized bed systems and fabrication services available
Plant Manager: Mark Castle
Purchasing Manager: Joe Malloy
Estimated Sales: $50 Million
Number Employees: 72
Number of Brands: 1
Square Footage: 30000
Parent Co: Idaho Energy Partnership

27080 Outterson, LLC
7747 Woodstone Drive
Cincinnati, OH 45244-2855 513-474-3521
www.fermentationbiz.com
Specializes- brew pubs, wineries and microdistilleries
Estimated Sales: $1.5 Million
Number Employees: 1

27081 Ovalstrapping
120 55th St NE
Fort Payne, AL 35967 256-845-1914
Fax: 256-845-1493 info@ovalstrapping.com
www.ovalstrapping.com
Strapping and strapping machines
Marketing Assistant: Jolie Martin
Plant Manager: Howard G Owen
Estimated Sales: $5-10 Million
Number Employees: 20-49

27082 Oven Deck Shop
11560 184th Pl
Orland Park, IL 60467-4904 708-478-6032
Fax: 708-849-3186 ovendeckshope@aol.om
Baking stones for deck pizza ovens and revolving pizza and bagel ovens
Sales Director: Mike Casey
Manager: Mark Otoole

Estimated Sales: Below $5 Million
Number Employees: 1-4
Number of Brands: 2
Number of Products: 1
Square Footage: 8000
Type of Packaging: Private Label

27083 Ovenworks
8300 Austin Avenue
Morton Grove, IL 60053-3209 847-965-3700
Fax: 847-965-8585 800-899-OVEN
infor@ovenworks.com
www.ovenworkspizza.com
Revolving tray ovens, rotating rack ovens, small specialty oven proofers
Estimated Sales: $10-20 Million
Number Employees: 50-99

27084 Overnight Labels
151 W Industry Ct Ste 15
Deer Park, NY 11729 631-242-4240
Fax: 631-242-4385 800-472-5753
custservice@overnightlabels.com
www.overnightlabels.com
US-based manufacturer specializing in labels, shrink sleeves, and flexible packaging. Multiple award winner, including awards for print and environmental excellence
President: Don Earl
Marketing Director: Carrie Houghton
Sales Director: Diane Pannizzo
Number Employees: 20-49
Type of Packaging: Consumer, Food Service, Private Label, Bulk

27085 Oxidyn
3712 Summer Pl
Raleigh, NC 27604-4252 919-790-6767
Fax: 919-790-6768
Custom contract assembling
Owner: Melvin Rogers
Estimated Sales: $500,000-$1 Million
Number Employees: 5-9

27086 Oxo International
601 West 26th St
Suite 1050
New York, NY 10011
Fax: 717-709-5350 800-545-4411
suggestionbox@oxo.com www.oxo.com
Manufacturer and exporter of vegetable peelers and kitchen utensils;high end speciality and gourmet outlets
President: Alex Lee
Marketing Director: Michelle Sohn
Sales: Kelly Yau
Public Relations: Gretchen Holt
Estimated Sales: $2.5-5 Million
Number Employees: 20-49
Number of Products: 600
Parent Co: General Housewares
Type of Packaging: Consumer
Brands:
Oxo Goodgrips

27087 Oxoid
Suite 100
Nepean, ON K2G 1E8
Canada 613-226-1318
Fax: 613-226-3728 800-567-8378
webinfo.ca@oxoid.com www.oxoid.ca
A manufacturer and distributor of diagnostic test and control in microbiology
Marketing Director: Brian Kemp
Sales Director: Jeff Crawford
Estimated Sales: $15 Million
Number Employees: 50-100
Parent Co: Oxoid

27088 Oystar North America
523 Raritan Center Parkway
Raritan Center
Edison, NJ 08837 732-343-7600
Fax: 732-343-7601 sales@oystarusa.com
www.oystar-group.com
Solutions for packaging machines.
President/CEO: Barry Shoulders
VP Finance: Suzanne Zeitler
VP Sales/Marketing: Tom Riggins
VP Manufacturing Operations: Frederick Priester
VP Purchasing: Linda Petersen
Number Employees: 235
Square Footage: 10228

27089 Oyster Bay Pump Works
78 Midland Avenue
PO Box 725
Hicksville, NY 11802-0725 516-933-4500
Fax: 516-933-4501 info@obpw.com
www.obpw.com
Manufacturer and exporter of dispensers including single channel, multi-channel and conveyor systems for metering fluids
President: Patrick Gaillard
Sales/Marketing: Michael Dedora
Estimated Sales: $5 - 10 Million
Number Employees: 20-49
Square Footage: 20000
Type of Packaging: Consumer, Food Service, Private Label, Bulk

27090 Ozark Tape & Label Company
2061 E McDaniel St
Springfield, MO 65802 417-831-1444
Fax: 417-831-1424
www.ozarktapeandlabelcoofspringfield.ylsonline.com
Printed pressure sensitive tapes, tags and labels
R&D: Steve Lane
Manager: Steve Lane
Production Manager: Steve Lane
Estimated Sales: $1 - 2.5 Million
Number Employees: 10-19
Square Footage: 5000

27091 Ozonia N.A.
491 Edward H Ross Dr
Elmwood Park, NJ 07407-3197 201-794-3100
Fax: 201-794-3358 info@ozonia.com
www.ozonia.com
Water treatment specializing in ozone, CIP, rinsing, UV, sterilizing
President: Joseph Giannone
CFO: John Palmer
CEO: Shyam Bhan
Marketing Director: Gastar Leszmik
Estimated Sales: $250 - 500 Million
Number Employees: 20-49

27092 Ozotech
2401 E Oberlin Rd
Yreka, CA 96097 530-842-4189
Fax: 530-842-3238 ozotech@ozotech.com
www.ozotech.com
Manufactures ozone generators, air preparation and water treatment systems for commercial, industrial and home uses
President: Ken Mouw
Administration Director: Nancy Mouw
Marketing Director: Kat Hoag
Sales Manager: Steve Christopher
Purchasing Manager: Cari Burke
Type of Packaging: Consumer, Private Label

27093 P & L System
819 Pickens Industrial Drive
Suite 5
Marietta, GA 30062-3159 678-355-9809
Fax: 678-354-7253 nstyrin@hotmail.com
www.pandl.co.uk
CEO: Chris Lee
Estimated Sales: Below $5 Million
Number Employees: 6

27094 P&A Food Industry Recruiters
188 Liberty Way
Deptford, NJ 08096-6822 856-384-4774
Fax: 856-384-8074 foodrecruit@comcast.net
www.pandafoodrecruit.com
Executive search firm specializing in permanent selection and placement of executive, managerial and technical personnel in the food industry only
President: Paul Sundstrom
VP and Partner: Andrew Sundstrom
Operations Manager: Dieter Sievers
Estimated Sales: Below $500,000
Parent Co: Winston Franchise Corporation

27095 P&E
108 Marcia Dr
Altamonte Spgs, FL 32714-2913 407-857-3888
Fax: 407-857-0900 800-438-0674
stewheistpe@compuserve.com
Packaging equipment including bag-in-box and cases
Office Manager: Beverly Smith
Estimated Sales: $5-10,000,000
Number Employees: 50-99

27096 P&F Metals
301 S Broadway
Turlock, CA 95380 209-667-4716
Fax: 209-667-4945 eparker@pfmetals.com
www.pfmetals.com
Manufacturer and exporter of custom engineered and fabricated food, poultry and wine processing equipment
Purchasing Agent: Jim Wells
Estimated Sales: less than $500,000
Number Employees: 50-99

27097 P&H Milling Group
1060 Fountain Street North
Cambridge, ON N3E 0A1 519-650-6400
Fax: 519-650-6429 info@dovergrp.com
www.dovergrp.com
Freshly baked goods and ingredients
President: Sheila LaLang

27098 P&L Specialties
1650 Almar Pkwy
Santa Rosa, CA 95403 707-573-3141
Fax: 707-573-3140 888-313-7947
sales@pnlspecialties.com
www.pnlspecialties.com
Winery equipment
President: Edwin L Barr
Estimated Sales: $10-20 Million
Number Employees: 20-49

27099 P.F. Harris Manufacturing Company
PO Box 1122
Alpharetta, GA 30009 904-389-5686
Fax: 904-384-0979 800-637-0317
info@pfharris.com www.pfharris.com
Manufacturer, importer and exporter of insecticides and pest control devices including roach tablets
General Manager: Franklin Goodman
Estimated Sales: $300,000-500,000
Number Employees: 4
Square Footage: 24000
Brands:
Harris Bug Free
Harris Famous

27100 P.L. Thomas & Company
119 Headquarters Plaza
Morristown, NJ 07960 973-984-0900
Fax: 973-984-5666 www.plthomas.com
Supplier of extracts, natural color and flavorings, herbs and probiotics.
President: Paul Flowerman

27101 PAC Equipment Company
PO Box 8
Garfield, NJ 07026-0008 973-478-1008
Fax: 973-478-1008
Solid waste equipment, compactors and roll offs
President: Walter Johns
Number Employees: 10

27102 PAK 2000
189 Governor Wentworth Hwy
Mirror Lake, NH 03853 603-569-3700
Fax: 603-569-5478 sales@pak2000.com
www.pak2000.com
World's leading producer of high quality shopping bags and tamper evidence security bags targeting major brands in sectors such as luxury, cosmetics, fashion & retail, fine food and beverage worldwide. We are equipped to provide acomplete service from concept development through to production, logistics and customer support worldwide
CEO: Nina Virga
Marketing Director: Veronique Aboohe
VP Sales/Marketing: Mary Sieninmer
Estimated Sales: $20-50 Million
Number Employees: 50-99
Number of Products: 56
Parent Co: Asia Pulp and Paper
Brands:
Cartier
Chanel
Estee Lauder
Guerlain
Nordstrom
Tiffany

27103 PAL Marking Products
10 Princess Street
Sausalito, CA 94965-2210 415-332-2596
Fax: 415-332-2598

Wine industry labelers
Estimated Sales: less than $500,000
Number Employees: 1-4

27104 PAR Visions Systems Corporation
8375 Seneca Tpke
New Hartford, NY 13413-4957 703-433-6300
Fax: 315-768-3838 800-448-6505
sales@orbcomm.com www.parlms.com
X-ray inspection systems
VP: John W Sammon Iii
Estimated Sales: $1 - 5 Million
Number Employees: 10-19

27105 PARTA
2000 Summit Rd
Kent, OH 44240 330-678-7745
Fax: 330-678-7751 800-543-5781
CustService@partaonline.org
www.partaonline.org
Set-up paper boxes, vacuum formed parts, plastic lids and folding cartons
Secretary, Treasurer, General Manager, P: John Drew
Estimated Sales: $5-10 Million
Number Employees: 50-99
Square Footage: 200000

27106 PBC
185 Route 17 North
Mahwah, NJ 07430 201-512-0387
Fax: 201-512-1459 800-514-2739
brewing@pubbrewing.com
www.pubbrewing.com
Stainless steel tanks; importer of beer and wine filters; exporter of microbrew systems
President: Erwin Eibert
CFO: David Generso
VP: Ralph Eibert
Design Engineer: Dino Benvenuto
Estimated Sales: $3.5 Million
Number Employees: 10-19

27107 PBC Manufacturing
185 Route 17 North
Mahwah, NJ 07430-1212 201-512-0387
Fax: 201-512-1459 800-514-2739
brewing@pubbrewing.com
www.pubbrewing.com
Wine industry SS vessels, packaging, filtration
Owner: Erwin Eibert
Manager: Mat Swanson
Production Manager: Ralph Eivert
Estimated Sales: $1 - 5 Million
Number Employees: 10-19

27108 PBI Dansensor America
139 Harristown Rd # 102
Glen Rock, NJ 07452-3326 201-251-6490
Fax: 201-251-6491 jm@pbi-dansensor.com
www.pbi-dansensor.com
President: Jim Margiotta
Chief Executive Officer, Managing Direct: Jesper Bilde
Marketing Director: Karsten Kejlhof
Estimated Sales: Below $5 Million
Number Employees: 10-19

27109 PBM
1070 Sandy Hill Rd
Irwin, PA 15642 724-863-0550
Fax: 724-864-9255 800-967-4PBM
info@pbmvalve.com www.pbmvalve.com
Valve manufacturing
Owner: Stuart Zarembo
CEO: Stuart Zarembo
Controller: Nancy Mayer
Engineering/Manufacturing Manager: Jeff Kerr
Quality Control: Ed Docherty
Marketing/Sales Manager: Jay Giffen
COO: Mark Nahorski
Plant Manager: Mark Nahorski
Purchasing Manager: Phil Kochasic
Estimated Sales: $15 Million
Number Employees: 70

27110 PC/Poll Systems
3162 Cedar Crest Rdg
Suite B
Dubuque, IA 52003 563-556-2323
Fax: 563-556-0835 800-670-1736
sales2004@pcpoll.com www.pcpoll.com
Manufacturer and exporter of software providing the ability to connect a PC to a cash register; compatible with all Casio ECR's NCR 2170, 2113, CRS 2000 and 3000 and Samsung 6500; also, provides collection, display, printing, export ofreports, etc
Support: Gary Bishop
Estimated Sales: $2.5-5 Million
Number Employees: 5-9
Square Footage: 1200

27111 PCA Denver
4221 Monaco St
Denver, CO 80216 303-331-0400
Fax: 303-331-9455 www.coloradocontainer.com
Corrugated and fiber boxes
President/CEO/Treasurer: Bruce Kelley
Chief Financial Officer: Russell Shurts
Chief Information Officer: Chris Kenzel
Marketing Manager: Eric Braaten
Vice President, Sales: Bob Staffen
Plant Engineer: Russ Herrick
Purchasing Manager: Carrie Winter
Estimated Sales: $21 Million
Number Employees: 125
Square Footage: 250000
Parent Co: Packaging Corporation of America

27112 PCI Inc.
10800 Baur Blvd
Saint Louis, MO 63132 314-872-9333
Fax: 314-872-9104 800-752-7657
sales@pcistl.com www.purochem.com
Toilet bowl cleaners and drain openers
President: Charles Vondoerston
Technology: Scott Kretzer
Estimated Sales: $5-10 Million
Number Employees: 20-49
Square Footage: 42000
Brands:
Acid Free
Brite Bowl
Chief 90
Drain Power
Jet White
Scout 20

27113 PCI Membrane Systems
1615 State Route 131
Milford, OH 45150-2667 513-575-3500
Fax: 513-575-7393 pcims@itt.com
www.pcims.com
Membrane filtration
CEO: Sandy Maxwell
Vice President: David Pearson
Estimated Sales: $500,000-$1 Million
Number Employees: 10-20

27114 PCM Delasco
11940 Brittmoore Park Dr
Houston, TX 77041 713-896-4888
Fax: 713-896-4806 www.pcmdelasco.com
Designer and manufacturer in Progressive Cavity, Peristaltic and hose pump and offers solutions for a wide range of applications
President: Bruno Lafont
Estimated Sales: Less than $500,000
Number Employees: 1-4

27115 (HQ)PDC International
1106 Clayton Ln # 521w
Austin, TX 78723-2489 512-302-0194
Fax: 512-302-0476 sales@pdc-corp.com
www.pdceurope.com/
Manufacturer and exporter of heat shrinkable tamper-evident seal and sleeve label machinery.
President: Neal Konstantin
Chief Executive Officer: Anatole Konstantin
VP: Alcyr Coelho
Marketing & Sales Director North America: Alcyr Coelho
Sales Representative: Reid Vail
Purchasing: Paul Strauss
Estimated Sales: $20 - 50 Million
Number Employees: 50-99
Square Footage: 17000
Other Locations:
PDC International Corporation
Austin TX

27116 PDMP
105 Loudoun St SW
Leesburg, VA 20175-2910 703-777-8400
Fax: 703-777-8430 wmt@pdmpinc.com
www.pdmpantiqueprints.com
Contract manufacturer of packaging materials including foam extrusions and molding
President: William Teringo
Estimated Sales: Below $5 Million
Number Employees: 5-9

27117 PDQ Plastics
PO Box 1001
Bayonne, NJ 07002 201-823-0270
Fax: 201-823-0345 800-447-7141
hartson@pdqplastics.com www.pdqplastics.com
Plastic pallets
President: Barry Nathans
VP/General Manager: Harston Poland
Estimated Sales: $1-2.5 Million
Number Employees: 10-19
Square Footage: 200000

27118 PE Applied Biosystems
850 Lincoln Centre Dr
Foster City, CA 94404-1128 650-638-5800
Fax: 650-638-5884 800-345-5224
info@perkin-elmer.com/ab
www.appliedbiosystems.com
PCR technology and automated genetic analysis systems
VP Human Resources: Barbara Kerr
CEO: Gregory T Lucier
Estimated Sales: $200 - 500 Million
Number Employees: 1,000-4,999

27119 PEAK Technologies, Inc.
10330 Old Columbia Rd
Columbia, MD 21046 410-312-6000
Fax: 410-309-6219 800-926-9212
info@peaktech.com www.peaktech.com
Systems integrator of automatic identification and data collection equipment and systmes
Estimated Sales: $52 Million
Number Employees: 777
Square Footage: 7350
Parent Co: Moore Corporation
Other Locations:
PEAK Technologies-North East
Hasbrouck Heights NJ
PEAK Technologies
Dover NH
PEAK Technologies NYC
New York NY
PEAK Technologies-North Central
Itasca IL
PEAK Technologies-New England
Nashua NH
PEAK Technologies Canada Limited
Mississauga, ON, Canada

27120 PFI Displays
40 Industrial Street
PO Box 508
Rittman, OH 44270 330-925-9015
Fax: 330-925-8520 800-925-9075
jtricomi@pfidisplays.com www.pfidisplays.com
Manufacturer and exporter of point of purchase displays, exhibits and store fixtures
Chairman of the Board: Anthony Tricomi
Chairman of the Board: Vincent Tricomi
Vice President of Sales: Jim Tricomi
Estimated Sales: $5 - 10 Million
Number Employees: 20-49
Square Footage: 70000

27121 PFI Prasence From Innovation
2290 Ball Dr
St Louis, MO 63146-8602 314-423-9777
Fax: 314-423-0420 info@pfinnovation.com
www.paulflumideas.com
Manufacturer and exporter of universal gravity feed systems, ice barrel coolers and display and merchandising equipment
President: Jim Watt Jr
Number Employees: 100-249
Brands:
Iceman
Ultra Glide

27122 PFM Packaging MachineryCorporation
1271 Ringwell Drive
Newmarket, ON L3Y 8T9
Canada 905-836-6709
Fax: 905-836-7763 info@pfmnorthamerica.com
www.pfmnorthamerica.com

PFM has over 40 years of experience in manufacturing over 35 different models of flow wrappers - both vertical and horizontal.
President: Elizabeth Fioravanti
Engineering Manager: Mike Borza
Marketing Director: Jackie Pineau
Sales Director: Lana Pratt
Estimated Sales: $4.5 Million
Number Employees: 40
Square Footage: 200000

27123 PHD
P.O.Box 9070
Fort Wayne, IN 46899-9070 260-747-6151
Fax: 260-479-2312 800-324-8511
phdinfo@phdinc.com www.phdinc.com
Grippers, cylinders, escapements, slides, rotary actuators, sheet metal clamps
CEO: Harry Neff
Estimated Sales: $40 Million+
Number Employees: 250-499

27124 PHF Specialists
P.O.Box 7697
San Jose, CA 95150-7697 408-275-0161
Fax: 408-280-0979 phfspec@pacbell.net
www.phfspec.com
HACCP programs for vegetables, meats, seafood and food service, thermal process design and validation and third party audits
Owner: Pamela Hardt-English
Estimated Sales: Below 1 Million
Number Employees: 1-4

27125 PHI Enterprises
12832 Garden Grove Boulevard
Suite E
Garden Grove, CA 92843-2014 714-537-7858
Fax: 714-537-8228 800-971-9955
phienterprises@aol.com
www.phienterprises.com

27126 PIAB USA
65 Sharp St
Hingham, MA 02043-4311 781-337-7309
Fax: 781-337-6864 800-321-7422
info@piab.com www.piabusa.com
President: Chuck Weilbrenner
Vice President of Business Development: Ed McGovern
Estimated Sales: $10 - 20 Million
Number Employees: 50-99

27127 PIAB Vacuum Conveyors
65 Sharp Street
Hingham, MA 02043-4311 781-792-0003
Fax: 781-337-6864 800-321-7422
info@piab.com www.piab.com
Material handling/processing systems: pneumatic vacuum conveyor
Vice President of Business Development: Ed McGovern
CEO: Donald Spradlin
Estimated Sales: $10 - 20 Million
Number Employees: 45

27128 PIECO, Inc.
P.O. Box 86
Manchester, IA 52057 563-927-3352
Fax: 563-927-2310 800-334-3929
sales@pieco.com www.pieco.com
Circular blade sharpeners and rotary surface grinders, grinder parts, wheels, knives and also reconditon mechanical deboning equipment.

27129 PILZ Automation Safety
7150 Commerce Blvd
Canton, MI 48187 734-354-0272
Fax: 734-354-3355 888-650-7450
info@pilzusa.com www.pilz.com
CEO: Thomas Pilz
Estimated Sales: Below $5 Million
Number Employees: 20-49

27130 PLI (Plasticard-Locktech International
605 Sweeten Creek Industrial Park
Asheville, NC 28803 828-210-4754
Fax: 828-210-4755 800-752-1017
info@hotelkeycard.com www.plicards.com
Key cards and lock systems
Sales Representative: Tom Smith
Estimated Sales: $2.5-5 Million
Number Employees: 20-49

27131 PLM Trailer Leasing
5722 Naylor Ave
Livemore, CA 94551 925-245-0056
Fax: 925-245-0185 877-736-8756
pyata@plmtrailer.com www.plmtrailer.com
President, Chief Executive Officer: Keith Shipp
CEO: Hugh Fehrenbach
Vice President of Sales: Mark Domzalski
Estimated Sales: $3 - 5 Million
Number Employees: 20

27132 PM Chemical Company
5319 Grant Street
San Diego, CA 92110-4010 619-296-0191
Manufacturer and exporter of detergents, soaps and food processing cleaners
President: John Mehren
CEO: Bernard Mehren
Estimated Sales: $1-2.5 Million
Number Employees: 5-9
Square Footage: 20000
Brands:
Astro
Pure Chem
Red X
Sofwite

27133 PM Plastics
627 Capitol Dr
Pewaukee, WI 53072 262-691-1700
Fax: 262-691-4405 jkildow@pmplastic.com
www.pmplastic.com
Molded plastic signs, diplays and packaging products
Engineering: John Matejcik
Quality Control: Ryan Ford
Sales: Jeff Kildow
Manager: William E Ford Jr
Plant Manager: William Ford, Jr.
Estimated Sales: $10-20 Million
Number Employees: 100-249

27134 PM Plastics
3970 Parsons Rd
Howell, MI 48855-9617 517-546-9900
Fax: 517-546-7097 800-854-2920
pump@ismi.net www.pmpnet.com
President: Don Verna
Estimated Sales: $10-20 Million
Number Employees: 50-99

27135 PMC Industries
275 Hudson St
Hackensack, NJ 07601 201-342-3684
Fax: 201-342-3568 pmcindustries@verizon.net
www.pmc-industries.com
Capping equipment
President: Kazmier Wysocki
VP: Peter Wysocki
Estimated Sales: Below $5 Million
Number Employees: 20-49

27136 PME Equipment
230 Route 206
Suite 405
Flanders, NJ 07836 973-927-2700
Fax: 973-927-4411 info@pmeequipment.com
www.pmeequipment.com
Representatives
Estimated Sales: $1-2.5 Million
Number Employees: 5-9
Square Footage: 1200

27137 PMI Cartoning
850 Pratt Blvd.
Elk Grove Village, IL 60007 847-437-1427
Fax: 847-437-1627 btisma@pmicartoning.com
www.pmicartoning.com
Custom designed carton packaging machinery and systems
President: Branko Tisma
Vice President of Sales: Tony BLESS
Vice President of Sales: Tony Bless
Estimated Sales: $2.5 - 5 Million
Number Employees: 50-99

27138 PMI Food Equipment Group
701 S Ridge Ave
Troy, OH 45374-0001 937-332-3000
Fax: 937-332-2852 www.hobartcorp.com
Equipment and systems including ovens, salad bars, electronic weighing, wrapping and labeling systems, etc
President: John McDonough
VP: Ken Kessler
Vice President: Jack Gridley
Research Director of Research: David Sprinkle
Business Development Manager: John Davis
Number Employees: 1,000-4,999
Parent Co: Premark International
Brands:
Adamatic
Foster
Hobart
Stero
Tasselli
Vulcan
Wolf

27139 POM Wonderful LLC
11444 W Olympic Blvd
2nd Fl
Los Angeles, CA 90064 310-966-5800
kredfield@pomwonderful.com
www.pomwonderful.com
Pomegranates, pomegranate products and ingredients.
Owner: Lynda Resnick
CFO: Sarah Hermatti
VP/CIO: Richard Scheitler
Director Research & Development: Malcolm Knight
Quality Assurance Director: Barbara Larson
Director Enterprise Applications: Kalyan Ayyaswamy
Director of Sales: Trent McKay
Director of Sales North America: Mark Orsi
Director of International Sales: Gerhard Leodolter
Manager Interactive Marketing: Andrea Scott
VP/General Manager: Paul Sheppard
Sr Director Supply Chain: George Misso
Estimated Sales: $60 Million
Number Employees: 296
Type of Packaging: Bulk

27140 (HQ)POS Pilot Plant Corporation
118 Veterinary Road
Saskatoon, SK S7N 2R4
Canada 306-978-2800
Fax: 306-975-3766 800-230-2751
pos@pos.ca www.pos.ca
Wide variety of industries served, including food and ingredients, fats and oils, nutraceutical and functional food, cosmetics, cosmeceuticals and fragrances, feeds and biotechnology. Total capability under one roof, including fullsolvent extraction, algae and yeast based biomass extraction,analytical services and custom processing. services supported by in-house analytical,methods, development, logistics, and information research.
President: Robert Morgan
VP: Paul Fedec
Manager of Quality: Grace Varga
VP, Operations and Corporate Affairs: Heather Ryan
Public Relations: Marilyn Huber
Manager of Operations: Doug Karlson
Purchasing: Sandra Bodnar
Number Employees: 87

27141 POSitively Unique
591 Boxford Lane
Columbus, OH 43213-2603 614-755-2469
Fax: 614-575-2578
Windows based POS Systems for the hospitality industry
President: Gary Zomonski
Number Employees: 6

27142 (HQ)PPG Industries
3938 Porett Dr
Gurnee, IL 60031-1244 847-244-3410
Fax: 724-325-5342 aronson@ppg.com
www.ppg.com
Manufacturer and exporter of precipitated silica for anticaking and carrier applications
President: Michael Horton
Vice President: Anup Jain
Vice President of Research and Developme: Charles Kahle
Marketing Manager: Paul Brown
Vice President of Operations: John Richter
Vice President of Purchasing: Stephen Lampe

Estimated Sales: $20-50 Million
Number Employees: 100-249
Type of Packaging: Food Service, Bulk
Brands:
Flo-Gard

27143 PPG Industries
3938 Porett Dr
Gurnee, IL 60031-1244 847-244-3410
Fax: 847-249-6331 aronson@ppg.com
www.ppg.com
Organic surfactants, defoamers, emulsifiers, silicones and silicone emulsions
President: Michael Horton
Vice President: Anup Jain
Vice President of Research and Developme: Charles Kahle
Vice President of Operations: John Richter
Vice President of Purchasing: Stephen Lampe
Estimated Sales: $50-100 Million
Number Employees: 100-249

27144 PPG Industries, Milford
500 Techne Center Dr
Milford, OH 45150-2763 513-576-3100
Fax: 513-576-3032 www.ppg.com/packaging
Pretreatment chemicals, interior and exterior coatings for the metal packaging industry
President: Michael Horton
Human Resources: Casandra Tembo
Vice President of Research and Developme: Charles Kahle
Vice President of Operations: John Richter
Vice President of Purchasing: Stephen Lampe
Estimated Sales: $20-50 Million
Number Employees: 50-99

27145 PPI Printing Press
3008 Main St
Union Gap, WA 98903-1758 509-453-6130
Fax: 509-453-4159 www.packagingplusllc.com
Manufactures thermoform packaging— blisters, blisterboard and skinboard, clamshells, food trays and printed inserts
Manager: Jim Burde
Estimated Sales: $5-10 Million
Number Employees: 50-99

27146 PPI Technologies Group
1610 Northgate Blvd
Sarasota, FL 34234 941-359-6678
Fax: 941-359-6804 rcmpp@aol.com
www.ppitechnologies.com
Manufacturer and supplier of stand up pouch machinery
President: Stuart Murray
CEO: R Charles Murray
CFO: Karena Thomas
Vice President: Sandra Christensen
Research & Development: Rudi Kleer
Quality Control: Gary Bush
Marketing: Richard Murray
Marketing/Sales: Robert Libera
Public Relations: Debbie Reed
Operations Manager: Peter Aeberhard
Production Manager: Pete Ceconci
Plant Manager: Sean Reed
Purchasing Manager: Tom Richard
Estimated Sales: $20 Million
Number Employees: 40
Number of Brands: 7
Number of Products: 10
Square Footage: 60000
Parent Co: Profile Packaging Inc - Paksource Group LLC
Type of Packaging: Food Service
Brands:
Laudenberg
Nishibe
Psgjme
Psglee

27147 PQ Corporation Speciality Chemicals
P.O.Box 840
Valley Forge, PA 19482-0840 610-651-4200
Fax: 610-651-4504 ed.myszak@pqcorp.com
www.pqcorp.com
President: Stanley W Silverman
CEO: Michael R Boyce
Number Employees: 1,000-4,999

27148 PR Farms
2917 E Shepherd Ave
Clovis, CA 93619-9152 559-299-0201
Fax: 559-299-7292 pat@prfarms.com
www.prfarms.com
CEO: Pat V Ricchiuti
Estimated Sales: $10-20 Million
Number Employees: 100-249

27149 PROMA Technologies
24 Forge Pkwy
Franklin, MA 02038 508-541-7700
Fax: 508-541-7777 800-343-6977
promainfo@promamail.com
www.promatechnologies.com
Holographic metallized paper
President: Frank Sereno
CFO: Robert Kynoch
Marketing Director: Harry Mann
Estimated Sales: $20 - 50 Million
Number Employees: 1-4
Square Footage: 140000

27150 PSI
1901 S. Meyers Road
Suite 400
Oakbrook Terrace, IL 60181 817-640-4162
Fax: 800-548-7901 analytical@psiusa.com
www.psiusa.com
Consultant specializing in nutritional labeling testing, sanitation audits and microbiological and chemical food testing
Executive Vice President: Tom Boogher
Manager: Rodney Ortega
Sales Manager: Sharon Winders
District Manager: John Southerland
Number Employees: 60
Square Footage: 40000
Parent Co: PSI

27151 PSI Preferred Solutions
7819 Broadview Road
Cleveland, OH 44131-6146 216-642-1200
Fax: 216-642-1166 800-522-4522
www.stayflex.com
Fiberglass wall and ceiling paneling, floor and wall coating materials, paints, enamels and coating, insulated building panels, insulation-floors, ceilings, refrigerated structures and corrosion control
President: John Stahl
Estimated Sales: $500,000-$1 Million
Number Employees: 5-9

27152 PTI Packaging
1055 Saddle Rdg
Portage, WI 53901 920-623-3566
Fax: 920-623-5659 800-501-4077
protech@powerweb.net
Manufacturer and exporter of palletizers, conveyors, sheet dispensers, pallet dispensers/conveyors and package accumulators
President: John Wildner
Estimated Sales: $2.5-5,000,000
Number Employees: 1-4

27153 PTI-Packaging Technologies & Inspection
145 Main St
Tuckahoe, NY 10707-2906 914-337-2005
Fax: 914-337-8519 info@ptiusa.com
www.ptiusa.com
President: Tony Stauffer
Vice President: Oliver Stauffer
Sales Manager: Jesse Sklar
Estimated Sales: $10 - 20 Million
Number Employees: 20-49

27154 PTI-Packaging Technologies & Inspection LLC
145 Main Street
Tuckahoe, NY 10707-2906 914-337-2005
Fax: 914-337-8519 800-532-1501
info@ptiusa.com www.ptiusa.com
Food packaging, filling, sealing equipment and inspection systems, both visual and package integrity systems. Also, leak testing equipment for filled and empty packages, off-line/SPC and 100% on-line systems, vision inspectionequipment for packages and air-borne ultrasonic systems for seal integrity
President and CEO: Tony Stauffer
R & D: Mike Noller
Vice President: Oliver Stauffer
Marketing Director: Sylvia Stauffer
Sales Manager: Jesse Sklar
Operations Manager: Heinz Wof
Estimated Sales: $5-10 Million
Number Employees: 20-49

27155 PTR Baler and CompactorCompany
2207 E Ontario St
Philadelphia, PA 19134-2615 215-533-5100
Fax: 215-533-8907 800-523-3654
sales@ptrco.com www.ptrco.com
Manufacturer and exporter of vertical recycling balers and waste compaction systems
President/CEO: Michael Savage
Estimated Sales: $30 Million
Number Employees: 100-249
Number of Brands: 3
Square Footage: 135000
Parent Co: RJR Enterprises
Brands:
Trampak

27156 PURA
9848 Glenoaks Boulevard
Sun Valley, CA 91352-1045 818-768-0451
Fax: 661-257-6385 800-292-7872
eroberts@hyrdtechology.com www.pura.com
Manufacturer and exporter of ultraviolet and filtration water treatment products
Vice President: Edwin Roberts
Regional Sales Manager: Brad Hess
Estimated Sales: $1-2.5 Million
Number Employees: 10-19
Square Footage: 320000
Parent Co: Hydrotech
Brands:
Pura

27157 PURAC America
111 Barclay Blvd
Lincolnshire, IL 60069 608-752-0449
Fax: 847-634-1992 pam@purac.com
www.purac.com
President: Gerrit Vreeman
Estimated Sales: $20 - 50 Million
Number Employees: 20-49

27158 PVI Industries
3209 Galvez Ave
Fort Worth, TX 76111-4509 817-335-9531
Fax: 817-332-6742 800-784-8326
pbothner@pvi.com www.pvi.com
Hot water generation for sanitation and process
President: Craig Adams
CFO: Lynn Meadows
R & D: Frank Myers
Quality Control: John Calland
Sales: Chris Bollas
Number Employees: 10-19

27159 Pac Strapping Products
307 National Rd
Exton, PA 19341 610-363-8805
Fax: 610-363-7349 800-523-7752
info@strapsolutions.com
www.strapsolutions.com
Plastic strapping and accessories for strapping
President: Edwin A Brownley Jr
Estimated Sales: $20 - 50 Million
Number Employees: 50-99

27160 PacMoore
1844 Summer St
Hammond, IN 46320 855-413-2780
Fax: 219-932-0879 866-610-2666
solutions@pacmoore.com www.pacmoore.com

Kosher foods
President & CEO: William J. Moore
Corporate Controller: Lee Randall
Director of IS & Technology: Lee Randall
VP Quality Assurance: Giri Veeramuthu
VP Sales & Marketing: Chris Bekermeier
National Sales Director: Tony Weber
VP Human Resources: Susan Bondy
VP Operations: Scott Reid
VP Engineering: Brent Ness
Estimated Sales: $3.4 Million
Number Employees: 50+
Type of Packaging: Consumer, Food Service, Private Label, Bulk

27161 PacTech Engineering
4444 Carver Woods Drive
Cincinnati, OH 45242-5532 513-792-1090
Fax: 513-891-4232 teckert@pactech.com
www.pactech.com
Engineering consultant specializing in packing systems including feasibility, conceptual, design, installation, etc
CEO: Sam Pantano
Business Development Manager: Tina Eckert
Estimated Sales: $1 - 5 Million
Number Employees: 20-49
Square Footage: 20000

27162 Pace Labels
104 Twenty Nine Court
Williamston, SC 29697 864-855-0313
Fax: 864-855-3637 800-789-1592
pace@pacelabels.com www.pacelabels.com
Pressure sensitive labels
Owner: Stuart Pace
CEO: W Stuart Pace
Estimated Sales: $1-2.5 Million
Number Employees: 5-9
Square Footage: 40000
Type of Packaging: Consumer, Food Service, Private Label, Bulk

27163 Pace Packaging Corporation
3 Sperry Rd
Fairfield, NJ 07004 973-227-1040
Fax: 973-227-7393 800-867-2726
sales@pacepackaging.com www.pacepkg.com
Manufacturer and exporter of high speed plastic bottle unscramblers
President/CFO: Kenneth F Regula
Vice President-Sales: Glenn G. Kelley
Quality Control: Mike Regula
Sales Manager: Glenn Kelley
VP Manufacturing: Ken Regula
Estimated Sales: $5 - 10 Million
Number Employees: 20-49
Square Footage: 30
Brands:
Omni-Line

27164 Pace Products
2764 N.Green Valley Pkwy
Henderson, NV 89014 702-272-0048
Fax: 702-272-0668 800-796-2675
pacecork@msn.com www.pacecork.com
Special packaging
Owner: Michael Piluso
Estimated Sales: $1-5 Million
Number Employees: 1-4

27165 Pacemaker Packaging Corporation
7200 51st Rd
Flushing, NY 11377-7631 718-458-1188
Fax: 718-429-2907
info@pacemakerpackaging.com
www.pacemakerpackaging.biz
Bag closers and fillers
President: Emil Romotzki
Sales Coordinator: Gene Cignoli
Estimated Sales: $1-2.5 Million
Number Employees: 5-9
Brands:
Pacemaker
Unibagger

27166 Pacer Pumps
41 Industrial Cir
Lancaster, PA 17601 717-656-2161
Fax: 717-656-0477 800-233-3861
sales@pacerpumps.com www.pacerpumps.com
Manufacturer and exporter of pumps including self-priming centrifugal nonmetallic, hand operated and powered drum
Manager: Glenn Geist
General Manager: Denzel Stoops
Marketing: Art Foster
Sales: Ron Hock
Purchasing Manager: Ernie Stoltzfus
Estimated Sales: $5 - 10 Million
Number Employees: 20-49
Square Footage: 144000
Parent Co: Serfilco
Brands:
Camelot
Pacer

27167 Pacific Bag
15300 Woodinville Redmond Road NE
Suite A
Woodinville, WA 98072 425-455-1128
Fax: 425-455-1886 800-562-2247
bags@pacificbag.com www.pacificbag.com
Flexible packaging and packaging equipment
CEO: Mark Howley
Estimated Sales: $5-10 Million
Number Employees: 20-49

27168 Pacific Bearing Company
P.O.Box 6980
Rockford, IL 61125-1980 815-389-5600
Fax: 815-389-5790 800-962-8979
marketing@pacific-bearing.com
www.pacific-bearing.com
CEO: Robert Schroeder
President: Glen Michalske
Quality Control: Paul Bertolasi
Estimated Sales: $10 - 20 Million
Number Employees: 100-249

27169 Pacific Choice Seafood
1 Commercial St
Eureka, CA 95501 707-442-1113
Fax: 707-442-2985 info@pacseafood.com
www.pacseafood.com
Processor and deliverer of various seafood such as halibut, salmon, bottomfish, farmed fish, shellfish, and exotics
Director: Drew Jacobs
Sales Manager: Jim Lanter
Marketing Director: Bob O Bryant
Estimated Sales: $20-50 Million
Number Employees: 100-249
Brands:
Pacific Seafood
Steelhead
Snowmist
Newport
Sea Passion

27170 Pacific Coast Container
11010 NE 37th Cir
Suite 110
Vancouver, WA 98682 360-892-3451
Fax: 360-892-4955 pccinfo@calglass-pcc.com
www.saxco.com
Wine industry glass containers
Manager: Mark Petays
Estimated Sales: $2.5-5 Million
Number Employees: 10-19

27171 Pacific Espresso
716 Frederick St
Santa Cruz, CA 95062 831-429-1920
Fax: 831-459-0798 888-429-1920
info@pacificespresso.com
www.pacificespresso.com
Artisan Coffees Roasted to Order. Pacific Espresso has a long standing tradition of excellent customer service to supplement their high quality coffees, teas and espresso machines.
President: Tim O'Connor
Operations: Paula Berman
Estimated Sales: $500,000 - $1 Million
Number Employees: 5-9

27172 Pacific Handy Cutter
2968 Randolph Ave
Costa Mesa, CA 92626 714-662-1033
Fax: 714-662-7595 800-229-2233
info@pacifichandycutter.com www.go-phc.com
Tool and blade manufacturer: safety carton cutters, point blades, and specialized hook knives
President/CEO: Mark Marinovich
Sales: Dave Puglisi
Estimated Sales: $10-20 Million
Number Employees: 50-99

27173 Pacific Harvest Products
13405 SE 30th Street
Bellevue, WA 98005-4454 425-401-7990
www.pacificharvestproducts.com
Dry blends, sauces, dressings, bases. Custom packaging offers a diverse range of sizes
Number Employees: 20-49
Type of Packaging: Consumer, Food Service, Private Label, Bulk
Brands:
Firmenich

27174 Pacific Isles Trading
465 Monroe Avenue
Township of Washington, NJ 07676-4928 201-666-8849
Fax: 201-666-6053 jzberkman@aol.com
Gift containers and specialty packaging made of abaca

27175 Pacific Merchants Trading Company
149 S Burlington Avenue #507
Los Angeles, CA 90049 818-988-8999
Fax: 818-988-6999 info@pacificmerchants.com
www.pacificmerchants.com
Accessories/supplies i.e. picnic baskets, cooking implements/housewares.
Marketing: Bruce Mannis

27176 Pacific Northwest Wire Works
3250 International Pl
Dupont, WA 98327-7707
Fax: 425-656-9090 800-222-7699
www.pwesterngroup.com
Wire shelving for refrigerators, stoves, etc
Manager: James Bennett
Estimated Sales: Below $5 Million
Number Employees: 10-19

27177 Pacific Oasis Enterprises
8413 Secura Way Ste B
Santa Fe Springs, CA 90670 562-698-9146
Fax: 562-698-9147 800-424-1475
POEUS@PacificOasis.com
www.pacificoasis.com
Manufacturer, importer and exporter of stainless steel scouring pads for the cleaning of pans, grills, ovens, etc.; also, disposables including aprons and gloves
President: S C Chen
Quality Control: Nick Sumgsun
General Manager: Daisy Reyes
Manager: Nely Go
Estimated Sales: $2.5 - 5 Million
Number Employees: 9

27178 Pacific Ozone Technology
6160 Egret Ct
Benicia, CA 94510 707-747-9600
Fax: 707-747-9209 info@pacificozone.com
www.pacificozone.com
President: Chris Rombach
CFO: Karen Johnson
Head of Engineering: Rob Mullaney
Estimated Sales: $500,000 - $1 Million
Number Employees: 20-49

27179 Pacific Packaging Machinery
1284 Puerta Del Sol
San Clemente, CA 92673 949-369-2425
Fax: 949-369-2429 sales@pacificpak.com
www.pacificpak.com
Packaging machinery liquid fillers for all industries
Estimated Sales: $5-10 Million
Number Employees: 20-49

27180 Pacific Packaging Systems
2125 Williams St
San Leandro, CA 94577-3224 510-352-1070
Fax: 510-352-8535 800-272-7774
Wine industry shrink wrap equipment
Estimated Sales: $5 - 10 Million
Number Employees: 5-9

27181 Pacific Pneumatics
8576 Red Oak Avenue
Rancho Cucamonga, CA 91730-4822 909-481-8300
Fax: 909-481-8308 800-221-0961
sales@pacpneu.com www.pacpneu.com

Chillers, pneumatic and portable conveyors, vacuum pumps, dryers and material handling equipment
Estimated Sales: $1 - 5 Million
Number Employees: 6

27182 Pacific Press Company
1215 Fee Ana St.
Anaheim, CA 92807 714-525-0630
Fax: 714-525-2664 800-878-8029
sales@pacpress.com www.pacpress.com
Wine industry frame filters
Owner: Sean Duby
Estimated Sales: $2.5-5 Million
Number Employees: 20-49

27183 Pacific Process Machinery
2062 Stonefield Lane
Santa Rosa, CA 95403-0951 707-523-4122
Fax: 707-523-4418
Dealer of rebuilt and used centrifuges dryers, evaporators, presses, and other processing equipment
Estimated Sales: $1 - 5 Million

27184 Pacific Process Technology
7370 Cabrillo Avenue
La Jolla, CA 92037-5201 858-551-3298
Fax: 858-459-2362
Filtration and pasteurization systems, separators, clarifiers, pump feeders/stuffers and cheese processing equipment including grinders and mixers
President: Bill Loy
VP Engineering: John Perlman
VP Marketing: Jeff Campbell

27185 Pacific Refrigerator Company
328 S Mountain View Avenue
San Bernardino, CA 92408-1415 909-381-5669
Fax: 909-888-1203 www.pacificrefrigerator.com
Manufacturer and exporter of walk-in cooler and freezers
President: John Gomez
Estimated Sales: Below $5 Million
Number Employees: 10

27186 Pacific Scale Company
16002 SE 106th Ave
Clackamas, OR 97015 503-657-7500
Fax: 503-657-5561 800-537-1886
psco@pacifier.com www.pacificscale.com
Steel, stainless steel and aluminum platform floor, livestock and lift truck scales; also, tank mounts and batching meters
President: Harry Baughn
VP: Joel Offield
Secretary: Lee Offield
Estimated Sales: $2.5-5 Million
Number Employees: 5-9
Square Footage: 7300
Brands:
Lift-N-Weigh
Tuf-N-Low

27187 Pacific Scientific
201 W Rock Rd
Radford, VA 24141-4026 815-226-3100
Fax: 815-226-3080
rockford.customerservice@danahermotion.com
www.pacsci.com
Generator motors
President: David Burnworth
Quality Manager: Shaz Bashir
Vice President of Sales: Ross Hamilton
Director of Operations: Arnold Pinto
Estimated Sales: $50-100 Million
Number Employees: 250-499

27188 Pacific Scientific Instrument
481 California St
Grants Pass, OR 97526 541-479-1248
Fax: 541-479-3057 800-866-7889
infogp@hachultra.com www.pacsciinst.com
Manufacturer and exporter of instruments for detecting and measuring minute particles
President: Simon Appleby
Production Manager: Brian Bosch
Production Manager: Joe Gecsey
Estimated Sales: $50-100 Million
Number Employees: 100-249
Square Footage: 10000
Brands:
Hiac Royco

27189 Pacific Sign Construction
12339 Oak Knoll Rd
Poway, CA 92064-5319 858-486-8006
Fax: 858-486-8124 pacsign@pacificsign.com
www.pacificsign.com
Manufacturer and exporter of luminous signs
President: Roy Flahive
Estimated Sales: $500,000-$1 Million
Number Employees: 5-9

27190 Pacific Southwest Container
P.O.Box 3351
Modesto, CA 95353-3351 209-526-0444
Fax: 209-522-8746 800-772-0444
bsmith@teampsc.com www.teampsc.com
Wine industry point of purchase packaging
President: John Mayol
President: John Mayol
Executive Vice President of Sales and Ma: Bryan Smith
Estimated Sales: $20 - 50 Million
Number Employees: 250-499

27191 Pacific Spice Company
6430 E Slauson Ave
Commerce, CA 90040 323-726-9190
Fax: 323-727-9442 800-281-0614
info@pacspice.com www.pacspice.com
Established in 1966. Importer and manufacturer of spices and herbs
Director of Operations: Elias n Pflaster
Sales/Customer Service: Raquel Becerra
Account Executive: Tam Nguyen
Estimated Sales: $20 Million
Number Employees: 90
Square Footage: 150000
Type of Packaging: Consumer, Food Service, Private Label, Bulk
Brands:
Pacific Natural Spices

27192 Pacific Steam Equipment, Inc.
10648 Painter Ave
Santa Fe Springs, CA 90670 562-906-9292
Fax: 562-906-9223 800-321-4114
sales@pacificsteam.com www.pacificsteam.com
Manufacturer and exporter of boilers; distributor of food processing machinery
Owner: David Ken
President: William Shanahan MD
Vice President: Shin King
Marketing Manager: Simon Lee
Sales Manager: Santiago Kuan
Estimated Sales: $2.9 Million
Number Employees: 25
Square Footage: 90000

27193 Pacific Store Designs
11781 Cardinal Cir
Garden Grove, CA 92843 714-636-4440
Fax: 714-636-4442 800-772-5661
psd4cmiller@sbcglobal.net
www.pacificstoredesigns.com
Manufacturer and exporter of retail store fixtures including shelving, general contractor, architecturer and desgin services trade show exhibits and custom woodworking items specializing in small to medium sized convenience, gourmetand health food stores; also, installation services available
President: Chris Miller
Sr. Vice President: James Raynor
Research & Development: Sonia Quintana
Quality Control: Erv Miller
Plant Manager: Ken Kasper
Estimated Sales: $2 Million
Number Employees: 10-19
Square Footage: 6600
Type of Packaging: Private Label

27194 Pacific Tank
17177 Muskrat Ave
Adelanto, CA 92301 760-246-6136
Fax: 760-246-6062 800-449-5838
pactankltd@aol.com www.pacifictank.com
Double wall, fiberglass and storage tanks, food processing equipment and material handling equipment
President: Norvald Farestveit
CFO: Robert Clanton
Estimated Sales: Below $5,000,000
Number Employees: 10-19
Square Footage: 10000

27195 Pack & Process
309 136th Ct E
Bradenton, FL 34212
Fax: 302-658-6928 877-777-8425
w.orris@packandprocess.com
www.packandprocess.com
Contract packaging for food, ingredients. Horizontal and vertical form-fill, standup pouching, sachet
President: Steven A Ames
Estimated Sales: Less than $500,000
Number Employees: 10

27196 Pack Air
449 S Green Bay Rd
Neenah, WI 54956 920-727-3000
Fax: 920-727-3010 salesis@packairinc.com
www.packairinc.com
Accumulating conveyors
President: Pete Calder
CEO: Pete Clater
Sales Manager: Rob McCarry
Manager: Ron Mc Carry
Estimated Sales: $10 Million
Number Employees: 50-99

27197 Pack Line Corporation
3026 Phillips Ave
Racine, WI 53403 262-635-6966
Fax: 262-634-0512 800-248-6868
packrite@packrite.com www.packrite.com
Manufacturer, importer and exporter of semi-automatic and automatic fillers and capping, and sealing machinery
Manager: Dave Bornhuepter
CFO: Michael Beilinson
Vice President: Nick Maslovets
Marketing Director: Erica Kosinski
Estimated Sales: $1 Million
Number Employees: 5-9
Square Footage: 8000
Parent Co: Pack Line

27198 Pack Process Equipment
17025 N Scottsdale Rd # 100
Scottsdale, AZ 85255-5887 480-513-7676
Fax: 480-513-7677 fnuttelln@packprocess.com
www.packprocess.com
Agitators, bag forming machines, bar formers, batch kneaders, blanchers, blenders, brushes, wrapping, foiling, carton machines: closing, filling, forming, handling, sealing, chocolate equipment
Manager: Lisa Smoke
Estimated Sales: $3 - 5 Million
Number Employees: 10-19

27199 Pack Rite
3026 Phillips Avenue
Racine, WI 53403-3585 262-635-6966
Fax: 262-634-0521 800-248-6868
packrite@packrite.com www.packrite.com
Manufacturer and exporter of bag sealing equipment
Sales Director: Dave Bornhuetter
Public Relations: Eileen Pulice
Production Manager: Dale Klinkhammer
Estimated Sales: Below $5 Million
Number Employees: 5-9
Number of Products: 10
Square Footage: 20000
Parent Co: Mettler-Toledo

27200 Pack West Machinery Company
5316 N Irwindale Avenue
Irwindale, CA 91706 626-814-4766
Fax: 626-814-1615 sales@packwest.com
www.packwest.com
Manufacturer and exporter of packaging machinery including top driven and in-line cappers
Owner: Bill Ellison
Marketing/General Manager: Loren Lauxen
Estimated Sales: $2.5-5,000,000
Number Employees: 20-49

27201 Pack'R North America
1921 W Wilson Street
Suite A171
Batavia, IL 60510-1680 630-761-3104
Fax: 630-761-3105 packrna@comcast.net
www.filling-equipment.com
Net weight liquid fillers and software
General Manager: Pierre Guillon
Estimated Sales: $1 - 5 Million
Number Employees: 1-4

27202 **Pack-A-Drum**
862 Hawksbill Island Drive
Satellite Beach, FL 32937-3850 321-773-1551
Fax: 321-779-3816 800-694-6163
profits@packadrum.com www.pack-a-drum.com
Manufacturer and exporter of manually operated trash compactors/deflators, waste containers and platform carts with free waste management consulting for customers.
President: Bill Wagner
CFO: Kelli Wagner
VP Marketing: Erik Wagner
VP Sales: Mark Wagner
Director Customer Service: Kirk Wagner
Estimated Sales: $2 Million
Number Employees: 5-9
Number of Brands: 1
Number of Products: 10
Square Footage: 200000
Brands:
Pack-A-Drum

27203 **Pack-All**
3003 W Hirsch Street
Melrose Park, IL 60160-1738 708-410-1140
Fax: 708-410-1137 888-806-9800
laurac@pack-all.com www.pack-all.com
Packaging equipment: shrink packaging machinery and tamper evident neck banding
President: Tom Nolan
Office Administrator: Laura Cannata
Estimated Sales: $1 - 3 Million
Number Employees: 5-9

27204 **Pack-Rite**
95 Day Street
Newington, CT 06111-1299 860-953-0120
Fax: 860-953-3354
Wooden boxes; also, packaging services available
Sales Manager: Oleg Ouchakof
Estimated Sales: $1-2.5 Million
Number Employees: 10-19

27205 **Pack-Rite**
3026 Phillips Ave
Racine, WI 53403 262-635-6966
Fax: 262-634-0521 800-248-6868
packrite@packrite.com www.packrite.com
Manufacturer and exporter of bag closing, and packaging machinery
Manager: Dave Bornhuepter
General Manager: Dave Bornhuetter
Estimated Sales: $3 - 5 Million
Number Employees: 5-9
Square Footage: 24000
Parent Co: Mettler-Toledo
Brands:
Pack Rite

27206 **PackRite**
3026 Phillips Avenue
Racine, WI 53403 262-635-6966
Fax: 262-634-0521 800-248-6868
packrite@packrite.com www.packrite.com
Manufactures and distributes sealing and handling products including poly sealers, thermo sealers, band sealers, conveyors & accumulating tables.
Marketing Executive/General Manager: Dave Bornhuetter
Manufacturing Supervisor: Dale Klinkhammer
Number Employees: 6
Square Footage: 10410
Parent Co: Mettler-Toledo, Inc

27207 **Package Automation Corporation**
53016 Highway 60, Acheson Industrial
Spruce Grove, AB T7X 3L3
Canada 780-962-6265
Fax: 780-962-6215 sales@pacauto.com
www.packageautomation.com

27208 **Package Concepts & Material**
1023 Thousand Oaks Blvd
Greenville, SC 29607-5642 864-458-7291
Fax: 864-458-7295 800-424-7264
www.packageconcepts.com
Films, polyester, flexible packages, netting plastics
Owner: Peter D Bylenga
Estimated Sales: $10-20 Million
Number Employees: 50-99

27209 **Package Containers**
777 NE 4th Ave
Canby, OR 97013 503-266-2721
Fax: 503-266-8650 800-266-5806
sales@packagecontainers.com
www.packagecontainers.com
Specialty paper converting. Produce merchandising paper totes and wire ties. Importer/distributor of poly products.
President/CEO: Robert Degnan
Director of Operations: John Stupfel
CFO/Controller: Rolland Royce
MW Regional Sales: Mary Pytko
NE Regional Sales: P R Morris
Director of Sales & Marketing: Scott Koppang
Estimated Sales: F
Number Employees: 50-99
Number of Brands: 6
Number of Products: 5
Square Footage: 80000
Type of Packaging: Food Service, Private Label
Brands:
Adver-Tie
Home Toter
Insta-Tie
Skirt Tie

27210 **Package Converting Corporation**
PO Box 6183
Holyoke, MA 01041 413-533-2992
Fax: 413-533-5201
Flexible packages, vacuum packaging materials, vacuum packaging equipment, beef, lamb, meat
Estimated Sales: $1-2.5 Million
Number Employees: 1-4

27211 **Package Conveyor Company**
123 S Main St
Fort Worth, Fo 76104 817-332-7195
Fax: 817-334-0855 800-792-1243
wapowers@flash.net www.apowers.com
Manufacturer and exporter of conveying equipment including flat, inclined and floor-to-floor belts
Owner: Jack Powers
President: Doyle Powers
Estimated Sales: $2.5-5 Million
Number Employees: 20-49
Parent Co: W.A. Powers Industries

27212 **(HQ)Package Machinery Company**
380 Union St Ste 58
West Springfield, MA 01089 413-732-4000
Fax: 413-732-1163
customerservice@packagemachinery.com
www.packagemachinery.com
Manufacturer and exporter of rebuilt packaging and injection molding equipment; also, parts
President: Katherine E Putnam
Marketing Manager: Meg Cook
General Manager: Paul Stiebel
Estimated Sales: $2.5-5 Million
Number Employees: 10-19
Square Footage: 22000
Brands:
Package

27213 **Package Nakazawa**
16233 Hartsook Street
Encino, CA 91436-1304 818-708-3771
Fax: 818-907-9756
yokuaki@americanaccessusa.com
www.packagenakazawa.com
President: Yokoaki Nazakwa
Sales Contact: Yoko Okuaki
Estimated Sales: $300,000-500,000
Number Employees: 3

27214 **Package Products**
3126 Preble Avenue
Pittsburgh, PA 15233-1084 412-766-1234
Fax: 412-766-6335 maryjo.fox@menasha.com
www.packageproducts.com
Estimated Sales: $10 - 20 Million
Number Employees: 50-99

27215 **Package Service Companyof Colorado**
1800 NW Vivion Rd
Northmoor, MO 64150-9611 816-891-8300
Fax: 816-891-9032 800-748-7799
www.lsod.net
Pressure sensitive labels, printed packaging and promotional coupons
CEO: Mike Reed
CEO: Russ Jones
Chairman: Jeff Nedblake
Quality Control: Bill Krumrei
R & D: Larry Johnson
Marketing Director: Mike Steczak
VP Sales: Dennis Shannon
Estimated Sales: $20-50 Million
Number Employees: 100-249
Square Footage: 57000

27216 **Package Supply Equipment**
P.O.Box 19021
Greenville, SC 29602 404-344-8551
Fax: 864-277-0957 info@packagesupply.com
www.packagesupply.com
Wine industry corks and closures
President: Gary Daniels
CEO: Gary Daniels Sr
Estimated Sales: $50-75 Million
Number Employees: 5-9

27217 **Package Systems Corporation**
109 Connecticut Mills Avenue
Danielson, CT 06239-1653 860-774-0363
Fax: 860-774-5326 800-522-3548
psc@labels-ps.com www.labels-ps.com
Pressure sensitive rolls and sheets, labels, label machinery and grease proof polystyrene inserts for meats, poultry, etc.; importer of cellophane; exporter of labels
Sales/Marketing Executive: Charles Pingeton
VP Sales: Randall Duhaime
Estimated Sales: $2.5-5 Million
Number Employees: 20-49
Square Footage: 132000

27218 **Packagemasters**
52 Sindle Avenue
Little Falls, NJ 07424-1619 973-890-7511
Fax: 973-890-0470
Tea and coffee bags and packaging film supplies, pouch materials

27219 **(HQ)Packaging & Processing Equipment**
121 Earl Thompson Road
Ayr, ON N0B 1E0
Canada 519-622-6666
Fax: 519-622-6669 ppetinc@netcom.ca
Manufacturer and exporter of new, used, rebuilt and custom built blister packagers, bottle sorters, cappers, cartoners, case packers and sealers, cleaners, conveyors, fillers, heat sealers, kettles, labelers, mixers, palletizerstanks, etc
President: P Wiese
CEO: Peter Weise
Other Locations:
Packaging & Processing Equipm
Windhagen

27220 **Packaging Aids Corporation**
P.O.Box 9144
San Rafael, CA 94912-9144 415-454-4868
Fax: 415-454-6853 sales@pacaids.com
www.pacaids.com
Manufacturer, importer and exporter of sealing machinery for meat, produce, poultry and seafood; also, vacuum chambers and form/fill machinery
President: Serge Berguig
Quality Control: Dana McDaniel
National Sales/Marketing Manager: R Perrone
Sales Manager (Eastern Region): Jerry Henry
Estimated Sales: $5-10 Million
Number Employees: 20-49
Brands:
Audion

27221 **Packaging Associates**
4 Middlebury Boulevard
Randolph, NJ 07869-1121 973-252-8890
Fax: 973-252-8894 cliffbridge@msn.com
Tamper-evident and CT plastic closures and bottles including PET, PP and HDPE; also, contract packaging of powders and liquids available
President: Charles Bridge
Estimated Sales: $3 - 5 Million
Number Employees: 15
Square Footage: 10000
Type of Packaging: Consumer, Food Service, Private Label, Bulk

27222 Packaging By Design
1460 Bowes Rd
Elgin, IL 60123 847-741-5600
Fax: 847-741-5666
mike@packaging-by-design.com
www.packaging-by-design.com
Flexographic packaging for the food industry product line of which includes roll-stock surface printed films; roll-stock custom laminations; roll-stock reverse printed and laminated, and preformed bags
VP: Charles Graziano
Sales Manager: Michael Graziano
General Manager: Ira Krakow
Type of Packaging: Consumer

27223 Packaging Concept Company
1801 N Kentucky Avenue
Evansville, IN 47711-3853 812-464-2525
Fax: 812-464-8080 pcc@plasticclosures.com
www.plasticclosures.com
Design and development of plastic bottle closure
President: Bruno Zumbuhl
Estimated Sales: Below $5 Million
Number Employees: 10

27224 Packaging Consultants Associated Inc
7820 Airport Hwy
Pennsauken, NJ 08109 856-488-0277
Fax: 856-488-0957 info@thenewpca.com
www.thenewpca.com
Packaging equipment, heat seal
President: Joseph R Morgan
CFO: Vincent Giannetti
Estimated Sales: $2.5 - 5 Million
Number Employees: 5-9

27225 Packaging Corporation of America
1955 West Field Court
Lake Forest, IL 60045
800-456-4725
www.packagingcorp.com
Corrugated cartons
Manager: George Mc Caffrey
CEO: Mark W. Kowlzan
SVP and CFO: Richard B. West
EVP: Thomas A. Hassfurther
SVP Sales and Marketing: Thomas W. H. Walton
Estimated Sales: $1 - 5 Million
Number Employees: 50-99
Square Footage: 1000000

27226 Packaging Corporation of America
1955 West Field Court
Lake Forest, IL 60045
800-456-4725
www.packagingcorp.com
Manufacturer and exporter of foil and plastic containers
Manager: John Mc Caffrey
Investor Relations Contact: Barb Sessions
Estimated Sales: $5-10 Million
Number Employees: 50-99
Brands:
Hefty

27227 Packaging Corporation of America
1955 West Field Court
Lake Forest, IL 60045
Fax: 847-482-4545 800-456-4725
www.packagingcorp.com
Boxes in all sizes
Chief Executive Officer: Mark Kowlzan
SVP/Chief Financial Officer: Richard West
EVP, Corrugated Products: Thomas Hassfurther
SVP, Mill Operations: Charles Carter
SVP, Paper: Judith Lassa
SVP/General Counsel/Secretary: Kent Pflederer
SVP, Sales & Marketing, Corrugated Prod.: Thomas W.H. Walton
Plant Manager: Richard Thomas
Purchasing Agent: Julie Valle
Estimated Sales: $50-100 Million
Number Employees: 100
Square Footage: 60827
Parent Co: Packaging Corporation of America

27228 Packaging Design Corporation
101 Shore Dr
Burr Ridge, IL 60527 630-323-1354
Fax: 630-323-2802 info@pack-design.com
www.pack-design.com
Corrugated boxes
President: Scott Jones
Vice President: Scott Jones
Sales Director: Benjamin Gercone
Production Manager: Don Hlavac
Estimated Sales: $6 Million
Number Employees: 20-49
Square Footage: 35000

27229 Packaging Distribution Services, Inc
2308 Sunset Road
Des Moines, IA 50321 800-747-2699
Fax: 515-243-1741 mail@pdspack.com
www.pdspack.com
Wiping cloths
Manager: Marty Robinson
Number Employees: 47

27230 (HQ)Packaging Dynamics
PO Box 5332
Walnut Creek, CA 94596-1332 925-938-2711
Fax: 925-938-2713 dlehm19148@aol.com
Manufacturer, importer and exporter of packaging machinery including horizontal and vertical form/fill/seal machinery, liquid fillers and bottling lines, cartoners, wrappers, bundlers and tea baggers
President: Richard Novak
Engineering Manager: Mike Sanchez
Marketing: Banchez
Sales Manager: Fred Wermuth
Estimated Sales: $2.5-5 Million
Number Employees: 5-9
Square Footage: 10000

27231 (HQ)Packaging Dynamics
3900 W 43rd St
Chicago, IL 60632-3421 773-843-8000
Fax: 773-254-8136 www.pkdy.com
Manufacturer and exporter of packaging machinery including liquid filling
Vice President of Human Resources: Paul Christensen
Estimated Sales: $2.5-5 Million
Number Employees: 1,000-4,999
Square Footage: 40000
Other Locations:
Packaging Dynamics Ltd.
Hartwell GA

27232 Packaging Dynamics
35B Carlough Rd
Bohemia, NY 11716 631-563-4499
Fax: 631-563-4893 dlehm19148@aol.com
www.packagingdynamics.com
Liquid filling and packaging equipment
Owner: Eric Lehmann
Estimated Sales: $2.5-5 Million
Number Employees: 10-19

27233 Packaging Dynamics Corporation
3900 W 43rd St
Chicago, IL 60632-3421 773-843-8000
Fax: 773-254-8204 www.pkdy.com
Food Service and supermarket packaging
Chief Executive Officer & Director: Roger Prevot
Estimated Sales: $393.10 Million
Number Employees: 2500

27234 Packaging Dynamics International
17153 Industrial Hwy
Caldwell, OH 43724-9779 740-732-5665
Fax: 740-732-7515
laminations@ici-laminating.com
www.ici-laminating.com
Manufacturer and exporter of aluminum beverage and can liners, containers for biscuits and sandwich wrap; also, laminated paper
President: Darin Barton
VP: Gerry Medlin
Estimated Sales: $15 - 20 Million
Number Employees: 50-99
Parent Co: Alupac
Brands:
I-Rap

27235 Packaging Enterprises
12 N. Penn Ave
Rockledge, PA 19046 215-379-1234
Fax: 215-379-1166
fillers@packagingenterprises.com
www.packagingenterprises.com
Manufacturer and exporter of plastic bags and pouches
President: Lee Sanford
Estimated Sales: $1-2.5 Million
Number Employees: 1-4
Square Footage: 36000
Type of Packaging: Private Label, Bulk
Brands:
Sobo

27236 Packaging Enterprises
10 N Penn Ave
Jenkintown, PA 19046 320-209-3152
Fax: 218-464-1527 763-257-3687
jgibbs4321@aol.com
www.packagingenterprises.com
Manufacturer and exporter of filling machinery for liquids and viscous food products
President: Terrence Geyer
VP: Timothy Geyer
Estimated Sales: $2.5-5 Million
Number Employees: 10-19
Number of Products: 15
Square Footage: 6800
Type of Packaging: Private Label
Brands:
Geyer

27237 Packaging Equipment & Conveyors, Inc
52853 County Road 7
Elkhart, IN 46514-9522 574-266-6995
Fax: 574-264-6210 peac@peacinc.com
www.peacinc.com
Manufacturer and exporter of liquid and aerosol filling line equipment; also, modular conveying systems, bi-directional accumulation tables, flight-bar sorters, tube taping machines, orienting systems, de-palletizers, can de-elevatorsand product hoppers
Manager: Dennis Kline
Vice President: Brenda Arbogast
Research & Development: Brad Wegner
Sales Director: Chuck Reed
Operations Manager: Dennis Kline
Estimated Sales: $3 Million
Number Employees: 5-9
Number of Products: 16
Square Footage: 40000
Type of Packaging: Private Label
Brands:
Connect-A-Veyor

27238 Packaging Graphics Corporation
60 Delta Dr
Pawtucket, RI 02860 401-725-7700
Fax: 401-727-2700 www.packgraph.com
Blister cards
Manager: Gary Stiffler
Estimated Sales: $20-50 Million
Number Employees: 250-499
Square Footage: 250000

27239 Packaging Group
360 Spinnaker Way
Concord, ON L4K 4W1
Canada 905-761-7040
Fax: 905-761-7266 info@thepackaginggroup.com
Supplier of flexible packaging materials. Cello-Foil Holdings has acquired the company as of September 2005
President: Ted Hue
CFO: Frank Petti
Parent Co: Cello-Foil Holdings, Corp

27240 Packaging Machine Service Company
2260 Lithonia Industrial Boulevard
Suite C
Lithonia, GA 30058-4668 770-482-4808
Fax: 770-482-9371 800-871-4764
pmscom@aol.com
Gluefomer, in-line tri-seal closer, autoload end load cartoner
Estimated Sales: $1-2.5 Million
Number Employees: 10-19

27241 Packaging Machinery
2303 W Fairview Ave
Montgomery, AL 36108 334-265-9211
Fax: 334-265-9218
Manufacturer and exporter of material handling equipment, designer packaging machinery, conveyors, etc
Finance/Treasurer: Bruce Murchison
Estimated Sales: $1-2.5 Million
Number Employees: 5-9
Type of Packaging: Bulk

27242 Packaging Machinery & Equipment
179-181 Watson Ave
West Orange, NJ 07052 973-325-2418
Fax: 973-325-6937 packmach@aol.com
www.packagingmachineryandequipment.com
Manufacturer and exporter of cartoners and machinery including marking, printing, dating and coding; also, rebuilding of packaging equipment available
President: James Lyle Clark
Secretary: Mary Cameron
Quality Control: Dennis McDermott
Estimated Sales: Below $5 Million
Number Employees: 1-4

27243 Packaging Machinery International
1260 Lunt Avenue
Elk Grove Village, IL 60007-5618 847-640-1512
Fax: 847-640-8732 800-871-4764
pmiinc@pmi-intl.com www.pmi-intl.com
Manufacturer and exporter of packaging machinery and equipment including shrink wrappers and bundlers
President: Branko Vukotic
CFO: Branko Vukotic
VP: Randy Spahr
Estimated Sales: $5 - 10 Million
Number Employees: 20-49
Square Footage: 56000

27244 Packaging Machinery Service Company
4217 E Jefferson Avenue
Fresno, CA 93725-9707 559-834-4400
Fax: 559-834-4835 877-402-1404
pmsc@bellsouth.net
www.packagingmachineryservicecompany.com
Owner: Ken Libby
Estimated Sales: $1 - 5 Million
Number Employees: 10-19

27245 Packaging Machines International
9511 River St
Schiller Park, IL 60176-1019 847-640-1512
Fax: 847-640-8732 800-871-4764
pmiinc@pmi-intl.com www.pmi-intl.com
President: Branko Vukotic
CFO: Randy Swpahr
Estimated Sales: $5 - 10 Million
Number Employees: 10

27246 Packaging Materials
PO Box 731
Cambridge, OH 43725 740-432-6337
Fax: 740-439-4718 800-565-8550
Polyethylene film and bags including shrink, bundle wrap, form-fill-seal, on rolls, etc.; also, six color printing available
CFO: Amanda Johnson
VP Manufacturing: Ron Funk
VP Sales: Bill Funk
VP Production: Ron Funk
Estimated Sales: $5 - 10 Million
Number Employees: 20-49
Type of Packaging: Food Service, Private Label, Bulk

27247 Packaging Materials Corporation/PM Label Corporation
6995 Industrial Ave
El Paso, TX 79915-1116 915-772-9012
Fax: 915-779-8751 800-325-4195
dbarron@writeme.com
www.packagingmaterials.com
Pressure sensitive labels including heat seal, dry gum and bar code
President: Armando Barron
VP: Larry Muther
Estimated Sales: $3-5 Million
Number Employees: 10-19
Square Footage: 64000

27248 Packaging Partners, Ltd.
951 Thorndale Avenue
Bensenville, IL 60106-1139 630-238-1964
Fax: 630-238-2801 hbrkd2@aol.com
Founder: Grover L. Foote
Sales Representative: Hoyt Diehl
Type of Packaging: Consumer

27249 Packaging Parts & Systems
22831 Avenida Empresa
Rcho Sta Marg, CA 92688 949-888-7221
Fax: 949-888-7112
info@extreme16packaginc.com
www.extremepkg.com
Owner: Ray Uttaro
Estimated Sales: $1 - 3 Million
Number Employees: 1-4

27250 (HQ)Packaging Products Corporation
6820 Squibb Rd
Mission, KS 66202 913-262-3033
Fax: 913-789-8698
ppcsales@packagingproductscorp.com
www.packagingproductscorp.com
Manufacturer and exporter of printed and converted flexible packaging materials including sheet and roll
President: Jack Joslin
Sales/Marketing: Laird Dowgray
Sales Manager: Tom Zammit
COO: Jack Joslyn
Billing & Accounts Receivable: Cindy Hansen
Number Employees: 50-99
Square Footage: 37000
Other Locations:
Packaging Products Corp.
Rome GA

27251 Packaging Progressions
102 G P Clement Drive
Collegeville, PA 19426-0244 610-489-8601
Fax: 610-489-8394 sales@pacproinc.com
www.pacproinc.com
A full line of stainless steel packaging/processing equipment for the food industry; alignment, centralizer, interleaver, counter stacker
President: Larry Ward
Sales Director: Drew Ward
Estimated Sales: $2.5-5,000,000
Number Employees: 20-49
Type of Packaging: Food Service, Private Label, Bulk

27252 Packaging Service Company
1904 Mykawa Rd
Pearland, TX 77581 281-485-1457
Fax: 281-485-3242 800-826-2949
sales@packserv.com www.packserv.com
Contract packager and exporter of charcoal starter, all-purpose cleaners, lamp oil and household chemicals; private labeling available
President: Gabriel Baizan
Quality Control: Carl Caldwell
VP/General Manager: Jean-Pierre Baizan
Manager Grocery/Sales: Larry Lubs
Export Manager: George Foster
Plant Manager: Luis Dela Cruz
Estimated Sales: $20-25 Million
Number Employees: 100-249
Square Footage: 150000

27253 Packaging Solutions
11600 Magdalena Avenue
Los Altos Hills, CA 94024-5150 650-917-1022
Fax: 510-791-7606
Trays, cartons, labels, inserts and cold temperature shippers
President: Clayton Bussey
Co-Owner: Jerry Chaine
Estimated Sales: $1-2.5 Million
Number Employees: 5-9

27254 Packaging Specialties
P.O.Box 360
Fayetteville, AR 72702 479-521-2580
Fax: 479-521-2748 800-247-3446
gmathews@psi-ark.com www.psi-ark.com
Flexographic printing
President: Kaaren Biggs
Estimated Sales: $20-50 Million
Number Employees: 100-249

27255 Packaging Store
1255 Howard St
San Francisco, CA 94103 415-558-8100
Fax: 415-558-0625
sales@the-packaging-store.com
www.the-packaging-store.com
Wine industry foam carriers
President: Richard Neill
Estimated Sales: $1-2.5 Million
Number Employees: 20-49

27256 Packaging Systems Automation
2200 Niagara Ln N
Plymouth, MN 55447 763-473-1032
Fax: 763-473-1204 sales@psautomation.com
www.psautomation.com
Continuous motion cartoner, pouch flattener
Owner: Steven Swanlund
Estimated Sales: $20-50 Million
Number Employees: 20-49

27257 (HQ)Packaging Systems International
4990 Acoma St
Denver, CO 80216 303-296-4445
Fax: 303-296-2164 sales@pkgsys.com
www.pkgsys.com
Manufacturer and exporter of bag filling and weighing machinery, portable flexible conveyors, bag openers, stackers, palletizers and material handling machinery
Executive Director: Tony Melton
Chairman of the Board: H Lott
Quality Control: Jenee Jenee
Sr. VP Sales/Marketing: A Guyton
Estimated Sales: $5-10 Million
Number Employees: 10-19
Square Footage: 75000
Parent Co: St. Regis Paper Company

27258 Packaging Technologies
P.O.Box 3848
Davenport, IA 52808-3848 563-391-1100
Fax: 563-391-4951 800-257-5622
sales@packt.com www.ptipacktech.com
Manufacturer and exporter of packaging, food processing and analyzing machinery
President: Barry Shoulders
Marketing: Julie Doty
Sales: Tom Riggins
Estimated Sales: $37 Million
Number Employees: 100-249
Square Footage: 200000
Parent Co: WKA

27259 Packexpo.Com
11911 Freedom Drive
Suite 600
Reston, VA 20190 703-243-8555
Fax: 703-243-8556 expo@pmmi.org
www.pmmi.org
President: Charles Yuska
Executive Assistant: Corinne Mulligan
CFO: Marry N Japour
Director, Tradeshow Marketing: Jeannine Gibson
Director, Business Intelligence: Paula Feldman
Senior Director, PR/Communications: Julie Ackerman
Director, Operations: Caroline Abromavage
Vice President, Administration: Katie Bergmann
Number Employees: 20

27260 Packing Material Company
PO Box 252
Southfield, MI 48037 248-489-7000
Fax: 248-489-7009 info@packingmaterial.com
www.packingmaterial.com
Manufacurer of boxes, cases, skids, wooden pallets, packaging films and foams used for temperature sensitivity. Also corrugated products, forest products, strapping, plastic fabrication and thermal pak
President: James Foster
VP: Gary Turnbull
VP: Gary Turnbull
General Manager: Jack Smylie
Controller: James Gross
Estimated Sales: $1 - 2.5 Million
Number Employees: 10-19
Number of Products: 11
Type of Packaging: Private Label, Bulk

Brands:
Thermalpak

27261 Packing Specialities
11350 Kaltz Ave
Warren, MI 48089 586-758-5240
Fax: 586-758-3557 sales@packspec.net
www.packspec.net
Corrugated containers
President: Kurt Tabor
Manager: Joe Zehel
Estimated Sales: $5-10 Million
Number Employees: 20-49
Parent Co: Ecorse Packaging Specialties

27262 Packrite Packaging
3900 Comanche Drive
Archdale, NC 27263 336-431-1111
Folding boxes
General Manager: Hollis Kelley, Sr.
Estimated Sales: $5-10 Million
Number Employees: 50-99
Square Footage: 75000
Parent Co: Caraustar Industries

27263 Packtive Corporation
801 5th Ave
Belvidere, IL 61008-5196 815-547-1200
Fax: 815-547-1255 www.packtive.com
Manufacturer and exporter of oven and microwaveable trays
Plant Manager: Scott Anderson
General Manager: Joe Deal
Plant Manager: Charles Parmenter
Estimated Sales: $20 - 50 Million
Number Employees: 100-249
Parent Co: Champion International Corporation
Type of Packaging: Food Service

27264 Packworld USA
539 S Main St
Nazareth, PA 18064 610-746-2765
Fax: 610-746-2754 sales@packworldusa.com
www.packworldusa.com
Sealing machinery including heatseal presses for tray lidding and irregular shapes, bag/pouch, rotary belt, etc
President: Charles H Trillich
CFO: Kathy Feyti
VP: Helma Young
Quality Control and R&D: Gabe Munoz
General Manager: Frank Welles
Estimated Sales: Below $5 Million
Number Employees: 10-19
Number of Products: 10

27265 Packworld USA
539 South Main Street
Nazareth, PA 18064-2728 610-746-2765
Fax: 610-746-2754 sales@packworldusa.com
www.packworldusa.com
Precision validatable heat sealers for accurate temperature control
President: Charles Trillich
Estimated Sales: $5-10 Million
Number Employees: 10-19

27266 Pacmac
1501 S Armstrong Ave
Fayetteville, AR 72701 479-521-0525
Fax: 479-521-2448 joe@pacmac.com
www.pacmac.com
Manufacturer and exporter of vertical form/fill/seal machinery
Administrator: Joe Terminella
Estimated Sales: $2.5-5,000,000
Number Employees: 20-49
Square Footage: 100000
Brands:
Ter-A-Zip

27267 Pacmaster by Schleicher
130 Wicker St
Sanford, NC 27330-4265 919-775-7318
Fax: 919-774-8731 800-775-7570
soa@interpath.com www.intimus.com
President: Jack Costelloe
Sales: Kathy Ainsworth
Estimated Sales: $10 - 20 Million
Number Employees: 50-99

27268 Pacmatic Corporation
8325 Green Meadows Drive N
Lewis Center, OH 43035-9451 740-657-8283
Fax: 740-657-8483 800-468-0440
uspacmatic@aol.com www.pacmatic.com
Automatic horizontal bagger from film roll, pallet stretch wrapper, flowpack wrapping machine
Estimated Sales: $5-10 Million
Number Employees: 10-19

27269 Paco Label Systems
PO Box 6502
Tyler, TX 75711 903-561-2125
Fax: 903-561-3455 800-346-4185
info@pacolabel.com www.pacolabel.com
Labels
President: David Anderson
General Manager: Rowe Anderson
Office Manager: Mary June Goodson
Estimated Sales: Below $5 Million
Number Employees: 1-4
Type of Packaging: Bulk

27270 Paco Manufacturing Company
2120 Addmore Ln
Clarksville, IN 47129 888-283-7963
Fax: 812-283-7992 sales@pacomfg.com
www.pacomfg.com
Stretch wrap
General Manager/VP: G Morris
Estimated Sales: $10-20 Million
Number Employees: 20-49
Square Footage: 35000
Parent Co: Precision Automation Company

27271 Pacquet Oneida
1600 Westinghouse Boulevard
Charlotte, NC 28273-6327 973-777-5600
Fax: 973-777-2155 800-631-8388
pacquet@sprintmail.com
Laminations for snack food, confectionery, pasta, bakery and coffee markets
President: Pet Matthais
Number Employees: 200
Parent Co: Butler & Smith
Brands:
Ful-Lok

27272 Pactiv
2023 Encino Vista Street
San Antonio, TX 78259-2431 210-481-3280
Fax: 210-481-3281
Territory Manager: Lawrence Treger
Type of Packaging: Consumer

27273 Pactiv LLC
1900 West Field Court
Lake Forest, IL 60045 847-482-2000
888-828-2850
www.pactiv.com
Manufacturer and exporter of bags, cartons, containers, film, trays, etc.
Chairman/Chief Executive Officer: Richard Wambol
Senior VP/Chief Financial Officer: Andrew Campbell
Vice President/Chief Information Officer: Richard Proszowski
Vice Pres./Chief Human Resources Officer: Henry Wells III
Estimated Sales: $7.3 Billion
Number Employees: 25,000
Parent Co: Tenneco Packaging

27274 Pacur
3555 Moser St
Oshkosh, WI 54901 920-236-2888
Fax: 920-236-2882 rknapp@pacur.com
www.pacur.com
Manufacturer and exporter of packaging materials; extruder of PET, PP, PETG, CPET, APET, RPET and recycled materials
President: Ron Johnson
R&D: Tim Wiycha
Director Sales/Marketing: Richard Knapp
Estimated Sales: $20 - 50 Million
Number Employees: 50-99
Square Footage: 80000
Parent Co: Rexham

27275 Padinox
489 Brackley Point Road
P.O. Box 20106
Winsloe, PE C1A 9E3
Canada 902-629-1500
Fax: 902-629-1502 800-263-9768
paderno@padinox.ca www.paderno.com
Manufacturer and exporter of stainless steel cookware including pots, pans,gadgets, utensils and bakeware
President: Jim Casey
VP: Tim Casey
Marketing: Scott Chandler
Production: Ernie Bremman
Number Employees: Oover 200
Brands:
Chaudier
Paderno

27276 Pafra/Veritec
260 Us Highway 46
Fairfield, NJ 07004-2324 973-575-2752
Fax: 973-575-2649 800-357-2372
Hot and cold adhesive equipment, noncontact gun assemblies, glue detection, bar code verification
Estimated Sales: $1 - 5 Million
Number Employees: 20-49

27277 Page Slotting & Saw Company
3820 Lagrange St
Toledo, OH 43612 419-476-5131
Circular blade machine knives, perforators and slitters for paper, leather and plastic food packaging
General Manager: Bill Gibbons
Estimated Sales: $5-10 Million
Number Employees: 10-19
Square Footage: 8000

27278 Paget Equipment Company
P.O.Box 369
Marshfield, WI 54449-0369 715-384-3158
Fax: 715-387-0720 paget@northsidecomp.com
www.pagetequipment.com
Manufacturer and exporter of process control systems, spray dryers, evaporators, tanks, heat exchangers, wet separators, blenders and conveyors
President: James Reigel
CFO: James Reigel
Quality Control: Steve Desmet
Sales: Richard Wermersen
Project Engineer: Brian Johnson
Estimated Sales: $5 - 10 Million
Number Employees: 50-99
Square Footage: 88000
Parent Co: JBL International

27279 Pagoda Products
777 Commerce St
Sinking Spring, PA 19608 610-678-8096
Fax: 610-678-8036
Industrial detergents and degreasers including floor cleaners and equipment cleaners
President: David Weaver
VP Sales: Blair Weaver
Estimated Sales: Below $5 Million
Number Employees: 1-4
Number of Products: 50
Square Footage: 4000

27280 Pak Sak Industries
122 S Aspen St
Sparta, MI 49345 616-887-8837
Fax: 616-887-7411 800-748-0431
www.packagingpersonified.com
Plain and printed polyethylene film and plastic bags
Marketing: Dave Rimer
Marketing Manager: Tom Wright
Business Manager: Doug Dolder
Estimated Sales: $20 - 50 Million
Number Employees: 100-249
Square Footage: 80000
Parent Co: Maxco

27281 Pak-Rapid
1050 Colwell Ln Bldg 4
Conshohocken, PA 19428 610-828-3511
Fax: 610-828-4290 sales@pakrapid.com
www.pakrapid.com
Vertical and horizontal packaging machinery for vitamins, liquids and powders
Sales: Jim Wallace
Sales: Lisa Crawford

Estimated Sales: $1-2.5 Million
Number Employees: 10-19
Square Footage: 10000

27282 Pak-Sher Company
2500 N Longview St
Kilgore, TX 75662 800-642-2295
Fax: 903-984-1524 www.paksher.com
Carry out, deli, bakery, seafood and hot food bags, interfolded sheets, drink carriers and sine wave bags; also, custom packaging available
President: Don James
VP Sales/Marketing: Tom Croninn
Estimated Sales: $20-50 Million
Number Employees: 100-249

27283 Paket Corporation
9165 S Harbor Ave
Chicago, IL 60617 773-221-7300
Fax: 773-221-7316 info@paketcorp.com
www.paketcorp.com
Contract packager of private label items
President: Mark K. O'Malley
Vice President: Mike Hintz
Estimated Sales: $3 - 5 Million
Number Employees: 20-49
Square Footage: 105000
Type of Packaging: Private Label

27284 Paket Corporation/UniquePack
9165 S. Harbor Avenue
Chicago, IL 60617-4436 773-221-7300
Fax: 773-221-7316 inf@paketcorp.com
www.paketcorp.com
Packaging service
President: Mark O'Malley
Controller: Stella Diaz
Vice President of Manufacturing: Mike Hintz
Estimated Sales: $3 - 5 Million
Number Employees: 20-49

27285 Pakmark
PO Box 228
Chesterfield, MO 63006-0228 636-532-7877
Fax: 636-532-9634 800-423-1379
pakmark@pakmark.com
Manufacturer and exporter of decorative pressure sensitive labels and tapes; also, hot-stamped and embossed foil
Estimated Sales: $1-2.5 Million
Number Employees: 10-19
Brands:
Signette

27286 Paktronics Controls
7415 Whitehall St Ste 124
Richland Hills, TX 76118 817-284-5241
Fax: 817-284-1712 info@maxitrol.com
www.maxitrol.com
Manufacturer, importer and exporter of temperature controls
President: David Sundberg
Inside Sales: Toni Thompson
Purchasing Manager: Linda McCleskey
Estimated Sales: $2.5-5 Million
Number Employees: 10
Square Footage: 10800
Parent Co: Maxitrol Company
Brands:
Beta Series
Pakstat
Paktronics
Trakstat

27287 Palace Packaging Machines
4102 Edges Mill Rd
Downingtown, PA 19335 610-873-7252
Fax: 610-873-7384 palace@unscramblers.com
www.unscramblers.com
Plastic bottle handling and cap/lid feeding systems. Component feeding and counting systems also available for food, beverage, and medical applications
President/CEO: Paul Taraschi
Marketing: Stephen Taraschi
Estimated Sales: $5-10 Million
Number Employees: 20-49
Square Footage: 35000

27288 Paley-Lloyd-Donohue
125 Bayway Ave
Elizabeth, NJ 07202-3006 908-352-5835
Fax: 908-352-8042 www.cleaning-supplies.net
Janitorial supplies including cheesecloth and germicidal multi-purpose cleaners
President: Bill Paley
CFO: Bill Paley
VP: Rick Paley
Estimated Sales: $5 - 10 Million
Number Employees: 5-9
Square Footage: 40000
Brands:
Lemon Kleen 32

27289 Palintest USA
1455 Jamike Avenue
Suite 100
Erlanger, KY 41018 859-341-7423
Fax: 859-341-2106 info@palintestusa.com
www.palintestusa.com
Water testing equipment
President: John Lever
VP: David Miller
VP: David Miller
Estimated Sales: $1-2.5 Million
Number Employees: 5-9
Parent Co: The Halma Group

27290 Pall Corporation
25 Harbor Park Dr
Port Washington, NY 11050 516-484-5400
Fax: 516-484-3651 800-876-7255
piannucci@pall.com www.pall.com
President: Franl Overli
Estimated Sales: $100+ Million
Number Employees: 500-999

27291 Pall Corporation
25 Harbor Park Dr
Port Washington, NY 11050 516-484-5400
Fax: 516-484-3651 800-717-7255
piannucci@pall.com www.pall.com
President & Chief Executive Officer: Lawrence Kingsley
Chief Financial Officer: Akhil Johri
Estimated Sales: $2.67 Billion
Number Employees: 10800

27292 Pall Corporation
25 Harbor Park Dr
Port Washington, NY 11050 516-484-5400
Fax: 516-484-3651 866-905-7255
foodandbeverage@pall.com www.pall.com
The largest and most diverse filtration, separations and purifications company in the world. For the food and beverage industries, Pall has developed filtration and advanced filtration systems that meet market needs for reliability andcost effectiveness.
President/CEO/CFO: Lawrence D. Kingsley
President, Life Sciences: Yves Baratelli
President, Industrial: Ruby Chandy
Vice President, Finance & Treasurer: R. Brent Jones
Chief Technology Officer: Michael Egholm, Ph.D
Senior Vice President, Business Developm: H. Alex Kim
Chief Human Resources Officer: Linda Villa
Senior Vice President, Global Operations: Kenneth V. Camarco
Number Employees: 250-499

27293 Pall Filtron
50 Bearfoot Rd # 1
Northborough, MA 01532-1551 508-393-1800
Fax: 508-393-1874 800-345-8766
piannucci@pall.com www.pall.com
Filtration and separation systems for food and beverage applications
Sr. VP: Jamie Monat
VP Sales: Piers O'Donnell
VP Sales: Gerard Gach
Estimated Sales: $20 - 50 Million
Number Employees: 50-99
Parent Co: Pall Group
Other Locations:
Pall Filtron
Shinagawa-Ku
Brands:
Emflon
Fluorodyne
Hdc Ii
Pallcell
Pallsep
Profile Ii Plus
Ultipleat
Ultipor Gf/Gf Plus
Ultipor N66

27294 Pall Food and Beverage
25 Harbor Park Drive
Port Washington, NY 11050 516-484-3600
Fax: 516-801-9548 866-905-7255
foodandbeverage@pall.com www.pall.com
Researching and developing filtration and advanced separation systems that will help improve the quality of products for the food and beverage processor.
Chairman & Chief Executive Officer: Lawrence Kingsley
Chief Financial Officer: Akhil Johri
CEO: Eric Krasnoff
Chief Technology Officer: Michael Egholm
SVP, Corporate Strategy: H. Alex Kim
Market Sales Manager: Kathleen Berry
Senior Vice President, Operations: Richard Jackson
Estimated Sales: $5 - 10 Million
Number Employees: 10,000

27295 Pallet Management Systems
PO Box 339
Lawrenceville, VA 23868-0339 804-848-2164
Fax: 804-848-4888 800-446-1804
sales@palletnet.com
www.pallet-management.com
New and used wooden, metal and plastic pallets; also, pallet repair, management, distribution and recovery services available
Chairman/CEO: Johnary Lucy III
Director: Donald Norwood
Estimated Sales: $20-50 Million
Number Employees: 100-249
Square Footage: 63000

27296 Pallet Masters
655 E Florence Ave
Los Angeles, CA 90001 323-758-6559
Fax: 323-758-9600 800-675-2579
info@palletmasters.com www.palletmasters.com
Pallets
President: Stephen Anderson
Inside Sales Manager: Bridgette Lathem
General Manager/Controller: Tim Hwang
Estimated Sales: Below $5 Million
Number Employees: 20-49
Parent Co: Trojan Transportation

27297 Pallet One
1470 Highway 17 South
PO Box 819
Bartow, FL 33830 863-533-1147
Fax: 863-533-3065 800-771-1148
sales@palletone.com www.palletone.com
Manufacturer and exporter of wooden pallets and harvesting bins
CEO/President/Chairman: Howe Wallace
Vice President/CFO: Casey A. Fletcher
Vice President of Sales: Keith M. Reinstetle
Estimated Sales: $10 - 20 Million
Number Employees: 100-249
Parent Co: IFCO

27298 Pallet Pro
9980 Clay County Hwy
Moss, TN 38575-6333 931-258-3661
Fax: 931-258-3280 800-489-3661
barkybeaver@info-ed.com www.barkybeavr.com
Pallets
Manager: Mary Strong
CEO: J Smith
Quality Control: Jackie Trent
VP Manufacturing: J Wix
VP Marketing: K Donaldson
Estimated Sales: $10 - 20 Million
Number Employees: 20-49
Square Footage: 15000

27299 Pallet Reefer International LLC
4000 Highway 56
Houma, LA 70363-7817 731-616-2219
Fax: 985-868-3715 800-259-3693
lsaia@palletreefer.com www.pallatreefer.com
Member of the Board: Louis P Salia III
Number Employees: 10,000+

27300 Pallet Service Corporation
11201 90th Ave N
Maple Grove, MN 55369 763-391-8020
Fax: 763-391-8026 888-391-8020
sales@palletservice.com www.palletservice.com

Pallets; also, recycling of cardboard available
President: Robert Wenner
Sales: Tom Saari
Manager: Scott Wicklund
Estimated Sales: $5-10 Million
Number Employees: 50-99

27301 PalletOne, Inc.
1470 Highway 17 South
Bartow, FL 33830
Fax: 863-533-3065 800-771-1148
sales@PalletOne.com www.palletone.com
Pallets
Chairman, President, CEO: Howe Wallace
VP and CFO: Casey Fletcher
VP and CFO: Casey Fletcher
Vice President of Sales: Keith Reinstetle
Chief Operating Officer: Al Holland
Estimated Sales: Less than $500,000
Number Employees: 50-99
Square Footage: 160000

27302 Pallets
99 1/2 East Street
PO Box 326
Fort Edward, NY 12828 518-747-4177
Fax: 518-747-3757 800-PLT-SKID
sales@pltsinc.com www.palletsincorporated.com
Wooden pallets, skids and crates
President: Clint Binley
Sales Manager: Clinton Binley
Estimated Sales: $2.5-5 Million
Number Employees: 20-49

27303 Pallister Pallet
14035 70th Street
Wapello, IA 52653-9596 319-523-8161
Fax: 319-523-5429
Wooden pallets
Secretary/Treasurer: Heather Pallister
VP: Ted Pallister
Estimated Sales: $3 Million
Number Employees: 20-49
Square Footage: 45000

27304 Pallox Incorporated
7221 Hickory Ln
Onsted, MI 49265 517-456-4101
Fax: 517-456-7821 pallox@veriozon.net
Manufacturer and exporter of wooden pallets, skids and boxes; also, pallet repair and design available; also heat treat pallets for ISPM-15 standard
President: R J Moore
Estimated Sales: $2.5 Million
Number Employees: 20-49
Number of Products: 100
Square Footage: 18000

27305 Palmer Displays
704 Whitney St
San Leandro, CA 94577 510-632-8597
Fax: 510-632-1545 paldispla@aol.com
www.adamsscreenprint.com
Decals and screen printing and metal finishing available
Owner: Mark Adams
Estimated Sales: $300,000-500,000
Number Employees: 5-9
Square Footage: 6000

27306 (HQ)Palmer Distributors
23001 W Industrial Dr
St Clair Shores, MI 48080-1187 586-498-2900
Fax: 586-772-4627 800-444-1912
www.palmerpromos.com
Manufacturer and exporter of display cases, card holders, bowls, tray covers, light boxes and syrup bottles
President: James Palmer
VP: Mark Armstrong
Food Service Sales Manager: Michael Lacoursiere
Estimated Sales: $10 - 20 Million
Number Employees: 50-99
Square Footage: 50000
Type of Packaging: Food Service
Brands:
Pdi
Ppp

27307 Palmer Fixture Company
1255 Winford Ave
Green Bay, WI 54303-3707 950-884-8698
Fax: 920-884-8699 800-558-8678
info@palmerfixture.com
www.palmerfixture.com
Manufacturer, importer and exporter of paper towel, tissue, and napkin dispensers including a universal hands-free towel dispenser
Owner: Bill Palmer
Vice President: Greg Kampschroer
Purchasing Manager: Chris Worth
Estimated Sales: $820,000
Number Employees: 7
Square Footage: 44000
Brands:
Economy
Holdit
Natures Plumber

27308 Palmer Snyder
400 N Executive Drive
Brookfield, WI 53005-6068 262-780-8780
Fax: 262-780-8790 800-762-0415
lpage@palmersnyder.com
www.palmersnyder.com
Manufacturer and exporter of plywood and plastic folding tables, wooden folding chairs maintenence free, galerie series chairs and transport cars for tables and chairs
CEO: Richard Bibler
VP Sales: Craig Clarke
Sales Representative: Chelsea Stecker
Estimated Sales: $1-2.5 Million
Number Employees: 100-250
Square Footage: 600000
Parent Co: Palmer Snyder
Other Locations:
Palmer Snyder
Elkhorn WI
Brands:
Palmer Snyder

27309 Palmer Wahl TemperatureInstruments
234 Old Weaverville Road
Asheville, NC 28804 828-658-3131
Fax: 828-658-0728 800-421-2853
info@palmerwahl.com www.palmerwahl.com
Manufactures temperature and pressure instrumentation. Process Industrial and RTD thermometers, Bimetal, Dial and Sanitary thermometers, infrared thermal imagers, Temperature Recording Labels and Chart Recorders, Pressure gauges andThermowells.
Owner: Stephen Santangelo
Vice President: Schuyler Tilly
Quality Control: Paul Lankford
VP Sales: Gary Lux
Brands:
All Star
Cleanliners
Digi-Stem
Heat Prober
Heat Spy
Temp-Plate

27310 Palmetto Canning Company
PO Box 155
3601 US Highway 41
Palmetto, FL 34220 941-722-1100
Fax: 941-729-1934
pcanning@palmettocanning.com
www.palmettocanning.com
Manufacturer and exporter of jams, jellies, preserves, marmalades and barbecue sauce
Owner: Jonathan C Greenlaw Jr
Estimated Sales: $5-10 Million
Number Employees: 10-19
Square Footage: 128000
Type of Packaging: Consumer, Private Label
Brands:
Palmalito

27311 Palmetto Packaging Corporation
1131 Edwards Cir
Florence, SC 29502-4740 843-662-5800
Fax: 843-662-5668
CustomerService@palmettopackaging.com
www.palmettopackaging.com
Corrugated and fiber boxes
President: David Searcy
Estimated Sales: $5-10 Million
Number Employees: 50-99

27312 Palmland Paper Company
708 NE 2nd Ave
Fort Lauderdale, FL 33304 954-764-6910
Fax: 954-779-3849 800-266-9067
Paper place mats, dinner and cocktail napkins, etc
Chairman of the Board: Bernard Beauregard
Secretary: Linda Dunn
Estimated Sales: $2.5-5 Million
Number Employees: 5-9
Square Footage: 8000

27313 Palo Alto Awning
750 W San Carlos
San Jose, CA 95126 650-968-4270
Fax: 650-968-3676 800-400-4270
info@PaloAltoAwning.com
www.paloaltoawning.com
Commercial awnings
President: John Ashman
Estimated Sales: $1-2.5 Million
Number Employees: 10-19

27314 Paltier
1701 Kentucky St
Michigan City, IN 46360 219-872-7238
Fax: 219-872-9480 800-348-3201
paltier@paltier.com www.paltier.com
Manufacturer and exporter of engineered storage rack systems including cantilever and drive-in/drive-thru
VP/General Manager: James Washington
Plant Manager: Glenn Clark
Estimated Sales: $20-50 Million
Number Employees: 100-249
Square Footage: 110000
Parent Co: Lyon Metal Products
Type of Packaging: Food Service
Brands:
Interchange
Pal Dek
Pal Gard
Paltier

27315 Pam Fastening Technology
1108A Continental Blvd
Charlotte, NC 28273 704-394-3141
Fax: 704-394-9339 800-699-2674
sales@pamfast.com www.pamfast.com
Hot-melt adhesives and hot-melt applicators, autofeed system
President: Edward Minchew
VP: Edward Minchew
Estimated Sales: $5 - 10 Million
Number Employees: 10-19

27316 Pamco Printed Tape & Label Company
2200 S Wolf Rd
Des Plaines, IL 60018-1934 847-803-2200
Fax: 847-803-2209 info@pamcolabel.com
www.pamcolabel.com
Pressure sensitive tape and labels
Controller: Maureen Brandes
CEO: Alan M Berkowitz
Vice President of Operations: Dave Heaster
Estimated Sales: $10 Million
Number Employees: 100-249
Square Footage: 26000

27317 Pan American Papers
5101 NW 37th Ave
Miami, FL 33142-3232 305-635-2534
Fax: 305-635-2538 jvl@panampap.com
www.panampap.com
Distributors of paper
President: Jesus A Roca
Sr. VP: Jesus Roca
Executive VP: Francisco Valdes
Estimated Sales: $20-50 Million
Number Employees: 10-19
Square Footage: 80000

27318 Pan Pacific Plastics Manufacturing
26551 Danti Ct
Hayward, CA 94545-3917 510-785-6888
Fax: 510-785-6886 888-475-6888
panpacplastics@aol.com www.pppmi.com
Manufacturer, exporter and importer of plastic bags
President: Ying Wang
Marketing/Sales: Mike Tan
Estimated Sales: $20-50 Million
Number Employees: 20-49

Square Footage: 40000
Parent Co: Pan Pacific Group Companies
Type of Packaging: Consumer, Food Service, Private Label, Bulk

27319 Panasonic Commercial Food Service
1 Panasonic Way
Secaucus, NJ 07094-2999 201-348-7000
Fax: 201-348-5310 800-553-0384
megarrk@panasonic.com www.panasonic.com
Commercial microwave ovens, vacuum cleaners, compact fluorescent light bulbs and ventilating fans; importer of rice cookers
Founder: Konosuke Matsushita
CEO: Yoshi Yamada
Marketing Specialist: Clare Morse
National Sales Manager: Paul Garber
General Manager: Ray Leibman
Estimated Sales: $300,000-500,000
Number Employees: 10,000
Brands:
Panasonic

27320 Panhandler, Inc.
PO Box 1329
Cordova, TN 38088-1329 800-654-7237
Fax: 901-336-6377 panhandlerpads@yahoo.com
www.panhandlerinc.com
Manufacturer and exporter of pot holders, bakers' gloves and bakery oven pads
Owner: Don White
CEO: Sherrie Nischwitz
Vice President: Christy Graves
Number Employees: 8
Square Footage: 24000
Type of Packaging: Food Service
Brands:
Panhandler Safety-Wall
Panhandler Twin-Terry

27321 Panoramic
1500 N Parker Dr
Janesville, WI 53545 608-754-8850
Fax: 608-754-5703 800-333-1394
packages@panoramicinc.com
www.panoramicinc.com
Food, Retail and Industrial Packaging, Stock PET Food Tubs/Containers. Thermoformed Plastic Clamshells, Blisters, Trays, Containers, Custom Packaging Designs, Rigid Set-Up Boxes (Box/Tray Combinations). Contract Packaging/Fulfillment.In-House Design, Tooling, Prototypes
CEO: Rick Holznecht
Estimated Sales: $20-50 Million
Number Employees: 100-249

27322 Panther Industries
8990 Barrons Blvd.
Highlands Ranch, CO 80129 303-703-9876
Fax: 720-283-9462 800-530-6018
sales@print-n-apply.com
www.print-n-apply.com
Supplies labeling equipment for the food industry
President: James Thompson
CFO: James Thompson
R&D: James Thompson
Quality Control: Jim Thompson
Estimated Sales: $1 Million
Number Employees: 5-9

27323 Papelera Puertorriquena
PO Box 119
Utuado, PR 00641-0119 787-894-2098
Fax: 787-894-0517
Paper and plastic bags
President: Jose A Rios Montalvo
Manager: Jose Rios
Number Employees: 80
Parent Co: All Plastic Products

27324 Paper Bag Manufacturers
4131 NW 132nd St
Opa Locka, FL 33054 305-685-1100
Fax: 305-685-2200 888-678-2247
baglady@paperbag.com www.paperbag.com
Bags for packaging tea, coffee and more
President: Joseph Greenspan
Owner: Adam Cohen
VP: Susan Hernandez
Estimated Sales: $1 Million
Number Employees: 17

27325 Paper Bleyer
400 Audubon Rd
Wakefield, MA 01880-1204 781-245-8201
Fax: 781-245-8209 www.alcoa.com
Paper converting, padding for candy boxes, baking cups and candy cups
Manager: Rick Holbrook
Estimated Sales: $20-50 Million
Number Employees: 50-99

27326 Paper Box & Specialty Company
1505 Sibley Ct
Sheboygan, WI 53081 920-459-2440
Fax: 920-459-2463 888-240-3756
Linda.quast@paperboxandspecialty.com
www.paperboxandspecialty.com
Manufacturer and exporter of set-up and folding cartons, poly-coated cheese liners and gift boxes
President: David Van Der Puy
Contact: Nicole Spielvogel
Estimated Sales: $2.5 - 5 Million
Number Employees: 20-49
Square Footage: 75000

27327 Paper Converting Machine Company Aquaflex
899 Old Route 220 North
Duncansville, PA 16635 814-695-5521
Fax: 814-695-0860 www.pcmc.com
Manufacturer and exporter of flexographic printing machinery and printing presses
President: E A Smithe Jr
VP Sales/Marketing: Mac Rosenbaum
Number Employees: 300
Square Footage: 880000
Parent Co: Barry-Wehmiller Companies Inc
Other Locations:
Aquaflex
Boucherville, PQ Canada
Brands:
Aquaflex
Chromas
Els
Fpc
Instaprep

27328 Paper Converting MachineCompany
P.O.Box 19043
Green Bay, WI 54307 920-336-4300
Fax: 920-494-8865 mikegigl@pcmc.com
www.pcmc.com
Printing presses print narrow to wide flexographic printing on film, paper, labels, non woven board stock.
President: Tim Sullivan
Estimated Sales: $237 Million
Number Employees: 500-999
Number of Brands: 20

27329 Paper Machinery Corporation
8900 W Bradley Rd
Milwaukee, WI 53224 414-354-8050
Fax: 414-354-8614 info@papermc.com
www.papermc.com
Paperboard cup and package forming machines
President: John Baumgartner
CFO: Scott Koehler
CEO: Donald W Baumgartner
Estimated Sales: $20 - 50 Million
Number Employees: 100-249

27330 (HQ)Paper Pak Industries
1941 White Avenue
La Verne, CA 91750 909-392-1750
Fax: 909-392-1760
salesinfo@paperpakindustries.com
www.pp-industries.com
Supplier of absorbent product packaging to the leading food processors, supermarket chains, and packaging manufacturers and distributors
President/CEO: Ron Jensen
VP/General Counsel: Marty Michael
Director of Technology: Sayandro Versteylen
VP Sales/Marketing: John Terrien
Estimated Sales: $15-$18 Million
Number Employees: 100
Type of Packaging: Food Service, Bulk

27331 Paper Product Specialties
PO Box 363
Waukesha, WI 53187-0363 262-549-1730
Fax: 262-549-3614
lauterbachgroup@lauterbachgroup.com
www.lauterbachgroup.com
Pressure sensitive labels and tags; also, heat seal paper and flexible packaging
President: Shane Lauterbach
Marketing/Sales: Dean Dimitriou
Estimated Sales: $20-50 Million
Number Employees: 50-99
Square Footage: 50000

27332 Paper Products Company
1543 Queen City Ave
Cincinnati, OH 45214 513-921-4717
Fax: 513-251-5553
info@paperproductscompany.com
www.paperproductscompany.com
Folding cartons and foil laminated, poly coated nested bakers' trays
President: Dennis Smith
Sales Manager: Jim Davis
Estimated Sales: $5 - 10 Million
Number Employees: 20-49
Brands:
Bakers' Gold

27333 Paper Service
PO Box 45
Hinsdale, NH 03451-0045 603-239-6344
Fax: 603-239-8861 paperservice@top.monad.net
www.paperservice.com
Manufacturer and exporter of paper napkins, wrapping and tissue paper
CEO: G O'Neal
Operations Manager: R O'Neal
Estimated Sales: $10-20 Million
Number Employees: 20-49
Square Footage: 200000
Type of Packaging: Food Service, Private Label

27334 Paper Systems
6127 Willowmere Dr
Des Moines, IA 50321 515-280-1111
Fax: 515-280-9219 800-342-2855
nate@paper-systems.com
www.paper-systems.com
Manufacturer and exporter of pallets and disposable and returnable bulk containers for food grade liquids and powders
Owner: William Chase
Estimated Sales: Below $5 Million
Number Employees: 10-19
Type of Packaging: Bulk
Brands:
Ez-Bulk
Ez-Flow
Ez-Pak
Ez-Pallet
Stack-Sack

27335 Paper-Pak Products
9740 Canterbury Street
Leawood, KS 66206-2106 913-341-7524
Fax: 913-341-7553 rcrossland@paperpak.com
Regional Sales Manager: Robin Crossland

27336 Paper-Pak Products
1941 N White Ave
La Verne, CA 91750 909-392-1200
Fax: 909-392-1732
Meat and poultry absorbent pads
COO: Dennis Murphy
VP Packing Products: Jim Gillispie
Estimated Sales: $20-50 Million
Number Employees: 250-499
Brands:
Dri-Sheet
Securely Yours
Zap Soakers

27337 Papertech
108-245 Iell Avenue
North Vancouver, BC V7P 2K1
Canada 604-990-1600
Fax: 604-990-1606 877-787-2737
info@papertech.ca www.papertech.ca
Manufacturer and exporter of dairy processing equipment including clean-in-place systems, milk processors and process control instruments
President: Kari Hilden
Marketing Coordinator: Tanja Kannisto

Number Employees: 30
Brands:
Optec

27338 Paperweights Plus
3661 Horseblock Road
Suite Q
Medford, NY 11763-2232 631-924-3222
Fax: 631-345-0752
Manufacturer, importer and exporter of advertising specialties including emblems, ID badges, name plates, lapel pins, key rings and paperweights
President: Darlene Reynolds
Estimated Sales: Less than $500,000
Number Employees: 1-4
Square Footage: 1700

27339 Papillon Ribbon & Bow
35 Monhegan Street
Clifton, NJ 07013 973-928-6128
Fax: 973-246-1065 800-229-2998
sales@papillonusa.com www.papillonusa.com
Packaging ribbons and bows
President: Wong Vinci
Vice President Finance: Jimmy Cheung
Marketing: Dan Schwatzbach
Estimated Sales: $7.6 Million
Number Employees: 40

27340 Pappas Inc.
575 E Milwaukee St
Detroit, MI 48202 313-873-1800
Fax: 313-875-7805 800-521-0888
info@pappasinc.com www.pappasinc.com
Makers of fine cutlery, emulsifying equipment, blades, parts and supplies.

27341 Paques ADI
182 Main St
Unit 6
Salem, NH 03079 603-890-5434
Fax: 603-898-3991 acocci@adi.ca
www.paquesadi.com
Supplier of wastewater treatment systems:, anaerobic, UASB, aerobic, hybrid
VP: Al Cocci
Estimated Sales: $1 - 5 Million
Number Employees: 5-9

27342 Par Systems
707 County Road E W
Saint Paul, MN 55126 651-484-7261
Fax: 651-483-2689 800-464-1320
info@par.com www.par.com
A leader in the design, construction, installation and support of large-scale, as well as small and precise, high-precision robotic and matieral handling equipment and systems.
President: Mark A Wrightsman
CFO: Brad Yopp
Research & Development: Albert Sturm
Quality Control: Jenny Conlin
Marketing Director: Karen Knoblock
Sales Director: Brian Behm
Production Manager: Wayne Skiba
Purchasing Manager: Kallie Swartz
Estimated Sales: $80 Million
Number Employees: 100-249
Square Footage: 60000
Brands:
Cimroc
Ederer
Jered
Mec
M"Zak
Nr
Pr
Ssi Robotics
Tr
Vector
Xr

27343 Par-Kan Company
2915 W 900 S
Silver Lake, IN 46982 260-352-2141
Fax: 260-352-0701 800-291-5487
info@par-kan.com www.par-kan.com
Manufacturer and exporter of recycled grease containers, lids, screens and caster frames
President: David Caldwell
Marketing: Todd Sheets
Sales: Carolyn Montel
Estimated Sales: $10 - 20 Million
Number Employees: 50-99
Brands:
Par-Kan

27344 (HQ)Par-Pak
14345 Northwest Freeway
Houston, TX 77040 713-686-6700
Fax: 713-686-5553 888-272-7725
clearsells@houston.parpak.com
www.parpak.com
Manufacturer and exporter of clear plastic containers for food packaging; also, catering trays
President: Sajjad Ebrahim
VP Technical: Dominic DiDomizio
VP Sales: David Goralski
Estimated Sales: $5 - 10 Million
Number Employees: 20-49
Square Footage: 105000
Brands:
Cake-Mix
Ebony
Invisi-Bowl
Invisible Packaging
Quartz Collection

27345 Par-Pak
3450 Lang Rd
Houston, TX 77092 713-686-6700
Fax: 713-686-5553
clearsells@houston.parpak.com
www.parpak.com
Rigid plastic containers
Owner: Mohammed Ebrahim
VP Sales: David Goralski
Operations Manager: Ali Virani
Estimated Sales: $5-10 Million
Number Employees: 20-49
Square Footage: 48000
Parent Co: Par-Pak

27346 ParTech
8383 Seneca Tpke # 2
New Hartford, NY 13413-4991 315-738-0600
Fax: 315-738-0562 800-448-6505
askpar@partech.com www.partech.com
Manufacturer and exporter of computerized cash registers
President and CEO: Dr John W Sammon Jr
CFO: Ronald Casciano
Vice President of Client Services: John Darby
Chief Technical Officer: Scott Langdoc
Director of Investor Relations: Christopher R Byrnes
Chief Marketing Officer: Peter Wolf
Senior Vice President of Sales and Marke: Tim Votaw
Public Relations: Christopher Byrnes
Plant Manager: William Williams
Purchasing Manager: Peter Cougan
Estimated Sales: $118 Million
Number Employees: 500-999
Type of Packaging: Food Service

27347 Parachem Corporation
2733 6th Ave
Des Moines, IA 50313 515-280-9445
Fax: 515-280-7600
Manufacturer and exporter of hand soap, hand soap dispensers, anti-bacterial soap systems in leaf form, etc
President: Beryl Halterman
Marketing Manager: Carla Stephens
Office Manager: Dean Blum
Purchasing Manager: Dean Blum
Estimated Sales: Below $5 Million
Number Employees: 1-4
Square Footage: 24000
Parent Co: Flightags
Brands:
Cleaf
Jardin Savon

27348 Paraclipse
2271 East 29th Ave
Columbus, NE 68601 402-563-3625
Fax: 402-564-2109 800-854-6379
ljochen@paraclipse.com www.paraclipse.com
Manufacturer and exporter of decorative indoor lighted fly traps and industrial fly traps for public dining areas, kitchen and food preparation areas. Outdoor lighted mosquito trap for restaurant outside serving areas and patios.
CFO: Cheryl Ditter
Sales Manager: Len Jochens
Estimated Sales: $3-6 Million
Number Employees: 1-4
Square Footage: 216000
Brands:
Insect Inn Iv

27349 Parade Packaging
333 Washington Blvd
Mundelein, IL 60060 847-566-6264
Fax: 847-566-2017
ssilverstein@fortuneplastics.com
www.fortuneplastics.com
Plastic bags and films
General Manager: Jerry Alexander
Manager: Scott Silverstein
Estimated Sales: $10-20 Million
Number Employees: 50-99
Parent Co: Parade Packaging Materials

27350 Paradigm Technologies
PO Box 25540
Eugene, OR 97402-0457 541-345-5543
Fax: 541-345-5549 paratech@presys.com
Food and dairy processing equipment and material handling equipment
Owner: Charles Nutter
Brands:
Alan Bradley
Ge

27351 Paradise
PO Box 4230
1200 Dr. Martin Luther King Jr. Blvd.
Plant City, FL 33563-0021 813-752-1155
Fax: 813-754-3168 800-330-8952
paradisefruit@hotmail.com
www.paradisefruitco.com
Manufacturer, importer and exporter of candied fruits used in fruitcakes and strawberries
Chairman/CEO: Melvin Gordon
President/Director: Randy Gordon
Senior Vice President: Tracy Schulis
Executive Vice President: Mark Gordon
VP/Corporate Sales: Ron Peterson
Estimated Sales: $21 Million
Number Employees: 250-499
Square Footage: 275000
Type of Packaging: Consumer, Food Service, Private Label, Bulk
Brands:
Dixie
Mor-Fruit
Sun-Ripe

27352 Paradise Plastics
116 39th St
Brooklyn, NY 11232
Fax: 718-965-4030 www.paradiseplastics.com
Plastic garbage bags
President: George Grossberger
Estimated Sales: $20 - 50 Million
Number Employees: 20-49

27353 Paradise Products
PO Box 568
El Cerrito, CA 94530-0568 510-524-8300
Fax: 510-524-8165 800-227-1092
paradise-party@worldnet.att.net
www.partymaster.com
100 page catalog of theme decorations and party supplies for special events and sales promotions cateterias and clubs
Controller: Alice Rickey
Sales: Shirley Imai
Number Employees: 14
Number of Products: 3000
Square Footage: 80000
Brands:
Fling Decorating Kits

27354 Paragon Electric Company
PO Box 28
Two Rivers, WI 54241-0028 920-793-1161
Fax: 920-793-3736 www.paragonelectric.com
Refrigeration defrost controls for walk-in and reach-in coolers and refrigerated display cases
VP/General Manager: Bob Stalder
Sales Manager: Mike Simino
Estimated Sales: $20 - 50 Million
Number Employees: 500

27355 **Paragon Films**
3500 W Tacoma St
Broken Arrow, OK 74012-1164 918-250-3456
Fax: 918-355-3456 800-274-9727
jpt@paragon-films.com www.paragon-films.com
Manufacturer and exporter of packaging materials including stretch and specialty films and hand applied and pallet stretch wrap
President: Mike Baab
Estimated Sales: $20 - 50 Million
Number Employees: 100-249

27356 **Paragon Group USA**
3433 Tyrone Boulevard N
St Petersburg, FL 33710-1136 727-341-0547
Fax: 727-302-9816 800-835-6962
info@zontec.com www.paragon-usa.com
Manufacturer and exporter of ozone generators designed to electronically eliminate odors without the use of chemicals; also, food preservation equipment
President: David Kocksten
R & D: Phillip Rod
VP Sales: Susan Duffy
Purchasing Manager: Chuch Pacino
Estimated Sales: $1-2.5 Million
Number Employees: 10
Square Footage: 20800
Brands:
Zontec

27357 **Paragon International**
P.O.Box 560
Nevada, IA 50201 515-382-8000
Fax: 515-382-8001 800-433-0333
info@manufacturefun.com
www.manufacturedfun.com
Manufacturer and exporter of popcorn machines and carts
Owner: Dave Swegle
Quality Control: Bill Tierce
VP Sales/Marketing: Tom Berger
Manager Customer Service: Sandra Holubar
Estimated Sales: $3 - 5,000,000
Number Employees: 10-19
Square Footage: 25000
Brands:
1911 Originals
Thrifty Pop

27358 **Paragon Labeling Systems**
1607 9th St
White Bear Lake, MN 55110-6717 651-429-7722
Fax: 651-429-6006 800-429-7722
info@paragonlabeling.com
www.paragonlabeling.com
Manufacturer and exporter of printing machines and supplies and custom labeling systems
Director of Label Manufacturing Operatio: Karla Bridgeman
CFO: Ed Clarke
Vice President: Craig Blonigen
VP: Craig Blonigen
Sales/Marketing: Craig Blonigen
Operations Manager: Ken Koehler
Production Manager: Matt Thoreson
Plant Manager: Ken Koehler
Estimated Sales: $5 Million
Number Employees: 50-99
Square Footage: 160000
Parent Co: Lowry Computer Products Company
Brands:
Paragon

27359 **Paragon Labeling Systems**
1607 9th St
White Bear Lake, MN 55110-6717 651-429-7722
Fax: 651-429-6006 800-429-7722
info@paragonlabeling.com
www.lowrycomputer.com
Labels, labeling machines, print and apply labelers, ribbons, printers, and scanners
Director of Label Manufacturing Operatio: Karla Bridgeman
Sr. VP: David Heiff
VP: Craig Boligen
Estimated Sales: $12 Million
Number Employees: 50-99

27360 **(HQ)Paragon Packaging**
7700 Centerville Rd
Ferndale, CA 95536 707-786-4004
Fax: 707-786-4014 888-615-0065
info@paragonpackaging.com
www.paragonpackaging.com
Gift packaging including boxes and plastic containers
Owner: Ron Cohn
Production Manager: Ed Davis
Estimated Sales: $1-2.5 Million
Number Employees: 1-4
Square Footage: 1500

27361 **Parallel Products**
401 Industry Rd
Louisville, KY 40208 502-634-1014
Fax: 813-289-4283 800-883-9100
CustomerServices@parallelproducts.com
www.parallelproducts.com
Developer and manufacturer of technologies for the processing of food and beverage wastes. Specific product areas include that of: brewery, winery, distillery services; soft drink, juice services; candy, sugar services; and also thatof pharmaceutical, cosmetic services.
President/Chief Executive Officer: Gene Kiesel
Controller: David Kenney
Vice President of Business Development: Tim Cusson
Vice President Sales and Marketing: Ken Reese
National Sales Manager: Ed Stewart
Corporate HR Manager, Director of Corpor: Hal Park
Vice President of Operations: Bob Pasma
National Customer Service Manager: Denise Gibson
Plant Manager: Russ Hohn

27362 **Paramount Industries**
304 N Howard Ave
PO Box 259
Croswell, MI 48422 810-679-2551
Fax: 810-679-4045 800-521-5405
piisales@paramountlighting.com
www.paramountlighting.com
High performance lighting for specialized environments
President: Craig Bailey
VP Sales: Derryl Fewins
Sales: Angie Smiley
Plant Manager: Jim Jarchow
Estimated Sales: Below $5 Million
Number Employees: 50-99
Square Footage: 45000
Brands:
Aerolux
Cleanroom
Craft Lite
Guardcraft
Techniseal
Vandalume

27363 **(HQ)Paramount ManufacturingCompany**
353 Middlesex Ave
Wilmington, MA 01887 978-657-4300
Fax: 978-658-5215
info@paramountmanufacturing.com
www.paramountmanufacturing.com
Store fixtures, cafeteria counters and table and wall units
Owner: Louis Tarantino
Estimated Sales: $2.5-5 Million
Number Employees: 10-19

27364 **Paramount Packaging Corp.**
1221 Old Walt Whitman Road
Melville, NY 11747 516-333-8100
Fax: 516-333-9720 ppc735@aol.com
www.paramountpackagingcorp.com
Designer and builder of custom food equipment and machinery that include sanitary conveyor system, reciprocating nose conveyor/feeder system, high speed bread product slicing and separating, and band saw bread products slicing andseparating
President: Joe Zabala

27365 **Paramount Packing & Rubber**
4012 Belle Grove Rd
Baltimore, MD 21225 410-789-2233
Fax: 410-789-2238 866-727-7225
info@paramountpacking.com
www.paramountpacking.com
Gaskets
President: William Huber
CEO: James Huber
Vice President: Byron Huber
Quality Control: Joe Kammerzel
Sales Director: Joel Hayer
Estimated Sales: $500,000-$1 Million
Number Employees: 5-9
Number of Brands: 100
Number of Products: 85
Square Footage: 7500
Type of Packaging: Consumer

27366 **Parasol Awnings**
4834 Hickory Hill Rd
Memphis, TN 38141 901-368-4477
Fax: 901-368-1798 sales@parasolawnings.com
www.parasolawnings.com
Commercial awnings
Manager: Michael Folk
Chief Manager: Michael Fold
Estimated Sales: $2.5-5 Million
Number Employees: 10-19

27367 **Paratherm Corporation**
31 Portland Rd
Conshohocken, PA 19428 610-941-4900
Fax: 610-941-9191 800-222-3611
info@paratherm.com www.paratherm.com
Manufacturer and exporter of food-grade heat transfer fluids for precise and uniform temperature control in food processing applications
President: John Fuhr
Research & Development: Jim Oetinger
Marketing Director: Andy Andrews
Sales Director: Jim Oetinger
Public Relations: Greg Gaul
Purchasing Manager: Anne Grabowski
Estimated Sales: $2.5-5 Million
Number Employees: 1-4
Number of Brands: 1
Number of Products: 9
Square Footage: 10000
Brands:
Paratherm Nf
Paratherm Or

27368 **Pariser Industries**
91 Michigan Ave
Paterson, NJ 07503 973-569-9090
Fax: 973-569-9101 800-370-7627
info@pariserchem.com www.pariserchem.com
Manufacturer and exporter of warewashing detergents, water-treatment chemicals and institutional maintenance products. Products include laundry chemicals, soaps and detergents
Owner: Andrew Pariser
VP: Andrew Pariser
VP: Scott Pariser
Estimated Sales: $10-20 Million
Number Employees: 20-49
Type of Packaging: Consumer, Food Service, Private Label, Bulk

27369 **Parish Manufacturing**
7430 New Augusta Rd
Indianapolis, IN 46268 317-872-0172
Fax: 317-872-1242 800-592-2268
www.parishmfg.com
Manufacturer and exporter of bag-in-box liquid packaging systems
President: Dan Cunningham
Estimated Sales: $10-20 Million
Number Employees: 20-49
Square Footage: 28000
Type of Packaging: Consumer, Food Service, Bulk

27370 **Parisi/Royal Store Fixture**
305 Pheasant Run
Newtown, PA 18940-3423 215-968-6677
Fax: 215-968-3580 sales@parisi-royal.com
www.parisi-royal.com
Manufacturer and exporter of bars, booths, counters, tabletops and buffet equipment; also, bakery, confectionery and deli display cases
President: Joseph Parisi
CFO: Gary Graf
Marketing Director: Eleanor Parisi
Sales Director: Dave Moore
Sales: Bill Matnias
Operations Manager: Steve Dickier
Estimated Sales: $10 - 20 Million
Number Employees: 20-49
Square Footage: 90000

27371 **(HQ)Parisian Novelty Company**
17859 Tipton Ave
Homewood, IL 60430 773-847-1212
Fax: 773-847-2608

Printed plastic signs and labels
General Manager: Norman Weinberg
Estimated Sales: less than $500,000
Number Employees: 50-100

27372 **Parity Corporation**
11812 N Creek Pkwy N Ste 204
Bothell, WA 98011 425-408-9511
Fax: 425-487-2317 Info@ParitCorp.com
www.paritycorp.com
Manufacturer and exporter of accounting, systems integration and inventory control software
Owner: Arvid Tellevik
R & D: John Ratliff
VP: George Fletcher
Office Administrator: Cindy Kouremetis
Estimated Sales: $5-10,000,000
Number Employees: 20-49
Square Footage: 2000

27373 **Parity Corporation**
11812 N Creek Pkwy N
Suite 204
Bothell, WA 98011-8202 425-408-9511
Fax: 425-487-2317 Info@ParityCorp.com
www.paritycorp.com
Develops specialized software and related services for the food industry; industry specific business management tools
Owner: Arvid Tellevik
Estimated Sales: $5-10 Million
Number Employees: 20-49

27374 **Park Custom Molding**
940 S Park Avenue
Linden, NJ 07036-1646 908-486-8882
Fax: 908-486-1376
Plastic packaging products
VP Sales: Edward Joffe
Estimated Sales: $2.5-5 Million
Number Employees: 20-49

27375 **Park Place Machinery**
2120 Addmore Ln
Clarksville, IN 47129-9151 812-283-7963
Fax: 812-283-7992
in@precisionautomationinc.com
www.precisionautomation.com
Estimated Sales: $1 - 3 Million
Number Employees: 1-4

27376 **Parker Hannifin Corporation/Industrial Hose Products Division**
17295 Foltz Industrial Parkway
Strongsville, OH 44149-5525 440-268-2120
Fax: 440-268-2230 800-272-7537
epic@parker.com www.parker.com
Food and beverage hoses with internally expanded couplings; internal expansion crimpers available
President: Donald Washkewicz
Vice President: Michael Hiemstra
Principal: Robert Griffin
VP (OEM Sales): Jake Boland
Sales Manager: Joe Lepone
Operations Manager: Jack Myslenski
Number Employees: 30
Parent Co: Mark IV Industries

27377 **Parker Hannifin Corporation**
6035 Parkland Blvd
Cleveland, OH 44124 609-586-5151
Fax: 216-896-4000 www.parker.com
Motion control technologies and systems, providing precision-engineered solutions
President & Chief Executive Officer: Donald Washkewicz
Executive VP Finance/Admin. & CFO: Jon Marten
Executive VP Human Resources: Daniel Serbin
Executive VP & Chief Operating Officer: Lee Banks
Estimated Sales: $13.1 Billion
Number Employees: 59,300

27378 **Parker Hannifin Corporation**
6650 Telecom Dr Ste 165
Indianapolis, IN 46278 317-275-8300
Fax: 317-275-8410 800-272-7537
dperorazio@parker.com www.parker.com
Filtration products including filter bags, cartridges and systems
Controller: Dave Gordon
Market Sales Manager: Jim Schmitz
General Manager: David Perorazio
Estimated Sales: $10-20,000,000
Number Employees: 20-49
Parent Co: Parker Hannifin Corporation
Brands:
Fulflo

27379 **Parker Hannifin Corporation**
PO Box 1262
Tewksbury, MA 01876-0962 800-343-4048
Fax: 978-858-0635 800-343-4048
info@puredraft.com www.puredraft.com
Hydraulic, pneumatic and electrochemical motion control components and systems including filtration devices, fittings, valves, etc
OEM Sales: Robert Daly
Number Employees: 500-999

27380 **Parker Sales & Service**
69 Parker Lane
Sparta, NC 28675-8341 336-372-2812
Fax: 336-372-4119 filtersrus@skybest.com
www.psasinc.com
Dust collection filters
Owner: Sam Walker
Estimated Sales: $5-10 Million
Number Employees: 20-49
Square Footage: 40000

27381 **Parkland**
PO Box 266342
Houston, TX 77207-6342 713-926-5055
Fax: 713-926-7358
Manufacturer and exporter of air conditioners, refrigerators and heating and ventilation equipment
President: J P Landers
Office Manager: John Rosales
Number Employees: 10
Type of Packaging: Food Service

27382 **Parkson Corporation**
PO Box 408399
Fort Lauderdale, FL 33340-8399 954-974-6610
Fax: 954-974-6182 www.parkson.com
Supplier of innovative, cost effective solutions for potable water, process water, and industrial and municipal wasterwater problems.
President/CEO: Zain Mahmood
Estimated Sales: G
Number Employees: 250-499
Parent Co: Axel Johnson Company

27383 **(HQ)Parkson Corporation**
368 Timber Dr
Berkeley Heights, NJ 07922-1764 908-464-0700
Fax: 908-464-0703
Manufacturer and exporter of bulk material conveyors, bucket elevators and slide and diverter gates; importer of shaftless spirals
Owner: Steven Lombardi
Director Marketing: Charlene Low
Estimated Sales: $1-2.5 Million
Number Employees: 10-19
Square Footage: 60000
Parent Co: Conelco
Brands:
Corra-Trough

27384 **Parkson Illinois**
562 E Bunker Court
Vernon Hills, IL 60061-1831 847-816-3700
Fax: 847-816-3707 technology@parkson.com
www.parkson.com
Provider of equipment and systems for water/process water and wastewater treatment including screens, sand filters, dewatering presses, inclined plate clarifiers, conveyors, filter presses, sludge thickeners and thermodryers andaeration
President: Axel Johnson, Inc
CEO: William Acton
Marketing Director: Charlene Low
Sales Director: Michael Miller
Number Employees: 100
Parent Co: Parkson Corporation
Brands:
American Bulk Conveyors
Hycor Screening & Dewatering Equip.
Parkson Dynasand Gravity Filters
Parkson Lamella Plate Settlers

27385 **Parkway Plastics**
561 Stelton Rd
Piscataway, NJ 08854-3868 732-752-3636
Fax: 732-752-2192 sales@parkwayjars.com
www.parkwayjars.com
Manufacturer and exporter of polystyrene, linear polyethylene and polypropylene jars, bottles, boxes and caps
President: Edward Rowan
Estimated Sales: $10 - 20 Million
Number Employees: 50-99

27386 **Parlor City Paper Box Company**
PO Box 756
Binghamton, NY 13902-0756 607-772-0600
Fax: 607-772-0806 parcitybox@aol.com
Manufacturer and exporter of trays and printed folding boxes
President: David Culver
Sales/Marketing: Jeffrey Culver
Office Manager: Juanita Mendez
Estimated Sales: $5-10 Million
Number Employees: 20-49
Square Footage: 102000

27387 **Parsons Manufacturing Corp.**
1055 Obrien Dr
Menlo Park, CA 94025 650-324-4726
Fax: 650-324-3051
Manufacturer and exporter of sample cases, tote boxes, travel cases and shipping cases
Owner: Alan Parsons
VP Sales/Marketing: Steve Wurzer
Estimated Sales: $20-50 Million
Number Employees: 20-49

27388 **Partex Corporation**
G-4415 Richfield Road
Flint, MI 48506 810-736-5656
Fax: 810-736-5100 partexcorp@msn.com
Parts for ice cream dispensing equipment
Number Employees: 5

27389 **Particle Sizing Systems**
8203 Kristel Circle
Port Richey, FL 34668 727-846-0866
Fax: 727-846-0865 sales@pssnicomp.com
www.pssnicomp.com
Particle sizers
President: David Nicoli
Finance Manager: Carrey Hasapidis
Bookkeeper: Inge Griffith
Head Marketing: Patrick Ohagen
Head Production: Chris Rowan
Purchasing Manager: Ray Ruttan
Estimated Sales: $2.5 - 5 Million
Number Employees: 20-49
Square Footage: 12000

27390 **Partner Pak**
5322 Oceanus Dr # 101
Huntington Beach, CA 92649-1031 714-799-7879
Fax: 714-799-2858 info@partnerpak.com
www.partnerpak.com
Owner: Paul Appelbaum
Estimated Sales: $1 - 3 Million
Number Employees: 1-4

27391 **Partners International**
PO Box 27
Hanover, NH 03755-0027 603-643-8574
Fax: 603-643-3835
Consultant specializing in international acquisitions and export development
VP: Joan Drape
Estimated Sales: $1 - 5 Million

27392 **Partnership Resources, Inc.**
1069 10th Avenue SE
Minneapolis, MN 55414 612-331-2075
Fax: 612-331-2887 www.partnershipresources.org
Manufacturer and exporter of electric infrared heating systems and based power controllers
Manager: Dan Mc Calister
Chief Executive Officer: Norm Munk
Marketing Manager: James Lee
Chief Operating Officer: Julie Zbaracki
Number Employees: 50-99
Square Footage: 360000
Brands:
Chambir
Controlir
Hi-Tempir
Lineir

Paneir
Spotir
Stripir

27393 Partola Packaging
40 Shuman Blvd Ste 220
Naperville, IL 60563-8483 877-801-9169
Fax: 724-657-8597 800-727-8652
fjanz@portpack.com www.portpack.com
Manufacturer and exporter of tamper evident plastic bottle closures and related capping machinery
President: Tom Blaskow
CEO: Jack Watts
R&D: Borilla
Quality Control: Jee Book
Director: Bill Lauderbaugh
Sales/Marketing Manager: Don Kirk
General Manager: Alex Williams
Estimated Sales: $10 - 20 Million
Number Employees: 50-99
Parent Co: Partola Packaging
Other Locations:
Partola Packaging
Chino CA

27394 Party Linens
7780 S Dante Ave
Chicago, IL 60619 773-731-9281
Fax: 773-731-7669 800-281-0003
www.partylinens.com
Manufacturer and importer of specialty linens and table skirting for various table shapes
Owner: Ed Denormandie
Estimated Sales: $2.5-5 Million
Number Employees: 10-19
Square Footage: 10000
Parent Co: DeNormandie Towel & Linen

27395 Party Perfect Catering
3030 Audley Street
Houston, TX 77098-1926 713-522-3932
Fax: 713-522-1746 800-522-5440
rmeric@partyperfect.net www.partyperfect.net
Catering, event and kitchen production software
Owner: Ruth Meric
Sales Manager: Kelly Folk

27396 Party Yards
950 S Winter Park Drive
Suite 101
Casselberry, FL 32707-5451 407-696-9440
Fax: 407-696-6963 877-501-4400
partyyards@aol.com www.partyyards.com
Manufacturer, importer and exporter of plastic cups
VP: Andrew Baron
Sales Contact: Peter Dorney
Estimated Sales: $2.5-5 Million
Number Employees: 5-9
Square Footage: 48000
Parent Co: Party Yards
Brands:
Glow
Glow Shots
Party Yards

27397 Parvin Manufacturing Company
6033 W Century Blvd # 1180
Los Angeles, CA 90045-6424 310-645-4411
Fax: 323-585-0427 800-648-0770
www.parvinmfg.com
Manufacturer, importer and exporter of protective clothing and supplies including oven/barbecue mitts, aprons, skillet handle covers and insulated pizza delivery bags
Owner: Michael Provan
VP: Rick Resnick
Estimated Sales: $10-20 Million
Number Employees: 5-9
Square Footage: 34000
Brands:
Flameguard
Footguard
Pro-Cut

27398 Pasco
2600 S Hanley Rd Ste 450
Saint Louis, MO 63144 314-781-2212
Fax: 314-781-9986 800-489-3300
pasco@pascosystems.com
www.pascosystems.com
Manufacturer and exporter of packaging machinery including slipsheet and pallet dispensers and bag, drum, pail and case palletizers
President: Tim Elfrink
CFO: Teresa Ovelgoenner
Executive VP: Sandy Elfrink
Sales Manager: Darin Everett
Estimated Sales: $10-20,000,000
Number Employees: 20-49
Square Footage: 25000

27399 Pasco Poly Tank
407 River Dock Rd
Weiser, ID 83672-5819 208-549-1861
Fax: 208-549-0530 www.pascopoly.com
Wine industry tanks
Chairman of the Board: David D Rule
Estimated Sales: $1 - 5 Million
Number Employees: 5-9

27400 Pasquini Espresso
1501 W Olympic Blvd
Los Angeles, CA 90015-3803 213-739-0480
Fax: 213-385-8774 800-724-6225
pasquini@pasquini.com www.pasquini.com
Manufacturer and exporter of commercial espresso equipment
President: Ambrose Pasquini
VP: Guy Pasquini
National Sales Manager: Sergio Laganiere
Estimated Sales: Below $5 Million
Number Employees: 20-49
Square Footage: 24000
Type of Packaging: Food Service

27401 Pasta Filata International
154 Pine Street
Montclair, NJ 07042-4910 973-744-6640
Fax: 973-744-1488
Estimated Sales: $1 - 5 Million
Number Employees: 2

27402 Pasta Montana
1 Pasta Pl
Great Falls, MT 59401 406-761-1516
Fax: 406-761-1403
comments@pastamontana.com
www.pastamontana.com
24 dry pastas ranging from petite shells and orzo to fettuccine
President: Yasuhiko Harada
CFO: Craig Smith
Vice President: Randy Gilbertson
Quality Control: John Lacanilao
Sales Director: Buzz Weisman
Operations Manager: Kelly Easley
Plant Manager: Stephen SaPerite
Purchasing Manager: Tony Koslosky
Estimated Sales: $10-20 Million
Number Employees: 100-249
Square Footage: 30000
Type of Packaging: Consumer, Food Service, Private Label, Bulk

27403 Pate International
2350 Taylor St
Suite 1
San Francisco, CA 94133 415-928-4400
Fax: 415-928-0690 info@pateinternational.com
www.pateinternational.com
Wine industry packaging
President: Susan Pate
Estimated Sales: Below $5 Million
Number Employees: 1-4

27404 Pater & Associates
P.O.Box 54884
Cincinnati, OH 45254 513- 24- 215
Fax: 513-474-4829 payday11@aol.com
Printed and plain flexible packaging films, pouches, and bags; folding paperboard cartons; bag closing equipment and loks
Owner: James Pater Jr
CFO: James Pater Jr
Sales: James Pater Jr
Purchasing Director: James Pater Jr

27405 Patio Center Inc
1507 Eraste Landry Rd
Lafayette, LA 70506 337-233-9896
Fax: 337-232-7178 patiocenter@patiocenter.com
www.patiocenter.com
Commercial awnings
President: Herman D Richard
VP: Ryan Richard
Estimated Sales: Below $5 Million
Number Employees: 20-49

27406 Patio King
10744 SW 190th St
Cutler Bay, FL 33157 786-258-8508
www.patioking.com
Gas and charcoal outside and commercial barbecues for restaurants
Supervisor: Humberto Gonzalez
Secretary: Edith Garcia
Estimated Sales: $1-2.5 Million
Number Employees: 1
Square Footage: 3000

27407 Patlite Corporation
20130 S. Western Ave
Torrance, CA 90501 310-328-3222
Fax: 310-328-2676 888-214-2580
sales@patlite.com www.patlite.com
Visual and audible warning devices
President: Fumio Sawamura
Sales: Sandra Rodriguez

27408 Patrick & Company
2100 Stemmons Freeway
Suite 2927
Dallas, TX 75207 214-761-0900
Fax: 800-397-4647
info@patrickandcompany.com
www.patrickandcompany.com
Metal signs, name plates, badges, office supplies, stationery and furniture
Owner: James M Patrick
Sales Manager: Mark Rodby
Estimated Sales: $500,000-$1 Million
Number Employees: 10-19

27409 Patrick E. Panzarello Consulting Services
8001 Grove Street
Sunland, CA 91040-2111 818-353-0431
Fax: 818-951-6638 panzpaar@aol.com
www.patrickpanzarello.com
Consultant specializing in architectural design services, health department permits
President: Patrick Panzarello
CEO: Mike Hess
CFO: Ed Navaratte
Estimated Sales: 200000

27410 Patrick Signs
5411 Randolph Rd
Rockville, MD 20852 301-770-6200
Fax: 301-770-0083 jpn123@prodigy.net
www.patricksigns.com
Signs; also, installation services available
Owner: Constance Nusbaum
Estimated Sales: $1 - 5 Million
Number Employees: 20-49

27411 Patterson Fan Company
1120 Northpoint Blvd
Blythewood, SC 29016-8873 803-691-4750
Fax: 803-691-4751 800-768-3985
info@pattersonfan.com www.pattersonfan.com
Industrial fans, air movement equipment
President: Vance Patterson
Regional Manager: Albert Howell
Vice President, Chief Operating Officer: Thomas Salisbury
Estimated Sales: $10-20 Million
Number Employees: 50-99

27412 Patterson Industries
250 Danforth Road
Scarborough, ON M1L 3X4
Canada 416-694-3381
Fax: 416-691-2768 800-336-1110
process@pattersonindustries.com
www.pattersonindustries.com

Designers, engineers and manufacturers of quality time proven equipment for the food industries; Ribbon and Paddle mikers, ThoroBlender Double Cone Blenders, Conaform Double Cone Vacuum Dryers, Ribbon and Paddle type round bodydryers, pressure vessels and heat exchangers and general mixing and agitation equipment
President: H Haischt
CFO: Seth Mendonza
Research & Development: Mike Lindsey
Sales Director: M Lindsey
Estimated Sales: $2,500,000
Number Employees: 10-20
Square Footage: 120000
Brands:
Conaform
Thoroblender

27413 **(HQ)Patterson Laboratories**
11930 Pleasant Street
Detroit, MI 48217-1620 313-843-4500
Fax: 313-843-9416
Industrial chemicals and cleaners including bottled ammonia, bleaches, window cleaners and detergents
VP Produce: Darrell Cardwell
Administration: Richard Hodgkinson
Estimated Sales: $1 - 5 Million
Number Employees: 50-99
Square Footage: 90000
Brands:
Blue Ribbon
Ful-Value
Steer Clear

27414 **(HQ)Patterson-KelleyHars Company**
PO Box 458
East Stroudsburg, PA 18301-0458 570-421-7500
Fax: 570-421-8735 www.patkelco.com
Batch and continuous blenders, dryers, compact water heaterand gas fired boilers for commercial, institutional and industrial applications
Manager: Mark Lasewicz
Marketing Director: Ruth Ann Rocchio
Sales Manager: Jef Potters
Estimated Sales: $35 Million
Number Employees: 100-249
Square Footage: 200000
Brands:
Cross-Flow
Twin-Shell
Zig-Zag

27415 **Patty Paper, Inc.**
1955 North Oak Drive
Plymouth, IN 46563 574-935-8439
Fax: 574-936-6053 800-782-1703
www.pattypaper.com
Manufacturer and supplier of specialty papers for wrapping meat, cheese and deli items, bakery style picking paper and waxed paper.

27416 **Patty-O-Matic**
PO Box 404
Farmingdale, NJ 07727-0404 732-938-2757
Fax: 732-938-5809 877-938-5244
info@pattyomatic.com www.pattyomatic.com
Molding equipment for meat, seafood, vegetables, etc.; also, meat preparation machinery, portion control equipment and weight control equipment
President: Bernard Miles
Sales Director: Daniel Miles
Estimated Sales: $1-2.5 Million
Number Employees: 5-9
Brands:
Patty-O-Matic

27417 **Paul G. Gallin Company**
222 Saint Johns Avenue
Yonkers, NY 10704-2717 914-964-5800
Fax: 914-964-5293 cgctradingintl@aol.com
Manufacturer and exporter of uniforms and accessories
Estimated Sales: $25-50 Million
Number Employees: 18
Square Footage: 12000
Type of Packaging: Bulk

27418 **Paul Hawkins Lumber Company**
RT 2 Box 387A
Mannington, WV 26582 304-986-2230
Wooden lift truck pallets
Owner: Paul Hawkins
Estimated Sales: $2.5-5 Million
Number Employees: 19-Oct

27419 **Paul Mueller Company**
P.O.Box 828
Springfield, MO 65801 417-831-3000
Fax: 417-575-9669 800-683-5537
processing@muel.com www.muel.com
Specializes in the design and manufacture of stainless steel processing systems and equipment for the food, dairy, beverage, chemical, pharaceutical, biotechnology, and pure water industries. Also the erection of vessels in the fieldexpanded scope, transportation and electrical controls.
Chairman Emeritus/Founder: Paul Mueller
CEO/President: Matt Deterson
CFO/VP: Don Gosik
R&D: William Allison
Quality Control: Duane Shaw
Marketing: Paul Hume
Public Relations: Kim Pridgeon
Operations/Production: Jerry Cedutti
Plant Manager: Roger Smith
Estimated Sales: $200 Million
Number Employees: 900
Square Footage: 975000
Other Locations:
Osceola IA
Brands:
Accu-Therm
Avalanche
Maximice
Pyropure
Sentry Ii
Temp Plate
Vapure

27420 **Paul O. Abbe**
P.O.Box 80
Bensenville, IL 60106-0080 630-350-2200
Fax: 630-350-9047 sales@pauloabbe.com
www.aaronequipment.com
Manufacturer and exporter of tumble and agitated mixers and blenders for powders and solids; also, batch vacuum and fluidized dryers and ball and pebble mills
VP: Alan Cohen
Vice President of Business Development: Bruce Baird
Estimated Sales: $5-10 Million
Number Employees: 20-49
Square Footage: 140000
Brands:
Fluidized
Forberg Ii
Rota-Blade
Rota-Cone

27421 **Paul O. Abbe**
139 Center Avenue
Little Falls, NJ 07424-2220 973-256-4242
Fax: 973-256-0041 sales@pauloabbe.com
www.pauloabbe.com
Chemical processing equipment: ball and pebble mills, vacuum dryers, blenders and mixers
VP: Allen Cohen
Estimated Sales: $10-20 Million
Number Employees: 4

27422 **Paul T. Freund Corporation**
P.O.Box 130
Palmyra, NY 14522 315-597-4873
Fax: 315-597-4188 800-333-0091
info@ptfreund.com www.ptfreund.com
Set-up, paper covered and candy boxes
CEO: Paul Freund Jr
VP Marketing: Thomas Farnham
Estimated Sales: $10-20 Million
Number Employees: 100-249

27423 **Pavailler Distribution Company**
232 Pegasus Avenue
Northvale, NJ 07647-1904 201-767-0766
Fax: 201-767-1723 gerard@pavailler-usa.com
www.pavailler-usa.com
Bakery equipment
Estimated Sales: $2.5-5 Million
Number Employees: 9
Square Footage: 22400

27424 **Pavan USA, Inc.**
PO Box 505
Emigsville, PA 17318 717-767-4889
Fax: 717-767-4656 infor@pavanusainc.com
www.pavan.com
President: Dave C Parent
VP/General Manager: David Parent
Estimated Sales: $1-3 Million
Number Employees: 1-4
Square Footage: 20000
Parent Co: Pavan SrL
Brands:
Mapimpianti
Pavan
Toresani

27425 **Paxall**
7300 Monticello Ave
Skokie, IL 60076-4025 847-677-7800
Fax: 847-677-7139
Tea and coffee industry packaging machines
Estimated Sales: $1 - 5 Million
Number Employees: 1-4

27426 **Paxar**
500 E 35th Street
Paterson, NJ 07504-1720 973-684-6564
Fax: 973-684-0235
Woven labels
Estimated Sales: $20-50 Million
Number Employees: 20-49

27427 **Paxon Polymer Company**
Baton Rouge
Baton Rouge, LA 70892 225-775-4330
Fax: 225-774-6632
Estimated Sales: $1 - 5 Million

27428 **Paxton Corporation**
86 Tupelo St
Unit 5
Bristol, RI 02809
Fax: 203-925-8722 paxton@paxtoncorp.com
www.paxcor.com
Food processing machines such as cutters, slicers, shredders, dicers, graters, and strip cutters, for vegetables, fruits, cheeses, and nuts
CFO: Monica Wingard
Sales Director: Steven King
Estimated Sales: $3 - 5 Million
Number Employees: 12
Square Footage: 15000
Brands:
Alexanderwerk
Hallde
Paxton

27429 **Paxton North America**
5300 Port Royal Road
Springfield, VA 22151 703-321-7600
Fax: 703-321-9426 800-336-4536
info@paxton.com www.paxton.com
Plastic tote containers and bulk boxes
Estimated Sales: Below $500,000
Number Employees: 7

27430 **Paxton Products**
10125 Carver Rd
Cincinnati, OH 45242 513-891-7474
Fax: 513-891-4092 800-441-7475
sales@paxtonproducts.com
www.paxtonproducts.com
Manufacturer and exporter of air delivery systems for drying and blowoff during packaging, coding and labelling. High efficiency centrifugal blowers, air knives and nozzles.
National Sales Manager: Rick Immell
Estimated Sales: $20 - 50 Million
Number Employees: 20-49
Parent Co: Illinois Tool Works
Brands:
Cold Air Gun
Cold Pump
Curtain Transvector
Hand-E-Vac
Round Transvector
Vortex Cooler

27431 **Paxton Products**
10125 Carver Rd
Cincinnati, OH 45242 513-891-7485
Fax: 513-891-4092 800-441-7475
sales@paxtonproducts.com
www.paxtonproducts.com

A leader in energy saving, application-specific air systems. Designs and manufactures compact, energy-efficient compressors, blowers, air knives and drying systems.
General Manager: Barbara Stefl
Engineering Manager: Steve Pucciani
Quality Control: Charlie Hertel
International Sales Manager: Rick Immell
Customer Service: Anne Tomsic
Operations Manager: Stan Coley
Buyer: Sherry Driskell
Number Employees: 20-49

27432 Payne Engineering
PO Box 70
Scott Depot, WV 25560 304-757-7353
Fax: 304-757-7305 800-331-1345
info@PaynEng.com www.payneng.com
Manufacturer and exporter of motor controls for material handling equipment and SCR controls for ovens and process temperature controls
President: Henry Payne
Manager Marketing Services: Jean Miller
Estimated Sales: $5-10 Million
Number Employees: 10-19
Square Footage: 36000
Brands:
Sentrol 31
Sentrol Em3

27433 Peace Industries
1100 Hicks Rd
Rolling Meadows, IL 60008-1016 847-259-9236
Fax: 847-259-9236 800-873-2239
pchartier@spotnails.com www.spotnails.com
Manufactures a wide range of industrial fastening products including nails, staples, pins, brads and tools for use in packaging, furniture/woodworking, construction, factory-built housing and many other industries.
President: Mark R Wilson
CFO: Rex Janderman
Vice President: Win Waterman
Marketing Director: Candi Mortenson
Sales Director: Win Waterman
Plant Manager: Sy Akbari
Purchasing Manager: Alice Mortenson
Estimated Sales: $10 - 20 Million
Number Employees: 50-99
Type of Packaging: Bulk

27434 (HQ)Peacock Crate Factory
225 Cash St
PO Box 1110
Jacksonville, TX 75766 903-586-0988
Fax: 903-586-7476 800-657-2200
peacockdisplay@suddenlink.net
www.peacockdisplay.com
Manufacturer and exporter of wood veneer gift, fruit and vegetable baskets; also, store fixtures and displays
President: Richard S Peacock
CFO: Claudia Vastal
Vice President: Speedy Peacock
Estimated Sales: Below $5 Million
Number Employees: 20-49
Other Locations:
Peacock Crate Factory
Jacksonville TX

27435 Pearson Packaging
8120 W. Sunset Hwy.
Spokane, WA 99224 509-838-6226
Fax: 509-747-8532 800-732-7766
sales@goodmanpkg.com www.goodmanpkg.com
Case/tray packaging equipment
CEO: James A Goodman
President, Chief Executive Officer: Michael Senske
Vice President of Engineering: Leo Robertson
President: Billy Goodman
Vice President of Sales and Marketing: Randy Denny
Number Employees: 50-99

27436 Pearson Packaging Systems
8120 W Sunset Hwy
Spokane, WA 99224-9048 509-838-6226
Fax: 509-747-8532 800-732-7766
info@pearsonpkg.com www.pearsonpkg.com
Manufacturer and exporter of case forming, case packing, tray forming, bottom, top or end sealing, carrier erecting, multipacking, partition and bag inserting machinery, and magazine feeding machinery
President: Michael Senske
CEO: Michael Senske
CFO: Randy Bell
Vice President of Engineering: Leo Robertson
Marketing/Sales: Mark Ewing
Vice President of Sales and Marketing: Randy Denny
Estimated Sales: $10 - 20 Million
Number Employees: 100-249
Square Footage: 110000
Type of Packaging: Food Service, Private Label, Bulk

27437 Pearson Research
PO Box 1778
Santa Cruz, CA 95061 831-429-9797
Fax: 831-426-7010 info@pearsonresearch.com
www.pearsonresearch.com
Consultant specializing in market research, survey design, consumer tests, sensory evaluation, focus groups, etc
Owner: Adrian Pearson
Number Employees: 1-4

27438 Pearson Signs Service
2031 Hanover Pike
Hampstead, MD 21074-1336 410-239-3838
Fax: 410-239-3848 tshaffer7@aol.com
Signs including metal, wood, paper, plastic and neon
Owner: Herb Shaffer
Estimated Sales: $1 - 5 Million
Number Employees: 5-9
Square Footage: 3000

27439 Pecan Deluxe Candy Company
2570 Lone Star Dr
Dallas, TX 75212 214-631-3669
Fax: 214-631-5833 800-733-3589
pdcc_info@pecandeluxe.com
www.pecandeluxe.com
Processor and exporter of ingredients for frozen desserts and baked goods including toffees, praline nuts, chocolate coated items, flavor bases, sauces, etc.; also, nonfat and nonsugar ingredients available
President: Jay Brigham
Chairman of the Board: Bennie Brigham
Chief Financial Officer: Keith Hurd
Chief Operating Officer: Tim Markowicz
VP Quality Assurance: Rick Hintermeier
VP Operations: Mike Cavin
Inventory/Production Coordinator: Wayne Miller
Plant Manager: Mike Cavin
Purchasing Manager: James Mitchell
Estimated Sales: $20 - 50 Million
Number Employees: 100-249
Number of Products: 2000
Square Footage: 63000
Type of Packaging: Bulk

27440 Pechiney Plastic Packagiing
716 Tanager Lane
West Chicago, IL 60185-5949 630-293-8050
Fax: 630-293-8064 davequinn@pechiney.com
www.alcan.com
Food Sales/Marketing: David Quinn
Estimated Sales: $1 - 5 Million
Type of Packaging: Consumer

27441 Pechiney Plastic Packaging
8770 W Bryn Mawr Ave
Chicago, IL 60631 773-399-0255
Fax: 773-399-8549
webmaster@pechineyplasticpackaging.com
www.pechineyplasticpackaging.com
Flexible packaging and plastic bottles
President: Ilene Gordon
CFO: Robert Mosesian
Quality Control: Rey Brunelle
Estimated Sales: $20 - 50 Million
Number Employees: 250-499

27442 (HQ)Peco Controls Corporation
48041 Fremont Blvd
Modesto, CA 95351 510-226-6686
Fax: 510-226-6687 800-732-6285
info@pecocontrols.com www.pecocontrols.com
Manufacturer and exporter of monitors for inspecting fill and vacuum/pressure levels, contents and labels of packages; also, automatic container sampling systems and two-piece can metrology systems
President: F Allan Anderson
Vice President: Aslam Khan
Quality Control: Cheong Chan
Estimated Sales: $3 - 5 Million
Number Employees: 35
Square Footage: 32000
Type of Packaging: Consumer, Private Label
Other Locations:
Peco Controls Corp.
Pershore, Wozos
Brands:
Criterion
Gamma 101p
Sample Trac
Vac Trac
Valv-Chek

27443 Peekskill Hair Net
201 S Division Street
Peekskill, NY 10566-3611 914-737-1524
Fax: 914-788-3890
Acetate, nylon and rayon protective hair nets and caps
President: John Kotowski
Secretary/Bookkeeper: Gertrude DeFazio
Treasurer: John Kotowski
Number Employees: 10
Square Footage: 6000

27444 Peerless Cartons
1073 Martingale Drive
Bartlett, IL 60103-5676 312-226-7952
Fax: 312-226-6861
Folding cartons
President: Larry Mitchell
Estimated Sales: $2.5-5 Million
Number Employees: 19

27445 Peerless Conveyor and Manufacturing Corporation
201 E Quindaro Blvd
Kansas City, KS 66115 913-342-2240
Fax: 913-342-2237 www.peerlessconveyor.com
Conveyors and conveying equipment for bulk materials including grain sugar
President: William S Walker
Sales Director: Chuck Leonard
Production Manager: Seth Rodriquez
Estimated Sales: $2.5 - 5 Million
Number Employees: 20-49
Square Footage: 80000

27446 Peerless Dough Mixing and Make-Up
P.O.Box 769
Sidney, OH 45365-0769 937-492-4158
Fax: 937-492-3688 800-999-3327
sales@peerlessgroup.us
www.thepeerlessgroup.us
Dough machinery
President: Dane Belden
Chairman/CEO: Robert Zielsdorf
Estimated Sales: $20 - 50 Million
Number Employees: 100-249

27447 Peerless Food Equipment
500 S Vandemark Road
Sidney, OH 45365-0769 937-492-4158
Fax: 937-492-3688 info@petersmachinery.com
www.thepeerlessgroup.us
Manufacturer and exporter of food processing machinery including stackers and cookie sandwiching and wrapping equipment
General Manager: George Hoff
Controller: David Alexander
Director, Marketing And Customer Support: Sherri Swabb
Sales Director: Richard Taylor
Human Resource Manager: Kathy Weldy
Plant And Materials Manager: Mike Gniazdowski
Estimated Sales: $7 Million
Number Employees: 100-249
Parent Co: Peerless Group

27448 Peerless Food Inc
500 S Vandemark Road
Sidney, OH 45365-0769 937-494-2870
www.peerlessfood.com

Manufacturer and exporter of snack food and bakery processing equipment including conveyors, coolers, depositors, icers, mixers, pumps, topping applicators and bagel machinery
General Manager: George Hoff
Director of Marketing: Sherri Swabb
Director of Sales: Richard Taylor
Estimated Sales: 5-10 Million
Number Employees: 50-99
Square Footage: 208000

27449 **Peerless Lighting Corporation**
PO Box 2556
Berkeley, CA 94702-0556 510-845-2760
Fax: 510-845-2776 www.peerless-lighting.com
Manufacturer and exporter of institutional and commercial fluorescent lighting fixtures
President: Douglas Herst
VP: Jim Young
Manager Marketing Services: Margaret Einhorn
Public Relations/Events Manager: Megan Seluate
Estimated Sales: $10-20 Million
Number Employees: 50-99

27450 **Peerless Machine & ToolCorporation**
1804 West Second Street
Marion, IN 46952-0385 765-662-2586
Fax: 765-662-6067
peerlessmt@peerlessmachine.com
www.peerlessmachine.com
Paper converting machinery, paper plates and trays
Owner: Jeff Carson
Estimated Sales: $2.5-5 Million
Number Employees: 20-49

27451 **(HQ)Peerless Machinery Corporation**
PO Box 769
Sidney, OH 45365 937-492-4158
Fax: 937-492-3688 800-999-3327
webbing@peerlessgroup.us
www.thepeerlessgroup.us
Manufacturer and exporter of bakery mixers, dividers, blenders and rounders
President: Dane Belden
Director Marketing: Terry Bartsch
VP Sales: Michael Booth
Estimated Sales: $20-50 Million
Number Employees: 100-249
Square Footage: 75000
Other Locations:
Peerless Machinery Corp.
Odessa FL
Brands:
Hallmark
Peerless
Royal
Supergrain

27452 **Peerless Ovens**
PO Box 859
Sandusky, OH 44870 419-625-4514
Fax: 419-625-4597 800-548-4514
www.peerlessovens.com
Manufacturer and exporter of bakery and pizza ovens, griddles and ranges
President: Bryan Huntley
Estimated Sales: $1-2.5 Million
Number Employees: 5-9
Square Footage: 200000
Type of Packaging: Food Service

27453 **Peerless Packages**
23600 Mercantile Rd # A
Cleveland, OH 44122-5971 216-464-3620
Fax: 216-464-3440 info@peerlesspackages.com
www.peerlesspackages.com
Plastic and paper bags and boxes
Sales: Lynn Harmon
Sales Manager: Lynn Harmon
Estimated Sales: $1-2.5 Million
Number Employees: 5-9

27454 **Peerless of America**
109 Schelter Rd
Lincolnshire, IL 60069-3603 847-634-7500
Fax: 847-634-7506 poa@effingham.net
www.ceu-inc.com
Manufacturer and exporter of refrigeration and air conditioning equipment including evaporators, finned coils, heat transfer products and unit and flash coolers
Owner: Igor Gordon
VP Sales/Marketing: Michael Schopf
Estimated Sales: $20-50 Million
Number Employees: 100-249
Square Footage: 395000

27455 **Peerless-Premier Appliance Company**
PO Box 387
Belleville, IL 62222 618-233-0475
Fax: 618-235-1771 info@premierrange.com
www.premierrange.com
Manufacturer and exporter of gas and electric ranges
President: Joseph Geary
CEO: Alex Volansky
Chairman of the Board: William T Sprague
VP Marketing: Allan Gramlich
National Sales Manager: Robert Volkmann
Estimated Sales: $20 - 50 Million
Number Employees: 250-499
Square Footage: 300000
Brands:
Eagle
Heritage By Orbon
Mark Royal
Modern Chef
Premier

27456 **Peerless-Winsmith**
172 Eaton St
Springville, NY 14141 716-592-9310
Fax: 716-592-9546 winsmith@winsmith.com
www.winsmith.com
Manufacturer and exporter of worm gear speed reducers for material handling conveyors and machinery; also, food processing and bottling machinery
Manager: William Sutton
Quality Control: Demont Bruce
Manager: David McCann
Sales/Marketing Manager: Bill Sutton
Estimated Sales: $100 - 500 Million
Number Employees: 250-499

27457 **Pel-Pak Container**
1107 Dowzer Ave
Pell City, AL 35125 205-338-2993
Fax: 205-338-6120 800-239-2699
Corrugated boxes
President: Jeanette L Chasteen
Plant Manager: Mike Richerzhagen
Number Employees: 19

27458 **Pelco Packaging Corporation**
269 Mercer St.
Stirling, NJ 07980 908-647-3500
Fax: 908-647-1868
customerservice@pelcopackaging.com
www.pelcopackaging.com
Plastic material handling equipment and packaging including boxes
President: Arthur J Brinker
Estimated Sales: $1 - 2.5 Million
Number Employees: 15

27459 **Pelican Displays**
109 E 1st St
Homer, IL 61849-1101 217-896-2628
Fax: 217-896-2628 800-627-1517
mrpelican@net66.com
Wood, polyethylene and acrylic bulk food display bins
Owner: David Lucas
Estimated Sales: $1 - 5 Million
Number Employees: 1-4
Square Footage: 8500

27460 **Pelican Products Company**
1049 Lowell St
Bronx, NY 10459 718-860-3220
Fax: 718-860-4415 800-552-8820
info@pelicanproducts.com
www.pelicanproducts.com
Manufacturer and exporter of molded plastic advertising specialties, imprinted premiums and promotional give-aways including coasters, stirrers, cocktail forks, corkscrews and ball point pens
President: Kenneth Silver
CEO: Harold Silver
Vice President: Dave Silver
Estimated Sales: $2.5 - 5 Million
Number Employees: 20-49
Square Footage: 20000

27461 **Pell Paper Box Company**
PO Box 584
Elizabeth City, NC 27907-0584 252-335-4361
Fax: 252-335-9639 murry@series2000.com
www.pellpaper.com
Set-up and folding boxes for frozen foods, baked goods and promotional and specialty products
COO: P Murry Pitts
General Manager: Tony Rossi
Estimated Sales: $10-20 Million
Number Employees: 50-99
Square Footage: 85000

27462 **Pellenc America**
955 S Virginia Street
Suite 116
Reno, NV 89502-0413 702-853-3455
Fax: 702-853-4554 pellenc@accurek.com
Wine industry pruning equipment

27463 **Pellerin Milnor Corporation**
PO Box 400
Kenner, LA 70063-0400 504-467-9591
Fax: 504-712-3782 800-469-8780
milnorinfo@milnor.com www.milnor.com
A leading commercial and industrial laundry equipment manufacturer. Washer-extractors range in size from 25 lb to 700 lb capacity; dryers from 30-550 lb. These models are available with a variety of controls from very simple to quitesophisticated, depending upon your food and beverage linen needs.
President: James Pellerin
VP: Richard Kelly
Estimated Sales: $100+ Million
Number Employees: 530
Square Footage: 400000
Brands:
E-P Plus
System 7

27464 **Pelouze Scale Company**
7400 W 100th Place
Bridgeview, IL 60455-2438 708-430-8330
Fax: 800-654-7330 800-323-8363
www.pelouze.com
Manufacturer and exporter of mechanical and electronic timers, food thermometers and food portion, dietetic, electronic digital and shipping and receiving scales
VP: Dan Maeir
VP: Dan Maeir
National Sales Manager: Jack Kramer
Customer Service Manager: Laura Anton
Estimated Sales: $50 - 100 Million
Number Employees: 140
Parent Co: Sunbeam
Type of Packaging: Consumer, Food Service

27465 **Pemberton & Associates**
3610 Nashua Drive
Mississauga, ON L4V 1X9
Canada 905-678-8900
Fax: 905-678-8989 800-668-6111
pemco@pemcom.com www.pemcom.com
President: Dennis Hicks
R&D: Keith Tse
Vice President: Bill Froggatt
Number Employees: 20

27466 **Pemberton & Associates**
152 Remsen Street
Brooklyn, NY 11201
Canada 718-923-1111
Fax: 718-923-6065 800-736-2664
career@pencom.com www.pencom.com
Manufacturers full service representative of meat and poultry processing, and packaging equipment
Founder, President: Wade Saadi
Vice President of Operations: Jim Kenner
Number Employees: 15

27467 **Penasack Contract Manufacturer**
49 Sanford St
PO Box 396
Albion, NY 14411-1117 585-589-7044
Fax: 585-589-0046 penasack@rochester.rr.com
www.penasack.com

Manufacturer and fabricator of stainless steel products
President: Gerard Da More
Engineering Manager: Jeff Kinser
Operations: Mike Hrycelak
Estimated Sales: $3-5 Million
Number Employees: 20-49
Square Footage: 40000
Parent Co: GDM Enterprises
Type of Packaging: Food Service, Private Label, Bulk

27468 **Penco Products**
P.O.Box 158
Skippack, PA 19474 610-666-0500
Fax: 610-666-7561 800-562-1000
customerservice@pencoproducts.com
www.pencoproducts.com
Manufacturer and exporter of shelving, work benches, storage cabinets, pallet racks and lockers
President: Greg Grogan
VP Sales/Marketing: Bill Vain
Estimated Sales: $20-50 Million
Number Employees: 250-499
Brands:
Clipper
Erectomatic
Hi-Performance
Rivit Orite

27469 **Pengo Corporation**
13369 60th St SW
Cokato, MN 55321 320-286-5581
Fax: 320-286-5583 800-599-0211
sales@pengocorp.com
www.pengoattachments.com
Custom fabricated conveyor screws for food applications
VP: Brian Richards
Engineering Manager: Eric Matthias
Vice President-Sales/Marketing: Dana Scudder
Human Resources Manager: Connie Groat
Operations Manager: Jim Groat
Product Manager: Mary Pohlman
Division Controller: John Ricke
Estimated Sales: $10-20 Million
Number Employees: 20-49
Square Footage: 42000
Parent Co: Crown Holdings

27470 **Peninsula Plastics Compny**
2800 Auburn Ct
Auburn Hills, MI 48326-3203 248-852-3731
Fax: 248-852-5482 800-394-8698
www.peninsulaplastics.com
Custom vacuum formed packaging products
President: Richard Jositas
Controller/CFO: Grace McKinney
General Manager: Roderick Zielinski
Estimated Sales: $10 - 20 Million
Number Employees: 50-99
Square Footage: 30000

27471 **Penley Corporation**
PO Box 277
West Paris, ME 04289-0277 207-674-2501
Fax: 207-674-2510 800-368-6449
penley@megalink.net
Manufacturer, importer and exporter of wooden toothpicks, matches, chopsticks, etc.; also, plastic cutlery and drinking straws
Owner: Richard Penley
Director Sales/Marketing: Stephen Gilman
Director Manufacturing: Robert Warrington
Estimated Sales: $5-10 Million
Number Employees: 10-19

27472 **Penn Barry**
605 Shiloh Road
Plano, TX 75074 972-212-4700
Fax: 972-212-4701
pennbarrysales@pennbarry.com
www.pennbarry.com
Single source for commercial and industrial ventilation product solutions.
Square Footage: 120000
Parent Co: Air System Components, Inc.
Brands:
Supreme
Bayley Fan
Penn Ventilation
Barry Blower
Industrial Air

27473 **Penn Bottle & Supply Company**
7150 Lindbergh Boulevard
Philadelphia, PA 19153-3008 215-365-5700
Fax: 215-365-2320
Plastic and glass bottles
CEO and President: Richard Probinsky
VP Finance and Administration: Paul Silverman

27474 **Penn Products**
91 Main Street
Portland, CT 06480 860-342-2500
Fax: 860-342-5563 800-490-7366
service@pennproductsusa.com
www.pennproductsusa.com
Custom injection molded plastic boxes and containers
VP Operations: Ray Pennoyer III
Administrator: Raymond Pennoyer Iii
Estimated Sales: $2.5-5 Million
Number Employees: 20-49
Number of Brands: 1
Square Footage: 20000
Type of Packaging: Private Label, Bulk

27475 **Penn Refrigeration Service Corporation**
P.O.Box 1261
Wilkes Barre, PA 18703-1261 570-825-5666
Fax: 570-825-5705 800-233-8354
sales@pennrefrig.com www.pennrefrig.com
Manufacturer and exporter of refrigeration equipment and systems including walk-in coolers and freezers
President: Albert Finarelli Jr
Plant Manager: John Gosciewski
Estimated Sales: $5 - 10 Million
Number Employees: 50-99

27476 **Penn Scale ManufacturingCompany**
150 W Berks St
Philadelphia, PA 19122 215-739-9644
Fax: 215-739-9640 sales@pennscale.com
www.pennscale.com
Scales and scoops
President: Larry Biren
Owner: Andy Levin
Quality Control: Andy Levin
Estimated Sales: $300,000
Number Employees: 5-9
Square Footage: 12000
Brands:
Penn Scale

27477 **Penn-Wheeling Closure**
1701 Wheeling Ave
Glen Dale, WV 26038-1728 304-845-3402
Fax: 304-843-5475 800-999-2567
lcomadena@p-wc.com www.penn-wheeling.com
President: Louis Comadena
CFO: Al Morack
Quality Control: P D Simpson
Estimated Sales: $100+ Million
Number Employees: 100-249

27478 **PennBarry**
605 Shiloh Rd.
Plano, TX 75074 972-212-4700
pennbarrysales@pennbarry.com
www.pennvent.com
Fans and ventilation equipment
Number Employees: 45
Parent Co: Air System Components, Inc.

27479 **PennPac International**
8200 Flourtown Avenue
Suite 6b
Wyndmoor, PA 19038-7969 215-836-1380
Fax: 215-836-7885 rushbs@gateway.net
Plastic containers
*Estimated Sales:*less than $500,000
Number Employees: 1

27480 **Penny Plate**
PO Box 3003
Haddonfield, NJ 08033 856-429-7583
Fax: 856-429-7166 mmiller@pennyplate.com
www.pennyplate.com
Aluminum food service containers
Assistant to CEO: George Buff IV
CEO: George Buff
Estimated Sales: $30 - 50 Million
Number Employees: 100-249

27481 **Pensacola Rope Company**
PO Box 1926
Slidell, LA 70459-1926 850-968-9760
Fax: 850-968-1669
Solid braided nylon cord and rope
President: Thomas Fields
Estimated Sales: $500,000-$1 Million
Number Employees: 4

27482 **Penske Truck Leasing**
P.O.Box 563
Reading, PA 19603 610-775-6000
Fax: 610-775-5064 800-221-3040
ralph.stockmayer@penske.com www.penske.com
President: Brian Hard
Estimated Sales: K
Number Employees: 1,000-4,999

27483 **Pentad Group Inc**
7234 Francisco Bend Dr
Delray Beach, FL 33446 561-362-8678
Fax: 561-495-9777 labelsaver@aol.com
www.labeloff.com
Logos on any item, wine related products such as wine label removers, wine label albums, glassware, coolers, aprons, posters, etc
CEO: Marvin Pesses
Vice President: Marvin Pesses
Estimated Sales: $2.5-5 Million
Number Employees: 5
Number of Products: 46
Type of Packaging: Consumer, Private Label
Brands:
Labeloff Wine Label Removers

27484 **Pentwater Wire Products**
474 S Carroll St
Pentwater, MI 49449 231-869-6911
Fax: 231-869-4020 877-869-6911
carl@pentwaterwire.com
www.pentwaterwire.com
Racks, displays, containers, assemblies, shelving and baskets
Chairman of the Board: Jay C Petter
Vice President: Dwight Swanson
Sales Director: Mike Piper
Estimated Sales: $5-10 Million
Number Employees: 50-99
Square Footage: 100000
Brands:
On Guard

27485 **PeopleSoft USA**
2727 Paces Ferry Rd SE # Ii900
Atlanta, GA 30339-4053 404-439-5500
Fax: 404-439-5367 800-380-7638
sales@distinction.com www.oracle.com
Manufacturer and exporter of supply chain planning software
President: Craig A Conway
EVP: Nanci Caldwell
CEO: Patrick Brandt
EVP: Ram Gupta
Manager Marketing Development: Sandy Skrobis
Vice President of Corporate Communicatio: Carol Sato
Estimated Sales: $100-500 Million
Number Employees: 500-999

27486 **Peoria Packing**
1300 W Lake St
Chicago, IL 60607 312-738-1800
Fax: 312-738-1180 www.peoriapacking.com
Packaging
Owner: Harry Katsiavlos
Estimated Sales: $10 - 20 Million
Number Employees: 20-49

27487 **Peoria Tent & Awning**
P.O.Box 1315
Peoria, IL 61654 309-674-1128
Fax: 309-673-0338 info@peoriaawning.com
www.peoriaawning.com
Commercial awnings
Owner: Breck Nelson
Estimated Sales: $1-2,500,000
Number Employees: 20-49

27488 **Pepetti's Hygrade Egg Product**
100 Trumbull Street
Elizabeth, NJ 07206-2105 908-351-9618
Fax: 908-351-7528 www.papetti.com
Estimated Sales: $.5 - 1 million
Number Employees: 1-4

27489 Pepper Mill Company
558 S Broad St
Mobile, AL 36603-1124 251-433-7919
Fax: 251-433-3364 800-669-5175
Trivet boards and brushes including wire and bristle
President: Scott Gonzalez
VP Finance: Siobhan Gonzalez
Estimated Sales: $.5 - 1 million
Number Employees: 1-4
Square Footage: 1000
Brands:
Fajita Trivet
Monster
Roughneck

27490 Pepper+Fuchs
1600 Enterprise Pkwy
Twinsburg, OH 44087-2245 330-425-3555
Fax: 330-425-4607 sales@us.pepperl-fuchs.com
www.am.pepperl-fuchs.com
Industrial controls and sensors
President: Wolfgang Mueller
R&D: Hurman Witch
CEO: Wolfgang Mueller
Estimated Sales: $20 - 50 Million
Number Employees: 100-249

27491 PepperWorks
303 Industrial Way
Suite 5
Fallbrook, CA 92028 760-723-0202
Fax: 760-723-2227 info@wine-master.com
Wine industry tasting room supplies
Manager: Biby Zeledon

27492 Pepperell Paper Company
9 S Canal Street
Lawrence, MA 01843-1412 978-433-6951
Fax: 978-433-6427 www.merimacpaper.com
Manufacturer and exporter of specialty papers including acid free, beater dyed colors, packaging, supercalendered, grease, mold and flame resistant, crepe, flour bag, kraft, etc
Sales Manager: Steve Ulicny
Number Employees: 4
Square Footage: 400000
Parent Co: James River Corporation
Brands:
Strypel
Styprint
Stysorb

27493 Per Pak/Orlandi
131 Executive Boulevard
Farmingdale, NY 11735 631-756-0110
Fax: 631-756-0256 Info@orlandi-usa.com
www.orlandi-usa.com
Contract packager offering high-speed over wrapping, form fill and seal for liquids, powders and cartoning
President: Sven Dobler
COO: Per Dobler
Controller: David Hays
VP Marketing: Dale Beal
Plant Manager: Mike Cheff
Estimated Sales: $5 - 10 Million
Number Employees: 50-99
Parent Co: Jefferson Smurfit Corporation

27494 Per-Fil Industries Inc
PO Box 9
Riverside, NJ 08075 856-461-5700
Fax: 856-461-0741 sales@per-fil.com
www.per-fil.com
Manufacturer and exporter of filling machinery for liquids, powder, paste, granules and food products
President: Shari Becker
Director/Chairman: Horst Boellmann
Service Manager: Tobin Wrice
National and International Sales: Shari Becker
Estimated Sales: Below $5 Million
Number Employees: 25
Square Footage: 14500
Brands:
Micro-Recharger
Rotary Recharger

27495 Perception
3307 S College Avenue
Unit 113
Fort Collins, CO 80525-4196 970-226-1941
Fax: 970-221-4809

27496 Peregrine
5301 N 57th St Ste 102
Lincoln, NE 68507-3164 402-466-4011
Fax: 402-466-1639 800-777-3433
info@peregrine-inc.com www.peregrine-inc.com
Manufacturer and exporter of material handling equipment including four-wheel steering trailers
President: Troy Rivers
Office/Sales Manager: Joyce Schiermann
Estimated Sales: $1 - 2,500,000
Number Employees: 5-9
Type of Packaging: Bulk
Brands:
Quad-Steer

27497 Perfecseal
9800 Bustleton Ave
Philadelphia, PA 19115 215-673-4500
Fax: 215-676-1311 800-568-7626
mediplus@bemis.com www.perfecseal.com
Heat seal coated materials, coated paper and laminations, laminated films, tubing, header bag packaging
President: Paul Verbeten
CEO: Alan McClure
R&D: Richard Craig
Quality Control: Gail Turner
CFO: Ben Travey
Plant Manager: Gail Turner
Estimated Sales: $83.8 Million
Number Employees: 100-249

27498 Perfect Fit Glove Company
85 Innsbruck Dr
Cheektowaga, NY 14227 716-668-2000
Fax: 716-668-3224 800-245-6837
perfectfitglove@perfectfitglove.com
www.perfectfitglove.com
Safety equipment and hand protection
Manager: Greg Wall
Estimated Sales: $50 - 75 Million
Number Employees: 50-99

27499 Perfect Fry Company
615 71st Avenue SE
Calgary, AB T2H 0S7
Canada 403-255-7712
Fax: 403-255-1725 800-265-7711
profits@perfectfry.com www.perfectfry.com
Manufacturers ventless countertop deep fryers designated for commercial deep-frying without the instalation of hoods and vents
Vice President of Business Development: Gary Calderwood
CFO: Sharon Hyasdick
Vice President, General Manager: Greg Moyer
Research & Development: Shaun Calderwood
Senior Manager of Sales: Bonnie Bolster
Vice President of Operations: Steve Reale
Plant Manager: Jeff Scott
Estimated Sales: Below $5 Million
Number Employees: 20
Square Footage: 60000
Parent Co: Perfect Fry Corporation
Type of Packaging: Food Service
Brands:
Perfect Fry

27500 Perfect Packaging Company
26974 Eckel Road
PO Box 286
Perrysburg, OH 43551 419-874-3167
Fax: 419-874-8044
perfectpackaging@netzero.com
www.exportpackagingohio.com
Manufacturer and exporter of custom wooden boxes for machinery and related equipment and domestic, export and military packaging; also, heated warehousing available
President: Donald Hartman Sr
Estimated Sales: Below $5 Million
Number Employees: 1-4
Square Footage: 14000

27501 Perfect Plank Company
2850 South 5th Avenue
Oroville, CA 95965 530-533-7606
Fax: 530-533-2814 800-327-1961
info@perfectplank.com www.perfectplank.com
Laminated wood countertops, butcher blocks, tabletops and sign blanks
Sales Manager: Terry Horne
General Manager: Jim Horne
Production Manager: Bob Horne
Sales and Accounts Payable: Adam Horne
Estimated Sales: $1-2.5 Million
Number Employees: 10-19
Square Footage: 60000

27502 Perfect Score Company
9326 Garfield Blvd
Cleveland, OH 44125-1313 216-883-8000
Fax: 216-883-8800 sales@theperfectscore.com
www.theperfectscore.com

27503 Perfection Equipment
4259 Lee Ave
Gurnee, IL 60031 847-244-7200
Fax: 847-244-7205 800-356-6301
info@perfectequip.com www.perfectequip.com
Manufacturer and exporter of beverage and condiment dispenser systems, custom fabricated stainless steel bar and restaurant equipment including underbar and portable and back bar units, glycol units and water chillers
President: Sanford Hahn
CEO: Kay Hahn
Sales Manager: Robert Barnhisel
Plant Manager: Alan Hale
Purchasing: Gene Wood
Estimated Sales: $5-10,000,000
Number Employees: 20-49
Square Footage: 14000
Type of Packaging: Food Service

27504 Perfex Corporation
32 Case St
Poland, NY 13431 315-826-3600
Fax: 315-826-7471 800-848-8483
perfex@perfexonline.com
www.perfexonline.com
Manufacturer and exporter of PVC floor and neoprene rubber squeegees, polypropylene, chemical resistant and hygienic brooms and brushes, shovels and stainless steel clean room flat mopping systems
President: Michael Kubick
Marketing Manager: Mike Dougherty
Sales: Irene Gouthier
Customer Service Supervisor: Trudy Pickerd
Estimated Sales: $1-2.5 Million
Number Employees: 10-25

27505 Performance Contracting
16400 College Boulevard
Lenexa, KS 66219 913-888-8600
Fax: 913-492-8723 800-255-6886
info@pcg.com www.pcg.com
Construction of specialized facilities for cold storage, food processing and distribution
President/Chief Executive Officer: Craig Davis
Executive Manager: Lori Weddle
Vice President/Chief Financial Officer: Dan Hefferon
Senior Vice President, Corporate Affairs: Michael Matthews Sr
Director, Marketing: Carson Dorsey
Project Manager: Tatyana Wentzel
Estimated Sales: $871 Million
Number Employees: 4,000
Square Footage: 36000

27506 Performance Imaging
5392 Leon St
Oceanside, CA 92057 760-721-2925
Fax: 760-721-2925 800-266-5742
info@performanceimaging.com
www.performanceimaging.com
Specializing in machine vision inspection systems offering complete package inspection. Capabilities include label inspection, character recognition and verification, cap inspection and fill level; custom application softwareavailible
Estimated Sales: $2.5-5 Million
Number Employees: 10-19

27507 Performance Packaging
6430 Medical Center St
Suite 102
Las Vegas, NV 89148 702-240-3457
Fax: 702-240-3453 ppsales@pplv.co
www.pplv.co
President: Robert Reinders
CFO: Bruce Moore
Estimated Sales: Below $5 Million
Number Employees: 5-9

27508 **Performance Packaging**
251 N Roeske Avenue
Trail Creek, IN 46360-5072 219-874-6226
Fax: 219-874-3011
Corrugated boxes and packaging materials
VP Sales/Marketing: Will Childers
Estimated Sales: $5-10 Million
Number Employees: 2
Square Footage: 100000

27509 **Perkin-Elmer Inc.**
710 Bridgeport Ave
Shelton, CT 06484-4794 203-925-4600
Fax: 203-944-4904 800-762-4000
info@perkin-elmer.com www.perkinelmer.com
Analytical instruments and life science systems used in biotechnology, pharmaceutical, environmental testing, food, agriculture and chemical manufacturing
Chairman and Chief Executive Officer: Robert F. Friel
SVP and Chief Financial Officer: Frank A. Wilson
Estimated Sales: $2.5-5 Million
Number Employees: 20-49

27510 **Perky's Pizza**
4029 Tampa Rd
Oldsmar, FL 34677-3206 813-855-7700
Fax: 813-855-0014 800-473-7597
perky@perkys.com www.perkys.com
Pizza producer of Perky's pizza products, program and product sales
President: Jim Howell
CEO: Frank Rozel
R&D: Bill Sweet
Marketing Manager: Anne Reilley
Sales: Rick White
Estimated Sales: $2.5-5 Million
Number Employees: 10-19
Square Footage: 8000
Type of Packaging: Food Service, Private Label
Brands:
Perky's Fresh Bakery

27511 **Perl Packaging Systems**
80 Turnpike Dr # 2
Middlebury, CT 06762-1830 203-598-0066
Fax: 203-598-0068 800-864-2853
david@perlpackaging.com
www.perlpackaging.com
Manufacturer and exporter of straight line liquid filling machines, piston fillers, portable cappers, rotary unscramblers, cap and bottle orienter feeders and labelers
President: David Baker
Estimated Sales: $3 - 5 Million
Number Employees: 5-9
Square Footage: 40000

27512 **Perley-Halladay Associates, Inc.**
1037 Andrew Dr
West Chester, PA 19380 610-296-5800
Fax: 610-647-1711 800-248-5800
sales@perleyhalladay.com
www.perleyhalladay.com
Manufacturer and exporter of refrigerated buildings, walk-in coolers and process freezers
Owner: Harry Holiday
Office Mngr.: Jim Sonvogni
Estimated Sales: $2.5-5 Million
Number Employees: 10-19

27513 **Perlick Corporation**
8300 W Good Hope Rd
Milwaukee, WI 53223 414-353-7060
Fax: 414-353-7069 800-558-5592
perlick@perlick.com www.perlick.com
Manufactuer of bar and beverage dispensing equipment for the foodservice industry.
President, CEO: Paul Peot
CFO: Mike Pitialip
VP of Manufacturing: Tim Carpenter
VP of Marketing & Business Development: Tim Ebner
VP of Commercial Sales: Jim Koelbl
Number Employees: 250-499
Square Footage: 1112000
Type of Packaging: Food Service

27514 **Perma USA**
2129 Center Park Dr
Charlotte, NC 28217 704-377-3100
Fax: 704-377-3106 800-997-3762
info@permausa.com www.permausa.com
Manager: Kevin Keating
Estimated Sales: $5 - 10 Million
Number Employees: 5-9
Parent Co: perma-tec GmbH u. Co. KG

27515 **Perma-Vault Safe Company**
72 Ash Cir
Warminster, PA 18974-4800 215-293-9951
Fax: 215-293-9952 800-662-3360
sales@perma-vault.coom www.perma-vault.com
Largest manufacturer of cash protection systems units. Product line includes rotary hopper despository safes, wall safes, in-room safe deposit boxes, cash boxes, pistol boxes, through the wall/door depository safes, hotel guest safescustom built safes, and in-floor safes.
President: Robert Johnson
Marketing: Norman Bartwink
Sales Manager: Norman Bartwink
Operations: Tina Williams
Production: Tina Williams
Purchasing: Tina Williams
Estimated Sales: $3 - 5 Million
Brands:
Perma-Vault

27516 **PermaCold Engineering**
3005 NE Argyle St
Portland, OR 97211 503-249-8190
Fax: 503-249-8322 800-455-8585
info@permacold.com www.permacold.com
Refrigeration contractors: parts, service, overhaul and construction
Owner: Steve Jackston
Vice President: Randy Clelokit
Marketing: Lindsay Jackson
Sales Director: Randy Cieldna
Operations Manager: Steve Jackson
Estimated Sales: $20 - 50 Million
Number Employees: 90

27517 **Permaloc Security Devices**
PO Box 4699
Silver Spring, MD 20914 301-681-6300
Fax: 301-681-7552
Installation and monitoring of alarm systems
Owner: James Wolfe
Secretary/Treasurer: John Goetz
Vice President: Berthol Harbrant
Estimated Sales: $500,000-$1 Million
Number Employees: 20-49
Square Footage: 3500

27518 **Perplas**
4073 Shoreside Cir
Tampa, FL 33624-2373 610-268-1620
Fax: 610-268-1621 800-898-0378
sales@perplascorp.com www.perplascorp.com
Estimated Sales: $1 - 5 Million

27519 **Perry Industries**
412 N. Smith Avenue
Corona, CA 92880-6903 951-734-9838
Fax: 951-734-2454 sales@moperry.com
www.moperry.com
Powder fillers, liquid fillers
President: Phillip Osterhaus
Estimated Sales: $5-10 Million
Number Employees: 20-49

27520 **Perry Videx Llc**
25 Mount Laurel Rd
Hainesport, NJ 08036 609-267-1600
Fax: 609-267-4499 info@perryvidex.com
www.perryvidex.com
Wholesaler/distributor, importer and exporter of used food processing equipment; serving the food service market
President: Gregg Epstein
Sales Representative: Luis Mencado
Estimated Sales: $5-10 Million
Number Employees: 20-49

27521 **Perten Instruments**
6444 S 6th Street Rd
Springfield, IL 62707 217-585-9440
Fax: 217-585-9441 888-773-7836
lblack@perten.com www.perten.com
Manufacturer, importer and exporter of spectrometers, gluten and alpha analysis testing equipment, laboratory sample mill grinders and NIR analyzers
Manager: Gavin O'Reilly
Manager Western: Carl Meuser
Manager Eastern: Walter Munday
Sales/Marketing Manager: Wes Shadow
Estimated Sales: $2.5-5 Million
Square Footage: 16000
Parent Co: Perten Instruments AB
Brands:
Da 7000
Skcs

27522 **Perten Instruments**
PO Box 7398
Reno, NV 89510-7398 702-829-8199
Fax: 775-829-8196 info@perten.com
www.perten.com
Tea and coffee industry moisture analyzers, quality control instruments
Chief Executive Officer: Sven Holmlund
Sales/Marketing Manager: Wes Shadow
Number Employees: 110

27523 **Perten Instruments**
6444 S 6th Street Rd
Springfield, IL 62712 217-585-9440
Fax: 217-585-9441 jpowers@perten.com
www.perten.com
Analytical laboratory services, analyzing fat testing
Founder: Harald Perten
CEO: Sven Holmlund
Manager: Gavin O'Reilly
Estimated Sales: $2.5 - 5 Million
Number Employees: 10-19

27524 **Peryam & Kroll ResearchCorporation**
6323 N Avondale Ave
Suite 211
Chicago, IL 60631 773-774-3100
Fax: 773-774-7956 800-747-5522
info@pk-research.com www.pktesting.com
President/CEO: James M. Ondyak
Chairman of the Board: Beverley J. Kroll
CFO: Eric Maddux
Senior Vice President: Dr. Richard Popper
Estimated Sales: $5 - 10 Million
Number Employees: 250-499

27525 **Peskin Neon Sign Company**
3991 Simon Rd
Youngstown, OH 44512-1390 330-783-2470
Fax: 330-783-9704
Plastic and neon signs
President: Marvin Peskin
VP: Jerry Peskin
Estimated Sales: Below $5 Million
Number Employees: 10-19

27526 **Pestcon Systems**
1808 Firestone Parkway
Wilson, NC 27893-7991 509-233-9732
Fax: 252-243-1832 800-548-2778
info@pestcon.com www.pestcon.com
Marketer of stored commodity pesticide protection products
VP Sales: George Hunt
Estimated Sales: $1 - 5 Million
Number Employees: 16
Other Locations:
Pestcon Systems
Wilson NC

27527 **Pester-USA**
110 Commerce Drive
Allendale, NJ 07401-1656 201-327-7009
Fax: 201-327-7824 pester-usa@pester.com
www.pester.com/en
End-of-line equipment, overwrapping, stretch/shrink bundling, case packing, palletizing
Vice President: Joachim Eckart
Estimated Sales: $5 - 10 Million
Number Employees: 10-19

27528 **Petal**
30 W 31st St
New York, NY 10001 212-947-3662
Fax: 212-279-5107 petal@aol.com.net/il
www.petal.com

Consultant specializing in research and development for beverage flavors
Estimated Sales: Below $500,000
Number Employees: 1-4

27529 Peter Drive Components
5148 Kennedy Rd
Suite 600
Fayetteville, GA 30214 678-904-0853
Fax: 770-371-5063 faudius@aol.com
Solutions for shaft/hub connections
Estimated Sales: $1 - 3 Million
Number Employees: 1-4

27530 Peter Gray Corporation
44 Park St
Andover, MA 01810-3692 978-470-0990
Fax: 978-475-6663 davequinn@pechiney.com
www.westwoodcorp.com
Stainless steel stampings, deep drawn parts, cylinders, pans, burners, barbecue housings and thermoset molded plastics, etc
Chairman, President, Chief Executive Off: Michael Strianese
Executive Vice President of Corporate St: Curtis Brunson
Director Sales: Mark Marchessault
Senior Vice President of Operations: Richard Cody
Estimated Sales: $1 - 5 Million
Number Employees: 1-4
Square Footage: 320000
Parent Co: Peter Gray Corporation

27531 Peter Kalustian Associates
239 Reserve Street
Boonton, NJ 07005-1301 973-334-3008
Fax: 973-334-2757 pk/pka@aol.com
Consultant specializing in manufacturing management, engineering, construction and marketing for the fat, margarine, shortening, cocoa butter substitute, fatty acid and derivative industries
President: Peter Kalustian
Number Employees: 3
Square Footage: 900

27532 Peter Pepper Products
P.O.Box 5769
Compton, CA 90224-5769 310-639-0390
Fax: 310-639-6013
customerservice@peterpepper.com
www.peterpepper.com
Trash receptacles, reusable containers, displays, store fixtures and tables
President: Sigi Pepper
CFO: Michael Pepper
Quality Control: Bob Caceres
Marketing/Sales: Kip Pepper
Purchasing Manager: Chuck Martlaro
Estimated Sales: $10 - 20 Million
Number Employees: 50-99
Brands:
Minimint
Peppermint
Tasque

27533 (HQ)Peterboro Basket Company
130 Grove St
PO Box 120
Peterborough, NH 03458 603-924-3861
Fax: 603-924-9261 www.peterborobasket.com
Insulated coolers and baskets including fruit, vegetable and shopping
CEO: Russell E Dodds
Estimated Sales: $10-20 Million
Number Employees: 50-99
Square Footage: 36000

27534 Peterson Fiberglass Laminates
PO Box 158
Shell Lake, WI 54871-0158 715-468-2306
Fax: 715-468-7923 macman@spacestar.net
Brine tanks, flume and canal brining systems, cheese conveyors and fiberglass tanks for live fish transport
Vice President: Wayne Peterson
Estimated Sales: $500,000-$1 Million
Number Employees: 9
Square Footage: 16000

27535 Peterson Manufacturing Company
24133 W 143rd St
Plainfield, IL 60544 815-436-9201
Fax: 815-436-2863 800-547-8995
callpmc@peterson-mfg.com
www.peterson-mfg.com
Manufacturer and exporter of metal storage racks
President: Gerry Kusiolek
CFO: Dicks Jenkins
Chairman of the Board: David Peterson
Estimated Sales: $5 - 10 Million
Number Employees: 50-99

27536 Peterson Sign Company
660 Mapunapuna Street
Honolulu, HI 96819-2031 808-521-6785
petersonsignco@cs.com
www.petersonsign.com
Signs including magnetic, engraved and silk screened
Owner: Arlene Patterson
Estimated Sales: $1-2.5 Million
Number Employees: 1-4

27537 (HQ)Petro Moore Manufacturing Corporation
3641 Vernon Blvd
Long Island City, NY 11106-5123 718-784-2516
Fax: 718-784-7099 www.petromoore.com
Manufacturer and exporter of steel folding legs and folding and stackable tables
President: Robert Murphy
Secretary: Jan DeRosa
Estimated Sales: Below $5 Million
Number Employees: 5-9
Square Footage: 40000
Type of Packaging: Food Service

27538 Petro-Canada America Lubricant
4087 Lower Valley Rd
Parkesburg, PA 19365 610-593-2669
Fax: 610-593-2705 888-284-4572

27539 Petro-Canada Lubricants
2310 Lakeshore Road
Mississauga, ON L5J 1K2
Canada 866-335-3369
Fax: 905-822-7450 www.petro-canada.ca
Petro-Canada is a world class producer of more than 350 advanced lubricants, specialty fluids, food grade grease and lubricants
Number Employees: 10
Number of Products: 350
Parent Co: Suncor Energy Inc
Type of Packaging: Consumer, Food Service, Private Label, Bulk

27540 Petrochem Insulation
110 Corporate Pl
Vallejo, CA 94590 707-644-7455
Fax: 707-644-4908 800-520-2705
corp@petrocheminc.com
www.petrocheminc.com
Petrochem is your premier single source specialty contractor.providing mechanical isulation,heat tracing, removable pad fabrication, fireproofing, scaffolding,floor coatings and abatement services. working nationwide fromsevenregional offices.
President: Art Lewis
Marketing Director: Brian Benson
Sales Director: Brian Benson
Estimated Sales: $1 - 5 Million
Number Employees: 250-499

27541 Pexco Packaging Corporation
PO Box 6540
Toledo, OH 43612 419-470-5935
Fax: 419-470-5940 800-227-9950
www.pexcopkg.com
Bags including plain and printed polyethylene, polypropylene and styrene recloseable; also, roll stock available
President: William Buri
Controller: Gene Roach
Production Manager: Thomas Jesionowski
Estimated Sales: $5-10 Million
Number Employees: 20-49
Square Footage: 40000

27542 Pfankuch Machinery Corporation
5885 149th St W Ste 101
Apple Valley, MN 55124 952-891-3311
Fax: 952-891-5168 pfankuchmachine@msn.com
www.pnedc.org
Manufacturer, importer and exporter of packaging machinery including feeders, collators, counters and wrappers
CEO: Claus Pfankuch
Estimated Sales: $3 - 5,000,000
Number Employees: 5-9
Square Footage: 11000
Parent Co: Pfankuch Maschinen

27543 Pfeil & Holing
5815 Northern Blvd
Flushing, NY 11377-2297 718-545-4600
Fax: 718-932-7513 800-247-7955
info@cakedeco.com www.cakedeco.com
Bakery decorations
President: Sy Stricker
Estimated Sales: $5-10 Million
Number Employees: 20-49

27544 (HQ)Pfeil & Holing, Inc.
5815 Northern Blvd
Flushing, NY 11377 718-545-4600
Fax: 718-932-7513 800-247-7955
info@cakedeco.com www.cakedeco.com
Supplier and exporter of bakers' equipment and utensils including edible sugar cake decorations, chocolate flowerpots with icing roses, holiday novelties, birthday candles, pastry bags, pans, tubes, icing roses and plastic tierseparators
President: Sy Stricker
CEO: Sy Stricker
Sales Director: Jenn Covalluzzi
Estimated Sales: $5-10 Million
Number Employees: 20-49
Number of Products: 7000
Square Footage: 200000
Brands:
Affordable Elegance
Party Hits
Pop-Ons
Simplicity

27545 PhF Specialist
P.O.Box 7697
San Jose, CA 95150-7697 408-275-0161
Fax: 408-280-0979 phfspec@pacbell.net
www.phfspec.com
Owner: Pamela Hardt-English
Estimated Sales: $300,000-500,000
Number Employees: 1-4

27546 Pharmaceutic Litho & Label Company
3990 Royal Ave
Simi Valley, CA 93063 818-882-8884
Fax: 818-882-4234 paul@pharmaceuticlitho.com
www.pharmaceuticlitho.com
President: Tom Moore
President: Tom Moore
Quality Control: Adriene Charatca
Estimated Sales: $100-200 Million
Number Employees: 50-99

27547 Pharmaceutical & Food Special
P.O.Box 7697
San Jose, CA 95150-7697 408-275-0161
Fax: 408-280-0979 phfspec@pacbell.net
www.phfspec.com
Importer and exporter of temperature sensing equipment; also, consulting services available including plant and process design, training, seminars and FDA/USDA regulation compliance packaging design
President: Pamela Hardt-English
Quality Control: Peter Cocotas
Vice President: Peter Cocotas
Food Tecnologist: Kim Cortes
Estimated Sales: Below $5 Million
Number Employees: 1-4
Square Footage: 10000

27548 Phase Fire Systems
2685 S Melrose Drive
Vista, CA 92081 760-741-2341
Fax: 760-741-2218 888-741-2341
pkgmachy@aol.com www.phasefiresystems.com

Shrink packaging machinery including sleevers and banders; also, tunnel ovens
President: Noel Perez
Secretary/Accounts Payable: Nicole Perez
Purchasing Manager: John Edgar
Estimated Sales: $1-2.5 Million
Number Employees: 9

27549 **Phase II Pasta Machines**
55 Verdi St
Farmingdale, NY 11735 631-293-4259
Fax: 631-293-4572 800-457-5070
pastamachine@aol.com www.pastamachines.net
Manufacturer, exporter and importer of commercial pasta equipment
President: Michael Wilson
Estimated Sales: $500,000-$1 Million
Number Employees: 1-4
Square Footage: 5500
Brands:
Pastamagic
Pastamatic

27550 **Phelps Industries**
P.O.Box 190718
Little Rock, AR 72219-0718 501-568-5550
Fax: 501-568-3363 psales@phelpsind.com
www.phelpsfan.com
Manufacturer and exporter of platform dump trucks and live floor hoppers for bulk handling
Owner: Donald Phelps
Vice President: John Phelps
Estimated Sales: $10 - 20 Million
Number Employees: 50-99

27551 **Phenix Label Company**
11610 S Alden St
Olathe, KS 66062 913-327-7000
Fax: 913-327-7010 800-274-3649
info@phenixlabel.com www.phenixlabel.com
Manufacturer and exporter of custom printed labels
President: Hans Peter
CFO: Mark Volz
VP: Mike Darpel
Quality Control: Gina Waltmire
Estimated Sales: $10-20 Million
Number Employees: 50-99
Square Footage: 35000
Parent Co: Phenix Box & Label Company
Type of Packaging: Consumer, Food Service, Private Label

27552 **Philadelphia Glass Bending Company**
2520 Morris Street
Philadelphia, PA 19145-1716 215-726-8468
Fax: 215-336-3002
Lighting fixtures
Estimated Sales: $20-50 Million
Number Employees: 50-99
Parent Co: Seagull Lighting Products

27553 **Philipp Lithographing Company**
1960 Wisconsin Ave.
PO Box 4
Grafton, WI 53024 262-377-1100
Fax: 262-377-6660 800-657-0871
help@philipplitho.com www.philipplitho.com
Manufacturer and exporter of labels and point of purchase displays
President/CEO: Peter Buening
CFO/Treasurer: Dave Kaehny
Vice President/General Counsel: Stacy Buening
Estimated Sales: $5-10 Million
Number Employees: 50-99
Square Footage: 35000
Type of Packaging: Private Label

27554 **Philips Lighting Company**
PO Box 6800
Somerset, NJ 08875-6800 732-563-3000
Fax: 732-563-3641 www.lighting.philips.com
Manufacturer and exporter of lamps including incandescent, fluorescent, HID, specialty, miniature, etc
CEO: Ed Crawford
Director Channel Marketing: Paul Lienesch
Estimated Sales: $30 - 50 Million
Number Employees: 10,000

27555 **Phillips Gourmet, Inc**
1011 Kaolin Rd
PO Box 190
Kennett Square, PA 19348 610-925-0520
Fax: 610-925-0527 info@phillipsgourmetinc.com
www.phillipsgourmetinc.com
Fresh, organic, stuffed and dried wild mushrooms
President: R M Phillips
COO/CFO: Bill Steller
General Manager: Rick Angelucci
Quality Assurance Manager: Bill Green
Estimated Sales: $1 Million
Number Employees: 10
Square Footage: 21540
Type of Packaging: Consumer, Food Service
Brands:
Bella

27556 **Phillips Plastics and Chemical**
3200 Southwest Fwy
suite 3200
Houston, TX 77027-7538 713-552-9595
Fax: 713-552-0231 800-537-3746
www.phillipsakers.com
Food packaging, industrial packaging, conventional equipment, clear rigid and flexible packaging, conventional equipment
Number Employees: 100-249

27557 **Phillips Refrigeration Consultants**
4014 Balmoral Drive
Champaign, IL 61822-8552 217-355-0319
Fax: 217-355-0324 boyitscold@worldnet.att.net
President: John Phillips
Number Employees: 3

27558 **(HQ)Philmont Manufacturing Co.**
370 Overpeck Pl
Englewood, NJ 07631 201-816-5867
Fax: 201-569-3426 888-379-6483
info@philmontmfg.com www.philmontmfg.com
Table padding and tablecloths
President: Bruce Strongwater
Quality Control: Jason Strongwater
Executive VP: Michael Rattner
CFO: Catherine Maren
VP Marketing: Adrian Trautman, Jr.
National Sales Manager: Bill Sarna
Estimated Sales: $20 - 30 Million
Number Employees: 100
Square Footage: 35000

27559 **Phoenix & Eclectic Network**
172 N York St
Elmhurst, IL 60126-2762 630-530-4373
Fax: 630-530-0651 info@hm-na.com
www.hm-na.com
Consultant providing packaging design services to food processors
Estimated Sales: $1 - 5 Million
Number Employees: 5-9

27560 **Phoenix Closures**
1899 High Grove Ln
Naperville, IL 60540 630-544-3475
Fax: 630-420-4774
greatcaps@phoenixclosures.com
www.phoenixclosures.com
Manufacturer and exporter of caps and seals
President: Bert Miller
CFO: Rich Classen
Quality Control: Jim Twohij
VP Sales/Marketing: Jeff Davis
Sales Director: Tim Ferrel
Estimated Sales: $20 - 50 Million
Number Employees: 250-499
Number of Products: 1000
Square Footage: 100000
Brands:
Accugard
Accuseal
Sealgard
Softseal
Sureseal
Torkgard
Tritab

27561 **Phoenix Coatings**
19893 Berenda Blvd
Madera, CA 93638 559-675-8122
Fax: 559-673-2571 800-464-1958
tburk@phoenixcoatings.com
www.phoenixcoatings.com
Decorative wine bottles
President/CEO: Tom Burk
Owner: Bob Pricer
Controller: Gordon Begman
Office Manager: Craig Alton
Safety Officer: Mark Pankratz
Estimated Sales: $500,000-$1 Million
Number Employees: 5-9

27562 **Phoenix Contact**
P.O.Box 4100
Harrisburg, PA 17111 717-944-1300
Fax: 717-944-1625 800-586-5525
info@phoenixcon.com www.phoenixcon.com
President: Jack Nehlig
CEO: Jack Nehlig
Estimated Sales: $50 - 100 Million
Number Employees: 100-249

27563 **Phoenix Design & Engineering LLC**
8162 Market St
Suite H
Boardman, OH 44125 330-726-3477
Fax: 608-827-5898 www.phoenixdesigneng.com
Filling and heat sealing equipment

27564 **Phoenix Engineering**
13208 Arctic Circle
Santa Fe Springs, CA 90670-5510 562-407-0512
Fax: 562-407-0518 800-991-1395
sales@pouchmachines.com
www.pouchmachines.com
Resins for cast and blown films for food packaging
President and CFO: Lynn Worthington
Estimated Sales: $1 - 2.5 Million
Number Employees: 1-4

27565 **Phoenix Process Equipment Company**
2402 Watterson Trl
Louisville, KY 40299 502-333-9623
Fax: 502-499-1079 phoenix@dewater.com
www.dewater.com
President: Gary L Drake
CFO: Stephen Kovaka
Estimated Sales: $5 - 10 Million
Number Employees: 20-49

27566 **Phoenix Sign Company**
112 Clemons Rd
Aberdeen, WA 98520-0112 360-532-1111
Fax: 360-637-8557
Neon, electric, wooden and plastic signs
Owner: Faron Lash
Estimated Sales: $.5 - 1 million
Number Employees: 1-4

27567 **Photo-Graphics Company**
5100 Martha Truman Rd # C
Grandview, MO 64030 816-761-3333
Fax: 816-761-3032 pgcinc@worldnet.att.net
www.nameplate.thomasregister.com
Industrial name plates and labels
Manager: Andy Ortbals
Production Manager: Andrew Ortbals
Estimated Sales: $1 - 3 Million
Number Employees: 1-4
Square Footage: 19200
Brands:
Metalphoto

27568 **Phytotherapy Research Laboratory**
W Fourth S
PO Box 627
Lobelville, TN 37097-0627 931-593-3780
Fax: 931-593-3782 800-274-3727
newherbs@netease.net
Certified organic herb extracts; also, research, development and production of specialty herbal products in the area of immune and vital organ support
President: Brent Davis
Estimated Sales: $500,000-$1 Million
Number Employees: 1-4
Square Footage: 25000
Type of Packaging: Private Label
Brands:
Forest Center
Hahg
Prl

27569 **Piab USA**
65 Sharp St
Hingham, MA 02043-4311 781-337-7309
Fax: 781-337-6864 800-321-7422
info-usa@piab.com www.piab.com
N.A. distributor and manufacturer of vacuum conveyors and pumps for company based in Sweden
President: Chuck Weilbrenner
Estimated Sales: $10 - 20 Million
Number Employees: 50-99

27570 **Piab Vacuum Products**
65 Sharp St
Hingham, MA 02043 781-792-0003
Fax: 781-337-6864 800-321-7422
info@piab.com www.piabusa.com
Vacuum pumps, suction cups, vacuum filters, pneumatic conveyors, etc
President: Chuck Weilbrenner
CEO: Don Spradlin
Marketing Director: Ed McGraven
Sales: Jack Gray
Estimated Sales: $10 - 20 Million
Number Employees: 50-99

27571 **Piacere International**
1101 Air Way
Glendale, CA 91201-2403 818-240-7335
Fax: 818-240-0558 800-432-3288
piacere@kiweb.com www.piacerecoffees.com
Espresso machines and accessories, pre-brewed espresso, roasters, powders
Manager: Dick Forque
Estimated Sales: $1.5 Million
Number Employees: 30

27572 **Picard Bakery Equipment**
1325 E Notre-Dame Estate
Victoriaville, QC G6P 4B8
Canada 819-758-1883
Fax: 819-758-1465 info@picardinc.com
www.picardinc.com
Picard Ovens, Inc is the proud manufacturer of the REVOLUTION HYBRID OVEN, moduler deck oven, LP200 baking stone, SPITFIRE pizza oven, PRG rotisserie ovenm and much more.
President: Gilles Picard
Chief Financial Officer: Isabella Dupua
Vice President: Guy Picard
Research: Phillipe Lamay
Quality Control: Francis Picard
Marketing: Kristina Marchelli
Sales: Eric Ambrosio
Public Relations: Kristina Marchelli
Operations: Francis Picard
Estimated Sales: $5-10 Million
Number Employees: 10

27573 **Pick Heaters**
P.O.Box 516
West Bend, WI 53095 262-338-1191
Fax: 262-338-8489 800-233-9030
info1@pickheaters.com www.pickheaters.com
Manufacturer and exporter of direct steam injection liquid heating systems including heat exchangers, water heaters, hose stations and clean-in-place; also, cookers including food/starch, fruit and vegetable purees, etc
President: Prudence Hway
CEO: Prudence Hway
Executive VP: Michael Campbell
Estimated Sales: $2.5 - 5 Million
Number Employees: 25
Brands:
Constant Flow
Pick
Sanitary
Variable Flow

27574 **Pick Heaters Inc.**
PO Box 516
West Bend, WI 53095 262-338-1191
Fax: 262-338-8489 800-233-9030
info1@pickheaters.com www.pickheaters.com
Steam injection equipment such as custom fabricated heaters and indirect heaters, hotwater jacketed heating equipment, meat and poultry scalder application, gelatin candy application, bakery pan cleaning applications.

27575 **Pickard**
782 Pickard Ave
Antioch, IL 60002 847-395-3800
Fax: 847-395-3827 finest@pickardchina.com
www.pickardchina.com
Manufacturer and exporter of stock and custom fine china
President: Andrew P Morgan
International Sales VP: Larry Smith
Estimated Sales: $5-10 Million
Number Employees: 50-99
Square Footage: 60000
Brands:
Pickard

27576 **Pickney Molded Plastics**
3970 Parsons Rd
Howell, MI 48855-9617 517-546-9900
Fax: 517-546-7097 800-854-2920
www.pmpnet.com
Food transport systems
President: Don Verna
Estimated Sales: $10-20 Million
Number Employees: 50-99

27577 **Pickwick Company**
4200 Thomas Dr SW
Cedar Rapids, IA 52404-5055 319-393-7443
Fax: 319-393-7456 800-397-9797
wcorey@pickwick.com www.pickwick.com
Manufacturer and exporter of poultry processing equipment including batch scalders, pickers and conveyorized eviscerating lines
CEO: Jeff McEachron
CEO: Walter F Corey
Estimated Sales: $20-50 Million
Number Employees: 50-99
Square Footage: 100000
Brands:
Dunkmaster
Econo System
Hom-Pik
Pickwick
Spin-Pik

27578 **Picnic Time**
5131 Maureen Ln
Moorpark, CA 93021 805-529-7400
Fax: 805-529-7474 888-742-6429
info@picnictime.com www.picnictime.com
Picnic baskets
President: Mario Tagliati
Managing Partners: Paul Cosaro
Managing Partners: Danny Corbucci
Vice President/Founder: Gustavo Cosaro
Marketing: Danny Corbucci
Estimated Sales: $5.4 Million
Number Employees: 30

27579 **Pieco**
P.O.Box 86
Manchester, IA 52057-0086 563-927-3352
Fax: 563-927-2310 800-334-3929
sales@pieco.com www.pieco.com
Cutting and boning devices, sharpening machines and services, sharpening and overhaul equipment, bone chips and cartilage removal, emulsifiers, accessories
Owner: Jerry York
Estimated Sales: $1-2.5 Million
Number Employees: 5-9

27580 **Piedmont Label/Smyth Company**
311 W Depot St
Bedford, VA 24523-1937 540-586-2311
Fax: 540-586-0549 800-950-7011
www.smythco.com
Pressure sensitive, sheeted, in-mold and PET labels; also, graphic design services available
Manager: Ben Witt
Marketing Communications Manager: Bill Orme
VP Sales/Marketing: Bill Bumgarner
Estimated Sales: $20 - 50 Million
Number Employees: 100-249
Square Footage: 125000

27581 **Piepenbrock Enterprises**
919 State Route 33
Freehold, NJ 07728-8454 732-683-0991
Fax: 732-683-0992 800-942-0052
piepenbrock@earthlink.com www.siebler.de
Pouching machine for tablets, caplets and capsules
Estimated Sales: $1 - 5 Million

27582 **Pier 1 Imports**
453 Chestnut Ridge Rd
Woodcliff Lake, NJ 07677-7679 201-666-4500
Fax: 201-666-8525 800-448-9993
www.pier1.com
Espresso machines, wood burning ovens and pasta equipment; importer of pasta and espresso equipment
Manager: Lauren Sanders
Estimated Sales: $1 - 3 Million
Number Employees: 10-19
Type of Packaging: Food Service
Brands:
Cap-O-Mat

27583 **Pierce Laminated Products**
2430 N Court St
Rockford, IL 61103 815-968-9651
Fax: 815-968-7601 piercelaminated@prodigy.net
www.piercelaminated.com
Countertops and store fixtures
President: Eric Lindroth
President: Eric Lindroth
Vice President: Eric Lindroth
Estimated Sales: $2.5-5 Million
Number Employees: 30
Square Footage: 35000

27584 **Pierrepont Visual Graphics**
15 Elser Ter
Rochester, NY 14611 585-235-5620
Fax: 585-235-8376 info@pvgrochester.com
www.pvgrochester.com
Signs, directory boards, vinyl letters, pressure sensitive decals, banners, posters and T-shirts
President: Scott Zappia
Vice President: Terry Zappia
Estimated Sales: $1-2.5 Million
Number Employees: 10-19
Square Footage: 34000
Type of Packaging: Private Label

27585 **Pike Tent & Awning Company**
7300 SW Landmark Ln
Portland, OR 97224 503-624-5600
Fax: 503-968-5440 800-866-9172
sales@pikeawning.com www.pikeawning.com
Commercial awnings
Owner: Tony Spear
Vice President: Ken Spearing
Estimated Sales: $2.5-5 Million
Number Employees: 20-49

27586 **Pilgrim Plastic ProductsCompany**
1200 W Chestnut Street
Brockton, MA 02301-5574 508-436-6300
Fax: 508-580-3542 800-343-7810
pilgrimsales@pilgrimplastics.com
www.pilgrimplastics.com
Manufacturer and exporter of plastic point of purchase displays, including window displays, door displays, counter change mats, shelf displays, membership cards, change cashing cards, promotional items, rulers, luggage tags, etc
President: Mark Abrams
CFO: Mark Abrams
Quality Control: Jason Abrams
Estimated Sales: Below $5 Million
Number Employees: 85
Square Footage: 320000

27587 **Pillar Technologies**
475 E Industrial Dr
PO Box 110
Hartland, WI 53029-0110 262-912-7200
Fax: 262-912-7272 888-PIL-LAR6
www.pillartech.com
Induction sealers
Sales: Brad Budde
General Manager: Mark Stohl
Parent Co: Illinois Tool Works Inc

27588 **Pilot Brands**
PO Box 10107
Zephyr Cove, NV 89448 775-588-8850
Fax: 775-588-8380 800-621-5262
info@pilotbrands.com www.pilotbrands.com
President: Kitt Barkley

27589 **Pinckney Molded Plastics**
3970 Parsons Rd
Howell, MI 48855 517-546-9900
Fax: 517-546-7097 800-854-2920
pmp@ismi.net www.pmpnet.com
Cases, crates, dollies, trays, totes, pallets
President: Don Verna
Chairman of the Board: Leland Blatt
Sales Manager: Dave Heyink
Estimated Sales: $10 - 20 Million
Number Employees: 50-99

27590 **Pine Bluff Crating & Pallet**
2600 S Persimmon St
Pine Bluff, AR 71603 870-879-2287
Fax: 870-879-1190 866-415-1075
www.pinebluffcrating.com
Wooden pallets and skids
Owner: Leonard Brazil
Operations Manager: Zach Thicksten
Pallet Production Manager: Robert Ferguson
Customer Accounts/office operations: Mark Thicksten
Estimated Sales: $2.5 - 5 Million
Number Employees: 20-49

27591 **Pine Point Wood Products**
PO Box 1900
Dayton, MN 55327 763-428-4301
Fax: 763-428-4304 pineptwood@msn.com
www.pinepointwoodproducts.com
Custom cut wooden pallets, skids, crates and containers
President: James R Talbot
Quality Control: Larry Corbin
Sales Manager: Don Lenz
Sales: Larry Corbin
Estimated Sales: $10 - 20 Million
Number Employees: 20-49

27592 **Pinnacle Furnishing**
10564 Nc Highway 211 E
Aberdeen, NC 28315 910-944-0908
Fax: 910-944-0920 866-229-5704
sales@pinnaclefurnishing.com
www.pinnaclefurnishings.com
Manufacturer and exporter of chairs and tables for restaurants, casinos, hotels and banquets
President: Jack Berggren
R&D: Jack Berggren
Vice President: Steve Laufer
Quality Control: Sarah Swanson
Regional Sales Representative: Bunnie Strauh
Estimated Sales: $2.5 - 5,000,000
Number Employees: 20-49
Square Footage: 40000

27593 **Pino's Pasta Veloce**
1903 Clove Road
Staten Island, NY 10304-1607 718-273-6660
Fax: 718-720-5906
Pasta sauce; manufacturer of pasta heaters for portion control and food preparation
Manager Marketing: Joe Klaus
VP Operations: Al Cappillo
Estimated Sales: $2.5-5,000,000
Number Employees: 1-4
Parent Co: AEI
Type of Packaging: Consumer, Food Service
Brands:
Pino's Pasta Veloce

27594 **Pinquist Tool & Die Company**
63 Meserole Avenue
Brooklyn, NY 11222 718-389-3900
Fax: 718-349-3168 800-752-0414
info@pinquisttool.com www.pinquisttool.com
Metal stampings, display hardware, banner stands and wire and tubing racks
President: Richard Pinquist
Sales Director: C Oshinsky
Estimated Sales: Below $5 Million
Number Employees: 20-49
Square Footage: 10000

27595 **Pioneer Chemical Company**
13717 S Normandie Ave
Gardena, CA 90249 310-366-7393
Fax: 310-366-7193
customerservice@pioneerchem.com
www.pioneerchem.com
Janitorial supplies, disinfectants, soaps and cleaning equipment
President: Jose Alvarez
Manager: Mary Alvarez
Estimated Sales: Below $5 Million
Number Employees: 10-19

27596 **Pioneer Labels**
1195 S Lipan St
Suite C
Denver, CO 80223 303-744-1606
Fax: 303-744-2443 877-744-1606
kevin@pioneerlabels.com
www.pioneerlabels.com
Labels
President: Kevin Daly
Estimated Sales: $500,000-$1 Million
Number Employees: 1-4

27597 **(HQ)Pioneer Manufacturing Company**
4529 Industrial Pkwy
Cleveland, OH 44135 216-671-5500
Fax: 216-671-5502 800-877-1500
www.pioneer-mfg.com
Aerosol insecticides, dustless chemical floor polishing mops, liquid quick drying floor wax and patching material for freezer and cooler floors
President: James Schattinger
Estimated Sales: $20 - 50 Million
Number Employees: 100-249
Square Footage: 68000
Brands:
Advance
Kent

27598 **Pioneer Marketing International**
188 Westhill Drive
Los Gatos, CA 95032-5032 408-356-4990
Fax: 408-356-2795 edesoto@jps.net
www.pioneer.com
Export and import broker of confectionery products, snacks and private label items. Consultant in marketing, sales and product promotion in England and Africa
Partner: Russ Tritomo
Director Sales: Ed DeSoto
Estimated Sales: $1 - 5 Million
Number Employees: 4

27599 **Pioneer Packaging**
220 Padgette St
Chicopee, MA 01022 413-378-6930
Fax: 413-378-6963 www.pioneerpackaginginc.com
Vacuum formed folding cartons
Owner: Jeffrey Shinners
Estimated Sales: $5-10 Million
Number Employees: 50-99

27600 **Pioneer Packaging**
PO Box 6
Dixon, KY 42409-0006 270-639-9133
Fax: 270-639-5882 800-951-1551
sales@pioneerplastics.com
www.pioneerplastics.com
Manufacturer and exporter of rigid molded clear plastic containers including round, square, oval and rectangular
President: Edward Knapp
CFO: Edward Knapp Jr
Marketing Manager: Wayne Fiester
Customer Service: David Fiester
Estimated Sales: $5 - 10 Million
Number Employees: 65
Type of Packaging: Consumer, Food Service

27601 **Pioneer Packaging & Printing**
1220 Lund Blvd
Anoka, MN 55303-1092 763-323-8308
Fax: 763-323-8207 800-708-1705
www.pioneerpack.com
Folding paper boxes
President: Greg Polack
President/CEO: Greg Pollack
CFO: Richard Hall
Quality Control: Jon Maguessen
Estimated Sales: $10 - 20 Million
Number Employees: 100-249

27602 **Pioneer Packaging Machinery**
135 Farrs Bridge Rd
Pickens, SC 29671 864-878-4999
Fax: 864-878-8642 mail@pioneerpackmach.com
www.pioneerpackmach.com
President: Howard Frist
Estimated Sales: $5 - 10 Million
Number Employees: 10

27603 **Pioneer Sign Company**
PO Box 583
Lewiston, ID 83501-0583 208-743-1275
Signs; crane installation service available
Owner: Bradley Keller
Estimated Sales: $1-2.5 Million
Number Employees: 19
Parent Co: Pioneer Sign Company

27604 **(HQ)Piper Products**
300 S 84th Ave
Wausau, WI 54401 715-842-2724
Fax: 715-842-3125 800-544-3057
info@piperonline.net www.piperonline.net
Aluminum racks, transport cabinets, dollies, proofer cabinets, hot boxes, pans and accessories; exporter of aluminum racks and transport cabinets
President: Roger D Sweeney
National Sales Manager: R Joseph Graf
Customer Service: Evelyn Yakich
Estimated Sales: $10 - 20 Million
Number Employees: 50-99
Type of Packaging: Food Service
Other Locations:
Piper Products
Wausau WI

27605 **Piper Products**
300 S 84th Ave
Wausau, WI 54401 715-842-2724
Fax: 715-848-1870 800-544-3057
medaniels@adelphia.net www.piperonline.net
Manufacturer and exporter of ovens, proofers, combination oven/proofers, transport and heated cabinets and bakery racks, cafeteria, buffet lines, tray delivery carts and support equipment
CEO: Tony Sweeney
Estimated Sales: $10 - 20 Million
Number Employees: 50-99
Type of Packaging: Food Service
Brands:
Piper Products
Super Systems

27606 **Pitco Frialator**
PO Box 501
Concord, NH 03302 603-225-6684
Fax: 603-230-5548 800-258-3708
dpacka@maytag.com www.pitco.com
Manufacturer and exporter of commercial cooking equipment including standard, high capacity, doughnut/bakery and high efficiency fryers, pasta cookers, frying filters and baskets
President: Dave Brewer
Director Materials: Steve Karas
VP/General Manager: Robert Granger
VP Engineer: George McMahon
Estimated Sales: $20-50 Million
Number Employees: 250-499
Parent Co: G.S. Blodgett Corporation
Type of Packaging: Food Service
Brands:
Frialator
Pitco

27607 **Pittsburgh Corning Corporation**
800 Presque Isle Drive
Pittsburgh, PA 15239-2799 724-327-6100
Fax: 724-325-9701 www.pittsburghcorning.com
Manufacturer and exporter of moisture resistant glass insulation for floors, walls and roofs of food and beverage buildings, coolers and freezers
Manager: Erik Elthiele
Chief Financial Officer/VP, Finance: Joseph Kirby
Vice President: Jean Collet
Vice President, Information Technology: Peter Atherton
Sales Manager: Steve Oslica
Director, Global Supply Chain: John Holzwarth
Estimated Sales: $45 Million
Number Employees: 490
Brands:
Foamglas

27608 Pittsburgh Tank Corporation
1500 Industrial Dr
Monongahela, PA 15063 724-258-0200
Fax: 724-258-7350 800-634-0243
sales@pghtank.com www.pghtank.com
Aluminum, carbon steel and stainless steel storage tanks
President: James Bollman
Vice President: Phil Duvall
Research & Development: Jeff Farrar
Sales Director: John Thompson
Purchasing Manager: Tracie Doman
Estimated Sales: 5-10 Million
Number Employees: 50-99
Number of Products: 6
Square Footage: 70000
Type of Packaging: Bulk

27609 Pittsfield Weaving Company
PO Box 8
Pittsfield, NH 03263 603-435-8301
Fax: 603-435-6753 www.pwcolabel.com
Woven labels
President: Gilbert Bleckmann
Controller: Robert Russell
Estimated Sales: $10-20 Million
Number Employees: 50-99

27610 Pizzamatic Corporation
130 E 168th St
South Holland, IL 60473-2836 708-331-0660
Fax: 708-331-0663 888-749-9279
sandy@pizzamaticusa.com
www.pizzamaticusa.com
Pizza production systems and pizzeria equipment
President: Cliff Fitch Iii
Co-founder: Clifford E. Fitch Jr
Sales: Sandy Johnson
Estimated Sales: $1-5 Million
Number Employees: 10-19

27611 Placemat Printers
Old Rt. 22 & 863
P.O. Box 699
Fogelsville, PA 18051-0699 610-285-2255
Fax: 610-285-2607 800-628-7746
sales@mastercraftprinting.com
www.mastercraftprinting.com
Full scale commercial print e-design shop
President: Darlene Pinto
Estimated Sales: Below $5 Million
Number Employees: 10-19

27612 Placon Corporation
6096 McKee Rd
Fitchburg, WI 53719 608-271-5634
Fax: 608-271-3162 800-541-1535
betterdesign@placon.com www.placon.com
Thermoformed plastic packages, blister packages, box inserts, medical disposables and food container trays
President: Jan Acker
CEO: Dan Mohs
CFO: Rick Terrin
Estimated Sales: $50 - 75 Million
Number Employees: 250-499

27613 (HQ)Plaint Corporation
4100 W Profile Pkwy
Bloomington, IN 47404-2546 812-323-7565
Fax: 317-392-4772 800-366-3525
info@pliantcorp.com www.pliantcorp.com
Manufacturer and exporter of custom and stock recloseable and polyethylene bags
Manager: Peter Lenzen
Executive VP: Ronald Thieman
VP Sales: Dick Zurich
Estimated Sales: $3 - 5 Million
Number Employees: 5-9
Square Footage: 1400000
Other Locations:
KCL Corp.
Dallas TX

27614 (HQ)Plainview Milk ProductsCooperative
130 Second St. SW
Plainview, MN 55964 507-534-3872
Fax: 507-534-3992 800-356-5606
dmoe@plainviewmilk.com
www.plainviewmilk.com
Butter, powdered whey and dry milk including non-fat, whole and buttermilk. Whey protein concentrates, custom agglomeration and spray drying
General Manager: Dallas Moe
Controller: Janna Van Rooyen
Sales Manager: Darrell Hanson
Plant Manager: Donny Schreiber
Number Employees: 5
Square Footage: 18060
Type of Packaging: Consumer, Food Service, Private Label, Bulk
Other Locations:
Plainview Milk ProductsCoop.
Plainview MN
Brands:
Greenwood Prairie

27615 Planet Products Corporation
4200 Malsbary Rd
Blue Ash, OH 45242 513-984-5544
Fax: 513-984-5580 info@planet-products.com
www.planet-products.com
Manufacturer and exporter of sausage and frankfurter loading, cheese stick equipment. Manufacturer of turnkey systems in automating sandwich assembly and other ready to eat products
Owner: Kathy Randolph
CEO: Mike F
VP: John Abraham
Marketing: Jennifer Coromel
Estimated Sales: $10-20 Million
Number Employees: 50-99
Brands:
Link N Load
Servo-Pak

27616 Plas-Ties
14272 Chambers Rd
Tustin, CA 92780 714-542-4487
Fax: 714-972-2978 800-854-0137
info@plasties.com www.plasties.com
Tie-matic hd twist-tying machines and materials; also cable ties.
Owner: Lou Contreras
Marketing Manager: Stephanie O'Neill
Estimated Sales: $2.5-5 Million
Number Employees: 1-4
Square Footage: 200000
Type of Packaging: Consumer, Private Label, Bulk
Brands:
Plas-Ties
Tie-Matic

27617 Plas-Ties, Co.
14272 Chambers Road
Tustin, CA 92780 714-547-8288
Fax: 714-972-2978 800-854-0137
info@plasties.com www.plasties.com/
Strip and air curtains and food service doors
President: Mike Bell
Sales Manager: Jesse Garcia
Estimated Sales: $5-10 Million
Number Employees: 10
Square Footage: 240000

27618 Plascal Corporation
361 Eastern Parkway
PO Box 590
Farmingdale, NY 11735 516-249-2200
Fax: 516-249-2256 800-899-7527
plascal@aol.com www.plascal.com
Manufacturer and exporter of plain, printed, laminated and PVC plastic film and sheeting
CEO: Mark Hurd
President: Fred Hurd
Estimated Sales: $10-20 Million
Number Employees: 100-249

27619 Plaskid Company
PO Box 162841
Austin, TX 78716-2841 512-328-7785
Fax: 714-972-2978 800-854-0137
Coatings to frictionize plastics, application systems for films and foam

27620 Plassein International
200 S Biscayne Boulevard
Suite 900
Miami, FL 33131-5344 860-429-5070
Fax: 860-429-5071 866-752-7734
jdoak@plassein.com www.plassein.com

27621 Plasseint International
920 Wilshire Drive
Libertyville, IL 60048-1858 847-680-5835
Fax: 847-680-1478 rickk101@aol.com
A packaging firm, manufacture plastic packaging materials in US and Canada

27622 Plast-O-Matic Valves
1384 Pompton Ave
Suite 1
Cedar Grove, NJ 07009 973-256-3000
Fax: 973-256-4745 info@plastomatic.com
www.plastomatic.com
Thermoplastic valves
VP: Bob Sinclair
Estimated Sales: $10-25 Million
Number Employees: 50-99

27623 Plastech
205 W Duarte Rd
Monrovia, CA 91016-4529 626-358-9306
Fax: 626-303-6288 mbonio@plastechspec.com
www.plastechspec.com
Manufacturer and exporter of plastic point of purchase displays
Owner: Pat Delaney
CFO: Pat Delaney
Estimated Sales: Below $5 Million
Number Employees: 10-19
Type of Packaging: Consumer, Bulk

27624 Plastech Corporation
2080 General Truman St NW
Atlanta, GA 30318 404-355-9682
Fax: 404-355-5410 info@plastech.com
www.plastech.com
Thermoformed plastic products including blister and clamshell packaging, trays and signs; also, in-house product design and tool making, computerized trimming, finishing and decorating, assemblies and prototypes available
President: Larry W Lee
Quality Control: Darius Lee
Sales/Marketing: David Lee
Estimated Sales: Below $5 Million
Number Employees: 20-49

27625 Plasti-Clip Corporation
38 Perry Rd
Milford, NH 03055 603-672-1166
Fax: 603-672-6637 800-882-2547
sales@plasticlip.com www.plasticlip.com
Manufacturer and exporter of point of purchase clips and fasteners including displays, price tags, tickets, etc; also, coupon holders, employee (and visitor) ID badging software and supplies
President: Daniel Faneuf
Estimated Sales: $1-2.5 Million
Number Employees: 5-9
Number of Brands: 50
Number of Products: 1000
Square Footage: 7000
Brands:
3m
Anchor
Arrow Clip
Crystal View
Dc Uni-Clip
E-Z Rak-Clip
Flex-Holder
Grip Clip
Gt Uni-Clip
Magnaclamp
Mid-Trak
Plasti-Rivet
Premium Trak-Clip
Presto Galaxy
Snap'n Clip
Springrip
Take-1
The Messenger
Thum-Screw
Trak Clip
Uni-Badge
Uni-Strap
Wobblers

27626 Plasti-Line
445 S Gay Street
Suite 100
Knoxville, TN 37902-1133 865-938-1511
Fax: 865-947-8531 800-444-7446
info@plasti-line.com www.plasti-line.com

Manufacturer and exporter of plastic, metal, interior and exterior illuminated signs including menu boards and point of purchase displays
VP Marketing: Mickey Davis
Marketing Manager: Mary Ann Herrick
Estimated Sales: $20 - 50 Million
Number Employees: 500-999

27627 Plasti-Mach Corporation
704 Executive Blvd # G
Valley Cottage, NY 10989-2023 845-267-2985
Fax: 845-267-2825 800-394-1128
plastimach@plastimach.com
www.plastimach.com
Manufacturer and exporter of used equipment including thermoforming, extrusion and heat sealing
President: Robert Rosen
VP: Jerry Hammerman
Estimated Sales: $1 - 5 Million
Number Employees: 5-9
Square Footage: 40000

27628 Plasti-Print
1620 Gilbreth Rd
Burlingame, CA 94010 650-652-4950
Fax: 650-652-4954 plastiprint@compuserve.com
www.plasti-print.com
Plastic pressure-sensitive labels and shelf strips
President: Peter Vigil
CEO: Helen Vigil
VP: Rodney Vigil
Estimated Sales: Below $5 Million
Number Employees: 5-9
Square Footage: 4500

27629 Plastic Arts Sign Company
3931 W Navy Blvd
Pensacola, FL 32507 850-455-4114
Fax: 850-455-5033 866-662-7060
www.passignspensacola.com
Neon and plastic signs
President: Joe Navarro
Estimated Sales: $500,000-$1 Million
Number Employees: 10-19

27630 Plastic Assembly Corporation
1 Sculley Rd. Unit A
Ayer, MA 01432-632 978- 77- 472
Fax: 978-772-6096 patrickmagmus@aol.com
Plastic containers
President: Regis M Magnus
R & D: Patric Magnus
Estimated Sales: Below $5 Million
Number Employees: 10
Square Footage: 75000
Brands:
Blinky

27631 Plastic Container Corporation
2508 N Oak St
Urbana, IL 61802 217-352-2722
Fax: 217-352-2822 jgentles@netpcc.com
www.netpcc.com
Plastic Container Corporation (PCC) manufactures plastic bottles for numerous industries including that of food and beverage. PCC utilizes extrusion blow molding machines to produce containers from any common extrusion blow moldingmaterial.
CEO: Ronald Rhoades
Sales Manager: Jo Ellen Gentles
Sales Representative: John Foote
Square Footage: 500000
Type of Packaging: Consumer

27632 Plastic Equipment
305 Rock Industrial Park Drive
Bridgeton, MO 63044-1214 800-645-5439
Fax: 314-739-3240 800-270-6225

27633 Plastic Fantastics/BuckSigns
823 Siskiyou Boulevard
Ashland, OR 97520-2168 541-482-2223
Fax: 541-482-2223 800-482-1776
Push-type portion control food dispensers, brochure holders, picture frames, signs, magazine holders, grocery displays, medical appliances, bulk food dispensers, display boxes, acrylic wine racks, engraved and sand blasted woodsigns
Owner: Michael Buckley
CEO: Barbara Buckley
CFO: Issac Reed
Estimated Sales: $2.5-5 Million
Number Employees: 4
Square Footage: 1400

27634 Plastic Industries
213 Dennis St
Athens, TN 37303 951-277-4800
Fax: 951-894-0124 800-894-4876
www.pi-inc.com
Blowmolded plastic bottles
President: Nicholas Rende
VP Sales/Marketing: Dennis Niles
Estimated Sales: $10 - 20 Million
Number Employees: 1-4
Square Footage: 65000

27635 Plastic Ingenuity, Inc.
1017 Park St
Cross Plains, WI 53528 608-798-3071
Fax: 608-798-4452 www.plasticingenuity.com
Thermoformed packaging, tooling & extrusion services for the food packaging industry.
President: Tom Kuehn

27636 Plastic Packaging Corporation
750 S 65th St
Kansas City, KS 66111-2301 913-287-3383
Fax: 913-287-9420 800-468-0029
info@plaspack.com www.plaspack.com
President: David Staker
CFO: Deena Staus
Quality Control: John Seevers
R&D: John Seevers
Number Employees: 100-249

27637 Plastic Packaging Corporation
PO Box 2029
Hickory, NC 28603-2029 828-328-2466
Fax: 828-322-1830 www.ppi-hky.com
Manufacturer and exporter of flexible packaging including drawstring and sideweld bags,rollstock laminations and sleeve labels pouches.
President: Bert Brinkley
General Manager: Mark Coffey
Quality Control: Ron Windley
Marketing: David Anderson
VP: Gary Boetsch
Operations: Preston Bryant
Estimated Sales: $10-20 Million
Number Employees: 100-249
Square Footage: 99000

27638 Plastic Packaging Corporation
1227 Union Street
PO Box 548
West Springfield, MA 01090 413-785-1553
Fax: 413-731-5952 800-342-2011
info@plasticpkg.com www.plasticpkg.com
Injection molded plastic food containers and lids
President: Susan Weiss
CFO: Edd Katotlam
Estimated Sales: $10-25 Million
Number Employees: 100-249

27639 Plastic Packaging Inc
1246 Main Avenue SE
Hickory, NC 28602 828-328-2466
Fax: 828-322-1830 800-333-2466
solutions@ppi-hky.com www.ppi-hky.com
Manufacturer and exporter of flexible packaging including drawstring and sideweld bags, rollstock, laminations and sleeve labels pouches
President: Bert Brinkley
VP Sales: Bill Lipscomb
Operations Manager: Dan Chamley
Estimated Sales: less than $500,000
Number Employees: 100-249
Square Footage: 740000

27640 Plastic Printing
320 Clay St
Dayton, KY 41074 859-581-5700
Fax: 859-291-2112 877-581-7748
csr@plasticprintinginc.com
www.plasticprintinginc.com
Plastic advertising items
Manager: Shawn Davis
Estimated Sales: Below $5 Million
Number Employees: 5-9
Square Footage: 6327

27641 Plastic Suppliers
2400 Marilyn Ln
Columbus, OH 43219 614-475-8010
Fax: 614-471-9033 800-722-5577
moore@plasticsuppliers.com
www.plasticsuppliers.com
Complete line of unsupported film substracts for the label market including Labelflex, a biaxially oreinted polysterne label stock film, polyester film, polypropylene films for labeling, packaging and lamination applications, PVC andsynthetic papers; also new shrink label films. Whether your products call for durability, printability or over all appearance, Plastic suppliers is your total films solution
CEO: Theodore Riegert
Marketing: Roger Brown
Sales: Rich Ekhfeld
Operations: Bob Scholz
Purchasing: Joyce Blocker
Estimated Sales: $100 - 200 Million
Number Employees: 250-499
Brands:
Labelflex
Polyflex
Tip-On

27642 Plastic Supply Incorporated
735 E Ind Park Dr
Suite 1
Manchester, NH 03109 603-669-2727
Fax: 603-668-1691 800-752-7759
sales@plasticsupply.com
www.plasticsupply.com
Lobster tanks
President: Richard Dutile
General Manager: Bill Johnson
Estimated Sales: $2.5-5 Million
Number Employees: 11
Square Footage: 11500
Parent Co: Plastic Supply Inc
Brands:
Atlantic Lobster

27643 Plastic Systems
465 Cornwall Avenue
Buffalo, NY 14215 716-835-7555
Fax: 716-835-7776 800-604-7159
plastics@plasticsystems.com
www.plasticsystems.com
Custom molding of vacuum formed parts
President: Daniel E McNamara
Estimated Sales: $1-2.5 Million
Number Employees: 5-9

27644 Plastic Tag & Trade Check Company
1201 Woodside Ave
Essexville, MI 48732 989-892-7913
Fax: 989-892-7988
Plastic badges and tags
President: Earl J Mast
President: Earl J Mast
Office Manager: Alice Brennan
Estimated Sales: $10-20 Million
Number Employees: 10-19

27645 Plastic Turning Company
331 Hamilton Street
Leominster, MA 01453-2313 978-534-8326
Plastic signs and canopies
Proprietor: Ruth Nickel
Estimated Sales: Less than $500,000
Number Employees: 4
Square Footage: 2500

27646 Plastic-Craft Products Corp
744 West Nyack Rd
PO Box K
West Nyack, NY 10994
Fax: 845-358-3007 800-627-3010
pc@plastic-craft.com www.plastic-craft.com
Plastic film and acrylic signs
President: Mark Brecher
VP Sales: Mark Brecher
Operations Manager: Yung Nguyen
Estimated Sales: $2.5-5 Million
Number Employees: 20-49
Square Footage: 33000

27647 Plastican Corporation
271 Us Highway 46
Suite G110
Fairfield, NJ 07004-2489 973-227-7817
Fax: 973-227-6821
Plastic containers
President: John Carrico
Manager: Kathy Gaiser
Estimated Sales: $5-10 Million
Number Employees: 5-9

27648 Plastics
PO Box 159
Greensboro, AL 36744 334-624-8801
Fax: 334-624-4889
Plastic milk containers
President: W E Burt
Estimated Sales: $10-20 Million
Number Employees: 50-99

27649 Plastilite Corporation
P.O.Box 12457
Omaha, NE 68112 402-453-7500
Fax: 402-571-6739 800-228-9506
info@plastilite.com www.plastilite.com
Foam coolers designed to keep products frozen during shipping
Sales Representative: Greg Montgomery
Principal: Tom Colligan
Estimated Sales: $10+ Million
Number Employees: 50-99
Square Footage: 150000
Brands:
Chubby 7 Day Cooler

27650 Plastimatic Arts Corporation
3622 N Home St
Mishawaka, IN 46545 574-254-9000
Fax: 574-254-9001 800-442-3593
sales@pacbannerworks.com
www.pacbannerworks.com
Coding, dating and marking equipment and plastic signs
Owner: Tim Rink
Estimated Sales: $5-10 Million
Number Employees: 20-49
Parent Co: Rink Riverside Printing

27651 (HQ)Plastipak Industries
30 Taschereau Boulevard
Suite 210
La Prairie, QC J5R 5H7
Canada 800-387-7452
Fax: 450-619-1444
normand.tanguay@plastipak.ca
www.plastipak.ca
Rigid plastic packaging
President: Normand Tanguay
CFO: Guy Bellemare
Vice President: Yves Gosselin
Estimated Sales: $80,000,000
Number Employees: 400
Number of Products: 5000
Type of Packaging: Food Service, Private Label

27652 Plastipak Packaging
41605 Ann Arbor Road
Plymouth, MI 48170 734-354-3510
Fax: 734-455-0556 info@plastipak.com
www.plastipak.com
Manufacturer and exporter of PET and HDPE bottles and containers
President/CEO: William C Young
Estimated Sales: $5-10 Million
Number Employees: 100-249

27653 Plastipro
205 Yuma Street
Denver, CO 80223-1001 417-325-7182
Fax: 303-934-4835 800-654-0409
Plastic insulated jacketing systems for pipes, tanks, vessels, walls, etc
General Manager: Bill Bitterman
VP: Christy Gonzales
Estimated Sales: $2.5-5,000,000
Number Employees: 19
Square Footage: 15000
Brands:
P.I.C. Plastics, Inc.

27654 Plastiques Cascades Group
Suite 400
Montreal, QC H3A 1G1
Canada 514-284-9850
Fax: 514-284-9866 888-703-6515
fmclean@cascades.com
www.cascadesreplast.com
Manufactures meat trays, pre-padded trays, plates and ProZorb meat pads. Specializes in plastic thermoforming and operates in the retail and industrial markets under the brand names of Plastichange Benpac and Deli-Tray
President: Mario Plourve
General Manager: Mario Lacharite
R & D: Claude Cossette
Marketing Assistant: Barbara Hogg
Sales/Marketing Executive: Sandra Hudon
Estimated Sales: $30-50 Million
Number Employees: 10
Parent Co: Plastiques Cascades
Type of Packaging: Consumer, Food Service, Private Label, Bulk
Brands:
Frig-O-Seal
Gourmet
Maxima
Plastichange
Pro-Zorb

27655 Plastocon
1200 W 2nd St
Oconomowoc, WI 53066 262-569-3131
Fax: 262-569-3135 800-966-0103
hottray@plastocon.com www.plastoconinc.com
Manufacturer and exporter of temperature-maintaining meal delivery systems including insulated food trays, mugs, delivery carts, bowls, tray inserts, lids and hot and cold carts; also, rethermalizers and drying and storage racks
President: Joe Camielewski
National Sales Manager: Jerry L. Marks
Type of Packaging: Food Service, Private Label
Other Locations:
Hot Tray Division
Columbia SC
Brands:
Hot Tray

27656 Plaxall
5-46 46th Ave
Long Island City, NY 11101 718-784-4800
Fax: 718-784-4611 800-876-5706
info@plaxall.com www.plaxall.com
Custom thermoformed plastic clamshells, cups and trays; also, experimental model workshop, machine shop and in-plant sheet extrusion of plastic materials
President: James M Pfohl
Vice President: Andrew Kirby
Estimated Sales: $10-20 Million
Number Employees: 50-99
Square Footage: 90000
Parent Co: Design Center

27657 Plaxicon
1300 Nuclear Dr
West Chicago, IL 60185-1652 630-231-0850
Fax: 630-562-5858 www.liquidcontainer.com
Stock and custom rigid plastic containers and bottles
President: Bill Williams
CFO: Bill Williams
R&D: Bills Williams
VP Sales: Robert Harmony
Estimated Sales: $100+ Million
Number Employees: 500-999
Square Footage: 350000
Parent Co: Liquid Container LP

27658 Playtex Products, LLC
890 Mountain Ave.
New Providence, NJ 07974
888-310-4290
www.playtexproductsinc.com
Protective neoprene and latex gloves
CEO: Michael Gallagher
Estimated Sales: $1 - 5 Million
Number Employees: 1750

27659 Plaze
105 Bolte Ln
Saint Clair, MO 63077 636-629-3400
800-986-9509
info@plaze.com www.plaze.com
Contract packager of aerosol and liquid pan coating products
President: John Ferring IV
VP Sales: Hugh Davison
VP Manufacturing: Dennis Bullock
Plant Manager: Bob Thornton
Purchasing Manager: Denise Steen
Number Employees: 100-249
Square Footage: 200000
Type of Packaging: Private Label

27660 PlexPack Corp
1160 Birchmount Road
Unit 2
Toronto, ON M1P Z08
Canada 416-291-8085
Fax: 416-298-4328 855-635-9238
info@emplex.com www.plexpack.com
Bag sealing and automated bagging equipment and the bamark line of shrink and sleeve wrapping equipment
President/CEO: Paul Irvine
Vice President: John Lewitt
Number Employees: 20-49
Type of Packaging: Consumer, Food Service, Private Label

27661 Plicon Corporation
4949 Schatulga Road
Columbus, GA 31907-1945 706-561-9999
Fax: 706-563-0567
Coffee industry pouch materials (cellophane, paper, films)
Estimated Sales: $10-30 Million
Number Employees: 20-50

27662 Plitek
69 Rawls Rd
Des Plaines, IL 60018 847-827-6680
Fax: 847-827-6733 800-966-1250
sales@plitek.com www.plitek.com
Tea and coffee industry valve applications
President: Karl Hoffman
Estimated Sales: $10 - 20 Million
Number Employees: 50-99

27663 PlusPharma, Inc.
2460 Coral Street
Vista, CA 92081 760-597-0200
Fax: 760-597-0734 info@pluspharm.com
www.pluspharm.com
Herbs, gelatin and vegetarian capsules

27664 Pluto Corporation
PO Box 391
French Lick, IN 47432 812-936-9988
Fax: 812-936-2828
alan.friedman@plutocorp.com
www.plutocorp.com
Contract packager and exporter of household cleaners; also blowmold HDPE plastic bottles
President: Alan J Friedman
Plant Manager: Dennis Kaiser
Estimated Sales: $5-10 Million
Number Employees: 100-249
Square Footage: 120000
Parent Co: AHF Industries

27665 Plymold
615 Centennial Dr
Kenyon, MN 55946-1297 507-789-5111
Fax: 507-789-8315 800-759-6653
seating@plymold.com www.foldcraft.com
Manufacturer and exporter of tabletops, booths, indoor/outdoor clusters, millwork, tables, chairs, waste receptacles, salad bars and cabinets
Founder: Harold Nielsen
CEO: Chuck Mayhew
Marketing Coordinator: John Price
Estimated Sales: $20 - 50 Million
Number Employees: 100-249
Square Footage: 275000
Parent Co: Foldcraft
Brands:
Dur-A-Edge
Plymold

27666 (HQ)Plymouth Tube Company
2061 Young St
East Troy, WI 53120 262-642-8201
Fax: 262-642-8486 sales@plymouth.com
www.trent-tube.com
Specialty manufacturer of precision steel tubing, steel and titanium near-net shapes, and steel and titanium cold drawn shapes.
President: Donald Van Pelt
VP Development: Scott Curnel
VP Marketing/Sales: Steve Bohnenkamp
Number Employees: 250-499

27667 Pneumatic Conveying, Inc.
960 East Grevillea Court
Ontario, CA 91761-5612 909-923-4481
Fax: 909-923-4491 800-655-4481
sales@pneu-con.com
www.pneumaticconveyingsolutions.com
Manufacturer and exporter of customized pneumatic conveying equipment
President: Wayland Gillrspie
Sales Engineer: David Gordon
Sales Administrator: Jennifer Edmondson
Estimated Sales: $2.5-5 Million
Number Employees: 1-4
Square Footage: 120000
Parent Co: Pneumatic Conveying
Brands:
Pneu-Con

27668 Pneumatic Scale Corporation
10 Ascot Pkwy
Cuyahoga Falls, OH 44223 330-923-0491
Fax: 330-923-5570 sales@pneumaticscale.com
www.pneumaticscale.com
Manufacturer and exporter of liquid and dry fillers, cappers, and can seamers
President: William Morgan
Marketing Director: Bethany Hilt
Sales Director: Paul Kearney
Sales: Bethany Hilt
Operations Manager: Paul Kelly
Purchasing Manager: Dave Bellet
Estimated Sales: $30 - 50 Million
Number Employees: 100-249
Square Footage: 130000
Parent Co: Barry-Wehmiller Company
Type of Packaging: Consumer, Food Service, Private Label, Bulk

27669 Poblocki
922 S 70th St
Milwaukee, WI 53214 414-453-4010
Fax: 414-453-3070 jdm@poblocki.com
www.poblocki.com
Exhibition cases, exterior and interior custom signs and message boards; custom design services available
President: David Drury
VP: Mark Poblocki
Estimated Sales: $10-20 Million
Number Employees: 100-249
Square Footage: 100000

27670 Pocono PET
512 Forest Rd
Hazle Twp, PA 18202-9389 570-459-1800
Fax: 570-459-6462 petjars@aol.com
www.pretiumpkg.com
Clear polyester food jars and bottles
President: Keith Harbison
Human Resources: Jane Mindler
Sales Manager: Bob Plesnicher
VP Manufacturing: Raymond Eble
Estimated Sales: $20 - 50 Million
Number Employees: 100-249
Square Footage: 63000
Parent Co: Pretium Packaging

27671 Pod Pack International
11800 Industriplex Blvd Ste 9
Baton Rouge, LA 70809 225-752-1110
Fax: 225-752-1163 tmartin@podpack.com
www.podpack.com
Espresso coffee pods and filter pack
Owner: Thomas Martin
Quality Control: Gary Kennington
Executive VP/COO: Tom Martin
Estimated Sales: $10-20 Million
Number Employees: 10-19
Type of Packaging: Consumer, Food Service, Private Label

27672 Podnar Plastics
1510 Mogadore Rd
Kent, OH 44240 330-673-2255
Fax: 330-673-2273 800-673-5277
Manufacturer and exporter of injection blow-molded plastic products including bottles and point-of-purchase containers
President: Jack Podnar
Marketing Director: Jack Podnar
Sales Director: C Allen Clarke
Plant Manager: Scott Podnar
Estimated Sales: $5-10 Million
Number Employees: 20-49
Square Footage: 47000
Type of Packaging: Bulk

27673 Pohlig Brothers
8001 Greenpine Rd
Richmond, VA 23237 804-275-9000
Fax: 804-275-9900 info@pohlig.com
www.pohlig.com
Custom folding and rigid set-up paper boxes
President: Mike Gaffney
Estimated Sales: $9 Million
Number Employees: 55
Square Footage: 110000

27674 Pointing Color
2526 Baldwin Street
Saint Louis, MO 63106-1949 651-770-7888
Fax: 651-770-7999
Dyes, dispersions for food products

27675 Polanis Plastic of America
820 Freeway Drive N
Suite 208
Columbus, OH 43229-5404 614-848-5560
Fax: 614-848-5570 polinas@worldnet.att.net
www.polinas.com
Biaxially oriented polypropylene films, food and confectionery films, antifog films, metallized films, lamination and tape base films

27676 (HQ)Polar Bear
1471 N Perry Hwy
Mercer, PA 16137 724-475-2327
Fax: 724-475-2344 800-538-2327
polarbear@usa.net
Distributor of commercial refrigeration freezers, ice cubers, ice dispensers and ice storage bins
Owner: Michael Kennis
General Manager Sales/Distribution: Vic Lemieux
General Manager Production Plant: Dwayne Whitehill
Estimated Sales: $5-10,000,000
Number Employees: 5-9
Type of Packaging: Private Label

27677 Polar Beer Systems
26035 Palomar Rd
Sun City, CA 92585 951-928-8171
Fax: 619-449-0464
admin@polarbeersystems.com
www.polarbeersystems.com
Manufacturer and exporter of food service equipment including beverage dispensers, servers and preparation equipment; also, carts
President: Sandra Blais
Estimated Sales: $2.5-5 Million
Number Employees: 1-4
Type of Packaging: Food Service

27678 Polar Hospitality Products
2046 Castor Ave
Philadelphia, PA 19134 215-535-6940
Fax: 215-535-6971 800-831-7823
bradk@the-polar.com www.the-polar.com
Manufacturer and exporter of menu covers and wine list covers, check presenters and coasters
President: Brad Karasik
National Sales Manager: Lisa Dale
Customer Service Manager: Arlinda Candelaria
Estimated Sales: $1 Million
Number Employees: 20-49
Square Footage: 72000
Parent Co: Polar Manufacturing
Brands:
Polar

27679 Polar Ice
2423 W Industrial Park
Bloomington, IN 47404-2601 812-333-1528
Fax: 812-333-1591 800-733-0423
Packaged ice
President: Don Kinser
Treasurer: Pam Kinser
Number Employees: 10
Square Footage: 10000

27680 Polar King International
4410 New Haven Ave
Fort Wayne, IN 46803 260-428-2530
Fax: 260-428-2533 800-752-7178
info@polarking.com www.polarking.com
Constructed and ready to operate walk-in coolers and freezers for outdoor use
Marketing Director: Kris Markham
Manager: Mike Lovett
Number Employees: 20-49
Square Footage: 75000
Brands:
Polar King

27681 Polar Peaks
16845 N 29th Avenue
Suite I-303
Phoenix, AZ 85053-3053 480-949-4787
Fax: 602-547-8939

27682 Polar Plastics
314 Mooresville Blvd
Mooresville, NC 28115 704-660-6600
Fax: 704-660-7604 info@polarplastic.ca
www.wincup.com
Plastic cutlery, plates, bowls, tumblers, stemware and take-out containers; also, custom molded items for the food service and consumer markets
Director: Don Towne
CEO: Eric Cohen
VP Marketing: Dave Hicks
Plant Manager: Philip Goudreault
Estimated Sales: $31.1 Million
Number Employees: 250-499
Brands:
Alpha
Belle
Gild
Infinity
Legend
Pro
Perfection
Polar Pal
Polaronde
Prodigy
Signature
Xl

27683 Polar Plastics
4210 Thimens Blouevard
St Laurent, QC H4R 2B9
Canada 514-331-0207
Fax: 514-331-7604 info@polarplastic.ca
www.polarplastic.ca
Manufacturer and exporter of disposable plastic tableware including plates, cups, utensils and dish covers
President: David Stevenson
Plant Manager: Claude Jacques
Estimated Sales: $30 - 50 Million
Number Employees: 250
Type of Packaging: Consumer, Food Service

27684 Polar Process
PO Box 190
Plattsville, ON N0J 1S0
Canada 519-896-8077
Fax: 519-896-1850 877-896-8077
info@polarprocess.com www.polarprocess.com
Manufactures sanitary equipment meeting 3A/USDA standards. Pumps, pump feeders, extruders, depositors, and on-line blenders for viscous products. Ultrasonic cutting systems. Conveyors, rental units available. Free testing.
CEO/President: Roger Venning
Sales: Tim Venning
Operations: Peter Solomon
Plant Manager: Mark Karlsen
Estimated Sales: $1-5 Million
Number Employees: 20-49
Number of Products: 10
Brands:
P0lar Pump
Polar Extruder
Polar Ultrashear

27685 Polar Tech Industries
415 E Railroad Ave
Genoa, IL 60135 815-784-9000
Fax: 815-784-9009 800-423-2749
info@polar-tech.com www.polar-tech.com

At the forefront of temperature controlled and protective packaging innovation since 1984. Polar Tech industries is the largest manufacturer of temperature assured packaging materials. Offering over 100 sizes of insulated containersnew dry ice making equipment, a complete line of ICE-BRIX refrigerants and cold packs, insulated totes and wine shippers, specialized cakes, candy, sausage and meat shippers, large insulated transports, pallet covers, packaging tape, labels andshipping supplies.
General Manager: Autumn Santeler
Account Representative: Leann Schuman
Account Representative: Liz Suobata
Account Representative: Allen Cole
Customer Service Manager: Lora Evans
Inside Sales: Angie Dellinger
Estimated Sales: E
Number Employees: 20-49

27686 Polar Ware Company
2806 N 15th St
Sheboygan, WI 53083-3943 920-458-3561
Fax: 920-458-2205 800-237-3655
customerservice@polarware.com
www.polarware.com
Manufacturer and exporter of deep drawn and stainless steel items including steam table pans and covers, trays, pans, pots, bowls, containers, smallwares, bar supplies, etc.; importer of smallwares, barware, chafers, beverage serversaccessories and sinks
CEO: Jerry Baltus
Executive VP: Rick Carr
Marketing Director: Steph Wittmus
National Sales Manager: Dick Ballwahn
Production Manager: Peter Hansen
Purchasing Manager: Tom Kennedy
Estimated Sales: $20-50 Million
Number Employees: 100-249
Square Footage: 250000
Brands:
Polar Ware
Yukon

27687 Polaris Industrial Corporation
7 Dayton Wire Pkwy
Dayton, OH 45404-1282 937-236-8000
Fax: 937-236-8300 dwppic@aol.com
www.daytonwireproducts.com
Wire store display racks
Owner: Brian Schissler
Estimated Sales: $10 - 20 Million
Number Employees: 50-99

27688 Polibak Plastics: America
113 Executive Drive
Suite 116
Sterling, VA 20166 703-709-3004
Fax: 703-709-1012 888-765-4225
info@polibakusa.com www.polibakusa.com
Bioriented polypropylene film, cast polypropylene film, metalized films, polyethylene.
President: Bora Porabaki
VP: Tolga Baki
Sales Manager: Erdogan Alkan
Estimated Sales: $3 Million
Number Employees: 5-9

27689 Poliplastic
415 Rue Saint-Valier
Granby, QC J2G 7Y3
Canada 450-378-8417
Fax: 450-378-0220
Plastic bags including plain, printed and shopping
President: Michael Friedman
Number Employees: 70

27690 Pollard Brothers Manufacturing
5504 N Northwest Hwy
Chicago, IL 60630 773-763-6868
Fax: 773-763-4466 info@pollardbros.com
www.pollardbros.com
Individual lunch tables
President: Steve F Hein
Marketing Director: Will Hein
Estimated Sales: Below $5 Million
Number Employees: 10-19

27691 Pollinger Company
8100 Nathanael Greene Lane
Charlotte, NC 28227-0654 704-535-2177
Fax: 704-535-4572 pollingerd@aol.com
Batching and blending systems
President: Don Pollinger
Estimated Sales: $30-50 Million
Number Employees: 10

27692 Poly Plastic Products
21 Schultz Drive
PO Box 220
Delano, PA 18220-0220 570-467-3000
Fax: 570-467-3001 www.polyplasticproducts.com
Plastic bags and film
President: Steven Redlich
Chairman of the Board: Alfred Teo
Accounting Manager: Donna Petri
VP Sales: Vince Oberto
Vice President of Operations: Tim McGowan
Production Manager: Brad Smith
Plant Manager: John Boyer
Purchasing Manager: Donna McGowan
Number Employees: 100-249
Square Footage: 312000

27693 Poly Processing Company
8055 Ash St
French Camp, CA 95231 209-982-4904
Fax: 209-982-0455 877-325-3142
sales@polyprocessing.com
www.polyprocessing.com
Manufacturer and exporter of molded plastic tanks
Quality Control: John Bnnlanco
Sales Manager: Del Mann
Manager: John Blanco
Estimated Sales: $2.5 - 5 Million
Number Employees: 50-99

27694 Poly Shapes Corporation
41740 Schadden Rd
Elyria, OH 44035
Fax: 847-428-8869 800-605-9359
Printed and plain plastic bags including custom shaped
Vice President: Don Harreld
Sales Manager: Tom Drake
Operations Manager: Don Paulson
Estimated Sales: $5-10 Million
Number Employees: 20-49
Square Footage: 45000

27695 Poly-Clip System
1000 Tower Rd
Mundelein, IL 60060 847-949-2800
Fax: 847-949-2815 800-872-2547
gil@polyclip-usa.com www.polychip.com
Package closure systems
President: Eggo Haschke
Senior Executive Assistant: Pat Mangioni
VP Sales/Marketing: Gil Williams
Estimated Sales: $20 - 50 Million
Number Employees: 50-99

27696 Poly-Seal Corporation
1810 Portal St
Baltimore, MD 21224 410-633-1990
Fax: 410-633-6311 pscapinfo@poly-seal.com
www.barryplastic.com
Manufacturer and exporter of plastic bottle closures and flow-control plastic plugs and overcaps
President: William Herdrich
CFO: Robert Weilminsger
Vice President: Robert Weilminster
Quality Control: Dess Gallows
Marketing Director: Frank Cassidy
Sales Director: Randy Hobson
Plant Manager: Bill Fryer
Estimated Sales: $100+ Million
Number Employees: 250-499
Square Footage: 450000
Parent Co: Berry Plastics Corporation
Brands:
Poly-Seal
Poly-Tab

27697 PolyConversions
505 E Condit Dr
Rantoul, IL 61866 217-893-3330
Fax: 217-893-3003 888-893-3330
info@polycoUSA.com
www.polyconversions.com
Personal protective apparel for industrial safety, food procedding, controlled environment and much more.
Owner: Dennis Smith
Estimated Sales: $10-20 Million
Number Employees: 10-19
Number of Brands: 2
Number of Products: 15
Square Footage: 47000
Type of Packaging: Consumer, Food Service, Private Label, Bulk
Brands:
Diposables
Protecting Wear
Polywear
Vr

27698 PolyMaid Company
PO Box 1466
Largo, FL 33779-1466 727-507-9321
Fax: 727-524-8271 800-206-9188
Manufacturer and exporter of food mixers and coffee flavoring tumble mixers with removable plastic liners
President: Ken Orthner
VP Operations: Susan Orthner
Number Employees: 4
Square Footage: 10000
Brands:
Polymaid

27699 PolyScience
6600 W Touhy Ave
Niles, IL 60714 800-229-7569
Fax: 847-647-1155 800-229-7569
culinary@polyscience.com
www.cuisinetechnology.com
Producer of constant temperature control equipment
President: Philip Preston
Marketing: Bob Bausone
Sales: Jason Sayers
Operations: Wayne Walter
Estimated Sales: $10-20 Million
Square Footage: 64000
Parent Co: Preston Industries

27700 Polyair
330 Humberline Drive
Toronto, ON M9W 1R5
Canada 416-679-6600
Fax: 416-679-6610 888-765-9847
marketing@polyair.com www.polyair.com
Estimated Sales: $1 - 5 Million

27701 Polyair Packaging
808 E 113th St
Chicago, IL 60628 773-995-1818
Fax: 773-995-7725 888-pol-yair
marketing@polyair.com www.polyair.com
Protective packaging and insulation
President: Alan Castle
CFO: Henry Schriback
Plant Manager: Carl Honaker
Estimated Sales: $20-50 Million
Number Employees: 50-99

27702 Polybottle Group
303 Orenda Road
Brampton, ON L6T 5C3
Canada 905-450-3600
Fax: 905-450-0027
Stock and custom plastic containers including wide and narrow mouth
CEO: Chris Hornsby
Sales Manager: Percy Goslang
Number Employees: 205
Square Footage: 80000
Parent Co: ABC Group

27703 Polychem Corporation
6277 Heisley Rd
Mentor, OH 44060 440-357-1500
Fax: 440-352-9553 800-548-9557
tcorbo@polychem.com www.polychem.com
Plastic strapping
CEO: Thomas Jeckering
Chairman of the Board: Charles Bolton
Estimated Sales: $50 - 75 Million
Number Employees: 100-249

27704 Polychem International
6277 Heisley Rd
Mentor, OH 44060-1899 440-357-1500
Fax: 440-352-9553 intl@polychem.com
www.polychem.com
Polyester strapping/polypropylene strapping.
President: Brian Jeckering
Estimated Sales: $100 Million
Number Employees: 50-99

27705 Polyclutch
457 State Street
North Haven, CT 06473-3094 203-248-6397
Fax: 262-786-3280 800-298-2066
sales@aaman.com www.polyclutch.com
Mechanical and pneumatic slip clutches for overload protection and torque control
President: Gerald H Shaff
CEO: Gerald Shaff
Number Employees: 20-49

27706 Polycon Industries
1001 E 99th Street
Chicago, IL 60628-1693 773-374-5500
Fax: 773-374-9805
Manufacturer and exporter of plastic bottles and containers; also, various types of labeling and silk screening available
VP: Dan Faro
Plant Manager: Fred Palmer
Estimated Sales: $1 - 5 Million
Number Employees: 100-250
Square Footage: 105000

27707 Polyfoam Corporation
2355 Providence Road
PO Box 906
Northbridge, MA 01534 508-234-6323
Fax: 508-234-2123 info@polyfoamcorp.com
www.polyfoamcorp.com
Plastic foam products
President: Thomas L Coz
Estimated Sales: $5-10 Million
Number Employees: 50-99

27708 Polyfoam Packers Corporation
3930 N Ventura Dr # 450
Arlington Hts, IL 60004-7432 847-398-0110
Fax: 847-398-0653 800-323-7442
info@polyfoam.com www.polyfoam.com
Foam containers, hot and cold food transporters, portable dry ice block makers and ice chests
President: Ron Leach
CEO: Ken Harris
CFO: Dan Maeir
VP New Business: Kevin Grogan
Marketing Director: Leora Rosen
Plant Manager: Paul Chanberlain
Purchasing Manager: Joanne Kaysen
Estimated Sales: $20 - 50 Million
Number Employees: 20-49
Square Footage: 260000
Brands:
Freezesafe
Insta-Ice
Thermosafe

27709 Polymer Solutions International
15 Newtown Woods Road
PO Box 310
Newtown Square, PA 19073
877-444-7225
info@prostack.com www.prostack.com
Bottled water racks
President: Daniel Kelly
Estimated Sales: $170,000
Number Employees: 1
Square Footage: 1706

27710 Polymercia
609 Fertilla Street
Carrollton, GA 30117-3927 770-830-7434
Fax: 770-830-7377 800-762-1678
info@polymerica.com www.polymerica.com
Estimated Sales: $1 - 5 Million
Number Employees: 10-19

27711 (HQ)Polypack
3301 Gateway Centre Blvd
Pinellas Park, FL 33782-6108 727-578-5000
Fax: 727-578-1300 info@polypack.com.com
www.polypack.com
Engineer and manufacturer of shrink packaging equipment including shrink-wrap robotic infeeds and collation, continuous motion form fill seal machines
President/Founder: Alain Cerf
Estimated Sales: $10-20 Million
Number Employees: 50-99
Type of Packaging: Consumer, Food Service, Private Label, Bulk
Other Locations:
Polypack
Shanghai

27712 Polyplastic Forms, Inc
49 Gazza Blvd
Farmingdale, NY 11735 631-249-5011
Fax: 631-249-8504 800-428-7659
sales@polyplasticforms.com
www.polyplasticforms.com
Advertising signs and letters including plastic, foam, wood, metal, vinyl, etc
CEO: Diane Garrett
Marketing Director: Richard Garrett
Sales Director: Wayne Maciura
Plant Manager: Jim Dietz
Estimated Sales: $2.5-5 Million
Number Employees: 20-49

27713 Polyplastics
10201 Metropolitan Dr
Austin, TX 78758 512-339-9293
Fax: 512-339-9317 800-753-7659
sales@1polyplastics.com
www.1polyplastics.com
Manufacturer, exporter and wholesaler/distributor of rigid and flexible foamed plastics
President: Dave McArthur
VP: Tim Buckley
Sales Director: Tim Buckley
Manufacturing Manager: Harry Stevens
Estimated Sales: $2.5-5 Million
Number Employees: 20-49
Square Footage: 28000
Parent Co: Buckley Industries
Brands:
Avi
Monarch
Rubatex
Sealed Air
Sentinel
Specialty Composites Ear
Uniroyal Ensolite

27714 Polypro International
7300 Metro Blvd # 570
Minneapolis, MN 55439 952-835-7717
Fax: 952-835-3811 800-765-9776
polypro@polyprointl.com www.polyprointl.com
Processor, importer and exporter of guar and cellulose gums
President: Mark Kieper
Controller: Jennifer Jansson
Senior Account Manager, Sales/Technical: Louise Polizzotto
Customer Service/Logistics: Janet Burger
Estimated Sales: $2.5-5 Million
Number Employees: 1-4
Type of Packaging: Bulk
Brands:
Procol
Progum
Viscol

27715 Polysource
555 East Statler Road
PO Box 916
Piqua, OH 45356 937-778-9500
Fax: 937-778-9300 800-290-6323
ewehtje@polysource.com www.polysource.com
Innovative plastic foam solutions for applications
President: Erick Wehtje
Sales/Product Development Manager: Randy Dickerson
Number Employees: 20-49

27716 Polyspec
6614 Gant Rd
Houston, TX 77066 281-397-0033
Fax: 281-397-6512 888-797-0033
info@polyspec.com www.polyspec.com
Estimated Sales: $5 - 10 Million
Number Employees: 20-49

27717 (HQ)Polytainers
197 Norseman Street
Toronto, ON M8Z 2R5
Canada 416-239-7311
Fax: 416-239-0596 800-268-2424
www.polytainersinc.com
Designer and manufacturer of thinwall rigid plastic containers for the food and dairy industry
President: Robert Barrett
Number Employees: 600
Square Footage: 1000000

27718 Polytop Corporation
P.O.Box 68
Slatersville, RI 02876 401-767-2400
Fax: 401-765-2694 sales@polytop.com
www.polytop.com
Dispensing closures
President: Steve B Wilson
CFO: Kevin Rowles
Estimated Sales: $20 - 50 Million
Number Employees: 250-499

27719 Polytype America Corporation
10 Industrial Ave
Suite 4
Mahwah, NJ 07430-3530 201-995-1000
Fax: 201-995-1080 usa@wifag-polytype.com
www.wifag-polytype.com
Dry offset printing equipment for plastic containers, cups, lids, tubes, jars, vials, metal cans and can ends.
President: Pieter S Vander Griendt
VP Sales Converting North America: Glenn Whitmore
Senior Sales Representative: Rod Brynildsen
VP Sales Wifag USA: Joseph Ondras
Operations Manager: Jim Dominico
Sales Manager Decorating: Felix Gomez
Number Employees: 1000
Parent Co: wifag//polytype

27720 (HQ)Pomona Service & SupplyCompany
PO Box 2733
Yakima, WA 98907-2733 509-452-7121
Fax: 509-576-3942
Manufacturer and exporter of produce handling and packaging equipment
President: John Muller
Estimated Sales: $1-2.5 Million
Number Employees: 5-9

27721 Ponce Carribian Distributors
PO Box 11946
San Juan, PR 00922-1946 787-840-0404
Fax: 787-840-9474 info@ablesales.com
www.ablesales.com
Candy
General Manager: Luis Bornes
Estimated Sales: Under $500,000
Number Employees: 20-49

27722 Pop Tops Company
10 Plymouth Dr
South Easton, MA 02375 508-238-8585
Fax: 508-230-2851
sales@poptopssportswear.com
www.poptopssportswear.com
Sportswear for employee uniforms and advertising promotions; also, canvas bags; screenprinting and embroidering available
President: James Fine
VP Marketing: Jim Fine
Estimated Sales: $2.5 - 5 Million
Number Employees: 20-49

27723 Pop n Go
12429 East Putnam St
Whittier, CA 90602 562-945-9351
Fax: 562-945-6341 888-476-7646
info@popngo.com www.popngo.com
Popcorn vending machines
CEO: Melvin Wyman
Estimated Sales: Below $500,000
Number Employees: 10-19
Brands:
Pop N Go

27724 Popcorn Connection
7615 Fulton Avenue
North Hollywood, CA 91605-1805 818-764-3279
Fax: 818-765-0578 800-852-2676
popcornconnection@earthlink.net
www.popcornconnection.com
Gourmet popcorn confections and nuts
Owner: Kevin Needle
VP: Ross Wallach
Estimated Sales: $300,000
Number Employees: 3
Number of Brands: 15
Number of Products: 20
Square Footage: 14000
Type of Packaging: Consumer, Food Service, Private Label, Bulk
Brands:
Corn Appetit

Corn Appetit Ultimate
Fruit Corn Appetit
Video Munchies

27725 Porcelain Metals Corporation
400 South 13th Street
PO Box 7069
Louisville, KY 40210 502-635-7421
Fax: 502-635-1200 www.porcelainmetals.com
Manufacturer and exporter of cooking equipment including barbecue and charcoal grills, domestic cooktops and accessories
Manager: Randy Smitley
OEM Sales Management: Bob Miller
Estimated Sales: $10-20 Million
Number Employees: 20-49
Square Footage: 175000
Type of Packaging: Consumer, Private Label
Brands:
Barbecue Bucket
Gourmet Grid
Kingsford

27726 Port Erie Plastics
909 Troupe Rd
Harborcreek, PA 16421 814-899-7602
Fax: 814-899-7854 jconnole@porterie.com
www.porterie.com
Lightweight plastic pallets and custom modling
President: John Johnson
Quality Control: Mike Malin
CEO: William C Witkowski
Marketing/Sales Manager: John Connole
Estimated Sales: $20 - 50 Million
Number Employees: 250-499
Parent Co: Port Erie Plastics

27727 Port of Pasco
1110 Osprey Pointe Blvd
Suite 201
Pasco, WA 99301 509-547-3378
Fax: 509-547-2547 portofpasco@portofpasco.org
www.portofpasco.org
Director of Finance & Administration: Linda O'Brien
Executive Director: James Toomey
Executive Assistant & Public Information: Vicky Keller
Number Employees: 20-49

27728 Portable Cold Storage
860 Us Route One
Edison, NJ 08540 609-252-1105
Fax: 609-252-1107 800-535-2445
sales@portablecoldstorage.com
www.portablecoldstorage.com
Rent refrigerated trailers and containers. All electric three phase equipment. -15F to +75F indoors or outdoors
Operations Manager: N Kewley
Estimated Sales: $1 Million+

27729 Portco Corporation
3601 SE Columbia Way Ste 260
Vancouver, WA 98661 360-696-4167
Fax: 360-695-4849 800-426-1794
info@portco.com www.portco.com
Paper and polyethylene bags for fruit, vegetables, grains, pasta products and fish; also, printed film rollstock for form and fill; custom printing available
President: Howard M Wall Jr
CEO: Andy Stewart
Controller: Chip Nipschke
VP: Brian Williamson
Estimated Sales: $20-50 Million
Number Employees: 100-249
Square Footage: 240000

27730 Portec Flowmaster
PO Box 589
Canon City, CO 81215-0589 719-275-7471
Fax: 719-269-3750 800-777-7471
rcw@portec.com www.portecgroup.com
Curved belt conveyors, curved spiral conveyors, chutes, straight conveyors.Rollers for conveyors motorized pulleys for conveyors
President/CEO: Lawrence Weber
CEO: Kirk Mortin
Marketing: Dick Watkins
Sales: Ken Cline
Estimated Sales: $20 - 50 Million
Number Employees: 100-249
Square Footage: 80000
Parent Co: J. Richard Industries
Brands:
Portec Flowmaster
Portec Pathfinder

27731 Porter & Porter Lumber
PO Box 157
Fort Gay, WV 25514 304-648-5133
Fax: 304-648-7283
Wooden pallets and skids
Owner: H S Porter Iii
Estimated Sales: $1 - 5 Million
Number Employees: 10-19

27732 (HQ)Porter Bowers Signs
3300 101st Street
Des Moines, IA 50322-3866 515-253-9622
Fax: 515-253-9915 porterbowerssign@aol.com
Manufacturer and exporter of signs including neon, painted, indoor and outdoor
Estimated Sales: $1-2.5 Million
Number Employees: 5-9

27733 Portion-Pac Chemical Corp.
400 N Ashland Ave
Suite 1
Chicago, IL 60622 312-226-0400
Fax: 312-226-5400 info@portionpaccorp.com
www.portionpaccorp.com
Manufacturer/exporter of cleaning products including pre-measured floor cleaners and detergents, bathroom and glass cleaner, air freshener odor counteractant, carpet shampoo, final rinse sanitizers, extraction detergent andstrippers/degreasers
President: Marvin Klein
Vice President: John Miller
SFS Pac Division Manager: Chuck Ainsworth
Estimated Sales: $10-20 Million
Number Employees: 20-49
Type of Packaging: Consumer, Food Service
Brands:
Base Pac
Bowlpack
Depotpac
Foam Pac
Germicidal
Glass Pac
Mop Pac
Mop Paclite
Neutrapac
Pot & Pan Pac
Restore Pac
Sani Pac
Scrub Pac
Steam Pac
Strip Pac

27734 Portland Paper Box Company
226 SE Madison St
Portland, OR 97214-3317 503-233-6271
Fax: 503-232-4922 800-547-2571
Folding paper boxes
Estimated Sales: $5-10 Million
Number Employees: 20-49

27735 Portola Allied
275 Commerce Ave
New Castle, PA 16101-7625 724-658-4306
Fax: 724-657-8597 800-521-1368
alliedsales@portpack.com www.portpack.com
Molds for blow molding
Manager: John Piezer
R&D: Pat Taylor
CFO: Bill Stoewer
Estimated Sales: $50 - 100 Million
Number Employees: 50-99

27736 (HQ)Portola Packaging
40 Shuman Blvd.
Suite 220
Naperville, IL 60563 877-801-9169
Fax: 630-369-4583 800-767-8652
info@portpack.com www.portpack.com
Manufacturer and exporter of capping equipment and closures
President: James Taylor
CFO: Deniss Berk
CEO: Brian Bauerbach
Quality Control: Jo Beni Kisto
VP Sales/Services: Ross Markely
Number Employees: 100-249
Other Locations:
Portola Packaging
Guadalajara
Brands:
Cap Snap
Nepco
Portola Packaging

27737 Poser Envelope
1999 Harrison St # 100
Oakland, CA 94612-3517 510-251-6100
Fax: 510-444-5253 800-208-6100
Die cut envelopes; also, printing services available
Manager: Heidi Crouch
Sales/Marketing Manager: Doug Drendel
Production Manager: Rick Pallas
Plant Manager: Brain Stee
Estimated Sales: $3 - 5 Million
Number Employees: 10-19

27738 Posimat
1646 NW 108 Ave
Doral Miami-Dade, FL 33172 305-477-2029
Fax: 305-477-8044 888-767-4628
miami@posimat.com www.posimat.com
Bottle unscramblers, storage silos and bulk conveyors
President: Jaime Mart¡
Estimated Sales: Below $5 Million
Number Employees: 1-4
Number of Brands: 10
Number of Products: 5
Square Footage: 1600

27739 Positech
191 N Rush Lake Rd
Laurens, IA 50554 800-831-6026
Fax: 712-841-4765 800-831-6026
sales@positech-solutions.com
www.positech-solutions.com
Material handling machinery including manipulators, rotary manifolds and torque arms; exporter of manipulators
President: Peter Hong
CFO: Kent Radford
Quality Control: Kent Radford
Sales/Marketing Manager: Brett Stumbo
Purchasing Agent: Kay Anderson
Estimated Sales: $50 - 75 Million
Number Employees: 50-99
Square Footage: 65000
Parent Co: Columbus McKinnon Corporation
Brands:
Reaction Arm
Sam
Taurus

27740 (HQ)Positive Employment Practice
1 Muller Court
New City, NY 10956-3508 845-638-6442
scaccavo@aol.com
Consultant specializing in business coaching and problem solving support including project design, marketing strategies, organization building, financial performance, etc
Business Coach: Steven Caccavo
Number Employees: 1-4

27741 Poss USA
6643 Cupecoy Drive
Salt Lake City, UT 84121-3242 801-453-1996
Fax: 801-943-1670

27742 Posterloid Corporation
4862 36th St
Long Island City, NY 11101-1918 718-729-1050
Fax: 718-786-9310 800-651-5000
gbroder@posterloid.com www.posterloid.com
Manufacturer and exporter of menu boards and displays
President: Robert Sudack
Sales Manager: Allied Collins
Estimated Sales: $10 - 20 Million
Number Employees: 100-249

27743 Potdevin Machine Company
26 Fairfield Place
West Caldwell, NJ 07006 201-288-1941
Fax: 201-288-3770 sales@potdevin.com
www.potdevin.com
Wine industry labeling machines
President: Robert S Potdevin
Director/Sales: James Barnes
Estimated Sales: $5-10 Million
Number Employees: 20-49

27744 **Potlatch Corporation**
601 West First Avenue
Suite 1600
Spokane, WA 99201 509-835-1500
www.potlatchcorp.com
Manufacturer and exporter of paper products including napkins, toilet paper, paper towels and facial tissues
Executive Director: Mark Ohleyer
Manager: Mike Lappa
Director Marketing: Cynthia Dickerson
National Sales Manager: Mike Redden
Estimated Sales: $50-100 Million
Number Employees: 20-49
Parent Co: Potlatch Corporation
Brands:
Potlatch
Spa
Velure

27745 **Powdersize**
20 Pacific Dr
Quakertown, PA 18951-3601 215-536-5605
Fax: 215-536-6630 thigley@powdersize.com
www.powdersize.com
Contract micronizing, milling and classification and processing of pharmaceutical, food, cosmetic, and industrial dry powders in compliance with current Good Manufacturing Practices, and adherence to the principles of Total QualityManagement
President: Wayne Sigler
Founder: Lowell Histand
Partner: Thomas Moran
Estimated Sales: $1 - 5 Million
Number Employees: 10-19
Number of Products: 30
Square Footage: 40000
Type of Packaging: Private Label

27746 **Powell Systems**
162 Churchill Hubbard Rd
Youngstown, OH 44505 330-759-9220
Fax: 330-759-9434 leah@powell-systems.com
www.powellsystems.com
Materials handling containers, metal stampings, bulk packaging equipment and scales
President: Bill Powell
Founder: Willaim J. Powell
Estimated Sales: Below $5 Million
Number Employees: 1-4

27747 **Power Brushes, Inc**
756 S Byrne Rd
Toledo, OH 43609 419-385-5725
Fax: 419-382-0756 800-968-9600
president@powerbrushes.com
www.powerbrushes.com
Manufacturer and exporter of custom designed brushes for harvesting, cleaning, peeling and packing of fruits and vegetables
President: Tom Parseghian
Sales Director: Scott Dunckel
Estimated Sales: $3 Million
Number Employees: 17

27748 **Power Electronics International**
561 Plate Dr Ste 8
East Dundee, IL 60118 847-428-9494
Fax: 847-428-7744 800-362-7959
pei@peinfo.com www.peinfo.com
Manufacturer and exporter of variable speed and AC powered drives
President: Victor Habisohn
Sales Manager: Michael Habisohn
Service Manager: Adam Jezek
Estimated Sales: $20 - 50 Million
Number Employees: 50-99

27749 **Power Flame**
2001 S 21st St
Parsons, KS 67357 620-421-0480
Fax: 620-421-0948 800-862-4256
csd@powerflame.com www.powerflame.com
Small immersion tube gas, drier and oven burners
President: Bill Wiener
Sales/Marketing Executive: Bob Rizza
Customer Service Manager: Mark Dunlap
Purchasing Agent: Jerry Cruz
Estimated Sales: $10-20 Million
Number Employees: 100-249
Square Footage: 100000

27750 **(HQ)Power Group**
40w222 Old Lafox Rd
St Charles, IL 60174 630-587-3770
Fax: 630-377-4603 info@powerpackaging.com
www.powergroup.com
Dedicated and multi-customer manufacturing, packaging and logistics facilities in the food industry. Operates 25 facilities in four countries and has been providing manufacturing outsourcing and integrated supply chain solutions toFortune 100 customers since 1968
Chairman of the Board: Wayne K Sims
CEO: Wayne Sims
Sr. VP: Ken Battista
VP Sales: Jay Toelkes
Estimated Sales: $.5 - 1 million
Number Employees: 1-4
Square Footage: 14000000
Type of Packaging: Consumer, Food Service, Private Label, Bulk
Other Locations:
Power Group
Guildford Surrey

27751 **Power Industrial Supply**
80 Sebastopol Road
Santa Rosa, CA 95407-6929 707-544-3994
Fax: 707-544-3996 sppwrind@sonic.net
Boiler, control and process piping equipment
Estimated Sales: $2 Million
Number Employees: 16

27752 **Power Industries**
520 Barham Ave
Santa Rosa, CA 95404 707-545-7904
Fax: 707-541-2200 sales@powerindustries.com
www.powerindustries.com
Wine industry hoses, pipes, fittings, stainless steel tanks and construction
President: Rick Call
CFO: Kem Thangvall
Estimated Sales: $20 - 50 Million
Number Employees: 10-19

27753 **Power Logistics**
1200 Internationale Pkwy
Suite 300
Woodridge, IL 60517-4976 815-936-1800
Fax: 815-936-1970 info@powergroup.com
www.powergroup.com
Warehouse offering cooler, freezer and dry storage for frozen, refrigerated and nonperishable food products
VP Business Development: Ken Battista
Director Operations: Drew Walker
Estimated Sales: $1-2.5 Million
Number Employees: 19
Parent Co: Power Group

27754 **Power Machine Company**
118 Brookfield Drive
Moraga, CA 94556-1747 510-658-9661
Fax: 510-653-3848 carol@powermachineco.co
www.power-machine.net
Wine industry pumps and compressors
VP: Christopher Adam
CEO: Elfriede Knight
VP/General Manager: Christopher Adam
Marketing Manager: Henry Zacata
Public Relations Manager: Caral Frawman
Estimated Sales: $5-10 Million
Number Employees: 10-19

27755 **Power Packaging**
525 Dunham Rd Ste 3
St Charles, IL 60174 630-377-3838
Fax: 630-377-4603 sales@powerpackaging.com
www.powerpackaging.com
President: Randy Merigith
CEO: Wayne Sims
Operations: Gregg King
Estimated Sales: $50 - 100 Million
Number Employees: 30

27756 **Power Packaging, Inc.**
570 Polaris Parkway
Westerville, OH 43082 614-865-8500
Fax: 614-865-8875 877-272-1054
media.inquiries.excel.com
www.powerpackaging.com
Full-service contract manufacturer for dry foods, beverage mixes, bulk blending and filling, hot fill, organic, nutraceuticals, aseptic and commissary. Designs, owns and operates multi-customer and dedicated food manufacturingfacilities nationwide
President: Kevin Bauer
Chief Information Officer: Domenic Dilalla
Chief Financial Officer: Scot Hofacker
Chief Development Officer: Michael Gardner
Chief Commercial Officer: Ted Nikolai
Vice President, Communications: Lynn Anderson
VP/General Counsel/Compliance Officer: Mark Smolik
SVP, Human Resources: Tim Sprotsy
Chief Operating Officer: Scott Sureddin
Estimated Sales: $153 Million
Number Employees: 1,600
Square Footage: 10050000
Parent Co: Exel Inc.

27757 **Power Ramp**
W194n11481 McCormick Dr
Germantown, WI 53022-3035 262-255-1510
Fax: 262-255-4199 800-643-5424
sales@poweramp.com www.docksystemsinc.com
Manufacturer and exporter of dock levelers including pit-style, edge of dock, truck, truck restraining systems, dock seals and shelters, etc
President: Edward McGuire
Vice President: Mike Pilgrim
Estimated Sales: $25 Million
Number Employees: 50-99
Square Footage: 100000
Parent Co: Systems

27758 **Power Soak by Metcraft**
13910 Kessler Drive
Grandview, MO 64030-2810 816-761-3250
Fax: 816-761-0544 info@powersoak.com
www.powersoak.com
President: John Cantrell
Vice President of Distribution: Barry Bergstein
Sales Manager: Mary Cunningham
Vice President of Operations: John McCreight
Manufacturing Manager: Monty Patton
Estimated Sales: $10 - 15 Million
Number Employees: 50-100

27759 **Power-Pack Conveyor Company**
38363 Airport Pkwy
Willoughby, OH 44094 440-975-9955
Fax: 440-975-0505
ppcc@power-packconveyor.com
www.power-packconveyor.com
Belt conveyors
President: Jim Ensinger
CFO: Jim Ensinger
VP: Jim Ensinger
R&D: Jim Ensinger
Estimated Sales: $5 - 10 Million
Number Employees: 20-49

27760 **Powertex**
1 Lincoln Blvd
Suite 101
Rouses Point, NY 12979 518-297-4000
Fax: 518-297-2634 800-769-3783
seabulk@powertex.com www.powertex.com
Manufacturer and exporter of dry powder and bulk plastic liners for use in ocean containers and truck trailers
President: Stephen Podd
Chariman/CEO: Victor Podd
Sales Manager: Patricia Olsen
Estimated Sales: $10 - 20 Million
Number Employees: 50-99
Square Footage: 65000
Brands:
Powerbulk
Powerliner
Powertex Meatstrap
Seabulk Powerliner

27761 **Powertex**
1 Lincoln Blvd
Suite 101
Rouses Point, NY 12979 518-297-4000
Fax: 518-297-2634 seabulk@powertex.com
www.powertex.com
Tea and coffee container liners
President: Stephen Podd
Sales/Marketing: Patricia Olsen
Estimated Sales: $10-20 Million
Number Employees: 50-99

27762 **Prairie View IndustriesFood Service Inc**
P.O.Box 575
Fairbury, NE 68352-0575 402-729-4055
Fax: 402-729-4058 800-554-7267
info@pvifs.com www.pvifs.com
Accessories, benches, can racks, carts, dollies, drip catcher, dunnage racks, equipment stands, hotshelves, organizers, pan racks, picnic table, pizza racks, platform trucks, ramps, shelving carts, sinks, tables
Owner: Richard Allen

27763 **(HQ)Prater Industries**
2 Sammons Ct
Bolingbrook, IL 60440 630-679-3200
Fax: 630-759-6099 800-451-6958
info@praterindustries.com
www.praterindustries.com
Sizing, separation, particle reduction/enlargement equipment
President/CEO: R Scott Prater
CFO: David Utterback
Marketing: Katie Meyers
Estimated Sales: $5-10 Million
Number Employees: 50-99
Square Footage: 55000
Other Locations:
Prater Industries
Sterling IL
Brands:
Mega-Mill
Rota-Sieve

27764 **Pratt Industries**
220 Plantation Rd
New Orleans, LA 70123 504-733-7292
Fax: 504-734-8920 www.prattindustries.com
Manufacturer and marketer of advanced intermodal equipment
President: Jim Hale
CFO: Gary Byrd
R&D: Mark Nay
Estimated Sales: $10 - 20 Million
Number Employees: 1-4

27765 **(HQ)Pratt Poster Company**
3001 E 30th Street
Indianapolis, IN 46218-2850 317-545-0842
Fax: 317-927-0653 tpratt@prattcorp.com
www.prattcorp.com
Point of purchase advertising signs, flags, pennants and banners
CEO: Sarah Pratt
National Sales Manager: Thomas Pratt
Estimated Sales: $10-20 Million
Number Employees: 100-249
Type of Packaging: Bulk

27766 **Prawnto Shrimp Machine Company**
4770 Interstate 30 W
Caddo Mills, TX 75135-7634 903-527-4149
Fax: 903-527-4951 800-426-7254
sales@prawntomachine.com
www.prawntomachine.com
President: Don Morris
Estimated Sales: Below $5 Million
Number Employees: 1-4

27767 **Prawnto Systems**
4770 Interstate 30 W
Caddo Mills, TX 75135 903-527-4149
Fax: 903-527-4951 800-426-7254
sales@prawntomachine.com
www.prawntomachine.com
Manufacturer and exporter of shrimp processing equipment including cutters, processing stations and deveiners
President/CEO: Don Morris
CEO: Don Morris
VP: Derrell Sawyer
Sales: Derrell Sawyer
Estimated Sales: $1,000,000
Number Employees: 1-4
Number of Brands: 2
Number of Products: 7
Square Footage: 3500
Brands:
Prawnto
Shrimperfect

27768 **Praxair**
39 Old Ridgebury Rd Ste 7
Danbury, CT 06810 203-837-2000
Fax: 800-772-9985 800-772-9247
www.praxair.com
Manufacturer and exporter of nitrogen freezing systems for food packaging
President: Wayne Yakich
CEO: Stephen F Angel
Estimated Sales: $11.22 Billion
Number Employees: 26,500
Brands:
Linde

27769 **(HQ)Praxair**
39 Old Ridgebury Rd Ste 7
Danbury, CT 06810 203-837-2000
Fax: 203-837-2532 800-772-9247
info@praxair.com www.praxair.com
Industrial gases and refrigeration equipment including cooling and water treatment systems, freezers, gas spargers and packaging processes
Chairman/President/CEO: Dennis Reilly
Sr. VP/CFO: James Swayer
Estimated Sales: $11.22 Billion
Number Employees: 26539

27770 **Praxair Food Technologies**
7000 High Grove Blvd
Burr Ridge, IL 60527-7595 630-320-4000
Fax: 630-320-4001 www.praxair.com
Cryogenic freezing and chilling systems for the food and beverage industries.
Parent Co: Nu-Star, Inc.

27771 **Precision**
1135 NW 159th Dr
Miami, FL 33169-5882 305-625-2451
Fax: 305-623-0475 800-762-7565
sales@atlasfoodserv.com
www.atlasfoodserv.com
Food transport carts, heated and refrigerated conveyors, buffet equipment, milk and ice cream units and modular serving systems
President: David Meade
VP Sales: Howard Bolner
VP Manufacturing: Mark Siegfriedt
Estimated Sales: $10 - 20 Million
Number Employees: 100-249
Parent Co: Atlas Metal Industries

27772 **Precision Automation**
1841 Old Cuthbert Rd
Cherry Hill, NJ 08034 856-428-7400
Fax: 856-428-1270
sales@precisionautomationinc.com
www.precisionautomationinc.com
Chairman of the Board: G Frederick Rexon Sr
Estimated Sales: $10-20 Million
Number Employees: 50-99

27773 **Precision Automation Company**
1841 Old Cuthbert Road
Cherry Hill, NJ 08034 856-428-7400
Fax: 856-428-1270
sales@precisionautomationinc.com
www.precisionautomationinc.com
President: Glen A Morris
Founder: Fred. Rexon Sr
Chairman: Fred Rexon Sr
Estimated Sales: $3.5 Million
Number Employees: 20-49
Square Footage: 45

27774 **Precision Brush Company**
6700 Parkland Blvd
Cleveland, OH 44139 440-542-9600
Fax: 800-252-0834 800-252-4747
info@precisionbrush.com
www.precisionbrush.com
Manufacturer and exporter of custom metal channel strip brushes in various shapes and sizes
President: Jim Benjamin
General Manager: Mike Porter
Estimated Sales: $2.5-5 Million
Number Employees: 10-19
Square Footage: 18000

27775 **Precision Component Industries**
5325 Southway St SW
Canton, OH 44706 330-477-6287
Fax: 330-477-1052
tricia@precision-component.com
www.precision-component.com
Manufacturer and exporter of special production machinery, tools, dies, fixtures, short and long run production machining, stamping services and cans
CEO: Patricia Gerak
President: Tony Gerak
Sales Manager: Lewis Page
Purchase Manager: George Melson
Estimated Sales: Below $5 Million
Number Employees: 20-49
Parent Co: Brennan Industrial Group
Type of Packaging: Bulk

27776 **Precision Foods**
11457 Olde Cabin Rd
Suite 100
Saint Louis, MO 63141 314-567-4700
Fax: 314-567-7421 800-442-5242
info@precisionfoods.com
www.precisionfood.com
Processor and contract packager of pickle and tomato mixes, pectins, jams, jellies, fruit preservatives, blended spices and seasonings, dry dessert preparations and mixes, exporter of dry soft serve and dessert mixes
President: Jerry Fritz
VP: Marilyn Romine
R&D: Bob Bonardi
Quality Control: Tyson Koch
Marketing: Janet Brooks
Sales: Jerry Wright
Operations: Andy Balafas
Purchasing Director: Chuck Pombert
Estimated Sales: $5 - 10 Million
Number Employees: 10-19
Square Footage: 100000
Type of Packaging: Consumer, Food Service, Private Label, Bulk
Brands:
Frostline

27777 **Precision Microcontrol**
2075-N Corte del Nogal
Carlsbad, CA 92011-1415 760-930-0101
Fax: 760-930-0222 info@pmccorp.com
www.pmccorp.com
Four axis packaged controller with motion control features
Head Marketing Team: David Clark
Number Employees: 50-99

27778 **Precision Plastics Inc.**
6405A Ammendale Rd
Beltsville, MD 20705 301-937-1317
Fax: 301-937-4184 800-922-1317
info@preciousplastics.com
www.precisionplastics.com
Plastic food service products including sneeze guards, heat shields, condiment racks, menu/card holders, ice trays, buffet bars, signage, etc. Also a 3M product distributor
Owner: Oliver Hofe
Administrator Assistant: Vicki Juneau
Marketing Manager: Chris Marshall
Estimated Sales: $2.5-5 Million
Number Employees: 20-49
Square Footage: 15000

27779 **Precision Plus Vacuum Parts**
6416 Inducon Drive W
Sanborn, NY 14132 716-297-2039
Fax: 716-297-8210 800-526-2707
info@precisionplus.com www.precisionplus.com
Vacuum pump replacement parts
Manager: Joseph Miller
Estimated Sales: $7 Million
Number of Brands: 15
Number of Products: 2000
Square Footage: 80000
Parent Co: BOC Group, Inc.
Type of Packaging: Food Service
Brands:
Alcatel
Boc Edwards
Boce Stokes
Busch
Ebara
Kinney
Leybold
Precision Scientific
Ristschic
Varian
Welch

27780 Precision Pours
12837 Industrial Park Blvd
Plymouth, MN 55441 763-694-9291
Fax: 763-694-9343 800-549-4491
ricksandvik@precisionpours.com
www.precisionpours.com
Manufacturer and exporter of pour spouts for liquor, syrups and cooking oils; wholesaler/distributor of pour cleaning systems
President: Richard Sandvik
Accounting: Patrick Sandvik
VP Sales: Duane Nording
Estimated Sales: Below $5,000,000
Number Employees: 10-19
Square Footage: 4800
Brands:
Rack & Pour
Sure Shot

27781 Precision Printing & Packaging
801 Alfred Thun Rd
Clarksville, TN 37040 931-920-9000
Fax: 931-920-9001 800-500-4526
Metallized and paper glue-applied labels
Chairman of the Board: Joseph Sellinger
National Sales Manager: Reba Meek
Plant Manager: Rod Stough
Estimated Sales: $50 - 100 Million
Number Employees: 250-499
Parent Co: Anheuser-Busch Companies

27782 Precision Solutions
2525 Tollgate Rd
Quakertown, PA 18951 215-536-4400
Fax: 215-536-4096
info@precisionsolutionsinc.com
www.precisionsolutionsinc.com
Representative for many manufacturers of scale and measurement equipment
Owner: Dan Kendra
Technical Service Consultant: Trevor Filipowicz

27783 Precision Stainless
501 N Belcrest Ave
Springfield, MO 65802 417-865-8724
Fax: 417-865-0906 info@precision.itt.com
www.precisionstainless.com
Wine industry aseptic processing equipment, bins and blenders and equipment fabrication
Sales Engineer: Bert Adams
Estimated Sales: $25-50 Million
Number Employees: 10-19

27784 Precision Systems
16 Tech Cir
Suite 100
Natick, MA 01760 508-655-7010
Fax: 508-653-6999 precisionsystems@msn.com
www.precisionsystemsinc.com
Milk cryoscopes manufacturing, testing, incoming inspection and final Q.C oeomerers and chemistry analyzers
President: Charles Bell
CFO: Ann Rogers
VP: Jennifer Knapp
Quality Control: Bob Atwood
Estimated Sales: $1-5 Million
Number Employees: 20-49
Number of Brands: 20
Number of Products: 100
Square Footage: 45600
Type of Packaging: Private Label
Brands:
Analette
Cryoscopes
Osmette

27785 Precision Temp
11 Sunnybrook Drive
Cincinnati, OH 45237 513-641-4446
Fax: 513-641-0733 800-934-9690
service@precisiontemp.com
www.precisiontemp.com
Manufacturer and exporter of gas booster heaters for high temperature water
President: Gerry Wolter
CEO: Rick Muhlhauser
Vice President: Fred Rohtzeid
Estimated Sales: $2-4,000,000
Number Employees: 10-19
Square Footage: 20000
Type of Packaging: Food Service
Brands:
Precision Temp

27786 (HQ)Precision Wood Products
PO Box 529
Vancouver, WA 98666-0529 360-694-8322
Fax: 360-696-1530 palletmfg@aol.com
Manufacturer and exporter of wooden pallets and containers
President: Marley Petersen Jr
Estimated Sales: $5-10 Million
Number Employees: 50-99

27787 Precision Wood of Hawaii
PO Box 529
Vancouver, WA 98666-0529 808-682-2055
Fax: 808-682-2465
Pallets, wooden boxes and crates; also, rebuilder of recycled wooden pallets
VP/General Manager: T Ross
Estimated Sales: $1-2.5 Million
Number Employees: 50-100

27788 Precit
710 Tech Park Drive
La Vergne, TN 37086-3622 615-287-8255
Fax: 615-287-8355 800-338-4585
jeff.watson@franke.com www.precit.com
Parent Co: Franke

27789 Preco Inc
500 Laser Dr
Somerset, WI 54025 715-247-3285
Fax: 715-247-5650 800-775-2737
sales@precoinc.com www.precoinc.com
President/CEO: Tim Burns
Estimated Sales: $1 - 5 Million
Number Employees: 100-249

27790 Preferred Freezer Services
900 East M Street
Wilmington, CA 90744 310-984-1800
Fax: 310-518-1870
jzarrella@preferredfreezer.com
www.preferredfreezer.com
Supplier of recipe management software for product development and nutritional labeling.
President: Brian Beattie
Chief Executive Officer: John J. Galiher
CFO: Samuel Hensley
VP Finance: Jim Glades
IT: B Vasquez
Director, Health, Safety Environmental: Mark Sens
Marketing Manager: Gail Hannagan
Executive Vice President, Sales: Dan DiDonato
Director, HR: L Fashan
VP, Operations: R Williams
Warehouse/Plant Administrator: Jamie Walton
Estimated Sales: $5 - 10 Million
Number Employees: 10-19
Number of Brands: 3
Number of Products: 3
Parent Co: Preferred Freezer
Brands:
Colorsoft
Colortec-Pcm
Formulator

27791 Preferred Machining Corporation
3730 S Kalamath Street
Englewood, CO 80110-3493 303-761-1535
Fax: 303-789-9300 sales@pmc1.net
www.preferredcorporation.com
Manufacturer and exporter of fillers, pumps/stuffers, formers and vacuumizers for poultry, beef, etc. As well as end liners and accessories for the can making industry
Vice President: Jim Abbott
Marketing Director: Tom Hoffmann
Estimated Sales: $10 - 20 Million
Number Employees: 50
Brands:
Prc Weight Control Filler
Versaform

27792 Preferred Packaging
PO Box 700
Mount Gilead, NC 27306 336-884-0792
Fax: 336-884-5829
preferredmichael@northstate.net
Folding paper boxes
President: William H Drummond
VP Sales/Marketing: Michael Drummond
Estimated Sales: $5 - 10 Million
Number Employees: 30
Square Footage: 43000
Type of Packaging: Consumer, Food Service, Private Label

27793 Preferred Packaging Systems
440 S Lone Hill Avenue
San Dimas, CA 91773
Fax: 909-592-5640 800-378-4777
info@ghlpackaging.com www.ghlpackaging.com
Manufactures, engineers and designs packaging equipment.
Estimated Sales: $10-15 Million
Number Employees: 15
Square Footage: 30000

27794 Premier Brass
255 Ottley Dr NE Ste A
Atlanta, GA 30324-3926 404-873-6000
Fax: 404-873-9993 800-251-5800
info@premierbrass.com www.premierbrass.com
Manufacturer, importer and exporter of brass and chrome components for custom foodguards, display cases and railing systems
President: Alex Mazingue
Vice President: Pep Matus
General Manager: Fred Boyajian
Estimated Sales: $1-2.5 Million
Number Employees: 10-19
Square Footage: 25000
Parent Co: Great Eastern Distributors
Type of Packaging: Food Service
Brands:
Premier Brass

27795 Premier Foods
871 Harbour Way S
Richmond, CA 94804-3612 707-554-4623

27796 Premier Glass & PackageCompany
PO Box 5612
Napa, CA 94581 707-224-1660
Fax: 707-224-1660 tremglass@interx.net
Wine bottles and packaging
President: Kent Robert
Owner: Stuart Humpert
Estimated Sales: Less than $500,000
Number Employees: 1-4

27797 Premier Industries
5721 Dragon Way
Suite 113
Cincinnati, OH 45227-4518 859-581-1390
Fax: 859-581-5525 800-354-9817
jtaylor@premierindustry.com
Manufacturer and exporter of paper plates, hot dog holders, food trays and foil laminated ashtrays
VP/General Manager: J Paul Taylor
Sales: Lori Roberts
VP Operations: Viea Gerwin
Plant Manager: Mike McCann
Estimated Sales: $5-10 Million
Square Footage: 40000
Type of Packaging: Private Label
Brands:
Teddy Bear

27798 Premier Manufactured Systems
8716 W Ludlow Dr Ste 1
Peoria, AZ 85381 623-931-1977
Fax: 623-866-5666 800-752-5582
mail@premierh2o.com www.wattspremier.com
Manufacturer and exporter of water purification equipment
VP: Shannon Murphy
Estimated Sales: $5-10 Million
Number Employees: 20-49
Parent Co: Watts Water Technologies Co.

27799 (HQ)Premier Packages
9438 Watson Industrial Park
Saint Louis, MO 63126-1523 314-961-6588
Fax: 314-961-6589 800-466-6588
info@premierpackages.com
www.premierpackages.com
Bakery boxes, folding cartons and trays; also, die cutting available
Co-Owner: Jeff Petroski
Estimated Sales: $1-2.5 Million
Number Employees: 5-9
Square Footage: 32000

27800 Premier Plastics Company
1225 Pearl St
Waukesha, WI 53189-7478 262-547-4582
Fax: 262-547-1373 800-878-8430
Thin gauge packaging for short runs
Owner: Keith Wein
Sales Manager: Franklin Berry
Customer Service Manager: Elizabeth Laska
Estimated Sales: $3 - 5 Million
Number Employees: 10-19
Square Footage: 15000

27801 Premier Restaurant Equipment
7120 Northland Ter N
Minneapolis, MN 55428 763-544-8800
Fax: 763-544-7949 info@premiereq.com
www.premiereq.com
Provider of design and production services
Owner: Rob Jocob
Estimated Sales: $5 - 10,000,000
Number Employees: 20-49

27802 Premier Skirting Products
241 Mill St
Lawrence, NY 11559 516-239-6581
Fax: 516-239-6810 800-544-2516
info@premierskirting.com
www.premierskirting.com
Manufacturer and exporter of table and skirting cloths, napkins, chair covers and place mats
Owner: Ross Yudin
CEO: C VanDewater
CFO: Linda Ehrlich
Plant Manager: Wayne Rizzo
Estimated Sales: $1 - 2.5 Million
Number Employees: 10-19
Square Footage: 10000

27803 Premier Southern TicketCompany
7911 School Rd
Cincinnati, OH 45249 513-489-6700
Fax: 513-489-6867 800-331-2283
sales@premiersouthern.com
www.premiersouthern.com
Coupons and numbered pressure sensitive labels
President: Kirk Schulz
Sales Manager: Bill Reilly
Estimated Sales: $5 - 10 Million
Number Employees: 20-49
Parent Co: Price Chopper

27804 Premium Air Systems
1051 Naughton Dr
Troy, MI 48083 248-680-8800
Fax: 248-680-8808 877-430-0333
leonardf@premiumair.net www.premiumair.net
Custom stainless steel food service tables, sinks, hoods, custom ventilation systems, refrigeration and HV/AC equipment; also, installation available
President: Leonard Framalin
Sales Manager: Gilbert St.Louis
Engineer Manager: Ken Comito
Estimated Sales: $5-10 Million
Number Employees: 50-99

27805 Premium Foil Products Company
PO Box 32309
Louisville, KY 40232 502-459-2820
Fax: 502-454-5488 www.premiumfoil.com
Manufacturer and exporter of aluminum foil containers
President: A J Kleier
VP/General Manager: Robert Moses
Estimated Sales: $5-10 Million
Number Employees: 20-49
Type of Packaging: Food Service, Bulk

27806 Premium Ingredients International US, LLC
285 E Fullerton Ave
Carol Stream, IL 60188-1886 630-868-0300
Fax: 630-868-0310 info@prinovausa.com
www.prinovausa.com
Food ingredients and aroma chemicals
President: Donald Thorp
CEO: Richard Thorp
CFO: Donald Cepican
VP: Daniel Thorp
Research/Development Director: Suzanne Johnson
VP Sales/Marketing: Richard Calabrese
Estimated Sales: $30-35 Million
Number Employees: 100
Parent Co: AMC Chemicals
Other Locations:
Premium Ingredients International
Holladay UT
Premium Ingredients International
Ellisville MO
Premium Ingredients International
Cranford NJ
Premium Ingredients Int'l(UK)
London, England

27807 Premium Pallet
5000 Richmond Street
Philadelphia, PA 19137-1815 215-535-2559
Fax: 215-535-2570 800-648-7347
Skids and pallets
President: Erik Bronstein
Number Employees: 40
Square Footage: 990

27808 Prengler Products
P.O.Box 2305
Sherman, TX 75091 903-892-0242
Fax: 903-893-9536 craig@prenglerproducts.com
www.prenglerproducts.com
Point of purchase displays
President: Craig S Prengler
Estimated Sales: $500,000-$1 Million
Number Employees: 1-4
Square Footage: 28000

27809 Prent Corporation
P.O.Box 471
Janesville, WI 53547-0471 608-754-0276
Fax: 608-754-2410 prent@prent.com
www.prent.com
Custom thermal former
Owner: Joseph T Pregont
Marketing Director: Vicki Damron
Estimated Sales: $50-100 Million
Number Employees: 250-499

27810 Prentiss
3600 Mansell Rd Ste 350
Alpharetta, GA 30022 770-552-8072
Fax: 770-552-8076 info@prentiss.com
www.prentiss.com
Manufacturer, importer and exporter of pesticides, insecticides and rodenticides
President: Richard A Miller
VP/Purchasing: Jeffery Miller
Sales Director: Larry Eichler
Estimated Sales: $10 - 20 Million
Number Employees: 5-9
Square Footage: 50000
Type of Packaging: Private Label, Bulk
Brands:
Prentox

27811 Pres-Air-Trol Corporation
1009 W Boston Post Rd
Mamaroneck, NY 10543-3329 914-698-2026
Fax: 914-698-9456 800-431-2625
presair@aol.com www.presair.com
Manufacturer and exporter of foot pedals and switches including pneumatic/electric and shock, explosion and water-proof; pressure and vacuum switches, thermometers, thermostats
President: Arthur Blumenthal
Vice President: Doreen Bassin
Sales: Juana Magana
Production/Plant Manager: Chris Felon
Purchasing: Marie Schuartz
Estimated Sales: $10 - 20 Million
Number Employees: 20-49
Square Footage: 12000
Brands:
Control Safe
Disposertrol
Magictrol
Pres-Air-Trol
Tinytrol

27812 Pres-On Products
21 W Factory Rd
Addison, IL 60101 630-543-9370
Fax: 630-628-8025 800-323-7467
Manufacturer and exporter of liners including induction seal, PE, styrene and self-sealing
Division VP: Tom Cummins
VP Manufacturing: Frank Edes
Estimated Sales: $20-50 Million
Number Employees: 15

27813 Pres-On Tape & Gasket Corporation
2600 E. 107th Street
Bolingbrook, IL 60440 630-628-1205
Fax: 630-628-8025 800-323-7467
industrial@pres-on.com www.pres-on.com
Induction and pressure sealed cap liners, gasketing tapes of vinyl foam
Founder: Henry L. Gianatasio
Estimated Sales: $10 Million
Number Employees: 1-4

27814 Prescolite
695 Walnut Ave
Vallejo, CA 94592-1134 707-562-3500
Fax: 510-577-5022 www.prescolite.com
Manufacturer and exporter of lighting fixtures including electric, incandescent, mercury and outdoor
Marketing Manager: John Taylor
Estimated Sales: $20-50 Million
Number Employees: 250-499
Parent Co: US Industries

27815 Presentation Packaging
870 Louisiana Ave S
Minneapolis, MN 55426 763-540-9544
Fax: 763-540-9522 800-818-2698
customerservice@presentationpackaging.com
www.presentationpackaging.com
Stock boxes in matched colors, graphics, textures, structures, and sizes
Manager: Lori Corder
General Manager: Carol Sylvester
Estimated Sales: $100-500 Million
Number Employees: 10-19

27816 Presentations South
4748 Jetty St
Orlando, FL 32817-3183 407-657-2108
Fax: 407-849-0930 psixpo@evcom.net
Manufacturer, designer and exporter of industrial displays, attraction exhibits, etc
Estimated Sales: $2.5-5 Million
Number Employees: 1-4
Square Footage: 60000

27817 President Container
PO Box 387
Wood Ridge, NJ 07075-0387 201-933-7500
Fax: 201-933-8990
pcsales@presidentcontainer.com
www.presidentcontainer.com
Corrugated boxes
President: Marvin Grossbard
Vice President: Richard Grossbard
General Manager: Larry Grossbard
Vice President of Production: Joe Restifo
Estimated Sales: $20 - 50 Million
Number Employees: 250-499
Square Footage: 200000

27818 Pressed Paperboard Technologies LLC
30400 Telegraph Rd
Bingham Farms, MI 48025-4537 248-646-6500
Fax: 248-646-6532 sales@papertrays.com
www.papertrays.com
Press formed, dual-ovenable paperboard trays for the frozen food, school and institutional feeding and pizza industries.
Owner: Lawrence Epstein
Vice President Sales: Al Fotheringham

27819 Pressure Pack
PO Box 3007
Williamsburg, VA 23187-3007 757-220-3693
Fax: 757-229-7612 rwfox@widamaker.com
Asceptic, food processing, heat sealing and can filling machinery
Owner: Robert Fox
VP Technology: Joseph Marcy
Estimated Sales: $1 - 5,000,000
Number Employees: 1-4

27820 Prestige Label Company
151 Industrial Dr
Burgaw, NC 28425 910-259-3600
Fax: 910-259-6312 800-969-4449
info@prestigelabel.com www.prestigelabel.com
Labels including thermal, thermal transfer, laser, computer, styrene inserts, prime, bar code and consecutive numbers
Manager: Terie Syme

Estimated Sales: $5-10 Million
Number Employees: 20-49
Square Footage: 18000
Type of Packaging: Private Label

27821 Prestige Metal Products
885 Anita Ave
PO Box 700
Antioch, IL 60002 847-395-0775
Fax: 847-395-0792 rfq@prestigemetals.com
www.prestigemetals.com
Custom sheet metal fabrication
President: Gordon Miller
Estimated Sales: $2.5-5 Million
Number Employees: 20-49
Square Footage: 19000

27822 Prestige Plastics Corporation
8207 Swenson Way
Delta, BC V4G 1J5
Canada 604-930-2931
Fax: 604-930-2936 jberry@prestigeplas.com
www.prestigeplas.com
Manufacturer, importer and exporter of bins, tote and plastic boxes, cartons, point of purchase displays and signs; also, die cutting and design services available
President: Bill Schoenbaum
Sales Manager: James Berry
Estimated Sales: $10-20 Million
Number Employees: 10-19

27823 Prestige Skirting & Tablecloths
60 Dutch Hill Rd # 4a
Orangeburg, NY 10962-1722 845-358-6900
Fax: 845-359-2287 800-635-3313
prestigeskirting@aol.com
www.prestigeskirting.com
Manufacturer and exporter of tablecloths, napkins, banquet skirting, clips with Velcro, skirt hangers, chair covers, working racks and custom made linens
President: Marilyn Enison
Office Manager: Emily Valerie Ross
Sales Manager: Paul Tessler
Customer Service: Jane Smithers
Estimated Sales: $5-10 Million
Number Employees: 10-19
Square Footage: 20000
Brands:
Hangars

27824 Presto Tek Corporation
2229 S Yale St
Santa Ana, CA 92704-4401 714-540-4914
Fax: 714-968-7311 800-639-7678
info@newportus.com www.newportus.com
NEWPORT® is known for designing and manufacturing the world's most accurate industrial intrumentation. Prestotek brand of products includes: pH, ORP, conductivity, Resistivity, salt, and much more. Offered as panel mount ofhandheld instruments.
President: Milton Hollander
Estimated Sales: $1 - 3 Million
Number Employees: 10-19
Parent Co: Newport Electronics
Type of Packaging: Private Label
Brands:
Pocket Pal
Presto-Tek

27825 Prestolabels.Com
31 Industry Park Court
Tipp City, OH 45371
Fax: 937-667-5687 800-201-7120
andy.heinl@prestolabels.com
www.prestolabels.com
Digital labels and tags
President: Tony Heinl
CEO: Rick Heinl
CFO: Gene Harris
R&D/Sales: Andy Heink
QControl/Operations/Plant Manager: Gary Packott
Marketing/Public Relations: Pat Larson
Production: Rob Sloan
Purchasing: Heidi Ponlman
Estimated Sales: $35 Million
Number Employees: 160
Parent Co: Repacorp, Inc
Type of Packaging: Consumer, Food Service, Private Label, Bulk

27826 Preston Scientific
1450 N Hundley St
Anaheim, CA 92806-1322 714-632-3700
Fax: 714-632-7355
baspear@prestonscientific.com
www.prestonscientific.com
Manufacturer and exporter of computer systems including data acquisition sub-systems
President and CEO: Bernard Spear
Executive VP: Phillip Halverson
President: Bill Boston
Sales Manager: Charles McGuire
Plant Manager: Amber Brideisca
Purchasing Manager: Robert Exley
Estimated Sales: $1 - 2.5 Million
Number Employees: 1-4
Square Footage: 48000
Parent Co: Halear
Brands:
Presys1000

27827 Pretium Packaging
PO Box 230
Hermann, MO 65041 573-486-2811
Fax: 573-486-2443 www.pretiumpkg.com
Manufacturer and exporter of custom packaging and mustard bottles
President: Keith Harbison
Plant Manager: Bob Gillig
Estimated Sales: $20 - 50 Million
Number Employees: 50-99

27828 Pretium Packaging
2230 D Ave E
Seymour, IN 47274 812-522-8177
Fax: 812-522-9441 www.pretiumpkg.com
Blow molded plastic bottles in HDPE, PVC, LPDE and EPET; also, labeling and decorating available
CFO: Bob Mohrmann
Manager: John Cannaday
Plant Manager: Joe Wolf
Estimated Sales: $10-20 Million
Number Employees: 50-99

27829 Pretium Packaging, LLC.
15450 S. Outer 40 Drive
Suite 120
Chesterfield, MO 63017-2062 314-727-8200
Fax: 314-727-0249 www.petriumpkg.com
Manufacturer and exporter of plastic bottles and containers used for syrup
Manager: John Cannaday
Plant Manager: Joe Wolf
Estimated Sales: $232.23 Million
Number Employees: 1200
Parent Co: Harrison
Type of Packaging: Bulk

27830 Pri-Pak
P.O.Box 4010
Lawrenceburg, IN 47025-4010 812-537-7300
Fax: 812-537-7310 ssassaman@pripak.com
www.pripak.com
Wine coolers
Plant Manager: Gary Dunn
Estimated Sales: $50 - 75 Million
Number Employees: 100-249

27831 Pride Container Corporation
4545 W Palmer St
Chicago, IL 60639 773-227-6000
Fax: 773-227-2645 info@strivegroup.com
www.strivegroup.com
Corrugated containers
President: Jeff Sharfstein
CFO: Jeff McReynolds
Chairman of the Board: Richard Sharfstein
VP Sales: Michael Weiss
Estimated Sales: $20-50 Million
Number Employees: 100-249

27832 Pride Neon
3010 W 10th St
Sioux Falls, SD 57104 605-336-3563
Fax: 605-336-6938 signs@prideneon.com
www.prideneon.com
Indoor and outdoor signs including neon and back-lit; also, awnings
Owner: George Menke Jr
Secretary/Treasurer: Dick Menke
Vice President: Bob Menke
Service Manager: Mitch Menke
Sales: Gale Mudder
Assistant Financial Manager: Dan Menke
Production Manager: Nick Menke
Estimated Sales: $1,800,000
Number Employees: 20-49

27833 Pride Polymers
1111 No. 20th Avenue
Yakima, WA 98902 509-452-3330
Fax: 509-452-8850 info@pridepolymers.com
www.pridepolymers.com
Owner: Joe O'Malley

27834 Primary Liquidation Corporation
80 Orville Dr
Bohemia, NY 11716-2534 631-244-1410
Fax: 516-229-2741 primaryl@aol.com
Supplier of surplus closeout liquidation inventories of a food and grocery nature. Over 29 years of experience
President: Paul Klein
Estimated Sales: $2.5-5,000,000
Number Employees: 1-4
Type of Packaging: Consumer, Food Service

27835 Prime Equipment
10201 E Buckeye Ln
Spokane Valley, WA 99206-4270 509-928-8947
Fax: 509-928-0690 custserv@primequipusa.com
Packaging machinery
Estimated Sales: $1-2.5 Million
Number Employees: 5-9

27836 Prime Inc.
P.O.Box 4208
Springfield, MO 65808
Fax: 417-521-6878 800-321-4552
www.primeinc.com
Trucking service that provides refrigerated, flatbed, and tanker carrier services to an international customer base.
President/Founder: Robert E Low
Director, Finance: Dean Hoedl
General Counsel: Steve Crawford
Director, Technology: Rodney Rader
Director, Marketing: Keith McCoy
Vice President, Sales & Marketing: Steve Wutke
Director, Operations: Pat Leonard
Manager, Special Projects: Chad Clay
Director, Logistics: Rich Gallagher
Estimated Sales: $500 Million
Number Employees: 500-999

27837 Prime Label Consultants
536 7th St SE
Washington, DC 20003 202-546-3333
Fax: 202-543-4337 800-766-5225
info@primelabel.com www.primelabel.com
Consulting services to processors affected by Federal food labeling regulations
President: Joe Bechtold
Owner/CEO: Elizabeth Bechtold
Director, Software Development: Fred Mosher
Food Technologist: Ames Perry
Office Manager: Pat Yingling
Estimated Sales: $1-2.5 Million
Number Employees: 5-9

27838 Prime ProData
800 N Main St
North Canton, OH 44720 330-497-2578
Fax: 330-430-1776 877-497-2578
Support@PrimePro.com www.primepro.com
Accounting systems software with consultants specializing in computer systems software analysis
President: Susan Caghan
Estimated Sales: $1 - 3 Million
Number Employees: 5-9
Brands:
Pcas
Prime Prodata

27839 Prime Tag & Label
1516 F Ave SE
Hickory, NC 28602 828-327-4012
Fax: 828-327-4018 887-710-7771
sales@victrix-groupusa.com www.ptlabel.com
Manager: Monica Commisso

Estimated Sales: Below 1 Million
Number Employees: 5-9

27840 PrimeSource Equipment
PO Box 2389
Addison, TX 75001-2389 214-273-4900
Fax: 214-273-4999 800-737-8567
sales@primesourcefse.com
www.buyprimesource.com
A wholesale food service distribution company
CEO: Charles James III

27841 Primepak Company
133 Cedar Ln # 104
Teaneck, NJ 07666-4416 201-836-5060
Fax: 201-836-3275 info@primepak.com
www.primepakcompany.com
Manufacturer, importer and exporter of HDPE and LLDPE poly bags, sheeting, box and trash can liners, T-sacks and plain and printed bags
Chief Financial Officer: Mike Heilferty
VP Sales: William Heilferty
VP Operations: Chris Poppe
Estimated Sales: $20 - 50 Million
Number Employees: 32
Square Footage: 120000
Brands:
Prime Liner
Primeliner Sacks
Primeliners

27842 Primera Technology
2 Carlson Pkwy N
Plymouth, MN 55447 763-475-6676
Fax: 763-475-6677 800-797-2772
sales@primeralabel.com www.primeralabel.com
Labels
Estimated Sales: $13.3 Million
Number Employees: 90

27843 Primex Plastics Corporation
1235 N F St
Richmond, IN 47374 765-966-7774
Fax: 765-935-1083 800-222-5116
sales@primexplastics.com
www.primexplastics.com
Rolls and sheets of polystyrene
Chairman of the Board: Paul J Bertch
VP: John Kittner
Estimated Sales: $75 - 100 Million
Number Employees: 500-999

27844 Primlite Manufacturing Corporation
407 S Main St
Freeport, NY 11520 516-868-4411
Fax: 516-868-4609 800-327-7583
sales@primelite-mfg.com
www.primelite-mfg.com
Manufacturer and exporter of outdoor lighting fixtures, plastic globes and store fixtures including custom designed prismatic glass ceiling and wall fixtures
President: Benjamin Heit
Quality Control Manager: Joanne Heit
Estimated Sales: $3 - 5 Million
Number Employees: 10-19
Square Footage: 60000

27845 Primo Piatto
7300 36th Ave N
Minneapolis, MN 55427 763-531-9194
Fax: 763-536-0100 www.dakotagrowers.com
Pasta, pasta products and services
President: Tim Dodd
Executive: Tom Mac Cani
Estimated Sales: $100+ Million
Number Employees: 100-249

27846 Primo Roasting Equipment
1309 S Lyon St
Santa Ana, CA 92705 714-556-5259
Fax: 714-556-5690 800-675-0160
dion@primoroasting.com
www.primoroasting.com
Coffee roaster manufacturing
CEO: Dion Humpreys
Estimated Sales: $500,000-$1 Million
Number Employees: 5-9

27847 Primus Laboratories
2810 Industrial Parkway
Santa Maria, CA 93455-1880 805-922-0055
Fax: 805-922-2462 800-779-1156
sales@primus.com www.primuslabs.com
Wine industry analytical services
President: Bob Stovicek
Estimated Sales: $5 - 10 Million
Number Employees: 250-499

27848 Prince Castle
355 East Kehoe Blvd
Carol Stream, IL 60188 630-462-8801
Fax: 630-462-1460 800-722-7853
info@princecastle.com www.princecastle.com
Manufacturer and exporter of preparation and holding equipment including warming and toasting equipment, electronic cooking timers and computers, grill tools, high chairs, fry baskets and shortening filters, dispensers, drink mixerscutters and slicers
President: Randy Garvin
Product Marketing Manager: Richard Blauvelt
VP Sales/Marketing: William Kinney
Number Employees: 100-249
Square Footage: 120000
Parent Co: Marmon Group
Type of Packaging: Food Service
Brands:
Comfortline
Excalibur
Fasline
Frequent Fryer
Merlin
Multi Mixer
Portion-All
Redi-Grill

27849 Prince Industries
5635 Thompson Bridge Rd
Murrayville, GA 30564 770-536-3679
Fax: 770-535-2548 800-441-3303
www.princeindustriesinc.com
Manufacturer and exporter of poultry processing equipment including deboners, grinders and meat pumps
President: Jesse Prince
CFO: Jesse Prince
Vice President: Dottie Prince
National Sales Manager: Jesse Prince
General Manager: Kam Singh
Estimated Sales: $2.5 - 5 Million
Number Employees: 5-9
Square Footage: 8000

27850 Prince Seating
1355 Atlantic Ave
Brooklyn, NY 11216-2810 718-363-2300
Fax: 718-363-9800 800-577-4623
info@PrinceSeating.com
www.princeseating.com
Wood and metal chairs, tables and barstools
Owner: Abe Belsky
VP: Abe Belsky
Contract Sales: Peri Lissauer
Estimated Sales: $5 Million
Number Employees: 20-49
Square Footage: 260000

27851 Princeton Shelving
873 Center Point Road NE
Cedar Rapids, IA 52402-4664 319-369-0355
Fax: 319-369-0387
Dealer rep. and distributor of pallet racks, wire decking and containers, POP displays, carts (hand, service), racks, steel and wire shelving. Over 500 different companies
Estimated Sales: $1 - 5,000,000

27852 Print & Peel
620 12th Ave
New York, NY 10036-1004 212-226-7007
Fax: 212-226-7174 800-451-0807
www.printandpeel.com
Printed and nonprinted pressure sensitive paper labels, film, paper, etc
President: Linda Owen
VP/Sales: Ronald Steinberg
Estimated Sales: $5 - 10 Million
Number Employees: 20-49

27853 Print Ons/Express Mark
505 Cuthbertson St
Monroe, NC 28110-3809 704-289-8261
Fax: 704-289-2158
Printed and embroidered shirts
Director Sales Marketing: John Schnader
Estimated Sales: $500,000-$1,000,000
Number Employees: 1-4
Brands:
Express Mark
Print Ons

27854 Print Pack
2800 Overlook Parkway, NE
Atlanta, GA 30339 404-460-7000
info@printpack.com
www.printpack.com
Manufacturer and exporter of flexible packaging materials including printed and laminated rollstock
Estimated Sales: $50-100 Million
Number Employees: 100-249
Parent Co: James River Corporation

27855 Print Pack
210 Kansas City Ave
Shreveport, LA 71107-6637 318-226-8661
Fax: 318-222-0701 800-884-3101
www.printpack.com
Polyethylene bags for bakeries
Manager: Stacy Hall
Manager: Travis Shepard
Estimated Sales: $50 - 100 Million
Number Employees: 100-249
Parent Co: Print Pac

27856 Print Source
128 Main Street
Wakefield, RI 02879 401-789-9339
Fax: 401-789-1750 csr@printsource.com
www.printsource.com
Decals, labels, name plates and advertising signs including magnetic, vinyl and hot die cut, printing on plastic containers
President, Chief Executive Officer: Donald Shortman
Sr. Account Manager: Deb Saccoccio
Production Manager: Bruce Gibbs
Estimated Sales: $5 - 10 Million
Number Employees: 50-99
Square Footage: 140000
Type of Packaging: Private Label, Bulk

27857 Print-O-Tape
755 Tower Rd
Mundelein, IL 60060 847-362-1476
Fax: 847-949-7449 800-346-6311
customerservice@printotape.com
www.printotape.com
Pressure sensitive labels and tapes
President: Carl J Walliser
CFO: Marty Justin
R&D: Roger Haase
Quality Control: Ron Quba
Marketing Manager: Eddie Walschner
Estimated Sales: $10 - 20 Million
Number Employees: 50-99

27858 Print-Tech
330 E Kilbourn Avenue
Suite 1085
Milwaukee, WI 53202-3146 608-241-5027
Fax: 608-249-7760 800-682-7746
signpro@ptptpromo.com www.ptpromo.com
President: Ryan Simons
R&D: Ryan Simons
Quality Control: Randy Agisv
Estimated Sales: $5 - 10 Million
Number Employees: 50

27859 Printape Corporation ofAmerica
174 Passaic St
Garfield, NJ 07026-1358 973-815-1880
Fax: 973-815-1882
Printed, pilfer proof, carton sealing, paper tapes
President: Jerry Bialick
Estimated Sales: $20-50 Million
Number Employees: 50-99

27860 Printcraft Marking Devices
1193 Military Rd
Buffalo, NY 14217 716-873-8181
Fax: 716-873-2751 pmdinc@banet.net

Engraved and rubber stamps
Owner: Lynn Wuertzer
Manager: Ruff Wuertzer
Estimated Sales: less than $500,000
Number Employees: 1-4

27861 Printex Packaging Corporation
555 Raymond Dr
Islandia, NY 11749 631-234-4300
Fax: 631-234-4840 info@printexpackaging.com
www.printexpackaging.com
President: Joel Heller
R & D: Joe Heller
Estimated Sales: $20-30 Million
Number Employees: 50-99

27862 Printpack
2800 Overlook Pkwy NE
Atlanta, GA 30339 404-460-7000
info@printpack.com
www.printpack.com
Manufacturer and converter of printed, coated, laminated and flexible film, rolls, sheets and heat sealing paper; also, candy bar and meat wrappers
President/CEO/Director: Dennis Love
Founder And Ceo: Brian Stearns
VP Finance/CFO: R Michael Hembree
VP/General Manager/Director: James Love III
Marketing And Communication Manager: Lisa Preston
VP/General Manager: Rick Williams
Estimated Sales: $522 Million
Number Employees: 3,800

27863 Printpak
14651 Dallas Pkwy
Suite 320
Dallas, TX 75254-1639 972-392-3101
Fax: 972-392-1129 iharris@indpkg.com
www.printpakllc.com
President: Dennis Love
Estimated Sales: $1 - 3 Million
Number Employees: 1-4
Type of Packaging: Consumer

27864 Printpak
14651 Dallas Pkwy
Suite 320
Dallas, TX 75254-1639 972-392-3101
Fax: 404-691-8143 800-451-9985
www.printpak.com
President: Dennis Love
Estimated Sales: $1 - 3 Million
Number Employees: 1-4

27865 Printsafe Inc.
12125 Kear Place
Poway, CA 92064 858-748-8600
Fax: 858-748-8640 info@printsafe.com
www.printsafe.com
President: Tom Hittle
Estimated Sales: $5 - 10 Million
Number Employees: 20-49

27866 Priority Food Processing
635 Oakwood Rd
Lake Zurich, IL 60047 847-438-1338
Fax: 847-438-1599
Contract dry food blending and packaging
President: Andy Burke
Quality Control: Rodney Hart
Estimated Sales: $50 - 100 Million
Number Employees: 100-249

27867 Priority One America
815 Bridge Street
Waterloo, ON N2V 1V7
Canada 519-746-6950
Fax: 519-746-3578
general@priorityonepackaging.com
www.priorityonepackaging.com
Manufacturer, exporter and importer of palletizers, conveyors, depalletizers and packaging machinery
President: Colin Cunningham
Controller: Carolyn Schnefer
Estimated Sales: $10 - 20 Million
Number Employees: 100
Square Footage: 15000
Parent Co: Priority One Packaging

27868 Priority One Packaging
815 Bridge Street
Waterloo, ON N2V 2M7
Canada 519-746-6950
Fax: 519-746-3578 800-387-9102
general@priorityonepackaging.com
www.priorityonepackaging.com
Number Employees: 10

27869 Priority One Packaging
815 Bridge Street
Waterloo, ON N2V 2M7
Canada 519-746-6950
Fax: 519-746-3578 800-387-9102
products@priorityonepackaging.com
www.priorityonepackaging.com
Priority One is a manufacturer of palletizing and depalletizing equipment. Included in the product range are both high and low level palletizers, small footprint palletizers, multi-line (shuttle and rotary) palletizers, pailpalletizers, bulk palletizers, high and low depalletizers, table-top and mat-top conveyor systems, pressured and pressureless single filers, bottle and case elevators/lowerators, rinsers, magnetic elevators, cable track, full load stackers, labellersand line integration
Owner/CEO: Colin Cunningham
President: Brian Webster
VP: Drew Cameron
Estimated Sales: $30 Million
Number Employees: 120
Square Footage: 100000
Brands:
Langguth
Pro-Pal

27870 Priority One Packaging Machinery
124 N Columbus Street
Randolph, WI 53956
Canada 800-882-4995
Fax: 920-326-6551 800-387-9102
inquiry@arrowheadsystems.com
www.priorityonepackaging.com

27871 Prism
8300 NW 53rd St
Suite 103
Miami, FL 33166-7710 305-599-9033
Fax: 305-594-9280
Sanitation supplies and services
Manager: Manny Gonzalez
Estimated Sales: Less than $500,000
Number Employees: 1-4

27872 Prism Visual Software
1 Sagamore Hill Dr
Port Washington, NY 11050-2137 516-944-5920
Fax: 516-944-5243 info@prismvs.com
www.prismvs.com
Routing/scheduling software
Owner: David Cullen
CEO: Marc J. Eisenberg
CFO: Robert G. CostantiniVP: John J Stolte, Jr
VP Marketing: Lynn Keating
Vice President of Sales: Andrew Kuneth
Estimated Sales: $3 Million

27873 Prism Visual Software, Inc
1 SAGAMORE HILL DRIVE
Port Washington, NY 11050 516-944-5920
Fax: 516-944-5243 sales@prismvs.com
www.prismvs.com
Readquest, Prisms route management/palm pilot solution for food and beverage companies
Owner: David Cullen
CEO: Lorraine Keating
CEO: Lorraine Keating
Marketing: Lynn Keating
Sales Director: Michael Del Colle
Operations: Chris Heinrich
Estimated Sales: $1.5 Million
Number Employees: 5-9

27874 Pro Bake
2057 E Aurora Rd
Suite Pq
Twinsburg, OH 44087 330-425-4427
Fax: 330-425-9742 800-837-4427
probake@probake.com www.probake.com
Bakery equipment reconditioning
President: Kevin Wallace
Sales Promotion Manager: Jeff Salenger
Estimated Sales: $5-10 Million
Number Employees: 10-19

27875 Pro Controls
1312 Gordon Rd
Yakima, WA 98901 509-457-3386
Fax: 509-457-3491 800-488-3386
sales@proctrl.com www.proctrl.com
Process control systems
President: Doug Tilton
Estimated Sales: $1-2,500,000
Number Employees: 10-19

27876 Pro Mach
6279 Tri Ridge Blvd Ste 410
Loveland, OH 45140 513-831-8778
Fax: 513-831-5795 info@promachinc.com
www.promachinc.com
CEO: J P Richard
CEO: Mark W Anderson
Estimated Sales: $100 - 200 Million
Number Employees: 1,000-4,999

27877 Pro Media
W127 N8690 Westbrook Xing
Menomonee Falls, WI 53051 262-532-2600
Fax: 800-951-5955 800-328-0439
info@promediaus.com
www.promedia-streff.com
Specializing in manufacturer, distributor, and operator frequency programs
President: Tom Collier
Executive VP: Rick Stolowski
VP Incentive Sales: Jim Egan
Estimated Sales: $10-20,000,000
Number Employees: 10-19
Square Footage: 9000

27878 Pro Pack Systems
1354-A Dayton Street
Salinas, CA 93901 831-771-1300
Fax: 831-771-1303 dz@propacksystems.com
www.propacksystems.com
Adhesive systems, wax systems for wineries, ink jet coding, cave/tray packing
President: David Zurlinden
Estimated Sales: Below $5 Million
Number Employees: 5-9
Square Footage: 8

27879 Pro Scientific
99 Willenbrock Rd
Oxford, CT 06478 203-267-4600
Fax: 203-267-4606 800-584-3776
sales@proscientific.com www.proscientific.com
Manufactures laboratory homogenizers from handheld to larger benchtop programmable models. North American distributor of Andreas Hettich Centifuges which range in size from micro to floor-model. Also distribute a full line ofincubators, water and oil baths and ovens
Owner: Richard Yacko
Sales/Marketing: Holly Yacko
Estimated Sales: $5 - 10 Million
Number Employees: 10-19
Number of Brands: 3
Number of Products: 40
Brands:
Hettich
Memmert
Pro
Riebosam

27880 Pro Scientific
PO Box 448
Monroe, CT 06468-0448 203-452-9431
Fax: 780-452-9753 prosci@aol.com
www.proscientific.com/chef.html
Handheld and bench top mechanical homogenizers, laboratory and custom homogenizers
Estimated Sales: $1-2.5 Million
Number Employees: 10-19

27881 Pro Sheet Cutter
705 S Electric Avenue
Alhambra, CA 91803-1639 626-576-0785
Fax: 626-576-8895 dhabel@schobers.com
www.schobers.com

Extrusion fabrication systems, sawing systems, low-level radioactive and mixed waste containers, transloader, grinders, computer controlled slit mask fabricator and electronically integrated control system bandsaw

27882 **Pro-Ad-Company**
655 N Tillamook St
Portland, OR 97227 503-288-5885
Fax: 503-281-8725 800-287-5885
sales@proadco.com www.proadco.com
Labels, screen printed decals, signs, point of purchase displays, bumper stickers and metal and engraved name plates
President: Clif Overholt
Estimated Sales: $5-10 Million
Number Employees: 10-19

27883 **Pro-Com Security Systems**
136 Stevens Avenue
Mount Vernon, NY 10550-2604 914-667-8400
Fax: 914-668-1822
Long range radio security systems
Parent Co: Sonitrol Company

27884 **Pro-Dex, Inc.**
2361 McGaw Ave.
Irvine, CA 92614 503-629-8081
Fax: 503-629-0688 800-562-6204
sales@omsmotion.com www.pro-dex.com
Motion controllers, motors, drives
VP: Phil Brown
Chief Executive Officer, President: Michael Berthelot
Vice President of Regulatory Affairs: Joseph Rotino
Marketing: Julie Kealy
Vice President of Sales and Marketing: Frank Noone
Estimated Sales: $5-10 Million
Number Employees: 20-49

27885 **Pro-Flo Products**
30 Commerce Rd
PO Box 390
Cedar Grove, NJ 07009 973-239-2400
Fax: 973-239-5817 800-325-1057
pro-flo@att.net
Manufacturer, importer and exporter of water treatment and filtration equipment, drinking water coolers, chillers and dispensers
President: Louis Reyes
Quality Control: Nicaolas Iannaccio
Estimated Sales: $657,000
Number Employees: 5-9
Square Footage: 4200

27886 **Pro-Gram Plastics**
700 Pro-Gram Pkwy
Geneva, OH 44041 440-466-8080
Fax: 440-466-8099 sales@programplastics.com
www.programplastics.com
Blow-molded plastic bottles
President: Walter Sargi
Sales Director: Bob Sweitzer
Production Manager: Robert Sweitzer
Estimated Sales: $5-10 Million
Number Employees: 50-99
Square Footage: 64000

27887 **Pro-Line**
10 Avco Rd # E
Haverhill, MA 01835-6975 978-556-1695
Fax: 978-374-4885 bench@1proline.com
www.1proline.com
Manufacturer and exporter of ergonomic workstations for production and lab areas
Owner: Derek Coughlin
President, Chief Executive Officer: Robert W Hatfield
Sr. VP: Bob Simmons
Estimated Sales: $3 - 5 Million
Number Employees: 20-49
Type of Packaging: Bulk

27888 **Pro-Tex-All Company**
210 S Morton Ave
Evansville, IN 47713 812-424-8268
Fax: 812-424-8330 800-755-5458
drm@protexall.com www.protexall.com
Facility maintenance chemicals, supplies and equipment for industry and commerce
Owner: Richard Kuhn
President: James Kuhn
Vice President: Mike Kuhn
Customer Service: Carla Richards
Estimated Sales: $5 - 10 Million
Number Employees: 20-49
Square Footage: 29500

27889 **Pro-Western Plastics**
30 Riel Drive
PO Box 261
St Albert, AB T8N3Z7
Canada 780-459-4491
Fax: 800-428-4756 800-661-9835
wayne.hunt@pro-westernplastics.com
www.pro-westernplastics.com
President: Wall Lacroix
Quality Control: Trevor Hansen
CFO: Wall Lacroix
R&D: Wall Lacroix
Number Employees: 275

27890 **ProAct, Inc.**
3195 Neil Armstrong Blvd
Eagan, MN 55121 651-686-0405
Fax: 651-686-0312 877-245-0405
info@proactinc.org www.proactinc.org
Sub-contract packager of food products
President,CEO: Steven Ditschler
Controller: Pat McGuire
Director of Production: David Cavalier
Estimated Sales: $$2.5-5 Million
Number Employees: 100-249
Square Footage: 120000

27891 **ProActive Solutions**
301 Bridge Street
Green Bay, WI 54303 800-279-7761
Fax: 732-329-1192 800-411-6734
chemunexinc@msn.com www.chemunex.com
Rapid method for microbial contamination detection
Estimated Sales: $2.5-5 Million
Number Employees: 5-9

27892 **(HQ)ProBar Systems Inc.**
92 Caplan Ave.
Suite 607
Barrie, ON L4N 0Z7
800-521-7294
info@probarsystems.com
www.probarsystems.com
Manufacturer and exporter of beverage dispensing machines including computer controlled bar pouring and inventory systems, juice dispensers and soft drink machines
President: Charles M Stimac Jr
CFO: John Hornbeck
Research & Development: Mike Smith
Quality Control: Greg Gemmell
Marketing: Chris Burden
Sales Director: Kris Croft
Operations Manager: Carlos DeMelo
Production/Plant Manager/Purchasing: Jimmy Neuman
Estimated Sales: $300,000-500,000
Number Employees: 1-4
Number of Brands: 3
Number of Products: 3
Type of Packaging: Private Label
Brands:
Ultra Bar

27893 **ProMinent Fluid Controls**
136 Industry Dr
R.I.D.C. Park West
Pittsburgh, PA 15275-1014 412-787-2484
Fax: 412-787-0704 sales@prominent.us
www.prominent.us
Manufacturer disinfection equipment, chlorine dioxide and ozone generators
General Manager: Mike Weber
Finance Director: Fran Perfett
VP: Garth Debruyn
Marketing Director: Noel Twyman
National Sales Manager: Mike St Germain
Operations Director: Jim DiNardo
Estimated Sales: $34 Million
Number Employees: 120
Number of Products: 25
Square Footage: 32500

27894 **ProMinent Fluid Controls**
136 Industry Dr
Pittsburgh, PA 15275-1014 412-787-2484
Fax: 412-787-0704 sales@prominent.cc
www.prominent.us
Manufacture chemical feed equipment, metering pumps, process controllers, sensors, desinfection equipment
President: Victor Dulger
President, Chief Executive Officer: Andreas Dulger
Executive Vice President of Manufacturin: Rainer Dulger
CFO: Fran Persett
Director of Marketing: Noel Twyman
Director of Sales and Marketing: Mike St
Director of Operations: Jim DiNardo
Estimated Sales: $10 Million
Number Employees: 50-99
Number of Products: 75
Parent Co: ProMinent DosierTechnick GmbH

27895 **ProRestore Products**
1016 Greentree Road
Suite 115
Pittsburgh, PA 15220 412-264-8340
Fax: 412-920-2905 800-332-6037
sales@prorestoreproducts.com
www.prorestoreproducts.com
Manufacturer and exporter of deodorants, cleaners and disinfectants
President: Cliff Zlotnik
Estimated Sales: $5 - 10 Million
Number Employees: 20-49
Parent Co: RPM International Inc.
Type of Packaging: Food Service, Private Label, Bulk
Brands:
Mediclean
Microban
Unikleen
Unsmoke

27896 **ProTeam**
12438 W Bridger Street
Boise, ID 83713 208-377-9555
Fax: 208-377-8444 800-541-1456
customerservice.proteam@emerson.com
www.pro-team.com
ProTeam became a global phenomenon in the commercial cleaning world after introducing a game-challenging design innovation, the lightweight backpack vacuum. Today ProTeam offers a full range of innovative vacuums, including the newProGuard wet/dry line.
CEO: Matt Wood
Estimated Sales: $50-100 Million
Number Employees: 50
Square Footage: 5000

27897 **Probat Burns, Inc.**
601 Corporate Woods Parkway
Vernon Hills, IL 60061-7924 847-415-5293
Fax: 847-793-8611 877-683-8113
info@probatburns.com www.probatburns.com
Bin silo systems, bin vibrators, blending and mixing equipment, cleaners, afterburners, augers, automatic controls, bag emptier, bulk silo servicees, magnetic separation, moisture analyzers, quality control instruments and cuppingequipment.
President: Karl Schmidt
Vice President of Sales & Marketing: Launtia Taylor
Estimated Sales: $5-10 Million
Number Employees: 20-49

27898 **Probiotic Solutions**
1331 W. Houston Ave.
Gilbert, AZ 85233 480-961-1220
Fax: 480-961-3061 800-961-1220
info@probiotic.com www.probiotic.com
President: Lyndon Smith
Sales Director: Diana Burtrum
Estimated Sales: $1 - 5 Million
Number Employees: 10-19
Parent Co: Bio Huma Netics, Inc.

27899 **Procedyne Corporation**
11 Industrial Dr
New Brunswick, NJ 08901-3657 732-249-8347
Fax: 732-249-7220 mail@procedyne.com
www.procedyne.com

Manufacturer and exporter of fluidized bed systems including dryers, granulators and thermal processors. Engineering and research and development facility with laboratory and pilor plant. Offer process design, process development andscale-up testing
President: H Kenneth Staffin
VP Process Technology: Thomas Parr
VP Products: Bob Archibald
Chairman of the Board: Dr H Kenneth Staffin
Estimated Sales: $10 - 20 Million
Number Employees: 50-99
Square Footage: 60000
Type of Packaging: Bulk
Brands:
Mikrodyne

27900 **Procell Polymers**
PO Box 33
Baton Rouge, LA 70821-0033 225-978-8069
Fax: 866-860-1269 info@procellpolymers.com
www.procellpolymers.com
Cellulose gum, guar gum, xanthan gum and other specialty products.
Manager: David Hatcher
Manager: Harry Steeghs
Type of Packaging: Bulk

27901 **Procesamiento De Carne**
122 S Wesley Ave
Mt Morris, IL 61054-1451 815-734-4171
Fax: 815-734-4201 tuten@wattmm.com
www.wattnet.com
Equipment for meat processors
President: Gregory A Watt
Estimated Sales: $15 Million
Number Employees: 50-99

27902 **Process Automation**
P.O.Box 457
Hurst, TX 76053 817-488-9546
Fax: 817-283-1813 800-460-9546
www.processauto.net
Process controls and stainless steel manufacturing for food and beverage industries
President: Scott Carlson
CFO: Steppnie Duelm
Estimated Sales: $30-50 Million
Number Employees: 20-49

27903 **Process Displays**
5800 S Moorland Rd
New Berlin, WI 53151 262-782-3600
Fax: 262-782-3857 800-533-1764
www.pdisplays.com
Manufacturer and exporter of point of purchase displays, vacuum form trays, case dividers, rail strips, counter mats, menu board and deli signs and decals
President: Bob Zanotti
Vice President: Brendon Rowan
Estimated Sales: $2.5 - 5 Million
Number Employees: 50-99
Square Footage: 100000
Parent Co: Process Retail Group

27904 **Process Engineering & Fabrication**
20 Hedge Ln
Afton, VA 22920 540-456-8163
Fax: 540-456-8171 800-852-7975
bob@processengineeringinc.com
www.processengineeringinc.com
Manufacturer and exporter of custom industrial refrigeration systems, spiral conveyor systems and stainless steel food processing equipment; also, installation services available
President: Bart Shellabarger
CEO: Bob Amacker
CFO: Bruce Neidlinger
Chief Freezing Officer: Charley Marckel
Sales: Jimmy Sokora
Estimated Sales: Below $5 Million
Number Employees: 10
Square Footage: 20000

27905 **Process Heating Company**
2732 3rd Avenue South
PO Box 84585
Seattle, WA 98124 206-682-3414
Fax: 206-682-1582 866-682-1582
inquire@processheating.com
www.processheating.com
Manufacturer and exporter of industrial immersion heaters, circulation heating systems and fuel oil preheaters
President: Rick Jay
CEO: Ron Jay
Marketing: Mike Peringer
Sales/Industrial: Eric Olden
Estimated Sales: $3 - 5 Million
Number Employees: 10-19
Number of Products: 15
Square Footage: 7500
Brands:
Lo-Density

27906 **Process Heating Corporation**
547 Hartford Tpke
Shrewsbury, MA 01545 508-842-5200
Fax: 508-842-9418 proheat@gis.net
www.proheatcorp.com
Manufacturer and exporter of ovens, furnaces, air pollution control incinerators and process heating equipment; also, rebuilding and remodeling available
President: Bradford Green
Estimated Sales: Below $5,000,000
Number Employees: 5-9

27907 **Process Plus**
5320 S 39th Street
Phoenix, AZ 85040 602-470-8051
Fax: 602-470-1654
President: Gerald Schneerer

27908 **Process Sensors Corporation**
113 Cedar St Ste S1
Milford, MA 01757 508-473-9901
Fax: 508-473-0715 info@processsensors.com
www.processsensors.com
Manufacturer, importer and exporter of moisture measuring instruments
President: Robert Winson
Estimated Sales: $5 - 10,000,000
Number Employees: 5-9

27909 **Process Solutions**
6701 Garden Rd Unit 1
Riviera Beach, FL 33404 561-840-0050
Fax: 561-840-0070 sales@processsolutions.net
www.processsolutions.net
Manufacturer and exporter of drum lifters and inverters, stainless steel drums, bins, tanks, control panels and systems, etc.; importer of stainless steel bins and butterfly valves
President: Howard Rosenkranz
Vice President: H Rosenkranz
Estimated Sales: $5-10 Million
Number Employees: 20-49
Brands:
Ergoscoop
Omegalift
Pharmaseal

27910 **Process Systems**
102 Covington Drive
Barrington, IL 60010-6611 847-842-8618
Fax: 847-842-8619 IlliniPick@aol.com
Sanitary process equipment including modelsam steam jacketed and vacuum/pressure kettles, high and low shear mixers
Estimated Sales: $3-5 Million
Number Employees: 20-50
Square Footage: 15000
Brands:
Model Sam

27911 **Processing Machinery & Supply**
1108 Frankford Ave
Philadelphia, PA 19125 215-425-4320
Fax: 215-426-2034 icecream@gowcb.com
www.wcbicecream.dk
Manufacturer and exporter of fillers, sealers, fittings, freezers, homogenizers, pumps, tanks and frozen novelty equipment
Manager: John Dorety
Office Manager: Susie Margolis
Plant Manager: Vince Somers
Estimated Sales: $2.5-5 Million
Number Employees: 20-49

27912 **Processors Co-Op**
1110 Powers Pl
Alpharetta, GA 30009-8389 770-664-1516
Fax: 770-636-3006 alan@cutyourfoodcost.com
www.cutyourfoodcost.com
Seafood, meats, poultry
President, CEO: Alan Brown
Director of Marketing: Terrie Bradley
Operations Manager: Robert Bragg
Director of Purchasing: Bill Larsen
Estimated Sales: $10 - 20 Million
Number Employees: 10-19

27913 **Procon Products**
910 Ridgely Rd
Murfreesboro, TN 37129 615-890-5710
Fax: 615-896-7729 mail@proconpump.com
www.procon.com
Manufacturer and exporter of positive displacement rotary vane pumps
President: Paul Roberts
Purchasing Agent: Tracy Harris
Estimated Sales: $10-25 Million
Number Employees: 50-99
Parent Co: Standex International
Type of Packaging: Food Service

27914 **(HQ)Proctor & Gamble Company**
1 Proctor & Gamble Plaza
Cincinnati, OH 45202 513-983-1100
Fax: 513-983-9369 www.pg.com
Variety of foods and snack foods.
Chairman/President/CEO: Bob McDonald
Chief Financial Officer: Jon Moeller
Global External Relations Officer: Christopher Hassall
Vice Chairman/Global Operations: Werner Geissler
Global Product Supply Officer: R Keith Harrison Jr
Estimated Sales: $84 Billion
Number Employees: 126,000
Square Footage: 15000
Type of Packaging: Consumer
Other Locations:
Procter & Gamble Co.
Boca Raton FL
Brands:
100 Calorie Packs
Actonel
Always
Ariel
Bounty
Charmin
Clairol
Crest
Downy
Folgers
Head & Shoulders
Iams
Lenor
Olay
Pampers
Pantene
Pringles
Tide
Whisper

27915 **Prodo-Pak Corporation**
77 Commerce St
Garfield, NJ 07026 973-777-7770
Fax: 973-772-0471 sales@prodo-pak.com
www.prodo-pak.com
Manufacturer, importer and exporter of form/fill/seal packaging machines for pouches and tube fillers; also, conveyor systems and labeling equipment
President: John Mueller
Research & Development: Rudy Degenars
Operations/Plant/Purchasing Manager: Ralph Isler
Estimated Sales: $5 - 10 Million
Number of Brands: 1
Number of Products: 10
Square Footage: 20000

27916 **Product Dynamics**
10608 W. 163rd Place
Orland Park, IL 60467 708-364-7060
Fax: 708-364-7061 pdd@rqa-inc.com
www.productdynamicsdivision.com
Product Dynamics offers Product design and formulation, consumer and product research, qualitative insight and analytical sensory testing. They collabrate with your marketing business planning and research and development teams toaddress your strategic and tatical product issues.
President: Lawrence Platt
Executive Vice President: Mary Ann Platt
Vice President/General Manager: Judy Lindsey

Estimated Sales: $1 - 3 Million
Number Employees: 10-19
Parent Co: RQA, Inc

27917 Product Saver
12838 Stainless Drive
Holland, MI 49424 616-399-2220
Fax: 616-399-7365 jswiatlo@nbe-inc.com
www.productsaver.com
Bag openers, fillers and closers, reclaiming machinery and recovery systems
President: Ed Swiatlo
General Manager: Jess Swiatlo
Estimated Sales: $1 - 5 Million
Number Employees: 10-19

27918 Product Solutions
N Street
220
Wilkes Barre, PA 18701-1706 570-825-0600
Fax: 570-825-0600 888-776-3765
prodsol@aol.com
Consultant providing design and engineering of food service equipment; also, aesthetic and engineering improvements to existing equipment available
President: Robert Cohn
Sales Director: Sandee Cohn
Estimated Sales: $1-2.5 Million
Number Employees: 1-4
Square Footage: 5000

27919 Production Equipment Company
401 Liberty St
Meriden, CT 06450
Fax: 800-563-4150 800-758-5697
peco@peco1938.com
www.productionequipmentcompany.com
Manufacturer and exporter of overhead cranes and hoists; also, steel fabricators
President: Rebecca Davis
VP Sales/Marketing: Rosewell Davis
Estimated Sales: $5-10 Million
Number Employees: 20-49

27920 Production Packaging & Processing Equipment Company
1450 E Van Buren St
Phoenix, AZ 85006 602-254-7878
Fax: 602-254-2630 sales@kettles.com
www.kettles.com
Manufacturer, exporter and wholesaler/distributor of new and rebuilt packaging and processing equipment including mixers, fillers, cap tighteners, labeling, cappers, kettles and tanks
President: Louis R Klein
CEO: Jeff Klein
Estimated Sales: $2.5-5 Million
Number Employees: 5-9
Square Footage: 50000
Brands:
P3

27921 Production Systems
850 Mountain Industrial Dr NW
Marietta, GA 30060 770-424-9784
Fax: 770-424-8392 800-235-9734
solutions@productionsystemsinc.com
www.productionsystemsinc.com
Manufacturer and exporter of package and case conveyors and packaging and palletizing systems; also, integrated control systems for production and processing plants
President: Michael Anderson
Manager Marketing Serives: Sharon Phillips
Engineer Manager: Wayne Marlow
Estimated Sales: $5-10 Million
Number Employees: 20-49
Square Footage: 50000
Brands:
Package To Pallet

27922 Productos Familia
1511 Calle Loiza
Santurce, PR 00911-1846 787-268-5929
Fax: 787-268-7717 info@sca.com
www.nosotrasonline.com
Supplier of soft paper tissues; wholesaler/distributor, importer and exporter of toilet paper, paper towels and napkins; serving the food service market
President: Fabio Posada
VP: Carlos Upegui
Number Employees: 7
Square Footage: 12000
Parent Co: Productos Familia SA
Type of Packaging: Food Service

27923 Profamo Inc
7506 Albert Tillinghast Dr
Sarasota, FL 34240 941-379-8155
Fax: 941-379-8699 info@profamo.com
www.profamo.com
Provides sales and services for manufacturers of quality assurance and process control equipment for the brewing and beverage industries.
President: Klaus Nimptsch
Technical Information Specialist: Chris Nimptsch
Estimated Sales: $300,000-500,000
Number Employees: 1-4

27924 Professional Bakeware Company
11739 N Highway 75
Willis, TX 77378-5740 866-710-1936
Fax: 936-890-8760 800-440-9547
customerservice@professionalbakeware.com
www.professionalbakeware.com
Bakeware, cookware, servingware, displayware and indestructable alumaware
President: David Beauregard
Vice President: Jennifer Beauregard
Marketing/Design: Judy Beck
Public Relations: Stephanie Samudio
Plant Manager: Sterling Samudio
Estimated Sales: $10 - 20,000,000
Number Employees: 20-49
Number of Brands: 5
Number of Products: 500
Square Footage: 15000
Type of Packaging: Food Service, Bulk

27925 Professional EngineeringAssociation
8007 Vine Crest Ave
Suite 5
Louisville, KY 40222 502-429-0432
Fax: 502-429-0552
Automated parts feeding systems, feeders, conveyors, screens and process system dryers/coolers
President: Virgil Plummer
Sales Manager: Neal Plummer
Estimated Sales: $2.5-5 Million
Number Employees: 5-9

27926 Professional Image Inc
12437 E 60th Street
Tulsa, OK 74146 918-461-0609
Fax: 918-249-2602 800-722-8550
sales@calvertco.com www.pi-pkg.com
Printing and packaging
President/Owner: Cynthia Calvert-Copeland
Marketing: Jennifer Giebel
Estimated Sales: $8 Million
Number Employees: 48

27927 Professional Marketing Group
912 Rainier Avenue S
Seattle, WA 98144-2840 206-322-7303
Fax: 206-322-4351 800-227-3769
support@vacuumpacker.com
www.vacuumpackers.com
Importer, exporter and wholesaler/distributor of commercial grade flush and nonflush vacuum packing machinery
Owner: Thom Dolder
Estimated Sales: $2.5-5 Million
Number Employees: 5-9

27928 Proffitt Manufacturing Company
404 Mitchell Street
Dalton, GA 30721-2705 706-278-7105
Fax: 706-225-4419 800-241-4682
Manufacturer and exporter of dust control mats
CEO: John R Proffitt Jr
VP: W Masters
Manager: Fred Lester
Estimated Sales: $3 - 5 Million
Number Employees: 50
Square Footage: 66000
Brands:
Endurance
Master Turf
New Age
Rib Tred
Ruff N Tuff

27929 Profire Stainless SteelBarbecue
9621 S Dixie Hwy
Miami, FL 33156 305-665-5313
Fax: 305-666-3315 info@profirebbq.com
www.profirebbq.com
Outdoor barbecues, built-in-grills, portable grills and other accessories
President and CFO: David Zisman
Estimated Sales: $10 - 20 Million
Number Employees: 10

27930 Progress Lighting
P.O. Box 6701
Greenville, SC 29606 864-678-1000
www.progresslighting.com
Manufacturer and exporter of commercial, interior and exterior lighting
Warehouse Manager: Grant Barrett
Director, Purchasing: Jeff Pickens
Estimated Sales: $77 Million
Number Employees: 899
Square Footage: 35000
Parent Co: Hubbell Incorporated
Type of Packaging: Bulk

27931 Progressive Flexpak
1138 Pond Road
Glencoe, MO 63038-1322 800-565-3407
Bottle label, snack, candy, coffee printing films, process, flexo, roto and bag making

27932 Progressive Packaging
14700 28th Avenue N
Suite 35
Plymouth, MN 55447 763-541-1440
800-844-7889
info@progressivepackaging.com
www.progressivepackaging.com
Packaging materials and equipment.
President: John Mork
VP: C J Mork
Estimated Sales: $1.4 Million
Number Employees: 8
Square Footage: 12000

27933 Progressive Plastics
14801 Emery Ave
Cleveland, OH 44135 216-252-5595
Fax: 216-252-6327 800-252-0053
marketing@progressive-plastics.com
www.progressive-plastics.com
Manufactures and design plastic containers for the food and beverage industries. PET, HDPE, PP, PVC, FDA, CGMP, 150 9001 compliant
President: A J Busa
Executive VP/CEO: Duke Busa
CEO: Brian Gill
Quality Control: Mary Anne Golba
Operations Manager: Jason Castro
Purchasing Manager: Glen Maringer
Estimated Sales: $20 - 50 Million
Number Employees: 250-499
Square Footage: 300000
Type of Packaging: Bulk

27934 Progressive Software
6836 Morrison Blvd Ste 104
Charlotte, NC 28211 704-295-7000
Fax: 704-849-6401 info@xpient.com
www.progressivesoftware.com
Point of sale and back office software
Marketing Manager: Ryan Willis
VP Global Sales/Marketing: Karen Holick
Estimated Sales: $1 - 3,000,000
Number Employees: 50-99
Parent Co: Tridex Corporation
Brands:
Iris

27935 Progressive Technology International
3826a Branch River Road
Manitowoc, WI 54220-9479 920-683-2000
Fax: 920-683-9276 888-683-2003
dale@progressivetechnology-biz.com
www.progressivetechnology-biz.com
Food processing equipment manufacturers
President: Dale Gehrig
Vice President: Mark Kugsh
Sales Director: Julio Rivera
Estimated Sales: $1-2.5 Million
Number Employees: 4

27936 **Proheatco Manufacturing**
3427 Pomona Boulevard
Suite D
Pomona, CA 91768-3260 909-598-7445
Fax: 909-598-3514 800-423-4195
proheatco@earthlink.net www.proheatco.com
Manufacturer and exporter of ovens, heaters and steam heated systems; exporter of heaters
President: Ralph J Schaefer
Estimated Sales: $1-2.5 Million
Number Employees: 10-19
Square Footage: 24000

27937 **Prolon**
P.O.Box 568
Port Gibson, MS 39150 601-437-4211
Fax: 601-437-3068 888-480-9828
mhyman@prolon.biz www.prolon.biz
Melamine dinnerware, tote boxes, food storage containers, school trays, etc
VP: Steve Gluck
Sales/Marketing: Sylvia Saxon
Estimated Sales: $20-50 Million
Number Employees: 50-99
Square Footage: 116000
Parent Co: Perstorp
Brands:
Prolon Products

27938 **Proluxe**
PO Box 869
Paramount, CA 90723-0869 562-531-0305
Fax: 562-869-7715 800-594-5528
scott@doughpro.com www.proluxe.com
Manufacturer and exporter of pizza and tortilla presses, dough and vending carts, pizza slicing guides, clam shell and tortilla warming grills, pan racks, conveyor and tray ovens and sauce rings; also, custom stainless steelfabrication available
President: Eugene Raio
VP/General Manager: Daniel Raio
Director of Marketing: Michael Cole
Vice President of Sales: Mike Cervantes
Number Employees: 50
Square Footage: 180000
Brands:
Doughcart
Doughpro
Hotslot
Personnal
Pizzacart

27939 **Promac**
PO Box 9818
Fresno, CA 93794-0818 559-271-9222
Fax: 559-271-9312 888-776-6220
roxi@promacstainless.com
Wine, food and beverage industry process machinery
Estimated Sales: $20-50 Million
Number Employees: 20-49

27940 **Promarks, Inc.**
1915 E. Acacia Street
Ontario, CA 91761 909-923-3888
Fax: 909-923-3588 www.promarksvac.com
Vacuum sealing and vacuum packaging machines. Also manufacture dicer, stuffer, tumbling and brine injector machines.

27941 **Promega Corporation**
2800 Woods Hollow Rd
Fitchburg, WI 53711 608-274-4330
Fax: 608-277-2516 www.promega.com
DNA purification kit for testing genetically modified organisms in food
President: William Linton
Estimated Sales: I
Number Employees: 500-999

27942 **Promens**
100 Industrial Drive
PO Box 2087
St. John, NB E2L 3T5 506-633-0101
Fax: 506-658-0227 800-295-3725
info@promensstjohn.ca www.promens.com
Trays, cups, jars and plastic packaging for the food and beverage industry. Also manufacture bins, bin liners, ingredient bins and dump tubs.

27943 **Promo Edge**
5029 Industrial Road
Wall Township, NJ 07727-3651 732-938-4242
Fax: 732-938-3301
Pressure sensitive labels
Customer Relations: Joanne Switzer
Plant Manager: Ray Mass

27944 **Promotion in Motion Companies**
PO Box 558
Closter, NJ 07624-0558 201-784-5800
800-369-7391
mail@promotioninmotion.com
www.promotioninmotion.com
Manufacturers and marketers of popular brand name confections, fruit snack and other fine foods.
President/CEO: Michael Rosenberg
Executive Director: Frank McSorley
COO: Basant Dwivedi
Number Employees: 250-499
Type of Packaging: Private Label

27945 **Promotional Packaging Group**
4556 Sunbelt Drive
Addison, TX 75001 972-733-3199
Fax: 972-733-3790
karen_johnson@propacmarketing.com
www.propacmarketing.com
Packaging for promotional materials including marketing materials, coupons, literature, table tents, etc.; also, demonstration kits
President: Charles Daigle
Senior Account Director: Arthur Kaplan
Account Executive: Charles Daigle
Estimated Sales: $1 - 2.5 Million
Number Employees: 20-49

27946 **Pronova Biopolymer**
135 Commerce Way
Suite 201
Portsmouth, NH 03801-3200 603-433-1231
Fax: 603-433-1348 800-223-9030
bess.mosley@pronova.com www.pronova.com
Processor, importer and exporter of industrial ingredients including alginates, propylene glycol alginates, chitin and chitosan
General Manager: Sandra Platt
Manager Customer Service: Bess Mosley
Number Employees: 5-9
Parent Co: Pronova Biopolymer
Brands:
Pro Floc
Seacure

27947 **Pronova Biopolymer**
1735 Market Street
Philadelphia, PA 19103-7501 603-433-1231
Fax: 603-433-1348 800-223-9030
bess.mosley@hydro.com www.pronova.com
Solutions for the world's food and pharmaceutical markets (Omega-3 fatty acids and ultra pure, high concentrate alginates); onsite electrolytic hydrogen/oxygen gas supply systems and cooling/heating solutions based on Transcritical C-2technology
Information and Internet and HES: Age Wik
Finance/IT: Richard Clemm
Business Development: Kenneth Bern
Business Development: Carl Christian Bachke
Business Development: Bjorn Poul Ringvold
Finance/Divisional Accounting: Kirsti Botheim
Number Employees: 200

27948 **Pronto Products Company**
11765 Goldring Rd
Arcadia, CA 91006 626-358-5718
Fax: 626-358-9194 800-377-6680
prontoprod@earthlink.net
www.prontoproducts.com
Wire products including chrome and stainless steel dispensers and frying baskets
President: William Parrott
VP: Martha Wagner
Estimated Sales: $20-50 Million
Number Employees: 20-49

27949 **Propak**
5230 Harvester Road
Burlington, ON L7L 4X4
Canada 905-681-2345
Fax: 905-681-1023 800-263-4872
Sheets, cookie liners, displays and containers including point of purchase and corrugated shipping
President: H Keith Munt
CFO: Cris Gumbs
Sales Director: John Nadon
Plant Manager: Colin Carr
Number Employees: 100
Square Footage: 157000

27950 **Prospero Equipment Corporation**
123 Castleton St
Pleasantville, NY 10570-3405 914-769-6252
Fax: 914-769-6786 888-732-1222
www.prosperoequipment.com
President: Tony Prospero
Estimated Sales: $10 - 20 Million
Number Employees: 10-19

27951 **Prosys Innovative Packaging Equipment**
422 E 17th Street
Webb City, MO 64870-2956 417-673-3870
Fax: 417-673-7971 800-231-3455
info@prosysfill.com www.prosysfill.com
Cartridges, squeeze tubes and containers, automatic filling equipment, automatic metal tube filler
Division Manager: Don Sonntag
Estimated Sales: $10-20 Million
Number Employees: 20-49

27952 **Protectowire Company**
60 Washington Street
Pembrook, MA 02559 781-826-3878
Fax: 781-826-2045 pwire@protectowire.com
www.protectowire.com
Manufacturer and exporter of fire detection systems for refrigerated storage
President: Andrew Sullivan
CFO: Steve Loughlin
VP North American Sales: John Whaling
Chairman of the Board: Carol M Sullivan
Quality Assurance Manager: Richard Twigg
Sales Engineer: John Whaling
Sales Engineer: James Roussel
Estimated Sales: $5-10 Million
Number Employees: 20-49
Brands:
Firesystem 2000
Protectowire

27953 **Protein Research Associates**
1852 Rutan Dr
Livermore, CA 94551-7635 925-243-6300
Fax: 925-243-6308 800-948-1991
info@proteinresearch.com
www.proteinresearch.com
Processor and exporter of nutritional, amino acid and vitamin/mineral supplements
President: Robert Matheson
Director: Theodore Aarons
VP Operations: Daniel Aarons
Estimated Sales: $5-10 Million
Number Employees: 5-9
Number of Products: 12
Square Footage: 132000
Type of Packaging: Private Label, Bulk

27954 **Protex International Corp.**
180 Keyland Ct
Bohemia, NY 11716-2657 631-563-4250
Fax: 631-563-4206 800-835-3580
b.kennedy@protex-intl.com
www.protex-intl.com
Camera domes, simulated surveillance and cash boxes, safety and detection mirrors, high security locks and annunciators
President: David Wachsman
CFO: Bill Ciccareli
CEO: Steve Migliorino
VP Sales: Bob Frazier
Estimated Sales: $20 - 50 Million
Number Employees: 50-99
Square Footage: 34000

27955 **Protexall**
1025 S. Fourth St
Greenville, IL 62246 618-664-6990
Fax: 877-776-8397 800-334-8939
sales@protexallinc.com
www.protexalluniforms.com
Manufacturer and exporter of uniforms
President: Wayne Williams
CEO: Lois Williams
Vice President: Wade Williams
Sales Rep Coordinator: Dona Tredge
Operations Head: Randy Woods
Estimated Sales: $5-10 Million
Number Employees: 50-99
Square Footage: 100000
Parent Co: DeMoulin Bros. and Co.

27956 (HQ)Prototype Equipment Corporation
1601 Northwind Blvd
Libertyville, IL 60048-9613 847-680-4433
Fax: 847-816-6374 prototy1@ix.netcom.com
www.prototypecorp.com

Manufacturer, exporter and importer of robotic packaging equipment including flexible bag packers, case formers, pick and place packers, bulk case packers, top sealers and vertical snack food packers
Owner: Matthew Clatch
Director Sales/Marketing: Bruce Larson
VP Production: William Goodman
Estimated Sales: $300,000-500,000
Number Employees: 5-9
Square Footage: 168000
Brands:
Goodman
Pouch Pak
Universal

27957 Prototype Equipment Corporation
1081 S Northpoint Blvd
Waukegan, IL 60085-8215 847-596-9000
Fax: 847-596-9001 sales@goodmanpkg.com
www.goodmanpkg.com
Custom packaging machinery, case erectors, case and tray packers and sealers, packaging integration, electronic equipment and supplies
President: James Goodman
President, Chief Executive Officer: Michael Senske
Vice President of Engineering: Leo Robertson
Vice President of Sales and Marketing: Randy Denny
Estimated Sales: $10-25 Million
Number Employees: 50-99

27958 Providence Packaging
143 Barley Park Ln
Mooresville, NC 28115 704-660-1469
Fax: 704-660-0988 866-779-4945
info@providencepackaging.com
www.providencepackaging.com
Molded foam containers, reflective foil packaging, refrigerants (ice packs), corrugated shipping containers, paper products, tapes, poly, plastic and supplies
Secretary: Deby King
Marketing: David Vance
Estimated Sales: $400,000
Number Employees: 3

27959 Provisioner Data Systems
3467 W Hillsboro Boulevard
Suite 6
Deerfield Beach, FL 33442-9473 800-611-6592
Fax: 954-427-7007 800-611-6592
www.provdata.com
Computer systems for the food industry. Meat and seafood processing systems
Number Employees: 15

27960 Provisur Technologies
9150 191st Street
Mokena, IL 60448 708-479-3500
Fax: 708-479-3598 formaxinfo@provisur.com
www.provisur.com
Grinders, mixers, separators and material handling units.

27961 Provisur Technologies/Weiler
1116 East Main Street
Whitewater, WI 53190 262-473-5254
Fax: 262-473-5867 800-558-9507
www.weilerinc.com
Poultry & meat grinders, mixers and food processing equipment.
President & CEO: Mel Cohen
Vice President, Sales & Marketing: Kevin Howard

27962 (HQ)Prudential Lighting Corporation
1737 E 22nd St
Los Angeles, CA 90058 213-746-0360
Fax: 213-746-8838 800-421-5483
info@prulite.com www.prulite.com
Custom and standard fluorescent lighting fixtures with wet, damp and clean room applications; also, linear systems
Vice President: Jeff Ellis
Quality Control: Albert Pastina
Sales Director: Jon Steele
Manager: Alice Elliott
Estimated Sales: $10-20 Million
Number Employees: 5-9
Square Footage: 100000
Brands:
Galv
Pru Lites

27963 Pruitt's Packaging Services
2201 Kalamazoo Avenue SE
Grand Rapids, MI 49507-3783 616-243-0553
Fax: 616-243-4424 800-878-0553
pruitpak@aol.com
Wooden pallets and boxes, watermelon bins, skids and grocery wraparounds
President: John Pruitt
Secretary/Treasurer: Ruby Gilewski
Sales/Marketing Executive: Brian Hager
Supervisor: James McNitt
Estimated Sales: Below $5 Million
Number Employees: 8
Square Footage: 16000

27964 Prystup Packaging Products
101 Prystup Drive
PO Box 1039
Livingston, AL 35470-1039 205-652-9583
Fax: 205-652-2696 info@prystup.com
www.prystup.com
Folding boxes
President: J Leslie Prystup
CFO: Kathryn Prystrup
VP: James Emroy
R&D: Ronald Harwell
Quality Control: Jason Guin
Marketing: Rick Framer
Sales: Paul Sparkman
Public Relations: Suzanne McGahey
Production: Roy Rainer
Plant Manager: Craig Ray
Purchasing: Rickey Rogers
Estimated Sales: $10 - 20 Million
Number Employees: 100-249
Number of Brands: 6
Square Footage: 110000
Type of Packaging: Consumer, Private Label

27965 Psion Teklogix
1810 Airport Exchange Blvd
Erlanger, KY 41018-3196 859-372-4100
Fax: 859-371-6422 800-322-3437
americas.marketing@teklogix.com
www.psionteklogix.com
President: Ron Caines
Chief Executive Officer: John Conoley
Vice President of Human Resources: Maija Michell
Chief Technical Officer: Mike Doyle
Chief Marketing Officer: Nick Eades
Vice President of Operations: Rob Gayson
Estimated Sales: $50 - 75 Million
Number Employees: 100-249

27966 Publix Supermarkets
3300 Publix Corporate Parkway
PO Box 407
Lakeland, FL 33802-0401 863-688-1188
800-242-1227
www.publix.com
Largest employee-owned supermarket chain in the United States. Has 39 manufacturing facilities with the five major facilities listed below. Founded in 1930 by George W. Jenkins.
President: Randall Jones
Director/Founder: Howard Jenkins
Chief Financial Officer: David Phillips
Director: William Crenshaw
Estimated Sales: $27.0 Billion
Number Employees: 152,000
Other Locations:
Bakery Manufacturing
Atlanta GA
Dairy/Fresh Foods Manufacturing
Deerfield Beach FL
Fresh Foods Manufacturing
Jacksonville FL
Bakery/Deli/Dairy Manufacturing
Lakeland FL
Dairy Manufacturing
Lawrenceville GA

27967 Pucel Enterprises
1440 E 36th St
Cleveland, OH 44114 216-881-4604
Fax: 216-881-6731 800-336-4986
pucel-grizzly@att.net www.pucel-grizzly.com
Manufacturer and exporter of material handling equipment, stock carts, drum lifters and hand, shop and platform trucks, benches and cabinets
President: Anthony F Mlakar
Vice President: Robert Mlakar
Plant Manager: Ronald Cook
Estimated Sales: $5-10,000,000
Number Employees: 50-99
Square Footage: 105000

27968 Puget Sound Inline
300 Chestnut Ridge Road
Woodcliff Lake, NJ 07677-7731 253-983-9390
Fax: 253-627-2029 800-831-1117
sales@pugetsoundinline.com
www.pugetsoundbmw.com
Manufactures thermoforming blister packaging—trays, computer, clamshell packaging, electrical, retail display and food
President: Bob Shupe
Estimated Sales: $1-2.5 Million
Number Employees: 10-19

27969 Pulse Systems
422 Connie Avenue
Los Alamos, NM 87544 505-662-7599
Fax: 505-662-7748 pulsesystems@psilasers.com
www.psilasers.com
Manufacturer and exporter of laser marking and coding systems
President: Edward J McLellan
VP: Linda McLellan
Chief Operating Officer: Linda Mclellan
Estimated Sales: $1 - 3 Million
Number Employees: 1-4
Type of Packaging: Consumer, Private Label, Bulk
Brands:
Pulseprint

27970 Pulsetec Products Corporation
1100 S Kimball Ave
Southlake, TX 76092-9009 817-329-6099
Fax: 817-329-5914 800-580-7554
ppc@pulsetech.net www.pulsetech.net
Battery maintenance systems, digital battery analyzers, battery chargers and conditioning systems
President: Pete Smith
VP/Sales/Marketing: Scott Schilling
Business Manager: Rick Gregory
Business Development Manager: Rick Gregory
Manager: Shawn Doonan
Public Relations: Kevin Hosey
VP/Military Programs: Mark Witt
Director Military Programs: Mark Abelson
Estimated Sales: $500,000-$1 Million
Number Employees: 20-49

27971 Pulva Corporation
P.O.Box 427
Saxonburg, PA 16056-0427 724-898-3000
Fax: 724-898-3192 800-878-5828
sales@pulva.com www.pulva.com
Grinding mills, parts and feeders
President: Edward Ferree
R&D: Bruce Dene
Quality Control: Bruce Dene
Sales Director: L Ward
Estimated Sales: $20 - 50 Million
Number Employees: 20-49

27972 Purac America
111 Barclay Blvd
Lincolnshire, IL 60069 608-752-0449
Fax: 847-634-1992 pam@purac.com
www.purac.com
Producer of lactic acid, lactates and lactitol
President: Gerrit Vreeman
Vice President: Peter Kooijman
Marketing Manager: Casper Ravesteijn
VP Sales: Peter Hooijman
Estimated Sales: $20 - 50 Million
Number Employees: 20-49
Type of Packaging: Bulk

27973 Puratos Corporation
1941 Old Cuthbert Rd
Cherry Hill, NJ 08034 856-428-4300
Fax: 856-428-2939 800-654-0036
info@puratos.com www.puratos.com
Baking ingredients
President: Denis Wellington
Marketing Manager: Sheila Caufield
Estimated Sales: $500,000-$1 Million
Number Employees: 100-249

27974 Purdy Products Company
1255 Karl Court
Wauconda, IL 60064 847-526-5505
Fax: 847-526-5271 800-726-4849
sales@purdyproducts.com
www.purdyproducts.com
Chemicals, sanitizers, cleaners and degreasers for food service equipment
President: Robert D Husemoller
Estimated Sales: $5-10 Million
Number Employees: 1-4

27975 Pure & Secure, LLC
4120 NW 44th St
Lincoln, NE 68524 402-467-9300
Fax: 402-467-9393 800-875-5915
info@mypurewater.com www.mypurewater.com
Manufacturer and exporter of water treatment equipment; also, bottling and molding equipment
President: A E Meder
Sales Manager: Jason Harrington
Sales Manager: Alan Billups
Estimated Sales: $5-10 Million
Number Employees: 10-19
Square Footage: 45000
Brands:
Pure Water
Ultima

27976 Pure Fit
924 Marcon Boulevard
Allentown, PA 18109-9538 949-679-7997
Fax: 949-679-7998 866-787-3348
info@purefit.com www.purefit.com
Manufacturer and exporter of fittings, hoses and assemblies
President/CEO: Robb Dorf
Vice President: Robert Elbich
Sales Manager: John Cooling
Number Employees: 10-19
Parent Co: Nalge Process Technologies

27977 Pure-1 Systems
25 Coligni Ave
New Rochelle, NY 10801-2605 914-576-5800
Fax: 914-235-8849 sales@pure1.com
www.pure1.com
Plumbed water colors, point-of-use water color products, hot and cold bottled water colors with patented Everfull self-filling bottle
Owner: Frank Pisano
Estimated Sales: $1 - 5 Million
Number Employees: 1-4

27978 Pure-Chem Products Company
8371 Monroe Ave
Stanton, CA 90680 714-995-4141
Fax: 714-527-7802 www.pure-chem.com
President: Bill King
Estimated Sales: $2.5-5 Million
Number Employees: 10-19

27979 PureCircle USA
915 Harger Rd
Suite 250
Oak Brook, IL 60523 630-361-0374
Fax: 630-361-0384 info.usa@purecircle.com
www.purecircle.com
High purity stevia products.
CEO: Magomet Malsagov
CFO: William Mitchell
Type of Packaging: Bulk

27980 Purico USA Ltd
497 Bransom Court
Suite 202
Mt. Pleasant, SC 29464 843-881-6684
Fax: 843-881-6492 sales@puricousa.com
www.purico.com
Complete range of papers for all types of tea and coffee bags
Manager: Joe Szorc
Estimated Sales: $5-10 Million
Number Employees: 5-9

27981 Puridec Irradiation Technology
175 E. Hawthorn Parkway
Suite 142
Vernon Hills, IL 600061 847-795-8822
Fax: 847-680-5159 puridecna@reviss.com
www.puridec.co.uk
Irradiation
Number Employees: 35

27982 Puritan Manufacturing
1302 Grace St
Omaha, NE 68110 402-341-3753
Fax: 402-341-4508 800-331-0487
purmfg@ixnetcom.com www.purmfg.com
Custom fabricated conveyors, mixers, hoppers, tanks, cereal puffing machinery and catwalks; exporter of cereal puffing machinery
President: Bill Water
CEO: William Waters
CEO: Joseph F Waters
Quality Control: Jack Parr
Estimated Sales: $5-10 Million
Number Employees: 50-99
Square Footage: 175000
Brands:
Puritan

27983 Puritan/Churchill Chemical Company
1341 Capital Circle SE
Suite E
Marietta, GA 30067-8718 404-875-7331
800-275-8914
Manufacturer and exporter of deodorants, warewash systems and chemicals, disinfectants and cleaners including kitchen, industrial laundry and window
President: Richard Bruce
VP Finance: Regina Crothers
Director Marketing: Adam Gould
Number Employees: 240
Parent Co: Gibson Chemical Industries

27984 Purity Foods
417 S. Meridian Road
Hudson, MI 49247 517-448-2050
Fax: 517-448-2070 800-997-7358
info@purityfoods.com www.purityfoods.com
Products include beans, grains, seeds; cereals; cookbooks; flours; granola; pastas; pretzels; and sesame sticks.
President: Donald Stinchcomb
Regional Sales Manager: Hezeden Graye
Estimated Sales: $5-10 Million
Number Employees: 5-9
Square Footage: 60000

27985 Purity Products
200 Terminal Dr
Plainview, NY 11803 800-471-9206
Fax: 516-767-1722 800-256-6102
customercare@purityproducts.com
www.purityproducts.com
Sauces, mayonnaise, vinegar, mustard, salad dressings, vegetable oils, jellies, pickles
President: William Schroeder
President, Chief Executive Officer: Jahn Levin
CFO: Bruce Morecroft
Vice President of Quality Assurance: Richard Conant
Marketing: Al Rodriquez
Sales VP: Al Rodriquez
Operations: Ricky Montejo
Plant Manager: Rick Montejo
Purchasing Director: Charles Menezes
Estimated Sales: $1 - 3 Million
Number Employees: 20-49
Square Footage: 400000
Parent Co: Sea Specialties Company
Type of Packaging: Food Service, Private Label, Bulk
Brands:
Chef's Choice
Cheryl Lynn
Ideal
Purity

27986 Purolator Products Company
8439 Triad Dr
Greensboro, NC 27409-9018 336-668-4444
Fax: 336-668-4452 800-852-4449
info@purolator-facet.com
www.purolator-facet.com
Manufacturer and exporter of self-cleaning and sterilizable stainless steel filters for viscous fluids, food and steam
President: Ross Stellfox
Program Manager: Mark Willingham
Director Sales/Marketing: Kevin Nelson
Number Employees: 100-249
Square Footage: 360000
Parent Co: Dayco Products
Brands:
Metaledge
Poromesh
Poroplate

27987 Puronics Water Systems Inc
5775 Las Positas Rd
Livermore, CA 94551-7819 925-456-7000
Fax: 925-456-7010 service@ionicsfidelity.com
www.ionicsfidelity.com
Water treatment systems for the consumer and commercial markets. Puronics solutions include technologies such as water conditioning, filtering, micro-filtration, filtration, carbon filtration, reverse osmosis and ultra violetdisinfection.
Chief Financial Officer: Mark Cosmez II
Director of Commercial Sales: Roy Esparza

27988 Put-Ons USA
7308 Aspen Lane N
Suite 149
Brooklyn Park, MN 55428-1020 763-425-9216
Fax: 763-425-9211 888-425-1215
Uniforms
President: Brian Peterson
Sales Director: Varlerie Peterson
Estimated Sales: Less than $500,000
Number Employees: 4
Square Footage: 3000
Brands:
Put-Ons U.S.A.

27989 Putnam Group
35 Corporate Dr
Trumbull, CT 06611-6319 203-452-7270
Fax: 203-268-8071 sales@bowmanhandbags.com
www.putnamgroup.com
Importer and wholesaler/distributor of promotional items; also, marketing consultant services available
VP: Ann Rerat
Estimated Sales: Less than $500,000
Number Employees: 1-4

27990 Putsch
PO Box 5128
Asheville, NC 28813-5128 828-684-0671
Fax: 828-684-4894 800-847-8427
info@putschusa.com www.putschusa.com
Beet refinery equipment
CFO/R&D: Dieter Mergner
Engineering: Henning Wedemeyer
Sales: Jon E. DeBuvitz
Customer Service: Jeanne West
Manager: Dieter Mergner
Parts/ Supply Chain: Olav Seimer
Plant Superintendent: Dieter Mergner
Estimated Sales: $2.5 - 5 Million
Number Employees: 10-19
Parent Co: H. Putsch & Company

27991 Pyramid Flexible Packaging
120 E La Habra Boulevard
La Habra, CA 90631-5475 562-690-2208
Fax: 562-690-7892
info@pyramidflexiblepackaging.com
www.pyramidglobal.com
Estimated Sales: $1 - 3 Million
Number Employees: 30

27992 Pyro-Chem
1 Stanton St
Marinette, WI 54143 715-732-3465
Fax: 715-732-3569 800-526-1079
charding@tycoint.com www.pyrochem.com

Manufacturer and exporter of pre-engineered fire fighting systems
CEO: John Fort
Technical Services Engineer: Curt Harding
Technical Services Engineer: Brian Chernetski
General Manager Sales/Marketing: William Vegso
Customer Service Representatives: Carol Kakuk
Product Manager: Katherine Adrian
Estimated Sales: $1 - 5 Million
Number Employees: 12
Square Footage: 30000
Parent Co: Borg-Warner/Wells Fargo Alarm
Brands:
Kitchen Knight

27993 **Pyromation**
5211 Industrial Rd
Fort Wayne, IN 46825 260-484-2580
Fax: 260-482-6805 sales@pyromation.com
www.pyromation.com
Manufacturer and exporter of 3A compliant CIP thermocouples. RTDs, temperature sensors, thermowells, transmitters, connection heads, wire and cable
President: Peter Wilson
Marketing Manager: Greg Craghead
Sales Manager: Scott Farnham
Estimated Sales: $25-30 Million
Number Employees: 187
Square Footage: 40000

27994 **Pyrometer Instrument Company**
92 N Main St, Bldg 18-D
PO Box 479
Windsor, NJ 08561-0479 609-443-5522
Fax: 609-443-5590 800-468-7976
information@pyrometer.com
www.pyrometer.com
Manufacturer, importer and exporter of controllers, sensors, chart recorders, indicators, alarms and portable pyrometers; also, pressure transmitters and temperature measurement systems
Owner: Dave Crozier
CEO: D Crozier
Marketing: Mickey Otto
Estimated Sales: $2.4 Million
Number Employees: 19
Number of Brands: 2
Number of Products: 12
Square Footage: 30000
Brands:
Philips/Pma
Pyro

27995 **Q Laboratories**
1400 Harrison Ave
Cincinnati, OH 45214-1606 513-471-1300
Fax: 513-471-5600
mmcdonough@qlaboratories.com
www.qlaboratories.com
Consultant providing laboratory testing services including microbiology and analytical chemistry support, QC/release, antimicrobial efficacy and GMP testing, plant sanitation audits, nutrition labeling and preservative analysis
President: David Goins
Microbiology Group Leader: Meghan McDonough
Marketing: Mark Goins
Estimated Sales: $2.5-5 Million
Number Employees: 20-49
Square Footage: 13000

27996 **Q Pak Corporation**
2145 McCarter Hwy
Newark, NJ 07104 973-483-4404
Fax: 973-484-7896 qpak@earthlink.net
www.qpakcorp.com
Plastic bottles
President: Michael Formica
Estimated Sales: $2.5-5 Million
Number Employees: 20-49

27997 **Q Vac**
1973 E. Via Aradoÿ
Rancho Dominguez, CA 90220 310-898-3400
Fax: 310-898-3430 888-879-7822
Sales@Newaypkg.com www.qvac.com
Skin packaging machines, roller press die cutting, automatic conveyor belt blistering sealers, and vacuum forming machines
Estimated Sales: $1-2.5 Million
Number Employees: 5-9

27998 **Q&B Foods**
15547 1st St
Irwindale, CA 91706 626-334-8090
Fax: 626-969-1587 www.qbfoods.com
Contract packer and exporter of glass and plastic packed salad dressings and mayonnaise; also, sauces including taco and teriyaki
COO: Vern Robinius
CEO: Kuniaki Ishikawa
Estimated Sales: $20-50 Million
Number Employees: 50-99
Square Footage: 50000

27999 **Q-Matic Technologies**
355 East Kehoe Boulevard
Carol Stream, IL 60188-1817 847-263-7324
Fax: 847-263-7367 800-880-6836
info@qinfraredovens.com
www.q-maticovens.com
Manufacturer and exporter of conveyor ovens
Sales Manager: David Cook
Production Manager: Frank Agnello
Estimated Sales: $1-2.5 Million
Number Employees: 7
Square Footage: 20000
Type of Packaging: Food Service
Brands:
Q-Matic

28000 **QA Supplies, LLC**
1185 Pineridge Road
Norfolk, VA 23502 757-855-3094
Fax: 757-855-4155 800-472-7205
info@QAsupplies.com www.qasupplies.com
Supplier of insulated refrigiwear insulated clothing, boots and gloves, hot/cold transport bags & covers, temperature measurements, thermometers and alarms.
Sales: Russ Holt

28001 **QAD**
100 Innovation Pl
Santa Barbara, CA 93108 805-566-6000
Fax: 805-565-4202 www.qad.com
Meat industry computer systems, software, consultants, data processing
CEO: Karl F Lopker
Estimated Sales: $20-50 Million
Number Employees: 1,000-4,999

28002 **(HQ)QBD Modular Systems**
5255 Steven Creeks Blvd
#187
Santa Clara, CA 95051
Canada 408-890-8924
Fax: 905-459-1478 800-663-3005
daryl@qpd.com www.qpd.com
Manufacturer and exporter of merchandising coolers and modular display cases
President: Jeff Jaffer
CFO: Mohammed Chowdhary
Number Employees: 40
Brands:
Qbd

28003 **QC**
P.O.Box 514
Southampton, PA 18966-0514 215-355-3900
Fax: 215-355-7231 ejpcsolar@qclaboratories.com
www.qclaboratories.com
Consultant specializing in the testing of food and dairy products; also, environmental testing available
President: Thomas Heins
Quality Control: Rich Royer
Estimated Sales: $20 - 50 Million
Number Employees: 100-249
Square Footage: 30000
Parent Co: Land O'Lakes

28004 **QC Industries**
4057 Clough Woods Dr
Batavia, OH 45103-2587 513-753-6000
Fax: 513-753-6001 mail@qcindustries.com
www.qcindustries.com
Conveyors, washdowns, timing belts
President: David Dornbach
Marketing Supervisor: Chris Thompson
Estimated Sales: $10-20 Million
Number Employees: 20-49

28005 **QDC Plastic Container Company**
111 W Mount Hope Ave
Lansing, MI 48910-9093 517-319-4194
Fax: 517-319-4304 800-652-2330
qdcplastics@acd.net www.qdcplastics.com
Supplier of plastic bottles for beverages
President: Stan Martin
Operations Manager: Ken David
Estimated Sales: $10-20 Million
Number Employees: 50-99
Type of Packaging: Bulk

28006 **QMI**
426 Hayward Ave N
St Paul, MN 55128-5379 651-501-2337
Fax: 651-501-5797 qmi2@aol.com
www.qmisystems.com
Manufacturer and exporter of aseptic sampling and transfer systems for liquids; also, sampling system for bioreactors
President: Darrell Bigalke
Manager: Gwen Raddatz
Estimated Sales: Below $5 Million
Number Employees: 1-4
Square Footage: 8000
Parent Co: Quality Management
Brands:
Qmi
Qmi Safe Septum

28007 **QMS International, Inc.**
1833 Folkway Drive
Mississauga, Ontario, ON
Canada 905-820-7225
Fax: 905-820-7021 info@qmsintl.com
www.qmsintl.com
Manufacturer and supplier of new and refurbished tying machines and supplies for the meat, poultry and seafood industries.

28008 **QNC**
12021 Plano Rd Ste 160
Dallas, TX 75243 972-669-8993
Fax: 972-669-8990 888-668-3687
sales@q-n-c.com www.q-n-c.com
Hot air ovens
President/Founder: Paul R Artt
Estimated Sales: Below $5,000,000
Number Employees: 1-4
Brands:
Quik 'n Crispy

28009 **QPF**
601 E Lake Street
Streamwood, IL 60107-4101 630-830-6900
Fax: 630-213-6209 800-323-6963
wterrell@qpf.com www.qpf.com
Manufacturer and exporter of flexible polypropylene films
CEO: Robert Dea
Director Marketing: Mark Montsinger
Director Sales: Bill Rowe
Number Employees: 100-249
Square Footage: 1800000
Parent Co: Hood Industries
Brands:
Mirage
Qlam
Qpet

28010 **QSR Industrial Supply**
1888 W Point Drive
Cherry Hill, NJ 08003-2850 856-427-4270
Fax: 856-427-6736 800-257-8282
sales@qsrind.com www.qsrind.com
Industrial lighting with shatter-resistant and protective coated bulbs including fluorescent, incandescent and outdoor
President: David Diamondstein
Manager: Dave Drake
Sales Manager: Rick Jackson
Estimated Sales: $5-10 Million
Number Employees: 20-49
Square Footage: 3500
Brands:
Permalux Shatter-Kote

28011 **QST**
550 West Adams Street
Suite 200
Chicago, IL 60661 312-930-9400
Fax: 312-648-0312 carlevato.jeff@qst.com
www.qst.com
Regional Sales Manager: Sue Wech

Type of Packaging: Consumer

28012 QUIKSERV Corporation
PO Box 40466
Houston, TX 77240-0466 713-849-5882
Fax: 713-849-5708 sales@quikserv.com
www.quikserv.com

28013 (HQ)Qosina Corporation
150 Executive Dr Ste Q
Edgewood, NY 11717 631-242-3000
Fax: 631-242-3230 info@qosina.com
www.qosmedix.com
We are an oem components supplier to the medical, cosmetic, cleanroom & veterinary & pharmaceutical industries
President: Stuart Herskovitz
Estimated Sales: $100+ Million
Number Employees: 50-99

28014 Quadra-Tech
864 E Jenkins Avenue
Columbus, OH 43207-1317 614-443-0630
Fax: 614-737-5429 800-443-2766
info@quadra-techinc.com
www.quadra-techinc.com
Work tables, fry baskets and specialty smallwares
Manager: Tim Mc Cormick
General Manager: Tim McCormick
Sales Director: Rob Zigler
Estimated Sales: $10-20,000,000
Number Employees: 100-249

28015 Quadrant
2710 American Way
PO Box 9086
Fort Wayne, IN 46809 260-479-4100
Fax: 219-478-1074 800-628-7264
americas.epp@qplas.com
www.quadrantplastics.com
Standard and custom food grade components and wear resistant UHMW-PE conveying equipment
President: Roland Finch
Vice President: Mark Edele
Marketing Communication Manager: Connie Brown
National Sales Manager: Robert Blackwood
Plant Manager: Lonnie Crump
Number Employees: 250
Square Footage: 337712
Other Locations:
Scranton PA
Delmont PA
Reading PA
Wytheville VA
Brands:
Redirail
Tivar

28016 Quadrel Labeling Systems
7670 Jenther Dr
Mentor, OH 44060 440-602-4700
Fax: 440-602-4701 800-321-8509
labeling@quadrel.com www.quadrel.com
Manufacturer and exporter of labeling equipment
President: Lon Deckard
VP/General Manager: Charles Wepler
Marketing: Joe Uhlir
Sales: Christine Burrier
Operations: Shirley Chambers
Estimated Sales: $15-20 Million
Number Employees: 15
Square Footage: 40000
Type of Packaging: Consumer, Food Service
Brands:
Moduline
Premier
Q31
Q32
Rotary
Table Line
Versaline

28017 Quadro Engineering
613 Colby Drive
Waterloo, ON N2V-1A1
Canada 519-884-9660
Fax: 519-884-0253 quadrosales@idexcorp.com
www.quadro.com
Manufactures and markets an innovative line of size reduction mills, emulsifiers, powder dispertion units and vacuum conveyors for the food industry
President: Keith McIntosh
Marketing Manager: Richard Franzke
Number Employees: 100
Number of Brands: 3
Number of Products: 6
Other Locations:
Millburn NJ
Brands:
Quadro

28018 Quaker Chemical Company
PO Box 554
Columbia, SC 29202-0554 803-765-9520
Fax: 803-765-9522 800-849-9520
quakerchemical@quakerchemical.com
www.quakerchem.com
Janitorial supplies and equipment including mops and floor finish-acrylics for high speed buffers and general use; exporter of cleaning chemicals
President: Josie Hendrix
Estimated Sales: $5-10 Million
Number Employees: 5-9
Square Footage: 40000
Brands:
Fibercare 5000
Panther Power
Perma Glo
Sunburst
Superwear

28019 (HQ)Quaker Oats Company
555 W Monroe St, 1st Floor
PO Box 049003
Chicago, IL 60661-3716 312-821-1000
Fax: 312-222-7057 800-367-6287
www.quakeroats.com
Leading manufacturer, processor and exporter of cookies, oats, oatmeal, farina, granola bars, puffed wheat, puffed rice, barley, groats, rice, shredded wheat, pancake syrups and mixes, flour, corn syrups, baking mixes, pasta and cornmeal.
President: Michael Andrews
Chief Executive Officer: Jeffrey Hummel
Estimated Sales: $1.85 Billion
Number Employees: 10000
Square Footage: 300000
Type of Packaging: Consumer, Food Service
Brands:
Kretschmer Wheat Germ
Quaker
Quaker Rice Snacks
Quisp Cereal

28020 Quali-Tech Tape & Label
6695 Grove St
Denver, CO 80221-2126
Fax: 303-431-4405 glomanufacturing@aol.com
Grocery store and pressure sensitive labels; also, paper tape
President: Gloria Schlaht
Estimated Sales: $500,000 - $1 Million
Number Employees: 1-4

28021 Qualicon
PO Box 80357
Wilmington, DE 19880-0357 302-695-5300
Fax: 302-695-5301 800-863-6842
info@qualicon.com www.qualicon.com
Automated instruments that performs ribotyping to get genetic fingerprints that can identify an organism below species level, microbial charecterization, gmo detection and measurement, food safety and quality management services
President: Kevin Huttman
Chief Executive Officer: Eldon Roth
CFO: Beth Peck
Senior Vice President, General Counsel: Thomas Sager
R & D: Lance Bolton
Quality Control: Shawn Anderson
Marketing Manager: Megan DeStefano
Director of Sales: Craig Drinkwater
Number Employees: 10

28022 Qualiform, Inc
689 Weber Drive
Wadsworth, OH 44281 330-336-6777
Fax: 330-336-3668
contactsales@qualiform-inc.com
www.qualiformrubbermolding.com
Manufacturer and exporter of custom molded rubber stoppers
President: Nick Antonino
CFO: Andy Antonino
Quality Control: Duane Lawrence
Estimated Sales: Below $5 Million
Number Employees: 10

28023 Qualita Paper Products
3101 West MacArthur Boulevard
Santa Ana, CA 92704 714-540-0994
Fax: 714-540-1077 800-611-4010
info@qualitapaper.com www.qualitapaper.com
Paper baking molds, baking cups, carboard trays, doilies, cake boxes, ice cream containers and cups, cake boards, panettone molds and boxes, hard-bottom bags
President: Omar Aguirre
Vice President: Fabrice Clement
Estimated Sales: $860,000
Number Employees: 5
Parent Co: A.B.M. Inc.

28024 Quality Aluminum & Canvas
1514 Gardner Blvd.
P.O.Box 2569
Columbus, MS 39702 662-329-2525
Fax: 662-329-3725
www.qualityaluminumandcanvas.com
Commercial awnings
President: Winford Mattison
Estimated Sales: $1-2,500,000
Number Employees: 5-9

28025 Quality Assured Label
1600 5th St S
Hopkins, MN 55343 952-933-7800
Fax: 952-939-2092 sales@qal.com
www.qal.com
Custom pressure sensitive labels
Chairman: Robert Westmeyer
CEO: Robert Westnever
VP: Joe Farnko
Research & Development: Joe Farnko
Marketing Head: Petero Cattori
Estimated Sales: $20 - 50 Million
Number Employees: 50-99

28026 Quality Assured Packing
568 S Temperance Avenue
Fresno, CA 93727-6601 209-931-6700
Fax: 209-931-0286
Industrial tomato ingredient processor and supplier
Estimated Sales: $10-25 Million
Number Employees: 60

28027 Quality Bakers of America
1275 Glenlivet Drive
Suite 100
Allentown, PA 18106-3107 973-263-6970
Fax: 973-263-0937 info@qba.com
www.qba.com
Wholesale bakers' cooperative providing consulting services including marketing, sales, product development, research and development, nutritional analysis, etc
Chairman: Sherman Strider II
President/Manager: Norman Trapp
VP/Finance: Donald J. Cummings
Director: Judith Moderacki
Research & Development: Andrew Maier
Estimated Sales: $1.6 Million
Number Employees: 20-49
Brands:
Sunbeam

28028 (HQ)Quality Cabinets & Fixtures Company
885 Gateway Center Way
San Diego, CA 92102-4541 619-266-1011
Fax: 619-266-0878 quality1@qcfc.com
www.qcfc.com
Manufacturer, exporter and importer of store fixtures and wood cabinets
President: Tim Paradise
Sales/Marketing: Laura Cohen
Estimated Sales: $10-20 Million
Number Employees: 100-249

28029 Quality Container Company
1236 Watson St
Ypsilanti, MI 48198 734-481-1373
Fax: 734-481-8790
sfabiyan@qualitycontainer.com
www.qualitycontainer.com
Manufacturer and exporter of high density polyethylene containers
Manager: Rob Salemi
CFO: Jamie Barche
Quality Control: Robert Johnson
VP Sales/Marketing: Robert Bell

Estimated Sales: $20 - 50 Million
Number Employees: 50-99
Square Footage: 160000
Other Locations:
Quality Container Company
Thomasville GA

28030 Quality Containers
128 Milvan Drive
Weston, ON M9L 1Z9
Canada 416-749-6247
Fax: 416-749-3293
Manufacturer and exporter of tin cans and slip cover, friction top and open top containers
President: Patrick Henry
Number Employees: 20
Square Footage: 16000

28031 Quality Containers of New England
83 Portland St
Yarmouth, ME 04096 207-846-5420
Fax: 207-846-3755 800-639-1550
sales@qualitycontainersne.com
www.qualitycontainersne.com
Packaging and containerizing products
President: Gregory H Leonard
VP/Treasurer: Kevin Burns
Plant Manager: David Holub
Estimated Sales: $1-2.5 Million
Number Employees: 10-19
Square Footage: 12000

28032 Quality Control Equipment Company
4280 E 14th St
Des Moines, IA 50313 515-266-2268
Fax: 515-266-0243 sales@qcec.com
www.qcec.com
Manufacturer and exporter of automatic wastewater and dry material samplers, open channel flow meters and flumes
Quality Control: Tim Johnston
Sales Director: Joyce Hanson
Manager: Mike Wright
Purchasing Manager: Tim Johnston
Estimated Sales: $1-3 Million
Number Employees: 20-49
Type of Packaging: Bulk

28033 Quality Controlled Services
11971 Westline Industrial Drive
Suite 200
St. Louis, MO 63146ÿ 314-851-3100
Fax: 636-827-6761 800-325-3338
postmaster@delve.com www.delve.com
Data collection firm for marketing and sensory research
President: Laura Livers
CEO: Noel Sitzmann
Controller: Doug Ortwerth
Senior Vice President, Operations: Kim Reale
Account Manager: Jessica Lynch
Senior Vice President of Operations: Kim Reale
Estimated Sales: $1 - 5 Million

28034 Quality Corporation
2401 S Delaware St
Denver, CO 80223-4322 303-777-6608
Fax: 303-777-6488 www.donkeyforklift.com
Manufacturer and exporter of truck-carried forklifts
President: Kc Ensor
CFO: Kenton C Ensor Jr
Estimated Sales: $10 - 20 Million
Number Employees: 50-99
Type of Packaging: Bulk

28035 Quality Cup Packaging Machinery Corporation
5408 3M Drive N.E.
Menomonie, WI 54751 800-732-4624
Fax: 715-235-1111 info@qualitycup.com
www.qualitycup.com
President: Jeff James
Estimated Sales: $300,000-500,000
Number Employees: 5

28036 Quality Fabrication & Design
955 Freeport Pkwy Ste 400
Coppell, TX 75019 972-393-0502
Fax: 972-745-4244
AlexPier@quality-fabrication.com
www.quality-fabrication.com
Manufacturer and exporter of stainless steel food processing equipment including corn handling, fryers, seasoning systems, corn cooking systems, conveyors, etc
President: Alex Pier
VP: Vondel Kremeier
Technical Sales: Harvey Norman
Operations Manager: Roger Pier
Estimated Sales: $12-15 Million
Number Employees: 50-99
Square Footage: 85300

28037 Quality Films
19459 Thompson Ln
Three Rivers, MI 49093-9089 269-679-5263
Fax: 616-679-4261 qfi@qualityfilmsinc.com
www.qualityfilms.com
Polyolefin packaging film
President: Blaine Rabbers
Assistant General Manager: Carol Huskey
Marketing/Sales: Bowie Grant
VP Operations: Richard Rabbers
Estimated Sales: $5 - 10 Million
Number Employees: 10
Square Footage: 132000

28038 Quality Food Equipment
10935 Weaver Ave
South El Monte, CA 91733 626-442-9281
Fax: 626-442-8386 800-423-3744
www.qualityfoodequipment.com
Blenders, grinders, massagers and tumblers, pickle injectors and slicers
Sales/Marketing Manager: Mo Fikry
Manager: Bob Maxwell
Estimated Sales: $1 - 2.5 Million
Number Employees: 5-9

28039 Quality Highchairs
13461 Van Nuys Blvd
Pacoima, CA 91331-3059 818-896-3620
Fax: 818-896-3532 800-969-9635
qualityhigchairs12@sbcglobal.net
www.qualityhighchairs.com
Hardwood high/youth chairs, booster seats, and tray stands
President: Gilbert Raynosa
Estimated Sales: Less than $500,000
Number Employees: 1-4
Square Footage: 20000
Brands:
Classi-Tray Stand
His-470
Saferstep
Versa-Chair

28040 Quality Industries
3716 Clark Ave
Cleveland, OH 44109 216-961-5566
Fax: 216-961-5569 qirolls@stratos.net
Rolls and precision parts for packaging and processing equipment
President: Jerald Kaplan
Vice President: Jim Kaplan
Estimated Sales: $500,000-$1 Million
Number Employees: 5-9
Square Footage: 10000

28041 (HQ)Quality Industries
130 Jones Blvd
La Vergne, TN 37086 615-793-3000
Fax: 615-793-2347 www.qualityind.com
Manufacturer and exporter of food service equipment, stainless steal sifter cabinets; also, custom metal fabrication available
President: Fred Apple
CFO: Jeff Mayfield
CEO: Jeff Mayfield
Quality Control: Terry Tidwell
R&D: Micheal Taylor
Estimated Sales: $20 - 50 Million
Number Employees: 250-499
Square Footage: 190000

28042 Quality Mop & Brush Manufacturers
341 Great Plain Avenue
Needham, MA 02492-4130 617-884-2999
Fax: 617-884-3999 www.manufacturingma.com
Mops, brooms, brushes, mop/broom handles and gloves
President: Donald Ferris
Estimated Sales: $1-2.5 Million
Number Employees: 5-9
Brands:
Telescopic

28043 Quality Natural Casing
P.O.Box 229
Hebron, KY 41048-0229 859-689-5311
Fax: 859-689-5177 800-328-8701
www.qualitycasing.com
Casings: collagen, fibrous, natural
President: Robert Novachich
Estimated Sales: $5-10 Million
Number Employees: 10-19

28044 Quality Packaging, Inc.
851 Sullivan Drive
PO Box 1720
Fond du Lac, WI 54936-1720 920-923-3633
Fax: 920-923-2749 800-923-3633
www.qpack.com
Offers experience in package design, materials and equipment for various types of packaging.
President: Larry Wills
Plant Manager: Kevin Graham
Estimated Sales: $14.1 Million
Number Employees: 75

28045 Quality Partition Manufacturing
869 State Route 12
Frenchtown, NJ 08825-4223 908-782-0505
Fax: 908-782-0583
Wine industry corrugated partitions
Manager: Jeff Connlain
Estimated Sales: $25-50 Million
Number Employees: 100-249

28046 Quality Plastic Bag Corporation
3430 56th Street
Flushing, NY 11377-2122 718-429-1632
Fax: 718-429-1634 800-532-2247
Plastic bags
Estimated Sales: $2.5-5 Million
Number Employees: 10-19
Square Footage: 15000
Type of Packaging: Bulk

28047 Quality Seating Company
4136 Logan Way
Youngstown, OH 44505-5703 330-747-0181
Fax: 330-747-0183 800-765-7096
Manufacturer and exporter of furniture including booths, chairs and tables
CEO: Roger Gasser
CFO: Frank Joy
Vice President: Marylou Joy
Research & Development: Mel Textoris
Marketing Director: Anthony Johntony
Sales Director: Paula Rapone
Operations Manager: Jim Humparies
Purchasing Manager: Paula Rapone
Estimated Sales: $2.5-5 Million
Number Employees: 20-49
Number of Brands: 1
Number of Products: 100
Square Footage: 100000
Parent Co: Quality Upholstering Company

28048 Quality Transparent Bag
PO Box 486
Bay City, MI 48707-0486 989-893-3561
Fax: 989-893-3004 bagcentral@aol.com
www.qualitybag.com
Polyethylene bags
President: Stephen Kessler
CEO: Leonard Kessler
Director Corporation Services: Tony Bloenk
Quality Control: Mery Carey
Estimated Sales: $5 - 10 Million
Number Employees: 20-49
Square Footage: 248000
Other Locations:
Quality Transparent Bag
Lawrenceburg TN
Brands:
Best Buy
Valu Pak

28049 Qualtech
1880, Rue L,on-Harmel
Quebec, QC G1N 4K3
Canada 418-686-3802
Fax: 418-686-3801 888-339-3801
info@qualtech.ca www.qualtech.ca

Specializing in stainless steel components and fabrications equipment
President: Andre Giguere
Customer Service: Andre Turcotte
Other Locations:
Saint-Laurent, QC
Scarborough, ON

28050 Quanex Building Products
1800 West Loop South
Suite 1500
Houston, TX 77027 713-961-4600
Fax: 216-910-1505 www.truseal.com
Glass doors and display units designed to improve thermal performance for refrigerated products, also glass sealant for same
CEO: August J Coppola
President, Chief Executive Officer: Dave Petratis
Vice President, Controller: Deborah Gadin
Quality Manager: Christoph Rubel
Director of Marketing: Erin Johnson
Sales Manager: Andreas Schultheiss
Executive Vice President, Chief Operatin: Curtis Stevens
Estimated Sales: $5-10 Million
Number Employees: 20-49

28051 Quantek Instruments
183 Magill Dr
Grafton, MA 01519 508-839-3940
Fax: 508-819-3444
sales@quantekinstruments.com
www.quantekinstruments.com
Oxygen and carbon dioxide analyzers
Estimated Sales: $3 - 5 Million
Number Employees: 10-19

28052 Quantem Corporation
1457 Lower Ferry Rd
Ewing, NJ 08618 609-883-9191
Fax: 800-800-1531 609-883-9879
info@quantemcorp.com www.quantemcorp.com
Production Manager: S Sunderland
Estimated Sales: $2 Million
Number Employees: 20-50
Square Footage: 15000
Brands:
Analog Thermostats
Data Loggers
Defrost Controllers
Digital (Appliance) Thermometers
Digital Thermostats
Temperature Sensors
Ventilation Controllers

28053 Quantis Secure Systems
7255 Standard Drive
Hanover, MD 21076-1389 410-712-6020
Fax: 410-712-0329 800-325-6124
Security, fire alarm and intercom systems
President: Kevin Robison
Estimated Sales: $2.5-5 Million
Number Employees: 20-49
Parent Co: BET

28054 Quantum Net
PO Box 49
Sewickley, PA 15143 704-376-0509
Fax: 704-551-0941
Netting plastics, netting and tying machines
President: George Seal
Estimated Sales: $500,000-$1 Million
Number Employees: 6

28055 Quantum Storage Systems
15800 NW 15th Avenue
Miami, FL 33169 305-687-0405
Fax: 305-688-2790 800-685-4665
sales@quantumstorage.com
www.quantumstorage.com
Plastic storage containers, metal shelving and mobile storage cabinets and carts
President: Larry Groll
VP: Dean Cohen
Marketing: Jose Babani
Sales: Elizabeth Faller
Estimated Sales: $3 - 5,000,000
Number Employees: 250
Square Footage: 150000
Parent Co: M&M Plastics
Type of Packaging: Consumer

28056 Quantum Topping SystemsQuantum Technical Services Inc
9524 West Gulfstream Road
Frankfort, IL 60423 815-464-1540
Fax: 815-464-1541 888-464-1540
information@q-t-s.com www.q-t-s.com
Manufacturer and designer of manual and automated portion control, cheese, IQF meat, and IQF vegetable. Topping application equipment and pepperoni slicing equipment
President: David White
CEO: Mark Freudinger
Sales Manager: Jim Machura
Estimated Sales: $3 - 5 Million
Number Employees: 20
Square Footage: 76000

28057 Quasar Industries
1911 Northfield Drive
Rochester Hills, MI 48309 248-852-0300
Fax: 248-852-0442 sales@quasar.com
www.quasar.com
Microwave ovens
CEO: Denise Higgins
VP Sales: Dave Bearden

28058 Queen City Awning
7225 E Kemper Rd
Cincinnati, OH 45249 513-530-9660
Fax: 513-530-0662 info@queencityawning.com
www.queencityawning.com
Commercial awnings
President: Peter Weingartner
Estimated Sales: Below $5,000,000
Number Employees: 20-49

28059 Quest
PO Box 73381
San Clemente, CA 92673-0113 949-643-1333
Fax: 949-362-4937 foods4you@aol.com
Consultant specializing in nutrition analysis and labeling services for dry, frozen and refrigerated products
President: Harry Messersmith

28060 Quest Corporation
12900 York Rd
North Royalton, OH 44133 440-230-9400
Fax: 440-582-7765 info@2quest.com
www.2quest.com
Electronic scales, weighing and batching systems and data acquisition/transmission systems; exporter of weighing and batching systems
Sales/Marketing Manager: Daniel Donovan
Operations Manager: Jerome Kelly
Estimated Sales: $2.5-5 Million
Number Employees: 19

28061 Quetzal Foods International Company
3419 Iberville Street
New Orleans, LA 70119-5322 504-486-0830
Fax: 504-486-0830

28062 Quick Label Systems
600 E Greenwich Ave
West Warwick, RI 02893-7526 401-828-4000
Fax: 401-822-2430 877-757-7978
info@quicklabel.com
www.quicklabelsystems.com
CFO: Joseph Oconnell
CEO: Albert W Ondis
Estimated Sales: G
Number Employees: 250-499

28063 Quick Label Systems
600 E Greenwich Ave
West Warwick, RI 02893-7526 401-828-4000
Fax: 401-822-2430 877-757-7978
info@quicklabelsystems.com
www.quicklabelsystems.com
Digital color thermal transfer printers, barcode label printers, labelers, print and apply systems, labels, thermal transfer ribbon
President: Edward Kizzuti
CFO: Joseph O'Connell
CEO: Albert W Ondis
CEO: Albert Ondis
Marketing Director: April Ondis
Sales Director: Eric Pizzuti
Estimated Sales: $50 Million
Number Employees: 250-499
Square Footage: 125000
Parent Co: Astro-Med
Type of Packaging: Consumer, Food Service, Private Label, Bulk
Other Locations:
Astro-Med
Longucuil, Quebec
Astro-Med
Slough, United Kingdom
Astro-Med
Trappes, France
Astro-Med
Rodgau, Germany
Astro-Med
Milano, Italy

28064 Quick Point
1717 Fenpark Dr
Fenton, MO 63026 636-343-9400
Fax: 636-343-3587 800-638-1369
sales@quickpoint.com www.quickpoint.com
Manufacturer, supplier and exporter of advertising specialties
President: John Goessling, Jr Jr
CEO: John Goessling Sr
CFO: Doug Bozler
Vice President: Duane Mayer
Marketing Director: Duane Mayer
Sales Director: Joe Keely
Operations Manager: Rick Smith
Production Manager: Bryan Frenzel
Purchasing Manager: Dave Miller
Number Employees: 100-249

28065 Quick Stamp & Sign Mfg
805 General Mouton Ave
P. O. Box 3272
Lafayette, LA 70501-3272 337-232-2171
Fax: 337-232-4561 sales@qrstamp.com
www.qrstamp.com
Manufacturer and wholesaler/distributor of regular and self-inking rubber stamps, grocery marking ink, price markers for deposit stamps, daters and numberers
President: Patrick Gaubert
Estimated Sales: Less than $500,000
Number Employees: 1-4
Square Footage: 7200

28066 Quickdraft
1525 Perry Dr SW
Canton, OH 44710 330-477-4574
Fax: 330-477-3314 www.quickdraft.com
Hot dog/sausage casing removal systems, draft inducer's to vent out the heat produced from ovens & boilers and food conveying systems.

28067 Quickie Manufacturing Corp.
1150 Taylors Ln
Suite 2
Cinnaminson, NJ 08077 856-829-7900
Fax: 856-786-9318 help@quickie.com
www.quickie.com
Mops, brushes, brooms, sponges and scourers
President: Peter Vosbikian
Sr. VP Sales: David Vosbikian
Executive VP Sales/Marketing: Vince Cella
Estimated Sales: $10-20 Million
Number Employees: 50-99

28068 Quickserv Corporation
11441 Brittmoore Park Dr.
PO Box 40466
Houston, TX 77041 713-849-5882
Fax: 713-849-5708 800-388-8307
sales@quikserv.com www.quikserv.com
Manufacturer and exporter of food service drive-thru windows, security transaction drawers, BR glass, and air curtains; custom fabrications available
President, Chairman: Jason T. Epps
CEO: Jason T. Epps
Marketing/Sales: Ray Epps
Sales Director: Sophia Navarro
Plant Manager: Jack Weaver
Purchasing Manager: Jason Epps
Number Employees: 40
Square Footage: 152000
Brands:
Quikserv

28069 (HQ)Quik-Stik Labels
PO Box 490100
Everett, MA 02149 617-389-7570
Fax: 617-381-9280 800-225-3496
rkaress@qsxlabels.com www.qsxlabels.com
Manufacturer and exporter of labels including thermal, laser, pin feed, graphic, bar code, etc.; also, label applicators and dispensers
President and CEO: Mike Karess
Vice President: Robert Karess
Marketing: Robert Karess
Plant Manager: Peter Kozowylt
Estimated Sales: $5-10 Million
Number Employees: 50-99
Square Footage: 120000
Type of Packaging: Private Label
Brands:
Quikstik

28070 QuikWater, Inc.
8939 W 21st St
Sand Springs, OK 74063 918-241-8880
Fax: 918-241-8718 sales@quikwater.com
www.quikwater.com
QuikWater manufactures a 99% thermal efficient direct contact water heater that provides potable hot water on demand. Water heated with a QuikWater can be used for domestic purposes, as a food ingredient and for sterilization andsanitation processes. With tremendous thermal efficiency, QuikWater can create up to 40% fuel savings compared to traditional methods.
President: Dana Weber
Marketing: Kay Weiman
Sales: Tammy Collins
Number of Brands: 3
Number of Products: 1
Brands:
Econowater
Quikwater
Twintower

28071 Quintex Corporation
3808 N Sullivan Rd
Bldg 8a
Spokane Valley, WA 99216 509-924-7900
Fax: 509-924-7991 sales@qntx.com
www.qntx.com
Custom and stock plastic bottles; also, printing services available
President: Dorothea Christiansen
Regional Sales Manager: Bruce McElwain
Customer Service: George Ferriola
Estimated Sales: $10-20 Million
Number Employees: 50-99
Square Footage: 72000

28072 Quintex Corporation
3808 N Sullivan Rd Bldg 8a
Spokane Valley, WA 99216 509-924-7900
Fax: 509-924-7991 www.qntx.com
Manufactures blow mold plastic containers
President: Dorochea Christiansen
CFO: Bob Pullis
Quality Control: Bill Massey
Estimated Sales: $10 - 20 Million
Number Employees: 50-99

28073 Quipco Products
1401 Mississippi Avenue
Suite 5
Sauget, IL 62201 314-993-1442
Fax: 618-271-2311
Manufacturer and exporter of custom and standard service food equipment including counters, racks, sinks and tables; also, custom stainless steel fabrication available
President: James Nations
VP/Owner: Jerry Chervitz
Office Manager: Tena Holmes
Estimated Sales: $1 - 3 Million
Number Employees: 17
Square Footage: 20000

28074 Qwik Pack Systems
16571 Saddlebrook Ln
Moreno Valley, Mo 92551 951-232-2507
Fax: 909-242-6019
qwikpacksystemsinc@yahoo.com
www.qwikpacksystemsinc.com
Automatic and semiautomatic carton sealing and taping machines. Robotics, L-Sealers, automatic stretch wrap machines, strapping machines and adhesive tapes
President: James Mahoney
Estimated Sales: $10-20 Million
Number Employees: 1-4
Number of Brands: 1
Number of Products: 31
Square Footage: 500000
Type of Packaging: Food Service
Brands:
Qwik Pack Systems

28075 Qyk Syn Industries
8527 NW 66th Street
Miami, FL 33166-2636 305-594-3366
Fax: 305-594-0075 800-354-5640
bobbiebridge@aol.com
Formed plastic and custom neon signs, faces, letters,architectural panels and menu boards
CEO: Ernest Hunt
Estimated Sales: $1 - 5 Million
Number Employees: 10
Square Footage: 3600

28076 (HQ)R F Schiffmann Associates
149 W 88th St
New York, NY 10024-2424 212-362-7021
Fax: 212-769-4630 microwaves@juno.com
www.microwaveinnovations.com
Consultant specializing in new products, process and packaging research anddevelopment, product testing and microwave technology
President: Robert Schiffmann
CFO: Ernest Stein
VP: Marilyn Schiffmann
Estimated Sales: $500,000-$1 Million
Number Employees: 1-4
Square Footage: 8000

28077 R on I Automation Solutions
9319 Forsyth Park Drive
Charlotte, NC 28273 704-714-4699
Fax: 704-714-5317 866-543-8635
info@roni.com www.roni.com
Offers automated processes and equipment
President: Gunnar Lofgren
Estimated Sales: $5 - 10 Million
Number Employees: 10-19

28078 R&C Pro Brands
1655 Sally Road
Wayne, NJ 973-633-7374
Disinfectants, washing compounds, polishes and cleaners including glass, hand, carpet and windows
President: John Culligan
VP Marketing: Karen Messer
National Sales Manager: Michael Tracy
Parent Co: Reckitt & Colman PLC

28079 R&D Brass
25 Sprout Creek Court
Wappingers Falls, NY 12590 845-831-6900
Fax: 845-223-6195 800-447-6050
RDBRASSINC@AOL.COM www.rdbrass.com
Brass sneeze guards, booth dividers, railings, glass racks and crowd control products
Estimated Sales: Less than $500,000
Number Employees: 1-4
Square Footage: 20000

28080 R&D Glass Products
1808 Harmon Street
Berkeley, CA 94703-2496 510-547-6464
Fax: 510-547-3620 www.angelfire.com
Wine industry labware
President: Doug Dobson
Estimated Sales: Below $5 Million
Number Employees: 10-19

28081 R&G Machinery
7204 Beckwith Road
Morton Grove, IL 60053-1723 847-966-1530
Fax: 773-265-6311 www.r&gmachinery.com
Tanks, kettles
President: Sofi Rahmon
Estimated Sales: $1-2.5 Million
Number Employees: 4
Square Footage: 100000

28082 R&I Automation Solutions
9319 Forsyth Park Drive
Charlotte, NC 28273 704-714-4699
Fax: 704-714-5317 866-543-8635
info@roni.com www.roni.com
Material handling applications including rollhandling, clean room, product pouring and weighing
President: Gunnar Lofgren
Owner: Gunner Lofgren
Estimated Sales: $1 - 2.5 Million
Number Employees: 10-19

28083 R&R Corrugated Container
PO Box 399
Terryville, CT 06786-0399 860-584-1194
Fax: 860-582-5051
Corrugated boxes
President: Richard Braverman
CFO: Wayne
Estimated Sales: $10 - 20 Million
Number Employees: 50-99

28084 R&R Industries
1000 Calle Cordillera
San Clemente, CA 92673 949-361-9238
Fax: 949-361-9360 800-234-1434
rrosen@rrind.com www.rrind.com
Embroidered and printed promotional clothing
President: Richard Rosen
Marketing Manager: Richard Rosin
Production Manager: Robin Grohman
Estimated Sales: $20-50 Million
Number Employees: 50-99

28085 R-K Electronics
7405 Industrial Row Dr
Mason, OH 45040 513-489-4060
Fax: 513-489-0043 800-543-4936
info@rke.com www.rke.com
Manufacturer and exporter of relays and voltage suppressors for HVAC applications
President: John L Keller
Estimated Sales: $5 - 10 Million
Number Employees: 10-19

28086 R-TECH Laboratories
4001 Lexington Ave N
Saint Paul, MN 55126 651-481-2207
Fax: 651-486-0837 800-328-9687
kkinn@landolakes.com www.rtechlabs.com
Research laboratory offering focus groups, analytical testing, sensory evaluation, nutrition labeling, pilot plant facilities, etc
Business Development Manager: Carle Shanks
Sales: Annette Sass
Estimated Sales: $5 - 10 Million
Number Employees: 100-249
Square Footage: 17000
Parent Co: Land O'Lakes

28087 R. Markey & Sons
5 Hanover Sq
Rm 1202
New York, NY 10004 212-482-8600
Fax: 212-344-5838
rmarkeycoffee@compuserve.com
www.keymar.com
Tea and coffee samplers and weighers
President: Michael Steele
Estimated Sales: $1 - 2.5 Million
Number Employees: 20-49
Parent Co: R Markey & Sons

28088 R. Murphy Company
13 Groton Harvard Rd
Ayer, MA 01432 978-772-3481
Fax: 978-772-7569 888-772-3481
sales@rmurphyknives.com
www.rmurphyknives.com
Industrial knives including carving, butchers', fish scaling and slitting
President: Douglas Bethke
Plant Manager: Charles Liebfried
Estimated Sales: $2.5 - 5 Million
Number Employees: 10-19

28089 (HQ)R. Wireworks
PO Box 1118
Elmira, NY 14902 607-733-7169
Fax: 607-734-8859 800-550-4009
sales@rwireworks.com
www.shoprwireworks.com

Point of purchase displays and fixtures
President: Ned Rubin
Quality Control: Terry Cosgelo
Marketing Manager: Deb Eighmey
Estimated Sales: $2.5 - 5 Million
Number Employees: 20-49

28090 (HQ)R.C. Keller & Associates
14 Passage Lane
Suite 110
Barnegat, NJ 08005-3340 973-694-8810
Fax: 973-649-3535 rkeller@kellerpackaging.com
www.kellerpackaging.com
Consultant specializing in packaging, processing and automation systems integration, facilities design, project management, industrial engineering and operations research
Estimated Sales: $1 - 5 Million
Number Employees: 1

28091 R.C. Smith Company
14200 Southcross Dr W
Burnsville, MN 55306 952-854-0711
Fax: 952-854-8160 800-747-7648
info@rcsmith.com www.rcsmith.com
Store fixtures
President: Peter Smith
Marketing Manager: Sarah Dunne
Estimated Sales: $2.5-5 Million
Number Employees: 20-49

28092 R.F. Hunter Company
113 Crosby Rd Ste 9
Dover, NH 03820 603-742-9565
Fax: 603-742-9608 800-332-9565
info@rfhunter.com www.rfhunter.com
Manufacturer and exporter of filtration equipment for edible oils
President: Richard Santoro
Estimated Sales: $500,000 - $1 Million
Number Employees: 5-9
Brands:
Ecco One
Hunter Filtrator Hf Series
Mini Max Iii

28093 R.F. MacDonald Company
10261 Matern Pl
Santa Fe Springs, CA 90670 714-257-0900
Fax: 714-257-1176
jim.macdonald@rfmacdonald.com
www.rfmacdonald.com
Wine industry pumps
Manager: Christopher Sentner
VP Pump Division: Robert Sygiel
VP Boiler Division: Chris Sentner
Co-President: James T McDonald
Estimated Sales: $20 - 50 Million
Number Employees: 20-49

28094 R.G. Stephens Engineering
707 W 16th Street
Long Beach, CA 90813-1410 562-435-6244
Fax: 562-435-1664 800-499-3001
Food processing equipment and supplies, conveyor systems, waste handling equipment and systems and process control systems; also, engineering, design, fabrication and installation services available
General Manager: Ralph Stephens
Manager: Ken Diehl
VP: Diane Stephen
Number Employees: 6

28095 R.H. Chandler Company
1040 Claridge Pl
Saint Louis, MO 63122-2431 314-962-9353
Fax: 314-962-1661 rhc493@netscape.net
Manufacturer and importer precision machined parts
President: Robert H Chandler
Number Employees: 7
Square Footage: 11600

28096 R.H. Saw Corporation
28386 W Main Street
Barrington, IL 60011-0707 847-381-8777
Fax: 847-381-9492 rhsaw@aol.com
Manufacturer, importer and exporter of cutlery, blades, grinder plates and knives including metal, wood and plastic
President: Ralph Hirsch
CEO: Larry Adler
Estimated Sales: $500,000-$1 Million
Number Employees: 1-4

28097 R.I. Enterprises
PO Box 351
Hernando, MS 38632-0351 662-429-7863
Fax: 662-429-2561
Wire display racks
President: R Gates
Secretary/Treasurer: B Gates
VP: L Gates
Estimated Sales: $500,000-$1 Million
Number Employees: 19
Square Footage: 22000

28098 R.L. Instruments
16009 Arminta Street
Van Nuys, CA 91406 818-780-1800
Fax: 818-780-1978 rlinstruments@earthlink.net
www.rlinstruments.com
Refractometer products, spectrophotometers, pH meters and related products, and microwave moisture and solids analyzer
Owner: April Hodges
Estimated Sales: Below $5 Million
Number Employees: 1-4

28099 R.P. Adams Company
P.O.Box 963
Buffalo, NY 14240-0963 716-877-2608
Fax: 716-877-9385 800-896-8869
info@rpadams.com www.rpadams.com
Manager: David Shull
VP: Dan Petko
Estimated Sales: $9 Million
Number Employees: 50-99

28100 R.P. Childs Stamp Company
161 Prokop Av
Ludlow, MA 01056 413-733-1211
Fax: 413-737-6865
Marking devices, rubber stamps, parts, pads, numbering machines and time recorders
President: Roland Stebbins
Estimated Sales: Below $5 Million
Number Employees: 2 to 4

28101 R.R. Scheibe Company
29 Westgate Rd
Newton Center, MA 02459 508-584-4900
Fax: 508-580-2644 info@scheibeco.com
www.scheibeco.com
Serving trays, snack tables and tray stands
Owner: Alan Hackel
Estimated Sales: Below $5 Million
Number Employees: 30

28102 R.R. Street & Co., Inc.
215 Shuman Blvd, Suite 403
Naperville, IL 60563 630-416-4244
Fax: 630-416-4150 email@4streets.com
www.4streets.com
Manufacturer and exporter of dry cleaning detergents, fabric finishes, spotters and filtration products
CEO: Ross Beard
CFO: James Beecher
Estimated Sales: $5 - 10 Million
Number Employees: 5-9

28103 RA Jones & Company
2701 Crescent Springs Road
Covington, KY 41017 859-341-0400
Fax: 859-341-0519 www.rajones.com
Manufacturer and exporter of automatic carton loading machines, case and tray packers, continuous web form, fill and seal machinery, bottle uncasers, pouch makers, fillers and robotic solutions; also provide complete partial lineintegration services
Estimated Sales: $300,000-500,000
Number Employees: 1-4
Parent Co: The Coesia Group

28104 RA Jones & Company
7800 Cooper Rd # 102
Cincinnati, OH 45242-7733 513-891-7800
Fax: 859-341-0519 holmesp@rajones.com
www.rajones.com
Cartoners, pouch/sachet machines, multipackers, case packers, robotics, integrated systems
President: Bonsild Gordon
Estimated Sales: $80 Million
Number Employees: 1-4

28105 RACO Manufacturing
1400 62nd St
Emeryville, CA 94608-2099 510-658-6713
Fax: 510-658-3153 800-722-6999
sales@racoman.com www.racoman.com
Controlled atmosphere monitors, alarms, controls and probes
President: Constance Brown
VP Sales/Marketing: James Brown
Estimated Sales: $20 - 50 Million
Number Employees: 100-249
Brands:
Chatterbox
Verbatim

28106 RAM Center
5140 Moundview Dr
Red Wing, MN 55066-1100 651-388-1821
Fax: 651-385-2180 800-762-6842
isg.sales@ram-center.com
www.autoequipllc.com
Manufacturer and exporter of systems for robotic packaging and material handling; including palletizers for cold room and washdown applications
General Manager: Steve Halverson
R&D: Cory Doln
Executive VP: Dave Muelken
Quality Control: Dave Mulken
Director Sales/Marketing: Steve Valade
Estimated Sales: $10 - 20 Million
Number Employees: 20-49
Parent Co: RAM Center
Brands:
Ram Center

28107 RAM Equipment
W227n913 Westmound Dr
Waukesha, WI 53186-1647 262-513-1114
Fax: 262-513-1115 info@tiefmach.com
www.tiemach.com
Confectionery extruders, high viscosity pump feeders
President: James E Tiefenthaler Jr.
Vice President: Norman Searle
Estimated Sales: Below $5 Million
Number Employees: 1-4

28108 RAM Machinery Corporation
PO Box 1199
Burlington, CT 06013 860-673-5511
Fax: 860-675-9419
miller@rammachinerycorp.com
www.rammachinerycorp.com
Used packaging and production equipment
President: Richard Miller
Estimated Sales: $1-2.5 Million
Number Employees: 1-4

28109 RAO Contract Sales
94 Fulton Street
Paterson, NJ 07501 201-652-1500
Fax: 973-279-6448 888-324-0020
info@rao.com www.rao.com
Manufacturer and exporter of menu and bulletin boards, pedestal displays, etc
Owner: Brian Bergman
Account Executive: George Cross
Account Executive: Marsha Holland
Estimated Sales: $1 - 5 Million
Number Employees: 20-49
Square Footage: 20000
Brands:
Tak-Les

28110 RAPAC
30 Industrial Park Road
Oakland, TN 38060
Fax: 901-465-1181 800-280-6333
ecosix@rapac.com
www.ringcompanies.com/rapachome
Plastic bottles and jars
Estimated Sales: $32 Million
Number Employees: 102
Square Footage: 50000

28111 RAS Process Equipment
324 Meadowbrook Rd
Robbinsville, NJ 08691 609-371-1000
Fax: 609-371-1200 sales@ras-inc.com
www.ras-inc.com

Manufacturer and exporter of process equipment including pressure vessels, heat exchangers, reactors, columns and storage tanks
Owner: John Bonacorda
Director: John Bonacorda
VP: John Bonacorda
Estimated Sales: $5 - 10 Million
Number Employees: 20-49
Square Footage: 80000

28112 RBA-Retailer's Bakers Association
14239 Park Center Drive
Laurel, MD 20707-5261 301-725-2149
Fax: 301-725-2187 301-725-2187
rba@rbanet.com www.rbanet.com
Communications Director: Dawn Rivera
Estimated Sales: $1 - 5 Million
Number Employees: 15

28113 RBM Manufacturing Company
1570 West Mission Boulevard
Pomona, CA 909-620-13 909-620-6119
Fax: 800-367-7260 info@rbmcsi.com
www.rbmcsi.com
Art technology for the bulk material handling industry; conveying, surge and distribution systems, vibratory conveyors, belt conveyors, bucket elevators, controlled by the most advanced electronic instrumentation, either withconventional or computerized
President: Roobik Kureghian
Estimated Sales: Below $5 Million
Number Employees: 10-19

28114 RBS Fab
230 Hoernerstown Rd
Hummelstown, PA 17036 717-566-9513
Fax: 717-566-9268 www.rbsfab.com
Custom designed food processing equipment
President: Terry Smith
CEO: Joann Smith
Office Manager: Denise Ajala
Production: Edward Rupp
Estimated Sales: $2.5-5 Million
Number Employees: 10-19
Square Footage: 24000

28115 RC Molding Inc.
19 Freedom Ct
Greer, SC 29650 864-879-7279
Fax: 864-879-7309
customerservice@rcmolding.com
www.rcmolding.com
Thermoplastic injection molded parts for boxes
President: William Humphrey
Estimated Sales: $1-2.5 Million
Number Employees: 10-19
Square Footage: 80000

28116 RCS Limited
1301 Commerce Street
Birmingham, AL 35217-3603 205-841-9955
Fax: 205-841-2106 brentmarshall@rcands.com
www.rcands.com
Designs and builds contractor for cold storage warehouses
Marketing/Sales: Laura Williams

28117 RDA Container Corporation
70 Cherry Rd
Gates, NY 14624 585-247-2323
Fax: 585-247-5680 info@rdacontainer.com
www.rdacontainer.com
Corrugated boxes
President: Alan Brant
Founder: Peter R. Brant
President: Peter R Brant
Sales Manager: Jack Fennell
Mngr.: Bob Bardeen
Estimated Sales: $10-20 Million
Number Employees: 50-99

28118 RDM International
11643 Otsego Street
North Hollywood, CA 91601-3628 818-985-7654
Fax: 818-760-2376 bobmoore@rdmintl.com
www.rdmintl.com
Processor, importer and exporter of fruits including frozen, dried, powderes, flakes and canned; also, fruit concentrates and purees, oils, nuts, pumpkin, sweet potatoes/yams and coconut
President/Sales: Bob Moore
Operations: Peri Abel
Number of Brands: 135
Number of Products: 280
Square Footage: 276000
Type of Packaging: Food Service, Private Label, Bulk
Brands:
Beesweet Blueberries
Berry Fine Raspberries
Big Banana Perfet
Big Boy Blazin Berries
Big Red Rhubarb
Bubba's Yams
Fruit To the World
Gourmet Brand Blackberries
Mountain Mats' Apples
Pacific Coconut
Perfect Peach
Petes Pumpkin
Rain Sweet
Rippin Cherries
Tru Blue Blueberries

28119 RDM Technologies
4711 East 355 Street
Willoughby, OH 44094
Canada 440-954-3500
Fax: 440-954-3501 sales@bevcorp.com
www.bevcorp.com
Estimated Sales: C
Parent Co: Bevcorp LLC

28120 RDM-Sesco
4711 East 355 Street
Willoughby, OH 44094 440-954-3500
Fax: 440-954-3501 sales@bevcorp.com
www.bevcorp.com
President: David Kemp Sr
CFO: Tim Frantz
Quality Control: Jim Hannah
Number Employees: 60

28121 RDS of Florida
13170 92nd St # 303
6302 Benjamin Rd
Largo, FL 33773-1319
Fax: 407-831-0833 sales@rdsflorida.com
www.rdsflorida.com
Restaurant point of sale systems including table and quick service, wireless headsets and close circuit t.v
President: Joe Pollock
Account Manager: David Henderson
Estimated Sales: $5 - 10 Million
Number Employees: 10-19

28122 RE Systems
45335 Vintage Park Plaza
Sterling, VA 20166 703-480-9100
Fax: 703-689-4680 info@reisystems.com
www.reisystems.com
Custom-designed conveyor equipment and systems
Estimated Sales: $1 - 5 Million
Number Employees: 5-9

28123 REA Elektronik
7307 Young Dr
Suite B
Cleveland, OH 44146-5369 440-460-0552
Fax: 440-232-5335 rturchi@rea-jet.com
www.rea-systeme.com
Owner: Ray Turchi
Estimated Sales: $.5 - 1 million
Number Employees: 1-4

28124 RER Services
19431 Business Center Dr # 17
Northridge, CA 91324-6408 818-993-1826
Fax: 818-993-0016 rerserv@flash.net
Manufacturer and exporter of packaging machinery
Owner: Rick Ray
Estimated Sales: $2.5-5,000,000
Number Employees: 5-9

28125 RES & Associates
300 N Wolf Rd
Suite B
Wheeling, IL 60090-2900 847-541-0080
Fax: 847-541-0212 800-741-5919
President: Ralph E Squaglia Jr
Estimated Sales: $500,000-$1 Million
Number Employees: 1-4

28126 RETROTECH, Inc
610 Fishers Run
Victor, NY 14564 585-924-6333
Fax: 585-924-6334 info@retrotech.com
www.retrotech.com
Automated warehousing systems
Vice President: Len DeWeerdt
Tactical Marketing Specialist: Cynthia Hamann
VP Operations: Peter Hartman
Estimated Sales: $10-20 Million
Number Employees: 100-249
Number of Brands: 2
Number of Products: 3

28127 REYCO Systems
1704 Industrial Way
Caldwell, ID 83605 208-795-5700
Fax: 208-795-5749 info@reycosys.com
www.reycosys.com
Manufacturer and exporter of pneumatic waste conveying, dewatering and fryer oil recovery equipment
General Manager: Rex McArthur
Account Manager: Marilyn McGrew
Design Manager: Jeff Denkers
Sales Director: Kathryn Brown
Plant Manager: Rex McArthur
Purchasing Manager: David Lethcoe
Estimated Sales: $5 - 10,000,000
Number Employees: 10-19
Brands:
Cornell Pumps and Pumping Systems
Dynavac and Watervac Water Systems
Oil Miser Oil Recovery Systems
Pneumatic Conveying Systems
Ventilation & Process Air Systems

28128 RGF Environmental Group
1101 West 13th Street
West Palm Beach, FL 33404 561-848-1826
Fax: 561-848-9454 800-842-7771
requests@rgf.com www.rgf.com
CEO: Ron Fink
Estimated Sales: $1 - 5 Million
Number Employees: 50-99

28129 RGN Developers
44 Gales Dr Apt 4
New Providence, NJ 07974
Fax: 908-665-6901 rgnsoft@aol.com
Design engineer specializing in software development, technology transfers, engineering specifications and start-up in food, dairy and pharmaceutical plants
President: Raja Nori
Estimated Sales: $2.5-5 Million
Number Employees: 4

28130 RH Forschner
P.O.Box 1212
Monroe, CT 06468-8212 203-929-6391
Fax: 203-925-2933 800-243-4032
web.orders@swissarmy.com
www.swissarmy.com
Cutlery, knives, scabbards for cutting and deboning, safety apparel professional swiss knives
President: Susanne Recher
CEO: Carl Elsener
CFO: Thomas M Lupinski
CEO: Rick Taggart
Estimated Sales: $1-2.5 Million
Number Employees: 100-249

28131 RJ Jansen Company
10831 1st St
Highway KR
Sturtevant, WI 53177 262-884-0511
Fax: 262-884-0512 richard@rjjansen.com
www.rjjansen.com
Chocolate equipment: decorating, enrobing, pumping systems. Cluster machine, coaters, cutting machines: carmel, cream centers; depositors: chocolate, liquid, portable, wire-cut
President: Richard Jansen
Estimated Sales: $3 - 5 Million
Number Employees: 5-9

28132 RJ Jansen Confectionery
10831 1st Street
Sturtevant, WI 53177-3338 262-884-0511
Fax: 262-884-0512 richard@rjjansen.com
www.rjjansen.com

Enrobers, depositors, coaters and packaging equipment, bag and pouch sealers, bag filling and sealing machines, bag forming machines
President: Richard Jansen
Estimated Sales: Below 1 Million
Number Employees: 5-9

28133 **RJO Produce Marketing**
1177 West Shaw Avenue
Fresno, CA 93711-3704 559-222-7200
Fax: 559-222-7277 www.rjoproduce.com
Procurement, inspection and delivery of fruits and berries. Also market analyses reports, marketing, and inventory control
Owner: John O'Rourke
Estimated Sales: $3 - 5 Million
Number Employees: 5-9

28134 **RJR Executive Search**
11999 Katy Freeway
Suite 585
Houston, TX 77079 281-368-8550
Fax: 281-368-8560 sschorejs@rjrsearch.com
www.rjrsearch.com
Executive search firm specializing in selection and placement of consumer packaged goods and services personnel
Research Assistant: Sherry Schorejs
VP: Ray Schorejs
VP: Bob O Dell
Industrial Sales / Operations: Vince Lyden
Estimated Sales: $1 - 3 Million
Number Employees: 5-9

28135 **RJR Packaging, Inc.**
7875 Edgewater Drive
Oakland, CA 94621 510-638-5901
Fax: 510-638-5958 Service@rjrpolymers.com
www.rjrpolymers.com
Manufacturer and exporter of flexible packaging products including folding foil cartons, barrier films and aluminum foil; also, printing and lamination available
President & CEO: Wil Salhuana
CFO: Tony Bregante
Estimated Sales: $1 - 5 Million
Number Employees: 1,000-4,999

28136 **RJS Carter Company**
251 5th St NW #D
New Brighton, MN 55112-6864 651-636-8818
Manufacturer and exporter of synthetic rubber balls for sifter and screener cleaning
President: John Galt
Estimated Sales: Less than $500,000
Number Employees: 1 to 4
Brands:
Screwballs

28137 **RL Instruments**
9 Main St # 2e
Douglas, MA 01516 508-476-1935
Fax: 508-476-1927 800-427-4361
rlinstruments@earthlink.net
www.rlinstruments.com
Refractometers, spectrophotometers, moisture balances, pH meters, and parts and service
Owner: April Hodges
Sales Manager: Todd Hodges
Estimated Sales: Below $5 Million
Number Employees: 5-9

28138 **RLS Equipment Company**
PO Box 282
Egg Harbor City, NJ 08215-0282 609-965-0074
Fax: 609-965-2509 800-527-0197
rls.equip@att.net www.rlsequipment.com
Winery and fruit processing equipment
President: Robert L Stollenwerk
Estimated Sales: $.5 - 1 million
Number Employees: 7

28139 **RLS Logistics**
Rosario Leo Building
2185 Main Road
Newfield, NJ 08344 856-694-2500
800-579-9900
info@rlslogistics.com www.rlslogistics.com
Transportation, warehousing and fulfillment to the frozen and refrigerated food industry.
Chief Executive Officer, President: Anthony Leo
Vice President of Development: John Gaudet
Director of Operations: Greg Deitz

28140 **RM Waite Inc**
45 6th Street
Clintonville, WI 54929 715-823-4327
Fax: 715-823-7311 rmwaite@frontiernet.net
www.rmwaiteinc.com
Replacement parts and rebuiling machinery for meat processors
President: Rick Waite
VP: Marsha Waite
Estimated Sales: $768,000
Number Employees: 6
Square Footage: 400

28141 **RMF Freezers**
4417 East 119th Street
Grandview, MO 64030 816-765-4101
Fax: 816-765-0067 www.rmff.com
Freezing/cooling systems, mixers, blenders, frozen patty stackers, conveyors and packaging systems.
President: John Robertson
Executive Vice President: Bill Norman
Marketing Manager: Scott Robertson
Vice President, Sales: Ron Mickey
Chief Engineer: Sam Elliott
Production Manager: Terry Rozell

28142 **(HQ)RMF Steel Products**
4417 E 119th St
Grandview, MO 64030 816-765-4101
Fax: 816-765-0067 sales@rmfsteel.com
www.rmfsteel.com
Manufacturer and exporter of food processing and vacuum packaging equipment engineering services include turnkey systems and plant design.
President: John Robertson
VP: Anthony Skevington
Number Employees: 50-99
Brands:
Challenge
Meissner
Snorkel-Vac

28143 **RMF Steel Products Company**
4417 E 119th St
Grandview, MO 64030 816-765-4101
Fax: 816-765-0067 sales@rmfsteel.com
www.rmfsteel.com
Stainless steel food processing and vacuum packaging machines, conveyors, bulk handling equipment and fabricated steel products
Chairman: John Robertson
CFO: Jony Skezington
Estimated Sales: $10 - 20 Million
Number Employees: 50-99

28144 **RMI-C/Rotonics Manaufacturing**
736 Birginal Dr
Bensenville, IL 60106-1213 630-773-9510
Fax: 630-773-4274 chicago@rotonics.com
www.rotonics.com
Manufacturer and exporter of polyethylene containers molded from FDA/USDA approved resin including material handling, shipping and storage; also, barrels, drums, tilt trucks, mobile bins, totes and custom molded parts available
Manager: Jay Rule
Sales Director: Michael Morrison
Estimated Sales: $20 - 50 Million
Number Employees: 50-99
Square Footage: 38000
Parent Co: Rotonics Manufacturing
Type of Packaging: Bulk
Brands:
Bulkatilt
Bulkitank
Gripper
Tabletote

28145 **RMX Global Logistics**
35715 U.S.
Highway 40 Building B
Evergreen, CO 80439 888-824-7365
Fax: 303-674-3803 888-824-7365
generalinquiries@rmxglobal.com
www.rmxglobal.com
Shelf stable, high barrier food packaging
President: Steve Whaley

28146 **ROE**
8030 Broadstone Rd
Perrysburg, OH 43551-4856 419-666-6789
Fax: 419-666-4020 robinvogel@roeinc.com
www.dillin.com
Engineered conveyor systems, vertical accumulators, case lifts and compression belts
President: David Smith
Estimated Sales: $10-20 Million
Number Employees: 50-99

28147 **ROHA USA, Llc.**
5015, Manchester Avenue,
St. Louis, MO 63110 636-305-9538
Fax: 888-531-0461 888-533-7642
roha.usa@rohagroup.com www.roha.com
Distributors of synthetic colors, lake pigments and dye blends. Custom blends. Patent pending, dust free colors
CEO: Rohit Tebrewala
CEO: Rohit Tibrewala
CEO: Rohit Tiberwala
Research & Development: Mike Chin
Estimated Sales: $2.5-5 Million
Number Employees: 1-4
Number of Brands: 3
Parent Co: Roha Dyechem
Brands:
Dust Free Form of Fd&C Colors

28148 **ROI Software, LLC**
P.O.Box 2747
Knoxville, TN 37901-2747 865-522-2211
Fax: 865-522-7907 patkrimmel@resourceopt.com
www.resourceopt.com
Software; also, consulting services available
President: T Brient Mayfield
Estimated Sales: Below $5 Million
Number Employees: 10-19

28149 **RPA Process Technologies**
PO Box 1087
Marblehead, MA 01945-5087 781-631-9707
Fax: 781-631-9507 800-631-9707
signware@rosedisplays.com
www.rosedisplays.com
Manufacturer and exporter of displays including 3-D hanging, hanging sign, window and hall; also, price card holders
President: Michael Hoffman
Assistant to President: Carol Jones
Sales Manager: Tracy Hatfield
Number Employees: 15
Square Footage: 12800
Brands:
Biclops Installation Tool
Clearly Invisible Hooks
Gotcha - Sure Snap Sign Holder
One-Up
Perfect Hanging System
Ropole
Smartbox
Supergotcha

28150 **(HQ)RQA**
10608 W 163rd Place
Orland Park, IL 60467 708-364-7060
Fax: 708-364-7061 info@rqa-inc.com
www.rqa-inc.com
Consultant providing quality assurance evaluations of consumer products and competitive product comparison; also, consumer complaint, domestic and international product retrievals, product recalls, quality consulting services, etc;product development, sensory evaluation and consumer research at new state of the art facility.
President: Lawrence Platt
Executive VP: Mary Ann Platt
Sales: Pamela Vaillancourt
Number Employees: 10-19
Other Locations:
RQA
Calabasas CA

28151 **RR Donnelley**
111 South Wacker Drive
Chicago, IL 60606-4301 312-326-8000
Fax: 312-326-8001 800-742-4455
www.rrdonnelley.com
Signs including permanent point of purchase, plastic and neon; also, displays and merchandising systems, pressure sensitive labels, rotary letterpress and screens
President, CEO: Thomas J. Quinlan, III
Number Employees: 57000
Square Footage: 800000
Other Locations:
Banta Specialty Converting
Sturtevant WI

28152 **RSI ID Technologies**
I-94 at McKnight Road
St. Paul, MN 55144-1000 619-656-2515
Fax: 619-872-0662 888-364-3577
info@rsiidtech.com
solutions.3m.com/wps/portal/3M/en_US/WW3/Country/
President: John Freund
CEO: Wolff Bielas
Chief Technical Officer: Bruce Roesner
Estimated Sales: $1 - 5 Million
Number Employees: 50-99
Parent Co: 3M

28153 **RTC Industries**
2800 Golf Rd
Rolling Meadows, IL 60008 847-640-2400
Fax: 847-640-5175 gcohen@rtc.com
www.rtc.com
Manufacturer and exporter of merchandising displays, signs, nonmechanical coolers and interactive, electronic, in store point of purchase displays
President: Bruce Vierck
CEO: Richard Nathan
Sr VP: Howard Topping
Estimated Sales: $500,000-$1 Million
Number Employees: 100-249
Square Footage: 350000

28154 **RTI Laboratories Inc**
31628 Glendale Street
Livonia, MI 48150 734-422-8000
Fax: 734-422-5342 information@rtilab.com
www.rtilab.com
Laboratory facility specializing in environmental, chemical, metallurgical, and industrial hygiene analyses
President: Jerry Singh
CFO: Ralph Davis
VP: Fred Hoitash
Quality Control: Charles O'Bryan
Sales Director: Patricia Jennings
Number Employees: 20-49
Square Footage: 12000

28155 **RTI Shelving Systems**
40-19 80th Street
Elmhurst, NY 11373 212-279-0435
Fax: 212-465-1795 800-223-6210
info@rtishelving.com www.rtishelving.com
Manufacturer and exporter of steel filing systems, steel and wire shelving, racks, bins and storage systems
Owner: Bhim Motilal
Office Manager: Darryl Buyckes
Estimated Sales: $5 - 10 Million
Number Employees: 10-19

28156 **RTS Packaging**
250 N Mannheim Rd
Hillside, IL 60162 708-338-2800
Fax: 708-338-2882 webmaster@rocktenn.com
www.rocktenn.com
Corrugated paper and fiberboard box partitions
Manager: Mary Sachs
CFO: Nancy Garner
Estimated Sales: $20 - 50 Million
Number Employees: 100-249
Parent Co: Sonoco Products Company

28157 **RTS Packaging**
250 N Mannheim Rd
Hillside, IL 60162 708-338-2800
Fax: 708-338-2882 800-558-6984
webmaster@rocktenn.com www.rocktenn.com
Wine industry fiber partitions
Manager: Mary Sachs
Manager: Betch Cambell
Estimated Sales: $20 - 50 Million
Number Employees: 100-249

28158 **RVS**
5151 Allendale Lane
Taneytown, MD 21787-2155 410-756-2600
Fax: 410-756-6450 marketing@evapco.com
www.evapco.com
Architecture and engineering firm providing facility planning, design and construction services to the food and beverage industries.we ofer architecture planning and design and civil structural mechanical and electrical design formanufacturing warehouse and distribution facilities.
President: Bill Bartley
Estimated Sales: E
Number Employees: 5-9

28159 **(HQ)RW Products**
101 Heartland Blvd
Edgewood, NY 11717-8315 631-349-8400
Fax: 516-349-8407 800-345-1022
rw@rwproducts.com www.rwproducts.com
Retail displays, racks and fixtures
General Manager: Jon Scott
VP Sales: Martin Baum
Estimated Sales: $.5 - 1 million
Number Employees: 1-4

28160 **RWH Packaging**
PO Box 6335
Oakland, CA 94603-0335 510-535-0700
Fax: 510-535-0702 haight@aol.com
Wine industry packaging
President: Randy Haight
Estimated Sales: Below $5 Million
Number Employees: 10

28161 **RWI Resources**
3401 Old Wagon Rd
Marietta, GA 30062-5513 770-977-3950
Fax: 770-973-4299 866-545-4794
info@rwiproducts.com www.rwiresources.com
Developer and marketer of carbonated beverage
Estimated Sales: Below $500,000
Number Employees: 5-9

28162 **RXI Silgan Specialty Plastics**
541 Technology Dr
Triadelphia, WV 26059-2711 304-547-9100
Fax: 304-547-9200
silgan_sales@silganplastics.com
www.silganplastics.com
Manufacturer and exporter of plastic caps, jar covers, sifter and plug fitments and bottles; custom injection molding available
VP Engineering: Vice Exner
VP Sales: Tony Marceau
Operations Manager: Phil Sanderson
Estimated Sales: $36 Million
Number Employees: 100-249
Square Footage: 168400
Parent Co: Silgan Plastics
Type of Packaging: Consumer, Food Service, Private Label, Bulk
Other Locations:
RXI Plastics
Richmond VA
Brands:
Cs Assembled

28163 **Rabbeco**
22900 Miles Rd
Cleveland, OH 44128 212-564-0664
Fax: 973-529-0224 mb@packlinecorp.com
www.packline.com
Automatic and semiautomatic filling, sealing and capping systems, cup filling and sealing, bag forming, filling and sealing, bottle lines, shrink wrapping machines, fillers for liquid and paste products
President: Michael Beilinson
Estimated Sales: $.5 - 1 million
Number Employees: 1-4

28164 **Rabin Worldwide**
731 Sansome St
2nd Floor
San Francisco, CA 94111 415-522-5700
Fax: 415-522-5701 info@rabin.com
www.rabin.com
Owner: Irving Rabin
Estimated Sales: $15 Million
Number Employees: 20-49

28165 **Raburn**
1060 Thorndale Ave
Elk Grove Vlg, IL 60007-6747 847-350-2229
Fax: 847-350-2657 www.ecolab.com
Manager: Mark Swisher
Estimated Sales: $50 - 100 Million
Number Employees: 50-99
Parent Co: ECOLAB

28166 **Racine Company**
730 Wisconsin Avenue
Racine, WI 53403
Fax: 262-636-3733 800-242-4202
RCPurchasing@GoRacine.org
www.racineco.com
Labels including litho printed, pressure sensitive, die-cut and gummed; also, commercial printing services available
President: James A. Ladwig
Estimated Sales: Below $5 Million
Number Employees: 10-19

28167 **Racine Paper Box Manufacturing**
3522 W Potomac Ave
Chicago, IL 60651 773-227-3900
Fax: 773-227-3983
Manufacturer and exporter of boxes including set-up, fancy and folding
President: Navnit Patel
Estimated Sales: $1-2.5 Million
Number Employees: 10-19

28168 **Racket Group**
713 Walnut Street
Kansas City, MO 64106 816-842-2380
Fax: 816-842-8998 mail@racketgroup.com
www.racketgroup.com
Tableware for the airline catering industry
President and CFO: Joseph Hoagland
Estimated Sales: $5 - 10 Million
Number Employees: 10-19

28169 **Racks**
7684 St. Andrews Avenue
San Diego, CA 92154 619-661-0987
Fax: 619-661-0988 williamschiffman@cox.net
www.racksinc.com
Point of Purchase displays.
President: Doug Wall
CFO: Don Wall
VP: Doug Wall
Sales: William Schiffman
Production Manager: Mark Kleffel
Estimated Sales: $20-50 Million
Square Footage: 100000

28170 **Radcliffe System**
Suite 305
Toronto, ON M2J 4R4 416-493-3844
Fax: 416-493-1616 info@radsystems.com
www.radcliffesystems.com
Estimated Sales: $1 - 5 Million
Number Employees: 5-9

28171 **Radding Signs**
PO Box 4653
Springfield, MA 01101 413-736-5400
signs@RaddingAssociates.com
www.raddingassociates.com
Illuminated and nonilluminated signs including custom made electric, office building, directional, garage and outdoor advertising
Estimated Sales: $1-2.5 Million
Number Employees: 10-19
Parent Co: Rador

28172 **Rademaker USA**
5218 Hudson Dr
Hudson, OH 44236 330-650-2345
Fax: 330-656-2802
rademaker@rademakerusa.com
www.rademaker.nl
President: Ronald Gates
Vice President: William Palumbo
Estimated Sales: $5 - 10 Million
Number Employees: 10-19

28173 **Radiant Industrial Solutions, Inc.**
10801 Kempwood Drive
Houston, TX 77043 713-972-0196
Fax: 713-974-0253 sales@radiantuv.com
www.radiantuv.com
Waste water management.
President: Troy Smith
Technical Manager: John Shol

28174 **Radiant Systems**
1233 Quarry Lane
Suite 145
Pleasanton, CA 94566-8475 925-417-8600
Fax: 925-417-8612 800-767-4554
retailsales@radiantsystems.com
www.counterpointpos.com
Consultant providing point of sale, back office and headquarter solutions for quick and full service establishments
President: Andrew Heyman
Chief Executive Officer: John Heyman

Estimated Sales: $343 Million
Number Employees: 180
Square Footage: 7500

28175 Radiation Processing Division
P.O.Box 5064
Parsippany, NJ 07054-6064 973-267-5660
Fax: 973-267-5667 800-442-1969
martinw@karibafarms.com
www.realestateconsultants.com
Manufacturer and exporter of radiation sanitation and pathogen elimination equipment for the removal of bacteria from raw materials and food ingedients
President: Robert Solotist
President: Bruce Welt PhD
Estimated Sales: $1 - 5 Million
Number Employees: 20-49
Square Footage: 120000
Parent Co: Alpha Omega Technology

28176 Radio Cap Company
1331 N Pine St
San Antonio, TX 78202-1219 210-472-1649
Fax: 800-766-4812
Advertising promotion caps
VP: Christopher Edelen
VP Sales: Eileen Guina
Estimated Sales: $1 - 5 Million
Number Employees: 1-4
Parent Co: Norwood Promotional Products

28177 Radio Frequency Company
150 Dover Rd
Millis, MA 02054 508-376-9555
Fax: 508-376-9944 rfc@radiofrequency.com
www.radiofrequency.com
Manufacturer and exporter of radio frequency post-baking dryers and pasteurization equipment.
President/CEO: Timothy Clark
Estimated Sales: $5 - 10 Million
Number Employees: 20-49
Square Footage: 26
Parent Co: Radio Frequency Company
Brands:
Macrowave

28178 Radius Display Products
800 Fabric Xpress Way
Dallas, TX 75234 972-406-1221
Fax: 972-406-1321 888-322-7429
info@radiusdp.com www.radiusdp.com
Manufacturer and exporter of table skirting and clips.
President/CFO/Quality Control/R&D: Tim Lightfoot
CEO: Michelle Stacy
VP Sales: Sherry Day
Estimated Sales: $2.5 - 5 Million
Number Employees: 50-99
Brands:
Omniclip Ii

28179 Rafael Soler
135 Walworth Avenue
White Plains, NY 10606-2720 914-761-4609
Fax: 914-683-3755 info@deprosa.dk
www.derprosa.es
Laminations, labels, acrylic and PVDC coatings, bottle labels, food packing
President: Raphael Hernandez Soler

28180 Ragtime
4218 Jessup Rd
Ceres, CA 95307 209-634-8475
Fax: 209-634-2667 ragtimewest@earthlink.net
www.ragtimewest.com
Manufacturer and exporter of coin and floppy disk operated pianos, monkey organs, animated food dispensers and dioramas and calliopes; importer of decorative plastic pipe
Owner: Kenneth B Caulkins
Manager: Glenn Kern
Estimated Sales: $1-2.5 Million
Number Employees: 5-9
Square Footage: 20000
Brands:
Active Magnetics

28181 Rahmann Belting & Industrial Rubber Products
3100 Northwest Blvd
Gastonia, NC 28052-1167 704-864-0308
Fax: 704-868-4651 888-248-8148
info@rahmannbelting.com
www.rahmannbelting.com
Manufacturer and exporter of industrial conveyors and transmission belting including oriented nylon, monofilament and food, etc
Owner: Ron Dayton
CEO: Ronald Dayton
Estimated Sales: $2.5 - 5 Million
Number Employees: 5-9
Square Footage: 60000

28182 Railex Corporation
8902 Atlantic Ave
Jamaica, NY 11416-1497 718-845-5454
Fax: 718-738-1020 800-352-3244
tech@railexcorp.com www.railexcorp.com
Supplier and exporter of electric and stationary coat and hat check equipment; also, garment racks
President: Abe Rutkovsky
VP: Sam Rutkovsky
Sales: Bill Quirke
Estimated Sales: $10 - 20 Million
Number Employees: 50-99
Square Footage: 35000
Brands:
Railex

28183 RainSoft Water TreatmentSystem
2080 Lunt Ave
Elk Grove Vlg, IL 60007 847-437-9400
Fax: 847-437-1594 comments@rainsoft.com
www.rainsoft.com
Manufacturer and exporter of water treatment equipment including filters, purifiers, reverse osmosis systems and ultraviolet
President: Robert Ruhstorfer
Commercial Department: Bob Krinner
Estimated Sales: $1 - 5 Million
Number Employees: 100-249
Square Footage: 140000
Brands:
Amazon
Classic Apollo
P-12 Hydefiner
Ultrefiner

28184 Rainbow Industrial Products
825 Morgantown Rd
Reading, PA 19607-9533 610-373-1400
Fax: 610-373-7448 800-426-5751
info@kvp-inc.com www.kvp-inc.com
Manufactures modular plastic belt and flat top chains and markets a full line of stainless/carbon steel, case conveyor and multi-flex chains, custom molded rubber inserts
President: Christopher Nigon
Estimated Sales: $5-10 Million
Number Employees: 500-999

28185 Rainbow Neon Sign Company
257 W 3300 S
Salt Lake City, UT 84115 801-466-7856
Fax: 801-466-1144 vince@rainbowsign.com
www.rainbowsign.com
Neon signs
Owner/Sales: Vincent Coley
Office Manager: Barbara Barnes
Estimated Sales: $1 - 2.5 Million
Number Employees: 10-19

28186 Rainbow Neon Sign Company
202 S Lockwood Dr
Houston, TX 77011-3198 713-923-2759
Fax: 713-923-2875
Advertising signs including neon, plastic and flex face lighted
President: Louis Freund
VP/Secretary: Naida Freund
Estimated Sales: $500,000-$1 Million
Number Employees: 5-9
Square Footage: 9000

28187 (HQ)Ralcorp Holdings
800 Market Street
St Louis, MO 63101 314-877-7000
Fax: 314-877-7900 800-772-6757
investorrelations@ralcorp.com www.ralcorp.com
Supplier of private label cereal, producing both ready-to-eat and hot cereals. Organic cereals, snack mixes, cereal and nutrition bars and more
President, CEO & Director: Kevin Hunt
Corporate VP & Chief Accounting Officer: Thomas Granneman
Director of Marketing: John Sterling
Operations Director: Otis Thaxton
Manufacturing Director: David Jerome
Estimated Sales: $4.74 Billion
Number Employees: 11000
Type of Packaging: Consumer, Private Label
Brands:
American Italian Pasta Company
Bloomfield Bakers
Bremner
Carriage House
Harvest Manor Farms
J.T. Bakeries
North American Baking
Nutcracker
Parco Foods
Post Cereals
Ralston Foods
Sepp's Gourmet Foods

28188 Ralph L. Mason
8344 Patey Woods Rd
Newark, MD 21841 410-632-1766
Fax: 410-632-1142
Wooden pallets
VP: Tom Mason
Plant Manager: Bruce Wood
Estimated Sales: $1 - 5 Million
Number Employees: 10-19
Square Footage: 120000

28189 Ralphs-Pugh Company
3931 Oregon St
Benicia, CA 94510 707-745-6222
Fax: 707-745-3942 800-486-0021
sales@ralphs-pugh.com www.ralphs-pugh.com
Manufacturer and exporter of rollers, idlers and bearings for conveyors
President: William Pugh
Vice President: Tom Anderson
Estimated Sales: $5 - 10 Million
Number Employees: 20-49

28190 Ralston Analytical Laboratories
824 Gratiot St
St Louis, MO 63102-1024 314-982-1310
Fax: 314-982-1078 800-423-6832
npal@purina.nestle.com www.npal.com
Chemical and microbiological testing services
Executive Director: Lynn Loudermilk
Research & Development: Dorene Rist
Estimated Sales: $5 - 10 Million
Number Employees: 5-9

28191 Ram Equipment
W227n913 Westmound Dr
Waukesha, WI 53186-1647 262-513-1114
Fax: 262-513-1115 tiefmach@execpc.com
Manufacturer and exporter of baking, blending and batching equipment, bins, control systems, enrobers, extruders and feeders; manufacturer of custom, pump feeding systems for pumping high viscosity products for food and industrialapplications
President: James E Tiefenthaler
VP: Norman Searle
Estimated Sales: $1 - 3 Million
Number Employees: 1-4
Number of Brands: 2
Number of Products: 20
Square Footage: 4800

28192 Ram Industries
PO Box 610
Erwin, TN 37650-0610 423-743-6126
Fax: 423-743-6128 800-523-3883
Heat sealed plastic and vinyl products including advertising novelties, bags, date code label pouches, 3-ring binders, menu covers and ticket, notepad and guest check holders
VP: Keith Patton
Director Sales: Jack Degatis
Estimated Sales: $1 - 5 Million
Parent Co: Plasco Products

28193 (HQ)Ramco Systems Corporation
3150 Us Highway 1 Ste 130
Lawrence Township, NJ 08648
Fax: 609-620-4860 800-472-6461
www.ramco.com
Computer software services and prepackaged software
Vice Chairman/Managing Director/CEO: P R Venketrama Raja
CFO: K Ramachandran
Senior VP: Bivek Luthra
Chief Marketing Officer: Barbara Angius Saxby
COO: Kamesh Ramamoorthly
Estimated Sales: $20.7 Million
Number Employees: 20-49
Other Locations:
San Jose CA
Frankfurt, Germany
Central Milton, UK
Basel, Switzerland
New Delhi, India
Malaysia, Asia
Singapore, Asia
Durban, South Africa
Dubia, Middle East

28194 Ramondin U.S.A.
2557 Nv Corporate Dr
Suite G
Napa, CA 94558 707-944-2277
Fax: 707-257-1408 ramondin@ramondinusa.com
Wine industry capsules
Manager: Steve Galvan
Estimated Sales: $1 - 3 Million
Number Employees: 5-9

28195 Ramoneda Brothers
PO Box 893
Culpeper, VA 22701 540-825-9166
Fax: 540-547-3271 ramonedabro@aol.com
Manufacturer and exporter of oak staves
Partner: Vincent Ramoneda
Manager: Vincent Ramoneda
Estimated Sales: $5 - 10 Million
Number Employees: 5-9

28196 Ramsay Signs
9160 SE 74th Ave
Portland, OR 97206-9345 503-777-4555
Fax: 503-777-0220 info@ramsaysigns.com
www.ramsaysigns.com
Neon and electrical indoor and outdoor advertising signs
Owner: Darryl Paulsen
General Manager: Joe Gibson
VP: John Olds
Estimated Sales: $2.5-5 Million
Number Employees: 20-49

28197 Ramsey
P.O.Box 581510
Tulsa, OK 74158-1510 918-438-2760
Fax: 918-438-6888 info@ramsey.com
www.ramseystore.com
Checkweighers, conveyor accesories including belt tracking, conveyors and metal detecting
CEO: Bruce Barron
Chairman of the Board: Robert Heffron
Estimated Sales: $25-50 Million
Number Employees: 1-4

28198 Rancolio North America
8102 Lemont Rd # 1200
Woodridge, IL 60517-7773 630-427-1703
Fax: 630-493-4265 info@rancilio-na.com
www.rancilio.com
VP: Glenn Surlet
Estimated Sales: $300,000-500,000
Number Employees: 1-4

28199 Rand-Whitney Container Corporation
166 Corporate Drive
Suite 200
Portsmouth, NH 03801 603-822-7300
Fax: 603-822-7396 www.randwhitney.com
Corugated containers
President/CEO: Edwin Davis
VP (Rand-Whitney): Dwight Hamlin
Operations Manager: Raymond Hey
Estimated Sales: $10-20 Million
Number Employees: 50-99
Square Footage: 80000
Parent Co: Rand-Whitney Group LLC

28200 (HQ)Rand-Whitney Container Corporation
1 Agrand St
Worcester, MA 01607-1699 508-791-2301
Fax: 508-792-1578 joconnor@randwhitney.com
www.randwhitney.com
Corrugated boxes, containers, displays and protective packaging
President: Robert Kraft
CEO: Edwin Davis
Sales Manager: Jerry O'Connor
Estimated Sales: $20 - 50 Million
Number Employees: 500-999

28201 Rand-Whitney Container Corporation
One Agrand Street
Worcester, MA 01607 508-791-2301
www.randwhitney.com
Folding paper boxes, cartons and containers
Estimated Sales: H
Number Employees: 5
Parent Co: Kraft Group LLC

28202 Randall Manufacturing
722 N Church Rd
Elmhurst, IL 60126 630-782-0001
Fax: 630-782-0003 800-323-7424
info@randallmfg.com www.randallmfg.com
Manufacturer and exporter of bulkheads for refrigerator trailer partitions, plastic strip curtains for coolers and freezers and insulated pallet covers and curtain walls
President: Fred Jevaney
CFO: Philip Pick
VP: Fred Jevaney
Number Employees: 20-49
Square Footage: 40000
Type of Packaging: Food Service, Bulk
Brands:
Conservador
Insul-Wall
Tough One

28203 Randall Printing
707 Centre Street
Brockton, MA 02302-3310 508-588-3830
Fax: 508-588-3830
Labels, forms and booklets
Estimated Sales: Less than $500,000
Number Employees: 1-4

28204 Randell ManufacturingUnified Brands
252 South Coldwater Road
Weidman, MI 48893
Fax: 888-864-7636 888-994-7636
cs@unifeidbrands.com www.unifiedbrands.com
Stainless steel preparation tables, custom equipment, refrigerators, freezers, precise temperature solutions, equipment stands, and hot food tables.
Estimated Sales: $50 - 100 Million
Number Employees: 250-499
Parent Co: Dover Corporation
Brands:
Rancraft
Randell
Ranserve

28205 Randware Industries
P.O.Box 414
Prospect Heights, IL 60070-0414 847-299-8884
Fax: 847-299-8885 info@randware.com
www.randware.com
Food display items including chafing dishes with logos
Manager: Neal Katz
Estimated Sales: $3 - 5 Million
Number Employees: 1-4
Brands:
Chafer Shield

28206 Ranger Blade Manufacturing Company
PO Box 205
1561 South Main
Traer, IA 50675
Fax: 319-478-8298 800-377-7860
info@rangerblade.com www.rangerblade.com
Household and professional metal cutlery including processing and packaging machinery blades
President: Rex Betts
CFO: Louis Rausch
Quality Control: Matt Devick
Sales Manager: Steve Droste
Estimated Sales: $5 - 10 Million
Number Employees: 20-49
Square Footage: 32000
Parent Co: Clearline Cutlery

28207 Ranger Tool Company
5786 Ferguson Rd
Memphis, TN 38134 901-213-0458
Fax: 901-386-8088 800-737-9999
Manufacturer and exporter of peelers which remove cellulose casing from frankfurters and sausages
President: Eleanor Kiss
Estimated Sales: $2.5-5 Million
Number Employees: 20-49
Brands:
Apollo Peeler

28208 Rankin-DeLux
3245 Corridor Dr Ste B
Eastwale, CA 91752-1030 951-685-0081
Fax: 951-685-0082 www.rankindelux.com
Broilers, griddles, hot plates, cheese melters, stock pot and oriental ranges, etc
President/CEO: Dick Jones
Chairman: William Rankin
VP: Peggy Jones
Estimated Sales: $2.5-5 Million
Number Employees: 20-49

28209 Ranpak Corporation
P.O.Box 8004
Painesville, OH 44077 440-354-4445
Fax: 440-639-2198 800-726-7257
inquiries@ranpak.com www.ranpak.net
Packaging, cushioning
President: David Gabrielsen
Estimated Sales: $20 - 50 Million
Number Employees: 100-249

28210 Ransco Industries
1655 Mesa Verde Avenue
Suite 250
Ventura, CA 93003-6518 805-487-7777
Fax: 805-486-7024 talktous@ransco.com
www.ransco.com
Industrial refrigeration and freezing equipment; also, design and construction services available
VP Product: Robert Briner
Marketing Manager: Taylor Hobson
Sales Manager: Lou Coppo
Production Manager: Jim Topp
Estimated Sales: $10-20 Million
Number Employees: 50-99

28211 Rao Design International
9451 Ainslie St
Schiller Park, IL 60176 847-671-6182
Fax: 847-671-9276 raodesign@aol.com
www.raodesign.com
Turn-key operation setup, PET machines, engineering and consulting, blow mold making, blow-fill seal machines, blow molding
CEO: Kumar Murkurthy
Marketing Director: David Muiukurthy
Estimated Sales: $5-10 Million
Number Employees: 50-99

28212 Rapa Products (USA)
1 Depot Lane
Seabrook, NH 03874-4492 603-474-5508
Fax: 603-474-3919 www.portalnewhampshire.com
Natural casings
Estimated Sales: $1-5 Million
Number Employees: 8

28213 Rapak
1201 Windham Parkway
Suite D
Romeoville, IL 60446 630-296-2000
Fax: 630-296-2195 www.rapak.com
Bag-in-Box liquid packaging systems for dairy, edible oil, fruits/purees, juices, liquid egg, post mix/syrup, sauces, water, wine
Owner/President: Mark Smith
SVP: Paul Petriekis
Marketing/Sales Director: Pierre Ferrai
VP Sales: Joe Pranckus

Number Employees: 140
Square Footage: 121000
Parent Co: DS Smith Group

28214 Rapat Corporation
919 O'donnel St
Hawley, MN 56549-4310 218-483-3344
Fax: 218-483-3535 800-325-6377
www.rapat.com
Manufacturer and exporter of material handling equipment including conveyors and conveyor belting
President: Thomas E Sparrow
Sales Manager: Greg Deal
Estimated Sales: $10-20 Million
Number Employees: 50-99

28215 (HQ)Rapid Displays
4300 W 47th St
Chicago, IL 60632 773-927-5000
Fax: 773-927-9281 800-356-5775
info@rapiddisplays.com www.rapiddisplays.com
Manufacturer and designer of advertising point of purchase displays
Chairman: Earl Abramson
President: David Abramson
VP: Brian Mc Cormick
Quality Control: Jim Guadgnola
VP/Sales Manager: Pierre Pype
Estimated Sales: $20 - 50 Million
Number Employees: 250-499
Square Footage: 360000

28216 Rapid Industries
P.O.Box 19259
Louisville, KY 40259-0259 502-968-3645
Fax: 502-968-6331 800-787-4381
info@rapidindustries.com www.rapidi.com
Manufacturer, importer and exporter of conveyors including trolley, enclosed track, power, free and floor
President: Mary Sheets
Controller: Jansen Nally
Marketing Manager: Paul McDonald
Sales Manager: Walt Hiner
Estimated Sales: $20 - 50 Million
Number Employees: 100-249
Type of Packaging: Bulk

28217 Rapid Pallet
100 Chestnut St
Jermyn, PA 18433-1433 570-876-4000
Fax: 570-876-4002
Manufacturer and exporter of lumber pallets
President: Rose Moran
Estimated Sales: $10-20 Million
Number Employees: 50-99

28218 Rapid Rack Industries
14421 Bonelli St
City of Industry, CA 91746 626-333-7225
Fax: 626-333-5265 800-736-7225
customerservice@rapidrack.com
www.rapidrack.com
Racks and mobile aisle and mezzanine systems; importer of wire storage racks; exporter of wire and storage rack
CEO: William Marvin
CEO: Vaughn Sucevich
Marketing Director: Clara Banegas
VP Sales: Steve Painter
Operations Manager: Rosemarie Kodarte
Production Manager: Alfredo Calderon Kodarte
Plant Manager: Ed Sledge
Purchasing Manager: Dennis Fachler
Estimated Sales: $30 - 50 Million
Number Employees: 250-499
Square Footage: 192000
Parent Co: Hampshire Equity Partners
Type of Packaging: Consumer

28219 RapidPak
932 Development Drive
PO Box 260
Lodi, WI 53555 608-592-3211
Fax: 608-592-4039
daryl.shackelford@rapidpak.com
www.rapidpak.com
Form/fill/seal horizontal packaging equipment, rollstock machines
President: Dave Smith
CFO: Dave Smith
R&D: Bob Hanson
Quality Control: Dave Brathorst
Regional Sales Manager: Mike McCann
Estimated Sales: $5 - 10 Million
Number Employees: 100-249

28220 Rapistan Systems
507 Plymouth Ave NE
Grand Rapids, MI 49505 616-451-6700
Fax: 616-913-7701 info.sdma.us@siemens.com
www.siemens-dematic.us
Materials handling systems for in-process and distribution operations
Marketing Manager: Esther Land
Estimated Sales: Over $1 Billion
Number Employees: 1,000-4,999

28221 Raque Food Systems
P.O.Box 99594
Louisville, KY 40269-0594 502-267-9641
Fax: 502-267-2352 sales@raque.com
www.raque.com
Food processing equipment
President: Glenn Raque
VP: Ed Robinson
Director Marketing: Tim Kent
Estimated Sales: $20 - 50 Million
Number Employees: 20-49

28222 Rasco Industries
730 Tower Drive
Hamel, MN 55340 763-478-5100
Fax: 763-478-5101 800-537-3802
bschless@rasco.com www.rasco.com
Screen sectional loading dock doors used with existing commercial rolling, high, vertical, standard lift and side sliding doors; also, overhead screen door systems and service door screen inserts
VP/Sales Manager: Rick Brown
Inside Sales Manager: Victoria Scully
Estimated Sales: $3-6 Million
Number Employees: 22
Square Footage: 100000
Brands:
The Bug Blocker

28223 Ratcliff Hoist Company
1655 Old County Rd
San Carlos, CA 94070-5205 650-595-3840
Fax: 650-595-5687 bruce@ventureprime.com
www.ventureprime.com
Material handling equipment including hoists
President: Bruce Ratcliff
Chairman: Ralph A Ratcliff
Estimated Sales: $1-2.5 Million
Number Employees: 10-19

28224 Rath Manufacturing Company
P.O.Box 389
Janesville, WI 53547 608-754-2222
Fax: 608-754-0889 800-367-7284
rathmfg@inwave.com www.rathmfg.com
Manufacturer and exporter of stainless steel pipes and tubing
President: Harley Aplan
CEO: Michael G Schwartz
VP Sales: James Coenen
Estimated Sales: $50 - 100 Million
Number Employees: 100-249

28225 Rathe Productions
555 W 23rd Street
New York, NY 10011-1011 212-242-9000
Fax: 212-242-5676 www.rathe.com
Displays and exhibits
Estimated Sales: $10 - 20 Million
Number Employees: 50-99

28226 Ratioflo Technologies
1284 Puerta Del Sol
San Clemente, CA 92673 949-369-2425
Fax: 949-369-2429 ratioflo@pacificpak.com
www.ratioflo.com
Fillers, pail lidders, and denesters
OWNER: Dale Tanner
Estimated Sales: Below $5 Million
Number Employees: 10
Number of Products: 5

28227 Rational Cooking Systems
895 American Lane
Schaumburg, IL 60173-4575 847-755-9583
Fax: 847-755-9584 888-320-7274
info@rationalusa.com www.rational-usa.com
Manufacturer and importer of combination ovens
President: Peter Schon
Marketing Director: Werner Jochem
Sales Director: Robert Bratton
Estimated Sales: $2.5-5 Million
Number Employees: 20-49
Parent Co: Rational AG
Brands:
Clima Plus Combi
Climaplus Control
Rational Combi-Steamers

28228 Ray C. Sprosty Bag Company
323 E Liberty St
Wooster, OH 44691 330-264-8559
Fax: 330-263-4621
Film and bags including multi-wall, woven polypropylene, burlap, cotton and paper
President: Ray C Sprosty Iii III
CFO: Pam Farthing
Quality Control: Tom Catamzarite
General Manager: Tom Catanzarite
Estimated Sales: $10 - 20 Million
Number Employees: 10-19
Square Footage: 15000

28229 Ray-Craft
2067 W 41st St
Cleveland, OH 44113 216-651-3330
Fax: 216-651-8714 arrow@arrowpublicity.com
www.thercline.com
Manufacturer and exporter of advertising novelties and promotional materials
President: Thomas Topp
Office Manager: Agnes Milter
Estimated Sales: $500,000-$1 Million
Number Employees: 9

28230 RayPress Corporation
380 Riverchase Pkwy E
Birmingham, AL 35244 205-989-3731
Fax: 205-989-7203 800-423-3731
sales@raypress.com www.raypress.com
Pressure sensitive labels and tags
President: Thomas Ray
Estimated Sales: $5-10 Million
Number Employees: 50-99

28231 (HQ)Raymond Corporation
P.O.Box 130
22 S. Canal St
Greene, NY 13778 607-656-2311
Fax: 607-656-9005 800-235-7200
www.raymondcorp.com
Manufacturer and exporter of electric forklift trucks
President Operations & Engineering: Michael Field
Chief Financial Officer: Ed Rompala
Vice President, Marketing: David Furman
Vice President, Sales: Timothy Combs
Vice President, Human Resources: Stephen VanNostrand
Vice President, Distribution Development: Patrick McManus
Estimated Sales: $130,000
Number Employees: 2500
Square Footage: 500000

28232 Rayne Plastic Signs
813 S Adams Ave
Rayne, LA 70578 337-334-4276
Fax: 337-334-4263 www.rayneplasticsigns.com
Plastic signs including illuminated outdoor
President: Hilman Meche
Secretary: Verline Meche
Manager: Blaine Meche
Estimated Sales: $1-2.5 Million
Number Employees: 5-9

28233 Raypak
2151 Eastman Ave
Oxnard, CA 93030 805-278-5300
Fax: 805-278-5489 www.raypak.com
Manufacturer and exporter of water heating equipment including boosters
Manager: Peter Reynolds
VP: Louis Falzer
Number Employees: 50
Parent Co: Rheem

Other Locations:
Raypak
Victoria

28234 (HQ)Raytek Corporation
P.O.Box 1820
Santa Cruz, CA 95061-1820 831-458-1110
Fax: 831-425-4561 800-866-5478
solutions@raytek.com www.raytek.com
Monitor hot and cold holding, reheating, cooling, and storage temperature instantly in steam tables, warming ovens, freezers, display cases and coolers with the new Raytek Mini Temperature Food Safety infrared thermometer
President: Carl Pickard
VP: Jim Love
Marketing: Fernando Lisboa
Sales: Bob Bader
Public Relations: Kate McGuire
Estimated Sales: $20-50 Million
Number Employees: 100-249
Number of Brands: 1
Type of Packaging: Private Label

28235 Raytheon Company
870 Winter Street
Waltham, MA 02451-1449 617-522-3000
Fax: 781-522-3001 www.raytheon.com
Manufacturer and exporter of dehydration equipment for sugar, minerals, chemicals, corn and grain; also, evaporators, vacuum pans, dryers, crystallizers, granulators and coolers; engineering design services available
Chief Executive Officer: Thomas A. Kennedy
SVP and Chief Financial Officer: David C. Wajsgras
Senior Vice President: Keith J. Peden
Number Employees: 250-499
Square Footage: 1200000
Brands:
Stearns-Roger

28236 Razor Edge Systems
303 N 17th Ave E
Ely, MN 55731 218-365-6419
Fax: 218-365-5360 800-541-1458
sales@razoredgesystems.com
www.razoredgesystems.com
Cutting and boning devices, sharpening machines and services, general packinghouse equipment, maintenance, sharpening and overhaul equipment
Service Technician: Jim Dally
Sales/Service Representative: Robert Sanders
Manager: Joann O'Reilly
Estimated Sales: $1-2.5 Million
Number Employees: 5-9

28237 ReMACS
877 W Park Avenue
Ocean, NJ 07712-7205 732-493-9596
Fax: 732-493-1061
Computer software including menu planning, inventory, labor and payroll control systems
Manager: Steve Gasperini
Number Employees: 5
Parent Co: ReMACS

28238 Rea UltraVapor
665 Tradewind Drive
Unit 10
Ancaster, ON L9G 4V5
Canada 905-572-0946
Fax: 905-304-3067 800-323-3865
mail@ultravapor.com www.ultravapor.com
Food equipment sanitation and infection control.

28239 Read Products
3615 15th Ave W
Seattle, WA 98119 206-283-2510
Fax: 206-282-8339 800-445-3416
info@cuttingboards.com
www.cuttingboards.com
Manufacturer and exporter of food preparation cutting boards and tools
President: Charles R Read
Marketing Manager: Chuck Read
Marketing Manager: Chuck Read Jr
Inside Sales/Production Manager: Robert Read
Estimated Sales: $5-10 Million
Number Employees: 10-19
Square Footage: 40000
Type of Packaging: Food Service
Brands:
Read Woodfiber Laminate

28240 Readco Kuimoto, LLC
460 Grim Lane
York, PA 17406 717-848-2801
Fax: 717-848-2811 800-395-4959
readco@readco.com www.readco.com
Manufacturer and exporter of containerized batch and continuous processing mixers
President: David Sieglitz
Estimated Sales: $5-10 Million
Number Employees: 20-49
Brands:
Cbm

28241 Reading Bakery Systems
380 Old West Penn Ave
Robesonia, PA 19551 610-693-5816
Fax: 610-693-5512 info@readingbakery.com
www.readingbakery.com
Manufacturer and exporter of extruders, cookers, topical seasoning applicators, multifuel ovens, guillotine dough cutters, dough handling systems and biscuit, cookie and cracker sheeters and laminators
Chairman/President/CEO: E. Terry Groff
President: Joseph Zaleski
Chairman: Tom Lugar
VP Finance/Operations: Chip Czulada
Director of Engineering: Tremaine Hartranft
Director, Science & Innovation Center: Ken Zvoncheck
VP Sales/Marketing: David Kuipers
Human Resources Manager: Roseann Reinhold
Vice President of Operations: Travis Getz
Estimated Sales: $10-20 Million
Number Employees: 50-99
Square Footage: 31000

28242 (HQ)Reading Box Company
250 Blair Ave
Reading, PA 19601 610-372-7411
Fax: 610-372-2143
Wooden boxes
President: Brent Atkins
Estimated Sales: Below $5 Million
Number Employees: 5-9

28243 Reading Plastic Fabricators
PO Box 10
Temple, PA 19560 610-926-3245
Fax: 610-926-7026 r.p.f.@readingplastic.com
www.readingplastic.com
Custom fabricated plastic wear materials including tanks, hoods, covers and guards; also, clear acrylic and polycarbonate displays and nylon and derlin conveyor parts
President: Tom Funk
Quality Control Manager: Kenny Williams
National Sales Manager: Patty Alagna
HR Controller: Tracie Smith
General Manager: Tim Long
Office Manager: Susan Laird
Estimated Sales: $2.5-5 Million
Number Employees: 20-49
Square Footage: 10000

28244 Reading Technologies
1031f Macarthur Rd
Reading, PA 19605 610-372-9200
Fax: 610-372-1984 800-521-9200
info@driair.com www.driair.com
President: Paul Flynn
Estimated Sales: $3 - 5 Million
Number Employees: 10-19

28245 Ready Access
1815 Arthur Rd
West Chicago, IL 60185 630-876-7766
Fax: 630-876-7767 800-621-5045
ready@ready-access.com www.ready-access.com
Manufacturer and exporter of pass-thru windows and air curtain systems for fast food establishments
President: John Radek
CFO: Robert McKeever
R & D: Scott Hammac
Marketing/Sales/Public Relations: Kristy Rivera
Sales Director: Vince Asta
Operations/Production: Bob McKeever
Estimated Sales: $5 - 10 Million
Number Employees: 20-49
Square Footage: 35000

28246 Ready White
532 Main St # 4
Holyoke, MA 01040-5647 413-534-4864
Fax: 413-534-4864
Wiping rags
Owner: Leon E Barlow
Estimated Sales: Less than $500,000
Number Employees: 1-4

28247 Real Foods Group
300 E Auburn Ave
Springfield, OH 45505-4703 937-322-2040
Fax: 937-322-2254
therealfoodsgroup@therealfoodsgroup.com
www.therealfoodsgroup.com
Sales and sales management; representing a wide range of packaged goods like confections, salted snacks, natural foods
President: Jeff Kreidenweis
Estimated Sales: $3 - 5 Million
Number Employees: 1-4
Type of Packaging: Food Service, Private Label

28248 Rebel Stamp & Sign Company, Inc.
307 Choctaw Drive
Baton Rouge, LA 70805 225-387-4634
Fax: 225-344-1218 800-860-5120
orders@rebelstamp.com www.rebelstamp.com
Marking devices including stamps, daters, etc.; also, interior and exterior office signage including name plates, name badges, etc
President: Lewis Roeling
Estimated Sales: $500,000-$1 Million
Number Employees: 5-9
Square Footage: 12000
Brands:
Royal Mark

28249 Recco Tape & Label
3940 Platt Springs Rd
West Columbia, SC 29170-1606 803-356-4003
Fax: 803-356-4439 800-334-3008
sales@reccointernational.com
www.reccointernational.com
Manufacturer and exporter of printed labels and tapes
Owner: John Etters
General Manager: Craig Hall
Estimated Sales: $20 - 50 Million
Number Employees: 20-49

28250 Red Kap Industries
P.O.Box 140995
Nashville, TN 37214-0995 615-565-5000
Fax: 615-565-5284 www.vfc.com
Uniforms
Vice President of Corporate Relations: Cindy Knoebel
Account Executive: Ray Hoff
Director of Corporate Communications: Carole Crosslin
Estimated Sales: $20-50 Million
Number Employees: 250-499
Brands:
Red Kap

28251 (HQ)Red Lion Controls
20 Willow Springs Cir
York, PA 17406 717-767-6511
Fax: 717-764-0839 sales@redlion.net
www.redlion-controls.com
A range of control devices that include process measurement and control, and digital measurement and control
President: Mike Granby
Development: Vincent Paolizzi
Sales Director: George Simok
Estimated Sales: $20-$50 Million
Number Employees: 100-249
Square Footage: 100000

28252 Red River Lumber Company
2959 Saint Helena Highway N
Saint Helena, CA 94574-9703 707-963-1251
Fax: 707-963-3142 redriver@napanet.net
Manufacturer and exporter of redwood boxes
Estimated Sales: $5-10 Million
Number Employees: 20-49

28253 Red Star BioProducts
433 E Michigan Street
Milwaukee, WI 53202-5104 414-347-3936
Fax: 414-347-3912 800-528-3388
Number Employees: 50-99

28254 Red Valve Company
P.O.Box 548
Carnegie, PA 15106 412-279-0044
Fax: 412-279-7878 valves@redvalve.com
www.redvalve.com
A complete line of pinch valves and control valves for use in the food industry; aeration and sparging products, flexible connectors, and instrument protection devices
Owner: Spiros Raftis
Chairman: Spiros G Raftis
Marketing Manager: David Schneider
Estimated Sales: $20 - 50 Million
Number Employees: 50-99
Type of Packaging: Bulk

28255 Red-Ray Manufacturing Company
10 County Line Rd
Suite 22
Branchburg, NJ 08876 908-722-0040
Fax: 908-722-2535 burners@red-ray.com
www.red-ray.com
Gas-fired and infrared process burners
President: Thomas Bannos
Chairman of the Board: Robert S Adelson
Vice President, Product & Applications M: Tim O'Neal
Applications Engineering: Mike Strand
Controller: Jorge Acosta
Estimated Sales: $5 - 10 Million
Number Employees: 10-19

28256 Reddi-Pac
215 W Church Rd
Suite 112
King of Prussia, PA 19406-3203 610-265-1827
Fax: 610-992-1407 reddipac@aol.com
www.naturalfertilitycenter.com
Laminated and formed paperboard
Owner: Meredith L Murphy

28257 Redding Pallet
5323 Eastside Rd
Redding, CA 96001 530-241-6321
Fax: 530-241-3475
Manufacturer and exporter of hardwood and softwood pallets
President: Don Lincoln
Estimated Sales: $1 - 5 Million
Number Employees: 10-19

28258 Reddy Ice Holdings, Inc.
8750 North Central Expressway
Suite 1800
Dallas, TX 75231 214-526-6740
Fax: 410-219-5685 800-683-4423
information@reddyice.com www.reddyice.com
Processor and warehouse providing cooler and freezer storage of ice; also, distribution services available
Owner: Joe Reden
Chief Executive Officer, President: Gilbert Cassagne
Quality Control: Patricia Shana
Executive Vice President: William Tolany
Executive Vice President, Chief Operatin: Paul Smith
Plant Manager: Rob Webber
Estimated Sales: Below $5 Million
Number Employees: 10-19

28259 Redex Packaging Corporation
860 E State Pkwy
Schaumburg, IL 60173-4529 847-882-9500
Fax: 847-882-9570 redex@kwom.com
www.redex.net

28260 Redi-Call, Incorporated
PO Box 18361
Reno, NV 89511 775-331-0183
Fax: 775-331-2730 800-648-1849
sales@redi-callusa.com www.redi-callusa.com
Manufacturer, importer and exporter of stainless steel cup and lid dispensers, condiment holders for bars, circular wheel check holders for restaurant kitchens, stainless steel pump units, squeeze bottles, waitress/waiter paging/callstations, etc
President: Melinda James
VP: Eric Seltzer
Purchasing Agent: Dave Schankin
Estimated Sales: $.5 - 1 million
Number Employees: 1-4
Square Footage: 80000
Brands:
Redi-Call
Speed-Rak
Top O' Cup

28261 Redi-Print
49 Mahan St
Unit B
West Babylon, NY 11704 631-491-6373
Fax: 631-491-6372 rediprint1@aol.com
Manufacturer and exporter of pre-printed menu paper and menu designing software
President: Tom Vlahakis
Estimated Sales: $300,000-500,000
Number Employees: 10
Square Footage: 2500

28262 Redicon Corporation
2824 Woodlawn Ave NW
Canton, OH 44708-1424 330-477-2100
Fax: 330-477-2101 www.redicon.com
Systems supplier for beverage and food can manufacturers: complete systems for draw, redraw, cans, shell (lid) systems for beverage cans, end systems for CWI cans, die sets for existing systems; both low and high volume requirements
Owner: Tracee Mc Afee-Gates

28263 Redlake Imaging Corporation
11633 Sorrento Valley Road
San Diego, CA 92121-1039 858-481-8182
Fax: 858-792-3179 800-462-4307
sales@redlake.com www.redlake.com
Packaging production, manufacturing, inspection
Estimated Sales: $10.5 Million
Number Employees: 20-49

28264 Redlake MASD
6295 Ferris Sq
Suite A
San Diego, CA 92121-3248 858-481-8182
Fax: 858-350-9390 800-462-4307
sales@redlake.com www.redlake.com
President: Stephen Ferrell
Estimated Sales: $15 - 20 Million
Number Employees: 100-250

28265 Reed & Barton Food Service
144 West Brittania Street
Taunton, MA 02780 508-824-6611
Fax: 508-822-7269 800-797-9675
information@reedbarton.com
www.reedbartonfoodservice.com
Flatware and hollowware
President/Chief Executive Officer: Timothy Riddle
Manager: Jill Pedro
VP, Finance/CFO/Treasurer/Controller: Stephen Normandine
Vice President, Information Technology: Paul Bartlet
SVP, Sales & Marketing: Joe D'Allessandro
Director, Sales: Angie Miller
Director, Purchasing & Planning: Rocco Davanzo
Estimated Sales: $25 Million
Number Employees: 98
Number of Brands: 5
Square Footage: 500000
Parent Co: Reed & Barton Silversmiths
Type of Packaging: Food Service

28266 Reed Ice
2642 Double Branches Rd
Lincolnton, GA 30817-2321 706-359-3127
Fax: 706-359-5465 800-927-9619
sales@reedice.com www.reedice.com
Manufacturer, wholesaler and distributor of ice; serving the food service market
President: Talmadge Reed
Owner: Talmadge Reed
Estimated Sales: $20-50 Million
Number Employees: 10-19
Type of Packaging: Private Label, Bulk

28267 Reed Oven Company
1720 Nicholson Ave
Kansas City, MO 64120 816-842-7446
Fax: 816-421-0422 reedoven@mindspring.com
www.reedovenco.com
Manufacturer and exporter of revolving shelf and rack ovens, proofers, retarders, fermentation rooms and steam cabinets
President: Kay Davies
Marketing Director/ IT Supervisor: Chris Davies
Operations: Brad Mitchell
Administrative Assistant: Linda Zeller
Plant Manager/ Engineer: Tim Davies
Purchasing Manager: Linda Zeller
Estimated Sales: $2.5-5 Million
Number Employees: 20-49
Square Footage: 36000
Brands:
Reed

28268 Reef Industries
9209 Almeda Genoa Rd
Houston, TX 77075 713-507-4250
Fax: 713-507-4295 800-231-6074
ri@reefindustries.com www.reefindustries.com
Reinforced film laminates and plastics.
Owner: Phillip Cameron
Sales Manager: Jeff Garza
Number Employees: 100-249
Brands:
Armorlon
Banner Guard
Griffolyn
Permalon
Roll-A-Sign
Terra Tape

28269 Reelcraft Industries
2842 E Business 30
Columbia City, IN 46725 260-248-8188
Fax: 260-248-2605 800-444-3134
reelcraft@reelcraft.com www.reelcraft.com
Manufacturer and exporter of industrial-grade hose, cord and cable reels, including stainless steel.
President: Walter Sterneman
Estimated Sales: Over $50 Million
Number Employees: 100-249
Square Footage: 130000
Type of Packaging: Consumer, Food Service

28270 Reeno Detergent & Soap Company
9421 Midland Boulevard
Saint Louis, MO 63114-3327 314-429-6078
Fax: 314-429-6078
Manufacturer, importer and exporter of powder and liquid laundry detergents and industrial cleaners
President: Colleen Trotter
VP Sales: Tim Trotter
VP Purchasing: Brad Trotter
Estimated Sales: $1-2.5 Million
Number Employees: 5-9
Brands:
Borax-Splash
Borax-Sudz
Woolmaster

28271 Rees
405 S Reed Rd
Fremont, IN 46737 260-495-9811
Fax: 260-495-2186 sales@reesinc.com
www.reesinc.com
Manufacturer and exporter of industrial control switches including cable, palmbutton and stop-start
President: Daniel Breeden
Estimated Sales: $1 - 5 Million
Number Employees: 20-49
Square Footage: 35000

28272 Reese Enterprises
16350 Asher Ave
PO Box 459
Rosemount, MN 55068-0459 651-423-1126
Fax: 651-423-2662 800-328-0953
info@reeseusa.com www.reeseusa.com
Manufacturer, importer and exporter of plastic doors and door strips, aluminum roll-up mats, aluminum stair treads, floor mats and grates, weatherstrips and thresholds
President: Chester W Ellingson Iii III
National Sales/Marketing Manager: Edward Green
Estimated Sales: $10-20 Million
Number Employees: 50-99
Number of Products: 4
Square Footage: 80000
Parent Co: Astro Plastics

28273 Reeve Store Equipment Company
9131 Bermudez St
Pico Rivera, CA 90660 562-949-2535
Fax: 562-949-3862 800-927-3383
info@reeveco.com www.reeveco.com
Manufacturer and exporter of point of purchase displays, tags, card holders and fixtures
President: John Frackelton
Manager Sales/Marketing: Robert Frackelton
Estimated Sales: $20 - 50 Million
Number Employees: 100-249
Square Footage: 160000

28274 Reeves Enterprises
1350 Palomares Ave
La Verne, CA 91750 909-392-9999
Fax: 909-392-0124 reevesrack@dslextreme.com
www.dreevesinc.com
Store fixtures; also, woodworking services available
President and CFO: Dennis Reeves
Accounting: Michelle Scherer
Vice President: Brad Reeves
Engineering: Al Gonzaga
Sales: Joe Greco
Estimated Sales: Below $5,000,000
Number Employees: 5-9

28275 Refcon
335 Chestnut St
Norwood, NJ 07648 201-750-5060
Fax: 201-750-5066 sales@refconcase.com
www.refconcase.com
Manufacturer and exporter of curved display cases for candy, baked goods, deli meat, fish and poultry
President: Herman Jakubowski
Manager/Manufacturing: Len Pushkantser
Engineer: Rapael Colon
Estimated Sales: $3-5 Million
Number Employees: 20-49
Square Footage: 44000

28276 Refinishing Touch
9350 Industrial Trace
Alpharetta, GA 30004 770-751-7227
Fax: 770-475-4782 800-523-9448
sales@therefinishingtouch.com
www.therefinishingtouch.com
Firm providing refinishing and refurbishing services for furniture
Founder, President: Mario Insenga
National Sales Manager: Roberta Bernhardt
Estimated Sales: $500,000-$1 Million
Number Employees: 5-9

28277 Reflectronics
3009 Montavesta Road
Lexington, KY 40502-2907 888-415-0441
Fax: 888-415-0442 info@reflectronics.com
www.reflectronics.com
Optical sensors for process monitoring and control
Estimated Sales: Below $500,000
Number Employees: 2
Number of Products: 2

28278 Reflex International
6624 Jimmy Carter Boulevard
Norcross, GA 30071-1727 770-729-8909
Fax: 770-729-8805 800-642-7640
jbd@reflexintl.com www.reflexinternational.org
Point of purchase software, touch screen monitors, peripheral printers, mag card readers, kiosk cabinets, scanners and rack mounted open and close chassis displays
Marketing Director: John Dodrill
Sales Manager: Bryan Graves
Estimated Sales: $5-10 Million
Number Employees: 45
Square Footage: 180000
Parent Co: CTX International

28279 Refractron TechnologiesCorporation
5750 Stuart Ave
Newark, NY 14513-9798 315-331-6222
Fax: 315-331-7254 info@refractron.com
www.refractron.com
Manufacturer, importer and exporter of advanced porous ceramic filters including water, process, gas, micro, cross-flow, ceramic membrane, air, etc.; also, diffusers including liquid and gas
President: Robert Stanton
Director R & D: Gregg Crume
Sales/Marketing Executive: Thomas Kinton
Estimated Sales: $10-20 Million
Number Employees: 50-99
Square Footage: 65000
Type of Packaging: Private Label
Brands:
Durasieve
Refractite
Solidome

28280 Refrigerated Design Texas
P.O.Box 622
Waxahachie, TX 75168-0622 972-937-3215
Fax: 972-937-0970 800-736-9518
randall@rdtonline.com www.rdtonline.com
Custom made refrigeration equipment and systems
President: Randall Dyess
Quotations: Brent Dyess
Purchasing: Jim Wright
Estimated Sales: $2.5-5 Million
Number Employees: 10-19
Parent Co: RJS Company

28281 Refrigerated Warehouse Marketing Group
PO Box 530
La Verne, CA 91750-0530 909-625-4512
Fax: 909-625-4612 botterell@earthlink.net
www.warehousesales.net

28282 Refrigerated Warehousing
198 High Trail Vista Cir
Jasper, GA 30143 770-894-4012
Fax: 706-692-3749 800-873-2008
dshine@rwizero.com www.rwizero.com
Designer and constructor of refrigeration warehouses and processing facilities
President: Dennis Shine
Estimated Sales: $1-2.5 Million
Number Employees: 1-4

28283 Refrigeration Design & Service
14 Union Hill Road
West Conshohocken, PA 19428-2719610-834-1264
Fax: 610-834-0807 bschadler@refdesign.com
www.refrigerationdesign.com
President: Micheal Zion
Estimated Sales: $10 - 20 Million
Number Employees: 35

28284 Refrigeration Engineering
3123 Wilson Dr NW
Grand Rapids, MI 49534-7565 616-453-2441
Fax: 616-453-0750 800-968-3227
Commercial refrigeration equipment including cases and walk-in coolers; also, sales and services available
Manager: John Atsma
Parts Manager: Carl Boltz
Estimated Sales: $10-20 Million
Number Employees: 10-19

28285 (HQ)Refrigeration Research
525 N 5th St
PO Box 869
Brighton, MI 48116 810-227-1151
Fax: 810-227-3700 info@refresearch.com
www.refresearch.com
Manufacturer and exporter of component parts for commercial refrigeration systems
Chairman of the Board: Edward Bottum Sr
Vice President: M Ramalia
Estimated Sales: $5-10 Million
Number Employees: 100-249
Type of Packaging: Bulk

28286 Refrigeration Systems Company
1770 Genessee Ave
Columbus, OH 43211 614-263-0913
Fax: 614-263-6660 columbus@rsc-gc.com
www.rsc-gc.com
President: Robert Appleton
CEO: Tom Leighty
Estimated Sales: $10 - 20 Million
Number Employees: 50-99

28287 Refrigeration Technology
595 Portal Street
Cotati, CA 94931-3023 707-792-1934
Fax: 707-792-1417 800-834-2232
rti2000@rpnet.net
Wine industry refrigeration units

28288 Refrigerator Manufacturers LLC
17018 Edwards Rd
Cerritos, CA 90703 562-926-2006
Fax: 323-838-5510 sales@rmi-econocold.com
www.rmi-econocold.com
Manufacturer, importer and exporter of walk-in cold storage rooms and environmental chambers
President: Lawrence Jaffe
VP: Leo Lewis
Estimated Sales: $10-20 Million
Number Employees: 20-49
Square Footage: 40000
Brands:
Econocold
Rmi

28289 RefrigiWear
54 Breakstone Dr
Dahlonega, GA 30533 706-864-5757
Fax: 706-864-5898 800-645-3744
customerservice@refrigiwear.com
www.refrigiwear.com
President/CFO: Ronald Breakstone
Vice President: Scotty Depriest
Marketing Manager: Kate Bishop
Chief Operating Officer: Mark Silberman
Estimated Sales: $10 - 20 Million
Number Employees: 50-99

28290 Refrigiwear
P.O.Box 39
Dahlonega, GA 30533 706-864-5757
Fax: 706-864-5898 800-645-3744
keepmewarm@refrigiwear.com
www.refrigiwear.com
Manufacturer and exporter of insulated and protective work clothing, head, hand, and footwear, thermal insulated blankets and carts and pallet covers
President: Ronald Breakstone
Vice President: Mark Silberman
Quality Control: Kate Bishop
Marketing: Kristy Chrisciaske
VP Sales: Don Byerly
Vice President/Operations: Scotty Depriest
Estimated Sales: $25 Million
Number Employees: 110
Square Footage: 80000
Brands:
Iron Tuff
Refrigiwear
Storm Trac
Weatherguard

28291 Refrigue USA
3845 Shopton Rd
Suite 350
Charlotte, NC 28217-3030 704-347-1511
Fax: 704-347-1448
Safety equipment and apparel

28292 Regal - Pinnacle Manufacturing
220 Route 70
Medford, NJ 08055-9522 609-714-2330
Fax: 609-714-2331 www.regalpinnacle.com
Founder: Luis Mora
Estimated Sales: $5-10 Million
Number Employees: 100-249

28293 Regal Box Company
923 E Garfield Ave
Milwaukee, WI 53212 414-562-5890
Fax: 414-562-0341
Corrugated boxes
President: John J Schwartz
Estimated Sales: Below $5 Million
Number Employees: 1-4

28294 Regal Custom Fixture Company
22 Burrs Rd., Bldg. C
PO Box 446
Westampton, NJ 08060-0446 609-261-3323
Fax: 609-261-4929 800-525-3092
regalcustom@rcn.com
Manufacturer and exporter of display cases including bakery, deli and candy
VP: Mike Rainbolt
National Sales Manager: Shawn Adair
Number Employees: 20-49
Type of Packaging: Food Service
Brands:
Regal

28295 **Regal Equipment**
4171 State Route 14
Ravenna, OH 44266-8739 330-325-9000
Fax: 330-325-7900 sales@regalequipment.com
www.regalequipment.com
Dealer of used and rebuilt cutters, dicers, blanchers, centrifuges grinders, and other food processing equipment
President: Kenneth Regal
Estimated Sales: $1 - 3 Million
Number Employees: 5-9

28296 **Regal Manufacturing Company**
5438 W Roosevelt Road
Chicago, IL 60644-1495 773-921-3071
Fax: 773-921-3076
Metal and wooden bar stools and dining chairs
President: Gerald Saviano
Estimated Sales: $5-10 Million
Number Employees: 20-49
Square Footage: 35000

28297 **Regal Plastic Company**
5310 Canterbury Road
Mission, KS 66205-2611 816-483-3040
Fax: 816-483-7948 800-852-1556
haber@regplas.com www.regplas.com
Thermoformed FDA approved tote boxes and freezer spacers
President: A Bashor
CFO: J Streeter
VP Sales: L Haber
Plant Manager: Doug Meyer
Estimated Sales: $50-100 Million
Number Employees: 50-99

28298 **Regal Plastics**
1500 Burlington
North Kansas City, MO 64116 816-471-6390
Fax: 816-221-5822 jnorman@regalplastic.com
www.regalplastic.com
Acrylic items including food containers, store fixtures, advertising signs and name plates
President: Harry R Greenwald
CEO: Enzo Castelli
Estimated Sales: $1-2.5 Million
Number Employees: 1-4
Square Footage: 5000

28299 **(HQ)Regal Ware**
1675 Reigle Dr.
Kewaskum, WI 53040 262-626-2121
Fax: 262-626-8504 www.regalware.com
Manufacturer, importer and exporter of frying and sauce pans, coffee makers and urns
President/CEO: Jeffery Reigle
Chairman: James Reigle
SVP/Chief Financial Officer: Gerald Koch
SVP/Chief HR Officer: David Lenz
Sales Director: Jim Dorn
SVP Operations: Joe Swanson
Purchasing: John McCormack
Estimated Sales: $36.8 Million
Number Employees: 421
Square Footage: 500000
Other Locations:
Regal Ware
Jacksonville AR
Brands:
Kitchen Pro
La Machine
Poly Perk
Regal

28300 **Regency Label Corporation**
217 Berger Street
Wood Ridge, NJ 07075-1802 201-342-2288
Fax: 201-438-3439
Printed labels including pressure sensitive
VP Marketing: Mike Pagano
*Estimated Sales:*less than $500,000
Number Employees: 1-4

28301 **Reggie Ball's Cajun Foods**
501 Bunker Rd
Lake Charles, LA 70615 337-436-0291
Fax: 337-433-9851 reggieball@cox-internet.com
www.ballscajunfoods.com
Cajum seasonings and mixes. Contract packaging and private labeling is available.
Owner/President: Reginald Ball Jr
Estimated Sales: $500,000-$1 Million
Number Employees: 20-49
Type of Packaging: Private Label

28302 **Regina USA, Inc**
305 Mahn Ct
Oak Creek, WI 53154-2155 414-571-0032
Fax: 414-571-0225 sales.us@reginachain.net
www.reginachain.net
Manufacturer, of metal and plastic power transmission chains, conveying chains and plastic belts
President: Carlo Garbagnati
VP Sales/Marketing: Michael Hager
Sales: Brian Kelley
Estimated Sales: $20 Million
Number Employees: 30
Square Footage: 65000
Parent Co: Regina Industria SPA
Brands:
Regina

28303 **Regina-Emerson**
1604 S West Avenue
Waukesha, WI 53189-7434 262-521-1790
Fax: 262-521-1790
Belting

28304 **Rego China Corporation**
200 Broadhollow Road
Suite 400
Melville, NY 11747-4806 516-753-3700
Fax: 516-753-3728 800-221-1707
www.oneida.com
Manufacturer, importer and exporter of chinaware
President, CEO: Foster Sullivan
Sales Manager: Frank Fan
Estimated Sales: $300,000-500,000
Number Employees: 40
Parent Co: Oneida
Type of Packaging: Food Service

28305 **Reheis**
235 Snyder Ave
Berkeley Heights, NJ 07922 908-464-1500
Fax: 908-464-7726 rduffy@reheis.com
www.reheis.com
Chemicals and pharmaceuticals
General Manager: Douglas McF+R2441arlend
Plant Manager: Gerry Kirwan
Estimated Sales: $20-50 Million
Number Employees: 100-249
Parent Co: General Chemicals

28306 **Rehrig Pacific Company**
4010 E. 26th St.
Los Angeles, CA 90023 323-262-5145
Fax: 323-269-8506 800-421-6244
info@rehrigpacific.com www.rehrigpacific.com
Plastic injection molding, returnable plastic crates and pallets
President: Will Rehrig
Estimated Sales: $101.4 Million
Number Employees: 1100

28307 **Reichert Analytical Instruments**
3362 Walden Avenue
Depew, NY 14043 716-686-4500
Fax: 716-686-4545 www.reichertai.com
Hand held digital refractometers.

28308 **Reid Boiler Works**
920 10th St
Bellingham, WA 98225 360-714-6157
Fax: 360-734-6660
Canning retorts and pressure vessels
President: Robert Reid
Office Manager: Shirley Maytag
Estimated Sales: Less than $500,000
Number Employees: 1-4

28309 **Reid Graphics**
7 Connector Rd
Andover, MA 01810-5922 978-474-1930
Fax: 978-474-1931 pzackular@reidgraphics.com
www.reidgraphics.com
Labels and decals
President: Stephen Dunlevy
General Manager: Robert Stewart
Estimated Sales: $10-20 Million
Number Employees: 20-49

28310 **Reidler Decal Corporation**
264 Industrial Pk. Road
PO Box 8
Saint Clair, PA 17970 570-429-1528
Fax: 570-429-1528 800-628-7770
marketing@reidlerdecal.com
www.reidlerdecal.com
Manufacturer and exporter of decals, plastic safety signs, fleet graphics, reflective markings, reflective striping and roll labels
President: Edward Reidler
Marketing Coordinator: Maralynn Hudock
Estimated Sales: $5 - 10 Million
Number Employees: 20-49
Square Footage: 50000
Brands:
Ad Vantage
Fleet Mark

28311 **Reilly Foam Corporation**
1101 E Hector St # 1
Conshohocken, PA 19428-2382 610-834-1900
Fax: 610-834-0769 info@reillyfoam.com
www.reillyfoam.com
Plastic foam sheets including die cut, laminated and pressure sensitive
Owner: Charles Reilly
VP Marketing: Stephen Phillips
Estimated Sales: $20-50 Million
Number Employees: 100-249
Square Footage: 249000

28312 **Reiner Products**
196 Mill St
Waterbury, CT 06706-1208 203-574-2666
Fax: 203-755-8178 800-345-6775
info@reinerproducts.com
www.reinerproducts.com
Manufacturer, importer and exporter of salt and pepper shakers
Owner: Patrick Bergin
Estimated Sales: $2.5-5 Million
Number Employees: 10-19

28313 **Reinhold Sign Service**
2070 Holmgren Way
Green Bay, WI 54304 920-494-7161
Fax: 920-494-8720 sales@reinholdsigns.com
www.reinholdsigns.com
Interior and exterior signage, truck and trailer lettering and vinyl letters
President: John Gage
Sales & Service Manager: Robert Ott
Estimated Sales: $1 - 5 Million
Number Employees: 10-19
Square Footage: 32000

28314 **Reinke & Schomann**
3745 N Richards St
Milwaukee, WI 53212 414-964-1100
Fax: 414-964-1995
sales@reinkeandschomann.com
www.reinkeandschomann.com
Manufacturer and exporter of steel and stainless steel screw conveyors and components
President: Frederick Schomann
VP Engineering/Sales: Ken Buchholz
Estimated Sales: Below $5,000,000
Number Employees: 5-9
Square Footage: 30000

28315 **Reis Robotics**
1320 Holmes Rd
Elgin, IL 60123-1202 847-741-9500
Fax: 847-888-2762 800-358-4245
dchece@reisrobotics.com
www.reisroboticsusa.com
Manufacturer and importer of automated robotic material handling and palletizing systems and system integrators
Manager: Peter Stellbrink
Business Manager: Anja Waaga
Vice President: Don Seary
Operations Manager: Hans Volkhart
Estimated Sales: $1-5 Billion
Number Employees: 10-19
Square Footage: 45000
Parent Co: Reis Gmbh Maschinenfabrik

28316 **(HQ)Reiser**
725 Dedham St
Canton, MA 02021-1450 781-575-9941
Fax: 781-821-1316 sales@reiser.com
www.reiser.com

High-quality food processing and packaging equipment that includes tray sealing, vacuum and form/fill/seal packaging equipment as well as processing machines used for stuffing, portioning, grinding, injecting, extruding and slicing.Equipment can be used as stand-alone machines or as complete systems.
President/CEO: Roger Reiser
Engineering/R&D Technician: Dan Flaherty
Estimated Sales: $23 Million
Number Employees: 100-249
Brands:
Amfec
Fomaco
Holac
Ross
Seydelmann
Vemag

28317 Reit-Price ManufacturingCompany
532 W Chestnut St
Union City, IN 47390 765-964-5343
Fax: 765-964-5343 800-521-5343
sales@reitprice.com www.reitprice.com
Wet and dust mops, squeegees, push brooms, floor brushes and handles
President: Roger Stewart
Sales Manager: R Stewart
Estimated Sales: $10-20 Million
Number Employees: 20-49
Square Footage: 50000
Brands:
Black Cat

28318 Relco Unisystems Corporation
2281 3rd Ave SW
Willmar, MN 56201 320-231-2210
Fax: 320-231-2282
lorencorle@relcounisystems.com
www.relco.net
Provides dairy and food plants with customized cheese, whey, soy, and processing equipment and systems through design, engineering, fabrication, installation, and commissioning. Relco process and control systems are recognized asindustry leaders because of their application knowledge, understanding of sanitary and regulatory requirements, and focus on consumer needs
President: Loren Corle
VP: M Douglas Rolland
Estimated Sales: $20-50 Million
Number Employees: 20-49

28319 (HQ)Reliable Container Corporation
12029 Regentview Ave
Downey, CA 90241-5517 562-745-0200
Fax: 562-861-3969 www.reliablecontainer.com
Manufacturer and exporter of corrugated boxes and foil-lined, coated, printed and plain cake circles and pads
President: Dan Brough
VP: Andrew Rosen
VP: Robert Schwartz
VP: Bob Schwartz
Estimated Sales: $20 - 50 Million
Number Employees: 100-249
Square Footage: 112500
Other Locations:
Reliable Container Corp.
Tijuana, Baja CA

28320 Reliable Fire EquipmentCompany
12845 S Cicero Ave
Alsip, IL 60803-3083 708-597-4600
Fax: 708-389-1150 fire@reliablefire.com
www.reliablefire.com
Wholesaler/distributor of restaurant fire supression and security systems, alarm monitoring, fire alarms, portable, industrial and special hazard fire extinguishers, emergency lights, smoke detectors and first aid equipment, servingthe food service market.
President: Debra Horvath
Vice President: Barbara Horvath
VP Sales: Robert Marek
Purchasing Manager: Tim Zurek
Estimated Sales: $22 Million
Number Employees: 50-99
Number of Brands: 30
Number of Products: 200
Square Footage: 40000

28321 Reliable Food Service Equipment
Units 5,7,8
Concord, ON L4K 1L3
Canada 416-738-6840
Fax: 416-739-7271
sales@restaurantequipmentdepot.com
www.restaurantequipmentdepot.com
Steam tables, ovens, freezers, sinks, etc
President: Frank Gambino
Number Employees: 8

28322 Reliable Tent & Awning Co.
501 N 23rd St
Billings, MT 59101 406-252-4689
Fax: 406-252-6508 800-544-1039
sales@reliabletent.com www.reliabletent.com
Commercial awnings
President: Robert Nemer
Estimated Sales: $1-2,500,000
Number Employees: 10-19
Type of Packaging: Private Label

28323 Reliance Product
1093 Sherwin Road
Winnipeg, MB R3H 1A4
Canada 204-633-4403
Fax: 204-694-5132 800-665-0258
www.relianceproducts.com
Shipping containers including HDPE pails and bottles includesCamping lines
President: Charles Schiele
CFO: Arla Ervett
VP General Manager: Linda Lemer
Sales Manager: Peter Harvey
Number Employees: 10
Parent Co: Moll Industries

28324 Reliance-Paragon
2070 Wheatsheaf Lane
Philadelphia, PA 19124-5041 215-743-1231
Fax: 215-742-1584
Packaging products including set-up, paper and folding boxes; also, plastic boxes
VP: Larry Chatzkel
Plant Supervisor: William Scnappor
Estimated Sales: $1 - 5 Million
Number Employees: 50-99
Square Footage: 60000

28325 Rem Ohio
11530 Century Boulevard
Cincinnati, OH 45246 513-878-8188
www.rem-oh.com
Chemical cleaners, sanitizers and detergents
President: Gary Farraria
VP: B Nelson
Controller: Larry Schirmann
Sales Manager: E Newman
Estimated Sales: $2.5 - 5 Million
Number Employees: 1-4
Square Footage: 200000

28326 (HQ)Remco Industries International
PO Box 480008
Fort Lauderdale, FL 33348-0008 954-462-0000
Fax: 954-564-0000 800-987-3626
remco2mill@aol.com www.remcousa.com
Manufacturer and exporter of cooking equipment including wood burning and infrared rotisseries and pizza ovens; also, spit racks, bagel ovens and warming carts; manufacturer and importer of wood burning, infrared and carousel brickpizza ovens; manufacturer of grease free chicken wing roaster the Wing King and BBQ Boy
President/CEO: Romano Moreth
CFO: Susan Test
Vice President: Rob Moreth
R&D/Plant Manager: Remy Moreth
Quality Control: Wayne Wilkenson
Marketing/Public Relations: Pascal Ledesma
Sales Director: Joe Obrien
Operations: David Finch
Production Manager: Vean George
Plant Manager: Sean Harker
Purchasing Manager: Ed Moreth
Estimated Sales: $7-8 Million
Number Employees: 20-49
Number of Brands: 3
Number of Products: 6
Square Footage: 160000
Type of Packaging: Food Service

28327 Remco Products Company
4735 W 106th St
PO Box 698
Zionsville, IN 46077 317-876-9856
Fax: 317-876-9858 800-585-8619
annb@remcoproducts.com
www.remcoproducts.com
Ice and beverage dispensing products
Founder: Richard Garrison
President: David Garrison
Accounting: Cristal Garrison
Vice President Sales & Marketing: Steve Hawhee
Sales Representative: Paula Pearson
Operations: Mike Garrison
Customer Service: Amye Kersey
Number Employees: 250-499

28328 Remco Products Corporation
4735 West 106th Street
Zionsville, IN 46077 317-876-9856
Fax: 317-876-9858 800-585-8619
sales@remcoproducts.com
www.remcoproducts.com
Remco Products sells a high quality line of products to the food processing, sanittation, pharmaceutical, safety, and material handling industries. Our tubs and polyropylene shovels have been used in these areas for over 30 years. TheVikan line of cleaning brooms, brushes, and squeegees is specifically designed to meet the stringent hygienic requirements of these different industries. We can also provide you with other hand tools such as scoops, scrapers, mixing paddles, forkkand rakes.
President: Richard L. Garrison
Marketing/Sales Support: Richard L. Williams
Director/Sales and Marketing: Chuck Bush Jr
President of Operations: Richard L. Garrison
Estimated Sales: $2.5-5 Million
Number Employees: 20
Number of Brands: 2
Number of Products: 737
Square Footage: 96000
Brands:
Remco

28329 Remcon Plastics
208 Chestnut St
West Reading, PA 19611 610-376-2666
Fax: 610-375-4750 800-360-3636
info@remcon.com www.remcon.com
ISO 9001 certified material handling equipment, including bulk bins, liquid shippers, drums, pallets, tanks, aseptic packaging equipment, lockers, tote boxes, safety barriers, hoppers and candy trays. Structural foam molding androtational molding
President: Peter J Connors
Marketing/Inside Sales Manager: Sylvie Mackenzie
Regional Sales Manager: Michael Pierotti
Purchasing Manager: Susan Cook
Estimated Sales: $10-20 Million
Number Employees: 100-249
Square Footage: 140000
Type of Packaging: Private Label, Bulk
Brands:
Remcon

28330 Remcraft Lighting Products
12870 NW 45th Ave
PO Box 54-1487
Miami, FL 33054 305-687-9031
Fax: 305-687-5069 800-327-6585
customerservice@remcraft.com
www.bacimirrors.com
Manufacturer and exporter of electric and fluorescent lighting fixtures
President: Jeffrey Robboy
CEO: Michell Roboy
Estimated Sales: $1 - 2.5 Million
Number Employees: 20-49
Square Footage: 40000
Type of Packaging: Consumer, Private Label
Brands:
Baci
Remcraft

28331 Remel
P.O.Box 14428
Shawnee Mission, KS 66285-4428 913-888-0939
Fax: 913-888-5884 800-255-6730
icustomersupport@remel.com www.remel.com

Manufacturer and exporter of microbiology products including culture media, dehydrated culture media identification kits, reagents and stains
President: Rodney Smith
Chairman of the Board: Frank H Jellinek Jr
VP Marketing/Sales: Gary Pearson
Sales Director: Greg Candelmo
VP Operations: Gerald Lillian
Estimated Sales: K
Number Employees: 10,000
Brands:
Chrisope
Ids
Remel

28332 **Reminox International Corporation**
7207 Bay Drive
Apt 13
Miami, FL 33141-5457 305-865-0925
infocreminox.com
www.creminox.com
Sales Manager: Roberto Garcia
Estimated Sales: $1 - 5 Million

28333 **Remmele Engineering**
677 Transfer Rd
Saint Paul, MN 55114 651-643-3700
Fax: 651-642-5665 800-854-7742
automation@remmele.com
www.aspectautomation.com
Packaging and filling
President: Terry Johnson
Quality Control: Jim Schaefer
Chairman of the Board: William J Saul
Estimated Sales: $75 - 100 Million
Number Employees: 100-249

28334 **Remmey Wood Products**
PO Box 1020
Southampton, PA 18966-0720 215-355-3335
Fax: 215-355-3781
Packaging and shipping products including wood pallets, boxes, skids, crates, etc
VP Marketing: Donald Remmey Jr
Estimated Sales: $2.5-5 Million
Number Employees: 20-49

28335 **Remote Equipment Systems**
11390 Old Roswell Road
Alpharetta, GA 30004-2058 770-777-2627
Fax: 770-777-2662 800-803-9488
info@requipsystems.com
www.remotemagazine.com
Data loggers for material handling systems
VP Sales: Doug Reed
Estimated Sales: $5-10 Million
Number Employees: 20-49

28336 **Rempak Industries**
2125 Center Avenue #200
Fort Lee, NJ 07024-5810 201-585-9007
Fax: 201-585-0918
Contract packager of portion control powders, liquids and solids
President: Gene Cohen
Estimated Sales: Less than $500,000
Number Employees: 14
Type of Packaging: Consumer, Food Service, Private Label

28337 **Remstar International**
41 Eisenhower Dr
Westbrook, ME 04092 207-854-1861
Fax: 207-854-1610 800-639-5805
info@remstar.com www.remstar.com
Manufacturer, importer and exporter of automated storage and retrieval systems
President: Gary Gould
Marketing Director: Ed Romaine
Estimated Sales: $20-50 Million
Number Employees: 20-49
Parent Co: Kardex A.G.

28338 **Renard Machine Company**
PO Box 19005
Green Bay, WI 54307-9005 920-432-8412
Fax: 920-432-8430 www.renardmachine.com
Manufacturer and exporter of packaging machinery including fillers, sealers, labelers, weighers and wrappers; also, paper converting equipment including folding, cutting, etc
Division Controller: Gary Rossman
Production Manager: Carl Strebel
Plant Manager: Ken Harvey
Estimated Sales: $5-10 Million
Number Employees: 50-99
Square Footage: 300000
Parent Co: Paper Converting Machine Company

28339 **Renato Specialty Product**
3612 Dividend Drive
Garland, TX 75042 972-272-4800
Fax: 972-272-4848 866-575-6316
renatos@renatos.com www.renatos.com
Manufacturer and exporter of food service equipment including broilers, ovens, griddles, grills and rotisseries
President, Founder: Renato Riccio
Estimated Sales: $1-2.5 Million
Number Employees: 5-9
Type of Packaging: Consumer, Food Service

28340 **Renau Corporation**
9309 Deering Ave
Chatsworth, CA 91311-5858 818-341-1994
Fax: 818-341-8063 info@renau.com
www.renau.com
President: Karol Renau
Estimated Sales: $10 - 20 Million
Number Employees: 20-49

28341 **Render**
1800 Elmwood Avenue
Buffalo, NY 14207-2410 716-447-1010
Fax: 716-447-8918 888-446-1010
info@renderint.com www.renderat.com
Bakery display cases with solid wood construction, rearload options, adjustable shelving and accesory bins, and an internal lighting system specifically to enhance bakery products
President: Robert Nehin
Number Employees: 10

28342 **Renfro-Franklin**
525 Brooks St
Ontario, CA 91762-3702 909-984-5500
Fax: 909-984-2322 800-334-0937
rfcmark@verizon.net www.rfcwireforms.com
Soft drink backs, displays and display cases, cooler displays, cooler racks, custom design and manufacturing of displays and racks
President: Donald Kemby
CFO: Jay Munoz
Vice President: Don Kemby
Research & Development: Greg Lunsmann
Quality Control: Donald Kemby
Sales Director: Mark Arriola
Production Manager: Jesse Dunn
Purchasing Manager: Mike Manning
Estimated Sales: $20-30 Million
Number Employees: 50-99
Square Footage: 30000

28343 **Rennco**
PO Box 116
Homer, MI 49245 517-568-4121
Fax: 517-568-4798 800-409-5225
sales@rennco.com www.rennco.com
Manufacturer and exporter of vertical L-Bar sealers
VP/General Manager: Eric Vorm
Marketing Director: Jeanne George
Director of Operations: Terry Draper
Number Employees: 70
Parent Co: Pro Mach
Type of Packaging: Consumer, Food Service, Bulk
Brands:
Renwrap

28344 **Reno Technology**
PO Box 457
Hutchinson, KS 67504 620-663-6542
Fax: 620-665-5793 800-562-8065
bkneufeld@megamfg.com www.marlen.com
President: Adam Anderson
Estimated Sales: $10 - 20 Million
Number Employees: 50-99

28345 **Renold Ajax**
100 Bourne St
Westfield, NY 14787
Fax: 716-326-6121 800-879-2529
sales@renoldhaax.com www.renold.com
Custom design vibratory materials handling equipment: dewatering units, conveyors, feeder, screeners, bulk bab and box weigh filling systems, bulk bag unloading stations
President: Thomas J Murrer
Estimated Sales: $20 - 50 Million
Number Employees: 100-249

28346 **Renold Products**
P.O.Box A
Westfield, NY 14787-0546 716-326-3121
Fax: 716-326-6121 800-879-2529
ainfo@renoldajax.com www.renold.com
Manufacturer and exporter of material handling equipment including mechanical power transmission products and packer weigh scales and conveyors.
President: Thomas Murrer
Business Development Director: Alan Dean
Estimated Sales: $20-50 Million
Number Employees: 100-249
Square Footage: 120000
Parent Co: Renold PLC
Brands:
Ajax
Renold

28347 **Renovator's Supply**
PO Box 2515
Conway, NH 03818 800-659-0203
Fax: 603-447-1717
Manufacturer and exporter of hardware, lighting, plumbing and gift accessories; also, solid brass, iron, porcelain and stainless steel sinks and work centers
President: Cindy Harris
Estimated Sales: $10-20 Million
Number Employees: 100-249
Brands:
Renovator's Supply

28348 **Reotemp Instrument Corporation**
10656 Roselle St
San Diego, CA 92121 858-784-0710
Fax: 858-784-0720 800-648-7737
sales@reotemp.com www.reotemp.com
Manufactures temperature and pressure instrumentation. Provide bimetal thermometers, pressure gauges, diaphragm seals, transmitters, RTD's and thermocouples and related accessories.
President: Michael Oleary
VP/General Manager: John Sisti
Quality/Engineering Manager: Cora Marsh
Marketing Manager: Nathan O'Connor
Sales Manager, Global Sales: Mark Leonelli
Purchasing Associate: Stacy Munoz
Estimated Sales: $6 Million
Square Footage: 7500

28349 **Replacements Ltd.**
P.O.Box 26029
Greensboro, NC 27420-6069 336-697-3000
Fax: 336-697-3100 800-737-5223
inquire@replacements.com
www.replacements.com
Manufacturer and exporter of household and institutional cutlery
Director Marketing: Maron Atkins
General Manager: James Robellard
Estimated Sales: $5-10 Million
Number Employees: 20-49
Square Footage: 70000
Parent Co: Syratech

28350 **Republic Blower Systems**
5131 Cash Rd
Dallas, TX 75247-5805 214-631-8070
Fax: 214-631-3673 800-847-0380
sales@rebulicsales.com www.republicsales.com
President: George Goff
Vice President: Dan Marlett
Regional Manager: Michael McFerren
Estimated Sales: $10 - 20 Million
Number Employees: 50-99

28351 **Republic Foil**
55 Triangle St
Danbury, CT 06810 203-743-2731
Fax: 203-743-8838 800-722-3645
john.jehle@garmcousa.com
www.garmcousa.com

Manufacturer and exporter of aluminum foil on coils
President: John Jehle
CFO: Fred Wallace
Estimated Sales: $20 - 50 Million
Number Employees: 50-99
Square Footage: 100000
Type of Packaging: Bulk
Brands:
Republic High Yield

28352 Republic Refrigeration IInc.
2890 Gray Fox Rd
Monroe, NC 28110 704-282-0399
Fax: 704-283-2180
info@republicrefrigeration.com
www.republicrefrigeration.com
Design, install and maintain industrial refrigereation systems.
President: Rodney L. Helms
CEO: Walter F. Teeter
Founder: Henry Saye
Vice President: Robert G. Belanger
Director of Process Refrigeration: Joe Ramsey
Director of Business Development: Wayne Donaldson
Regional Manager: Banks Thomas
Insulation Project Manager: Jamie R. Foster

28353 Republic Sales & Manufacturing
5131 Cash Rd
Dallas, TX 75247 214-631-8070
Fax: 214-631-3673 800-847-0380
info@republicsales.com www.republicsales.com
President: George Goff
Vice President/International: Dan Marlett
Marketing: Nicole Taylor
Sheet Metal Sales: Andrew Servais
Production: Raul Maldonado
Estimated Sales: $1 - 5 Million
Number Employees: 50-99

28354 Republic Storage Systems LLC
1038 Belden Ave NE
Canton, OH 44705 330-438-5800
Fax: 330-454-7772 800-477-1255
sales@republicstorage.com
www.republicstorage.com
Steel storage products including lockers, shelving and storage racks. Also shop furniture
President: Chris Carr
CFO: Eric Cook
CEO: James T Anderson
Marketing Director: Cathy Maxin
Sales Director: Ed Meek
Estimated Sales: $20 - 50 Million
Number Employees: 500-999
Square Footage: 1300000
Brands:
Mondrian
Wedge Lock

28355 Research & Development Packaging Corporation
1221 Us Highway 22
Suite 1
Lebanon, NJ 08833 908-236-2111
Fax: 908-236-7013 key-pak@worldnet.att.net
www.key-pak.com
President: Donald Bogut
Estimated Sales: $1 - 3 Million
Number Employees: 5-9

28356 Research Products Company
1835 E North St
Salina, KS 67401 785-825-2181
Fax: 785-825-8908 info@researchprod.com
www.researchprod.com
Insecticides
President: Monte White
Marketing Coordinator (Flour Division): Edna Richard
Estimated Sales: $20-50 Million
Number Employees: 50-99
Parent Co: McShares

28357 Resina
1900 51st St
Brooklyn, NY 11204-1335 718-252-4242
Fax: 718-624-4339 800-207-4804
sales@resina.com www.resina.com
Manufacturer and exporter of container capping machines
CEO: Micheal Tom
Director Sales: Andrew May
Sales Director: Tina Tricome
Estimated Sales: $10-20 Million
Number Employees: 1-4
Square Footage: 35000
Brands:
Resina

28358 Resource Equipment
1547 Palos Verdes Mall
Walnut Creek, CA 94597-2228 925-825-5536
Fax: 925-687-5513 800-324-1030
sales@reisite.net www.reisite.net
President: Jeff Slamal
Owner: Kenneth Gottfried
Estimated Sales: Below $5 Million
Number Employees: 2

28359 Resource One/Resource Two
6900 Canby Ave # 106
Reseda, CA 91335-8729 818-343-3451
Fax: 818-343-3405 info@resourceone.com
www.resourceoneinc.com
Table cloths, napkins and chair covers
President: Roberta Karsch
Estimated Sales: $5-10,000,000
Number Employees: 20-49

28360 Resource Optimization
P.O.Box 2747
Knoxville, TN 37901-2747 865-522-2211
Fax: 865-522-7907 sales@resourceopt.com
www.resourceopt.com
Software for quantification of ingredients in multi-level products
President: T Brient Mayfield
R&D: Bill Walter
Estimated Sales: Below $5 Million
Number Employees: 10-19

28361 Resources in Food & FoodTeam
222 S Central Ave # 202
St Louis, MO 63105-3509 314-727-0002
Fax: 314-727-5590 800-875-1028
rif@primary.net www.rifood.com
Professional placement service for the food industry
President: Bonnie Pollock
VP Sales/Marketing: Mike Bray
Marketing Secretary: Marylynn Hayes
Estimated Sales: $300,000-500,000
Number Employees: 1-4
Parent Co: Resources In Food And Food Team

28362 Respirometry Plus, LLC
PO Box 1236
Fond Du Lac, WI 54937-7527
Fax: 920-922-1085 800-328-7518
operations@respirometryplus.com
www.respirometryplus.com
Manufacturer and exporter of bench and on-line respirometer
Owner: Louis Sparagarto
CEO: Robert Arthur
Estimated Sales: $1 - 2,500,000
Number Employees: 10

28363 Restaurant Development Services
7404 Helmsdale Rd
Bethesda, MD 20817 301-263-0400
Fax: 301-263-0151
info@restaurantdevelopment.com
www.restaurantdevelopment.com
Consultant specializing in business planning for restaurants
Estimated Sales: less than $500,000
Number Employees: 10-19

28364 Restaurant Partners
1030 N Orange Ave # 200
Orlando, FL 32801-1030 407-839-5070
Fax: 407-839-3388
contact@restaurantpartnersinc.com
www.restaurantpartnersinc.com
Consultant providing strategic and expansion planning services for restaurants
President, CEO: David Manuchia
Sr Consultant: George Cheros
VP, Operations: Eric Sheen
Estimated Sales: $500,000-$1 Million
Number Employees: 1-4

28365 Restaurant Technologies
2250 Pilot Knob Rd
Suite 100
Saint Paul, MN 55120-1127
Fax: 651-379-4914 888-796-4997
customercare@rti-inc.com www.rti-inc.com
President: Paul Plooster
CEO: Jeffrey R. Kiesel
CFO: Robert E. Weil
VP: Brad Schoendauer
Vice President, Engineering & Quality As: Bradley J. Schoenbauer
Vice President, Sales/Marketing: Sara Sampson
Vice President, Operations: Leanne E. Branham
Estimated Sales: $1 - 3 Million
Number Employees: 20-49

28366 Restaurant Technology
1325 Williams Dr
Marietta, GA 30066-6287 770-590-4300
Fax: 770-590-4313 sales@internetrt1.com
www.restauranttechnology.com
Point of purchase and inventory software
Owner: James Clutter
Sales/Marketing Executive: Greg Waddell
Estimated Sales: $10-20 Million
Number Employees: 20-49

28367 Retail Automations Products
45 W 38th Street
New York, NY 10018
Fax: 212-391-0575 800-237-9144
SALES@RAP-POS.COM
www.alohapos4me.com
Reseller of aloha computer point of sale, inventory tracking, smart card, automated delivery, touch screen and accounting systems; also, catering software, internet security. Also the tri-state area's premiere integrator of foodservice automation technologies. Through Aloha POS software, we serve NYC, Long Island and Southern CT. POS Inventory-tracking, seurity cameras, automated delivery, touch screen and accounting systems.
Estimated Sales: $500,000 - $1 Million
Number Employees: 10
Square Footage: 12000
Brands:
Aloha
Business Works Accounting
Cater Ease

28368 Retail Decor
PO Box 4019
Ironton, OH 45638-4019 740-532-9559
Fax: 740-532-5288 800-726-3402
Decor packages for commercial interiors including aisle directories, end display pricers, check lane signal lights, chalk, menu and bulletin boards, signage, custom wall graphics, etc.; installation services available
Estimated Sales: $500,000-$1,000,000
Number Employees: 6
Square Footage: 10000

28369 Retalix
2490 Technical Dr
Miamisburg, OH 45342 937-384-2277
Fax: 937-384-2280 800-533-2277
infousa@retalix.com www.retalix.com
Manufacturer and exporter of computer software including point of sale backoffice and headquarters systems for supermarkets, grocery stores and convenience stores
President: Ronen Levkovich
CEO: Shuky Sheffer
CFO: Sarit Sagiv
Head Innovation & Portfolio Strategy: Dr,Gill Roth
Marketing: Oren Betzaleli
Sales Director: Rick Cumberland
HR: Irit Ben-Ari
Operations Manager: Eli Spirer
Estimated Sales: $10 - 20 Million
Number Employees: 50-99
Square Footage: 30000
Parent Co: Retalix, Ltd
Type of Packaging: Consumer
Brands:
Consumer Scan

28370 **Retrotec**
W197n7577 F and W Ct
Lannon, WI 53046 262-253-9677
Fax: 262-253-9685 info@retrotecinc.com
www.retrotecinc.com
Full line of still and end over end rotating batch retorts, processes and style of hermetically sealed package in full or partial water immersion
President: Henry Cathers
Estimated Sales: $1-2.5 Million
Number Employees: 5-9

28371 **Revent**
100 Ethel Rd W
Piscataway, NJ 08854 732-777-9433
Fax: 732-777-1187 info@revent.com
www.revent.com
Manufacturer and exporter of ovens including deck, mini and bake and roast rack; also, proof boxes
President: Torvjorn Alm
Quality Control: Tom Parker
Estimated Sales: $1 - 3 Million
Number Employees: 1-4
Square Footage: 200000
Parent Co: Revent International
Brands:
Do-Sys
Revent

28372 **Revere Group**
9310 4th Avenue S
PO Box 80157
Seattle, WA 98108 206-545-8150
Fax: 206-545-3676 info@rvgroup.com
www.rvgroup.com
Packaging supplies (accessories, bags, boxes, confectionery supplies, equipment, gift asket supplies, wrapping film, box pads and trays, ribbons, tissue, thermal transfer ribbon and gift wrap)

28373 **Revere Packaging**
39 Pearce Industrial Rd
Shelbyville, KY 40065 502-633-1404
Fax: 502-633-9547 inforp@reverepackaging.com
www.reverepackaging.com
Plant Manager: John Wherry
Estimated Sales: $20 - 30 Million
Number Employees: 50-99
Type of Packaging: Consumer

28374 **Revere Packaging**
39 Pearce Industrial Road
Shelbyville, KY 40065 502-633-1404
800-626-2668
www.reverepackaging.com
Foil containers and polystyrene plastic items
Estimated Sales: $61 Thousand
Number Employees: 50-99
Square Footage: 2178

28375 **Rewdco & Hanson Brass Products**
7530 San Fernando Road
Sun Valley, CA 91352-4344 818-767-3501
Fax: 818-767-7891 888-841-3773
info@hansonbrass.com www.hansonbrass.com
Sneeze guards, copper carts and brass, chrome and copper lamps; exporter of carving units, food displays; wholesaler/distributor of restaurant equipment and supplies; serving the food service market, alto shaam test kitchen
President: Tom Hanson Jr
VP: Jim Hanson
CFO: Tom Hanson Sr
Vice President: Robert Hanson
Plant Manager: Mark Denny
Estimated Sales: $6-7 Million
Number Employees: 10-12
Number of Brands: 2
Square Footage: 32000
Brands:
Hanson Brass

28376 **Rex Art Manufacturing Corp.**
655 N Queens Avenue
Lindenhurst, NY 11757-3004 631-884-4600
Fax: 631-884-4611
Point of purchase displays including plastic wood and steel; also, metal specialties and aluminum sheet metal and tubing; custom rack fabrications available
President/General Manager: Robert Santangelo
Number Employees: 50
Square Footage: 40000

28377 **Rex Carton Company**
4528 W 51st St
Chicago, IL 60632 773-581-4115
Fax: 773-581-4120 info@rexcarton.com
www.rexcarton.com
Corrugated boxes
President: Ronald Lemar
VP/Plant Manager: Sal Arena
Customer Service: Greg Fleck
Controller: Diane Green
Estimated Sales: $5-10 Million
Number Employees: 20-49

28378 **Rex Chemical Corporation**
2270 NW 23rd St
Miami, FL 33142-8488 305-634-2471
Fax: 305-634-5546 rexchem@bellsouth.net
www.rexchemical.com
Liquid and powder cleaners; wholesaler/distributor of janitorial supplies
President: Beatriz Granja
Estimated Sales: $10-20 Million
Number Employees: 20-49

28379 **Rexam Beverage Can Company**
8770 West Bryn Mawr Ave.
Chicago, IL 60631 773-399-3000
Fax: 773-399-8088 www.rexam.com
Metal cans, flexible packaging, plastic bottles and tubes for the beverage, food and personal care markets
Chief Executive Officer: Graham Chipchase
Finance Director: David Robbie
Group Director, Marketing: Ollie Graham
Group Director, Human Resources: Nikki Rolfe
Group Director, Operations: Malcolm Harrison
Estimated Sales: $384 Million
Number Employees: 3,000
Square Footage: 250000
Parent Co: Rexam PLC

28380 **Rexam Containers**
743 Westgate Road
Deerfield, IL 60015-3136 847-945-2249
Fax: 847-945-4938 carrollpjx@aol.com
Director Sales: Patrick Carroll

28381 **Rexam Food Containers**
4201 Congress Street
Suite 340
Charlotte, NC 28209 704-551-1500
Fax: 636-583-5565 800-933-4220
jamie.meyer@rexam.com www.rexam.com
Sales: Kenneth Corbett

28382 **Rexcraft Fine Chafers**
4139 38th Street
Long Island City, NY 11101-3617 718-361-3052
Fax: 718-361-3054 888-739-2723
rexchafer@aol.com
Manufacturer and exporter of banquetware including chafers, coffee/tea brewers and urns, hollowware, steam table inserts, serving trays and food warmers
President: Ahsan Ullaha
VP: John Berman
EngineeR & Designer: David Berman
Number Employees: 40
Square Footage: 18000
Brands:
Rexcraft

28383 **Rexford Paper Company**
5802 Washington Ave
Suite 102
Racine, WI 53406-4088 262-886-9100
Fax: 262-886-9130
Manufacturer, wholesaler/distributor and exporter of gummed, and reinforced paper and tapes including plain and printed, heat seal coated, lightweight meat packaging, gummed stay and pressure sensitive carton closure
CFO: Muriel Fincle
Sales Service Manager: James Carse
Sales Manager: Rory Wolf
Estimated Sales: $5 - 10 Million
Number Employees: 10-19
Parent Co: Inland Paperboard & Packaging
Type of Packaging: Consumer, Food Service
Brands:
Lok-A-Box
Redcore
Rexford
Safe-T-Seal

28384 **Rexnord Corporation**
4701 W Greenfield Ave
Milwaukee, WI 53214-5310 414-643-3000
Fax: 414-643-3078 866-739-6673
www.rexnord.com
Manufacturer, importer and exporter of belt, bottle and chain conveyors
President: Robert Hitt
Estimated Sales: $2.01 Billion
Number Employees: 7300
Brands:
Link-Belt
McC
Marbett
Mattop
Rex
Stearns
Table Top
Thomas

28385 **Rexnord Tabletop**
4701 W. Greenfield Avenue
Milwaukee, WI 53214-5310 262-376-4600
Fax: 262-376-4740 www.rexnord.com
President and Chief Executive Officer: Todd Adams
Senior Vice President and Chief Financia: Mark Peterson
Director of Engineering: Andy Flaherty
Quality Manager: Mary Strutzenberg
Marketing Manager: Gary Nass
Executive Vice President-Corporate & Bus: Praveen Jeyarajah
Plant Manager: Tom Amhart
Estimated Sales: $50,000,000
Number Employees: 100-249

28386 **Rexroth Corporation**
5150 Prairie Stone Pkwy
Hoffman Estates, IL 60192-3707 847-645-3600
Fax: 847-645-0804 steveg@godfrey.com
www.boschrexroth-us.com
Manufacturer and importer of servodrives and controls for motion control of processing and packaging machinery
President, Chief Executive Officer: Berend Bracht
VP Sales/Marketing: Richard Huss
Estimated Sales: $20-50 Million
Number Employees: 1,000-4,999
Square Footage: 50000
Parent Co: Rexroth Corporation
Brands:
Indramat

28387 **Reynolds Metals Company**
2125 Reymet Rd
Richmond, VA 23237 804-743-6723
Fax: 804-281-3289 stwalker@rmc.com
www.alcoa.com
Manufacturer and exporter of can manufacturing equipment
Owner: Leon Reynolds
Inside Sales/Marketing Manager: D Gillespie
Customer Service Manager: G Barbour
Estimated Sales: $1 - 5 Billion
Number Employees: 1-4
Square Footage: 100000
Parent Co: Reynolds Metal Company

28388 **Reynolds Water Conditioning Company**
24545 Hathaway St
Farmington Hills, MI 48335 248-888-5000
Fax: 248-888-5005 800-572-9575
info@reynoldswater.com
www.reynoldswater.com
Water softeners, filters and purifiers
President: James Reynolds
VP: James Reynolds Jr
Estimated Sales: $500,000-$1 Million
Number Employees: 1-4
Square Footage: 11000
Type of Packaging: Consumer
Brands:
Clearstream
Oxy-Catalytic
Soft-Sensor
Softstream
Turbo Sensor
Twin-Stream

28389 Rez-Tech Corporation
1510 Mogadore Rd
Kent, OH 44240 330-673-4009
Fax: 330-673-2273 800-673-5277
info@rez-tech.com www.rez-tech.com
Blow and injection molded clear plastic food containers
Chairman Of Board: Tom Podnar
Co-President/CEO: Jack Podnar
CEO: Scott Podnar
VP: Craig Podnar
CEO: Jack Podnar
Purchasing Manager: Martha Sth
Estimated Sales: $2.5 - 5 Million
Number Employees: 20-49
Square Footage: 45000
Type of Packaging: Consumer, Food Service, Private Label

28390 Rhee Brothers
7461 Coca Cola Dr
Hanover, MD 21076 410-799-6656
Fax: 410-381-9080 www.rheebros.com
Asian food products
President: Syng Rhee
CFO: Ha Chang
Estimated Sales: $20-50 Million
Number Employees: 100-249
Type of Packaging: Private Label

28391 Rheo-Tech
640 Sanders Ct
Gurnee, IL 60031-3135 847-367-1557
mowli@fbcgobal.net
USDA certified pumps and extruders for cheese, licorice candy, ground meat, sausage meat, fillings, peanut butter, etc
President: John Mowli
Estimated Sales: $1-2.5,000,000
Number Employees: 1-4

28392 Rheometric Scientific
109 Lukens Drive
New Castle, DE 19720-2765 732-560-8550
Fax: 732-560-7451 marketing@rheosci.com
www.rheosci.com
Rheometers, viscometers, thermal analyzers and process controllers
VP: Joseph Musanti
Managing Director: Don Becker
Marketing Manager: Joyce Altauia
Director Sales: Sean Kohl
Sales Manager: Michael Goliner
District Manager of Rheology: Howard Eubanks
Number Employees: 100-249

28393 Rheon
445 Holly Street
Laguna Beach, CA 92651-1746 949-497-3150
Fax: 949-497-3951 cnaess@home.com
Manufacturer, importer and exporter of food processing equipment including automated mass production lines and flexible compact tables

28394 Rheon USA
13400 Reese Blvd W
Huntersville, NC 28078 704-875-9191
Fax: 704-875-9595 rheonusa@earthlink.net
www.rheonusa.com
Manufacturer, importer and exporter of food processing equipment including automated mass production lines and flexible compact tables
General Manager: Kiyo Kamiyama
Sales Coordinator: Terry Smith
Manager Engineering Sales: Kazu Onuki
Estimated Sales: $500,000-$1 Million
Number Employees: 1-4
Brands:
Cwc System
Ez Table

28395 Rheon, U.S.A.
9490 Toledo Way
Irvine, CA 92618 949-768-1900
Fax: 949-855-1991 usinfo@rheon.com
www.rheon.com
Dough sheet & pastry equipment, bread equipment and encrusting machines.

28396 Rhino Foods
79 Industrial Pkwy
Burlington, VT 05401 802-862-0252
Fax: 802-865-4145 800-639-3350
info@rhinofoods.com www.rhinofoods.com
Founded in 1981. Manufacturer of frozen desserts including ice cream novelties, brownies, cookie dough batter, cakes, truffles, low fat, no fat, reduced sugars/NSA, trans fat free
President/Owner: Ted Castle
Marketing Director: Dan Kiniry
Sales Manager: Gillian Bell
Director of Operations: Gene Steinfeld
Estimated Sales: $25 Million
Number Employees: 120
Square Footage: 29000
Type of Packaging: Consumer, Food Service, Private Label, Bulk
Brands:
Chessters
Vermont Velvet

28397 Rhoades Paper Box Corporation
PO Box 1666
Springfield, OH 45501 937-325-6494
Fax: 937-324-1597 800-441-6494
mikem@rhoades-paper-box.com
www.3g-graphics.com
Paper set-up boxes used for fine candies
Owner: Jeanie Lape
Sales Manager: Pat Hays
Estimated Sales: $2.5 - 5 Million
Number Employees: 20-49
Square Footage: 50000
Parent Co: Graphic Paper Products Corporation

28398 Rhode Island Label Works
14 Clyde St
West Warwick, RI 02893 401-828-6400
Fax: 401-828-8884 sales@rilabel.com
www.rilabel.com
Seals and labels including UPC/bar code, pressure sensitive, gum, ungummed and transfer
President: William H Cole
Estimated Sales: Below $5 Million
Number Employees: 1-4
Square Footage: 5000

28399 Rhodes Bakery Equipment
14330 SW McFarland Boulevard
Portland, OR 97224-2906 503-232-9101
Fax: 503-232-9206 800-426-3813
sales@kook-e-king.com www.kook-e-king.com
Manufacturer and exporter of cookie depositors and cutters
Marketing/Sales: Jan Duncan
Number Employees: 10-19
Square Footage: 120000
Brands:
Kook-E-King

28400 Rhodes Machinery International
1350 S 15th St
Louisville, KY 40211-2002 502-778-7377
Fax: 502-778-8526 r7727282@aol.com
www.rsisystemsinc.net
Manufacturer and exporter of tow line conveyors
President: William Rhodes
Plant Manager: Mark Wolford
Estimated Sales: $1 - 3 Million
Number Employees: 5-9
Parent Co: Rhodes Systems Worldwide
Type of Packaging: Bulk

28401 (HQ)Rhodia
8 Cedar Brook Dr
Cn 7500
Cranbury, NJ 08512 609-860-4000
Fax: 609-409-8652 800-343-8324
www.rhodia.us
Processor, importer and exporter of food and beverage ingredients including phosphates, bicarbonates, hydrocolloids, xanthan, guar and locust bean gum, vanillin, antioxidants, low/no fat systems, emulsifiers, stabilizers, startercultures, colors, etc
President/North America: James Harton
CFO: Mark Dahlinger
Plant Manager: William McConnell
Purchasing Performance & Quality Mgr.: Bill Kehayes
Estimated Sales: $324.8 Million
Number Employees: 1800
Square Footage: 90000
Parent Co: Rhodia SA
Brands:
Rhovanil® Natural
Rhodiarome®
Rhovanil®
Rhovea™

28402 Ricca Chemical Co.
1490 Lammers Pike
Batesville, IN 47006-8631 817-461-5601
Fax: 812-689-4061 888-467-4222
redbirdser@aol.com www.riccachemical.com
Laboratory chemicals used for quality control
President: Peter J Ricca
Estimated Sales: $5-10 Million
Number Employees: 10-19

28403 Rice Lake Weighing Systems
230 West Coleman Street
Rice Lake, WI 54868
Fax: 715-234-6967 www.ricelake.com
Manufacturer and exporter of electronic scales, weighing instrumentation and process control systems
Manager: Mark Patty
VP: Doro Maffia
Marketing Manager: Mark Patty
Number Employees: 10-19
Square Footage: 120000
Brands:
Flexi-Weigh

28404 (HQ)Rice Lake Weighing Systems
230 West Coleman Street
Rice Lake, WI 54868 715-234-9171
Fax: 715-234-6967 800-472-6703
prodinfo@ricelake.com www.ricelake.com
Manufacturer and exporter of heavy capacity scales and computer interface equipment; also, full metal services available
VP: Rick Tyree
Regional Sales Director: Matt Crawford
Estimated Sales: $2.5-5 Million
Number Employees: 20-49
Square Footage: 100000

28405 Rice Lake Weighing Systems
P.O.Box 272
Rice Lake, WI 54868
Fax: 715-234-6967 800-472-6703
prodinfo@ricelake.com www.ricelake.com
Manufacturer and exporter of stainless steel scales, indicators, load cellsand related weighing equipment; also, thermal direct label printers
President: Mark Johnson
Sales: Chris Olsen
Estimated Sales: $20 - 50 Million
Number Employees: 250-499
Square Footage: 225000
Brands:
Cw
Iq Plus
Survivor
Survivor Sst

28406 Rice Packaging
356 Somers Rd
Ellington, CT 06029 860-872-8341
Fax: 860-872-0880 800-367-6725
info@ricepackaging.com
www.ricepackaging.com
Custom printed folding cartons, stock boxes, point of purchase displays and pressure sensitive and embossed foil labels
President: Clifford B Rice
Sales Manager: Angelo Salvatore
Estimated Sales: $10-20 Million
Number Employees: 50-99

28407 Rice Paper Box Company
PO Box 62096
1187 East 68th Avenue
Colorado Springs, CO 80962-2096 303-733-1000
Fax: 303-733-6789
info@riceridgeboxcompany.com
www.ridgeridgeboxcompany.com
Rigid set up, folding and transparent paper boxes
President: Douglas E Miller
CFO: David Rice
VP: Eugene Rice
Sales/Marketing: Michael Porter
Director of Operations: Matt Juhasz
Estimated Sales: Below $5 Million
Number Employees: 45

28408 Riceselect
1925 FM 2917
Alvin, TX 77511 281-393-3502
Fax: 281-393-3811 800-993-7423
reception@ricetec.com www.riceselect.com

Aromatic rice, texmati, organic, whole grain, royal blend, world rice, couccous, orzo, rice medleys, and side dishes.
President: John Nelsen
Ceo: John Zimmerman
VP Finance: Tena Bressler
VP Marketing: Lewis Fernandez
Human Resources Director: Jim Walker
COO/VP Sales & Marketing: Mark Denman
Production Manager: Richard Pittman
Estimated Sales: $23081227
Number Employees: 200
Square Footage: 1260
Type of Packaging: Consumer, Food Service, Private Label, Bulk
Brands:
Chef's Original
Jasmati Rice
Rice Select
Texmati Rice

28409 Rich Xiberta Excell Corks
450 Aaron Street
Cotati, CA 94931-3016 707-795-1800
Fax: 707-795-1667 rxusa@xiberta.com
www.xiberta.com
Natural, high-end quality cork manufacturers
President: Ferran Botifoll
Estimated Sales: Below $5 Million
Number Employees: 5-9

28410 Richard Read Construction Company
302 North First Avenue Suite #2
Arcadia, CA 91006 626-445-3002
Fax: 626-445-1027 888-450-7343
RRCCO@Pacbell.net www.rrcco.net
Plastic containers and bottles
Owner: Richard Read
Estimated Sales: $1 - 5 Million
Number Employees: 1-4

28411 Richards Industries Systems
4 Fairfield Cres
West Caldwell, NJ 07006 973-575-7480
Fax: 973-575-6783 www.rifab.com
Bucket Z-type conveyors, dumpers, skip hoists and material lifts; also, steel fabricators for all shapes and forms of industrial equipment
Owner: Chuck Wampler
VP: Chuck Wampler
Sales: Paul Verrengia
Estimated Sales: $5 - 10 Million
Number Employees: 10-19
Square Footage: 25000

28412 Richards Packaging
4721 Burbank Rd
Memphis, TN 38118-6302 901-360-1121
Fax: 901-360-0050 800-583-0327
richardspkg-memphis@worldnet.att.net
www.richardsmemphis.com
Manufacturer, exporter and importer of glass and plastic bottles and jars; also, droppers, sprayers and closures
President: Robert Boord
CEO: Robert Boord
Estimated Sales: $10 Million
Number Employees: 10-19
Number of Brands: 100
Number of Products: 1000
Square Footage: 30000

28413 Richards Packaging
4721 Burbank Rd
Memphis, TN 38118-6302 901-360-1121
Fax: 901-360-0050 800-361-6453
richardspkg-memphis@worldnet.att.net
www.richardsmemphis.com
Manufacturer, importer and exporter of glass and plastic containers; also, plastic and metal closures; wholesaler/distributor of packaging containers and accessories
President: Robert Boord
VP Operations: Benoit Lavictoire
Estimated Sales: $5 - 10 Million
Number Employees: 10-19
Square Footage: 168000

28414 Richardson Oilseed Ltd.
2800 One Lombard Pl
Winnipeg, MB R3B 0X8
Canada 204-934-5287
Fax: 204-943-6065 800-635-3296
sharon.jones@richardson.ca www.richardson.ca
Canola-based oils, margarine and shortening supplying retail, foodservice, food processors and industrial bakeries worldwide.
President: Curt Vossen
Manager: Patrick Van Osch
Estimated Sales: $149.39 Million
Number Employees: 1600+
Type of Packaging: Consumer, Food Service, Private Label, Bulk

28415 Richardson Researches
480 Grandview Drive
South San Francisco, CA 94080 650-589-5764
Fax: 510-785-6857 info@richres.com
www.richres.com
Consultant for new products and process development; also, courses available in chocolate and confectionery technology
President: Terence Richardson
CEO: Rose Marie Richardson
VP: RM Richardson
Estimated Sales: $1-2.5 Million
Number Employees: 5-9

28416 Richardson Seating Corporation
2545 W Arthington St
Chicago, IL 60612 312-829-4040
Fax: 312-829-8337 800-522-1883
sales@richardsonseating.com
www.richardsonseating.com
Bar and counter stools, logo seating and stack, dining, upholstered and club chairs and consumer furniture
Owner/CEO: Earl Lichtenstein
National Sales Manager: Jim Spatzek
Estimated Sales: $10-20 Million
Number Employees: 50-99
Square Footage: 75000

28417 Richardson's Stamp Works
8566 Katy Fwy
Suite 124
Houston, TX 77024-1811 713-973-0300
Fax: 713-973-0314 nmame@ezi.zip
Stamp pad ink, name plates and badges, signs and rubber and plastic stamps
President: Marjorie Waltman
Estimated Sales: $300,000-500,000
Number Employees: 5-9

28418 (HQ)Richmond Corrugated BoxCompany
PO Box 7715
Richmond, VA 23231 804-222-1300
Fax: 804-222-4897 chuckw@richbox.com
www.richbox.com
Corrugated boxes and die cut products
President: Mark Williams
Vice President/General Manager: Chuck White
Structural Design: Wayne Johnson
Quality Control: Walters Spence
Sales: George Bayer
Customer Service Mgr: Shawn Ways
Sales Manager: Mike Kelly
Production Manager: Mark Lawrence
Estimated Sales: $2.5 - 5 Million
Number Employees: 20-49
Square Footage: 48000
Other Locations:
Richmond Corrugated BoxCo.
Wilmington NC

28419 Richmond Printed Tape &Label
1901 N Penn Road
Hatfield, PA 19440-1961 804-798-4753
Fax: 804-798-0632 800-522-3525
rptl@eathlink.net www.rptl.com
Pressure sensitive tapes and labels
President: Scott Moeller
Quality Control: Kevin Moller
Manager Sales/Marketing: Mark Moeller
Estimated Sales: Below $5 Million
Number Employees: 15

28420 Richway Industries
504 N Maple St
PO Box 508
Janesville, IA 50647 319-987-2976
Fax: 319-987-2251 800-553-2404
info@richwayind.com www.richway.com
Chemicals and equipment
President: Richard Borglum
Estimated Sales: $5-10 Million
Number Employees: 20-49

28421 Rico Packaging Company
3617 S Ashland Avenue
Chicago, IL 60609-1320 773-523-9190
Fax: 773-523-7965
Manufacturer and exporter of printed flexible packaging
President: William Wrigeyjr
CFO: Carol Riley
Manager: Don Bicking
R & D: William Wrigeyjr
Estimated Sales: $10-20 Million
Number Employees: 10
Parent Co: Wrigley

28422 Ricoh Technologies
1022 Santerre St
Grand Prairie, TX 75050-1937 972-602-0210
Fax: 972-602-3126 800-585-9367
Commercial fryers
President: Mac Shinagawa
Sales Representative: David Coronado
Estimated Sales: $2.5-5,000,000
Number Employees: 20-49
Parent Co: Sivex Corporation
Brands:
Aqua Pro

28423 Ridg-U-Rak
120 South Lake Street
North East, PA 16428-1232 814-725-8751
866-479-7225
www.ridgurak.com
Racks including storage, flow, pushback, structural and cold-formed; custom designing available
National Sales Manager: Dave Olson
Estimated Sales: $27 Million
Number Employees: 350
Square Footage: 200000

28424 RidgeView Products LLC
2527 East Avenue S
La Crosse, WI 54601-6759 608-781-5946
Fax: 608-781-4408 888-782-1221
info@ridgeviewproducts.com
www.ridgeproducts.com
Manufacurer of brush and broom products
President: Keith Martin
Marketing/Sales: Roshelle Easterday
Number Employees: 4

28425 Rieke Packaging Systems
500 W 7th St
Auburn, IN 46706 260-925-3700
Fax: 260-925-2493 sales@riekecorp.com
www.riekepackaging.com
Manufacturer and exporter of dispensing equipment including pumps, pourspouts and faucets
CEO: Lynn Brooks
CFO: Chris Baron
VP: Don Laipple
Marketing Director: Wayne Schmidt
Director Of Sales: William Heimach
Purchasing Manager: Jim Szink
Estimated Sales: $1 - 5,000,000
Number Employees: 250-499
Type of Packaging: Consumer, Food Service
Brands:
Englass
Flexspout
Flo-King
Flo-Rite
Fnd-30
Hybrid
Maxi
Multi-Meter
R-30

28426 Rietschle
1800 Gardner Expy
Quincy, IL 62305
Fax: 410-712-4148 800-247-2158
info@rietschlepumps.com
www.rietchlepumps.com

Vacuum pumps and compressors
President: Stephen J Lovell
Marketing Manager: Ron Heller
Estimated Sales: $10 - 20 Million
Number Employees: 60

28427 Rig-A-Lite
8500 Hansen Road
PO Box 12942
Houston, TX 77217-2942 713-943-0340
Fax: 713-943-8354 garybarber@azz.com
www.azz.com/rigalite
Innovative and energy efficient lighting solutions for food processing environments, where rugged lighting products are required. Offer a complete line of high pressure hose down and corrosion resistant lighting products for severeenvironments suitable for almost any applications using florescent, HID, incandescent and LED lamping.
R&D: Syed Hasan
Marketing: Ross Blanford
Sales: Paul Markee
Operations: Walter Despain
Purchasing: Gordon Logan
Estimated Sales: $10-25 Million
Number Employees: 100
Parent Co: AZZ incorporated

28428 Rigidized Metals Corporation
658 Ohio St
Buffalo, NY 14203 716-849-4760
Fax: 716-849-0401 800-836-2580
rmcsales@rigidized.com www.rigidized.com
Manufacturer, importer and exporter of embossed metal parts for conveyors, packaging machinery and food processing equipment
Manager: Os Putman
VP Sales: Louis Martin
Estimated Sales: $2.5-5,000,000
Number Employees: 20-49
Brands:
Rigid-Tex
Rigidized

28429 Riley & Geehr
2205 Lee Street
Evanston, IL 60202-1559 847-869-8100
Fax: 847-869-4765 www.rileyflex.com
Flexible pouches, stand-up pouches, shaped pouches, zipper pouches
CEO: Tom Riley
Sales Director: Diane Riley
Estimated Sales: $5-10 Million
Number Employees: 80
Type of Packaging: Consumer, Food Service, Private Label, Bulk

28430 Riley Cole ProfessionalRecruitment
4110 Redwood Road
Suite 201
Oakland, CA 94619-2370 510-336-2333
Fax: 510-428-2072
Executive search firm
Co-Partner: Donald Cole
Co-Partner: James Riley
Partner: James Riley
Estimated Sales: Below $5 Million
Number Employees: 2

28431 Rimex Metals
2850 Woodbridge Ave
Edison, NJ 08837-3616 732-549-3800
Fax: 732-549-6435 sales@rimexusa.com
www.rimexmetals.com
President: John Horbal
Estimated Sales: $10 - 20 Million
Number Employees: 20-49

28432 Rio Syrup Company
2311 Chestnut Street
Saint Louis, MO 63103-2298 314-436-7701
Fax: 314-436-7707 800-325-7666
flavors@riosyrup.com www.riosyrup.com
Manufacturer and exporter of syrups, extracts and concentrates for shaved ice, sno cones, slush flavors and bases and fountain syrups; also manufacturer of liquid food colors
President: Phillip Tomber
CEO: Bill Tomber
Operations/Public Relations: William Tomber
Estimated Sales: $500,000-$1 Million
Number of Brands: 3
Number of Products: 1200
Square Footage: 92000
Type of Packaging: Consumer, Food Service, Bulk
Brands:
Rio

28433 Ripon Manufacturing Company
652 S Stockton Ave
Ripon, CA 95366 209-599-2148
Fax: 209-599-3114 800-800-1232
sales@riponmfgco.com www.riponmfgco.com
Manufacturer and exporter of edible nut processing equipment and conveyance systems
President: Glenn Navarro
VP: Ernst Boesch
Sales: Bruce Boyd
Purchasing: Denise Judd
Estimated Sales: $6 Million
Number Employees: 20-49
Square Footage: 63000

28434 Risco USA Corporation
60 Bristol Dr
PO Box 198
South Easton, MA 02375 508-230-3336
Fax: 508-230-5345 888-474-7267
info@riscousa.com www.riscousa.com
Equipment manufacturer to the meat and poultry industry which includes; stuffers, vacuum stuffers and systems
President: Alan Miller
VP: P Kean
Technician: Victor Silva
Estimated Sales: $2.5-$5 Million
Number Employees: 20-49

28435 Rite-Hite Co.
8900 N Arbon Dr
Milwaukee, WI 53223 414-355-2600
Fax: 414-355-9248 888-841-4283
info@ritehite.com www.ritehite.com
Doors for industrial freezers and coolers.
Owner/Chairman: Michael White

28436 Rite-Hite Corporation
8900 North Arbon Drive
Milwaukee, WI 53223 414-355-2600
Fax: 414-355-9248 888-841-4283
info@ritehite.com www.ritehite.com
Industrial impact and power doors; also, dock safety equipment including seals and shelters
Chairman: Mike White
President: Mark Petri
CEO: Jeff Schwager
Number Employees: 100-249

28437 Rite-Hite Doors
P.O.Box 245020
Milwaukee, WI 53224-9520 414-355-2640
Fax: 414-355-9248 800-456-0600
info@ritehite.com www.ritehite.com
President: Glenn Manich
CEO: Michael White
Estimated Sales: I
Number Employees: 500-999

28438 Ritt-Ritt & Associates
5105 Tollview Drive
Suite 110
Rolling Meadows, IL 60008-3724 847-827-7771
Fax: 847-827-9776 info@rittsearch.com
Executive search firm specializing in job placement for the food and hospitality industries
Chairman: Art Ritt
President: William Morris
Estimated Sales: Less than $500,000
Number Employees: 1-4
Square Footage: 2200

28439 Ritz Packaging Company
54 Knickerbocker Avenue
Brooklyn, NY 11237-1636 718-366-2300
Fax: 631-476-4358
Paper boxes for ravioli, pasta, doughnuts, breadsticks and candy
*Estimated Sales:*less than $500,000
Number Employees: 1-4

28440 (HQ)Rival Manufacturing Company
800 E 101st Terrace
Suite 100
Kansas City, MO 64131-5308 816-943-4100
Fax: 816-943-4123 www.rivco.com
Manufacturer and exporter of can openers, vegetable and fruit shredders/slicers, mini choppers, slow cookers and ice cream freezers
Number Employees: 100-249
Other Locations:
Rival Manufacturing Co.
Kansas City MO
Brands:
Chop 'n Shake
Crock Pot
Dolly Madison

28441 River City Sales and Marketing Company
11700 Congo Ferndale Rd
Alexander, AR 72002-7007 501-316-3663
Fax: 501-794-0605
Owner: Vick Pannell
Estimated Sales: $1 - 5 Million
Number Employees: 1-4

28442 River Road Vineyards
5220 Ross Rd
Sebastopol, CA 95472-2158 707-887-2243
Fax: 707-887-8160
wine@riverroadvineyards.com
www.riverroadvineyards.com
Wine; custom labels available
Estimated Sales: Under $500,000
Number Employees: 1-4
Type of Packaging: Private Label
Brands:
River Road Vineyards

28443 Riverside Industries
PO Box D
St Helens, OR 97051-0280 503-397-1922
Fax: 503-397-1527
riverside@columbia-center.com
Contract packager of liquids, powders, creams and solids
Executive Director: Cindy Stockton
Director Marketing: John Briggs
Number Employees: 50-99
Square Footage: 8000

28444 (HQ)Riverside ManufacturingCompany
301 Riverside Drive
P.O. Box 460
Moultrie, GA 31776-0460
800-841-8677
www.riversideuniforms.com
Manufacturer and exporter of industrial uniforms and clothing for bottlers, bakers, dairy workers, security officers and distillers
President/Chief Executive Officer: Lisa Vereen Zeanah
Estimated Sales: $104 Million
Number Employees: 2,000
Square Footage: 1000000
Brands:
Riverside

28445 Riverside ManufacturingCompany
3405 N Arlington Heights Rd
Arlington Hts, IL 60004-1581 847-577-9300
Fax: 847-577-9318 800-877-3349
info@flagmaster.org
www.riversidemedicalsc.com
Manufacturer and exporter of custom made plastic and fluorescent display pennants, flags and banners
VP Marketing: Andy Krupp
Estimated Sales: $1 - 5 Million
Number Employees: 20-49
Square Footage: 80000
Type of Packaging: Food Service
Brands:
Flagmaster

28446 Riverside Wire & Metal Co.
PO Box 122
Ionia, MI 48846-0122 616-527-3500
Fax: 616-527-8550
Wire racks and baskets
Owner: Don Shephard
Estimated Sales: $500,000-$1 Million
Number Employees: 5-9
Parent Co: Col-Mell
Type of Packaging: Consumer, Food Service

28447 **Riverwood International**
3350 Riverwood Pkwy SE
Atlanta, GA 30339-6401 770-984-5477
Fax: 770-644-2620
suzanne.johnson@graphicpkg.com
www.riverwood.com
Packaging systems and machinery for beverages, produce, etc
President: Stephen Humphrey
CEO: Stephen Humphrey
CFO: Don Baldwin
Estimated Sales: $50 - 100 Million
Number Employees: 100-249

28448 **Riverwood International**
814 Livingston Ct SE
Marietta, GA 30067-8940 770-644-3000
Fax: 770-644-2962
investor.relations@graphicpkg.com
www.riverwood.com
Paperboard and paperboard packaging machinery company
President: Thomas H Johnson
CEO: David W Scheible
Marketing Manager: Hous King
Estimated Sales: $50-100 Million
Number Employees: 10,000

28449 **(HQ)Riviana Foods**
2777 Allen Parkway
PO Box 2636
Houston, TX 77019-2141 713-529-3251
Fax: 713-529-1866 sales@riviana.com
www.riviana.com
Rice and rice products.
President & CEO: Bastiaan de Zeeuw
VP Industrial, Foodservice & Exp. Sales: Enrique Zaragoza
Vice President & CFO: Gregory Richardson
Vice President of Logistics: Joseph Marelli
VP Sales & Customer Development: R. Shane Faucett
Vice President of Marketing: Paul Galvani
Vice President of Retail Sales: Joseph DeMarco
Vice President Human Resources: Gerard Ferguson
Vice President of Operations: Brett Beckfield
Estimated Sales: $302.7 Million
Number Employees: 2752
Square Footage: 57500
Type of Packaging: Consumer, Food Service, Private Label, Bulk
Other Locations:
Carlisle AR
Clearbrook MN
Brands:
Carolina
Gourmet House
Mahatma
Minute
River
Success
Water Main

28450 **Rjo Associates**
3645 Cortez Rd W Ste 140
Bradenton, FL 34210 941-756-3001
Fax: 941-756-0027 admin@mriflorida.com
Search consultants for technical product development and marketing in food and food ingredient manufacturing
President: R Rush Oster
Estimated Sales: Less than $500,000
Number Employees: 1-4
Parent Co: Management Recruiters

28451 **Ro-An Industries Corporation**
6420 Admiral Ave
Flushing, NY 11379 718-366-8971
Fax: 718-821-3838 800-255-7626
www.roan.com
Plastic bag machinery
President: Angelo Cervera
Estimated Sales: $10-20 Million
Number Employees: 100-249

28452 **RoMatic Manufacturing Company**
1200 Main St S
Southbury, CT 06488 203-264-8203
Fax: 203-264-3442
Metal caps for bottles, cans and jars
President: Roger Hebert
CEO: Rob Pecci
Estimated Sales: $20-50 Million
Number Employees: 100-249

28453 **RobaTech USA**
1005 Alderman Dr
Suite 108
Alpharetta, GA 30005 770-663-8380
Fax: 770-663-8381 info@robatechusa.com
www.robatechusa.com
President: Marcel Lynch
CEO: Marcel Leuthner
Estimated Sales: $1 - 3 Million
Number Employees: 1-4

28454 **RobaTech USA**
1005 Alderman Dr
Suite 108
Alpharetta, GA 30005 770-663-8380
Fax: 770-663-8381 info@robatechusa.com
www.robatechusa.com
Hot melt and cold adhesive application equipment, patten controls
CEO: Marcel Leuthner
CEO: Beat Stauble
Marketing Director: Beat Stauble
Estimated Sales: $500,000-$1 Million
Number Employees: 1-4
Parent Co: Robatech Group

28455 **Robar International**
3013 N 114th St
Milwaukee, WI 53222 414-259-1104
Fax: 414-259-0842 800-279-7750
rhoelzl@robarinternational.com
www.robarinternational.com
Dispoza-Pak trash compactors.
President: Robert Hoelzl
VP: Daniel Hoelzl
Estimated Sales: Below $5 Million
Number Employees: 5-9
Brands:
Dispoza-Pak

28456 **Robbie Manufacturing**
10810 Mid America Dr
Shawnee Mission, KS 66219 913-492-3400
Fax: 913-492-1543 800-255-6328
www.robbiemfg.com
Packaging equipment and materials
President/CEO: Irv Robinson
COO: Pepper Stokes
Executive VP Sales/Marketing: Doug Larson
Product Development Director: Jeff Linton
Estimated Sales: $20 - 50 Million
Number Employees: 100-249
Square Footage: 94596
Type of Packaging: Food Service, Private Label

28457 **Robby Vapor Systems**
10224 NW 47th Street
Sunrise, FL 33351-7970 954-746-3080
Fax: 954-746-0036 800-888-8711
robbyvapor@aol.com www.robbyvapor.com
Manufacturer, importer and exporter of stainless steel vapor cleaning systems and carts
President: Fran Vogt-Strauss
Office Manager: Lisa Skewes
Estimated Sales: $500,000-$1 Million
Number Employees: 9
Square Footage: 22240
Brands:
Robby Vapor Systems
Vapor Dragon

28458 **Robecco**
99 Park Ave # 7
New York, NY 10016-1506 212-286-8585
Fax: 212-490-8966 sales@robecoinc.com
www.robecoinc.com
Supplier of vinyl sheeting
President: Maurice Rosenthal
Estimated Sales: $10-20 Million
Number Employees: 20-49

28459 **Robelan Displays**
395 Westbury Blvd
Hempstead, NY 11550 516-564-8600
Fax: 516-564-8077 865-564-8600
main@robelan.net www.robelan.net
Merchandising fixture and food display units; importer of theme props
President: Andrew Abatemarco
CFO: John Didiovanni
VP Sales: Rob Abutemarco
Customer Service: Carol Kirk
Estimated Sales: $5 - 10 Million
Number Employees: 50-99
Type of Packaging: Food Service

28460 **Robert Bosch Corporation**
P.O.Box 4601
Carol Stream, IL 60197 708-865-5200
Fax: 708-865-6430 www.boschusa.com
Filling and sealing equipment
President: Kurt W Liedtke
VP Food Confectionary Operation: John Staruch
CEO: Peter Marks
Marketing Manager: Marc Wortman
Estimated Sales: K
Number Employees: 10,000
Parent Co: Robert Bosch GmbH
Brands:
Svk
Trans-Zip

28461 **Robert C. Vincek DesignAssociates LLC**
30 Eric Trail
Sussex, NJ 07461 973-702-8553
Fax: 973-702-8553 rcvdes@warwick.net
www.rcvdes.com
Consulting firm providing packaging design, development, engineering, graphics, validation, source reduction, troubleshooting and project management services
Estimated Sales: Below $500,000
Number Employees: 5

28462 **Robert's Packaging**
424 Howard Avenue
Des Plaines, IL 60018 847-390-9410
Fax: 847-390-6170 800-707-5070
rapidstart@robertspackaging.com
www.robertspackaging.com
Contract packager and manufacturer of high speed pouch packaging equipment
President: Robert G Koppe
Director Sales/Marketing: Michael Boyd
Estimated Sales: $2.5-5 Million
Number Employees: 20-49
Square Footage: 40000

28463 **Robert-James Sales**
699 Hertel Ave
Buffalo, NY 14207-2341 716-871-0091
Fax: 716-871-0923 800-777-1325
RJSales@RJSales.com www.RJSales.com
Manufacturer and exporter of fittings, pipes, tubing, hose clamps and sanitary stainless steel valves
Sales Manager: Thomas Callahan
Estimated Sales: $50-100 Million
Number Employees: 100-249

28464 **Robertet Flavors, Inc.**
201 Circle Drive N.
Suite 108
Piscataway, NJ 08854-3723 732-981-8300
Fax: 732-981-1717
robertetFlavors@robertetUSA.com
www.robertet.com
Aromatic products mainly used for food flavouring industry
Chairman & CEO: Philippe Maubert
Head of the Flavourings Division: Olivier Maubert
CFO: Gilles Audoli
General Manager of Flavourings Division: Antoine Kastler
Head of Development: Jean-Daniel Dor
Industrial Dir. for Perfume & Flavour: Herve Bellon
Estimated Sales: $480.05 Million
Number Employees: 1,059
Number of Brands: 5+
Square Footage: 16805
Parent Co: Robertet SA
Type of Packaging: Food Service
Other Locations:
Robertet Culinary
Schoten, Belgium
Brands:
Citra-Next®
Natur-Cell®

Flavour Sensations
Smart® Flavours
Accord® Flavours

28465 Roberts Gordon
P.O.Box 44
Buffalo, NY 14240 716-852-4400
Fax: 716-852-0854 800-828-7450
www.rg-inc.com
Gas-fired infrared heaters and energy management systems
CEO: Paul Dines
R & D: Mak Murdlch
Marketing Director: Madonna Courtney
Sales Director: Kevin Mahoney
Plant Manager: Roy Wyzykowski
Purchasing Manager: Judith Cloon
Estimated Sales: $20-50 Million
Number Employees: 100-249

28466 Roberts Pallet Company
PO Box 790
Ellington, MO 63638 573-663-7877
Fax: 573-663-7873
Wooden pallets
President: Jack Roberts
VP: Wes Roberts
Estimated Sales: Less than $500,000
Number Employees: 5-9
Square Footage: 9000

28467 Roberts PolyPro
5416 Wyoming Ave
Charlotte, NC 28273 704-588-1794
Fax: 704-588-1821 800-269-7409
info@robertspolypro.com
www.robertspolypro.com
Manufacturer and exporter of converting equipment and systems including folder/gluers, case packers, prefeeders, turntables, stack turners, etc.; also, plastic packaging components and machinery including label and pour spoutapplicators, etc
President: Allan Sutherland
VP Engineering: Claude Monsees
Estimated Sales: $5-10 Million
Number Employees: 50-99
Square Footage: 70000
Parent Co: Pro Mach

28468 Roberts Systems
8506 S Tryon St # A
Charlotte, NC 28273-3549 704-588-5210
Fax: 704-588-8199 800-269-7409
sales@robertssystems.com
www.robertssystems.com
Motion cartoner and automatic inserter
Estimated Sales: $.5 - 1 million
Number Employees: 1-4

28469 Roberts Technology Group
120 New Britain Blvd
Chalfont, PA 18914 215-822-0600
Fax: 215-822-0662 info@rtgpkg.com
www.rtgpkg.com
Quality Control: Debby Read
CEO: Robert S Cheatle Jr
CEO: Robert S Cheatle Jr
Sales: Tom Cheatle
Customer Service: Angela Frattone
Production Manager: Kevin Joyce
Estimated Sales: Below $5 Million
Number Employees: 10-19

28470 Roberts Technology Group
120 New Britain Blvd
Chalfont, 18 18936-9637 215-822-0600
Fax: 215-822-0662 info@rtgpkg.com
www.rtgpkg.com
Bandages bundling, shrink

28471 Robertson Furniture Company
890 Elberton St
Toccoa, GA 30577 706-886-1494
Fax: 706-886-8998 800-241-0713
tzirkle@robertson-furniture.com
www.robertson-furniture.com
Manufacturer and importer of chairs, tables, booths, steel frame seating and casegoods
President: Scott Hodges
Director Sales/Marketing: Tim Zirkle
Estimated Sales: $10 - 20 Million
Number Employees: 50-99
Square Footage: 200000
Type of Packaging: Food Service, Private Label

28472 Robin Shepherd Group
500 Bishopgate Ln
Jacksonville, FL 32204 904-359-0981
Fax: 904-359-0808 888-447-2823
www.trsg.net
Consultant providing food product development, point of purchase display design, public relations and marketing services; importer, exporter and packager of specialty foods including condiments and sauces
President: Robin Shepherd
VP Marketing: Tom Nuijens
Estimated Sales: $5-10 Million
Number Employees: 20-49
Square Footage: 10000
Type of Packaging: Consumer, Food Service, Private Label

28473 Robinett & Associates
2011 N Collins Blvd
Suite 701
Richardson, TX 75080-2689 972-234-1945
Consultant providing designing and engineering of heating, ventilation, air conditioning, plumbing, electrical, security, fire, smoke detection and alarm and energy management facilities
President: Robert Robinett
Estimated Sales: Less than $500,000
Number Employees: 1-4
Square Footage: 1600

28474 (HQ)Robinette Company
PO Box 3567
Bristol, TN 37625 423-968-7800
Fax: 423-968-7982 www.therobinetteco.com
Printed paper for flour, cornmeal, sugar, construction industry, and food industry
President: Joseph Robinette
CFO: Gary Hunt
Vice President: Gary Hunt
Quality Control: Payne Greg
Customer Service: Laura Mann
Estimated Sales: $20-50 Million
Number Employees: 250-499
Square Footage: 200000
Type of Packaging: Consumer, Food Service, Private Label
Other Locations:
Robinette Co.
Bristol TN
Brands:
Shinglgard
Shinglwrap

28475 Robinson Cone
PO Box 758
4350 Harvester Rd
Burlington, ON L7R 3Y7
Canada 905-333-1515
Fax: 905-333-1584 www.dovergrp.com
Cake and sugar ice cream cones, plastic and flex straws, stir sticks, paperboard pails and popcorn containers
VP: Chuck Gouett
Estimated Sales: $30 - 50 Million
Number Employees: 500-999
Parent Co: Dover Industries

28476 Robinson Industries
3051 W Curtis Rd
Coleman, MI 48618 989-465-6111
Fax: 989-465-1217 info@robinsonind.com
www.robinsonind.com
Manufacturer and exporter of thermoformed and injection molded plastic pallets, trays and totes. Also, consumer items. Custom designed.
President: Bin Robinson
CEO: Inez Kaleto
CFO: Kurt Schefka
Research & Development: Jeff Sankler
Quality Control: Rod Crites
Marketing: Ronda Robinson
VP Sales/Sales Manager: Mark Weidner
Production: Tom Roberts
Plant Manager: Melissa Jellum
Purchasing: Jason Pahl
Estimated Sales: $40 Million
Number Employees: 200
Square Footage: 152005

28477 Robinson Tape & Label
32 Park Drive East
Branford, CT 06405 203-481-5581
Fax: 203-481-6076 800-433-7102
robinson.tape@snet.net
www.robinsontapeandlabel.com
Pressure sensitive tapes and labels; wholesaler/distributor of tape machines and shipping supplies
President: Edward Pepe
Marketing: Sarah Yale
Sales: Mike Dellavalle
Production: Anthony Martone
Purchasing: Dennis Smith
Estimated Sales: $5-10 Million
Number Employees: 10-19
Square Footage: 11000
Type of Packaging: Consumer, Food Service, Private Label, Bulk

28478 Robinson/Kirshbaum Industries
8915 S La Cienega Boulevard
Suite F
Inglewood, CA 90301-7420 310-645-4993
Fax: 310-645-2034 800-929-3812
rkindustry@aol.com
Beverage equipment including dispensers, water filtration, etc
VP: Bruce Kirshbaum
Estimated Sales: $1-2,500,000
Number Employees: 5-9

28479 Robinson/Kirshbaum Industries
261 E 157th St
Gardena, CA 90248 310-354-9948
Fax: 310-354-9921 support@rki-inc.com
www.rki-inc.com
Beverage equipment including dispensers, water filtration, etc
President: Jon Robinson
Executive VP: Bruce Kirshbaum
R&D: Bruce Kirshbaum
Estimated Sales: Below $5 Million
Number Employees: 1-4

28480 Robocom Systems International
1111 Broadhollow Road
Suite 100
Farmingdale, NY 11735 631-753-2180
Fax: 516-795-6933 800-795-5100
info@robocom.com www.robocom.com
Develops and implements logistic warehouse solutions designed to maximize productivity and streamline warehouse operations. Services provide inlcude software development and installation, and support
CEO: Irwin Balaban
COO: Judy Frenkel
Vice President: Richard Adamo
President: Irwin Balaban
Estimated Sales: Below $5 Million
Number Employees: 25

28481 Robot Coupe USA
P.O.Box 16625
Jackson, MS 39236-6625 601-898-8411
Fax: 601-898-9134 800-824-1646
info@robotcoupeusa.com
www.robocoupeusa.com
Manufactures commercial food processors, vegetable preparation units, and combination processing units.
President: Jay Williams
VP: David Mouck
VP/Controller: C Redding
VP Marketing: David Mouck
National Accounts Manager: David Mouck
Estimated Sales: $10-20 Million
Number Employees: 50-99
Square Footage: 30000
Type of Packaging: Food Service
Brands:
Robot Coupe

28482 Robot Coupe USA, Inc.
P.O. Box 16625
Jackson, MS 39236-6625 601-898-8411
Fax: 601-898-9134 800-824-1646
nfo@robotcoupeusa.com
www.robotcoupeusa.com
Superior quality food processors, power mixers and vegetable prep machines.
MarketÿSolutions Advisor: Ron Snyder
Sales: Kevin Keith

28483 **(HQ)Robotic Vision Systems**
486 Amherst Street
Nashua, NH 03063-1224 781-821-0830
Fax: 781-828-8942 800-646-6664
info@rvsi.net www.roboticvisionsystems.com
Bar code scanners, data collection systems, decoders, machine vision, and scanners
Senior VP: John Agapakis
Estimated Sales: $1 - 5 Million
Number Employees: 100-249

28484 **Rocheleau Blow Molding Systems**
117 Industrial Road
Fitchburg, MA 01420-4697 978-345-1723
Fax: 978-345-5972 sales@rocheleautool.com
www.rocheleautool.com
Extrusion blow molding and plastic blow molding machinery
President: Steven Rocheleau
Number Employees: 10-19

28485 **Rochester Midland**
155 Paragon Dr
Rochester, NY 14624 585-336-2377
Fax: 909-548-4907 800-387-7174
barr@rochestermidland.com
www.rochestermidland.com
Deli and butcher paper and latex and poly gloves
Chairman/ CEO: H.D. Calkins
key person: Brenda Barr
National Sales Manager: Bob Guberman
Manager: Brenda Barr
National Account Manager: Matt Willoughby
Estimated Sales: $10 - 20 Million
Number Employees: 20-49

28486 **(HQ)Rochester Midland Corporation**
155 Paragon Drive
Rochester, NY 14624 585-336-2200
Fax: 585-266-8919 800-535-5053
webmaster@rochestermidland.com
www.rochestermidland.com
Cleaning/sanitary equipment and supplies including dish washing compounds, detergents, disinfectants, floor polish, chemicals, etc.; also, insecticides and insect control systems
CEO: Harlan D Calkins
Estimated Sales: $2.5-5 Million
Number Employees: 500-999

28487 **Rochester Midland Corporation**
155 Paragon Drive
Rochester, NY 14624 585-336-2200
800-836-1627
www.rochestermidland.com
Manufacturer and exporter of production cleaning and sanitizing chemicals for food and beverage processing facilities; also, water and wastewater treatment chemicals
President/Chief Operating Officer: Michael Coyner
Chief Financial Officer: Lisa Steel
Senior Vice President: Al Swierzewski
Senior Vice President, Marketing: Owen Foster
Vice President, Sales: Mike Burroughs
Senior Vice President, Operations: Howard Shames
Purchasing Manager: Richard Roy
Estimated Sales: $83 Million
Number Employees: 425
Square Footage: 190000
Brands:
Brandguard

28488 **Rock Tenn/Alliance Group**
411 E Carroll Street
Tullahoma, TN 37388-3947 931-455-3535
Fax: 931-393-6003 www.rocktenn.com
Manufacturer graphic laminated corrugated packaging
Operations-Production: Jim Vance
General Manager: Jim Vance
Manager Sales: Don Stanford
Manager Production: Bryan Dodson
Estimated Sales: $10-20 Million
Number Employees: 50-99
Square Footage: 88000
Parent Co: Rock-Tenn Company

28489 **Rock Valley Oil & Chemical Company**
1911 Windsor Rd
Rockford, IL 61111 815-654-2400
Fax: 815-654-2428 www.rockvalleyoil.com
'Today, Rock Valley has grown to be recognized as an international manufacturer and supplier of superior quality industrial lubricants, metalworking and hydraulic fluids, as well as reference oils and calibrating fluids tailored to theautomotive and heavy truck industry'. www.rockvalleyoil.com
President: Roger Schramm
Estimated Sales: $12.5 Million
Number Employees: 50-99
Brands:
Sun Oil
Viscor
Viscosity

28490 **Rock-Tenn Company**
16 Washington Ave
Scarborough, ME 04074-8311 207-883-8921
Fax: 207-883-5189 www.rocktenn.com
Packaging
General Manager: David Boudreau
Estimated Sales: $20 - 50 Million
Number Employees: 50-99

28491 **Rock-Tenn Company**
504 Tasman St
Norcross, GA 30071 608-223-6272
Fax: 608-246-1145 www.rocktenn.com
Manufacturer and exporter of folding paper cartons, boxes and displays
Owner: Bill Rock
General Manager: Gary Adrian
Estimated Sales: $5-10 Million
Number Employees: 1-4

28492 **(HQ)Rock-Tenn Company**
504 Thrasher Street
Norcross, GA 30071 770-448-2193
Fax: 770-291-7666 www.rocktenn.com
Produces containerboard and paperboard packaging for food, hardware, apparel and other consumer goods.
President & Chief Operating Officer: Steven Voohees
Chairman & Chief Executive Officer: James Rubright
Chief Accounting Officer: A. Stephen Meadows
Executive Vice President Human Resources: Jennifer Graham-Johnson
Estimated Sales: $9.2 Billion
Number Employees: 26,300
Type of Packaging: Consumer, Food Service, Private Label, Bulk

28493 **Rock-Tenn Company**
PO Box 64260
St Paul, MN 55164-0260 651-641-4874
Fax: 651-641-4149 investorrel@rocktenn.com
www.rocktenn.com
Indoor and outdoor electric and plastic signs
Manager: Greg Johnson
Manager: Ray Liorca
Estimated Sales: $100-500 Million
Number Employees: 500-999

28494 **Rockaway Baking**
PO Box 392
Rockaway, NJ 07866-0392 973-625-3003
Fax: 973-625-4271 877-762-5225
rockbake@aol.com
www.rockawaybakingmachine.com
Automatic equipment for baking industry; specializing in English muffin systems, materials handling conveyors, spiral conveyors for freezing, proofing and cooling
Estimated Sales: $1 Million
Number Employees: 2

28495 **Rocket Man**
2501 Maple St
Louisville, KY 40211-1163 502-775-7502
Fax: 502-775-7519 800-365-6661
sales@rocketman.com www.rocketman.com
Manufacturer, importer and exporter of backpack drink dispensers and portable beverage dispensing equipment
Owner: Mike Hinson
Estimated Sales: $1-3 Million
Number Employees: 10-19
Square Footage: 20000
Brands:
Rocket Man

28496 **Rockford Chemical Company**
915 W Perry St
Belvidere, IL 61008 815-544-3476
Fax: 815-544-0532
Boiler compounds
President: Vann Rossmiller
Estimated Sales: $1-2.5 Million
Number Employees: 1-4

28497 **Rockford Sanitary Systems**
5159 28th Ave
Rockford, IL 61109 815-229-5077
Fax: 815-229-5108 800-747-5077
rssem@inwave.com www.rkfdseparators.com
Grease, oil, sand and lint separators; also, trench drains
President: Merritt Mott
CEO: James Griffin
VP Engineering: Bryce Russell
Quality Control: Jim Griffin
Estimated Sales: $5 - 10 Million
Number Employees: 10-19
Square Footage: 34000

28498 **Rockford-Midland Corporation**
1715 Northrock Ct
Rockford, IL 61103 815-877-0212
Fax: 815-877-0419 800-327-7908
info@rockfordmidland.com
www.rockfordmidland.com
Manufacturer and exporter of fully and semi-automatic case packers and sealers including hot melt, cold glue and tape
President: Adrienne Murphy
Sales Director: Donna Bonetti
Production Manager: Tim Vronch
Purchasing Manager: Karen Steiner
Estimated Sales: $5-10 Million
Number Employees: 20-49
Square Footage: 40000
Brands:
Casestar
Sealstar

28499 **Rockland Foods**
300 Corporate Drive
Suite14
Blauvelt, NY 10913-1162 845-358-8600
Fax: 845-358-9003 800-962-7663
rfi@rfiingredients.com www.rfiingredients.com
Owner: Jeff Wuagneux
Quality Control: Pi-Yu Hsu
Estimated Sales: $1 - 5 Million
Number Employees: 10-19

28500 **Rockland Technology**
817 S Mill Street
Suite 104
Lewisville, TX 75057-4637 972-221-6190
Fax: 972-420-0055 support@rocklandtech.com
www.rocklandtech.com
President: Thomas Bronson
Estimated Sales: Below $5 Million
Number Employees: 20

28501 **Rockline Industries**
PO Box 1007
Sheboygan, WI 53082-1007 920-459-4160
Fax: 920-452-3611 800-558-7790
sales@rocklineind.com www.rocklineind.com
'Rockline is the largest supplier of coffee filters and private label baby wipes in North America'. from www.rocklineind.com
President: Randy Rudolph
VP Sales/Marketing: Ron Kerscher
Sr. VP Sales: Sam Salm
Estimated Sales: $100-500 Million
Number Employees: 250-499
Square Footage: 800000
Brands:
Bake Fresh
Brew Rite
Fresh'n Up
Natural Brew
Star

28502 **Rockwell Automation**
1201 S 2nd St
Milwaukee, WI 53204 414-382-2000
Fax: 414-382-4444 www.rockwellautomation.com

Industrial automation equipment, machinery and componets
Chairman/CEO: Keith Nosbusch
Senior Vice President/CFO: Theodore Crandall
Senior VP, Global Sales/Marekting: John McDermott
Senior VP, Operations/Engineering Servic: Marty Thomas
Estimated Sales: $6.2 Billion
Number Employees: 22,000

28503 Rockwell Automation
1201 S 2nd St
Milwaukee, WI 53204 414-382-2000
Fax: 414-382-4444
communication@rsc.rockwell.com
www.rockwellautomation.com
Controls, energy management
President: Keith Nosbusch
Quality Control: Pat Zolkmann
Senior VP: Theodore Crandell
R & D: Ram Pai
Estimated Sales: $1 Billion+
Number Employees: 10,000

28504 Rockwell Automation Software
1130 S 93rd St
Milwaukee, WI 53214-2709 414-321-8000
Fax: 414-321-9647 info@rockwellsoftware.com
www.softwarerockwell.com
Speed reducers, drives, gears, mounted bearings and mechanical transmission products; electric, electronic and industrial controls, converters, motors and telecommunications equipment
Owner: April Batchelor
Estimated Sales: $30 - 50 Million
Number Employees: 250-499

28505 Rockwell Automation, Inc.
1201 S. 2nd St.
Milwaukee, WI 53204-2496 414-382-2000
Fax: 414-382-4444 www.rockwellautomation.com
Power transmission and conversion products manufacturer
President: Joseph D Swann
Public Relations: Susan Trayler
Estimated Sales: $6.26 Billion
Number Employees: 22000
Brands:
Dodge & Reliance Electric

28506 Rockwell Automation/Electro
6950 Washington Ave S
Eden Prairie, MN 55344-3450 952-942-3600
Fax: 952-942-3636 800-328-3983
bjcasey@ra.rockwell.com
www.rockwellautomation.com
Servo systems and motors
President: Bob Becker
Chairman: Keith Nosbusch
Senior Vice President of Solutions: Blake Moret
Global Marketing Director: Brain Casey
Senior Vice President of Sales and Marke: John McDermott
Estimated Sales: $20 - 50 Million
Number Employees: 100-249
Parent Co: Rockwell International Corporation
Brands:
Electro-Craft

28507 Rocky Shoes & Boots
39 E Canal St
Nelsonville, OH 45764-1247 740-753-1951
Fax: 740-753-4024 www.rockyboots.com
Nonslip service shoes and boots
President: Mike Brooks
R&D: Mark Recchi
CFO: Jim McDonald
Quality Control: Kris Lewson
Director Sales: Don Johnson
Estimated Sales: I
Number Employees: 1,000-4,999
Brands:
4 Way Step

28508 Roddy Products PackagingCompany
PO Box 164
Aldan, PA 19018 610-623-7040
Fax: 610-623-0521 joearoddy@aol.com
www.roddypkg.com
Manufacturer and exporter of wooden shipping crates
President: Joseph Masticola Sr
CFO: Joseph Masticola Sr
Estimated Sales: $1 - 2.5 Million
Number Employees: 20-49

28509 Rodem Process Equipment
5095 Crookshank Rd
Cincinnati, OH 45238 513-922-6140
Fax: 513-922-1680 sales@rodem.com
www.rodem.com
Agitation systems, curd, milk, silo, tank, analyzers/tests, plant operations,chlorine, total solids, chillers, clean rooms and equipment, custom fabrication, deaerators, dispensers, milk, ice equipment, ingredient feeders, laddersvat, margarine process
President: Chris Diener
R&D: Stan Pritchart
Chairman of the Board: Robert Diener
Estimated Sales: $30 - 50 Million
Number Employees: 50-99

28510 Rodes Professional Apparel
4938 Brownsboro Road
Louisville, KY 40222 502-584-3112
Fax: 502-584-8840 info@rodes.com
www.rodes.com
Uniforms, aprons and shoes
President: Lawrence Smith
Number Employees: 80
Parent Co: Lithgow Industries

28511 Rodo Industries
44 Meg Drive
London, ON N6E 3R4
Canada 519-668-3711
Fax: 519-668-3257 rodo@rodoinc.com
www.rodoinc.com
Stacking and regular chairs, fast food seating, cushions, pads, bar/counter stools, tables including legs, bases and booths
President: Randy Snow
CFO: Gary Forgrade
R&D: Gary Forgrade
Quality Control: Gary Forgrade
Sales: Hugh Crosby
Estimated Sales: $3.5 Million
Number Employees: 45

28512 Roechling Engineered Plastics
PO Box 2729
Gastonia, NC 28053-2729 704-922-7814
Fax: 704-922-7651 800-541-4419
paul-krawczyk@roechling-plastics-us
www.roeplast.com
Manufacturer and exporter of conveyor components, industrial plastics, HDPE, PP, UHMW and PVDF; also, sheets, tubes and profiles
President: Lewis Carter
Quality Control: Brychan Griffiths
Marketing: Tim Brown
Sales: Paul Krawczyk
Number Employees: 50-99
Square Footage: 560000
Brands:
Polystone Cut-Rite
Sustamid
Sustarin
Sustatec

28513 Roechling Machined Plastics
1551 Woodward Drive Ext
Greensburg, PA 15601 724-834-1340
Fax: 724-834-5822 www.roechling-plastics.us
Fiberglass plastic machining
Estimated Sales: $20-50 Million
Number Employees: 20-49

28514 Roesch
P.O.Box 328
Belleville, IL 62222-0328 618-233-2760
Fax: 618-233-1186 800-423-6243
sales@roeschinc.com www.roeschinc.com
Enameling of steel and cast iron, stoves, refrigerators and specialty parts, including high temperature ceramic coatings and metal fabrications of sheet metal parts
President: Pauline Voges
Executive Vice President: Debbie Voges-Schneider
Sales Manager: Debbie Thomas
Estimated Sales: $10-20 Million
Number Employees: 100-249

28515 Roeslein & Associates
9200 Watson Rd
Suite 200
Saint Louis, MO 63126 314-729-0055
Fax: 314-729-0070 sales@roeslein.com
www.roeslein.com
President: Rudi Roeslein
CFO: Fritz Dickmann
Estimated Sales: $5 - 10 Million
Number Employees: 20-49

28516 Rofin-Baasel
68 Barnum Rd
Devens, MA 01434 978-635-9100
Fax: 978-635-9199 ctatosian@rofin-baasel.com
www.rofin-baasel.com
President: Walter Volkmar
Number Employees: 10

28517 Roflan Associates
5314 S Yale Avenue
Suite 1100
Tulsa, OK 74135-6251 978-475-0100
Fax: 978-475-4144
Lighting fixtures
VP/Manager: Mike Lacharite
Number Employees: 22

28518 Rohm America Inc.
2 Turner Place
Piscataway, NJ 08855 732-981-5250
Fax: 732-981-5382
Estimated Sales: $1 - 5 Million

28519 Rohrer Corporation
1800 Enterprise Drive
P.O. Box 1800
Buford, GA 30515 770-945-1050
Fax: 770-945-1121 800-243-6640
www.rohrer.com
Manufacturer and exporter of skin packaging, blister cards and stretch pack cards
Estimated Sales: $50-100 Million
Number Employees: 100-249
Type of Packaging: Bulk

28520 Rohrer Corporation
717 Seville Rd
Wadsworth, OH 44281 330-335-1541
Fax: 330-336-5147 droberts@rohrer.com
www.rohrer.com
Skin and blister packaging and die cutting service. Our additional capabilites include custom and combo run clamshell inserts, foldover polybag header cards, folding cartons, and specialty die cut cards
President: John Rohrer
VP: David Rohrer
Treasurer: Joanne Rohrer
Estimated Sales: $20-50 Million
Number Employees: 100-249
Number of Products: 9
Square Footage: 86000
Type of Packaging: Private Label, Bulk

28521 Rolfs @ Boone
1773 219th Ln
P.O. Box 369
Boone, IA 50036 515-432-2010
Fax: 515-432-5262 800-265-2010
info@boonegroup.com www.boonegroup.com
Manufacturer and exporter of dust systems, high and low bag filters, cyclones, ducting, fittings, bearing and belt alignment instrumentation and hazard and motion monitoring controls
President: Kevin Miles
Sales: Greg Knoxx
Dust Control: Delmar Mains
Production Manager: Brian Huffman
Estimated Sales: $5 - 10 Million
Number Employees: 10-19
Square Footage: 112000

28522 Roll Rite Corporation
26265 Research Road
Hayward, CA 94545-3725 510-293-1444
Fax: 510-293-1450 800-345-9305
info@rollrite.com www.roll-rite.net
Material handling equipment including factory hand trucks, wheels, casters, skewing racks and nonpowered equipment; exporter of wheels and casters
CEO/President: Mario Sequeira

Estimated Sales: $1-2.5 Million
Number Employees: 5-9
Square Footage: 8900
Brands:
Alumiflex
Areo
Bassick
Colson
Dutro
Hamilton
Magliner
Roll Rite Super Caster
Roll-Rite Corp.
Wesco

28523 Roll-O-Sheets Canada
130 Big Bay Point Road
Barrie, ON L4N 9B4
Canada 705-722-5223
Fax: 705-722-7120 888-767-3456
info@roll-o-sheets.com www.roll-o-sheets.com
Manufacturer, importer and exporter of converted PVC film; wholesaler/distributor of vacuum pouches, table covers, Cellophane and plastic sandwich and ovenable containers
General Manager: Bryce Atkinson
Number Employees: 20
Square Footage: 88000
Brands:
Row L
Row S
Wrap It

28524 Rolland Machining & Fabricating
43 Ventnor Avenue
Moneta, VA 24121-5350 973-827-6911
Fax: 973-827-5699
Custom fabricated plastic materials including ducts, fittings, tanks, trays, etc.; also, general machining in soft metals and plastic
President: Mary Rolland
Number Employees: 10
Square Footage: 4000

28525 Rollhaus Seating Products
2109 Borden Avenue
Long Island City
New York, NY 11101 718-729-9111
Fax: 718-729-9117 800-822-6684
info@seatingproducts.com
www.seatingproducts.com
Booths, chairs and folding tables
President: Michael Rollhaus
Estimated Sales: $2.5 - 5,000,000
Number Employees: 20-49

28526 Rollon Corporation
30 Wilson Dr Ste A
Sparta, NJ 07871 973-300-5492
Fax: 973-300-9030 877-976-5566
infocom.usa@rollon.com www.rollon.com
Estimated Sales: $5 Million
Number Employees: 5-9

28527 Rollprint Packaging Products
320 S Stewart Ave
Addison, IL 60101 630-458-9752
Fax: 630-628-8510 800-276-7629
mail@rollprint.com www.rollprint.com
Manufacturer and exporter of flexible food packaging materials including lidding, pouches, peelable and non-peelable composites. FlexForm and ClearForm line of forming webs provide tough, puncture resistant substrates that provideuniform film draw without snapback for frozen food applications including: poultry, meat, seafood, bakery, pizza, vegetables, fruits, and bakery goods.
President: Robert Dodrill
CFO: David Reed
Marketing Manager: Edward Verkuilen
Estimated Sales: $20-50 Million
Number Employees: 100-249
Square Footage: 198000
Type of Packaging: Consumer, Food Service, Private Label, Bulk
Brands:
Allegro
Clearfoil
Flexform
Forte
Multimix
Propapeel
Propaseal

28528 Rollstock
5720 Brighton Ave.
Kansas City, MO 64130 616-570-0430
Fax: 616-570-0430 800-295-2949
rollstockkc@aol.com www.rollstock.com
Horizontal form, fill and seal machine, vacuum, map, cap
Plant Manager: Gary Filippone
Estimated Sales: $1 - 5 Million
Number Employees: 10-19

28529 Rollstock, Inc.
5720 Brighton Ave
Kansas City, MO 64130 616-570-0430
Fax: 616-570-0430 800-954-6020
rollstockkc@aol.com www.rollstock.com
Vacuum packaging machines for the meat industry.
Parent Co: Azzar Group

28530 Romaco
6 Frassetto Way
Unit D
Lincoln Park, NJ 7035 973-605-5370
Fax: 973-605-1360 usa@romaco.com
www.romaco.com
Printing and labeling systems for bottles
Estimated Sales: $5-10 Million
Number Employees: 20-49

28531 Romanow Container
346 University Ave
Westwood, MA 02090 781-320-9200
Fax: 781-461-5900 www.romanowcontainer.com
Corrugated fiber boxes
Owner: Theodore Romanow
President: Theodore Romanow
Executive VP: Richard Romanow
Estimated Sales: $20-50 Million
Number Employees: 100-249
Square Footage: 145000

28532 Romanow Container Inc
346 University Ave
Westwood, MA 02090 781-320-9200
www.romanowcontainer.com
Manufacturer and exporter of corrugated and wooden boxes, foam converters and fabricators; also, contract packaging available
President: Barry Steinberg
Estimated Sales: $5-10 Million
Number Employees: 20-49

28533 Rome
P.O.Box 186
Sheldon, IA 51201-0186 712-324-5391
Fax: 712-324-5394 800-443-0557
rome@ncn.net www.rome.com
Processing equipment
President: Michael Weaver
Quality Control: Tim McDonald
Sales Director: Jim Justi
Estimated Sales: $10 - 20 Million
Number Employees: 20-49

28534 Rome Machine & Foundry Company, Inc
906 Walnut Ave
PO Box 5383
Rome, GA 30162-5383 706-234-6763
Fax: 706-232-0337 800-538-7663
jburnett@romemachine.com
www.romemachine.com
Manufacturer and exporter of custom fabricated conveyors and food processing machinery
President: Albert Berry
Sales/Marketing Manager: Willis Rogers
Chief Engineer: Jay Burnett
Purchasing Manager: Ted Porterfield
Estimated Sales: $1-2.5 Million
Number Employees: 10-19
Square Footage: 129600

28535 Romicon
1300 W Lodi Avenue
Suite 19a
Lodi, CA 95242-3000 209-333-8100
Fax: 209-333-2947
Wine industry filtration equipment
Estimated Sales: $500,000-$1 Million
Number Employees: 5-9

28536 Rommelag USA
P.O.Box 2530
Evergreen, CO 80437-2530 303-674-8333
Fax: 303-670-2666 mail@rommelag.com
www.rommelag.com
Supplier of packaging machinery specializing in blow/fill/seal machines for the aseptic filling of liquids in plastic
Manager: Tim Kram
President and General Manager: Anke Henke
Estimated Sales: Less than $500,000
Number Employees: 1-4

28537 Ron Teed & Associates
26W325 Menomini Dr
Wheaton, IL 60189-5987 630-462-7662
Fax: 630-462-7669 ronteed@aol.com
Owner: Ronald Teed
Estimated Sales: $.5 - 1 million
Number Employees: 1

28538 Ron Ungar Engineering
1595 Walter St
Suite 4
Ventura, CA 93003 805-642-3555
Fax: 805-642-0326 800-235-5644
uron21@sbcglobal.net www.ime-co.net
Owner: Ron Ungar
Estimated Sales: $1 - 3 Million
Number Employees: 5-9

28539 Ron Vallort & Associates
502 Forest Mews Dr
Oak Brook, IL 60523 630-734-3821
Fax: 630-734-3822 ronvallort@aol.com
Engineering and building consultants specializing in site planning, facility design, construction management and operational analysis for the food industry including processing, freezing, storage and distribution
President: Ron Vallort

28540 Ron Vallort AndAssociates,Ltd
2 S. Atrium Way
606
Elmhurst, IL 60126 630-334-3821
Fax: 630-734-3822 ronvallort@aol.com
www.ronvallort.com
Engineering and building consultants specializing in site planning,process design,facility design,construction management,expert investigation and building analysis for the food industry including processingfreezing,storage/distribution, sanitation and refrigeration.
President: Ron Vallot
Estimated Sales: Below $5 Million
Number Employees: 10

28541 RonI, Inc.
8026 Tower Point Drive
Charlotte, NC 28227 704-847-2464
Fax: 704-847-6739 866-543-8635
www.liftoflex.com
Automated ergonomic material handling systems and equipment.

28542 Ronchi America
63 Duncan Circle
Hiram, GA 30141 678-395-7413
Fax: 770-694-6071 info@ronchiamerica.com
www.ronchi.it
Plastic bottle unscramblers, bottle fillers, advanced flowmeter filling technology, pump cappers, case packaging, and integrated lines
VP: Frank Chitg
Estimated Sales: $2.5-5 Million
Number Employees: 9
Square Footage: 60000
Parent Co: Ronchi Mario

28543 Rondo Inc.
51 Joseph St
Moonachie, NJ 07074 201-229-9700
Fax: 201-229-0018 800-882-0633
info@us.rondo-online.com www.rondo-inc.com
Manufacturer, importer and wholesaler/distributor of high volume bakery equipment including mixers and sheeters
President: Jerry Murphy
VP Sales: Andrea Henderson
Estimated Sales: $2.5-5 Million
Number Employees: 10-19

28544 **Rondo of America**
209 Great Hill Rd
Naugatuck, CT 06770 203-723-7474
Fax: 203-723-5831
custserv@rondopackaging.com
www.rondopackaging.com
Manufacturer and exporter of protective packaging, automatic packaging machinery and paper boxes
Owner: James Sinkins
Estimated Sales: $5-10 Million
Number Employees: 20-49
Parent Co: Interrondo

28545 **Ronell Industries**
298 Cox St
Roselle, NJ 07203-1798 908-245-5255
Fax: 908-241-4244
www.ronellmanagedservices.com
Environmental services including cleaning and sanitation
President: Ronald Globerman
VP: John Carroll
Estimated Sales: $5 - 10 Million
Number Employees: 10-19

28546 **Ronnie Dowdy**
1839 Batesville Blvd
Batesville, AR 72501 870-251-3222
Fax: 870-251-3763 800-743-5611
www.ronniedowdy.com
Transportation firm providing refrigerated trucking services including local, long and short haul
Owner: Ronnie Dowdy
Owner: Sandra Dowdy
Number Employees: 250-499

28547 **Ronnie's Ceramic Company**
5999 3rd St
San Francisco, CA 94124 415-822-8068
Fax: 415-822-8966 800-888-8218
ronnie8@ronnie-ceramics.com
www.ronnie-ceramics.com
Manufacturer and exporter of tableware, platters, coffee mugs and water pitchers
President: Risly Cheung
Vice President: Risly Chin
Estimated Sales: $3 - 5,000,000
Number Employees: 15
Square Footage: 8500
Brands:
Ronnie's Ocean
Terramoto

28548 **Roofian**
8605 Kewen Ave
Sun Valley, CA 91352 818-768-9945
Fax: 818-768-9285 800-431-3886
roofian@juno.com www.roofian.com
Gift and floral baskets
President/Owner: Mayer Roofian
VP: Shahla Roofian
Estimated Sales: $1.1 Million
Number Employees: 8

28549 **(HQ)Rooto Corporation**
3505 W Grand River Ave
Howell, MI 48855 517-546-8330
Fax: 517-548-5162 rootocorp2@aol.com
www.rootocorp.com
Manufacturer and exporter of ammonia, liquid soap and chemical cleaners for drains, toilets and septic tanks
Manager: Penny Rulason
National Sales Manager: Roger Sheets
Plant Manager: Ken Wood
Purchasing Manager: Dennis West
Estimated Sales: $2.5-5 Million
Number Employees: 10-20
Square Footage: 1000000
Type of Packaging: Consumer, Food Service, Private Label
Brands:
Blue Ribbon
Rooto

28550 **Ropak**
1515 W.22nd Street
Suite 550
Oak Brook, IL 60523
Canada
800-527-2267
sales@bwaycorp.com www.ropakcorp.com
Manufacturer and exporter of polyethylene containers
President: Greg Toft
Sales Representative: Ricahrd Harrison
Operations Manager: Nevin McKay
Number Employees: 110
Parent Co: Bway Corporation
Type of Packaging: Food Service, Bulk

28551 **Ropak Manufacturing Company**
1019 Cedar Lake Rd SE
Decatur, AL 35603 256-350-4241
Fax: 256-350-1611 sales@ropak.com
www.ropak.com
Manufacturer and exporter of form/fill/seal, liquid/dry and vertical/horizontal packagers, stik-pak packager
President: Ralph Matthews
Sales: Norm Spires
Sales Manager: Norm Spires
VP Operations: Ernest Matthrews
Purchasing Manager: Ken Ray
Estimated Sales: $5-10,000,000
Number Employees: 20-49
Brands:
Expresspak

28552 **Roplast Industries Inc.**
3155 S 5th Ave
Oroville, CA 95965 530-532-9500
Fax: 530-532-9576 800-767-5278
sales@roplast.com www.roplast.com
Integrated domestic manufacturer of plastic (LDPE/LLDPE) film and bags.
President: Robert Bateman
COO: Chris Mann
Director of Sales: Roxanne Vaughan
Sales Manager: Erik Johansen
Estimated Sales: $20 - 30 Million
Number Employees: 100-249
Square Footage: 130000
Type of Packaging: Food Service, Private Label

28553 **(HQ)Rosco, Inc**
14431 91st Ave
Jamaica, NY 11435-4302 718-526-2601
Fax: 718-297-0323 800-227-2095
www.roscomirrors.com
Manufacturer and exporter of acrylic and glass convex safety mirrors
President: Sol Englander
Quality Control: George Lewandowski
VP and Finance: Danny Englander
VP Engineering and Ops: Ben Englander
National Sales Manager: Dave Mostel
Sales Manager: Joe Liberman
Estimated Sales: $5 - 10 Million
Number Employees: 100-249
Square Footage: 140000

28554 **Rose City Awning Company**
1638 NW Overton St
Portland, OR 97209-2481 503-226-2761
Fax: 503-222-5060 800-446-4104
sales@rosecityawning.com
www.rosecityawning.com
Canvas products, vinyl door strips, moving pads, solar screen transparent shades, tarpaulin, awnings, cloth and polythylene taper, polyethylene film and rope including nylon, sisal, manilas, poly, twine, etc
Owner: Pam Butcher
Sales Department: Ida Pfenning
Factory Manager: Mike Pedersen
Estimated Sales: Below $5 Million
Number Employees: 20-49
Square Footage: 2000

28555 **Rose City Label Company**
7235 SE Label Ln
Portland, OR 97206 503-777-4711
Fax: 503-777-4799 800-547-9920
info@rclabel.com
www.labelprintingportland.com
Labels including pressure sensitive, flexo, hot stamped, embossed, sheet fed and custom printed
President: Scott Pillsbury
CFO: Whitney Pillsbury
Marketing: Scott Pillsbury
Sales Manager: Walt Ostergard
Estimated Sales: $5-10 Million
Number Employees: 20-49

28556 **Rose City Printing & Packaging**
900 SE Tech Center Dr
Suite 100
Vancouver, WA 98683 503-241-6486
Fax: 503-241-3604 800-704-8693
info@rcpp.com www.rcpp.com
Folding cartons, blister cards and beverage carriers
President: Richard L Safranski
CEO: Chuck Parsons
CFO: Chris Farm
Quality Control: Steve Rautenbach
Marketing Director: Kathryn Rautenbach
Sales Director: Dave Wehrman
Operations Manager: Ken Karallis
General Manager: Steve Lobis
Estimated Sales: $5 - 10 Million
Number Employees: 100-249
Square Footage: 62000

28557 **Rose Forgrove**
1 Illinois St Ste 300
Suite 400
Saint Charles, IL 60174 630-443-1317
Fax: 630-377-3069
flowpak@rose-forgrove-inc.com
Manufacturer and exporter of flow wrappers for food and candy
VP Sales: Liam Buckley
Number Employees: 3
Square Footage: 2500
Parent Co: Howven
Brands:
Flowpak

28558 **Rose Forgrove**
1 Illinois St
Suite 300
Saint Charles, IL 60174 630-443-1317
Fax: 630-377-3069
Hermatic seals and other high quality wrapping applications

28559 **Rose Plastic USA**
P.O.Box 698
California, PA 15419-0698 724-938-8530
Fax: 724-938-8532 inforose-plastic.us
www.rose-plastic.us/850.0.html
President: Ken Donahue
Executive Vice President Technical and M: Peter Hess
Western Sales Director: Lisa Montgomery
Director of Human Resources: Jen Capozza
Estimated Sales: $300,000-500,000
Number Employees: 1-4

28560 **Rosemount Analytical**
2400 Barranca Pkwy
Irvine, CA 92606 949-757-8500
Fax: 949-757-3001 800-543-8257
jumana.sweis@emersonprocess.com
www.emersonprocess.com
Liquid analyzers including pH, conductivity, ORP, residual chlorine, dissolved ozone and oxygen refractometers, water activity measurement systems and gas analyzers and systems
President: Ram Krishnam
President: Ken Biele
Marketing Manager: John Wright
Sales Manager: Ken Partridge
Estimated Sales: $50 - 100 Million
Number Employees: 100-249
Parent Co: Fisher-Rosemont

28561 **Rosenthal Manufacturing**
1840 Janke Dr
Northbrook, IL 60062 847-714-0404
Fax: 847-714-0440 800-621-1266
411@rosenthalmfg.com www.rosenthalmfg.com
Sheeting machines
Owner: Lorelei Rosenthal
Estimated Sales: $10-20 Million
Number Employees: 20-49

28562 **Rosenwach Tank Company**
40-25 Crescent St
Long Island City, NY 11101 718-729-4900
Fax: 718-482-0661 info@rosenwachgroup.com
www.rosenwachgroup.com
Manufacturers of wooden and steel water towers, wooden cheese vats, tanks, planters and benches
Chairman of the Board: Wallace Rosenwach
Estimated Sales: $5-10 Million
Number Employees: 50-99
Parent Co: Rosenwach Group

28563 Roseville Charcoal & Manufacturing
PO Box 160
Zanesville, OH 43702 740-452-5473
Fax: 740-452-5474
Manufacturer and exporter of industrial and commercial charcoal briquettes including hardwood, granular and lump
President: Timothy Longstreth
Estimated Sales: $1-2.5 Million
Number Employees: 1-4

28564 Roskamp Champion
2975 Airline Cir
Waterloo, IA 50703 319-232-8444
Fax: 319-232-4040 800-366-2563
www.cpmroskamp.com
Manufacturer and exporter of particle sizeing equipment including roller and hammer mills, flakers, crushers, pallet mills, coolers and crumblers for food processing; also, testing/lab facility available
President: Ted Waitman
CEO: Heath Hartwig
CFO: Doug Ostrich
Research & Development: Ron Fuller
Marketing Director: Scott Anderson
Sales Director: Linda Kruckenberg
Operations Manager: Jim Hughes
Plant Manager: Terry Tackenberg
Purchasing Manager: Stuart Downs
Estimated Sales: $20 Million
Number Employees: 50-99
Square Footage: 50000
Parent Co: California Pellet Mill
Brands:
Champion
Roskamp

28565 Ross & Son Company
P.O.Box 12308
Hauppauge, NY 11788-0615 631-234-0500
Fax: 631-234-0691 800-243-7677
sales@mixers.com www.mixers.com
Emulsifying equipment
President: Richard Ross
Executive Vice President: Bogard Lagman
Product Manager: Shannon Wolf
Regional Sales Manager: Chip Nipps
Estimated Sales: $20-50 Million
Number Employees: 100-249

28566 Ross & Wallace Paper Products
204 Old Covington Hwy
Hammond, LA 70403
Fax: 985-345-1370 800-854-2300
rwpp@i-55.com www.rossandwallace.com
Manufacturer and exporter of paper and plastic bags and wrappings
President: Ken Ross
Chairman: Albert Ross
Estimated Sales: $10-20 Million
Number Employees: 50-99
Square Footage: 175000
Type of Packaging: Consumer, Bulk

28567 Ross Computer Systems
214 S Peters Rd Ste 208
Knoxville, TN 37923 865-690-3008
Fax: 865-690-1089 moreinfo@rossusa.com
www.rossusa.com
Manufacturer and exporter of computer hardware and software; also, consulting services available
President: Louis Schumacher
Executive VP: Louis Schumacher
VP Sales: Greg Roberts
Estimated Sales: Below $5 Million
Number Employees: 10-19

28568 Ross Computer Systems
19 W 44th St
Suite 715
New York, NY 10036 212-221-7677
Fax: 212-221-0362 moreinfo@rossusa.com
www.rossusa.com
Software for route accounting and manufacturing, handheld sales tracking-ordering-route settlement systems and host systems including Bakers Dozen and PrepMaster
Owner: Seymour Weiss
Estimated Sales: $1-2.5 Million
Number Employees: 10-19

28569 Ross Cook
1551 Las Plumas Avenue
San Jose, CA 95133-1611 408-929-9955
Fax: 408-929-9944 800-233-7339
prumpit@rosscook.com www.rosscok.com
Centrifugal blowers and exhausters and industrial vacuum systems
President: Mike Fisher
VP Operations: Bill Splinder
Estimated Sales: $10-20 Million
Number Employees: 20-49
Square Footage: 44000

28570 Ross Engineering
32 Westgate Blvd
Savannah, GA 31405 912-238-3300
Fax: 912-238-5983 800-524-7677
sales@rossengineering.com www.mixers.com
Manufacturer and exporter of food processing equipment including mixing, blending and dispersion machinery
President: Richard Ross
Vice President: David Hathaway
Estimated Sales: $10-20,000,000
Number Employees: 20-49
Square Footage: 60000
Parent Co: Charles Ross & Son Company

28571 Ross Industries
5321 Midland Rd
Midland, VA 22728 540-439-3271
Fax: 540-439-2740 800-336-6010
sales@rossindinc.com www.rossindinc.com
President: Phil Tribel
Estimated Sales: $20 - 50 Million
Number Employees: 100-249

28572 Ross Industries
5321 Midland Rd
Midland, VA 22728 540-439-3271
Fax: 540-439-2740 800-336-6010
sales@rossindinc.com www.rossindinc.com
Manufacturer and exporter of food processing and packaging equipment including pre-formed tray seal machines, tunnel freezers, mechanical tenderizers and meat presses.
Director Of Sales: Mark Douglas
Estimated Sales: $20-50 Million
Number Employees: 100-249

28573 Ross Systems
34 Westgate Blvd
Savannah, GA 31405 912-238-5800
Fax: 912-238-1905 866-797-2660
mail@rosssyscon.com www.rosssyscon.com
Owner: Paul Rose
Account Executive: Mike Ellis
Estimated Sales: $1 - 5 Million
Number Employees: 1-4

28574 Ross Systems
2 Concourse Pkwy NE # 800
Atlanta, GA 30328-5588 770-351-9600
Fax: 770-351-0036 info@rossinc.com
www.keops.com
Computer software design and programming service
President: J Patrick Tinley
CEO: Peter Yip
Estimated Sales: $30 - 50 Million
Number Employees: 50-99

28575 Rosson Sign Company
3071 Broadway
Macon, GA 31206 478-788-3905
Fax: 478-788-8020 jrosson@rossonsign.com
www.rossonsign.com
Electric, neon, painted and plastic signs
President: Jack Rosson
Estimated Sales: $1-2.5 Million
Number Employees: 10-19

28576 Roth & Associates PC
554 E Maple Rd # 100
Troy, MI 48083-2805 248-583-1221
Fax: 248-583-3221 rmroth@rothassocpc.com
www.rothassocpc.com
President: Robet Roth Jr
Estimated Sales: $5 - 10 Million

28577 Roth Sign Systems
606 Lakeville Street
Petaluma, CA 94952-3324 707-778-0200
Fax: 707-765-6079 800-585-7446
sales@rothsigns.com www.rothsigns.com
Manufacturer and exporter of menu, black and chalk boards; also, signs including changeable letter, advertising, luminous tube, plastic, etc
Owner: Lary Mathews
Estimated Sales: $500,000-$1 Million
Number Employees: 10
Square Footage: 80000
Parent Co: Rothcoast Company

28578 Roth Young Bellevue
PO Box 3306
Bellevue, WA 98009-3306 425-454-0677
Fax: 425-453-4552 rothyoung@wolfenet.com
www.rothyoungseattle.com
Executive search firm
Owner: B K Lee
Division Manager: Robert Richardson
CFO: David Salzberg
VP: C Salzberg
R&D: Bob Richardson
Estimated Sales: Below $5 Million
Number Employees: 5-9

28579 Roth Young Chicago
1100 W Northwest Highway
Suite 106
Mount Prospect, IL 60056 847-797-9211
Fax: 847-797-9303
Employment agency/executive search firm specializing in permanent selection and placement of food industry personnel
Number Employees: 10
Square Footage: 1800
Parent Co: Winston Franchise Corporation

28580 Roth Young Farmington Hills
31275 Northwestern Hwy
Farmington Hills, MI 48334-2558 248-539-9242
Fax: 248-626-7079 rydetroit@worldnet.att.net
Executive search firm specializing in the selection and placement of food industry personnel
President: Samuel Skeegan
Number Employees: 5-Jan
Square Footage: 2000
Parent Co: Winston Franchise Corporation

28581 Roth Young Hicksville
P.O.Box 7365
Hicksville, NY 11802-7261 516-822-6000
Fax: 516-822-6018 careers@rothyoung-li.com
www.rothyoung-li.com
Executive search firm specializing in selection and placement of food industry personnel
Owner: George Jung
Estimated Sales: Below $500,000
Number Employees: 1-4
Square Footage: 2960
Parent Co: Winston Franchise Corporation

28582 Roth Young Minneapolis
6212 Vernon Court S
Minneapolis, MN 55436-1669 952-932-0769
Fax: 952-831-7413 800-356-6655
info@rymn.com www.rymn.com
Executive search firm specializing in selection and placement of professional and managerial personnel in the retail and grocery industries
Estimated Sales: $500,000
Number Employees: 6
Square Footage: 6400
Parent Co: Winston Franchise Corporation

28583 Roth Young Murrysville
3087 Carson Ave
Murrysville, PA 15668-1814 724-733-5900
Fax: 724-733-0183 rothyoungpit@cs.com
www.rothyoung.com
Employment agency/executive search firm specializing in selection and placement of food industry personnel
President: Leonard Di Naples
Director (Health Care): Ann Marie Panzek
VP: Len DiNaples Jr
Estimated Sales: Below $5 Million
Number Employees: 1-4
Parent Co: Winston Franchise Corporation

28584 Roth Young New York
122 E 42nd Street Room 320
New York, NY 10168-0300 212-557-8181

Employment agency/executive search firm specializing in selection and placement of food industry personnel; See our ad on the spine of the print product
VP: David Silver
VP: Eric Kugler
Number Employees: 2
Parent Co: Winston Franchise Corporation

28585 **Roth Young Washougal**
24 S A Street
Suite A
Washougal, WA 98671-2101 360-835-3136
Fax: 360-835-9383 info@ruthyoung.com
www.rothyoung.com
Employment agency/executive search firm specializing in selection and placement of food industry personnel
President: David Salzberg
Estimated Sales: Less than $500,000
Number Employees: 4
Parent Co: Winston Franchise Corporation

28586 **Roth Young of Tampa Bay**
14914 Winding Creek Ct
Tampa, FL 33613-1603 813-269-9889
Fax: 813-269-9919 800-646-1513
pbarry97@tampabay.rr.com
www.rothyoungoftampabay.com
Employment agency/executive search firm specializing in selection and placement of food industry personnel
President: Barry Cushing
Estimated Sales: $400,000
Number Employees: 1-4
Square Footage: 1000
Parent Co: Winston Franchise Corporation

28587 **(HQ)Rothchild Printing Company**
7920 Barnwell Ave
Flushing, NY 11373-3727 718-899-6000
Fax: 718-397-1921 800-238-0015
www.rothchildprinting.com
Coupons, tags and labels including multiple page, paper, foil, flat, rolls and die-cut
VP: Paul Rothchild
Estimated Sales: $10-20 Million
Number Employees: 50-99
Square Footage: 40000

28588 **Rotisol France Inc**
341 North Oak St
Inglewood, CA 90302 310-671-7254
Fax: 310-671-8171 800-651-5969
info@rotisolusa.com www.rotisolusa.com
Manufacturer, importer and exporter pizza and rotisserie ovens; also, grills
President/CEO: Jack Kramer
Head Accounts: Milene Berry
Business Development Manager: Orlane Parsons
Director Sales: Alain Lebret
Sales Coordinator: Cedric Dauphin
Office/Customer Service Manager: Kate Gramcko
Estimated Sales: $2.5 - 5 Million
Number Employees: 7
Parent Co: Rotisol S.A.

28589 **Roto-Flex Oven Company**
135 E Cevallos
San Antonio, TX 78204-1795 210-222-2278
Fax: 210-222-9007 877-859-1463
info@rotoflexoven.com www.rotoflexoven.com
Manufacturer and exporter of food service equipment and pizza ovens
President: Richard Dunfield
CEO: Richard Dunfield
CFO: Ed Dunfield
Vice President: Doug Dunfield
Marketing Director: Marijke Carey
Plant Manager: Jose Briano
Estimated Sales: $2 Million
Number Employees: 10-19
Number of Brands: 2
Number of Products: 10
Square Footage: 25000
Type of Packaging: Consumer, Food Service
Brands:
Dual-Flex
Js-1
Roto-Flex Oven
Roto-Smoker

28590 **Roto-Jet Pump**
P.O.Box 209
Salt Lake City, UT 84110-0209 801-359-8731
Fax: 801-355-9303 info@rotojet.com
www.rotojet.com
Specialty pumps including high pressure washing, centrifugal screw impeller and abrasive/corrosive resistant
CEO: Joseph W Roark
Director Marketing: Steven Osborn
Sales Manager: Sebastien Dumas
Estimated Sales: $1 - 5 Million
Number Employees: 500-999
Brands:
Ash
Galigher
Roto Jet
Wemco

28591 **Rotonics Manufacturing**
736 Birginal Dr
Bensenville, IL 60106 630-773-9510
Fax: 630-773-4274 877-768-6642
chicago@rotonics.com www.rotonics.com
Manager: Jay Rule
Estimated Sales: $30 - 50 Million
Number Employees: 50-99

28592 **(HQ)Rotonics Manufacturing**
17038 S Figueroa St
Gardena, CA 90248 310-327-5401
Fax: 310-538-5579 corporate@rotonics.com
www.rotonics.com
Manufactures FDA approved containers, bins, totes, hoppers, pallets for the food industry
Chairman/CEO: Sherman McKinniss
CFO: Doug Russell
VP: Dawn Whitney
Number Employees: 50-99
Other Locations:
Rotonics Manufacturing
Bensenville IL
Rotonics Manufacturing
Commerce City CO
Rotonics Manufacturing
Bartow FL
Rotonics Manufacturing
Gardena CA
Rotonics Manufacturing
Caldwell ID
Rotonics Manufacturing
Gainesville TX
Rotonics Manufacturing
N Las Vegas NV
Rotonics Manufacturing
Brownwood TX
Rotonics Manufacturing
Knoxville TN
Rotonics Manufacturing
Miami FL

28593 **Rotronic Instrument**
135 Engineers Road
Suite 150
Hauppauge, NY 11788 631-427-3898
Fax: 631-427-3902 800-628-7101
sales@rotronic-usa.com www.rotronic-usa.com
Water activity measuring instrumentation
Manager: David P Love
Vice President: David Love
Marketing Director: Rose Mannarino
Estimated Sales: $2.5-5 Million
Number Employees: 10-19

28594 **Rotronics Manufacturing**
736 Birginal Dr
Bensenville, IL 60106-1213 630-773-9510
Fax: 630-773-4274 chicago@rotonics.com
www.rotonics.com
Storage containers and systems, tanks, drums
Manager: Jay Rule
Estimated Sales: $20 - 50 Million
Number Employees: 50-99

28595 **Round Noon Software**
14785 Preston Road
Suite 550
Dallas, TX 75254-7899 972-789-5191
info@roundnoon.com
www.roundnoon.com
Restaurant management software
Estimated Sales: $1 - 5 Million

28596 **Round Paper Packages**
511 Enterprise Dr
Erlanger, KY 41017 859-331-7200
Fax: 859-331-7285
Fiber and paper cans, tubes and cores
President: James Meier
VP: Linda Meier
Marketing: David Meier
Estimated Sales: $20-50 Million
Number Employees: 20-49

28597 **Roundup Food Equipment**
180 Kehoe Blvd
Carol Stream, IL 60188-1814 630-784-1000
Fax: 630-784-1650 800-253-2991
customerservice@roundupfoodequip.com
www.ajantunes.com
Manufacturer and exporter of toasters, steamers and hot dog grills
President: Glenn Bullock
Chairman of the Board: Virginia M Antunes
CFO: Bill Nelson
R & D: Tom Goodman
VP Marketing: Thomas Krisch
Estimated Sales: $5 - 10 Million
Number Employees: 250-499
Parent Co: A.J. Antunes & Company

28598 **Rovema**
650 Hurricane Shoals Rd NW
Lawrenceville, GA 30045-4460 770-513-9604
Fax: 770-513-0814 jnielsen@rovema.com
www.rovemausa.com
Vertical form-fill-seal machines, horizontal form-fill-seal machines, zipper applicators, cartoners, end-packing machines
President: Klaus Kraemer
Research & Development: Donald Harmon
Sales Director: Charlotte Koellner
Operations Manager: Ronald Kahlmann
Purchasing Manager: Dave Henninger
Estimated Sales: $10-20 Million
Number Employees: 50-99

28599 **Rowe International**
2517 Shadowbrook Drive SE
Grand Rapids, MI 49546-7457 616-246-0483
www.roweinternational.com
Manufacturer and exporter of currency changers, bill acceptors, under-the-counter safes, jukeboxes and vending machines including refrigerated food, snack and popcorn
Controller: Scott Van Dam
Senior Vice President, Sales & Marketing: John Margold
Human Resources Executive: Linda Roer
Purchasing: Chris Steffes
Estimated Sales: $160 Thousand
Number Employees: 3
Square Footage: 3096
Brands:
Rowe
Rowe Ami

28600 **Rowland Technologies**
320 Barnes Rd
Wallingford, CT 06492 203-269-9500
Fax: 203-265-2768 info@rowtec.com
www.rowlandtechnologies.com
Manufacturer and exporter of decorative plastic and polycarbonate packaging film
President: Peter Connerton
Sales Manager: Carl Heflin
Estimated Sales: $5 - 10 Million
Number Employees: 20-49
Square Footage: 60000

28601 **Rowlands Sales Company**
Butler Industrial Park
PO Box 552
Hazleton, PA 18201-0552 570-455-5813
Fax: 570-454-4790 800-582-6388
rowlands@rowlands.com www.rowlands.com
Aseptic processing equipment, batch control systems, cheese equipment, blenders, heat exchangers, plate, scraped surfaces, tubular, homogenizers, ice equipment, ingredient feeders
President: William Rowlands
CEO: David Rowlands
Estimated Sales: $10-20 Million
Number Employees: 20-49

28602 Rownd & Son
PO Box 1495
Dillon, SC 29536-1495 803-774-8264
Vegetable shipping containers
CEO: Annie Dollison
VP Sales: Harry Rownd
Estimated Sales: $2.5-5 Million
Number Employees: 20-49

28603 Rox America
PO Box 5561
Spartanburg, SC 29304-5561 864-463-4352
Fax: 864-463-4670 800-458-3194
info@roxenergy.com www.zimmer-usa.com
Flavor and taste assessment and stability for analytical services and instrumentation
President: Roland Zimmer
Vice President of Technology: Juergen Merz
National Sales Director: Bob Patterson
Estimated Sales: $1 Million
Square Footage: 3500

28604 (HQ)Roxanne Signs
23413 Woodfield Rd
Gaithersburg, MD 20882 301-428-4911
Fax: 301-253-5833 rox_signs@yahoo.com
Custom designed menu signs, menus and advertising specialty items including logos, banners, neon signs, window lettering, etc
President: Roxanne Riley
Estimated Sales: Below $5 Million
Number Employees: 1-4

28605 (HQ)Roxide International
24 Weaver St
Larchmont, NY 10538 914-630-7700
Fax: 914-235-5328 800-431-5500
roxide@aol.com www.roxide.com
Manufacturer and importer of insecticides, repellents, swatters, traps, fly paper, baits and muldicides; also, graffiti removers, organic cleaners and lubricants; exporter of fly paper and insecticides
President: James Cowen
Estimated Sales: $2.5-5 Million
Number Employees: 10
Type of Packaging: Food Service
Brands:
Aeroxon
Revenge
Roxo

28606 Roy's Folding Box
5140 Richmond Rd
Cleveland, OH 44146-1331 216-464-1191
Fax: 216-464-1562
Paper folding boxes
Owner: Sue Harky
Controller: Jeff Stuteman
Estimated Sales: $1 - 3 Million
Number Employees: 5-9

28607 Royal Acme Corporation
3110 Payne Ave
Cleveland, OH 44114 216-241-1477
Fax: 216-241-1479 sales@royalacme.com
www.royalacme.com
Rubber stamps
President: Theodore D Cutts
Estimated Sales: $1-2.5 Million
Number Employees: 10-19

28608 Royal Box Group
1301 S 47th Ave
Cicero, IL 60804 708-656-2020
Fax: 708-656-2108 kenh@royalbox.com
www.royalbox.com
Corrugated cartons, graphic packaging and packaging supplies
Sales Manager: Ken Hirsh
Estimated Sales: $50-75 Million
Number Employees: 100-249
Square Footage: 350000
Parent Co: Schwarz Partners, L.P.

28609 Royal Broom & Mop Factory
5717 Plauche Ct
Harahan, LA 70123 504-818-2244
Fax: 504-818-2266 800-537-6925
sales@royalbroom.com www.royalbroom.com
Brooms and mops; wholesaler/distributor of brushes and paint sundries
Owner: William Staehle III
CEO: Donald Staehle
CFO: Donald Staehle
Estimated Sales: $5 - 10 Million
Square Footage: 18000
Type of Packaging: Consumer, Private Label

28610 Royal Chemical of Carolina
204 Memory Ln
Albemarle, NC 28001-5402 704-982-5513
Fax: 704-982-3018 800-650-6346
Janitorial and industrial cleaning compounds
President: Joyce Morton
Sales/Marketing Executive: Madilyn Lampley
Purchasing Agent: Boyce Hill
Estimated Sales: $500,000
Number Employees: .

28611 (HQ)Royal Cup Coffee
160 Cleage Dr
Birmingham, AL 35217-1461 205-849-5836
Fax: 205-271-6071 800-366-5836
samantha@royalcupcoffee.com
www.royalcupcoffee.com
Coffee and tea; wholesaler/distributor of coffee equipment; serving the food service market
Vice President: Nelson Wilbanks
Marketing Coordinator: Anita Morgan
Operations Executive: Lorene Farley
Product Development Manager: David Strahl
Manager, Purchasing: Philip Naro
Estimated Sales: $79 Million
Number Employees: 635
Square Footage: 260000
Type of Packaging: Food Service
Other Locations:
Royal Cup
Birmingham AL

28612 Royal Display Corporation
725 Main St
Middletown, CT 06457 860-344-9988
Fax: 860-344-1045 800-569-1295
service@royaldisplay.com
www.royaldisplay.com
Custom wire display racks, point of purchase displays and signs and shelves
President: Rick Wright
VP: Laurie Ambrose
Estimated Sales: $2.5-5 Million
Number Employees: 20-49
Square Footage: 50000

28613 Royal Ecoproducts
119 Snow Boulevard
Vaughan, ON L4K 4N9
Canada 905-761-6406
Fax: 905-761-6419 800-465-7670
Manufacturer and exporter of plastic pallets
President: Burno Casciato
President: Maircein Tarascandalo
Director Sales/Marketing: Anthony DiNunzio
Sales Coordinator: Vince Franze
Number Employees: 30

28614 Royal Industries
4100 W Victoria St
Chicago, IL 60646 773-478-6300
Fax: 773-478-4948 800-782-1200
rylininc@aol.com www.royalindustriesinc.com
Wholesaler/distributor of restaurant supplies; serving the food service market
Chairman: Irving Naiditch
CFO: Joe Lewis
VP: Jay Johnson
Estimated Sales: $10-20 Million
Number Employees: 20-49
Square Footage: 200000

28615 Royal Label Company
50 Park St
Boston, MA 02122 617-825-6050
Fax: 617-825-2678 sales@royallabel.com
www.royallabel.com
Manufacturer and exporter of pressure sensitive labels, price tags, decals, name plates and panels
Owner/President: Paul Clifford Jr.
Director of QA: Craig DiGiovanni
VP: Paul Ryan
Business Development: Marychristine Clifford
Operations Manager: Paul Pelletier
Operations & Scheduling: Steve Gefteas
Plant Manager: Paul Pelletier
Controller: Eileen Clifford
Estimated Sales: Below $5 Million
Number Employees: 20-49
Square Footage: 25000

28616 Royal Oak Enterprises
One Royal Oak Avenue
Roswell, GA 30076 770-393-1430
Fax: 770-393-0313
Manufacturer and exporter of instant light charcoal briquettes and natural lump charcoal
VP Sales/Marketing: Harold Ovington
Sales Manager: Brian Kerrigan
Estimated Sales: $1 - 5 Million

28617 Royal Paper Box Companyof California
1105 South Maple Avenue
Montebello, CA 90640 323-728-7041
Fax: 323-722-2646 www.royalpaperbox.com
Paper boxes
Estimated Sales: $50-100 Million
Number Employees: 250-499

28618 Royal Paper Products
PO Box 151
Coatesville, PA 19320 610-384-3400
Fax: 610-384-5106 800-666-6655
sales@royalpaper.com www.royalpaper.com
Manufacturer and importer of place mats, coasters, bibs, napkin bands, chef hats, aprons, gloves, toothpicks, sword picks, arrow picks, skewers, coffee stirrers, griddle blocks/screens, scouring pads and metal sponges
President: David Milberg
CEO/CFO: Vince Mazzei
Executive VP: Fred Leibowitz
Quality Control: Debbie Sumka
Marketing Director: Todd Straves
Sales Director: Mark LaRusso
Plant Manager: Ross Glazer
Estimated Sales: $5 - 10 Million
Number Employees: 20-49
Number of Brands: 1
Number of Products: 300
Square Footage: 240
Type of Packaging: Food Service, Private Label, Bulk
Brands:
Royal Land

28619 Royal Prestige Health Moguls
1025 Old Country Road
Suite 206
Westbury, NY 11590-5654 516-997-1775
Fax: 516-759-1997 888-802-7433
Servicioalcliente@royalprestige.com.mx
www.royalprestige.com
Cookware, water and air purifcation equipment, china, crystal, tableware and cutlery
President: Steven Pollack
District Manager: Matt Rubin
Estimated Sales: $1 - 3 Million
Number Employees: 10
Square Footage: 800
Parent Co: Royal Prestige Distribution Center
Type of Packaging: Consumer

28620 Royal Range Industries
1768 W 1st Street
Irwindale, CA 91702-3259 626-812-4434
Fax: 626-812-4437
Estimated Sales: $3 - 5 Million
Number Employees: 20-49

28621 Royal Silver Company
3300 Chesapeake Blvd
Norfolk, VA 23513-4099 757-855-6004
Fax: 757-855-0017 contact@royalsilver.com
www.royalsilver.com
Stainless steel flatware
Chairman Of Board: Lloyd Gilbert
President: Lloyd Gilbert Jr
Secretary and Treasurer: Edward Landreth
President: Alan Gilbert Jr
Estimated Sales: $2.5 - 5 Million
Number Employees: 10-19
Square Footage: 144000

28622 Royal Welding & Fabricating
1000 East Elm Ave
Fullerton, CA 92831 714-680-6669
Fax: 714-680-6646 info@royalwelding.com
www.royalwelding.com

Manufacturer and exporter of custom stainless steel process tanks; also, vacuum chambers, mixers and cookers, also aluminum, inconel, titanium.
President: Wallace Cook
CFO: Sekyung Kim
Vice President/Chief Engineer: Brad Card
Quality Control: Merritt Read
Chief Engineer: Collie Janda
General Manager: Wallace Cook
Estimated Sales: $4.0 Million
Number Employees: 32
Square Footage: 116000
Parent Co: Cook & Cook
Brands:
Dimple Plate

28623 **Royalton Foodservice Equipment**
9981 York Theta Dr
Cleveland, OH 44133-3512 440-237-0806
Fax: 440-237-1694 800-662-8765
sales@mayind.com www.royalton.cc
Food service equipment including baking, roasting and holding ovens and cabinets
President: Leonard May
Service Engineer: Fred McKinney
CFO: Pat Tatton
Quality Control: David Kinshaw
Estimated Sales: $10-20 Million
Number Employees: 50-99

28624 **Royce Phoenix**
PO Box 729
Glendale, AZ 85311-0729
Canada 602-256-0006
Fax: 623-435-2030 info@roycemasonry.com
www.roycecorp.net
Manufacturer and exporter of wire and metal shelving, production line trucks, warehouse bins, point of purchase displays and racks; also, custom designed for chip, beverage, soups and biscuits
President: George Knowles
General Manager: Glenn Millar
Customer Service: Dave Haywood
Manager Operations: John Fox
Number Employees: 50
Square Footage: 212000
Parent Co: Royce Corporation
Type of Packaging: Consumer, Food Service, Private Label, Bulk
Brands:
Royce

28625 **Royce-Rolls Ringer Company**
16 Riverview Terrace N.E.
Grand Rapids, MI 49505 616-361-9266
Fax: 616-361-5976 800-253-9638
info@roycerolls.net www.roycerolls.net
Manufacturer and exporter of stainless steel mopping equipment, multi and single roll toilet paper dispensers, restroom fixtures and janitorial cleaning carts
President: Charles Royce Jr
VP: Charles Royce
Marketing Director: William Swartz
Estimated Sales: $1-3 Million
Number Employees: 20-49
Square Footage: 117200

28626 **Rtech Laboratories**
4001 Lexington Ave N
Arden Hills, MN 55126-2998 651-481-2207
Fax: 651-486-0837 800-328-9687
awdotterweich@landolakes.com
www.rtechlabs.com
Microbiology and chemistry testing, sensory, evaluation and custom processing services for the retail, food service and food development markets
Sales: Annette Sass
Estimated Sales: $5 - 10 Million
Number Employees: 100-249
Parent Co: Land O'Lakes

28627 **RubaTex Polymer**
PO Box 1050
Middlefield, OH 44062-1050 440-632-1691
Fax: 440-632-5761 www.universalpolymer.com
Manufacturer and exporter of plastic straws, can coolers and stoppers
President: Joe Colebank
VP: Andy Cavanagh
Sales/Marketing Manager: Philip Moses
Estimated Sales: $3 - 5 Million
Number Employees: 5-9

28628 **RubbAir Durr**
100 Groton Shirley Road
Ayer, MA 01432-1050 978-772-0480
Fax: 978-772-7114 800-966-7822
info@rubbair.com www.rubbair.com
Vinyl and plastic interior and exterior double impact doors
Manager: Alex Eckel
CEO: Alan Eckel
CFO: Joe Tunneva
Sales Director: Randy Gowld
General Manager: Alex Eckel
Purchasing Manager: John Waldron
Estimated Sales: $1 - 5 Million
Number Employees: 20-49
Number of Products: 12
Parent Co: Eckel Industries

28629 **Rubber Fab**
26 Brookfield Drive
Sparta, NJ 07871 973-579-2959
Fax: 973-579-7275 866-442-2959
sales@rubberfab.com www.rubberfab.com
Hygienic seals, sanitary gaskets, hose assemblies, valve, pump and filler machine components in a wide range of high purity elastomer materials
President: Patrick Parisi
Chief Executive Officer: Bob DuPont, Sr.
Chief Financial Officer: Daniel Licini, CPA
Quality Assurance: Allison Luke
Marketing Department: Laura Schnitzer
Sales Manager: Gary Johnson
Materials Manager: Kellie Cash
Estimated Sales: $6.5 Million
Number Employees: 20-49

28630 **Rubber Stamp Shop**
PO Box 610
Accokeek, MD 20607-610
Fax: 301-423-2208 800-835-0839
runstamp@erols.com
www.dcfagowees.com/news/benevolent/benevolent
Rubber stamps; also, letter press printing services available
President: Carl Harlow
VP: Carl Harlow
Estimated Sales: less than $500,000
Number Employees: 1-4
Square Footage: 1250
Parent Co: Rubber Stamp Shop

28631 **Rubbermaid Canada**
2562 Stanfield Road
Mississauga, ON L4Y 1S5
Canada 905-279-1010
Fax: 905-279-5254 chpcanada@rubbermaid.com
www.rubbermaidcommercial.com
Commercial dinnerware
Estimated Sales: $1 - 5,000,000
Parent Co: Rubbermaid Commercial Products
Brands:
Rubbermaid

28632 **Rubbermaid Commercial Products**
3124 Valley Ave
Winchester, VA 22601 540-667-8700
Fax: 540-542-8770 800-336-9880
rcpcomments@webrcp.com
www.rcpworksmarter.com
Manufacturer and exporter of food service, sanitary maintenance and material handling products
President: Larry McIsaac
Estimated Sales: $150 Million
Number Employees: 1,000-4,999
Type of Packaging: Consumer, Food Service

28633 **(HQ)Rubbermaid Commercial Products**
2000 Overhead Bridge Road NE
Cleveland, TN 37311-4692 423-476-4544
Fax: 423-476-1533 www.rubbermaid.com
Manufacturer and exporter of mops and cleaning aids
President: Neil Eibeler
Finance Manager: Kevin Rogers
Operations Manager: Frank McNeely
Production Manager: Phillip Carlton
Plant Manager: Steve Jones
Purchasing Senior Specialist: Jack Burke
Estimated Sales: $50-100 Million
Number Employees: 250-499
Parent Co: Newell Rubbermaid Inc.

28634 **(HQ)Rubbermaid Specialty Products**
29 E. Stephenson Rd.
Freeport, IL 61032-4235 815-235-4171
info@rubbermaid.e-mail.com
www.rubbermaid.com
Manufacturer and exporter of ice coolers and chests, thermal jugs and containers, re-freezable ice substitutes and lunch kits,also hummingbird feeders and accessories
Manager: Joesph Galli Jr.
Estimated Sales: $114.70 Million
Number Employees: 1460
Number of Products: 15
Type of Packaging: Food Service
Other Locations:
Rubbermaid Specialty Products
Winchester VA
Brands:
Blue Ice
Hi & Dri
Tote

28635 **(HQ)Rubicon Industries Corporation**
848 E 43rd St
Brooklyn, NY 11210 718-434-4700
Fax: 718-434-6174 800-662-6999
sales@rubiconhx.com www.rubiconhx.com
Stainless, carbon and high alloy steel and tube heat transfer equipment; also, pressure vessels, stainless steel tanks, reactors and ribbon blenders
President: Michael Rubinberg
Estimated Sales: $500,000-$1,000,000
Number Employees: 20-49

28636 **Ruby Manufacturing**
9853 Alpaca St
South El Monte, CA 91733 626-443-1171
Fax: 626-443-0028 info@rubymfg.com
www.rubymfg.com
Manufacturer and exporter of vegetable juice extractors
President: Daniel Turner
Estimated Sales: $500,000-$1 Million
Number Employees: 5-9
Type of Packaging: Food Service

28637 **Rudd Container Corporation**
4600 S Kolin
Chicago, IL 60632 773-847-7600
Fax: 773-847-7930 ruddbox@aol.com
www.ruddcontainer.com
Corrugated cartons and point of purchase displays
President: Darrell Rudd
Vice President: Ted Bihun
Design Manager: Lynna Cavallo
Sales Manager: Errol Dolin
Customer Service: Ann Rudd
Plant Manager: Ken Coyle
Estimated Sales: $15 Million
Number Employees: 20-49
Square Footage: 50000

28638 **Rudolph Industries**
1176 Cardiff Boulevard
Mississauga, ON L5S 1P6
Canada 905-564-6160
Fax: 905-564-6155 info@rudolphind.com
www.rudolphind.com
Machine knives and injector needles for food processors
President: Bill Rudolph
Number Employees: 10
Square Footage: 80000
Parent Co: W. Rudolph Investments

28639 **Rudy's L&R**
432 W 38th St
New York, NY 10018-2816 212-245-4966
Fax: 212-262-4815 info@rudys-espresso.com
www.rudys-espresso.com
Suppliers of expresso and capuccino machines
President: Louis Martinez
Estimated Sales: Less than $500,000
Number Employees: 1-4

28640 **Rueff Sign Company**
1530 E Washington St
Louisville, KY 40206 502-582-1714
Fax: 502-584-6427 sales@rueffsigns.com
www.rueffsigns.com
Signs including electric, plastic, metal and wooden
Owner: Bob Rueff

Estimated Sales: Below $5 Million
Number Employees: 20-49

28641 Ruffino Paper Box Manufacturing
63 Green St
Hackensack, NJ 07601-4082 201-487-1260
Fax: 201-487-3926 ruffino@foldingboxes.com
www.foldingboxes.com
Folding paper boxes
President: Rosario Ruffino
VP: Raymond Ruffino
Director Sales/Marketing: Rosanne Baleccny
Estimated Sales: $1 - 2.5 Million
Number Employees: 10-19

28642 Ruggles Sign Company
308 Crossfield Dr
Versailles, KY 40383 859-879-1199
Fax: 859-873-1697 info@rugglessign.com
www.rugglessign.com
Neon and plastic signs
President: Tim Cambron
CFO: Anna Cambron
Design Development: Jason Elmore
Local Sales: Tony Shaw
Office Manager: Lisa Smith
Production Manager: John Ratcliff
Account Manager: Elizabeth Pitchford
Purchasing: Brad Turpin, Jr
Estimated Sales: $5-10 Million
Number Employees: 50-99
Square Footage: 55000

28643 (HQ)Ruiz Flour Tortillas
1200 Marlborough Ave
Riverside, CA 92507 909-947-7811
Fax: 909-947-2338 info@ruizflourtortillas.com
www.ruizflourtortillas.com
Traditional and specialty, ethnic and gourmet flour tortillas serving food manufacturers, foodservice industry, restaurant distributors, retail food brokers, and specialty retail outlets
Founder: Edward Ruiz
CFO: Uriel Maciaf
Vice President: Vickie Salgado
R&D: David Rodriguez
Manager: Maria Lopez
Purchasing: Carmen Sandoval
Type of Packaging: Food Service, Private Label, Bulk

28644 Ruland Manufacturing Company
6 Hayes Memorial Drive
Marlborough, MA 01752 508-485-1000
Fax: 508-485-9000 800-225-4234
sales@ruland.com www.ruland.com

28645 (HQ)Rupp Industries
3700 W Preserve Blvd
Burnsville, MN 55337-7746 952-707-5000
Fax: 952-707-5292 800-836-7432
rleritz@rupp-inc.com www.temp-air.com
Chemical-free pest control, environmental air systems and air cleaners
CEO: Jim Korn
Product Manager: Mimoun Abaraw
Technical Field Representive: Warren Barich
Marketing Manager: Jessica Anderson
National Sales Manager: Tom Danley
Estimated Sales: $20 - 50 Million
Number Employees: 50-99

28646 Rusken Packaging
PO Box 2100
Cullman, AL 35056 256-734-0092
Fax: 256-734-3008 www.rusken.com
Corrugated containers
President: Greg Rusk
Office Manager: Robin Marty
Sales Manager: Joy Jackson
Estimated Sales: $20-50 Million
Number Employees: 250-499

28647 Russell
221 S Berry St
Brea, CA 92821-4829 714-529-1935
Fax: 714-529-7203 mike.michk@carrier.utc.com
www.russellcoil.com
Commercial refrigeration systems
Manager: Joe Berry
CFO: Gary Beale
Technical Manager: David Vallbracht
Quality Control: Steve Wellander
Accounts Manager: Dara Wilson
Estimated Sales: $100 - 250 Million
Number Employees: 50-99
Parent Co: Ardco

28648 Russell Finex
625 Eagleton Downs Dr
Pineville, NC 28134 704-588-9808
Fax: 704-588-0738 800-849-9808
sales@russellfinexinc.com
www.russellfinex.com
Sieving, filtering, separation equipment
President: John Edwards
Managing Director: Ray Singh
Estimated Sales: $1 - 2.5 Million
Number Employees: 10-19
Parent Co: Russell Group

28649 Russell T. Bundy Associates
P.O.Box 728
Urbana, OH 43078-0728 937-652-2151
Fax: 937-653-3546 sales@rtbundy.com
www.rtbundy.com
Bakery machinery rebuilding services, remanufactured baking equipment, reconditioned baking equipment and pans
CEO: Russell T Bundy
Estimated Sales: $20-50 Million
Number Employees: 50-99

28650 Russell-Stanley Corporation
14 Convery Blvd
Woodbridge, NJ 07095-2649 732-634-6000
Fax: 732-634-2927 800-229-6001
info@russell-stanley.com
www.russell-stanley.com
Steel and poly industrial drums and containers with tight and open heads
President: Dan Miller
Plant Manager: Herman Graff
Quality Control: Giovanni Valsano
District Sales Manager: Frank Luthe
Plant Manager: Herman Graff
Estimated Sales: $20-50 Million
Number Employees: 100-249
Square Footage: 13000
Parent Co: Russell-Stanley Corporation

28651 Russell-William
1710 Midway Rd
Odenton, MD 21113-1128 410-551-3602
Fax: 410-551-9076 greg@rwl.com
www.rwl.com
Store fixtures and point of purchase displays
CEO: Robert Williams
CEO: Robert Williams
Sales Manager: Rick Sauer
Estimated Sales: $20 - 50 Million
Number Employees: 100-249

28652 Rust-Oleum Corporation
11 Hawthorn Pkwy
Vernon Hills, IL 60061 847-367-7700
Fax: 847-816-2330 800-553-8444
www.rustoleum.com
Flooring, floor and wall coating materials, paints, enamels and coatings
President: Michael D Tellor
Human Resources: Stephen J Gillmann
Estimated Sales: $199.80 Million
Number Employees: 1146

28653 Rutan Polyethylene Supply Bag & Manufacturing Company
39 Siding Place
Mahwah, NJ 07430-1828 201-529-1474
Fax: 201-529-4440 800-872-1474
sales@rutanpoly.com www.rutanpoly.com
Polyethylene film, bags, tubing and sheeting
President and CEO: Arnold Tanowitz
Vice President: Esther Tanowitz
Estimated Sales: $5 - 10 Million
Number Employees: 20-49
Square Footage: 92800
Type of Packaging: Food Service

28654 Rutherford Engineering
1731 Apaloosa
Rockford, IL 61107 815-623-2141
Fax: 815-623-7170
Manufacturer and exporter of fillers, valves and packaging equipment
President: Ashwin Patel
Estimated Sales: $950,000
Number Employees: 15
Square Footage: 13500
Brands:
Akra-Pak
Rutherford

28655 Rutler Screen Printing
169 Belview Rd
Phillipsburg, NJ 08865 908-859-3327
Fax: 908-859-2138 sales@rutler.com
www.rutler.com
Garments, point of purchase displays, posters, decals, bumperstickers, T-shirts, etc
Owner: John Shubert
Estimated Sales: $1-2.5 Million
Number Employees: 10-19

28656 Rx Honing Machine Corporation
1301 E 5th St
Mishawaka, IN 46544 574-259-1606
Fax: 574-259-9163 800-346-6464
rxhoning@michiana.org www.rxhoning.com
Manufacturer and exporter of honing and sharpening machines for restaurant knives
President: R J Watson
Estimated Sales: $5-10 Million
Number Employees: 5-9
Square Footage: 5500
Brands:
Mini Rx Hone

28657 Ryan Instruments
P.O.Box 599
Redmond, WA 98073-0599 425-883-7926
Fax: 425-883-3766 ryan@ryaninst.com
www.sensitech.com
Manufacturer and exporter of time/temperature and humidity monitors for perishable commodities in transit, storage or processing
Manager: Mike Hanson
CFO: Mike Hurton
Senior Director of Quality Assurance: Dave Ray
Director Marketing: Susan Milant
VP Sales: Dan Vache
Estimated Sales: $10-20 Million
Number Employees: 50-99

28658 Ryan Technology
2705 SE 39th Loop
Suite B
Hillsboro, OR 97123-8415 503-640-9200
Fax: 503-640-3846 800-277-2290
info@ryanslicer.com www.ryanslicer.com
Rotary table and in line horizontal slicers for products such as bagels, buns, croissants, sub rolls, etc. Rolling stands for model 872 kwiklok machines.
President: John Ryan
Sales: Sandra Ryan
Estimated Sales: Below $5 Million
Number Employees: 1-4

28659 (HQ)Ryder - Logistics and Transportation Worldwide
P.O.Box 20816
Miami, FL 33102-0816 305-500-3726
Fax: 305-500-3390 800-297-9337
david_bruce@ryder.com www.ryder.com
Transportation firm providing leasing and transportation management services; also, vehicle maintenance and inventory deployment services available
PRESIDENT: Raymond Greer
CEO/PRES/CHR: Gregory Swienton
EVP/CFO: Art Garcia
EVP: Thomas Mc Kinnon
Estimated Sales: $5.0 Billion
Number Employees: 7,500
Parent Co: Ryder System
Other Locations:
Ryder Integrated Logistics
Birmingham AL

28660 Ryowa Company America
555 Bonnie Ln
Elk Grove Village, IL 60007 847-952-8363
Fax: 847-952-8309 800-700-9692
contact@ryowaamerica.com
www.ryowaamerica.com
Conveyors, conveyor merge units and accessories for packaging and slicers and slicer applications for processing
President: Hiroshi Hayashi
Technical Sales Manager: Bill Linahan

Estimated Sales: Less than $500,000
Number Employees: 1-4

28661 Ryson International
300 Newsome Drive
Yorktown, VA 23692-5006 757-898-1530
Fax: 757-898-1580 sales@ryson.com
www.ryson.com
Materials handling equipment
President: Ole B Rygh
CFO: Ragnhild Rygh
Estimated Sales: Below $5 Million
Number Employees: 5-9

28662 Rytec Corporation
780 N Water St
Milwaukee, WI 53202-3512 414-273-3500
Fax: 414-273-5198 888-467-9832
info@rytecdoors.com
www.rytecdoors.com/welcome2
Manufacturer and exporter of high-speed, rolling and folding doors including cold storage
Chairman: Donald Grasso
Regional Manager: Jamie Lilly
Marketing Manager: Scott Blue
Estimated Sales: $20-50 Million
Number Employees: 250-499
Brands:
Bautam
Clean-Roll
Fast-Fold
Fast-Seal
Preda

28663 Ryter Corporation
32732 730th Avenue
Saint James, MN 56081-5516 507-642-8529
Fax: 507-642-3692 800-643-2184
ryter@prairie.lake.com
Bacteria and enzyme products for waste water treatment, drains, grease traps and odor control
President: Terry Etter
Sales Manager: Barb Nelson
Estimated Sales: $1-2.5 Million
Number Employees: 9
Brands:
Odormute

28664 Ryther-Purdy Lumber Company
174 Elm Street
PO Box 622
Old Saybrook, CT 06475 860-388-4405
Fax: 860-388-9401 tpurdy@rytherpurdy.com
www.rytherpurdy.com
Lighting standards and fixtures
President: Timothy Purdy
Estimated Sales: $1-2.5 Million
Number Employees: 10-19

28665 S Hochman Company
PO Box 1204
Danville, CA 94526-8204 925-838-9990
Fax: 925-743-1234 800-999-9511
sandy@shcauction.com www.shcauction.com
Food and beverage industry
Owner: Shayel M Hochman Jr

28666 S Howes Company
25 Howard St
Silver Creek, NY 14136 716-934-2611
Fax: 716-934-2081 888-255-2611
sales@showes.com www.showes.com
Bins for bulk storage; hoppers, conveyors, bucket elevators
President: Wayne Mertz
VP: Fred Mertz
Sales Head: Dave Augustine
Estimated Sales: $10 - 20 Million
Number Employees: 10-19
Parent Co: MetalWorks

28667 S Walter Packaging Corporation
2900 Grant Avenue
Philadelphia, PA 19114
Fax: 215-698-7119 888-429-5673
shop@swalter.com www.swalter.com
Bags, boxes, ribbons, bows, gift wrap, tissue paper and labels for packaging supplies.
President/CEO: Andrew Wilson
Finance Executive: Maury Jaffe
EVP: James Leddy
SVP Marketing/Sales: Paula Wilmer
Human Resources Manager: Barbara Guido
VP Operations: Marc Leventhal
Purhcasing Agent: Beth Lopergola
Estimated Sales: $70 Million
Number Employees: 135
Square Footage: 200000

28668 S&G Resources
266 Main St
Olde Medfield Square
Medfield, MA 02052 508-359-7771
Fax: 508-359-7775 877-359-7776
sandg@sandgresources.com
www.sandgresources.com
President: Michael I Goldman
Estimated Sales: Below $5 Million
Number Employees: 1-4

28669 S&H Uniform Corporation
1 Aqueduct Rd
White Plains, NY 10606 914-937-6800
Fax: 914-937-0741 800-210-5295
info@sandhuniforms.com
www.sandhuniforms.com
Uniforms, aprons, smocks, caps and visors
President: Glen Ross
Vice President: Kevin Ross
Sales Manager: Pat Kraft
Estimated Sales: $35 Million
Number Employees: 50-99
Square Footage: 50000
Type of Packaging: Private Label
Brands:
S&H Uniforms

28670 S&J Laboratories
4669 Executive Dr
Portage, MI 49002 269-324-7383
Fax: 269-324-7384 sandjlab.mc@worldnet.att.net
www.sandjlab.com
Food laboratory service providing chemical, microbiological and physical analysis for food, feed and ingredients
President: Sheree Lin
Estimated Sales: $500,000-$1 Million
Number Employees: 5-9
Square Footage: 8000

28671 S&L Store Fixture Company
3755 NW 115th Ave
Miami, FL 33178 305-592-8672
Fax: 305-599-8906 800-205-4536
info@slstoredisplays.com
www.slstoredisplays.com
Manufacturer and exporter of store fixtures including metal shelving
President: Ronald Maier
VP: Ron Maier
Estimated Sales: $2.5 - 5 Million
Number Employees: 10-19
Square Footage: 128000
Brands:
Kent Supermatic

28672 (HQ)S&M Manufacturing Company
PO Box 1637
Cisco, TX 76437-1637 254-442-1380
Fax: 254-442-1643 800-772-8532
Mops and brooms
President: George Owens
Executive VP: Gail Hogan
VP: Sandy Boyett
Estimated Sales: Below $5 Million
Number Employees: 5-9
Brands:
Sheen Master

28673 S&O Corporation
527 Layton Rd
Gallaway, TN 38036 901-867-2223
Fax: 901-867-3760 800-624-7858
Garbage bags
President: Terry Draughon
VP: Tommy White
Estimated Sales: $5-10 Million
Number Employees: 20 to 49

28674 S&P Marketing, Inc.
11100 86th Ave
Maple Grove, MN 55369 763-559-0436
Fax: 763-557-1318 info@snpmarketing.com
snp-marketing.com
Fruit ingredients including tropical and temperate fruit juices, purees, dried fruits, powders and more. Niche products include tamarind, coconut cream, alphonso mango puree, prickly pear juice, puree, powder, fiber and oil.
President: Chareonsri Srisangnam PhD
Marketing/R&D: Vinod Padhye PhD
Type of Packaging: Food Service, Bulk

28675 S&R Machinery
943 Underwood Rd
Olyphant, PA 18447-2619 570-489-1212
Fax: 570-489-2572 800-229-4896
timm@sandrindustries.com
www.sandindustries.com
Manufacturing automated packaging machinery for your business
President: Brain McCarthy
Sales: Tim McAndrew
Production: Tim Mcandrew
Plant Manager: Tim Mc Andrew
Estimated Sales: $1-2.5 Million
Number Employees: 1-4
Number of Brands: 12
Number of Products: 1
Square Footage: 28000
Type of Packaging: Food Service

28676 S&R Products/Mr. Party
765 Oak Rd
Bronson, MI 49028-9353 517-369-2351
Fax: 517-369-2424 800-328-3887
Manufacturer and wholesaler/distributor of automatic liquor control pourers
Owner: Scot Kubasiak
Sales Manager: Rick Sandvik
Estimated Sales: $2.5-5 Million
Number Employees: 1-4
Square Footage: 7000
Parent Co: Kazico
Brands:
Cheapshot

28677 S&S Metal & Plastics
3740 Morton St
Jacksonville, FL 32217-2206 904-731-4655
Fax: 904-739-1394 c.strickland@ssmetal.com
www.ssmetal.com
Plastic signs
President: Garland Strickland
VP: Tim Clifton
Estimated Sales: $5-10 Million
Number Employees: 20-49

28678 S&S Service Parts
409 St. Croix Avenue
New Richmond, WI 54017-2609 715-246-3299
Fax: 715-246-3212 sales@bagcloser.com
www.bagcloser.com
Hand sealers, band sealers, bagging scales, conveyors, palletizers and vertical form fill and seal systems
Owner: Mike Preece
Sales Director: Tim Tonkson
Estimated Sales: $500,000-$1 Million
Number Employees: 5-9

28679 S&S Soap Company
815 E 135th St
Bronx, NY 10454 718-585-2900
Fax: 718-585-2902 info@sssoap.com
www.sssoap.com
Powdered, liquid and hand soap; also, detergents
Owner: Joseph Sebrow
Estimated Sales: $10 - 20 Million
Number Employees: 10-19
Square Footage: 40000
Brands:
Pink Magic
White Magic

28680 S&W Pallet Company
2120 Dividr and Natchez Trc Rd
Camden, TN 38320 731-584-4540
Fax: 731-584-2664 800-640-0522
sales@swpallet.com www.swpallets.com
Wooden pallets and skids
Manager: Jackie Wimberly

Estimated Sales: $5-10 Million
Number Employees: 50-99

28681 S-F Analytical Labs
2345 South 170th Street
New Berlin, WI 53151-2701 262-754-5300
Fax: 262-754-5310 800-300-6700
sales@sflabs.com www.sflabs.com
Laboratory performing chemical analysis and microbiological testing of food and food related products. Nutritional labeling anf USDA Fat Claims are specialties.
President/CEO: David Kliber
Number Employees: 20-49
Type of Packaging: Food Service

28682 S-H-S International of Wilkes
1124 Highway 315 Blvd
Wilkes Barre, PA 18702-6943 570-825-3411
Fax: 570-825-7790 contact@shstechstaffing.com
www.shstechstaffing.com
Recruiter of technical and managerial personnel for the food industry
Owner: Christopher Hackett
President: Chris Hackett
Estimated Sales: $1 - 3 Million
Number Employees: 10-19

28683 S. B. C. Coffee
19529 Vashon Highway SW
Vashon, WA 98070-6029 206-463-5050
Fax: 206-463-5051
Import and retail coffee equipment and supplies
President: J Stewart
Estimated Sales: $500,000-$1 000,000
Number Employees: 5-9
Type of Packaging: Private Label, Bulk

28684 S. Howes
25 Howard St
Silver Creek, NY 14136 716-934-2611
Fax: 716-934-2081 888-255-2611
sales@showes.com www.showes.com
Manufacturer and exporter of job engineered processing and materials handling equipment including classifiers, conveyors, crushers, rotary cutters, horizontal/vertical mixers, continuous liquid mixers and feeders, sifters, elevatorsauger packers and scales
President: Wayne Mertz
Vice President: Frederick Mertz
Estimated Sales: $10-20,000,000
Number Employees: 10-19

28685 S.I. Jacobson Manufacturing Company
1414 Jacobson Dr
Waukegan, IL 60085-7600 847-623-1414
Fax: 847-623-2556 800-621-5492
plzang@sij.com www.sij.com
CEO: Larry Futterman
Estimated Sales: $50 - 100 Million
Number Employees: 250-499

28686 S.L. Canada Packaging Machine
1391 Kebet Way
Port Coquitlam, BC V3C 6G1
Canada 604-941-6538
Fax: 604-941-2924 info@marpak.ca
www.marpakpackaging.com
President: George Davis
Number Employees: 20-40

28687 S.L. Doery & Son Corporation
299 Rockaway Tpke
Lawrence, NY 11559-1269 516-239-8090
Fax: 516-239-0696
Commerical awnings
President: Tom Peppe
Estimated Sales: Less than $500,000
Number Employees: 5-9

28688 S.S.I. Schaefer System International Limited
140 Nuggett Court
Brampton, ON L6T 5H4
Canada 905-458-5399
Fax: 905-458-7951 sales@ssi-schaefer.ca
www.ssi-schaefer.ca
Plastic, steel, stacking and nesting storage containers
General Manager: Otto Fasthuber
Number Employees: 25

28689 S.V. Dice Designers
1836 Valencia Street
Rowland Heights, CA 91748-3050 909-869-7833
Fax: 909-869-0515 888-478-3423
pdoyle@svdice.com www.svdice.com
Manufacturer and exporter of packaging machinery including case packers, erectors and sealers
President: Todd Dice
VP: Don Jameson
Engineer: Kent Martins
Estimated Sales: $2.5-5 Million
Number Employees: 1-4
Square Footage: 60000

28690 SA Wald Reconditioners
534 Foothill Road
Bridgewater, NJ 08807-2236 908-218-0627
Fax: 201-433-0098
Tea and coffee industry equipment and machinery reconditioning
Estimated Sales: $1 - 5 Million
Number Employees: 7

28691 SAF Products
433 E Michigan St
Milwaukee, WI 53202-5104 414-221-6333
Fax: 414-615-4000 800-641-4615
www.safbankproducts.com
CEO: John Riesch
Estimated Sales: $10-20 Million
Number Employees: 50-99

28692 SAN-AIRE Industries
101 E Felix St
Fort Worth, TX 76115 817-924-8105
Fax: 817-921-3963 800-757-1912
sales@san-aire.com www.san-aire.com
Manufacturer and exporter of commercial dish, trayware, pot and pan dryers
Manager: Bruce Barker III
VP Sales/Marketing: Bruce Barker
Estimated Sales: $1 - 2.5 Million
Number Employees: 1-4
Brands:
Powerdry

28693 SASA Demarle
8 Corporate Dr
Cranbury, NJ 08512-3630 609-395-0219
Fax: 609-395-1027 sales@demarleusa.com
www.demarleusa.com
President: Hatsuo Takeuchi
Finance & Administration Manager: Andrew Rozek
Vice President: Pierre Bonnet
Marketing & Sales Administrator: Brandon Iacometta
Estimated Sales: $5 - 10 Million
Number Employees: 10-19

28694 SASIB North America
808 Stewart Dr
Plano, TX 75074-8197 972-422-5808
Fax: 972-424-5041 800-558-3814
dhamilto@sasib-na.com www.sasib-bev.it
Designs and manufactures a wide variety of packaging and processing equipment for all industries, with a particular emphasis on fruits and vegetables, beer and softdrinks, consumer foodstuffs, household goods, and petroleum products
Estimated Sales: $20 - 30 Million
Number Employees: 5-9

28695 SASOL North America
900 Threadneedle
Suite 100
Houston, TX 77079 281-588-3000
Fax: 281-588-3144 info@us.sasol.com
www.sasolnorthamerica.com
Medium chain triglycerides, release agents, emulsifiers, fats
President: Charles Putnik
SNA Finance Manager: Patrick Cain
Vice President, Sasol US Operations: Mike Thomas
Research & Development Manager: Holger Ziehe
Marketing: Barbara Pagliocca
Sales: Barbara Pagliocca
Manager O&S US Operations: Paul Hippman
Estimated Sales: $5 - 10 Million
Number Employees: 500-999

28696 SATO America
10350 Nations Ford Rd Ste A
Charlotte, NC 28273 704-644-1650
Fax: 704-644-1662 888-871-8741
satosales@satoamerica.com
www.satoamerica.com
Manufacturer and exporter of bar code printers
President: Robert Linse
Marketing Manager: Nikki Aunn
Type of Packaging: Consumer, Food Service, Private Label, Bulk
Brands:
Sato

28697 SBA Software
10460 NW 29th Ter
Doral, FL 33172-2527 305-477-7366
Fax: 305-477-7175 800-222-8324
sales@restez.com www.pintodesigns.net
Point of sale hospitality and back office software
Owner: Pelia Pinto
Director Development: Roman Teller
Technical Services Director: Brad Sherman
Estimated Sales: $5 - 10 Million
Number Employees: 1-4
Brands:
Rest Ez

28698 SBB & Associates
4708 S Old Pch Rd Ste 100a
Norcross, GA 30071 770-449-7610
Fax: 770-449-1839 mark@sbbassoc.com
Executive personnel search firm
President: Mark Barlow
Estimated Sales: Below $5 Million
Number Employees: 1-4

28699 SBN Associates
5702 Larchmont Drive
Erie, PA 16509-2918 814-454-6326
Fax: 814-459-3359
Computer systems and software for the meat industry

28700 SBS of Financial Industries
28 New Hampton Road
Washington, NJ 07882-4002 908-689-5520
Fax: 908-689-5774
Electronic card processing and check verification services for the food service industry
CEO: Joe Kaplan
Director New Business Development: Linda Booth
VP: Tim Jochner
Parent Co: Superior Bankcard Service (SBS)

28701 SCA Hygiene Paper
PO Box 719
San Ramon, CA 94583-5719 925-830-2970
Fax: 925-830-0628 800-992-8675
Industrial food wipes, toilet tissue, towels, polishing cloths and soaps
EVP: Dan Filippini
Marketing Specialist: Debbie Allyn
Estimated Sales: $1 - 5 Million
Number Employees: 100-250
Brands:
Mevon
Tork

28702 SCA Tissue
PO Box 2400
Neenah, WI 54957 920-725-7031
Fax: 920-727-8801 866-722-6659
nfo.tissue-na@sca.com www.torkusa.com
Paper products including napkins, table cloths, place mats, tray covers, towels and toilet and facial tissue
President: Joe Raccuia
Director Marketing: Greg Linnemanstons
Sr. VP Sales/Marketing: Pete Chiericozzi
VP Distribution Sales: Joe Selzer
Estimated Sales: $5-10 Million
Number Employees: 250-499
Parent Co: Chesapeake Corporation
Brands:
Main Street
Park Avenue
Park Avenue Ultra
Second Nature Plus

28703 (HQ)SDIX
111 Pencader Dr
Newark, DE 19702 302-456-6789
Fax: 302-456-6770 800-544-8881
sales@sdix.com www.sdix.com
SDIX is a leader in developing accurate, simple, and rapid tests for pathogens. Our Rapidchek Tests for E.coli 0157, Listeria and Salmonella Enteritidis give you confidence in test reslutls, shortened product hold times and loweroverall testing costs. Rapidchek is Simply Accurate.
President/CEO: Fran DiNuzzo
R&D: Klaus Linopaintner
Marketing: Tim Lawink
Estimated Sales: $30 Million
Number Employees: 200
Brands:
Inquest
Rapid Assays
Rapid Prep

28704 SEAL-IT
70 Schmitt Blvd
Farmingdale, NY 11735 516-935-3965
Fax: 516-935-3967 800-325-3965
info@sealitinc.com www.sealitinc.com
President: Sharon Gonzales
CFO: Yvonne Gonzales
Estimated Sales: $100+ Million
Number Employees: 100-249

28705 SEC
106 N Main St
Plymouth, MI 48170 734-455-4500
Fax: 734-455-1026 secwireguards@aol.com
Ceiling fan, light fixture and protective wire guards; also, industrial ceiling-suspended fans
President: Donald Keeth
National Sales Manager: Patricia Keeth
Estimated Sales: $1-2.5 Million
Number Employees: 10-19

28706 SECO Industries
6858 Acco Street
Commerce, CA 90040 323-726-9721
Fax: 323-726-9776 sales@seco-ind.com
www.seco-ind.com
CEO: Charles De Heras
Estimated Sales: $1 - 5 Million
Number Employees: 100-249

28707 SEM - Systems Engineering & Manufacturing
2660 Perrowville Road
Forest, VA 24551-1859 434-525-7707
Fax: 434-525-7739 800-488-6055
info@se-m.com se-m.com
President: Jack Balrd
CFO: Jack Balrd
Estimated Sales: Below $5 Million
Number Employees: 10

28708 SEMCO
1211 W. Harmony
PO Box 505
Ocala, FL 34478-0505 800-451-3383
Fax: 352-351-3088 800-749-6894
salesatsemco@aol.com www.semcodisplay.com
Spinner racks, grid systems, peg hooks, dump bins, pegboard and slatwall fixtures; also, custom display items
VP: Adrian Simonet
Marketing: Tammy Robinson
Sales: Tammy Robinson
Public Relations: Fran Smith
Estimated Sales: $1 - 5 Million
Number Employees: 100-250
Square Footage: 540000
Parent Co: Leggett & Platt

28709 SEMCO Systems
6355 Kestrel Road
Mississauga, ON L5T 1Z5
Canada 905-670-9301
Fax: 905-670-9367 800-730-5859
info@semcotbs.com www.semcotbs.com

28710 SERCO Laboratories
2817 Anthony Lane S
Suite 104
St. Anthony, MN 55418 612-782-9716
Fax: 612-782-9782 800-388-7173
serco@sl-ser.com www.sl-ser.com
Environmental testing laboratory
CEO: David Allen
Project Manager: Diane Anderson
Estimated Sales: $500,000 - $1 Million
Number Employees: 5-9

28711 (HQ)SERFILCO Ltd
2900 MacArthur Boulevard
Northbrook, IL 60062-2007 847-509-2900
Fax: 847-559-1995 800-323-5431
sales@serfilco.com www.serfilco.com
Designs, manufactures and markets a broad line of corrosion resistant high performance pumps, agitators, filtration systems and instruments.
Founder: Jack Berg
Marketing: Chuck Schultz
Operations: Mike Berg
Production Manager: Jerry Swooda
Estimated Sales: $10 - 20 Million
Number Employees: 100
Other Locations:
Serfilco Ltd.
Lancaster PA
Brands:
Guardian
Space'saver
Titan '90

28712 SEW Eurodrive
1295 Old Spartanburg Hwy
Lyman, SC 29365 864-439-8792
Fax: 864-439-0566 mktg@seweurodrive.com
www.seweurodrive.com
Manufacturer and exporter of drives, motors and accessories
CEO: Bruce King
CEO: Juegon Blicke
Marketing Coordinator: JoAnn Greenup
Estimated Sales: I
Number Employees: 250-499
Parent Co: SEW Eurodrive
Brands:
Movidrive
Movidyn
Movimot
Movitrac
Snuggler

28713 SEW-Eurodrive
1295 Old Spartanburg Hwy
Lyman, SC 29365 864-439-8792
Fax: 864-439-0566 800-601-6195
cslyman@seweurodrive.com
www.seweurodrive.com
High performance, constant speed gearmotors and reducers, mechanical and electrical variable speed drives
VP: Bruce King
CEO: Juegon Blicke
CEO: Juergen Blickle
Estimated Sales: I
Number Employees: 250-499

28714 SFB Plastics
P.O.Box 533
Wichita, KS 67201-0533 316-262-0409
Fax: 316-712-0112 800-343-8133
sales@sfbplastics.com www.sfbplastics.com
Manufacturer and exporter of polyethylene air flow separators, pallets, pallet equipment and industrial blow molded plastic containers
President: David Long
Quality Control: Debbie Speven
Marketing: John Fosse
Sales: John Fosse
Estimated Sales: $10 - 20 Million
Number Employees: 50-99
Square Footage: 84000

28715 SFB Plastics
P.O.Box 533
Wichita, KS 67201-0533 316-262-0409
Fax: 316-712-0112 800-343-8133
sales@sfbplastics.com www.sfbplastics.com
Packaging equipment
President: David Long
CFO: David Long
R&D: David Long
Quality Control: Debbie Stevens
Estimated Sales: $10 - 20 Million
Number Employees: 50-99

28716 (HQ)SFBC, LLC dba Seaboard Folding Box
P.O Box 547
Fitchburg, MA 01420 978-342-8921
Fax: 978-342-1105 800-225-6313
info@seaboardbox.com www.cjfox.com
Boxes, cards, labels and tags
President: Robert Starr
Quality Control: Les Coster
Marketing Manager: Joe Wescott
VP Marketing: Jill Fox-Tabak
Public Relations: Joe Wescott
Estimated Sales: $1 - 2.5 Million
Number Employees: 100-249
Square Footage: 260000
Type of Packaging: Private Label
Other Locations:
C.J. Fox Co.
Providence RI

28717 SFK Danfotech, Inc.
8301 N.W. 101st Terrace #7
Kansas City, MO 64153 816-891-7357
Fax: 816-891-0550 www.sfk.com
www.sfkdanfotech.com
Automated cutting, slaughtering, deboning and processing machines for the meat industry.

28718 SFS intec, Inc
Spring Street & Van Reed Rd
Wyomissing, PA 19610 610-376-5751
Fax: 610-376-8551 610-376-8551
info@intecvrt.com www.sfsintecusa.com
Freezing, material handling, chilling, automated freezing, automated chilling
Managing Director: R John Smith
Estimated Sales: $5-10 Million
Number Employees: 10-19

28719 SG Frantz Company
PO Box 1138
Trenton, NJ 08606-1138 215-943-2930
Fax: 215-943-2931 800-227-7642
sales@sgfrantz.com www.sgfrantz.com
Magnetic separation equipment and industrial processing equipment including dry materials, liquids and slurries and laboratory equipment
VP: Steve Fortunate
Estimated Sales: $1-5 Million
Number Employees: 1

28720 SGS International
201 State Rt 17 # 2
Rutherford, NJ 07070-2597 201-935-1500
Fax: 201-508-3193 800-747-9047
greg_hansa@sgs.com www.sgsicsus.com
Environmental and social accountability management systems registration; ISO 14001 training includes IRCA-accredited lead assessor and internal auditing courses, EMS implementation, environmental laws and regulations
Chairman of the Board: Ernani Perez
VP: Michael J Brigante
Estimated Sales: $2.5-5 Million
Number Employees: 20-49

28721 SHURflo
5900 Katella Ave
Cypress, CA 90630 562-795-5200
Fax: 562-795-7564 800-854-3218
customer_service@shurflo.com
www.shurflo.com
Manufacturer and exporter of pumps including gas operated demand, liquid, electric and dual inlet gas systems for beverage syrups and condiments
President: J Russell Phillips
CFO: Norman Alexander
CEO: Steve Pilla
Quality Control: John Morey
Marketing Manager (Beverage): Tom Hardesty
National Sales Manager: John Obert
Estimated Sales: $100+ Million
Number Employees: 250-499
Parent Co: WICOR Company
Type of Packaging: Food Service

28722 SI Systems
600 Kuebler Rd
Easton, PA 18040 610-252-7321
Fax: 610-252-3102 800-523-9464
casey@sihs.com www.sihs.com

Material handling equipment including horizontal transport, order fulfillment and sortation systems
Chief Executive Officer: Ron Casey
Chief Financial Officer: Ron Semanick
CEO: Bill Casey
Director Marketing: James Walter
Operations: Bob Leidy
Purchasing: Tony Franco
Estimated Sales: $10 - 20 Million
Number Employees: 33
Brands:
Sps 3000

28723 (HQ)SICO America
7525 Cahill Rd
Minneapolis, MN 55439-2745 952-941-1700
Fax: 952-941-6688 800-328-6138
sales@sicoinc.com www.sicoinc.com
Manufacturer and exporter of room service carts and mobile folding banquet and buffet tables; also, fuel-powered and electric food warmers. Also manufacture portable dance floors, and portable stages, and bellmans carts and trucks
Chairman: Harold Wilson
President: Ken Steinbauer
CFO: Keith Dahlen
Vice President, Global Sales: Jerry Danielson
Marketing: Joel Mondshane
National Sales Manager: Heidi Niesen
Vice President, Operations: James Kline
Plant Manager: Pam Heller
Estimated Sales: $20-50 Million
Number Employees: 10-19
Type of Packaging: Food Service
Other Locations:
SICO America
Singapore
Brands:
Sico

28724 SICOM Systems
4434 Summer Meadow Dr
Doylestown, PA 18902
Fax: 215-489-2769 800-547-4266
sales@sicompos.com www.sicompos.com
The SL18, a Linux-based color touch screen, point of sale ssytem for the quick service restaurant environment.
President: William Doan
Estimated Sales: $10-20,000,000
Number Employees: 50-99

28725 SIG Combibloc
5327 Fisher Road
Columbus, OH 43228-9511 614-347-9971
Fax: 614-876-8678 800-843-2562
sales@combiblocusa.com
www.sigcombibloc.com
Aseptic packaging systems, aseptic filling equipment
President: Stphen Walliser
Estimated Sales: $50 - 100 Million
Number Employees: 25

28726 SIG Combibloc USA, Inc.
2501 Seaport Drive
River Front Suite 100
Chester, PA 19013-9791 610-546-4200
Fax: 610-546-4201 sales@combiblocusa.com
www.sigcombibloc.com
Manufacturer and exporter of aseptic carton filling and packaging systems for liquid foods and beverages
President: Yerry Derrico
Director Marketing: Bob Abamson
VP Sales/Marketing: Geoff Campbell
Estimated Sales: $50-100 Million
Number Employees: 100-249
Parent Co: PKL Verpackungssysteme GmbH

28727 SIG Doboy
869 S Knowles Ave
New Richmond, WI 54017 715-246-6511
Fax: 715-246-6539 sales@doboy.com
www.doboy.com
Manufacturer and exporter of carton and tray forming and sealing machines, horizontal wrappers and bag closing machines
President: William Heilhecker
CFO: Julie Foss
Sales: Mike Wilcox
Director Sales: John Bowerman
Director Operations: Mark Hanson
Estimated Sales: $30 - 50 Million
Number Employees: 250-499
Parent Co: SIG
Brands:
At
Bd-Iii
Cbs-B
Cbs-Ch
Hd-900
J-Series
Microtronic
Mustang
Mustang Iv
Pc-1200
S-Ch
Scotty Ii
Servotronic
Super H
Super Mustang

28728 SIG Pack Eagle Corporation
2107 Livingston Street
Oakland, CA 94606-5218 510-533-1400
Fax: 510-534-3000 800-824-3245
butlerp@parsons-eagle.com
www.sigpack-usa.com
Manufacturer and exporter of vertical form/fill/seal machinery, linear scales and combination weighers
Regional Sales Manager: Pete Butler
Production Manager: Gary Barlettano
Estimated Sales: $1 - 5 Million
Number Employees: 50-100
Square Footage: 160000
Parent Co: SIG Pack International
Brands:
Golden Eagle
Infinity
Phasor

28729 SIG Pack Eagle Corporation
2107 Livingston Street
Oakland, CA 94606-5218 510-533-1400
Fax: 510-534-3000 butlerp@parsons-eagle.com
www.sigpack-usa.com
Automatic weighing and packaging machinery: vertical form fill and seal machines, augers, baggers and scales
Regional Sales Manager: Pete Butler
Estimated Sales: $10-25 Million
Number Employees: 100

28730 SIG Pack Services
2401 Brentwood Rd
Raleigh, NC 27604-3686 919-872-5561
Fax: 919-877-0887 info@sigpack-usa.com
www.sigpack.com
Tea and coffee industry, bag and pouch sealers, bag filling and sealing machines, brushes, wrapping, foiling, carton machines: closing, filling, forming, sealing, closing equipment: bag closure, heat seal, conveyor accesories
President: Harold Carr
Estimated Sales: Below $5 Million
Number Employees: 20-49

28731 SIG Packaging Technologies
PO Box 5838
Norwalk, CT 06856-5838 203-845-8900
Fax: 203-846-3792
Packaging machinery
Estimated Sales: $1 - 5 Million
Number Employees: 20-50

28732 SIGHTech Vision Systems
2953 Bunker Hill Lane
Suite 400
Santa Clara, CA 95054 408-282-3770
Fax: 408-413-2600 sales@sightech.com
www.sightech.com
Manufacturer and exporter of quality control and assurance machinery for visual inspection
Chairman, Chief Executive Officer: Art Gaffin
Director Marketing Communications: Jeanette Hazelwood
VP Sales/Marketing: Francis Tapon
Estimated Sales: $1-2.5 Million
Number Employees: 4
Brands:
Sightech

28733 SIMS Manufacturing
134 N 1st Ave
Yakima, WA 98902 509-453-7690
Fax: 509-457-8606 dau@simsmfg.com
www.simsmfg.com
Estimated Sales: $10 - 20 Million
Number Employees: 20-49

28734 SIPROMAC Inc.
240 Industriel Boulevard
Saint-Germain-de-Grantha, QC J0C 1K0 819-395-5151
Fax: 819-395-5343 855-395-5252
sipromac@sipromac.com www.sipromac.com
President: Dave Couture
Vice President/Mktg & Sales Mgr.: Andre Francoevr
Research & Development: Yoann Frechette
Purchasing Manager: Richard Tremblay
Estimated Sales: $1 - 5 Million
Number Employees: 27

28735 SIT Indeva
3630 Green Park Circleÿÿ
Charlotte, NC 28217-2866 704-357-8811
Fax: 704-357-8866 info@sit-indeva.com
www.sit-indeva.com
Lifting devices for payloads
VP: Stefania Zanardi
Estimated Sales: Below $5 Million
Number Employees: 5-9

28736 SJ Controls
2248 Obispo Ave
Suite 203
Signal Hill, CA 90755-4026 562-494-1400
Fax: 562-494-1066 info@sjcontrols.com
www.sjcontrols.com
Manufacturer and exporter of blending and batching equipment, process control systems, flow meters and level detectors; also, engineering services available
President: Dave Olszewski
CFO: Cindy Pawn
Engineer: Steve Czaus
Estimated Sales: Below $5 Million
Number Employees: 10-19

28737 SJ Industries
7217 Lockport Place
Suite 101
Lorton, VA 22079-1596 703-751-5400
Fax: 703-370-3672
inquiry@arrowheadsystems.com
www.sjii.com
Accumulating conveyors, bottle rinsers, both twist and positive gripper type, can rinsers using ionized air and water, bidirectional accumulation tables, can and bottle warmer, can and bottle pasteurizer and coolers, plastic casewasher, preheater for ho
Estimated Sales: $5-10 Million
Number Employees: 30

28738 SK Food International
4666 Amber Valley Pkwy
Fargo, ND 58104 701-356-4106
Fax: 701-356-4102 skfood@skfood.com
www.skfood.com
Import/export trading company and demestic bulk ingredient supplier. Ingredients include soybeans, grains, seeds, dry edible beans, vegetable oils, precooked powders/flakes, peas & lentils, flours and meals
Owner/President & CEO: David Skyberg
VP: Beverly Skyberg
Marketing: Tara Froemming
Sales & Marketing: Aaron Skyberg
Estimated Sales: $2.9 Million
Number Employees: 17
Other Locations:
SK Food Specialty Processing
Moorhead MN

28739 SKC America
850 Clark Dr
Budd Lake, NJ 07828 973-347-7000
Fax: 973-347-7775 800-526-2717
jbrown@skcfilms.com www.skcfilms.com
Polyester film
President: Y J Joon
Number Employees: 50

28740 (HQ)SKD Distribution Corp
130-10 180th Street
Jamaica, NY 11434 718-525-6000
Fax: 718-276-4595 800-458-8753
rachel@skdparty.com www.skdparty.com

Manufacturer and exporter of plastic molders and fabricators, rigid foam fillers, wedges and foam packing inserts for boxes
Manager: Richard Mark
VP: Jack Schnitt
Marketing: Bill Stephan
Estimated Sales: $5-10 Million
Number Employees: 50-99
Square Footage: 1080000

28741 SKW Biosystems
2021 Cabot Blvoulevard
Langhorne, PA 19047-1810 215-702-1000
Fax: 215-702-1015
Estimated Sales: $10-20 Million
Number Employees: 50-99

28742 SKW Gelatin & Specialties
PO Box 234
Waukesha, WI 53187-0234
Canada 262-650-8393
Fax: 262-650-8456 800-654-2396
gelatin.usa@rousselot.com www.rousselot.com
Food processing equipment manufacturer specializing in vacuum packaging machines (table top, single/double chamber, automatic and belted chambers) shring tunnels, tray sealers, thermoforming machines, injectors, tumblers, massagers andsmokehouses. Exports internationally to more than 50 countries.
President: Geoge Masson
CFO: Steve Smith
Estimated Sales: C
Number Employees: 10

28743 SKW Industrial Flooring
23700 Chagrin Boulevard
Cleveland, OH 44122-5506 216-831-5500
800-537-4722
Polymer flooring systems with exceptional chemical impact and wear resistance
Estimated Sales: $1 - 5 Million
Number Employees: 250-499

28744 SL Sanderson & Company
173 Sandy Springs Ln
Berry Creek, CA 95916 530-589-3062
Fax: 530-589-3062 800-763-7845
Manufacturer and exporter of handheld capsule fillers and tampers; wholesaler/distributor of gelatin capsules
President: Stuart Sanderson
Estimated Sales: Less than $500,000
Number Employees: 1-4
Number of Products: 6
Brands:
Cap. M. Quik

28745 SLM Manufacturing Corpation
215 Davidson Avenue
Somerset, NJ 08873-4190 732-469-7500
Fax: 732-469-5546 800-526-3708
slminfo@slmcorp.com www.slmcorp.com
Semi-rigid plastic cut to size roll form tubing that can be combined with stock end caps to form complete tooling-free packages
President: Thomas Vhatay
Estimated Sales: $2.5-5 Million
Number Employees: 10-19

28746 SLX International
3453 Empresa Drive
Suite A
San Luis Obispo, CA 93401-7328 805-541-8356
Fax: 805-541-8320 800-883-9121
sales@slxinc.com www.slxinc.com
Reusable shipping containers
President and CEO: Edward De Temple
VP Engineering: Thomas DeTemple
Estimated Sales: $5-10 Million
Number Employees: 19

28747 SMC Corporation of America
10100 SMC Blvd.
Noblesville, IN 46060 317-899-4440
Fax: 317-899-3102 800-762-7621
dbrushi@smcusa.com www.smcusa.com
Estimated Sales: $1 - 5 Million
Number Employees: 10-19

28748 SMC Pneumatics
10100 SMC Blvd.
Noblesville, IN 46060 317-899-4440
Fax: 317-899-3102 800-726-7621
mrhode@smcusa.com www.smcusa.com
Low to high speed packing machines including shrink wrappers, multi packers, wrap around case packers, handle applicators and turn key complete lines.
VP: Steve Lefevre
Sales Representative: Mike Rhode
Estimated Sales: $1 - 5 Million
Number Employees: 100-249

28749 SMI USA
5500 South Cobb Dr. Building 400
Suite 5
Smyrna, GA 30080 404-799-9929
Fax: 860-688-5577 sales.us@smigroup.net
www.smigroup.it
General Manager: Walter Gallo
Number Employees: 10-19

28750 SMP Display & Design Group
4215 Cromwell Rd
Chattanooga, TN 37421 423-892-3720
Fax: 423-855-1869 800-251-6308
smp-display@smp-display.com
www.smp-display.com

28751 SNUX Sensors
P.O.Box 65310
West Des Moines, IA 50265-0310 515-225-6933
Fax: 515-225-6933 800-280-6933
www.ramcoinnovations.com
President: Brian Reelitz
Estimated Sales: $10 - 20 Million
Number Employees: 50-99

28752 SOCO System
1931 Mac Arthur Rd
Waukesha, WI 53188 262-547-5551
Fax: 262-547-4707 800-441-6293
info2@jphnmayecompany.com
www.johnmayecompany.com
Owner: John Maye
Accounts: Don Mertins
Sales: Jeff Devorse
Customer Service: Gail Pludeman
Operations: John Maye
Estimated Sales: $5 - 10 Million
Number Employees: 5-9
Type of Packaging: Consumer

28753 SONOCO
1 N 2nd St
Hartsville, SC 29550-3300 843-383-7000
Fax: 843-383-7008 800-576-6626
lisa.marshall@sonoco.com www.sonoco.com
Round and nonround composite cannisters (i.e. Pringles can, Minute Maid frozen orange juice, coffee, cleaning powders, powdered beverages and infant formulas)
President: Harris Deloch
CEO: Harris Delouch
CFO: Charles Hupfer
Executive Vice President: Charles Sullivan
R&D: David Hodge
Quality Control: Thomas Wallis
Marketing Director: Patrick Keese
Sales Director: Joe Lucas
Estimated Sales: $100 Million
Number Employees: 1,000-4,999
Square Footage: 70000
Type of Packaging: Consumer, Food Service, Private Label, Bulk

28754 SOPAKCO Foods
215 S Mullins St
Mullins, SC 29574-3207 843-464-0121
Fax: 423-639-7270 800-276-9678
www.sopakco.com
Pasta sauces; also, retortable pouch manufacturer, canner and contract packager of poultry, meat, fish, pasta, vegetable, bean, fruit and dessert products, flexible, semi-rigid and glass containers
CEO: Al Reitzer
CFO: Steve Keight
R&D: Jim Dukes
Quality Control: Phyllis Calhoun
General Manager: Wynn Pettibone
Plant Manager: Carl Whitmore
Purchasing Director: Beverly Stacey
Estimated Sales: $5-10 Million
Number Employees: 100
Square Footage: 400000
Parent Co: Unaka Corporation
Type of Packaging: Consumer, Food Service, Private Label

28755 SP Graphics
PO Box 1591
Santa Rosa, CA 95402-1591 707-542-9492
Fax: 707-542-9492 spgraphx@aol.com
Wine industry label design

28756 SP Industries
935 Mearns Rd
Warminster, PA 18974-2811 215-672-7800
Fax: 215-672-7807 800-523-2327
cs@spindustries.com www.spindustries.com
Manufactures Wilmad-LabGlass NMR & EPR tubes, hotpack incubators, chambers and glassware washers, VirTis Laboratory to production scale freeze dryers, FTS Smart Freeze Dryers Technology anf Precision Thermal Control Equipment, Genevacevaporator systems, and Hull Luophilization Systems.
CEO: Chuck Grant
CEO: Charles Grant
Marketing Director: Jennifer Colaiacomo
Sales: Robert Hoesly
Number Employees: 100-249
Square Footage: 280000

28757 (HQ)SP Industries
2982 Jefferson Rd.
Hopkins, MI 49328 269-793-3232
Fax: 269-793-7451 800-592-5959
info@sp-industries.com www.sp-industries.com
Manufacturer and exporter of hydraulic cart/dumpers, vertical balers, recycling equipment and refuse, precrusher and self-contained compactors
Owner/President: Denny Pool
Vice President: Roger Arndt
Marketing Mgr: David Jackiewicz
Sales Manager: Gene Koelsch
Office Manager: Elise Pool
Production Mgr: Julie Tahaney
Estimated Sales: $10-20 Million
Number Employees: 20-49
Square Footage: 50000

28758 (HQ)SPG International LLC
11230 Harland Drive
Covington, GA 30014 678-823-4001
Fax: 404-296-3040 877-503-4774
info@spgusa.com www.kelmax.com
Manufacturer and exporter of aluminum and stainless steel carts, racks and bakery shelving
President: Max Oyler
President, Chief Executive Officer: Steven DarnelL
VP Mfg.: Jose Lopez
Vice President of Business Development: Dave Mack
Vice President of Operations: Bob Buehler
Number Employees: 50-99
Square Footage: 320000
Parent Co: Keggerr & Platt Storage Products Group
Type of Packaging: Food Service
Other Locations:
Kelmax Equipment Co.
San Luis Potosi

28759 SPI's Film and Bag Federation
1667 K St., NW
Suite 1000
Washington, DC 20006-1620 202-974-5200
Fax: 202-296-7005 ddempsey@socplas.org
www.plasticsindustry.org
President: William Cartuaex
CFO: John Maguire
R&D: Tommy Fouthall
Number Employees: 100-249

28760 SPX Corporation
13515 Ballantyne Corporate Place
Charlotte, NC 28277 704-752-4400
Fax: 704-752-4505 www.spx.com
Manufactures a wide range of food process technologies from control valves to integrated food processing equipment.
Chairman, President & CEO: Christopher Kearney
EVP, CFO & Treasurer: Patrick O'Leary
VP, Flow Technology: Jeremy Smeltser
Estimated Sales: $5.46 Billion
Number Employees: 200
Square Footage: 10411
Brands:
Anhydro
Apv
Bran+Luebbe

Clydeunion Pumps
Copes-Vulcan
Delair
Deltech
Dollinger
Gd Engineering
Gerstenberg Schroder
Hankison
Jemaco
Johnson Pump
Lightnin
M&J Valve
Plenty
Pneumatic Products
Waukesha Cherry-Burrell

28761 SPX Flow Technology
13320 Ballantyne Corporate Place
Charlotte, NC 28277 262-728-1900
Fax: 262-728-4904 800-252-5200
ftamer.info@spx.com www.spxft.com
Manufacturer, importer and exporter of fat crystallization machinery for the processing of mayonnaise, salad dressings, margarine and shortening
Marketing: Scott Dillner
Sales Manager: Bjarne Buchert
Customer Service Manager: Robert Ladd
Number Employees: 15,000

28762 SRC Vision
PO Box 1666
Medford, OR 97501 541-776-9800
Fax: 541-779-4104 sales@srcvision.com
www.srcvision.com
Computerized optical sorting systems for the detection and automatic removal of defects from food processing lines; specialists in vision automated systems
Estimated Sales: $1 - 5 Million
Number Employees: 1-4

28763 SRI
203 Frances Ln
Barrington, IL 60010 847-382-3877
Fax: 847-382-3878 abean5452@aol.com
www.srimatch.com
Owner: Alan Bean
CEO: Allen Bean
Estimated Sales: $300,000-500,000
Number Employees: 1-4

28764 SSE Software Corporation
P.O. Box 384
Buckner, KY 40010 502-553-8653
Fax: 888-866-1931 contact@ssestandards.com
www.ssesoftware.com
Sanitary CAD/Design software
President: James Wynn
Number Employees: 12

28765 SSOE Group
1001 Madison Ave Ste A
Toledo, OH 43604 419-255-3830
Fax: 419-255-6101 lslusher@ssoe.com
www.ssoe.com
Engineering consultant specializing in the design of food plants and food process design
Senior Project Manager: Joe Badalomenti
Executive Vice President: Bob Howell
Senior Vice President: Mike Murphy
Division Manager: Ken Gruenhagen
Estimated Sales: $100-150 Million
Number Employees: 500-999

28766 SSW Holding Company, Inc.
1100 West Park Road
Elizabethtown, KY 42701 270-769-5526
Fax: 270-769-0105 info@sswholding.net
www.sswholding.net
Manufacturer and exporter of wire racks and refrigerator and freezer shelving and baskets
President: Paul Kara
Marketing: Brad Nall
VP Sales/Marketing: Mark Gritton
Marketing Manager: Brad Nall
Product Development Manager: Jeff Ambrose
Number Employees: 1,000-4,999
Square Footage: 1120000
Parent Co: SSW Holding Company
Other Locations:
SSW Holding Co.
Fort Smith AR

28767 ST Restaurant Supplies
#1 - 1678 Fosters Way
Delta, BC V3M 6S6
Canada 604-524-0933
Fax: 604-524-0633 888-448-4244
sales@strsupplies.com www.strsupplies.com
Manufacturer, importer and wholesaler/distributor of chef hats, hairnets, gloves and aprons; also, woodenware and nylon/metal scrubbers
President: Terry Kuehne
CEO: Sandy Lee
Sales: Sabastien Lachat
Purchasing: Sandy Lee
Number Employees: 21
Number of Products: 220
Square Footage: 160000
Type of Packaging: Food Service, Private Label, Bulk
Other Locations:
ST Restaurant Supplies
Dallas TX

28768 STA Packaging Tapes
100 S Puente St
Brea, CA 92821-3813 714-255-7888
Fax: 800-235-8273 800-258-8273
www.sta-tape.com
Carton sealing tape, hand dispensers, case sealers
President: Ikusuke Shimizu
CEO: Ernest J Wong
CFO: Matt Minami
VP: Stephen Wilson
R&D: Dinesh Shah
Marketing: Melissa Morris
Editorial Chief: Melissa Morris
Plant Manager: C Fang
Estimated Sales: $20 - 50 Million
Number Employees: 100-249
Square Footage: 185000

28769 STARMIX srl
Via dell'Artigianato, 5
Marano, VI 36035 044- 57- 659
Fax: 044- 57- 203 info@starmix.it
www.starmix-srl.com
Food service equipment including meat slicers
Estimated Sales: $300,000-500,000
Number Employees: 1-4
Brands:
Fleetwood

28770 STD Precision Gear & Instrument
318 Manley St
West Bridgewater, MA 02379-1087 508-580-0035
Fax: 888-329-4783 888-783-4327
sales@stdgear.com www.stdgear.com
Manufacturer and exporter of corrosion-proof precision gears, sprockets, ratchets, splines, pulleys, etc
President: James Manning
CFO: Doug Grant
Sales Director: Susan Dauwer
Estimated Sales: $1-2 Million
Number Employees: 20-49
Square Footage: 26000
Brands:
Std Precision Gear & Instrument

28771 STM Graphics
2626 Cole Ave
Dallas, TX 75204-1083 214-665-9544
Fax: 214-634-9219 800-766-7861
sales@stmgraphics.com www.stmgraphics.com
Commercial specialty printing: fleet graphics and P.O.P and architectural and digital products
Controller: Terry Thomas
CFO: Robert Schlezier
VP: Tim Allen
Customer Service Manager: Larry Morrow
Plant Manager: Mark Kitzman
Estimated Sales: $5-10 Million
Number Employees: 5-9

28772 STRAPEX Corporation
2601 Westinghouse Blvd
Charlotte, NC 28273 704-588-2510
Fax: 704-588-6838 800-346-1804
contactus@aidcoint.com www.itwpbna.com
Plastic strapping equipment for the security of loads during transport
General Manager: Bill Drake
Controller: Glenn Boyd
Estimated Sales: $10 - 20 Million
Number Employees: 20-49

28773 SV Dice Designers
1836 Valencia Street
Rowland Heights, CA 91748-3050 909-869-7833
Fax: 909-869-0515 888-478-3423
pdoyle@svdice.com www.svdice.com
Bag in box system, case packers, high speed case erectors, case semers
Owner: S Virgil Dice
Estimated Sales: $2.5-5 Million
Number Employees: 19-Oct

28774 SV Research
7429 Allentown Blvd
Harrisburg, PA 17112-3609 717-540-0370
Fax: 717-540-0380 info@svresearch.com
www.svresearch.com
Optical character recognition and optical character verification system designed to provide complete inspection on labeling and packaging lines and fully automatic spray nozzle monitoring system for quick and easy retrofit into mostcoating machines
President: Ron Lawson
manager: Ron Lawson
Sales Director: Bob Leiby
Estimated Sales: Below $5 Million
Number Employees: 20-49

28775 SWECO
2029 US Highway 25
PO Box 1509
Florence, KY 41042 859-371-4360
Fax: 859-283-8469 800-807-9326
info@sweco.com www.sweco.com
Manufacturer and exporter of FDA approved separation/screening equipment
President: David M Sorter
VP Engineering: Brad Jones
Marketing Manager: Jeff Dierig
Number Employees: 100-249
Parent Co: M-I LLC
Brands:
Supertaut Plus Ii
Vibro-Energy

28776 SWF Companies
1949 E Manning Ave
Reedley, CA 93654 559-638-8484
Fax: 559-638-7478 800-344-8951
cfriesen@swfcompanies.com
www.swfcompanies.com
President: Roland J Parker
VP: Ed Suarez
VP Sales/Marketing: Bob Williams
Product Manager: Craig Friesen
Number Employees: 100-249

28777 SWF McDowell
5505 Carder Road
Orlando, FL 32810-4738 407-291-2817
Fax: 407-293-7054 800-877-7971
www.swfmachinery.com
Manufacturer and exporter of carton forming and packaging systems including case, inverted bottle and drop packers, top sealers and case erectors
Service Manager: David Robertson
Operations Manager: Dennis Ramey
Estimated Sales: $1 - 5 Million
Number Employees: 50-99
Square Footage: 72000
Parent Co: SWF Machinery

28778 SWF/Dyna-Pak
1949 East Manning Avenue
Reedley, CA 93654-0548 559-638-8484
Fax: 559-638-7478 800-344-8951
info@swfcompanies.com www.thieletech.com
Flexible bags, case loaders, horizontal tray formers, lidding equip
VP: Ed Suarez
Number Employees: 100-249

28779 Saatitech
247 Route 100
Somers, NY 10589 914-767-0100
Fax: 914-767-0109 800-719-7130
info.US@saatitech.com www.saatiamericas.com
Manager: Todd Burt
Number Employees: 10-19

28780 Sabate USA
902 Enterprise Way # M
Napa, CA 94558-6288 707-256-2830
Fax: 707-256-2831 sabateusa@sabate.com
www.sabate.com

Wine and spirits corks and closures
President: Eric Mertier
CFO: Olivier Poissonnier
Estimated Sales: Below $5 Million
Number Employees: 5-9

28781 **Sabel Engineering Corporation**
1010 East Lake Street
Villard, MN 56385 320-554-3611
Fax: 320-554-2650 info@massmanllc.com
www.massmanllc.com
Manufacturer and exporter of automatic case packers and tiering mechanisms for collating multiple layers
President: Herbert Sabel
Engineering Manager: Stan Lundguist
Sales Director: Gary Ensey
Manager: Dave Rosenburg
General Manager: Noel Barbulesco
Estimated Sales: $5 - 10 Million
Number Employees: 20-49
Square Footage: 14400
Parent Co: Massman Automation Designs, LLC
Brands:
Carousel Caser
Descender

28782 **(HQ)Sabert Corporation**
2288 Main St Extension
Sayreville, NJ 08872 732-721-5546
Fax: 732-721-0622 800-722-3781
sabert@sabert.com www.sabert.com
Plastic disposable plates, platters, containers and bowls; exporter of disposable platters and bowls
President: Albert Salama
Marketing Director: Mark Seckinger
Sales Director: Bob Shemming
Estimated Sales: $5-10 Million
Number Employees: 100-249
Square Footage: 100000
Other Locations:
Sabert Corp.
Brussels
Brands:
Freshpack Bowls
Roma Gold
Roma Marble
Roma Silver
Ultima

28783 **Sable Technologies**
1628 norwood drive
Eagan, MN 55122 604-232-1290
Fax: 510-293-8553 800-722-5390
info@sabletechnology.com
www.sabletechnology.com
Manufacturer and exporter of compact point of sale systems for table and quick service restaurants
Executive VP: Adrian Bryan
VP Sales: James Files
Estimated Sales: $1 - 5 Million
Number Employees: 20-50
Square Footage: 8000
Type of Packaging: Food Service

28784 **Sackett Systems**
1033 Bryn Mawr Avenue
Bensenville, IL 60106-1244 630-766-5500
Fax: 630-766-5631 800-323-8332
sales@sackett-systems.com
www.sackett-systems.com
Lift trucks, carriers, racks, etc
President: Leonard Maniscalco
Director of Sales: Chris Lareau
Regional Accounts Manager: Andy Kerrins
Estimated Sales: $5 - 10 Million
Number Employees: 20-49

28785 **(HQ)Sacramento Bag Manufacturing**
440 N Pioneer Ave
Suite 300
Woodland, CA 95776-1788 530-662-6130
Fax: 530-662-6381 800-287-2247
tiffanyj@sacbag.com www.sacbag.com
Bags including raschel knit, polyethylene, burlap, polypropylene and cotton
Sales: Larry Deman
Customer Service Reps: Kathy Anderson
General Manager/Controller: Paresh Shah
Accounts Receivables: Suvo Lahiri
Plant Manager: Dennis Joost
Estimated Sales: $2.5 - 5 Million
Number Employees: 20-49
Square Footage: 55000
Parent Co: Acme Bag Company
Other Locations:
Sacramento Bag Manufacturing
Vernon CA

28786 **(HQ)Sadler Conveyor Systems**
1845 William Street
Montreal, QC H3J 1R6
Canada 519-941-4858
Fax: 519-941-7339 888-887-5129
info@sadler-conveyor.com
www.sadler-conveyor.com
Custom conveying systems for case and pallet handling from horizontal to vertical applications
President: Stephen Sadler
Vice President: Neil Sadler
R & D: Neil Sadler
Marketing Director: Luc Martineau
Sales Director: Chris Morin
Production Manager: Marcel Richard
Engineering: Eric Allard
Estimated Sales: Below $5 Million
Number Employees: 10
Square Footage: 144000
Other Locations:
Sadler Conveyor Systems
Hartford CT
Brands:
Hercules
Ls-Q50
Sadler
Uni-Flo

28787 **Saeco**
7905 Cochran Rd # 100
Cleveland, OH 44139-5470 440-528-2000
Fax: 440-542-9173 estronic@aol.com
www.saeco-usa.com
Manufacturer and importer of espresso and cappuccino machines including self-grinding, fully automatic and manual
President: John Mc Cann
Marketing Manager (Commercial Products): Julianna Benedick
Sales Manager (Housewares): Elizabeth Will
Senior Manager of Corporate Communicatio: Kathryn Cars
Estimated Sales: $2.5-5 Million
Number Employees: 20-49
Square Footage: 80000
Parent Co: Estro/Saeco
Type of Packaging: Consumer, Food Service
Brands:
Estro Da-Line
Saeco Housewares

28788 **Saeplast Canada**
PO Box 2087
St John, NB E2L 3T5
Canada 506-633-0101
Fax: 506-658-0227 800-567-3966
saeplast@saeplastcanada.com
www.saeplastcanada.com
Manufacturer and exporter of plastic pallets and insulated containers for transporting fruits, vegetables, frozen foods and fresh fish
President: Torfi Gudmundsson
CFO: Dave Burnan
Number Employees: 50-60
Brands:
Dynoplast

28789 **Saf-T-Gard International**
205 Huehl Rd
Northbrook, IL 60062-1972 847-291-1600
Fax: 847-291-1610 800-548-4273
safety@saftgard.com www.saftgard.com
Disposable gloves, mesh gloves
President: Richard Rivkin
Quality Control: Tom Rearer
Chairman of the Board: Norman Rivkin
Estimated Sales: $10 - 20 Million
Number Employees: 50-99

28790 **Safe T Cut**
97 Main St
Monson, MA 01057 413-267-9984
Fax: 413-267-9585 info@safetcut.com
www.safetcut.com
Manufacturer and exporter of safety knives for cutting films, foams and cartons
President: Richard Baer
CEO: Mary Clark
CFO: Debra Baer
Number of Products: 10
Brands:
Safe T Cut

28791 **Safety Fumigant Company**
197 Beal St
Hingham, MA 02043-1506 781-749-1199
Fax: 781-740-4996 800-244-1199
safetyfumigant@aol.com
www.safetyfumigant.com
Insecticides
President: John Hall
Estimated Sales: Less than $500,000
Number Employees: 10-19

28792 **Safety Light Corporation**
4150 Old Berwick Rd
Suite A
Bloomsburg, PA 17815 570-784-4344
Fax: 570-784-1402 info@safetylight.com
www.safetylight.com
Self-luminous nonelectric exit and safety signs
President: C Richter White
Plant Manager: Larry Harmon
Estimated Sales: $2.5-5 Million
Number Employees: 20-49

28793 **Safety Seal Industries**
447 Main Street
Catskill, NY 12414-1317 518-943-1300
Fax: 518-943-0873
customer-service@tmi-pvc.com
www.stripdoors.com

28794 **Safeway Solutions**
2804 SE Loop 820
Fort Worth, TX 76140-1012 817-237-6373
Fax: 817-237-2613 info@safewaysolutions.com
www.safewaysolutions.com
Chief Executive Officer: Randall Price

28795 **Sage Automation**
4925 Fannett Rd
Beaumont, TX 77705 409-842-8040
Fax: 409-842-9141 800-731-9111
rbeller@sagerobot.com www.sagerobot.com
Custom material handling and case packing
President: Don W Cawley
Applications Engineer: Greg White
Marketing/Technology: Jason Blake
Business Development: Randy Beller
Public Relations: Rodney Gonzalez
Estimated Sales: $10-20 Million
Number Employees: 50-99

28796 **Saint Charles Lumber Products**
1225 N Saginaw St
St Charles, MI 48655-1024 989-865-9915
Fax: 989-865-9037
Wooden skids, pallets and boxes
President: Rick Lorentzen
Sales: Duane Schneider
Sales: Dan McGee
Estimated Sales: $5-10 Million
Number Employees: 50-99

28797 **Saint-Gobain Containers**
P.O.Box 4200
Muncie, IN 47307-4200 765-741-7000
Fax: 765-741-7012 www.sgcontainers.com
Designs and manufactures glass containers for the food and beverage industries in North America.
CEO: Joe Grewe
Marketing Director: Marilyn LaGrange
Sales Director: Jarrell Reeves
Number Employees: 1,000-4,999
Parent Co: Ardagh Group S.A.

28798 **Saint-Gobain PerformancePlastics**
1199 S Chillicothe Rd
Aurora, OH 44202 216-245-0529
Fax: 330-562-3933 800-562-5151
hosesupport@saint-gobain.com
www.plastics.saint-gobain.com
Soft drinks, beer, and alcohol beverage dispensing, clear, natural and colored tubings, barrier and nonbarrier reinforced hose, specialty grade hose and tubing, fire retardent bundles
General Manager: Phil Corvo
Vice President: Phil Corvo
Marketing Director: Dave Tersigni
Sales Director: Doug Fisher
Plant Manager: Gary Wolny

Estimated Sales: $50 - 100 Million
Number Employees: 100-249
Parent Co: Saint-Gobain
Type of Packaging: Private Label, Bulk
Brands:
Premier Python
Synflex

28799 (HQ)Salem China Company
1000 S Broadway Avenue
Salem, OH 44460-3773 330-337-8771
Fax: 330-337-8775 salem-urfic@worldnet.att.net
Custom manufacturer and exporter of chinaware, dinner sets, teapots, beer steins, stainless flatware and mugs; importer of dinnerware sets
Secretary: Carolyn Brubaker
Estimated Sales: $500,000-$1 Million
Number Employees: 10-19

28800 Salem-Republic Rubber Company
P.O.Box 339
Sebring, OH 44672 330-938-9801
Fax: 330-938-9809 800-686-4199
srr@salem-republic.com
www.salem-republic.com
Manufacturer, importer and exporter of FDA approved hoses and hose assemblies, rubber tubing and pipes
President: Drew Ney
VP Corporate Development: Anthony Kindler
Sales Manager: Raymond Willis
Estimated Sales: $10-20 Million
Number Employees: 50-99
Brands:
Champion
Flexrite
Vol-U-Flex

28801 Sales Building Systems
9325 Progress Pkwy
Mentor, OH 44060 440-639-9100
Fax: 440-639-9190 800-435-7576
jzaback@workplaceprint.com
www.workplaceprint.com
Consultant specializing in restaurant chain database marketing
President: Pat White
CEO: Tim McCarthy
CFO: Jack Zaback
CEO: Stephanie Molnar
Founder: Tim McCarthy
VP Sales: Cindy Venable
Operations Manager: Shelly Furness
Estimated Sales: $5 - 10,000,000
Number Employees: 50-99
Number of Products: 2

28802 Sales Partner System
789 S Nova Rd
Ormond Beach, FL 32174 386-672-8434
Fax: 386-673-4730 800-777-2924
spsmkt@spsi.com www.spsi.com
Computer software for sales automation
CEO: Larry Frank
VP/General Manager: Ken Yontz
President: Jal Belix
Number Employees: 10-19

28803 SalesData Software
6340 San Ignacio Avenue
San Jose, CA 95119-1209 408-281-5811
Fax: 408-281-3736
Computer software for the food service industry including point of sale management systems, cash and sale analysis, menu costing, marketing tools, inventory control and purchase ordering; also, installation and training servicesavailable
President: Binh Nguyen
Parent Co: Aureflam Corporation
Brands:
Restaurant Basics
Retail Basics

28804 Salient Management Company
203 Colonial Dr
Horseheads, NY 14845 607-739-4511
Fax: 607-739-4045 info@salient.com
www.salient.com
Developer of strategic sales management solutions for high volume businesses, Windows-based software and sales management software tools for sales data online, service rep productivity and a high-power work-order tracking system
President: Guy Amisano
Sales Director: Larry Beuter
Marketing Director: John Shannon
Business Development: Mike Dzikowski
Operations Manager: Sandy Houper
Estimated Sales: $5-10 Million
Number Employees: 20-49

28805 Salinas Valley Wax PaperCompany
PO Box 68
Salinas, CA 93902-0068 831-424-2747
Fax: 831-424-5883
Manufacturer and importer of printed and plain packaging paper including kraft, laminated, waxed, tissue, pads, box liners, etc
President: Chas Nelson
VP: Bill Zimmerman
Plant Manager: Richard Johnson
Estimated Sales: $10 - 20 Million
Number Employees: 20-49
Number of Brands: 1
Square Footage: 40000
Type of Packaging: Private Label, Bulk
Brands:
Ratan
Salinas Valley Wax Paper Co.

28806 Salonika Imports
3509 Smallman Street
Pittsburgh, PA 15201
800-794-2256
info@solanika.net www.salonika.net
Mediterranean culinary products
President/Owner: Chris Balouris

28807 Salvajor Company
4530 E 75th Ter
Kansas City, MO 64132 816-363-1030
Fax: 816-363-4914 800-821-3136
sales@salvajor.com www.salvajor.com
Manufacturer, importer and exporter of commercial food waste disposal and waste handling systems
President: Chris Hohl
Vice President: Don Misenhelter
Research & Development: Chris Hohl
VP Sales/Marketing: Gregory Wait
Purchasing Manager: P Cooper
Estimated Sales: $10 - 20 Million
Number Employees: 20-49
Square Footage: 40000
Brands:
Scrapmaster
Troughveyor

28808 Salwasser ManufacturingCompany
1949 E Manning Ave
Reedley, CA 93654 559-638-8484
Fax: 559-638-7478 800-344-8951
cfriesen@swfcompanies.com
www.swfcompanies.com
Vice President, General Manager: Ed Suarez
Product Manager: Craig Friesen
Estimated Sales: $1 - 5 Million
Number Employees: 5-9

28809 Salwasser ManufacturingCompany
1949 E Manning Ave
Reedley, CA 93654 559-638-8484
Fax: 559-638-7478 800-344-8951
cfriesen@swfcompanies.com
www.swfcompanies.com
Manufacturer and exporter of automatic case and tray loading machinery
VP: Ed Suarez
Director Engineering: Dan Nourian
Sales/Marketing Executive: Gregory Cox
Product Manager: Craig Friesen
Special Project Manager: Dennis Decker
Estimated Sales: $10-20 Million
Number Employees: 100-249
Square Footage: 200000
Parent Co: Thiele Technologies
Brands:
Sure Way

28810 Sam Pievac Company
14044 Freeway Dr
Santa Fe Springs, CA 90670 562-404-5590
Fax: 562-404-7566 800-742-8585
lhansenspc@bwsys.net
www.sampievaccompany.com
Store fixtures and displays
President/COO: Matt Johnson
Chairman/CEO: Scott Pievac
VP Sales: Robin Hess
VP: Michael Pievac
Sales Representative: Bill Polack
Estimated Sales: $10-20 Million
Number Employees: 20-49
Square Footage: 14500

28811 Sambonet USA/Paderno USA
1180 McLester St # 8
Elizabeth, NJ 07201-2931 908-351-4800
Fax: 908-351-3351 america@sambonet.it
www.sambonet.it
Wholesaler/distributor and importer of general merchandise including cutlery, trays, coffee and tea service equipment, chafing dishes, etc.; serving the food service market
President: Pierre Luigi Coppo
CFO: Harish Patel
VP: Andrea Viannello
Quality Control: Harish Patel
Estimated Sales: $2.5 - 5 Million
Number Employees: 5-9
Parent Co: Paderno SpA

28812 Samco Freezewear Company
3499 Lexington Ave N
Ste 205
St Paul, MN 55126-7070 651-638-3888
Fax: 651-638-3896 dbramwell@freezewear.com
www.freezewear.com
Insulated industrial clothing including pants, jackets, full suits, hoods, vests, safety boots and light and heavy weight
President: Thomas Bramwell Sr
CEO: Tom Bramwell Jr
CFO: Richard Schuster
VP: Dave Bramwell
Quality Control: David Bramwell
Estimated Sales: $12-18 Million
Number Employees: 130
Square Footage: 80000

28813 Samsill Corporation
5740 Hartman Road
Fort Worth, TX 76119 817-429-8093
Fax: 817-535-6900 800-255-1100
www.samsill.com
Presentation and storage products including binders, sheet protectors and menu covers
Executive Director: Michelle McLaughlin
CFO: Dave Paton
Executive VP Marketing/Sales: Bob Schultz
Type of Packaging: Food Service

28814 Samson Controls
4111 Cedar Boulevard
Baytown, TX 77523-8588 281-383-3677
Fax: 281-383-3690 samson@samson-usa.com
www.samson-usa.com
Manufacturer and exporter of controls and control systems, flow regulators, valves and valve operators
President: Siegfried Hanicke
Estimated Sales: $2.5-5 Million
Number Employees: 20-49
Parent Co: Samson Controls

28815 Samsung Electronics America, Inc.
85 Challenger Road
Ridgefield Park, NJ 07660 201-229-4000
Fax: 864-752-1632 800-726-7684
www.samsungusa.com

President/Chief Executive Officer: Kim Yangkyu
Managing Director: Peter Altuch
Director, Tax: Nancy Abbott
Executive Vice President: Mas Fukomoto
Senior Principal Engineer: Jin Kyu Han
Quality Manager: Steve English
Executive Vice President, Marketing: S Hong Steel
Vice President, Sales: Kevin Moreton
Public Relations Director: Richard Johnson
Senior Vice President, Operations: Michael Noblit
Technology Architect: Jounyong Park
Purchasing Manager: Xiaofang Xia
Estimated Sales: $9.4 Billion
Number Employees: 1,700

28816 **Samuel P. Harris**
55 Pawtucket Avenue
Rumford, RI 02916 401-438-4020
Fax: 401-438-8980
Vacuum formed plastic packaging materials
President: Kenneth Hatch
Treasurer: David Brower
VP Operations: Suzanne Manzak
Estimated Sales: $5-10 Million
Number Employees: 100-249

28817 **Samuel Strapping Systems**
1401 Davey Rd # 300
Woodridge, IL 60517-4991 630-783-8900
Fax: 630-783-8901 800-323-4424
information@samuelstrapping.com
www.samuelstrapping.com
Manufacturer and exporter of steel and plastic straps; also, carton closing machines
President: Robert Hickey
CFO: Richard Louis
Controller: Dick Louis
Sales/Marketing: Tom Gould
Marketing Manager: Cy Slifka
Purchasing Manager: Joe Capoccio
Estimated Sales: $30 - 50 Million
Number Employees: 20-49
Parent Co: Samuel Manu-Tech

28818 **Samuel Strapping Systems**
2000 K Boyer S Drive
Fort Mill, SC 29173 803-802-3203
Fax: 803-802-3209 smt@samuelmanutech.com
www.samuelstrapping.com
Plastic strapping
President: Robert Hickey
Quality Control: Donna Shicely
Estimated Sales: $1-5 Million
Number Employees: 10
Parent Co: Samuel Manu-Tech

28819 **Samuel Underberg**
1784 Atlantic Ave
Brooklyn, NY 11213-1208 718-363-0787
Fax: 718-363-0786
Wire butter and cheese cutters, electric graters, meat hooks, box openers and fish scalers
President: David Chalom
CEO: David Chalom
Estimated Sales: $1-2.5 Million
Number Employees: 1-4
Number of Brands: 100
Number of Products: 2100

28820 **Samuels Products**
9851 Redhill Dr
Cincinnati, OH 45242 513-891-4456
Fax: 513-891-4520 800-543-7155
sampro@juno.com www.samuelsproducts.com
Computer and pressure sensitive labels and printed bags
Owner: Millard Samuels
National Sales Manager: Tim Kroger
Purchasing Manager: Rick Helton
Estimated Sales: $5-10 Million
Number Employees: 50-99
Square Footage: 60000

28821 **San Diego Health & Nutrition**
PO Box 1318
Bonita, CA 91908-1318 619-470-3345
Fax: 619- 47- 382 www.sdhnsclasses.com
Consultant providing food safety and sanitation training
Partner: Jack Ezroj
Estimated Sales: $100,000
Number Employees: 1-4

28822 **San Diego Paper Box Company**
PO Box 1219
Spring Valley, CA 91979-1219 619-660-9566
Fax: 619-660-9570 richard.chapman@sdpbc.com
www.sdpbc.com
Folding cartons
President: Sidney B Chapman
CFO: Richard Chapman
R&D: Richard Chapman
Vice President of Sales and Marketing: Jeff Shipman
Production Manager: Gilbert Bernal
Estimated Sales: $20 - 50 Million
Number Employees: 50-99

28823 **San Fab Conveyor Systems**
2000 Superior Street
Sandusky, OH 44870 419-626-4465
Fax: 419-626-6376 www.sanfab.com
Manufacturer, importer and exporter of package and bulk conveying components and systems including stainless, pallet handling and table top conveyors, carton sealers and stainless case tapers
President: Timothy Shenigo
Manager (Packaging Equipment): Don Williams
Engineering Manager: Charles Wheeler
Estimated Sales: $5-10 Million
Number Employees: 10-19
Square Footage: 320000
Brands:
San Fab

28824 **San Jamar**
555 Koopman Ln
Elkhorn, WI 53121 262-723-6133
Fax: 262-723-4204 800-248-9826
customercare@sanjamar.com
www.sanjamar.com
Manufacturer and exporter of built-in dispensing units for condiments and disposable paper products including cups, towels and napkins; also, bar supplies and check management systems
President: Charles Colman
CFO: Andy Skerkowitz
Marketing Manager: Topper Woelfer
Senior Sales Coordinator: Michael Johnson
Estimated Sales: $10 - 20 Million
Number Employees: 50-99
Number of Brands: 3
Number of Products: 600
Type of Packaging: Consumer, Food Service
Brands:
Classic
Gourmet

28825 **San Joaquin Supply Company**
PO Box 692422
Stockton, CA 95269-2422 209-952-0680
Fax: 209-466-1080
Soaps, disinfectants and sterilizers
VP: Mick Albright
Regional Sales Manager: Mike Valasquez
Estimated Sales: $1 - 5 Million
Number Employees: 1-4

28826 **San Jose Awning Co., Inc.**
755 Chestnut St
San Jose, CA 95110 408-350-7000
Fax: 408-350-7001 800-872-9646
sales@sanjoseawning.com
www.sanjoseawning.com
Commercial awnings
President: Michael Yaholkovsky
Estimated Sales: $1 - 2.5 Million
Number Employees: 10-19

28827 **San Juan Signs**
736 E Main St
Farmington, NM 87401 505-326-5511
Fax: 505-326-5513 sjsigns@fisi.net
www.sanjuansigns.com
Advertising displays and signs
President: Clint L Roper
VP: Teri Roper
Office Manager: Phyllis Davis
Estimated Sales: $1-2.5 Million
Number Employees: 20-49
Square Footage: 5600

28828 **San Marco Coffee, Inc.**
3120 Latrobe Dr
Suite 280
Charlotte, NC 28211-2186 704-366-0533
Fax: 704-366-0534 800-715-9298
www.sanmarcocoffee.com
American coffee, espresso, cappuccino
Chief Executive Officer: Marc Decaria
Number Employees: 5-9
Type of Packaging: Consumer, Food Service, Private Label
Brands:
San Giorgio

28829 **San Miguel Label Manufacturing**
PO Box 1401
Ciales, PR 00638-1401 787-871-3120
Fax: 787-871-0443 smlabels@caribe.net
Labels and plastic bags
Estimated Sales: $1 - 5 Million
Number Employees: 20-50
Square Footage: 20000

28830 **San-Rec-Pak**
9995 SW Avery St
PO Box 3210
Tualatin, OR 97062-3210 503-692-5552
Fax: 503-692-4477 www.tihi.net
Manufacturer and exporter of maltsters' machinery
Manager: Karla Mc Combs
Estimated Sales: $3 - 5 Million
Number Employees: 10-19
Parent Co: Kloster Corporation

28831 **SanSai North America Franchising, LLC**
1365 E. Gladstone Street
Suite 300
Glendale, CA 91203-2678 909-599-9456
Fax: 818-244-2470 800-368-5594
mark.stegeman@us.nestle.com
www.sansaiusa.com
Ingredients for chocolate making
Owner: Peter Han
Estimated Sales: $1 - 5 Million
Number Employees: 10-19
Parent Co: Nestle USA

28832 **Sanchelima International**
1783 NW 93rd Ave
Doral, FL 33172 305-591-4343
Fax: 305-591-3203 sales@sanchelimaint.com
www.sanchelimaint.com
Manufacturer and exporter of dairy and cheese making equipment, fillers and sealers, homogenizers, molds, centrifugal separators, bottle unscramblers, pasteurizers, tanks and valves; processor and exporter of cultures
President: Juan A Sanchelima
Technical Director: Jesus Gonzalez
CFO: Maximo Questa
Estimated Sales: $5-10 Million
Number Employees: 10-19

28833 **Sanchelima Intl. Inc.**
1783 NW 93rd Ave
Miami, FL 33172 305-591-4343
Fax: 305-591-3203 sales@sanchelimaint.com
www.sanchelimaint.com
Processing units for the dairy, yogurt and cheese industries.

28834 **Sanco Products Company**
330 Harrison Ave
Greenville, OH 45331 937-548-2225
Fax: 937-548-0132
Disinfectants, insecticides, etc
President: Philip R Saylor
Quality Control: John Saylor
Estimated Sales: Below $5 Million
Number Employees: 5-9

28835 **Sancoa International**
92 Ark Rd
Lumberton, NJ 08048 609-953-5050
Fax: 856-273-2710 mbrennan@sancoa.com
www.sancoa.com
Manufacturer, exporter and importer of pressure sensitive labels and shrink sleeves
President: Joseph Sanski
Controller: Roger Spreen
CFO: Kevin Austin
Quality Assurance Manager: Bob Zimmerman

Estimated Sales: $20 - 50 Million
Number Employees: 250-499

28836 Sanden Vendo America Inc
10710 Sanden Dr
Dallas, TX 75238 214-765-9066
Fax: 800-541-5684 800-344-7216
www.vendoco.com
Automatic and manual vending machines for bottles and cans
President: Bernt Voelkel
CEO: Frank Kabei
Number Employees: 500-999
Parent Co: Sanden Corporation

28837 Sanders Manufacturing Company
1422 Lebanon Pike
Nashville, TN 37210 615-254-6611
Fax: 615-242-3732 866-254-6611
sales@samcoline.com www.samcoline.com
Advertising specialties
President: Jimmy Sanders Iii III
Manager: Paul Cowan
Mngr.: Paul Cowan
Estimated Sales: $10-20 Million
Number Employees: 5-9
Square Footage: 46000
Brands:
Samco

28838 Sanderson Computers
450 W Wilson Bridge Road
Worthington, OH 43085-2237 614-781-2525
Fax: 614-781-2755 zebra@sandersonusa.com
www.sandersonusa.com
Software for the process, food and formulations industries
Owner: Gary Sanderson
Marketing (US): David Lee
President US Operations: Carl Parker
Parent Co: Sanderson Group PLC
Brands:
Formul8

28839 Sandler Seating
1175 Peachtree Street NE
Suite 1850
Atlanta, GA 30361 404-982-9000
Fax: 404-321-7882 sales@sandlerseating.com
www.sandlerseating.com
Manufacturer and exporter/importer of tables and chairs for hotels, restaurants, and food courts
U.S. Director of Sales: Rusty Wolf
Chief Executive Officer: Roy Sandler
Sales Manager: Anita Haslett
Estimated Sales: $5 - 10 Million
Number Employees: 5-9
Brands:
Sandler Seating

28840 Sandusky Plastics
400 Broadway Street
Sandusky, OH 44870-2006 419-626-8980
Fax: 419-616-1803 800-234-7587
spi@lrbcg.com www.whirley.com
Thermoformed plastic containers
President: Lincoln Sokolski
Administrator: Holly Colvin
Human Resources: DiAnn Savko
Estimated Sales: $50-100 Million
Number Employees: 250-499

28841 Sandvik Process Systems
21 Campus Rd
Totowa, NJ 07512 973-790-1600
Fax: 973-790-9247 spsusa.info@sandvik.com
www.sandvik.com
Manufacturer and exporter of food processing equipment including dryers, coolers, freezers, drop-formers and steam cookers
Manager: Craig Bartsch
General Manager: Greg Burnham
Marketing Manager: Craig Bartsch
Estimated Sales: $1 - 5 Million
Number Employees: 55
Parent Co: Sandvik
Brands:
Roto-Former

28842 Sandvik Process Systems
21 Campus Rd
Totowa, NJ 07512 973-790-1600
Fax: 973-790-9247 spsusa.into@sandvik.com
www.sandvik.com
Process equipment for drying vegetables, fruits, and rice, roasters for nuts and beans, freezers for seafood and slurries for freeze drying, melt solidification systems, cooling tunnels and dropformers for chocolate and steam cookingtunnels for meat
Marketing Director: Craig Batsbh
Manager: Craig Bartsch
Estimated Sales: $1 - 5 Million
Number Employees: 50-99

28843 Sandy Butler Group
1375 Jackson St
Suite 401
Ft Myers, FL 33901 239-357-6162
Fax: 239-333-0481
jerome@sandybutlergroup.com
www.sandybutlergroup.com
Balsamic, oilve oil, flavored olive oil, pasta, vegetables, wine vinegar and salts

28844 Sanford Redmond
780 E 134th St
Bronx, NY 10454-3527 718-792-7000
Fax: 718-292-0010
Small disposable containers for cream, jams, ect
Estimated Sales: $1-2.5 Million
Number Employees: 10-19

28845 Sanford Redmond Company
65 Harvard Ave
Stamford, CT 06902 203-351-9800
Fax: 718-292-0010
Manufacturer and exporter of wrapping, food processing and packaging machinery
President: S Redmond
Estimated Sales: $1-2,500,000
Number Employees: 5-9

28846 Sangamon Mills
PO Box 467
Cohoes, NY 12047 518-237-5321
Fax: 518-237-6282 sangamonmill@aol.com
www.sangamonmills.com
Knit wash and dish cloths
President: Ella Fisher
Estimated Sales: Below $5 Million
Number Employees: 10-19
Brands:
Sunflower
White Swan

28847 Sani-Fit
620 S Raymond Avenue
Suite 9
Pasadena, CA 91105-3261 626-395-7895
Fax: 626-395-7899
Manufacturer, importer and exporter of stainless steel sanitary fittings, diaphragm valves and food processing fitting components
Estimated Sales: $1 - 5,000,000
Brands:
Bradford Cast Metals
Garitech
Sanifit
Topline

28848 Sani-Matic
P.O.Box 8662
Madison, WI 53708-8662 608-222-1935
Fax: 608-222-5348 800-356-3300
info@sanimatic.com www.sanimatic.com
Cleaning systems for the food and pharmaceutical industries. Product lines include clean-out-of-place parts washers, clean-in-place systems, rinse/foam/sanitize pressure systems, conveyorized wash tunnels, and a variety of cabinetwashers to clean vats, racks, pallets, ibc, bin, totes and other product handling items.
President: Ted Lingard
Marketing: Kelsy Boyd
Sales: Chad Dykstra
Plant Manager: Wayne Huebner
Estimated Sales: $20 Million
Number Employees: 100-249
Number of Products: 10
Square Footage: 40000
Brands:
Sani-Matic
Ultra Flow

28849 Sani-Pure Food Laboratories
178-182 Saddle River Rd
Saddle Brook, NJ 07663-4619 201-843-2525
Fax: 201-843-4934 sanipure.labs@verizon.net
www.sanipure.com
Quality control lab testing facility specializing in microbiological, extraneous matter, packaging materials, pesticide residue, pharmalogical, water and effluent testing services
Owner: Ronald Snitcher
Estimated Sales: $1-2.5 Million
Number Employees: 10-19
Square Footage: 5000

28850 Sani-Tech Group
PO Box 1010
Andover, NJ 07821-1010 973-579-1313
Fax: 973-579-3908

28851 Sani-Top Products
PO Box 117
De Leon Springs, FL 32130-0117 386-985-4667
Fax: 386-985-0202 800-874-6094
Manufacturer and exporter of plastic trays, bowls, servers and food covers; also, acrylic specialty display cases
President: A David Logan
CEO: Joyce Monaco
Purchasing Manager: Walt Houdeshell
Estimated Sales: $1 - 3 Million
Number Employees: 10-19
Parent Co: Mastercraft Products Corporation

28852 SaniServ
451 E County Line Rd
Mooresville, IN 46158 317-831-7030
Fax: 317-831-7036 800-733-8073
sdowling@saniserv.com www.saniserv.com
Manufacturer and exporter of batch machines, freezers and dispensers for ice cream, shakes, frozen beverages/cocktails, yogurt and custard; processor of cappuccino; importer of visual slush machines
President: Robert Mc Afee
CFO: Allen McCormick
Number Employees: 50-99
Square Footage: 150000
Parent Co: MD Holdings
Type of Packaging: Consumer, Food Service, Private Label
Brands:
Saniserv

28853 Sanifab
P.O.Box 86
Stratford, WI 54484-0086 715-687-4332
Fax: 715-687-3225
greatsolutions@abprocess.com
www.abprocess.com
Manufacturer and exporter of ASME U and R stamps, process systems, tanks, vessels and custom components
President: Anthony Hilgemann
CEO: Ajay Hilgemann
CFO: Paul Kinate
Quality Control: Brian Folv
VP Sales/Marketing: Jim Banks
Estimated Sales: $10 - 20 Million
Number Employees: 100-249
Square Footage: 35000
Parent Co: A&B Process Systems Corporation

28854 Sanitary Couplers
275 S Pioneer Boulevard
Springboro, OH 45066-1180 513-743-0144
Fax: 513-743-0146 reseal@compuserve.com
www.reseal.com
Manufacturer and exporter of high purity sanitary hoses, fittings and hose assemblies
General Manager: Jeffrey Zornow
Manager: Mark Hess
Sales Manager (Western Region): Jason Parks
Customer Service: Tracy Brandenburg
Estimated Sales: $2.5-5 Million
Number Employees: 9
Square Footage: 80000
Parent Co: Norton Performance Plastics
Brands:
Challenger
Cleargard
Gladiator
Permaseal
Protector
Reseal

Sanigard
Sentry

28855 (HQ)Sanitech Corporation
7207 Lockport Pl # H
Lorton, VA 22079-1534 703-339-7001
Fax: 703-339-6848 800-486-4321
info@sanitechcorp.com www.sanitechcorp.com
Manufacturing sanitation systems for food processing and food service operations
President/CEO: Mano Sharma
CFO: Pash Bhalla
VP: Bill Hannigan
Director Marketing: Sumeer Sharma
Production: Tom Wines
Plant Manager: J R Bhalla
Purchasing Manager: Mike Sherman
Estimated Sales: $5 Million
Number Employees: 20-49
Square Footage: 10000
Brands:
Sanitech Mark Series Systems

28856 (HQ)Sanitek Products, Inc
3959 Goodwin Ave
Los Angeles, CA 90039 323-245-6781
Fax: 818-242-1071 818-242-1071
info@sanitek.com www.sanitek.com
Manufacturer and exporter of floor finishes, hand cleaners and industrial chemicals; also, liquid soap and specialty chemicals available
President: Robert L Moseley
VP: David Moseley
R&D and QC: Ronald Ostroff
Estimated Sales: $5 - 10 Million
Number Employees: 10-19
Square Footage: 160000
Type of Packaging: Consumer, Private Label

28857 Sanitor Manufacturing Company
1221 W Centre Ave
Portage, MI 49024 269-327-3001
Fax: 269-327-4562 800-379-5314
customerservice@sanitorusa.com
www.sanitorusa.com
Paper toilet seat covers and dispensers
President: David J Dietrich
Director Sales/Marketing: Mike Fawley
Estimated Sales: $5-10 Million
Number Employees: 10-19
Square Footage: 25000
Brands:
Neat Seat

28858 Sanolite Corporation
26 Papetti Plz
Elizabeth, NJ 07206 908-353-8500
Fax: 908-353-6752 800-221-0806
webmaster@sanolite.com www.sanolite.com
Manufacturer and exporter of dishwashing and laundry products
President: Norman Lubin
Vice President: Mark Sherman
Estimated Sales: $10-20 Million
Number Employees: 50-99
Type of Packaging: Food Service
Brands:
Sanolite

28859 Santa Fe Bag Company
4950 E 49th Street
Vernon, CA 90058-2736 323-585-7225
Fax: 323-585-0313
Multi-wall and paper bags
President: David Sugarman
Estimated Sales: $10-20 Million
Number Employees: 20-49

28860 Santa Ynex Trading Company
500 N 8th Street
Suite B
Lompoc, CA 93436-4946 805-737-7967
Fax: 805-737-1844
Wine industry corks and capsules

28861 Santana Products
801 E Corey St
Scranton, PA 18505-3523 570-343-7921
Fax: 570-348-2959 800-368-5002
inforequest@hinyhider.com www.hinyhider.com
Storage systems
Estimated Sales: $20-50 Million
Number Employees: 100

28862 Sapac International
PO Box 2035
Fond Du Lac, WI 54936-2035 920-921-5060
Fax: 920-921-0822 800-257-2722
Palletizers; importer of bag filling and sealing equipment
Project Manager: Henry Brown
President/National Sales Manager: Bruce McMurry
Controls Manager: Jerome Haser
Number Employees: 1-4
Parent Co: Sapac

28863 Sapat Packaging Industry
PO Box 65723
Albuquerque, NM 87193-5723 505-275-9251
Fax: 505-271-8830
Estimated Sales: $.5 - 1 million
Number Employees: 1-4

28864 Sarasota Restaurant Equipment
2651 Whitfield Ave Ste 101
Sarasota, FL 34243 941-924-1410
Fax: 941-923-1510 800-434-1410
sales@floridafoodservicespecialists.com
www.sarasotarestaurantequipment.com
Manufacturer and wholesaler/distributor of restaurant and kitchen equipment
Owner: Marylin Snodell
Project Manager: Thomas Moon
Sales Manager: Joe Todd
Estimated Sales: $2.5-5 Million
Number Employees: 10-19
Square Footage: 10000

28865 Sardee Industries
2211 W Washington St
Orlando, FL 32805 407-295-2114
Fax: 407-297-6362 sales@sardee.com
www.sardee.com
Container and lid conveyor handling systems including air, vacuum, magnetic and mechanical; also, PET bottle palletizers/depalletizers
Manager: Bill Bryer
Estimated Sales: $1-2.5 Million
Number Employees: 20-49
Square Footage: 100000

28866 Sardee Industries
5100 Academy Drive
Suite 400
Lisle, IL 60523 630-824-4200
Fax: 630-824-4225 sales@sardee.com
www.sardee.com
Manufacturer and exporter of palletizers, depalletizers and pallet, container and end handling equipment
Manager: Bill Bryer
Sales Director: Gary Bishop
Estimated Sales: $5 - 10 Million
Number Employees: 20-49
Square Footage: 50000
Parent Co: Sardee Industries

28867 Sargent & Greenleaf
P.O.Box 930
Nicholasville, KY 40340-0930 859-885-9411
Fax: 859-885-3063 800-826-7652
custserv@sglocks.com www.sglocks.com
Security products including money safe locks and exit devices with alarms
President: Bill Demtsey
R&D: Mike Clarke
CEO: Jerry A Morgan
Quality Control: Wayne Landa
Director Marketing: Gary Kepler
Customer Services Manager: Brian Costley
Estimated Sales: $20 - 50 Million
Number Employees: 100-249
Brands:
Arm-A-Dor
Secure Panic Hardware

28868 (HQ)Sargento Foods Inc.
1 Persnickety Place
Plymouth, WI 53073 920-893-8484
Fax: 920-893-8399 800-243-3737
www.sargentocheese.com
Founded in 1949. Natural and processed cheese
Chairman/CEO: Lou Gentine
CFO: George Hoff
Senior Research Scientist R&D: Craig Hackl
Senior Packaging Development Manager: Guy Turnbull
VP Foodservice Sales/Marketing: Sam Colson
Consumer Products Division Sales Rep: Mike Ruhland
EVP/COO: Mark Rhyan
Corporate Chef: Guy Beardsmore
Estimated Sales: $534 Million
Number Employees: 1,000-4,999
Type of Packaging: Consumer, Food Service, Private Label, Bulk
Brands:
Sargento

28869 Sartorius Corporation
131 Heartland Blvd
Edgewood, NY 11717 631-254-4249
Fax: 631-254-4253 800-635-2906
info.investor@sartorius.com www.sartorius.com
Filtration and weighing products including lab and moisture determination balances and industrial scales
VP: Maurice Knapp
Director Marketing Communications: Arnold Breisblatt
Estimated Sales: $50-100 Million
Number Employees: 100-249
Square Footage: 35000
Parent Co: Sartorius AG
Other Locations:
Sartorius Corp.
Mississauga ON

28870 Sartorius Corporation
131 Heartland Blvd
Edgewood, NY 11717 631-254-4249
Fax: 631-254-4253 800-635-2906
custserv@sartoriuscorp.com www.sartorius.com
Wine industry filtration and weighing equipment
President: Mary Layin
VP: Maurice Knapp
Estimated Sales: $50-100 Million
Number Employees: 100-249

28871 Sasib Beverage & Food North America
808 Stewart Drive
Plano, TX 75074-8101 800-558-3814
sasibbeverage@worldnet.att.net
Manufacturer and exporter of high speed beverage fillers and processing systems, labelers, bottle washers, rinsers, casers, palletizers and turnkey beverage production facilities
President: Claudia Salvi
VP Manufacturing: Robert Prescott
Estimated Sales: $20-50 Million
Number Employees: 186
Square Footage: 300000
Parent Co: Sasib Beverage
Brands:
Alfa
Meyer
Mojonnier
Pama
Sarcmi
Simonazzi

28872 Sasib North America
808 Stewart Dr
Plano, TX 75074-8197 972-422-5808
Fax: 972-424-5041
jim.makins@stewart-systems.com
www.stewart-systems.com
Conveyors, ovens and proofers
Vice President: Jim Makins
Estimated Sales: $20-50 Million
Number Employees: 5-9
Parent Co: Sasi B. Baking

28873 Sasser Signs
750 Craghead St
Danville, VA 24541 434-792-2696
Fax: 434-793-8964 800-752-6091
www.sassersigns.com
Electric signs and billboards including neon
Owner: Cindy Sasser-Hill
VP: Diane Sasser
Estimated Sales: $1-2.5 Million
Number Employees: 10-19
Square Footage: 15000

28874 **Satake USA**
10905 Cash Rd
Stafford, TX 77477 281-276-3600
Fax: 281-494-1427 cvincent@satake-usa.com
www.satake-usa.com
Manufacturer and exporter of sorters including color, nut meat and tomato; also, rice processing and cereal milling equipment available
President: J J Naoki
VP Marketing: Peter Cawthorne
Marketing Specialist: Sandra Langlois
Estimated Sales: $20-50 Million
Number Employees: 100-249
Parent Co: Satake Corporation
Other Locations:
Satake (USA)
Cheshire, UK
Brands:
3vision
Colorwatch
Scanmaster
Shell-Ex
Summa-6

28875 **Saticoy Lemon Cooperative**
600 E Third Street
Oxnard, CA 93030 805-654-6543
Fax: 805-654-6510
webmaster@saticoylemon.com
www.saticoylemon.com
Agricultural Cooperative that is owned by the lemon grower members of which the marketing of the fruit is handled through their affiliation with Sunkist Growers, Inc.
President: Glenn Miller
Chief Financial Officer: Mike Dillard
Exchange/Business Development Manager: John Eliot
Field Manager: David Coert
Sales Coordinator: Jose Mendez
MIS Director: Lee Raymond
Personnel Director: Michael Dennington
Production Manager: Ron Davis
Plant Superintendent: Albert Rivera
Shipping Supervisor: Albert Palacio Sr
Type of Packaging: Food Service

28876 **Sato America**
10350 Nations Ford Rd Ste A
Charlotte, NC 28273 704-644-1650
Fax: 704-644-1662 satosales@satoamerica.com
www.satoamerica.com
Manufactures bar code printers and software
President: Robert Linse
VP: Richard Armstrong
VP: Bob Karb
VP: Bob Lindsay
Estimated Sales: $50 - 75 Million
Number Employees: 20-49

28877 **Satoris America**
1403 Heritage Drive
Suite B
Northfield, MN 55057 507-663-6100
Fax: 507-663-6123 877-603-6100
info@satoris-america.com
www.satoris-america.com
Company's products and services includes autoclaves and retorts, customer service, sales and replacement parts for German technology food safety systems. sales of new retorts, as well as replacement parts for stock retorts used insterilization of commercial food products. Official supplier of OEM parts for retort brnads stock, satori stocktec, satoris.
President: Oliver Barth
CEO: Oliver Barth
Sales: Pam Tidona
Estimated Sales: $4,000,000
Brands:
Satori Stocktec
Satoris
Stock

28878 **Saturn Engineering Corporation**
10 Main St
Newark, NJ 07105 973-465-0224
Fax: 973-465-4219 h.heller@saturneng.com
www.saturneng.com
Hoists including overhead electric wire and rope
President: Steven Gordon
CFO: Debbie Swerdlow
Quality Control: Gert Martens
Estimated Sales: Below $5 Million
Number Employees: 48

28879 **Sauereisen**
160 Gamma Dr
Pittsburgh, PA 15238 412-963-0303
Fax: 412-963-7620 questions@sauereisen.com
www.sauereisen.com
Corrosion-resistant material of construction, corrosion and skid-resistant flooring
CEO: Eric Sauereisen
Quality Control: Craig Maloney
Number Employees: 40

28880 **Saunder Brothers**
Bacon Street
Bridgton, ME 04009 207-647-3331
Fax: 207-647-2064
Manufacturer and exporter of wooden candy sticks, skewers and plain dowels
Co-Owner/President/General Manag: Read Grover
Co-Owner/VP: Robert Berry
Sales Manager/Treasurer: Terri Grover
Number Employees: 24

28881 **Saunders Corporation**
975 N Todd Ave
Azusa, CA 91702 626-691-1111
Fax: 626-691-0116 888-932-8836
west@saunderscorp.com www.saunderscorp.com
Pressure sensitive and adhesive tapes; also, die cutting of roll stock available
CEO: Robert McCollum
Sales Manager: Mike Hibbard
Manager: John Sciacca
Manager: Jon Tarian
General Manager: Wilson Wong
Estimated Sales: $10-20 Million
Number Employees: 1-4
Square Footage: 21000
Parent Co: R.S. Hughes Company

28882 **Saunders Manufacturing Co.**
PO Box 12539
N Kansas City, MO 64116-0539 816-842-0233
Fax: 816-842-1129 800-821-2792
goldenstar@goldenstar.com
www.goldenstar.com
Manufacturer and exporter of regular and dust mops including antimicrobial, cotton wet, disposable and rayon; also, mop handles and frames and carpet mats and mattings
President: Gary Gradinger
National Sales Manager: Ssteve Lewis
VP Manufacturing: Mike Julo
Estimated Sales: $20 - 50 Million
Number Employees: 20-49
Square Footage: 100000
Parent Co: Golden Star
Type of Packaging: Consumer, Food Service, Private Label, Bulk

28883 **Sausage Shoppe**
4501 Memphis Ave
Cleveland, OH 44144 216-351-5213
cheinle@sausageshoppe.com
www.sausageshoppe.com
Sausage and luncheon meat
President/Owner: Norm Heinle
VP/Owner: Carol Heinle
Plant Manager: Alan Heinle
Number Employees: 1-4
Type of Packaging: Consumer, Bulk
Brands:
Sheffler Ham

28884 **Sauvagnat Inc**
12200 Herbert Wayne Court
Suite 180
Huntersville, NC 28078-6396 704-948-0440
Fax: 704-948-0190 800-258-5619
www.evolutiffurniture.com
Outdoor furniture including chairs, tables and lounges
President: Bradford Elliot
CEO: John Menas
Marketing Director: Shannon Lowe
Number Employees: 15
Parent Co: Groupe Sauvagnat
Brands:
Allibert
Triconfort

28885 **Sauve Company Limited**
151 Mill St
Amherst, WI 54406 715-824-2502
Fax: 715-824-2192 ontrack@scltd.com
www.scltd.com
Executive recruiters for the food and dairy industry
President: Gordon Sauve
Vice President: Diane Sauve
Estimated Sales: Less than $500,000
Number Employees: 10

28886 **Savage Brothers Company**
1125 Lunt Ave
Elk Grove Vlg, IL 60007 847-981-3000
Fax: 847-981-3010 800-342-0973
info@savagebros.com www.savagebrothers.com
Supplier of cookers, mixers, stoves, chocolate melting and processing tanks, kettles, mixing bowls and pumps for food depositing, transferring and metering
President: David Floreani
Marketing Manager: Robert Parmley
Estimated Sales: $2.5-5,000,000
Number Employees: 20-49
Square Footage: 20000
Type of Packaging: Food Service
Brands:
Firemixer
Hi-Speed Cooker
Liftiltruk

28887 **Savanna Pallets**
106 E 1st Ave
PO Box 308
McGregor, MN 55760 218-768-2077
Fax: 218-768-3112 pallets@frontiernet.net
www.savannapallets.com
Skids and pallets
President: Allen Raushel
VP: Al Raushel
Estimated Sales: $1 - 5 Million
Number Employees: 50-99
Square Footage: 10000

28888 **Savasort**
6811 Garden Rd
West Palm Beach, FL 33404 561-848-8744
Fax: 800-835-8515 800-255-8744
info@savasort.com www.savasort.com
Document sorting equipment
President: Phillip Elmore
Estimated Sales: Below $5 Million
Number Employees: 1-4
Square Footage: 18000

28889 **Save-A-Tree**
1338 Berkeley Way
P.O.Box 862
Berkeley, CA 94701 510-843-5233
Fax: 510-843-4906 lolalone@yahoo.com
Organic cotton bags
Properietor: Penny Marienthal
Estimated Sales: Below $5,000,000
Number Employees: 1

28890 **Save-O-Seal Corporation**
PO Box 553
Elmsford, NY 10523-0553 914-592-3031
Fax: 914-592-4511 800-831-9720
www.save-o-seal.com
Manufacturer and exporter of bagging machines and heat sealing equipment; also, coated slitting blades
President: Tullio Muscariello
Sales: Anna DeLuca
Estimated Sales: $2.5 - 5 Million
Number Employees: 5-9

28891 **Saverglass**
841 Latour Court
Suite B
Napa, CA 94558 707-259-2930
Fax: 707-259-2933 fgc@savgerglass.com
www.saverglass.com
Wine and spirits bottles
VP Fainance: Michael Graham
Manager: Mike Graham
Estimated Sales: $500,000-$1 Million
Number Employees: 5-9
Parent Co: Saverglass group

28892 Savogran Company
259 Lenox St
Norwood, MA 02062 781-762-2371
Fax: 781-762-1095 800-225-9872
contactus@savogran.com www.savogran.com
Paint remover and cleaning powder
Estimated Sales: $20-50 Million
Number Employees: 20-49
Brands:
Dirtex

28893 Savoye Packaging Corporation
645 Edison Way
Reno, NV 89502 775-857-3600
Fax: 775-857-3601 info@savoyepackaging.com
www.savoyepackaging.com
Wine industry polyaluminum capsules
Owner: Hanna Lasilla
Estimated Sales: $10-20 Million
Number Employees: 1-4

28894 Saxco International
200 Gibraltar Rd # 101
Horsham, PA 19044-2385 215-443-8100
Fax: 215-443-8370 800-245-1016
info@saxcointl.com www.saxcointl.com
Wine industry packaging materials
President: Herb Sachs
Estimated Sales: $5 - 10 Million
Number Employees: 10-19

28895 Saxco Plastics
200 Gibraltar Rd # 101
Horsham, PA 19044-2385 215-443-8100
Fax: 215-443-8370 info@saxcointl.com
www.saxcointl.com
Wine industry closures
President: Herbert L Sachs
Estimated Sales: $5 - 10 Million
Number Employees: 10-19

28896 Sayco Yo-Yo Molding Company
2 Sunset Ave
Cumberland, RI 02864 401-724-5296
Manufacturer and exporter of advertising promotions and novelties including yo-yos, yo-yo promotions
President: Lawrence Sayegh
Plant Manager: Leroy Sayegh
Purchasing Manager: Larry Sayco
Estimated Sales: Under $300,000
Number Employees: 5
Square Footage: 1500
Parent Co: L.J. Sayegh & Company
Type of Packaging: Consumer, Private Label
Brands:
Sayco
Sayco Tournament

28897 Scafati Uniforms
417a W 44th St
New York, NY 10036-4402 212-695-4944
Fax: 212-695-4944 sca.fati@horizon.net
Doorman, bellboy, waiter uniforms
President: Joe Itkowitz
Estimated Sales: Below $5 Million
Number Employees: 1-4

28898 Scaglia America
3630 Green Park Cir
Charlotte, NC 28217 704-357-8811
Fax: 704-357-8866 szanardi@scaglia.us
www.sit-indeva.com
Manufacturer and importer of material handling equipment including balancers
President: Alessandro Scaglia
VP: Stefania Zanardi
Estimated Sales: $2.5-5 Million
Number Employees: 5-9
Parent Co: Scaglia America
Type of Packaging: Bulk
Brands:
Liftronic Balancer

28899 Scaltrol
PO Box 609
Norcross, GA 30091-0609 404-261-4272
Fax: 404-262-7679 800-868-0629
scaltrol@mindspring.com www.scaltrolinc.com
Manufacturer and exporter of water treatment units for removal of scale and staining
Owner: Austin Hansen
Business Manager: Hilda Epsten
Operations Manager: Sunday Christopher
Number Employees: 6
Square Footage: 5000
Brands:
Scaltrol

28900 Scan Coin
20145 Ashbrook Pl # 110
Ashburn, VA 20147-3375 703-729-8600
Fax: 703-729-8606 800-336-3311
info@scancoin-usa.com www.scancoin-usa.com
Manufacturer and importer of coin and currency handling equipment including counting, sorting and packing
President: Per Lundin
CFO: Per Lundin
CEO: Lloyd Kaiser
R&D: Per Lundin
Quality Control: Per Lundin
Estimated Sales: Below $5 Million
Number Employees: 5-9
Parent Co: Scan Coin AB
Type of Packaging: Consumer

28901 Scan Corporation
110 Lithia Pinecrest Rd Ste G
Brandon, FL 33511 813-653-2877
Fax: 813-654-3949 800-881-7226
sales@scancorporation.com
www.scancorporation.com
Manufacturer and exporter of point of sale systems including touch screen p.c.'s and terminals, membrane keyboards and scanning equipment
President: Frank Harrison
Estimated Sales: $10-20 Million
Number Employees: 10-19

28902 Scan Group
1820 S Mohawk Dr
Appleton, WI 54914-4732 920-730-9150
Fax: 920-730-8991 muller@scangroup.net
www.scangroup.net
Paper tableware including plates, cups and napkins
Manager: Steve Mueller
Estimated Sales: $5-10 Million
Number Employees: 1-4

28903 Scandia Packaging Machinery Company
15 Industrial Rd
Fairfield, NJ 07004 973-473-6100
Fax: 973-473-7226 jbrown@scandiapack.com
www.scandiapack.com
Manufacturer and exporter of automatic packaging equipment for overwrapping, bundling, banding, multipacking, cartoning and collating
President: Bill I Bronander II III
Finance: Cecelia G. Bronander
Engineering: Arthur Goldberg
Sales Representative: Carolyn Placentino
Customer Service: Maria Van Ness
Sales Manager: James J. Brown
Parts Department: Lewis D'Allegro
Estimated Sales: $10-20 Million
Number Employees: 20-49
Square Footage: 30600

28904 Scanning Devices
31 Dunham Rd.
Unit 1
Billerica, MA 01821 978-362-1123
Fax: 978-362-8693 mail@scanningdevices.com
www.scanningdevices.com
Photoelectric control and optical activated counters, optical sensors and scanners Force Measurement instrumentation,Display devices
Estimated Sales: $2.5 - 5 Million
Number Employees: 20-49

28905 Scattaglia Farms
10400 E Avenue U
Littlerock, CA 93543-3121 661-944-3880
Fax: 661-944-5790 www.scattagliafarms.com
President: Louis Scattaglia
Estimated Sales: $50 - 100 Million
Number Employees: 50-99

28906 Schaefer Machine Company Inc.
200 Commercial Dr
Deep River, CT 06417 860-526-4000
Fax: 860-526-4654 800-243-5143
schaefer@schaeferco.com www.schaeferco.com
Manufacturer and exporter of label gluing and cementing machinery
Owner: Robert Gammons
Estimated Sales: $1-3 Million
Number Employees: 5-9
Square Footage: 40000
Brands:
Schaefer Ms Label

28907 Schaefer Technologies
4901 W Raymond St
Indianapolis, IN 46241 317-241-9444
Fax: 317-240-1273 800-435-7174
kjs@indy.net www.schaefer-technologies.net
Distributor of quality equipment specialized in the fit the needs of the pharmaceutical, health, food and cosmetic industries
President: Steven Schaefer
Estimated Sales: $5-10 Million
Number Employees: 50-99
Number of Products: 19

28908 Schaeff
8657 Beloit Ave
Bridgeview, IL 60455-1776 708-598-9099
Fax: 712-944-5115 www.schaafequipment.com
Fork lift trucks, tow tractors and electric rider material transport vehicles
Owner: Bill Schaaf
Sales Manager: Melanie Bohle
Estimated Sales: $10-20 Million
Number Employees: 5-9
Square Footage: 144000

28909 Schaeffler Group USA
308 Springhill Farm Rd
Fort Mill, SC 29715 803-548-8500
Fax: 803-548-8599 info.us@schaeffler.com
www.inausa.com
CEO: Bruce Warmbold
Estimated Sales: $1 - 5 Million
Number Employees: 1,000-4,999

28910 Schaerer Corporation
2900 Orange Ave # 102
Signal Hill, CA 90755-1821 562-989-3004
Fax: 562-989-5815 info@schaererusa.com
www.schaererusa.com
Supra-automatic espresso machines
President: Steven Eckenhausen
Estimated Sales: $5 Billion
Number Employees: 20-49
Parent Co: M. Schaerer AG
Brands:
Schaerer

28911 Schaffer Poidometer Company
5421 Claybourne Street
Pittsburgh, PA 15232-1623 412-281-9031
Fax: 412-281-1911
Poidometers for weighing and blending large quantities of raw ingredients
Owner: Joseph Pfenninger
Estimated Sales: Less than $500,000
Number Employees: 4
Square Footage: 10000

28912 Schanno Transportation
837 Apollo Rd
Eagan, MN 55121-2387 651-457-9700
Fax: 651-552-5835 800-544-6172
Estimated Sales: $1 - 5 Million
Number Employees: 100-249

28913 Scheb International
27 Clarington Way
North Barrington, IL 60010-6932 847-381-2573
Fax: 847-381-2573 schebltd@aol.com
www.schebltd.com
Manufacturer and exporter of tote, storage and material handling boxes; also, bulk carbon dioxide storage and delivery systems for beverage use; importer of carbon dioxide bulk delivery systems
Estimated Sales: $1 - 5 Million
Number Employees: 3
Parent Co: Carbo Carbonation Company
Type of Packaging: Food Service
Brands:
Carbo Mizers
Econ-O-Totes

28914 Schebler Company
5665 Fenno Rd
Bettendorf, IA 52722 563-359-0110
Fax: 563-359-8430 schebler@schebler.com
www.schebler.com

Conveying and weighing equipment, vibratory feeders and food eqiupment
President: Gerald W McClure
CEO: Gerald McClure
CFO: Jim Booe
Quality Control: Ron Wildermuth
Marketing Director: Don Gbeault
Sales Director: John Guinta
Production Manager: Larry Jones
Purchasing Manager: Barbara Welsch
Estimated Sales: $20 - 30 Million
Number Employees: 100-249
Square Footage: 190000

28915 Scheidegger
345 Kear St Ste 200
Yorktown Heights, NY 10598 914-245-7850
Fax: 914-243-0976 scheidseal@aol.com
Manufacturer, importer and exporter of tamper evident sealing and full body sleeving machinery
VP Sales/Marketing: Dipak Modi
Number Employees: 2
Parent Co: Sch. S.A.

28916 Schenck AccuRate
746 E Milwaukee St
Whitewater, WI 53190 262-473-2441
Fax: 262-473-2489 800-558-0184
mktg@accuratefeeders.com www.sarinc.com
Dry material feeders
President: Dirk Maroske
Marketing Manager: Gary Kuehneman
Estimated Sales: $20-50 Million
Number Employees: 100-249

28917 Schenck Process LLC
746 E. Milwaukee Street
P.O.Box 208
Whitewater, WI 53190-0208 262-473-2441
Fax: 262-473-2489 888-742-1249
mktg@accuratefeeders.com
www.accuratefeeders.com
Vibratory feeders with loss-in-weight batch control systems and loss-in-weight continuous flow systems; also, portable universal bin and feeder combination, bulk bag discharger, box dumps, weightbelts, and screw feeders
President: Dirk Maroske
CEO: Jay Brown
Research & Development: Bob Stephenson
Marketing Director: Mike Koras
Sales Director: Chris Isom
Regional Sales Manager: Rick Pruden
Plant Manager: Bill Samborski
Purchasing Manager: Angie Adams
Estimated Sales: $3-4 Million
Number Employees: 100-249
Square Footage: 128000
Parent Co: Schenck Process
Brands:
Accuflow
Solidsflow

28918 Schermerhorn
165 Front St # D12
Chicopee, MA 01013-1270 413-598-8348
Fax: 413-594-8439
Paper set-up boxes
President: Mark Farsi
Estimated Sales: $20-50 Million
Number Employees: 20-49
Square Footage: 37000

28919 Scherping Systems
PO Box 10
Winsted, MN 55395-0010 320-485-4401
Fax: 320-485-2666 mail@scherpingsystems.com
www.scherpingsystems.com
Custom stainless steel tanks, cheese making machinery and clean-in-place systems; also, design installation and control services available
President: Tim High
CFO: Cindy Tellinghuisen
Sales Manager: George Schwinghammer
Plant Manager: Harvey Dvorak
Number Employees: 100-249

28920 Schiefer Packaging Corporation
160 Beverly Rd
Syracuse, NY 13207-1302 315-422-0615
Fax: 315-478-4140
Boxes for food products
President: Charles Simek
Estimated Sales: $1-2.5 Million
Number Employees: 1-4

28921 Schiff & Company
1120 Bloomfield Ave
Ste 103
West Caldwell, NJ 07006 973-227-1830
Fax: 973-227-5330 schiffandcompany@aol.com
www.schiffandcompany.com
Regulatory services for the food and cosmetic industry.
President: Robert Schiff
VP: Jack Parker
Business Development: John Round
Estimated Sales: $2.5 - 5 Million
Number Employees: 5-9
Square Footage: 3000

28922 (HQ)Schiffenhaus Industries
2013 McCarter Hwy
Newark, NJ 07104 973-484-5000
Fax: 973-484-8628
Corrugated paper boxes and P.O.P. displays
President: J Anton Schiffenhaus
CEO: Steven Grossman
Estimated Sales: $28.7 Million
Number Employees: 100-249

28923 Schiffmayer Plastics Corp.
1201 Armstrong St
Algonquin, IL 60102 847-658-8140
Fax: 847-658-0863
fritz@schiffmayerplastics.com
www.schiffmayerplastics.com
Capping and closing supplies
President: Karl F Schiffmayer
Quality Control: Gary Hunt
Estimated Sales: $20 - 30 Million
Number Employees: 70

28924 Schlagel
491 N Emerson
Cambridge, MN 55008 763-689-5991
Fax: 763-689-5310 800-328-8002
sales@schlagel.com www.schlagel.com
Manufacturer and exporter of feed and grain equipment
CEO: Chris Schlagel
Sales Manager: Jeff Schwab
Purchasing Manager: Drew Stoffell
Estimated Sales: $10-20 Million
Number Employees: 50-99

28925 Schleicher & Company ofAmerica
5715 Clyde Rhyne Drive
Sanford, NC 27330-9563 919-775-7318
Fax: 919-774-8731 800-775-7570
soa@interpath.com www.intlmus.com
Distributor and supplier of compactors and balers, paper shredders
President: Jack Costelloe
VP: John Ulam
Marketing Manager: Libby Nelson
Estimated Sales: $10 - 20 Million
Number Employees: 20
Square Footage: 50000
Brands:
Intimus
Olympia
Schleicher

28926 Schleicher & Schuell MicroSience
800 Centennial Ave # 1
Piscataway, NJ 08854-3911 973-245-8300
Fax: 973-245-8301 800-645-2302
sales@biopathinc.com www.whatman.com
Microbiological media, membranes, monitors, HACCP kits, MI agar & broth, Coliform broth, Listeria swabs, E coli media, paper filtration, glass filtration, sample preparation filtration, ultra filtration for pharmaceutical research andproduction, cell counters
President: Keith Jaythaward
Quality Control: Berni Reedes
Senior VP: Richard Dool
VP Marketing: John Perini
VP Sales: Joseph Murdock
Operations Manager: Louis Gugliotta
Estimated Sales: $9 - 12 Million
Number Employees: 10-19
Parent Co: Schleicher & Schuell MicroScience, GmbH
Brands:
Biopath

28927 Schloss Engineered Equipment
10555 E Dartmouth Ave
Suite 230
Aurora, CO 80014 303-695-4500
Fax: 303-695-4507
Drum and bar screens, compactors, grit and sludge collectors, flocculators and conveyors
President: Kristy Schloss
Estimated Sales: $5-10 Million
Number Employees: 5-9

28928 (HQ)Schlueter Company
PO Box 548
Janesville, WI 53547-0548 608-755-5444
Fax: 608-755-5440 800-359-1700
www.schlueterco.com
Manufacturer and exporter of dairy and food plant equipment including process tanks, conveyors, hoppers, sanitizing systems (CIP-COP-HY pressure-foam), liquid/solid separators, strainers, filters, rotary drums, etc.; also, carts andwork tables
President: Brad Losching
VP: H Losching
Marketing Manager: C Benskin
Estimated Sales: $10-20 Million
Number Employees: 50
Square Footage: 100000
Other Locations:
Schlueter Co.
Fresno CA
Brands:
Safgard

28929 Schlueter Company
310 N Main St
Janesville, WI 53545 608-755-5444
Fax: 608-755-5440 800-359-1700
schlueter@socket.net www.schlueterco.com
Custom plastic blow molding, recreational, medical, toys, industrial and others all under the category if custom moulding. also post moulding and resins under the category of plastic moulding
President: Bradley W Losching
Estimated Sales: $5-10 Million
Number Employees: 50-99

28930 Schlueter Company
310 N. Main Street
PO Box 548
Janesville, WI 53545 608-755-5444
Fax: 608-755-5440 800-359-1700
www.schlueterco.com
Clean rooms and equipment, custom fabrication, flow diversion stations
President: Brad Losching
Marketing: Charles Benskin
Plant Manager: Erik Eide
Estimated Sales: $10-20 Million
Number Employees: 35
Square Footage: 80000
Type of Packaging: Food Service

28931 Schmalz
5200 Atlantic Avenue
Raleigh, NC 27616-5008 919-713-0880
Fax: 919-713-0883 schmalz@schmalz.us
www.schmalz.com
Supplier of; vacuum lifting equipment, vacuum components & gripping systems
President: Volker Schmitz
CFO: Kevin Saylor
Estimated Sales: $10 Million
Number Employees: 26
Parent Co: Schmalz

28932 Schmersal
660 White Plains Road
Suite 160
Tarrytown, NY 10591-9994 914-347-4775
Fax: 914-347-1567 888-496-5143
salesusa@schmersal.com www.schmersal.com
Man and machine safeguarding devices
President: Peter Engstrom
CFO: Mario Tucci
Manager: John Monahan
Estimated Sales: $3 - 5 Million
Number Employees: 20

28933 Schmidt Progressive, LLC
360 Harmon Ave
P.O. Box 380
Lebanon, OH 45036 513-934-2600
Fax: 513-932-8768 800-272-3706
steve@schmidtprogressive.com
www.schmidtprogressive.com

Design, engineering and manufacturing display fixtures for the supermarket, bakery, concession, food service and floral industries.
Owner/CEO: Julia Rodenbeck
VP Sales/Marketing: Stephen Moore
VP Sales/Marketing: Stephen Moore
VP Administration: Joseph Perdy
VP Manufacturing: Don Blades
Plant Manager: Robert Newton
Purchasing Manager: Don Blades
Estimated Sales: $2-5 Million
Number Employees: 20-49
Square Footage: 240000
Brands:
Food Furniture
Schmidt

28934 Schneider Automation
1 High St Ste 5
North Andover, MA 01845 978-691-1400
Fax: 978-975-9400 www.schneiderautomation.com
Manufacturer and exporter of programmable logic controllers and software
President: Ray Sansouci
CEO: Ed Mueskes
Marketing Manager: Fred Curieck
Estimated Sales: I
Number Employees: 500-999
Parent Co: Groupe Schneider
Brands:
Modicom
Square D
Telemechanique

28935 Schneider Electric Sensor Competency Center
1875 Founders Dr
Dayton, OH 45420 937-252-2121
Fax: 937-258-5830 800-435-2121
customer-support-us@sesensors.com
www.tesensors.com
Manufacturer and exporter of controls and ultrasonic sensors for food processing machinery and conveyors
President: Greg Nelson
CFO: Benjamin Berner
Quality Control: Mark Waggoner
Marketing Manager: Erin Weckesser
Sales: Greg Welson
Operations Manager: Michael Edmiston
Purchasing Manager: William Denlinger
Estimated Sales: $5 - 10 Million
Number Employees: 50-99
Number of Brands: 2
Square Footage: 30000
Brands:
Microsonic
Superprox

28936 Schneider Packaging Equipment Company
P.O.Box 890
Brewerton, NY 13029 315-676-3035
Fax: 315-676-2875 sales@schneiderequip.com
www.schneiderequip.com
CEO: Dick Schneider
Estimated Sales: $20 - 50 Million
Number Employees: 100-249

28937 Schneider Packaging Equipment
PO Box 890
Brewerton, NY 13029 315-676-3035
Fax: 315-676-2875 info@schneiderequip.com
www.schneiderequip.com
Case packers, robotic palletizers, conveyors, pallet dispersers, tray packers, turnkey systems and line packaging integration
President: Richard Schneider
Director Sales/Marketing: Paul Burdick
Sales: Paul Burdick
Estimated Sales: $20-50 Million
Number Employees: 100-249
Square Footage: 88000

28938 Schneider Packing Equipment Company
PO Box 890
5370 Guy Young Rd
Brewerton, NY 13029-0890 315-676-3035
Fax: 315-676-2875 sales@schneiderequip.com
www.schneiderequip.com
Manufacturers case packing and robotic palletizing equipment and integrates conveyors, case elevators/lowerators, pallet dispensers, slip sheet dispensers and shuttle transfer cars for full unit loads.
Founder, Chief Executive Officer: Dick Schneider
Founder, Chief Executive Officer: Dick Schneider
Estimated Sales: $500,000-$1 Million
Number Employees: 100-249
Square Footage: 400000

28939 Schnuck Markets, Inc.
11420 Lackland Road
PO Bix 46928
St Louis, MO 63146-6928 314-994-9900
800-829-9901
consumer@schnucks.com www.schnucks.com
Supermarket chain with 100 stores in five states: Missouri, Illinois, Indiana, Wisconsin, and Iowa. Founded in 1939. Has two manufacturing facilities listed below.
Chairman/CEO: Scott Schnuck
Estimated Sales: $2.1 Billion
Number Employees: 15,000
Other Locations:
Manufacturing Facility
O Fallon MO
Manufacturing Facility
Bridgeton MO
Brands:
Valutime
Schnucks
Full Circle
Top Care
Schnucks
Culinaria

28940 Schober USA
4690 Industry Dr
Fairfield, OH 45014 513-489-7393
Fax: 513-489-7485 800-344-8324
solutions@schoberusa.com
www.schoberusa.com
Rotary die cutting equipment
CFO: Marion Hixon
Manager: Marion Hixson
Estimated Sales: $1 - 2.5 Million
Number Employees: 1-4

28941 Schoeneck Containers
2160 S 170th St
New Berlin, WI 53151 262-786-9360
Fax: 262-786-0772 www.schoeneck.com
Plastic bottles
President: Paul Schoeneck
Chairman: Robert Schoeneck
CFO: Jim Anderson
Estimated Sales: Below $5 Million
Number Employees: 100-249
Square Footage: 120000

28942 (HQ)Scholle Corporation
19520 Jamboree Rd.
Suite 250
Irvine, CA 92612 949-955-1750
Fax: 949-250-1462 www.scholle.com
Supplier of bag-in-box packaging, metallized plastics and paper, flexible shipping containers, industry leading bag-in-box tap and filling technology, marine salvage devices and battery electrolyte
President/CEO: William Scholle
Estimated Sales: $227.30 Million
Number Employees: 1900
Square Footage: 35000
Brands:
Rhino

28943 (HQ)Scholle Corporation
200 W North Ave
Northlake, IL 60164 708-562-7290
Fax: 708-562-6569 888-224-6269
scholle@scholle.com www.scholle.com
Bag-in-box packaging solutions with molded spouts and barrier films for hot fill, extended shelf life, particulated liquids and aseptic foods
President: Leon Gianeschi
CFO: Jim Samson
Quality Control: Ed Kajiwara
R&D: Jeff Jessers
Director Marketing: Jeff Jeffers
Estimated Sales: $185 Million
Number Employees: 250-499

28944 Schoneman, Inc
4540 Park Avenue
Ashtabula, OH 44004 440-998-2273
Fax: 440-998-2285 800-255-4439
steve@schoneman.com www.schoneman.com
Software for meat, poultry, seafood and produce companies

28945 School Marketing Partners
32302 Camino Capistrano # 207
San Juan Cpstrno, CA 92675-4506 949-487-1515
Fax: 949-661-7778 800-565-7778
tooned-in@schoolmenu.com
www.schoolmenu.com
Menus for school cafeterias
Manager: Lana Huie
Estimated Sales: Below $5 Million
Number Employees: 5-9
Brands:
B.J. Spot
Tooned-In Menus

28946 Schreck Software
1420 Interlachen Cir
Woodbury, MN 55125-8859 651-731-6822
www.schrecksoftware.com
Food costing, inventory and margin management software

28947 (HQ)Schreiber Foods Inc
425 Pine St
Green Bay, WI 54301 920-437-7601
Fax: 920-437-1617 800-344-0333
schreiberweb@schreiberfoods.com
www.schreiberfoods.com
Founded in 1945. Natural cheese, processed cheese, cream cheese, specialty cheese, substitute/imitation cheese, string cheese, yogurt and butter blends
President/CEO: Mike Haddad
VP Finance/CFO: Matt Mueller
VP Foodservice Sales: John O'Connor
Estimated Sales: $3 Billion
Number Employees: 6,800
Type of Packaging: Consumer, Food Service, Private Label, Bulk
Other Locations:
Tempe AZ
Gainesville GA
Carthage MO
Clinton MO
Monett MO
Mt Vernon MO
Ravenna NE
Shippensburg PA
Nashville TN
Stephenville TX
Logan UT
Smithfield UT
Wisconsin Rapids WI
Brands:
American Heritage
Clearfield
Cooper
Laferia
Lov-It
Menu
Raskas
Ready-Cut
School Chioce
Schreiber

28948 Schroeder Sewing Technologies
165 Balboa Street
Ste C-2
San Marcos, CA 92069 760-591-9733
Fax: 760-591-4019 sales@ssmci.com
www.schroedermachinetechnologies.com
Manufacturer and exporter of automatic case packing and erecting machines
President: Carl Fahrenkrug
CFO: Richard Jones
Chief Mechanical Engineer: Patrick Burton
Marketing: Sandy Delepovitz
Sales Manager: Matt Brown
Public Relations: Sandy Delepovit
Operations: David Barriello
Estimated Sales: $1 Million
Number Employees: 50-99
Square Footage: 160000
Type of Packaging: Private Label
Brands:
Formnumatic
Quadnumatic

28949 **Schroter, USA**
508 Clinton Street
Defiance, OH 43512-2635 419-782-2430
Fax: 419-784-9717
Air pollution control and environmental services, drying rooms, ovens, smokehouses, refrigeration systems, tempering systems and accessories

28950 **Schubert Packaging Systems**
4505 Excel Pkwy
Addison, TX 75001-5677 972-233-6665
Fax: 972-233-3422
sales@schubertpackaging.com
www.schubertpackaging.com
Casing equipment, packers
Manager: Doug Granowski
Head of Sales: Gerald Grad
Estimated Sales: $500,000-$1 Million
Number Employees: 10-19

28951 **Schurman's Wisconsin Cheese Country**
7786 County U East
PO Box 176
Beetown, WI 53802 608-794-2422
Fax: 608-794-2194 info@schurmanscheese.com
www.schurmanscheese.com
Broker of health foods, natural cheeses, packaging and private label items
President: Lorraine Schurman
CEO: Jim Morgan
CFO: Jim Morgan
R&D: John Schurman
Quality Control: Jim Morgan
Estimated Sales: $10 - 20 Million
Number Employees: 20-49
Type of Packaging: Private Label

28952 **Schutte-Buffalo HammermilLl**
61 Depot Street
Buffalo, NY 14206 716-855-1555
Fax: 716-855-3417 800-447-4634
info@hammermills.com www.hammermills.com
Hammer mills including crushers, pulverizers, and grinders .
President, Chief Executive Officer: Thomas Warne
General Manager/Co-Owner: Jim Guarino
Estimated Sales: $5 - 10 Million
Number Employees: 25
Square Footage: 100000

28953 **Schwaab, Inc**
11415 W. Burleigh Street
Milwaukee, WI 53222
Fax: 800-935-9866 800-935-9877
schwaab@schwaab.com www.schwaab.com
Rubber and steel stamps, corporate and notary seals and name plates
President, Chief Executive Officer: Doug Lane
Vice President and Controller: Bill Yentz
Vice President and Controller: Bill Yentz
VP Sales: Sara Wagner
Chief Operating Officer: Jeremiah McNeal
Estimated Sales: Below $5 Million
Number Employees: 100-249

28954 **Schwab Paper Products Company**
636 Schwab Circle
Romeoville, IL 60446-1144 815-372-2233
Fax: 815-372-1701 800-837-7225
info@schwabpaper.com www.schwabpaper.com
Manufacturer and exporter of layerboards, wax paper and steak paper for bakery, confectionery, frozen meat, seafood and poultry packaging
President: Kathy Schwab
CEO: Michael Schwab
Estimated Sales: Below $5 Million
Number Employees: 30
Square Footage: 60000
Brands:
Econo-Board
Frees-It
Ovenable
Quilon Bakeable Paper

28955 **Schwartz ManufacturingcoCompany**
1000 School St
PO Box 328
Two Rivers, WI 54241 920-793-1375
Fax: 920-793-2235 service@schwartzmfg.com
www.schwartzmfg.com
Filters and filter systems for the dairy, food, beverage and brewery industries.

28956 **Schwarz**
8338 Austin Ave
Morton Grove, IL 60053-3209 847-966-4050
Fax: 847-966-1271 careers@schwarz.com
www.schwarz.com
Food service packaging including take-out and pizza boxes
CFO: Warren Kelleher
CEO: Christopher Donnelly
Estimated Sales: $100-500 Million
Number Employees: 100-249

28957 **Schwerdtel Corporation**
530 van Buren Street
Ridgewood, NJ 7450 201-485-8160
Fax: 201-485- 815 info@schwerdtel.com
www.schwerdtel.de
Automatic filling machines for sealants and food concentrates
President & CFO: Cay Werner
Senior Sales Manager: Florian Mendheim
Estimated Sales: $1 - 2.5 Million
Number Employees: 1-4

28958 **Science Applications International**
221 3rd St
Newport, RI 02840-1087 401-847-4210
Fax: 401-849-1585 800-729-4210
info@saic-epak.com www.saic.com
Inventory and measurement services, package reduction consulting and customized data managment software. Global environmental packaging services
President: Anthony Moraco
President, Chief Executive Officer: John Jumper
Executive Vice President of Human Resour: Brian Keenan
Chief Technical Officer: Amy Alving
Marketing: Janie Harris
Chief Operating Officer: Stuart Shea
Estimated Sales: $10-20 Million
Number Employees: 50-99

28959 **Scienco Systems**
3240 N Broadway
Saint Louis, MO 63147-3515 314-621-2536
Fax: 314-621-1952 fastsandl@primary.net
www.sciencofast.com
Manufacturer and exporter of food and preservative tablets, oil/water separators, grease traps and waste water treatment equipment
General Manager: Jim Predeau
Sales Manager: Gary Wotli
Estimated Sales: $2.5 - 5 Million
Number Employees: 10-19
Parent Co: Smith Loveless

28960 **Scientech, Inc**
5649 Arapahoe Ave
Boulder, CO 80303-1399 303-444-1361
Fax: 303-444-9229 800-525-0522
inst@scientech-inc.com www.scientech-inc.com
Electronic balances and scales
President: Tom O'Rourke
VP/COO: Tom Campbell
Estimated Sales: $2 Million
Number Employees: 10-19
Number of Brands: 6
Number of Products: 75
Square Footage: 52000
Brands:
Astral Laser Power
Mentor Laser Power
Sa Analytical
Sg General
Sl Laboratory
Sp Precision
Synergy Laser Power
Ultra Laser Power
Vector Laser Power

28961 **Scientific Fire Prevention**
627 Union Ave
Brooklyn, NY 11222-2421 718-389-3260
Fax: 718-389-7315 516-222-1715
Fire prevention and exhaust systems; also, indoor air quality testing services available
President: Roy Leonard
Marketing Director: Jeffrey Schwartz

28962 **Scientific Process & Research**
P.O.Box 5008
Kendall Park, NJ 08824-5008 732-846-3477
Fax: 732-846-3029 800-868-4777
info@spar.com www.spar.com
Manufacturer and exporter of extruder, timing and conveyor screws and extruder barrels; exporter of extruder screws and software
Production Manager: Felicia Cappo
Estimated Sales: $2.5-5 Million
Number Employees: 10-19
Square Footage: 80000

28963 **Scitt Turbon Mixer**
9351 Industrial Way
Adelanto, CA 92301-0160 760-246-3430
Fax: 760-246-3505 800-285-8512
sales@scottmixer.com www.scottmixer.com
President: Bill Scott
Estimated Sales: $5 - 10 Million
Number Employees: 20-49

28964 **Scope Packaging**
PO Box 3768
Orange, CA 92857 714-998-4411
Fax: 714-998-5323 www.scopepackaging.com
Manufacturer and exporter of corrugated boxes
President: Michael Flinn
VP Marketing: Cindy Baker
Estimated Sales: $20-50 Million
Number Employees: 50-99
Type of Packaging: Bulk

28965 **(HQ)Scorpio Apparel**
3318 Commercial Avenue
Northbrook, IL 60062-1909 847-559-3100
Fax: 847-559-3103 800-559-3338
lewkscorpio@aol.com www.scorpioapparel.com
Manufacturer and exporter of uniforms
President: Allan L Klein
CEO: Lew Klein
Vice President: Carolyn Philips
Sales Director: Juli Shapiro
Estimated Sales: $2 Million
Number Employees: 34
Square Footage: 14000
Type of Packaging: Private Label
Other Locations:
Scorpio Products
Chicago IL
Brands:
9th Wave
Scorpio
Vespron

28966 **Scot Young Research**
503 Renick St
Saint Joseph, MO 64501 816-232-4100
Fax: 816-232-3701
inquiry@entiprise-manufactureing.com
www.syrclean.com
Manufacturer and exporter of ergonomic and color coded mopping systems
General Manager: Myong Stracener
Estimated Sales: $5-10,000,000
Number Employees: 100-249
Brands:
Syr

28967 **Scotsman Beverage System**
2007 Royal Lane
Suite 100
Dallas, TX 75229-3279 972-488-1030
Fax: 972-243-8075 800-527-7422
www.booth.com
Parent Co: ENODIS

28968 **Scotsman Ice Systems**
75 Corporate Woods Parkway
Vernon Hills, IL 60061 847-215-4500
Fax: 847-913-9844 800-726-8762
customer.relations@scotsman-ice.com
www.scotsman-ice.com
Manufacturer, importer and exporter of ice machines including flakers and nugget makers and hotel dispensing bins, drink dispensers, water filtration systems, etc
President: Mark McClanahan
Controller: Jo Rendino
Director, Quality Assurance: Robert Lee
Vice President, Marketing: Mark Hardy
VP Sales/Marketing: Jim Weaks
Purchasing Agent: Becky Martin
Estimated Sales: $92 Million
Number Employees: 800

Square Footage: 36000
Parent Co: Scotsman Industries
Type of Packaging: Consumer, Food Service
Other Locations:
Scotsman Ice Systems
La Verne CA
Brands:
Cm3 Cubers
Dc33 Luxury
Fme Flakers
Nme Nugget
Scotsman
Slim Line Cubers
Tde Dispensers

28969 Scotsman Ice Systems
775 Corporate Woods Parkway
Vernon Hills, IL 60061 847-215-4500
Fax: 847-913-9844 800-726-8762
sales@scotsman-ice.com www.scotsman-ice.com
Commercial ice making equipment for 50 years including cubers, flakers, dispensers, bins and accessories. Provides equipment for restaurants, bars, hotels/motels, hospitals, etc
Vice President: Robert Weeks
Marketing Director: JoAnn Leach
Sales Director: Jon Noble
Number Employees: 200
Square Footage: 720000
Brands:
Booth
Crystal Tips

28970 Scott & Daniells
264 Freestone Ave
Portland, CT 06480-1640 860-342-1932
Fax: 860-342-2436 info@pharmagraphics.com
www.scottanddaniells.com
Folding cartons
VP: Robert Papa
VP Operations: Kevin Robrge
Plant Manager: Robert Papa
Estimated Sales: $10-20 Million
Number Employees: 50-99
Square Footage: 120000

28971 Scott Equipment Company
605 4th Ave NW
New Prague, MN 56071-1121 952-758-2591
Fax: 952-758-4377 800-264-9519
dave.lucas@scottequipment.com
www.scottequipment.com
Mixers, dryers, high speed blenders, size reduction, de-packaging, turbo dominator, and horizontal batch mixers, available in carbon or stainless steel
President: Dave Lucas
CEO: Richard Lucaas
Estimated Sales: $20 - 50 Million
Number Employees: 50-99

28972 Scott Laboratories
P.O.Box 4559
Petaluma, CA 94955-4559 707-765-6666
Fax: 905-839-0738 800-797-2688
info@scottlabsltd.com www.scottlab.com
Wine industry equipment and supplies
President: Bruce Scott
President: Bruce Scott
Senior Vice President: Tom Anders
Sales Representative: Peter Anderson
Vice President of Sales: Bob Fithian
Vice President of Operations: Bruce Edwards
Estimated Sales: $5 - 10 Million
Number Employees: 50-99

28973 Scott Packaging Corporation
340 N 12th St
Philadelphia, PA 19107-1102 215-925-5595
Packaging products including thermoformed trays, blisters and clamshells
Owner: Scott Page
Estimated Sales: $300,000-500,000
Number Employees: 1-4
Square Footage: 12000
Parent Co: Supplies Unlimited

28974 Scott Pallets
PO Box 657
Amelia Court House, VA 23002 804-561-2514
Fax: 804-561-2664 800-394-2514
scottpallets@tds.com
Wooden pallets
President: Joanne Scottwebb
Quality Control: Joanne Scott
Manager: Ray Hoerger

Estimated Sales: $2.5 - 5 Million
Number Employees: 20-49
Square Footage: 20000
Brands:
Gma
Gpc

28975 Scott Process Equipment& Controls
15 Southgate Drive
Guelph, ON N1G 3M5
Canada 519-836-6902
Fax: 519-836-3325 888-343-5421
info@scottpec.com www.scottpec.com
Processing equipment and controls.
President: Ladislav Rudik
Estimated Sales: $1.3 Million
Number Employees: 5
Square Footage: 4855

28976 Scott Sign Systems
7525 Pennsylvania Ave Ste 101
PO Box 1047
Sarasota, FL 34270-1047 941-355-5171
Fax: 941-351-1787 800-237-9447
mail@scottsigns.com www.scottsigns.com
Manufactures signs and sign systems including letters, logos, graphics and architectural signs.
President: Steve Evans
Estimated Sales: $1-5 Million
Number Employees: 50-99
Square Footage: 75000
Parent Co: Identity Group
Brands:
Brailldots
Braillplaques
Scotslants
Scott-A.D.A.'s Brailleters
Scott-Elites
Scott-Thins
Scott-Trax
Snap-Ins
Tabbee

28977 Scott Turbon Mixer
9351 Industrial Way
Adelanto, CA 92301 760-246-3430
Fax: 760-246-3505 800-285-8512
sales@scottmixer.com www.scottmixer.com
Manufacturer and exporter of sanitary mixing equipment for dairy, beverage and meat; also, complete systems including tanks, platforms and piping, lab and pilot plant mixers
Owner: William Scott
Sales Director: Tim Moore
Estimated Sales: $1 - 5 Million
Number Employees: 20-49
Square Footage: 25000
Brands:
Scott Turbon

28978 (HQ)Scott's Liquid Gold
PO Box 39s
Denver, CO 80239-0019 303-373-4860
Fax: 303-576-6151 800-447-1919
www.scottsliquidgold.com
Household and industrial polishes and air fresheners
Chairman of the Board: Mark Goldstin
R&D and Quality Control: Sharon Moore
CEO: Mark E Goldstein
VP Marketing: Jeff Hinkle
Sales Operations Manager: Linda Melphy
Estimated Sales: $20 - 30 Million
Number Employees: 50-99
Brands:
Touch of Scent

28979 Scranton Lace Company
PO Box 121
Forest City, PA 18421 570-344-1124
Fax: 570-344-1125 800-822-1036
slclace@icontech.com www.scrantonlace.com
Cotton and lace tablecloths, window curtains, place mats and accessories
President: Robert Hyne
CEO: Jennifer Herman
VP Sales: Carol Rabe
Office Manager/EDI COOrd: Wendy Yannuzzi
Estimated Sales: $10-20 Million
Number Employees: 50-99
Square Footage: 600000
Parent Co: Jerry's SportCenter

Brands:
Black Tie Collection
Classic Home Collection

28980 Screen Print, Etc.
1081 N Shepard St # E
Anaheim, CA 92806-2819 714-630-1100
Fax: 714-630-3719 screenprintetc@excitr.com
Display and exhibit boards, decals, flags, pennants, banners and signs; also, commercial printing, graphic design and plastic printing services available
Owner: Raymond Lynch
Estimated Sales: $530 Million
Number Employees: 5-9
Square Footage: 4000
Type of Packaging: Private Label, Bulk

28981 (HQ)Screw Conveyor Corporation
700 Hoffman St
Hammond, IN 46327-1894 219-931-1450
Fax: 219-931-0209 sales@screwconveyor.com
www.screwconveyor.com
Screw conveyors and accessories, elevator buckets, industrial and grain bucket elevators, hydraulic truck dumpers, screw lifts, tube screws and belt conveyor idlers
Owner: Garry M Abraham
Manager of Engineering & Procurement: Steve Rauhut
VP Marketing/Sales: Randy Block
Sales Manager: Anita Kozlowski
Customer Service Supervisor/Sales Engine: Robert Belko
Senior Applications Engineer: Barry Stacy
Estimated Sales: $10 - 20 Million
Number Employees: 20-49
Other Locations:
SCC Industries
Guadalajara, Jal.
Brands:
Enduro-Flo
Enduro-Roll
Exacta-Flo
Kewanee
Rigid-Flo
Screw-Lift
Super-Flo

28982 Scrivner Equipment Company
1811 Hopoca Road
Carthage, MS 39051-9449 601-267-7614
Industrial equipment and supplies
Owner: Martin Scrivner
Estimated Sales: $200,000
Number Employees: 2
Square Footage: 2625

28983 Se-Kure Controls
3714 Runge St
Franklin Park, IL 60131-1112 847-678-3188
Fax: 847-288-9999 800-250-9260
info@se-kure.com www.se-kure.com
Manufacturer, importer and exporter of safes, vaults, security mirrors and cameras and anti-shoplifting devices
Founder/President/CEO: Roger Leyden
Executive VP Administration & Finance: Laura Greenwell
National Sales Manager: John Mangiameli
Estimated Sales: $20-50 Million
Number Employees: 100-249
Number of Products: 500
Square Footage: 200000

28984 Sea Breeze Fruit Flavors
441 Main Road
Towaco, NJ 07082-1201 973-334-7777
Fax: 973-334-2617 800-732-2733
info@seabreezesyrups.com
www.seabreezesyrups.com
Syrups including chocolate, pancake and fountain; also, sundae toppings, bar mixes, juice concentrates and beverage dispensing equipment
President: Steven Sanders
Vice President: Josh Sanders
Research/Development/QC: Frank Maranino
Estimated Sales: $25-49.9 Million
Number Employees: 50-99
Type of Packaging: Consumer, Food Service, Private Label
Brands:
Bosco
Sea Breeze
Tropic Beach

28985 Sea Gull Lighting Products, LLC
306 Elizabeth Lane
Corona, CA 92880-2504 951-273-7380
Fax: 800-877-4855 800-347-5483
Info@SeaGullLighting.com
www.seagulllighting.com
Lighting fixtures
Vice President, Marketing: Ace Rosenstein
Estimated Sales: $1-2.5 Million
Number Employees: 5-9

28986 Seaboard Bag Corporation
3412 Moore St
Richmond, VA 23230-4444
Fax: 804-355-9100 jedge@seaboardbag.com
www.seaboardbag.com
Multi-walled and pasted paper valve bags
Owner: Jim Edge
Estimated Sales: $10-20 Million
Number Employees: 50-99
Parent Co: Morgan Brothers Bag Company

28987 Seaboard Carton Company
1140 31st Street
Downers Grove, IL 60515-1212 708-344-0575
Fax: 708-344-4058
Folding cartons
Estimated Sales: $10-20 Million
Number Employees: 50-99
Square Footage: 90000

28988 Seaboard Folding Box Company
Po Box 547
Fitchburg, MA 01420 978-342-8921
Fax: 978-342-1105 800-255-6313
info@seaboardbox.com www.seaboardbox.com
Manufacturer and exporter of paper boxes
President: Alan Rabinow
Number Employees: 100-249

28989 Seaga Manufacturing
700 Seaga Dr
Freeport, IL 61032 815-297-9500
Fax: 815-297-1700 info@seaga.com
www.seaga.com
Vending equipment for cold beverage merchandisers, soda and beverage vendors, e-cigarette vending equipment, custom vending equipment
President: Steven Chesney
Chairman of the Board and Owner: Steven Chesney
Estimated Sales: $30 - 50 Million
Number Employees: 100-249
Parent Co: Seaga Manufacturing

28990 Seajoy
6619 S Dixie Hwy
PO Box 344
Miami, FL 33143 305-669-0108
Fax: 302-663-0312 877-537-1717
peder@seajoy.com www.seajoy.com
Shrimp including raw head-on whole shrimp, raw shell-on tails, raw shell-on E-Z peel meats, raw peeled & deveined tail on or off, uncut, raw peeled, butterfly meat, raw breaded shrimp meat, and raw peeled & deveined meat on skewers
Administrative President: Peder Jacobson
VP Sales & Operations: Brad Price
Estimated Sales: $220 Thousand
Brands:
Seajoy®
Cjoy®
Bluefield®
Seabrook®

28991 Seal King North America
21720 Hamburg ave
Lakeville, MN 55044 952-469-6639
Fax: 803-364-5008 800-582-4372
info@sealking.com www.sealking.com
Bag sealing tape, double coated foam tapes, tissue tapes and polyester tape, spooled tapes, fingerlift tapes for plastic and paper envelopes and siliconised release liners
President/Founder: Ben Nelson
Number Employees: 12

28992 Seal Science
17131 Daimler St
Irvine, CA 92614 949-253-3130
Fax: 949-253-3141 800-576-7325
westernsales@sealscience.com
www.sealscience.com
Manufactures gaskets, molded rubber products, engineered seal systems, O-rings, teflon seals, vacuum cups and diaphragms; custom plastic machining
CEO: Rick Tuliper
Marketing/Sales: Doug Albin
Purchasing Manager: Christy Seastedt
Estimated Sales: $5-10 Million
Number Employees: 50-99
Square Footage: 25000
Parent Co: Seal Science East

28993 Seal-A-Tron Corporation
3815 SE Naef Rd
Portland, OR 97267 503-652-5200
Fax: 503-905-1331 800-487-3257
drehs@seal-a-tron.com www.seal-a-tron.com
Industrial shrink wrap equipment
President: Werner Duemmer
Technical Assistance: Werner Duemmer
Customer Service Officer: John Borich
Estimated Sales: Below $5 Million
Number Employees: 20-49

28994 Seal-O-Matic Company
2542 Humbug Creek Rd
Jacksonville, OR 97530 970-532-0333
Fax: 541-846-1004 800-631-2072
info@sealomatic.com www.sealomatic.com
Manufacturer, importer and exporter of shrink wrap and packaging equipment including gummed tape dispensers, safety knives, shipping room equipment, price labeling guns, staplers, staples, etc
President: Mel Ortner
Vice President: Janine Ortner
Marketing Director: Greg Sparre
Purchasing Manager: Kim Westmoreland
Estimated Sales: $1 - 3 Million
Number Employees: 4
Square Footage: 5000
Brands:
Flash
Labelmaster
Lewis
Pricemaster

28995 Seal-Tite Bag Company
4324 Tackawanna St
Philadelphia, PA 19124 717-917-1949
Fax: 215-288-5664
Transparent and flexible packaging, plastic and heat sealed and plastic bags; also, plastic film and poly labels
Estimated Sales: $1-2.5 Million
Number Employees: 8
Brands:
Seal-Tite

28996 Sealant Equipment & Engiineering
45677 Helm St
PO Box 701460
Plymouth, MI 48170 734-459-8600
Fax: 734-459-8686 sales@sealantequipment.com
www.sealantequipment.com
Manufacturer and exporter of adhesive and food dispensing machinery
President/Chairman: Carl Schultz
Sales/Marketing/Public Relations: James Schultz
Estimated Sales: $10-20 Million
Number Employees: 50-99

28997 Sealed Air Corporation
200 River Front Blvd
Elmwood Park, NJ 07407 201-791-7600
Fax: 203-791-3618 800-648-9093
ppd.mkt@sealedair.com www.sealedair.com
Flexible plastic packaging materials including film, food packaging and shrink wrap.
Chairman/Chief Executive Officer: William Hickey
President/Chief Operating Officer: Jerome Peribere
Senior VP/ Chief Financial Officer: Carol Lowe
Estimated Sales: $7.6 Billion
Number Employees: 25,000
Parent Co: Sealed Air Corporation

28998 Sealed Air Corporation
200 Riverfront Boulevard
Elmwood Park, NJ 07407 201-791-7600
www.sealedair.com
Manufacturer and exporter of foam-in-place packaging materials and systems
President/Chief Operating Officer: Jerome Peribere
Chief Financial Officer: Carol Lowe
CTO/Research & Development: Dr. Robert Tatterson
VP/General Counsel/Secretary/HR: Norman Finch Jr.
VP, Corporate Communications: Jim Whaley
Estimated Sales: $7.65 Billion
Number Employees: 25000
Square Footage: 11839

28999 Sealed Air Corporation Saddle Brook
200 Riverfront Boulevard
Elmwood Park, NJ 7407 201-791-7600
Fax: 201-703-4205 800-648-9093
cryovac.mkt@sealedair.com www.sealedair.com
Protective packaging materials and systems including inflatable packaging system, foam-in-bag packaging system, ultra-thin shrink film, soft shrink, multipacking and merchandising films
President: William V Hickey
Marketing Manager: Andy Brewer
Estimated Sales: Below $5 Million
Number Employees: 50-99

29000 Sealeze
8000 Whitepine Rd
Richmond, VA 23237 804-275-1675
Fax: 804-271-3428 800-787-7325
industrial@sealeze.com www.sealeze.com
Strip brush for selaing out debris, shielding, guiding on conveyors, positioning products during production and static dissipation.
President: Doug Pollak
Number Employees: 20-49

29001 Sealpac USA LLC
5901 School Avenue
Richmond, VA 23228 804-261-0580
Fax: 804-261-0581 sealpacusa@sealpacusa.com
www.sealpacusa.com
Sealpac tray sealing equipment for meats, cheeses, fruits and vegetables.

29002 Sealpac USA LLC
5901 School Avenue
Richmond, VA 23228 804-261-0580
Fax: 804-261-0581 info@sealpac-us.com
www.sealpac-us.com
Distributor of tray sealers

29003 Sealstrip Corporation
200 N Washington St
Boyertown, PA 19512-1115 610-367-6282
Fax: 610-367-7727 info@atsealstrip.com
www.sealstrip.com
Manufacturer and exporter of resealable packaging equipment and materials
President: Joanne Forman
Owner: Harold Forman
R&D: Ajrlod Forman
Sales: Heather Hartman
Manufacturing Manager: Jacob Greth
Estimated Sales: Below $5 Million
Number Employees: 20-49
Square Footage: 28000
Brands:
Everfresh
Fresh Pak
Sealstrip
Serv & Seal

29004 Sealstrip Corporation
103 Industrial Drive
Gilbertsville, PA 19525 610-367-6282
Fax: 610-367-7727 888-658-7997
hhartmann@tearstripsystems.com
www.tearstripsystems.com
Shrinkable teartape, shrink tape applicators, resealable bags and systems
Director of Product Development: Jo Anne Forman
Manufacturing Manager: Jacob Greth
Estimated Sales: $2.5-5 Million
Number Employees: 20-49

29005 SeamTech
24231 Fuhrman Rd
Acampo, CA 95220-9766 209-464-4610
Fax: 209-464-1438 sales@seamtech.net
www.seamtechpk.com
Service parts and sales of fillers, seamers and warehouse equipment
President: Pete Saavedra
CFO: Pete Saavedra
Quality Control: Jason Saavedra
Estimated Sales: Below $5 Million
Number Employees: 5

29006 Seaquist Closures
711 Fox St
Mukwonago, WI 53149 262-363-7191
Fax: 262-363-3658
shawn.storbakken@sequistclosures.com
www.aptar.com
President: Eric Ruskoski
R & D: Jim Hammond
Data Processing: Michael Wedge
Number Employees: 250-499
Parent Co: Aptar Group

29007 Search West
PO Box 641609
Los Angeles, CA 90064-6609 310-203-9797
www.searchwest.com
Executive search firm recruiting middle to upper level managers, professionals and executives in sales, administrative and technical areas
President: Bob Cowan
Estimated Sales: $500,000-$1 Million
Number Employees: 50-100

29008 Season's 4
4500 Industrial Access Rd
Douglasville, GA 30134 770-489-0716
Fax: 770-489-2938 jkodobocz@seasons4.net
www.seasons4.net
Manufacturer and exporter of custom engineered HVAC systems for supermarkets
President: Lewis Watford
VP Sales: Todd Smith
Purchasing Manager: Rick Rothschild
Estimated Sales: $50 - 100 Million
Number Employees: 250-499
Square Footage: 145000

29009 Seatex Ltd
445 TX-36
Rosenberg, TX 77471 713-357-5300
Fax: 713-357-5301 800-829-3020
kaimes@seatexcorp.com www.seatexcorp.com
Providers of turn key chemical compounding, toll manufacturing and private label packaging services. Areas of expertise included the food service, food processing, automotive, institutional and industrial laundry, janitorialindustrial and oilfield service markets.
President/CEO: Jim Nattier
CFO: John Nowak
VP: Kelly Aimes
R&D: Don Trepel
Director QA/QC: Don Trepel
Sales/Marketing: Tom Austin
Sales/Marketing: Kelly Aimes
Public Relations: Kelly Aimes
Operations/Production: Dan Boone
Warehouse/Logistics: Jim Dockery
VP Purchasing: Larry Brown
Estimated Sales: $26 Million
Number Employees: 85
Number of Products: 400
Square Footage: 220000
Type of Packaging: Consumer, Food Service, Private Label, Bulk

29010 Seating Concepts
125 Connell Ave
Rockdale, IL 60436 815-730-7980
Fax: 815-730-7969 800-421-2036
sales@seating-concepts.com
www.seating-concepts.com
Manufacturer and exporter of chairs, booths, cafeteria counters, tables and waste receptacles; importer of chairs
President: Bill Overton
Sales Director: Chris Mazzoni
Estimated Sales: $3,000,000
Number Employees: 20-49
Type of Packaging: Food Service

29011 Seattle Boiler Works
500 S Myrtle St
Seattle, WA 98108 206-762-0737
Fax: 206-762-3516 jgesell@seattleboiler.com
www.seattleboiler.com
Manufacturer and exporter of boilers, heat exchangers and pressure vessels; also, stainless steel fabrication, pipe and tube bending services available
President: Frank H Hopkins
VP: Craig Hopkins
Estimated Sales: $5-10 Million
Number Employees: 20-49
Square Footage: 70000
Type of Packaging: Bulk

29012 Seattle Menu Specialists
5844 South 194th Street
Kent, WA 98032 206-784-2340
Fax: 206-782-7778 800-622-2826
customerservice@seattlemenu.com
www.seattlemenu.com
Manufacturer and designer of menu, wine and guest check covers and placemats; exporter of menu covers
President: Dale Phelps
Operations Manager: Lonnie Axtell
Purchasing Manager: George Rought
Estimated Sales: Below $5 Million
Number Employees: 10
Brands:
Duracrafic

29013 Seattle Plastics
309 S. Cloverdale St.
#E7
Seattle, WA 98134 206-233-0869
Fax: 206-233-0874 800-441-0679
info@seattleplastics.com
www.seattleplastics.com
Display cases, bagel and coffe bins and lid holders; also, custom fabrication available
President: Mike Albanese
Estimated Sales: $1-2,500,000
Number Employees: 5-9

29014 Seattle Refrigeration &Manufacturing
1057 S Director St
Seattle, WA 98108 206-762-7740
Fax: 206-762-1730 800-228-8881
seattlerefrigeration@msn.com
www.seattlerefrigeration.com
Manufacturer and importer of compressors, pressure vessels, belt and spiral freezers, condensers, heat exchangers, ice makers, chillers, freezers, hoses, pumps, etc.; importer of compressors, plate freezers and valves; exporter ofcompressors, and ice makers
President: Tracy Abbott
R&D: Frank Kanpp
Quality Control: Bob Petersen
Service Manager: Don Irons
Estimated Sales: $5 - 10 Million
Number Employees: 10-19
Square Footage: 15300
Parent Co: Seattle Refrigeration
Brands:
Alco
Asme
C.P.
Carrier
Copeland
Dunham-Bush
Eagle Signal
F.E.S.
Frick
Fuller
Grasso
Henry
Howden
Howe
Johnson (Penn)
Paragon
Ranco
Sabroe
Shank
Sporian
Sullair
Tecumseh
Vitter
Wolf Linde
York

29015 Seattle's Best Coffee
18870 103rd Avenue
Vashon, WA 98070-5229 206-463-5050
Fax: 206-463-5764
Tea and coffee industry, bags (brick packs, flexible, and valve packs)
Estimated Sales: $1-5 Million
Number Employees: 6

29016 Seattle-Tacoma Box Co.
23400 71st Pl S
Kent, WA 98032-2994 253-854-9700
Fax: 253-852-0891 www.seattlebox.com
Custom designed corrugated boxes and wood boxes. Skids, pallets, wooden containers, plastic bags, styrofoam and other packaging supplies.
Owner: Jacob Nist
Sales: Joseph Nist

29017 Seattle-Tacoma Box Company
23400 71st Pl S
Kent, WA 98032 253-854-9700
Fax: 253-852-0891 info@seattlebox.com
www.seattlebox.com
Manufacturer and exporter of wooden produce and corrugated boxes
President: Ferdinand Nist
Vice President: Mike Nist
Marketing Director: Rob Nist
Estimated Sales: $30 - 50 Million
Number Employees: 20-49

29018 Sebesta Blombeg
2381 Rosegate
Roseville, MN 55113 651-634-0775
877-706-6858
info@sebesta.com www.sebesta.com
President: James Sebasta
Number Employees: 120
Square Footage: 160000

29019 Sebring Container Corporation
PO Box 359
Salem, OH 44460 330-332-1533
Fax: 330-332-2205 www.sebringcontainer.com
Flat corrugated containers
President: William Mc Devitt
Sales Manager: John Berlin
Estimated Sales: $10-20 Million
Number Employees: 20-49

29020 Seco-Grahatech
6858 Acco Street
Commerce, CA 90040 323-726-9721
Fax: 323-726-9776 sales@seco-ind.com
www.seco-ind.com
Barrier packaging, heat sealing equipment, and vacuum sealers
CEO: Charles De Heras
Vice President: Jerome Druss
Estimated Sales: $5-10 Million
Number Employees: 38
Square Footage: 120000

29021 Security Link
816 N Gilbert Street
Danville, IL 61832 217-446-4871
Fax: 309-685-7161
Alarm systems
General Manager: Deborah Morris
Estimated Sales: Less than $500,000
Number Employees: 1-4

29022 Security Packaging
PO Box 892
North Bergen, NJ 07047-0892 201-854-1955
Fax: 201-854-1978
Corrugated boxes
President: Norbert Mester
Estimated Sales: $1-2.5 Million
Number Employees: 5-9
Square Footage: 1500

29023 Sedalia Janitorial & Paper Supplies
4211 S 65 Highway
Sedalia, MO 65301 660-826-9899
Janitorial and paper supplies
Estimated Sales: $1 - 5 Million
Number Employees: 1

29024 **Sedex Kinkos**
PO Box 1198
Tualatin, OR 97062-1198 503-692-3550
Fax: 503-692-1860 800-800-6271
www.fineartsgraphics.com
Wine industry label printing
Estimated Sales: $5-10 Million
Number Employees: 10

29025 **Sediment Testing SupplyCompany**
7366 N Greenview Ave
Chicago, IL 60626 773-465-3634
Fax: 773-465-4309 800-853-7323
info@sedimenttesting.com
www.sedimenttesting.com
Sediment testing equipment and supplies recommended for scorch-particles testing of reconstituted nonfat dry milk and coffee, determining sediment or extraneous matter in milk products and batch sample testing when quality-controlstandards have been est
President: Kathleen S Fox
Estimated Sales: $.5 - 1 million
Number Employees: 1-4

29026 **Seepex**
511 Speedway Dr
Enon, OH 45323 937-864-7150
Fax: 937-864-7157 800-695-3659
sales@seepex.net www.seepex.com
Designs, manufactures, and sells Progressive Cavity Pumps and Pump accessories.
President: Michael Dillon
VP: Francis Harris
R&D: Mathew Brown
Quality Control: Robert Mentz
Marketing/Public Relations: Daniel Lakovic
Director, Sales: Mark Murphy
Product Manager: Joe Zinck
Purchasing: Robert Mentz
Estimated Sales: $30 Million
Number Employees: 90
Number of Brands: 1
Number of Products: 1000
Square Footage: 40000
Parent Co: Seepex
Brands:
Map
Seepex
Tricam

29027 **Sefar America**
111 Calumet St
Depew, NY 14043-3734 716-683-4050
Fax: 716-683-4053 rgaiser@sefaramerica.com
www.sefaramerica.com
CEO: Art Alex
R & D: Richard Gaiser
Number Employees: 10

29028 **Sefi Fabricators**
50 Ranick Drive E
PO Box 338
Amityville, NY 11701 631-842-2200
Fax: 631-842-2203 info@sefifabricators.com
www.imcteddy.com
Custom stainless steel food service equipment, countertops, cabinets, floordrains, lab furniture, shelving, grating sinks and tables
President: Asit Majumdar
Sales Manager: Louis Stanley
Sales Engineer: Barry Greene
Customer Service: Maria Fernandez
Estimated Sales: $2.5-5 Million
Number Employees: 20-49
Square Footage: 17000
Type of Packaging: Consumer, Food Service, Private Label, Bulk

29029 **Seiberling Associates**
655 3rd Street
Suite 203
Beloit, WI 53511-6269 608-313-1235
Fax: 608-313-1275 craig.guyse@seiberling.com
www.seiberling.com
Consultant providing engineering services and project management; also, installation and start-up services available
President: John Miller
CFO: Don Hewitt
VP: Don Huett
Estimated Sales: $2.5-5 Million
Number Employees: 20-49

29030 **Seidenader Equipment**
25 Hanover Rd # 210
Florham Park, NJ 07932-1424 973-301-9800
Fax: 973-301-9090 800-342-6910
scalabrese@seidenader.com www.seidenader.de
Manufacturers of fully automatic inspection machines for parental products, semi-automatic inspection machines, exterior vial washers, and tray loaders
Manager: Eileen Scanlon
Marketing Manager: Sara Savastano
Estimated Sales: $500,000 - $1 Million
Number Employees: 1-4

29031 **Seidman Brothers**
25 Sixth Street
Chelsea, MA 02150 617-884-8110
Fax: 617-884-4284 800-437-7770
info@seidmanbros.com www.seidmanbros.com
Commercial kitchen exhaust systems. custom stainless steel, and distributors of food service equipment.
President: Allen Seidman
President: Allen Seidman
General Manager: Jack Seidman
Sales: Gina Venezia
Operations Manager: Rick Seidman
Estimated Sales: $5-10 Million
Number Employees: 10-19

29032 **Seiler Plastics Corporation**
9750 Reavis Park Dr
Saint Louis, MO 63123 314-815-3030
Fax: 314-815-3025 rjones@seilerpc.com
www.seilerpc.com
Plastic products including tubing profiles, sheets, etc.; die cutting and thermoforming services available
Owner: John Sieler
VP: Paul Benson
Sales Manager: Paul Dyer
Estimated Sales: $5-10 Million
Number Employees: 20-49
Square Footage: 24000

29033 **Seitz Memtec America Corporation**
635 Shannon Corners Rd
Dundee, NY 14837-9158 607-243-7568
Fax: 607-243-5251
Wine industry equipment
Owner: Joe Gibson

29034 **Seitz Schenk Filter Systems**
2118 Greenspring Drive
Lutherville, MD 21093-3112 443-322-2494
Fax: 443-322-2496 877-716-8778
info@benelogic.com www.benelogic.com
Filters and filtration equipment
CEO: Matthew T Oros
Estimated Sales: $5-10 Million
Number Employees: 250-499

29035 **Seitz Stainless**
17578 400th St
Avon, MN 56310 320-746-2781
Fax: 320-746-2782 sales@seitzstainless.com
www.seitzstainless.com
Custom fabrication, dryers, spray, heat recovery systems, heat exchangers, pasteurizers, tubular
President: Jeff Haviland
Estimated Sales: $10-20 Million
Number Employees: 25

29036 **Seiz Signs Company**
1231 Central Ave
Hot Springs, AR 71901 501-623-3181
Fax: 501-623-4595 david@seizsigns.com
www.seizsigns.com
Advertising signs
President: David Hamilton
VP & Billboard Sales: Tammy Hamilton
Office Manager: Shannon McLean
Estimated Sales: $1-2.5 Million
Number Employees: 10-19

29037 **Sekisui TA Industries**
100 S Puente St
Brea, CA 92821-3813 714-255-7888
Fax: 800-235-8273 800-258-8273
www.sta-tape.com
Manufacturer and exporter of FDA approved B.O.P.P. pressure sensitive tapes and semi and fully automatic carton sealing machinery
President: Ikusuke Shimizu
CEO: Ernest J Wong
CFO: Matt Minami
VP: Stephen J Wilson
R&D: Dinesh Shan
Marketing Administrator: Melissa Morris
Plant Manager: C P Fang
Estimated Sales: $20 - 50 Million
Number Employees: 100-249
Square Footage: 185000
Parent Co: Sekisui Chemical
Brands:
Sta Series
Sta-Pack
Supreme

29038 **Selby Sign Company**
2138 Bypass Road
PO Box 127
Pocomoke City, MD 21851 410-957-1541
Fax: 410-957-1074 www.selbysign.com
Exterior and interior illuminated signs including electronic message centers, time/temperature units, neon, etc.; also, installation and maintainence available
Owner: David Selby
VP: Steve Selby
Production Manager: Doug Dryden
Estimated Sales: $1-2.5 Million
Number Employees: 20-49
Square Footage: 6000

29039 **Selby/Ucrete IndustrialFlooring**
26383 Broadway Ave
Cleveland, OH 44146-6516 440-232-6644
Fax: 216-839-8822 800-445-6182
webmaster@selby-ucrete.com
www.selby-ucrete.com
Owner: Chuck Slaby
Estimated Sales: $1 - 5 Million
Number Employees: 1-4

29040 **Selco Products Company**
605 S East St
Anaheim, CA 92805-4842 714-917-1333
Fax: 714-917-1355 800-257-3526
sales@selcoproducts.com
www.selcoproducts.com
Selco offers mechanical and electronic temperature controls, control knobs, and digital and analog panel meters
President: Tim Wilkinson
CEO: Tim Wilkinson
Marketing Manager: Michelle Blakeslee
Sales Manager: Russell Kido
Estimated Sales: $5-10 Million
Number Employees: 50-99

29041 **Select Appliance Sales,Inc.**
159 West Harris Avenue
San Francisco, CA 94080 650-588-9100
Fax: 650-588-9108 888-235-0431
customercare@selectappliance.com
www.selectappliance.com
President: Russell Zipkin
Marketing Manager: Ming Chu
Estimated Sales: 3MM
Number Employees: 4

29042 **Select Stainless**
11145 Monroe Rd
PO Box 158
Matthews, NC 28105 704-843-2334
Fax: 704-843-1757
generalinfo@selectstainless.com
www.selectstainless.com
President: Ben Williams
Vice President: Mike Auten
President: Ben Williams
National Sales Manager: Doug Joyner
Estimated Sales: $3 - 5 Million
Number Employees: 20-49

29043 **Select Technologies Inc.**
8093 Graphic Dr NE
Belmont, MI 49306 616-866-6700
Fax: 616-866-6770 www.select-technologies.com

Designer, builder and installer of plant facility & utility systems and production lines for processing and material handling.

29044 Selecto
1400 Market Place Blvd # 109
Cumming, GA 30041-7925 770-205-0800
Fax: 770-448-7021 www.selectcareerchoices.com
Tea and coffee industry, filtration equipment
Owner: Kirk Sherrill
Number Employees: 5-9

29045 (HQ)Selecto Scientific
3980 Lakefield Ct
Suwanee, GA 30024 678-475-0799
Fax: 678-475-1595 800-635-4017
mainserve.service@mainserveinstall.com
www.selectoinc.com
Manufacturer and exporter of water filters for scale reduction, taste and odor and sediment for fountain dispensing equipment, coffee makers, ice equipment and steamers
Owner: Terry Libin
VP Sales/Marketing: Terry Libin
Customer Service: Sandra White
Purchasing Manager: Kenny Powell
Estimated Sales: $1 - 3 Million
Number Employees: 10-19
Square Footage: 68000
Brands:
Leadout
Supraplus
Uptaste

29046 Selig Chemical Industries
1100 Spring St NW # 550
Atlanta, GA 30309-2848 404-876-5511
Fax: 404-875-2629 www.seligenterprises.com
Disinfectants, insecticides, household cleaners, soaps, sanitizers and polishes
President: S Stephen Selig
Chief Financial Officer: Ronald J. Stein, CPA
Co-Owner & Senior Vice President: Cathy Selig
Director Marketing: Tom Graves
Estimated Sales: $5-10 Million
Number Employees: 50-99

29047 Selkirk Metalbestos
14801 Quorum Drive
Dallas, TX 75254-7589 972-560-2100
Fax: 877-393-4145 800-992-8368
info@selkirkcorp.com www.selkirkinc.com
Number Employees: 100-249
Type of Packaging: Food Service

29048 Sellers Cleaning Systems
420 3rd St
Piqua, OH 45356-3918 937-778-8947
Fax: 937-773-2238 seller@internetMCI.com
Wine industry, sanitation processing unit
Manager: Mike Kemp
Estimated Sales: $500,000-$1 Million
Number Employees: 250-499

29049 Sellers Engineering Division
PO Box 48
Danville, KY 40423-0048 859-236-3181
Fax: 859-236-3184
john@greenboilertechnologies.com
www.greenboilertechnologies.com
Manufacturer and exporter of boiler feed systems, steam and hot water boilers, water heaters and deaerators
President & Public Relations: G. Miller
CEO/CFO: S Miller
Controller: J. Sizemore
VP Research & Development: Bill Doughty
Quality Control: L Gambrel
Marketing Director: R Larson
Sales Director: R Larson
Production/Plant Manager: R Woolum
Plant Manager: R Woolum
Purchasing Manager: P Coffman
Estimated Sales: $20-50 Million
Number Employees: 78
Square Footage: 64000
Type of Packaging: Food Service
Other Locations:
Sellers
Dallas TX
Weestern Engineering
Danville KY
Brands:
Sellers

29050 Selma Wire Products Company
County Road 700 E
Selma, IN 47383 765-282-3532
Fax: 765-282-4428
Wire store display racks
Estimated Sales: $1-2.5 Million
Number Employees: 20-49
Parent Co: Mid-West Metal Products Company

29051 Selo
196 120th Ave # A
Holland, MI 49424-3309 616-392-7849
Fax: 616-392-2262 sales@cnhenterprises.com
www.cnhenterprises.com
Equipment for materials handling, processing, slaughtering and temperature control
Owner: Paul Sale
Estimated Sales: $1 - 5 Million
Number Employees: 5-9

29052 Seltzer Chemicals
5927 Geiger Ct
Carlsbad, CA 92008 760-438-0089
Fax: 760-438-0336 800-735-8137
sci@seltzerchemicals.com
www.seltzerchemicals.com
Wholesaler/distributor of custom blended bulk fine chemicals, vitamin pre-mixes and colors
EVP: Trent Seltzer
Executive VP: Trent Seltzer
Estimated Sales: $50-100 Million
Number Employees: 50-99
Square Footage: 60000
Type of Packaging: Bulk

29053 Semanco International
500 Clanton Road
Suite H
Charlotte, NC 28217-1310 704-527-9010
Fax: 704-527-8290 fbcp@bellsouth.net
www.semanco.com
Electronic process evaluation systems for soft drink bottlers, bottling lines, all blended products, wine processing, packaging lines and fruit and juices
Number Employees: 20-49

29054 Semco Manufacturing Company
705 E Us Highway 83
PO Box 1686
Pharr, TX 78577 956-787-4203
Fax: 956-781-0620 www.semcomfgco.com
Manufacturer and exporter of mobile/portable ice plants, slush ice makers, hydro coolers, freezers and vegetable harvesting and packing equipment
President: James Hatton
Sales Director: Jason Hatton
Purchasing Manager: Rod Bradley
Estimated Sales: Below $5 Million
Number Employees: 20-49
Square Footage: 30000
Brands:
Semco

29055 Semco Plastic Company
5301 Old Baumgartner Rd
Saint Louis, MO 63129 314-487-4557
Fax: 314-487-4724 sales@semcoplastics.com
www.semcoplastics.com
Manufacturer and exporter of plastic products including drinking straws, boxes and advertising novelties
President: Marvin Skaggs
CFO: Marvin Skaggs
R&D: Chuck Voelkel
Quality Control: Jerry Leiberoff
Estimated Sales: $100 - 500 Million
Number Employees: 250-499

29056 Semi-Bulk Systems
159 Cassens Ct
Fenton, MO 63026 636-343-4500
Fax: 636-343-2822 800-732-8769
info@semi-bulk.com www.semi-bulk.com
Manufacturer and exporter of mixers including batch and continuous; also, dry ingredient handling interface systems
President: Jeff Doherty
CEO: Charles Attack
Chief Financial Officer: Al Moresi
Vice President: Ron Bentley
Research/Development: Iris Freidel
Controller: All Moresi
Sales/Marketing: Ronald Bentley
Public Relations: Diana McMahon
Operations/Production/Purchasing: Bernie Klipsch
Estimated Sales: $10 Million
Number Employees: 30
Square Footage: 220000
Brands:
Vacucam

29057 Sencon
6385 W 74th St
Chicago, IL 60638-6128 708-496-3100
Fax: 708-496-3105 sales@senconinc.com
www.sencon.com
Specialized control devices, sensors, and quiality instruments to the metal packaging industry; tooling protective systems, line control devices and a range of manual and automatic quality gauges
Owner: Winston Shields
Technical Manager: Ian Blackledge
Estimated Sales: $10-20 Million
Number Employees: 50-99

29058 Sencorp Systems
400 Kidds Hill Rd
Hyannis, MA 02601-1850 508-771-9400
Fax: 508-790-0002 sales@sencorp-inc.com
www.sencorp-inc.com
Plastic packaging machinery
President: Brian Urban
Estimated Sales: $25 - 50 Million
Number Employees: 100-249

29059 SencorpWhite
400 Kidds Hill Rd
Hyannis, MA 02601 508-771-9400
Fax: 508-790-0002 info@sencorpwhite.com
www.whitesystems.com
Storage and retrieval systems, vertical and horizontal carousels, transporters, robots and power columns
VP Operations: John Molloy
VP Marketing: Richard Frye
Estimated Sales: Less than $500,000
Number Employees: 1-4

29060 Seneca Environmental Products
Airport Industrial Park 1685 S. County
PO Box 429
Tiffin, OH 44883 419-447-1282
Fax: 419-448-4048
sepinc@senecaenvironmental.com
www.senecaenvironmental.com
Manufacturer and exporter of sanitary type dust collectors including stainless steel, carbon steel, reverse jet, cartridge, cyclone, shaker and cylindrical; also, noise pollution control equipment, miscellaneous sanitary and steelfabrication
President: C Harple
Sales Manager: Don Harple
Estimated Sales: $1 - 3 Million
Number Employees: 20-49
Square Footage: 50000

29061 Seneca Printing & SalemLabel
P.O.Box 1211
Franklin, PA 16323-5211 814-432-7890
Fax: 814-432-8050 800-372-1313
www.senecaprinting.com
Commercial offset printing and labels
President: Randy Hicks
Estimated Sales: $10-20 Million
Number Employees: 100-249

29062 Seneca Tape & Label
13821 Progress Pkwy
Cleveland, OH 44133-4396 440-237-1600
Fax: 440-237-0427 800-251-0514
sales@senecalabel.com www.senecalabel.com
Pressure sensitive labels
President: Mike Hoopingarner
VP Finance: John Hoopingarner
Estimated Sales: $2.5-5 Million
Number Employees: 50-99

29063 **Senior Flexonics**
300 E Dvon Ave
Bartlett, IL 60103 690- 83- 181
Fax: 815-886-4550 800-473-0474
www.sinior -flexonics.com
Deep fryer hoses and filters
President: John Divine
Sales Manager: Gerry Blanchet
Estimated Sales: $5-10,000,000
Number Employees: 50-99
Parent Co: Senior Flexonics
Brands:
Filter-Master
Fryer Pro

29064 **(HQ)Senior Housing Options**
1510 17th St
Denver, CO 80202 303-595-4464
Fax: 303-595-9225 800-659-2656
info@seniorhousingoptions.org
www.seniorhousingoptions.org
Plain and printed plastic bags; also, plastic film
President: James A. Roberts
Controller: Vicky Campbell
Vice-President: Teri Romero
Quality Assurance Director: Jennifer Marcols
Estimated Sales: $1 - 3 Million
Number Employees: 20-49

29065 **Senomyx, Inc.**
4767 Nexus Centre Dr
San Diego, CA 92121 858-646-8300
Fax: 858-404-0752 www.senomyx.com
Flavor ingredients
President/COO: John Poyhonen
Chairman/CEO: Kent Snyder
Executive Director: Fred Shinnick
VP/CFO: Anthony Rogers
Estimated Sales: $28 Million
Number Employees: 100-249

29066 **Sensaphone**
901 Tryens Road
Aston, PA 19014-1597 610-558-2700
Fax: 610-558-0222 877-373-2700
sales@sensaphone.com www.sensaphone.com
Wine industry security systems
President: Kenneth E Blanchard
VP Marketing/Sales: Mary Ellen Gomeau
Vice President of Sales and Marketing: Bob Douglass
Estimated Sales: $5 - 10 Million
Number Employees: 20-49
Square Footage: 60000

29067 **Sensidyne**
16333 Bay Vista Dr
Clearwater, FL 33760 727-530-3602
Fax: 727-539-0550 800-451-9444
info@sensidyne.com www.sensidyne.com
Manufacturer and exporter of gas detection and air sampling systems
President: Howie Mills
VP: Glenn Warr
Quality Control: George Mason
Marketing: Mary Slattery
National Sales Manager: Gary Queensberry
Human Resources Executive: Stephanie Stock
Estimated Sales: $10-20 Million
Number Employees: 50-99

29068 **Sensient Flavors**
5600 W Raymond St
Indianapolis, IN 46241 317-243-3521
Fax: 317-243-2820 800-445-0073
flavors@sensient-tech.com
www.sensient-tech.com
Flavoring extract and syrups
President/COO: Douglas Pepper
SVP/CFO: Richard Hobbs
CEO: Ken Manning
Estimated Sales: $100 - 200 Million
Number Employees: 1,000-4,999
Parent Co: Sensient Technologies Corporation

29069 **(HQ)Sensient Technical Colors**
24-08 Broadway
Fair Lawn, NJ 07410-3065 201-794-3800
Fax: 201-797-4660 stc@sensient-tech.com
www.triconcolors.com
Processor, importer and exporter of colors
Owner: Debra Aiello
Office Manager: Linda Bradley
Estimated Sales: $12900000
Number Employees: 50-99
Square Footage: 20000
Type of Packaging: Consumer, Food Service, Private Label, Bulk

29070 **(HQ)Sensient Technologies**
777 East Wisconsin Ave
Milwaukee, WI 53202-5304
800-558-9892
corporate.communications@sensient.com
www.sensient.com
Colors for food and beverage industry and pharmaceuticals
President, CEO & Chairman: Kenneth Manning
President, Flavors & Fragrances Group: James McCarthy
SVP & CFO: Richard Hobbs
VP & Treasurer: John Collopy
Estimated Sales: $1.43 Billion
Number Employees: 3887
Square Footage: 10124

29071 **Sensitech**
800 Cummings Ctr Ste 258x
Beverly, MA 01915 978-927-7033
Fax: 978-921-2112 800-843-8367
info@sensitech.com www.sensitech.com
Temperature monitoring systems and electronic temperature monitors and recorders for perishable products; also, hand-held HACCP compliance systems
COO: Eric Schultz
CFO: Mike McKerson
Senior VP of Engineering: Tom Weir
Senior VP of Quality: Dave Ray
Sennior VP of Mktg/Business Development: Elizabeth Darragh
Senior VP Sales: David Vaught
Marketing Coordinator: Elizabeth Darragh
VP Operations: Scott Hubley
Estimated Sales: $100 Million
Number Employees: 307
Square Footage: 6000
Brands:
Quickcheck
Temptale
Temptale 2
Temptale 3
Temptale 4

29072 **Sensitech**
P.O.Box 599
Redmond, WA 98073-0599 425-883-7926
Fax: 425-883-3766 800-999-7926
info@sensitech.com www.sensitech.com
Temperature and humidity measurement in food and beverages
Manager: Mike Hanson
Estimated Sales: $10-25 Million
Number Employees: 50-99
Parent Co: Sensitech

29073 **Sensormatic ElectronicsCorporation**
6600 Congress Ave
Boca Raton, FL 33487-1213 561-912-6000
Fax: 561-989-7017 www.sensormatic.com
Manufacturer and exporter of safety systems including closed circuit television, electronic article surveillance and access control.
Estimated Sales: $300 Million
Number Employees: 5700
Brands:
Sensorvision
Ultramax

29074 **Sensors Quality Management**
156 Duncan Mill Road
Suite 19
Toronto, ON M3B 3N2
Canada 416-444-4491
Fax: 416-444-2422 800-866-2624
sqm@sqm.ca www.sqm.ca
Consultant specializing in the evaluation of company operations including quality assurance, competition analysis, integrity inspections, training programs, research and surveys, marketing, promotions, etc
President: David Lipton
VP: Craig Henry
VP: Craig Henry
Number Employees: 10

29075 **Sensortech Systems**
8929 Fullbright Ave
Chatsworth, CA 91311-6179 818-341-5366
Fax: 818-341-9059 info@sensorantennas.com
www.sensorantennas.com
Moisture measurement and control instrumentation
President: Mary E Bazar
Director of Sales and Marketing: Mike Crow
Estimated Sales: $1-2.5 Million
Number Employees: 1-4

29076 **Sensory Computer Systems**
144 Summit Avenue
Berkeley Heights, NJ 7922 908-665-6464
Fax: 908-665-6493 800-579-7654
johnream@sensorysims.com
www.sensorysims.com
Sensory testing and market research software used for laboratory, central location and point-of-sale testing of consumer survey data
Director: John Ream
Account Manager of Logistics, Chief Oper: Elena Keegan
Estimated Sales: $500,000-$1 Million
Number Employees: 5-9

29077 **Sensory Spectrum**
554 Central Ave
New Providence, NJ 07974 908-376-7000
Fax: 908-376-7040
spectrum@sensoryspectrum.com
www.sensoryspectrum.com
Consultant specializing in sensory evalutation techniques applied to the understanding of consumer products through descriptive analysis, advanced sensory methodology, qualitative and quantitative consumer research, experimentaldesign, etc
President: Gail Vance-Civille
Marketing Executive: Emily Engler
Sales Executive: Marie Rudolph
Estimated Sales: $5 - 10 Million
Number Employees: 40

29078 **Sentinel Lubricants Corporation**
15755 NW 15th Ave
PO Box 694240
Miami, FL 33269-1240 305-625-6400
Fax: 305-625-6565 800-842-6400
info@sentinelsynthetic.com
www.sentinelsynthetic.com
Manufacturer and exporter of food grade synthetic lubricants including nontoxic oil and grease
President: R Chaban
CEO: R Chaban
VP: J C Barroso
Research & Development: Charles Clay
Quality Control: Phil Sauder
Marketing Director: Emile Freidman
Sales: Raul Oquendo
Public Relations: Marta Garcia
Operations Manager: Randye Chaban
Production Manager: Juanillo Barroso
Plant Manager: Philip Sauder
Purchasing Manager: Martha Garcia
Estimated Sales: $18 Million
Number Employees: 20-49
Number of Brands: 200
Number of Products: 400
Square Footage: 25000
Type of Packaging: Consumer, Private Label
Brands:
Biosyn
Sentinel
Sentishield
Sl Nt

29079 **Sentinel Polyolefins**
P.O.Box 355
West Hyannisport, MA 02672-0355 508-775-5220
Fax: 508-771-1554 800-457-3234
cellect@cellectfoam.com
www.sentinelproducts.net
Crosslinked polyethylene foam and specialty elastomers for packaging applications including multi-density lamination for end-caps packaging
Estimated Sales: $1 - 3 Million
Number Employees: 1-4

29080 **Sentron**
7117 Stinson Ave # C
Gig Harbor, WA 98335-4902 253-851-7881
Fax: 253-851-7899 800-472-4361
info@sentronph.com www.sentron.ca

Nonglass, ion sensitive field effect transistor(ISFET) and pH measurement equipment
Marketing: Eric Amundson
Technical Sales Manager: Eric Amundson
Number Employees: 5-9
Square Footage: 24000
Other Locations:
Sentron
9300 AC Roden
Brands:
Sentron

29081 Sentry Equipment Corporation
966 Blue Ribbon Cir N
Oconomowoc, WI 53066 262-567-7256
Fax: 262-567-4523 sales@sentry-equip.com
www.sentry-equip.com
Manufacturer and exporter of sanitary samplers for milk, cream, whey, orange juice, viscous food products, wastewater liquids and slurries
President: Michael Farrell
Marketing Director: Lynn Castrodale
Sales Director: Doris Hoeft
Number Employees: 20-49
Brands:
Isolok

29082 Sentry Equipment Erectors
13150 E Lynchburg Salem Tpke
Forest, VA 24551-4328 434-525-0769
Fax: 434-525-1701 sales@sentryequipment.com
www.sentryequipment.com
Conveyor belts and equipment
President: Adam Vinoskey
Estimated Sales: $50-100 Million
Number Employees: 250-499

29083 Sentry/Bevcon North America
16630 Koala Road
PO Box 578
Adelanto, CA 92301-0578 800-854-1177
Fax: 760-246-4044 800-661-3003
sales@ici.us www.ici.us
Manufacturer and exporter of portable bars and dispensers including soda, juice, coffee, liquor and beer
President: Joe Suarez
Quality Control: Jerry Wheeler
R & D: Jerry Wheeler
Marketing: Ken Wogberg
Sales: Amber Micham
Public Relations: Ken Wogberg
Technical Support: Jerry Wheeler
President: Joe Suarez
Number Employees: 35
Square Footage: 224000
Parent Co: International Carbonic
Type of Packaging: Consumer, Food Service, Private Label
Brands:
Bevcon
Ici

29084 Separators
5707 W Minnesota St
Indianapolis, IN 46241 317-484-3745
Fax: 317-484-3755 800-233-9022
separate@sepinc.com www.separatorsinc.com
Leader in the sale and repair of reconditioned centrifuges.
President/CEO: Joe Campbell
COO/CFO: Joe Mansfield
Director of Manufacturing: Dan Goss
Estimated Sales: $10-20 Million
Number Employees: 20-49
Square Footage: 30000

29085 Sepragen Corporation
1205 San Luis Obispo St
Hayward, CA 94544 510-475-0650
Fax: 510-475-0625 info@sepragen.com
www.sepragen.com
Manufacturer and exporter of process control systems and instruments and separation machinery for the dairy industry
CEO: Vinit Saxena
President: James Spradling
CFO: Henry Edmunds
Quality Control: Salah Ahmed
Number Employees: 10-19

29086 Septimatech Group
106 Randall Drive
Waterloo, ON N2V 1K5
Canada 519-746-7463
Fax: 519-746-3464 888-777-6775
sales@septimatech.com www.septimatech.com
Septimatech is the total solution provider in line changeover products, innovation, services, research and development. Specializing in Quick Change Tooling solutions, Customer Container Handling solutions and enhancements, andproviding RXNT®, Unison® Guide Rails, and OEM parts.
President & CEO: Sharron Gilbert
VP Engineering/Innovation: Glenn Bell
VP Marketing/Sales/Service: Gord Beaton
VP Manufacturing/Quality: Quinn Martin
Number Employees: 50-99
Number of Brands: 2

29087 Septipack
2313 Benson Mill Rd
Sparks Glencoe, MD 21152-9420 410-472-2575
Fax: 410-771-1528
Aseptic packaging systems
President: Herve Franceschi
Estimated Sales: $300,000-500,000
Number Employees: 1-4

29088 Sequa Can Machinery
6949 S Potomac St
Englewood, CO 80112
Fax: 201-933-9029 sales@sequacan.com
www.sequacan.com
Machinery for the 2-piece can industry: cuppers, rutherford decorators and base coaters, can industry products tooled, cuppers, shell presses and DRD systems and FM&S replacement parts
President: Gus Reall
CFO: Bob Mayone
Quality Control: John Agar
Number Employees: 175

29089 Sequoia Pacific
20940 Avenue 296
Exeter, CA 93221-9713 559-562-3726
Fax: 415-442-0563 www.seqpac.com
Wine industry, label printing
Chairman: James Matthews
CEO: Michael Marino
CFO: Ruth Damsker
Estimated Sales: $20-50 Million
Number Employees: 1-4

29090 SerVaas Laboratories
5240 Walt Pl
Indianapolis, IN 46254 317-636-7760
Fax: 317-264-2192 800-433-5818
www.barkeepersfriend.com
Manufacturer and exporter of powdered and liquid cleansers for the removal of rust, lime, stains and mildew; also, polishes, bathroom and toilet bowl cleaners
President: Matt Selig
VP Sales: Tony Patterson
Estimated Sales: $20 - 50 Million
Number Employees: 20-49
Square Footage: 30000
Parent Co: SerVaas
Type of Packaging: Consumer, Private Label
Brands:
Bar Keepers Friend
Copper Glo
Just 'n Time
Shiny Sinks Plus

29091 SerVend International
2100 Future Drive
Sellersburg, IN 47172-1868 812-246-7000
Fax: 812-246-9922 800-367-4233
williamsk@servend.com www.servend.com
Manufacturer and exporter of ice makers, beverage, cup and ice dispensers, ice storage bins and beverage dispensing valves
CEO: Terry Growcock
VP Sales/Marketing: Lonnie Shafer
Director Marketing: Elaine Momson
Communication Manager: Susan Reed
Estimated Sales: $20 - 30 Million
Number Employees: 250
Square Footage: 155000
Parent Co: Manitowoc Foodservice Group
Other Locations:
SerVend International
Clackamas OR
Brands:
Flomatic
Servend

29092 Serac
300 Westgate Drive
Carol Stream, IL 60188 630-510-9343
Fax: 630-510-9357 serac@serac-usa.com
www.serac-usa.com
Filling and packaging machinery
President: Christopher Lebraun
Number Employees: 20-49

29093 Serco Company
1612 Hutton Drive
Suite 140
Carrollton, TX 75006 800-933-4834
Fax: 972-389-4769 sales@sercocompany.com
www.sercocompany.com
Estimated Sales: C
Number Employees: 100-249

29094 Sermatech ISPA
2915 Wilmarco Ave
Baltimore, MD 21223-3223 410-644-4500
Fax: 410-644-1766 800-882-4772
svogt@ispaco.com www.appcoat.com
Applicator of nonstick coatings for food processing and handling equipment including mixers, enrobers, chutes, dryers, etc
Owner: Ron Kaufmann
VP: Scott Vogt
Sales Director: Paul Kellogg
Sales: Rob Aldave
Purchasing Manager: Wes Prince
Estimated Sales: $10-20 Million
Number Employees: 20-49
Square Footage: 70000
Parent Co: Sermatech International
Brands:
Fluoroshield-Magna
Teflon

29095 Sermia International
100-742 Boulevard Industrial
Blainville, QC J7C 3V4
Canada 450-433-7483
Fax: 450-433-7484 800-567-7483
info@sermia.com www.sermia.com
Manufacturer and exporter of filters for liquids
Number Employees: 10
Brands:
Sermia

29096 Serpa Packaging Solutions
7020 W Sunnyview Ave
Visalia, CA 93291 559-651-2339
Fax: 559-651-2345 800-348-5453
sales@serpapkg.com www.serpapkg.com
Manufacturer and exporter of cartoners and case packers and erectors; also, custom designs and turnkey applications available
President/CEO: Fernando M Serpa
Director Of Marketing: Rich James
Estimated Sales: $10,000,000
Number Employees: 50-99
Square Footage: 46000

29097 Serr-Edge Machine Company
4471 W 160th St
Cleveland, Cl 44135-2625 216-267-6333
Fax: 216-267-2929 800-443-8097
Manufacturer and exporter of industrial and commercial sharpening machines for scissors, knives and shears
President: Linda Ribar Oakley
Owner: Matthew Oakley
Estimated Sales: Below $5 Million
Number Employees: 5-9
Brands:
Easisharp
Keenedge
Tru-Hone

29098 Sertapak Packaging Corporation
PO Box 1500
Woodstock, ON N4S 8R2
Canada 519-539-3330
Fax: 519-539-4499 800-265-1162
think@sertapak.com www.sertapak.com

Manufacturer and exporter of returnable and expandable packaging systems, containers, pallets and sealed edge plastic corrugated slip sheets
President: C J David Nettleton
CEO: Alison Clarke
CFO: Bruce Orr
Number Employees: 10
Brands:
Rak Pak
Sertote

29099 Serti Information Solution
7555, Beclard Street
Montreal, QC H1J 2S5
Canada 514-493-1909
Fax: 514-493-3575 800-361-6615
info@serti.com www.serti.com
Consulting services providing software and solutions for a solid foundation on completing-achieving all your information technology projects
President: LOUIS LAPORTE
Vice-President, finance & operations: MAURICE LANTHIER
Vice-President, IT Consulting Services: ODILE PATRY
Vice-President, Business Development: FRANCIS GINGRAS

29100 (HQ)Servco Co.
3189 Jamieson Ave
St Louis, MO 63139-2595 314-781-3189
Fax: 314-645-7003 hgage@servco-stl.com
www.servco-stl.com
Manufacturer and exporter of conveyors and under and back bar refrigerators
President: Earl Gates Jr
President: Earl Gates Jr
Estimated Sales: $5-10 Million
Number Employees: 20-49
Square Footage: 56000
Brands:
Gates
Servco

29101 Server Products
3601 Pleasant Hill Road
PO Box 98
Richfield, WI 53076 262-628-5600
Fax: 262-628-5110 800-558-8722
spsales@server-products.com
www.server-products.com
Manufacturer and exporter of small pumps, food dispensers and warmers, bars and accessories, rails and pizza ovens
President: Paul Wickesberg
VP Sales: Ron Ripple
VP Production: Carol Miller
Estimated Sales: $10 - 20 Million
Number Employees: 20-49
Square Footage: 125000

29102 Service Brass & AluminumFittings
190 N Wiget Lane
Suite 202
Walnut Creek, CA 94598-2440 925-977-8320
Fax: 925-256-0318
Wine industry, hose fittings
Estimated Sales: Under$500,000
Number Employees: 25-49

29103 Service Ideas
2354 Ventura Dr
Woodbury, MN 55125 651-730-8800
Fax: 651-730-8880 800-328-4493
sales@serviceideas.com www.serviceideas.com
Manufacturer, importer and exporter of insulated serving plates, beverage servers, dispensers, pitchers and buffet bowls
President: Patrick Murray
VP: Christina Brandt
Operations Director: Mark Bolowiak
Estimated Sales: $10 - 20 Million
Number Employees: 20-49
Square Footage: 40000
Brands:
Aero-Serv
Brew'n'pour Lid
Eco-Serv
Magnetag
Metallic Luster
New Generation
Sculptured Ice
Thermo-Plate
Thermo-Serv
Thermo-Serv Sculptured Ice

29104 Service Manufacturing
1601 Mountain Street
Aurora, IL 60505-2402 630-898-6800
Fax: 630-898-7800 888-325-2788
tvickers@theramp.net www.servicemfg.com
Manufacturer, importer and exporter of custom packaging products including insulated coolers, cases and bags
President: Camerina Torres
Vice President: David Goodman
Marketing/Sales: Matthew Sheridan
Plant Manager: Octavio Serrano
Purchasing Manager: Clarence Eisernman
Estimated Sales: $10-20 Million
Number Employees: 50-99
Square Footage: 188000
Type of Packaging: Bulk
Brands:
Service Manufacturing
Sun Valley

29105 Service Master
860 Ridge Lake Blvd Ste 101
Memphis, TN 38120
Fax: 630-271-5709 800-937-4949
customercare@servicemaster.com
www.servicemaster.com
Facilities management, plant operations and maintenance, ground and landscaping management, custodial services, energy management
President: Michael M Isakson
Vice President: Richard Sabol
Estimated Sales: $5 Billion+
Number Employees: 250-499

29106 Service Neon Signs
6611 Iron Pl
Springfield, VA 22151 703-354-3000
Fax: 703-354-5810 sales@snsigns.org
www.snsigns.org
Neon, plastic and aluminum on-site identification signs
President: Mark Luxenburg
CEO: Mark Luxenburg
VP/General Manager: Robert Gray
Sales: George Marino, Jr.
Plant Manager: Jack Evans
Purchasing Manager: Mike Volpe
Estimated Sales: $5 - 10 Million
Number Employees: 50-99
Square Footage: 75000

29107 Service Stamp Works
1227 W Jackson Boulevard
Chicago, IL 60607-2895 312-666-8839
Fax: 312-666-4167 marionk@hsonline.net
Rubber stamps, printing plates and food inks
Operations Manager: Peter Haack
Estimated Sales: $500,000-$1 Million
Number Employees: 5-9

29108 Service Tool International
39 S La Salle St
Suite 1410
Chicago, IL 60603 847-439-7000
Fax: 847-439-7009 loren.scheel@stieoe.com
www.stieoe.com
Easy-open conversion systems, shell manufacturing systems, and integrated manufacturing lines for ends, shells, or EOE; partial product list: carbide scroll dies, tab dies, lane dies, single, double and multi-dies, beader tooling, andcurler tooling
President: Loren Scheel
CEO: John Tensland
R & D: Just Klingel
Quality Control: Mike Fries
Estimated Sales: $10-20 Million
Number Employees: 20-49

29109 Servin Company
51518 Industrial Dr
Suite E
New Baltimore, MI 48047 586-725-5571
Fax: 586-725-5573 800-824-0962
support@servinco.com www.information.com
Reusable coated nylon bags
VP: Charles Clandinen
Sales Manager: Charles Clendinen
Estimated Sales: $.5 - 1 million
Number Employees: 5-9

29110 Servomex
525 Julie Rivers Dr # 185
Sugar Land, TX 77478-2845 281-295-5800
Fax: 281-295-5899 800-862-0200
info@servomex.com www.servomex.com
Servomex food pack analyzers offer simple, fast and accurate analysis of oxygen and carbon dioxide in soft packages or rigid containers
VP: Claire Lucarino
Marketing: Jane Hammond
Sales: Susan Harris
Plant Manager: Ed Arestie
Purchasing Director: Jon Pryer
Estimated Sales: $10 - 20 Million
Number Employees: 20-49
Brands:
1450 Food Pack Analyzer
574 Portable Oxygen Analyzer

29111 Servomex Company
4 Constitution Way
Woburn, MA 01801-1087 781-935-4600
Fax: 781-938-0531 800-433-2552
americas_sales@servomex.com
www.servomex.com
Oxygen and carbondioxide CAP/MAP analyzers
Estimated Sales: $10-20 Million
Number Employees: 20-49

29112 Servpak Corporation
5844 Dawson Street
Hollywood, FL 33023 954-962-4262
Fax: 954-962-5776 800-782-0840
info@serv-pak.com www.servpakcorp.com
Manufacturer and exporter table-topheat seal packaging machinery forrigid and semi rigid trays covered by pre-cut lids or lid film on a roll
President: Peter Knobel
Estimated Sales: Less than $500,000
Number Employees: 1-4
Square Footage: 2000

29113 Sesame Label System
1501 Third Ave
New York, NY 10028 212-989-3020
Fax: 212-989-3021 800-551-3020
orders@seslbl.com www.seslbl.com
Labels, decals and name plates; also, custom printing available
Purchasing: Tony Jackson
Estimated Sales: $2.5-5 Million
Number Employees: 10
Square Footage: 4000

29114 Sessions Company
PO Box 311310
Enterprise, AL 36331 334-393-0200
Fax: 334-393-0240 www.sessionspeanuts.com
Chairman: H Moultrie Sessions
CEO: H Moultrie Sessions Jr
Estimated Sales: $2.5-5 Million
Number Employees: 100-249

29115 Set Point Paper Company
31 Oxford Rd
Mansfield, MA 02048-1126 508-339-0700
Fax: 508-339-9929 800-225-0501
Food containers, cups, specialty bags and folding cartons
Manager: Elizabeth Dudley
VP: Michael Keneally
VP: Richard Madigan Jr
Estimated Sales: $300,000-500,000
Number Employees: 1-4
Square Footage: 125000
Brands:
Smart Cup
Smart Seal

29116 Setaram/SFIM
210 Lakeview St
Grand Prairie, TX 75051-4998 972-262-4900
Fax: 972-641-3711
sales@stormlawnandgarden.com
www.stormlawnandgarden.com
Thermal analysis instrumentation for fats, liquids, etc
Owner: R L Storm
Estimated Sales: $2.5-5 Million
Number Employees: 5-9

29117 Setco
P.O.Box 68008
Anaheim, CA 92817-0808 714-777-5200
Fax: 714-777-5355 www.setcobottle.com
Stock and custom plastic bottles
President: Don Parodi
VP Sales/Marketing: Thomas Dunn
Estimated Sales: $1 - 5 Million
Number Employees: 250-499
Parent Co: McCormick & Company
Other Locations:
Setco
Monroe Township NJ

29118 Setco
34 Engelhard Dr
Monroe Twp, NJ 08831 609-655-4600
Fax: 609-655-0225 www.setco.com
Manufacturer and exporter of plastic bottles
Plant Manager: Ray Agondo
Estimated Sales: $50-100 Million
Number Employees: 250-500
Parent Co: APL Company

29119 Seton Identification Products
20 Thompson Rd
PO Box 819
Branford, CT 06405-0819 203-488-8059
Fax: 203-488-5973 800-571-2596
seton_mailroom@seton.com www.seton.com
Signs, tags, labels, identification and safety products
Manager: Pascal Deman
Estimated Sales: Less than $500,000
Number Employees: 250-499
Brands:
Set Mark

29120 Setter, Leach & Lindstrom
730 2nd Ave S # 1100
Minneapolis, MN 55402-2455 612-338-8741
Fax: 612-338-4840 www.leoadaly.com
Consultant specializing in design and project management of food distribution centers
President: Bob Egge
Chairman: Leo Daly
Vice President: Charles Dalluge
Estimated Sales: $20-50 Million
Number Employees: 100-249

29121 Setterstix Corporation
261 S Main St
Cattaraugus, NY 14719 716-257-3451
Fax: 716-257-9818 nan@setterstix.com
www.setterstix.com
Manufacturer and exporter of rolled paper sticks for the confectionery industry
President: Christopher Cadigam
CFO: Ron Wasmund
Sales: Nan Mikowicz
Plant Manager: Eric Pritchard
Estimated Sales: $10 - 15 Million
Number Employees: 55
Square Footage: 60000
Parent Co: Knox Industries
Brands:
Setterstix

29122 Seven B Plus
46161 SE Wildcat Mountain Dr
Sandy, OR 97055 503-668-5079
Fax: 503-668-6347
Smokers

29123 Seven Mile Creek Corporation
315 S Beech St
Eaton, OH 45320-2311 937-456-3320
Fax: 937-456-3320 800-497-6324
sevenmile@voyager.net
www.sevenmilecreek.com
Industrial and promotional aprons; also, silk screening available
President: William Cressell
Estimated Sales: $500,000 - $1 Million
Number Employees: 1-4
Square Footage: 80000

29124 Severn Newtrent
2660 Columbia St
Torrance, CA 90503-3802 310-618-9700
Fax: 310-618-1384 800-777-6939
www.severntrentservices.com
Manufactures machines and equipment for use in service industries, water purification systems
President, Chief Executive Officer: Martin Kane
VP: Marwan Nesicolaci
Estimated Sales: $10-20 Million
Number Employees: 100-249

29125 (HQ)Severn Trent Services
580 Virginia Dr
Suite 300
Fort Washington, PA 19034 215-646-9201
Fax: 215-283-3487
wjohnson@severntrentservices.com
www.severntrentservices.com
Supplier of water and wastewater treatment solutions
President/CEO: Martin Kane
Senior VP/CFO: Stephane Bouvier
VP Marketing/Business Development: Thomas Mills
Operations Director: Alex Lloyd
Estimated Sales: $2 Million
Number Employees: 10,000

29126 Seville Display Door
27495 Diaz Road
Temecula, CA 92590-3414 951-676-6161
Fax: 951-676-7728 800-634-0412
www.displaydoors.com
Glass refrigerator and PVC sliding doors
Owner: Randy Fitzpatrick
Estimated Sales: $2.5-5 Million
Number Employees: 10-19
Square Footage: 120000

29127 (HQ)Seville Flexpack Corporation
PO Box 246
Oak Creek, WI 53154 414-761-2751
Fax: 414-761-3140
kskempk@sevilleflexpack.com
www.sevilleflexpack.com
Manufacturer and exporter of flexible packaging materials, stand-up pouches and cold seal coatings
President: Walter Yakich
Director Sales: Jay Yakich
VP Manufacturing: James Yakich
Estimated Sales: $20-50 million
Number Employees: 50-99
Square Footage: 12000000
Other Locations:
Seville Flexpack Corp.
Waco TX
Brands:
Fastseal
Flexfilm
Hide-A-Winner
Up-Right

29128 Seville Flexpack Corporation
P.O.Box 246
Oak Creek, WI 53154 414-761-2751
Fax: 414-761-3140
kskempka@sevilleflexpack.com
www.sevilleflexpack.com
Flexible packages, packaging materials
President: Walter Yakich
CFO: Cris Mercener
VP: Jim Yakich
VP Marketing and Sales: Jay Yakich
Marketing Manager: Mark Hoffman
Sales Manager: J Yakich
Operations Manager: Jim Yakich
Production Manager: Dave Gras
Purchasing Manager: Roger Kline
Estimated Sales: $20 - 50 Million
Number Employees: 50-99
Parent Co: Seville Flexpack Corporation

29129 Sewell Products
P.O.Box 660
Salem, VA 24153-0660 540-389-5401
Fax: 540-387-1747 www.kikcorp.com
Household and commercial 5.25% sodium hypochlorite bleach, ammonia and dilute fabric softener
President, Chief Executive Officer: Jeffrey Nodland
Executive Vice President of Legal Affair: Mark Halperin
Plant Manager: Jerry Doggett
Estimated Sales: $10-20 Million
Number Employees: 50-99
Square Footage: 120000
Brands:
Blue Ridge

29130 Sexton Sign
PO Box 5555
Anderson, SC 29623-5555 864-226-6071
Fax: 864-226-4074 sextonsign@statecom.net
Commercial electric signs
Estimated Sales: $1 - 5 Million

29131 Seymour Housewares
885 N Chestnut St
Seymour, IN 47274 812-522-5130
Fax: 812-522-5294 800-457-9881
Shopping carts, ironing tables, pad and cover sets and laundry products
President: Norman Bouvier
Director Marketing: Kurt Tyler
VP Sales: Tony Taggart
Estimated Sales: $20 - 50 Million
Number Employees: 100-249

29132 Seymour Woodenware Company
522 Seymour St
Seymour, WI 54165 920-833-6551
Fax: 920-833-7698 qadamski@new.rr.com
Wooden boxes and baskets including cheese, wine, coffee, gift, veneer, etc
President: Quintin J Adamski
General Manager: Steven Adamski
Estimated Sales: $1-2.5 Million
Number Employees: 10-19
Square Footage: 25000

29133 Shade Foods
400 Prairie Village Dr
New Century, KS 66031 913-780-1212
Fax: 913-780-1720 800-225-6312
pvd@shadefoods.com
www.kerryingredients.com
Liquid chocolate, hard candy, chocolate and yogurt chips, flakes, cereal particles, nuggets, pralines, granola, coated raisins, nuts and candy
CFO: Yves Gedert
R&D: Andrew Nelson
Vice President: Addison Bergfalk
VP: Jim White
VP Sales/Marketing: Bob Blefko
Plant Manager: Miles Miller
Purchasing Manager: Lynn Christian
Estimated Sales: $25 - 49.9 Million
Number Employees: 240
Square Footage: 145000
Parent Co: Norfoods
Type of Packaging: Private Label, Bulk
Brands:
Chewy Chunks
No Boil Pasta
Shade Icings & Fillings
Wayfels

29134 Shae Industries
PO Box 1268
Healdsburg, CA 95448 707-431-2337
Fax: 707-431-8060 shae@shaeind.com
www.shaeind.com
Manufacuring quality stainless steel products for the winery, microbrewery and dairy industries
Owner: Darrell Beer
Estimated Sales: $300,000-500,000
Number Employees: 1-4

29135 Shafer Commercial Seating
4101 E 48th Ave
Denver, CO 80216 303-322-7792
Fax: 303-393-1836 sales@shafer.com
www.shafer.com
Manufacturer and exporter of booths, chairs, cushions, pads, stools and tables including legs and bases
President: Randall Shafer
CFO: Dick Gish
CEO: Richard Gish
R & D: Dennis Trutcman
Marketing Director: Richard Howard
Purchasing Manager: Carla Rembolt
Estimated Sales: $18 Million
Number Employees: 100-249
Type of Packaging: Food Service

29136 Shaffer Manufacturing Corporation
1186 Walter St
Lemont, IL 60439 630-257-5200
Fax: 630-257-3434 800-652-2151
service@shaffermixers.com shaffermixers.com

Dough feeding equipment
Owner: Terry Bartsch
CEO: George Dunbar
Vice President: Kirk Lang
Director of Engineering: Mike Hall
Sales Manager: Terry Bauer
Estimated Sales: $10 - 20 Million
Number Employees: 10-19

29137 Shaffer Manufacturing Corporation
1186 Walter St
Lemont, IL 60439 630-257-5200
Fax: 630-257-3434 info@dunbarsystems.com
www.shaffermanufacturing.com
Mixers
Owner: Terry Bartsch
Estimated Sales: $5-10 Million
Number Employees: 10-19

29138 Shaffer Sports & Events
601 W 6th Street
Houston, TX 77007 713-699-0088
Fax: 713-426-1672 shaffers@coshocton.com
www.shaffersports.com
Commercial awnings
Manager: Robert Hamilton
Estimated Sales: $1 - 5 Million
Number Employees: 20-49

29139 Shakespeare Company
19845 Us Highway 76
Newberry, SC 29108 803-276-5504
Fax: 803-276-8940 800-800-9008
jprochak@bellsouth.net
www.shakespeare-ce.com
Fiberglass lighting poles including breakaway, ornamental and transmission
Director Sales/Marketing: Bill Griffin
Operations-Production: Ray Jeffords
Plant Manager: Scott Burriss
Estimated Sales: $1 - 5 Million
Number Employees: 250-499
Parent Co: K 2

29140 (HQ)Shambaugh & Son
P.O.Box 1287
Fort Wayne, IN 46801-1287 260-487-7777
Fax: 260-487-7701
mshambaugh@shambaugh.com
www.shambaugh.com
Construction/engineering services for industrial, commercial and institutional industries
President/CEO: Mark Shambaug
CFO: Mark Veerkamp
CEO: Mark P Shambaugh
Estimated Sales: $100-250 Million
Number Employees: 1,000-4,999
Square Footage: 100000
Parent Co: EMCOR Group, Inc.

29141 Shammi Industries/Sammons Equipment
390 A Meyer Circle
Corona, CA 92879-6617 951-340-3419
Fax: 951-340-2716 800-417-9260
ÿinfo@sammonsequipment.com
www.sammonsequipment.com
Manufacturer, importer and exporter of banquet and transport equipment including carts, heated cabinets, racks, tables, dollies and shelving
President: Bhupinder Saggu
Estimated Sales: $1-2.5 Million
Number Employees: 10-19
Square Footage: 21000
Brands:
Queen Mary's
Samco

29142 Shamrock Paper Company
1201 S Wharf St
Saint Louis, MO 63104 314-241-2370
Fax: 314-241-9230 info@shamrockpaper.com
www.shamrockpaper.com
Butcher, locker and kraft wrapping paper
President: William Firestone
Vice President: Rick Bliss
VP Sales: Sally Lippmann
Estimated Sales: $5 - 10Million
Number Employees: 10-19
Square Footage: 50000
Type of Packaging: Consumer, Food Service, Private Label, Bulk
Brands:
Somethin' Special
Sun Bright

29143 Shamrock Plastics
633 Howard St
Mount Vernon, OH 43050 740-392-5555
Fax: 740-392-3555 800-765-1611
shamrockplasticsinc@ecr.net
www.shamrockplastics.com
Plastic packaging and containerizing products including wicketed and bakery bags
Owner: Tom Ruffner
Account Representative: Susan Orlando
Estimated Sales: $3 - 5 Million
Number Employees: 10-19
Square Footage: 85000

29144 Shamrock Technologies
255 Pacific St
Newark, NJ 07114 973-242-3859
Fax: 732-242-8074
marketing@shamrocktechnologies.com
www.shamrocktechnologies.com
Manufacturer and exporter of powdered waxes and PTFE (polytetrafluoroethylene); also, dispersions and emulsions including carnauba, PE, PP, paraffin, microcrystalline and blends
Owner: William B Neuberg
President: Bill Neueerg
Marketing Manager: Melanie McCarroll
Estimated Sales: $20 - 50 Million
Number Employees: 50-99

29145 Shanghai Freemen
977 Hoes Ln
Suite 240
Piscataway, NJ 08854 732-981-1288
Fax: 732-981-0302 li.haisong@freemen.sh.cn
www.sflifescience.com
Dietary supplements, and food and beverage ingredients including vitamins, stevia, natural beta carotene, energy beverage ingredients, amino acids and joint health products
Chairman: Dong Zhang
Manager: Xinchun Zhang
Estimated Sales: $341.95 Million
Parent Co: Shanghai Freemen-Zhucheng Haotian
Type of Packaging: Bulk

29146 Shanker Industries
301 Suburban Avenue
Deer Park, NY 11729 631-940-9889
Fax: 631-940-9895 877-742-6561
sales@shanko.com www.shanko.com
Manufacturer and exporter of decorative wall and ceiling tiles for hotels and restaurants
President: John Shanker
VP Advertising and Finance: Francine Shanker
VP Sales: David Shanker
Estimated Sales: $500,000 - $1 Million
Number Employees: 5-9
Square Footage: 60000
Type of Packaging: Food Service

29147 Shanklin Corporation
100 Westford Rd
Ayer, MA 01432 978-772-3200
Fax: 978-772-5660 info@shanklincorp.com
www.shanklincorp.com
Manufacturer and exporter of shrink wrapping and bundling equipment
President: Norman D Shanklin
CEO: William V Hickey
VP Sales: William Rand
Estimated Sales: $20-50 Million
Number Employees: 10,000
Square Footage: 160000
Brands:
Shanklin

29148 Shanzer Grain Dryer
PO Box 2371
Sioux Falls, SD 57101-2371 605-336-0439
Fax: 605-336-9569 800-843-9887
sales@dwindustries.us
Manufacturer and exporter of grain dryers
Owner: Marian Leuning
Secretary/Tresaurer: Dave Leuning
VP: Marian Leuning
Estimated Sales: $3 - 5 Million
Number Employees: 20-49
Parent Co: D&W Industries

29149 Shaped Wire
900 Douglas Road
Batavia, IL 60510-2294 630-406-0800
Fax: 630-406-0003 sales@shapedwire.com
www.shapedwire.com
Packaging materials
President: William Wolford
Estimated Sales: $20-50 Million
Number Employees: 50-99

29150 Shared Data Systems
P.O.Box 7787
Charlotte, NC 28241-7787 704-588-2233
Fax: 704-588-7154 800-622-2140
info@sdnglobal.com www.shareddata.com
Custom-made software for material handling systems
President: Larry Jones
CFO: Doug Yoder
Estimated Sales: $5 - 10 Million
Number Employees: 20-49

29151 Sharon Manufacturing Company
540 Brook Avenue
Deer Park, NY 11729
Fax: 631-586-6822 800-424-6455
info@sharonmfg.com www.sharonmfg.com
Manufacturer and exporter of replacement parts for gable top and reconditioned fillers for dairy and juice products

29152 Sharp Brothers
201 Orient St
Bayonne, NJ 07002 201-339-0404
Manufacturer and exporter of yeast extruders and cutters
Owner: Basem Abdelnour
Estimated Sales: $500,000-$1 Million
Number Employees: 1-4
Square Footage: 4375

29153 (HQ)Sharp Electronics Corporation
Sharp Plaza
Mahwah, NJ 07495 201-529-8200
Fax: 201-529-8425 800-237-4277
philippr@sharpsec.com www.sharp-usa.com
Manufacturer and importer of commercial microwave ovens
President: Joel Biterman
CEO: Raymond Philippon
Chairman: Toshiaki Urushisako
Senior VP: Robert Scaglione
Number Employees: 1,000-4,999
Square Footage: 300000
Type of Packaging: Consumer, Food Service, Private Label
Other Locations:
Sharp Electronics Corp.
Romeoville IL

29154 Sharp Packaging Systems
N62w22632 Village Dr
Sussex, WI 53089 262-246-8815
Fax: 262-246-8885 800-634-6359
info@sharppackaging.com
www.sharpackaging.com
Pre-opened plastic bags on a roll, specialty films, and automatic bagging machines
President: Paul Scarberry
CEO: Jim Kornfeld
Estimated Sales: $20 - 50 Million
Number Employees: 250-499

29155 Sharpe Measurement Technology
97 West Avenue
Stratford, CT 06615-6112 203-380-1776
Fax: 203-386-0087 info@smt-usa.com
www.smt-usa.com
Continuous thickness gauges and rolling mill control systems
Estimated Sales: $2.5-5 Million
Number Employees: 9

29156 Sharpsville Container
600 W Main St
Sharpsville, PA 16150 724-962-1100
Fax: 724-962-1226 800-645-1248
sales@scacon.com
www.sharpsvillecontainer.com

Stainless steel and plastic tanks, stock pots, drums, hoppers, mixing and steaming kettles, etc.; also, plastic boxes and stainless steel hand carts; custom fabrication available
President: Thom Rigsby
Controller: Joe Higgins
Sales/Customer Service: Laura Puskar
Plant Manager: Michel Altenor
Estimated Sales: $10-20 Million
Number Employees: 50-99
Square Footage: 100000
Parent Co: Spartanburg Stainless Products

29157 Sharpsville Container
600 W Main St
Sharpsville, PA 16150 724-962-1100
Fax: 724-962-1226 800-645-1248
sales@scacon.com
www.sharpsvillecontainer.com
Stainless steel and rotationally molded plastic vessels
President: Rick Mallat
Controller: Joe Higgins
Plant Manager: Michel Altenor
Estimated Sales: $10-20 Million
Number Employees: 50-99

29158 Shashi Foods
55 Esandar Dr
Toronto, ON M4G 4H2 416-645-0611
Fax: 416-645-0612 866-748-7441
www.shashi.ca
Spices, herbs, seasoning blends and specialty flours, also, custom grinding, blending, bottling, and bagging.
President: Sujay Shah
VP: Ajay Shah
Estimated Sales: $7.37 Million
Number Employees: 30
Brands:
Elephant Brand
Shashi
King of Spice
Patak's

29159 Shat-R-Shield
116 Ryan Patrick Dr
Salisbury, NC 28147 704-633-2100
Fax: 704-633-3420 800-223-0853
ayost@shatrshield.com www.shat-r-shield.com
Manufacturer and exporter of plastic-coated and shatter-proof fluorescent lamps and Teflon-coated 125 and 250 watt infrared heat lamps
Owner: Bob Nolan
Marketing Coordinator: Anita Yost
VP Sales/Marketing: Marty Pint
Marketing/Communications Manager: Bill Hahn
Estimated Sales: Below $5 Million
Number Employees: 20-49
Square Footage: 42000
Type of Packaging: Food Service
Brands:
Shat-R-Shield

29160 (HQ)Shaw & Slavsky
13821 Elmira St
Detroit, MI 48227-3099 313-834-3990
Fax: 313-834-2680 800-521-7527
sales@shawandslavsky.com
www.shawandslavsky.com
POP signs for grocery retailers. Also manufacture a wide variety of metal sign holders, poster floor stands, large-format graphics and signage, checkout lights, custom light boxes and custom fixtures.
President: Tom Smith
Estimated Sales: $10 - 20 Million
Number Employees: 50-99
Square Footage: 100000
Other Locations:
Shaw & Slavsky
Detroit MI
Brands:
Tube-Lok

29161 Shaw-Clayton Corporation
90 Montecito Road
San Rafael, CA 94901-2378 415-472-1522
Fax: 415-472-1599 800-537-6712
scorp@shaw-clayton.com
www.shaw-clayton.com
Manufacturer and exporter of small hinged lid containers
President: H Shaw
Sales: L Smith
Public Relations: S Hanson
Estimated Sales: Less than $500,000
Square Footage: 8000
Type of Packaging: Consumer
Brands:
Flex-A-Top

29162 Shawans Specialty Papers
W7575 Poplar Rd
Shawano, WI 54166
800-543-5554
paper@littlerapids.com
www.shawanospecialtypapers.com
Manufacturer and exporter of paper including glazed, wet crepe, dry crepe tissue and serim reinforced tissue
Estimated Sales: $50-100 Million
Number Employees: 100-249
Parent Co: Little Rapids Corporation
Type of Packaging: Consumer, Bulk

29163 Sheahan Sanitation Consulting
424 Hazelnut Drive
Oakley, CA 94561-2404 925-625-9683
Fax: 925-625-2310 800-554-4243
mike@sheahanconsulting.com
www.sheahanconsulting.com
Sanitation and food safety consultant providing training, surface hygiene testing and chemical and hygiene audits and inspections
Estimated Sales: $500,000-$1 Million
Number Employees: 1

29164 Shear Kershman Laboratories
701 Crown Industrial Ct
Suite F
Chesterfield, MO 63005 636-519-8900
Fax: 636-519-0959 info@shearkershman.com
www.shearkershman.com
Research and development consultant for the food and confectionery industries; also, sourcing for material and co-packing available
President & Co-Founder: Jeff L. Shear
Executive Vice President & Co-Founder: Al Kershman
VP Pharmaceuticals Division: Arthur B. Hermelin
Research & Development: Harold Cole
Office Manager: Sue Wagoner
Estimated Sales: $570,000
Number Employees: 7
Square Footage: 12000

29165 Sheboygan Paper Box Company
PO Box 326
Sheboygan, WI 53082-0326 920-458-8373
Fax: 920-458-2901 800-458-8373
jschmitz@spbox.com www.microflute.com
Folding cartons, displays, blister cards. Specializing in polycoated and microflute packaging
Chairman: Jack R Liebl
Branch Manager: Tom Van De Kreeke
Executive VP: Larry Schneider
Director Sales/Marketing: David Moga
Estimated Sales: $10 - 20 Million
Number Employees: 100-249
Square Footage: 206000
Type of Packaging: Consumer, Food Service, Private Label, Bulk

29166 Sheffield Lumber & Pallet Company
165 Turkey Foot Rd
Mocksville, NC 27028 336-492-5565
Fax: 704-492-5682
Wooden pallets and skids
Estimated Sales: $1 - 5 Million
Number Employees: 50-99
Parent Co: Palex Company

29167 Sheffield Plastics
119 Salisbury Rd
Sheffield, MA 01257 413-229-8711
Fax: 413-229-8717 800-628-5084
www.sheffieldplastics.com
Extruded plastic sheets for window glazing, signs, displays, architectural products and industrial applications
President: Dennis Duff
CFO: David Martin
Quality Control: Sherley Alarie
Estimated Sales: $20 - 50 Million
Number Employees: 100-249
Square Footage: 160000
Parent Co: Bayer Corporation

29168 Sheffield Platers
9850 Waples Street
San Diego, CA 92121 858-546-8484
Fax: 858-546-7653 800-227-9242
mwatkins@sheffieldplaters.com
www.sheffieldplaters.com
Coffee urns; wholesaler/distributor of punch bowls, chaffing sets, trays, etc.; serving the food service market; repair and replating services available
President: Dale L. Watkins Jr
VP: Mark E. Watkins
Director, Business Development: Vincent Noonan
VP, Marketing: Mark Watkins
VP, Sales: Mark Watkins
Estimated Sales: $2.5-5 Million
Number Employees: 20-49
Square Footage: 68000

29169 Shelburne Systems
8 Harbor View Rd
South Burlington, VT 05403-7850 802-658-6588
Fax: 802-658-6596 sarah@shelburneplastics.com
www.shelburneplastics.com
Plastic bottles
President: Eugene Torvend
Vice President of Sales: John Wolfgang
Estimated Sales: $10-20 Million
Number Employees: 50-99

29170 Shelby Pallet & Box Company
PO Box 27
Shelby, MI 49455-0027 231-861-4214
Fax: 231-861-0054
Pallets and skids
President: Brad Smith
Number Employees: 9

29171 Shelby Williams Industries
810 W Highway 25 70
Newport, TN 37821 423-586-7000
Fax: 866-319-9371 800-873-3252
swisales@shelbywilliams.com
www.shelbywilliams.com
President: David Morley
CFO: Jean Fleetwood
R & D: Terry Roche
Quality Control: Marriane Carter
Plant Manager: Bob Drey
Number Employees: 1,000-4,999
Parent Co: Falcon Products

29172 (HQ)Shelby Williams Industries
810 W Highway 25 70
Newport, TN 37821 423-586-7000
Fax: 866-319-9371 800-873-3252
swisales@shelbywilliams.com
www.shelbywilliams.com
Manufacturer and exporter of seating; importer of wicker chairs
President: David Morley
Chairman and CEO: Franklin Jacobs
VP Operations: Marty Blaylock
Plant Manager: Bob Drey
Number Employees: 1,000-4,999
Parent Co: Falcon Industries
Other Locations:
Williams, Shelby, Industries
Statesville NC

29173 Shelcon
2081 S Hellman Ave
Suite J
Ontario, CA 91761 909-947-4877
Fax: 909-947-1083
Soiled tray, tray assembly and plating conveyors; also, display rotisseries
President: Jon Clark
CEO: John Silvas
Estimated Sales: $1-2.5 Million
Number Employees: 5-9
Square Footage: 7400

29174 (HQ)Shelden, Dickson, & Steven Company
6114 Country Club Road
Omaha, NE 68152-2020 402-571-4848
Manufacturer and exporter of vending machines, fluorescent light fixtures, wall safes, etc
President: Richard Lebron
Estimated Sales: $.5 - 1 million
Number Employees: 16
Square Footage: 100000

29175 **Sheldon Wood Products**
PO Box 339
Toano, VA 23168-0339 757-566-8880
Fax: 757-566-2230
Wooden pallets and skids
President: S Sheldon
Number Employees: 25

29176 **Shell Oil Products Company**
910 Louisiana St
Houston, TX 77002-4934 713-241-6161
Fax: 713-241-6418 MRBINGHAM@SHELL.com
www.shell.com
Senior VP: Roxanne J Decyk
Technology Director: Matthias Bichsel
Account Manager: John Hamilton
Estimated Sales: K
Number Employees: 10,000

29177 **Shelley Cabinet Company**
1407 N 630 E
Shelley, ID 83274 208-357-3700
Fax: 208-357-7447 sccdan@srv.net
Custom cabinets and counter tops
President: Dan Tschikof
Purchasing Manager: Greg Wilklund
Estimated Sales: $500,000-$1 Million
Number Employees: 10-19
Square Footage: 10000

29178 **Sheman Tov Corporation**
150 Oakwood Ave
Orange, NJ 07050-3912 973-673-2350
President: Lee Saal
Estimated Sales: Below $5 Million
Number Employees: 1-4

29179 **(HQ)Shen Manufacturing Company**
40 Portland Rd
W Conshohocken, PA 19428-2717 610-825-2790
Fax: 610-834-8617 johnritz@aol.com
Manufacturer, importer and exporter of placemats, chair pads, pot holders, oven mitts, aprons, bar mops, dish towels and cloths inclduing table, dish, scrub, dusting and polishing
President: Howard Steidle Jr
CFO: Robert Steidle
VP Sales/Marketing: Howard Steidle Jr
Estimated Sales: $5-10 Million
Number Employees: 20-49

29180 **Shenandoah Vineyards**
12300 Steiner Rd
Plymouth, CA 95669 209-245-4455
Fax: 209-245-5156 info@sobowine.com
www.sobonwine.com
Wines
President: Leon Sobon
CEO: Shirley Sobon
Estimated Sales: Below $5 Million
Number Employees: 10-19

29181 **Shenck AccuRate**
PO Box 208
Whitewater, WI 53190-0208 262-473-2441
Fax: 262-473-2489 888-742-1249
mktg@accuratefeeders.com www.sarinc.com
Manufacturing and supplying superior volumetric and gravimetric feeders, weighfeeders, solids flow meters, bulk bag discharging systems, and vibratory feeders to a wide variety of markets throughout the world.
President: Dirk Maroske
CFO: Neal Mueller
Number Employees: 100-249
Parent Co: Schenck AccuRate
Brands:
Mechatron Gravimetric Feeders
Mechatron Volumetric Feeders
Sac Master Bulk Bag Dischargers
Solid Flow Vibratory Feeders
Tuf-Flex Volumetric Series Feeders

29182 **Shep Company**
P.O.Box 385
Lawrence, MA 01842-0785 978-686-0632
Fax: 978-683-5202 info@shepcompany.com
www.shepcompany.com
Adhesives
Owner: Craig Allard
Quality Control: Craig Aalard
Estimated Sales: $20-50 Million
Number Employees: 20-49

29183 **Shepard Brothers**
503 S Cypress St
La Habra, CA 90631 562-697-1366
Fax: 562-697-4421
remy-luthra@shepardbros.com
www.shepardbros.com
Manufacturer and exporter of cleaners, sanitizers and water treatment and waste treatment systems; also, consultant specializing in sanitation
Manager: Valerie Saldana
CEO: Ron Shepard
VP Sales: Tony Terranova
Estimated Sales: $15 - 20 Million
Number Employees: 50-99

29184 **Shepard Niles**
220 N Genesee St
Montour Falls, NY 14865 607-535-7323
Fax: 607-535-7323 800-481-2260
kim.messersmith@us.konecranes.com
www.shepard-niles.com
Hoists and genuine Shepard Niles replacement parts
Manager: Michael Baker
Number Employees: 15
Type of Packaging: Bulk
Brands:
Cleveland Tramrail
Enduro
Liftabout
Safpowrbar

29185 **Sheridan Sign Company**
124 Wilson St
Salisbury, MD 21801-4100 410-749-7441
Fax: 410-749-4179 signs@bwave.com
Signs including painted, electric and neon
President: Eugene F Trapkin
Manager: Marlynn R Schaeffer
Estimated Sales: Below $5 Million
Number Employees: 10-19

29186 **Sherwood Tool**
10100 Reisterstown Road
Owings Mills, MD 21117-3815 860-828-4161
Fax: 860-828-5387 info@sherwoodtool.com
www.sherwoodtool.com
Manufacturer and exporter of packaging machinery
President: Paul R Corazzo Sr
Parent Co: Sherwood Industries
Type of Packaging: Food Service, Private Label
Brands:
Shercan

29187 **Shibuya International**
1070 Reno Avenue
Modesto, CA 95351-1176 209-529-6466
Fax: 209-529-1834 sales@shibuya-int.com
www.shibuya-international.com
Importer of food processing and packaging machinery including aseptic filling systems, cappers, cartoners, unscramblers, casers, uncasers, washers, cleaners, pasteurizers, warmers, coolers, conveyors and labelers
President: Ken Saisho
CEO: Ian Greenland
Estimated Sales: $1 - 3 Million
Number Employees: 4
Square Footage: 66800
Parent Co: Shibuya Kogyo Company

29188 **Shick Tube-Veyor Corporation**
4346 Clary Blvd
Kansas City, MO 64130 816-861-7224
Fax: 816-921-1901 info@shicktube.com
www.shickusa.com
Manufacturer and exporter of ingredient handling systems and components including liquid systems process control/diverter valves, sifters, bag dump stations, hoppers and dust collectors; installation and service available
President: Joseph Ungashick
Executive VP: Mark Ungashick
Marketing Communication Manager: Kerwin Brown
VP Sales/Marketing: Rob Merrill
Estimated Sales: $10 - 20 Million
Number Employees: 100-249

29189 **Shields Bag & Printing Company**
1009 Rock Avenue
Yakima, WA 98902 509-248-7500
Fax: 509-248-6304 800-541-8630
sales@shieldsbag.com http://web.shieldsbag.com
Manufacturer and exporter of plain and printed mono and co-extrusion polyethylene, nylon and polypropylene film and bags; also, commercial printing services available.
Estimated Sales: $50-100 Million
Number Employees: 500-999
Square Footage: 300000

29190 **Shields Products**
530 Exeter Ave
West Pittston, PA 18643-1735 570-655-4596
Fax: 570-655-0262
Packaging materials including shredded cellophane, tissue, waxed paper and parchment
Owner: Warren Hemmelwright
Estimated Sales: $500,000-$1 Million
Number Employees: 1-4

29191 **Shiffer Industries**
41 Moana Ave
Kihei, HI 96753-7170 216-524-6546
800-642-1774
shiffer@clevelandindustry.com www.shiffer.com
Manufacturer and exporter of assemblers, handlers, formers, feeders, index transferers, sorters, orienters, fillers, meters, markers, cutters, counters, loaders, unloaders, dispatchers, dedimplers, deburrers, labelers, etc.; customdesigning available
Office Manager: L Mangal
President: Stuart Shiffer
Estimated Sales: $2.5-5 Million
Number Employees: 20-49

29192 **Shild Company**
9 Lispenard St
New York, NY 10013-2290 212-431-7489
Fax: 212-941-1702 866-435-2949
shild1@aol.com www.shieldpress.com
Advertising specialties, wine list covers, manufacturers Of corporate excutive leather goods
Owner: Steven Shield
VP: Abe Horawitzch
Marketing: Abe Horowitz
Sales: Abe Horowitz
Purchasing: Abe Horowitz
Estimated Sales: $500,000-$1,000,000
Number Employees: 05to10
Number of Products: 75
Type of Packaging: Consumer, Food Service

29193 **Shillington Box Company**
3501 Tree Court Ind Blvd
Saint Louis, MO 63122 636-225-5353
Fax: 636-225-5306 info@shillingtonbox.com
www.shillingtonbox.com
Corrugated boxes
Estimated Sales: $18 Million
Number Employees: 50-99
Square Footage: 56000

29194 **Shimadzu Scientific Instruments**
7060 Koll Center Pkwy
Suite 328
Pleasanton, CA 94566 925-417-2090
Fax: 925-462-7348 800-482-0253
tichi@shimadzu.co.jp www.ssi.shimadzu.com
Wine industry analytical instruments
Manager: Will Bankert
Estimated Sales: $1-2.5 Million
Number Employees: 10-19
Parent Co: Shimadzu Corporation

29195 **Shingle Belting**
420 Drew Ct
Suite A
King of Prussia, PA 19406 610-239-6667
Fax: 610-239-6668 800-345-6294
belting@shinglebelting.com
www.shinglebelting.com
Manufacturer and exporter of flat sheet and profile thermoplastic conveyor belting including PU, PVC and polyester and bakery belts
President: Ronnie Keating
Marketing Coordinator: Monica Berry
Sales VP: Bob Frasetto
Operations: Frank Manley
Plant Manager: Bob Bolan
Estimated Sales: $5-10 Million
Number Employees: 20-49
Square Footage: 30000
Brands:
European Monofilements
Polyflex

Rounthane
Veethane

29196 Ship Rite Packaging
161 Woodbine Street
Bergenfield, NJ 07621-2839 201-385-4747
Fax: 201-385-2448 800-721-7447
sales@shipritebags.com www.shipritebags.com
Flexible polyethylene film; also, bags including flexible polyethylene, ziplock, rollstock and wicketted; custom printing available
President: Mayer Schlisser
Estimated Sales: $1-2.5 Million
Number Employees: 1-4

29197 Shipley Basket Inc
191 Shipley Ln
Dayton, TN 37321-5415 423-775-2051
Fax: 423-775-2145 800-251-0806
shipleybasket@aol.com www.shipleybasket.com
Manufacturer and exporter of fruit and vegetable baskets
President: Diane Shipley
Estimated Sales: $5-10 Million
Number Employees: 20-49

29198 Shipmaster Containers Ltd.
380 Esna Park Drive
Markham, ON L3R 1G5
Canada 416-493-9193
Fax: 416-493-6223 info@shipmaster.com
www.shipmaster.com
Corrugated paper containers
Estimated Sales: $10 - 15 Million
Number Employees: 50-99

29199 Shippers Paper Products
808 Blake Rd
Sheridan, AR 72150 870-942-2151
Fax: 870-942-5933 800-468-1230
inquiry@itwshippers.com www.itwshippers.com
Manufacturer and exporter of paper and plastic dunnage bags
Plant Manager: Jeff Maness
Number Employees: 100-249

29200 Shippers Paper Products
808 Blake Rd
Sheridan, AR 72150 870-942-2151
Fax: 931-379-7735 800-933-7731
inquiry@itwshippers.com www.itwshippers.com
Manufacturer and exporter of air bags, void filler, bulk heads and slip sheets
President: Jeff Maness
Vice President: Tom Keenan
Marketing Director: Eric Lott
Estimated Sales: $20 - 50 Million
Number Employees: 100-249
Parent Co: ITW
Type of Packaging: Food Service

29201 Shippers Supply
2815A Cleveland Avenue
Saskatoon, SK S7K 8G1
Canada 306-242-6266
Fax: 306-933-4333 800-661-5639
saskatoon@shipperssupply.com
www.shipperssupply.com
Manufacturer and wholesaler/distributor of printed labels, pressure sensitive tapes, corrugated boxes, material handling equipment, stretch and shrink film and shipping supplies
President: Ron Brown
CFO: Miles Jern
Branch Manager: Neil Nutter
Number Employees: Oover 200
Square Footage: 400000

29202 Shippers Supply
2815A Cleveland Avenue
Saskatoon, SK S7K 8G1
Canada 306-242-6266
Fax: 306-933-4333 800-661-5639
saskatoon@shipperssupply.com
www.shipperssupply.com
Manufacturer, wholesaler/distributor and importer of printed labels, pressure sensitive tapes, corrugated boxes, material handling equipment, stretch film and shipping supplies; exporter of labels and printed tape
President: Ron Brown
Branch Manager: Ken Nordyke
Number Employees: Oover 200
Square Footage: 400000

Brands:
Labelgraphics
Redeman

29203 Shippers Supply
102 King Edward Street E
Winnipeg, NB R3H 0N8
Canada 204-772-9800
Fax: 204-772-9834 800-661-5639
winnipeg@shipperssupply.com
www.shipperssupply.com
Printed labels, pressure sensitive tapes, corrugated boxes, material handling equipment, stretch film and shipping supplies
President: Ron Brown
Branch Manager: Bob Letchford
Number Employees: 10
Square Footage: 400000

29204 Shippers Supply, Labelgraphic
8-3401 19 Street NE
Calgary, AB T2E 6S8
Canada 403-291-0450
Fax: 403-291-3641 800-661-5639
airways@shipperssupply.com
www.shipperssupply.com
Manufacturer and wholesaler/distributor of printed labels, pressure sensitive tapes, corrugated boxes, material handling equipment, stretch film and shipping supplies
President: Ron Brown
General Manager: Dennis Rhind
Branch Manager: Jerry Pierce
Number Employees: Oover 200
Square Footage: 400000
Parent Co: Shippers Supply

29205 Shivvers
613 W English St
Corydon, IA 50060 641-872-1007
Fax: 641-872-1593 shivvvers@shivvrs.com
www.shivvers.com
Manufacturer and exporter of continuous flow drying equipment and computer controls for dryers
President: Carl Shivvers
Quality Control: Bobby Wilson
VP: Carl Shivvers
Assistant Sales Manager: Jim Ratliff
Estimated Sales: $20-50 Million
Number Employees: 100-249
Square Footage: 120000
Parent Co: Shivvers Manufacturing

29206 Sho-Me Container
704 Pinder Ave
Grinnell, IA 50112 641-236-4798
Fax: 641-236-3478 800-798-3512
lawrence@sho-me.com www.showme.com
Custom silk screened printed plastic canisters and plastic bottles; exporter of plastic bottles
President: Lawrence Den Hartog
Plant Manager: Gary Vowels
Estimated Sales: $20 - 50 Million
Number Employees: 20-49
Square Footage: 28000
Brands:
Sho-Me

29207 ShockWatch
1111 W Mockingbird Ln Ste 1050
Dallas, TX 75247 214-630-9625
Fax: 214-638-4512 800-527-9497
info@shockwatch.com www.shockwatch.com
Damage prevention products for shipping and handing of fragile and environmentally sensitive gods.
President/CEO: Gerard Smith
VP/CFO: David Chisum
VP/CIO: Tim Hegwood
VP Marketing: Jeff Kilpatrick
VP Sales, North America: Dennis Raymond
VP Operations: Danny Goldsmith
Estimated Sales: $10-15,000,000
Number Employees: 50-99
Brands:
Shock Switch
Shock Watch

29208 Shoes for Crews/Mighty Mat
1400 Centrepark Blvd # 31
West Palm Beach, FL 33401-7402 561-683-5090
Fax: 561-683-3080 800-667-5477
scotts@shoesforcrews.com
www.shoesforcrews.com
Shoes for Crews Slip-Resistant Footwear will provent your slips and falls with over 38 styles to choose from at prices starting at $24.98. We offer the exclusive $5000 Slip & Fall Warranty: If any employee slips and falls wearing SHOESFOR CREWS, we will reimburse your company up to $5000 on the paid workers comp claim. Call us at 1-877-667-5477 for details
Chairman of the Board: Stanley Smith
Estimated Sales: $5 - 10 Million
Number Employees: 1-4
Type of Packaging: Private Label
Brands:
Shoes For Crews

29209 Shook Design Group
2151 Hawkins St # 400
Charlotte, NC 28203-6904 704-377-0661
Fax: 704-377-0953
stacywegner@shookkelley.com
www.shookkelley.com
We are a brand strategy, architecture and design consultancy, specializing in food retailing and consumption environments. Includes supermarkets, restaurants, C-stores, etc. Focus on influencing consumer perception to drive sales
President: Charlesshook Shook
VP: Kevin Kelley
Marketing Director: Jason Mink
Public Relations: Jonathan Scott
Estimated Sales: $350 Million
Number Employees: 1-4

29210 Shoppers Plaza USA
PO Box 450
Dewitt, MI 48820-0450 517-327-9949
Fax: 517-886-9633 jay@spusa.com
www.spusa.com
Retailer of industrial food equipment
Estimated Sales: Below 1 Million
Number Employees: 5

29211 Shore Distribution Resources
18 Manitoba Way
Marlboro, NJ 07746-1219 732-972-1711
Fax: 732-972-7669 800-876-9727
shordist@aol.com www.sdronline.com
Wholesaler/distributor of packaging materials and equipment including plastic containers, polyester film, cellophane and polypropylene; also, carry out platters, bowls, disposable thermometers and food safety products
President: Elaine Shore
CEO: Harvey Shore
Sales: Harvey Shore
Operations: Scott Shore
Estimated Sales: $1-2.5 Million
Number Employees: 5-9
Square Footage: 12000
Type of Packaging: Food Service

29212 Shore Paper Box Company
9821 Riverton Rd
PO BOX 149
Mardela Springs, MD 21837-0149 410-749-7125
Fax: 410-860-2188 office@shorepaperbox.com
www.shorepaperbox.com
Set-up paper boxes; also, die cutting and hot stamping available. made to order only
President: Rennie Keating
Chairman: Vernon Taylor
CFO: Vernon Taylor
Vice President: Mary Thompson
Quality Control: Mary Thompson
Estimated Sales: Below $5 Million
Number Employees: 10-19

29213 Shorewood Engineering
865 Industrial Blvd
Waconia, MN 55387 952-442-2526
Fax: 952-442-4036
sales@shorewoodengineering.com
www.shorewoodengineering.com
Packaging machinery
Owner: Ken Good
Estimated Sales: $1-2.5 Million
Number Employees: 5-9

29214 Shorewood Packaging
1 Kero Rd
Carlstadt, NJ 07072-2604 201-933-3203
Fax: 203-754-6020
shorewoodmarketing@ipaper.com
www.shorewoodpackaging.com

Set-up fancy boxes
President: Mark Shore
Chairman: John Faraci
Senior Vice President of Corporate Devel: Cato Ealy
Estimated Sales: $20-50 Million
Number Employees: 100-249

29215 Shouldice Brothers SheetMetal
400 W Dickman Rd
Battle Creek, MI 49037 269-962-5579
Fax: 269-962-8114
shobro@shouldicebrothers.com
www.shouldicebrothers.com
Bins, ovens and material handling equipment including conveyors, hoppers and carts
President: Dave Shouldice
Secretary and Treasurer: Dave Shouldice
VP: Dave Middlesworth
Estimated Sales: $2.5-5 Million
Number Employees: 20-49

29216 Showeray Corporation
2028 E 7th St
Brooklyn, NY 11223 718-965-3633
Fax: 718-965-3647
Manufacturer, importer and exporter of tablecloths
Estimated Sales: $1 - 5 Million
Number Employees: 50-99
Square Footage: 60000

29217 Shrinkfast Marketing
460 Sunapee St
Newport, NH 03773 603-863-7719
Fax: 603-863-6225 800-867-4746
info@shrinkfast-998.com
www.shrinkfast-998.com
Manufacturer and exporter of portable propane operated heat guns for shrinkwrap and palletizing applications
Manager: Chuck Milliken
CFO: Chuck Milliken
Manager Sales/Marketing: Douglas Barton Jr
Estimated Sales: $5 - 10 Million
Number Employees: 50-99

29218 Shure-Glue Systems
600 Vine Street
Suite 1004
Cincinnati, OH 45202 513-333-0014
Fax: 513-874-3612 sales@shure-glue.com
www.suhrelaw.com
Owner: Joe B Suhre Iv
Estimated Sales: Below $5 Million
Number Employees: 1-4

29219 Shurflo Pump Manufacturing
12650 Westminster Avenue
Santa Ana, CA 92706-2139 714-554-7709
Fax: 714-265-2127 800-854-3218
u2689@shurflo.com www.shurflo.com
Beverage, beer, condiment dispensing, water filtration, pumps
CEO: James Phillips
Estimated Sales: $79.4 Million
Number Employees: 250-499

29220 Shurtape Technologies
1506 Highland Ave. NE
Hickory, NC 28601 828-322-2700
Fax: 828-322-7899 888-442-8273
www.shurtape.com
Commodity, industrial grade and specialty adhesive tapes
CEO: Jim Shuford
Estimated Sales: $113.20 Million
Number Employees: 1100

29221 Shuster Corporation
4 Wright St
New Bedford, MA 02740 508-999-3261
Fax: 508-991-8585 info@shustercorp.com
www.shustercorp.com
Specialty ball and roller bearings including ceramic anticorrosive bearings for harsh applications;
President: Steven Shuster
Quality Control: John Sinlk
Estimated Sales: $5-10 Million
Number Employees: 20-49
Parent Co: Genuine Parts Company

29222 Shuster Laboratories
85 John Rd
Canton, MA 02021-2826 781-821-2200
Fax: 781-821-2200 800-444-8705
info@shusterlabs.com www.shusterlabs.com
Consultant and contract research and development firm providing research and development for product development, sensory testing, nutrition analysis/labeling, HACCP, GMP, audits, regulatory liaison, shelf-life studies andmicrobiological and analytical testing
President: Philip Katz
CEO: Roy Lamothe
Director Marketing: Patricia Baressi
Estimated Sales: $10 - 20 Million
Number Employees: 100-249
Square Footage: 42000
Parent Co: Hauser Chemical Research Company
Other Locations:
Shuster Laboratories
Smyrna GA

29223 Shuster Laboratories
85 John Rd
Canton, MA 02021-2826 781-821-2200
Fax: 781-821-2200 800-444-8705
info@shusterlabs.com www.shusterlabs.com
Product development, product formulation, sensory evaluation, market research, quality assurance, analytical and microbiological testing
President: Thil Katz
Manager: Ed Sarcione
CEO: Roy Lamothe
National Sales Manager: Eric Wieland
Estimated Sales: $10 - 20 Million
Number Employees: 100-249
Square Footage: 42000

29224 (HQ)Shuttleworth
10 Commercial Rd
Huntington, IN 46750 260-356-8500
Fax: 260-359-7810 800-444-7412
inc@shuttleworth.com www.shuttleworth.com
Custom engineered solutions, conveyors, devices and material handling systems
President: Carol Shuttleworth
Estimated Sales: $10-20 Million
Number Employees: 50-99
Number of Brands: 4
Square Footage: 4600
Parent Co: Shuttleworth
Other Locations:
Shuttleworth
Petaling Jaya
Brands:
Clean Glide
Slip-Torque
Slip-Trak
Zone Control

29225 Shyrflo Pump Manufacturing Company
12650 Westminster Avenue
Santa Ana, CA 92706-2139 714-554-7709
Fax: 714-265-2127
customer_service@shurflo.com
www.shurflo.com
Manufactures pumps—positive displacement up to 10 GPM
Estimated Sales: $50-100 Million
Number Employees: 250-499

29226 Si-Lodec
4611 S 134th Place
Tukwila, WA 98168-3202 206-244-6188
Fax: 714-731-2019 800-255-8274
Manufacturer and exporter of scales including mobile, portable axle and force measurement
President: Rick Beets
Director International Sales: Arthur Tyson
Number Employees: 80
Square Footage: 30000

29227 Sicht-Pack Hagner
Musbacher Str. 21-23
Dornstetten/ Hallwangen, QC D-72280
Canada 004- 7-43 2
Fax: 004- 74-3 31 800-454-5269
info@sicht-pack-hagner.de
www.sicht-pack-hagner.de
President: Heirich Hagner
Number Employees: 10

29228 Sick Inc.
6900 West 110th Street
Minneapolis, MN 55438 952-941-6780
Fax: 952-941-9287 800-325-7425
info@sick.com www.sickusa.com
A global manufacturer of sensors, safety systems, machine vision and automatic identification products for industrial applications. Including: 2D and 2D machine vision cameras, Color Vision Sensors (CVS), and capacitative sensors.
President: Albert Bertomeu
Managing Director: Renate Sick-Glaser
Marketing Director: Maria Mueller
Sales Manager: Marion Bentin
Number Employees: 200
Parent Co: SICK, Inc

29229 Sick, Inc.
6900 W 110th St
Bloomington, MN 55438 952-946-6800
Fax: 952-941-9287 800-325-7425
info@sick.com www.sickusa.com
Sick is one of the worlds leading manufacturers of sensors,safety systems,and automatic identification products for industrial applications. whether automating factories or optimizing distribution centers,sick provides fast effectivesolutions. the company now has more than 4,000 employees around the world. sick north america is headquartered in minneapolis, mn.
President: Alberto Bertomeu
Marketing Director: Maria Moeiler
Estimated Sales: $20-50 Million
Number Employees: 100-249

29230 Sidel, Inc.
5600 Sun Ct.
Norcross, GA 30092-2892 678-221-3000
Fax: 678-221-3571 800-453-7439
www.sidelsystems.com
Filling machines, mixers, conveyors, and line engineering
President: Philippe Bartissol
Estimated Sales: $19.60 Million
Number Employees: 350

29231 Sidney Manufacturing Company
405 N. Main Ave.
PO Box 380
Sidney, OH 45365 937-492-4154
Fax: 937-492-0919 800-482-3535
sbaker@sidneymfg.com
www.sidneymanufacturing.com
Equipment used in handling wet and dry bulk materials with a customer base in industries such as grain, wood byproducts, cellulose fibers, animal feeds, pet foods, flour, pellets, powders, food products and the line. ALso manufacture aline of industrial personnel elevators from 300lbs to 1000lbs capacity four passengers.
President: Steve Baker
Executive Vice President: Paul Borders
Engineering Manager: Tom Gross
Design Engineer: Josh Hicks
Sales Engineer/Customer Service: Joe Swartz
Purchasing Agent: Ward Cartwright
Estimated Sales: Below $5 Million
Number Employees: 20-49
Square Footage: 50000
Brands:
Smc
Sidney

29232 Sielt Stone
6965 Union Park Center
Midvale, UT 84047-6008 801-268-9100
Fax: 801-268-9114 800-688-9781
Number Employees: 10

29233 Siemens Dematic
507 Plymouth Ave NE
Grand Rapids, MI 49505 616-913-7700
Fax: 616-913-7701 877-725-7500
usinfo@dematic.com www.dematic.com
Chief Executive Officer: Alan Bradley
CEO: John K Baysore
Estimated Sales: $3 - 5 Million
Parent Co: Siemens AG

29234 Siemens Energy & Automation
3333 Old Milton Pkwy
Alpharetta, GA 30005 770-751-2000
Fax: 770-751-4333 800-743-6367
juergen.brandes@sea.siemens.com
www.usa.siemens.com
AC/DC drives, programmable controllers and industrial systems
CEO: Denis Sadlowski
CFO: Harry Volande
Contact Person in USA: Andreas Klenke
Estimated Sales: Less than $500,000
Number Employees: 10,000
Parent Co: Siemens

29235 Siemens Measurement Systems
1000 Pittsford Victor Rd
Pittsford, NY 14534-3822 585-248-3050
800-568-7721
verax_info@moore-solutions.com
www.sea.siemens.com
Data collection and analysis systems and software for statistical process control applications for food and beverage processors
President: Aubert Martin
Senior Vice President, Chief Information: Craig Berry
Executive Vice President of Global Sales: Paul Vogel
Number Employees: 20-49
Square Footage: 24000
Brands:
Focus Plus
Sentinel
Sentry/Sentry Plus

29236 Siemens Water Technologies Corp.
181 Thorn Hill Rd
Warrendale, PA 15086 724-772-0044
Fax: 724-722-1360 866-926-8420
www.water.siemens.com
Supplier of water and wastewater treatment systems and services
Chief Executive Officer: Dr. Lukas Loeffler
Vice President Hub Management: Ursula Boehm
VP Global Research & Development: Ruediger Knauf
Estimated Sales: K
Number Employees: 5700

29237 Sierra Converting Corporation
1400 Kleppe Ln
Sparks, NV 89431 775-331-8221
Fax: 775-331-8385 800-332-8221
info@sierraconventing.compark.nv.us
www.sierraconverting.com
Manufactures, prints and laminates packaging for the food and snack industries; zippered pouches and pouch bags
President: Robert Yarhi
VP: Daniel Yarhi
Quality Control: Victor Seballes
Sales: Jim Harmon
Public Relations: Norman Robins
Operations: Bill Anglos
Productions: Ron Vurwip
Plant Manager: Otis Wilson
Purchasing: Chris Back
Estimated Sales: $20 - 30 Million
Number Employees: 75
Type of Packaging: Consumer, Food Service, Private Label

29238 Sierra Dawn Products
P.O.Box 513
Graton, CA 95444-0513 707-535-0172
Fax: 707-588-0757 sierradawn@ap.net
www.sierradawn.com
Manufacturer and exporter of liquid soaps, recycled packaging and household cleaning products with vegetable-based ingredients
President: Chris Maurer
VP: Janet Jenkins
Estimated Sales: $1-2.5 Million
Number Employees: 1-4
Brands:
Lifetree

29239 Sifters Parts & Service
29807 State Road 54
Wesley Chapel, FL 33543 813-991-9400
Fax: 813-991-9700 800-367-3591
Info@SifterParts.com www.sifterparts.com
Filters and sifters
President: Karen Williams
CFO: Tim Robinson
CEO: Bob Williams
Quality Control: Derek Williams
Estimated Sales: $5 - 10 Million
Number Employees: 10-19

29240 Sig Pack Systems Division
2440 Sumner Blvd
Raleigh, NC 27616-3275 919-877-0886
Fax: 919-877-0887 888-546-5744
info@sigpack-usa.com www.siggroup.com
Bag and pouch sealers, bag filling and sealing machines, brush wrapping, foiling, carton machines: closing, filling, forming, horizontal form and fill, sear machines, robotics, pharmaceutical packaging
President: Harold Carr
VP: Tod Torey
Estimated Sales: $5 - 10 Million
Number Employees: 20-49

29241 Sigma Engineering Corporation
39 Westmoreland Ave
White Plains, NY 10606 914-682-1820
Fax: 914-682-0599 info@sigmaus.com
www.sigmaus.com
Manufacturer and exporter of drum pumps and forming extruders
President: Edward Derrico
Estimated Sales: $5 - 10 Million
Number Employees: 5-9
Square Footage: 40000

29242 Sigma Industrial Automation
5450 Fm 1103
Cibolo, TX 78108 210-659-5000
Fax: 210-659-3443 800-578-5060
dean@sigma-usa.com www.sigma-usa.com
Data collection in washdown environments, washdown computers, food processing-SPC, high speed and manual box labeling
Owner: Kathleen Chinni
Director - SPC/QA: Dr. Guy Gibson
VP - Systems Engineering: Jeff Chinni
Engineering Manager: Rick Curcio
GM - Sales Director: Dean Chinni
Applications Development Manager: Doug Lansdowne
Accounts Receivable: Anita Torres
Estimated Sales: $1-2.5 Million
Number Employees: 10-19

29243 Sigma Industries
4325 Mann Rd
Concord, MI 49237-9534 517-857-6520
Fax: 517-857-3292 ww.sigmawire.com
Manufacturer and exporter of material handling equipment including pallets, pallet racks, decking and steel wire mesh containers
President: Stanley Jurasek
CFO: Stanley Jurasek
Sales Director: Jan Richardson
Estimated Sales: $2.5 - 5 Million
Number Employees: 10-19
Brands:
Junior
Palletainer
Rigitainer

29244 Sign Classics
1014 Timothy Dr
San Jose, CA 95133-1042 408-298-1600
Fax: 408-298-3177 info@signclassics.com
www.signclassics.com
Manufacturer and exporter of custom signs and designs including restaurant
President: Kenneth Fisher
Sales Manager: Clare Wild
Estimated Sales: $1-2.5 Million
Number Employees: 10-19

29245 Sign Experts
2044 Rose
Pacific, MO 63069
Fax: 877-688-1863 800-874-9942
sales@signexperts.com www.signexperts.com
Manufacturer and exporter of advertising signs
President: Paul Stojeba
CFO: Deb Stojeba
Estimated Sales: Less than $500,000
Number Employees: 1-4

29246 Sign Factory
13905 Artesia Blvd
Cerritos, CA 90703 562-809-1443
Fax: 562-809-1435 info@1signfactory.com
www.1signfactory.com
Flags, pennants, banners and signs; lettering service available
Owner: Ernst Dinkel
Estimated Sales: Less than $500,000
Number Employees: 1-4
Square Footage: 8000

29247 Sign Graphics
2317 E Florida St
Evansville, IN 47711 812-476-9151
Fax: 812-479-5147 graphics@sigecom.net
www.signgraphicsinc.com
Signs and custom directory systems; also, vehicle and window lettering engraving and decals
President: Brad Nash
Plant Manager: Kerry Dubuque
Estimated Sales: $500,000-$1 Million
Number Employees: 5-9
Square Footage: 4000

29248 Sign Products
1664 Terra Ave Unit 1
Sheridan, WY 82801 307-672-3145
Fax: 307-672-9829 800-532-4753
54663signprod@aol.com
Restaurant signage including neon and road boards
Manager: Terry Reimers
Sales: Paul Cox
Estimated Sales: Less than $500,000
Number Employees: 1-4
Parent Co: Billings Neon

29249 Sign Shop
9223 Archibald Ave Ste A
Rancho Cucamonga, CA 91730 909-945-5888
Fax: 909-941-7395 sales@signshoporfc.com
www.signshopofrc.com
Custom vinyl banners, wood and metal signs, name plates, labels, etc.; also, screen printing and lettering services available
Owner: Terri Hart
Estimated Sales: $500,000-$1,000,000
Number Employees: 5-9
Brands:
The Bob-O-Bear

29250 Sign Systems, Inc.
23253 Hoover Road
Warren, MI 48089 586-758-1600
service@signssystemofmichigan.com
www.signsystemsofmichigan.com
Manufacturer and exporter of metal and plastic advertising signs
Manager: Barbara Warren
Type of Packaging: Consumer, Food Service, Bulk

29251 Sign Warehouse, Inc.
2614 Texoma Drive
Denison, TX 75020 903-462-7704
Fax: 800-966-6834 800-699-5512
www.signwarehouse.com
Signs
Owner: Claude West
Sales/Design: Gary Gale
Manager: Rhonda Cummings
Estimated Sales: $1-2.5 Million
Number Employees: 5-9

29252 SignArt Advertising
PO Box 2
Van Buren, AR 72957-0002 479-474-8581
Fax: 479-474-4708
Interior and exterior signs
President: Charles Jannen
VP: Gene Jennen
In-House Sales Manager: Linda Jennen
Estimated Sales: Below $5 Million
Number Employees: 10-19
Square Footage: 9000

29253 Signal Equipment
3616 E Marginal Way S.
Seattle, WA 98134-1130 206-324-8400
Fax: 206-623-0510 800-542-0884
Fire and security systems and emergency generator systems
President: Tony Hastings

Estimated Sales: $5-10 Million
Number Employees: 5-9
Square Footage: 8000
Brands:
Edwards
Energy Dynamics
F.G. Wilson
Generac

29254 **Signart**
6225 Old Concord Rd
Charlotte, NC 28213 704-597-9801
Fax: 704-597-9808 800-929-3521
randy.souther@signartsign.com
www.signartsign.com
Electric signs; installation services available
Owner: Randy Souther
Director Project Management: Sue Prince
CFO: Randy Souther
Sales Leader: Earl Floyd
General Manager: Bill Sundberg
Estimated Sales: $2.5 - 5 Million
Number Employees: 20-49

29255 **Signature Packaging**
18 Dockery Dr
West Orange, NJ 07052 973-324-1838
Fax: 973-884-1909 800-376-2299
sigpak@aol.com
Plain and printed polyethylene bags for chicken, potatoes, fruits, etc.; also, paper and turkey tags, closures, packaging machinery, paper wrap, etc.; wholesaler/distributor of produce and specialty foods
*Estimated Sales:*less than $500,000
Number Employees: 1-4
Square Footage: 2500

29256 **Signco**
3113 Merriam Ln
Kansas City, KS 66106 913-722-1377
Fax: 913-722-3614 signs@signcokc.com
www.signcokc.com
Signs and decals; also, screen printing, vinyl graphics available
President: Mike Sailer
Estimated Sales: $500,000-$1 Million
Number Employees: 1-4

29257 **Signco/Stylecraft**
2611 Crescentville Rd
Cincinnati, OH 45241 513-771-9090
Fax: 513-326-3090 800-733-0045
info@signcoscreenprinting.com
www.signcoscreenprinting.com
Printed T-shirts for food service vendors
President/Owner: Craig Howell
Vice President: Scott Howell
Head of the Art Department: Steve Diedling
Sales: Mary Beth
Estimated Sales: $1 - 2.5 Million
Number Employees: 10-19

29258 **Signet Graphic Products**
9037 Saint Charles Rock Rd
St Louis, MO 63114-4253 314-426-0200
Fax: 314-426-3535
Signs, banners and decals; fleet graphics available
Corporate Secretary: Ilene Leichtle
Manager: Bill Jones
Estimated Sales: $10-20 Million
Number Employees: 10-19
Square Footage: 70000

29259 **Signet Marking Devices**
3121 Red Hill Ave
Costa Mesa, CA 92626 714-549-0341
Fax: 714-549-0972 800-421-5150
sales@signetmarking.com
www.signetmarking.com
Manufacturer and exporter of steel type marking equipment
President: Deirdre Mc Giffin
Operations Manager: Brian McGiffin
Estimated Sales: Below $5,000,000
Number Employees: 10-19

29260 **Signets/Menu-Quik**
7280 Industrial Park Boulevard
Mentor, OH 44060-5383 440-946-8676
Fax: 440-946-4646 800-775-6368
menuboardsales@signets.com
www.menu-quik.com
Menu boards
President: Robert Ledenican
Vice President: Terence Zuik
Marketing/Sales: Brenda Rolf
Number Employees: 25

29261 **Signmasters**
18421 Gothard St # 300
Huntington Beach, CA 92648-1236 949-364-9128
Fax: 949-364-6743
Banners, signs, flags and pennants
Owner: Mike Suzanski
Estimated Sales: Less than $500,000
Number Employees: 1-4

29262 **Signode Corporation**
3650 West Lake Avenue
Glenview, IL 60026-1273 847-657-5283
Fax: 847-657-5323 800-323-2464
ccunningham@signode.com www.signode.com
President: Russell Flaum
CFO: John Mayfield
Number Employees: 10

29263 **Signode Packaging Systems**
3650 West Lake Avenue
Glenview, IL 60026 847-821-8930
Fax: 847-657-5323 800-323-2464
cs@signode.com www.signode.com
Manufacturer and exporter of protective packaging systems, equipment and consumables for steel and plastic strapping, stretch film and tape
Director National Sales: Jeff Osisek
Manager: George Heller
Estimated Sales: $3 - 5 Million
Number Employees: 5-9
Parent Co: Illinois Tool Works
Brands:
Apex
Contrax
Gemini
High Strength Tenex
Magnus
Octopus
Spiral Grip
Tenax

29264 **Signs & Designs**
620 E Rancho Vista Blvd
Palmdale, CA 93550 661-947-4473
Fax: 661-947-3559 888-480-7446
sales@signsanddesigns.tv
www.signsanddesigns.tv
Wood, metal, plastic, electrical and neon signs
Owner: Craig Mc Nabb
Estimated Sales: $1-2.5 Million
Number Employees: 10-19

29265 **Signs & Shapes International**
2320 Paul St
Omaha, NE 68102 402-331-3181
Fax: 402-331-2729 800-806-6069
sales@signandshapes.com
www.signsandshapes.com
Manufacturer and exporter of standard and custom cold air-inflated walk-around costumes; also, signs and character shapes; grand opening packages available
President: Lee Bowen
Estimated Sales: Below $5 Million
Number Employees: 20-49
Square Footage: 13000
Type of Packaging: Food Service

29266 **Signs O' Life**
45 Bodwell St
Avon, MA 02322 800-750-1475
Fax: 508-583-9780 www.signsolife.com
Illuminating and nonilluminating signs and graphics
Owner: Alvin Barber
VP: Steven Supinski
Estimated Sales: $1-2.5 Million
Number Employees: 10-19

29267 **Signtech Electrical Advertising Inc**
4444 Federal Blvd
San Diego, CA 92102 619-527-6100
Fax: 866-275-6115 sales@signtechusa.com
www.signtechusa.com
Commercial awnings
President: David Schauer
CEO: Harold Schauer Jr.
CFO: Kimra Schauer
VP Sales: Art Navarro
Estimated Sales: Less than $500,000
Number Employees: 20-49

29268 **Siko Products**
2155 Bishop Cir E
Dexter, MI 48130 734-426-3476
Fax: 734-426-3453 800-447-7456
sales@sikoproducts.com www.sikoproducts.com
Position, feedback devices
President: Maurizio Masullo
IT / Web Admin: Peter Crist
Sales Engineer: Cary Mulvany
Customer Service/Sales: Jim Schnebelt
Office Manager/Returns: Terry Miller
Shipping: Lisa LaRoe
Estimated Sales: $1 - 2.5 Million
Number Employees: 5-9

29269 **Silent Watchman Security Services LLC**
P.O. BOX 3017
Danbury, CT 06813 203-743-1876
Fax: 203-743-9814 800-932-3822
info@silentwatchman.net
www.silentwatchman.net
Manufacturer and exporter of smoke and infrared intrusion detectors, recording door locks, CCTV and multiplex security systems
President: Vincent Dascano
General Manager: Gary Sherman

29270 **Silesia Grill Machines**
4770 County Road 16
Saint Petersburg, FL 33709 727-544-1340
Fax: 727-544-2821 800-267-4766
silesia@tampabay.rr.com www.veloxgrills.com
Manufacturer and exporter of high speed contact grills, crepe machines and bucket openers
President: Maria Hermansson
Estimated Sales: $300,000-500,000
Number Employees: 1-4
Type of Packaging: Food Service

29271 **Silesia Velox Grill Machines, Inc.**
4770 County Road 16
Saint Petersburg, FL 33709 727-544-1340
Fax: 727-544-2821 800-237-4766
sales@veloxgrills.us www.veloxgrills.com
Manufacturer and exporter of high speed contact grills, crepe makers, panini grills and bucket openers
President: Maria Hermansson
Type of Packaging: Food Service
Brands:
Silesia

29272 **Silgan Containers**
21800 Oxnard Street
Suite 600
Woodland Hills, CA 91367 818-710-3700
www.silgancontainers.com
Plastic and aluminum closures for bottles and aluminum containers, capping machinery and feed systems
Estimated Sales: $50 - 100 Million
Number Employees: 100-249
Type of Packaging: Bulk
Brands:
Drop-Lok
Jetflow
Magna Torq
Pharma-Lok
Plasti-Lug
Ro
Wing-Lok

29273 **Silgan Plastics**
14515 N. Outer Forty
Suite 210
Chesterfield, MO 63017 314-542-9223
Fax: 314-469-5387 800-274-5426
www.silganplastics.com
HDPE bottles and stock/private containers, closures and fitments
President: Russell Gervais
CEO: Derek Schmidt
Estimated Sales: $61.5 Million
Number Employees: 266
Square Footage: 265000

Other Locations:
Silgan Plastics
Ottawa OH

29274 **Silgan Plastics Canada**
14515 North Outer Forty
Suite 210
Chesterfield, MO 63017
Canada 416-293-8233
Fax: 314-469-5387 800-274-5426
silgansales@silganplastics.com
www.silganplastics.com
Manufacturer and exporter of plastic jars, bottles and closures including standard screw cap, child resistant and dispensing
National Sales Manager: David Meharg
Estimated Sales: $1 - 5 Million
Number Employees: 100
Square Footage: 460000
Parent Co: Silgan Plastics Corporation

29275 **(HQ)Sillcocks Plastics International**
PO Box 421
Hudson, MA 01749-0421 978-568-9000
Fax: 978-562-7128 800-526-4919
Sarah@428Main.com www.428main.com
Manufacturer and exporter of advertising novelties including plastic credit, debit and photo/ID cards; also, mag stripe signature panels, holography and security printing available
CEO and President: John Herslow
VP Sales/Marketing: Michele Logan
Estimated Sales: $3 - 5 Million
Number Employees: 10-19
Square Footage: 244000
Brands:
Silcard

29276 **Silliker Canada Company**
90 Gough Road
Markham, ON L3R 5V5
Canada 905-479-5255
Fax: 519-822-0132
customercare@sillikercanada.com
www.silliker.com/canada
Technical Sales Manager: Greg Forster
Number Employees: 90
Parent Co: M□RIEUX NUTRISCIENCES CORPORATION

29277 **Silliker Laboratories**
6390 Hedgewood Dr
Allentown, PA 18106 312-938-5151
Fax: 610-366-9357 silliker@silliker.com
www.silliker.com
Food consultant providing plant sanitation, microbiological research and analysis of foods and infestation
Microbiology Manager: Kathy Jost-Keating
VP: Bob Colvin
Estimated Sales: $5-10 Million
Number Employees: 50-99
Parent Co: Silliker Laboratories Group

29278 **Silliker Laboratories**
2057 Builders Pl
Columbus, OH 43204 614-486-0150
Fax: 614-486-0151 silliker@silliker.com
www.silliker.com
Consultant offering analytical services for food processors
Manager: Amitha Miele
Estimated Sales: $5 - 10 Million
Number Employees: 20-49
Parent Co: Silliker Laboratories

29279 **Silliker Laboratories**
2169 W Park Ct Ste G
Stone Mountain, GA 30087 770-469-2701
Fax: 770-469-2883
kurt.westmoreland@silliker.com
www.silliker.com
Consultant for sanitation, testing, analysis, etc
Manager: Robert Yemm
Regional Manager: Kurt Westmoreland
Estimated Sales: $2.5-5 Million
Number Employees: 20-49
Parent Co: Silliker Laboratories

29280 **Silliker, Inc**
111 E Wacker Dr
Suite 2300
Chicago, IL 60601 312-938-5151
info@silliker.com
www.silliker.com
Laboratory providing food testing, microbiological and chemical analysis, technical consulting and audits for HACCP/GMPs employee training services and custom research
President: James Ondyak
VP: Jim Hayes
Marketing Communications Manager: Jessica Sawyer-Lueck
Number Employees: 50-99
Parent Co: BioMerieux Alliance

29281 **Silver King**
1600 Xenium Ln N
Minneapolis, MN 55441-3706 763-923-2441
Fax: 763-553-1209 800-328-3329
info@silverking.com www.silverking.com
Manufacturer and exporter of refrigerators, freezers, prep tables, ice cream cabinets, bulk milk and salad dispensers, display cases and fountainettes
General Manager: Korey Kohl
Executive VP: Benjamin Rubin
Estimated Sales: $15 - 20 Million
Number Employees: 100-249
Parent Co: Prince Castle
Type of Packaging: Food Service
Brands:
Silver King

29282 **Silver Mountain Vineyards**
P.O.Box 3636
Santa Cruz, CA 95063 408-353-2278
Fax: 408-353-1898 info@silvermtn.com
www.silvermtn.com
Wine
President: Jerold O'Brien
Estimated Sales: $1-2.5 Million
Number Employees: 1-4
Type of Packaging: Private Label
Brands:
Silver Mtn Vineyards

29283 **(HQ)Silver Spur Corporation**
16010 Shoemaker Ave
Cerritos, CA 90703 562-921-6880
Fax: 562-921-7916 vivian@silverspurcorp.com
www.silverspurcorp.com
Manufactures glass bottles, glass containers, HDPE (High Density Polyethlene) Packers, PET (polyethylene terephthalare) containers and closures. 1
President: James Hao
Marketing: Alvin Hao
Operations Manager: Vivian Chu
Plant Manager: James Wilder
Estimated Sales: $9 Million
Number Employees: 20-49
Square Footage: 200000

29284 **Silver State Plastics**
2626 8th Ave
Greeley, CO 80631-1404 970-346-8667
Fax: 970-346-9191 800-825-2247
silverstateplastics@comcast.net
www.silverstateplastics.com
Plain and printed polyethylene bags
Owner: James Cornforth
Sales: Vickie Walker
Plant Manager: Richard Dailey
Estimated Sales: $5 - 10 Million
Number Employees: 20-49
Square Footage: 40000
Type of Packaging: Private Label

29285 **Silver Weibull**
14800 E Moncrieff Place
Aurora, CO 80011-1211 303-373-2311
Fax: 303-373-2319
Manufacturer and exporter of sugar centrifugals, reheaters and crystallizers
Manager Technical Process: Tommy Persson
Business Unit Manager (Worldwide): Derrald Houston
Manager: Randy Copsey
Estimated Sales: Below $5 Million
Number Employees: 3
Square Footage: 100000
Parent Co: Consolidated Process Machinery
Brands:
Silver-Weibull

29286 **Silverson Machines**
355 Chestnut St E
PO Box 589
East Longmeadow, MA 01028 413-525-4825
Fax: 413-525-5804 800-204-6400
fran@silverson.com www.silverson.com
Manufacturer, supplier and exporter of food processing equipment including blending and batching equipment, high shear mixers, colloid mills and homogenizers; also, laboratory equipment and supplies
President: Harold Rothman
Clerk/VP: David Rothman
VP: Anne Rothman
Sales Manager: Brian Martin
General Manager: Michael Boyd
Estimated Sales: $2.6 Million
Number Employees: 16
Parent Co: Silverson Machines
Brands:
Flashblend
Silverson

29287 **Simco Industrial StaticControl**
2257 N Penn Road
Hatfield, PA 19440 215-822-6401
Fax: 215-822-3795 800-203-3419
sales@simco.biz www.simco-static.com
President: Gary Swink
Number Employees: 50-99

29288 **Simco/Herbert IndustrialStatic Control**
2257 North Penn Road
Hatfield, PA 19440-1906 215-822-6401
Fax: 215-822-3795 800-203-3419
sales@simco.biz www.simco-static.com
Packaging, static control, electrostatic charging, web cleaning
President: Gary Swink
Sales: Lou Gieleonora
Estimated Sales: $1-2.5 Million
Number Employees: 50-99

29289 **(HQ)Simkar Corporation**
700 Ramona Ave
Philadelphia, PA 19120 215-831-7700
Fax: 215-831-7703 800-523-3602
lighting@simkar.com www.simkar.com
Manufacturer and exporter of lighting fixtures including fluorescent, vaporproof, H.I.D., parabolic deep cell, waterproof, strip, undershelf display and overhead
President: William Eagle
CFO: Wayne Romambzuk
CEO: Glen Grunewald
R&D: Yorum Weiff
Regional Sales Manager: Jim Talbot
VP Sales/Marketing: Robert McCully
VP Sales (Power Products): Howard Ferraro
Estimated Sales: $100+ Million
Number Employees: 500-999
Square Footage: 300000
Type of Packaging: Consumer, Food Service, Private Label, Bulk
Other Locations:
Simkar Corp.
Philadelpia PA
Brands:
Channelites
Fashion Fluorescent
Para-Spec
Ultratensity
Vangard

29290 **Simkins Industries**
317 Foxon Rd.
East Haven, CT 06513-2038 203-787-7171
Fax: 203-782-6324 www.simkinsindustries.com
Folding boxes; also, glassine and greaseproof paper and paperboard
President: Leon Simkins
Chief Financial Officer: Anthony Battaglia
Estimated Sales: $89 Million
Number Employees: 950
Square Footage: 1600

29291 **(HQ)Simmons Engineering Corporation**
1200 Willis Ave
Wheeling, IL 60090 847-419-9800
Fax: 847-419-1500 800-252-3381
sales@simcut.com www.simcut.com

Manufacturer and exporter of cutting knives and blades for bread, cake, fish, fruit, vegetables and meat products
President: Bruce Gillian
Estimated Sales: $5 - 10 Million
Number Employees: 50-99
Square Footage: 30000
Brands:
Tru-Trak

29292 **Simolex Rubber Corporation**
14505 Keel St
Plymouth, MI 48170 734-453-4500
Fax: 734-453-6120 info@simolex.com
www.simolexrubber.com
Manufacturer and exporter of rubber products including beverage hoses, juice tubing, milk hoses, gaskets, seals and bottle stoppers
President: Bob Dungarani
Estimated Sales: $10-20 Million
Number Employees: 30
Square Footage: 25000
Type of Packaging: Food Service

29293 **Simon S. Jackel Plymouth**
684 Hidden Lake Drive
Tarpon Springs, FL 34689-2600 727-942-3991
Consultant specializing in product and ingredient development and improvement for companies supplying baking ingredients and products
Director: Simon Jackel PhD

29294 **Simonds International**
135 Intervale Road
PO Box 500
Fitchburg, MA 01420
Canada 978-424-0100
Fax: 978-424-2212 nlaflamme@simondsint.com
www.simonds.cc
Manufacturer, exporter and importer of knives for packaging and food processing equipment, cryovac, etc
President: Fred Adams
Sales Manager: Fred Adams
Number Employees: 10
Square Footage: 30000
Parent Co: IKS International

29295 **Simonds International**
135 Intervale Road
P.O. Box 500
Fitchburg, MA 01420 978-424-0100
Fax: 978-424-2212 800-343-1616
www.simondsinternational.com
Manufacturer and exporter of band and hack saws and saw blades, circular machine knives, files and investment castings
President: Raymond Martino
Chairman: John Consentino
Chief Financial Officer: Henry Botticello
Vice President: Chip Holm
Engineering & R&D Manager: Rick Brautt
Vice President, Sales & Marketing: David Miles
Sales Manager: Tim House
Operations Supervisor: Dick Vain
Plant Manager: Roy Erdwins
Purchasing Agent: Valerie Johnson
Estimated Sales: $83 Million
Number Employees: 960
Square Footage: 400000

29296 **Simonson Group**
35 Washington Street
Winchester, MA 01890-2927 781-729-8906
Fax: 781-729-5079 jsimonson-nfp@attgi.com
Consultant specializing in marketing research and product development; serving food service manufacturers and restaurants
Executive VP: Barbara Simonson
Estimated Sales: $1 - 5 Million
Number Employees: 1-4

29297 **Simplex Filler Company**
640 Airpark Rd Ste A
Napa, CA 94558 707-265-6801
Fax: 707-265-6868 800-796-7539
simplex@simplexfiller.com
www.simplexfiller.com
Manufacturer and exporter of piston and pressure fillers for bottle, can, jar and bag filling; also, conveyors, unscramblers, lid droppers, accumulators and heated hoppers
President: G Donald Murray Iii III
CEO: G Donald Murray
Estimated Sales: $1-5 Million
Number Employees: 10-19
Square Footage: 15000
Parent Co: Wild Horse Industrial Corporation
Brands:
Simplex

29298 **Simplex Time Recorder Company**
1936 E Deere Avenue
Suite 120
Santa Ana, CA 92705-5732 949-724-5000
Fax: 978-630-7856 www.simplexnet.com
Manufacturer and exporter of fire alarms and time recorders
General Manager: Russell Stafford
Area/Branch Manager: Gary Holmes
Estimated Sales: $1 - 5 Million
Number Employees: 100
Brands:
Simplex

29299 **Simplex Time Recorder Company**
1936 E Deere Avenue
Suite 120
Santa Ana, CA 92705-5732 949-724-5000
Fax: 978-630-7856 800-746-7539
www.simplexnet.com
Manufacturer and exporter of fire alarm and security systems
General Manager: Russell Stafford
Estimated Sales: $1 - 5 Million
Number Employees: 20

29300 **Simply Manufacturing**
E11259 County Road Pf
Prairie Du Sac, WI 53578 608-643-6656
www.simplymfg.com
Meat processing accessories and replacement parts such as vats, meat sticks, ham press towers, screens, and portable racks.

29301 **Simply Products**
RR 5
Box 5299
Kunkletown, PA 18058-9696 610-681-6894
Fax: 610-681-6885 info@simplyproducts.com
www.simplyproducts.com
Software for point of sale and back office systems
President: Dave Rottkamp
VP Operations: Allison Ohl
Number Employees: 6
Square Footage: 8000
Brands:
Simply Food

29302 **Simpson**
2916 Kelly Dr
Elgin, IL 60124-4349 847-697-2260
Fax: 847-697-2272
cservice@simpsonelectric.com
www.simpsonelectric.com
Process control systems
Founder: Ray Simpson
Estimated Sales: $20-50 Million
Number Employees: 100-249

29303 **Sims Machinery Company**
3621 45th St SW
Lanett, AL 36863 334-576-2101
Fax: 334-576-3116
fabrication@simsmachinery.com
www.simsmachinery.com
Manufacturer and exporter of stainless steel food grade tanks; also, custom stainless steel fabrications available
Owner: Lynn Duncan
CEO: Lynn Duncan
Sales Manager: Bryant Hollon
Estimated Sales: $5-10 Million
Number Employees: 1-4
Square Footage: 40000

29304 **Sims Superior Seating**
P.O.Box 284
Locust Grove, GA 30248 770-957-9667
Fax: 770-954-1935 800-729-9178
manager@simseating.com www.simseating.com
Restaurant hospitality seating, booths, tabletops and bases, kitchen equipment covers and plantters
President: Charles Sims Sr
CFO: Kathryn Sims
VP: Charles Sims Jr
Sales: T Wonder
Plant Manager: T Wonder
Estimated Sales: $5-10 Million
Number Employees: 20-49
Square Footage: 28000

29305 **Sinco**
3965 Pepin Avenue
Red Wing, MN 55066-1837 860-632-0500
Fax: 860-632-1509 800-243-6753
sales@sinco.com www.sinco.com
Manufacturer and exporter of safety netting systems for guarding material handling equipment including conveyors, pallet racks, etc
President: David Denny
Estimated Sales: $10 - 20 Million
Number Employees: 40

29306 **Sine Pump**
14845 W 64th Ave
Arvada, CO 80007-7523 303-425-0800
Fax: 303-425-0896 888-504-8301
pumps@sundyne.com www.sinepump.com
Manufacturer and exporter of sanitary positive displacement pumps for the food and dairy industries including low-shear, low-pulsation and high-suction. designs, manufactures and supports industrial pump and compressor products for theprocess fluid and gas industries
President: William Taylor
Human Resources: Christine Lopez
Area Sales Manager: Brad Juntunen
After Market Specialist: Chuck Zachrich
Number Employees: 500-999
Parent Co: Sundyne Corporation
Brands:
Sine Pump

29307 **Sinicrope & Sons**
1124 Westminster Ave
Alhambra, CA 91803 323-283-5131
Fax: 323-283-3399 info@sinicropeandsons.com
www.sinicropeandsons.com
Store fixtures
President: Gary Sinicrope
VP: Sandra Sinicrope
Estimated Sales: Below $5,000,000
Number Employees: 20-49

29308 **Sioux Corporation**
1 Sioux Plz
Beresford, SD 57004 605-763-3333
Fax: 605-763-3334 888-763-8833
email@sioux.com www.sioux.com
Manufacturer and exporter of hot, cold and combination pressure washers and steam cleaners; also, all-electric and explosion-proof units available
President/Owner: Jack Finger
Marketing Manager: Jessica Johnson
Sales Manager: Meg Andersen
Regional Manager - International Sales (: David Nelson
Estimated Sales: $2.5-5 Million
Number Employees: 20-49
Number of Products: 500+
Brands:
Dakota
Sioux
Steam-Flo

29309 **Sioux Falls Rubber StampWork**
212 S Main Ave
Sioux Falls, SD 57104 605-334-5990
Fax: 605-334-0750 www.sfrubberstamp.com
Rubber stamps
President: Paul Brue
Estimated Sales: $1 - 5 Million
Number Employees: 1-4

29310 **Sipco**
12610 Galveston Road
Webster (Houston), TX 77598 281-480-8711
Fax: 281-480-8656 info@sipco-mls.com
www.sipco-mls.com
Mechanical linkage solutions
Manager: Tom Jones
Accountant: Marissa Reise
Estimated Sales: $10 - 20 Million
Number Employees: 20-49
Parent Co: Standalone
Type of Packaging: Private Label, Bulk

29311 Sipco Products
4301 Prospect Road
Peoria Heights, IL 61616-6537 309-682-5400
Fax: 309-637-5120 terry@sipcoproducts.com
www.pnduniforms.com
Ashtray receptacles, smoking urns, safety related items, wire racks and plastic bag holders; exporter of ashtray receptacles
President: Eileen Grawey
Office Manager: Audrey Wylie
Estimated Sales: $3 - 5 Million
Number Employees: 1-4
Square Footage: 40000
Type of Packaging: Food Service
Brands:
Rack-A-Bag
Sipco Dunking Station

29312 Sirco Systems
2828 Messer Airport Highway
Birmingham, AL 35203 205-731-7800
Fax: 205-731-7885 sircocs@sircosys.com
Manufacturer and exporter of food storage equipment including steel drums
VP Sales: Jack Matheson
Estimated Sales: $5-10 Million
Number Employees: 50-99
Parent Co: Jemison Investment Company

29313 Sirman Spa/IFM USA
9490 Franklin Ave
Franklin Park, IL 60131-2833 847-288-9500
Fax: 847-288-9501 info@sirman.com
www.ifmusa.com
CEO: Alessandro Lorengato
Estimated Sales: $1 - 5 Million
Number Employees: 1-4

29314 Sitka Store Fixtures
PO Box 410247
Kansas City, MO 64141-0247 816-531-8290
Fax: 816-753-5701 800-821-7558
Wooden retail store fixtures including customer service centers and bakery, deli, produce and feature display
President: Patrick Clifford
Sales/Design: Brian Kipper
Project/Production Manager: Dave Sellers
Number Employees: 21
Square Footage: 34000
Parent Co: Cliff-Stan Industries

29315 Sitma USA
Via Vignolese
Spilamberto, MO 41057 390-597-8031
Fax: 390-597-8030 800-728-1254
sitmausa@sitma.com www.sitma.com
Manufacturer and importer of packaging equipment including horizontal form, fill and seal systems and bundle wrappers
President: Aris Ballestrazzi
CEO/Managing Director: Pete Butikis
National Sales Manager: Al Lindsay
Estimated Sales: $2.5 - 5 Million
Number Employees: 10-19
Square Footage: 33000
Parent Co: Sitma Machinery SPA
Other Locations:
Sitma USA
BP 28-77013 Melun Cedex

29316 Sitram/Global Marketing
PO Box 5503
Parsippany, NJ 07054-6503 973-515-0085
Fax: 973-515-3467 800-515-8585
glbmktg@opontine.net www.sitram.com
Manufactures stainless steel cookware with new surface technology, cybernox
President: Christopher D Boyhan
Vice President: Allan Wolk
Estimated Sales: $1-2.5 Million
Number Employees: 19
Parent Co: Sitram France
Brands:
Catering
Cybernox
Magnum
Profiserie

29317 Sivetz Coffee
349 SW 4th St
Corvallis, OR 97333-4622 541-753-9713
Fax: 541-757-7644 info@sievtzcoffee.com
www.sivetzcoffee.com
Roasted coffee beans, extracts, almond kernels, hazelnut kernels, and coffee roasting machines
President: Mike Sivetz
Number Employees: 1-4
Type of Packaging: Consumer, Bulk
Brands:
Sivetz Coffee Essence

29318 Six Hardy Brush Manufacturing
1172 East St S
Suffield, CT 06078-2410 860-623-8465
Specialty bakers' and confectioners' brushes
President: Steven Pierz
Estimated Sales: $2.5-5 Million
Number Employees: 5 to 9
Square Footage: 3200

29319 Skalar
5012 Bristol Industrial Way
Suite 107
Buford, GA 30518
Fax: 770-416-6718 800-782-4994
info@skalar-us.com www.skalar.com
Wine industry lab equipment, flow analyzers, process analyzers, robotic analyzers
President: Lel Seruyzken
CFO: Sjaak Surrer
Quality Control: Jomen Ting
Estimated Sales: Below $5 Million
Number Employees: 100

29320 Skinetta Pac-Systems
55742 Currant Road
Mishawaka, IN 46545-4808 574-254-1950
Fax: 219-254-1955 info@skinetta.com
www.skinetta.com
Packaging machinery: end-of-line machines
Estimated Sales: $2.5-5 Million
Number Employees: 4

29321 Skinner Sheet
3536 Bee Cave Road
Suite 211
West Lake Hills, TX 78746-5474 512-328-7785
Fax: 512-328-7786 larkin@io.com
Corrugated board products

29322 (HQ)Skrmetta Machinery Corporation
3536 Lowerline Street
New Orleans, LA 70125-1004 504-488-4413
Fax: 504-488-4432
Manufacturer and exporter of shrimp peeling and deveining machinery
President: Eric Skrmetta
VP: Dennis Skrmetta
Estimated Sales: $5800000
Number Employees: 55
Square Footage: 20000
Other Locations:
Skrmetta Machinery Corp.
New Orleans LA

29323 Slautterback Corporation
11475 Lakefield Drive
Duluth, GA 30097-1511 831-373-3900
Fax: 831-373-0385 800-827-3308
marcom@slautterback.com
www.slautterback.com
Manufacturer and exporter of hot melt adhesive packaging equipment
President: Fred Erler
President, Chief Executive Officer: Michael Hilton
Marketing Manager: Jim Pagnella
Vice President of Systems: Douglas Bloomfield
Number Employees: 135
Square Footage: 252000
Parent Co: Nordson Corporation

29324 SleeveCo Inc
103 Lumpkin Campground Rd N
Dawsonville, GA 30534 706-216-3110
Fax: 706-216-3116 info@sleeveco.com
www.sleeveco.com
Manufacturer and exporter of packaging materials including full body shrink labels, multi-pak sleeves, tamper evident bands, stretch sleeve labels, and stretch sleeve application equipment.
President: Martin Wilson
CEO: David Johnson
CEO: David Johnson
Research & Development: Jay Johnson
Marketing Director: Martin Wilson
Sales Director: Martin Wilson
Operations Manager: Eric Grabau
Estimated Sales: $100 Million
Number Employees: 100-249
Square Footage: 100000
Type of Packaging: Consumer, Food Service, Private Label, Bulk

29325 SleeveCo, Inc
103 Lumpkin Campground Rd N
Dawsonville, GA 30534 706-216-3110
Fax: 706-216-3116 info@sleeveco.com
www.sleeveco.com
Manufacturer and exporter of packaging materials including shrink film, full bodu shrink labels, multi-pack sleeves, bands and shrink bags, stretch sleeve labels and stretch sleeve application equipment.
CEO: David Johnson
Number Employees: 50-99
Type of Packaging: Consumer, Food Service, Private Label, Bulk

29326 Slidell
PO Box 39
New Market, MN 55054-0039 507-451-0365
Fax: 507-451-2405 800-328-1769
info@slidell.com www.slidellinc.com
Packaging equipment for paper or plastic needs
Estimated Sales: $20-50 Million
Number Employees: 100

29327 Slip-Not Belting Corporation
PO Box 386
Kingsport, TN 37662 423-246-8141
Fax: 423-246-7728
Manufacturer and exporter of leather, plastic and perlon transmission and conveyor belting
President/CEO: David Shivell
CEO: Phill Shivell
Marketing: David Shivell
Estimated Sales: $3 - 5 Million
Number Employees: 5-9

29328 Slipnot Metal Safety Flooring
2545 Beaufait St
Detroit, MI 48207 313-923-0400
Fax: 313-923-4555 800-754-7668
info@slipnot.com www.slipnot.com
SlipNOT manufactures NSF registered stainless steel slip resistant flooring products from floor plates, drain covers, bar grating, ladder rungs/covers, to stair treads/covers, perforated and expanded metal retrofit plates. SlipNOTproducts can withstand the extreme cold of cyrogenics and heat of cookers, as well as caustic cleaning agents.
President: William S Molnar
National Sales Manager: Brian Pelto
Estimated Sales: $.5 - 1 million
Number Employees: 1-4
Parent Co: WS Monar Comapany
Brands:
Flex-Grip
Grid-Grip
Grip-Grate
Grip-Plate
Slipnot

29329 Smalley Manufacturing Company
PO Box 22788
Knoxville, TN 37933-0788 865-966-5866
Fax: 865-675-1618 droberto@smalleymfg.com
www.smalleymfg.com
Conveyor, feeder and storage systems
President: Dale Roberto
VP Sales: Mike Green
Sales Engineer: Keith Iddins
Sales: Mark Kipfer
Estimated Sales: $10-20 Million
Number Employees: 50-99
Square Footage: 46000

29330 **Smalley Package Company**
PO Box 231
Berryville, VA 22611 540-955-2550
Fax: 540-955-4590 sales@smalleypackage.com
www.smalleypackale.com
Wooden, pallets, pallet boxes, baskets; also, recycled/remanufactured pallets
President: Robert W Smalley Jr
Vice President: James Livengood
Sales Director: William Hair
Estimated Sales: $5-10 Million
Number Employees: 1-4

29331 **Smartscan, Inc**
33083 Eight Mile Road
Livonia, MI 48152 248-477-2900
Fax: 248-477-7453 ussales@smartscan.com
www.smartscaninc.com
Variable beam spacing, link systems, marshaling boxes, and light curtaining
President: Paul Budesheim
CFO: Paul Budesheim
Quality Control: Paul Budesheim
General Manager: Paul Budesheim
Estimated Sales: $20 - 50 Million
Number Employees: 20-49
Number of Products: 4

29332 **Smetco**
PO Box 560
14633 Ottaway Rd NE
Aurora, OR 97002 503-678-3081
Fax: 503-678-3095 800-253-5400
www.smetco.com
Manufacturer and exporter of pallet handling systems for sorting and repair; also, conveyors, scissor lifts, dispensers, stackers and turn tables
President: John Smet
CFO: Kelly Wick
Vice President: John Smets
Marketing Director: Ken Butler
Estimated Sales: $1-3 Million
Number Employees: 20-49
Square Footage: 116000
Brands:
Smetco
Stackers

29333 **Smico Manufacturing Company**
6101 Camille St.
Valley Brook, OK 73149 405-946-1461
Fax: 405-946-1472 800-351-9088
jmurray@smico.com www.smico.com
Manufacturer and exporter of vibrating screens and gyratory sifters
President: Randall Stoner
CEO: Erick Held
VP: Tim Douglass
Sales: Holly Lindsey
Operations: Randall Stoner
Purchasing Director: Jane Wenk
Estimated Sales: $5 - 10 Million
Number Employees: 20-49
Square Footage: 46000

29334 **Smith & Loveless**
14040 Santa Fe Trail Dr
Shawnee Mission, KS 66215 913-888-5201
Fax: 913-888-2173 800-898-9122
answers@smithandloveless.com
www.smithandloveless.com
Water and wastewater treatment and transfer equipment
President: Robert Rebori
CFO: David Ferbezar
Estimated Sales: $30 - 50 Million
Number Employees: 250-499

29335 **Smith & Taylor**
1071 Howell Mill Rd NW
Atlanta, GA 30318-5557 404-872-8135
Fax: 404-872-0471 sunlow1@aol.com
Owner: Danny Graham
Sales Director: Jerry Hernnebaul
Estimated Sales: $3 - 5 Million
Number Employees: 10-19

29336 **Smith Design Associates**
205 Thomas St
Bloomfield, NJ 07003 973-429-2177
Fax: 973-429-7119 laraine@smithdesign.com
www.smithdesign.com
Package design and brand identity
President: Laraine Smith
CFO: James C Smith
Estimated Sales: $5 Million
Number Employees: 10-19
Type of Packaging: Consumer, Private Label

29337 **Smith Packaging**
6045 Kestrel Road
Mississauga, ON L5T 1Y8
Canada 905-564-6640
Fax: 905-564-5681
www.smithpackagingandequipment.com
Manufacturer and exporter of boxes, cartons and containers
President: Mervin Hillier
Operations Manager: Gerard Gregoire
Number Employees: 100
Type of Packaging: Consumer, Bulk

29338 **Smith Pallet Company**
159 Polk Road 29
PO Box 207
Hatfield, AR 71945 870-389-6184
Fax: 870-389-6194 spallet@windstream.net
www.smithpallet.com
Skids, crating, dunnage, boxes and hooked and softwood pallets
President: Jim Wilson
Sales Manager: Tate Mendoza
Sales: Jim Mabry
General Manager: Lyle Wilson
Controller: Bryan Schoeppey
Plant Manager: Dalton Doughty
Estimated Sales: Below $5 Million
Number Employees: 100-249

29339 **Smith, RD, Company**
PO Box 186
Eau Claire, WI 54702 715-832-3479
Fax: 715-832-7456 800-826-7336
bobk@rdsmithco.com www.rdsmithco.com
Centrifuges, cheese equipment, flow diversion stations, heat exchangers, ladders, vats
President: Frederick Smith
Controller: Steve Burk
Vice President of Administration: Joan Bliesener
Vice President of Operations: Bob Kutchera
Estimated Sales: $5 - 10 Million
Number Employees: 10-19

29340 **Smith-Berger Marine**
7915 10th Ave S
Seattle, WA 98108 206-764-4650
Fax: 206-764-4653 sales@smithberger.com
www.smithberger.com
Processing machinery for pacific salmon prior to canning; leasing available
President: Bonnie Warrick
President: Bonnie Warrick
CFO: Bonnie Warrick
Estimated Sales: $1 - 2.5 Million
Number Employees: 20-49
Square Footage: 15000
Brands:
Berger
Smith Berger

29341 **Smith-Emery Company**
781 E Washington Blvd
Los Angeles, CA 90021 213-745-5333
Fax: 213-741-8620 www.smithemery.com
Consultant specializing in air pollution analysis
President: James E Partridge
VP Marketing: Fred Partridge
Estimated Sales: $10-20 Million
Number Employees: 50-99

29342 **Smith-Lee Company**
2920 N Main St.
PO Box 2038
Oshkosh, WI 54901 315-363-2500
Fax: 315-363-9573 800-327-9774
marketing@hoffmaster.com
www.hoffmaster.com
Manufacturer and exporter of paper plates, place mats, napkins, bottle caps and packaged lace and linen doilies
President: Jonathan M Groat
VP Sales: Thomas Hennessey
VP Manufacturing: Alan Mattei
Estimated Sales: $10-20 Million
Number Employees: 50-99
Parent Co: Hoffmaster Group, Inc
Brands:
Serv-Ease

29343 **Smith-Lustig Paper Box Manufacturing**
2165 E 31st St
Cleveland, OH 44115 216-621-0454
Fax: 216-621-0483 www.smithlustigbox.com
Manufacturer and exporter of paper boxes
President: Richard Ames
Estimated Sales: $5-10 Million
Number Employees: 20-49

29344 **Smokaroma**
62 Bar-B-Que Avenue
P.O.Box 25
Boley, OK 74829-0025 918-667-3341
Fax: 918-667-3935 800-331-5565
www.smokaroma.com
Manufacturer and exporter of barbecuing, smoking and cooking equipment for hamburgers, hot dogs, sausage patties, chicken fillets, etc.; also, spices for meat and barbecue sauce mix
Owner: Maurice W Lee Iii
CEO: Maurice Lee Jr
Marketing Director: Tonia Guess
Estimated Sales: $5-10 Million
Number Employees: 10-19
Square Footage: 160000
Brands:
Bar B O Boss Sauce Mix
Bar Bq Boss
Instant Burger
One Step Prep Mix
Red Rub

29345 **Smoke Right**
4602 S Pulaski Rd
Chicago, IL 60632-4038 647-933-0623
Fax: 312-425-0020 888-375-8885
sales@smokeright.com www.smokeright.com
Smoke-free ashtrays
Owner: Anna Greengurg
Circulation Coordinator: Envija Svanberga
Marketing Director: Roseanna Mazzei
Production Manager: Lynne Campbell
Estimated Sales: $300,000-500,000
Number Employees: 1-4
Brands:
Smoke Right

29346 **Smokehouse Limited**
4867 NC Highway 22 N
Franklinville, NC 27248 336-824-1424
Fax: 336-824-1026 800-554-8385
info@smokehouselimited.com
www.smokehouselimited.com
Supplies pneumatic seals and foam over door gaskets for smokehouses, brine chillers and other processing equipment.

29347 **Smoot Company**
1250 Seminary St
Kansas City, KS 66103-2599 913-362-1710
Fax: 913-362-7863 800-748-7000
smootco@aol.com www.smootco.com
President: Leo Ribich
Estimated Sales: $10 - 20 Million
Number Employees: 50-99

29348 **Smurfit Flexible Packaging**
7074 W Parkland Ct
Milwaukee, WI 53223 414-355-2700
Fax: 414-355-1925 www.graphicpkg.com
Polyethylene bags
VP Sales/Marketing: John Sorman
Plant Manager: Jim Bradach
Estimated Sales: $10 - 20 Million
Number Employees: 100-249
Parent Co: Smurfit Corporation

29349 **Smurfit Stone Container**
8182 Maryland Ave
Suite 1100
St Louis, MO 63105-3915 314-679-2300
Fax: 314-679-2300
Folding cartons, corrugated containers and labels including printed paper, foil and heat transfer; exporter of linerboard
VP Corporate Sales/Marketing: Jack Straw
Marketing: James P Duncan
Estimated Sales: $1 - 5 Million
Number Employees: 20-49
Parent Co: Jefferson Smurfit Group

29350 Smurfit Stone Container
7393 Shawnee Rd
North Tonawanda, NY 14120 716-692-6510
Fax: 716-694-9262 www.smurfit-stone.com
Packaging materials including corrugated boxes
General Manager: Andrew Giambroni
Estimated Sales: Below $5 Million
Number Employees: 50-99
Parent Co: Jefferson Smurfit

29351 Smurfit Stone Container
1980 S 7th St
San Jose, CA 95112 408-925-9391
Fax: 408-293-1022 www.smurfit-stone.com
Containerboard and corrugated containers, point-of-purchase displays, specialty boxes, consumer packaging, recycled materials packaging and containers and packaging
Executive Secretary: Karen Korienek
Executive Secretary (Carol Stream): Janelle Lenza
VP Sales/Marketing (Carol Stream): James Duncan
Manager E-Commerce: Greg St Laurent
Executive Secretary (Procurement): Ronald Daniels
Manager: Chad Wilson
VP (Procurement): Mark O'Bryan
Estimated Sales: $10 - 20 Million
Number Employees: 20-49
Square Footage: 110000
Parent Co: Jefferson Smurfit Group
Type of Packaging: Consumer, Private Label, Bulk

29352 Smurfit Stone Container
1980 S 7th St
San Jose, CA 95112 408-925-9391
Fax: 408-293-1022
Folding cartons, corrugated containers and plastic and fiber drums
Manager: Chad Wilson
Estimated Sales: $20-50 Million
Number Employees: 20-49
Parent Co: Jefferson Smurfit Corporation

29353 Smurfit Stone Container
1980 S 7th St
San Jose, CA 95112 408-925-9391
Fax: 408-293-1022 888-254-6696
Case erector/bottom sealer, case packer, corrugated boxes
Manager: Chad Wilson
Estimated Sales: $10 - 20 Million
Number Employees: 20-49

29354 Smurfit Stone Container
1980 S 7th St
San Jose, CA 95112 408-925-9391
Fax: 408-293-1022 888-801-2579
bags@smurfit.com www.smurfit-stone.com
Valve bag filling systems, force air packers, jet flow impeller packers, easiflow screw packers, gravity fill bags, bulk bag fillers, bag sealer
Manager: Chad Wilson
Estimated Sales: $10 - 20 Million
Number Employees: 20-49

29355 Smurfit-Stone ContainerCorporation
4364 SW 34th St
Orlando, FL 32811 407-843-1300
Fax: 407-843-8459 888-254-6696
pkequipment@smurfit.com
www.smurfit-stone.com
President: Tom Graham
Estimated Sales: $20 - 50 Million
Number Employees: 20-49

29356 Smyrna Container Company
4676 S Atlanta Rd SE
Smyrna, GA 30080 404-794-4305
800-868-4305
customerservice@smyrnacontainer.com
www.smyrnacontainer.com
Paper folding boxes for bakeries, pizza and carry-out
President: Ed R Whiteman Jr
Estimated Sales: $1-2.5 Million
Number Employees: 10-19

29357 (HQ)Smyth Companies, LLC
1085 Snelling Avenue North
Saint Paul, MN 55108 651-646-4544
Fax: 651-646-8949 800-473-3464
info@smythco.com www.smythco.com
Manufacturer of sheet-fed and pressure sensitive labels, coupons, and high speed labelers for consumer goods packaging.
President: Jim Lundquist
Chief Executive Officer: John Hickey
Chief Financial Officer: David Baumgardner
Executive Vice President: Daniel Hickey
Quality Control Manager: Donna Niedenfuer
Purchasing Manager: Tom Schoolmeesters
Estimated Sales: $41 Million
Number Employees: 380
Square Footage: 110000
Parent Co: G.G. McGuiggan Corporation
Other Locations:
Smyth Companies
Bedford PA

29358 Snap Drape International
2045 Westgate Dr
Suite 100
Carrollton, TX 75006 972-466-1030
Fax: 972-466-1049 800-527-5147
info@snapdrape.com www.snapdrape.com
President: Darrin Garlish
CEO: Felton Norris
CFO: John Phillips
Vice President: Ray Belknap
Marketing Manager: Tammy Brazeal
Sales Manager: Kevin Burns
Operations Manager: Jose Aguado
Estimated Sales: $10 - 20 Million
Number Employees: 50-99

29359 Snap-Drape
2045 Westgate Dr # 100
Carrollton, TX 75006-9478 972-466-1030
Fax: 972-466-1049 800-527-5147
exhibits@snapdrape.com www.snapdrape.com
Manufacturer and exporter of table skirting and drapes
President: Darrin Garlish
Contact: Daielon Sasser
Sales Manager: Kevin Burns
Estimated Sales: $10-20 Million
Number Employees: 50-99
Type of Packaging: Food Service

29360 Snapware
4101 Bonita Place
Fullerton, CA 92835-1007 714-446-9212
Fax: 714-446-9217 800-334-3062
georgeg@snapwareusa.com www.snapware.com
Manufacture of Food Service containers, caps, and closures
President: John Lown
VP: Jim Spillane
Marketing: Heidi Slocumb
Sales: George Ghesquiere
Estimated Sales: $20-46 Million
Number Employees: 50-100
Number of Brands: 6
Number of Products: 15
Square Footage: 90000
Brands:
Living Hinge
Make a Gift Products
Sandcap
Snap'n Stack
Snap-N-Serve
Snapware

29361 Snee Chemical Company
5565 Pepsi St
Harahan, LA 70123 504-734-7633
Fax: 504-734-5221 800-489-7633
sales@sneechemical.com
www.sneechemical.com
Janitorial supplies including detergents and soaps
President: Mitchell Mark
Estimated Sales: $5-10 Million
Number Employees: 20-49

29362 Sneezeguard Solutions
2508 B Paris Rd
Columbia, MO 65202 573-443-5756
Fax: 573-449-7126 800-569-2056
info@sneezeguardsoultions.com
www.sneezeguard-solutions.com
Manufacturer and exporter of sneeze guards
President: Sydney Baumgartner
CFO: Susan Baumgaltner
Marketing: Bill Pfeiffer
Plant Manager: John Bazzell
Estimated Sales: $1 - 3 Million
Number of Brands: 14
Number of Products: 14
Square Footage: 40000
Brands:
Magic Buss
Next Generation Magic Buss
Plexus
Sampler
Sneezeguard

29363 Snow Craft Company
200 Fulton Ave
PO Box 829
Garden City Park, NY 11040 516-739-1399
Fax: 516-739-1637 snowcraft1@aol.com
www.snowcraft.com
Insulated shipping containers
President: Kirk Guton
Secretary: William Hess
Estimated Sales: $5-10 Million
Number Employees: 20-49

29364 Snowden Enterprises
PO Box 751
Fresno, CA 93712 559-237-5546
Fax: 559-237-6383 www.snowdenenterprises.com
SO2 dispensers
President: Kirk Snowden Shermer
Estimated Sales: $10-20 Million
Number Employees: 10-19

29365 Snyder Crown
602 Industrial St
Marked Tree, AR 72365-1909 870-358-3400
Fax: 870-358-3140
Manufacturer and exporter of custom, rotational-molded plastic transport tanks, storage bins and containers
Director Marketing: David Kelley
Director Operations: Dale Givens
Plant Manager: Ronnie Stone
Estimated Sales: $10-20 Million
Number Employees: 20 to 49

29366 Snyder Industries Inc.
4700 Fremont Street
P.O. Box 4583
Lincoln, NE 68504
Fax: 402-465-1220 800-351-1363
info@snyderplasticsolutions.com
www.snyderplasticsolutions.com
Custom rotational molded plastic containers
President: David Fair
Production Manager: Claretta Jo Segura
Number Employees: 20-49

29367 Sobel Corrugated Containers
18612 Miles Rd
Cleveland, OH 44128 216-475-2100
Fax: 216-475-2107
Corrugated containers
President: Arthur Sobel
Executive VP: Terry Sobel
Estimated Sales: $20-50 Million
Number Employees: 20-49

29368 Soco System
1931 Mac Arthur Rd
Waukesha, WI 53188-5702 262-547-0777
Fax: 262-547-4707 800-535-SOCO
info@socosysteminc.com
www.johnmayecompany.com
End-of-line packing and handling systems, case sealers and palleters
Owner: John Maye
Service Manager: Tage Peterson
Sales Director: Hans Sondersted
Estimated Sales: $5-10 Million
Number Employees: 5-9

29369 Sodexho Marriott Services
9801 Washingtonian Blvd
Gaithersburg, MD 20878-5355 301-987-4000
Fax: 301-987-4444 800-763-3946
pr@sodexhousa.com www.sodexhousa.com
Food Service management business
CEO: George Chavel
Estimated Sales: $5 Billion
Number Employees: 10,000

29370 Sohn Manufacturing
PO Box X
Elkhart Lake, WI 53020-0427 920-876-3361
Fax: 920-876-2952
info@sohnmanufacturing.com
www.smi-div.com

Label printing and die-cutting machines, automatic label dispensers and paper converters; also, inks, printing plates, label stocks and printed labels
President: Wallace Beaudry
Estimated Sales: $20-50 Million
Number Employees: 100-249
Square Footage: 100000

29371 Sokol & Company
5315 Dansher Rd
Countryside, IL 60525 708-482-8250
Fax: 708-482-9750 800-328-7656
bparoubek@solofoods.com www.solofoods.com
Cake and pastry fillings, almond paste and marzipan, pie and dessery fillings, marshmallow and toasted marshmallow creme, fruit butters, Asian dipping sauces and marinades, seasoning mixes.
Chairman: John Sokol Novak
President/CEO: John Novak Jr
Research & Development: Larry Lepore
Quality Control: Galina Mann
Marketing Director: Eva Karnezis
Sales Director: Bobby Paroubek
Plant Manager: Mark Kiefhaber
Purchasing Manager: Andy Kaminski
Estimated Sales: $16 Million
Number Employees: 50-99
Number of Brands: 5
Square Footage: 25000
Type of Packaging: Consumer, Food Service, Private Label
Brands:
Baker
Bohemian Kitchen
Dobla
Simon Fischer
Solo

29372 Solae
4300 Duncan Avenue
Saint Louis, MO 63110 314-982-1983
Fax: 314-982-2461 800-325-7108
dschmidt@protein.com www.solae.com
Chairman: Craig F. Binetti
CFO: Terry Fox
Regional Vice President: Reinhart Schmitt, Ph.D.
Senior Director, Research and Developmen: Phil. Kerr, Ph.D
Vice President, Global Strategy & Market: Michele Fite
Vice President, Human Resources: Lindell R. Bean
Vice President Global Operations: Ricky Jack
Parent Co: DuPont

29373 Solapak
8219 Saint James Avenue
Elmhurst, NY 11373-3720 718-457-9589
Fax: 718-396-2875
Automatic wrapping machines
President: Wang
Number Employees: 10-19

29374 Solar Group
Taylorsville, MS 39168
800-647-7063
www.gibraltarmailboxes.com/solarstory.php
Shelving
Estimated Sales: $50-75 Million
Number Employees: 250-499
Parent Co: Gibraltar Industries

29375 Solarflo Corporation
22901 Aurora Road
Bedford, OH 44146-0391 440-439-1680
Fax: 440-439-8612 mailbox@solarflo.com
www.solarflo.com
President: Bill Thompson
Production & Chief Technician: Dave Frederick
Purchasing: Mike Kane
Estimated Sales: $3 - 5 Million
Number Employees: 10-19

29376 Solazyme Roquette Nutritionals
225 Gateway Blvd
S San Francisco, CA 94080 650-243-5500
Fax: 650-989-1284 contact@srnutritionals.com
www.srnutritionals.com
Microalgae-based healthy food ingredients and oils. Microalgae-derived lipid, protein and fiber-based products for nutrition, taste, texture and functionality.
President, CTO & Director: Harrison Dillon
CEO & Director: Jonathan Wolfson
CFO: Tyler Painter
EVP Research & Development: Peter Licari
Sr Director of Marketing: Philippe Caillat
VP Sales & Marketing: Jeff Avila
VP Communications: Genet Garamendi
Director of Operations: Kieran Furlong
SVP Manufacturing: Adrian Galvez
General Manager Nutritionals: Michael Golembieski
Estimated Sales: $39 Million
Type of Packaging: Bulk

29377 Solbern
8 Kulick Rd
Fairfield, NJ 07004 973-227-3030
Fax: 973-227-3069 sales@solbern.com
www.solbern.com
Manufacturer and exporter of container filling and dough folding equipment
President: Gil Foulon
VP: Jorge Espino
VP: Tom Berger
Marketing Director: Jorge Espino
Sales: Jorge Espino
Operations: Tom Berger
Estimated Sales: $5-10,000,000
Number Employees: 20-49
Square Footage: 24000

29378 Solganik & Associates
116 N Jefferson St
Dayton, OH 45402-1385 937-438-1666
Fax: 937-433-2354 800-253-8512
solganik@aol.com www.solganik.com
Consultant specializing in retail food service and product development
VP: Carin Solganik
Estimated Sales: $500,000-$1 Million
Number Employees: 50-99
Square Footage: 20000

29379 Solid Surface Acrylics
800 Walck Rd # 14
North Tonawanda, NY 14120-3500 716-743-1870
Fax: 716-743-0475 888-595-4114
info@ssacrylics.com www.ssacrylics.com
Acrylic solid surface tabletops, cutting boards, serving trays, planters, logo tops
President: Jack Tillotson
CEO: Robert Barenthaler
Designer: Melissa Aldrich
VP Sales: Allen Vaillancourt
Shipping Manager: Barb Smith
Plant Manager: Mark Lawrence
Estimated Sales: $2.5-5 Million
Number Employees: 10-19
Square Footage: 120000
Brands:
Dinelle

29380 Solka-Floc
1 Park 80 Plaza W
Saddle Brook, NJ 07663-5808 201-712-1188
Fax: 201-712-1250

29381 Sollas Films & PackagingSystems
146 Keystone Drive
Montgomeryville, PA 18936-9637 215-283-3250
Fax: 215-283-3254 film@rtgpkg.com
www.rtgpkg.com
Acrylic coated, shrinkable, and co-ex polypropylene, polyethylene films, polyolefin films, and printed, pearlescent, mettalized, barrier, laminations, cellophane, mylar and tear-tape specialty films, wrapping equipment, bandingequipment and cartostretch

29382 Solo Cup Canada
2121 Markham Road
Toronto, ON M1B 2W3
Canada 416-293-2877
Fax: 416-332-3489 800-465-9696
info@solocup.com www.solocup.com
Paper, plastic and foam cups and plates; also, plastic knives, forks and spoons
President, Chief Executive Officer: Robert Korzenski
Executive Vice President, General Counse: Jan Reed
Vice President of Sales: Jeff Lombardo
Executive Vice President, Chief Operatin: George Chappelle
Plant Manager: Vince Castro
Number Employees: 400+
Parent Co: Dart Container Corp.
Brands:
Lily

29383 Solo Cup Company
150 Spouth Saunders Rd.
Lake Forest, IL 60045 847-444-5000
Fax: 847-236-6049 800-367-2877
info@solocup.com www.solocup.com
Single-use cups, plates, cutlery, take-out contaiers
Estimated Sales: $1.6 Billion
Number Employees: 6400
Parent Co: Dart Container Corporation

29384 (HQ)Solo Cup Company
PO Box 5012
Lake Forest, IL 60045 847-831-4801
Fax: 847-579-3245 800-367-2877
info@solocup.com www.solocup.com
Solo is a leading global producer and marketer of disposable foodservice products. Solo manufactures on of the broadest products lines of cups, lids, food containers, plates, bowls, portion cups, stirres, straws, cutlery, napkinsplacemats, tablecovers and disposable food packaging containers in the industry, with products available in plastic, paper and foam.
CEO: Robert M Korzenski
Estimated Sales: $2.4,000,000
Number Employees: 5,000-9,999
Type of Packaging: Consumer, Food Service, Private Label
Other Locations:
Solo Cup Plant
El Cajon CA
Solo Cup Plant
Conyers GA
Solo Cup Plant
Augusta GA
Solo Cup Plant
Twin Falls ID
Solo Cup Plant
Highland Park IL
Solo Cup Plant
Wheeling IL
Solo Cup Plant
Urbana IL
Solo Cup Plant
Goshen IN
Solo Cup Plant
Goshen IN
Solo Cup Plant
Shreveport LA
Solo Cup Plant
Leominster MA
Solo Cup Plant
N Andover MA
Solo Cup Plant
Federalsburg MD
Brands:
Creative Expressions
Flex Style
Flex-E-Fill
Hoffmaster
Mtrene
Sensations
Solo Grips
Solo Ultra
Super Flex Ii

29385 (HQ)Solo Cup Company
10100 Reisterstown Rd
Owings Mills, MD 21117 410-363-1111
Fax: 410-998-2319 800-800-0300
info@solocup.com www.solocup.com
Foodservice disposables, paper, foam and plastic cups, containers, plates, bowls, dishes, carryout containers, cutlery, straws
President: Robert Korzenski
Chairman/CEO Solo Cup: Robert Hulseman
Estimated Sales: $400 Million
Number Employees: 5-9
Type of Packaging: Food Service
Other Locations:
Solo Cup Company

Chicago IL
Solo Cup Company
Urbana IL
Solo Cup Company
Wheeling IL
Solo Cup Company
Federalsburg MD
Solo Cup Company
Lubbock TX
Solo Cup Company
Belen NM
Solo Cup Company
Roseville CA
Solo Cup Company
Leominster MA
Solo Cup Company
Shreveport LA
Solo Cup Company
Ada OK
Solo Cup Company
Twin Falls ID
Solo Cup Company
Dallas TX
Brands:
Atlas
Basix
Guildware
Highlights
Maximizers
Sweetheart

29386 **Solon Manufacturing Company**
7 Grasso Ave
North Haven, CT 06473 203-230-5300
Fax: 207-474-7320 800-341-6640
sales@solonme.com www.solonme.com
Wooden spoons and sticks for ice cream novelties
President: Steve Clark
CEO/CFO: Larry Feinn
Marketing Director: Jayne Norman
Sales Director: Grover Kilpatrick
Estimated Sales: $10-20 Million
Number Employees: 100-249
Type of Packaging: Private Label, Bulk

29387 **Solus Industrial Innovations**
30152 Aventura
Rcho Sta Marg, CA 92688-2019 949-589-3900
Fax: 949-858-0300 solusteam@solusii.com
www.solusii.com
CEO: Garland Jones
Estimated Sales: $50 - 100 Million
Number Employees: 100-249

29388 **Solutions Plus**
2275 Cassens Drive
Suite 147
Fenton, MO 63026-2574 636-349-4922
Fax: 636-349-8027 solnplus@inlink.com
Analytical standards and testing reagents
President: Nancy Brinner
Partner: Peter Ricca
Estimated Sales: $1-5 Million
Number Employees: 15
Square Footage: 8500

29389 **Solutions by Design**
451 Clovis Avenue
Suite #130
Clovis, CA 93612 559-436-8380
Fax: 559-436-5263 800-888-4084
support@solutionsbydesign.com
www.solutionsbydesign.com
Wine industry research
Owner: William Poss
Marketing Director: Sherry Netto
Estimated Sales: $2.5-5 Million
Number Employees: 10-19

29390 **Solvay Specialty Polymers**
4500 McGinnis Ferry Rd
Alpharetta, GA 30005-3914 770-772-8200
Fax: 770-772-8213 888-765-3378
engpolymers@solvay.com
www.solvayplastics.com
Polyvinylidene chloride extrusion resins, polyvinylidene chloride soluble resins, and polyvinylidene chloride aqueous dispensions
President: Roger Kurne
CEO: George Corbin
Number Employees: 100-249
Parent Co: Solvay Group

29391 **Solve Needs International**
10204 Highland Rd
White Lake, MI 48386 248-698-3200
Fax: 248-698-3070 800-783-2462
sales@solveneeds.com www.solveneeds.com
Manufacturer, importer and exporter of corrugated bins, boxes, dividers, drawers, shelving, cantilever and pallet racks, hydraulic and scissor lifts, pallet jacks, stairways, rolling ladders, casters, wheels, carts, platform andutility trucks, new equipment and repair parts, etc
President: Don Burski
Estimated Sales: $3 - 5 Million
Number Employees: 5-9
Square Footage: 200000
Brands:
Ecoa
Equipment Company of America

29392 **Solvit**
7001 Raywood Rd
Monona, WI 53713 608-222-8624
Fax: 608-222-8733 888-314-1072
solvit1@aol.com
Solvit all-purpose pine cleaner including window, toilet bowl cleaner, warewashing compounds, degreasers and rat and mouse bait stations
President: John Kelly
Estimated Sales: $550,000
Number Employees: 1-4
Square Footage: 10000
Type of Packaging: Consumer, Food Service, Private Label
Brands:
Solvit

29393 **Solvox Manufacturing Company**
PO Box 26506
Milwaukee, WI 53226 414-774-5664
Fax: 414-774-0888
Food grade defoamers including kosher; manufacturer of food grade cleaning compounds, sanitizers, food ingredients commoditites, processing aids and waste water tratment
VP: Glen Polzin
Marketing: Bill McCoy
Sales: Kim Ireland
Operations: Shane Ireland
Purchasing: Shane Ireland
Estimated Sales: $20-50 Million
Number Employees: 10
Number of Products: 100
Square Footage: 58000
Parent Co: Hydrite Chemical Company

29394 **Somat Company**
3200 Lakeville Hwy
Petaluma, CA 94954-5675 707-762-0071
Fax: 707-762-5036 kstero@sonic.net
www.stero.com
Director of Operations: Terry Goodfellow
General Manager: Lin Sensening
Parts Department: Wendy Grado
Director of Operations: Terry Goodfellow
Estimated Sales: D
Number Employees: 10,000

29395 **Somat Company**
165 Independence Court
Lancaster, PA 17601 610-384-7000
Fax: 610-380-8500 800-237-6628
info@somatcomapny.com www.somatcorp.com
Manufacturer and exporter of waste pulping and dewatering systems for processing and reduction of food service wastes
General Manager: Lin Sensenig
R&D: Steve Eno
Marketing: Lin Sensenig
Production: Barry Alexander
Number Employees: 25
Square Footage: 39000
Brands:
Somat Classic
Somat Evergreen

29396 **Somerset Industries**
1 Esquire Rd
Billerica, MA 01862 978-667-3355
Fax: 978-671-9466 800-772-4404
somerset@smrset.com www.smrset.com
Manufacturer and exporter of bakery equipment including dough sheeters, rollers, fillers, depositors, bread molders and croissant machines
CEO: Andrew Voyatzakis
Estimated Sales: $2.5-5 Million
Number Employees: 10
Brands:
Cdr
Gpf-1
Somerset
Spm-45

29397 **Somerville Packaging**
7830 Tranmere Drive
Mississauga, ON L5S 1L9
Canada 905-678-8211
Fax: 905-678-7462 info@cascades.com
www.somervillepackaging.com
Aluminum foil and cartons for milk, frozen foods, juice and cereal
Estimated Sales: $1 - 5 Million
Number Employees: 1800
Parent Co: Paperboard Industries Corporation

29398 **Somerville Packaging**
1845 Birchmount Road
Scarborough, ON M1P 2J4
Canada 416-291-1161
Fax: 416-291-4909
Folding cartons and packaging systems
Customer Service Manager: D Hayes
Plant Manager: K Mucha
Estimated Sales: $1 - 5 Million
Number Employees: 100-250
Parent Co: Paperboard Industries Corporation

29399 **Something Different Linen**
474 Getty Ave
Clifton, NJ 07011 973-772-8019
Fax: 973-772-6519 800-422-2180
inforequest@tablecloths.net www.tablecloths.net
Manufacturer and exporter of tablecloths, skirting and napkins; custom sizes available
President: Mitchell Smith
Quality Control: Micheal Gates
Sales Manager: Wally Rachmaciej
Estimated Sales: $20 - 50 Million
Number Employees: 50-99
Parent Co: Something Different Linen

29400 **Sommer Awning Company**
8888 Keystone Xing # 1400
Indianapolis, IN 46240-4622 317-844-4744
Fax: 317-257-4307
Commercial awnings
President: Stephen Sommer
Estimated Sales: $300,000-500,000
Number Employees: 1-4

29401 **Sommers Plastic ProductsCompany**
31 Styertowne Rd
Clifton, NJ 07012 973-777-7888
Fax: 973-777-7890 800-225-7677
sales@sommers.com www.sommers.com
Manufacturer and exporter of plastic packaging products including sheeting, fabrics, cloths and film
President: Ed Schecter
VP: Fred Schecter
R&D: Fred Schecter
Estimated Sales: $5 - 10 Million
Number Employees: 20-49

29402 **Sonderen Packaging**
2906 N Crestline St
PO Box 7369
Spokane, WA 99207 509-487-1632
Fax: 509-483-2964 800-727-9139
steveag@sonderen.com www.sonderen.com
Paper folding boxes
Owner: Mark Sonderen
Sales Manager: Steve Agen
Estimated Sales: $5-10 Million
Number Employees: 50-99
Square Footage: 85000

29403 **Sonic Air Systems**
1050 Beacon St
Brea, CA 92821 714-255-0124
Fax: 714-255-8366 800-827-6642
asksonic@sonicairsystems.com
www.sonicairsystems.com
Drying systems, air knives, blowers
Owner: Dan Vander Pyl
Estimated Sales: $5-10 Million
Number Employees: 20-49

29404 Sonic Corporation
1 Research Dr
Stratford, CT 06615 203-375-0063
Fax: 203-378-4079 866-493-1378
kurt.limbacher@sonicmixing.com
www.sonicmixing.com
Manufacturer and exporter of food processing machinery including propeller mixers, agitators, continuous inline multiple-feed liquid blending systems, colloid mills and homogenizing systems.
President: R Brakeman
Sales Manager: Kurt Limbacher
Estimated Sales: $2.5-5 Million
Number Employees: 15
Square Footage: 13000
Brands:
Sonolator
Tri-Homo
Typhoon
Wizard

29405 Sonicor Instrument Corporation
14 Connor Ln
Deer Park, NY 11729 631-842-3344
Fax: 631-842-3389 800-864-5022
sonicor@sonicor.com www.sonicor.com
Ultrasonic and nonultrasonic cleaning equipment for processing machinery
President: Mike Parker
Marketing Manager: Gary Levanti
VP Sales: Ed Parker
Estimated Sales: $2.5 - 5 Million
Number Employees: 50

29406 Sonics & Materials, Inc
53 Church Hill Rd
Newtown, CT 06470-1699 203-270-4600
Fax: 203-270-4610 800-745-1105
info@sonics.com www.sonics.com
Manufacturer and exporter of liquid processing systems, food processing equipment, and food cutting equipment.
President/CEO: Robert Soloff
Quality Control: Dan Grise
Sales Manager: Lois Baiad
Biotechnology Manager: Mike Donaty
North Am. Sales Mngr., Welding Products: Brian Gourley
Estimated Sales: $10-20 Million
Number Employees: 50-99
Square Footage: 90000
Brands:
Vibra-Cell

29407 Sonoco
1 N 2nd St
Hartsville, SC 29550-3300 843-383-7000
Fax: 843-383-7008 800-377-2692
corporate.communications@sonoco.com
www.sonoco.com
Global manufacturer of consumer and industrial packing products and provider of packaging services.
Chairman/President/CEO: Harris Deloch Jr
Owner: Dennis Close
SVP/CFO: Charles Hupfer
Senior Vice President: Jim Brown
VP/Chief Information Officer: Bernard Campbell
Vice President Corporate Planning: Kevin Mahoney
Senior Vice President Human Resources: Cynthia Hartley
Estimated Sales: $3.7 Billion
Number Employees: 16,500

29408 Sonoco
10 Quinter St
Pottstown, PA 19464 610-323-9221
Fax: 610-323-6146 800-377-2692
www.sonoco.com
Manufacturer and exporter of disposable paper products including coasters: cellulose, pulpboard, budgetboard, nonwoven, etc.; also, placemats and sanitary caps for drinking glasses
President: Tom Johnson
VP Sales/Marketing: Smitty Thomas
VP Operations: Kent Adicks
Plant Manager: Lee Burg
Estimated Sales: $5 - 10 Million
Number Employees: 20-49
Parent Co: Engraph
Type of Packaging: Food Service
Brands:
Cupkin
Rixcaps
Sof-Ette

29409 Sonoco Engraph Labels
104 N Gold Dr
Trenton, NJ 08691-1602 609-586-1332
Fax: 856-631-8137 www.ccllabel.com
Printed and die-cut pressure sensitive labels
Manager: Ray Mass
Estimated Sales: $20 - 50 Million
Number Employees: 100-249
Parent Co: Sonoco Products Company

29410 Sonoco Engraph Labels
2635 Century Pkwy NE
Suite 90
Atlanta, GA 30345-3153 770-423-2500
Fax: 770-423-2509 800-377-2692
www.sonoco.com
Pressure sensitive labels

29411 Sonoco Fibre Drum
P.O.Box 160
Hartsville, SC 29551-0160 843-383-7000
Fax: 843-383-6501 800-377-2692
www.sonoco.com
Packaging supplies
CEO: Harris Deloach
Estimated Sales: $1 - 5 Million

29412 Sonoco Flexible Packaging
PO Box 160
Hartsville, SC 29551 843-383-7000
Fax: 843-383-6501 800-377-2692
www.sonoco.com
Manufacturer and exporter of flexible packaging materials
CEO: Harris Deloach
CEO: Jack Sanders
Sales/Marketing Manager: Brad Ross
Manager: Dana Mooring
Number Employees: 1,000-4,999
Parent Co: Sonoco Products
Type of Packaging: Consumer

29413 Sonoco Flexible Packaging
1 North Second Street
Hartsville, SC 29550 843-383-7000
Fax: 843-383-7008 800-377-2692
www.sonoco.com
Manufacturer and exporter of packaging products including greaseproof bread and pastry bags, cello roll stock, cellophane and polyethylene bags, folding cartons, inserts, blister cards, roll labels, etc
Estimated Sales: $50-100 Million
Number Employees: 50-99

29414 Sonoco Paper BoardSpecialties
3150 Clinton Ct
Norcross, GA 30071-1643 770-476-9088
Fax: 770-476-0765 800-264-7494
stancap@sonoco.com
www.sononcospecialties.com
Manufacturer and exporter of biodegradable and recyclable paperboard glassware caps used in the lodging, food and hospital industries for sanitary purposes
General Manager: Smitty Thomas
CEO: Harris DeLouch
General Manager: Smitty Thomas
Regional Sales Manager: Ralph Ward
Plant Manager: Kelly Mowen
Purchasing Manager: Gus Copeletti
Estimated Sales: $5 - 10 Million
Number Employees: 1-4
Square Footage: 132000
Parent Co: Sonoco Products Company
Type of Packaging: Consumer, Food Service, Private Label, Bulk

29415 Sonoma Pacific Company
1540 S Greenwood Avenue
Montebello, CA 90640-6536 323-838-4374
Fax: 323-838-4381
Manufacturer and recycler of pallets and skids including hardwood, softwood and plywood
Regional Manager: Tony Serge
District Manager: Len Spitzer
Number Employees: 60
Square Footage: 250000
Parent Co: Palex

29416 Sonoma Signatures
4381 17th Street
San Francisco, CA 94114-1804 415-864-2582
Fax: 415-864-2582
Tea and coffee industry jars (glass)

29417 Soodhalter Plastics
PO Box 21276
Los Angeles, CA 90021 213-747-0231
Fax: 213-746-8125
soodhalterplastics@yahoo.com
Manufacturer, importer and exporter of party and bar accessories including plastic cocktail forks, stirrers and picks
President: Jackie Wolfson
CFO: Jackie Wolfson
Estimated Sales: $5-10 Million
Number Employees: 10-19

29418 Sooner Scientific
1501 Riverbluff Rd
PO Box 180
Idabel, OK 74745 405-237-0302
Fax: 580-286-4268 800-991-1974
sonrsci@ionet.net www.soonersci.com
DNA electrophoresis products
Estimated Sales: $1-2.5 Million
Number Employees: 1-4

29419 Sopralco
6991 W Broward Blvd
Plantation, FL 33317-2907 954-584-2225
Fax: 954-584-3271 sopralco@aol.com
Ready-to-drink espresso
Owner: Peter Marciante
VP: Arcelia De Battisti
Marketing: Ana Ordaz
Estimated Sales: $1,500,000
Number Employees: 1-4
Square Footage: 1250
Parent Co: Sopralco
Type of Packaging: Consumer, Food Service
Brands:
Espre
Espre-Cart
Espre-Matic

29420 Sorensen Associates
999 NW Frontage Rd
Suite 190
Troutdale, OR 97060 503-665-0123
Fax: 503-666-5113 800-542-4321
james.sorensen@saiemail.com www.tns.com
Market research consultant specializing in in-store shopper surveys and new product development for the packaged goods industry
President: Herb Sorensen
CFO: Jack Birnbach
Sr. VP: James Sorensen
VP Marketing: Bill Hruby
Estimated Sales: $2.5-5 Million
Number Employees: 20-49
Square Footage: 5000

29421 Sorenson
632 NW California Street
Chehalis, WA 98532 360-748-8877
Fax: 360-748-1288 800-332-3213
dsorenseon@sorensontransport.com
www.sorensontransport.com
Owner: Darrell E Sorensen
Estimated Sales: $5 - 10 Million
Number Employees: 10-19

29422 Sorg Paper Company
901 Manchester Avenue
Middletown, OH 45042 513-420-5300
Fax: 513-420-5324
Paper products: abrasive coating, bactericides, cotton furnish, deeptone colors, fiberglass pulp matrix, flame retardant, latex, moisture barrier, recycled/post consumer, wet strength resin, specialty pulps, u.v. coatings and watermarking
VP Sales/Marketing: Joe Piela
Production Manager (Tissue): Carl Eisenmenger
Production Manager (Decorative): Bill Huggins
Number Employees: 200

29423 Sortex
39161 Farwell Dr
Fremont, CA 94538-1050 510-797-5000
Fax: 510-797-0555 sales@sortex.com
www.sortex.com

Manufacturer and exporter of color sorters and vision systems
VP Sales: Mike Evans
Sales Director of Product: Christoph Naef
Head of Corporate Communications: Corina Atzli
Number Employees: 20-49
Square Footage: 80000
Parent Co: Buhler
Brands:
Sortex

29424 Sortie/Kohlhaas
PO Box 534
Monee, IL 60449-0534 708-534-3940
Fax: 708-534-8013
Sorting devices

29425 Sossner Steel Stamps
180 Judge Don Lewis Blvd
Elizabethton, TN 37643 423-543-4001
Fax: 423-543-8546 800-828-9515
info@sossnerstamps.com
www.sossnerstamps.com
Manufacturer and exporter of marking stamps
President: Neil Friedman
International Sales: Vianney Cabrera
General Manager: Russel Lacy
Estimated Sales: $5 - 10 Million
Number Employees: 20-49
Square Footage: 47000
Parent Co: Sossner Steel Stamps
Brands:
2-In-1 Time-Saver
Roll-A-Matic
Shal-O-Groove
True-Sharp

29426 Soten
21572 Surveyor Cir
Huntington Beach, CA 92646-7067 714-969-9510
Fax: 714-969-9520 film@soten.it
www.soten.it

29427 Sould Manufacturing
PO Box 21064
Winnepeg, NB R3R 3R2
Canada 204-339-3499
Fax: 204-334-6844
Concession carts
Number Employees: 9

29428 Source Distribution Logistics
2s700 Horseshoe Dr
Batavia, IL 60510 630-761-1231
Fax: 630-761-2974 info@sourcedl.com
www.sourcedl.com
Sales and marketing consultant for the warehousing industry
President: Thomas Peters
Estimated Sales: $300,000-500,000
Number Employees: 1-4

29429 Source Marketing
761 Main Avenue
Norwalk, CT 6851 203-291-4000
Fax: 203-229-0865 800-536-1235
info@source-marketing.com
www.source-marketing.com
Textile screen printing
President: Janie Goldberg
Estimated Sales: $1-5 Million
Number Employees: 10
Type of Packaging: Bulk

29430 Source Packaging
215 Island Road
Mahwah, NJ 07430-2117 201-831-0005
Fax: 201-831-0009 888-665-9768
contact@sourcepackaging.com
www.sourcepackaging.com
Manufacturer of custom and stock carrying cases and transport care.
President: Alan Alder
Sales Director: Veronica Knipping
Estimated Sales: $5 - 10 Million
Number Employees: 10-19
Square Footage: 80000

29431 Source for Packaging
227 E 45th Street
New York, NY 10017-3306 212-687-4700
Fax: 212-687-4725 800-223-2527
Manufacturer and exporter of shopping bags, promotional items, labels, foil, pressure sensitive tapes; also, packaging design services available
President: Jay Raskin
VP Sales/Operations: Louis Cruz
Estimated Sales: $50-100 Million
Number Employees: 250-499

29432 South Akron Awning Company
763 Kenmore Blvd
Akron, OH 44314 330-848-7611
Fax: 330-753-4224 info@southakronawning.com
www.southakronawning.com
Commercial awnings and renter of tents and party supplies.
President: Ranell Minear
Vice President: Mike Halgaga
Sales: Jack Carroll
Estimated Sales: $1-2.5 Million
Number Employees: 12

29433 South Jersey Awning
101 Oak Avenue
Egg Harbor Township, NJ 08234-221609-646-2002
Fax: 609-646-2656
Commercial awnings
President: Steve Alberts
Estimated Sales: $500,000-$1,000,000
Number Employees: 5-9

29434 South Jersey Store Fixture & Refrigeration
773 Kaighns Ave
Camden, NJ 08103 856-365-6664
Fax: 856-365-9010
Wholesaler/distributor of food service equipment including broilers, bar equipment, barbecues, chairs, beverage coolers, dishwashers, freezers, shelving, slicers, stools, toasters, kitchen ventilating systems, etc.; serving the foodservice market
President: George Fatlowitz
CEO: Edward Fatlowitz
Estimated Sales: Below $5 Million
Number Employees: 1-4
Square Footage: 100000

29435 South River Machine
115 S River Street
Hackensack, NJ 07601-6909 201-487-1736
Fax: 201-487-1508
Mixing/kneading mixers and pasta machinery for ravioli, cavatelli, manicotti, noodles, etc
Estimated Sales: $500,000-$1 Million
Number Employees: 4

29436 South Valley Citrus Packers
9600 Road 256
Terra Bella, CA 93270 559-906-1033
Fax: 559-525-4206 vcpg@vcpg.com
www.vcpg.com/gvh.htm
Packinghouse and licensed shipper of Sunkist Growers Inc. citrus products.
Manager: Cliff Martin
Grower Service Representative: Maribel Nenna
General Manager Visalia Citrus Packing: Bob Walters
Parent Co: Visalia Citrus Packing Group
Type of Packaging: Food Service

29437 South Valley Manufacturing
PO Box 1595
Gilroy, CA 95021-1595 408-842-5457
Fax: 408-842-1097
Food processing equipment including brine tanks, kettles, steam blanchers, atmospheric can cookers, coolers, deaerators, sterilizers, tubular heat exchangers
President: Paul L Jennings
Estimated Sales: Below $5 Million
Number Employees: 5-9
Square Footage: 9000
Brands:
South Valley Manufacturing

29438 SouthPack
One Hartford Square
New Britain, CT 06052 860-224-2242
Fax: 860-224-2445 spc@southpack.com
www.southpack.com
Custom thermoforming and contract packaging
President: Lynn Robertson
VP: Kurt Mogielnicks
Number Employees: 25-35
Square Footage: 60000
Type of Packaging: Food Service, Private Label, Bulk

29439 Southbend Company
1100 Old Honeycutt Rd
Fuquay Varina, NC 27526 919-762-1000
Fax: 919-552-9798 800-348-2558
sbgeneral@southbendnc.com
www.southbendnc.com
Manufacturer and exporter of commercial cooking equipment including broilers, fryer systems, restaurant ranges, convection, steamers, kettles, braising pans and cabinets
President: Nestor Ibrahim
COO: Selim Bassaul
CFO: Dave Baker
VP: Rob August
Research & Development: Ray Wi
VP Sales: Jonette Wylie
National Sales Manager: Mitch Cohen
Estimated Sales: $50 Million
Number Employees: 100-249
Square Footage: 135000
Parent Co: Middleby Corporation
Brands:
Southbend

29440 Southeastern Filtration& Equipment
158 Railroad St
Canton, GA 30114 770-720-2800
Fax: 770-720-2900 800-935-8500
gerhard@sfes.com www.sfes.com
Water treatment systems for high and low temperature applications
Owner: John Brandreth Iii
VP Marketing: Gerhard Zamorano
Estimated Sales: $1-2,500,000
Number Employees: 10-19
Square Footage: 22000
Brands:
Hydroblend
Microlene
Scalestick

29441 Southend Janitorial Supply
11422 S Broadway
Los Angeles, CA 90061 323-754-2842
Fax: 323-779-5457 leday@aol.com
www.southendjanitorial.com
Janitorial supplies and equipment
President: John Leday
Estimated Sales: $5-10 Million
Number Employees: 5-9

29442 Southern Ag Company
942 N Main St
Blakely, GA 39823 229-723-4262
Fax: 229-723-3223
Manufacturer and exporter of conveyors, elevators, sizers and separators for peanuts; also, grain bins
Estimated Sales: $2.5-5 Million
Number Employees: 10-19

29443 Southern Atlantic LabelCompany
1300 Cavalier Blvd
Chesapeake, VA 23323 757-487-2525
Fax: 757-487-9712 800-456-5999
info@salinc.com www.southernatlanticlabel.com
Pressure sensitive roll labels, coupons, tags, polystyrene inserts, 4 color process, 9 color in line printing, 16-inch web capacity, static cling and screen printed point of purchase, foil stamping and bar codes
CEO: Chil Daper
President: James Cumming
CEO: Phillip W Draper
Sales Manager: Kurt Webber
Estimated Sales: $20 - 50 Million
Number Employees: 100-249
Square Footage: 33000

29444 Southern Automatics
2845 Brooks Street
Lakeland, FL 33803-7379 863-665-1633
Fax: 863-665-2500 800-441-4604
Manufacturer, importer and exporter of high-volume fruit and vegetable packing machinery; also, compact optic sorters and sizers
President: Hugh Oglesby
VP: Scott Oglesby
Estimated Sales: $1 - 3 Million
Number Employees: 20
Square Footage: 20000
Parent Co: Future Alloys

29445 **Southern Awning & Sign Company**
532 Industrial Drive
Woodstock, GA 30189-7214 770-516-8652
Fax: 770-516-3940
Commercial awnings
President: Ron Dinsmore
Number Employees: 5

29446 **Southern Bag Corporation**
25 Woodgreen Pl
Madison, MS 39110-9531 662-746-3631
Fax: 662-746-3673 www.hoodpackaging.com
Multi-wall paper shipping bags
Manager: Ray Brown
Sales: Paul Rusche
Customer Service Manager: Mike Boughman
Plant Manager: Kevin McCarthy
Estimated Sales: $20-50 Million
Number Employees: 100-249

29447 **(HQ)Southern Champion Tray**
220 Compress Street
PO Box 4066
Chattanooga, TN 37405 423-756-5121
Fax: 423-756-5163 800-468-2222
cchapellin@sctray.com www.sctray.com
Manufacturer and exporter of paperboard folding cartons
CEO: John Zeiser
CEO: Mark Lonqnecker
National Sales Manager: Paul Powell
Operations Manager: Jim Skidmore
Number Employees: 100-249
Square Footage: 325000
Type of Packaging: Consumer, Food Service, Private Label, Bulk
Other Locations:
Southern Champion Tray L.P.
Chattanooga TN

29448 **Southern Container Corporation**
140 W Industry Ct
Deer Park, NY 11729 631-586-6006
Fax: 631-586-6068
deerpark.webcontact@southern-container.com
www.southern-container.com
Corrugated packaging including die cut, pre-print and hi-graphic; also, point-of-purchase displays
CEO: Steven M Grossman
Sales Manager: Barry Kolevzon
Estimated Sales: $20-50 Million
Number Employees: 100-249

29449 **Southern Express**
2305 N Broadway
Saint Louis, MO 63102-1405 770-662-0220
800-444-9157
Manufacturer and designer of restaurant kiosks, mobile merchandisers and mobile carts
Manager: Michael Samborn
Number Employees: 20
Parent Co: Duke Manufacturing Company

29450 **Southern Film Extruders**
2327 English Road
High Point, NC 27262 336-885-8091
Fax: 336-885-1221 800-334-6101
sales@southernfilm.com www.southernfilm.com
FDA polythylene packaging films
Owner: Joseph Martinez
Chief Financial Officer: John Barnes
Quality Control Manager: Tom Vanpelt
Vice President, Sales: Lanny Rampley
Warehouse Manager: Austin Fisher
Estimated Sales: $24 Million
Number Employees: 145
Square Footage: 115000
Type of Packaging: Private Label

29451 **Southern Garden Citrus Corporation**
1820 County Road 833
Clewiston, FL 33440-9222 863-983-3030
Fax: 863-983-3060 800-339-6025
dtope@ussugar.com www.southerngardens.com
Citrus juices, not-from-concentrate and concentrated citrus by-products
Finance Executive: Ginny Pena
Estimated Sales: $25-50 Million
Number Employees: 100-249

29452 **Southern Imperial**
1400 Eddy Ave
Rockford, IL 61103 815-986-1709
Fax: 815-877-7454 800-747-4665
grothmeyer@southernimperial.com
www.southernimperial.com
Manufacturer and exporter of scanning hooks, display hooks, wire racks and baskets, clip strips, J-hooks, paper and adhesive labels and merchandising accessories
President: Stanley Valiulis
CFO: Dean Zanseil
Quality Control: Denise Bermingham
R&D: Tom Zeliulis
Marketing Manager: Tom Valiulis
Estimated Sales: $20 - 30 Million
Number Employees: 100-249
Square Footage: 320000

29453 **Southern Metal Fabricators**
1215 Frazier Road
Albertville, AL 35950 256-891-4343
Fax: 256-891-0922 800-989-1330
sales@southernmetalfab.com
www.southernmetalfab.com
Manufacturer and exporter of ventilating systems, ducts, hoods, blowpipes, fittings, tanks, hoppers, railings, funnels, racks, boxes, vats and conveyors
President/CEO: Charles Bailey
CFO: Teresa Hammett
Vice President: Regenia Bailey
Quality Control: Donnie Buchanan
Sales Manager: Bud Weed
Operations Manager: Danny Murray
Estimated Sales: $5 Million
Number Employees: 50
Square Footage: 189000

29454 **(HQ)Southern Missouri Containers**
PO Box 4306
Springfield, MO 65808 417-831-2685
Fax: 417-831-7912 800-999-7666
www.smcpackaging.com
Corrugated boxes
Chairman/CEO/Secretary: Kevin Ausburn
Finance Manager: Ron Thomas
Vice President: Benjamine Jones
Quality Control Director: Galen Perry
Chief Operating Officer: John Pojunos
Estimated Sales: $63 Million
Number Employees: 300
Square Footage: 153000
Other Locations:
Southern Missouri Containers
Kansas City MO

29455 **Southern Packaging & Bottling**
P.O.Box 112
Athens, GA 30603-0112 706-208-0814
Fax: 706-208-0815
sales@southernpackaging.com
www.southernpackaging.com
Horizontal form/fill/seal pouch packaging machinery
Owner: Roy Miller
Engineering Manager: Mike Rupert
Director, Sales: Vince Tamborello
Estimated Sales: $5-10 Million
Number Employees: 20-49
Type of Packaging: Food Service

29456 **Southern Packaging Corporation**
PO Box 993
Bennettsville, SC 29512 843-479-7154
Fax: 843-479-1909
Corrugated paper containers
CEO: Don Evans
Estimated Sales: $2.5-5 Million
Number Employees: 20-49

29457 **Southern Packaging Machinery**
P.O. Box 112
Athens, GA 30603-0112 706-208-0814
Fax: 706-208-0815 800-922-8030
sales@southernpackaging.comÿ
www.southernpackaging.com
Owner: Roy Miller
Engineering Manager: Mike Rupert
Regional Sales Manager: Jay Cavanaugh

29458 **Southern Pallet**
PO Box 807
Memphis, TN 38101 901-942-4603
Fax: 901-942-4613
Wooden shipping crates and pallets
Manager: Verna Frye
Production Manager: Louis Ratchford
Estimated Sales: $500,000-$1 Million
Number Employees: 5-9

29459 **Southern Perfection Fabrication Company**
232 Ga Highway 49 S
Byron, GA 31008 478-956-4442
Fax: 478-956-4001 800-237-4726
brochure@southernperfection.com
www.southernperfection.com
President/CFO: Gordon Hale
Estimated Sales: Below $5 Million
Number Employees: 50-99

29460 **Southern Pride Distributing**
5003 Meadowland Pkwy
Marion, IL 62959-5892 618-997-9348
Fax: 618-993-5960 800-851-8180
sopride@midwest.net www.southern-pride.com
Manufacturer and exporter of ovens including mobile, revolving and warming; also, commercial barbecue equipment, smokers and rotisseries
President/CEO: Mike Robertson
VP: Jared Robertson
Quality Control: Bret Robertson
Marketing Director: Jack Griggs
Operations Manager: Jerry Cadle
Plant Manager: Marty Degrini
Purchasing: Rich Rowell
Estimated Sales: $10 Millions
Number Employees: 20-49
Square Footage: 65000
Type of Packaging: Food Service
Brands:
Southern Pride

29461 **Southern Rubber Stamp Company**
2637 E Marshall St
Tulsa, OK 74110 918-587-3818
Fax: 918-587-3819 888-826-4304
sales@southernmark.com
www.southernmark.com
Manufacturer and exporter of rubber stamps, seals, numbering machines, embossers, special inks, etc
President: Mike Forehand
VP: David Parnell
Estimated Sales: $500,000-$1 Million
Number Employees: 5-9
Type of Packaging: Consumer, Food Service, Bulk
Brands:
Perfect Seal

29462 **(HQ)Southern Store Fixtures**
275 Drexel Rd SE
Bessemer, AL 35022 205-428-4800
Fax: 205-428-2552 800-552-6283
chughes@southerncasearts.com
www.southerncasearts.com
Manufacturer, exporter and designer of mobile and modular refrigerated cases for deli, bakery, salads, produce and floral; store and fixture design and installation services available
President: Gene Cary
National Sales Manager: Joe Moore
Estimated Sales: $10 - 20 Million
Number Employees: 100-249
Square Footage: 108000

29463 **Southern Tailors**
1862 Marietta Blvd NW
Atlanta, GA 30318 404-367-8660
Fax: 404-367-8654 877-655-2321
www.southerntailors.com
Custom flags, banners, ribbons, buttons and other advertising specialties; also, engraving available
President: Neal Zucker
Estimated Sales: $1 - 2.5 Million
Number Employees: 10-19
Square Footage: 7000
Parent Co: Southern Tailors

29464 Southern Testing & Research Labs
3809 Airport Dr NW
Wilson, NC 27896 252-237-4175
Fax: 252-237-9341
jyakupkovic@southerntesting.com
www.southerntesting.com
Analytical laboratory specializing in chemical and microbiological analysis of food samples. Nutritional label analysis, nutraceutical analysis, and camera ready nutirtional labels
Executive Director: Robert Dermer
Marketing/Sales: Walter Nogg
Department Manager: Martin Donenco
Estimated Sales: $10 - 20 Million
Number Employees: 50-99
Square Footage: 21000
Parent Co: Microbac Laboratories

29465 Southern Tool
738 Well Road
West Monroe, LA 71292-0138 318-387-2263
Fax: 318-387-5372
Manufacturer and exporter of packaging equipment
President: Dale Doty
Plant Manager: Buck Carlisle
Number Employees: 65
Square Footage: 100000
Parent Co: Southern Tool

29466 Southland Packaging
303 E Alondra Boulevard
Gardena, CA 90248-2809 213-532-3720
Estimated Sales: $2.5-5 Million
Number Employees: 10-19

29467 Southline Equipment Company
P.O.Box 8867
Houston, TX 77249 713-869-6801
Fax: 713-869-2875 800-444-1173
www.eqdepot.com
Wholesaler/distributor of material handling equipment including new and used forklift trucks, parts, service and rental in addition to industrial sweepers/scrubbers.
Manager: Jeff Jones
Finance: F Rigell
Marketing Director: Bob McClelland Sr
Sales Manager: M Zinda
Operations Manager: M Gunter
Estimated Sales: $20 Million
Number Employees: 50-99
Square Footage: 60000

29468 Southwest Endseals
4323 South Drive
Houston, TX 77053-4820 832-399-3900
Fax: 832-399-3903 866-832-1454
info@swformseal.com www.swformseal.com
Ceiling jaws for packaging machines
President: John Deterling
Number Employees: 10-19

29469 Southwest Fixture Company
8909 Chancellor Row
Dallas, TX 75247-5324 214-634-2800
Fax: 214-634-2847 sales@swfdc.com
www.swfdc.com
Store fixtures
President: Daniel W Thor
VP: A Winkler
Estimated Sales: $2.5-5 Million
Number Employees: 5-9

29470 Southwest Indiana and American Cold Storage
P.O.Box 875
Newburgh, IN 47629-0875 812-858-3555
Fax: 812-858-3558 bhasler@warrick-edd.org
www.warrick-edd.org
Manager: Larry Taylor
Number Employees: 1-4

29471 Southwest Neon Signs
7208 S Ww White Rd
San Antonio, TX 78222-5204 210-648-3221
Fax: 210-648-4709 800-927-3221
www.southwestsigns.com
Indoor and outdoor advertising and electric signs
President: Chad Jones
Sales Manager: Greg Burkette
Estimated Sales: $10-20 Million
Number Employees: 50-99

29472 Southwest Vault Builders
596 Bennett Ln
Lewisville, TX 75075 469-671-5800
Fax: 214-671-5812 800-749-1431
www.southwestvault.com
Specializes in cold storage construction
President: Larry Nolan

29473 (HQ)Southwestern Porcelain Steel
201 E Morrow Road
Sand Springs, OK 74063-6531 918-245-1375
Fax: 918-241-7339 jdbigelo@swbell.net
www.swporcelain.com
Porcelain enamel tops for steel tables, counters and signs; importer of cast iron stove top grates; also, silk screen porcelain graphics available
Vice President: Jim Bigelow
Plant Superintendent: Don Bushnell
Estimated Sales: $5-10 Million
Number Employees: 20-50
Square Footage: 512000

29474 Southworth Products Corporation
P.O.Box 1380
Portland, ME 04104-1380 207-878-0700
Fax: 207-797-4734 800-743-1000
salesinfo@southworthproducts.com
www.southworthproducts.com
Material handling equipment including lift tables, dock lifts, container tilters, vertical conveyors, manual palletizers, elevating transporters, rotators, upenders and adjustable workstations
Owner: Lewis P Cabot
CFO: Mike Nordman
Marketing Program Manager: Meredith Herzog
Sales Manager: Randy Moore
Director Product Support: James Galante
Estimated Sales: $5 - 10 Million
Number Employees: 50-99
Parent Co: Southworth International Group

29475 SoyNut Butter Company
4220 Commercial Way
Glenview, IL 60025
Fax: 847-635-6801 800-288-1012
www.soynutbutter.com
Peanut free peanut butter, made from roasted soy.
President: Steve Grubb
Estimated Sales: Below $5 Million
Number Employees: 5-9

29476 Soyatech
1369 State Highway 102
Bar Harbor, ME 04609-7019 207-288-4969
Fax: 207-288-5264 800-424-7692
peter@soyatech.com www.soyatech.com
Consultant specializing in soybean processing and product development services
President: Peter Golbitz
Chief Executive Officer: Chris Erickson
Publisher & Operations Director: Keri Hayes
Marketing/Sales: Susan Bradley
Regional Sales Manager: Mark Phillips
Publisher & Operations Director: Keri Hayes
Estimated Sales: Below $5 Million
Number Employees: 1-4

29477 Space Guard Products
711 South Commerce Dr
Seymour, IN 47274 812-523-3044
Fax: 812-523-3362 800-841-0680
WebSales@SpaceGaurdProducts.com
www.spaceguardproducts.com
Woven wire partitions
Owner: Ed Murphy
VP Sales: Gary Myers
Estimated Sales: $5-10 Million
Number Employees: 20-49
Brands:
Ford Logan Wire
Space Guard 2000

29478 Spacekraft Packaging
1811 W Oak Pkwy
Marietta, GA 30062-2216 770-429-3500
Fax: 770-429-3535 800-483-1168
info@spacekraft.com www.spacekraft.com
Manufacture of laminated panels.
Estimated Sales: $1 - 5 Million
Number Employees: 10-19
Square Footage: 20000

29479 Spacekraft Packaging
4901 W. 79th Street
Indianapolis, IN 46268 317-871-6999
Fax: 317-871-6993 800-599-8943
rdaly@mbpi.com www.spacekraft.com
Packaging containers for liquid, semi-bulk products
Estimated Sales: $5-10 Million
Number Employees: 20-50

29480 Spacesaver Corporation
1450 Janesville Ave
Fort Atkinson, WI 53538 800-492-3434
Fax: 920-563-2702 800-492-3434
ssc@spacesaver.com www.spacesaver.com
Manufacturer and exporter of mobile high-density storage systems
President: Paul Olsen
R&D: David Klumb
Vice President: Bill Wettstein
CFO: Ryan Bittner
Marketing Director: Christopher Batterman
Sales Director: Kevin Carmody
Public Relations: Karen King
Operations Manager: Jim Muth
Purchasing Manager: Patricia Cropp
Estimated Sales: $75 - 100 Million
Number Employees: 250-499
Parent Co: KI
Type of Packaging: Bulk

29481 Span Tech
P.O.Box 369
Glasgow, KY 42142-0369 270-651-9166
Fax: 270-651-7533 billy_miller@spantechllc.com
www.spantechllc.com
USDA and BISSC approved modular side flexing conveyor systems with plastic belting
President: James Layne
CEO: James Layne
Engineering Director: Lavon Riegel
Quality Control: Paul Chambers
Marketing/Sales: Genia Johnson
Operations: Jimmy Wiley
Production/Plant Manager: Phillip Coleman
Purchasing: Alf McDougal
Estimated Sales: $20 - 50 Million
Number Employees: 50-99
Square Footage: 50000
Brands:
Designer System
Minispam
Maxispan
Monospan
Multispan

29482 Spanco
604 Hemlock Rd Ste 2
Morgantown, PA 19543 610-286-7200
Fax: 610-286-0085 800-869-2080
www.spanco.com
Manufacturer and exporter of stainless steel material handling equipment including cranes and conveyor systems and components
VP: George Nolan
Sales Manager: George Nolan
Estimated Sales: $20 - 50 Million
Number Employees: 50-99

29483 Spann Sign Company
PO Box 546
Kenosha, WI 53141-0546 262-658-1288
Fax: 262-658-1878
Electric, neon and plastic signs
President: Duane Laska
Number Employees: 6
Brands:
Spann Signs

29484 Sparkler Filters
101 N Loop 336 E
Conroe, TX 77301 936-756-4471
Fax: 936-539-1165 sales@sparklerfilters.com
www.sparklerfilters.com

Manufacturer and exporter of filter systems including fryer oil and liquid; also, manual and automatic
President/CEO: James Reneau Jr
CFO: Robert Thompson
VP: Jose Sentmanat
Quality Control: James Dunklin
Marekting: Jose Sentmanat
Sales: Tom Buttera
Public Relations: Norm Hofer
Operations/General Manager: Link Reneau
Plant Manager: Alan Powell
Purchasing: Phil Lawson
Estimated Sales: $5-5.5 Million
Number Employees: 20-49
Number of Brands: 2
Square Footage: 70000
Type of Packaging: Food Service
Brands:
Sparklaid
Sparkler

29485 Sparks Belting Company
3800 Stahl Dr SE
Grand Rapids, MI 49546 616-949-2750
Fax: 616-949-8518 800-451-4537
sbcinfo@sparksbelting.com
www.sparksbelting.com
Wholesaler/distributor of food-approved and package handling conveyor belting; manufacturer of motorized pulleys; importer of thermoplastic belting, motorized pulleys and rollers
President: Steven Swanson
CFO: Martha Vrias
VP: Steven Bayus
Quality Control: Dave Vanderwood
Marketing: Frank Kennedy
Operations: Bruce Dielema
Production: Joe Graver
Plant Manager: John Grasmeyer
Purchasing Director: Mark White
Estimated Sales: $20 - 50 Million
Number Employees: 100-249
Square Footage: 52000
Brands:
Dura-Drive Plus
Microrollers

29486 Sparks Companies
P.O.Box 17339
Memphis, TN 38187 901-766-4600
Fax: 901-766-4462 info@informaecon.com
www.sparksco.com
Agriculture research and consulting company
Chairman of the Board: Willard Sparks
Estimated Sales: $10 - 15 Million
Number Employees: 100-249

29487 Spartan Flag Company
PO Box 248
Northport, MI 49670 231-386-5150
Fax: 231-386-5904
Flags, pennants and banners
President: Cheryl Feipke
VP: Milt Seipke
Estimated Sales: Below $5 Million
Number Employees: 10-19

29488 Spartan Showcase
702 Spartan Showcase Dr
Union, MO 63084 636-583-4050
Fax: 636-583-4067 800-325-0775
sales@spartanshowcase.com
www.spartanshowcase.com
Manufacturer and exporter of bakery and deli wallcases, merchandising and self-serve display cases and dry and refrigerated showcases; also, custom glass and wood fixtures
CEO: Mike Lause
VP Marketing: Steve Lause
Sales Director: Royce Buehrlen
Manager: Greg Hall
Estimated Sales: $14 Million
Number Employees: 140
Square Footage: 200000
Parent Co: Leggett & Platt Inc

29489 Spartan Tool
P.O.Box 950
Mendota, IL 61342-0950 815-539-7411
Fax: 815-539-9786 800-435-3866
hmiller@spartantool.com www.spartantool.com
Drain and sewer cleaning equipment
Member of the Board: Tom Pranka
Advertising Manager: Nancy Dessing
Sales Manager: Bill Madden
Estimated Sales: $10 - 20 Million
Number Employees: 20-49

29490 Spartanburg Stainless Products
121 Broadcast Drive
Spartanburg, SC 29303-4711 864-699-3200
Fax: 864-699-3250 800-974-7500
info@ssprod.com www.ssprod.com
Pressurizable stainless steel beverage, beer, and chemical containers
President: Richard Dye
CEO: Dick Dye
CFO: Barry Whipple
Quality Control: Daniel Ahein
VP Sales/Marketing: Del Strandburg
Operations: Buck Wiggins
Production: Chuck Manahan
Purchasing: Tyler Evans
Estimated Sales: $3 - 5 Million
Number Employees: 150
Square Footage: 800000
Parent Co: Reserve Group

29491 Spartanics
3605 Edison Pl
Rolling Meadows, IL 60008 847-394-5700
Fax: 847-394-0409 sales@spartanics.com
www.spartanics.com
Blanking and die-cutting systems, optical and mechanical counters, laser cutting machines, digital printing equipment, converting systems, finishing equipment, material handling machinery, screen printing systems.
Vice President of Sales & Marketing/Inte: Mike Bacon
Marketing Coordinator: Jeanette DesJardins
National Sales Manager - US: Rick Roberts
Estimated Sales: E
Number Employees: 20-49
Type of Packaging: Food Service

29492 Spartec Plastics
PO Box 620
Conneaut, OH 44030-0620 440-599-8175
Fax: 440-593-2003 800-325-5176
Manufacturer and exporter of extruded low and high density polyethylene and polypropylene products including thermoplastic and rolled sheets, rods, textured cutting boards and sanitary paneling systems with antibacterial additives
Operations Manager: Ernie Szydlowski
Estimated Sales: $2.5-5 Million
Number Employees: 19
Square Footage: 95000
Brands:
Arp
Permaclean
Resinol

29493 Spartech Industries
260 Rexdale Boulevard
Etobicoke, ON M9W 1R2
Canada 416-744-4220
Fax: 416-744-2464
Buckets, pails and containers
President: Robert Hanlin
VP: Bob Connely
Number Employees: 100-249
Parent Co: Hamlin

29494 Spartech Plastics
1444 S Tyler Rd
Wichita, KS 67209 316-722-8621
Fax: 316-722-4875 www.spartech.com
Sheet and roll plastics and plastic film
Plant Manager: Steve Zubke
Estimated Sales: $20-50 Million
Number Employees: 100-249
Square Footage: 60000
Parent Co: Atlas Alchem
Type of Packaging: Bulk

29495 Spartech Plastics
1325 Adams St
Portage, WI 53901 608-742-7123
Fax: 608-745-1703 800-998-7123
www.spartech.com
Extruder of plastic sheet and rollstock
VP: Steven J Ploeger
Quality Control: Tim Hofp
Marketing: Kurt Kassner
Sales: Scott Eaton
Operations: Don Asch
Plant Manager: Don Asch
Purchasing: Jay Eggleston
Estimated Sales: $20-50 Million
Number Employees: 100-249
Square Footage: 170000
Parent Co: Spartech Plastics

29496 Spartech Poly Com
120 South Central Avenue
Suite 1700
Clayton, MI 63105-1705 314-721-4242
Fax: 314-721-1447 888-721-4242
mark.garretson@spartech.com
www.spartech.com
Compounder of PVC for tubing & other applications
Manager: Nate Sofer
CEO: Natehen Sofer
Marketing/Sales: Mark Garretson
Estimated Sales: $10-20 Million
Number Employees: 20-49
Number of Products: 250
Parent Co: Spartech Corporation

29497 Spear Label
5510 Courseview Dr
Mason, OH 45040-2385 513-459-1100
Fax: 513-459-1362 800-627-7327
info@spearsystem.com www.spearsystem.com
Pressure-sensitive labeling systems, self-adhesive film
VP Marketing: Dan Muenzer
Estimated Sales: $200 Million
Number Employees: 700

29498 SpecTape, Inc.
2771 Circleport Dr
Erlanger, KY 41018 859-283-2044
Fax: 859-283-2068 www.spectape.com
Pressure sensitive tape
President: Maurice J Halpin Iv
Quality Control: Maury Halpin Jr
Production Manager: Leo Henrichs
Estimated Sales: Below $5 Million
Number Employees: 10-19
Square Footage: 120000

29499 Special Events Supply Company
P.O.Box 12415
Hauppauge, NY 11788
Fax: 631-436-7715 specialevt@aol.com
www.specialevt.com
Promotional goods including display equipment, banners and pennants
Estimated Sales: $300,000-500,000
Number Employees: 1-4

29500 Special Products
1526 South Enterprise
Springfield, MO 65804 417-881-6114
Fax: 417-881-7314 cs@fhfoodequipment.com
www.fhfoodequipment.com
Brushes, centrifuge parts and fittings, flow meters, homogenizers, pumps, thermometers and valves
Owner: Wilbur Feagan
Manager: Dennis Wiggins
Inside Sales Manager: Stacy Toal
Purchasing Manager: Bob Collins
Estimated Sales: Below $5 Million
Number Employees: 1-4
Parent Co: Mid-America Dairymen

29501 Specialized Packaging London
5 Cuddy Boulevard
London, ON N5W 5R6
Canada 519-659-7011
Fax: 519-452-3197 robert.gariepy@spgroup.com
www.spgroup.com
Litho-printed cutter boxes and folding cartons for food, beverage, paper and personal care products
President: Carlton Highsmith
Site Manager: Don Gray
CFO: Lamaemig Rosekrans
Quality Control: Scott Laking
Director Operations: Robert Gariepy
Number Employees: 200
Parent Co: Lawson Mardon Group
Brands:
Pakastrip

29502 Specialty Blades
9 Technology Drive
PO Box 3166
Staunton, VA 24402-3166 540-248-2200
Fax: 540-248-4400 sales@specialtyblades.com
www.specialtyblades.com
Manufacturer and exporter of custom made industrial-duty food blades including stainless, high-speed and tool steel or carbide; also, prototyping available
President: Alan Connor
Chairman: Martin Lightsey
President, Chief Executive Officer: Peter Harris
Vice President of Quality: Jeff Crist
Vice President of Marketing: Chip Harvill
Account Manager: Jim Kivlighan
Estimated Sales: $8.5 Million
Number Employees: 50-99
Square Footage: 160000
Type of Packaging: Consumer, Food Service, Private Label, Bulk

29503 Specialty Box & Packaging Company
1040 Broadway
Albany, NY 12204 518-465-7344
Fax: 518-465-7347 800-283-2247
wrapit@acmenet.net www.specialtybox.com
Packaging
President: Eric Fialkoff
Vice President: Jason Fialkoff
Graphic Design/Print Media: Jessica L. Jones
Business Office Manager: Daphne Playotes
Estimated Sales: $5-10 Million
Number Employees: 5-9

29504 Specialty Cheese Group Limited
24 King Street
Apt 4
New York, NY 10014-4937 212-243-7274
Fax: 212-243-0807 cheesenyc@aol.com
Consultant specializing in new product development for cheese; also, retail buying, training and merchandising services for supermarkets, wholesalers and manufacturers available
President: Lynne Edelson
Number Employees: 1

29505 Specialty Commodities Inc.
1530 47th St N
Fargo, ND 58102 919-606-4868
cinman@sci-fargo.com
www.specialtycommodities.com
Manufacturer and importer of specialty ingredients for snack food, dairy, bakery, cereal, energy bar and confectionery. Products include dehydrated, dried fruit, legumes, nuts, seeds, spices and grains.
CEO/Merchandiser: Larry Leitner
Import/Export Documentation: Rose Althoff
Export Sales: Mia Macatula
VP Sales & Marketing: Carole Inman
Warehouse/Transportation Manager: Dean Schwab
Estimated Sales: $18 Million
Number Employees: 35
Type of Packaging: Private Label, Bulk

29506 Specialty Equipment Company
1415 Mendota Heights Rd
Mendota Heights, MN 55120 651-452-7909
Fax: 651-452-0681 sales@specialtyequip.com
www.specialtyequip.com
Manufacturer, importer and exporter of high pressure washing equipment
CEO: Sheldon Russell
President: Bryan Russell
Estimated Sales: $20-50 Million
Number Employees: 20-49
Square Footage: 70000
Type of Packaging: Consumer, Bulk

29507 (HQ)Specialty Equipment Company
Ste 301
3 Farm Glen Blvd
Farmington, CT 06032-1981 630-585-5111
Fax: 630-585-9450
jrhodenbaugh@specialty-equipment.com
www.specialtyequipment.com
Manufacturer and exporter of commerical and catering food service, worldwide
Director Financial Services: Doug Johnson
Estimated Sales: $257 Million
Number Employees: 1
Type of Packaging: Food Service
Other Locations:
Specialty Equipment Cos.
Etten-leur
Brands:
Beverage Air
Bloomfield Industries
Carter Hoffmann
Gamko
Nova
Taylor Company
Wells Manufacturing
World Dryer

29508 Specialty Equipment Corporation
1221 Adkins Rd
Houston, TX 77055 713-467-1818
Fax: 713-467-9130 800-654-1792
info@specialtyequipment.com
www.specialtyequipment.com
Manufacture of conveyors and liquid/solids filling systems
Owner: Mike Seiver
VP: Carlton Rickard
Sales Manager: Kevin Calelly
Operations: Francis Kryst
Plant Manager: Dennis Mayo
Number Employees: 20-49

29509 Specialty Films & Associates
2000 Arbor Tech Dr
Hebron, KY 41048 859-647-4100
Fax: 859-647-4105 800-984-3346
info@specialtyfilms.com
www.specialtyfilms.com
Plastic flexible packaging products including vacuum, zipper and stand-up pouches; also, forming and nonforming film including vertical form/fill/seal
President: Jane Dirr-Cherot
CEO: Tony Cherot
Estimated Sales: $20 - 50 Million
Number Employees: 50
Square Footage: 40000
Brands:
Spec-Bar
Spec-Flex
Spec-Plus
Spec-Up
Spec-Vac
Spec-Zip

29510 Specialty Food America
5055 Huffman Mill Rd
Hopkinsville, KY 42240 270-889-0017
888-881-1633
customerservice@specialtyfoodamerica.com
www.specialtyfoodamerica.com
Herbs and spices; cooking related supplies and contract packaging
Owner: Tom Marshall
Estimated Sales: Below $5 Million
Number Employees: 1-4
Square Footage: 4800
Type of Packaging: Consumer, Private Label
Brands:
Lucini Honestete
Sonoma Syrups

29511 Specialty Lubricants Corporation
8300 Corporate Park Dr
Macedonia, OH 44056 330-425-2567
Fax: 330-425-9637 800-238-5823
steve@speclubes.com www.speclubes.com
Food grade lubricants; contract packaging for private labeling
Manager: Kathy Turner
COO: Sherry Bugenske
R&D: Stve Bugenske
Quality Control: Keith Lahrmer
Marketing Director: Steve Bugenske
Sales Director: Rick Beichner
Plant Manager: Chuck Turner
Purchasing Manager: Marge Bugenske
Estimated Sales: $10 - 20 Million
Number Employees: 1-4
Number of Brands: 1
Number of Products: 8
Square Footage: 34520
Type of Packaging: Private Label
Brands:
Huskey Specialty Lubricants

29512 Specialty Packaging
3250 W Seminary Dr
Fort Worth, TX 76133 817-922-9727
Fax: 817-922-8262 800-284-7722
www.bagsandwrap.com
Food service paper bags and wrap
President: Hank Dorris IV
R&D: Herman Chenezert
Estimated Sales: $10 - 20 Million
Number Employees: 50-99

29513 Specialty Paper Bag Company
537 Tiffany Street
Bronx, NY 10474-6615 718-893-8888
Fax: 718-893-5662
Plain and printed bags including bread, food, kraft paper and plastic
Foreman: Brian Birchall
Number Employees: 18

29514 Specialty Saw
30 Wolcott Rd
Simsbury, CT 06070 860-658-4419
Fax: 860-651-5358 800-225-0772
info@specialtysaw.com www.specialtysaw.com
Band saws, carbide-tipped saw and high speed steel blades, saw machinery and coolants
Owner: David B Nagy
Estimated Sales: $3 Million
Number Employees: 10-19

29515 (HQ)Specialty Wood Products
PO Box 455
Clanton, AL 35046 205-755-6016
Fax: 205-755-3678 800-322-5343
info@specwood.com www.specwood.com
Store fixtures and gift baskets
President: Bonny Smith
Estimated Sales: Below $5 Million
Number Employees: 20-49
Type of Packaging: Food Service

29516 Specific Mechanical Systems
6848 Kirkpatrick Crescent
Victoria, BC V8M 1Z9
Canada 250-652-2111
Fax: 250-652-6010 info@specific.net
www.specificmechanical.com
Manufacturer and exporter of stainless steel process and storage tanks, pressure vessels and mixers
President and CEO: Phil Zacharias
CFO: Bill Cumming
Engineering Manager: Tom Goldbach
Quality Control: Darren Combs
Sales Director: Blaine Clouston
Plant Manager: Bill Cummings
Estimated Sales: Below $5 Million
Number Employees: 40
Square Footage: 72000

29517 Spectratek Technologies
5405 Jandy Pl
Los Angeles, CA 90066 310-822-2400
Fax: 310-822-2660 888-442-6567
mkelem@spectratek.net www.spectratek.net
Holographic film and glitter
President: Michael Wanlass
CFO: Michael Dedonaco
Estimated Sales: $10 - 20 Million
Number Employees: 20-49

29518 Spectro
1515 Us Highway 281
Marble Falls, TX 78654-4507 830-798-8786
Fax: 830-798-8467 800-580-6608
inquiry@spectro-tx.com www.spectro.com
Manufacturer and exporter of X-ray fluorescent elemental analyzers
Manager: Robert Bartek
Marketing Communications Manager: Gisela Becker
VP Sales/Marketing: Phil Almquist
Estimated Sales: $3 - 5 Million
Number Employees: 5-9
Square Footage: 120000

29519 Spectronics Corporation
P.O.Box 483
Westbury, NY 11590 516-333-4840
Fax: 516-333-4859 800-274-8888
www.spectroline.com
Manufactures a variety of ultraviolet lamps useful to the foodand beverage industry
President: Jonathan Cooper

Estimated Sales: $30 Million
Number Employees: 200

29520 Spectrum Ascona
1305 Fraser St
Suite D2
Bellingham, WA 98229-5800 360-647-0877
Fax: 360-734-8106 800-356-1473
mail@asconapkg.com www.asconapkg.com
Bags, boxes, ribbons, cups, gift basket supplies, shrink wrapping equiment, and films
Owner: Bruce Maynard
Estimated Sales: $1-2.5 Million
Number Employees: 1-4

29521 Spectrum Enterprises
3220 Kratzville Road
Evansville, IN 47710-3357 812-425-1771
Fax: 812-425-1637
Rubber stamps and pads
General Manager: Thomas Evans
Estimated Sales: Less than $500,000
Number Employees: 4

29522 Spectrum Plastics
3311 S Jones Boulevard
Suite 209
Las Vegas, NV 89146-6775 702-876-8650
Fax: 702-876-8260
Custom and standard plastic bags

29523 Spee-Dee Packaging Machinery
P.O.Box 656
Sturtevant, WI 53177 262-886-4402
Fax: 262-886-5502 877-387-5212
info@spee-dee.com www.spee-dee.com
Manufacturer and exporter of volumetric cup-type and auger filling equipment for powders, granulars and pastes
President: James P Navin
Vice President: Timm Johnson
Operations Manager: Paul Navin
Estimated Sales: Below $5 Million
Number Employees: 20-49
Square Footage: 10000
Brands:
Digitronic
Spee-Dee

29524 Speedrack Products GroupLtd.
7903 Venture Ave NW
Sparta, MI 49345-9427 616-887-0002
Fax: 616-887-2693 sales@speedrack.net
www.speedrack.net
Storage racks including adjustable tubular and structural steel
Owner: Ron Ducharme
CFO: H W Baird
CEO: Ron Ducharme
Marketing Director: Butch Newland
Estimated Sales: $30 - 50 Million
Number Employees: 20-49
Square Footage: 280000

29525 Speedways Conveyors
PO Box 9
Lancaster, NY 14086-0009 716-893-2222
Fax: 716-893-3067 800-800-1022
dbuckley@speedwaysconveyors.com
www.speedwaysconveyors.com
Aluminum conveyors including gravity, powered, pallet flow and line shaft; exporter of pallet flow systems
Executive VP: John Jacobowitz
VP Sales: Daniel Buckley
Estimated Sales: $5-10 Million
Number Employees: 50-99
Square Footage: 440000
Type of Packaging: Consumer, Food Service
Brands:
C-Square
Clean Wheel
Q-50

29526 Spencer Business Form Company
PO Box 229
Spencer, WV 25276 304-372-8877
Fax: 304-372-8902 sbfco@aol.com
Rubber stamps and office supplies
President: Milton S Griffith
Estimated Sales: $300,000-500,000
Number Employees: 5

29527 Spencer Research
1290 Grandview Ave
Columbus, OH 43212-3439 614-488-3123
Fax: 614-421-1154 800-488-3242
www.spencerresearch.com
Consultant specializing in consumer testing for technical product development providing sensory testing, statistical experimental design and analysis
Owner: George Maynard
President: Betty Spencer
Estimated Sales: $5 - 10 Million
Number Employees: 20-49
Square Footage: 30000

29528 Spencer Strainer Systems
6205 Gheens Mill Rd
Jeffersonville, IN 47130 812-282-6300
Fax: 812-282-7272 800-801-4977
spencer@spencerstrainer.com
www.spencerstrainer.com
MIG and TIG welding, general machining, drilling, boring, cutting, surface grinding, mill and lathe work; stainless steel filtration systems; Spencer strainer system
President: Glenn Spencer
Number Employees: 5-9

29529 Spencer Turbine Company
600 Day Hill Rd
Windsor, CT 06095 860-688-8361
Fax: 860-688-0098 800-232-4321
marketing@spencer-air.com
www.spencerturbine.com
Manufacturer and exporter of central vacuum systems, tubing, fittings and centrifugal blowers; also, air and gas handling equipment, air knives and pressure fans
President/CEO: Mike Walther
VP: Paul Burdick
Marketing Manager: Janis Cayne
Sales: Jim Yablonski
Estimated Sales: $20 - 50 Million
Number Employees: 130
Square Footage: 200000
Brands:
Dirt Eraser
Fume Eraser
Industravac
Jet-Clean
Power Mizer
Sump-Vac
Top Hat
Vortex

29530 Sperling Boss
51 Station Street
Box 100
Sperling, MB R0G 2M0 204-626-3401
Fax: 204-626-3252 877-626-3401
sperling@sperlingind.com www.sperlingind.com
Designs, manufactures, and installs equipment and building for the beef and hog processing industry.
Manager: Jeff Nicolajsen

29531 Sperling Industries
2420 Z St
Omaha, NE 68107-4430 402-556-4070
Fax: 402-556-2927 800-647-5062
sperling@sperlingind.com www.sperlingind.com
Meat and food processing equipment; exporter of meat packing house equipment
President: Craig Ellett
Manager: Jeff Nicolajsen
Estimated Sales: $3 - 5 Million
Number Employees: 10-19
Square Footage: 3500
Parent Co: Cincinnati-Boss Company

29532 Sperling Industries U.S.A.
2420 Z Street
Omaha, NE 68107-4430 402-556-4070
Fax: 402-556-2927 800-647-5062
ronb@sperlingomaha.com www.sperlingind.com
Meat rail equipment and accessories, conveyor systems and accessories, architects and engineers, consultants, on-rail kill systems and accessories
President: Craig Ellett
CFO: Craig Ellett
R & D: Russel Nicolajsen
Estimated Sales: $3 - 5 Million
Number Employees: 10-19

29533 Sphinx Adsorbents
53 Progress Ave
Springfield, MA 01104 413-736-5020
Fax: 413-736-8257 800-388-0157
info@muthassociates.com muthassociates.com
Wholesaler/distributor of adsorbent materials
President: Douglas C Muth
CEO: Doug Muth
CFO: Sandra Peterson
Estimated Sales: $5-10 Million
Number Employees: 1-4
Number of Products: 300
Square Footage: 26000
Type of Packaging: Private Label, Bulk
Brands:
Desi-Pak
Sorb-It
Tri-Wall

29534 Spicetec Flavors & Seasonings
11 Conagra Drive
Omaha, NE 68102 402-240-4005
800-921-7502
jaime.emanuel@conagrafoods.com
www.spicetec.com
President/Consumer Foods: Andr, Hawaux
CEO: Gary Rodkin
EVP/CFO: John Gehring
EVP: Colleen Batcheler
EVP, Research, Quality & Innovation: Al Bolles
President/Commercial Foods: Paul Maass
EVP/Chief Marketing Officer: Joan Chow
President/ConAgra Foods Sales: Doug Knudsen
SVP/Human Resources: Nicole Theophilus
Plant Manager: Liam Doherty
Number Employees: 10-19
Parent Co: ConAgra Foods

29535 Spin-Tech Corporation
1024 Adams St
Suite A
Hoboken, NJ 07030 201-659-6110
Fax: 201-963-7674 800-977-4692
spinware_products@worldnet.att.net
www.spinwareproducts.com
Beverage fountains, candelabra, serving trays and liquid fuel candles; exporter of beverage fountains, table candles and floral holders
Owner: Frank Pasquale
Estimated Sales: $1-2.5 Million
Number Employees: 5-9
Square Footage: 25000

29536 Spinco Metal Products
1 Country Club Dr
Newark, NY 14513 315-331-6285
Fax: 315-331-9535 cthayer@spincometal.com
www.spincometal.com
Manufacturer and exporter of copper refrigeration components, brass flow metering devices and stainless steel beverage lines, welded and brazed assemblies, cut to length tubing
President: Robert C Straubing
Engineering/Quality Manager: David Gardner
Quality Assurance Coordinator: Craig Thayer
Inside Sales: Connie Rios
Estimated Sales: $10-20 Million
Number Employees: 100-249
Square Footage: 60000

29537 Spinzer
799 Roosevelt Road
Bldg 6
Glen Ellyn, IL 60137-5908 630-469-7184
Fax: 630-469-7185 spinzer@earthlink.net
www.spinzer.us/
Stirrers for hot and cold beverages, drinking straws
Estimated Sales: 100000
Number of Brands: 1
Number of Products: 2
Parent Co: SPINZER OFFICE SUPPLIES
Type of Packaging: Consumer, Bulk

29538 Spir-It/Zoo Piks
200 Brickstone Sq # G05
Andover, MA 01810-1439 978-964-1551
Fax: 978-964-1552 800-343-0996
www.spiritbrands.us

Manufacturer and exporter of plastic cutlery, picks, sticks, stirrers, straws and other food service accessories; importer of wooden stirrers and toothpicks
President: Donald McCann
CFO: Peter Maki
VP Sales/Marketing: Joe Pierro
Sales/Marketing Manager: Marva White
Number Employees: 100-249
Square Footage: 320000
Type of Packaging: Food Service
Other Locations:
Spir-It/Zoo Piks
Dallas TX
Brands:
Glassips
Hob Nob
Oakhill
Spir-It

29539 **Spiral Biotech**
2 Technology Way
Norwood, MA 02062 781-320-9000
Fax: 781-320-8181 800-554-1620
mail@aicompanies.com www.spiralbiotech.com
Manufacturer and exporter of laboratory equipment including fast sample dilutors, spiral platers, automated plate counters and colony counting systems; importer of microbial air samplers and filter bags; wholesaler/distributor ofmicrobial air samplers
President: John Coughlin
VP Operations: P Emond
Estimated Sales: $10 - 20 Million
Number Employees: 50-99
Square Footage: 3000
Parent Co: Advanced Instruments
Brands:
Autoplate 4000
Casba Ii
Casba Iv
Labpro Gravimetric

29540 **Spiral Manufacturing Company**
11419 Yellow Pine St NW
Minneapolis, MN 55448 763-755-7677
Fax: 763-755-6184 800-426-3643
info@spiralmfg.com www.spiralmfg.com
Manufacturer and exporter of commercial and industrial HVAC, ventilation, air conditioning and pneumatic conveying, dust and fume collection distribution systems
President: Tom Menth
Estimated Sales: $5 - 10 Million
Number Employees: 10-19

29541 **Spiral Slices Ham Market**
1930 Division St
Detroit, MI 48207-2153 313-259-6262
Fax: 313-259-4219
Manufacturer and distributor of vertical ham slicing machines
Owner: Don Bonanno
Estimated Sales: Below $5 Million
Number Employees: 1-4

29542 **Spiral Systems**
8630 Farley Way
Fair Oaks, CA 95668 916-852-0177
Fax: 916-966-7771 800-998-6111
info@spiralsystems.com www.spiralsystems.com

29543 **Spiral-Matic**
7772 Park Pl
Brighton, MI 48116 248-486-9700
Fax: 248-486-5081 contact@spiralmatic.com
www.spiralmatic.com
Slicing blades, slicers
Manager: Bill Mc Phail
Estimated Sales: $1-2.5 Million
Number Employees: 1-4
Square Footage: 20

29544 **Spirax Sarco**
1150 Northpoint Blvd.
Blythewood, SC 29016 412-310-9911
Fax: 803-714-2222 800-575-0394
insidesalesleads@spirax.com
www.spiraxsarco.com/usa
Air eliminators
Regional Manager: Ed Beedle
Branch Manager: Steve Williams
Estimated Sales: Below $5 Million
Number Employees: 1-4
Number of Products: 12
Square Footage: 103000
Type of Packaging: Private Label

29545 **Spirit Foodservice, Inc.**
200 Brickstone Square
Suite G-05
Andover, MA 01810 978-964-1551
Fax: 978-964-1552 800-343-0996
sales@spir-it.com www.spiritfoodservice.com
Manufacturer and exporter of plastic swizzle sticks, picks, napkin holders, tip trays, napkins, drinking straws and disposable drinkware; also, custom imprinting available
Estimated Sales: $5-10 Million
Number Employees: 100-249
Brands:
Zoo

29546 **Spirocut Equipment**
3005 Bledsoe Street
Fort Worth, TX 76107 817-877-3266
Fax: 817-877-3742 888-887-4267
info@spirocut.com www.spirocut.com
Meat slicers
President: Thomas Misfeldt
Estimated Sales: $1 Million
Number Employees: 8
Square Footage: 2200

29547 **Spiroflow Systems**
1609 Airport Road
Monroe, NC 28110 704-246-0900
Fax: 704-291-9594 info@spiroflowsystems.com
www.spiroflowsystems.com
Manager: Marline Carlisle
Estimated Sales: Below $5 Million
Number Employees: 20-49

29548 **Spokane House of Hose**
5520 E Sprague Ave
Spokane Valley, WA 99212-0880 509-535-3638
Fax: 800-541-4673 800-541-6351
sales@spokanehose.com www.spokanehose.com
Full color menu cards
Owner: Larry Hayden
Estimated Sales: $1-2.5 Million
Number Employees: 5-9

29549 **Spontex**
100 Spontex Dr
Columbia, TN 38401 931-388-5632
Fax: 931-490-2105 800-251-4222
sales@mapaglove.com www.spontexusa.com
Cellulose sponges, scrubbers, and rubber gloves
President: Peter Moeller
CFO: Greg Grmez
Quality Control: Dewitt Loexton
R&D: Rick Mallernebb
VP Sales: T Gladfelter
VP Manufacturing: R Schmidt
Purchasing Manager: Cindy Brindley
Estimated Sales: $50 - 75 Million
Number Employees: 100-249
Square Footage: 193000
Parent Co: Hutchinson SA
Brands:
Spontex

29550 **Sportsmen's Cannery & Smokehouse**
182 Bayfront Loop
Winchester Bay, OR 97467 541-271-3293
Fax: 541-271-9381 800-457-8048
karch@presys.com www.sportsmenscannery.com
Processor and canner of salmon, albacore tuna, sturgeon and shellfish
Manager: Brandy Roelle
Owner: Mikayle Karcher
Number Employees: 1-4
Type of Packaging: Consumer, Private Label
Brands:
Winchester

29551 **Spot Wire Works Company**
413 Green St
Philadelphia, PA 19123 215-627-6124
Fax: 215-627-0950
Stainless steel and wire shelves, trays and display racks; also, wire parts and guards
President: Eli Brownstein
Estimated Sales: $10-20 Million
Number Employees: 10-19
Square Footage: 10000

29552 **Spray Drying Systems**
5320 Enterprise St Ste J
Eldersberg, MD 21784 410-549-8090
Fax: 410-549-8091 sales@spraydrysys.com
www.spraydrysys.com
Manufacturer and exporter of spray dryers
President: Ronald Bayliss
Quality Control: Jess Bayliss
Vice President: Jeff Bayliss
Estimated Sales: Below $5 Million
Number Employees: 10-19
Square Footage: 3500

29553 **Spray Dynamics, Ltd**
108 Bolte Ln
Saint Clair, MO 63077 636-629-7366
Fax: 636-629-7455 800-260-7366
spraydynamics@heatandcontrol.com
www.spraydynamics.com
Manufacturer and exporter of liquid and dry ingredient applicators and dispensers for food processing machinery.
Owner: Dave Holmeyer
Accounts Payable: Melanie Booher
Marketing Coordinator: Stephanie Butenhoff
Sales Representative: George Wipperfurth
Service Manager: Craig Booher
Estimated Sales: $2.5-5 Million
Number Employees: 20-49
Brands:
Clog-Free Slurry Spray Encoater
Delta Dry
Delta Liquid
Econoflo
Enhancer
Master Series
Meter Master
Micro-Meter Airless
Powder Xpress
Soft Flight
Unispense

29554 **Spray Master Technologies**
112 E Linden St
Rogers, AR 72756-6035 479-636-5776
Fax: 479-636-3245 800-548-3373
steve@assembledproducts.com
www.assembledproducts.com
President: George Panter
Estimated Sales: $1 - 5 Million
Number Employees: 100-249

29555 **Spray-Tek**
344 Cedar Ave
Middlesex, NJ 08846 732-469-0050
Fax: 732-302-0866
Spray drying
CEO and President: Mark Epstein
VP: David Brand
Estimated Sales: $20 - 50 Million
Number Employees: 50-99

29556 **SprayMaster Technologies**
112 E Linden St
Rogers, AR 72756-6035 479-636-5776
Fax: 479-636-3245 800-548-3373
apc@assembledproducts.com
www.assembledproducts.com
Manufacturer and exporter of pressure washers
President: George Panter
Vice President: Bob Sage
Marketing Director: Steve Scroggins
Sales Director: Kent Langum
Plant Manager: R Smith
Purchasing Manager: Don McKenzie
Estimated Sales: $20 - 30 Million
Number Employees: 100-249
Square Footage: 123000
Parent Co: Assembled Pro Corporation
Brands:
Spraymaster

29557 **Spraying Systems Company**
North Avenueand Schmale Road
PO Box 7900
Wheaton, IL 60187 630-655-5000
Fax: 630-260-0842 info@spray.com
www.spray.com

Manufacturer and exporter of nozzles, spray guns, portable spray systems and spray nozzle accessories including connectors, ball fittings, valves, regulators, etc
President/CEO: James Bramsen
VP Manufacturing: Don Fox
VP/COO: Dave Smith
Sr Applications Engineer: Wes Bartell

29558 Spraymation
5320 NW 35th Ave
Fort Lauderdale, FL 33309-6314 954-484-9700
Fax: 954-484-9778 800-327-4985
sales@spraymation.com www.spraymation.com
Standard and Custom designed hot melt, cold adesive and fluid dispensing equipment, featuring Electromatic Applicator Heads for the application of beads, dots, spray patterns and slot coating; DC Pattern Controllers, Pumping Systemsand Temperature Control Units
President: Eric J Cocks Sr
R&D: David Kerzel
Quality Control: Ken Jones
Estimated Sales: Below $5 Million
Number Employees: 20-49

29559 Sprayway
1005 S Westgate St
Addison, IL 60101 630-628-3000
Fax: 630-543-7797 800-332-9000
ohernandez@spraywayinc.com
www.spraywayinc.com
Manufacturer and exporter of aerosol products including all purpose and glass cleaners, dust control sprays and insecticides
President: Michael Rohl
VP Sales/Marketing: Bob Potvin
Estimated Sales: $10 - 20 Million
Number Employees: 100-249
Number of Brands: 1
Square Footage: 80000
Type of Packaging: Private Label
Brands:
Crazy Clean
Dust Up
Sprayway
Tru-Nox

29560 Spring Air Systems
1464 Cornwall Road
Unit 9
Oakville, ON L6J 7W5
Canada 905-338-2999
Fax: 905-338-0179 866-874-4505
info@springairsystemsinc.com
www.springairsystems.com
Specializes in kitchen ventilation systems
Number Employees: 10

29561 Spring Cove Container
PO Box 12
Roaring Spring, PA 16673 814-224-2222
Fax: 814-224-5783 scc@roaringspring.com
www.springcove.com
Corrugated cartons
Sales: P Adams
Plant Manager: Johnathen Sneed
Estimated Sales: $20-50 Million
Number Employees: 20-49
Parent Co: Roaring Spring Blank Book Company

29562 Spring USA Corporation
127 Ambassador Dr Ste 147
Naperville, IL 60540 630-527-8600
Fax: 630-527-8677 800-535-8974
springusa@springusa.com www.springusa.com
Products range from chafing dishes to professional cookware, from induction ranges to coffee urns.
President: Tom Brija
Sales/Marketing Supervisor: Kelly Boyle
Estimated Sales: $2.5-5,000,000
Number Employees: 5-9
Parent Co: Spring Switzerland
Brands:
Blackline
Brigade
Brigade +
Endurance
Flix
Mr. Induction
Vulcano

29563 Spring Wood Products
4267 Austin Rd
Geneva, OH 44041 440-466-1135
Fax: 440-466-1138
Wooden pallets and shipping containers
CEO: Jacob Castrilla
VP: Gregory Castrilla
VP: Thomas Castrilla
Estimated Sales: $2.5-5 Million
Number Employees: 20-49

29564 (HQ)Springer-Penguin
PO Box 199
Mount Vernon, NY 10552-0199 914-699-3200
Fax: 914-699-3231 800-835-8500
jspringer21@juno.com
www.springerpenguin.com
Manufacturer and exporter of refrigerators, file cabinets and wood office furniture including conference tables, bookcases, etc.; importer of wooden bookcases
Number Employees: 10
Square Footage: 80000
Brands:
Penguin

29565 Springfield Metal Products Company
8 Commerce St
Springfield, NJ 07081-2983 973-379-4600
Fax: 973-379-7314
jd.sommer@springfieldmetalproducts.com
www.springfieldmetalproducts.com
Sheet metal and structural fabrications in stainless steel and aluminum
President: John D Sommer
VP/Secretary: Irene Powell
Estimated Sales: Below $5 Million
Number Employees: 10-19
Square Footage: 6000

29566 Springport Steel Wire Products
4325 Mann Rd
Concord, MI 49237 517-857-3010
Fax: 517-857-3292 info@sigmawire.com
www.sigmawire.com
Manufacturer and exporter of handling equipment including containers, pallets, wire and mesh shelving and conveyor guards
Estimated Sales: $2.5-5 Million
Number Employees: 20-50
Brands:
Wire Dek
Wiretainer

29567 Springprint Medallion
1431 Marvin Griffin Road
Augusta, GA 30906-3852 800-543-5990
Fax: 800-982-6434
Custom printed place mats, napkins, coasters and tray covers
VP Sales/Marketing: Layne Allen
VP Converting Operations: Eric Simmons
Number Employees: 2
Parent Co: Marcal Paper Mills

29568 Sprinkman Corporation
PO Box 390
Franksville, WI 53126-0390 262-835-2390
Fax: 262-835-4325 800-816-1610
info@sprinkman.com www.sprinkman.com
Wholesaler/distributor of dairy and food processing equipment and supplies; consultant specializing in the design processing systems; also, installation and reconditioning services available
Chief Operating Officer: Robert Sprinkman
CFO: Dale Metcoff
President: Brian Sprinkman
Vice President: Merlin Winchell
Estimated Sales: $30 Million
Number Employees: 100
Square Footage: 35000
Parent Co: W.M. Sprinkman Corporation

29569 Sprinter Marking
1805 Chandlersville Rd
Zanesville, OH 43701 740-453-1000
Fax: 740-453-6750 sales@sprintermarking.com
www.sprintermarking.com
Automatic ink code dating and marking machinery for cups
President: Bob Bishop
CEO: Bob Bishop
Estimated Sales: $1-5 Million
Number Employees: 1-4
Square Footage: 6000
Brands:
Sprinter

29570 Sprouts Farmers Market
11811 N. Tatum Rd.
Suite 2400
Phoenix, AZ 85028 480-814-8016
Fax: 480-814-8017 888-577-7688
www.sprouts.com
Specialty and natural foods supermarket chain with over 100 stores in Arizona, California, Colorado, and Texas. Founded in 2002. Has two manufacturing facilities listed below.
President & Chief Executive Officer: Doug Sanders
Director: Shon Boney
Chief Financial Officer: Amin Maredia
Chief Operating Officer: Jim Nielsen
Estimated Sales: $1.8 Billion
Number Employees: 13200
Square Footage: 28000
Other Locations:
Manufacturing Facility
Chandler AZ
Manufacturing Facilty - Dairy
El Cajon CA
Brands:
Country Kitchen Meals
Henry's Heritage Bread
Sprouts
Sunflower

29571 Spudnik Equipment
584 West 100 North
PO Box 1045
Blackfoot, ID 83221-1045 208-785-0480
Fax: 208-785-1497 www.spudnik.us
Manufacturer and exporter of potato handling equipment and parts including pliers, scoopers, conveyors, sorters, bins, bulk beds, van unloaders, semi-trailers, etc
CEO: Rolf Geier
Sales Manager: Dennis Schumacker
Engineering Manager: Andrew Blight
Estimated Sales: $10-20 Million
Number Employees: 10-19
Square Footage: 100000

29572 Spurgeon Company
1330 Hilton Rd
Ferndale, MI 48220 248-547-3805
Fax: 248-547-8344 800-396-2554
Manufacturer and exporter of conveyors, unscramblers, aluminum casting and stacking equipment; importer of aluminum casting and stacking equipment
VP: Thomas Woodbeck
VP: Bernie Makie
Estimated Sales: $10-20 Million
Number Employees: 50-99
Square Footage: 100000
Parent Co: Overhead Conveyor Company

29573 (HQ)Spurrier Chemical Companies
PO Box 2812
Wichita, KS 67201-2812 316-265-9491
Fax: 316-265-9518 800-835-1059
info@spurrierchemical.com
www.spurrierchemical.com
Cleaning products including institutional and industrial chemicals and detergents
President: Robin Spurrier
CEO: Robin Spurrier
CFO: Tony DiStefano
Vice President: Donald Ryel
Research & Development: Bruce Lavery
Quality Control: Karen Rowe
VP Distribution Sales & Kansas/Missouri: Marshall Ryel
Sales Director: Kurt Luhmann
Operations Manager: Marcia Ryel
Production Manager: Marcia Ryel
Plant Manager: Todd Hardesty
Purchasing Manager: Jeff Alfaro
Estimated Sales: $10 - 20 Million
Number Employees: 50-99
Square Footage: 60000
Type of Packaging: Food Service, Private Label
Other Locations:
Spurrier Chemical Companies
Clwyd, North Wales

29574 **Squar-Buff**
1000 45th Street
Oakland, CA 94608-3314 510-655-2470
Fax: 510-652-0969 800-525-6955
Manufacturer and exporter of floor and rug cleaning machinery
Number Employees: 5

29575 **Squid Ink Manufacturing**
7041 Boone Avenue North
Brooklyn Park, MN 55428 763-795-8856
Fax: 763-795-8867 800-877-5658
info@squidink.com www.squidink.com
Ink jet coding and inks, coding and marking equipment, and date codes batch numbers product identification
President: William Hoagland
Vice President: Loyd Tarver
Engineering: Chris Miller
Marketing Manager: Chad Carney
Estimated Sales: $5 - 10 Million
Number Employees: 20-49

29576 **(HQ)Squire Corrugated Container Company**
PO Box 405
South Plainfield, NJ 07080 908-561-8550
Fax: 908-561-2791 info@squirebox.com
www.squirebox.com
Corrugated packaging
President: James Beneroff
Sales Manager: James Benneroth
Estimated Sales: $10-20 Million
Number Employees: 100-249

29577 **Squire-Cogswell**
1111 Lakeside Dr
Gurnee, IL 60031 847-855-0500
Fax: 847-855-6391 800-448-0770
mjindra@squire-cogswell.com
www.ohiomedical.com
Filters, air
President: James Koppa
Chairman of the Board: Craig R Schifter
Sales: Martin Jindra
Estimated Sales: $20-50 Million
Number Employees: 100-249

29578 **Squirrel Systems**
3157 Grandview Highway
Vancouver, BC V5M 2E9
Canada 604-412-3300
Fax: 604-434-9888 800-388-6824
squirrel@squirrelsystems.com
www.squirrelsystems.com
Manufacturer and exporter of electronic point of sale terminals
Vice President of Research and Developme: Joe Cortese
Vice President of Corporate Sales: David Atkinson
Estimated Sales: $20 - 30 Million
Number Employees: 100-250
Brands:
Squirrel

29579 **St Joseph Packaging Inc**
PO Box 579
St Joseph, MO 64502-0579 816-233-3181
Fax: 816-233-2475 800-383-3000
www.stjpkg.com
Custom industrial packaging offset/flexo printing, diecut/cello windowing, laminating and direct print on mini-flute corrigated
President: C Hamilton Jr
CFO: Patty Waitkoss
CEO: Brad Keller
Quality Control: Don Kragel
Marketing: Pam Hurley
Plant Manager: Josh Hamilton
Purchasing: Kenny Hayter
Estimated Sales: $15 Million
Square Footage: 110000
Type of Packaging: Consumer, Food Service, Private Label

29580 **St Onge Ruff & Associates**
2400 Pershing Road
Ste 400
Kansas City, MO 64108 816-329-8700
Fax: 816-329-8701 800-800-5261
marketing@transystems.com www.sora.com
Engineering firm specializing in the planning, design and construction of processing and distribution facilities
Number Employees: 5-9

29581 **St. Clair Pakwell**
120 25th Ave
Bellwood, IL 60104-1201 708-547-7500
Fax: 708-547-9052 800-323-1922
www.stclairepakwell.com
Manufacturer and exporter of decorative packaging including wrapping paper
Estimated Sales: $20-50 Million
Number Employees: 100-249
Parent Co: Field Container Corporation
Type of Packaging: Food Service, Bulk

29582 **St. Elizabeth Street Display Corporation**
21 Main Street
West Wing, Suite 349
Hackensack, NJ 07601 201-883-0333
Fax: 201-883-1333 bill@stelizdisp.com
www.stelizdisp.com
Point of sale displays
President: William Talaia
Estimated Sales: Below $5 Million
Number Employees: 20-49

29583 **St. George Crystal**
1101 William Flynn Hwy
Glenshaw, PA 15116-2637 724-523-6501
Fax: 724-523-0707 800-677-0261
www.stgeo.com
Wine industry glassware
President: Richard Rifenburgh
Estimated Sales: $50 - 100 Million
Number Employees: 275

29584 **St. Gobain Performance Plastics**
407 East Street
New Haven, CT 06511-5017 203-777-2822
Fax: 203-787-1725
Pressure sensitive industrial and electrical tapes
Production: Scott Yudkin
Estimated Sales: $10-20 Million
Number Employees: 50-99
Parent Co: Furon

29585 **St. Louis Carton Company**
1620 N Jefferson Ave
Saint Louis, MO 63106 314-241-0990
Fax: 314-241-0991 bobg@stlcarton.com
www.stlcarton.com
Folding paper boxes
President: Bonnie Green
Estimated Sales: $1-2.5 Million
Number Employees: 1-4

29586 **St. Louis Stainless Service**
1736 Rudder Industrial Park Dr
Fenton, MO 63026 636-343-3000
Fax: 636-343-1925 888-507-1578
maryc@stlouisstainless.com
www.stlouisstainless.com
Tables, cabinets, counters, sinks and floor troughs
President: Don Durham
Estimated Sales: $5-10,000,000
Number Employees: 5-9

29587 **St. Pierre Box & LumberCompany**
66 Lovely St
Canton, CT 06019 860-693-2089
Fax: 860-693-6155
Wooden boxes, pallets and steel skids
President: John St Pierre
Estimated Sales: $500,000-$1 Million
Number Employees: 5-9

29588 **St. Tobain Containers**
5801 E Marginal Way S
Seattle, WA 98134-2413 206-762-0660
Fax: 206-768-6266 www.saint-gobain.com
Manufacturer and exporter of glass containers including jars and bottles
Plant Manager: Doug Coburn
Estimated Sales: $100+ Million
Number Employees: 500-999
Type of Packaging: Food Service, Bulk

29589 **Sta-Rite Ginnie Lou**
245 E South 1st St
PO Box 435
Shelbyville, IL 62565 217-774-3921
Fax: 217-774-5234 800-782-7483
sales@sta.riteginnielou.com
www.sta-riteginnielou.com
Manufacturer, importer and exporter of nylon hair nets, hairpins, bobbypins and haircare accessories.
Chairman: Robert Bolinger
CEO: Noel Bolinger
Sales Director: Linda Stewardson
Estimated Sales: $1 Million
Number Employees: 10-19
Number of Brands: 10
Number of Products: 1300
Square Footage: 16000
Type of Packaging: Consumer, Food Service, Private Label, Bulk
Brands:
Ginnie Lou
Sta-Rite

29590 **StaVin**
PO Box 1693
Sausalito, CA 94966 415-331-7849
Fax: 415-331-0516 info@stavin.com
www.stavin.com
Wine industry oak infusion systems
President: Allan Sullivan
General Manager: Jemie Zenk
Estimated Sales: $500,000 - $1 Million
Number Employees: 10-19
Type of Packaging: Private Label

29591 **Staban Engineering Corporation**
65 N Plains Industrial Rd
PO Box 8
Wallingford, CT 06492 203-294-1997
Fax: 203-294-0583 888-782-2261
sales@staban.com www.staban.com
Packaging machinery
President: Dennis Formal
Estimated Sales: $2.5-5 Million
Number Employees: 10-19

29592 **Stablized Products**
1832 W Square Drive
High Ridge, MO 63049-1968 636-677-5764
Fax: 636-376-5811 800-546-7349

29593 **Stackbin Corporation**
29 Powder Hill Rd
Lincoln, RI 02865-4424 401-333-1600
Fax: 401-333-1952 800-333-1603
stackbin@worldnet.att.net www.stackbin.com
Stackable storage systems for small parts
President: William A Shaw
Quality Control and VP: Scott Shaw
Sales Supervisor: Andrew Porter
Estimated Sales: $10 - 20 Million
Number Employees: 10-19

29594 **Stadia Corporation**
691 Corporate Cir
Golden, CO 80401-5622 303-273-0336
Fax: 303-273-1414 800-765-6600
sales@cognitive.com www.cogsol.com
Print and apply labeling equipment
President: Patrick Frinat
Marketing Manager: Vic Barczyk
Number Employees: 100-249

29595 **Staff Lighting**
3300 Us Highway 9w
Highland, NY 12528-2630 845-691-6262
Fax: 845-691-6289
Manufacturer, importer and exporter of lighting fixtures
President: Wolfgang Egger
Sales: Allison Craig
Estimated Sales: $50 - 100 Million
Number Employees: 100-249

29596 **(HQ)Stafford - Smith**
3414 S Burdick St
Kalamazoo, MI 49001 269-343-1240
Fax: 269-343-2509 800-968-2442
djs@staffordsmith.com www.staffordsmith.com
Freezers, dishwashers, ranges, slicers, fryers, refrigeration equipment, etc
President: David J Stafford Sr
Estimated Sales: $50 - 75 Million
Number Employees: 100-249

Other Locations:
Stafford - Smith
Lansing MI

29597 Stahlman Group
P.O.Box 245
New London, NH 03257 603-526-2585
Fax: 603-526-9468 866-526-2585
spribula@stahlman.net www.stahlman.net
Full service engineering, architectural and construction management firm specializing in the food and beverage industry
President: Robert Stahlman
VP: Scott Pribula
Marketing: Scott Pribula
Estimated Sales: $5-10 Million
Number Employees: 50-99
Square Footage: 7500

29598 Stainless
305 Tech Park Drive
Suite 115
La Vergne, TN 37086-3633 954-421-4290
Fax: 954-421-4464 800-877-5177
www.stainless.com
Manufacturer and exporter of stainless steel kitchen and dining room equipment including tables and sinks
VP/General Manager: Edward Umphlette
VP Sales: Tom Kassab
Estimated Sales: Less than $500,000
Number Employees: 4
Square Footage: 920000
Parent Co: Franke USA Holding
Other Locations:
Stainless
Holland MI

29599 Stainless Equipment Manufacturing
5950 Cedar Springs Road
Suite 125
Dallas, TX 75235-6816 214-357-9600
Fax: 214-358-4959 800-736-2038
Metal sinks, counters and work tables for hotels and restaurants
Shop Foreman: Rex Riddle
Plant Manager: Bill Cross
Purchasing Agent: Patricia Corder
Estimated Sales: $5 - 10 Million
Number Employees: 35
Parent Co: White Swan

29600 Stainless Fabricating Company
860 Navajo St
Denver, CO 80204-4317 303-573-1700
Fax: 303-573-3776 800-525-8966
stafadball@stafad.com www.stafad.com
Stainless steel counters, tabletops, dish tables, shelving and sinks
President: Jeff Manion
Estimated Sales: $5-10 Million
Number Employees: 20-49

29601 Stainless Fabrication
4455 W. Kearney
PO Box 1127
Springfield, MO 65801 417-865-5696
Fax: 417-865-7863 800-397-8265
sfi-info@stainlessfab.com www.stainlessfab.com
Design and manufacture high quality, custom, shop and field fabricated stainless steel processing equipment including tanks, dryers, reaactors, columns, sanitary processing tunnels and other vessels
President: Claude Mizell
Estimated Sales: $16 Million
Number Employees: 100-249
Square Footage: 45000

29602 Stainless International
2650 Mercantile Dr Ste C
Rancho Cordova, CA 95742 916-638-7370
Fax: 916-638-1172 888-300-6196
www.all-stainless.com
Stainless steel hoods, under counter bar equipment, sinks, dish tables and counters; also, custom fabrication services available
President: Ted Lambertson
CFO: Monica Lambertson
Estimated Sales: $2.5-5 Million
Number Employees: 20-49

29603 Stainless Motors Inc
7601 Nita Place NE
Rio Rancho, NM 87144 505-867-0224
info@stainlessmotors.com
www.stainlessmotors.com
Stainless steel power transmission equipment
Engineering: John Oleson
Sales/Customer Service: Gene Filion
Marketing/Human Resources: Lori Costa
Estimated Sales: $1.2 Million
Number Employees: 12
Square Footage: 22000

29604 Stainless One DispensingSystem
790 Eubanks Drive
Vacaville, CA 95688-9470 800-722-6738
Fax: 707-448-1521 888-723-3827
autobar@aol.com www.stainlessone.com
Manufacturer and exporter of beer dispensing equipment
VP: Clark Smith
Number Employees: 3
Brands:
Perfect Pour
Stainless One

29605 Stainless Products
1649 72nd Ave
P O Box 169
Somers, WC 53171 262-859-2826
Fax: 262-859-2871 800-558-9446
sales@stainless-products.com
www.stainless-products.com
Manufacturer and exporter of stainless steel fabrications including O-rings, pumps, gauges, welding and valves; also, clean-in-place systems
President: Cindy Gross
President: Cindy Gross
Sales/Purchasing: Mike Shoop
Estimated Sales: $1 - 5 Million
Number Employees: 20-49
Type of Packaging: Bulk

29606 Stainless Specialists
P.O.Box 687
Wausau, WI 54402-0687 715-675-4155
Fax: 715-675-9096 800-236-4155
info@stainlessspecialists.com
www.stainlessspecialists.com
Manufacturer installation and exporter of stainless steel food processing and equipment, conveyors, tanks and work platforms
President: Roger Prochnow
CFO: Paul Kinate
Sr VP Sales: Mike Slattery
R&D: Steve Radant
Quality Control: Brian Stoffel
Marketing/Sales/Public Relations: Roger Prochnow
Operations: Keith Christian
Production: Shannon Herdt
Plant Manager: Keith Christian
Purchasing: Corey Eimmer
Estimated Sales: $20 Million
Number Employees: 100-249
Square Footage: 15000

29607 Stainless Steel
800 Aviation Parkway
Smyrna, TN 37167 888-437-2653
Fax: 954-421-4464 800-877-5177
frankefs@franke.com www.stainless.com
Manufacturer and distributor of french fry dispensers and food service equipment
Parent Co: Franke
Brands:
Robofry

29608 Stainless Steel Coatings
835 Sterling Road
P.O.Box 1145
South Lancaster, MA 01561 978-365-9828
Fax: 978-365-9874 info@steel-it.com
www.steel-it.com
Manufacturer and exporter of anti-corrosion and stainless steel pigmented paint coatings
President: Michael Faigen
Estimated Sales: $1-2,500,000
Number Employees: 10-19
Number of Brands: 2
Number of Products: 14
Square Footage: 10000
Brands:
Steel It
Steel It Lite

29609 Stainless Steel Fabricators
P.O.Box 4549
Tyler, TX 75712-4549 903-595-6625
Fax: 903-592-8819 info@ssftexas.com
ssftexas.com
Stainless steel, corrugated, copper and brass vent hood systems, countertops, sinks, tables and shelving
President: Greg King
Estimated Sales: $5-10,000,000
Number Employees: 10-19

29610 (HQ)Stainless Steel Fabricators
15120 Desman Rd
La Mirada, CA 90638 714-739-9904
Fax: 714-739-0502 info@ssfab.net
www.ssfab.net
Food processing machinery
President: Craig Miller
Sales Representative: Dick Naess
Estimated Sales: $20-50 Million
Number Employees: 50-99

29611 StainlessDrains.com
PO Box 1278
Greenville, TX 75403 888-785-2345
Fax: 877-785-2342 www.stainlessdrains.com
Manufactures a full line of stainless steel drains and drain products, from roof drains to sanitary floor drains.

29612 Stamfag Cutting Dies
2 Braley Point Road
Po Box 1249
Bolton Landing, NY 12814-1249 518-644-2054
Fax: 518-644-2546 sales@stamfag-usa.com
www.stamfag-usa.com
Manufacturing and cutting dies for label printers and lithographers
Type of Packaging: Consumer, Food Service, Private Label, Bulk

29613 Stampendous
1122 N Kraemer Pl
Anaheim, CA 92806 714-688-0288
Fax: 714-688-0297 800-869-0474
stamp@markenterprises.com
www.stampendous.com
Manufacturer and exporter of stain and spot removers
Owner: Fran Sieford
General Manager: Mark Bruhns
Product Manager: Regina Ashbaugh
Estimated Sales: $5 - 10 Million
Number Employees: 50-99
Square Footage: 40000
Brands:
Spoto

29614 Stancase Equipment Company
165 Chubb Ave
Suite 3
Lyndhurst, NJ 07071 201-434-6300
Fax: 201-434-1508 casings@standardcasing.com
www.standardcasing.com
Cheese equipment, agitators, cutters, forks, knives
President: Michael Koss
Executive: Joel Koss
Estimated Sales: $5 - 10 Million
Number Employees: 50-99

29615 Stand Fast Packaging Products
350 S Church St
Addison, IL 60101 630-600-0900
Fax: 630-543-6390 scott@standfastpkg.com
www.standfastpkg.com
Corrugated boxes and dispaly packaging
Owner: John Carman Sr
CEO: John Carmen
Research & Development: Keith Carman
Quality Control: John Carman
Sales Manager: Scott Carmen
Plant Manager: Jon Clair
Purchasing Manager: Phil Lynch
Estimated Sales: $20-25 Million
Number Employees: 50-99
Square Footage: 90000
Type of Packaging: Consumer

29616 (HQ)Standard Casing Company
165 Chubb Ave
Lyndhurst, NJ 07071-3503 201-434-6300
Fax: 201-434-1508 800-847-4141
sales@standardcasing.com
www.standardcasing.com
Manufacturer, importer and exporter of sausage processing equipment including stuffers as well as sausage casings
President: Michael Koss
Executive VP: Joel Koss
Manager Sales: Richard Theise
Estimated Sales: $10-20 Million
Number Employees: 50-99
Square Footage: 35000
Type of Packaging: Bulk
Brands:
Gold Hog Casings
Platinum Hog Casings
Stancase
Standard

29617 Standard Folding Cartons
7520 Astoria Blvd # 100
Flushing, NY 11370-1645 718-335-5500
Fax: 718-507-6430 stanfold@aol.com
www.thestandardgroup.com
Manufacturer and exporter of folding cartons
President: Louis Cortes
Estimated Sales: $20-50 Million
Number Employees: 100-249

29618 Standard Paper Box Machine Company
347 Coster St # 2
Bronx, NY 10474-6813 718-328-3300
Fax: 718-842-7772 800-367-8755
SPBM@prodigy.net
www.standardmachineco.com
Manufacturer and exporter of box making machinery
President: Bruce Adams
Sales: Ronnie Nadel
Estimated Sales: $5 - 10 Million
Number Employees: 20-49
Square Footage: 200000
Brands:
Standard Econocut Die Cutters
Standard Excalibur Die Cutters
Standard Folder Gluers

29619 Standard Pump
1540 University Dr
Auburn, GA 30011 770-307-1003
Fax: 770-307-1009 866-558-8611
info@standardpump.com
www.standardpump.com
Barrel and container pumps and flow control systems are commonly used through out the food processing, cosmetics, pharmaceutical, bio-tech, chemical processing, waste water treatment, plating, medical, semi-conductor, agriculture andpetroleum industries.
President: Don Murphy
Vice President: Christopher Murphy
Estimated Sales: $2-$3 Million
Number Employees: 5-9
Square Footage: 80000

29620 Standard Rate Review
PO Box 23415
San Antonio, TX 78223 210-532-6000
Fax: 210-532-6200 info@standardratereview.com
www.standardratereview.com
President: Alan Ziperstein

29621 Standard Refrigeration Company
321 Foster Avenue
Wood Dale, IL 60191 708-345-5400
Fax: 708-345-3513
stanref.customerservice@alfalaval.com
www.stanref.com
Manufacturer and exporter of heat exchangers for refrigeration applications
Materials & Logistics Manager: Frank Nimesheim
Senior Vice President, Equipment: Mark Larsen
Research and Development Manager: Gary Kaiser
Quality Control Manager: Kevin Lenihan
Market Unit Manager, Refrigeration: Dan Aiken
Business Development Manager: Yao Jeppsson
General Manager: Phil Lucas
Product Portfolio Manager: Mark Hetherington
Factory Manager: Therese Huff
Estimated Sales: $50-100 Million
Number Employees: 50-99

29622 Standard Signs
9115 Freeway Dr
Macedonia, OH 44056 330-467-2030
Fax: 330-467-2076 800-258-1997
marianne@standardsigns.com
www.lumacurve.com
Manufacturer and exporter of porcelain top tables
President: John A Messner
Quality Control: Craig Fussner
R&D: Dane Scholz
Sales: Neil Messner
Estimated Sales: Below $5,000,000
Number Employees: 20-49
Type of Packaging: Food Service
Brands:
Logotop

29623 Standard Terry Mills
38 Green St
Souderton, PA 18964-1702 215-723-8121
Fax: 215-723-3651
Manufacturer and exporter of knitted and woven dish cloths, kitchen towels, oven mitts, aprons, food covers and pot holders; importer of kitchen towels
President: Kerry Gingrich
VP Production: G Nam
Estimated Sales: $10-20 Million
Number Employees: 1-4
Square Footage: 100000

29624 Standard-Knapp
63 Pickering St
Portland, CT 06480 860-342-1100
Fax: 860-342-1557 800-628-9565
info@standard-knapp.com
www.standard-knapp.com
Automated packaging machinery including vertical case, continuous motion tray, shrink and bottle packers
President: Arthur Tanner
CFO: Michael Montano
CEO: Robert Reynolds
R&D: Mike Weaver
Quality Control: David Lou
VP Marketing: Kristofer Kolstad
Estimated Sales: $5 - 10 Million
Number Employees: 100-249

29625 (HQ)Standex International Corporation
11 Keewaydin Drive
Salem, NH 03079 603-893-9701
Fax: 603-893-7324 www.standex.com
Food service equipment, air distribution products, casters, supermarket cart wheels, pumps, point of purchase displays, hydraulic cylinders, etc
Chairman: Edward Trainor
President/Chief Executive Officer: David Dunbar
Chief Financial Officer: Thomas DeByle
VP/Chief Legal Officer/Secretary: Deborah Rosen
Chief Accounting Officer: Sean Valashinas
Estimated Sales: $635 Million
Number Employees: 3,900
Brands:
Bki Wordwide
Federal Industries
Master-Bilt
Procon Products

29626 Stanford Chemicals
12640 E Northwest Hwy # 411
Dallas, TX 75228-8091 972-682-5600
Fax: 972-682-9553
Industrial cleaning compounds
President: Ted Egerton
Customer Service: Lynnette Ladd
Chemist: Kenn Gretz PhD
Estimated Sales: $1 - 3 Million
Number Employees: 5-9
Square Footage: 20000

29627 Stanfos
3908 69th Avenue NW
Edmonton, AB T6B 2V2
Canada 780-468-2165
Fax: 780-465-4890 800-661-5648
info@stanfos.com www.stanfos.com
Manufacturer, exporter and wholesaler/distributor of dairy, food and meat processing equipment including pasteurizers
President: Lang Jameson
Sales Manager: Shawna Bungax
Number Employees: 10-19

29628 Stanley Access Technologies
65 Scott Swamp Rd
Farmington, CT 06032 860-677-2861
Fax: 877-339-7923 800-722-2377
S-SAT-SatInfo@sbdinc.com
www.stanleyaccesstechnologies.com
Manufacturer and exporter of automatic doors including fireproof, sliding, swinging and electrical; also, access control systems and door operating devices
President: Justin Boswell
International Sales/Marketing: Jennifer Loranger
Customer Service: Susan Martin
Administrative Assistant: Jennifer Almeida House
Estimated Sales: Below $500,000
Number Employees: 100-249
Parent Co: Stanley Works
Brands:
Dura-Glide
Magic-Access
Magic-Swing
Sentrex
Stan-Ray

29629 Stanley Black & Decker
1000 Stanley Drive
New Britain, CT 06053 860-225-5111
Fax: 860-827-3895
www.stanleyblackanddecker.com
Fastening equipment and hand tools manufacturer
President & Chief Operating Officer: James Loree
Chairman & Chief Executive Officer: John Lundgren
Senior VP & Chief Financial Officer: Donald Allan Jr.
Estimated Sales: $10 Billion
Number Employees: 45500
Number of Brands: 30
Number of Products: 30
Parent Co: Stanley Works
Type of Packaging: Private Label, Bulk

29630 Stanley Roberts
501 Hoes Ln Ste 108
Piscataway, NJ 08854 973-778-5900
Fax: 973-778-8542 stanleyroberts@erols.com
Flatware
President: Edward Pomeranz
Estimated Sales: $20-50 Million
Number Employees: 20-49

29631 Stanly Fixtures Company
PO Box 616
Norwood, NC 28128 704-474-3184
Fax: 704-474-3011 sandeel@cvnc.net
www.stanlyfixtures.com
Store fixtures
President: Todd Curlee
Quality Control/CFO: Boyce Thompson
Manager: Kenny Bowers
Senior Project Manager/Estimator: Harold Thompson
Estimated Sales: $10 - 20 Million
Number Employees: 100-249

29632 Stanpac, Inc.
Spring Creek Road
R.R. # 3
Smithville, ON L0R 2AO
Canada 905-957-3326
Fax: 905-957-3616 info2ustampacnet.com
www.stanpacnet.com
Ice cream packaging, refillable glass milk bottles and closures, and glass bottles for the beverage and wine industries.
President: Steve Witt
Vice President, Marketing: Murray Bain
Vice President, Sales: Andrew Witt
Vice President, Operations: Ian Killins
Purchasing: Barry Kirk

29633 Stapling Machines Company
41 Pine St # 30
Rockaway, NJ 07866-3139 973-627-4400
Fax: 973-627-5355 sncllc@erols.com
www.smcllc.com

Manufacturer and exporter of packaging machinery for wirebound containers
President: Dough Halkenhauser
Estimated Sales: $10 - 20 Million
Number Employees: 10-19
Parent Co: Stapling Machines Company

29634 Star Container Company
2635 E Magnolia St
Phoenix, AZ 85034 480-281-4200
Fax: 480-281-4201 davenrobertson@techrp.com
www.starcontainercompany.com
Biaxillary-oriented PET containers including wide mouth, narrow neck, custom and stock
VP and General Manager: Paul Ellis
Project Engineer: Phil Blank
Purchasing Agent: Earnest LaFrance
Estimated Sales: $20-50 Million
Number Employees: 1-4
Parent Co: Tech Group

29635 Star Container Corporation
175 Pioneer Dr
Leominster, MA 01453 978-537-1676
Fax: 978-537-9119
Corrugated boxes
President: Nick Campagna
General Manager: Bill Ferzoco
Human Resources: Marlene Nazare
Estimated Sales: $20-50 Million
Number Employees: 100-249
Square Footage: 180000

29636 Star Filters
PO Box 518
Timmonsville, SC 29161-0518 843-346-3101
Fax: 843-346-3736 800-845-5381
invest@hilliard.com www.hilliard.com
Manufacturer and exporter of disposable filters and stainless steel plate and frame filter presses for process filtration applications; also, polypropylene dewatering presses for wastewater applications
Regional Sales Manager: Scott Thomas
Regional Sales Manager: Frank Reid
Sales/Marketing Executive: Howard Reed
Estimated Sales: $2.5-5 Million
Number Employees: 20-49
Square Footage: 140000
Parent Co: Hillard Corporation
Brands:
Carbon Comet
Easy Earth
Star

29637 Star Glove Company
106 S Oak St
Odon, IN 47562 812-636-7395
Fax: 812-636-8038 800-832-7101
starglov@dmrtc.net www.starglove.com
Gloves including industrial knitted, canton flannel, hot mill, double palm and cut resistant
VP: Eric Moll
Sales: Marc Gebhart
Estimated Sales: $10-20 Million
Number Employees: 50-99
Parent Co: Star Glove Company

29638 Star Industries, Inc.
P.O. Box 178
La Grange, IL 60525 708-240-4862
Fax: 708-240-4915 bob@starhydrodyne.com
www.starhydrodyne.com
Manufacturer and exporter of automatic floor scrubbing systems
Executive Director: Susan Frassato
Regional Sales Manager: Scott O'Brien
Estimated Sales: $2.5-5 Million
Number Employees: 50-100
Square Footage: 160000
Brands:
Star Hydrodyne

29639 Star Labels Products
42 Newbold Road
Fairless Hills, PA 19030-4308 215-295-3340
Fax: 215-295-1994 800-394-6900
info@starlabel.com www.starlabel.com
President: Sevket Okumus
CFO: Sevket Okumus
Estimated Sales: $2.5 - 5 Million
Number Employees: 20-49

29640 Star Manufacturing International
10 Sunnen Dr
PO Box 430129
Saint Louis, MO 63143-3800 314-781-2777
Fax: 314-781-4344 800-264-7827
technical@star-mfg.com www.star-mfg.com
Manufacturer and exporter of food service equipment including gas and electric cooking equipment, sandwich grills, toasters/waffle bakers, hot dog equipment, condiment dispensers, popcorn equipment, specialty warmers, dispensing anddisplay/merchandising equipment
President/CEO: Frank Ricchio
VP Sales/Marketing: Tim Gaskill
VP Engineering: Doug Vogt
VP: Mike Barber
Marketing Director: Cindi Benz
Sales Director: Phil Kister
Public Relations: Paulette Bellistri
Estimated Sales: $1 - 3 Million
Number Employees: 5-9
Square Footage: 190000
Type of Packaging: Food Service
Brands:
Chromemax
Galaxy
Jetstar
Starmax

29641 Star Micronics
1150 King Georges Post Rd
Edison, NJ 08837-3731 732-623-5500
Fax: 732-623-5590 800-782-7636
sales@starmicronics.com
www.starmicronics.com
Miniature electronic buzzers, audio transducers and dot matrix, thermal and P.O.S. printers utilized in retail and restaurant applications
President: Takayuki Aoki
Marketing Manager: Patty McCarthy
Number Employees: 1,000-4,999
Parent Co: Star Micronics Company

29642 Star Pacific
1205 Atlantic St
Union City, CA 94587 510-471-6555
Fax: 510-471-4339 800-227-0760
starpac7@aol.com
Manufacturer and exporter of cleaning compounds including household/consumer detergents
Chairman of the Board: Joon Moon
General Manager: Ed Kubiak
Estimated Sales: $5 - 10 Million
Number Employees: 10-19
Square Footage: 57000
Type of Packaging: Consumer
Brands:
Blue Ribbon
Blue Ribbon Classic

29643 Star Poly Bag, Inc.
200 Liberty Ave.
Brooklyn, NY 11207 718-384-3130
Fax: 718-384-2342 rachel@starpoly.com
www.starpoly.com
Manufacturer and exporter of plastic bags including shopping, food, confectioners', heat sealed, etc.; also, packaging materials including cellulose acetate film and garbage and ice cream can liners
President: Rachel Posen
Production: Hershy Rosenfeld
Estimated Sales: Below $5 Million
Number Employees: 10-19
Square Footage: 100000

29644 Star Restaurant Equipment & Supply Company
6178 Sepulveda Blvd
Van Nuys, CA 91411 818-782-4460
Fax: 818-782-8179 sales@starkitchen.com
www.starkitchen.com
Wholesaler/distributor of food service equipment and supplies; serving the food service market
President/Owner: Les Birken
Purchasing: Lee Siegel
Estimated Sales: $5 -10 Million
Number Employees: 10-19
Square Footage: 15000

29645 Star-K Kosher Certification
122 Slade Avenue
Suite 300
Baltimore, MD 21208 410-484-4110
Fax: 410-653-9294 star-k@star-k.org
www.star-k.org
International Kosher certification service for the food industry. The Star-K Kosher symbol assures worldwide acceptance
President: Dr. Avrom Pollak
Executive Vice President: Patricia (Pesi) Herskovitz
Development Director: Steve Sichel
Estimated Sales: $3.5 Million
Number Employees: 250

29646 Starbrook Industries Inc
325 S Hyatt St
Tipp City, OH 45371-1241 937-473-8135
Fax: 937-473-0331 Richard@StarbrookInd.com
www.starbrookind.com/
Product line includes forming and non-forming food packaging films designed for Bi-Vac, Dixie Pak and Multi Vac machines.
Sales Manager: Richard Anderson

29647 Starflex Corporation
204 Turner Rd
Jonesboro, GA 30236 770-471-2111
Fax: 770-478-1304 www.starflexcorp.com
Poultry packing and processing
Chairman of the Board: Ollie Wilson Jr
VP: Bob Polkinghorne
Estimated Sales: $5-10 Million
Number Employees: 20-49

29648 Starkey Chemical ProcessCompany
PO Box 10
La Grange, IL 60525 708-352-2565
Fax: 708-352-2573 800-323-3040
www.starkeychemical.com
Rubber cement, duplicating fluids, printing chemicals, hand cleaners, toners and gelled alcohol cooking and heating fuels; exporter of ink marking and duplicating fluids
President: Linda K Yates
President: Linda Yates
Estimated Sales: $1-2.5 Million
Number Employees: 20-49
Square Footage: 27000
Brands:
Bantam
Perf
Starkey
Super Key

29649 Starlite Food Service Equipment
9200 Conner St
Detroit, MI 48213-1238 313-521-6600
Fax: 313-521-2400 888-521-6603
Stainless steel food service equipment including work tables, refrigerators, freezers, canopies, hoods, shelving, storage units, sinks, etc
Owner: Rodney Gullett
VP Operations: Ettore Commisso
Controller: Maria Kraft
Estimated Sales: Below $5 Million
Number Employees: 5-9
Square Footage: 16000

29650 Start International
4270 Airborn Dr
Addison, TX 75001-5182 972-248-1999
Fax: 972-248-1991 800-259-1986
info@startinternational.com
www.startinternational.com
Industrial tape and label dispensers - semiautomatic, use photosensors, heavy duty contruction.
President: Dan Sternberg
Vice President: Todd Sternberg
Marketing Director: Melanie Riddick
Production Manager: Mike Pfattenberger
Brands:
The Label Dispenser
The Tape Dispenser

29651 Start International
4270 Airborn Drive
Addison, TX 75001-5182 972-248-1999
Fax: 972-248-1991 800-259-1986
info@startinternational.com
www.startinternational.com

Tape and label dispensers, hand-held label applicators, semi-automatic bottle labeler
President: Dan Sternberg
Estimated Sales: $1-2.5 Million
Number Employees: 10-19

29652 Starview Packaging Machinery
1840 St Regis Blvd
Dorval, QC H9P 1H6
Canada 514-920-0100
Fax: 514-920-0092 888-278-5555
info@starview.net www.starview.net
Plastic packaging machinery.
Technical Director: Iwan Heynen
Number Employees: 15
Square Footage: 36216
Type of Packaging: Private Label
Brands:
Starview

29653 (HQ)Statco Engineering & Fabricators
7595 Reynolds Cir
Huntington Beach, CA 92647-6752 714-375-6300
Fax: 714-375-6314 800-421-0362
www.statco-engineering.com
Distributor and systems integrators for the sanitary processing marketing in North America. Products include pumps, valves, heat exchangers, homogenizers, separators, fillers, conveyor systems, instrumentation/controls and otherpackaging and processing equipment
Manager: Kathleen Hall
CFO: James Statham
Vice President: David Statham
Marketing Director: Randy Smith
Sales Director: Eric Perkins
Estimated Sales: $50 Million
Number Employees: 100-249

29654 State Container Corporation
111 West Commercial Avenue
Moonachie, NJ 07074 201-933-5200
dawn@statecontainer.com
Corrugated and fiber boxes
President: John Smith
Director, Administration & Finance: Jane Smith
Estimated Sales: $50-100 Million
Number Employees: 50-99

29655 (HQ)State Industrial Products
5915 Landerbrook Drive
Suite 300
Mayfield Heights, OH 44124 216-861-7114
877-747-6986
www.stateindustrial.com
Disinfectants and soap
President/Chief Executive Officer: Hal Uhrman
Corporate Controller: Scott Moore
Vice President, Research & Development: Tammy Westerman
Senior Marketing Executive: Watson Boxley
Sales Manager: Jamie Montague
Operations Manager: Chrystal Singer
Director, Warehouse Operations: Keith Clouston
Estimated Sales: $96 Million
Number Employees: 1,100
Square Footage: 240000

29656 State Products
4485 California Avenue
Long Beach, CA 90807-2417 562-495-3688
Fax: 562-495-5788 800-730-5150
Manufacturer and exporter of standard baking pans, cookie sheets, French bread frames and fiberglass fabric liners coated with silicon rubber
Chairman: Arthur Haskell
Estimated Sales: $1-2.5 Million appx.
Number Employees: 20
Square Footage: 53000

29657 Statex
3947 Street Hubert
Montreal, QC H2L 4A6
Canada 514-527-6039
Fax: 514-524-0343 guillet@statex.qc.ca
Wholesaler/distributor of sensory analysis software; consultant offering training, technical support and quality control services
Vice President: Michel Guillet
Estimated Sales: $1 - 5,000,000

29658 Stay Tuned Industries
8 W Main St
Clinton, NJ 08809-1290 908-730-8455
Fax: 908-735-8180
Wholesaler/distributor and exporter of steel and aluminum cans and easy-open ends; also, consultant for can manufacturers
Owner: Ray Slocum
Estimated Sales: $500,000-$1 Million
Number Employees: 1-4
Square Footage: 900

29659 Steamway Corporation
2128 S Leslie Ln
Scottsburg, IN 47170 812-889-0896
Fax: 812-889-2269 800-259-8171
hopkins@scottsburg.com
www.steamwaytech.com
Microwavable food containers
President/CEO: Gary Hopkins Sr
CFO: Drusilla Hopkins
VP: Gary Hopkins II
R&D: Gary Hopkins Sr
Quality Control: Gary Hopkins II
Marketing/Sales: Tim Barrett
Estimated Sales: $50 Million
Number Employees: 5-9
Number of Brands: 1
Number of Products: 15
Square Footage: 100000
Type of Packaging: Food Service, Private Label

29660 Stearns Packaging Corporation
PO Box 3216
Madison, WI 53704-0216 608-246-5150
Fax: 608-246-5149 www.stearnspkg.com
Cleaning supplies including detergents
President: John Everitt
Controller: Dennis Stuart
Product Manager: Darla Steinborn
Vice President of Sales and Marketing: Bill Bestmann
Purchasing Manager: Jeff Hanson
Estimated Sales: $20-50 Million
Number Employees: 20-49
Square Footage: 500000
Brands:
Stearns
Vallley View

29661 Stearns Technical Textiles Company
100 Williams Street
Cincinnati, OH 45215-4602 513-948-5292
Fax: 513-948-5281 800-543-7173
Manufacturer and exporter of hot oil filters for deep fryers and medium and heavy duty nonabrasive scrub pads; manufacturer of milk filters
Director Sales: Kevin Finn
Customer Service Manager: Joanne Heidotting
Estimated Sales: $20-50 Million
Number Employees: 100-249
Square Footage: 50000
Brands:
Ffc
Scrubbe
Stearns

29662 Stearnswood
320 3rd Ave NW
PO Box 50
Hutchinson, MN 55350-0050 320-587-2137
Fax: 320-587-7646 800-657-0144
info@stearnswood.com www.stearnswood.com
Manufacturer and exporter of corrugated cartons, wooden boxes, crates, plastic pallets and bulk shipping cartons and bins
Owner: Paul Stearns
Sales Director: Paul Stearns
Plant Manager: Corey Stearns
Estimated Sales: 100000
Number Employees: 1-4
Square Footage: 30000
Type of Packaging: Bulk
Brands:
Flow Max
Ultra Bin

29663 Steel Art Company
189 Dean Street
Norwood, MA 02062 617-566-4079
Fax: 888-783-5335 800-322-2828
info@steelartco.com www.steelartco.com
Manufacturer and exporter of metal signs, letters and plaques
President: John Borell
Director of Sales/Marketing: Charles Blanchard
CFO: Stew Dobson
Vice President: Stewart Dobson
Manager of Design & Engineering: Ciaran Dalton
Sales Director: Charles Blanchard
Customer Service: Catherine O'Neill
Project Manager: Jim Rosicky
Manufacturing Manager: Zeyn Saloojee
A/R-Credit Manager: Robert Smith
Estimated Sales: $5 - 10 Million
Number Employees: 50-99

29664 Steel Art Signs
37 Esna Park Drive
Markham, ON L3R 1O9
Canada 905-474-1678
Fax: 905-474-0515 800-771-6971
thrivnak@steelart.com www.steelart.com
Electric signs
President: Tom Hrivnak
Sales Manager: Gene Mordaunt
Operations Manager: Jorge Dasilva
Number Employees: 90
Square Footage: 348000

29665 (HQ)Steel City Corporation
PO Box 1227
Youngstown, OH 44501-1227 330-792-7663
Fax: 330-792-7951 800-321-0350
jsmith@scity.com www.scity.com
Manufacturer, wholesaler/distributor, importer and exporter of plastic bags, plastic and wire racks and coin operated vending machines; manufacturer and importer of rubber bands
President: C Kenneth Fibus
CFO: Mike Janak
Quality Control: Steve Speece
National Sales Manager: Jim Smith
VP Sales: Lee Rouse
Sales Department: Erika Flaherty
Estimated Sales: $30 - 50 Million
Number Employees: 100-249
Square Footage: 150000

29666 Steel Craft FluorescentCompany
191 Murray St
Newark, NJ 07114-2751 973-349-1614
Fax: 973-824-0825
Manufacturer and exporter of fluorescent lighting fixtures

Estimated Sales: $1 - 3 Million
Number Employees: 10-19

29667 Steel King Industries
2700 Chamber St
Stevens Point, WI 54481 715-341-3120
Fax: 715-341-8792 800-553-3096
info@steelking.com www.steelking.com
Manufacturer and exporter of racks including pallet, pushback, flow, cantilever and portable. Products also inlcude steel containers and guard railing
President: Jay Anderson
Marketing Director: Don Heemstra
National Sales Manager: Skip Eastman
Plant Manager: Ralph Gagas
Estimated Sales: $20-50 Million
Number Employees: 100-249
Parent Co: VCI
Brands:
Sk 2000
Sk 2500
Sk 3000
Sk 3400
Sk 3600 Rock

29668 Steel Products
750 44th Street
Marion, IA 52302-3841 319-377-9451
Fax: 319-377-4580 800-333-9451
Hot chocolate and cappuccino dispensers; exporter of hot chocolate dispensers and parts
Customer Service: Lori Pickart
Operations Manager: Bryce Sandell
Estimated Sales: $1-2.5 Million
Number Employees: 5-9
Square Footage: 33000
Parent Co: ConAgra Foods

29669 Steel Specialty Equipment Corporation
1644 Summerfield Street
Ridgewood, NY 11385-5748 718-366-2131
Fax: 718-366-2865 800-521-7732
ssec.thomasregister.com
Manufacturer and exporter of steel and stainless steel fabricated hand carts and trucks
President: Mark Abeles
Estimated Sales: $1 - 3 Million
Number Employees: 5-9
Square Footage: 15000

29670 Steel Storage Systems
6301 Dexter St
Commerce City, CO 80022 303-287-0391
Fax: 303-287-0159 800-442-0291
info@steelstorage.com www.steelstorage.com
Manufacturer and exporter of material handling equipment including roller conveyors, sheet racks and drawers
President: Brian Mc Callin
Estimated Sales: $5-10 Million
Number Employees: 10-19
Type of Packaging: Bulk
Brands:
Spacesaver

29671 Steele & Marshall
19 Elltee Cir
Thomaston, ME 04861 207-594-7655
Fax: 207-594-7790
General Manager: Mike Young
Manager: Dave Wyllie
Estimated Sales: $3 - 5 Million
Number Employees: 10-19

29672 Steelite International USA
4041 Hadley Rd
South Plainfield, NJ 07080-1111 908-755-0357
Fax: 908-755-7185 800-367-3493
usa@steelite.com www.steelite.com
Importer of ceramic commercial china
CEO: R J Chadwick
Marketing Director: Karen Gowarty
Estimated Sales: $5-10 Million
Number Employees: 10-19
Parent Co: Steelite International
Type of Packaging: Food Service

29673 Steelmaster Material Handling
503 Commerce Park Drive SE
Suite B
Marietta, GA 30060-2745 770-425-7244
Fax: 770-423-7545 800-875-9900
rakman@mindspring.com
Manufacturer and exporter of new and used warehouse equipment including pallet racks and shelving
President: Mike Miller
CEO: Deborah Molley
Plant Manager: James Young
Estimated Sales: $1-2.5 Million
Number Employees: 5-9
Square Footage: 20000
Brands:
Bilt

29674 Steep & Brew Coffee Roasters
855 E Broadway
Monona, WI 53716-4012 608-223-0707
Fax: 608-223-0355 coffee@steep-n-brew.com
www.steep-n-brew.com
Espresso machines and accessories, grinders,roast coffees, wholesale and resale of coffee
Owner: Mark Ballering
Vice President: Mark Mullee
Estimated Sales: $10 - 20 Million
Number Employees: 10-19

29675 Stefanich & Company
1933 N Farris Avenue
Fresno, CA 93704-5912 559-237-2295
Fax: 559-237-2299 stefanich@aol.com
Stainless steel fittings
President: Steven Stefanich

29676 (HQ)Stegall Metal Industries
2800 5th Ave S
Birmingham, AL 35233-2820 205-251-0330
Fax: 205-328-1988 800-633-4373
ajarvis@stegallmechanical.com
www.stegallmechanical.com
Manufacturer and exporter of food service ventilation equipment including ventilation/exhaust hoods and fans; also, custom fabrications in stainless steel and wood available
President: Greg Smith III
Estimated Sales: $10 - 15 Million
Number Employees: 50-99
Type of Packaging: Food Service

29677 Stein DSI
1622 1st St
Sandusky, OH 44870-3902 419-626-0304
800-447-2630
stein.info@fmcti.com www.fmcfoodtech.com
Manufacturer and exporter of ovens, fryers, air filters, hot oil filters, breading machinery, batter mixers, batter applicators, conveyors and broilers; also, product and process testing consultation services available
Manager: Charlie Rogers
Director Sales/Service: Don Mather
Director Marketing: Jan Gaydos
Estimated Sales: $20-50 Million
Number Employees: 250-499
Square Footage: 120000
Parent Co: FMC
Brands:
Procontrol

29678 Steiner Company
401 W Taft Drive
Holland, IL 60473-2015 708-333-2003
Fax: 800-578-2507 800-222-4638
Manufacturer and exporter of waterless hand and skin soaps; also, soap dispensers
President: Guy Marchesi
Director OEM Sales: Craig Brown
Marketing Director: Karen Siravo
VP Sales: Greg Fachet
Estimated Sales: $10-20 Million
Number Employees: 50-99
Parent Co: Steiner Company
Type of Packaging: Private Label
Brands:
Bulkmaster
Change-O-Matic
Economaster
Handmaster
Papermaster
Swiss Air
Wesco

29679 Steiner Company
5801 N Tripp Ave
Chicago, IL 60646-6013 773-588-3444
Fax: 773-588-3450 800-222-4638
www.steinerindustries.com
Manufacturer and exporter of air freshener and soap dispensers; also, garment lockers, soaps, lotions and hand cleaners
President: R J Steiner
Marketing: Karen Siravo
Sales Director: Greg Fachet
Estimated Sales: $10 - 20 Million
Number Employees: 50-99
Parent Co: Steiner Corporation
Type of Packaging: Consumer, Food Service, Bulk
Brands:
Bulkmaster
Change-O-Matic
Economaster
Handmaster
Papermaster
Swiss Air
Wesco

29680 Steingart Associates
5211 Main Street
South Fallsburg, NY 12779 845-434-4321
Fax: 845-436-8609 info@sterlingnets.com
www.steingartprinting.com
Advertising specialties, envelopes, brochures, letterheads, business cards, posters, etc
President: Ira Steingart
VP: Cindy Perlmutter
Estimated Sales: $1-2,500,000
Number Employees: 10-19

29681 Steinmetz Machine Works
44 Homestead Ave
Stamford, CT 06902-7226 203-327-0118
Fax: 203-327-4942 smwct@aol.com
Machinery for the baking industry
President: John Michelotti
Estimated Sales: $3 - 5 Million
Number Employees: 10-19

29682 (HQ)Stellar Group
2900 Hartley Rd
Jacksonville, FL 32257-8221 904-260-2900
Fax: 904-268-4932 800-260-2900
stellar@thestellargroup.com
www.stellargroupindia.com
Provides design, engineering, construction and mechanical services on design/build, general contracting and construction management projects.
Chairman: Ronald Foster Sr
President/CEO: Ronald Foster Jr
SVP/CFO: Scott Witt
CEO: Ronald H Foster Jr
Senior VP Sales/Marketing: Ernest Veale
Estimated Sales: $240 Million
Number Employees: 250-499

29683 Stellar Steam
276 E Allen St
Suite 5
Winooski, VT 05404 802-654-8603
Fax: 802-654-8618 info@colburtreat.com
www.colburtreat.com
Boilerless steamers
President: Michael G Colburn
Quality Control: Steven Bogner
Estimated Sales: Below $5 Million
Number Employees: 20-49

29684 Stello Products
840 W Hillside Ave
PO Box 89
Spencer, IN 47460 812-829-2246
Fax: 812-829-6053 800-868-2246
stello@ccrtc.com www.stelloproducts.com
Signs including metal and silk screen
President: John A. Hackworthy
Foreman: John Summerlot
Estimated Sales: $500,000-$1 Million
Number Employees: 10-19
Square Footage: 18000

29685 (HQ)Stelray Plastic Products, Inc.
50 Westfield Ave
Ansonia, CT 06401 203-735-2331
Fax: 203-735-9412 800-735-2331
sales@stelray.com www.stelray.com
Plastic injection molded products
President: Lawrence D Saffran
General Manager: John Therriaelt
Estimated Sales: $2.5-5 Million
Number Employees: 20-49

29686 Step Products
1500 Chisholm Trail
Round Rock, TX 78681 512-255-0888
Fax: 815-646-4896 800-777-7837
www.stepproducts.com
Fluorinated HDPE containers and plastic components
General Manager: Jim Niemeyer
Sales: Scott Ellison
Sales: Diane Sherin
Number Employees: 35
Square Footage: 20000

29687 Stephan Machinery GmbH
1385 Armour Blvd.
Mandelein, IL 60060 847-247-0182
Fax: 847-247-0184 www.sympak-usa.com
Processing lines and machines for the food, dairy, meat, confectionary and convenience food industries.

29688 Stephan Machinery, Inc.
1385 Armour Blvd
Mundelein, IL 60060 224-360-6206
Fax: 847-247-0184 800-783-7426
weirich@stephan-machinery.com
www.stephan-machinery.com
Designs, engineers and builds the finest food processing equipment available.
CEO: Olaf Pehmoller
CFO: Gunter Dahling
Sales Manager: Eric Weirich
Operations Director: Dirk Kuhnel
Estimated Sales: $7 -10 Million
Number Employees: 5-9
Square Footage: 28000

Brands:
Microcut
Stephan

29689 Stephen Paoli Manufacturing Corporation
2531 11th St
Rockford, IL 61104-7219 815-965-0621
Fax: 815-965-5393 info@stephenpaoli.com
www.stephenpaoli.com
Manufacturer and exporter of one-step deboners and desinewers for meat, poultry and seafood
President: Lowes Paoli
CFO: Louis Paoli
Sales: Neal Ryan
General Manager: Shawn Lee
Estimated Sales: $5 - 10 Million
Number Employees: 20-49
Square Footage: 760000
Brands:
Paoli One Step

29690 Steri Technologies
857 Lincoln Ave
Bohemia, NY 11716 631-563-8300
Fax: 631-563-8378 800-253-7140
steri@steri.com www.steri.com
Manufacturer, importer and exporter of dryers including vacuum shelf, lab and band; also, pressure leaf and vacuum filters
President: Clemens Nigg
Estimated Sales: $10 - 20 Million
Number Employees: 10-19
Square Footage: 15000
Type of Packaging: Private Label
Brands:
Funda
Zwag Nutsche

29691 Steri Technologies
857 Lincoln Ave
Bohemia, NY 11716 631-563-8300
Fax: 631-563-8378 800-253-7140
steri@steri.com www.steri.com
Stainless steel motors and worm reducers for sanitary applications, continuous vacuum band dryers, pressure extractors and Aseptomag aseptic valves
President: Clemens Nigg
Estimated Sales: $10-20 Million
Number Employees: 10-19

29692 Steril-Sil Company
1050 Commonwealth Avenue
Boston, MA 02215 717-405-2258
Fax: 617-739-5063 800-784-5537
orders@sterilsil.com www.sterilsil.com
Manufacturer and exporter of condiment and silverware dispensers, containers and covers
President: David Stiller
CFO: Laura McEachern
VP: Bernard Chiccariello
Estimated Sales: $500,000-$1 Million
Number Employees: 1-4
Parent Co: Stiller Equipment Corporation

29693 Steris Corporation
5960 Heisley Rd
Mentor, OH 44060 440-354-2600
Fax: 440-354-7078 peter_burke@steris.com
www.steris.com
President: Les Vinney
CFO and VP: Laurie Brlas
CEO: Walter M Rosebrough Jr
Estimated Sales: K
Number Employees: 5,000-9,999

29694 Steritech Food Safety &Environmental Hygiene
7600 Little Avenue
Charlotte, NC 28226 704-971-4725
Fax: 704-544-8705 800-868-0089
contact@steritech.com www.steritech.com
Consultant providing food safety audits, pest prevention and food safety training to the food processing and hospitality industries
Executive Chairman, Founder: John Whitley
Chief Executing Officer: Rich Ennis
Chief Financial Officer: Mike Lynch
Vice President of HR: Jennifer Courtney-Trice
Board Member: Mark Jarvis
VP Pesticides (Mid-Atlantic Region): Eric Eicher
Chief Operating Officer: Rich Ennis
Number Employees: 30

29695 Sterling
2900 S. 160th St.
PO Box 245018
New Berlin, WI 53151 262-641-8610
Fax: 262-641-8653 sterlco@corpemail.com
www.sterlco.com
Manufacturer and exporter of temperature control units & other heating & cooling equipment
President: Thomas Breslin
VP: Mike Zvolanek
Marketing: Bill Desrosiers
Sales: Wayne Lange
Public Relations: Nichole Saccomonto
Operations Manager: Rich Cramer
Number Employees: 2
Parent Co: Sterling
Type of Packaging: Private Label

29696 Sterling Alarm Company
2001 E Gladstone St # B
Glendora, CA 91740-5381 909-305-0968
Fax: 909-981-1441 800-932-9561
Manufacturer and importer of security equipment including fire and burglar alarms and systems; also, installation services available
Manager: Bill Jones
Estimated Sales: $2.5-5,000,000
Number Employees: 5-9

29697 Sterling Caviar LLC
Sterling Sturgeon
Sacramento, CA 916-991-4420
Fax: 916-991-4334 800-525-0333
info@sterlingcaviar.com
www.sterlingcaviar.com
Caviar
Manager: Peter Struffenegger
Type of Packaging: Private Label

29698 Sterling China Company
511 12th Street
Wellsville, OH 43968-1303 330-532-1609
Fax: 330-532-4587 800-682-7628
www.sterlingchina.com
Vitrified china
Vice President: Bruce Hill
National Sales Manager: Brian Lewis
Estimated Sales: $10-20 Million
Number Employees: 250-500
Square Footage: 125000

29699 Sterling Controls
24711 Emerson Rd.
Sterling, IL 61081 815-625-0852
Fax: 815-625-3103 800-257-7214
info@praterindustries.com
www.prater-sterling.com
Manufacturer, importer and exporter of batching and weighing process controls for dry and liquid products; also, weighing systems for poultry and meat
President: Don Goshert
VP/General Manager: Don Goshert
Western Sales: Bob Rogan
South/Southeastern Sales: Dean Considine
Northeastern Sales: Marty Gustafson
Estimated Sales: $2.5-5 Million
Number Employees: 10-19
Square Footage: 10500
Parent Co: Prater Industries

29700 (HQ)Sterling Electric
7973 Allison Ave
Indianapolis, IN 46268 317-872-0471
Fax: 800-474-0543 800-654-6220
websales@sterlingelectric.com
www.sterlingelectric.com
Production of customized/standard AC induction motors along with drive products such as; AC adjustable frequency controls, DC permanent magnet motors and controls, mechanical adjustable speed transmissions, shaft mounts and screwconveyors, and cycloidal reducers and gearmotors
Sales: Roman Wiggins
Manager: Walter Mashburn
Number Employees: 20-49
Other Locations:
Sterling Distribution Center
Indianapolis IN
Sterling Power Systems
Hamilton, ON

29701 Sterling Net & Twine Company
P.O.Box 411
Cedar Knolls, NJ 07927 973-783-9800
Fax: 973-783-9808 800-342-0316
info@sterlingnets.com www.sterlingnets.com
Manufacturer and exporter of nets and netting, conveyors, pallets and custom bags for produce and customer packaging
President: James Van Loon
Sales Manager: Jerry Eick
Estimated Sales: $5 - 10,000,000
Number Employees: 20-49
Square Footage: 32000

29702 Sterling Novelty Products
1940 Raymond Dr
Northbrook, IL 60062-6715 847-291-0070
Fax: 847-291-0120
Manufacturer and exporter of U.S. flag sets, nylon mesh scouring cloths and plastic food bags
President: Marvin Glasser
Secretary/Treasurer: Michael Glasser
Estimated Sales: $1 - 3 Million
Number Employees: 10-19
Square Footage: 5000
Parent Co: Sterling Novelty

29703 Sterling Packaging Company
2531 Thomas St
Jeannette, PA 15644-1876 724-523-5565
Fax: 724-527-3575 rruskin@sterlingpkg.com
www.sterlingpackaginginc.com
Paper boxes for pasta, frozen poultry, pizza, etc
Manager: Tracey Moranduzzo
Estimated Sales: $20-50 Million
Number Employees: 10-19

29704 Sterling Paper Company
2155 Castor Ave
Philadelphia, PA 19134-2799 215-744-5350
Fax: 215-533-9577 www.sterling-paper.com
Manufacturer, exporter and importer of paper plates, Chinese food pails and food trays; also, boxes including cake, pizza, doughnuts, sausage, steak, pastry, etc
President: Martin Stein
Secretary: John Paul
VP: Suzy Faigen
Estimated Sales: $10-20 Million
Number Employees: 50-99
Square Footage: 325000
Brands:
Aristocrat

29705 Sterling Process Engineering
333 McCormick Blvd
Columbus, OH 43213 614-868-5151
Fax: 614-868-5152 800-783-7875
sales@sterlingpe.com www.sterlingpe.com
Stainless steel process tanks, pipe/tubing, clean-in-place systems, stainless steel conveyor, platforms, skid mounted process equipment, design, fabrication and installation of food and beverage process system
President: Jerry Martin
Sales Director: Jack Selvages
Operations Manager: Russ Flax
Estimated Sales: $10-20 Million
Number Employees: 20-49
Square Footage: 35000

29706 Sterling Rubber
675 Woodside Street
Fergus, ON N1M 2M4
Canada 519-843-4032
Fax: 519-843-6587
Manufacturer and exporter of rubber gloves
President: Robert Joyce
Manager Quality Assurance: Norma Ford
Number Employees: 30
Square Footage: 27000

29707 (HQ)Sterling Scale Company
20950 Boening Dr
Southfield, MI 48075-5737 248-358-0590
Fax: 800-556-9931 800-331-9931
sales@sterlingscale.com www.sterlingscale.com

Manufacturer, importer, exporter and wholesaler/distributor of industrial scales; manufacturer of engineering software for weighing equipment
President: E Donald Dixon
CFO: J Dixon
Vice President: Tom Ulicny
Research & Development: T Klauinger
Quality Control: Jeff Shultz
Marketing Director: Tom Ulicny
Plant Manager: J Holcomb
Purchasing Manager: S Latucca
Estimated Sales: $2-3 Million
Number Employees: 20-49
Number of Brands: 5
Number of Products: 100
Square Footage: 112000
Brands:
Sterling
Sterling Eliminator

29708 Sterling Truck Corporation
4747 N Channel Ave
Portland, OR 97217-7613
Fax: 440-269-5979 800-785-4357
www.sterlingtrucks.com
Senior VP: John Merrifield
Sales: Richard Saward
Estimated Sales: $20 - 30 Million
Number Employees: 100-249

29709 Sterner Lighting Systems
7575 Corporate Way
Eden Prairie, MN 55344-2022 952-906-7300
Fax: 320-485-2881 800-328-7480
adman@sternerlighting.com
www.sternerlighting.com
Manufacturer and exporter of indoor and outdoor lighting equipment
General Manager: Mike Naylor
Marketing Manager: Sherry Thomson
Plt Mgr: Ken Lehner
Estimated Sales: $10 - 20 Million
Number Employees: 20-49
Parent Co: Hubbel Lighting
Type of Packaging: Food Service
Brands:
Softform

29710 Sterno
1064 Garfield Street
Lombard, IL 60148 630-792-0080
Fax: 630-792-9914 www.candlecorpfs.com
Manufacturer and exporter of candles, including table, birthday, tapers, and table lamps
President: Richard T Browning
Number Employees: 50-99
Parent Co: Sterno
Type of Packaging: Food Service
Brands:
Chafing Fuels
Handy Fuel Brand
Tabie Lamps & Stereo Brand

29711 Stero Company
3200 Lakeville Hwy
Petaluma, CA 94954 707-762-0071
Fax: 707-762-5036 800-762-7600
kstero@sonic.net www.stero.com
Commercial dish, glass, pot/pan and tray washers
Manager: Terry Goodfellow
VP Sales/Marketing: Lars Noren
Estimated Sales: $20-50 Million
Number Employees: 10,000
Square Footage: 66000
Parent Co: PMI
Brands:
Stero

29712 Steven Label Corporation
11926 Burke St
Santa Fe Springs, CA 90670 562-698-9971
Fax: 562-698-1507 800-752-4968
slc4you@stevenlabel.com www.stevenlabel.com
Labels including bar code and pressure sensitive; also, decals
President: Steve Stong
Estimated Sales: $20-50 Million
Number Employees: 100-249

29713 Steven's International
15800 W Overland Dr
New Berlin, WI 53151-2882 262-827-3800
Fax: 262-827-3911 www.zerand.com
Manufacturer and exporter of paper board printing and packaging machinery
VP: Paul Capper
Director Sales/Marketing/Administration: Bill Dennis
Estimated Sales: $10 - 20 Million
Number Employees: 50-99

29714 Stevens Linen Association
137 Schofield Ave
Suite 5
Dudley, MA 01571 508-943-0813
Fax: 508-949-1847
www.co-store.com/stevenslinen
Manufacturer and exporter of linen goods, pot holders and place mats
President: Gregory Kline
VP Sales/Marketing: Nancy Dalrymple
Estimated Sales: $10-20 Million
Number Employees: 100-249
Square Footage: 75000

29715 Stevens Transport
9757 Military Pkwy
Dallas, TX 75227 972-288-8928
Fax: 972-289-8545 800-823-9369
www.stevenstransport.com
Transportation firm providing refrigerated and dry rail and long haul TL and LTL services
President: Clay Aaron
Chairman and CEO: Steven Aaron
Executive Vice President: Michael Richey
Number Employees: 250-499

29716 Stevenson-Cooper, Inc.
1039 W. Venango Street
PO Box 46345
Philadelphia, PA 19160 215-223-2600
Fax: 215-223-3597 waxcooper@aol.com
www.stevensoncooper.com
Manufacturer and exporter of oils including cottonseed and palm oils; also, manufacturer of paraffin and sealing wax
President: Dennis Cooper
R&D: Tammy Pullins
Estimated Sales: Below $5 Million
Number Employees: 5-9

29717 (HQ)Stewart Assembly & Machining
7234 Blue Ash Rd
Cincinnati, OH 45236 513-891-9000
Fax: 513-891-0449 sales@stewartam.com
www.stewartindustries.com
Manufacturer and exporter of packaging machinery
President: Jim Weckenbrock
VP Sales: Ray Meyer
Estimated Sales: $5-10 Million
Number Employees: 20-49
Type of Packaging: Bulk

29718 Stewart Laboratories
PO Box 27048
Golden Valley, MN 55427-0048 763-545-8905
Fax: 612-782-0506 800-820-2333
Laboratory glassware detergents
Owner: Stanley Segelbaum
National Sales Manager: Stanley Stewart
Customer Service Manager: Joyce Berk
Estimated Sales: $2.5-5 Million
Number Employees: 1-4
Square Footage: 5000
Brands:
Labkol
Labkolax
Labkolite

29719 Stewart Marketing Services
11122 NE 41st Drive
Apt 31
Kirkland, WA 98033-7725 425-889-2455
Fax: 425-889-8786
Consultant specializing in sales and advertising for the frozen food market in the Pacific Northwest
President: Bill Stewart

29720 Stewart Mechanical Seals & Supply
3600 Pegasus Drive
Suite #10
Bakersfield, CA 93308 661-391-9332
Fax: 661-391-9336 bill@stewartseals.com
www.stewartseals.com
Supplier of sealing and packing parts for machinery used in the foodservice packing industry
Estimated Sales: $450,000
Number Employees: 3
Square Footage: 8800
Type of Packaging: Consumer, Private Label, Bulk
Brands:
Four Aces
M&R

29721 Stewart Sutherland
5411 E V Ave
Vicksburg, MI 49097 269-649-5489
Fax: 269-649-3961 www.ssbags.com
Sandwich wraps and bags including bakery, french bread, candy, doggie, foil insulated, french fry, sandwich, pizza, etc
President: John Stewart
CEO/VP/Pub Relations & Operations: Tom Farrell
Quality Control: Anna Liggett
Research & Devel/Marketing & Sales: Shelley Averill
Quality Control: Irene Carroll
VP Sales: Jack Bailey
VP Production: William Moran
Plant Manager: Dick Vandrestradten
Purchasing: Loretta Johnson
Estimated Sales: $42 Million
Number Employees: 125

29722 Stickney Hill Dairy
15371 County Road 48
Kimball, MN 55353 320-398-5360
Fax: 320-398-5361 sales@stickneydairy.com
www.stickneydairy.com
Goat cheeses
General Manager: Cheryl Willenbring
Quality Assurance Manager: Kathy Ratka
Estimated Sales: $2 Million
Number Employees: 19

29723 Stik-2 Products
41 Oneil St
Easthampton, MA 01027-1103 413-527-7120
Fax: 413-527-7249 800-356-3572
sales@stik-2.com www.stik-2.com
Manufacturer and exporter of pressure sensitive foam cloth adhesive tapes
Manager: Dave Premo
Sales Manager: David Premo
Sales Specialist: Judette Savino
Estimated Sales: $10 - 20 Million
Number Employees: 20-49
Parent Co: October Company

29724 Stiles Enterprises
114 Beach St.
PO Box 92
Rockaway, NJ 07866 973-625-9660
Fax: 973-625-9346 800-325-4232
www.stilesenterprises.com
Packaging machine replacement parts-rubber parts, conveyor belts, drive belts, fabricated belts, resurface rubber rollers, parts for cappers, fillers, labelers, bottle unscramblers, case tapers, form/fill/seal baggers , heattunnels.
President: Richard Stiles
CFO: Nancy Stiles
R&D: John Dubowchik
Sales: Ken Stiles
Estimated Sales: $5-10 Million
Number Employees: 10-19

29725 Stober Drives
1781 Downing Dr
Maysville, KY 41056 606-759-5090
Fax: 606-759-5045 800-711-3588
sales@stober.com www.global.stoeber.de
President: Peter Feil
CFO: Peter Fiel
R&D: Shane Art
Quality Control: Mick Michelle
Estimated Sales: $5 - 10 Million
Number Employees: 20-49

29726 (HQ)Stock America Inc
900 Cheyenne Ave
Suite 700
Grafton, WI 53024 262-375-4100
Fax: 262-375-4101 michaelg@stockamerica.com
www.stockamerica.com

Wholesaler/distributor of full-water and steam retorts, temperature and pressure monitoring equipment, fillers, packaging containers and sealing equipment.
President: Michael Galvin
Vice President: Victoria Schlegger
CEO: Michael Galvin
Vice President: Tim Schurr
Marketing: Donette Lambert
Sales Manager: Rick Eleew
Estimated Sales: $5 - 10 Million
Number Employees: 10-19
Number of Brands: 8
Number of Products: 5
Square Footage: 72000
Type of Packaging: Consumer
Other Locations:
Stock America
Montreal PQ
Stock America
Cary NC

29727 Stoffel Seals Corporation
P.O.Box 217
Tallapoosa, GA 30176 770-574-2382
Fax: 770-574-7937 800-422-8247
info-ga@stoffel.com www.stoffel.com
Stoffel Seals is a key supplier for product identification and branding systems, packaging enhancements, advertising premiums/promotional products, employee identification badges, tamper evident security seals and many other custommanufactured products. Our specialty items for the food and beverage industry include ham bone guards, trussing loops, rotisserie tags, tray pack inserts, pricing/shellfish tags, metal seals, string
Quality Control: Henry Bosshard
Marketing: Valerie Cates
Sales: Mark Swan
Production: Mike Brown
Plant Manager: Norbert Falk
Purchasing: James Westmoreland
Estimated Sales: $40 Million
Number Employees: 250-499
Square Footage: 180000
Parent Co: Stoffel Seals
Type of Packaging: Consumer, Food Service, Private Label, Bulk
Brands:
Prestige

29728 Stoffel Seals Corporation
P.O.Box 217
Tallapoosa, GA 30176 770-574-2382
Fax: 770-574-7937 800-422-8247
info@stoffel.com www.stoffel.com
We are the supplier of choice for product identification and branding systems, packaging enhancements, advertising premiums/promotional products, employee identification badges, tamper evident security seals and many other custommanufactured products. Our specialty include ham bone guards, trussing loops, rotisserie tags, turkey lifters, tray pack inserts, pricing/shellfish tags, metal seals for kosher foods, elastic string tags, bottle neckers and cohes
President and CEO: Charles Fuehrer
Executive VP: Norbert Falk
Vice President: Joe Williams
Marketing Director: Pat Renz
Sales Director: Joe Cusack
Plant Manager: Norbert Falk
Estimated Sales: $50 - 100 Million
Number Employees: 250-499
Square Footage: 40000
Type of Packaging: Consumer, Private Label, Bulk
Brands:
Prestige

29729 Stogsdill Tile Company
14316 Harmony Rd
Huntley, IL 60142 847-669-1255
Fax: 847-669-1278 800-323-7504
info@stogsdilltile.com www.stogsdilltile.com
Manufacturer and exporter of stainless steel floor drains; also, acid brick and monolithic flooring installation services available
Owner: William Stogsdill
Operations Manager: Ivan Gonzalez
Estimated Sales: $1 - 5 Million
Number Employees: 20-49
Square Footage: 16000

29730 Stokes
400 Kitts Hillroad
Hyannis, MA 02601 215-788-3500
Fax: 215-781-1122 800-635-0036
info@stokesdti.com www.stokesdti.com
Tablet presses, tabletting dedusters, tooling, granulators, metal detectors, automated control systems, encapsulation equipment and size reduction equipment
President: Brayan Urban
Marketing: Barb McPeditt
Number Employees: 100

29731 Stokes Material HandlingSystems
1000 Crosskeys Dr
Doylestown, PA 18902 215-340-2200
Fax: 215-230-9280 nwfeigles@stokesmhs.com
www.stokesmhs.com
Conveyor systems; custom designing available - specializing in USDA/FDA approved systems
President: Ronald Feigles
Marketing Director: Steve Heinel
VP Operations: Neal Feigles
Estimated Sales: $8,500,000
Number Employees: 10-19
Square Footage: 6000

29732 Stolle Machinery Company, LLC
6949 S. Potomac Stree
Centennial, CO 80112-4036 303-708-9044
Fax: 303-708-9045 tooling@formatec.com
www.stollemachinery.com
High-speed wide and narrow coil and sheet-fed shell systems for D-I and D-R-D cans, complete draw-redraw can systems and air cup conveyors; other services include complete rebuilds, speed-ups and retolling of shell and cuppingpresses
President: Ralph P Stodd
VP: David Bolek
CFO: Jimm Miceli
Estimated Sales: $2.5 - 5 Million
Number Employees: 5-9

29733 Stoltz Enterprises
429 South St
Slidell, LA 70460 985-781-1015
Fax: 985-781-1025 800-738-1000
info@seihq.com www.food6000.com
Software for food processing, packing and distribution
President: James Stolt
VP Sales/Marketing: Donald Tyler
Estimated Sales: Less than $500,000
Number Employees: 1-4
Brands:
Sei

29734 Stoncor Group
1 Park Ave
Maple Shade, NJ 08052 856-779-7500
Fax: 856-321-7510 800-854-0310
stonhard.marketing@stonhard.com
www.stoncor.com
President: David P Reif
Estimated Sales: $100 - 250 Million
Number Employees: 100-249

29735 Stone Container
12112 Greens Ferry Road
Moss Point, MS 39562-8836 502-491-4870
Fax: 502-491-7283
Corrugated boxes
General Manager: Michael Cash
Estimated Sales: $5-10 Million
Number Employees: 20-49

29736 Stone Container
150 N Michigan Ave # 1700
Chicago, IL 60601-7597 312-346-6600
Fax: 312-580-2299 www.smurfit-stone.com
Manufacturer and exporter of envelopes, plastic film and bags: multi-wall, paper and plastic
President: Pat Moore
Estimated Sales: $10 - 20 Million
Number Employees: 10,000
Parent Co: Stone Container

29737 Stone Container
13833 Freeway Dr
Santa Fe Springs, CA 90670 714-774-0100
Fax: 562-921-0620 www.smurfit.com
Corrugated boxes and displays
CFO: Paul Hailey
President: Dale McClurgh
Quality Control: Debra Heyeen
Sales Manager: Morgan Welch
Production Manager: Paul Smith
Estimated Sales: $30 - 50 Million
Number Employees: 100-249
Square Footage: 250000
Parent Co: Stone Container Corporation

29738 Stone Enterprises Inc.
10011 J St
Suite 3
Omaha, NE 68127 402-753-0500
Fax: 402-502-8102 877-653-0500
sales@stoneent.net www.stoneent.net
Designer and manufacturer of custom built machinery, refurbished machines and replacement parts.

29739 Stone Soap Company
2000 Pontiac Dr
Sylvan Lake, MI 48320 248-706-1000
Fax: 248-706-1001 800-952-7627
sales@stonesoap.com www.stonesoap.com
Manufacturer, importer and exporter of cleaning products including hand cleaners, detergents and soaps
President: Kenneth Stone
National Sales Manager: Patty Muskat
Purchasing Agent: Jacqueline ElChemmas
Estimated Sales: $5-10 Million
Number Employees: 20-49
Square Footage: 100000
Brands:
Sport Mate

29740 Stoner
1070 Robert Fulton Hwy
Quarryville, PA 17566 717-786-7355
Fax: 717-786-9088 800-227-5538
timesaver@stonersolutions.com
www.stonersolutions.com
FDA approved specialty lubricants
President: Rob Ecklin
Owner: John H Stoner
Sales Manager: Tim Bupp
Customer Service Manager: Dave Scranto
Estimated Sales: $5 - 10 Million
Number Employees: 1-4
Brands:
Food Grade

29741 Stoneway Carton Company
3047 78th Ave SE # 203
Mercer Island, WA 98040-2847 206-232-2645
Fax: 206-232-2725 800-498-2185
cartonco@stonewayctn.com
www.stonewayctn.com
Manufacturer and exporter of cartons, pads, and parts. Also graphic and structural design
President: Charles E Farrell
General Manager: Russ Salger
Sr. Account Executive Sales: Art Wical
Purchasing Manager: Troy Giesinger
Estimated Sales: $2.5-5 Million
Number Employees: 1-4
Square Footage: 240000

29742 Stonhard
P.O.Box 308
Maple Shade, NJ 08052-0308 856-321-2033
Fax: 856-321-7510 800-257-7953
stonhard.marketing@stonhard.com
www.stonhard.com
Manufacturer and installer of polymer floors, high performance epoxy floors
CEO: Dave Reis
Estimated Sales: $175 Million
Number Employees: 250-499

29743 Stor-Loc
880 N Washington Ave
Kankakee, IL 60901 815-936-0700
Fax: 815-936-0767 sales@storloc.com
www.storloc.com
High density storage equipment, drawer cabinets and workstations
President: Michael J Ryan
Quality Control: Ed Ryan
Estimated Sales: Below $5 Million
Number Employees: 20-49
Brands:
Stor-Frame

29744 **Storad Tape Company**
126 Blaine Ave
Marion, OH 43301-0493 740-382-6440
Fax: 740-383-3241 sales@storadlabel.com
www.storadlabel.com
Pressure sensitive labels
President: Bob Hord
Estimated Sales: $5-10 Million
Number Employees: 10-19

29745 **Storage Unlimited**
1001 N Kenneth Street
Nixa, MO 65714-8401 417-725-3014
Fax: 417-725-5750 800-478-6642
Manufacturer and exporter of racks including can, storage, dunnage, pan, tray; also, dish mobiles
President: Glenn Scott
Secretary: Mary Van Noy
Office Manager: Lisa Lewellen
Estimated Sales: 700000
Number Employees: 5-9
Square Footage: 12000
Brands:
Always Can

29746 **Storax**
72 Sherwood Road
Bromsgrove, UK B60 3DR 845-130-3090
Fax: 152-757-6144 info@storaxsystems.com
www.storaxsystems.com
Mobile rack systems
VP Operations: Jim McLain
Number Employees: 10
Parent Co: Barpro Group

29747 **Stork Food Dairy Systems**
P.O.Box 1258
Gainesville, GA 30503-1258 770-535-1875
Fax: 770-536-0841 jan.kuiper@stork.com
www.sfds.com
Sales and service of various integrated processing and packaging systems for food, dairy, juice and beverage industry
CEO: Bath Dowdy
VP: Jan Lucas-Kuiper
Executive VP: Ben Hamer
Quality Control: Robert Terhaar
Estimated Sales: Below $5 Million
Number Employees: 10-19

29748 **Stork Food Machinery**
3525 W Peterson Ave
Suite 611
Chicago, IL 60659-3318 773-583-7793
Fax: 773-583-8155 800-81S-TORK
Automatic warehouse systems, aseptic packaging systems and aseptic processing equipment
Manager: Nicole Stack
Estimated Sales: $.5 - 1 million
Number Employees: 1-4

29749 **Stork Gamco**
PO Box 1258
Gainesville, GA 30503-1258 770-532-7041
Fax: 770-532-5672 titan@stork-gamco.com
www.stork-gamco.com
Manufacturer and exporter of poultry processing equipment
President: Frank Nicoletti
Executive VP: Frank Nicoletti
Manager Domestic Sales: Bryon Lovingood
Estimated Sales: $20-50 Million
Number Employees: 100-249
Square Footage: 145000

29750 **Stork Townsend Inc.**
PO Box 1433
Des Moines, IA 50306-1433 515-265-8181
Fax: 515-263-3333 800-247-8609
info.townsendusa@stork.com
www.townsendeng.com
Manufacturer and exporter of meat processing machinery including pork, fish and poultry skinners, sausage stuffers, linkers, bacon injectors, sausage coextrusion, sausage loaders and meat harvesting systems.
President: Theo Bruinsma
Regional Sales Manager: David Bertelsen
Estimated Sales: $20-50 Million
Number Employees: 100-249
Type of Packaging: Food Service
Brands:
Townsend

29751 **Storm Industrial**
PO Box 14666
Shawnee Mission, KS 66285-4666 913-599-3650
Fax: 559-277-9580 800-745-7483
Manufacturer and exporter of plastic and brass valves including pilot mini, automatic drain, speed control exhaust, solenoid, hydraulic nonelectric, slip, pressure regulating, electric and barbed drain; also, wire connectors
Number Employees: 50
Square Footage: 40000
Parent Co: Imperial Valve Company
Brands:
Imperial

29752 **Stormax International**
90 Manchester St
Concord, NH 03301-5129 603-223-2333
Fax: 603-223-2330 800-874-7629
egestewitz@stormax-usa.com www.stormax.com
Manufacturer, importer and exporter of filling, sealing and lidding machinery for cups, trays, tubs and paper containers
President: Earl Gestewitz
Estimated Sales: Below $5 Million
Number Employees: 1-4
Parent Co: Stormax International A/S

29753 **Storopack**
12007 Woodruff Ave
Downey, CA 90241 562-803-5582
Fax: 562-803-4462 800-827-7225
info@storopackinc.com www.storopackinc.com
Manufacturer, converter and recycler of EPS (Expanded Polystyrene) with primary activities that include the conversion of EPS, natural starch, paper and plastic cushioning materials
Manager: John Melat
VP Marketing: Paul Deis
Estimated Sales: $20-50 Million
Number Employees: 50-99
Type of Packaging: Private Label, Bulk

29754 **Storsack**
7111 Perimeter Park Dr # 300
Houston, TX 77041-4048 713-461-0840
Fax: 713-461-0654 800-841-4982
info@storsack.com www.storsack.com
Global manufacturer of flexible intermdiate bulk bags
CEO: Bruce Boyd
CEO: Bruce Boyd
Sales Director of Public Relations: Sonja GrAger
Estimated Sales: $10-25 Million
Number Employees: 50-99
Brands:
Cleanmaster
Guardmaster
Safemaster
Spacemaster
Tripmaster

29755 **Stout Sign Company**
6425 W Florissant Ave
Saint Louis, MO 63136-3622 314-385-4600
Fax: 314-385-9412 800-325-8530
john-woods@stoutmarketing.com
www.stoutsign.com
Manufacturer and exporter of point of purchase signs and displays; silk screening available
President: Patrick Conners
Sales Manager: Randall Simonian
VP Operations: Lee Witt
Estimated Sales: $15 - 20 Million
Number Employees: 100-249
Square Footage: 70000
Parent Co: Stout Industries of Delaware

29756 **Strahl & Pitsch**
230 Great East Neck Rd
West Babylon, NY 11704 631-669-0175
Fax: 631-587-9120 info@strahlpitsch.com
www.strahlpitsch.com
Confectionery waxes, custom blending
President: William Deluca
Marketing Manager: Dan Damico
Estimated Sales: $20-50 Million
Number Employees: 20-49

29757 **Strahman Valves**
Lehigh Valley Industrial Park VI
Bethlehem, PA 18020 610-867-0516
Fax: 484-893-5099 877-787-2462
strahman@strahman.com
www.strahmanvalves.com
Manufacturer and exporter of cleaning products, hoses and valves
VP: Kevin Carroll
Sales Director: Kevin Carroll
Estimated Sales: $10-20 Million
Number Employees: 50-99
Type of Packaging: Bulk

29758 **Straight Line Filters**
701 Christiana Ave
Wilmington, DE 19801-5842 302-654-8805
Fax: 302-655-5038 www.straightlinefilters.com
Food-processing vacuum belt filters
Manager: Kenneth Seibert
Estimated Sales: $1-2.5 Million
Number Employees: 10-19

29759 **Straits Steel & Wire Company**
PO Box 589
Ludington, MI 49431 231-843-3416
Fax: 231-843-8096 www.sswholding.net
Wire shelves, racks, fruit and vegetable baskets and displays
President: Paul Kara
VP: James Boals
Estimated Sales: $20 - 50 Million
Number Employees: 100-249

29760 **Strand Lighting**
10911 Petal St
Dallas, TX 75238
Fax: 714-899-0042 support@strand.ca
www.strandlight.com
Manufacturer and exporter of electric and incandescent lighting fixtures
President: Tim Burnham
VP Marketing: Peter Rogers
Estimated Sales: $20 - 30 Million
Number Employees: 50-99
Parent Co: Rank Industries America
Type of Packaging: Food Service

29761 **Strapack**
30860 San Clemente St
Hayward, CA 94544-7135 510-475-6000
Fax: 510-475-6090 800-475-5006
hayward@strapack.com www.strapack.com
Strapping machines, corrugated converting machine
Owner: Keisho Yamamoto
Estimated Sales: $10-20 Million
Number Employees: 10-19

29762 **Strapex Corporation**
2601 Westinghouse Blvd
Charlotte, NC 28273 704-588-2510
Fax: 704-588-6838 800-346-1804
info@strapexusa.com www.itwpbna.com
Bottle and can containers
Estimated Sales: $10-20 Million
Number Employees: 20-49

29763 **Strasburger & Siegel**
7249 National Dr Ste 2
Hanover, MD 21076 410-712-7373
Fax: 410-712-7378 888-726-3753
theoffice@sas-labs.com www.eurofinsus.com
Consultant to food technologists for product formulation, evaluation, analysis, etc
President: Rick Gjesdal
Director: Tom Light
Estimated Sales: $1-2.5 Million
Number Employees: 20-49

29764 **Stratecon**
5215 Mountain View Road
Winston Salem, NC 27104-5117 336-768-6808
Fax: 336-765-5149 cbeckstc@bellsouth.net
www.stratecon-intl.com
Consultant specializing in strategic planning, start-up feasibility, marketing research, technology assessment, project management, etc. for the food industry
Estimated Sales: Below $500,000
Number Employees: 2
Square Footage: 4000

29765 Stratecon InternationalConsultants
5215 Mountain View Road
Winston Salem, NC 27104-5117 336-768-6808
Fax: 336-765-5149
weck@foodbusinessresource.com
www.stratecon-intl.com
We combine the experience of twelve seasoned food industry professionals who work together to fulfill client needs. Members have skills in processed foods and ingredients. Specialties: business development, coffee manufacturingdietary fibers, due diligence, food safety, fortification, process and equipment development, product introduction, strategic planning, and training. See website for individual consultant locations
Coordinator: Catherine Side
Estimated Sales: Below $500,000
Number Employees: 2

29766 Strategic Equipment & Supply
8360 E Via De Ventura
Scottsdale, AZ 85258-3172 480-905-5530
Food service equipment
Estimated Sales: Less than $500,000
Number Employees: 1-4

29767 Stratis Plastic Pallets
5677 W 73rd St
Indianapolis, IN 46278 317-328-8000
Fax: 317-328-8080 800-725-5387
sales@pallets.com www.pallets.com
Plastic pallets
President: Andrew Elder
Estimated Sales: $300,000-500,000
Number Employees: 1-4

29768 (HQ)Stratix Corporation
4920 Avalon Ridge Pkwy # 600
Norcross, GA 30071-1572 770-326-7580
Fax: 770-326-7591 800-883-8300
info@stratixcorp.com www.stratixcorp.com
Bar code generation software, bar code verification equipment, bar code pressure sensitive labels, verification/label printing systems and thermal transfer/direct thermal printers
President: David Knowlton
CEO: Bonney Shuman
CEO: Bonney S Shuman
Marketing Director: Kathryn Fraas
Sales Director: Tim Burkett
Estimated Sales: $10 - 20 Million
Number Employees: 50-99
Other Locations:
Stratix Corporation
St. Leonards
Brands:
Bar Code Creator
Symart Systems
Xaminer

29769 Straub Company
2238 Florida Ave So
Minneapolis, MN 55426 952-546-6686
Fax: 215-672-8092 clinsep@cs.com
www.straubdesign.com
Manufacturer and exporter of hand and electric grinding mills for dry and oily materials including beans, nuts and herbs and for preparing laboratory samples for analysis
President: William Clinton
Office Manager: Judy Haag
Number Employees: 10
Parent Co: Clinton Separators, Inc.
Brands:
Quaker City

29770 Straub Design Company
2238 Florida Ave S
Suite A
Minneapolis, MN 55426 952-546-6686
Fax: 952-546-3056 800-959-3708
www.straubdesign.com
Manufacturer and exporter of packaging and taping machinery
President: Dennis Schuette
Sales: Mark Baillie
Sales: Glenn Baillie
Estimated Sales: $2.5-5 Million
Number Employees: 20-49
Square Footage: 20000

29771 Straubel Company
1891 Commerce Dr
De Pere, WI 54115 920-336-1412
Fax: 920-336-1308 888-336-1412
sharil@straubelcompany.com
www.straubelcompany.com
Disposable plastic and paper products including table covers; also, plastic banquet tables, drop cloths, and laminations
President: Thomas Tess
Vice President: Craig Nothstine
Human Resources: Diane Biersteker
VP Operations: Paul Piikila
Production Planning: Brenda Scray
Plant Manager: John Westcott
Supply Chain Management: Shari Linksens
Estimated Sales: Below $5 Million
Number Employees: 10-19
Square Footage: 40000
Brands:
Breez Proof
Picnic Time
Table Mate

29772 Streamfeeder
315 27th Ave NE
Minneapolis, MN 55418 763-502-0000
Fax: 763-502-0100 info@streamfeeder.com
www.streamfeeder.com
Electromechanical products and friction feeders for inserting, feeding and collating
President: Mitch Speicher
Estimated Sales: $10-20 Million
Number Employees: 20-49

29773 Streater LLC
411 S 1st Ave
Albert Lea, MN 56007 507-373-0611
Fax: 507-373-7630 800-527-4197
salesinfo@streater.com www.streater.com
Store fixtures including gondolas and wall cases
President: Thomas Stensrude
Finance Executive: Dan Juntunen
Marketing: Dan Heckmann
Sales: Dave Sprunt
Estimated Sales: $1 - 3 Million
Number Employees: 1-4
Square Footage: 2240000
Parent Co: Joyce International

29774 Streator Dependable Manufacturing
1705 N Shabbona St
Streator, IL 61364 815-672-0551
Fax: 815-672-7631 800-798-0551
sales@streatordependable.com
www.streatordependable.com
Manufacturer and importer of material handling equipment including containers, pallets, stacking racks, skids and spools
President: Paul A Walker
Marketing: Bill Bontemps
Sales: Nathan Hovious
Number Employees: 100-249
Square Footage: 100000

29775 Stretch-Vent Packaging System
PO Box 51462
Ontario, CA 91761-1062 909-947-3993
Fax: 909-947-0579 800-822-8368
Manufacturer, importer and exporter of vented produce wrap
VP Sales/Marketing: T Lasker
Director Sales/Operations: Phil Beach
Estimated Sales: $10-20 Million
Number Employees: 50-99
Type of Packaging: Consumer, Bulk
Brands:
Stretch-Vent
Vex-Cap

29776 Stretchtape
18460 Syracuse Ave
Cleveland, OH 44110 216-486-9400
Fax: 216-486-9444 888-486-9400
info@stretchtape.com www.stretchtape.com
President: Sean Mc Donald
Estimated Sales: $1 - 5 Million
Number Employees: 20-49

29777 Stricker & Company
PO Box 667
La Plata, MD 20646 301-934-8346
Fax: 301-870-3112
Signs, printed labels and point of purchase displays
Owner: Susan Stiles
Estimated Sales: Below $5 Million
Number Employees: 1-4
Square Footage: 5000

29778 Stricklin Company
1901 W Commerce St
Dallas, TX 75208-8104 214-637-1030
Fax: 214-747-7872 tjohnson@baldwinmetals.com
www.stricklincompany.com
Manufacturer and exporter of blenders, cookers and mixers; also, repair services available
President: Tom Johnson
Controller: Don Smith
Engineer: Mitch Withem
Estimated Sales: Below $5 Million
Number Employees: 20-49
Square Footage: 120000
Parent Co: Baldwin Metals
Brands:
Stricklin
Strico

29779 Stripper Bags
121 Quail Run Road
Henderson, NV 89014-2129 800-354-2247
Fax: 702-898-9938
Manufacturer and exporter of preprinted poly bags for food portioning and rotation; also, labels including peel/stick and disposable for food rotation
President: Mark Tenner

29780 Strohmeter & Arpe Company
106 Allen Road
Basking Ridge, NJ 07920-3851 908-580-9100
Fax: 908-580-9300 800-628-2374
sales@strohmeyer.com www.strohmeyer.com
Natural waxes including beeswax, carnauba, candelilla, ouricouri and Japan wax, bulk honey, private label canned fruits, vegetables and seafood
President: Charles Kocot
Estimated Sales: $5 - 10 Million
Number Employees: 5-9

29781 (HQ)Strong Group
163 Western Ave
Gloucester, MA 01930-4042 978-281-4443
Fax: 978-281-6321 800-332-6025
custsvc@strong-holster.com
www.strong-holster.com
Custom made leather menu covers, wine lists, check presenters and ID badges
Owner: Don Strong
CEO: Rich Cutter
Marketing Director: Larry Angello
Operations Manager: Steve Kaity
Purchasing Manager: Brian Cutter
Estimated Sales: $5 Million
Number Employees: 1-4
Number of Products: 250
Square Footage: 232000
Type of Packaging: Bulk

29782 Strong Hold Products
PO Box 9043
Louisville, KY 40209-0043 502-363-4175
Fax: 502-363-3827 800-880-2625
info@strong-hold.com www.strong-hold.com
Industrial welded storage cabinets and shelving
President: Thomas Diebold
VP: Tina Gillenwoater
Vice President: Tom Diebold
Sales Director: Peggy Drake
Plant Manager: Dannis Hughbanks
Estimated Sales: $10-20 Million
Number Employees: 100-249
Square Footage: 108000
Parent Co: Fabricated Metals

29783 Strongarm
425 Caredean Drive
Horsham, PA 19044 215-443-3400
Fax: 215-443-3002 sales@strongarm.com
www.strongarm.com
Operator interface mountings and systems
President: Tom Holden
Sales Manager: Bill Flemming

29784 Stronghaven Inc.
11135 Monroe Rd
Matthews, NC 28105 704-847-7743
Fax: 704-847-5871 800-222-7919
info@stronghaven.com www.stronghaven.com

Manufacturer and exporter of corrugated boxes
Estimated Sales: $1 - 5 Million
Number Employees: 5-9
Square Footage: 500000

29785 Strongwell
2911 Industrial Park Dr
Lenoir City, TN 37771 865-986-5533
Fax: 865-986-4186 800-346-3061
quazite@strongwell.com www.strongwell.com
Polymer concrete drain systems
General Manager: John Downey
Finance Executive: David Redman
Estimated Sales: $20 - 50 Million
Number Employees: 100-249

29786 Stroter Inc
PO Box 892
Freeport, IL 61053 815-616-2506
Fax: 815-244-2102 diane@stroter.com
www.stroter.com
Spare parts, electric motors and complete replacement units

29787 Structural Concepts Corporation
888 E Porter Rd
Norton Shores, MI 49441 231-798-8888
Fax: 231-798-4960
dscripps@structuralconcepts.com
www.structuralconcepts.com
President: David P Geerts
Quality Control: Jeff Cimnes
Chairman: James Doss
Estimated Sales: $30 - 50 Million
Number Employees: 250-499

29788 (HQ)Structure Probe
PO Box 656
West Chester, PA 19381-0656 610-436-5400
Fax: 610-436-5755 800-242-4774
spi3spi@2spi.com www.2spi.com
Independent laboratory offering problem solving and analysis
President and Chairman of the Board: Violet Garber
Corporate Secretary and Vice President: Kim Murray
Vice President: Eugene Rodek
Vice President, Technical: Andrew W. Blackwood, Ph.D.
Quality Officer: Andrew W. Blackwood, Ph. D.
Office Manager: Nancy Blackwood
Estimated Sales: $1 - 2.5 Million
Number Employees: 10-19
Square Footage: 80000
Other Locations:
Structure Probe
Fairfield CT

29789 Stryco Wire Products
1110 Flint Road
North York, ON M3J 2J5
Canada 416-663-7000
Fax: 416-663-7001 info@strycowire.com
www.strycowire.com
Wire baskets and shelving, cooler shelves, slide guards and barbecue grills
President: Calford Robinson
CFO: Jana Bonder
Quality Control: Ken Duffney
R&D: Ede Zendai
Number Employees: 30-40

29790 Stuart W. Johnson & Company
1002 Mobile St
Lake Geneva, WI 53147-0999 262-248-8851
Fax: 262-248-0277 800-558-5904
sales@stuartjohnsonco.com
www.stuartjohnsonco.com
Aseptic processing equipment, centrifuges, cheese equipment, filtration equipment, clean rooms and equipment, cutting equipment, fillers, pin, milk, steam, flow diversion stations, heat exchangers, plate, tubular, homogenizersladders, vat, meters, flow
President: Robert T Morava Jr
Estimated Sales: $5-10 Million
Number Employees: 10-19

29791 Stubblefield Screen Print Company
2323 1ST ST. NW
Albuquerque, NM 87102 505-202-9802
Fax: 505-243-4187 ana@stubblefieldprint.com
www.stubblefieldprint.com
Emblems and decals
Owner: Ana Segura
Estimated Sales: Below $5 Million
Number Employees: 1-4

29792 Studd & Whipple Company
PO Box 17
Conewango Valley, NY 14726-0017 716-287-3791
Fax: 716-287-3309
Wooden pallets and pre-cut pallet materials
Branch Manager: Lynn Emley
Estimated Sales: $10 - 20 Million
Number Employees: 8
Parent Co: Crawford Manufacturing Company

29793 (HQ)Sturdi-Bilt Restaurant Equipment
7150 Nollar Rd
Whitmore Lake, MI 48189 313-231-4911
Fax: 800-444-2895 800-521-2895
sbrei@juno.com www.sturdibilt.com
Kitchen equipment and ventilation systems
Chairman: Arnold H Robinson
Secretary: Ruth Ann Robinson
Sales Director: Shirley Van Reuter
Estimated Sales: $2.5-5 Million
Number Employees: 5-9

29794 Stutz Products Corporation
606 S Walnut St
Hartford City, IN 47348 765-348-2510
Fax: 765-348-1001 info@stutzproducts.com
www.stutzproducts.com
Food processing machine knives
President: Bill Musselman
Purchasing Manager: Helen Musselman
Estimated Sales: $500,000
Number Employees: 5-9
Square Footage: 6000

29795 Suburban Corrugated BoxCompany
6363 Keokuk Rd
Indianhead Park, IL 60525-4341 630-920-1230
Fax: 630-920-1353 subcorr1@aol.com
Corrugated boxes
VP: Gene Mazurek
Estimated Sales: $2.5-5 Million
Number Employees: 10-19

29796 Suburban Laboratories
4140 Litt Dr
Hillside, IL 60162 708-544-3260
Fax: 708-544-8587 800-783-5227
sublabsinc@aol.com www.suburbanlabs.com
Consultant and analyst for the food and sanitation industries providing analytical, enviromental and microbiological testing, nutritional assays and water and sterility testing
President: Ray Thomas
Laboratory Manager: Jarrett Thomas
Sales Manager: Larry Horn
Estimated Sales: $2.5-5 Million
Number Employees: 20-49

29797 Suburban Sign Company
19611 Jasper Street NW
Anoka, MN 55303-9642 763-753-8849
Fax: 763-753-8225
Signs including advertising, plastic, painted and wooden
Owner: Burt Pfeifer
Number Employees: 2

29798 Suburban Signs
5051 Greenbelt Rd
College Park, MD 20740 301-474-5051
Fax: 301-345-1196 info@suburbansigns.com
www.suburbansigns.com
Signs
President: Robert E Wells
President: Robert Wells
VP: Joel Hurst
Estimated Sales: Below $5 Million
Number Employees: 1-4
Square Footage: 2100

29799 Success Systems
45 Church St P.O. Box 2457
st. 106
Stamford, GA 06906 404-252-6002
Fax: 203-921-1660 800-653-3345
mkt@success-systems.com
www.success-systems.com
Computer systems and software
VP: Howard Spiller
Estimated Sales: $1 - 5 Million
Number Employees: 20-49
Square Footage: 40000

29800 Sudmo North America, Inc
1330 Anvil Road
Machesney Park, IL 61115 815-639-0322
Fax: 815-639-1135 800-218-3915
snainfo@petair.com www.sudmona.com
Supplier of valves and components to the food, dairy, beverage and pharmaceutical industries
Director of Sales: Jim Banks
Estimated Sales: $5-10 Million
Number Employees: 10-19
Parent Co: Pentair

29801 Suffolk Iron Works
418 E. Washington Street
PO Box 1943
Suffolk, VA 23434 757-539-2353
Fax: 757-539-1520
info@suffolkironworks.com""
www.suffolkironworks.com
Manufacturer and exporter of peanut machinery and bulk material handling systems
President: Clifton Harrell
VP: Jenny Winslow
Senior Project Engineer: John Harrell
General Manager: Kenny Johnson
Project Manager/Estimator: Bill Hatter
Safety Administrator: Tiffany Youker
Estimated Sales: $5-10 Million
Number Employees: 20-49

29802 Sugarplum Desserts
20381 62nd Avenue
Building 5
Langley, BC V3A SE6 604-534-2282
Fax: 604-534-2280 info@sugarplumdesserts.com
www.sugarplumdesserts.com
Thaw and serve cheesecakes and thaw and bake cookies
President: Leslie Goodman
Number Employees: 15
Square Footage: 32000

29803 Suhner Manufacturing
S Suhner Drive
Rome, GA 30162 706-235-8046
Fax: 706-235-8045 info@suhnerusa.com
www.suhnerusa.com
Chairman of the Board: Otto Suhner
Estimated Sales: $20 - 30 Million
Number Employees: 100-250

29804 Suitt Construction Company
201 E McBee Ave Ste 400
Greenville, SC 29601 864-250-5000
Fax: 864-250-5101 design-build@suitt.com
www.suitt.com
Construction and maintenance, specilizing in bakeries, poultry, frozen foods, dairy, bottling plants, prepared foods, etc
CEO: John Cronin
President and CEO: Donald Warren
VP/COO: Donald Nickell
Marketing/Public Relations: Donald White
Sales Director: Karl Kelly
Operations Manager: Donald Nickell
Purchasing Manager: W Tony Masters
Estimated Sales: $200-500 Million
Number Employees: 100-249
Parent Co: BE & K
Other Locations:
Suitt Construction Corporation
Richmond VA
Suitt Construction Corporation
Atlanta GA
Suitt Construction Corporation
Orlando FL
Suitt Construction Corporation
Lincoln RI
Suitt Construction Corporation
Raleigh NC
Suitt Cosntruction Corpoation
Birmingham AL

29805 **Sultan Linens**
313 5th Ave
New York, NY 10016-6518 212-689-8900
Fax: 212-689-8965
Manufacturer and exporter of decorative linens, towels, table cloths, place mats and aprons
President: Joseph Sultan
Sales Manager: Daniel Sultan
Estimated Sales: $500,000 - $1 Million
Number Employees: 1-4
Parent Co: SLI Home Fashions

29806 **Sumitomo Machinery Corporation of America**
4200 Holland Blvd
Chesapeake, VA 23323-1529 757-485-3355
Fax: 757-485-0643 800-SMC-YCLO
customercare@suminet.com www.smcyclo.com
Mechanical and electrical adjustable speed drives, parallel shaft and right angle reducers, shaft mounted gear motors, and helical, planetary, spiral bevel, gear reducers
President: Ron Smith
Executive VP: James Magee
CFO: Nobuhiao Kawamusa
Estimated Sales: $50 - 75 Million
Number Employees: 250-499

29807 **Summit Appliance Division**
770 Garrison Ave
Bronx, NY 10474-5603 718-893-3900
Fax: 718-842-3093 800-932-4267
sales@summitappliance.com
www.summitappliance.com
Manufacturer, importer and exporter of beer taps, wine coolers, ice cream freezers and beverage merchandisers, minibars and coolers
President: Felix Stroch
Vice President of Marketing: Steve Ross
R&D: Phil Yacht
Quality Control: Jeff Musnikow
Sales Director: Stephen Ross
Vice President: Paul Storch
Estimated Sales: $25 Million
Number Employees: 50-99
Square Footage: 140000
Parent Co: Felix Storch
Brands:
Summit

29808 **Summit Commercial**
770 Garrison Ave
Bronx, NY 10474-5603 718-893-3900
Fax: 718-842-3093 800-932-4267
info@summitappliance.com
www.summitappliance.com
Equipment
President: Felix Storch
Vice President: Paul Storch
Vice President: Paul Storch
Estimated Sales: $40-50 Million
Number Employees: 100
Number of Brands: 1
Number of Products: 170
Square Footage: 150000
Parent Co: Storch, Felix
Brands:
Summit

29809 **Summit Industrial Equipment**
930 Riverside Pkwy # 30
Broderick, CA 95605-1511 916-372-5890
Fax: 916-372-1973 www.summitindustrial.com
Air compressors
Manager: Mark Kabnick
Communications Director: Chris Fisher
Vice President of Corporate Communicatio: Annika Berglund
Estimated Sales: $5-10 Million
Number Employees: 5-9

29810 **Summit Machine BuildersCorporation**
550 W 53rd Place
Denver, CO 80216-1612 303-294-9949
Fax: 303-294-9622 800-274-6741
smb@summitmb.com www.summitmb.com
Manufacturer and exporter of automation and automated assembly equipment including dry and fibrous product feeding, filling and dispensing systems; also, ingredients dispensing and automatic micro weighing equipment
President: Scott Harris
Director Sales: Mike Schmehl
Estimated Sales: $5-10 Million
Number Employees: 85
Square Footage: 200000
Brands:
Sro Feeder
Vibra-Meter Feeder

29811 **Summitville Tiles**
P.O.Box 73
Summitville, OH 43962-0073 330-223-1511
Fax: 330-223-1414 info@summitville.com
www.summitville.com
Ceramic tiles
President: David Johnson
CFO: Rich Finnicun
Estimated Sales: $20-50 Million
Number Employees: 500-999

29812 **Sun Industries**
PO Box 379
Goodland, IN 47948-0379 219-297-3010
Fax: 219-297-3010 sunind@ffni.com
Packaging machinery and equipment
Estimated Sales: $1-2.5 Million
Number Employees: 5-9

29813 **Sun Paints & Coatings**
4701 East 7th Avenue
PO Box 75070
Tampa, FL 33605 813-367-4444
Fax: 813-367-0263
james-lowery@warrior-group.net
www.suncoatings.com
Manufacturer and exporter of window, tile and mildew cleaners
President: Barton Malina
Estimated Sales: $5-10 Million
Number Employees: 20-49
Square Footage: 100000

29814 **Sun Plastics**
PO Box 37
Clearwater, MN 55320-0037 320-558-6130
Fax: 320-558-6119 800-862-1673
www.sunplastics.biz
Thermoformed plastic packaging for food
President: Paul Amundson
Plant Manager: Ken Doble
Estimated Sales: $2.5-5 Million
Number Employees: 20-49
Square Footage: 48000

29815 **Sun-Ray Sign & Glass**
376 Roost Ave
Holland, MI 49424-2032 616-392-2824
Fax: 616-392-5797
Signs
Owner: Scott Tardiff
Estimated Sales: $500,000-$1 Million
Number Employees: 1-4

29816 **Sunbeam Health & Safety**
7400 W 100th Place
Bridgeview, IL 60455-2406 708-598-9100
Fax: 708-233-5472 www.sunbeam.com
Manufacturer and exporter of food scales
Estimated Sales: $50-100 Million
Number Employees: 250-499
Type of Packaging: Consumer, Food Service

29817 **Sunbeam Product**
PO.Box 8097
Toledo, OH 43605-0097 419-691-1551
Soap and detergents
Partner: George Stoycheff
Estimated Sales: $1-2.5 Million
Number Employees: 1-4

29818 **Sundance Architectural Products, LLC**
4249 L B McLeod Rd
Orlando, FL 32811 407-297-1337
Fax: 407-296-4330 800-940-1337
info@sdap.com www.sdap.com
Commercial awnings and fabric structures
President: Raymond Toot
Estimated Sales: $5 - 10 Million
Number Employees: 50-99

29819 **(HQ)Sundyne Corporation**
14845 W 64th Ave
Arvada, CO 80007 303-425-0800
Fax: 303-425-0896 www.sundyne.com
Air/gas compressor pumps and pumping equipment
President: Phillip Ruffner
CFO: John O'Toole
VP/General Manager: Jeff Wiemelt
Human Resources Director: Marie Weiss-Rich
Estimated Sales: $41.8 Million

29820 **Sunflower Packaging**
8952 NW 24th Ave
Miami, FL 33147 305-591-3388
Fax: 305-591-9356 lungmeng@lung-meng.com
www.lung-meng.com
Packaging machinery
Manager: Allen Tsai
General Manager: Allen Tsai
Estimated Sales: $5-10 Million
Number Employees: 10-19

29821 **Sungjae Corporation**
Po Box 6525
Irvine, CA 92616 949-757-1727
Fax: 949-757-1723 minhee@sungjaecorp.com
Printed flexible packaging,packing materials, bags, films, wrap, wrapping zipper bag,stand up bag and shrink film.
President: Kim Eunhee
Marketing Director: Vin Eun Hee
Estimated Sales: $5 - 10,000,000
Number Employees: 8
Parent Co: Sungjae Corporation

29822 **Sungjae Corporation**
27 Highpoint
Irvine, CA 92603 949-757-1727
Fax: 949-757-1723 sjpackaging@msn.com
Rotogravure printed flexible packaging, packaging materials, bags, film, wrap, wrapping, printers, printing
Owner: Minhee Kim
Marketing Head: Min Hee
Estimated Sales: Less than $500,000
Number Employees: 1-4

29823 **(HQ)Sunkist Growers**
14130 Riverside Drive
Sherman Oaks, CA 91423-2313 818-986-4800
Fax: 818-379-7405 www.sunkist.com
Sunkist Growers Trademark Licensing Operations Division provides branded products services. Sunkist licensed products are available in the following categories: Fruit Juices, Fruit Drinks, Healthy Snacks, Baking Mixes, CarbonatedBeverages, Confections, Vitamins, Frozen Novelties, Salad Toppings, Freshly Peeled Citrus, Chilled Jellies and even Nonfood products.
President/Chief Executive Officer: Russell Hanlin II
Chairman: Mark Gillette
Vice Chairman: James Finch
Vice President: Charles Brown
Vice President, Sales & Marketing: Kevin Fiori
Director, Corporate Communications: Claire Smith
Manager, Operations: Robert Quinn
Purchasing Manager: George Garcia
Estimated Sales: $1 Billion
Number Employees: 500
Type of Packaging: Food Service, Private Label
Other Locations:
Sunkist Growers
Toronto Canada ON
Sunkist Growers
Cary NC
Sunkist Growers
Pittsburgh PA
Sunkist Growers
Buffalo NY
Sunkist Growers
Stafford TX
Sunkist Growers
Visalia CA
Sunkist Growers
Cherry Hill NJ
Sunkist Growers
West Chester OH
Sunkist Growers
Detroit MI
Sunkist Growers
Long Valley NJ
Sunkist Growers
Phoenix AZ
Sunkist Growers
Clackamas OR
Sunkist Growers
Anjou Canada QC

29824 **Sunland Manufacturing Company**
1658 93rd Ln NE
Minneapolis, MN 55449 763-785-2247
Fax: 763-785-9667 800-790-1905
www.sunlandmfg.com
Polyethylene bags
Owner: Pat Haley
Estimated Sales: $2.5-5 Million
Number Employees: 10-19
Square Footage: 8000

29825 **Sunmaster of Naples**
900 Industrial Blvd
Naples, FL 34104 239-261-3581
Fax: 239-261-7499 www.sunmasterinc.com
Commercial awnings
President: John Wilkinson
Vice President: David Rinker
Estimated Sales: $2.5-5,000,000
Number Employees: 50-99

29826 **Sunny Cove Citrus LLC**
1315 E Curtis Ave
Reedley, CA 93654-9317
Fax: 559-626-7210
customer.service@sccitrus.com
www.sccitrus.com
Packinghouse and licensed shipper of citrus products for Sunkist Growers Inc.
President: Tom Clark
Field Manager: Justin Kulikov
Controller: Warren Lee
Office Manager: Vera Fast
Square Footage: 340000
Type of Packaging: Food Service

29827 **Sunpoint Products**
PO Box 567
Lawrence, MA 01842-1267 978-794-3100
Fax: 978-685-7840 bokane@sunpointinc.com
www.sunpointinc.com
Disinfectants, anti-bacterial soaps, etc
President: Brooks O Kane
Sales Manager: Bob Monroe
Number Employees: 3
Brands:
Red Cross Nurse

29828 **(HQ)Sunroc Corporation**
PO Box 13150
Columbus, OH 43213-0150 302-678-7800
Fax: 302-678-7809 800-478-6762
literature@sunroc.com www.sunroc.com
Manufacturer and exporter of electric and bottled water coolers,drinking fountains and point-of-use coolers
President: Anthony Salamone
CFO: Mark Whitaker
Director Engineering: Ronald Greenwald
Quality Control: Tom Huber
VP Sales/Marketing: John Ott
Estimated Sales: $20-50 Million
Number Employees: 100-249
Square Footage: 250000
Brands:
Softtouch

29829 **Sunset Paper Products**
3148 Divernon Avenue
Simi Valley, CA 93063-1611 323-587-4488
Fax: 323-587-1313 800-228-7882
info@sunsetpaper.com www.sunsetpaper.com
Manufactures baking and candy cups
President: Alan Newman
Estimated Sales: $20-50 Million
Number Employees: 50-99

29830 **Sunset Sales**
PO Box 446
Hurricane, UT 84737-0446 435-635-3199
Fax: 435-635-0205
Commercial food packaging and processing machinery
Estimated Sales: $1-5 Million
Number Employees: 9

29831 **Sunshine Restaurant Supply**
24833 Commercial Ave
Orange Beach, AL 36561 251-974-5000
Fax: 251-974-5640
www.pleasureislandrestaurants.net
Owner: J Schenck
Vice President: J Hall Schenck
Estimated Sales: Below 1 Million
Number Employees: 10-19

29832 **Supelco**
595 N Harrison Rd
Bellefonte, PA 16823 814-359-3441
Fax: 814-359-5459 800-247-6628
techservice@sial.com www.sigmaaldrich.com
Chromatography products for analysis and purification
President: J Russel Gant
Vice President: Russel Gant
Research & Development: Mark Robillard
Marketing Director: Don Hobbs
Sales Director: Marty McCoy
Public Relations: Diane Lidgett
Operations/Production: Rod Datt
Production Manager: Tom Henderson
Plant Manager: Rod Datt
Purchasing Manager: Jim Heiserl
Estimated Sales: $50 - 75 Million
Number Employees: 250-499
Parent Co: Sigma-Aldrich Corporation

29833 **Super Beta Glucan, Inc.**
5 Holland #109
Irvine, CA 92618 949-264-2888
Fax: 626-203-0655
service@superbetaglucan.com
www.superbetaglucan.com
Mushroom Beta Glucan (Immulink MBG)
Founder: Dr. S.N. Chen

29834 **Super Cooker**
6049 Peterson Rd
PO Box 1009
Lake Park, GA 31636 229-559-1662
Fax: 229-559-1611 800-841-7452
sales@supercooker.com www.supercooker.com
Manufacturer and exporter of portable barbecue grills and smokers including charcoal, wood and gas
Owner: Ben Futch
Estimated Sales: $3 - 5,000,000
Number Employees: 10-19

29835 **Super Radiator Coils**
451 Southlake Blvd
Richmond, VA 23236 804-794-2887
Fax: 804-379-2118 800-229-2645
vainfo@superradiatorcoils.com www.srcoils.com
Coils and heat exchangers; exporter of coils, evaporators and condensors
Estimated Sales: $30+ Million
Number Employees: 130
Square Footage: 112000
Parent Co: Super Radiator Coils
Other Locations:
Super Radiator Coils
Phoenix AZ
Brands:
Super

29836 **Super Seal ManufacturingLimited**
670 Rowntree Dairy Road
Woodbridge, ON L4L 5T8
Canada 905-850-2929
Fax: 905-850-4440 800-337-3239
info@supersealmfg.com www.supersealmfg.com
Manufacturer and exporter of energy saving devices, retail and industrial impact traffic, P.V.C. and bi-folding doors, dock seals, truck shelters and inflatable seals and shelters
President: Renato Torchetti
Director Sales (USA): Paul Ricci
Number Employees: 10
Square Footage: 160000
Brands:
Atmo

29837 **(HQ)Super Steel Products Corporation**
7900 W Tower Ave
Milwaukee, WI 53223 414-355-4800
Fax: 414-355-0372
heather.krugler@supersteel.com
www.supersteel.com
Fabricated metal parts
Chief Financial Officer: Brad Nennig
Director, Quality Assurance: Dan Klumpyan
Sales Manager: Dale Wilson
Public Relations Contact: Heather Krugler
General Manager: Greg Gaberino
Director, Project Management: Dan Brook
Plant Manager: Joe Rouse
Director, Engineering & Purchasing: Jason Gaare
Estimated Sales: $50-100 Million
Number Employees: 250-499
Square Footage: 650000
Other Locations:
Super Steel Products Corp.
Troy OH

29838 **Super Sturdy**
200 Rock Fish Drive
Weldon, NC 27890-2106 252-536-4833
Fax: 252-536-2118 800-253-4833
Custom stainless steel mobile carts, sinks, tables and cabinets
VP: Salvatore Pirruccio
Estimated Sales: $2.5-5 Million
Number Employees: 17
Square Footage: 33000
Parent Co: Marlo Manufacturing Company

29839 **Super Systems**
300 S 84th Ave
Wausau, WI 54401-8460 715-842-2724
Fax: 715-848-1870 800-558-5880
www.piperonline.net
Bakery ovens and proofers, barbecue rotisseries, self-service food warmers/merchandisers, transport cabinets and racks; exporter of bakery ovens and proofers
President: Roger Sweeney
Estimated Sales: $20-50 Million
Number Employees: 50-99
Square Footage: 30000
Parent Co: Piper Products
Brands:
Piper Products
Super Systems

29840 **Super Vision International**
9400 Southridge Park Ct # 200
Orlando, FL 32819-8643 407-857-9900
Fax: 407-857-0050 kingstone@svision.com
www.svision.com
Manufacturer and exporter of signs, lighting and lighting fixtures
President: Mike Bauer
Chairman of the Board: Brett M Kingstone
Sales (USA): Rick Hunter
International Sales: Paula Vega
Number Employees: 50-99
Square Footage: 320000
Brands:
Endglow
Sideglow
Supervision

29841 **Super-Chef Manufacturing Company**
9235 Bissonnet Street
Houston, TX 77074 713-729-9660
Fax: 713-729-8404 800-231-3478
www.superchefmfg.com
Manufacturer and exporter of broilers, fryers, griddles, warming units, ovens, hoods, ranges, hot plates, food concession trailers and compact kitchens with recirculating filter hoods
President: Chris Pappas
CEO: Regina Seale
CFO: Isabel Repka
VP: Ed Seale
R&D: Chris Pappas
Quality Control: Ed Seale
Marketing: Regina Seale
Sales: Isabel Repka
Public Relations: Regina Seale
Operations: Chris Pappas
Production: Barry Berg
Plant Manager: Barry Berg
Purchasing: Ed Seale
Number Employees: 20-49
Number of Brands: 2
Square Footage: 160000
Brands:
Fat Mizer
Kompact Kitchen
Super Chef

29842 Superflex
152 44th St
Brooklyn, NY 11232 718-768-1400
Fax: 718-768-5065 800-394-3665
sales@superflex.com www.superflex.com
Manufacturer and exporter of P.V.C. flexible suction and discharge reinforced hoses, liquid tight conduit and electrical tubing used for pumps, refrigerators, dairy equipment, beverage dispensers, etc
President: Simon Elbaz
VP: Y Elbaz
Estimated Sales: $2.5-5 Million
Number Employees: 1-4
Brands:
Rollerflex
Sealproof
Superflex

29843 Superfos Packaging
11301 Superfos Dr SE
Cumberland, MD 21502 804-240-1793
Fax: 301-759-4905 800-537-9242
jim.mason@superfos.com www.superfos.com
Rigid open top plastic containers
President: James Mason
CFO: John Mathews
Sales Manager: Stephen Towl
Estimated Sales: $10-$20 Million
Number Employees: 100-249
Parent Co: Superfos Emballagelas
Brands:
Flex Off
Ring Lock
Vapor Lock

29844 Superior Belting Company
6 Andrews St
PO Box 8678
Greenville, SC 29601 864-605-0076
Fax: 864-269-9754
salesdepartment@superiorbelt.com
www.superiorbelt.com
Conveyor belting for the food processing industry
President: Leonard Sandy Chace
CFO: Allan Thompson
R&D: Sandy Chace
Estimated Sales: Below $5 Million
Number Employees: 10-19

29845 (HQ)Superior Brush Company
3455 W 140th St
Cleveland, OH 44111 216-941-6987
Fax: 216-252-8838 www.superiorbrush.com
Manufacturer and exporter of metal strip brushes; also, custom design services available
VP Sales/Marketing: Richard Mertes
Estimated Sales: $10-20 Million
Number Employees: 20-49
Square Footage: 11000

29846 Superior Distributing
2501 Maple St
Louisville, KY 40211 502-778-6661
Fax: 502-775-7519 800-365-6661
www.superiordisplayboards.com
Manufacturer and exporter of FDA approved wiping cloths, polyethylene bags, hairnets, beard guards, gloves and butchers' paper
Owner: Michael Hinson
Sales Manager: Susan Thrapp
Estimated Sales: $5-10 Million
Number Employees: 10-19

29847 Superior Food Machinery
7635 Serapis Ave
Pico Rivera, CA 90660 562-949-0396
Fax: 562-949-0180 800-944-0396
info@Superiorinc.com www.superiorinc.com
Manufacturer, importer, exporter and designer of tortilla and tortilla chip processing equipment; also, corn feeders, ovens and washers
Owner: Polo Reyes
General Sales Manager: Rick Rangel
Customer Service Manager: Mark Reyes
Estimated Sales: $5-10 Million
Number Employees: 20-49
Square Footage: 7000

29848 Superior Imaging Group
22710 72nd Ave S
Kent, WA 98032-1926 253-872-7200
Fax: 253-872-7202 888-872-7200
sales@superiorimaging.com
www.superiorimaging.com
Commercial screen printing on nontextiles
Owner: Eric Richards
CFO: Michelle McKenzie
Estimated Sales: $2.5 - 5 Million
Number Employees: 20-49

29849 Superior Industries
315 State Highway 28
Morris, MN 56267 320-589-2406
Fax: 320-589-2260 800-321-1558
info@superior-ind.com www.superior-ind.com
Manufacturer and exporter idlers and portable conveying equipment
President: Paul Schmidgall
Estimated Sales: $15 - 20 Million
Number Employees: 100-249

29850 Superior Label Company
625 Gotham Pkwy
Carlstadt, NJ 07072-2403 201-438-4500
Fax: 201-438-8126 800-877-3795
superior95@aol.com www.superiorpack.com
Pressure sensitive label application equipment including primary labeler or bar code printer and applicator

29851 Superior Linen & Work Wear
3001 Cherry St
Kansas City, MO 64108-3124 816-931-4477
Fax: 816-931-0504 800-798-7987
sales@superiorlinen.com
www.superiorlinen.com
Table covers, uniforms, aprons,towels, table cloths, table skirts, chef wear, oxford shirts, and polo shirts
Chairman of the Board: William G Kartsonis
Estimated Sales: $20-50 Million
Number Employees: 50-99
Type of Packaging: Consumer, Private Label

29852 Superior Neon Sign, Inc.
2515 N Oklahoma Ave
Oklahoma City, OK 73105 405-528-5515
Fax: 405-528-5535 jim@superiorneon.com
www.superiorneon.com
Sign manufacturer
President: Dan Lorant
Estimated Sales: $1-2.5 Million
Number Employees: 20-49

29853 Superior Packaging Equipment Corporation
3 Edison Pl
Suite 4
Fairfield, NJ 07004 973-575-8818
Fax: 973-890-7295 info@superiorpack.com
www.superiorpack.com
Manufacturer and exporter of cartoning machinery including forming, gluing, inserting, closing, sealing and opening
President: Glenn Rice
Executive VP: Russell Rice
Mngr.: Edwin Santiago
Estimated Sales: $5 - 10 Million
Number Employees: 10
Square Footage: 38000

29854 Superior Product PickupServices
5707 W Howard Street
Niles, IL 60714-4012 847-647-4720
Fax: 847-647-4739 www.productpickup.com
Consultant offering market research on consumer products
Estimated Sales: $1 - 5 Million
Number Employees: 20
Square Footage: 5000

29855 Superior Products Company
P.O.Box 64177
Saint Paul, MN 55164 651-636-1110
800-328-9800
comments@superprod.com www.superprod.com
Wholesale Distributor of foodservice equipment and supplies
Number Employees: 1-4
Type of Packaging: Food Service
Other Locations:
Alexandria VA
Anaheim CA
Atlanta GA
Baltimore MD
Boston MA
Charlotte NC
Cleveland OH
Dallas TX
Hartford CT
Orlando FL
Pennsauken NJ
Reno NV
San Diego CA
Brands:
Next Day Gourmet
Superior Monogram

29856 Superior Quality Products
602 Potential Pkwy
Schenectady, NY 12302 518-831-6800
Fax: 518-831-6890 800-724-1129
info@superiorqualityproducts.com
www.superiorqualityproducts.com
Tissue, paper food trays, plastic straws and stirrers, napkins, chicken boxes and paper hinged takeouts
VP: Richard Bonaker
Plant Manager: Barbara Flaming
National Sales Manager: William Gnatek
Sales Manager: Richard Bonaker
Plant Manager: Larry Meyers
Estimated Sales: $20-50 Million
Number Employees: 100-249
Type of Packaging: Bulk
Brands:
Valay

29857 Superior Tank & Trailer
P.O.Box 500
Beach City, OH 44608 330-756-2030
Fax: 330-756-2015 superiortank@yahoo.com
www.superiortankinc.com
Wine industry stainless steel tanks
Owner: Thomas Burkey
VP: Byron Kovalaske
VP Sales: Byron Kovalaske
Estimated Sales: $20-50 Million
Number Employees: 20-49

29858 Superior-Studio Specialties Ltd
2239 South Yates Ave
Commerce, CA 90040-1948 323-278-0100
Fax: 323-278-0111 800-354-3049
jake@superiorstudio.com
www.superiorstudio.com
Decorative items, lighting and theme props
Estimated Sales: $1 - 5 Million
Parent Co: Superior Specialties LLC

29859 Superklean Washdown Products
1550 Bryant Street
Suite 750
San Francisco, CA 94103-4877 415-252-2861
Fax: 415-255-2032 superkln@aol.com
www.sverdrup.com/opeos/facilities.html
Spray nozzles, hot and cold water mixer-hose stations, steam and cold water mixer-hose stations, swivel fittings, 3-piece fittings, and accessories

29860 Supermarket Associates
4209 Pin Oak Drive
Durham, NC 27707-5270 919-493-0994
Fax: 919-493-0994
Consultant specializing in advertising, marketing and management services for the food retailing industry
President: Sheldon Sosna
VP: Charles Ebner
Estimated Sales: $500,000-$1 Million
Number Employees: 1-4
Square Footage: 1000

29861 SuppliesForLess
905 G St
Hampton, VA 23661 757-245-7675
Fax: 757-244-4819 800-235-2201
www.suppliesforless.com
Floating advertising balloons and blimps and flexible neon rope lights
Estimated Sales: $1 - 3 Million
Number Employees: 10-19
Square Footage: 243000
Brands:
Bend-A-Lite
Blimpy
Giant

29862 Supply Corporation
P.O.Box 100
Lake Geneva, WI 53147 262-248-8837
Fax: 800-325-9404 800-558-2455
supplies@supplycorp.com www.supplycorp.com

Industrial safety, sanitation supplies, lubricants and tools for maintence, food processing supplies, cleaning supplies, brushes, mops, gloves, containers and material handling products
President/Owner: Rex Anderson
CEO: Roland Johnson
Sales: Rex Anderson
Number Employees: 10
Parent Co: Stand Alone Company

29863 Supply One
11401 East 27th Street North
Suite D
Tulsa, OK 74116 918-446-4428
Fax: 918-445-7448 800-832-4725
www.supplyone.com
Meat and produce boxes
Manager: Dave Jones
President, Chief Executive Officer: Bill Leith
Manager: J R Clonts
Estimated Sales: $1-2.5 Million
Number Employees: 10-19

29864 Supramatic
3313 Lakeshore Boulevard West
Toronto, ON M8W 1M8
Canada 416-251-3266
Fax: 416-251-1433 877-465-2883
info@supramatic.com www.supramatic.com
Manufacturer and importer of espresso, coffee and cappuccino machines; importer of coffee beans
President: Rene Peterson
Estimated Sales: Below $5 Million
Number Employees: 3

29865 Supreme Corporation
2572 East Kercher Road
PO Box 463
Goshen, IN 46527 574-533-0331
Fax: 574-642-4729 800-642-4889
info@supremecorp.com www.supremeind.com
Manufacturer and exporter of refrigerators, freezers and refrigerated truck cars
CEO: Herbert M Gardner
VP Marketing/Sales: Rick Horn
Estimated Sales: $10 - 20 Million
Number Employees: 2
Type of Packaging: Bulk

29866 Supreme Corporation
5901 S 226th St
Kent, WA 98032-4861 253-395-8712
Fax: 253-395-8713 info@supremecorp.com
www.supremediamondtools.com
Synthetic wine closures, synthetic closures for specialty food bottles
President: Robert Anderson
CEO: Bob De Monte
Estimated Sales: $5 - 10 Million
Number Employees: 50-99

29867 Supreme Fabricators
19127 Pioneer Blvd Spc 18
Artesia, CA 90701 323-583-8944
Fax: 323-583-8946
Stainless steel tanks and automatic storage and handling systems
President: Dean Graves
Estimated Sales: $500,000-$1,000,000
Number Employees: 1-4

29868 Supreme Metal
3125 Trotters Parkway
Alpharetta, GA 30004-7746
Fax: 770-740-6010 800-645-2526
www.suprememetal.com
Manufacturer and exporter of stainless steel hot food tables, sinks, ice storage equipment and wait stations; also, bars, bins and glass racks
President: Rick Schwartz
VP Sales: Lisa Finegan
National Sales Manager: Sandy Hill
Type of Packaging: Food Service

29869 Supreme Murphy Truck Bodies
4000 Airport Dr NW
Wilson, NC 27896 252-291-2191
Fax: 252-291-9183 800-334-2298
Refrigerated truck, trailer and van bodies
Estimated Sales: $10-25 Million
Number Employees: 100

29870 Supreme Products
PO Box 154308
Waco, TX 76715-4308 254-799-4941
Fax: 254-799-4943 sales@supremeproducts.com
www.supremeproducts.com
Food and beverage concession trailers and vending carts.
President: Pat Hood
VP: Hugh Hood
Number Employees: 10
Square Footage: 35000
Brands:
Supreme

29871 (HQ)Surco Products
290 Alpha Dr
RIDC Industrial Park
Pittsburgh, PA 15238 412-252-7000
Fax: 412-252-1005 800-556-0111
odorstop@earthlink.com www.surcopt.com
Manufacturer and exporter of air fresheners, deodorants and insecticides
President: Arnold Zlotnik
CEO: Bernard Surloff
Estimated Sales: $10 - 20 Million
Number Employees: 50-99
Square Footage: 57000
Type of Packaging: Consumer, Private Label, Bulk
Brands:
2-In-One Deodorizer
24 Hour Odor Absorber
Air-Savers
Air-Scent
Ban-O-Dor
End Smoke
Fresh As a Baby
Garb-O-Flakes
Odomaster
Oh No!
Potty Fresh
Round the Clock
Rug Aroma
Sani-Aire
Sani-Flakes
Sani-Scent
Scatter
Scent-Flo
So-Fresh
Sta-Fresh
Surco
Surcota
Zorb-It-All

29872 Sure Beam Corporation
9276 Scranton Rd Ste 600
San Diego, CA 92121 858-795-6300
Fax: 858-552-9973 invest@surebeamcorp.com
www.surebeamcorp.com
Provider of electronic pasteurization systems and services
President: Terrance Bruggeman
Number Employees: 50-99

29873 Sure Clean Corporation
PO Box 1
Two Rivers, WI 54241-0001 920-793-3838
Fax: 920-793-1555 jimkonop@charter.net
Detergent, soap, household cleaners, etc
Estimated Sales: $1 - 5 Million

29874 Sure Shot Dispensing Systems
100 Dispensing Way
Lower Sackville, NS B4C 4H2
Canada 902-865-9602
Fax: 902-865-9604 888-777-4990
sales@sureshotdispensing.com
www.sureshotdispensing.com
President: Michael Duck
VP: David Macaulay
R&D: Ian Maclean
Quality Control: Peter Black
Marketing: Chad Wiesner
Sales: William Morris
Operations: Garth I
Production: Dennis Dickinson
Plant Manager: Ken Lawrence
Purchasing Director: Tracey S
Number Employees: 90
Square Footage: 260000

29875 Sure Torque
1461 Tallevast Rd
Sarasota, FL 34243 941-753-1095
Fax: 941-756-8425 800-387-6572
spearson@suretorque.com www.suretorque.com
Manufacturer and exporter of container closure torque measurement instruments including near and on-line, automatic and electronic
Owner: Michelle Bergeron
R&D: Steve Pearson
Technical Engineer: Tibor Szenti
Sales/Technical: Gloria LaCroix
Director Operations: Jeff Dubrow
Estimated Sales: Below $5 Million
Number Employees: 1-4
Square Footage: 2500
Brands:
Torque Tester

29876 Sure-Feed Engineering
12050 49th St N
Clearwater, FL 33762 727-571-3330
Fax: 727-571-3443 sales@sure-feed.com
www.pb.com
Feeders, attaching systems
Sales/Marketing: Abe Mammau
Manager: Joe Springer
Estimated Sales: $1-2.5 Million
Number Employees: 100-249

29877 Sure-Kol Refrigerator Company
490 Flushing Ave
Brooklyn, NY 11205 718-625-0601
Fax: 718-624-1719 surekol@hughes.net
www.surekol.com
Walk-in refrigerators
President: Steven Waslin
Estimated Sales: $2.5 - 5 Million
Number Employees: 10-19
Square Footage: 16000
Brands:
Sure-Kol

29878 Surekap
579 Barrow Park Dr
Winder, GA 30680 770-867-5793
Fax: 770-867-5799 support@surekap.com
www.surekap.com
Manufacturer and exporter of liquid filling and bottle and capping equipment including plastic, metal, tamper evident, CRC, etc
President: Greg Raines Jr
Estimated Sales: $10-20 Million
Number Employees: 20-49

29879 Surface Measurement Systems
2125 28th Street SW
Suite 1
Allentown, PA 18103 610-798-8299
Fax: 610-798-0334 sales@smsna.com ÿÿÿ
www.smsna.com
Automated laboratory systems measuring all materials for food industry
Manager: Joe Domingue
Director Sales/Marketing: Joe Domingue
Estimated Sales: $1 - 5 Million
Number Employees: 5-9

29880 Surfine Central Corporation
PO Box 5698
Pine Bluff, AR 71611-5698 870-247-2387
Fax: 870-247-9830
Paper bags
President: Bob Ratchford
Number Employees: 45

29881 Surtec, Inc.
1880 N Macarthur Dr
Tracy, CA 95376 209-820-3700
Fax: 209-820-3793 800-877-6330
orderdesk@surtecsystem.com
www.surtecsystem.com
Manufacturer, importer and exporter of floor cleaning systems, chemicals and high-speed buffing machines
President: W Fields
CFO: Bill Haag
VP/Director Reaserch/Development: Don Fromm
Manager Sales: Kurt Grannis
Estimated Sales: $5 - 10 Million
Number Employees: 50-99
Square Footage: 140000

29882 **Sus-Rap Protective Packaging**
4010 Suburban Drive
Danville, VA 24540-6116 434-836-1666
Fax: 434-836-7606 800-558-7078
www.multiwall.com
Supplier of paper products
Manager: Melvin Shumate

29883 **Sussman Electric Boilers**
4320 34th St
Long Island City, NY 11101 718-937-4500
Fax: 718-937-4676 800-238-3535
seb@sussmanboilers.com
www.sussmanboilers.com
Manufacturer and exporter of electric boilers including steam, hot water, stainless steel and humidification, also, steam superheaters and steam-to-steam generators
President: Charles Monteverdi
Marketing: Louise Mound
Sales: Louise Mound
Production: Ben Cavanna
Plant Manager: Ben Cavanna
Purchasing Manager: Arthur Perlman
Estimated Sales: $10 - 20 Million
Number Employees: 50-99
Parent Co: Sussman-Automatic Corporation
Brands:
Sussman

29884 **Sutherland Stamp Company**
PO Box 151319
San Diego, CA 92175-1319 858-233-7784
Fax: 858-233-0105
Badges, medals, plastic signs and rubber stamps
Owner: Richard Branch
Number Employees: 3

29885 **Sutter Process Equipment**
P.O.Box 5459
Walnut Creek, CA 94596-1459 925-937-1405
Fax: 707-642-2288 888-254-2060
juvenaldirect@juvenaldirect.com
www.juvenaldirect.com
Wine presses
Owner: Jerry Denham
Number Employees: 10-19
Square Footage: 88000
Parent Co: S.A. Juvenal
Type of Packaging: Private Label

29886 **(HQ)Sutton Designs**
215 N Cayuga Street
Ithaca, NY 14850-4329 607-277-4301
Fax: 607-277-6983 800-326-8119
mmiller@cuttondesigns.com
Plexiglass counter cards, menu holders and displays
CFO: L Karro
VP Marketing: Dan Steele
Sales Director: Mark Miller
Purchasing Manager: Ned Ficher
Estimated Sales: $7.5 Million
Number Employees: 42
Number of Products: 350
Square Footage: 10000

29887 **Suzhou Chem, Inc.**
396 Washington St
#318
Wellesley, MA 02481 781-433-8618
Fax: 781-433-8619 joanni@suzhuchem.com
www.suzhouchem.com
Food and beverage ingredients including ascorbic acid, sodium ascorbate, calcium ascorbate, sodium saccharin granular, sodium saccharin dehydrate, sodium saccharin powder, calcium saccharin, insoluble saccharin, acesulfame-kaspartame, caffeine, potassium, sorbic acid, etc.
Director: Fenggen Ye
Manager: Weilin Hu
Estimated Sales: $302 Million
Type of Packaging: Bulk

29888 **Svedala Industries**
621 S Sierra Madre St
Colorado Springs, CO 80903-4016 719-471-3443
Fax: 719-471-4469 denversala@aol.com
www.metso.com
Manufacturer and exporter of thermal heat exchangers
Manager: Kirk Smith
Production Manager (Thermal Equipment): Siegfried Nierenz
Estimated Sales: $20 - 50 Million
Number Employees: 20-49
Brands:
Holo Flite

29889 **Svedala Industries**
621 S Sierra Madre St
Colorado Springs, CO 80903-4016 719-471-3443
Fax: 719-471-4469 denversala@aol.com
www.metso.com
Manufacturer and exporter of belt conveyor components for bulk material handling systems
Manager: Kirk Smith
Manager: Rick Pummell
Manager Sales Administration: Jim Danielson
Estimated Sales: $20 - 50 Million
Number Employees: 20-49
Parent Co: Svedala Industries

29890 **Sverdrup Facilities**
801 N 11th Blvd
Saint Louis, MO 63102-1815 314-552-8339
Fax: 314-552-8453 800-325-7910
vicarywc@sverdrup.com www.sverdrup.com
Consultant specializing in architecture, construction and engineering design services for sanitary processing facilities, etc
VP: Bill Vicary

29891 **Sverdrup Facilities**
222 S Riverside Plz # 1400
Chicago, IL 60606-6001 312-416-0990
Fax: 312-416-1700 800-337-3239
www.sverdrup.com/opeos/facilities.html
Engineers, architects, planners, food technologists, sanitation specialists and construction experts, processing plants and productions systems
Estimated Sales: $5 - 10 Million
Number Employees: 20-49

29892 **Svresearch**
7429 Allentown Blvd
Harrisburg, PA 17112-3609 717-540-0370
Fax: 717-540-0380 info@svresearch.com
www.svresearch.com
President: Ron Lawson
Estimated Sales: $3 - 5 Million
Number Employees: 20-49

29893 **Swan Label & Tag**
929 Second Avenue
PO Box 308
Coraopolis, PA 15108 412-264-9000
Fax: 412-264-7259 info@swanlabel.com
www.swanlabel.com
Manufacturer and exporter of pressure sensitive labels and tags
President: Jon Swan
Art/Graphic Department: Justin Kevish
Sales: Jill Clendening
Customer Service: Gilda Clendenning
General Manager: Mike Chieski
Sales/Office Manager: Mike Chieski
Estimated Sales: $10-20 Million
Number Employees: 5-9

29894 **Swancock Designworks**
755 Sherri Court
Bosque Farms, NM 87068-9770 603-465-2015
Fax: 603-465-2015
Wine industry label design

29895 **Swander Pace & Company**
100 Spear St Ste 1900
San Francisco, CA 94105-1529 415-477-8500
Fax: 415-477-8510 info@spcap.com
www.spcap.com
Consultant offering strategy development, acquisitions and divestitures, market and competitive assessments, category management, salesforce optimization, etc
President: Bill Tace
Managing Director: Bill Pace
Managing Director: Todd Hooper
VP: Pete Boylan
Estimated Sales: $5-10 Million
Number Employees: 20-49

29896 **Swanson Wire Works Industries, Inc.**
4229 Forney Rd
Mesquite, TX 75149 972-288-7465
Fax: 972-285-3030 swwind@prodigy.net
www.swansonwireworks.com
Powder coated and regular wire shelves, display racks and barbecue grills
President: David J Burroughs
VP: Ken Brunson
Estimated Sales: $5-10 Million
Number Employees: 20-49
Square Footage: 200000

29897 **Sweet Manufacturing Company**
2000 E Leffel Lane
PO Box 1086
Springfield, OH 45501 937-325-1511
Fax: 937-322-1963 800-334-7254
sales@sweetmfg.com www.sweetmfg.com
Specialize in bulk material handling, conveying and processing equipment.
President/CEO: Alicia Sweet Hupp
VP Marketing: Mike Gannon
VP Sales: Julio Contreras
Number Employees: 50-99
Square Footage: 70000
Brands:
Calormatic®
Filte-Veyor®
Gollath®
Quick-Key®
Silver-Grip®
Silver-Span®
Silver-Sweet®

29898 **SweetWARE**
2821A Chapman Street
Oakland, CA 94601 510-436-8600
Fax: 510-436-8601 800-526-7900
inquiries@sweetware.com www.sweetware.com
Manufacturer and exporter of inventory control, order entry, invoicing, accounts receivable, recipe formula costing and nutrition analysis software
Manager: John Morin
Estimated Sales: $500,000-$1 Million
Number Employees: 1-4
Brands:
Nutra Coster
Smallpics
Stock Coster

29899 **Sweetener Supply Corporation**
9501 Southview Avenue
Brookfield, IL 60513 708-588-8400
Fax: 708-588-8460 888-784-2799
sales@sweetenersupply.com
www.sweetenersupply.com

29900 **Sweeteners Plus**
5768 Sweeteners Blvd
Lakeville, NY 14480 858-346-2318
Fax: 585-346-2310 www.sweetenersplus.com
Manufacturer and distributor of liquid and dry sweeteners including white and brown sugar, organic and kosher products, fructose, maltitol, corn syrup, and invert syrups. Also bottling, custom blending, and liquid fondants. Shippedregionally long haul by rail and short haul by trucks and nationally by distribution products
President & CEO: Carlton Myers
Quality Assurance Manager: Mark Rudolph
VP Sales: Mark Whitford
Operation Manager: Bill Devine
Estimated Sales: $14.7 Million
Number Employees: 70
Type of Packaging: Food Service, Bulk

29901 **Swift Creek Forest Products**
PO Box 507
Amelia Court Hse, VA 23002-0507 804-561-4498
Fax: 804-561-6137
Pallets and skids
President: Jerry Long
Estimated Sales: $2.5-5 Million
Number Employees: 20-49

29902 **(HQ)Swing-A-Way Manufacturing Company**
4100 Beck Ave
St Louis, MO 63116-2694 314-773-1488
Fax: 314-773-5187
Manufacturer, importer and exporter of corkscrews, ice crushers and can and jar openers
President: Dorothy Rhodes
Estimated Sales: $10-20 Million
Number Employees: 50-99
Square Footage: 125000
Type of Packaging: Consumer

Other Locations:
Swing-A-Way Manufacturing Co.
Saint Louis MO
Brands:
Swing-A-Way

29903 Swirl Freeze Corp
1261 S Redwood Rd Unit H
Salt Lake City, UT 84104 801-972-0109
Fax: 800-262-4275 800-262-4275
swirlfreeze@swirlfreeze.com swirlfreeze.com
Manufacturer and exporter of ice cream and frozen yogurt blending machinery
President: D Heinhold
Vice President: K Heinhold
Marketing Director: D Savage
Estimated Sales: $1 Million
Number Employees: 5-9
Number of Brands: 1
Number of Products: 6
Square Footage: 15000
Type of Packaging: Consumer
Brands:
Swirl Freeze

29904 Swirl Freeze Corporation
1261 S Redwood Rd Ste H
Salt Lake City, UT 84104 801-972-0109
Fax: 801-973-7620 800-262-4275
swirlfreeze@swirlfreeze.com swirlfreeze.com
Supplier of ice cream and frozen yogurt blending machinery
President: Duane Heinhold
VP: Ken Heinhold
Estimated Sales: $.5 - 1 million
Number Employees: 1-4
Square Footage: 15000

29905 Swissh Commercial Equipment
5520 Chabot 203
Montreal, QC H2H 2S7
Canada 514-524-6005
Fax: 514-524-3305 888-794-7749
info@swissh.ca www.swissh.com
President: Bruno O Frank
Marketing: Elyse Pastor
Production: Miguel Viche
Number Employees: 7
Number of Brands: 4
Number of Products: 50
Square Footage: 16000
Brands:
Swissh

29906 Swisslog
161 Enterprise Dr
Newport News, VA 23603 757-820-3400
Fax: 757-887-5588 800-783-9840
wds.us@swisslog.com www.swisslog.com
President: Karl Puehringer
Chairman: Hans Ziegler
CFO: Christian M,,der
Estimated Sales: $5 - 10 Million
Number Employees: 20-49

29907 (HQ)Swivelier Company
600 Bradley Hill Rd Ste 3
Blauvelt, NY 10913 845-353-1455
Fax: 845-353-1512 info@swivelier.com
www.swivelier.com
Manufacturer and exporter of lighting including track, low-voltage display,clamp-on, display and accent, lighting fixtures, light converters and extenders
President: Michael Schwartz
VP Manufacturing: Gerard Phelan
Estimated Sales: $5 - 10 Million
Number Employees: 20-49
Square Footage: 480000
Brands:
Convert-A-Lite
Cozy-Lite
Litestrip
Star Track
Swivelier

29908 Sybo Composites
404 South Riberia Street
St. Augustine, FL 32084 904-599-7093
Fax: 937-746-9706 800-874-4088
info@sybocomposites.com
www.sybocomposites.com
Manager: Martin South
Sales Director: Pam South
Estimated Sales: E
Number Employees: 50-99
Square Footage: 20000

29909 Sycamore Containers
215 Fair St
Sycamore, IL 60178 815-895-2343
Fax: 815-895-5555 www.landsberg.com
President: Lawrence Kendzora
Manufacturing Executive: Marvin Barnes
Estimated Sales: $10 - 15 Million
Number Employees: 20-49

29910 (HQ)Syfan USA Corporation
PO Box 203
Everetts, NC 27825-0212 877-792-2547
Fax: 252-792-3185 syfansales@syfranusa.com
www.syfanusa.com
Packaging, shrink films, over wrap, bread bags, skin films
Executive V.P: Ramy Diga
President: Frank Marrowitz
Product Development Manager: Alan Castle
Regional Manager: Bruce Paster
Estimated Sales: $1 - 2.5 Million
Number Employees: 10
Type of Packaging: Consumer, Food Service, Private Label

29911 Symbol Technologies
116 Wilbur Pl
Bohemia, NY 11716 631-244-3503
Fax: 631-653-5494 www.symbol.com
Barcode scanners and terminals
EVP: Ron Goldman
Estimated Sales: $1 - 5 Billion
Number Employees: 250-499

29912 Symmetry Products Group
55 Industrial Cir
Lincoln, RI 02865-2606 401-365-6272
Fax: 401-365-6273 ftmktg@ids.net
www.symmetryproducts.com
Manufacturer and exporter of signs; also, theme and architectural designing available
President: Steven Lancia
Marketing Director: Justine Ruizzo
Sales Director: Rich Dowd
Plant Manager: Tony Chernasky
Estimated Sales: $20 - 50 Million
Number Employees: 100-249
Square Footage: 150000
Parent Co: Lance Industries

29913 Sympak, Inc.
1385 Armour Blvd.
Mundelein, IL 60060 847-247-0182
Fax: 847-247-0184 sympak-usa@sympak.com
www.sympak-usa.com
Processing and packaging equipment for the dairy, confectionery/baking industries and convenience stores.
Number Employees: 600

29914 Symtech,Inc
P.O. Box 2627
Spartanburg, SC 29304-2627 219-477-4554
Fax: 219-464-3352 tgowan@symtech-usa.com
www.strayfieldfastran.co.uk

29915 Synchro-Systems Technology
4563 Nance Road
Stanfield, NC 28163-8630 704-888-6407
Fax: 704-888-5080
Indexing, collating, and accumulating machinery, auto-loaders

29916 Syndett Products
201 Boston Tpke
Bolton, CT 06043-7203 860-646-0172
Fax: 860-645-6070 wgorra@simonizusa.com
www.simonizusa.com
Manufacturer and exporter of waterless hand cleaners, soap and specialty chemicals
President: William Gorra
CFO: Mark Kershw
CEO: Mark Kershaw
Quality Control: Mark Kershw
VP Marketing: Michele O'Neal
Estimated Sales: F
Number Employees: 50-99

29917 Synthron
420 W Fleming Drive
Suite C
Morganton, NC 28655-3966 828-437-8611
Fax: 828-437-4126 synthron@hci.net
Processor and exporter of detergents and oil and wax emulsifying agents
President: Raymond Pinard
Estimated Sales: $5-10 Million
Number Employees: 10-19
Type of Packaging: Bulk

29918 Syracuse China Company
2801 Court St
Syracuse, NY 13208-3241 315-455-5671
Fax: 315-455-6763 800-448-5711
www.libbey.com
China
President: Charles S Goodman
Estimated Sales: Below $500,000
Number Employees: 500-999
Parent Co: Libbey

29919 Syracuse Label Company
110 Luther Ave
Liverpool, NY 13088 315-422-1037
Fax: 315-422-6763 sales@syrlabel.com
www.syrlabel.com
Pressure sensitive labels
President: Kathy Alamio
Estimated Sales: $20-50 Million
Number Employees: 100-249

29920 (HQ)Sysco Corporation
1390 Enclave Pkwy
Houston, TX 77077-2099 281-584-1390
Fax: 281-584-1737 800-337-9726
www.sysco.com
Food service distributor
President/CEO: Bill DeLaney
Chairman: Manny Fernandez
EVP/CFO: Chris Kreidler
SVP/Chief Information Officer: Twila Day
SVP/Sysco Business Services: Kirk Drummond
EVP/Foodservice Operations: Larry Pulliam
SVP/Corporate Multi-Unit Sales: Kent Humphries
EVP/Business Transformation: Jim Hope
SVP/Merchandising: Alan Hasty
EVP/US Foodservice Operations: Mike Green
EVP/Merchandising & Supply Chain: Bill Day
Estimated Sales: $37 Billion
Number Employees: 10,000

29921 Systech
2540 US Highway 130
Suit 128
Cranbury, NJ 08512 609-395-8400
Fax: 609-395-0064 800-847-7123
support@systech-tips.com.
www.systech-tips.com
President: Robert Dejean
CFO: Kenith Kirktatrick
Director of Sales: Paulo Machado
Number Employees: 10-19

29922 Systech Illinois
2401 Hiller Rdg
Suite A
Johnsburg, IL 60051 815-344-6212
Fax: 815-344-6332
illinstr@illinoisinstruments.com
www.systechillinois.com
President: Brian Cummings
Estimated Sales: $5 - 10 Million
Number Employees: 20-49

29923 System Concepts, Inc/FOOD-TRAK
15900 N 78th St
Scottsdale, AZ 85260-1215 480-951-8011
Fax: 480-951-2807 800-553-2438
ftsales@foodtrak.com www.foodtrak.com
SCI's FOOD-TRAK® System is a food & beverage management system that enables foodservice operations to increase purchasing and accounting efficiencies; reduce cost of goods and increase asset security.
President/Founder: William Schwartz
Estimated Sales: Below $5 Million
Number Employees: 20-49
Brands:
Food-Trak

29924 System Packaging
28905 Glenwood Rd
PO Box 109
Perrysburg, OH 43552 419-666-9712
Fax: 419-666-8072 sales@systempackaging.com
www.systempackaging.com
Owner: Tom Ziems
Estimated Sales: $1 - 5 Million
Number Employees: 100-249

29925 System Plast
130 Wicker St
Suite B
Sanford, NC 27330-4265 919-775-5716
Fax: 919-775-5720 800-726-2630
info@systemplast.com www.solusii.com
CEO: Garland Jones
Estimated Sales: $1 - 5 Million
Number Employees: 10-19

29926 System-Plast
2000 Boone Trail Rd
Sanford, NC 27330 919-775-5716
Fax: 919-775-5720 info@systemplast.com
www.systemplast.com
Conveyor components
Member: Sergio Marcitti
CEO: Garland Jones
Vice President - Finance: Marco Manzoni
Director of Engineering: Ted Van Der Hoeven
VP Marketing & Sales: Dick Overtoom
Procurement Manager: Stephan Petzold
Estimated Sales: $5-10 Million
Number Employees: 10-19

29927 Systemate Numafa
6390 Hickory Flat Hwy
Canton, GA 30115-9224 770-345-1055
Fax: 770-345-5926 800-240-3770
peter@numafa.com www.carnetts.com
Industrial washing systems, tote washers, pallet washers, tray washers, rack washers, drum washers, vat washers
Manager: Michael Warren
National Sales Manager: Scott Hazenbroek
Number Employees: 20-49

29928 Systems Graphics
1530 S Kingshighway
Saint Louis, MO 63110 314-773-4151
Fax: 314-773-3338 800-221-7858
labels@systemsgraphics.com
www.systemsgraphics.com
Pressure sensitive and paper labels for food products
President: Martin Daly
Estimated Sales: $2.5-5 Million
Number Employees: 20-49

29929 Systems IV
6641 W Frye Rd
Chandler, AZ 85226 480-961-1225
Fax: 480-961-1247 800-852-4221
sales@systemsiv.com www.systemsiv.com
Manufacturer and exporter of food service water treatment systems for ice makers, steamers, coffee machines, proofers, misters and post mix systems
President: Leroy Terry
Quality Control: Dave Terry
Manager Sales/Marketing: Sean Terry
Number Employees: 20-49
Brands:
System Iv

29930 Systems Modeling Corporation
504 Beaver St
Sewickley, PA 15143 412-741-3727
Fax: 412-741-5635 www.rockwell.com
Simulation and scheduling software
President: Keith Bush
Estimated Sales: $20-50 Million
Number Employees: 10

29931 Systems Online
1001 NW 62nd St
Fort Lauderdale, FL 33309-1900 954-840-3467
Fax: 954-376-3338 support@sysonline.com
www.sysonline.com
EZ Trade, the ultimate forms based e-trading solution/distribution management software DiMan for Windows95/98,2000; e-commerce, inventory, sales, purchasing, accounting
Estimated Sales: $1-2.5 Million
Number Employees: 1-4

29932 Systems Technology
1351 Riverview Dr
San Bernardino, CA 92408 909-799-9950
Fax: 909-796-8297
info@systems-technology-inc.com
www.systems-technology-inc.com
STI, Systems Technology has been a worldwide leader in packing machinery for over 30 years. Our high-speed wraparound cartoning technology for the automated packaging of books, CDs, DVD's videos, and a varitey of other products in arange of protective corrugated carton blanks has made us a preferred supplier in the fulfillment industry
President: John St John
Controller: Steve Fox
Estimated Sales: $20 - 50 Million
Number Employees: 50-99

29933 T&A Metal Products Company
PO Box 5410
Deptford, NJ 08096 856-227-1700
Fax: 856-227-1805
Stainless steel kitchen equipment
Owner: Nicholas Demarco
Estimated Sales: $5-10 Million
Number Employees: 10-19

29934 T&C Stainless
1016 Progress Rd
Mount Vernon, MO 65712 417-466-4704
Fax: 417-466-4705 Sales@TC-Stainless.com
www.tc-stainless.com
President: Terry L Cook
Estimated Sales: $5-10 Million
Number Employees: 20-49

29935 T&G Machinery
Unit 5
Orangeville, ON L9W 4N6
Canada 519-940-3527
Fax: 519-940-4558 sales@tandgmachinery.com
www.tandgmachinery.com

29936 T&H Trading Corporation
15036 NE 95th St Ste C
Redmond, WA 98052 425-883-2131
Fax: 425-497-8311 www.emeraldcc.com
Manufacturer, importer and exporter of induction ranges and ovens
Owner: John Pearson
Purchasing Manager: Winston Chiu
Estimated Sales: $2.5-5 Million
Number Employees: 1-4
Square Footage: 15000
Type of Packaging: Food Service, Private Label
Brands:
Fuji Electric

29937 T&M Distributing Company
12 Sunset Way
Henderson, NV 89014-2003 702-458-1962
Fax: 702-458-1160 www.rallyshirts.com
Flags, pennants and banners
Owner: Tom Almassy
Estimated Sales: Less than $500,000
Number Employees: 1-4

29938 T&S Blow Molding
117 Simott Road
Scarborough, ON M1P 4S6
Canada 416-752-8330
Fax: 416-752-1909 sales@tsblowmoulding.com
www.tsblowmoulding.com
Manufacturer and exporter of plastic bottles and jars
President: Donald Seaton
CEO: Peter Barker
CFO: Eric Lakien
Sales: Donna Strong
Plant Manager: Grant Ross
Estimated Sales: $14 Million
Number Employees: 10
Number of Brands: 5
Number of Products: 300
Square Footage: 68000
Type of Packaging: Consumer, Food Service, Private Label, Bulk

29939 T&S Brass & Bronze Works
2 Saddleback Cv
PO Box 1088
Travelers Rest, SC 29690 864-834-4102
Fax: 800-868-0084 800-476-4103
tbrass@tsbrass.com www.tsbrass.com
T&S produces a full line of faucets, fittings and specialty products for the foodservice, industrial, commercial plumbing, and laboratory markets.
President: Claude Theisen
Type of Packaging: Consumer, Food Service, Private Label, Bulk

29940 (HQ)T&S Brass & Bronze Works
2 Saddleback Cv
Travelers Rest, SC 29690 864-834-4102
Fax: 864-834-3518 800-476-4103
tsbrass@tsbrass.com www.tsbrass.com
T&S produces a full line of faucets, fittings, and specialty products for the food service, industrial, commercial plumbing, and laboratory markets all across the world.
President: I Claude Theisen
CEO: Claude Theisen
Vice President: Craig Ashton
Research & Development: Jeff Baldwin
Quality Control: Gary Cole
Marketing Director: Eva Fox
Sales Director: Ken Gallagher
Public Relations: Mary Alice Bowers
Operations Manager: Bob Clemment
Assembly Supervisor: David Whitlock
Purchasing Manager: Steve Abercrombie
Estimated Sales: $20-50 Million
Number Employees: 250-499
Type of Packaging: Consumer, Food Service, Private Label, Bulk
Brands:
Sage
T&S Brass and Bronze

29941 T&T Industries
5070 Highway 95
Fort Mohave, AZ 86426-7200 928-768-4511
Fax: 928-768-4766 800-437-6246
tandtinc@pacbell.net www.twistems.com
Manufactures paper, foil & plastic twist ties
President: John Vaughan
COO: John Mayberry
CFO: John Mayberry
R&D: Pat Clemmons
Quality Control: Art Vigil
Director Sales/Marketing: Jim Doherty
Number Employees: 10-19
Brands:
Twis-Tags
Twist-Ems

29942 T&T Valve & Instruments
1181 Quarry Ln
Suite 150
Pleasanton, CA 94566 925-484-4898
Fax: 925-484-4727 sales@tt-valve.com
www.tt-valve.com
Wine industry valves
President: Sanford B Wolfe
Engineering Support, Design & Major Proj: Sanford Wolfe
Sales Manager: Delain Murphy
Inventory Control, Purchasing: Javier Cendejas
Estimated Sales: $1 - 5 Million
Number Employees: 5-9

29943 T-Drill Industries
1740 Corporate Drive
Norcross, GA 30093 770-925-0520
Fax: 770-925-3912 800-554-2730
sales@t-drill.com www.t-drill.com
Pipe and tube fabricating equipment
President: James Peters
Vice President: Mark Sanders
Industrial Sales: John Hodges
Estimated Sales: $2.8 Million
Number Employees: 10-19

29944 T.D. Rowe Company
18890 S Susana Road
Compton, CA 90221-5706 310-639-6710
Fax: 310-604-3227
Vending machines
VP Sales: John Hulick
Estimated Sales: $2.5-5 Million
Number Employees: 20-49

29945 T.D. Sawvel Company
5775 Highway 12 West
Maple Plain, MN 55359 763-479-4322
Fax: 763-479-3517 877-488-1816
www.tdsawvel.com

Manufacturer and exporter of denesters, fillers, sealers and lidders for plastic and paper containers for dairy and nondairy products; also, blenders, variegators, inline and rotary machines; custom design services available
President: Troy Sawvel
Estimated Sales: $1-3 Million
Number Employees: 10
Square Footage: 32000
Brands:
Bottomup

29946 T.E. Ibberson Company
828 5th St S
Hopkins, MN 55343-7750 952-938-7007
Fax: 952-939-0451 tei@ibberson.com
www.ibberson.com
Consultant specializing in design, engineering and construction services for new or expanding food and oil seed processing plants
President/Owner: Steve Kimes
Vice President: Gerry Leukam
Marketing: Glenn Higgins
Estimated Sales: $1 - 5 Million
Number Employees: 1-4
Square Footage: 90000
Parent Co: The Industrial Company

29947 T.J. Smith Box Company
515 South I Street
PO Box 1643
Fort Smith, AR 72902 479-782-8275
Fax: 479-782-8276 877-540-7933
sales@tjsmithbox.com
www.foldingcartonpackaging.com
Folding and set-up paper boxes
President: R Hahn
Estimated Sales: $2.5-5 Million
Number Employees: 20-49
Type of Packaging: Consumer, Food Service, Private Label, Bulk

29948 T.J. Topper Company
2734 Spring St
Redwood City, CA 94063 650-365-6962
Fax: 650-368-4547
Institutional and antique coffee makers; also, urns including coffee, hot chocolate, iced tea, tea and hot water
President: Willard Dann
Estimated Sales: $2.5-5 Million
Number Employees: 20-49
Parent Co: Tilley Manufacturing Company

29949 T.K. Designs
2551 State Street
Carlsbad, CA 92008 760-434-6225
Fax: 760-434-0058
Indoor-outdoor countertops, wall and easel, chalk-crayon boards

29950 T.K. Products
1565 N Harmony Cir
Anaheim, CA 92807-6003 714-621-0267
Fax: 714-693-3762 tkproducts@earthlink.net
Manufacturer, importer and exporter of high speed and high shear mixers, dispersers and kneaders
President: Hisashi Furuichi
Marketing Director: Masaki Mori
Estimated Sales: $1-2,500,000
Number Employees: 4
Parent Co: T.K. Japan

29951 T.O. Plastics
1325 American Boulevard E
Suite 6
Minneapolis, MN 55425-1152 952-854-2131
Fax: 952-854-2154 www.toplastics.com
Manufacturer and exporter of plastic sheeting and thermoformed and foam packaging materials
CFO: Doug Cundell
National Sales Manager: Jeff Smesmo
Estimated Sales: $20-50 Million
Number Employees: 10
Type of Packaging: Bulk

29952 TA Instruments
159 Lukens Dr
New Castle, DE 19720 302-427-4000
Fax: 302-427-4001 info@tainst.com
www.tainst.com
Thermal analysis and rheology instruments
President: Terry Kelly
CFO: Randy Mercner
Vice President: Terry Kelly
R&D: Jan Wenstrut
Quality Control: John Gaito
Marketing Director: George Dallas
Estimated Sales: $75 - 100 Million
Number Employees: 100-249
Brands:
Ar Series Rheometers
Q Series Thermal Analysis

29953 TAC-PAD
1370 Reynolds Avenue
Irvine, CA 92614 949-851-4337
Fax: 949-252-8079 800-947-1609
Pressure sensitive labels and warehouse and bin tags
Estimated Sales: $1 - 5 Million
Number Employees: 5-9

29954 TC/American Monorail
12070 43rd St NE
Saint Michael, MN 55376 763-497-7000
Fax: 763-497-7001 sales@tcamerican.com
www.tcamerican.com
Manufacturer and exporter of cranes and monorail systems
President: Paul Lague
Sales/Marketing: Beth Keene
Sales Administration Manager: Bill Swanson
Number Employees: 100-249
Square Footage: 90000

29955 TCC Enterprises
16310 Arthur Street
Cerritos, CA 90703-2129 562-802-0998
Fax: 562-802-5069 800-725-8233
www.paktcce.com
Heat sealers, product bag sealers and reclosable bags
Estimated Sales: $10-25 Million
Number Employees: 46

29956 TCG Technologies
1050 Thomas Jefferson Stree
NW-Suite 2300
Washington, DC 20007 972-820-4759
Fax: 703-847-5041 800-226-9999
info@domin-8.com www.tcgtechnologies.com
Rotary cappers, retorquers, torque release chucks
Owner: Tim Flachman
CEO: Bob Franseth
Number Employees: 5-9
Square Footage: 8000

29957 TCT&A Industries
308 E Anthony Drive
Urbana, IL 61802 217-328-5749
Fax: 217-328-5759 800-252-1355
info@awning-tent.com www.awning-tent.com
Commercial awnings
President: Byron Yonce
CEO: Kevin Yonce
Vice President, Chief Financial Officer: Wanda Yonce
Chairman: Wayne Yonce
Vice President of Sales: Ron Crick
Office Administrator: Mary Crider
Production Manager: Byron Yonce
Director of Installations: Matthew Steinkruger
Estimated Sales: $3 - 5 Million
Number Employees: 20-49

29958 (HQ)TDF Automation
PO Box 816
Cedar Falls, IA 50613-0040 319-277-3110
Fax: 319-277-7023 800-553-1777
sales@doerfer.com www.doerfercompanies.com
Manufacturer and exporter of display cartoning and casepacking systems; also, collaters/loaders and product handling machinery; consultant specializing in designing automated systems; custom fabricating services available
President: David Takes
Chairman: Sunder Subbaroyan
Plant Manager: Curt Barfels
Estimated Sales: $1-2.5 Million
Number Employees: 10
Square Footage: 320000
Type of Packaging: Consumer, Food Service
Other Locations:
Doerfer Engineering
Eagan MN

29959 TDH Manufacturing
P.O.Box 957
Sand Springs, OK 74063-0957 918-241-8800
Fax: 918-241-8884 888-251-7961
tdhmeginc@earthlink.net
Manufacturer and exporter of mixers, presses, pumps and automation equipment
President: Johnnie Owens
VP: J Owens
VP: R Owens
Estimated Sales: $500,000-$1 Million
Number Employees: 1-4
Square Footage: 8000

29960 TE Ibberson Company
828 5th Street South
Hopkins, MN 55343-7750 952-938-7007
Fax: 952-939-0451 tei@ibberson.com
www.ibberson.com
Design, engineering and construction services
Manager: Dennis Gries
Estimated Sales: $1 - 3 Million
Number Employees: 1-4

29961 TEC
P.O.Box 1086
Gualala, CA 95445-1086 707-884-9655
Fax: 707-884-9656 vickitec@aol.com
www.kirkdenson.com
Winery equipment
Owner: Anthony Agliolo
Partner: Vicki Mastbaum
Estimated Sales: Less than $500,000
Number Employees: 1-4

29962 TEC America
4401 Bankers Cir
Atlanta, GA 30360 770-453-0868
Fax: 770-449-1152 guzikp@tecamerica.com
www.toshibatecusa.com
Electronic cash registers, scales, point of sale systems and scanners for grocery stores, restaurants, convenience stores, etc.; also, thermal transfer/direct printers
President: Harry Murata
CFO: K Fujii
Executive VP: Ken Fujii
Quality Control: Jeff Warren
Sales Director: Mike Calderwood
Estimated Sales: $50 - 100 Million
Number Employees: 50-99
Parent Co: Toshiba TEC Corporation

29963 TEI Analytical
7177 N Austin Ave
Niles, IL 60714 847-647-1345
Fax: 847-647-0844 gayle@teianalytical.com
www.teianalytical.com
Laboratory offering chemical testing
President: Gayle E O'Neill
Estimated Sales: $500,000-$1 Million
Number Employees: 5-9

29964 TEMP-AIR
3700 W Preserve Blvd
Burnsville, MN 55337 952-707-5000
Fax: 952-707-5292 800-836-7432
info@temp-air.com www.temp-air.com
Provide chemical pest management for milling operations and processors
Chairman of the Board: Ruth E Rupp
CEO: Jim Korn
Sales Director: Mimoum Abaraw
Number Employees: 10-19
Square Footage: 140
Parent Co: Rupp Industries

29965 TEMP-TECH Company
PO Box 2941
Springfield, MA 01101-2941 413-783-2355
Fax: 413-782-7220 800-343-5579
sales@temp-tech.com www.temp-tech.com
Heatstones, thermal bags, tray totes and plastic smallwares including trays, plates and covers; exporter of trays
President: Jack Anderson
VP: Chuck Attridge
Purchasing Agent: Layla O'Shea
Estimated Sales: $2 Million
Number Employees: 5-9
Square Footage: 24000
Type of Packaging: Food Service
Brands:
Temp-Tech

29966 TENTE CASTERS
2266 S Park Dr
Hebron, KY 41048 859-586-5558
Fax: 859-586-5859 800-783-2470
info@tente-us.com www.tente.com
NSF listed casters; importer of casters
President: Brad Hood
Vice President: Renne Beltramo
Marketing Director: Sabine Batsche
Sales Director: Aaron Romer
Production Manager: Sue Dinkel
Estimated Sales: $10 - 20 Million
Number Employees: 100-249
Square Footage: 65000
Parent Co: TENTE-ROLLEN Gmbh

29967 TEQ
11320 E Main St
Huntley, IL 60142 847-669-5291
Fax: 847-669-2720 800-874-7113
info@tekpackaging.com www.teqnow.com
Plastic containers and blister skin packaging materials
President: Randall Loga
Director of Sales/Marketing: Todd McDonald
Director of Operations: Darrel Blocksom
VP Finance and Administration: Paul Sepe
Estimated Sales: $10 - 20 Million
Number Employees: 50-99
Parent Co: ESCO Technologies
Brands:
Combo/Combo

29968 TES-Clean Air Systems
2021 Las Positas Ct Ste 119
Livermore, CA ÿ94551 510-656-5333
Fax: 510-656-5335 sales@pacaids.com
www.tesinc.com
President: James Harris

29969 TESTO
P.O.Box 1030
Sparta, NJ 07871-5030 973-579-3400
Fax: 973-579-3222 800-227-0729
info@testo.com www.ita.cc
Manufacturer and importer of thermometers, probes and data loggers
Manager: Melissa Curro
VP: Andrew Kuezkuda
Marketing/Sales: John Bickers
Estimated Sales: $3 - 5 Million
Number Employees: 10-19
Square Footage: 20000
Parent Co: TESTO GMBH
Type of Packaging: Consumer, Food Service
Brands:
Testoterm

29970 TGI Texas
8700 Clay Road
Suite 100
Houston, TX 77080-8104 909-772-6658
Fax: 626-574-8123 joecwenyahoo.com

29971 TGR Container Sales
2374 Davis Street
San Leandro, CA 94577-2206 510-562-2251
Fax: 510-562-3226 800-273-6887
Storage containers; also, leasing services available
Manager: Nelio Fernandes

29972 TGS Engineering & Conveying
6100 Cunningham Rd
Houston, TX 77041 713-466-0426
Fax: 713-896-8830 www.kindermorgan.com
Conveyor systems including overland, radial, stackers and portable screening plants
Manager: Ron Smith
VP: Ronald Smith
manager: Ronlad Smith
Estimated Sales: $20 - 30 Million
Number Employees: 50-99
Square Footage: 54000

29973 TGW International
5 Spiral Dr Ste 3
Florence, KY 41042 859-647-7383
Fax: 859-647-7877 800-407-0173
sales@tgwint.com www.tgwinc.com
Circular and straight machine knives and cutters for food processing and packaging equipment
President: Jeff Littmer
Vice President: Jeff Litmer
Marketing Director: Debbie Busching
Estimated Sales: Below $5 Million
Number Employees: 5-9
Parent Co: Wolstenholme Machine Knives

29974 (HQ)THARCO
2222 Grant Ave
San Lorenzo, CA 94580-1892 510-276-8600
Fax: 510-317-2728 800-772-2332
sales-slz@tharco.com www.tharco.com
Corrugated boxes, packaging materials and displays; exporter of corrugated boxes and foam cushion packaging
President: Oscar Fears
Marketing Manager: Steve Malmquist
Sales Manager: Don Godshall
Estimated Sales: $20-50 Million
Number Employees: 1,000-4,999
Square Footage: 550000
Other Locations:
THARCO
Algona WA

29975 THARCO
2222 Grant Ave
San Lorenzo, CA 94580-1892 510-276-8600
Fax: 510-317-2728 800-446-6676
sales-slz@tharco.com www.tharco.com
Shipping containers
President: Oscar Fears
Estimated Sales: $20-50 Million
Number Employees: 1,000-4,999

29976 THE Corporation
PO Box 445
Terre Haute, IN 47808-0445 812-232-2151
Fax: 800-783-2534 800-783-2151
corpies@thecorp.org www.thecorp.com
Graphic design, prepress, printing plates for packaging primary foods
CEO: Kenneth Williams
Sales Director: Dave Bryan
Estimated Sales: $3 Million
Number Employees: 31
Square Footage: 128000

29977 THERMO-KOOL/Mid-South Industries
PO Box 989
Laurel, MS 39441-0989 601-649-4600
Fax: 601-649-0558 sales@thermokool.com
www.thermokool.com
Manufacturer and exporter of self-contained, remote, quick connect and walk-in refrigeration equipment
President: Randolph McLaughlin
CEO: Patricia McLaughlin
VP: Randplph McLaughlin
Sales: Gary Crocker
Plant Manager: Duane Eldridge
Purchasing: Lee Thames
Estimated Sales: $20-50 Million
Number Employees: 100-249
Square Footage: 123000
Brands:
Thermo-Kool

29978 TKF
726 Mehring Way
Cincinnati, OH 45203 513-241-5910
Fax: 513-651-2792 sales@tkf.com
www.tkf.com
Manufacturer, designer and exporter of custom vertical conveyor systems, including continuous vertical lift conveyors, reciprocating vertical lift conveyors, pallet handling conveyors, zero-pressure accumulating conveyors, and overheadmonorail conveyors
President: Ron Eubanks
VP Sales: Jim Walsh
Estimated Sales: $20 - 50 Million
Number Employees: 50-99

29979 TKO Doors
N56w24701 N Crporate Cir Ste A
Sussex, WI 53089 262-820-1217
Fax: 262-820-1273 800-575-3366
tkosales@dockproducts.spx.com
www.tkodoors.com
Automatic doors and accessories, loading dock equipment
Manager: Wayne Strauss
Marketing Manager: Rob Innps
Estimated Sales: $5 - 10 000,000
Number Employees: 50-99

29980 (HQ)TLB Corporation
150 Willard Avenue
Newington, CT 06111-1293 203-233-5109
Fax: 203-233-1268
Manufacturer, importer and exporter of pre-fabricated waste water treatment plants and pumping stations; also, effluent can be sanitized for reuse
President/Chief Engineer: Thomas Bond
Finance: Russell Correll
Production Manager: Thomas Farrell
Number Employees: 20-49
Square Footage: 30000
Brands:
Hart Boost
Hart Treat
Hartlift
Oxy Tower

29981 TLC & Associates
5600 Bell Street
Suite 105, PMB 167
Amarillo, TX 79109 806-353-1517
Fax: 806-335-4321 charles-kin@msn.com
Management consulting in the food service industry.
President: Charles King

29982 TLF Graphics
235 Metro Park
Rochester, NY 14623-2699 585-272-5500
Fax: 585-272-5525 800-356-2701
sales@tlfgraphics.com www.tlfgraphics.com
Label printing
Owner: Ronald Le Blanc
Estimated Sales: $10-20 Million
Number Employees: 50-99

29983 TMB Baking Equipment
480 Grandview Drive
South San Francisco, CA 94080 650-589-5724
Fax: 650-589-5729 contact@tmbbaking.com
www.tmbbaking.com
President: Michel Suas
Estimated Sales: $3 - 5 Million
Number Employees: 10-19

29984 TMF Corporation
850 West Chester Pike
Suite 303
Havertown, PA 19083 610-853-3080
Fax: 610-789-5168 info@tmfcorporation.com
www.tmfcorporation.com
Pallets
Number Employees: 4
Square Footage: 3016

29985 TMI-USA
11491 Sunset Hills Rd
Suite 310
Reston, VA 20190 703-668-0114
Fax: 703-668-0118 qi.xiangyu@tmigi.com
www.tmi-orion.com
Manufacturers of data loggers for sterilization processors
President: Guillaume Favre
VP: Guillaume Favre
Sales Manager: Emmanuel Cisternino
Operations Manager: Myriam Vidal

29986 TMS
2 Lombard Street
San Francisco, CA 94111-6206 415-665-2565
Fax: 415-362-1756 800-447-7223
www.tmsstorage.com
Refrigerated and nonrefrigerated cargo and storage containers
President: Robert Skinner
General Manager: Scott Weiser
Estimated Sales: $300,000-500,000
Number Employees: 1-4

29987 TMT Software Company
6114 Fayetteville Rd
Suite 106
Durham, NC 27713 919-493-4700
Fax: 919-489-1449 800-401-6682
solutions@tmwsystems.com
www.tmtsoftware.com

Manufacturer and developer of fleet and equipment maintenance management software including PM scheduling, fuel, parts, tire, warranty, bar coding, shop planner, mechanics workstation and accounting programs; software operates on LANWAN, PCs and IBM AS/400
President: Richard Rosenberg
Vice President: Renaldo Adler
Marketing Head: Chrissie Spillarf
Sales Director: Mark Ashdown
Estimated Sales: $3 - 5 Million
Number Employees: 20-49
Number of Products: 3
Square Footage: 7000
Brands:
Tmt Transman

29988 TMT Vacuum Filters
407 S. College
Danville, IL 61832 217-446-0742
Fax: 217-446-0744
www.modernmachinebaggers.com
Bag filling machinery; also, industrial maintenance and repair available
President: Manny Mechalas
CFO: Manny Mechalas
Estimated Sales: $1 - 2.5 Million
Number Employees: 10-19

29989 TNA Packaging Solutions
702 S Royal Lane
Suite 100
Coppell, TX 75019-3800 972-462-6500
Fax: 972-462-6599
mark.lozano@tnasolutions.com
www.tnasolutions.com
Manufacturer and exporter of packaging systems including vertical form/fill/seal machinery; importer of multi-head scales and metal detectors
Founder & Director: Nadia Taylor
Founder & CEO: Alf Taylor
Group Finance Manager: Peter Calopedis
VP - Americas: Alfredo Blanco
Group Marketing Manager: Shayne De la Force
Group Sales Manager: Patrick Avelange
Group Operations Manager: Natasha Avelange
Group Manufacturing Manager: Andrew Smith
Estimated Sales: $3.5 Million
Number Employees: 240
Square Footage: 192000
Brands:
Robag

29990 TNI Packaging
333 Charles Ct Ste 101
West Chicago, IL 60185 630-293-3030
Fax: 630-293-5303 800-383-0990
sales@tnipackaging.com
www.TNIPackaging.com
Manufacturer and exporter of open mesh netting bags, pre-tied elastic poultry trusses and mechanical meat tenderizers
President: Jerry J Marchese
Marketing Director: Ana Tirado
Sales Director: Jane Larsen
Plant Manager: Victor Castijelo
Estimated Sales: $3-5 Million
Number Employees: 12
Number of Brands: 7
Number of Products: 4
Square Footage: 48000
Type of Packaging: Consumer, Food Service, Private Label, Bulk
Brands:
Chicken-Tuckers
Mister Tenderizer
Net-All
Tie-Net

29991 TNN-Jeros USA
697 N Colfax Street
PO Box 12
Byron, IL 61010 815-978-2210
jens_hedegaard@tnn-jeros.com
www.tnn-jeros.com
Supplier of cleaning and washing equipment for food manufacturers
Partner: Jens Hedegaard

29992 TNN-Jeros, Inc.
P.O. Box 12
Byron, IL 61010 815-978-2210
Fax: 815-234-5915 www.tnn-jeros.com
Cleaning and washing equipment for the baking and food service industries.

29993 TNT Container Logistics
10751 Deerwood Park Blvd # 200
Jacksonville, FL 32256-4836 904-928-1400
Fax: 904-928-1410 800-272-3129
pallecon@compuserv.com www.tntlogistics.com
Dairy industry packaging containers
Senior VP: Mark Johnson
Director: Joseph Keller
Number Employees: 100-249

29994 TNT Container Logistics
10751 Deerwood Park Blvd # 200
Jacksonville, FL 32256-4836 904-928-1400
Fax: 904-928-1410 800-272-2129
mal_perry@tnt.com.au www.tntlogistics.com
Senior VP: Mark Johnson
Director: Joseph Keller
Number Employees: 100-249

29995 TOPS Software Corporation
275 W Campbell Rd
Suite 600
Richardson, TX 75080 972-739-8677
Fax: 972-739-9478 800-889-2441
info@topseng.com www.topseng.com
Offers packaging software and truck loading software for packaging and distribution professionals.
President: Bill Rehring
Manager: Reet Randhawa
Estimated Sales: $1-2.5 Million
Number Employees: 10-19

29996 TPS International
7650 Binnacle Lane
Owings, MD 20736-3102 301-855-3541
Fax: 301-855-0474 info@bagging.com
www.tpsintl.com
Forming tubes and shoulders for form full seal bagging machines
Founder: Don Wooldridge
Estimated Sales: $2.5-5 Million
Number Employees: 19

29997 TQ Constructors
911 Second St
Dayton, KY 41074 859-655-6700
Fax: 859-655-6704 888-655-0300
mail@tqconstructors.com
www.tqconstructors.com
TQ provides total quality mechanical process system fabrication and installation for the food, beverage, cosmetic, and pharmaceutical industries.
President: Kent Fennell Sr
Project Director: Kent Fennell Jr
National Account Manager: David Cauley
Vice President: John Bardo
Project Engineer: Greg Dennis
Local Account Manager: Larry Schuler
Regional Account Manager: Tom Burkhart
Operations Manager: Bill Sharkey

29998 (HQ)TRC
15005 Enterprise Way
Middlefield, OH 44062 440-834-0078
Fax: 440-834-0083
customerserv@trcmanufacturing.com
www.globalplastictechnologies.com
Manufacturer and exporter of staple set brushes; also, custom injection molding of thermoplastic materials
Owner: Terry Ross
VP Sales/Marketing: Dan Armstrong
Plant Manager: William O'Donnell
Estimated Sales: $10-20 Million
Number Employees: 100-249
Square Footage: 40000

29999 TREIF USA
50 Watreview Drive
Suite 130
Shelton, CT 06484-6160 203-929-9930
Fax: 203-929-9949 info@treif.com
www.treif.com
High-speed slicing machines, bone in or boneless high volume dicing machines
President: Guenter Becker
Vice President: Bill Render
Marketing Director: Alicia Kidd Jr.
Estimated Sales: $6.0 Million
Number Employees: 14
Parent Co: Treif Machinery GmbH

30000 TRICOR Systems
1650 Todd Farm Drive
Elgin, IL 60123 847-742-5542
Fax: 847-742-5574 800-575-0161
info@tricor-systems.com
www.tricor-systems.com
TRICOR is ISO 90001-2008 Certified, ISO 13485:2003 Certified, Mil Spec Certified and FDA registered manufacturer. TRICOR also offers products designed and manufactured by TRICOR which include: DOI/Haze Meter, gloss meters, videophotometers, imaging spectrophotometers, switch testers, life cycle tester and chocolate temper meters.
President: Tim Allen
VP of Sales: Thomas Allen
Estimated Sales: $5 - 10 Million
Number Employees: 45
Square Footage: 96000

30001 TRITEN Corporation
3657 Briarpark
Houston, TX 77042 713-690-9050
Fax: 713-690-9080 832-214-5000
pswitzer@triten.com www.triten.com
Manufacturer and exporter of plunger pumps, water blasting equipment and accessories
Chairman of the Board/President/ Chief E: John Scott Arnoldy
President/Chief Executive Officer: Thomas Amonet
Executive Vice President/Chief Financial: Donald O. Bainter
Executive Vice President and Chief Opera: Gary J. Baumgartner
Product Manager: John Matlock
Estimated Sales: $1-2.5 Million
Number Employees: 100-249
Square Footage: 25000
Brands:
Hydro-Laser

30002 TSA Griddle Systems
395 Penno Road
Suite 100
Kelowna, BC VIX 7W5
Canada 250-491-9025
Fax: 250-491-9045 info@griddlesystems.com
www.griddlesystems.com
Manufacturer and exporter of food processing equipment including pancake, waffle, french toast, egg patty and baked goods; also, mixers, blenders, depositors and cooling systems
President: Kevin Forrest
Estimated Sales: Below $5 Million
Number Employees: 10
Square Footage: 40000

30003 TSE Industries
4370 112th Ter N
Clearwater, FL 33762-4902 727-573-7676
Fax: 727-572-0487 800-237-7634
inquire@tse-industries.com
www.tse-industries.com
Custom rubber molding
President: Robert Klingel
Vice Chairman/Director: Helen Klingel
Director: Diane Klingel
CEO: Robert R Klingel Sr
VP Rubber Products Division: Louis Mirra
VP Speciality Chemicals Division: William Stephens
VP Plastics/Machine Shop Division: Gary Reese
VP Materials: Mark Neuman
Estimated Sales: $10 - 20 Million
Number Employees: 100-249
Square Footage: 150000

30004 TSG Merchandising
410 E Walnut Street
Perkasie, PA 18944-1618 215-453-9220
Fax: 215-453-7710
Designer of point of purchase displays, store fixtures, etc
President: Paul Schmidt
Number Employees: 10-19

30005 TTS Technologies
160 Farm Hill Cir
Roswell, GA 30075-4263 770-640-7808
Fax: 770-622-9183 admin@ttstechnologies.com
www.ttstechnologies.com

30006 TURBOCHEF Technologies
4240 Intrntnl Pkwy Ste 105
Carrollton, TX 75007 972-247-9624
Fax: 972-379-6073 800-908-8726
sales@turbochef.com www.turbochef.com
Designs, develops, manufactures and markets speed cooking solutions
Chairman: Richard Perlman
CEO: James Price
CFO: Al Cochran
COO: Paul Lehr
Sr VP Global Sales/Business Development: Peter Ashcraft
Plant Manager: Jeanean Weaver
Estimated Sales: $10 - 20 Million
Number Employees: 10
Square Footage: 11000
Brands:
Turbochef

30007 TURCK Inc
3000 Campus Drive
Minneapolis, MN 55441-2619 763-694-2327
Fax: 763-694-2399 888-546-5880
philip.andersen@turck.com www.turck.com
Leader in providong bus network products. Providing smart stations, junctions, connectorized cable and accessories for unique plug-and-play concept to distributed process control and automation solutions. These plug-and-play componentsallow for quick installation of new plant layouts and easy retrofits to existing plants
President: Murray Death
Number Employees: 10
Brands:
Busstop

30008 (HQ)TVC Systems
284 Constitution Ave
Portsmouth, NH 03801 603-431-5251
Fax: 603-431-8909 888-431-5251
info@tvcsystems.com www.tvcsystems.com
Turnkey process control and information systems
CEO: Nels Tyring
Operations Manager: Linda Tyring
Estimated Sales: $5 - 10 Million
Number Employees: 10-19
Square Footage: 7000

30009 TW Metals
760 Constitution Dr # 204
Exton, PA 19341-1149 610-458-1300
Fax: 610-458-1399 www.twmetals.com
Steel, nickel alloys, aluminum, copper, brass, carbon alloys in all metal configurations. Processing equipment services for cutting, shearing, leveling, and slitting, distributor of fittings and flanges
President, CEO: Jack Elrod
Estimated Sales: I
Number Employees: 50-99

30010 TWM Manufacturing
1960 Concession 3
Leamington, ON N9Y 2E5
Canada 519-326-0014
Fax: 519-326-7746 888-495-4831
sales@tugweld.com www.tugweld.com
Premium quality custom made food processing machinery and automated mechanical systems/specialists in stainless steel
President: John Friesen
VP: Jake Friesen
Estimated Sales: $2-3 Million
Number Employees: 13
Square Footage: 88000
Brands:
Cluster Buster
Tugweld
Twm

30011 TXS
124 Commercial Avenue
B
Rogers, AR 72757 501-631-1363
Fax: 501-631-1294 800-562-6552
txs@ipa.net www.tsxinc.com

30012 Table De France: North America
373 Park Avenue S
Floor 4
New York, NY 10016-8805 212-725-3461
Fax: 212-447-9270
Silver utensils and tabletop supplies
VP: James Fagan
Parent Co: Christoff Silver
Brands:
Christoff

30013 Table Talk Pies
120 Washington Street
Worcester, MA 01610 508-798-8811
Fax: 508-798-0848 ttula@tabletalkpies.com
www.tabletalkpies.com
Mini 4 inch pies in a variety of dessert and fruit flavors
Director of Sales/Marketing: Bob Littlefield
Inside Sales: Tara Tula
Sales/Marketing: Louise Lindberg
Logistics: Valdemar Siquiera
Estimated Sales: $40 Million
Brands:
Table Talk

30014 Tablecheck Technologies, Inc
13276 Research Blvd # 103
Austin, TX 78750 512-219-9711
Fax: 512-219-6964 800-522-1347
info@tablecheck.com www.tablecheck.com
Manufacturer and exporter of electronic seating systems
President: Barbara Horan
Estimated Sales: $1 - 5 Million
Number Employees: 5-9
Number of Brands: 1
Number of Products: 1
Square Footage: 3200
Brands:
Tablecheck

30015 Tablecraft Products
801 Lakeside Drive
Gurnee, IL 60031 847-855-9000
Fax: 847-855-9012 800-323-8321
info@tablecraft.com www.tablecraft.com
Manufacturer, importer and exporter of smallwares, salt and pepper shakers, condiment and beverage dispensers, bar supplies, kitchen utensils, coffee equipment, baskets, salad bowls, rangettes, etc
President: Glenn Davis
CFO: Ron Kostrewa
Vice President: Larry Davis
General Manager: Ted Rutkowski
Marketing Director: Amy Garrard
Sales Director: Dave Burnside
Plant Manager: Ted Rotkowski
Purchasing Manager: Larry Davis
Number Employees: 150
Square Footage: 400000
Parent Co: Hunter Manufacturing Company
Brands:
Kenket
Seattle Series
Superlevel
Tablecraft

30016 Tables Cubed
2305 Manor Ridge Drive
Chesterfield, MO 63017 314-843-3001
Fax: 314-843-2127 800-878-3001
cubed@tablescubed.com www.tablescubed.com
Occasional tables for hospitality environment.
President: Don Depke
Sales: Seth Lieberman
Estimated Sales: C
Number Employees: 5-9

30017 Tablet & Ticket Company
1120 Atlantic Dr
West Chicago, IL 60185 630-231-6611
Fax: 630-231-0211 800-438-4959
sales@tabletandticket.com
www.tabletandticket.com
Custom menu display boards including stainless steel, brass, aluminum, illuminated and nonilluminated; also, matching bulletin boards available
President: Brian Blair
CFO: Tom Evans
Estimated Sales: $5 - 10 Million
Number Employees: 10-19
Square Footage: 15000

30018 Taconic
P.O.Box 69
Petersburg, NY 12138 518-658-3202
Fax: 518-658-3988 800-833-1805
info@4taconic.com www.4taconic.com
Manufacturer, importer and exporter of PTFE and silicone coated fiberglass fabrics and tapes; also, reusable and nonstick coated cake rings and liners for trays, bagel boards, ovens, roasting and proofing
Executive: Philippe Heffley
Sales: Al Hepp
Estimated Sales: $20 - 50 Million
Number Employees: 100-249
Brands:
Tefbake

30019 Tafco-TMP Company
PO Box 269
Hyde, PA 16843-0269 814-765-9615
Fax: 814-765-5410 800-233-1954
bridgettwhite@walkins.com www.walkins.com
Walk-in coolers and freezers
President/CEO: William Carr
VP: Gary Brannon
Vice President of Sales: Bridgett White
Estimated Sales: $20-50 Million
Number Employees: 100-249

30020 Tag & Label Corporation
2800 W Whitner St
Anderson, SC 29626-1035 864-224-2122
Fax: 864-261-3684 www.advancedlabelworx.com
Pressure sensitive roll labels and printed tape, foils and tags
VP Marketing: Dennis Burt
VP Sales: Paul Neerhof
Plant Manager: John Kaser
Estimated Sales: $10-20 Million
Number Employees: 50-99
Square Footage: 62500

30021 Tag-Trade Associated Group
1730 W Wrightwood Ave
Chicago, IL 60614-1972 773-871-1300
Fax: 773-871-8432 800-621-8350
mail@tagltd.com www.tagltd.com
Napkins, place mats, tablecloths, wine racks and buckets and candles
CEO and President: Norman Glassperg
CEO: Norman Glassburg
National Sales Manager: Nancy Mathyer
Estimated Sales: $20-50 Million
Number Employees: 50-99

30022 Talbert Display
5713 Hart St
Fort Worth, TX 76112-6918 817-429-4504
Fax: 817-457-4066
Store fixtures and cabinets
Owner: Mark Talbert
Estimated Sales: Less than $500,000
Number Employees: 1-4
Square Footage: 12000

30023 (HQ)Talbot Industries
1211 W Harmony St
Neosho, MO 64850 417-451-5900
Fax: 417-451-7830 www.talbotindustries.com
Point of purchase displays, store displays and steel wire products
President: Jerral Downs
VP (National Accounts): Mike Howley
Quality Control: Greg Harris
Human Resources: Beth Foust
VP Sales: Jeff Talbot
Number Employees: 250-499
Square Footage: 400000
Other Locations:
Talbot Industries
Point TX

30024 TallyGenicom
15345 Barranca Parkway
Irvine, CA 92618 714-368-2300
800-665-6210
printers@tally.com www.tally.com
Manufacturer and provider of industrial and back-office enterprise printing solutions for office/industrial marketplace and distribution supply chain.
Chief Executive Officer: Randy Eisenbach
Chief Financial Officer: Rhonda Longmore-Grund
VP, Worldwide Engineering/CTO: Bill Matthews
SVP, Global Sales Marketing: Mark Edwards
VP, Sales & Marketing, Asia-Pacific: Albert Ching
Vice President, Global Operations: Sean Irby
Estimated Sales: $50-100 Million
Number Employees: 100-249

Square Footage: 140000
Parent Co: Printronix
Brands:
Computer Printers
Tally Printer Corporation

30025 Tam Packaging Systems
871 Range End Road
Dillsburg, PA 17019 717-432-9738
Fax: 717-432-8389 800-826-2775
tampackaging@att.net www.tamsystems.com
Bagging machines
Estimated Sales: $1 Million

30026 Tamanet (USA) Inc
16541 Gothard St
Suite 112
Huntington Beach, CA 92647 714-698-0990
Fax: 714-842-5600 800-441-8262
jeff@tamanetusa.com www.tamanetusa.com
Knited net for wrapping pallets
President: Nackem Dorou
Estimated Sales: $5-10 Million
Number Employees: 1-4
Parent Co: TAMA Plastic Industry

30027 Tamarack Products
1071 N Old Rand Rd
Wauconda, IL 60084 847-526-9333
Fax: 847-526-9353 info@tamarackproducts.com
www.tamarackproducts.com
Manufacturer and exporter of printing, labeling and die cutting equipment
President: David Steidinger
Estimated Sales: $2.5-5 Million
Number Employees: 20-49

30028 Tampa Bay Copack
15052 Ronnie Dr # 100
Dade City, FL 33523-6011 352-567-7400
Fax: 352-567-2257 scot@tampabaycopack.com
www.tampabaycopakc.com
Contract manufacturing beverage bottling, pastuerizer, formulation, private label, product development.
President: Scot Ballantyne
Research & Development: Vince Curetto
Number Employees: 5-9
Square Footage: 34000
Type of Packaging: Private Label

30029 Tampa Corrugated CartonCompany
3517 N 40th Street
Tampa, FL 33605-1641 813-623-5115
Fax: 813-626-2153
Manufacturer and exporter of custom and stock boxes including corrugated, paper and paper folding; also, cartons
General Manager: Ron Pollard
Estimated Sales: $10-20 Million
Number Employees: 50-99

30030 Tampa Pallet Company
PO Box 310386
Tampa, FL 33680 813-626-5700
Fax: 813-623-5180
TAMPAPALLET@AOL.COM
www.tampapallet.com
Manufacturer and exporter of wooden pallets, crates and boxes
Owner, President: Fred Haman
Estimated Sales: $5-10 Million
Number Employees: 5-9

30031 Tampa Sheet Metal Company
1402 W Kennedy Blvd
Tampa, FL 33606-1847 813-251-1845
Fax: 813-254-7399 sales@tampasheetmetal.com
www.tampasheetmetal.com
Aluminum, steel and stainless steel cabinets, hoppers, pipes, tanks, etc
President: John L Jiretz
General Manager: J Jiretz
Estimated Sales: $1 - 2,500,000
Number Employees: 10-19

30032 Tanaco Products
3465 Bonnie Hill Dr
Los Angeles, CA 90068-1325 360-332-6010
Fax: 360-332-0936 info@tanacoproducts.com
www.tanacoproducts.com
Manufactures conventional Tanaco plastic plug valves and rebuilding of all types of plug valves, also manufacturers tanaco in-line automatic and hand actuated plug valves
President: Annelie Hoyer
Owner: Annelie Hoyer
Estimated Sales: Less than $500,000
Number Employees: 1-4
Other Locations:
Tanaco Products
Vancouver, B.C., Canada

30033 Tangent Systems
8030 England Street
B
Charlotte, NC 28273-5978 704-554-0830
Fax: 704-554-0820 800-992-7577
sales@versid.com www.versid.com
Manufacturer and exporter of temperature measurement and data logging instruments
Sales Manager: Mary Lynn Rogers
Estimated Sales: $1-2.5 Million
Number Employees: 10
Brands:
Tempest
Versid

30034 Tangerine Promotions
900 Skokie Blvd
Suite 275
Northbrook, IL 60062 847-313-6000
Fax: 847-313-6092
info@tangerinepromotions.com
www.tangerinepromotions.com
Promotional products and marketing agency
President/CEO: Steve Friedman
CFO/COO: Adam Rosenbaum
Sales Director: Michael Gertz
Director of Production: Carolyn Boehm
Estimated Sales: $2.8 Million
Number Employees: 18
Square Footage: 28000

30035 Tangible Vision
320 Billingsly Court
Suite 50
Franklin, TN 37067 615-771-7177
Fax: 630-969-7523 800-763-8634
sales@tangiblevision.com
Software for customer service, accounting, manufacturing, etc
VP Marketing: Kathy Harmon
Estimated Sales: $2.5-5 Million
Number Employees: 10-19

30036 Tango Shatterproof Drinkware
P.O.Box 737
Walpole, MA 02081 888-898-2646
Fax: 508-668-0543 Kpicchi@IslandOasis.com
www.tango-shatterproof.com
Shatterproof glasses, tumblers and pitchers
General Manager: Paul Shilo
Sales: Marie Sandre
Parent Co: Island Oasis
Brands:
Tango Shatterproof

30037 Tank Temp Control
23275 NE Dayton Ave
Newberg, OR 97132 503-538-8267
Fax: 503-538-1837 888-960-9090
info@tanktempcontrol.com
www.tanktempcontrol.com
Wine industry temperature monitoring
Owner: Curt Jungwirth
Estimated Sales: Less than $500,000
Number Employees: 1-4

30038 Tanner Industries
735 Davisville Rd Ste 3
Southampton, PA 18966 215-322-1238
Fax: 215-322-7725 800-643-6226
sales@tannerind.com www.tannerind.com
Anhydrous ammonia and aqua ammonia for uses including refrigeration applications, metal treating, chemical, pharmaceutical and petroleum industries, agriculture, reprographincs, resins, polymers, acid neutralization, water treatmentand explosives
Chairman of the Board: Raymond C Tanner
CEO: Raymond Tanner
VP: Greg Tanner
Estimated Sales: $30 - 50 Million
Number Employees: 20-49

30039 Tantec
630 Estes Avenue
Schaumburg, IL 60193-4403 847-524-5506
Fax: 847-524-6956 mrtantec@aol.com
www.tantecusa.com
Industrial equipment including static control, corona treating and surface measuring
President: Waltraud Legat
Estimated Sales: $2.5 - 5 Million
Number Employees: 20

30040 Tape & Label Converters
8231 Allport Avenue
Santa Fe Springs, CA 90670 562-945-3486
Fax: 562-696-8198 888-285-2462
tlcstickers@stickybiz.com www.stickybiz.com
Printer of high quality short run digital and large run flexographic pressure sensitive lavels. 35+ years of experience with food and beverage labels. Customers are small family owned companies to Fortune 500.
Owner: Robert Varela
CEO: Robert Varela Sr.
Research & Development: Robert Varela Jr.
Quality Control: Roger Varela
Marketing: Mas Crawford
Sales: Mas Crawford
Public Relations: Mas Crawford
Operations: Robert Varela Sr.
Production: Roger Varela
Plant Manager: Randy Varela
Purchasing: Robert Varela Jr.
Estimated Sales: $1-2.5 Million
Number Employees: 15
Square Footage: 24000
Type of Packaging: Consumer, Food Service, Private Label

30041 Tape & Label Engineering
2950 47th Avenue N
St Petersburg, FL 33714-3132 727-527-6686
Fax: 727-526-0163 800-237-8955
customerservice@tle.net www.tle.net
Die-cut cloth, foil, mylar, paper and pressure-sensitive labels; wholesaler/distributor of pressure sensitive application equipment
Manager: Bob White
Marketing Director: Chuck Pullich
Sales Director: Charlie Goldson
Production Manager: Tom Bowers
Purchasing Manager: Michael Summers
Estimated Sales: $10-20 Million
Number Employees: 50-100
Square Footage: 84000
Parent Co: Weber Marking Systems
Type of Packaging: Consumer, Private Label

30042 Tapesolutions
1217 Rabas Street
Algoma, WI 54201-1985 847-776-8880
Fax: 847-776-8890 800-323-6026
marketing@wlgroup.com www.wlgroup.com
Manufacturers of security tapes and labels
CEO: Terrence Fulwiler
Estimated Sales: $5-10 Million
Number Employees: 5-9
Square Footage: 10000
Parent Co: W.S Packaging

30043 Taprite-Fassco Manufacturing
3248 Northwestern
San Antonio, TX 78238-4043 210-523-0800
Fax: 210-520-3035 800-779-8488
sales@taprite.com www.taprite.com
CO2 regulators, BIB packs, portable bars, and assessory items for the beverage industry
President: Craig Swanson
CFO: Scott Cary
Estimated Sales: $20 - 50 Million
Number Employees: 100-249

30044 Tar-Hong Melamine USA
780 Nogales St
City of Industry, CA 91748-1306 626-935-1612
Fax: 626-585-1609 cservice@tarhong.com
www.tarhong.com
Plastic dinnerware, stainless steel flatware and tumblers
Owner: Eddie Liu
Manager: Ralph Liu
Manager: Joe Wen
Estimated Sales: $5 - 10 Million
Number Employees: 10-19

30045 **Tara Communications**
698 Litchfield Lane
Dunedin, FL 34698-7429 303-417-9602
Fax: 303-413-1869 taracomm@earthlink.net
Consultant specializing in sales and advertising for the natural products industry
Partner: Joel Packman
Partner: Tish Packman
Number Employees: 1-4

30046 **Tara Linens**
PO Box 1350
Sanford, NC 27331-1350 919-774-1300
Fax: 919-774-3525 800-476-8272
info@taralinens.net
www.atlanticinteractions.com/gallery/taralinens/index.htm
Manufacturer and exporter of table linens including cloths, napkins, place mats, skirting, runners, aprons and tray and chair covers; importer of table aprons
President: Brooks Pomeranz
Number Employees: 100-249
Square Footage: 480000
Parent Co: Cascade Fibers Company
Brands:
Checkmate
Classic
Nouveau
Queens Linen
Windsor

30047 **Tara Tape**
250 Canal Rd
Fairless Hills, PA 19030 215-736-3644
Fax: 215-428-4510 800-366-8272
sales@taratape.com www.taratape.com
Filament tape, strapping tape, tearstrip tape, printed tape, overlaminate, laminated label stocks
President: Tom Dodd
Estimated Sales: $2.5-5 Million
Number Employees: 50-99

30048 **Tarason Packaging, LLC.**
1101 Keisler Road
Conover, NC 28613 828-464-4743
Fax: 828-465-5517 tarason@tarason.com
www.tarason.com
Pressure sensitive labels, hang tags and cloth printed labels
President: Kevin McKenna
Operations Manager: Ronnie A. Caldwell
Estimated Sales: Below $5 Million
Number Employees: 10-19

30049 **Target Industries**
PO Box 810
Flanders, NJ 07836 973-927-0011
Fax: 973-927-0005 targetind@bellatlantic.net
www.targetlabel.com
Extruded plastic bags, sheetings, discs, liners and tubings; also, converter of polyamide/plastic casings for processed meat, cheese and poultry; importer of plastic casings
President: Tom Fox
CFO: Warren Greenberg
Sales Manager: Guy Eric
Estimated Sales: $10-20 Million
Number Employees: 50-99
Square Footage: 53000

30050 **Tartaric Chemicals Corporation**
515 Madison Ave Rm 1902
New York, NY 10022 212-752-0727
Fax: 212-207-8037 www.tartarics.com
President: Alessandro Bonecchi
Estimated Sales: $2.5-5 Million
Number Employees: 5-9

30051 **Task Footwear**
1251 1st Ave
Chippewa Falls, WI 54729-1408 715-723-1871
Fax: 715-720-4260 800-962-0166
Steel toe, nonsteel and slip resistant shoes
Wholesale Manager: Linda Jackson
CEO: Daniel Hunt
VP Marketing: Herb Steinmetz
Estimated Sales: $1 - 5,000,000
Number Employees: 250-499
Brands:
Mason

30052 **Tasler**
1804 Tasler Dr
Webster City, IA 50595 515-832-5200
Fax: 515-832-2721 amaxon@tasler.com
www.tasler.com
Wooden pallets
President: Greg Tasler
Estimated Sales: $20-50 Million
Number Employees: 250-499

30053 **Tate Western**
36 Aero Camino
Goleta, CA 93117-3105 805-685-5544
Fax: 805-685-3695 800-903-0200
info@tatewestern.com www.tatewestern.com
Manufacturer, importer and exporter of automatic chemical dispensers including warewash, laundry and metering pumps
President: Russ Kovacevich
Sales Manager: Glen Kent
Estimated Sales: $5-10 Million
Number Employees: 25
Square Footage: 34000
Parent Co: Shurflo Pump Manufacturing
Brands:
Gorilla Bowl
Tate Western
Versa Pro

30054 **Tawi USA**
683 Executive Dr
Willowbrook, IL 60527 630-655-2905
Fax: 630-655-2907 sales@tawiusa.com
www.tawi.us
Vacumove lifting device
Estimated Sales: $2 Million
Number Employees: 1-4

30055 **Taylor Box Company**
293 Child St
PO Box 343
Warren, RI 02885 401-245-5900
Fax: 401-245-0450 800-304-6361
info@taylorbox.com www.taylorbox.com
Manufacturer and exporter of specialty paper and metal boxes for consumer goods and confectionery items
President: Daniel Shedd
Design/Engineering: Julie Passey
Sales/Marketing: Daniel Shedd
Administration: Martha Lemoi
Production: Donna Costa
Estimated Sales: $10 - 20 Million
Number Employees: 20-49

30056 **Taylor Made Custom Products**
66 Kingsboro Ave
Gloversville, NY 12078 518-725-0681
Fax: 518-725-4335
tmginfo@taylormadegroup.com
www.taylormadegroup.com
Commercial awnings
President: Dennis Flint
Estimated Sales: $1 - 3,000,000
Number Employees: 5-9
Parent Co: Taylor Made Group

30057 **Taylor Manufacturing Company**
128 Talmadge Dr
PO Box 625
Moultrie, GA 31776 229-985-5445
Fax: 229-890-9090 tmc@peasheller.com
www.peasheller.com
Manufacturer and exporter of motor driven shelling machinery for peas and beans
President/CFO: Terry Taylor Sr
VP: Terry Taylor
Estimated Sales: Below $5 Million
Number Employees: 5-9

30058 **Taylor Precision Products**
2220 Entrada del Sol
Suite A
Las Cruces, NM 88001 866-843-3905
info@taylorusa.com
www.taylorusa.com
Thermometers including digital and mechanical, instant read, pocket and hand-held; for meat, candy, jelly, scales, portion control, receiving and utility
Chief Financial Officer/COO: Donald Robinson
Controller: Robert Haddock
Director, Information Technology: Nancy Carson
Quality Assurance Manager: Steve Mowad
Director, Marketing: Liz Wentland
Estimated Sales: $50 Million
Number Employees: 45
Square Footage: 85000
Other Locations:
Taylor Precision Products
Juarez, Mexico
Taylor Precision Products
Las Cruces NM
Brands:
Bi-Therm
Taylor
Tru-Temp

30059 **Taylor Precision Products**
2220 Entrada del So
Suite A
Las Cruces, NM 88001 630-954-1250
Fax: 630-954-1275 info@taylorusa.com
www.taylorusa.com
CFO: Donald Robinson
VP: Donald Robinson
Director Sales/Marketing: Kent Beaverson
Estimated Sales: $1-2,500,000
Number Employees: 10-19
Type of Packaging: Consumer, Food Service, Private Label, Bulk

30060 **(HQ)Taylor Products CompanyA Division Of Magnum Systems**
2205 Jothi Ave
Parsons, KS 67357-8477 620-421-5550
Fax: 620-421-5586 888-882-9567
sales@magnumsystems.com
www.magnumsystems.com
Manufacturer and exporter of bag filling and unloading bagging scales, applicable for open mouth, valve, drum/box and bulk bags
President: Gary Saunders
CEO: Gary Saunders
CFO: Debra Weidert
Sales Manager: Brad Schultz
Estimated Sales: $20-50 Million
Number Employees: 75-200
Square Footage: 208000
Other Locations:
Taylor Products Co.
Decatur AL
Brands:
Avatar
Weigh Trac

30061 **Taylor-Made Labels**
P.O.Box 2189
Lake Oswego, OR 97035 503-699-5000
Fax: 503-699-0408 800-878-8654
dtaylor@taylormadelabels.com
www.taylormadelabels.com
Manufacture of custom pressure sensitive labels and tags. Distributor of label application equipment.
President: Paul Taylor
Vice President: Dan Taylor
Plant Manager: Mike Summers
Estimated Sales: $20 - 50 Million
Number Employees: .

30062 **Taymar Industries**
4-151 Monterey Ave
Palm Desert, CA 92201-2388 760-775-2424
Fax: 760-775-2420 800-624-1972
Plastic product display cases; also, stock and custom pieces available
VP: Bob Stevens
Marketing: Dave Parkinson
Sales Manager: Bonnie Miller
Estimated Sales: $1-2.5 Million
Number Employees: 30

30063 **Teaco**
5800 Monroe Rd
Charlotte, NC 28212-6104 704-535-5305
Fax: 704-531-5801 globaoco2K@cs.com
Teabag wire, threads
President: Steven Cropp
Estimated Sales: $1-2.5 Million
Number Employees: 5-9

30064 **Teamwork Technology**
7700 Riverside Drive
Dublin, OH 43016-9044 419-782-4990
Fax: 419-782-3577 billh@defnet.com
www.fessmann.com
Continuous and batch smokehouses, smoke generators and chill equipment
Number Employees: 2

30065 Tec Art Industries Inc
46925 West Rd
Wixom, MI 48393-3654 248-624-8880
Fax: 248-624-8066 800-886-6615
mwear@tecarinc.com www.tecartinc.com
Back lit signs, banners, poster and banner stands, metal tackers, counter stools, custom floor mats and neon. Over 300 in stock - Title Signs available.
CEO: Steve Bolin
COO/CFO: Kimberly Perrigan
VP Sales/Marketing: Michele Wehr
Estimated Sales: $5 Million +
Number Employees: 20-49
Square Footage: 32000
Brands:
Alumitec Elite
Alumtec
Tec Frames
Tecneon
Tectwo

30066 Tec-Era Engineering Corporation
1860 Altamont Dr
Felton, CA 95018 831-438-1930
Fax: 831-438-1939
Water treatment equipment
President: Gerald G Green
Estimated Sales: Less than $500,000
Number Employees: 5-9

30067 Tech Development
6800 Poe Ave
Dayton, OH 45414 937-898-9600
Fax: 937-898-8431 www.tdi-turbotwin.com
Turbo machinery, propulsion simulators, pumps, industrial air motors and engine air starters
Manager: Tom Jacobs
Field Service Engineer: Mike Briscoe
Marketing Coordinator: Anita Hamilton
Northern Regional Sales Manager: Bob Englet
Customer Service: Deanne Hartman
General Manager: William Nordby
Estimated Sales: $10 - 20 Million
Number Employees: 100-249

30068 Tech Pak Solutions
85 Bradley Drive
Westbrook, ME 04092-2013 207-878-6667
Fax: 425-883-9455
Temperature controlled management for food products.
Vice President: Richard Brown

30069 Tech Pak Solutions
2 5th St
Peabody, MA 01960 978-532-3500
Fax: 978-532-9135 800-832-4725
sales@techpak.com www.techpak.com
Packaging; insulated foam boxes and refrigerated jello packs
President: Bruce Trusdale
Estimated Sales: $10-20 Million
Number Employees: 100-249

30070 Tech-Roll, Inc.
P.O. Box 959
Blaine, WA 98231-0959 360-371-4321
Fax: 360-371-0752 888-946-3929
www.tech-roll.com
Hyrdaulic motorized pulleys for the meat, poultry and food processing equipment industries.

30071 Techform
PO Box 270
Mount Airy, NC 27030 336-789-2115
Fax: 336-789-2118 tfinfo@techforminc.com
www.plasticingenuity.com/techform/
Custom thermoformed plastic products including blisters, clamshells, trays, cups, lids, etc.; also, contract packaging services available
President: Richard Wimbish
Quality Control: Allan Hick
Sales/Administrative: Shannon Branch
Estimated Sales: $5 - 10 Million
Number Employees: 10-19
Square Footage: 57000
Type of Packaging: Consumer, Food Service, Private Label, Bulk

30072 Technetics Industries
1201 N Birch Lake Boulevard
St. Paul, MN 55110-5246 651-777-4780
Fax: 651-777-5582 800-536-4880
info@tecweigh.com www.tecweigh.com
Weighing systems and equipment
President: Jon Madgett
CFO: Dteven Fiank
Service Manager: Chuck Svoboda
Marketing Director: Andrew Holloway
Regional Manager: Jeff Desjardin
Estimated Sales: $1 - 5 Million
Number Employees: 20-49
Type of Packaging: Private Label

30073 Techni-Chem Corporation
1 N Maple Grove Rd
Boise, ID 83704-8265 208-375-7200
Fax: 208-376-3605 800-635-8930
brencher@mindspring.com
www.technichemcorp.com
Liquid and dry cleaning compounds for restaurant stove hoods
President: Brian Rencher
Estimated Sales: $750,000
Number of Brands: 200
Number of Products: 1
Square Footage: 10000
Brands:
Technichem

30074 TechniQuip
530 Boulder Ct.
Suite 103
Pleasanton, CA 94566 925-251-9030
Fax: 925-251-0704 888-414-0789
blue@techniquip.com www.techniquip.com
Digital refractometers
Estimated Sales: $2.5-5 Million
Number Employees: 20-49

30075 TechniStar Corporation
7825 Fay Avenue
Suite 200
La Jolla, CA 92037 858-454-1400
Fax: 858-300-5118 info@technistar.com
www.technistar.com
Robotic carton loaders, casing equipment, packers, conveyor or accessories, belt tracking

30076 Technibilt/Cari-All
700 E P St
Newton, NC 28658 828-464-7388
Fax: 828-464-7603 800-233-3972
custserv@technibilt.com www.technibilt.com
Manufacturer and exporter of wire shelves, carts, stacking baskets, dunnage and display racks, security units, stock trucks, containers, utility/shopping carts and high density storage sytems
President: Pierre Lafleur
General Manager: Marcel Bourgeoys
Sales Manager: Charles Nicely
Estimated Sales: $20-50 Million
Number Employees: 250-499
Square Footage: 260000
Parent Co: Cari-All Products
Type of Packaging: Food Service
Brands:
Adapta-Flex
Adapta-Plus

30077 Technical
3445 North Causeway Blvd
Suite 1001
Metairie, LA 70002-6867 504-733-0300
Fax: 504-733-0345 support@tcal.com
www.tcal.com
President: Scott Cabes
Founder/CEO: Leon Cabes
Estimated Sales: $.5 - 1 million
Number Employees: 5-9

30078 Technical Instrument SanFrancisco
7545 Carroll Rd
San Diego, CA 92121-2401 858-578-1860
Fax: 858-578-2344 800-765-1860
www.tsystemsinternational.com
Wine industry laboratory equipment
President: David Everitt
Chairman, Chief Executive Officer: Samuel Allen
Vice President: Aaron Wetzel
Manager of Marketing: Brett Bedard
Vice President of Sales and Marketing: Christoph Wigger
Vice President of Public Affairs: Charles Stamp
Senior Vice President of Operations: Lawrence Sidwell
Estimated Sales: $50 - 100 Million
Number Employees: 100-249

30079 (HQ)Technical Oil Products
93 Spring St Ste 303
Newton, NJ 07860-2079
Fax: 973-335-1952 orders@technicaloil.com
www.technicaloil.com
Pan release agents, vegetables oil blends, divider and mineral oils, and cake and bread emulsifiers. Available is custom blending services of liquid, dry and paste type products
Owner: Alan Geisler
Number Employees: 5-9
Brands:
Sursweet

30080 Technical Tool Solutions Inc.
766 Oakwood Ave
Lake Forest, IL 60045 847-235-5551
Fax: 847-574-2506 sales@techtoolsolutions.com
www.techtoolsolutions.com
Portable machining and welding equipment.
Manager: Carl Middelegge
Manager: Carl Middelegge
Number Employees: 1-4

30081 Technipack, Inc.
31515 Cambria Ave.
Le Sueur, MN 56058
Canada 507-665-6658
Fax: 507-665-2870 technipack@qc.aira.com
www.technipacinc.com
Wooden boxes, containers, skids and pallets
President: Mark Steele
VP of Sales & Development: Greg Melchoir
VP of Sales & Development: Greg Melchoir
Estimated Sales: Below $5 Million
Number Employees: 6

30082 Technistar Corporation
1725 Gaylord Street
100
Denver, CO 80206-1208 303-651-0188
Fax: 303-651-5600 support@ew3.com
www.technistar.com
Manufacturer and exporter of flexible robotic packaging equipment including carton loaders, case packers, palletizers, kit assembly, vision inspection and system integration
Chief Engineer: Rick Tallian
Sales Manager: Mike Weinstein
Number Employees: 85
Square Footage: 172000
Brands:
Galileo
Standard Systems

30083 Technium
68 Stacy Haines Road
Medford, NJ 08055 609-702-5910
Fax: 609-702-5915 rob@techjuice.com
www.techjuice.com
Manufacturer, exporter and importer of juice machines
Chief Executive Officer: Ian Bell
Vice President of Product Development: Jeronimo Barrera
Chief Technical Officer: Dan Gaul
Vice President of Sales: Sean Cullinane
Estimated Sales: $1-3 Million
Number Employees: 10
Square Footage: 32000
Brands:
Power Glide
Technium

30084 Techno-Design
11 Erie St Ste 1
Garfield, NJ 07026-2302 973-478-0930
Fax: 973-478-0575
Machinery for frozen pasta products including manicotti, lasagna, ravioli, stuffed rigatoni, etc.; also, blanchers
Owner: Ruben Diaz
Estimated Sales: $500,000-$1 Million
Number Employees: 1-4
Square Footage: 8000

30085 Technomic
300 S Riverside Plz # 1200
Chicago, IL 60606-6637 312-876-0004
Fax: 312-876-1158 foodinfo@technomic.com
www.technomic.com

Research and consulting firm specializing in emerging channel/segment analyses, new product research, strategic planning, acquisition studies and local market planning
President: Ronald N Paul
Estimated Sales: $5-10 Million
Number Employees: 20-49

30086 Technoquip
19515 Wied Rd
Suite A
Spring, TX 77338 281-350-1970
Fax: 281-350-4239 sales@technoquip.com
www.technoquip.com

Filtration systems

30087 Tecogen
45 1st Ave
Waltham, MA 02451 781-466-6400
Fax: 781-466-6466 800-678-0550
products@tecogen.com www.tecogen.com
Natural gas engine-driven refrigeration systems
Chairperson: Angelina M. Galiteva
Chief Executive Officer: Dr. John N. Hatsopoulos
Chief Financial Officer: Bonnie Brown
Principal Engineer: Joseph Gehret
Vice President of Sales: Jeffrey Glick
Estimated Sales: $5-10 Million
Number Employees: 50-99

30088 Tecton/Divercon
9684 N 109th Ave.
Omaha, NE 68122-9703 402-571-5115
Fax: 402-571-1742 www.scottent.com
Consultant specializing in the design and engineering of food manufacturing, warehouse and distribution facilities
President: Scott Seaton
Executive VP: S Shain Humphrey
Vice President: Tim Wood
Estimated Sales: $5-10 Million
Number Employees: 20-49
Square Footage: 40000

30089 Tectonics
PO Box 27
Westmoreland, NH 03467 603-352-8894
Fax: 603-352-8897
Plastic sheets and boxes
President: Kenneth Bergmann
Estimated Sales: Less than $500,000
Number Employees: 1-4
Square Footage: 10000

30090 (HQ)Tecumseh Products Company
5683 Hines Drive
Ann Arbor, MI 48108 734-585-9500
Fax: 734-352-3700 www.tecumseh.com
Refrigeration compressors, condensing units and gasoline engines, power train components and centrifugal pumps; exporter of ice making, refrigerating and cooling machinery
Chairman/President/CEO: Todd Herrick
CFO: David Kay
CEO: Edwin L Buker
Estimated Sales: $854 Million
Number Employees: 7,700
Square Footage: 7176000
Other Locations:
Tecumseh Products Co.
Paris
Brands:
Tecumseh

30091 Tecweigh/Tecnetics Industries
1811 Buerkle Rd
White Bear Lake, MN 55110-5246 651-233-1923
Fax: 651-777-5582 800-536-4880
info@tecweigh.com www.tecweigh.com
Manufacturer and exporter of volumetric and gravimetric feeders, weigh belts, belt scales, batching systems and bulk bag dischargers
CFO: John Madgett Jr
Quality Control: Steve Frank
President: John P Madgett Sr
Regional Manager: Jeff Desjardin
Estimated Sales: $10 - 20 Million
Number Employees: 20-49
Square Footage: 30000
Brands:
Flex-Feed
Multi-Weigh
Tec Line
Tecweigh

30092 Tedea-Huntliegh
20630 Plummer street
Chatsworth, CA 91311 818-701-2750
Fax: 818-701-2799 800-423-5483
info@celesco.com www.celesco.com
Load cells and indicators
President: Michael Katz
Quality Control: Tony Roblen
Marketing: Mark Armstrong
Sales: Mark Armstrong
Estimated Sales: $2.5 - 5 Million
Number Employees: 35

30093 Tee-Jay Corporation
415 Howe Ave
Suite 202
Shelton, CT 06484 203-924-4767
Fax: 203-924-2967
Manufacturer and exporter of industrial sponge rubber products
Owner: Thomas J Mc Queeney Jr
Estimated Sales: Less than $500,000
Number Employees: 1-4

30094 (HQ)Teepak LLC
1011 Warrenville Rd # 255
Lisle, IL 60532-0910 630-493-9080
Fax: 630-719-3805 800-621-0264
uscustomer.service@teepak.com
www.viscofan.com
Meat casings and plastic films
President/CEO: Paul Murphy
Sales Director: Joseph Wallner
Estimated Sales: $2 Million
Number Employees: 20-49

30095 Teilhaber ManufacturingCorporation
2360 Industrial Ln
Broomfield, CO 80020 303-466-2323
Fax: 303-469-9183 800-358-7225
www.teilhaber.com
Manufacturer and exporter of pallet racks, shelving and storage accessories
President: Don Dunshee
VP Sales: Don Rutkowski
Estimated Sales: $.5 - 1 million
Number Employees: 1-4
Square Footage: 70000
Brands:
C.U.E.

30096 Tekmar-Dohrmann
4736 Socialville Foster Rd
Mason, OH 45040 513-229-7000
Fax: 513-229-7050 800-874-2004
tekmarinfo@teledyne.com
www.teledynetekmar.com
Manufacturer and exporter of equipment used for flavors and fragrance analysis, bacterial count analysis and food packaging material studies
Manager: Charlie Fulmer
CFO: Cindy Reed
Chairman of the Board: Robert Mehrabian
Director Operations: Ron Uchtman
Estimated Sales: $20-50 Million
Number Employees: 20-49
Parent Co: Rosemount
Brands:
3100 Sample Concentrator
7000 Ht High Temperature Headspace
Vector Chns/O Analyzer

30097 Tekmatex
375 Lexington Ave
New York, NY 10017-5644 704-394-5131
Fax: 704-391-0641 800-392-9890
www.tekmatex.jp
Commercial fryers and griddles
Estimated Sales: $1 - 5 Million
Number Employees: 20-50
Brands:
Magnastar
Tekmastar

30098 Teknor Apex Co
420 S 6th Ave
City of Industry, CA 91746-3128 626-968-4656
Fax: 626-968-4040 800-556-3864
www.teknorapex.com
PVC film
VP Marketing: Wayne Small
Plant Manager: Bill Boseman
Number Employees: 100-249

30099 Teksem LLC
19 Wayne Street
Jersey City, NJ 07302-3614 646-552-5807
Fax: 503-213-9627 barikan@teksem.com
www.teksem.com
President: Burak Arikan
VP Marketing: Burak Arikan
Estimated Sales: $5 Million
Type of Packaging: Private Label, Bulk
Other Locations:
Fruit Acres Farm Market
Coloma MI

30100 Tekvisions California
40970 Anza Rd
Temecula, CA 92592-9368 951-506-9709
Fax: 951-506-4035 800-466-8005
tekv@primenet.com www.tekvisions.com
Manufacturer, importer and exporter of touch monitors, PCs and POS systems. TechVisions specializes in fast-loading, quickly-developed and memorable Web sites that are within any budget!
President/Director Sales: Thomas Cramer
VP, Sales: Nick Christie
Tech Support Engineer: Fred Meyerhofer
VP, Sales: Tom Cramer
Estimated Sales: $5-10 Million
Number Employees: 20-49

30101 Tel-Tru Manufacturing Company
408 St Paul Street
Rochester, NY 14605 585-232-1440
Fax: 585-232-3857 800-232-5335
info@teltru.com www.teltru.com
Manufactures and distributes instrumentation products such as Bimetal Thermometers, Digital Thermometers, Temperature and Pressure Transmitters, pressure gauges, and accessory products that are designed and manufactured for worldwidedistribution to sanitary, industrial OEM, HVAC, and food service markets.
President: Andy Germanow
Marketing Manager: Kati Chenot
Sales Manager: Yvonne O Brien
Estimated Sales: $20-50 Million
Number Employees: 100-249
Square Footage: 100000
Brands:
Check-Temp Ii
Tel-Tru

30102 TeleTech Label Company
113 Commerce Dr
Fort Collins, CO 80524-2764 970-221-2275
Fax: 970-221-2530 888-403-8253
randyh@labeltecllc.com www.teletech.com
Manufacturer and exporter of pressure sensitive and extended format promotional labels and weather and ultra-violet resistant tags; also, digital printing on films and hot stamping available
President: Carol Hargadine
Director Sales/Marketing: Lindsay Woods
Estimated Sales: $3 - 5 Million
Number Employees: 5-9
Brands:
Polytech

30103 Telechem Corporation
6477-D Peachtree Industrial
Atlanta, GA 30360 770-451-7117
Fax: 770-451-7758 800-637-0495
carson@telechem.com www.telechem.com
Water treatment chemicals, hand cleaners, detergents and sanitation chemicals; also, project services available
CEO/Founder: Les Washington
Director: Les Washington
Marketing: Dena Stacks
Estimated Sales: $2.5-5 Million
Number Employees: 10-19
Square Footage: 9000
Parent Co: Sun Mar

30104 Teledyne Benthos Incorporated
49 Edgerton Dr
North Falmouth, MA 02556 508-563-1000
Fax: 508-563-6444 800-423-4044
www.benthos.com

President: Ronald Marsiglio
CFO: Frank Dunne
Vice President: Richard Martin
Estimated Sales: F
Number Employees: 5,000-9,999

30105 Teledyne Taptone
49 Edgerton Drive
North Falmouth, MA 02556-2826 508-563-1000
Fax: 508-664-9945 taptone@teledyne.com
www.taptone.com
Manufacturer and exporter of package inspection equipment and leak detectors
General Manager: Francois Leroy
CFO: Franke Dunne
Director of Research: Bob Melvin
Director of QC/QA: Andrew Bonacker
Marketing Manager: Melissa Rossi
Sales/Marketing Director: Doug McGowen
Director of Production: Rick Martin
Estimated Sales: $5-10 Million
Number Employees: 50-99
Parent Co: Teledyne Technologies
Type of Packaging: Bulk

30106 Telesonic Packaging Corporation
805 East, 13th Street
Wilmington, DE 19802 302-658-6945
Fax: 302-658-6946 telesonics@aol.com
www.telesoniconline.com
Manufacturer and exporter of flexible and shrink packaging equipment, form/fill/seal and bagging machinery and horizontal flow wrappers
Estimated Sales: $1 - 5,000,000
Number Employees: 20
Square Footage: 20000
Brands:
Versapak

30107 (HQ)Televend
111 Croydon Rd
Baltimore, MD 21212 410-532-7818
Fax: 410-532-7818 krauses@erols.com
www.televendtrionics.com
Manufacturer and exporter of computer terminal systems and custom application software including supermarket incentive gaming; importer of computer software
President: Stephen R Krause
CEO: Nat Miller
CFO: Sam Katz
VP: George Panda
R&D: SR Krause
Quality Control: Earl Davis
Marketing/Sales: Nat Miller
Public Relations: Sam Katz
Operations: RM Martin
Production: Charles Caplan
Plant Manager: Earl Davis
Purchasing: Geroge Panda
Estimated Sales: $1-3 Million
Number Employees: 50-99
Number of Brands: 12
Number of Products: 11
Square Footage: 2500
Type of Packaging: Bulk
Brands:
Chain-Data
Prize Box

30108 Tema Systems
7806 Redsky Dr
Cincinnati, OH 45249-1632 513-489-7811
Fax: 513-489-4817 salesinfo@tema.net
www.tema.net
Centrifuge parts, filtration and recycling equipment, separators, clarifiers and whey processing equipment; exporter of centrifuges and separators
President: Michael Mullins
Technical Manager: Mike Vastola
Estimated Sales: $10-20 Million
Number Employees: 20-49
Square Footage: 15000
Parent Co: Tema BV
Brands:
Conidur
Conturbex

30109 Temco
2100 Dennison St
Oakland, CA 94606 707-746-5966
Fax: 707-746-5965 sales@temcoscales.com
www.temcoscales.com
Manufacturer and exporter of packaging machinery including weighers, bag openers, fillers, sealers and case and can fillers
President: David Travis
Engineer: Rob Vincent
Plant Manager: Bob Breitenstein
Estimated Sales: Below $5 Million
Number Employees: 10
Square Footage: 18000

30110 Tempco Electric Heater Corporation
607 N Central Ave
Wood Dale, IL 60191 630-350-2252
Fax: 630-350-0232 888-268-6396
info@tempco.com www.tempco.com
Manufacturer and exporter of industrial and commercial electric heating elements including air, band, bolt and cartridge heaters, temperature sensors and controls including thermocouples and RTDs
President: Fermin A Adames Sr
CFO: Paul Wickland
R&D: Monika Hunter
Quality Control: Tony Dcosta
Sales Director: Nick Ospina
Estimated Sales: $10 - 20 Million
Number Employees: 250-499
Square Footage: 130000

30111 Tempera/Sol
74 Hightland Cir
Suite 126
Wayland, MA 01778-1731 508-358-0090
Fax: 978-358-0099 tempera-sol@mediaone.net
Industrial equipment to temper, thaw, chill, crust, freeze, or cook food
President: Ronald Snider

30112 Temple-Inland
6400 Poplar Avenue
Memphis, TN 38197 901-419-9000
internationalpaper.comm@ipaper.com
www.templeinland.com
Shipping containers
Estimated Sales: $50-100 Million
Number Employees: 100-249
Parent Co: International Paper

30113 Templock Corporation
The Vercal Building 170
Santa Barbara, CA 93130 805-983-4400
Fax: 805-983-4401 800-777-1715
sales@templock.com www.templock.com
Manufacturer and exporter of PVC heat shrinkable tubing for tamper-evident seal, label and sleeve applications
President: William Spargur
Executive VP: Paul Montgomery
Sales Manager: Kristine Hille
Estimated Sales: $5-10 Million
Number Employees: 20-49
Square Footage: 30000
Brands:
Templock

30114 Tenchy Machinery Corporation
P.O.Box 284
Eastpointe, MI 48015 586-773-8822
Fax: 586-445-1358 sales@techmachinery.com
www.techimachinery.com
Manufacturer and distributor of twistwrapping, pillowpack and overwrap packaging machinery
Brands:
Tenchi

30115 Tenent Laboratories
6555 Quince Road
Suite 202
Memphis, TN 38119-8214 901-272-7511
Fax: 901-272-2926 800-880-1038
loverstreet@compuserve.com www.wtlabs.com
Analytical chemistry services for food industry, nutrition labeling, microbiology, lipid analysis, fatty acid profiles, proximate chemistry, vitamin and mineral
Estimated Sales: $1 - 5 Million
Number Employees: 100-250

30116 Tenka Flexible Packaging
5418 Schaefer Ave
Chino, CA 91710 909-628-2788
Fax: 909-902-0097 888-836-5255
info@tenkapack.com www.tenkapack.com
Coffee bags; bags for snack foods, pet foods, gourmet items, specialty foods and various other products; stand up pouches, flat pouches, foil bags and paper bags
Sales Executive: Angie Ramirez
Regional Manager: Corrine Douglas

30117 Tennant Company
701 North Lilac Drive
P.O. Box 1452
Minneapolis, MN 55440 763-540-1200
Fax: 763-513-2142 800-553-8033
info@tennantco.com www.tennantco.com
Manufacturer and exporter of clean room and sanitation equipment and supplies, power sweeper/scrubbers, floor coatings and flooring
President/CEO/Director: Chris Killingstad
Managing Director: Junzo Tsuda
Vice President/Chief Financial Officer: Thomas Paulson
Vice President, Global Operations: Don Westman
Vice President, Technology: Thomas Bruce
Director, Public Relations: Michael Buckley
Vice President, Operations: Steven Weeks
Plant Manager: Chris Ferris
Estimated Sales: $739 Million
Number Employees: 2,816
Type of Packaging: Bulk

30118 Tenneco Packaging
777 Oakmont Lane
Westmont, IL 60559-5511 630-850-7034
Fax: 303-452-0430
Corrugated boxes and interior cushion packaging
Sales Manager: Michael Farmer
Estimated Sales: $1 - 5 Million
Parent Co: Tenneco Packaging

30119 Tenneco Packaging/Pressware
500 North Field Drive
Lake Forest, IL 60005 847-482-5000
Fax: 847-482-5940 800-403-3393
crhoads@ix.netcom.com www.tenneco.com
Manufacturer and exporter of dual oven pressed paperboard trays
Chairman: Gregg Sherrill
CEO: Hari N Nair
CFO/EVP: Kenneth R Trammell
SVP, General Counsel & Corp. Secretary: James Harrington
Marketing Administration: Carly Rhoads
VP Sales North America: William Read
SVP, Global HR & Administration: Gregg A Bolt
Estimated Sales: $1 - 5 Million
Number Employees: 100-249
Square Footage: 1172000
Parent Co: Tenneco Packaging
Type of Packaging: Food Service
Brands:
Pressware

30120 Tenneco Specialty Packaging
2907 Log Cabin Drive SE
Smyrna, GA 30080-7013 404-350-1300
Fax: 404-350-1489 800-241-4402
Manufacturer and exporter of foam and barrier modified atmosphere packaging trays, disposable tableware, plastic utensils and foam cups
Manager: Ross Eckerman
Number Employees: 1500
Parent Co: Tenneco
Type of Packaging: Consumer, Food Service

30121 Tennessee Mills
5546 Clay County Highway
Red Boiling Springs, TN 37150-5265 615-699-2253
Fax: 615-699-2033
Wooden pallets
Owner: W White
VP Marketing/Sales: David White
Estimated Sales: $2.5-5 Million
Number Employees: 20-49

30122 Tennessee Packaging
1500 Elizabeth Lee Parkway
PO Box 418
Loudon, TN 37774 865-988-2761
Fax: 865-988-2780 800-968-6894
swinfield@tnpkg.com www.tenpack.com
Corrugated boxes
Division President: Scott Winfield
Sales Manager: Scott Barnett
Administrative Operations Manager: Terri Wall
Production Manager: Don Laurie

Estimated Sales: $10-20 Million
Number Employees: 50-99
Parent Co: BCI Companies

30123 Tennsco Corporation
P.O.Box 1888
Dickson, TN 37056 615-446-8000
Fax: 615-446-7224 800-251-8184
info@tennsco.com www.tennsco.com
Manufacturer and exporter of wire shelving systems, lockers and cabinets
Chairman Of the Board: Lester Speyer
CEO: Lester Speyer
VP Sales: Hal McCalla
Plant Manager: Johnnie Morris
Purchasing Manager: Mickey Self
Estimated Sales: $80 Million
Number Employees: 500-999
Square Footage: 1400000
Type of Packaging: Food Service
Brands:
Logic

30124 Tenor Controls Company
2120 S Calhoun Rd
New Berlin, WI 53151-2218 262-782-3800
Fax: 262-782-3880 800-468-4494
tenor@execpc.com
Timers, relays and controls
Estimated Sales: $1-5 Million
Number Employees: 5-9

30125 Tente Casters
2266 S Park Dr
Hebron, KY 41048 859-586-5558
Fax: 859-586-5859 800-783-2470
info@tente-us.com www.tente.com
Company is a manufacturer of NSF Certified casters and wheels.
President: Brad Hood
CEO: Brad Hood
Marketing/Public Relations: Sabine Batasche
Sales Director: Aaron Romer
Plant Manager: Sue Dinkel
Estimated Sales: $20 Million
Number Employees: 100-249
Square Footage: 65000

30126 Tente Casters
2266 S Park Dr
Hebron, KY 41048 859-586-5558
Fax: 859-586-5859 800-783-2470
info@tente-us.com www.tente.com
NSF certified casters and wheels.
President: Brad Hood
CEO: Brad Hood
Marketing: Sabine Batsche
Sales: Aaron Romer
Plant Manager: Sue Dinkel
Estimated Sales: $20 Million
Number Employees: 100-249
Square Footage: 65000

30127 Tepromark International
7518 Saint Louis Ave
Suite 1047
Skokie, IL 60076 847-329-7881
Fax: 847-329-7882 800-645-2622
info@tepromark.com www.tepromark.com
Floor mats, corner guards and railings
VP: Harold Klein
Sales Associate: Diane Mazuelerich
Manager: Alvin Templeton
Estimated Sales: $10 - 20 Million
Number Employees: 10-19

30128 Terkelsen Machine Company
Airport Road
Hyannis, MA 02601 508-775-6229
Fax: 508-778-4441
Manufacturer and exporter of baling wire for bulk packaging
President: Russell Terkelsen
Number Employees: 4

30129 Terlet USA
520 Sharptown Rd
Swedesboro, NJ 08085 856-241-9970
Fax: 856-241-9975 info@terletusa.com
www.terletusa.com
Aseptic and sterile process equipment and systems.
Founder: J.W. Terlet
CEO: Philip Stibbe
Estimated Sales: $1-2 Million
Parent Co: Stibbe Management Group

30130 Terminix Commercial Services
3050 Whitestone Expy # 303
Flushing, NY 11354-1995 718-939-4064
Fax: 718-939-4161 866-319-6528
www.terminix.com
Manufacturer and exporter of waste disposal and pest control systems
President: Bill Derwin
Chief Operating Officer: Larry Pruitt
VP, Customer Experience: Phil Barber
Chief Marketing Officer: Kevin Kovalski
Vice President of Sales: Steve Good
VP, Communications: Valerie Middleton
Vice President of Operations: Larry Pruitt
Estimated Sales: $2.5-5 Million
Number Employees: 20-49
Parent Co: Terminix Commercial Services
Brands:
Terminix

30131 Terphane
2754 W Park Dr
Bloomfield, NY 14469-9385 585-657-5800
Fax: 585-657-5838 mail@terphane.com
www.terphane.com
Manufacturer, importer and exporter of polyester film
General Manager: Brian Small
Sales/Marketing Manager: Brian Ochsner
Plant Manager: Chuck Mac Cary
Estimated Sales: $10-20 Million
Number Employees: 50-99
Square Footage: 160000
Brands:
Terphane

30132 Terracon Corporation
1376 West Central Street
Suite 130
Franklin, MA 02038-7100 508-429-9950
Fax: 508-429-8737 sales@terracon-solutions.com
www.terracon-solutions.com
Wine industry plastic tanks. These tanks are also used in water/waste treatment, biotech, pharmaceutical, plating/etching, food, medical, ceramics, aquaculture and semiconductor markets
President: Rob Jewett
Technical Sales: Joe Bolandrino
Sales Manager: Bernie Lanaham
Ccustomer Service: Ben Olsen
Operations Manager: Rob Jewett
Estimated Sales: $5-10 Million
Number Employees: 10-19

30133 Terriss Consolidated Industries
807 Summerfield Avenue
Asbury Park, NJ 07712-6519 732-988-0909
Fax: 732-502-0526 800-342-1611
terriss@terriss.com www.terriss.com
Laboratory equipment: testing equipment, stainless steel fabricators, mixing tanks, tables, and sinks
Owner: Judith Bodnovich
Research and Development: Marc Epstein
Sales: Edward DellaZanna
Estimated Sales: $1.8 Million
Number Employees: 15
Square Footage: 25000

30134 Terry Manufacturing Company
PO Box 130041
Birmingham, AL 35213-0041 205-250-0062
Fax: 334-863-8835
Manufacturer and exporter of uniforms
President: Roy Terry
Estimated Sales: $1-2.5 Million
Number Employees: 1-4
Type of Packaging: Food Service

30135 Tesa Tape
5825 Carnegie Blvd
Charlotte, NC 28209 704-554-0707
Fax: 704-553-5677 800-429-8273
customercare@tesatape.com www.tesatape.com
Manufacturer and exporter of pressure sensitive adhesive tape
CEO: Torsten Schermer
Estimated Sales: H
Number Employees: 250-499
Parent Co: tesa AG
Type of Packaging: Consumer, Food Service, Private Label, Bulk
Brands:
Nopi
Tesa
Tuck

30136 Testing Machines, Inc
40 McCullough Dr
New Castle, DE 19720 631-439-5400
Fax: 631-439-5420 800-678-3221
info@testingmachines.com
www.testingmachines.com
Manufacturer and exporter of crush, permeation, humidity, thickness and printability testing machinery
President: John Sullivan
CEO: John Sullivan
Vice President: Richard Young
Marketing Director: Dave Muchorski
Sales Director: Richard Young
Estimated Sales: $10-20,000,000
Number Employees: 50-99
Brands:
Lab Master

30137 Testo
P.O. Box 1606
Berlin, MA 21811 410-777-8555
Fax: 973-579-3222 800-227-0729
info@testo.com www.ita.cc
Digital thermometers, data loggers, portable instruments for humidity, air velocity and water quality
Manager: Melissa Curro
VP: Andrew Kuczkuda
Quality Control: Cate Mariott
Marketing Manager: Lori Lyonn
Estimated Sales: Below $5 Million
Number Employees: 10-19

30138 Tetosky Plastics
5725 Commerce Blvd
Morristown, TN 37814-1096 423-586-8917
Fax: 423-587-1524 www.petoskeyplastics.com
Open zipper/recloseable and take-out food bags
President: Paul Keiswetter
General Manager (Morristown): Gary Ramsey
General Manager (Santa Fe Springs): Dennis Waggoner
Vice President of Sales and Marketing: Charles Lee
Director of Operations: Steven Smith
Plant Manager: Gordon Thompson
Number Employees: 50-99

30139 Tetra Pak
101 Corporate Woods Pkwy
Vernon Hills, IL 60061 847-955-6000
Fax: 847-955-6500 800-358-3872
infomedia.us@tetrapak.com www.tetrapak.com
Supplier of packaging and processing for liquid food products. Provides aseptic, ESL, and pasteurized packaging systems in both carton and plastic, as well as complete processing lines or individual components
President: Dennis J"nsson
Director Engineer: Alan Murray
Number Employees: 50-99
Parent Co: Tetra Pak
Type of Packaging: Consumer, Food Service, Private Label
Brands:
Tetra Alblend
Tetra Albrix
Tetra Alcarb Spark
Tetra Alcip
Tetra Alcross
Tetra Aldose
Tetra Alvac
Tetra Alvap
Tetra Alwin
Tetra Brik Aseptic
Tetra Centri
Tetra Classic
Tetra Fino
Tetra Plantcare
Tetra Plantmaster
Tetra Plantopt
Tetra Plex
Tetra Prisma
Tetra Rex
Tetra Spiraflo
Tetra Tebel
Tetra Therm
Tetra Top
Tetra Wedge
Treta Alex

Treta Alfast
Treta Almix
Treta Alrox
Treta Alsafe
Treta Alscreen

30140 **Tetra Pak**
10 S La Salle St # 35
Chicago, IL 60603-1002 312-553-9200
Fax: 312-553-5151 www.tpus.com
Components and systems for processing, packaging and distribution of liquid foods; serving the dairy and beverage industries
CFO: Brian Kennell
Sr. VP Technical/Operations: Lars-Erik Jonsson
Estimated Sales: $100 - 200 Million
Number Employees: 1,000-4,999
Brands:
Tetra Brik Aseptic
Tetra Rex

30141 **Tetra Pak Inc.**
101 Corporate Woods Parkway
Vernon Hills, IL 60061 847-955-6000
Fax: 847-955-6500 www.tetrapak.com
President: Gustav Korsholm
Estimated Sales: $5-10 Million
Number Employees: 20-49
Square Footage: 600000

30142 **Tew Manufacturing Corporation**
470 Whitney Rd
PO Box 87
Penfield, NY 14526 585-586-6120
Fax: 585-586-6083 800-380-5839
info@tewmfg.com www.tewmfg.com
Manufacturer and exporter of fruit and vegetable cleaning equipment
Owner: Hank Tew
Estimated Sales: $1 - 3 Million
Number Employees: 1-4
Square Footage: 8000

30143 **Texas Baket Company**
100 Myrtle Drive
Jacksonville, TX 75766-1110 903-586-8014
Fax: 903-586-0988 800-657-2200
sales@texasbasket.com www.texasbasket.com
Wooden baskets, display racks and hand-painted baskets
President: Mardin Swanson
CFO and R&D: Troy Parker
Quality Control: David Habberle
Estimated Sales: Below $5 Million
Number Employees: 100-249

30144 **Texas Corn Roasters**
3300 X.A. Meyer Rd
Granbury, TX 76049 817-561-9987
Fax: 817-561-5006 800-772-4345
cornroaster@live.com www.cornroaster.com
Mobile corn roasters and concession trailers
Owner: Ken O'Keefe

30145 **Texas Hill Country Barbacue**
919 State Highway 46 E
Boerne, TX 78006-5758 830-336-2858
Fax: 830-336-2991 866-302-7289
sales@texashillcountrybarbecue.com
www.texashillcountrybarbecue.com/Merchant2/merchant.mvc
Barbacued foods and smoked meats, product line of which includes smoked beef brisket, smoked sausage, chopped beef BBQ with sauce, pulled pork with sauce, whole smoked chicken, whole smoked turkey, spiral cut ham and smoked BBQsauce.
CEO: Jesse Tindall
Sales & Marketing: Hal McCall
Type of Packaging: Food Service

30146 **Texas Neon Advertising Company**
245 W Josephine St
San Antonio, TX 78212 210-734-6694
Fax: 210-734-6697
Indoor and outdoor signs including neon
President: George Ryan
Estimated Sales: $1 - 2.5 Million
Number Employees: 10-19

30147 **(HQ)Texas Refinery Corporation**
PO Box 711
Fort Worth, TX 76101 817-332-1161
Fax: 817-332-6110 trc711@texasrefinery.com
www.texasrefinery.com
Food machinery lubricants
President: Jerry Hopkins
CEO: A M Pate III
CFO: Chuck Adamson
VP: Jim Peel
R&D: Seth Davis
Sales: Dennis Parks
Purchasing: Barbara Main
Estimated Sales: $20-50 Million
Number Employees: 120

30148 **Texas Spice Company**
2709 Sam Bass Rd.
Round Rock, TX 78681 512-255-8816
Fax: 512-255-4189 800-880-8007
contact@texas-spice.net www.texas-spice.net
Wholesale and retail custom blending, spices, seasoning blends, bases, extracts, flavors, coffee & tea
Owner: Beckie Forsyth
Estimated Sales: Below $5 Million
Number Employees: 1-4
Type of Packaging: Food Service
Brands:
Texas Spice

30149 **Texican Specialty Products**
10900 Brittmoore Park Dr Ste H
Houston, TX 77041 713-896-9924
Fax: 713-896-9925 800-869-5918
customerservice@texicanspecialty.com
www.texicanspecialty.com
Tostada dispensers and warming cabinets
President: Donald J Spilger
Vice President: V Spilger
Estimated Sales: $500,000
Number Employees: 1-4
Number of Brands: 1
Number of Products: 2
Square Footage: 3800

30150 **Texpak Inc**
892 Route 73 N
Suite 1
Marlton, NJ 08053-1228 856-988-5533
Fax: 856-988-5524 texpak@bellatlantic.net
Roasters (machines), bin silo systems and storage, blending and mixing equipment (coffee), computer systems, grinders
Estimated Sales: $1 - 5 Million

30151 **Textile Buff & Wheel Company, Inc.**
511 Medford St
Charlestown, MA 02129-0001 617-241-8100
Fax: 617-241-7280 waste@textilebuff.com
www.textilebuff.com
Manufacturer and exporter of wiping cloths, mill remnants, cheesecloths and cotton gloves
Owner: Jerold Wise
Partner: Andrew Wise
Estimated Sales: $5-10 Million
Number Employees: 20-49
Square Footage: 200000

30152 **Textile Chemical Company**
P.O.Box 13788
Reading, PA 19612-3788 610-926-4151
Fax: 610-926-4160 800-523-8402
customerservice@textilechem.com
www.textilechem.com
Chemicals used for the beverage, dairy, bakery and meat industries
President: Markus Klaehn
Estimated Sales: $100 - 500 Million
Number Employees: 100-249

30153 **Textile Products Company**
2512-2520 W Woodland Drive
Anaheim, CA 92801-2636 714-761-0401
Fax: 714-761-2928
Manufacturer and exporter of cheesecloth wiping rags and disposable rags
Marketing Director: Pearl Seratelli
Estimated Sales: $1 - 5 Million
Parent Co: Textile Products

30154 **Texture Technologies Corporation**
18 Fairview Rd
Scarsdale, NY 10583 914-472-0531
Fax: 914-472-0532
marcj@texturetechnologies.com
www.texturetechnologies.com
Manufacturer, importer and exporter of measurement instrumentation and software for testing food texture; also, bloom gel testers
President: Boine Johnson
CEO: Marc Johnson
CFO: Sue Perko
Quality Control: Joseph Piperis
Public Relations: Lucca Piaggesi
Estimated Sales: $5 Million
Brands:
Ta-Xt2
Texture Expert For Windows

30155 **Texwrap/Stork Fabricators**
P.O.Box 185
Washington, MO 63090-0185 636-239-7424
Fax: 636-239-7322 sales@texwrap.com
www.texwrap.com
Fully automatic shrink wrap machinery including; horizondal side seals, tunnels, L-sealers, belted and flighted conveyors and high speed wrappers, our machines are touchscreen operated for easy set-up
President: Robert Stork
CFO: David Hood
VP & R&D: Brian Stork
Quality Control: Steve Angell
Marketing: Tom Dickman
Estimated Sales: $10 - 20 Million
Square Footage: 72000

30156 **Thamesville Metal Products Ltd**
2 London Road
Thamesville, ON N0P 2K0
Canada 519-692-3963
Fax: 519-692-5213 bulldogsteelwool@kent.net
www.bulldogsteelwool.ca
Steel wool scouring pads
President: Robert Schieman
CFO: Greg Schieman
Estimated Sales: Below $5 Million
Number Employees: 10
Square Footage: 240000
Brands:
Bulldog

30157 **Tharo Systems, Inc**
2866 Nationwide Pkwy
PO Box 798
Brunswick, OH 44212-0798 330-273-4408
Fax: 330-225-0099 800-878-6833
info@easylabel.fr www.tharo.com
Manufacturer and exporter of computer software for custom designing and printing bar code, RFID and food ingredient labels, printers and printer/applicators, ribbons, labels, label rewinds, unwinds, and dispensers
President: Thomas Thatcher
VP Marketing: Lauren Shaarda
Sales Director: James Danko
Operations: Randy Thatcher
Estimated Sales: $5 - 10 Million
Number Employees: 20
Number of Brands: 1000
Number of Products: 4
Brands:
Cab Produkttechnik
Datamax Corporation
Dispensa-Matic
Easylabel
Sony Chemicals
Tharo

30158 **Thayer Scale**
PO Box 669
Pembroke, MA 02359-0669 781-826-8101
Fax: 781-826-7944 mail@thayerscale.com
www.thayerscale.com
Manufacturer and exporter of continuous scale weighing systems, flow aid devices, volumetric feeders and pre-blending and continuous compound feeder networks for extrusion processes
Owner: Frank Hyer
CFO: Bruce Edward
R & D: Rick Tolles
VP Sales/Marketing: Charles Wesley
Purchasing Agent: Lou Sawyer
Estimated Sales: $10-20 Million
Number Employees: 100-249
Square Footage: 82000
Parent Co: Hyer Industries

30159 The Canvas Exchange Inc
2324 Dennison Avenue
Cleveland, OH 44109 216-749-2233
Fax: 216-749-0987 ceiawning@sbcglobal.net
www.ceiawning.com
Founded in 1984. Manufacturer of commercial awnings.
President: Hank Proctor
Account Rep.: Kevin Potoczak
Estimated Sales: $500,000-$1 Million
Number Employees: 5-9

30160 The Clyde Bergemann Power Group
3700 Koppers St
Baltimore, MD 21227-1019 410-368-6800
Fax: 410-368-6721 www.cbpg.com
Air cleaning systems and air filters
President, Chief Executive Officer: Franz Bartels
Vice President & CFO: Graham Lees
VP Finance & Chief Operating Officer: Patrick von Hagen
Estimated Sales: $1 - 5 Million
Number Employees: 100-249

30161 The Funny Apron Company
PO Box 1780
Lake Dallas, TX 75065-1780 940-498-3308
Fax: 800-515-8076 800-835-5802
info@funnyaprons.com
www.funnyaproncompany.com
Imprinted aprons with humorous food themed designs
President: Ellice Lovelady
CFO: Charles Lovelady
Sales Director: Terri Whiting
Estimated Sales: Under $1 Million
Number Employees: 6
Number of Products: 90+
Parent Co: The Imagination Association LLC
Type of Packaging: Consumer

30162 The Ingredient House
120 Applecross Rd
2nd Fl
Pinehurst, NC 28374 910-693-0037
Fax: 877-542-4844 info@theingredienthouse.com
www.theingredienthouse.com
Supplier of food ingredients to food manufacturers such as high intensity sweeteners, soluble fibers, hydrocolloids, agave syrup, polyols, insoluble fibers, sugar alcohols, cooling compounds
President, COO: Rudi Van
CEO: Graham Hall
Vice President Quality Assurance: Jeff Lewis
VP Marketing: Peter Brown
VP Sales: Janet Timko
Customer Service Director: Ann Hall
VP Operations: Kevin Lovett
Estimated Sales: $300 Thousand
Number Employees: 2

30163 The National Provisioner
155 N. Pfingsten Rd.
Suite 205
Deerfield, IL 60015 847-763-9534
Fax: 847-763-9538
nationalprovisioner@bnpmedia.com
www.provisioneronline.com
Manufacturer and exporter of material handling products including conveyors and laser guided automated vehicle systems
Owner: Elmer Hartford
COO: Kevin Donahue
Engineer Manager: Todd Frandsen
Vice President of Services: Tom Egan
Sales Manager: Diana Rotman
Number Employees: 100-249
Square Footage: 300000
Brands:
Pulverlaser

30164 The Orelube Corporation
20 Sawgrass Drive
Bellport, NY 11713 631-205-9700
Fax: 631-205-9797 800-645-9124
info@orelube.com www.orelube.com
Manufacturer and exporter of lubricants including aluminum complex EP grease, chain oil and synthetic grease
Purchasing Agent: Donna Klempka
Estimated Sales: $5-10 Million
Number Employees: 10-19
Square Footage: 132000
Brands:
Bakesafe 500
Boelube Aerospace
Et-2a
Et-2s
Ht-1001
Ht-500
Ocean 7
Orelube Industrial

30165 The Original Lincoln Logs
5 Riverside Drive
PO Box 135
Chestertown, NY 12817 330-343-7671
Fax: 330-343-9709 800-833-2461
info@lincolnlogs.com www.lincolnlogs.com
Wooden pallets, boxes, crates and skids; also, used and reconditioned pallets and crates
President: Caroline Hawk
Plant Manager: Robert Rust
Estimated Sales: $500,000-$1 Million
Number Employees: 1-4
Square Footage: 24000

30166 The Phytopia Garden
6947 Forest Glen Dr
Dallas, TX 75230-2358 214-750-7322
Fax: 214-750-7910 888-750-9336
barbara@phytopia.com www.phytopia.com
Culinary trained registered dietitian specializing in low-fat recipe development and nutritional analysis
Owner: Barbara Gollman, MS, RD
Estimated Sales: $1 - 5 Million
Number Employees: 1-4

30167 The Piqua Paper Box Company
616 Covington Ave
PO Box 814
Piqua, OH 45356 937-773-0313
Fax: 937-773-0142 800-536-2136
sales@piquapaperbox.com
www.piquapaperbox.com
Rigid and folding cartons, vinyl and specialty packaging
President: Brian T Gleason
Estimated Sales: $5-10 Million
Number Employees: 50-99
Square Footage: 85000

30168 The Pub Brewing Company
EAST COAST
185 Route 17 North
Mahwah, NJ 07430 201-512-0387
Fax: 201-512-1459 brewing@pubbrewing.com
www.pubbrewing.com
President: Erwin Eibert
Estimated Sales: $5 - 10 Million
Number Employees: 10-19

30169 The Pub Brewing Company
WEST COAST
3600 C Standish Avenue
Santa Rosa, CA 95407 707- 58- 179
Fax: 201-512-1459 brewing@pubbrewing.com
www.pubbrewing.com
President: Erwin Eibert
Estimated Sales: $5 - 10 Million
Number Employees: 10-19

30170 The Revere Group
Po Box 80157
9310 4th Ave SO
Seattle, WA 98108 866-747-6871
Fax: 206-545-3676 info@rgroup.com
www.rgroup.com
Specialty food packaging i.e. gift wrap/boxes/containers.
Marketing: Bill Revere
Estimated Sales: $190,000
Number Employees: 3

30171 The Royal Group
1301 S 47th Ave
Cicero, IL 60804 262-723-6900
Fax: 262-723-3706 www.royalbox.com
Corrugated fiber shipping containers
President: Ken Johnson
CFO: Cleary Scott
Estimated Sales: $5-10 Million
Number Employees: 20-49
Square Footage: 48325

30172 (HQ)The Shelby Company
865 Canterbury Rd
Cleveland, OH 44145 440-871-9901
Fax: 440-871-0326 800-842-1650
info@shelbycompany.com
www.shelbycompany.com
Printed folding cartons and point of purchase advertising signs
President: Richard Rapacz
Controller: Wayne McGan
Executive VP: Sue Hintze
Plant Manager: Brian Charlton
Estimated Sales: $5-10 Million
Number Employees: 50-99
Square Footage: 200000
Type of Packaging: Consumer

30173 The Sherwin-Williams Co.General Polymers Brand
145 Caldwell Dr
Cincinnati, OH 45216 513-761-0011
Fax: 513-761-1330 800-543-7694
info@generalpolymers.com www.sherwin.com
One of the worlds leading suppliers engaged in the manufacture,distribution and sale of architecural and industrial coatings and resinous floor systems.
President: John Durig
Marketing Director: Gina Atzinger
Sales Director: Jim Ratliff
Estimated Sales: $1 - 5 Million
Number Employees: 50-99

30174 The Southwell Company
928 N. Alamo
San Antonio, TX 78215 210-223-1831
Fax: 210-223-8517 sales@southwellco.com
www.southwellco.com
Pre-inked rubber stamps for check endorsement
Owner: Wilson P Southwell Jr
CEO: Wilson P Southwell Jr
Estimated Sales: $2.5 - 5 Million
Number Employees: 20-49
Brands:
Super-Stamp

30175 (HQ)The Staplex Company
777 5th Ave
Brooklyn, NY 11232-1626 718-768-3333
Fax: 718-965-0750 800-221-0822
info@staplex.com www.staplex.com
Electric staplers for packaging applications. Made in the U.S.A.
President: C Stevens
CEO: Phil Reed
Estimated Sales: $5 - 10 Million
Number Employees: 20-49
Brands:
Accuslitter
Staplex
Tabster

30176 The Sugar Plum
5756 West Main Street
Houma, LA 70360 985-872-9524
customerservice@thesugarplum.com
www.thesugarplum.com
Designer cakes, wedding cakes, holiday cakes, confectionary, and various other desserts
President/Owner: Cindy Stahler
Number Employees: 7
Square Footage: 10000

30177 The Swiss Colony, LLC
1112 7th Ave
Monroe, WI 53566
800-544-9036
www.swisscolony.com
Cakes, tortes & pies; cookies & bars; pastries; tetits fours; postpaid gifts; candy; chocolate; boxed assortments of all kinds; cheeses; sausage, ham and other meats; nuts & pre-mixed snacks; sugar free candy, chocolate, cakestortes/pies, cookies, bars, and snacks
Chairman: Pat Kubly
Director of Strategic Planning: Ryan Kubly
Estimated Sales: $160,000
Square Footage: 13236
Parent Co: Colony Brands, Inc.
Brands:
Swiss Colony Foods

30178 (HQ)The Tin Box Company
216 Sherwood Avenue
PO Box 9068
Farmingdale, NY 11735 631-845-1600
Fax: 631-845-1610 800-888-8467
info@tinboxco.com www.tinboxco.com
Decorative metal boxes
Owner: Lloyd Ross
Director of Sales: Andy Siegel
Sales Manager: Richard Spitz
Estimated Sales: $5 - 10 Million
Number Employees: 20-49
Square Footage: 40000

30179 The Tombras Group
830 Concord Street
Knoxville, TN 37919 865-524-5376
Fax: 865-524-5667 jwelsch@tombras.com
www.tombras.com
President: Charles P Tombras Jr
Estimated Sales: $5 - 10 Million
Number Employees: 100+

30180 The WL Jenkins Company
1445 Whipple Ave SW
Canton, OH 44710-1321 330-477-3407
Fax: 330-477-8404 info@wljenkinsco.com
www.wljenkinsco.com
Manufacturer and exporter of mechanically operated fire alarm systems; also, bells and gongs
Owner: Susan Jenkins
Estimated Sales: $2.5-5 Million
Number Employees: 20-49
Parent Co: W.L. Jenkins Company

30181 Theimeg
58 W Shenango St
Sharpsville, PA 16150-1154 724-962-3571
Fax: 724-962-4310 theimeg@pwshift.com
www.cattron.com
Remote control systems for cranes, locomotives and other industrial machinery
President: John Paul
Estimated Sales: $10 - 15 Million
Number Employees: 10-19
Parent Co: Theimeg

30182 (HQ)Theochem Laboratories
7373 Rowlett Park Dr
Tampa, FL 33610 813-237-6463
Fax: 813-237-2059 800-237-2591
johnt@theochem.com www.theochem.com
Manufacturer and exporter of chemical cleaners and inorganic cleaning compounds
COO and President: John Theofilos
Director Operations: Lenny Wydotis
Estimated Sales: $20-50 Million
Number Employees: 5-9
Square Footage: 250000
Brands:
Solutions For a Cleaner World

30183 Theos Foods
119 N Duke St
Hummelstown, PA 17036-1310 717-566-5622
Fax: 717-566-5592 800-755-8436
info@theosfoods.com www.theosfoods.com
Cost effective bulk packaged items such as Theo's Stromboli, and pre-baked sandwiches also available
President and CFO: Ted Atanasoff
Manager: Barry Broadwater
Estimated Sales: $5 - 10 Million
Number Employees: 20-49

30184 Therm Tec, Inc
PO Box 1105
Tualatin, OR 97062 503-625-7575
Fax: 503-625-6161 800-292-9163
thermtec@earthlink.net www.thermtec.com
Manufacturer and exporter of solid, animal and human crematories, and hospital waste incinerators; also air pollution control equipment
Owner: Dean Robbins
Estimated Sales: Below $5 Million
Number Employees: 10-19
Square Footage: 160000
Brands:
Therm-Tec

30185 Therm-L-Tec Building Systems LLC
15115 Chestnut Street
Basehor, KS 66007 913-728-2662
Fax: 913-724-1446 sales@therm-l-tec.com
www.thermltec.com
Insulated commercial cold storage panels, partitions, doors and liners
Sales: Dennis Bixby
Estimated Sales: $5-10 Million
Number Employees: 20-49
Square Footage: 300000
Brands:
Therm-L-Bond

30186 ThermPhos USA, Corporation
21 E Front St
Suite 5
Red Bank, NJ 07701 732-383-8405
Fax: 732-383-8407 info@thermphos.com
www.thermphos.com
Sodium, potassium, aluminum and ammonium phosphates, in addition to a variety of specialty phosphate blends for specific applications including food and potable water.
Managing Director: R. Milke
Estimated Sales: $501 Million
Number Employees: 1,200

30187 Therma-Kleen
10212 S Mandel St Ste A
Plainfield, IL 60585 630-718-0212
Fax: 630-305-8696 800-999-3120
steamtk@aol.com www.therma-kleen.com
Manufacturer and exporter of steam cleaners and pressure washers
President: Andy Heller
VP: Linda Heller
Estimated Sales: $500,000-$1 Million
Number Employees: 5-9
Square Footage: 2800
Brands:
Therma-Kleen

30188 Thermaco
646 Greensboro St
PO Box 2548ÿ
Asheboro, NC 27203 336-629-4651
Fax: 336-626-5739 800-633-4204
info@thermaco.com www.big-dipper.com
Manufacturer and exporter of pre-treatments and automatic solid and grease/oil removal units for restaurants and food processing plants
President: William Batten
Estimated Sales: $1-2.5 Million
Number Employees: 10-19
Square Footage: 6000
Brands:
Big Dipper
Big Flipper
Superceptor

30189 Thermafreeze
776 Lakeside Drive
Mobile, AL 36693-5114 251-666-2011
Fax: 251-666-5660
Solutions for the safe shipment of temperature-critical media
President: J Murray

30190 Thermal Bags by Ingrid
131 Sola Dr
Gilberts, IL 60136 847-836-4400
Fax: 847-836-4408 800-622-5560
info@thermalbags.com www.thermalbags.com
Manufacturer and exporter of thermal food bags, racks, thermal hoods, insulated carrying bags, pizza delivery pouches and catering bags. Also lightweight insulated bags for the carry-out market and advertising specialites
President: Ingrid Kosar
Marketing Director: Fred Kosar
Estimated Sales: $2.5-5 Million
Number Employees: 10-19
Type of Packaging: Food Service
Brands:
Food Carriers
Thermal Bags By Ingrid

30191 Thermal Engineering Corporation
P.O.Box 868
Columbia, SC 29202-0868 803-783-0750
Fax: 803-783-0756 800-331-0097
tecontrol@aol.com www.tecinfrared.com
Under-fired infrared gas charbroilers and griddles for the consumer and food service industry
President: Bill Best
CFO: Tony Stihom
Sales/Marketing Exeuctive: Johnny Johnson
Sales Manager: Jack Whitten
Public Relations: Renee Pecks
Estimated Sales: $20-50 Million
Number Employees: 100-249
Parent Co: Thermal Engineering Corporation
Type of Packaging: Food Service

30192 Thermal Package TestingLaboratory
41 Pine Street
Rockaway, NJ 07866-3139 973-627-4405
Fax: 973-627-5355 800-432-5909
info@package-testing.com
www.package-testing.com
Testing: ASTM, ISTA, Unidot, vibration, drop; inafine impact, compression, environmental chambers, pallet loads, supersacks, drums
President: David Dixon
Estimated Sales: $.5 - 1 million
Number Employees: 5-9

30193 Thermal Technologies
630 Park Way
Broomall, PA 19008-4209 610-353-8887
Fax: 610-353-8663
Produce repening systems for the fruit industry. Also design, engineering and construction of cold rooms
Estimated Sales: $.5 - 1 million
Number Employees: 1-4

30194 Thermaline
1531 14th St NW
Auburn, WA 98001-3518 253-833-7118
Fax: 253-833-7168 800-767-6720
info@thermaline.com www.thermaline.com
Plate heat exchangers, tubular heat exchangers, skid mounted pasteurization systems, boiler packages and CIP systems
President: Jerry Sanders
Estimated Sales: $1-2.5 Million
Number Employees: 5-9

30195 Thermalogic Corporation
22 Kane Industrial Dr
Hudson, MA 01749-2922 978-562-5974
Fax: 978-562-6753 sales@thlogic.com
www.thermalogic.com
Temperature control systems including analog, digital indicating and microprocessor based
Owner: Lou Grein
Estimated Sales: $20 - 50 Million
Number Employees: 20-49

30196 Thermalrite Refrigeration
6514 E 26th St
Commerce, CA 90040-3240 323-724-3700
Fax: 323-724-5685 800-290-7073
davej@thermalrite.com www.thermalrite.com
Manager: Dave Jett
Estimated Sales: $100+ Million
Number Employees: 50-99

30197 Thermedics Detection
220 Mill Road
Suite 1
Chelmsford, MA 01824-4127 978-251-2002
Fax: 978-251-2010 888-846-7226
sales@thermedics.com www.thermedics.com
Sorting systems, soft rejectors, moisture analysis and inspection equipment including fill level, net content, package integrity, foreign particle and chemical
Chairman, President, Chief Executive Off: James Hambrick
Corporate Vice President of Human Resour: Andrew Panega
Corporate Vice President of Research and: Robert Graf
Director Sales (North America): Ron Pokraka
Corporate Vice President of Operations: Mike Vaughn
Production Manager: George McNeil
Parent Co: Thermedics

30198 **Thermex Thermatron**
10501 Bunsen Way
Suite 102
Louisville, KY 40299 502-493-1299
Fax: 502-493-4013
sales@thermex-thermatron.com
www.thermex-thermatron.com
Industrial microwave equipment and RF heat sealing equipment.
President: Raymond Lund
VP Marketing: John Hokanson
Sales Director: Robert Dachert
Sales: Mark Isgrigg
Operations Manager: Zoly Bogdan
Estimated Sales: $7 Million
Number Employees: 50-99
Number of Brands: 2
Square Footage: 144000
Brands:
Thermatron
Thermex

30199 **Thermo BLH**
75 Shawmut Rd
Canton, MA 02021-1408 781-821-2000
Fax: 781-828-1451 sales@blh.com
www.blh.com
Weighing system, scales, and web tension measurement systems
President: Robert Murphy
CEO: Bob Murphy
Vice President: Rainer Halmberg
Quality Control: Jay Bailey
Marketing Director: Art Koehler
Estimated Sales: $16 Million
Number Employees: 1-4
Parent Co: Thermo Electron

30200 **Thermo Detection**
27 Forge Pkwy
Franklin, MA 02038-3135 508-520-0430
Fax: 508-520-1732 866-269-0070
sales@thermedics.com www.thermo.com
Manufacturer and exporter of moisture and other consistent process analyzers and monitors
Administrator: Michael Nemergut
VP Sales/Marketing: Terry Rose
National Sales Manager: Don Piatt
Inside Sales: Jill Holman
Number Employees: 50-99
Square Footage: 80000
Parent Co: Thermedics Detection
Brands:
Micro Lab
Micro Quad
Quadra Beam 6600

30201 **Thermo Fisher Scientific, Inc.**
81 Wyman St
Waltham, MA 02454 781-622-1000
Fax: 781-622-1207 800-678-5599
www.thermofisher.com
Laboratory equipment including quality control supplies/machinery.
President & CEO: Marc Casper
SVP/President Customer Channels: Edward Pesicka
SVP & CFO: Peter Wilver
EVP: Alan Malus
SVP/President Laboratory Products: Tom Loewald
SVP/President Specialty Diagnostics: Andrew Thomson
Estimated Sales: $12.5 Billion
Number Employees: 38900

30202 **Thermo Instruments**
84 Horseblock Rd
Unit D
Yaphank, NY 11980 631-924-0880
Fax: 631-924-0923
Hydrometers and thermometers
President: Michael Charzuk
Estimated Sales: $500,000-$1 Million
Number Employees: 1-4
Brands:
Thermo

30203 **Thermo Jarrell Ash Corporation**
27 Forge Pkwy
Franklin, MA 02038-3135 508-520-1880
Fax: 508-520-1732 www.thermo.com
Instruments used to analyze water, oil and metal content
General Manager: Mark Whiteman
Number Employees: 400

30204 **Thermo King Corporation**
314 W 90th St
Minneapolis, MN 55420 952-887-2200
Fax: 952-887-2615
bridgeton_contact_center@irco.com
www.thermoking.com
Freezers, heaters, refrigeration equipment, temperature indicators and controllers, and refrigeration trucks
President: Steven Shawley
VP: John Cobb
Number Employees: 50
Parent Co: Westinghouse

30205 **Thermo Pac LLC**
1609 Stone Ridge Dr
Stone Mountain, GA 30083 770-492-5105
pnaiman@thermopacllc.com
www.thermopacllc.com
Wide range of thin-to-thick viscosity liquids including processed cheese sauces, tomato-based sauces and other savory or sweet sauces. Also peanut butter, in pouches, single serve cups and dried powder sticks.
Manager: Dave Barnes
Controller/Director: Leticia Simbach
IS Manager: Glenn Corbin
Administrative Assistant: Jean Williams
Plant Manager: John Stevens
Purchasing Manager: Buddy Wilson
Estimated Sales: $12.4 Million
Square Footage: 120000
Parent Co: AmeriQual Group LLC
Type of Packaging: Consumer, Food Service, Private Label, Bulk

30206 **Thermo Ramsey**
501 90th Ave NW
Coon Rapids, MN 55433 763-783-2500
Fax: 763-783-2525 sales@thermogoringkerr.com
www.thermo.com
Weighing and inspection manufacturer and exporter of checkweighers; metal detectors; weighbelt, loss-in-weight and gravimetric feeders; level indicators; flow monitors; and blending control systems
President: Ralph Sperrazza
VP Finance: Dan Walsh
VP: Joergen Olsson
Estimated Sales: $3 - 5 Million
Number Employees: 10
Square Footage: 125000
Parent Co: Thermo Electron
Brands:
Ac 8000
Ac 9000 Rx
Metal Scout Iie

30207 **Thermo Sentron Goring Kerr**
501 90th Ave NW
Coon Rapids, MN 55433-8005 763-783-2741
Fax: 763-780-2315 info@thermoramsey.com
www.thermo.com
President: Mike Jost
R&D: Rick Cast
Quality Control: Shanda Osiecki
Estimated Sales: $50 - 100 Million
Number Employees: 100-249

30208 **Thermo Wisconsin**
PO Box 5030
De Pere, WI 54115-5030 920-766-7200
Fax: 920-766-5211 www.thermo.com
Stainless steel tanks and vessels
Manager Custom Fabrication: Jeff Loker
Designer: Scott Brauer
Estimated Sales: Less than $500,000
Number Employees: 1-4
Square Footage: 560000
Parent Co: Thermo Electron Corporation

30209 **Thermo-Serv**
3901 Pipestone Rd
Dallas, TX 75212-6017 214-631-0307
Fax: 214-631-0566 800-635-5559
samples@thermoserv.com www.thermoserv.com
Molded plastic servingware and insulated beverage ware and speciality cups and mugs
President: Joe Betras
CEO: Jay Rigby
Marketing Director: Peggy Hock
National Sales Director: Jon Hock
COO: Tom Morris
Purchasing: Beverly Robbins
Estimated Sales: $40 Million
Parent Co: New Thermo Serv, Ltd.

30210 **ThermoQuest**
2215 Grand Avenue Pkwy
Austin, TX 78728-3812 512-251-1400
Fax: 512-251-1596 800-876-6711
dclay@thermofinnigan.com www.thermo.com
Manufacturer and exporter of laboratory equipment including gas chromatographs and GC/MS systems for research and quality control applications
Manager: Andrew Walder
General Manager: Dennis Orr
Product Marketing Manager: Duncan Carmichael
Operations Manager: Ken Davis
Production Manager: Randy Bullock
Estimated Sales: $75 - 100 Million
Number Employees: 50-99
Square Footage: 140000
Parent Co: ThermoQuest
Brands:
Cei Instruments
Finnigan
Tremetrics

30211 **ThermoWorks**
1762 W 20 S
Suite 100
Lindon, UT 84042 801-756-7705
Fax: 801-756-8948 800-393-6434
randyvowen@thermoworks.com
www.thermoworks.com
President: Randy Owen
Estimated Sales: Below $5 Million
Number Employees: 5-9

30212 **Thermodynamics**
6780 Brighton Blvd
Commerce City, CO 80022
Fax: 918-251-2826 800-627-9037
info@okpallets.com www.okpallets.com
Reusable plastic pallets, bins, boxes, containers and trays including standard and custom; exporter of plastic pallets
CEO: Sheri Orlowitz
General Manager: Robert Lux
Production Manager: Shawn Harley
Plant Manager: Robert Luxtwood
Purchasing Manager: Ray Carr
Estimated Sales: $5 - 10 Million
Number Employees: 20-49
Square Footage: 35000
Parent Co: Shan Industries

30213 **Thermodyne Food Service**
4418 New Haven Ave
Fort Wayne, IN 46803-1650 260-428-2535
Fax: 260-428-2533 800-526-9182
tellinger@vptag.com www.tdyne.com
Manufacturer and exporter of conduction ovens
President: Vincent Tippmann Sr
General Manager: Sue Brown
Number Employees: 10-19
Square Footage: 600000
Parent Co: Polar King International

30214 **Thermodyne International**
1841 S Business Pkwy
Ontario, CA 91761-8537 909-923-9945
Fax: 909-923-7505
sales@thermodyne-online.com
www.thermodynecases.com
Manufacturer and exporter of reusable plastic containers and instrument shipping and carrying cases; also, custom vacuum forming services available
President: Gary Ackerman
Sr. VP: Gary Ackerman
Chairman of the Board: Gary S Ackerman
Estimated Sales: $10 - 20 Million
Number Employees: 50-99
Brands:
Rack-Pack
Shok-Stop

30215 **Thermoil Corporation**
7 Franklin Avenue
Brooklyn, NY 11211-7801 718-855-0544
Fax: 718-643-6691
Manufacturer and exporter of industrial oils and greases
Estimated Sales: $10-20 Million
Number Employees: 10-19

30216 **Thermolok Packaging Systems**
5050 Prince George Drive
Prince George, VA 23875-2623 452-001- 001
Fax: 804-452-2011 thermolok7@aol.com
www.strapmc.com
Manufacturers of plastic strapping equipment, stretch film machines and tape machines
Estimated Sales: $1-2.5 Million
Number Employees: 1-4

30217 **Thermomass**
1000 Technology Drive
PO Box 950
Boone, IA 50036-0950 515-433-6075
Fax: 515-433-6088 800-232-1748
info@thermomass.com www.thermomass.com
Composite sandwich walls used for cold or frozen storage units, also wineries
President: Tom Stecker
R&D: Rex Donahey
Estimated Sales: $5 - 10 Million
Number Employees: 50-99

30218 **Thermoquest**
3661 Interstate Park Road N
Riviera Beach, FL 33404-5906 800-532-4752
Manufacturer and exporter of stainless steel pots and pans
General Manager: Ralph Kearney
Number Employees: 50
Parent Co: Floaire
Type of Packaging: Food Service
Brands:
Floware

30219 **Thermos Company**
475 N Martingale Road
Suite 1100
Schaumburg, IL 60173 847-439-7821
Fax: 847-593-5570 800-243-0745
customer@grilllovers.com www.thermos.com
Vacuum insulated bottles and carafes, stainless steel thermal cookware, ice buckets, coffee presses and airpot coffee dispensers
Chairman: Shouji Toida
Executive VP: Rick Dias
Director Special Marketing Division: Nedda Glenn
Estimated Sales: $1-2,500,000
Number Employees: 500-999
Brands:
Thermos

30220 **Thermoseal**
1310 Highway 287 S
Suite 105
Mansfield, TX 76063-5705 817-453-0813
Fax: 817-453-0594
tscustomercare@therm-o-seal.com.
www.therm-o-seal.com
Sealers
President: Shawn Kennedy

30221 **Theta Sciences**
11835 Carmel Mountain Road
Suite 1304
San Diego, CA 92128-4609 760-745-3311
Fax: 760-745-5519
Manufacturer, importer and exporter of electronic instruments specializing in food process control and personnel hazard monitoring
President: Hal Buscher
VP: Bob LeClair
VP: Dave Furuno
Estimated Sales: $1-2.5 Million
Number Employees: 9
Square Footage: 9600
Brands:
Theta Sciences

30222 **Thiel Cheese & Ingredients**
N7630 County Hwy BB
Attn: Kathy Pitzen
Hilbert, WI 54129 920-989-1440
Fax: 920-989-1288 kathyp@thielcheese.com
www.thielcheese.com
Manufacturer and custom formulator of processed cheeses that are used primarily as ingredients in other food products
President: Steven Thiel
Sales: Kathy Pitzen
Number Employees: 50-99
Type of Packaging: Consumer, Food Service, Private Label, Bulk
Brands:
Thiel

30223 **Thiele Engineering Company**
810 Industrial Park Boulevard
Fergus Falls, MN 56537 218-739-3321
Fax: 218-739-9370 info@swfcompanies.com
www.thieletech.com
Manufacturer and exporter of cartoners and case packers
VP Sales: Wayne Slaton
Number Employees: 260
Square Footage: 86950
Parent Co: Barry-Wehmiller Company

30224 **Thiele Technologies**
1949 E. Manning Avenue
PO Box 548
Reedley, CA 93654 559-638-8484
Fax: 559-638-7478 800-344-8951
info@swfcompanies.com www.thieletech.com
Manufacturer and exporter of corrugated box forming and sealing machinery, case erectors, automatic case packers, case openers/positioners, cartoners and robotics automation.
President: Larry Smith
VP: Ed Suarez
Sales Director: Craig Friesen
Number Employees: 250-499
Square Footage: 200000
Parent Co: Barry-Wehmiller
Other Locations:
SWF Machinery
Orlando FL

30225 **Thieley Technolgies**
315 27th Ave NE
Minneapolis, MN 55418-2715 612-782-1200
Fax: 612-782-1203 www.thieletech.com
Packaging and palletizing equipment
CEO: Laurence P Smith
Sales/Marketing Manager: Todd Sandell
Estimated Sales: $20-50 Million
Number Employees: 500-999

30226 **Thielmann Container Systems**
6301 Gravel Ave
Alexandria, VA 22310 703-836-4003
Fax: 703-836-4070 www.via-mailing.com
Cylindrical and cubic containers
Estimated Sales: $1 - 3 Million
Number Employees: 5-9

30227 **Thinque Systems Corporation**
4130 Cahuenga Boulevard
Suite 128
Toluca Lake, CA 91602-2847 818-752-1350
Fax: 818-752-1355 sales@thinque.com
www.thinque.com
President: George Bayz
VP Business Development: Rich Love
VP Marketing: Ellen Libenson
Estimated Sales: $27 Million
Number Employees: 150

30228 **Thirstenders**
11518 Bedford Street
Houston, TX 77031-2108 713-664-8050
Fax: 713-664-8008 www.thirstenders.com
Manufacturers proprietary, mobile delivery systems for food, beverages and consumer products.
President: Fred Ash
Quality Control: Lee Grover
R&D: Fred Ash
Estimated Sales: Below $5 Million
Number Employees: 1-4

30229 **Thirty Two North Corporation**
32north Corporation16 Pomerleau Street
Biddeford, ME 04005 800-782-2423
Fax: 207-284-5015 800-782-2423
info@32north.com www.32north.com
Safety shoes, detachable anti-slip soles
Owner: Anne Gould
Estimated Sales: Below $5 Million
Number Employees: 10

30230 **Thomas J. Payne Market Development**
865 Woodside
San Mateo, CA 94401 650-340-8311
Fax: 650-340-8568 tpayne@tjpmd.com
www.tjpmd.com
Consultant specializing in marketing development and food technology
President: Tom Payne
Market Development Activities: Edith Nagy
Estimated Sales: $500,000-$1 Million
Number Employees: 5-9

30231 **Thomas L. Green & Company**
380 Old West Penn Ave
Robenosia, PA 19551 610-693-5816
Fax: 610-693-5512 info@readingbakery.com
www.readingbakery.com
Manufacturer and exporter of bakery machinery including automatic band ovens, dough mixers, conveyors for crackers and cookies, biscuit cutters, dough formers and dough sheeters
Chairman: Thomas Lugar
President: Terry Groff
CEO: Terry Groff
CFO: Charles Czulada
Quality Control: Mike Johnson
Sr. VP Engineering: Don Smith
Estimated Sales: $5 - 10 Million
Number Employees: 10-19

30232 **Thomas Lighting Residential**
10275 W Higgins Rd, 8th Floor
Rosemont, IL 60018
Fax: 800-288-4329 800-825-5844
info@thomaslighting.com
www.thomaslighting.com
Manufacturer and exporter of outdoor lighting fixtures
Sales Manager: Sheryl Fraga
Number Employees: 350

30233 **Thomas Precision, Inc.**
3278 S Main St
Rice Lake, WI 54868-8793 715-234-8827
Fax: 715-234-6737 800-657-4808
sales@tpm-inc.com www.tpm-inc.com
Manufacturer and exporter of stainless steel and alloy replacement parts for food processing equipment including grinder plates, blades and screens; also, build and rebuild separating machines and augers
Owner: Roger Norberg
CEO: Roger Norberg
Sales: Jerry Klasen
Plant Manager: Kevin Nyra
Purchasing Agent: Rod Stoyke
Estimated Sales: $10 Million
Number Employees: 60
Square Footage: 24000
Brands:
Tpm

30234 **Thomas Pump & Machinery**
120 Industrial Drive
Slidell, LA 70460 985-649-3000
Fax: 985-649-4300 www.thomaspump.com
Cleaning and washing equipment, pressure washers, heaters-water, heat reclaiming systems, automobile products
President: Jim Thomas
VP of Finances: Rebecca Rhoto
VP of Inside Sales: Craig Robinson
VP of Operations: Joe Galey
Estimated Sales: $1 - 3 Million
Number Employees: 10-19

30235 **Thomas Pump & Machinery**
120 Industrial Dr
Slidell, LA 70460 985-649-3000
Fax: 985-649-4300 tpump@thomaspump.com
www.thomaspump.com
Owner: Jim Thomas

Estimated Sales: $2.5-5 Million
Number Employees: 20-49

30236 Thomas Tape Company
PO Box 207
Springfield, OH 45501-0207 937-325-6414
Fax: 937-325-2850 sales@thomastape.com
www.thomastape.com
Manufacturer and exporter of sealing tape including paper, cloth, reinforced glass fiber, gummed, and pressure sensitive tape
President: David Simonton
Sales/Marketing Executive: Kevin Amidon
Estimated Sales: $300,000-500,000
Number Employees: 1-4
Square Footage: 120000
Brands:
Paxrite
Raycord

30237 Thomas Technical Services
P.O.Box 28
Neillsville, WI 54456-0028 715-743-4666
Fax: 715-743-2062 TTSRandy@netscrape.net
Ultrafiltration and reverse osmosis systems for the dairy industry; wholesaler/distributor of replacement parts
President: R L Thomas
CEO: Theresa Thomas
CFO: Randy Thomas
Estimated Sales: Below $5 Million
Number Employees: 1-4
Square Footage: 9000
Brands:
Thomas Fractioner

30238 Thomas Technical Services
W4780 US Highway 10
Neillsville, WI 54456-6213 715-743-4666
Fax: 715-743-2062
Ultra filtration, reverse osmosis, membrane systems
Owner: Randy L Thomas
*Estimated Sales:*less than $500,000
Number Employees: 1-4

30239 Thomasen
1303 43rd St
Kenosha, WI 53140 262-652-3662
Fax: 262-652-3526 sales@lcthomsen.com
www.lcthomsen.com
Custom fabrication, filters, milk, flow diversion stations
President: Wayne Borne
Sales: Joyce Saftig
Estimated Sales: $1-5 Million
Number Employees: 20-49

30240 Thombert
P.O.Box 1123
Newton, IA 50208-1123 641-792-4449
Fax: 641-792-2390 800-433-3572
thombert@thombert.com www.thombert.com
Polyurethane wheels and tires for forklift trucks
Chairman of the Board: Walter Smith
President: Dick Davidson
VP Manufacturing: Terry Beckham
Estimated Sales: $10-20 Million
Number Employees: 50-99
Brands:
Dyalon
Vulkollan

30241 (HQ)Thompson Bagel Machine MFg. Corp.
8945 Ellis Ave
Los Angeles, CA 90034-3380 310-836-0900
Fax: 310-836-0156 sales@bagelproducts.com
www.bagelproducts.com
Manufacturer and exporter of one and two bank bagel machines including horizontal and vertical; also, two and four row rotary dividers.
President: Stephen Thompson
Research & Development: Dan Thompson
Marketing/Sales: Charles Ducat
Operations Manager: Craig Thompson
Estimated Sales: $1-5 Million
Number Employees: 1-4
Number of Products: 10
Type of Packaging: Private Label
Brands:
Thompson Bagel Machines

30242 Thompson Scale Company
9000 Jameel
Suite 190
Houston, TX 77040 713-932-9071
Fax: 713-932-9379 info@thompsonscale.com
www.thompsonscale.com
Weighing systems and packaging machinery controls
President: Bobbie Thompson
Estimated Sales: $2 Million
Number Employees: 13
Square Footage: 9000

30243 Thomsen Group, LLC
1303 43rd St.
Kenosha, WI 53140 262-652-3662
Fax: 262-652-3526 800-558-4018
sales@lcthomsen.com www.lcthomsen.com
Wine industry pumps and valves
President: Wayne Borne
Sales: Joyce Saftig
Number Employees: 10-19

30244 (HQ)Thomson-Leeds Company
450 Park Avenue S
2nd Floor
New York, NY 10016-7320 914-428-7255
Fax: 914-428-7047 800-535-9361
info@thomson-leeds.com
www.thomson-leeds.com
Manufacturer, importer and exporter of displays, fixtures, package designs and point of purchase merchandising materials. Broker of specialty displays
President: Vince Esposito
CEO: Douglas Leeds
Director Marketing: Peter Weiller
Estimated Sales: $2.5-5 Million
Number Employees: 50-99
Square Footage: 80000
Brands:
Fiberpoptics
Freelight
Greenpop
Security Peg Hook
Stockpop

30245 Thorco Industries LLC
1300 E 12th St
Lamar, MO 64759 417-682-3375
Fax: 417-682-1326 800-445-3375
sales@thorco.com www.thorco.com
Manufacturer and exporter of point of purchase displays, wire grids, store fixtures, bag holders and baskets
President: John Kuhahl
CFO: Jeff Gardener
Quality Control: Rodney Walters
Estimated Sales: E
Number Employees: 500-999
Parent Co: Marmon Corporation

30246 Thoreson-McCosh
1885 Thunderbird
Troy, MI 48084-5472 248-362-0960
Fax: 248-362-5270 800-959-0805
sales@thoresonmccosh.com
www.thoresonmccosh.com
Manufacturer and exporter of dryers, hoppers, loaders and loading systems, tilters and bulk handling systems
President: David Klatt
Estimated Sales: $10-20 Million
Number Employees: 20-49
Type of Packaging: Bulk

30247 Thorn Smith Laboratories
7755 Narrow Gauge Rd
Beulah, MI 49617 231-882-4672
Fax: 231-882-4804 auric@thornsmithlabs.com
www.thornsmithlabs.com
Manufacturer and exporter of temperature specific sterilizer controls for use in quality assurance programs
President: Robert Brown
Plant Manager: Melanie Cederholm
Estimated Sales: Below $5 Million
Number Employees: 1-4
Square Footage: 17200
Brands:
Diack
Vac

30248 Thornton Plastics
745 Pacific Ave
Salt Lake City, UT 84104 801-322-3413
Fax: 801-359-2800 800-248-3434
sales@thorntonplastics.com
www.thorntonplastics.com
Transparent plastic snap-cap vials
President: Briton Mc Conkie
VP: Jean Eastham
Estimated Sales: Below $5 Million
Number Employees: 5-9
Square Footage: 17000

30249 Thorpe & Associates
227 N Chatnam Ave
Siler City, NC 27344-3443 919-742-5516
Fax: 919-742-4657
Manufacturer and importer of chairs and tables
President: Bill Thorpe
VP Design: William Thorpe
VP Sales: Van Thorpe
Estimated Sales: Less than $500,000
Number Employees: 500
Square Footage: 200000

30250 Thorpe Rolling Pin Company
336 Putnam Ave
Hamden, CT 06517-2744 203-562-6866
Fax: 203-230-2753 800-344-6966
Rolling and pizza pins
President: Timothy Pagnam
Estimated Sales: $1-2.5 Million
Number Employees: 5-9

30251 Three P
333 Andrew Ave
Salt Lake City, UT 84115-5113 801-486-7407
Fax: 801-571-4896
Manufacturer and exporter of custom printed and pressure sensitive decals, labels, tags, signs, etc
Owner: Edd Lancaster
Quality Control: Ernie Ashcroft
Marketing: Denise Lancaster
Sales: Edd Lancaster
Estimated Sales: $500,000-$1 Million
Number Employees: 5-9
Type of Packaging: Private Label, Bulk

30252 Three-A Sanitary Standards Symbol
1500 2nd Avenue SE
Suite 209
Cedar Rapids, IA 52403-2371 319-286-9221
Fax: 319-286-9290

30253 Threshold Rehabilitation Services
1000 Lancaster Ave
Reading, PA 19607 610-777-7691
Fax: 610-777-1295 trsincmail@trsinc.org
www.trsinc.org
Founded in 1973. Contract packagers
President: Ronald Williams
Sales/Marketing: Nancy Benjamin
VP Program Operations: Tom McNelis
Estimated Sales: $20 - 50 Million
Number Employees: 250-499
Square Footage: 20000

30254 Thunder Pallet
625 North Menomonee Street
PO Box 298
Theresa, WI 53091 920-488-4211
Fax: 920-488-4306 800-354-0643
ann@thunderpallet.com www.thunderpallet.com
Wooden pallets, skids, boxes, crates, etc
President: Ben Mahsem
Estimated Sales: Below $5 Million
Number Employees: 50

30255 Thunderbird Food Machinery
PO Box 4079
Blaine, WA 98231 360-366-9328
Fax: 360-366-0998 800-764-9377
tbfm@tbfm.com www.thunderbirdfm.com
Importer and wholesaler/distributor of food processing equipment including mixers, dough sheeters, vegetable and bread slicers, meat grinders, etc
Owner: Ky Lin
Marketing Director: Kara M
Estimated Sales: $1-2.5 Million
Number Employees: 5-9

30256 **Thunderbird Label Corportion**
70 Clinton Road
Fairfield, NJ 07004-2928 973-575-6677
Fax: 973-575-4970 sales@thunderbirdlabel.com
www.thunderbirdlabel.com
Pressure sensitive labels including prime, coupon, tamper-evident and four color process
President: Karl Beierle
VP Sales: George Coughlin
Estimated Sales: $2.5-5 Million
Number Employees: 19
Square Footage: 48000

30257 **Thurman Scale**
4025 Lakeview Crossing
Groveport, OH 43125 614-221-9077
Fax: 614-221-8879 800-688-9741
thurmanscales@fancor.com
www.thurmanscale.com
Weighing equipment
Estimated Sales: $.5 - 1 million
Number Employees: 1-4
Parent Co: Fancor

30258 **Thwing-Albert InstrumentCompany**
14 W Collings Ave
West Berlin, NJ 08091 856-767-1000
Fax: 856-767-2615 info@thwingalbert.com
www.thwingalbert.com
Thwing-Albert Instrument Company provides a complete offering of tensile testers and other materials testing instruments for quality control, research & development and process control applications worldwide.
President: Joseph Raab
VP/Sales/Marketing: Steven Berg
Estimated Sales: $5 - 10 Million
Number Employees: 50-99

30259 **Tiax LLC**
35 Hartwell Ave
Lexington, MA 02421 781-879-1200
Fax: 617-498-7200 800-677-3000
lupien.bernard@tiaxllc.com www.tiaxllc.com
Consultant specializing in technology, product and marketing services, health, safety, product formulation, and research and development.
President: Kenan Sahin
VP: Arthur Schwope
VP Sales: Bernard Lupien
VP Operations: Boyd Boucher
Purchasing Manager: Jose Bairos
Estimated Sales: $20 - 50 Million
Number Employees: 120
Square Footage: 120000
Other Locations:
Cupertino CA
Irvine CA

30260 **Tibersoft Corporation**
2200 West Park Dr
Westborough, MA 01581 508-898-9555
Fax: 508-898-1820 888-888-1969
info@tibersoft.com www.tibersoft.com
Founder: Christopher Martin
Vice President, Founder: Mary Wilson
Estimated Sales: $1 - 5 Million
Number Employees: 1-4

30261 **Tidland Corporation**
2305 SE 8th Ave
Camas, WA 98607 360-834-2345
Fax: 360-834-5865 800-426-1000
tidlandmarketing@tidland.com www.tidland.com
Manufactures air expanding shafts, chucks, air brakes, slitting knife holders and electronic slitting positioning machines
President: Quino Lorente
Director International Marketing: John Rupp
Estimated Sales: Below $5 Million
Number Employees: 100-249

30262 **Tieco-Unadilla Corporation**
22 Depot Street
Unadilla, NY 13838 607-369-3236
Fax: 607-369-2011 877-889-6540
tieco@tyups.com www.tyups.com
Manufacturer and exporter of tying devices for securing bundles and pallets
President: Scott McLean
Estimated Sales: Below $500,000
Number Employees: 5-9
Brands:
Ty-Up

30263 **Tiefenthaler Machinery Co, Inc**
W227 N913 Westmound Dr
Waukesha, WI 53186 262-513-1111
Fax: 262-513-1113 www.tiefmach.com
President: James Tiefenthaler Jr
Estimated Sales: $5 - 10 Million
Number Employees: 5-9

30264 **Tier-Rack Corporation**
425 Sovereign Ct
Ballwin, MO 63011 636-527-0700
Fax: 636-256-4901 800-325-7869
info@tier-rack.com www.tier-rack.com
Manufacturer and exporter of portable storage racks
Owner: Scott Ten Eyck
General Manager: George Willis
Controller: Ward Wilson
Estimated Sales: $1 - 2.5 Million
Number Employees: 10-19
Square Footage: 75000
Brands:
Tier-Rack

30265 **Tifa (CI)**
109 Stryker Lane
Building 3, Suite 4&5
Millington, NJ 8844 908-829-3230
Fax: 908-829-3240 go@tifausa.com
www.tifausa.com
Manufacturing of aeorsol fogging equipment for public health
President: Gamel Osman
Chairman: Vladimir Alexanyan
Vice President: Deirdre Cerciello
Estimated Sales: $1-2.5 Million
Number Employees: 10-19

30266 **Tiffin Metal Products**
450 Wall St
Fort Seneca, OH 44883 419-447-8414
Fax: 419-447-8512 800-537-0983
tiffin@bpsom.com www.tiffinmetal.com
Stainless steel lockers and special sheet metal fabrication, ergonomic seating, stainless, plated polyurethane seats for washdown areas, adjustable work tables, packing stands and anti-fatigue matting
President/CEO: Will Heddles
Chief Financial Officer: Timothy Demith
VP Outdoor/Custom & OEM Products: Ron Myers
VP Security Products & Marketing: Andrew Beebe
Marketing Manager: Mike Wittman
National Sales Manager Custom/OEM: Rodney Osmena
Estimated Sales: $5 - 10 Million
Number Employees: 50-99

30267 **Tiger-Vac (USA)**
73 S.W. 12 Ave. Bldg.1, Unit 7
Dania, FL 33004 954-925-3625
Fax: 954-925-3626 800-668-4437
sales@tiger-vac.com www.tiger-vac.com
Industrial vacuum cleaners, specializes in systems for clean manufacturing areas and contamination controlled environments, foodgrade vacuums, continuous duty vacuums, vacuums with high efficiency
President: Rocco Mariani
Estimated Sales: $1 - 2.5 Million
Number Employees: 1-4
Number of Products: 15

30268 **Tilly Industries**
4210 Blvd Poirier
St Laurent, QC H4R 2C5
Canada 514-331-4922
Fax: 514-331-4924
infotilly@mavencorporation.com
www.tillyindustries.com
Manufacturer and exporter of aluminum foil dies for pie plates and containers
VP: Dagmar Tilly
Estimated Sales: $1 - 5 Million
Number Employees: 8
Square Footage: 18000
Parent Co: Maven Engineering Corporation

30269 **Timberline Consulting**
3333 S Bannock St
Suite 800
Englewood, CO 80110-2450 303-781-3977
www.timberlineconsulting.com
President: David Daniel
Estimated Sales: $810,000
Number Employees: 11

30270 **Timbertech Company**
1055 White Mountain Highway
Milton, NH 03851-4443 603-669-7743
Fax: 603-669-2024 800-572-5538
rodvans@aol.com
Pallets including new and rebuilt 48 x 40 grocery; also, disposal
Owner and President: Rod Van Sciver
Office Manager: Nancy Boudreau
Estimated Sales: $2.5-5 Million
Number Employees: 20-49
Square Footage: 25000

30271 **Timco**
2 Greentown Rd
Buchanan, NY 10511 914-736-0206
Fax: 914-736-0395 800-792-0030
sales@timco-eng.com www.timco-eng.com
Rigging gear, hardware, jacks and rollers: sheaves, chain guides
Chairman: Rudolf Walter
Sales: Joe Yaniv
Plant Manager: Barry Volaski
Estimated Sales: $6 Million
Number Employees: 20-49
Number of Brands: 3
Number of Products: 30

30272 **Time Products**
3780 Browns Mill Rd SE
Atlanta, GA 30354 404-767-7526
Fax: 404-767-7010 800-241-6681
tymebill@aol.com www.timeproducts.com
Cleaning compounds
VP and General Manager: Bill Drew
CEO: John Theophilis
Chairman of the Board: Steve Theofilos
Marketing Director: Stan Lanch
Production Manager: Rod Abrahansen
Estimated Sales: $20-50 Million
Number Employees: 20-49
Square Footage: 100000
Parent Co: Theochem Laboratories
Brands:
Time-Saver

30273 **Timely Signs**
2135 Linden Blvd
Elmont, NY 11003 516-285-5339
Fax: 516-285-9637 800-457-4467
sales@timelysigns.net www.timelysigns.net
Manufacturer and exporter of labels, marketing signs and banners; wholesaler/distributor of computerized sign making equipment
President: Eugene Goldsmith
Estimated Sales: $1-2.5 Million
Number Employees: 5-9
Square Footage: 2000
Brands:
Duracast
Timely Signs
Ulta Mag

30274 **Timemed Labeling Systems**
27770 N Entertainment Drive
Suite 200
Valencia, CA 91355 818-897-1111
Fax: 818-686-9317 intl@pdcorp.com
www.pdchealthcare.com
Manufacturer and exporter of pressure-sensitive labels, embossed seals and printed gummed tapes
President: Jerry Nerad
General Manager: Lee Smith
Plant Manager: Dave Luther
Estimated Sales: $10 - 20 Million
Number Employees: 20-49
Parent Co: Timemed Labeling Systems

30275 **TinWerks Packaging**
1237 West Capitol Drive
Addison, IL 60101 630-628-8600
Fax: 630-628-0330 sales@tinwerks.com
www.tinwerks.com

Tins
President/Owner: James Giusto V
VP: Peter Goschi
Sales: Joseph Marlovits
Number Employees: 10

30276 Tinadre
15310 Amberly Dr Ste 180
Tampa, FL 33647 813-866-0033
Fax: 813-866-0462 tinadre@gte.net
www.tinadre.com
Turnkey customer frequency pre-paid private label cards, electronic gift certificates and payment processing services for food service operators; also, POS software and hardware
Owner: Michael Crochet
VP: Mike Crochot
VP: Zachary Tapp
Production: Steven Malcanas
Estimated Sales: $500,000-$1 Million
Number Employees: 1-4

30277 Tindall Packaging
1150 E U Ave
Vicksburg, MI 49097 269-649-1163
Fax: 616-649-1163
information@tindallpackaging.com
www.tindallpackaging.com
Manufacturer and exporter of filling equipment for dairy, deli and cultured products; also, single and two-flavor variegators
President: Marianne Tindall
VP: Marianne Tindall
Quality Control: Frank Tindall
Number Employees: 5

30278 Tipper Tie
2000 Lufkin Road
Apex, NC 27539 919-362-8811
Fax: 919-303-4839 sales@tippertie.com
www.tippertie.com
Clippers, aluminum clips, aluminum wire products, electric fence supplies and netting
President: Gernot Foerster
Chief Financial Officer: Roman Steiger
Vice President: Robert Cleveland
Directory, Quality: Tim Downes
Marketing Executive: Emy Mooffitt
Sales Manager: Bryan Wilkins
Officer Manager: Ashley Gideon
Purchasing: Sue Chandler
Estimated Sales: $35 Million
Number Employees: 180
Square Footage: 130000
Parent Co: Dover Corporation
Brands:
Tipper Clippers

30279 (HQ)Tippmann Group
9009 Coldwater Road
Fort Wayne, IN 46825-2072 260-490-3000
Fax: 260-490-1362
tippsales@tippmanngroup.com
www.tippmanngroup.com
Design and building construction of refrigerated warehouses/facilities
CEO: John V Tippmann Sr
Number Employees: 10-19

30280 Tisma Machinery Corporation
1099 Estes Avenue
Elk Grove Village, IL 60007-4907 847-427-9525
Fax: 847-427-9550
bwilliams@swfcompanies.com
www.tisma.com
Manufacturer and exporter of automatic cartoning machinery and systems
Estimated Sales: $10-20 Million
Number Employees: 50-99
Square Footage: 88000

30281 Titan Corporation
3033 Science Park Rd
San Diego, CA 92121 858-552-9565
Fax: 858-535-3609 www.titan.com
Markets technology for the electronic irradation of food products
President: Andy Ivers
Number Employees: 250-499
Brands:
Surebean

30282 Titan Industries
735 Industrial Loop Rd
New London, WI 54961-2600 920-982-6600
Fax: 920-982-7750 800-558-3616
sales@titanconveyors.com
www.titanconveyors.com
Manufacturer and exporter of conveyors
President: Dan Baumbach
Estimated Sales: $5-10 Million
Number Employees: 20-49
Square Footage: 42000

30283 Titan Plastics
433 Murray Hill Pkwy
East Rutherford, NJ 07073 201-935-7700
Fax: 201-935-1584 www.titanplasticsgroup.com
Plastic containers
President: Rich Probinsky
Estimated Sales: $10-20 Million
Number Employees: 10-19
Square Footage: 100000
Parent Co: Penn Bottle & Supply Company

30284 Titan Ventures International, Inc
170 Millennium Blvd
Moncton, NB E1E 2G8
Canada 506-858-8990
Fax: 506-859-6929 800-565-2253
sales@bakemax.com www.bakemax.com
Wholesaler/distributor of Planetary Mixers, Hot Dog Roller Grills, Slicers, Spiral Mixers, Water Meters, Bakery Equipment, Countertop Pizza or Pie Sheeter, Electric Display Food Warmers, Deli or Meat Equipment, Bread SlicersReversible Sheeters, Bun Dividers and more
Chief Financial Officer: Cathy Flanagan
Sales: Shawn Melanson
Estimated Sales: $3-5 Million
Number Employees: 5
Square Footage: 48000
Type of Packaging: Bulk

30285 Tnemec Company
123 W 23rd Ave
Kansas City, MO 64116 816-474-3400
Fax: 816-483-2951 800-TNE-MEC1
www.tnemec.com
High performance paints, coatings and floor toppings, industrial steel maintenance paints and primers, concrete, brick and masonry waterproofing materials, chemical resistant coatings for steel
President: Lbpete Portlyou
CEO: Pete Cortelyou
Marketing Director: Mark Thomas
Estimated Sales: H
Number Employees: 50-99

30286 Toastmaster
1400 Toastmaster Drive
Elgin, IL 60120-9274 847-741-3300
Fax: 847-741-0015 mww@middleby.com
www.toastmastercorp.com
Manufacturer and exporter of broilers, fryers, griddles, grills, hot plates, ovens, ranges, rotisseries and toasters
President: Mark Sieron
Estimated Sales: $1 - 5 Million
Number Employees: 5-9
Parent Co: Middleby Corporation

30287 Todd Construction Services
1206 Price Ave
Pomona, CA 91767-5840 909-469-6242
Fax: 909-469-6241 todd@toddconst.com
www.toddconst.com
Designers, engineers and planners for the food production and cold storage industry
President: Glenn Todd
Estimated Sales: $5-10 Million
Number Employees: 5-9

30288 Todd Uniform
PO Box 29107
Saint Louis, MO 63126-0107 800-458-3402
Fax: 800-231-8633
Uniforms
Sales: Robin Berry

30289 Todd's
PO Box 4821
Des Moines, IA 50305 515-266-2276
Fax: 515-266-1669 800-247-5363
sales@toddsltd.com www.toddsltd.com
Variety of food products, wet and dry, kosher and organic certified.
President/CEO: Alan Niedermeier
Quality Control: Diana Burzloff
Public Relations: Alissa Douglas
Operations: Duane Hettkamp
Production: Jeff Sullivan
Plant Manager: John Routh
Purchasing: Danielle Robinson
Estimated Sales: $1 - 3 Million
Number Employees: 30
Number of Brands: 40
Number of Products: 200
Square Footage: 320000
Type of Packaging: Consumer, Food Service, Private Label, Bulk
Brands:
Butcher's Friend
Papa Joe's Specialty Food

30290 Token Factory
2131 South Ave
La Crosse, WI 54601 608-785-2439
888-486-5367
custserv@tokenfactory.com
www.tokenfactory.com
Manufacturer and exporter of plastic tokens and swizzle sticks
President: Dale Stevens
Sales Manager: Rosie Hundt
Estimated Sales: $1-2.5 Million
Number Employees: 11

30291 Tokheim Company
560 31st St
Marion, IA 52302 319-362-4847
Fax: 319-377-7953 800-747-3442
info@tokheimco.com www.tokheimco.com
Manufacturer and exporter of liquid level gauges for large storage tanks
President: Vicky Barnes
Quality Control: Chris Peyton
VP: Thomas Barnes
Sales: Barb Riffey
Estimated Sales: Below $5 Million
Number Employees: 1-4
Square Footage: 20000

30292 (HQ)Tolan Machinery Company
PO Box 695
Rockaway, NJ 07866 973-983-7212
Fax: 973-983-7217 sales@tolanmachinery.com
www.tolanmachinery.com
Manufacturer and exporter of tanks, reactors, hoppers, bins, heat exchangers, storage vessels and fermentors
President: John Tolpa
Chief Engineer: Bill Ebbinghouser
VP Sales/Marketing: Thomas Spencer
Estimated Sales: $10 - 20 Million
Number Employees: 20-49
Square Footage: 40000

30293 Tolas Health Care Packaging
905 Pennsylvania Blvd
Feasterville Trevose, PA 19053 215-322-7900
Fax: 215-322-9034 marketing@tolas.com
www.tolas.com
Printed and converted paper, foil and plastics for packaging; exporter of paper, barrier films and foils
President: Carl D Marotta
CFO: Chuck Klink
Quality Control: Skip Peacock
R & D: Chris Perry
Marketing Team Leader: Denise Dilissio
Sales Director: Leslie Love
Operations Manager: Dave Preikszas
Purchasing Manager: Jim McNally
Estimated Sales: $20 Million
Number Employees: 100-249
Square Footage: 50000

30294 Tolco Corporation
1920 Linwood Ave
Toledo, OH 43604 419-241-1113
Fax: 419-241-3035 800-537-4786
tolco@tolcocorp.com www.tolcocorp.com
Funnels, soap dispensers, spouts, containers, scoops, pumps and trigger spray and plastic bottles
President: William E Spengler Sr
VP Sales/Marketing: George Notarianni
VP Operations: W Spengler
Purchasing Agent: T Denker

Estimated Sales: $5-10 Million
Number Employees: 50-99
Square Footage: 50000
Brands:
Spraymist

30295 Toledo Sign
2021 Adams St
Toledo, OH 43604 419-244-4444
Fax: 419-244-6546 tsigns@toledosign.com
www.toledosign.com
Changeable, letter, electric, luminous tube, interchangeable, point of purchase and plastic signs
President: Brian Heil
Estimated Sales: $2.5-5 Million
Number Employees: 20-49

30296 Toledo Ticket Company
PO Box 6876
Toledo, OH 43612 419-476-5424
Fax: 419-476-6801 rcarter@toledoticket.com
www.toledoticket.com
Manufacturer and exporter of labels and coupons
VP Sales and Marketing: Tom Carter
Estimated Sales: $5-10 Million
Number Employees: 20-49

30297 Toledo Wire Products
3601 Expressway Dr S
Toledo, OH 43608 419-729-5446
Fax: 419-729-0241 888-430-7445
info@toledowire.com www.toledowire.com
Wire display racks
President: Ann Obertacz
Contact: Ken Obertacz
VP Sales: Rick Breivik
Production Manager: Ken Obertacz
Estimated Sales: $2.5-5 Million
Number Employees: 10-19

30298 Tom Lockerbie
1023 County Highway 20
Edmeston, NY 13335-2524 315-737-5612
Fax: 315-737-5183
Air agitated ice builders
Estimated Sales: $500,000-$1 Million
Number Employees: 3

30299 Tom McCall & Associates
6 Nanticoke Crossing Plaza
Millsboro, DE 19966-9511 410-539-0700
Fax: 212-689-5761
Recruiting and placement agency specializing in sales and management personnel
Manager: Charley Greene
Assistant Manager: Emma Jean Smith
Estimated Sales: $500,000-$1 Million
Number Employees: 10-19
Square Footage: 700

30300 (HQ)Tomac Packaging
271 Salem Street
Unit G
Woburn, MA 01801-2004 781-938-1500
Fax: 781-938-7536 800-641-3100
Automatic weighing and bagging equipment for the produce industry; also, repairing and operating services available
President: Richard Gold
VP: Thomas Gold
VP: Hans Van Der Sande
Estimated Sales: $.5 - 1 million
Number Employees: 40
Square Footage: 4000
Other Locations:
Tomac Packaging
Idaho Falls ID

30301 Tomco Equipment Company
3340 Rosebud Rd
Loganville, GA 30052-7341 770-979-8000
Fax: 770-985-9179 800-832-4262
tomco@tomcoequipment.com
www.tomcoequipment.com
Tomco equipment company has developed products and services to suit all phases of co2 usage with storage. delivery and co2 application-driven equipment.tomco2's full range of products matches any carbon dioxide requirements. EPAcertified professional parts and service technicians are availible 24hrs a day 7 days a week. the company has supplied co2 storage and applications equipment since 1970.
President: John Toepke
Cfo: Lynn Brown
Quality Control: Louis Pittaluga
Vice President Sales: Dan Tenpleton
Operations: Ken Mercer
Purchasing: Rayna Hewitt
Estimated Sales: $20-50 Million
Number Employees: 100-249

30302 Tomlinson Industries
13700 Broadway Ave
Cleveland, OH 44125 216-587-3400
Fax: 216-587-0733 800-945-4589
jengle@tomlinsonind.com
www.tomlinsonind.com
Manufacturer and exporter of faucets and fittings, kettles, warmers and dispensers for cups, cones, lids, straws, napkins and condiments; also, table top organizers, thermal platters and cook and serve skillets;foodservice glovescutting boards and anti-fatigue mats.
President: Michael Figas
CEO: H Meyer
CFO: Donald Calkins
VP: Louis Castro
Quality Control: John Silcox
Marketing: Jeanne Engle
Operations: Kenneth Sidoti
Purchasing: Michael Ritley
Estimated Sales: $20 - 50 Million
Number Employees: 100-249
Square Footage: 120000
Parent Co: Meyer Company
Brands:
Frontier Kettle
Glenray
Melco
Modular Dispensing Systems
No-Drip
Tomlinson

30303 Tomric Systems
85 River Rock Dr
Suite 202
Buffalo, NY 14207 716-854-6050
Fax: 716-854-7363 sales@tomric.com
www.tomric.com
Custom molds, supplies, equipment and packaging for chocolate
President: Timothy M Thill
Estimated Sales: $1-5 Million
Number Employees: 20-49

30304 Tomsed Corporation
420 McKinney Pkwy
Lillington, NC 27546 910-814-3800
Fax: 910-814-3899 800-334-5552
sales@tomsed.com www.tomsed.com
Manufacturer and exporter of access control equipment including high security and waist-high turnstiles, handicapped gates, portable posts and sign holders; wholesaler/distributor of portable and fixed crowd railing
President: Robert Sedivy
CEO: Thomas Sedivy
CFO: Karin Sedivy
Sales: Russell Socles
Estimated Sales: $15 Million
Number Employees: 100-249
Number of Brands: 9
Number of Products: 100
Square Footage: 110000
Brands:
Entry Gard
Lawrence Model 88
Roto Gard
Round Nose
Safesec
Tomsed
Tut-50e
Tut-50r

30305 Tonnellerie Mercier
171 Spring Grove Avenue
San Anselmo, CA 94960-2410 415-453-2069
Fax: 650-463-5485 www.tonnellerie-mercier.com
Wine industry cooperage
Partner: Ken Deis

30306 Tonnellerie Montross
139 Jenkins Point Road
Montross, VA 22520-3524 804-493-9186
Fax: 804-493-0435 lilreeht@aol.com
www.tonnellerie-mercier.com
Wine industry cooperage and French oak barrels of all sizes
President: Jackqus Reche
Number Employees: 10

30307 Tonnellerie Radoux
480 Aviation Blvd
Santa Rosa, CA 95403-1069 707-284-2888
Fax: 707-284-2894 800-755-4393
www.tonnellerieradoux.com
Wine industry cooperage
Manager: Norm Leighty
Quality Control: Lee Iller
President, Chief Executive Officer, Pres: Michel Tapol
Estimated Sales: $5 - 10 Million
Number Employees: 10-19
Square Footage: 100000
Parent Co: Radoux

30308 Tonnellerie Remond
793 Broadway Street
Sonoma, CA 95476-5920 707-935-2176
Fax: 707-935-4774 remondsonona@aol.com
Wine industry cooperage
Manager: Todd Stanfield
Estimated Sales: $1 - 3 Million
Number Employees: 1-4

30309 Tooterville Trolley Company
5422 Bice Lane
Newburgh, IN 47630-8815 812-858-8585
Fax: 812-858-8580
Manufacturer and exporter of mobile carts including shaved ice, fruit and salad bar; also, soda vending machines
Owner: Thomas Rennels
Number Employees: 1
Square Footage: 1200
Brands:
Jolly Trolley
Tooterville Express

30310 (HQ)Tootsie Roll Industries,Inc.
7401 South Cicero Avenue
Chicago, IL 60629 773-838-3400
Fax: 415-401-0087 866-972-6879
tootiseroll@worldpantry.com www.tootsie.com
Manufacturer and exporter of all types of candy, sold in a wide variety of venues, including supermarkets, warehouse and membership stores, vending machines, dollar stores, drug stores, and convenience stores.
Chairman/CEO: Melvin Gordon
President/COO/Director: Ellen R Gordon
VP Finance & CFO: G. Howard Ember Jr.
VP: George Rost
Research & Development: Terri Sons
Director QA & Research and Development: Tony Luksas
Director, Marketing: Frank Thometz
Sales & Marketing Manager: Greg Miller
Operations Executive: Pete Mealus
Plant Manager: Steve Green
Director of Purchasing: David Perez
Estimated Sales: $550 Million
Number Employees: 2200
Square Footage: 2375000
Type of Packaging: Consumer, Food Service, Bulk
Brands:
Andes Creme De Menthe
Andes Cherry Jubilee
Andes Toffee Crunch
Andes Mint Parfait
Andes Creme De Menthe Sugar Free
Candy Carnival
Caramel Apple Pops
Cella Cherries
Charleston Chew
Charms Blow Pops
Charms Flat Pops
Charms Mini Pops

Child's Play
Cry Baby
Dots & Crows
Dubble Bubble
Fluffy Stuff
Frooties
Junior Mints
Nik-L-Nip
Razzles
Sugar Babies
Sugar Daddy
Tootsie Pops
Tootsie Roll
Wack-O-Wax

30311 (HQ)Top Line Process Equipment Company
PO Box 264
Bradford, PA 16701 814-362-4626
Fax: 814-362-4453 800-458-6095
topline@toplineonline.com
www.toplineonline.com
Supplier of hygienic stainless steel process equipment
CEO: Dan McCone
VP: Kevin O'Donnell
Marketing: Debra Fowler
Sales: John Quteri
Operations: Tom Wilson
Plant Manager: Tim Fox
Purchasing: Marlene Raszmann
Number Employees: 5-9
Brands:
Top Flo

30312 Top Source Industries
503 S Westgate St
PO Box 1246
Addison, IL 60101-8246
Fax: 630-543-2076 800-362-9625
gene@quickdisplay.net www.quickdisplay.net
Clear acrylic display cases, floor, counter and wall displays, trade show displays, counters, cabinets and custom plastic products
President: Viola Wycislak
VP Sales: Gene Wycislak
Estimated Sales: $350,000
Number Employees: 1-4
Square Footage: 10000

30313 (HQ)Topco
7711 Gross Point Rd
Skokie, IL 60077-2697 847-676-3030
Fax: 847-676-4949 webmaster@topco.com
www.topco.com
Grocery, frozen, dairy, and bakery, branded meat, equipment and supplies, business services, world brands and diverting.
President: Steve Lowery
CEO: Steve K Lauer
Estimated Sales: $50 - 100 Million
Number Employees: 250-499
Type of Packaging: Consumer, Food Service, Private Label
Other Locations:
Topco
Skokie IL
Brands:
Clear Value
Dining In
Food Club
Full Circle
Paws
Price Saver
Shur Fine
Top Care
Top Crest
Valu Time
World Class

30314 Topflight Grain Company
400 E Bodman St
Bement, IL 61813 217-678-2261
Fax: 217-678-8113 www.topflightgrain.com
Stores and distributes corn and grains
Manager: Derrick Bruhn
Estimated Sales: $10 - 20 000,000
Number Employees: 5-9

30315 Topos Mondial Corporation
600 Queen Street
Pottstown, PA 19464 610-970-2270
Fax: 610-970-1619 Sales@toposmondial.com
www.toposmondial.com
President: Michael Angelo Morabito Jr
Vice President: Damian Morabito
Estimated Sales: $5 - 10 Million
Number Employees: 20-49

30316 Tops Manufacturing Company
83 Salisbury Rd
Darien, CT 06820 203-655-9367
Coffee and tea equipment including percolators, knobs, handles, carafes, coffee makers and filters, tea infusers, liquid coffee flavors, glass cups, instant and ground coffee dispensers, measuring spoons, etc
President: Mitch Himmel
VP: Pat Himmel
Sales Manager: Ernie Hurlbut
Estimated Sales: Less than $500,000
Number Employees: 1-4
Square Footage: 15700
Type of Packaging: Consumer, Food Service
Brands:
Brick-Pack Clip
Fitz-All
Flav-A-Brew
Kaf-Tan
Measure Fresh
Perma-Brew
Rapid Brew
Tops

30317 Tor Rey USA
3737 Yale St
Houston, TX 77018 713-884-1988
Fax: 713-564-3246 800-867-7391
sales@tor-rey.com www.tor-rey-usa.com
Wholesaler/distributor of meat grinders and parts, saws, slicers, scales and bandsaw blades
Owner: Jesus Iglecis
Estimated Sales: $10-20 Million
Number Employees: 20-49

30318 Tor Rey USA
3737 Yale St
Houston, TX 77018 713-884-1988
Fax: 713-564-3246 sales@tor-rey.com
www.tor-rey-usa.com
Chopper plates and knives, choppers, grinder plates and knives, grinders and scales
Owner: Jesus Iglecis
Estimated Sales: $10 - 20 Million
Number Employees: 5-9

30319 Toray Plastics America
50 Belver Ave
North Kingstown, RI 02852 401-294-4511
Fax: 401-294-2154 becky.shaw@toraytpa.com
www.toraytpa.com
Biaxially oriented film, polyprolylene film, metallized
CEO: Richard Schloesser
Estimated Sales: $110 Million
Number Employees: 500-999

30320 Torbeck Industries
355 Industrial Dr
Harrison, OH 45030-1483 513-367-0080
Fax: 513-367-0081 800-333-0080
sales@torbeckind.com www.torbeckind.com
Producer of material handling and safety equipment used inmanufacturing, distribution and warehousing facilities throughout North America.
President: R L Torbeck Jr
Estimated Sales: $10,000,000 - $49,900,000
Number Employees: 50-99
Square Footage: 40000
Brands:
Astrodeck
Quik-Space
Saf-T-Rail

30321 Toroid Corporation
PO Box 1435
Huntsville, AL 35807 256-837-7510
Fax: 256-837-7512 toroidcorp@hotmail.com
toroidcorp.com
Custom weighing equipment, load cells and repairing load cells.
President: Anne Paelian
Vice President/Sales Manager: Paul Paelian
Estimated Sales: $1 Million
Number Employees: 15
Square Footage: 80000
Brands:
Lowboy
Omniflex

30322 Toromont Process Systems
395 W 1100 N
North Salt Lake, UT 84054-2621 801-292-1747
Fax: 801-292-9908 sales@toromontprocess.com
www.toromontpowersystems.com
Manufacturer and exporter of custom designed industrial and chemical refrigeration systems
President: Hugo Sorenson
CFO: Jerry Frailec
Manager: Jim Shepherd
Estimated Sales: $30-50 Million
Number Employees: 10
Square Footage: 70000
Parent Co: Toromont Industries
Other Locations:
Toromont Process Systems
Malden MA

30323 Toronto Fabricating & Manufacturing
1021 Rangeview Road
Mississauga, ON L5E 1H2
Canada 905-891-2516
Fax: 905-891-7446 sales@tfmc.com
www.tfmc.com
Manufacturer and exporter of tables, chairs, table tops and bases, benches, barstools and decorative lighting sconces and fixtures
Manager: Allan Farnum

30324 Toronto Kitchen Equipment
1150 Barmac Drive
North York, ON M9L 1X5
Canada 416-745-4944
Fax: 416-745-3217
Stoves, ovens, hoods, mixers, slicers and grills
General Manager: Paul Antolin
Number Employees: 20-49

30325 Torpac Capsules
333 Route 46
Fairfield, NJ 07004 973-244-1125
Fax: 973-244-1365 info37@torpac.com
www.torpac.com
Processor, importer and exporter of gelatin capsules; manufacturer and exporter of capsule filling machinery
President: Raj Tahil
Quality Control: Ajay Varma
Estimated Sales: Below $5 Million
Number Employees: 10
Square Footage: 40000
Type of Packaging: Consumer
Brands:
Torpac

30326 Tosca Ltd
1032 Bay Beach Road
Green Bay, WI 54302 920-617-4000
Fax: 920-465-9198 info@toscaltd.com
www.toscaltd.com
Plastic containers for food storage
President: John Frey
Business Development: Robin Last
VP: Michael Fechter
VP Operations: Greg Gorske
Plant Manager: Curt Dhein
Estimated Sales: $40 Million
Number Employees: 180
Square Footage: 21000

30327 Toscarora
2901 W Monroe Street
Sandusky, OH 44870-1810 419-625-7343
Fax: 419-625-1171
Manufacturer and exporter of custom designed plastic thermoformed food trays; also, custom designed cookie trays
Operations Manager: Joe Knight
Plant Manager: Mike LaFond
Estimated Sales: $10-20 Million
Number Employees: 50-99
Square Footage: 100000

30328 Toska Foodservice Systems
W197n7577 Fw Court
Lannon, WI 53046 262-253-4782
Fax: 262-253-9685 info@toskainc.com
www.toskainc.com

Designer and manufacturer of commercial modular combination kitchens serveries. Supplier of customer operated order and payment system. Supplier of prepaid card systems
President: Guenter Toska
Sales Manager: Thomas Conlan
Estimated Sales: Below $5 Million
Number Employees: 10

30329 **Toss Machine Components**
539 S Main St
Nazareth, PA 18064 610-759-8883
Fax: 610-759-1766 info@tossheatseal.com
www.tossheatseal.com
Heatsealing plastic materials, temperature controllers, dataloggers, heatseal bands, transformers, back-up materials, heatseal bars
President: Charles Trillich
Vice-President: Helma Young
Sales Manager: Andy Becan
Estimated Sales: $5-10 Million
Number Employees: 10-19
Square Footage: 400000
Type of Packaging: Consumer, Food Service

30330 **Total Control Products**
2001 Janice Avenue
Melrose Park, IL 60160-1010 708-345-5500
Fax: 708-345-5670 www.total-control.com
Electronic controls
Estimated Sales: $10-20 Million
Number Employees: 50-99

30331 **Total Foods Corporation**
6018 W Maple Rd
West Bloomfield, MI 48322-4404 248-851-2611
Fax: 248-737-2035
Manager: Dave Owens
Estimated Sales: $50-100 Million
Number Employees: 5-9

30332 **(HQ)Total Identity Group**
255 Pinebush Road
Cambridge, ON N1T 1B9 519-622-4040
Fax: 519-622-4031 877-551-5529
info@pridesigns.com www.pridesigns.com
Custom signs and awnings
Manager: David Kurty
CFO: Dan Cass
Marketing Director: Lara Fedele
Operations Manager: Joel Shenton
Purchasing Manager: Denise Carroll
Number Employees: 100-249

30333 **Total Lubricants**
5 N Stiles St
Linden, NJ 07036-4208 908-862-9300
Fax: 908-862-1647 IBU-CSR@total-us.com
http://keystonelubricants.com/keystone/index.htm
Product lines includes food machinery lubricants; air compressor fluids; metalworking lubricants; and maintenance lubricants.
Human Resources: Steve Daubert
Food Industry Sales Specialist: Jim Cancila
Food Industry Sales Specialist: Bruce Wolfe
Food Industry Sales Specialist: Rob Stevenson
International Food Industry Specialist: Christine Richard
Estimated Sales: H
Number Employees: 10,000

30334 **Total Quality Corporation**
PO Box 723
Branford, CT 06405-0723 203-483-7447
Fax: 203-483-7449 800-453-9729
tqcinfo@totalqualitycorp.com
www.totalqualitycorp.com
X-ray inspection service for raw and finished products
Office Manager: Kymberly Seneco
Estimated Sales: $1-2.5 Million
Number Employees: 4
Square Footage: 20000

30335 **Total Quality Corporation**
320 Soundview Road
Guilford, CT 6437 888-608-8291
Fax: 203-483-7449 800-453-9729
tqcinfo@totalqualitycorp.com
www.totalqualitycorp.com
Off-line inspection for contamination, container equipment, inspection and systems division
Marketing Director: Kimberly Seneco
Estimated Sales: $1-2.5 Million
Number Employees: 4

30336 **Total Scale Systems**
1040 N Dutton Avenue
Santa Rosa, CA 95401-5042 707-526-2221
Fax: 707-526-0644
Wine industry scales
Estimated Sales: $1 - 5 Million
Number Employees: 6

30337 **Toter**
P.O.Box 5338
Statesville, NC 28687 704-872-8171
Fax: 704-878-0734 800-772-0071
toter@toter.com www.toter.com
Manufacturer and exporter of carts and lifter systems
President: Jeff Gilliam
VP Sales: Rick Hoffman
Estimated Sales: $50-100 Million
Number Employees: 250-499
Brands:
Toter Worksaver

30338 **Touch Controls**
520 Industrial Way
Fallbrook, CA 92028 760-723-7900
Fax: 760-723-7910 800-848-4385
support@touchcontrols.com
www.touchcontrol.com
Rugged sized touch screens, industrial computers, industrial enclosures, fiberoptic transmission systems
Estimated Sales: $5-10 Million
Number Employees: 20-49

30339 **Touch Menus**
1601 116th Ave NE # 111
Bellevue, WA 98004-3010 425-881-3100
Fax: 425-881-2980 800-688-6368
info@towermenus.com www.towermenus.com
Manufacturer and exporter of touch screen point of sale systems and software; also, credit card services available
VP: Darrin Howell
Marketing Manager: Gill Gilman
Estimated Sales: $5-10 Million
Number Employees: 5-9
Square Footage: 8000
Type of Packaging: Private Label
Brands:
Cats
Editpro
Touch Menus
Trapr

30340 **Tourtellot & Company**
43 Haswell Street
Providence, RI 02905 401-331-2385
Fax: 401-351-1260
Wholesaler/distributor of produce; serving the food service market; also, retail consultation services available
President: Irving Sigal
VP Operations: Andrew Sigal
Estimated Sales: $20-50 Million
Number Employees: 20-49
Square Footage: 65000

30341 **Tower Pallet Company**
5211 County Road X
PO Box 5006
De Pere, WI 54115 920-336-3495
Fax: 920-336-3025
towerpalletcompany@aycomwi.com
www.towerpallet.com
Pallets and skids
President: William Koltz
VP/Treasurer: Randy Koltz
Estimated Sales: $2.5-5 Million
Number Employees: 20-49

30342 **Town Food Service Equipment Company**
72 Beadel Street
Brooklyn, NY 11222 718-388-5650
Fax: 718-388-5860 800-221-5032
customerservice@townfood.com
www.townfood.com
Asian barbecue equipment, cooking utensils, china, soup stoves, ovens, ranges, smokers and electric rice cookers; importer of hand hammered woks and gas rice cookers; exporter of rice cookers, ranges and smokers
President: Charles Suss
Founder: Morris Suss
VP: Sada Nair
R&D/Quality Control: Ken Trosterman
Marketing Executive: Marianne Suss
Sales: Mary Ann Balk
Equipment Specialists: Sincere Chan
Production: Ken Tosterman
Purchasing Director: Sada Nair
Estimated Sales: $5-10 Million
Number Employees: 20-49
Square Footage: 100000
Type of Packaging: Consumer, Private Label
Brands:
Rice Master
York & Masterrange

30343 **Townsend-Piller Packing**
719 19 4th Avenue
Cumberland, WI 54829 715-822-4910
Packing supplies and equipment
President: Robert Townsend

30344 **Toyo Seikan Kaisha**
707 Skokie Blvd # 670
Northbrook, IL 60062-2857 847-509-3080
Fax: 847-509-3088
Total packaging system, from material to processing
Owner: Masa Morotomi
Estimated Sales: $1 - 5 Million
Number Employees: 1-4

30345 **Toyota Tshusho America,Inc.**
700 Triport Road
Georgetown, KY 40324 502-868-3450
www.taiamerica.com
International trading, supply-chain services, intermediate goods processing. Engages in business opportunities related to industrial and consumer products and services.
President/Chief Executive Officer: Nobuyuki Minowa
Vice President: Larrey Keiser
Vice President, Sales: Arthur Harrison
Estimated Sales: $5.3 Billion
Number Employees: 1,100
Square Footage: 16234
Parent Co: Toyota Tshusho Corporation

30346 **Traco Manufacturing**
620 S 1325 W
Orem, UT 84058 801-225-8040
Fax: 801-226-1509 866-516-1205
info@traco-mfg.com www.tracopackaging.com
Shrink film, tamper-resistant packaging, heat sealer machines
President: John Palica
CFO: John Hiatt
Quality Control: Craig Johnson
VP Sales: Ron Moore
Purchasing Manager: Craig Johnson
Estimated Sales: Below $5 Million
Number Employees: 50-99
Square Footage: 40000
Brands:
Impulse Heat Sealer
Shrink Bags
Shrink Bands & Preforms

30347 **Trade Fixtures**
1501 Westpark Dr Ste 5
Little Rock, AR 72204 501-664-1318
Fax: 501-664-9253 800-872-3490
cservice@tradefixtures.com
www.tradefixtures.com
Manufacturer and exporter of molded displays for bulk food items including gravity and scoop bins
Manager: Scott Johnson
Quality Control: Walter Baumgarten
President: Scott Johnson
VP Sales: Clay Odom
VP Sales: Doug Holland
General Manager: Joe Herrmann
Purchasing Manager: Roy Jackson
Estimated Sales: $5 - 10 Million
Number Employees: 50-99
Square Footage: 56000
Parent Co: Display Technologies

30348 **Trade Wings**
4929 Wyaconda Rd
Rockville, MD 20852-2443 301-770-8770
Fax: 301-770-8771
Owner: Nader Dibiglari
Estimated Sales: Under$500,000
Number Employees: 5-9

30349 **Tradeco International**
1107 S Westwood Ave
PO Box 1155
Addison, IL 60101 630-628-1112
Fax: 630-628-6616 800-628-3738
ventura@tradecointl.com www.tradecointl.com
Manufacturer and importer of chinaware including plates, cups, saucers and hollowware
President: Leslie D Plass
Estimated Sales: $1 - 3,000,000
Number Employees: 10-19
Type of Packaging: Consumer
Brands:
Ventura China

30350 **Trademarx Inc**
1443 E Washington Blvd.,
Pasadena, CA 94110 626-795-0587
Fax: 626-795-0548 sales@trademarx.net
www.trademarx.net
Manufacture disposable plastic and paper products for the foodservice industry.
President/CEO: Scott James
CFO/Public Relations: Jenny Wang
VP/R&D: Peter Song
Quality Control: Shelly Lu
Marketing/Sales: Scott James
Estimated Sales: $5 Million
Number Employees: 250-499
Number of Brands: 3
Number of Products: 100
Square Footage: 680000
Type of Packaging: Consumer, Food Service, Private Label, Bulk
Brands:
Jay
Purex
Trademarx

30351 **Tradepaq Corporation**
30 Montgomery Street
Jersey City, NJ 07302 201-716-2665
Fax: 201-435-9916 info@tradepaq.com
www.tradepaq.com
Supplier of commodity trading software
CFO: Charles Griffs
Sales: Deborah Laska
Estimated Sales: $5-10 Million
Number Employees: 10-19

30352 **Traeger Industries**
1385 E College St
Mount Angel, OR 97362 503-845-9234
Fax: 503-845-6366 800-872-3437
traeger@traegerindustries.com
www.traegergrills.com
Manufacturer and exporter of wood pellet smokers and cooking appliances
President: Joseph Traeger
VP Sales/Marketing: Randy Traeger
VP Production: Mark Traeger
Estimated Sales: $5 - 10 Million
Number Employees: 50-99
Square Footage: 54000
Brands:
Traeger

30353 **Traex**
101 Traex Dr
Dane, WI 53529 608-849-2500
Fax: 608-849-2580 800-356-8006
sotraxdl@wanadoo.fr www.libbey.com
Manufacturer, importer and exporter of food trays, straw dispensers, portion control and napkin dispensers, bus boxes, dishracks and tabletop accessories
Marketing: Lori Barger
Marketing Service Manager: Tammy Blied
Plant Manager: Steve Boeder
Purchasing Agent: Rose Ohlert
Estimated Sales: $10-20 Million
Number Employees: 100-249
Square Footage: 15000
Parent Co: Menasha Corporation
Brands:
Barkeep
Batter Boss
Cupro
Dripcut
Kondi-Keeper
Lidpro Lid Dispenser
Quik-Pik
Rackmaster
Sauce Boss
Self Service System
Straw Boss
T-Rex

30354 **(HQ)Tragon Corporation**
350 Bridge Pkwy
Redwood Shores, CA 94065 650-412-2100
Fax: 650-412-2101 800-841-1177
info@tragon.com www.tragon.com
Consultant specializing in product testing, market research and management consultation services. Quantitative and qualitative market research
President/CEO: Douglas Vort
Co-Founder: Herbert Stone
VP: Rebecca Bleibaum
Marketing: Joseph Salerno
COO: Brian Adkins
Estimated Sales: $2.5-5 Million
Number Employees: 20-49
Square Footage: 7000
Other Locations:
Tragon Corporation
Buffalo Grove IL
Brands:
Prop
Prop Plus
Qda
Qda Software

30355 **Traitech Industries**
100 Four Valley Drive
Unit C
Vaughan, ON L4K 4T9
Canada 905-695-2800
Fax: 905-695-0737 877-872-4835
info@traitech.com www.traitech.com
Manufacturer and exporter of ventilated merchandising trays, baskets and displays custom manufacturer
President: Tom Penton
VP: Ryan Slight
Type of Packaging: Consumer, Food Service, Private Label, Bulk
Brands:
California
California Trays

30356 **Trak-Air/Rair**
555 Quivas St
Denver, CO 80204-4915 303-779-9888
Fax: 303-694-3575 800-688-8725
sales@trak-air.com www.trak-air.com
Manufacturer and exporter of hot air and greaseless countertop fryers; also, pizza ovens
President: Dale Terry
Estimated Sales: $1 - 2 Million
Number Employees: 20-49
Square Footage: 64000
Type of Packaging: Food Service
Brands:
Rair 2000
Rair 7000
Trak-Air Ii
Trak-Air V

30357 **Tramontina USA**
12955 W Airport Blvd
Sugar Land, TX 77478 281-340-8400
Fax: 281-340-8410 800-221-7809
tusa@tramontina-usa.com
www.tramontina-usa.com
Cutlery, cookware and servingware
President: Antonio Galafassi
Manager Food Service Sales: Steve Kozicki
Sales Assistant (Food Service): Debbie Rademacher
Manager Customer Service: Donna Parke
Estimated Sales: $10-20,000,000
Number Employees: 250-499

30358 **Trane Company**
2313 20th St S
La Crosse, WI 54601 608-787-2000
Fax: 608-787-3262 www.trane.com
Manufacturer and exporter of roof top and self-contained air conditioner; also, heat pumps including water-source
President/CEO: Fred Poses
VP: Bob Shuman
Estimated Sales: $348 Million
Number Employees: 2600
Parent Co: American Standard
Brands:
Aire Systems
Centravac
Earthwise Systems
Integrated Comfort Systems
Intellipack
Service First
Tracer Summit
Tracker
Trag
Trane
Unit Trane
Varitrac
Varitrane

30359 **(HQ)Trans Container Corporation**
PO Box 10
Upland, CA 91785-0010 909-985-2750
Fax: 909-985-8463 www.paradigmpackaging.com
Injection blow-molded plastic containers and injection molded closures
President: Robert Donnahoo
VP: Mike Mc Allister
Customer Service: Sophia Ibara
Estimated Sales: $10-20 Million
Number Employees: 1-4
Other Locations:
Trans Container Corp.
West Valley City UT
Brands:
Trc

30360 **Trans Flex Packagers**
34 Burnham Ave
PO Box 127
Unionville, CT 06085 860-673-2531
Fax: 860-673-6238 www.tfpackagers.com
Flexible plastic bags including cellulose, polyethylene and polypropylene
President: M Kaplan
Estimated Sales: $5-10 Million
Number Employees: 20-49
Square Footage: 25000

30361 **Trans World Services**
72 Stone Pl
Melrose, MA 02176-6016 781-665-9200
Fax: 781-665-6649 800-882-2105
twsinc@gis.net wwwt-stick.com
Manufacturer and exporter of thermometers and sandwich packaging materials including crystal wrap and cellophane; also, packaging machinery. Consumer, institution and processor packaging of T-shirts, USDA/FSIS partner
President: Thomas E Ford
CFO: Thomas Foid
Vice President: Dan Tuono
R&D: Thomas Foid
Quality Control: Thomas Foid
Sales/Marketing: Ira Siegal
Estimated Sales: $10 - 20 Million
Number Employees: 10-19
Square Footage: 104000
Type of Packaging: Food Service

30362 **(HQ)Trans-Chemco**
19235 84th St
Bristol, WI 53104 262-857-2363
Fax: 262-857-9127 800-880-2498
info@trans-chemco.com www.trans-chemco.com
Manufacturer, importer and exporter of chemicals including defoamers and antifoamers; also, laboratory research and development for products and special needs
President: Susanne Gardiner
CFO: Irene Swan
VP/Director: Merle Gardiner
VP R&D: Merle Gardiner
Operations Manager: Sheila Cleveland
Estimated Sales: $1 - 3 Million
Number Employees: 10-19
Square Footage: 30000
Brands:
Trans-10

Trans-100
Trans-30

30363 Transbotics Corporation
3400 Latrobe Dr
Charlotte, NC 28211 704-362-1115
Fax: 704-364-4039 info@trnasbotics.com
www.transbotics.com
Design, development, support and installation of Automatic Guided Vehicles, or transportation robots, with an emphasis on complete customer satisfaction. Supplier of Automatic Guide Vehicle Systems, AGV controls technology, engineeringservices, AGV batteries, charges and other related products
CEO: Claude Imbleau
VP: Lennart Johansson
Marketing: Ryan Willis
Sales: Chuck Rossell
Public Relations: Ryan Willis
Operations: Mark Ramsey
Purchasing Manager: David Melton
Estimated Sales: $1 - 5,000,000
Number Employees: 20-49
Parent Co: NDC Automation
Type of Packaging: Bulk

30364 Transition Equipment Company
444 Laguna Vista Road
Santa Rosa, CA 95401 707-537-7787
Fax: 707-537-7174 vickitec@aol.com
www.transitionequipment.com
Used equipment, winery, packaging and beverage
Fiscal Operations Manager: Eileen Paul
Director of Sales: Vicki Mastbaum
Estimated Sales: Below $500,000
Number Employees: 3

30365 Transnorm System
1906 S Great Southwest Pkwy
Grand Prairie, TX 75051-3580 972-606-0303
Fax: 972-606-0768 800-259-2303
sales@transnorm.com www.transnorm.com
Manufacturer and exporter of belt curve conveyors including mini edge, power, spiral, straight, etc
Chief Financial Officer: Kay Lynn Wolfe
VP: Rick Lee
Estimated Sales: $20-50 Million
Number Employees: 10
Square Footage: 80000
Parent Co: Transnorm System GmBH
Brands:
F.R.P.
Safeglide

30366 Transparent Container Company
325 S Lombard Rd
Addison, IL 60101 708-449-8520
Fax: 708-449-1341
marketing@transparentcontainer.com
www.transparentcontainer.com
Containers
President: Dan Greiwe
CFO: Ron Pranger
VP/Sales: Dan Wyss
General Manager: Steve Fifer
Estimated Sales: $5-10 Million
Number Employees: 50-99

30367 Tranter Pite
P.O.Box 2289
Wichita Falls, TX 76307-2289 940-723-7125
Fax: 940-723-5131 sales@tranter.com
www.tranterphe.com
Surface and plate heat exchangers, cabinet liners for walk-in refrigerator/freezing rooms, freezing storage units, cold and hot food displays; exporter of heat exchangers
President: Charles Monachello
CEO: Roy Mason
CFO: Arnold Downes
VP: Roy Mason
Research & Development: Jeff Mathur
Marketing Director: Ronald Stonecipher
Sales Director: Frank Kierzkowski
Purchasing Manager: Czeech Richardson
Number Employees: 100-249
Square Footage: 480000
Parent Co: Tranter
Brands:
Colbank
Freeztand
Maxchanger
Platecoil
Snobanc
Snopan
Steempan
Superchanger

30368 Trap Zap Environmental Systems
255 Braen Avenue
Wyckoff, NJ 07481 201-251-9970
Fax: 201-251-0903 800-282-8727
labelle@trapzap.com www.trapzap.com
Biological products for greasetraps, drains and septic systems, septic system additives and floor and surface cleaners; also, consultant providing wastewater management, turnkey programs and greasetrap maintenance
National Accounts Manager: Rick Albano
Estimated Sales: $2.5-5 Million
Number Employees: 25-49
Square Footage: 10000
Brands:
Bio-Zap
D-Grade
Trap-Zap Plus

30369 Traub Container Corporation
22475 Aurora Road
Cleveland, OH 44146-1270 216-475-5100
Fax: 216-475-5015
Corrugated displays, shipping containers and fiberboard sheets
Sales Manager: Bob Mavity
General Manager: Donald Colombo
Plant Manager: Dale Kiaski
Estimated Sales: $10 - 20 Million
Number Employees: 135
Square Footage: 125000
Parent Co: MacMillan Bloedel Packaging

30370 Traulsen & Company
4401 Blue Mound Rd
Fort Worth, TX 76106 817-625-9671
Fax: 817-624-4302 800-825-8220
www.traulsen.com
Manufacturer and exporter of commercial refrigerators and freezers including display, stainless steel, anodized aluminum, vinyl, reach-in, roll-in and pass-through
Manager: Gary Hoying
Vice President: Pepe Griffo
Marketing Director: Mark Kauffman
Operations: Gary Hoying
Purchasing: John Hebert
Estimated Sales: $20-50 Million
Number Employees: 250-499
Square Footage: 300000
Parent Co: ITW
Other Locations:
Traulsen & Co.
New Troy MI
Brands:
Show-Off
Traulsen
Ultima
Ultra

30371 Travaini Pumps USA
200 Newsome Dr
Yorktown, VA 23692 757-988-3930
Fax: 757-988-3975 800-535-4243
customerservice@travaini.com
www.travaini.com
Liquid ring vacuum pumps
President: Dominic Gemmiti
Estimated Sales: $10-20 Million
Number Employees: 20-49

30372 Travelon
700 Touhy Ave
Elk Grove Vlg, IL 60007 847-621-7000
Fax: 847-621-7001 800-537-5544
travelon@travelonbags.com
www.travelonbags.com
Manufacturer, importer and exporter of metal displays and carts
Owner: Don Godshaw
VP Marketing: Kathy Novak
Estimated Sales: $1 - 5 Million
Number Employees: 100-249
Square Footage: 50000
Type of Packaging: Consumer

30373 Travis Manufacturing Company
13231 Salem Church St NE
Alliance, OH 44601 330-875-1661
Fax: 330-875-4240
Custom fabricated stainless steel tables, shelving
President: Roger W Oberlin
VP: Brian Taranto
Estimated Sales: Less than $500,000
Number Employees: 1-4
Square Footage: 8500

30374 Tray Pak
PO Box 14804
Reading, PA 19612 610-926-5800
Fax: 610-926-9140 info@traypak.com
www.traypak.com
Thermoformed plastic trays
President: John Rusnock
CEO: Randy Simcox
Marketing: William Mosier
Estimated Sales: $20-50 Million
Number Employees: 250-499

30375 Traycon
555 Barell Ave
Carlstadt, NJ 07072 201-939-5555
Fax: 201-939-4180 info@traycon.com
www.traycon.com
Manufacturer and exporter of conveyors and carts for dish and tray handling systems
President: Nicholas Pisto
CEO: Nicholas Pisto
VP: Candice Pisto
Estimated Sales: $5-10 Million
Number Employees: 20-49
Square Footage: 20000
Brands:
Dw
Ra
Rdb
Rdl
Sdb
Sdl
Ssw
Traycon

30376 Tree Saver
2830 S Shoshone Street
Englewood, CO 80110-1204 303-781-2646
Fax: 303-762-8616 800-676-7741
Reusable bags including cloth grocery, trash liner and produce
Operations Manager: Carol Sweet
Estimated Sales: $500,000-$1 Million
Number Employees: 19
Brands:
Tree Saver Bags

30377 Tree of Life East Region
PO Box 9000
St Augustine, FL 32085-9000 904-940-2100
Fax: 904-940-2553 800-223-2910
contactus@kehe.com www.treeoflife.com
Wholesaler/distributor of general merchandise, organic pastas and frozen and specialty foods, smoked tofu, rice milk, dijon mustard.
Chairman/President/CEO: Richard Thorne
SVP Finance/CFO: Tom Wissbaum
CEO: Richard Lane
SVP Sales: George Schuetz
Estimated Sales: $1.9 Million
Number Employees: 5,000-9,999
Parent Co: Wessanen
Other Locations:
Tree of Life
Louisville KY
Brands:
American Natural
Annie's Homegrown
Blue Diamond
Hain Pure Foods
Harmony Farms
Horizon Organic
Kraft Foods
Manischewitz
McCormick
Naturade
Nestle
Peanut Wonder
Seeds of Change
Soy Wonder
World Finer Foods

30378 Tree of Life Midwest
225 N Daniels Way
Bloomington, IN 47404-9772 812-333-1511
Fax: 812-335-6219 800-999-4200
CustSvcMW@TreeofLife.com
www.treeoflife.com

Wholesaler/distributor of natural health food, groceries, dairy items, frozen food, private label items, and specialty/gourmet foods.
President: John Mc Curry
VP Finance: Perry Dunmire
VP Sales: Mike Weger
VP Operations: Gene Carter
Human Resources: Felice Herrera
Purchasing Director: Scott McCulloch
Estimated Sales: $100-500 Million
Number Employees: 250-499
Square Footage: 85000
Parent Co: Tree of Life
Brands:
Annie's Homegrown
Bella Good
Blue Diamond
Hain Pure Foods
Horizon Organic
Kraft Foods
Manischewitz
McCormick
Naturade
Nestle
Seeds of Change
World Fine Foods

30379 Treen Box & Pallet Corporation
1950 Street Rd Ste 400
Bensalem, PA 19020 215-639-5100
Fax: 215-639-8530 treen@cris.com
www.pallet-mall.com
Wooden boxes, pallets and skids
President: George P Geiges
VP: A Geiges
Estimated Sales: $30 Million
Number Employees: 20-49
Square Footage: 30000

30380 Treier Popcorn Farms
16793 County Line Rd
Bloomdale, OH 44817 419-454-2811
Fax: 419-454-3983 ptreier@wcnet.org
Popcorn including bagged, natural, buttered and microwaveable; wholesaler/distributor of commercial popcorn poppers and other concession supply equipment; serving the food service market
President: Don Treier
Secretary/Treasurer: Peggy Treier
Estimated Sales: $500,000-$1 Million
Number Employees: 15
Number of Brands: 2
Number of Products: 6
Square Footage: 12000
Parent Co: Treier Family Farms
Type of Packaging: Consumer, Food Service, Bulk
Brands:
Lake Plains
Pelton's Hybrid Popcorn

30381 Treif USA
230 Long Hill Cross Rd
Shelton, CT 06484-6160 203-929-9930
Fax: 203-849-8517 treifusa@treif.com
www.treif.com
High speed, high-output slicing and dicing equipment
President: Robert Linke
Estimated Sales: $1-2.5 Million
Number Employees: 5-9

30382 Trent Corporation
PO Box 2650
Trenton, NJ 08690 609-587-7515
Fax: 609-586-9710 trentboxmfgco@aol.com
www.trentbox.com
Packaging materials including bikini packs, box lids and corrugated containers
President: Carl A Angelini
Quality Control: Bob Campbell
Sales/Marketing Executive: Charles Baumann
Purchasing Agent: Lynda Saganowski
Estimated Sales: $10 - 20 Million
Number Employees: 10-19
Brands:
Kwik-Pak
Twin-Pak

30383 Trenton Mills
400 Factory St
PO Box 107
Trenton, TN 38382-0107 731-855-1323
Fax: 731-855-9000 sales@trentonmills.com
www.trentonmills.com
Stockinette knit for meat packing and filters
Owner: Richard Donner
Operations: Bubby Blakely
Estimated Sales: $3 - 5 Million
Number Employees: 20-49
Square Footage: 260000
Parent Co: Dyersburg Fabrics

30384 Treofan America, LLC
6001 Gun Club Road
Winston-Salem, NC 27103 336-766-9448
Fax: 336-766-8260 800-424-6273
www.treofan.com
Packaging films and labels for snacks, bakery items, pasta, and confectionery items.

30385 (HQ)Trepte's Wire & Metal Works
14822 Lakewood Boulevard
Bellflower, CA 90706-2857 562-630-6798
Fax: 562-630-5901 800-828-6217
rontrepte@hotmail.com www.treptewire.com
Skewers, hot pan grips, spoons and racks including roasting, baking and broiling
President and CEO: A Ron Trepte Sr
Secretary: E Trepte
Number Employees: 10
Square Footage: 48000
Brands:
E-Z-V

30386 Trevor Industries
8698 S Main St
Eden, NY 14057 716-992-4775
Fax: 716-992-4788 sales@trevorindustries.com
Manufacturer, importer and exporter of plastic drinking straws and cocktail stirrers
Owner: Gary Ballowe
VP Administration: Karen Amico
Plant Manager: Robert Martin
Estimated Sales: $5 - 10 Million
Number Employees: 20-49
Square Footage: 75000

30387 Trevor Owen Limited
80 Barbados Boulevard
Unit 5
Scarborough, ON M1J 1K9
Canada 416-267-8231
Fax: 416-267-1035 866-487-2224
sales@trevorowenltd.com
www.trevorowenltd.com
Manufacturer and exporter of banners and insulated food delivery bags
President: Pierre Barcik
Sales Executive: Trevor Owen
Number Employees: 10
Square Footage: 40000

30388 Tri-Boro Shelving & Partition
300 Dominion Dr
Farmville, VA 23901 434-315-5600
Fax: 434-315-0139 sales@triboroshelving.com
www.triboroshelving.com
Shelving, bin units, mobile shelf trucks and service carts
Owner: Fred De Maio
CFO: Tony De Maio
Estimated Sales: $2.5 - 5 Million
Number Employees: 20-49
Square Footage: 200000
Brands:
Boxer
Rivet Rak
Stor-It
Sturdi-Frame

30389 Tri-Clover
PO Box 7731
Richmond, VA 23231-0231 804-545-8120
Fax: 804-545-0194 800-558-4060
customerservice@alfalaral.com
www.alfalaral.com
Pumps, valves, fittings, blenders, filter, batch control systems, cheese equipment, fillers, gravity, milk, flow diversion stations
Marketing Director: Chip Bresette
Public Relations: Joyce Bergh
Estimated Sales: $1 - 5 Million
Number Employees: 250-499

30390 Tri-Connect
111 Frank Lloyd Wright Lane
Oak Park, IL 60302-2644 708-660-8190
Fax: 312-951-6243 triconnect@aol.com
Wholesaler of England Farmhouse Biscuits packaged in gift tins and boxes, d'Orsay Chocolatier featuring imported Belgian chocolate and petit four desserts. Private labeling available
President: Tony Birbeck
CEO: Linda Murphy
CFO: Anthony Cioffi
Estimated Sales: Below $5 Million
Number Employees: 5
Type of Packaging: Private Label, Bulk
Brands:
Farmhouse Biscuits

30391 Tri-K Industries
2 Stewart Court
PO Box 10
Denville, NJ 07834 973-298-8850
Fax: 973-298-8940 rebecca.morton@tri-k.com
www.tri-k.com
Owner: Reno Deldotto
Number Employees: 50-99

30392 Tri-Pak Machinery, Inc.
1102 North Commerce Street
Harlingen, TX 78550 956-423-5140
Fax: 956-423-9362
dfitzgerald@tri-pakmachinery.com
www.tri-pak.com
Manufacturer and exporter of fruit and vegetable processing machinery including belt and chain conveyors, graders, sizers, cleaners, packers and wax coaters; also, graders for shrimp
President: David A Fitzgerald
VP: Charles M. Kilbourn
Director of Sales and Marketing: James W. Fitzgerald
Sales: Robert E. Fitzgerald
Director of Operations: Daniel J. Groves
Purchasing: Chuck Kilbourn
Estimated Sales: $5 - 10 Million
Number Employees: 100-249
Square Footage: 516000

30393 Tri-Seal
900 Bradley Hill Rd
Blauvelt, NY 10913 845-353-3300
Fax: 845-353-3376
LinersNorthAmer@tekni-plex.com
tri-seal.tekni-plex.com
Manufacturer and exporter of coextruded thermoplastic bottle cap liners and extruded rigid and flexible PVC tubing and profiles
CEO: F Smith
President: Bruce Burus
VP Sales/Marketing: Walter Burgess
Estimated Sales: $5 - 10 Million
Number Employees: 50-99
Square Footage: 440000
Brands:
Tri-Foil
Tri-Gard
Tri-Lam
Tri-Seal

30394 (HQ)Tri-State Plastics
PO Box 337
Henderson, KY 42419-0337 270-826-8361
Fax: 270-826-8362
Manufacturer and exporter of injection molded food containers
Owner: Mike Walden
VP/Secretary/Treasurer: Mike Walden
Estimated Sales: less than $500,000
Number Employees: 1-4
Square Footage: 35000
Type of Packaging: Private Label, Bulk

30395 Tri-State Plastics
PO Box 496
Glenwillard, PA 15046-0496 724-457-6900
Fax: 724-457-6901
Manufacturer and exporter of vacuum formed plastic products including trays, covers, guards, material handling components, etc.
President: Dave Mitchell
General Manager: Michael Lopez

30396 **Tri-Sterling**
1050 Miller Dr
Altamonte Spgs, FL 32701-7505 407-260-0330
Fax: 407-260-7096 sales@swfsoutheast.com
www.sfwcompanies.com
Manufacturer and exporter of packaging equipment and shrink wrappers
VP: Ken Schilling
Marketing: Thomas Jimenez
Estimated Sales: $20-50 Million
Number Employees: 100-249
Brands:
Genesis Ii

30397 **Tri-Tool**
3041 Sunrise Blvd
Rancho Cordova, CA 95742 916-351-0144
Fax: 916-351-0372 800-345-5015
customer.service@tritool.com www.tritool.com
Manufactures pipe cutting and welding preparation equipment
President: George Wernette
CEO: Jerry VanDer Pol
Chairman: George J Wernette
CFO: Tom Meyer
R & D: Dale Flood
Sales: Daryl Anderson
Production: Jim Bergstrand
Purchasing: Barbara Porter
Estimated Sales: $20-50 Million
Number Employees: 100-249
Type of Packaging: Bulk

30398 **Tri-Tronics Company**
7705 Cheri Court
PO Box 25135
Tampa, FL 33622 813-886-4000
Fax: 813-884-8818 800-237-0946
info@ttco.com www.ttco.com
Manufacturer and exporter of material handling and automation application controls including photoelectric sensors, registration scanners, photoelectric eyes and flexible plastic/glass fiber optic light guides
President: David Hacquebord
VP/Sales Manager: Dennis Henderson
Estimated Sales: $10-20 Million
Number Employees: 50-99
Square Footage: 28000
Brands:
Color Mark
D.C. Eye
Mity-Eye
Smarteye
Tiny-Eye
U.S. Eye
Visioneye

30399 **TriCore**
6921 Mariner Drive
Racine, WI 53406 262-886-3630
Fax: 262-886-1676 infoHQ@TriCore.com
www.tricore.com
Software engineering for the food, dairy, beverage industries
President: David Mc Carthy
President, Chief Executive Officer: David McCarthy
Engineering/Business Development VP: Steve Reiter

30400 **TriEnda Corporation**
N7660 Industrial Rd
Portage, WI 53901 608-742-5303
Fax: 608-742-9153 800-356-8150
hbreezer@trienda.com www.trienda.com
Plastic thermoformed pallets, self-palletizing shipping systems and material handling devices
President: Curtis Zamec
VP Sales/Marketing: Rob Klinko
Number Employees: 250-499
Square Footage: 500000
Brands:
Dc Distribution Center
Enviropal/Recy
Load Locker
Weight Lifter
Wolf Pak

30401 **TriEnda Products**
N7660 Industrial Rd
Portage, WI 53901-9451 608-742-5303
Fax: 608-742-9153 800-356-8150
bklimko@wilbertinc.com www.wilbertinc.com
President: Curtis Zamec
Marketing Manager: Paul Schoeder
Sales Director: Rick Sasse
Estimated Sales: $1 - 5 Million
Number Employees: 250-499
Square Footage: 1200000
Parent Co: Wilbert

30402 **Triad Pallet Company**
4910 Bartlett St
Greensboro, NC 27409 336-292-8175
Fax: 336-292-8175
Wooden skids and pallets
President/CFO: B Bare
Estimated Sales: $5 - 10 Million
Number Employees: 5-9
Square Footage: 4000

30403 **Triad Products Company**
1913 Commerce Circle
Springfield, OH 45504-2011 937-323-9422
Fax: 937-328-6463
Aprons
President: Louis Jung
Number Employees: 20

30404 **Triad Scientific**
6 Stockton Lake Blvd
Manasquan, NJ 08736 732-886-3366
Fax: 732-292-1961 800-867-6690
triadscientific@gmail.com www.triadsci.com
Manufacturer and exporter of laboratory equipment including balances, analysis instrumentation, filtration, incubators, lamps, microscopes, monitoring systems, ovens, sterilizers, spectrophotometers, etc.; also, analysis, designservice and repair available
VP: Tom Leskow
Estimated Sales: $3 - 5 Million
Number Employees: 5-9
Square Footage: 10000
Type of Packaging: Food Service, Bulk

30405 **Triad Scientific**
6 Stockton Lake Blvd
Manasquan, NJ 08736 732-886-3366
Fax: 732-292-1961 800-867-6690
triadscientific@gmail.com
www.triadscientific.com
President: Tom Leskow
Vice-President: Bill Aronoff

30406 **Triangle Package Machinery Company**
6655 W Diversey Ave
Chicago, IL 60707 773-889-0200
Fax: 773-889-4221 800-621-4170
wcray@trianglepackage.com
www.trianglepackage.com
Manufacturer and exporter of bag and carton making, closing, filling, packing, weighing and sealing machinery
President: John Muskat
R&D: Jerone Lasky
Quality Control: Roger Gaw
Director Sales: John Michalson
Purchasing Agent: John Musso
Estimated Sales: $20 - 50 Million
Number Employees: 100-249
Square Footage: 10000000
Brands:
Acceleron Advantage
Proline
Selectacom
Selectech 32 Controls

30407 **Triangle Sign Service Company**
PO Box 24186
Halethorpe, MD 21227-0686 410-247-5300
Fax: 410-247-1944 rlea@trianglesign.com
www.trianglesign.com
Neon and plastic signs
President: Robert Altshuler
Estimated Sales: $10 - 20 Million
Number Employees: 100-249

30408 **Tribology/Tech-Lube**
35 Old Dock Rd
Yaphank, NY 11980-9702 631-345-3000
Fax: 631-345-3001 800-569-1757
info@tribology.com www.tribology.com
Manufacturer and exporter of synthetic and specialty lubricants
President: William Krause
Sales: Paul Anderson
Operations/General Manager: Terence Tierney
Purchasing: Gail Moore
Estimated Sales: $50-100 Million
Number Employees: 20-49
Number of Products: 300
Square Footage: 35000
Type of Packaging: Private Label, Bulk

30409 **Trico Converting**
1801 Via Burton
Fullerton, CA 92831-5340 714-563-0701
Fax: 714-772-7528
Manufacturer and exporter of flexible packaging; also, printing and laminating available
President: John Clemmons
VP: Tim Love
Estimated Sales: $10 - 20 Million
Number Employees: 20-49
Square Footage: 20000
Type of Packaging: Consumer, Food Service, Private Label, Bulk

30410 **Tricor Systems**
1650 Todd Farm Dr
Elgin, IL 60123 847-742-5542
Fax: 847-742-5574 800-575-0161
info@tricor-systems.com
www.tricor-systems.com
Specialized test instruments including gloss, color and texture analysis systems aand chocolate temper meters
President: Jack Jereb
Sales Director: Thomas Allen
Estimated Sales: $5 - 10 Million
Number Employees: 20-49
Square Footage: 18500

30411 **Trident**
1114 Federal Rd
Brookfield, CT 06804 203-740-9333
Fax: 203-775-9660 hq@trident-itw.com
www.trident-itw.com
Print heads and inks for industrial applications
Manager: Juan Lopez
General Manager: Jean-Marie Gutierrez
Marketing/Sales: Robert Donofrio
Estimated Sales: $1 - 5,000,000
Number Employees: 50-99
Parent Co: ITW
Brands:
A 3000
Allwrite
Hi-Def
Jetwrite
Microcoder
Pixeljet
Ultrajet
Versaprint

30412 **Trident Plastics**
1009 Pulinski Rd
Ivyland, PA 18974 215-672-5225
Fax: 215-672-5582 800-222-2318
pasales@tridentplastics.com
www.tridentplastics.com
Manufacturer and exporter of plastic tubes, sheets, rods, ducts, films, slabs and signs
President: Ronald Cadic
Sales Manager: Michael Peroni
Estimated Sales: $1-2.5 Million
Number Employees: 10-19

30413 **Tridyne Process Systems Inc.**
80 Allen Rd
South Burlington, VT 05403-7801 802-863-6873
Fax: 802-860-1591 sales@tridyne.com
www.tridyne.com
Manufacturer and exporter of automatic weighing and counting systems including net weighers and weigh counters; also, baggers, cartoners, conveyors, etc
President: Susith Wijetunga
Estimated Sales: $1 - 5 Million
Number Employees: 7
Square Footage: 44000
Parent Co: Tridyne Process Systems, Inc
Type of Packaging: Consumer, Food Service, Private Label, Bulk
Brands:
Tridyne

30414 **Trienda Corporation**
N7660 Industrial Rd
Portage, WI 53901 608-742-5303
Fax: 608-742-9153 800-356-8150
hbreezer@trienda.com www.trienda.com
Plastic, material handling products
President: Curtis Zamec
CFO: Jim Masterangelo
VP Marketing: Bob Shimmel
Plant Mgr: David Fiddes
Number Employees: 250-499

30415 **Trilla Steel Drum Corporation**
2959 W 47th St
Chicago, IL 60632-1998 773-847-7588
Fax: 773-847-5550 ltrilla@trilla.com
www.trilla.com
Steel shipping barrels and drums
Owner: Lester Trilla
CFO: Andy Perpetual
Quality Control: Chris Racawski
Sales Manager: Robert Craven
Estimated Sales: $20-50 Million
Number Employees: 5-9

30416 **Trilogy Essential Ingredients, Inc.**
1304 Continental Dr
Abingdon, MD 21009 410-612-0691
Fax: 410-612-9401 info@trilogyei.com
www.trilogyei.com
Flavors, seasonings, liquid spice extracts, proprietary delivery systems and functional ingredients.
CTO: John Cavallo
Estimated Sales: $500 Thousand
Type of Packaging: Bulk

30417 **Trimen Foodservice Equipment**
1240 Ormont Drive
North York, ON M9L 2V4
Canada 416-744-3313
Fax: 416-744-3347 877-437-1422
paul_cesario@trimen.net www.trimen.net
Manufacturer and exporter of ovens, broilers, tables, booths and refrigeration equipment
President: Paul Cesario
Finance Manager: Grace Giulano
Head Operations: Mario Dipiede
Purchasing Manager: Mario Dipiede
Estimated Sales: $50-75 Million
Number Employees: 10
Type of Packaging: Food Service

30418 **Trimline Corporation**
PO Box Q
Elkhart Lake, WI 53020-0366 920-876-3611
Fax: 920-876-3527 www.plyco.com
Insulated utility doors including food service and plastic
Plant Manager: Blend Luedtk
CFO: Tom Blend
CEO: Gary Matz
President: Gary Matz
Estimated Sales: $10 - 20 Million
Number Employees: 20-49
Brands:
Plyco

30419 **Trine Corporation**
1421 Ferris Pl
Bronx, NY 10461-3698 718-828-5200
Fax: 718-828-4052 800-223-8075
info@trinecorp.com www.trinecorp.com
OEM manufacturer of factory direct original F-series baffle grease filters, aluminum, galvanized, stainless steel, all sizes-large inventory, UL/MEA/USA
President: Frank Rella
Plant Manager: James Lange
Estimated Sales: $5-10 Million
Number Employees: 20
Square Footage: 264000
Type of Packaging: Private Label
Brands:
Trine Baffle

30420 **Triner Scale & Manufacturing Co., Inc.**
8411 Hacks Cross Rd
Olive Branch, MS 38654 662-890-2385
Fax: 901-363-3114 800-238-0152
info@trinerscale.com www.trinerscale.com
Manufacturer and exporter of scales including electronic, postage and platform; stainless steel, washdown and USDA approved
President: John Wendt
Estimated Sales: $1 - 2.5 Million
Number Employees: 10-19
Square Footage: 120000
Brands:
Triner

30421 **Trinidad Benham Corporation**
3650 S Yosemite
Suite 300
Denver, CO 80237 303-220-1400
Fax: 303-220-1490 info@trinidadbenham.com
www.trinidadbenham.com
Dry beans, rice, popcorn, and peas
President: Pat Horrigan
CEO/ Chief Technology Officer: Carl Hartman
CFO/ VP of Finance: Gary Peters
Vice President: Larry Cotham
VP of Logistics: Steve Dipasquale
Quality Control Manager: Sandy Schmidt
VP Packaging Operations: Charlie Lewie
Director of Sales Marketing: Jim Pike
Director Human Resources: Diane Lockard
Operations Manager: Kevin Jolly
Risk Manager: Mike McKenna
Plant Manager: Dan Nightengale
National Account Manager: Tracy Page
Estimated Sales: $36.3 Million
Number Employees: 500
Square Footage: 35000
Type of Packaging: Consumer, Food Service, Private Label, Bulk
Brands:
Jack Rabbit
Siler's
Green Earth Organics
Budget Buy
Everyday Chef
Wonder Foil
Peak
Master Wrap
Solfresco
Diamond
Cookquik Ranch Wagon
Sabor Del Campo

30422 **Trinkle Signs & Displays**
24 5th Ave
Youngstown, OH 44503 330-747-9712
Fax: 330-747-9712
Manufacturer and exporter of signs and displays
Owner: Robert Page
Estimated Sales: Below $5 Million
Number Employees: 1-4

30423 **(HQ)Trio Packaging Corporation**
90 13th Ave Unit 10
Ronkonkoma, NY 11779 631-588-0800
Fax: 631-467-4690 800-331-0492
sales@triopackaging.com
www.triopackaging.com
Manufacturer, importer and exporter of form/fill/seal packaging equipment and films
President: John Bolla
Vice President: Frederick Kramer
Sales Director: Anthony Carris
Estimated Sales: $20 - 50 Million
Number Employees: 20-49
Square Footage: 20000
Other Locations:
Trio Packaging Corp.
Ronkonkoma NY

30424 **Trio Products**
250 Warden Ave
Elyria, OH 44035 440-323-5457
Fax: 440-323-3247
Manufacturer and exporter of plastic food packaging materials including regular and thermoforming sheets and bacon boards
National Sales Representative: C Derringer
Engineering/Technical: Mike Linner
Estimated Sales: $10-20 Million
Number Employees: 10-19
Type of Packaging: Consumer, Private Label, Bulk

30425 **Triple A Containers**
16069 Shoemaker Ave
Buena Park, CA 90621 714-521-2820
Fax: 714-521-8781 bruce@tripla.com
www.tripla.com
Corrugated shipping containers
Owner: Brad McCroskey
Purchasing: Bob Ryan
Estimated Sales: $20-50 Million
Number Employees: 100-249

30426 **Triple A Neon Company**
12325 Califa Street
Valley Village, CA 91607-1106 323-877-5381
Fax: 818-763-6255
Neon signs
President: Todd Showalter
Estimated Sales: Less than $500,000
Number Employees: 4

30427 **Triple Dot Corporation**
3302 S Susan St
Santa Ana, CA 92704-6841 714-241-0888
Fax: 714-241-9888 info@triple-dot.com
www.triple-dot.com
Plastic containers, dessicant packages and neck bands; importer of glass containers
President: Tony Tsai
VP: Jason Tsai
Estimated Sales: $5-10 Million
Number Employees: 20-49
Square Footage: 140000
Brands:
Seca-Pax
Tdc

30428 **Triple X Packaging Company**
2100 Commonwealth Avenue
North Chicago, IL 60064 847-689-2200
Fax: 847-689-8470 information@emcochem.com
www.emcochem.com
Contract packager of detergents
President/Chief Executive Officer: Edward Polen
Quality Assurance Manager: David Jepsen
National Sales Manager: Bill Bishop
Operations Manager: Janet Pederson
Maintenance Facilities Manager: Mike Perreault
Purchasing Manager: Brad Polen
Estimated Sales: $31 Million
Number Employees: 385
Square Footage: 650000
Parent Co: Emco Chemical Distributors, Inc.

30429 **Triple-A Manufacturing Company**
44 Milner Avenue
Toronto, ON M1S 3P8
Canada 416-291-4451
Fax: 416-291-1292 800-786-2238
www.rivalstores.com
Manufacturer and exporter of storage systems, shelving, steel work benches, modular storage drawers, plastic and corrugated bins, welded wire partitions and mezzanines; also, racks including bottle, can, cold storage room, palletwine, wire, barrel, drum, etc
President: Joe Harnest
VP Finance: A Lerman
VP Sales: R Gasner
Buyer: T Kelly
Estimated Sales: $10 - 20 Million
Number Employees: 35
Square Footage: 120000
Other Locations:
Triple-A Manufacturing Co. Lt
Exeter NH

30430 **Triple/S Dynamics**
P.O.Box 151027
Dallas, TX 75315 214-828-8600
Fax: 214-828-8688 800-527-2116
sales@sssdynamics.com www.sssdynamics.com
Manufacturer and exporter of conveyors, separators and vibrating screens
Marketing: Jim Tatum
Estimated Sales: $10-20,000,000
Number Employees: 100-249
Square Footage: 125000
Brands:
Slipstick

30431 **Trisep Corporation**
95 S La Patera Ln
Goleta, CA 93117 805-964-8003
Fax: 805-964-1235 sales@trisep.com
www.trisep.com

Manufactures membrane filters and separators, spiral wound reverse osmosis elements
President: James Bartlett Jr
Sr. Vice President -Commercial: Jon Goodman
SpiraSep UF Marketing Mgr.: Mike Snodgrass
International Sales Director: John Waring
Estimated Sales: $8 Million
Number Employees: 50-99

30432 Triune Enterprises
13711 S Normandie Ave
Gardena, CA 90249 310-719-1600
Fax: 310-719-1800 www.triuneent.com
Films, polypropylene, polyester, gas packaging materials, shrink packaging materials, vacuum packaging materials
President: John Jerry Christman
CFO: John Jerry Christman
Estimated Sales: $4 Million
Number Employees: 20-49

30433 (HQ)Trojan
PO Box 850
Mount Sterling, KY 40353 859-498-0526
Fax: 859-498-0528 800-264-0526
sales@trojaninc.com www.trojaninc.com
Manufacturer and exporter of lighting including long life, energy-efficient incandescent, fluorescent, HID, NSF approved, shatter-resistant, lamps, etc.; also, adapters and plate and exit sign retrofit kits
President: Edward Duzyk
CEO: Dennis Duzyk
Estimated Sales: $3 - 5 Million
Number Employees: 10-19
Square Footage: 170000
Type of Packaging: Food Service
Other Locations:
Trojan
Meadville PA
Brands:
Hytron
Hytronics
Powersaver
Saf-T-Cote

30434 (HQ)Trojan Commercial Furniture Inc.
163 Van Horne
Montereal, QC H2T 2J2
Canada 514-271-3878
Fax: 514-271-8960 877-271-3878
info@trojanproducts.com
www.trojanproducts.com
Manufacturer and exporter of wooden restaurant furniture including tables, chairs, booths and counters
President: Dennis Petsinis
Co-President: Chris Petsinis
Number Employees: 10
Square Footage: 24000
Type of Packaging: Food Service, Bulk
Brands:
Trojan Commercial

30435 Trola Industries
2360 N George St
York, PA 17406 717-848-3700
Fax: 717-848-6993 tbarton@trolaindustries.com
www.trolaindustries.com
Design, build, install control systems and panels (UL508A)
President: Thomas Barton PE
Vice President: Steve Halweski
Sales Director: Jim Schneider
Estimated Sales: $10-20 Million
Number Employees: 20-49
Square Footage: 23000

30436 Tromner
201 Wolf Drive
Thorofare, NJ 08086 570-278-9700
Fax: 570-278-3868 856-686-1600
web@troemner.com www.troemner.com
Manufacturer and exporter of laboratory stirrers and mixers for research and development and quality assurance applications
Sales/Marketing: Linda Sears
Estimated Sales: $1-2.5 Million
Number Employees: 9
Brands:
T-Line

30437 Tronex Industries
1 Tronex Centre
Denville, NJ 07834 800-833-1181
Fax: 973-625-7630 800-833-1181
information@tronexcompany.com
www.tronexhealthcare.com
Manufacturer and distributor of disposable gloves and apparel including bouffant cups, aprons, beard and sleeve covers
CFO: John Prail
Executive VP: Poyee Tai
Marketing Director: Carol Fletcher
Sales Director: Robert Larsen
Operations Manager: Mike Rowe
Number Employees: 20
Square Footage: 320000
Parent Co: Tronex International
Brands:
Choice
Tronex

30438 Tronics America
1434 East 86th Place
Merrillville, IN 46410-6342 866-465-3415
Fax: 219-769-0962 sales@TronicsAmerica.com
www.tronicsamerica.com
Pressure sensitive labeling machines and heat transfer decorators
Manager: Richard Dew
Estimated Sales: $1-2.5 Million
Number Employees: 5-9

30439 Tropic-Kool EngineeringCorporation
1232 Donegan Rd
Largo, FL 33771-2904 727-581-2824
Fax: 727-587-7973 www.tropickool.com
Metal parts for vents and air conditioning systems
President: Kenneth W. Bray
General Manager: Ken Bray
Estimated Sales: $5-10 Million
Number Employees: 20-49
Square Footage: 72000

30440 Tropical Soap Company
1512 Silverleaf Dr.
PO Box 112220
Carrollton, TX 75011-2220 972-492-7939
Fax: 972-233-1955 800-527-2368
Coconut oil soap including liquid and bar
Brands:
Sirena

30441 Trout Lake Farm Company
PO Box 181
Trout Lake, WA 98650 509-395-2025
Fax: 509-395-2749 800-655-6988
herbs@troutlakefarm.com
www.troutlakefarm.com
Quality Control: Angie Brackhahn
Sales Manager: Martha Jane Hylton
Operations Supervisor: Danielle Hawkins
General Manager: Lloyd Scott
Number Employees: 50

30442 Trowelon
973 Haven Place
Green Bay, WI 54313-5207 920-499-8778
Fax: 920-499-9065 800-975-8778
Floor and wall coating materials
CEO: Lewis Krueger
Estimated Sales: $5-10 Million
Number Employees: 50-99

30443 (HQ)Troxler Electronic Laboratories
3008 E. Cornwallis Rd
PO Box 12057
Research Triangle Park, NC 27709 919-549-8661
Fax: 919-549-0761 www.troxlerlabs.com
Moisture and density testing equipment
President: William F Troxler Jr
Director Product Service: Bill Worrell
Estimated Sales: $10-20 Million
Number Employees: 100-249
Square Footage: 125000

30444 (HQ)Troy Lighting
14508 Nelson Ave
City of Industry, CA 91744-3514
Fax: 626-330-4266 800-533-8769
Manufacturer, exporter and importer of electric lighting fixtures including decorative interior, track and recessed; also, exterior including wall, hanging, flush and post lanterns
President: David Littman
VP Sales/Marketing: Steve Nadell
Estimated Sales: $20-50 Million
Number Employees: 100-249
Square Footage: 100000

30445 Tru Hone Corporation
1721 NE 19th Ave
Ocala, FL 34470 352-622-1213
Fax: 352-622-9180 800-237-4663
www.truhone.com
Knife sharpeners and accessories for industrial operations, meat, fish, poultry and produce plants.

30446 Tru Hone Corporation
1721 NE 19th Ave
Ocala, FL 34470 352-622-1213
Fax: 352-622-9180 800-237-4663
truhone@truhone.com www.truhone.com
Manufacturer and exporter of knife sharpeners
President: James Gangelhoff
CEO: Fred R Gangelhoff
Estimated Sales: $1-2.5 Million
Number Employees: 11-50
Square Footage: 6600
Brands:
Tru Hone

30447 Tru-Form Plastics
17809 S Broadway
Gardena, CA 90248 310-327-9444
Fax: 310-878-1107 800-510-7999
www.tru-formplastics.com
Food processing/service equipment and supplies, air conditioning and vents, lighting fixtures, point of purchase displays, uniform hats and caps, refrigeration equipment, sinks, etc
President: Douglas Sahm
CEO: Mario Guzman
National Sales Manager: Doug Sahm
Customer Service: Yolanda Cardenas
VP Operations: Mario Guzman
Estimated Sales: $1-2,500,000
Number Employees: 20-49

30448 TruHeat Corporation
P.O.Box 190
Allegan, MI 49010-0190 269-673-2145
Fax: 269-673-7219 800-879-6199
jkaylor@truheat.com www.truheat.com
Manufacturer and exporter of electric heating elements and assemblies for warming, broiling, frying, steaming and defrosting
President: Larry Nameche
Marketing/Sales: Jim Jennings
Estimated Sales: $10-20 Million
Number Employees: 100-249
Square Footage: 52000

30449 True Food Service Equipment, Inc.
2001 E Terra Ln
O Fallon, MO 63366-4434 636-240-2400
Fax: 636-272-2408 800-325-6152
truefood@truemfg.com www.truemfg.com
Manufacturer and exporter of commercial refrigeration equipment including deli cases, refrigerators, freezers and coolers; also, beer dispensers and pizza prep tables
President: Robert J Trulaske
Estimated Sales: $.5 - 1 million
Number Employees: 1-4
Brands:
True

30450 True Manufacturing Company
2001 E Terra Ln
O Fallon, MO 63366-4434 636-240-2400
Fax: 636-272-2408
truefoodservice@truemfg.com
www.truemfg.com
President: Robert Trulaske
Estimated Sales: $.5 - 1 million
Number Employees: 1-4

30451 True Pack Ltd
420 New Churchmans Rd
New Castle, DE 19808-6271 302-326-2222
Fax: 302-326-9330 800-825-7890
info@truepack.com www.truepack.com

Manufacturer and exporter of insulated shipping containers
Manager: Joan Carter
Estimated Sales: $1 - 5 Million
Number Employees: 20-50

30452 Truesdail Laboratories
14201 Franklin Ave
Tustin, CA 92780-7008 714-730-6239
Fax: 714-730-6462 www.truesdail.com
Consultant offering laboratory testing and sanitary analysis
Owner: John Hill
Chief Scientist: Steve Roesch
Estimated Sales: $10-20 Million
Number Employees: 50-99
Square Footage: 40000

30453 Truitt Brothers Inc
1105 Front Street NE
PO Box 309
Salem, OR 97308-0309 503-362-3674
Fax: 503-588-2868 800-547-8712
truittbros@truittbros.com www.truittbros.com
Canned green beans, cherries, pears and plums; also, shelf stable entrees
CFO: Alan Wynn
Quality Control: David Stump
Human Resources: Sue Meier
Cannery Operations Manager: Sue Root
Purchasing: Chet Thomas
Estimated Sales: $20 - 50 Million
Number Employees: 500-999
Type of Packaging: Consumer, Food Service, Private Label
Brands:
Truitt Bros.

30454 Truly Nolen
438 E Brandon Blvd
Brandon, FL 33511-5318 813-684-6665
Fax: 813-643-1615
Pest control systems
Manager: Patty Mc Intire
Estimated Sales: $1-2.5 Million
Number Employees: 20-49

30455 Trumbull Nameplates
1101 Sugar Mill Dr
New Smyrna Beach, FL 32168 386-423-1105
Signs and pressure sensitive labels
General Manager: Frank Tisler
Number Employees: 1-4
Square Footage: 1800

30456 Trump's Fine Foods
646 Powell Street
Vancouver, BC V6A 1H4
Canada 604-732-8473
Fax: 604-732-8433 info@trumpsfood.com
www.trumpsfood.com
Cakes, cookies, bars, buffet cakes, cheese cakes, loaves, and biscotti.
Number Employees: 20
Square Footage: 16000
Brands:
Banana Slims
Cocoa Slims
Omega Slims

30457 Try Coffee Group
320 Carlisle Street
Harrisburg, PA 17104-1226 717-238-8381
Fax: 717-238-9173 www.trycoffee.com
Brewers, grinders
Estimated Sales: $5-10 Million
Number Employees: 10

30458 Tryco Coffee Service Annex Warehouse
3146 Corporate Place
Hayward, CA 94545-3916 510-293-9199
Fax: 510-293-0971 annextryco@aol.com
www.annextryco.net
Blending and mixing equipment (coffee), cleaners (green coffee), reconditioners, samplers, weighers, storage, consolidations, and packaging
CEO: Terry Sloat
Number Employees: 40

30459 TuWay American Group
PO Box 306
Rockford, OH 45882-0306 419-363-3191
Fax: 419-363-2129 800-537-3750
info@tuwayamerican.com www.tuwaymops.com
Manufacturer, importer and exporter of dust cloths and mops, carpet cleaning pads and bonnets, scouring pads, wall washing supplies and handles
President: Trudy Koster
Director Sales: M Healy
National Sales Manager: Steve Grimes
Plant Manager: John Feeney
Estimated Sales: $20 - 50 Million
Number Employees: 50-99
Parent Co: Tu-Way Products Company
Brands:
Dustmaster
Dustroyer
Speed Trek
Wide Track

30460 Tubesales QRT
800 Roosevelt Road
suite 410
Glen Ellyn, IL 60137-5839 800-545-5000
Fax: 800-545-5883
www.plumbingnet.com/listt.html

30461 Tucel Industries, Inc.
2014 Forestdale Rd.
Forestdale, VT 05745-0146 802-247-6824
Fax: 802-247-6826 800-558-8235
info@tucel.com www.tucel.com
Manufacturer and exporter of produce sponges and food preparation brushes including pastry; also, janitorial supplies including brushes, brooms, scours and squeegees
President: John Lewis Jr
CEO: Joanne Raleigh
Estimated Sales: $3 - 5 Million
Number Employees: 20-49
Square Footage: 180000
Type of Packaging: Consumer, Food Service, Private Label, Bulk
Brands:
Cycle Line
Fused
Hygienic Fusedware
Sponge 'n Brush
Tu-Scrub
Tucel

30462 Tuchenhagen
6716 Alexander Bell Drive
Suite 125
Columbia, MD 21046-2186 410-910-6000
Fax: 410-910-7000 info@tuchenhagen.com
www.tuchenhagen.com
Manufacturer and exporter of compact modular skid-mounted processing units and systems including blending, mixing, yeast pitching, etc.; also, valves, in-line flow measuring instruments and sanitary fittings, etc.; also, consultationservices available
Marketing Coordinator: Mads Michael Skaarenborg
Sales Director: Dave Medlar
Estimated Sales: $2.5-5 Million
Number Employees: 20-49
Parent Co: Tuchenhagen North America

30463 Tuchenhagen-Zajac
90 Evergreen Dr
Portland, ME 04103-1066 207-797-9500
Fax: 207-878-7914 szajac@zajac-inc.com
www.gea-l-div.com
Liquid processing
President: Dave Metler
CFO: Ralf Brockman
COO: David Harding
Estimated Sales: $5 - 10 Million
Number Employees: 5-9

30464 Tuckahoe Manufacturing Company
327 Tuckahoe Rd
Vineland, NJ 08360-9243 856-696-4100
Fax: 856-691-7312 800-220-3368
Strip doors; wholesaler/distributor of vinyl strip, sheet and panel materials and soft impact doors
President/Owner: John Tombleson
Estimated Sales: $1 - 3 Million
Number Employees: 1-4
Square Footage: 1800

30465 Tucker Industries
2835 Janitell Road
Colorado Springs, CO 80906-4104 719-527-4848
Fax: 719-527-1499 800-786-7287
action@burnguard.com www.burnguard.com
Manufacturer and exporter of burn protective garments including oven mitts, aprons and hot pads
President: Vincent A. Tucker
Safety Director: Les Burns
CFO: Hathy Tucker
Quality Control: Hathy Tucker
VP Marketing: Paul Weklinski
Estimated Sales: Below $5 Million
Number Employees: 20-49
Square Footage: 172000
Brands:
Burnguard
Safestep
Vaporguard

30466 Tucker Manufacturing Company
P.O.Box 848
Cedar Rapids, IA 52406 319-363-3591
Fax: 319-366-7792 800-553-8131
info@tuckerusa.com www.tuckerusa.com
High level window washers, aluminum telescoping handles, brushes, detergent tablets, window and awning cleaning systems, spot free water
President: Irvin Lee Tucker
VP/General Manager: Robin Bradley Tucker
CFO: Robin Tucker
R&D: Robin Tucker
Quality Control: Robin Tucker
Estimated Sales: $5 - 10,000,000
Number Employees: 10-19
Brands:
Tucker

30467 (HQ)Tucson Container Corporation
6601 S Palo Verde Rd
Tucson, AZ 85756 520-746-3171
Fax: 520-741-0962 www.tucsoncontainer.com
Manufacturer and exporter of fiber and corrugated boxes; also, packaging materials and foam products
President: John Widera
Manager: Daniel Robinson
Controller: Christel Widera
Sales Service Manager: Karina Walters
Production Supervisor: Eladios Cortez
Plant Manager: Joaquin Rivadeneyra
Purchasing Agent: Chris Woolridge
Estimated Sales: $16 Million
Number Employees: 85
Square Footage: 160000
Other Locations:
Tucson Container Corp.
El Paso TX

30468 Tudor Pulp & Paper Corporation
17 White Oak Dr
Prospect, CT 06712 203-758-4494
Fax: 203-758-4498
Manufacturer and importer of specialty paper for packaging including grease resistant, oil resistant, industrial and electric
VP Sales: Stephen Hansen
Manager: Brad Russell
Estimated Sales: $1 - 5 Million
Number Employees: 10-19

30469 Tudor Technology
5145 Campus Drive
Plymouth Meeting, PA 19462-1129 610-828-5910
Fax: 610-828-0635 800-777-0778
Manufacturer and exporter of temperature controls and sensors and process control systems
President: Jose Broker
CFO: Paul Boyle
Sales Manager: Alan Breckenridge
Estimated Sales: $2.5 - 5 Million
Number Employees: 5-9

30470 Tufco International
P.O.Box 456
Gentry, AR 72734-0456 479-736-2201
Fax: 479-736-2947 800-364-0836
info@tufcoflooring.com www.tufcoflooring.com
Flooring
President: Brent Mills
VP Sales: Russell Cox
Estimated Sales: Below $5 Million
Number Employees: 50-99

30471 Tufty Ceramics
47 South Main Street
PO Box 785
Andover, NY 14806 607-478-5150
ktufty@infoblvd.net
www.tuftyceramics.com
Manufacturer and exporter of terracotta bakeware including nonstick, microwaveable and dishwasher safe
President: Karen Tufty
Estimated Sales: Below $500,000
Number Employees: 1-4
Brands:
Alfred Bakeware

30472 Tulip Corporation
714 E Keefe Ave
Milwaukee, WI 53212 414-963-3120
Fax: 414-962-1825 tulip@tulipcorp.com
www.tulipcorp.com
CFO: Mike Araco
Principal: Courtland Hientze
Senior VP: Alan Schmidt
Estimated Sales: $20-50 Million
Number Employees: 250-499

30473 Tulox Plastics Corporation
P.O.Box 984
Marion, IN 46952 765-664-5155
Fax: 765-664-0257 800-234-1118
sales@tulox.com www.tulox.com
Tubes and toppers that are available in rounds, squares, rectangulars, triangulars, and custom shapes, transparent, opaque, colored, or striped
President: John Sciaudone
Vice President: Bill Patuzzi
National Sales Director: Christopher Sciaudone
Type of Packaging: Consumer

30474 Tulsa Plastics Company
6112 E 32nd Pl
Tulsa, OK 74135 918-664-0931
Fax: 918-622-2943 888-273-5303
sales@tulsaplastics.com www.tulsaplastics.com
Store fixtures, sky lights, plastic sheet materials, plastic signs and displays
President: Jim Blakemore
CFO: Jim Blakemore
Estimated Sales: Below $5 Million
Number Employees: 10-19

30475 Tulsack
5400 S Garnett Rd
Tulsa, OK 74146 918-664-0664
Fax: 918-664-0849 www.tulsack.com
Handled paper bags
President: Jarrod Dyess
Estimated Sales: $10-20 Million
Number Employees: 100-249
Parent Co: Denmar Products

30476 Tupperware Brand Corporation
14901 South Orange Blossom Trail
Orlando, FL 32837 407-826-5050
Fax: 407-826-8268 800-366-3800
www.tupperwarebrands.com
Plastic storage containers and cookware.
President & Chief Operating Officer: Simon Hemus
Chairman & Chief Executive Officer: E.V. Rick Goings
Executive VP & Chief Financial Officer: Michael Poteshman
EVP & Chief Human Resources Officer: Lillian Garcia
Estimated Sales: $2.6 Billion
Number Employees: 13,000
Brands:
Tupperware

30477 Turbo Refrigerating Company
P.O.Box 396
Denton, TX 76202-0396 940-387-4301
Fax: 940-382-0364 info@turboice.com
www.turboice.com
Manufacturer and exporter of ice making, storage and distribution systems; processor of ice
President: El Beard
CFO: Chris Worghington
VP: Dan Aiken
VP Sales/Marketing: T Baker
Estimated Sales: $20 - 50 Million
Number Employees: 20-49
Parent Co: Henry Vogt Machine Company
Other Locations:
Turbo Refrigerating Co.
Louisville KY

30478 Turbo Systems
4 Glenberry Ct.
Phoenix, MD 21131 410-527-2800
Fax: 954-925-4190 rubosysfl@aol.com
www.turbosystemsusa.com
Aerators, bar formers, bottomers, chocolate equipment, vermicelli machines, coaters, conveyors, cookers
President: Michael Thorz
Sr. Vice President: Joost J. de Koomen
Estimated Sales: $.5 - 1 million
Number Employees: 1-4

30479 Turck
3000 Campus Dr
Minneapolis, MN 55441 763-553-7300
Fax: 763-553-0708 800-544-7769
grant.bistram@turck.com www.turck-usa.com
Provides sensing solutions and related components by manufacturing and marketing proximity sensors, cordsets, connection products and automation devices. The company's products are primaly used in manufacturing automationapplications
President: William Scheneider
CFO: Bill Chrisianson
CEO: David Lagerstrom
R&D: Boss
Quality Control: Bamian Pike
Marketing Director: Grant Bistram
Production Manager: Hanz Ziesch
Estimated Sales: $50 - 100 Million
Number Employees: 250-499

30480 Turner & Seymour Manufacturing
100 Lawton St
Torrington, CT 06790 860-489-9214
Fax: 800-676-3197 888-856-4864
sales@turnerseymour.com
www.turnerseymour.com
Manufacturers welded and weldless chains and chain accessories. Also, upholstery nails, furniture glides, escutcheon pins and commercial can openers
President: Tom Pretak
VP Human Resources: Carol Soliani
CFO: Ken Rizzi
Chairman of the Board: Allen M Sperry Sr
VP Sales: Frank Silano
Estimated Sales: $10 - 20 Million
Number Employees: 50-99
Square Footage: 100000
Type of Packaging: Food Service

30481 Turtle Wax
PO Box 247
Westmont, IL 60559-0247 905-470-6665
Fax: 708-563-4302
distributorinfo@turtlewax.com
www.turtlewax.com
Manufacturer and exporter household cleaners, dressings and polishes
CEO: Denis J Healy
Chairman: Sondra A Healy
Estimated Sales: $5 - 10 Million
Number Employees: 1,000-4,999

30482 Tuscarora
PO Box 448
New Brighton, PA 15066 724-847-2601
Fax: 724-843-4845 packagingna@sca.com
www.tuscarora.com
Packaging and containerizing products including polystyrene coolers
President: Rob Beeson
Plant Manager: Jeff Weingart
Estimated Sales: $20-50 Million
Number Employees: 1,000-4,999
Square Footage: 122000

30483 Tuscarora
800 5th Ave
New Brighton, PA 15066 724-843-8200
Fax: 724-843-0326 packagingna@sca.com
www.tuscarora.com
Packaging and material handling trays, containers, and pallets
Marketing Director: Rachel Coltin
Sales Director: Ken Harris
Estimated Sales: $300 Million
Number Employees: 2000
Type of Packaging: Consumer, Food Service, Bulk

30484 Tuthill Vacuum & BlowerSystems
P.O.Box 2877
Springfield, MO 65801-2877 417-865-8715
Fax: 417-865-2950 800-825-6937
vacuum@tuthill.com www.tuthillvacuum.com
Manufacturer and exporter of positive displacement rotary lobe blowers mechanical vacuum boosters, rotary piston vacuum pumps, liquid ring vacuum pumps and complete systems
President: John Ermold
Controller: James Ashcraft
Sales/Marketing Director: Mike Branstetter
Estimated Sales: $10-20 Million
Number Employees: 250-499
Number of Brands: 10
Number of Products: 6
Square Footage: 65000
Parent Co: Tuthill Corporation
Brands:
Acousticair
Competitor Plus
Equalizer
Pd Plus

30485 Tuxton China
21011 Commerce Point Drive
Walnut, CA 91789-3052 909-595-2510
Fax: 909-595-5353 info@tuxton.com
www.tuxton.com

30486 Twelve Baskets Sales & Market
5200 Phillip Lee Dr SW
Atlanta, GA 30336 404-696-9922
Fax: 404-696-9099 800-420-8840
www.twelvebaskets.com
Wholesaler/distributer of general line items; also, packer of edible oils
Owner: Ken Mc Millan
President: Kirk McMillen
Sales: Bob Quinet
Estimated Sales: $20 - 50 Million
Number Employees: 20-49
Square Footage: 15000

30487 Twenty First Century Design
1008 Madison Ave
Albany, NY 12208-2600 518-446-0939
Designer of restaurant interiors, mechanical and electrical systems; also, architectural and engineering services available
Owner: Menglin Liu
Estimated Sales: $500,000-$1 Million
Number Employees: 5-9
Square Footage: 5000

30488 Twenty/Twenty Graphics
7895 Cessna Ave # S
Gaithersburg, MD 20879 240-243-0511
Fax: 240-243-0512 123@20-20GRAPHICS.COM
www.20-20graphics.com
Signs, displays and decals; screen printing available
President: Luclere Lee
Estimated Sales: $2.5-5 Million
Number Employees: 10-19

30489 Twi-Laq Industries
1345 Seneca Ave
Bronx, NY 10474 718-638-5860
Fax: 718-789-0993 800-950-7627
customerservice@twi-laq.com www.twi-laq.com
Manufacturer and exporter of cleaning chemicals including soaps, degreasers, detergents, marble care chemicals and floor finishes
President: Lorin Wels
VP: Robert Wels
VP Operations: Michael Wels
Estimated Sales: $5-10 Million
Number Employees: 10-19
Brands:
Stone Glo
Sun-Glo
Top-Guard
Welsite

30490 Twin City Bottle
1227 E Hennepin Ave
Minneapolis, MN 55414 612-331-8880
Fax: 612-379-5118 800-697-0607
sales@kaufmancontainer.com
www.twincitybottle.com
Major supplier of all types of containers
CEO: Roger Seid

Estimated Sales: $20-50 Million
Number Employees: 50-99

30491 **Twin City Pricing & Label**
744 Kasota Cir SE
Minneapolis, MN 55414-2883 612-378-1055
Fax: 612-379-0112 800-328-5076
www.twincityproduce.com
Custom printed labels
President: John Rotondo
Production Manager: Curtis James
Estimated Sales: $10 - 20 Million
Number Employees: 20-49
Square Footage: 13000

30492 **Twin State Signs**
14 Gauthier Dr
Essex Junction, VT 05452 802-872-8949
Fax: 802-878-0200 twinsign@together.net
www.twinstatesigns.com
Signs including neon, electric, indoor, outdoor, wooden, etc.; also, signage repair and installation services available
President: Mary Denault
CFO/R&D: Ray Denault
VP: Raymond Denault
Sales Manager: Suzanne Denault
Estimated Sales: Below $5 Million
Number Employees: 5-9
Brands:
Gerber Edge
Scotch Print

30493 **Two Rivers Enterprises**
490 River St W
Holdingford, MN 56340 320-746-3156
Fax: 320-746-3158 joeh@stainlesskings.com
www.stainlesskings.com
Restaurant and food service equipment; also provides renovations of processing plants and on-site equipment.
President: Robert Warzecha
Midwest Regional Sales: Joe Herges
Sales Engineer: Jeff Jones
Midwest Regional Sales: Steve Bairett

30494 **Tyco Fire Protection Products**
1400 Pennbrook Parkway
Lansdale, PA 19446 215-362-0700
Fax: 800-877-1295 800-558-5236
sales@starsprinkler.com www.starsprinkler.com
Manufacturer and exporter of automatic self-adjusting fire sprinkler systems including concealed and recessed
Marketing Manager: John Corcoran
International Sales Manager: Patti Kowalski
Number Employees: 12
Parent Co: Tyco Corporation
Brands:
Quasar
Starmist

30495 **Tyco Plastics**
8235 220th St W
Lakeville, MN 55044-8059 952-469-8771
Fax: 952-469-5337 800-328-4080
www.tycoplastics.com
Manufacturer and exporter of packaging supplies including barrier bags, films and pouches for meats, cheeses, etc
Sales/Marketing: Mike Baarts
Business Unit Manager (Food): Dennis Leisten
Business Unit Manager (Industrial): Tom Lundborg
Purchasing Manager: Gordon Raway
Estimated Sales: $20-50 Million
Number Employees: 100-249
Brands:
Rexfit
Rextape
Startex
Starvac
Starvac Ii
Starvac Iii

30496 **Tyco Plastics**
1401 W 94th St
Minneapolis, MN 55431 952-884-7281
Fax: 952-884-6438 800-276-4628
shrrelations@melloninvestor.com
www.tycoplastics.com
Packaging films and bags, polyethylene shrink film, polyethylene bags, polyethylene stretch film
President: Brian Strauss
Estimated Sales: $500 - 750 Million
Number Employees: 250-499

30497 **Tycodalves & Controls**
1010 N Edward Ct
Anaheim, CA 92806-2601 714-575-9201
Fax: 714-575-9206 800-972-8926
westcoastusa@tycovalves.com
www.tycovalves.com
Wine industry valves
Manager: Eddie Kim
Estimated Sales: $10 - 20 Million
Number Employees: 10-19

30498 **Tyler Refrigeration Corporation**
1329 Lake St
Niles, MI 49120-1297 269-683-2000
Fax: 269-684-9802 800-992-3744
tylercorp@carrier.utc.com
www.tylerrefrigeration.com
Manufacturer and exporter of commercial refrigeration equipment and display cases
VP: Dave Cangelosi
Estimated Sales: $260 Million
Number Employees: 1,000-4,999
Square Footage: 750000
Parent Co: Carrier Corporation
Brands:
Tyler

30499 **Tyson Foods**
2545 E Ozark Ave
Gastonia, NC 28054-1423 704-865-2108
Fax: 704-866-0674 www.tyson.com
Meat, produce, dairy products, frozen foods, baked goods, equipment and fixtures, general merchandise and specialty foods serving the food service market.
Chairman: John Tyson
President/CEO: Donnie Smith
EVP/CFO: Wade Miquelon
EVP/General Counsel: J Alberto Gonzalez-Pita
SVP/Research & Development: Howell Carper
VP/Investor Relations: Ruth Ann Wisener
SVP/Human Resources: Kenneth Kimbro
Estimated Sales: $10-20 Million
Number Employees: 10-19
Square Footage: 10000
Parent Co: Tyson Foods

30500 **U Mec Food Processing Equipment**
548 Claire St
Hayward, CA 94541-6412 510-537-4744
Fax: 510-537-9564 800-933-8632
sales@umec.net www.umec.net
Elevators, loaders, lifters and dumpers, belt conveyors, blenders, chup separators, massagers and tumblers, mixers, screw conveyors
President: Barry Brescia
CEO: Benny Brescia
CEO: Ralph Creech
Sales Director: Dennis Dennings
Estimated Sales: $2.5 - 5 Million
Number Employees: 20-49
Type of Packaging: Food Service, Private Label

30501 **U Roast Em**
16778W US Highway 63
Hayward, WI 54843 715-634-6255
Fax: 715-934-3221 info@u-roast-em.com
www.u-roast-em.com
Supplier of green coffee beans, bulk teas, home roasting supplies and coffee flavorings
Type of Packaging: Consumer
Brands:
Bodum
Fresh Beans

30502 **U-Line Corporation**
PO Box 245040
Milwaukee, WI 53224-9540 414-354-0300
Fax: 414-354-0349 sales@u-line.com
www.u-line.com
Manufacturer and exporter of ice making machinery, compact freezers and compact, built-in and under counter refrigerators
President: Philip Uline
VP: Jennifer Seraszewski
CEO: Jennifer U Straszewski
Quality Control: Dean Bycnski
Sales/Marketing Manager: Henry Uline
Vice President of Operations: Andrew Doberstein
Estimated Sales: $20 - 50 Million
Number Employees: 250-499

30503 **U.B. Klem Furniture Company**
3861 E Schnellville Rd
Saint Anthony, IN 47575 812-326-2236
Fax: 812-326-2525 800-264-1995
info@ubklem.com www.ubklem.com
Chairs, barstools, booths, tables, pedestals and trash receptacles
President: U Klem
CEO: U Butch Klen
Estimated Sales: $10-20 Million
Number Employees: 100-249
Square Footage: 75000

30504 **UAA**
2561 N Greenview Avenue
Chicago, IL 60614-2028 773-755-4545
Fax: 773-755-4555 800-813-1711
info@restaurantpagers.com
www.restaurantpagers.com
Paging and surveillance systems including two-way radios; consulting services available
President: Joe Grody

30505 **UCB Films**
1950 Lake Park Dr SE
Smyrna, GA 30080-7648 770-432-0062
Fax: 770-970-8482 877-822-3456
margaret.boggess@ucb-group.com
www.films.ucb-group.com
Cellulose and polypropylene specialty films that are supplied into packaging, industrial and label markets
Quality Control: Jeff Fricks
CEO: Fabrice Egros
Marketing Director: S Laing
Sales Director: J Bonk
Estimated Sales: $100+ Million
Number Employees: 250-499
Parent Co: UCB S.A.
Type of Packaging: Consumer, Food Service, Private Label
Brands:
Cellophane
Celloplus
Cellotherm
Natureflex
Optitwist
Propafilm
Propafiol
Propaream
Ratoface
Startwist

30506 **UDEC Corporation**
271A Salem Street
Woburn, MA 01801 781-933-7770
Fax: 781-933-5366 800-990-8332
info@udeccorp.com www.udeccorp.com
Manufacturer and exporter of solid-state fluorescent emergency, exit and night lights; also, electronic ballasts for back lighting
President: Eugene P. Brandeis
CFO: Janice Ferro
Purchasing Manager: J Ferro
Estimated Sales: Below $5 Million
Number Employees: 1-4
Square Footage: 9200
Type of Packaging: Food Service, Private Label

30507 **UDY Corporation & AlphaPlastic & Design**
201 Rome Ct
Fort Collins, CO 80524 970-482-0937
Fax: 970-482-2067 info@UDYOne.com
www.udycorp.com
Manufacturer and distributor of protein analyzers, shakers, sample mills, hay samplers and other general lab equipment. Also custom plastic fabrication for science and general industries.
President: William Lear
CFO: William Lear
Estimated Sales: Below $5 Million
Number Employees: 5-9
Number of Brands: 3
Number of Products: 20
Brands:
Colorado Hay Products
Cuclone Sample Mills
Dairy Tester Ii
Plastic Fabrication
Protein Color Meter
React-R-Mill

30508 UFE
520 Industrial Way
Fallbrook, CA 92028-2244 760-723-7900
Fax: 760-723-7910 touchsupport@dolch.com
www.touchcontrols.com
Ruggedized solutions for harsh conditions, clean rooms and NEMA4X, power touch displays and workstations feature enhanced infrared
Marketing Manager: Christopher McDonald
VP Sales: Tony Faint
Manager Information Systems: Michael McGinley
Estimated Sales: $1 - 5 Million
Number Employees: 100-250

30509 UFE Incorporated
1850 Greeley St S
Stillwater, MN 55082 651-351-4273
Fax: 651-351-4272 ask@ufeinc.com
www.ufeinc.com
Caps and closures specializing in custom thermoplastic injection molds and molding
President: Martin N Kellogg
CEO: Greg Willis
Estimated Sales: $20 - 50 Million
Number Employees: 100-249

30510 UFP Technologies
1521 Windsor Drive
Clinton, IA 52732-6611 888-671-7774
Fax: 415-474-0430 888-638-3456
info@ufpt.com www.moldedfiber.com
Design, prototyping, tooling, testing and manufacturing of protective packaging made from 100% recycled paper
CFO: Ron Latiaille
Estimated Sales: $500,000-$1 Million
Number Employees: 4

30511 UL Lighting Fixtures Corp.
3443 10th St
Long Island City, NY 11106-5107 718-726-7500
Fax: 718-626-8812
Manufacturer and importer of lighting fixtures
CEO: Kyries Papastylianou
Estimated Sales: $2.5 - 5,000,000
Number Employees: 10-19
Square Footage: 10000

30512 ULMA Packaging Systems,Inc.
3035 Torrington Drive
Ball Ground, GA 30107 770-345-5300
Fax: 770-345-5322 www.ulmapackaging.com
Packaging machines and packaging solutions such as traysealers, vertical and side seal packaging, blister packaging and film.

30513 UNEX Manufacturing
50 Progress Pl
Jackson, NJ 08527 732-928-2800
Fax: 732-928-2828 800-695-7726
span@unex.com www.unex.com
Carton flow track and carton flow accumulating conveyors
President: Brian Neuwirth
CEO: Mark Newrith
CEO: Frank Neuwirth
Vice President Sales: Mark Neuwirth
Marketing Manager: Mike Levine
Southern Regional Sales Manager: Bill McKenzie
Product Manager: David Scelfo
Estimated Sales: $10-25 Million
Number Employees: 50-99

30514 UNIMAR, Inc
3195 Vickery Rd.
N. Syracuse, NY 13212 315-699-4400
Fax: 315-699-3700 800-739-9169
sales@unimar-ny.com www.unimar.com
Refrigerators, freezers, beverage dispensers, snack bars, C-stoves, and heaters
Estimated Sales: $2.5-5 Million
Number Employees: 1-4

30515 UPM Raflatac Inc
400 Broadpointe Dr
Mills River, NC 28759 828-651-4800
Fax: 800-452-4127 www.upmraflatac.com
Supplier of self-adhesive label materials and producer of HF and UHF radio frequency identification (RFID) tags and inlays.
President: Dan O'Connell
VP: Jan Forssgrom
Media Relations: Paula Morri
Director Environmental Affairs: Paivi Salpakivi-Salomaa
Product Manager: Petteri Stromberg
Manager: Steve Egland
Estimated Sales: $1.3 Billion
Number Employees: 2600

30516 UPN Pallet Company
305 N Virginia Ave
Penns Grove, NJ 08069 856-299-1192
Fax: 856-299-5824
Wooden pallets
Office Manager: Mano Massari
Estimated Sales: $500,000-$1 Million
Number Employees: 5-9
Square Footage: 8000

30517 UPS Logistics Technologies
849 Fairmount Ave # 400
Towson, MD 21286-2601 410-823-0189
Fax: 410-847-6246 800-762-3638
market@upslogistics.com www.upslogistics.com
Street routing and scheduling software, wireless dispatch software
COO: Len Kennedy
COO: Len Kennedy
Director Customer Services: George Evans
Vice President of Product Management: Cyndi Brandt
Sales Director: Charlie Virden
Public Relations: Lisa Beck
Purchasing Manager: Donna Blizzard
Estimated Sales: $20 - 50 Million
Number Employees: 100-249
Number of Products: 5
Parent Co: United Parcel Service

30518 US Bottlers Machinery Company
11911 Steele Creek Road
PO Box 7203
Charlotte, NC 28273 704-588-4750
Fax: 704-588-3808 sales@usbottlers.com
www.usbottlers.com
Manufacturer and exporter of bottling machinery including liquid filling, bottle rinsing, container cleaning and capping equipment
President: Thomas Risser
VP Sales: Jack Harding
Estimated Sales: $10-20 Million
Number Employees: 50-99

30519 (HQ)US Can Company
1101 Todds Lane
Rosedale, MD 21237-2905 410-686-6363
Fax: 410-391-9323 800-436-8021
specialtysales@uscanco.com www.uscanco.com
Manufacturer and exporter of aluminum and tin cans
VP Sales/Marketing: David West
Sales Director: Jack Finnell
Estimated Sales: $20-50 Million
Number Employees: 20-49
Type of Packaging: Consumer, Food Service, Private Label, Bulk

30520 US Cap Systems Corporation
111 Elm St
Suite 204
Worcester, MA 01609-1967 508-754-7283
Fax: 508-752-5546 800-727-5555
President: Emanuel Wohlgemuta
Estimated Sales: $1 - 5 Million
Number Employees: 1-4

30521 US Chemical
316 Hart St
Watertown, WI 53094-6631 920-261-3453
Fax: 920-206-3979 800-558-9566
info@uschemical.com www.uschemical.com
Specialty chemicals including warewashing, laundry, maintenance, carpet and floor care chemicals; exporter of cleaning products and dispensing systems
General Manager: Bill Moody
Technical Manager: Cheryl Maas
QC Lab: Brian Truman
Sales Leader: David Kohnke
Plant Manager: Dennis Bollhurst
Estimated Sales: $30-50 Million
Number Employees: 100-130
Square Footage: 150000
Parent Co: Diversey, Inc

30522 US Coexcell
400 West Dussel Drive
Maumee, OH 43537-1636 419-897-9110
Fax: 419-897-9112 info@uscoxl.com
www.uscoxl.com
Owner: Bob Huebner
President, Chief Executive Officer: Harley Cramer
VP: Mark Woltell
Estimated Sales: $2.5-5 Million
Number Employees: 20-49

30523 US Cooler Company
401 Delaware St
Quincy, IL 62301 217-228-2421
Fax: 217-228-2424 800-521-2665
admin@uscooler.com www.uscooler.com
Walk-in coolers and freezers
President/Owner: Allen Craig
Marketing Director: Kristin Peters
Number Employees: 50-99
Square Footage: 40000
Parent Co: Craig Industries

30524 US Filter
40004 Cook Street
Palm Desert, CA 92211-3299 760-340-0098
Fax: 760-341-9368 information@usfilter.com
www.usfilter.com
Water and wastewater treatment systems and equipment
President: Richard Heckmann
President, Chief Executive Officer: Eric Spiegel
Vice President: Alison Taylor
Corporate Marketing Manager: Mike Markovsky
Executive Vice President of Global Sales: Paul Vogel
Estimated Sales: $1 - 5 Million
Number Employees: 50-99
Square Footage: 4000000

30525 US Filter
40004 Cook Street
Palm Desert, CA 92211-3299 760-340-0098
Fax: 760-341-9368 information@usfilter.com
www.usfilter.com
Water purification equipment
President: Richard Heckmann
President, Chief Executive Officer: Eric Spiegel
Vice President: Alison Taylor
Executive Vice President of Global Sales: Paul Vogel
Estimated Sales: $50-100 Million
Number Employees: 100-249

30526 US Filter Corporation
2330 Scenic Highway
P.O. Box is 871329
Snellville, GA 30078 518-758-2179
Fax: 518-758-2182 info@usfilter.com
www.usfilterco.com
President, Chief Executive Officer: Eric Spiegel
Vice President: Alison Taylor
Executive Vice President of Global Sales: Paul Vogel
Estimated Sales: $1 - 5 Million

30527 US Filter Davco Products
1828 Metcalf Ave
Thomasville, GA 31792-6845 229-226-5733
Fax: 229-226-4793 800-841-1550
info@davcoproducts.com
Water and wastewater treatment equipment.
CEO: Roger Radke
Marketing Manager: Doug Davis
Estimated Sales: $50 - 100 Million
Number Employees: 100-249
Square Footage: 40000

30528 US Filter Dewatering Systems
2155 112th Ave
Holland, MI 49424-9609 616-772-9011
Fax: 616-772-4516 800-245-3006
dewatering@usfilter.com.net
www.usfilterdsg.com

Manufacturer and exporter of filter presses and other dewatering equipment for processing and waste treatment
President: Ken Hollidge
President, Chief Executive Officer: Eric Spiegel
CEO: Chuck Gordon
Executive Vice President of Global Sales: Paul Vogel
Estimated Sales: $20 - 50 Million
Number Employees: 100-249
Square Footage: 140800
Brands:
J-Press

30529 US Filter/Continental Water
5413 Bandera Road
Suite 405
San Antonio, TX 78238-1955 210-523-8181
Fax: 210-523-8393 800-426-3426
information@usfilter.com www.usfilter.com
Water purification equipment
President, Chief Executive Officer: Eric Spiegel
Vice President: Alison Taylor
Executive Vice President of Global Sales: Paul Vogel
Estimated Sales: Less than $500,000
Number Employees: 1-4
Parent Co: US Filter/Continental Water

30530 US Flag & Signal Company
802 Fifth Street
Portsmouth, VA 23704 757-497-8947
Fax: 757-497-1819 flagmaker@flagmaker.com
www.flagmaker.com
Flags, pennants and banners
Number Employees: 25

30531 US Industrial Lubricants
3330 Beekman St
Cincinnati, OH 45223 513-541-2225
Fax: 513-541-2293 800-562-5454
info@usindustriallubricants.com
www.usindustriallubricants.com
Manufacturer and exporter of vegetable oil and liquid soap, synthetic liquid detergent and lubricants including petroleum and synthetic
Co-Owner: Don Mattcheck
R & D: Ted Korzep
Facilities Engineer: Adam Freeman
Inside Sales: Jenny Anderson
USIL National Sales Manager: Dave Darling
Controller: Shannon Schlichte
Estimated Sales: $5-10 Million
Number Employees: 10-19
Number of Brands: 3
Number of Products: 250
Square Footage: 35000
Brands:
Nusheen
Oilkraft
Usil

30532 (HQ)US Label Corporation
2118 Enterprise Rd
Greensboro, NC 27408-7004 336-332-7000
Fax: 336-275-7674 sales@uslabel.com
www.uslabel.com
Manufacturer and exporter of printed cloth, woven and paper labels; also, label tape
CFO: Charlie Davis
VP Marketing: Phil Koch
Sales Manager: James Grant
Number Employees: 250-499

30533 US Lace Paper Works
PO Box 2038
Oshkosh, WI 54903-2038
Fax: 203-937-4583 800-873-6459
brooklace.inc@worldnet.att.net
Manufacturer and exporter of strip lace, place mats, baking cups, tray covers and doilies including paper lace, linen, glassine, grease-proof and foil
Customer Service Manager: Lori Hart-Noyes
General Manager: Wayne Grant
Number Employees: 50
Square Footage: 25000
Type of Packaging: Consumer, Private Label, Bulk
Brands:
Gay 90's

30534 US Line Company
16 Union Avenue
Westfield, MA 01085-2497 413-562-3629
Fax: 413-562-7328 www.usline.com
Manufacturer and exporter of specialized industrial braided synthetics
President: Brad Gage
CFO: Brad Gage
Quality Control: Brad Gage
R&D: Brad Gage
Marketing Director: Bradley Gage
Estimated Sales: Below $5 Million
Number Employees: 15

30535 US Magnetix
7140 Madison Ave. W.
Golden Valley, MN 55427 763-540-9497
Fax: 763-540-0142 800- 3-0
sales@usmagnetix.com www.usmagnetix.com
Magnetic products; specializing in promotional magnetic products. The company's core competencies include printing, die cutting, assembly, packaging, promotional marketing and graphic design
President: John Condon
Sales Business Development Director: Chris Ryder
Art Director: Dean Vaccaro
Lead Production Operator: Neil Deonarain
Production Manager: Keith Johnson
Estimated Sales: $1-2.5 Million
Number Employees: 10-19

30536 US Plastic Corporation
PO Box 104
Swampscott, MA 01907-0104 781-595-1030
Fax: 781-593-6440
Polyethylene and plastic film bags
Estimated Sales: $20-50 Million
Number Employees: 100-249

30537 US Product
1101 Todds Ln
Baltimore, MD 21237-2905 410-686-6364
Fax: 410-687-6741 specialtysales@uscanco.com
www.ball.com
Custom and stock decorated tins, cups and closures
President: Bernie Salles
Estimated Sales: $50 - 100 Million
Number Employees: 100-249

30538 US Rubber Supply Company
238 N 9th St
Brooklyn, NY 11211-2160 718-782-7888
Fax: 718-782-8788 www.usrubbersupply.com
Manufacturer and exporter of food hoses, tubing and conveyor belts
Chairman of the Board: Martin Auster
Estimated Sales: $10-20 Million
Number Employees: 20-49

30539 US Seating Products
1715 S Orange Blossom Trl
Apopka, FL 32703-7746 407-884-4411
Fax: 407-884-0911 usseat@earthlink.net
www.usseating.com
Manufacturer and exporter of aluminum and vinyl benches, chairs, cushions and pads, tray stands, tables and booths including legs and bases
President: Peter Villella
Estimated Sales: $10-20 Million
Number Employees: 10
Type of Packaging: Food Service

30540 US Standard Sign Company
11400 W. Addison Ave
Franklin Park, IL 60131 847-455-7446
Fax: 847-455-3330 800-537-4790
sales@usstandardsign.com
www.usstandardsign.com
Aluminum sign blanks
President: Rick Mandel
CFO: Steve Fallon
Estimated Sales: $1 - 2.5 Million
Number Employees: 50-99
Parent Co: Mandel Metals

30541 US Tag & Label
2208 Aisquith St
Baltimore, MD 21218 410-962-2676
Fax: 410-889-1227 800-638-1018
72723.1042@compuserve.com
Labels
Estimated Sales: $1-5 Million
Number Employees: 50-99

30542 US Tsubaki
301 E Marquardt Dr
Wheeling, IL 60090 847-459-9500
Fax: 847-459-9515 800-323-7790
bobcallahan@ustsubaki.com www.ustsubaki.com
Precision roller chains
President: Yoshi Kitayama
Estimated Sales: $290 Million
Number Employees: 800

30543 USA Canvas Shoppe
2435 Glenda Lane
Dallas, TX 75229 972-484-7633
Fax: 972-620-0364 877-626-8468
awnings@usacanvas.com www.usacanvas.com
Commercial awnings and back-lit awnings
President: Gary Cozart
Estimated Sales: $1-2.5 Million
Number Employees: 10-19
Parent Co: Four Seasons Patio and Awning Company

30544 (HQ)USDA-NASS
1400 Independence Ave SW
Washington, DC 20250-0002 202-690-8122
Fax: 202-720-9013 800-727-9540
nass@nass.usda.gov www.nass.usda.gov
The mission is to research and develop knowledge and technology needed to solve technical agricultural problems of broad scope in order to ensure adequate production of high quality food and agricultural products
Administrator: Cynthia Clark
Director of Research and Development: Mark Harris
Director of Operations: Kevin Barnes
Number Employees: 250-499

30545 USECO
P.O.Box 20428
Murfreesboro, TN 37129-0428 615-893-4820
Fax: 615-893-8705 info@useco.com
www.useco.com
Manufacturer and exporter of stainless steel and aluminum food service equipment including hot and cold food service carts, tray line refrigerators, blast chillers, tray lifters, pellet heaters, etc
President: John Westbrook
VP (Food Service Systems Tech.): Sara Hurt
VP Sales/Marketing (USECO): Paul Murphy
Estimated Sales: $20-50 Million
Number Employees: 50-99
Square Footage: 100000
Parent Co: Standex International Corporation
Type of Packaging: Food Service
Brands:
Catr
Remotaire
Rota-Chill
Unitray
Unitron
Useco

30546 Uhrden
750 Edelweiss Dr.
PO Box 705
Sugarcreek, OH 44681 330-852-2411
Fax: 330-852-2415 800-852-2411
sales@tubar2.com www.tubar2.com
Bulk dumping equipment and vertical reciprocating conveyors
Chairman of the Board: Kenneth L Cook
General Manager: Mike Sigma
Sales: Rod Synder
Purchasing Agent: Lois Harig
Estimated Sales: Below $5 Million
Number Employees: 20-49
Square Footage: 65000
Brands:
Tubar

30547 Uhtamaki Foods Services
242 College Ave
Waterville, ME 04901-6226 207-873-3351
Fax: 207-877-6504 www.chinet.com
Biodegradable disposable tableware; serving the food service industry
Manager: Steve Bosse
CEO: Mark Staton
Estimated Sales: $1 - 5 Million
Number Employees: 500-999
Parent Co: Royal Packaging Industries

30548 Ulcra Dynamics
3000 Advance Lane
Colmar, PA 18915-9432 201-489-0044
Fax: 201-489-9229 800-727-6931
Manufacturer and exporter of water treatment systems
Estimated Sales: $500,000-$1 Million
Number Employees: 10-19
Parent Co: Severn Trent Services

30549 Ullman Company
299 Broadway # 17
New York, NY 10007-1914 212-571-0068
info@ullmanco.com
www.ullmancompany.com
Manufacturer and exporter of platters, plates, bowls, tumblers and pitchers
Partner: Marc Ullman
Chief Executive Officer: Zev Weiss
Executive VP: Marvin Lipkind
Estimated Sales: $10-20 Million
Number Employees: 1-4
Square Footage: 150000

30550 Ulma Packaging Systems
175 John Quincy Adams Road
Taunton, MA 2780 508-884-2500
Fax: 508-884-2501 info@ulmapackaging.us
www.ulmapackaging.com
Flexible packaging machinery
Manager: Candy Curtis
VP: Harvey Fine
Number Employees: 10-19
Type of Packaging: Consumer, Food Service, Private Label, Bulk
Brands:
Ulma

30551 Ulmer Pharmacal Company
PO Box 408
Park Rapids, MN 56470 218-732-2656
Fax: 218-732-5300 www.lobanaproducts.com
Vitamins, disinfectants, chemical detergents and soaps
President: Al Trudeau
National Sales Manager: Rick Dressler
Estimated Sales: $1-2.5 Million
Number Employees: 5-9
Parent Co: Ulmer Pharmacal Company
Brands:
Derm Ade
Lobana
Peri Garde

30552 Ultimate Textile
18 Market St
Paterson, NJ 07501-1721 973-523-5866
Fax: 973-523-5460 pecata@aol.com
www.ultimatetextile.com
Tabletop accessories including napkins, table cloths and skirting
President: Roger Glicman
Estimated Sales: $20-50 Million
Number Employees: 50-99

30553 Ultra Cool International
PO Box 57844
Sherman Oaks, CA 91413-2844 818-908-9208
Fax: 818-908-4058

30554 Ultra Industries
2801 Carlisle Ave
Racine, WI 53404 262-633-5070
Fax: 262-633-5102 800-358-5872
info@ultradustcollectors.com
www.ultradustcollectors.com
Dust collection equipment, cartridge collectors and pneumatic filter receivers
President: Ko Kryger
CFO: Evone Hagerman
General Manager: Dave Cleveland
Sales and Marketing Manager: Tom Meyer
Application/Sales Engineer: Daniel Hahn
Product Manager: Norman Pratt
Estimated Sales: $2.5-5 Million
Number Employees: 1-4
Square Footage: 2000

30555 Ultra Lift Corporation
475 Stockton Ave Ste E
San Jose, CA 95126 408-287-9400
Fax: 408-297-1199 800-346-3057
info@ultralift.com www.ultralift.com
Powdered material handling equipment products are specially designed for food and beverage equipment movers and installers
President: George Dabb
VP: Charae Hewphill
Estimated Sales: $1-2.5 Million
Number Employees: 5-9
Brands:
Kegmaster
Ultra Lift

30556 Ultra Pac
21925 Industrial Blvd
Rogers, MN 55374 800-324-8541
Fax: 763-428-2754 www.alcoa.com
Manufacturer and exporter of thermoform plastic packaging
President: Cal Krupa
Plant Manager: Rob Davis
Number Employees: 250-499
Parent Co: IVEX
Type of Packaging: Bulk

30557 Ultra Packaging
534 N York Rd
Bensenville, IL 60106 630-595-9820
Fax: 630-595-9710 ultrapkg@aol.com
www.ultrapackaging.com
Cartoning machines
President: Robert Stockus
Estimated Sales: $1-2.5 Million
Number Employees: 5-9

30558 Ultra Process Systems
733 Emory Valley Road
Oak Ridge, TN 37830-7017 865-483-2772
Fax: 865-483-2979 info@UltraProcess.com
www.ultraprocess.com
High temperature process equipment and services to the dairy and food processors

30559 Ultrafilter
3560 Engineering Drive
Norcross, GA 30092-2819 770-942-5322
Fax: 770-448-3854 800-543-3634
jtocio@ultrafilter-us.com www.ultrafilter-us.com
Worldwide supplier of compressed gas, steam and liquid purification equipment. Process filtration: culinary steam filters, sterile gas filters, process liquid filters, tank vent filters, 3-A approved sanitary filter housings, microfiltration cartridges. Compressed air filters and dryers, on-site compressed air quality testing: ultra-survey programs
President: Keith Hayward
Sales/Marketing: Jeff Touo
Number Employees: 20-49
Square Footage: 132000
Parent Co: Ultrafilter GmBH
Other Locations:
Ultrafilter
Scarborough ON
Brands:
Boreas
Buran
Ufmt
Ultrafilter
Ultrair
Ultrapac
Ultraqua
Ultrasep
Ultratoc
Ultrex

30560 Ultrafryer Systems
302 Spencer Ln
San Antonio, TX 78201 210-731-5000
Fax: 210-731-5099 800-545-9189
ultrafryersales@ultrafryer.com
www.ultrafryer.com
Manufacturer and exporter of gas and electric fryers, filters, breading tables, warmers, cookers and hoods
President: Ed Odmark
National Manager Sales: Steve Ricketson
General Manager: William Collins
Estimated Sales: $10-20 Million
Number Employees: 50-99
Square Footage: 75000
Type of Packaging: Consumer, Food Service
Brands:
Ultrafryer

30561 Ultrak
6252 W 91st Avenue
Westminster, CO 80031-2909 303-428-9480
Fax: 303-429-6609
Closed-circuit surveillance equipment
Managing Director: Tom Verzuh
Marketing Coordinator: Linda Pohl
Sales Manager: Chris Staniforth
Number Employees: 24
Square Footage: 7000

30562 Ultralight Plastic
6700 E Rogers Cir
Boca Raton, FL 33487 561-988-1676
Fax: 561-988-0928 palletbox@hotmail.com
Plastic pallets, pallet bases
CEO: Geoffrey Bourne
Estimated Sales: $12 Million
Number Employees: 5
Parent Co: Ultralight Plastic

30563 Ultrapar
13 Flintlock Drive
Warren, NJ 07059-5014 908-647-6650
Fax: 908-647-1281 800-647-6315
chrisparkinson@ultrapar.com www.ultrapar.com
Wholesaler/distributor of steam filters, culinary steam filtration systems, air sterilizing filters and filtration systems
President: Chris Parkinson
Vice President: Nancy Siconolfi
Estimated Sales: $500,000-$1 Million
Number Employees: 9
Square Footage: 7200

30564 Ultratainer
910 Industrial Boulevard
St Jean-Sur-Richelie, QC J3B 8J4
Canada 514-359-3651
Fax: 514-359-3653 ultra@ultratainer.com
www.ultratainer.com
Collapsible, reusable, stackable, stainless steel and wire mesh containers
CEO: Bert Gaumond
Plant Manager: Dave Lapierre
Purchasing Manager: Lina Levert
Estimated Sales: $10 Million
Number Employees: 30
Square Footage: 50000
Type of Packaging: Bulk

30565 Unarco Industries
400 SE 15th St
Wagoner, OK 74467 918-485-9531
Fax: 918-485-2131 800-654-4100
susan.tidwell@unarco.com www.unarco.com
Manufacturer and exporter of shopping carts, retail display fixtures, stainless steel tables and accessories, food service containers and carts and warehousing and stocking carts
President: Randy Garvin
Sales: Richard Wilkinson
VP International Sales: David Warneke
VP Sales: Richard Wilkinson
Estimated Sales: $50-100 Million
Number Employees: 250-499
Square Footage: 650000
Type of Packaging: Food Service

30566 Underwriters Laboratories
2600 N W Lake Rd
Camas, WA 98607-8542 877-854-3577
Fax: 360-817-6278 cec.us@us.ul.com
www.ul.com
Testing and certification service for product, environmental and public safety of appliances and equipment
President: Loring W Knoblauch
CFO: Michael Saltzmen
CEO: Keith E Williams
VP Sales/Marketing: Stuart Paul
Number Employees: 1,000-4,999

30567 Uneco Systems
8412 Autumn Drive
Woodridge, IL 60517 630-910-0505
Fax: 630-910-0558 800-700-6894
junewitz@att.net www.uneco.com
President: John Unewitz
Estimated Sales: $1-2.5 Million
Number Employees: 1-4

30568 Unette Corporation
1578 Sussex Turnpike
Building #5
Randolph, NJ 07869 973-328-6800
Fax: 973-584-4794 info@unette.com
www.unette.com

Contract packager of food colors, condiments, groceries, etc
President: Carol Ann Hark
Sales Service Coordinator: Dawn Stone
Estimated Sales: $4400000
Number Employees: 50-99
Square Footage: 240000

30569 Unex Manufacturing
50 Progress Pl
Jackson, NJ 08527 732-928-2800
Fax: 732-928-2828 800-695-7726
span@unex.com www.unex.com
Carton flow truck and storage products
President: Brian Neuwirth
CEO: Frank Neuwirth
CFO: Eilean Brant
VP Sales: Mark Neuwrith
R&D: Haward McIbaine
Marketing Director: Carolann Neuwirth
Northwest Sales Manager: Bill Link
Estimated Sales: $5 - 10 Million
Number Employees: 50-99
Brands:
Pathline
Spantrack

30570 Unger Company
12401 Berea Rd
Cleveland, OH 44111 216-252-1400
Fax: 216-252-1427 800-321-1418
info@ungerco.com www.ungerco.com
Supplier of packaging for bakery and deli products. Importer of polyethylene, polyprop and plastic shopping bags, and boxes. Consulting services available
President/CEO: Gerald Unger
Controller: Scott Smith
VP: Diane Tracy
Estimated Sales: $5-10 Million
Number Employees: 10-19
Type of Packaging: Food Service
Brands:
Bake'n Show
Deleez
Ungermatic

30571 Uni-Chains Manufacturing
Hjulmagervej 21
Vejle, DK 7100 457-572-3100
Fax: 457-572-3348 800-937-2864
admin@unichains.com www.unichains.com
Manufactures a comprehensive programs for internal transport offering chains in both steel and plastic, modular plastic belt and conveyor accessories.
President: Soren Pedersen
Number Employees: 10-19
Parent Co: Uni Chains

30572 UniFirst Corporation
68 Jonspin Rd
Wilmington, MA 01887 978-658-8888
800-455-7654
ufirst@unifirst.com www.unifirst.com
Supplier of workwear and textile services. Rent, lease, and sell uniforms, protective clothing, custom corporate workwear, floorcare, and other facility services products to all kinds of businesses.
President/CEO: Roland Croatti
Estimated Sales: $7.5 Million
Number Employees: 325

30573 UniMac
Shepard Street PO Box 990
Ripon, WI 54971-0990 920-748-3121
Fax: 920-748-4431 800-587-5458
sales@alliancels.com www.uniwash.com
Washer extractor, tumblers, topload washers, dryers
CEO: Thomas L Esperance
CEO: Thomas F L'Esperance
CFO: Bruce Roundf
Number Employees: 500-999

30574 UniMac Company
Shepard Street PO Box 990
Ripon, WI 54971-0990 920-748-3121
Fax: 920-748-4431 800-587-5458
www.uniwash.com
CEO: Thomas F L'Esperance

30575 UniPak
715 E Washington St
West Chester, PA 19380 610-436-6600
Fax: 610-436-6069 info@unipakinc.com
www.unipakinc.com
Paper boxes; also, printing services available
President: Steve Frain III
Structural / Graphic Design: Nicole Dana
Sales/Marketing: Teddy Frain
Customer Service: Angela Marchetti
Operations: Mike Golas
Supply Chain and Operations: Zak Allen
Purchasing/Estimating: Jenn Correa
Estimated Sales: $5 - 10 Million
Number Employees: 50-99

30576 (HQ)UniTrak Corporation
299 Ward Street
PO Box 330
Port Hope, ON L1A 3W4
Canada 905-885-8168
Fax: 905-885-2614 866-883-5749
info@unitrak.com www.unitrak.com
Manufacturer and exporter of bucket elevators, packaging machinery and conveyors
President: W Gorsline
Engineering Team Leader: Keith Douglas
Scheduling and Special Project: D Snoddon
Marketing Team Leader: Marie Lytle
Operations Manager: D Snoddon
Plant Manager: Ivan Patton
Number Employees: 10
Square Footage: 40000
Other Locations:
UniTrak Corp. Ltd.
Furness Vale, High Peak
Brands:
Bagstarder
Efficia
Tiptrak

30577 Unibloc-Pump Inc
1701 Spinks Dr SE
Marietta, GA 30067-8925 770-218-8900
Fax: 770-218-8442 info@flowtechdiv.com
www.flowtechdiv.com
Sanitary lobe pumps and valves
President/Owner: Harry Soderstrom
Estimated Sales: $4-8 Million
Square Footage: 25000

30578 Unibloc-Pump, Inc.
1701 Spinks Drive SE
Marietta, GA 30067 770-218-8900
Fax: 770-218-8442 info@uniblocpump.com
www.flowtechdiv.com
Aseptic processing equipment

30579 Unichema North America
4650 S Racine Ave
Chicago, IL 60609-3321 773-650-7600
Fax: 773-376-0095
Industrial chemicals, oleic, stearic and fatty acids, lubricating oils and greases
Estimated Sales: $50 - 100 Million
Number Employees: 100-249

30580 Unidex
2416 North Main Street
Warsaw, NY 14569 585-786-3170
Fax: 585-786-3223 800-724-1302
sales@unidex-inc.com www.unidex-inc.com
Lifting, positioning and manipulating devices including pallet lifting tables, adjustable height work benches, stainless steel lifts and carts, roll handling
President: Arthur Crater
CFO: Tom Baldwin
Quality Control: Don Cunningham
Sales: Sue Gardner
Estimated Sales: $2.5-5 Million

30581 Unifill Division of Elopak
30000 S Hill Rd
New Hudson, MI 48165-9828 248-486-4600
Fax: 248-486-4601 elopak@elopakus.com
www.elopak.com
Thermofilling
President: Robert B Gillis
Executive VP: Jorg Thiels
Estimated Sales: $40 Million
Number Employees: 100-249

30582 Unifiller Systems
7621 MacDonald Road
Delta, BC V4G 1N3
Canada 604-940-2233
Fax: 604-940-2195 888-733-8444
worldsales@unifiller.com www.unifiller.com
Manufacturs of stainless steel food grade filling and portioning systems for the baking and food service industries. Extensive line of bakery depositors, pumps/depositors and fully automated cake assembly/finishing lines
President: Kuno Kurschner
CEO: Markÿ Soares
CFO: Ballard Client
Vice President: Benno Bucher
R&D: Andy Fillers
Quality Control: Chris Moora
VP Marketing: Stewart MacPherson
Sales Director: Nickÿ Frost
Number Employees: 50
Brands:
Deco-Mate
Handi-Matic
Uni-Versal

30583 Unifoil Corporation
12 Daniel Rd
Fairfield, NJ 07004-2536 973-244-9900
Fax: 973-244-5555 www.unifoil.com
Manufacturer and exporter of laminated and coated aluminum foil; also, metallized and holographic paper and boards
President: Joseph Funicelli
CFO: William Mulooney
Quality Control: Robert Galloino
Sales Director: Robert Rumer
Plant Manager: Dwight Penrell
Estimated Sales: $20-50 Million
Number Employees: 50-99

30584 Uniforms to You & Company
5600 W 73rd Street
Chicago, IL 60638-6273 708-563-8932
Fax: 708-563-5003 800-864-3676
Uniforms and special clothing
Sr. VP Sales/Marketing: Michael DiMino
General Manager: Keith Nacker
Number Employees: 500-999

30585 Uniloy Milacron
10495 Highway M-52
Manchester, MI 48158 734-428-8371
Fax: 734-428-7095 800-666-8852
adinfo@uniloy.com www.uniloy.com
Blowmolding and structural foam machinery. Included are stretch blowmolding systems for PET. Molds, tooling, parts, training and technical support
President: Martin Lakes
Marketing Director: Doug Svik
VP Sales/Marketing: Dwayne Phillips
Human Resources Director: Michael Arnold
Operations Manager: Bob Spagnoli
Business Unit Manager: Jeff Newman
Purchasing Manager: Daryll Garton
Estimated Sales: $140 Million
Number Employees: 500-999

30586 Unimove, LLC
1145 C Little Gap Road
Palmerton, PA 18071 610-826-7855
Fax: 610-826-8422 unimove@ptd.net
www.unimove.com
Manufacturer and exporter of vacuum tube lifting systems
Director: Robert Shannon
VP: Vincent Julian Jr
Director Marketing: Ken Kasick
Operations: Alan Zimmermann
Purchasing: Charles Kistler
Estimated Sales: 1,000,000
Number Employees: 10
Number of Brands: 1
Square Footage: 140000
Brands:
Unimove

30587 Union Camp Corporation
5050 Ironton Street
Denver, CO 80239-2412 303-371-0760
Fax: 303-375-0718
Inner packaging materials including fiber corrugated boxes; also, enhanced graphics and pre-print available
Sales Manager: Ron Wise
General Manager: Paul Areson
Number Employees: 130
Square Footage: 130000
Parent Co: Union Camp Corporation

30588 **Union Carbide Corporation**
39 Old Ridgebury Rd
Danbury, CT 06817-0001 203-794-2000
Fax: 203-794-5664 800-568-4000
www.dow.com
Processor and exporter of ethylene oxide/ethylene glycol,coating materials,industrial performance chemicals,polyolefin resins and compounds, solvents intermediates and monomers, UCAR emulsion systems, speciality polymers andproducts
President: John Dearborn
CFO: Pedro Reinhardt
Estimated Sales: $5 Billion
Number Employees: 15,000
Type of Packaging: Bulk

30589 **Union Cord Products Company**
900 Estes Court
Schaumburg, IL 60193-4426 877-237-9098
Fax: 847-524-0811
Manufacturer and exporter of gaskets including braided, knitted, rubber insert and poly-jacketed cellulose
Estimated Sales: $1 - 5,000,000

30590 **Union Industries**
10 Admiral St
Providence, RI 02908 401-274-7000
Fax: 401-331-1910 800-556-6454
mike.kauffman@unionind.com
www.unionind.com
Manufacturer and exporter of flexible packaging
President: Harley Frank
Chairman: H Alan Frank
CFO: John Wilbur
Sales Director: Michael Kauffman
Estimated Sales: $23.5 Million
Number Employees: 125
Square Footage: 125000
Type of Packaging: Food Service, Private Label

30591 **Union Pen Company**
PO Box 220
Hagaman, NY 12086 518-842-6000
Fax: 203-531-0681 www.imprintsonline.com
Writing instruments including fine point, felt tip and ball point pens; also, advertising specialties including calendars, mugs, etc.; importer of roller ball pens
President: Robert Rosenthal
Sales/Marketing: Jim Zuzzolo
Purchasing Manager: David Laemle
Estimated Sales: $10-20 Million
Number Employees: 50-99
Square Footage: 26000

30592 **Union Plastics Company**
132 E Union St
Marshville, NC 28103 704-624-2112
Fax: 704-624-6119
Plastic and vinyl hose and tubing
President: Carroll H Osborn
Plant Manager: C Osborn
Estimated Sales: Below $5 Million
Number Employees: 5-9

30593 **Union Process**
1925 Akron Peninsula Rd
Akron, OH 44313 330-929-3333
Fax: 330-929-3034 eli@unionprocess.com
www.unionprocess.com
Manufacturers a broad line of wet and dry milling attritors and small media mills. Also offer a wide assortment of grinding media and provide toll milling and refurbishing services. Also the meading manufacturer of rubber inks forballoons, swim caps and other rubber products.
President: Arno Szegvari
National Sales Manager: Robert Schilling
Plant Manager: Ron Sloan
Estimated Sales: $5 - 10 Million
Number Employees: 20-49
Square Footage: 28000
Brands:
Attritor

30594 **Unipac International**
22 Chateau Square
Rochester, NY 14618-5135 716-244-6451
Fax: 434-817-0155 800-586-2711
Absorbent pads for pre-packaging meats, poultry, fish, sprouts, asparagus, apples, pizza, etc
President: Richard Engel
Number Employees: 20
Square Footage: 60000

30595 **Uniplast Films**
1017 Wilson Street
Palmer, MA 01069-1137 413-283-8365
Fax: 413-283-8278 800-343-1295
Film laminates and plastic and coextended film; exporter of plastic film
VP: Fredy Steng
Customer Service: Diane Fihal
Estimated Sales: $1 - 5 Million
Number Employees: 100
Square Footage: 80000
Parent Co: Uniplast Industries

30596 **Unique Boxes**
6548 N Glenwood Ave
Chicago, IL 60626 773-743-6617
Fax: 773-254-1023 800-281-1670
rrchagin@aol.com
Box partitions, set-up paper boxes and folding cartons
President: R Chagin
CFO: Rafael Chagin
Estimated Sales: Below $5 Million
Number Employees: 5

30597 **Unique Manufacturing**
1920 W Princeton Ave Ste 17
Visalia, CA 93277 559-739-1007
Fax: 559-739-7725 888-737-1007
unique@lightspeed.net
www.visalia-online.com/unique
Manufacturer and importer of silverware sleeves, paper napkin bands, beverage coasters, menu covers, chopsticks, flag food picks and paper parasols
President: Irwin Smith
Marketing: Paul Smith
Sales: Erwin Smith
Number Employees: 5-9
Square Footage: 4000

30598 **Unique Manufacturing Company**
1050 Corporate Ave
Suite 108
North Port, FL 34289 941-429-6600
Fax: 253-669-7645 sales@uniquemanuf.com
www.uniquemanuf.com
Importers and manufacturing of hospitality items. Custom printed stock flag food picks, beverage stirs, paper/foil parasols, napkins bands, silverware sleeves, chenille and foil decorator picks, plastic food picks, chop stickscoasters, paper glass covers, placemats, tray covers, and menu covers and binders
Owner: Michael Jakubowski
Estimated Sales: Below $5 Million
Number Employees: 1-4
Number of Products: 500
Square Footage: 2000
Type of Packaging: Consumer, Private Label
Brands:
American Ingredients
Dole Packaged Foods
Nakand
Nutrin Corp
Qa Products
Quick Dry Foods
Vita Foods

30599 **Unique Plastics**
372 Rio Rico Drive
Rio Rico, AZ 85648-3517 520-377-0595
Fax: 520-377-0696 800-658-5946
uniqueplas@aol.com
Round plastic trays
Estimated Sales: $1 - 5,000,000
Number Employees: 20-50
Square Footage: 14000

30600 **Unique Solutions**
2836 Corporate Parkway
Algonquin, IL 60102 847-540-1200
Fax: 847-540-1431 info@unique-solutions.com
www.unique-solutions.com
Product line includes inserting and labeling equipment produced in a continuous, perforated bandolier format in addition to that of two or three-dimensional premiums and labels that are inserted (In-Pakrs) or attached to the outside ofprimary packaging (On-Pakrs).
President: Mark Ulan
Chairman/CEO: Joyce Witt
CEO: C J Witt
Business Development Manager: Brian Dawson
VP Sales: Walter Peterson
COO: Jason Raasch
Production Manager: Norman Hendle Jr
Customer Service Representative: Christie Haack
Estimated Sales: $2.5-5 Million
Number Employees: 20-49
Square Footage: 52000
Parent Co: Unique Coupons

30601 **Unirak Storage Systems**
7620 Telegraph Rd
Taylor, MI 48180-2237 313-291-7600
Fax: 313-291-7605 800-348-7225
sales@unirak.com?subject=Inquiry%20from%20Website www.unirak.com
Manufacturer and exporter of racks including adjustable storage, pallet, galvanized, refrigerated, selective, drive-in/thru, deck, pallet flow, push-back and carton flow
Sales Director: Eric Gonda
Estimated Sales: $3 - 5 Million
Number Employees: 10-19
Number of Brands: 4
Number of Products: 110
Square Footage: 400000
Type of Packaging: Bulk
Brands:
Unirack Drive-In Rack
Unirak Pallet Rack

30602 **Unisoft Systems Associates**
4890 Trailpath Drive
Dublin, OH 43016 614-791-1592
Fax: 614-791-1592 800-448-1574
info@unisoft-systems.com
www.unisoft-systems.com
Food management software including inventory, recipe, invoicing, forecasting, nutrient, diet office management, bid list and daily activity
Technical Support: Robert Davis
Research & Development: Diane Clapp
Estimated Sales: $2.5-5 Million
Number Employees: 19
Square Footage: 4800
Brands:
Food System 4 Windows

30603 **Unisource**
5786 Collett Road
Farmington, NY 14425-9536 585-742-1110
Fax: 585-742-1171 800-864-7687
www.unisourcelink.com
Manufacturer and exporter of packaging materials; wholesaler/distributor of disposable food service products
Estimated Sales: Below $5 Million
Number Employees: 10
Parent Co: Unisource

30604 **Unisource Converting**
330 Stevens St
Jacksonville, FL 32254-6619 904-783-0550
Fax: 904-783-0968
Envelopes, paper, drinking straws and special extrusions
Marketing Director: Michael Skaff
Estimated Sales: $20-50 Million
Number Employees: 250-499
Brands:
Cardinal
Jaguar
Signet

30605 **Unisource Manufacturing**
8040 NE 33rd Drive
Portland, OR 97211 503-281-3781
Fax: 503-287-4818 800-234-2566
info@unisource-mfg.com
www.unisource-mfg.com

Manufacturer and engineering of industrial hoses and related products
President: Joseph Thompson
Quality Mgr.: Blu Matsell
National Sales Mgr.: Joseph Thompson
General/Human Resources Mgr: Dan Christiansen
Operations/Purchasing Mgr.: Ron Bateman
Purchasing Manager: Ralph Lorusso

30606 Unisource Worldwide
6600 Governors Lake Pkwy
Norcross, GA 30071 770-447-9000
Fax: 770-734-2000 800-864-7687
www.unisourceworldwide.com
Packaging systems, portioner and auto loader, tray denester and feeder with a Weiler ground beef grinder and Bizerba weigh scale and labeler, map bulk pack systems equipment, modified atmosphere packaging, tray and filmdistributors
President: Newell Holt
CEO: Al Dragone
Estimated Sales: $4.5 Billion
Number Employees: 4500
Square Footage: 1100
Parent Co: Georgia Pacific

30607 Unitech Scientific
12026 Centralia Rd Ste H
Hawaiian Gardens, CA 90716 562-924-5150
Fax: 562-809-3140 info@unitechscientific.com
www.unitechscientific.com
Glucose, fructose, L-malic acid, acetic acid, primary amino nitrogen and other food testkits
Member of the Board: Geoffrey Anderson
CEO: Lee Anderson
R & D: Ted Chou
Quality Control: Jim Sisowth
Estimated Sales: Below $5 Million
Number Employees: 5-9

30608 United Ad Label
3075 Highland Parkway
Suite 400
Downers Grove, IL 60515-5560 714-990-2700
Fax: 800-962-0658 800-423-4643
Manufacturer and exporter of pressure sensitive labels
President: Cal Laird
VP Marketing: Brad Baylies
New Markets Manager: Cheryl Hall
Estimated Sales: $1 - 5 Million
Number Employees: 100-250
Type of Packaging: Consumer, Bulk

30609 (HQ)United Air Specialists
4440 Creek Rd
Cincinnati, OH 45242-2832 513-891-0400
Fax: 513-891-4171 800-992-4422
uas@uasinc.com www.uasinc.com
Manufacturer and exporter of air filtration media including electrostatic precipitators, liquid coating and dust collection systems
President: Rich Larson
VP Marketing: Lynne Laake
Estimated Sales: G
Number Employees: 250-499
Square Footage: 152500
Other Locations:
United Air Specialists
Cincinnati OH
Brands:
Crystal-Aire
Dust-Cat
Dust-Hog
Smog-Hog
Smokeeter
Total-Stat

30610 United Bags
2508 N Broadway
Saint Louis, MO 63102 314-421-3700
Fax: 314-421-0969 800-550-2247
customerservice@unitedbags.com
www.unitedbags.com
Manufacturer and importer of bags including bulk, burlap, multi-wall, polypropylene, paper and cotton
CEO: Herbert Greenberg
CFO: Ruth Allen
VP: Todd Greenberg
Estimated Sales: $2.5-5 Million
Number Employees: 20-49
Square Footage: 300000

30611 United Bakery EquipmentComapny
19216 S Laurel Park Rd
Rancho Dominguez, CA 90220 310-635-8121
Fax: 310-635-8171 sales@ubeusa.com
www.ubeusa.com
VP: Mike Bastasch
Director of Domestic/nternational Sales: Tom Sheffield
Estimated Sales: $10 - 20 Million
Number Employees: 20-49

30612 United Bakery EquipmentCompany
15815 W 110th St
Shawnee Mission, KS 66219 913-541-8700
Fax: 913-541-0781 www.ubeusa.com
Manufacturer and exporter of slicers and baggers for breads, buns, tortillas, muffins, bagels, etc
President: Frank Bastasch
Vice President: Paul Bastasch
Sales Director: Bob Plourde
Estimated Sales: $20 - 50 Million
Number Employees: 50-99
Square Footage: 32000
Parent Co: United Bakery Equipment Company
Type of Packaging: Food Service, Private Label

30613 United Barrels
1303 Jefferson Street no. 210a
Napa, CA 94559-2470 707-258-0795
Fax: 707-259-5324
Wine barrels, French oak wine barrels
President: Scott Harrop
Estimated Sales: Below $5 Million
Number Employees: 1-4

30614 United Basket Company
58-01 Grand Avenue
Maspeth, NY 11378 894-545- 555
Fax: 718-326-3378 ubsales@verizon.net
www.unitedbasketco.com
Wholesale baskets and wholesale gift basket supplies and packaging supplies
Founder: Max Hanfling
CEO: Phil Hanfling
Square Footage: 56

30615 United Commercial Corporation
20 Avenue At the Cmn
Shrewsbury, NJ 07702-4801 732-935-0025
Fax: 732-935-0022 800-498-7147
wpearl@verizon.net
We supply plastic fabrication for dispensing hot and cold food merchandising equipment and menu systems
President: Wade Pearlman
Estimated Sales: $2 Million

30616 United Desiccants
PO Box 32370
Louisville, KY 40232-2370 505-864-6691
Fax: 505-864-9296
Manufacturer and exporter of desiccant absorption packs; also, humidity indicators for packaging
President: William Monin
General Manager: George Klett
Business Unit Manager: Richard Greenlaw
Number Employees: 300
Parent Co: United Catalysts
Brands:
Adsormat
Container Dri
Desi Pak
Desi View
Sorb Pak
Sorb-It
Tri-Sorb

30617 (HQ)United Electric ControlsCompany
PO Box 9143
Watertown, MA 02471-9143 617-926-1000
Fax: 617-926-4354 techsupport@ueonline.com
www.ueonline.com
Manufacturer and exporter of temperature control and detection devices including thermostats, pressure and temperature switches, transducers and sensors for general purpose and sanitary service
CEO: Dave Reis
Vice President: Peter Godfrey
CFO: Dennis Lonigro
Marketing Director: K Kotwal
Plant Manager: Mark Tardiff
Purchasing Manager: Cheryl O'Connell
Estimated Sales: $100+ Million
Number Employees: 200
Other Locations:
United Electric Controls Co.
Milford CT

30618 United Fabricators
1110 Carnall Avenue
Fort Smith, AR 72901-3756 479-782-9169
Fax: 479-783-5901 800-235-4101
Custom stainless steel food service equipment including chef's counters, canopies, sinks, work tables, etc
EVP: Jerry Bollin Jr
Sales Manager: Greg Donald
Office Manager: Jeanne Emery
Estimated Sales: $3.6 Million
Number Employees: 35
Square Footage: 160000
Type of Packaging: Food Service
Brands:
Unifab

30619 United Filters
PO Drawer 9417
Amarillo, TX 79105 806-373-8386
Fax: 806-371-7783 info@unitedfilters.com
www.unitedfilters.com
Manufacturer and exporter of string wound filter cartridges and vessels
Manager: David Otwell
Sales Manager (South): David Otwell
Sales Manager (North): Lynn Love
Estimated Sales: $500,000-$1 Million
Number Employees: 5-9
Square Footage: 50000
Parent Co: Perry Equipment Corporation
Brands:
United Filters

30620 United Fire & Safety Service
979 Saw Mill River Rd.
PO Box 53
Yonkers, NY 10710-0053 914-968-4459
Fax: 914-747-3983
Safety equipment, exhaust hoods and fans and fire suppression systems
President: Maureen Ulley
Estimated Sales: $1-2.5 Million
Number Employees: 5-9

30621 United Flexible
900 Merchants Concourse
Westbury, NY 11590-5142 516-222-2150
Fax: 516-222-2168 captivepackaging@aol.com
Manufacturer and exporter of plastic bags, printed roll stock and shrink packaging and lamination
President/CEO: Aldel Englander
Marketing Head: Elen Blonett
Estimated Sales: $5-10,000,000
Number Employees: 1-4

30622 United Floor Machine Company
7715 S South Chicago Ave
Chicago, IL 60619 773-734-0848
Fax: 773-734-0874 800-288-0848
unico1946@aol.com
www.unitedfloormachine.com
Manufacturer and exporter of burnishers, heavy duty floor polishers and scrubbers, carpet shampooers
President/Owner: Richard Leitelt
VP: David Leitelt
Estimated Sales: Below $5 Million
Number Employees: 5-9
Square Footage: 3000
Brands:
Aero
Floor Magic
Floorite
Glo-Pro
Uni-Vac
Unico

30623 **United Industries**
1546 Henry Ave
Beloit, WI 53511 608-365-8891
Fax: 608-365-1259 paulk@unitedindustries.com
www.unitedindustries.com
Stainless steel sanitary finishing and welding equipment; also, tubing and pipe
President: John Robb
Estimated Sales: $50-100 Million
Number Employees: 100-249

30624 **United Industries Group**
P.O.Box 8009
Newport Beach, CA 92658 949-759-3200
Fax: 949-759-3425 info@unitedind.com
www.unitedind.com
Manufacturer and exporter of storage tanks and wastewater treatment and water purification systems; also, designer of water bottling and water purification package plants
Manager: Jim Mansour
Quality Control: John Mansell
VP: M Mulvaney
Estimated Sales: $20-30 Million
Number Employees: 5-9

30625 **United Insulated Structures Corporation**
5430 Saint Charles Rd
Berkeley, IL 60163 708-544-8200
Fax: 708-544-8274 800-821-5538
office@unitedinsulated.com unitedinsulated.com
Design build firm specializing in architecture, engineering and contruction for the food industry
President: Lawrence L. Lantero
CEO: Frank Maratea Sr
VP: Rich Maleczka Jr
Marketing Director: Connie Maratea
Public Relations: Frank Maratea
Estimated Sales: $10-20 Million
Number Employees: 10-19
Square Footage: 70000

30626 **United Label Corporation**
65 Chambers St
Newark, NJ 07105 973-589-6500
Fax: 973-589-4465 800-252-0917
info@unitedlabelcorp.com
www.unitedlabelcorp.com
Labels
President: Joe Cic
Sales Manager: Harry Stillman
Estimated Sales: $2.5-5 Million
Number Employees: 10-19

30627 **United McGill Corporation**
One Mission Park
Groveport, OH 43081-1508 614-829-1200
Fax: 614-829-1291 personnel@unitedmcgill.com
Vacuum drying equipment
General Manager: James Beset
Sales Manager: Don Crockett

30628 **United Natural Trading Company**
96 Executive Avenue
Edison, NJ 08817-6016 732-650-9905
Fax: 732-650-9909 www.unfi.com
Importer, processor, packager, and wholesale distributor of nuts, dried fruit, seeds, trail mixes, natural and organic products, and confections.
President: Eric Zitelli
Controller: Bill Armstrong
Quality Assurance Manager: Celso Paguntalan
Marketing Staff: Irma Esparza
Director, Sales: John Anthony
Vice President, Operations: Robert Buzga
Operations & Productions Manufacturing: John Hochuli
Director, Purchasing: Vince Thaner
Estimated Sales: $15 Million
Number Employees: 100
Square Footage: 100000
Parent Co: United Natural Foods
Type of Packaging: Consumer, Food Service, Private Label, Bulk
Brands:
Expressnacks
Woodfield Farms

30629 **United Pentek**
8502 Brookville Road
Indianapolis, IN 46239-9427 317-359-3858
Fax: 317-353-9845 800-357-9299
sales@unitedpentek.com
Conveyor systems
Sales Manager: Jeffrey Smeathers
Estimated Sales: $10,000,000 - $25,000,000
Number Employees: 100-249

30630 **United Products & Instruments**
182 Ridge Rd # E
Dayton, NJ 08810-1594 732-274-1155
Fax: 732-274-1151 upii@worldnet.att.net
www.unico1.com
Spectrophotometers for food and beverage labs
Owner: Albert Chang
Estimated Sales: $3 - 5 Million
Number Employees: 10-19

30631 **United Receptacle**
1400 Laurel Blvd
Pottsville, PA 17901 570-622-7715
Fax: 570-622-3817 800-233-0314
united@unitedrecept.com www.unitedrecept.com
Manufacturer and exporter of fiberglass, steel aluminum, marble and cement waste receptacles; also, smokers' urns, planters and restroom accessories
President/CEO: Richard Weiss
CFO: Rick Piger
Vice President: Layton Dodson
Marketing Director: Tom Palangio
Plant Manager: George Derosa
Purchasing Manager: Margaret Zimmerman
Estimated Sales: $50-100 Million
Number Employees: 100-249
Square Footage: 145000

30632 **United Ribtype Company**
1319 Production Rd
Fort Wayne, IN 46808 260-424-8973
Fax: 260-424-0635 800-473-4039
sales@ribtype.com www.ribtype.com
Manufacturer and exporter of rubber stamps
Owner: Tom Beaver
VP Sales: John Peirce
Estimated Sales: $3,000,000
Number Employees: 20-49
Square Footage: 20000
Parent Co: Indiana Stamp Company
Brands:
Ribtype

30633 **United Seal & Tag Corporation**
1544 Market Cir
Building 8
Port Charlotte, FL 33953 941-625-6799
Fax: 941-625-3644 800-211-9552
info@unitedlabelcorp.com
www.unitedsealandtag.com
Manufacturer and exporter of pressure sensitive, embossed, hot stamp, acetate and vinyl foil labels; also, foil tags
Owner: Robert Freda
Estimated Sales: $500,000-$1 Million
Number Employees: 10-19
Square Footage: 10000

30634 **United Showcase Company**
PO Box 145
Wood Ridge, NJ 07075-0145 201-438-4100
Fax: 201-438-2630 800-526-6382
info@unitedshowcase.com
www.unitedshowcase.com
Manufacturer and exporter of stainless steel and brass showcases, nonrefrigerated salad cooler cases, collapsible cutting board brackets, pot and pan racks, sneeze guards, guide rails, tray slides, tray slide brackets and salad barshields
President/CEO: Robert Cline
CFO: Doris Cline
VP: Robert Cline II
R&D: Robert Cline
Quality Control: William Stevick
Marketing: Robert Cline II
Sales/Public Relations: Robert Cline
Operations/Production/Plant Manager: William Stevick
Plant Manager: Bill Stevick
Estimated Sales: $1-2.5 Million
Number Employees: 20-49
Square Footage: 60000

30635 **United Sign Company**
4900 Lister Ave
Kansas City, MO 64130 816-923-8208
Fax: 816-923-9512 unitsignkc@aol.com
Signs including metal, plastic and neon
President: David Pickett
Owner: Dave Pickett
Estimated Sales: $2.5-5 Million
Number Employees: 20-49

30636 **United Silicone**
4471 Walden Ave
Lancaster, NY 14086-9778 716-681-8222
Fax: 716-681-8789 info@unitedsilicone.com
www.unitedsilicone.com
Designer and manufacturer of product decorating and packaging equipment, supplies, tooling and heat seal solutions.
President: Kim Jackson
Marketing Manager: Laura Baumann
Sales Director: Eric Steinwachs
Estimated Sales: $20-50 Million
Square Footage: 18000
Parent Co: Illinois Toolworks
Type of Packaging: Consumer, Food Service

30637 **United Specialty Flavors**
999 Willow Grove Street
Suite 2-12e
Hackettstown, NJ 07840-5001 908-850-1118
Fax: 908-850-6099
Flavors and custom flavor delivery systems
President/CEO: William May
Number Employees: 30

30638 **United States Systems**
PO Box 5218
Kansas City, KS 66119 913-281-1010
Fax: 913-281-2901 888-281-2454
gregahawkins@aol.com
www.unitedstatessystems.com
Manufacturer and exporter of portable and stationary pneumatic conveyor systems for dry bulk goods including railcar unloading systems and in-plant transfers; also, storage silos, dust filters and bulk bag/box filling machines
President: Greg Hawkins
General Manager: Mark Aron
Sales Manager: Greg Hawkins
Estimated Sales: $2.5-5 Million
Number Employees: 5-9
Square Footage: 5000
Brands:
A/F Pot
Fwp - 7000
P/D Pot
Uss In-Tank Filter System
Vactank
Venturi 25 Air Conveyor
Venturi 30
Vibracone

30639 **United Steel Products Company**
P.O.Box 407
East Stroudsburg, PA 18301-0407 570-476-1010
Fax: 570-476-4358 usp@usprack.com
www.usprack.com
Manufacturer and exporter of roll-formed and structural steel storage rack systems
President: Martin A Skulnik
Sales: Mary Petronio
Plant Manager: Bob Micco
Purchasing Manager: Maria Sosa
Estimated Sales: $50-100 Million
Number Employees: 100-249
Square Footage: 390000
Parent Co: United Steel Enterprises
Brands:
Storage Rack-Steel-Clad

30640 **United Textile Distribution**
350 Shipwash Drive
Garner, NC 27529
Fax: 919-779-6065 800-262-7624
joel@uti-rags.com
www.unitedtextiledistribution.com
Manufacturer and exporter of disposable food service wipers including cloth and paper; also, towels and absorbent traffic mats; importer of towels
Owner: Rick EtheridgeGradin
Sales Representatives: Dave Shelton
Estimated Sales: $1 - 5 Million
Number Employees: 100-249
Number of Brands: 20
Number of Products: 4000
Brands:
Absorbant Rugs & Pads

Envirotex
Industrial Traffic Mats

30641 Unitherm Food Systems
502 Industrial Rd
Bristow, OK 74010 918-367-0197
Fax: 918-367-5440
unitherm@unithermfoodsystems.com
www.unithermfoodsystems.com
Manufactures a full range of stainless steel cooking, chilling, and pasteurizing systems, including spiral ovens, impingement ovens, continuous water cookers, vertical crusters, branders, and infra-red surface pasteurization, waterpasteurization and combination pasteurization systems, as well as a full range of clean room equipment, inclusing hands-free sinks, automatic bootwashers and drains.
President: David Howard
Marketing Director: Tom Van Doorn
Estimated Sales: Below $5 Million
Number Employees: 20-49

30642 Unitherm Food Systems Innc.
502 Industrial Rd
Bristow, OK 74010 918-367-0197
Fax: 918-367-5440
www.unithermfoodsystems.com
Steamers & spiral ovens, roasters, smokehouses and grilling systems, pasteurization equipment and chillers.

30643 Universal Aqua Technologies
2660 Columbia St
Torrance, CA 90503 310-618-9700
Fax: 310-618-1384 800-777-6939
avw@bottledwaterweb.com
www.severntrentservices.com
CFO: Howard Halem
VP: Marwan Nesicolaci
Quality Control Manager: Mark Wright
Estimated Sales: $10 - 20 Million
Number Employees: 100-249

30644 Universal Beverage Equipment
100 Leland Ct Ste B
Bensenville, IL 60106 630-227-0250
Fax: 630-227-0253 800-627-0026
www.ubeuniversal.com
Owner: Ed Morarty
Engineering/Technical: Gino Notardonato
Purchasing Executive: Joy Claffey
Estimated Sales: $5-10 Million
Number Employees: 10-19

30645 Universal Coatings
8511 Tower Park Dr
Twinsburg, OH 44087-2088 330-963-6776
Fax: 330-963-6743
Manufacturer and applicator of electrostatic powder paints, fluid bed, plastic dip, corrosion resistant and F.D.A. approved coatings
President: Ken Palik
VP Sales: Ken Palik
VP Operations: John Palik
Estimated Sales: $20-50 Million
Number Employees: 10-19
Square Footage: 40000

30646 Universal Container Corporation
11805 State Road 54
Odessa, FL 33556-3469 727-376-0036
Fax: 727-372-1957 800-582-7477
www.universalcontainer.com
Plastic drink containers
President: Kent Bissell
VP: Chip Williams
Estimated Sales: $2.5-5 Million
Number Employees: 18

30647 (HQ)Universal Die & Stamping
735 15th St
Prairie Du Sac, WI 53578 608-643-2477
Fax: 608-643-2024 breunigb@unidie.com
www.unidie.com
Manufacturer and exporter of stainless steel conveyor belts for tab conversion systems: for food, beer and beverage
Owner: Carol Baier
Research & Development: Bryan Jaedike
Quality Control: Steve Heyn
Sales Director: Gene Everson
Plant Manager: Karl Anderson
Estimated Sales: $5-10 Million
Number Employees: 20-49
Square Footage: 40000

30648 Universal Dynamics Technologies
100-13700 International Place
Richmond, BC V6V 2X8
Canada 604-214-3456
Fax: 604-214-3457 888-912-7246
info@brainwave.com
Manufacturer and exporter of software for automation process control equipment
Sales/Marketing Executive: Steve Crotty
Product Manager: Bill Gough

30649 Universal Folding Box
181 S 18th Street
East Orange, NJ 07018-3902 973-482-4300
Fax: 973-676-3628 info@disbrowmfg.com
www.disbrowmfg.com
Folding paper display boxes
President: Frank Pauza
General Manager: Steve Carretero
Estimated Sales: $20 - 30 Million
Number Employees: 100-250

30650 Universal Folding Box Company
555 13th Street
Hoboken, NJ 07030-6414 201-659-7373
Fax: 201-798-4126
info@universalfoldingbox.com
www.universalfoldingbox.com
Folding paperboard cartons
VP Manufacturing: Richard Berkey
Number Employees: 100-249
Square Footage: 520000

30651 Universal Handling Equipment
PO Box 3488, Station C
Hamilton, ON L8H 7L5
Canada 905-547-0161
Fax: 905-549-6922 877-843-1122
twalker@uhecl.com www.universalhandling.com
Waste disposal units and refuse compactors
President: David Gerard
CFO: James Hreljac
Director Sales/Marketing: Richard Kool
Estimated Sales: $20-50 Million
Number Employees: 10
Square Footage: 80000
Type of Packaging: Food Service

30652 Universal Industries, In
5800 Nordic Dr
Cedar Falls, IA 50613 319-277-7501
Fax: 319-277-2318 800-553-4446
sales@universalindustries.com
www.universalindustries.com
Manufacturer and exporter of bucket elevators and belt conveyors
President: Dean Bierschenk
Marketing: Drew McConnell
Sales: Mike Giaaratmnd
Operations: Carolyn Peterson
Purchasing: Gail Snyder
Estimated Sales: $9 Million
Number Employees: 70
Square Footage: 240000

30653 Universal Jet Industries
PO Box 70
Hialeah, FL 33011 305-887-4378
Fax: 305-887-4370
Manufacturer and exporter of air curtains
Chairman: L Bass
General Manager: B Warshaw
Number Employees: 12
Square Footage: 18000
Brands:
Uji

30654 Universal Labeling Systems
3501 8th Ave S
St Petersburg, FL 33711 727-327-2123
Fax: 727-323-4403 877-236-0266
sales@universal1.com www.universal1.com
A complete line of pressure sensitive labeling equipment
President: L Douglas Hall
Director Business Development: Michael Bieda
CFO: Ivan Campbell
Estimated Sales: $5 - 10 Million
Number Employees: 50-99
Square Footage: 40000

30655 Universal Machine Company
645 Old Reading Pike
Pottstown, PA 19464-3733 610-323-1810
Fax: 610-323-9343 800-862-1810
www.umc-oscar.com
Custom built machinery, general and CNC machining, drilling, boring, cutting, honing, welding, lathe and mill work
President: Richard Francis
Estimated Sales: $10-20 Million
Number Employees: 100-249

30656 Universal Marketing
1647 Pilgrim Ave
Bronx, NY 10461-4807 914-576-5383
Fax: 914-576-1711 800-225-3114
sales@unimar-ny.com www.unimar-ny.com
Wholesaler/distributor, importer and exporter of commercial kitchen equipment including freezers, refrigerators, coolers and fast food cooking equipment; serving the food service market
President: James Deluca
VP: Henry Muench
Estimated Sales: Below $5 Million
Number Employees: 7
Square Footage: 12000

30657 Universal Overall Company
1060 W Van Buren St
Chicago, IL 60607 312-226-3336
Fax: 312-226-1986 800-621-3344
email@universaloverall.com
www.universaloverall.com
Food handlers' shirts, butchers' frocks and beef luggers
President: Sanford Eckerling
Estimated Sales: $10-20 Million
Number Employees: 100-249
Brands:
Stone-Cutter
Universal

30658 Universal Packaging
PO Box 79769
Houston, TX 77279-9769 713-461-2610
Fax: 713-461-1459 800-324-2610
sales@upiweb.com www.upiweb.com
Manufacturer and exporter of vertical form/fill/seal machinery, conveyors, flexible packaging equipment, augers, coders and indexers
President: John Wylie
R & D: Bill Huhn
Sales: Jim Hooper
Estimated Sales: Below $5 Million
Number Employees: 10
Brands:
Mark Ii
Mark Iii

30659 Universal Packaging Machinery
965 Shadick Dr
Orange City, FL 32763 386-775-2969
Fax: 386-774-4900 800-351-8263
www.universal-ultraspeed.com
Industrial bottling machinery soft drink filling valves
Quality Control: Michael Purvis
Sales: Elihu Rivera
Purchasing/Shipping: Thomas Neff
Estimated Sales: $1-2 Million
Number Employees: 9

30660 Universal Paper Box
644 NW 44th St
Seattle, WA 98107 206-782-7105
Fax: 206-782-3817 800-228-1045
info@paperboxco.com www.paperboxco.com
Manufacturer and exporter of boxes including rigid, set-up and die-cut; also, PVC lids and bases
Owner: Greg Donald
Estimated Sales: Below $5 Million
Number Employees: 20-49
Square Footage: 36000
Type of Packaging: Consumer, Food Service, Private Label

30661 Universal Plastics
PO Box 8362
Greenville, SC 29604-8362 864-277-3623
Plastic bags
President: Richard Tollison
Estimated Sales: $2.5-5 Million
Number Employees: 20-49

30662 Universal Sanitizers & Supplies
PO Box 50305
Knoxville, TN 37950-0305 865-584-1936
Fax: 865-584-3203 888-634-3196
info@universalsanitizers.com
www.universalsanitizers.com
Consulting services including sanitation testing and analysis, employee training and vendor audits; wholesaler/distributor of industrial cleaners and sanitizers, water treatment products and conveyor lubricant/santizer systems
President: Amy Rigo
VP: Emilia Rico
Estimated Sales: $5 - 10 Million
Number Employees: 5-9
Square Footage: 8000

30663 Universal Sign Company and Manufacturing Company
PO Box 62032
Lafayette, LA 70596 337-234-1466
Fax: 337-234-2180 unisign@aol.com
www.unisignco.com
Neon and illuminated plastic signs
Owner: Dewey Boudreaux
Marketing Director: Michael Taylor
Estimated Sales: $1 - 3 Million
Number Employees: 10-19
Square Footage: 15000

30664 Universal Sign Company and Manufacturing Company
PO Box 62032
Lafayette, LA 70596 337-234-1466
Fax: 337-234-2180 unisign@aol.com
www.unisignco.com
Signs including neon, plastic and electric
Owner: Dewey Boudreaux
Marketing Director: Michael Taylor
Estimated Sales: $1 - 3 Million
Number Employees: 10-19
Square Footage: 15000

30665 Universal Stainless
14002 E 33rd Pl
Aurora, CO 80011 303-375-1511
Fax: 303-375-1626 800-223-8332
info@lpstorage.com
Stainless steel sinks, utlity cabinets, counters, racks, tables and shelving
Manager: Robert Buehler
Number Employees: 50-99
Square Footage: 40000
Parent Co: Leggett & Platt Storage Products Group
Brands:
Universal Stainless

30666 Universal Stainless
121 Caldwell St
Titusville, PA 16345 814-827-9723
Fax: 303-375-1626 800-295-1909
info@lpstorage.com www.univstainless.com/
Stainless steel sinks, shelving, utility cabinets, counters, tables and racks
Manager: Robert Buehler
Number Employees: 50-99
Square Footage: 60000
Parent Co: Leggett & Platt

30667 Universal Strapping
630 Corporate Way
Valley Cottage, NY 10989 845-268-2500
Fax: 845-268-7999 800-872-1680
info@universalstrapping.com
www.universalstrapping.com
Manufacturer and sells a complete line of non-metallic and steel strapping. This includes everything from hand grade, all the way up to machine grade strapping, which runs on the most sophisticated strapping machinery availabletoday.
President: Sol Obelander
Number Employees: 20-49

30668 Universal Tag
36 Hall Rd
PO Box 1518
Dudley, MA 01571-1518 508-949-2411
Fax: 508-943-0185 800-332-8247
info@universaltag.com www.universaltag.com
Printed labels and tags including pressure sensitive and nonpressure sensitive; also, printed specialties available
President: Armand Mandeville
Sales Director: Robert Meyers
VP Operations: Paul Mandeville
Estimated Sales: $3 - 5 Million
Number Employees: 20-49
Square Footage: 40000

30669 (HQ)University Products
PO Box 101
Holyoke, MA 01041-0101 413-532-3372
Fax: 413-532-9281 800-628-9281
www.universityproducts.com
Pressure sensitive labels
President: John Magoon
CFO: Bruce Riggott
Assistant Marketing Manager: Linda McInerney
Advertising Sales Manager: John Dunphy
President, Chief Operating Officer: Scott Magoon
Estimated Sales: $20 - 50 Million
Number Employees: 50-99

30670 University-Brink
131 Morse Street
Foxboro, MA 02035-5220 617-926-4400
Fax: 617-924-7965 ubmaint@prodigy.net
Electric, neon and plastic signs
Estimated Sales: $1 - 5 Million
Number Employees: 10

30671 Univex Corporation
3 Old Rockingham Rd
Salem, NH 03079 603-893-6191
Fax: 603-893-1249 800-258-6358
info@univexcorp.com www.univexcorp.com
Manufacturer and exporter of food preparation machines including ground beef fat analyzers, vertical, electric bench and floor model mixers, electric bench model vegetable peelers, slicers and shredders and gravity feed electric meatslicers
President: Dick Pereira
VP Marketing: Richard McIntosh
National Sales Manager: John Tsiakos
Estimated Sales: $10-20 Million
Number Employees: 50-99
Type of Packaging: Food Service
Brands:
Perfect Peeler

30672 Univogue
12091 Forestgate Dr
Suite 120
Dallas, TX 75243 214-341-7300
Fax: 214-341-7306 800-527-3374
info@univogue.com www.univogue.com
Manufacturer and designer of health care, restaurant, hospitality and chef uniforms
President: Curtis Hougland
Executive VP: David Barr
VP: Sylvia Hougland
Estimated Sales: $5 - 10 Million
Number Employees: 10-19
Square Footage: 40000

30673 Uniweb
222 S Promenade Ave
Corona, CA 92879 951-279-7999
Fax: 951-279-7989 800-486-4932
brietdyke@uniwebinc.com www.uniwebinc.com
Metal store fixtures and displays
CEO: Karl Weber
Estimated Sales: $20-50 Million
Number Employees: 100-249
Square Footage: 45000

30674 Upaco Adhesives
4105 Castlewood Rd
Richmond, VA 23234 804-275-9231
Fax: 804-743-8366 800-446-9984
info@worthenind.com
www.worthenindustries.com
Water-based, solvent-based and hot melt adhesives and coatings
President/CEO: Robert Worthen
Quality Control: Ralph Roane
Marketing/Sales: Steven Adams
Plant Manager: Dave Smith
Estimated Sales: $20-30 Million
Number Employees: 20-49
Square Footage: 40000
Parent Co: Worthen Industries

30675 Update International
5801 S. Boyle Ave
Los Angeles, CA 90058-3926 323-585-0616
Fax: 323-585-4021 800-747-7124
stephen@update-international.com
www.update-international.com
Manufacturer, importer and exporter of stainless steel kitchenware and utensils; also, air pots and steam table pans
Controller: Herman Yu
VP: Andrew Lazar
Marketing: Charles Arjavac
Vice President of Sales and Marketing: Steven Linzy
Operations: Jose Aleman
Estimated Sales: $5 - 10 Million
Number Employees: 20-49
Square Footage: 320000

30676 Upham & Walsh Lumber
2155 Stonington Ave.
Hoffman Estates, IL 60169 847-519-1010
Fax: 847-519-3434
contactus@uphamwalshlumber.com
www.uphamwalshlumber.com
Manufacturer and importer of wooden, steel and plastic pallets; also, skids and watermelon and onion bins
Partner: Chris Hayden
Office Manager: Lauren Kowalski
Sales Manager: Sean Hayden
Estimated Sales: $7 Million
Number Employees: 5-9

30677 Upper Limits EngineeringCompany
5662 La Ribera Street
Suite F
Livermore, CA 94550-2528 510-538-8500
Fax: 510-538-8533 888-700-0717
orenm@aol.com
Net weight filler, bag filler sealer
Estimated Sales: $5-10 Million
Number Employees: 10-19

30678 Upright
10715 Kahlmeyer Dr
St Louis, MO 63132-1621 314-426-4347
Fax: 314-426-0145 800-248-7007
sales@uprightinc.com www.wyksorbents.com
Manufacturer and exporter of sorbents, anti-slip compounds and spill response products
President: James Dunn
Sales Manager: James Meador
Production: James Callaham
Estimated Sales: $1-3 Million
Number Employees: 10-19
Square Footage: 80000
Brands:
Upright
Wyk

30679 Urania Engineering Company
198 S Poplar St
Hazleton, PA 18201 570-455-7531
Fax: 570-455-0776 800-533-1985
info@uraniaeng.com www.uraniaeng.com
Pouch handling system, heat sealer
President/CEO: Joe Zoba
Estimated Sales: $5-10 Million
Number Employees: 20-49

30680 Urnex Brands, Inc.
700 Executive Boulevard
Elmsford, NY 10523 914-963-2042
Fax: 914-963-2145 800-222-2826
info@urnex.com www.urnex.com
Manufacturer and exporter of coffee and tea equipment cleaning compounds, urn brushes, lemon covers, lemon wedge bags and shellfish steamer bags
President: Joshua Dick
R & D: Jason Dick
Quality Control: Bill Colter
Sales Manager: Joshua Dick
General Manager: Jay Lazarin
Assist. Mngr: Frankie Dominiquez
Estimated Sales: $5-10 Million
Number Employees: 10-19
Square Footage: 15000
Brands:
Urnex

30681 **Urschel Laboratories**
2503 Calumet Avenue
PO Box 2200
Valparaiso, IN 46384-2200 219-464-4811
Fax: 219-462-3879 info@urschel.com
www.urschel.com
Manufacturer and supplier of high capacity food cutting equipment
President: Robert Urschel
CFO: Dan Marchetti
VP Sales: Tim O'Brien
Regional Manager: Alan Major
Plant Manager: Dave Whitenack
Number Employees: 250-499
Square Footage: 250000
Type of Packaging: Food Service
Brands:
Comitrol
Urschalloy
Urschel

30682 **Ursini Plastics**
RR 2 High Falls Road
Bracebridge, ON P1L 1W9
Canada 705-646-2701
Swizzle sticks
Owner: John Ursini
Number Employees: 1-4

30683 **Useco/Epco Products**
P.O.Box 20428
Murfreesboro, TN 37129-0428 615-893-8432
Fax: 615-890-3196 800-251-1429
info@useco.com www.useco.com
Number Employees: 10-19
Parent Co: Standex International

30684 **Utah Paper Box Company**
340 W 200 S
Salt Lake City, UT 84101-1272 801-363-0093
Fax: 801-363-9212 info@upbslc.com
www.upbslc.com
Set-up boxes and folding cartons
President: Paul Keyser
CFO: Richard Seversln
VP: Mike Bean
Quality Control: Gordon Lambert
Production Manager: Paul Keyser
Purchasing Manager: Tom Boner
Estimated Sales: $20 - 50 Million
Number Employees: 100-249

30685 **(HQ)Utica Cutlery Company**
820 Noyes St
PO Box 10527
Utica, NY 13503-1527 315-733-4663
Fax: 315-733-6602 800-879-2526
info@uticacutlery.com www.uticacutlery.com
Manufacturers of pocket knives and importers of stainless steel cutlery
President: David Allen
CFO: Jess Gouger
VP (Walco): Kathleen Allen
International Sales Manager: Dave Meislin
Estimated Sales: $10 - 20 Million
Number Employees: 100-249

30686 **Utility Refrigerator Company**
7355 E Slauson Avenue
Los Angeles, CA 90040-3626 323-267-0700
Fax: 323-728-2318 800-884-5233
www.utilityrefrigerator.com
Manufacturer and exporter of commercial cooking equipment, refrigerators and freezers
Customer Service: Larry Gomez
Customer Service: Mark Parra
Customer Service: Martha Gonzalez
General Manager: Mark Champaigne
Estimated Sales: $.5 - 1 million
Number Employees: 160
Square Footage: 800000
Parent Co: Stery Manufacturing Company
Brands:
Dynasty
Jade Range
Utility

30687 **V&R Metal Enterprises**
272 39th St
Brooklyn, NY 11232-2820 718-768-8142
Fax: 718-768-0921
Lighting fixtures and metal fabrications including pizza pans
Owner: Hon Ng
Estimated Sales: $1 - 3,000,000
Number Employees: 1-4
Square Footage: 3000

30688 **V. Loria & Sons**
1876 Central Park Ave
Yonkers, NY 10710-2998 914-779-3377
Fax: 914-779-3587 800-540-2927
customerservice@loriaawards.com
www.loriaawards.com
Awards, stemware and name plates; also, imprinting available
Owner: Roger Loria Sr
VP: Roger Loria Jr
Production Manager: David DiPietro
Estimated Sales: $1-2.5 Million
Number Employees: 10-19
Square Footage: 120000

30689 **VC Menus**
P.O.Box 71
Eastland, TX 76448-0071 254-629-2626
Fax: 254-629-1134 800-826-3687
menusales@vcmenus.com www.vcmenus.com
Manufacturer and exporter of menus and covers
President: Cary Meeks
Secretary and Treasurer: Donald Eaves
Corporate Sales/Marketing: Trent Smith
Estimated Sales: $5-10 Million
Number Employees: 20-49
Brands:
Euro-Menu
Poly-Menu

30690 **VC999 Packaging Systems**
419 E 11th Ave
Kansas City, MO 64116 816-472-8999
Fax: 816-472-1999 800-728-2999
Sales.US@VC999.com www.vc999.com
Vacuum packaging machines, vacuum chamber machines, shrink systems, dryers, vacuum skin pack machines, automatic rollstock machines, preformed tray sealing machines, packaging accessories, packaging material and custom equipment related topackaging
Owner: Silvio Weder
Number Employees: 250

30691 **VCF Specialty Films**
1100 Sutton Street
Howell, MI 48843-1716 517-546-2300
Fax: 517-546-2984 888-823-4141
contactus@vcffilm.com www.vcffilm.com
Manufacturer and marketer of plastic flexible packaging materials to industrial manufacturers, packagers, distributors, and retailers in North America and internationally
Owner: Reva Kamins
Estimated Sales: $5-10 Million
Number Employees: 50-99

30692 **VCG Uniform**
5050 Weat Irving Park Road
Chicago, IL 60641 773-545-3676
Fax: 773-545-0876 800-447-6502
info@vcguniform.com www.vcguniform.com
In-stock and custom uniforms
CEO: Vince Gerage
Estimated Sales: $1-2.5 Million
Number Employees: 10-19
Parent Co: VCG
Other Locations:
Carlson-Murray
Chicago IL

30693 **VICAM, A Waters Business**
34 Maple Street
Milford, MA 01757 508-482-4935
Fax: 508-482-4972 800-338-4381
vicam@vicam.com www.vicam.com
Mycotoxin testing equipment
Estimated Sales: $2.5-5 Million
Number Employees: 20-49
Type of Packaging: Bulk

30694 **VIFAN**
1 Rue Vifan
Lanoraie, QC J0K 1E0
Canada 514-640-1599
Fax: 514-640-1577 800-557-0192
joseph.basa@vifan.com www.vifan.com
Manufacturer and exporter of BOPP film including metallized, coex, homopolymer, and specialty white films.
CEO: Vittoriano DiLuzio
Marketing: J Basa
Sales: Joseph Basa
Plant Manager: Greg Gillis
Estimated Sales: $185 Million
Number Employees: 245
Number of Brands: 78
Number of Products: 78
Square Footage: 130000
Parent Co: Vibac International BV
Type of Packaging: Food Service
Brands:
Vifan Bt
Vifan Cl/Cls
Vifan Cz

30695 **VINITECH**
1611 N Kent St
Suite 903
Arlington, VA 22209 703-522-5000
Fax: 703-522-5005 888-522-5001
usa@promosalons.com
Viticulture, viniculture, bottling equipment
Owner: Philippe Bazin
Number Employees: 1-4

30696 **VIP Real Estate Ltd**
3945 S Archer Ave
Chicago, IL 60632 773-376-5000
Fax: 773-376-5091 www.viprealestateltd.com
Manufacturer and exporter of folding boxes, printed folding cartons, point of purchase displays and polylined, freezer-coated boxes for frozen foods. Items manufactured to order
Owner: Sammy Cruz
VP: Ray Maza
Marketing: James Coen
Estimated Sales: $5-10 Million
Number Employees: 20-49
Square Footage: 212000
Type of Packaging: Consumer, Food Service, Private Label

30697 **(HQ)VMC Signs Inc.**
PO Box 3944
Victoria, TX 77903-3944 361-575-0548
Fax: 361-575-8464 vmcsigns@txcr.net
www.vmcsigns.com
Interior and exterior neon signs and menus; also, water filtration and air filtration systems
Owner: Tom Willis
General Manager: Aibie McLeroy
Estimated Sales: $1-2.5 Million
Number Employees: 10-19
Square Footage: 100000
Other Locations:
VMC Signs
Victoria TX
Brands:
Vmc-Nsa

30698 **VPI**
P.O.Box 138
Sheboygan Falls, WI 53085-0138 920-467-6422
Fax: 920-467-2692 vpi@vpicorp.com
www.spartech.com
Plastic film and sheet
President: P Gregory Mickelson
Senior Vice President - Human Resources: Robert Lorah
Estimated Sales: $10-20 Million
Number Employees: 100-249

30699 **VPI Manufacturing**
11814 S. Election Rd
Ste 200
Draper, UT 84020 801-495-2310
Fax: 866-307-0033 request@vpiengineering.com
www.vpimanufacturing.com
Manufacturer and exporter of heat shrinkable polyethylene cook-in bags for meat, poultry, etc
President: Aron Perlman
VP: Hessa Tary
Estimated Sales: $4114713
Number Employees: 20-49

30700 **VPI Mirrex Corporation**
105 Carson Dr
Bear, DE 19701-1319 302-836-5950
Fax: 302-836-7622 800-488-7608
www.networkflooring.net

PVC film and sheet products
President: Linda Pargoe
VP: Kevin Kerchner
Marketing: Gregory Pagonakis
Director Sales: Bob Kramer
Estimated Sales: $100-500 Million
Number Employees: 250-499
Square Footage: 181000
Brands:
Mirrex

30701 VR Food Equipment
7 Bush Park Ln
Penn Yan, NY 14527 315-531-8133
Fax: 315-531-8134 800-929-9367
info@vrfoodequipment.com
www.vrfoodequipment.com
Processing, packaging equipment; fruit, vegetable, aseptic processes
President: Steve Von Rhedey
Vice President: Steven Von Rhedey
Marketing Director: David Von Rhedey
Estimated Sales: $1 - 2.5 Million
Number Employees: 5-9
Number of Brands: 8
Number of Products: 30
Square Footage: 10000

30702 VRAM Solids
620 South Broadway
Albert Lea, MN 56007
Fax: 507-373-5937 888-373-3996
sales@vram.com www.vram.com
Pumps designed for the meat industry.
Parent Co: Olson Manufacturing Company

30703 (HQ)VT Industries
1000 Industrial Park
P.O. Box 490
Holstein, IA 51025 712-368-4381
Fax: 712-368-4111 800-827-1615
jfell@vtindustries.com www.vtindustries.com
Manufacturer and exporter of post-formed laminated and solid surface countertops; also, laminated multi-use components
President/Chief Executive Officer: Douglas Clausen
Chief Financial Officer: Randy Gerritsen
Vice President: Elizabeth Hansch
Director, Information Technology: Teri Luebeck
Vice President, Marketing: Trisha Schmidt
Vice President, Sales & Marketing: John Bowling
Vice President, Operations: Bruce Campbell
Plant Manager: Gary Henry
Estimated Sales: $32 Million
Number Employees: 534
Square Footage: 300000
Brands:
Casemate
Curvflo
Durallure

30704 VWR International LLC
Radnor Corporate Center, Bldg. 1, #200
P.O. Box 6660, 100 Matsonford Road
Radnor, PA 19087-8660 610-431-1700
Fax: 610-431-9174 www.vwr.com
Distributor of scientific products
Vice President, Finance: Michael Kinzler
SVP/General Counsel/Secretary: George Van Kula
Chief Information Officer: Charles Patel
Vice President, Marketing: Doug Ward
Vice President, Sales: Frank Iafrato
SVP, Human Resources: Paul Dumas
Manager, Purchasing: Melanie Bartleson
Estimated Sales: $665 Million
Number Employees: 6,500

30705 VWR Scientific
3745 Bayshore Blvd
Brisbane, CA 94005 415-468-7150
Fax: 415-468-1105 800-932-5000
solutions@vwr.com www.vwr.com
Distributors of scientific equipment, supplies, chemicals and furniture
President: Walter Zywottek
VP: Arne Brandon
Number Employees: 250-499

30706 Vac Air
5254 N 124th St
Milwaukee, WI 53225 414-353-5270
Fax: 414-353-5289 www.vac-airinc.com
Cutting and boning devices, vacuum systems, slaughtering equipment, dehairing machines and equipment, hock cutters
President: Lee Baertlein
CFO: Mary Baertlein
Quality Control: Lee Baertlein
Estimated Sales: $1 - 2.5 Million
Number Employees: 5-9
Brands:
Vac Airr

30707 Vac-U-Max
69 William St
Belleville, NJ 07109 973-759-4400
Fax: 973-759-6449 800-822-8629
info@vac-u-max.com www.vac-u-max.com
Manufacturer, importer and exporter of pneumatic conveying systems and ingredient storage systems; also, handling and batching systems
President: Stevens Pendelton
CEO: H Kadel
VP: Doan Pendleton
Estimated Sales: $10 - 20 Million
Number Employees: 50-99
Square Footage: 100000
Brands:
Vac-U-Max

30708 Vacuform Industries
1877 E 17th Ave
Columbus, OH 43219-1006 614-564-1300
Fax: 614-564-1399 800-366-7446
harned@totalimagespecialists.com
www.vacuform.com
Manufacturer and importer of interior and exterior signs, menus and image products including point of purchase displays
President: Kenneth Galloway
CEO: Dennis Kaufman
CEO: Dennis E Kaufman
Estimated Sales: $10-20 Million
Number Employees: 100-249
Square Footage: 200000
Type of Packaging: Food Service

30709 Vacumet Corp
20 Edison Dr
Wayne, NJ 07470 973-628-1067
Fax: 973-628-0491 bfoley@vacumet.com
www.vacumet.com
Manufacturer and exporter of metallized and holographic films and papers; also microwave susceptor and barrier films for flexible packaging, label stock available.
President: Robert Korowicki
Estimated Sales: G
Number Employees: 50-99
Parent Co: Scholle Corporation
Brands:
Barrier-Met

30710 Vacumet Corporation
7929 Troon Cir
Austell, GA 30168-7759 404-432-6300
Fax: 404-505-8984 800-776-0865
www.vacumet.com
Plain and metallized flexible packaging films and microwaveable interactive packaging
President: Raymond Woody
Manager: Steve Eulieno
Executive VP: Andy Terakawa
VP Staff/Marketing: Dave McKae
Plant Manager: Steve Euliano
Estimated Sales: $10 - 20 Million
Number Employees: 20-49
Square Footage: 41000
Parent Co: Marubeni America Corporation
Brands:
Himac
Himet

30711 Vacuum Barrier Corporation
4 Barten Ln
Woburn, MA 01801 781-933-3570
Fax: 781-932-9428 sales@vacuumbarrier.com
www.vacuumbarrier.com
Manufacturer, importer and exporter of cryogenic pipe systems including liquid nitrogen injection equipment for pressurizing hot filled beverages, food, etc
President: Russell Blanton
CFO: Leonard Gardner
Vice President: David Gorham
Quality Control and R&d: David Tucker
VP Sales: Edward Hanlon Jr
Purchasing Manager: Douglas Vanaruem
Estimated Sales: $5 - 10 Million
Number Employees: 20-49
Square Footage: 42000
Brands:
Linerter
Linjector
Semiflex

30712 Vacuum Depositing
1294 Old Fern Valley Rd
Okolona, KY 40219 502-969-4227
Fax: 502-969-3378
Sputter and vapor metallized film for solar control, microwave and anti-static products
President: David Bryant
Sales Manager: Teeny Lee
Estimated Sales: $5-10 Million
Number Employees: 20-49
Square Footage: 70000

30713 Vaisala
10 Gill St # D
Woburn, MA 01801 781-537-1000
Fax: 781-933-8029 888-824-7252
james.tennermann@vaisala.com
www.vaisala.com
Supplier of humidity measurement instrumentation for process and environmental monitoring. In addition to relative humidity and dewpoint, offers innovative measurement solutions for carbon dioxide, ammonia, and barometric pressure.Global organization that is ISO9002 certified and committed to excellence in all facets of the business
President: Steve Chansky
CEO: Steve Chansky
Marketing Director: Elizabeth Mann
Sales Director: Gerry Ducharme
Estimated Sales: $20 - 30 Million
Number Employees: 50-99

30714 Val-Pak Direct Market Systems
8605 Largo Lakes Dr
Largo, FL 33773-4912 727-393-1270
Fax: 727-399-3061 pat_fridley@coxtarget.com
www.valpak.com
Supplier and exporter of coupons
President: Joe Bourdow
Number Employees: 1,000-4,999
Parent Co: Cox Industries
Type of Packaging: Consumer, Bulk

30715 Valad Electric Heating Corporation
PO Box 577
Tarrytown, NY 10591
Fax: 914-631-4395 www.valadelectric.com
Manufacturer and exporter of food warming ovens, hot plates and food warming cabinets
President: Dante Cecchini
VP: Arthur Cecchini
Sales: Mike Sona
Estimated Sales: Below $5 Million
Number Employees: 10-19
Square Footage: 35000
Type of Packaging: Consumer, Food Service

30716 Valco
411 Circle Freeway Dr
Cincinnati, OH 45246-1284 513-874-6550
Fax: 513-874-3612
sales@valcocincinnatiinc.com
www.valcocincinnatiinc.com
Manufacturer and exporter of hot melt and cold glue dispensers
President: Greg Amond
CFO: Scott Soutar
CEO: Gregory Amend
Purchase: Jim Epp
Sales Manager: Paul Chambers
Estimated Sales: $5 - 10 Million
Number Employees: 100-249
Square Footage: 200000

30717 Valeo
555 taxter Road
Suite 210
Elmsford, Ny 10523 800-634-2704
Fax: 800-831-9642 800-634-2704
valeoinfo@valeonic.com www.valeoinc.com
Manufacturer and exporter of safety accessories including back support belts, wrist supports, knee supports, elbow support, and material handling gloves
President: Lisa Yewer
Estimated Sales: $5 - 10 Million
Number Employees: 20-49
Square Footage: 240000

30718 Valley City Sign Company
5009 West River Dr NE
Comstock Park, MI 49321 616-784-5711
Fax: 616-784-8280 www.valleycitysign.com
Plastic and illuminated signs
Owner: Sam Kovalak
CEO: Judson Kovalak Jr
CFO: Sam Kovalak
Sales Representative: Jack Vos
Sales Representative: Jean Hughes
Sales Representative: Jeff Surman
Estimated Sales: $5 - 10 Million
Number Employees: 50-99
Square Footage: 75000

30719 (HQ)Valley Container
850 Union Ave
Bridgeport, CT 06607 203-336-6100
Fax: 203-367-5266 flutedpartition@aol.com
www.valleycontainer.com
Manufacturer and exporter of corrugated shipping containers
President: Arthur Vietze Jr
CEO: Rudy Niederneier
VP Sales: Richard Jackson
Estimated Sales: $20 - 50 Million
Number Employees: 50-99

30720 Valley Container Corporation
858 Kingsland Avenue
Saint Louis, MO 63130-3112 314-652-8050
Fax: 314-652-2719
Corrugated boxes
General Manager: John Clark Sr
Estimated Sales: $5-10 Million
Number Employees: 20-49

30721 Valley Craft
2001 S Highway 61
Lake City, MN 55041 651-345-3386
Fax: 651-345-3606 800-328-1480
customer@valleycraft.com www.valleycraft.com
Manufacturer and exporter of hand and delivery trucks, trailers and forklift attachments, and storage equipment, custom-designed manufacturing and production equipment.
Owner: Dennis Campbell
Manager: Roger Goff
R&D: Josh Rodewald
Marketing: Daria Dalager
Sales: Dave Minck
Production: Tom Balow
Plant Manager: Roger Goff
Estimated Sales: $10-20,000,000
Number Employees: 100-249
Number of Brands: 6
Number of Products: 300+
Square Footage: 166000
Parent Co: Liberty Diversified International
Type of Packaging: Consumer, Private Label, Bulk
Brands:
Dura-Lite
Proline
Viking

30722 Valley Fixtures
171 Coney Island Drive
Sparks, NV 89431-6317 775-331-1050
Manufacturer and exporter of cabinet fixtures for bars, restaurants, casinos, hotels and stores
Sales Manager: Dillon Moore
Estimated Sales: $10-20 Million
Number Employees: 100-249
Square Footage: 50000

30723 Valley Lea Laboratories
4609 Grape Road
D4
Mishawaka, IN 46545-8259 574-272-8484
Fax: 574-273-0370 800-822-1283
Laboratory offering quality assurance and microbiological testing for food, dairy and water
President: Mary E. Nimtz
Number Employees: 10

30724 Valley Packaging SupplyCompany, Inc.
3181 Commodity Ln
Green Bay, WI 54313 920-336-9012
Fax: 920-336-3935
general@valleypackagingsupply.com
www.valleypackagingsupply.com
Manufacturer and exporter of pouches and bags for food and industry
President: Lance Czachor
Treasurer: Richard Czachor
Sales Director: Lance Czachor
Operations Manager: Ty Parsons
Purchasing Manager: Jean Rottier
Estimated Sales: $5 Million
Number Employees: 20-49
Square Footage: 272000
Type of Packaging: Bulk
Brands:
Valley

30725 Valspar Corporation
8725 W Higgins Rd Fl 10
Chicago, IL 60631-2717 800-845-9061
Fax: 847-541-2752 800-637-7793
flooringmarketing@valspar.com
www.valspar.com
Industrial and commercial floor coatings including solvent and water based epoxies and urethanes.
President: Greg McGreg
R & D: Vasant Kale
Technical Sales Representative: Jeff Fleming
Plant Manager: Vuk Trivanovic
Estimated Sales: $5-10 Million
Number Employees: 100-249
Square Footage: 164000
Parent Co: Valspar Corporation

30726 Valspar Corporation
P.O.Box 1461
901 3rd Avenue South
Minneapolis, MN 55402 612-851-7000
Fax: 612-851-3535 www.valspar.com
Provides coatings and metal decorating inks for food cans, beverage cans, aerosol, paint cans and paper, film and foil markets
Chief Executive Officer: Gary Hendrickson
EVP & Chief Financial Officer: James Muehlbauer
Executive Vice President: Steven Erdahl
Estimated Sales: $4.02 Billion
Number Employees: 9800

30727 Valu Guide & Engineering
1a Morgan
Irvine, CA 92618-1917 949-472-7336
Fax: 949-837-3481 800-825-8364
www.firstteam.com
Packaging equipment components
President: Joe Duenas
Number Employees: 100

30728 Valvinox
650 1st Rue
Iberville, QC J2X 3B8
Canada 450-346-1981
Fax: 450-346-1067 www.valvinox.it
Manufacturer and exporter of fittings, pumps, stainless steel valves, tubing and pipe
Administrator: Chantal Allard
Number Employees: 10,000
Parent Co: SQRM
Type of Packaging: Bulk

30729 Van Air Systems
2950 Mechanic St
Lake City, PA 16423 814-774-2631
Fax: 814-774-3482 800-840-9906
vanair@vanairsystems.com
www.vanairsystems.com
Manufacturer and exporter of compressed air dryers, condensation drain valves, after coolers, filters, oil/water separators, etc.; importer of filters
President: James Ourrie
CEO: J Currie
CFO: Mark Sunseri
VP: Jeff Mace
Sales: W J Ulrich
Estimated Sales: $20 Million
Number Employees: 55
Number of Brands: 8
Square Footage: 65000
Brands:
Dry-O-Lite

30730 Van Blarcom Closures
156 Sandford St
Brooklyn, NY 11205 718-855-3810
Fax: 718-935-9855 caps2lugs@aol.com
Manufacturer and exporter of metal and plastic caps
Chairman of the Board: Vincent Scuderi Jr
VP Sales/Marketing: John Scuderi
Estimated Sales: $20-50 Million
Number Employees: 100-249

30731 Van Dam Machine Corporation
81-B, Walsh Drive
Parsippany, NJ 07054-1010 973-257-7050
Fax: 973-257-7398 info@vandammachine.com
www.vandammachine.com
Printer
President: Andy Stobb
Chief Financial Officer: Kim Filippone
Estimated Sales: $5 - 10 Million
Number Employees: 50

30732 Van Der Graaf Corporation
1481 Trae Lane
Lithia Springs, GA 30122 770-819-6650
Fax: 770-819-6675 www.vandergraaf.com
Drum motors for conveyor belts.

30733 Van Leer Containers, Inc.
4300 W 130th St
Alsip, IL 60803-2094 708-371-4777
Fax: 708-371-2047 800-233-0004
www.greif.com
Steel and plastic shipping containers and drums, specialty containers, stainless steel batch containers and process drums
President: Tony Riley
Estimated Sales: $49.5 Million
Number Employees: 700

30734 Van Leer Flexibles
9505 Bamboo Rd
Houston, TX 77041 713-462-6111
Fax: 713-690-2746 800-825-3766
info@valeron.com www.valeron.com
High density polyethylene film for packaging
Estimated Sales: $25-50 Million
Number Employees: 250-499

30735 Van Lock Company
6834 Center St
Cincinnati, OH 45244 513-561-9692
Fax: 513-561-0314 800-878-1826
vanlock@excite.com www.vanlock.com
Locks, padlocks, cam locks and alarm systems
President: James Padjen
Owner: Chris Padjen
CFO: John Sali
Estimated Sales: $1-2.5 Million
Number Employees: 1-4

30736 Van Nuys Awning Company
5661 Sepulveda Blvd
Van Nuys, CA 91411 818-780-4868
Fax: 818-782-6837
awnings@vannuysawning.com
www.vannuysawning.com
Commercial awnings
President: James Powell
Estimated Sales: $5 - 10 Million
Number Employees: 50-99

30737 Van Pak Corporation
1188 Walters Way Lane
Saint Louis, MO 63132-2200 314-432-2224
Fax: 314-432-2227 800-811-7710
sales@vanpak.com www.vanpak.com
All types of conveyors, palletizers/depalletizers
President: Jon Vaninger
Estimated Sales: $5-10 Million
Number Employees: 10

30738 Van Waters & Roger
2256 Junction Avenue
San Jose, CA 95131-1290 800-659-5908
Fax: 408-456-9196 www.vwr-inc.com

Chemical compounding and manufacturing, coatings, inks and adhesives, electronics and precision cleaning, food and pharmaceutical, forest products, mining, oil, gas and CPI, professional pest control, waste management and watertreatment
General Manager: Jamie Hanks
President, Chief Executive Officer: Erik Fyrwald
Branch manager: Bob Crandall
Executive Vice President, General Counse: Amy Weaver
Number Employees: 83

30739 Van der Pol Muller International
4801 Harbor Pointe Dr.
Suite 1305
North Myrtle Beach, SC 29582 803-691-8941
Fax: 803-240-1384
benmuller@mullerinternational.com
www.mullerinternational.com
Engineering and consulting company for the food industry, specializing in the baking industry
President: Ben Muller
Estimated Sales: Below $5 Million
Number Employees: 2

30740 VanSan Corporation
16735 E Johnson Dr
City of Industry, CA 91745-2469 626-961-7211
Fax: 626-369-9510 info@vansan.com
www.vansan.com
President: Mark E Vanlandingham
Estimated Sales: $1 - 5 Million
Number Employees: 10-19

30741 Vance Metal Fabricators
251 Gambee Road
Geneva, NY 14456
Fax: 315-789-1848 800-234-6752
sales@vancemetal.com www.vancemetal.com
Stainless, structural and aluminum steel tanks
President: Joseph Hennessy
Vice President of Sales: Chris Jennings
Quality and Safety Manager: Brian Mott
Business Development Specialist - Sales: Wade Woodworth
Operations Manager: Len Visco
Purchasing Associate: Laura Gute
Estimated Sales: $10-25 Million
Number Employees: 50-99
Square Footage: 70000

30742 Vanco Products Company
1269 Massachusetts Avenue
Dorchester, MA 02125 617-265-3400
Bakery supplies
President: Chris Anton
Production Manager: Carl Hogenda
Estimated Sales: $5 - 10 Million
Number Employees: 10-19
Square Footage: 15000
Parent Co: Johnson's Food Products Corporation
Type of Packaging: Consumer

30743 Vancouver Manufacturing
765 S 32nd Street
Washougal, WA 98671-2519 360-835-8519
Fax: 360-835-8521
Wooden pallets
Owner: Al Ely
General Manager: Rob Burnett
Estimated Sales: $20-50 Million
Number Employees: 20-49

30744 Vande Berg Scales
770 7th St NW
Sioux Center, IA 51250-1918 712-722-1181
Fax: 712-722-0900 info@vbssys.com
www.vbssys.com
Conveyor scales, meat/produce sortation systems
Owner: David Vande Berg
Office Manager: Diane Vande Berg
Estimated Sales: $5 Million
Number Employees: 46
Brands:
Bicerba
Duran
Gse
Vande Berg Scales
Weigh-Tranix

30745 Vandereems ManufacturingCompany
40 Schoon Ave
Hawthorne, NJ 07506 973-427-2355
Fax: 973-427-2356
Wooden store fixtures including skids, boxes and laminated workbenches
President: John Vandereems
Estimated Sales: Below $5 Million
Number Employees: 1-4
Square Footage: 10000

30746 Vanguard Packaging Film
9970 Lakeview Ave
Shawnee Mission, KS 66219-2502 913-599-1111
Fax: 913-599-0096 800-772-1187
www.okurausa.com
President: John Campbell
Estimated Sales: $1 - 3 Million
Number Employees: 5-9

30747 Vanguard Technology
29495 Airport Rd
Eugene, OR 97402 541-461-6020
Fax: 541-461-6023 800-624-4809
vti1999@aol.com
www.vanguardtechnologyinc.com
High-efficiency gas fired domestic hot water heaters, gas fired booster water heaters
President: Stephen Kujawa
Estimated Sales: $1 Million
Number Employees: 5-9
Square Footage: 10000
Type of Packaging: Food Service
Brands:
Firepower
Powermax
Powerpac

30748 Vanmark Corporation
300 Industrial Pkwy
Creston, IA 50801 641-782-6575
Fax: 641-782-9209 800-523-6261
vmsales@vanmarkcorp.com
www.vanmarkequipment.com
Manager: Tom Mathues
Sales: Tom Jones
Operations: Rich Shafar
Estimated Sales: $5-10 Million
Number Employees: 20-49
Square Footage: 60000
Brands:
Vanmark

30749 Vanmark Equipment LLC
4252 S Eagleson Rd
Boise, ID 83705 208-362-5588
Fax: 208-362-3171 800-523-6261
sales@vanmarkequipment.com
www.vanmarkequipment.com
Manufacturer and exporter of food processing equipment for produce including tension blades and wedge, square and rectangular tension cutters
Owner: George Mendenhall
Estimated Sales: $2.5-5 Million
Number Employees: 10-19

30750 Vansco Products
2652 Lashbrook Avenue
South El Monte, CA 91733-1598 626-448-7611
Fax: 626-448-0221 sales@vansco.com
www.vansco.com
Manufactures adhesive application systems, cold glue, hot glue, hand and automatic and carton sealing
President/CEO: Gregory Amend
CFO: Scott Soutar
Vice President: Fred Van Loben Sels
R & D: Eric Sueyoshi
Sales Manager: Richard Goennier
Plant Manager: Grek Ameg
Estimated Sales: Below $5 Million
Number Employees: 10-19
Square Footage: 32000

30751 Vantage Pak International
221 South St
New Britain, CT 06051-3650 860-832-8766
Fax: 860-832-8766 800-839-9030
vpinorth@aol.com www.vantagepak.com
Packaging equipment: high speed, multi-size tray packer of cans and bottles, wrap around tray/case packers, integrated tray, shrink wrapping systems
Estimated Sales: $5 Million
Number Employees: 20-49

30752 Vantage USA
4740 S Whipple St
Chicago, IL 60632 773-247-1086
Fax: 708-401-1565 help@vantageusa.net
www.VantageUSA.net
Organic/natural & commodity wholesaler consolidator/supplier and logistics provider. Specializing in natural and private label products planning & development.
Owner: Dan Gash
Type of Packaging: Food Service, Private Label, Bulk
Brands:
Applegate Farms
Cargill
Colavita
Cucina Viva
Eberly
Excalibur
Excel
Gotham
Great Plains
Honeysuckle
Norbest
Prairie Grove
Reichert
Roma
Smart Choice
Taste It
Turano

30753 Vapor Corporation
551 S County Line Rd
Franklin Park, IL 60131-1013 630-694-5500
Fax: 630-694-2230 888-874-9020
info@vaporpower.com www.vaporpower.com
Manufacturer and exporter of steam generators and liquid phase heaters
Chief Operating Officer: Jim Pawlak
CEO: Bob Forslund
Sales Manager: B Corrigan
Number Employees: 250-499
Parent Co: Westinghouse Air Brake Company

30754 Varco Products
PO Box 915
Chardon, OH 44024-0915 216-481-6895
Fax: 216-481-6897
Fluorescent light fixtures and signs
President: Edward Vlack
VP: Norman Arnos
Number Employees: 8
Square Footage: 14000

30755 (HQ)Variant
7169 Shady Oak Road
Eden Prairie, MN 55344-3516 612-927-8611
Fax: 612-927-4624 info@variantinc.com
Manufacturer, importer and exporter of advertising products
President: Jerry Gruggen
Operations: Jan Davis
Controller: Tom Fournelle
Plant Manager: Ted Fors
Square Footage: 15000
Other Locations:
Variant
Minneapolis MN

30756 Varick Enterprises
P.O.Box 84
Winchester, MA 01890-0184 781-729-9140
Fax: 781-729-9143 800-882-7425
sales@euromachines.com
www.euromachines.com
Bar formers, bar take-off machines, batch kneaders, batch spinners, belting, cooling tunnel, plastic, steel, wire mesh, conveying, bars, hard candy, cookers, cooking equipment, cooling equipment
Estimated Sales: Below 1 Million
Number Employees: 3

30757 Variety Glass
201 Foster Ave
Cambridge, OH 43725 740-432-3643
Fax: 740-432-8693

Manufacturer and exporter of drug and laboratory glassware
President: Thomas Mosser
VP: Tim Mosser
Estimated Sales: $2.5 - 5,000,000
Number Employees: 10-19

30758 Varimixer
14240 South Laes Drive
Charlotte, NC 28273 800-222-1138
Fax: 704-583-1703 800-221-1138
mixer@varimixer.com www.varimixer.com
Commercial mixers and food preparation equipment
President: Richard Aversa
Sales Manager: Linda Dunn
Operations: Charlie Strate
Plant Manager: Charlie Strate
Number Employees: 5-9
Square Footage: 200000
Parent Co: ENODIS
Type of Packaging: Food Service

30759 Varitronic Systems
6835 Winnetka Cir
Brooklyn Park, MN 55428 763-536-6400
Fax: 763-536-0769 www.varitronicsystem.com
Manufacturer and exporter of electronic lettering systems and labels
Manager: David Grey
President: Cathy Hudson
Estimated Sales: $20 - 30 Million
Number Employees: 5-9
Parent Co: W.H. Brady

30760 Vasconia Housewares
6391 De Zavala Rd # 301
San Antonio, TX 78249-2159 210-545-4241
Fax: 210-558-9568 800-377-6723
vasconia@iamerica.net
Aluminum cookware including pots, pans and pressure cookers
Manager: Jack Nimmo
President: Olivia Lozano
Estimated Sales: Less than $500,000
Number Employees: 1-4
Brands:
Vasconia

30761 Vaughan Company
364 Monte Elma Rd
Montesano, WA 98563 360-249-4042
Fax: 360-249-6155 888-249-2467
info@chopperpumps.com
www.chopperpumps.com
Heavy duty chopper pumps for chopping and pumping solids in wastewater without plugging
President: Larry Vaughan
President: Dale Vaughan
CFO: Pattcornwell Cornwell
Sales Manager: Bob Simonetti
Chief Engineer: Glenn Dorsch
Estimated Sales: $10 - 20 Million
Number Employees: 50-99

30762 Vaughan-Chopper Pumps
1989 Peabody Road
Suite 235
Vacaville, CA 95687-6286 707-447-6300
Fax: 707-447-6400
info@rockwellengineering.com
www.rockwellengineering.com
Wine industry chopping pumps

30763 Vaughn Belting Company
200 Northeast Dr
PO Box 5505
Spartanburg, SC 29304 864-574-0234
Fax: 864-574-4258 800-325-3303
sales@vaughnbelting.com
www.vaughnbelting.com
Hoses and belts including conveyor, food grade, timing, nylon core, etc
VP: Brian Schachner
Manager: Amanda Hash
Estimated Sales: $5 - 10 Million
Number Employees: 10-19

30764 Vc999 Packaging SystemsInc.
419 E 11th Ave
Kansas City, MO 64116 816-472-8999
Fax: 816-472-1999 800-728-2999
Sales.US@VC999.com www.vc999.com
Manufacturer and supplier of packaging equipment, materials and supplies such as trays, bags/pouches, containers and film.
Founder: Bernhard Inauen
Number Employees: 250

30765 (HQ)Vector Corporation
675 44th St
Marion, IA 52302 319-377-8263
Fax: 319-377-5574
vector.sales@vectorcorporation.com
www.vectorcorporation.com
Designs, manufactures, and markets processing equipment for the processing of solid dosage form materials.
President: Steven Jensen
CFO: Tatsuo Matsugaki
VP Marketing: Greg Smith
Sales: Greg Smith
Production: Mike Douglas
Purchasing Director: Keith Wenndt
Estimated Sales: $25-50 Million
Number Employees: 100-249
Square Footage: 75000
Other Locations:
Vector Corp.
Huxley IA

30766 (HQ)Vector Packaging
2021 Midwest Road
Suite 307
Oak Brook, IL 60523 888-227-4647
Fax: 630-434-9650 800-435-9100
info@vectorpackaging.com
www.vectorpackaging.com
Packaging materials
President/CEO: Brian Samuels
VP Sales/Marketing: Dave McCaffrey
Sales Director: Dave Hugg
VP Operations: David Fiedler
Operations Director: Cyndi Christel
Number Employees: 10

30767 Vector Technologies
6820 N 43rd St
Milwaukee, WI 53209 414-247-7100
Fax: 414-247-7110 800-832-4010
sales@vector-vacuums.com
www.vector-vacuums.com
Manufacturer and exporter of dust collectors and vacuum cleaners and conveying systems
President: Stebe Schonberger
CFO: Chris Koe
Operations Manager: Bruce Kolb
Estimated Sales: $5 - 10 Million
Number Employees: 20-49
Square Footage: 45000
Parent Co: Vector Technologies
Brands:
Hepavac
Invader
Klean Scrub
Mdc
Rapid Response
Spartan
Titan
Vec Loader

30768 Vee Gee Scientific
13600 NE 126th Pl Ste A
Kirkland, WA 98034-8720 425-823-4518
Fax: 425-820-9826 800-423-8842
sales@veegee.net www.veegee.com
Manufacturer and importer of laboratory products including refractometers, volumetric glassware, porcelain and microscopes
Owner: Guy Mc Farland
Chairman of the Board: Guy McFarland
Estimated Sales: $5-10,000,000
Number Employees: 10-19

30769 Vega Mfg Ltd.
Unit 112-1647 Broadway Street
Port Coquitlam, BC V3C 6P8
Canada 604-941-0761
Fax: 604-941-0781 800-224-8342
sales@vegacases.com www.vegacases.com
Bakery Showcases
President: Walter Kollenberg

30770 Vegetarian Resource Group
PO Box 1463
Baltimore, MD 21203 410-366-8343
Fax: 410-366-8804 vrg@vrg.org
www.vrg.org
Nonprofit specializing in marketing vegetarian products
Executive Director: Debra Wasserman PhD
CEO: Debra Wasserman MD
CFO: Suzanne Havala DrPH
Number Employees: 5-9

30771 Velcro USA
P.O.Box 4806
Manchester, NH 03108 603-669-4892
Fax: 603-669-9271 800-225-0180
marketing@velcro.com www.velcro.com
Hook and loop industrial fasteners
President: Joan Cullinane
Estimated Sales: I
Number Employees: 500-999

30772 Vendome Copper & Brass Works
729 East Franklin St
Louisville, KY 40202 502-587-1930
Fax: 502-589-0639 888-384-5161
office@vendomecopper.com
www.vendomecopper.com
Manufacturer and exporter of copper and confectioners' kettles, distilling apparatus, vacuum pans, evaporators, coils, etc
President: Thomas Sherman
Estimated Sales: $5-10 Million
Number Employees: 50-99
Type of Packaging: Food Service

30773 Vent Master
1021 Brevik Place
Mississauga, ON L4W 3R7
Canada 905-624-0301
Fax: 800-665-2438 800-565-2981
nmozurkewich@delfield.com
www.ventmaster.com
Manufacturer and exporter of exhaust fans, air filters, fire safety equipment, heat recovery units, hoods and utility distribution and ventilating systems
Vice President: Mark Meulenbeck
Sales Director: Dan O'Brien
Operations Manager: Barry Carter
Estimated Sales: $1 - 5 Million
Parent Co: ENODIS
Type of Packaging: Food Service

30774 (HQ)Vent-A-Hood Company
PO Box 830426
Richardson, TX 75083-0426 972-235-5201
Fax: 972-231-0663 www.ventahood.com
Manufacturer and exporter of hoods
President: Miles Woodall Iii
CEO: Mileas Woodall
Quality Control: David Stiles C
Limited Partner: Miles Woodall III
National Sales Manager: Ed Gober
Estimated Sales: $10 - 20 Million
Number Employees: 100-249

30775 Ventura Foods
14840 Don Julian Rd
City of Industry, CA 91746-3111 626-937-0136
Fax: 626-336-3229 800-327-3906
www.venturafoods.com
Produces and extensive line of branded and private label products including: shortenings; oils; margarine; salad dressings; mayonnaise; sauces and syrups. Also contract packaging and export site.
Plant Manager: John Collie
Parent Co: Ventura Foods LLC
Type of Packaging: Consumer, Food Service, Private Label
Brands:
Gold N Sweet
Louana
Saffola

30776 (HQ)Venture Measurement Company
150 Venture Blvd
Spartanburg, SC 29306 864-574-8960
Fax: 864-578-7308 sales@venturemails.com
www.venturemeas.com
Manufacturer and exporter of level sensors
President: Mark Earl
CFO: Michael Hallinan
d: Roy Zielinski
Sales Manager: Rick Ayers
Estimated Sales: $30-50 Million
Number Employees: 50-99
Square Footage: 42000

Brands:
Bin-Dicators
Cap Level Iia
Pulse Point
Roto-Bin-Dicator

30777 **Venture Packaging**
311 Monroe St
Monroeville, OH 44847 419-465-2539
Fax: 419-465-2702 www.berryplastics.com
Plastics containers
Manager: Howard Weatherwax
Marketing Manager (Container Division): Brent Beeler
Estimated Sales: $20-50 Million
Number Employees: 250-499

30778 **Venturetech Corporation**
10720 Lexington Dr
Knoxville, TN 37932 865-966-2532
Fax: 865-675-2532 800-826-4095
venturet@aol.com
www.venturetechcorporation.com
Soap, detergents, bleaches, etc.; also, insecticides and insect control systems
President: Richards Wills
VP/GM: Brandon Wills
Graphics Manager/Web Development: Justin Marion
Estimated Sales: $2.5-5 Million
Number Employees: 10-19

30779 **Venus Corporation**
302 Industrial Dr
Blytheville, AR 72315 870-763-3830
Fax: 870-763-4529
Custom fabricated sheet metal including full CNC punching, forming and laser cutting
President: Clifford Carver Sr
CEO: Clifford Carver Sr
Engineer: Chris Carver
Plant Manager: Clifford Carver Jr
Estimated Sales: $2.5-5 Million
Number Employees: 10-19

30780 **(HQ)Verax Chemical Company**
PO Box 803
Bothell, WA 98041 360-668-2431
Fax: 360-668-5186 800-637-7771
info@veraxproducts.com
www.veraxproducts.com
Maintenance chemicals and supplies including hand and toilet bowl cleaners, disinfectants, mops, soap and floor polish; importer of cocoa mats
President: Julie Curkendall
Secretary/Treasurer: Sue Copeland
Estimated Sales: Below $5 Million
Number Employees: 5-9
Square Footage: 15000

30781 **VeriFone**
11700 Great Oaks Way Ste 210
Alpharetta, GA 30022 770-410-0890
Fax: 770-754-3422 www.verifone.com
Payment processing/transaction automation systems
Manager: Robbie Lopez
Director Marketing: Mike Matthis
Industry Marketing Manager: Kathy LeNoir
Product Marketing Manager: Ida Wu
Estimated Sales: $20-50 Million
Number Employees: 100-249

30782 **Verify Brand Inc**
7277 Boone Ave N
Brooklyn Park, MN 55428 763-235-1400
Fax: 763-235-1401 888-896-7882
verify@verifybrand.com www.verifybrand.com/
Verify Brand, Inc. provides product authentication system based on mass serialization. Verify Brand works with brand owners to design, construct, install and support turnkey product serialization and data formation, supply chainauthentication, unauthorized event management and product tracking, and reporting solutions based on the concept of mass serialization.
President: Kevin Erdman
Director Project Management: Curt Tomhave

30783 **Verilon Products Company**
452 Diens Dr
Wheeling, IL 60090 847-541-1920
Fax: 847-541-4525 800-323-1056
sales@verilonvinyl.com www.verilonvinyl.com
Vinyl strips for freezers and coolers
President: Sy Levine
VP: Kim Pullen
Marketing Director: Linda Mallon
VP Sales: Dorine Hanson
Estimated Sales: Below $5 Million
Number Employees: 10-19
Brands:
Verilon

30784 **Vermillion Flooring Company**
1207 S Scenic Ave
Springfield, MO 65802-5124 417-862-3785
Fax: 417-862-3789 sales@vermillionco.com
www.vermillion-flooring.com
Manufacturer and exporter of serving trays, pantryware, wood-chopping blocks, cedar accessories and wall decor; also, racks including wine, cookbook and mug trees
President: Art Thomas
VP: Gary Robinson
Special Markets Manager: Steve Baker
Estimated Sales: $10-20 Million
Number Employees: 100-249
Square Footage: 80000
Brands:
10th St. Bakery
Chef's Select
Classic Images

30785 **Vermont Bag & Film**
PO Box 135
Bennington, VT 05201-0135 802-442-3166
Fax: 802-442-3167
Plastic bags including sandwich, shopping, etc
Sales Manager: James Comi
Estimated Sales: $1 - 5 Million
Number Employees: 12

30786 **Vermont Container**
473 Bowen Rd
Bennington, VT 05201 802-442-5455
Fax: 802-442-6910
Corrugated boxes
VP: Gerald Lambert
Estimated Sales: $5 - 10 Million
Number Employees: 20-49
Parent Co: K&H Corrugated Corporation

30787 **Vermont Tent Company**
14 Berard Dr
South Burlington, VT 05403 802-863-6107
Fax: 802-863-6735 800-696-8368
www.vttent.com
Event rental and manufacturer of commercial gas convection ovens
Owner: John Crabbe
VP: Mike Lubas
Marketing: Krita Washburn
Estimated Sales: $5-10,000,000
Number Employees: 50-99

30788 **Vermont Tissue Paper Company**
RR 67a
North Bennington, VT 05257 802-447-7558
Fax: 802-447-8673
Tissue paper
President: Edward Woodard
Estimated Sales: $5 - 10 Million
Number Employees: 6

30789 **Vern's Cheese**
312 W Main St
Chilton, WI 53014 920-849-7717
Fax: 920-849-7883 info@vernscheese.com
www.vernscheese.com
Cheeses
President: Vern Knoespel
Estimated Sales: $20-50 Million
Number Employees: 20-49

30790 **Vernon Plastics**
25 Shelley Road
Haverhill, MA 01835-8033 978-373-1551
Fax: 978-373-6562 blair@victoryplastics.com
www.vernonplastics.com
Commercial awnings, plastic materials
President: Blair McIntosh
CFO: Joe Juliano
R&D: Dave Morse
VP: Mark Delaney
Marketing Manager: Steve Giaquinta
Estimated Sales: $50 - 100 Million
Number Employees: 25
Parent Co: Bordon

30791 **Veronica's Treats**
31 West Grove Street
Middleboro, MA 02346 508-946-4438
Fax: 508-946-4460 866-576-1122
info@veronicastreats.com
www.veronicastreats.com
Personalized cookies, brownies, and cupcakes
President: Hillary Souza
Number Employees: 5
Square Footage: 24000
Type of Packaging: Private Label

30792 **Versa Conveyor**
PO Box 899
London, OH 43140-0899 740-852-5609
Fax: 740-869-2839 versa@versaconveyor.com
www.versaconveyor.com
Manufacturer and exporter of gravity and power conveyor
President: Andrew Petitt
Chief Executive Officer: Chris Cole
Vice President of Project Management: Alfred Rebello
Chief Technical Officer: Ray Neiser
Senior Vice President of Sales and Marke: Jim McKnight
Vice President of Operations: Chris Arnold
Estimated Sales: $20-50 Million
Number Employees: 100-249
Parent Co: Tomkins Industries

30793 **Versa-Matic Pump Company**
800 North Main Street
Mansfield, OH 44902 419-526-7296
Fax: 419-526-7289 800-843-8210
customerservice.versamatic@idexcorp.com
www.versamatic.com
Line of air-operated, double diaphragm pumps and replacement parts, air decompression pumps, 3A sanitary pumps, and food processing pumps
Estimated Sales: $5-10 Million
Number Employees: 20-49

30794 **(HQ)Versailles Lighting**
1305 Poinsettia Dr Ste 6
Delray Beach, FL 33444 561-278-8758
Fax: 561-278-8759 888-564-0240
www.versailleslighting.com
Manufacturer, importer and exporter of lighting fixtures and metal tables
President: Max Guedj
CEO: Maurine Locke
CFO: Tung Nguyen
Quality Control: Rajendrauth James
Sales: Samantha Basdeo
Estimated Sales: $3 - 5 Million
Number Employees: 10-19
Square Footage: 20000
Other Locations:
Versailles Lighting
Delnay FL

30795 **Versatile Systems**
19105 36th Ave W Ste 101
Lynnwood, WA 98036 425-778-8577
Fax: 425-712-0326 800-262-1633
info@versatilemobile.com
www.versatilemobile.com
President: Bob Polychron
Finance Executive: Brenda McKena
Chairman of the Board: John Hardy
Estimated Sales: $100 - 250 Million
Number Employees: 50-99

30796 **Vertex China**
135 Brea Canyon Rd
Walnut, CA 91789 909-595-2429
Fax: 909-595-1993 800-483-7839
info@vertexchina.com www.vertexchina.com
Manufacturer, importer and exporter of dinnerware, chinaware and tableware including lead-free, microwave/dishwasher safe, cups, saucers, bowls, dishes, platters and mugs; custom decoration available
President: Hoi Shum
Sales: Ken Joyce
Estimated Sales: $10-20 Million
Number Employees: 10-19
Square Footage: 25000
Brands:
Alpine
City Square

Crystal Bay
Kentfield
Market Buffet
Rubicon
Sausalito
Vertex

30797 Vertex Interactive
23 Carol Street
Clifton, NJ 07014-1490 973-777-3500
Fax: 973-472-0814 www.vertexinteractive.com
Manufacturer and exporter of balances, weights, bar code and magnetic strip card readers, industrial scales and data collection software
Chairman: James Maloy
CEO/President: Ron Byer
Number Employees: 60
Parent Co: Vertex Industries
Brands:
Torbal

30798 Vertical Systems
2126 Chamber Center Drive
Ft. Michelle, KY 41017 859-485-9650
Fax: 859-485-9654 sales@vsilift.com
www.vsilift.com
Manufacturer and exporter of vertical lifts, stackers, conveyors, dumpers, and autostore units
President: Daniel Quinn
Member: Daniel Quinn
VP Sales: Steve Templeton
Estimated Sales: $5 - 10 Million
Number Employees: 20-49
Square Footage: 88000

30799 Vertique Inc
115 Vista Blvd
Arden, NC 28704-9457 828-654-7500
Fax: 828-654-8908 contactus@vertique.com
www.vertique.com
Vertique specializes in warehouse distribution equipment (Vertique systems and VPS picking and loading software) for the beverage and food industry, providing complete product services specifically designed to meet any manufacturingand distribution need.
Owner: Jay Stingel
VP: John Stingel
Senior Engineer: James Smith
Vice President Sales: Jeff Stingel
Estimated Sales: $20-50 Million
Number Employees: 20-49
Type of Packaging: Bulk

30800 Vesco
9 Camden Pl
New Hyde Park, NY 11040-3601 516-746-5139
Fax: 516-747-6911
Manufacturer, importer and exporter of recycling systems for food wastes including feeders, shredders, weight controllers, screeners, conveyors, packers and dust collection systems
Owner: Robert Vrabel
Estimated Sales: $300,000-500,000
Number Employees: 1-4
Square Footage: 500

30801 Vetrerie Bruni
3101 W Mcnab Rd
Pompano Beach, FL 33069 954-590-3990
Fax: 954-590-3991 800-432-4825
Glass containers for wine, champagne and food
Estimated Sales: $10-20 Million
Number Employees: 10-19

30802 Vetter Vineyards Winery
8005 Prospect Station Rd
Westfield, NY 14787 716-326-3100
Fax: 716-326-3100 wine@cecomet.net
www.vettervineyards.com
Wines
Co-Owner: Mark Lancaster
Co-Owner: Barbara Lancaster
Estimated Sales: $300,000-500,000
Number Employees: 1-4
Type of Packaging: Private Label
Brands:
Vetter Vineyards

30803 Viacam
313 Pleasant Street
Watertown, MA 02472-2418 617-926-7045
Fax: 617-923-8055 800-338-4381
viacom@viacom.com www.viacom.com
Rapid myocotoxin testing kits, tests for the detection of DON, fumonisin, ochratoxin and zearalenone and tests for the detection of listeria, salmonella and salmonella enteritidis
President and Chief Executive Officer: Philippe Dauman
CFO: Wade Davis
Senior Vice President of Investor Relati: James Bombassei
CFO: Majoire Radlo
Estimated Sales: $2.5 - 5 Million
Number Employees: 20-49

30804 Viatec
1230 W State St
Hastings, MI 49058 269-948-3860
Fax: 269-945-2357 800-942-4702
sales@viatec.com www.viatec.com
Manufacturer and exporter of dairy processors, cookers, coolers, stainless and fiberglass tanks, mixers and valves
Sales/Marketing Executive: Monte Ball
Sales (Stainless): Bob Johnson
Estimated Sales: $10-20 Million
Number Employees: 50-99
Square Footage: 52000
Brands:
Chemtek
Duratek
Permasan
Resinfab

30805 Viatec Process Storage System
500 Reed St
PO Box 99
Belding, MI 48809-1532 616-794-1230
Fax: 616-794-2487 klk@viatec.com
www.viatec.com
Manufacturer and exporter of dairy processors, cookers, coolers, stainless and fiberglass tanks, mixers and valves
Sales Director: Bob Johnson
Plant Manager: Ron Timmer
Estimated Sales: $5,000,000 - $9,900,000
Number Employees: 20-49
Square Footage: 52000
Parent Co: Viatec
Brands:
Chemtek
Duratek
Permasan
Resinfab

30806 Viatran Corporation
3829 Forest Park Way
Suite 500
North Tonawanda, NY 14120 716-773-1700
Fax: 716-773-2488 800-688-0030
solutions@viatran.com www.viatran.com
Sanitary, flush/CIP, solid state pressure, level and flow transmitters
Number Employees: 50-99

30807 Vibrac Corporation
19 Columbia Drive
Amherst, NH 03031 603-882-6777
Fax: 603-886-3857 sales@vibrac.com
www.vibrac.com
Cap torque testing laboratory and on-line
President: Tom Rogers
CEO: Quentin Searle
Vice President of Engineering: Bob Searle
General Manager: Tom Rogers
VP of Operations: Lisa Rogers
Production Manager: Scott Whipple
Plant Manager: Richard Brams
Estimated Sales: $3 Million
Number Employees: 10-19
Number of Brands: 2
Number of Products: 6
Square Footage: 15000
Brands:
Gold Bottle
Torgo

30808 VibroFloors World
1415 Highway 85 N
Suite 310-361
Fayetteville, GA 30214 770-632-9701
Fax: 770-632-9710 info@vibrofloorswg.com
www.vibrofloorsworldgroup.com
High performance and maintenance free flooring for commercial and industrial work facilities
President: Jackie Smith Jr
CEO: Dejana Gavrilovic
Project Manager: T Freddy Venos
Parent Co: VibroFloors WorldGroup, LLC

30809 Vicksburg Chemical Company
5100 Poplar Ave Fl 24
Memphis, TN 38137-4000 901-747-0234
Fax: 901-747-4031 800-227-2798
jhreeves@aol.com
Processor, importer and exporter of potassium nitrates, potassium carbonates, monammonium phosphates and monopotassium phosphates
Sales Manager/Distributor: John Reeves
Estimated Sales: $1 - 5 Million
Number Employees: 100-250
Type of Packaging: Private Label

30810 Vicmore Manufacturing Company
20 Grand Avenue
Brooklyn, NY 11205-1317 718-855-7758
Fax: 718-852-3768 800-458-8663
Manufacturer and exporter of double polished clear tablecloths, and vinyl and chemical aprons
President: Morris Steinberg
Estimated Sales: $5-10 Million
Number Employees: 50-99

30811 Victone Manufacturing Company
726 W 19th St
Chicago, IL 60616-1024 312-738-3211
Fax: 312-738-3214
Wire racks and stands
President: Joe Di Monte
Plant Manager: Raymond Di Monte
Estimated Sales: $2.5-5 Million
Number Employees: 10-19

30812 Victor Associates
514 Creekside Ct
Golden, CO 80403-1903 720-379-6850
Fax: 303-526-5069 mikesvictor@msn.com
Food consulting
C.E.O: Michael S Victor
Estimated Sales: $1 - 5 Million
Number Employees: 1

30813 Victoria Porcelain
7790 NW 67th St
Miami, FL 33166-2702 305-593-2353
Fax: 305-593-8363 888-593-2353
sales@victoriaporcelain.com
www.victoriaporcelain.com
Porcelain cups, bowls, plates, gravy boats, saucers, mugs, ovenware, teapots, etc.; importer and exporter of flatware and knives
President: Jose Espejo
VP Sales: David Yablin
Customer Service Manager: Phyllis Halpern
Estimated Sales: $2.5 - 5 Million
Number Employees: 1-4
Square Footage: 40000

30814 Victory Box Corporation
645 W 1st Ave
Roselle, NJ 07203 908-245-5100
Fax: 908-245-5670
Corrugated boxes
President: Alex Landy
VP Sales: Paul Bell
Estimated Sales: $20 - 50 Million
Number Employees: 100-249

30815 Victory Packaging, Inc.
3555 Timmons Lane
Suite 144
Houston, TX 77027 713-961-3299
Fax: 800-778-7210 800-486-5606
www.victorypackaging.com
Custom and stock corrugated boxes
President: Bryan Burnett
CFO: Vic Samuels
Estimated Sales: $62 Million
Number Employees: 900

30816 Victory Refrigeration
110 Woodcrest Rd
Cherry Hill, NJ 08003 856-428-4200
Fax: 856-428-7299 victory@victory-refrig.com
www.victory-refrig.com

Commercial refrigerators and freezers
President: Mark Whalen
CFO: Eileen Kurskin
R&D and Quality Control: Robert Hettinger
Director Sales Marketing: Jim Hurston
Estimated Sales: $30 - 50 Million
Number Employees: 1-4
Square Footage: 240000
Parent Co: Middleby Corporation
Brands:
Victory

30817 Videojet Technologies, Inc
1500 N Mittel Blvd
Wood Dale, IL 60191 630-860-7300
Fax: 630-616-3623 800-843-3610
info@videojet.com www.videojet.com
Manufacturer and exporter of coding and labeling equipment, printing inks and printing equipment; also, material handling equipment
President: Matt Trerotola
CEO: Robert Willett
VP Finance: Ranjana Bhagwakar
VP AR&D: John Folkers
VP Marketing: Adrian Fernandez
VP North American Sales: Kevin O'Connor
Public Relations: Theresa DiCanio
Operations: Dave Pratt
Purchasing: Lou Vidopivec
Estimated Sales: $395.4 Million
Number Employees: 2600
Square Footage: 250000
Parent Co: Donaher Corporation
Brands:
Cheshire
Excel
Inksource
Maxum
Sigmark
Totalsource
Triumph
Videojet

30818 Videx, Inc.
1105 NE Circle Blvd
Corvallis, OR 97330 541-758-0521
Fax: 541-738-5501 support@videx.com
www.videx.com
Manufacture portable bar code scanners and ibutton readers in addition to access control and security products, electronic locks
Marketing Director: Stephanie Ulrich
Sales Director: Tish Phillips
Number Employees: 59
Number of Brands: 25
Number of Products: 226
Brands:
Authorizer
Barcode Labeler
Cyber Key
Cyber Lock
Cyber Point
Duratrax
Duraward
Laserlite Mx
Laserlite Pro
Omni Wand
Pulse Star
Time Wand I
Time Wand Ii
Touch Access
Touch Alert
Touchprobe

30819 View-Rite Manufacturing
455 Allan St
Daly City, CA 94014 415-468-3856
Fax: 415-468-4784
Manufacturer and exporter of store fixtures
President: Brad Somberg
VP: Nha Nguyen
Number Employees: 10
Square Footage: 80000

30820 Vifan USA
1 Vifan Dr
Morristown, TN 37814 423-581-6990
Fax: 423-581-9998 866-843-2668
sales@vifan.com www.vifan.com
Bi-axially polypropylene films, film for industrial and flexible packaging applications
President: Pietro Battista
CFO: Thomas Mohr
Executive VP: Vittoriano Di Luzio
Estimated Sales: $10 - 20 Million
Number Employees: 100-249
Number of Products: 4
Square Footage: 280000

30821 Viking Corporation
210 Industrial Park Dr
Hastings, MI 49058 269-945-9501
Fax: 269-945-4495 800-968-9501
techsvcs@vikingcorp.com www.vikingcorp.com
Manufacturer and exporter of fire protection systems including wet and dry pipe, deluge and fire cycle; also, valves, sprinklers, spray nozzles and alarm devices
CEO: Tomdra Groos
CEO: Kevin Ortyl
Marketing Director: Sandra Wake
Sales Director: Bill Phair
Purchasing Manager: Jerry Dinges
Estimated Sales: $20 - 30 Million
Number Employees: 100-249
Parent Co: Tyden Seal Company

30822 Viking Identification Product
8964 Excelsior Blvd
Hopkins, MN 55343 952-935-5245
Fax: 952-935-3764 info@vikingid.com
www.intersearchsystems.com
Pressure sensitive, foil and silk-screened labels
Owner: Tim Paulson
Estimated Sales: Below $5 Million
Number Employees: 5-9

30823 Viking Industries
489 Tumbull Bay Rd
New Smyma Beach, FL 32168 386-428-9800
Fax: 386-409-0360 888-605-5560
info@thomasregional.com
www.thomasregional.com/gfl/viking
Manfacturer and exporter of hot melt adhesive application equipment for carton and case sealings; also, hot wax dispensing systems for wine bottle seals, cheese products and hot candy
Owner: Walter Warning Jr
VP Sales/Marketing: Douglas White
Estimated Sales: $2.5-5,000,000
Number Employees: 10-19
Square Footage: 40000
Brands:
Sys-Clean
Titan

30824 Viking Label & Packaging
5652 County Road 18
Nisswa, MN 56468 218-963-2575
Fax: 218-963-4849 info@vikinglabel.com
www.vikinglabel.com
Labels
Owner: Tom Wetrosky
Sales Manager: Kim Larson
Estimated Sales: $5-10 Million
Number Employees: 20-49

30825 Viking Machine & Design
1408 Viking Lane
De Pere, WI 54115-9265 920-336-1190
Fax: 920-336-2970 888-286-2116
sales@vikingmachine.com
www.vikingmachine.com
Cheese processing equipment for processing of mozzarella, provolone, and blue cheese
President, Founder: Don Lindgren Sr
Engineer and CFO: Dan Lindgren
Founder: Don Lindgren
Quality Control: Rick Felchlin
Sales Director: Rick Felchlin
Plant Manager: Rick Felchlin
Shop Foremanÿ/ÿProject Coordinator / Pur: Rick Felchlin
Estimated Sales: $1 - 2.5 Million
Number Employees: 10-19
Square Footage: 128640
Brands:
Hydra Form
Hydra Mold

30826 Viking Packaging & Display
620 Quinn Avenue
San Jose, CA 95112-2604 408-998-1000
Fax: 408-293-8162
Corrugated containers, protective foam packaging and point of purchase displays
President: Peter Keady
Production: Ed Hirle
Estimated Sales: $20-50 Million
Number Employees: 20-49
Square Footage: 80000

30827 Viking Pallet Corporation
9188 Cottonwood Lane
PO Box 167
Osseo, MN 55369 763-425-6707
Fax: 763-425-4400 sales@vikingpallet.com
www.vikingpallet.com
Wooden pallets
President: Tim Logan
CFO: Tim Logan
R&D/Quality Control: Tim Logan
Estimated Sales: Below $5 Million
Number Employees: 22

30828 Viking Pump
406 State St
Cedar Falls, IA 50613 319-266-1741
Fax: 319-273-8157 info.viking@idexcorp.com
www.vikingpump.com
Stainless steel rotary pumps and equipment
President: Paul Schwar
CEO: Jason Struthrs
CFO: Steve Huan
Sales Director: Kevin Rhodes
Number Employees: 1,000-4,999
Square Footage: 154
Parent Co: IDEX Corp.
Brands:
Acculobe
Classic Rotary Lobe Pumps
Concept Sq
Duralobe
Sterilobe

30829 Vilter Manufacturing Corporation
5555 S Packard Ave
Cudahy, WI 53110 414-744-0111
Fax: 414-744-3483 custserv@vilter.com
www.vilter.com
Compressors, condensors, air untis and custom packaged systems
President/CEO/COO: Ron Prebish
VP Business Development: Wayne Wehber
VP Sales/Marketing: Mark Stencel
VP Operations: John Barry
Estimated Sales: $43 Million
Number Employees: 100-249
Number of Brands: 4
Number of Products: 7
Square Footage: 400000
Brands:
450xl
Econ-O-Mizer
Power Pincher
Steady-Mount
Super Separator
Tri-Micro
V-Plus
Vmc
Vilter

30830 Vimco Inc.
300 Hansen Access Rd
King of Prussia, PA 19406 610-768-0500
Fax: 610-768-0586 www.vimcoinc.com
Lighting and lamp fixtures including food heating, industrial task, bench and assembly
President: Vic Maggitti, Jr
Sales Manager: Dave Gyuris
Administration: Brandon O'Brien
Plant Manager: Max DiRado
Estimated Sales: $1 - 3 Million
Number Employees: 5-9

30831 Vin-Tex
1 Mount Forest Drive
Ontario, CA N0G-2L2 519-323-0300
Fax: 519-323-4777 800-846-8399
sales@vintex.com www.vin-tex.com
Reusable packaging bags
Estimated Sales: $5-10 Million
Number Employees: 20-49

30832 Vincent Commodities Corporation
7182 US Highway 14
Middleton, WI 53562 608-831-4447
Fax: 608-833-0555 800-279-4447
vcc20@msn.com
President: Ronald Vincent
Estimated Sales: $2.5-5 Million
Number Employees: 5-9

30833 **Vincent Corporation**
2810 E 5th Ave
Tampa, FL 33605 813-248-2650
Fax: 813-247-7557 vincent@vincentcorp.com
www.vincentcorp.com
Manufacturer and exporter of screw presses for dewatering; also, pectin peel and citrus by-product machinery for liquids separation/solids concentration
President: Robert Johnston
Project Engineer: Bob Johnston
Estimated Sales: $2.5-5 Million
Number Employees: 20-49
Square Footage: 160000
Brands:
Vincent

30834 **Vine Solutions**
200 Tamal Plaza
Suite 100
Corte Madera, CA 94925-1172 415-927-3308
Fax: 415-485-6011 tnikaidoh@vinesolutions.com
www.vinesolutions.com
Consultant specializing in accounting services, strategic market planning, restructuring and restaurant start-up
Owner: Edward Vine
Chief Executive Officer: Edward Levine
Executive Vice President: John Priest
Director, Accounting: Takashi Nikaidoh
Estimated Sales: Below $5 Million
Number Employees: 1-4
Square Footage: 3600

30835 **Vineco International Products**
27 Scott Street W
St Catharines, ON L2R 1E1
Canada 905-685-9342
Fax: 905-685-9551 info@vineco.on.ca
www.vineco.on.ca
Manufacturer and wholesaler/distributor of wine and beer making kits
President: Rob Van Wely
CFO: Jason Hough
R&D: Sandra Sartor
Quality Control: Sandra Sartor
Marketing: Michael Hind
Estimated Sales: $5 - 10 Million
Number Employees: 45
Parent Co: Andres Wines
Type of Packaging: Consumer
Brands:
Bin 49
Brew Canada
California Connoisseur
European Select
Kendall
Lagacy
Ridge Classic
Ridge Showcase
V.I.P. Series

30836 **Vintage**
225 Clay Street
P.O.Box 231
Jasper, IN 47547 812-482-3204
Fax: 812-936-9979 800-992-3491
humanresources@jaspergroup.us.com
www.jaspergroup.us.com
Bar stools, tables, chairs and benches
President: Mike Elliott
Technical Services Manager: Amilcar Ubiera
Marketing Director: Lisa Kieffner
Sales Territory Manager: Jimi Barreiro
Operations Manager: Ronald Beck
Plant Manager: Mark Kluemper
Purchasing Manager: Dan Herman
Number Employees: 100-249
Parent Co: Jasper Seating Company

30837 **Virgin Cola USA**
3600 Wilshire Blvd
Los Angeles, CA 90010-2603 213-380-3433
Fax: 213-487-3631 www.virgincola.com
Owner: Virgil Sy

30838 **Virginia Industrial Services**
P.O.Box 532
Waynesboro, VA 22980-391
Fax: 540-943-7192 800-825-3050
Manufacturer and exporter of food processing equipment; also, repair and modification available
President: William Merrill
Estimated Sales: Below $5,000,000
Number Employees: 10-19
Square Footage: 20000

30839 **Virginia Plastics**
3453 Aerial Way Dr
Roanoke, VA 24018-1503 540-981-9700
Fax: 540-981-2022 800-777-8541
sales@vaplastics.com www.vaplastics.com
Manufacturer and exporter of packaging materials including polyethylene film and tubing
President: Mike Callister
Estimated Sales: $5-10 Million
Number Employees: 10-19

30840 **Virtual Packaging**
530 South Nolen Dr
Southlake, TX 76092 817-328-3900
Fax: 817-328-3901 888-868-7848
sales@virtualpackaging.com
www.virtualpackaging.com
Mock-ups, full-color bags, boxes, cans, labels, shrink film and wrappers
President: Monty Patterson
Marketing Manager: Paul Ferreris
Estimated Sales: Less than $500,000
Number Employees: 1-4

30841 **Viscofan USA**
50 County Ct
Montgomery, AL 36105 334-396-0092
Fax: 334-396-0094 800-521-3577
www.viscofan.com
Manufacturer and distributor of artifical casings for the meat industry
President: Jose Maria Fernandez
Sales VP: David Hambert
Product Manager: Tripp Ferguson
Estimated Sales: $1.2 Million
Number Employees: 100-249
Type of Packaging: Consumer, Food Service, Bulk

30842 **Visionary Design**
620 Wolfs Hollow Dr
Atglen, PA 19310 610-408-0540
Fax: 610-408-0541 vdi@epix.net
www.visionarydesign.com
Out of the box innovative creativity for the food industry
President: Eugene Gadlardi
Quality Control: Frank Oas
Estimated Sales: Below $5 Million
Number Employees: 3

30843 **Visions Epresso Service**
2737 First Avenue South
Seattle, WA 98134-1823 206-905-4381
Fax: 206-623-6710 800-277-7277
info@visionsespresso.com
www.visionsespresso.com
Espresso machine cleaners, espresso machines/accessories, filtration equipment, service espresso machines
Owner: Dawn Loraas
Manager: Bethanie Fritz
Estimated Sales: $500,000-$1 Million
Number Employees: 20-49

30844 **Visipak**
209 N Kirkwood Rd
St Louis, MO 63122-4029 314-984-8100
Fax: 314-984-0021 800-949-1171
marylou-pudlowski@sinclair-rush.com
www.visipak.com
Clear plastic tubing
Manager: Mike Boysen
Estimated Sales: $20-50 Million
Number Employees: 100-249

30845 **Viskase Companies**
8205 S Cass Ave Ste 115
Darien, IL 60561 630-874-0700
Fax: 630-874-0178 800-323-8562
info@viskase.com www.viskase.com
Manufacturer and exporter of nonedible, fibrous and cellulosic food casings and film including barrier, polypropylene and cook-in
President/CEO: Robert Weisman
VP/COO: Henry Palacci
VP/CFO/Secretary/Treasurer: Charles Pullin
VP Sales, North America: Maurice Ryan
VP Worldwide Operations: Bernard Lemoine
Estimated Sales: $20 Million
Number Employees: 1,000-4,999
Other Locations:
Viskase Manufacturing Plant
Kentland IN
Viskase Manufacturing Plant
Loudon TN
Viskase Manufacturing Plant
Osceola AR
Viskase Manufacturing Plant
Escobedo, Mexico
Viskase Manufacturing Plant
Sao Paulo, Brazil

30846 **Vista International Packaging, Inc.**
1126 88th Place
Kenosha, WI 53143
Fax: 262-694-4824 800-558-4058
sales@vistapackaging.com
www.vistapackaging.com
Forming and non-forming films, shrink bags, and tubular plastics for the poultry, meat and cheese industries.

30847 **Vista International Packaging**
1126 88th Pl
Kenosha, WI 53143-6538 262-694-2276
Fax: 262-694-4824 800-558-4058
sales@vistapackaging.com
www.vistapackaging.com
Custom food packaging for meat, poultry and cheese
President/CEO: David Hagman
CFO: Mike Mader
R & D: Lloyd Wallenslager
Quality Control: Marie McMahon
VP Marketing: David Jaeger
VP Sales: Paul Walter
Operations Manager: Mike Schultz
Estimated Sales: $10-20 Million
Number Employees: 100-249
Type of Packaging: Consumer, Food Service, Private Label, Bulk

30848 **Visual Marketing Associates**
9560 Pathway St Ste 1
Santee, CA 92071-4181 619-258-0393
Fax: 619-258-0790
Backlit and nonbacklit menu display systems and retro-fit menu systems; also, transparency illuminators
President: Dale Godfrey
Estimated Sales: Below $5 Million
Number Employees: 1-4
Square Footage: 17000
Brands:
Broadway Menu
Light Hawk

30849 **Visual Packaging Corporation**
91 4th Ave
Haskell, NJ 07420 973-835-7055
Fax: 973-835-0445
visualpackaging@optimum.net
www.visualpackagingcorp.com
Transparent plastic candy containers and boxes
President: Don Stackhouse
Estimated Sales: $500,000-$1 Million
Number Employees: 10-19

30850 **Visual Planning Corp**
1320 Route 9 #3314
Champlain, NY 12919 518-298-8404
Fax: 518-298-2368 800-361-1192
info@visualplanning.com
www.visualplanning.com
Scheduling boards-magnetic, perforated, T-card, boardmaster, fixed, rotating, planner sheets, PC software & accessories, AV equipment & supplies-easels, pads, lecterns, bulletin boards, conference cabinets, electronic boardsprojectors, screens, markers, Graphic Arts materials-templates, portfolios, filing systems, precision knives; Signs-labels, badges, nameplates, directory boards, magnetic, etc; office supplies.
President: Joseph Josephson
Marketing: Boris Polanski
Plant Manager: Stefan Neciorek
Purchasing Manager: Paul Harrison
Estimated Sales: $1 - 3 Million
Number Employees: 20-49
Type of Packaging: Private Label
Brands:
All Ways
Kling
Lecturers' Marker
Liquid Chalk

Magnetically Aligned
Overlay/Underlay
Triple Erasability System
Visitint
Visutate
Visutype

30851 Vita Craft Corporation
11100 W 58th St
Shawnee, KS 66203 913-631-6265
Fax: 913-631-1143 800-359-3444
info@vitacraft.com www.vitacraft.com
Manufacturer and exporter of stainless steel and multi-ply cooking utensils
CEO: Mamoru Imura
VP: John Ratigan
Estimated Sales: $10-20 Million
Number Employees: 100-249
Parent Co: Rena-Ware Distributors
Type of Packaging: Consumer, Food Service

30852 Vita Juice Corporation
10725 Sutter Ave
Pacoima, CA 91331-2553 818-899-1195
President: Fred Farago
Estimated Sales: $1 - 5 Million
Number Employees: 1-4

30853 Vita Key Packaging
6975 Arlington Ave
Riverside, CA 92503 909-355-1023
Fax: 909-355-1070 vitakey@earthlink.net
www.vitaminpackaging.com
Full service contract packaging, custom formulation and overflow packaging for the food and nutritional supplement industries
Owner: Douglas Delia
Director Operations: Robert Lockovich
Estimated Sales: $2.5-5,000,000
Number Employees: 20-49
Type of Packaging: Private Label, Bulk

30854 Vita-Mix Corporation
8615 Usher Rd
Cleveland, OH 44138 440-235-4840
Fax: 440-235-3726 800-437-4654
foodservice@vitamix.com www.vitamix.com
Manufactures highly engineered, high performance commercial food blenders and drink mixers built for outstanding durability and versatility
President: John Barnard
Marketing Director: D Scott Hinckley
Estimated Sales: $20 - 50 Million
Number Employees: 100-249
Brands:
Bar Boss
Blending Station
Mix'n Machine
Rinse-O-Latic
Touch and Go Blending Station
Vita-Mix Drink Machine
Vita-Prep
Vita-Pro

30855 VitaMinder Company
23 Acorn St
Providence, RI 02903-1066 401-273-0444
Fax: 401-273-0630 800-858-8840
sales@vitaminder.com www.medportllc.com
Manufacturer and exporter of multi-compartment vitamin containers, portable blenders for powdered drink mixes and food scales; importer of scales, tablet splitters/crushers and blenders
President: Larry Wesson
CFO: Larry Weffon
Quality Control: Vanessa Honwybhan
VP Sales: James Shuster
Sales Manager: Ken Michaels
Number Employees: 10-19
Parent Co: Ocean Group
Brands:
Vitaminder

30856 Vitakem Neutraceutical Inc
811 West Jericho Turnpike
Smithtown, NY 11787 855-837-0430
www.vitakem.com
Vitamins and supplements
President/CEO: Bret Hoyt Sr

30857 Vitatech International
2802 Dow Ave
Tustin, CA 92780-7212 714-832-9700
Fax: 714-731-8482 vitatech@vitatech.com
www.vitatech.com
Vitamins
President: Thomas Tierney
CFO: Toni Clubb
VP Sales/Client Services: Greg Williford
Estimated Sales: $20-50 Million
Number Employees: 200
Type of Packaging: Private Label

30858 Vitex Packaging
1137 Progress Rd
Suffolk, VA 23434 757-538-3115
Fax: 757-538-3120 www.vitexpackaging.com
Paper based flexible packaging tea tags and envelopes
President: Anthony Maclaurin
Estimated Sales: $20 Million
Number Employees: 100-249

30859 Vitro Packaging
5200 Tennyson Pkwy Ste 100
Plano, TX 75024 469-443-1100
Fax: 469-443-1258 800-766-0600
Dhesche@vitro.com
www.vitro.com/vitro_packaging/ingles/
Stock and private design glass containers.
President: John Shaddox
Vice President Finance: Kevin Jackson
Vice President Sales & Marketing: Doug Hesche
Business Manager: Gabriel Gentile
Estimated Sales: $20-50 Million
Number Employees: 50-99
Parent Co: Vitro S.A.

30860 Vitro Packaging
3700 Preston Rd
Plano, TX 75093-7440 972-596-6483
Fax: 972-960-1076 800-766-0600
evprbelk@vto.com www.vto.com
Glass bottles in all shapes, sizes and colors
Estimated Sales: $20-50 Million
Number Employees: 50-99

30861 Vitro Seating Products
201 Madison St
Saint Louis, MO 63102 314-241-2265
Fax: 314-241-8723 800-325-7093
mail@vitroseating.com www.vitroseating.com
Manufacturer and exporter of hotel, restaurant and bar furniture including fountain and bar stools, booths, chairs and tables
CEO: Stephen Scott
VP of Admin./National Sales Mngr: Mike Scott
Senior Designer: Kim Luce
CSR/Sales: Linda Meadows
Accounts Receivable Manager: Lauren Rush
VP of Manufacturing: Steve Scott Jr.
Purchasing Mngr./CSR: Matt Schleicher
Estimated Sales: $5-10 Million
Number Employees: 50-99
Square Footage: 225000
Type of Packaging: Food Service

30862 Vivid Packaging Inc
26055 Emery Road
Suite K
Cleveland, OH 44128 216-595-1563
Fax: 216-595-1564 877-752-2250
sales@vividpackaging.com
www.vividpackaging.com
Packaging supplies
Owner: Allan Saltz
Executive: Cheryl Piccirilli
Sales Director: Glen Bloomberg
Estimated Sales: $1.4 Million
Number Employees: 7
Square Footage: 10000

30863 Vivolac Cultures
6108 W. Stoner Drive
Greenfield, IN 46140 317-359-9528
Fax: 317-356-8450 800-848-6522
vivolac@iquest.net www.vivolac.com
Laboratory specializing in dairy and food microbiological testing, consultation and sanitation
Owner, President & CEO: Wesley D. Sing Ph. D.
Chief Marketing Officer: Philip Reinhardt
Technical Sales Manager: Rossana Reyes
Estimated Sales: $1-2.5 Million
Number Employees: 20-49

30864 Vogel Lubrication Corporation
1008 Jefferson Ave
Newport News, VA 23607-6197 757-380-8585
Fax: 757-380-0709 www.vogel-lube.com
Centralized lubrication systems and liquid pumps for industry
President: Robert Amen
Quality Control: Thomas Steinhoff
Estimated Sales: $10 - 20 Million
Number Employees: 50-99

30865 Vogt-Tube Ice
1000 W Ormsby Ave Unit 19
Louisville, KY 40210 502-635-3000
Fax: 502-634-0479 800-853-8648
info@vogtice.com www.vogtice.com
Manufacturer and exporter ice machines including cubers and crushers
President/CEO: Mark Barter
Chairman: J.T Sim
CEO: Mark Barter
Commercial Marketing Manager: Tim Burke
Sales Support Manager: John Whitmer
Estimated Sales: $5 - 10 Million
Number Employees: 100-249
Type of Packaging: Food Service
Brands:
Vogt Tube-Ice

30866 Voigt Lighting Industries Inc.
135 Fort Lee Road
Suite 10
Leonia, NJ 07605-2247 201-461-2493
Fax: 201-461-7827 voigtlight@aol.com
FDA compliant lighting fixtures for food processing areas and warehouses
President: Frank Stein
CFO: Frank Stein
Estimated Sales: Below $5 Million
Number Employees: 4
Brands:
Asym-A-Lyte
Frugalume
Korode-Not

30867 Volckening
6700 3rd Ave
Brooklyn, NY 11220-5296 718-748-0294
Fax: 718-748-2811 info@volckening.com
www.volckening.com
Manufacturer and exporter of replacement parts for beverage filling machinery; also, industrial brushes
Chairman: William Schneider
CEO: F Schneider
Estimated Sales: $10-20 Million
Number Employees: 100-249
Square Footage: 25000

30868 (HQ)Volk Corporation
23936 Industrial Park Dr
Farmington Hills, MI 48335 248-477-6700
Fax: 248-478-6884 800-521-6799
sales@volkcorp.com www.volkcorp.com
Manufacturer and exporter of signs, rubber stamps, markers, name badges, envelopes, tapes, tape dispensers, advertising novelties, printing dies, zinc plates, steel stamps, ink cartridges, etc
President: Bill Woolfall
Marketing Director: Todd Cruthfield
Sales Director: Ron Harper
Plant Manager: Donald Schultz
Purchasing Manager: Scott Szumanski
Estimated Sales: $5-10 Million
Number Employees: 50-99
Other Locations:
Volk Corp.
Grand Rapids MI

30869 Volk Enterprises
1335 Ridgeland Pkwy
Suite 120
Alpharetta, GA 30004 770-663-5400
Fax: 770-663-5411 sales@volkenterprises.com
www.volkenterprises.com
President: Tony Volk
Vice President: Daniel J. Volk (DAN)
Regional Sales Manager: Burt Hewitt
Estimated Sales: $500,000-$1 Million
Number Employees: 1-4

30870 Volk Packaging Corporation
11 Morin St
Biddeford, ME 04005 207-282-6151
Fax: 207-283-1165 800-341-0208
vpc@volkboxes.com www.volkboxes.com

Manufacturer and exporter of packaging and containerizing supplies including corrugated, fiber and wooden boxes, cartons and containers
President: Douglas Volk
CEO: Kenneth Volk
Sales Manager: Greg Milligan
VP Operations: Michael Rousselle
Estimated Sales: $20 - 50 Million
Number Employees: 100-249
Square Footage: 140000

30871 Vollrath Company
P.O.Box 611
Sheboygan, WI 53082 920-457-4851
Fax: 920-459-6570 vollrathfs@vollrathco.com
www.vollrathco.com
Manufacturer, importer and exporter of mobile serving equipment and food carriers, buffet service, stainless steel and aluminum pots and pans, plastic spoons, ladles, whips and tongs
President: Thomas G Belot
CFO: Marty Crneckly
CFO: Marty Crneckiy
Vice President: David Wasserman
R&D: Jeff Madson
Quality Control: Rich Velten
Marketing Director: Cathy Fitzgerald
Operations Manager: Dennis Heaney
Purchasing Manager: Peggy Pettersen
Estimated Sales: $100 - 500 Million
Number Employees: 500-999
Type of Packaging: Food Service
Brands:
Impressions
New York, New York
Super Pan Ii

30872 Volta Belting Technology, Inc.
11 Chapin Road
Pine Brook, NJ 07058 973-276-7905
Fax: 973-276-7908 sales@voltabelting.com
www.voltabelting.com
Food conveyor belts, power transmission & timing belts and belt welding tools.

30873 Volumetric Technologies
401 Cannon Industrial Blvd #1
Cannon Falls, MN 55009 507-263-0034
www.volumetrictechnologies.com
Filling and packaging equipment including conveyors, cup machines, piston fillers/depositors, complete turn key filling lines, dispensing nozzles and net weight filling lines. Applications include meats, soups, dipstaco/burrito/tamale filling, chili, pizzas, bakery items, dairy products, condiments/sauces, precooked dinners, deli products and creamed meats.
President: Timothy Piper
VP: Keith Piper
VP/Secretary: Bruce Piper
Number Employees: 6
Type of Packaging: Bulk

30874 Vomela/Harbor Graphics
444 Fillmore Avenue East
St Paul, MN 55107 651-228-2200
Fax: 651-228-2295 800-645-1012
sales@vomela.com www.vomela.com
Screen and digital printing of graphics and signage for retail , fleet, P.O.P., vehicle, tradeshow and event marketing
President: Thomas Auth
President: Mark Auth
Marketing/Sales: Jeff Noren
Plant Manager: Mark Gillen
Estimated Sales: $1 - 3 Million
Number Employees: 5-9

30875 Von Gal
3101 Hayneville Rd
Montgomery, AL 36108-3900 334-261-2700
Fax: 334-261-2801 800-542-6570
jason.bennett@vongal.com www.vongal.com
Palletizers for baking, bottling and brewing industries
Manager: Paul Probst
Sales Manager: Jason Bennett

30876 Vonco Products
201 Park Ave
Lake Villa, IL 60046 847-356-2323
Fax: 847-356-8630 800-323-9077
sales@vonco.com www.vonco.com
Poly and laminated bags
President: L Lawrence Laske
VP Sales: Les Laske
Sales Representative: Gary Link
Estimated Sales: $10-20 Million
Number Employees: 100-249
Square Footage: 38000

30877 Voorhees Rubber Manufacturing Co., Inc.
PO Box 27
Newark, MD 21841 410-632-1582
Fax: 410-632-1522 info@voorheesrubber.com
www.voorheesrubber.com
Manufacturer, exporter and wholesaler/distributor of rubber candy molds
President: Richard Jackson
Vice President: Teresa Jackson
Estimated Sales: Below $5 Million
Number Employees: 5-9
Brands:
Voorhees

30878 Vorti-Siv
36165Salem GangaRoad
PO Box 720
Salem, OH 44460-0720 330-332-4958
Fax: 330-332-1543 800-227-7487
info@vorti-siv.com www.vorti-siv.com
Manufacturer and exporter of gyrating sieves and tanks; self-cleaning filters
President: Barbara Maroscher
CFO: Barb Groppe
VP: Vic Maroscher
Sales: Dennis Ulrich
Plant Manager: Kevin Penner
Estimated Sales: $3 - 5,000,000
Number Employees: 10-19
Square Footage: 35000
Parent Co: MM Industries
Brands:
Vorti-Siv

30879 Vortron Smokehouse/Ovens
120 South Main Street
Iron Ridge, WI 53035 608-362-0862
Fax: 608-362-9012 800-874-1949
sales@vortronsmokehouses.com
www.vortronsmokehouses.com
Manufacturer and exporter of food processing machinery, ovens, smokehouses, drying rooms and smoke generators
VP: Dan Mertes
Plant Manager: Dan Mertes
Estimated Sales: $2.5-5 Million
Number Employees: 10-19
Parent Co: Apache Stainless Equipment
Other Locations:
Vortron Smokehouse/Ovens
Beaver Dam WI

30880 Voss Belting
6965 North Hamlin Avenue
Lincolnwood, IL 60712-2598 847-673-8900
Fax: 847-673-1408 info@vossbelting.com
www.vossbelting.com
Rubber and thermoplastic conveyor belting; neoprene and urethane timing belts; high temperature silicone/teflon conveyor belting
President: Richard A Voss
Estimated Sales: $5-10 Million
Number Employees: 20-49

30881 Voxcom Web Printing
102 Clover Grn
Peachtree City, GA 30269 770-487-7575
Fax: 770-487-3230 www.wspackaging.com
Pressure sensitive labels
President: Ken Young
Sales Representative: Linda Brass
Estimated Sales: $5 - 10 Million
Number Employees: 50-99

30882 Vrymeer Commodities
PO Box 545
St Charles, IL 60174-0545 630-377-2584

30883 Vulcan Electric Company
28 Endfield St
Porter, ME 04068 207-625-3231
Fax: 207-625-8938 800-922-3027
sales@vulcanelectric.com
www.vulcanelectric.com
Manufacturer and exporter of heaters including immersion, strip and fin strip, radiant cartridge, band and flexible; also, tubular elements, thermocouples, programmable/mechanical temperature controls and sensors
President: Michael Quick
General Manager: Stan Haupt
CFO: Jenet Floyd
Quality Control: Bob Doglus
Estimated Sales: $20 - 30 Million
Number Employees: 50-99
Square Footage: 50000
Brands:
Cal-Stat

30884 Vulcan Industries
300 Display Dr
Moody, AL 35004 205-640-2400
Fax: 205-640-2412 888-444-4417
hello@vulcanind.com www.vulcanind.com
Manufacturer and exporter of point of purchase display fixtures and products including tubular, sheet metal, hard board, plastic and wire
VP: J Whitley
Quality Control: Steve Brugge
Manager Sales/Marketing: Douglas Stockham
Accountant: Virgil Wells
Plant Manager: James Raynor
Number Employees: 100-249
Square Footage: 165000
Parent Co: Ebsco Industries

30885 Vulcan Materials Company
1200 Urban Center Drive
P.O. Box 385014
Birmingham, AL 35242-5014 205-298-3000
www.vul.com
Foam cleaner, sanitizer, hard surface disinfectants, chlorine dioxide water treatment and odor control agents
Chairman, Chief Executive Officer: Don James
EVP, Chief Financial Officer: John R. McPherson
VP, Marketing Support Services: Sidney F. Mays
National Sales Director: Richard Higby
EVP, Chief Operating Officer: J. Thomas Hill
Number Employees: 50-99
Square Footage: 240000
Brands:
Absorb
Akta Klor
Bioslide
Dura Klor
Rio Klor

30886 Vulcan-Hart Company
2006 Northwestern Pkwy
Louisville, KY 40203 502-778-2791
Fax: 502-772-7831 800-814-2028
dreiter@wch-mktg.com
www.vulcanequipment.com
Manufacturer and exporter of broilers, steam cookers, ranges, fryers and warmers; also, bakery, food processing, hotel, restaurant and pizza ovens
President: Tim Murray
VP Sales National Accounts: Tom Cassin
VP: Jim Cullinane
Director Sales: Dennis Ball
National Accounts Manager: Jim Thompson
Estimated Sales: $10 - 20 Million
Number Employees: 50-99
Parent Co: ITW Food Equipment Group LLC
Type of Packaging: Food Service

30887 Vulcanium Metals International, LLC
3045 Commercial Avenue
Northbrook, IL 60062-1997 847-498-3111
Fax: 847-498-2810 888-922-0040
titanium@vulcanium.com www.vulcanium.com
Manufacturer and exporter of titanium caustic food processing equipment and machine parts including scrapper, tubing and pipe coils
President: Richard Leopold
Senior Vice President: Dave Yoho
Marketing Director: Joanie Leopold
Sales: Steve Gerzel
Operations: Adelberto Cordova
Estimated Sales: $9000000
Number Employees: 35
Parent Co: United Performance Metals

30888 Vynatex
7 Carey Pl
Suite 2
Port Washington, NY 11050 516-944-6130
Fax: 516-767-7056 vynatex@vynatex.com
www.vynatex.com
Custom menu covers, wine books, check presentation folders, guest service directories and in-room hotel products including ice buckets, promotional items, etc.
President: Angela Lamagna
Sales Manager: Alexander Juarez
Estimated Sales: $1-2.5 Million
Number Employees: 5-9
Square Footage: 30000
Brands:
Compu-Check
Dynahyde
Sculptathane
Scultahyde

30889 W H Wildman Company
P.O.Box 42
New Hampshire, OH 45870 419-568-7531
Fax: 419-568-7531 scott@wildmanspice.com
www.wildmanspice.com
Wholesale packager; general groceries
Owner: Scott Gray
Estimated Sales: Less than $300,000
Number Employees: 1-4
Type of Packaging: Consumer, Food Service, Private Label, Bulk
Brands:
Wildman's

30890 W&H Systems
120 Asia Pl
Carlstadt, NJ 07072 201-933-9849
Fax: 201-933-2144 dbetman@whsystems.com
www.whsystems.com
Provider of distribution logistics service emphasizing conveyor and computer system and integration including visual control, manifesting and paperless picking
President: Don Betman
Executive VP: Ron Quackenbush
CFO: Frank Artizone
VP: Ken Knapp
Estimated Sales: $20-50 Million
Number Employees: 100-249
Square Footage: 31000
Brands:
Buschman
Promech

30891 W.A. Golomski & Associates
N9690 County Road U
Algoma, WI 54201-9528 920-487-9864
Fax: 920-487-7249
Consultant specializing in product introductions, motivation programs and total quality management programs
President: William Golomski
Estimated Sales: Less than $500,000
Number Employees: 4

30892 (HQ)W.A. Powers Company
125 S Main St
Fort Worth, TX 76104-1293 817-332-7151
Fax: 817-334-0855 800-792-1243
info@wapowers.com www.wapowers.com
Conveyor systems including gravity, wheel and roller powered
President: Doyle Powers
Estimated Sales: $2.5-5 Million
Number Employees: 1-4
Other Locations:
Powers, W.A., Co.
Fort Worth TX

30893 W.A. Schmidt Company
99 Brower Ave
Oaks, PA 19456 215-721-8300
Fax: 215-721-5890 800-523-6719
www.pencoproducts.com
Manufacturer and exporter of storage systems and racks
President: Greg Grogan
Estimated Sales: $20-50 Million
Number Employees: 100-249
Square Footage: 246000
Brands:
H.F. Cradle System

30894 W.F. Cosart Packing Company
1145 E Firebaugh Ave
Exeter, CA 93221 559-592-2821
Fax: 559-592-6259
Fresh fruits and vegetables
President: Keith Cosart
Estimated Sales: $50 - 100 Million
Number Employees: 50-99

30895 W.G. Durant Corporation
9825 Painter Ave # A-E
Whittier, CA 90605-2700 562-946-5555
Fax: 562-946-5577 www.premier.tech.com
Manufacturer and exporter of palletizers, bag packers, conveyors and system electrical controls
Owner: Zara Badalian
Sales Manager: Jack Schreyer
Estimated Sales: $3 - 5 Million
Number Employees: 5-9
Square Footage: 600000
Parent Co: Westmont Industries
Brands:
Hy-Ac Iv

30896 W.J. Egli Company
P.O.Box 2605
Alliance, OH 44601 330-823-3666
Fax: 330-823-0011 info@wjegli.com
www.wjegli.com
Manufacturer and exporter of wire, wood and tube display racks
President: William Egli
Marketing Director: Jeff Egli
Estimated Sales: $2.5 - 5 Million
Number Employees: 20-49
Square Footage: 100000

30897 W.M. Barr & Company
PO Box 1879
Memphis, TN 38101-1879 901-775-0100
Fax: 901-775-5468 800-238-2672
klnstrip@wmbarr.com www.wmbarr.com
Aerosols and liquid cleaners including glass and hand cleaners
CEO: Richard Loomis
VP Marketing/Administration: Mike Davis
Marketing Services Coordinator: Averi Dunkle
Estimated Sales: $100-500 Million
Number Employees: 500-999
Parent Co: W.M. Barr & Company
Brands:
Citrus Solvent
Klean Hand
P&D
Pane Relief

30898 W.M. Sprinkman Corporation
1002 Academy Street
P.O.Box 57
Elroy, WI 53929-0057 608-462-8456
Fax: 608-462-8774 800-816-1610
sales@sprinkman.com www.sprinkman.com
Agitation systems, milk, silo, tank, agitators, cutters, drainers, fines savers, forks, presses, manual, tanks, starter, custom fabrication, flow diversion stations, and ladders
General Manager: Larry Willer
Estimated Sales: $1 - 2.5 Million
Number Employees: 10-19

30899 W.R. Grace & Company
7500 Grace Dr
Columbia, MD 21044-4098 410-531-4000
Fax: 410-531-4367 getinfo@paragon-md.com
www.grace.com
Processor and exporter of silica gel absorbents; also, clarifying and anticaking agents
President & Chief Operating Officer: Gregory Poling
Chairman & Chief Executive Officer: Fred Festa
Senior VP & Chief Financial Officer: Hudson La Force
VP & Chief Human Resources Officer: Pamela Wagoner
Estimated Sales: $3.16 Billion
Number Employees: 6,500
Brands:
Condensation Gard
Sycoid
Trisyl

30900 W.T. Nickell Label Company
4360 Winding Creek Blvd
Batavia, OH 45103 513-752-2191
Fax: 513-752-2354 888-899-1991
labels@wtnickell.com www.wtnickell.com
Custom pressure sensitive labels, printer ribbons and stock labels.
Owner: Ray Meyer
Vice President: Jaime Kinkade
Estimated Sales: Under $1 Million
Number Employees: 10-19
Type of Packaging: Private Label

30901 W.W. Babcock Company
36 Delaware Ave
Bath, NY 14810-1607 607-776-3341
Fax: 607-776-7483
Manufacturer and exporter of small wooden crates
President: Marc Mc Connell
Sales/Marketing Executive: A Cranmer
Estimated Sales: $2.5-5 Million
Number Employees: 100-249
Square Footage: 77000

30902 WA Brown & Son
209 Long Meadow Dr
Salisbury, NC 28147 704-636-5131
Fax: 704-637-0919 wid@wabrown.com
www.wabrown.com
Manufacturer, importer and exporter of walk-in coolers, freezers, and structural insulated panels
President: Ed Brown
Vice President: Paul Brown
Sales Director: Dave Morris
Operations Manager: Deric Skeen
Estimated Sales: $25-50 Million
Number Employees: 100-249
Square Footage: 250000
Type of Packaging: Food Service, Private Label
Brands:
W.A. Brown

30903 WCB Ice Cream
267 Livingston Street
Northvale, NJ 7647 201-784-1101
Fax: 201-784-1116 800-252-5200
wcbice@wcbicecream.com
www.wcbicecream.com
Cheese equipment, firesavers, heat exchangers, scraped surface, ice cream equipment, ingredient feeders
President: Ken Rodi
CFO: Ken Rodi
Quality Control: Harry Colber
Number Employees: 10,000

30904 WCB Ice Cream USA
267 Livingston Street
Northvale, NJ 07647 215-425-4320
Fax: 215-426-2034 800-644-4320
wcbice@wcbicecream.dk www.wcbicecream.dk
Dairy equipment and food processing machinery repair and rebuilding
Manager: John Dorety
Estimated Sales: $1-5 Million
Number Employees: 20-49
Parent Co: Udi And Spx.

30905 WCR
221 Crane St
Dayton, OH 45403 937-223-0703
Fax: 937-223-2818 800-421-4927
info@wcr-regasketing.com
www.wcr-regasketing.com
Plate heat exchangers
Owner: Brad Stevens
Applications Engineer: Heather Comer
Director of Sales and Technical Support: Jeremy Foley
Production Coordinator: Jenna Grigsby
Estimated Sales: $5-10 Million
Number Employees: 20-49

30906 WCS Corporation
2498 American Ave
Hayward, CA 94545-1810 510-782-8727
Fax: 510-783-6843
Cleaning compounds, liquids and powders
Executive VP: Jeanette Conde
Estimated Sales: $20-50 Million
Number Employees: 20-49
Parent Co: Royal Chemical Company

30907 WE Killam Enterprises
PO Box 741
Waterford, ON N0E 1Y0
Canada 519-443-7421
Fax: 519-443-6922
Manufacturer, importer and exporter of packaging equipment including inkjet printers, case coding, full wrap and spot labelers, case and tray packing and sealing machinery and can ejectors, standard knapp, burt, fmc, ace/kore, ualcosystems.
President: Roger Elliott
Number Employees: 1-4
Square Footage: 2500
Brands:
Ace & Icore
Labellett
Mateer-Burt
Sauven
Standard Knapp
Valco

30908 WE Lyons Contruction
1301 Ygnacio Valley Rd
Walnut Creek, CA 94598 925-658-1600
Fax: 925-658-1604 800-493-5966
info@welyons.com www.welyons.com
Design-build construction; manufacturing, food service, food processing, distribution, and USDA design and construction
President: Greg Lyon
CFO: Debora Allan
Estimated Sales: $10 - 20 Million
Number Employees: 50-99

30909 WEI Equipment
207 Evergreen Ave
Haddon Township, NJ 08108-3508 856-863-9577
Fax: 856-863-9641
Materials handling equipment, elevators, loaders, lifters and dumpers, used and rebuilt equipment, frozen meat slicers, flakers and breakers, grinders, mixers, screw conveyors
President: John Camp
Estimated Sales: $1-2.5 Million
Number Employees: 9

30910 WEI Equipment
4312 Jade Avenue
Cypress, CA 90630 714-827-9510
Fax: 714-209-0023 800-934-4934
a.anderson@wei-inc.com www.wei-inc.com
Used food processing equipment for the red meat industry
Estimated Sales: $1-2.5 Million
Number Employees: 9

30911 WES
6389 Tower Ln
Sarasota, FL 34240 941-371-7617
Fax: 941-378-5218 800-881-9374
info@wesinc.com www.wesinc.com
Water treatment equipment
Owner: Anthony De Loach
Estimated Sales: $10-20 Million
Number Employees: 50-99

30912 WES Plastics
561 Edward Avenue
Richmond Hill, ON L4C 9W6
Canada 905-508-1546
Displays, boxes, stands; also, custom fabrication available for acrylic items
Owner: Wayne Simpson
Number Employees: 1-4

30913 WGN Flag & Decorating
7984 South Chicago Ave
Chicago, IL 60617 773-768-8076
Fax: 773-768-3138 sales@wgnflag.com
www.wgnflag.com
Flags, pennants, banners and signs
President: Carl "Gus" Porter III
VP: Gus Porter
Estimated Sales: $1-2.5 Million
Number Employees: 10-19

30914 WH Cooke & Company
6868 York Road
P.O.Box 893
Hanover, PA 17331-0893 717-630-2222
Fax: 717-637-9999 800-772-5151
sales@whcooke.com www.whcooke.com
Temperature and RH sensors, temperature and RH controls, dough temperature boxes, proofer control systems
President: Wayne Cooke
Estimated Sales: Below $5 Million
Number Employees: 10-19

30915 WMF/USA
85 Price Parkway
Farmingdale, NY 11735-1305 704-882-3898
Fax: 631-694-0820 800-999-6347
consumer@WMFAmericas.com
www.wmf-usa.com
Wholesaler/distributor of flatware, hollowware, cookware, china and crystal
President: Stefan Nisi
VP Sales and Marketing: Peter Braley
National Sales Manager: Emma Popolow
Parent Co: WMF/AG

30916 WNA Hopple Plastics
7430 Empire Drive
Florence, KY 41042-2924 859-283-1570
Fax: 859-283-0061 800-446-4622
www.hopple.com
Extruded and thermoformed custom plastic packaging including food trays and containers; also, design consultation services available
VP Sales: Brett York
Estimated Sales: $20-50 Million
Number Employees: 250-499
Square Footage: 185000
Parent Co: John Waddington

30917 WNA-Comet West
1135 Samuelson St
City of Industry, CA 91748-1222 626-913-0724
Fax: 626-913-1776 800-225-0939
karwna@aol.com www.wna-inc.com
Disposable plastic dinnerware including cutlery, tumblers, plates, bowls, etc
manager: Kurt Rogstad
Executive VP: R Greer
Sales Manager: Michael Sharpe
Estimated Sales: $20-50 Million
Number Employees: 10-19
Square Footage: 200000
Parent Co: WNA-Waddington North America

30918 WNA-Cups Illustrated
2155 W Longhorn Dr
Lancaster, TX 75134 972-228-6318
Fax: 972-224-3067 800-334-2877
www.cupsillustrated.com
Manufacturer and importer of plastic fabrications, containers and cups
CEO: Mike Evans
Plant Manager: Alex Yarocoy
Estimated Sales: $20-50 Million
Number Employees: 10-19
Parent Co: WNA Waddington
Brands:
Celebrity Cups

30919 WNC Pallet & Forest Products
1414 Smoky Park Hwy
Candler, NC 28715 828-667-5426
Fax: 828-665-4759 wncpallet@bellsouth.net
www.wncpallet.com
Wooden and recycled pallets, skids and boxes; also, pallet recycling
President: Tom Orr
VP: T Orr
Sales: Cyndi Commozi
Manager: Brent Orr
Estimated Sales: $10 - 20 Million
Number Employees: 5-9

30920 WP Bakery Group
3 Enterprise Drive
Suite 108
Shelton, CT 06484 203-929-6530
Fax: 203-929-7089 pat@kemperusa.com
www.kemperusa.com
Bakery equipment
President: Patricia Kennedy
Controller: Karen Smith
VP Marketing/Mixer Product Manager: Shawna Goldfarb
Vice President of Sales: Bruce Gingrich
Estimated Sales: $5 Million
Number Employees: 5-9

30921 WR Grace & Company
7500 Grace Dr
Columbia, MD 21044-4029 410-531-4000
Fax: 410-531-4367 888-398-4646
www.grace.com
Specialty chemicals
President: Fred Festa
CEO: Paul Loren
Estimated Sales: K
Number Employees: 5,000-9,999
Type of Packaging: Private Label, Bulk

30922 WR Key
4770 Sheppard Avenue E
Scarborough, ON M1S 3V6
Canada 416-291-6246
Fax: 416-291-4882 sales@wrkey.com
www.wrkey.com
Manufacturer and exporter of stainless steel serving carts, cash boxes, desk trays and card cabinets
President and CEO: Gw Key
R&D and QC: Lisa Key
Sales Manager: Lisa Key
Estimated Sales: $5 - 10 Million
Number Employees: 40
Type of Packaging: Consumer, Food Service, Private Label

30923 WS Packaging & Systems
2571 S. Hemlock Road
Green Bay, WI 54229 513-459-2400
Fax: 513-459-8815 800-818-5481
www.wspackaging.com
Pressure sensitive labelers, printer applicators, pressure sensitive labels
CEO: Kenneth Kidd
Estimated Sales: $5-10 Million
Number Employees: 100-249

30924 WS Packaging Group
950 Breezewood Lane
Neenah, WI 54956 920-751-1600
Fax: 920-751-1464 888-532-3334
www.wspackaging.com
Estimated Sales: $300,000-500,000
Number Employees: 10

30925 (HQ)WS Packaging Group Inc
2571 S Hemlock Rd
Green Bay, WI 54229 920-866-6300
Fax: 920-866-6480
mmoorhead@wspackaging.com
www.wspackaging.com
Manufacturer and exporter of labels, tags, folded cartons, instant redeemable coupons, F.D.A. packaging and tape; also, offset printing available
President: Terry Fulwiler
CFO: Jay Tomcheck
VP: Becky Smith
Estimated Sales: $400 Million
Square Footage: 110000
Type of Packaging: Private Label
Other Locations:
WL Group-Wisconsin Label
Tulsa OK
Brands:
Xl

30926 WS Packaging Group, Inc.
950 Breezewood Lane
Neenah, WI 54956 920-751-1600
Fax: 920-751-1464 888-532-3334
www.wspackaging.com
Roll labels and in-store promotional materials
General Manager: Jeff Buchta
Marketing Manager: Patricia Mulvey
Operations Manager: Jeff Nyman
Estimated Sales: $300,000-500,000
Number Employees: 1-4

30927 (HQ)WS Packaging-Superior Label
2571 S. Hemlock Rd.
Green Bay, WI 54229 920-866-6300
Fax: 920-866-6480 800-818-5481
www.wspackaging.com
Labels and label application equipment; printing available
CEO: Terry Fulwiler
Estimated Sales: $230 Million
Number Employees: 2098
Number of Products: 150
Type of Packaging: Consumer, Food Service, Private Label

Brands:
Accorista
Genisis
Roll Tax 200
Supergard

30928 Wabash Power Equipment Company
444 Carpenter Ave
Wheeling, IL 60090-0427 847-541-5600
Fax: 847-541-1279 800-704-2002
info@wabashpower.com
www.wabashpower.com
Deaerators, boilers, power generation equipment and technical energy services
Owner: Richard Caitung
Estimated Sales: $10-20 Million
Number Employees: 20-49

30929 Waco Broom & Mop Factory
PO Box 1656
Waco, TX 76703-1656 254-753-3581
Fax: 254-753-3595 800-548-7716
msimon7760@aol.com
Mops, brooms and handles
President: Mark Simon
Number Employees: 15
Square Footage: 18000
Brands:
Crown

30930 Waddington North America
6 Stuart Rd
Chelmsford, MA 01824-4108 978-256-6553
Fax: 978-256-1614 888-962-2877
www.wna-inc.com
Manufacturer and exporter of disposable plastic dinnerware, drinkware, servingware, cutlery, cutlery packets, straws and stirrers
President: Mike Evans
CEO: Dave Gordon
CFO: Steve Morehouse
Quality Control: Tom Whitcumb
Marketing Director: Al Madonna
Public Relations: Mary Ryan
Operations Manager: Jim Messeder
Estimated Sales: $25-100 Million
Number Employees: 250-499
Square Footage: 12000
Parent Co: Waddington PLC
Brands:
Classic Crystal
Classicware
Comet
Crystal Flex
Designerware
Frost Flex

30931 Waddington North AmericaCups Illustrated
2155 W Longhorn Dr
Lancaster, TX 75134-2105 972-224-8407
Fax: 972-224-3067 800-334-2877
iregister@cupsillustrated.com
www.cupsillustrated.com
Manufacturer and exporter of injection molded plastic disposables including platters, bowls, utensils and specialty items
Manager: Dave Gordon
VP Sales: Jon Naulgasch
Plant Manager: Alex Yarocoy
Estimated Sales: $10-20 Million
Number Employees: 50-99
Parent Co: Avon Plastics

30932 Wade Manufacturing Company
PO Box 23666
Tigard, OR 97281-3666 503-692-5353
Fax: 503-692-5358 800-222-7246
sales@waderain.com www.waderain.com
Manufacturer and exporter of agricultural irrigation systems including handrove, poweroll and center pivot; also, micro irrigation products and aluminum casters
President: Ed Newbegin
VP: Cliff Warner
Estimated Sales: $20-50 Million
Number Employees: 50-99
Parent Co: R.M. Wade & Company
Brands:
Wade Rain

30933 Wag Industries
4117 Grove Street
Skokie, IL 60076-1713 773-638-7007
Fax: 773-533-6951 800-621-3305
blunt232@aol.com www.cateringtrucks.com
Manufacturer and exporter of mobile catering truck units including bar and hot dog carts
President: Gail Gilbert
CEO: Doris Gilbert
CFO: George Gilbert
Quality Control: Gavin London
Purchasing Manager: Gavin Lendan
Estimated Sales: $5-10 Million
Number Employees: 10

30934 Wagner Brothers Containers
4101 Ashland Ave
Baltimore, MD 21205-2924 410-354-0044
Fax: 410-354-3125
Corrugated boxes
President: Lawrence K Wagner
VP: Lawrence Wagner Jr
Estimated Sales: $10 - 20 Million
Number Employees: 50-99

30935 Wahlstrom Manufacturing
15235 Boyle Ave
Fontana, CA 92337-7254 909-822-4677
Fax: 909-822-1675
Wire point-of-purchase display racks
Owner: Zach Fener
Estimated Sales: 700000
Number Employees: 5-9
Square Footage: 8000

30936 Wako Chemicals, U.S.A.
1600 Bellwood Rd
Richmond, VA 23237 804-271-7677
Fax: 804-271-7791 labchem@wakousa.com
www.wakousa.com
Specialty chemicals
Manager: Ed Sata
R&D: Hiramatsu Max
CFO: Ed Sata
Estimated Sales: $20 - 50 Million
Number Employees: 50-99

30937 Wal-Vac
900 47th St SW
Suite A
Wyoming, MI 49509 616-241-6717
Fax: 616-241-1771 walvac@walvac.com
www.walvac.com
Manufacturer and exporter of built-in central vacuum cleaning systems
President: David Mol
VP Operations: David Mol
Estimated Sales: $2.5-5 Million
Number Employees: 5-9
Square Footage: 9600
Brands:
Wal-Vac

30938 Walco Stainless
820 Noyes St
Utica, NY 13502-5053 315-733-4663
Fax: 315-733-6602 800-879-2526
sales@walcostainless.com
www.uticastainless.com
Manufacturer, importer and exporter of stainless steel flatware, steak knives, hollow ware, buffetware, and chafers
President: David S Allen
Sales/Marketing: Philip Benbenek
Estimated Sales: $10 - 20 Million
Number Employees: 100-249
Square Footage: 125000
Parent Co: Utica Cutlery Company
Type of Packaging: Food Service
Brands:
Walco

30939 Walco-Linck Company
PO Box 5643
Bellingham, WA 98227-5643 845-353-7600
Fax: 845-353-8056 800-338-2329
williamburge@b2badvantage.net
www.walcolinck.com
Manufacturer and exporter of aerosol insecticides, ant and roach baits and fly paper
President: William Burge
Executive VP: Richard Bozzo
CFO and QC: Richard Bozzo
Estimated Sales: $5 - 10 Million
Number Employees: 15
Brands:
Tat

30940 Wald Imports
11200 Kirkland Way
Suite 300
Kirkland, WA 98033 425-822-0500
Fax: 425-828-4201 800-426-2822
alsnel@waldimports.com www.waldimports.com
Decorative containers for gift baskets and floral
President: Lou Wald
Controller: Greg Best
VP: Martin Sippy
Sales Coordinator: Andria Blizzard
Order Entry & Invoicing: Gwen McClellan
Estimated Sales: $3.8 Million
Number Employees: 23

30941 Wald Wire & Manufacturing Company
846 Witzel Ave
Oshkosh, WI 54901 920-231-5590
Fax: 920-231-2212 800-236-0053
waldwire@waldwire.com www.waldwire.com
Wire racks for refrigerators and displays, wire forms, shelving, guards
President: Randy Stark
Estimated Sales: Below $10 Million
Number Employees: 50

30942 Waldon Equipment, LLC
201 W Oklahoma Ave
Fairview, OK 73737 580-227-3711
Fax: 580-227-2165 800-486-0023
waldon@mobileproductsinc.com
www.waldonequipment.com
Forklift trucks, lift truck attachments and compact wheel loaders
President: Michael Bossetti
CEO: Don Collins Jr
Sales Director: Tim Carroll
Public Relations: Kent Tyler
Operations Manager: Ricky Heflin
Number Employees: 10-19
Brands:
Lay-Mor
Waldon

30943 Walker Bag ManufacturingCompany
11198 Ampere Ct
Louisville, KY 40299 502-266-5696
Fax: 502-266-9823 800-642-4949
bagmann@aol.com www.printex-usa.com
Custom designed burlap, canvas, cotton, jute, paper, tote and polypropylene bags; importer of polypropylene bags
CEO: Steve Dutton
VP: Steve Dutton
Estimated Sales: $5-10 Million
Number Employees: 20-49

30944 Walker Brush
82 East Main Street
Webster, NY 14580 585-467-7850
Fax: 585-342-2264 pgtaft@frontiernet.net
www.brushmfg.com
Brushes
President: Thomas R Erb
Sales Director: Timothy Mura
Estimated Sales: $500,000-$1 Million
Number Employees: 4

30945 Walker Companies
121 NW 6th St
Oklahoma City, OK 73102 405-235-5319
Fax: 405-235-1698 800-522-3015
info@walkercompanies.com
www.walkercompanies.com
Signs, banners and marking devices including rubber stamps
Manager: Sue Stephens
Quality Control: Sue Steven
VP: Kenny Walker
Estimated Sales: Below $5 Million
Number Employees: 20-49

30946 Walker Magnetics
20 Rockdale St
Worcester, MA 01606 508-853-3232
Fax: 508-852-8649 800-962-4638
sales@walkermagnet.com
www.walkermagnet.com
Designer and manufacturer of magnetic workholding chucks, lifting, material handling, and separation applications.
Owner: Eric Englested
Plant Manager: Dick Isabell
Estimated Sales: Below $5 Million
Number Employees: 50-99

30947 Walker Magnetics
20 Rockdale St
Worcester, MA 01606-1922 508-853-3232
Fax: 508-852-8649 800-962-4638
info@walkermagnet.com
www.walkermagnet.com
Suppliers of conveying systems tailored to the canmaking and can filling industries, magnetic cable conveyors, elevators, loverators, palletizing heads, magnetic twist conveyors, end handling conveyors, magnetic rails, rollers andcomplete turnkey systems
Owner: Eric Englested
Estimated Sales: $10 - 20 Million
Number Employees: 5-9

30948 Walker Sign Company
9255 San Fernando Rd
Sun Valley, CA 91352-1416 818-252-7788
Fax: 818-252-7785 rufs-v@spcglobal.net
www.walkerairsep.com
Signs, awnings, canopies, flags, pennants and banners
President: Russ Walker
Estimated Sales: Below $5 Million
Number Employees: 20-49
Type of Packaging: Bulk

30949 Walker Stainless Equipment
625 W State St
New Lisbon, WI 53950 608-562-7500
Fax: 608-562-7549 800-356-5734
spgsales@walker.carlisle.com
www.walkerstainless.com
Manufacturer and exporter of stainless steel transportation and plant equipment tanks for the dairy industry
President: D Nick
CEO: Doug Chapple
Plant Manager: Nilo Buan
Treasurer: Nelly Buan
Estimated Sales: $250 - 500 Million
Number Employees: 10-19
Square Footage: 200000
Parent Co: Carlisle Companies
Brands:
Norman Machinery
Walker

30950 Wall Conveyor & Manufacturing
PO Box 7664
Huntington, WV 25778-7664 304-429-1335
Fax: 304-429-1337 800-456-1335
wallcon@ezwv.com
Package handling conveyors including rebuilt; also, accessories
Owner: Jim Fankhanel
Office Manager: Liz Rexroad
Estimated Sales: $1-2.5 Million
Number Employees: 1-4
Square Footage: 6000

30951 Wallace & Hinz
P.O.Box 708
Blue Lake, CA 95525-0708 707-668-1825
Fax: 707-826-0224 800-831-8282
tomh@whbars.com www.whbars.com
Manufacturer and exporter of bars including portable and modular
Owner: Tom Tellez
Sales Manager: Richard Cook
Estimated Sales: $10-20 Million
Number Employees: 20-49
Square Footage: 15000

30952 Wallace Computer Services
1550 E Higgins Rd
Elk Grove Vlg, IL 60007-1699 847-734-0000
Fax: 847-734-0070 888-925-8324
cwilson2@wallace.com www.wallace.com
Prime, pressure sensitive and linerless labels, bar code and ingredient labeling software and printers including automatic label applicators and dispensers and bar code
Owner: Tushar Pandya
President, Chief Executive Officer: Thomas Quinlan
VP: David Jones
General Sales Manager: Chuck Wilson
Senior Vice President of Public Affairs: Gian-Carlo Peressutti
Estimated Sales: $10-20 Million
Number Employees: 1-4
Parent Co: Wallace Computer Services
Other Locations:
Wallace Computer Services
Hinsdale IL
Brands:
Label-Aire
Printware

30953 Wallace Computer Services
2275 Cabot Dr
Lisle, IL 60532 630-588-5000
Fax: 630-588-5115 800-323-8447
webmaster@wallace.com www.wallace.com
Printed business forms, packaging labels, automatic applicators and bar coding software, direct mail, point of purchase products and product collateral
President: Mike Duffield
Estimated Sales: $50-100 Million
Number Employees: 250-499

30954 Walle Corporation
600 Elmwood Park Blvd
New Orleans, LA 70123 504-734-8000
Fax: 504-733-2513 800-942-6761
www.walle.com
Manufacturer and exporter of labels for cans, bottles, plastics, etc.; also, lithographic and flexographic printing available
Vice Chairman/CEO: Michael Keeney
VP: Colleen Rottmann
Estimated Sales: $20-50 Million
Number Employees: 100-249
Square Footage: 300000

30955 Walnut Packaging
450 Smith St
Farmingdale, NY 11735 631-293-3836
Fax: 631-293-3878 info@wpiplasticbags.com
www.wpiplasticbags.com
Manufacturer and exporter of polyethylene bags; also, print designers
Owner: Jose Alvarado
Estimated Sales: $2.5-5 Million
Number Employees: 10-19

30956 Walsh & Simmons Seating
2511 Iowa Ave
Saint Louis, MO 63104 314-664-1215
Fax: 314-664-0703 800-727-0364
sales@walshsimmons.com
www.walshsimmons.com
Manufacturer and exporter of benches, booths, chairs and cushion pads, stools and tables including legs and bases
President: Bill Simmons
Estimated Sales: $10 - 20 Million
Number Employees: 100-249
Square Footage: 200000
Type of Packaging: Food Service

30957 Walsroder Packaging
7330 South Madison Street
Willowbrook, IL 60527-5588
Fax: 630-789-8489 800-882-9987
sales@walsroder.com
www.walsroderpackaging.com
Plastic and fibrous food casings for sausages and deli meats.

30958 Waltco Truck Equipment Company
285 Northeast Ave
Tallmadge, OH 44278 330-633-9191
Fax: 330-633-1418 800-211-3074
sales@waltco.com www.waltco.com
Truck and hydraulic cylinder electrohydraulic tailgate lifts
CEO: Rod Robinson
Director Marketing/Sales: Ray Thompson
Estimated Sales: $30 - 50 Million
Number Employees: 100-249

30959 Walter Molzahn & Company
1050 W Fullerton Avenue
Chicago, IL 60614 312-528-0550
Cake ornaments and decorations
Type of Packaging: Private Label

30960 Walters Brothers LumberManufacturing
10489 W State Road 27 70
Radisson, WI 54867-7084 715-945-2217
Fax: 715-945-2878
Brite stack pallets
President: William Walters
Vice President: Timothy Walters
Estimated Sales: $7 Million
Number Employees: 20-49
Square Footage: 10000

30961 Waltham Fruit Company
105 2nd St
Chelsea, MA 02150-1803 617-354-1994
Fax: 617-354-8423 www.baldor.com
Owner: Pat Pizzuto
Chief Executive Officer: Ronald Tucker
Vice President of Materials: Amy Lakin
Vice President of International Sales: Joe Maloney
Estimated Sales: $10-20 Million
Number Employees: 20-49

30962 Wang Cheong CorporationUSA
193 6th Street
Brooklyn, NY 11215-3104 718-222-0880
Fax: 718-222-9037
Adhesive, stationary and printed tape

30963 Ward Ironworks
2 Broadway Avenue
Welland, ON L3B 5G4
Canada 905-732-7591
Fax: 905-732-3310 888-441-9273
info@ward.on.ca www.ward.on.ca
Manufacturer, importer and exporter of material handling machinery including bucket elevators, regular and vibrating conveyors, empty bag compactors, vibrating feeders and screens
President: Guy Nelson
Estimated Sales: $5-10 Million
Number Employees: 10
Square Footage: 200000
Parent Co: Ward Automation

30964 Wardcraft Conveyor
1 Wardcraft Dr
Spring Arbor, MI 49283 517-750-9100
Fax: 517-750-2244 800-782-2779
info@wardcraft.net
www.wardcraftconveyor.com
Manufacturer and exporter of pneumatic conveyors and quick die change systems
President: John Richard
VP: Pat Sprague
National Sales: Paul Miner
Estimated Sales: $5 - 10 Million
Number Employees: 20-49
Square Footage: 72000

30965 Waring Products
314 Ella Grasso Ave
Torrington, CT 06790 860-496-3100
Fax: 860-496-9008 800-492-7464
waring@conair.com www.waringproducts.com
Manufacturer, exporter and importer of commercial food processors, blenders, juice extractors, bar glass washers, rod mixers, food choppers, slicers, ice crushers and glass and can crushers
Manager: Richard Dombroski
CFO: James McCooskey
Consultant: Larry Casalino
Estimated Sales: $5 - 10 Million
Number Employees: 50-99
Parent Co: Dynamics Corporation of America
Type of Packaging: Food Service
Brands:
Acme
Qualheim
Waring

30966 Warner Electric
449 Gardner St
South Beloit, IL 61080 800-825-6544
Fax: 815-389-2582 800-234-3369
info@warnerelectric.com
www.warnerelectric.com

The Colfax Power Transmission Group is a leading supplier of mechanical and electrical power transmission products to the food processing and packaging industries. With hundreds of years of industry experience, Colfax PT has developedsome of the premier products, delivery programs and services available today.
Marketing VP: Craig Schuele
Sales Manager: Jan Dixon
Number Employees: 1,000-4,999
Type of Packaging: Bulk

30967 Warren Analytical Laboratory
650 O St
Greeley, CO 80631 970-475-0252
Fax: 970-351-6648 800-945-6669
info@warrenlab.com www.warrenlab.com
Analytical food testing laboratory offering services for nutritional labeling, microbiological testing, chemistry and residue analysis
President: Rob Yemm
Vice President: Michael Aaronson
Sales Director: Kristen Peter
Estimated Sales: $2.5-5 Million
Number Employees: 20-49
Square Footage: 12000
Parent Co: ConAgra Foods

30968 Warren E. Conley Corporation
1099 3rd Ave SW
Carmel, IN 46032-2564 317-846-5890
Fax: 317-846-5899 800-367-7875
Manufacturer and wholesaler/distributor of maintenance and cleaning products including brooms, brushes, cleaning polish and concentrates, hand soap, window cleaners, insecticides, kitchen degreasers, lime/rust remover, bowl cleansersdrain openers and squeegees
President: Kevin Conley
Estimated Sales: $1-2.5 Million
Number Employees: 1 to 4
Brands:
Blue Satin
Butter Better
Butter Up
Cut-Off
Dapper Actor
Dapper Duster
Drain Warden
Kleenitol
Kleenzup
Leplus Ultra
Lime Lite
Miss Kriss
One-For-All
Pastry Pal
Power Quota
Reveal
Satin Doll
Satin Fan
Showtime
Softasilk
Sparkle 'n' Glo
Sqyer
Star Guard
Swab 'n' Smile
Terminator
Tyle Style
W C Insect Finish One
Warcon Out

30969 Warren Packaging
879 East Rialto Avenue
San Bernardino, CA 92408 909-888-7008
Fax: 714-690-2905 phil@warrenpkg.com
warrenpackaging.com
Folding cartons, marketing displays and packaging solutions
Estimated Sales: $300,000-500,000
Number Employees: 1-4

30970 Warren Pallet Company
601 County Road 627
Bloomsbury, NJ 08804 908-995-7172
Fax: 908-995-4146 contact@warrenpallet.com
www.warrenpallet.com
Reconditioned wooden pallets; various sizes available
President/CEO: Donald Tigar
Owner: Donald Tigar Sr
VP Marketing (Special Projects): J Bernard Noll Jr
Estimated Sales: $10-20 Million
Number Employees: 10-19

30971 (HQ)Warren Rupp
800 North Main St
Mansfield, OH 44902 419-524-8388
Fax: 419-522-7867
info@warrenrupp@idexcorp.com
www.warrenrupp.com
Air-operated, double-diaphragm pumps and accessories
President: John Carter
Co-Founder: Charles Young Jr
District Manager: Tim Zetzman
Estimated Sales: D
Number Employees: 250-499
Parent Co: IDEX Corporation
Brands:
Sandpiper

30972 Warrenton Products
1410 E Old Us Highway 40
Warrenton, MO 63383-1316 636-456-3492
Fax: 636-456-3422
Contract packaging
Estimated Sales: $50-100 Million
Number Employees: 100-249

30973 Warsaw Chemical Company
PO Box 858, Argonne Road
Warsaw, IN 46580 574-267-3251
Fax: 574-267-3884 800-548-3396
wcc@warsaw-chem.com
www.warsaw-chem.com
Manufacturer and exporter of sanitary chemicals and compounds
President: Donald Sweatland
R & D: Jeff Rufner
Quality Control: Scott Ware
Estimated Sales: $10-20 Million
Number Employees: 50-99

30974 Warther Museum
331 Karl Avenue
Dover, OH 44622 330-343-7513
Fax: 330-343-1443 info@warthers.com
www.warthers.com
Cutlery
President: David Warther
CFO: Juanne Warther
Quality Control: Dale Warther
Estimated Sales: $1 - 3 Million
Number Employees: 10-19
Square Footage: 10000
Brands:
Warther Handcrafted Cutlery

30975 Warwick Manufacturing &Equipment
1112 12th St
North Brunswick, NJ 08902 732-241-9263
Fax: 732-729-1235
sales@warwickequipment.com
www.warwickequipment.com
Manufacturer and exporter of new, used and rebuilt packaging and bakery food processing equipment
Managing Director: Gregory Pantchenko
Estimated Sales: Below $500,000
Number Employees: 5-9
Square Footage: 25000

30976 Warwick Products Company
5350 Tradex Pkwy
Cleveland, OH 44102 216-334-1200
Fax: 216-334-1201 800-535-4404
info@warwickproducts.com
www.warwickproducts.com
Bulk food and bakery displays, barrels, store fixtures and bins including bagel, bulk and candy
President: Matthew Beverstock
Sales Manager: Jon Murray
Estimated Sales: $1-2.5 Million
Number Employees: 20-49

30977 Washing Systems
167 Commerce Drive
Loveland, OH 45140
Fax: 513-870-4850 800-272-1974
sales@washingsystems.com
www.washingsystems.com
Pallet and tote washers
VP: Gary Turnbull
Sales Manager: James Smylie
Estimated Sales: $1 - 3 Million
Number Employees: 25
Brands:
The Eliminator

30978 Washington Frontier
PO Box 249
Grandview, WA 98930-0249 509-469-7662
Fax: 509-469-7739 www.wfj.net
Used process equipment sales and fruit and vegetable juice sales
Manager General Operations: Joe Stoops
Estimated Sales: $10 - 15 Million
Number Employees: 50-100

30979 Washington Group International
500 Corporate Pkwy
Birmingham, AL 35242-5448 205-995-7878
Fax: 205-995-7777 800-877-0980
Design consultant providing engineering, procurement, construction and environmental services
VP: Charles Dietz
Marketing/Sales: Bill Lott
Estimated Sales: $1 - 5 Million
Number Employees: 500-999
Square Footage: 1000000
Parent Co: Washington Group International

30980 Washington Group International
1020 31st St # 300
Downers Grove, IL 60515-5578 630-829-3000
Fax: 630-829-3513 www.wgint.com
Worldwide design and construction of manufacturing plants for: processed/packaged foods, beverages, agro-industrial
Manager: Robert Nickel
Marketing: Paul Kervan
Sales Director: Gail Luttinen
Estimated Sales: $50-100 Million
Number Employees: 250-499

30981 Washington State Juice
10725 Sutter Ave
Pacoima, CA 91331-2553 818-899-1195
Fax: 818-899-6042
Manufactures and processes fruit concentrates, blends and natural flavors. Custom blending is available
President: Fred Farago
Estimated Sales: $.5 - 1 million
Number Employees: 100-249
Type of Packaging: Food Service, Private Label, Bulk

30982 Wasserman Bag Company
26 Frowein Road
Center Moriches, NY 11934 631-909-8656
Fax: 631-878-1569
kwasserman@imperialbag.com
www.wassermanbag.com
Master distributor of bags including paper, burlap, mesh, polyethylene and polyproylene; also, tapes, wire and waxed and dry boxes as well as packaging equipment
President: Karen Wasserman
Operations Manager: Charlie Greco
Estimated Sales: $2.5 - 5 Million
Number Employees: 10-19
Type of Packaging: Consumer, Food Service, Bulk

30983 Waste Away Systems
132 South 30th Street
Newark, OH 43055 740-349-2783
Fax: 813-222-0220 800-223-4741
info@wasteawaysystems.com
www.wasteawaysystems.com
Compactors, balers and waste reduction and recycling equipment for hospitals, schools and restaurants
President: Dennis Calnan
VP Sales: David Fagan
Office Manager: Glenda O'Hara
Estimated Sales: $1-2.5 Million
Number Employees: 9
Square Footage: 80000
Brands:
Advance 2000
Convenience Pac 1000
Custom Pac 2000
Twin Chamber 3002
Twin Pac 2203
Twin Pac 2204
Twin Pac 2205

30984 Waste King Commercial
PO Box 4146
Anaheim, CA 92803-4146 714-524-7770
Fax: 714-996-7073 800-767-6293
cs@anaheimmfg.com www.anaheimmfg.com

President: Thomas P Dugan
Number Employees: 100-249

30985 Wastequip
6525 Morrison Blvd
Suite 300
Charlotte, NC 28211 877-468-9278
sales@wastequip.com
www.wastequip.com
Manufacturer and exporter of waste handling equipment including compactors, hoists, balers, etc
Manager: Bram Chappell
VP Sales/Marketing: Donald Sharp
Owner: Roy Holt
Estimated Sales: $5 - 10 Million
Number Employees: 50-99
Square Footage: 308000
Type of Packaging: Bulk

30986 Wastequip Teem
PO Box 99
Eagleville, TN 37060 605-336-1333
Fax: 605-334-8704 800-843-3358
www.wastequip.com
Manufacturer and exporter of rear-end loading refuse containers
Manager: Val Bochenek
Estimated Sales: $2.5-5 Million
Number Employees: 20-49
Parent Co: Wastequip

30987 Water & Oil Technologies
52 Eastfield Road
Montgomery, IL 60538 630-892-2007
Fax: 630-892-7472 800-841-6580
fuelalternatives@sbcglobal.net
www.wateroiltech.com
Waste treatment and by-product use equipment including natural florculents, systhetic cationic, nonionic florculents and equipment and by-product recovery and marketing assistance
President: Ed Laurent
Estimated Sales: $500,000-$1 Million
Number Employees: 6

30988 (HQ)Water & Power Technologies
P.O.Box 27836
Salt Lake City, UT 84127 801-974-5500
Fax: 801-973-9733 888-271-3295
cberg@wpt.com www.a-wpt.com
Manufacturer and exporter of custom designed skid-mounted and mobile water purification systems including reverse osmosis, demineralization, electrodeionization, ultrafiltration, manganese, greensand filters, softners, carbon towersand in-line filtration, etc.
General Manager: Jim Laraway
Controller: Tom Kirkland
Sales: Bryan Schillar
Purchase Manager: Chuck Gendre
Sales/Marketing: James Laraway
Operations: Fred Farmer
Plant/Production Manager: Emma Anderson
Purchasing: Lee Courtney
Estimated Sales: $10 - 20 Million
Number Employees: 50-99
Square Footage: 42000
Type of Packaging: Consumer
Other Locations:
Water & Power Technologies
Portland OR
Water & Power Technologies
Denver CO
Water & Power Technologies
Dallas TX
Water & Power Technologies
Columbia SC
Water & Power Technologies
Houston TX
Water & Power Technologies
Ontario, Canada
Brands:
Smart-Ro
Superskids
Waterpro

30989 Water Management Resources
PO Box 219
Overton, NV 89040 702-397-8440
Fax: 702-397-8450 800-552-5797
lpg@watermr.com www.watermr.com
Providing food safety and water conservation
Design & Engineering: Terry Griffiths
Field Sales: Greg Bilyeu
General Manager: Larry Griffiths

30990 Water Savers Worldwide
PO Box 1101
Santa Barbara, CA 93102 916-354-0718
Wine industry water treatment
Owner: Bill Wampler
Owner: Lori Wampler

30991 Water Sciences Services,Inc.
280 Emmans Road
PO Box 5000-364
Jackson, TN 38302 973-584-4131
Fax: 731-660-4115
Manufacturer and exporter of ice cubing/bagging machinery, bottled water sanitizers, bottled spring water, descaling equipment and water filters
President: Elizabeth Reed
Vice President: Paul Reed
Estimated Sales: $1-2.5 Million
Number Employees: 15
Square Footage: 18000
Brands:
Crystal Clean

30992 Water System Group
27737 Bouquet Canyon Rd # 126
Santa Clarita, CA 91350-3743 661-297-6294
Fax: 818-597-9923 800-350-9283
Reverse osmosis, carbon filtration and water softening systems
Owner: Miguel Alvarez
VP: Martin Swanson
Estimated Sales: $1 - 5,000,000
Number Employees: 1-4

30993 Waterfurnace International
9000 Conservation Way
Fort Wayne, IN 46809-9794 260-478-5667
Fax: 260-747-2828 bill_dean@waterfurnace.com
www.waterfurnace.com
Manufacturer and exporter of geothermal heating and cooling systems
CEO: Bruce Ritchey
Director Sales: Mike Murphy
Estimated Sales: G
Number Employees: 250-499
Type of Packaging: Food Service

30994 Waterlink Technologies
3610 Quantum Blvd
Boynton Beach, FL 33426-8637 561-684-6300
Fax: 561-697-3342 800-684-4844
wet@waterlink.com www.wetpurewater.com
Water purification systems, filters
General Manager: Audrey Pinkerton
Engineering Manager: Mike Mudrick
Operations Manager: Jason Gallegly
Estimated Sales: $10-25 Million
Number Employees: 50-99

30995 Waterlink/Sanborn Technologies
4100 Holiday Street NW
Canton, OH 44718-2556 330-649-4000
Fax: 330-649-4008 800-343-3381
waterlink@waterlink.com www.waterlink.com
Manufacturer and exporter of liquid/solid separation equipment and systems, wastewater pretreatment and food waste dewatering systems
VP Operations: Steve Friedman
Estimated Sales: Below $500,000
Number Employees: 4
Square Footage: 180000

30996 Waterloo Container
2311 State Route 414
Waterloo, NY 13165 315-539-3922
Fax: 315-539-9380 888-539-3922
wcbottles@flare.net
www.waterloocontainer.com
Wine industry bottles and packaging
President: Bill Lutz
CFO: William Lutz
Sales: Mike Shaffer
Chief Operating Officer: John Dixon
Estimated Sales: $1 - 2.5 Million
Number Employees: 10-19

30997 Waters Corporation
34 Maple St
Milford, MA 01757 508-478-0941
Fax: 508-872-1990 800-252-4752
info@waters.com www.waters.com
Biological products
Chairman: Douglas Berthiaume
CFO: John Ornell
Estimated Sales: K
Number Employees: 5,000-9,999

30998 (HQ)Watlow
12001 Lackland Rd
St Louis, MO 63146-4039 314-878-4600
Fax: 314-878-6814 800-492-8569
info@watlow.com www.watlow.com
Designer and manufacturer of heaters, sensors, controllers and software.
President: Thomas LaMantia
Chairman & Chief Executive Officer: Peter Desloge
Chief Financial Officer: Steve Desloge
Estimated Sales: $330 Million
Number Employees: 2000
Parent Co: Watlow Electric
Type of Packaging: Food Service

30999 Watlow
5710 Kenosha St
Richmond, IL 60071-9411 815-678-2211
Fax: 815-678-3961 info@watlow.com
www.watlow.com
Manufacturer and exporter of controler, heaters, sensors and software
Manager: Greg Wagner
Marketing Director: Rich Wilkening
Plant Manager: Mark Lehmann
Estimated Sales: $20 - 30 Million
Number Employees: 250-499
Parent Co: Watlow
Type of Packaging: Food Service
Other Locations:
Watlow
Columbia MO
Watlow
Winona MN
Brands:
Xactpak

31000 Watlow Anafaze
141 Albright Way
Los Gatos, CA 95032-1801 831-724-3800
Fax: 831-724-0302 www.watlow.com
Process control equipment
General Manager: William Hyatt
Number Employees: 20-49

31001 Watson-Marlow
37 Upton Dr
Wilmington, MA 01887-1018 978-658-6168
Fax: 978-658-0041 800-282-8823
info@wmbpumps.com www.watson-marlow.com
Peristaltic hose pumps for metering, transferring and dispensing
CEO and CFO: James Whalen
Estimated Sales: $20 - 50 Million
Number Employees: 20-49
Parent Co: Spirax Sarco Engineering Group
Brands:
Bioprene
Marprene
Watson-Marlow

31002 Watts Regulator Company
815 Chestnut St
North Andover, MA 01845-6098 978-688-1811
Fax: 978-688-2976 www.wattsind.com
Valves, grease interceptors and drains
President & Chief Executive Officer: David Coghlan
Executive Vice President & CFO: Dean Freeman
Estimated Sales: $224 Million
Number Employees: 2250
Parent Co: Watts Industries
Type of Packaging: Food Service, Private Label

31003 WattsRadiant Floors & Snmelting
4500 E. Progress Place
Springfield, MO 65803 800-276-2419
Fax: 417-831-8161 800-255-1996
www.wattsradiant.com
President: Mike Chiles
Estimated Sales: $1 - 5 Million
Number Employees: 1-4

31004 Waukesha Cherry-Burrell
2025 S Hurstbourne Pkwy
Louisville, KY 40220-1623 502-491-4310
Fax: 502-491-4312 800-252-5200
custserv@gowcb.com www.halfpricebooks.com

Fluid handling and process equipment including PD pumps, centrifugal pumps, valves, heat exchangers, and ice cream equipment
Manager: Jeff Comara
VFO and VP Finance: Ken Rod
Estimated Sales: $1 - 3 Million
Number Employees: 10-19
Number of Brands: 10
Number of Products: 50
Parent Co: SPX
Brands:
Heat Exhangers
Positive Displacement Pumps
Universal
Votatr

31005 **Waukesha Cherry-Burrell**
2025 S Hurstbourne Pkwy
Louisville, KY 40220-1623 502-491-4310
Fax: 502-491-4312 www.gowcb.com
Manufacturer and exporter of aseptic processing equipment, colloid mills, coopers/kettles, fittings, freezers, ingredient feeders, pumps and tanks
Manager: Jeff Comara
National Sales Manager: Tony Mazza
Sales Manager (Process Prod.): Paul Duddleson
Estimated Sales: $20-50 Million
Number Employees: 10-19
Parent Co: United Dominion Company

31006 **Waukesha Foundry**
1300 Lincoln Ave
Waukesha, WI 53186-5389 262-542-0741
Fax: 262-549-8440
spfeiffer@waukeshafoundry.com
www.waukeshafoundry.com
Anti-galling alloys and stainless steel castings
President: Ken Kurek
VP Sales/Marketing: Gary Evans
Manager Sales/Advertising: Thomas Kerwin
Estimated Sales: $10-20 Million
Number Employees: 100-249

31007 **Waukesha Specialty Company**
N3355 Us Highway 14
PO Box 160
Darien, WI 53114-5014 262-724-3700
Fax: 262-724-5120
Manufacturer and exporter of fittings, stainless steel hinges and sanitary valves
President: Stephen Miller
VP: Malcom Miller
Estimated Sales: $1 - 2.5 Million
Number Employees: 2

31008 **Wave Chemical Company**
350 5th Avenue
Suite 1806
New York, NY 10118-1806 973-243-5852
Fax: 973-243-5853
Cleaning chemicals and dishwashing detergents
Assistant Manager: Mark Lim
VP: Charles Lim

31009 **Wawona Packing Company**
12133 Avenue 408
Cutler, CA 93615 559-528-9729
Fax: 559-528-4696 sales@wawonapacking.com
www.wawonapacking.com
Apricots, plums, figs, grapes, peaches, and nectarines
President: Brent Smittcamp
Sales Manager: Tony Supino
Estimated Sales: $35 Billion
Number Employees: 1400
Brands:
Sweet 2 Eat

31010 **Waxine**
65 River Rd
Suite A
Bow, NH 03304 603-228-8241
Fax: 603-228-2324 mrsrptng@aol.com
Dustless sweeping compounds
President: Richard Seymour
VP/Treasurer: Richard Seymour
*Estimated Sales:*less than $500,000
Number Employees: 1-4
Square Footage: 2000

31011 **Waymar Industries**
14400 Southcross Dr W
Burnsville, MN 55306 952-435-7100
Fax: 952-435-2900 888-474-1112
billz@waymar.com www.waymar.com
Manufacturer and exporter of restaurant, cafeteria and industrial seating, table tops and trash containers
President: Dick Koehring
CFO: Greg Klingler
Director Manufacturing: Bill Smith
Marketing/Sales: Bill Ziegler
Operations Manager: Bob Haugen
Plant Manager: Mike Boegeman
Purchasing Manager: Doug Schultz
Estimated Sales: $10 - 20 Million
Number Employees: 50-99
Square Footage: 140000
Parent Co: Foldcraft Co
Brands:
Waymar

31012 **Wayne Automation Corporation**
605 General Washington Ave
Norristown, PA 19403 610-630-8900
Fax: 610-630-6116 sales@wayneautomation.com
www.wayneautomation.com
Automatic packaging equipment including partition inserters, case erectors, case packers and tray formers; exporter of partition inserters and case erectors
President: A David Johnson Jr
CFO: Dorothy Schlosser
Sales Director: Harry Dudley
Estimated Sales: $5-10 Million
Number Employees: 20-49
Square Footage: 30000
Brands:
Ce-15/22
Cpt-25
Sf-400
Wr-25

31013 **Wayne Combustion Systems**
801 Glasgow Ave
Fort Wayne, IN 46803-1344 260-425-9200
Fax: 260-424-0904 clagemann@waynecs.com
www.waynecombustion.com
Manufacturer and exporter of custom gas and oil burners; also, oven, fryer and griddle design analysis available
Manager: Karen Myrice
R & D: Dan Voorhis
Marketing: Karen Wygant
Sales: Dennis Parda
Purchasing: Phil Fenker
Estimated Sales: $10 - 20 Million
Number Employees: 50-99
Square Footage: 280000
Parent Co: Scott Fetzer Company
Brands:
Blue Angel
Premix Technology
Wayne

31014 **Wayne Engineering Corporation**
701 Performance Dr
Cedar Falls, IA 50613 319-266-1721
Fax: 319-266-8207 info@wayneusa.com
www.wayneusa.com
Manufacturer and exporter of mobile material handling equipment and refuse equipment
CEO: Kevin Watje
Sales Manager: Dave Severson
Sales Coordinator: Sherry Berak
Estimated Sales: $20-50 Million
Number Employees: 50-99
Square Footage: 60000
Brands:
Cargomaster

31015 **Wayne Group**
110 Sutter St
San Francisco, CA 94104-4002 415-421-2010
Fax: 415-421-2060 jjw@waynegroup.com
www.waynegroup.com
Executive search firm
*Estimated Sales:*less than $500,000
Number Employees: 1-4
Parent Co: Wayne Group

31016 **Wayne Industries**
1400 8th St N
Clanton, AL 35045 205-755-2365
Fax: 205-755-1516 800-225-3148
info@wayneindustries.com
www.wayneindustries.com
Indoor and outdoor signs and displays; also, lighted and nonlighted menu boards
National Sales: Bill Weston
Sales Manager: Monte Easterling
Operations Manager: Mike Cooper
Manager: Steve Hill
Manager: Stevde Hill
Estimated Sales: Below $5 Million
Number Employees: 50-99
Square Footage: 125000
Parent Co: Ebsco Industries

31017 **WePackItAll**
2745 Huntington Dr.
Duarte, CA 91010 626-301-9214
Fax: 626-301-9216 jackb@wepackitall.com
www.wepackitall.com
Contract packager of food supplement tablets and powders in pakettes and blister cards
President: Jack Bershtel
General Manager: Sharla Hughes
Plant Manager: Sharla Hughes
Estimated Sales: $5-10 Million
Number Employees: 20-49
Square Footage: 120000

31018 **Wearwell/Tennessee Mat Company**
P.O.Box 100186
Nashville, TN 37224-0186 615-254-8381
Fax: 615-255-4428 info@wearwell.com
www.wearwell.com
Safety and ergonomic matting
President: Elliot Greenberg
CEO: Steve Goldsmith
National Sales Manager: Nick Mead
Estimated Sales: $20 - 50 Million
Number Employees: 100-249

31019 **Weatherchem Corporation**
2222 Highland Road
Twinsburg, OH 44087 330-425-4206
Fax: 330-425-4586
marketing@weatherchem.com
www.weatherchem.com
A packaging company that designs, develops, and delivers innovative dispensing closures.
President: Jennifer Altstadt
CEO: Jennifer Altstadt
CFO: Bill Wolf
Research & Development: Barry Daggett
VP Marketing: Anna Fedova-Levi
Director of Sales: Jack Hotz
VP Operations: Carol Rinder
Estimated Sales: $10-20 Million
Square Footage: 40000
Parent Co: Weatherhead Industries
Type of Packaging: Consumer, Food Service, Private Label
Brands:
Agricap
Flapper
Tec-Loc
Top-Squeeze

31020 **Weavewood, Inc.**
7520 Wayzata Blvd
Golden Valley, MN 55426-1622 763-544-3136
Fax: 763-544-3137 800-367-6460
info@weavewood.com www.weavewood.com
Manufacturer and exporter of woodenware including bowls, plates, trays, coasters, tongs, susans, fork, spoon and magnetic server sets, etc.; also, aluminum and stainless steel steak platters
President: Howard Thompson
Quality Control: Tim Zanor
R&D: Tim Zanor
CFO: Howard Thompson Jr
Marketing Director: Peter Meyer
Estimated Sales: Below $5 Million
Number Employees: 20-49
Square Footage: 120000
Type of Packaging: Consumer, Food Service, Private Label, Bulk
Brands:
Weavewood

31021 Web Industries
377 Simarano Drive
Suite 220
Marlborough, MA 01752 508-898-2988
Fax: 508-898-3329 800-932-3212
askus@webindustries.com
www.webindustries.com
Suppliers of precision slitting, rewinding, spooling, sheeting, coating/printing, spooling
President: Don Romine
Chief Financial Officer: Carl Rubin
Executive Vice President: Dennis Latimer
Chief Operations Officer: Mark Pihl
Number Employees: 10

31022 Web Label
600 Hoover St NE
Suite 500
Minneapolis, MN 55413 612-588-0737
Fax: 612-706-3757 www.weblabel.com
Manufacturer and exporter of pressure sensitive labels
Owner: John Coldwell
Sales Manager: Dave Olson
Estimated Sales: $5 - 10 Million
Number Employees: 20-49
Type of Packaging: Consumer, Bulk

31023 Webb's Machine Design Company
2251 Montclair Rd
Clearwater, FL 33763 727-799-1768
Fax: 727-791-1639
Citrus processing equipment
Owner: John D Webb
CFO: Jon Weber
R&D: Jon Weber
Quality Control: Jon Weber
Estimated Sales: Below $5,000,000
Number Employees: 5-9

31024 (HQ)Webb-Stiles Company
675 Liverpool Dr
PO Box 464
Valley City, OH 44280 330-225-7761
Fax: 330-225-5532 webb-stiles@webb-stiles.com
www.webb-stiles.com
Manufacturer and exporter of custom designed conveyor systems for custom package and pallet handling
President: Donald G Stiles Jr
CEO: Donald Stiles Jr
Vice President: Larry Birchler
Sales Director: Matthew Weisman
Estimated Sales: $10-20 Million
Number Employees: 100-249
Square Footage: 300000
Other Locations:
Webb-Stiles Co.
Gadsden AL

31025 Webb-Triax Company
34375 W 12 Mile Rd
Farmington Hills, MI 48331 248-553-1000
Fax: 440-285-1878 info@jerviswebb.com
www.asrs-webbtriax.com
Manufacturer and exporter of automated storage and retrieval systems, including cooler and freezer storage systems and deep lane flow rack systems
Sales Director: Fred Cirino
Estimated Sales: $1 - 5,000,000
Number Employees: 20-49
Parent Co: Jervis B. Webb Company
Type of Packaging: Bulk
Brands:
Ms/Rv
Retriever

31026 (HQ)Webber/Smith Associates
1857 William Penn Way Ste 200
Lancaster, PA 17601 717-291-2266
Fax: 717-291-4401 800-231-0392
gsmith@webbersmith.com
www.webbersmith.com
Engineering design firm specializing in the design and construction of food processing, storage and distribution facilities throughout the usa.
President: Keith Shollenberger
Chairman: Garry Smith
VP: Joe Shaffer
Marketing & Public Relations Manager: Don Landis
Estimated Sales: $5 - 10 Million
Number Employees: 20-49

31027 Weber Display & Packaging
3500 Richmond St
Philadelphia, PA 19134 215-426-3500
Fax: 215-634-3073 www.weberdisplay-pkg.com
Corrugated shipping boxes
President: Jim Doherty
Estimated Sales: $20-50 Million
Number Employees: 100-249

31028 Weber Inc.
10701 N Ambassador Dr
Kansas City, MO 64153 816-891-0072
Fax: 816-891-0074 800-505-9591
usasales@weberslicer.com
www.weberslicer.com
Slicers for the meat, pork, poultry and cheese processing industries.

31029 Weber North America
10701 N. Ambassador Drive
Kansas City, MO 64153-1239 816-891-0072
Fax: 816-891-0074 www.weberslicer.com
Manufacturer and supplier of slicing machines for the meat and cheese industry
President: Scott Scariven
Estimated Sales: $2.5-5 Million
Number Employees: 20-49

31030 (HQ)Weber Packaging Solutions, Inc.
711 W Algonquin Rd
Arlington Hts, IL 60005 800-843-4242
Fax: 847-364-8575 800-843-4242
info@packaging.comcom
www.weberpackaging.com
Manufacturer and exporter of labeling equipment, labels and software
CEO: G Gillyth
Marketing Director: T Michalsen
Sales Director: M Campbell
Public Relations: R Stake
Plant Manager: J. O'Leary
Purchasing Director: L McGrath
Estimated Sales: $125 Million
Number Employees: 300
Number of Products: 100+
Square Footage: 320000
Type of Packaging: Consumer, Food Service, Private Label, Bulk
Other Locations:
Tape & Label Engineering
St. Petersburg FL
Brands:
Legijet
Legitronic

31031 Weber Scientific
2732 Kuser Road
Hamilton, NJ 08691 609-584-7677
Fax: 609-584-8388 800-328-8378
info@weberscientific.com
www.weberscientific.com
Products for dairy, food and water testing.
Owner/President: Fred Weber
VP: Joyce Arcarese
Account Manager: MaryBeth Karczynski
National Accounts Manager: Sharon Wilson
Account Manager: Nancy Silvester
Purchasing Manager: John Santillo
Estimated Sales: $1-2.5 Million
Number Employees: 28
Square Footage: 100000

31032 Weber-Stephen Products Company
200 E Daniels Rd
Palatine, IL 60067 847-934-5700
Fax: 847-407-8900 800-446-1071
support@weberstephen.com www.weber.com
Gas, charcoal, and electric grills. Useful for smoked products or grilled foods in restaurants or events.
President & CEO: James Stephen
Executive VP & CFO: Leonard Gryn
Quality Control Manager: Steve Butirro
Quality Control Manager: Dave Lohbauer
Marketing Manager: Brooke Jones
Media Contact: Melanie Hill
Executive VP Sales, Americas: Dale Wytiaz
Director of Public Relations: Sherry Bale
Operations Manager: Ken Stephen
Product Manager: Trace Weskamp
Plant Manager: Stan Gucwa
Director of Purchasing: Christoher Stephen
Square Footage: 1200000
Brands:
Weber

31033 Webster Packaging Corporation
715 S Riverside Ave
Loveland, OH 45140 513-683-5666
Fax: 513-683-0535
Corrugated products including shipping containers and displays
President: Denny Philips
Sales Manager: Susan Terlau
Estimated Sales: $20-50 Million
Number Employees: 50-99

31034 Wedgwood USA
1330 Campus Pkwy
Wall Township, NJ 07753-6811 732-938-5800
Fax: 732-938-7108 800-999-9936
consumer@wwusa.com
www.waterfordwedgwood.com
Manufacturer and importer of fine bone china tableware
Sales Manager: Michael Durao
Director Hotel/Restaurant Sales: Kathy Santangelo
Estimated Sales: $20-50 Million
Number Employees: 250-499
Square Footage: 368000
Parent Co: Waterford Wedgwood USA
Brands:
Johnson Brothers
Mason's Ironstone
Waterford Crystal
Wedgwood

31035 Wedlock Paper ConvertersLtd.
2327 Stanfield Road
Mississauga, ON L4Y 1R6
Canada 905-277-9461
Fax: 905-272-1108 800-388-0447
info@wedlockpaper.com
www.wedlockpaper.com
Manufacturer and exporter of paper bags
Customer Service: Scott Wedlock
Number Employees: 100
Type of Packaging: Consumer

31036 Wega USA
524 North York Road
Bensenville, IL 60106-1607 630-350-0066
Fax: 630-350-0005 info@expressoshoppe.com
www.expressoshoppe.com
Manufacturer, exporter and importer of coffee grinders and espresso equipment
President: David Dimbert
Estimated Sales: $500,000-$1 Million
Number Employees: 1-4
Square Footage: 20000
Type of Packaging: Food Service
Brands:
Bunn
Carioca
Jura
Pavoni
Ranulio
Saeco
Wega

31037 Weigh Right Automatic Scale Company
612 Mills Rd # A
Joliet, IL 60433 815-726-4626
Fax: 815-726-7638 800-571-0249
mikep@weighright.com www.weighright.com
Net weigh scales, volumetric fillers, wiegh/count scales. Industries serviced: fresh cut produce, IQF foods, confectionery, coffee, petfood, meat, spice, pharmaceutica, hardware, snack food, nuts, and more
President and CEO: Stephen Almberg
Marketing Director: Mike Phillips
Estimated Sales: Below $5 Million
Number Employees: 5-9
Square Footage: 20000

31038 WeighPack Systems/PaxiomGroup
2525 Louis Amos
Montreal, QC H8T 1C3
Canada 514-422-0808
Fax: 514-932-8118 888-934-4472
info@weighpack.com www.weighpack.com

Manufacturer and exporter of net-weighing systems; also, micro-processors and bagging systems
National Sales Manager: Anthony Delviscio
Number Employees: 30
Square Footage: 400000
Brands:
Aef-1
Aef-25
Aef-7
B-1
Bbf
Multi-Trix
Vs Bagger
Weigh Pack Systems
Zippy Bagger

31039 **Weighpack Systems**
2525 Louis Amos
Montreal, QC H8T 1C3
Canada 514-422-0808
Fax: 514-422-0834 888-934-4472
info@weighpack.com www.weighpack.com
Packaging machinery and conveying systems
President: Louis Taraborelli
Sales/Marketing Coordinator: John Brown
Sales Director: Nicholas Taraborelli

31040 **(HQ)Weiler & Company**
1116 E Main St
Whitewater, WI 53190 262-473-5254
Fax: 262-473-5867 800-558-9507
sales@weilerinc.com www.weilerinc.com
Manufacturer and exporter of meat, poultry and seafood processing equipment including grinders, mixers, screw and belt conveyors, portioning systems, meat/bone separtators and mixers/grinders; also, special equipment and designservices available
CEO: Nick Lesar
Corporate Director Equipment Sales: Jim Schumacher
International Sales Manager: Dave Schumacher
Customer Support/Sales: Jeremy Niemuth
General Manager: John Allred
Estimated Sales: $10-20 Million
Number Employees: 100-249
Square Footage: 72000
Other Locations:
Weiler & Co.
Sandy UT
Brands:
Beehive
Weiler

31041 **Weiler Equipment**
1116 E Main Street
Whitewater, WI 53190 262-473-5254
Fax: 262-473-5867 800-558-9507
www.weilerinc.com
Premier meat grinders and integrated food processing systems
President/CEO: Mel Cohen
VP Sales/Marketing: Kevin Howard

31042 **Weinbrenner Shoe Company**
108 S Polk St
Merrill, WI 54452 715-536-5521
Fax: 715-536-1172 800-826-0002
wsc@weinbrennerusa.com
www.weinbrennerusa.com
Manufacturer, importer and exporter of slip resisting safety shoes
President: L Nienow
CFO: David Giffleman
VP Sales/Marketing: Fred Girsky
Manager Sales: Shane Baganz
Estimated Sales: $20 - 50 Million
Number Employees: 100-249
Parent Co: Weinbrenner Shoe Company
Brands:
Mainstream
Thorogard
Thorogood

31043 **Weinman/Midland Pump**
420 3rd St
Piqua, OH 45356-3918 937-773-2442
Fax: 937-773-2238
cranepumps@cranepumps.com
www.cranepumps.com
Manufacturer and exporter of pumps for the agricultural and food processing industries
President: Lynn White
CFO: Mike Koon
CEO: Tom Pozda
R&D: Steve Palsey
Marketing VP: Rich Griffin
Operations: Tim Erwin
Plant Manager: Tim Adams
Estimated Sales: $100+ Million
Number Employees: 250-499
Square Footage: 400000
Parent Co: Crane Pumps & Systems
Brands:
Midland
Weinman

31044 **Weis Markets**
1000 South Second Street
PO Box 471
Sunbury, PA 17801 570-286-4571
Fax: 570-286-3286 866-999-9347
www.weismarkets.com
Supermarket chain with 159 stores in the U.S. states of Maryland, New York, New jersey, and West Virginia. Founded in 1912. Has two manufacturing facilities listed below.
President: Brian Kramer
CEO: Norman Rich
Owner: Frank Fantalucia
General Counsel: Martin Burt
VP Sales/Marketing: Lynn Thogun
Director/Public Relations: Dennis Curtin
Estimated Sales: $1 Billion
Number Employees: 25,000
Other Locations:
Manufacturing Facility - Market St
Sunbury PA
Manufacturing Facility - N 4th St
Sunbury PA
Brands:
Weis Five Star
Weis Quality
Full Circle

31045 **Weiss Instruments**
905 Waverly Avenue
Holtsville, NY 11742 631-207-1200
Fax: 631-207-0900 sales@weissinstruments.com
www.weissinstruments.com
Manufacturer and exporter of thermometers and pressure gauges
President: John Weiss
OEM Sales Manager: Stephen Weiss
Industrial Sales Manager: Thomas Keefe
Number Employees: 100
Square Footage: 200000

31046 **Weiss Sheet Metal**
105 Bodwell St
Avon, MA 02322 508-583-8300
Fax: 508-588-5690
stainlessfab@weiss-sheetmetal.com
www.weiss-sheetmetal.com
Custom stainless steel work tables, counters, sinks and wall mounted stacked shelves
President: Wayne G De Lano
Vice President: Brian De Lano
Shop Foreman: James Warfield
Estimator: Al Quieto
Estimated Sales: $3 Million
Number Employees: 10-19
Square Footage: 26000
Type of Packaging: Food Service

31047 **(HQ)Welbilt Corporation**
500 Summer St # 4
Stamford, CT 06901-4301 203-325-8300
Fax: 203-323-4550 www.aquent.com
Manufacturer and exporter of ventilators, ice machines and commercial cooking, warming and refrigeration equipment including broilers, fryers, ovens, toasters, rotisseries, mixers, etc
Manager: Maggie Patterson
Vice President of Services: Deb McCusker
Account Director: Damien Rocherolle
Estimated Sales: $5 - 10 Million
Number Employees: 1-4
Square Footage: 7200000
Other Locations:
Welbilt Corp.
Shreveport LA
Brands:
Belshaw
Clark
Cleveland
Contempo
Dean
Euro
Frymaster
Garland
Ice-O-Matic
Lincoln
Merco
Mercury
Panorama
Savory
Titan
Us Range
Varimixer

31048 **(HQ)Welch Brothers**
9 N 325 Rt. 25
Bartlett, IL 60103 847-741-6134
Fax: 847-697-0123 www.welchbrothers.com
Packer of steaks and portion-controlled meats; also, slaughtering and locker services available
President and CEO: Ron Hards
VP: Robert Welch
VP/Sales Manager: Jack Welch
Estimated Sales: $2.5-5 Million
Number Employees: 5-9
Square Footage: 12000
Type of Packaging: Consumer, Food Service

31049 **Welch Packaging**
1020 Herman St
Elkhart, IN 46516-9028 574-295-2460
Fax: 574-295-1527 www.welchpkg.com
Corrugated cartons and pallets
President: M Scott Welch
Estimated Sales: $20-50 Million
Number Employees: 100-249

31050 **Welch Stencil Company**
7 Lincoln Ave.
Scarborough, ME 04074 207-883-6200
Fax: 207-883-8588 800-635-3506
customerservice@welchusa.com
www.welchusa.com
Rubber stamps and engraved signs
President: Terry Davis
VP: Kathy Davis
Estimated Sales: $3 - 5 Million
Number Employees: 10-19

31051 **WellSet Tableware Manufacturing Company**
201 Water Street
Brooklyn, NY 11201-1111 718-624-4490
Fax: 718-596-3959 sales@wellset.com
www.wellset.com

31052 **Welliver Metal ProductsCorporation**
672 Murlark Ave NW
Salem, OR 97304 503-362-1568
Fax: 503-585-3374 del@wellivercorp.com
www.wellivercorp.com
Manufacturer and exporter of case packagers, size graders, steam kettles, tanks, size sorters, etc
Manager: John Layton
CEO/General Manager: Del Starr
Engineer Manager: Gray Johnson
Quality Control: John Hell
CEO: Del Starr
Estimated Sales: $3 - 5 Million
Number Employees: 20-49
Square Footage: 27000

31053 **Wells Lamont Industrial**
6640 W Touhy Avenue
Niles, IL 60714 847-647-8200
Fax: 847-470-1026 800-247-3295
wligcs@wellslamont.com
www.wellslamontindustrial.com
Hand protection including cut resistant, heat resistant, general purpose, liquid/chemical resistant, leather gloves and more.
President/CEO: Philippe Milliet
Marketing Coordinator: Dena Riccio
VP Human Resources: Lawrence Rist
Operations Executive: Heat Mathias
Number Employees: 130
Square Footage: 82000

31054 **Wells Lamont Industry Group**
6640 W. Touhy Avenue
Niles, IL 60714-4587 847-647-8200
Fax: 847-647-6943 800-323-2830
kmeger@wellslamont.com
www.wellslamont.com
Hand protection including cut-resistant heat resistant, leather and general purpose. Products include cut-resistant gloves, bakers pad, terry gloves, leather gloves, jersey gloves, canvas gloves, cut-resistant and heat resistantsleeves
VP: William Trainer
Marketing Coordinator: Michelle Kurtz
Sales Director: Jim Buckingham
Public Relations: Michelle Kurtz
Operations Manager: Bruce Smith
Estimated Sales: Below $500,000
Number Employees: 1,000-4,999
Type of Packaging: Private Label, Bulk

31055 **Wells Manufacturing Company**
P.O.Box 280
Verdi, NV 89439 775-345-0444
Fax: 775-345-8220
kevin.g.clark@carrier.utc.com
www.wellsbloomfield.com
Estimated Sales: $30 - 50 Million
Number Employees: 250-499
Parent Co: Carrier Commercial Refrigeration

31056 **Wells Manufacturing Company**
P.O.Box 280
Verdi, NV 89439 775-345-0444
Fax: 775-345-8220 800-777-0450
kevin.g.clark@carrier.utc.com
www.wellsbloomfield.com
Manufacturer and exporter of commercial griddles, fryers, broilers, warmers, coffee and tea brewers, espresso machines and accessories, dispensers, decanters, etc
President: Paul Angrick
President: Paul Angrick
Quality Control: Terry Mees
Sales Manager: Jeanine Blue
Number Employees: 250-499
Square Footage: 154000
Parent Co: Specialty Equipment Companies
Type of Packaging: Food Service

31057 **Wells-Lamont Corporation**
6640 W Touhy Ave
Niles, IL 60714 847-647-8200
Fax: 847-647-6943 800-323-2830
cservice@wellslamont.com
www.wellslamont.com
Vinyl impregnated gloves
CFO: Tom Palzer
VP: William Trainer
VP: R Stoller
Marketing Director: Jace Suttner
Estimated Sales: $5 - 10 Million
Number Employees: 1,000-4,999
Parent Co: A Marmon Group / Berkshire Hathaway Company
Brands:
Golden Gripper
Grips
Handy Andy
No Sweat
Nob Nob
Sure Gard
Tuff Guys
Wells Lamont
White Mule

31058 **Welltep International**
138 Palm Coast Pkwy NE # 192
Palm Coast, FL 32137-8241 386-437-5545
Fax: 386-437-5546
julie.rand@livelyartscenter.org
www.welltep.com
Broker of grocery related products
President: Luis Lopez
Estimated Sales: $1 - 3 Million
Number Employees: 1-4

31059 **Wemas Metal Products**
636 36th Avenue NE
Calgary, AB T2E 2L7
Canada 403-276-4451
Fax: 403-277-0725 sales@wemas.com
www.wemas.com
Manufacturer and exporter of custom stainless steel, aluminum and exotic metal food processing machinery
General Manager: Dave Swedak
Sales: Enno Ziemann
Sales: Joanne McCaughey
Number Employees: 44
Square Footage: 180000

31060 **Wemco Pumps**
P.O.Box 209
Salt Lake City, UT 84110-0209 801-359-8731
Fax: 801-355-9303 info@wemcopump.com
www.wemcopump.com
Wine industry pumps
CEO: Joseph W Roark
Marketing Director: Dave Borrowman
Production Manager: Gary Pearson
Estimated Sales: $50-100 Million
Number Employees: 500-999

31061 **Wen-Don Corporation**
PO Box 12127
Roanoke, VA 24023-2127 540-982-1061
Fax: 540-982-1066 800-223-1284
Specialty chemicals including municipal, institutional and industrial maintenance
President: Linda Jones III
Estimated Sales: $2.5-5 Million
Number Employees: 1-4

31062 **Wenda America, Inc.**
1823 High Grove Ln
Suite 103
Naperville, IL 60540 630-527-9800
Fax: 630-527-9200 sales@wendaingredients.com
www.wendaingredients.com
Meat ingredients including phosphates, soy protein, sodium alginate binding systems and more.
President: Wei Xiong
Sales Manager: Chad Boeckman
Operations Manager: Li Huamin
Type of Packaging: Bulk
Brands:
Wendaphos®
Wbs®
Novaprom®
Prosur
Safeplate™ Spices
Soypura®
Koolgel®
Savorphos™

31063 **Wendell August Forge**
1605 South Center Street
PO Box 109
Grove City, PA 16127 724-450-8700
Fax: 724-458-0906 800-923-1390
info@wendell.com www.wendellaugust.com
Hand-hammered aluminum, bronze, pewter and sterling silver advertising specialties, collector's items and gifts
CEO: F W Knecht Iii
Marketing Director: George Kenyon
Sales Director: Erin Pisano
Sales: Carol Snyder
Estimated Sales: $10-20 Million
Number Employees: 100-249
Number of Brands: 1
Number of Products: 100

31064 **Wenglor**
2280 Grange Hall Rd
Beavercreek, OH 45431 937-320-0011
Fax: 937-320-0033 877-936-4567
info.us@wenglor.com www.wenglor.com
Analog sensors, laser sensors, color sensors, line and optical sensors, reflex sensors and proximity sensors
General Manager: Tobiaf Schmitt
Estimated Sales: $500,000 - $1 Million
Number Employees: 5

31065 **Wepackit**
1-16 Tideman Drive
Orangeville, ON L9W 4N6
Canada 519-942-1700
Fax: 519-942-1702 sales@wepackitinc.com
www.wepackitinc.com
Manufacturer and exporter of case packers, erectors, sealers, de-casers and tray formers
President: David Wiggins
Number Employees: 55-60
Number of Products: 7
Square Footage: 80000

31066 **Werthan Packaging**
605 Highway 76
White House, TN 37188 615-672-3336
Fax: 615-581-5414 sales@werthan.usa.com
www.werthan.com
Multi-wall bags
Chairman of the Board: Anthony Werthan
Vice President, Finance/CFO: Jerry Gregg
Quality Control Manager: Tisha Stokes
Paper Mill Manager: Mike Palmer
Procurement Manager: Gary Parker
Estimated Sales: $50 Million
Number Employees: 273
Square Footage: 5000

31067 **Wesco Industrial Products**
1250 Welsh Rd
North Wales, PA 19454 215-699-7031
Fax: 800-346-5511 800-445-5681
bmunion@wescomfg.com www.wescomfg.com
Material handling products
President: Allen Apter
President: Jamie Johnson
Director of Sales: Mike Esris
Estimated Sales: $10-25 Million
Number Employees: 50-99

31068 **Wescor**
370 W 1700 S
Logan, UT 84321 435-752-6011
Fax: 435-752-4127 800-453-2725
biomed@wescor.com www.wescor.com
Manufacturer and exporter of osmometers and thermometers
President: Wayne K Barlow
Estimated Sales: $5-10,000,000
Number Employees: 50-99

31069 **Wesley International Corporation**
3680 Chestnut St
Scottdale, GA 30079 404-292-7441
Fax: 404-292-8469 800-241-8649
sales@wesleyintl.com
www.wesleyinternational.com
Manufacturer and exporter of electric vehicles, burden and personnel carriers and trucks including hand hydraulic pallets, skids and straddles
Sales/Marketing: Lee Gatins
Manager: Vanessa Holiday
Estimated Sales: $5 - 10 Million
Number Employees: 20-49
Square Footage: 25000
Brands:
Pack Mule
Pallet Mule

31070 **Wesley-Kind Associates**
200 Old Country Rd
Suite 364
Mineola, NY 11501-4240 516-747-3434
Fax: 516-248-2728
Management consultant specializing in plant and warehouse layouts and operating systems for the movement, storage and control of materials and products
Executive Director: Daniel Kind
Director Engineer: Oliver Wesley
Marketing Director: Daniel Kind
Estimated Sales: Less than $500,000
Number Employees: 1-4

31071 **West Agro**
11100 N Congress Ave
Kansas City, MO 64153 816-891-1600
Fax: 816-891-1595 list.tom@delaval.com
www.universaldairy.com
Manufacturer and exporter of cleaning and sanitation supplies including clean-in-place systems; also, sanitation control system consultant
President: Walt Maharay
VP: Thomas Fahey
Number Employees: 100-249
Parent Co: Tetra Laval Group

31072 **(HQ)West Carrollton Parchment Company**
PO Box 49098
West Carrollton, OH 45449 937-859-3621
Fax: 937-859-7610 wcp@wcparchment.com
www.wcparchment.com

Manufacturer and exporter of paper including printing, rewinding, sheeting, die cutting, creping and coating
President: Cameron Lonergan
CEO: Pierce Lonergan
VP Finance: Alan Berens
Quality Control: Brandon Carpenter
Sales/Marketing: Larry Teague
Operations: Bob Scancella
Production: Tom Bray
Purchasing Director: Jerry Lienesch
Estimated Sales: $30 Million
Number Employees: 100-249
Number of Products: 150
Square Footage: 260000
Parent Co: Friend Group
Type of Packaging: Food Service
Brands:
Gvp-100

31073 (HQ)West Chemical Products
1000 Herrontown Rd Ste 2
Princeton, NJ 08540 609-921-0501
Fax: 609-924-4308 www.upe.com
Manufacturer and exporter of sanitizing agents including detergents and disinfectants; also, insecticides including liquid and fly killing
President: Elwood Phares II
CEO: Elwood W Phares Ii
Estimated Sales: G
Number Employees: 100-249
Other Locations:
West Chemical Products
Tenefly NJ

31074 West Coast Industries
10 Jackson St
San Francisco, CA 94111 415-621-6656
Fax: 415-552-5368 800-243-3150
info@westcoastindustries.com
www.westcoastindustries.com
Restaurant and contract furniture including counters, tables, etc
President: Rob Liss
Secretary/Treasurer: Ron Liss
VP: Norman Sobel
Estimated Sales: $5-10 Million
Number Employees: 10-19

31075 West Coast Specialty Coffee
71 Lost Lake Lane
Campbell, CA 95008 650-259-9308
Fax: 650-259-8024 rh@specialtycoffee.com
www.specialtycoffee.com
Coffee and coffee equipment and supplies
President: Robert Hensley
Estimated Sales: $500,000
Number Employees: 2
Type of Packaging: Consumer, Food Service, Bulk

31076 West Hawk Industries
1717 S State St
Ann Arbor, MI 48104-4601 734-761-3100
Fax: 734-761-8430 800-678-1286
sales@westhawkpromo.com
www.westhawkind.com
Manufacturer and exporter of advertising novelties, decals, signs, banners, calendars, imprinted matches, bags and custom printed cups; also, imprinted mints and chocolates
President: Jan Hawkins
CEO: Harry Hawkins
Vice President: Sarah Spratt
Sales Director: Harry Hawkins
Estimated Sales: $2.5-5 Million
Number Employees: 5-9
Number of Products: 800
Square Footage: 15000
Type of Packaging: Private Label

31077 West Louisiana Ice Service
PO Box 1507
Leesville, LA 71496-1507 337-239-4530
Fax: 337-238-5095
Owner: James S Shapkoff Jr

31078 West Metals
463 Nightingale Avenue
London, ON N5W 4C4
Canada 519-457-0603
Fax: 519-457-7960 800-300-6667
sales@westmetals.com www.westmetals.com
Glass display cases, cocktail mix and beverage units, sinks, prep and steam tables, work centers, exhaust hoods and fans
Number Employees: 10

31079 West Oregon Wood Products
P.O.Box 249
Columbia City, OR 97018 503-397-6707
Fax: 503-397-6887 mross@wowpellets.com
www.wowpellets.com
A manufacturer of premium wood fuel pellet, all 100 percent wood fire logs, animal bedding, firestarter, and BBQ pellets. The quality products combined with a strong value proposition has provided us the platform to build categoryleading products. We continue to lead the industry in innovation, product development, and service.
President: Chris Sharron
General Manager: Mike Knobel
Director Marketing/Sales: Mark Ross
Estimated Sales: $1-2.5 Million
Number Employees: 45-50
Square Footage: 560000
Brands:
Blazers
Lil' Devils

31080 West Penn Oil Company
2305 Market St
Warren, PA 16365 814-723-9000
Fax: 814-723-9003 lang@westpenn.com
www.westpenn.com
Contract packager of lubricating oils
President: Larry Lang
Estimated Sales: $20 - 50 Million
Number Employees: 20-49
Brands:
Emblem

31081 West Star Industries
4445 E Fremont St
Stockton, CA 95215 209-955-8220
Fax: 209-955-8250 800-326-2288
wsi1@aol.com
Stainless steel products including sinks, tables, exhaust hoods and refrigeration equipment
President: Richard Hackett
VP: William George
Estimated Sales: $5-10 Million
Number Employees: 20-49
Square Footage: 30000
Brands:
West Star

31082 West Texas Untilities Company
301 Cypress St
Abilene, TX 79601-5820 325-674-7000
Fax: 325-674-7611 800-360-7483
www.aeptexas.com
Plant Manager: Greg W Blair
Estimated Sales: $200 - 500 Million
Number Employees: 250-499

31083 West-Pak
PO Box 763847
Dallas, TX 75376 214-337-8984
Fax: 214-337-8988
Protective packaging
President: Edwin Monroe
Estimated Sales: $10 - 20 Million
Number Employees: 20-49

31084 Westec Tank & Equipment
1402 Grove St.
Healdsburg, CA 95448 707-431-9342
Fax: 707-431-8669 joe@westectank.com
www.westectank.com
Wine industry valves and fittings
President: Wanda Alary
Estimated Sales: $5 - 10 Million
Number Employees: 100

31085 Westech Engineering
3625 S West Temple Ste 200
Salt Lake City, UT 84115 801-265-1000
Fax: 801-265-1080 info@westech-inc.com
www.westech-inc.com
Wastewater and water treatment systems; solid and liquid separators
President: Rex Plaizier
VP: Rex Plaizier
Marketing Manager: Marshall Palm
Sales Director: Jeff Easton
Estimated Sales: $30 - 50 Million
Number Employees: 100-249
Brands:
Cop
Simarotor

31086 Westeel
PO Box 1370
Saskatoon, SK S7K 3P5
Canada 306-931-2855
Fax: 306-931-2786 www.westeel.com
Storage bins
President: Robert Skull
CFO: Ray Anderson
Quality Control: Linda Thurston
R & D: Bruce Allen
Operations Manager: Bruce Allen
Number Employees: 10
Parent Co: Jenisys

31087 Westerbeke Fishing Gear
400 Border St
East Boston, MA 02128 617-561-9967
Fax: 617-561-3752 800-536-6387
westerbeke@prodigy.net wfg1.com
Wholesaler/distributor of boots, clothing, cutlery, shovels, netting, forks, containers, gloves, etc.; serving the seafood industry; liferaft annual inspections and netting & vinyl products.
President: Christopher Halligan
Sales Director: Ed Creamer
Purchasing Manager: Ed Creamer
Estimated Sales: $1 Million
Square Footage: 12000

31088 Western Carriers
2220 91st Street
North Bergen, NJ 07047-4713 800-631-7776
201-869-3300
wine@westerncarriers.com
www.westerncarriers.com
Warehouse providing storage for wines and spirits, and the alcoholic beverage industry.
President: Michael Hodes
Estimated Sales: $5-10 Million
Number Employees: 50-99
Square Footage: 3600000
Other Locations:
Vallejo 1,000,000 Sq Ft CA

31089 Western Combustion Engineering
640 E Realty St
Carson, CA 90745 310-834-9389
Fax: 310-834-4795
info@westerncombustion.com
www.westerncombustion.com
Manufacturer, exporter of ovens, oil fryers and food processing equipment
President: Marcia Paul
Vice President: Marcia Paul
Estimated Sales: $1-2,500,000
Number Employees: 10-19
Square Footage: 10000

31090 (HQ)Western Container Company
4323 Clary Blvd
Kansas City, MO 64130 816-924-5700
Fax: 816-924-7032
richardh@westerncontainer.com
www.westerncontainer.com
Manufacturer and exporter of cartons including folding, cellophane window and plastic coated
President: Richard Horton
CFO: Allen Booe
Quality Control: Charlie Palmer
Estimated Sales: $20 - 50 Million
Number Employees: 100-249

31091 Western Exterminator Company
1732 Kaiser Avenue
Irvine, CA 92614-5706 800-698-2440
Fax: 949-474-7767 mlawton@west-ext.com
www.west-ext.com
Pest control systems
Founder: Carl Strom
Vice President of Administration: Debbie Byrne
Vice President of Sales: Michael Britt
Estimated Sales: $2.5-5 Million
Number Employees: 50-99

31092 Western Foods
4717 Asher Avenue
Little Rock, AR 72219-4060 501-562-4646
Fax: 501-568-3447

Wholesaler/distributor of groceries, frozen foods, meats, cleaning supplies, disposables, table top needs, etc.; serving the food service market
President: Tony Huffman
Vice President: Ed Fason
Estimated Sales: $20-50 Million
Number Employees: 100-249

31093 Western Laminates
431 S 91st Cir
Omaha, NE 68114 402-556-4600
Fax: 402-556-4601
Laminated doors, cabinets and counter tops
President: Bennett Wagner
Estimated Sales: Below $5 Million
Number Employees: 10-19

31094 Western Lighting
2349 17th St
Franklin Park, IL 60131-3432 847-451-7200
Fax: 847-451-7275 www.westerlightinginc.com
Light fixtures and illuminated signs
Owner: Norma Heen
Number Employees: 1-4

31095 (HQ)Western Manufacturing Company
149 9th St
Suite 210
San Francisco, CA 94103-2662 415-431-1458
Fax: 415-431-5980
Manufacturer and exporter of leather goods including menu covers
Owner: Craig Storek
Office Manager: Lorraine Storek
Estimated Sales: $2.5-5 Million
Number Employees: 1-4

31096 Western Pacific Oils, Inc.
201 S Anderson St
Los Angeles, CA 90033 213-232-5117
Fax: 213-232-5102 info@westpacoils.com
www.westpacoils.com
Palm oils and coconut oil.
Manager: Y Neman
Estimated Sales: $900 Thousand
Type of Packaging: Food Service, Bulk
Brands:
Golden Palm Shortening
Golden Joma Palm Oil
Golden Palm Margarine
Golden Palm Cake & Icing
Golden Coconut Oil

31097 Western Pacific StorageSystems
300 E Arrow Hwy
San Dimas, CA 91773 909-451-0303
Fax: 909-451-0311 800-888-5707
trogers@wpss.com www.wpss.com
Manufacturer and exporter of steel and boltless shelving, carton flow racks and mezzanine systems
President: Tom Rogers
Marketing Manager: Diane Gowgill
Estimated Sales: $5-10,000,000
Number Employees: 100-249
Brands:
Deluxe
Industrial Structures
Pacific
Quik Pik
Rivetier

31098 (HQ)Western Plastics
P.O.Box 1636
Calhoun, GA 30703 706-625-5260
Fax: 706-625-0003 800-752-4106
calhoun@wplastics.com www.wplastics.com
Manufacturer and exporter of packaging materials including plastic film and aluminum foil
President: Thomas Cunningham
CEO: Frederick Young
CFO: George Schultz
Vice President: Frederick Young
Marketing Director: Paul O'Loghlen
Operations Manager: Bobby Hyde
Purchasing Manager: Jeff Silvers
Estimated Sales: $40 Million
Number Employees: 1-4
Square Footage: 100000
Type of Packaging: Food Service, Private Label, Bulk
Other Locations:
Brands:
Eldorado

31099 Western Plastics
2399 US 41 SW
Calhoun, GA 30701 706-625-5260
Fax: 706-625-0003 800-752-4106
calhoun@wplastics.com www.wplastics.com
Foil, foodfilm, pallet stretch film, meat and produce film
President: Tom Cunningham
Estimated Sales: $10-20 Million
Number Employees: 1-4

31100 Western Plastics California
105 Western Dr
Portland, TN 37148-2018 615-325-7331
Fax: 615-325-4924 sales@wplastic.com
www.wplastic.com
Manufacturer, importer and exporter of aluminum foil rolls, PVC film cutter-boxes, pallet stretch wrap, perforated food wrap and shrink film
President/General Manager: Steve Nichols
VP: Gene Ketter
Sales Manager: David Sullender
Estimated Sales: $5-10 Million
Number Employees: 100-249
Square Footage: 120000
Brands:
Air Flow
Ez Bander
Eco Wrap
Indenti-Film
Securi Seal
Strong Bow
Wp
Wp Foodfilm
Wp Handywrap
Wrapnet

31101 Western Polymer Corporation
32 Road R SE
Moses Lake, WA 98837-9303 509-765-1803
Fax: 509-765-0327 800-362-6845
sales@westernpolymer.com
www.westernpolymer.com
Processor, exporter and importer of starch; manufacturer of starch recovery systems
Owner: Sheldon Townsend
CEO: Sheldon Townsend
Marketing: Mike Markillie
Estimated Sales: $20-50 Million
Number Employees: 50-99
Parent Co: Moses Lake
Type of Packaging: Bulk

31102 Western Precoolingn
43990 Fremont Blvd
Fremont, CA 94538-0133 510-656-2220
Fax: 510-656-1137 www.westernprecooling.com
Wine industry refrigeration
President: Carig Miller
CFO: Jerry Nopis
Estimated Sales: Below $5 Million
Number Employees: 20-49

31103 Western Pulp Products Company
P.O.Box 968
Corvallis, OR 97339-0968 541-757-1151
Fax: 541-757-8613 800-547-3407
sales@westernpulp.com www.westernpulp.com
Wine industry pulp byproducts
President: Mel Kelsey
CFO: Brad McIntyre
Estimated Sales: $10 - 25 Million
Number Employees: 50-99

31104 Western Refrigerated Freight Systems
8238 W Harrison Street
Phoenix, AZ 85043 602-254-9922
www.westernrefrigerated.com
Handles all temperature sensitive shipping and distribution needs throughout California, Arizona & Nevada
President: Jeff Boley
Estimated Sales: $6 Million
Number Employees: 50
Other Locations:
Las Vegas NV

31105 Western Square Industries
1621 N Broadway
Stockton, CA 95205 209-944-0921
Fax: 209-944-0934 800-367-8383
info@westernsquare.com
www.westernsquare.com
Racks to hold bottled water
President: Trygve Mikkelsen
Accounts Payable / Receivables: Joan Mikkelsen
Chief Engineer: Larry Bartko
Southern Coast Sales: Bobby Fox
Plant Manager: Robert Craven
Purchasing Agent: Russell Danero
Estimated Sales: $6 Million
Number Employees: 40
Square Footage: 44000

31106 Western Stoneware
521 W 6th Ave
Monmouth, IL 61462 309-734-2161
Fax: 309-734-5942
contact@westernstoneware.com
www.westernstoneware.com
Manufacturer and exporter of stoneware bean pots, cheese crocks, canister sets, cups, mugs, soup bowls and steins
Owner: Jack Horner
CFO: Jean Wiseman
VP: Gene Wiseman
Estimated Sales: Below $5 Million
Number Employees: 20-49

31107 Westfalia Separator
100 Fairway Ct
Northvale, NJ 07647 201-767-3900
Fax: 201-784-4313 800-722-6622
www.us.westfalia-separator.com
Equipment for clarifying suspensions, separating liquids with removal of solids, separating liquid mixtures of differing densities of viscosities, extracting of active substances, classifying substances, and concentrating anddewatering of solids.
President: Michael Vick
COO: Hanno Lehmann
CFO: Norbert Breuer
Lab Director: Pete Malanchuk
Quality Control Director: Bill Taylor
Marketing Manager: Frank Kennedy
Sales: Michael Rohr
Human Resources Manager: Pam Pekar
VP Operations: Joseph Pavlosky
Purchasing Manager: John Nayancsik
Estimated Sales: $36.7 Million
Number Employees: 530
Square Footage: 105000
Brands:
Westfalia

31108 (HQ)Westfalia-Surge, Inc.
1880 County Farm Drive
Naperville, IL 60563 630-548-8374
Fax: 630-369-9875 www.westfaliasurge.com
Manufacturer and exporter of dairy farm equipment including cleaners
Manager: Ralph Rottier
CEO: Dirk Hejnal
CFO: Dr. Ulrich Hullman
Sales: Vern Foster
Business Unit, Milking & Cooling: Dr. Armin Tietjen
Estimated Sales: Below $5 Million
Number Employees: 100-249
Other Locations:
Babson Brothers Co.
Galesville WI
Brands:
Surge

31109 Westfield Sheet Metal Works
North 8th St & Monror Ave
PO Box 128
Kenilworth, NJ 07033 908-276-5500
Fax: 908-276-6808
info@westfieldsheetmetal.com
www.westfieldsheetmetal.com

Stainless steel belt guards, bins, booths, cabinets, canopies, gloves boxes, consoles, carts, casings, chutes, conveyors, cooling towers, cornices, dampers, ducts, dust collectors, exhaust systems, flues, guardrails, hoods, hoppersOSHA machine guards, pressure vessels, U&R racks, skids, tanks. Also a consultant for engineering, fabrication, and installation
President: C Johnstone
CEO: Tom Johnstone
CFO: Gregg Wheatley
VP/Office Manager: Lorraine Carine
Quality Control/R&D: William Nicolson
Marketing: Walter Basilone
Sales Director: Hubert Plungis
Chief Engineer: William Nicolson
VP/Manager Production: Thomas Johnstone
Plant Manager: Mike McElroy
Purchasing Manager: Stanley Guididas
Estimated Sales: $10-20 Million
Number Employees: 50-99
Square Footage: 50000

31110 Weston Emergency Light Company
11 Fox Rd
Waltham, MA 02451 781-890-6606
Fax: 781-890-6607 800-649-3756
Manufacturer and importer of exit signs, lamps and lighting fixtures; also, emergency light batteries, portable rechargeable hand lights and flashlights
President: Peter Palmgren
Manager: Thomas Silveira
Clerk: Paul Amsden
Estimated Sales: $5-10 Million
Number Employees: 10-19
Square Footage: 5000

31111 Westra Construction
1263 12th Ave E
Palmetto, FL 34221 941-723-1611
Fax: 920-324-5957 800-388-3545
info@westraconst.com www.westraconst.com
Building and construction contractor, design/builder, construction management and consultants
President and CEO: Don Thayer Jr
CFO: Patrick Flynn
Vice President: Peter Roehrig
VP Operations: Scott Heaze
Marketing Director: Gena Herwig
Sales Director: Scott Clark
Operations Manager: Rick Bickert
Estimated Sales: $1.7 Million
Number Employees: 240

31112 Westrick Paper Company
3011 Mercury Rd
Jacksonville, FL 32207 904-737-2122
Fax: 904-737-9129 info@westrickpaper.com
www.westrickpaper.com
Envelopes, writing tablets and other paper specialties
President: Jack Lamb
Estimated Sales: $5-10 Million
Number Employees: 10-19

31113 Westvaco Corporation
2000 Ogletown Road
Newark, DE 19711-5439 302-453-7200
Fax: 302-453-7280
Folding cartons and MAP packaging; exporter of ovenware packaging
Business Development Manager: Rufus Miller
Manager (Frozen Foods): Shelly Dicken
National Account Manager: Richard De Ruiter
Estimated Sales: $1-2.5 Million
Number Employees: 9
Square Footage: 60000

31114 Westvaco Corporation
320 Hull St
Richmond, VA 23224 804-233-9205
Fax: 804-232-3975 www.meadwestvaco.com
Contract packager of microwaveable entrees, baked goods, etc
Sales Manager: John McInerney
Sales: Bob London
Estimated Sales: $20 - 50 Million
Number Employees: 250-499
Parent Co: Westvaco Corporation

31115 Wetterau Wood Products
1600 Deleglise St
PO Box 429
Antigo, WI 54409 715-623-7907
Fax: 715-623-4399 wetterauwood@yahoo.com
www.wetterauwoodproductsinc.homestead.com
Pallets and skids
President: Michael Wetterau
VP: Deborah Wetterau
Number Employees: 10

31116 Wexler Packaging Products
777-M Schwab Road
Hatfield, PA 19440 215-631-9700
Fax: 215-631-9705 800-878-3878
sales@wexlerpackaging.com
www.wexlerpackaging.com
Paper/poly banding machines
Marketing Manager: Joseph Ambrose
Estimated Sales: $5-10 Million
Number Employees: 10-19

31117 Wexxar Corporation
3851 W Devon Avenue
Chicago, IL 60659-1024 630-983-6666
Fax: 630-983-6948 sales@wexxar.com
www.wexxar.com
Manufacturer and exporter of packaging equipment including tray and case formers and sealers
Vice President of Sales: Jim Stoddard
Estimated Sales: Less than $500,000
Number Employees: 4
Square Footage: 200000
Parent Co: Wexxar Packaging Machinery
Brands:
Wexxar

31118 Wexxar Packaging Inc
13471 Vulcan Way
Richmond, BC V6V 1K4
Canada 604-930-9500
Fax: 604-930-9368 888-565-3219
sales@wexxar.com www.wexxar.com
Case forming, case sealing by hot glue, cold glue, tape. Poly bag insertors stainless steel wash down corrosion resistant machinery
President: William Chu
Marketing Director: Melissa Montague
Parent Co: ProMach Inc
Type of Packaging: Food Service
Brands:
Bel Line

31119 Weyerhaeuser Company
P.O. Box 9777
Federal Way, WA 98063-9777 253-924-2345
800-525-5440
www.weyerhaeuser.com
Corrugated boxes
Chairman: Charles Williamson
President/CEO/Director: Daniel Fulton
EVP/Chief Financial Officer: Patricia Bedient
Vice President, Information Technology: Kevin Shearer
SVP, Research & Development/CTO: Miles Drake
Director, Quality Assurance: Jason Smitherman
Director, Marketing: Jason McIntosh
Director, Sales: Mike Spath
Public Affairs Manager: Anthony Chavez
Operations Manager: Walt Shriver
Production Manager: Linor Williams
Plant Manager: William Snyder
Purchasing Manager: Karen Andrus-Hughes
Estimated Sales: $50-100 Million
Number Employees: 13,200
Square Footage: 14672
Parent Co: Wayerhaeuser Company

31120 Whallon Machinery
205 N Chicago St
PO Box 429
Royal Center, IN 46978 574-643-9561
Fax: 574-643-9218 info@whallon.com
www.whallon.com
Manufacturer and exporter of palletizers and depalletizers for cans, cases and pails
President: Leslie Whallon Smith
Engineering Manager: Jeff Tevis
Sales Manager: Bruce Ide
Purchasing Manager: Judy Roudebush
Estimated Sales: $10-20 Million
Number Employees: 45
Square Footage: 35000

31121 Whatman
PO Box 8223
Haverhill, MA 01835-0723 978-374-7400
Fax: 978-374-7070
Manufacturer and exporter of filters, analytical instruments and laboratory equipment and supplies
VP Sales/Marketing: David Largesse
Estimated Sales: $500,000-$1 Million
Number Employees: 50-99
Type of Packaging: Bulk

31122 Whatman
800 Centennial Ave # 1
Piscataway, NJ 08854-3911 973-245-8300
Fax: 973-245-8301 info@whatman.com
www.whatman.com
Provides separations technology and in known throughout the scientific community for providing innovative products and solutions.
CEO: Bob Thein
Senior VP: Richard Dool
Product Manager: Tiana Gorham
Estimated Sales: $7 Million
Number Employees: 50-99
Other Locations:
Sanford ME
Brands:
Whatman

31123 Wheaton Plastic Containers
1101 Wheaton Ave
Millville, NJ 08332-2003 856-825-1400
Fax: 856-825-1368 wheaton.com
Plastic and glass containers, plastic bottles, caps and closures
President, Chief Executive Officer: Stephen Drozdow
Vice President of Global Marketing: Michael Blazes
Vice President of Quality: Nicholas DeBello
Regional Manager: Al Lancto
Vice President of Operations: Gregory Bianco
Number Employees: 250-499

31124 Wheel Tough Company
1597 E Industrial Drive
Terre Haute, IN 47802-9265 812-298-8606
Fax: 812-298-1166 888-765-8833
wheeltough@aol.com www.wheeltough.com
Manufacturer and exporter of aluminum bar and restaurant furniture including stools, chairs and tables; also, gas and charcoal grills, deep fryers and steamers
President: Rudolph J Stakeman Jr
Estimated Sales: $1 Million
Number Employees: 5
Square Footage: 272000
Brands:
Driver's Seat, The
Trackside Cookery

31125 Whey Systems
PO Box 1689
Willmar, MN 56201-1689 320-905-4122
Fax: 320-231-2282 roshsner@wheysystems.com
www.wheysystems.com
Provides edible whey processing equipment and systems to the dairy industry. Each system and component is specifically designed to efficiently process the desired whey fraction. Recognized as the world leader in providing lactosedrying systems, with the lowest capital and operating cost to produce high quality edible powder. Providing systems for whey, WPC, lactose, permeate, demineralization, and ammonium lactate.
President: Loren Corle
Product Manager: Jay Gilbert
Number Employees: 20-49

31126 Whirl Air Flow Corporation
20055 177th St NW
Big Lake, MN 55309 763-262-1200
Fax: 763-262-1212 800-373-3461
whirlair@whirlair.com www.whirlair.com
Dense and dilute phase pneumatic conveyors including pressure and vacuum
President: Edward Mueller
Marketing Director: Gregg Hedtke
Sales Director: Gregg Hedtke
Plant Manager: Ken Hanley
Purchasing Manager: Wendy Holland
Estimated Sales: $6-7 Million
Number Employees: 1-4

Number of Brands: 45
Square Footage: 50000

31127 Whirley Industries
PO Box 988
Warren, PA 16365 814-723-7600
Fax: 814-723-3245 800-825-5575
klabarbera@whirley.com www.whirley.com
As the world's leading manufacturer of plastic promotional drink containers, Whirley Industries offers a diverse line of products ranging from 12-128 oz
Owner/CEO: Lincoln Sokolski
CFO: Greg Aross
Marketing: Andrew Solkoski
Sales: William Turner
Estimated Sales: $20-50 Million
Number Employees: 250-499
Type of Packaging: Bulk

31128 (HQ)Whisk Products
130 Enterprise Dr
Wentzville, MO 63385 636-327-6261
Fax: 636-327-6288 800-204-7627
whisk@whiskproducts.com
www.whiskproducts.com
Manufacturer and exporter of hand cleaners, germicidal hand soap and dishwashing detergents; also, soap dispensers
President: Raymond A LaMantia
Sales: Brad LaMantia
Plant Manager: Scott Berg
Purchasing: Lisa Thess
Estimated Sales: $3 - 5 Million
Number Employees: 10-19
Number of Brands: 1
Number of Products: 32
Square Footage: 23000
Brands:
Metalife
Sir
Whisk
Xcel

31129 Whit-Log Trailers Inc
PO Box 668
Wilbur, OR 97494 541-673-0651
Fax: 541-673-1166 800-452-1234
brett@whitlogtrailers.com
www.whitlogtrailers.com
Manufacturer and exporter of hydraulic material handling equipment including truck mounted and pedestal electric stationary cranes
Owner: Gene Whitaker
Sales Manager: Jim Davidson
Estimated Sales: $300,000-500,000
Number Employees: 1-4

31130 White Cap
1140 31st St
Downers Grove, IL 60515 630-515-8383
Fax: 630-515-5326 800-515-1565
Manufacturer and exporter of metal and plastic vacuum closures and related sealing equipment including cappers
VP Sales: George Sullivan
Estimated Sales: $10-20 Million
Number Employees: 5-9
Square Footage: 10000
Parent Co: Schmalbach Lubecca
Type of Packaging: Bulk
Brands:
Plast-Twist
Twist-Off

31131 White Mop Wringer Company
P.O.Box 16647
Tampa, FL 33687-6647 813-971-2223
Fax: 813-971-6090 800-237-7582
customerservice@pullmanholtcorp.com
www.pullmanholtcorp.com
Manufacturer and exporter of janitorial equipment including burnishers, carts, floor and carpet care products and waste baskets and receptacles
Chief Financial Officer: Thomas Halluska
Estimated Sales: $50 - 100 Million
Number Employees: 100-249
Type of Packaging: Food Service
Brands:
Gator
Microscrub
Mipro
Propak
Pullman-Holt Gansow
Rugboss
Smartbasket

31132 White Mountain Freezer
800 E 101st Terrace
Kansas City, MO 64131-5322 816-943-4100
Fax: 816-943-4123
Manufacturer and exporter of ice cream and fruit processing machinery including freezers, parers and pitters
VP Marketing: Phil Gyori
Marketing Manager: Lori Baker
Production Manager: Melea Burghart
Parent Co: Rival Company

31133 White Mountain Lumber Company
30 East Milan Road
PO Box 7
Berlin, NH 03570 603-752-1000
Fax: 603-752-1400 www.whitemtnlumber.com
Wooden pallets
President: Barry J Kelley
Treasurer: Mark Kelley
Sales Director: Phil Bedard
General Manager/Wholesale Manager: Barry Kelley
Estimated Sales: $10-20 Million
Number Employees: 50-99
Square Footage: 25000

31134 White Oak Frozen Foods LLC
2525 Cooper Ave.
Merced, CA 95348 209-725-9492
Fax: 209-725-9441
www.whiteoakfrozenfoods.com
Reduced Moisture™ IQF vegetables.
President: Jack Sollazzo
VP Sales: Jim McKendry
Quality Assurance Manager: Gilbert Garza
Sales Manager: Dan Wilkinson
Operations Manager: Brian DiCiano
Estimated Sales: $3 Million
Number Employees: 25
Parent Co: Cascade Specialties, Inc.

31135 White Rabbit Dye Company
4265 Meramec St
Saint Louis, MO 63116 314-664-6563
Fax: 314-664-5563 800-466-6588
info@whiterabbitdye.com
www.whiterabbitdye.com
Easter egg dyes, kits and food colors; also, wire dippers; exporter of dry food colors
Co-Owner: Julie Consolino
Co-Owner: Jeff Petroski
Estimated Sales: $5-10 Million
Number Employees: 5-9
Square Footage: 32000
Parent Co: Premier Packaging
Type of Packaging: Consumer
Brands:
White Rabbit

31136 White Stokes International
3615 South Jasper Place
Chicago, IL 60609 773-523-7540
Fax: 773-523-0767 800-978-6537
info@whitestokes.com www.whitestokes.com
Quality ingredients for bakery, confectionary, and ice cream. Founded in 1906.
President: Nicholas Tzakis
Vice President: George Tzakis
Number Employees: 26

31137 White Swan Fruit Products
1200 W Drive M L King
Plant City, FL 33563-0021 813-752-1155
Fax: 813-754-3168 800-330-8952
paradisefruitco@hotmail.com
www.paradisefruitco.com
Processor and exporter of candied fruit and peels; manufacturer of custom plastic molders
President: Randy Gordon
CEO: Melvin Gordon
Estimated Sales: 20-50 Million
Number Employees: 250-499
Parent Co: Paradise Beverages
Type of Packaging: Consumer, Food Service, Private Label, Bulk
Brands:
Queen Anne
White Swan

31138 White Way Sign & Maintenance
451 Kingston Ct
Mt Prospect, IL 60056 847-391-0200
Fax: 847-642-0272 800-621-4122
sales@whiteway.com www.whitewaysign.com
Manufacturer and exporter of electronic message displays
President: Robert B Flannery Jr
VP of Sales: Robert Flannery III
Plant Mgr: Pete Tomaselli
Estimated Sales: $20 - 50 Million
Number Employees: 100-249

31139 (HQ)Whitford Corporation
33 Sproul Rd
Frazer, PA 19355 610-296-3200
Fax: 610-647-4849 sales@whitfordww.com
www.whitfordww.com
Manufacturer and exporter of nonstick coatings designed for food contact and food associated applications
President: David Willis Jr
Chief Administrative Officer: Joan Eberhardt
CFO: Brian Kilty
Marketing Director: John Badner
Plant Manager: Scott De Bourke
Purchasing Manager: Jill Schultz
Estimated Sales: $30 - 50 Million
Number Employees: 100
Square Footage: 60000
Brands:
Excalibur
Quantanium
Quantum
Ultralon
Xylac
Xylan
Xylan Eterna
Xylan Plus

31140 Whiting & Davis
PO Box 1270
Attleboro Falls, MA 02763-0270 508-699-0214
Fax: 508-643-9303 800-876-6374
radimarzio@aol.com
www.whitinganddavis.com/
Manufacturer, exporter and importer of stainless steel ring mesh safety protective clothing including gloves, aprons, arm and body gear
Director Sales/Marketing: Ron DiMarzio
Customer Service: Karen Laushway
Estimated Sales: $5-10 Million
Number Employees: 100
Square Footage: 400000
Parent Co: WDC Holdings
Brands:
3-Step
Aegis
Ultra Guard
Whiting & Davis

31141 Whitley Manufacturing Company
PO Box 112
Midland, NC 28107 704-888-2625
Fax: 704-888-3023 www.whitleyhandle.com
Mop, broom and shovel handles; importer of dowels
President: Arlene Whitley
CEO: A Whitley
Quality Control: Arlene Whitley
Estimated Sales: $20 - 50 Million
Number Employees: 20-49
Square Footage: 35000

31142 (HQ)Whitlock Packaging Corporation
1701 S Lee St
Fort Gibson, OK 74434 918-478-4300
Fax: 918-478-7360 mollerd@whitlockpkg.com
www.whitlockpkg.com
Contract packager providing glass, steel, aluminum can, PET and plastic packaging services for noncarbonated beverages
President: David Moller
Vice President: Fred Ahrens
VP Marketing/Sales: Terry Milan
VP Sales & Private Label: Bill Towler
VP Human Resource: Ted Smith
VP Manufacturing: Abraham Jospeh
Plant Manager: Joe Tomaskovic
Purchasing Manager: Tammy Sanders
Number Employees: 250-499
Square Footage: 281

31143 Whitmire Micro-Gen Research
3568 Tree Court Indstrl Blvd
St Louis, MO 63122-6682 636-225-5371
Fax: 636-225-3739 800-777-8570
www.wmmg.com
Pest control equipment and chemicals
CEO: Tony Accurso
National Sales Manager: Larry Sharp
Director Manufacturing/Logistics: Chuck Sutton
Estimated Sales: $15 Million
Number Employees: 50-99
Parent Co: S.C. Johnson & Son
Brands:
Advance
Allure
Ascend
Avert
Mouse Master
Vector

31144 Whittle & Mutch
712 Fellowship Rd
Mount Laurel, NJ 08054 856-235-1165
Fax: 856-235-0902 jmutch3d@wamiflavor.com
www.wamiflavor.com
President: John C Mutch Jr
Estimated Sales: $10-20 Million
Number Employees: 10-19

31145 Wholesome Classics
1224 Rimer Dr
Moraga, CA 94556-1727
Fax: 408-292-2394
carol@wholesomeclassics.com
www.wholesomeclassics.com
Low fat and wheat free baking mixes; private labeling available
Research & Development: Carol Zelinski
Number Employees: 1-4
Type of Packaging: Consumer, Private Label
Brands:
N-Dur-Enzo

31146 Wichita Stamp & Seal
807 N. Main
Wichita, KS 67203 316-263-4223
Fax: 316-263-9738 stamps@feist.com
www.wichitastampandseal.com
Notary and corporate seals, rubber stamps, interior signs, etc.; also, ink jet printers, coders and FDA approved inks
President: Melvin Bird
CFO: Linne Bird
Marketing Director: Martha Hays
Estimated Sales: Below $5 Million
Number Employees: 5-9

31147 Wick's Packaging Service
7545 S State Road 75
Cutler, IN 46920 574-967-3104
Fax: 765-268-2729 info@wickspackaging.com
www.wickspackaging.com
Manufacturer and exporter of rebuilt vertical form/fill/seal packaging machinery. Distribute plastic pouch making machinery: T-shirt, standup zip lock pouch, and wicketed bags
Owner: Steven Wickersham
Vice President: Barb Wickersham
Research & Development: Craig Wickersham
Public Relations: Jerry Ellis
Packaging Engineer: Shawn Wickersham
Production Manager: Jerry Reef Jr
Estimated Sales: $2.5-5 Million
Number Employees: 1-4
Square Footage: 28000
Type of Packaging: Consumer, Food Service, Private Label, Bulk

31148 Wick's Packaging Service
7545 South State Road 75
Cutler, IN 46920-9670 574-967-3104
Fax: 765-268-2729 info@wickspackaging.com
www.wickspackaging.com
Vertical form seal bag makers
President: Steve Wickersham
Estimated Sales: Below $5 Million
Number Employees: 1-4

31149 (HQ)Wico Corporation
7847 N Caldwell Avenue
Niles, IL 60714-3375 847-583-1320
Fax: 847-583-1043 800-367-9426
www.wicothesource.com
Parts and supplies for coin-operated vending and amusement equipment

31150 Wiegmann & Rose
9131 San Leandro Street
Oakland, CA 94603 510-632-8828
Fax: 510-632-8920
jlogan@wiegmannandrose.com
www.wiegmannandrose.com
Designer and manufacturer of ammonia flooded, spray shell and tube chillers for food and wine processing
President: Scott E. Logan
CEO: Scott E. Logan
Executive VP: R Trent
VP Quality: Jon E. Hammons
Sales: Scott E. Logan
Sales: K Gardner
Administration, Personnel: Suzette I. Logan
Plant Manager: Gary D. Keeler
Purchasing: Will O' Bryant
Estimated Sales: $2.5-5 Million
Number Employees: 20-49
Square Footage: 212000
Parent Co: Xchanger Manufacturing Corporation
Brands:
Thermxchanger
Wiegmann & Rose

31151 Wifag Group Polytype America Corp
10 Industrial Ave
Mahwah, NJ 07430-2205 201-995-1000
Fax: 201-995-1080 info@polytype-usa.com
migration.opencloudapi.com/data/www.polytypeamerica.com/aboutus.html
Dry offset printing on plastic containers
President: Pieter S. van der Griendt
VP Sales: Thomas Stuart
Sales Manager: Felix Gomez
Operations Manager: Jim Dominico
Estimated Sales: $1-5 Million
Number Employees: 25
Parent Co: wifag//polytype

31152 Wiginton Fire Sprinklers
699 Aero Ln
Sanford, FL 32771-6699 407-831-3414
Fax: 407-585-3280 www.wiginton.net
Automatic fire sprinkler systems
Chairman, Chief Executive Officer: Don Wiginton
Sr. Project Manager: Bob Lyle
Manager of Sales: Kenny Trevino
Estimated Sales: $20-50 Million
Number Employees: 50-99

31153 Wika Instrument Corporation
1000 Wiegand Blvd
Lawrenceville, GA 30043 770-513-8200
Fax: 770-338-5118 800-645-0606
info@wika.com www.wika.com
Full line of mechanical and electronic pressure instruments, temperature instruments and diaphram seals manufactured to stric ISO 9001 standards
President: Michael Gerster
Estimated Sales: $20 - 50 Million
Number Employees: 500-999
Square Footage: 225000
Parent Co: Wika Instrument Corporation
Brands:
Trend

31154 Wika Instrument LP
1000 Wiegand Blvd
Lawrenceville, GA 30043 770-513-8200
Fax: 770-338-5118 888-945-2872
info@wika.com www.wika.com
President: Michael Gerster
Chief Financial Officer: Steve McCullough
Chief Revenue Officer: Drew Firestone
Quality Control: Bernett Bigts
Estimated Sales: $5 - 10 Million
Number Employees: 500-999

31155 Wil-Mac Container Corporation
1975 Sarasota Business Pkwy NE
Conyers, GA 30013 770-483-8744
Fax: 770-607-1473 800-428-9269
info@wil-mac.com www.prattindustries.com
Corrugated boxes
Sales: Michael Wilkie
Estimated Sales: $20-50 Million
Number Employees: 50-99

31156 Wilbur Curtis Company
6913 W Acco St
Montebello, CA 90640 800-421-6150
Fax: 323-837-2401 800-421-6150
info@wilburcurtis.com www.wilburcurtis.com
Manufacturer and exporter of coffee and tea brewing equipment
COO: Joe Laws
Estimated Sales: $30 - 50 Million
Number Employees: 250-500
Square Footage: 105000
Brands:
Advanced Digital System
Alpha
Curtis
Gemini
Mercury
Polaris
Primo Cappaccino
Thermologic

31157 Wilch Manufacturing
1345 SW 42nd Street
Topeka, KS 66609-1267 785-267-2762
Fax: 785-267-6825
Manufacturer and exporter of ice cream blenders, cooking grills, freezers and dispensers including slush, cocktail, yogurt and soft serve
President: Bill Young
Sales: Dave White
Purchasing Manager: Dee Kuhn
Number Employees: 45
Square Footage: 51000
Brands:
Wilch

31158 Wilco Distributor
P.O.Box 291
Lompoc, CA 93438-0291 805-735-2476
Fax: 805-735-3629 800-769-5040
williewilc@aol.com www.wilcodistributors.com
Manufacture and distributor of rodenticides in ther Western portion of the United States and Canada.
President/Owner: Brent Hazen
Chief Executive Officer, Founder: Donald Willis
VP: Blake Hazen
Estimated Sales: $3 - 5 Million
Number Employees: 15

31159 Wilco Precision Testers
145 Main St
Tuckahoe, NY 10707-2906 914-337-2005
Fax: 914-337-8519 info@ptiusa.com
www.ptipacktech.com
Specialty packaging and inspection machinery for the pharmaceutical, food, container and automotive industries including total container inspection, package integrity testing, e-z open peelable can ends, and filling and heat sealing
Member of the Board: Anton Stauffer
Estimated Sales: $10 - 20 Million
Number Employees: 20-49

31160 Wilco, USA
181 Woodland Valley Drive
Woodland Park, CO 80863-9314 719-686-0074
Fax: 719-686-0112
gc-schramm@compuserve.com
Leak inspection equipment for all products

31161 Wilcox Canvas Awning
3217 Genoa Road
Perrysburg Wood, OH 43551 419-837-2821
Fax: 419-837-2814 donr@wilcoxawning.com
www.wilcoxawning.com
Commercial awnings
President: Don Reinbolt
Estimated Sales: $1-2.5 Million
Number Employees: 1-4
Parent Co: Toledo Tarp Service

31162 Wild Flavors
1261 Pacific Ave
Erlanger, KY 41018 859-342-3744
Fax: 859-342-3610 888-945-3352
marketing@wildflavors.com
www.wildflavors.com

Develops, manufactures, and distributes flavors, flavor systems, colors, health ingredients and systems to the food and beverage industry.
Owner: Dr Hans-Peter Wild
CEO: Michael Ponder
CFO: Gary Massie
Assistant Director Regulatory: Greg Betsch
Senior Director, Quality Control: Karen Eberts
Senior Director, Marketing: Donna Hansee
VP Sales: Reed Lynn
Senior Director, Public Relations: Donna Hansee
Chief Operating Officer: Erik Donhowe
Director, Operations: Dan Holtzleiter
Senior Director, Procurement: Tony Sizemore
Estimated Sales: $7.4 Million
Square Footage: 760000
Type of Packaging: Consumer, Food Service, Private Label, Bulk

31163 Wilden Pump & Engineering LLC
22069 Van Buren St
Grand Terrace, CA 92313-5607 909-422-1700
Fax: 909-783-3440 www.wildenpump.com
Air operated double diaphragm pumps.
President: John Allen
VP Finance: William Barton
VP Sales/Marketing: Martino Valela
VP Operations: Denny Buskirk
VP Engineering: Gary Lent
Estimated Sales: $2.4,000,000
Number Employees: 20-49
Brands:
Pro-Flow

31164 Wilder Manufacturing Company
41 Mechanic St
Port Jervis, NY 12771 845-856-5188
Fax: 845-856-1950 800-832-1319
wilder@warwick.net www.wildermfg.com
Manufacturer and exporter of holding, warming and transporting equipment including proofing cabinets, bins, racks, utility tables, etc
VP Sales/Marketing: Ray Addington
Estimated Sales: $1 - 5 Million
Parent Co: Win-Holt Equipment Group
Type of Packaging: Food Service
Brands:
Wilder

31165 Wildes - Spirit Design & Printing
PO Box 1510
4321 Charles Crossing Drive
White Plains, MD 20695-1510 301-870-4141
Fax: 301-932-7495 info@wildes-spirit.com
www.wildes-spirit.com
General commercial markers and stamps
Owner: Katie Stickel
CEO: Katie Stickel
Owner: Katie Stickel
Estimated Sales: $2.5 - 5 Million
Number Employees: 20-49
Brands:
Crown Marketing

31166 Wilen Professional Cleaning Products
3760 Southside Industrial Pkwy
Atlanta, GA 30354-3219 404-366-2111
Fax: 404-361-8832 800-241-7371
vperry@wilen.com www.wilen.com
Manufacturer and exporter of cleaning equipment and supplies including brushes, scouring and hand pads and floor/carpet products
President: Vance Perry
Quality Control: Rachael Alexander
VP Marketing/Customer Relations: Rhonda Lassiter
Production Manager: John Akin
Purchasing Manager: Norris Minnis
Estimated Sales: $75 - 100 Million
Number Employees: 100-249
Square Footage: 150000

31167 Wilevco
10 Fortune Dr
Billerica, MA 01821-3996 978-667-0400
Fax: 978-670-9191 sales@wilevco.com
www.wilevco.com
Manufacturer and exporter of automatic batter control systems, rotary atomization spray applicators and swept surface heat exchangers for process chilling systems
President/CEO: Leverett Flint
Chairman/Founder: Putnam Flint
Vice President: John Whitmore
Estimated Sales: Below $5 Million
Number Employees: 10-19
Square Footage: 16000
Brands:
Cryolator
Wilevco

31168 Wilheit Packaging
1527 May Dr
Gainesville, GA 30507 770-532-4421
Fax: 770-532-8956 bedwards@wilheit.com
www.wilheit.com
Corrugated boxes
President and CFO: Philip Wilheit
Marketing: Barbara Edwards
Estimated Sales: $20 - 50 Million
Number Employees: 50-99

31169 Wilhelmsen Consulting
455 Falcato Dr
Milpitas, CA 95035-6113 408-946-4525
Fax: 413-235-0121 ewilhel@klarify.com
www.klarify.com
Consultant providing analytical and business development services; also, food safety and training available
Owner: Eric Wilhelmsen
Estimated Sales: $300,000-500,000
Number Employees: 1-4

31170 Wilhite Sign Company
218 S High Ave
Joplin, MO 64801-2075 417-623-1411
Fax: 417-623-2223
information@wilhitesigns.com
www.wilhitesigns.com
Signs including neon, plastic and painted
President: Jeplin Hipple
Estimated Sales: $500,000-$1 Million
Number Employees: 5-9

31171 Wilkens-Anderson Company
4525 W Division St
Chicago, IL 60651 773-384-4433
Fax: 773-384-6260 800-847-2222
waco@wacolab.com www.wacolab.com
Laboratory and quality control equipment, supplies instruments and chemicals can testing equipment, can seam evaluation equipment
President/CEO: Bruce Wilkens
Marketing Director: Peter Thomases
Sales Director: Don Hartman
Operations Manager: Eric Jensen
Production Manager: Don Lamonica
Estimated Sales: $6-8 Million
Number Employees: 20-49
Square Footage: 220000
Brands:
Waco

31172 (HQ)Wilkie Brothers Conveyors
1765 Michigan
PO Box 219
Marysville, MI 48040 810-364-4820
Fax: 810-364-4824 info@wilkiebros.com
www.wilkiebros.com
Manufacturer and exporter of new and reconditioned overhead conveyor systems and equipment including chains, trolleys, attachments and structural components
Owner: Paul Naz
Sales Manager: Robert Wilkie
Sales: John Moews
Estimated Sales: $2.5-5 Million
Number Employees: 20-49
Square Footage: 120000
Type of Packaging: Bulk
Brands:
Bluewater Mfg., Inc.
J.B. Webb Co.
R.W. Zig Zag
Unibuilt

31173 (HQ)Wilkinson ManufacturingCompany
PO Box 490
Fort Calhoun, NE 68023 402-468-5511
Fax: 402-468-5521 info@wilkmfg.com
www.wilkinsonindustries.com
Manufacturer and exporter of aluminum foil pans
President: Bob Dalziel
R&D: Ray Massey Jr
Quality Control: Claude Weimcr
Director Marketing: Ray Salinas
Estimated Sales: $30 - 50 Million
Number Employees: 250-499
Type of Packaging: Consumer, Food Service

31174 Wilks Precision Instrument Company
PO Box 1080
Union Bridge, MD 21791 410-775-7917
Fax: 410-775-7919 info@wilksprecision.com
www.wilksprecision.com
Custom plastic injection molded boxes, trays and funnels
President: Tom Wilks
Estimated Sales: $1-2.5 Million
Number Employees: 10-19

31175 Will & Baumer
PO Box 2992
Syracuse, NY 13220 315-451-1000
Fax: 315-451-0120 info@willbaumer.com
www.willbaumer.com
Manufacturer, importer and exporter of candles, processed beeswax and candlelamps
President: Marshall Ciccone
Sales Director: John Dowd
Estimated Sales: $5-10 Million
Number Employees: 50-99
Square Footage: 200000
Type of Packaging: Food Service
Brands:
Brite-Lite
Mood Lite

31176 Will-Pemco
P.O.Box 1146
Sheboygan, WI 53082-1146 920-458-2500
Fax: 920-458-1265 wpemco@willpemco.com
www.pemco.kpl.net
Sheeting and packaging
President: Kevin Witter
CFO: Jim Wanalstine
CEO: Lee Sleiter
Estimated Sales: $50 - 100 Million
Number Employees: 250-499

31177 Willamette Industries
PO Box 666
Beaverton, OR 97075-0666 503-641-1131
Fax: 503-526-8830 www.weyerhaeuser.com
Corrugated shipping containers
President: Michael Miller
General Manager: Richard Knapton
Sales Manager: Larry Brill
Estimated Sales: $20-50 Million
Number Employees: 100-249
Square Footage: 240000
Parent Co: Willamette Industries

31178 Willamette Industries
PO Box 666
Beaverton, OR 97075-0666 503-641-1131
Fax: 503-526-8830 www.weyerhaeuser.com
Manufacturer and exporter of corrugated boxes and folding cartons
Plant Manager: David Dickey
Sales Manager: Brent Wagner
Estimated Sales: $20-50 Million
Number Employees: 100-249
Parent Co: Willamette Industries

31179 Willamette Industries
P.O.Box 666
Beaverton, OR 97075-0666 503-641-1131
Fax: 503-526-8830 www.weyerhaeuser.com
Custom shipping containers and full color floor/counter displays
Sales Manager: Rick Lantello
Assistant Sales Manager: Jim Weiks
Plant Manager: David Dickey
Estimated Sales: $20-50 Million
Number Employees: 100-249
Square Footage: 300000
Parent Co: Willamette Industries

31180 **Willamette Industries**
2300 Greene Way
Louisville, KY 40220-4040 502-753-0264
Fax: 502-753-0276 800-465-3065
Manufacturer and exporter of liquid bulk one-way disposable containers
Manager: Jim Woolums
General Manager: Larry Ogle
Sales Manager (Liquid Systems): H Edwin Cross
Estimated Sales: $50-100 Million
Number Employees: 5-9
Brands:
Willpak Liquid Systems

31181 **Willamette Industries**
23950 NW Huffman Street
Hillsboro, OR 97124-5833 503-620-6672
Fax: 503-684-9048 www.weyerhaeuser.com
Wine cartons
Manager: Andy Rivinus
Sales: Barry Greig
Estimated Sales: $1-5 Million
Number Employees: 20-49

31182 **Willard Packaging**
PO Box 27
Gaithersburg, MD 20884-0027 301-948-7700
Fax: 301-963-2375 www.willardpackaging.com
Corrugated boxes, foam parts and packaging supplies
President: Dana Salkeld
Chairman of the Board: Raymond W Salkeld Jr
Sales Manager: H Harper
Estimated Sales: $20 - 50 Million
Number Employees: 50-99
Square Footage: 86000

31183 **Willett America**
1500 N Mittel Boulevard
Wood Dale, IL 60191-1072 817-222-2233
Fax: 817-222-0466 800-259-2600
carver@willett.com www.willett-us.com
Ink jet coding systems
President: Wes Lansford
VP Sales: Wayne Moore
Marketing Manager: Terri Carruth

31184 **William Brown Company**
6429 Hegerman St
Philadelphia, PA 19135 215-331-2776
Fax: 215-333-4231 800-962-7696
www.wmbrownco.com
Cutting systems for food processing
President: William Black
Vice President: Kevin Beck
Sales Director: Benjamin Rickards
Estimated Sales: $2.5 - 5 Million
Number Employees: 5-9

31185 **William Hecht**
508 Bainbridge Street
Philadelphia, PA 19147 215-925-6223
Fax: 215-923-6798
Display cases and store fixtures; also, architectural millwork and casework available
President: Stuart Hecht
Number Employees: 49
Square Footage: 50000

31186 **William J. Mills & Company**
74100 W Front St
P.O.Box 2126
Greenport, NY 11944 631-477-1500
Fax: 631-477-1504 800-477-1535
info@millscanvas.com www.millscanvas.com
Commercial awnings
Owner: William Willets III
Estimated Sales: Below 1 Million
Number Employees: 20-49

31187 **William Willis Worldwide**
310 W Lyon Farm Drive
PO Box 4444
Greenwich, CT 06831-4356
Fax: 203-532-1919 wwwinc@aol.com
www.williamwillisworldwide.com
Executive search firm
Estimated Sales: $1-2.5 Million
Number Employees: 3
Square Footage: 1500

31188 **Williams & Mettle Company**
14309 Sommermeyer Street
Houston, TX 77041-6204 713-939-1830
Fax: 713-939-1337 800-526-4954
Filters and extruder pack screens
President and COO: Alan Arterbury
Chairman/CEO: Ken Howard
VP Finance: Allan Goertz
Number Employees: 140
Square Footage: 95000
Parent Co: WMW Industries

31189 **Williams Pallet**
9154 Port Union Rialto Rd
West Chester, OH 45069 513-874-4014
Fax: 513-874-5438
Wooden pallets and skids
Estimated Sales: $10-20 Million
Number Employees: 10

31190 **Williams Refrigeration**
65 Park Ave
Hillsdale, NJ 07642-2109 201-358-6005
Fax: 201-358-0401 800-445-9979
williamsref@msn.com
www.williams-refrigeration.co.uk
Manufacturer and exporter of commercial refrigeration equipment including blast chillers and reach-in, roll-in and counter refrigerators
Owner: William Gesner
VP: Nicholas Williams
Engineering Director: Steve Bernard
Marketing Director: Malcolm Harling
Sales Manager: Andy Ward
Purchasing Manager: Lynette Wixey
Number Employees: 250-499
Square Footage: 1400000
Parent Co: Williams Refrigeration
Type of Packaging: Food Service
Brands:
Williams

31191 **Williams Shade & AwningCompany**
4834 Hickory Hill Rd
Memphis, TN 38116-3252 901-368-5055
Fax: 901-396-2327
Commercial awnings
President: R Allen Gray
Number Employees: 20

31192 **Williamsburg Metal Spinning & Stamping Corporation**
263 Kent Ave
Brooklyn, NY 11211-4120 718-782-7040
Fax: 718-384-7424 888-535-5402
williamsburgmetal@hotmail.com
www.williamsburgmetal.com
Round baking pans, heat lamp reflectors and aluminum cooking items
President: Thomas Desanti
Estimated Sales: $1-2.5 Million
Number Employees: 10-19
Square Footage: 10000

31193 **Williamsburg Millwork Corporation**
PO Box 427
Bowling Green, VA 22427 804-994-2151
Fax: 804-994-5371 atlaspal@ncinfi.net
www.atlaspallets.com
Wooden pallets
President: M R Piland Iii III
VP: M Piland
Estimated Sales: $20 - 50 Million
Number Employees: 50-99
Square Footage: 40000

31194 **Williamson & Company**
9 Shelter Dr
Greer, SC 29650 864-848-1011
Fax: 864-848-4310 800-849-3263
Manufacturer and exporter of automated packaging, data collection and material handling systems, transport trucks and jacks.
President: Dan Williamson
Chief Financial Officer: Larry Williamson
VP: Lester Collins
Operations: Gene Settles
Estimated Sales: $5 - 10 Million
Number Employees: 20-49

31195 **Williamson, Lannes, Pallets**
17168 Kanawha Valley Rd
Southside, WV 25187 304-675-2716
Fax: 304-675-6124 lwilliamson@citynet.net
www.millwoodinc.com
Pallets and industrial blockings
President: Lanny Williamson
CEO: Larry Supple
CPA/Controller: Mark Price
Estimated Sales: $5 - 10 Million
Number Employees: 20-49

31196 **Willow Specialties**
34 Clinton St
Batavia, NY 14020 585-344-2900
Fax: 585-344-0044 800-724-7300
info@willowspecialties.com
www.willowgroupltd.com
Baskets and packaging supplies
Owner: Bernie Skalny

31197 **Willson Industries**
1003 Tuckahoe Road
P.O.Box 8
Marmora, NJ 08223 609-390-0756
Fax: 609-390-0757 800-894-4169
willson@will-lan.com www.will-lam.com
Point-of-purchase displays and custom advertising specialties
President: Edward Willson
Estimated Sales: $1 - 2.5 Million
Number Employees: 4
Square Footage: 16000

31198 **Wilson Steel Products Company**
PO Box 70214
Memphis, TN 38107 901-527-8742
Fax: 901-527-8779
Structural steel bins, chutes, hoppers and bucket elevators
President: Robert Wilson
Estimated Sales: $2.5-5 Million
Number Employees: 10-19

31199 **Wiltec**
P.O.Box 367
Leominster, MA 01453-0367 978-537-1497
Fax: 978-537-7806 sales@wiltecplastics.com
www.wiltecplastics.com
Plastic tabletop, partyware and food service products including cafeteria bowls, ladles, trays, cups, tumblers, utensils, tongs, plates, etc
President: Amy Ullman
Sales/Marketing: Diane Holloway
Estimated Sales: $3 - 5 Million
Number Employees: 10-19
Number of Brands: 2
Number of Products: 100
Type of Packaging: Consumer, Food Service, Private Label, Bulk
Brands:
Galaware
Wiltec

31200 **Wilton Armetale Company**
PO Box 600
Mount Joy, PA 17552 717-653-4444
Fax: 717-653-6573 800-779-4586
kadams@armetale.com www.armetale.com
Manufacturer and exporter of metal tabletop ware and salad bar accessories
President: Kenneth Lefever
Estimated Sales: $1 - 5 Million
Number Employees: 1-4
Brands:
Armetale

31201 **(HQ)Wilton Industries**
2240 75th St
Woodridge, IL 60517-2333 630-963-1818
Fax: 630-963-7299 info@wilton.com
www.wilton.com
Manufacturer and exporter of kitchenware including bakeware, cake decorating supplies, tools and gadgets; also, picture frames
President: Danielle Detten
Chief Financial Officer: Tom Kasvin
Chief Operating Officer: Mary Merfeld
Estimated Sales: $50 Million
Number Employees: 755
Square Footage: 1000000
Brands:
Copco
Rowoco

Weston Gallery
Wilton

31202 **Wilton Industries CanadaLtd.**
98 Carrier Drive
Etobicoke, ON M9W 5R1
Canada 416-679-0790
Fax: 416-679-0798 800-387-3300
canadasales@wilton.ca www.wilton.com
Cake, candy and cookie decorating and making supplies
President: Jeff McLaughlin
General Manager: Steve Curtis
Number Employees: 45
Square Footage: 30000

31203 **Win-Holt Equipment Group**
865 Merrick Avenue
Westbury, NY 11590-6694 516-222-0335
Fax: 516-222-0371 800-444-3595
winholt@winholt.com www.winholt.com
Material and food handling equipment, food service equipment and heating, holding and transporting equipment
President: Howard Lind
Chairman, Chief Executive Officer: Jonathan Holtz
R&D: Nancy Korista
Marketing Director: Bruce Schwartz
Sales Director: Jeff Herbert
Sales: Tim Sullivan
President, Chief Operating Officer: Dominick Scarfogliero
VP Operations: John Jameson
Purchasing Manager: Glen Stein
Estimated Sales: $10 - 20 Million
Number Employees: 300-500
Number of Brands: 4
Number of Products: 200

31204 **WinCup Holdings, LLC**
4640 Lewis Rd.
Stone Mountain, GA 30083 770-938-5281
www.wincup.com
Styrofoam bowls, cups and food containers; also, custom design and printing available
President & Chief Executive Officer: Jack Brucker
Executive VP & Chief Financial Officer: Mark Thomas
Estimated Sales: $101.8 Million
Number Employees: 1100
Square Footage: 125000
Brands:
Compac
Profit Pals
Simplicity
Styrocups

31205 **Winchester Carton**
P.O.Box 597
Eutaw, AL 35462-0597 205-372-3337
Fax: 205-372-9226 www.rocktenn.com
Boxes including recycled paper
President: Ben Williams
Plant Manager: Willie Carpenter
Estimated Sales: $20 - 50 Million
Number Employees: 100-249
Parent Co: Rock Tenn Company

31206 **Windhorst Blowmold**
P.O.Box 696
Euless, TX 76039-0696 817-540-6639
Fax: 817-540-0271 www.windhorstblowmold.com
Retrofitter and installer of electrical and mechanical components for the blowmolding industry
Owner: Michael Windhorst
Vice President: Gerry Trainque
Estimated Sales: $500,000-$1 Million
Number Employees: 20-49

31207 **Windmill Electrastatic Sprayers**
PO Box 220
Hughson, CA 95326-1490 209-883-4405
Fax: 209-883-9565 800-426-5615
info@valleytoolmfg.com www.vrisimo.com
Wine industry sprayers
President and Owner: Fred Brenda
Estimated Sales: $1 - 3 Million
Number Employees: 5-9

31208 **Windmoeller & HoelscherCorporation**
23 New England Way
Lincoln, RI 02865 401-334-0965
Fax: 401-333-6491 800-854-8702
info@whcorp.com www.whcorp.com
A supplier of flexographic and gravure printing press, blown and cast film extrusion systems, multiwall equipment, plastic sack and bag making machines, as well as form-fill-seal machinery for the converting and packaging industry.
President: Hans Deamer
Corporate Controller: Walter Kaehler
Vice President: Andrew Wheeler
Advertising/Public Relations: Lindsay Morriss
Estimated Sales: $50 - 75 Million
Number Employees: 20-49

31209 **Windsor Industries**
1351 W Stanford Ave
Englewood, CO 80110
Fax: 866-271-0520 800-444-7654
pete.dewlaney@windsorind.com
www.windsorind.com
Manufacturer and exporter of carpet and floor maintenance equipment including wet/dry vacuums, automatic scrubbers, carpet extractors, pressure washers and polishers
Financial Services Manager: Pete Dewlaney
Technical Support Manager: Joel Yourzek
Distribution Manager: Mary Millibrandt
Estimated Sales: $75-100 Million
Number Employees: 250-499
Parent Co: Alfred Karcher GmbH & Co. KG
Type of Packaging: Food Service
Brands:
Fastraction
Lightening Polishers
Mr. Steam
Powertree Scrubbers
Versamatic

31210 **(HQ)Windsor Wax Company**
PO Box 76
Carolina, RI 02812 401-364-5941
Fax: 401-364-3729 800-243-8929
windsorwax@cox.net www.windsorwax.com
Manufacturer and exporter of floor care products including wax, polymer finishes, cleaning compounds, carpet cleaner and concrete coatings; importer of natural wax and paraffin
Office Manager: M Wojcik
CEO: D Kahn
CEO: David Kahn
Brands:
Konkrete
Wincoat
Windsor
Woodee

31211 **Wine Analyst**
23230 Ravensbury Avenue
Los Altos Hills, CA 94024-6429 650-949-5929
Fax: 650-941-1892 rysmith@arthill.com
www.arthill.com
Wine industry analyst software
President: Ray Smith
Number Employees: 10

31212 **Wine Appreciation Guild**
360 Swift Ave # 34
S San Francisco, CA 94080-6220 650-866-3020
Fax: 650-866-3029 info@wineappreciation.com
www.wineappreciation.com
Wine industry tasting room supplies
Manager: James Mackey
Estimated Sales: $10 Million
Number Employees: 1-4

31213 **Wine Cap Company**
PO Box 1784
Santa Rosa, CA 95402-1784 707-535-1950
Fax: 707-939-3934 pstaehle@winecap.com
www.winecap.com
Wax Cap and B-Cap bottle closure systems
CEO: Dwight Pate
Estimated Sales: $500,000-$1 Million
Number Employees: 4

31214 **Wine Chillers of California**
1104 E 17th St Ste F
Santa Ana, CA 92701 714-541-5795
Fax: 714-541-3139 800-331-4274
winechillers@earthlink.net

President: R Sizemore
CEO: D Sizemore
Estimated Sales: $.5 - 1,000,000
Number Employees: 1-4
Square Footage: 2000000
Brands:
Cruvinet
Vimo Cave
Vino Temp
Vinotheque
Wine Well
Winekeeper

31215 **Wine Concepts**
135 Mason Cir
Suite K
Concord, CA 94520 925-521-9001
Fax: 925-521-9006 800-560-0105
stemware@pacbell.net www.wineconcepts.com
Wine industry tasting room supplies
Owner: Gerry Dodd
Estimated Sales: $1-2.5 Million
Number Employees: 10-19

31216 **Wine Country Cases**
995 Vintage Ave
Saint Helena, CA 94574 707-967-4805
Fax: 707-967-4807 info@winecountrycases.com
www.winecountrycases.com
Wine industry wooden wine boxes
Owner: Dan Pina
Owner: Ignacio Delgadillo
Estimated Sales: $2 Million
Number Employees: 20-49

31217 **Wine Things Unlimited**
PO Box 1349
Sonoma, CA 95476 707-935-1277
Fax: 707-935-3403 800-447-3983
sales@winethings.com www.winethings.com
Wine industry tasting room supplies
President: David Liberstein
Estimated Sales: $1 - 5 Million
Number Employees: 5-9

31218 **Wine Thingsÿ**
1006 S. Milpitas Blvd.
Milpitas, CA 95035 408-262-1898
Fax: 408-262-1890 800-796-7797
service@winethings.com www.winethings.com
Wine racks
President: David Lieberstein
Estimated Sales: $1 - 5 Million
Number Employees: 5-9

31219 **Wine Well Chiller Company**
301 Brewster Rd
Suite 3c
Milford, CT 06460-3700 203-878-2465
Fax: 203-878-2466 winewellchiller@aol.com
www.wine-well.com
Manufacturer and exporter of high-speed beverage chillers including wine
Chairman/Owner: James Fisher
CEO/President: Anabel Fisher
Sales: Melissa Lawless
Production: Tyrone P
Estimated Sales: $1 - 3 Million
Square Footage: 2000
Brands:
Microchiller
Wine Well

31220 **Winekeeper**
625 E Haley St
Santa Barbara, CA 93103 805-963-3451
Fax: 805-965-5393 winekeeper@earthlink.net
www.winekeeper.com
Wome dispensing and wine cellaring equipment
President: Norman Grant
Number Employees: 5-9
Parent Co: Winekeeper
Brands:
Cruvinet
Winekeeper

31221 **Wineracks by Marcus**
PO Box 2713
Costa Mesa, CA 92628-2713 714-546-4922
Fax: 714-549-8238
marcu@wineracksbymarcus.com
www.wineracksbymarcus.com

Wineracks By Marcus; a strong, accessible, space-efficient aluminum racks with a sharp, clean look for restaurants, serious collectors and retail. Manufactured to order, custom sizes and layout drawings available
President: Steve Marcus
Estimated Sales: $300,000-500,000
Number Employees: 1-4

31222 **Winkler USA**
88 South State Street
Hackensack, NJ 07601 201-525-0775
Fax: 201-525-0771 info@winklerusa.com
www.winklerusa.com
Sales Director: Cindy Chananie

31223 **Winmark Stamp & Sign**
2284 S West Temple
Salt Lake City, UT 84115 801-486-2011
Fax: 801-467-6265 800-438-0480
sales@winmarkinc.com www.winmarkinc.com
Signage, badges, name plates, notary seals, marking devices and rubber stamps including pre-inked and self-inking
Owner: Traci Szwedko
CFO: Traci Szwedko
Estimated Sales: Below $5 Million
Number Employees: 5-9
Square Footage: 16000

31224 **Winn-Sol Products**
PO Box 978
Oshkosh, WI 54903-0978 920-231-2031
Lime, rust, scale and milkstone solvents and removers used in dishwashers
President: James Driessen Sr
Secretary: Jenece Driessen
VP: Connie Hart
Estimated Sales: $300,000-500,000
Number Employees: 1-4
Brands:
Dairi-Sol
Industri-Sol
Lime-Elim

31225 **Winnebago Sign Company**
PO Box 662
Fond Du Lac, WI 54936-0662 920-922-5930
Fax: 920-922-5930
Luminous tube and plastic signs; also, servicing of signs available
Owner: Donald E Gross
Sign Installer: Bob Samp
Office Manager: Laura Leichtfuss
Estimated Sales: Less than $500,000
Number Employees: 1-4
Parent Co: Barber Graphix

31226 **Winpak Lane**
998 S Sierra Way
San Bernardino, CA 92408 909-885-0715
Fax: 909-381-1934 800-804-4224
info@wli.winpak.com www.winpak.com
Manufatures vertical-form-fill-seal packaging for flexible pouches and cups through innovative machine building and design. Our expertise in liuid filling (ranges 1.5m-19ml and hot-fill capabilities up to 90 degrees excelsiors)mbinedwith a commitment to never compromise on quality makes Winpak equipment one of the standards in the industry
President: Ted Torrens
Marketing/Sales: John Schcfer
Estimated Sales: $10-20 Million
Number Employees: 50-99
Parent Co: Wipak Group

31227 **Winpak Portion Packaging**
1 Summit Sq Ste 200
Langhorne, PA 19047 267-685-8200
Fax: 267-685-8243 800-841-2600
info@wppwinpak.com www.winpak.com
Manufacturer and exporter of pre-formed portion controlled plastic packaging. Diecut for lidding and filling equipment
President: Thomas Herlihy
Vice President: Jim McMacken
Marketing Director: Debbie Calvarese
Number Employees: 225
Parent Co: Winpak
Type of Packaging: Consumer, Food Service, Private Label

31228 **Winpak Technologies**
85 Laird Drive
Toronto, ON M4G 3T8
Canada 416-421-1700
Fax: 416-421-7957
Manufacturer and exporter of flexible packaging materials
Director Sales/Marketing: L de Bellefeuille
Manufacturing: J Millwrad
Estimated Sales: $1 - 5 Million
Number Employees: 250
Square Footage: 300000
Parent Co: Winpak

31229 **Wins Paper Products**
321 Murray Road
Springtown, TX 76082-6520 817-281-6550
Fax: 817-281-0560 800-733-2420
www.winspaper.com
Manufacturer and wholesaler/distributor of paper bags; serving the food service market
President: Douglas Wiley
Chairman: Gordon Wiley
Estimated Sales: Below $5 Million
Number Employees: 10
Square Footage: 78000

31230 **Winston Industries**
2345 Carton Dr
Louisville, KY 40299 502-495-5400
Fax: 502-495-5458 800-234-5286
winston@winstonind.com www.winstonind.com
Manufacturer and exporter of stainless steel ovens, pressure cookers and holding cabinets
President: Barry Yates
CEO: David Shelton
Quality Control: Tina Thompson
CEO: David B Shelton
CFO: Bob Leavitt
VP Marketing: D Paul Haviland
VP Sales: Barry Yates
VP Administration: John Heigl
VP Manufacturing: Leo Gutgsell
Estimated Sales: $10 - 20 Million
Number Employees: 100-249
Type of Packaging: Food Service
Brands:
C-Vap
C-Vat
Collettramatic

31231 **Winston Laboratories**
100 N Fairway Drive
Suite 134
Vernon Hills, IL 60061 847-362-8200
Fax: 847-362-8394 800-946-5229
info@winstonlabs.com www.winstonlabs.com
Consultant specializing in nutritional and laboratory testing for food additives, pesticide residues, MSG, sulfites, etc.; also, FDA liaison service, HACCP plans, food plant inspections and certification of acidified foods and thermalprocesses available
President: Marvin Winston
CEO: Joel E Bernstein
CFO: Barry Hollingsworth
Vice President: David A Henninger
Senior Scientist: Porus Aria PhD
Estimated Sales: $500,000-$1 Million
Number Employees: 9
Square Footage: 6500

31232 **Winzen Film**
P.O.Box 677
Sulphur Springs, TX 75483-0677 903-885-7595
Fax: 903-885-4702 800-779-7595
info@winzen.com www.winzen.com
Manufacturer and exporter of plastic container materials
Manager: Frank Neidhart
CEO: Robert Williamson
Estimated Sales: $10 - 20 Million
Number Employees: 20-49
Parent Co: BAG Corporation

31233 **Wipe-Tex**
110 E 153rd St
Bronx, NY 10451 718-665-0013
Fax: 718-665-0787 800-643-9607
www.wipe-tex.com
Washed and sterilized cloths including wiping rags, cotton cleaning remnants, kitchen and new hemmed towels; also, cheesecloth
Owner: Alex Fudder
VP Sales Marketing: Richard Chesney
Number Employees: 20-49
Square Footage: 200000

31234 **(HQ)Wipeco, Inc.**
250 N. Mannheim Rd., Unit B.
Hillside, IL 60162 708-544-7247
Fax: 708-544-7248 info@wipeco.com
www.wipeco.com
Wiping rags and nonwoven wipers
President: Jeff Shanken
Chief Executive Officer: Sandy Woycke
Estimated Sales: $370,000
Number Employees: 5-9

31235 **Wire Belt Company of America**
154 Harvey Rd
Londonderry, NH 03053 603-644-2500
Fax: 603-644-3600 sales@wirebelt.com
www.wirebelt.com
Stainless steel open-mesh conveyor belting
President: David Greer
Marketing Director: Richard Spiak
Sales: Richard Spiak
Operations: Scott Monk
Estimated Sales: $20-50 Million
Number Employees: 100-249
Brands:
Eye-Flex
Flat-Flex El
Flat-Flex
Flat-Flex Xt
Flex-Turn

31236 **Wire Products Corporation**
1319 W Lee St
Greensboro, NC 27403 336-275-0515
Fax: 336-274-4284 800-334-0807
displays@wireproductscorp.com
www.wireproductscorp.com
Manufacturer and exporter of point-of-purchase displays including stock and special designs, powder coated and wire formed
President: Louise M Neese
VP: Gilbert Luck
Sales Manager: Jim Plumb
Estimated Sales: $2.5-5 Million
Number Employees: 20-49

31237 **Wire Products Manufacturing Company**
PO Box 407
Merrill, WI 54452-0407 715-536-7144
Fax: 715-536-1476
Manufacturer and exporter of wire racks including display and fryer
President: Roger C Dupke
Estimated Sales: $20-50 Million
Number Employees: 20-49
Type of Packaging: Consumer, Food Service, Bulk

31238 **Wire Way Husky**
P.O.Box 645
Denver, NC 28037-0645 704-483-1900
Fax: 704-483-1911
productinfo@wirewayhusky.com
www.wirewayhusky.com
Material handling equipment including pallet racks and cable reel racks
President: Ron Young
VP: Gregory Young
Estimated Sales: $10 - 20 Million
Number Employees: 100-249
Parent Co: Husky Systems

31239 **Wirefab**
75 Blackstone River Rd
Worcester, MA 01607 508-754-5359
Fax: 508-797-3620 877-877-4445
info@wirefab.com www.wirefab.com
Manufacturer and exporter of wire baskets, shelving and racks including doughnut and bagel baskets and deep-fry crumb screens
Owner: A B Zakarian
CEO: A Zakarian
VP: M M Zakarian
R & D: Larry Clough
Sales: William Binson
Public Relations: Michael Murdock
Operations: John Michaels
Production: Christopher Bousbouras
Plant Manager: James Hall
Purchasing: Barbara Vasdagalis

Estimated Sales: $5-10 Million
Number Employees: 50-99
Square Footage: 80000
Type of Packaging: Bulk

31240 Wiremaid Products
11711 W Sample Rd
Coral Springs, FL 33065-3155
Fax: 954-545-9011 800-770-4700
info@vutec.com www.vutec.com
Manufacturer and exporter of wire and metal products including displays, racks, shelves, etc
Manager: Bryan Sciullo
CEO: Howard L Sinkoff
CFO: Jeff Chanoff
VP: Allen Axman
R&D: Hai Nguyen
Marketing: John Cavanaugh
Sales: Allen Axman
Production: Raul Passalaqua
Plant Manager: Raul Passalaqua
Purchasing: Robert Ciarletto
Estimated Sales: $20-50 Million
Number Employees: 50-99
Square Footage: 100000
Parent Co: Vutec Corporation
Brands:
Vutec Usa
Wiremaid Usa

31241 Wisco Industries
955 Market St
Oregon, WI 53575 608-835-3300
Fax: 608-835-7399 800-999-4726
info@wiscoind.com www.wiscoind.com
Counter top ovens and warmers for pizza, pretzels and cookies; exporter of pizza ovens, food warmers, toasters and sandwich grills
Chairman of the Board: Elving J Kjellstrom
CEO: Elving Kjellstrom
Marketing Director: Donald Porkner
Sales Director: Randy Kjellstrom
Estimated Sales: $20 - 30 Million
Number Employees: 100-249
Square Footage: 200000

31242 Wisco Signs
2502 Melby St
Eau Claire, WI 54703 715-835-6189
Fax: 715-835-6868 wiscosigns@charter.net
www.wiscosigns.com
Indoor and outdoor signs including electric, painted, vinyl lettering and neon
VP: Gregory Mitchell
Estimated Sales: $1-2.5 Million
Number Employees: 5-9

31243 Wisconsin Aluminum Foundry Company
838 S. 16th Street
Manitowoc, WI 54221-0246 920-682-8286
Fax: 920-682-7285 inquiries@wafco.com
www.wafco.com
Manufacturer and exporter of griddles,grills, can sealers, sterilizers, pressure cookers, cookware, etc... importer of cookware.
President: Jim Hatt
CEO: Philip Jacobs
Quality Control: Don Noworatsky
Estimated Sales: $5 - 10 Million
Number Employees: 20-49
Number of Brands: 1
Type of Packaging: Consumer
Brands:
Chef's Design
Chef-Way

31244 Wisconsin Bench
507 E Grant St
Thorp, WI 54771 715-669-5360
Fax: 715-669-5929 800-242-2303
www.wisconsinbench.com
Bench tops
General Manager: Steve Burgess
CEO: Phillip Jeska
Estimated Sales: $5-10 Million
Number Employees: 50-99
Square Footage: 35000

31245 Wisconsin Box Company
929 Townline Rd
PO Box 718
Wausau, WI 54402-0718 715-842-2248
Fax: 715-842-2240 800-876-6658
garyl@tcrllc.com www.wisconsinbox.com
Manufacturer and exporter of wirebound and collapsible pallet boxes and crates
Owner: Jeff Davis
CEO: Gary LeMaster
Sales Manager: Dennis Maxson
Controller / Human Resources: Michael Shipway
Estimated Sales: $10 - 20 Million
Number Employees: 50-99
Square Footage: 75000

31246 Wisconsin Converting ofGreen Bay
1689 Morrow St
Green Bay, WI 54302 920-437-6400
Fax: 920-436-4964 800-544-1935
sc@wisconsinconverting.com
www.wisconsinconverting.com
Mailers and bags including paper, lined, candy and nut bags and self opening food sacks
President: Richard Bierman
CEO: Charles Johns
Marketing Director: Jill Walschinski
VP Operations: Bob McGee
Estimated Sales: $10 - 20,000,000
Number Employees: 20-49

31247 Wisconsin Film & Bag
3100 E Richmond St
Shawano, WI 54166 715-524-2565
Fax: 715-524-3527 800-765-9224
greggreene@wifb.com www.wifb.com
Polyethylene sheeting and bundling films and bags
President: Jim Feeney
Director of Sales Operations: Leann Gueths
CFO: Al Johnson
V.P. of Major Accounts: Greg Greene
VP: Ian Anderson
Inside Sales Representative: Kristin Gehm
Regional Sales Manager: Tony Hindley
Estimated Sales: Below $5 Million
Number Employees: 100-249
Square Footage: 59000
Brands:
Atlas
Inflation Fighter

31248 Wisconsin Precision Casting Corporation
W405 County Road L
East Troy, WI 53120-2406 262-642-7307
Fax: 262-642-4115 866-642-7307
cliff@wisconsinprecision.com
www.wisconsinprecision.com
Owner: Clyde Klemowits
VP - Manufacturing: Cliff Fischer
VP - Engineering: Claude Klemowits
Sales and Marketing Manager: Dean Kirschner
Estimated Sales: $10-20 Million
Number Employees: 50-99
Square Footage: 40

31249 Wisconsinbox
929 Townline Road
PO Box 718
Wausau, WI 54402-0718 715-842-2248
Fax: 715-842-2240 www.wisconsinbox.com
Manufacturer and exporter of wooden shipping containers and crates
President: W Jeff Davis
CFO: Michael Shipway
Vice President of Sales: Gene Davis
Customer Service: Jim Geise
Plant Manager: Bob Schultz
Plant Manager: Charley Ewell
Estimated Sales: $5 - 10 Million
Number Employees: 20
Type of Packaging: Bulk

31250 Wisdom Adhesives Worldwide
1575 Executive Drive
Elgin, IL 60123 847-841-7002
Fax: 847-841-7009 info@wisdomadhesives.com
www.wisdomadhesives.com
Water-based adhesives, animal glue, hot melts and custom adhesives
Chief Executive Officer: Jeff Wisdom
Vice President of Technologies: Tom Rolando
Vice President of Sales: Paul Preston
Vice President of Operations: Linda Wisdom
Estimated Sales: $1-5 Million
Number Employees: 12

31251 Wishbone Utensil Tableware Line
15 Paramount Pkwy
Wheat Ridge, CO 80215-6615 303-238-8088
Fax: 253-595-7673 866-266-5928
rfkltd1@mindspring.com
www.wishboneutensil.com
Forever replaces chopsticks. One piece tong, skewer & ergonomic utensil. Child safe. Dishwasher friendly. Assisted living compatible. Solution for the chopstick challenged. Popular among hotel/resorts, restaurateur and occupationalhealth. Ten motif-friendly colors. FDA approved. Stylish, durable, reusable, fun. Sanitized and individually wrapped. Gourmet quality Feng Shui tableware
CEO: R Farlan Krieger Sr
Estimated Sales: Under $300,000
Number Employees: 9
Number of Brands: 4
Number of Products: 8
Square Footage: 50000
Parent Co: RF Krieger, LLC
Type of Packaging: Consumer, Food Service, Private Label, Bulk
Brands:
Wishbone Utensil Tableware Line

31252 Witt Industries
4600 N. Mason-Montgomery Road
Mason, OH 45040 800-543-7417
Fax: 877-891-8200 800-543-7417
sales@witt.com www.witt.com
Manufacturer and exporter of wastebaskets and firesafe steel, outside, torpedo and fiberglass waste receptacles; importer of structural foam lockers
President: Tim Harris
President: Tim Harris
Chairman: Marcy Wydman
Director Sales/Marketing: Chris Adams
Purchasing Manager: Rick Royce
Estimated Sales: $10-20 Million
Number Employees: 100-249
Square Footage: 75000
Type of Packaging: Food Service

31253 Witt Plastics
P.O.Box 808
Greenville, OH 45331-0808 937-548-7272
Fax: 937-547-6046 800-227-9181
wp-info@wittplastics.com www.wittplastics.com
Roll and sheet high impact polystyrene and polypropylene for container and lid stock thermoforming
President: Bob Kramer
Owner/CEO: John Witt
Purchasing Manager: Bill Simmons
Estimated Sales: $10 - 20 Million
Number Employees: 50-99
Square Footage: 100000

31254 Wittco Food Service Equipment
7737 N 81st St
Milwaukee, WI 53223 414-365-4400
Fax: 414-354-2821 800-367-8413
custserv@wittco.com www.wittco.com
Manufacturer and exporter of heated food holding equipment and cook/hold ovens
General Manager: Steve Jensen
CEO: Tim Murray
VP: Jeff Smith
Marketing: Joe Burns
Operations Manager: Dave Braun
Estimated Sales: $5-10 Million
Number Employees: 1,000-4,999

31255 Wittco Foodservice Equipment, Inc.
7737 North 81st Street
Milwaukee, WI 53223 414-434-4713
Fax: 414-354-2821 800-821-3912
Custserv@wittco.com www.crimsco.com
Manufacturer and exporter of carts including hot/cold food delivery and insulated tray; also, cook/chill equipment
Estimated Sales: $5 Million
Number Employees: 50-100

Square Footage: 180000
Parent Co: Nichols Industries
Type of Packaging: Food Service
Brands:
Meals-On-Wheels

31256 Witte Brothers Exchange
575 Witte Industrial Ct
Troy, MO 63379 314-219-4200
Fax: 314-219-4700 800-325-8151
info@wittebros.com www.wittebros.com
Warehousing, transportation and distribution for refrigerated and frozen products including LTL, TL (also dry), consolidation, freight pooling, rail service, and full freight management capabilities. Full in ventory management. Temprange to -15F 2,000,000 cubic feet warehouse with 34 doors and 20,000 square feet refrigerated cross dock.
President: Brent Witte
Sr. Director of Business Development: Laura Wort
Director Of Operations: Shane Carter
Number Employees: 100-249

31257 Witte Company
P.O.Box 47
Washington, NJ 07882-0004 908-689-6500
Fax: 908-537-6806 info@witte.com
www.witte.com
Manufacturer and exporter of vibrating screens, conveyors, fluid bed dryers and coolers
President: Richard Witte
Sales/Marketing: Jim Schak
Engineering Manager: Larry Stoma
Purchasing Manager: Marilyn March
Estimated Sales: $10 - 20,000,000
Number Employees: 20-49
Square Footage: 60000
Type of Packaging: Private Label
Brands:
Witte

31258 Wittemann Company
1 Industry Dr
Palm Coast, FL 32137 386-445-4200
Fax: 386-445-7042 co2@wittemann.com
www.wittemann.com
Manufacturer and exporter of carbon dioxide generation and recovery systems; also, dryers, cylinder filling units and dry ice systems
President: William Geiger
General Manager: Bill Gieyer
CFO: Cara Brammer
Sales Manager: Gabreil Dominguez
Regional Sales Manager: Daniel Gruber
Product Manager: Jay Soto
Estimated Sales: $3 - 5 Million
Number Employees: 10-19
Square Footage: 60000

31259 (HQ)Wittern Group
8040 University Boulevard
Clive, IA 50325 515-274-3641
Fax: 515-271-8530 855-712-8729
contact@vending.com www.vending.com
Manufacturer and exporter of vending machines for snacks, canned and hot beverages, refrigerated and frozen foods, desserts, etc
Chairman of the Board: Francis Wittern III
President/CEO/Secretary/Treasurer: John Bruntz
Chief Financial Officer: Craig Mile
Vice President, Data Processing: Dave Twedale
Chief Marketing Officer: Mike McGillis
Vice President, Sales: Mike Frye
Purchasing Manager: Ron Harter
Estimated Sales: $9 Million
Number Employees: 50
Square Footage: 420000
Parent Co: 8040 Holdings, Inc.
Brands:
Servomatic

31260 Wizard Art Glass
9721 Mason Avenue
Chatsworth, CA 91311-5208 818-709-2007
Fax: 818-709-5068 800-438-9565
thewzrd@msn.com
Manufacturer and importer of etched glass separators and screens, brass posts, traffic control systems, liscourts and sneeze guards
Metal Sales/Operations: Steve Bolens
Estimated Sales: $1-2.5 Million
Number Employees: 10-19
Square Footage: 8500
Type of Packaging: Bulk

31261 Woerner Wire Works
3008 Evans Street
PO Box 11449
Omaha, NE 68111 402-451-5414
Fax: 402-451-5415 www.woernerwireworks.com
Established in 1892. Structural Steel Manufacturer, ornamental metal work, wholesale wire, fabricated wire, manufacturers, metal fabricator.
President: Daniel Scanlan
VP: Sandor Horvath
Project Manager: Rick Weitkemper
Estimated Sales: Below $5 Million
Number Employees: 10-19
Square Footage: 40000

31262 Wohl Associates
50 Floyds Run
Bohemia, NY 11716 631-244-7979
Fax: 631-244-6987 info@wohlassociates.com
www.wohlassociates.com
Dealer of used and rebuilt scrubbers, blanchers, steamers, labelers, and other food processing equipment
President: Angrew Wohl
Estimated Sales: $5 - 10 Million
Number Employees: 10-19

31263 Wohl Associates
50 Floyds Run
Bohemia, NY 11716 631-244-7979
Fax: 631-244-6987 info@wohlassociates.com
www.wohlassociates.com
Buyer and seller of surplus equipment including blanchers, dicers, mixers, dryers and coolers
President: David Wohl
CFO: Anndy Wohl
Estimated Sales: $5 - 10 Million
Number Employees: 10-19

31264 Wolens Company
PO Box 560964
Dallas, TX 75356-0964 214-634-0800
Fax: 214-634-0880 www.morganplasticsigns.com
Manufacturer and exporter of plastic letters and signs
President: Steve Schwartz
Estimated Sales: $1-2.5 Million
Number Employees: 1-4

31265 Wolf Packaging Machines
9310 SW 100th Avenue Road
Miami, FL 33176-1724 305-274-3641
Fax: 305-274-3685 ralphs@inlandtrade.com
Packaging machines, such as vertical f/f/s machines
Estimated Sales: $1 - 5 Million

31266 Wolf Range Company
3101 S 2nd St
Louisville, KY 40208-1446 502-637-3737
Fax: 310-637-7931 800-366-9653
info@wolfrange.com www.beefobradys.com
Manufacturer and exporter of commercial gas broilers, fryers, griddles, ranges and ovens; also, household ranges and slide-ins
Manager: Denny Thompson
General Manager (Gourmet Products): Harvey Wolsky
VP Sales: Tom Egan
Estimated Sales: $100-500 Million
Number Employees: 250-499
Square Footage: 150000
Parent Co: PMI Food Equipment Group

31267 Wolf Works
167 Vard Loomis Court
Arroyo Grande, CA 93420-2919 805-489-2920
Fax: 805-239-1787 800-549-3806
wolfworkswood@hotmail.com
Wine industry wine gift boxes/crates/tasting room items
President: Mark Wolf
Co-Owner: Christina Wolf
Estimated Sales: less than $500,000
Number Employees: 2
Square Footage: 1200

31268 Wolf-Tec
20 Kieffer Ln
Kingston, NY 12401 845-340-9727
Fax: 845-340-9732 sales@wolf-tec.com
www.wolf-tec.com
Massagers and tumblers, pickle injectors, sausage linkers
CEO: Ralf Ludwig
Estimated Sales: $20-50 Million
Number Employees: 50-99

31269 Wolfkiny
PO Box 30970
Columbus, OH 43230-0970 614-863-3144
Fax: 614-863-3296 800-292-3144
www.wolfking.com
Analyzing fat testing, continuous sausage processing systems, emulsifiers, accessories, grinders, massagers and tumblers, pickle injectors, belt and screw conveyors, handling systems for ground meats, dry sausages, hams, pizzatoppings, patties and poultry
Estimated Sales: $5-10 Million
Number Employees: 50-99

31270 (HQ)Wolverine Proctor & Schwartz
121 Proctor Lane
Lexington, NC 27292 336-248-5181
Fax: 336-248-5118 sales@wolverineproctor.com
www.wolverineproctor.com
Manufacturer and exporter of energy efficient equipment including conveyor dryers, roasters, toasters, coolers, ovens and the JETZONE fluidized dryers, puffers and toasters for the processing of fruits, vegetables, nuts, bakery, snackfoods, meat, poultry, pet foods, etc. Also offers batch drying equipment including tray, truck and laboratory dryers. Fully equipped Tech Centers available for demonstration purposes and development of new products and processes.
CEO: Steven Chilenski
CFO: Mark Brown
VP: Paul E Smith
Sales: Terry Midden
Estimated Sales: $15-25 Million
Number Employees: 200-300
Square Footage: 30000
Brands:
Jetzone
Proctor

31271 Womack International
451 Azuar Ave
Vallejo, CA 94592 707-647-2370
Fax: 707-562-1010 info@womack.com
www.womack.com
Manufacturer and exporter of food processing filters including multiple plate, vertical stack and pressure
President: Thomas H. Womack
VP Engineer: Michael Oakes
VP Sales: Stanley Jennings
Estimated Sales: $3 - 5 Million
Number Employees: 10-19
Square Footage: 50000
Brands:
Filter-Max
Micron One

31272 Wonderware Corporation
26561 Rancho Pkwy S
Lake Forest, CA 92630 949-727-3200
Fax: 949-727-3270 press@wonderware.com
www.wonderware.com
Industrial automation software, enterprise asset management and maintenance software and enterprise resource planning (ERP) software
President: Sudipta Bhattacharya
Branch Manager: Roy Slavin
Estimated Sales: $43.4 Million
Number Employees: 500-999

31273 Wood & Jones Printers
66 Waverly Drive
Pasadena, CA 91105-2512 626-797-5700
Fax: 626-797-6858
Labels; also, printing available
Estimated Sales: $1 - 5 Million
Number Employees: 20-50

31274 Wood & Laminates
102 Us Highway 46 E
Lodi, NJ 07644 973-773-7475
Fax: 973-773-8344 gabriels@wlbars.com
www.wlbars.com
Custom-made bars
Owner: Gabriel Salacar
Estimated Sales: $2.5 - 5 Million
Number Employees: 10-19

31275 **Wood Stone Corporation**
1801 W Bakerview Rd
Bellingham, WA 98226 360-650-1111
Fax: 360-650-1166 800-988-8103
info@woodstone-corp.com
www.woodstone-corp.com
Stone-health cooking equipment
President: Wade C. Bobb
CEO: Kurt I. Eickmeyer
VP - Finance: Justin Mitchell
Marketing Director: Tamra Nelson
VP - Sales: Phil Eaton
VP Client Relations: Kurt Eickmeyer
Chief Operating Officer: Harry E. Hegarty
Purchasing Agent: Matt Laninga
Estimated Sales: $10 - 20 Million
Number Employees: 20-49

31276 **Wood Stone Corporation**
1801 W Bakerview Rd
Bellingham, WA 98226 360-650-1111
Fax: 360-650-1166 800-988-8103
info@woodstone.net www.woodstone-corp.com
Manufacturer and exporter of broilers, stone hearth ovens, pizza equipment and rotisseries; cast ceramic available
President: Wade C. Bob
CEO: Keith R. Carpenter
COO: Harry E. Hegarty
VP Sales: K Carpneter
President Manufacturing: Harry Hegarty
Estimated Sales: $5 - 10 Million
Number Employees: 20-49
Square Footage: 50000

31277 **Woodard**
210 S Delaney Rd
PO Box 1037
Coppell, TX 75019-1037 989-725-4500
Fax: 989-725-4221 800-877-2290
ÿretail3@woodard-furniture.com
www.woodard-furniture.com
Restaurant furnishings including wrought iron and cast and extruded aluminum
President: Dean Engelage
VP Contract Sales/International Sales: Eric Parsons
Estimated Sales: $10-20 Million
Number Employees: 3
Square Footage: 1000000

31278 **Woodfold-Marco Manufacturing**
PO Box 346
Forest Grove, OR 97116-0346 503-357-7181
Fax: 503-357-7185 info@woodfold.com
www.woodfold.com
Manufacturer and exporter of wood roll up and accordion doors and custom shutters; also, laminated kitchen and machined hardwood products
President: Mark Lewis
Vice President: Randall Roedl
Estimated Sales: $10-20 Million
Number Employees: 100-249
Square Footage: 160000

31279 **Woodgoods Industries**
407 S Duncan St
Luck, WI 54853-9082 715-472-2226
Fax: 715-472-8708 info@woodgoods.com
www.woodgoods.com
Table tops and bases for the contract, hospitality and institutional trades
President: Brad Johnson
CFO: Brad Johnson
Quality Control: Brad Johnson
Customer Service/Purchasing: David Corredato
Estimated Sales: $5 - 10 Million
Number Employees: 50-99
Square Footage: 120000

31280 **Woodhead**
3411 Woodhead Drive
Northbrook, IL 60062-1812 847-272-7990
Fax: 847-272-8133 888-456-1990
info@domino.danielwoodhead.com
www.danielwoodhead.com
Wiring devices, portable lighting, portable power, cable reels, cord grips, push buttoms, and pendants
President: Terry Spandet
Estimated Sales: $2.5-5 Million
Number Employees: 100-249

31281 **Woods Fabricators**
2759 Old State Highway 113
P.O.Box 167
Taylorsville, GA 30178 770-684-5377
Fax: 770-684-8850 info@woodsfab.com
www.woodsfab.com
Cooling tunnels and conveyors
Owner/ President: Rickey Woods
Engineering Manager: Nevin Harne
Safety Manager: Henry Mathews
Sales Manager: John Dodson
Office Manager: Allen Wilson
Procurement: Tim McGinnis

31282 **Woodson**
7 Wynfield Drive
Lititz, PA 17543-8001 717-627-6990
Fax: 717-627-6920 888-627-6990
info@woodsoninc.com www.woodsoninc.com
Automatic storage and retrieval systems (AS/RS) specifically designed for high density, deep lane storage warehouses. The AS/RS accommodate pallet and palletless applications and include a fully functional automated warehousemanagement system. For frozen food, dairy and bakery applications
President: J Thomas Woodson III
Vice President: Richard Troy
Sales Director: Mark Linesay
Estimated Sales: $5-10 Million
Number Employees: 10-19
Number of Products: 4
Square Footage: 15000

31283 **Woodson Pallet**
PO Box 38
Anmoore, WV 26323-0038 304-623-2858
Fax: 304-623-2865
Pallets and corrugated boxes
President: Lorena Woodson
CFO: William T Woodson
Estimated Sales: Below $5 Million
Number Employees: 10-19

31284 **Woodson-Tenent Laboratories**
5659 Brentlinger Dr
Dayton, OH 45414 937-236-5756
Fax: 937-236-5756 billhirt@compuserve.com
www.eurofinsus.com
Laboratory specializing in nutritional analysis with amino acid, dietary fiber, microbiological, proximate and vitamin analyses; pesticide and residue testing and mycotoxin screening
Manager: Michael Muse
Vice President of Corporate Development: Joseph Dunham
Operations Manager, Director of Client S: Jules Skamarak
Estimated Sales: $1-2.5 Million
Number Employees: 1-4
Parent Co: Woodson-Tenent Laboratories

31285 **Woodson-Tenent Laboratories**
2035 Atlas Circle
Gainesville, GA 30501-6135 770-536-5909
Fax: 770-536-6909
Laboratory specializing in nutritional analysis with amino acid, dietary fiber, microbiological, proximate and vitamin analyses; pesticide and residue testing and mycotoxin screening available
Manager: Robert W Brooks
Estimated Sales: $500,000-$1 Million
Number Employees: 5-9
Parent Co: Woodson-Tenent Laboratories

31286 **Woodson-Tenent Laboratories**
P.O.Box 1292
Des Moines, IA 50306-1292 515-265-1461
Fax: 515-266-5453 www.eurofinsus.com
Laboratory specializing in nutritional analysis of amino acids, dietary fibers, microbiologicals, proximates and vitamins; also, mycotoxin screening
Manager: Ardin Backous
Branch Manager: Cecil Bogy
Vice President of Corporate Development: Joseph Dunham
Operations Manager, Director of Client S: Jules Skamarak
Estimated Sales: $1-2.5 Million
Number Employees: 50-99
Parent Co: Woodson-Tenent Laboratories

31287 **Woodson-Tenent Laboratories**
P.O.Box 1292
Des Moines, IA 50306-1292 515-265-1461
Fax: 515-266-5453 www.eurofinsus.com
Laboratory specializing in nutritional analyses including amino acids, dietary fibers, microbiological proximates and vitamins; also, pesticide and residue testing and mycotoxin screening
Manager: Ardin Backous
Vice President of Corporate Development: Joseph Dunham
Operations Manager, Director of Client S: Jules Skamarak
Estimated Sales: $2.5 - 5 Million
Number Employees: 50-99
Parent Co: Woodson-Tenent Laboratories

31288 **Woodstock Line Company**
83 Canal St
Putnam, CT 06260 860-928-6557
Fax: 860-928-1096 info@woodstockline.com
www.theanglersconnection.com
Manufacturer and exporter of braided cordage and twine
Owner: Burney Phaneuf
Estimated Sales: $2.5-5 Million
Number Employees: 10-19
Square Footage: 25000

31289 **Woodstock Plastics Company**
22511 W Grant Hwy
Marengo, IL 60152 815-568-5281
Fax: 815-568-5339 sales@woodstockplastics.com
www.woodstockplastics.com
Manufacturer and exporter of fabricated plastic displays, dump bins, containers, clamshell and vinyl pouches including sealed, vacuum formed, molded and blow molded
President: Brain Jenkner
CFO: Matthew Jenkner
Vice President: John Jenkner
Quality Control: Jude Jons
Estimated Sales: $10 - 20 Million
Number Employees: 50-99
Square Footage: 45000

31290 **Woodward Manufacturing**
299 Forest Ave
Suite F
Paramus, NJ 07652 201-262-6700
Fax: 201-262-1322
Packaging machinery
President: Cyril H T Woodward
VP: Joseph Giorgio
National Sales Director: Louis Cannizzaro
Estimated Sales: $1-2.5 Million
Number Employees: 10
Brands:
Vac-U-Pac

31291 **Woody Associates**
844 E South St
York, PA 17403 717-843-3975
Fax: 717-843-5829 info@woody-decorators.com
www.woody-decorators.com
Manufacturer and exporter of automatic confectionery and bakery decorating machinery
President: Harry Reinke
VP: Kerrie Reinke
Sales: Harry Reinke
Estimated Sales: $1 - 3 Million
Number Employees: 2
Square Footage: 1000
Brands:
Woody Stringer

31292 **Wooster Novelty Company**
45 Washington Street
Floor 6a
Brooklyn, NY 11201-1029 718-852-8934
Fax: 718-624-6925
Cutting board underliners for hot plates
President: Stephen Winaker
Partner: Scott Kail
Estimated Sales: $500,000-$1 Million
Number Employees: 9

31293 **Worcester Envelope Company**
22 Millbury St
Auburn, MA 01501 508-832-5394
Fax: 508-832-5870 www.worcesterenvelope.com
Commercial and official envelopes
President: Eldon D Pond Iii

Estimated Sales: $20-50 Million
Number Employees: 250-499

31294 Worcester Industrial Products
7 Brookfield St
Worcester, MA 01605-3901 508-757-5161
Fax: 508-831-9990 800-533-5711
sales@shortening-shuttle.com
www.shortening-shuttle.com
Waste oil transfer systems used to transport waste shortening from fryers to grease dumpsters
President: Martha Hawley
Marketing: Elaine Liad
Vice President of Sales: Jeremiah Hawley
Estimated Sales: $2.5-5 Million
Number Employees: 10-19
Number of Products: 5
Type of Packaging: Food Service
Brands:
Shortening Shuttle

31295 Work Well Company
861 Taylor Road
Unit C
Gahanna, OH 43230-6275 614-759-8003
Fax: 614-759-8013
Manufacturer and exporter of safety gloves and oven mitts
Estimated Sales: $1 - 5 Million

31296 Workman Packaging Inc.
345 Montee de Liesse
Saint-Laurent, QC H4T 1P5
Canada 514-344-7227
Fax: 514-737-4288 800-252-5208
info@multisac.com www.multisac.com
Manufacturer and exporter of woven and laminated polyethylene and polypropylene bags, covers and wraps
President: Mark Kraminer
CFO: Luc Dumont
Quality Control: Bryan Morton
Director Marketing: Mark Kraminer
Number Employees: 100
Brands:
Multisac
Plastex
Stretch-Tite
Toss 'n' Tote

31297 Worksafe Industries
130t W 10th Street
Huntington Station, NY 11746-1616 516-427-1802
Fax: 516-427-1840 800-929-9000
info@charkate.com www.charkate.com
Manufacturer and exporter of protective clothing including gloves, respirators, goggles and industrial safety equipment
President: Larry Densen
Number Employees: 300

31298 World Division
11929 Denton Dr
Dallas, TX 75234 972-241-2612
Fax: 972-247-8807 800-433-9843
info@worlddivision.com
www.worlddivisionusa.com
Manufacturer and exporter of banners, pennants, streamers and signs
President: John Adams
Sr. VP: Francois Louis
Operations Director: David Fry
Estimated Sales: $5-10,000,000
Number Employees: 1-4

31299 World Dryer Corporation
5700 McDermott Dr
Berkeley, IL 60163 708-449-6950
Fax: 708-449-6958 800-323-0701
sales@worlddryer.com www.worlddryer.com
Warm air push button and automatic hand dryers, baby changing tables, automatic soap dispensers, 3-in-1 towel dispenser/hand dryer systems and ADA compliant/handicapped approved hand dryers.
President: Tom Vic
CFO: Tom Bic
Vice President: Chris Berl
Marketing Director: Stacey Hefford
Sales Director: Erin Eddy
Estimated Sales: $10 - 20 Million
Number Employees: 20-49
Square Footage: 50000
Parent Co: Specialty Equipment Companies
Brands:
Airspeed
Electric Aire
Sensamatic
World

31300 World Finer Foods
1455 Broadacres Dr Ste 100
Bloomfield, NJ 07003 973-338-0300
Fax: 973-338-0382 www.worldfiner.com
President: Frank Muchel
CFO: Jon Beer
Estimated Sales: Less than $500,000
Number Employees: 1-4

31301 World Food Tech Services
153 Cherry St
Malden, MA 02148-1603 781-321-3750
Fax: 781-321-3750 worldfood@comcast.com
Aids in developing the import/export and product development of spruce in the US market
President: Daniel Casper
VP: Jane Casper
Sales: Jersy Moytasch

31302 World Kitchen
PO Box 1555
Elmira, NY 14902-1555 607-377-8000
Fax: 607-377-8962 800-999-3436
www.worldkitchen.com
Manufacturer and exporter of glassware including bottles, jars, cookware, trays, urns, etc
President/ CEO: Carl Warschausky
CFO: Stephen Earhart
SVP, Human Resources & Chief Legal Offic: Ed Flowers
VP Marketing: Clark Kinlin
SVP/ General Manager, Global Business: Lee Mui
Estimated Sales: $5 - 10 Million
Number Employees: 10-19
Brands:
Corningware
Pyrex
Visions

31303 World Kitchen
5500 Pearl St Ste 400
Rosemont, IL 60018 847-678-8600
Fax: 847-678-9424 www.worldkitchen.com
Manufacturer and exporter of plastic containers; wholesaler/distributor and exporter of bakery racks and food trays; serving the food service market
President: Jim Sharman
CEO: Joe Mallof
Estimated Sales: $20 - 50 Million
Number Employees: 100-249
Parent Co: Borden Inc.
Type of Packaging: Food Service
Brands:
Bakers Secret
Chicago Cutlery
Corelle
Corningware
Cuisinart
Ekco
Farberware
Grilla Gear
Oxo
Olfa
Pyrex
Regent Sheffield
Revere
Visions

31304 World Pride
PO Box 41463
St Petersburg, FL 33743-1463 727-522-5020
Fax: 727-522-2317 800-533-2433
info@ablebrands.com www.ablebrands.com
Kitchen apparel including aprons, chef coats and hats; also, ice carvers
President: Douglas S Fyvolent
VP Marketing: Douglas Fyvolent
Estimated Sales: $1-2.5 Million
Number Employees: 4
Brands:
Kitchen Wise
Laural
Noble
Pro-Icer
Progold
Provell
Sterling

31305 World Tableware
P.O.Box 10060
Toledo, OH 43699-0060 419-727-2100
Fax: 419-325-2749 800-678-9849
stock@libbey.com www.libbey.com
Importer, exporter and wholesaler/distributor of tabletop supplies including flatware, dinnerware and hollowware; serving the food service market
President: John Myer
Quality Control: Allwyn Cahoun
CEO: John Meier
R & D: Bill Herp
Number Employees: 20-49
Parent Co: Libbey
Type of Packaging: Food Service

31306 World Technitrade
PO Box 72
Villanova, PA 19085-0072 610-525-1600
Fax: 610-525-1600 www.worldtechnitradeltd.com
Confectionery, bakery, and pressure and vacuum vessels import and export
President: Erwin Von Allmen
Estimated Sales: $1 - 5 Million

31307 World Variety Produce
Po Box 514599
Los Angeles, CA 90021 323-588-0151
Fax: 323-588-9774 800-588-0151
www.melissas.com
Importer and distributor of specialty produce
President & CEO: Joe Hernandez
CFO: Lee Zeller
Director of Marketing: Bill Schneider
VP Sales: Peter Steinbrick
Director Public Relations: Robert Schueller
Estimated Sales: $20.4 Million
Number Employees: 325
Type of Packaging: Consumer, Food Service, Bulk
Brands:
Don Enrique
Jo San
Melissas

31308 World Water Works
4 Vernon Lane
Elmsford, NY 800-607-7873
sales@worldwaterworks.com
www.worldwaterworks.com
Designs, builds and installs a line of wastewater treatment systems
President: Mark Fosshage
Vice President of Technology: Greg Parks
Director of Sales and Marketing: John Schnecker
Estimated Sales: $10 Million
Number Employees: 4

31309 World Water Works Inc.
4000 SW 113th St
Oklahoma City, OK 73173 405-943-9000
Fax: 405-943-9006 800-607-7973
info@worldwaterworks.com
www.worldwaterworks.com
Wastewater treatment.

31310 World Wide Beverage
P.O.Box 191
Glencoe, IL 60022-0191 847-835-3444
Fax: 847-835-3434
Manufacturers of accumulating table conveyors, bag-in-box filling equipment, bag-in-box dispensers, bottle, can warmers, bottle rinsers and washers
President: Howard Buckner
Estimated Sales: $1-2.5 Million
Number Employees: 1-4
Type of Packaging: Bulk

31311 World Wide Fittings
7501 N Natchez Ave
Niles, IL 60714 847-588-2200
Fax: 847-588-2212 800-393-9894
sales@worldwidefittings.com
www.worldwidefittings.com
Pneumatic and hydraulic fittings for food processing machinery
Chairman of the Board: Joseph D Mc Carthy
VP Sales: Mike Casey
VP Production: Sean McCarthy
Estimated Sales: $5-10,000,000
Number Employees: 20-49

31312 **World Wide Hospitality Furniture**
7311 Madision Street
Paramount, CA 90723 562-630-2700
Fax: 562-630-2227 800-728-8262
wrldwideh@aol.com www.wwhfurniture.com
Manufacturer and importer of tables, chairs and booths
President: Isaac Gonshor
CEO: Isaac Gonshor
Estimated Sales: $1 - 5,000,000
Number Employees: 20-50
Type of Packaging: Food Service
Brands:
World Wide

31313 **World Wide Safe Brokers**
112 Cromwell Court
Woodbury, NJ 08096 856-863-1225
Fax: 856-845-2266 800-593-2893
info@worldwidesafebrokers.com
www.worldwidesafebrokers.com
Fire safes, electronic safes, gun safes, safe deposit boxes, hotel room safes, insulated files, burglary safe, vaults, vault doors, in-floor safes, depository safes, custom designed and manufactured safes.
President: Edward Dornisch
VP: Mildred Dornisch
Estimated Sales: $.5 - 1 million
Number Employees: 3
Square Footage: 16000

31314 **Worldwide Dispensers**
1201 Windham Parkway
Suite D
Romeoville, IL 60446 630-296-2000
Fax: 630-296-2195 info@dssplastics.com
www.dssmith.com
Fun, fabulous ceramic products. All are bright and bold with witty sentiments, all designed by artist Lorrie Veasey. Lead free ceramic, dishwasher and microwave safe
Estimated Sales: D
Number Employees: 250-499
Number of Products: 200
Type of Packaging: Consumer

31315 **Wornick Company**
PO Box 55
McAllen, TX 78505-0055 561-227-0765
Fax: 956-631-0857
Meals Ready to Eat (MRE). Humanitarian Daily Rations (HDR)

31316 **(HQ)Worthen Industries**
3 E Spit Brook Rd
Nashua, NH 03060-5783 603-888-5443
Fax: 603-888-7945 info@worthenind.com
www.worthenindustries.com
Manufacturer and exporter of labels and adhesive tapes
President: Robert Worthen
CEO: Eileen Morin
Estimated Sales: $1 - 3 Million
Number Employees: 5-9

31317 **Wrap-Pak**
1728 Presson Pl
Yakima, WA 98903-2238 509-453-2830
Fax: 509-453-3653 800-879-9727
glbraden@fruitwrap.com www.fruitwrap.com
Fruit wrappers and packing needle holders
President: Lance Braden
CFO: Ted Smith
General Manager: G Lance Braden
Plant Manager: Shane May
Estimated Sales: $2.5 - 5 Million
Number Employees: 20-49

31318 **Wrapade Packaging Systems, LLC**
27 Law Dr.
Suite B/C
Fairfield, NJ 07004 973-773-6150
Fax: 973-773-6010 888-815-8564
sales@wrapade.com www.wrapade.com
Manufacturer and exporter of vertical, horizontal and stand-up pouch packaging machinery
President: Bill Beattie
Estimated Sales: $2.5-5 Million
Number Employees: 10-19
Square Footage: 88000

31319 **Wraps**
810 Springdale Avenue
East Orange, NJ 07017-1298 973-673-7873
Fax: 973-673-2240 sales@wrapsinc.com
www.wrapsinc.com
Manufacturer and exporter of flexible packaging materials, heat sealers and packaging machinery
President: Ralph Barone
General Manager: Michael Mikulis
Sales Manager: Brian Guidera
Estimated Sales: $2.5-5 Million
Number Employees: 20-49
Square Footage: 192000
Brands:
Clamco

31320 **Wright Brothers Paper Box Company**
800 Morris St
Fond Du Lac, WI 54935 920-921-8270
Fax: 920-921-8384 info@wbpaperbox.com
www.wbpaperbox.com
Rigid set-up paper boxes and folding cartons
President: Joan Pennau
President: Victor Pupo
Chairman: Frank Erdman
Sales / Customer Service: Amy Goebel
Sales / Customer Service: Diane Seibel
Estimated Sales: $5-10 Million
Number Employees: 50-99

31321 **Wright Global Graphic Solutions**
5115 Prospect St
Thomasville, NC 27360 800-678-9019
Fax: 336-476-8554 800-678-9019
salesinfo@wrightlabels.com
www.wrightglobalgraphics.com
Labels and labeling materials
President/CEO: Greg Wright
Vice President of Marketing: Vicki Fishman
Vice President of Sales: Carol Phillips
Estimated Sales: A
Number Employees: 200

31322 **(HQ)Wright Metal Products**
PO Box 6763
Greenville, SC 29606 864-297-6610
Fax: 864-281-0594
jcamden@wrightmetalproducts.com
www.wrightmetalproducts.com
Machine parts for food handling equipment
President: Paul Hoeft
VP: Jim Camden
General Manager: Jim Camden
Estimated Sales: $10-20 Million
Number Employees: 50-99
Square Footage: 40000
Other Locations:
Wright Metal Products
Greenville SC

31323 **Wright Plastics Company**
1107 Doster Road
Prattville, AL 36067-4329 334-365-9494
Fax: 334-365-9559 800-874-7659
sales@wrightplastics.com
www.wrightplastics.com
Polyethylene bags and film
Estimated Sales: $10-20 Million
Number Employees: 19

31324 **Wright-Bernet**
2605 Zimmerman Ave
Hamilton, OH 45015 513-874-1800
Fax: 513-874-5899 info@wrightbernet.com
www.dqb.com
Manufacturer and exporter of brooms and brushes
Manufacturing Manager: Mike Lindemoth
Estimated Sales: $2.5-5 Million
Number Employees: 20-49
Square Footage: 100000
Parent Co: Erco Housewares
Type of Packaging: Consumer, Food Service, Private Label, Bulk

31325 **Wylie Systems**
1190 Fewster Drive
Mississauga, ON L4W 1A1
Canada 905-238-1619
Fax: 905-238-5623 800-525-6609
info@wyliemetals.com www.wyliemetals.com
Manufacturer and exporter of railings and partitions for hotels, restaurants, etc.; also, sneeze guards
President: Michael Wylie
Brands:
Decorail

31326 **Wyssmont Company**
1470 Bergen Blvd
Fort Lee, NJ 07024 201-947-4600
Fax: 201-947-0324 sales@wyssmont.com
www.wyssmont.com
Manufacturer, designer and exporter of food processing equipment including rotating tray dryers, lumpbreakers, fixed and rotating bars and self-cleaning airlock feeders; also, solid handling equipment
President: Ed Weisselberg
VP: Joseph Bevacqua
R&D: J Ulrich
VP Sales: Joseph Henderson
Estimated Sales: $2.5-5 Million
Number Employees: 10-19
Square Footage: 20000
Brands:
Turbo-Dryer

31327 **Wythe Will Tzetzo**
3612 La Grange Parkway
Toano, VA 23168 757-566-5360
800-296-0273
www.wythewill.com
Distributor of specialty foods and fine confections across the US
President: Keith McDaniel
Owner: John McCurry
CFO & VP Finance: Rod Hogan
VP: Belton Joyner
Director of Sales & Marketing: David Mastricola
Director of Human Resources: Lisa Weakland
Operations Manager: Bill Hall
Purchasing Manager: Nanette Ross
Estimated Sales: $8.9 Million
Number Employees: 400
Square Footage: 200000
Type of Packaging: Consumer, Bulk

31328 **X-Press Manufacturing**
271 Fm 306
New Braunfels, TX 78130 830-629-2651
Fax: 830-620-4727 sales@x-pressmfg.com
www.x-pressmfg.com
Display tortilla cookers, pressers and warmers
Owner: Charles Smith
President/Owner: Rex Wilson
Customer Service: Anne Sowell
Shop Manager: Charlie Smith
Estimated Sales: $.5 - 1 million
Number Employees: 1-4
Square Footage: 3750
Parent Co: Copprex
Brands:
X-Press

31329 **X-Ray Industries**
1961 Thunderbird
Troy, MI 48084-5467 248-362-2242
Fax: 248-362-4422 800-973-4800
foodx@aol.com www.xritesting.com
Manufacturer and exporter of in-line and off-line X-ray inspection equipment; also, X-ray inspection services available
President: Scott Thams
Estimated Sales: $30 - 50 Million
Number Employees: 1-4
Square Footage: 30000
Parent Co: X-Ray Industries

31330 **X-Rite, Inc.**
4300 44th St SE
Grand Rapids, MI 49512 616-803-2100
Fax: 616-534-0723 info@xrite.com
www.xrite.com
Portable hand-held spectrophotometers and colorimeters with supporting computer software for color control applications and color formulation
President: Michael Ferrara
CEO: Richard Cook
CFO: Mary Koueing
Estimated Sales: $237.55 Million
Number Employees: 747
Parent Co: Foresight Enterprises
Brands:
Qa-Master
Sp68

31331 **XL Corporate & ResearchServices**
62 White Street
New York, NY 10013-3593 212-431-5000
Fax: 212-431-5111 800-221-2972
Consultant providing product, company or industry research including trademark research on product names, company names and logos, preparation and filing of trademarks and credit reports
President: Robert Blumerang
Counsel: Marc Moel
General Counsel: Arthur McGuire
Estimated Sales: $20 - 50 Million
Number Employees: 30
Square Footage: 5000
Parent Co: Julius Blumberg

31332 **XanGo LLC**
2889 Ashton Blvd
Lehi, UT 84043 801-816-8000
Fax: 801-816-8001 877-469-2646
service@xango.net www.xango.net
Markets daily dietary supplemental juice beverage made from the mangosteen fruit.
President/Chief Executive Officer: Aaron Garrity
Chairman: Gary Hollister
President Intnl Distributor Relations: Joe Morton
EVP International Relations: Bryan Davis
Quality Assurance Manufacturing: Wayne Davis
Chief Marketing Officer: Gordon Morton
President Operations: Ken Wood

31333 **Xcel Tower Controls**
1600 W 6th St
PO Box 187
Gilbertsville, NY 13776 574-259-7804
Fax: 574-259-5769 800-288-7362
info@xcel.com www.xcel.com
Manufacturer and exporter of control and process control systems, universal programmers, programmable control systems and industrial computers, tower light controllers and monitoring systems
President: Bruce Shepard
CEO: John Brickley
Sales Director: Bruce Shepard
Estimated Sales: $2.5-5 Million
Number Employees: 10-19
Square Footage: 15000

31334 **Xcell International**
16400 Est 103rd Street
Lemont, IL 60439 630-323-0107
Fax: 630-323-0217 800-722-7751
info@xcellint.com www.xcellint.com
Spice blends, confectionery dessert toppings, coffee flavors and creamers, teas and coffee and tea accessories.
CEO: Raymond Henning
Estimated Sales: $20-50 Million
Number Employees: 50-99

31335 **Xela Pack**
8300 Boettner Road
Saline, MI 48176 734-944-1300
Fax: 734-429-4714 800-742-7225
info@xelapack.com www.xelapack.com
Single and multi-dose packaging alternative to bottles and tubes
President: Aliseo Gentile
Estimated Sales: $2.5 - 5Million
Number Employees: 20-49

31336 **Xiaoping Design**
73 Hudson Street
New York, NY 10013-2870 212-962-4080
Fax: 212-962-4071 800-891-9896
support@xiaopingdesign.com
www.develop4u.com
Custom furniture including tables and chairs also designs for custom furniture
President: Xiaoping Zao
VP/Marketing/Sales/Operations: David Chang
Estimated Sales: $1 Million
Number Employees: 2
Number of Brands: 1
Number of Products: 45

31337 **Xpander Pak**
1045 Technology Park Drive
Glen Allen, VA 23059-4500 804-266-5000
Fax: 804-266-4474 800-720-1777
sales@xpander.com www.xpander.com
Projective packaging: Xpander Pak super protective shippers, Safe-T Shipper, Safe-T Shipper ESD
CEO: Joseph Sullivan
Estimated Sales: $1-2.5 Million
Number Employees: 9

31338 **Xpedx**
50 E Rivercenter Boulevard
Covington, KY 41011-1683 859-655-2000
Fax: 859-655-8983 imac@earthnet.net
www.xpedx.com
Paper products, sanitation supplies, janitorial supplies
Marketing Director: Michael Feenan
Estimated Sales: $6.5 Million
Number Employees: 9000
Number of Brands: 600
Type of Packaging: Food Service

31339 **Xtreme Beverages, LLC**
32565-B Golden Lantern
#282
Dana Point, CA 92629
Canada 949-495-7929
Fax: 949-495-8015 xtremebeverages@cox.net
www.xtremebeverages.com
Wood and bamboo box; wood and bamboo tea chest; wine box; baskets; tea and coffee accessories; wine accessories; MDF box; cardboard box; wooded tea dispenser; wrought iron tea can rack; wood and bamboo products, candles; candleholders; gourmet gift packaging and food and beverage gift packaging
President: William Quinley
VP: James Moffitt
Estimated Sales: $5 Million
Number Employees: 4
Type of Packaging: Consumer, Food Service, Private Label, Bulk

31340 **Xylem, Inc.**
1133 Westchester Avenue
White Plains, NY 10604 914-323-5700
Fax: 914-323-5800 www.xyleminc.com
Field, portable, online and laboratory analytical instrumentation.
President & Chief Executive Officer: Gretchen McClain
Senior VP & Chief Financial Officer: Mike Speetzen
Estimated Sales: $3.79 Billion
Number Employees: 12700
Type of Packaging: Bulk

31341 **Y-Pers**
PO Box 9559
Philadelphia, PA 19124 215-289-6507
Fax: 215-289-6811 800-421-0242
info@ypers.com www.ypers.com
Manufacturer and exporter of cheesecloths and uniforms including disposable clothing, hairnets and gloves
President: David Blum
CFO: David Blum
R&D: David Blum
Estimated Sales: Below $5 Million
Number Employees: 10-19

31342 **Y-Z Sponge & Foam Products**
811 Cundy Avenue
Delta, BC V3M 5P6
Canada 604-525-1665
Fax: 604-525-1081
Polyurethane foam

31343 **YBB Flexible Automation**
2487 S Commerce Dr
New Berlin, WI 53151-2717 262-785-3400
Fax: 262-785-0342 414-785-9915
ann.r.smith@us.abb.com
www.abb.com/automation
Robotic system solutions for packaging and palletizing
Estimated Sales: $25-50 Million
Number Employees: 250-499

31344 **YCU Air/York International**
1519 Highway 13 E
Burnsville, MN 55337-2917 952-707-1286
Fax: 952-707-0914 info@york.com
www.york.com
Clean rooms and equipment
Estimated Sales: $1 - 5 Million

31345 **YSI**
1725 Brannum Ln
Yellow Springs, OH 45387 937-767-7241
Fax: 937-767-9320 800-765-4974
support@ysi.com www.ysi.com
Instrumentation for the analysis of carbohydrates, organic acids, sugars, dissolved oxygen, etc.; also, conductivity meters and temperature devices
President: Richard Omlor
CFO: Lee Erdman
VP: Jim Smith
Quality Control: Marek Jezior
Estimated Sales: $50-75 Million
Number Employees: 100-249

31346 **YW Yacht Basin**
8341 Black Dog Alley
Easton, MD 21601-6329 410-822-0414
Fax: 410-822-1090
Material handling conveyors; also, custom metal, structural and steel fabrications of stairs and handrails available
President: Douglas Weinmann
VP Sales: David Weinmann
Number Employees: 6
Square Footage: 25000

31347 **Yakima Wire Works**
1949 E. Manning Avenue
PO Box 9995
Reedley, CA 93654 509-248-6790
Fax: 509-452-5862 www.swfcompanies.com
Manufacturer and exporter of fully and semi-automatic bagging, weighing and batching, modular net dispensers, check-weighers, dual-belt conveyors and blowers
President: Gary Germunson
Chairman/VP: Tim Main
Estimated Sales: $.5 - 1 million
Number Employees: 1-4

31348 **Yaloom Marketing Corporation**
51 James St
South Hackensack, NJ 07606-1438 201-488-3535
Fax: 201-488-8056 jzzmc@aol.com
www.surimiseafood.com
Consultant specializing in marketing, promotion and food technology; importer of seafood products including imitation crab meat
President: Roy Zaloom
Estimated Sales: $10-20 Million
Number Employees: 10-19

31349 **Yamada America**
1575 Highpoint Drive
Elgin, IL 60123-9303 847-697-1878
Fax: 847-697-2794 800-990-7867
sales@yamadapump.com
www.yamadapump.com
Air-operated, double diaphragm pump
President: Steve Kameyama
Estimated Sales: Below $500,000
Number Employees: 3

31350 **Yamato Corporation**
1775 S. Murray Blvd.
Colorado Springs, CO 80916-4513 719-591-1500
Fax: 719-591-1045 800-538-1762
www.yamatocorp.com
Manufacturer and exporter of electronic and mechanical scales, electronic weight printers and computerized weighing systems
President: Sadao Nakamura
CEO: Sado Nakamura
Marketing Director: Gary Mendenhall
Sales Director: Prague Mehta
Estimated Sales: $2.5 - 5 Million
Number Employees: 20-49
Square Footage: 96000
Brands:
Accuweigh
Yamato

31351 **Yardney Water ManagementSystems**
6666 Box Springs Blvd
Riverside, CA 92507 951-656-6716
Fax: 951-656-3867 800-854-4788
info@yardneyfiopro.com
www.yardneyfilters.com
Manufacturer and exporter of water quality improvement and filtration systems
President: Kenneth Phillips
CFO: Kenneth Phillips
Quality Control: Janie Weissberg
Industrial Field Sales Manager: Ron Gamble
Estimated Sales: $5 - 10 Million
Number Employees: 20-49
Square Footage: 200000

Brands:
Yardney

31352 Yargus Manufacturing
12285 E Main St
Marshall, IL 62441 217-826-6352
Fax: 217-826-8551 layco@yargus.com
www.yargus.com
Stainless steel equipment including conveyors, hopper scales, blenders and bucket elevators; exporter of conveyor and blender systems
President: Larry Yargus
Sales: Lyle Yargus
Estimated Sales: $5-10 Million
Number Employees: 50-99
Square Footage: 30000
Brands:
Layco

31353 Yates Industries
23050 E Industrial Dr
Saint Clair Shores, MI 48080 586-778-7680
Fax: 586-778-6565 sales@yatesind.com
www.yatesind.com
Pneumatic and hydraulic cylinders including stainless steel, food grade and epoxy paint
President: William Yates III
Sales/Marketing Manager: Fred Cormier
Estimated Sales: $10+ Million
Number Employees: 20-49
Square Footage: 60
Parent Co: Yates Cylinder

31354 Yeager Wire Works
620 Broad St
Berwick, PA 18603 570-752-2769
Fax: 570-752-2934
Display racks including wire and sheet-metal
President: David Ungemach
VP: Robert Ungemach
Estimated Sales: Below $5 Million
Number Employees: 1-4

31355 Yerecic Label Company
701 Hunt Valley Rd
New Kensington, PA 15068 724-335-2200
Fax: 724-335-8872 experts@yereciclabel.com
www.yereciclabel.com
Pressure sensitive labels; printing services available
President: Arthur Yerecic
VP: Arthur Yerecic Jr
Estimated Sales: $2.5 - 5 Million
Number Employees: 10-19
Square Footage: 7500

31356 Yerger Wood Products
3090 Wentling Schoolhouse Road
East Greenville, PA 18041-2313 215-679-4413
Fax: 215-679-8797 sue@yergerwood.com
www.yergerwood.com
Wooden pallets
President: James Yerger Jr
CEO/Sales: Susan Klolz
Estimated Sales: Below $5 Million
Number Employees: 10

31357 Yeuell Nameplate & Label
8 Adele Rd
Woburn, MA 01801 781-933-2984
Fax: 781-933-3569 tbarry@yeuell.com
www.yeuell.com
Nameplates and labels; also, metal etching services available
President: Andrew F Hall Iii
Estimated Sales: $2.5-5 Million
Number Employees: 20-49

31358 (HQ)Yohay Baking Company
146 Albany Ave
Lindenhurst, NY 11757 631-225-0300
Fax: 631-225-4278 www.yohay.com
Processor, importer and exporter of wafer rolls, specialty cookies, biscotti, and fudge mix, kosher and all natural products. Retail packaging available
Owner: Michael Soloman
Number Employees: 20-49
Type of Packaging: Consumer, Food Service, Private Label, Bulk
Brands:
Fudge Gourmet
Gourmet Cookie Place
Sweetheart Fudge

31359 York Container Company
PO Box 3008
York, PA 17402 717-757-7611
Fax: 717-755-8090 www.yorkcontainer.com
Corrugated shipping containers
President: Chuck Wolf
CFO: Bill Ludwid
Executive VP: Charles Wolf Jr
Estimated Sales: $20 - 50 Million
Number Employees: 100-249
Square Footage: 200000

31360 York Refrigeration Marine US
4401 23rd Avenue W
Seattle, WA 98199-1212 206-285-0904
Fax: 206-285-0965 800-282-0904
smservice@york.com www.york.com
Reciprocating and screw compressors and customized LT pump recirculation packages; also, freezers
President: Thomas Berfenfeldt
Sales: Slawonir Tabaczynski
Estimated Sales: $10-20 Million
Number Employees: 20-49
Parent Co: York Refrigeration A/S
Brands:
Sabroe
Unisab
Unisafe

31361 York River Pallet Corporation
PO Box 191
Shacklefords, VA 23156 804-785-5811
Fax: 804-785-3702
Wooden pallets and pallet materials
President/CEO: James Potts
Estimated Sales: Below $5 Million
Number Employees: 5-9

31362 York Saw & Knife Company
P.O.Box 733
York, PA 17405 717-764-2345
Fax: 717-764-2768 800-233-1969
info@yorksaw.com www.yorksaw.com
Manufacturer and exporter of circular and straight knives for food processing; custom and standard specifications available
President: Michael Pickard
CFO: Todd Gladfeltzer
Quality Control: Tim Wentz
Estimated Sales: $10 Million
Number Employees: 50-99
Square Footage: 65000

31363 York Tape & Label Company
P.O.Box 1309
York, PA 17405-1309 717-266-9675
Fax: 717-266-9837 yorkwebsite@yorklabel.com
www.yorklabel.com
Labels and tags, nameplates, commercial printing and bar coding
President: Timothy Hare
CFO: Dennis Cole
Sales: Karen S Chavez
Quality Control: Tom Walko
VP Sales: John Attayek
Estimated Sales: $50 - 100 Million
Number Employees: 250-499

31364 York Tent & Awning Company
7 E 7th Ave
York, PA 17404 717-854-3806
Fax: 717-843-6555 800-864-3510
sales@yorktentandawning.net
www.yorktentandawning.com
Commercial awnings
President: Joseph Musti
Estimated Sales: $1-2,500,000
Number Employees: 10-19

31365 Yorkraft
2675a Eastern Boulevard
York, PA 17402-2905 717-845-3666
Fax: 717-846-3213 800-872-2044
sales@yorkcraft.com www.yorkraft.com
Food service equipment including cabinetry products, salad bars, buffet lines and merchandising carts; also, decorative lighting panels available
President: David Imhoff
VP Operations: Jack Smith
VP: William Imhoff
Estimated Sales: $5-10 Million
Number Employees: 10
Square Footage: 360000

31366 YottaMark
203 Redwood Shores Parkway
Suite 100
Redwood City, CA 94065 650-264-6200
Fax: 650-264-6220 866-768-7878
info@yottamark.com www.yottamark.com
Product fingerprint solution detects and deters counterfeiting, diversion and fraud and allows manufacturers, brand protection personnel, law enforcement officials-even consumers- to authenticate individual products anytimeanywhere.
President/CEO: J Scott Carr
President, Chief Executive Officer: Scott Carr
Engineering VP: Matthew Self
Founder, Chief Marketing Officer: Elliott Grant
Senior Vice President of Sales: Michael Bromme
Chief Operating Officer: Paul Gifford

31367 Young & Associates
8915 58th Pl
Kenosha, WI 53144-7802 262-657-6394
Fax: 262-657-4306 sales@youngassoc.net
www.youngassoc.net
Manufacturer and supplier of food product machinery
President: William B Young
CEO: Bill Young
Public Relations: Nancy Beck

31368 Young & Swartz
39 Cherry St
Buffalo, NY 14204 716-852-2171
Fax: 716-852-5652 800-466-7682
info@youngandswartz.com
www.youngandswartz.com
Brushes, brooms and janitorial supplies
President: Raphael Winzig
Estimated Sales: $1-2.5 Million
Number Employees: 10-19
Square Footage: 15000

31369 Young Electric Sign Company
1605 Gramercy Rd
Salt Lake City, UT 84104 801-487-8481
Fax: 801-467-3447 800-444-3847
info@yesco.com www.yesco.com
Manufacturer and exporter of electric signs
President: Michael Young
CFO: Duane Wardle
Sales Manager: Susan Ward
Estimated Sales: $30 - 50 Million
Number Employees: 250-499

31370 Young Industries
16 Painter Street
Muncy, PA 17756-1423 570-546-3165
Fax: 570-546-1888 mktinfo@younginds.com
www.younginds.com
Tea blending equipment, conveying equipment (elevators, machines and buckets), blending and mixing equipment, portioning equipment, bin silo systems and storage, safety/occupational health/environment, listing of equipment, fieldservice, quality assurance, manufacturing, technical information
CFO: Jerry Stauffer
R&D: John Pfeiffer
Estimated Sales: $10 - 20 Million
Number Employees: 45

31371 Young's Lobster Pound
2 Fairview St.
Belfast, ME 04915 207-338-1160
Fax: 207-338-1656
raymond@youngslobsterpound.com
youngslobsterpound.webs.com
Sea food supplier
President: Raymond Young
CEO: Katrina Young
Vice President: Diane Young
Quality Control: Joe Young
Estimated Sales: $500,000-$1 Million
Number Employees: 20-49
Type of Packaging: Consumer, Food Service, Private Label, Bulk

31372 Your Place Menu Systems
2600 Lockheed Way
Carson City, NV 89706-0717 775-882-7834
Fax: 775-882-5210 800-321-8105
joneil@pymramid.net www.yourplacemenus.com

Manufacturer and exporter of outdoor and indoor illuminated and nonilluminated menu boards
President, Sales Manager: John O Neil
Operations Manager, Product Design: Matt Stutsman
Number Employees: 20-49
Square Footage: 280000
Parent Co: Impact International

31373 **Yuan Fa Can-Making**
PO Box 14016
Torrance, CA 90503-8016 310-532-5829
Fax: 310-536-4216
Tea and coffee cans

31374 **Z 2000 The Pick of the Millenium**
819 S Madison Boulevard
Bartlesville, OK 74006-8534 918-335-2030
Fax: 918-335-1789 800-654-7311
z20001989@cabkone.net
Manufacturer and exporter of 45 degree angled dental cleaners
President: Mack Blevins
VP: Pamela Blevins
Estimated Sales: $1 - 5 Million
Number Employees: 1-4
Square Footage: 7500
Parent Co: Mack Blevins Enterprises
Type of Packaging: Consumer, Food Service, Private Label, Bulk
Brands:
Angled Pro Picks

31375 **Z-Loda Systems Engineering**
1010 Summer
Suite 101
Stamford, CT 06905 203-325-8001
Fax: 203-978-0104
Manufacturer and exporter of vertical lift systems
President: Clifford Mollo
Estimated Sales: $1-2.5 Million
Number Employees: 1-4

31376 **Z-Trim Holdings, Inc**
1101 Campus Drive
Mundelein, IL 60060 847-549-6002
Fax: 847-549-6028 customerservice@ztrim.com
www.ztrim.com
Ingredients
Sales Director: Rick Harris
VP Sales/Applications: Lynda Carroll
Applications Project Manager: Aili Young
Research Chef: Erin Ryan

31377 **ZMD International**
600 W 15th St
Long Beach, CA 90813 562-628-0071
Fax: 562-628-0080 800-222-9674
info@zmd.com www.zmd.com
Temperature controlling and trimming equipment
President: Yosi Cohen
VP Marketing: Jacob Horev
Manager Sales: David Maciel
Estimated Sales: $5-10,000,000
Number Employees: 20-49
Number of Products: 7
Square Footage: 46000

31378 **Zacmi USA**
2391 Zanker Road
Suite 320
San Jose, CA 95131-1145 408-433-0100
Fax: 408-433-0224 zacmiUS@aol.com
Processing machinery sales, fillers for all products
President: Charles Hoffman
Estimated Sales: $500,000-$1 Million
Number Employees: 4

31379 **Zahm & Nagel Company**
210 Vermont Street
PO.Box 400
Holland, NY 14080 716-537-2110
Fax: 716-537-2106 800-216-1542
info@zahmnagel.com www.zahmnagel.com
Quality control equipment: CO2 and air testers, pilot plants, carbonating equipment, batch tester filter
President: David Koch
Estimated Sales: $5 - 10 Million
Number Employees: 5-9

31380 **Zanasi USA**
8601 73rd Ave No. # 38
Brooklyn Park, MN 55428 763-593-1907
Fax: 763-593-1941 800-627-2633
info@zanasiusa.com www.zanasiusa.com
Coding and marking equipment
President: Gianni Zanasi
CFO: Dana Paige
Marketing Director: Jenny Worre
National Sales Manager: Mark Koethe
Estimated Sales: Below $5 Million
Number Employees: 5-9
Square Footage: 8000
Brands:
Jet 2000
Modul Print
Z Jet

31381 **Zander**
ÿÿ 212 Oceola Avenue
Nashville, TN 37209 770-381-7846
Fax: 615-352-2850 ÿ80- 35- 428
info@zanderins.com www.zanderins.com
Compressed air and industrial gas purification products
Estimated Sales: $2.5 - 5 Million
Number Employees: 20-49

31382 **Zapata Industries**
2699 S Bayshore Drive
Miami, FL 33133 305-856-8804
Fax: 305-856-3046
110173.1012@compuserve.com
Metal crowns, aluminum closures, plastic closures, lining compounds
President: Claudio Zapata
Estimated Sales: $1-2.5 Million
Number Employees: 1-4

31383 **Zealco Industries**
PO Box 809
Calvert City, KY 42029-0809 800-759-5531
Fax: 270-395-9522 zealco@purlanco.com
www.purlanco.com
Manufacturer and exporter of high pressure commercial and industrial washing equipment
Parent Co: Purlanco

31384 **Zebra Technologies Corporation**
30 Plan Way
Warwick, RI 02886-1012 401-739-5800
Fax: 401-732-0145 800-556-7266
ri_jobs@zebra.com www.zebra.com
Portable, desktop and tranportable printing solutions for automatic identification systems
CEO: Paul Karpizz
CEO: Alfred Petteruti
R & D: Majid Amani
Vice President, General Manager: Andrew Tay
Director of Marketing: Jim Pattermann
Vice President of Sales: Stephen Logue
Plant Manager: Steven Seagrave
Estimated Sales: $20-50 Million
Number Employees: 100-249
Square Footage: 45000
Parent Co: Zebra Technologies Corporation

31385 **Zebra Technologies Corporation**
475 Half Day Road
Suite 500
Lincolnshire, IL 60069 847-634-6700
Fax: 847-913-8766 866-230-9494
www.zebra.com
Manufacturer and exporter of bar code equipment including printers, supplies and software for point-of-application labeling and performance thermal transferring.
Executive Vice President/Director: Gerhard Cless
Chief Executive Officer: Anders Gustafsson
Chief Financial Officer: Michael Smiley
Senior VP, Corporate Development: Michael Cho
Senior VP, Human Resources: Terrance Collins
Senior VP, New Growth Platforms: Philip Gerskovich
Senior VP/General Counsel/Secretary: Jim Kaput
Senior VP, Global Sales & Marketing: Michael Terzich
Vice President, Finance: Todd Naughton
Senior VP, Engineering & Operations: Hugh Gagnier
VP/General Manager, North America: Dean Dalesandro
Estimated Sales: $996 Million
Number Employees: 2,544
Square Footage: 167600
Brands:
Zebra
Zebra Value-Line
Zebra Xii

31386 **Zed Industries**
3580 Lightner Road
PO Box 458
Vandalia, OH 45377 937-667-8407
Fax: 937-667-3340 info@zedindustries.com
www.zedindustries.com
Manufacturer and exporter of vacuum and pressure thermoforming equipment, heat sealers, formers/fillers/sealers, blister packers and custom engineered plastic packaging systems
President: Mark Zelnick
CFO: Helen Zelnick
VP: Peter Zelnick
Sales: Leonard Loomis
Estimated Sales: $10-20 Million
Number Employees: 50-99
Type of Packaging: Consumer, Food Service, Bulk

31387 **Zeeco**
22151 E 91st St S
Broken Arrow, OK 74014 918-258-8551
Fax: 918-251-5519 sales@zeeco.com
www.zeeco.com
Manufacturer and exporter of gas and oil food burners used for heating and drying; also, fume/liquid incinerators used for hazardous waste disposal
President: Darton Zink
Chairman: John Zink
Sales Manager: D Caho
Purchasing Manager: D Updike
Estimated Sales: $20-50 Million
Number Employees: 100-249
Square Footage: 42000

31388 **Zeier Plastic & Manufacturing**
2203 Leo Circle
Madison, WI 53704 608-244-5782
Fax: 608-244-1810 DZ@Zeierplastic.com
www.zeierplastic.com
Manufacturer and exporter of thermoplastic injection molded trays and funnels; also, custom injection molded parts available
Owner: Dennis Zeier
VP: Dennis Zeier
Estimated Sales: $2.5-5 Million
Number Employees: 10-19

31389 **Zelco Industries**
110 Haven Ave
Mount Vernon, NY 10553 914-699-6230
Fax: 914-699-7082 800-431-2486
office@zelco.com www.zelco.com
Lighting fixtures, cooking and barbecuing utensils, stainless steel cutlery and coffee brewers
Chairman of the Board: Noel E Zeller
CEO: Noel Zeller
CFO: Mike Ronan
Vice President: Nicole Zeller
Marketing Director: Terri Manganelli
Sales Director: Mike Boylan
Operations Manager: Robert Jacobs
Estimated Sales: $2.5-5,000,000
Number Employees: 20-49
Square Footage: 55000
Type of Packaging: Consumer, Private Label

31390 **Zeltex**
130 Western Maryland Parkway
Hagerstown, MD 21740 301-791-7080
Fax: 301-733-9398 800-732-1950
canders@zeltex.com www.zeltex.com
Manufacturer and exporter of near-infrared analyzers for the food, grain and patrochemical industries
President: Todd Rosenthal
Director of Sales: Chris Anders
Number Employees: 20
Brands:
Zeltex

31391 **Zeltex**
130 Western Maryland Pkwy
Hagerstown, MD 21740-5116 301-791-7080
Fax: 301-733-9398 800-732-1950
canders@zeltex.com www.zeltex.com
Near infrared instrumentation for moisture and product constituents
President: Todd Rosenthal
Director of Sales: Chris Anders
Estimated Sales: $1-5 Million
Number Employees: 24

31392 Zenar Corporation
7301 S 6th St
PO Box 107
Oak Creek, WI 53154-0107 414-764-1800
Fax: 414-764-1267 mail@zenarcrane.com
www.zenarcrane.com
Manufacturer and exporter of electric overhead cranes and hoist units
President: John Maiwald
Estimated Sales: $10 - 20 Million
Number Employees: 40

31393 Zenith Cutter Company
5200 Zenith Pkwy
Loves Park, IL 61111-2735 815-282-5200
Fax: 815-282-5232 800-223-5202
toddg@zenithcutter.com www.zenithcutter.com
Manufacturer and exporter of machine knives and cutters; also, custom manufacturing and duplicating available
Personnel: Bob Yocum
VP: Robert Yocum
Quality Control: Tim Greve
Director Sales/Marketing: Tim Schoenecker
Production Manager: Terry Willis
Estimated Sales: $20 - 50 Million
Number Employees: 100-249
Square Footage: 140000
Type of Packaging: Bulk

31394 Zenith Specialty Bag Company
17625 Railroad St
City of Industry, CA 91748-0445 626-912-2481
Fax: 800-284-8493 800-925-2247
cust.serv@zenithbag.com www.zsb.com
Manufacturer and exporter of paper products including custom print, pan liners, wax paper bags and grease resistant sheets
President: Scott Anderson
CEO: Betty Anderson
CFO: Jack Grave
Vice President: Ron Anderson
VP: Ron Anderson
Marketing Director: Susan Washle
Sales Director: Scott Apperson
Operations Manager: Jeff Behrends
Estimated Sales: $10 - 20 Million
Number Employees: 100-249
Square Footage: 85000
Brands:
Sta-Fresh
The Cubby
Thermal Gard

31395 Zep Superior Solutions
1310 Seaboard Industrial Dr
Atlanta, GA 30318 404-352-1680
Fax: 404-350-2742 webmaster@zepmfg.com
www.zepmfg.com
Owner: Marty Zappa
CFO: John Ehrie
Quality Control: Bruce Dunkley
Estimated Sales: $300,000-500,000
Number Employees: 1-4

31396 Zepf Technologies
5320 140th Ave N
Clearwater, FL 33760-3743 727-535-4100
Fax: 727-539-8944 sales@zepf.com
www.pneumaticscale.com
Manufacturer and exporter of shrink wrappers, case packers, bundlers, tray formers, straw applicators, rotary uncasers, combiners and laners
President: Michael Mc Laughlin
Estimated Sales: $20-50 Million
Number Employees: 50-99
Square Footage: 45000
Brands:
Akron
Akron Hawk
Akron Spartan
Flex-Packer
Flexwrap
Iac 2000
Pilot Divider
Tampco
Universal

31397 Zephyr Manufacturing
200 Mitchell Rd
Sedalia, MO 65301 660-827-0352
Fax: 660-827-0713 info@zephyrmfg.com
www.zephyrmfg.com
Processor and exporter of brushes, floor and carpet cleaners, wet mops, handles, mopsticks, sponges, frames, squeegees
President: John A Lindstrom
Estimated Sales: $20-50 Million
Number Employees: 50-99
Brands:
Dover Grill Scraper
Zephyr

31398 Zero Corporation
288 Main Street
Monson, MA 01057-1314 413-267-5561
Fax: 413-267-3179 sales@apwi.com
www.zerocorporation.com
Vacuum and thermoformed plastic reusable shipping containers and closures; also, aluminum and steel modular electronic cabinets and racks
Estimated Sales: $10-20 Million
Number Employees: 100-249
Parent Co: Zero Corporation

31399 Zero-Max
13200 6th Ave N
Minneapolis, MN 55441 763-546-4300
Fax: 763-546-8260 800-533-1731
zero-maz@zero-maz.com www.zero-max.com
Servoclass couplings, composite disk couplings, torque limiters
President: Doug Moore
Estimated Sales: $20-50 Million
Number Employees: 50-99

31400 Zero-Temp
2510 N Grand Ave
Suite 112
Santa Ana, CA 92705-8753 714-538-3177
Fax: 714-538-1531 gflassoc@aol.com
www.zerotempinstallation.com
Manufacturer and exporter of turn key refrigerated warehouses, walk-in freezers, walk-in coolers, controlled environment rooms and clean rooms
President: Gary Lyons
CEO: Michael Lyons
CFO: Donna Lyons
R&D: David Pinillos
Operations: Pat McBride
Production: Gary Lyons
Estimated Sales: $6 Million
Number Employees: 10-19
Square Footage: 3000
Parent Co: Garry F Lyons & Associates

31401 Zeroll Company
PO Box 999
Fort Pierce, FL 34954 772-461-3811
Fax: 772-461-1061 800-872-5000
sales@zeroll.com www.zeroll.com
Manufacturer and exporter of scoops, dishers and spades
Plant Manager: Thomas Funka Sr
General Manager/CEO: Lenny Van Valkenburg
Plant Manager: Thomas Funka, Jr.
Estimated Sales: $10 Million
Number Employees: 20-49
Number of Brands: 5
Number of Products: 40
Square Footage: 30000
Type of Packaging: Consumer, Food Service, Private Label, Bulk
Brands:
Nuroll
Roldip
Universal
Zeroll
Zerolon

31402 Zeroloc
9757 NE Juanita Dr # 119
Kirkland, WA 98034-8966 425-823-4888
Fax: 425-820-9749 sales@zeroloc.com
www.zeroloc.com
Insulated panel and door systems
Number Employees: 1-4
Other Locations:
Zeroloc Manufacturing Plant
Brantford, ON
Zeroloc Manufacturing Plant
Langley, BC

31403 Zesto Food Equipment Manufacturing
6450 Hutchison Street
Montreal, QC H2V 4C8
Canada 514-278-4621
Fax: 514-278-4622 info@zesto.ca
www.zesto-ovens.com
President: George Moshonas
Number Employees: 20

31404 Zimmer Custom Made Packaging
P.O.Box 1869
Columbus, OH 43216-1869 614-294-4931
Fax: 614-299-0538 800-338-7465
gbrinkman@norse.com www.norse.com
Sugar cones for ice cream, sleeves, paper tubes and cups for packaging, all-purpose fillers and cup collator that automatically counts, stacks and collates cups
President: Scott Fullbright
CFO: Randy Harvey
CEO: Scot Fulbright
R&D: Gunther Brinkman
Human Resources: Brian McGinney
Estimated Sales: $20 - 50 Million
Number Employees: 100-249

31405 Zimmer Custom-Made Packaging
1450 E 20th St
Indianapolis, IN 46218 317-263-3436
Fax: 317-263-3427 info@zcmp.com
www.zcmp.com
A leading supplier in the worldwide flexible packaging industry. ZCMP has focused on frozen novelty, butter/margarine, candy, confectionary and other food markets and is currently beginning to supply die cut cone sleeves and die cutlids.
President: Mark Lastovich
CFO: Chuck Bollard
Quality Assurance Manager: Herbert Henson
VP Marketing/Sales: Mike DoBosh
VP Operations: David Brown
Estimated Sales: $20-50 Million
Number Employees: 20-49
Square Footage: 60000
Other Locations:
Zimmer Custom-Made Packaging
Indianapolis IN

31406 Zimmerman Handling Systems
29555 Stephenson Hwy
Madison Heights, MI 48071 248-398-6200
Fax: 248-398-1374 800-347-7047
seekinfo@irco.com www.irhoist.com
Manufacturer and exporter of ergonomic lifting systems
President: Gerard Geraghty
National Accounts Manager: Stephen Klostermeyer
Estimated Sales: $10 Million
Number Employees: 50-99
Parent Co: Ingersol-Rand

31407 Ziniz
3955 E Blue Lick Road
Louisville, KY 40229-6047 502-955-6573
Fax: 502-955-6960
Manufacturer and exporter of package handling conveyors including chain, gravity belt live roller and overhead trolley; also, installation available
President: Ronny Grant
Marketing/Sales: Paul McDonald
Estimated Sales: $50-100 Million
Number Employees: 250-499
Square Footage: 50000

31408 Zip-Net
801 William Ln
Reading, PA 19604 610-929-9426
Fax: 610-921-1588 info@zip-net.com
www.zip-net.com
President: Andrew Wicklow
Estimated Sales: $20 - 50 Million
Number Employees: 50-99

31409 Zip-Pak
1800 W Sycamore Rd
Manteno, IL 60950-9369 815-468-6500
Fax: 815-468-6550 info@zippak.com
www.zippak.com

Recloseable zipper products that can be used for storing a variety of products within the food industry.
Chairman/Chief Executive Officer: David Speer
VP/Investor Relations: John Brooklier
SVP/Chief Financial Officer: Ronald Kropp
Finance Executive: Roger Geckner
VP/Research and Development: Lee Sheridan
Senior Vice President: Allan Sutherland
SVP/General Counsel & Secretary: James Wooten
Senior Vice President Human Resources: Sharon Brady
Vice President Patents & Technology: Mark Croll
Parent Co: Illinois Tool Works
Type of Packaging: Consumer

31410 **Zip-Pak**
4250 NE Expressway
Atlanta, GA 30340 888-866-8091
Fax: 770-454-7350 800-241-1833
howiej@ami-recpro.com www.zippak.com
Recloseable plastic zipper on the top and short side of the package in-line with any vertical f/f/s machine, in-line sealing of webless zipper for recloseable overwrap operations
Vice President: Howie Johnson
Sales/Marketing Manager: Geoff Griffin
Estimated Sales: $5-10 Million
Number Employees: 50-99
Square Footage: 228000

31411 **Zipskin**
3108 Baker Rd
Dexter, MI 48130-1119 734-426-5559
Fax: 734-426-0899
Sanitary hand coverings
President: Gary Gochanour
Estimated Sales: $1 - 5,000,000
Number Employees: 1-4
Brands:
Zipkin

31412 **Zitropack Ltd**
240 S La Londe Ave
Addison, IL 60101 630-543-1016
Fax: 630-543-7216 info@zitropack.com
www.zitropack.com
Remanufactured and repaired food processing equipment, fillers, filling equipment and sealers
VP: Rafael Ortiz
Number Employees: 10-19

31413 **Zoia Banquetier Company**
4700 Lorain Ave
Cleveland, OH 44102 216-631-6414
Fax: 216-961-5119
Food banquet covers, brushes, dollies and carts; exporter of food banquet covers
Owner: Lorraine Hangauer
Secretary: Donald Hangauer
Estimated Sales: $500,000-$1 Million
Number Employees: 1-4
Square Footage: 25000

31414 **Zojirushi America Corporation**
1149 W., 190th Street
Suite 1000
Gardena, CA 90248 310-769-1900
Fax: 310-323-5522 800-264-6270
www.zojirushi.com
Zojirushi offers a complete line of quality NSF approved vacuum insulated coffee, serving products and a wide variety of restaurant equipment including commerical grade rice cookers and warmers, vacuum insulated carafes, Air Pot®beverage dispensers, Gravity Pot® beverage dispensers, vacuum insulated creamers and electric soup warmers.
President: Norio Ichikawa

31415 **Zol-Mark Industries**
470 Logan Avenue
Winnipeg, NB R3A 0R8
Canada 204-943-7393
Fax: 204-943-9803 zolmark@ilos.net
Commercial steel furniture including chairs, tables and bar stools for the hospitality industry
Marketing: Hart Goldman
Sales: Aaron Goldman
Plant Manager: Aaron Goldman
Number Employees: 20-49

31416 **Zumbiel Packaging**
2339 Harris Ave
Cincinnati, OH 45212 513-531-3600
Fax: 513-531-0072 www.zumbiel.com
Boxes, cartons, beverage carriers, transparent plastic lids and tubes
President: Robert Zumbiel
CFO: Mark Hausfeld
Quality Control: Dennis Richardson
Marketing: Charles Mace
Estimated Sales: $250 - 500 Million
Number Employees: 250-499

31417 **Zurn Industries**
1801 Pittsburgh Ave
Erie, PA 16502 905-405-8272
Fax: 814-875-1402 855-663-9876
www.zurn.com
Commercial, institutional and industrial building products
President: Alex Marini
Vice President: Craig Wehr
Sales/Marketing Manager: Jerry Dill
Number Employees: 1,000-4,999

31418 **iVEX Packaging Corporation**
1805 50e Avenue
Lachine, QC H8T 3C8
+32 514-636-7951
Fax: 514-636-9545 www.ivexpackaging.com
Manufacturer and exporter of packaging materials including corrugated paper and trays
President: Paul Gaulin
Estimated Sales: $710 Million
Brands:
Grand Stands
Ivex
M&R
Prime Time
Reflections
Selectware
Sho-Bowls
Ultra Pac

31419 **iVEX Packaging Corporation**
1550 South Champagne Avenue
Ontario, CA 91761 909-390-4422
Fax: 909-605-2795 800-238-1550
www.ivexpackaging.com
President: Paul Gaulin
General Manager: Steve Darby
Estimated Sales: $500 Million
Square Footage: 29559
Parent Co: Group Emballage Specialise

31420 **optek-Danulat, Inc**
N118 W18748 Bunsen Drive
Germantown, WI 53022 262-437-3600
Fax: 262-437-3699 800-371-4288
info@optek.com www.optek.com
In-line photometric equipment

Numeric

A

D

E

F

G

H

I

N

Q

R

S

T

U

V

W

X

Y

Z

Alabama

Alaska

Alberta

Arizona

Arkansas

British Columbia

California

Colorado

Connecticut

Delaware

District of Columbia

Florida

Georgia

Hawaii

Idaho

Illinois

Indiana

Iowa

Kansas

Kentucky

Louisiana

Maine

Manitoba

Maryland

Massachusetts

Michigan

Minnesota

Mississippi

Missouri

Montana

Nebraska

Nevada

New Brunswick

New Hampshire

New Jersey

New Mexico

New York

Newfoundland and Labrador

North Carolina

North Dakota

Nova Scotia

Ohio

Oklahoma

Ontario

Oregon

Pennsylvania

Prince Edward Island

Puerto Rico

Quebec

Rhode Island

Saskatchewan

South Carolina

South Dakota

Tennessee

Texas

Utah

Vermont

Virginia

Washington

West Virginia

Wisconsin

Wyoming

Grey House Publishing

Grey House Publishing

2014 Title List

Visit **www.GreyHouse.com** for Product Information, Table of Contents and Sample Pages

General Reference

America's College Museums
American Environmental Leaders: From Colonial Times to the Present
An African Biographical Dictionary
An Encyclopedia of Human Rights in the United States
Constitutional Amendments
Encyclopedia of African-American Writing
Encyclopedia of the Continental Congress
Encyclopedia of Gun Control & Gun Rights
Encyclopedia of Invasions & Conquests
Encyclopedia of Prisoners of War & Internment
Encyclopedia of Religion & Law in America
Encyclopedia of Rural America
Encyclopedia of the United States Cabinet, 1789-2010
Encyclopedia of War Journalism
Encyclopedia of Warrior Peoples & Fighting Groups
From Suffrage to the Senate: America's Political Women
Nations of the World
Political Corruption in America
Speakers of the House of Representatives, 1789-2009
The Environmental Debate: A Documentary History
The Evolution Wars: A Guide to the Debates
The Religious Right: A Reference Handbook
The Value of a Dollar: 1860-2009
The Value of a Dollar: Colonial Era
This is Who We Were: A Companion to the 1940 Census
This is Who We Were: The 1920s
This is Who We Were: The 1950s
This is Who We Were: The 1960s
US Land & Natural Resource Policy
Working Americans 1770-1869 Vol. IX: Revolutionary War to the Civil War
Working Americans 1880-1999 Vol. I: The Working Class
Working Americans 1880-1999 Vol. II: The Middle Class
Working Americans 1880-1999 Vol. III: The Upper Class
Working Americans 1880-1999 Vol. IV: Their Children
Working Americans 1880-2003 Vol. V: At War
Working Americans 1880-2005 Vol. VI: Women at Work
Working Americans 1880-2006 Vol. VII: Social Movements
Working Americans 1880-2007 Vol. VIII: Immigrants
Working Americans 1880-2009 Vol. X: Sports & Recreation
Working Americans 1880-2010 Vol. XI: Inventors & Entrepreneurs
Working Americans 1880-2011 Vol. XII: Our History through Music
Working Americans 1880-2012 Vol. XIII: Education & Educators
World Cultural Leaders of the 20th & 21st Centuries

Business Information

Complete Television, Radio & Cable Industry Directory
Directory of Business Information Resources
Directory of Mail Order Catalogs
Directory of Venture Capital & Private Equity Firms
Environmental Resource Handbook
Food & Beverage Market Place
Grey House Homeland Security Directory
Grey House Performing Arts Directory
Hudson's Washington News Media Contacts Directory
New York State Directory
Sports Market Place Directory

Education Information

Charter School Movement
Comparative Guide to American Elementary & Secondary Schools
Complete Learning Disabilities Directory
Educators Resource Directory
Special Education

Health Information

Comparative Guide to American Hospitals
Complete Directory for Pediatric Disorders
Complete Directory for People with Chronic Illness
Complete Directory for People with Disabilities
Complete Mental Health Directory
Diabetes in America: A Geographic & Demographic Analysis
Directory of Health Care Group Purchasing Organizations
Directory of Hospital Personnel
HMO/PPO Directory
Medical Device Register
Older Americans Information Directory

Statistics & Demographics

America's Top-Rated Cities
America's Top-Rated Small Towns & Cities
America's Top-Rated Smaller Cities
American Tally
Ancestry & Ethnicity in America
Comparative Guide to American Hospitals
Comparative Guide to American Suburbs
Profiles of America
Profiles of... Series – State Handbooks
The Hispanic Databook
Weather America

Financial Ratings Series

TheStreet.com Ratings Guide to Bond & Money Market Mutual Funds
TheStreet.com Ratings Guide to Common Stocks
TheStreet.com Ratings Guide to Exchange-Traded Funds
TheStreet.com Ratings Guide to Stock Mutual Funds
TheStreet.com Ratings Ultimate Guided Tour of Stock Investing
Weiss Ratings Consumer Guides
Weiss Ratings Guide to Banks & Thrifts
Weiss Ratings Guide to Credit Unions
Weiss Ratings Guide to Health Insurers
Weiss Ratings Guide to Life & Annuity Insurers
Weiss Ratings Guide to Property & Casualty Insurers

Bowker's Books In Print® Titles

Books In Print®
Books In Print® Supplement
American Book Publishing Record® Annual
American Book Publishing Record® Monthly
Books Out Loud™
Bowker's Complete Video Directory™
Children's Books In Print®
El-Hi Textbooks & Serials In Print®
Forthcoming Books®
Law Books & Serials In Print™
Medical & Health Care Books In Print™
Publishers, Distributors & Wholesalers of the US™
Subject Guide to Books In Print®
Subject Guide to Children's Books In Print®

Canadian General Reference

Associations Canada
Canadian Almanac & Directory
Canadian Environmental Resource Guide
Canadian Parliamentary Guide
Financial Services Canada
Governments Canada
Health Services Canada
Libraries Canada
Major Canadian Cities
The History of Canada

Grey House Publishing | Salem Press | H.W. Wilson
4919 Route, 22 PO Box 56, Amenia NY 12501-0056

SALEM PRESS

SALEM PRESS

2014 Title List

Visit **www.SalemPress.com** for Product Information, Table of Contents and Sample Pages

Literature

American Ethnic Writers
Critical Insights: Authors
Critical Insights: New Literary Collection Bundles
Critical Insights: Themes
Critical Insights: Works
Critical Survey of Drama
Critical Survey of Graphic Novels: Heroes & Super Heroes
Critical Survey of Graphic Novels: History, Theme & Technique
Critical Survey of Graphic Novels: Independents & Underground Classics
Critical Survey of Graphic Novels: Manga
Critical Survey of Long Fiction
Critical Survey of Mystery & Detective Fiction
Critical Survey of Mythology and Folklore: Heroes and Heroines
Critical Survey of Mythology and Folklore: Love, Sexuality & Desire
Critical Survey of Mythology and Folklore: World Mythology
Critical Survey of Poetry
Critical Survey of Poetry: American Poetry
Critical Survey of Poetry: British, Irish & Commonwealth Poets
Critical Survey of Poetry: European Poets
Critical Survey of Poetry: European Poets
Critical Survey of Poetry: Topical Essays
Critical Survey of Poetry: World Poets
Critical Survey of Science Fiction & Fantasy Literature
Critical Survey of Shakespeare's Sonnets
Critical Survey of Short Fiction
Critical Survey of Short Fiction: American Writers
Critical Survey of Short Fiction: British, Irish & Commonwealth Poets
Critical Survey of Short Fiction: European Writers
Critical Survey of Short Fiction: Topical Essays
Critical Survey of Short Fiction: World Writers
Cyclopedia of Literary Characters
Introduction to Literary Context: American Post-Modernist Novels
Introduction to Literary Context: American Short Fiction
Introduction to Literary Context: English Literature
Introduction to Literary Context: World Literature
Magill's Literary Annual 2014
Magill's Survey of American Literature
Magill's Survey of World Literature
Masterplots
Masterplots II: African American Literature
Masterplots II: Christian Literature
Masterplots II: Drama Series
Masterplots II: Short Story Series
Notable African American Writers
Notable American Novelists
Notable Playwrights
Short Story Writers

Science, Careers & Mathematics

Applied Science
Applied Science: Engineering & Mathematics
Applied Science: Science & Medicine
Applied Science: Technology
Biomes and Ecosystems
Careers in Chemistry
Careers in Communications & Media
Careers in Healthcare
Careers in Hospitality & Tourism
Careers in Law & Criminology
Careers in Physics
Computer Technology Inventors
Contemporary Biographies in Chemistry
Contemporary Biographies in Communications & Media
Contemporary Biographies in Healthcare
Contemporary Biographies in Hospitality & Tourism
Contemporary Biographies in Law & Criminology
Contemporary Biographies in Physics
Earth Science
Earth Science: Earth Materials & Resources
Earth Science: Earth's Surface and History
Earth Science: Physics & Chemistry of the Earth
Earth Science: Weather, Water & Atmosphere
Encyclopedia of Energy
Encyclopedia of Environmental Issues
Encyclopedia of Global Resources
Encyclopedia of Global Warming
Encyclopedia of Mathematics and Society
Encyclopedia of the Ancient World
Forensic Science
Internet Innovators
Introduction to Chemistry
Magill's Encyclopedia of Science: Animal Life
Magill's Encyclopedia of Science: Plant life
Magill's Medical Guide
Notable Natural Disasters
Solar System

Health

Addictions & Substance Abuse
Cancer
Complementary & Alternative Medicine
Genetics & Inherited Conditions
Infectious Diseases & Conditions
Magill's Medical Guide
Psychology & Mental Health
Psychology Basics

SALEM PRESS

2014 Title List

Visit **www.SalemPress.com** for Product Information, Table of Contents and Sample Pages

History and Social Science

A 2000s in America
50 States
African American History
Agriculture in History (check)
American First Ladies
American Heroes
American Indian Tribes
American Presidents
American Villains
Ancient Greece
Bill of Rights, The
Cold War, The
Defining Documents: American Revolution 1754-1805
Defining Documents: Civil War 1860-1865
Defining Documents: Emergence of Modern America, 1868-1918
Defining Documents: Exploration & Colonial America 1492-1755
Defining Documents: Manifest Destiny 1803-1860
Defining Documents: Reconstruction, 1865-1880
Defining Documents: The 1920s
Defining Documents: The 1930s
Defining Documents: World War I
Eighties in America
Encyclopedia of American Immigration
Fifties in America
Forties in America
Great Athletes
Great Events from History: 17th Century
Great Events from History: 18th Century
Great Events from History: 19th Century
Great Events from History: 20th Century, 1901-1940
Great Events from History: 20th Century, 1941-1970
Great Events from History: 20th Century, 1971-200
Great Events from History: Ancient World
Great Events from History: Middle Ages
Great Events from History: Modern Scandals
Great Events from History: Renaissance & Early Modern Era
Great Lives from History: 17th Century
Great Lives from History: 18th Century
Great Lives from History: 19th Century
Great Lives from History: 20th Century
Great Lives from History: African Americans
Great Lives from History: Ancient World
Great Lives from History: Asian & Pacific Islander Americans
Great Lives from History: Incredibly Wealthy
Great Lives from History: Inventors & Inventions
Great Lives from History: Jewish Americans
Great Lives from History: Latinos
Great Lives from History: Middle Ages
Great Lives from History: Notorious Lives
Great Lives from History: Renaissance & Early Modern Era
Great Lives from History: Scientists & Science
Historical Encyclopedia of American Business
Immigration in U.S. History
Magill's Guide to Military History
Milestone Documents in African American History
Milestone Documents in American History
Milestone Documents in World History
Milestone Documents of American Leaders
Milestone Documents of World Religions
Musicians & Composers 20th Century
Nineties in America
Seventies in America
Sixties in America
Survey of American Industry and Careers
Thirties in America
Twenties in America
U.S. Court Cases
U.S. Laws, Acts, and Treaties
U.S. Legal System
U.S. Supreme Court
United States at War
USA in Space
Weapons and Warfare
World Conflicts: Asia and the Middle East

2014 Title List

Visit **www.HwWilsonInPrint.com** for Product Information, Table of Contents and Sample Pages

Current Biography
Current Biography Cumulative Index 1946-2013
Current Biography Magazine
Current Biography Yearbook-2004
Current Biography Yearbook-2005
Current Biography Yearbook-2006
Current Biography Yearbook-2007
Current Biography Yearbook-2008
Current Biography Yearbook-2009
Current Biography Yearbook-2010
Current Biography Yearbook-2011
Current Biography Yearbook-2012
Current Biography Yearbook-2013
Current Biography Yearbook-2014

Core Collections
Senior High Core Collection
Middle & Junior High School Core
Children's Core Collection
Fiction Core Collection
Public Library Core Collection: Nonfiction

Sears List
Sears List of Subject Headings
Sears: Lista de Encabezamientos de Materia

The Reference Shelf
Aging in America
Revisiting Gender
The U.S. National Debate Topic, 2014/2015
Embracing New Paradigms in education
Marijuana Reform
Representative American Speeches 2013-2014
Reality Television
The Business of Food
The Future of U.S. Economic Relations: Mexico, Cuba, and Venezuela
Sports in America
Global Climate Change
Representative American Speeches, 2012-2013
Conspiracy Theories
The Arab Spring
U.S. National Debate Topic: Transportation Infrastructure
Families: Traditional and New Structures
Faith & Science
Representative American Speeches 2011-2012
Social Networking
Dinosaurs
Space Exploration & Development
U.S. Infrastructure
Politics of the Ocean
Representative American Speeches 2010-2011
Robotics
The News and its Future
American Military Presence Overseas
Russia
Graphic Novels and Comic Books
Representative American Speeches 2009-2010

Readers' Guide
Readers Guide to Periodicals Literature
Abridged Readers' Guide to Periodical Literature
Short Story Index

Indexes
Short Story Index
Index to Legal Periodicals & Books

Facts About Series
Facts About the Presidents, Eighth Edition
Facts About China
Facts About the 20th Century
Facts About American Immigration
Facts About World's Languages

Nobel Prize Winners
Nobel Prize Winners, 2002-2013

World Authors
World Authors 2000-2005
World Authors 2006-2013

Famous First Facts
Famous First Facts, Seventh Edition
Famous First Facts About American Politics
Famous First Facts About Sports
Famous First Facts About the Environment
Famous First Facts, International Edition

American Book of Days
The American Book of Days, Fifth Edition
The International Book of Days

Junior Authors & Illustrators
Tenth Book of Junior Authors & Illustrations

Monographs
The Barnhart Dictionary of Etymology
Celebrate the World
Indexing from A to Z
Radical Change: Books for Youth in a Digital Age
The Poetry Break
Guide to the Ancient World

Wilson Chronology
Wilson Chronology of Asia and the Pacific
Wilson Chronology of Human Rights
Wilson Chronology of Ideas
Wilson Chronology of the Arts
Wilson Chronology of the World's Religions
Wilson Chronology of Women's Achievements

Book Review Digest
Book Review Digest, 2014